THE
INTERNATIONAL
AUTHORS AND WRITERS
WHO'S WHO

THE INTERNATIONAL AUTHORS AND WRITERS WHO'S WHO

Hon. General Editor
ERNEST KAY
Author of Biographical and Other Works
Editor and Publisher (London)

Publisher:
Nicholas S. Law

Consultant Editor:
M. J. Shields, FIInfsc, MITI

Editorial/Production Manager:
Jocelyn Timothy

Assistant Editors:
Sheryl Rigby
Rebecca Thompson
Brenda White

All communications to: International Authors and Writers Who's Who
International Biographical Centre
Cambridge CB2 3QP, England

THE
INTERNATIONAL
AUTHORS AND WRITERS
WHO'S WHO

THIRTEENTH EDITION

Consultant Editor
M. J. Shields FIInfSc, MITI

International Biographical Centre
Cambridge England

First published 1934
Second Edition 1935
Third Edition 1948
Fourth Edition 1960
Fifth Edition 1963
Sixth Edition 1972
Reprinted 1972
Seventh Editon 1976
Eighth Edition 1977
Ninth Edition 1982
Tenth Edition 1986
Eleventh Edition 1989
Twelfth Edition 1991
Thirteenth Edition 1993

ISBN 0 948875 51 8

Printed and bound in the UK by The Bath Press Ltd, Lower Bristol Road
Bath BA2 3BL, Avon, England

FOREWORD

Taking over the Consultant Editorship of a major work of reference is no easy task, especially when that work is in the process of change. It is however a task I have welcomed, because I feel very strongly that a directory such as this is a major requirement not only in the literary world, but also as a reference work in its own right. I also strongly support the Publisher's policy of gradual change, and hope I have managed to implement positive changes in the compilation of this edition.

These changes consist partly of redefining what constitutes an author or writer. This is quite difficult, because most professionals in the course of their careers produce writing, some of which may be published. Furthermore, books are sometimes produced by, or on behalf of, people who have achieved fame in other spheres, but who are not themselves writers in any meaningful sense of the word. Obviously, in a book of manageable size, it is impossible to include everyone who writes, and therefore we have to look more closely at entry criteria. This has meant that some who were included in previous editions have had to be left out of this one, a regrettable necessity if we are to continue the process of refinement.

We have also had to consider the definition of the terms 'author' and 'writer' themselves, because they are to some extent synonymous in English. We have chosen to ignore etymological quibbles, and to consider the terms as incorporating all those who produce as a main activity books, plays, articles, or journalistic contributions, whether literary, commercial, technical, or scientific. This interpretation will inevitably be somewhat subjective, and we will therefore be interested in any comments readers or reviewers might have as to our selection criteria, which of course we will be refining over future editions.

One specific decision that was taken was the inclusion of translators. My own association with the translation profession might be thought to be a factor in the decision, but in fact by far the most important consideration is the internationalism of this volume. Without translators, there would be no such concept as 'world literature'. One has only to think of great cultural works such as the Bible, the Koran, the books of Homer or Confucius, of authors such as Shakespeare, Voltaire, Goethe, Pushkin, or of great scientific endeavours from Leonardo da Vinci through Freud and Darwin to modern texts on subjects from astronomy to zoology, to appreciate the immense contribution made by translators to the dissemination of human knowledge. It is a contribution a reference work such as this could not legitimately ignore.

The internationalism of the work also presents special problems for the editor. No one person can be conversant with the state of literature in all the countries of the world, and I certainly make no such claims for myself. We are therefore very dependent on the degree of assistance obtainable from the literary authorities of various countries. Regrettably, not all countries look after their writers, nor apparently hold them in very high regard. While therefore we are most grateful for the assistance we have had from those embassies, writers associations, and libraries that have been able to co-operate with us, we must also record our regret at a lack of coverage in certain areas, and hope we will find ways of overcoming this in the future.

Despite all these changes, revisions, reservations, and unavoidable deficiencies, we think we have managed to produce a reference work valuable to all who need information on writers and their product. We have amassed over 8,000 entries in the main list, with a wealth of personal and career information on each. Unlike previous editions, this one includes all pseudonyms in the main sequence, so that users can go directly to the person they wish to look up without having to refer to appendices. At the same time, a comprehensive set of appendices has been provided to provide extra information on all aspects of the world of literature, appropriate to an international work of reference.

In conclusion, I would like to record my thanks to the staff of Melrose Press for their patience and friendly understanding, especially to Jocelyn Timothy, who is as near to indispensable as makes no difference; also to my son Richard, who came to my aid when I was about to be overwhelmed by paper, and to all the many individuals and organizations who acted as direct and indirect suppliers of information.

M J Shields, FIInfSc, MITI, Consultant Editor, Versailles, May 1993.

INTERNATIONAL BIOGRAPHICAL CENTRE
RANGE OF REFERENCE TITLES

From one of the widest ranges of contemporary biographical reference works published under any one imprint, some IBC titles date back to the 1930's. Each edition is compiled from information supplied by those listed, who include leading personalities of particular countries or profession. Information offered usually includes date and place of birth; family details; qualification; career histories; awards and honours received; books published or other creative work; other relevant information including postal address. Naturally there is no charge or fee for inclusion.

New editions are freshly compiled and contain on average 80-90% new information. New titles are regularly added to the IBC reference library.

Titles include:

Dictionary of International Biography

Who's Who in Australasia and the Far East

Who's Who in Western Europe

Dictionary of Scandinavian Biography

Dictionary of Latin American and Caribbean Biography

International Who's Who in Art and Antiques

International Authors and Writers Who's Who

International Leaders in Achievement

International Who's Who in Community Service

International Who's Who in Education

International Who's Who in Engineering

International Who's Who in Medicine

International Who's Who in Music and Musicians' Directory

International Who's Who of Professional and Business Women

Men of Achievement

The World Who's Who of Women

The World Who's Who of Women in Education

International Youth of Achievement

Foremost Women of the Twentieth Century

International Who's Who in Poetry and Poets' Encyclopaedia

Enquiries to:

International Biographical Centre

Cambridge, CB2 3QP

England

CONTENTS

CONTENTS

A

AARDEMA Verna Geneva, b. 6 June 1911, New Era, Michigan, USA. Elementary Teacher; Journalist. m. (1) Albert Aardema, 30 May 1936 (dec.1974), 1 son, 1 daughter, (2) Dr Joel Vugteveen, 3 Aug 1975. *Education:* BA, Michigan State College (now University), 1934. *Appointments:* Publicity Chairman, Juvenile Writers' Workshop, 1955-69; Staff Correspondent, Muskegon Chronicle. *Publications:* Why Mosquitoes Buzz in People's Ears, 1975; Who's In Rabbit's House?, 1977; Riddle of the Drum, 1978; Bringing the Rain to Kapiti Plain, 1981; What's So Funny, Ketu?, 1982; The Vinganaee & the Tree Toad, 1983; Oh, Kojo! How Could You!, 1984; Bimwili & the Zimwi, 1985; Behind the Back of the Mountain, 1973, Tales for the Third Ear, 1969; Forthcoming books: Princess Gorilla and a New Kind of Water, 1988; Rabbit Makes a Monkey of Lion; Pedro and the Padre, 1991; Traveling to Tondo, 1991; Borreguita and the Coyote, 1991; Anansi Finds a Fool, 1992; Forthcoming, The Misoso Storybook, and This For That; books published in Japan, France, South America, England, Canada and USA. *Contributions To:* Instructor, Cricket and Christian Life. *Honours:* Caldecott Award, 1976; Lewis Carroll Shelf Award, 1978; Parents' Choice Awards, 1984, 1985; Parents' Choice, 1989, 1991; Junior Library Guild Selection, 1991; Redbook Award, 1991; ALA Notable Book, 1991. *Memberships:* Juvenile Writers' Workshop; Children's Reading Round Table, Chicago; National & Michigan Education Associations; Womens National Book Association. *Literary Agent:* Curtis Brown Ltd. *Address:* 784 Via Del Sol, North Fort Myers, Florida, USA.

AARON David (Laurence), b. 21 Aug 1938, California, USA. Company President; Writer. m. Chloe Wellingham, 1 son. *Education:* BA, Occidental College 1960; MA, Princeton University, 1962. *Appointments:* US Foreign Service, diplomatic postings in South America, Washington DC and the US mission to the North Atlantic Treaty Organization in Paris, 1962-68; US Arms Control and Disarmament Agency, Washington DC, served on the US Delegation to the United Nations General Assembly, 1968 and on the US Delegation to the first Strategic Arms Limitation Talks, 1969-72; National Security Council, Washington DC, senior member, 1972-74; US Senate, Washington DC, task force director of Intelligence Committee, 1974-77; deputy national security advisor, 1977-81; Oppenheimer & Co (investment banking firm) New York, New York, Vice-President for mergers and acquisitions 1981-; President, D L Aaron & Co (consulting firm); writer. Presidential emissary to Europe, Africa and China, 1977-81; member of the board of directors of Oppenheimer International 1981-; Quest for Value Fund. *Publications:* State Scarlet (novel) 1987; Agent of Influence (novel) 1989. *Contributions to:* Articles for periodicals and newspapers, including Foreign Affairs, Foreign Policy, the New York Times and the Los Angeles Times. *Address:* c/o The Lantz Office, 888 Seventh Avenue, New York, NY 10106, USA.

ABASS *See:* **ASSENSOH Akwasi Bretuo.**

ABBAS Ahmad (Khwaja), b. 1914, India. Writer; Journalist; Film Director; Film Producer. *Literary Appointments:* Reporter, Sub-Editor, 1936-39, Editor, Sunday Edition, Columnist, 1939-47, The Bombay Chronicle; Contributing Columnist, Blitz Magazine, Bombay, 1947-. *Publications:* Outside India: The Adventures of a Roving Reporter, 1940; An Indian Looks at America, 1943; Tomorrow Is Ours!, 1943; Defeat for Death: A Story Without Names, 1944; Report to Gandhiji (with N.G. Yog), 1944; Invitation to Immortality (play), 1946; Blood and Stones, 1947; Rice and Other Stories, 1947; I Write As I Feel, 1948; Kashmir Fights for Freedom, 1948; Cages of Freedom and Other Stories, 1952; In the Image of Mao Tse-Tung, 1953; Inqilab, 1955; One Thousand Nights on a Bed of Stones and Other Stories, 1957; Face to Face with Krushchev, 1960; Til We Reach the Stars: The Story of Yuri Gagarin, 1961; Black Sun and Other Stories, 1963; Indira Gandhi: Return of the Red Rose, 1966; The Most Beautiful

Woman in the World, 1968; When Night Falls, 1968; Mera Naam Joker, 1970; Maria, 1971; That Woman: Her Seven Years in Power, 1973; I Am Not an Island, 1977.

ABBENSETTS Michael, b. 8 June 1938, British Guiana (now Guyana), became British citizen, 1974. Writer. *Education:* Queen's College, Guyana, 1952-56; Stanstead College, Quebec; Sir George Williams University, Montreal, 1960-61. *Appointments:* Security Attendant, Tower of London, 1963-67; Staff Member, Sir John Soane Museum, London, 1968-71; Resident playwright, Royal Court Theatre, London 1974; Visiting Professor of Drama, Carnegie Mellon University, Pittsburgh, 1981. *Publications:* Plays: Sweet Talk (produced London, 1973, New York, 1974). London, Eyre Methuen, 1976; Alterations (produced London and New York, 1978; revised version produced London 1985); Samba (produced London 1980) London, Eyre Methuen, 1980; In the Mood (produced London, 1981); Outlaw (produced Leicester and London, 1983); El Dorado (produced London, 1984). Writer for radio and television. Novel: Empire Road (novelization of television series, London, Panther, 1979. *Honours:* George Devine award, 1973; Arts Council bursary, 1977; Afro-Caribbean award, 1979. *Literary Agent:* Anthony Sheil Associates, London. *Address:* Anthony Sheil Associates, 43 Doughty Street, London WC1N 2LF, England.

ABBEY Edward, b. 1927 Writer; Farmer. *Publications:* Jonathan Troy, 1954; The Brave Cowboy, 1958; Fire on the Mountain, 1962; Desert Solitaire (personal history), 1968; Black Sun, 1970 (in United Kingdom as Sunset Canyon); Cactus Country, 1973; Appalachian Wilderness, 1973; The Monkey Wrench Gang, 1975; The Journey Home, 1977; The Hidden Canyon (with J. Blaustein), 1977; Back Roads of Arizona, (with E. Thollander), 1978; Abbey's Road, 1970; Desert Images (with D. Muench), 1979; Good News, 1980; Down the River, 1982; Beyond the Wall, 1984; Slumgullion Stew: A Reader, 1985; The Fool's Progress, 1988. *Address:* Box 1690, Oracle, AZ 85623, USA.

ABBOT Rick. *See:* **SHARKEY Jack.**

ABBOTT John B. Jr. b. 25 Feb 1956, Plainfield, New Jersey, USA. Mystery Writer. m. Maria G Di Tommaso, Oct 3 1992. *Education:* BA, English, Rutgers University, 1985. *Appointments:* Writing Tutor, English Department, Rutgers University, New Brunswick, New Jersey, 1988-; Visiting Professional Lecturer, Rutgers University, 1989-. *Publications:* Knight Moves, 1990; Interactive Murder Mystery Scripts: All in the Game; Two for the Money; The Botsford Inn Mystery; The Kris Kringle Kaper; How the West was Fun and Birthdays Can Be Murder; Smithson's Knight, 1992. *Contributions to:* Short stories/Editor in Chief, Untitled, Rutgers University, 1984-85; Cooking with Malice Domestic, 1991. *Memberships:* Active Member, Mystery Writers of America. *Address:* 22 Church Street, PO Box 439, Kingston, NJ 08528-0439, USA.

ABERBACH David, b. 17 Oct 1953, London, England. Univ Prof. m. Miriam Skelker, 29 June 1980, 1 daughter. *Education:* Talmudical Academy of Baltimore, Maryland, 1971; BA, Univ Coll, London, 1975; M Litt, Oxford Univ, 1977; D Phil, 1980. *Appointments:* Univ Lecturer, Oxford Univ, Cambridge Univ, Leo Baeck College, Cornell Univ, 1982-85; Visiting Professor, McGill Univ, 1986-87; Associate Professor, 1987-. *Publications:* At The Handles of The Lock; Bialik; Surviving Trauma; A Shoot From A Severed Bough. *Contributions to:* Articles in TLS; THES; Encounter Commentary; Intl Review of Psychoanalysis; The Yimes; Hebrew Union; College Annual Jewish Chronicle Literary Supplement; Observer; Moznayim Miostream. *Address:* 32 Ravenshurst Avenue, London NW4 4EG, England.

ABLEMAN Paul, b. 1927. Writer. *Publications:* Even His Enemy (with Gertrude Macauley), 1948; I Hear

Voices, 1958; As Near As I Can Get, 1962; Green Julia (play), 1966; Tests (playlets), 1966; Vac, 1968; Blue Comedy: Madly in Love, Hawk's Night, 1968; The Twilight of the Vilp, 1969; Bits: Some Porse Poems, 1969; Tornado Pratt, 1977; Shoestring (novelization of TV play), 1979; Porridge (novelization of screen play), 1979; Shoestring's Finest Hour, 1980; County Hall (novelization of TV series), 1981; The Anatomy of Nakedness, 1982; The Doomed Rebellion, 1983. *Address:* Flat 37, Duncan House, Fellows Road, London NW3, England.

ABRAHAM Claude Kurt, b. 1931. Writer. *Literary Appointments:* Faculty Member, University of Illinois, 1959-64; Professor of French, University of Florida, Gainesville, 1964-75; Professor of French, University of California, Davis, 1975-. *Publications:* Gaston d'Orleans et sa Cour, 1963, 1964; Bourgeois Gentilhomme, 1966; The Strangers, 1966; J. Mesnard: Pascal, (translated with M. Abraham), 1969; Enfin Malherbe, 1971 (SAMLA Studies Award); Corneille, 1972; Tristan L'Hermite: Theatre Complet (with J. Schweitzer and J. van Baelen), 1974; J Racine, 1977; Tristan L'Hermite, 1980; Norman Satrists of the Age of Louis XIII, 1983; Moliere's Comedies - Ballets, 1984, 1985. *Address:* 1604 Westshore Street, Davis, CA 95616, USA.

ABRAHAM Henry J, b. 1921. *Appointments:* Assistant Professor, 1953-57, Associate Professor, 1957-62, Professor of Political Science, 1962-72, University of Pennsylvania, Philadelphia; James Hart Professor of Government and Foreign Affairs, University of Virginia, Charlottesville, 1971-. *Publications:* Compulsory Voting, 1955; Government as Entrepreneur and Social Servant, 1956; Courts and Judges: An Introduction to the Judical Process, 1959; Elements of Democratic Government, 4th Edition (with J.A. Cory), 1964; Essentials of American National Government (with J.C. Phillips), 1971; Freedom and the Court: Civil Rights and Liberties in the United States, 5th Edition, 1988; The Judiciary: The Supreme Court in the Governmental Process, 6th Edition, 1983, 7th Edition, 1986, 8th Edition, 1991; Justices and Presidents: A Political History of Appointments to the Supreme Court, 1975, 1985, 1992; American Democracy, 3rd Edition (with W.E. Keefe), 1989; The Judical Process: An Introductory Analysis of the Courts of the United States, England and France, 5th Edition, 1986, 6th Edition, 1992. *Address:* 906 Fendall Terrace, Charlottesville, VA 22903, USA.

ABRAHAMS Peter, b. 1919, South Africa. Author; Journalist. *Literary Appointments:* Regular Contributor, The Observer, London and The Herald Tribune, New York City, Paris, 1952-64; Editor, West Indian Economist and Controller, West Indian News, Jamaica, 1955-64; Chairman, Radio Jamaica, 1977-80. *Publications:* Dark Testament (Short Stories), 1942; Song of the City, 1945; Mine Boy, 1946; The Path of Thunder, 1948; Wild Conquest, 1950; Return to Goli (reportage), 1953; Tell Freedom: Memories of Africa, 1954; A Wreath for Udomo, 1956; An Island Mosaic, 1957; A Night of Their Own, 1965; This Island Now, 1966; The View from Coyaba, 1985. *Address:* Red Hills, P.O. Box 20, St Andrew, Jamaica.

ABRAHAMS Roger David, b. 1933, United States of America. Writer. *Appointments:* Professor of English and Anthropology, 1969-79, Chairman, Department of English, 1974-79, University of Texas, Austin; Kenan Professor of Humanities and Anthropology, Scripps and Pitzer Colleges, Claremont, 1979-. *Publications:* Deep Down in the Jungle, 1964, revised edition 1970; Anglo-American Folksong Style (with G.W. Foss Jr.), 1968; Jump Rope Rhymes: A Dictionary, 1968; Positively Black, 1970; A Singer and Her Songs, 1970; Language and Cultural Diversity in American Education (with R.C. Troike), 1972; Deep the Water, Shallow the Shore, 1974; Talking Black, 1975; Afro-American Folk Culture: An Annotated Bibliography (with J. Szwed), 1977; Between the Living and the Dead: Riddles Which Tell Stories, 1980; Counting Out Rhymes: A Dictionary (with Lois Rankin), 1980; And Other Neighborly Names (with Richard Bauman), 1981; Performers, Performances and Enactments, 1983; After Africa (with John Szwed), 1983; African Folktales, 1983; The Man-of-Words in the West Indies, 1983; Afro-American Folktales, 1985.

ABRAHAMSON David, b. 7 May 1947, Washington DC, USA. Writer. *Education:* BA, History, Johns Hopkins University, 1969; M.Journalism, University of California, 1971; CertA/ES, Worcester College, Oxford University, 1983. *Appointments:* Managing Editor, Car and Driver Magazine, 1973-77; Adjunct Faculty, School of Visual Arts, New York, 1985-, Adjunct Asst. Professor of Publishing, New York University, 1987-; Adjunct Faculty, Pratt Institute, 1987-. *Contributor To:* New York Times Sunday Magazine; Science Magazine; Playboy Magazine; International Wildlife Magazine; Car and Driver Magazine, Magazine Editing Workbook, 1988. *Honours:* Sea Scribe Award, Northern California, SBRA, 1972; Purdy Memorial Award, International Motor Press Association, 1978. *Memberships:* American Society of Journalists & Authors; History of Science Society; Society for History of Discoveries; Chairman, Board of Education, Appalachian Mountain Club; Chairman, Foundation for Educational Development, New York. *Address:* 165 East 32nd St., New York, NY 10016, USA.

ABRAHAMSON Irving, b. 21 Dec 1925, Chicago, IL, USA. Professor of English. m. Perle Cirulnikov Herzog, 4 Feb 1967. *Education:* BA, Roosevelt University, 1948; MA, University of Chicago, 1949; PhD, 1956. *Appointments:* Elie Wiesel Research Fellow, Spertus College of Judaica, Chicago, 1977, 1978. *Publications:* Against Silence: The Voice and Vision of Elie Wiesel; Articles in Dictionary of American Biography & Encylopaedia Britannica; Annotated Bibliography in Confronting the Holocaust: The Impact of Elie Wisel; Essay-chapter in Elie Wiesel: Between Memory and Hope. *Contributions to:* Midstream; Present Tense; Reform Judaism; Martyrdom & Resistance; Chicago Tribune; Chicago Sun-Times; JUF News. *Memberships:* National Book Critics Circle. *Address:* 1230 Linden Avenue, Highland Park, IL 60035, USA.

ABRAMS Karin L Von, b. 23 Aug 1952, Oregon, USA. Writer; Translator. *Education:* BA Hons 1974, University of California, Santa Cruz; MA with distinction 1975, University College London; PhD 1983, Kings College, London; all in German & English. *Publications:* A Voice from Germany, 1986; Paul Maenz Köln 1970-80-90, 1991; For Museum of Modern Art, Stuttgart, 1991: Peter Roehr; Christian Boltanski; Gerhard Graubner. *Contributions to:* Opera Now (of which Managing Editor for 2 years); Translations for Contemporary Music Review; other academic journals. *Memberships:* Society of Authors; Translators Association. *Address:* 3 Frognal, London, NW3 6AL, England.

ABSALOM John Henry, b. 11 Nov 1927, PT Augusta, South Australia. Professional Artist. m. Mary Elizabeth Wills, 4 Aug 1951, 2 sons, 3 daughters. *Education:* Correspondence Schooling. *Publications:* Safe Outback Travel; Outback Cooking in the Camp Oven; Absaloms Outback Paintings; Jack Absaloms Barbeque Cook Book. *Contributions to:* Save the Earth. *Honours:* Australian Achiever of the Year. *Memberships:* Press Club in Canberra. *Address:* 638 Chapple Street, Broken Hill, NSW 2880, Australia.

ABSE Dannie, b. 22 Sept 1923, Cardiff, Glamorgan, Wales. Medical Specialist; Writer. m. Joan Mercer, 1951, 1 son, 2 daughters. *Education:* St Illtyd's College, Cardiff; University of South Wales and Monmouthshire, Cardiff; King's College, London; Westminster Hospital, London; qualified as physician 1950, MRCS, LRCP. Served in the RAF 1951-54: Squadron Leader. *Career:* Specialist in charge of chest clinic, Central London Medical Establishment, 1954-; Senior Fellow in Humanities, Princeton University, New Jersey, 1973-74. *Publications:* Verse includes: Corgi Modern Poets in Focus 4, with others, edited by Jeremy Robson, 1972;

Funland and Other Poems, London and New York, 1973; Lunchtime, 1974; Penguin Modern Poets 26, with D J Enright and Michael Longley, 1975; Collected Poems 1948-76, London and Pittsburgh, 1977; Way Out in the Centre, London 1981, as One-Legged on Ice, Athens, University of Georgia Press, 1981. Recordings: Poets of Wales, Argo, 1972; The Poetry of Dannie Avse, McGraw Hill; Dannie Abse, Canto, 1984; Plays include: Gone in January (produced London, 1978) Published in Madog, 1981; Various plays for radio. Novels: Ash on a Young Man's Sleeve, London 1954, New York 1955; Some Corner of an English Field, London 1956, New York 1957; O Jones, O Jones, 1970; Voices in the Gallery, 1986; The Music Lover's Literary Companion, 1988; The Hutchinson Book of Post-War British Poets, 1989; Various other published works. Honours: Foyle Award 1960; Welsh Arts Council award for verse, 1971, for play 1980. Membership: President, Poetry Society, 1978-. Literary Agent: Anthony Sheil Associates Ltd, 2-3 Morwell Street, London WC1B 3AR. Address: 85 Hodford Road, London NW11 8NH, England.

ABSHIRE David Manker, b. 1926, United States of America. Politic. Appointments: Executive Director, 1962-70, Chairman, 1973-82, President, 1982-83, Center for Strategic and International Studies, Georgetown University, Washington, DC; Assistant Secretary of State for Congressional Relations, 1970-73; Permanent US Representative to NATO, 1983-. Publications: International Broadcasting: A New Dimension of Western Diplomacy, 1976; Foreign Policy Makers: President vs Congress, 1981. Memberships: Congressional Committee on the Organization of Government for the Conduct of Foreign Policy, 1973-75; Chairman, US Board for International Broadcasting, 1974-77; Director, National Security Group, Transition Office of President-Elect Reagan, 1980-81.

ACHEBE Chinua, b. 16 Nov 1930, Ogidi, Anambra State. Writer. m. Christie C. Okoli, 1961, 2 sons, 2 daughters. Education: University College, Ibadan. Appointments include: Producer, Nigerian Broadcasting Corporation, Lagos, 1954-58; Regional Controller, Enugu, 1958-61, Director, Voice of Nigeria, Lagos, 1961-66; Senior Research Fellow, University of Nigeria, 1967-72; Founding Editor, Okike, 1971-; Professor, English, University of Massachusetts, 1972-75, University of Connecticut, 1975-76, University of Nigeria, 1976-81; Professor Emeritus, 1985-. Publications: Things Fall Apart, 1958; No Longer at Ease, 1960; The Sacrificial Egg and Other Stories, 1962; Arrow of God, 1964; A Man of the People, 1966; Chike and the River, 1966; Poems, 1971; Girls at War, 1972; Beware Soul Brother, 1972; How the Leopard Got His Claws, 1973; Morning Yet on Creation Day, 1975; The Flute, 1978; The Drum, 1978; Don't Let Him Die (co-ed), 1978; The Trouble With Nigeria, 1983; Hopes and Impediments, 1987; Nigerian Topics, 1987. Honours: Numerous honours and awards including: Honorary Degrees; Margaret Wrong Memorial Prize, 1959; Nigerian National Trophy, 1960; Jock Campbell New Statesman Award, 1965; Commonwealth Poetry Prize, 1972; The Lotus Prize, 1975; Order of the Federal Republic (Nigeria), 1979; Nigerian National Merit Award, 1979. Memberships include: Hon. Member, American Academy of Arts & Letters; Fellow, Modern Language Association of America; Fellow, Ghana Association of Writers. Address: PO Box 53, Nsukka, Anambra State, Nigeria.

ACHUGAR Hugo J, b. 9 Feb 1944, Uruguay. m. Marta Del Huerto Diaz, 23 Jan 1967, 1 son, 3 daughters. Education: Professor, Literature, IPA, Uruguay, 1969; PhD, University of Pittsburgh, USA, 1980. Appointment: Editor, Brecha, 1968-69; Editorial Board, Fragmentos, 1976-83; Editorial Board, Revista de Estudios Hispanicos, 1985-; Editorial Board, Cuadernos de Marcha, 1986-. Publications: Poetry:Las Mariposas Tropicales, 1987; Con Bigote Triste, 1971; El Derrumbe, 1969; Textos Para Decir María, 1976; Todo Lo Que Es Solido Se Disuelve En El Aire, 1989, (Poetry). Contributor To: Marcha; Casa de Las Americas; Eco; Triquarterly. Honours: Literary price, Banda Oriental, 1969; National Literary Award, Poetry, 1969, Feria de Libros, 1973; Jry, Cuba, 1978; National Jury Uruguay, 1986. Memberships: ASESUR; PEN; MMLA: LASA. Address: Hispanic Studies, Northwestern University, Evanston, IL 60208, USA.

ACKERMAN Diane, b. 7 Oct 1948, Waukegan, Illinois, USA. Writer. Education: BA, English, Pennsylvania State University, 1970; MFA Creative Writing 1973, MA English 1976, PhD 1978, Cornell University. Appointments include: Writer-in-residence, College of William & Mary 1982, Ohio University 1983, Washington University 1983; Director, Writers programme, Washington University, St Louis, 1984-86; Visiting Writer, Cooper Union 1984, New York University 1986, Columbia University 1986, Cornell 1987, Columbia 1987. Publications: Poetry: Jaguar of Sweet Laughter, 1990; Lady Faustus, 1984; Wife of Light, 1978; The Planets: A Cosmic Pastoral, 1976. Prose: On Extended Wings, 1985, 1987; Twilight of the Tenderfoot, 1980, Reverse Thunder, 1989; A Natural History of the Senses, 1990; The Moon by Whale Light, 1990. Contributions to: Newyorker; Life; New York Times; Parade; National Geographic. Honours include: NEA, 1986; Peter I.B.Lavan Award, Academy of American Poets, 1985; Advisory Board, Planetary Society, 1980-; Board of Directors, Associated Writing Programmes, 1982-85; Poetry panel, NY Foundation for the Arts, 1985. Poetry judge, various awards & festivals; Panellist, various bodies. Literary Agent: Morton Janklow, 598 Madison Avenue, New York, NY 10022.

ACKROYD Peter, b. 5 Oct 1949, London, England. Writer. Education: MA, Cambridge University, 1971; Mellon Fellowship, Yale University, USA, 1971-73; Hon D.Litt, Exeter University, 1992. Appointments: Literary Editor, Spectator, 1973-77; Lead Reviewer, The Times, 1976-. Publications: The Great Fire of London, 1982; The Last Testament of Oscar Wilde, 1983; T.S. Eliot, 1984; Hawksmoor, 1985; Chatterton, 1987; Ezra Pound and His World, 1981; The Diversions of Purley, 1987; First Light, 1989; Dickens, 1990; Introduction to Dickens, 1991; English Music, 1992; The House of Doctor Dee, 1993. Honours: Somerset Maugham Award, 1984; Whitbread Prize for Biography, 1985; Royal Society of Literature's W.E. Heinemann Award, 1985; Whitbread Prize for Fiction, 1986; Guardian Fiction Award, 1986. Memberships: Fellow, Royal Society of Literature. Literary Agent: Anthony Sheil Associates. Address: c/o Anthony Sheill Ltd., 43 Doughty St., London WC1N 2LF, England.

ACKROYD Peter (Runham), b. 1917. Appointments: Samuel Davidson Professor of Old Testament Studies, 1961-82; Professor Emeritus, 1982, Dean, Faculty of Theology, 1968-69, Fellow of King's College, 1969-, University of London; Minister, Roydon Congregational Church, Essex, 1943-47; Minister, Balham Congregational Church, London, 1947-48; Lecturer in Old Testament and Biblical Hebrew, University of Leeds, Yorks, 1948-52; Lecturer in Divinity, Cambridge University, 1952-61; Ordained Anglican Priest, 1958; President, Society for Old Testament Study, 1972. Publications: Freedom in Action, 1951; The People of the Old Testament, 1959; Continuity, 1962; The Old Testament Tradition, 1963; Exile and Restoration, 1968; Words and Meanings, 1968; The Cambridge History of the Bible, 1970; Israel Under Babylon and Persia, 1970 (New Clarendon Bible); The Age of the Chronicler, 1970; I Samuel (Cambridge Bible Commentary), 1971; I and II Chronicles, Ezra, Nehemiah (Torch Bible Commentaries), 1973; II Samuel (Cambridge Bible Commentary), 1977; Doors of Perception, 1978, 1983; Studies in the Religious Tradition of the Old Testament, 1987; The Chronicler in his Age, 1991. Address: 155 Northumberland Road, North Harrow, HA2 7RB, England.

ACLAND Alice (Anne Marreco), b. 1912. Author; Freelance Writer. Publications: Caroline Norton, 1948; Templeford Park. 1954; A Stormy Spring, 1955; A

Second Choice, 1956; A Person of Discretion, 1958; (As Anne Marreco): The Charmer and the Charmed, 1963, The Boat Boy, 1964, The Rebel Countess, 1967; The Corsican Ladies, 1974; The Secret Wife, 1975; The Ruling Passion, 1976. *Address:* c/o Curtis Brown Limited, 162-168 Regent Street, London, W1, England.

ACZEL Tamas, b. 16 Dec 1921, Budapest, Hungary. Novelist; Professor of English. m. 5 Aug 1959, 1 son, 1 daughter. *Education:* BA, University of Budapest, 1948; MA, Eotvos Lorant University, Budapest, 1950; D.Litt, 1992. *Appointments:* Editor in Chief: Szikra, 1948-59, Csillag, 1950-52; Secretary, Hungarian Writers Association, 1953-54; Editor, Hungarian Literary Gazette, London, 1957-63; Profesor, English, University of Massachusetts. *Publications:* Novels: In the Shadow of Liberty, 1948; Storm and Sunshine, 1950; The Revolt of the Mind, 1959; The Ice Age, 1966; Underground Russian Poetry, 1973; Illuminations, 1980; The Hunt, 1991; Poetry: Song on the Ship, 1941; Vigilance and Faith, 1948; In Lieu of a Report, 1950; Flames and Ashes, 1955; On the Secret, 1956. *Contributor to:* Preuves; Encounter; Poesie; Monat; Forum; Massachusetts Review. *Honours:* Kossuth Prize for Literature 1949; Stalin Prize for Literature, 1952; NEA Award, 1977; Fulbright Scholar, Hungary, 1991-92. *Memberships:* Vice President, PEN in Exile, American Branch. *Literary Agents:* The Richard Parks Agency, New York. *Address:* Department of English, University of Massachusetts, Amherst, MA 01003, USA.

ADAIR Ian (Hugh), b. 1942. Writer. *Appointments:* Writer, Partner, Supreme Magic Company, Devon; President, Ideas Associated; Former Television Announcer and Presenter, STV, Westward Television. *Publications:* Adair's Ideas, 1958; Magic with Doves, 1958; Dove Magic, Parts 1 and 2, 1959; Dove Magic Finale, 1960; Ideen, 1960; Television Dove Magic, 1961; Television Card Manipulations, 1962; Television Puppet Magic, 1963; Doves in Magic, 1964; Doves from Silks, 1964; New Doves from Silks, 1964; Dove Classics, 1964; More Modern Dove Classics, 1964; Further Dove Classics, 1964; Classical Dove Secrets, 1964; Diary of a Dove Worker, 1964; Magic on the Wing, 1965; Balloon-o-Dove, 1965; Spotlite on Doves, 1965; Watch the Birdie, 1965; Dove Dexterity, 1965; Rainbow Dove Routines, 1965; Heads Off!, 1965; Tricks and Stunts with a Rubber Dove, 1965; Television Dove Steals, 1965; A La Zombie, 1966; Pot Pourri, 1966; Magical Menu (3 vols), 1967; Encyclopedi of Dove Magic, vols 1 and 2, 1968, vol 3, 1973, vol 4, 1977, vol 5, 1980; Magic with Latex Budgies, 1969; Paddle Antics, 1969; Conjuring as a Craft, 1970; Magic Step by Step, 1970; Party Planning and Entertainment, 1972; Oceans of Notions, 1973; Papercraft-Step by Step, 1975; Card Tricks, 1975; Glove Puppetry, 1975; The Know How Book of Jokes and Tricks, 1977; Complete Party Planner, 1978; Complete Guide to Conjuring, 1978; Magic, 1979; Complete Guide to Card Conjuring, 1980; Swindles: The Cheating Game, 1980. *Address:* 20 Ashley Terrace, Bideford, Devon, England.

ADAIR Jack. *See:* **PAVEY Don.**

ADAIR James R(adford), b. 1923, United States of America. Writer. *Appointments:* Editor, Power for Living, Free Way, Teen Power and Counselor weekly churchpapers, 1949-77; Senior Editor, Victor Books Division, Scripture Press Publications Inc, Wheaton, 1970-. *Publications:* Saints Alive, 1951; Editor, God's Power Within, 1961; We Found Our Way (edited with T. Miller), 1964; Editor, Teen with a Future, 1965; Editor, God's Power to Triumph, 1965; The Old Lighthouse, 1966; The Man from Steamtown, 1967, 1988; Editor, Tom Skinner, Top Man of the Lords and Other Stories, 1967; M.R. DeHaan: The Man and His Ministry, 1969; Editor, Hooked on Jesus, 1971; Escape from Darkness (edited with Ted Miller), 1982; Surgeon on Safari (autobiography, Paul J Jordon, MD), 1976, 1985; A Greater Strength (autobiography, Paul Anderson; co-authored W/Jerry Jenkins), 1975, 1990; 101 Days in the Gospels, Oswald Chambers, compiled with Harry

Verploegh, 1992. *Address:* 703 Webster Avenue, Wheaton, Il 60187, USA.

ADAM Hans Christian, b. 19 May 1948, Bad Munder, Germany. Picture Reseacher. m. Renate Adam-Ellinger, 7 May 1975, 1 son, 1 daughter. *Education:* Diplom Psychologe, 1974. *Publications:* Fruhe Reisen mit Ddr Kamera; Bilder vom Krieg; Reiseerinnerungen von damals; Bretagne; Menschen im Wasser; Wildes Korsika; Malta-Nabel des Meeres; Goldenes Burgund; Hundert Jahre Metall im Bild; Zypern-Insel der Aphrodite Normandie. *Contributions to:* Fotogeschichte (Frankfurt/M.); History of Photography (London); Ausloser; Architecture, Landschafts, Und Reisefotografie; Philippos Margaritis And Some Early Daguerreo Types of Athens. *Memberships:* International Advisory Board, History of Photography quarterly; Deutsche Gesellschaft fur Photographie; European Society for the History of Photography; Daguerreian Society. *Address:* Am Feuerschanzengraben 14, D-37083 Gottingen, Germany.

ADAM Helen. *See:* **JACOBS Barbara.**

ADAM Helen (Douglas), b. 1909. Play, Screen Writer; Poet. *Publications:* The Elfin Pedlar and Tales Told by Pixy Pool, 1923; Charms and Dreams from the Elfin Pedlar's Pack, 1924; Shadow of the Moon, 1929; The Queen o' Crow Castle, 1958; San Francisco's Burning (play with Pat Adam), 1963; Ballads, 1964; Counting-Out Rhyme, 1972; Selected Poems and Ballads, 1974; Ghosts and Grinning Shadows (short stories), 1977; Turn Again to Me and Other Poems, 1977; Gone Sailing, 1980; Songs with Music, 1982; The Bells of Dis, 1984; Stone Cold Gothic (with Auste Adam), 1984.

ADAM-SMITH Patricia Jean. *See:* **ADAM-SMITH Patsy.**

ADAM-SMITH Patsy (Patricia Jean Adam-Smith), b. 1924, Australia. Author. *Appointments:* Adult Education Officer, Hobart, Tasmania, 1960-66; Manuscripts Field Officer, State Library of Victoria, 1970-82; President, Federal Fellowship of Australian Writers, 1973-75. *Publications:* Hear the Train Blow, 1963; Moon-Bird People, 1964; There was a Ship, 1965; Tiger Country, 1966; The Rails Go Westward, 1967; Folklore of Australia's Railmen, 1969; No Tribesmen, 1970; Tasmania Sketchbook, 1972; Launceston Sketchbook, 1972; Port Arthur Sketchbook, 1973; Barcoo Salute, 1973; The Desert Railway, 1974; Romance of Australian Railways, 1974; The Anzacs, 1978; Outback Heroes, 1981; The Shearers, 1982; Australian Women at War, 1984; Heart of Exile, 1986; Prisoner of War from Gallipoli to Korea, 1992. *Honour:* OBE; Winner of Triennial award, Order of Australia Association for Prisoners of War from Gallipoli to Korea. *Address:* 47 Hawksburn Road, South Yarra, Victoria 3141, Australia.

ADAMS Alice, b. 1926. Author. *Publications:* Careless Love (in United Kingdom as The Fall of Daisy Duke), 1966; Families and Survivors, 1975; Listening to Billie, 1978; Beautiful Girl (short stories), 1979; Tich Rewards, 1980; Superior Women, 1984. *Address:* 2661 Clay Street, San Francisco, CA 94115, USA.

ADAMS Chuck. *See:* **TUBB E C.**

ADAMS Clifton (Jonathan Gant, Matt Kinkaid, Clay Randall), b. 1919. Author; Musician; Freelance Writer. *Publications:* Western Novels: The Desperado, 1950; A Noose for the Desperado, 1951; Six Gun Boss (As Clay Randall), 1952; The Colonel's Lady, 1952; When Oil Ran Red (As Clay Randall), 1953; Two Gun Law, 1954; Gambling Man, 1955; Law of the Trigger, 1956; Outlaw's Son, 1957; Boomer, (as Clay Randall), 1957; Killer in Town, 1959; Stranger in Town, 1960; The Legend of Lonnie Hall, 1960; Day of the Gun, 1962;

Reckless Men, 1962; The Moonlight War, 1963; The Dangerous Days of Kiowa Jones, 1963; The Oceola Kid (As Clay Randall), 1963; Hardcase for Hire, (As Clay Randall), 1963; Amos Flagg Series, 6 vols (As Clay Randall), 1963-69; Doomsday Creek, 1964; The Hottest Fourth of July in the History of Hangtree County, 1964, (in United Kingdom as The Hottest Fourth of July, 1965); The Grabhorn Bounty, 1965; Shorty, 1966; A Partnership with Death, 1867; The Most Dangerous Profession, 1967; Dude Sheriff, 1969; Tragg's Choice, 1969; The Last Days of Wolf Garnett, 1970, (in United Kingdom as Outlaw Destiny, 1972); Biscuit-Shooter, 1971; Rogue Cowboy, 1971; The Badge and Harry Cole, 1972, (in United Kingdom as Lawman's Badge, 1973); Concannon, 1972; Hard Times and Arnie Smith, 1972; Once an Outlaw, 1973; The Hard Time Bunch, 1973; Hasle and the Medicine Man, 1973; Crime Novels: Whom Gods Destroy, 1953; Hardcase (As Matt Kinkaid), 1953; Death's Sweet Song, 1955; The Race of Giants (As Matt Kinkaid), 1956; Never Say No to a Killer (as Jonathan Gant), 1956; The Very Wicked, 1960; The Long Vendetta (As Jonathan Gant), 1963. *Address:* c/o Ace Books, Berkeley Publishing Group, 200 Madison Avenue, New York, NY 10016, USA.

ADAMS Daniel. *See:* **NICOLE Christopher Robin.**

ADAMS Deborah, b. 22 Jan 1956, Tennessee, USA. Writer. *Publications:* Poetry: Propriety, 1976; Looking for Heroes, 1984; Mystery: All the Great Pretenders, 1992; All the Crazy Winters, 1992; All the Dark Disguises, 1993; All the Hungry Mothers, 1994. *Memberships:* Sisters in Crime; MWA; Appalachian Writers' Association. *Address:* Rt 4, Box 664, Waverly, TN 37185, USA.

ADAMS Douglas (Noel), b. 11 March 1952. Writer; Producer. *Education:* BA, MA, St John's College, Cambridge. *Appointments:* Radio Producer, BBC, London, 1978; Script Editor, Doctor Who, BBC-TV, London, 1978-80. *Publications:* The Hitch Hiker's Guide to the Galaxy, radio series, 1978, novel, 1979; The Restaurant at the End of the Universe, 1980; Life, The Universe and Everything, 1982; The Meaning of Liff (with John Lloyd), 1984; So Long, and Thanks for All the Fish, 1984; The original Hitch Hiker Radio Scripts, 1985; The Utterly Utterly Merry, 1986; Comic Relief Christmas Book (co-author), 1986. Dirk Gently's Holistic Dectective Agency, 1987; The Long Dark Tea-Time of the Soul, 1988; Last Chance to See, 1990; The Deeper Meaning of Liff, 1990; Mostly Harmless, 1991. *Address:* c/o Ed Victor Limited, 162 Wardour Street, London, W1V 3AT, England.

ADAMS Harold, b. 20 Feb 1923, Clard, South Dakota, USA. Executive. m. Betty E Skossbergh, 17 Sept 1959 (div April 1965), 1 daughter. *Education:* BA, University of Minnesota, 1950. *Publications:* Murder, 1981; Paint the Town Red, 1982; The Missing Moon, 1983; The Naked Liar, 1985; The Fourth Widow, 1986; When Rich Men Die, 1987; The Barbed Wire Noose, 1987; The Man Who Met The Train, 1988; The Man Who Missed The Party, 1989; The Man Who Was Taller Than God, 1992. *Memberships:* Author's Guild; Mystery Writers of America. *Literary Agent:* Ivy Fischer Stone. *Address:* 12916 Greenwood Road, Hopkins, MN 55343, USA.

ADAMS Hazard, b. 15 Feb 1926, Cleveland, Ohio, USA. University Professor. m. 17 Sept 1949, 2 sons. *Education:* BA, Princeton University, 1948, MA 1949, PhD 1953, University of Washington. *Appointments:* Instructor, Cornell University, 1952-56; Assistant Professor, University of Texas, 1956-59; Associate Professor to Professor, Michigan State University, 1959-64; Professor and Founding Chair of English, University of California, Irvine, 1964-77; Byron W and Alice L Lockwood Professor of Humanities, University of Washington 1977-; Fulbright Lecturer, Trinity College, Dublin, 1961-62; Professor of English, University of California, Irvine, 1990-. *Publications include:* (ed) poems by Robert Simeon Adams, 1952; Blake and Yeats: The Contrary Vision, 1955; William Blake - A Reading,

1963; The Contexts of Poetry, 1963; Poetry: An Introductory Anthology, 1968; (ed) Fiction as Process, 1968; The Horses of Instruction (novel), 1968; The Interests of Criticism, 1969; The Truth About Dragons (novel), 1971; (ed) Critical Theory Since Plato, 1972 (rev ed 1992); Lady Gregory, 1973; Philosophy of the Literary Symbolic, 1983; The Book of Yeats' Poems, 1990; Antithetical Essays on literary Criticism and Liberal Education, 1990; (ed) Critical Essays on William Blake. *Contributor to:* Numerous scholarly and critical journals, 1954-. *Memberships:* American Society of Aesthetics, American Conference for Irish Studies; Society for Critical Exchange. *Address:* 3930 N E 157th Place, Seattle, WA 98155, USA.

ADAMS Henry, b. 12 May 1949, Boston, Mass. Museum Curator; Teacher; Writer. m. Marianne Berardi, 15 Apr 1992. *Education:* Harvard University, BA, 1971; Yale University, MA, 1977; PhD, 1980. *Appointments:* Samuel Sosland Curator of American Art, Nelson atkins Museum of Art; Adjunct Professor, University of Kansas; Adjunct Professor, University of Missouri Kansas City. *Publications:* Thomas Hart Benton, An American Original; Thomas Hart Benson, Drawing From Life; American Paintings; John La Farge; American Drawings & Watercolours; Over 100 Scholarly Articles. *Contributions to:* Smithsonian; The Burlington Magazine. *Honours:* Frances Blanshard Proze; Arthur Kingsley Prize; William F Yates Distinguished Service Medallion. *Memberships:* Massachusetts Historical Society; College Art Association; Association of American Museums; Midwest Art History Society; association of Historians of American Art. *Address:* Nelson Atkins Museum of Art, 4525 Oak Street, Kansas City, MO 64111, USA.

ADAMS Jack, b. 15 Sept 1952, Lakehurst, New Jersey, USA. Screenwriter; Producer; Director; Educator. m. Shirley Janulewicz, 28 June 1975, 2 sons, 2 daughters. *Education:* MusB in Music Education 1974, University of Delaware. *Appointments:* President, Koala Studio, Valencia 1977-; Vice President Development, Unifilms Inc, North Hollywood 1984-; Co-Founder, ScripTip, 1990; Instructor, Film, TV Writing and Script Analysis: College of the Canyons, Valencia 1988-; LA City College 1989-; Every Woman's Village, Van Nuys Info Exchange, LA, Learning Tree University, Chatsworth, Info Network, S Pasadena 1990-; University of Wisconsin-Madison, USIA, Washington DC, Moorpark College, Oxnard College, Northwestern University, Classes Unlimited, S Pasadena, Glendale Community College 1991-; University of Hawaii 1992-; Founding Member, Board of Directors, LA Filmmakers Workshop 1989-91; Founder, Santa Clarita Scriptwriters' Workshop; Member, Larry Wilson Development Workshop, Paramount Studios; Member, Storyboard Development Group, Paramount Studios, 1989-, Le Group; President, Entertainment Writers' Workshop, 1990; President, NBC Writers' Workshop; Member, KNX Speakers Bureau, CBS Radio, 1989-; Member, Independent Feature Project West. *Publications:* Composer, film, EAT, 1980; Writer, Co-Creator, sitcom pilot Lola, Universal Studios, 1991; Writer, Developer, sitcom pilot Fat Farm; Writer, Producer, Director, sitcom pilot Box 22; Line Producer, sitcom pilots Zebra and It's Not My Fault. *Memberships:* American Film Institute, Alumni Association Writers Workshop; Scriptwriters' Network, Board of Advisors; Film Artists' Network; Independent Writers of Southern California Scriptwriters' Caucus; Association of Information Systems Professionals, Board 1983; Freelance Screenwriters' Forum, Founding Board, TV Editor, FFS Newsletter 1990-; Columnist, Screenwrite New magazine 1991-; Comedy Writers Co-op, Founding ABC; Wisconsin Screenwriters Forum, Consultant, Advisor 1989-. *Address:* 22931 Sycamore Creek Drive, Santa Clarita, CA 91354, USA.

ADAMS James MacGregor David, b. 22 April 1951, Newcastle, England. Journalist; Author. m. Rene Thatcher Riley, 1 July 1990, 1 daughter. *Education:* Harrow, 1964-69; Neuchatel Univerity, 1970-71. *Publictions:* The Unnatural Alliance, 1984; The

Financing of Terror, 1986; Secret Armies, 1988; Ambush (the War Between the SAS and the IRA) with Robin Morgan and Anthony Bambridge, 1988; Merchants of Death, 1990; The Final Terror, 1991; Bull's Eye, 1992; Taking the Tunnel, 1993. *Contributions to:* The Sunday Times; Washington Post; Los Angeles Times; Atlantic. *Literary Agent:* Janklow Nesbit. *Address:* c/o The Sunday Times, 1 Pennington Street, London E1 9XW, England.

ADAMS John Kenneth, b. 3 June 1915. Editor, Country Life. m. Margaret, 1944. *Education:* Balliol College, Oxford. *Appointments:* Assistant Master, Stonyhurst College, 1939-40; Served with RAFVR, 1940-41 (invalided); Assistant Master, Wellington College, 1941-44; attached to Manchester Guardian as Leader Writer, 1942-44; Leader-Writer, The Scotsman, 1944-46; joined Editorial Staff, Country Life 1946, Assistant Editor, 1952, Deputy Editor, 1956, Editor 1958-73, Editorial Director, 1959-73. *Address:* 95 Alleyn Park, West Dulwich, London, SE21 8AA, England.

ADAMS Richard George, b. 9 May 1920, Newbury, Berkshire, England. Author. m. Barbara Elizabeth Acland, 26 Sept 1949, 2 daughters. *Education:* MA, Worcester College, Oxford, 1948. *Publications:* Watership Down, 1972; Shardik, 1974; The Plague Dogs, 1977; The Girl in a Swing, 1980; Maia, 1984; Nature through the Seasons; The Tyger Voyage (narrative poem), 1976; The Ship's Cat, (narrative poem), 1977; Nature Day and Night, 1978; The Iron Wolf, (anthology of short stories), 1980; Voyage Through the Antarctic, 1982; Maia, 1984; The Bureaucats, 1985; A Nature Diary, 1985; Traveller, 1988; The Day Gone By, (autobiography) 1990; Editor, Contributor to, Occasional Poems, 1986; The Legend of Te Tuna, (narrative poem) 1986; Traveller, 1988. *Contributions to:* numerous journals and magazines. *Honours:* Carnegie Medal, 1972; Guardian Award of Children's Literature, 1972; Medal, California Young Readers Association, 1977. *Memberships:* Fellow, Royal Society of Literature; RSPCA, President 1980-82. *Literary Agent:* David Higham Associates Limited. *Address:* Benwell's, 26 Church Street, Whitchurch, Hants RG28 7AR, England.

ADAMSON Donald, b. 30 Mar 1939, Culcheth, Cheshire, England. Author; Bookdealer. m. Helen Freda Griffiths, 24 Sept 1966, 2 sons. *Education:* Magdalen College, Oxford, 1956-59; University of Paris, 1960-61; MA, 1963; MLitt, 1979; DPhil, 1971. *Publications:* The Genesis of 'Le Cousin Pons', 1966; (trans) The Black Sheep by Balzac, 1970; The House of Nell Gwyn (co-author), 1974; Balzac: Illusions Perdues, 1981; (ed) T S Eliot: A Memoir by R Sencourt; Two translations of Balzac novels; Various publications on museums. *Contributions to:* Various magazines and journals. *Honours:* Chevalier de L'Ordre des Palmes Academiques, 1986; Justice of the Peace, City of London, 1983; Visiting Fellow, Wolfson College, Cambridge, 1989-90. *Memberships:* Fellow, Royal Society of Literature; PEN. *Literary Agent:* Watson, Little Limited. *Address:* Dodmore House, The Street, Meopham, Kent DA13 0AJ, England.

ADAMSON Iain, b. 22 Aug 1928, Strathclyde, Scotland. Author; Principal, London Art College. *Education:* Glasgow Academy, Scotland; Institute of Political Science, University of Paris, France. Winner of Open Scholarship. *Appointments:* Served with Seaforth Highlanders, Malay Regiment, 1st/2nd Gurka Rifles, Malaya, 1947-48. *Publications include:* The Old Fox; The Forgotten Men; A Man of Quality; The Great Detective; The Promised Messiah; A Man of God; Profitable Art. *Contributor to:* Numerous papers and magazines in UK, USA, Canada, Australia; TV Spokesman, Reporter, Farming News; Scottish Daily Express; Sunday Express; Daily Mirror; Daily Express; Santa Monica Outlook, Los Angeles, USA; Foreign Correspondent, France, Spain, Germany, USA, Mexico, India, Pakistan. *Address:* Iain Adamson & Partners, PO Box 934, Bristol, BS99 5PR, England.

ADAMSON Robert, b. 17 May 1943, Sydney, New South Wales, Australia. Publisher; Designer; Writer. m. Cheryl Adamson, 1973. *Appointments:* Worked as a pastry cook, fisherman and journalist in the 1960's; Associate Editor, 1968-70, Editor 1970-75 and Assistant Editor 1975- 77, New Poetry magazine, Sydney; Editor and Director, Prism Books, Sydney 1970-77; Founding Editor and Director, with Dorothy Hewett, Big Smoke Books, Sydney, 1979-; Designer for Prism Books and New Poetry magazine, 1970-; Designer for Big Smoke Books, 1979-. *Publications:* Verse: Canticles on the Skin, 1970; The Rumour, 1971; Swamp Riddles, 1974; Theatre I-XIX, 1976; Cross the Border, 1977; Selected Poems, 1977; Where I Come From, 1979; The Law at Heart's Desire, 1982. Novel: Zimmer's Essay, with Bruce Hanford, 1974. *Honours:* Australia Council fellowship, 1976, 1977; Grace Leven Prize, 1977. *Address:* Big Smoke Books, 1/2 Billyard Avenue, Elizabeth Bay, NSW 2011, Australia.

ADAMSSON Slade. See: **KOWALCZYK David Theodore.**

ADCOCK Fleur, b. 1934, New Zealand. Poet. *Publications:* The Eye of the Hurricane, 1964; Tigers, 1967; High Tide in the Garden, 1971; The Scenic Route, 1974; The Inner Harbour, 1979; Below Loughrigg, 1979; Editor, The Oxford Book of Contemporary New Zealand Poetry, 1982; Selected Poems, 1983; The Virgin and the Nightingale: Medieval Latin Poems, 1983; The Incident Book, 1986; Editor, The Faber Book of 20th Century Women's Poetry, 1987; Time-Zones, 1991. *Membership:* F.R.S.L. *Address:* 14 Lincoln Road, London, N2 9DL, England.

ADDINGTON Arthur Charles, b. 1939. Genealogist. *Publications:* Royal House of Stuart: The Descendants of King James VI of Scotland, James I of England, vol 1, 1969, vol II, 1971, vol III, 1975, (Editor); The Lineage and Ancestry of H.R.H. Prince Charles, Prince of Wales, by Gerald Paget, 2 vols, 1977; (with Zenaide Burke) Origine et Famille de Felix Nicolaievitch Elston, Comte Soumarokov-Elston, 1983. *Address:* 6 Fairfield Close, Harpenden, Herts, England.

ADDINGTON Larry Holbrook, b. 1932, United States of America. Writer; Historian. *Appointments:* Assistant Professor of History, 1962- 64; San Jose State College. Consultant to the Institute of Advanced Studies, U.S.Army War College, Carlisle, 1968-69; Assiociate Professor, Professor of History, The Citadel, 1970-; Head, History Department, The Citadel, 1989-, The Military College of South Carolina, Charleston, 1964-; Visiting Professor, Duke University, 1976-77. *Publications:* From Moltke to Hitler: The Evolution of German Military Doctrine, 1865-1939, 1967; The Blitzkrieg Era and the German General Staff, 1865-1941, 1971; The Patterns of War since the 18th Century, 1984; The Patterns of War through the Eighteenth Century, 1990. *Address:* History Department, The Citadel, Charleston, SC 29409, USA.

ADELBERG Doris. See: **ORGEL Doris.**

ADES Dawn, b. 1943. Art Historian. *Appointment:* Professor the Department of Art History and Theory, University of Essex, Colchester, 1968-. *Publications:* Dada and Surrealism, 1974; Photomontage, 1976; Dada and Surrealism Reviewed, 1978; Salvador Dali, 1982, The Twentieth Century Poster: Design of the Avant Garde, 1984, Art in Latin America the Modern era 1820-1980, 1989. *Address:* Department of Art History and Theory, University of Essex, Wivenhoe Park, Colchester, Essex, England.

ADHIKARI Santos Kumar, b. 24 Nov 1923, India. Writer; Author; Retired College Principal. m. Sadhona. *Education:* Calcutta University; Associate, Indian Institute of Bankers; Diplomas, Industrial Finance, Management. *Appointments include:* Vidyasager Lecturer, University of Calcutta. *Publications include:*

Ekla Chalo Re (Go Thou Alone), 1948; Clouds on the Horizon, 1960; At Some Other Domain, 1973; Blossoms in the Dust, 1980. Novels: Rakta Kamal, 1967; Nirjan Sikhar, 1971. 4 books, Benghali essays: Adhunik Manasikata D.Vidyasagar, 1984; Vidyasagar; Saheed Jatin Vas O Bharater Bipab Andolan; Santarasbad & Bhagat Singh (in English). Also: Vidyasagar & the Regeneration of Bengal; Banking Law & Practice; Lending Banker; Editor, Spark, anthology of Indian poetry in English; Paari, collection of poems, 1986. Contributions to: Major journals, Calcutta; All India Radio, Calcutta. Honours include: PRASAD Award, poetry, 1986. Memberships: Former Honorary Secretary, West Bengal Branch, PEN; Honorary General Secretary, Vidyasagar Research Centre; Asiatic Society, Calcutta. Address: Vidyasagar Research Centre, 81 Raja Basanta Roy Road, Calcutta 700 029, India.

ADISA Opal Palmer, b. 6 Nov 1954, Kingston, Jamaica. Teacher. m. V. K Tarik Farrar, 12 Aug 1989, 1 son, 2 daughters. Education: BA, Hunter College, City of New York University, 1975; MA, English, San Francisci State University, 1981; MA, Drama, 1986; PhD, University of California, 1992. Appointments: Head Teacher, Booker T Washington Child Development center, San Francisco, 1978-79; Teacher, Counselor, Lucinda Weeks Center, San Francisco, 1979-81; Instructor, City College of San Francisco, 1980-84; Lecturer, San francisco State University, 1981-87; Writer, Developmental Studies Center, San Ramon, CA, 1991; Lecturer, University of California, Berkeley, 1992. Publications: Tamarind & Mango Women; Traveling Women; Bake Face & Other Guava Stories; Pina The Many Eyed Fruit; Essays inc, Womens Studies International Forum; This Poem Knows You; Book Reviews inc, The Maidu Indian Myths & Stories of Hanc'ibyim; This Childs Gonna Live; No Telephone to Heaven. Contributions to: Fronters; The Berkeley Poetry Review. Honours include: Master Folk Artist; Push Cart prize; Affirmative Action Dissertation Year Fellowship; Merit Certificate; Bronze Medal; Feminist Institute & Gender Study Research Grant; Winner, PEN Oakland/ Josephine Miles Award for Tamarind and Mango Women. Memberships: Modern Language Association; The Society for the Study of Multi Ethnic Literature of the United States; Diasponic Represtative of CAFRA. Address: PO Box 10625, Oakland, CA 94610, USA.

ADKINS Arthur William Hope, b. 1929. Appointments: Assistant, Humanity Department, University of Glasgow, 1954-56; Lecturer in Greek, Bedford College, University of London, 1956-61; Fellow, Classical Languages and Literature, Exeter College, Oxford, 1961-65; Professor of Classics, University of Reading, 1966-74; Visiting Senior Fellow, Society for the Humanities, Cornell University, Ithaca, New York, 1969-70; Edward Olson Professor, Depts of Classical Languages, Literature, Philosophy and Early Christian Literature; Chairman, Committee on Ancient Mediterranean World, University of Chiacgo, 1974-82. Publications: Merit and Responsibility: A Study in Greek Values, 1960; From the Many to the One: A Study of Personality and Views of Human Nature in the Context of Ancient Greek Society, Values and Beliefs, 1970; Moral Values and Political Behaviour in Ancient Greece, 1972; Poetic Craft in the Early Greek Elegists, 1985; Joint Editor, University of Chicago, Readings in Western Civilization, Vol I, The Greek Polis. Memberships: American Philological Association; Classical Association of Great Britain; Society, Promotion of Hellenic Studies; American Philosophical Association. Address: Department of Classics, University of Chicago, 1050 E 59th Street, Chicago, IL 60637, USA.

ADKINS Patrick H, b. 9 Jan 1948, New Orleans, Louisiana, USA. Technical Writer and Editor; Novelist. m. Dixie Wagoner, 28 Dec 1971, 2 sons, 1 daughter. Education: Attended University of New Orleans, 1966-70. Appointments: Technical Editor, Naval Biodynamics Laboratory, New Orleans, Louisiana 1990-; Mail Order Specialty Bookseller, PDA Enterprises, New Orleans, Louisiana, 1971-82; Purchasing and Inventory Manager, Midland Inc, New Orleans, 1983-88; Security

Guard 1976-83; Editor and Publisher of small press science fiction and fantasy books, 1977-80. Publications: Novels: Lord of the Crooked Paths, 1987; Master of the Fearful Depths, 1989; Sons of the Titans, 1990. Work represented in anthologies, including Chrysalis 9, edited by Roy Torgeson, 1981. Literary Agent: Ralph M Vicinanza Ltd, New York. Address: c/o Ralph M Vicinanza Ltd, 111 Eighth Avenue S, Suite 1501, New York, NY 10011, USA.

ADLER C S. See: **ADLER Carole.**

ADLER Carole, (C S Adler), b. 23 Feb 1932, Long Island, New York, USA. Children's Book Author. m. Arnold R Adler, 22 June 1952, 3 sons. Education: BA 1952, Hunter College; MS 1964, Russell Sage College. Publications: The Magic of the Glits, 1979; The Silver Coach, 1979; In Our House Scott is My Brother, 1980; The Cat That Was Left Behind, 1981; Down By the River, 1981; Shelter on Blue Barns Road, 1981; Footsteps on the Stairs, 1982; The Evidence That Wasn't There, 1982; The Once in a While Hero, 1982; Some Other Summer, 1982; The Shell Lady's Daughter, 1983; Get Lost Little Brother, 1983; Roadside Valentine, 1983; Shadows on Little Reef Bay, 1984; Fly Free, 1984; Binding Ties, 1985; With Westie and the Tin Man, 1985; Good-Bye Pink Pig, 1985; Split Sisters, 1986; Kiss The Clown, 1986; Cary's Buck, 1987; Always and Forever Friends, 1988; If You Need Me, 1988; Eddie's Blue Winged Dragon, 1988; One Sister Too Many, 1989; The Lump in the Middle, 1989; Help, Pink Pig!, 1990; Ghost Brother, 1990; Mismatched Summer, 1991; A Tribe for Lexi, 1991; Tuna Fish Thanksgiving, 1992; Daddy's Climbing Tree, 1993; Willie, the Frog Prince, forthcoming. Honours: William Allen White Award and the Golden Kite Award for The Magic of the Glits; The Shell Lady's Daughter chosen by ALA as Best Young Adult Book of 1984; With Westie and the Tin Man won the Children's Book Award of the Child Study Committee in 1986; That committee has commended several of her books; Split Sisters in 1987 and Ghost Brother in 1991 were IRA Children's Choices selections; One Sister Too Many was on 1991 Young Adults' Choices list; Always and Forever Friends and Eddie's Blue Winged Dragon were on a 1991 IRA 99 Favourite Paperbacks List; Many of her books have been on state lists; She has been widely published in Japan, Germany, England, Denmark, Austria, Sweden and Norway. Memberships: SCBW; Authors Guild. Address: 1350 Ruffner Road, Schenectady, NY 12309, USA.

ADLER Joyce, (Joyce Sparer Adler), b. 2 Dec 1915, New York City. USA. Teacher; Writer; Critic. m. Irving Adler, 16 Sept 1968, 2 daughters. Education: BA, Brooklyn College, City University of New York, 1935; MA, 1951. Appointments: Teacher, English public High Schools, NYC, 1940-54; Acting Chairman, Dept of English, 1950-52; Editor Blood Journal Hematology, NYC, 1954-55; Teacher, English, 1956-63; Teacher, English, Ramaz High School, NYC, 1960-63; Founding Member, University Guyana, Georgetown, 1963-68; Professor, Literature, 1963- 68; Editor, University Newsletter, 1964-68. Publications include: War in Melvilles Imagination; Attitudes Towards 'Race' in Guyanese Literature; Langauage and Man; Essays on Wilson Harris & Melville; Dramatization of Three Melville Novels: with an Introduction on Dramatization as Criticism, 1991. Contributions to include: Essays, PMLA Journal of Commonwealth Literature; American Literature. Honours: National Second Prize Award by National Council of Teachers of English; Fellow of The Vermont Academy of Arts & Science. Memberships: Modern Language Association of America; President, Melville Society, 1988; Commonwealth Literature Association; American Literature Association; Vermont Association of arts & Science; Teachers Union. Address: RR1 Box 532, North Bennington, VT 05257, USA.

ADLER Joyce Sparer. See: **ADLER Joyce.**

ADLER Margot Susanna, b. 16 Apr 1946, Little Rock, Arkansas, USA. Journalist; Radio Producer; Talk Show

Host. *Education:* BA, University of California, Berkeley, 1968; MS, Columbia School of Journalism, 1970; Nieman Fellow, Harvard University, 1982. *Publication:* Drawing Down the Moon: Witches, Druids, Goddess-Worshippers & Other Pagans in America Today, 1979, paperback 1981, revised 1986. *Memberships:* Authors Guild; AFTRA. *Literary Agent:* Jane Rotrosen. *Address:* 333 Central Park West, New York, NY 10025, USA.

ADLER Mortimer J(erome), b. 1902, United States of America. Writer. *Appointments:* Director, Institute for Philosohical Research, Chicago, 1952-; Editor, The Great Ideas Today series, 1962-; Gateway to the Great Books series, 1963-; The Annals of America series, 1968-; Chairman, Board of Editors, 1974-, Editor-in-Chief, Great Books of the Western World (2nd edition), 1990-. Encyclopaedia Britannica, Chicago; Secretary to Editor, New York Sun, 1915-17. *Publications include:* Dialectic, 1927; Crime, Law and Social Science (with Jerome Michael), 1933; Art and Prudence: A Study in Practical Philosophy, 1937 revised edition as Poetry and Politics, 1965; What Man Has Made of Man, 1937; Problems for Thomists: The Problem of Species, 1940; How To Read a Book: The Art of Getting a Liberal Education, 1940, revised edition with Charles Van Doren, 1972; The Difference of Man and the Difference It Makes, 1967; The Idea of Freedom, 2 vols., 1958; 1961; Some Questions About Language: A Theory of Human Discourse, 1976; Philosopher at Large: An Intellectual Autobiography, 1977; The Common Sense of Politics, 1971; Aristotle for Everybody, 1978; Six Great Ideas, 1981; Ten Philosophicl Mistakes, 1985; A Guidebook to Learning: For the Lifelone Pursuit of Wisdom, 1986; We Hold These Truths: Understanding the Ideas and Ideals of the Constitution, 1987; Reforming Education, 1989; Intellect: Mind over Matter, 1990; Truth in Religion, 1990; Haves Without Have-Nots, 1991; Desires, Right and Wrong, 1991; A Second Look in the Rearview Mirror, 1992; The Great Ideas: A Lexicon of Western Thought, 1992. *Address:* Institute for Philosophical Research, 101 E. Ontario Street, Chicago, IL 60611, USA.

ADLER Renata, b. 1938. United States of America. Writer. *Appointments:* Writer, Reporter, The New Yorker, since 1963. *Publications:* Toward a Radical Middle: Fourteen Pieces of Reporting and Criticism, 1970; A Year in the Dark: Journal of a Film Critic 1968-69, 1970; Speedboat, 1976; Pitch Dark (novel), 1984; Reckless Disregard: Westmoreland v. CBS et al., Sharon v. Time, 1986. *Memberships:* Member Editorial Board., American Scholar, 1968-73; PEN. Executive Board, 1964-70; Judge in arts and letters, National Book Awards, 1969; Fellow, Trumbull Coll., Yale University, 1969-72. *Address:* c/o The New Yorker, 25 West 43rd St., New York, NY 10036, USA.

ADLER Warren, b. 16 Dec 1927. New York City, USA. Novelist; Playwright; Lyricist; Screenwriter. m. Sonia Kline, 5 May 1951, 3 sons. *Education:* Ba, New York University. *Appointments:* Chairman of Board, Washington Dossier Magazine. *Publications:* The War of the Roses; The Sunset Gang; Trans-siberian Express; The Housewife Blues; Private Lies; Others inc, Thw Witch of Watergate; Banguest Before Dawn; Twilight Child; Random Hearts; Senator Love. *Contributions to:* Rescuing David From the Moonies. *Memberships:* Authors Guild; Mysters Writers of America. *Literary Agent:* Peter Lampack. *Address:* 45 Huckleberry Drive, Jackson Hole, WY 83001, USA.

ADNAN Etel, b, 24 Feb 1925, Bey South, USA. Poet; Writer; Painter. *Education:* Liecence es Lettres, Lyon University, France, 1949; University of Paris, France, 1950; University of California, Berkeley, 1955-57; Harvard University, USA, 1957-58. *Publications:* Sitt Marie Role; Ine Indian Never Had a Horse; Journey to Mount Tamalpais; The Arab A Pocalypse; Th Sprint Flowers Own & The Manifestations of the Voyage; From A to Z; Moonshots. *Contributions to:* Quixate; S B Gazette; Mawakig Karmel; AVEC. *Address:* 35 Marie Street, Sausalito, CA 94965, USA.

ADOFF Arnold, b. 1935. Writer; Poet. *Appointments:* Teacher, New York Public Schools, 1957-69; Literary Agent, Yellow Springs, Ohio, 1977-. *Publications:* Poetry for Children: MAnDA LA, 1971; Black Is Brown Is Tan, 1973; Make a Circle, Keep Us In: Poems for a Good Day, 1975; My Sister Tells Me That I'm Black, 1976; Tornado, 1977; Under the Early Morning Trees, 1978; Where Wild Willy, 1978; Eats, 1979; I Am the Running Girl, 1979; Friend Dog, 1980; Today We Are Brother and Sister, 1981; OUTside INside Poems, 1981; Birds, 1982; All the Colors of the Race, 1982; The Cabbages are Chasing the Rabbits; 1985; Sports Pages; 1986; Green: Poems; 1988; Chocolate Dreams; 1989; Hard T Be Six; 1991; In for Winter, Out for Spring; 1991; other: Malcolm X, 1970; Flamboyan; 1988. Editor: I am the Darker Brother: An Anthology of Modern Poems by Negro Americans, 1968; Black on Black: Commentaries by Negro Americans, 1968; City in All Directions: An Anthology of Modern Poems, 1969; Black Out Loud: An Anthology of Modern Poems by Black Americans, 1970; Brothers and Sisters: Modern Stories by Black Americns, 1970; It Is the Poem Singing into Your Eyes: An Anthology of New Young Poets, 1971; The Poetry of Black America: An Anthology of the 20th Century, 1973; My Black Me: A Beginning Book of Black Poetry, 1974; Celebrations: A New Anthology of Black American Poetry, 1977. *Address:* Box 293, Yellow Springs, OH 45387, USA.

ADORJAN Carol (Kate Kenyon), b. 17 Aug 1934, Chicago, Illinois, USA. Writer; Teacher. m. William W. Adorjan, 17 Aug 1957, 2 sons, 2 daughters. *Education:* BA, English Literature, Magna Cum Laude, Mundelein College, 1956. *Appointments:* Fellow, Midwest Playwrights Lab, 1977; Writer in Residence, Illinois Arts Council, 1981; Writer in Residence, National Radio Theatre, 1980-81. *Publications:* Someone I Know, 1968; The Cat Sitter Mystery, 1972; Eighth Grade to the Rescue (as Kate Kenyon), 1987; A Little Princess (abridgment), 1987; Those Crazy Eighth Grade Pictures (as Kate Kenyon), 1987; WKID: Easy Radio Plays, (co Author: Yupi Rasovsky), 1988; The Copy Cat Mystery, 1990; Thats What Friends Are For, 1990; Radio & Stage Plays: Julian Theater, BBC, National Radio Theatre, etc. *Contributor to:* Redbook; Woman's Day; North American Review; Denver Quarterly; Four Quarters; Yankee; etc. *Honours:* Josephine Lusk Fiction Award, Munderlein, 1955; Earplay, 1972; Illinois Arts Council Completion Grant, 1977-78; Dubuque Fine Arts Society National One-Act Playwriting competition, 1978; Ohio State Award, 1980. *Memberships:* Dramatists Guild; Society of Midland Authors; Poets & Writers; Children's Reading Roundtable. *Literary Agent:* Denise Marcil; Shelly Power (Abroad). *Address:* 812 Rosewood Ave, Winnetka, IL 60093, USA.

ADRIAN Arthur Allen, b. 1906, United States of America. Writer. *Appointments:* English Teacher, High Schools in Kansas, 1929-35; Instructor in English, University of Kansas, Lawrence, 1935-39, Oregon State College, 1940-44; Assistant Professor of English, 1946-51, Associate Professor, 1951-61; Professor, 1962-74, Professor Emeritus, 1974-, Case Western Reserve University, Cleveland, Ohio. *Publications:* Georgina Hogarth and the Dickens Circle, 1957; Mark Lemon: First Editor of Punch, 1965; Charles Dickens and the Parent-Child Relationship, 1984. *Address:* 1099 Mount Vernon Boulevard, Cleveland Heights, OH 44112, USA.

ADRIAN Frances. *See:* **POLLAND Madeleine Angela.**

AFRICANO Lillian (Nora Ashby, Lila Cook, Jessica March), b. 7 June 1935, USA. Author; Columnist. divorced. 2 sons, 1 daughter. *Education:* BA, summa cum laude, Barnard College, 1953-57; Columbia University Graduate School, 1958. *Literary Appointments:* Arts Editor, The Villager, 1971; News Editor, Penthouse/Forum, 1973; Columist, New York Times Syndicate, 1977; Columnist, Woman's World, 1980. *Publications:* Businessman's Guide to the Middle East, 1977; Doctor's Walking Book (co-authored), 1980; Something Old, Something New, 1983; Passions, 1985;

Gone From Breezy Hill (as Nora Ashby), 1985; Illusions (as Jessica March), 1988; Consenting Adults (as Lila Cook), 1988. Temptations, (as Jessica March) 1989; Obsessions, 1990. *Contributions to:* New York Times; New York News; Readers' Digest; Harper's Bazaar; Woman's Day; Woman's World; National Review; The Nation. *Honour:* Phi Beta Kappa, 1956. *Memberships:* Drama Desk, Vice President, Secretary; Outer Critics' Circle; American Society of Journalists & Authors, Authors Guild. *Address:* 1 Roseld Avenue, Deal, New Jersey 07723, USA.

AGEE Jonis, b. 31 May 1943, Omaha, USA. m. Paul McDonough, 1 daughter. *Education:* BA, University of Iowa, 1966; MA, Suny Binghamton, English, 1969; PhD, 1976. *Appointments:* Teacher, College of St Catherine, St Paul, Minnesota, 1975-; Literaery Consultant, Performing Arts Program, Walker Arts Center, Minneapolis, 1978-84; Chair, Midwestern Writers Festival & Small Press Book Fair, Minnesota, 1976-80; Adjunct Teacher, Macalester College, 1980-88; Literary Post Program, Senior Citizen Writers, 1986-89. *Publications:* Strange Angels; Sweet Eyes; Pretend We've Never Met; Bend This Heart; Two Poems; Mercury; Houses; Anthologies, Stillers Pond; After A While; In The Blood. *Contributions to:* Resume; Kya; What The Fall Brings. *Honours:* Loft McKnigh Award of Distinction; Loft McKnight Award in Fiction; National Endowment for the Arts Fellowship; Minnesota State Arts Board Award; Faculty Excellence Award in Teaching. *Memberships:* Literary Guild; Society of American Poets. *Literary Agent:* Ned Leavitt Agency. *Address:* 1926 Lincola Avenue, St Pual, MN 55105, USA.

AGNEW-BROWN Ronald, b. 10 May 1916, Murwillumbah, New South Wales, Australia. Retired NT Police Officer. m. Mona Jessie McKenzie Evens, 26 Dec 1942, 1 son, 1 daughter. *Education:* Matriculalion, ICS, 1932. *Appointments:* Editor, Northern Territory, Police Association Journals, 1940-41. *Publications:* Bush Justice; Darwin Dilemmas. *Memberships:* Oral History Association of Australia; Masonic Lodge, Probus Club; Historical Societies of Murwillumbah & Tween Head NSW; Tweed River Agricultural Society; Justice of the Peace, Kingscliff Branch National Party. *Literary Agent:* Peter Bridge Hesperian Press, 65 Oats Street, Calisle, WA 6101. *Address:* 6 Quirk Place, Kingscliff 2487, NSW, Australia.

AGRI Shirin. *See:* **LAIZER Sheri J.**

AGUIRRE Eugenio, b. 31 July 1944, Mexico City, Mexico. Writer. m. 6 Aug 1971, 1 son, 1 daughter. *Education:* BA Law, MA Literature, Universidad Nacional Autonoma de Mexico. *Appointments include:* Lecturer: University of Lawrence, Kansas, USA; Wabash College, Indianapolis, Indiana, USA; Writers Association of Panama; Several bank & government offices, Mexico. *Publications include:* Novels: Jesucristo Perez, 1973; Pajar de Imaginacion, 1975; El caballero de las espudas, 1978; Gonzalez Guerrero, 1980; El testamento del diablo, 1981; En el campo, 1982; Cadaver exquisito, 1984; El rumor quillego del mar, 1985; Pajuror de guego, 1986; Un mundo de nino lleno de mar, 1986. *Contributions to:* Excelsior; Uno & Uno; El Cuento; Plural; Vaso Comunicante; Contenido; El Buho; etc, all Mexico City. Also Angoleta, Venezuela; Paris Atlantic, France. *Honours:* Great Silver Medal, International Academy of Lutece, Paris, France, 1981; Finalist, 1st crime novel, Plaza de Janes, 1985; Finalist, Fuentes Mares Prize for Literature, 1986; Finalist, 1st International Award, Diana Publishers, 1986. *Memberships:* Past president, Asociacion de Escritores de Mexico; Board, Sociedad General de Escritores de Mexico; International PEN Club. *Address:* Buhos no.32, Fracc. Loma de Guadalupe, Mexico DF 01720, Mexico.

AHERNE Owen. *See:* **CASSILL Ronald Verlin.**

AHLSEN Leopold, b. 12 Jan 1927, Munich,

Germany. Author. m. Ruth Gehwald, 1964, 1 son, 1 daughter. *Publications:* 13 Plays, 23 radio plays, 42 television plays, 5 novels. *Honours:* Gerhart Hauptmann Prize; Schiller-Forderungspreis; Golden Bildschirm; Horspielpreis der Kriegsblinden; Silver Nymph of Monaco. *Address:* Waldschulstrasse 58, 8000 Munich 82, Gemany.

AIDOO (Christina) Ama Ata, b. 1942 Ghana. 1 daughter. Writer. *Appointments:* Lecturer, University of Cape Coast, Ghana, 1970-83; Minister of Education, Ghana, 1982-83; Chair, Africa Regional Panel of Connomwealth Writers Prize, 1990-91. *Publications include:* Changes, A Love Story; The Dilemma of a Ghost; Anowa; No Sweetness Here; Our Sister Killjoy; Someone Talking to Somtime; The Eagle And The Chickens; Birds And Other Poems; Short Stories inc, To Be a Women. *Contributions to:* BBC African Service; MS Magazine; South Magazine; Kumapipi; Rapport; The Chapman Review. *Address:* PO Box 4930, Harare, Zimbabwe.

AIKEN Joan Delano, b. 4 Sept 1924, Rye, Sussex, England. Writer. m. (1) Ronald George Brown (dec. 1955), 1 son, 1 daughter, (2) Julius Goldstein, 2 Sept 1976. *Appointments include:* Features editor, Argosy magazine, 1955-60; Copywriter, J Walter Thompson advertising agency, 1960-61. Freelance writer, full time, 1961-. *Publications:* 21 books for adults, over 50 for children. Adult fiction includes: The Fortune Hunters, 1965; Hate Begins at Home, 1967; The Windscreen Weepers, fantasy & horror stories, 1969; Died on a Rainy Sunday, 1972; Last Movement, 1977; The Smile of the Stranger, 1978; A Whisper in the Night, 1982; Mansfield Revisited, 1985; Deception (US title, If I Were You), 1987. Children's fiction includes: Smoke from Cromwell's Time, stories, 1970; A Harp of Fishbones, stories, 1972; The Mooncusser's Daughter, play, 1973; Tale of a One-Way Street, stories, 1978; The Skin Spinners, poems, 1976; Mortimer & the Sword Excalibur, 1979; The Mystery of Mr Jones' Disappearing Taxi, 1982; Last Slice of Rainbow Cape, 1985; Dido & Pa, 1986; The Moon's Revenge, 1987; The Teeth of the Gale, 1988; The Erl King's Daughter, 1988; A Goose on Your Grave, 1987; Voices, 1989; Blackground, 1989; Give Yourself a Fright, 1989; A Foot in the Grave, 1990; A Fit of Shivers (horror stories), 1990; Is, 1992; The Haunting of Lamb House, 1991; Morningquest, 1992; Mortimer and Arabel, 1992; Published UK & USA. *Contributions to:* New Statesman; Times Literary & Educational Supplements; Washington Post; Good Housekeeping; Woman's Journal; Children's Literature in Education; Quarterly Bulletin of Library of Congress. *Honour:* Guardian Award, children's fiction, 1969; Lewis Carroll Award, 1970. *Memberships:* Society of Authors; Writers Guild; Mystery Writers of America; Crime Writers Association. *Literary Agent:* A.M.Heath Ltd. *Address:* The Hermitage, East Street, Petworth, West Sussex, GU28 0AB, England.

AINSWORTH Mary Dinsmore (Mary D Salter, Mary D Salter Ainsworth), b. 1913, Canada. *Appointments:* Senior Research Psychologist, Tavistock Clinic, London, 1950-54; Senior Research Fellow, East African Institute of Social Research, Kampala, Uganda, 1954-55; Lecturer, 1956-58, Associate Professor, 1958-63, Professor, 1964-75, Johns Hopkins University, Baltimore; Commonwealth Professor, 1975-84, Emeritus Professor of Psychology, 1984-, University of Virginia, Charlottesville. *Publications:* Doctor in the Making (as Mary D. Salter with A.W. Ham), 1943; Developments in the Rorschach Technique, vole 1 (with B.Klopfer, W.F. Klopfer and R.R. Holt), 1954; Measuring Security in Personal Adjustment (with L.H. Ainsworth), 1958; Child Care and the Growth of Love (with J. Bowlby), 1965; Infancy in Uganda, 1967; Patterns of Attachment (with M.C. Blehar, E. Waters, S. Wall), 1978. *Address:* Department of Psychology, Gilmer Hall, University of Virginia, Charlottesville, VA 22901, USA.

AINSWORTH Mary D Salter. *See:* **AINSWORTH Mary Dinsmore.**

AINSWORTH Patricia. *See:* BIGG Patricia Nina.

AJIBADE Adeyemi Olanrewaju, (Yemi Ajibade), b. 28 July 1939, Nigeria. Actor; Playwright; Director. m. Gwendoline Augusta Ebonywhite, May 1973, 2 daughters. *Education:* Diplomas, Dramatic Arts Film Technique; British Drama League Diploma, Theatre Production; Associate of Drama Board; MA, London University, 1985. *Appointments:* Tutor, Producer, Drama, Panel of Inner London Education Authority; Visiting Director, Actors Workshop, London; Artistic Director, Pan-African Players, Keskidee Centre, (London); Assistant Advisor to Earl of Snowdon on Mary Kingsley; Senior Arts Fellow & Artistic Director, Unibadan Masques, Acting Company of Ibadan University, Nigeria; Artist in Residence, Colby College, Waterville, Maine, USA, 1987. *Publications:* Lagos, Yes Lagos, BBC Radio; Award (Keskidee Centre); The Black Knives (ORTF, Paris); The Big One, Parcel Post, (Royal Court, London); Behind the Mountain, Mokai, The Girl from Bulawayo (Arts Theatre, Ibadan University); Fingers Only (Black Theatre Cooperative, London); Para Ginto (black version Peer Gynt), commissioned by Birmingham Repertory Theatre; Waiting for Hannibal (Black Theatre Co-Op), 1986; etc. *Honours:* 4 Times Recipient, British Arts Council Bursary Award for Playwriting, 1976, 1977, 1981, 1984. *Memberships:* Fellow, Royal Society of Arts; British Kinematographic Society; Theatre Writers Union; Black Writers Association. *Literay Agent:* Michael Imison Playwrights (London). *Address:* 29 Seymour House, Churchway, London NW1, England.

AJIBADE Yemi. *See:* AJIBADE Adeyemi Olanrewaju.

AKAVIA Miriam, b. 20 Nov 1927, Krakow, Poland. Novelist; Translator. m. 3 Dec 1946. 2 daughters. *Appointments:* Co-editor of some bulletins; Hebrew Writers Ass; Pen-Israel; The World Literary Academy; Acum; Ass. Intern Trust for Secular Humanistic Judaism; The Israeli Society for the Right to Die with Dignity. *Publications:* Adolescence of Autumn, 1975; Ha mechir (The Price), 1978; Galia & Miklosh, 1982; Karmi Sheli, (My Own Vineyard), 1984; Adventure on a Bus, 1986; Ma Vigne A Moi, 1992; The Other Way, The Story of a Group, in Hebrew, 1992. Written in Hebrew, trans. to Polish and other languages. *Contributions to:* Various literary magazines. *Honours:* Dvorsecki Prize; Korczak-Prize, SEK-Prize (Sociéte Européen de Culture); (Amicus Polonie; Cracovians Prize). *Literary Agent:* Lipman, AG, CH-8044 Zürich. *Address:* P.O.B. 53050, 61530 Tel-Aviv, Israel.

AKEN Paul Van, b. 20 Nov 1948, Reet, Belgium. Teacher; Literary Critic. *Education:* Free University, Brussels, 1966-70. *Publications:* Features of the essay; Lettermarker, A History of Dutch Literature; Paul De Wispelaere; About Sugar by Hugo Claus; About Lucifer By Vondel; About The Wall by Jos Vandeloo. *Contributions to:* Nieuw Vlaams Tydschrift; De Vlaamse Gids; Yang; Kunst & Cultuur; Kruispunt; Ons Erfdeel; Creare; Septentrion. *Memberships:* PEN; FLANDERS. *Address:* Dirk Martensstraat 60, 9300 Aalst, Belgium.

AKERS Alan Burt. *See:* BULMER Henry Kenneth.

AL-AZM Sadik J, b. 7 Nov 1934, Damascus, Syria. University Professor. m. Fawz Touqan, 2 July 1957, 2 sons. *Education:* Gerard Institute Highschool, Sidon, 1949-53; American University, Berut, 1953-57; Yale Univserity, New Haven, Connecticut, 1957-61. *Publications:* Kants Theory of Time; The Origins of Kants Arguments in the Antinoics; Critique of Religious Thought; Studies in Modern Western Philosophy; Of Love & Arabic Courtly Love; Materialism & History: A Defense. *Contributions to:* Orientalism & Orientalism in Reverse; Sionisme Une Enterprise de Colonisation; Der Palastinensiche Widerstand neu durchdacht; Palestintian Zionism; The Importance of Being Earnest About Salman Rushdie. *Address:* Dept of Philosophy, Faculty of Letters, Damarcus Univeristy, Damascus, Syria.

AL-KHARRAT Edwar, b. 16 Mar 1926. Writer. 2 sons. *Education:* LLB 1946, Alexandria University. *Appointments:* Editor, Gallery 68 magazine 1968; Editor, Afro Asian Writings magazine 1968; Editor, Afro Asian Publications 1970; Edited a special issue on Egyptian Literature of Al-Karmal magazine 1984. *Publications:* High Walls, 1959; Hours of Pride, 1972; Ramah and the Dragon, 1980; Suffocations of Love and Mornings, 1983; The Other Time, 1985; City of Saffron, Arabic 1986, English 1989, French 1990, German 1991, Spanish 1992; Girls of Alexandria, 1990; Waves of Nights, 1991; Appollo's Ruins, 1992. *Contributions to:* Many of the Arab literary magazines. *Honours:* Arts & Letters Medal, 1st class, 1972; State Prize for the Short Story, 1972; Franco-Arab Friendship Award, 1989. *Memberships:* The Egyptian Writer's Union; Gezira Sporting Club. *Address:* 45 Ahmed Hishmat Street, Zamalak 11211, Cairo, Egypt.

AL-SHAYKH Hanan, b. 12 Nov 1945, Beirut. Author. m. Fouad Malouf, 22 June 1986, 1 son, 1 daughter. *Education:* The American College for Girls. *Publications:* The Suicide of a Dead Man; The Praying Mantis; The story of Zahra; Women of Sand & Myrrh; A Desert Rose; Poste Restante Beirut. *Contributions to:* An Nahar Newspaper; Al Hasna Women Magazine; English Anthologies & Magazines. *Memberships:* PEN International. *Literary Agent:* Anthony Goff, David Higham Associates. *Address:* 7 Grosvenor Square, Flat 16, London W1X 9LA, England.

ALAMI Ahmad, b. 24 Oct 1939. Librarian. m.(1) Zenat, 1969, (2) Salma, 1980, (3) Samiva, 1988. 1 son, 1 daughter. *Education:* Sophomore Diploma, 1957; MBBCH, Ain Shams Medical School Cairo, 1966. *Appointments:* Literary Director, College of Islamic Studies, 1979-. *Publications include:* War of 1948, 1980; War of 1956, 1982; Bloody Days, 1983; Waqt of Saladin, 1981; Waqt of the Moroccans, 1982; Catalogue of Arabic Manuscripts, 1986; The Palestine State, (translation), 1984; New Violence, (translation), 1987; War of 1967, 1990; numerous contributions to journals and magazines. *Address:* P.O. Box 19859, Jerusalem, Israel.

ALBANY James. *See:* CRAUFORD Rae.

ALBEE Edward Franklin, b. 12 Mar 1928, Virginia, USA. Playwright. *Education:* Pennsylvania Choale School, Connecticut, 1946; Trinity College, Hartford, Connecticut, 1946-47. *Appointments:* Radio Writer, WNYC, Office Boy, Warwick & Ledler Record Salesman, Bloomingdales Book Salesman, G Schirmer Counterman, Manhattan Towers Hotel, Messenger, 1955-58; Producer, Richard Barr & Clinton Wilder, Playwrighters Univ, Alberwild Theatre Arts & Albar Productions, Founder, William Flanagan Center for Creative Persons, 1971. *Publications:* Plays inc, Whos Afraid of Virginia Woolf; The Zoo Story; The Death of Bessie Smith; The Sandbox; The American Dream; Tiny Alice; Seascape; Everything in the Garden; Screenplay, A Delicate Balance. *Honours include:* London Evening Standard Award; Tony Award; Morgo jones award; Pulitzer Proze; American Academy Gold Medal; Brandeis University Creative Arts Award. *Membership:* American Academy. *Literary Agent:* William Morris Agency. *Address:* 14 Harrison Street, New York, NY 10013, USA.

ALBERT Gabor, b. 30 Oct 1929, Hungary. Writer; Essayist. m. Zsuzsanna Marek, 30 Oct 1954, 1 son, 1 daughter. *Education:* Eotvos Lorand University, Budapest, 1955. *Appointments:* Editor in Chief, Uj Magyarorszag, 1991-92; Editor in Chief, Magyarok Vilaglapja, 1992-. *Publications:* Dragon And Octahedron; After Scattering, Essays; Where Are Those Columns; In A Shell; Book of Kings; Heros of the Failures; Atheist; Final Settlement of A Wedding. *Memberships:* Association of Hungarian Writers; Association of D

Berzsenyi. *Address:* Bimbo ut 3 IV5, H-1022 Budapest, Hungary.

ALBERT Linda I, b. 15 Nov 1939, New York City, USA. Writer. div, 2 sons, 1 daughter. *Education:* BS 1968, MS 1972, State University of New York; PhD, Psychology, Lyon International University, 1984. *Publications:* Coping with Kids, 1982; Coping With Kids & School, 1984; Co-author: Coping With Kids & Vacation, 1986; Strengthening Stepfamilies, 1986; Quality Parenting, 1987, Cooperative Discipline, 1990; An Administrator's Guide to Cooperative Discipline: Strategies for Schoolwide Implementation, 1992. *Contributions to:* Syndicated columnist for: Changing Families; Gannett News Service; Coping with Kids, monthly column in Working Mother Magazine; Parent and Child, monthly column in Family magazine. *Membership:* American Society of Journalists & Authors. *Literary Agent:* Pam Bernstein, William Morris Agency. *Address:* 3405 Ellenwood Lane, Tampa, Florida 33618, USA.

ALBERT Marvin H, (Nick Quarry, Anthony Rome, Tony Rome), b. USA. Author; Freelance Writer. *Publications include:* Lie Down with Lions, 1955; The Law and Jake Wade, 1956; Apache Rising, 1957; Party Girl (novelization of screenplay), 1958; The Bounty Killer, 1958; The Girl with No Place to Hide (as Nick Quarry), 1959; All the Young Men (novelization of screenplay), 1960; My Kind of Game, 1962; Lover Come Back (novelization of screenplay), 1962; Move Over, Darling (novelization of screenplay), 1963; Palm Springs Weekend, 1963; Honeymoon Hotel, 1964; What's New Pussycat? (novelization of screenplay), 1965; Strange Bedfellows (novelization of screenplay), 1965; The Divorce (non-fiction), 1965; Come September, 1971; Hidden Lives, 1982; Operation Lila, 1983; The Warmakers, 1985; Stone Angel, 1986; Back in the Real World, 1986; Get Off At Babylon, 1987; Long Teeth, 1987.

ALBEVERIO MANZONI Solvejg, b. 6 Nov 1939, Arogno, Switzerland. Painter; Writer. m. Sergio Albeverio, 7 Feb 1970, 1 daughter. *Education:* Textile Designer Diploma, Como, Italy, 1960; Art Courses, Kunstgewerbeschule Zurich, 1969; Drawing & Etching, Statens Kunstindustriskole, Oslo, 1972-77. *Publications:* Da Stanze Chiuse (drawings and poems); 11 Pensatore Con Il Mantello Come Meteora (novel); Controcanto Al Chiuso (drawings, with Bianca Maria Frabotta, poetry); Ip fiore, il frutto, triandro donna (poems, with K. Fusco and C Ragni). *Contributions to:* Poems & Drawings, Literary Journals & Reviews; Exhibitions & Group Exhibitions, Many Countries. *Honours:* Premio Ascona, 1987 for Unpublished Narrative. *Memberships:* Swiss Society of Painters, Sculptors & Architects; Swiss Society of Womens Painters & Scupltors; PEN Club; Associazione Scrittori della Svizzera Italiana. *Address:* Auf dem Aspei 55, D 4630 Bochum, Germany.

ALBRIGHT Daniel, b. 29 Oct 1945, Chicago, IL, USA. Professor. m. Karin Larson, 18 June 1977, 1 daughter. *Education:* BA, Rice University, 1967; M Phil, Yale University, 1969; PhD, 1970. *Appointments:* Assistance Professor, University of Virginia, 1970-75; Associate Professor, 1975-81; Professor, 1981-86; Visiting Professor, University of Munich, 1986-87; Professor, University of Rochester, 1987-. *Publications:* The Poems; The Music Box & The Nightingale; The Muses, Tug of War; Lyricality in Englush Literature; Representation & The Imagination; Personality & Impersonality; The Myth Against Myths. *Honours:* Phi Beta Kappa; NEH Fellow; Guggenheim Fellow. *Address:* Dept of English, University of Rochester, Rochester, NY 17627, USA.

ALBROW Desmond, b. 22 Jan 1925. Assistant Editor, Sunday Telegraph, 1976-. m. Aileen Mary Jennings, 1950, 1 son, 3 daughters. *Education:* MA, Keble College, Oxford. *Appointments:* Editorial Staff, Yorkshire Observer, 1950-51, Manchester Guardian, 1951-56, Daily Telegraph 1956-60, Sunday Telegraph 1960-66; Chief Sub Editor, News Editor, Night Editor, Editor, Catholic Herald, 1966-71; Features Editor, Sunday Telegraph, 1971-76. *Address:* Totyngton Cottage, Victoria Road, Teddington, Middlesex, TW11 0BG, England.

ALCOCK (Garfield) Vivien, b. 23 Sept 1924, Worthing, England. Author. m. Leon Garfield, 23 Oct 1948, 1 daughter. *Education:* Oxford School of Art. *Publications:* The Haunting of Cassie Palmer, 1980; The Stonewalker, 1981; The Sylvia Game, 1982; Travellers by Night, 1983; Ghostly Companions, 1984; The Cuckoo Sister, 1985; The Mysterious Mr Ross, 1987; The Monster Garden, 1988; The Trial of Anna Cotman, 1989; A Kind of Thief, 1991. *Membership:* Authors Society. *Literary Agent:* John Johnson. *Address:* 59 Wood Lane, London N6 5UD, England.

ALDCROFT Derek Howard, b. 25 Oct 1936, North Wales. Professor of Economic History. *Education:* Manchester University 1955-60, BA (Econ) 1958, PhD 1962. *Publications:* The European Economy 1914-1990, 1993; Full Employment the Elusive Goal, 1984; The British Economy 1920-1951, 1986; Education, Training and Economic Performance in the UK 1944-1990, 1992. *Contributor to:* Numerous academic journals. *Memberships:* Economic History Society, Council Member 1982-88; Editorial Advisory Board of The Economic Review, 1984-; The Advisory Board of Independent Research Services. *Address:* 10 Linden Drive, Leicester LE5 6AH, England.

ALDISS Brian Wilson, b. 18 Aug 1925, East Dereham, England, Writer. m. (1) 1 son, 1 daughter, (2) Margaret Manson, 11 Dec 1965, 1 son, 1 daughter. *Appointment:* Literary Editor, Oxford Mail, 1958-69. *Publications include:* The Brightfount Diaries, 1955; Non-Stop, 1958; Hothouse, 1962; Greybeard, 1964; Barefoot in the Head, 1969; The Horatio Stubbs trilogy, 1970, 1971, 1978; Frankenstein Unbound, 1973; The Malacia Tapestry, 1976; Life in the West, 1980; The Helliconia Trilogy, 1982, 1983 & 1985; Forgotten Life, 1988; Space, Time and Nathaniel, 1957; The Canopy of Time, 1959; Best SF Stories of Brian W Aldiss, 1965, revised 1971; Last Orders, 1977; New Arrivals, Old Encounters, 1979; Seasons in Flight, 1984; Best SF Stories of Brian W Aldiss, 1988; A Romance of the Equator, Best Fantasy Stories, 1989; A Tupoleu Too Far, 1993. Cities and Stones, A Traveller's Yugoslavia, 1966; The Shape of Further Things, 1970; Billion Year Spree: The History of Science Fiction, 1973; This World and Nearer Ones, 1979; Trillion Year Spree, 1986; Bury My Heart at W H Smith's: a Writing Life, 1990; Dracula Unbound, 1991; Rememberance Day, 1993 *Contributor to:* Numerous magazines, periodicals & newspapers, including Penguin SF Omnibus, Space Opera Series, Best SF Series, Hell's Cartographers, 1975, Decades series. *Honours include:* Observer Book Award Science Fiction, 1956; Ditmar Award for Best Contemporary Writer, Science Fiction, 1969; First James Blish Award for SF Criticism, 1977; Pilgrim Award, 1978; First Award for Distinguished Scholarship, International Association for the Fantastic in the Arts, Houston, 1986; Guest of Honour, World SF Convention, London, 1965, Brighton, 1979; Fellow of the Royal Society for Literature. *Literary Agent:* Michael Shaw, Curtis Brown, United Kingdom; Robin Straus, USA. *Address:* Woodlands, Foxcombe Road, Boars Hill, Oxford OX1 5DL, England.

ALDRIDGE (Harold Edward) James, b. 10 July 1918. Author; Journalist. m. Dina Mitchnik, 1942, 2 sons. *Appointments:* Herald and Sun, Melbourne, Australia, 1937-38, Daily Sketch, Sunday Dispatch, London, 1939; with Australian Newspaper Service and North American Newspaper Alliance (as war correspondent), Finland, Norway, Middle East, Greece, USSR 1939-45; Correspondent for Time and Life, Teheran, 1944. *Publications:* Signed With Their Honour, 1942; The Sea Eagle, 1944; Of Many Men, 1946; The Diplomat, 1950; The Hunter, 1951; Heroes of the Empty View, 1954; Underwater Hunting for Inexperienced Englishmen, 1956; I Wish He Would Not Die, 1958; Gold and Sand (short stories), 1960; The Last Exile,

1961; A Captive in the Land, 1962; The Statesman's Game, 1966; My Brother Tom, 1966; The Flying 19, 1966; Living Egypt, (with Paul Strand), 1969; Cairo : Biography of a City, 1970; A Sporting Proposition, 1973; The Marvellous Mongolian, 1974; Mockery in Arms, 1974; The Untouchable Juli, 1975; One Last Glimpse, 1977; Goodbye Un-America, 1979; The Broken Saddle, 1982; The True Story of Lilli Stubek, 1984; The True Story of Spit MacPhee, 1986. *Honours:* Rhys Memorial Award, 1945; Lenin Peace Prize, 1972. *Address:* c/o Curtis Brown, 162-168 Regent Street, London W1R 5TA, England.

ALDRIDGE John Watson, b. 26 Sept 1922, Sioux City, Iowa, USA. Literary Critic; Educator. m. (2) Patricia McGuire Eby, 16 July 1983. 5 sons, previous marriage. *Education:* BA, University of California, Berkeley, 1947. *Appointments include:* Lecturer, Christian Gauss seminars in criticism, Princeton University 1953-54; Breadloaf Writers Conference 1966-69; Rockefeller Humanities Fellowship, 1976; Book critic, MacNeil/Lehrer TV News, 1983-84. *Publications include:* After the Lost Generation, criticism, 1951; In Search of Heresy, criticism, 1956; The Party at Cranton, novel, 1960; Time to Murder & Create, criticism, 1966; In the Country of the Young, social commentary, 1970; The Devil in the Fire, criticism, 1972; The American Novel & the Way We Live Now, criticism, 1983; Talents and Technicians, Criticism, 1992; Classics and Contemporaries, Criticism, 1992. *Contributions to:* Harper's; Saturday Review; New York Times Book Review; New York Herald Tribune Book Week; Chicago Tribune Book World. *Honours:* Fulbright Senior Lectureships, 1958-59, 1962-63; Berg Professorship, New York University, 1958; Writer-in-residence, Hollins College, 1960-62; Special Advisor, American Studies, American Embassy, Germany, 1972-73. *Memberships:* PEN Club; Authors League of America; National Book Critics Circle. *Literary Agent:* Gerard F. McCauley. *Address:* 1050 Wall Street no.4-C, Ann Arbor, Michigan 48105, USA.

ALEGRIA Claribel. *See:* **ALEGRIA FLAKOLL Claribel.**

ALEGRIA FLAKOLL Claribel, (Claribel Alegria), b. 12 May 1924, Esteli, Nicaragua. Writer. m. Darwin J Flakoll, 29 Dec 1947, 1 son, 3 daughters. *Education:* BA Philosophy & Letters, George Washington University, Washington DC, USA. *Publications include:* Cenizas de Izalco, novel, co-author, 1966; Suma y Siqua, poetry, 1982; Nicaragua: la revolucion sandinists, history, 1982; No me agarran viva, testimony, 1983; Woman of the River, poetry, 1989; Y esta poema-rio, poetry, 1989; Family Album, 3 novellas, 1990; Total of 30 books in five languages. *Contributions to:* Many magazines and journals. *Honour:* Casa de las Americas poetry prize for Sobrevivo 1978. *Literary Agent:* Alexander Taylor, Curbstone Press. *Address:* Aptdo Postal A-36, Managua, Nicaragua.

ALESHKOVSKY Joseph, (Aleshkovsky Yuz), b. 21 Sept 1929, Russia. Writer. m. Kanton Dektor Irina, 3 Feb 1976, 2 sons. *Publications:* Kangaroo; The Hand; Nikolaj Nikolajevich; Death in Moscow; The Flea Tango; 12 Books Published in Russian; 2 in English; 2 in French, German, Hebrew & Dutch. *Contributions to:* Many. *Honour:* Guoqenheim. *Literary Agent:* Joan Daves. *Address:* 16 Willoe Court, Cromwell, CT 06416, USA.

ALESHKOVSKY Yuz. *See:* **ALESHKOVSKY Joseph.**

ALEXANDER Caroline Elizabeth, b. 13 Mar 1956, Florida, USA. Writer. *Education:* Florida State University, BA, 1977; Oxford University, BA, 1980; Columbia University, PhD, 1992. *Appointments:* Editorial Board, American Oxarian. *Publication:* One Dry Season. *Contributions to:* Sunday Telegraph Magazine; North Borneo Expedition; Vital Covers; The White Goddess of the Wangna; An Ideal State; New Yorker Magazine;

Traveler Magazine. *Honours:* Mellan Fellowship in the Humanities; Rhodes Scholarship. *Memberships:* Authors Guild; American Philological Association; Royal Geographical Society; University Womens Club. *Literary Agent:* Anthony Sheil. *Memberships:* c/o Anthony Sheil, 43 Doughty Street, London WC1 N2LF, England.

ALEXANDER Christine Anne, b. 9 July 1949, Hastings, New Zealand. University Lecturer, English Literature. m. Peter Fraser Alexander, 18 June 1977, 1 son, 1 daughter. *Education:* BA 1970, MA 1st Class Honours 1971, University of Canterbury, New Zealand; PhD, University of Cambridge, UK, 1978. *Appointments:* Assistant lectureship, English, University of Canterbury, 1972; Tutor 1978-83, Lecturer 1986-88, Senior Lecturer, 1988-92; Associate Professor, 1993-, School of English, University of New South Wales, Australia. *Publications include:* Bibliography of the Manuscripts of Charlotte Brontë, 1982; The Early Writings of Charlotte Brontë, 1983; Something About Arthur, by Charlotte Brontë, editor, 1981; An Edition of the Early Writings of Charlotte Brontë, volume I, 1987; volume II (parts 1 & 2), 1991. *Contributions to:* Books: Charlotte Brontë at Roe Head, Norton Critical Edition; Charlotte Bronte, Jane Eyre, Norton Critical Edition, 1987; Search after Love, in Critical Perspective: Charlotte Bronte, 1987. Articles & reviews in various journals. *Honours:* New Zealand Postgraduate Scholarships, 1974-76; New Zealand University Womans Fellowship, 1976-77; Travel Grants and Special Research Grants, 1975-88; British Council Grant, 1983; British Academy Rose Mary Crawshay Prize, 1984; Australian Research Council Grants, 1986- 93; Visiting Scholar, Pembroke College Cambridge, 1990-1991. *Memberships include:* Brontë Society; Australasian Language & Literature Association; Australasian Victorian Studies Association; Australasian & Pacific Society for 18th Century Studies; Bibliographical Society of Australia; etc. *Literary Agent:* Basil Blackwell, UK. *Address:* School of English, University of NSW, PO Box 1, Kensington, NSW 2033, Australia.

ALEXANDER Gary Roy, b. 18 Jan 1941, Bremerton, WA, USA. Writer. m. Shari, 9 Aug 1969, 3 daughters. *Publications:* Pigeon Blood; Unfunny Money; Kiet And The Golden Peacock; Kiet And The Opium War; Deadly Drought; Kiet Goes West; A Novel Set in Yucatan; Blood Sacrifice. *Contributions to:* Approx 75 Short Stories, Various Magazines. *Memberships:* Mystery Writers of America. *Literary Agents:* Fox Chase Agency (Al Hart). *Address:* 122 SW 104th Street, Seattle, WA 98146, USA.

ALEXANDER Louis George, b. 1932. Writer. *Publications include:* Sixty Steps, 1962; Poetry and Prose Appreciation, 1963; A First Book in Comprehension, 1965; Essays and Letter Writing, 1965; The Carters of Greenwood, 1966; Detectives from Scotland Yard, 1966; April Fools Day, 1966; New Concept English (4 vols), 1967; Worth a Fortune, 1967; Question and Answer, 1967; For and Against, 1968; Look, Listen and Learn, Sets 1-4, 1968- 71; Reading and Writing English, 1969; Car Thieves, 1969; K's First Case, 1975; Good Morning, Mexico!, 1975; Operation Janus, 1976; Clint magee, 1976; Dangerous Game, 1977; Some Methodological Implications of Waystage and Threshold Level, Council of Europe, 1977; Follow Me, 1979; Survive in French/Spanish/German/Italian, 1980; Conversational French/Spanish/German/Italian, 1981; Excel, 1985-87; Plain English, 1987-88; Longman English Grammar, 1988-89; Longman English Grammar Practice, 1990; Step by Step 1-3, 1991; Longman Advanced Grammer, 1993; The Essential English Grammer, 1993. *Address:* Garden House, Weydown Road, Haslemere, Surrey, England.

ALEXANDER Robert McNeill, b. 7 July 1934, Lisburn, N Ireland. Professor of Zoology. m. Ann Elizabeth Coulton, 29 July 1961. *Education:* Tonbridge School; Cambridge University, BA, 1955; PhD, 1958; MA, 1959; University of Wales, DSc, 1969. *Publications:* Animal Mechanics; The Chordates; Elastic Mechanisms in Animal Movement; Dynamics of Dinosaurs And Other

Extinct Giants; Optima for Animals; Functional Design in Fishes; Size and Shape; Biomechanics; The Invertebrates; Locomotion of Animals; Animals; The Human Machine; Exploring Biomechanics. *Contributions to:* About 200 Papers in Scientific Journals. *Honours:* Scientific Medal Zoological Society of London; Linnean Medal for Zoology; Muybridge Medal. *Memberships:* Fellow in the Royal Society; American Scoiety of Zoologists; Institute of Biology; Zoological Society of London. *Address:* Dept of Pure & Applied Biology, University of Leeds, Leeds, LS2 9 JT, England.

ALEXANDER Sue, b. 1933, United States of America. Writer. *Publications:* Small Plays for You and a Friend, 1973; Nadir of the Streets, 1975; Peacocks Are Very Special, 1976; Witch, Goblin and Sometimes Ghost, 1976; Small Plays for Special Days, 1977; Marc the Magnificent, 1978; More Witch, Goblin and Ghost Stories, 1978; Seymour the Prince, 1979; Finding Your First Job, 1980; Whatever Happened to Uncle Albert? and Other Puzzling Plays, 1980; Witch, Goblin and Ghost in the Haunted Woods, 1981; Witch, Goblin and Ghost's Book of Things to Do, 1982; Nadia the Willful, 1983; Dear Phoebe, 1984; World Famous Muriel, 1984; Witch, Goblin and Ghost Are Back, 1985; World Famous Muriel and the Scary Dragon, 1985; America's Own Holidays, 1986; Lila on the Landing, 1987; There's More - Much More, 1987; World Famous Muriel and the Magic Mystery, 1990; Who Goes Out On Halloween?, 1990; Ellsworth and Millicent, 1993. *Address:* 6846 McLaren, Canoga Park, CA 91307, USA.

ALEXANDER III. *See:* **KIMBROUGH Robert.**

ALKALAY-GUT Karen, b. 29 Mar 1945, London, England. m. Ezra Gut, 26 July 1980, 2 sons, 2 daughters. *Education:* University of Rochester, BA, 1966; MA, 1967; PhD, 1975. *Publications:* Alone in the Dawn; Between Bombardments; Ignorant Armies; Mechitza; Butter Sculptures; Making Love. *Contributions to:* Prairie Schooner; The American Voice; Massachusetts Review. *Honours:* BBC World Service Poetry Award; Rosenberg Poetry Award. *Memberships:* Israel Association of Writers in English; PEN; Federation of Writers in Israel; Poetry Society of America. *Memberships:* Israel Association of American Studies. *Address:* Dept of English, Tel Aviv University, Ramat Aviv, Israel.

ALLABY John Michael, b. 18 Sept 1933, Belper, Derbyshire, England. Author. m. Ailsa Marthe McGregor, 3 Jan 1957. 1 son, 1 daughter. *Appointments:* Editor, The Oxford Dictionary of Natural History, 1980; Co-Editor, The Concise Oxford Dictionary of Earth Sciences (with Ailsa Allaby), 1986; Editor, Series of Official Guides to All the National Trails in England and Wales, 1987. *Publications:* Guide to Gaia, 1989; Dictionary of the Environment, 1977, 1983, 1988; Green Facts, 1989; A Year in the Life of a Field, 1981; The Great Extinction (with James Lovelock), 1983; The Greening of Mars (with James Lovelock), 1984; Animal Artisans, 1982; The Food Chain, 1984; Conservation at Home, 1988; Inventing Tomorrow, 1976. *Contributions to:* Newspapers and magazines. *Memberships:* Society of Authors; New York Academy of Sciences. *Literary Agent:* Peters Fraser & Dunlop. *Address:* Penquite, Fernleigh Road, Wadebridge, Cornwall PL27 7BB, England.

ALLADIN Bilkiz, b. Bombay, India. Journalist; Dramatist; Writer of children's books. m. Mr Iqbal Alladin, 6 June 1954, 2 sons, 1 daughter. *Education:* Queen Mary High School; Elphinstone College, Bombay. *Publications:* Barbie's Wonderful Holiday, 1972; Prayers for All Occasions, religious, 1972; Qasida Borda, co-author, religious, 1973; Thank You Jane Austen, 1975; Shankar and the Mountain of Secrets, 1976; The Life of Shivaji, retold for children, 1976; The Story of Muhammed the Prophet, 1977; Know Your Lord, 1980; The Mahabharata, retold for children, 1989; For the Love of a Begum, historical, 1989; Lazzat-e-Khas, cookery, 1989; Plays: Hyder Mahal, 1976; The Nabob, 1977;

Chanda, 1990; Children's plays: A Man of Peace, 1970; To Light a Candle, 1973; Plant a Tree, 1989; To Catch a Tiger, 1982; The Willow Pattern. *Contributions to:* The Times of India; The Evening News; The Illustrated Weekly of India; Star & Style; Eve's Weekly; Femina; New Delhi; The Deccau Chronicle; Citizen's Evening; Deccay Herald; Indian Express; Mid-Day; A P Journal; Hindustan Times; Channel 6; Siasat; Trend; Onlooker; Gentleman; India Magazine; Aside; Swagat; United Asia; Khaleej Times; Elegant. *Honours:* Hon Cultural Doctorate from University of Louisiana, USA; Chevalier de l'Ordre des Arts et Lettres from French Government; Distinguished Service Award, Intercontinental Poetry Society, Phoenix, Arizona, USA, National Unity Award, India. *Memberships include:* PEN; Mehfu-e- Khawateen, Founder President; Poetry Society (India), President. *Address:* Shangrila, Road No 9, Banjara Hills, Hyderabad 500034, India.

ALLAN Elkan, Journalist. *Appointments:* Writer, Odhams Press, 1950-55; Writer, Producer, Executive and Head of Entertainment, Rediffusion Television, 1955-66; Television Columnist, Sunday Times, 1966-82; Editor, Video Viewer, 1982-83; Columnist, Video Week, 1983-; Listings Editor, The Independent, 1986-88; Senior Editor, 1988-. *Publications:* Quiz Team, 1945; Editor, Living Opinion, 1946; Good Listening: A Survey of Broadcasting, with D.M. Robinson, 1948; The Sunday Times Guide to Movies on Television, with A. Allan, 1973, 1980; Editor, Video Year Book, 1984, 1985; 10 monographs on Silent Films Makers, 1990-. *Contributions to:* Senior Editor, The Independent. *Honours:* Triple Berlin TV Awards, 1965; British Press Awards, 1988. *Address:* The Independent, 40 City Road, London EC1Y 2DB, England.

ALLAN George Gordon, b. 4 Sept 1934, Aberdeen, Scotland. Sports Journalist. m. Joyce Ward, 22 Mar 1980. *Appointments:* Sub-Editor, Aberdeen Journals, 1951-60, (National Service, 1952-54), Daily Telegraph, 1960-61, The Scotsman, 1961-62, North London Press, 1962-63, Press Association, 1963-65; Sports Sub-Editor, Reporter, The Times, 1965-73; Freelance Reporter, Columnist, 1973-. *Contributions to:* The Times; World Bowls; Scottish Rugby. *Membership:* National Union of Journalists. *Address:* 18 Carshalton Park Road, Carshalton, Surrey, SM5 3SS, England.

ALLAN Mabel Esther, (Jean Estoril, Priscilla Hagon, Anne Pilgrim), b. 11 Feb 1915, Wallasey, Cheshire, England. Author. *Publications:* A Dream of Hunger Moss, 1983; The Pride of Pine Street, 1985; The Road to Huntingland, 1986; The Crumble Lane Mystery, 1987; Up the Victorian Staircase, 1987; First Term at Ash Grove, 1988; Drina Ballerina, 1991; over 150 other books. *Contributions to:* Over 320 short stories for young people many adult travel and other articles; poetry. *Honours:* Recipient, various honours and awards. *Literary Agent:* Curtis Brown & John Farquharson Ltd., London, England. *Address:* 11 Oldfield Way, Heswall, Wirral L60 6RQ, England.

ALLAN Ted, (William Maxwell), b. 1916, Canada. Author; Playwright. *Publications:* This Time a Better Earth (novel), 1939; The Scalpel, The Sword: The Story of Dr. Norman Bethume, 1952; Double Image (with Roger MacDougall), 1957; Quest for Pajaro (novel as William Maxwell), 1961; Oh What a Lovely War, 1964; Fuse (screenplay), 1970; Chu Chem: A Zen Buddhist-Hebrew Novel, 1973; Lies My Father Told Me (novel), 1975; My Sister's Keeper, 1976; Willie the Squowse (juvenile), 1977; Love Is a Long Shot (novel), 1985; Don't You Know Anybody Else (short stories), 1986.

ALLARDYCE Paula. *See:* **TORDAY Ursula.**

ALLBEURY Ted. *See:* **ALLBURY Theo Edward Le Bouthillier.**

ALLBURY Theo Edward Le Bouthillier (Ted Allbeury, Richard Butler, Patrick Kelly), b. 1917.

Author. *Publications:* A Choice of Enemies, 1973; Snowball, 1974; Palomino Blonde, 1975; The Special Collection, 1975; Moscow Quadrille, 1976; The Only Good German, 1976; The Man with the President's Mind, 1976; The Lantern Network, 1977; The Alpha List, 1978; Consequence of Fear, 1979; The Twentieth Day of January, 1980; The Reaper, 1980; The Other Side of Silence, 1981; The Secret Whispers, 1981; Shadow of Shadows. 1982; All Our Tomorrows, 1982; Pay Any Price, 1983; The Girl from Addis, 1984; No Place to Hide, 1984; The Judas Factor, 1984; Children of Tender Years, 1985; The Choice, 1986; The Seeds of Treason, 1986; The Crossing, 1987; A Wilderness of Mirrors, 1988; Deep Purple, 1989; A Time Without Shadows, 1990; Other Kinds of Treason, 1990; The Dangerous Edge, 1991; Show me a Hero, 1992; The Line-Crosser, 1993; As Richard Butler: Where All the Girls are Sweeter, 1975, Italian Assets, 1976; As Patrick Kelly: Codeword Cromwell, 1980, The Lonely Margins, 1981. *Membership:* Society of Authors. *Literary Agent:* Blake Friedmann Literary Agency. *Address:* Cheriton House, Furnace Lane, Lamberhurst, Kent, England.

ALLCOT Guy. *See:* **POCOCK Tom.**

ALLDRITT Keith, b. 10 Dec 1935, Wolverhampton, England. Professor of English; Writer. m. Joan Hardwick, 10 Apr 1980, 1 son, 1 daughter. *Education:* BA, MA, St Catharine's College, Cambridge. *Publications:* The Making of George Orwell, 1969; The Visual Imagination of D H Lawrence, 1970; The Good Pit Man, 1975; The Lover Next Door, 1977; Elgar on the Journey to Hanley, 1978; Poetry as Chamber Music, 1978; Modernism in the Second Word War, 1989; Churchill The Writer: His Life as a Man of Letters, 1992. *Honour:* Fellow, Royal Society of Literature. *Memberships:* Arnold Bennett Society; Society of Authors; D H Lawrence Society; International Churchill Society; Modern Language Association. *Address:* 48 Church Street, Lichfield, Staffordshire WS13 6ED, England.

ALLEN Blair H, b. 2 July 1933, Los Angeles, California, USA. Writer; Poet; Artist. m. Juanita Aguilar Raya, 27 Jan 1968, 1 son, 1 daughter. *Education:* AA San Diego City College, 1964; Studied, University of Washington, 1965-66; BA, San Diego State University, 1970. *Appointments:* Book Reviewer, Los Angeles times, 1977-78; Special Feature Editor, Cerulean Press & Kent Publications, 1982-. *Publications:* Televisual Po-ums for Bloodshot Eyeballs; Malice in Blunderland; The Atlantis Trilogy; Dreamwish of the Magician; Right through the Silver Lined, 1984; Looking Glass; The Magical World of David Cole; Snow Summits in the Sun; Trapped in a Cold War, Travelogue, 1991; May Burning into August, 1992; The Subway Poems, 1992; (Ed) The Cerulan Anthology of Sci-Fi/Outer Space/ Fantasy/Poetry and Prose Poems, 1992; 5 Other Small Chapbooks & Poetry. *Contributions to:* Numerous US Journals, Magazines & Reviews, Los Angeles Times. *Honours:* Various Honors & Awards. *Memberships:* Beyond Baroque Foundation; Medina Foundation, California State Poetry Society; Association of Applied Poetry. *Address:* 9651 Estacia Court, Cucamonga, CA 91730, USA.

ALLEN Diogenes, b. 17 Oct 1932, Lexington, Kentucky, USA. Clergy; Professor. m. Jane Mary Billing, 8 Sept 1958, 3 sons, 1 daughter. *Education:* BA with high distinction, University of Kentucky, 1954; BA Honours, 1957, MA, 1961, Oxford University, England; BD, 1959, MA, 1962, PhD, 1965, Yale University. *Publications:* Reasonableness of Faith, 1968; Finding Our Father, 1974, re-issued as Path of Perfect Love, 1992; Temptation, 1977; Between Two Worlds, 1977; Traces of God, 1981; Three Outsiders, 1983; Mechanical Explanations and the Ultimate Origin of the Universe According to Leibniz, 1983; Philosophy for Understanding Theology, 1985; Love, 1987; Christian Belief in a Postmodern World, 1989; Quest, 1990. *Contributions to:* About 40 Magazines and Journals. *Honours:* Phi Beta Kappa, 1953; Rhodes Scholar, 1955-57; Rockefeller Doctoral Fellow, 1962-64; Outstanding Educator of America, 1974; Research Fellowship,

Association of Theological Schools, 1975-76; PEW Evangelical Scholar, 1991-92. *Memberships:* Executive Board, Society of Christian Philosophers; Executive Board, American Weil Society; Advisory, Committee of Center of Theological Inquiry; Leibniz Gesellschaft. *Address:* Princeton Theological Seminary, Princeton, NJ 08542, USA.

ALLEN John. *See:* **PERRY Ritchie John Allen.**

ALLEN Oliver E, b. 29 June 1922, Cambridge, Mass, USA. Writer. m. Deborah Hutchison, 8 May 1948, 3 sons, 2 daughters. *Education:* Harvard, AB, 1943. *Publications:* New York, New York; Gardening With the New Small Plants; Wildflower Gardening; Decorating With Plants; Pruning & Grafting; Shade Gardens; Winter Gardens; The Windjammers; The Airline Builders; The Pacific Navigators; Building Sound Bones & Muscles; The Atmosphere; Secrets of a Good Digestion; The Vegetable Gardener's Journal. *Contributions to:* Horticulture Magazine; American Heritage & Smithsonian. *Literary Agent:* Curtis Brown Ltd. *Address:* 42 Hudson street, New York, NY 10013, USA.

ALLEN Pamela, b. 3 Apr 1934, Devonport, Auckland, New Zealand. Writer and Illustrator. m. William Robert Allen, 12 Dec 1964, 1 son, 1 daughter. *Education:* Diploma in Fine Art, Elam School of Art (now Auckland University), 1954; Attended Auckland Teachers Training College, 1955- 56. *Appointments:* Art teacher, Pio Pio District High School, New Zealand, 1956; Art Teacher, Rangitoto College, Auckland, New Zealand, 1957-58, 1960-64; Writer and illustrator, 1979-. *Publications:* Self-illustrated children's books: Mr Archimedes' Bath, 1980; Who Sank the Boat? 1982, 1983; Bertie and the Bear 1983, 1984; A Lion in the Night, 1985, 1986; Simon Said, 1985; Watch Me, 1985; Herbert and Harry, 1986; Mr McGee, 1987; Hidden Treasure, 1987; Fancy That! 1988; Simon Did, 1989; Watch Me Now, 1989; I Wish I Had a Pirate Suit, 1989; My Cat Maisie, 1990; Black Dog, 1991; Mr McGee Goes to Sea, 1992; Belinda, 1992. Illustrator of books including: Farr, Big Sloppy Dinosaur Socks, 1977; Farr, Mummy, Are Monsters Too Big for Their Boots? 1977; N L Ray, The Pow Toe, 1979; Sally Fitzpatrick, A Tall Story, 1981. *Honours:* Picture Book of the Year commendation for Children's Book Council of Australia and New South Wales Premier's Literary Award in children's book category, both 1981 and Book Design Award commendation from Australian Book Publishers Association 1980-81, all for Mr Archimedes' Bath; Children's Book of the Year Award from Children's Book Council of Australia and New South Wales Premier's Literary Award om children's book category, both 1983, and honor diploma for illustration from International Board on Books for Young People, 1984, all for Who Sank the Boat?; Children's Book of the Year Award from Children's Book Council of Australia, 1984, for Bertie and the Bear. *Memberships:* Australian Society of Authors, Children's Book Council of Australia. *Literary Agent:* Curtis Brown Ltd, Sydney, Australia. *Address:* c/o Curtis Brown Ltd, 27 Union Street, Paddington, Sydney, New South Wales 2021, Australia.

ALLEN Roberta, b. New York City, USA. Writer. *Appointments:* Creative Writing Instructor, Parsons School of Design, 1986; Guest Lecturer, Murdoch University, Perth, Australia 1989; Workshop Instructor, The Writer's Voice, New York City 1992. *Publications:* The Traveling Woman, 1986; The Daughter, 1992; Amazon Dream, 1993; Anthologies: Contemporary American Fiction, 1983; Wild History, 1985; Between C & D, 1988; Mondo Barbie, 1993; Stories: House Hunting; Certain People. *Contributions to:* Fiction International, 1991; Chelsea, 1991; Die Reisende, Akzente, Munich, 1992. *Honours:* LINE (NEA & NYS Council) grant 1985; Yaddo 1987. *Literary Agent:* Glen Hartley. *Address:* 5 West 16th Street, New York, NY 10011, USA.

ALLEN Stephen Valentine, (Steve Allen, William Christopher Stevens), b. 26 Dec 1921, New York, USA.

Entertainer. m. Jayne Meadows, 4 sons. *Education:* First year: Drake University, Des Moines, Iowa; Second Year: Arizona University. *Publications include:* Dumbth, 1989; Meeting of Minds, Vol I 1978, Vol II 1979, Vol III 1989, Vol IV 1989; Murder on the Glitter Box, 1989; Murder in Manhattan, 1990; Passionate Nonsmokers' Bill of Rights, 1989; The Public Hating, 1990; Steve Allen on the Bible, Religion and Morality, 1990; Murder in Vegas, 1991; Hi-Ho, Steverino: My Adventures in the Wonderful Wacky World of TV, 1992; How To Be Funny (re-release), 1992; The Murder Game, 1993; More Steve Allen on the Bible, Religion & Morality, Book Two, 1993. Compositions: Written over 4,000 Songs. *Contributor to:* Numerous articles to magazines and newspapers. *Address:* Meadowlane Ent Inc, 15201 Burbank Boulevard, Suite B, Van Nuys, CA 91411, USA.

ALLEN Steve. *See:* **ALLEN Stephen Valentine.**

ALLEN Woody. *See:* **KONIGSBERG Allen Stewart.**

ALLENDE Isabel, b. 2 Aug 1942, Lima, Peru. Writer. m. Willim C Gordon, 17 July 1988, 1 son, 1 daughter. *Publications:* The House of the Spirits; Of Love And Shadows; Eva Luna; Stories of Eva Luna; The Infinite Plan; Several Childresn Stories. *Contributions to:* Too Numerous. *Literary Agents:* Carmen Balcells. *Address:* c/o Carmen Balcells, Diagonal 580, Barcelona 21, Spain.

ALLIBONE Thomas Edward, b. 11 Nov 1903. Scientist. m. Feb 1931, 2 daughters. *Education:* DSc, PhD, D Eng, Sheffield; PhD, cambridge; DSc, Reading; DSc, City University. *Publications:* Cockcroft And The atom; The Royal Society & Its Dining Clubs; Rutherford Ecyl Britannia; Philately And The Royal Society; Cambridge Physics In The Thirties; The Making of Physics. *Contributions to:* Scientific Journals. *Memberships include:* FRS; FENG; Hon FIEE. *Address:* York Cottage, Winkfield, Windsor, England.

ALLISON Gaylene Dolores, b. 2 Aug 1948, Saskatchewan, Canada. English and E.S.L. Teacher; Editor; Poet. m. Geoff Hancock, 6 Aug 1983, 1 daughter. *Education:* BA, BEd., University of British Columbia; MA, University of Toronto. *Appointments:* Co-Founder, Woman's Writing Collective, 1975; Poetry Editor, Landscape, 1976; Founding Editor, Fireweed Feminist Journal, 1977; Poetry Editor, Waves Literary Journal, 1983; Fiction Editor, The Canadian Forum: Literary and Political Magazine, 1984; Advisory Board: Tiger Lily, 1985. *Publications:* Women and Their Writing 1 and II, anthology, 1975, 1976; Landscape, Anthology, 1977; Life : Still, Poetry, 1981; The Unravelling, 1987; In the Valley of the Butterflies, 1989; Fungus Lady, forthcoming. *Contributions to:* Landscape; Fireweed; Canadian Literature; Island; The Canadian Forum; Women and their Writing I/II; PCR; Writers' Quarterly; Femme Plurielle; Prairie Fire; Dandelion; Poetry Toronto; Waves; Room of One's Own etc. Anthologies: Sp/elles; Women and Words, 1984; Canadian Poetry by Women, 1986; Canadian Women Studies, 1987. *Honours:* Poetry Award, Ontario Teachers Federation, 1982; 1987. Nominated for Pat Lowther Poetry Award, 1987. *Memberships:* The League of Canadian Poets; Amnesty International. *Address:* Fiction Editor, 109 Brunswick Street, Stratford, Ontario, Canada N5A 3L9.

ALLOTT Miriam, b. 16 June 1920, London, England. University Lecturer. m. Kenneth Allott, 2 June 1951 (dec.1973). *Education:* MA, Liverpool University, 1946; Ph D 1949. *Literary Appointments:* William Noble Felowship, English Literature, 1946-48; Lecturer, Senior Lecturer, Reader, English Literature, Liverpool University, 1948-73; Andrew Cecil Bradley Professor, Modern English Literature, 1973-81; Professor of English, Birkbeck College, London University, 1981-85; Honorary Senior Fellow, Liverpool University; Professor Emeritus, London University. *Publications:* The Art of Graham Green, with Kenneth Allott, 1951; Novelists on the Novel, 1959; Complete Poems of John Keats,

1970; Complete Poems of Matthew Arnold, 2nd edition 1979 (1st edition, Kenneth Allott, 1965); Matthew Arnold, with R.H.Super, 1986. Numerous essays & articles on 19th & 20th century novelists & poets, notably Keats, Shelley, Arnold, Clough, the Brontes, George Eliot, Henry James, James Joyce, Graham Greene, Iris Murdoch, William Golding; Currently completing: Poems of Matthew Arnold, co-editor with Nicholas Shrimpton; Critical biography of Clough. *Membership:* Executive Committee, English Association. *Address:* 21 Mersey Avenue, Liverpool L19 3QU, England.

ALLSOPP (Harold) Bruce, b. 4 July 1912, Oxford, England. Author; Artist. m. Florence Cyrilla Woodroffe, 29 Dec 1936 (dec 1991), 2 sons. *Education:* B Arch, 1933; Dip C D, 1935, Liverpool University. *Appointments:* Senior Lecturer, History of Architecture, University of Newcastle Upon Tyne, 1969-73; Reader 1973-77. *Publications include:* General History of Architecture, 1955; Art and the Nature of Architecture, 1952; Civilization, The Next Stage, 1969, A Modern Theory of Architecture, 1970; The Country Life Companion to British and European Architecture, 1977; Social Responsibility and the Responsible Society, 1985. *Contributions to:* Various journals. *Memberships:* Athenaeum; Art Workers Guild Mater, 1970; MRTPI, FSA, Chairman - Society of Architectural Historians, 1959-65. *Address:* Woodburn, 3 Batt House Road, Stocksfield, Northumberland NE43 7QZ, England.

ALLWOOD Martin Samuel, b. 13 Apr 1916, Jonkoping, Sweden. Author; Professor. m. Enelia Paz Gomez, 20 Dec 1976, 2 sons, 3 daughters by previous marriage. *Education:* MA Cantab; MA Columbia, 1949; Dr.rer.pol, Technische Hochschule Darmstadt, 1953. *Appointments:* President, Anglo American College, Sweden; Professor, Mass Media Nordic College of Journalism, Sweden. *Publications:* More than 80 books in Swedish and English including Middlevillage, 1943; The Cemetery of the Cathedrals, 1945; Scandinavian Songs and Ballads, 1953; Eilert Sundt, 1957; Toward a New Sociology, 1964; The Swedish Crime, play, 1976; He collected Poems of Edith Sodergran, translations, 1980; New English Poems, 1981; Modern Scandinavian Poetry, 1982; Valda Svenska Dikter, 1982; A dream of Poland, 1982; The Academy, a play, 1984; Meet Will Shakespeare, Nine Scences from the Life of Shakespeare, 1985; Snapshots of more or less famous people, 1985; Indiska dikter, by Octavio Paz, 1986 and 1990; Essays on Contemporary Civilization, 1988; Something Like Aphorisms, 1989; The Black Hat, Short Stories, 1990; The Roots of Western Civilization, 1990; Fundamentalism in Islam and Christianity; The Religious Principles of Ayatollah Khomeiny, 1992; The Empress and Her Lover; Plays, 1993. *Contributor to:* numerous articles in professional journals. *Memberships:* Founding Member, Gothenburgh Society of Authors; Swedish Society of Immigrant Authors; Life Member, Plesse Academy, Gottingen, West Germany. *Address:* Anglo-American Center, 56532 00 Mullsjö, Sweden USE.

ALMQUIST Gregg Andrew, b. 1 Dec 1948, Minneapolis, Minnesota, USA. Actor; Novelist; Playwright. *Education:* BA, University of Minnesota, 1971. *Publications:* Beast Rising, 1988, Pocket Books, Inc (published in France under the title L'eveil de la bete); Wolf Kill, 1990, Pocket Books, Inc Plays (produced): The Duke; The Eve of Saint Venus (adapted from Burgess); The Winter That Ended in June; Pavan for a Dead Princess. *Literary Agent:* Lisa Bankoff, c/o ICM, New York. *Address:* ICM, 40W 57th Street, New York, NY 10019, USA.

ALPERS Antony, b. 1919, New Zealand. Writer. *Appointments:* Journalist, Editor, New Zealand, 1936-66; Professor of English, Queen's University, Kingston, Ontario, 1966-82 (now Emeritus). *Publications:* Katherine Mansfield: A Biography, 1953; Dolphins, 1960; Maori Myths and Tribal Legends, 1964; Legends of the South Sea, 1970, as The World of the Polynesians, 1987; The Life of Katherine Mansfield, 1980; The Stories of Katherine Mansfield, 1984. *Address:* 46 Memorial Avenue, Christchurch 5, New Zealand.

ALPHONSO-KARKALA John B, b. 1923, India. Author; Poet. *Appointments:* Member, Indian Foreign Missions, Geneva, London, United Nations, New York City, 1953-60; Teaching Fellow, Oriental Studies Programme, Columbia University, New York City, 1962-64; Assistant Professor, 1964-65, Associate Professor, 1965-68, Professor of Literature, 1969-, State University of New York, New Platz. *Publications:* Indo-English Literature in the Nineteenth Century, 1970; An Anthology of Indian Literature: Selections from Vedas to Tagore, 1972; Passions of the Nightless Nights (novel), 1974; Bibliography of Indo-English Literature 1800-1966 (with Leena Karkala), 1974; Studies in Comparative Literature: Essays, 1974; Jawaharial Nehru: A Literary Portrait, 1975; Vedic Vision, 1980; When Night Falls (verse with Leena Karkala), 1980; Joys of Jayamagara (novel), 1981. *Memberships:* Modern Language Association, USA; American Comparative Literature Association. *Address:* 20 Millrock Road, New Paltz, NY 12561, USA.

ALSTON Charles. *See:* **MOTT Michael.**

ALTER Robert B, b. 2 Apr 1935, New York City, USA. Professor; Literary Critic. m. Carol Cosman, 17 June 1974, 3 sons, 1 daughter. *Education:* BA, Columbia College, 1957; MA, 1958, PhD, 1962, Harvard University. *Appointments:* Instructor, Assistant Professor, English, Columbia University, 1962-66; Associate Professor, Hebrew & Comparative Literature, University of California, Berkeley, 1967-69; Professor of Hebrew & Comparative Literature, 1969-89; Class of 1937 Professor, 1989-. *Publications:* Partial Magic, 1975; Defenses of the Imagination, 1978; Stendhal : A Biography, 1979; The Art of Biblical Narrative, 1981; Motives for Fiction, 1984; The Art of Biblical Poetry, 1985; The Pleasures of Reading in an Idealogical Age, 1989; Necessary Angels, 1991; The World of Biblical Literature, 1992. *Contributions to:* Commentary; New Republic; New York Times Book Review. *Honours:* English Institute Essay Prize, 1965; National Jewish Book Award for Jewish Thought, 1982; Present Tense Award for Religious Thought, 1986; American Academy of Arts and Sciences, 1986. *Memberships:* American Comparative Literature Association; Council of Scholars of the Library of Congress; American Academy of Arts and Sciences. *Literary Agent:* Georges Borchardt. *Address:* 1475 Le Roy Avenue, Berkeley, CA 94708, USA.

ALTHER Lisa, b. 1944, United States of America. Author. *Appointments:* Staff Member, Atheneum Publishers, New York City; Lecturer, St Michael's College, Burlington, 1980. *Publications:* Kinflicks, 1976; Original Sins, 1981; Other Women, 1984; Bedrock, 1990. *Contributions to:* NY Times Magazine, NY Times Book Review, Natural History, New Society, Arts and Antiques. *Memberships:* PEN; Authors Guild; National Writers Union. *Literary Agent:* Gloria Loomis, Watkins-Loomis, 150 E. 35th St, NY, NY 10016, USA. *Address:* c/o Gloria Loomis, Watkins-Loomis, 150 E. 35th St, NY, NY 10016, USA.

ALTICK Richard Daniel, b. 1915, United States of America. Writer. *Appointments:* Faculty, 1945, Regent's Professor of English, 1968-82, Regent's Professor Emeritus of English, 1982-, Ohio State University, Columbus. *Publications:* Preface to Critical Reading, 1946, 6th revised edition, 1984; The Cowden Clarkes, 1948; The Scholar Adventurers, 1950; The English Common Reader: A Social History of the Mass Reading Public, 1800-1900, 1957; The Art of Literary Research, 1963, 4th revised edition 1992; Lives and Letters: A History of Literary Biography in England and America, 1965; (ed.) Carlyle: Past and Present, 1965; Browning's Roman Murder Story (with J.F. Loucks), 1968; To Be in England, 1969; Victorian Studies in Scarlet, 1970; (ed.) Browning: The Ring and the Book, 1971; Victorian People and Ideas: A Companion for the Modern Reader

of Victorian Literature, 1973; The Shows of London, 1978; Paintings from Books: Art and Literature in Britain 1760-1900, 1985; Deadly Encounters: Two Victorian Sensations (as Evil Encounters in UK), 1986; Writers, Readers and Occasions, 1989, (Lit Criticism); The Presence of the Present: Topics of the Dau in the Victorian Novel, 1991. *Honour:* Winner, Phi Beta Kappa's Christian Gauss Award, 1991. *Address:* Department of English, Ohio State University, 164 West 17th Avenue, Columbus, Ohio 43210, USA.

ALTMAN Dennis, b. 16 Aug 1943, Sydney, New South Wales, Australia. Lecturer. *Education:* BA (Hons), Tasmania; MA, Cornell University, USA. *Appointments:* Currently Reader in Politics, La Trobe University, Melbourne. *Publications:* Homosexual: Oppression and Liberation, 1972; Rehearsals for Change, 1980; The Homosexualization of America, 1982; AIDS in the Mind of America, 1986; AIDS and the New Puritanism, 1986; Paper Ambassadors, 1991. *Memberships:* PEN, Delegate to 1989 Conference. *Literary Agent:* Curtis Brown. *Address:* c/o Politics Department, La Trobe University, Bundoora, Victoria 3083, Australia.

ALTMAN Philip L, b. 6 Jan 1924, Kansas City, Missouri, USA. Editor; Administrator. m. Lillian Berlinsky, 1 Sept 1946, 1 son, 1 daughter. *Education:* BA, University of Southern California, 1948; MSc, Western Reserve University, 1949. *Appointments:* Director, Editor, Office of Biological Handbooks, 1959-79; Executive Editor, Biology Databook Series, 1983-86; Executive Director, Council of Biology Editors, 1981-. *Publications:* Handbook of Respiration, 1958; Handbook of Circulation, 1959; Blood and Other Body Fluids, 1961; Growth, 1962; Biology Data Book, 1st edition, 1964; Environmental Biology, 1966; Metabolism, 1968; Respiration & Circulation, 1971; Biology Data Book, 2nd Edition, Volume 1, 1972, Volume II, 1973, Volume III, 1974; Cell Biology, 1976; Human Health and Disease, 1977; Inbred and Genetically Defined Strains of Laboratory Animals, 1979; Pathology of Laboratory Mice and Rats 1985. *Contributor to:* Scientific journals; Zoology CODATA Directory of Data Sources for Science and Technology, in CODATA Bulletin No. 38, 1980; Council of Biology Editors : A 25 Year Chronology of Events, in CBE Views, Volume 4, 1981; Publications of the Council of Biology Editors, in CBE Views Volume 6, 1983; The Council of Biology Editors, in Scholarly Publishing, Volume 20, 1989. *Address:* Council of Biology Editors, 9650 Rockville Pike, Bethesda, MD 20814, USA.

ALUKO Timothy Mofolorunso, b. 1918, Nigeria. Author. *Appointments:* Town Engineer, Lagos Town Council, 1956-60; Director and Permanent Secretary, Ministry of Works and Transport, Western Nigeria, 1960-66; Senior Research Fellow, Municipal Engineering, University of Lagos, 1966-78; Associate Professor, Public Health Engineering, University of Lagos, 1978; Partner, Scott Wilson Kirkpatrick, Lagos, 1979-88. *Publications:* One Man, One Wife, 1959; One Man, One Matchet, 1964; Kinsman and Foreman, 1966; Chief the Honourable Minister, 1970; His Worshipful Majesty, 1973; Wrong Ones in the Dock, 1982; A State of Our Own, 1986. *Address:* 53 Ladipo Oluwole Road, Apapa, Lagos, Nigeria.

ALVAREZ Alfred, b. 5 Aug 1929. Poet; Author. m. 7 Apr 1966, 2 sons, 1 daughter. *Education:* Oundle School; Corpus Christi College, Oxford, BA, 1952; MA, 1956. *Literary Appointments:* Poetry Critic and Editor, The Observer, 1956-66; Advisory Editor, Penguin Modern European Poets, 1964-76. *Publications Include:* The Shaping Spirit (in US: Stewards of Excellence), 1958; The School of Donne, 1961; The New Poetry (Editor and Introduction), 1962; Under Pressure, 1965; Beyond All The Fiddle, 1968; Lost (Poems), 1968; Penguin Modern Poets No. 18, 1970; The Savage God, 1971; Beckett, 1973; Hers, 1974; Autumn To Autumn and Selected Poems, 1978; Hunt, 1978; Life After Marriage, 1982; The Biggest Game In Town, 1983; Offshore, 1986; Feeding the Rat, 1988; Rain Forest, 1988; Day of Atonement, 1991; The Faber Book of

Modern European Poetry, 1992 (editor amd introduction). *Contributions To:* Numerous Magazines and Journals. *Honours:* Vachel Lindsay Prize for Poetry (from Poetry, Chicago), 1961. *Memberships:* Climbers; Alpine; Beefsteak. *Literary Agent:* Gillon Aitken. *Address:* c/o Aitken and Stone, 29 Fernshaw Road, London, SW10 0TG, England.

ALVERSON Marianne, b. 11 Oct 1942, Shanghai, China. Ethnographer: Research on Dual Diagnosis (schizophrenia and substance abuse) Clients in Mental Health Care; Public Speaker; Writer. m. Hoyt Sutliff Alverson, 6 June 1964, 2 sons. *Education:* BA, George Washington University, 1964. *Appointments:* Ethnographer, Community & Family Medicine, Dartmouth College, 1989-; Administrative Assistant on Asian Studies Programme, Dartmouth College, Hanover, New Hampshire, 1980-; Volunteer for Head Start Association, 1968-70; Public speaker on the women of Botswana, 1986-. *Publications:* Under African Sun, 1987; Editor of Orient Express, a newsletter of Dartmouth College Asian Studies Programme, 1981-86. *Honours:* Under African Sun was named to Choice magazine's Outstanding Academic List for 1988. *Address:* RR1, Box 138, Lyme, NH, USA.

AMADI Elechi, b. 1934, Nigeria. Author; Playwright. *Publications:* The Concubine, 1966; The Great Ponds, 1969; Isiburu (play), 1973; Sunset in Biafra, 1974; Peppersoup and The Road to Ibadan (play), 1977; The Slave, 1978; Dancer of Johannesburg (play), 1979; Ethics in Nigerian Culture, 1982; Estrangement (novel), 1986. *Address:* Box 331, Port Harcourt, Nigeria.

AMADO Jorge, b. 10 Aug 1912. Novelist. m. Zelia Gattai, 1945, 1 son, 1 daughter. *Publications include:* Mar Morto; Jubiaba; The Violent Land; Sao Jorge dos Ilheus; Cacau; Suor; Capitaes da Areia; ABC de Castro Alves; Bahia de Todos os Santos; O Amor do Soldado; Seara Vermelha; O Cavaleiro da Esperanca; O Mundo da Paz; os Subterraneos da Liberdade; Gabriela Cravo e Canela; Os velhos marinheiros; Os pastores da noite; Dona Flor e seus dois maridos!; Tenda dos Milagres; Teresa Bautista Cansada de Guerra; Tieto do Agreste e Farda; Fardao; Camisola de Dormir; O Menino Grapiuna; Tocaia Grande. *Honours:* Calouste Gulbenkian Prize, Academy du Monde Latin, 1971; National Literary Prize, Brazil; Nonnino Literary Prize, Italy; Commander, Legion d'Honneur, France. *Address:* Rua Alagoinhas 33, Rio Vermelho-Salvador, Bahia, Brazil.

AMANSHAUSER Gerhard, b. 2 Jan 1928, Salzburg, Austria. Writer. *Education:* Technical University of Graz; Universities of Vienna, Austria & Marburg/Lahn, Germany. *Publications:* Aus der Leben der Quaden, novel, 1968; Der Deserteur, short stories, 1970; Satz und Gegensatz, essays, 1972; Argenisse eines Zauberers, satires & marginalia, 1973; Schloss mit spaten Gasten, novel, 1975; Grenzen, essays, 1977; Aufzeichnungen einer Sonde, parodies, 1979; List der Illusionen, commentaries, 1985; Gedichte, 1986; Fahrt zur Verbotenen Stadt, satires & capriccios, 1987; Der Ohne-Namen-See, Chinese Impressions, 1988; Moloch Horridus (Aufzeichnungen 1989); Lekrüre, 1991; Gegensätze, 1993. *Contributions to:* Literatur und Kritik; Neues Forum; Protokolle; Neue Rundschau. *Honours:* Georg Trakl Promotion Prize, 1952; Theodor Korner Prize, 1970; Rauriser Literaturpreis, 1973; Forderungspreis der Stadt Salzburg, 1975; Preis der Salzburger Wirtschaft, 1985; Alma Johanna Koenig Preis, 1987. *Address:* Brunnhausgasse 10, 5020 Salzburg, Austria.

AMBLER Eric (Eliot Reed), b. 28 June 1909, London, England. Novelist; Screenwriter. *Education:* London University. *Publications include:* A Kind of Anger, 1964; Dirty Story, 1967; The Levanter, 1972; Doctor Frigo, 1974; Send No More Roses, 1977; Here Lies (autobiog), 1985. *Honours:* OBE, 1981; MWA, Grand Master, 1975; CWA Gold and Diamond Daggers. *Memberships:* Society of Authors, Council; Writers Guild of America

(West), Council 1961-62. *Literary Agent:* Campbell Thomson & MacLaughlin Ltd. *Address:* c/o Campbell Thomson & MacLaughlin Ltd., 1 King's Mews, London WC1N 2JA, England.

AMERY Carl, b. 9 Apr 1922, Munich, Germany. Writer m. Marijane Gerth, 10 Apr 1950, 3 sons, 2 daughters. *Education:* Humanistisches Gymnasium (Abitur 1940); Literary and Language Studies in Munich and Washington 1946-50. *Literary Appointments:* Director of Munich City Library System, 1967-71; Editor of Bavarian Broadcasting Station, 1950 and 1962 (temporary). *Publications include:* Die Kapitulation, Essay, 1963; Die Grosse Deutsche Tour, Novel 1959; Das Ende der Vorsehung, Essay, 1972; Natur als Politik, Essay, 1976; Das Koenigsprojekt, Novel, 1974; Die Wallfahrer, Novel, 1986; Das Geheimnis der Krypta, Novel, 1990. *Honours:* German Federal Cross of Merit, 1988; Honorary Citizen Nr 9 of the village of Granit, South Bulgaria. *Memberships:* VS (German Writers' Association affiliated to the Media trade union); PEN Center of Germany, President. E f Schumachgesellschaft fuer politische Oekologie, Munich, President; ECOROPA member. *Address:* Draechslstr 7, D-8 Muenchen 90, Germany.

AMERY H. Julian, (Rt Hon), b. 27 Mar 1919. Member of Parliament, UK (Conservative, Preston North, 1950-66, Brighton Pavilion 1969-). *Education:* Eton; Balliol College, University of Oxford, England. *Publications:* Sons of the Eagle, 1948; The Life of Joseph Chamberlain: Vol IV 1901-03, At the Height of His Power, 1951, Volumes V & VI, Joseph Chamberlain & The Tariff Reform Campaign 1901-14, 1969; Approach March (autobiography), 1973. *Contributions to:* Various newspapers and journals. *Honours include:* Privy Councillor, 1960; Knight Commander of the Order of the Phoenix; Order of Oman 1st Class; Life Peer of Preston, 1992. *Address:* 112 Eaton Square, London SW1 9AE, England.

AMES Leslie. *See:* **RIGONI Orlando Joseph.**

AMES Sarah Rachel, (Sarah Gainham) b. 1 Oct 1922, London, England. Writer. m. Kenneth Robert Ames, 14 Apr 1964, dec 1975. *Publications:* Time Right Deadly, 1956; Cold Dark Night, 1957; The Mythmaker, 1957; Stone Roses, 1959; Silent Hostage, 1960; Night Falls on the City, 1967; A Place in the Country, 1968; Takeover Bid, 1970; Private Worlds, 1971; Maculan's Daughter, 1973; To the Opera Ball, 1975; The Habsburg Twilight, 1979; The Tiger, Life, 1983. *Contributions to:* Encounter, Atlantic Monthly, BBC, and others. *Address:* Altes Forsthaus, Schlosspark, A2404 Petronell, Austria.

AMIN Sayed Hassan, b. 25 Nov 1948, Persia. Professor of Law; Author; Advocate. m. 1 son, 1 daughter. *Education:* LLB, 1970; LLM, 1975; PhD, 1979; Scottish Bar Exams, 1980-82. *Appointments:* Lecturer, 1979; Senior Lecturer, 1981; Reader, 1984; Professor, 1991, Glasgow Caledonian University. *Publications:* International And Legal Problems of the Gulf; Middle East Legal Systems; Law & Justice in Contemporary Yemen; Islamic Law And Its Implications for the Modern World; Legal System of Iraq, Legal System of Kuwait, Law of Intellectual Property in Developing Countries. *Contributions to:* International & Comparative Law Quarterly; Oil & Gas Law & Taxation Review. *Memberships:* Society of Authors; Royal Institute of International Affairs; Faculty of Advocates; Scottish Institute of International & Comparative Law; Council for National Academic Awards. *Address:* Dept of Law, Caledonian University, Cowcaddens Road, Glasgow, G4 0BA, Scotland.

AMIS Kingsley Sir, (Robert Markham) b. 16 Apr 1922, London, England. Author. m. (1) Hilary A. Bardwell, 1948, 2 sons, 1 daughter, (2) Elizabeth Jane Howard, 1965, divorced 1983. *Education:* St John's College, Oxford. *Appointments:* Lecturer, English, University College, Swansea, 1949-61; Fellow,

Peterhouse, Cambridge, 1961-63; Visiting Professor, various Universities in USA. *Publications:* A Frame of Mind, 1953; Lucky Jim, 1954; That Uncertain Feeling, 1955; A Case of Samples, 1956; I Like It Here, 1958; New Maps of Hell, 1960; Take a Girl Like You, 1960; My Enemy's Enemy, 1962; One Fat Englishman, 1963; The James Bond Dossier, 1965; The Egyptologists (with Robert Conquest), 1965; The Anti-Death league, 1966; A Look Around the Estate, (poems 1957-67), 1967; Colonel Sun, 1968 (As Robert Markham); What Became of Jane Austen?, 1970; Girl, 20, 1971; On Drink, 1972; The Riverside Villas Murder, 1973; Ending Up, 1974; Rudyard Kipling and His World, 1975; The Alteration, 1976; Jake's Thing, 1978; Collected Poems 1944-1979, 1979; Russian Hide and Seek, 1980; Collected Short Stories, 1980; Every Day Drinking, 1983; Stanley and the Women, 1984; How's Your Glass, 1984; The Old Devils, 1986; Difficulties with Girls, 1988. Editor, New Oxford Book of Light Verse, 1978, Faber Popular Reciter, 1978, The Golden Age of Science Fiction, 1981; Crime of the Century, 1987; The Folks That Live On The Hill, 1990; We Are All Guilty, 1991; The Russian Girl, 1992. *Honours;* Somerset Maugham Award; John W. Campbell Memorial Award; Booker Prize for Fiction; Hon. Fellow, University College, Swansea; CBE, 1981; Kt, 1990; Hon. Fellow St. John's Oxford. *Address:* c/o Jonathan Clowes and Co, 22 Prince Albert Road, London NW1, England.

AMIS Martin Louis, b. 25 Aug 1949. Author. *Education:* Exeter College, Oxford. *Appointments:* Fiction and Poetry Editor, Times Literary Supplement, 1974; Literary Editor, New Statesman, 1977-79; Special Writer, The Observer Newspaper, 1980-. *Publications:* The Rachel Papers, 1973; Dead Babies, 1975; Success, 1978; Other People: a Mystery Story, 1981; Invasion of the Space Invaders, 1982; Money, 1984; London Fields, 1989; Time's Arrow. *Honours:* Somerset Maugham Award, 1974. *Address:* c/o Peters Fraser & Dunlop, 5th Floor, The Chambers, Chelsea Harbour, Lots Road, London SW10 0XP, England.

AMMONS A(rchie) R(andolph), b. 18 Feb 1926, Whiteville, North Carolina, USA. Professor of English; Poet. m. Phyllis Plumbo, 1949, 1 son. *Education:* BS, Wake Forest College, North Carolina, 1949; University of California, Berkeley, 1950-52. Served in the US Naval Reserve, 1944-46. *Appointments:* Principal, Hatteras Elementary School, North Carolina, 1949-50; Executive Vice-President, Friedrich and Dimmock Inc, Millville, New Jersey, 1952-62; Assistant Professor 1964-68, Associate Professor 1969-71; Professor of English 1971-; Goldwin Smith Professor of English, Cornell University, Ithaca, New York, 1973-; Visiting Professor, Wake Forest University, 1974-75; Poetry Editor, Nation, New York, 1963. *Publications:* Verse includes: The Snow Poems, 1977; The Selected Poems 1951-1977, 1977; Highgate Road, 1977; For Doyle Fosco, 1977; POem, 1977; Six-Piece Suite, 1979; Selected Longer Poems, 1980; A Coast of Trees, 1981; Worldly Hopes, 1982; Lake Effect Country, 1983. *Honours:* Bread Loaf Writers Conference scholarship, 1961; Guggenheim Fellowship, 1966; American Academy Travelling Fellowship, 1967 and award 1977; Levinson Prize (Poetry, Chicago) 1970; National Book Award, 1973; Bollingen Prize, 1975; MacArthur Fellowship, 1981; National Book Critics Circle Award, 1982; D Litt: Wake Forest University, 1972, University of North Carolina, Chapel Hill, 1973; Fellow, American Academy of Arts and Sciences, 1982. *Memberships:* Elected Member, Fellowship's of Southern Writers, 1989; Inducted Member, American Academy and Institute of Arts and Letters, 1990. *Address:* Department of English, Cornell University, Ithaca, NY 14850, USA.

AMOS James H, b. 10 Apr 1946, Missouri, USA. Chief Operating Officer. m. Janice, 27 Aug 1966, 2 daughters. *Education:* University of Missouri, AB; Course Work for Masters in Hunam Relations. *Publications:* The Memorial; Trens & Developments in International Franchising; European Franchising. *Contributions to:* International Business Franchising Update; Franchising World. *Honours:* National Library

Association, Best Works. *Memberships:* National Authors Guild; National Speakers Association; National Handball Association; 3rd Marine Division Association; Military Order of the Purple Heart. *Literary Agent:* Jan Miller, Dupree Miller. *Address:* 3404 Leigh Court, Plano, TX 75025, USA.

AN Tai Sung, b. 3 Feb 1931, Seoul, Korea. College Professor; Author. m. Sihn Ja Lee, 23 Aug 1969, 2 daughters. *Education:* Bach of Arts, Indiana University, Bloomington, 1956; Master of Arts, Yale University, New Haven, 1957; PhD, University of Pennsylvania, 1963. *Appointments:* Professor of Political Science, Washington College, Chestertown, 1963-73; Everett E Nuttle Professor, Political Science at Washington College, Chestertown, 1973-. *Publications:* Mao Tse Tung's Cultural Revolution; The Sino Soviet Territorial Dispute; The Lin Piao Affair; North Korea in Transition: From Dictatorship to Dynasty; North Korea: A Political Handbook; The Vietnam War. About 80 Articles. *Honours:* Lindback Award for Distinguished Teaching; Sears Roebuck Foundation Teaching Excellence & Campus Leadership Award. *Memberships:* American political Science Association; Association for Asian Studies; Asia Society; Korean association of Oriental History & Civilization; American Association of University Professors. *Address:* Dept of Pol Science & Internal Studies, Washington College, 300 Washington Avenue, Chestertown, MD 21620, USA.

ANANIA Michael (Angelo), b. 1938, United States of America. Author; Poet. *Literary Appointments:* Co-ordinating Council of Litery Magazines, Bibliographer, Lockwood Library, State University of New York, Buffalo, 1963-64; Editor, Audit, 1963-64; Co-Editor, Audit/ Poetry, Buffalo, 1963-67; Instructor in English, State University of New York, Fredonia, 1964- 65, Northwestern University, Evanston, Illinois, 1965-68; Literary Editor, Swallow Press, Chicago, 1968-; Professor of English, University of Illinois, Chicago, 1970-. *Publications:* New Poetry Anthology I and II, 1969, 1972; The Colour of Dust, 1970; Set/Sorts, 1974; Riversongs, 1978; The Red Menace, 1984; Constructions/Variations, 1985; The Sky at Ashland, 1986; In Plain Sight, 1991. *Address:* Department of English, University of Illinois at Chicago, Chicago, IL 60680, USA.

ANCONA George Efraim, b. 4 Dec 1929, New York City, USA. Photographer; Author. m. Helga Von Sydow, 20 July 1968, 2 sons, 4 daughters. *Education:* Cooper Union, Academia de San Carlos, Escuela del Arte del Libro, Mexico City, Art Students League. *Publications include:* Handtalk, 1974; It's a Baby, 1979; Dancing Is, 1981; Sheepdog, 1985; Helping Out, 1985; Turtle Watch, 1987; Handtalk Birthday, 1987; Riverkeeper, 1989. *Contributor to:* Photographs appeared in: Esquire, New York Magazine, Vogue Children, McCalls, Popular Mechanics. *Honours include:* Junior Literary Guild Selection: for And What Do You Do? 1976, for It's A Baby, 1979, for Dancing Is 1981, for Monster Movers 1983; Notable Children's Book in Social Science for Sheepdog, 1985; ALA Notable Book, Sheepdog, 1985; AIGA 50 Best Books, Handtalk, 1974; Children's Science Book Award, Handtalk, 1975; NY Academy of Science Award, Turtle Watch, 1987; Junior Literary Guild Selection for Turtle Watch, 1987; NY Times Year's Best Illustrated Children's Books, Handtalk Birthday, 1987; Ny Art Directors Club Award, I Feel, 1978; Various film awards. *Address:* Route 10 Box 94G, Santa Fe, NM 87501, USA.

ANDENAES Johannes Bratt, b. 7 Sept 1912, Innvik, Norway. Professor of Law. m. Ida, 10 June 1939, 2 sons, 2 daughters. *Education:* University of Oslo, 1935, 1943. *Publications:* Criminal Law, General Part; The Constitution of Norway; Norwegian Criminal Procedure; Punishment And Deterrence; Norway and The Second World War. *Contributions to:* Many Papers. *Honours:* Norwegian Academy of Science & Letters; Universities of Uppsala & Copenhagen; Award for for International Contributions to Criminology; Prize for Outstanding Legal Scholarship; Honorary Gold Medal, University of

Copenhagen. *Address:* Generallunden 23, 0381 Oslo, Norway.

ANDERSEN Benny Allan, b. 7 Nov 1929, Copenhagen. Author. m. Cynthia La Touche Andersen, 28 Dec 1981, Lyngby. *Publications:* Den musikalske al, 1960; Kamera med Kokkenadgang, 1962; Den indre bowlerhat, 1964; Puderne, 1965; Portraetgalleri, 1966; Tykke-Olsen Det sidste M.fl., 1968; Oh, 1969; Tykke-Olsen M.Fl., 1968; Det sidste Oh, 1969; Her i reservatet, 1971; Svantes viser, 1972; Personlige papirer, 1974; Under begge ojne, 1978; Himmelspraet, 1979; Pa broen, 1981; Tiden og storken, 1985; Over Skulderen, 1983; Chagall & skorpiondans, 1991. *Contributor to* Anthologies: Niet noodzakelijk met insteeming, Dutch, 1967; Poesia moderna danese, Italian, 1971; Norraen Ljod, Icelandic, 1972; Anthologie de la poesie danoise contemporaine, French, 1975; Anegdoty Losu, Polish, 1976; Skumju Druva, Latvian, 1977; Dan Elbeszelok, 1978, Hungarian; N3 Cobpemehhonoatckon Mo33NN, Russian, 1983. Also Malahat Review; Mundus Artium; Contemporary Literature in Translation; Poetry Now; Prism International; West Coast Review; Literary Review; Scandinavian Review; Liberte; Svetova Literatura; Complete works translated: Kuddarna, 1969; Selected Poems, 1975; Livet är smalt och högt, 1988 Das Leben ist schmal und hoch, 1977; The Pillows, 1983; Selected Prose, 1983; Ma velka doba byla mala, 1983; Over axeln, 1985; Tlustóch Olsen aj. 1989. *Address:* Kaerparken 11, 2800 Lyngby, Denmark.

ANDERSON Daphne Margaret, b. 27 Oct 1919, Harare, Zimbabwe. m. 30 Nov 1942, 3 sons. *Education:* Dominican Convent; Harare, Zimbabwe, 1923-35. *Publications:* The Toerags; The Toerags Paperback. *Literay Agent:* James Sharkey Associates. *Address:* Mulberry Cottage, Hoxne, Nr Eye, Suffolk IP21 5AZ, England.

ANDERSON David Daniel, b. 1924, United States of America. Writer. *Appointments:* Dinstinguished University Professor, Department of American Thought and Language, Michigan State University, East Lansing, 1957-; Editor, Midwestern Miscellany Annual; Executive Secretary, Society for the Study of Midwestern Literature, 1971-73. *Publications:* Louis Bromfield, 1964; Critical Studies in American Literature, 1964; Sherwood Anderson, 1967; Sherwood Anderson's Winesburg, Ohio, 1967; Brand Whitlock, 1968; Editor-in-Chief, The Black Experience, 1969; Abraham Lincoln, 1970; The Literary Works of Abraham Lincoln, 1970; The Dark and Tangled Path (with R. Wright), 1971; Sunshine and Smoke, 1971; Robert Ingersoll, 1972; Mid-America I-XIV, 1974-87; Sherwood Anderson: Dimensions of His Literary Art (essays), 1976; Woodrow Wilson, 1978; Sherwood Anderson: The Writer at his Craft, 1979; Ignatius Donnelly, 1980; William Jennings Bryan, 1981; Critical Essays on Sherwood Anderson, 1981; Michigan: A State Anthology, 1982; Route Two, Titus, Ohio, 1993. *Address:* Department of American Thought and Language, Michigan State University, East Lansing, MI 48824, USA.

ANDERSON Jan Rosemary, b. 26 Sept 1944, Sydney, Australia. Scientific Writer and Editor. m. Donald Orrock Anderson, 30 Nov 1968, 3 daughters. *Education:* Bachelor of Science, Sydney University; Master of Science, Sydney University. *Appointments:* Freelance Writer, Editor, D O Anderson & Co Pty Limited, Melbourne, 1984-93. *Publications:* The Days of the Dinosaurs; Spare Parts for People; Antarctica The World's Biggest Desert; Towns of Australia; The Children's Book of Australia; Your World — Communications; Others inc. MacMillan Science and Technology Encyclopedia. *Contributions to:* Journal of Chemical Society, London; Kids Times. *Memberships:* Australian Society of Authors; Society of Editors (Victoria, Australia); Lyceum Club, Melbourne. *Address:* 39 King Street, East Ivanhoe, Vic 3079, Australia.

ANDERSON Jessica (Margaret), b. Australia. Author. *Publications:* An Ordinary Lunacy, 1963; The Last Man's Head, 1970; The Commandant, 1976; Tirra Lirra by the River, 1978; The Impersonators (in United States of America and United Kingdom as The Only Daughter), 1980; Stories from the Warm Zone, 1987; Taking Shelter, 1989. *Address:* c/o Elaine Marson, Agent, 44 Greenwich Avenue, New York, NY 10011, USA.

ANDERSON Kenneth Norman, b. 1921, United States of America. Writer. *Appointments:* Executive Editor, Publishers Editorial Services; President, Editorial Guild; Editor, Holt Rinehart and Winston, Inc. New York, 1965-70; Executive Director, Coffee Information Institute, New York, 1970-. *Publications:* Co-Author, Lawyer's Medical Cyclopedia, 1962; The Family Physician (with Robert Addison), 1963; Today's Health Guide (with William Baver), 1965; Pictorial Medical Guide (with Robert Addison), 1967; Field and Stream Guide to Physical Fitness, 1969; Home Medical Encyclopedia (with Paul Kuhn), 1973; Sterno Guide to the Outdoors, 1977; Eagle Claw Fish Cookbook, 1977; The Newsweek Encyclopedia of Family Health and Fitness, 1980; Banham Medical Dictionary (with Walter Glanze), 1980, 1982; How Long Will You Live, 1981; Dictionary of Dangerous Pollutants, Ecology and Environment (with David Tver), 1981; The Pocket Guide to Coffees and Teas, 1982; Orphan Drugs, 1983; Longman Dictionary of Psychology and Psychiatry (with Walter Glanze and Robert Goldenson), 1984; History of the US Marines (with Jack Murphy), 1984; Prentice-Hall Dictionary of Nutrition and Health (with Lois Harmon Anderson), 1985; Mosby Medical Encyclopedia (with Lois Harman Anderson and Walter Glanze), 1985. *Address:* Coffee Information Institute, 60 East 42nd Street, New York, NY 10017, USA.

ANDERSON Leone Castell, b. 12 Aug 1923, Los Angeles, California, USA. Free-lance writer; Owner and operator of Lee's Booklover's. m. J Eric Anderson, 17 Aug 1946, 3 sons. *Education:* Attended Austin Academy of Music, 1942-43. *Appointments:* Copy-writer, Russell Seeds Advertising, Chicago, Illinois, 1944-46; Free-lance writer, 1946-49; Member of library staff, Elmhurst Public Library, Elmhurst, Illinois, 1969-74; Free-lance writer 1974-; Owner and operator of Lee's Booklover's, 1979-. *Publications:* Publications for children include: The Good-By Day, 1984, reprinted as Moving Day, 1987; My Friend Next Door, 1984; Contributor to Christmas Handbook, 1984; Surprise at Muddy Creek, 1984; How Come You're So Shy? 1987; My Own Grandpa, 1987; Other works: Glendenna's Dilemma (readers' theatre), first performed in Chicago, Illinoios at Performance Community, 1979; Come-Uppance (readers' theatre) first performed in Stockton, Illinois at Stockton Unitarian-Universalist Church, 1986. *Contributions to:* Columns in Elmhurst Press and Stockton Herald News (Author); Magazines and Newspapers. *Memberships:* Society of Children's Book Writers (Midwest representative 1981-87), Children's Reading Round Table, Authors Guild, Off-Campus Writer's Workshop. *Address:* Lee's Booklover's, 127 South Main, Stockton, IL 61085, USA.

ANDERSON Matthew Smith, b. 23 May 1922, Perth, Scotland. Retired University Teacher. m. Olive Ruth Gee, 10 July 1954, 2 daughters. *Education:* Perth Academy, 1929-40; University of Edinburgh 1940-42, 1945-47, MA, History, 1947. PhD 1952. *Publications:* Europe in the Eighteenth Century 1713-1783, 1961, 1976, 1987; The Eastern Question 1774- 1923, 1966; The Ascendency of Europe 1815-1914, 2nd edition 1985; Peter the Great, 1978; Historiana and Eighteenth-Century Europe, 1979; War and Society in Europe of the Old Regime 1618-1789, 1988; Britain's Discovery of Russia 1553-1815, 1961; The Great Powers and the Near East, 1774-1923, 1966. *Contributor to:* Numerous articles in historical periodicals, notably the English Historical Review, the Slavonic and East European Review and the American Slavic and East European Review. *Memberships:* Fellow, Royal Historical Society; Economic History Society; Past and Present Society.

Address: 45 Cholmeley Crescent, Highgate, London N6 5EX, England.

ANDERSON Michael Falconer, b. 16 Jan 1947, Aberdeen. Author; Journalist. m. Hildegarde Becze, 16 Apr 1970, 2 sons. *Appointments:* Newspaper and Magazine Editor; Chief Sub-Editor of a national weekly; Sub-Editor of a daily newspaper; Showbusiness Writer; Reporter; Correspondent in newspapers, television and radio. *Publications:* The Woodsmen, 1986; The Unholy, 1987; God of a Thousand Faces, 1987; The Covenant, 1988; Black Trinity, 1989; The Clan of Golgotha Scalp, 1990; Numerous short stories and plays for radio and television. *Contributions to:* Feature articles on everything from travel to history, the environment to books, in newspapers and magazines around the world. *Memberships:* Society of Authors; National Union of Journalists. *Address:* Portlethen, Aberdeen, Scotland.

ANDERSON Mignon Holland. *See:* **ANDERSON Mignon Karin Holland.**

ANDERSON Mignon Karin Holland, (Mignon Holland Anderson), b. 20 Jan 1945, Nassawadox, Virginia, USA. College Instructor in English. m. George S Anderson, 26 Nov 1971, div, 1 son, 1 daughter. *Education:* BA 1966, Fisk University, Nashville; MFA 1970, Columbia University School of the Arts, Writing Division, New York. *Publications:* Mostly Womenfolk and a Man or Two: a Collection, short fiction,1976; Customs of Bereavement, essay, 1990. *Contributions to:* Negis Digest/Black World; Freedom Ways; Galliman Fry Press; The Maryland Review; Short Story International. *Honours:* Columbia University Ford Foundation Fellowship for the Arts; Nominee- Second Governors Awards for Virginia; Exceptional Performance, US Department of Justice; Dedication Poem Post, C D Hylton High School, Woodbridge, Virginia. *Address:* Department of English and Modern Language, University of Maryland Eastern Shore, Princess Anne, MD 21853, USA.

ANDERSON Nancy Fix, b. 23 Aug 1941, Dallas, Texas, USA. Professor. m. Clifford H Anderson, 1 son, 1 daughter. *Education:* BA, Stanford University, 1965; MA, University of California, 1967; PhD, Tulane University, 1973. *Publications:* Woman Against Women in Victorian England. *Contributions to:* Journal of British studies; Journal of Family History; Psychohistry Review; Dicken Studies Annual; Victorian Reriodicals Review. *Memberships:* American Historical Association; National Womens Studies Association; Southern Conference in British Studies. *Address:* Dept of History, Loyola University, 6363 St Charles Avenue, New Orleans, LA 70118, USA.

ANDERSON Olive Ruth, b. Mar 1926, Edinburgh, Scotland. University Professor. m. Matthew Smith Anderson, July 1954, 2 daughters. *Education:* King Edward VI Grammar School, Louth; BA, Modern History, Class 1, 1947, B Litt 1949, MA 1951, St Hugh's College, Oxford. *Appointments:* Assistant Lecturer in History, Westfield College, University of London, 1949-56; Lecturer, 1958-69; Reader 1969-86; Professor and Head of Department of History, 1986-89; Deputy Head of Department of History, Queen Mary and Westfield College, University of London 1989-91; Professor Emeritus and Honorary Research Fellow, 1991. *Publications:* Suicide in Victorian and Edwardian England, 1987; A Liberal State at War: English Politics and Economics during the Crimean War, 1967. *Contributor to:* Numerous articles and reviews in Past & Present; English Historical Review; Historical Journal; Economic History Review and many other historical journals. *Membership:* Fellow of Royal Historical Society, 1968, member of Council 1986-90; Vice Xhairman, 1991. *Address:* Department of History, Queen Mary and Westfield College, Mile End Road, London, E1 4NS, England.

ANDERSON Poul William, b. 25 Nov 1926, Bristol,

Pennsylvania, USA. Writer. m. Karen Kruse, 12 Dec 1953, 1 daughter. *Education:* BS, University of Minnesota, 1948. *Publications:* Brain Wave, 1954; The High Crusade, 1960; Guadians of Time, 1961; Three Hearts & Three Lions, 1961; Tau Zero, 1971; The Broken Sword (revised edition), 1971; Hrolf Kraki's Saga, 1973; A Midsummer's Tempest, 1974; The Atavar, 1978; The Merman's Children, 1979 Orion Shall Rise, 1983; The Boat of a Million Years, 1989. *Contributor to:* Analog; Magazine of Fantasy & Science Fiction; Destinies; National Review; Boy's Life and others. *Honours:* Hugo Awards, 1961, 1964, 1968, 1971, 1973, 1978, 1982; Nebula Awards, 1971, 1972, 1981; Knight of Mark Twain, 1971; Mythopoeic Award, 1975; J R R Tolkien Memorial Award, 1978. *Memberships:* Science Fiction Writers of America, President 1972-73; Baker Street Iregulars. *Literary Agent:* Scott Meredith, New York. *Address:* 3 Las Palomas, Orinda, CA 94563, USA.

ANDERSON Quentin, b. 1912, United States of America. Writer. *Appointments:* Columbia University, 1939-82; University of Sussex, 1966-67; Univeristy of Barcelona, 1985. *Publications:* Selected Short Stories by Henry James, 1950; The American Henry James, 1957; The Proper Study: Essays on Western Classics, (with Joseph A. Mazzeo), 1962; The Imperial Self: An Essay in American Literary and Cultural History, 1971; Art, Politics and Will: Essays in Honor of Lionel Trilling (with others), 1977; Making Americans: an Essay on Individualism and Money, 1992. *Honours:* National Endowment for the Humanities, Senior Fellow, 1973; Paley Lecturer, Hebrew University of Jerusalem, 1982; Fellow, National Humanities Center, 1979-93. *Address:* 29 Claremont Avenue, New York, NY 10027, USA.

ANDERSON Rachel, b. 1943. Writer: Novels, Short Stories, Plays. m. David Bradby. 4 Children . *Publications:* Books for adults: Pineapple, 1965; The Purple Heart Throbs, A Survey of Popular Romantic Fiction, 1850-1972, 1974; Dream Lovers, 1978; For the Love of Sang, 1990; Books for small children: Tim Walks, 1985; The Cat's Tale, 1985; Wild Goose Chase, 1986; Jessy Runs Away, 1988; Best Friends, 1991; Jessy and The Long-Short Dress, 1992; Tough as Old Boots, 1991; Little Lost Fox, 1992; For older children: Moffatt's Road, 1978; The Poachers' Son, 1982; The War Orphan, 1984; Little Angel Comes to Stay, 1985; Little Angel, Bonjour, 1988; Happy Chrtistmas, Little Angel, 1991; French Lessons, 1988; Renard The Fox (with David Bradby), 1986; The Boy Who Laughed, 1989; The Bus People, 1989; Paper Faces, 1991; When Mum Went to Work, 1992; Forthcoming: The Working Class, 1993; Jessy and the Long Short Dress, 1993. *Honours:* Medical Journalists Association Award for For The Love Of Sang, 1990; 25th Anniversary Guardian Children's Fiction Award for Paper Faces, 1992. *Address:* c/o Oxford University Press, Oxford OX2 6DP, England.

ANDERSON Robert Woodruff, b. 28 Apr 1917, NYC, USA. Playwright; Screenwriter; Novelist. *Education:* AB, Magna cum laude, 1939, MA 1940, Harvard University. *Publications:* Tea and Sympathy, 1953; All Summer Long, 1954; Silent Night Lonely Night, 1959; The Days Between, 1965; You Know I Can't Hear When the Water's Running, 1967; I Never Sang for My Father, 1968; Solitaire/Double Solitaire, 1971; Free and Clear, 1983; Co-author, Elements of Literature, 1988. Novels: After, 1973; Getting Up and Going Home, 1978. Screenplays: The Nun's Story, 1959; The Sand Pebbles, 1966; Play: The Last Act is A Solo, TV, 1991; Absolute Strangers, TV, 1991. *Honours:* Recipient Awards for, I Never Sang for My Father, Writers' Guild, 1970. *Memberships:* President, Dramatists Guild, 1971-73; Authors League Counc; Writers Guild of America; W.Am. Playwrights Theatre, Board of Trustees; Theatre Hall of Fame, 1981; P.E.N.; V.P, Authors League of America. *Literary Agent:* ICM. *Address:* Transylvania Rd, Roxbury, Connecticut 06783, USA.

ANDERSON William C., b. 7 May 1920, La Junta, Colorado, USA. Author. m. Dortha Marie Power, 10 July 1948, 1 son, 2 daughters. *Education:* Mesa Community College; San Diego University, Maryland. *Publications:*

Bomber Crew 369, 1986; Bat-21, 1980; Home Sweet Home has Wheels, 1979; When the Offspring have Sprung, 1978; Penelope the Damp Detective, 1974; Headstrong Houseboat, 1972; Adapted for TV, Hurricane Hunters, 1972; Adapted for Films, Bat-21, 1987. *Contributions to:* Readers Digest. *Membership:* Screen Writer's Guild. *Literary Agent:* Shirley Burke. *Address:* 4857 Lake Shore Place, Boise, ID 83703, USA.

ANDRE Robert, b. 30 Aug 1920, Paris. Professor; Writer. m. Maie Therese Poirier, 10 Aug 1950, 2 sons, 1 daughter. *Education:* Licence, 1945; Markers, 1948; PhD, 1950; Doctor, 1980. *Publications include:* L'Enfant Miroir; L'Amour et la Vie d'une Femme; Les Vertes Fenillantines; L'Amours à l'Avengle; A La Belle Saison. *Contributions to:* La Nonvelle Rivue Francaise. *Honours:* Grand prix du Roman de la Société des Gens de Lettres; prix Mediterranée; Prix de 1Acadmic Francaise. *Memberships:* President International Association of Literary Critics; Societe des Gens de Lettres. *Address:* 58 Rue Claude Bernard, 75005 Paris, France.

ANDRESKI Stanislav Leonard, b. 18 May 1919, Czestochowa. Poland. Writer, 2 sons, 2 daughters. *Education:* BSc, 1st Class Honours, 1943, MSc 1947, Economics, PhD 1953. *Appointments:* Prof. Em. University of Reading and Polish University in London, Editorial Board, Journal of Strategic Studies. *Publications include:* Military Organisation & Society, 1954, 2nd ed. 1968; Elements of Comparative Sociology, 1964; The Uses of Comparative Sociology (American Edition of 2) 1965, paperback 1969, Spanish Edition, 1973, 1972; Parasitism & Subversion: The Case of Latin America, 1966; 2nd ed. 1969. Argentinian Edition in Spanish, 1967; The African Predicament: A Study in Pathology of Modernisation, 1968; Social Sciences as Sorcery, 1972, Spanish translation, 1973; German translation, 1974 2nd ed. 1977, French translation 1975, Japanese translation 1981, Italian translation 1977, The Prospects of a Revolution in the USA, 1973; Max Weber's Insights & Errors, 1984; Polish Translation, 1992, Syphilis, Puritanism and Witch Hunts: Historical Explanations in the Light of Medicine and Psychoanalysis with a Forecast About Aids 1989; Wars, Revolutions, Dictatorships, 1992; Editor: Herbert Spencer: Principles of Sociology, 1968; Herbert Spencer: Structure, Function and Evolution, 1971; The Essential Comte, 1974; Max Weber on Capitalism, Bureaucracy and Religion, 1984; Reflection on Inequality. 1975; Co-Editor, Class Structure and Social Development, 1964 (in Polish). *Contributions to:* Approximately 90 articles in learned journals. *Memberships:* Writers' Guild; Institute of Patentees and Inventors. *Address:* Farriers, Village Green, Upper Basildon, Berkshire RG8 8LS, England.

ANDREW Prudence, b. 1924. Author. *Publications:* The Hooded Falcon, 1960; Ordeal by Silence, 1961; Ginger Over the Wall, 1962; A Question of Choice, 1963; Ginger and Batty Billy, 1963; The Earthworms, 1964; Ginger and No. 10, 1964; The Constant Star, 1964; A Sparkle from the Coal (Novel), 1964; Christmas Card, 1966; Mr. Morgan's Marrow, 1967; Mister O'Brien, 1972; Rodge, Sylvie and Munch, 1973; Una and Grubstreet, 1973; Goodbye to the Rat, 1974; The Heroic Deeds of Jason Jones, 1975; Where Are You Going To, My Pretty Maid?, 1977; Robinson Daniel Crusoe, 1978 (in United States of America as Close Within My Own Circle, 1980); The Other Side of the Park, 1984. *Address:* c/o Heinemann Limited, 10 Upper Grosvenor Street, London, W1X 9PA, England.

ANDREWS Allen, b. 1913. Author. *Publications include:* Proud Fortress: Gibralter, 1958; Earthquake (sociology), 1963; The Mad Motorists (exploration), 1964; Those Magnificent Men in their Flying Machines (humour), 1965; Monte Carlo or Bust (humour), 1969; Quotations for Speakers and Writers, 1969; I Did It My Way (biography as Billy Cotton), 1970; Intensive Inquiries (criminology), 1973; The Follies of King Edward VII, 1975; Kings and Queens of England and Scotland, 1976; The Whisky Barons (biography), 1977; An Illustrated Dictionary of Classical Mythology, 1978; The

Cards Can't Lie, 1978; The Royal Coats of Arms of England, 1982; Catle Crespia (novel), 1982; Castle Crespin (novel), 1982; The People of Rome (verse), 1984; Straight Up, 1984; Impossible Loyalties (novel), 1985. *Address:* 4 Hazelmere Road, London, NW6 6PY, England.

ANDREWS Elmer, b. 26 Jan 1948, Northern Ireland. University Lecturer. m. 20 June 1976, 2 daughters. *Education:* Dalriada School, Ballymoney, 1952-66; Queens University of Belfast, 1966-76; BA, 1970; MA, 1973; PhD, 1976. *Appointments:* Thessa Loniki University, Greece, 1972- 74; Mohammed V University Rabat, Morocco, 1976-80; Queens University Belfast, 1980-81; University of Vister, 1981-88; University of Ulster, 1988-. *Publications:* The Poetry of Seamus Heaney: All The Realms of Whisper; Seamus Heaney: A Collection of Critical Essays; Contemporary Irish poetry. *Contributions to:* Many Articles, Journals & Magazines. *Honours:* Porter Scholarship; Foundation Scholarship. *Address:* Dept of English, University of Ulster, Coleraine, Northern Ireland.

ANDREWS Lucilla Matthew, (Diana Gordon, Joanna Marcus), Writer. *Publications:* The Print Petticoat, 1954; The Secret Armour, 1955; The Quiet Wards, 1956; The First Year, 1957; A Hospital Summer, 1958; My Friend the Professor, 1960; Nurse Errant, 1961; The Young Doctors Downstairs, 1963; Flowers for the Doctor, 1963; The New Sister Theatre, 1964; The Light in the Ward, 1965; A House for Sister Mary, 1966; Hospital Circles, 1967; A Few Days in Endel (as Diana Gordon), 1968; Highland Interlude, 1968; The Healing Time, 1969; Edinburgh Excursion, 1970; Ring o' Roses, 1972; Silent Song, 1973; In Storm and in Calm, 1975; No Time for Romance: An Autobiographical Account of a Few Moments in British and Personal History (non-fiction), 1977; The Crystal Gull, 1978; One Night in London, 1979; Marsh Blood (as Joanna Marcus), 1980; A Weekend in the Garden, 1981; In an Edinburgh Drawing Room, 1983; After a Famous Victory, 1984; The Lights of London, 1985. *Address:* c/o Heinemann Limited, 10 Upper Grosvenor Street, London, W1X 9PA, England.

ANDREWS Lyman, b. 1938, United States of America. Poet. *Appointments:* Lecturer, American Literature, University of Leicester, 1965-1988; Visiting Professor of English, Indiana University, Bloomington, 1978- 79; Poetry Critic, The Sunday Times, London, 1968-79. *Publications:* Ash Flowers, 1958; Fugitive Visions, 1962; The Death of Mayakovsky and Other Poems, 1968; Kaleidoscope: New and Selected Poems, 1973. *Address:* Flat 311, 4 Shakespeare Street, Nottingham, NG1 4FG, England.

ANDREWS Wendy. *See:* **SHARMAT Marjorie Weinnman.**

ANDREYEVA Victoria, b. 21 Jan 1942, Omsk, Russia. Writer; Editor. m. Arkady Rovner, 5 Aug 1969, 1 son. *Education:* MA Russian Philology 1965, Moscow University; Diploma of Literary Editor 1967, Moscow Polygraphic Institute; Completed course work for PhD in Comparative Literature 1981-83, New York University. *Appointments:* Editor, Gnosis Press 1978- . *Publications:* Son Tverdii, 1987; Dream of the Firmament, 1989; The Telephone Novel, 1992; P Ya Tschaadaeyen, co-collaborator, 1989; In a Small Circle of Poetry, 1978; Tolstoy and Fet: An Experiment of Life-Building, 1978; Kizeyersky & Tchaadaeyer, 1978; The Time of the Numbers, 1979; Khlopka, 1983; The Meeting of Bely & Blok in Solovyovian Ideas, 1991; The Third Literature, co-collaborator, 1990; Charchoune Whom I Knew, 1982; 1000 Russian Verbs, dictionary, 1991; and others. *Contributions to:* Gnosis Anthology of Contemporary American and Russian Literature; Almanack, Appollo-77; Crossroads; Russian Literary Triquarterly; Spring; Echo; Man and Nature; This and That. *Honours:* Cummington Community of the Art, 1983; Community of International Writers of Mme

Karolgy, Vance, France, 1984. *Address:* PO Box 42, Prince Street Station, New York, NY 10012, USA.

ANDRIJIC Zdenka, b. 25 May 1953, Zagreb, Croatia. Economist. m. Timo Andrjic, 4 Sept 1971, 2 sons, 1 daughter. *Appointments:* Freelance. *Publications:* Kockanje; Staklapcua; Astrolojki Rjacniky; Ova Sedma Kvoay; Sto Donosi. *Contributions to:* Many. *Honours:* Young Poets of Croatia. *Memberships:* PEN. *Address:* 50260 Korcula, Cujetuo Maseljebb, Croatia.

ANGEL Heather, b. 21 July 1941, Buckinghamshire, England. Biological Photographer; Author; Lecturer. m. Martin V. Angel, 3 Oct 1964, 1 son. *Education:* BSc Honours, Zoology, 1962, MSc 1965, Bristol University. *Publications:* 28 nature books, 12 photography books. Titles include: Nature Photography: Its Art & Techniques, 1972; Photographing Nature, 5 volumes on Trees, Insects, Seashore, Flowers, Fungi, 1975; Natural History of Britain & Ireland, co-author, 1981; Book of Nature Photography, 1982; Book of Close-Up Photography, 1983; Heather Angel's Countryside, 1983; A Camera in the Garden, 1984; A View from a Window, 1988; Nature in Focus, 1988; Landscape Photography, 1989; Animal Photography, 1991; Kew: A World of Plants, 1993. *Contributions to:* Numerous wildlife, photographic, gardening magazines & journals; Monthly column, Amateur Photographer. *Honour:* DSc, Bath University, 1986. *Memberships:* Past President, Fellow, Royal Photographic Society; Fellow, British Institute of Professional Photographers; Fellow, Linnean Society; Various conservation organisations. *Address:* Highways, 6 Vicarage Hill, Farnham, Surrey GU9 8HJ, England.

ANGEL Leonard Jay, b. 20 Sept 1945. Writer; Lecturer. m. Susan, 1 son, 1 daughter, 1 step-daughter. *Education:* BA Philosophy 1966, McGill University; MA Philosophy 1968, MA Creative Writing & Theatre 1970, PhD Philosophy 1974, University of British Columbia. *Appointments:* Department of Creative Writing, University of British Columbia 1981-82; Department of Creative Writing, University of Victoria 1984-86. *Publications:* After Antietam, 1975; Isadora and G B, 1976; The Unveiling, 1981; The Silence of the Mystic, 1983; Eleanor Marx, 1985; How to Build a Conscious Machine, 1989. *Contributions to:* Dialogue & Dialectic, Dialogue, 1991; Six of One, 1985. *Honours:* 1st Prize, Short Fiction, McGill Daily, 1963; 1st Prize (joint) Playhouse Theatre Award, 1971; Canada Council Artist B Grants 1979, 1982; Nominee Jessie Award, Best New Play, 1982. *Memberships:* Playwrights Canada 1976-88; Chairman, BC Region, Guild of Canadian Playwrights 1978-79, Regional Representative 1980-81. *Address:* 865 Durward Avenue, Vancouver, BC, Canada V5V 2Z1.

ANGELOU Maya, b. 1928, St Louis, Missouri, USA. University Professor; Writer; Black Activist; Singer. 1 son. *Appointments include:* Toured Europe and Africa in Porgy and Bess in her twenties; Night Club singer and performer in Genet's The Blacks; Involved in Black struggles in 1960s; spent several years in Ghana as editor of African Review; Life-time appointment as Reynolds Professor of American Studies at Wake Forest University, North Carolina. *Publications:* Five volumes of autobiography: I Know Why The Caged Bird Sings, Gather Together In My Name, Singin' and Swingin' and Gettin' Merry Like Christmas, The Heart of a Woman, All God's Children Need Travelling Shoes; Several collections of poetry including: And Still I Rise; Just Give Me A Cool Drink of Water 'Fore I Dine; Now Sheba Sings The Song, verse by Maya Angelou and illustrations by Tom Feelings. *Address:* c/o Virago Press, 20-23 Mandela Street, Camden Town, London NW1 0HQ, England.

ANGLESEY Henry (The Marquess of), b. 8 Oct 1922, London, England. Peer of the Realm. *Publications:* Editor: The Capel Letters 1814-1817, 1955; One-Leg: the Life & Letters of 1st Marquess of Anglesey, 1961; Editor, Sergeant Pearman's Memoirs, 1968; Editor, Little Hodge, 1971; A History of the British Cavalry,

1816-1919, Volume 1, 1973, Volume II, 1975, Volume III, 1981, Volume IV, 1986. *Contributor to:* Sunday Telegraph (reviews). *Honours:* Hon D Litt; FRHist S; FSA; FRSL; Hon FRIBA. *Literary Agent:* Curtis Brown. *Address:* Plas Newydd, Anglesey, Llanfairpwll, North Wales.

ANGLUND Joan Walsh, b. 1926, United States of America. Children's Writer. *Publications:* A Friend is Someone Who Likes You, 1958; Look Out the Window, 1959; The Brave Cowboy, 1959; Love Is a Special Way of Feeling, 1960; In a Pumpkin Shell: A Mother Goose ABC, 1960; Christmas Is a Time of Giving, 1961; Cowboy and His Friend, 1961; Nibble Nible Mousekin: A Tale of Hansel and Gretel, 1962; Cowboy's Secret Life, 1963; Spring Is a New Beginning, 1963; Childhood Is a Time of Innocence, 1964; A Pocketful of Proverbs (verse), 1964; A Book of Good Tidings from the Bible, 1965; What Color Is Love?, 1966; A Year Is Round, 1966; A Cup of Sun: A Book of Poems, 1967; A Is for Always: An ABC Book, 1968; Morning Is a Little Child (verse), 1969; A Slice of Snow: A Book of Poems, 1970; Do You Love Someone?, 1971; The Cowboy's Christmas, 1972; A Child's Book of Old Nursery Rhymes, 1973; Goodbye, Yesterday: A Book of Poems, 1974; Storybook, 1978; Emily and Adam, 1979; Almost a Rainbow, 1980; A Gift of Love, 5 volumes, 1980; A Christmas Cookie Book, 1982; Rainbow Love, 1982; Christmas Candy Book, 1983; A Christmas Book, 1983; See the Year, 1984; Coloring Book, 1984; Memories of the Heart, 1984; Teddy Bear Tales, 1985; Baby Brother, 1985; All About Me!, 1986; Christmas is Here!, 1986; Tubtime for Thaddeus, 1986. *Address:* c/o Random House, 201 E. 50th Street, New York, NY 10022, USA.

ANGREMY Jean Pierre. *See:* **REMY Pierre Jean.**

ANGUS Ian. *See:* **MACKAY James Alexander.**

ANGUS Tom. *See:* **POWELL Geoffrey Stewart.**

ANMAR Frank. *See:* **NOLAN William Francis.**

ANNANDALE Barbara. *See:* **BOWDEN Jean.**

ANOUILH Jean, b. 23 June 1910, Bordeaux. Dramatic Writer. m. Nicole Lançon, 1953, 1 son, 2 daughters. *Publications:* Plays Include: L'Ermine, 1934; Y'avait un prisonnier, 1935; Le Voyageur sans bagages, 1937; Le Bal des Voleurs, 1938; Le Sauvage, 1938; Cavalcade d'Amour, 1941; Le Rendez-vous de Senlis, 1942; Leocadia, 1942; Eurydice, 1942; humulus le Niuet, 1945; Oreste, 1945; Antigone, 1946; jezebel, 1946; Romeo et Jeannette, 1946; L'Invitation au Chateau, 1948; Ardele ou la Marguerite, 1949; le Repetition ou l'amour puni, 1950; Colombe, 1950; La Valse des toreadors, 1952; L'Alouette, 1953; Ornifle, 1955; L'Hurluberlu, 1958; La Foire d'Empigne, 1960; Becket, 1961; Pauvre Bitos, 1963-64; Cher Antoine, 1969; Les Poissons Rouges, 1969; Ne Reveille Pas, Madame, 1970; Tu etais si gentil quand tu etais petit, 1974; Chers Zoiseaux, 1976; Vive Henri IV, 1977; La Culotte, 1978; Le Nombril, 1981; Films Include: Monsieur Vincent; Pattes blanches; Caprice de Caroline. *Address:* c/o Les Editions de la Table Ronde, Rue Huyshans, 75007, Paris, France.

ANSCOMBE Isabelle Mary, b. 4 Oct 1954. Author and Journalist. m. Howard Grey, 17 Dec 1981, 1 daughter. *Education:* Malvern Girls' College; MA, English, Newnham College, Cambridge. *Publications:* Arts and Crafts in Britain and America, 1978; Omega and After: Bloomsbury and the Decorative Arts, 1981; A Woman's Touch: Women in Design from 1860 to the Present Day, 1984; Novel entitled Angel published under her married name, Belle Grey, 1990. *Contributor to:* The Times; Sunday Times; Cosmopolitan; Company; Country Living. *Membership:* National Union of Journalists. *Literary Agent:* A M Heath Ltd. *Address:*

c/o A M Heath, 79 St Martin's Lane, London WC2N 4AA, England.

ANTHONY James R, b. 1922, United States of America. Professor of Music; Writer. Professor of Musicology, University of Arizona, Tucson, 1952-; Regional Associate of American Council of Learned Societies, 1956-60; Contributor, Grove's Dictionary of Music and Musicians, 1972-; Consultant, National Endowment for the Humanities, 1974-. *Publications:* French Baroque Music from Beaujoyeulx to Rameau, 1973, 1978; Cantatas, Book III, by Monteclair, 1978; De profundis , by Delalande, 1980; La Musique en France a l'Epoque Baroque, 1981; 40 articles in The New Grove; The New Grove French Baroque Masters, 1986. *Address:* School of Music, University of Arizona, Tucson, AZ 85721, USA.

ANTHONY Peter. *See:* **SHAFFER Peter.**

ANTHONY Piers. *See:* **JACOB Anthony Dillingham.**

ANTOKOLETZ Elliott Maxim, b. 3 Aug 1942, Jersey City, NJ, USA. Professor of Musicology. m. Juana Canabal, 28 May 1972, 1 son. *Education:* Juilliard School of Music, 1960-65; Hunter College, AB, 1967-68; MA, 1968-70; PhD, 1970-75. *Appointments:* Queens College, Instructor of Music Theory, 1973-76; University of Texas, Austin, Professor of Musicology, 1976-. *Publications:* The Music of Bela Bartok; Bela Bartok: A Guide to Research; Twentieth Century Music. *Contributions to:* Journal of the American Musicological Society; College Music Symposium; Tempo; Studia Musicologica; Musik und Dichtung; Musica Realta; Moment Magazine; Discovery; Texas MLA Quarter Notes; Music Analysis. *Honours include:* Bela Bartok Memorial Plaque; PhD Alumni Award. *Memberships:* Editor of International Journal of Musicology; American Music, Editorial Board; American Musicological Society; College Music Society; Sonneck Society; Society of Ethnomusicology; International Alban Berg Society; South Central Modern Language Association; AMS Council. *Address:* Dept of Music, The University of Texas, Austin, TX 78712, USA.

ANTOLSKI Zdislaw Henryk, b. 16 Jan 1953, Skallomierz. Educator. Divorced. *Education:* Pegagogical College, Kielce, 1971-72; Graduate, Culture & Education, Pedagogical College, Kielce, 1976. *Appointment:* Editorial Assistant, Gossip, 1987-. *Publications:* Self-Lynch, 1978; Alone in the Crowd, 1980; To Bed I Disguise Myself as my Double, 1981; Joseph's Side, 1984. *Contributions To:* Poetry; New Books; Creation; New Word; Here and Now. *Honours:* Red Rose Award, 1982; Bursa's Award, 1986. *Membership:* Polish Writers' Association. *Address:* ul. Walhelmq Piecka 3m 4, Kielce, 25-001, Poland.

ANTONOV Sergei Petrovich, b. 1915. Soviet Writer; Critic. *Publications include:* Novels and Stories: Lena, 1948; Rains, 1951; The Penkova Affair, 1956; Empty Journey, 1960; Alenka, 1960; Petrovich, 1964; Torn Rouble Note, 1966; Silver Wedding, 1972; The Three Warrior Knights, 1973; Criticism: Letters about the Short Story, 1964; First-Person Narrative, 1973; The Word, 1974; Vaska, 1987; Ravines, 1988. *Honours:* State Prize, 1951. *Address:* 125252 Moscow, Concord of Independent Stats, CIS, Novopeschanaja str. N16, ap 72, Russia.

ANTROBUS John, b. 2 July 1933, Woolwich, London. Writer. m. Margaret McCormick, 1958 (divorced 1980) 2 sons, 1 daughter. *Education:* King Edward VII Nautical College; Royal Military Academy, Sandhurst, Camberley, Surrey. *Appointments:* Apprentice Deck Officer, Merchant Navy 1950-52; Served in British Army, East Surrey Regiment, 1952-55; Supply Teacher and Waiter 1953-54; Freelance writer 1955-. *Publications:* Plays include: The Bed-Sitting Room, with Spike Milligan (also co-director; produced London, 1963) Walton on Thames, Surrey, Hobbs, 1970, revised version as The Bed-Sitting room 2 (also director, produced, London 1983). Crete and Sergeant Pepper, 1972, 1974. Captain Oates Left Sock, 1969, 1974. Jonah (also director, produced cambridge 1979); Hitler in Liverpool, One Orange for the Baby, Up in the Hide (produced London, 1980), London, Calder and New York, Riverrun Press, 1983. When Did You Last See Your Trousers? with Ray Galton, adaptation of a story by Galton and Alan Simpson (produced Mold, Clwyd, 1986, London 1987, Samuel French, 1988). Screenplays: Carry on Sergeant, with Norman Hudis, 1958; Idol on Parade, 1959; The Wrong Arm of the Law, with others, 1962; The Big Job, with Talbot Rothwell, 1965; The Bed-Sitting Room, with Charles Wood, 1969. Children's Books: The Boy with Illuminating Measles, 1978; Help I'm a Prisoner in a Toothpaste Factory, 1978; Ronnie and The Haunted Rolls Royce, 1982; Ronnie and the Great Knitted Robbery, 1982; Ronnie and the High Rise, 1992; Ronnie and the Flying Fitted Carpet, 1992; Writer for radio and television. *Honours:* George Devine Award, 1970; Writers Guild award, 1971; Arts Council bursary, 1973, 1976, 1980, 1982; Room at the Bottom 1 with Ray Galton, BANFF TV Festival Award, Best Comedy, 1987; Finalist, International Emmy Awards, 1987. *Memberships:* Writers Guild of Great Britain; Writers Guild of America, West Inc. *Literary Agent:* c/o Pat White, Rogers Coleridge and White. *Address:* 20 Powis Mews, London, W11 1JN, England.

APFEL Necia H., b. 31 July 1930, Mt Vernon, New York, USA. Science Writer. m. Donald A. Apfel, 7 Sept 1952, dec., 1 son, 1 daughter. *Education:* BA magna cum laude, Tufts University, 1952; Radcliffe College Graduate School, 1952-53; Northwestern University Graduate School, 1962-69. *Publications:* Astronomy One (with J Allen Hynek), 1972; Architecture of the Universe (with J Allen Hynek), 1979; It's All Relative: Einstein's Theory of Relativity, 1981; The Moon and Its Exploration, 1982; Stars and Galaxies, 1982; Astronomy and Planetology, 1983, Soft-cover Edition, Astronomy Projects for Young Scientists, 1984; Calendars, 1985; It's All Elementary: From Atoms to the Quantum World of Quarks, Leptons, and Gluons, 1985; Space Station, 1987; Space Law, 1988; Nebulae: The Birth and Death of Stars, 1988; Voyager to the Planets, 1991. *Contributions to:* Various articles to Odyssey magazine; Ask Ulysses, and I/O Port monthly columns. *Honours:* Phi Beta Kappa, 1952; Nebulae chosen as 1 of 100 Best Children's Books, 1988. *Memberships:* Society of Midland Authors; Society of Children's Book Writers; Astronomical Society of the Pacific; American Association for the Advancement of Science; Planetary Society. *Address:* 3461 University Avenue, Highland Park, IL 60035, USA.

APODACA Rudy Samuel, b. 8 Aug 1939, Las Cruces, New Mexico, Appelate Judge. m. Nancy Ruth, 16 Jan 1967, 1 son, 3 daughters. *Education:* New Mexico State University, Bachelor of Science, 1961; Georgetown University Law Center, 1964. *Appointments:* Poets & Writers, 1978; PEN New Mexico, 1982. *Publications:* The Waxen Image; Screenplay, A Rare Thing. *Honours:* Phi Kappa Phi; Distinguished Alumns. *Memberships:* Citizens Bank of Las Cruces; NMSU Board of Regents; NMSU Pesidents Association; American Southwest Theatre Co; Coordinating Council, Higher Education; NM Bar; Institute Judical Administration. *Address:* 829 Canterbury Arc, Las Cruces, NM 88005, USA.

APODACA-RUDY S. *See:* **APODACA Rudy Samuel.**

APOSTOLOU John L, b. 4 Jan 1930, Brooklyn, New York, USA. Audiovisual Manager. *Education:* City College, New York, 1948-50; Columbia University, 1950-51; University of Southern California, BA, 1956. *Publications:* Murder in Japan, 1987; The Best Japanese Science Fiction Stories, 1989. *Contributions to:* Detective & Mystery Fiction, 1985; Twentieth Century Crime & Mystery Writers, 1991; Armchair Detective;

Extrapolation. *Address:* 425 South Kenmore Avenue 310, Los Angeles, CA 90020, USA.

APPIAH Peggy, b. 1921. Children's Writer. *Publications:* Ananse the Spider, 1966; Tales of an Ashanti Father, 1967; The Pineapple Child and Other Tales from Ashanti, 1969; Children of Ananse, 1969; A Smell of Onions, 1971; Why Are There So Many Roads?, 1972; Gift of the Mmoatia, 1973; Ring of Gold, 1976; A Dirge Too Soon, 1976; Why the Hyena Does Not Care for Fish and Other Tales, 1977; Young Readers: Afua and The Mouse, Alena and the Python, Kofi and the Crow, The Twins, 1991; Poems of Three Generations, 1978. Literary Agent: David Higham Associates. *Address:* PO Box 829, Kumasi, Ashanti, Ghana.

APPLE Jacki, b. New York City, USA. Writer; Artist; Producer. *Education:* Syracuse University; Parsons School of Design. *Publications:* Trunk Pieces; Doing It Right in LA; The Mexican Tapes; Swan Lake; Voices in the Dark; The Culture of Disappearance; The Garden Planet Revisited; The Amazon, The Mekong, The Missouri & The Nile; Palisade. *Contributions to:* High Performance; Artweek; LA Weekly; Media Arts; Visions. *Honour:* WESTA Award. *Memberships:* International Association of Art Critics; National Writers Union. *Address:* 3827 Mentone Avenue, Culver City, CA 90232, USA.

APPLEBY John Hilary, b. 8 Nov 1938, Burma. Writer. *Education:* General degree, Danish 1962; BA Hons Russian 1963; MA Literary Translation 1967; ICS Diploma, Freelance Journalism & Speciality Writing 1968; ICS Diploma, Television Scriptwriting 1978; PhD British Doctors in Russia 1979. *Appointments:* Press Coverage, Foreign Office Research Department 1963-65; Press Monitor, Foreign Broadcast Information Service 1967-70; British Industrial Publicity Overseas Ltd 1970-73. *Publications:* Translator, I I Brekhman: Man & Biologically Active Substances, 1980; Translator, A S Batuev: Higher Integrative Systems of the Brain, 1987; Index to Siberian, &c.Materia Medica, 1987; Translator, Yu P Altukhov: Population Genetics, 1990; Dictionary of National Biography: Missing Persons, Entries, 1993. *Contributions to:* Study of Russian History from Archival Sources, 1986; The Caledonian Phalanx, 1987; Book Reviews and Research Paper Reviews: Ambix; Annals of Science; Archives of the Bibliotheck; The Library; Medical History; Notes & Records of the Royal Society; Oxford Slavonic Papers; RSA Journal; Slavonic Review. *Honour:* Gideon De Laune Medallist, 1982. *Memberships:* Society of Authors; Translators Association. *Address:* 16 Pine Close, Upton Road, Norwich, Norfolk NR4 7PU, England.

APPLEMAN Philip, b. 8 Feb 1926, Indiana, USA. Distinguished Professor Emeritus of English, Indiana University. m. Marjorie Haberkorn, 19 Aug 1950. *Education:* PhD 1955, Northwestern University. *Publications:* The Silent Explosion, nonfiction, 1965; Kites on a Windy Day, poetry, 1967; Summer Love and Surf, poetry, 1968; In the Twelfth Year of the War, novel, 1970; Open Doorways, poetry, 1976; Shame the Devil, novel, 1981; Darwin's Ark, poetry, 1984; Darwin's Bestiary, poetry, 1986; Apes and Angels, novel, 1989; Let There Be Light, poetry, 1991; Edited: Victorian Studies, founding co-editor and first General Editor 1956-64; 1859: Entering an Age of Crisis, co-editor, 1959; Darwin, 1970, revised ed 1979; The Origin of Species, 1975; Malthus: An Essay on the Principle of Population, 1976. *Contributions to:* Poems published in many periodicals including: American Review; Antioch Review; Beloit Poetry Journal; Dryad; Harper's Magazine; Kentucky Poetry Review; The Nation; New York Times; Poetry; Poetry Northwest; Pushcart Prize; Southern Poetry Review; Spectator; West Coast Review; Yale Review; Poetry readings at many colleges, universities and forums. *Honours:* National Endowment for the Arts, Fellowship in Poetry; Poetry Society of America: Castagnola Award; Christopher Morley Award; Society of Midland Authors, Midland Poetry Award;

Friends of Literature, Ferguson Memorial Award. *Address:* PO Box 39, Sagaponack, NY 11962, USA.

APPLEWHITE Cynthia, b. St Louis, Missouri, USA. Novelist. m. Louis Zamperini, 25 May 1946, 1 son, 1 daughter. *Education:* Bennett College, Millbrook, New York; American Academy of Dramatic Arts, New York City. *Publications:* Sundays, 1978; Summer Dreams & The Kleig Light Gas Company, 1982. *Membership:* PEN. *Literary Agent:* Barbara Lowenstein. *Address:* 2338 Hollyridge Drive, Hollywood Hills, CA 90068, USA.

APTHEKER Bettina Fay, b. 2 Sept 1944. Teacher; Writer. 1 son, 1 daughter. *Education:* BA, University of California, Berkeley, 1967; MA, San Jose State University, 1976, PhD, University of California, Santa Cruz, 1983. *Publications:* Tapestries of Life: Women's Work, Women's Consciousness and the Meaning of Daily Experience, 1989; Woman's Legacy: Essays on Race, Sex and Class in American History, 1982; The Morning Breaks: The Trial of Angela Davis, 1976; Academic Rebellion in the US: A Marxist Appraisal; With Angela Y Davis: If They Come in the Morning: Voices of Resistance, 1971. *Contributor to:* Imagining Our Lives: The Novelist as Historian, Woman of Power, Vol 16, 1990; How to Do Meaningful Work in Women's Studies in Women's Studies: An Interdisciplinary Journal 17: 1-2, 1989. *Address:* Women's Studies, Kresge College, University of California, Santa Cruz, CA 95064, USA.

ARCHER Fred, b. 1915. *Publications:* The Distant Scene, 1967; Under the Parish Lantern, 1969; Hawthorn Hedge Country, 1970; The Secrets of Bredon Hill, 1971; A Lad of Evesham Vale, 1972; Muddy Boots and Sunday Suits, 1973; Golden Sheaves and Black Horses, 1974; The Countryman Cottage Life Book, 1974; When Village Bells were Silent, 1975; Poachers Pie, 1976; By Hook and By Crook, 1978; When Adam was a Boy, 1979; A Hill Called Bredon, 1983; Fred Archer Farmer's Son, 1984; The Village Doctor, 1986; Evesham to Bredon in Old Photographs, 1988; The Village of my Childhood, 1989; Country Sayings, 1990. *Address:* 54 Stanchester Way, Curry Rivel, Langport, Somerset TA10 09U, Gloucestershire, England.

ARCHER Jeffrey Howard, b. 15 Apr 1940, Mark, Somerset, England. Author; Politician. m. Mary Weeden, 2 sons. *Education:* Brasenose College, Oxford. *Publications:* Plays: Beyond Reasonable Doubt, Queen's, 1987; Exclusive, Queen's, 1990; Not A Penny More, Not a Penny Less, 1975; Shall We Tell the President?, 1977; Kane & Abel, 1979; A Quiver Full of Arrows, 1980; The Prodigal Daughter, 1982; First Among Equals, 1984; A Matter of Honour, 1986; A Twist in the Tale, 1988; As The Crow Flies, 1991. *Contributions to:* Numerous journals & magazines. *Literary Agent:* Vanessa Holt Assoc Ltd, Essex, England. *Address:* Alembic House, 93 Albert Embankment, London SE1 T91, England.

ARCHIBALD Rupert Douglas, b. 1919, Trinidad and Tobago. Author; Playwright. *Appointments:* Editor, Progress Magazine, 1952; Member, Editorial Board, Clarion Newspaper, 1954-56. *Publications:* Junction Village, 1954; Anne Marie, 1958; The Bamboo Clump, 1962; The Rose Slip, 1962; Old Maid's Tale, 1965; Island Tide, 1972; Defeat with Honour, 1973; Isidore and the Turtle (novel), 1973. *Address:* 7 Stephens Road, Maraval, Trinidad and Tobago, West Indies.

ARDAI Charles, b. 25 Oct 1969, New York City, USA. Author; Editor. *Education:* BA English summa cum laude 1991, Columbia University. *Appointments:* Contributing Editor, Computer Entertainment and K-Power 1985; Editor, Davis Publications 1990-91. *Publications include:* Great Tales of Madness & The Macabre, 1990; Kingpins, 1992; Futurecrime, 1992. *Contributions to:* Alfred Hitchcock's Mystery Magazine; Ellery Queen's Mystery Magazine; Twilight Zone; The Year's Best

Horror Stories; Computer Gaming World; and others. *Honour:* Pearlman Prize for Fiction, Columbia University, 1991. *Membership:* Active member, Mystery Writers of America. *Address:* 350 East 52 Street, New York, NY 10022, USA.

ARDEN John, b. 26 Oct 1930. Playwright. m. Margaretta Ruth D'Arcy, 4 sons (1 son deceased). *Education:* King's College, Cambridge; Edinburgh College of Art. *Publications:* Plays Produced: All Fall Down, 1955; The Life of Man, 1956; The Waters of Babylon, 1957; Live Like Pigs, 1958; Serjeant Musgrave's Dance, 1959; Soldier, Soldier, 1960; Wet Fish, 1962; The Workhouse Donkey, 1963; Ironhand, 1963; Armstrong's Last Goodnight, 1964; Left Handed Liberty, 1965; The True History of Squire Jonathan and his Unfortunate Treasure, 1968; The Bagman, 1970; Pearl, 1978; To Put it Frankly, 1979; Don Quixote, 1980; Garland for a Hoar Head, 1982; The Old Man Sleeps Alone, 1982; The Business of Good Government, 1960; The Happy Haven, 1960; Ars Longa Vita Brevis, 1964; Friday's Hiding, 1966; The Royal Pardon, 1966; The Hero Rises Up, 1968; Island of the Mighty, 1972; The Ballygombeen Bequest, 1972; The Non-Stop Connolly Cycle, 1975; Vandaleur's Folly, 1978; The Little Gray Home in the West, 1978; The Manchester Enthusiasts, 1984; Whose is the Kingdom?, 1988; To Present the Pretence, 1977; Silence Among the Weapons, 1982; with Margaretta D'Arcy (Essays) Awkward Corners, 1988; (Novel) Books of Bale, 1988; (Novel) Cogs Tyrannic, 1991. *Address:* c/o Casarotto Ramsay Ltd, National House, 60-66 Wardour St, London W1V 3HP, England.

ARDEN William. *See:* LYNDS Dennis.

ARDIES Tom, b. 1931 United States of America. Author. *Appointments:* Reporter, Columnist, Editorial Writer, Vancouver Sun, 1950-64; Telegraph Editor, Honolulu Star Bulletin, 1964-65; Special Assistant to Government of Guam, 1965-67. *Publications:* Their Man in the White House, 1971; This Suitcase Is Going to Explode, 1972; Pandemic, 1973; Kosygin Is Coming, 1974 (in United Kingdom paperback as Russian Roulette, 1975); In a Lady's Service, 1976; Palm Springs, 1978.

ARDLEY Neil Richard, b. 26 May 1937, Wellington, Surrey. Writer. m. Bridget Mary Gantley, 3 Sept 1960, Marnhull, Dorset. 1 daughter. *Education:* BSc Bristol University, 1959. *Publications include:* How Birds Behave, 1971; Atoms and Energy, 1975; Birds of Towns, 1975; Birds Of The Country, 1975; Birds Of Coasts, Lakes and Rivers, 1976; Birdwatching, 1978; Man and Space, 1978; Birds, 1978; Birds of Britain and Europe, 1978; Birds and Birdwatching, 1980; 1001 Questions and Answers (with Bridget Ardley) 1981; The World of Tomorrow Series, 1981-82; Transport On Earth, 1981; Out Into Space, 1981; Tomorrow's Home, 1981; School, Work and Play, 1981; Our Future Needs, 1982; Health and Medicine, 1982; Future War and Weapons, 1982; Fact or Fantasy? 1982; Computers, 1983; Action Science Series, 1983-84; Working With Water, 1983; Using the Computer, 1983; Hot and Cold, 1983; Sun and Light, 1983; Making Measurements, 1983; Exploring Magnetism, 1983; Making Things Move, 1984; Discovering Electricity, 1984; Air and Flight, 1984; Sound and Music, 1984; Simple Chemistry, 1984; Force and Strength, 1984; My Favourite Science Encyclopedia, 1984; Just Look At...Flight, 1984; Sinclair ZX Spectrum User Guide, 1984; Just Look At...The Universe, 1985; The Science of Energy, 1985; Music-An Illustrated Encyclopedia, 1986. My Own Science Encyclopedia, 1987; The Universe - Exploring the Universe, 1987; The Inner Planets; The Outer Planets; The Way Things Work, 1988; The World of the Atom, 1989; Music (Eyewitness Guide), 1989; India, 1989; Greece, 1989; Twentieth Century Science, 1989; The Giant Book of the Human Body, 1989; How we Build-Bridges; Dams Oil Rigs, 1989; Language and Communications, 1989; Sound Waves to Music, 1990; Wings and Things, 1990; Snap Happy, 1990; Tune In, 1991; Bits and Chips, 1991; How It Works, 1991; The Way It Works, Light, 1991; The

Way It Works, Heat, 1991; The Way It Works, Electricity, 1991; A Series of 15 Science Books, 1991-92. *Contributions to:* Caxton Yearbook; Macmillan Children's Encyclopedia; Collins Music Dictionary; Joy of Knowledge, Children's Illustrated Encyclopedia. *Honours:* Fellow, Royal Society of Arts, 1982; Science Book Prize (under 16), 1989, shared with David Macaulay for the The Way Things work; Times Educational Supplement Senior Information Book Award, 1989, for The Way Things Work with David Macaulay. *Address:* Lathkill House, Youlgrave, Derbyshire DE45 1WL England.

ARDMORE Jane Kesner, b. 12 Sept 1915, Chicago, Illinois, USA. Author; Journalist. m. Albert Ardmore, 10 Nov 1951, 1 daughter. *Education:* PhB, University of Chicago. *Publications:* Novels: Women Inc., 1946; Julie, 1952; To Live Is To Listen, 1967. Biographies: Take My Life, Eddie Cantor, 1957; The Self Enchanted, Mae Murray, 1959; The Dress Doctor, Edith Head, 1959; Portrait of Joan, Joan Crawford, 1962. *Contributions to:* Good Housekeeping; McCall's; Family Circle, Redbook, Woman, UK; Woman's World, UK; Woman's Own, UK. *Honours:* Fiction prize, Indiana Writers Conference, 1942; Fiction Award, California Press Women, 1967; Headliner Award, Women in Communications, 1968. *Membership:* Hollywood Women's Press Club. *Literary Agents:* McIntosh & Otis, New York; Heath & Company, London, UK. *Address:* 10469 Dunleer Drive, Los Angeles, California 90064, USA.

ARGYLE Michael, b. 1925. Psychologist; Writer. *Appointments:* University Lecturer in Social Psychology, 1952-69, Acting Head, Department of Experiemental Psychology, 1978-80, Reader in Social Psychology, 1969-92, Fellow of Wolfson College, 1966-, Vice-gerent, 1989-91, Emeritus Professor of Psychology, 1992-, Oxford University; Social Psychology Editor, British Journal of Social and Clinical Psychology, 1961-67; Editor, Pergamon International Series in Experimental Social Psychology, 1979-92. *Publications:* The Scientific Study of Social Behaviour, 1947; Religious Behaviour, 1959; Training Managers (with M. Kirton and T. Smith), 1962; Society (with A.T. Welford, D.Glass and J.N. Morris), 1962; Social Psychology Through Experiment (with G. Humphrey), 1962; Psychology and Social Problems, 1964; The Psychology of Interpersonal Behaviour, 1967, 4th Edition 1983; Social Interaction, 1969; The Social Psychology of Work, 1972, 2nd edition 1989; Skills with People A Guide for Managers (with E Sidney and M Brown), 1973; Social Encounters, 1973; Bodily Communication, 1974, 2nd edition 1988; The Social Psychology of Religion (with B Beit-Hallahmi), 1975; Gaze and Mutual Gaze (with M Cook), 1975; Social Skills and Mental Health (with P Trower and B Bryant), 1978; Person to Person (with P Trower), 1979; Social Situations (with A Furnham and J A Graham), 1981; The Psychology of Social Situations (with A Furnham), 1981; Social Skills and Work (Health) 2 vols, 1981; The Anatomy of Relationships (with M Henderson), 1985; The Psychology of Happiness, 1987; Cooperation, 1991; The Social Psychology of Every Day Life, 1992. *Address:* Department of Experimental Pychology, South Parks Road, Oxford, England.

ARKIN Frieda, b. 4 Sept 1917. Writer. m. 4 Sept 1943, 1 son, 1 daughter. *Education:* University of Chicago, BA, 1940; Columbia University, MA, 1945. *Publications:* The Dorp; The Essential Kitchen Gardener; Kitchen Wisdom; Soup Wisdom; More Kitchen Wisdom; The Cooks Companion; Kitchen Digest. *Contributions to:* The Yale Review; McCalls; Yankee Magazine; American Short Fiction; The Transatlantic Review; The Kenyon Review; The Colorado Review; New Mexico Quarterly; The Massachusetts Review; California Quarterly. *Honours:* Best American Short Shories. *Membership:* National Writers Union. *Address:* 1 Winthrop Street, Essex, MA 01929, USA.

ARKOW Philip S, b. 30 Apr 1947, Philadephia, USA. Education & Publicity Director. m. Melody Meyer, 18 Sept 1982, 1 daughter. *Education:* University of

Pennsylvania, BA, 1969. *Publications:* The Loving Bond; Pet Therapy; The Luckiest Pets in the World Calendar. *Contributions to:* Too Numerous. *Memberships:* Society for the Preservation & Enhancement of the Recognition of Millard Fillmore; Delta Society; American Veterinary Medical Association; Animal Welfare Committee; National Animal Control Association; American Humane Association. *Address:* PO Box 187, Colorado Springs, CO 80901, USA.

ARLEN Leslie. *See:* **NICOLE Christopher Robin.**

ARLEN Michael John, b. 9 Dec 1930, London, England. Author. m. Alice Albright, 1972, 4 daughters. *Education:* BA, Harvard University, USA, 1952. *Publications:* Exiles, 1970; Passage to Ararat, 1974; Living-Room War, 1969; Thirty Seconds, 1980; The Camera Age, 1982; An American Verdict, 1972; The View from Highway One, 1975; Say Goodbye to Sam, 1984. *Contributions To:* New Yorker, 1957-. *Honours:* National Book Award, 1975; Le Prix Bremond, 1976; D.Litt., 1984. *Memberships:* Authors Guild; PEN; Century Association. *Literary Agent:* Candida Donadio & Associates. *Address:* 1120 Fifth Avenue, New York, NY 10128, USA.

ARMES Roy, b. 1937. Author. *Appointments:* Reader in Film, Middlesex Polytechnic; Film Critic of London Magazine. *Publications:* French Cinema since 146 (2 vols), 1966, 1970; The Cinema of Alain Resnais, 1968; French Film, 1970; Patterns of Realism, 1972; Film and Reality, 1974; The Ambiguous Image, 1975; A Critical History of British Cinema, 1978; The Films of Alain Robbe-Grillet, 1981; French Cinema, 1985; Patterns of Realism, 1985. *Address:* 19 New End, Hampstead, London, NW3, England.

ARMITAGE Gary. *See:* **EDRIC Robert.**

ARMITAGE Ronda (Jacqueline), b. 1943, New Zealand. Children's Writer. *Appointments:* Infant Teacher, Duvauchelles, 1964-66, Auckland, 1968-69; Supply Teacher, London, 1966; Adviser on Children's Books, Dorothy Butler Limited, Booksellers, Auckland, 1970-71; Assistant Librarian, Lewes Priory Comprehensive School, Sussex, 1976-77; Supply Teacher, East Sussex County Council, 1978-81; Family Counsellor - Hastings, 1985-. *Publications:* The Lighthouse Keeper's Lunch, 1977; The Trouble with Mr. Harris, 1978; Don't Forget Matilda, 1979; The Bossing of Josie, 1980, as The Birthday Spell, 1981; Ice Creams for Rosie, 1981; One Moonlight Night, 1983; Grandma Goes Shopping, 1985; The Lighthouse Keepers Catastrophe, 1986; The Lighthouse Keepers Rescue, 1989; When Dad Did the Washing, 1990; Watch the Baby, Daisy, 1991; A Quarrel of Koalas, 1992; Looking After Chocolates, 1992. *Address:* Old Tiles Cottage, Church Lane, Hellingly, East Sussex, BN27 4HA, England.

ARMOUR Peter James, b. 19 Nov 1940, Fleetwood, Lancashire, England. University Professor. *Education:* PhL, English College & Gregorian University, Rome, Italy, 1961; BA (Hons), University of Manchester, 1966; PhD, Leicester, 1980. *Publications:* The Door of Purgatory, 1983; Dante's Griffin and the History of the World, 1989; Chapters in: G Aquilecchia et al, Collected Essays. K Speight, 1971; D Nolan, Dante Commentaries, 1977 and Dante Soundings, 1981; RA Cardwell & J Hamilton, Virgil in a Cultural Tradition, 1986; G Barblan, Dante e la Bibbia, 1988; T O'Neill, The Shared Horizon, 1990; JR Dashwood & JE Everson, Writers and Performers in Italian Drama, 1991; JC Barnes & J Petrie, Word and Drama in Dante, 1993. *Contributions to:* The Year's Work in Modern Language Studies; Italian Studies, volumes 34 and 38; Lectura Dantis; Dertsches Dante-Jahrbuch, vol 67; Reviews in Italian Studies; Modern Language Review; Medium Aevum; Filologia e Critica; Translations in Journal of Garden History, volumes 1, 3 and 5; The Genius of Venice. *Memberships:* Società Dantesca Italiana; Dante Society of America;

Society for Italian Studies; Modern Humanities Research Association; London Medieval Society; Middlesex County Cricket Club. *Address:* Department of Italian, Royal Holloway, University of London, Egham Hill, Egham, Surrey TW20 0EX, England.

ARMSTRONG Alice Catt, b. Fort Scott, Kansas, USA. Author; Editor; Publisher. 1 son. *Education:* Litt D, St Andrews University, England, 1969; St Pauls College & Seminary, Italy, 1970. *Publications:* 17 books including: California Biographical & Historical Series, 1950-; Dining & Lodging on the North American Continent, 1958; And They Called It Society, 1961-62; Editor, special issue, 200th Anniversary of California, 1968. Also radio skits, travel guides, children's stories including Princess McGuffy & the Little Rebel. *Honours:* Numerous Honours & Awards including: National Travel Guide Award, National Writers Club, 1958; Dame Grand Cross, Order of St Jaurent; Outstanding citizen. *Memberships include:* National Society of Magna Charta Dames; Los Angeles World Affairs Council; National Writers Club; Historial Los Angeles Association; Art Patrons Association of America. *Address:* Cordell Views 1331, Cordell Place, Los Angeles, California 90069, USA.

ARMSTRONG Diane Julie, b. 18 July 1939, Krakow, Poland. Freelance Writer. m. Michael Lawrence Armstrong, 20 Dec 1959, 1 son, 1 daughter. *Education:* BA, Sydney University, Australia. *Contributor to:* Reader's Digest; Playboy; Vogue; Harper's Bazaar; Good Housekeeping; Cosmopolitan; Cleo; The Australian; The Sydney Morning Herald; Financial Review; Melbourne Age; Sun-Herald. *Honours:* Pluma de Plata, Award given by Mexican Government, 1983, for the best travel article written about Mexico, 1982; Winner, PATA Gold Award for best travel story, 1987. *Address:* 181 Military Road, Dover Heights, Sydney 2030, Australia.

ARMSTRONG John Alexander, b. 4 May 1922, Saint Augustine, Florida, USA. Professor Emeritus of Political Science; Author; Consultant. m. Annette Taylor, 14 June 1952, 3 daughters. *Education:* PhB 1948, MA 1949, University of Chicago; Frankfurt University, West Germany 1949-50 (no degree); PhD, Public Law and Government, 1953, Certificate of Russian Institute, 1953, Columbia University, New York, USA. *Appointments:* Research Analyst, War Documentation Project, Alexandria, Virginia, USA 1951, 1953-54; Assistant Professor, University of Denver, Colorado, 1952; Visiting Assistant Professor, Russian Institute, Columbia University, 1957; Assistant Professor to Philippe de Commynes Professor of Political Science (presently Emeritus), University of Wisconsin, Madison, 1954-86. *Publications include:* Ukrainian Nationalism, 1955, 1963, 1990; Nations Before Nationalism, 1982; The European Administrative Elite, 1973; Ideology, Politics and Government in the Soviet Union, 1962, 1967, 1974, 1978; The Politics of Totalitarianism, 1961; The Soviet Bureaucratic Elite, 1959; Soviet Partisans in World War II (ed) 1964. *Contributor to:* International Affairs, Soviet Studies; Soviet Jewish Affairs (UK); Osteuropa (German); American Historical Review; Slavic Review; American Journal of History etc. *Honours:* Guggenheim Fellow, 1967, 1975; (US) National Endowment for the Humanities Research Grant 1980 and Publication Grant 1981; Co-awardee of Ralph J Bunche Award for Nations Before Nationalism by American Political Science Association, 1983 (best book on ethnic and cultural pluralism). *Memberships:* President, American Association for Advancement of Slavic Studies, 1965-67; Council Member, International Political Science Association, 1979-82; American Historical Association. *Address:* 40 Water Street, Saint Augustine, FL 32084, USA.

ARMSTRONG Michael Allen, b. 10 May 1956, Charlottesville, Virginia, USA. Writer. *Education:* BA, New College of the University of South Florida, 1977; Master of Fine Arts, University of Alaska, Anchorage, 1986. *Publications include:* After The Zap (Book), 1987; Going After Arviq (Story), 1985; Between The Devil and The Deep Blue Sea (Story), 1987; Various other articles and stories including first publication, Absolutely The Last Pact With The Devil Story, in The Magazine of Fantasy and Science Fiction, 1981; Agviq: The Whale, 1990. *Contributions to:* We Alaskans, 1981-; Anchorage Daily News, 1982; The Magazine of Fantasy and Science Fiction, 1981, 1987. *Honours:* Alaska Press Club Award of Excellence, First Place, Best Newspaper Feature Story, 1983, Best Magazine Story, 1984, Daily and Non-Daily Newspapers; Alaska State Council on The Arts Writing Fellowship, 1987. *Memberships:* Science Fiction Writers of America, 1981-; Alaskan Sled Dog and Racing Association. *Literary Agent:* Perry Knowlton, Curtis Brown, Ltd. *Address:* 15032 Snowshoe Lane, Anchorage, AK 99516, USA.

ARMSTRONG Patrick Hamilton, b. 10 Oct 1941, Leeds, Yorkshire, England. University Lecturer. m. Moyra E.J. Irvine, 8 Aug 1964, Altcar, Lancashire, England. 2 sons. *Education:* BSc, Honours, 1963, Dip.Ed., 1964, MA, 1966, Univeristy of Durham, England; PhD, (CNAA), 1970. *Publications:* Discovering Ecology, 1973; Discovering Geology, 1974; The Changing Landscape, 1975; a series of childrens' books for Ladybird Books, 1976-79; Ecology, 1977; Reading & Interpretation of Australian & NZ Maps, 1981; Living in the Environment (with L.T. Miller), 1982; The Earth: Home of Humanity, (with N. Jarvis), 1984; Charles Darwin in Western Australia, 1985; Ecology and Ecosystems, 1986; A Sketch-Map Geography of Australia, 1988; A Sketch-Map Physical Geography for Australia, 1989; Darwin's Desolate Islands, 1992. *Contributions to:* New Scientist; Geographical Magazine; East Anglian Magazine; Geography; Cambridgeshire Life; Eastern Daily Press; Hemisphere; Journal of Biogeography; The Expatriate; Work & Travel Abroad; West Australian Newspaper; Weekly Telegraph and others. *Memberships:* Geographical Association; British Ecological Society; Institute of Australian Geographers. *Literary Agent:* Curtis Brown. *Address:* Department of Geography, University of Western Australia, Nedlands, WA 6009, Australia.

ARNDT C C. *See:* **HOEPPNER Iona Ruth.**

ARNDT Heinz Wolfgang, b. 1915, Germany, resident and national of Australia. *Literary Appointment:* Editor, Bulletin of Indonesian Economic Studies, 1965-84, Asian-Pacific Economic Literature. 1987- *Publications:* The Economic Lessons of the Nineteen-Thirties, 1944; Labour and Economic Policy, 1956; The Australian Trading Banks, 1957-77, The Banks and the Capital market, 1960; The Australian Economy: A Volume of Readings, vol 1 (with W.M.Corden), 1963, 1972, vol 2 (with A Boxer) 1972; Co- Author: Taxation in Australia: Agenda for Reform, 1964; Co-Author: Some Factors in Economic Growth in Europe During the 1950's, 1964; The Indonesian Economy: Facing a New Era? (with J. Panglaykim), 1966; A Small Rich Industrial Country: Studies in Australian Development, Aid and Trade, 1968; Australia and Asia: Economic Essays, 1972; Co-Author: Australia: OECD Annual Survey, 1972; Development and Equality: Indonesia during the New Order, 1983; The Rise and Fall of Economic Growth, 1978, 1984; The Indonesian Economy: Collected Papers, 1984; A Course through Life: Memoirs of an Australian Economist, 1985; Economic Development: The History of an Idea, 1987; Asian Diaries, 1987; Indonesian Economic Development: As Seen by a Neighbour, 1991. *Memberships:* President, Economic Society of Australia & New Zealand, 1957-59; Fellow, Academy of the Social Sciences in Australia, 1954-. *Address:* Australian National University, Canberra, ACT 0200, Australia.

ARNER Betty Anne. *See:* **CAMPION Joan Berengaria.**

ARNOLD Arnold, b. 6 Feb 1928, Germany. m. (1) Eve Arnold, 1942, (2) Alison Pilpel, 1982. *Education:* St Martins School of Art, London, 1937-38; Pratt Institute, New York, 1938-39; New York University & Columbia University, 1939-42. *Appointments:* graphic, toy & industrial designer, 1946; Director, Workshop School, New York, 1949-52; President, Arnold Arnold Design Inc, 1960-66; President, Manuscript Press Inc, 1963-66; Designer of childrens play, learning matericals & progams; Consultant Editor, Rutledge Books, NY, 1962-65; Cyberneticist, Writer & Consultant, Systems Analysis & Operational Research, London, 1980-. *Publications include:* How to Play With Your Child; The Arnold Arnold Book of Toy Soldiers; Your Childs Play; Your Child & You; The World Book of Children's Games; The World Book of Arts & Crafts for Children; Winners & Other Losers in War & Peace; The Corrupted Sciences; The I Ching and the Theory of Everything, in progress. *Contributions to:* Syndicated Newspaper, Parents & Children; Woman's Journal; The Guardian; The Times; Computer Weekly; Far Eastern Technical Review; Science Policy; The New European. *Honours:* Fellow of Boston University; Leverhulme Fellow. *Memberships:* American Management Association Educational Conference; Youth Committee, US Office of Child Development. *Literary Agent:* Tina Betts. *Address:* c/o Andrew Mann Ltd, 1 Old Compton Street, London W1V 5PH, England.

ARNOLD Guy, b. 1932. Freelance Writer. *Appointments:* Adviser on Youth Problems, Government of Northern Rhodesia, 1963-64; Researcher, Overseas Development Institute, London, 1965-66; Director, Africa Bureau, London, 1968-72. *Publications:* Longhouse and Jungle, 1959; Towards Peace and a Multiracial Commonwealth, 1964; Economic Co-Operation in the Commonwealth, 1967; Kenyatta and the Politics of Kenya, 1974; The Last Bunker, 1976; Modern Nigeria, 1977; Strategic Highways of Africa (with Ruth Weis), 1977; Britain's Oil, 1978; Aid in Africa, 1979; Held Fast for England: G.A. Henty, Imperialist Boys' Writer, 1980; The Unions, 1981; Modern Kenya, 1981; Datelines of World History, 1983; Aid and the Third World, 1985; Third World Handbook, 1989; Down the Danube, 1989; Britain Since 1945, 1989; Journey Round Turkey, 1990; Wars in the Third World Since 1945, 1991; South Africa: Crossing The Rubicon, 1992; Brainwash: The Cover-up Society, 1992. *Literary Agent:* Mike Shaw, Curtis Brown and John Farquharsom. *Address:* 163 Seymour Place, London, W1H 5TP, England.

ARNOLD Heinz Ludwig, b. 29 Mar 1940, Essen/Ruhr, Federal Republic of Germany. Writer; Critic; Editor. *Education:* Studied Literary Science, University of Göttingen. *Appointments:* Editor: Text und Kritik, 1963; Kritisches Lexikon zur deutschsprachigen Gegenwartsliteratur, 1978-; Kritisches Lexikon zur fremdsprachigen Gegenwartslieratur, 1983-. *Publications:* Brauchen wir noch die Literatur?, 1972; Gespräche mit Schriftstellern, 1975; Deutsche über dieDeutschen, 1975; Gespräch mit F Dürrenmatt, 1976; Handbuch der deutschen Arbeiterliteratur, 1977; Tagebuch einer Chinareise, 1978; Als Schriftsteller leben, 1979; Literaturbetrieb in der Bundesrepublik Deutschland, 1981; Vom Verlust der Scham und dem allmühlichen Verschwinden der Demokratie, 1988. *Contributor To:* Die Zeit; Deutsches Allgemeines Sonntagblatt; various radio stations, Germany. *Memberships:* Association of German Writers; PEN; Ohio Tuölip Order. *Address:* Tuckermannweg 10, 3400 Göttingen, Germany.

ARNOTT Margaret Anne, b. 1916. Author. *Appointments:* Justice of the Peace, Newcastle-upon-Tyne and Weston-Super-Mare Bench, 1964-73; Former Teacher in Grammar and High Schools. *Publications:* The Brethren (in United States of America as Turbulent Water), 1969; Journey into Understanding: Portrain of a Family, 1971; The Secret Country of C.S. Lewis, 1974; Wife to the Archbishop, 1976; Fruits of the Earth, 1979; The Unexpected Call, 1981; Valiant for Truth: The Story of John Bunyan, 1986.

AROND Miriam, b. 31 Oct 1955, USA. Writer. m. 11 June 1981, 2 daughters. *Education:* University of Pennsylvania, BA, 1977; New YorK University, MA, 1981. *Publications:* The First Year of Marriage. *Contributions to:* Child Magazine; Lilith Magazine; CV

Magazine; Brides Magazine; New York Daily News. *Honour:* The dealine Clerk Award. *Memberships:* Sigma Delta Phi; The Authors Guild. *Literary Agent:* Vicky Bijur. *Address:* Forest Hills, New York, USA.

ARONSON Theo, b. 13 Nov 1930, South Africa. Writer. *Education:* BA, University of Cape Town, 1950. *Publications:* The Golden Bees, 1965; The Kaisers, 1971; Grandmama of Europe, 1973; Victoria and Disraeli, 1977; Princess Alice, 1981; Royal Family, 1983; Royal Vendetta, 1967; The Coburgs of Belgium, 1968; The Fall of the Third Napoleon, 1970; Queen Victoria and the Bonapartes, 1972; A Family of Kings, 1975; Crowns in Conflict, 1986; Kings Over the Water, 1979; The King in Love, 1988; Napoleon and Josephine, 1990; Heart of a Queen, 1991; The Royal Family at War, 1993. *Contributions to:* Various journals and magazines. *Literary Agent:* Andrew Lownie.*Address:* North Knoll Cottage, 15 Bridge Street, Frome, Somerset BA11 1BB, England.

ARRABAL Fernando, b. 11 Aug 1932, Melilla, Spain. Writer, Poet, m. Luce Moreau, 1 Feb 1958, 2 children. *Publications include:* (Novels) Baal Babylone, 1959; The Burial of Sardine, 1952; Fetes et Rites de la Confusion, 1965; La Torre Herida por el Rayo, 1983; (Poetry) Pierre de Folie, 1963; 100 Sonnets, 1966; Un nuage, 1966; L'Odeur de saintete, 1975; Les eveques se noient, 1969; Reves d'insectes, 1987; Lanzarote, 1988; Le voyage est le feu, 1985; Sur les cimes, 1986; Peches maudits 1987; La Nature est le maitre, 1976; Anges et taupes, 1979, Cinco sonetos, 1980, Poemes 1982 and numerous others; Numerous plays include: The Architect and the Emperor of Assyria; And They Put Handcuffs on the Flowers; Garden of Delights; The Automobile (essays); The Panic; The New York of Arrabal; Letter to General Franco; Fishcher 1973; Writer Director, Films: Viva la Muerte; Jairai comme in Cheval fou; Larbre de Guernica; Odyssey of the Pacific. *Honours:* Grand Prix du Theatre, 1967; Grand Prix Humour Noir, 1968; Prix de l'Humour Noir, 1969. *Memberships:* Founder, Panique Movement with Topor, Jodorowsky and others; Political Prisoner, Spain, 1967. *Address:* 22 Rue Jouffroy, Paris 75017, France.

ARRIENS Jan, b. 31 July 1943, Esher, England. Freelance Translator. m. Pamela Wood, 17 Feb 1967, 2 sons, 1 daughter. *Education:* BA Hons 1964, Melbourne University; PhD (Cantab) 1968. *Publications:* Bearers of Bad Tidings, Translator, M T Hart, 1984; The Mother of David S., Translator, Y Keuls, 1985; A Flight of Curlews, Translator, M T Hart, 1986; Welcome to Hell, 1991. *Memberships:* Translators Association, Committee 1987-89; Chairman, Lifelines (US Death Row Correspondence Organisation). *Address:* 3 Middlemoor Road, Whittlesford, Cambridge CB2 4PB, England.

ARTHUR Elizabeth Ann, b. 15 Nov 1953, New York, USA. m. Steven Bauer, 19 June 1982. *Education:* BA, English, University of Victoria, 1978; Diploma, Education, 1979. *Appointments:* Visiting Instructor, Creative Writing, University of Cincinnati, 1983-84; Assistant professor, English, Miami University, 1984-85; Assistant Professor, English, IUPUI, Indianapolis, 1985-. *Publications:* Island Sojourn, 1980; Beyond the Mountain, 1983; Bad Guys, 1986; Bindig Spell, 1988. *Contributor to:* New York Times; Outside; Backpacker; Ski-XC; Shenandoah. *Honours:* William Sloane Fellowship, Bread Loaf Writers' Conference, 1980; Writing Felowshi, Ossabaw Island Project, 1981; Grant in Aid, Vermont Council on the Arts, 1982; Fellowship in Prose, NEA, 1983; Artists' Fellowship, Indiana Arts Council, 1988; Fellowship from the National Endowment for the Arts, 1989. *Memberships:* Poets & Writers. *Literary Agent:* Jean Naggar. *Address:* Bath, Indiana 47010, USA.

ARTHUR Rasjid Arthur James, b. 7 June 1928, Stirling, Scotland. Journalist. *Education:* MA Hons., English, Edinburgh University, 1950. *Appointments:* Leader Writer, The Scotsman, 1955-64; Features Editor,

News Editor, Writer, Central Office of Information, London, 1965- 78. *Contributions to:* London Press Service; Spectrum (scientific); Industrial Waste Management; Water and Waste Treatment; Water and Environment International. *Membership:* Chartered Institute of Journalists. *Address:* 32 Midway, Middleton Cheney, Banbury OX17 2QW, England.

ARYA Anita Nahal, b. 3 Apr 1958, New Delhi, India. Teacher; Senior Assistant Professor. m. Jagjit Singh Arya, 25 Mar 1985, 1 son. *Education:* BA Hons 1978, Lady Shri Ram College, New Delhi; MA 1980, M Phil 1988, Delhi University. *Appointments:* Managing Editor, The Humanities Review 1978-81; Assistant Professor of History, Kamala Nehru College, New Delhi 1981-86; Senior Assistant Professor, Sri Venkateswara College, New Delhi 1987-. *Publications:* Initiations, collection of poems, 1988; Hawaii: An Ethnic Synthesis, 1993; Nursery Rhymes Book I and Book II, 1993. *Contributions to:* The National Herald; Choice India; Indian Author; Women's Era; The Humanities Review; India International Centre Journal; poems, book reviews, features. *Memberships:* The Poetry Society of India; Indian History Congress; India International Centre; American Studies Research Centre. *Address:* 2/1 Kalkaji Extension, New Delhi - 110 019, India.

ASCH Frank, b. 1946, American. *Publications:* George's Store, Linda, 1969; Elvira Everything, 1970; The Blue Balloon, Yellow Yellow, Rebecka, 1971; I Met a Penguin, 1972; In the Eye of the Teddy, 1973; Gia and the $100 Worth of Bubblegum, 1974; Good Lemonade, 1975; The Inside Kid, Monkey Face, 1977; Macgoose's Grocery, Moon Bear, Turtle Tale, City Sandwich, 1978; Country Pie, Little Devil's ABC, Popcorn, Sand Cake, Little Devil's One Two Three, Running with Rachel, 1979; The Last Puppy, Starbaby, 1980; Just Like Daddy, Goodnight Horsey, 1981; Happy Birthday Moon, Milk and Cookies, Bread and Honey, 1982; Mooncake, 1983; Moongame, Pearl's Promise, Skyfire, 1984. *Address:* c/o McGraw-Hill Incorporated, 1221 Avenue of the Americas, New York, NY 10020, USA.

ASCHER Sheila, (Ascher Straus), b. New York, USA. Writer. *Education:* MA Slavic Literature and Languages, Columbia University. *Publications:* Letter to an Unknown Woman, 1979; The Menaced Assassin, 1982, revised 1989; Red Moon/Red Lake, 1988; The Other Planet, 1988; Long fictions in anthologies: Pushcart Prize III; Likely Stories; Chelsea: A 25 Year Retrospective; Top Top Stories; Exile: The Fifteen Years. *Contributions to:* Chicago Review; Paris Review; Epoch; Top Stories; Chelsea; Exile; Calyx; Zone. *Honours:* Panache Experimental Fiction Prize, 1973; Pushcart Prize, 1982; CAPS Fellowship, NY State, 1983. *Address:* Ascher/Straus, PO Box 176, Rockaway Park, NY 11694, USA.

ASCHER STRAUS. *See:* **ASCHER Sheila and STRAUS Dennis David.**

ASH Brian (Henry Dorland), b. 1936, British. *Appointments:* Assistant, Bank of England, 1953-58; Administration Officer, Royal National Lifeboat Institution, 1959-65; Advertising Executive, Kodak Limited, 1965-66; Head of Editorial Services, Esso Petroleum Company, 1966-70; Public Relations Officer, London Borough of Camden, 1971-72; Publicity Officer, H G Wells Centenary, 1966; General Secretary, H G Wells Society, 1967-70. *Publications:* H G Wells: A Comprehensive Bibliography (ed), 1966; The Last Books of H G Wells (ed), 1968; Tiger in Your Tank, 1969; Faces of the Future: The Lessons of Science Fiction, 1975; Who's Who in Science Fiction, 1976; The Visual Encyclopaedia of Science Fiction (ed), Who's Who in H G Wells, 1977. *Address:* 21 Fawe Park Road, Putney, London SW15, England.

ASH John, b. 29 June 1948, England. *Appointments:* Primary school teacher, 1970-71; Research Assistant 1971-75. *Publications:* Verse: Casino, 1978; The Bed and Other Poems, 1981; The Goodbyes, 1982; The Branching Stairs, 1984. *Address:* c/o Carcanet Press Ltd, 208 Corn Exchange Buildings, Manchester M4 3BQ, England.

ASH William, b. 30 Sept 1917. m. 29 Sept 1955, 1 son 1 daughter. *Education:* BA, University of Texas, Phi Beta Kappa; MA, Oxford University. *Publications:* The Lotus in the Sky, 1961; Choice of Arms, 1962; The Longest Way Round, 1963; Ride a Paper Tiger, 1968; Incorporated, 1980; Right Side Up, 1984; A Red Square (autobiography) 1978; The Way to Write Radio Drama, 1985; Marxist Morality, 1988. *Literary Agent:* M.B.A.

ASHANTI Baron James, b. 5 Sept 1950, New York, USA. Freelance Writer. m. Brenda Cummings, 11 Sept 1979, 1 son, 1 daughter. *Literary Appointments:* Literary editor, Impressions Magazine, 1972-75; City editor, Liberation News Service, 1974-79; Contributing editor, The Paper, 1978; Literary Editor, New Heat Magazine, 1980-82. *Publications:* Nova, 1990, nominated for Pulitzer Prize in Poetry; The Candy Marine, novel; The Journeyman, novel. *Contributions to:* Liberation News Service; Pan African Journal; Presance Africaine; Essence Magazine; Greenfield Review; Maintrend; Race Today; Nethula II & III; Hoodoo VII; Blacks on Paper, III & IV. *Honours:* Killen Prize, poetry, St Peters College, New York, 1982; PEN Fellowships, 1985, 1987. *Memberships:* Griots Society; Society of African Poets; Harlem Writers Guild; New Renaissance Writers Guild; John Oliver Killens Writers Workshop, Calabash Poets Workshop. *Literary Agent:* Mari Brown Associates, New York. *Address:* 4343 North 9th Street, Philadelphia, Pennsylvania 19140, USA.

ASHBY Gwynneth Margaret, b. 1 May 1922, Birmingham, England. Children's Author; Photographer; Lecturer. *Education:* Brownhills High School, Stoke-on-Trent, 1933-39; Teaching Diploma, Hereford College, 1939-42. *Literary Appointment:* Editorial Staff (Education) of A & C Black, 1948-50. *Publications include:* Looking at Norway: 1967, 1969, 1971, 1975; Looking at Japan, 1969, 1971, 1976; Korean Village 1986; A Family in South Korea (US) 1987; Yung Mee o Dde Korea (Welsh) 1988; Dorp in Zuid Korea (Dutch) 1988. *Contributor to:* Various journals, magazines etc. *Honour:* Winner of Photographic Prize (Travel) Seoul 14th Annual Photographic Contest held under the auspices of the Korean National Tourism Corporation. *Memberships:* Society of Authors (on Educational Executive Committee 1975-79); Society of Women Writers and Journalists; Tunbridge Wells Writer Circle (period as Vice-Chairman); Royal Geographical Society. *Address:* 12 D Blenheim Drive, De Havilland Way, Christchurch, Dorset BH23 4JH, England.

ASHDOWN Dulcie Margaret, b. 24 Feb 1946, London, Great Britain. Writer; Editor. *Education:* BA (Hons) History, Bristol University, 1967. *Publications:* Christmas Past, 1976; Ladies-in-Waiting, UK and USA Editions, 1976; Princess of Wales, UK and USA Editions, 1976; Royal Children, 1980; Royal Weddings, 1981; Victoria and the Coburgs, 1981; 4 other books, UK and USA. *Contributions to:* Majesty; Heritage; Writers Monthly; The Lady. *Address:* c/o National Westminster Bank, 1302 High Road, Whetstone, London N20, Great Britain.

ASHE Geoffrey Thomas, b. 29 Mar 1923, London, England. Writer; Lecturer. m. Dorothy Irene Train, 3 May 1946 (dec), 4 sons, 1 daughter. (2) Maxine Lefever, 8 Dec 1992. *Education:* BA, University of British Columbia, Canada, 1943; BA, Trinity College, Cambridge University, UK, 1948. *Appointments include:* Associate editor, Arthurian Encyclopaedia, 1986. *Publications include:* King Arthur's Avalon, 1957; From Caesar to Arthur, 1960; Land to the West, 1962; The Land & the Book, 1965; Gandhi, 1968; The Quest for Arthur's Britain, 1968; Camelot & the Vision of Albion, 1971; The Art of Writing Made Simple, 1972; The Finger & the Moon, 1973; Do What You Will, 1974; The Virgin, 1976; The Ancient Wisdom, 1977; Miracles, 1978;

Guidebook to Arthurian Britain, 1980; Kings & Queens of Early Britain, 1982; Avalonian Quest, 1982; The Discovery of King Arthur, 1985; Landscape of King Arthur, 1987; Mythology of the British Isles, 1990; King Arthur: The Dream of a Golden Age, 1990; Dawn Behind the Dawn, 1992; Atlantis, 1992. *Contributions to:* Associate Editor, The Arthurian Encyclopedia, 1986; Numerous magazines & journals. *Honour:* Fellow, Royal Society of Literature, 1963. *Memberships:* Medieval Academy of America; Secretary, Camelot Research Committee. *Address:* Chalice Orchard, Well House Lane, Glastonbury, Somerset BA6 8BJ, England.

ASHER Jane, b. 5 Apr 1946, London, England. Actress. m. Gerald Scarfe, 2 sons, 1 daughter. *Publications:* Jane Asher's Party Cakes, 1982; Jane Asher's Fancy Dress, 1983; Silent Nights for You and Your Baby, 1984; Jane Asher's Quick Party Cakes, 1986; The Moppy Stories, 1986; Easy Entertaining, 1987; Keep Your Baby Safe, 1988; Jane Asher's Children's Parties, 1988; Jane Ashers Calender of Cakes, 1989; Eats for Treats, 1990; Complete Book of Cake Decorating, 1993. *Contributions to:* Numerous articles for Newspapers and Magazines. *Literary Agent:* Mark Lucas, Fraser & Dunlop. *Address:* c/o I.C.M., 76 Oxford Street, London, W1R 1RB, England.

ASHLEY Bernard, b. 2 Apr 1935, London, England. Teacher. *Education:* Teacher's Certificate; Advanced Diploma, Cambridge Institute of Education. *Publications include:* The Trouble with Donovan Croft, 1974; Terry on the Fence, 1975; All my Men, 1977; A Kind of Wild Justice, 1978; Break in the Sun, 1980; Dodgem, 1982; High Pavement Blues, 1983; Janey, 1985; Running Scared, 1986; Bad Blood, 1988; The Country Boy (TV), 1989; The Secret of Theodore Brown (Stage Play), 1989. *Contributions to:* Books for Your Children; Junior Education; Books for Keeps; Times Educational Supplement. *Honours:* The Other Award, 1976; Runner-up, Carnegie Medal, 1979, 1986. *Memberships:* Writers Guild. *Address:* 128 Heathwood Gardens, London SE7 8ER, England.

ASHLEY Leonard R(aymond) N(elligan), b. 5 Dec 1928, Miami, Florida, USA. Professor of English; Author; Editor. *Education:* BA, McGill University, 1949; MA, 1950; AM Princeton University, 1953; PhD, 1956. *Appointments:* Instructor, University of Utah, 1953-56; Assistant to The Air Historian RCAF, 1956-58; Instructor, University of Rochester, 1958-61; Faculty, The New School for Social Research (part-time), 1962-72; Faculty, Brooklyn College of The City University, New York, 1961-. *Publications:* Whats in a Name?; Elizabethan Popular Culture; Colley Cibber; Nineteenth-Century British Drama; Authorship & Evidence in Renaissance Drama; Mirrors for Man; Other People's Lives; The Wonderful World of Magic & Witchcraft; Shakespeare's Jest Book; George Peele: The Man and His Work. *Contributions to:* Great Writers of the English Language; Reference Guide to American Literature; British Women Writers; Encyclopeadia of British Humor, Encyclopeadia of World Drama, Cyclopeadia of Short Fiction; Regular reviewer for Bibliotheque d'Humarisme et Renaissance, Names, etc. *Honours:* The Shakespeare Gold Medal; American Name Society Best Article Award; Fellowships & Grants. *Memberships include:* The American Name Society (past president); International Linguistics Association (former secretary); American Association of University Professors (former president, Brooklyn College Chapter); American Society of Geolinguistics (president); Princeton Club of New York. *Address:* 1901 Avenue H, Brooklyn, NY 11230, USA.

ASHMORE Owen, b. 1920, British. *Appointments:* Resident Staff Tutor 1950-62, Deputy Director 1962-69, Associate Director 1969-73, Acting Director 1973-76, Director of Extra-Mural Studies 1976-83, University of Manchester. *Publications:* The Development of Power in Britain, 1967; Industrial Archaeology of Lancashire, 1969; The Industrial Archaeology of Stockport, 1975; Historic Industries of Marple and Mellor (ed), 1977; The Industrial Archaeology of North West England, 1982.

ASHOKAMITRAN (Jagadisan Thyagarajan), b. 22 Sept 1931, Secunderabad, India. Writer. m. Rajeswari, 5 July 1963, 3 sons. *Education:* BSc Maths Physics, Chemistry. *Publications:* Dissolved Shadows, 1969; Once in a lifetime, 1971; Today, 1985; A Lake, 1990; Appavin Snehidar, 1991; Water, 1973; Otran!, 1986; Iruvar, 1988. *Contributions to:* Almost all the reading magazines, newspapers and journals of India published in English and several other Indian langauges. *Honours:* Book of the Year, 1977, 1983; Govt of Tamilnadu Fiction of the year award, 1986, 1988, 1990; Santhome Award for Values, 1983. *Memberships:* Authors Guild of India. *Address:* 23 Damodara Reddy St, T Nagar, Madras 600017, India.

ASHTON Christina Julia Allen, b. 16 Sept 1934, Brooklyn, New York. Writer; Teacher. m. 21 Aug 1954, 1 daughter. *Education:* BA English 1957, Washington State University; MS Special Education 1975, Dominican College. *Publications:* Words Can Tell, A Book About Our Language, 1988; Codes and Ciphers: Hundreds of Unusual and Secret Ways to Send Messsages, 1993; The First Defender of France, article, 1991; The Deer, short story, prize winner, not yet published, 1991. *Contributions to:* Calliope Magazine. *Honours:* English Honours, University of Oregon, 1954; Second Prize, California Writers Club, short story, 1991; Second Prize, National Writers Club, short story, 1991; Honorable Mention, National Writers Club, nonfiction book, 1992. *Memberships:* National Writers Club; California Writers Club, member, Secretary Peninsular Branch. *Literary Agent:* Norma Lewis Agency, New York. *Address:* 4009 Kingridge Drive, San Mateo, CA 94403, USA.

ASHTON Robert, b. 21 July 1924, Chester, England. Retired University Professor. m. Margaret Alice Sedgwick, 30 Aug 1946, 2 daughters. *Education:* Magdalen College School, Oxford, 1938-40; 1946-49 University College, Southampton, BA (Lond) 1st Class Honours, 1949-52 London School of Economics, PhD (London) 1953. *Appointments:* Assistant Lecturer, Lecturer and Senior Lecturer in Economic History, Nottingham University 1952-63; Visiting Associate Professor, University of California, Berkeley, 1962-63; Professor of English History, University of East Anglia, 1963-89; Emeritus Professor of English History, University of East Anglia, 1989-; Visiting Fellow, All Souls College, Oxford 1974-75, 1987. *Publications:* The English Civil War: Conservatism and Revolution, 1603-49, 1978, 2nd edition 1989; The Crown and the Money Market 1603-1640, 1960; James I by his Contemporaries, 1969; The City and the Court 1603-1643, 1979; Reformation and Revolution 1558-1660, 1984. *Contributor to:* Articles in Economic History Review; Bulletin of Institute of Historical Research; Past and Present; Historical Journal. *Memberships:* Fellow of Royal Historical Society, Vice President 1984-86. *Address:* The Manor House, Brundall, Norwich NR13 5JY, England.

ASIMOV Isaac, (Dr A, Paul French), b. 2 Jan 1920, USSR. Writer. m. Janet Opal Jeppson, 30 Nov 1973, 1 son, 1 daughter (previous marriage). *Education:* BSc, Chemistry, 1939, MA 1941, PhD 1948, Columbia University, USA. *Publications:* Prelude to Foundations, 1989, (Fiction); Nemesis, 1989, (Fiction). Author of 434 Books. *Contributor to:* About 3,000 publications. *Honours:* Recipient, numerous honours and awards including The Grand Master Award for Science Fiction Writers of America, 1987. *Memberships:* Science Fiction Writers of America; Mystery Writers of America, etc. *Address:* 10 West 66th Street, New York, NY 10023, USA.

ASIMOV Janet O. Jeppson, b. 6 Aug 1926, Ashland, Pennsylvania, USA. Physician; Writer. m. Isaac Asimov, 30 Nov 1973. *Education:* BA, Stanford University, 1948; MD, New York University College of Medicine, 1952; Diploma, Psychoanalysis, William Alanson White Institute, 1960. *Publications include:* The Second Experiment, 1974; The Last Immortal, 1980; The Mysterious Cure, 1985; Mind Transfer, 1988. With Isaac Asimov: How to Enjoy Writing; Laughing Space, 1982; Norby, the Mixed-Up Robot, 1983; Norby's Other Secret, 1984; Norby & the Lost Princess, 1985; Norby & the Invaders, 1985; Norby & the Queen's Necklace, 1986; Norby Finds a Villain, 1987; The Package in Hypcrspace, 1988; Norby and Yobo's Great Adventure, 1989. *Contributions to:* Several journals. *Honour:* Phi Beta Kappa 1948. *Memberships:* Science Fiction Writers of America; William Alanson White Society; American Academy of Psychoanalysis; American Psychiatric Association. *Address:* 10 West 66th Street, New York, NY 10023, USA.

ASPINWALL Dorothy Brown, b. 21 Oct 1910, Regina, Saskatchewan, Canada. Teacher; University Professor. m. Albion Newton Aspinwall, 10 Jan 1942, 1 son. *Education:* BA, University of Alberta, 1933; MA, 1939; PhD, University of Washington, 1948. *Publications:* The Portico of the Mystery of the Second Virtue; French Poems in English Verse; Modern Verse Translations from French; Recitatif Translated under the Title The Party is Over; Choice Poems of Ilarie Voronca. *Contributions to:* The Atlantic Monthly; Modern Language Journal; PMLA; The Mexico Quarterly; The Explicator; The Husk; The Lantern; Poet Lore; Paradise of the Pacific; Webster Review; Poesie USA. *Honours:* Carnegie Hero Fund Commission award; French Government Bursary; Ford Foundation Grant for Research; Danforth Foundation Summer Workshop; NDEA Institute Director. *Memberships:* Modern Language Association; American Association of Teachers of French; Hawaii Association of Language Teachers. *Address:* 2003 Kalia Road, 9-I Honolulu, HI 96815, USA.

ASPLER Tony, b. 12 May 1939, London, England. Writer. m. 11 July 1971, 1 son, 1 daughter. *Education:* BA, McGill University, Canada, 1959. *Publications:* With Gordon Page: Chain Reaction, 1978. The Scorpion Sanction, 1980; The Music Wars, 1983. Sole author: Streets of Askelon, 1972; One of my Marionettes, 1973; Vintage Canada, 1983; The Wine Lover Dines, International Guide to Wine; Titanic, 1989. *Contributions to:* Wine Tidings; Wine Spectator. *Membership:* Founding Chairman 1982-84, Crime Writers of Canada. *Literary Agent:* MGA. *Address:* 202 Keewatin Avenue, Toronto, Canada M4P 1Z8.

ASPREY Robert B, b. 16 Feb 1923, Sioux City, Iowa, USA. Writer. *Education:* University of Iowa, New College, Oxford University; University of Vienna, Austria, University of Nice, France. *Publications:* The Panther's Feast; The First Battle of the Marne; Once a Marine; At Belleau Wood; Semper Fidelis; War in the Shadows; Operation Prophet; Frederick the Great - The Magnificent Enigma, 1986; The German High Command at War - Hindenburg and Ludendorff Conduct and World War One, 1991. *Contributions to:* Marine Corps Gazette; Ency. Britannica; New Yorker; Naval Institute Proceedings; Brassey's Annual; Army Quarterly; New York Times. *Memberships include:* Authors Guild; Oxford University Society; New College Society; Frilford Heath Golf Club (Oxford); Clun de Golf Sotogrande; Army & Navy Club, Washington, DC; Special Forces Club, London. *Literary Agent:* Robert Gottlieb, William Morris Agency, 1350 Avenue of The Americas, New York, NY 10019, USA.

ASPRIN Robert (Lynn), b. 1946. American. Writer. *Appointments:* Accounts Clerk, 1966-70, Payroll Analyst, 1970-74 and Cost Accountant, 1974-78, University Microfilm, Ann Arbor; Freelance Writer since 1978. *Publications:* The Cold Cash War, 1977; Another Fine Myth, 1978; The Bug Wards, 1979; Tambu, 1979; (with George Takei) Mirror Friend, Mirror Foe, 1979; (ed.) Thieves World, 1979; Myth Conceptions, 1979; (ed.) Storm Seasons, 1982; Hit or Myth, 1983; Myth-ing Persons, 1984; The Face of Chaos, 1984; (ed. with Lynn Abbey) Birds of Prey, 1984; (ed. with Lynn Abbey) Wings of Omen, 1984; Myth Adventures Two, 1986; (with Kay Reynolds) Myth Inc. Link, 1986. *Address:* c/o Kirby MccCauley Ltd., 425 Park Ave. South, NY 10016, USA.

ASSELINEAU Roger Maurice, b. 24 Mar 1915, Orleans, France. Emeritus Professor, American Literature. *Education:* Licence es Lettres, Agregation, English, 1938, Docteur es Lettres 1953, Sorbonne. *Publications include:* L'Evolution de Walt Whitman, 1954; The Literary Reputation of Mark Twain, 1964, USA 1971; Poesies Incompletes, 1959; Evolution of Walt Whitman, 1960-62; E.A. Poe, 1970; Transcendentalist Constant in American Literature, 1980; Incomplete Poems, 1984; St John de Crevecoeur: The Life of an American Farmer, with Gay Wilson Allen, 1987; Poésies incomplètes (II), 1989. *Contributions to:* Etudes Anglaises; Revue de Litterature Comparee; Forum; Dialogue; Calamus; Walt Whitman Review. *Honours:* Walt Whitman Prize, Poetry Society of America; Honorary doctorate, University of Poznan. *Memberships include:* Honorary president, French Association for American Studies; Honorary member, Modern Language Association; Hemingway Society; International Association of University Professors of English; Societe des Gens de Lettres. *Address:* 114 Avenue Leon Blum, 92160 Antony, France.

ASSENSOH Akwasi Bretuo, (A Bretuo) b. Ghana, West Africa. Historian; Journalist. m. Irenita Benbow, 19 Mar 1981, 1 son, 1 daughter. *Education:* University of Stockholm, 1978; School of Journalisim, Frilsham, 1968-69; Swedish Language Certification, University of Stockholm, Sweden, 1975-76; BA, Dillard University, 1981; MA, New York University, 1982; PhD, New York University, 1984. *Appointments:* Writers Society of Liberia, Secretary, 1968-69; Editor, Daily Listener, 1989-71; Associate Editor, The Pioneer, 1971-72; Associate Editor & Head of Research, M L King, Jr Papers Project, Stanford University/King Center, Atlanta, USA, 1988-1990; Assoc Prof, Southern University, USA, 1991-. *Publications:* Kwame Nkrumah, Six Years in Exile; Black Woman, Black Woman; Campus Life; Essays on Contemporary International Topics; Martin Luther King Junior and Americas Quest for Racial Intergration; Kwame Nkrumah of Africa; Africa in Retrospect; Topics in Socio Historical Studies. *Contributions to:* Pen International; African Commentary Journal; Journal of Third World Studies; West Africa Magazine of London; African Studies Review; Africa Magazine; African Development. *Honours:* Dillard University Social science Plaque for Literary Achievement; Listed Contemporary Authors. *Memberships:* International PEN; Press Club of Liberia; Press Club of New Orleans; American Historical Association; African Studies Association of America. *Address:* Department of History, Southern University, PO Box 10281, Baton Rouge, LA 70813, USA.

ASTLEY Thea (Beatrice May), b. 1925, Australian. *Appointments:* Senior Tutor, Fellow, School of English, Macquarie University, Sydney, 1968-. *Publications:* Girl with a Monkey, 1959; A Descant for Gossips, 1960; The Well-Dressed Explorer, 1962; The Slow Natives, 1965; A Boat Load of Home Folk, 1968; Coast to Coast (ed), 1969-70, 1971; The Acolyte, 1972; A Kindness Cup, 1974; Hunting the Wild Pineapple, 1979; An Item from the Late News, 1983; Beachmasters, 1985.

ASTON Athina Leka, b. 14 Nov 1934, New York City, USA. Author; Publisher. m. Daniel Astbury Aston, 5 May 1962, 2 sons. *Education:* BA, Marymount Manhattan College, New York, 1956; Columbia University, 1957-58. *Appointments:* Publisher, Editor, Play, Toys, Life Lifestyle, Food. *Publications:* How to Play with Your Baby, 1971, Reprints, 1977, 1984; Toys That Teach Your Child, 1984, Reprint 1985; Today He Can - Toy Guide, Birth-Two Years, 1977; A Child at Play. *Contributions to:* Fountain Publishing, The Learning Child Series, Play Guides for Child Development Series, Birth-6 Years; Articles in Parent Guide Magazine; Publisher of A Child at Play and American Feasts and Festivals. *Memberships:* Women's National Book Association, American Society of Journalists & Authors; Authors Guild; Women's Direct Response Group. *Address:* 86-15 Ava Place, Jamaica Estates, NY 11432, USA.

ASTOR Gerald, American. *Publications:* The Charge is Rape, Capitol Hell, A Question of Rape, 1974; Brick Agent (with A Villano), 1978; The Disease Detectives: Deadly Medical Mysteries and the People Who Solve Them, 1983; The Last Nazi: The Life and Times of Dr Joseph Mengele, 1985.

ATHANASSIADIS Tassos, b. 1 Nov 1913, Salichli of Asia Minor, Turkey. Author; Novelist; Essayist; Biographer. m. Maria Dimitropoulou, 1979. *Education:* Law and Foreign Languages, Law School of Athens University 1931-36. *Publications:* The Panthei Saga, IV vols, novel, 1948-61; The Guards of Achaia, II vols, novel, 1974; Dostojevsky from prison to passion, novel 1953-55; The Last Grandchildren, II vols, novel, 1981-84; Niobe's Children, IV vols, novel, 1985-88; Julian the apostate, the Sun's Son, biography; Voyage to loneliness, biography of Greek statesman, John Kapodistrias, 1938-42; Albert Swaitzer, biography, 1966; Three Children of their century - Dostojevsky, Tolstoi, Hugot; Essays: Recognitions, 1965; Certainties and Doubts, 1980; From ourself to others, 1992; His novels have been translated into: French, Italian; Swedish, Portuguese, Romanian and German. *Honours:* Literary State Award for Dostojevsky from prison to passion, 1955; The Athens Academy Award for The Panthei Saga, 1961; State Literary Award for Albert Sveitzer, 1963; Literary Award for The Throne Hall, 1969; Athens Academy Award for The Guards of Achaia, 1975; State Literary Award for the Sun's Son, 1978; State Literary Award for The Last Grandchildren, 1984; Ipeski Prize of Greek- Turkish Friendship for Niobe's Children, 1989. *Memberships:* Full member of Athens Academy, Chair of Literature 1986; President, PEN club 1992; President, Greek Lyric Opera, 1980; General Secretary and Administrative Director, Greek National Theatre. *Literary Agent:* Estia Publishing House, Athens. *Address:* 83 Drossopoulou Str, Athens 112 57, Greece.

ATKINS Meg Elizabeth (Elizabeth Moore), British. *Publications:* (As Elizabeth Moore) - Something to Jump For, 1960; The Gemini, 1963; Shadows of the House, 1968; By the North Door, 1975; Samain, 1976; Kestrels in the Kitchen, 1979; Haunted Warwickshire, 1981; Palimpset, 1982; The Folly, 1987. *Address:* 40 Moseley Road, Kenilworth, Warwickshire, England.

ATKINSON Anthony Barnes, b. 4 Sept 1944, Caerleon. Economist. m. Judith Mary Mandeville, 11 Dec 1965, 2 sons, 1 daughter. *Education:* BA, 1966; MA, 1969. *Publications:* Poverty in Britain, 1969; Unequal Shares, 1972; Lectures On Public Economics, 1980; Social Justice and Public Policy, 1982; Economics of Inequality, 1983; Parents and Children (with A Maynard and C Trinder), 1985; Poverty and Social Security, 1989. *Memberships:* Fellow, British Academy; President, Econometric Society, 1988; President, International Economics Association, 1989-92; Fellow of Churchill College, Cambridge, 1992. *Address:* 33 Hurst Green, Brightlingsea, Colchester, Essex CO7 0HA, England.

ATKINSON James, b. 27 Apr 1914, Tynemouth, Northumberland. Retired Professor of Theology. m. Laura Jean Nutley (deceased 5 July 1967), 1 son, 1 daughter. *Education:* BA 1936, MA 1938, M Litt 1950, University of Durham; Doctor of Theology, University of Muenster, Germany, 1955. *Publications:* Library of Christian Classics Vol XVI, 1962; Rome and Reformation, 1965; Luther's Works Vol 44, 1966; Luther and the Birth of Protestantism, 1968, translated into Spanish and Italian; The Reformation Vol 4 in Protestant Church History, 1968; The Trial of Luther, 1971; Martin Luther - Prophet to Church Catholic, 1983; The Darkness of Faith, 1987. *Contributor to:* Contributions to learned journals; Part author of several books; Many articles in Encyclopaedias and Dictionaries. *Memberships:* Society for the Study of Theology (President 1978-80); Society for the Study of Ecclesiastical History; Member, L'Academie Internationale des Sciences Religieuses (Brussels). *Address:* Leach House, Hathersage. Sheffield S30 1BA, England.

ATKINSON Mary. *See:* **HARDWICK Mollie.**

ATLAN Liliane, b. 14 Jan 1932, Montpellier, France. Writer. m. June 1952, divorced 1976, 1 son, 1 daughter. *Education:* Diploma in Philosophy; CAPES Modern Literature. *Publications include:* Plays: Mr Fugue or Earth Sick, The Messiahs, The Carriage of Flames and Voices (all translated into English); Poetry: L'amour èlémentaire: (Elementary Love), 1985; Lapsus, poems, 1971; Videotext: Même les oiseaux ne peuvent pas toujours planer, 1979; Play: Les Musiciens, les emigrants; Un opera pour Terezin (An Opera for Terezin); Novels: Les Passants (The Passersby), 1989, Le Reve des animaux rongeurs (The Dream of the Rodents). Many books and plays have been broadcast by France Culture (Radio). *Honours:* Prix Habimah, 1972; Prix Wizo 1989; Chevalier de l'Ordre des Arts et des Lettres, 1984; Prize Villa Medicis Outside The Walls, 1992. *Memberships:* Writers Union of France; AMOAL (Association of Members of the Order of Arts and Literature) Paris. *Address:* 70 rue du javelot, 75645 Paris, Cedex 13, France.

ATTENBOROUGH David Frederick. b. 8 May 1926, London, England. Broadcaster and Naturalist. m. Jane Elizabeth Ebsworth Oriel, 11 Feb 1950, 1 son, 1 daughter. *Education:* Wyggeston Grammar School, Leicester; Clare College, Cambridge. *Publications:* Zoo Quest to Guiana, 1956; Zoo Quest for a Dragon, 1957; Zoo Quest in Paraguay, 1959; Quest in Paradise, 1960; Zoo Quest to Madagascar, 1961; Quest Under Capricorn 1963; The Tribal Eye, 1976; Life on Earth, 1979; The Living Planet 1984; The First Eden 1987; Atlas of Living World, 1989; The Trials of Life, 1990. *Honours:* Silver Medal, Zoological Society of London, 1966; Gold Medal, Royal Geographical Society; Kalinga Prize, UNESCO; Honorary Degrees: Leicester, London, Birmingham, Liverpool, Heriot-Watt, Sussex, Bath, Ulster, Durham, Bristol, Glasgow, Essex, Cambridge, Oxford. *Memberships:* Fellow, Royal Society; Honorary Fellow, British Academy of Film and Television Arts. *Address:* 5 Park Road, Richmond, Surrey, England.

ATTICUS. *See:* **HATAR Victor Gyozo George John.**

ATWATER P M H, b. 19 Sept 1937, Twin Falls, Idaho, USA. Author; Reseacher; Public Speaker; Workshop Leader; Psychic Counselor. m. Terry Y Atwater, Apr 1980, 3 Children from Previous Marriage. *Education:* Boise State University, 1976; Semmary Doctorate (Lh.D) from International College Seminary (SSF) in Montreal, Canada, 1992. *Publications:* Coming Back to Life: The Aftereffects of the Near Death Experience; The Magical Language of Runes; Audio books: Coming Back to Life and As You Die; The After Effects of the Near Death Experience. *Contributions to:* Over 200 Articles in national magazines; Appeared on most major television talk shows in the USA and Canada. *Honours:* Most Influential Newspaper Columnist, state of Idaho; Prize Writer of the Year, 1973; Most Outstanding Low Budget Shopping Center Promotion; Governors Meritorius Wage Increase for Outstanding Service to Idaho; Numerous Writing awards; Cooking Award. *Memberships:* Idaho writers League; Boise Chapter of Idaho Writers League; Virginia Writers Club; The Authors League of America; The Authors Guild; American Dowsers Society; Association for Research & Enlightenment; International Institute of Intergral Human Sciences; American Federation of Astrologers; New Frontiers Fellowship; Board Member of International Association Near Death Studies. *Literary Agent:* Stephany Evans & David Morgan. *Address:* PO Box 7691 Charlottesville, VA 22906, USA.

ATWOOD Margaret, b. 18 Nov 1939, Ottawa, Canada. Author; Lecturer. *Education:* BA, University of Toronto, 1961; AM, Radcliffe College, Cambridge, Mass, 1962; Lecturer in English, Harvard University, Cambridge Mass, University of BC, Vancouver, 1964-65; Instructor in English, Sir George Williams University, Montreal, 1967-68; University of Alberta, University of Toronto, 1972-73; Tuscaloosa, Alabama, 1985; Berg Professor, New York University, 1986; Macquarie University, Australia, 1987; Holds Honours Degrees from Universities and Colleges. *Publications include:* Poetry: Double Persephone, 1961; Kaleidoscopes Baroque, 1965; Talismans for Children, 1965; Speeches for Doctor Frankenstein, 1966; The Circle Game, 1966; Two Headed Poems, 1978; Snake Poems, 1983; Selected Poems II, 1986; Selected Poems, 1966-84, 1990; Margaret Atwood Poems, 1991; Fiction: The Edible Woman, 1979; Bodily Harm, 1981; Encounters with the Element Man, 1982; Murder in the Dark, 1983; Cat's Eyes, 1989; The Best American Short Stories, 1989; Wilderness Tips, (short stories), 1991; For Children: Up in the Tree, 1978; Anna's Pet, 1980; For The Birds, 1990; Non-Fiction: Survival: a thematic guide to Canadian Literature, 1972; Days of the Rebels, 1815-1840, 1977; TV Scripts: The Servant Girl, 1974; Heaven on Earth, 1986; Radio Script: The Trumpets of Summer, 1964. *Honours:* Recipient of Awards, Medals and Prizes for Writing; Honorary D.Litt, Trent University, 1973, Concordia, 1980; LL.D Queen's University. *Address:* c/o Jonathan Cape, 32 Bedford Square, London, WC1B 3EL, England.

AUCHINLOSS Louis Stanton, b. 27 Sept 1917, USA. Lawyer; Author. m. Adele Lawrence, 1957, 3 sons. *Education:* Yale University; University of Virginia; Admitted, New York Bar, 1941. *Publications include:* The Indifferent Children, 1947; The Injustice Collectors, 1950; Sybil, 1952; A Law for the Lion, 1953; The Romantic Egoists, 1954; The Great World & Timothy Colt, 1956; Venus in Sparta, 1958; Pursuit of the Prodigal, 1959; House of Five Talents, 1960; Reflections of a Jacobite, 1961; Portrait in Brownstone, 1962; Powers of Attorney, 1963; The Rector of Justin, 1964; Pioneers & Caretakers, 1965; The Embezzler, 1966; Tales of Manhattan, 1967; A World of Profit, 1969; Motiveless Malignity, 1969; Edith Wharton: A Woman in her Time, 1971; I Come as a Thief, 1972; Richelieu, 1972; The Partners, 1974; A Winter's Capital, 1974; Reading Henry James, 1975; The Winthrop Covenant, 1976; The Dark Lady, 1977; The Country Cousin, 1978; Persons of Consequence, 1979; Life, Law & Letters, 1979; The House of the Prophet, 1980; The Cat & the King, 1981; Watchfires, 1982; Exit Lady Masham, 1983; The Book Clan, 1984; Honorable Men, 1985; Diary of a Yuppie, 1987; The Golden Calves, 1989; Fellow Passengers, 1990. *Membership:* National Institute of Arts & Letters. *Address:* 67 Wall Street, New York, NY 10005, USA.

AUCHTERLONIE Dorothy. *See:* **GREEN Dorothy.**

AUCKETT Amelia Daphne, b. 8 June 1929, San Remo, Australia. Nursing Sister; Author; Film Producer. m. Edmond Auckett, 10 May 1958, div, 2 sons. *Education:* General Nursing Diploma, 1950; Midwifery Cerficiate, 1952; Infant Welfare Certificate, 1957. *Publications:* Baby Massage; Films: Family Massage; Being In Touch. *Contributions to:* Australian Nurses Journal; Parent and Child Magazine; First steps Magazine; You and Your Baby, newspaper column. *Memberships:* Australian Society of Authors; Australian Song Writers Association; Australian Nursing Federation. *Address:* Melbourne, Victoria 3194, Australia.

AUEL Jean M, b. 18 Feb 1936, Chicago, Illinois, USA. Writer. m. Ray Bernard Auel, 19 Mar 1954, 2 sons, 3 daughters. *Education:* MBA 1976, University of Portland. *Publications:* The Clan of the Cave Bear, 1980; The Valley of Horses, 1982; The Mammoth Hunters, 1985; The Plains of Passage, 1990. *Honours include:* Excellence in Writing, The Pacific Northwest Booksellers Association Award, 1980; Vicki Penziner Matson Memorial Award, The Clan of the Cave Bear, The Friends of Literature, 1980; Nominee, The American Book Award, Best First Novel, 1981; Award for Excellence in Literature, Scandinavian Kaleidoscope of Art & Life, 1982; University of Portland, Doctor of Letters h.c. 1984; University of Maine, Doctor of Humanities h.c. 1986; Mt Vernon College, Doctor of Humane Letters h.c. 1986; Golden Plate Award, American Academy of

Achievement, 1986; Woman Who Made a Difference Award, International Women's Forum, 1988; Silver Trowel Award, Sacramento Archaeological Society, 1990; Persie Award, WIN/WIN, 1990; Waldo Award, Waldenbrooks Bestselling Book of 1990; Most Popular Foreign Language Novel, Holland, 1990; Award for Contributions to Cultural Resource Management, Department of the Interior, Secretary Manuel Lujan and the Society for American Archaeology, 1990; National Zoo Award, Centennial Medal, Smithsonian Institution, 1990; International MENSA, Honorary Vice President 1991. *Memberships include:* Authors Guild; PEN American Centre, Northwest Branch; International MENSA; Academy of American Poets; Willamette Writers; Oregon Writers Colony; Society for American Archaeologists; Institute of Human Origins; Pacific Northwest Archaeological Society; Oregon High Desert Museum; Oregon Historical Society. *Literary Agent:* Jean V Naggar. *Address:* c/o Jean V Naggar Literary Agency, 216 East 75th Street, New York, NY 10021, USA.

AUGARDE Anthony John, b. 10 Apr 1936, Tunbridge Wells, Kent, England. Lexicographer. m. Anna Fleur Whitwell, 30 Sep 1961, 1 son, 1 daughter. *Education:* MA Honours, St Peter's Hall, Oxford. *Appointments:* Lexicographer, 1960-, Manager, English Dictionary Department, 1984-91, Oxford University Press; Arts Editor, Oxford Times, 1983-; Campaign Organiser, Peace Pledge Union, 1991. *Publications:* Oxford Guide to Word Games, 1984; Oxford Intermediate Dictionary, 1981; Oxford School Dictionary, Editor, 1981; Peace is the Way, (co-author), 1990; Oxford Dictionary of Modern Quotations, 1991; pamphlets on Gandhi, Disarmament, etc for the Peace Pledge Union. *Contributions to:* Oxford Times; Contemporary Review; The Pacifist. *Address:* 18 Carlton Road, Oxford, OX2 7SA, England.

AUMBRY Alan. *See:* **BAYLEY Barrington John.**

AUSTIN Brett. *See:* **FLOREN Lee.**

AUSTIN William W., b. 1920, American. *Appointments:* Assistant Professor 1947-50, Associate Professor 1950-60, Professor 1960-69, Goldwin Smith Professor of Musicology 1969-80, Given Foundation Professor of Musicology 1980-90, Professor Emeritus 1990, Cornell University. *Publications:* Music in the Twentieth Century, 1966; New Looks at Italian Opera (ed), 1968; Debussy's Prelude to the Afternoon of a Faun (ed), 1970; Susanna, Jeanie and the Old Folks at Home: Meanings and Contexts of the Songs of Stephen C Foster from His Time to Ours, 1975, 1987; Esthetics of Music by Carl Dahlhaus (trans), 1982. *Address:* Department of Music, Cornell University, Ithaca, NY 14853, USA.

AUTTON Norman, (William James), b. 1920, British. *Appointments:* Chaplain, St George's Hospital, 1961-67; Director of Training, Hospital Chaplaincies Council of General Synod, London, 1967-72; Chaplain, University Hospital of Wales, Cardiff, 1972-90. Chancellor of Llandaff Cathedral, 1977-90, Chaplain, Marie Curie Centre, Penarth, South Glam, 1990-; Tutor in Pastoral Studies, St Michael's Theological College, Llandaff, Cardiff, 1990. *Publications:* The Pastoral Care of the Mentally Ill, 1963; The Pastoral Care of the Dying, 1964; The Pastoral Care of the Bereaved, 1967; The Pastoral Care In Hospitals, 1968; From Fear to Faith (ed), 1970; Christianity and Change (ed), 1971; When Sickness Comes, 1973; A Guide to Oncological Nursing (contribution), 1974; The Dying Patient (contribution), Visiting Ours, 1975; Readings in Sickness (compiler), Watch with the Sick (compiler), Getting Married, 1976; Understanding Cancer (contributor), 1977; Peace at Last, 1978; Visiting the Sick, 1980; A Handbook of Sick Visiting, 1981; Doctors Talking, 1984; Pain: An Exploration, 1986; Touch: An Exploration, 1988. *Address:* 112 St Anthony Road, Health, Cardiff, CF4 4DJ, Wales.

AVALLONE Michael Angelo, Jr, (James Blaine, Nick Carter, Troy Conway, Priscilla Dalton, Mark Dane, Jean-Anne De Pre, Dora Highland, Steve Michaels, Dorothea Nile, Ed Noon, Edwina Noone, John Patrick, Vance Stanton, Sidney Stuart) b. 27 Oct 1924, Manhattan, New York, USA. m. 27 May 1960, 2 sons, 1 daughter. *Appointments:* Editor, Republic Features 1956-58, Cape Publications 1958-60, The Third Degree (house organ, Mystery Writers of America), 1961-65; Chairman, Motion Picture Committee 1964-70, TV Committee 1962-64, ibid. *Publications:* Over 200 books including: The Tall Dolores, 1953; The Man from U.N.C.L.E., 1964; Beneath the Planet of the Apes, 1970; Tales of the Frightened, 1963; The Haunted Hall, 1970; Run Spy Run (Nick Carter), 1964. Also: Ed Noon private detective series, 1953-88; Satan Sleuth series, 1973-75; Craghold Hotel series, 1971-73; Hawaii Five-O; Krakatoa East of Java; The Coffin Things; Missing!; A Woman Called Golda; The Beast with the Red Hands; All The Way, When Were You Born? Red Roses Forever, Sound of Dying Roses, The Silent Silken Shadows, The Darkening Willows, Treasure Island, The Last of the Mohicans, etc. Articles, short stories. *Contributions to:* Numerous magazines, films, mystery, general. *Honours:* Author Award, New Jersey Association of Teachers of English, 1969; Literary Luminary of New Jersey, NJ Literary Hall of Fame, NJ Institute of Technology, 1977; Over 20 scrolls for yearly novels; etc. *Memberships:* Board, Mystery Writers of America, 1958-70; Authors League, 1975-78. *Address:* 80 Hilltop Boulevard, East Brunswick, NJ 08816, USA.

AVERY Gillian (Elise), b. 1926, British, Writer - children's fiction, literature. *Appointments:* Junior Reporter, Surrey Mirror, Redhill, Surrey, 1944-47; Staff Member, Chambers Encyclopaedia, London 1947-50; Assistant Illustrations Editor, Clarendon Press, Oxford, 1950-54. *Publications:* (ed) A Great Emergency and a Very Ill-Tempered Family, by Juliana Horatia Ewing, 1967; (ed) The Gold of Fairnilee and Other Stories, by Andrew Lang, 1967; (ed) Village Children, by Charlotte Younge, 1967; (ed) Banning and Blessing, by Margaret Roberts, 1967; (ed) The Hole in the Wall and Other Stories, 1968; (ed) Victoria Bess and Others, by Brenda, Mrs Gatty and Frances Hodgson Burnett, 1968; (ed) The Wallypug of Why, by G E Farrow, 1968; (ed) Froggy's Little Brother, by Brenda 1968; (ed) My New Home, by Mary Louisa Molesworth, 1968; (ed) The Life and Adventures of Lady Anne (anonymous) 1969; (ed) Stephanie's Children by Margaret Roberts, 1969; (ed) Anne's Terrible Good Nature and Other Stories for Children, by E V Lucas, 1970; (ed) The Rival Kings, by Annie Keary, 1970; Victorian People in Life and Literature, 1970; A Likely Lad, 1971; Ellen's Birthday, 1971; Jemima and the Welsh Rabbit, 1972; The Echoing Green Memories of Victorian and Regency Youth, 1974; Ellen and the Queen, 1974; Book of Strange and Odd, 1975; Childhood's Pattern A Study of the Heroes and Heroines of Children's Fiction, 1770-1950, 1975; Freddie's Feet, 1976; Huck and Her Time Machine, 1977; Mouldy's Orphan, 1978; Sixpence, 1979; The Lost Railway, 1980; Onlookers, 1983; The Best Type of Girl, 1991. *Address:* 32 Charlbury Road, Oxford OX2 6UU, England.

AVEY Ruby Doreen, (Vicki Page, Lita Bidwell), b. 29 Jan 1927, Hove, Sussex, England. Author; Lecturer; Broadcaster. *Education:* St Mary's Convent, Portslade; Hove Secretarial College. *Appointments include:* Part-time tutor, creative writing, Hove Adult Further Education Centre 1971-82, Ford Open Prison 1974-76. *Publications include:* House of Harron, 1977; Shadows on the Snow, 1978; Wedding in Winter, 1978; Love is for Tomorrow, 1979; Lord of the Watchtower, 1980; Call for Nurse Hope, 1980; Bracelet for a Bride, 1980; Nurse in Deep Water, 1981; Love & Nurse Jeni, 1981; Arabian Love Story, 1981; As One Small Candle, 1982; Because I Loved You, 1982; Jo Lane, Store Nurse, 1983; Miranda, 1983; To Love & Cherish, 1985; Silken Cord of Love, 1987; Winter of the Heart, 1988; Flower That Fades, 1988; Seven Steps to Love, 1989; A Demon called Love, 1990; No Formula for Love, 1990; House of Strangers, 1990; (All as Vicki Page.) A Rainbow in

Hawaii, 1990; (as Lita Bidwell).*Contributions to:* Various newspapers, magazines, local radio. *Membership:* Romantic Novelists, Association. *Address:* 53 Norway Street, Portslade, Brighton, Sussex BN41 1AE, England.

AVGERINOS Cecily T. Grazio, b. 16 Apr 1945, New York, USA. Poet; Novelist. m. Robert T. Avgerinos, 24 May 1969, 2 sons, 1 daughter. *Education:* BA, New York University, 1966. *Publications:* Poems: My Tatterdemalion, 1985; Sunrises, 1985, 1987; Eternity, 1986; Summer Fantasy, 1986; My Prayer, 1986; Lunch in the Park, 1986; Circle of Gold, 1986; Lord, I wonder, 1986; The Fig Tree, 1987; Fishing, 1987; Septecential, 1987; Loss, 1987; Bridge Across Tomorrow, 1987; To My Children, 1987; The Stringless Guitar, 1988; Pink Socks, 1988; My Dogwood-Love's Analogy, 1989, Merry-Go-Round, 1989; Strawsticks, 1989. *Contributions to:* Numerous anthologies. *Honours:* 25 Awards of Merit, World of Poetry, 1985-; 4 Golden Poet Awards, 1985-. *Memberships:* Board, Alumni Association, New York University; Vice President, Parent Organisation. *Literary Agent:* Scott Meredith. *Address:* 173 Momar Drive, Ramsey, New Jersey 07446, USA.

AWDRY Christopher Vere, b. 2 July 1940, Devizes, Wiltshire, England. Author. m. (1) Elaine Margaret Checkley, 15 Apr 1968, 1 daughter, (2) Diana Wendy Scott, 7 July 1979, 1 son. *Education:* Worksop College, Worksop, Notts. *Publications:* 11 titles in 'Railway Series' up to 1993, many other connected titles; Encyclopaedia of British Railway Companies, 1990; Branch Lines Around Huntingdon, 1991; Brunel's Broad Gauge Railway, 1992; Branch Lines Around March, 1993; Over The Summit, 1993. *Contributions to:* Cambridgeshire Life; Steam Railway; Railway Magazine; Railways South-East, British Railway Modelling. *Membership:* Society of Authors. *Address:* Oundle, Peterborough, England.

AWDRY W(ilbert) V(ere), b. 1911, British. *Appointments:* Anglican Clergyman: Rector, Elsworth and Knapwell, Cambridge, 1946-63; Vicar of Emneth, Wisbech, 1953-65. *Publications:* The Three Railway Engines, 1945; Thomas the Tank Engine, 1946; James the Red Engine, 1948; Tank Engine Thomas Again, 1949; Troublesome Engines, 1950; Henry the Green Engine, 1951; Toby the Tram Engine, 1952; Gordon the Big Engine, 1953; Edward the Blue Engine, 1954; Four Little Engines, 1955; Percy the Small Engine, 1956; The Eight Famous Engines, 1957; Duck and the Diesel Engine, Belinda the Beetle, 1958; The Little Old Engine, 1959; The Twin Engines, 1960; Branch Line Engines, Belinda Beats the Band, 1961; Gallant Old Engine, 1962; Stepney the Blue Bell Engine, 1963; Mountain Engines, 1964; Very Old Engines, 1965; Main Line Engine, 1966; Small Railway Engines, 1967; Duke the Lost Engine, 1970; Map of the Island of Sodor, 1971; Tramway Engines, 1972; Industrial Archaeology in Gloucestershire (ed), 1974, 3rd edition 1983; A Guide to Steam Railways of Great Britain, 1979, 1984. *Address:* Sodor, 30 Rodborough Avenue, Stroud, Gloucestershire GL5 3RS, England.

AWOONOR Kofi Nyidevu, b. 13 Mar 1935, Wheta, Ghana. Diplomat. 4 sons, 1 daughter. *Education:* Zion College of West Africa 1951-54; Achimota Secondary School 1955-56; University College of Ghana 1957-60; University of College of London 1967-68; University of the State of New York at Stony Brook 1969-72. *Publications:* Rediscovery, 1964; Night of My Blood, 1971; This Earth My Brother, 1972; Ride Me Memory, 1973; Guardian of the Sacred Word, 1974; Breast of the Earth, essays, 1974; House By the Sea, 1978; Until The Morning After, poetry, 1988; Ghana: A Political History, history, 1990; Comes the Voyager At Last, fiction, 1992; Latin American and Caribbean Notebook, poetry, 1993. *Honours:* Translation Award, Columbia University, 1972; Ghana Book Award, 1978; Dillons Commonwealth Award, 1989; Ghana Association of Writers Distinguished Authors Award, 1992. *Literary Agent:* Harold Ober Associates. *Address:* Permanent Mission of Ghana to the United Nations, 19 East 47th Street, New York, NY 10017, USA.

AXTON David. *See:* **KOONTZ Dean R.**

AYARS Albert Lee, b. 1917, American. *Appointments:* Teacher, Davenport High School, 1940-42; Principal, Colville High School, 1942-45; Superintendent, Omak Public School, 1945-49, Sunnyside Public School, 1949-52, WA; Associate Director, Joint Council on Economic Education, 1952-53; Director, Education Department, Hill and Knowlton Incorporated, 1953-65; Vice-President, John W Hill Foundation, 1956-65; Superintendent, Spokane Public School, WA, 1965-72; Consulting Editor, Journal of National Open Education and Editorial Advisory Board, 1960-65; Superintendent 1972-83, Superintendent Emeritus 1983-, Norfolk Public School, VA. *Publications:* How to Plan Your Community Resources Workshop, 1954; Administering the People's Schools, 1957; The Teenager and Alcohol (with Gail Milgram), 1970; How to Plan a Community Resources Workshop, 1974; The Teenager and the Law (with John Ryan), 1978.

AYCKBOURN Alan, b. 1939, London, England. Theatre Director; Playwright; Artistic Director, Stephen Joseph Theatre, Scarborough. *Plays:* Mr Whatnot, 1963; Relatively Speaking, 1965; How the Other Half Loves, 1969; Time and Time Again, 1971; Absurd Person Singular, 1972; The Norman Conquests (Trilogy), 1973; Absent Friends, 1974; Confusions, 1975; Bedroom Farce, 1975; Just Between Ourselves, 1976; Ten Times Table, 1977; Joking Apart, 1978; Sisterly Feelings, 1979; Taking Steps, 1979; Season's Greetings, 1980; Way Upstream, 1981; Intimate Exchanges, 1982; A Chorus of Disapproval, 1984; Woman in Mind, 1985; A Small Family Business, 1986; Henceforward..., 1987; Man of the Moment, 1988; The Revengers' Comedies, 1989; Mr A's Amazing Maze Plays, 1989; Invisible Friends, 1991; (Children's Plays) Time of My Life, 1992; Radio Drama Producer, British Broadcasting Corporation Leeds, 1965-70. *Honours:* Hon. DLitt (Hull), 1981; (Keele), 1987; (Leeds), 1987; (York), 1992; Cameron Mackintosh Professor of Contemporary Theatre, Oxford, 1992; CBE, 1987. *Membership:* Garrick Club; Fellow of the Royal Society of Arts. *Literary Agent:* Margaret Ramsay Limited. *Address:* c/o Casarotto Ramsay Ltd, National House, 60-66 Wardour St, London, W1R 3HP, England.

AYDY Catherine. *See:* **TENNANT Emma.**

AYERS Mary Alice, b. New York, USA. Fiction Writer. *Education:* AB, Hunter College, New York; MEd, Georgia State University, Atlanta, Georgia. *Publication:* Anthology: Life on the Line, 1992. *Contributions to:* Stories: Partisan Review; Paris Review; Literary Review; Numerous quarterlies; National newspaper syndication; Featured on National Public Radio series, The Sound of Writing, 1988 (PEN prize story). *Honours:* PEN Syndicated Feature Award 1986, 1988; Ingram Merrill Foundation Grant 1989; Fellowship, Millay Colony for the Arts 1979. *Memberships:* Poets and Writers; Phi Beta Kappa; Sigma Tau Delta. *Address:* Miami, Florida, USA.

AYERST David, (George Ogilvy), b. 1904, British. *Appointments:* Editorial Staff Member 1929-34, Historian 1964-73, The Guardian, Manchester and London; H M Inspector of Schools, 1947-64. *Publications:* Europe in the 19th Century, 1940; Understanding Schools, 1967; Records of Christianity (ed with A S T Fisher), 1970, 1977; Guardian: Biography of a Newspaper (in US as The Manchester Guardian), 1971; The Guardian Omnibus (ed), 1973; Garvin of the Observer, 1985. *Address:* Littlecote, Burford, Oxford OX18 4SE, England.

AYLEN Leo, b. Vryheid, Zululand, South Africa. Poet; Author; Film Director. m. Annette Battam. *Education:* MA, 1st Class Honours, New College, Oxford University; PhD Bristol University. *Appointment:* Television Producer, BBC, 1965-70; Writer. *Publications:* Poetry: Discontinued Design; I, Odysseus; Sunflower; Return to Zululand; Red Alert: this is a god warning; Jumping-Shoes; Rhymoceros. Non-Fiction: Greek Tragedy and the Modern World; Greece for Everyone; The Greek Theater; Children's Opera: The Apples of Youth. Films for TV include: The Drinking Party; 1065 and All That; Dynamo; Who'll Buy a Bubble?; ''Steel, be my Sister''; Soul of a Nation. *Honours:* Nominated for British Academy Television Awards, 1966; Poet-in-Residence, Fairleigh Dickinson University, New Jersey, USA, 1972-74; Cecil Day Lewis Fellowship, London 1979-80; Hooker Distinguished Visiting Professor, McMaster University, Ontario, Canada, 1982. *Memberships:* Poetry Society of Great Britain; Poetry Society of USA; British Actors Equity; Association of Cinema and Television Technicians; Writers Guild of Great Britain; Writers Guild of USA; British Academy of Film and Television Arts. *Address:* 13 St Saviour's Road, London SW2 5HP, England.

AYLING Stanley Edward, b. 15 Mar 1909, London, England. Biographer. m. 17 Dec 1936, 2 sons. *Education:* Strand School, London 1920-28; Emmanuel College, Cambridge, 1928-31. *Publications:* George the Third, 1972; The Elder Pitt, Earl of Chatham, 1976; John Wesley, 1979; A Portrait of Sheridan, 1985; Edmund Burke, his Life and Opinions, 1988. *Honour:* Fellow of the Royal Society of Literature, 1980. *Address:* The Beeches, Middle Winterslow, Salisbury, Wilts., England.

AYLMER G(erald) E(dward), b. 1926, British. *Appointments:* J E Proctor Visiting Fellow, Princeton University, NJ, 1950-51; Junior Research Fellow, Balliol College, Oxford, 1951-54; Assistant Lecturer in Modern History, 1954-57; Lecturer, University of Manchester, 1957-62; Professor of History, Head of Department, University of York, 1963-78; Master of St Peter's College, Oxford, 1978-91; On Editorial Board, History of Parliament, 1968-, Chairman, 1989-; Royal Commission on Historical Manuscripts, 1977-, Chairman, 1989-; Vice- President 1973-77, President 1984-88, Hon. Vice-President, 1988-; Royal Historical Society; Hon Vice-President, Historial Association 1992-. *Publications:* The King's Servants: The Civil Service of Charles I 1625-1642, 1961, revised edition, 1974; The Diary of William Lawrence (ed), 1961; The Struggle for the Constitution 1603-1689 (in US as A Short History of 17th-Century England) (ed), 1963; The Interregnum: The Quest for Settlement 1646-1660 (ed), 1972; The State's Servants: The Civil Service of the English Republic 1649-1660, 1973; The Levellers in the English Revolution, 1975; A History of York Minster (ed with R Cant), 1977; Rebellion or Revolution? England 1640-1660, 1986-, rev. adm., 1987. *Address:* 18 Albert Street, Jericho, Oxford, OX2 6A2, England.

AYRES Philip James, (Diana Lakehurst), b. 28 July 1944, South Australia, University Professor. m. (1) Maruta Sudrabs, 11 Dec 1965, (2) Patricia San Martin, 28 Nov 1981, 1 son. *Education:* BA, 1965; PhD, 1971; FR Hist S, 1989. *Appointments:* Tutor, University of Adelaide, 1969-71; Lecturer, Senior Lecturer, Monash University, 1972-. *Publications:* Malcolm Fraser, A Biography; Ben Jonson, Sejanus; Cyril Tourneur, The Revengers Tragedy; Anthony Munday, The English Roman Life. *Contributions to:* Studies in Philology; Modern Philology; Studies in English Literature; Studies in Bibliography; English Literary Renaissance; Short Stories. *Honours:* Royal Historical Society; Visiting Professor, Vassar College. *Address:* 13 Harris Avenue, Glen Iris, Victoria 3146, Australia.

B

BAARS Hermanus Dirk, Retired, Director, Chamber of Commerce Northern Europe. *Education:* MO Staathuishoudkunde & Statistiek, Amsterdam; Sociale Geografie & Geschidenis, Utrecht. *Publications:* Gedichten; Scandinavie, Verwant Cultuurgebied; Denemarken, Land Volk Cultuur; Noorwegen Land Volk Cultuur; Neem Het gerust in, Novellen; Rurik Van Trajectum, Graaf van de Zeekust. *Contributions to:* Tot Jaron, NRC; Nederland Noord Europa. *Membership:* PEN. *Literary Agent:* Auteursbureau Greta Baars Jelgersma. *Address:* Den Heuvel 73, NL 6881 VD Velp (G), The Netherlands.

BAARSCHERS Mary Rose, b. 24 May 1930, Broken Hill, New South Wales, Australia. Retired Teacher; Author. m. (1) N Grant, 6 May 1950, (2) Herman Baarschers, 21 Jan 1970. 1 daughter. *Education:* Teaching Certificate, 1941-51; School Administration, 1976-77; Educational Studies, 1981-82; PhD, 1987. *Publications:* Poems for Special Days And Seasons; I Like to Write Stories; My Life, By Lass; Sound Blending Words Kit; Double Sounds in verse; Fun with Sounds; Creative Fairy Tales and Folk Dances; Fun With Music; Understanding What You Read; Music Appreciation Precussion; Classical Stimulus Readers 1983-1993. *Contributions to:* Education; Education Gazette; Waggly. *Memberships:* Australian Society of Authors; Society of Australian Songwriters; Australian Performing Rights Association; Retired Teachers Association. *Address:* 11 Mittabah Road, Hornsby 2077, Australia.

BABE Thomas, b. 1941, American. *Appointments:* Operated the Summer Players, Agassiz Theatre, Cambridge, MA, with Timothy S Mayer, 1966-68; Speechwriter for John Lindsay, Mayor of NY, 1968-69. *Publications:* Rebel Women, 1976; A Prayer for My Daughter, 1977; Taken in Marriage, 1979; Kid Champion, Fathers and Sons, Salt Lake City Skyline, 1980; Great Solo Town, 1981; Burried Inside Extra, 1983.

BABINECZ Friedrich Karl, (Karl Frientius, Friedrich Schroder), b. 29 Apr 1925, Vienna, Austria. Writer; Photographer; Ethologist. m. Adele Blodi, 15 Jan 1955. *Education:* University of Vienna. *Publications:* Timon; Menschenachter Timon; Australian Nature in Focus. *Contributions to:* Homunkulus Humor; Outdoors; Overlander; Travel & Adventure; GEO. *Memberships:* Biological Institute. *Literary Agent:* Heinz Körner, Rotenburg, Germany. *Address:* 89 Griffith Street, Oak Flats, NSW 2529, Australia.

BABINGTON Anthony Patrick, b. 4 Apr 1920, Cork, Ireland. *Education:* Reading School; Inms of Court Law School; Called to the Bar, 1948. *Publications:* For the Sake of Example; No Memorial; Military Intervention in britain; A House in Bow Street; The Rule of Law in Britain; The Devil to Pay; The Power to Silence; The English Bastille. *Memberships:* PEN; The Society of Authors; Garrick. *Literary Agent:* David Fletcher. *Address:* 3 Gledhow Gardens, Kensington, London SW5 0BL, England.

BABSON Marian, American. Writer. *Appointment:* Secretary, Crime Writers Association, London, 1976-86. *Publications:* Cover-Up Story, 1971; Murder on Show, 1972; Pretty Lady, 1973; The Stalking Lamb, Unfair Exchange, 1974; Murder Sails at Midnight, There Must Be Some Mistake, 1975; Untimely Guest, 1976; The Lord Mayor Death, Murder Murder Little Star, 1977; Tightrope for Three, 1978; So Soon Done For, The Twelve Deaths of Christmas, 1979; Dangerous to Know, Queue Here for Murder, 1980; Bejewelled Death, 1981; Death Warmed Up, Death Beside the Seaside, 1982; A Fool for Murder, 1983; The Cruise of a Deathtime, A Trail of Ashes, Death Swap, 1984; Death in Fashion, Weekend for Murder, 1985; Reel Murder, 1986; Fatal Fortune, 1987; Guilty Party; Encore Murder, 1989; Past Regret, 1990. *Address:* c/o William Collins Sons & Co Ltd, 8 Grafton Street, London W1X 3LA, England.

BACHMAN Richard. *See:* **KING Stephen Edwin.**

BACON Margaret, b. Leeds. Writer. Widower, 2 daughters. *Education:* MA, The Mount School, York. *Publications:* Journey to Gyana; The Episode; Kitty; The Unentitled; The Package; A Packetful of Trouble; Others inc, Snow in Winter; The Chain. *Contributions to:* Translation into Dutch, Snow in Winter; Articles. *Memberships:* PEN; Society of Authors; The Arts Club, London. *Literary Agent:* Carote Fredman.

BADAWI Mohamed Mustafa, b. 1925, British. Lecturer. *Appointments:* Research Fellow 1947-54, Lecturer 1954-60, Assistant Professor of English 1960-64, Alexandria University, Egypt; Lecturer, Oxford University and Brasenose College, 1964-; Fellow, St Antony's College, Oxford, 1967-; Ed. Journal of Arabic Literature, Leiden, 1970-; Advisory Board Member, Cambridge History of Arabic Literature. *Publications:* An Anthology of Modern Arabic Verse, 1970; Coleridge Critic of Shakespeare, (trans) The Saint's Lamp and Other Stories by Yahya Haqqi, 1973; A Critical Introductioin to Modern Arabic Poetry, 1975; (trans) Sara, by AM El Aqqad, 1978; Background to Shakespeare, 1981; (co-trans) The Thief and the Dogs, by Naguib Mahfouz, 1984; Modern Arabic Literature and the West, 1985; Modern Arabic Drama in Egypt, 1987; Early Arabic Drama, 1988; Ed, Cambridge History of Arabic Literature: Modern Arabic Literature, 1992; A Short History of Modern Arabic Literature, 1993. *Memberships:* Committees of Ministry of Culture, Egypt, 1961; Unesco Expert on Modern Arabic Culture, 1974; Awarded King Faisal International Prize for Arabic Literature in 1992. *Address:* St Antony's College, Oxford, England.

BADCOCK Christopher Robert, b. 13 May 1946, Plymouth, England. Reader in Sociology. m. Lenis Gee, 17 June 1967, 2 sons. *Education:* BA Hons, Sociology & Social Anthropology (First Class), 1967; PhD, 1973. *Publications:* Essential Freud, 1988; Oedipus In Evolution, 1990; The Problem of Altruism, 1986; Madness & Modernity, 1983; The Psychoanalysis of Culture, 1980; Levi-Strauss, 1975. *Contributions to:* London School of Economics Quarterly. *Memberships:* European Sociobiological Society; The American Society for Human Behavior & Evolution. *Address:* The London School of Economics, Houghton Street, Aldwych, London WC2A 2AE, England.

BADER-MOLNAR Katarina Elisabeth, b. Berlin, Germany. Retired Teacher/Professor; Freelance Writer. m. Imre Molnar, (div 1985). *Education:* Diploma, Librarian, Berlin, 1934; English Literature Studies, Liverpool, England; MA, French Philology, Kopernikus University, graduation 1950; English Philology Diploma, 1950. *Appointments:* Diploma Librarian, Professor and Librarian, Torun, Grudziadz, Dantzig; Zurich; Switzerland; Freelance Writer. *Publications include:* L'idée d'humanité dans l'oeuvre de Voltaire jusqu'en, 1970; 1950; Lyriden, (poems), 1976; Romantisches Gefuege, (poems & stories), 1978; Teufelskreis und Lethequelle, (novel), 1979; Karola contra Isegrim und Reineke, (story), 1980; Da waren Träume noch süss, (novel), 1988; Vom Leuchten der Liebe, (novel), 1990; Gehn und Sein (selected poems), 1991; Various poems, stories for journals, for children, and for anthologies in 3 languages. *Honours include:* Gold Medal, Diploma, Académie Internationale de Lutèce, Paris, 1984, 1986; Silver Medal, Académie Int. Universalle de Lausanne, 1984. *Memberships include:* Schweizerischer Schriftsteller-Verband Zürich; PEN Zentrum Bern; Zurcher Schrisftsteller-Verband Zurich, Literarisher Club, Zürich; Mozart Gesellschaft; Academie Internationale der Lutèce Paris, Life Fellow. *Address:* Tobelshofstr. 6, CH 8044, Zürich, Switzerland.

BAERWALD Hans H, b. 1927, American. Professor. *Appointments:* Assistant Professor 1956-61, Associate Professor of Government 1961- 62, Miami University, Oxford, OH; Lecturer 1962-65, Associate Professor 1965-69, Professor of Political Science, 1969-,

University of California at Los Angeles. *Publications:* The Purge of Japanese Leaders Under the Occupation, 1959; American Government: Structure, Problems, Policies (with Peter H Odegard), 1962; Chinese Communism: Selected Documents (with Dan N Jacobs), 1963; The American Republic, Its Government and Politics (with P Odegard), 1964, revised edition with William Harvard, 1969; Japan's Parliament: An Introduction, 1974; Party Politics in Japan, 1986. *Address:* 10538 Edgeley Pl, Los Angeles, CA 90024, USA.

BAGGS Sydney Allison, b. 15 July 1930, Sydney, Australia. Architect; Landscape Architect; Environment Cons; Urban Designer. m. Joan Constance Baggs, 2 Feb 1952, 1 son, 2 daughters. *Education:* Diploma Arch, 1952; Bach Arch, 1968; M Arch, 1975; PhD, 1982. *Appointments:* Editor, Geotecture Journal, 1981-92; Environmental Consultant, Nature and Health Magazine, 1990-93. *Publications:* Australian Earth Covered Building; Introduction to Earth Covered Housing; A Method of Environmental Impact Assessment & Evaluation; Earth Integrated and Earth Covered Building for Aust. Conditions; Research Methods and Thesis Writing. *Contributions to:* Underground Space; Solar Energy; Journal Architecture & Planning; Royal Institute British Architecture Journal; Landscape Planning; Future; Nature and Health; Home Beautiful; Womens Day; House & Garden. *Honours:* Excellence in House Design Award; Certificate Merit National Energy Management Aust Award; Most Innovative Design Award. *Memberships:* Royal Aust Institute Architects; Aust Institute Landscape Architects; International Association for Impact Assessment; Environment Institute of Australia; National Environmental Law Association; Underground Space Association. *Address:* Managing Director, PEOPL, PO Box 1814, Chatswood 2067, Australia.

BAGLEY John Joseph, b. 1908, St Helens, Lancashire, England. Reader in History (retired). *Education:* MA, University of Liverpool. *Publications:* History of Lancashire, 1956; Life in Medieval England, 1960; Henry VIII & His Times, 1962; Historical Interpretation (2 volumes), 1965 & 1971; Poor Law (with A J Bagley), 1966; Lancashire Diarists, 1975; Medievil People, 1978; The Earls of Derby 1485-1985, 1985; Lancashire: A History of the County Palatine In Early Maps (with A G Hodgkiss), 1985. *Contributions to:* Historical Society of Lancashire & Cheshire; Lancashire Life. *Memberships:* Association of University Teachers; Tutors Association; Vice President, Historic Society of Lancashire & Cheshire. *Address:* 10 Beach Priory Gardens, Southport, Merseyside PR8 1RT, England.

BAI Hua, b. 20 Nov 1930, He Nan, China. Writer. m. Wang Pei, 30 Dec 1956, 1 son. *Education:* Fine Arts Department, Hsin Yang College of Education. *Literary Appointments include:* Cultural propaganda, People's Liberation Army, 1947-52; Literary & creative activities, General Office of Political Affairs of the Army, 1955-58; Skilled worker, Shanghai film equipment company 1958-62; Editor, Shanghai Movies Production Company; Army writer, 1964-66; Writer, Shanghai Writers Association, 1985-. *Publications include:* Mama, Mama, novel, 1980; Little Birds Can't Understand the Songs Big Tree Sings, novel, 1984; Hometown in the Distance, novel, 1979; Death of a Skilled Fisherman, novel, 1982; The Princess of Peacock, poem, 1957; A Flock of Eagles, poem, 1956. Numerous screen plays including The Sun & The People. *Contributions to:* Numerous magazines & journals. *Honours:* National Best Poems Award, 1981. *Memberships:* Director, vice chairman, Hu Bei Province Branch, Council of Chinese Writers Association; Council of Chinese Film Artists Association; Beijing Pen Centre, Chinese Opera Artists Association. *Address:* Room 706, no 4, Lane 83, Jiangning Road, Shanghai, China.

BAIGELL Matthew, b. 1933, American. Professor. *Appointments:* Instructor, Assistant Professor, Associate Professor, 1961-68, Ohio State University, Columbus; Professor 1968, Distinguished Professor of Art History, Rutgers 1978-, The State University of NJ, New Brunswick. *Publications:* A Thomas Hart Benton

Miscellany, A History of American Painting, 1971; Thomas Hart Benton, The American Scene: American Painting in the 1930s, 1974; Charles Burchfield, Frederick Remington, 1976; Dictionary of American Art, 1979; Thomas Cole, Albert Bierstadt, 1981; A Concise History of American Painting and Sculpture, 1984; The Papers of the American Artists' Congress (1936), 1985. *Address:* Art History Department, Rutgers University, New Brunswick, NJ 08903, USA.

BAIGENT Beryl, b. 16 Dec 1937, Writer/Teacher. m. Alan H Baigent, 19 Jan 1963, 3 daughters. *Education:* Grove Park Grammer School, Wrexham, Wales; BA, Physical Education; MA, English Literature, University of Western Ontario, London, Canada. *Appointments:* Judge, Woodstock Library Contest, 1982, 1985; Judge, United Amateur Press Laureate Awards, 1978; Editor, PomSeed, University of Western Ontario, 1980-; Editor, Public Works, University of Western Ontario, 1990. *Publications include:* The Quiet Village, 1972; Pause, 1974; In Counter Point, 1976; Ancestral Dreams, 1981; The Sacred Beech, 1985; Mystic Animals, 1988; Absorbing the Dark, 1990; Undress Stress, 1991. *Contributor to:* Poetry Toronto; Poetry Canada Review; Canadian Author and Bookman; Canadian Humanist; Poet; Ploughman; Pom Seed; Poets Gallery; Public Works. *Honours:* Ontario Weekly Newspaper Award, 1979; Canadian Authors Association (Fritch Memorial) Award, 1982; Kent Writers Award, 1986; Ontario Arts Council, 1983, 1985, 1987; Canada Council, 1990, 1992, 1993; Judge League of Canadian Poets, Pat Lowelles Award, 1992. *Memberships:* League of Canadian Poets; Canadian Poetry Association; World Poetry Association Intercontinental; Celtic Arts Association; Internaitonal Cultural Relations: External Affairs Award, 1991; Federation of Ontario Yoga Teachers; Kripalu Yoga Teachers Association. *Address:* 137 Byron Avenue, Thamesford, Ontario N0M 2M0, Canada.

BAILEY Anthony Cowper, b. 5 Jan 1933, Portsmouth, England. Author and Journalist, Staff Writer, The New Yorker, 1956-92. *Publications include:* In the Village, 1971; America, Lost and Found, 1980 (memoir); Rembrandt's House, 1978; Along the Edge of the Forest, 1983; England, First and Last, 1985 (memoir); Major André, 1989 (novel); A Walk Through Wales, 1992; Responses to Rembrandt, 1993. *Honour:* Overseas Press Club Award, 1974. *Literary Agent:* Candida Donadio/Abner Stein. *Address:* c/o Candida Donadio, Donadio and Ashworth, 231 W 22nd Street, New York, NY 10011, USA.

BAILEY Charles Waldo II, b. 1929, American. *Appointments:* Editor, Minneapolis Star and Tribune; Washington Editorial, National Public Radio, 1984-. *Publications:* (with Fletcher Knebel), No High Ground, 1960; Seven Days in May, 1962; Convention, 1964; Conflicts of Interest: A Matter of Journalistic Ethics, 1984. *Address:* National Public Radio, 2025 M Street, NW, Washington, DC 20036, USA.

BAILEY David R Shackleton, b. 1917, British. Professor. *Education:* Litt.D, Cambridge; Hon D.Lit, Dublin. *Appointments:* Fellow 1944-55, Fellow, Deputy Bursar, Senior Bursar, 1964-68, Caius College; Lecturer in Tibetan, Cambridge University, 1948-68; Fellow, Jesus College, 1955-64; Professor of Latin, University of Michigan, Ann Arbor, 1968-74; Visiting Lecturer 1963, Professor of Greek and Latin 1975- 82, Pope Professor of Latin Language and Literature 1982-, Harvard University, Cambridge, MA; Editor, Harvard Studies in Classical Philology, 1980-85. *Publications include:* The Satapancasatka of Matrceta, Propertiana 1951; Ciceronis Epistulae ad Atticum IX-XVI, 1961; Cicero's Letters to Atticus (7 vols), 1965-70; Cicero, 1971; Two Studies in Roman Nomenclature, 1976; Cicero: Letters to His Friends, 1977; Cicero's Letters to Atticus, 1978; Cicero's Letters to His Friends (2 vols), 1978; Towards a Text of Anthologia Latina, 1979; Cicero: Epistulae ad Q Fratrem et M Brutum, 1981; Profile of Horace, Anthologia Latina I, 1982; Horatius, Cicero: Philippics, 1985; Lucanus, 1988; Martialis, 1990; Back from Exile, 1991. *Honours:* Recipient, Ch. J. Goodwin Award of Merit, 1978; Kenyon Medal of British Academy, 1986. *Memberships:* Fellow, British Academy; American Academy of Arts and Sciences; Member, Philos Society. *Address:* 303 North Division, Ann Arbor, MI 48104, USA.

BAILEY Donna. *See:* **BAILEY Veronica Anne.**

BAILEY Eva. Author. m. Dr Norman Bailey, 1 daughter. *Education:* BA; Certificate of Education, University of Bristol; Further Professional Studies Certificate in School Librarianship, University of Bristol. *Publications:* Churchill; Music and Musicians; Disease and Discovery; Montgomery of Alamein; Amy Johnson; Radio: Granville Sharp, BBC Schools; Achievement, BBC Short Story. *Contributions to:* Various maazines. *Memberships:* The Society of Authors; The Saciety of Women Writers and Journalists; The West Country Writers Association. *Address:* Wheel Gates, Southam Lane, Southam, Nr Cheltenham, Glos GL52 3NY, England.

BAILEY Fred Arthur, b. 28 Mar 1947, Dumas, Arkansas, USA. Historian. m. Bonnie Pitt, 22 Aug 1968, 2 sons, 1 daughter. *Education:* BA, Harding University, Searcy, Ark, 1970; MA, University of Tennessee, 1972; PhD, 1979. *Publications:* Class & Tennessees Confederate Generation. *Contributions to:* Numerous Articles inc: Tennessees Antebellum Culture from the Bottom Up, Journal of Southern Studies; Oliver Perry Temple and the Struggle for Tennessees Agricultural College, Tennessee Historical Quarterly. *Honours:* E Merton Coulter Award; Outstanding Paper in American History; Tennessee History Book Award; John Trotwood Moore Award; Marshall Wingfield Award. *Memberships:* Organization of American Historians; Southern Historical Association. *Address:* 1400 Compere, Abilene, TX 79601, USA.

BAILEY Gordon, (Keith Gordon), b. 1936, British. *Appointments:* Film Editor, 1956-59; Sales Manager, 1959-62; Voluntary Youth Worker, 1962-; Free-lance Broadcaster, 1968-; Gordon Bailey Series, ATV Network Limited, Birmingham, 1973-75. Executive Director of Educational Charity Schools Ostreach, 1985. *Publications:* Plastic World, 1971; Moth- balled Religion, 1972; Patchwork Quill, 1975; Can a Man Change?, 1979; 100 Contemporary Christian Poets, I Want to Tell You How I Feel God, 1983; Stuff and Nonsense, 1989. *Address:* 9 Wentworth Drive, Blackwell, Nr Bromsgrove, Worcestershire, England.

BAILEY Margaret. *See:* **MARKHAM Marion Margaret.**

BAILEY Martin, b. 26 Oct 1947, London, England. Journalist. *Education:* PhD, London School of Economics, 1974. *Appointments:* The Observer, 1983-. *Publications:* Freedom Railway, 1976; Oilgate: The Sanctions Scandal, 1979; A Green Part of the World, 1984; Young Vincent: Van Gogh's Years in England, 1990; Van Gogh: Letters from Provence, 1990; Van Gogh in England: Portrait of the Artist as a Young Man, 1992; . *Honour:* Journalist of the Year, 1979. *Literary Agent:* A.D. Peters. *Address:* The Observer, Chelsea Bridge House, Queenstown Rd, London, SW8 4NN, England.

BAILEY Paul, b. 1937, British. Actor; Writer. *Appointment:* Actor, 1953-63. *Publications:* At the Jerusalem, 1967; Trespasses, 1971; A Worthy Guest, A Distant Likeness, 1973; Peter Smart's Confessions, 1977; Old Soldiers, 1980; An English Madam: The Life and Work of Cynthia Payne, 1982; Gabriel's Lament, 1986; An Immaculate Mistake (autobiog), 1990; Hearth and Home, 1990. *Address:* 79 Davisville Road, London W12 9SH, England.

BAILEY Veronica Anne, (Donna Bailey, Veronica

Bonar),** b. 6 Dec 1938, Kuala Lumpur, Malaysia. Freelance Writer. m. George William Bailey, 1 son, 1 daughter. *Education:* MA 1960, Edinburgh University; Passed registration exams for the Library Association 1961. *Appointments:* Library Assistant, Sussex University 1962-64; Teacher of English, Margaret Tabor School, Braintree 1967; Senior Library Assistant & Assistant Russian Cataloguer, Essex University Library, 1967-69; EFL Teacher to company employees, Language Teaching Centre N V Philips, Eindhoven 1970-71; Senior Library Assistant, Cataloguer, London School of Economics 1972; Freelance Editor, Macmillan 1972-73; Various editorial and managerial posts with Macmillan 1974-84, Freelance Publisher & Consultant, Writer and Co-Author of children's information books 1984-. *Publications:* Over 200 titles; Developer and writer/publishing consultant of NEW WAY reading scheme, 70 titles; Developer and re-writer of Pan/ Macmillan reading scheme READ TOGETHER, 36 titles; Developer and writer of MY WORLD information series, 24 titles; Writer of DAYS TO REMEMBER, 6 titles; Writer and packager of SMALL WORLD, 6 book audio-visual course; Writer of HEALTH FACTS, 8 titles; Writer of a series about RUBBISH, 6 titles; Writer of The Story of..... information series, 12 titles; Writer of series Take a Square of..... 6 titles; Writer of What we can do about.... series, 6 titles; Writer of, 4 titles; Writer of Funfax Dictionary; The Science of Colour; Publishing Consultant and Developer of Computer Club series, 3 titles; Debates series, 6 titles; Originator and packager of Children in Conflict series, 4 titles; Reviser and Consultant of Starters (Places) plus audio tapes, 5 titles; For BBC English by Radio and Television: Publishing Consultant for non video materials (book and audio tape) for Muzzy Comes Back; Ghost Writer of Duncan Dares. *Memberships:* Society of Authors; Vice- Chairman, Board of Governors, Appleshaw Primary School; Parish Councillor, Appleshaw PC. *Address:* Reeds Cottage, Appleshaw SP11 9AA, England.

BAILLIE Allan Stuart, b. 29 Jan 1943, Prestwick, Scotland. Writer. m. Agnes Chow, 14 Jan 1971, 1 son, 1 daughter. *Appointments:* Member CBCA Delegation to China, 1987. *Publications:* Mask Maker, 1975; Adrift, 1983; Little Brother, 1985; Riverman, 1986; Eagle Island, 1987; Creature, 1987; Drae and the Gremlin, 1988; Megan's Star, 1988; Mates, 1989; Hero, 1990; Bawshou Rescues the Sun; Little Monster; The Boss; Magician; Rebel; The Bad Guys; China Coin. *Honours:* Kathleen Fidler Award; IBBY Honor Diploma; CBCA Picture Book of Year; Multicultural Childrens Book Award. *Memberships:* Australian Society of Authors; Childrens Book Council of Australia; Amnesty International; Wilderness Society. *Address:* 49 Prince Alfred Parade, Newport, NSW 2106, Australia.

BAILYN Bernard, b. 1922, American. Professor. Assistant Professor 1954-58, Associate Professor 1958-61, Professor 1961-66, Winthrop Professor of History 1966-81, Adams University Professor 1981-, Editor in Chief, John Harvard Library 1962-70, Harvard University; Director, Charles Warren Center for Studies in American History, Harvard University, 1983-; Treelyan Lecturer, Cambridge University, 1971; Pitt Professor, Cambridge University, 1986-1987; Trustee, Institute for Advanced Study, Princeton; Co-Editor, Perspectives in American History, 1967-76, 1984-86. *Publications:* The New England Merchants in the Seventeeth Century, 1955; Massachusetts Shipping 1697-1714, 1959; Education in the Forming of American Society, 1960; Pamphlets of the American Revolution, 1965; The Ideological Origin of the American Revolution, 1967; The Origins of American Politics, 1968; The Intellectual Migration, Europe and America 1930-1960 (Co-Editor), 1969; Law in American History (Co-editor), 1972; The Ordeal of Thomas Hutchinson, 1974; The Great Republic (Co- author), 1977; The Press and the American Revolution (Co-Editor), 1980; The Apologia of Robert Keayne: The Self Portrait of a Puritan Merchant, (editor), 1965; The Peopling of British North America: An Introduction, 1986; Voyagers to the West, 1986; Faces of Revolution, 1990. *Address:* 170 Clifton Street, Belmont, MA 02178, USA.

BAINBRIDGE Beryl (Margaret), b. 1934, British. *Appointments:* Actress in Repertory Theatres in UK, 1949-60; Clerk, Gerald Duckworth and Company Limited, London, 1971-73. *Publications:* A Weekend with Claude, 1967, 1981; Another Part of the Wood, 1968, 1979; Harriet Said, 1972; The Dressmaker (in US as The Secret Glass), 1973; The Bottle Factory Outing, 1974; Sweet William, 1975; A Quiet Life, Injury Time, 1976; Young Adolf, 1978; Winter Garden, 1980; English Journey or The Road to Milton Keynes, Watson's Apology, 1984; Mum & Mr Amitage, 1985; Forever England, 1986, (T.V. series 1986); Filthy Lucre, 1986; An Awfully Big Adventure, 1989; The Birthday Boys, 1991. *Address:* 42 Albert Street, London NW1 7NU, England.

BAINBRIDGE Cyril, b. 15 Nov 1928, Bradford, West Yorkshire, England. Author; Journalist. m. Barbara Hannan Crook, 20 Jan 1953, 1 son, 2 daughters. *Education:* Negus College, Bradford. *Appointments:* Reporter, Bingley Guardian, 1944-45; Reporter, Yorkshire Observer & Bradford Telegraph, 1945-54; The Press Association, 1954-63; The Times, Asstistant News Editor, 1963-88; News Editor, 1967-69; Regional News Editor, 1969-77; Managing News Editor, 1977-82; Assistant Managing Editor, 1982-88. *Publications:* Pavilions on the Sea; Brass Triumphant; The Brontes & Their Country; North Yorkshire & North Humerside; One Hundred Yeras of Journalism. *Contributions to:* Various Feature, Travel Articles; Book Reviews. *Memberships:* The Cronte Society; Chartered Institute of Journalists; Society of Authors. *Literary Agent:* Laurence Pollinger. *Address:* 6 Lea Road, Hemingford Grey, Huntingdon, Cambridgeshire, PE18 9ED, England.

BAIRD John Charlton, b. 24 June 1938, Pawtucket, Rhode Island, USA. Professor. 2 daughters. *Education:* AB, Dartmouth College, 1960; MA, University of Delaware, 1962; PhD, Princeton University, 1964. *Publications:* The Inner Limits of Outer Space, 1987; Mind Child Architecture, 1982; Fundamentals of Scaling and Psychophysics, 1978; Psychophysical Analysis of Visual Space, 1970. *Contributor to:* Environment International; Journal of Experimental Psychology. *Memberships:* American Psychological Society; Psychonomic Society. *Address:* Department of Psychology, Dartmouth College, Hanover, NH 03755, USA.

BAKER Betty (Lou), (Elizabeth Renier), b. 1928, American. *Publications:* The Sun's Promise, Little Runner of the Longhouse, 1962; Killer-of-Death, The Shaman's Last Raid, 1963; The Treasure of the Padres, 1964; Walk the World's Rim, 1965; The Blood of the Brave, 1966; The Dunderhead War, 1967; Do Not Annoy the Indians, 1968; The Pig War, Arizona, 1969; And One was a Wooden Indian, 1970; A Stranger and Afraid, The Big Push, 1972; At the Center of the World, 1973; The Spirit Is Willing, 1974; Three Fools and a Horse, 1975; Settlers and Strangers, 1977; No Help at All, Save Sirrushany!, Partners, 1978; Latki and the Lightning Lizard, 1979; All-by-Herself, Santa Rat, The Great Desert Rat, 1980; Rat Is Dead and Ant Is Sad, Danby and George, Worthington Botts and the Stream Machine, 1981; Seven Spells to Farewell, And Me Coyote!, 1982; The Turkey Girl, 1983; My Sister Says, The Night Spider Case, 1984. *Address:* 4127 East Indian School, Apartment 20, Phoenix, AZ 85018, USA.

BAKER David A, b. 27 Dec 1954, Bangor, Maine, USA. Professor; Poet; Editor. m. Ann Townsend, 19 July 1987. *Education:* BSE, 1976, MA 1977, Central Missouri State University; PhD, University of Utah, 1983 (all degrees in English). *Appointments:* Visiting Assistant Professor, Kenyon College, 1983; Assistant Professor, Denison University, 1984; Visiting Professor, Cornell University, 1985; Associate Professor, Denison University 1989-; Poetry Editor, Kenyon Review, 1989-. *Publications:* Haunts (poems) 1985; Laws of the Lane (poems) 1981; Sweet Home, Saturday Night (poems) 1991; Poetry Chapbooks: Summer Sleep, 1984; Rivers in the Sea, 1977; Looking Ahead, 1975. *Contributor to:* Poetry and criticism in: New Yorker, Poetry, Nation, New Republic, Kenyon Review, Southern Review, Sewanee Review, Gettysburg Review, 50 others. *Honours:* Utah Arts Council Poetry Award, 1981; James Wright Poetry Prize, 1982; Poetry Fellow, National Endowment for the Arts, 1985; Bread Loaf Poetry Fellow, 1989. *Memberships:* Poets and Writers; Associated Writing Programs; Poetry Society of America; Modern Language Association. *Address:* 135 Granview Road, Granville, OH 43023, USA.

BAKER Donna, (Nicola West), b. 4 July 1939, Gosport, Hants, England. Author. div, 1 son, 1 daughter. m. Peter Thomson, 13 Feb 1993. *Publications:* Classmaker Saga; Carpetmaker Trilogy; 26+ Books Mills & Boon; How To Write Stories for Magazines; Currently Working on, Bid Time Return; Walking Quakes, Tracking Through Mercia. *Contributions to:* Several Hundred Articles, Short Stories to Newspapers & Magazines. *Memberships:* Society of Authors; Romantic Novelists Association. *Literary Agent:* Caroline Sheldon.

BAKER Houston Alfred Jr, b. 1943, American. Professor. *Appointments:* Instructor, Howard University, WA, 1966; Instructor 1968-69, Assistant Professor 1969, Yale University, New Haven, CT; Associate Professor 1970-73, Professor of English 1973, University of Virginia, Charlottesville; Director of Afro-American Studies 1974-77, Professor of English 1977-82, Albert M Greenfield Professor of Human Relations 1982-, University of Pennsylvania, Philadephia. *Publications:* Black Literautre in America, 1971; Long Black Song: Essays in Black American Literature and Culture, Twentieth-Century Interpretations of Native Son, 1972; A Many-Colored Coat of Dreams: The Poetry of Countee Cullen, Singers of Daybreak: Studies in Black American Literature, 1974; Reading Black: Essays in the Criticism of African, Caribbean and Black American Literature, 1976; No Matter Where You Travel, You Still Be Black, 1979; The Journey Back: Issues in Black Literature and Criticism, 1980; Spirit Run, 1982; Blue, Ideology and Afro-American Literature: A Vernacular Theory, 1984; Blues Journeys Home, 1985; Modernism and the Harlem Renaissance, 1987. *Address:* Department of English, University of Pennsylvania, Philadelphia, PA 19104, USA.

BAKER James Webb, b. 20 Dec 1926, Virginia, USA. Retired Journalist; Author. m. Elaine Campton, 15 Dec 1951, 2 sons. *Education:* BA, College of William & Mary, Williamsburg, USA, 1951. *Publications:* Illusions Illustrated; Series of Holiday Magic Books. *Contributions to:* Articles for Off Duty Magazine; Topic Magazine; Al Majal Magazine; William & Mary Alumni Magazine. *Memberships:* Virginia Writers Club. *Address:* 510 Spring Trace, Williamsburg, VA 23188, USA.

BAKER Liliane L. *See:* BAKER Lillian.

BAKER Lillian, (Liliane L Baker), b. 12 Dec 1921, New York, USA. Author; Historian. m. Roscoe A Baker, 1 son, 1 daughter. *Education:* El Camino, Calif, 1951; UCLA, 1968-77. *Appointements:* Continuity Writer Sta, WINS, NYC, 1945-46; Columnist, Freelance Writer, Reviewer Gardena Valley News, 1964-76; Freelance Writer, Editor Gardena, 1971-; Founder, Editor, International Club for Collectors of Hatpins & Hatpin Holders, 1977-; Conv & Seminar Coord, 1979, 82, 84, 87, 90, 92. *Publications include:* Collectors Encyclopedia of Hatpins & Hatpin Holders; 100 Years of Collectible Jewelry, 1850-1950; Art Nouveau and Art Deco Jewelry; The Concentration Camp Conspiracy; Hatpins & Hatpin Holders: An Illustrated Value Guide; Creative & Collectible Miniatures; Fifty Years of Collectible Fashion Jewelry; Dishonoring America: The Collective Guilt of American Japanese; Twentieth Century Fashionable Plastic Jewelry; The Japanning of America: Redress; The Common Boom and Reparations demands by Japanese Americans; American and Japanese Relocation in WWII: Fact, Ficiton and Fallacy; Established Lillian Baker Collection, Archives Hoover Institution; Poetry. *Contributions to:* Numerous Radio & TV Appearances. *Honours:* Scholarship Category

Award of Merit; George Washington Honor Medal; Recipient Award, Freedoms Foundation; Monetary Award Hoover Institution; Pro-Am Award; Golden Poet Award. *Memberships:* IBA; National League Am Pen Women; National Writers Club; Society Jewelry Historians; National Trust Historic Preservation; Life Member, NY Art Students League. *Address:* 15237 Chanera Avenue, Gardena, CA 90249, USA.

BAKER Margaret J(oyce), b. 1918, English. *Publications:* The Fighting Cocks, Nonsense Said the Tortoise (in US as Homer the Tortoise), 1949; Four Farthings abd a Thimble, 1950; A Castle and Sixpence, 1951; Benbow and the Angels, The Family That Grew and Grew, Treasure Trove, 1952; Homer Sees the Queen, 1953; The Young Magicians, Lions in the Potting Shed (in US as Lions in the Woodshed), 1954; The Wonderful Wellington Boots, 1955; Anna Sewell and Black Beauty, Acorns and Aerials, 1956; The Bright High Flyer, 1957; Tip and Run, Homer Goes to Stratford, 1958; The Magic Seashell, 1959; The Birds of Thimblepins, 1960; Homer in Orbit, 1961; Into the Castle, The Cats of Honeytown, Away Went Galloper, 1962; Castaway Christmas, 1963; Cut Off from Crumpets, The Shoe Shop Bears, 1964; Homer Goes West, Hannibal and the Bears, 1965; Bears Back in Business, Porterhouse Major, 1967; Home from the Hill, 1968; Hi-Jinks Joins the Bears, 1968; Snails' Place, 1970; The Last Straw, 1971; Boots and the Ginger Bears, 1972; The Sand Bird, Prickets Way, 1973; Lock Stock and Barrel, 1974; Sand in Our Shoes, 1976; The Gift Horse, 1982; Catch as Catch Can, 1983; Beware of the Gnomes, 1985; The Waiting Room Doll, 1986; Fresh Fields for Daisy, 1987. *Address:* Prickets, Old Cleeve, Nr Minehead, Somerset TA24 6HW, England.

BAKER Paul R(aymond), b. 1927, American. Professor. *Appointments:* Professor of History and Director of American Civilization Program, New York University, 1965-. *Publications:* Views of Society and Manners in America, by Frances Wright D'Arusmont, 1963; The Fortunate Pilgrims: Americans in Italy 1800-1860, 1964; The Atomic Bomb: The Great Decision, 1968, 1976; (with William Hall)The American Experience, (volume I) The American People, (volume II) Growth of a Nation, 1976; (volume III) Organizing a Democracy, (volume IV) The American Economy, (volume V) The United States in World Affairs, 1979; Richard Morris Hunt, 1980, 1986; (Contributor) Around the Square, 1982; Master Builders, 1985; The Architecture of Richard Morris Hunt, 1986; Stanny: The Gilded Life of Stanford White, 1989. *Address:* C/o Department of History, New York University, 19 University Place, Room 523, New York NY 10003, USA.

BAKER Peter, b. 1926, British. *Appointment:* Editor, Films and Filming Magazine, London, 1955-68. *Publications:* To Win a Prize on Sunday, 1966; Cruise, Casino, 1968; The Antibodies, 1969; The Bedroom Sailors, 1970; Babel Beach, 1973; Clinic, 1982. *Address:* c/o Hilary Rubinstein, AP Watt and Son, Literary Agency, 26-28 Bedford Row, London WC1, England.

BAKER Sharon, b. 10 May 1938, San Francisco, California, USA. Writer. m. Gordon P.Baker, 28 Sept 1963, 4 sons. *Education:* BA, History & Government, Mills College, 1960; MA, Library Science, University of Washington, 1965. *Publications:* Quarrelling, They Met the Dragon, 1984; Journey to Membliar, 1987; The Burning Tears of Sassurum, 1988. Articles in small magazines, poetry, book chapter. *Contributions to:* SF & Fantasy Newsletter; Northwest Review of Books. Chapter in How to Write Horror, Fantasy, & Science Fiction. *Honours:* 3rd prize, novel contest, Pacific Northwest Writers Conference; 2nd prize, novel contest. *Memberships:* Treasurer, Seattle Free Lances; Science Fiction Writers of America. *Literary Agent:* Dominick Abel. *Address:* Box 392, Seahurst, WA 98062, USA.

BAKER Stephen, b. 1921, American. *Appointment:* President, Stephen Baker Associates Incorporated NY. *Publications:* Advertising Layout and Art Direction, 1959; How to Live with a Neurotic Dog, 1960; Visual Persuasion, 1961; How to Play Golf in the Low 120's, 1962; How to Look Like Somebody in Business without Being Anybody, 1963; How to Live with a Neurotic Wife, How to Live with a Neurotic Husband, 1970; How to be Analyzed by a Neurotic Psychoanalyst, 1971; Systematic Approach to Advertising Creativity, Games Dogs Play, 1979; Motorist Guide to New York, 1981; I Hate Meetings, 1983; Executive Mother Goose, 1984; How to Live with a Neurotic Cat, 1985; Advertiser's Mannual, 1987; How to Survive a Lawyer, 1991; Me and My Cat, 1992; How to Live With a Neurotic Cat Owner, 1993; forthcoming publication: Complete Cat Catalogue. *Address:* 5 Tudor City Place, New York, NY 10017, USA.

BAKER W James. *See:* **BAKER James Webb.**

BAKEWELL Kenneth Graham Bartlett, b. 13 July 1931, Dudley. Lecturer. m. Agnes Lawson, 9 June 1956, 2 daughters. *Education:* MA, Queen's University of Belfast, 1972. *Appointments:* Various posts in public and special libraries 1947-66; Liverpool John Moores University, 1966-1993, (successively Lecturer, Senior Lecturer, Principal Lecturer Reader in Librarianship and Information Studies and Professor of Information and Library Management. *Publications include:* Managing User-centred Libraries and Information Services, 1990; Business Information and the Public Library, 1987; How to Organize Information, 1984; A Manual of Cataloguing Practice, 1972; Management Principles and Practice: A Guide to Information Sources, 1977; Cataloguing (with E J Hunter) 3rd edition 1992. The Manager's Guide to Getting the Answers (with Gillian A Dare) 2nd edition 1983; How to Orgainse Information, 1984; Business Information and the Public Library, 1986; Managing User-Centred Libraries and Information Services, 1990. *Contributor to:* Many journals, symposia; Editor, Library Management (MCB University Press). *Honours:* Wheatley Medal for an outstanding index (to Anglo-American cataloguing rules 1978) in 1979; Carey Award for services to indexing, 1991. *Memberships:* Fellow, Library Association; Society of Indexers; Institute of Information Scientists; Institute of Management; Vice-President, Librarians' Christian Fellowship. *Address:* 9 Greenacre Road, Liverpool L25 0LD, England.

BAKOLAS Nikos, b. 26 July 1927, Thessalonik, Greece. Retired Journalist. m. Helene Issidorou, 6 Sept 1957, 2 sons. *Education:* University of Thessaloniki; University of Michigan. *Appointments:* Artistic Manager, National Theatre of Northern Greece, 1980-81, 1990-. *Publications:* The Big Square; Mythology; The Princes, Garden; Trespass; Dont Cry Darling; Marches; Death Sleep. *Contributions to:* Numerous. *Honours:* Plotin Literary Award; National Book Award. *Memberships:* Greek Literary Society; Journalists Union of Macedonia. *Address:* 16 Papadiamandi Str, 546 45 Thessaloniki, Greece.

BALAAM. *See:* **LAMB Geoffrey Frederick.**

BALABAN John, b. 2 Dec 1943, Philadelphia, Pennsylvania, USA. Professor of English. m. 28 Nov 1970, 1 daughter. *Education:* BA, 1966, Pennsylvania State University; MA, 1967, Harvard University. *Appointments:* English Faculty, Pennsylvania State University, 1969; Professor of English and Director of Creative Writing, University of Miami, Florida. *Publications:* Poetry: After Our War, 1974; Blue Mountain, 1982; Words For My Daughter, 1991. Translation: Ca Dao Vietnam, 1980. Fiction: Coming Down Again, 1985; The Hawk's Tale, 1988. Memoir: Remembering Heaven's Face, 1991. Prose: Vietnam: The Land We Never Knew, 1989. Co-editor, Poets of Bulgaria, 1986. *Contributions to:* Hudson Review; American Poetry Review; Southern Review; American Scholar. *Honours:* Lamont Selection, Academy of American Poets, 1974; Nomination, National Book Award, 1975; Fulbright, NEH, NEA Fellowships, 1976, 1971, 1978, 1986; National Poetry Series Selection, 1991. *Memberships:* American PEN; Poetry Society of

America; American Literary Translators Association. *Literary Agent:* Sanford Greenbuger Associates, New York. *Address:* University of Miami, Department of English, PO Box 248145, Coral Gables, Florida 33124, USA.

BALBIR Jagbans Kishore, b. 1 June 1921, Delhi, India. Professor; Author; Diplomat. m. Nicole Balbir de Tugny, 5 Jan 1955, 1 son, 1 daughter. *Education:* Delhi University, BA (Hons), 1941; MA, 1943; Docteur, University of Paris, 1949; Research Diploma, Ecole Pratique Des Hautes Etudes, 1962. *Publications:* Histoire De Rama En Tibetain; Bhasha; Aspects of Training And Research in Higher Education; Dictionnaire General Hindi Francais. *Contributions to:* Indo Iranian Journal; Agra University Journal; Annals of Bhandarkar Oriental Research Institute; Bibliographie Bouddhique; Hindi Sahitya Kosh; Allahabad. *Honours:* Chevalier Des Palmes Academiques; University of Delhi Medal for Best Student. *Memberships:* Indian PEN; Linguistic Society of India; Bhandarkar Oriental Research Institute. *Address:* 58-60 Rue Denfert Rochereau, 92100 Boulogne, France.

BALBIR DE TUGNY Nicole Christiane, b. 6 June 1924, Paris, France. University Professor. m. J K Balbir, 5 Jan 1955, 1 son, 1 daughter. *Education:* Licence, Teaching, 1949; Diploma of Higher Studies, English, 1953, Diploma, Oriental Languages (Hindi), 1963, Sorbonne; State Doctorate, Sorbonne-Nouvelle, 1974. *Publications:* Gange, O Ma Mere, 1966; Chants Mystiques de Mirabai, 1979; Les Bien Heureuses, translations from Hindi, 1989; Manuel de Hindi a l'Usage des Francophones, 1985; Inde (collection Monde et Voyages), 1990; Dictionnaire General Hindi-Francais, 1991. *Contributions to:* Encyclopaedia Universalis, Hindi Literature; Encyclopedie Larousse, 1974; Dictionnaire des Litteratures, PUF. *Memberships:* ssa 00Societe des Gens de Lettres et Auteurs Multimedias; Societe Asiatique de Paris. *Literary Agent:* Presses Universitaires de France, Paris 75006, France. *Address:* 58-60 rue Denfert-Rochereau, 92100 Boulogne, France.

BALDERSON Margaret, Australian. *Appointment:* Librarian, Sydney. *Publications:* When Jays Fly to Barmo, 1969; A Dog Called George, 1975; Blue and Gold Day, 1979. *Honours:* Australian Children's Book Council Book of the Year Award, 1969. *Address:* c/o Oxford University Press, Box 2784Y, Melbourne, Victoria 3001, Australia.

BALFOUR Michael (Leonard Graham), b. 1908, British. *Appointments:* Lecturer, Politics, Magdalen College, Oxford, 1932-36; Study Group Secretary, Royal Institute of International Affairs, 1936-39; Principal, Ministry of Information, 1939-42; Deputy Director of Intelligence, Political Warfare Executive, 1942-44; Deputy Chief, Intelligence Section, Psychological Warfare Division, SHAEF, 1944-45; Director of Information Services Control, British Control Commission for Germany, 1945-47; Chief Information Officer, Board of Trade, 1947-64; Professor of European History, University of East Anglia, Norwich, 1966-74. *Publications:* Nationalism, 1939; States and Mind, 1952; Four-Power Control in Germany 1945-6, 1956; The Kaiser and His Times, 1964; West Germany, 1968; Helmuth von Moltke: A Leader Against Hitler, 1972; Propaganda in War 1939-45, 1979; The Adversaries: America, Russia and the Open World 1941-62, 1981; West Germany: A Contemporary History, 1982; Britain and Joseph Chamberlain, 1985; Withstanding Hitler, 1988. *Honours:* CBE, 1963. *Address:* Waine's Cottage, Swan Lane, Burford OX8 4SH, England.

BALIAN Lorna, b. 1929, American. *Publications:* Author and Illustrator. Humbug Witch, 1965; I Love You, Mary Jane, 1967; The Animal, Where in the World is Henry?, 1972; Sometimes It's Turkey - Sometimes It's Feathers, 1973; Humbug Rabbit, 1974; The Sweet Touch, 1976; Bah! Humbug?, 1977; A Sweetheart for Valentine, 1979; Leprechauns Never Lie, 1980; Mother's Mother's Day, 1982; Humbug Potion, 1984;

A Garden for a Groundhog, 1985; Amelia's Nine Lives, 1986; Thee Socksnatchers, 1988; Wilbur's Space Machine, 1990. *Address:* 6698 Highway 83 South, Hartford, WI 53027, USA.

BALL B N. *See:* **BALL Brian Neville.**

BALL Brian Neville, (B N Ball, Brian Kinsey Jones), b. 1932, British. Staff Member, subsequently Senior Lecturer in English, Doncaster College of Education, 1956-; Chairman, Doncaster Prose and Poetry Society, 1968-70. *Publications:* Mr Tofat's Term, Tales of Science Fiction (as B N Ball), 1964; (as Brian Kinsey Jones) Sundog, 1965; Basic Linguistics for Secondary Schools, 3 vols (as B N Ball), 1966-67; Paris Adventures (as B N Ball), 1967; Timepiece, Timepivot and Timepit, 1968-71; Lay Down Your Wife for Another, Lesson for the Damned, 1971; Night of the Robots (in the US as The Regiments of Night), Devil's Peak, The Probability Man, 1972; Planet Probability, Singularity Station, 1973; Death of a Low Handicap Man, Montenegrin Gold, The Venomous Serpent (in the US as The Night Creature), 1974; The Space Guardians, Keegan: The No-Option Contract, Princess Priscilla (as B N Ball), 1975; Jackson's Friend, Jackson's House, Jackson's Holiday (as B N Ball), 1975-77; Keegan: The One-Way Deal, Witchfinder: The Mark of the Beast, 1976; Witchfinder: The Evil at Monteine, 1977; (as B N Ball), Jackson and the Magpies, 1978; The Witch in Our Attic, Young Person's Guide to UFO's, 1979; Dennis and the Flying Saucer, 1980; The Baker Street Boys, The Starbuggy, 1983; The Doomship of Drax, 1985; Truant from Space, 1985; Look Out, Duggy Dog!, 1987; BMX Billy, 1986; Frog Island Summer, 1987; I'm Lost, Duggy Dog!, 1987; The Quest for Queenie, 1988; Cat in the Custard, 1988; Stone Age Magic, 1989; Hop It, Duggy Dog!, 1989; Bella at the Ballet, 1990; Cat in the Classroom, 1990; Come Back, Duggy Dog, 1991; The Mermaid and the Dolphins, 1991; Mrs Potts' New Pets, in Let's Join In, The 'Jenny' tales, in Here Comes Pob and Pob and Friends and various others in anthologies in the US and the UK. Various reviews and articles for the Guardian and Times Educational Supplement, BBC, Jackanory...televising of The Witch in Our Attic, 1979; Channel 4, in Pob's Programme, televising of the Jenny's stories, 1987-88; BBC Education various playlets in the Let's Join In, programme, 1979. *Address:* c/o Hamish Hamilton Ltd, 27 Wrights Lane, London, W8 5TZ.

BALL John Bradley, b. 21 Aug 1932, England. Journalist; Publisher; Editor. *Education:* CGLI Full Tech Print, Trent Polytechnic; Diploma Course, Keble College, Oxford. *Contributions to:* Topic Magazine Group; Womens Journal; Holiday Inn Magazine; High Life; Debretts World Book of Travel, 1989. *Honours:* PATA Magazine Travel Writer of the Year, 1979; Liveryman, Coach & Coach Harness Makers, London; Freeman, City of London; Commandeur de Vins de Bordeaux. *Memberships:* British Guild of Travel Writers; Guild of Motoring Writers; Midlands Group of Motoring Writers. *Address:* Field House, Bank Hill, Woodborough, Nottingham, England.

BALLANTYNE Sheila, b. 26 July 1936, Seattle, Washington, USA. Writer; Teacher. m. Philip Spielman, 22 Dec 1963, 1 son, 1 daughter. *Education:* Mills College, Oakland, California, USA, BA. *Appointments:* Dominican College, 1983; Mills College, 1984-; Bay Area Writers Workshop, 1988,89. *Publications:* Norma Jean The Termite Queen; Imaginary Crimes; Life On Earth. *Contributions to:* The New Yorker; American Review; Prize Stories: The O Henry Awards; Short Story International; Aphra. *Honours include:* O'Henry award; MacDowell Colony Fellowship; John Simon Guggenheim Fellowship; National Womens Political Caucus Distinguished Achievement Award. *Memberships:* Authors Guild; National Writers Union; PEN. *Address:* Dept of English, Mills College, 5000 MacAuthur Building, Oakland, CA 94613, USA.

BALLARD James Graham, b. 15 Nov 1930, Shanghai, China. Novelist; Short story writer. m. Helen

Mary Mathews, 1954 (dec.1964), 1 son, 2 daughters. *Education:* King's College, Cambridge. *Publications:* The Drowned World, 1963; The 4-Dimensional Nightmare, 1963; The Terminal Beach, 1964; The Drought, 1965; The Crystal World, 1966; The Disaster Area, 1967; The Atrocity Exhibition, 1970; Crash, 1973; Vermilion Sands, 1973; Concrete Island, 1974; High Rise, 1975; Low-Flying Aircraft, 1976; The Unlimited Dream Company, 1979; Myths of the Near Future, 1982; Empire of the Sun, 1984; The Day of Creation, 1987; Running Wild, 1988; War Forever, 1990; The Kindness of Women, 1991. *Honours:* Guardian Fiction Prize, 1984; James Tait Black Prize, 1984 *Address:* 36 Old Charlton Road, Shepperton, Middlesex, England.

BALLARD Juliet Lyle Brooke, b. 6 Feb 1913. Poet; Editor; Prose Writer. *Education:* AB, Randolph-Macon Woman's College, 1934; Certificate of Social Case Work, Richmond Professional Institute, 1938. *Literary Appointments:* Associate Editor, Association for Research and Enlightenment Journal, 1966-70; Associate Editor, Association for Research and Enlightenment Children's Magazine, 1970; Editor, Treasure Trove (Association for Research and Enlightenment Children's quarterly), 1971- 73. *Publications Include:* Major Works, Under a Tropic Sun, 1945; Winter Has Come, 1945; The Ballad of the Widow's Flag (official poem of The Star-Spangled Banner Flag House Association, Baltimore, Maryland), 1956; Prose Works: The Hidden Laws of Earth, 1979; Treasures from Earth's Storehouse, 1980; The Art of Living, 1982; retitled Unto the Hills, 1987; Research Bulletin, Pilgrimage Into the Light, Vols I, II & III, issued by The Edgar Cayce Foundation, 1988, Vol IV, 1989; translation of The Hidden Laws of Earth into Japanese by Chuo Art Shuppan Sha, 1989. *Contributor to:* Composers, Authors and Artists of America; Wings; Nature Magazine; Canadian Poetry; Poems for our Time; Moccasin; Driftwind; The Raven; The Lantern; Blue Moon; Kaleidograph; L'Alouette; Silver Star; The Searchlight; With Rhyme and Reason; American Poet; Greetings; ARE Journal; Coronet and others. *Honours:* Participant in various radio programmes; Library exhibitions of books and poems; Winner of literary organization contests; 1st prize, Saucier Lyric Award, National Federation of State Poetry Societies, 1965; Juliet Brooke Ballard Collection at Syracuse University, 1964-; (now part of George Arents Research Library manuscript collections). *Memberships:* Composers, Authors and Artists of America. *Address:* 2217 Wake Forest Street, Virginia Beach, VA 23451, USA.

BALLEM John Bishop, b. 2 Feb 1925, New Glasgow, Nova Scotia, Canada. Lawyer. m. Grace Louise Flavelle, 31 Aug 1951, 2 sons, 1 daughter. *Education:* BA 1946, MA 1948, LLB 1949, Dalhousie University, Halifax, Nova Scotia; LLM 1950, Harvard University Law School, Boston, Massachusetts. *Publications:* The Devil's Lighter, 1973; Dirty Scenario, 1974; Judas Conspiracy, 1976; The Moon Pool, 1978; Sacrifice Play, 1981; Marigot Run, 1983; Oilpatch Empire, 1985; The Oil and Gas Lease in Canada, textbook, 2 ed 1985; Death Spiral, 1989; The Barons, 1991. *Contributions to:* Numerous legal articles in: The Canadian Bar Review; The Alberta Law Review; and others. *Honour:* Appointed Queen's Counsel in 1966; Awarded Honorary Doctor of Laws Degree, University of Calgary, 1993. *Memberships:* Writers Guild of Alberta; Writers' Union of Canada; Crime Writers of Canada; Calgary Writers Association; Member International Bar Association; the Bars of Nova Scotia, Ontario and Alberta; The Law Society of Alberta; Phi Delta Theta. *Address:* 4000, 150-6th Avenue SW, Calgary, Alberta, Canada T2P 3Y7.

BANCROFT Anne, b. 17 Apr 1923, London, England. Author. 2 sons, 2 daughters. *Publications:* Twentieth Century Mystics and Sages, 1976, Republished 1989; Religions of the East, 1974; Zen: Direct Pointing to Reality, 1980; The Luminous Vision, Republished 1989; Six Medieval Mystics, 1981; Chinese New Year, 1984; Festivals of the Buddha, 1984; The Buddhist World, 1984; The New Religious World, 1985; Origins of the Sacred: The Spiritual Way in Western Tradition, 1987;

Weavers of Wisdom, 1989. *Contributions to:* The Middle Way; Everyman's Encyclopedia; Women in the World's Religions. *Memberships:* The Society of Authors; Society of Women Writers and Journalists. *Address:* 1 Grange Villas, The Street, Charmouth, Bridport, Dorset DT6 6QQ, England.

BANCROFT Iris, (Julia Barnright, Iris Brent, Andrea Layton), b. 1922, American. Writer. *Appointments:* Bookeeper then Garment union organizer, Chicago, 1945-50; Teacher, Chicago area, 1957-62; Publishing, CA, 1962-77. *Publications:* The Sexually Exiting Female, The Sexually Superior Male (both as J. Barnright), 1971; Swinger's Diary (as I Brent), 1973; (as A Layton) Love's Gentle Fugitive, So Wild a Rapture, 1978; Midnight Fires, Love's Burning Flame, 1979; Rapture's Rebel, 1980; Rebel's Passion, Dawn of Desire, (Iris Bancroft) Whispering Hope, 1981; The Five Minute Phobia Cure (with Roger Callahan), Any Man Can (with William Hartman and Marilyn Fithian), 1984; Sex and Single Parent (with Mary Mattis), Reaching Intimacy (with Jerry DeHaan), 1986. *Address:* c/o Sandy Watt & Associates, 8033 Sunset Boulevard, Los Angeles, CA 90046, USA.

BANDELE THOMAS Biyi, b. 13 Oct 1967, Kafanchan, Nigeria. *Education:* Dramatic Arts, Obafemi Awolowo University, ILE-IFE, 1987- 90. *Appointments:* Associate writer, Royal Court Theatre, London, 1992- . *Publications:* The Man Who Came In From the Back of Beyound; The Sympathetic Undertaker And Other Dreams; Incantations On The Eve of An Execution; Plays inc, Rain; Marching for Fausa; Death Catches the Hunter; Screenplay: Not Even God is Wise Enough, BBC, 1993. *Contributions to:* West Africa. *Honours:* International Student Playscript Competition; Arts Council Writers Bursary. *Memberships:* Society of Authors; Writers Guild; PEN. *Literary Agent:* MBA. *Address:* 45 Fitzroy Street, London W1P 5HR, England.

BANERJI Sara Ann, b. 6 June 1932, Stoke Poges, Bucks, England. Novelist. m. Ranjit Banerji, 4 Mar 1957, 3 daughters. *Education:* Various Convents, Art Schools, Governnesses. *Publications:* Writing on Skin; Absolute Hush; Shining Agnes; The Teaplanters Daughter; The Wedding of Jayanthi Mandel; Cobweb Walking. *Memberships:* Society of Authors and Writers in Oxford; PEN. *Literary Agent:* Gina Murray Pollinger. *Address:* 7 London Place, Oxford, OX4 1BD, England.

BANISTER Judith, b. 10 Sept 1943, Washington, DC, USA. Demographer. m. Kim Woodard, 17 Dec 1966, 1 son, 1 daughter, *Education:* BA, Swarthmore College, 1965; PhD, Stanford University, 1978. *Publications:* Chinas Changing Population; The Population of North Korea; The Population of Vietnam; The Population Dynamics of Nepal. *Contributions to:* The American Enterprise; Nikkei Business; The Washington Post; Asian Survey; Numerous Manuscripts & Conference Papers; Media Apperances. *Honours:* Foremost Women of the Twentieth Century; Contemporary Authors; Various Who's Who Publications. *Memberships:* population Association of America; International Union for the Scientific Study of Population; Association of Asian Studies. *Address:* Center for International Research, US Bureau of Population the Census, Room 206, Washington Plaza II, Washington, DC 20233, USA.

BANKER James, b. 29 Apr 1938, Plattsburgh, New York, USA. University Professor. m. Maureen J, 24 June 1961, 2 daughters. *Education:* BA, Taylor University, 1961; MA, Boston University, 1962; PhD, University of Rochester, 1971. *Appointments:* Assistance Professor, North carolina State University, 1971-76; Associate Professor, 1976-86; Professor, 1986-. *Publications:* Death in the Community. *Memberships:* American Historical Association; Renaissance Society of America; Society for Italian Historical Studies. *Address:* Dept of History, North Carolina State University, Raleigh, NC 27675, USA.

BANKOFF George. See: **MILKOMANE George Alexis Milkomanovich.**

BANKS Brian R(obert), b. 4 Oct 1956, Carshalton, Surrey, England. Antiquarian Bookseller. m. Catherine Walton, 28 Sept 1987, 1 son, 2 daughters. *Education:* Westminister College; Middlesex Polytechnic. *Publications:* The Image of J-K Huysmans, 1990; Phantoms of the Belle Epoque, 1993 (Introduction by Colin Wilson); Atmosphere and Attitudes (poems), 1993; Contributor to Encylopeadia of the 1980's, 1993. *Contributions to:* 1890's Journal; Book World; Aklo; Celtic Dawn (Yeats Society); Nuit Isis; Book and Magazine Collector. *Memberships:* Societe de J K Huysmans, Paris; 1890's Society. *Address:* c/o 4 Meretune Court, Martin Way, Morden, Surrey SM4 4AN, England.

BANKS James Albert, b. 1941, American. Professor. *Appointments:* Assistant Professor 1969-71, Associate Professor 1971-73, Professor of Education, 1973-, Chairman of the Department of Curriculum and Instruction, 1982-, University of Washington, Seattle; National Council for the Social Studies, 1982. *Publications:* Teaching the Black Experience: Mehtods and Materials, March Toward Freedom: A History of Black Americans, 1970, 2nd edition (with Cherry A Banks), 1978; Teaching Social Studies to Culturally Different Children (edition with William W Joyce), Teaching the Language Arts to Culturally Different Children (with W Joyce), 1971; Black Self-Concept (edition with Jean D Grambs), 1972; Teaching Ethnic Studies, Teaching Strategies for the Social Studies, 1973, 3rd edition, 1985; Teaching Strategies for Ethnic Studies, 1975, 4th edition, 1987; Curriculum Guidelines for Multiethnic Education (with others), 1976; Multiethnic Education: Practices and Promises, 1971; Multiethnic Education: Theory and Practice, 1981, 1988; Education in the 80's: Multiethnic Education, 1981; We Americans: Our History and People, 2 volumes (with Sebesta), 1982; Multicultural Education in Western Societies (with James Lynch), 1986. *Address:* 115 Miller Hall-DQ-12, University of Washington, Seattle, WA 98195, USA.

BANKS Lynne Reid, b. 1929, London, England. Writer; Actress. m. Chaim Stephenson, 1965, 3 sons. *Education:* Royal Academy of Dramatic Art. *Publications include:* The L Shaped Room; An End to Running; Children At The Gate; The Backward Shadow; Two is Lonely; Dark Quartet; The Indian in the Cupboard; Return of the Indian; Secret of the Indian; Mystery of the Cupboard; Casualties; Melusine, A Mystery for Young Adults; 13 Other Books. *Contributions to:* Sunday Telegraph; Guardian; Times Educational Supplement; Times; Observer; The Spectator; Jewish Chronicle; McCalls; Ladies Home Journal; Good Housekeeping. *Honour:* Virginia Young Readers Contest; Rebecca Caudill Young Readers award; Arizona Young Readers Award; Indian Paintbrush Award; Yorkshire Arts Literary Award; Western Australia Young Librarians Award; California Young Readers Medal. *Literary Agent:* Watson Little Limited. *Address:* c/o Watson Little Ltd, 12 Egbert Street, London, NW1 8LJ, England.

BANKS Russell, b. 28 Mar 1940, Newton, Massachusetts, USA. Novelist. 4 daughters. *Education:* BA, highest honours, English, University of North Carolina. *Publications include:* Searching for Survivors, 1975; Family Life, 1975; Hamilton Stark, 1978; The New World, 1978; The Book of Jamaica, 1980; Trailerpark, 1982; The Relation of my Imprisonment, 1984; Continental Drift, 1985; Success Stories, 1986; Affliction, 1989. *Contributions to:* New York Times Book Review; Washington Post; American Review; Vanity Fair; Antaeus; Partisan Review; New England Review; Fiction International; Boston Globe Magazine; etc. *Honours include:* Best American Short Stories, 1971, 1985; Fels Award, fiction, 1974; Prize story, O.Henry Awards, 1975; Guggenheim Fellow, 1976; NEA Fellowships, 1977, 1983; St Lawrence Award, fiction, 1976; John dos Passos Award, 1986; Pulitzer Prize nominee, 1986; Award, American Academy of Arts &

Letters, 1986. *Memberships:* Executive, PEN American Centre; Board 1968-71, secretary 1970-71, Coordinating Council of Literary Magazines. *Literary Agent:* Ellen Levine. *Address:* c/o Ellen Levine Literary Agency, 432 Park Avenue South, Suite 1205, New York, NY 10016, USA.

BANNER Angela. See: **MADDISON Angela May.**

BANNON Paul. See: **DURST Paul.**

BANTOCK Gavin (Marcus August), b. 1939, British. Professor. *Appointment:* Professor of English, Reitaku University, Japan, 1969-. *Publications:* Christ: A Poem in Twenty-Six Parts, 1965; Juggernaut, The Last of the Kings: Frederick the Great, 1968; A New Thing Breathing, 1969; Anhaga, 1970; Gleeman, 1972; Eirenikon, 1973; Isles, 1974; Dragons, 1979. *Address:* c/o Peter Jay, 69 King George Street, London SE10 8PX, England.

BANTOCK Geoffrey Herman, b. 12 Oct 1914. Emeritus Professor of Education, University of Leicester. m. Dorothy Jean Pick, 6 Jan 1950. *Education:* BA 1936, MA 1942, Emmanuel College, Cambridge. *Publications:* Freedom & Authority in Education, 1952; L H Myers: A Critical Study, 1956; Education & Values, 1965; Education, Culture & the Emotions, 1967; Culture, Industrialisation & Education, 1968; Education in an Industrial Society, 1968; T S Eliot & Education, 1970; Dilemmas of the Curriculum, 1980; Studies in the History of Educational Theory, Vol.I, 1980, Vol.II, 1984; Parochialism of the Present, 1981. *Contributions to:* Scrutiny; Cambridge Journal; Essays in Criticism; ELH; JES; Listener and numerous other journals. *Honour:* Awarded Book Prize of Standing Conference on Education Studies for best book on education published in 1984. *Address:* Old Rectory, Melton Road, Rearsby, Leicestershire, England.

BANVILLE John, b. 8 Dec 1945, Wexford, Ireland. Author. m. Janet Dunham, 2 sons. *Education:* Christian Brothers School; St Peters College, Wexford. *Appointments:* Literary Editor, The Irish Times, Dublin, 1988. *Publications:* The Book of Evidence; Kepler; Doctor Copernicus; The Newton Letter. *Contributions to:* Reviews for the Observer; New York Review of Books; The Irish Times. *Literary Agent:* Anthony Sheil, Sheil Land Associates Limited *Addres:* 6 Church Street, Howth, Co Dublin, Ireland.

BARAKA Imamu Amiri. See: **JONES Le Roi.**

BARBALET Margaret Evelyn Hardy, b. 19 Dec 1949, Adelaide, South Australia. Writer; m. Jack Barbalet, 5 Dec 1970, 3 sons. Div. 1989. *Education:* MA, History, Adelaide University, 1973. *Publications:* Adelaide Children's Hospital 1876-1976, 1976; Far From a Low Gutter Girl, 1983; Blood in the Rain, novel, 1986; Various short stories published Canberra Tales, 1988; Steel Beach, novel, 1988; The Wolf, picture, Puffin, 1991; Lady, Baby Gypsy Queen, novel 1992. *Honours:* Literature grant, 1985; New Writers Fellowship, 1986. *Memberships:* Australian Society of Authors; Amnesty International. *Address:* c/o Penguin Books, PO Box 257, Ringwood, Victoria 3134, Australia.

BARBER Charles Laurence, b. 20 Apr 1915, Harold Wood, Essex, England. University Teacher (retired). m. Barbara Best, 27 July 1943, 2 sons, 2 daughters. *Education:* BA, St. Catharine's College, Cambridge University, 1937; MA, 1941; Teacher's Diploma, University of London Institute of Education, 1938; PhD, University of Gothenburg, Sweden, 1957. *Publications:* Best Known: The Idea of Honour in the English Drama, 1957; The Story of Language, 1964; Linguistic Change in Present-Day English, 1964; Early Modern English, 1976; Poetry in English; An Introduction, 1983; The Theme of Honour's Tongue, 1985; The English Language: a Historical Introduction, 1993; Others; Editor of works by Thomas Middleton, A Trick to Catch the Old One, 1968, Women Beware Women, 1969, and A Chaste Maid in Cheapside, 1969; Henry V, 1980, As You Like It, 1981, and Richard III, 1981 (York Notes on Shakespeare); Shakespeare's Richard II (Macmillan Master Guide), 1987. *Contributions to:* Numerous articles in learned journals in the field of English Language and Literature. *Address:* 7 North Parade, Leeds, West Yorkshire, LS16 5AY, England.

BARBER D(ulan) Friar, (David Fletcher), b. 1940, British. Freelance Writer. *Appointments:* Taught at Morley College, London, 1976-78; Creative Writing Teacher, City Literary Institute, London, 1978-79. *Publications:* A Loveable Man, 1974; A Respectable Woman, 1975; Don't Whistle 'Macbeth', 1976; Accomplices, 1976; Raffles, 1977; Only Children, 1977; Rainbow in Hell, 1083; Rainbow End in Tears, 1984; On Suspicion, 1985.

BARBER James David, b. 1930, American. Professor. *Appointments:* Research Staff, Industrial Relations Center, University of Chicago, 1951-53, 1955; Assistant Professor of Political Science, Stetson University, 1955-57; Instructor 1960-61, Associate Director, Political Science Research Library 1960-62, Assistant Professor 1961-65, Director of Graduate Studies 1965-67, Associate Professor 1965-68, Director, Office for Advanced Political Studies 1967-68, Professor 1968-72, Yale University; Professor and Chairman, Department of Political Science 1972-77, James B Duke, Professor of Political Science 1978-, Duke University, Durham; Series Editor, Harcourt Brace Jovanovich Incorporated, 1971-; Chairman, Board of Directors, Amnesty International, USA, 1984-86. *Publications:* Political Leadership in American Government, Part II Heritage of Liberty, 1964; The Lawmakers: Recruitment and Adaptation to Legislative Life, 1965; Power in Committees: An Experiment in the Government Process, 1966; An Introduction to Political Analysis (ed. with R E Lane and F I Greenstein), 1967; Citizen Politics, 1968; Power to the Citizen, 1971; The Presidential Character: Predicting Performance in the White House, 1972, 1977, 1985, 1992; Choosing the President, 1974; Race for the Presidency, 1978; The Pulse of Politics: Electing Presidents in the Media Age, 1980, 1992; Erasmus: A Play on Words, 1982; Women Leaders in American Politics (with others), 1985; Politics by Humans: Research on American Leadership, 1988. *Address:* Department of Political Science, Duke University, Durham, NC 27706, USA.

. **BARBER Lynn,** b. 22 May 1944, England. Journalist. m. David Cloudesley Cardiff, 1 Sept 1971, 2 daughters. *Education:* BA Honours, English, Oxford University. *Appointments:* Assistant Editor, Penthouse Magazine, 1968-73; Staff Feature Writer, Sunday Express Magazine, 1984-89; Feature Writer, Independent on Sunday, 1990-. *Publications:* How to Improve Your Man in Bed, 1970; The Penthouse Sexindex, 1973; The Single Women's Sexbook, 1975; The Heyday of Natural History, 1980. *Honours:* British Press Awards as Magazine Writer of the Year, 1986, 1987. *Address:* Independent on Sunday, 40 City Road, London, EC1Y 2DH, England.

BARBER Richard William, b. 30 Oct 1941. Publisher; Author. m. Helen Tolson, 7 May 1970, 1 son, 1 daughter. *Education:* Trevelyan Scholar, BA History, MA, PhD, 1982, Corpus Christi College, Cambridge University. *Publications:* The Knight and Chivalry, 1972; Arthur of Albion, 1961 (Revised as King Arthur 1974, 2nd edition 1986); Edward Prince of Wales and Aquitaine, 1976; Companion Guide to South West France, 1977; Tournaments, 1978; The Penguin Guide to Medieval Europe, 1984; Tournaments: Jousts, Chivalry and Pageants in the Middle Ages (with Juliet Barker) 1989; Editor, The Pastons, 1975, Aubrey's Brief Lives, 1981, The Arthurian Legends, 1979, Fuller's Worthies, 1987; The Worlds of John Aubrey, 1988. *Contributions to:* Editor, Arthurian Literature (Annual). *Honours:* Somerset Maugham award, 1972; Times Higher Educational Supplement Book Award, 1978.

Memberships: Royal Society of Literature; Royal Historical Society; Society of Antiquaries. *Address:* Stangrove Hall, Alderton, Nr. Woodbridge, Suffolk IP12 3BL, England.

BARBET Pierre Claude Avice, (David Maine, Olivier Sprigel), b. 16 May 1925, Le Mans, France. Science Fiction Writer. m. Marianne, 23 July 1952, 2 sons, 1 daughter. *Education:* Pharmacist, University of Paris, 1953; Diplomas of Bacteriology and Serology, Parasitology, University of Paris, 1954; PhD, Summa cum laude, Institut Pasteur, Faculte de Pharmacie, University of Paris, 1955. *Appointments:* Libraries Gallimard, 1962-63; Fleuve Noir, 1966-87; Albin Michel, 1972-82; Champs Elysees, 1976-78. *Publications:* 72 Novels published; Cosmic Crusaders; Games psyborgs Play; Napoleon and Emperor of Eridanus; Joan of Arc Replay; Enchanted Planet; Rome doit etre detruite and Carthage sera detruite; Survivants de l'apocalypse - Glaciation nucleaire; Cities de l'espace, serial; Venusine - Defense spatiale - Un Reich de 1000 ans; Invasion cosmique - Alex Courville, serial. *Contributor to:* Horizons de Fantastique; Grande Encyclopedie de Fantastique et de la SF, Italy. *Honours:* Prix, Ailes d'or du Fantastique, pour son oeuvre de SF; et pour son travail dans l'organisation de la Societe Europeenne de SF, International Institute of SF, Poznana, Poland. *Memberships:* Co-ordinator, European Society of Science Fiction, 1979-89; Vice President, Francophone Society of SF member of Board, World SF Society; Director, Overseas, The Science Fiction Writers of America; International Association of Critics; Secretary, The French Society of Doctours en Pharmacie; Corresponding Member, the European Academy of Arts, Letters, Science. *Address:* 4 Square de l'avenue du Bois, 75116 Paris, France.

BARBOSA Miguel, b. 22 Nov 1925, Lisbon, Portugal. Writer; Painter. *Education:* Economics & Finance, University of Lisbon. *Publications:* Short Stories: Retalhos de Vida, 1955; Manta de Trapos, 1962; Plays: O Palheiro, 1963; Os Carnivoros, 1964, 1973; O Piquenique, 1964, 1973; O Insecticida, 1965, 1974; A Mulher que Pariu a France, 1971; Los profetas de la Paja, 1973; How New York was Destroyed by Rats 1977; The Materialisation of Love, 1978; Novels: Trineu do Morro, 1972, 1975; Mulher Macumba, 1973; A Pileca no Poleiro, 1976; As Confissoes de Um Cacador de Dinossauros, 1981; Esta Louca Profissao de Escritor, 1983; Cartas a Um Fogo-Fatuo, 1985. *Contributor to:* various publications. *Honours:* 1st Prize, Maria Terza Alves Viana Theatre, Sao Paulo, Brazil; Prix Nu, Jubile Mondial d'arts Plastiques, Nice, France, 1984; Honourable Mention, 1e Quadriennale Mondiale des Beaux Arts, Lyon, France, 1985; Medaille D'Argent, Academie de Lutece, Paris, 1987; Prix de La Revue D'Art, La Côte des Arts, Cannes, 1990. *Address:* Avenue Joao Crisostomo 9-12, Lisbon 1000, Portugal.

BARBOUR Douglas, b. 1940, Canadian. Professor. *Appointments:* Assistant Professor 1969-77, Associate Professor 1977-81, Professor 1982-, University of Alberta, Edmonton; Poetry Editor, Canadian Forum, 1978-80; Former Editor, Quarry Magazine, Kingston, Ontario. *Publications:* Land Fall, A Poem as Long as the Highway, 1971; White, 1972; Songbook, 1973; He. &. She. &., 1974; Visions of My Grandfather, 1977; Shore Lines, 1979; Vision/Sounding, 1980; The Pirates of Pen's Chance (with Stephen Scobie), The Maple Laugh Forever: An Anthology of Canadian Comic Poetry, 1981; Writing Right: Poetry by Canadian Women, 1982; Three Times Five: Short Stories by Harris, Sawai, Stenson, 1983; Selected and New Poems by Richard Sommer, The Harbingers, Visible Visions: The Selected Poems of Douglas Barbour, 1984; Tesseracts II, 1987; Story for a Saskatchewan Night, 1990. *Address:* 11655-72 Avenue, Edmonton, Alberta Canada T6G 0B9.

BARCLAY Tessa. *See:* **BOWDEN Jean.**

BARCUCHELLO Gianfranco, b. 29 Aug 1924, Livorno. *Publications:* Numerous Publications from

1966-92 inc, Dall'archivio dei Cinque Cuori; Al Polo Nord, rotolando. *Creative Works:* 13 Film & Videos inc, Punto di Fuga; Cinque esercizi di Mesia Difficolta; Numeous One Man Exhibitions, 1963-92. *Address:* 18 Rue Linne, Paris, France.

BARDEN Thomas E, b. 5 Aug 1946, Richmond, Virginia, USA. Professor of English and Folklore. m. Rayna C Zacharias, 21 June 1981, 3 sons. *Education:* BA 1968, MA 1971, PhD 1975, University of Virginia. *Appointments:* Assistant, Associate, and now Full Professor of English and Folklore, University of Toledo, Ohio; Director, Programme in American Studies; President, Ohio Folklore Society, 1982. *Publications:* Weevils in the Wheat: Interviews with Virginia Ex-slaves, 1976; The Virginia WPA Folklore: An Index, 1979; The Travels of Peter Woodhouse, 1981; Virginia Folk Legends, 1991. *Contributions to:* Wisconsin Academy Review; Virginia Cavalcade; Heartland Journal; Contemporary Legend; Artemis; FFV. *Honours:* Virginia Foundation for the Humanities Fellow, 1990; Faculty Research Excellence Award, University of Toledo, 1992; Awarded, J William Fulbright Fellowship to lecture at University College, Swansea, Wales, 1993-94. *Memberships:* American Folklore Society; Ohio Folklore Society, Vice President 1981, President 1982; American Studies Association. *Literary Agent:* Craig Holden, Weber & Sobel Inc, New York. *Address:* 2841 Kenwood Boulevard, Toledo, OH 43606, USA.

BARDIS Panos Demetrios, b. 24 Sept 1924, Arcadia, Greece. Editor; Author; Professor; Poet. m. Donna Jean Decker, 26 Dec 1964, 2 sons. *Education:* Diploma, Lyceum, Langadia, Arcadia, 1942; Panteios Supreme School, Athens, 1945-47; BA magna cum laude, Bethany College, West Virginia, USA, 1950; MA, Notre Dame University, Indiana, 1953; PhD, Purdue University, Indiana, 1955. *Appointments include:* Currently Professor of Sociology, University of Toledo, Ohio; Editor, Book Review Editor, International Social Science Review; Editor-in-Chief, Book Review Editor, International Journal on World Peace; Associate Editor or Book Review Editor, about 40 other journals. *Publications:* Ivan and Artemis, novel, 1957; The Family in Changing Civilizations, 1967, 1969; Encyclopedia of Campus Unrest, 1971; History of the Family, 1975; Studies in Marriage and the Family, 1975, 1978; The Future of the Greek Language in the United States, 1976; The Family in Asia (edited with Man Das), 1978; History of Thanatology, 1981; Atlas of Human Reproductive Anatomy, 1983; Evolution of the Family in the West, 1983; Global Marriage and Family Customs, 1983; Dictionary of Quotations in Sociology, 1985; Marriage and Family, 1988; South Africa and the Marxist Movement, 1989; Poetry anthologies: Poetry Americas (co-editor), 1982; Nine Oriental Muses, 1983; A Cosmic Whirl of Melodies, 1985; First English translation of Archimedes's lost work On Balances, definitive study of Epidaurus, The Theatre of Epidaurus and the Mysterious Vanishing Vases. *Contributions to:* Hundreds of articles, reviews, poems in academic and professional journals, newspapers, magazines. *Honours:* Couphos Prize; Outstanding Alumnus, Bethany College, 1975; Outstanding Teacher, Toledo University, 1975; Composed more than 20 songs for the Mandolin; Poetic form, Pandebar; Poetry programme, The Silent Dr. X and Arcadian Echoes, in many countries; Numerous others. *Memberships include:* Alpha Kappa Delta; Fellow, American Association for the Advancement of Science; American Association of University Professors; International Sociological Association; Kappa Delta Pi; Life Member, Phi Kappa Phi; Pi Gamma Mu; Sigma Xi. *Address:* University of Toledo, Toledo, OH 43606, USA.

BARDONI Avril Ross Helen Mandeville, b. 9 Apr 1936, Merton, London. Translator. m. Giuliano Bardoni, 2 May 1958, 2 sons, 1 daughter. *Education:* BA, Reading University, 1957. *Appointments:* Translator, Vocal Editor, Decca Record Co, 1976-84. *Publications:* Sciascia: The Wine Dark Sea; Ginzburg: Valentino and Sagittarius; Luciano De Crescenzo; Anonymous: A Man of Respect. *Honours:* John Florio Prize. *Memberships:*

Translators Association; Society of Authors. *Address:* 16 Forest Gardens, Lyndhurst, Hants, SO43 7AF, England.

BAREHAM Terence, b. 17 Oct 1937, Clacton-on-Sea, Essex, England. University Professor. *Education:* Open Scholar & State Scholar 1959-62, BA (Hons) 1962, MA 1969, Lincoln College, Oxford University, England; DPhil, Ulster University, Northern Ireland, 1977. *Publications:* George Crabbe: A Critical Study, 1977; George Crabbe: A Bibliography (joint author), 1978; The Art of Anthony Trollope, 1980; Anthony Trollope (Casebook Series), 1982; Tom Stoppard (Casebook Series), 1989; Malcolm Lowry, 1989; Charles Lever: New Evaluations (ed), 1991; York Notes, Monographs on Robert Bolt, T S Eliot, Shakespeare. *Contributions to:* Numerous on literature of 17th - 20th Century. *Address:* c/o Dept of English, University of Ulster, Coleraine, Co Derry, Northern Ireland.

BARISH Evelyn, (Evelyn Barish Greenberger), b. 1 Nov 1935, USA. Writer; College Professor. m. Daniel Greenberger, 1969, div 1980. *Education:* AB magna cum laude English Hons 1956, Bryn Mawr College; MA 1960, New York University; Fulbright and AAUW Fellow, Oxford University, Linacre House 1962-64; PhD English 1966, New York University. *Publications:* Arthur Hugh Clough: Growth of a Poet's Mind, as Evelyn Barish Greenberger, 1970; Emerson: The Roots of Prophecy, 1989; Emerson in Italy, photographs by Evelyn Hofer, 1989. *Contributions to:* Numerous articles on above subjects. *Honours:* Christian Gauss Award of 1990 of Phi Beta Kappa for Best Work of Scholarship or Literary Criticism for Emerson: The Roots of Prophecy; awards from National Endowment for the Humanities, National Humanities Center, et al. *Memberships include:* PEN; Modern Language Association, American Studies Association; NOW, CWC. *Literary Agent:* Jauklow & Nesbit Associates, New York. *Address:* City University of New York, Graduate Center and College of Staten Island, Department of English, Staten Island, New York 10301, USA.

BARISH Jonas Alexander, 22 Mar 1922, New York City, USA. Teacher; Critic of Literature. m. Mildred Seaquist, 26 July 1964, 2 daughters. *Education:* AB 1942, MA 1947, PhD 1953, Harvard University. *Appointments:* Instructor in English, Yale, 1953-54; Assistant Professor of English 1954-60, Associate Professor 1960-66, Professor 1966-, Professor Emeritus, 1991-, University of California, Berkeley. *Publications:* Ben Jonson and the Language of Prose Comedy, 1960; The Antitheatrical Prejudice, 1981; (both critical studies). *Contributions to:* Essays on Renaissance English drama and other drama in various scholarly journals (e.g. PMLA, SEL, UTQ, EIC, MP, NLH, etc). *Honours:* Fulbright Research Fellowship, 1952-53, 1961-62; ACLS Fellowship 1961-62; NEH Fellowship 1973-74, 1986-87. *Memberships:* American Academy of Arts and Science, 1973; Shakespeare Association of America (President 1984-85, Trustee 1982-87). *Address:* Department of English, University of California, Berkeley, CA 94720, USA.

BARKER A(udrey) L(ilian), b. 13 Apr 1918, Kent, England. Author. *Education:* Secondary Schools, Kent and Surrey. *Appointments:* Staff, Amalgamated Press, 1936; Reader, Cresset Press, 1947; Secretary, sub-editor, BBC, London, 1949-78. *Publications:* Innocents, 1947; The Middling, 1967; John Brown's Body, shortlisted Booker Prize, 1969; Life Stories, 1981; No Word of Love, 1985; The Gooseboy, 1987; The Woman Who Talked to Herself, 1989. *Contributions to:* Short Story anthologies: Twelve Stories by Famous Women Writers; Tales to Make the Flesh Creep; Magazines including Harper's, US; Good Housekeeping; Botteghe Oscure; Woman and Beauty; etc. *Honours:* Atlantic Award in Literature, 1946; Somerset Maugham Award, 1947; Cheltenham Festival Award, 1963; Arts Council Award, 1970; SE Arts Creative Book Award, 1981. *Memberships:* Fellow, Royal Society of Literature; Executive Committee, 1981-85, English PEN. *Literary*

Agent: Jennifer Kavanagh. *Address:* 103 Harrow Road, Carshalton, Surrey, England.

BARKER Dennis, b. 21 June 1929, Lowestoft, England. Journalist; Novelist. m. Sarah Katherine Alwyn, 1 daughter. *Education:* National Diploma in Journalism, 1959. *Appointments:* Reporter and Sub-Editor, Suffolk Chronicle and Mercury, Ipswich 1947-48; Reporter, Feature Writer, Theatre and Film Critic, 1948-58, East Anglian Daily Times; Estates and Property Editor, Feature Writer, Radio and Theatre Critic and Columnist, 1958-63, Express and Star, Wolverhampton; Midlands Correspondent, 1963-67, Reporter, Feature Writer, Columnist, The Guardian, 1967-1991. *Publications:* Novels: Candidate of Promise, 1969; The Scandalisers, 1974; Winston Three Three Three, 1987; Non-fiction: The People of the Forces Trilogy (Soldiering On 1971, Ruling the Waves 1986, Guarding the Skies 1989); One Man's Estate, 1983; Parian Ware, 1985; Fresh Start, 1990. *Contributor to:* BBC; Punch; East Anglian Architecture and Building Review (editor and editorial director, 1956-58); The Guardian, 1991-. *Memberships:* National Union of Journalists, secretary Suffolk Branch 1953-58, Chairman 1958; chairman Home Counties District Council 1956-57; Life member, 1991; Life member, Newspaper Press Fund; Writers' Guild of Great Britain; Broadcasting Press Guild; The Society of Authors. *Address:* 67 Speldhurst Road, London, W4 1BY, England.

BARKER Elspeth, b. 16 Nov 1940, Edinburgh, Scotland. Writer. m. George Barker, 29 July 1989, 3 sons, 2 daughters. *Education:* Drumtochty Castle School, 1947-53; St Leonards School, Scotland, 1953-57; Somerville College, Oxford, 1958-61. *Publications:* O Caledonia. *Contributions to:* Sunday Independent; London Review of Books, Cosmopolitan; Articles in Guardian; Observer; Harpers & Queen. *Honours:* David Higham Prize; Angel Fiction Prize; Scottish Spring Book Award; Royal Society of Literature Winifred Holtby Prize; Shortlisted, Whitebread 1st Novel Prize. *Memberships:* PEN. *Literary Agent:* Bill Hamilton. *Address:* Bintry House, Itteringham, Aylsham, Norwich, Norfolk NR11 7AT, England.

BARKER Howard, b. 1946, British. *Appointment:* Resident Dramatist, Open Space Theatre, London, 1974-75. *Publications:* Stripwell, with Claw, 1977; Fair Slaughter, 1978; That Good Between Us with Credentials of a Sympathiser, The Love of a Good Man with All Bleeding, 1980; The Hang of the Gaol with Heaven, Two Plays for the Right: Birth on a Hard Shoulder and the Loud Boy's Life, No End of Blame: Scenes of Overcoming, 1981; The Castle/Scenes from an Execution, Victory, 1984; Crimes in Hot Countries/ Fair Slaughter, The Power of the Dog: Movements in History and Anti- History, A Passion in Six Days/ Downchild, 1985; Don't Exaggerate, 1986; The Possibilities, 1987; The Bite of the Night, 1987; The Last Supper, 1988; Women Beware Women, 1988; Seven Lears/Golgo, 1989; The Europeans/Judith, 1990; Collected Plays, Volume I, 1990; Poems - The Breath of the Crowd, 1987; Garry the Thief, 1988; Lullabies for the Impatient, 1988; The Ascent of Monte Grappa, 1990. *Address:* Judy Daish Ass., 83 Eastbourne Mews, Brighton, Sussex, England.

BARKER Keith George, b. 16 June 1947, Wolverhampton, England. Librarian. m. Elizabeth Anthony, 28 Dec 1968, dec 1990, 2 daughters. *Education:* Associate of Library Association, 1968; BA, 1982; Master of Librarianship, 1985. *Appointments:* Editor, Youth Library Review, 1988; Review Editor, School Librarian, 1989. *Publications:* In The Realms of Gold; Bridging The Gap; Information Book for Children; Dick King Smith. *Contributions to:* Numerous Articles on Childrens Literature. *Memberships:* Childrens Book Foundation; Library Association; Publications Officer, Youth Libraries Group. *Address:* 249 Franklin Road, Kings Norton, Birmingham B30 2EH, England.

BARKER Patricia Margaret, b. 8 May 1943, Thornaby-on-Tees, England. Writer. m. 29 Jan 1977, 1 son, 1 daughter. *Education:* BSc, Economics, London School of Economics, 1965. *Publications:* Union Street, 1982; Blow Your House Down, 1984; The Century's Daughter, 1986; The Man Who Wasn't There, 1989; Regeneration, 1991; The Eye in the Door, 1993. *Honours:* One of Best of Young British Novelists, 1982; Joint Winner, Fawcett Prize, 1982; Hon.M.Litt, University Teesside, 1993. *Memberships:* Society of Authors; PEN. *Literary Agent:* Curtis Brown, England. *Address:* c/o Curtis Brown, 162-168 Regent Street, London W1R 5TB, England.

BARKER Paul, b. 24 Aug 1935, Halifax, Yorkshire, England. Writer; Broadcaster. m. Sally Huddleston, 3 sons, 1 daughter. *Education:* MA, Oxford University. *Appointments include:* Editor, New Society, 1968-86; Associate Editor, The Independent Magazine, 1988-90, Director and advisory editor, Fiction Magazine, 1982-87; Social policy editor, Sunday Telegraph, 1986-88; Visiting Fellow, University of Bath, 1986-; Trustee, 1991-, Fellow, 1992-, Institute of Community Studies; Fellow, Royal Society of Arts (FRSA), 1990; Leverhulme Reserch Fellow, 1993-; Columnist, London Evening Standard, 1987-92. *Publications include:* Editor, A Sociological Portrait, 1972; Editor, contributor, One for Sorrow, Two for Joy, 1972; Editor, Social Sciences Today, 1975; Editor, contributor, Arts in Society, 1977; Editor, contributor, The Other Britain, 1982; Editor, Founders of the Welfare State, 1985; Contributor, Britain in the Eighties, 1989. *Address:* 15 Dartmouth Park Avenue, London NW5 1JL, England.

BARKHOUSE Joyce Carman, b. 3 May 1913, Nova Scotia, Canada. Teacher; Author. m. Milton Joseph, 16 Sept. 1942, 1 son, 1 daughter. *Publications:* George Dawson, The Little Giant, 1974; Abraham Geisner, 1980; Anna's Pet, with Margaret Atwood, 1980; The Witch of Port Lajoye (award), 1983; The Lorenzen Collection, 1986; A Name for Himself, biography of Thomas Head Raddall, 1986. *Contributions:* Travel articles, New York Times; Regular column, For Mothers & Others, Nova Scotia weeklies. *Honours:* Award, Cultural Federation of Nova Scotia, 1982; Notable Canadian children's book listing, National Library, Ottawa, 1985. *Memberships:* Former Atlantic representative, Writers Union of Canada; Canadian Society of Children's Authors, Illustrators & Performers; Council, executive, Writers Federation of Nova Scotia; International Board for Books for Young People. *Address:* 719-1472 Tower Road, Halifax, Nova Scotia, Canada B3H 4K8.

BARKS Coleman Bryan, b. 1937, American. Professor. *Appointments:* Instructor of English, University of Southern California, Los Angeles, 1965-67; Assistant Professor 1967-72, Associate Professor of English 1972-, University of Georgia, Athens. *Publications:* The Juice, 1972; New Words, 1976; We're Laughing at the Damage, 1977; Night and Sleep, Versions of Rumi (trans with Robert Bly), 1981; Open Secret, by Rumi (trans with John Moyne), 1984; Unseen Rain, by Rumi (trans with J Moyne), 1986; We Are Three, by Rumi (trans with J Moyne), 1987; These Branching Moments, by Rumi (trans with J Moyne), 1988; This Longing, by Rumi (trans with J Moyne), 1988; Delicious Laughter, by Rumi (trans with J Moyne), 1990; Like This, by Rumi (trans with J Moyne), 1990; Feeling the Shoulder of the Lion, by Rumi (trans with R Nicholson), 1991; One-Handed Basket Weaving, by Rumi (trans with R Nicholson), 1991. *Address:* 196 Westview Drive, Athens, GA 30606, USA.

BARLOW Frank, b. 19 Apr 1911, Wolstanton, England. Emeritus Professor of History. m. Moira Stella Brigid Garvey, 1 July 1936, 2 sons. *Education:* MA, D.Phil., Hon D.Litt., Exon.; St John's College, Oxford, 1929-36. *Publications:* The Feudal Kingdom of England, 1955; Edward the Confessor, 1970; William Rufus, 1983; Thomas Becket, 1986; The English Church, 1000-1066, 1963, 1066-1154, 1979; The Letters of Arnulf of Lisieux, Editor, 1939; Durham Annals and Documents of the Thirteenth Century, Editor, 1945; Durham

Jurisdictional Peculiars, 1950; Vita Aedwardi Regis, Editor, Translator, 1962; The Norman Conquest and Beyond, 1983; William I and the Norman Conquest, 1965; Thomas Beckett, 1986; Introduction to Devonshire Domesday Book, 1991. *Contributions to:* various professional journals. *Honours:* D.Litt., 1981; CBE 1989. *Memberships:* Fellow, British Academy; Fellow, Royal Society of Literature; Fellow, Royal Historical Society. *Address:* Middle Court Hall, Kenton, Exeter, EX6 8NA, England.

BARLTROP Robert Arthur Horace, b. 6 Nov 1922, Walthamstow, England, Writer. m. Mary Gleeson, 18 July 1947, 3 sons. *Appointments:* Editor, Socialist Standard, 1972-78; Editor, Cockney Ancestor, 1983-86. *Publications:* The Monument, 1974; Jack London: The Man, the Writer, the Rebel, 1977; The Muvver Tongue, 1980; My Mother's Calling Me, 1984; A Funny Age, 1985; Bright Summer, Dark Autumn, 1986; The Bar Tree, 1979; Revolution - Stories and Essays by Jack London, (Editor), 1981. *Contributor To:* Weekly columns and features, Recorder Newspapers, 1985-; Guardian Newspapers; Root; Essex Countryside. *Membership:* National Union of Journalists. *Address:* 77 Idmiston Road, Stratford, London E15 1RG, England.

BARMANN Lawrence (Francis), b. 1932, American. Professor. *Appointments:* Assistant Professor 1970-73, Associate Professor 1973-78, Professor of History 1978-, Director of American Studies 1983-, St Louis University. *Publications:* Newman at St Mary's, 1962; Newman on God and Self, 1965; Baron Friedrick von Hugel and the Modernist Crisis in England, 1972; The Letters of Baron Friedrich von Hugel and Professor Norman Kemp Smith, 1981.

BARNABY Charles Frank, b. 27 Sept 1927, Andover, Hampshire, UK. Author. m. 12 Dec 1972, 1 son, 1 daughter. *Education:* BSc 1951, MSc 1954, PhD 1960, London University. *Publications:* Man & the Atom, 1970; Nuclear Energy, 1975; Future Warfare, 1983; Prospects for Peace, 1981; The Automated Battlefield, 1986; Star Wars Brought Down to Earth, 1986; The Invisible Bomb, 1989; Tha Gaia Peace Atlas, 1989; The Role and Control of Arms in the 1990's, 1993. *Contributions to:* Ambio; New Scientist; Technology Review. *Honour:* Honorary doctorate, Free University, Amsterdam, Netherlands. *Literary Agent:* June Hall. *Address:* Brandreth, Station Road, Chilbolton, Stockbridge, Hampshire SO20 6HW, England.

BARNARD Christaan (Neething), b. 1922, South African. Professor. *Appointments:* Professor Emeritus, University of Cape Town, Head of Cardiac Research and Surgery, 1968-83; Developed the Barnard Valve used in open heart surgery; Performed first successful heart transplant, 1967; First double heart transplant, 1974. *Publications:* Surgery of the Common Congenital Cardiac Malformations, (C N Barnard and VV Schrire), 1968; One Life, (C N Barnard and Bill Pepper), 1970; Heart Attack - All You Have to Know About It, 1971; The Unwanted, (C N Barnard and S Stander), 1974; South Africa - Sharp Dissertion, 1977; In the Night Season, (C N Barnard and S Stander), 1977; The Best Medicine; 1979; Good Life-Good Death, 1980; The Body Machine, 1981; The Junior Body Machine, (with Christopher Fagg), 1983; The Living Body (with Karl Sabbagh), 1984; Christian Barnard's Programme for Living with Arthritis, (with Peter Evans), 1984; The Arthritis Handbook, 1984; The Living Body, (with Karl Sabbagh), 1984; The Faith, (with S Stander), 1984; The Best of Barnard, (with Bob Mooloy), 1984; Your Healthy Heart, (with Peter Evans), 1985. *Address:* PO Box 6143, Welgemoed, 7538 Cape Town, South Africa.

BARNARD Robert, b. 23 Nov 1936, Burnham-on-Crouch, Essex, England. Crime Writer. m. Mary Louise Tabor, 7 Feb 1963. *Education:* Balliol College, Oxford, 1956-59; Dr Philos, Bergen University, Norway, 1972. *Publications include:* Death Of An Old Goat, 1976; Sheer Torture, 1981; A Corpse In A Gilded Cage, 1984; Out of the Blackout, 1985; Skeleton In The Grass, 1987;

At Death's Door, 1988; Death and the Chaste Apprentice, 1989. *Honours:* Seven times nominated for Edgar Awards in USA. *Memberships:* Crime Writer's Association (Committee Member 1988-91); Bronte Society; Society of Authors. *Literary Agent:* Peters, Fraser and Dunlop. *Address:* Hazeldene, Houghley Lane, Leeds LS13 2DT, England.

BARNES Christopher John, b. 10 Mar 1942, Sheffield, England. University Professor. m. Alexa H Dey, 26 July 1975, 2 daughters. *Education:* Cambridge University, 1960-67; Moscow University, 1963-64; MA, 1967; PhD, 1970. *Appointments:* Lecturer, University of St Andrews, Scotland, 1967-89; Editor, Radio Liberty, 1974-75; Professor, Chairman, University of Toronto, 1989-. *Publications:* Boris Pasternak: A Literary Biography; Boris Pasternak: The Voice of Prose; Boris Pasternak: Complete Short Prose; Studies in Twentieth Century Literature; Others inc. The Blind Beauty; Pasternak & European Literature. *Contributions to:* Encounter; Scottish Slavonic Review; Irish Slavonic Studies; TLS; Slavica Hierosolymitana; La Pensee Russe; Forum for Modern Language Studies; Performance; Tempo. *Memberships:* British University Association of Slavists; Canadian Association of Slavists; American Association for Advancement of Slavic Studies; Royal Musical Association. *Address:* Dept of Slavic Languages & Literatures, University of Toronto, 21 Sussex Avenue, Toronto, Canada M5S 1A1.

BARNES Clive Alexander, b. 13 May 1927, London, England. Journalist; Dance & Theatre Critic. m., 2 children. *Education:* King's College, London; Oxford University. *Appointments include:* Town planning officer/freelance journalist, 1952-61; Chief dance critic, The Times, London, 1961-65; Executive editor, Dance & Dancers, Music & Musicians, Plays & Players, 1961-65; Dance critic, New York Times, 1965-78, also drama critic (weekdays) 1967-77; Associate editor, chief dance & drama critic, New York Post, 1978-; New York correspondent, Times (London), 1970. *Publications:* Ballet in Britain Since the War; Frederick Ashton & His Ballet; Ballet Here & Now; Dance As it Happened; Dance in the 20th Century; Dance Scene USA; Editor, Nureyev, 1983. *Honour:* CBE, 1975. *Address:* 825 West End Avenue, New York, NY 10025, USA.

BARNES Douglas, b. 1 July 1927, Twickenham, UK. Former Reader in Education, University of Leeds. m. Dorothy Raistrick, 30 Dec 1954, 1 son, 1 daughter. *Education:* MA, English Tripos, 1948, Certificate in Education 1949, Downing College, Cambridge University. *Publications:* Language, The Learner & The School, co-author, 1969, 4th edition 1990; From Communication to Curriculum, 1976, 2nd edition, 1992; Versions of English, co-author, 1984; Practical Curriculum Study, 1982; Communication & Learning in Small Groups, co-author, 1977; School Writing: Discovering the Ground Rules, Co-author, 1990. Numerous articles on topics in 'language & learning' curriculum interests. *Contributions To:* Various professional journals. *Honour:* Order of British Empire, 1983. *Address:* 4 Harrowby Road, Leeds, LS16 5HN, England.

BARNES Jane Ellen, b. 29 Dec 1943, Brooklyn, New York, USA. Poet; Fiction Writer. *Education:* BA, Georgia State University, 1966; MA, Boston University, 1978. *Appointments:* Board, Boston First Night Celebration, 1981; Boston Artists Collaborative, 1987. *Publications:* Blue Giant Mythologies, 1976; They Say I Talk in My Sleep, 1979; Extremes, 1981; Founder, Publisher, Dark Horse, 1974-80; Founder, Quark Pres, and Blue Giant Press. *Contributor to:* Harvard Magazine; Hanging Loose; Ploughshares; Dark Horse; 13th Moon; Poetry Now; etc. *Honours:* Honourable Mention, Fiction, Brace Prize, Boston University, 1978. *Memberships:* Co-ordinating Council, Literary Magazines; New England Small Press Association. *Address:* 24 Concord Avenue, Apt. 308, Cambridge, MA 02138, USA.

BARNES Julian Patrick, (Dan Kavanagh, Basil

Seal), b. 1946, British. *Appointments:* Lexicographer, Oxford English Dictionary Supplement, 1969-72; TV Critic 1977-81, Assistant Literary Editor 1977-79, New Statesman; Contributing Editor, New Review, 1977-78; Deputy Literary Editor, Sunday Times, 1979-81; TV Critic, The Observer, 1982-86. *Publications:* Metroland, Duffy (as D Kavanagh), 1980; Before She Met Me, 1982; Fiddle City (as D Kavanagh), 1983; Flaubert's Parrot, 1984; Putting The Boot In (as D Kavanagh), 1985; Staring at the Sun, 1986; A History of the World in Ten and a Half Chapters, 1989. *Address:* The Chambers, Chelsea Harbour, Lots Road, London SW10 0XF, England.

BARNES Peter, b. 10 Jan 1931, London, England. Writer. m. 28 Aug 1963. *Publications:* Collected Plays (Vol 1) 1989; The Ruling Class, 1969; Red Noses, 1985; Nobody Here But Us Chickens, 1990; The Spirit of Man, 1990; Sunsets and Glories, 1990. *Honours:* John Whiting Award, 1969; Evening Standard Award, 1969; Giles Cooper Award, 1981; Olivier Award, 1985; Royal Television Award, 1989. *Literary Agent:* Margaret Ramsay Ltd. *Address:* 7 Archery Close, Connaught Street, London W2, England.

BARNETT Arthur Doak, b. 1921, American. Professor. *Appointments:* Fellow, Institute of Current World Affairs in China and Southeast Asia, 1947-50, 1952-53; Correspondent, Chicago Daily News Foreign Service in China and Southeast Asia, 1947-50, 1952-53, 1953-55; Associate, American Universities Field Staff, Hong Kong and other Asian Areas, 1953-55; Program Associate, International Training and Research Program, The Ford Foundation, NYC and Asia, 1959-61; Associate Professor 1960-64, Professor 1964-69, Head of Contemporary China Program, 1960-69; Columbia University; Senior Fellow, The Brookings Institution, 1969-82, Emeritus, 1982; Professor, Johns Hopkins University School of Advanced International Studies, 1982-90, Emeritus, 1990. *Publications:* Turn East Towards Asia, 1958; Communist Economic Strategy: The Rise of Mainland China, 1959; Communist China and Asia: Challenge to American Policy, 1960; Communist China in Perspective, 1962; Communist Strategies in Asia: A Comparative Analysis of Governments and Parties, China on the Eve of Communist Takeover, 1963; Communist China: The Early Years 1959-1955, 1964; The United States and China in World Affairs, by Robert Blum (ed), 1966; China After Mao, Cadres Bureaucracy and Political Power in Communist China, 1967; Chinese Communist Politics in Action (ed), 1969; The United States and China: The Next Decade (ed with E O Reischauer), 1970; A New United States Policy Toward China, 1971; Uncertain Passage: China's Transition to the Post-Mao Era, 1974; China Policy: Old Problems and New Challenges, China and the Major Powers in East Asia, 1977; China's Economy in Global Perspective, The FX Decision, 1981; US Arms Sales: The China-Taiwan Tangle, 1982; The Making of Foreign Policy in China: Structure and Process, 1985; Modernizing China: Post-Mao Reform and Development (ed with Ralph N Clough), 1986; After Deng, What? Will China Follow the USSR?, 1991. *Address:* Johns Hopkins University, SAIS, 1740, Massachusetts Avenue, NW, Washington, DC 20036, USA.

BARNETT Correlli (Douglas), b. 1927, British. Author. Fellow of the Royal Society of Literature and the Royal Historical Society. *Appointments:* Keeper of the Churchill Archives Centre and Fellow, Churchill College, 1977-; Defence Lecturer, Cambridge University, 1980-84. *Publications:* The Hump Organisation, 1957; The Channel Tunnel (co-author), 1958; The Desert Generals, 1960, (new enlarged edition 1984); The Swordbearers, 1963; The Great War (co-author), 1964; The Lost Peace (co-author), 1966; Britain and Her Army, 1970; The Collapse of British Power, 1972; The Commanders, 1973; Marlborough, 1974; Strategy and Society, 1975; Bonaparte, 1978; The Great War, 1979; The Audit of War, 1986; Engage the Enemy More Closely: The Royal Navy in the Second World War, 1991. *Honours:* Best Television Documentary Script

Award, Screenwriter's Guild, for The Great War; Royal Society of Literature Award for Britain and Her Army; Chesney Gold Medal of the Royal United Services Institute for Defence Studies, 1991; Yorkshire Post Book of the Year Award for Engage the Enemy More Closely, 1991. *Address:* Catbridge House, East Carleton, Norwich NR14 8JX, England.

BARNETT Paul. *See:* BARNETT Paul le Page.

BARNETT Paul le Page, (Paul Barnett, Dennis Brezhnev, Eve Devereux, John Grant), b. 22 Nov 1949, Aberdeen, Scotland. Writer; Freelance Editor. m. Catherine Stewart, 7 July 1974, 1 daughter. *Education:* Kings & University Colleges, London (no degree), 1967-68. *Publications include:* As John Grant: Ed, Aries 1, 1979; Ed, Book of Time, with Colin Wilson, 1980; Directory of Discarded Ideas, 1981; Directory of Possibilities, with Colin Wilson, 1981; A Book of Numbers, 1982; Dreamers, 1983; Truth About the Flaming Ghoulies, 1983; Sex Secrets of Ancient Atlantis, 1985; Depths of Cricket, 1986; Encyclopeadia of Walt Disney's Animated Characters, 1987 (2nd edition 1993); Earthdoom, with David Langford, 1987; The Advanced Trivia Quizbook, 1987; Great Mysteries, 1988; Introduction to Viking Mythology, 1989; Great Unsolved Mysteries of Science, 1989; Eclipse of the Kai, with Joe Dever, 1989; Dark Door Opens, with Joe Dever, 1989; Sword of the Sun, with Joe Dever, 1989; Hunting Wolf, wtih Joe Dever, 1990; Albion, 1991; Unexplained Mysteries of the World, 1991; Claws of Helgedad, with Joe Dever, 1991; Sacrifice of Ruanon, with Joe Dever, 1991; The World, 1992; Monsters, 1992; Birthplace, with Joe Dever, 1992; Book of the Magnakai, with joe Dever, 1992; Legends of Lone Wolf Omnibus, with Joe Dever, 1992; Tellings, with Joe Dever, 1993; Lorestone of Varetta, with Joe Dever, 1993; Technical Editor, Encylopeadia of Science Ficiton, by John Clute and Peter Nicholls, 1993; As Eve Devereux: Book of World Flags, 1992. *Membership:* West Country Writers' Association; *Literary Agent:* Jane C Judd. *Address:* 17 Polsloe Road, Exeter, Devon EX1 2HL, England.

BARNETT Peter Leonard, b. 21 July 1930, Albany, Western Australia. Journalist; Broadcster. m. Siti Nuraini Jatim, 1970, 1 son. *Education:* University of Western Australia. *Appointments include:* Canberra representative, columnist, The Western Australian, 1953-57; Southeast Asia correspondent 1961, 1963, 1964, Jakarta representative 1962, New York & UN correspondent 1964-67, Washington correspondent 1967-70, Australian Broadcasting Commission; News editor, Melbourne 1971-72, Washington correspondent 1972-80, Controller, Melbourne 1980-84, Director 1984-, Radio Australia, Executive Director, Australian Broadcasting Corporation, 1984-. *Address:* 63 Lum Road, Wheelers Hill, Melbourne 3150, Australia.

BARNETT Ursula A, b. 25 Apr 1924, Maribor, Yugoslavia. Writer; Literary Agent. m. Hyman Barnett, 18 July 1956, 2 sons, 2 daughters. *Education:* Bach of Arts, 1944; Master of Arts, 1945; Master of Science, 1948; PhD, 1971. *Publications:* Ezekiel Mphahlele, 1977; Vision of Order: a survery of black South African Literature in English, 1984. *Contributions to:* Reviews Book Abroad; Contrast; Matato; World Literature Writer in English; Dictionary of Literary Biographies. *Memberships:* Society of Women Writers and Journalists; Women in Publishing. *Literary Agent:* Shelley Power. *Address:* 19 Avenue South, Surbiton, Surrey KT5 8PJ, England.

BARNHART Michael A, b. 8 June 1951, Hanover, Pennsylvania, USA. Historian. m. Janet G Barnhart, 30 Apr 1978, 1 son. *Education:* BS, Northwestern University, 1974; AM, Harvard University, 1974; PhD, 1980. *Appointments:* Editor, The Journal of Americn East Asia Relations, 1991-. *Publications:* Japan Prepares for Total War; Congress and US Foreign Polices. *Memberships:* Society for Historians of American Foreign Relations; Organization of American

Historians; Association for Asian Studies. *Address:* Dept of History, Suny, Stony Brook, NY 11794, USA.

BARNHART Robert K, b. 17 Oct 1933, Chicago, Illinois, USA. Author; Editor. m. Cynthia Ann Rogers, 16 Sept 1955, 3 sons, 2 daughters. *Education:* University of the South, BA, 1956. *Publications:* World Book Dictionary; Barnhart Dictionary of Etymology; Barnhart Dictionaries of New English; American Heritage Dictionary of Science. *Contributions to:* Dictionary; World Book Ency; International Encylopedia of Lexicography. *Honour:* Association of Publishers Award. *Memberships:* MLA Dict Society of N America Dialect Society. *Address:* Baanhart Books, Box 479, Brewster, NY 10509, USA.

BARNWELL William (Curtis), b. 1943, American. Professor; Writer. *Appointments:* Assistant Professor of English, University of South Carolina, Columbia, 1971-77; Writer-in-Residence, Columbia College, 1977-. *Publications:* The Blessing Papers, 1980; Imram, 1981; Writing for a Reason, 1983. *Address:* c/o Curtis Brown Limited, 575 Madison Avenue, New York, NY 10022, USA.

BARNWRIGHT Julia. *See:* **BANCROFT Iris.**

BAROLINI Teodolina, b. 19 Dec 1951, Syracuse , NY, USA. Professor. m. Douglas Caverly, 21 June 1980, 1 son. *Education:* Sarah Lawrence College, BA, 1972; Columbia University, MA, 1973; PhD, 1978. *Appointments:* Assistant Professor, University of California, Berkeley, 1978-83; Associate Professor, Professor, New York University, 1983-92; Professor, Columbia University, 1992-. *Publications:* Dante's Poets; The Undivine Comedy. *Contributions to:* PMLA; Modern Language Notes; Dante Studies; Romance Philology. *Honours:* John Nicholas Brown Prize; Howard R Marraro Prize. *Memberships:* Dante Society of America; Medieval Academy of America; Renassance Society of America; American Association of Teachers; MLA; International Dante Seninar. *Address:* Dept of Italian, Columbia University, New York, NY 10027, USA.

BARON Alec, b. Leeds, Yorkshire, England. Writer; Playwright. m. Judith Edelson, 21 Aug 1951, 1 son, 3 daughters. *Appointments:* Lecturer, Theatre Studies, Creative Writing; Administrator, Leeds Playhouse, 1970-71. *Publications:* Stage Plays: Groucho at Large; Momma Gola; For You My Sons; The Third Alternative. Television: Company Come; Groucho in Toto, etc; Radio Plays: The Element of Doubt; The Trouble With Mother; Luxury Weekend; The Scrapheap, etc. Published works: The Big Cats; Chimera; Dress Rehearsal; Company Come; Asylum. *Contributor to:* Cambridge Guide to World Theatre, many short stories and articles. *Honour:* Winner, BBC/Radio Leeds Playwrighting Competition. *Memberships:* Writers Guild of Great Britain; Yorkshire Playwrights Society. *Literary Agent:* Michael Sharland. *Address:* 19 Park View Crescent, Leeds LS8 2ES, Yorkshire, England.

BARON J W. *See:* **KRAUZER Steven M.**

BARON Suze, b. 29 June 1942, Port-au-Prince, Haiti. Registered Nurse. m. James Murray, 5 Apr 1975, 1 son, 1 daughter. *Education:* RN 1965, Jewish Hospital & Medical Centre School of Nursing; BA 1971, Brooklyn College. *Publications:* The PS 269 Fivers, 1987; When Black People Pray, 1990. *Contributions to:* Calapooya Collage II; Z-Miscellaneous; Haiti-en-March; Poetry Halifax; Dartmouth; The Raven Chronicles; The New Press; Pegassus Review. *Memberships:* International Women's Writing Guild; Brooklyn College Alumni Association; Jewish Hospital and Medical Centre of Brooklyn Nurses Alumni; Pi Delta Phi. *Address:* 549E 34th Street, Brooklyn, NY 11203, USA.

BARR Andrew T, b. 9 Apr 1961, London, England. Journalist; Author. *Education:* St Pauls School, London,

1974-78; Magdalen College, Oxford, 1979-83. *Publications:* Wine Snobbery; Guide to Pinot Noir. *Honour:* Glenfiddich Trade Writer. *Literary Agent.* Andrew Lownie. *Address:* c/o Andrew Lownie, 122 Bedford Court Mansions, Bedford Square, London WC1B 3AH, England.

BARR Densil, b. Harrogate, Yorkshire, England. Author. *Publications:* The Man With Only One Head, (novel), 1955; Death of Four, Presidents, (novel), 1991; Radio Plays Broadcast; The Clapham Lamp-Post Saga, 1967, 1968, 1969, 1981, 1990; Gladys on the Wardrobe, 1970, 1971, 1972, 1983, 1990; But Petrovsky Goes on for Ever, 1971, 1972, 1973, 1975, 1985; The Last Tramp, 1972, 1973; The Square at Bastogne, 1973, 1974; The Battle of Brighton Beach, 1974; To a Green World Far Away, 1975, 1976, 1977; With Puffins for Pawns, 1976, 1979; Anatomy of an Alibi, 1978, 1982; The Speech, 1979; Two Gaps in the Curtain, 1979, 1982; Klemps Diary, 1980; Who Was Karl Raeder? 1980; The Boy in the Cellar, 1981; The Glory Hallelujah Microchip, 1982; The Dog that was only a Prophet, 1982, 1983; The Mythical Isles, 1983; St Paul Transferred, 1983. *Contributor to:* Transatlantic Review; International Storyteller; Kolokon. *Memberships:* Fellow PEN. *Address:* 15 Churchfields, Broxbourne, Hertfordshire, EN10 7JU, England.

BARR Patricia Miriam, b. 25 Apr 1934, Norwich, Norfolk, England. Writer. *Education:* BA, English Literature, University of Birmingham; MA, English, University College, London. *Major Publications:* The Coming of the Barbarians, 1967; The Deer Cry Pavilion, 1968; A Curious Life for a Lady, 1970; To China with Love, 1972; The Memsahibs, 1976; Taming the Jungle, 1978; Chinese Alice, 1981; Uncut Jade, 1983; Kenjiro, 1985; Coromandel, 1988; The Dust in the Balance, 1989. *Honour:* Winston Churchill Fellowship for Historical Biography, 1972. *Membership:* Society of Authors. *Literary Agent:* Murray Pollinger, 222 Old Brompton Road, London SW5 0B2, England. *Address:* 6 Mount Pleasant, Norwich NR2 2DG, England.

BARRETT Cathlene Gillespie, b. 14 Aug 1962, Utah, USA. Publisher; Editor. m. Kevin Barrett, 29 Aug 1981, 1 son, 1 daughter. *Education:* Continuing College Education. *Appointments:* Chairwomen, Utah State Poetry Society Contest, 1991, 1992; Publisher, Editor, Midge Literary Magazine, 1991-; Judge, Pennsylvania Poetry Society, 1991. *Publications:* American Poetry Anthology; Treasured Poems of America; Bay Area poets Coalition; Utah State Poetry Society Anthology; Fall, Spring, Winter. *Contributions to:* Poets at Work; Midge Magazine; Archer: Pro Poets of Satem; Review: Portland University. *Honours:* Golden poet Award; Honorable mention, Utah State Poetry Society, Poet of the year; 3rd Place, Sparrowgrass Annual Contest; Poet Lawveate Contender. *Memberships:* Utah State Poetry Society; Utah Cavy Breeders Association. *Address:* 2330 Tierra Rose Drive, West Jordan, UT 84084, USA.

BARRETT Charles Kingsley, b. 4 May 1917, Salford, England. Retired University Professor. m. Margaret E. Heap, 16 Aug 1944, 1 son, 1 daughter. *Education:* BA, 1938, MA, 1942, BD, 1948, DD, 1956, Cambridge University. *Publications:* The Holy Spirit and the Gospel Tradition, 1947; The Epistle to the Romans, 1957 (new edition, 1991); From First Adam to Last, 1962; The First Epistle to the Corinthians, 1968; The Signs of an Apostle, 1970; The Second Epistle to the Corinthians, 1973; The Gospel according to St John, 1978; Freedom and Obligation, 1985. *Contributions to:* numerous learned journals. *Honours:* Fellow, British Academy, 1961; Burkitt Medal for Biblical Studies, 1966; Honorary D.D. Hull University, 1970, Aberdeen University, 1972; D.Theol., Hamburg University, 1981. *Memberships:* Studiorum Novi Testamenti Societas, President, 1973-74; Society for Old Testament Study; Member, Royal Norweigian Society of Sciences and Letters, 1991. *Address:* 22 Rosemount, Pity Me, Durham, DH1 5GP, England.

BARRETT Judi, b. 1941, American. *Appointments:* Children's Book Reviewer, New York Times, 1974-; Part-time children's Art Teacher and Free-lance Designer. *Publications:* Old MacDonald had an Apartment House, 1969; Animals Should Definitely Not wear Clothing, 1970; An Apple a Day, 1973; Benjamin's 365 Birthdays, Peter's Pocket, 1974; I Hate to Take a Bath, 1975; I Hate to Go to Bed, The Wind Thief, 1977; Cloudy with a Chance of Meatballs, 1978; I'm Too Small You're Too Big, Animals Should Definitely Not Act Like People, 1981; What's Left, A Snake is Totally Tail, 1983; Pickles Have Pimples, 1986. *Address:* 230 Garfield Place, Brooklyn, NY 11215, USA.

BARRETT Susan, b. 24 June 1938, England. Writer. m. Peter Barrett, 18 June 1960, 1 son, 1 daughter. *Publications:* Jam Today, novel, 1969; Travels with a Wildlife Artist, natural history, 1986; The Beacon, novel, 1980; Stephen & Violet, novel, 1988; Private View, novel, 1972; Moses, novel, 1970; Noah's Ark, novel, 1971; Rubbish, novel, 1974. *Literary Agent:* Toby Eady. *Address:* c/o Toby Eady, 18 Park Walk, London SW10 0AQ, England.

BARRIE Douglas Mitchell, b, 21 Mar 1916, Lismore, New South Wales, Australia. Commercial Artist; Advertising Executive. m. Bess Bowen, 18 Jan 1941, 1 son, 1 daughter. *Education:* J S Watkins Art School, 1933-38; East Sydney Technical College, 1936-37; El'D Fellow Advertising Institute. *Appointments:* Contributor to, Australian Encyclopaedia, 1960; Australian Dictionary of Biographies, 1970. *Publications:* The Austrlian Bloodhorse; Turf Cavalcade; Valley of Champions; Australias Thoroughbred Idols; Notable Australian Thoroughbreds. *Contributions to:* Country Life; Turf Monthly; Australian Racing Journals; Australian Encylopaedia. *Honours:* Book of the Year; Fletcher Watson Scholarship. *Memberships:* Australian Society of Authors; Australian Jockey Blub; Tattersalls Club. *Address:* 34 Waterview Crescent, Laurieton, NSW 2443, Australia.

BARRINGTON Judith Mary, b. 7 July 1944, Brighton, England. Poet; Critic. *Education:* BA 1978; MA, 1980. *Appointments:* West Coast Editor, Motheroot Journal, 1985-86; Poet in the Schools, Oregon, 1986-87. *Publications:* Deviation, 1975; Trying to Be an Honest Woman, 1985; History and Geography, 1989; Why Children, co-author, 1980; An Intimate Wilderness (editor), 1991; Anthologies Work in: One Foot on the Mountain, 1979; Hard Feelings, 1982; Beautiful Barbarians, 1986; The World Between Women, 1987. *Contributor to:* Contemporary Literary Criticism; Northwest Magazine; San Francisco Chronicle; Ottawa Citizen; MS. Magazine. *Honours:* Fairlie Place Essay Prize, 1963; Jeanette Rankin Award for Feminist Journalism, 1983; Metropolitan Arts Commission Grant, 1985, 1987; Oregon Institute of Literary Arts Fellowship (Creative Nonfiction, 1989 and Poetry, 1992). *Memberships:* Poetry Society of America; National Writers' Union; National Book Critics Circle. *Address:* 622 SE 29th Avenue, Portland, OR 97214, USA.

BARROS Joseph De, b. 22 July 1921, Goa. Hitory Research; Writer. *Education:* MA, PhD, D Litt. *Appointments:* Professor, Principal, National Lyceum Goa; Doctoral Research techaer, Goa University; General Secretary, Institute Menezes, Braganza. *Publications:* Geography of Goa; History of Goa; Buddhism And World Peace; Francisco Luis Gomes-The Historian; Local Collaborators of Albuquereque, Luis de Camoes; Luis Goan Contribution to Banaglore; Perspectivas do Ensino do Portugues em Goa. *Contributions to:* The Navhind Times; Herald; Institute Menezea Braganza; Bulletin; R C acau; Gomantak Times. *Memberships:* Indian Academy of Science; Academia Portuguesa da Historia; Academia Canadense de Historia; Geographic Society Lisbon; Royal Asiatic Society of London; Indian History Congress New Delhi; World Academy of Arts & Culture; Institute Menezes Braganza. *Honours:* Translation of Dr Jose Pizal Poem. *Address:* PO Box 221, Institute Menezes Braganza, Panaji Gao, India.

BARROW Iris Lena, b. 8 Oct 1933, Auckland, New Zealand. Head of Seminar/Counselling Agency - Psychological Counsellor); Author. Seminar presenter. m. Robert Barrow, 1 son 4 daughters. *Education:* ATCL, Speech and Communications, 1953. *Publications:* Books: From Strength to Strength, 1988; 15 Steps to Overcome Anxiety and Depression, 1985; Know Your Strengths and Be Confident, 1982; You Can Communicate, 1983; Your Marriage Can Work, 1979; Relax and Come Alive (with Professor Helen Place) 1981; Make Peace With Yourself, 1990; 8 Self-help personal and interpersonal skills-training tapes 1981-89; Children's books 1970-72, Hapi series; Radio plays, 1962-70; Video training tapes, Celebrating Life with Iris Barrow, 1990. *Contributor to:* Feature writer (psychological issues) New Zealand; Articles on developing personal skills, New Zealandia; Article on stress, Challenge Weekly; Articles on Self-assertion for Courier Newspaper, contributor to various magazines and journals. *Memberships:* New Zealand PEN Association; Associate, New Zealand Institute of Management; ex on-air counsellor. *Address:* 13 Hostel Access Road, Eastern Beach, Auckland, New Zealand.

BARROW Robin (St Clair), b. 1944, British. Professor. *Appointments:* Assistant Master, City of London School for Boys, 1968-72; Lecturer 1972-80, Reader in Education 1980-, University of Leicester; Professor of Curriculum Theory, Simon Fraser University, Burnaby BC, 1982-. *Publications:* Athenian Democracy, 1973; Moral Philosophy for Education, Introduction to Philosophy of Education (with R G Woods), Plato Utilitarianism and Education, Sparta, 1975; Common Sense and the Curriculum, Greek and Roman Education, Plato and Education, 1976; Plato: The Apology of Socrates, 1977; Radical Education, 1978; The Canadian Curriculum, 1979; Happiness, 1980; The Philosophy of Schooling, 1981; Injustice Inequality and Ethics, Language and Thought, 1982.

BARROWS Sydney (Biddle), b. 14 Jan 1952, Long Branch, New Jersey, USA. Writer and Television Producer. *Education:* Graduated from Fashion Institution of Technology, 1973. *Appointments:* Executive Trainee, Abraham & Strauss (department store), New York City, 1973-76; Assistant Buyer, Ladies Accessories, 1976-1978; Accessories Buyer, Young Innovators (boutique wholesaler), 1978; Proprietress of Cachet, Elan and Finesse (three escort/call girl services) New York City, 1979-84; Writer and Professional Speacker, 1986-. *Publications:* (with William Novak) Mayflower Madam; The Secret Life of Sydney Biddle Barrows (autobiography), 1986; Mayflower Manners (with Ellis Weiner), 1990; Creator of Weekly column, Just Between Us, in the Manhattan Spirit. *Honour:* Bergdorf Goodman Award, 1973, for academic excellence. *Membership:* American Federation of Television and Radio Artists; National Speakers Association. *Address:* 210 West 70th Street, New York, NY 10023, USA.

BARRY Jocelyn. *See:* **BOWDEN Jean.**

BARRY Margaret Stuart, b. 1927, British. *Appointment:* Full Time Writer. *Publications:* Boffy and the Teacher Eater and Boffy and the Mumford Ghosts, 2 volumes, 1971, 1974; Tommy Mac, 1972; Woozy, The Woozies Go to School, Bill Books, 1973; The Woozies on Television, Tommy Mac Battles On, 1974; Tommy Mac on Safari, 1975; Simon and the Witch, 1976; Woozy and the Weight Watchers, The Woozies Go Visiting, Woozies Hold a Frubard Week, The Monster in a Woozy Garden, 1977; The Return of the Witch, 1978; Maggy Gumption and Maggy Gumption Flies High, 2 volumes, 1979, 1981; The Witch of Monopolopy Manor, 1980; The Witch on Holiday, 1983; The Witch VIP, Diz and the Big Fat Burglar, 1987.

BARRY Mike. *See:* **MALZBERG Barry Norman.**

BARRY Sebastian, b. 5 July 1955, Dublin, Ireland.

Writer. *Education:* LCC, Newend, London; Catholic University School, Dublin; BA, Trinity College, Dublin, 1977. *Appointments:* Iowa International Writing Fellowship, 1984; Writer in Association, Abbey Theatre, Dublin, 1989-90; Director of Board, Abbey Theatre, 1989-90. *Publications:* Boss Grady's Boys (play) 1989; The Engine of Owl-Light, (novel) 1987; Fanny Hawke Goes to the Mainland Forever (verse) 1989. *Contributor to:* Antaeus; London Review of Books; Stand; Observer. *Honours:* Hawthornden International Fellowships 1985 and 1988; Arts Council Bursary, 1982; BBC/Stewart Parker Award, 1989. *Memberships:* Irish Writers' Union; Aosdana; Half Moon Swimming Club. *Literary Agent:* Curtis Brown Ltd, 162-168 Regent Street, London. *Address:* c/o The Abbey Theatre, Abbey Street, Dublin 1, Ireland.

BARRY Sheila Anne, b. New York City, USA. Editor; Writer. m. (1) Julian Barry, div, (2) Paul Weissman, div, 1 son, 1 daughter. *Education:* BFA, Columbia University; Master Practitioner, NLP, Neuro Linguistic Programing. *Appointments:* Taplinger Publishing Co, 1960-70; Sterling Publishing Co, 1971-. *Publications:* Super Colossal Book of Puzzles & Games; Tricks & stunts to Fool Your Friends; Test Your Wits; Worlds Best party Games; Worlds Best Travel Games; Worlds Most Spine Tingling True Ghost Stories; Worlds Best Card Games for One. *Memberships:* International association of NLP. *Address:* c/o Sterling Publishing Co Inc, 387 Park Avenue S, New York, NY 10016, USA.

BARSTOW Stan, b. 28 June 1928, Horbury, Yorkshire, England. Novelist; Scriptwriter. m. Constance Mary Kershaw, 8 Sept 1951, 1 son, 1 daughter. *Education:* Ossett Grammar School. *Publications:* A Kind of Loving; The Desperadoes; Ask Me Tomorrow; Joby; The Watchers On The Shore; A Raging Calm; A Season With Eros; The Right True End; A Brothers Tale; The Glad Eye; Just You Wait And See; B Movie; Give Us This Day; Next of Kin. *Honours:* Royal TV Society Writers Award; Honorary MA Open University. *Memberships:* PEN; Society of Authors; Writers Guild of Great Britain. *Literary Agent:* Lemon, Jnna & Dorbridge. *Address:* c/o Lemon, Jnna & Dorbridge Ltd, 24 Pottery Lane, London W11 4LZ, England.

BART Lionel, Composer, Lyricist. b. 1 Aug 1930. British. *Publications:* Lock Up Your Daughters, 1959; Music and lyrics for Fings Ain't Wot They Used t'be, 1959; Music, lyrics and book for Oliver!, 1960, Film 1968; Music, lyrics and direction of Blitz!, 1962; Music and lyrics of Maggie May, 1964; Film scores include: Serious Charge, In the Nick, Heart of a Man, Let's Get Married, Light Up the Sky, The Tommy Steele Story, The Duke Wore Jeans, Tommy the Toreador, Sparrers Can't Sing, From Russia With Love, Man in the Middle: many hit songs. *Contributions:* Written for many films as above. *Honours:* Antoinette Perry Award (Tony) for Oliver!, as best composer and lyricist, 1962, Ivor Novello Award, 1957, 59, 60; Variety Club Silver Heart for Show Bus, Personality of the Year, Broadway, USA, 1960; Gold Disc Award for soundtrack of Oliver!, 1969; Ivor Novello Jimmy Kennedy Award, 1985; Ivor Novello Award 1989; Best Theme from a TV/Radio Commercial, Golden Break Award, 1990; Best Original Music. *Address:* c/o 8-10 Bulstrode St, London, W1M 6AH, England.

BARTEK Edward J, b. 25 Nov 1921, Hartford, Connectict, USA. m. Eugenia R Redekas, 19 Nov 1948, 2 sons. *Education:* BA, M.Ed, University of Hartford. *Publications:* A Treasury of Parables, 1959; Mind of Future Man, 1965; Unifying Principles of the Mind, 1965; Ultimate Philosophy: Trinityism, 1968; Ultimate Principles: Morality, 1987; Ultimate Principles: Principles, 1987; Ultimate Principles: Theology, 1987; Ultimate Principles: Truth, 1987; Trinitarian Philosophy, 1988; Trinitarian Psychology, 1988; Trinitarian Universal Ethics, 1988; Trinityison Applied I, 1990; Trinitarian Philosophy of History, 1988; Dream-analysis for Self-analysis, 1988. *Memberships:* Wit and Wisdom Writers Club, President; Connecticut Poetry Society, Vice-President; American Philosophical Association; International Society for Comparative Study Civilizations; Institute of Religion in an Age of Science. *Address:* 68 Walnut Street, East Hartford, CT 06108, USA.

BARTH J(ohn) Robert, b. 1931, American. Professor. *Appointments:* Entered Society of Jesus; Ordained Roman Catholic Priest, 1961; Assistant Professor of English, Canisius College, Buffalo, 1967-70; Assistant Professor, Harvard University, 1970-74; Professor of English, University of Missouri, 1974-88; Dean, College of Arts and Science, Boston College, 1988-. *Publications:* Coleridge and Christian Doctrine, 1969; Religious Perspectives in Faulkner's Fiction: Yoknapatawpha and Beyond, 1972; The Symbolic Imagination: Coleridge and the Romantic Tradition, 1977; Coleridge and the Power of Love, 1988; Coleridge, Keats and the Imagination: Ramanticism and Adam's Dream (co-ed), 1989. *Address:* Gasson Hall 103, Boston College, Chestnut Hill, MA 02167, USA.

BARTH John, b. 27 May 1930, Cambridge, Maryland, USA. Novelist; Professor of English. m. (1) Harriette Anne Strickland, 1950, 2 sons, 1 daughter, (2) Shelly Rosenberg, 1970. *Education:* MA, Johns Hopkins University. *Appointments include:* Professor, State University of New York at Buffalo 1965-73, Johns Hopkins University 1973-. *Publications:* Novels: The Floating Opera, 1956; The End of the Road, 1958; The Sot-Weed Factor, 1960; Giles Goat-Boy, 1966; Sabbatical, 1982. The Tidewater Tales, 1987; Lost in the Funhouse, stories, 1968; Chimera, 1972; Letters, 1979; The Friday Book, essays, 1984. *Honours:* National Academy of Arts & Letters Award; National Book Award, 1973; Rockefeller Foundation Grant; Brandeis University Citation in Literature; Honorary DLitt, University of Maryland. *Address:* Johns Hopkins University, Baltimore, MD 21218, USA.

BARTHELME Frederick, b. 1943, American. *Appointments:* An Artist, Exhibitions at galleries including Houston, New York City, Seattle, Vancouver, Buenos Aires, 1965-; Architectural draftsman, Jerome Oddo and Associates and Kenneth E Bentsen Associates, Houston, 1965-66; Exhibition Organizer, St Thomas University, 1966-67; Assistant to the Director, Kornblee Gallery, NY, 1967-68; Creative Director, BMA Advertising, 1971-73; Senior Writer, GDL and W Advertising, 1973-76; Professor of English, Director of the Centre for Writers, Editor for Mississippi Review, University of Southern Mississippi, Hattiesburg, 1977-. *Publications:* Rangoon, 1970; War and War, 1971; Moon Deluxe, 1983; Second Marriage, 1984; Tracer, 1985; Chroma, 1987; Two Against One, 1988; Natural Selection, 1990. *Address:* 203 Sherwood Drive, Hattiesburg, MI 39401, USA.

BARTKOWIAK Tadeusz Ludwik, b. 19 Aug 1942, Tomaszow Mazowiecki, Poland. Journalist. m. 30 Dec 1968, 1 son. *Education:* Diploma, Poznan Teachers College, 1962; Diploma, Philosophical & Historical Faculty, Adam Mickiewicz University, Poznan, 1967; Diploma, Evening University of Marxism- Leninism, 1985. *Appointment:* Editorial Staff, Poznan Newspaper, 1972-. *Publications include:* The Western Watch-Tower, 1922-1939; New Materials on the Battle of Poznan, 1945; A Chronicle of Poznan City; The Polish Association of Philatelists in Poznan, 1969-74; The Poznan Newspaper, 2.V.87 -9.VI.87; The Union of Poles in Germany, 1922-87; Almanac of Polish Emigrants. *Contributions to:* Polish Panorama, monthly; Almanac of Polish Emigrants, annual; Chronicle of Poznan City, quarterly; Chronical of the Wielkopolska, quarterly; Western Review, bimonthly; Voice of Poland, bi-weekly, Recklinghausen, GFR; Red Flag, daily, USSR. *Honours include:* 40 Year Commemorative Medal, Polish Peoples Republic, 1984; Silver Medal, Protection of National Memorials, 1982; Medal, Polish Emigrants Society, 1985; 5 awards, Polish Journalists Association, 1976-85. *Memberships:* Polish Journalists Association; International Union of Philatelic Journalists; Polish Club of Marine Painters & Writers. *Address:* Osiedle Rzeczypospolitej 14 m.33, 61-397 Poznan, Poland.

BARTLETT Christopher John, b. 12 Oct 1931, Bournemouth, England. University Professor of International History. m. Shirley Maureen Briggs, 7 Aug 1958, 3 sons. *Education:* University College, Exeter, 1950-53; 1st Class Honours, History (London External), PhD, International History, London School of Economics. *Publications:* Great Britain and Sea Power, 1815-53, 1963; Castlereagh, 1966; The Long Retreat (British Defence Policy 1945-70) 1972; The Rise and Fall of the Pax Americana, 1974; A History of Postwar Britain, 1945-74, 1977; The Global Conflict, 1880-1970, 1984; British Foreign Policy in the Twentieth Century (1989); The Special Relationship: a political history of Anglo-American relations since 1945, 1992; Defence and Diplomacy: Britain and the Great Powers, 1815-1914, 1993; Editor: Britain Pre-eminent, 1969; The Mid-Victorian Reappraisal of Naval Policy in K Bourne and D C Watt Studies in International History, 1967. *Contributor to:* English Historical Review; History; Annual Register. *Memberships:* Fellow, Royal Historial Society; Fellow, Royal Society of Edinburgh. *Address:* History Department, The University, Dundee DD1 4HN, Scotland.

BARTLETT Eric George, b. 25 Aug 1920, Llanbradach, Wales. Retired Postal Officer. m. Pauline Nancy Lewis, 9 Feb 1974. *Education:* Newport (Isle of Wight) Secondary School 1933-37; Holder of 3rd Dan and Doshi Teaching Certificate in Judo; 1st Dan Budo. *Publications:* Judo and Self Defence, 1962; Basic Judo, 1974; Basic Karate, 1980; Weight Training, 1986; The Case of the 13th Coach, 1958; Healing Without Harm, 1985; The Complete Body Builder; Self Defence in the Home; Weight Training for Women; Weight Training for the Over 35's; Smoking Flax; Summer Day in Ajaccio; Strangers in Eden; Mysterious Stranger; JUDO; Basic Fitness; Master of Kung Fu; Jungle Nurse; Clouded Love; Beloved Hostage. *Contributor to:* Christian Herald (short stories); Budokwai Bulletin and IBC Bulletin (articles on Judo); FFT Bulletin (religious article). The Friend. *Membership:* Society of Authors. *Address:* 5, Bryngwyn Road, Cyncoed, Cardiff CF2 6PQ, Wales.

BARTLEY William Warren III, b. 1934, American. Professor. *Appointments:* Lecturer, University of London, 1960-63; Associate Professor, University of California, 1963-67; Fellow, Gonville and Caius College, Cambridge, England, 1966-67; Professor of Philosophy and of History and Philosophy of Science, Associate Director, Senior Research Associate of the Center for Philosophy and Science, University of Pittsburgh, PA, 1967-73; Professor of Philosophy, California State University, Harvard, 1970-; Visiting Scholar 1984, Senior Research Fellow 1985-, Hoover Institution, Stanford University. *Publications:* The Retreat to Commitment, 1962; Morality and Religion, 1971; Wittgenstein, 1973; Die Notwendigkeit des Engagements, 1974; Lewis Carroll's Symbolic Logic (author and ed), 1977; Werner Erhard: The Transformation of a Man: The Founding of Est, 1978; Karl Popper's Postscript to the Logic of Scientific Discovery, 1982; Evolutionary Epistemology, Rationality and the Sociology of Knowledge, 1987. *Address:* c/o Hoover Institution, Stanford University, Stanford, CA 94305, USA.

BARTOSZEWSKI Wladyslaw, b. 19 Feb 1922, Warsaw, Poland. Writer; Historian. *Education:* Doctor honoris causa, Polish University in exile, London, 1981; Doctor h.c. Baltimore Hebrew College, USA, 1984. *Appointments:* Vice President, Institute for Polish Jewish Studies, Oxford England; Visiting Professor, Munich, Eichstaett, Augsburg, 1983-89; Voted Chairman of the International Council of the Museum at Auschwitz, 1990; Appointed to the council for Polish-Jewish Relations by the President of the Republic of Poland, 1991. *Publications include;* Warsaw Death Ring, 1939-44, 2nd edition 1970; The Samaritans, Heroes of the Holocaust with Z Lewin, USA, 1970; 1859 Days of Warsaw, 1974; The Warsaw Ghetto As It Really Was, 1983; Days of the Fighting Capital: A Chronicle of the Warsaw Uprising, 1984; On the Road to Independence, 1987; Experiences of My Life, 1989. *Contributions to:*

Various Catholic Magazines and Papers. *Honours include:* Polish Military Cross, 1944; Medal and Title of The Righteous Among the Nations, The Martyrs and Heroes Remembrance Yad Vashem, Jerusalem, 1963; prize, Alfred Jurzykowski Foundation, New York, 1967; prize, Polish Pen, Warsaw, 1975; Herder Prize, Vienna, 1983; Peace Prize, German Publishers' and Booksellers' Association, 1986; Commander, Polonia Restituta (with Star), London, 1986; Honorary Citizen of the State of Israel, 1991; Distinguished Service Cross Order of Merit of Germany, 1991; Austrian Cross of Honour for Science and Art 1st Class, 1992. *Memberships:* Polish PEN, Secretary General, 1972-83; Board Member, 1988-; Associate Member, French PEN. *Address:* ul. Karolinki 12, 02-635, Warsaw, Poland.

BARTUSIAK Marcia Frances, b. 30 Jan 1950, Chester, Pennsylvania, USA. Science Writer; Author. m. Stephen A Lowe, 10 Sept 1988. *Education:* BA, Communications, American University, 1971; MS, Physics Old Dominion University, Norfolk, 1979. *Appointments:* Writer, Science News, 1979; Writer, Discover Magazine, 1980-82; Contributing Editor, Discover, 1990-; Contributer, The New York Times Book Review, 1986-. *Publications:* Thursday's Universe; Through a Universe Darkly. *Contributions to:* Over 100 Articles; Discover; Science Digest; Omni; Popular Science; Air & space; Readers Digest. *Honours:* American Institute of Physics Science Writing Award; Astronomy Book of the Year; Nasa Journalist in Space Finalist. *Memberships:* The Authors Guild; National Association of Science Writers; Sigma Xi Honor Society. *Literary Agent:* Scott Meredith Literary Agency. *Address:* c/o Scott Meredith 845 Third Avenue, New York, NY 10022, USA.

BASINGER Jeanine, b. 3 Feb 1936, Ravenden, Arkansas, USA. Professor; Curator, Founder, Wesleyan Cinema Archives. m. 22 Sept 1967, 1 daughter. *Education:* BS, 1957, MS, 1959, South Dakota State University. *Publications:* Anthony Mann, 1979; It's a Wonderful Life Book, 1986; World War II Combat Book, Anatomy of a Genre, 1986; Shirley Temple, 1975; Lana Turner, 1977; Gene Kelly, 1976; Working with Kazan, 1973. *Contributions to:* American Film Magazine; Bright Lights; Women and the Cinema; Bijou; Great Filmmakers; Great Films; Actors and Actresses; etc. *Honours:* Anthony Mann nominated as best Film book of year, National Film Society, 1979. *Memberships:* Trustee, American Film Institute, 1979; Trustee, National Centre for Film and Video Preservation; Board of Advisors, Association of Independent Video and Filmmakers, 1982-. *Address:* c/o Wesleyan Univeristy Cinema Archives, Wesleyan University, Middlletown, CT 06457, USA.

BASS Howard, b. 28 Oct 1923, Waltham Cross, England. Author; Journalist. *Appointments:* Sports Writer, Programme Publications Limited, London, 1947-48; Managing Director, Howard Bass Publications Limited, London, 1948-69; Editor, Winter Sports Magazine, 1948-69; Winter Sports Correspondent, Evening News, London, 1960-61; Daily Telegraph, 1961-; Sunday Telegraph, 1961-; London Standard, 1973-; Daily Mail, 1987-; Mail on Sunday, 1987-. *Publications:* The Sense in Sport, 1941; This Skating Age, 1958; The Magic of Skiing, 1959; Winter Sports, 1966, American edition 1968; Success in Ice Skating, 1970; International Encyclopaedia of Winter Sports, 1971; Let's Go Skating, 1974, American Edition 1976; Tackle Skating, 1978; Ice Skating for Pleasure,, 1979; Ice Skating, 1980; The Love of Skating, 1980, American edition, 1980; Elegance on Ice, 1980, American edition 1980; Skating for Gold, 1980; Glorious Wembley, 1982; Superbook of Skating, 1988. *Contributions to:* Sport & Recreation; Ski Racing, Denver, USA; Skating, Colorado Springs, USA; Canadian Skater, Ottawa; Daily and Sunday Telegraphs; Ice Hockey World, UK; London Standard; Daily Mail; Mail on Sunday; Winter Sports Text Authority; Encyclopaedia Britannica; Guinness Book of Records. *Memberships:* International Sports Press Association, Committee Member; Sports Writers Association of Great Britain; British Olympic

Association; British Ice Hockey Writers Association, Committee Member. *Address:* 256 Willow Road, Enfield, Middlesex EN1 3AT, England.

BASS Jack, b. 1934, American. *Appointments:* Bureau Chief, Knight Newspapers, Columbia, 1966-73; Visiting Research Fellow, Institute of Policy Sciences and Public Affairs, Duke University, Durham, 1973-75; Writer-in-Residence, South Carolina State College, Orangeburg, 1975-78; Research Fellow, Director of American South Special Projects, University of South Carolina, 1979-85. *Publications:* The Orangeburg Massacre (with Jack Nelson), 1970; You Can't Eat Magnolias (co-author), Porgy Comes Home, 1972; The Transformation of Southern Politics (with Walter DeVires), 1976; Unlikely Heroes, 1981; The American South Comes of Age, 1985.

BASS Thomas Alden, b. 9 Mar 1951, Chagrin Falls, Ohio, USA. Writer. *Education:* AB, University of Chicago, 1973; PhD, University of California, 1980. *Publications:* Camping with the Prince And Other Tales of Science in Africa; The Eudaemonic Pie' The Newtonian Casion; Reinventing the Universe, 1993. *Contributions to:* Smithsonian; Audubon; The New York Times. *Memberships:* PEN; Authors Guild. *Address:* 31 Rue Saint Placide, Paris 75006, France.

BASSERMANN Lujo. *See:* **SCHREIBER Hermann O L.**

BASSETT Elizabeth Ewing, (Libby), b. 22 July 1937, USA. Writer; Editor. *Education:* AA, Bradford College, Massachusetts. *Appointments include:* Editor, World Environment Report Newsletter, 1978-85; Writer, Editor, Designer, UNEP North American News and Environmental Sabbath, Newsletters (also UNEP); Shared Vision and Update Newsletters, and Press Officer, 1988 Oxford, 1990 Moscow Global Forum on Environment and Development, 1992 Parliamentary Earth Summit in Rio de Janerio and 1993 Kyoto Global Forum, for the Global Forum of Spiritual and Parliamentary Leaders on Human Survival, 1985-; Communications Coordinator, 1991 World Women's Congress for a Healthy Planet in Miami, Florida, and the Women's Environment and Development Organisation (WEDO), 1991-, (UN Environment Programme Newsletter), 1986-. *Publications include:* Growth of Environment in the World Bank, 1982; World Environment Handbook, 1985; Environment & Development Opportunities in Africa & Middle East, 1986. *Contributions to:* Newsweek; MidEast Markets; Near East Business; Scholastic Science World; Modern Africa; New Age; IDRC Reports; Issues before the 35th-45th Sessions, United Nations General Assembly. *Honour:* Journalism Award, Editorial Excellence, Newsletter Association of America, 1980. *Memberships:* Sigma Delta Chi (professional journalists); Society of Environmental Journalists; International Science Writers Association; Women's Foreign Policy Council. *Address:* 521 East 14th Street, no.4F, New York, NY 10009, USA.

BASSETT Lisa Jane, b. 26 Jan 1958, Winter Park, Florida, USA. Teacher. *Education:* Rollins College, BA, 1984; University of Texas, MA, 1986; PhD, 1992. *Publications:* A Clock for Beany; Beany and Scamp; Beany Wakes Up for Christmas; Very Truly Yours, Charles L Dodgson, Alias Lewis Carroll; Koala Christmas; The Bunnies' Alphabet Eggs, 1993; Ten Little Bunnies, 1993. *Honours:* Junior Literary Guild Selection; Childrens Choice of International Reading Association. *Memberships:* Modern Language Association. *Literary Agent.* Dilys Evans. *Address:* Department of Electrical and Computer Engineering, The University of Texas, Austin, ENS 116, Austin, TX 78712, USA.

BASSETT Ronald Leslie, (William Clive), b. 1924, British. *Appointments:* Served with King's Royal Rifle Corps 1938-39, Royal Navy 1940-54; Full-time Author,

documentary and medical film scriptwriter, 1958-. *Publications:* The Carthaginian, 1963; The Pompeians, 1965; Witchfinder General, 1966; Amorous Trooper, 1968; Rebecca's Brat, 1969; Kill the Stuart, 1970; Dando on Delhi Ridge (as W Clive), 1971; Dando and the Summer Palace (as W Clive), 1972; Dando and the Mad Emperor (as W Clive), 1973; The Tune That They Play (as W Clive), 1974; Blood of an Englishman (as W Clive), 1975; Fighting Mac (as W Clive), 1976; Tinfish Run, 1977; Pierhead Jump, 1978; Neptune Landing, 1979; Guns of Evening, 1980; Battle-Cruisers, 1982. *Address:* 19 Binstead Drive, Blackwater, Camberley, Surrey, England.

BASUBANDHU. *See:* **BHAUMIK Gopal.**

BASURTO Luis G., b. 11 Mar 1921, Mexico. Writer; Journalist; Playwright. 1 son. *Publications:* Cada Quien Suvida, Play, 1958, 4th edition 1984; Miercoles De Eniza, Play, 1957, 2nd edition 1986; Con La Frente en el Polvo, Play, 1986; Asesinato De Una Conciencia, Play, 1986; El Escandalo de la Verdad, 1960, 2nd edition 1984; El Candidato de Dios, play, 1986; Los Reyes Del Mundo, 1962; Adaptations for Films and TV. *Contributions to:* Editor, Excelsior; Columnist; numerous journals and magazines. *Honours:* National Prize for Theatre, Juan Ruiz De Alarcon, 1956, 1967, 1986; Theatre Prizes in Spain, 1981, Argentina, 1962. *Memberships:* SOGEM, Vice President; Writers of Mexico Association; PEN. *Address:* Sogem Jose Maria Velasco 59, Mexico 19, DF.

BATCHELOR David Brook Lockhart, b. 19 June 1943, London. Writer. 3 daughters. *Education:* Eton College. *Publications:* Brogan and Sons, 1976; A Dislocated Man, 1978; Children in the Dark, 1982; Why Tilbury? 1985. *Address:* 52 Onslow Square, London SW7 3NX, England.

BATCHELOR John Barham b. 15 Mar 1942, England. University Teacher. m. Henrietta Jane Letts, 14 Sept 1968, 2 sons 1 daughter. *Education:* MA 1964, PhD 1969, Magdalene College, Cambridge; MA, University of New Brunswick, 1965. *Appointments:* Lecturer in English, Birmingham University, 1968-76; Fellow and Tutor, New College, Oxford, 1976-90; Joseph Owen Professor of English Literature, University of Newcastle-upon-Tyne, 1990-. *Publications:* Mervyn Peake, 1974; The Edwardian Novelists, 1982; H G Wells, 1985; Lord Jim (Unwin Critical Library), 1988; Virginia Woolf, 1991; Joseph Conrad: A Critical Biography, 1993; Breathless Hush (novel) 1974; Lord Jim (World's Classics Edition) 1983; Victory (World's Classics Edition) 1986. *Contributor to:* Reviews for: Times Literary Supplement, The Observer, The Economist. Articles in English, The Yearbook of English Studies. *Literary Agent:* Felicity Bryan, 2a North Parade, Oxford. *Address:* Department of English, University of Newcastle, Newcastle-upon-Tyne, England.

BATCHELOR John Calvin, b. 1948, American. *Appointments:* Editor and Book Reviewer, SoHo Weekley News, 1975-77; Book Reviewer, Village Voice, 1977-80, NY. *Publications:* The Further Adventures of Halley's Comet, 1981; The Birth of the People's Republic of Antartica, 1983; American Falls, 1985.

BATES Milton J, b. 4 June 1945, Warrensburg, Missouri, USA. University Professor. m. 6 May 1972, 1 son, 1 daughter. *Education:* BA, Classical Literature, English, 1968; MA, English, 1972; PhD, English, 1977. *Appointments:* Assistant Professor of English, Williams College, 1975-81; Assistant-Associate and Full Professor of English, Marquette University, Milwaukee, Wisconsin, 1981-. *Publications:* Wallace Stevens: A Mythology of Self, 1985; Sur Plusieurs Beaux Sujects: Wallace Stevens' Commonplace Book (editor), 1989; Opus Posthumous, by Wallace Stevens (editor), 1989. *Contributions to:* Essays: American Literature; English Literary History; Modern Fiction Studies; The New York Times Book Review; The Southern Review; other periodicals. *Honours:* Danforth Kent Fellow, 1973; American Council of Learned Societies Fellow, 1980, 1986; Guggenheim Fellow, 1989; Wallace Stevens: A Mythology of Self named a Notable Book of the Year, New York Times Book Review, 1985. *Memberships:* Executive Committee, Division on 20th Century American Literature and Nominating Committee, American Literature Section, Modern Language Association of America; Editorial Board, The Wallace Stevens Journal; Advisory Board, Wallace Stevens Society. *Address:* Department of English, Marquette University, Milwaukee, WI 53233, USA.

BATTESTIN Martin Carey, b. 1930, American. Professor. *Appointments:* Instructor 1956-58, Assistant Professor 1958-61, Wesleyan University, Middletown, CT; Assistant Professor 1961-63, Associate Professor 1963-67, Professor 1967-75, Kenan Professor of English Literature 1975-, Chairman of Department 1983-86, University of Virginia, Charlottesville. *Publications:* The Moral Basis of Fielding's Art, 1959; Fielding's Joseph Andrews and Shamela, 1961; Fielding's Joseph Andrews, 1967; Twentieth Century Interpretations of Tom Jones, 1968; The Providence of Wit: Aspects of Form in Augustan Literature and the Arts, 1974, 1989 (reissued); Fielding's Tom Jones (co-ed), 1975; Fielding's Amelia, 1983; British Novelists 1660-1800, 1985; New Essays by Henry Fielding: His Contributions to the 'Craftsman' (1734-39) and other early Journalism, 1989; Henry Fielding: A Life, 1989, (Biography); The Correspondence of Henry and Sarah Fielding (co-editor), 1992. *Address:* 1832 Westview Road, Charlottesville, VA 22903, USA.

BATTIN B W, (S W Bradford, Alexander Brinton, Warner Lee, Casey McAllister), b. 15 Nov 1941, Ridgewood, New Jersey, USA. Writer. m. Sandra McCraw, 14 Feb 1976, Shreveport, Louisiana. *Education:* BA, University of New Mexico, 1969. *Publications:* as B W Battin: Angel of the Night, 1983; The Boogeyman, 1984; Satan's Servant, 1984; Mary, Mary, 1985; Programmed for Terror, 1985; The Attraction, 1986; The Creep, 1987; Smithereens, 1987; Demented, 1988; as Warner Lee: Into the Pit, 1989; It's Loose, 1990; Night Sounds, 1992; as S W Bradford: Tender Prey, 1990; Fair Game, 1992; as Alexander Brinton: Serial Blood, 1992; Carved in Blood, in progress; as Casey McAllister: Catch Me if You Can, 1993. *Literary Agent:* Dominick Abel, New York. *Address:* 711 North Mesa Road, Belen, NM 87002, USA.

BATTISCOMBE Georgina, b. 21 Nov 1905, London, England. Biographer. m. 1 Oct 1932, Lt Col C.F. Battiscombe, 1 daughter. *Education:* St Michael's School, Oxford; BA Honours, History, Lady Margaret Hall, Oxford. *Publications include:* Charlotte Mary Yonge, 1943; Mrs Gladstone, 1956; John Keble, 1963; Queen Alexandra, 1970; Lord Shaftesbury, 1974; Christina Rossetti, 1981. Also: Two on Safari; English Picnics; Reluctant Pioneer, Life of Elizabeth Wordsworth, 1978; The Spencers of Althorp, 1984; Winter Song, 1992. *Contributions:* Reviews & articles, numerous newspapers & magazines including: Times; Sunday Telegraph; Times Literary Supplement; Spectator; Country Life; Books & Bookmen; History Today; etc. *Honour:* James Tait Black Prize, 1963. *Memberships:* Fellow, Royal Society of Literature; Society of Authors. *Literary Agent:* A.M. Heath & Company. *Address:* 40 Phyllis Court Drive, Henley-on-Thames, Oxfordshire RG9 2HU, England.

BATTLES Roxy Edith Baker, b. 29 Mar 1921, Spokane, Washington, USA. Novelist; Children's Author; Teacher; Lecturer; Consultant. m. Willis Ralph Battles, 2 May 1941, 1 son, 2 daughters. *Education:* AA, Bakersfield Junior College, 1940; BA, Californian State University, 1959; MA, University of Pepperdine, 1976. *Appointments:* Editor, Renegade Rip, 1939-40; Stringer, Bakersfield, California 1938-40; Long Beach Press Telegramme 1954-55; Columnist, Manhattan Tide, 1958; Elementary Teacher, Torrance Unified Schools, 1959-85; Instructor, Torrance Adult School, 1968-88; Instructor, Pepperdine University, 1976-79.

Publications: Over the Rickety Fence, 1967; The Terrible Trick or Treat, 1970, 1973, Film cassette narrated by Mason Adams, 1975; The Terrible Terrier, 1972, 1973, 501 Balloons Sail east, 1971, 1979; One to Teeter Totter 1973, 1975, 1982, 1984, 1988, German, Danish, Norwegian, 1976; Eddie Couldn't Find the Elephants, 1974, 1982, 1984, 1988; What Does the Rooster Say, Yoshio? 1978, United Nations selection; The Secret of Castle Drai, 1980, adult gothic; The Witch in Room 6, 1987; Harper Trophy 1989 Optioned for television, nominee for Hoosier Award, Garden State Award, 1990; The Chemistry of Whispering Caves, 1989, Mystery with chemistry college text - Texas A & M. *Contributor to:* Articles, poetry, short stories in 48 American national and regional magazines 1945-60, many educational articles 1960-80. *Honours:* United Nations Award 1978; Literary Guild Selection, The Terrible Terrier, 1972; National Science Award, 501 Balloons Sail East, 1971; Selected Author-in-Residence, March 1991 (Madrid, Spain) American School of Madrid. *Memberships:* Chaired, Southwest Manuscripters, Shakespeare Study Club and Surfwriters. *Address:* 560 South Helberta Avenue, Redondo Beach, CA 90277, USA.

BAUDRIER Jacqueline, b. 16 Mar 1922. Journalist; Diplomatist. m. (1) Maurice Baudrier, divorced, (2) Roger Perriard, 1957. *Education:* University of Paris. *Appointments:* Political Reportr, Actualites de Paris, Foreign News Reporter and Presenter, various news programmes, Radiodiffusion-Television Francaise, 1950-60; Secretary General, Soutien fraternal des journalises, 1955-; Editor in Chief, news programmes, Office de Radiodiffusion-Television francaise, 1963-66, in charge main news programme 1966-68; Assistant Director Radio Broadcasting, 1968-69; Director, Information, 2nd TV Channel (A2), 1969-72; Director, 1st TV Channel (TF1), 1972-74; Chairman, Radio-Fance, 1975-81; Board of Directors, Telediffusion de France, 1975-81; President, Communaute radiophonique des programmes de langue francaise, 1977-79; Vice Chairman, programming Commission, Union Europeenne de radiodiffusion, 1978, re-elected 1980; Permanent Representative of France to UNESCO, 1981-85. *Honours:* Prix Maurice Bourdet, 1960; Prix Ondes, 1969; Chevalier, Legion d'honneur; Officer, Ordre nationale du Merite. *Address:* 1 rue Miollis, 75015 Paris, France.

BAUER Caroline Feller, b. 12 May 1935, Washington DC, USA. Author; Lecturer. m. 21 Dec 1969, 1 daughter. *Education:* BA, Sarah Lawrence; MLS Columbia University; PhD, University of Oregon. *Publications:* Handbook for Storytellers; This Way to Books; Celebrations; Presenting Reader's Theater; My Mom Travels a Lot; Midnight Snowman; Rainy day, Snowy Day, Windy Day; Halloween; Too Many Books. *Contributor to:* Cricket. *Honours:* ERSTED Award for Distinguished Teaching; Christopher Award for My Mom Travels a Lot; Dorothy McKenzie Award for Distinguished Contribution to Children's Literature. *Memberships:* Society of Children's Book Writers; American Library Association ALSC Chair Notable Books. *Address:* 10175 Collins Avenue, 201 Miami Beach, FL 33154, USA.

BAUER Steven Albert, b. 10 Sept 1948, Newark, New Jersey, USA. Associate Professor of English, Miami Univ, Oxford, OH. m. Elizabeth Arthur, 19 June 1982. *Education:* BA, with Honours, Trinity College, 1970; MFA, University of Massachusetts, 1975. *Publications:* Daylight Savings, poems, 1989; Amazing Stories, 1986; The River, 1985; Satyrday, a novel, 1980. *Contributions to:* Southwest Review; Missouri Review; Indiana Review; Massachusetts Review; The Nation; Prairie Schooner; North American Review. *Honours:* Fellowship, Fine Arts Work Center, 1978-79; Fellowship, Bread Loaf Writers' Conference, 1981; Indiana Master Artist Fellowship, 1988; Peregrine Smith Poetry Prize, 1989. *Memberships:* Poetry Society of America; Associated Writing Programs; Poets & Writers, Inc. *Literary Agent:* Jean V Naggar. *Address:* 14100 Harmony Road, Bath, IN 47010, USA.

BAUER Yehuda, b. 6 Apr 1926, Historian. 2 daughters. *Education:* BA Hons 1st Class, Cardiff University, 1950; PhD, Hebrew University, Jerusalem, 1960. *Appointments:* Jona M Machover Professor of Holocaust Studies, Hebrew University; Academic Chairman, Institute of Contemporary Jewry, Hebrew University; Chairman, Vidal Sassoon International Center for the Study of Antisemitism; Editor of Journal of Holocaust and Genocide Studies, Oxford University Press, New York. *Publications include:* Holocaust in Historical Perspective, 1978; American Jewry and the Holocaust, 1981; A History of the Holocaust, 1982; Flight and Rescue, 1970; Out of the Ashes, 1989; My Brother's Keeper, 1974; From Diplomacy to Resistance, 1970. *Contributor to:* About 100 articles to newspapers and journals. *Honour:* Honorary PhD, Hebrew Union College, New York, USA. *Memberships:* Editorial Board Member, Yad Vashem Studies; Judaism; Moreshet; Scientific Advisory Committee, Yad Vashem. *Address:* Kibbutz Shoval, Nagev 85320, Israel.

BAUGHAN Peter Edward, b. 26 Aug 1934, Richmond, Surrey. Retired Local Government Officer. m. Anne Catherine Silverlock, 19 Dec 1960, 1 son, 2 daughters. *Education:* Latymer Upper School, Hammersmith. *Publications:* North of Leeds (Leeds-Settle-Carlisle Railway), 1966; The Railways of Wharfedale, 1969; The Chester and Holyhead Railway, 1972; Regional History of the Railways of Great Britain, Vol 11 North and Mid Wales, 1980; The Midland Railway North of Leeds, 1987; The North Wales Coast Railway, 1988. *Contributor to:* The Railway Magazine. *Address:* 97 Royal George Road, Burgess Hill, West Sussex RH15 9SJ, England.

BAUGHMAN J. Ross, b. 7 May 1953, Dearborn, Michigan, USA. Photo- Journalist; Educator. m. Jonalyn S. Schuon, 9 May 1987. *Education:* BA cum laude, Kent State University, 1975. *Appointments include:* Photographer, Writer, Lorain Journal, Ohio, 1975-77; Contract Photographer, Writer, Africa & Middle East, 1977-78; Co-founder, Visions International Inc, 1978; President, Visions Photo Group, New York City, 1978-; Faculty, New School for Social Research, NYC, 1979-. *Publications:* Graven Images: Thematic Portfolio, 1976; Forbidden Images: Secret Portfolio, 1977. *Honours:* J. Winton Lemen photojournalism scholar, Kent State University, 1975; Pulitzer Prize, Journalism, (Feature Photography portfolio), 1978. *Memberships:* National Press Photographers Association; Photographers Gallery; Sigma Delta Chi; American Society of Magazine Photographers. *Literary Agent:* Mark Greenberg, Visions, 220 West 19th St, Suite 500, NY 10011, USA. *Address:* 23 Overlook Drive, Huntingdon, NY 11743, USA.

BAUMAN Janina, b. 18 Aug 1926, Warsaw, Poland. Writer. m. Zygmunt Bauman, 18 Aug 1948, 3 daughters. *Education:* Academy of Social Science, 1951. *University of Warsaw, 1959. Appointments:* Script Editor, Polish Film, 1948-68. *Publications:* Winter in the Morning; A Dream of Belonging; Various Other Publications. *Contributions to:* The Jewish Quarterly; Oral History; Polin; British Journal of Holocaust Education. *Honours:* Award by Polityka Polenol Weekly. *Address:* 1 Lawnswood Gardens, Leed, LS16 6HF, Yorkshire, England.

BAUMAN M Garrett, b. 7 Aug 1948, USA. Professor. m. 3 June 1978, 1 son, 3 daughters. *Education:* BA 1969, Upsala College; MA 1971, SUNY at Binghamton. *Publication:* Ideas and Details, 1992. *Contributions to:* New York Times; Yankee; National Forum; Story; The Chronicle of Higher Education; Sierra; Greensboro Review; Orion; Fine Homebuilding. *Honours:* SUNY Creative Writing Award, 1983; Brigham Young University Essay Award, 1984; Writer's Digest, 1985; Freedoms Foundation, 1988; H G Roberts Foundation, 1989. *Address:* Monroe Community College, Rochester, NY 14623, USA.

BAUMAN Zygmunt, b. 19 Nov 1925, Poznan, Poland.

Sociologist. m. Janina Bauman, 18 Aug 1948, 3 daughters. *Education:* MA, 1954, PhD, 1956. *Appointments:* Warsaw University, 1953-68; Tel Aviv University, 1968-75; University of Leeds, 1971-91. *Publications:* Modernly & the Holocaust; Legislators & Interpreters; Intimations of Postinedermity; Thinking Sociologically; Modernity & Ambivalence; Freedom; Memories of Class; Culture as Praxis; Between Class & Elite; Mortality, Immortality & Other Life Strategies. *Contributions to:* TLS; The New Statesman; Professional Periodicals. *Honours:* Amalfi European Prize for Sociology. *Memberships:* British Sociological Association; Polish Sociological Association. *Address:* Leeds, England.

BAUMBACH Jonathan, b. 5 July 1933, New York, USA. Writer; Professor. 3 sons, 1 daughter. *Education:* AB, Brooklyn College, 1955; MFA, Columbia University, 1956; PhD, stanford University, 1961. *Appointments:* Instructor, Stanford University, 1958-60; Assistant Professor, Ohio State University, 1961-64; Director of Writing, New York University, 1964-66; Professor, English, Brooklyn College, 1966-; Visiting Professorships, Tufts University, 1970, University of Washington, 1978, 1983. *Publications:* The Landscape of Nightmare, 1965; A Man to Conjure With, 1965; What Comes Next, 1968; Reruns, 1974; Babble, 1976; Chez Charlotte & Emily, 1979; (Stories): Return of Service, 1979; My Father More or Less, 1984; The Life and Times of Major Fiction, 1987; Separate Hours, 1990. *Contributions to:* Movie Critic, Partisan Review, 1973-82; Articles, Fiction in Esquire; New American Review; TriQuarterly; Iowa Review; North American Review; Fiction. *Honours:* National Endowment of the Arts Fellowship, 1978; Guggenheim Fellowship, 1980; O. Henry Prize Stories: included 1980, 1984, 1988; Best American Short Stories, included 1978. *Memberships:* Pen; Teachers & Writers Collaborative, Board of Directors; National Society of Film Critics, Chairman, 1982-84. *Literary Agent:* Robert Cornfield. *Address:* 320 Stratford Road, Brooklyn, NY 11218, USA.

BAWDEN Harry Reginald (Rex), b. 29 July 1921, Birkenhead, England. Journalist; Broadcaster. m. (1) Valerie Primrose Smith, 8 Sept. 1951, 1 daughter, (2) Sylvia Mary Richards, 2 March 1968. *Appointments:* Various Journalistic Posts, Birkenhead & Liverpool, 1938-40, 1946-50, Manchester, 1951-57; Deputy Editor, Newcastle Evening Chronicle, 1958; Editor, Aberdeen Evening Express, 1959-62; Assistant Editor, Sunday Times Colour Magazine, 1962-63; Chief Sub Editor, Liverpool Echo, 1963-67; News Editor, 1967-69, Manager, 1970-81, BBC Radio Merseyside; Chief Music Critic & Writer, Liverpool Daily Post, 1982-; Broadcaster on Music, BBC, 1967-. *Address:* 14 Kingsmead Road South, Oxton, Birkenhead, Merseyside, L43 6TA, England.

BAWDEN (KARK) Nina Mary, b. 19 Jan 1925. Novelist. m. (1) Henry Walton Bawden, 1946, (2) Austen Steven Kark, 1954, 2 sons 1 dec, 1 daughter, 2 stepdaughters. *Education:* MA Oxford 1946, Somerville College. *Publications:* Main Books: Carrie's War, 1975; Afternoon of a Good Woman, 1976; The Peppermint Pig, 1976; Circles of Deceit; Family Money, 1991; Total 21 novels, 18 children's books, 3 picture books. *Contributions to:* Reviews for: The Daily Telegraph; Evening Standard. *Honours:* Guardian Award Children's Books, 1975; Yorkshire Post Novel of the Year, 1976. *Memberships:* PEN, executive; Council, Royal Society Literature; President, Society of Women Writers & Journalists; Council, Society of Authors. *Literary Agent:* Curtis Brown. *Address:* 22 Noel Road, London N1 8HA, England.

BAXT George, b. 1923, American. *Publications:* Films: Circus of Horrors, The City of the Dead (Horror Hotel), 1960; The Shadow of the Cat, Payroll, 1961; Night of the Eagle (Burn Witch Burn), 1962; Strangler's Webb, Thunder in Dixie, 1965; Books: A Queer Kind of Death, 1966; Swing Low Sweet Harriet, A Parade of Cockeyed Creatures or Did Someone Murder Our Wandering Boys?, 1967; Topsy and Evil, 1968; II Said the Demon, 1969; The Affair at Royalties, 1971; Burning Sappho, 1972; Process of Eliminations, The Dorothy Parker Murder Case, 1984; The Alfred Hitchcock Murder Case: An Unauthorized Novel, 1986; The Tallulah Bankhead Murder Case, 1987; Who's Next? 1988; The Talking Picture Murder Case, 1990; The Greta Garbo Murder Case, 1992; The Noel Coward Murder Case, 1993; 40 short stories, Ellery Queen Mystery Magazine. *Address:* c/o St Martin Press, 175 Fifth Avenue, New York, NY 10010, USA.

BAXTER Craig, b. 16 Feb 1929, Elizabeth, New Jersey, USA. Professor; Author; Consultant. m. Barbara T Stevens, 28 May 1984, 1 son, 1 daughter. *Education:* BS, 1951, AM 1954, PhD, 1967, University of Pennsylvania. *Publications:* Bangladesh: A New Nation in an Old Setting, 1984; Co-author: Government and Politics in South Asia, 1987, 1990, 1993; Co-author: Zia's Pakistan: Politics and Stability in a Frontline State, 1985; Co-author: Pakistan Under the Military: Eleven Years of Zia ul-Haq, 1990; The Jana Sangh: Biography of an Indian Political Party, 1969; Co-author: From Martial Law to Martial Law, 1985; Co-author: Historial Dictionary of Bangladesh, 1989; Co-author: Pakistan Emerging Democracy, 1990. *Contributor to:* Publications including: Asian Survey; Journal of Asian Studies; Journal of Asian and African Studies; Current History; World Today; Washington Quarterly. *Memberships:* Association for Asian Studies; American Institute of Bangladesh Studies, President 1985-; American Institute of Pakistan Studies, Trustee 1986-; Foreign Service Association; Middle Atlantic Region/ Association for Asian Studies, Treasurer 1989-; Vice President, President Elect, 1992, Middle East Institute. *Address:* Department of Political Science, Juniata College, Huntingdon, PA 16652, USA.

BAXTER John. *See:* HUNT E(verette) Howard.

BAXTER John, b. 1939, Australian. *Appointments:* Director of Publicity, Australian Commonwealth Film Unit, Sydney, 1968-70; Lecturer in Film and Theatre, Hollins College, 1974-78; Freelance TV Producer and Screenwriter, 1978-87; Visiting Lecturer, Mitchell College, 1987. *Publications:* The Off Worlders, 1966; in Australia as The God Killers, Adam's Woman (adaptor), Hollywood in the Thirties, 1968; The Pacific Book of Australian Science Fiction, The Australian Cinema, Science Fiction in the Cinema, The Gangster Film, 1970; The Cinema of Josef von Sternburg, The Cinema of John Ford, The Second Pacific Book of Australian Science Fiction, 1971; Hollywood in the Sixties, 1972; Sixty Years of Hollywood, An Appalling Talent: Kent Russell, 1973; Stunt: The Story of the Great Movie Stunt Men, 1974; The Hollywood Exiles, The Fire Came By (with Thomas R Atkins), King Vidor, 1976; The Hermes Fall, 1978; The Bidders (in UK as Bidding), 1979; The Kid, 1981; The Video Handbook (with Brian Norris), The Black Yacht, 1982; Who Burned Australia? The Ash Wednesday Fires, 1984; Filmstruck, 1987. Feature Film Scripts: The Time Guardian, 1988. TV Series: The Cutting Room, 1986; First Take, 1986; Filmstruck, 1986. *Address:* c/o MBA Literary Agents, 45 Fitzroy St, London W1P 5HR, England.

BAXTER Raymond Frederic, b. 25 Jan 1922, London, England. Broadcaster; Writer. m. Sylvia Kathryn nee Johnson, 20 Sept 1945, Mulhouse, France. 1 son, 1 daughter. *Literary Appointments:* BBC Staff Commentator, Writer & Producer for Radio & TV, 1947-65, thereafter freelance. *Major Publications:* Tomorrow's World. Volumes 1 & 2 (with James Burke & Michael Latham), 1970, 1971; Farnborough Commentary, 1980. *Contributions to:* Numerous publications, including: Aeroplane; Flight; Autocar; Motor Boat & Yachting; Punch; Daily Telegraph; Radio Times; film commentaries, various radio & television programmes. *Honours:* Fellow, Royal Society of Arts, 1966; Harold Pemberton Trophy, 1966; Honorary Freeman of the City of London, 1968; Liveryman, Guild of Air Pilots, 1982; Vice President, RNLI, 1987; Companion RAes, 1991. *Memberships:* Guild of Motoring Writers (Committee 1961-65); Hon Admiral,

Assoc, Dunkirk Little Ships, 1982-. *Address:* The Green Cottage, Wargrave Road, Henley-on-Thames, Oxfordshire RG9 3HX, England.

BAYBARS Taner, (Timothy Bayliss), b. 18 June 1936, Cyprus, British, Writer; Winegrower. 1 daughter. *Education:* Private, Turkish Lycee. *Publications:* To Catch a Falling Man, 1963; A Trap for the Burglar, 1965; Plucked in a Far-Off Land, 1970; Narcissus in a Dry Pool, 1978; Pregnant Shadows, 1981; A Sad State of Freedom, 1990; Many others; Critical Quarterly, Ambit, Orte, Détours d'Ecritures, Hudson Review, Club de Vin d'Angoulême. *Memberships:* The Poetry Society of London. *Literary Agent:* MBA Literary Agents. *Address:* Les Epardeaux, St Amant de Bonnieure, 16230 Mansle, France.

BAYER William, (Leonie St John), b. 1939, American. *Appointment:* US Foreign Service, WA, 1963-68. *Publications:* Love with a Harvard Accent (as Leonie St John: with Nancy Harmon), 1962; In Search of a Hero, 1966; Breaking Through, Selling Out, Dropping dead and Other Notes on Filmmaking, 1971; The Great Movies, 1973; Stardust, 1974; Visions of Isabelle, 1976; Tangier, 1978; Punish Me with Kisses, 1980; Peregrine, 1981; Switch, 1984; Pattern Crimes, 1987; Blind Side, 1989; Wall Flower, 1991; Mirror Maze, 1993. *Honour:* Edgar Allan Poe Award. *Address:* P.O.Box 322, Newtown, CT 06470, USA.

BAYLEY Barrington John, (Alan Aumbry, P F Woods), b. 9 Apr 1937, Birmingham, England. Author. m. Joan Lucy Clarke, 31 Oct 1969, 1 son, 1 daughter. *Publications:* The Soul of the Robot, 1974; The Rod of Light, 1985; The Knights of the Limits, 1978; The Zen Gun, 1984; The Fall of Chronopolis, 1974; Collision with Chronos, 1973; The Garments of Caean, 1976; The Grand Wheel, 1977; Star Virus, 1970; Annihilation Factor, 1972; Empire of Two Worlds, 1972; Star Winds, 1978; The Pillars of Eternity, 1982; The Seed of Evil, 1979; The Forest of Peldain, 1985. *Contributions to:* New Worlds, Interzone. *Honours:* Seiun Award for Best Foreign Science Fiction Novel Published in Japan, 1984-85. *Memberships:* Science Fiction Foundation. *Literary Agent:* Michael Congdon, Don Congdon Associates Inc. *Address:* 48 Turreff Avenue, Donnington, Telford, Shropshire TF2 8HE, England.

BAYLEY Peter (Charles), b. 1921, British. *Appointments:* Fellow, University College 1947-72, Praelector in English 1949-72, University lecturer 1952-72, Oxford University; Master, Collingwood College, University of Durham, 1972-78; Berry Professor and Head of English Department 1978-85, Berry Professor Emeritus 1985-, University of St Andrews, Fife. *Publications:* (ed)The Faerie Queene, by Spenser, Book II 1965, Book I 1966, 1970; Edmund Spenser, Prince of Poets, 1971; Loves and Deaths, 1972; A Casebook on Spenser's Faerie Queene, 1977; Poems of Milton, 1982; An ABC of Shakespeare, 1985. *Address:* 63 Oxford Street, Woodstock, Oxford, OX20 1TJ, England.

BAYLISS Timothy. *See:* **BAYBARS Taner.**

BAYLY Joseph, b. 1920, American. *Appointments:* Member of New England Staff, East Coast Supervisor, HIS Editor and Director, Director, Inter-Varsity Christian Fellowship, 1944-60; Managing Editor 1963-72, Vice President 1972-, David C Cook Publishing Company, Elgin IL. *Publications:* The Gospel Blimp, 1960; Martyred, 1966; The Last Thing We Talk About, Psalms of My Life, 1969; What About Horoscopes?, Out of My Mind, 1970; How Silently (formerly I Saw Gooley Fry), 1973; Winterflight, 1981. *Address:* 29 W515 Orchard Lane, Bartlett, IL 60103, USA.

B B. *See:* **WATKINS-PITCHFORD Denys James.**

BEACH Edward Latimer, b. 20 Apr 1918, New York, USA. Naval Officer; Author. m. Ingrid Schenck, 4 June

1944, 2 sons, 2 daughters. *Education:* US Naval academy, 1939; The George Washington University, MA, 1963; American International University, SCD (H), 1962; Bridgeport University, LLD (H), 1963; National War College, 1963. *Publications:* Submarine!; Run Silent, Run Deep; Around The World Submerged; The Wreck of The Memphis; Dust on the Sea; Cold is The Sea; The United States Navy: 200 Years; Keepers of the Sea; Naval Terms Dictionary, ed 3, 4, 5. *Contributions to:* US Naval Institute Proceedings; National Geographic; Colliers; Argosy; Esquire; Town & Country; Readers Digest; Bluebook; Saturday Evening Post; American Heritage; Sea Power; The Washington Post; Shipmate. *Honours include:* US Navy League Alfred Thayer Mahan Award; Theodore Roosevelt Distinguished Service Medal; US Naval Institute Award of Merit; Theodore & Franlin D Roosevelt Award of Merit. *Memberships:* Authors League; US Naval Institute; National Geographic Society; Cosmos Club; Metropolitan Club, New York City; Naval Historical Foundation; Secretary of the Navys Historical Advisory Committee. *Literary Agent:* Sterling Lord Literistic. *Address:* 1622-29th NW, Washington, DC 20007, USA.

BEACHCROFT Ellinor Nina, b. 10 Nov 1931, London, England. Writer. m. Dr Richard Gardner, 7 Aug 1954, 2 daughters. *Education:* Wimbledon High School, 1942-49; 2nd Class Hons degree in English Literature, St Hilda's College, Oxford, 1953. *Publications:* Well Met by Witchlight, 1972; Under the Enchanter, 1974; Cold Christmas, 1974; A Spell of Sleep, 1975; A Visit to Folly Castle, 1976; The Wishing People, 1978; The Genie and her Bottle, 1983; Beyond World's End, 1985; A Farthing for the Fair, 1977. *Memberships:* Society of Authors, Children's Writers' Group, twice a Committee Member. *Literary Agent:* David Highams. *Address:* 9 Raffin Green Lane, Datchworth, Herts SG3 6RJ, England.

BEADELL Leonard, b. 21 Apr 1923, West Pennant Hills, New South Wales, Australia. Surveyor; Author. m. 1 July 1961, 1 son, 2 daughters. *Publications:* Too Long in the Bush, 1965; Blast the Bush, 1967; Bush Bashers; Still in the Bush, 1975; Beating About the Bush, 1976; Outback Highways, 1979; End of an Era, 1983; A Lifetime in the Bush, Limited edition, box set. *Contribution to:* The Australian Author. *Honours:* BEM, 1958; FIEMS, (Aust), 1987; OAM, 1988; Advance Australia Award, 1989. *Memberships:* Australian Society of Authors; Chief Savage and Committee Member, Adelaide Savage Club. *Literary Agent:* Weldon Oublishing, Sydney, NSW. *Address:* 15 Fleet Street, Salisbury, SA 5108, Australia.

BEALE Paul Christian, b. 13 Mar 1933, Five Ashes, East Sussex, England. Librarian; Retired. m. Daphne Margaret Hughes, 9 Sept 1967. *Education:* BA, Chinese, 1971; Library & Info Studies, 1975; Civil Service, Chinese, 1966. *Publications:* Partridge's Dict of Slang & Unconventional English; Partridge's Dict of Catch Phrases; Concise Dict of Slang & Unconventional English. *Address:* 131 Byron Street, Loughborough, Leics, LE11 0JN, England.

BEALES D(erek) E(dward) D(awson), b. 1931, British. *Appointments:* Research Fellow 1955-58, Fellow 1958-, Tutor 1961-70, Vice-Master 1973-75, Sidney Sussex College; Assistant Lecturer 1962-65, Lecturer 1965-80, Chairman, Faculty Board of History 1979-81, Professor of Modern History 1980-, Cambridge University; Member of Council, Royal Historical Society, 1984-87; Editor, Historical Journal, 1971-75. *Publications:* England and Italy 1859-60, 1961; From Castlereagh to Gladstone, 1969; The Risorgimento and the Unification of Italy, 1971; History and Biography, 1981; History, Society and the Churches (ed with G F A Best), 1985; Joseph II: In the Shadow of Maria Theresa 1741-1780, 1987. *Honours:* Doctor of Letters, 1988; Fellow of the British Academy, 1989; Stanton Lecturer, University of Reading, 1992; Birkbeck Lecturer, Trinity College, Cambridge, 1993. *Address:* Sidney Sussex College, Cambridge, CB2 3HU, England.

BEAR Greg(ory Dale), b. 1951, American. Writer. *Appointments:* Lecturer, San Diego Aerospace Museum, 1969-72; Writer and Planetarium Operator, Fleet Space Theatre, 1973; Freelance writer, 1975-. *Publications:* Hegira, Psychlone, 1979; Beyond Heaven's River, 1980; Strength of Stones, 1981; The Wind from a Burning Woman, 1983; Corona, The Infinity Concerto, 1984; Blood Music, Eon, 1985; The Serpent Mage, 1986; The Forge of God, 1987. *Address:* Lakeview Road, Alderwood Manor, Washington DC 98036, USA.

BEARDSLEY John Douglas, b. 27 Apr 1941, Montreal, Canada. Writer; Editor; Teacher; Reviewer. 1 daughter. *Education:* BA, University of Victoria, 1976; MA, English, 1st Class Honours, York University, Toronto, 1978. *Publications:* A Dancing Star, 1988; Country on Ice, 1987; Kissing the Body of my Lord, 1982; Play on the Water, 1978; The Only Country in the World Called Canada, 1976; Going Down into History, 1976; Six Saanich Poems, 1977; Premonitions & Gifts, 1979; Poems, 1979; Pacific Sands, 1980. *Contributor to:* American Poetry Review; Canadian Forum; Canadian Literature; Poetry Canada Review; etc. *Honours:* Canada Council Arts Award; Ontario Arts Council Award; Canada Council Short-term Grants, etc. *Memberships:* League of Canadian Poets; Amnesty International; PEN; International Council of Candians; Association of Canadian University Teachers of English. *Address:* 1074 Lodge Avenue, Victoria, BC V8X 3A8, Canada.

BEASLEY William Gerald, b. 1919, British. Professor. *Appointments:* Professor of History of the Far East, School of Oriental and African Studies, University of London, 1954-83, now Emeritus. *Publications:* Great Britain and the Opening of Japan 1833-1858, 1951; Select Documents on Japanese Foreign Policy 1853-1868 (ed and translator), 1955; Historians of China and Japan (ed with E G Pulleyblank), 1961; The Modern History of Japan, 1963, 3rd edition 1981; The Meiji Restoration, 1972; Modern Japan: Aspects of History, Literature and Society, 1975; Japanese Imperialism 1894-1945, 1987; The Rise of Modern Japan, 1990. *Address:* 172 Hampton Road, Twickenham TW2 5NJ, England.

BEASLEY-MURRAY George Raymond, 10 Oct 1916, London, England. Professor. m. Ruth Weston, 4 Apr 1942, 3 sons, 1 daughter. *Education:* London University, BD, 1941; M Th, 1945; PhD, 1952; Kings College, DD, 1963; Cambridge University, MA, 1954; DD, 1990. *Appointments:* Spurgeons College, London, Lecturer, 1950-56; Professor of Greek New Testament, Ruschlikon Zurich, 1956-58; Professor, Southern Baptist Seminary, Louisville, 1973-80; Senior Professor, 1980-. *Publications:* Jesus and the Future; A Commentary on Mark Thirteen; Baptism in the New Testament; The Book of Revelation, New Century Bible; Jesus and the Kingdom of God; John, in Word Biblical Commentary; Gospel of Life: Theology in the Fourth Gospel; Jesus and the Last Days. *Contributions to:* Numerous, Journal of Theological Studies;New Testament Studies; Evangelical Quarterly; Expository Times; Catholic Biblical Quarterly; Foundations; Scottish Journal of Theology; Theology Today; Review & Expositor; Baptist Quarterly. *Memberships:* Studiorum Novi Testament Societas; Society of Biblical Literature; Catholic Biblical Association. *Address:* 4 Holland Road, Hove, East Sussex, BN3 1JJ, England.

BEATTY Warren. *See:* BEATY Warren.

BEATY Arthur David, b. 28 Mar 1919, Hatton, Ceylon. Author. m. Betty Joan Campbell Smith, 29 Apr 1948, 3 Daughters. *Education:* MA History, Merton College, Oxford University, England, 1940; M Phil Psychology, University College London, 1965; Airline Transport Pilot's Licence; Navigation and Radio Licences. *Appointments:* R.A.F, 1940-46; British Overseas Airways Corporation, 1946-53; Foreign Office, 1966-74. *Publications:* The Take Off, 1948; The Heart of the Storm, 1954; The Proving Flight, 1956; Cone of Silence, 1958; Call Me Captain, 1959; Village of Stars,

1960; The Wind off the Sea, 1962; The Siren Song, 1964; Milk and Honey, 1964; Sword of Honour, 1965; The Human Factor in Aircraft Accidents, 1969; The Temple Tree, 1971; Electric Train, 1974; Excellency, 1977; The Complete Sky Traveller, 1978; The White Sea Bird, 1979; With Betty Beaty Wings of the Morning, 1982; Strange Encounters, 1982; The Stick, 1984; The Blood Brothers, 1987; Eagles, 1990. *Contributions to:* Many magazines and Radio plays. *Honours:* Distinguished Flying Cross, 1944; Bar to the Distinguished Flying Cross, 1945; Aero Club Award for Literature, 1959. *Memberships:* Society of Authors; Authors Guild; R.A.F. Club; Royal Aeronautical Society. *Literary Agent:* Mike Shaw; Curtis Brown. *Address:* Manchester House, Church Hill, Slindon, Near Arundel, West Sussex BN18 0RD, England.

BEATY Betty Smith, (Karen Campbell, Catherine Ross), British. *Appointments:* Former WAAF Officer; Airline Hostess; Medical Social Worker, London. *Publications:* Maiden Flight, South to the Sea, 1956; Amber Five, The Butternut Tree, 1958; From this Day Forward (as C Ross), 1959; The Colours of the Night (as C Ross), 1962; The Path of the Moonfish, The Trysting Tower (as C Ross), 1964; Miss Miranda's Walk, 1967; Suddenly In the Air (as K Campbell), 1969; Thunder on Sunday (as K Campbell), 1971; Wheel Fortune (as K Campbell), The Swallows of San Fedora, Love ad the Kentish Maid, 1973; Head of Chancery, 1974; Master at Arms, 1975; Fly Away Love, Death Descending (as K Campbell), 1976; Exchange of Hearts, 1977; The Bells of St Martin (as K Campbell), Battle Dress (as C Ross), 1979; Wings of the Morning (with David Beaty), 1982; The Missionary's Daughter, Matchmaker Nurse, 1983.

BEATY Warren (Warren Beatty). b. 30 Mar 1937, Richmond, Virginia, USA. *Education:* Attended Northwestern University, 1955-56 and Stella Adler Theatre School 1957. *Career:* Actor 1957-; Film Producer 1967-; Screen writer 1975-; Film Director, 1978-. Worked odd jobs in Washington DC and New York NY. Actor in stage plays, including: A Hatful of Rain; The Happiest Millionaire; Visit to a Small Planet; The Boy Friend and Compulsion during the late 1950s. and in the Broadway play, A Loss of Roses, 1959; actor in television programs, including The Many Loves of Dobie Gillis, 1959-60 and Studio One, Playhouse 90 and Kraft Theatre during the late 1950s; actor in motion pictures, including, Splendor in the Grass, 1961; The Roman Spring of Mrs Stone, 1961; All Fall Down, 1962; Lilith 1963; Mickey One 1965; Promise Her Anything 1966; Bonnie and Clyde 1967; Kaleidoscope 1968; The Only Game in Town 1970; McCable and Mrs Miller 1971; Dollars 1971; The Parallax View 1974; The Fortune 1975; Shampoo 1975; Heaven Can Wait 1978; Reds 1981 and Ishtar 1987. *Publications:* Screenplays: (with Robert Towne) Shampoo, Columbia, 1975; (with Elaine May and co-director) Heaven Can Wait, Paramount, 1978; (with Trevor Griffiths and director) Reds, Paramount, 1981. *Honours:* Academy Award nominations from Academy of Motion Picture Arts and Sciences for best actor, 1967, for Bonnie and Clyde, for best actor, best director, best screenplay and best film, 1978, for Heaven Can Wait and for best actor, best screenplay and best film, 1981, for Reds; Academy Award for best director, 1981, for Reds. *Memberships:* Writers Guild of America; Directors Guild of America; Screen Actors Guild. *Address:* c/o Traubner & Flynn, 1849 Sawtelle, Suite 500, Los Angeles, CA 90025, USA.

BEAUMONT Helen. *See:* **UPSHALL Helen Ruby.**

BEAVER Bruce (Victor), b. 1928, Australian. *Appointment:* Freelance Journalist. *Publications:* Under the Bridge, 1961; Seawall and Shoreline, 1964; The Hot Spring, 1965; You Can't Come Back, 1966; Open at Random, 1967; Letters to Live Poets, 1969; Lauds and Plaints 1968-1972, 1974; Odes and Days, 1975; Death's Directives, 1978; As It Was, Selected Poems, 1979; Prose Sketches, 1986; Charmed Lives, 1988; New and Selected Poems 1960-1990, 1991. *Honours:* FAW, Christopher Brennan Award; Patrick White Literary Award, 1982; NSW, State Special Literary Award, 1990;

Captain Cook Bi-Centenary Prize; Grace Leven Prize; Poetry Society of Australia Award; AM Award, 1991. *Address:* 14 Malvern Avenue, Manly, NSW 2095, Australia.

BEAVER (Jack) Patrick, b. 5 Feb 1923, London, England. Author; Producer & Director, Documentary Films. m. Amé Parr, 1969, 1 son. *Publications include:* The Big Ship, 1969; Crystal Palace, 1970; History of Lighthouses, 1971; History of Tunnels, 1972; Spice of Life, 1979; Wipers Times, 1973. Also: 12 company & corporate histories including: Matchmakers (Bryant & May); Yes! We Have Some (Fyffes); Pedlar's Legacy (Empire Stores). *Contributions to:* Many & various journals. *Memberships:* Society of Authors; Performing Rights Society. *Literary Agent:* Scott Ferris Associates. *Address:* 50 Great Russell Street, Bloomsbury, London WC1B 3BA, England.

BEAVER Paul Eli, b. 3 Apr 1953, Winchester, England. Journalist; Author and Broadcaster. m. Ann Middleton, 20 May 1978 (separated). *Education:* Sheffield City Polytechnic; Henley Management College. *Literary Appointments:* Editor: IPMS Magazine, 1976-80, Helicopter World, 1981-86, Defence Helicopter World, 1982-86, Jane's Videotape, 1986-87; Assistant Compiler Jane's Fighting Ships, 1987-88; Managing Editor, Jane's Defence Yearbooks, 1988-89; Publisher, Jane's Defence Weekly, 1989-93; Senior Publisher, Jane's SENTINEL, 1993-. *Publications include:* Ark Royal - A Pictorial History, 1979; U-Boats In The Atlantic, 1979; German Capital Ships, 1980; German Destroyers and Escorts, 1981; British Aircraft Carrier, 1982; Encyclopaedia of The Modern Royal Navy, 1982; Carrier Air Operations, 1983; Fleet Command, 1984; Invincible Class, 1984; British Aircraft Carrier (Second Edition), 1984; British Navel Air Power, 1985; Royal Navy of The 1980's, 1985; NATO Navies of the 1980's, 1985; Encyclopaedia of The Modern Royal Navy (Second Edition), 1985; Missile Systems, 1985; Nuclear-Powered Submarines, 1986; Modern British Missiles, 1986; Encyclopaedia of Aviation, 1986; Modern Royal Navy Warships, 1987; British Aircraft Carrier (Third Edition), 1987; Encyclopaedia of The Modern Royal Navy (Third Edition), 1987; Modern Military Helicopters, 1987; Attack Helicopters, 1987; Encyclopaedia of The Fleet Air Arm Since 1945, 1987; Today's Army Air Corps; The Modern Royal Navy; Today's Royal Marines; Jane's World Naval Aviation; General Editor for Volume 1 Military Aerospace, Videotape companion to Jane's All The World's Aircraft; Rescue, (with Paul Berriff). *Contributions to:* Various Aerospace, Defence, Naval, Travel and Associated Journals and Magazines; Nikkei Business (arms trade and international security); Nikkei/Japan Economic Journal (internaitonal security); The Guaridan (flashpoints/conflicts); The Observer (international security); Sky Television (resident defence specialist); Fuji TV (internationa; security correspondent). *Memberships:* Royal United Services Institute; Helicopter Club of Great Britain; Fleet Air Arm Officers' Association; Army Aviation Association of America; Royal Institution of Chartered Surveyors; Army Air Corps Association. *Address:* Poppy Cottage, Barfield, Beltchingley, Surrey, RH1 4RD, England.

BEBB Prudence, b. 20 Mar 1939, Catterick, England. Writer. *Education:* BA; Dip Ed. *Publications:* The Eleventh Emerald; The Ridgeway Ruby; The White Swan; The Nabob's Nephew; Life in Regency York. *Memberships:* English Centre of International PEN. *Address:* 12 Brackenhills, Upper Poppleton, York, YO2 6DH, England.

BECHKO Peggy Anne, (Bill Haller), b. 1950, American. *Appointments:* Former Artist's Model; Legal Secretary; Delivery Person; Gift Wrapper. *Publications:* Night of the Flaming Guns, Gunman's Justice, 1974; Blown to Hell, Sidewinder's Trail (as B Haller), Dead Man's Feud, 1976; The Winged Warrior 1977 (in UK as Omaha Jones 1979); Hawker's Indians, 1979; Dark Side of Love, 1983; Harmonie Mexicaine, 1984. *Address:* 402 B Linda Vista Road, Santa Fe, NM 87501, USA.

BECHMANN Roland Philippe, b. 1 Apr 1919, Paris, France. Architect; Historian; Writer. m. Martine Cohen, 18 July 1942, 6 daughters. *Education:* Licencie es Lettres 1938; Architect Diplome par le Couvenement 1944; Docteur (3C) en Geographie 1978. *Publications:* Villard de Honnecourt: la pensee technique au XIIIe siecle et sa communication, (technical knowledge in the 13th century and its transmission), 1991; Les Racines des Cathedrales, L'architecture gothique, expression des conditions du milieu, 1989, 1984, 1981; Trees and Man: The Forest in the Middle Ages, 1990; Le radici delle cattedrali, pocket book, 1989; Villard de Honnecourt: disegni, 1987, joint author; Le radici delle cattedrali, 1984; Des Arbres et des Hommes, La foret au Moyen Age, 1984. *Contributions to:* Pour la Science (French Scientific America); Science er Vie; Historia; La Revue des Armes; Chief Editor, Amenagement et Nature, 1966-. *Address:* 23 rue du Conseille Collignon, 75116 Paris, France.

BECK Ian Archibald. b. 17 Aug 1947, Hove, England. Author; Illustrator. m. Emma Gabrielle stone, 7 May 1977, 2 sons, 1 daughter. *Education:* Brighton College of Art, 1963-68. *Publications:* Round & Round the Garden; Babys First Years; The teddy Robber; Little Miss Muffet; Emily And The Golden Acorn; Pudding And Pie; Ride A Cock Horse; Oranges & Lemons; Five Little Ducks; Edible Architecture; Hush A Bye Baby. *Contributions to:* The Sunday Telegraph Newspaper. *Honours:* Smith Illustration Award. *Memberships:* The Art Workers Guild; Chelsea Arts Club; The Double Crown Club. *Literary Agent:* Jenni Stone. *Address:* 48 Northcote Road, St Margarets, Twickenham TW1 1PA, England.

BECK Tatyana, b. 21 Apr 1949, Moscow, C.I.S. Poetress; Writer. m. div. *Education:* Diploma of A Literary Editor, Moscow State University, Journalist Department 1967-72. *Appointments:* Znamya, 1992 N9, number of poems. *Publications:* Skvoreshniky, 1974; Snegir, 1980; Zamysel, 1987; Poetry: Mixed Forest, 1993. *Contributions to:* Poems and articles in: Novymir; Znamya; Oktyabr; Voprosy; Literatury; Literatyrnoe Obozrenie; Ogoniek; and others. *Memberships:* Writers Union (former USSR), Secretary and member; Russian PEN Centre. *Address:* Krasnoarmeiskaya Street, House No 23, Apartment 91, Moscow 125319, C.I.S.

BECK Warren Albert, b. 1918, American. Professor. *Appointments:* Professor of History, Augustana College, Sioux Falls SD, 1948-50, Capital University, Columbia, OH, 1950-55, Eastern New Mexico University, Portales, 1955-58, Santa Ana College, CA, 1958-61, California State University, Fullerton, 1961-. *Publications:* A History of New Mexico, 1962; Historical Atlas of New Mexico (co-author), 1968; California: A History of the Golden State (co-author), 1972; Understanding American History Through Fiction (co-author), Historical Atlas of California (co-author), 1975; The California Experience, 1976; Historical Atlas of the American West (co- author), 1987. *Address:* 537 Lee Place, Placentia, CA 92670, USA.

BECKER Jillian, b. 1932, British. *Publications:* The Keep, 1967; The Union, 1971; The Virgins, 1976; Hitler's Children, 1977; The PLO: The Rise and Fall of the Palestine Liberation Organization, 1984. *Address:* c/o Weidenfeld and Nicholson, 91 Clapham High Street, London SW4 7TA, England.

BECKER Lucille Frackman, b. 1929, American. Professor. *Appointments:* Lecturer in French, Columbia University, 1954-58; Instructor in French, Rutgers University, Newark, 1959-69; Professor of French, Drew University, Madison, 1969-. *Publications:* Le Maître de Santiago by Henry de Montherlant (ed with A della Fazia), 1965; Henry de Montherlant, 1970; Louis Aragon, 1971; Georges Simenon, 1978; Françoise Mallet-Joris, 1985; Twentieth Century French Women Novelists, 1988. Chapters in works: Georges Simenon, European Writers: The Twentieth Century, vol 12, 1990; Françoise Mallet-Joris, French Women Writers: A Bio-

Bibliographical Source Book, 1991. *Address:* Drew University, Madison, NJ 07940, USA.

BECKER Stephen David, b. 31 Mar 1927, Mt Vernon, New York, USA. Novelist; Translator. m. Mary Elizabeth Freeburg, 24 Dec 1947, Beijing, 2 sons, 1 daughter. *Education:* AB 1947, Harvard College; Yenching University, Beijing 1947-48. *Appointments:* Occasional teaching and lecturing at several universities. *Publications:* Novels: The Season of the Stranger, 1951; Shanghai Incident, 1955; Juice, 1959; A Covenant with Death, 1965; The Outcasts, 1967; When the War Is Over, 1970; Dog Tags, 1973, reissue 1987; The Chinese Bandit, 1975; The Last Mandarin, 1979; The Blue- Eyed Shan, 1982; A Rendezvous in Haiti, 1987; Non-fiction: Comic Art in America, 1959; Marshall Field III, 1964. *Translations:* The Colours of the Day, 1953; Mountains in the Desert, 1954; The Sacred Forest, 1954; Faraway, 1957; Someone Will Die Tonight in the Caribbean, 1958; The Last of the Just, 1961; The Town Beyond the Wall, 1964; The Conquerors, 1976; Diary of My Travels in America, 1977; Ana No, 1980; The Aristotle System, 1985; Cruel April, 1990; Between Tides, 1991; The Forgotten, 1992. *Contributions to:* Dozens of short stories, essays, reviews, columns, introductions. *Honours:* Rotary Fellowship to Peking, 1947; Guggenheim Fellowship, fiction, 1954; NEA grant in translation, 1984; Judge, Hopwood Awards, fiction, University of Michigan, 1989. *Literary Agent:* Russell & Volkening, NY. *Address:* 880 Benchwood Drive, Winter Springs, FL 32708, USA.

BECKERMAN Wilfred, b. 1925, British. *Appointments:* Lecturer in Economics, University of Nottingham, 1950-52; Paris with OEEC (later OECD), 1952-62; London with NIESR, 1963-64; Fellow and Tutor in Economics 1964-69, Fellow 1975-, Balliol College, Oxford; Professor of Political Economy, University College, 1969-75; Member of Staff 1962-64, Governor and Member of Executive Committee 1972-, National Institute of Economics and Social Research, London. *Publications:* The British Economy (with Associates) in 1975, 1965; International Comparisons of Real Income, 1966; An Introduction to National Income Analysis, 1968; The Labour Government's Economic Record 1964-70, 1972; In Defence of Economic Growth (in US as Two Cheers for the Affluent Society), 1974; Measures of Equality Leisure and Welfare, Poverty and the Impact of Income Maintenance Payments, Slow Growth In Britain: Causes and Consequences, 1979; Poverty and Social Security in Britain since 1961 (with S Clark), 1982. *Membership:* Royal Commission on Environmental Pollution, 1970-73. *Address:* Balliol College, Oxford OX1 3BJ, England.

BECKETT Kenneth Albert, b. 12 Jan 1929, Brighton, Sussex, England. Horticulturalist; Technical Advisor; Editor. m. Gillian Tuck, 1 Aug 1973, 1 son. *Education:* Diploma, Horticulture, Royal Horticulture Society. *Appointments:* Technical Editor, Gardeners' Chronicle, Readers Digest. *Publications:* The Love of Trees, 1975; Illustrated Dictionary of Botany, 1977; Concise Encyclopaedia of Garden Plants, 1978; Amateur Greenhouse Gardening, 1979; Growing Under Glass, 1981; Complete Book of Evergreens, 1981; Growing Hardy Perennials, 1981; Climbing Plants, 1983; The Garden Library, 4 volumes: Flowering House Plants, Annuals and Biennials, Roses, Herbs, 1984; The RHS Encyclopaedia of House Plants, 1987; Evergreens, 1990. *Contributor to:* The Garden; The Plantsman. *Membership:* Scientific Committee, Royal Horticultural Society. *Address:* Bramley Cottage, Stanhoe, King's Lynn, Norfolk PE31 8QF, England.

BECKLES WILLSON Robina Elizabeth, b. 1930, British. *Appointments:* Teacher, Liverpool School of Art 1952-56, Ballet Rambert Educational School 1956-58, London. *Publications:* Leopards on the Loire, 1961; A Time to Dance, 1962; Musical Instruments, 1964; A Reflection of Rachel, The Leader of the Band, 1967; Roundabout Ride, 1968; Dancing Day, 1971; The Last Harper, The Shell on Your Back, 1972; What a Noise, 1974; The Voice of Music, 1975; Musical Merry-go-

Round, 1977; The Beaver Book of Ballet, 1979; Eyes Wide Open, Anna Pavlova: A Legend among Dancers, 1981; Pocket Book of Ballet, Secret Witch, 1982; Square Bear, Merry Christmas, Holiday Witch, 1983; Sophie and Nicky series, 2 volumes, Hungry Witch, 1984; Music Maker, Sporty Witch, 1986. *Address:* 44 Popes Avenue, Twickenham, Middlesex TW2 5TL, England.

BECKWITH Lillian, b. 25 Apr 1916, Ellesmere Port, England. Author. m. Edward Thornthwaite Comber, 3 June 1937, 1 son, 1 daughter. *Education:* Ornum College, Birkenhead. *Publications:* The Hebridean Stories: The Hills is Lonely, 1959, The Sea for Breakfast, 1961, The Loud Halo, 1964, A Rope in Case, 1968, Beautiful Just! 1975, Lightly Poached, 1973; The Spuddy, 1974; Green Hand, 1967; About My Father's Business, 1971; The Lillian Beckwith Hebridean Cookbook (Anecdotes and recipes) 1976; Bruach Blend, 1978; A Shine of Rainbows, 1984; The Bay of Strangers, 1988; A Proper Woman, 1986; The Small Party, 1989; An Island Apart, 1992. *Contributor to:* The Countryman; Woman's Own and various other magazines for women. *Memberships:* Society of Authors; Mark Twain Society; Women of the Year Association, Consultative Committee. *Literary Agent:* Curtis Brown Ltd. *Address:* c/o Curtis Brown Ltd, 163-168 Regent Street, London W1R 5TB, England.

BEDAU Hugo Adam, b. 1926, American. Professor. *Appointments:* Associate Professor of Philosophy, Reed College, Portland, OR, 1962-66; Professor of Philosophy, Tufts University, Medford, MA, 1966-. *Publications:* Author: The Courts the Constitution and Capital Punishment, 1977; Death is Different, 1987; Editor: The Death Penalty in America, 1964, 1982; Civil Disobedience: Theory and Practice, 1969; Justice and Equality, 1971. Co-Author: Nomos VI: Justice, 1963; Nomos IX: Equality, 1967; The Concept of Academic Freedom, 1972; Philosophy and Political Action, 1972; Philosophy Morality and International Affairs, Victimless Crimes: Two Views, 1974; Justice and Punishment, 1977; Human Rights and US Foreign Policy, Making Decisions, The Imposition of Law, 1979; Matters of Life and Death, 1980; Ethical Issues in Government, 1981; And Justice for All, 1982; Group Decision Making, 1984; Nomos XXVII: Criminal Justice, 1985; Current Issues and Enduring Questions, 1987, 1990. *Address:* c/o Department of Philosophy, Tufts University, Medford, MA 02155, USA.

BEECHING Jack, b. 8 May 1922, Hastings, Sussex, England. Writer. *Publications:* Poetry: Aspects of Love, 1950; The Polythene Maidenhead in, Penguin Modern Poets, 1969; Twenty Five Short Poems, 1982; The View From The Balloon, 1990; Novels: Let Me See Your Face, 1958; The Dakota Project, 1967; Death of a Terrorist, 1982; Tides of Fortune, 1988. History: The Chinese Opium Wars, 1975; An Open Path: Christian Missionaries 1515-1914, 1979; The Galleys at Lepanto, 1982. *Literary Agent:* Tessa Sayle. *Address:* c/o Tessa Sayle, 11 Jubilee Place, London SW3 3CE, England.

BEER Patricia, b. 1924, British. Lecturer. *Appointments:* Lecturer in English, University of Padua, 1946-48, Ministero Aeronautica, Rome, 1950-53, Italy; Senior Lecturer in English, Goldsmiths' College, University of London, 1962-68. *Publications:* Loss of the Magyar and Other Poems, 1959; New Poems (ed with Ted Hughes and Vernon Scannell), 1962; The Survivors, 1963; Just Like the Resurrection, 1967; Mrs Beer's House, (auto biog), 1968; The Estuary, 1971; An Introduction to the Metaphysical Poets, 1972; Spanish Balcony, 1973; Reader, I Married Him, 1974; Driving West, 1975; Moon's Ottery, 1978; Poems 1967-1979, Selected Poems, 1979; The Lie of the Land, 1983; Wessex, 1985. *Contributions to:* The Listener; London Review of Books. *Address:* Tiphayes, Up Ottery, Nr Honiton, Devon, England.

BEERS Burton Floyd, b. 1927, American. Professor. *Appointments:* Instructor 1955-57, Assistant Professor 1957-61, Associate Professor 1961-66, Professor of History 1966-, Alumni Distinguished Professor 1970-, North Carolina State University, Raleigh. *Publications:* Vain Endeavour: Robert Lansing's Attempts to End the American-Japanese Rivalry, 1962; The Far East: A History of Western Impacts and Eastern Responses (with P H Clyde), 6th edition, 1976; China in Old Photographs, 1978; World History: Patterns of Civilization, senior writer, 1st - 6th editions, 1983-1993; N C State: A Pictorial History (with Murray S Downs), 1986; World History: Patterns of Civilizations (Senior Writer) 6th rev ed. *Memberships:* American Historical Association; World History Association. *Honour:* 1st Recipient of Alexander Quarles Holladay Medal of Excellence, by North Carolina University's Chancellor and Board of Trustees. *Address:* 629 South Lakeside Drive, Raleigh, NC 27606, USA.

BEERS V. Gilbert, b. 6 May 1928, Sidell, Illinois, USA. Editor; Author. m. 26 Aug. 1950, 2 sons, 3 daughters. *Education:* AB, Wheaton College; MRE, MDiv, Th.M, Th.D., Northern Baptist Theological Seminary; PhD, Northwestern Univerity, Evanston. *Appointments include:* Custom book development for 10 publishers, 1967-; Editor, Christianity Today Magazine, 1982-85, Senior Editor, 1985-. *Publications include:* Joy Is; Patterns for Prayer; The Victor Handbook of Bible Knowledge; Family Bible Library, 10 volumes; The Book of Life, 23 volumes; Childrens Books; A Child's Treasury of Bible Stories, 4 volumes; Cats and Bats and Things Like That; The ABQ Book; Coco's Candy Shop; The Magic Merry Go Round; Around the World with My Red Balloon; The House in the Hole in the Side of the Tree; A Gaggle of Green Geese; Honeyphants and Elebees; Through Golden Windows; Under the Tagalong Tree; With Sails to the Wind; Over Buttonwood Bridge; From Castles in the Clouds; With Maxi & Mini in Muffkinland; Out of the Treasure Chest; Along Thimblelane Trails; Treehouse Tales; Muffkins on Parade; Captain Maxi's Secret Island; The Children's Illustrated Bible Dictionary; Learning to Read from the Bible Series, 8 volumes; My Picture Bible; Choosing God's Way; Growing God's Way. *Contributor to:* numerous journals and magazines. *Honours:* Recipient, various honours and awards. *Address:* Rt 1, Box 321, Elgin, IL 60120, USA.

BEEVER Antony, b. 14 Dec 1946, London, England. Historian; Novelist. m. Artemis Cooper, 2 Feb 1986, 1 son, 1 daughter. *Education:* Winchester College; Grenoble University; Royal Military Academy, Sandhurst. *Publications:* Crete, The Battle & The Resistance; Inside The British army; The Spanish Civil War; The Enchantment of Christina Von Retzen; The Violent Brink; For Reasons of State; The Faustian Pact. *Contributions to:* Times Literary Supplement; Times; Telegraph; Spectator. *Memberships:* Society of Authors; Royal Geographical Society; Anglo Hellenic League. *Literary Agent:* Andrew Nurnberg. *Address:* 54 Saint Maur Road, London SW6 4DP, England.

BEGUIN Bernard, b. 14 Feb 1923, Sion, Valais, Switzerland. Journalist. m. Antoinette Waelbroeck, 1948, 2 sons, 2 daughters. *Education:* Les L., Geneva University; Graduate Institute of International Studies. *Appointments include:* Correspondent, UN European Headquarters 1946-70, foreign editor 1947, editor-in-chief 1959-70, Journal de Geneve; Diplomatic commentator, Swiss Broadcasting System 1954-59, Swiss TV 1959-70; Head of Programmes, Swiss French-Speaking TV, 1970-73; Deputy director, Radio & TV, 1973-86. *Honours:* Honorary member, Swiss Press Association, 1974-; Visiting Professor, Professional Ethics, University of Neuchatel, 1984-88. *Memberships include:* Central President, Swiss Press Association, 1958-60; President, Swiss Press Council, 1985-90; Federal Commission on Cartels, 1964-80; Board, Swiss Telegraphic Agency, 1968-71; President, Independent Authority on Complaints dealing with Radio and Television, 1991-92. *Address:* 41 avenue de Budé, 1202 Geneva, Switzerland.

BEHLEN Charles William, b. 29 Jan 1949, Slaton, Texas, USA. Poet in Residence. 1 daughter. *Education:*

New Mexico Junior College, 1968-70. *Appointments:* Literature Fair Coordinator, Texas Circuit, 1979. *Publications include:* Perdition's Keepsake; Three Texas Poets; Dreaming at the Wheel; Uirsche's First Three Decades; The Voices Under the Floor. *Contributions to:* The Bloomsbury Review; Cedar Rock; The New Mexico Humanities Review; Poetry Now; Puerto del Sol; The Smith; The Texas Observer. *Honours:* Pushcart Prize (nominee); Ruth Stephan Reader; Manuscripts Displayed and Placed, in Time Capsule by San Antonio Museum of Art. *Memberships:* Texas Association of Creative Writing Teachers; Texas Circuit. *Address:* 501 West Industrial Drive, Apt 503-B, Sulphur Springs, TX 75482, USA.

BEHR Edward, b. 7 May 1926, British. m. Christiane Wagrez, 4 June 1967. *Education:* MA. Cambridge, 1953. *Appointments:* Reuters Correspondent, 1951-54; Correspondent, Time Magazine, 1957-63; Contributing Editor, Saturday Evening Post, 1963-65; Newsweek Bureau Chief, South East Asia 1966-68, Paris Bureau Chief, 1968-73, European Editor 1973-83, Newsweek International 1984-, Paris, France. *Publications:* The Algerian Problem, 1961; The Thirty Sixth Way (with Sydney Liu), 1969; Bearings, 1978, (in UK as Anyone Here Been Raped - and Speaks English?, 1981); Getting Even, 1980; Roman (with Roman Polanski), 1984; 'The Last Emperor', 1988, 'Hirohito - behind the Myth', 1989; 'Les Miserables': History in the Making, 1989; Kiss The Hand You Cannot Bite - The Rise and Fall of the Ceausescus; The Making of Miss Saigon. *Honours:* Gutenberg Prize, 1988 for 'The Last Emperor'. *Address:* c/o Newsweek, 162 Faubourg Saint Honore, 75008 Paris, France.

BEHREND George Henry Sandham, b. 10 Jan 1922, London, England. Travel Writer. m. Jeanette D'Enyer, 19 July 1960 (dec 1992). *Education:* Marlborough College, Wilts 1935-39; Hertford College, Oxford University, 1939-41; MA Honour, Geography, Oxon, 1942. *Appointments include:* Chairman, Jersey Artists Ltd, 1966. *Publications include:* Pullman in Europe, 1962; Grand European Expresses, 1962; Gone with Regret (GWR), 3rd edition 1969, 4th edition 1992; Histoire des Trains Deluxe, 1977 Luxury Trains, 1982; Night Ferry, with Gary Buchanan, 1985; Orient Express, translation, Des Cars/Caracalla, 1987. Don't Knock The Southern, 1993; Also: Railway Holiday in France, 1962; Railway Holiday in Switzerland, 1965; Stanley Spencer at Burghclere, 1966; Yatakli-Vagon: Turkish Steam Travel, with Vincent Kelly, 1969. *Contributions to:* Railway Magazine; Railway World; International Railway Traveller; Steam Days; The European; In Britain. Previously to: Times Special Reports; Daily Telegraph; Various other newspapers; Old Motor Magazine. *Memberships:* Life Member, British Guild of Travel Writers; Chartered Institute of Transport; Life Fellow, Royal Geographical Society; Club Garrick. *Address:* St Martin, Jersey, Channel Islands.

BEI DAO b. 2 Aug 1949, Beijing, China. Poet. m. Shao Fei, 1 daughter. Experimental poet who first achieved prominence during Democracy Movement, 1978-79, through the unofficial literary magazine Today. *Address:* Flat 504, Building 1, Beijing Art Studio, Tuanjiehu, Beijing, People's Republic of China.

BEIER Ulli, b. 1922, German. Professor. *Appointments:* President and Tutor 1961-64, Associate Professor 1965-66, Extra-Mural Department, University of Ibadan; Senior Lecturer in Literature, University of Papua New Guinea, 1967-71; Director and Research Professor, Institute of African Studies, University of Ife, 1971-, Nigeria. *Publications:* Art in Nigeria, 1960; African Mud Sculpture, 1963; Contemporary Art in Africa, 1968; Ten Thousand Years in a Lifetime: A New Guinea Authobiography (with A M Kiki), 1968; Hohao (with A M Kiki), 1970; Home of Man (with P Cox), 1971; When the Moon Was Big, Words of Paradise, 1973; The Return of the Gods, 1975; Stolen Images, 1976; Introduction to African Literature, 1980. *Address:* Institute of African Studies, University of Ife, Ife, Nigeria.

BEIM Norman, b. Newark, New Jersey, USA. Playwright; Actor, Director. div. *Education:* Ohio State University; Hedegrow Theatre School, Philadelphia; Institute of Contemporary Art, Washington DC. *Publications:* The Deserter, 1979. Theatre includes 11 off-Broadway productions, 1950-70; Success (Holland), 1982, 1983; Pygmalion & Galatea (Holland), 1983; Archie's Comeback (California, 1986. *Honours:* 1st Prize, Double Image/Samuel French Award; On A Darkling Plain, Winner, David James Ellis Memorial Award, best play of season at Theatre Americana, 1990, Dreams, Winner, new play competition, No Empty Space Theatre, New York, 1992; Shakespeare Revisited, winner Maxim Mazumdar Competition, Alleyway Theatre, New York. *Memberships:* Dramatists Guild; Actors Equity Association; Literary Managers & Dramatists; Screen Actors Guild; Federation of TV & Radio Artists. *Literary Agent:* Francis Lonnee, International Drama Agency, Amsterdam, Holland. *Address:* 425 West 57th Street, Apt 2J, New York, NY 10019, USA.

BEISSEL Henry, b. 12 Apr 1929, Cologne, Germany. Author. m. Arlette Francière, 3 children. *Publications:* Poetry including: Witness The Heart, 1963; New Wings For Icarus, 1966; The World Is A Rainbow, A secular cantata based on collection of poems by the same title composed by Wolkgang Bottenberg, 1968; A Different Sun, translation of poems by Walter Bauer, 1976; Season Of Blood, 1984; Body Of Woman, translation of Pablo Neruda's Veinte Poemas de Amor y Una Cancion Desesperada; Where Shall Birds Fly?, 1988; Stones To Harvest, 1991, 1993; Several Play translations and adaptations including: Sacrifices, adaptation of a play by Shie Min, 1988; Improvisations For Mr X, Workshopped by Montreal Playwrights Workshop, 1978, Staged Reading, Actor's Studio, New York, 1979, Dunvegan: revised version, 1989; The Glass Mountain, play, 1990, publication, 1989; Fiction: The Apple Orchard, translation short-story by Walter Bauer, 1960; Munchlaw Maird/The Complete Censor/Honesty in Government, short stories; Forthcoming Juvenile novel, Indian Headband; Non-Fiction: Festschrift Für Werner Berg, 1974; Kanada, 1981; Der Flur, short story, 1985; Raging Like A Fire Festschrift For Irving Layton, 1993. *Contributions to:* Numerous professional journals. *Honours:* Epstein Award, 1958; Davidson Award, 1959; DAAD Fellowship, 1977; Recipient of numerous other honours and awards. *Memberships:* League of Canadian Poets, President 1980-81; International Academy of Poets; Playwrights Canada; Montreal Playwrights Workshop; Theatres Ontario; PEN. *Address:* c/o P O Box 339, Alexandria, Canada K0C 1A0.

BEJA Morris, b. 1935, American. Professor. *Appointments:* Instructor 1961, Professor and Chairman of English, Ohio State University. *Publications:* Virginia Woolf's To The Lighthouse: A Selection of Critical Essays, 1970; Epiphany in the Modern Novel, 1971; Psychological Fiction, 1971; James Joyce's Dubliners and A Portrait of the Artist as a Young Man: A Selection of Critical Essays, 1973; Film and Literature, 1979; Samuel Beckett: Humanistic Perspectives (ed with S E Gontarski and Pierre Astier), 1982; Critical Essays on Virginia Woolf, 1985; James Joyce: The Centennial Symposium (co-ed), 1987; Coping with Joyce: Essays from the Copenhagen Symposium (co-ed.) 1989; Joyce the Artist Manqué, and Indeterminacy, 1989; James Joyce: A Literary Life, 1992. *Honours:* Guggenheim Fellowship, 1972-73; Fulbright Lectureship, 1972-73. *Memberships:* President, 1982-90, Executive Secretary, 1990-, International James Joyce Foundation. *Address:* Department of English, Ohio State University, 164 West 17th Avenue, Columbus, OH 43210, USA.

BEK Wieslaw Marian, b. 2 Dec 1929, Lodz, Poland. Journalist; Publisher. m. 1 son. *Education:* Lodz University. *Appointments include:* Editor, later sub-editor, daily Glos Robotniczy, Lodz, 1949-64; Secretary, Voivodship Committee, Polish United Workers Party (PZPR), Lodz, 1964-68; Deputy head, later head, press Bureau of PZPR Central Committee, 1968-72; President, Ksiazka i Wiedza Publishers, Warsaw, 1972-73; 1st vice president, Workers Publishing Cooperative, Prasa-Ksiazka-Ruch, Warsaw, 1973-78; 1st Vice-Minister of Culture & Art, 1978-80; Head, Department for Ideology & Education, PZPR Central Committee, 1980; Editor-in-chief, Trybuna Ludu, daily of PZPR Central Committee, 1980-85. *Honours:*Commander's & Officer's Crosses, Order of Polonia Restituta. *Memberships include:* PZPR, 1954-; Central Party Control Committee, 1975-81; President, Polish-Mongolian Society. *Address:* c/o Redakcja Trybuny Ludu, Pl.Starynkiewicza 7, 02-015 Warsaw, Poland.

BEKEDEREMO J P Clark. *See:* **CLARK John Pepper.**

BEL GEDDES Joan, b. Los Angeles, California, USA. Author; Editor. m. Barry Ulanov, 16 Dec. 1939, divorced 1968, 1 son, 2 daughters. *Education:* BA, Barnard College, Columbia University, 1937. *Appointments:* Assistant Non-Fiction Editor, Today's Woman Magazine, 1952-53; Editor in Chief, My Baby and Congratulations Magazines, 1954-56; Public Information Officer, UNICEF, 1970-76; Chief of UNICEF's Editorial and Publications Services, 1976-79; Editorial Consultant, Freelance Writer. *Publications:* To Barbara with Love, 1974; A History of Baby Care, 1964; How to Parent Alone, 1974; English Translation of Last Essays of Georges Bernanos, 1955; Co-Author: Art, Obsenity and Your Children, 1969; American Catholics and Vietnam, 1970; Holiness and Mental Health, 1972; The Future of the Family, 1971; The Children's Rights Movement, 1977; And You, Who Do You Say I Am?, 1981. *Contributor to:* Editor, Bulletin of the Pate Institute for Human Survival, 1986-; Newspapers and magazines. *Honour:* Catholic Press Association, best Book of the Year on Christian Living, 1974. *Memberships:* Authors League of America; National Writers Club; International Council of International Institute of Rural Reconstruction; Board of Directors of Pate Institute for Human Survival; UN Representative of Indian Association for Children and Youth Welfare of the World; New York City Mission Society; Thomas More Society (President 1966); Association of Former International Civil Servants. *Address:* 60 East 8 Street, New York City 10003, USA.

BELFORD Barbara, b. 23 Nov 1935, Oakland, California, USA. Professor. m. Dr Frank G de Furia (dec), 23 Dec 1973, 1 daughter. *Education:* BA 1957, Vanderbilt University, Nashville, Tennessee; MS 1962, Columbia Graduate School of Journalism. *Appointments:* Reporter, Edinburgh Scotsman 1954-56; Editor, New York Herald Tribune 1962-66; Editor, Redbook 1974-78. *Publications:* Brilliant Bylines, 1986; Violet: the Story of the Irrepressible Violet Hunt and her Circle of Friends, 1990. *Contributions to:* New York Times; Edinburgh Scotsman; London Times. *Memberships:* PEN New York; Author's Guild; Biographical Seminar of New York University. *Literary Agent:* Elaine Markson Agency, New York. *Address:* 350 Central Park West, New York, NY 10025, USA.

BELITT Ben, b. 2 May 1911, New York City, USA. Writer. *Education:* BA, 1932 (Phi Beta Kappa), MA 1934, University of Virginia, Charlottesville. Served in the US Army Infantry, 1942-44. *Appointments:* Editor-Scenarist, Signal Corps Photographic Center Combat Film Section, 1945-46; Assistant Literary Editor, The Nation, New York, 1937-38; Member of English Department 1938-, currently Professor of Literature and Languages, Bennington College, Vermont. Taught at Mills College, Oakland, California 1939 and Connecticut College, New London, 1948-49. *Publications include:* Verse: The Five-Fold Mesh, 1938; School of the Soldier, 1949; Wilderness Stair, 1955; The Enemy Joy: New and Selected Poems, 1964; Nowhere But Light: Poems 1964-1969, 1970; The Double Witness: Poems 1970-1976, 1977; Possessions: New and Selected Poems, 1985. Other works: Adam's Dream: A preface to translation, 1978; Editor and/or translator of numerous other works. *Honours:* Shelley Memorial Award, 1937; Guggenheim Fellowship, 1945; Oscar Blumenthal Award, 1957; Union League Civic and Arts Foundation Prize, 1960 (Poetry, Chicago); Brandeis University Creative Arts Award, 1962; National Institute of Arts and Letters Award in Poetry, 1965; William/Derwood Award for Poetry, 1986; Bennington College Ben Lectureship Endowment, 1977; Rockerfeller Found. grantee Belllagio Italy, 1984; Fellow Vermont Academy of Arts and Sciences; Russell Loines Award, 1981; National Endowment for the Arts grant, 1967. *Address:* Department of English, Bennington College, Bennington, VT 05201, USA.

BELKIN Robyn Sarah, (Robyn Sarah), b. 6 Oct 1949, New York, USA. Writer. *Publications:* The Space Between Sleep and Waking, 1981; Anyone Skating on that Middle Ground, 1984; Becoming Light, 1987; The Touchstone, 1992; A Nice Gazebo, 1992; Shadowplay, 1978. *Address:* c/o Vehicule Press, PO Box 125, Place Station du Parc, Montreal, Quebec, Canada H2W 2M9.

BELL Barbara H, b. 7 May 1920. Journalist; Radio Commentator, retired 1983. m. David L Bell, 14 May 1939, Watkins Glen, New York. 1 son, 1 daughter. *Appointments include:* News Editor, Schuyler County, 1977-78; Feature Writer, Reporter, Photographer, Freelance, 1954-62; Feature Writer, Reporter, Photographer, Ithaca Journal, 1962-78; Editor, Schuyler County Historical Social Journal, 1964-. *Publications include:* Little Tales from Little Schuyler, 1962; Ballad of Bertie, 1966; More Tales from Little Schuyler, 1967; To My Grandson and Other Poems, 1969; Glance Backward, 1970; Letters to Suzanna, 1992. *Contributions to:* Mid Western Chaparral Poets; Blue River Poetry Magazine; The American Bard; Hoosier Challenge; Sunday Telegram; Chemung Valley Reporter; Hartford Times; Glance Backward, weekly History column, Ithaca Journal, 1967-78. *Honours:* B M Heith Award, 1958; Historic Ithaca; New York State Temporary Historic Commission; Retired Senior Volunteer Program. *Address:* 3460 Co. Road, 28 Watkins Glen, NY 14891, USA.

BELL Carolyn. *See:* **RIGONI Orlando Joseph.**

BELL Charles Greenleaf, b. 31 Oct 1916, Greenville, Mississippi, USA. Author; Educator. *Education:* BS, University of Viginia, 1936; BA 1938, M.Litt, 1939, University of Oxford, England; MA 1966. *Publications:* Verse: Songs for a New America, 1953, revised 1966; Delta Return, 1955, revised 1969; Five Chambered Heart, 1985; Novels; The Married Land, 1962; The Half Gods, 1968; (film) The Spirit of Rome, 1965; Symbolic History (41 slide-tape shows also on video VHS cassettes). *Contributor To:* Harper's Magazine; New Yorker; Atlantic Monthly. *Honours include:* Rhodes Scholarship; Ford Foundation Fellowship; Rockefeller Grant, 1948. *Address:* 1260 Canyon Road, Santa Fe, NM 87501, USA.

BELL Marvin Hartley, b. 3 Aug 1937, New York City, USA. Poet; Teacher. m. Dorothy Murphy, 2 sons. *Education:* BA, Alfred University, 1958; MA, Literature, University of Chicago, 1961; MFA, Literature, University of Iowa, 1963. *Appointments:* Visiting Lecturer, Goddard College, 1970; Visiting Professor, University of Hawaii, 1981-82; Professor, University of Iowa, 1965, Flannery O'Connor Professor of Letters, 1986-. *Publications include:* (Poetry): A Probable Volume of Dreams, 1969; The Escape into You, 1971; Residue of Song, 1974; Stars Which See, Stars Which Do Not See, 1977; These Green-Going-To-Yellow, 1981; Segues: A Correspondence in Poetry (with William Stafford), 1983; Old Snow Just Melting; Essays and Interviews, 1983; Drawn by Stones, by Earth, by Things That Have Been in the Fire, 1984; New and Selected Poems, 1987; Iris of Creation, 1990; The Book of the Dead Man, forthcoming. *Contributor to:* professional journals. *Honours include:* Lamont Award, Acadmy of American Poets, 1969; Bess Hokin Award, Poetry, 1969; National Book Award Finalist, 1977; Guggenheim Fellowship, 1977; NEA Fellowships, 1978, 1984; American Poetry Review Prize, 1982; Senior Fulbright Scholar, 1983,

1986. *Address:* Writers' Workshop, EPB, The University of Iowa, Iowa City, IA 52242, USA.

BELLAIRS John, b. 17 Jan 1938, Marshall, Michigan, USA. Writer. *Education:* AB, Notre Dame Univerity, 1959; AM, University of Chicago, 1960. *Publications:* The Face in the Frost, 1969; The House with a Clock in its Walls, 1973; The Figure in the Shadows, 1975; The Letter, the Witch & the Ring, 1976; The Treasure of Alpheus Winterborn, 1978; The Curse of the Blue Figurine, 1983; The Mummy, the Will & the Crypt, 1983; The Dark Secret of Weatherend, 1984; The Spell of the Sorcerer's Skull, 1984; The Revenge of the Wizard's Ghost, 1985; The Eyes of the Killer Robot, 1986; The Lamp from the Warlock's Tomb, 1987; The Trolley to Yesterday, 1989; The Chessmen of Doom, 1989. *Honour:* Recipient, Woodrow Wilson Fellowship, 1959. *Memberships:* Authors Guild; Authors League. *Address:* 28 Hamilton Avenue, Haverhill, MA 01830, USA.

BELLAMY David James, b. 18 Jan 1933, England. Botanist; Writer. m. Rosemary Froy, 1959, 2 sons, 3 daughters. *Education:* Chelsea College of Science & Technology; PhD, Bedford College, London University. *Appointments include:* Lecturer, then senior lecturer, Department of Botany, University of Durham, 1960-80; Honorary Professor, Adult & Continuing Education, ibid, 1980-88; Special Professor of Botany, University of Nottingham, 1988. TV & radio presenter, scriptwriter, series include: Life in Our Sea, 1970; Bellamy on Botany, 1973; Bellamy's Britain, 1975; Bellamy's Europe, 1977; Botanic Man, 1978; Up a Gum Tree, 1980; Backyard Safari, 1981; The Great Seasons, 1982; Bellamy's New World, 1983; Seaside Safari, 1985; The End of the Rainbow Show, 1986; Bellamy on Top of the World, 1987; Turning the Tide, 1987; Bellamy's Bugle, 1987-88; Bellamy's Birds Eye View, 1988; Moa's Ark, 1989-90; Visting Professor, Natural Heritage Studies, Massey Univ, New Zealand, 1989. *Publications include:* Peatlands, 1974; Life Giving Sea, 1977; Half of Paradise, 1979; The Great Seasons, 1981; Discovering the Countryside with David Bellamy, 4 volumes, 1982-83; The Mouse Book, 1983; The Queen's Hidden Garden, 1984; Bellamy's Ireland, 1986; Bellamy's Changing World, (4 Volumes), 1988; Englands Last Wilderness, 1989; How Green Are You?, 1991; Tomorrow's Earth, 1991; World Medicine, 1992; Various books connected with TV series . *Memberships:* Fellow, Linnaens Society; Founder Director, Conservation Foundation; President, WATCH, 1982-83; President, Youth Hostels Association, 1983; President of Population Concern; President of National Association Environmental Education; Patron of West Midlands Youth Ballet Siol & Health Association of New Zealand. *Address:* Mill House, Bedburn, Bishop Auckland, County Durham, DL13 3NW, England.

BELLOW Saul, b. 10 June 1915, Quebec, Canada. Writer. divorced, 3 sons, previous marriages. *Education:* BS, Northwestern University. *Appointments include:* Professor, University of Minnesota 1946-48, Princeton University 1952-53, University of Chicago 1964-. *Publications include:* Dangling Man, 1944; The Victim, 1947; The Adventures of Augie March, 1953, Seize the Day, 1956; Henderson the Rain King, 1959; Great Jewish Short Stories, 1963; Herzog, 1964; The Last Analysis, 1964; Mosby's Memoirs & Other Stories, 1968; Mr Sammler's Planet, 1969; Humboldt's Gift, 1975; To Jerusalem & Back: A Personal Account, (Non Fiction), 1976; The Dean's December, 1981; Him With His Foot In His Mouth & Other Stories, 1984; The Bellarosa Connection, 1989, (Fiction); Something To Remember Me By, three tales, 1991. *Contributions to:* Numerous magazines & journals. *Honours include:* National Book Award, Institute of Arts & Letters, 1953; Ford Foundation Grant, 1959; Prix Internationale de Litterature, 1965; US National Book Awards, 1954, 1965, 1971; Pulitzer Prize, 1976; Nobel Prize for Literature, 1976; Fellow, American Academy of Arts & Sciences; Croix de Chevalier des Arts et Lettres, 1968; Malaparte Literary Award, 1984; Commander of the Legion of Honor, 1983. *Memberships include:*

Committee on Social Thought, 1963-. *Address:* c/o Committee on Social Thought, University of Chicago, 1126 East 59th Street, Chicago, IL 60637, USA.

BELOFF Lord, (Max). b. 2 July 1913, London, England. Historian. m. Helen Dobrin, 20 Mar 1938, 2 sons. *Education:* St Paul's School, 1926- 32; Corpus Christi and Magdalen Colleges, Oxford, 1932-37, MA Oxon 1937, DLitt 1974. *Publications include:* The Foreign Policy of Soviet Russia, 1947, 1949; The American Federal Government, 1959; New Dimensions in Foreign Policy, 1961; Imperial Sunset - Vol 1 Britain's Liberal Empire, 1969; Imperial Sunset - Vol 2, Dream of Commonwealth, 1989; The Intellectual in Politics, 1970; The Intellectual in Politics, 1970; Wars and Welfare, Britain 1914-45, 1984; Joint author: The Government of the UK, 1985; An Historian in the Twentieth Century, 1992; Joint editor: L'Europe du X1X siecle et XX siecle (1960-66). *Contributor to:* Encounter. *Honours:* Kt 1980; Life Peer 1981; Six honorary doctorates. *Memberships:* Fellow, British Academy; Fellow, Royal Historical Society; Fellow, Royal Society of Arts. *Address:* House of Lords, London SW1A 0PW, England.

BELOFF Nora, b. 24 Jan 1919. Author; Journalist. *Education:* BA, Honours, History, Lady Margaret Hall, Oxford, 1940. *Appointments:* Political Intelligence Department, FO, 1941-44; British Embassy, Paris, 1944-45; Reporter, Reuters News Agency, 1945-46; Paris Correspondent, The Economist, 1946-48; Observer Correspondent, Paris, Washington, Moscow, Brussels, and others, 1948-78; Political Correspondent, 1964-76, Roving Correspondent, 1976-78. *Publications:* The General Says NO, 1963; Le General dit Non, 1965; The Transit of Britain, 1973; Freedom under Foot, 1976; No Travel like Russian Travel, 1979 (US as Inside the Soviet Empire, Myth and Reality, 1980); Tito's Flawed Legacy: Yugoslavia and the West 1939-1984, 1985, 1986; Tito Duori dalla Legggenda Fine di un mito, 1987. *Address:* 11 Belsize Road, London NW6 4RX, England.

BELTRAMETTI Franco, b. 7 Oct 1937, Poet, Writer; Visual Artist. m. Judith Danciger, 1966, 1 son. *Education:* Eth Zurich. *Publications:* Uno di Quella Gente Condor; Another Earthquake; Quarantuno; Airmail Postcards; Tutto Questo; In Transito; Face to face; Target; Surprise; Clandestins; Tout Ca. *Contributions to:* Coyote's Journal; Tam Tam; Docks; Abra ca dabra; Il Verri; Mgur; Schreibheft; Grosseteste Review, Mini. *Address:* PO Box 3, CH 6828 Riva S.V, Switzerland.

BENCE-JONES Mark, b. 29 May 1930, London, England. Writer. m. Gillian Pretyman, 2 Feb 1965, 1 son, 2 daughters. *Education:* BA 1952, MA 1958, Pembroke College, Cambridge University; MRAC, Royal Agricultural College, Cirencester, 1954. *Publications include:* Clive of India, 1974; The Viceroys of India, 1982; Twilight of the Ascendancy, 1987. Also: All A Nonsense, 1957; Paradise Escaped, 1958; Nothing in the City, 1965; The Remarkable Irish, 1966; Palaces of the Raj, 1973; The Cavaliers, 1976; Burke's Guide to Irish Country Houses, 1984; The British Aristocracy, co-author, 1979; Ancestral Houses, 1984; A Guide to Irish Country Houses, 1989. Introductory articles, Burke's genealogical publications . *Contributions to:* Irish Times; Country Life. *Memberships:* Fellow, Royal Society of Arts; Kildare Street & University Club, Dublin; Royal Irish Automobile Club. *Address:* Glenville Park, Glenville, County Cork, Ireland.

BENEDICT Rex, b. 27 June 1920, Jet, Oklahoma, USA. Writer m. Giusi M Usai, 6 Jan 1966. *Education:* BA, Northwestern State University, Alva, Oklahoma, 1949; University of Oklahoma, Norman, 1949-50. *Appointments:* Served with US Navy Air Corps, 1942-45, 1951-53, Lieutenant; Orchestra Director, Alva 1938-41, Orchestra Manager, San Diego, 1945-46; Film Dubber, 1953-57; Film Translator, Rome, Italy, 1957-60; Publisher's Reader, New York, 1960-65; Printer, Corsair Press, New York, 1967- 79; Reviewer, New York Times 1965-79. *Publications include:* Fiction: Good Luck

Arizona Man, New York 1972, London 1973, Stuttgart 1979; Goodbye to the Purple Sage, New York 1973, London 1975, Stuttgart 1979; Last Stand at Goodbye Gulch, New York 1974, London 1975; The Ballad of Cactus Jack, New York 1975, London 1976; Run For Your Sweet Life, New York, 1986; Verse: In the Green Grasstime, 1964; Moonwash 1969; Nights in the Gardens of Glebe, 1970; Epitaph for a Lady, 1970; Haloes for Heroes, 1971; Other: Oh...Brother Juniper, 1963, illustrated by Joan Berg; Various translations. *Literary Agent:* McIntosh and Otis Inc, New York. *Address:* POB 176, Jet, OK 73749, USA.

BENEDICT Stewart Hurd, b. 27 Dec 1924, Mineota, New York, USA. Writer; Editor. *Education:* AB summa cum laude 1944, Drew University; MA 1945, The Johns Hopkins University; Study at New York University 1946-49, 1961-64. *Appointment:* Entertainment Editor, Michael's Thing magazine, New York 1991. *Publications:* Tales of Terror and Suspense, ed, 1963; Revision of Harper's English Grammar, ed, 1965; The Crime Solvers, ed, 1966; Teacher's Guide to Senior High School Lit, 1966; Famous American Speeches, ed, 1967; Teacher's Guide to Modern Drama, 1967; Teacher's Guide to Poetry, 1969; Blacklash, ed, 1970; Literary Guide to the US, 1981; Street Beat, 1982. *Contributions to:* Book reviews for Publishers Weekly; Play and book reviews for The Jersey Journal; Play reviews for Michael's Thing. *Memberships:* Dramatists Guild; The Newspaper Guild. *Address:* Apt 4-A, 27 Washington Square N, New York, NY 10011, USA.

BENEDICTUS David (Henry), b. 1938, British. *Appointments:* Book Reviewer and Theatre Director; Drama Director 1964-65, Story Editor 1967, BBC Television; Assistant Director, Royal Shakespeare Company, 1970-71; Visiting Fellow, Churchill College, Cambridge, 1981-82; Commissioning Editor, Channel 4 Drama Series, 1984-86; Editor Readings BBC Radio, 1989-92, Readings and Radio 3 Drama, 1992-. *Publications:* The Fourth of June, 1963; You're a Big Boy Now, 1964; This Animal is Mischievous, 1966; Angels (Over Your Grave) and Geese (Over Mine), 1967; Hump: or Bone by Bone Alive, 1968; Dromedary, 1969; The Guru and the Golf Club, 1970; A World of Windows, What a Way to Run a Revolution!, 1972; The Rabbi's Wife, Junk, 1976; Betjemania, 1977; A Twentieth Century Man, 1978; The Antique Collector's Guide, 1980; Lloyd George, 1981; Whose Life Is It Anyway?, The Golden Key, Who Killed the Prince Consort?, 1982; Floating Down to Camelot, 1985; Little Sir Nicholas, 1990; Transplant, 1991; Sunny Intervals and Showers, 1992; The Stamp Collector, 1993; Numerous Radio, TV and Stage Credits. *Address:* 19 Oxford Road, Teddington, Middlesex TW11 0QA, England.

BENEDIKT Michael, b. 26 May 1935, New York City, USA. Writer; Poet; Consultant; Editor; Anthologist; Literary, Art; Theatre & Film Critic. *Education:* BA, New York University, 1956; MA, Columbia University, 1961. *Literary Appointments:* The Paris Review, poetry editior, 1974-78; American Poetry Review, contributing editor, 1973-; Professorships in Literature and Poetry, Boston University, 1977-79; Vassar College, 1976-77; Hampshire College, 1973-75; Sarah Lawrence College, 1969-73; Bennington College, 1968-69. *Publications:* The Badminton at Gt Barrington or Gustave Mahler & The Chattanooga Cho-Choo, poetry, 1980; Night Cries, prose poems, 1976; Mole Notes, prose poems, 1971; Sky, verse, 1970; The Body, verse, 1968; The Prose Poem: An International Anthology, 1976; The Poetry of Surrealism, anthology, 1975; Theatre Experiment, anthology, 1968; Modern Spanish Theatre, anthology (co-edited with George E Wellwarth), 1968; Post-War German Theatre, anthology (co-edited with George E Wellwarth), 1967; Modern French Theatre: The Avant-Garde, Dada and Surrealism, anthology (co-edited with George E Wellwarth), 1964; in UK as Modern French Plays: An Anthology from Jarry to Ionesco, 1965. *Contributions to:* Poetry; Partisan Review; The Paris Review; Massachusetts Review; Ambit; The London Magazine; Poesis (interview); Art News; Agni Review; New York Quarterly. *Honours:* Guggenheim Grant in

Poetry, 1968-69; Bess Hokin Prize for Best Poems in Poetry, 1969; National Endowment for the Arts prize for single poem, 1970; Fels award for excellence in magazine editing, 1976; New York State (CAPS) Grant in Poetry, 1975; National Endowment for the Arts Fellowship in Poetry, 1979-80; Subject: Retrospective at The Library of Congress, videotape, 1986; Benedikt: A Profile, critical monograph/festschrift, 1978. *Memberships:* PEN Club of America; Poetry Society of America. *Literary Agent:* Georges Borchardt, Inc, New York, NY, USA. *Address:* 315 West 98th Street, New York, NY 10025, USA.

BENFIELD Derek, b. 11 Mar 1926, Bradford, Yorkshire, England. Playwright; Actor. m. Susan Elspeth Lyall Grant, 17 July 1953, 1 son, 1 daughter. *Education:* Bingley Grammar School; Royal Academy of Dramatic Art. *Publications include:* Plays: Wild Goose Chase, 1956, Running Riot, 1958; Post Horn Gallop, 1965; Murder for the Asking, 1967; Off the Hook, 1970; Bird in the Hand, 1973; Panic Stations, 1975; Caught on the Hop, 1979; Beyond a Joke, 1980; In for the Kill, 1981; Look Who's Talking, 1984; Touch & Go, 1985; Fish Out of Water, 1986; Flying Feathers, 1987; Bedside Manners, 1988; A Toe in the Water, 1991; Don's Lose the Place, 1992. *Membership:* Society of Authors. *Literary Agent:* Harvey Unna & Stephen Durbridge Ltd, 24 Pottery Lane, Holland Park, London W11 4LZ, England.

BENFORD Gregory Albert, b. 30 Jan 1941, Mobile, USA. Physicist; Author. m. Joan Abbe, 26 Aug 1967, 1 son, 1 daughter. *Education:* BS, University of Oklahoma, 1963; MS 1965, PhD 1967, University of California, San Diego. *Appointments include:* Professor of Physics, University of California, Irvine, 1971-. *Publications:* Novels: Deeper than the Darkness, 1970; Jupiter Project, 1975; If the Stars are Gods, 1977; In the Ocean of Night, 1977; The Stars in Shroud, 1978; Find the Changeling, 1980; Timescape, 1980; Against Infinity, 1983; Across the Sea of Suns, 1984; Artifact, 1985; Heart of the Comet, 1986; In Alien Flesh, 1986; Great Sky River, 1988; Tides of Light, 1989; Beyond the Fall of Night, 1990. Also research papers on plasma physics, astrophysics, solid state physics. *Honours:* Nebula Awards, Science Fiction Writers of America, 1975, 1981; British Science Fiction Award, 1981; Australian Ditmar Award, International Novel, 1981; John W.Campbell Award, best novel, 1981. Woodrow Wilson Fellow, 1963-64; Various grants, Office of Naval Research, National Science Foundation, Army Research Organisation, Air Force Office for Scientific Research, California Space Office. *Memberships:* American Physical Society; Royal Astronomical Society; Science Fiction Writers of America; Phi Beta Kappa. *Literary Agent:* Ralph Vicinanza, 111 8trh Avenue, Suite 1501, New York, NY 10011, USA. *Address:* 1105 Skyline Drive, Laguna Beach, California 92651, USA.

BENGTSON Bo Nils, b. 22 June 1944, Ostersund, Sweden. Publisher; Editor; Writer. *Education:* Fil.Kand, Stockholm University, 1972. *Publications:* Familjehunden, 1966; Dogs of the World, 1973; The Whippet, 1985. *Contributions to:* Pet Column, Svenska Dagbladet, 1965-70, Expressen 1970-75; Editorial Staff, Swedish Kennel Club Magazine, 1964-; Editorial Staff, Kennel Review, USA, 1980-; Dog World, UK; Editorial Staff, National Dog, Australia, 1980-. *Honours:* Outstanding Journalist of the Year Nomination, Dog Writers Association of America, 1985, 1987. *Address:* 1912 Mission Ridge Road, Santa Barbara, CA 93105, USA.

BENITO RUANO Eloy, b. 1 Dec 1921, Madrid, Spain. Professor. m. Covadonga Beltron Rojo, July 1973. *Education:* Dr. por La Universidad de Madrid, 1956. *Publications:* Toledo en el siglo XV; Los Origenes del Problema Converso; Estudios Santiagnistas; El Libro del Limosnero de Isabel la Catolica. *Contributions to:* About 150 Articles of Medieval History. *Honours:* Premio Nacional Menendez Pelayo. *Memberships:* Royal Academy of History; Spanish Committee of Historical Sciences; Spanish Society of Medieval Studies;

International Committee of Historical Sciences. *Address:* Jose Ortega y Gasset 12, 28006 Madrid, Spain.

BENJELLOUN Tahar, b. 1 Dec 1944, Fes, Maroc, France. Ecrivain. m. 1986, 1 son, 1 daughter. *Education:* Licence de Philosophie, Rabet, 1968; Doctorat en Psychiatrie Sociale, Paris, 1975. *Publications:* Harrouda; La Reclusion Solitatire; Motia le Fou Moha Le Sage; La priere de l'absent; l'eĉuvain public; l'Enfaut de Sable; La Nuit Sacree; Jour de Silence á Tanger; Les Yeux Baisses; Poesie: Le Amandiers sont morts de leurs blessurs; Al'insu du Souvenir; La Remontée des Cendres. *Contributions to:* Le Monde; La Repubbilca; El Pais. *Honours:* Prix Goncourt; Prix des Hemyspheres; Docteur Honris Causa de l'université Catholique de Lourain. *Memberships:* Conseil de la Francophonie. *Address:* Editor le Sevil, 27 Rue Jacob, 75 Paris 6, France.

BENN Tony (Anthony Neil Wedgwood), b. 3 Apr 1925. London, England. Member of Parliament. m. Caroline Middleton De Camp, 1949, 3 sons, 1 daughter. *Education:* New College, Oxford, 1941-42, 1946-48, MA, Oxon; Hon D Phil; HonDSc; HonDTech; HonDCL. *Appointments:* Served RAFVR 1943-45, RNVR 1945-46, Joined Labour Party 1943; Unsuccessfully attempted to renounce his succession to the title of Viscount Stansgate in 1955 and 1960, won bye-election in May 1961 only to be prevented from taking his seat; instigated Act to make disclaimer possible and disclaimed title for life in 1963; Member, NEC 1959-60, 1962- (Chairman 1971-72); MP (Lab) Bristol SE, Nov 1950-60 and Aug 1963-83; Postmaster General 1964-66, recommended establishment of GPO as public corporation and founded Giro; Minister of Technology, 1966-70, assumed responsibility for Ministry of Aviation, 1967 and Minister of Power 1969-70; Appointed Privy Councillor 1964; Opposition spokesman on Trade and Industry, 1970-74; Secretary of State for Industry and Minister for Posts and Telecommunications, 1974-75; Secretary of State for Energy. 1975-79; President of the EEC Council of Energy Ministers, 1977; Contested (Lab) Bristol East, 1983; MP (Lab) Chesterfield, March 1984-. *Publications:* The Privy Council as a Second Chamber, 1957; The Regeneration of Britain, 1964; The New Politics, 1970; Speeches 1974; Arguments for Socialism, 1979; Arguments for Democracy, 1981; Parliament, People and Power, 1982; (ed), Writings on the Wall: a radical and socialist anthology 1215-1984, 1984; Sizewell Syndrome, 1984; Fighting Back, 1988; A Future for Socialism, 1991. Diaries: Out of the Wilderness - 1963-68, 1987; Office Without Power - 1968-72, 1988; Against the Tide - 1973-76, 1989; Conflicts of Interest, 1977-80, 1990; End of an Era - 1980-90, 1992. *Contributions to:* Various journals in the UK and abroad. *Literary Agent:* Curtis Brown, London. *Address:* House of Commons, London SW1 OAA, England.

BENNETT Alan, b. 9 May 1934, Leeds, England. Dramatist. *Education:* BA, Modern History, Oxford, 1957. *Publications:* Forty Years On, 1968; Getting On, 1971; Habeas Corpus, 1973; The Old Country, 1977; Enjoy, 1980; Kafka's Dick, 1986; Objects of Affection, 1983; Writer in Disguise, 1984; Talking Heads, 1988; Single Spies, 1989; The Lady in the Van, 1990; Poetry in Motion, 1990; The Wind in the Williows (adaption), 1991; The Madness of George III, 1992; Screenplays: A Private Function, 1984; Prick Up Your Ears, 1987. *Contributions to:* London Review of Books. *Literary Agent:* A.D. Peters. *Address:* c/o Peter, Fraser & Dunlop, The Chambers, Chelsea Harbour, London SW10 OXF, England.

BENNETT Bruce Harry, b. 23 Mar 1941, Perth, Australia. University Professor. m. Patricia Ann Staples, 8 July 1967, 1 son, 1 daughter. *Education:* BA, Western Australia, 1963; MA, Oxford, 1972; MA Ed, London, 1974; FACE, 1990. *Appointments:* Lecturer, University of Western Australia, 1968; Senior Lecturer, 1975; Associate Professor, 1985; Professor, Head of English, University College, Australian Defence Force Academy, 1993-. *Publications:* Spirit in Exile; An Australian Compass; Myths, Heroes and Anti-heroes; Western Australian Writing; A Sense of Exile; Place, Region and Community; Cross Currents; The Literature of Western Australia; Windows onto Worlds. *Contributions to:* Westerly; Overland; Meanjin; Australian Literary Studies; World Literature Written in English; Journal of Commonwealth Literature; Ariel; Journal of Canadian Studies. *Honours:* Rhodes Scholar; Western Australian Premier's Literary Award. *Memberships:* Association for the Study of Australian Literature; Association of Commonwealth Language and Literature Societies; Modern Language Association; Australian National Commission for UNESCO. *Address:* Department of English, University College, University of NSW, Australian Defence Force Academy, Canberra, ACT 2600, Australia.

BENNETT Dwight. *See:* **NEWTON Dwight Bennett.**

BENNETT Gertrude Ryder, b. United States of America. Poet. *Publications:* Etched in Words, 1938; The Harvesters, 1967; Ballads of Colonial Days, with Historical Background, 1972; The Fugitive, 1975; The Hessian Lieutenant Left His Name, 1976; Living in a Landmark, 1980; Turning Back the Clock, 1982. *Memberships:* Governing Board, Poetry Society of America, 1973-74, 1979-81; President, National League of American Pen Woman, New York City Branch, 1974-76. *Address:* 1669 East 22nd Street, Brooklyn, NY 11229, USA.

BENNETT Hal Zina, b. 29 Sept 1936, Detroit, Michigan, USA. Writer. *Education:* BA, Language Arts-Creative Writing, 1964; MS, Holistic Health Sciences, 1986; PhD, Psychology, 1988. *Publications:* The Well Body Book; Well Body, Well Earth; Lens of Perception; Mind Jogger; Peak Performance (with Charles M Garfield); Follow Your Bliss. *Address:* P O Box 60655, Palo Alto, CA 94306, USA.

BENNETT Paul, b. 10 Jan 1921, Ohio, USA. Teacher; Writer. m. Jeanne Leonhart, 31 Dec 1941, 2 sons. *Education:* BA, Ohio University, 1942; AM, Harvard University, 1947. *Appointments:* Instructor, Samuel Adams School of Social Studies, Boston, 1945-46; Teaching Assistant, Harvard University, 1945-46; Instructor, Professor, Denison University, 1947-86; Poet in Residence, 1986-. *Publications:* Fellow The River, 1987; The Living Things; Robbery on the Highway; A Strange Affinity; The Eye of Reason; Building A House. *Contributions to:* New York Times Magazine; Centennial Review; Beloit Poetry Journal; College English; Georgia Review; Ohio Journal; America; Christian Science Monitor. *Honours include:* Denison University, Director of Writing Program; Writing Fellowship; Significant Achievement Award. *Memberships:* Ohio Poetry Society; Phi Beta Kappa; Pi Delta Epsilon. *Address:* 1281 Burg Street, Granville, OH 43023, USA.

BENNETT-ENGLAND Rodney Charles, b. 16 Dec 1936, Romford, Essex, England. Journalist; Writer. *Appointments:* Editor, various local weekly papers, Essex, 1954-55; Reporter & Columnist, Sunday Express, 1961-68; Contributing Editor, Penthouse, 1967-70; Leisure Editor, Men Only, 1970-73; London Editor, B&E International, Houston, Texas, 1977-79; Editor, Care Magazine, 1988. *Publications:* Dress Optional-The Revolution in Menswear, 1967, 1968; As Young As You Look, 1970; Inside Journalism, 1967; The Dale Cottage Cookbook, 1981. *Contributions to:* Tatler; Playboy; Penthouse; Men Only; Private Eye; Punch; Signature; Evening Standard; Sunday Telegraph; The Guardian. *Honours:* First Fashion Writer of The Year (ICI Trophy), 1968; Freeman, City of London, 1967; Scripps Lecturer in Journalism, University of Nevada, Reno, USA, 1978; Woodward-Bromley Lecturer, Yale University, USA, 1982; Fellow, Institute of Journalists, 1972. *Memberships:* Fellow, Royal Society of Arts; President 1986-87, Honorary Treasurer 1979-84, 1987-, Institute of Journalists; Chairman 1968-69, 1977-79, 1984-85, National Council for the Training of Journalists; Secretary- Director, 1984-, The Media Society. *Address:*

Church Cottage, East Rudham, Norfolk PE31 8QZ, England.

BENNETT-SPEED Carolyn, b. 14 Mar 1945, Bakersfield, California, USA. Writer. div, 1 son dec. *Education:* Overfelt High San Jose, State University. *Publications:* Inside Black Hollywood 1980; Soapsuds to Champagne - The Georgette Harvy Story; Films inc, Abby; The Mack; New Centurions; Television inc, Girls of Huntington House; Julia; Tenafly. *Contributions to:* La Oferta; Los Angeles Sentinel; San Jose Mercury; Richmond Afro American; Freelance Star. *Memberships:* Associated Writers Norfolk, Virginia; Poets & Writers; American Library Association. *Literary Agent:* Agnes Birnbaum, Bleecker Street Associates, New York, NY 10012, USA. *Address:* PO Box 16523 Beverly Hills, CA 90209, USA.

BENNIS Warren, b. 1925, United States of America. Writer. *Publications:* The Planning of Change: Readings in Behavioral Sciences (with K.D. Benne and R. Chin), 1961, 4th Edition, 1985; The Role of the Nurse in the Out-Patient Department, 1961; The Marked Deck: A Non-Objective Playlet for Four Characters, 1963; Interpersonal Dynamics: Essays and Readings on Human Interaction, 1964, 3rd Edition, 1973; Changing Organizations: Essays on the Development and Evolution of Human Organization, 1966; Personal and Organizational Change through Group Methods: The Laboratory Approach (with E.H. Schein), 1965; Leadership and Motivation: Essays by Douglas McGregor (with E.H.Schein and C. McGregor), 1966; The Professional Manager, by Douglas McGregor (with C. McGregor), 1967; Readings in Group Development for Managers and Trainers, 1967; The Temporary Society (with P.E. Slater), 1968; Organization Development: Its Nature, Origins and Prospects, 1969; American Bureaucracy, 1970; Today, Tomorrow, and the Day After, 1972; Management of Change and Conflict (with J. Thomas), 1973; The Leaning Ivory Tower, 1973; Leadership, 1974; The Unconscious Conspiracy: Why Leaders Can't Lead, 1976, 1989; Leaders: Strategies for Taking Charge, 1985; On Becoming a Leader, 1989. *Address:* Distinguished Professor of Business Administration, University of Southern California, Los Angeles, CA 90089-1421, USA.

BENOIT Jean-Marie Jules, b. 4 Apr 1942, Paris, France. Author; Academic; Journalist; Senior Fellow, College de France. m. (1) N. Breaud, (2) Catherine Dewavrin, 29 Sept 1979. 4 sons, 1 daughter. *Education:* Licence es Letres (BA Honours, Arts) 1962, Licence (Honours) Philosophy 1964, Ecole Normale Superieure; Master of Philosophy, Sorbonne, 1965; Agregation, Philosophy, Paris, 1966. *Appointments include:* Head, Seris Croisees, Presses Universitaires de France, 1979-; Various editorial appointments. *Publications include:* Marx is Dead, 1970; Les Outils de la Liberte, 1985; La revolution structurale, 1975, 1978; Tyrannie du Logos, 1975; La Generation sacrifiee, 1980; Pavane pour une Europe defunte, 1976; Chronique de decomposition du PCF, 1979; Les Nouveaux Primaires, 1978; Un singulier programme, 1978; Le devoir d'opposition, 1982. *Contributions to:* XXth Century Studies; Cambridge Review; Le Figaro; Le Monde; Quotidien de Paris; Connaissance des Arts; La Quinzaine Litteraire; L'Express; Washington Post; Wall Street Journal. *Honours:* French Academy Awards, 1975, 1979, 1980. *Memberships:* British section, PEN Club; Savile Club, London; Travellers Club, Paris; Founder, Chairman, Centre Europeen de Relations Internationales de Strategies. *Address:* c/o College de France 11, Place Marcelin Berthelot, 75006 Paris, France.

BENSON Daniel. *See:* **COOPER Colin Symons.**

BENSON Mary, b. 9 Dec 1919, Pretoria, South Africa. Writer. *Publications:* Tshekedi Khama, 1960; The African Patriots, 1963, 1964; At the Still Point, 1969, 1986; South Africa: The Struggle for a Birthright, 1969;

Nelson Mandela, 1986; A Far Cry, (autobiography) 1989; Editor, Athol Fugard Notebooks, 1983. *Contributions to:* London Magazine; Observer; Yale Theatre; Granta; Botswana Notes & Records. BBC Radio Drama & Documentaries. *Literary Agent:* Curtis Brown. *Address:* 34 Langford Court, London NW8 9DN, England.

BENSON Peter, b. 26 Jan 1956, Broadstairs, England. Novelist. *Publications:* The Levels; A Lesser Dependency; The Other Occupant; Odd's Hanging. *Honours:* Guardian Fiction Prize; The Encore Award; Somerset Maughan Award. *Address:* c/o 11 Jubilee Place, London SW3 3TE, England.

BENSTOCK Bernard, b. 23 Mar 1930, New York, New York, USA. Professor of English and Editor of the James Joyce Literary Supplement. m. Shari Gabrielson, 6 May 1973, 2 children from previous marriage. *Education:* AB, Brooklyn College, 1950; MA, Columbia University, 1954; PhD, Florida State University, 1957. *Appointments:* Louisiana State University, 1957-65; Kent State University, 1965-74; University of Illinois, 1974-82; University of Tulsa, 1982-86; University of Miami 1986-. *Publications:* Narrative Con/Texts in Ulysses, 1990; James Joyce: The Undiscover'd Country, 1977; Paycocks and Others: The World of Sean O'Casey, 1976; Joyce-Again's Wake: An Analysis of Finnegans Wake, 1965; James Joyce, 1985; Who's He When He's At Home: A James Joyce Directory (with Shari Benstock) 1980; Narrative Con/Texts in Dubliners, 1993. *Contributor to:* PMLA; Joyce Studies Annual; Philological Quarterly; Modern Fiction Studies; James Joyce Quarterly; Journal of Modern Literature. *Honours:* Camargo Foundation Fellow, 1981-82; Fellow, University of Illinois Institute for Advanced Study, 1982; Donald Gallup Fellow, Beinecke Library, Yale University, 1991. *Memberships:* International James Joyce Foundation, President 1971-77, Board of Trustees 1967-; Modern Language Association. *Address:* Department of English, University of Miami, Coral Gables, FL 33124, USA.

BENTLEY Eric (Russell), b. 14 Sept 1916, Bolton, Lancashire, England. moved to the United States, 1939, became a citizen 1948. Writer. m. (1) Maja Tschernjakow (marriage dissolved); (2) Joanne Davis, 1953, twin sons. *Education:* Educated at Bolton School; BA 1938, B Litt 1939, Oxford University; PhD, Yale University, New Haven, Connecticut, 1941. *Appointments:* Teacher, Black Mountain College, North Carolina, 1942-44 and University of Minnesota, Minneapolis, 1944-48; Brander Matthews Professor of Dramatic Literature, Columbia University, New York, 1952-69; Freelance writer 1970-73; Katharine Cornell Professor of Theatre, State University of New York, Buffalo, 1974-82; Professor of Comparative Literature, University of Maryland, College Park, 1982-89; Charles Eliot Norton Professor of Poetry, Harvard University, Cambridge, Massachusetts, 1960-61; Fulbright Professor, Belgrade, 1980; Drama critic, New Republic, New York, 1952-56. *Publications:* Plays include: The Kleist Variations: Three Plays, Baton Rouge, Louisiana, Oracle Press, 1982: 1. Wannsee (produced Buffalo, 1978); 2. The Fall of the Amazons (produced Buffalo, 1979); 3. Concord (produced Buffalo, 1982); Larry Parks' Day in Court, (produced New York, 1979); Lord Alfred's Lover (produced Gainesville, Florida, 1979). Toronto, Personal Library, 1981, in Monstrous Martyrdoms, 1985; Monstrous Martyrdoms: Three Plays (includes Lord Alfred's Lover, H for Hamlet, German Requiem). Buffalo, Prometheus, 1985. Other publiscations include: The Brecht Commentaries 1943-1980. New York, Grove Press and London, Eyre Methuen, 1981; The Pirandello Commentaries. Lincoln, University of Nebraska, Department of Modern Languages and Literature, 1985; The Brecht Memoir. New York, Performing Arts Journal Publications, 1986; German Requiem, New York, 1990; Round 2 (play) 1991. *Contributions to:* Translations of many works. *Honours:* Guggenheim Fellowship 1948; Rockefeller Grant, 1949; American Academy Grant, 1953; Longview award for criticism, 1961; Ford Grant, 1964; George Jean Nathan Award for criticism, 1967; CBS fellowship, 1976; Obie award 1978; Theater

Festival gold medal, 1985; DFA; University of Wisconsin, Madison, 1975; Litt D, University of East Anglia, Norwich, 1979; a Festschrift in his honour entitled The Critic and The Play, 1986; a Theatre Festival in his name, presenting 3 of his plays and awarded a plaque, New World School of the Arts, Miami, Florida, 1992; Honorary Doctorate, New School for Social Research, New York, 1992; Robert Lewis Award for Life achievement in theatre, 1992. *Memberships:* American Academy of Arts and Sciences, 1969; American Academy and Institute of Arts and Letters, 1990. *Literary Agent:* Jack Tantleff, Suite 700, 375 Greenwich Street, New York, 10013, USA; Joy Westendarp, 22A Aubrey House, Maida Avenue, London W2 1TQ, England. *Address:* 194 Riverside Drive, Apartment 4-E, New York, NY 10025, USA.

BENTLEY Joanne, b. 7 Apr 1928, Poughkeepsie, New York, USA. Psychologist; Writer. m. Eric Bentley, 7 May 1953, 2 sons. *Education:* BA, Vassar College, 1950; MA, Columbia University, 1958. *Publications:* Hallie Flanagan: A Life In The American Theatre. *Contributions to:* Journal of Asthma Research; Various Articles. *Address:* 2 Castle Hts Avenue, Upper Nyack, NY 10960, USA.

BENTON Peggie, (Shifty Burke), b. 19 Oct 1906, Valetta, Malta. Writer. m. 2 Mar 1938, 3 sons. *Education:* Royal School, Bath; Neuchatel & Madrid Universities; Diploma, Neuchatel; Fellow, Institute of Linguists. *Publications:* Finnish Food, 1960; Cooking With Pomiane, 1961; Meat at any Price, co-author, 1963; Chicken & Game, co-author, 1964; Fish for all Seasons, 1966; Peterman, under pen-name, 1966; Eggs, Milk & Cheese, 1971; One Man Against the Drylands, 1972; Fight For The Drylands, 1977; Baltic Countdown, 1984. *Contributions to:* Forum World Features; Ideal Home Magazine; Observer Magazine. *Honours include:* Bronze Medals, Darmstadt 1963, Frankfurt 1966. *Memberships:* Crime Writers Association; Society of Authors. *Literary Agent:* Laurence Pollinger Ltd, 18 Maddox Street, London W1R 0EU. *Address:* 2 Jubilee Terrace, Chichester, West Sussex, PO19 1XL, England.

BENVENISTE Asa, b. 1925, United States of America. Poet; Playwright. *Appointments:* Co-Editor, Zero-Quarterly, Paris, Tangier, London, 1948-56; Correspondent, Nugget Magazine, London, 1956-57; Copy Editor, Doubleday and Company, Publishers, New York City, 1957-58; Senior Art Editor, Paul Hamlyn Limited, Publishers, London, 1959-61; Senior Editor, Studio Vista Limited, Publishers, London, 1961-63; Executive Editor, Trigram Press Limited, London. *Publications:* Tangier for the Traveller (radio play), 1956; Piano Forte(radio play), 1957; Poems of the Month, 1966; A Work in Your Season: A Portfolio of Six Seriagraphs (with Jack Hirschman), 1967; Count Three, 1969; The Atoz Formula, 1969; Free Semantic No. 2, 1970; Umbrella, 1972; Time Being (with Ray Di Palma and Tom Raworth), 1972; Blockmakers Black, 1973; Certainly Metaphysics, 1973; It's the Same Old Feeling Again, 1973; Autotypography: A Book of Design Priorities, 1974; Edge, 1975; Poems, 1976; Loose End, 1977; Colour Theory, 1977; Throw Out The Life Line, Lay Out the Corse: Poems 1965-1985, 1983. *Address:* 22 Leverton Street, London, NW5, England.

BER Andre Marie-Antoine, b. 23 Sept 1920, Bordeaux, France. Retired Engineer; Writer. m. 5 June 1943, 1 son. *Education:* Ecole Nationale de Navigation Maritime, 1937-39; Navire-Ecole pour Eleves-officiers, 1939-41; Officier-mecanicien de la Marine, 1941-48. *Publications:* Mystere des trois roches, 1961; Repaire des loups gris, 1962; Segoldiah, 1964; Fourmis en societe, 1964; Canadia, 1967; Cage aux fauves, 1981; Nouvelles parues dans magazine Mac-Lean, et Radio Canada. *Contributions to:* Mac-Lean Magazine. *Honours:* Finalist, Canadia du concours du Centenaire du Canada; Finalist, du Prix du Cercle de France. *Memberships:* Society of Canadian Writers; Literary Society of Laval. *Address:* 1033 Avenue J.J. Joubert, Duvernay Ville de Laval, Quebec, H7G 4J5, Canada.

BERCH Bettina, b. 25 May 1950, Washington DC, USA. Writer. 1 daughter. *Education:* BA, Barnard College, 1971; MA, University of Madison, 1973; PhD, 1976. *Publications:* The Endless Day: The Political Economy of Women & Work; Radical by Design: The Life & style of Elizabeth Hawes. *Contributions to:* Early Feminist Fashion; The Resurrection of Out Work; Belles Letters; Paradise of A Kind, Lost. *Literary Agent:* Malaga Baldi. *Address:* PO Box 772, Belize City, Belize.

BERESFORD Anne Ellen Hamburger, b. 10 Sept 1928, Redhill, Surrey, England. Poet. m. 28 July 1951. 1 son, 2 daughters. *Appointments:* Poetry Society, Member of General Council, 1976-78; Committee Member, Aldeburgh Poetry Festival, 1989. *Publications:* The Sele of the Morning, 1988; Songs Athracian Taught Me, 1980; The Curving Shore, 1975; The Courtship, 1972; Footsteps on Snow, 1972; The Lair, 1968; Walking Without Moving, 1967; The Songs of Almut, 1980; Translation, Alexandros Poems of Vera Lungu, 1975; Snapshots From An Album 1884-1895, 1992. Co-author of Struck By Apollo, radio play, 1965; Short story, The Villa, radio, 1968; Duet for 3 voices, Anglia TV, 1984. *Contributions to:* Agenda; Akzente; The Scotsman; New Statesman; Boston Journal; Hommage a Arp. *Address:* Marsh Acres, Middleton, Saxmundham, Suffolk IP17 3NH, England.

BERESFORD Elisabeth, b. Paris, France. Writer. 1 son, 1 daughter. *Appointments include:* Founder, Alderney Youth Trust. *Publications:* Historical, romance, gothic, childrens fiction including: The Television Mystery, 1957; Trouble at Tullington Castle, 1958; Gappy Goes West, 1959; Two Gold Dolphins, 1961; Paradise Island, romance, 1963; Escape to Happiness, romance, 1964; Game, Set & Match, 1965; The Hidden Mill, 1965; The Black Mountain Mystery, 1967; Sea-Green Magic, 1968; Stephen & the Shaggy Dog, 1970; The Wandering Wombles, 1970; Dangerous Magic, 1972; The Secret Railway, 1973; The Wombles at Work, 1973; The Wombles Annual, yearly, 1975-78; Snuffle to the Rescue, 1975; Orinoco Runs Away, 1975; Bungo Knows Best, 1976; Tobermory's Big Surprise, 1976; Wombling Free, 1978; The Happy Ghost, 1979; Curious Mgic, 1980; The Four of Us, 1982; The Animals Nobody Wanted, 1982; The Tovers, 1982; The Adventures of Poon, 1984; One of the Family, 1985; The Ghosts of Lupus Street School, 1986; The Secret Room, 1987; Emily and the Haunted Castle, 1987; The Oscar Puffin Book, 1987; Once Upon A Time Stories, 1988; The Island Railway Armada Adventure, 1989; Rose. Charlie's Ark. The Wooden Gun. *Literary Agent:* A.M.Heath; David Higham Associates, 5-8 Lower John Street, London W1R 4HA, UK. *Address:* Alderney, Channel Islands, UK.

BERESFORD-HOWE Constance, b. 10 Nov 1922. Professor of English; Novelist. m. 31 Dec 1960, 1 son. *Education:* BA 1945, MA 1946, McGill University; PhD 1950, Brown University. *Publications:* The Book of Eve, 1973; A Population of One, 1976; The Marriage Bed, 1980; Night Studies, 1984; Prospero's Daughter, 1989; A Serious Widow, 1990. *Honours:* Dodd Mead Intercollegiate Literary Fellowship, 1948; Canadian Booksellers Award, 1974. *Memberships:* Canadian Authors Association, past President, Montreal Branch; International PEN, past President, Montreal Branch; Writers Union of Canada; International PEN, Writers in Prison Committee. *Literary Agent:* Ms Bella Pomer. *Address:* c/o Macmillan of Canada, 29 Birch Avenue, Toronto, Canada M4V 1E2.

BERG David, b. 12 June 1920, New York, USA. Writer; Artist. m. 3 Mar 1949, 1 son, 1 daughter. *Education:* Cooper Union; Pratt Institute; New School of Social Research; Iona College; College of New Rochelle. *Appointments:* Will Eisner Prods, 1940; Captain Marvel, 1941; Timely Comics, 1945-56; Mad Magazine, 1956-; Signet Books, 1964; Warner Books, 1969; NBC TV, 1979. *Publications:* Mad's Dave Berg Looks At: The USA; People; Things; Our Sick World; Modern thinking; Living; Mad's Dave Berg Takes a Loving Look; Mad's Dave Berg Look, Listens and Laughs; Mad's Dave Berg Looks Around; Mad's Dave Berg Looks at You; Mad's Dave Berg Looks at the Neighborhood; Looks at Our Planet; Looks at Today; My Friend G-D; Roger Kaputnik & G-D. *Contributor To:* various journals & magazines. *Honours:* B'nai B'rith Youth Service Award, 1978; Dave Berg Day City of New Rochelle, and West Chester County, 1978; Chair of Great Cartoonists, UCLA Student Body; International Cultural Exchange Program, 1965; Nominated for Academy Humor Award, 1975. *Memberships:* Authors Guild; International Platform Society; National Cartoonists Society; Writers Guild West. *Address:* 14021 Marquessas Way No 307C, Marina Del Rey, CA 90292, USA.

BERG Jean Horton, b. 30 May 1913, Clairton, Pennsylvania, USA. Writer; Teacher. m. 2 July 1938, 1 son, 2 daughters. *Education:* BS, Education, 1935; AM, Latin, 1937. *Publications:* Miss Kirby's Room; Miss Tessie Tate; I Cry When the Sun Goes Down; Also: 50 other books for young people. *Contributions to:* Numerous magazines for young people, over 35 years. *Honours:* Follett Award; Distinguished Alumna Awards, University of Pennsylvania, Friends' Central School. *Memberships:* President, Chester County branch, Association of American Pen Women; ASCAP; Authors Guild; Authors League. *Literary Agent:* McIntosh & Otis Inc. *Address:* 207 Walnut Avenue, Wayne, PA 19087, USA.

BERG Leila Rita, b. 12 Nov 1917, Salford, Lancashire, England. Writer. 1 son, 1 daughter. *Publications include:* Risinghill, Death of a Comprehensive School, 1968; Look at Kids, 1972; The Train Back (with Pat Chapman), 1972; Reading and Loving, 1977; The Adventures of Chunky, 1950; Little Pete, 1952; Trust Chunky, 1954; Fire Engine by Mistake, 1955; The Hidden Road, 1958; Box for Benny, 1958; Folk Tales, 1966; My Dog Sunday, 1968; The Nippers Stories, 1968-76; Snap series 1977; Chatterbooks series, 1981; Small World series, 1983, 1985; Tales for Telling, 1983; Christmas, 1985; Hannuka, 1985; Time for One More, 1986; Steep Street Stories, 1987 and others. *Contributor to:* In 1960's and 1970's: The Guardian, Anarchy, Times Educational Supplement, Times Literary Supplement. *Honours:* Eleanor Farjeon Award, 1973 for Services to Children's Literature. *Literary Agent:* A J Watt. *Address:* Alice's Cottage, Brook Street, Wivenhoe, Nr. Colchester CO7 9DS, England.

BERGE Carol, b. 4 Oct 1928, New York City, USA. Writer; Dealer in Art & Antiques. m. Jack Henry Berge, 1955, 1 son. *Appointments include:* Visiting Professor, Thos Jefferson College, 1975; Visiting Professor, University of Southern Mississippi, 1978; Lectr, SUNY Albany, 1981; Lectr, University of New Mexico, 1987; Colorado Council, Arts Literary Grants Panel, 1992. *Publications include:* Editorships: Woodstock Review; Mississippi Review; Wing Bones; Paper Branches; Subterraneans; Fiction and Poetry Books include: Acts of Love: An American Novel, 1973; Rituals & Gargoyles, 1977; Alba Genesis, 1978; Secrets, Gossip & Slander, 1984; ZEBRAS, Collected Fiction, 1991. *Contributions to:* Iowa Review; TriQuarterly; Center: Fiction International; Measure; Another Chicago Magazine; Poetry Chicago; Fireweed. *Honours:* NY State Council on the arts CAPS Grant; National Endowment for the Arts Award in Fiction; Thirteen Grants of Publication for Center Press. *Address:* 307 Johnson Street, Santa Fe, NM 87501, USA.

BERGE Claude Van De. *See:* PAUWELS Rony.

BERGE Hans Cornelis ten, b. 24 Dec 1938, Netherlands. Writer; Poet. *Appointments include:* Lecturer, Art Academy, Arnhem; Writer-in-residence, University of Texas, USA; Editor, Raster, Grid, literary journals, Amsterdam. *Publications:* Gedichten, collection of 3 poetry books, 1969; White Shaman, 1973; Poetry of the Aztecs, 1972; Va-banque, 1977; Semblance of Reality, 1981; Texas Elegies, 1983. Novels: Zelfportret met witte muts, 1985; Het geheim van een opgewekt humeur, 1986; Songs of Anxiety and Despair, (poetry) 1988; The Defence of Poetry, (essays) 1988. Also: Numerous poetry translations, Pound, Ekelof, Tarn, White, Villaurrutia; 3 prose books; 3 books myths & fables of Arctic peoples; 1 book of essays. *Contributions to:* Raster; De Gids; Vrij Nederland; New Directions in Poetry & Prose; Chicago Review; Plural; Dimension; Les Lettres Nouvelles. *Honours include:* Prose prize, City of Amsterdam, 1971; Van der Hoogt Prize, 1968. *Memberships:* Maatschappij der Nederlandse Letterkunde (Society of Dutch Literature); PEN. *Address:* c/o Meulenhoff Publishers, PO Box 100, 1000 AC Amsterdam, Netherlands.

BERGEL Hans, b. 26 July 1925, Kronstadt, Romania. Author. *Education:* History of Arts, University Cluj-Napoca, Bucharest. *Publications:* Rumanien, Portrait einer Nation, 1969; Ten Southern European Short Stories, 1972; Die Sachsen in Siebenburgen nach dreissig Jahren Kommunismus, 1976; Der Tanz in Ketten, 1977; Siebenburgen, A Picture Book of Transylvania, 1980; Gestalten und Gewalten, 1982; A Picture Book of Transylvania, 1983; Hermann Oberth oder Der mythische Traum vom Fliegen 1984; Der Tod des Hirten, 1985; Literaturgeschichte der Deutschen in Siebenburgen, 1987; Das Venusherz, short novel, 1987; Weihnacht ist uberall, eleven short stories, 1988. *Contributor To:* Kulturpolitische Korrespondenz, Bonn; Rhein-Neckar Zeitung, Heidelberg; Sudost-deutsche Vierteljahresblatter, Munchen; Zeitbuhne, Munchen; Der Gemeinsam Weg, Bonn, and others. *Honours:* Short Story Prize, Bucharest, 1957; Short Story Prize, Bonn, 1972; Georg Dehio Prize, Esslingen, 1972; Goethe Foundation Prize, Basel, 1972; Medien Prize, Bavarian Broadcasting Company, 1983, 89; Bundesverdienstkreuz, 1987; Saxon of Tranlyvanians Culture-Prize, 1988; Geyphius-Prize, 1990, and others. *Memberships:* Kunstlergilde e V. Esslingen; PEN International. *Address:* Rabensteinstrasse 28, D-8000 Munchen 60, Germany.

BERGER Arthur A(sa), b. 1933, United States of America. Writer. *Appointment:* Professor, Broadcast Communication Arts Department, San Francisco State University. *Publications:* Li'l Abner: A Study in American Satire, 1970; The Evangelical Hamburger, 1970; Collaborator, Language in Thought and Action, 3rd edition 1972, 4th Edition 1978; Pop Culture, 1973; The Comic-Stripped American, 1974; About Man: An Introduction to Anthropology, 1974; The TV-Guided American, 1976; Television as an Instrument of Terror, 1980; Film in Society, 1980; Media Analysis Techniques, 1982; Signs in Contemporary Culture: An Introduction to Semiotics, 1984; Television in Society, 1987; Humor, The Psyche and Society, 1987; Visual Sociology and Semiotics, 1987; Agitpop: Political Culture & Communication Theory, 1990; Scripts: Writing for Radio & Television, 1990; Media Research Techniques, 1991; Reading Matter: Multidisciplinary Perspective on Material Culture, 1992; Popular Culture Genres, 1992; An Anatomy of Humor, 1993. *Address:* 118 Peralta Avenue, Mill Valley, CA 94941, USA.

BERGER David G, b. 23 May 1941, New York City, USA. Writer; Sociologist; Director. m. Holly Maxson, 19 Aug 1984, 1 son, 1 daughter. *Education:* University Wisconsin, BS, 1963; Vanderbilt University, MA, 1965; PhD, 1969. *Appointments:* Associate Professor, Temple University, 1968-. *Publications:* Bass Line, The stories & photographs of Milt Hinton; Overtime: The Jazz Photographs of Milt Hinton. *Contributions to:* Aministrative Science Quarterly; American Sociological Review; Journal of Commonications. *Address:* 4 E. 12th Street, No 1, NYC, NY10003, USA.

BERGER Fredericka Nolde, b. 9 May 1932, Philadelphia, USA. m. Bruce Sutton Berger, 14 Mar 1958, 2 sons. *Education:* Harvard University, MAT, 1957. *Publications:* Nuisance: Robots: What They Are, What The Do; The Green Bottle And The Silver Kite. *Honours:* Junior Literary Guild Selection. *Address:* 4209 Sheridan Street, University Park, MD 20782, USA.

BERGER Terry, b. 1933, United States of America.

Children's Writer. *Publications:* Black Fairy Tales (adaptation), 1969; I Have Feelings (psychology), 1971; Lucky, 1974; Being Alone, Being Together, 1974; Big Sister, Little Brother, 1974; A Friend Can Help, 1974; A New Baby, 1974; Not Everything Changes, 1975; The Turtles' Picnic, 1977; How Does It Feel When Your Parents Get Divorced?, 1977; Special Friends, 1979; Stepchild, 1980; Friends, 1981; Co-author: The Haunted Dollhouse, 1982; Ben's ABC Day, 1982; Country Inns: The Rocky Mountains, 1983. *Address:* 130 Hill Park Avenue, Great Neck, NY 11021, USA.

BERGONZI Bernard, b. 1929. Author; Poet. *Appointments:* Senior Lecturer, 1966-71, Professor of English, 1971-92, Emeritus, 1992-, University of Warwick, Coventry. *Publications:* The Early H G Wells, 1961; Heroes' Twilight, 1965, 1980; Innovations: Essays on Art and Ideas, 1968; T S Eliot: Four Quartets: A Casebook, 1969; The Situation of the Novel, 1970, 1979; T S Eliot, 1972, 1978; The Turn of a Century, 1973; H G Wells: A Collection of Critical Essays, 1975; Gerard Manley Hopkins, 1977; Reading the Thirties, 1978; Years: Sixteen Poems, 1979; Poetry 1870-1914, 1980; The Roman Persuasion (novel), 1981; The Myth of Modernism and Twentieth Century Literature, 1986; Exploding English, 1990; Wartime and Aftermath, 1993. *Address:* 19 St. Mary's Crescent, Leamington Spa, CV31 1JL, England.

BERGSON Leo. *See:* **STEBEL Sidney Leo.**

BERKELEY Humphry John, b. 1 Feb 1926, Marlow, England. Writer; Author; Former MP. *Education:* Dragon School, Oxford; Malvern College; Pembroke College, Cambridge (Exhibitioner) BA 1947, MA 1963. *Appointments:* Member of Parliament (Conservative) for Lancaster 1959-66, joined Labour Party 1970; Chairman, United Nations Association of Great Britain and Northern Ireland 1966-70. *Publications:* The Power of the Prime Minister, 1968; Crossing the Floor, 1972; The Life and Death of Rochester Sneath, 1974; The Odyssey of Enoch: a political memoir, 1977; The Myth that Will Not Die: the formation of the National Government, 1978; Faces of the Eighties (with Jeffrey Archer), 1987. *Contributor to:* Many articles in the Times; The Sunday Times; The Daily Telegraph; The Financial Times; The Spectator; The New Statesman. *Membership:* Savile Club. *Literary Agent:* Mark Hamilton, A M Heath, 79 St Martin's Lane, London WC2. *Address:* 3 Pages Yard, Church Street, Chiswick, London W4 2PA, England.

BERKOFF Steven, b. 3 Aug 1937, Stepney, London. Writer; Director; Actor. m. Shelley Lee, 1976. *Education:* Educated at schools in Stepney; Hackney Downs Grammar School, London; Webber-Douglas Academy of Dramatic Art, London, 1958-59; Ecole Jacques Lecoq, Paris, 1965. *Career:* Actor in repertory in Nottingham, Liverpool, Coventry, and at Citizens' Theatre, Glasgow for six years. Founding Director, London Theatre Group, 1973- *Publications:* Plays include: The Fall of the House of Usher, Produced Edinburgh, 1985; Agamemnon, produced London, 1973, Amber Lane Press, 1977; Harry's Christmas, produced London, 1985; Included in West, Lunch, London, 1983; Harry's Christmas, 1985; West, Lunch, Harry's Christmas, London, Faber and New York, Grove Press, 1985; Kvetch and Acapulco (Produced Los Angeles, 1986; Kvetch produced New York, 1987, London, 1991) London, Faber, 1986; New York, Grove Press, 1987; Sink the Belgrano!, produced London 1986; With Massage, London, Faber, 1987; Metamorphosis, London, 1969; The Trial, London, 1970; In The Penal Colony, London, 1968, Amber Lane Press, 1988; East, Edinburgh, 1975; West, London, 1983; Greek, London, 1980; Decadence, London, 1981; Faber, 1989; The Theatre of Steven Berkoff - Photographic Record, Methuen, 1992. Short stories: Gross Intrusion and Other Stories. London, Calder and Dallas, Riverrun Press, 1979. Director of plays and actor in many plays and films and for television. *Honours:* Los Angeles Drama Critics Circle award for directing, 1983; Evening Standard Award for Kvetch, Comedy of the Year, 1991. *Literary Agent:* Joanna Marston, Rosica Colin Ltd,

London. *Address:* c/o Joanna Marston, Rosica Colin Ltd, 1 Clareville Grove Mews, London SW7 5AH, England.

BERKSON Bill (William Craig), b. 30 Aug 1939, New York City, USA. Poet; Critic; Teacher; Editor. m. Lynn O'Hare, 17 July 1975. 1 son, 1 daughter. *Education:* Brown University, 1957-59; The New School for Social Research, 1959-60; Columbia College, 1959-60; New York University, Institute of Fine Arts, 1960-61. *Appointments:* Editor, Best & Company, 1969; Editor, Big Sky magazines & books, 1971-78; Professor, San Francisco Art Institute, 1984-; Contributing Editor, Zyzzyva, 1987-92; Corresponding Editor, Art in America, 1988-. *Publications:* Saturday Night: Poems 1960-61, 1961, 1975; Shining Leaves, 1969; Recent Visitors, 1973; Enigma Variations, 1975; Hymns to St Bridget, (with Frank O'Hara), 1975; Blue is The Hero, 1976; Homage to Frank O'Hara, editor, 1978; Start Over, 1983; Red Devil, 1983; Lush Life, 1983. *Contributions to:* Paris Review; Poetry (Chicago); This; Sun & Moon; Art Forum; Evergreen Review; O-Blek; Angel Hair; Big Table; The World; New American Writing. *Honours:* Dylan Thomas Memorial Award, The New School, 1959; Poets Foundation Grant, 1968; Yaddo Fellow, 1968; National Endowment for the Arts Fellowship, 1980; Briarcombe Fellowship, 1983; Marin Arts Council Poetry Award, 1987; Artspace Award for Art Criticism, 1990. *Membership:* International Association of Art Critics; PEN. *Address:* Box 389, Bolinas, CA 94924, USA.

BERMAN Claire, b. 1936, United States of America. Author; Journalist. *Appointments:* Senior Editor, Cosmopolitan, 1958-63; Contributing Editor, New York Magazine, 1972-78; Former Director of Public Education, Permanent Familes for Children, Child Welfare League of America. *Publications:* A Great City for Kids: A Parent's Guide to a Child's New York, 1969; We Take This Child: A Candid Look at Modern Adoption, 1974; Making It as a Stepparent, 1980, 1986; 'What Am I Doing in a Stepfamily?', 1982; Adult Children of Divorce Speak Out, 1991; Golden Cradles: How The Adoption Establishment Works, 1991. *Memberships:* Executive Council, American Society of Journalists and Authors. *Literary Agent:* Julian Bach. *Address:* 52 Riverside Drive, New York, NY 10024, USA.

BERMAN David, b. 20 Nov 1942, New York, USA. University Teacher. m. Aileen Jill Mitchell, 25 Dec 1970, 1 son, 1 daughter. *Education:* BA, New School for Social Research, 1965; MA, University of Denver, 1966; PhD, Trinity College, Dublin, 1972. *Publications:* History of Atheism in Britain; Berkeley's Alciphron in Focus; Essays & Replies. *Contributions to:* Oxford Companion to English Literature; Encyclopedia of Unbelief; Field Day Anthology of Irish Literature; Irish Mind; George Berkeley: Critical Assessments; Berkeley Newsletter; Dictionaire des Philosophes; Mind; Apollo; Journal of History of Ideas; Journal of History of Philosophy; Book Collector; Internationl Review of Psychaonalysis; Revue International De Philosophie; Idealistic Studies. *Address:* Philosophy Department, Trinity College, Dublin 2, Ireland.

BERMANT Chaim Icyk, b. 26 Feb 1929, Poland. Author. m. Judith Weil, 16 Dec 1962, 2 sons, 2 daughters. *Education:* MA Honours, MLitt, Glasgow University, UK; MSc, London School of Economics. *Publications include:* Troubled Eden, 1967; The Cousinhood, 1970; Coming Home, 1976; The Jews, 1977; The Patriarch, 1981; House of Women, 1982; Dancing Bear, 1984; What's the Joke, study of Jewish humour, 1986; Titch, 1987; The Companian; 1988; Lord Jakobovits, 1990; Murmurings of a Licensed Heretic, 1990. *Contributions to:* Innumerable publications.

BERMINGHAM Carmel Mary, (Carmel Brudenell), b. 20 Feb 1945, Victoria, Australia. Kindergarten, Primary School Teacher. 1 son. *Education:* Bachelor of Teaching, (ECE) Royal Melbourne Institute of Technology. *Publications:* Motley; The Spotted Pony Foal; Forthcoming, Shelty and the Race. *Contributions to:* Hoofs & Horns; Welsh Pony; Cob Society of Aust

Annual Journal. *Memberships:* Kindergarten Teachers Association of Victoria; Childrens Book Council of Australia. *Address:* PO Box 252, Whittlesea, Victoria 3757, Australia.

BERNARD André, b. 15 Apr 1956, Boston, Massachusetts, USA. Book Editor. m. Jennie F McGregor, 16 June 1990. *Education:* BA 1979, Franklin & Marshall College. *Appointments:* Editor, Viking Penguin, 1984-87; Executive Editor, David R Godine, Publisher, 1987-89; Senior Editor, Touchstone/Simon & Schuster 1989-91; Senior Editor, Book-of-the-Month Club 1991-. *Publication:* Rotten Rejections, 1990. *Memberships:* PEN; The Coffee House, Board of Directors 1991-. *Address:* 77 Euclid Avenue, Hastings-on-Hudson, NY 10706, USA.

BERNARD Christopher William, b. 6 May 1950, Burlington, New Jersey, USA. Writer; Editor. *Education:* New College of California, 1981. *Appointments:* Associate Editor, 1976; Co Editor, 1989-. *Publications:* Gilded Abattoir: Wreckage From a Journey. *Contributions to:* Several. *Memberships:* Poets & Writers; The American Academy of Poets; Playwright's Center of San Francisco. *Address:* 1655 1/2A Mason Street, San Francisco, CA 94133, USA.

BERNARD Oliver, b. 6 Dec 1925, Chalfont St Peter, Bucks, England. Writer. 2 sons, 2 daughters. *Education:* Westminster School; BA, Goldsmiths' College; ACSD, Central School of Speech and Drama. *Publications:* Rimbaud Coll. Poems, 1962; Apollinaire Selection, 1965; Country Matters (poems) 1961; Five Peace Poems, 1985; Poems, 1983; The Finger Points at the Moon, 1989; Moons and Tides, 1989; Getting Over It, 1992. *Contributor to:* Since 1955 - Botteghe Oscure, Times Literary Supplement, The Listener, Poetry (Chicago), Gemini, Spectator, New Statesman, Only Poetry, New Poetry. *Honour:* Poetry Society Gold Medal for Verse Speaking, 1982. *Memberships:* William Morris Society; Council Member, Poetry Society; BP Speak-a-Poem (Committee Member). *Address:* 1 East Church Street, Kenninghall, Norwich NR16 2EP, England.

BERNARD Robert. *See:* **MARTIN Robert Bernard.**

BERNARDINI Joseph Alfred, b. 19 June 1937, New York City, USA. Writer. m. Jane George, 25 Aug 1984, 2 sons. *Education:* BA, University of New York, 1959. *Publication:* Singapore, A Novel of the Bronx. *Literary Agent:* Gunther Stuhlmann. *Address:* PO Box 669, Greenwood Lake, NY 10925, USA.

BERNAT-CIECHAN Anna Marianna, b. 3 Dec 1946, Poland. Poet. m. 18 Nov 1978, 1 son, 1 daughter. *Education:* State Technical School, 1965-68. *Publications:* White Island, 1978; Troubles of an Old Night, 1984; Religious Poems in 6 Anthologies, 1972-86; Bezdomna Jaskolka, libretto opera music Szymon Laks TV, 1975; many records with religious songs and songs for children, with husband. *Contributions to:* Przewodnik Katolicki; Poezja; Regiony; Nowy Wyraz; Kierunki; Razem. *Honours:* Forum of Poets Hybrydes, 1970; Spring of Poets, Lodz, 1972, 1973, 1975, 1976; V Autumn of Poetry, 1975; Radio Poetry Competition, 1973. *Memberships:* Union of Polish Writers, 1972; Union of Authors and Composers, 1981; Society of Authors and Composers. *Address:* Ul. Nowotki 15 m.8, 00-159 Warsaw, Poland.

BERNAUW Patrick, b. 15 Apr 1962, Alost, Belgium. Writer. m. Elke Van der Elst, 24 Mar 1984, 1 daughter. *Appointments:* Scenarist Comic Books, Gucky, 1983-84; Producer and Director of Radio Plays, 1988-; Editor, Historische Verhalen (Historical Studies). *Publications:* Mijn Lieve Spooklidmaat, 1983; De Stillevens Van De Dood, 1985; Mysteries Van Hetlam Gods, 1991; Dromen Van Een Farao, 1991; Landru Bestaat Niet, 1992; Several plays and radio plays. *Contributions to:* Vlaamse Filmpjes; Kreatief; Bres; Plot; Crime; Ganymedes; short stories and essays. *Honour:* John Flanders Award 1987,

1991. *Address:* Brusselbaan 296, 9320 Erembodegem, Belgium.

BERNAYS Anne, b. 14 Sept 1930. Writer; Teacher. m. Justin Kaplan, 29 July 1954, 3 daughters. *Education:* BA 1952, Barnard College. *Appointments:* Jenks Professor of Contemporary Letters, College of the Holy Cross, Worcester, Massachusetts. *Publications include:* Growing Up Rich, 1975; Professor Romeo, 1989; The Address Book, 1983. *Contributions to:* The New York Times Book Review; American Heritage; Sports Illustrated; The Atlantis Monthly; Lears; and others. *Honours:* Edward Lewis Wallant Award, 1976; Residency, Beliagio, Rockefeller Foundation. *Memberships:* PEN New England, Executive Board; Writers' Union, Advisory Board; Fine Arts Work Centre in Provincetown, Chair, Board of Trustees; Member, Selection Committee, Nieman Foundation, 1993. *Literary Agent:* Gina Maccoby. *Address:* 16 Francis Avenue, Cambridge, MA 02138, USA.

BERNE Leo. *See:* **DAVIES Leslie Purnell.**

BERNE Stanley, b. 8 June 1923, Port Richmond, Staten Island, New York, USA. Research Professor. m. Arlene Zekowski, July 1952. *Education:* BS, Rutgers University, 1947; MA, New York University, 1950; Graduate Fellow, Louisiana State University, Baton Rouge, 1954-59. *Appointments:* Associate Professor, English, 1960-80, Research Professor, English, 1980-, Eastern New Mexico University, Portales; Host, Co-Producer, TV series Future Writing Today, KENW-TV, PBS, 1984-85. *Publications:* A First Book of the Neo-Narrative, 1954; Cardinals and Saints...On the aims and purposes of the arts in our time, criticism, 1958; The Dialogues, 1962; The Multiple Modern Gods and Other Stories, 1969; The New Rubaiyat of Stanley Berne, poetry, 1973; Future Language, criticism, 1976; The Great American Empire, 1981; Every Person's Little Book of P=L=U=T=O=N=I=U=M (with Arlene Zekowski), 1992. *Honours:* Literary research awards, Eastern New Mexico University, 1966-76. *Memberships:* PEN; COSMEP; New England Small Press Association; Rio Grande Writers Association; Santa Fe Writers. *Address:* Box 4595 Santa Fe, NM 87502, USA.

BERNER Urs, b. 17 Apr. 1944, Schafisheim, Switzerland. Writer. Divorced. *Education:* Teacher's Training; Studies in History, University of Zurich. *Appointments:* Editor, then Freelance Journalist. *Publications:* Friedrichs einsame Traume in der Stadt am Fluss, novel, 1977; Fluchtrouten, novel, 1980; Wunschzeiten, novel, 1985; Das Wunder von Dublin, stories, 1987; Die Lottokonige, novel, 1989. *Honours:* Werkjahrpreis der Stadt Zurich, 1980; Preis der Schweiz, Schillerstiftung, 1980; 1st Preis des Kurzgeschicntenwettbewerbs des Schweiz, Schriftstellerverbandes, 1985. *Memberships:* PEN; Schriftstellerverband; LG-Wort. *Address:* Scharerstrasse 9, CH-3014 Berne, Switzerland.

BERNSTEIN Charles, b. 4 Apr 1950, New York, USA. Poet; Essayist; Teacher. m. Susan Bee, 1977, 1 son, 1 daughter. *Education:* Harvard College, AB, 1972. *Appointments:* David Gray Professor, state University of New York, 1989. *Publications:* A Poetics; Rough Trades; Content, is Dream: Essays; Controlling Interests. *Honours:* National Endowment for the Arts; Guggenheim; New York Foundation for the Arts. *Address:* 306 Clemens Hall, English Department, Suny, Buffalo, NY 14260, USA.

BERNSTEIN Marcelle. *See:* **CLARK Marcelle Ruth.**

BERRIDGE Elizabeth, b. 3 Dec 1919, London, England. Author; Critic. m. Reginald Moore, 1940, 1 son, 1 daughter. *Appointments:* Editor, Peter Owen, 1956-61; Reviewer/Critic, BBC, Spectator, Books and Bookmen, Tribune, Country Life, 1952-74; Fiction Reviewer, Daily Telegraph, 1967-88. *Publications:*

Family Matters, story collection, 1981; People at Play, 1982; Across the Common, 1964; 1985, 1989, Rose Under Glass, 1967, 1985; Sing Me Who You Are, 1972, 1985; The Barretts at Hope End, Editor and Introduction, 1974; Family Matters (stories), 1981; People at Play, 1982; The Barnetts at Hope End, (Ed and Introduction); Run for Home, 1981; That Surprising Summer, 1973, 1975, (Children's Books). Honour: Yorkshire Post, Novel of the Year, 1964. Memberships: PEN; Trustee, Chase Charity. Address: c/o David Higham Association, 5-8 Lower John Street, London W1R 4HA, England.

BERRIGAN Daniel J S.J., b. 9 May 1921, Virginia, Minnesota. Writer. Education: Educated at Woodstock College, 1943-46; Weston (Jesuit) Seminary, Massachusetts; ordained Roman Catholic priest 1952; Teacher, St Peter's Preparatory School, Jersey City, New Jersey, 1945-49; auxiliary military chaplain, 1954; taught French and Philosophy, Brooklyn Preparatory School, 1954-57; Teacher of New Testament Studies, LeMoyne College, Syracuse, New York, 1957-63; Director of United Christian Work, Cornell University, Ithaca, New York, 1967-68; jailed for anti-war activities, 1968; Visiting Lecturer, University of Manitoba, Winnipeg, 1973, University of Detroit, 1975, University of California, Berkeley, 1976 and Yale University, New Haven, Connecticut, 1977. Publications include: Verse includes: Night Flight to Hanoi: War Diary with 11 Poems, 1968; Crime Trial, 1970; Trial Poems, 1970; Selected and New Poems, 1973; Prison Poems, 1973, 1974; May All Creatures Live, 1983; Journey to Black Island, 1984. Recording: Not Letting Me Not Let Blood: Prison Poems, National Catholic Reporter, 1976; Play: The Trial of the Catonsville Nine (produced Los Angeles, 1970, New York and London 1971) Boston, Beacon Press, 1970. Many other publications. Honours: Lamont Poetry Selection Award, 1957; Thomas More Association Medal, 1970; Melcher Book Award, 1971. Address: 220 West 98th Street, New York, NY 10025, USA.

BERRINGTON John. See: **BROWNJOHN Alan.**

BERRY Adrian M, b. 1937. Journalist and Writer (Science Fiction, Astronomy, Sciences). Appointments:Correspondent, Time Magazine, New York City, 1965-67; Science Correspondent, Daily Telegraph, London 1977-. Publications: The Next Ten Thousand Years: A Vision of Man's Future in the Universe, 1974; The Iron Sun: Crossing the Universe through Black Holes, 1977; From Apes to Astronauts, 1981; The Super Intelligent Machine, 1983; High Skies and Yellow Rain, 1983; Koyama's Diamond (fiction), 1984; Labvrinth of Lies, (fiction) 1985; Ice with Your Evolution, 1986; Computer Softwave: The Kings and Queens of England, 1985; Harrap's Book of Scientific Anecdotes, 1989. Honour: Hon Fellow of the Royal Geographic Society, 1984-. Memberships: Fellow, Royal Astronomical Society, London, 1973-; Senior Fellow, British Interplantetary Society, 1986-. Address: 11 Cottesmore Gardens, Kensington, London, W8, England.

BERRY Brian Joe Lobley, b. 1934, United States of America. Writer (Geography, Planning). Appointments: Professor, Harvard University, Cambridge, Massachusetts, 1976-81; Professor, Dean, School of Urban and Public Affairs, Carnegie Mellon University, Pittsburgh, 1981-. Publications: Growth Centers in the American Urban System, 1960-1970, 1973; The Human Consequences of Urbanization: Divergent Paths in the Urban Experience of the Twentieth Century, 1973; Land Use, Urban Form, and Environmental Quality, 1974; Urban Environmental Management: Planning for Pollution Control, 1974; The Open Housing Question: Race and Housing in Chicago 1966-76, 1979; Editor, numerous books. Memberships: Faculty, Brookings Institution, Washington DC, 1966-76.

BERRY Francis b. 23 Mar 1915, Ipoh, Malaya. Emeritus Professor. m. (1) Melloney Nancy Graham, 4

Apr 1947, 1 son, 1 daughter; m. (2) Eileen Marjorie Lear, 9 Apr 1970. Education: BA, University of London, 1947; MA, University of Exeter, 1949. Publications include: Poets' Grammar, 1958; The Iron Christ, 1938; Murdock and Other Poems, 1962; The Galloping Centaur, 1952; Poetry and the Physical Voice, 1962; The Shakespeare Inset, 1966; Morant Bay and Other Poems, 1961; Ghosts of Greenland, 1966; I Tell of Greenland, 1977; From the Red Fort, 1984. Contributions to: BBC; TLS; The Listener; New Statesman; The Observer; Critical Quarterly. Memberships: Fellow, Royal Society of Literature. Address: 4, Eastgate Street, Winchester, Hampshire SO23 8EB, England.

BERRY Ila F, b. 9 June 1922. Freelance Writer; Poet; Student of Creative Writing. Education: AA, Fullerton College, USA; BA, John F Kennedy University; MA, English and Creative Writing, San Francisco State University, 1985. Appointments: Long Distance Operator and Supervisor, Pacific Telephone Co, Los Angeles, California; Investigator, International Department, Bank of America, San Francisco, California. Publications: Poetry: Come Walk with Me, 1979; Re-arranging the Landscape, March 1986; Rowing in Eden, 1987; Behold the Bright Demons, 1993. Contributions to: The Los Angeles Times; Oakland Tribune; Blue Unicorns; Attention Please; Ideals; Haiku Highlights; Communicating Through Word and Image; Tunnel Road; The Sandpiper; Torchlight. Honours include: Jessamyn West Creative Award, 1969; Woman of Distinction, Fullerton College, 1969; Grand Prize, Poetry, Poets Dinner, 1974. Memberships: Ina Coolbrith Circle, President, 1977-79; California State Poetry Society; Robert Frost Chapter, Californian Federation of Chaparral Poets; The California Writers Club; The National League of American Pen Women. Address: 761 Sequoia Woods Pl, Concord, CA 94518, USA.

BERRY Jo(ycelyn), b. 1933, United States of America. Writer (Theology/Religion, Women). Appointments: Director, Children's and Women's Ministries, Grace Community Church, Sun Valley, California, 1972-76; Writer, Consultant, David C. Cook Publishing Company, Elgin, Illinois, 1973- 80; Editor, Glencoe Publishing Company, Encino, California. Publications: The Happy Home Handbook, 1976; Can You Love Yourself?, 1978; Growing, Sharing, Serving, 1979; Staying Dry, 1980; Proverbs for Easier Living, 1980; Beloved Unbeliever, 1981; The Priscilla Principle, 1984; Recipes for Remembrance, 1984; Managing Your Life and Your Time, 1986; Becoming God's Special Woman, 1986. Address: 12739 Deon Place, Granada Hills, CA 91344, USA.

BERRY Paul, b. 1919. Writer. Publications: Daughters of Cain (with Renee Huggett), 1956; By Royal Appointment: A Biography of Mary Ann Clarke, Mistress of the Duke of York 1803-07, 1970; Joint Editor, The Selected Journalism of Winifred Holtby and Vera Brittain, 1985; Vera Brittain: A Life (with Mark Bostridge), 1993. Address: 1 Bridgefoot Cottages, Stedham, Midhurst, Sussex, England.

BERSSENBRUGGE Mei-Mei, b. 10 May 1947, China. Poet. m. Richard Tuttle, 12 Jan 1988, 1 daughter. Education: MFA, Columbia University, 1973; BA, Reed College, 1969. Publications: Empathy; Heat Bird; Random Possession; Summits Move With The Tide. Contributions to: Consunctions; Sulfur; Oblek; Parnassus. Honours: Nea Grant; American Book Award; Pen West Book Award. Memberships: Poetry Society of America. Address: c/o Publisher, Station Hill Press, Barrytown, NY 12507, USA.

BERTHA Zoltan, b. 4 June 1955, Szentes, Hungary. Writer; Teacher; Scholar. m. Hajdu Csilla, 5 July 1985, 1 son. Education: University of Debrecen, BA, 1978; Doctor's Degree, 1982. Appointments: Scholar Debrecen University, 1978-90; Editorial Board, Alfold, 1991-; Holnap, 1990. Publications: Hungarian Literature in Rumania in the 70's; A Szellem Jelzofenyei;

Balint Tibor. *Contributions to:* Alfold; Tiszataj; Forras; Eletunk; Holnap; Kortars. *Honours:* Moricz Zsigmond Literary Scholarship. *Memberships:* Association of Hungarian Writers; Society of Young Writers; International Society of Hungarian Studies; Society of Hungarian Literary History. *Address:* Boszormenyi, ut 69, N 15, H-4032 Debrecen, Hungary.

BERTIN Jack. *See:* **GERMANO Peter B.**

BERTOLINO James, b. 4 Oct 1942, Wisconsin, USA. College Teacher. m. Lois Behling, 29 Nov 1966. *Education:* BS, University of Wisconsin, Oshkosh, 1970; MFA, Poetry Writing, American Literature, Cornell University, 1973. *Appointments:* Creative Writing Faculty, Cornell University, 1973; University of Cincinnati, 1974; Western Washington University, 1984; Skagit Valley College, 1985; Djerassi Foundation, 1987; Centrum Arts Foundation, 1989; Edmonds Community College, 1989. *Publications:* Volumes of poetry: Employed, 1972; Making Space For Our Living, 1975; The Alleged Conception, 1976; New and Selected Poems, 1978; Precinct Kali and The Gertrude Spicer Story, 1982; First Credo, 1986; Others: Drool, 1968; Stone Marrow, 1969; Becoming Human, 1970; Edging Through, 1972; Terminal Placebos, 1975; The Gestures, 1975. *Contributions to:* Poetry; Gargoyle; International Synergy Journal; In Context; The Amicus Journal; Wilderness; Organic Gardening. *Honours:* Book-of-the-Month Club Poetry Fellowship, 1970; National Endowment for the Arts Fellowship, 1974; Ohio Arts Council Award, 1979; International Colladay Book Award for First Credo, 1986. *Address:* PO Box 1157, Anacortes, WA 98221, USA.

BERTON Pierre Francis Demarigny, b. 12 July 1920, Whitehorse, Yukon, Canada. Author; Broadcaster. m. Janet Walker, 22 Mar. 1946. 3 sons, 5 daughters. *Education:* BA, University of British Columbia, 1941; Recipient of 12 honorary degrees. *Appointments:* City Editor, Vancouver (BC) News Herald, 1941-42; Feature Writer, Vancouver Sun, 1946-47; Successive positions to Managing Editor 1947-58, Contributing Editor 1963, Maclean's Magazine, Toronto, Ontario; Associate Editor, Daily Columnist, Toronto Daily Star, 1958-62; YB Panellist Front Page Challenge, CBC; Radio Commentator, CKey, Toronto; Host, TV Program. *Publications:* 31 books including: The Invasion of Canada 1812-1813, 1980; Flames Across the Border, 1981; Why We Act Like Canadians, 1982; Klondike Quest, 1983; The Promised Land, 1984; Masquerade, 1985; Screenwriter, narrator. *Contributions to:* Numerous magazines. *Honours:* Decorated Order of Canada; Recipient Governor General's Award for Creative Non-fiction, 1956, 1958, 1972; Stephen Leacock Medal for Humor, 1959; J B McAree Award for Columnist of Year, 1959; National Newspaper Awards for Feature Writing and Staff Corresponding, 1960; Stephen Leacock Medal of Humour, 1960; National Newspaper Awards, Feature Writing and Staff Corresponding, 1961; Association of Canadian Televeison and Radio Artists 'Nellie' for Integrity and Outspokenness in Broadcasting, 1972; Governor-General Award for Creative Non-Fiction 'The Last Spike', 1972; Association of Canadian Televisin and Radio Artists, 1978; Canadian Authors Association Literary Award for Non-Fiction, 1981; The Alumni Award of Distinction, UBC, 1981; Canadian Bookseller Award, 1982; Ontario History and Social Science Teachers Association Perspective Award, 1982; World Tourism Day Medal, 1982; Beefeater Club Prize for Literature, 1982; Grand Prix Film Awards; Beefeater Club Prize for Literature, 1982; Canadian Booksellers Award, 1982; Named to Canada Newspaper Hall of Fame, 1982. *Memberships:* Authors League America; Heritage Canada; Association of Canadian Radio and TV Artists. *Literary Agent:* Elsa Franklin. *Address:* 21 Sackville Street, Toronto, Ontario M5A 3E1, Canada.

BETHELL Nicholas (William) (Lord Bethell of Romford), b. 1938. Writer. *Appointments:* Sub-Editor, Times Literary Supplement, London, 1962-64; Script Editor, BBC, London, 1964-67. *Publications:* Editor and Translator, Elegy to John Donne and Other Poems, by Joseph Brodsky, 1967; Translation, Six Plays, by Slawomir Mrozek, 1967; Gomulka: His Poland and His Communism, 1969; Cancer Ward and The Love-Girl and the Innocent, by Alexander Solzhenitsyn,(play translated with David Burg), 1969; The War Hitler Won, 1973; The Last Secret: Forcible Repatriation to Russia 1944-1947, 1974; Russian Besieged, 1977; The Palestine Triangle, 1979; The Great Betrayal, 1984. *Memberships:* House of Lords Government Whip 1970-71); European Parliament, 1975-. *Address:* 73 Sussex Square, London, W2 2SS, England.

BETTELINI Lauro, b. 27 Aug. 1938, Lugano, Switzerland. Journalist. 1 son, 1 daughter. *Education:* Techn. Architect, 1957; Journalism Degree, Milan, Italy. *Appointments:* Gazzetta Ticinese, 1975; Swiss TV, 1979. *Publications:* (Narrative Poetry) Noi Della Piazza, 1987; Lo Zodiaco Del Nonno, 1987; Gli Orti Del Disgelo, 1987; JI Doppio Allo Specchio, 1988; TV Documentary. *Contributions to:* Numerous journals and magazines. *Honours:* Premio Nazionale Narrative, La Spezia Italy, 1985; Premio Letterario L'Autore Poesia, Firenze, 1986; Premio Nazionale Di Poesia, Pisa, 1987; Premio Ascona Finalista Narrativa, Ascona, 1987; Mondo Letterario (Finalista) Narrative, Milan, 1987. *Memberships:* Associazione Scrittori della Svizzera Italiana; PEN; Federation of Swiss Journalist. *Literary Agent:* Lucchini Cristina. *Address;* Via Crespera 50B, 6932 Breganzona, Switzerland.

BETTERIDGE Anne. *See:* **POTTER Margaret.**

BETTS Raymond Frederick, b. 1925, United States of America. Writer (History, Current Affairs). *Publications:* Assimilation and Association in French Colonial Theory 1890-1914, 1961; The Scramble of Africa, 1966; Europe Overseas: Phases of Imperialism, 1968; The Ideology of Blackness, 1971; The False Dawn: European Imperialism in the Nineteenth Century, 1975; Tricouleur: The French Colonial Empire, 1978; Europe in Retrospect: A Brief History of the Past Two Hundred Years, 1979; Uncertain Dimensions: Western Overseas Empires in the Twentieth Century, 1985; France and Decolonisation, 1991. *Address:* 311 Mariemont Drive, Lexington, KY 40505, USA.

BEVAN Alistair. *See:* **ROBERTS Keith John Kingston.**

BEVAN Gloria, b. New Zealand. Author. *Publications:* The Distant Trap, 1969; The Hills of Maketu, 1969; Beyond the Ranges, 1970; Make Way for Tomorrow, 1971; It Began in Te Rangi, 1971; Vineyard in a Valley, 1972; Flame in Fiji, 1973; The Frost and the Fire, 1973; Connelly's Castle, 1974; High Country Wife, 1974; Always a Rainbow, 1975; Dolphin Bay, 1976; Bachelor Territory, 1977; Plantation Moon, 1977; Fringe of Heaven, 1978; Kowhai Country, 1979; Half a World Away, 1980; Master of Mahia, 1981; Emerald Cave, 1981; The Rouseabout Girl, 1983; Southern Sunshine, 1985; Golden Bay, 1986. *Address:* c/o Mills and Boon Limited, 15-16 Brooks Mews, London, W1A 1DR, England.

BEVERIDGE William Ian Beardmore, b. 23 Apr 1908. Professor of Animal Pathology, University of Cambridge. m. Patricia Thomson, 23 May 1935, 1 son. *Education:* BVSc, 1931, DVSc 1940, University of Sydney; DVM (hc) Hannover, 1963; MA 1947, ScD 1974, University of Cambridge. *Publications:* The Art of Scientific Investigation, 1950; Frontiers in Comparative Medicine, 1972; Influenza, the Last Great Plague, 1977; Seeds of Discovery, 1980; Viral Diseases of Farm Livestock, 1981; Bacterial Diseases of Cattle, Sheep and Goats, 1983; Footrot of Sheep, CSIR Bulletin, No 140, 1941; Cultivation of Viruses and Richettsiac in the Chick Embryo (with F M Burnet) British Medical Research Council, Special Report No 256 1946. *Contributions to:* Many research reports in scientific journals. *Honours:* Honorary Associate, Royal College of Veterinary Surgeons, 1963; Fellow, Australian Veterinary

Association, 1963; Honorary Foreign Member, L'Academie Royale de Medicine de Belgique, 1970; Honorary Member, American Veterinary Medicine Association, 1973; Gamgee Gold Medal of World Veterinary Association, 1975; Honorary Member, World Veterinary Association; Gold Headed Cane Award, American Veterinary Epidemiological Society, 1971. *Memberships:* President, World Veterinary Association, 1957-75; Honorary Member, British Veterinary Association, 1970; Life Fellow, Australian College of Veterinary Scientists, 1971. *Address:* 5 Bellevue Road, Wentworth Falls, NSW 2782, Australia.

BEWES Richard Thomas, b. 1 Dec 1934, Nairobi, Kenya. Anglican Rector. m. Elisabeth Ingrid Jaques, 18 Apr 1964, 2 sons, 1 daughter. *Education:* Marlborough School 1948-53; MA, Emmanuel College, Cambridge, 1954-57; Ridley Hall Theological College, Cambridge, 1957-59. *Publications:* Talking About Prayer, 1979; The Pocket Handbook of Christian Truth, 1981; The Church Reaches Out, 1981; John Wesley's England, 1981; The Church Overcomes 1983; On the Way, 1984; Quest for Life, 1985; The Church Marches On, 1986; When God Surprises, 1986; A New Beginning, 1989; The Resurrection, 1989. *Contributor to:* The Church of England Newspaper. *Address:* 2 All Souls Place, London W1N 3DB, England.

BEYE Holly, b. 27 Feb 1922, Iowa City, Iowa, USA. Writer; Librarian. *Education:* BA, Swarthmore College, 1943; MLS, University of New York, Albany, 1967; Graduate, Rutgers University School of Alcoholism, New Jersey, 1981. *Appointments:* Performance and Workshop Writer and Director: The Heads, Cafe theatre political improvisation group, 1960's; WESAW Improvisation for Elementary School students, 1975-85; Holly's Comets Improvisation Group, 1985-. *Publications:* Do Keep Thee in the Stony Bowes, prose poem, 1951; In the City of Sorrowing Clouds, 1952; XVI Poems, 1953; Stairwells and Marriages, 1954; Monsters in World Folklore, filmstrips, 1970; Lives of the Comets, video, 1989; Refractions, video, 1990; Plays: Afternoon of the Spawn, 1961; Thus, 1963; It's All Yours!, 1963; The Banana Thief, 1965; About the Cast, 1989; Chance, 1989; Dilly, Dawn and Dell, 1990; The Bat Girl, 1992; Sisters, 1993. *Contributions to:* Quarterly Review of Literature; New Directions Annual. *Honours:* Prize, Quarterly Review of Literature, 1962. *Membership:* Dramatists Guild. *Address:* PO Box 1043, Woodstock, NY 12498, USA.

BEYFUS Drusilla, Writer. *Appointments:* Women's Editor, Sunday Express, London, 1952-53; Columnist, Daily Express, London, 1953-56; Associate Editor, Queen Magazine, London, 1959-63; Home Editor, The Observer, London, 1962-64; Associate Editor, Weekend Telegraph Magazine, London, 1963-71; Editor, Brides and Setting Up Home Magazine, London, 1971-79; Associate Editor, Vogue Magazine, London, 1980-87; Contributing Editor, Telegraph Magazine, 1991-; Visiting Tutor Central St. Martins College of Art, 1989-. *Publications:* Lady Behave (with Anne Edwards), 1956, 1969; The English Marriage, 1968; The Brides Book, 1981; Modern Manners, 1992. *Contributions to:* Sunday Times; Punch; New Statesman; Daily Telegraph; The Spectator. *Address:* 51g Eaton Square, London, SW1, England.

BEYNON Huw, b. 1942. Writer. *Publications:* Perceptions of Work (with R.M. Blackburn), 1972; Working for Ford, 1973, 1984; Living with Capitalism (with Theo Nichols), 1977; What Happened at Speke?, 1978; The Workers Report on Vickers Limited (with Hilary Wainwright), 1979; Born to Work (with Nick Hedges), 1982; Digging Deeper: Issues in the Miners Strike, 1985; A Tale of Two Industies: The Decline of Coal and Steel in the North of England, 1991; Master and Servants Class and Patronage in the Making of a Labour Organisation, 1991. *Address:* Department of Sociology, University of Manchester, Manchester, M13 9PL, England.

BHARATI S, (Vachaspati), b. 6 June 1943, Vijayawada, India. Journalist; Poet; Translator; Author; Scholar; Astrologer; Publisher; Social Worker. *Education:* Vidwan degree; BOL degree; MA; Printing Technology Diploma; Diploma in Journalism; Diploma in Translation. *Appointments:* Freelance Journalist, Poet, Critic, Writer; Editor-in-Chief, Jyothi International, English monthly, 1978. *Publications:* Shakuntala, translation from Kalisasa's Sanskrit into English, 1959; The Last Look, 1960; The Queer Three, 1961; Man and Superman, 1962; Veeragiti, collection of poems written between 1953 and 1962; Training in Translation, 1962; Nagarjunasagar, poems, 1975; Pushpanjali, poems; Gitanjali, poems; Prasamsa, poems; Neerajanam, poems; Others. *Contributions to:* Over 600 articles, poems, essays stories to several leading English and other language journals and periodicals. *Honours:* 11 titles and numerous awards including: Kavi Hamsa; Sahitya Visharada; Jyotisha Samratt; Bharata Jateeya Kavi (National Poet of India); MTA Award in recognition of Mastery in Astrology, Numerology and Palmistry. *Memberships:* PEN (World Association of Writers), All India Centre. *Address:* Post Bag 1205, Madras 600 040, India.

BHAT Yashoda, b. 21 July 1933, Dharwad, India. Lecturer. m. N P Bhat, 26 May 1957, 1 son. *Education:* MA, Karnatak University; phD, University of Indore; Summer School, Language Teaching, CIE Hyderabad, India. *Appointments:* Teacher, Nagpur, Belgaum, Surat, Indore Colleges; Designation, Reader, 1976-; Lecturer-Reader, KM College, University of Delhi. *Publications:* Afternoon Poems; Pebbles; Research; Aldous Huxley & George Orwell; The Agony & The Glory; Editor of The Image of Woman in India: a Compilation of papers presented at a seminar for women, including a paper by herself. *Contributions to:* Commonwealth Quarterley; Mysore India; Poetry Time, India; The Scibleian. *Memberships:* The Poetry Society of India; PEN; Sahitya Akademy, India. *Address:* 701 Ambika Apartments, Sector XIV, Rohini, Delhi 85, India.bblank

BHATIA Jamunadevi, (June Bhatia, June Edwards, Helen Forrester, J Rana), b. 6 June 1919, England. Writer. *Appointments:* Writer in Residence, Lethbridge Community College, Alberta, Canada; Writer-in-Residence & Edmonton Public Library. *Publications:* Alien There is None, 1959, republished as Thursday's Child, 1985; The Latchkey Kid, 1971; Twopence to Cross the Mersey, 1974; Most Precious Employee, 1976; Minerva's Stepchild, 1979; Liverpool Daisy, 1979; Anthology 80, 1979; By the Waters of Liverpool, 1981; Three Women of Liverpool, 1984; The Suicide Tower, 1981; Lime Street at Two, 1985; A Matter of Friendship, 1986; The Moneylenders of Shahpur, 1987; Yes, Mama, 1987; The Lemon Tree, 1990; The Liverpool Basque, 1993. *Contributions to:* Government of Alberta Heritage Magazine; Book Reviews; Canadian Author and Bookman, Edmonton Journal. *Honours:* Hudson's Bay Beaver Award, best unpublished manuscript, 1970, 1977; Edmonton Journal Literary Competition, Honourable Mention; Honoured by City of Edmonton for distinguished contribution to Literature and to life of the City, 1977; Government of Alberta Achievement Award for Literature, 1979; YWCA Woman of the Arts, 1987; Alberta Culture's Literary Award for Non-Fiction, Lime Street At Two, 1986; Writer's Guild Fiction Award, Yes Mama, 1989; Degree of Doctor of Letters, University of Liverpool, 1988; Degree of Doctor of Letters, University of Alberta, 1993. *Memberships:* Writers' Union of Canada; Society of Authors, London; Canadian Association of Children's Authors, Illustrators and Performers; Authors' lending and copywright Society Ltd., London. *Literary Agent:* Richard Simon, Richard Scott Simon Ltd. *Address:* c/o The Writers' Union of Canada, 24 Ryerson Street, Toronto, Ontario, Canada.

BHATIA June. *See:* **BHATIA Jamunadevi.**

BHATNAGAR Om Prakash, b. 30 May 1932, Agra, India. Professor. m. Parvati Bhatnagar, 21 Oct 1959, 1 son, 1 daughter. *Education:* MA, 1954; MA, 1956; D Litt, 1959; PhD, 1991. *Appointments:* Editorial Board,

Indian Journal of English Studies, 1979-86. *Publications:* Poetry, Thought Poems; Angles of Retreat; Oneiric Visions; Shadows in Floodlights; Audible Landscape; Perspectives on Indian Poetry in English; Studies in Indian Drama in English. *Contributions to:* 69 Literary & Research Articles. *Honours:* Plaque of Honor for Excellence in Poetry; G Ramachandran Award for International Understanding Through Literature. *Memberships:* Zonal Representative, Indian Association for English Studies; University English Teachers Association. *Address:* Rituraj, Camp, Amravati-444, 602 India.

BHATTACHARYYA Birendra Kumar, b. 14 Oct 1924, Suffry Sibsagar, Assam, India. Journalist; Writer. m. Binita Bhattacharyya, 1958, 2 sons, 1 daughter. *Education:* Calcutta University, Gauhati University; BSc, MA, PhD. *Appointments include:* Science teacher, Manipur; Editor, Ramdhenu 1951-61, Sadiniya Navayung 1963-67; Lecturer, journalism, Gauhati University, 1974-85. *Publications:* Novels: Iyaruingam; Rajpathe Ringiai (Call of the Main Street); Ai (Mother); Satagnai (Killer); Mrityunjay; Pratipad; Nastachandra; Ballari; Kabar Aru Phul; Ranga Megh; Daini. Collections, short stories: Kolongahioboi (Still Flows the Kolong); Satsari (Necklace). Aurobindo, biography; Survey of Assamese Modern Culture (in Assamese). *Honours:* Sahitya Akademi Award for Assamese Literature, 1961; Jnanpith Award, 1979. *Memberships:* President, Sahitya Academi, New Delhi; Ex-President Asam Sahitya Sabha. *Address:* Kharghuli Development Area, Guwahati-4, Assam, India.

BHAUMIK Gopal, (Basubandhu), b. 16 Mar 1916, Danistapur, Bangadesh. Journalist; Press Officer. m. Uma Bhaumik, 8 Mar 1947, 2 sons, 2 daughters. *Education:* BA, Bangabasi College, Calcutta, 1936-38; MA, Calcutta University, 1940. *Appointments:* Assistant Editor, Monthly Matri Bhumi, Daily Krishak, 1942-46; Assistant Editor, Daily Swaraj, 1946; Editor Daily Kishore; Assistant Editor, Peoples Weekly, 1947-48; Press Officer, BIS Calcutta, 1951; Director of Information, Retired, 1975; Chief Editor, Managing Director, Daily Basumati, 1978. *Publications:* Swakshara; Basanta Bahar; Samaj O Sahitya; Samay Samprika; Shei Chhaya Murti; Others in, Stories of Jack London, Novels of Henry James, Anton Chekov; Three Biographies. *Contributions to:* Journals & Magazines in Bengali; English Journals inc, Indian PEN. *Memberships:* PEN; indian Red Corss Soceity; Authors Guild of India. *Address:* 146A Sarat Ghosh Garden Road, Calcutta, 700 031, India.

BHYRAPPA Santeshivara Lingannaiah, b. 26 July 1934, Santeshivara, Karnataka, India. m. Saraswati, 13 Dec. 1958. 2 sons. *Education:* BA (Hons), 1957; MA Philosophy, 1958; PhD Aesthetics, 1963. *Publications:* 15 novels and 4 books on Literary Criticism including: Novels: Vamsha Vriksha, 1966; Grihabhanga, 1970; Daatu, 1974; Parva, 1979; Nele, 1983; Sakshi, 1986; Truth and Beauty, 1964; Story and its Substance, 1969; Why do I write and other Essays, 1982. *Contributions to:* Numerous journals. *Honours:* Best Book of the Year Award, 1967, 1975; Central Sahihya Akademi Award, 1975; Karnataka Government Rajyotsava Day Award. *Memberships:* Karnataka State Sahitya Akademi; Central Sahitya Akademi; Bharatiya Jnaanapeeth Foundation; Indian Philosophical Congress. *Address:* 1007 Kuvempunagar, Mysore 570023, India.

BIANCHI Eugene Carl, b. 1930, United States of America. Writer (Theology/Religion). *Publications:* John XXIII and American Protestants, 1968; Reconciliation: The Function of the Church, 1969 The Religious Experience of Revolutionaries, 1972; From Machismo to Mutuality (with Rosemary P Ruether), 1975; Aging As a Spiritual Journey, 1982; On Growing Older, 1985; A Democratic Catholic Chutch, co-ed with Rosemary Ruether, 1992. *Address:* Department of Religion, Emory University, Atlanta, GA 30322, USA.

BIANCHIN Helen Shirley, b. 20 Feb 1939, Dunedin,

New Zealand. Author. m. Danilo Bianchin, 24 Feb 1962, 2 sons, 1 daughter. *Publications:* The Willing Heart; Bewildered Haven; Avenging Angel; The Hills of Home; The Vines in Splendour; Stormy Possession; edge of Spring; Master of uluru; Devil in Command; The Savage Touch; Wildfire Encounter; Yesterdays Shadow; Savage Pagan; Sweet Tempest. *Memberships:* British Society of Authors; Australian Society of Authors; British Romantic Novelists Association; Romance Writers of America; Romance Writers of Australia. *Address:* PO Box 5737, Gold Coast Mail Centre, Queensland 4217, Australia.

BIBBY Peter Leonard, b. 21 Dec 1940, London, England. Poet; Playwright; Screenwriter. m. 15 Apr 1967, 2 sons, 2 daughters. *Education:* BA, University of Western Australia; Dip.Ed., Murdoch University. *Appointments:* Editor, Fellowship of Australian Writers; Editor, "MAGABALA BOOKS", Broome Publishing Project, Australian Bicentennial Authority. *Publications:* Island Weekend, 1960; Represented in Anthologies: Quarry; Breakaway; Summerland; Inprint W.A. Story; Poetry Australia; Laughing Cry; Broadcast Verse and Drama, ABC. *Contributions to:* Professional journals including: Bulletin Australia; Outrider; Overland; Poetry Australia. *Honours:* Tom Collins Literary awards, Verse, 1978, 1982; Lyndall Hadow National Short Story award, 1983; Donald Stuart, National Short Story Award, 1985. *Memberships:* Australian Writers Guild; Fellowship of Australian Writers; Australian Film Institute; Computer Graphics Association. *Address:* c/o PO Box 668, Broome, WA, Australia.

BIBERGER Erich Ludwig, b. 20 July 1927, Passau, Bavaria, Germany. Editor; Writer. *Education:* Examination Städt; Wirtschafsaubauschule Passau, 1944; Volkshochschule Passau. *Publications include:* Dreiklang der Stille (Poems), 1955; Rundgang über dem Nordlicht (Philosophy, Fairy Tales of Atomic Age), 1958; Die Traumwelle (novel), 1962; Denn im Allsein der Welt (poems), 1966; Duadu oder der Mann im Mond (radio plays), 1967; Gar mancher (satirical. verses), 1967; Anthology Quer, 1974; Anthology 3 (in 47 languages), 1979; Andere Wege bis Zitterluft (poems), 1982; Was ist hier Schilf, was Reiher (Haiku), 1984; Nichts als das Meer(Poems), 1984; Zwei Pfund Morgenduft (Feuilletons), 1987. *Honours:* Recipient several honours. *Memberships include:* Chairman, Regensburger Schriftslellergruppe International, Joint Association of Authors in 25 Countries of the World, 1960-; Founder, Director, Internationale Regensburger Literaturtage, 1967-; Internationale Jungautoren-Wettbewerbe, 1972-; Founder, Editor, Publication series RSG Studio International, 1973-, RSG-Forum 15/25, 1977-; Member of Humboldt-Gesllschaft für Wissenschaft und Kunst, 1993-. *Address:* Altmühlstr, D 903059 Regensburg, Germany.

BICKHAM Jack Miles, (Jeff Clinton, John Miles), b. 1930, USA, Writer - Novels, Short stories, Mystery, Crime, Suspense, Westerns, Adventure; Professor of Journalism, University of Oklahoma, Norman, 1969-. *Appointments:* Managing Editor, The Oklahoma Courier, 1966-69. *Publications include:* The Padre Must Die, 1967; (as Jeff Clinton), Wildcat's Witch Hunt, 1967; The War on Charity Ross, 1967; (as Jeff Clinton), Watch Out for Wildcat, 1968; The Shadowed Faith, 1968; (as Jeff Clinton), Wildcat Meets Miss Melody, 1968; Target Charity Ross, 1968; (as Jeff Clinton), Build a Box for Wildcat, 1969; Decker's Campaign (in UK as the Sheriff's Campaign), 1970; (as Jeff Clinton), Wildcat's Claim to Fame, 1970; (as Jeff Clinton), A Stranger Named O'Shea, 1970; Goin' 1971; (as Jeff Clinton), Bounty on Wildcat, 1971; The Apple Dumpling Gang, 1971; Fletcher, 1972; Jilly's Canal, 1972; Dopey Dan, 1972; (as Jeff Clinton), Hang High. O'Shae, 1972; Kate, Kelly and Heck, 1973; (as John Miles), The Night Hunters, 1973; (as John Miles), The Silver Bullet Gang, 1974; (as John Miles), The Blackmailer, 1974; (as Jeff Clinton), Emerald Canyon, 1974; Hurry Home, Davey Clock, 1974; A Boat Named Death, 1975; (as John Miles with T Morris), Operation Nightfall, 1974; (as Jeff Clinton), Showdown at Emerald Canyon, 1975;

(as Jeff Clinton), Kane's Odyssey, 1975; Twister, 1976; The Winemakers, 1977; The Excalibur Disaster, 1978; Dinah, Blow Your Horn, 1979; A Question of Ethics, 1980; The Regensburg Legacy, 1980; All the Days Were Summer, 1981; I Still Dream About Columbus, 1982; Ariel, 1984; Miracleworker, 1987. *Address:* School of Journalism, University of Oklahoma, Norman, OK 73019, USA.

BIDDISS Michael Denis, b. 15 Apr 1942, Farnborough, Kent, England. University Professor. m. Ruth Margaret Cartwright, 8 Apr 1967, 4 daughters. *Education:* MA, PhD, Queens' College, Cambridge 1961-66; Centre des Hautes Etudes Europeennes, University of Strasbourg, 1965-66. *Appointments:* Fellow in History, Downing College, Cambridge, 1966-73; Lecturer/Reader in History, University of Leicester, 1973-79; Professor of History, University of Reading, 1979-. *Publications:* Father of Racist Ideology, 1970; Gobineau: Selected Political Writings (editor) 1970; Disease and History (co-author) 1972; The Age of the Masses, 1977; Images of Race (editor) 1979; Thatcherism: Personality and Politics (co-editor) 1987; The Nuremberg Trial and the Third Reich, 1992. *Honours:* Fellow of the Royal Historical Society, 1974; Honorary Fellow of the Faculty of the History of Medicine, Society of Apothecaries of London, 1986; Visiting Professorships at Universities of Victoria BC, 1973; Cape Town 1976 and 1978; Cairo 1985; Monash, Australia 1989. *Memberships:* Council of the Historical Association 1985-; President of the Historical Association, 1991-; Council of the Royal Historical Society, 1988-92. *Literary Agent:* Curtis Brown. *Address:* Department of History, The University of Reading, Whiteknights, Reading RG6 2AA, England.

BIDWELL Lita. See: **AVEY Ruby Doreen.**

BIEGEL Paul Johannes, b. 25 Mar 1925, Bussum, The Netherlands. Author. *Publications:* The King of the Copper Mountains, 1969; The Seven Times Search, 1971; The Little Captain, 1971; The Twelve Robbers, 1974; The Gardens of Dorr, 1975; Far Beyond & Back Again, 1977; The Elephant Party, 1977; Letters from the General, 1979; The Looking-Glass Castle, 1979; The Dwarfs of Nosegay, 1978; Robber Hopsika, 1978; The Fattest Dwarf of Nosegay, 1980; The Tin Can Beast, 1980; The Curse of the Werewolf, 1981; Virgil Nosegay and the Cake Hunt, 1981; Crocodile Man, 1982; Virgil Nosegay and the Wellington Boots, 1984. *Honours:* Best Children's Book of the Year, 1965; Golden Pencil Award, 1972; Silver Pencil Award, 1972, 1974, 1981, 1988; Nienke van Hichtum prize for Children's Literature, 1973; State Prize, 1974; Woutertje Dieterse Prize, 1991. *Memberships:* Vereniging van Letterkudigen; Maatschappij van Letterkunde. *Address:* Keizersgracht 227, Amsterdam, The Netherlands.

BIELINSKA Izabela, b. 21 Jan 1925, Lublin, Poland. Writer. *Education:* Warsaw University. *Publications:* Margaret, novel, 1960, 1982; The Love not Will Be, stories, 1963; Don't Beat Your Fathers, 9 short stories, 1976; Le Petit Dejeuner, short story, 1980; Taste of the Wild Strawberry ice-cream, 1986; Harlequin's Costume, short story, 1990; Polish: Smak lodów poziomkowych, co-author Ewa Otwinowska; Literary, Film and Art Reviews; Radio Plays; Film Scripts. *Contributions to:* Literary and Film Magazines; Polish Radio. *Memberships:* Polish Writers Association; Polish Journalists Association; Film Critics Club. *Address:* Ul Nowowiejska 4 m 57, Poland, 00-649 Warsaw, Poland.

BIELSKI Alison Joy Prosser, b. 24 Nov 1925, Newport, Gwent, Wales. Secretary; Writer; Lecturer. m. (1) D. Treverton Jones, 19 June 1948, (2) A.E. Bielski, 30 Nov 1955, 1 son, 1 daughter. *Appointments:* Honorary Secretary, Welsh Academy, 10 years. *Publications:* Across the Burning Sand, 1970; The Story of the Welsh Dragon, 1969; Flower Legends of the Wye Valley, 1974; The Lovetree, 1974; Eagles, 1983; The Story of St Mellons, 1985; Tales and Traditions of Tenby. *Contributions to:* Anglo- Welsh Review; Poetry Wales;

Planet; Spectrum; Tribune; Poetry Review; Pembroke Magazine; Acumen; Doors; New Poetry; Outposts. etc. *Honours:* Anglo- Welsh Review Poetry Prize, 1970; Arnold Vincent Bowen Poetry Prize, 1971; Recipient, various other prizes and awards in poetry competitions. *Memberships:* Society of Women Writers and Journalists; Folklore Society; Traditional Cosmology Society; Welsh Union of Writers; Gwent Poetry Society; Welsh Academy. *Address:* 92 Clifton Road, Paignton, Devon, TQ3 3LD, England.

BIGGLE Lloyd Jr, b. 1923, United States of America. Author. *Publications:* The Angry Espers, 1961; All the Colors of Darkness, 1963; The Fury Out of Time, 1965; Watchers of the Dark, 1966; The Rule of the Door and Other Franciful Regulations (short stories), 1967 (in United Kingdom as The Silent Sky), 1979; The Still Small Voice of Trumpets, 1968; The World Menders, 1971; The Light That Never Was, 1972; Nebula Award Stories 7, (editor) 1972; The Metallic Muse (short stories), 1972; Monument, 1974; This Darkening Universe, 1975; A Galaxy of Strangers (short stories), 1976; Silence is Deadly, 1977; The Whirligig of Time, 1979; Alien Main (with T.L. Sherred), 1985; The Quallsford Inheritance, A Memoir of Sherlock Holmes, 1986; Interface for Murder, 1987; The Glendower Conspiracy, A Memoir of Sherlock Holmes, 1990; A Hazard of Losers, 1991. *Contributions to:* Critiques of Science Fiction Scholarship: Science-Fiction Goes To College, Riverside Quarterly, vol 6, no 2, 1974; The Morasses of Academe Revisited, Analog, XCVIII, no 9, 1978. *Memberships:* Founding Secretary Treasurer, 1965-67; Chairman of the Trustees, 1967-73, Science Fiction Writers of America; Founder and current President, Science Fiction Oral History Association, 1992. *Literary Agent:* Owlswick Literary Agency, 4426 Larchwood, Philadelphia, PA 19104, USA. *Address:* 569 Dubie Avenue, Ypsilanti, MI 48198, USA.

BIGGS Margaret Annette, (Margaret Key Biggs) b. 26 Oct 1933, Pike County, Alabama, USA. Writer. m. 1 Mar 1956. *Education:* BS, Troy State University, 1954; MA, California State University, 1979. *Publications:* Swampfire, 1980; Sister to the Sun, 1981; Magnolias & Such, 1982; Petals from the Womanflower, 1983; Plumage of the Sun, 1986. *Contributions to:* Numerous journals including: Panhandler; Earthwise Poetry Journal; Gryphon; International University Poetry Quarterly; Thoreau Journal Quarterly; Echos; Jump River Review; Pipe Dream; Valhalla; Vega; Modern Images; Encore; Black Jack; Unicorn; Taurus; Poetry Monthly; etc. Anthologies including: Peace is Our Profession; Meltdown; Crow Calls; Poets & Peace International; Macomb Fantasy Factory; Best Poems of 1982; Darkness Screams a Yellow Rose; Anthology I, Florida State Poets Association. *Honours:* Numerous awards for poetry including: Poetry Monthly First Poem Award, 1981; 4 awards, National League of American Pen Women, 1984; Pulitzer Prize nominee, 1986. *Memberships include:* Panhandle Writers Guild; National League of American Pen Women; Alabama & Florida State Poetry Societies; National Federation of State Poetry Societies. *Address:* PO Box 551, Port St Joseph, Florida 32456, USA.

BIGSBY Christopher William Edgar, b. 27 June 1941, Dundee, Scotland. University Professor; Broadcaster; Novelist. *Education:* BA, MA, Sheffield Univerity; PhD, Nottingham University. *Publications:* Confrontation & Commitment: A Study of Contemporary American Drama, 1967; Edward Albee, 1969; Dada & Surealism, 1972; Tom Stoppard, 1976; The Second Black Renaissance, 1980; Joe Orton, 1982, 1984, 1985; David Mamet, 1985; Editor, The Black American Writer, 1969; Three Negro Plays, 1969; Approaches to Popular Culture, 1975; Superculture, 1976; Edward Albee, 1976; Contemporary English Drama, 1981; The Radical Imagination and the Liberal Tradition, 1982; A Critical Introduction to 20th C American Drama, 3 volumes; Cultural Change in the United States since World War II, 1986; Plays by Sugan Glaspell, 1987; File on Miller, 1988; American Drama: 1945-1990, 1992; Hester (novel), forthcoming. *Contributor to:* Broadcaster, TV and

Radio Scriptwriter; Times Literary Supplement; Times Higher Education Supplement; The Sunday Independent; American Quarterly; Modern Drama; Theatre Quarterly; The Guardian. *Agent:* Curtis Brown; Anthony Sheil. *Literary Address:* 3 Church Farm, Colney, Norwich, England.

BILLING Graham John, b. 12 Jan 1936, Dunedin, New Zealand. Author. m. Rowan Innes Cunningham, 29 Aug 1978, 1 son, 1 daughter by previous marriage. *Education:* Otago University, 1955-58. *Appointments:* Staff, Dunedin Evening Star, 1958-62; Antarctic Division, DSIR, 1962-64; NZ Broadcasting Corporation News Service and TV Service, (various appointments), 1964-67; Staff, Dominion Sunday Times, 1967-69; Lecturer, writing, Mitchell College Advanced Education, Bathurst, Australia, 1974-75. *Publications:* Forbush and the Penguins, 1965; The Slipway, 1973; The Alpha Trip, 1969; Statues, 1971; The Primal Therapy of Tom Purslane, 1980; Changing Countries (poetry), 1980; (Non-Fiction)South: Man and Nature in Antarctica, 1965; New Zealand, the Sunlit Land, 1966; The New Zealanders, 1974; (Radio Plays) Forbush and the Penguins, 1965; Mervyn Gridfern versus the Babsons, 1965; The Slipway, 1976. *Contributions to:* Landfall. *Honours:* New Zealand Government Scholarship in Letters, 1970; Robert Burns Fellowship, 1973; Writer in Residence, Canterbury University, 1985. *Memberships:* PEN; New Zealand Salmon Anglers Association; North Canterbury Acclimatisation Society. *Literary Agent:* Elaine Markson Literary Agency, New York, USA. *Address:* 22 Bretts Road, St Albans, Christchurch 5, New Zealand.

BILLINGTON Michael, b. 16 Nov 1939. Drama Critic. m. Jeanine Bradlaugh, 1978. *Education:* BA, St Catherine's College, Oxford. *Appointments:* Trained, as Journalist with Liverpool Daily Post and Echo, 1961-62; Public Liaison Officer, Director, Lincoln Theatre Co., 1962-64; Reviewed Plays, Films and TV for The Times, 1965-71; Film Critic, Birmingham Post, 1968-78, Illustrated London News, 1968-81; Drama Critic, The Guardian, 1971-; London Arts Correspondent, New York Times, 1978-; Drama Critic of Country Life, 1987-. *Publications:* The Modern Actor, 1974; How Tickled I Am, 1977; Editor, The Performing Arts, 1980; The Guinness Book of Theatre Facts and Feats, 1982; Alan Ayckbourn, 1983; Peggy Ashcroft, 1989, (Biography); Twelfth Night, 1990. *Address:* 15 Hearne Road, London W4 3NJ, England.

BILLINGTON Monroe Lee, b. 4 Mar 1928, Duncan, USA. Historian. m. Mary Elizabeth Salter, 2 June 1951, 1 son, 2 daughters. *Education:* BA, Oklahoma Baptist University, 1945-50; MA, University of Oklahoma, 1950-51; PhD, University of Kentuck, 1952-55. *Publications:* New Mexico's Buffalo Soldiers; The American South: A brief History; Thomas P Gore, The Blind Senator from Oklahoma; The Political South in the Twentieth century; Southern Politics Since the Civil War; The South: A Central Theme. *Contributions to:* 50 Scholarly Articles in Journals; Journal of Negro History; The Historian; Journal of Church & State; Chronicals of Oklahoma; New Mexico Historical Review. *Honour:* Phi Beta Kappa. *Memberships:* Phi Alpha Theta; Southern Historical Association; Organization of American Historians; Western History Association; Historical Society of New Mexico. *Address:* 905 Conway 4, Las Cruces, NM 88005, USA.

BILLINGTON Rachel Mary,b. 11 Nov 1942, Oxford, England. Writer. m. 16 Dec 1967, 2 sons, 2 daughters. *Education:* BA, English, London University. *Publications:* All Things Nice; The Big Dipper; Beautiful; A Woman's Age; Occasion of Sin; The Garish Day; Lilacs out of the Dead Land; Cock Robin; A Painted Devil; Children's Books: Rosanna and the Wizard-Robot; Star-Time; The First Christmas; The First Easter; Loving Attitudes, 1988; Theo and Matilda, 1990; The First Miracles (for children), 1990; Bodily Harm, 1992; The Family Year, 1992. *Contributions to:* Reviewer for Financial Times, New York Times; Short stories for various publications; 2 plays for BBC TV; 4 plays for Radio. *Memberships:* PEN; Society of Authors. *Literary Agent:* David Higham Associates, London. *Address:* 30 Addison Avenue, London W11 4QR, England.

BINCHY Maeve, b. Dublin, Republic of Ireland. Writer. m. Gordon Snell. *Appointments:* Joined The Irish Times, 1969. *Publications:* Novels: Light A Penny Candle; Echoes; Firefly Summer, 1987; Silver Wedding, 1989. Collections of short stories: London Transport; Dublin 4; The Lilac Bus; Stage plays: End of Term; Half Promised Land; Deeply Regretted By, TV play. *Contributions to:* Travel articles. *Honours:* 2 Jacobs Award and Best Script Award, Prague Film Festival. *Address:* London, England.

BINGHAM Caroline Margery Conyers, b. 7 Feb 1938. Professional Writer. m. Andrew Bingham, 1958, divorced 1972, 1 daughter. *Education:* BA, Honours, History, University of Bristol. *Publications:* The Making of a King : the Early Years of James VI and I, 1968; James V, King of Scots, 1971; Contributor, The Scottish Nation : a History of the Scots from Independence to Union, 1972; The Life and Times of Edward II, 1973; The Stewart Kingdom of Scotland 1371-1603, 1974; The Kings and Queens of Scotland, 1976; The Crowned Lions : the Early Plantagenent Kings, 1978; James VI of Scotland, 1979; The Voice of the Lion, verse anthology, 1980; James I of England, 1981; Land of the Scots: A Short History, 1983; The History of Royal Holloway College, 1886-1986, 1987; Beyond The Highland Line: Highland History and Culture, 1991. *Literary Agent:* A M Heath Co Ltd, 79 St Martin's Lane, London WC2N 4AA. *Address:* 164 Regents Park Road, London NW1 8XN, England.

BINGHAM Charlotte Marie-Therese, b. 29 June 1942, Sussex, England. Playwright; Novelist. m. 15 Jan. 1964, 1 son, 1 daughter. *Education:* Educated in England and France. *Publications:* Coronet Among the Weeds; Lucinda; Coronet Among the Grass; Belgravia; Country Life; At Home, TV Series (with Terence Brady); Upstairs, Downstairs; Nanny; No Honestly; Yes Honestly; Play for Today; Pig in the Middle; Father Matthew's Daughter; Thomas and Sarah; Novels: To Hear A Nightingale, The Business, In Sunshine or in Shadow, Stardust, 1988-92; TV Film: Riders, 1992. *Contributions to:* Vogue; Tatler; Woman's Journal; Town and Country; and others. *Membership:* Society of Authors. *Literary Agent:* Murray Pollinger, c/o 222 Old Brompton Road, London SW5 OB2, England. *Address:* c/o 10 Buckingham Street, London, WC1, England.

BINGLEY Albert Norris, b. 22 Jan 1921, Kalgorrlie, Western Australia. Wholesale Jeweller. m. (1) 30 Apr 1942, dec, 3 daughters, (2) 18 June 1977. *Publications:* Back to the Goldfields; Adventures of Tidilee Winks; On the Game. *Contributions to:* Daily News; West Australian Sunday Times; Chamber of Commerce Business Journal. *Honours:* Fellow of Australia. *Memberships:* Fellowship of Australian writers; Australian Jewellers Association; Chamber of Commerce and Industry. *Literary Agent:* A N Bingley. *Address:* A N Bingley, 9B Aundale Crescent, Wembley Downs, Western Australia 6019, Australia.

BINHAM Philip Frank, b. 19 July 1924. Teacher (retired). m. Marja Sola, 21 June 1952, 1 son, 1 daughter. *Education:* Magdalen College, Oxford, 1935-41; Wadham College, Oxford, 1946-49; BA (Oxon), 1949; MA (Oxon), 1954. *Publications:* How To Say It, 1965, UK Edition, 1968; Executive English I-III, 1968-70; Speak Up, 1975; Snow in May: An Anthology of Finnish Literature 1945-72, 1978; Service with a Smile: Hotel English, Restaurant English, 1979, UK Edition, 1982; Team 7, 8, 9, 1983-85; Translation: Tamara (Eeva Kilpi), novel, 1972. *Contributions to:* Regularly to World Literature Today (formerly Books Abroad), 1972-. *Honours:* Order of Finnish Lion, 1972; Finnish State Prize for Foreign Translators, 1990. *Memberships:* Society of Authors; Finnish Society of Scientific Writers; Honorary Member, Finnish Literature Society. *Address:* Seunalantie 34A, 04200 Kerava, Finland.

BINION Rudolph, b. 18 Jan 1927. Professor of History, Brandeis University. *Education:* BA, 1945, PhD 1958, Columbia University; Diploma, Institut d'Etudes Politiques, Paris, 1949. *Publications:* Defeated Leaders, 1960; Frau Lou, 1968; Hitler Among the Germans, 1976; Soundings 1981; Introduction àla psycohistoire, 1982; After Christianity, 1986; Love Beyond Death, 1993. *Contributor to:* Numerous journals in America, France, Germany and Italy. *Address:* Department of History, Brandeis University, Waltham, MA 02254, USA.

BINKLEY Thomas Eden, b. 26 Dec 1931, Cleveland, Ohio, USA. *Education:* University of Illinois, BM, 1952-56; University of Munich, 1957-58; University of Illinois, 1958-59. *Appointments:* Director, Early Music Quartet, Germany, 1959-79; Teacher, Basil, Switzerland, 1973-77; Visiting Professor, stanford University, 1977, 1979; Professor, Early Music Institute, Indiana University, 1979-. *Publications include:* Le Luth et sa Musique; Italian Violin Music of the Seventeenth Century; Die Interpretation Mittelalterlicher Musik; Numerous Recordings inc, Camino de Santiago 1, 11; Bernart de Ventadorn/Martim Codax; Minnesang und Spruchdichting; Vox humana; Weltliche Musik um 1300; General Editor, Music: Scholarship and Performance and Publications of the Early Music Institute. *Honours:* Edison Award; Grand Prix du Disques, Paris; Preis der deutschen Schallplattenkritik, Berlin; Deutscher Schallplattenpreis, Baden Baden; Dickenson College Arts Award. *Address:* 1520 E Maxwell Lane, Bloomington, IN 47401, USA.

BINNEY Marcus Hugh Crofton. Writer; President, Save Britain's Heritage, 1984-. m. (1) Hon. Sara Ann Vanneck, 1966, divorced 1976, (2) Anne Carolyn, 1981, 2 sons. *Education:* BA, Magdalene College, Cambridge, 1966. *Publications:* (with Peter Burman): Change and Decay: the future of our Churches, 1977; Chapels and Churches: Who Cares?, 1977; (with Max Hanna), Preservation Pays, 1978; Editor Jointly: Railway Architecture, 1979; Our Past Before Us, 1981; (with Kit Martin) The Country House: To be or not to be, 1982; (with Max Hanna) Preserve and Prosper, 1983; Sir Robert Taylor, 1984; Our Vanishing Heritage, 1984; Great Railway Stations of Europe, 1984; Country Manors of Portugal, 1987. Contributor to: Satanic Mills, 1979; Elysian Gardens, 1979; Lost Houses of Scotland, 1980; Taking the Plunge, 1982; Save Gilbraltar's Heritage, 1982; Vanishing Houses of England, 1983. *Address:* Domaine des Vaux, St. Lawrence, Jersey, Channel Islands.

BIRCH Carol, b. 3 Jan 1951, Manchester, England. Writer. m. Martin Lucas Butler, 26 Oct 1990, 2 sons. *Education:* University of Keele, 1968-72. *Publications:* Life in the Palace; The Fog Line; The Unmaking. *Honours:* David Higham Prize; Geoffrey Faber Memorial Award. *Memberships:* Society of Authors. *Literary Agent:* Mic Cheetham, Sheilland Associates. *Address:* c/o Sheilland Associates, 43 Doughty Street, London WC1N 2LF, England.

BIRCHAM Deric Neale, b. 16 Dec 1934, Wellington, New Zealand, Chief Executive. m. Patricia Frances Simkin, 18 Apr 1960, 2 daughters. *Education:* BA; MBA; PhD; DLitt; LittD; Dr Bus Man', D.Sc, D.D. *Publications:* Seeing New zealand, 5 editions, 1971-75; Wattomo Tourist caves, 1973; Towards a More Just World, 1976; New Zealanders of Destiny, 1977; Old St Pauls, 1982; Rhapsody, 1984; Thirteen facets, 1976; A Day in the Life of New Zealand, 1982; Dunedin NZ's Best Kept secret, 1984; St Josephs Cathedral, 1986; Works of Gottfried Lindauer, 1986; 20 other book titles. *Honours:* Recipient of 11 International Knighthoods and 3 Professorships (Personal Chairs), USA Europe and Australia; World Parliament with status; Diplomatic Status. *Memberships:* New Zealand Institute of Management; ABIRA, Deputy Governor; UN and UNESCO appointments; *Address:* 131 Tirohansa Road, Lower Hutt, Wellington, New Zealand.

BIRD CARPENTER J Delores, b. 6 Dec 1942, Chattanooga, Tennessee, USA. m. Joe Keith Carpenter, 27 Dec 1959, div, 1 son. *Education:* University of Mississippi; Boston University, BA, 1967; University of Hartford, MA, 1973. *Appointments:* Ma English Teacher, Shrewsbury Junior High, 1967-70; Part Time Various Universities, Colleges; Full Professor, Cape Cod Community College, 1977-. *Publications:* The Life of Lidian Jackson Emerson, re-published in 1992; The Selected Letters of Lidian Jackson Emerson; The Early Days of Cape Cod Community College; First Encounters: Native Americans and Europeans in New England, forthcoming. *Contributions to:* Studies in the American Renaissance, 1980*Honours:* Summa Cum Laude; Phi Beta Kappa. *Memberships:* Thoreau Society; Emily Dickinson Society; Ralph Waldo Emerson Society; MLA. *Address:* 89 South Sandwich Road, Mashpee, MA 02649, USA.

BIRDSELL Sandra Louise, b. 22 Apr 1942, Manitoba, Canada. Writer. m. Stanley Vivian Birdsell, 1 July 1959, 1 son, 2 daughters. *Appointments:* Writer-in-Residence; University of Prince Edward Island; University of Alberta; University of Waterloo, Ontario. *Publications:* Night Travellers, 1982; Ladies of the House, 1984; The Missing Child, 1989; The Chrome Suite, 1992. *Contributions to:* Western Living; Canadian Living; Quarry; The New Quarterly; Prairie Fire; Event; Border Crossing; Grain. *Honours:* Nominated for Governor General Award, English Language Fictin, 1992; Joseph P Stauffer Award, Canada Council; W H Smith, Books in Canada, 1st Novel Award; Nationl Magazine Award; Canada Council Grant; Major Arts Award, Manitoba Arts Council. *Memberships:* Writers Guild of Canada; Writers Union of Canada; PEN International; Founding Member, President, Manitoba Writers Guild. *Literary Agent:* Lucinda Vardey Agency, Toronto, Ontario, Canada. *Address:* 755 Westminster Ave, Winnipeg, Manitoba, Canada R3G 1A5.

BIRLEY Julia, b. 13 May 1928, London, England. Writer. m. 12 Sept 1954, 1 son, 3 daughters. *Education:* BA, Classics, Oxon. *Publications:* Novels, The Children on the Shore; The Time of the Cuckoo; When You Were There; A Serpents Egg; Dr Spicer; Short Stories for Children. *Contributions to:* Articles in The Guardian. *Memberships:* PEN; Charlotte Young Society. *Literary Agent:* Curtis Brown. *Address:* Upper Bryn, Longtown, Hereford, HR2 0NA, England.

BIRN Raymond Francis, b. 1935, United States of America. Writer(history). *Appointments:* Instructor, 1961-64, Assistant Professor, 1963-66, Associate Professor, 1966-72, Head, Department of History, 1971-78, Professor of History, 1972-, University of Oregon, Eugene; Advisory Editor, Eighteenth Century Studies, 1974-. *Publications:* Pierre Rousseau and the Philosophes of Bouillon, 1964; Crisis, Absolutism, Revolution: Europe 1648-1789/91, 1977; The Printed Word in the Eighteenth Century, 1984. *Address:* 2140 Elk Avenue, Eugene, OR 97043, USA.

BIRNEY Alice Lotvin, b. 6 Mar 1938, New York City, USA. Literary/Theatre Specialist. m. Dr G. Adrian Birney, 4 June 1964, 1 daughter. *Education:* BA, Barnard College, Columbia University, 1959; MA, Ohio State University, 1962; PhD, University of California, San Diego, 1968. *Appointments:* English Literature Cataloger, Library of Congress 1973; American Literature and Theatre Manuscript Specialist, Library of Congress 1990. *Publications:* Satiric Catharsis in Shakespeare, 1973; The Literary Lives of Jesus: An International Bibliography, 1989. *Contributions to:* Poetry, in Falcon, Focus, Ardentia Verba, and others; essays and reviews in several newspapers; Bibliographer for World Shakespeare Bibliography, 1976-. *Honours:* Amy Loveman Poetry Prize, 1959; Dissertation Scholarship, 1967; Folger Library Fellowship, 1974. *Memberships:* Playwrights Forum, Washington; MENSA; Modern Language Association; Library of Congress Film Society, Treasurer 1980-. *Address:* 112 5th St. NE, Washington DC 20002, USA.

BIRO Balint Stephen (Val Biro), b. 6 Oct 1921, Budapest, Hungary. Author; Illustrator. m. (2) Marie-Louise Ellaway, 25 Sept 1970. 1 stepson, 1 daughter, 1 stepdaughter. *Education:* Central School of Art and Design, London, England, 1939-42. *Appointment:* Art Editor, John Lehmann Ltd, 1949-53. *Publications:* The Gumdrop series of picture books, first title published 1966, 23rd 1992; Fables from Aesop, 18 books, 1983-86; Hungarian Folk Tales, 1980; The Hobyahs, 1985; The Magic Doctor, 1982; Tobias and the Dragon, 1990; Miranda's Umbrella, 1990; Rub-a-Dub-Dub, nursery rhymes, 1991. *Contributions to:* Occasional articles. Illustrator of some 400 books by other authors. *Memberships:* Society of Authors; Vintage Sports Car Club. *Address:* Bridge Cottage, Brook Avenue, Bosham, West Sussex, PO18 8LQEngland.

BIRO Val. *See:* **BIRO Balint Stephen.**

BIRSTEIN Ann, United States of America. Author. *Publications:* Star of Glass, 1950; The Troublemaker, 1955; The Works of Anne Frank (with A. Kazin), 1959; The Sweet Birds of Gorham, 1967; Summer Situations, 1972; Dickie's List, 1973; American Children, 1980; The Rabbi on Forty-Seventh Street, 1982; The Last of the True Believers, 1988. *Address:* c/o Elaine Markson, 44 Greenwich Avenue, New York, NY 10011, USA.

BISCHOFF David F(rederick), b. 1951, United States of America. Author. *Appointments:* Staff Member, NBC-TV, Washington DC, 1974-; Associate Editor, Amazing Magazine. *Publications:* The Seeker (with Christopher Lampton), 1976; Quest (juvenile), 1977; Strange Encounters (juvenile), 1977; The Phantom of the Opera (juvenile), 1977; The Woodman (with Dennis R Bailey), 1979; Nightworld, 1979; Star Fall, 1980; The Vampires of the Nightworld, 1981; Tin Woodman (with Dennis Bailey), 1982; Star Spring, 1982; War Games, 1983; Mandala, 1983; Day of the Dragonstar (with Thomas F. Monteleone), 1983; The Crunch Bunch, 1985; Destiny Dice, 1985; Galactic Warriors, 1985; The Infinite Battle, 1985; The Macrocosmic Conflict, 1986; Manhattan Project, 1986; The Unicorn Gambit, 1986. *Address:* c/o Henry Morrison Inc, 320 Mclain Street, Bedford Hill, NY 10705, USA.

BISHER James Furman, b. 4 Nov 1918, Denton, North Carolina, USA. Journalist. Divorced, 3 sons. *Education:* BA, University of North Carolina, 1938; Dartmouth College, 1943. *Publications:* With a Southern Exposure, 1961; Miracle in Atlanta, 1966; Strange But True Baseball Stories, 1966; Aaron, (with Henry Aaron), 1972-74; Masters-Augusta Revisited, 1976; Arnold Palmer - The Golden Year, 1971; various Anthologies including: Grantland Rice Prize Sports Stories; Best Sports Stories of Year (22 times); Fireside Book of Baseball and others. *Contributions to:* Over 600 articles in Saturday Evening Post; Sport; Sports Illustrated; Collier's; Golf Digest; True; Southern Living; GQ; Esquire; Sky Magazine. *Honours:* Sportswriter of the Year, Georgia, 14 times; Furman University Distinguished Alumnus of Year, 1978; University of North Carolina Hall of Fame, 1985; President, Football Writers Association, US, 1959-60; President, National Sportscasters & Sportswriters of America, 1974-76; Sigma Delta Chi Awards for Commentary, 1981-82; Florida Turf Writing Award and others. *Memberships:* Turf Writers Association; Baseball Writers Association; Football Writers Association; Tennis Writers Association; National Sportscasters & Sportswriters Association. *Address:* 3135 Rilman Road NW, Atlanta, GA 30327, USA.

BISHOP Gavin John, b. 13 Feb 1946, New Zealand. Author; Picture-Book Artist. m. Vivien Carol Edwards, 27 Aug 1966, 3 daughters. *Education:* Diploma, Fine Arts, Honours in Painting, University of Canterbury, 1967; Teachers' College Diploma, Distinction, Christchurch Teachers College, 1968. *Publications:* Mr Fox, 1982; Mrs McGinty and the Bizarre Plant, 1981; Bidibidi, 1982; Chicken Licken, 1984; The Horror of Hickory Bay, 1984; Mother Hubbard, 1986; A Apple Pie, 1987; The Three Little Pigs, 1990; Katarina, 1990. Illustrations for, The Year of the Yelvertons, by Katherine O'Brien, 1981. *Contributor to:* various literary and library magazines in New Zealand. *Honours:* New Zealand Childrens picture book of the year, 1983; Russel Clark Medal for Illustration, 1982; Grand Prix, Noma Concours for Childrens Picture Book Art, Japan, 1984; Finalist, Noma Concours, Japan, 1982. *Membership:* PEN International. *Address:* 11 Cracroft Terrace, Christchurch 2, New Zealand.

BISHOP Ian Benjamin, b. 18 Apr 1927, Gillingham, Kent, England. University Teacher. m. Pamela Rosemary Haddacks, 14 Dec 1968. 2 daughters. *Education:* MA, MLitt, The Queen's College, Oxford, 1945-51. *Appointment:* Reader in English, University of Bristol, 1982. *Publications:* The Narrative Art of The Canterbury tales, 1988; Pearl In Its Setting, 1968; Chaucer's Troilus and Criseyde: A Critical Study, 1981. *Contributions to:* The Review of English Studies; Medium Aevum; The Times Higher Education Supplement; Notes and Queries. *Address:* 8 Benville Avenue, Coombe Dingle, Bristol BS9 2RX, England.

BISHOP James Drew, b. 18 June 1929, London, England. Journalist. m. 5 June 1959, 2 sons. *Education:* BA, History, Corpus Christi College, Cambridge, 1953. *Appointments:* Foreign Correspondent, The Times, 1957-64; Foreign News Editor, 1964-66, Features Editor, 1966-70, The Times; Editor, 1971-87, Editor-in-Chief, 1987-, The Illustrated London News. *Publications:* Social History of Edwardian Britain, 1977; Social History of the First World War, 1982; The Story of the Times, with Oliver Woods, 1983; Illustrated Counties of England, Editor, 1985. *Contributions to:* USA Chapter in Annual Register, 1960-; Articles in many Newspapers and Magazines. *Memberships:* Association of British Editors, Chairman. *Literary Agent:* David Higham. *Address:* 11 Willow Road, London NW3 1TJ, England.

BISHOP Michael Lawson, b. 12 Nov 1945, Lincoln, Nebraska, USA. Writer. m. Jeri Ellis Whitaker, 7 June 1969, 1 son, 1 daughter. *Education:* BA, English, 1967, MA 1968, University of Georgia. *Publications include:* Novels: Catacomb Years, 1979; No Enemy But Time, 1982; Ancient of Days, 1985; Transfigurations, 1979; Who Made Stevie Crye?, 1983; The Secret Ascension, 1987; Unicorn Mountain, 1988; Philip K Dick is Dead (Alas), (novel), 1987. Short story collections: Blooded on Arachne, 1982; Close Encounters With the Deity, 1986; One Winter in Eden, 1984. Also short stories, reviews, criticism, essays, poetry including book, Windows & Mirrors. *Contributions to:* Various 'Best of the Year' collections. Journals including: Playboy; Interzone; Isaac Asimov's; Analog; Fantasy & Science Fiction; Omni; Galaxy; If; Missouri Review; Weirdbook; Science Fiction Digest. *Honours Include:* 2 Nebula Awards, best novelette, best novel; Rhysling Award, science fiction poetry; various other regional/speciality awards; Dogs' Lives, appears in The Best American Short Stories 1985. *Memberships:* Science Fiction Writers of America; Science Fiction Poetry Association; Writers Guild of America. *Literary Agent:* Howard Morhaim. *Address:* PO Box 646, Pine Mountain, GA 31822, USA.

BISHOP Pike. *See:* **OBSTFELD Raymond.**

BISHOP Robert, b. 1938. USA. Antiques/Furnishings, Art/Crafts. Director, Museum of American Folk Art, New York, 1976-; Adjunct Professor, Department of Art and Art Education, New York University, New York City, 1980- Associate Editor, The Gray Letter and Antique Chairman, Museums Council of New York City, 1978-81. *Publications include:* (ed) Mechanical Arts at the Henry Ford Museum, 1974; American Folk Sculpture, 1974; New Discoveries in American Quilts, 1975; (with E Safanda), A Gallery of Amish Quilts, 1976; (with W Distin), The American Clock, 1976; The Borden Limner and His Contemporaries, 1976; (with P Coblentz), World

Furniture, 1979; Treasures of American Folk Art, 1979; (with P Coblentz), Folk Painters of America, 1979; (with P Coblentz), The World of Antiques, Art and Architecture in Victorian America, 1979; (with P Coblentz), A Gallery of American Weathervanes and Whirligigs, 1980; American Decorative Arts, 1620-1980, 1982; (ed) Collectors' Guide to Glass, Tableware, Bowls and Vases, 1982; (ed) Collectors Guide to Chests, Cupboards, Desks and Other Pieces, 1982; (ed) Collectors' Guide to Chairs, Tables, Sofas and Beds, 1982; (with W Secord and J R Weissman), Collectors Guide to Quilts, Coverlets, Rugs and Samplers, 1982; (with W Ketchum), Collectors Guide to Folk Art, 1983; (ed) Collectors Guide to Toys, 1984; (ed) Collectors Guide to Silver and Pewter, 1984; (with C Houck), All Flags Flying, 1986; (with J Lipman and E V Warren), Young American, A Folk Art History, 1986; Hands All Around, 1986; American Quilts, Giftwraps by Artists, 1986. *Address:* 213 W 22nd Street, New York, NY 10011, USA.

BISHOP Wendy S, b. 13 Jan 1953, Japan. English Professor. m. Marvin E Pollard Jr, 1 son, 1 daughter. *Education:* BA, English, 1975, BA, Studio Art, 1975, MA, English, 1976, MA, English, 1979, University of California, Davis; PhD, English (Rhetoric and Linguistics), Indian University of Pennsylvania, 1988. *Appointments:* Bayero University, Kano, Nigeria, 1980-81; Northern Arizona University, USA, 1981-82; Navajo Community College, 1982-85; University of Alaska, Fairbanks, 1985-89; Florida State University, Tallahassee, 1989-. *Publications:* Released into Language: Options for Teaching Creative Writing, 1990; Something Old, Something New: College Writing Teachers and Classroom Change, 1990; Working Words: The Process of Creative Writing, 1992; The Subject Is Writing, 1993. *Contributions to:* Poems, fiction, essays to: American Poetry Review; College English; High Plains Literary Review; Prairie Schooner; Western Humanities Review; Many other journals. *Honours:* Winner, Joseph Henry Jackson award, 1980. *Memberships:* Poetry Society of America; Associated Writing Programmes, member, Board of Directors; Conference on College Composition and Communication, Executive Committee Member; Modern Language Association, member, Delegate Assembly. *Address:* Department of English, Florida State University, Tallahassee, FL 32302, USA.

BISSELL LeClair, b. 18 May 1928, Virginia, USA. Physician; Author; Researcher. *Education:* BA, University of Colorado, 1950; MS, Columbia University, 1952; MD, 1963; School of Alcohol Studies, Yale University, 1960. *Publications:* Ethics for Addiction Professionals; The Cat that Drank Too Much; Alcoholism in the Professions; Chemical Dependancy- Nursing; To Care Enough. *Contributions to:* Over Eighty Articles, Abstracts, Book Chapters. *Honours:* Marty Mann Award; Mel Schulsted Award; SECAD Award. *Memberships include:* NIAAA; American Civil Liberties Union; American Medical Writers Association; JACS Foundation; National Abortion Rights Action League; American Medical Women's Association; Past President of the American Medical Society on Alcoholism. *Address:* 1932 Woodring Road, Sanibel, FL 33957, USA.

BISSET Donald, b. 1910. British. Writer; Actor. *Publications:* Anytime Stories, 1954; Sometime Stories, 1957; Next Time Stories, 1959; This Time Stories, 1961; Another Time Stories, 1963; Little Bear's Pony, 1966; Hullo Lucy, 1967; Talks with a Tiger, 1967; Kangaroo Tennis, 1968; Nothing, 1969; Upside Down Land, 1969; Benjie the Circus Dog, 1969; Time and Again Stories, 1970; Barcha the Tiger, 1971; Tiger Wants More, 1971; Yak series, 6 vols., 1971-78; Father Tingtang's Journey, 1973; Jenny Hopalong, 1973; The Happy Horse, 1974; The Adventures of Mandy Duck, 1974; Hazy Mountain, 1974; Oh Dear, Said the Tiger, 1975; Paws with Shapes, 1976; (with Michael Morris) Paws with Numbers, 1976; The Lost Birthday, 1976; The Story of Smokey Horse, 1977; This is Ridiculous, 1977; Jungle Journey, 1977; What Time Is It, When It Isn't, 1980; Cornelia and Other Stories, 1980; Johnny Here and There, 1981; The

Hedgehog Who Rolled Uphill, 1982; Snakey Boo Series, 2 vols. 1982-85; Please Yourself, 1991. *Address:* 43 Andrewes House, Barbican, London EC2Y 8AX, England.

BISSETT Bill, b. 1939, Canada. Poet; Artist. *Appointment:* Editor, Printer, Blewointmentpress, Vancouver, 1962-. *Publications:* The Jinx Ship and other Trips: Poems-drawings-collage, 1966; We Sleep Inside Each Other All, 1966; Fires in the Temple, 1967; Where Is Miss Florence Riddle, 1967; What Poetiks, 1967; Gossamer Bed Pan, 1967; Lebanon Voices, 1967; Of the Land/Divine Service Poems, 1968; Awake in the Red Desert!, 1968; Killer Whale, 1969; Sunday Work?, 1969; Liberating Skies, 1969; The Lost Angel Mining Company, 1969; The Outlaw, 1970; Blew Trewz, 1970; Nobody Owns the Earth, 1971; Air 6, 1971; Dragon Fly, 1971; Four Parts Sand: Concrete Poems, 1972; The Ice bag, 1972; Poems for Yoshi, 1972, 1977; Drifting into War, 1972; Air 10-11-12, 1973; Pass the Food, Release the Spirit Book, 1973; The First Sufi Line, 1973; Vancouver Mainland Ice and Cold Storage, 1973; Living with the Vishyan, 1974; What, 1974; Drawings, 1974; Medicine My Mouths on Fire, 1974; Space Travel, 1974; You Can Eat it at the Opening, 1974; The Fifth Sun, 1975; The Wind Up Tongue, 1975; Stardust, 1975; An Allusyun to Macbeth, 1976; Plutonium Missing, 1976; Sailor, 1978; Beyond Even Faithful Legends, 1979; Soul Arrow, 1980; Northern Birds in Color, 1981; Parlant, 1982; Seagull on Yonge Street, 1983; Canada Gees Mate for Life, 1985; Animal Uproar, 1987; What we Have, 1989; Hard & Beleev, 1990; Incorrect Thoughts, 1992. Vocalist with The Luddites, Dreaming of the Night, 1992. *Address:* Box 273, 1755 Robson Street, Vancouver, BC Canada V6G 387.

BISWAS Anil Ranjan, (Oneil), b. 1 Feb 1916, Bangladesh. Writer; Former Civil Servant and Teacher. m. Lily Mullick, 15 May 1941, 1 son. *Education:* BA (Hons), 1937; MA, 1942; LLM, 1968; PhD, 1976. *Appointments:* Editor: Eastern Law Reports, 1982; Laikhi (writing), 1985. *Publications:* Footsteps,, 1951; Twentieth century Bengali Literature, 1952; Curly waters, 1961; Shakespeare's Sonnets, 1966; Asutosh's thoughts on education, 1968; At whose bid the bell rings, 1972; Continuum becomes Calcutta, 1973, 1991; On the Shores of Anxiety, 1980; Bengali Prosody, 1992; Calcutta and Calcuttans, 1992. *Contributions to:* Purvase; Ananda Bazar Patrika; Calcutta Review; Economic weekly; Prabhat; Bharatvarsa; Desh; Amrita Bazar Patrika; Law Quarterly; Journal of the Indian Law Institute. *Honours:* Onauth Nauth Deb Gold Medal, 1971; Anandaram Borooah Medal, 1977; Griffith Memorial Prize, 1977; Poet Kumudranjan Memorial Lecture. *Memberships:* Life Member, Asiatic Society; Life Member, Bangiya Sahitya Parishad; President, Laikhi Sahitya Parishad (Writing Academy of Letters); Life Member, Indian Law Institute. *Address:* Gairick, 18 Cooperative Road, Calcutta 700070, India.

BJARKMAN Peter Christian, b. 19 May 1941, Hartford, USA. Author. m. (1) Mary Anita Whitworth, 5 May 1967, (2) Ronnie Bring Wilbur, 1 Feb 1985, 1 son, 1 daughter. *Education:* BS, University of Hartford, 1963; M Ed, 1970; MA, Trinity College, 1972; PhD, University of Florida, 1976. *Publications:* Baseball & The Game of Life; The Baseball Scrapbook; The Brooklyn Dodgers; Baseball's Great Dynasties: The Reds; Baseball's Great Dynasties: The Dodgers; The Toronto Blue Jays; Roberto Clemente; The History of the NBA; Encyclopedia of Major League Baseball Team Histories: American League; National League; Duke Snider; Ernie Banks. *Contributions:* Forgotten Americans and the National Pastime; Literature on Baseball's Ethnic, Racial & Religious Diversity in: Multi Cultural Review, 1992. *Memberships:* Society for American Baseball Research. *Address:* 2707 Sleepy Hollow Drive, Lafayette, IN 47904, USA.

BJELKHAGEN Teresa Grace, b. 28 June 1951, Poland. Linguist. m. twice. *Education:* BA, English and Russian, 1974; MA, Applied Linguistics, 1977; Diploma in Applied Descriptive and Theoretical Linguistics,

Exeter University, England, 1982. *Publications:* Poems in Pasque Petals: The Laughing Jacaranda, Why Once Again, Fleurs de la Cote d'Azur, All That's You is LIGHT, Encounters, 1988; Posh Array, 1989; Engele (poem) in Voices of South Dakota III anthology; Poems: Your Phantom of the Night; Lips of Scarlet; Squeezeling, 1992. *Membership:* South Dakota State Poetry Society. *Address:* Åsögatan 194, 116 32 Stockholm, Sweden.

BJERG Anne Marie, b. 17 Dec 1937, Copenhagen, Denmark. Translator; Writer. m. Chrenn Bjerg, 29 Dec 1962, div, 1 daughter. *Education:* BA, University of Copenhagen, 1970. *Appointments:* Regular reader Gyldendal's Publishing house, 1971-86. *Publications:* A Start in Life; Look at Me; Yltel du Lac; Family and Friends; A Friend from England; Latecomers; Lewis Percy by Anita Brookner. *Contributions to:* BLM. *Honours:* The Translators Award of the Danish Academy; Honorary Award of the Danish Translators' Association; Life long grant, Danish State Art Foundation. *Memberships:* James Joyce Society; Danish Writers Association; Danish PEN; Danish Dramatists Association. *Address:* Laerdalsgate 6A 1tv, DK2300 Copenhgen S, Denmark.

BLAAS Erika B, (E B Rockford), b. Austria. Professor, German, English Language and Literature, Historian of Art; Writer. *Education:* University of Prague, Graz, Innsbruck, PHD, 1949; University of Wisconsin, 1950-51. *Publications:* Der Wolf mit Den Drei Goldenen Schüsseln; Wie Rohr Im Ried; Salzburg Von A-Z; Dorfbuch von Natters; Radio, In den StraBen von New York; Eine Reise Durch Amerika. *Memberships:* Österreichischer Autorenverband, Wien; American Translator Association. *Address:* Elsenheimstr 14/12, A 5020 Salzburg, Austria.

BLACK David, b. 21 Apr 1945, Boston, Massachusetts, USA. Writer; Producer. m. Deborah Hughes Keehn, 22 June 1968, 1 son, 1 daughter. *Education:* BA magna cum laude, Amherst College, 1967; MFA, Columbia University, 1971. *Appointments:* Contributing Writer, New Times, 1975- 76; Writer-in-Residence, Mt Holyoke College, 1982-86; Contributing Editor, Rolling Stone, 1986-89. *Publications:* Books: Ekstasy, 1975; Like Father, 1978; The King of Fifth Avenue, 1981; Minds, 1982; Murder at the Met, 1984; Medicine Man, 1985; Peep Show, 1986; Feature scripts include: Murder At the Met, 1982; Falling Angel, 1984; Catching It, 1988; Passion, 1990; The Man In The Slouch Hat, 1992; Detectives of the Heart, 1992; TV scripts: Hill Street Blues, 1987; Send Me, 1987; Alaska, 1988-89; Gideon Oliver, 1988; H E L P, 1989; In Your Face, 1989; The Nasty Boys, 1989; Law and Order, 1990; Legacy of Lies, 1992; In The Year 2000, 1992. *Contributions to:* Over 150 stories and articles to numerous national and international magazines including: The New York Times Magazine; The Atlantic; Harper's; Playboy; Penthouse; The Village Voice; Rolling Stone; The Transatlantic Review; Granta; Cosmopolitan; New York. *Honours:* Honourable Mention, Best Essays of 1986, Harpers; National Magazine Award; National Association of Science Writers Award; Best Article of the Year Award, Playboy; National Endowment for the Arts Grant in Fiction; Firsts Award, short story, Atlantic Monthly; Notable Book of the Year, New York Times (2); Several others including 2 Edgar nominations, Pulitzer Prize nomination. *Memberships:* PEN; The Writers Guild-East; Mystery Writers of America; International Association of Crime Writers; Century Association; Williams Club. *Literary Agent:* Dave Wirtschafter. *Address:* c/o Dave Wirtschafter, ICM, 8899 Beverly Blvd, Los Angeles, CA 90048, USA.

BLACK David (Macleod), b. 1941. Poet. *Publications:* Theory of Diet, 1966; With Decorum, 1967; A Dozen Short Poems, 1968; Penguin Modern Poets 11 (with D.M. Thomas and Peter Redgrove), 1968; The Educators, 1969; The Old Hag, 1972; The Happy Crow, 1974; Gravitations, 1979.

BLACK Dorothy, (Kitty Black), b. 30 Apr 1914,

Johannesburg, South Africa. Author; Translator. *Appointments:* H M Tennent Ltd, 1937-53; Curtis Brown Ltd, 1953-59; Granada Television, 1960-62; Associated- Rediffusion, 1962-64; Producer, Editor, simultaneous translations, World Theatre Seasons, 1963-75; Secretary, Apollo Society, 1975-85. *Publications:* Upper Circle, 1984; Translations: Men Without Shadows (Sartre); The Respectable Prostitute (Sartre); Crime Passionnel (Sartie); Lucifer and the Lord (Sartre); Point of Departure (Anouilh); The Rehearsal (Anouilh) (with Pamela Hansford Johnson); Many plays by Simenon, Hochwaelder, Camus, Marcel Aymé, Félicien Marceau; Riding to Jerusalem (from Evelyn Coquet); Julie (from Comtesse Félicité de Choiseul-Meuse). *Memberships:* PEN; Society of Authors; Translators Association; Royal Mid-Surrey Golf Club; President, Ladies Stage Golfing Society. *Literary Agent:* Curtis Brown Ltd. *Address:* 16 Brunswick Gardens, London W8 4AJ, England.

BLACK Gavin. *See:* **WYND Oswald.**

BLACK Kitty. *See:* **BLACK Dorothy.**

BLACK Laura. *See:* **LONGRIGG Roger Erskine.**

BLACK Veronica. *See:* **PETERS Maureen.**

BLACKBOURN David Gordon, b. 1 Nov 1949, Spilsby, Lincs. Historian; University Teacher. m. Deborah Frances Langton, 13 Apr 1985, 1 son, 1 daughter. *Education:* Christs College, Cambridge, 1967-70; BA, 1970; MA, 1974; PhD, 1976. *Appointments:* Research Fellow, Jesus College Cambridge, 1973-76; Lecturer, Queen Mary College, University of London, 1976- 79; Lecturer, 1979-85; Reader, 1985-89; Professor, Birkbeck College, University of London, 1989-92; Professor, Harvard University, 1992-. *Publications:* Class, Religion & Local Politics; The Peculiarities of German History; Populists & Patricians; The German Bourgeoisie; Marpingen: Apparitions of the Virgin Mary in Bismarckian Germany. *Contributions to:* New Society; Maxism Today; History Today. *Honours:* Frequent Quest Lecturer. *Memberships:* Fellow, Royal Historical Society; Editorial Board, Past & Present; German History Society. *Literary Agent:* Margaret Hanbury UK/Robin Strauss. *Address:* Minda De Gunzburg Center for European Studies, Harvard University, 27 Kirkland Street, Cambridge, MA 02138, USA.

BLACKIN Malcolm. *See:* **CHAMBERS Aidan.**

BLACKMAN Sue Anne Batey, b. 21 June 1948, Hamilton Air Force Base, California, USA. m. Martin R Blackman, 7 Apr 1977, 1 daughter. *Education:* BA, University of Colorado, 1970. *Appointments include:* Senior Research Assistant, Department of Economics, Princeton University, 1987-. *Publications:* Perfect Markets & Easy Virtue; Productivity & American Leadership: The Long View; Economics, Environmental Policy & The Quality of Life. *Contributions to:* Challenge: The Magazine of Economic Affairs; Economic Impact: A Quarterly Review of World Economics; Land Economics; Journal of the American Society for Information Science; American Economic Review. *Honours:* Honorable Mention Social Sciences, Association of American Publishers, Awards for Excellence in Publishing. *Address:* Department of Economics, Princeton University, Princeton, NJ 08544, USA.

BLACKMORE Howard Loftus, b. 27 Oct 1917, Mitcham, Surrey, England. Author. *Publications:* British Military Firearms 1650-1850, 1961; Firearms, 1964; Arms and Armour, 1965; Guns and Rifles of the World, 1965; Royal Sporting Guns at Windsor, 1968; Hunting Weapons, 1971; The Armouries of the Tower of London, Volume 1, Ordnance, 1976; English Pistols, 1985; A Dictionary of London Gunmakers, 1350-1850, 1986. *Contributor to:* Connoisseur; Apollo; Country Life;

Saturday Book; British History Illustrated; American Rifleman; Gun Digest; Gazette des Armes; Times Literary Supplement; British Book News. *Memberships include:* Arms and Armour Society; Society of Antiquaries of London; American Society of Arms Collectors; Gemmological Association. *Address:* Wildwood, Upper Harestone, Caterham, Surrey CR3 6BN, England.

BLACKSTOCK Charity. *See:* **TORDAY Ursula.**

BLACKSTOCK Lee. *See:* **TORDAY Ursula.**

BLACKWOOD Caroline, b. 1931. Author. *Publications:* For All That I Found There (short stories and essays), 1973; The stepdaughter, 1976; Great Granny Webster, 1977; Darling, You Shouldn't Have Gone to So Much Trouble (cookbook with Anna Haycraft), 1980; The Fate of Mary Rose, 1981; Goodnight Sweet Ladies (stories), 1983; On the Perimeter, 1984; Corrigan, 1984. *Address:* c/o Heinemann Limited, 10 Upper Grosvenor Street, London, W1X 9PA, England.

BLAINE James. *See:* **AVALLONE Michael.**

BLAINEY Geoffrey Norman, b. 1930, Australia. Writer. *Publications:* The Peaks of Lyell, 1954; A Centenary History of the University of Melbourne, 1957; Gold and Paper, 1958; Mines in the Spinifex, 1960; The Rush That Never Ended, 1963; A History of Camberwell, 1965; If I Remember Rightly: The Memoirs of W S Robinson, 1966; Co-Author and Editor, Wesley College: The First Hundred Years, 1967; The Tyranny of Distance, 1966; Across a Red World, 1968; The Rise of Broken Hill, 1968; The Steel Master, 1971; The Causes of War, 1973; Triumph of the Nomads, 1975; A Land Half Won, 1980; The Blainey View, 1982; Our Side of the Country, 1984; All for Australia, 1984; The Great Seesaw, 1988; A Game of our Own: The Origins of Australian Football, 1990; Eye on Australia, 1991. *Memberships:* Chairman, Commonwealth Literary Fund, 1971-73; Australia Council, 1977-81.*Address:*PO Box 257, East Melbourne, Victoria 3002, Australia.

BLAIR Claude, b. 1922. Antiquary and Art Historian *Appointments:* Assistant, Tower of London Armouries, 1951-56; Honoury Editor, Journal of Arms and Armour Society, 1953-77; Assistant Keeper, 1966-72, Deputy Keeper, 1966- 72, Keeper, 1972-82, Metalwork, Victoria and Albert Museum, London; Consultant, Christie's, London, 1982-. *Publications:* European Armour, 1958; European and American Arms, 1962; Pistols of the World, 1968; Three Presentation Swords in the Victoria and Albert Museum, 1972; The James A de Rothschild Collection at Waddesdon Manor: Arms, Armour and Base-Metalwork, 1974; Pollard's History of Firearms, 1983; A History of Silver, 1987. *Contribution to:* Numerous articles and reviews in Archaeology. *Memberships:* Architectural Advisory Panel of Westminster Abbey; Redundant Churches Fund; A Liveryman of the Goldsmiths and Amourers & Brasiers Companies; Fellow of the Society of Antiquaries of London; Vice-President, (currently); Christies Consultant. *Address:* 90 Links Road, Ashtead, Surrey, KT21 2HW, England.

BLAIR Emma. *See:* **BLAIR Iain John.**

BLAIR Iain John, (Emma Blair), b. 12 Aug 1942, Glasgow, Scotland. Novelist. m. 26 Apr 1975, 2 sons. *Education:* Royal Scottish Academy of Music and Dramatic Art. *Publications:* Where No Man Cries, 1982; Nellie Wildchild, 1983; Hester Dark, 1984; This Side of Heaven, 1985; Jessie Gray, 1985; The Princess of Poor Street, 1986; Street Song, 1986; When Dreams Come True, 1987; A Most Determined Woman, 1988; The Blackbird's Tale, 1989; Maggie Jordan, 1990; Scarlet Ribbons, 1991; The Water Meadows, 1992. *Memberships:* Romantic Novelists Association; British

Actors Equity. *Literary Agent:* Rogers, Coleridge and White, 20 Powis Mews, London W11 1JN, England. *Address:* The Old Vicarage, Stoke Canon, Nr Exeter, Devon EX5 4AS, England.

BLAIR Jessica. *See:* **SPENCE William John Duncan.**

BLAIR Pauline Hunter (Helen Clare, Pauline Clarke), Author. m. Peter Hunter Blair, Feb 1969. *Education:* BA, Honours, Somerville College, Oxford. *Publications:* Works include: As Pauline Clarke: The Pekinese Princess, 1948; The Great Can, 1952; The White Elephant, 1952; Smith's Hoard, 1955; The Boy with the Erpingham Hood, 1956; Sandy the Sailor, 1956; James, the Policeman, 1957; James and the Robbers, 1959; Torolv the Fatherless, 1959, 2nd edition 1974, re-issued 1991; The Lord of the Castle, 1960; The Robin Hooders, 1960; James and the Smugglers, 1961; Keep the Pot Boiling, 1961; The Twelve and the Genii, 1962; Silver Bells and Cockle Shells, 1962; James and the Black Van, 1963; Crowds of Creatures, 1964; The Bonfire Party, 1966; The Two Faces of Silenus, 1972; As Helen Clare: Five Dolls in a House, 1953; Merlin's Magic, 1953; Bel, the Giant and Other Stories, 1956; Five Dolls and the Monkey, 1956; Five Dolls in the Snow, 1957; Five Dolls and Their Friends, 1959; Seven White Pebbles, 1960; Five Dolls and the Duke, 1963; The Cat and the Fiddle and Other Stories from Bel, the Giant, 1968. *Honours:* Library Association Carnegie Medal, 1962; Lewis Carroll Shelf Award, Deutsche Jugend Buchpreis, 1968. *Address:* Church Farm House, Bottisham, Cambridge CB5 9BA, England.

BLAKE Alfred. *See:* **HARRIS Laurence Mark.**

BLAKE Andrew. *See:* **HARRIS Laurence Mark.**

BLAKE Jennifer. *See:* **MAXWELL Patricia Anne.**

BLAKE Ken. *See:* **BULMER Henry Kenneth.**

BLAKE Leslie James, (Peter Tabard), b. 1913, Australia. Writer. *Publications:* Teaching Social Studies, 1957, 3rd Edition, 1964; Shaw Neilson in the Wimmera, 1961; Principles and Techniques of Teaching (with J. Cole), 1962, 3rd Edition, 1965; Patterns in Poetry, 1962; Wimmera Shire Centenary (with K. Lovett), 1962, 4th Edition, 1970; Lost in the Bush, 1964; Richard Hale Budd, 1968; Australian Writers, 1968; Geelong Sketchbook, 1970; Gold Escort, 1971; Co-Author, John Shaw Neilson, 1973; General Editor and Co-Author, Vision and Realisation: A Centenary History of State Education in Victoria, 3 vols., 1973; Wimmera, 1973; General Editor and Co-Author, Werribee Park, 1974; Letters of Charles Joseph La Trobe, 1975; Place Names of Victoria, 1976; Pioneer Schools of Australia, 1976; Gold Escorts in Australia, 1978; Covered Wagons in Australia, 1979; Tales from Old Geelong, 1979; Peter Lalor, The Man from Eureka,1979; Editor and Co-Author, A Gold Digger's Diaries, 1980; Aunt Spencer's Diaries by Mary Read and Mary Spencer, 1981; Tattyara: A History of the Kaniva District, Kaniva Shire, 1981; Schools of the Tattyara, Kaniva Shire, 1981; Captain Dana and the Native Police, 1982. *Memberships:* Foundation President, Western Victorian Association of Historical Societies, 1963-64; Chairman, State Education History Committee, Education Department, 1966-70; President, Royal Historical Society of Victoria, 1966-71; Vice President, Australian International PEN, Melbourne Centre 1971-72; Chairman, State Education Department, Centenary Celebration Committee, 1972-73. *Address:* 4 Anton Court, Karingal, Victoria, 3199, Australia.

BLAKE Norman Francis, b. 1934. Writer. *Publications:* Editor, Translator, The Saga of the Jomsvikings, 1962; The Phoenix, 1964; Caxton and His World, 1969; William Caxton's Reynard the Fox, 1970; Middle English Religious Prose, 1972; Selections from

William Caxton, 1973; Caxton's Own Prose, 1975; Caxton's Quattnor Sermones, 1973; Caxton: England's First Publisher, 1976; The English Language in Medieval Literature, 1977; Non- Standard Language in English Literature, 1981; Shakespeare's Language, 1983; Textual Tradition of the Canterbury Tales, 1985; William Caxton: a bibliographical guide, 1985; Traditional English Grammar and Beyond, 1988; Index of Printed Middle English Prose, 1985; (with R E Lewis and A S G Edwards); The Language of Shakespeare, 1989; The Phoenix, 2nd edn.,1990; An Introduction to the Language of Literature, 1990. *Address:* Dept of English Language and Linguistics, University of Sheffield, Sheffield S10 2TN, England.

BLAKE Patrick. *See:* **EGLETON Clive Frederick William.**

BLAKE Robert. *See:* **DAVIES Leslie Purnell.**

BLAKE Robert, (Norman William), (Lord Blake of Braydeston, Norfolk), b. 1916. British. History, Politics/ Government. *Appointments:* Lecturer, 1946-47; Student and Tutor in Politics, 1947-68; Christ Church, Oxford; Ford's Lecturer in English History, Oxford University, 1967-68; Provost of Queen's College, Oxford, 1968-87; Conservative Member, Oxford City Council, 1957-64. *Publications:* The Private Papers of Douglas Haig, (ed), 1952; The Unknown Prime Minister, The Life and Times of Andrew Bonar Law, 1955; Disraeli, 1966; The Conservative Party from Peel to Churchill, 1970, 2nd ed. as The Conservative Party from Peel to Thatcher, 1985; The Office of the Prime Minister, 1975; (ed. with John Patten) The Conservative Opportunity, 1976; A History of Rhodesia, 1977; Disraeli's Grand Tour, 1982; The English World, (ed), 1982; The Decline of Power, 1985; Churchill, a Major New Assessment of His Life in Peace and War, (ed with Roger Louis), 1993. *Address:* Riverview House, Brundall, Norwich, Norfolk.

BLAKELEY Denis, b. 5 Aug 1931, Dewsbury, Yorkshire, England. Journalist. m. 28 Oct 1971. *Education:* BA, Honours, Foreign Languages, London. *Appointments:* Journalism in Bonn, Munich, Vienna, Paris, Moscow; British Broadcasting Corporation; Economist. *Contributor to:* Times Literary Supplement; The Economist; International Management; Christian Science Monitor; Guardian. *Address:* 1 Stonefield, Moss Lane, Garstang, Preston PR3 1PD, Lancashire, England.

BLAKE Robin James, b. 12 Dec 1948, Preston, Lancs, England. Writer. m. Frances Mary Waugh, 23 Dec 1981, 3 sons. *Education:* Jesus College, Cambridge Univserity, 1967-70; BA, 1971-72; Chelsea College, London University, 1974-75. *Publications:* Mind over Medicine; Fat Mans Shaddow; The Gwailo; Compulsion. *Memberships:* Society of Authors; The Radio Academy; Association of Cinematographic & Television Technicians. *Literary Agent:* Rogers, Coleridge & White. *Address:* c/o Rogers, Coleridge & White, 20 Powis Mews, London W11 1N, England.

BLAKEMORE Colin, b. 1 June 1944, Stratford-upon-Avon, England. Waynflete Professor of Physiology, University of Oxford, Fellow of Magdalen College, Oxford. m. Andree Elizabeth Washbourne, 28 Aug. 1965, 3 daughters. *Education:* BA Class I, Corpus Christi, Cambridge, 1965; PhD (California) in Physiological Optics, 1968; MA (Cantab), 1969; MA (Oxon), 1979; ScD (Cantab), 1988; DSc (Oxon), 1989; FRS 1992; Hon DSc (Aston), 1992. *Appointments:* Member, various editorial boards, 1971-; Series Editor, Perspective in Vision Research Research, Plenum Press, New York, 1981-; Associate Editor, News in Physiological Sciences, 1985-88; Editor-in-Chief, IBRO News, 1986-; Member, UK Publication Advisory Panel, IRL Press, 1987-91; Associate Editor, NeuroReport, 1989-; Director, McDonnell-Pew Centre for Cognitive Neuroscience, 1990-; Vice-President, British Association for the Advancement of Science, 1990-. *Publications:* Handbook of Psychobiology (with M Gazzaniga), 1975; Mechanics of the Mind, 1977; Mindwaves (with S Greenfield), 1987; The Mind Machine, 1988; Vision: Coding and Efficiency, 1990; Images and Understanding (with H B Barlow and M Weston- Smith), 1990. *Contributions to:* Numerous to scientific journals including Journal of Physiology, Nature, Vision Research, Science; New Scientist; Guardian; New York Times Magazine. *Honours:* Robert Bing Prize, Research in Neurology and Neurophysiology (Swiss Academy of Medical Sciences), 1975; Phi Beta Kappa Award in Science for contribution to the literature of science, 1978; Prix du Docteur Robert Netter (prize from the French Academie Nationale de Médécine for research on developmental disorders of vision), 1984; Michael Faraday Award and Medal for contribution to the public understanding of science, Royal Society, 1989; John P. McGovern Science and Society Prize, Sigma Xi, 1990; Montgomery Medal (Royal College of Surgeons in Ireland and the Irish Ophthalmological Society), 1991. *Memberships:* Brain Research Association; Physiological Society; Experimental Psychology Society; European Brain and Behaviour Society; International Brain Research Organization; Cambridge Philosophical Society; European Neuroscience Association; Society for Neuroscience; Oxford Medical Society; Child Vision Research Society; International Society for Myochemistry; National Conference of University Professors; British Association for the Advancement of Science; American Association for the Advancement of Science; Sigma Xi; Professional Advisory Committee of SANE (Schizophrenia: A National Emergency), 1989-. *Address:* University Laboratory of Physiology, Parks Road, Oxford OX1 3PT, England.

BLAMIRES Harry, b. 6 Nov 1916, Bradford, England. Lecturer in Higher Education; Author. m. Nancy Bowles, 26 Dec 1940, 5 sons. *Education:* BA 1938, MA 1945, University College, Oxford. *Appointments:* Head of English Department 1948-72, Dean of Arts & Sciences, retired 1976, King Alfred's College, Winchester. *Publications:* A Short History of English Literature, 1974, revised 1984; The Bloomsday Book, Guide to Joyce's Ulysses, 1966, revised 1988; Twentieth-Century English Literature, 1982, revised 1986; The Christian Mind, 1963; Where Do We Stand?, 1980; On Christian Truth, 1983; Word Unheard, Guide through Eliot's Four Quartets, 1969; Milton's Creation, 1971; The Victorian Age of Literature, 1988; Guide to 20th Century Literature in England, 1983; Words Made Flesh, 1985 published in UK as The Marks of the Maker, 1987; Meat Not Milk, 1988; The Age of Romantic Literature, 1989; A Histiry of Literary Criticism, 1991. *Honour:* Clyde Kilby Visiting Professor of English, Wheaton College, Illinois, USA, 1987. *Membership:* Society of Authors. *Address:* Rough Close, Braithwaite, Keswick, Cumbria CA12 5RY, England.

BLAND Jennifer. *See:* **BOWDEN Jean.**

BLASHFORD-SNELL John Nicholas, b. 22 Oct 1936, Hereford, England, Soldier; Colonel and Commander Operation Raleigh; Explorer. *Education:* Victoria College Jersey, Channel Islands; Royal Military Academy, Sandhurst. *Publication include:* Where the Trail Runs Out; In the Steps of Stanley; Expeditions the Experts Way, co-author; A Taste for Adventure, 1978; Operation Drake, 1981, In the Wake of Drake, 1982, with M Cable; Mysteries - Encounters with the Unexplained, 1983; Operation Raleigh, The Start of an Adventure, 1985; Operation Raleigh, The Way Forward, 1988; with Ann Tweedy; Operation Raleigh, Adventure Challenge, 1990; Operation Raleigh Adventure Unlimited, 1990, with Ann Tweedy. *Contributions to:* Expedition; The Field; British Army Review; Gun Digest; Spectator; Yorks Post; Scotsman; Explorers Journal; Daily Telegraph. *Honours:* MBE, 1969; Livingstone Medal, 1975; Segrave Trophy, 1975; Freeman, City of Hereford, 1984; The Royal Geographical Society, Patrons Medal, 1993; Honorary DSc., Durham University. *Memberships:* Scientific Exploration Society, Chairman; Fellow Royal Scottish Geographical Society;

Chairman, British Chapter, ExplorersClub. *Literary Agent:* June Hall, England. *Address:* c/o The Scientific Exploration Soicety, Expedition Base, Motcombe, Dorset, SP7 9PB, England.

BLEAKLEY David Wylie, b. 1925. Writer. *Publications:* Co- Author, Ulster Since 1800, 1955; Young Ulster and Religion in the Sixties, 1964; Peace in Ulster, 1972; Faulkner: A Biography, 1974; Saidie Patterson, An Irish Peacemaker, 1980; In Place of Work: The Sufficient Society, 1981; The Shadow and Substance, 1983; Beyond Work - Free to Be, 1985; Will The Future Work?, 1988. *Honour:* CBE, 1984. *Address:* 8 Thorn Hill, Bangor, Co. Down, BT19 1RD, Northern Ireland.

BLEASDALE Alan, b. 23 Mar 1946. Playwright; Novelist. m. Julia Moses, 1970, 2 sons, 1 daughter. *Education:* Padgate Teachers Training College (Teachers Certificate). *Publications:* Scully, 1975; Who's Been Sleeping in my Bed, 1977; No More Sitting on the Old School Bench, 1979; Boys from the Blackstuff, 1982, (Televised); Are You Lonesome Tonight?, 1985; No Surrender, 1986; Having a Ball, 1986; It's a Madhouse, 1986; The Monocled Mutineer, 1986, (Televised); GBH (TV series), 1992. *Honours:* BAFTA Writer's Award, 1982; RTS Writer's Award, 1982; Broadcasting Press Guild TV Award for Best Series, 1982; Best Musical, London Standard Drama Awards, 1985. *Address:* c/o Harvey Unna & Stephen Durbridge Ltd., 24 Pottery Lane, Holland Park, London W11 4LZ, Englandd.

BLECHMAN Burt, b. 2 Mar 1927, New York, New York, USA. Writer. *Education:* BA, University of Vermont, 1949. *Publications:* How Much? 1962; The War of Camp Omongo, 1963; Stations, 1965; Octopus Papers, 1966; Maybe, 1967. *Honour:* I Merrill Foundation Writing Award, 1964. *Address:* 200 Waverly Place, New York, NY 10014, USA.

BLIGHT John, b. 1913, Australia. Poet. *Publications:* The Old Pianist, 1945; The Two Suns Met: Poems, 1954; A Beachcomber's Diary: Ninety Sea Sonnets, 1964; My Beachcombing Days: Ninety Sea Sonnets, 1968; Hart - Poems, 1975; Selected Poems 1939-1975, 1976; Pageantry for a Lost Empire, 1977; The New City Poems, 1979; Holiday Sea Sonnets, 1985. *Address:* 34 Greenway Street, The Grange, Brisbane, Qld 4051, Australia.

BLIGHT Rose. *See:* **GREER Germaine.**

BLINDERMAN Charles, b. 31 Oct 1930, New York City, USA. Professor of English. 2 daughters. *Education:* BA, New York University, 1952; MA, 1953; PhD, Indiana University, 1957. *Appointments:* Graduate Assistant, Indiana University, 1953-55; Assistant Professor, Southern Illinois University, 1957-62; Associate Professor, Clark University, 1962; Full Professor, 1967- ; Adjunct Professor, 1984-; Director, Clark University Criminal Justice Program. *Publications:* The Piltdown Inquest: Prometheus Books; Biolexicon: A Guide to the Language of Biology; Medilex: A Guide to the Language of Medicine. *Contributions to:* 50 Articles inc, Thomas Henry Huxley; The great Bone Case; The Ampullae of Lorenzini; Huxley, Pater & Pretoplasm; The Curious Case ob Nebraska Man: Dictionary of Literary Biology. *Honours:* Fulbright Grant, Imperial College of Science & Technology. *Literary Agent:* Spencer Literary Development, Thomaston, Maine. *Address:* 30 Cascade Road, Worcester, MA 01602, USA.

BLISHEN Edward, b. 29 Apr 1920, Whetstone, Middlesex, England. Author. m. Nancy Smith, 4 Nov 1948, 2 sons. *Publications:* Roaring Boys, 1955; A Cackhanded War, 1971; Sorry Dad, 1978; A Nest of Teachers, 1979; Lizzie Pye, 1982; The Outside Contributor, 1986; The Disturbance Fee, 1988; Also: This Right Soft Lot, 1969; Uncommon Entrance, 1974; Shaky Reactions, 1981; Donkey Work, 1983; A Second Skin, 1984; The Penny World, 1990. *Contributions to:*

Numerous magazines & journals. *Honours:* Carnegie Medal (with Leon Garfield), 1970; Travelling Scholarship, Society of Authors, 1979; J R Ackerley Prize, autobiography, 1981; Fellow, Royal Society of Literature. *Memberships:* Society of Authors; PEN. *Literary Agent:* A M Heath. *Address:* 12 Bartrams Lane, Hadley Wood, Barnet, London EN4 0EH, England.

BLIVEN Bruce, b. 31 Jan 1916. Los Angeles, California, USA. Writer. m. Naomi Horowitz, 26 May 1950, 1 son. *Education:* AB, Harvard College, 1937. *Publications:* The Wonderful Writing Machine, 1954; Battle for Manhattan, 1956; The Story of D-Day, 1956; The American Revolution, 1958; From Pearl Harbor to Okinawa, 1960; From Casablanca to Berlin, 1965; New York, with Naomi Bliven, 1969; Under the Guns, 1972; Book Traveller, 1975; Volunteers, One and All, 1976; The Finishing Touch, 1978; New York: A History, 1981. *Contributions to:* The New Yorker; many other national magazines. *Memberships:* Authors Guild, Council 1970-; Society of American Historians, Board, 1975-; PEN American Centre; American Society of Journalists and Authors. *Address:* The New Yorker, 25 West 43rd Street, New York, NY 10036, USA.

BLOCH Chana, b. 15 Mar 1940, New York City, USA. Professor; Poet; Critic; Translator. m. Ariel A Bloch, 26 Oct 1969, 2 sons. *Education:* BA, Cornell University, 1961; MA, Brandeis University, 1963; MA, 1965; PhD, University of Calif, Berkeley, 1975. *Appointments:* Hebrew University, Jerusalem, 1964-67; University of California, Berkeley, 1967-69; Mills College, 1973-; Mills College, Professor of English, 1987-. *Publications:* The Secrets of the Tribe; Spelling the Word: George Herbert and the Bible; Selected Poems of Yehuda Amichai; The Window: New & Selected Poems of Dahia Ravikovitch; The Past Keeps Changing. *Contributions to:* Poetry, Iowa Review; Ploughshares; Field; Tikkun. *Honours:* Discovery Award; Translation Award; National Endowment for the Humanities Fellowship; Book of the Year Award; Poets & Writers Exchange Writers Award; National Edowment for the Arts Fellowship. *Literary Agent:* Geroges Borchardt. *Address:* 12 Menlo Place, Berkeley, CA 94707, USA.

BLOCH Robert, (Tarleton Fiske, Will Folke, Nathan Hindin, Wilson Kane, John Sheldon), b. 5 Apr 1917, Chicago, Illinois, USA. Writer. *Publications:* Psycho, 1959; The Best of Robert Bloch, 1977; Cold Chills, 1977; The King of Terrors, 1977; Out of the Mouths of Graves, 1979; Such Stuff as Screams Are Made Of, 1979; There is a Serpent in Eden, 1979; Psycho II, 1982; Mysteries of the Worm, 1983; The Night of the Ripper, 1984; Unholy Trinity, 1986; Midnight Pleasures, 1987; Lefty Feep, 1987; Selected Short Stories of Robert Bloch, 1987; Lori, 1989; Fear and Trembling, 1989; Psycho House, 1990; Psycho Paths (editor), 1991; Psycho Paths II (editor), 1993; One More Story To Tell (autobiography), 1993. *Contributions to:* Playboy; Penthouse; Gallery; Cosmopolitan; Red Book; Blue Book; Weird Tales; Ellery Queen Mystery Magazine and various others. *Honours:* Hugo Award, 1958; Life Career Awards; 1st World Fantasy Convention, 1975; Atlanta Science Fiction Convention, 1984; World Science Fiction Convention, 1984; Bramstoker Award, Horror Writers of America, 1990; Grand Master Award, 1st World Horror Convention, 1991. *Memberships:* Past President, Mystery Writers of America; Science Fiction Writers of America; Writers Guild of America; Motion Picture Academy of Arts and Sciences; Horror Writers of America. *Literary Agent:* The Pimlico Agency, New York; Shapiro Lichtman Talent Agency, Los Angeles. *Address:* 2111 Sunset Crest Drive, Los Angeles, CA 90046, USA.

BLOCK Francesca Lia, b. 3 Dec 1962, Hollywood, California, USA. Writer. *Education:* BA, UC Berkeley, 1986. *Publications:* Ecsrasia; Cherokee Bat And The Boat Guys; Witch Baby; Weetzie Bat. *Honours:* Shrout Fiction Award; Phi Beta Kappa; ALA Best Book for Young Adults; ALA Booklist YA Editors Choice; Recommended Book for Reluctant. *Literary Agent:* Julie Fallowfield, McIntosh & Otis. *Address:* c/o McIntosh & Otis, 310 Madison Avenue, New York, NY 10017, USA.

BLOM Karl Arne, b. 22 Jan 1946, Nassjo, Sweden. Author. m. Karin Gyllen, 29 June, 1969. 1 son, 2 daughters. *Education:* BA, 1972. *Publications:* Moment of Truth, 1974; Limits of Pain, 1978. *Contributions to:* Armchair Detective; Mystery Fancier; Pinkerton; Jury. *Honours:* Sherlock Award, 1983; Lund Cultural Prize, 1980; Spangen Award, 1983;. Marten Award, 1984. *Memberships:* Asociacion Internacioal Escritores Policancos; Crime Writers of Scandinavia; Mystery Writers of America; Crime Writers Association; Poe Club, Denmark; Society of Crime Writers of Scandinavia; Honorary Chairman, Swedish Academy of Detection. *Literary Agent:* Lennart Sane Agency. *Address:* Smaskolevagan 22, S-224 67 Lund, Sweden.

BLOND Anthony, b. 1928, Author. *Appointments:* Director, Piccadilly Radio; Trustee LIBERTY Director The Chem & Company (civil liberties); Formerly Director, Blond and Briggs Limited, Publishers, London. *Publications:* The Publishing Game, 1971; Family Business, 1978; The Book Book, 1985. *Contributor to:* Spectator; The Literary Review. *Address:* 9 Rue Thiers, 87300 Bellac, France.

BLONDEL Jean Fernand Pierre, b. 26 Oct 1929, Toulon, France. University Professor. m.(1) Michele Hadet 1954, (div.), (2) Teresa Ashton, 1982, 2 daughters. *Education:* Diploma, Institut Etudes Politiques, Paris, 1953; BLitt, Oxford, England, 1955. *Publications:* Voters, Parties and Leaders, 1963; An Introduction to Conservative Government, 1969; Compartive Legislatures, 1973; World Leaders, 1980; The Discipline of Politics, 1982; Political Leadership, 1987; The Organisation of Governments, 1982; Government Ministers in the Contemporary World, 1985; Political Parties, 1978; Comparative Government, 1990. *Contributions to:* Political Studies; Revue Francaise de Science Politique; European Journal of Political Research. *Memberships:* Royal Swedish Academy of Sciences; American Political Science Association; British Political Studies Association of the UK; Asssociation Francaise de Science Politique. *Address:* 15 Marloes Road, London W8 6LQ, England.

BLONDIN Antoine, b. 11 Apr 1922, Paris, France. Writer. m. (1) Sylviane Dollfus, 1 son, 1 daughter, (2) Francoise Barrere, 1969. *Education:* L es L, University of Paris. *Publications:* L'Europe buissonniere; Les enfants du bon Dieu; L'Humeur vagabonde; Un singe en hiver; un garcon d'honneur; Nous reviendrons a pied; Quat'saisons; Vivre a Paris; Certificats d'etudes. Films scenarios for: La route Napoleon; Obsession; La foire aux femmes; Cran d'arret; Le Dernier Saut. *Contributions to:* Paris-Presse; Arts; La Parisienne. *Honours:* Prix des Deux-Magots, 1949; Prix Interallie, 1959; Grand Prix (Literature), Academie Francaise, 1979. *Address:* 72 rue Mazarine, 75007 Paris, France.

BLOOM Lynn Marie Zimmerman, b. 11 July 1934, Ann Arbor, Michigan, USA. Professor; Author. m. 11 July 1958, 2 sons. *Education:* BA, 1956; MA, 1957; PhD, 1963. *Appointments:* Assistant & Associate Professor, English, Butler University, 1970-74; Associate Professor, English, University of New Mexico, 1975-78; College of William and Mary, 1978-81; Professor, English, Viginia Commonwealth University, 1982-; Professor of English and Aetna (endowed) Chair of Writing, University of Connecticut, 1988-. *Publications:* Bear, Man and God, 1969, 1971; Doctor Spock, 1972; Forbidden Diary, (ed), 1980; The New Assertive Woman, (co-author), 1975; Fact and Artifact: Writing Non-fiction, 1985, 1994; The Essay Connection, (ed), 1984, revised 1988, 1991, 1995; The Lexington Reader, (ed), 1987; American Autobiography, 1945-80; A Bibliography, (co-author), 1982; Forbidden Family, (ed), 1989. *Contributions to:* Professional Journals. *Honours:* Phi Beta Kappa; Recipient of various other honours and awards; Aetna Chair of Writing, University of Connecticut, 1988-. *Memberships:* Modern Language Association, Executive Committee, Division of Teaching Writing, 1987-91; College Composition and Communication Executive Committee, 1980-82; Council of Writing Program Administrators, Vice-President, 1987-89, President, 1989-91. *Address:* English Department U-25, University of Connecticut, Storrs, CT 06269-1025, USA.

BLOOMFIELD Anthony John Westgate, (John Westgate), b. 1922. Author; Playwright. *Appointment:* Senior Editor, Television News, BBC, London. *Publications:* Russian Roulette, 1955; The Delinquents, 1958; The Tempter,1961; Throw, 1965; Turn Off If You Know The Ending (TV play), 1966; One Day It Could Be Different (TV play), 1966; As John Westgate: Victor, Victor (TV play), 1967, Life for a Life (TV play), 1967, Inventory for the Summer (TV play), 1967, Hand with the Magic Touch (TV play), 1970, Beneath the Tide (TV play), 1971; Life for a Life (novel), 1971, (screenplay), 1973; Reilly's Fire (novel), 1980. *Address:* 22 Montpelier Court, Montpelier Road, Ealing, London, W5 2QN, England.

BLOOMFIELD Barry Cambray b. 1 June 1931, London, England. Retired Librarian. m. Valerie Jean Philpot, 29 Dec 1958. *Education:* BA, University of Exeter, 1952; Diploma in Librarianship, 1955; MA, 1960, University of London. *Publications:* W H Auden: A Bibliography, (with E. Mendelson), 1972; Philip Larkin: A Bibliography, 1979; Theses on Asia, 1967; Author Index British Little Magazines; 1976. *Contributions to:* Numerous articles to Literary, Library and Bibliographical magazines. *Honour:* Fellow, Library Association, 1950. *Memberships include:* Bibliographical Society, former President; Oxford Bibliographical Society; Cambridge Bibliographical Society; Bibliographical Society of America; Royal Asiatic Society. *Address:* Brambling, 24 Oxenturn Road, Wye, Kent TN25 5BE, England.

BLOTNER Joseph, b. 1923, United States of America. Writer (Literature, Biography). *Appointments:* Assistant Professor, 1955-61, Associate Professor of English, 1961-68, University of Virginia, Charlottesville; Professor of English, University of North Carolina, Chapel Hill, 1968-71; Professor of English, University of Michigan, Ann Arbor, 1971-. *Publications:* The Political Novel, 1955; The Fiction of J.D. Salinger (with F.L. Gwynn), 1959; Faulkner in the University (with F.L. Gwynn), 1959; William Faulkner's Library: A Catalogue, 1964; The Modern American Political Novel 1900-1960, 1966; Faulkner: A Biography, 2 vols, 1974, 1984; Selected Letters of William Faulkner, 1977; Uncollected Stories of William Faulkner, 1979; Faulkner: A Biography (rev.) I vol, 1984; William Faulkner Novels: 1930-1935, 1986; William Faulkner Manuscripts, 1987; William Faulkner Novels: 1936-1940, 1990. *Address:* 1031 Belmont Road, Ann Arbor, MI 48104, USA.

BLUE Marian Vivian, b. 27 Mar 1947, Denver, Colorado, USA. Writer. *Education:* BS, Mankato State University, Mankato, Minnesota, 1986. *Appointments:* Editor, Tanners Creek Publishers, Norfolk, Virginia, 1992-; Poetry Editor, Ghent Magazine, Norfolk, 1992-. *Publications:* Southeast Writers' Handbook, 1992. *Contributions to:* North Country Anvil; Cruising World; The Amaranth Review; Mankato Poetry Review; Motor Boat and Yachting; Dominion Review; Christian Science Monitor. *Honours:* Art of Peace Award, 1983; Virginia Press Award, 1990; Poetry Society of Virginia, 1991. *Address:* 527 Delaware Avenue, Norfolk, VA 23508, USA.

BLUESTONE Irving J, b. 5 Jan 1917, New York City, New York, USA. Professor; Retired Vice-President, United Auto Workers Union. m. Zelda F Bluestone, 28 June 1940, 1 son, 2 daughters. *Education:* BA, City College of New York, 1937; Graduate study, University of Bern, Switzerland, 1937-38. *Publications:* Aging of the American Work Force (edited with John Owen and Rhonda Montgomery), 1988; Negotiating The Future (with Barry Bluestone), 1992. *Contributions to:* The New Track of US Labor Relations, to Workplace Democracy, 1987; The Presidential Primary: A Faulty Process (with Douglas Fraser), to New England Journal of Public Policy, 1990; Needed: Millions of Late Bloomers, to

Options, 1990. *Honours:* Certificate of Commendation, Michigan State Senate and House of Representatives, 1980; Walter P Reuthers Solidarity Award, 1980; Certificate of Merit, National Association for the Advancement of Colored People, 1981; Townsend Harris Award, City College of New York, 1985. *Memberships:* Phi Beta Kappa; Industrial Relations Research Association; American Association of University Professors. *Address:* Reuther Library, Wayne State University, 5401 Cass, Detroit, MI 48202, USA.

BLUM Lawrence Alan, b. 16 Apr 1943, Baltimore, Maryland, USA. Professor. m. Judith Ellen Smith, 22 June 1975, 1 son, 2 daughters. *Education:* BA, Princeton University, 1964; Linacre College, Oxford University, 1968-69; PhD Harvard University, 1974. *Publications:* Friendship, Altruism And Morality; A Truer Liberty: Simone Weil & Marxism. *Memberships:* American Philosophical Association. *Address:* 149 Prospect Street, Cambridge, MA 02139, USA.

BLUM Mark Emanuel, b. 17 July 1937, Philadelphia, USA. Cultural Historian; Educator. *Education:* BA, Government, Franklin and Marshall, 1959; MA, English History, 1961, PhD European History, 1970, University of Pennsylvania. *Publications:* The Austro-Marxists, 1890-1918, A Psychobiographical Study, 1985; Ethical Citzenship Education Policies and Programs: A National Survey of State Education Agencies, 1977; Developing Educational Programs for the High-Risk Secondary and Education Programs for the High-Risk Secondary and College Student, 1982. *Contibutor to:* various journals and magazines. *Honours:* Pi Gamma Mu; Fulbright Fellow, Austria, 1965; Visting Fellow Centre for Studies of the Person (Carl Rogers) 1971. *Memberships:* Executive Secretary Kentucky Conference; American Association of University Professors. *Address:* Dept of History, University of Louisville, KY 40292, USA.

BLUM Richard A, b. 28 July 1943, Brooklyn, New York, USA. Television Programme Development Executive; Writer; Educator. *Education:* BA, Fairleigh Dickinson University, 1965; MS, Boston University, 1967; PhD, University of Southern California, 1977. *Appointments:* Professor, Screenwriting, University of Maryland, 1983-; Visiting Professor, Screenwriting: Harvard University Summer School, 1984, 1985, 1986; American Film Institute, 1983, 1984, 1986; The Writers Centre, 1984-88. *Publications:* Television Writing: From Cencept to Contract, 1980, 1984; American Film Acting, 1984; Primetime: Network TV Programming, (co-author), 1987. *Contributions to:* The Writer; The Scriptwriter; Educational Editor; Journal of Performing Arts Review. Television Writer, Producer, PBS, NBC-TV, Universal Studios, Columbia Pictures-TV. *Honours:* Best Playwrite, FDU, 1964, 1965; Media Programme Supervisor, NEH, Washington DC, 1978-81; Creative and Performing Arts Award, University of Maryland, 1987; Judge, Nicholl Screenwriting Fellowships, Academy of Motion Pictures Arts & Sciences, 1987, 1988; Judge, Public Television Awards, Corporation for Public Broadcasting, 1988; Ford Foundation Fellowship, 1988. *Memberships:* Writers Guild of America; Academy of Television Arts and Sciences; University Film & Video Association; Broadcast Education Association; Washington Independent Writers. *Address:* 2208 Washington Avenue, Silver Spring, MD 20910, USA.

BLUMBERG Stanley A, b. 11 Apr 1912, USA. Writer. m. 2 Aug 1952. *Education:* University of Maryland, 1931; Johns Hopkins University, 1932. *Publications:* Energy and Conflict - The Life and Times of Edward Teller, 1976; The Survival Factor, Israeli Intelligence from World War I to the Present, 1981; Edward Teller, Giant of the Golden Age of Physics, 1990. *Contributions to:* The Nation; Baltimore Sun; USA Today; Hepkin Magazine; Human Events. *Membership:* Literary Guild. *Address:* 6000 Ivydene Terrace, Baltimore, MD 21209, USA.

BLUME Judy, b. 12 Feb 1938, Elizabeth, New Jersey, USA. Writer. 1 son, 1 daughter. *Education:* BS, New York University, 1961. *Publications:* Are You There, God? It's Me Margaret; Blubber; Deenie; Freckle Juice; Iggie's House; It's Not the End of the World; The One in the Middle is the Green Kangaroo; Otherwise Known as Sheila the Great; Starring Sally J. Freedman as Herself; Superfudge; Tales of a Fourth Grade Nothing; Then Again, Maybe I Won't; Tiger Eyes; The Pain and thee Great One; The Judy Blume Diary; Forever; Wifey; Smart Women; Letters to Judy: What Kids Wish They Could Tell You; Just as Long As We're Together. *Honours:* Recipient, numerous honours and awards. *Memberships:* Authors Guild Council; PEN; Board, Society of Children's Book Writers. *Address:* c/o Claire Smith, Harold Ober Associate Inc., 40 E. 49th Street, New York City, NY 10017, USA.

BLUMENTHAL John F, b. 5 Jan 1949, Middletown, New York, USA. Author; Screenwriter. m. Ingrid Van Eckert, 20 June 1983, 2 daughters. *Education:* BA, Tufts University, Cum Laude. *Publications:* Loves Reckless Rash; Case of the Tinseltown Murders; Case of the Hardboiled Dicks; History of Hollywood High; Official Hollywood Handbook; Screenplay, Short time. *Contributions to:* Playboy; Esquire; Oui; Punch; National Lampoon. *Memberships:* Writers Guild of America. *Literary Agent:* United Talent Agency. *Address:* 5123 Bellaire Avenue, North Hollywood, CA 91607. USA.

BLUNT Don. *See:* **BOOTH Edwin.**

BLY Robert (Elwood), b. 23 Dec 1926, Madison, Minnesota, USA. Poet; Writer; Translator. m. (1) Carolyn McLean, 1955 (divorced 1980), 4 children; (2) Ruth Counsell Ray, 1981. *Education:* St Olaf College, Northfield, Minnesota, 1946-47; BA, magna cum Laude, Harvard University, Cambridge, Massachusetts, 1950; MA, University of Iowa, Iowa City, 1956. Served in United States Naval Reserve 1944-46. *Appointments:* Founding Editor, The Fifties magazine (later The Sixties and The Seventies) and the Fifties Press (later The Sixties and The Seventies Press) Madison, Minnesota, 1958-. *Publications:* Verse includes: Finding an Old Ant Mansion, Bedford, Martin Booth, 1981; The Eight Stages of Translation, Boston, Rowan Tree, 1983; Four Ramages, Daleville, Indiana, Barnwood Press, 1983; Out of the Rolling Ocean, New York, Dial Press, 1984. Recording: Today's Poets 5, with others, Folkways. A Broadsheet Against the New York Times Book Review, Madison, Minnesota, Sixties Press, 1961; Talking All Morning: Collected Conversations and Interviews, Ann Arbor, University of Michigan Press, 1979. Editor and translator of numerous works. *Honours:* Fulbright Fellowship, 1956; Amy Lowell Travelling Fellowship, 1964; Guggenheim Fellowship, 1964, 1972; American Academy grant, 1965; Rockefeller Fellowship, 1967; National Book Award, 1968. *Address:* 308 First Street, Moose Lake, MN 55767, USA.

BLYTH Chay, b. 1940, England. Company Director; Managing Director. *Publications:* A Fighting Chance, 1967; Innocent Abroad, 1969; The Impossible Voyage, 1971; Theirs is the Glory, 1974. *Honours:* Holder, various records for sailing. *Address:* Penquite Farm, Rosecraddock, Liskeard, Cornwall, England.

BLYTH Myrna, b. 22 Mar 1939, New York City, USA. Editor. m. Jeffrey Blyth, 25 Nov 1962, 2 sons. *Education:* Bennington College, Vermont, 1960. *Appointments:* Senior Editor, Ingenue Magazine, New York, 1962-70; Senior Editor, Family Health Magazine, New York, 1972-73; Executive Editor, Family Circle, 1974-78; Publishing Director and Editor in Chief, Ladies' Home Journal, 1981-. *Publications:* For Better and For Worse, 1978; Cousin Suzanne, 1975. *Contributions to:* New Yorker; New York; Reader's Digest; McCall's; Cosmopolitan; redbook. *Memberships:* American Society of Magazine Editors, Executive Committee; Women's Media Group; Authors Guild; Board, Child Care Action Campaign. *Literary Agent:* Arthur Pine, New York. *Address:* 90 Riverside Drive, New York, NY 10024, USA.

BLYTHE Ronald George, b. 6 Nov 1922, Acton, Suffolk, England. Author. *Appointments:* Eastern Arts Association Literature Panel, 1975-84; Society of Authors Management Committee, 1979-84; Associate Editor, New Wessex Edition of The Works of Thomas Hardy, 1978. *Publications:* The Age of Illusion, 1963; Akenfield, 1969; The View in Winter, 1979; From the Headlands, 1982; Divine Landscapes, 1986; Each Returning Day, 1989; William Hazlitt: Selected Writings (edited), 1970; The Stories of Ronald Blythe, 1985; Divine Landscapes 1986; Each Returning Day, 1989; Private Words, 1991. Critical studies of Jane Austen, Thomas Hardy, Leo Tolstoy, Literature of the Second World War. *Contributions to:* Observer; Sunday Times; New York Times; The Listener; Atlantic Monthly; London Magazine; Tablet; New Statesman; Bottegue Oscure; Guardian. *Honours:* Fellow, Royal Society of Literature, 1969; Heinemann Award, 1969; Society of Authors Travel Scholarship, 1970; Angel Prize, 1986; Honorary MA, University of East Anglia, 1990. *Memberships:* Royal Society of Literature; Society of Authors; President, The John Clare Society; Fabian Society. *Literary Agent:* Deborah Rogers, London. *Address:* Bottengoms Farm, Wormingford, Colchester, Essex, England.

BOARD Joan, m. Michael Board, 12 Apr 1952, 2 daughters. *Education:* BA, 1950; Diploma in Education, 1951. Publications: Candles; A Country Christmas; Babworth A Celebration; The Old North Road; Poems for Infants. *Contributions to:* In The Gold of Flesh; Shorts from South Yorkshire; Poems & Stories Broadcast. *Honours:* Awards in Charnwood Competitions; 1st Prize Rotherham Long Poem Competition. *Memberships:* Sheffield Writers Club; Chairman Sheffield Writers Club. *Address:* 34 Lime Tree Avenue, Retford, Notts, DN22 7BA, England.

BOARDMAN John, b. 1927, United Kingdom. Professor of Classical Art and Archaeology. *Appointments:* Assistant Keeper, Ashmolean Museum, 1955-59, Reader in Classical Archaeology, 1959-78, Lincoln Professor of Classical Art and Archaeology, 1978-, University of Oxford; Editor, Journal of Hellenic Studies, 1958-65; Co-Editor, Oxford Monographs in Classical Archaeology; Delegate, OUP, 1979-89. *Publications:* S Marinatos and M Hirmer: Crete and Mycenae (translator), 1960; The Cretan Collection in Oxford, 1961; Island Gems, 1963; The Date of the Knossos Tablets, 1963; The Greeks Overseas, 1964, 1974, 1980; Greek Art, 1964, 1973; Excavations at Tocra (with J Hayes), 2 vols, 1966-73; Die Griechische Kunst (with J Dorig, W Fuchs, M Hirmer), 1966; Greek Emporio, 1967; Pre-Classical Style and Civilisation, 1967; Engraved Gems, the Ionides Collection, 1968; Archaic Greek Gems, 1968; Greek Gems and Finger Rings, 1970; The European Community in Prehistory (edited with M Brown and T Powell), 1971; Greek Burial Customs (with D C Kurtz), 1971; Athenian Black Figure Vases, 1974; Athenian Red Figure Vases: The Archaic Period: A Handbook, 1975; The Ralph Harari Collection of Finger Rings (with D Scarisbrick), 1978; Eros in Greece (with E la Rocca), 1978; Greek Sculpture, Archaic Period, 1978; Catalogue of Gems and Finger Rings (with M L Vollenweider), vol I, 1978; Castle Ashby Corpus Vasorum (with M Robertson), 1979; Greek Sculpture, Classical Period, 1985; The Parthenon and its Sculptures, 1985; Athenian Red Figure Vases: Classical Period, 1989. *Honours:* Kt, 1989; Professor of Ancient History, Royal Academy, 1989-. *Memberships:* Fellow, British Academy, 1969-. *Address:* 11 Park Street, Woodstock, Oxford, OX20 1SJ, England.

BOAST Philip James, b. 30 Apr 1952, London, England. Writer. m. Rosalind Thorpe, 20 June 1981, 2 sons, 1 daughter. *Education:* Mill Hill School, 1965-69. *Publications:* London's Child; London's Millionare; Watersmeet; Pride; London's Daughter; The Assassinators. *Contributions to:* Science Fiction Monthly. *Literary Agent:* Carol Smith. *Address:* Rhydda Bank Cottage, Trentishoe, Parracombe, Barnstaple, N Devon EX31 4PL, England.

BOCOCK Robert James, b. 29 Sept 1940, England. Senior Lecturer in Social Science. *Publications:* Freud and Modern Society, 1976; Sigmund Freud, 1983; Ritual in Industrial Society, 1974; Hegemony, 1986. *Contributor to:* British Journal of Sociology; Sociology. *Membership:* British Sociological Association. *Literary Agent:* A D Peters, London. *Address:* Department of Sociology, Faculty of Social Sciences, Crowther Building, The Open University, Walton Hall, Milton Keynes, Buckinghamshire, England.

BODA Laszlo (Ladislas), b. 23 Nov 1929, Dregelypalank, Hungary. Professor. *Education include:* Doctor of Theology, Budapest, 1955. *Appointments:* Professor of Philosophy, Esztergom, 1955-73; Professor ordinarius, of Moral Theology, Budapest, 1973-. *Publications:* Moral Theology (I-IV), 1980; Moral Theology of the Christian Maturity, 1986; Inner Performance, a postmodern epos adpated from Dante (Hungarian: Belso szinjatek), 1986; To be Human or to have?, 1990; Your Way to Marriage, for young people, 1990; Give to God what is God's, 1991; Inkulturation, Church, Europe (first book of the European inkulturation), forthcoming. *Contributions:* In Hungarian to: Vigilia; Teologia; Diakonia; Others; Articles to: New Man (Uj Ember); About 25 to various journals; About 50 to periodical reviews; In German to: Arzt und Christ; Folia Theologica; Others. *Memberships:* Conferences of European Moral Theology; Societas Ethica; European Theology; Society of Peace and Human Understanding; Society of St Stephen, Hungary; Society of Johannes Messner, Vienna, 1993. *Address:* David F u 7, Fsz 3, H-1113 Budapest XI, Hungary.

BODE Friedrich Andreas, b. 27 Dec 1942, Leipzig, Germany. Historian; Librarian. m. Nina Georgievna Kulikovsky, 22 Aug 1974, 1 daughter. *Education:* Magister Artium, University of Munich, 1971; Educational visits, Sweden and USSR, 1971-73; Dr phil, 1975. *Appointments:* Male Nurse, Federal Republic of Germany, 1965-66; Librarian, University of Bamberg, 1977-78; Chief Librarian, University of Arts, Berlin, 1978-83; Director, 1983-, Library Director, 1992-, International Youth Library, Munich; Researcher. *Publications:* Die Flottenpolitik Katharinas II und die Konflikte mit Schweden und der Turkei (1768-1792), 1979; Die Kunstlerin Ida Bohattalta-Morpurgo, 1988; Lászlo Reber-Illustrator und Buchkunstler, 1992. *Contributions to:* Suddeutsche Zeitung newspaper; Bruno Paul as Direktor der Unterrichtsanstalt des Kunstgewerbemuseums, 1982; Gluck einer fernen Gegenwart: Erinnerungen an das Landhaus des Verlegers Goschen, 1988; Humor in the Lyrical Stories for Children of Samuel Marshak and Korney Chukovsky, 1989; Leben im Thomanerchor, 1990. *Memberships:* Wilhelm- Busch-Gesellschaft; Verein deutscher Bibliothekare. *Address:* Dall'Armistr 44, D-8000 Munich 19, Germany.

BODLEY Harley Ryan Jr, b. 24 Nov 1936, Dover, Delaware, USA. Broadcaster; Writer. m. Patricia Jean Hall, 4 Dec 1981. *Education:* BA, University of Delaware, 1959; Graduate study, American University, 1960. *Appointments:* Sports editor, Delaware State News, Dover, 1959-60; Sports Writer, 1960-63, Night Sports Editor 1963-67, Assistant Sports Editor, 1967-71; Sports Editor 1971-82, News-Journal Papers, Wilmington, Delaware; Baseball Editor, USA Today, Washington DC, 1982-; Sports Director of WDOV-Radio, Dover, 1958-62; Daily Broadcaster of USA Today Radio Report; Commentator for NBC Sports. *Publications:* I Learned to Fly, So Can You, 1967; The Team That Wouldn't Die, 1981; Countdown to Cobb, 1985. *Contributor to:* Writer for Gannett News Service; Author of regular column in USA Today. *Honours:* Twelve Sportswriter of the Year Awards from National Sportscasters and Sportswriters Association, 1961-79; Mark Twain Award from Associated Press, 1980, for superior coverage of college basketball; Best of Gannett Award from Gannett Co, Inc, 1981, for a collection of columns written throughout the year; Twenty-Five-Year Award from the Commissioner of Baseball, 1983, for coverage of major league baseball on a regular basis for twenty-five years. *Memberships:* Associated Press Sports Editors, President 1981-82; Baseball Writers Association of America (Chairman of Philadelphia chapter 1977-78), Wilmington Sportswriters and Broadcasters, President 1963, Sigma Delta Chi. *Literary Agent:* Edward J Acton Inc, 928 Broadway, New York, NY 10010, USA. *Address:* USA Today, P O Box 500, Washington DC 20044, USA.

BOECKMAN Charles, b. 9 Nov 1920, San Antonio, Texas, USA. Author. m. Patricia Kennelly, 25 July 1965, 1 daughter. *Appointment:* Free Lance Writer, 1950-. *Publications:* Maverick Brand, 1961; Unsolved Riddles of the Ages, 1965; Cool, Hot and Blue, 1968; And the Beat Goes On, 1972; Surviving Your Parents' Divorce, 1980; Remember Our Yesterdays, 1991; House of Secrets, 1992; Author of over 1000 short stories and articles, and many anthologies. *Honours:* Mr Banjo, selected for Anthology, Best Detective Stories of the Year, 1979. *Membership:* American Society of Journalists and Authors. *Address:* 322 Del Mar Blvd, Corpus Christi, TX 78404, USA.

BOER Charles, b. 1939, USA. Professor of English and Comparative Literature. *Appointments:* Assistant Professor, 1966-70, Associate Professor, 1970-75, Professor of English and Comparative Literature, 1975-, University of Connecticut, Storrs. *Publications:* The Odes, 1969; The Homeric Hymns, translation, 1971; The Bacchae of Euripides, translation, 1972; Varmint Q: An Epic Poem on the Life of William Clarke Quantrill, 1972; The Maximus Poems of Charles Olson (edited with G Butterick), vol III, 1974; Charles Olson in Connecticut, 1975; Marsilio Ficino: The Book of Life, translation, 1980. *Address:* Box 69, Pomfret Center, CT 06259, USA.

BOESCH Hans, b. 13 Mar 1926, Frumsen, Sennwald, Switzerland. Traffic Engineer. m. Mathilde Kerler, 1 July 1950, 3 daughters. *Education:* HTL Winterthur, 1941-46. *Appointments:* Hed, Transport Planning, Baudirektion Kanton Aargau; Scientific Collaborator, Dozent, ORL-Institut, ETH Zurich. *Publications include:* Der junge Os, novel, 1957; Das Gerust, novel, 1960; Die Fliegenfalle, novel, 1968; Menschen im Bau, stories, 1970; Ein David, poems, 1980; Der Mensch im Stadtverkehr, essay, 1975; Der Kiosk, novel, 1978; Unternehmen Normkopf, satire, 1985; Der Sog, novel, 1988. *Contributions to:* Neue Zurcher Seitung, Zurich; Tages-Anzeiger, Zurich; Schweizer Monatshefte, Zurich. *Honours include:* C F Meyer Prize, 1954; Medal of Honour, City of Zurich, 1970, 1978; Prize for Literature, Canton of Aargau, 1983; Prize, Schillerstiftung, 1988; International Bodensee Prize for Literature, 1989; Various, Pro Helvetia and Canton of Zurich. *Address:* Eichstr 10a, 8712 Stafa, Switzerland.

BOGARDE Dirk, b. 1921, United Kingdom. Film Actor; Author. *Publications:* A Postillion Struck by Lightning, autobiography, 1977; Snakes and Ladders, autobiography, 1978; A Gentle Occupation, novel, 1980; Voices in the Garden, novel, 1981; An Orderly Man, autobiography, 1983; West of Sunset, novel, 1984; Backcloth, autobiography, 1986; A Particular Friendship Letters, 1989; Great Meadow, 1992. *Honour:* Kt, 1992. *Address:* c/o J A A, 2 Goodwins Court, London W1, England.

BOGDANOR Vernon, b. 16 July 1943, London, England. University Lecturer, Reader in Government Oxford University, 1990. m. Judith Beckett, 23 July 1972, 2 sons. *Education:* BA, 1st class Honours, Philosophy, Politics and Economics 1964, MA 1968, Oxford University. *Publications:* Devolution, 1979; The People and The Party System, 1981; Multi-Party Politics and The Constitution, 1983; What is Proportional Representation? A Guide to the Issues, 1984; (ed) Representatives of the Poeple, 1985; (ed) Blacknells Encyclopedia of Political Institutions, 1987; (ed) Constitutions in Democratic Politics, 1988. *Contributions to:* Encounter; Political Quarterly; Public Law; Government and Opposition. *Honours:* Fellow of Braserose College, Oxford, 1966. *Membership:* Council

of Hansard Society for Parliamentary Government; Fellow of Royal Society of Arts, 1992. *Literary Agent:* Caradoc King, A P Watt & Son. *Address:* Brasenose College, Oxford OX1 4AS, England.

BOGDANOVICH Peter, b. 30 July 1939, Kingston, New York, USA. Film Director; Writer; Producer; Actor. m. (1) Polly Platt, 1962, divorced 1970, 2 daughter. (2) L B Straten, 1988. *Appointments:* Film Feature-Writer, Esquire, New York Times, Village Voice, Cahiers du Cinema, Los Angeles Times, New York Magazine, Vogue, Variety, and others, 1961-. *Publications:* The Cinema of Orson Welles, 1961; The Cinema of Howard Hawks, 1962; The Cinema of Alfred Hitchcock, 1963; John Ford, 1968; Fritz Lang in America, 1969; Allan Dwan: The Last Pioneer, 1971; Pieces of Time (Picture Shows in UK): Peter Bogdanovich on the Movies 1961-85, 1973, enlarged 1985; The Killing of the Unicorn: Dorothy Stratten (1960-1980), 1984; A Year and A Day Calendar (edited with introduction), 1991; This is Orson Wells, 1992. Films: The Wild Angels, 1966; Targets, 1968; The Last Picture Show, 1971; What's Up, Doc?, 1972; Paper Moon, 1973; Daisy Miller, 1974; At Long Last Love, 1975; Nickelodeon, 1976; Saint Jack, 1979; They All Laughed, 1981; Mask, 1985; Illegally Yours, 1988; Texasville, 1990; Noises Off, 1992; The Thing Called Love, 1993. *Honours include:* New York Film Critics' Award for Best Screenplay, British Academy Award for Best Screenplay, 1971; Writer's Guild of America Award for Best Screenplay, 1972; Silver Shell, Mar del Plata, Spain, 1973; Best Director, Brussels Festival, 1974; Pasinetti Award, Critics Prize, Venice Festival, 1979. *Memberships:* Directors Guild of America; Writer's Guild of America; Academy of Motion Picture Arts and Sciences. *Address:* c/o William Peiffer, 2040 Avenue of the Stars, Century City, CA 90067, USA.

BOGGS Jean Sutherland, b. 1922. Chairman, Chief Executive Officer, Canadian Museums Construction Corporation. *Publications:* Portraits by Degas, 1962; The National Gallery of Canada, 1971. *Address:* PO Box 395, Station A, Ottawa, Ontario, Canada K1N 8V4.

BOHIGIAN Valerie, b. New York City, USA. Author. m. Haig Bohigian, 4 Aug 1970, 2 daughters. *Education:* BA, English; MA, English; Ph.D, Criminal Justice. *Appointments:* Editorial Consultant, Self Reliant Trader's Journal, Tradeworld News. *Publications:* Successful Flea Market Selling, 1981; How to Make Your Home-Based Business Grow, 1984; Real Money From Home, 1985; Ladybacks, 1987. *Contributions include:* Woman's Day; Woman; Nations Business; American Way; INC; Redbook; Self-Reliant; New Woman; Trader's Journal; Fifty Plus; Tradeworld News; The Writer. *Memberships:* American Society of Journalists and Authors. *Address:* 225 Hunter Ave, North Tarrytown, NY 10591, USA

BOISDEFRE Pierre Jules Marie Raoul (Neraud le Mouton de), b. 11 July 1926, Paris France. Writer; Diplomatist; Broadcasting Official. m. Beatrice Wiedemann-Goiran, 1957, 2 sons. *Education:* Ecole Libre des Sciences Politiques; Ecole Nationale d'Administration; Harvard University, USA. *Appointments:* Director of Sound Broadcasting, Office de Radiodiffusion et Television Francaise (ORTF), 1963-68; Cultural Counsellor, French Embassy, London 1968-71; Brussels, 1972-77; Ministry of Foreign Affairs 1977-78; Minister Plenipotentiary, 1979; Ambassador to Uruguay 1981-84, Colombia 1984-88. *Publications:* Metamorphose de la litterature, 2 volumes, 1950; Ou va le Roman?, 19662; Les ecrivains français d'aujourd'hui, 1963; Histoire de la litterature, 1930-85, 2 volumes, 1985; Lettre ouverte aux hommes de gauche, 1969; La foi des anciens jours, 1977; Le roman français depuis 1900, 1979; Les nuits, l'Ile aux livres, Paroles de vie, La Belgique, 1980, Various critical portraits. *Honours:* Numerous national awards, including Prix de la Critique, 1950; Doctor honoris causa, Universities of Hull (Great Britain) and Bogota (Colombia); Officier de la Legiòn d'honneur Commandeur de l'ordre national du Merite. *Address:* 5 cite Vaneau, 75007 Paris, France.

BOISSEVAIN Jeremy (Fergus), b. 1928, United Kingdom. Professor of Social Anthropology. *Publications:* Saints and Fireworks: Religion and Politics in Rural Malta, 1965, 2nd Edition, 1969; Hal-Farrug: A Village in Malta, 1969; The Italians of Montreal: Social Adjustment in a Plural Society, 1970; Network Analysis: Studies in Human Interaction (edited with J C Mitchell), 1973; Friends of Friends: Networks, Manipulators and Coalitions, 1974; Beyond the Community: Social Process in Europe (edited with J Friedl), 1975. *Address:* Sarphatiestraat 105A, 1018 6V Amsterdam, Netherlands.

BOLAND Michael John, b. 14 Nov 1950, Kingston, Surrey, England. Poet; Civil Servant. *Education:* Shene CountyGrammer School. *Publications:* The Midnight Circus. *Contributions to:* Poems in Envoi; Purple Patch; Various Anthologies. *Honours:* Patrica Chown Sonnet Award. *Memberships:* PEN; Penman Club; Society of Civil Service Authors; Keats Shelley Memorial Association; Wordsworth Trust; Friends of Coleridge; MIAP. *Address:* 30 Byron Court, Byron Road, Harrow, HA1 1JT, England.

BOLD Alan, b. 20 Apr 1943, Edinburgh, Scotland. Writer. m. Alice Howell, 29 June 1963. 1 daughter. *Education:* Edinburgh University. *Publications include:* To Find the New, verse, 1967; A Perpetual Motion Machine, verse, 1969; In This Corner: Selected Poems, verse, 1983; The Edge of the Wood, stories, 1984; MacDiarmid, biography, 1988; A Burns Companion, criticism, 1991; East is West, novel, 1991. *Contributions:* Weekly review for Glasgow Herald; Sunday Times; Modern Painters. *Honours:* McVitie's Prize for 1989 Scottish Writer of the Year; Arts Award, Royal Philosophical Society of Glasgow, 1990; Honorary President, Auchinleck Boswell Society, 1992. *Membership:* Society of Authors. *Address:* Balbirnie Burns East Cottage, nr Markinch, Glenrothes, Fife KY7 6NE, Scotland.

BOLT David Michael Langstone, b. 30 Nov 1927, Harrow, England. Literary Agent. m. Sally Hall, 8 Aug 1970, 3 sons, 3 daughters. *Education:* Dulwich College, Matric, 1935-39. *Appointments:* Publishers Reader, Hutchinson, 1954; Bookseller, Director, David Higham Association, Bolt Watson, Now Own Agency. *Publications:* Adam; Gurkhas; Samson; An Authors Handbook; The Albatross; A cry Ascending; The Man Who Did; Of Heaven, And Hope; The Moon princes. *Contributions to:* Womens Magazines; A Book of Peace; Great Lives of Antiquity; The Book of Books. *Memberships:* Savage Club. *Literary Agent:* David Bolt Associates. *Address:* 12 Heath Drive, Send, Surrey, GU23 7EP, England.

BOLT Robert (Oxton), b. 15 Aug 1924, Manchester, Lancashire, England. Playwright. m. (1) Celia Ann Roberts, 1949 (marriage dissolved 1967), 1 son, 2 daughters; (2) actress Sarah Miles, 1967 (divorced 1976), 1 son; (3) Ann, Lady Queensberry, 1980 (divorced 1985). *Education:* Graduated Manchester Grammar School, 1940; Manchester University, 1943, 1946-49, BA (hons) History, 1949; Exeter University, 1949-50, Teaching Diploma 1950. Served in the Royal Air Force, 1943-44, in the Royal West African Frontier Force, 1944-46, Lieutenant. *Appointments:* Office boy, Sun Life Assurance Company, Manchester, 1942; Schoolmaster, Bishopsteignton, Devon, 1950-15 and Millfield School, Street, Somerset, 1952-58. *Publications:* Plays include: A Man for All Seasons (broadcast 1954; produced London 1960, New York, 1961) London, Heinemann 1960, New York, Random House, 1962; Doctor Zhivago: The screenplay based on the novel by Boris Pasternak, London Harvill Press and New York, Random House, 1966; Brother and Sister (produced Brighton, 1967; revised version produced Bristol 1968); Vivat! Vivat Regina! (produced Chichester and London, 1970; New York, 1972) London, Heinemann, 1971, New York, Random House, 1972; State of Revolution (produced London, 1977) London, Heinemann, 1977. Screenplays: Lawrence of Arabia, 1962; Doctor Zhivago, 1965; A Man for All Seasons,

1966; Ryan's Daughter, 1970; Lady Caroline Lamb, 1973; The Bounty, 1984; The Mission, 1986. Director of film, Lady Caroline Lamb 1973. Author of radio plays. *Honours:* Evening Standard award 1957, for screenplay 1987; New York Drama Critics Circle award, 1962; BAFTA award 1962, 1966; Oscar 1966, 1967; New York Film Critics award. 1966; Golden Globe award for screenplay, 1967; LLD, Exeter University, 1977; CBE 1972. *Literary Agent:* Margaret Ramsay Ltd, London. *Address:* c/o Margaret Ramsay Ltd, 14A Goodwin's Court, St Martin's Lane, London WC2N 4LL, England.

BOLTON Elizabeth. *See:* **JOHNSTONE Norma.**

BOMBECK Erma Louise, b. 21 Feb 1927, Dayton, Ohio, USA. Author; Syndicated Columnist. m. William L. Bombeck, 13 Aug 1949, 2 sons, 1 daughter. *Education:* BA, University of Dayton, 1949. *Publications:* At Wit's End, 1967; Just Wait Till You Have Children of Your Own!, 1971; I Lost Everything in the Post-Natal Depression, 1974; The Grass is Always Greener over the Septic Tank, 1976; If Life is a Bowl of Cherries - What am I doing in the Pits, 1978; Aunt Erma's Cope Book, 1979; Motherhood: The Second Oldest Profession, 1983; Family - The Ties that Bind .. And Gag!, 1987; I Want to Grow Hair, I Want to Grow up, I Want to go to Boise, 1989; When You Look Like Your Passport Photo, It's Time to Go Home, 1991. *Honours:* Theta Sigma Phi Headliner Award, 1969; Mark Twain Award, 1973; 15 Honorary Doctorates, 1974-90; Golden Plate Award, American Academy of Achievement, 1978; Grand Marshal, Tournament of Roses Parade, 1986; American Cancer Society Medal of Honor, 1990. *Address:* Universal Press Syndicate, 4900 Main Street, Kansas City, MO 64112, USA.

BONAR Veronica. *See:* **BAILEY Veronica Anne.**

BOND Alma Halbert, b. 6 Feb 1923, Philadephina, USA. Author. m. Rudy Bond, 1 Feb 1948, 2 sons, 1 daughter. *Education:* BA, Temple University, 1944; Post Doctoral Training, NPAP, 1953-60; MA, NYU, 1951; PhD, Columbia University, 1961. *Publications:* Dream portrait; America's First Woman Warrior: The Courage of Deborah Sampson; Is There Life After Analysis?; Who Killed Vriginia Woolf?. *Contributions to:* Chapters inc, The Resolution of a Paranoid Episode in the First Year of a Lengthy First Year Treatment; Articles inc, International Journal of Psychoanalysis. *Honours:* Research grant; Honors in Psychology, Temple University; Honor award, Olney High school; Winner, Poetry Contest; Winner Oratorical Contest; Best Thespian Award. *Memberships:* International Psychoanalytic Association; Institute for Psychoanalytic Training & Research; American Psychological Association. *Literary Agent:* Jane Dystal. *Address:* 606 Truman Avenue 1, Key West, FL 33040, USA.

BOND Edward, b. 1934, United Kingdom. Playwright; Songwriter. *Publications:* Saved, 1966; Narrow Road to the Deep North, 1968; Early Morning, 1968; The Pope's Wedding and Other Plays, 1971; Lear, 1972; The Sea, 1973; Bingo: Scenes of Money and Death, 1974; Spring's Awakening (adaptor), 1974; The Fool, 1975; We Come to the River, libretto, 1976; A-A-America - The Swing and Grandma Faust, 1976; A-A-America, and Stone, 1976; Plays, 2 vols, 1977-78; The Woman, 1978; The Bundle, 1978; Theatre Poems and Songs, 1978; The Worlds, 1980; The Cat, libretto, 1980; The Restoration, 1981; Summer, 1982; Human Cannon, 1985; War Plays (Red, Black and Ignorant; The Tin Can Riots; Great Peace), 1985; Jackete, 1988; In The Company of Men, 1988; Notes on Post-Modernism, 1988; September, 1988; Olly's Prison (3 TV plays), 1992; Tuesday (TV Play), 1993. *Literary Agent:* Margaret Ramsay Ltd, England. *Address:* c/o Margaret Ramsay Ltd, 14A Goodwin's Court, London WC2N 4LL, England.

BOND Gillian. *See:* **MCEVOY Marjorie.**

BOND Michael, b. 1926. Author. *Publications:* A Bear

Called Paddington, 1958; More About Paddington, 1959; Paddington Helps Out, 1960; Paddington Abroad, 1961; Paddington at Large, 1962; Paddington Marches On, 1964; Paddington at Work, 1966; Here Comes Thursday, 1966; Thursday Rides Again, 1968; Paddington Goes to Town, 1968; Thursday Ahoy, 1969; Parsley's Tail, 1969; Parsley's Good Deed, 1969; Parsley's Problem Present, 1970; Parsley's Last Stand, 1970; Paddington Takes the Air, 1970; Thursday in Paris, 1970; Michael Bond's Book of Bears, 1971; Michael Bond's Book of Mice, 1971; The Day the Animals Went on Strike, 1972; Paddington Bear, 1972; Paddington's Garden, 1972; Parsley Parade, 1972; The Tales of Olga de Polga, 1972; Olga Meets her Match, 1973; Paddington's Blue Peter Story Book, 1973; Paddington at the Circus, 1973; Paddington Goes Shopping, 1973; Paddington at the Seaside, 1974; Paddington at the Tower, 1974; Paddington on Top, 1974; Windmill, 1975; How to Make Flying Things, 1975; Eight Olga Readers, 1975; Paddington's Cartoon Book, 1979; J D Polson and the Dillogate Affair, 1981; Paddington on Screen, 1981; Olga Takes Charge, 1982; The Caravan Puppets, 1983; Paddington at the Zoo, 1984; Paddington's Painting Exhibition, 1985; Elephant, 1985; Paddington Minds the House, 1986; Paddington at the Palace, 1986; Paddington's Busy Day, 1987; Paddington and the Magical Maze, 1987; (Adult Books) Monsieur Pamplemousse, 1983; Monsieur Pamplemousse and the Secret Mission, 1984; Monsieur Pamplemousse on the Spot, 1986; Monsieur Pamplemousse Takes the Cure, 1987; The Pleasures of Paris, Guide Book, 1987; Monsieur Pamplemousse Aloft, 1989; Monsieur Pamplemousse Investigates, 1990; Monsieur Pamplemousse Rest's His Case, 1991; Monsieur Pamplemousse Stands Firm, 1992. *Literary Agent:* Harvey Unna, London. *Address:* c/o Lemon Unna & Durbridge Ltd, 24 Pottery Lane, Holland Park, London W11 4LZ, England.

BOND Nancy Barbara, b. 8 Jan 1945, USA. Librarian; Writer. *Education:* BA, Mount Holyoke College, 1966; Dip Lib Wales, 1972, College of Librarianship Wales. *Appointment:* Instructor, part-time, Simmons College, Centre for the Study of Children's Literature, 1979-. *Publications:* A String in the Harp, 1976; The Best of Enemies, 1978; Country of Broken Stone, 1980; The Voyage Begun, 1981; A Place to Come Back To, 1984; Another Shore, 1988. *Honours:* A String in the Harp was awarded the International Reading Association Award 1976, Newbery Honour, 1976, Welsh Arts Council Tir na n'Og Award, 1976. *Address:* 109 The Valley Road, Concord, MA 01742, USA.

BOND Ruskin, b. 1934, India. Children's Writer. *Appointments:* Managing Editor, Imprint, Bombay, 1975-79. *Publications:* The Room on the Roof, 1956; Grandfather's Private Zoo, 1967; The Last Tiger, 1971; Angry River, 1972; The Blue Umbrella, 1974; Once upon a Monsoon Time, memoirs, 1974; Man of Destiny: A Biography of Jawaharlal Nehru, 1976; Night of the Leopard, 1979; Big Business, 1979; The Cherry Tree, 1980; The Road to the Bazaar, 1980; A Flight of Pigeons, 1980; The Young Vagrants, 1981; Flames in the Forest, 1981; The Adventures of Rusty, 1981; Tales and Legends of India, 1982; A Garland of Memories, 1982; To Live in Magic, 1982; Tigers Forever, 1983; Earthquakes, 1984; Getting Granny's Glasses, 1985; The Eyes of the Eagle, 1987; The Night Train at Deoli, short stories; Times Stops at Shamli, short stories, 1989; Ghost Trouble, 1989; Snake Trouble, 1990; Dust of the Mountain, 1990. *Address:* Ivy Cottage, Landour, Mussouri, UP 248179, India.

BONE J(esse) F, b. 1916, USA. Professor of Veterinary Medicine (retired); Science Fiction Writer. *Publications:* Observations of the Ovaries of Infertile and Reportedly Infertile Dairy Cattle, 1954; Animal Anatomy, 1958, Revised Edition, Animal Anatomy and Physiology, 1975, 1981, 1988; Canine Medicine (editor), 1959, 2nd Edition, 1962; The Lani People, 1962; Equine Medicine and Surgery (co-editor), 1963, 2nd Edition, 1972; Legacy, 1976; The Meddlers, 1976; Gift of the Manti (with R Myers), 1977; Confederation Matador, 1978;

Animal Anatomy and Physiology, 3rd revised edition, 1988. *Address:* 3017 Brae Burn, Sierra Vista, AZ 85635, USA.

BONESSIO di TERZET Ettore, b. Italy. Teaches Aesthetics at University of Genoa. *Education:* MA; PhD. *Literary Appointments:* Editor, Poetry, Art and Aesthetics Magazine, il Cobold. *Publications:* Solitudine e comunicazione estetica, 1974; Hegel e la poesia moderna, 1975; L'esperienza dell'arte, 1980; Il Principio della Parola (anthology of distinguished poetry after 1974), 1986; Configurazioni, 1990; Del Frammento organico, 1992; Lo Splendore del vuoto, 1993. *Contributions to:* Sulfur, USA; International Poetry, USA Tracce, Stilb, Spirali, Symbola, Il Farone, Altri Termini, Nuova Corrente, Artivisive, Studio Marconi, Filosofia Oggi, Italy; Vertice Portugal; XUL, Argentina; Differentia, USA; Anterem, Alfabeta, Italy; Effects, USA. *Address:* CP 707, 16100 Genova AD Italy.

BONHAM Barbara, (Sara North), b. 1926, USA. Author. *Publications:* Diagnosis: Love, 1964; Challenge of the Prairie, 1965; Army Nurse, 1965; Nine Stewart, R.N., 1966; Crisis at Fort Laramie, 1967; To Secure the Blessings of Liberty, 1970; Willa Cather, 1970; Heroes of the Wild West, 1970; Proud Passion, 1976; Sweet and Bitter Fancy, 1976; Passion's Price, 1977; Dance of Desire, 1978; Jasmine for My Grave (as Sarah North), 1978; The Dark Side of Passion, 1980; Green Willow, 1982; Bittersweet, 1984.

BONHAM Frank, b. 1914, USA. Author; Playwright. *Publications:* Lost Stage Valley, 1948; Bold Passage, 1950; Blood on the Land, 1952; Snaketrack, 1952; The Outcast of Crooked River, 1953; Night Raid, 1954; The Feud at Spanish Fort, 1954; Hardrock, 1956; Border Guns, 1956; Last Stage West, 1957; Tough Country, 1958; The Sound of Gunfire, 1960; One for Sleep, 1960; Burma Rifles: A Story of Merrill's Marauders, 1960; The Skin Game, 1961; Trago..., 1962; Defiance Mountain, 1962; War Beneath the Sea, 1962; By Her Own Hand, 1963; Deepwater Challenge, 1963; Honor Bound, 1963; The Loud, Resounding Sea, 1963; Cast a Long Shadow, 1964; Rawhide Guns, 1964; Logan's Choice, 1964; Speedway Contender, 1964; Durango Street, 1965; Mystery in Little Tokyo, 1966; Mystery of the Red Tide, 1966; The Ghost Front, 1968; Mystery of the Fat Cat, 1968; The Nitty Gritty, 1968; The Vagabundos, 1969; Viva Chicano, 1970; Chief, 1971; Cool Cat, 1971; The Friends of the Loony Lake Monster, 1972; Hey, Big Spender, 1972; A Deam of Ghosts, 1973; The Golden Bees of Tulami, 1974; The Missing Persons League, 1976; The Rascals from Haskell's Gym, 1977; The Forever Formula, 1979; Break for the Border, 1980; Gimme an H Gimme an E Gimme an L Gimme a P, 1980; Fort Hogan, 1980; Premonitions, 1984. *Honours:* George G Stone Center for Children's Books Award, 1967. *Address:* Box 130, Skull Valley, AZ 86338, USA.

BONHAM-CARTER Victor, b. 1913, United Kingdom. Author. *Appointments:* Historian, Records Officer, Dartington Hall Estate, 1951-65; Secretary, Royal Literary Fund, 1966-82; Joint Secretary, Society of Authors, London, 1971-78. *Publications:* The English Village, 1952; Dartington Hall (with W B Curry), 1958; Exploring Parish Churches, 1959; Farming the Land, 1959; In a Liberal Tradition, 1960; Soldier True, US Edition The Strategy of Victory, 1965; Surgeon in the Crimea (editor), 1968; The Survival of the English Countryside, US Edition Land and Environment, 1971; Authors by Profession, 2 vols, 1978-84; The Essence of Exmoor, 1991. *Memberships:* Fellow, Royal Society of Literature. *Literary Agent:* Curtis Brown. *Address:* The Mount, Milverton, Taunton, Somerset TA4 1QZ, England.

BONINGTON Christian John Storey, b. 6 Aug 1934, Hampstead, London, England. Mountaineer; Writer; Photographer. m. Wendy Marchant, Mar 1962, 2 sons. *Education:* Royal Military Academy, Sandhurst; Honorary DSc, Sheffield and Lancaster Universities; Honorary MA, Salford University. *Publications:* I Chose to Climb, 1966; Annapurna South Face, 1971; The Next Horizon, 1973; Everest South West Face, 1973; Changabang (joint author), 1975; Everest The Hard Way, 1976; Quest For Adventure, 1981; Kongur-China's Elusive Summit, 1982; Everest-The Unclimbed Ridge (joint author), 1983; The Everest Years, 1986; Mountaineer-30 years of Climbing, 1989; The Climbers, 1992; Sea, Ice and Rock, (co-author with Robin Knox-Johnson), 1992. *Contributions to:* Numerous to magazines and journals. *Honours:* CBE, 1976; Founder's Medal, Royal Geographical Society, 1991. *Memberships:* President, Lepra; Past President, British Mountaineering Council; President, British Orienteering Foundation; Vice-President, British Lung Foundation; Vice President, Youth Hostel Association. *Literary Agent:* John Farquharson Ltd, Regent Street, London, England. *Address:* Badger Hill, Nether Row, Hesket Newmarket, Wigton, Cumbria, England.

BONNEFOY Yves Jean, b. 24 June 1923, Tours, France. Writer. m. Lucille Vine, 1968, 1 daughter. *Education:* Faculte des Sciences, Politiers; Faculte des Lettres, Paris; L es L. *Appointments:* Professor, College de France, 1981-; Lectures/seminars, Brandeis, Johns Hopkins, Princeton, Geneva, Nive, Yale & other universities. *Publications:* Poems: Du mouvement et de l'immobilite de Douve, 1953; Pierre ecrit, 1964; Selected Poems, 1968; Dans le leurre du seuil, 1975; Poems, 1947-75, 1978. Essays: L'Improbable, 1959; Arthur Rimbaud, 1961; Un reve fait a Mantoue, 1967; Le nuage rouge, 1977; Rue traversiere, 1977. On art: Peintures murales de la France Gothique, 1954; Miro, 1963; Rome 1630, 1969; L'Arriere-Pays, 1972; Entretiens sur la poesie, 1981; La Presence et l'Image , 1983; Ce qui fut sans lumière, 1987; Rècits en rêve, 1987. Other work: Hier regnant desert, 1958; Co-editor, L'Ephemere; translations of Shakespeare, Many books also in English. *Contributions to:* Mercure de France; Critique; Encounter; L'Ephemere. *Honours:* Prix Montaigne, 1980; Grand Prix de Poesie, Academie Francaise, 1981; Grand Prix Sociètè des bens de Lettres, 1987. *Address:* c/o College de France, 11 Place Marcelin-Berthelot, 75005 Paris, France.

BONNER Raymond Thomas, b. 11 Apr 1942, USA. Author; Journalist. *Education:* AB, MacMurray College, 1964; JD, Stanford Law School, 1967. *Publications:* Weakness and Deceit; US Policy and El Salvador, 1984; Waltzing with a Dictator: The Marcoses and the Making of American Policy, 1987. *Contributions to:* Numerous professional journals. *Honour:* Robert F. Kennedy Memorial Book Award, 1985. *Literary Agent:* Gloria Loomis, New York, USA. *Address:* 110 Riverside Drive, 4C, New York, NY 10024, USA.

BONNER Terry Nelson. *See:* **KRAUZER Steven M.**

BONSALL Crosby Newell, (Crosby Newell), b. 1921, USA. Children's Writer. *Appointments:* Worked in advertising agencies. *Publications:* The Surprise Party, 1955; Captain Kangaroo's Book, 1958; Polar Bear Brothers (as Crosby Newell), 1960; Kippy the Koala (as Crosby Newell), 1960; Tell Me Some More, 1961; Listen, Listen, 1961; Hurry Up, Slowpoke, 1961; Who's a Pest, 1962; Look Who's Talking, 1962; The Case of the Hungry Stranger, 1963; What Spot, 1963; Let Papa Sleep, reader, 1963; It's Mine, 1964; I'll Show You Cats, 1964; The Case of the Cat's Meow, 1965; The Case of the Dumb Bells, 1966; Here's Jellybean Reilly, 1966; Whose Eye Am I, 1968; The Case of the Scaredy Cats, 1971; The Day I Had to Play with My Sister, 1972; Mine's the Best, 1973; Piggle, 1973; And I Mean It, Stanley, 1974; Twelve Bells for Santa, 1977; The Goodbye Summer, 1979; Who's Afraid of the Dark, 1980; The Case of the Double Cross, 1980. *Address:* c/o Harper & Row Inc, 10 East 53rd Street, New York, NY 10022, USA.

BONTLY Thomas John, b. 25 Aug 1939, Madison, Wisconsin, USA. Professor of English. m. Marilyn R Mackie, 25 Aug 1963, 1 son. *Education:* BA, University of Wisconsin, 1961; Research Student, Corpus Christi College, Cambridge University, 1961-62; PhD, Stanford University, 1966. *Appointments:* Professor, English, 1966-, Coordinator, Creative Writing, 1975-78, 1968-89, University of Wisconsin, Milwaukee. *Publications:* The Competitor, 1966; The Adventures of a Young Outlaw, 1974; Celestial Chess, 1979; The Grants' Shadow, 1989. *Contributions to:* Short stories to: Esquire; Redbook; McCall's; Other magazines. *Honours:* Maxwell Perkins Award, for The Competitor, 1966; Fulbright Lecturer, Germany, 1984. *Memberships:* Board of Directors, Council for Wisconsin Writers; Milwaukee Literary Society. *Literary Agent:* Curtis Brown Ltd. *Address:* Department of English, University of Wisconsin- Milwaukee, PO Box 413, Milwaukee, WI 53201, USA.

BOOHER Dianna Daniels, b. 13 Jan 1948, Hillsboro, Texas, USA. Writer; Writing Consultant. 1 son, 1 daughter. *Education:* BA, North Texas State University, 1970; MA, University of Houston, 1979. *Publications:* Would You Put That in Writing? 1983; Send Me a Memo, 1984; Cutting Paperwork in the Corporate Culture, 1986; Letter perfect, 1988; Good Grief, Good Grammer, 1988; The New Secretary, 1985; Love, Love, 1985; Making Friends with Yourself and Other Strangers, 1982; Rape: What Would You Do If?...?, 1983; Help, We're Moving!, 1978; Coping When Your Family Falls Apart, 1979; Not Yet Free, 1981; Boy Friends and Boyfriends, 1988; They're Playing our Secret, 1988; That Book's Not in Our Library, 1988; Musical Dramas: For Me, It Was Different, 1984; Christmases of Your Life, 1983. *Honours:* American Library Association Best Books for Young Adults for book Rape: What Would You Do If?, 1981. *Memberships:* American Society of Training and Development; National Speakers Association. *Literary Agent:* Mitch Douglas, International Creative Management. *Address:* Booher Writing Consultants, 12337 Jones Road, Suite 242, Houston, TX 77070, USA.

BOOKER Christopher John Penrice, b. 7 Oct 1937. Journalist, Author. m. Valerie, 1979, 2 sons. *Education:* Corpus Christi College, Cambridge. *Appointments:* Liberal News, 1960; Jazz Critic, Sunday Telegraph, 1961; Editor, Private Eye, 1961-63; Regular Contributor, 1965-; Resident Scriptwriter, That Was the Week That Was, 1962-63; Not So Much a Programme, 1963-64. *Publications:* The Neophiliacs: A Study of the Revolution in English Life in the 50's and 60's, 1969; (with Candida Lycett-Green) Goodbye London, 1973; The Booker Quiz, 1976; The Seventies, 1980; The Games War: a Moscow Journal, 1981; The Repatriations from Austria in 1945, 1990; A looking Glass Tragedy: The Controversy over repatriation from Austria, 1992. *Contributor to:* Spectator, 1962-; Daily Telegraph, 1959-, (Way of the World column, 1987-). Wrote extensively on property development, planning and housing, 1972-77; Private Eye; Anthologies. *Honours:* Campaigning Journalist of the Year, with Bennie Gray, 1973. *Address:* The Old Rectory, Litton, Bath BA3 4PW, Somerset, England.

BOONE Daniel Richard, b. 30 Oct 1927, Chicago, Illinois, USA. Professor Speech-Voice Pathology. m. Mary Mosenthal, 30 Dec 1954, 2 sons, 2 daughters. *Education:* BS, University of Redlands, California, 1951; MA, 1954; PhD, 1958, Western Reserve University. *Publications:* The Voice and Voice Therapy, 1988; Human Communication and its Disorders, 1993; Cerebral Palsy, 1973; An Adult has Aphasia, 1985; Is Your Voice Telling on You?, 1991. *Contributions to:* Over 80 articles to professional journals, 1953-90. *Honours:* American Speech-Language-Hearing Association, 1984. *Memberships:* President, American Speech-Language-Hearing Association, 1975-77; Academy of Aphasia Treasurer 1967-72. *Address:* 5715 N Genematas Drive, Tucson, AZ 85704, USA.

BOORSTIN Daniel Joseph, (Professor X), b. 1 Oct 1914, Atlanta, Georgia, USA. Author; Historian. m. Ruth Carolyn Frankel, 9 Apr 1941, 3 sons. *Education:* AB, summa cum laude, Harvard College, 1934; BA, Jurisprudence, 1st Class Honours, Rhodes Scholar, 1936; BCL, 1st Class Honours, 1937; Bailliol College,

Oxford University, England; Student, Inner Temple, London, 1934-37; JSD (Sterling Fellow), Yale, 1940. *Publications:* The Discoverers, 1985; The Americans (Triology), 1958, 1965, 1974; The Image, 1971; The Republic of Technology, 1978; The Exploring Spirit, 1976; The Lost World of Thomas Jefferson, 1960, 2nd Edition 1982; The Decline of Radicalism, 1969; America and the Image of Europe, 1960; The Genius of American Politics, 1953; The Mysterious Science of the Law, 1973; Editor, The Chicago History of American Civilization, (now 30 volumes); American Civilization, 1972; An American Primer, 2 volumes, 1966; A Lady's Life in the Rocky Mountains, 1960. Textbook for Highschools, A History of the United States, 1980, with Brooks M. Kelley; The Discoverers, 1983; The Creators, 1992. *Contributions to:* Numerous professional journals. *Honours:* Recipient, various honours and awards. *Memberships:* President, American Studies Association; Colonial Society of Massachusetts; Antiquarian Society; American Academy of Arts & Sciences; American Historical Society; American Philosophical Society; Royal Historical Society. *Address:* 3541 Ordway St., NW., Washington, DC 20016, USA.

BOOTH Edward, b. 16 Aug 1928. Catholic Priest. *Education:* Cambridge University, 1949-52, 1971-75; BA, 1952; MA, 1970; PhD, 1975. *Publications:* St Augustine's Notitia sui, related to Aristotle and the early neo-Platonists (series of articles); Aristotelian Aporetic Ontology in Islamic & Christian Thinkers; St Augustine and the Western Tradition of Self Knowing. *Contributions to:* Sant' Alberto Magno, l'uomo e il pensatore; La production du livre universitaire au moyen age, Exemplar et pecia; Kategorie und Kategorialitität; Articles in: Angelicum; Augustiniana; Augustinianum; Studia Patristica; The New Grove Dictionary of Music & Musicians; Reviews in: Faith; Blackfriars; The Journal of the British Society for Phenomenology. *Address:* St Anna Stift, Lohstrasse 16-18, D-4500 Osnabrück, Germany.

BOOTH Edwin, (Don Blunt, Jack Hazard), b. USA. Author. *Publications:* Showdown at Warbird, 1957; Jinx Rider, 1957; Boot Heel Range, 1958; The Man who Killed Tex, 1958; The Trail to Tomahawk, 1958; Wyoming Welcome, 1959; Danger Trail, 1959, UK Edition, Danger on the Trail, 1960; Lost Valley, 1960; The Broken Window, 1960; The Desperate Dude, 1960; Return to Apache Springs, 1960; Crooked Spur (as Jack Hazard), 1960; Reluctant Lawman, 1961; Outlaw Town, 1961; The Troublemaker, 1961; Short Cut (as Don Blunt), 1962; Valley of Violence, 1962; Sidewinder, 1962; Hardcase Hotel, 1963; John Sutter, California, biography, 1963; Dead Giveaway (as Don Blunt), 1963; Devil's Canyon, 1964; The Dry Gulchers, 1964; The Stolen Saddle, 1964; Renegade Guns, 1965; Trouble at Tragedy Springs, 1966; Triple Cross Trail, 1967; Shoot-Out at Twin Buttes, 1967; No Spurs for Johnny Loop, 1967; One Man Posse, 1967; The Man from Dakota, 1968; Stranger in Buffalo Springs, 1969; The Backshooters, 1969; The Prodigal Gun, 1971; Grudge Killer, 1971; Hardesty, 1971; Stage to San Felipe, 1972; Bushwack, 1974; Small Spread, 1974; The Colt-Packin' Parson, 1975; Ambush at Adams Crossing, 1976; Crossfire, 1977; The Colorado Gun, 1980; Leadville, 1980; Rebel's Return, 1980. *Memberships:* Western Writers of America, Secretary-Treasurer 1963-67, Vice-President 1970. *Address:* 1850 Alice Street, No 712, Oakland, CA 94612, USA.

BOOTH Martin, b. 7 Sept 1944, Lancashire, England. Writer. *Publications:* Hiroshima Joe, novel, 1985; The Jade Pavilion, 1986; Black Chameleon, novel, 1988; Carpet Sahib: A Life of Jim Corbett, biography and film, 1986; Dreaming of Samarkand, novel, 1989; A Very Private Gentleman, 1991; The Triads: A History of Chinese Secret Societies, 1990; The Humble Disciple, 1992; Rhino Road: the evolution, natural history and conservation of African rhinos, 1992; The Iron Tree, 1993; Books of verse and other fiction; Screenplays and critical books. *Honour:* Fellow, Royal Society of Literature, 1980. *Literary Agent:* A M Heath & Co Ltd,

London. *Address:* c/o A M Heath & Co Ltd, 79 St Martin's Lane, London WC2N 4AA, England.

BOOTH Philip, b. 8 Oct 1925, Hanover, New Hampshire, USA. Writer. m. Margaret Tillman, 1946, 3 daughters. *Education:* AB, Dartmouth College, Hanover, 1948 (Phi Beta Kappa); MA, Columbia University, New York, 1949; Served in the United States Army Air Force 1944-45. *Appointments:* Bowdoin College, Maine, 1949-50; Assistant to the Director of Admissions, 1950-51 and Instructor 1954, Dartmouth College; Assistant Professor, Wellesley College, Massachusetts 1954-61; Associate Professor 1961-65, Professor of English and Poet-in-Residence, 1965-85, Syracuse University, New York; Taught at the University of New Hampshire Writers Conference, Durham, 1955; Spencer Memorial Lecturer, Bryn Mawr College, Pennsylvania 1959; taught at Tufts University Poetry Workshop, Medford, Massachusetts, 1960, 1961; Phi Beta Kappa Poet, Columbia University 1962. *Publications:* Verse: Letter from a Distant Land, New York, Viking Press, 1957; The Islanders, New York, Viking Press, 1961; North by East, Boston, Impressions Workshop, 1966; Weathers and Edges, New York, Viking Press, 1966; Margins: A Sequence of New and Selected Poems, New York, Viking Press, 1970; Available Light, New York, Viking Press, 1976; Before Sleep, New York, Viking Press, 1980; Relations: Selected Poems, 1950-85, New York, Viking Press, 1986; Selves, New York, Viking Press and Penguin, 1990. Recordings: Today's Poets 4, with others, Folkways; The Cold Coast Watershed, 1985. Editor of other works. *Honours include:* Guggenheim Fellowships, 1958, 1965, Rockefeller Fellowship, 1986; Theodore Roethke Prize (Poetry Northwest) 1970; National Endowment for the Arts Fellowship, 1980; Academy of American Poets Fellowship, 1983; Friends of Witherle Library Award, 1985; Maurice English Poetry Award, 1987; Litt D, Colby College, Waterville, Maine, 1968. *Address:* Main Street, Castine, ME 04421, USA.

BOOTH Rosemary Sutherland, (Frances Murray), b. 1928, United Kingdom. History Teacher; Author. *Publications:* The Dear Colleague, 1972; The Burning Lamp, 1973; Ponies on the Heather, for children, 1973; The Heroine's Sister, 1975; Ponies and Parachutes, for children, 1975; Red Rowan Berry, 1976; Castaway, 1978; White Hope, for children, 1978; Payment for the Piper, US Edition Brave Kingdom, 1983; The Belchamber Scandal, 1985; Shadow over the Islands, 1986. *Litarary Agent:* David Higham Associates, England. *Address:* c/o David Higham Associates, 5-8 Lower John Street, London W1R 4HA, England.

BORCHARDT Frank L., b. 1938, USA. Associate Professor. *Appointments:* Assistant Professor of German, Northwestern University, Evanston, Illinois, 1965-68; Assistant Professor of German and Comparative Literature, Queens College, City University of New York, Flushing, 1968-71; Fulbright Research Fellow, University of Wurzburg, Federal Republic of Germany, 1971-72; Associate Professor of German, Duke University, Durham, North Carolina, 1971-. *Publications:* German Antiquity in Renaissance Myth, 1971. *Address:* 100 East Forest Boulevard, Durham, NC 27707, USA.

BORDEN Louise Walker, b. 30 Oct 1949, Cincinnati, Ohio, USA. Writer. m. Peter A Borden, 4 Sept 1971, 1 son, 2 daughters. *Education:* BA, Denison University, 1971. *Publications:* Caps, Hats, Socks and Mittens, 1989; The Neighborhood Trucker, 1990; The Watching Game, 1991; Albie the Lifeguard, 1993; Christmas in the Stable (contributing poet), 1990. *Contributions to:* Writer-Author, literacy poem, to The Reading Teacher, 1992. *Memberships:* Society of Children's Book Writers; The Authors Guild. *Address:* 628 Myrtle Ave, Terrace Park, OH 45174, USA.

BORDEN William Vickers, b. 27 Jan 1938, Indianapolis, Indiana, USA. Writer; Professor. m. Nancy Lee Johnson, 17 Dec 1960, 1 son, 2 daughters.

Education: AB, Columbia University, 1960; MA, University of California, Berkeley, 1962. *Appointments:* Fiction Editor, North Dakota Quarterly, 1986-. *Publications:* Superstoe, novel, 1968; I Want to be an Indian, play, 1990; Slow Step and Dance, poems, 1991; The Last Prostitute, 1993; Plays produced: Turtle Island Blues; Tap Dancing Across the Universe; Loon Dance; Hangman; Quarks; Jumping; Ledge. *Contributions to:* Poems and short stories to numerous magazines including: Milkweed Chronicle; Cincinnati Poetry Review; New Orleans Review; Louisville Review; Colorado State Review; Poets On; Zone 3; Dakotah Territory; Loonfeather. *Honours:* Winner, Playwriting Competitions: Unicorn Theatre, 1983; Towngate Theatre, 1983; Humboldt State University, 1985; Deep South, 1992; Great Platte River, 1992. *Memberships:* Dramatists Guild; American Society of Composers, Authors and Publishers; PEN; Associated Writing Programs. *Address:* Rt 6, Box 284, Bemidji, MN 56601, USA.

BORENSTEIN Audrey F, b. 7 Oct 1930, Chicago, Illinois, USA. Freelance Writer. m. Walter Borenstein, 5 Sept 1953, 1 son, 1 daughter. *Education:* AB, 1953, MA, 1954, University of Illinois; PhD, Louisiana State University, 1958. *Publications:* Custom: An Essay on Social Codes, translation of Tonnies' Die Sitte, 1961; Redeeming the Sin, 1978; Older Women in 20th-Century America, 1982; Chimes of Change and Hours, 1983; Through the Years: A Chronicle of Cong Ahavath Achim (with Walter Borenstein), 1989. *Contributions to:* Over 30 short fiction works to literary journals including: Ascent, 1975; Northwest Review, 1981; Webster Review, 1981; North Dakota Quarterly, 1984; Calyx, 1986; Oxalis, 1988; The Albany Review, 1988; The MacGuffin, 1989. *Honours:* National Endowment for the Arts Fellowship, 1976; Rockefeller Foundation Humanities Fellowship, 1978; Fiction Prize for New York State, National League of American Pen Women's annual competition in fiction, 1988. *Membership:* Poets and Writers. *Literary Agent:* Bertha Klausner International Literary Agency Inc. *Address:* Four Henry Court, New Paltz, NY 12561, USA.

BORIS Martin, b. 7 Aug 1930, New York City, New York, USA. Writer. m. Gloria Shanf, 13 June 1952, 1 son, 2 daughters. *Education:* BA, New York University, University Heights, 1951; MA, New York University, Washington Square, 1953; BA, Long Island University, Brooklyn College of Pharmacy, 1957. *Publications:* Two and Two, 1979; Woodridge 1946, 1980; Brief Candle, 1990. *Literary Agent:* Arthur Pine Literary Agency. *Address:* 1019 Northfield Rd, Woodmere, NY 11598, USA.

BORNSTEIN George, b. 25 Aug 1941. Professor; Author. m. Jane Elizabeth York, 22 June 1982, 2 son, 1 daughter. *Education:* BA, Harvard University, 1963; PhD, Princeton University, 1966. *Publications:* Yeats and Shelley, 1970; Transformations of Romanticism, 1976; Postromantic Consciousness of Ezra Pound, 1977; Ezra Pound Among The Poets, 1985; Poetic Remaking: The Art of Browning, Yeats & Pound, 1988; Editor of: Romantic and Modern, 1977; W B Yeats, The Early Poetry, Volume I, 1987; W B Yeats' Letters to the New Island, 1989. *Contributions to:* Numerous scholarly journals. *Honours:* ACLS Fellowship, 1972; NEH Fellowship, 1982; Guggenheim Fellowship, 1986; Warner Rice Prize for Research in the Humanities, 1988. *Membership:* Modern Language Association (Executive Committee for 20th Century English 1980-85, For Poetry 1988-). *Address:* 2020 Vinewood Blvd, Ann Arbor, Michigan 48104, USA.

BORODIN George. *See:* **MILKOMANE George Alexis Milkomanovich.**

BOSKOVSKI Jozo T, b. 1933, Ostrilci, Macedonia, Yugoslavia. Poet. m. Ljubinka Veljanova- Boskovska, 1961, 2 children. *Education:* Prof. Degree, University of Skopje. *Publications:* The Fight with Evil, 1963; A Poet - Speaker, 1966; A Macedonian Tragedy, 1963;

Blossoms/Blooms, 1969; The Wisdoms of the Sun-Skilfullness and Last Consequences, 1976; The Eternal Reiiver, 1980; Children Flowers and Stars, 1981. *Contributions to:* Anthologies and Journals, Worldwide including: Australia, Austria, Holland, England, USA, India, Canada, France, Czechoslovakia, Italy, Germany and Mexico. His works have been translated into Serbian, Turkish and Albanian. *Honours include:* International Acknowledgement Award, First European Parliament of the Review Teleuropa, Rome, 1979; Munich Prize, Littera Medal, 1985. *Memberships:* Union of Writers; Union of Artists; Union of Journalists. *Address:* University of Skopje, Skopje, Macedonia, Yugoslavia.

BOSLEY Keith Anthony, b. 16 Sept 1937, Bourne End, Buckinghamshire, England. Poet; Translator. m. Satu Salo, 27 Aug 1982, 3 sons. *Education:* BA Honours, French, Universities of Reading, Paris, Caen. *Publications:* A Chiltern Hundred, poems, 1987; The Kalevala, translation, 1989; I Will Sing of What I Know, Finnish ballads, 1990; The Kanteletar, translation, 1992; Camoes: Epic & Lyric, translations, 1990; From the Theorems of Master Jean de la Ceppede, 1983; Mallarme: The Poems, 1977; Finnish Folk Poetry: Epic, translations, 1977; Stations, poems, 1979. *Contributions to:* Numerous journals and magazines. *Honours:* Finnish State Prize for Translators, 1978; First Prize, British Comparative Literature Association Translation Competition, 1982; Knighthood First Class, Order of the White Rose of Finland, 1991. *Membership:* Corresponding Member, Finnish Literature Society, Helsinki. *Address:* 108 Upton Road, Slough SL1 2AW, England.

BOSQUET Alain, b. 28 Mar 1919, Odessa, Russia. Writer. *Education:* Free University of Brussels, Belgium, 1938-49; MA, University of Paris, Sorbonne, France. *Publications:* Poems: Poemes Un 1945-67, 1979; 100 Notes Pour Une Solitude, 1970; Notes Pour Un Amour, 1972; Notes Pour Un pluriel, 1974; Le Livre du Doute et de la Grace, 1977; Sonnets Pour Une Fun de Siecle, 1980; Poems Deux 1970-74, 1982; Un Jour apres la Vie, 1985; Le Tourment de Dieux, 1987; Bourreaux et acrobates, 1990; Le Gardien des Rosées (Aphorisms), 1991; Novels: La Grande Eclipse, 1952; Un Besoin de Malheur, 1963; La Confesion Mexicaine, 1965; Les Bonnes Intentions, 1976; Une Mère Russe, 1978; Jean-Louis Trabart Medicin, 1980; L'Enfant que tu étais, 1982; Ni Guerre Ni Paix, 1983; Les Fêtes Cruelles, 1984; Lettre à mon Pere qui aurait Eu 100 Ans, 1987; Les Solitudes (trilogy), 1992. Short Stories: Un homme pour un autre, 1985; Le Létier d'Otage, 1989; Comme un refus de la planete, 1989; Plays: Un détenu à Auschwitz, 1991. *Contributions to:* Le Quotidien De Paris; Magazine Litteraire; Le Figaro. *Honours:* Grand Prix de Poesio of French Academy, 1967; Grand Prix du Roman of French Academy, 1978. *Membership:* Vice President Mallarme Academy. *Address:* c/o Gallimand, 5 rue Sebastien-Bottin, 75007 Paris, France.

BOSTON Ray. *See:* **BOSTON Raymond Jack.**

BOSTON Raymond Jack, (Ray Boston), b. 24 Dec 1927, Manchester, England. Writer; Researcher. m. Elizabeth Isabella Horsfield, 6 Aug 1955, 2 daughters. *Education:* BA, New College, Oxford, 1951; MA, 1964; MA, University of Wisconsin, USA, 1969. *Appointments:* Reporter, Manchester Evening News Ltd, 1950-53; Talks Producer, BBC, London, 1953-56; Lecturer, Central London Polytechnic, 1956-67; Writer, Daily Mirror 1958-60; Sub Editor, The Times, 1960-65; Professor, University of Wisconsin, USA, 1967-69; Professor, Univ of Sciences, 1970-75; Director, Cardiff, Wales, 1975-85. *Publications:* The Essential Fleet Street, Cassell; the Newspaper press in Britain; British Chartists in America. *Contributions to:* Journalism Studies Review; British Journalism Review; Journalism Quarterly. *Honours:* American Studies Fellow; 1st Visiting Fellow, Australia. *Memberships:* Sigma Delta Chi; The H.A.L. Fisher Society, Founder-President. *Address:* 85 Severn Grove, Cardiff, CF1 9EQ, Wales.

BOSTWICK Dorothy Lee. *See:* **BOSTWICK Dorothy Vernell Bable.**

BOSTWICK Dorothy Vernell Bable, (Dorothy Lee Bostwick), b. 17 June 1927. Freelance Writer. 1 son, 1 daughter. *Education:* Practical Nursing, 1959. *Publications:* Under the Elmal; Rose Wind; The Great Treasury of Wold Poems; Twentieth Century Poetry; The Best of Poetry. *Contributions to:* Tiotes; Reach Out; Invictus; Spafaswap; Aphony; Dustry Road; Must A Poet Conform in Jackson Citizen Patriot. *Honours:* Merit Awards; Modern Poet Award. *Address:* 6513 N Lake Road, Clark Lake, Brooklyn, MI 49230, USA.

BOSWELL James. *See:* **KENT Arthur.**

BOSWORTH David, b. 26 Oct 1936, Richmond, Surrey, England. University Lecturer. m. Jenny Lawton, 9 Sept 1961, 1 son, 1 daughter. *Education:* BA, 1961; B.Phil, 1963; MA, 1968, St John's College, Oxford University. *Publications:* Logic & Arithmetic, Vol. 1. 1974, Vol. II, 1979; Plato's Phaedo, 1986; Plato's Theaetetus, 1988. *Contributions to:* Various Journals. *Address:* 5-6 Church Street, Twickenham, Middlesex, TW1 3NJ, England.

BOTT George, b. 1920, United Kingdom. Former Educator. *Appointments:* Formerly Senior English Master and Librarian, Cockermouth Grammar School; Editor, Scholastic Publications, 1960-68. *Publications:* George Orwell: Selected Writings (editor), 1958; Read and Relate (editor), 1960; Shakespeare: Man and Boy (editor), 1961; Sponsored Talk, 1971; Read and Respond, 1984; Read, Relate, Communicate, 1984; The Mary Hewetson Cottage Hospital, Keswick: Brief History, 1892-1992, 1991. *Address:* 16 Penrith Road, Keswick, Cumbria CA12 4HF, England.

BOTTIGHEIMER Ruth Elizabeth Ballenger, b. 14 July 1939, Salem, New Jersey, USA. Writer. Lecturer. m. Karl S Bottigheimer, 4 Aug 1960, 1 son, 1 daughter. *Education:* Wellesley College, University Munich; University California, Berkeley, BA, 1961; MA, 1964; University College, London, 1962-63; SUNY, Stony Brook, DA, 1981. *Publications:* Fairy Tales & Society; Grimms Bad Girls And Bold Boys. *Contributions to:* Numerous. *Honours:* Visiting Fellow, Clare Hall; Fulbright Fellow. *Memberships:* Modern Language Association; International Society for Folk Narrative Research; Societé Internationale de Recherche en Litt d'Enfance et de Jeunesse. *Address:* Department of Comparative Studies, SUNY SB, Stony Brook, NY 11794, USA.

BOTTING Douglas Scott, b. 22 Feb 1934, London, UK. Author. m. 27 Aug 1964, 2 daughters. *Education:* St Edmund Hall, Oxford University, 1958. *Publications:* Nazi Gold, 1984; In the Ruins of the Reich, 1985; Humbolt & the Cosmos, 1973; Wilderness Europe, 1976. Various other books of History, Biography, Travel including: Island of the Dragon's Blood, 1958; The Knights of Bornu, 1961; One Chilly Siberian Morning, 1965; Rio de Janeiro, 1977; The Pirates, 1978; The Second Front, 1978; The Giant Airships, 1980; The Aftermath in Europe, 1945, 1983; The U-Boats, 1979. *Contributions to:* BBC TV & Radio; Sunday Times; Sunday Telegraph; Geographical Magazine; Readers Digest. *Memberships:* Society of Authors; Royal Institute of International Affairs; Royal Geographical Society. *Literary Agent:* John Johnson Ltd, London. *Address:* 21 Park Farm Road, Kingston-on-Thames, Surrey, England.

BOUCHER David Ewart George, b. 15 Oct 1951, Wales. Senior Lecturer. m. Clare Mary Frewch Mullen, 8 Sept 1979, 2 daughters. *Education:* University College, Swansea, 1973-76; BA, 1976; London School of Economics, 1976-77; M.Sc, 1977; University of Liverpool, 1977-79; PhD, 1983. *Appointments:* Advisor, Oxford University Press, 1989; Member Editorial Board Australian Journal of Political Science, 1990. *Publications:* Texts in Context; The Political Philosophy; Essays in Political Philosophy; The New Leviathan; pure Citizenship; Political Argument in Britain; British Idealist Political Thought. *Contributions to:* Interpretation; New Literary History; Idealist Studies; History & Theory; Polity; Political Studies; History of Political Thought; Storia, Antropologia E Scienza del Linguagio. *Honours:* Tutorial Fellowship; Research fellowship; Fellow of the Royal Historical Society; Best Special Issue Award. *Memberships:* Australian Political Science Association; Editorial Board of Associations Journal. *Address:* Department of Political Theory & Government, University College, Singleton Park, Swansea, SA2 8PP, Wales.

BOULTON David, b. 3 Oct 1935, Richmond, Surrey, England. Author and TV Producer. m. Anthea Ingham, 14 Feb 1969, 2 daughters. *Education:* Hampton Grammar School, 1947-52. *Publications:* Objection Overruled, 1968; The UVF; Protestant Paramilitary Organizations in Ireland, 1973; The Lockheed Papers (in USA, The Grease Machine) 1980; Jazz in Britain, 1958; The Making of Tania Hearst, 1975; Early Friends in Dent, 1986. *Contributor to:* Publications including: Tribune; New Statesman; The Listener; The Guardian. *Honours:* Cyril Bennet Award, Royal Television Society, 1981, for creative services to television. *Literary Agent:* Curtis Brown. *Address:* Hobsons Farm, Dent, Cumbria LA10 5RF, England.

BOULTON James Thompson, b. 17 Feb 1924, Pickering, Yorkshire, England. University Professor, retired. m. Margaret Helen Leary, 6 Aug 1949, 1 son, 1 daughter. *Education:* BA, University College, University of Durham, 1948; BLitt, Lincoln College, University of Oxford, 1952; PhD, University of Nottingham, 1960. *Appointments:* Lecturer, Senior Lecturer, Reader in English Literature 1951-63, Professor 1964-75, University of Nottingham; Professor of English Studies and Head of Department 1975-88, Dean of Faculty of Arts, 1981-84, Public Orator 1984-88, Emeritus Professor 1989-, University of Birmingham. *Publications:* Edition of Edmund Burke's Sublime and Beautiful, 1958, 1967, 1987; The Language of Politics in The Age of Wilkes and Burke, 1963; Editor: The Letters of D H Lawrence, Volumes 1-7, 1979-93; Samuel Johnson: The Critical Heritage, 1971; Edition: Defoe, Memoirs of a Cavalier, 1972. *Contributions to:* Durham University Journal; Essays in Criticism; Modern Drama; English. *Honour:* Fellow, Royal Society of Literature; Hon D.Litt University of Durham, 1991. *Literary Agent:* Laurence Pollinger Ltd, Maddox Street, Mayfair, London. *Address:* Institute for Advanced Research in the Humanities, University of Birmingham, Egbaston, Birmingham B15 2TT, England.

BOUMELHA Penny, b. 10 May 1950, London, England. University Professor. 1 daughter. *Education:* BA, 1972; MA, 1981; D Phil, 1981. *Appointments:* Researcher, Compiler, Mansell Publishing, 1981-84; Lecturer, University of Western Australia, 1985-90; Jury Professor, University of Adelaide, 1990-. *Publications:* Thomas Hardy & Women: Sexualideology & Narrative Form; Charlotte Bronte; Index of English Literary Manuscripts, vol.3. *Contributions to:* Women Reading Womens Writing; Grafts: Feminist Cultural Criticism; Feminist Criticism: Theory & Practice; The Sense of Sex: Feminist Perspectives on Hardy. *Contributions to:* Southern Review; ILS; Australian Victorian Studies Association Conference Papers; Review of English Studies; English Australian Feminist Studies; London Review of Books. *Address:* Department of English, University of Adelaide, GPO Box 498, Adelaide, SA 5001, Australia.

BOUNDY Donna J, b. 4 Dec 1949, Framingham, USA. Journalist; Author. *Education:* BA, University of Connecticut, 1971; MSW, Hunter College, 1981. *Publications:* When Money is The Drug, 1993; Willpower's Not Enough, 1989 and Straight Talk About Cocaine & Crack, 1988; Filmstrip & Video Scripts: Parents with Alcoholism: Kids with Hope; Maybe I Am: Story of a Teenage Alcoholic; Sexual Assault Crimes: What Teens Should Know; Setting Your Own Limits;

Understanding Suicide, 1986; Crack!, 1986; Sexual Abuse Prevention: A Middle School Primer, 1987; Cocaine & Crack: Formula for Failure, 1987. *Contributions to:* New York Times; Woman's World Magazine. *Literary Agent:* Meredith Bernstein, New York, USA. *Address:* P.O.Box 1208, Woodstock, New York, NY 12498, USA.

BOURKE Vernon J(oseph), b. 1907, USA. Emeritus Professor of Philosophy. *Appointments:* Associate Editor: The Modern Schoolman, 1935-; Speculum, 1948-68; American Journal of Jurisprudence, 1954-; Augustinian Studies, 1969-. *Publications:* Augustine's Quest of Wisdom, 1945; St Thomas and the Greek Moralists, 1947; Ethics, 1951, Revised Edition, 1966; St Augustine's Confessions, translation, 1953; On the Truth of the Catholic Faith, Book Three: Providence, by St Thomas Aquinas, translation, 2 vols, 1956; St Augustine's City of God (editor), 1958; The Pocket Aquinas (editor), 1960; Will in Western Thought, 1964; The Essential Augustine (editor), 1964, Revised Edition, 1974; Augustine's View of Reality, 1964; Aquinas' Search for Wisdom, 1965; History of Ethics, 1968; Joy in Augustine's Ethics, 1978; Wisdom from St Augustine, 1984; Augustine's Love of Wisdom, 1992. *Address:* 638 Laven Del Lane, St Louis, MO 63122, USA.

BOURNE Lesley. *See:* **MARSHALL Evelyn.**

BOURNE Kenneth, b. 17 Mar 1930, Wickford, Essex. University Professor. m. Eleanor Wells, 1 Jan 1955, 1 son, 1 daughter. *Education:* BA (Hons), History, University of Exeter and London, 1951; Phd, London School of Economics, 1955. *Publications:* Palmerston: The Early Years, 1784-1841, 1982; Britain and the Balance of Power in North America, 1815-1908, 1967; The Foreign Policy of Victorian England, 1970; Studies in International History, (with D.C. Watt), 1967; The Blackmailing of the Chancellor, 1975; The Letters of the Third Viscount Palmerston to Laurence and Elizabeth Sulican, 1804-1863, 1979; British Documents on Foreign Affairs: Reports and Papers from the Foreign Office Confidential Prints, (General Editor with D. Cameron Watt), 1983-. *Contributions to:* various journals. *Honours:* Albert B. Corey of American and Canadian Historical Association, 1967-68; FBA, 1984. *Memberships:* FR History S; List and Index Society; Archives and Manuscripts Advisory Committee, University of Southampton. *Address:* 15 Oakcroft Road, London SE13 7ED, England.

BOURNE (Rowland) Richard, Journalist; Author; Director, Commonwealth Human Rights Institute. m. Juliet Mary Attenborough, 1966, 2 sons, 1 daughter. *Education:* BA, Brasenose College, Oxford. *Appointments:* Journalist, The Guardian, 1962-72; Assistant Editor, New Society, 1972-77; Evening Standard; Deputy Editor, 1977-78, London Columnist, 1978-79; Founder Editor, Learn Magazine, 1979; Consultant, International Broadcasting Trust, 1980-81; Advisom Council for Adult and Continuing Education, 1982; Deputy Director, Commonwealth Institute, 1983-89; Director, Commonwealth Human Rights Institute, 1990-. *Publications:* Political Leaders of Latin America, 1969; The Struggle for Education, (with Brian MacArthur), 1970; Getulio Vargas of Brazil, 1974; Assault on the Amazon, 1978; Londoners, 1981; Self-Sufficiency, 16-25 (with Jessica Gould), 1983; Lords of Fleet Street, 1990. *Literary Agent:* Murray Pollinger. *Address:* 36 Burney Street, London SE10 8EX, England.

BOURNE-JONES Derek, b. 4 Sept 1928, St Leonards-on-Sea, Sussex, England. Director, D J Tutorials; Writer. m. Hilary Clare Marsh, 2 Aug 1975. *Education:* St Edmund Hall, Oxford, 1951-54, BA (Hons) Modern Languages, 1954, MA (Oxon) 1958. *Appointments:* Editor, Downlander Publishing, 1978-. *Publications:* Senlac, Epic Poem on the Battle of Hastings, 1978; Floating Reefs, Poetry Collection, 1981; The Singing Days, Poetry Collection, 1986; Merrily to Meet (on Sir Thomas More), 1988; Behold The Man, Poetic Sequence illustrated, on the Stations of the Cross,

1990; Brief Candle, a poetic study of The Lady Jane Grey, illustrated, 1991. *Contributions to:* Various journals over the years. *Memberships:* Founder President, The Downland Poets Society of Sussex 1975-90; Fellow, Royal Society of Arts; The Oxford Society. *Address:* 88, Oxendean Gardens, Lower Willingdon, Eastbourne, East Sussex BN22 ORS, England.

BOUTS Axel. *See:* **VERHENNE Jan Frans.**

BOVA Ben(jamin William), b. 1932, Philadelphia, USA, Writer - Science fiction, Sciences (general), Social commentary, Phenomena; Author; Lecturer; Newspaper Reporter. *Education:* Currently studying for his PhD. BA, in Journalism from Temple University, Philadelphia, 1954. MA, State University of New York at Albany, 1987; *Appointments:* Former Technical Editor, Project Vanguard, Martin Co, Baltimore, Maryland and with Physics Department, Massachusetts Institute of Technology, Cambridge; Marketing Manager, Avco Everett Research Laboratory, Massachusetts, 1960-71; Editorial Director, Omni Magazine; Editor of Analog Magazine. *Publications:* (ed) The Analog Science Fact Reader, 1974; (with B Berson) Survival Guide for the Suddenly Single, 1974; The Weather Changes Man, 1974; Workshops in Space, 1974; (with G R Dickson) Gremlins, Go Home! 1974; End of Exile, 1975; Notes to a Science Fiction Writer, 1975; Through Eyes of Wonder, 1975; Science - Who Needs It? 1975; The Starcrossed 1975; Millenium, 1976; (ed) Analog Annual, 1976; Multiple Man, 1976; City of Darkness, 1976; The Seeds of Tomorrow, 1977; (with Trudy E Bell) Closeup: New Worlds, 1977; Viewpoint, 1977; Colony, 1978; (ed) Analog Yearbook, 1978; Maxwell's Demons, 1978; Kinsman, 1979; The Weathermakers, 1979; The Exiles Triology, 1980; (ed) Best of Omni Science Fiction, 1980-82; Voyagers, 1981; The High Road, 1981; Test of Fire, 1982; Vision of Tomorrow, 1982; Escape Plus Ten, 1984; Assured Survival: How to Stop the Nuclear Arms Race, 1984; The Astral Mirror, 1985; Privateers, 1985; Prometheus, 1986; Voyager Two: The Alien Within, 1986; Best of the Nebulas, (Anthology), 1989. *Contributions to:* Journalism, aerospace and magazine editing, articles, short fiction, opinion pieces and reviews. Various works have appeared in major science fiction magazines, science journals, periodicals: Psychology Today; Modern Bride; The New York Times; Penthouse. *Honours:* Distinguished Alumnus, 1981, Temple University; Alumni Fellow, 1982. *Memberships:* President Emeritus of the National Space Society, Fellow of the British Interplanetary Society, Member of Planetary Society American Association for the Advancement of Science, the Nature Conservancy, New York Academy of Sciences, National Space Club, Charter Member of the Science Fiction Writers of America; Editorial Boards of the World Future Society; PEN. International.*Literary Agent:* Barbara Bova.

BOVEY John Alden Jr, b. 17 Apr 1913, Minneapolis, Minnesota, USA. Retired Diplomat. m. Marcia Peterson, 31 July 1943, 1 daughter. *Education:* Blake School, Minneapolis, 1919-31; Harvard College, BA, 1935; MA, 1938. *Appointments:* Teaching Fellow, Instructor, Harvard, 1938-42; Instructor, US Naval Academy, 1943-45. *Publications:* Desirable Aliens; The Silent Meteor. *Contributions:* 35 Short Stories; 27 Articles; Virginia Quarterly; The Literary Review; Ploughshares; New England Review; Cornhill Magazine; New York Times; The London Magazine. *Honours:* Emily Green Balch Fiction Award; Kansas Arts Commission Award; Angoff Award; David Bruce Fiction Contest, 2nd Prize. *Address:* 19 Chauncy Street, Cambridge, MA 02138, USA.

BOWDEN Jean, (Barbara Annandale, Tessa Barclay, Jocelyn Barry, Jennifer Bland, Avon Curry, Belinda Dell, Lee MacKenzie), b. 1928, British. Writer - Historical, Romance, Gothic, Dance, Ballet; Editorial Consultant, Mills and Boon Ltd, London 1971-. *Appointments:* Editorial Assistant, Panther Books, 1957-59, Four Square Books, 1959-61 and Armada Books, 1961-62; Feature Writer, Woman's Mirror magazine, London 1962-64; Assistant Fiction Editor, Woman's Own magazine, London 1964-71.

Publications include: (with F and P Spencer), Come Dancing: The Ceaseless Challenge; (as Jocelyn Barry), Summer in the City, (as Belinda Dell), Where the Rata Blossoms (as Belinda Dell), The Cruise of Curacao; (as Avon Curry), A Place of Execution; (as Belinda Dell), Dancing on My Heart; (with B Irvine), The Dancing Years; (as Belinda Dell), The Vermillion Gatewya; (as Belinda Dell), Next Stop Gretna; (as Avon Curry), Shack Up, in US as The Girl in the Killer's Bed; (as Belinda Dell), Change Partners; (as Belinda Dell), Flowers for the Festival; (as Belinda Dell), The Darling Pirate; (as Belinda Dell), Lake of Silver; (as Avon Curry), Hunt for Danger; (as Jennifer Bland), Accomplice (as Jean Bowden), Nanny, 1981; (as Lee Mackenzie), Emmerdale Farm series, 22 vols, (as Tessa Barclay), The Craigallan Saga, 4 vols; (as Tessa Barclay), The Tramont Saga, 2 vols, (as Barbara Annandale), The Bonnet Laird's Daughter; (as Barbara Annandale), High Banbaree, *Address:* 138 Himley Road, London SW17, England.

BOWDEN Jim. *See:* SPENCE William John Duncan.

BOWDEN Mary W(eatherspoon), b. 1941, USA. University Educator. *Appointments:* Member, Board of Review, Public Programs Division, National Endowment for the Humanities. *Publications:* Philip Freneau, 1976; Washington Irving, 1981. *Address:* 3402 Hillview, Austin, TX 78703, USA.

BOWDEN Roland Heywood, b. 19 Dec 1916, Lincoln, England. Teacher. m. 2 Jan 1946, 1 son, 1 daughter. *Education:* School of Architecture, Liverpool University, 1934-39. *Publications:* Poems From Italy, 1970; Every Season is Another, 1986; Death of Pasolini, play produced Edinburgh, 1980; After Neruda, play produced Hammersmith Riverside, 1984; The Fence, play produced Brighton, Gardner Centre, 1985. *Contributions to:* Arts Review; London Magazine; Panurge; Words International. *Honours:* Arts Council Drama Bursary, 1978; Cheltenham Festival Poetry Prize, 1982; 1st Prize All-Sussex Poets, 1983. *Membership:* National Poetry Secretariat. *Address:* 2 Roughmere Cottage, Lavant, Chichester, West Sussex PO18 0BG, England.

BOWDRING Paul Edward, b. 24 Mar 1946, Bell Island, Newfoundland, Canada. Writer; Teacher; Editor. m. Glenda Ellsworth, 21 Apr 1990, 1 daughter. *Education:* Memorial University of Newfoundland, BA, 1970. *Appointments:* Adjudicator, Fiction, Newfoundland & Labrador Arts & Letters Competition, 1992; Juror, Writing, Newfoundland & Labrador Arts Council Grants, 1992. *Publications:* The Roncesvalles Pass; TickleAce Magazine. *Contributions to:* Poetry & Fiction in Canadian Fiction Magazine; Newfoundland Quarterly; TickleAce; Grain; Pottersfield Portfolio. *Honours:* 1st Prize Newfoundland Arts & Letters Competition. *Memberships:* Writers Alliance of Newfoundland & Labrador. *Address:* Academic Department, Cabot Institute of Applied Arts & Technology, PO Box 1693, St Johns, Nfld, Canada A1C 5P7.

BOWEN Barbara C, b. 4 May 1937, Newcastle, England. Professor of French and Comparative Literature. m. Vincent E. Bowen, 12 Jan 1963, 2 daughters. *Education:* BA, 1958; MA, 1962, Oxford; Doctorat d'Université Paris, 1962. *Appointments:* Instructor, 1962; Assistant Professor, 1963; Associatiate Professor, 1966; Professor, 1973-, University of Illinois; Professor of French and Comparative Literature, Vanderbilt University, 1987-. *Publications include:* Les Caracteristiques essentielles de la farce française, 1964; The Age of Bluff: Paradox and Ambiguity in Rabelais and Montaigne, 1972; Words and the Man in French Renaissance Literature, 1983; One Hundred Renaissance Jokes, 1988. *Contributions to:* Renaissance Quarterly; Comparative Drama; French Forum; Journal of Warburg and Courtauld Institutes, and others. *Honours:* Guggenheim Fellowship, 1974; NEH Fellowships, 1981, 1988; Villa I Tatti non-stipendiary Fellowship, 1981; ACLS travel grants, 1973, 1984; NEH Summer Seminar for College Teachers, 1980, 1991. *Memberships:* MLA, Executive Council 1978-81; Central Renaissance Conference, Organizing Committee 1973-87; Program Chairman 1980; Medieval Association of the Midwest, Executive Council, 1982-85. *Address:* Box 1647-B, Vanderbilt University, Nashville, TN 37235, USA.

BOWEN John Griffith, b. 5 Nov 1924, Calcutta, India. Writer; TV Producer. *Education:* MA, Oxford University. *Publication:* The Truth Will Not Help Us; After the Rain; The Centre of the Green; Storyboard; The Birdcage; A World Elsewhere; Squeak; The McGuffin; The Girls; Fighting Back; The Precious Gift; Plays: I Love You Mrs Patterson; Little Boxes; The Disorderly Women; The Corsican Brothers; Hail Caesar; Singles; The Inconstant Couple; Which Way Are You Facing?; The Geordie Gentleman. *Contributions to:* London Magazine; Times Literary Supplement; New York Times Book Review; New Statesman; Gambit; Journal of Royal Asiatic Society; Times Educational Supplement; Listener. *Honour:* Tokyo Prize, 1974. *Memberships:* Executive Committee, PEN; Committee of Management, Society of Authors; Executive Committee, Writers Guild of Great Britain. *Literary Agent:* Elaine Greene Ltd. *Address:* Old Lodge Farm, Sugarswell Lane, Edgehill, Banbury, Oxon OX15 6HP, England.

BOWERING George b. 1 Dec 1936, BC, Canada. Writer. m. Angela Luoma, 14 Dec 1963, 1 daughter. *Education:* BA, 1960; MA, 1963, University of British Columbia. *Publications include:* Burning Water, 1980; Caprice, 1987; Mirror on the Floor, 1967; A Short Sad Book, 1977; Flycatcher, 1974; A Place to Die, 1983; Harry's Fragments, 1990. *Contributions:* to several journals and magazines. *Honours:* Governor-General's Award, 1969, 1980. *Membership:* Assocation of Canadian Television and Radio Artists. *Literary Agent:* Denise Bukowski, Toronto. *Address:* 2499 West 37th Avenue, Vancouver, BC Canada, V6M 1P4.

BOWERING Marilyn, b. 13 Apr 1949, Winnipeg, Canada. Writer. m. Michael S Elcock, 3 Sept 1982. 1 daughter. *Education:* BA, First Class 1971, MA, first Class 1973, University of Victoria; University of New Brunswick, 1975-78. *Literary Appointments:* Editor, Noel Collins and Blackwells, Edinburgh, Scotland, 1980-82; Editor and Writer, Gregson/Graham; Full-time Writer, Killin, Scotland, 1977-78; Writer-in-Residence, Aegean School of Fine Arts, Paros, Greece, 1973-74; Script Assistant, film, 1972. *Publications:* Books: Winter Harbour, forthcoming; To All Appearances A Lady, novel, 1989; Calling All the World, 1989. Poetry: Anyone Can See I Love You, 1987; Grandfather Was A Soldier, 1987; The Sunday Before Winter, 1984; Giving Back Diamonds, 1982; Sleeping With Lambs, 1980; The Killing Room, 1977; One Who Became Lost, 1976; The Liberation of Newfoundland, 1973. Many Voices (co-edited with D Day), 1977; The Visitors have All Returned, fiction, 1979. Represented in Anthologies; Readings and/or Workshops; Drama; Radio. *Contributions to:* The Candian Forum; Exile; Prospice; Poetry Canada Review; The Moorlands Review; Trends; Toronto Life; Radio 3 Magazine; Canadian Literature; The Malahat Review; Landfall. *Honours include:* Canada Council project Award, 1972, 1986; Canada Council Short Term Award, 1977, 1980; Canada Council Arts Award, 1973, 1981, 1984; Ontario Arts Council Award, 1980, 1986; Canada Council Arts A Award, 1988; National Magazine Award for Poetry, Silver, 1988. *Memberships include:* Writers' Union of Canada; League of Canadian Poets; BC Federation of Writers; PEN; CAPAC. *Literary Agent:* Denise Bukowski, Toronto, Ontario, Canada. *Address:* c/o 3777 Jennifer Road, Victoria, BC, Canada V8P 3X1.

BOWKER John Westerdale, b. 1935, United Kingdom. Academic. *Appointments:* Fellow, Corpus Christi College, Cambridge, 1962-74; Lecturer, University of Cambridge, 1965-74; Professor of Religious Studies, University of Lancaster, 1974-85; Fellow, Dean, Trinity College, Cambridge, 1984-; Honorary Canon of Canterbury Cathedral, 1985-.

Publications: The Targums and Rabbinic Literature, 1969; Problems of Suffering in Religions of the World, 1970; Jesus and the Pharisees, 1973; The Sense of God: Sociological, Anthropological and Psychological Approaches to the Origin of the Sense of God, 1973; Uncle Bolpenny Tries Things Out, 1973; The Religious Imagination and the Sense of God, 1978; Worlds of Faith, 1983; Violence and Aggression (editor), 1984; The Meaning of Death, 1991; A Year to Live, 1991. *Address:* 14 Bowers Croft, Cambridge CB1 4RP, England.

BOWLER Peter John, b. 8 Oct 1944, Leicester, England. University Professor. m. Sheila Mary Holt, 24 Sept 1966, 1 son, 1 daughter. *Education:* Cambridge BA, 1963; University of Sussex, MSc, 1967; University of Toronto, PhD, 1971. *Publications:* The Eclipse of Darwinism; Evolution: The History of An Idea; Theories of Human Evolution; The Non Darwinian Revolution; Fossils & progress; The Mendlian Revolution; The Invention of Progress; Charles Darwin: The Man & His Influence; The Fontana History of the Environmental Sciences. *Contributions to:* Reviews in TLS; THES. *Memberships:* British Society for the History of Science; History of Science Society. *Address:* Department of Social Anthropology, Queens University, Belfast, BT7 1NN, Northern Ireland.

BOWLES Paul, b. 30 Dec 1910, New York, USA. Composer; Writer. m. Jane Auer, 1938. *Education:* University of Virginia; Berlin & Paris. *Appointments:* Music Critic, New York Herald Tribune, 1942-45. Music composed for Films, Theatre, Ballet, Opera also Sonatas, Cocertos. *Publications:* Novels: The Sheltering Sky; Let it Come Down; The Spider's House; Up Above the World. Non-fiction: Their Heads Are Green; Yallah!; Without Stopping; Points in Time. Numerous short story collections. Poetry; Translations. *Honours:* Guggenheim Fellowship; Rockefeller Grant. *Address:* c/o William Morris Agency Inc, 1350 Avenue of the Americas, New York, NY 10019, USA.

BOWLING Harry, b. 30 Sept 1931, Bermondsey, London, England. m. Shirley Burgess, 27 Jul 1957, 1 son, 2 daughters. *Publications:* Conner Street's War, 1988; Tuppence to Tooley Street, 1989; Ironmonger's Daughter, 1989; Paragon Place, 1990; Gaslight in Page Street, 1991; The Girl From Cotton Lane, 1992; Backstreet Girl, 1993. *Literary Agent:* Jennifer Kavanagh. *Address:* Headline Book Publishing PLC, Headline House, 79 Great Titchfield St., London W1P 7FN, England.

BOWLT John Ellis, b, 6 Dec 1943, London, England. Professor. m. Nicolette Misler, 25 Dec 1981. *Education:* BA, 1965; MA, 1966; PhD, 1971, University of Birmingham. *Appointments:* Professor, University of Texas, Austin, 1971-88; Visiting Professor, Wellesley College, 1980; Visiting Professor, University of Otago, New Zealand, 1982; Visiting Professor, Hebrew University, Jerusalem, 1985; Professor, USC, Los Angeles, 1988-. *Publications:* Russian Avant Garde; Silver Age; Pavel Filonov; On Condition of Soviet Art Criticism; Goncharova and Futurist Theatre. *Honours:* Brit Cncl Award to Moscow; National Humanities Institute; Am Co of Learned Societies to Paris; International Research & Exchanges Board to Moscow. *Memberships:* Am Association for Advancement of Slavic Studies. *Address:* Slavic Department, University of So, California, Los Angeles, CA 90089, USA.

BOX Edgan. *See:* **VIDAL Gore.**

BOXILL Roger Evan, b. 27 Mar 1928, Sydney, Australia. Professor of English. m. Edith Hillman, 1965, div 1976. *Education:* PhD, Columbia University, 1966; AB, Columbia College, 1953; Royal Academy of Dramatic Art, 1954. *Publications:* Tennessee Williams; Shaw & the Doctors. *Contributions to:* Shalespeare Quarterly. *Memberships:* New York Shavians; Modern Language Association. *Address:* 425 Riverside Drive, Apt 10J, New York, NY 10025, USA.

BOYD Brian David, b. 30 July 1952, Belfast, Northern Ireland. University Teacher. m. (1) Janet Bower Eden, 1974, div. 1980, (2) Bronwen Mary Nicholson, 1983, 3 stepdaughters. *Education:* BA, 1972, MA (Hons), 1974, University of Canterbury, Christchurch, New Zealand; PhD, University of Toronto, Canada, 1979; Postdoctoral Fellow, University of Auckland, 1979. *Appointments:* Lecturer, 1980, Senior Lecturer, 1985, Associate Professor, 1992-, University of Auckland, New Zealand; Editorial Board, Nabokov Studies. *Publications:* Nabokov's Ada: The Place of Consciousness, 1985; Vladimir Nabokov: The Russian Years, 1990; Vladimir Nabokov: The American Years, 1991. *Contributions to:* Biblion; Europe; Islands; James Joyce Quarterly; Landfall; Modern Fiction Studies; Nabokovian; New York Times Book Review; Scripsi; Shenandoah; Southern Review; Times Literary Supplement; Washington Post. *Honours:* Claude McCarthy Fellowship, 1981-82; Thomas H Carter Essay Prize, 1989; 3rd Prize, 1991, 2nd Prize, 1992, Goodman Fielder Wattie Book Award, 1991; Lawrence and Suzanne Weiss Fellow, 1992. *Memberships:* PEN; Modern Language Association. *Literary Agent:* Georges Borchardt, 136 E 57th St, New York, NY 10022, USA. *Address:* Department of English, University of Auckland, Private Bag 92019, Auckland, New Zealand.

BOYD Malcolm, b. 24 May 1932, Newcastle Upon Tyne, England. Retired University Lecturer. m. Beryl Gowen, 3 Apr 1956, 2 sons. *Education:* Dame Allan's School, Newcastle, 1943-50; Durham University, 1950-53; BA, 1953; MA, 1962. *Publications:* Bach; Domenico Scarlatti: Master of Music; Palestrina's Style; Harmonizing 'Bach' Chorales; Bach's Instrumental Counterpoint; Bach: The Brandenberg Concertos; Grace Williams. *Contributions to:* Musical Times; Music & Letters; Music Review; Early Music. *Honours:* Yorkshire Post Literary Award for Music. *Membership:* Royal Musical Association. *Address:* 211 Fidlas Road, Llanishen, Cardiff, CF4 5NA, Wales.

BOYD William, b. 1952, United Kingdom. Full-time Writer. *Appointments:* Lecturer in English Literature, St Hilda's College, Oxford, 1980-83; Television Critic, New Statesman, London, 1982-83. *Publications:* A Good Man in Africa, novel, 1981; On the Yankee Station, short stories, 1981; An Ice-Cream War, novel, 1982; Stars and Bars, novel, 1984; School Ties, screenplay, 1985; The New Confessions, novel, 1987; Brazzaville Beach, 1990. *Honours:* Whitbread Prize, 1981; Somerset Maugham Award, 1982; James Tait Black Memorial Prize, 1990; McVitie's Prize, 1991. *Address:* c/o Harvey Unna and Stephan Durbridge Ltd, 24 Pottery Lane, London W11 4LZ, England.

BOYLE T Coraghessan, b. 2 Dec 1948, Peekskill, New York, USA. Fiction Writer. m. Karen Kvashay, 25 May 1974, 2 sons, 1 daughter. *Education:* MFA, 1974, PhD, 1977, University of Iowa. *Publications:* Descent of Man, 1979; Water Music, 1982; Budding Prospects, 1984; Greasy Lake, 1985; World's End, 1987; If the River Was Whiskey, 1989; East Is East, 1990; The Road to Wellville, 1993. *Honours:* Faulkner Award, PEN, 1988. *Literary Agent:* Georges Borchardt, New York, USA. *Address:* c/o Georges Borchardt, 136 E 57th St, New York, NY 10022, USA.

BOYNTON Sandra, b. 3 Apr 1953, Orange, New Jersey, USA. Company Vice-President; Designer of Greetings Cards; Writer. m. James Patrick McEwan, 18 Oct 1978, 1 daughter. *Education:* BA, Yale University, 1974; Graduate study, University of California, Berkeley, 1974-75 and Yale University, 1976-77. *Appointments:* Author and illustrator of children's books; Recycled Paper Products, Inc, Chicago, Illinois, designer of greetings cards, 1974-, Vice-President 1980-. *Publications include:* Self-illustrated children's books include: But Not the Hippoppotamus, edited by Klimo, 1982; The Going to Bed Book, edited by Klimo, 1982; Opposites, edited by Klimo, 1982; Sounds, edited by Klimo, 1982; A Is for Angry: An Adjective and Animal Alphabet, 1983; Moo Baa La La La, edited by Klimo, 1983; Hey! Waht's That? 1985; Chloe and Maude, 1985;

Good Night, Good Night, 1985; Christmastime, 1987. Books of Cartoons: Gopher Baroque and Other Beastly Conceits, 1979; The Compleat Turkey 1980, revised edition published as Don's Let The Turkeys Get Youo Down, 1986; Chocolate: The Consuming Passion, 1982. Other publications. *Contributor to:* Magazines including Redbook. *Honours:* Irma Simonton Black Award, 1986 for Chloe and Maude. *Membership:* Cartoonists Guild.

BOZEMAN Adda Bruemmer, b. 17 Dec 1908, Geistershof, Latvia. Author; Teacher; Consultant, foreign affairs. m. (1) Virgil Bozeman, 28 Mar 1937 (div. 1947), 1 daughter, (2) Arne Barkhuus, 8 Feb 1951. *Education:* Diploma, Ecole Libre des Sciences Politiques, (section Diplomatique), 1934; Barrister, Middle Temple, 1936; JD, Southern Methodist University, Texas, 1937; Postgraduate work, Hoover Institution, Stanford, Stanford, California, 1938- 40. *Publications include:* Regional Conflicts Around Geneva, 1948; Politics and Culture in International History, 1960; The Future of Law in a Multicultural World, 1971; Conflict in Africa: Concepts & Realities, 1976; How to Think about Human Rights, 1978; Strategic Intelligence and Statecraft, 1990; numerous monographs, human rights, foreign affairs, comparative and international law. *Contributions to:* Books: Expansion of International Society, 1982; Hydra of Carnage, Ra'anan et al, 1985; Future of International Law, 1984; Essyas, reviews to various journals. *Honours include:* Research grants, Carnegie Endowment for Intern Peace 1959/60; Rockefeller Foundation, 1960/61; Award of Distinction, International Society for Educational Cultural and Scientific Interchanges, 1985; *Memberships include:*American Political Science Association; Autobiographical Reflections of Thirty-four Academic Travelers, 1989; International Studies Association; International Sociological Society; Armed Forces and Society; Society for Comparative Study of Civilization; Grotins Society;Consortium for Study of Intelligence; Committee on the Present Danger. On Editorial Boards include ORBIS, Comparative Strategy, Conflict: An International Journal: Comparative Civilizations Review; Editorial Board of Defense Intelligence Journal (US Department of Defense). *Address:* 24 Beall Circle, Bronxville, NY 10708, USA.

BRABAZON James. *See:* **SETH-SMITH Leslie James.**

BRACEGIRDLE Brian, b. 1933, United Kingdom. Museum Curator. *Appointments:* Keeper, Wellcome Museum of the History of Medicine, Science Museum, London, 1977-. *Publications:* An Atlas of Embryology (with W H Freeman), 1963; An Atlas of Histology (with W H Freeman), 1966; Photography for Books and Reports, 1970; An Atlas of Invertebrate Structure (with W H Freeman), 1971; An Atlas of Plant Structure (with P H Miles), vol I 1971, vol II, 1973; The Archaeology of the Industrial Revolution, 1973; Thomas Telford (with P H Miles), 1973; The Darbys and the Ironbridge Gorge (with P H Miles), 1974; An Advanced Atlas of Histology (with W H Freeman), 1976; An Atlas of Chordate Structure (with P H Miles), 1977; The Evolution of Microtechnique, 1978; Beads of Glass: Leeuwenhoek and the Early Microscope (editor), 1983. *Memberships:* Secretary, then Chairman, Institute of Medicine and Biological Illustration, 1971-75; Former Chairman, Fellowship and Associateship Panel, Royal Photographic Society. *Address:* Cold Aston Lodge, Cold Aston, Cheltenham, Glos GL54 3BN, England.

BRADBROOK Muriel Clara, b. 1909, United Kingdom. Professor Emeritus; Author. *Appointments:* Fellow, 1932-35, 1936-, Mistress, 1968-76, Girton College, Cambridge; Lecturer in English, 1945-62, Reader, 1962-65, Professor of English Literature, 1965-76, Professor Emeritus, 1976-, Cambridge University. *Publications:* Elizabethan Stage Conditions, 1932; Themes and Conventions of Elizabethan Tragedy, 1934; The School of Night, 1936; Andrew Marvell (with M G Lloyd Thomas), 1940; Joseph Conrad, 1941; Ibsen the Norwegian, 1946; T S Eliot, 1950; Shakespeare and Elizabethan Poetry, 1951; The Queen's Garland

(compiler), 1953; The Growth and Structure of Elizabethan Comedy, 1955; Sir Thomas Malory, 1957; The Rise of the Common Player, 1962; English Dramatic Form, 1965; That Infidel Place: History of Girton College, 1969; Shakespeare the Craftsman, 1969; Literature in Action, 1972; T S Eliot: The Making of the Waste Land, 1972; Malcolm Lowry: His Art and Early Life, 1974; Shakespeare, 1978; George Chapman, 1978; John Webster, 1980; Collected Papers, 3 vols, 1982-83; Muriel Bradbook on Shakespeare, 1984; Collected Papers, vol 1-4, 1982-89. *Honours:*Litt.D Cantab, 1955; FBA, 1990. *Address:* 91 Chesterton Road, Cambridge, CB4 3AP, England.

BRADBURY Malcolm Stanley, b. 1932, England. Author; Writer; Professor of American Studies. *Publications include:* Eating People is Wrong, 1959; All Dressed Up and Nowhere to Go, 1962; Evelyn Waugh, 1964; Two Poets, (with A. Rodway), 1966; The Social Context of Modern English Literature, 1971; The History Man, 1975; The Novel Today, 1977; The After Dinner Game: Stories and Parodes, 1982; Rates of Exchange, 1983; Cuts: A Novella, 1987; Doctor Griminale, 1992. *Honour:* CBE, 1991. *Address:* University of East Anglia, Norwich NR4 7TJ, England.

BRADBURY Ray (Douglas), b. 1920. USA, Writer - Novels, Short Stories, Science fiction, Fantasy, Children's fiction, Plays, Screenplays, Poetry. *Publications include:* Tomorrow Midnight, 1966; The Pedestrian (play) 1966; S is for Space, 1966; The Picasso Summer (screenplay) 1968; I Sing the Body Electric, 1969; Christus Apollo (play) 1969; Old Ahab's Friend, and Friend to Nosh Speaks His Piece: A Celebration, 1971; The Halloween Tree, 1972; The Wonderful Ice Cream Suit and Other Plays: For Today, Tomorrow and Beyond Tomorrow, 1972; When Elephants Last in the Dooryard Bloomed(poetry) 1972; The Small Assassin, 1973; Zen and the Art of Writing, 1973; Mars and the Mind of Man, 1973; The Son of Richard III, 1974; Long after Midnight (stories) 1976; Pillar of Fire and Other Plays, 1976; Where Robot Mice and Robot Men Run Round in Robot Towns: New Poems Both Light and Dark, 1977; Beyond 1984, 1979; The Stories of Ray Bradbury, 1980; The Ghosts of Forever, 1981; The Haunted Computer and the Android Pope, 1981; The Last Circus, 1981; The Complete Poems of Ray Bradbury, 1982; The Love Affair, 1983; Dinosaur Tales, 1983; A Memory for Murder, 1984; Forever and the Earth, 1984; Death is a Lonely Business, 1985; The Toynbee Convector, 1989; A Graveyeard for Lunatics, 1990. *Memberships:* President, Science-Fantasy Writers of America, 1951-53; Board of Directors, Screen Workers Guild of America, 1957-61. *Address:* 10265, Cheviot Drive, Los Angeles, CA 90064, USA.

BRADDIN George. *See:* **MILKOMANE George Alexis Milkomanovich.**

BRADDON Russell Reading, b. 25 Jan 1921, Sydney, Australia. Author; Broadcaster; Scriptwriter. *Education:* BA, Sydney University, 1940. *Publications include:* The Naked Island, 1952; Cheshire VC, 1954; Joan Sutherland, 1962; End Play, 1972; The Finalists, 1977; The Other Hundred Years War, 1982; The Inseparables, 1968; The Siege, 1968; The Progress of Private Lilyworth, 1971; The Predator, 1977; All the Queen's Men, 1977; Funnelweb, 1990. *Contributor to:* Many journals and magazines worldwide; TV documentaries 1980-88 Great River Journeys of the World (BBC), Images of Australia (ABC Australia). *Honour:* Premier's Literary Award, NSW Scriptwriting, 1985. *Literary Agent:* Vivienne Schuster, John Farquharson Ltd. *Address:* c/o John Farquharson Ltd, 162-168 Regent Street, London W1A 5TB, England.

BRADFORD Karleen, b. 16 Dec 1936, Toronto, Canada. Writer. m. James Creighton Bradford, 22 Aug 1959, 2 sons, 1 daughter. *Education:* BA, University of Toronto, 1959. *Publications:* A Year for Growing, 1977; reprinted as Wrong Again, Robbie, 1983; The Other Elizabeth, 1982; I Wish There Were Unicorns,

1983; The Stone in the Meadow, 1984; The Haunting at Cliff House, 1985; The Nine Days Queen, 1986; Write Now!, 1988; Windward Island, 1989. *Contributions include:* Short Stories, articles to school readers & magazines in USA & Canada, including: Ginn & Company; Nelson Canada; Holt; Rinehart & Winston; Laidlaw Brothers. Also: Cricket Magazine; Cricket & Company, UK; Canadian Children's Annual; The Instructor; Canadian Aviation. *Honours:* Grant, Ontario Arts Council, 1977; 1st prize, CommCept KidLit Contest, 1979; 1st prize 1978, 2nd prize 1984, short story, Juvenile Division, Canadian Authors Association (Ottawa branch) prose contest; Grants, Canada Council, 1983, 1985; Ottawa Citizen Award, 1st prize Juvenile/Teen Short Story, 1988. *Memberships:* Chairman, Curriculum Committee 1984-85, Writers Union of Canada; Canadian Society of Children's Authors, Illustrators & Performers; Newsletter editor 1984-85, Canadian Authors Association; Ottawa Independent Writers. *Literary Agent:* MGA Agency Inc., 10 St. Mary Street, Toronto, Ontario, Canada, M4Y 1P9.

BRADFORD S.W. *See:* **BATTIN B W.**

BRADLEY John Lewis, b. 5 Aug 1917, London, England. University Professor (retired). m. Elizabeth Hilton Pettingell, 4 Nov 1943, 1 daughter. *Education:* BA 1940, PhD 1950, Yale University; MA, Harvard University, 1946. *Publications:* An Introduction to Ruskin, 1971. Editor: Ruskin's Letters from Venice 1851-52, 1955; Ruskin's Letters to Lord & Lady Mount Temple, 1964; The Correspondence of John Ruskin and Charles Eliot Norton, (with Ian Ousby), 1987; The Cambridge Guide to Literature in English (ed. Ian Ousby), 1988; Lady Curzon's India, 1985; Ruskin: The Critical Heritage, 1984; Selections from Mayhew's London Labour & the London Poor, 1965; Ruskin's Unto This Last and Traffic, 1967. *Contributions to:* TLS; THES; Victorian Studies; Essays in Criticism; Studies in English Literature; Journal of English & Germanic Philology; Notes & Queries; Modern Language Review. *Honours:* Fellow and Grantee, American Philosophical Society; Guggenheim Fellow, 1961-62. *Address:* Church Cottage, Hinton St George, Somerset TA17 8SA, England.

BRADWAY Becky, b. 21 Nov 1957, Phoenix, USA. Writer; Editor. m. Jan 1985, 1 daughter. *Education:* MA, Sangamon State University; Columbia University, 1985. *Appointments:* Writer, Editor, Illinois Coalation Against Sexual Assault, 1986-. *Publications:* Eating Our Hearts Out; American Fiction Number One; American Fiction. *Contributions to:* Green Mountains Review, Beloit Fiction Journal; South Carolina Review; Sojourner; Other Voices; Ascent; Crescent Review; Greensboro Review; Soundings East; Four Quarters. *Honours:* 1st Prize, Willow Review; Artist Advancement Awards; American Fiction Competition. *Memberships:* Illinois Writers Inc; Poets & Writers Inc. *Address:* 924 Bryn Mawr Boulevard, Springfield, IL 62703, USA.

BRADWELL James. *See:* **KENT Arthur.**

BRADY Anne M (Cannon), b. 23 May 1926, Dublin, Ireland. Writer. m. 2 Feb 1957, 2 sons, 2 daughters. *Education:* BA, English Literature and Language, University College Dublin; Diploma in Hospital Administration, College of Commerce. *Appointments:* University Library Assistant, Dublin and Ottawa; Farm Secretary, Co Meath. *Publications:* The Winds of God (historical fiction) 1985; Honey Off Thorns (historical fiction) 1988; co-author with Brian Cleeve, The Biographical Dictionary of Irish Writers, 1985. *Contributor to:* short stories to women's magazines prior to 1985. *Memberships:* University College Dublin Graduates, Association; Royal Dublin Society. *Literary Agent:* Eleanor Corey. *Address:* Rosbeg, 12 Ard Mhuire Park, Dalkey, Co. Dublin, Ireland.

BRADY James Winston, b. 15 Nov 1928, New York, USA. Writer; Broadcaster. m. Florence Kelly, 12 Apr 1958, 2 daughters. *Education:* AB, Manhattan College, 1950; Graduate study, New York University. *Publications:* Novels: Paris One, 1977; Nielsen's Children, 1979; Press Lord, 1981; Holy Wars, 1983; Designs, 1986. Non-fiction, The Coldest War, 1990; Fashion Show, 1992; Various UK & foreign editions, all books. *Contributions to:* Parade; Esquire; New York; Advertising Age; TV Guide; People; Harpers Bazaar. *Honour:* Emmy Award, New York, TV, 1973-74. *Literary Agent:* Jack Scovil, Scott Meredity Literary Agency Inc, 13th Floor, 845 Third Avenue, New York, NY 10022, USA. *Address:* PO Box 1584, East Hampton, New York, 11937, USA.

BRADY John Mary, b. 10 July 1955, Dublin, Ireland. Teacher. m. Johanna Wagner, 1 Aug 1981, 1 son, 1 daughter. *Education:* BA, Trinity College, Dublin, 1980; BEd, University of Toronto, 1981; MEd, 1985. *Publications:* Kaddish in Dublin; Unholy Ground; A Stone of the Heart; All Souls, 1993. *Honours:* Arthur Ellis Award; Best First Novel. *Literary Agent:* MGA, Toronot. *Address:* c/o MGA Agency, 10 St Mary Street, Suite 510, Toronto, Ontario, Canada.

BRADY Patricia, b. 20 Jan 1943, Danville, Illinois, USA. Historian. 1 son, 1 daughter. *Education:* BA cum laude, with honours, Newcomb College, 1965; MA, History, 1966, PhD, History, 1977, Tulane University. *Appointments:* Member, Programme Committee, Tennessee Williams-New Orleans Literary Festival, 1991-. *Publications:* Nelly Custis Lewis's Housekeeping Book, 1982; Introduction, The WPA Guide to New Orleans, 1983; Encylopaedia of New Orleans Artists, 1718-1918, 1987; George Washington's Beautiful Nelly, 1991; Mollie Moore Davis: A Literary Life, 1992; The Cities of the Dead: Free Men of Color as Tomb Builders, 1993. *Contributions to:* Black Artists in Antebellum New Orleans, to Louisiana History, 1991; Lafcadio Hearn, to Tulanian, 1991; A Woman's Consequence: George Washington's Beautiful Nelly, to Virginia Cavcalcade, 1992. *Honours:* Scholar, 1961-65, Fellow, 1965-68, Tulane University; Phi Beta Kappa, 1965; Honorary Woodrow Wilson Fellow, 1965; National Defense Foreign Language Fellow, 1965-68; Fulbright-Hays Fellow, 1974. *Memberships:* Board of Directors, Programme Committee Chair, Tennessee Williams-New Orleans Literary Festival; Board of Directors, Friends of New Orleans Public Library; Board of Directors, Vice-President, New Orleans, Gulf South Booksellers Association; Board of Directors, Louisiana Historical Association; Association for Documentary Editing; Southern Historical Association. *Literary Agent:* Susan P Urstadt. *Address:* 1205 Valence St, New Orleans, LA 70115, USA.

BRADY Terence Joseph, b. 13 Mar 1939. Playwright; Novelist; Actor; Columnist. m. Charlotte Mary Therese Bingham, 1 son, 1 daughter. *Publications:* Writer for Radio; Lines from my Grandfather's Forehead, 1972; TV; Broad and Narrow; TWTWTW; With Charlotte Bingham; TV Series: Boy Meets Girl; Take Three Girls; Upstairs Downstairs; Away From it All; Play for Today; Plays of Marriage; No-Honestly; Yes-Honestly; Thomas and Sarah; Pig in the Middle; The Complete Lack of Charm of the Bourgeoisie; Nanny; Oh Madeline; Father Matthew's Daughter; A View of Meadows Green; Love with a Perfect Stranger, (TV Film); This Magic Moment, (TV Film); Stage: (Contributor) The Sloane Ranger Revue, 1985; I Wish, I Wish, (stage); Novel: Rehearsal, 1972; The Fight Against Slavery, 1976; with Charlotte Bingham: Victoria, 1972; Rose's Story, 1973; Victoria and Company; 1974; Yes-Honestly, 1977; (withh Michael Felton), Point to Point, 1990; Riders (TV Film); Oh Madeline! (USA TV Series). *Contributions to:* Daily Mail; Living; Country Homes and Interiors; Punch; Sunday Express. *Address:* c/o Peters, Fraser & Dunlop, 5th Floor, The Chambers, Chelsea Harbour, Lots Road, London, SW10 0XF, England.

BRADY Upton Birnie, b. 17 Apr 1938, Washington, District of Columbia, USA. Literary Agent; Editor. m. Sally Ryder, 17 Nov 1962, 3 sons, 1 daughter. *Education:* AB cum laude, Classics (Latin), Harvard College, 1959.

Appointments: College Field Editor, Random House-Alfred A Knopf, New York City, 1961-63; Editor, Gregg Division, 1963, Editor, Business, Economics, College Division, 1963-65, McGraw-Hill, New York City; Managing Editor, 1965-72, Associate Director, 1972-79, Director, 1979-84, Atlantic Monthly Press, Boston, Massachusetts; Executive Editor, Atlantic Monthly Press, New York City, 1985-88; Consulting Editor, Book Doctor, Literary Agent, 1988-; Has worked with numerous authors including Peter Ustinov, Geoffrey Household, Agnes de Mille, Enid Bagnold, Joseph Wambaugh, Frances FitzGerald, William Least Heat Moon, Vicki Hearn, Han Suyin. *Publications:* Midsummer Passion and Other Tales of Maine Cussedness by Erskine Caldwell (editor). *Memberships:* PEN. *Address:* 267 Dudley Road, Bedford, MA 01730, USA.

BRAESTRUP Peter, b. 8 June 1929, New York City, USA. Editor. m. Angelica Hollins, divorced, 1 son, 2 daughters. *Education:* BA, Yale University, 1951; Nieman Fellow, Harvard University, 1960. *Appointments:* Contributing Editor, 1953-55; Correspondent, 1955-57; Time Magazine; Reporter, New York Herald Tribune, 1957-59; Correspondent, New York Times, Algeria, 1962-65; Paris, 1965; Bangkok, Saigon, 1966-68; Saigon Bureau Chief, 1968-69, National Staff Writer, 1969-73, Washington Post; Founding Editor, Wilson Quarterly, 1975-. *Publications:* Big Story, 1977; Battle Lines, (co-author), 1985; Vietnam as History, 1984, (ed), 1984. *Contributions to:* Marine Corps Gazette; Atlantic; New Leader; various journals, magazines and newspapers. *Honours:* Woodrow Wilson International Centre for Scholars Fellow, 1973-75; Sigma Delta Chi Award, for Big Story, 1978. *Memberships:* Yale Alumni Publications, Board, 1977-; Visions Foundation, Board; Yale University Council, 1984-. *Address:* 600 Maryland Ave., SW Suite 430, Washington, DC 20024, USA.

BRAGG Melvin, b, 6 Oct 1939. Writer, Presenter, Editor. m. (1) Marie-Elisabeth Roche, 1961, deceased, 1 daughter, (2) Catherine Mary Haste, 1973, 1 son, 1 daughter. *Education:* MA Wadham College, Oxford. *Appointments:* Writer, Presenter, Editor, The South Bank Show for ITV, 1978-; Head of Arts, London Weekend Television, 1982-; Deputy Chairman, Border TV, 1985-. *Publications:* Plays: Mardi Gras, 1976; Orion, 1977; The Hired Man, 1984. Screenplays: Isadora; Jesus Christ Superstar; Clouds of Glory, with Ken Russell; Speak for England, 1976; Land of the Lakes, 1983; Laurence Olivier, 1984. Novels: For Want of a Nail, 1965; The Second Inheritance, 1966; Without a City Wall, 1968; The Hired Man, 1969; A Place in England, 1970; The Nerve, 1971; Josh Lawton, Autumn Manoeuvres, 1978; Kingdom Come, 1980; Love and Glory, 1983; The Life of Richard Burton, 1989, (Biography); A Time to Dance, 1990, Televised, 1992; Crystal Rooms, 1992. *Contributions to:* Weekly Column in Punch; articles, various English Journals. *Memberships:* Arts Council, Chairman, Literature, Panel of Arts Council; President, Cumbrians for Peace, 1962-; Northern Arts. *Address:* 12 Hampstead Hill Gardens, London NW3, England.

BRAGG Michael, b. 24 Oct 1948, Croydon, Surrey, England. Writer; Illustrator; Lecturer. m. Christine, 16 Aug 1975, 3 daughters. *Education:* Goldsmiths College, University London, 1967-70. *Publications:* Bettys Wedding; The Pet Cellar; Mondays Child. *Memberships:* Society of Authors. *Address:* 9 Middle Lane, Ringwood, Hampshire, BH24 1LE, England.

BRAITHWAITE Eustace Edward Adolphe Ricardo, b. 27 June 1922, British Guiana (now Guyana). Author; Diplomat. *Education:* New York University, USA; Cambridge University, UK; MSc. *Appointments:* Schoolteacher, London, UK, 1950-57; Welfare Officer, London County Council, 1958-60; Human Rights Officer, World Veterans Foundation, Paris, France, 1960-63; Lecturer, education consultant, UNESCO, Paris, 1963-66; Permanent Representative of Guyana to UN, 1967-68; Ambassador to Venezuela, 1968-69. *Publications:* To Sir, With Love, 1959, (film 1967); A

Kind of Homecoming, 1961; Paid Servant, 1962; A Choice of Straws, 1965; Reluctant Neighbours, 1972; Honorary White, 1976. *Honours:* Ainsfield Wolff Literary Award, 1959; Franklin Prize.

BRAM Christopher, b. 22 Feb 1952, Buffalo, New York, USA. Novelist. *Education:* BA, College of William and Mary, Virginia, 1974. *Publications:* Surprising Myself, 1987; Hold Tight, 1988; In Memory of Angel Clare, 1989; Screenplays: George and Al (short film) 1987; Lost Language of Cranes (unproduced adaptation) 1989. *Contributor to:* Book reviews in New York Times Book Review, Newsday, Lambda Book Report and Christopher Street; Movie reviews in New York Native and Premiere. *Membership:* Publishing Triangle. *Literary Agent:* Eric Ashworth. *Address:* c/o Donadio and Ashworth Associates, 231 West 22nd Street, New York, NY 10011, USA.

BRANCH Edgar Marquess, b. 21 Mar 1913, Chicago, Illinois, USA. University Professor; Educator; Editor; Author. m. Mary Josephine Emerson, 29 Apr 1939, 1 son, 2 daughters. *Education:* Beloit College, Beloit, Wisconsin, 1930-32, 1933-34; University College, University of London, England, 1932-33; BA, Beloit College, 1934; Brown University, 1934-35; MA, University of Chicago, 1938; PhD, University of Iowa, 1941. *Appointments:* Graduate Assistant, University of Iowa, 1938-41; Instructor, 1941-43, Assistant Professor, 1943-49, Associate Professor, 1949-57, Professor, 1957-64, Chairman, Department of English, 1959-64, Research Professor, 1964-78, Miami University, Oxford, Ohio; Visiting Associate Professor, University of Missouri, summer 1950; Independent Author and Editor, Mark Twain Project, University of California, Berkeley, 1978-. *Publications:* The Literary Apprenticeship of Mark Twain, 1950; A Bibliography of the Writings of James T Farrell, 1921-1957, 1959; James T Farrell, University of Minnesota Pamphlets on American Writers, 1963; Clemens of the Call, 1969; James T Farrell, 1971; The Great Landslide Case, 1972; The Grangerford-Shepherdson Feud: Life and Death at Compromise (with Robert H Hirst), 1985; Men Call Me Lucky, 1985; Mark Twain's Early Tales and Sketches, vols 1 and 2 (edited with Robert Hirst); Mark Twain's Letters. vol 1 (edited with Michael Frank and Kenneth Sanderson). *Contributions to:* Numerous articles in 17 magazines and journals; Chapters and sections in books, anthologies. *Honours:* Bellit Collect Junior Foreign Fellow, 1932-33; Leaves, Research Grants, Miami University, ACLS; Senior Fellow, National Endowment for the Humanities, 1971-72; Literary Executor for James T Farrell, 1975-; Senior Research Fellow, National Endowment for the Humanities, 1976-77; Benjamin Harrison Medallion, Miami University, 1978; Distinguished Service Citation, Beloit College, 1979; Guggenheim Fellow, 1978-79. *Memberships:* Phi Beta Kappa; Phi Kappa Psi; Modern Language Association of America; National Council of Teachers of English; Beta Theta Pi. *Address:* 4810 Bonham Road, Oxford, OH 45056, USA.

BRAND Oscar, b. 1920, Canada. Freelance Writer, Composer and Folk-Singer. *Appointments:* President, Harlequin Productions; President Gypsy Hill Music; Lecturer on Dramatic Writing, Hofstra University, Hempstead, New York; Coordinator of Folk Music, WNYC; Host, numerous TV folk-songs programmes; Curator, Songwriters Hall of Fame, New York City. *Publications:* Courting Songs, 1852; Folksongs for Fun, 1957; The Ballad Mongers, autobiography, 1957; Bawdy Songs, 1958; The Gold Rush (writer, composer), ballet, 1961; In White America (composer), play, 1962; A Joyful Noise (co-writer-composer), musical play, 1966; The Education of Hyman Kaplan (co-writer-composer), musical play, 1967; Celebrate (writer-composer), religious songs, 1968; How to Steal an Election (co-writer-composer), musical play, 1969; Songs of '76, music history, 1973; When I First Came To This Land, children, 1974; Thunder Rock (writer-composer), musical play, 1974; Party Songs, 1985. *Honours:* Laureate, Fairfield University, 1972; PhD, University of Winnipeg, 1989; Radio Pioneers of America, 1991;

Friends of Old Time Radio, 1991. *Memberships:* AFTRA, ACTRA, SAG, AFM, Dramatists Guild. *Address:* 141 Baker Hill, Great Neck, NY 11023, USA.

BRANDENBERG Aliki Liacouras, b. Wildwood Crest, New Jersey, USA. Writer & Illustrator, Children's Books. *Education:* Graduate, Philadelphia College of Art. *Publications:* Keep Your Mouth Closed Dear, 1966; My Fire Senses, 1962; At Mary Bloom's, 1976; The Two of Them, 1979; Mummies Made in Egypt, 1979; Digging Up Dinosaurs, 1981; We Are Best Friends, 1982; A Medievil Feast, 1983; Use Your Head Dear, 1983; Feelings, 1984; How a Book is Made, 1986; Welcome Little Baby, 1987; Dinosaur Bones, 1988; The King's Day, 1988; My Hands, 1990; My Feet, 1990; Manners, 1990; Christmas Tree Memories, 1991; I'm Growing, 1991; Communication, 1993; My Visit to the Aquarius, 1993. *Honours:* Junior Book Award, Boys Club of America, 1968; 1st prize, Children's Book Award, New York Academy of Sciences, 1977; Prix de Livre pour Enfants, Geneva, Switzerland, 1987; Drexel University, Free Library of Philadelphia Citation, 1991; Pennsylvania School Librarians Association Award, 1991. *Address:* 17 Regent's Park Terrace, London, NW1 7ED, England.

BRANDENBERG Franz, b. 1932, Switzerland. Children's Writer. *Publications:* I Once Knew a Man, 1970; Fresh Cider and Pie, 1973; A Secret for Grandmother's Birthday, 1975; No School Today, 1975; A Robber A Robber, 1976; I Wish I Was Sick Too, 1976; Nice New Neighbors, 1977; What Can You Make of It, 1977; A Picnic, Hurrah, 1978; Six New Students, 1978; Everyone Ready, 1979; It's Not My Fault, 1980; Cock-a-Doodle-Doo, 1986; Leo and Emily series, 3 vols, 1981-84; Aunt Nina series, 2 vols, 1983; Otto Is Different, 1985; The Hit of the Party, 1985; What's Wrong with a Van, 1987; Leo and Emily's Zoo, 1988; Aunt Nina, Good Night, 1989; A Fun Weekend, 1991. *Address:* 17 Regent's Park Terrace, London NW1 7ED, England.

BRANDER John Morran, b. 26 Jan 1932, San Francisco, California, USA. Lawyer. *Education:* BSc, 1954; LLB, 1967; LLM, 1971; MA, 1980. *Appointments:* Editor, California State Poetry Quarterly, 1985-91. *Publications:* Drawing Dreams; The Trail of the Moon; Black Sun; Dorset Green; Fractured Horizon; Darkness Over Paradise; Blue Silence; Wessex Downs; Ships in the Night; A Time of Geburah. *Honours:* Golden City Award. *Memberships:* PEN. *Address:* c/o David Alpaugh, Small Poetry Press, 362 Odin Place, Pleasant Hill, CA 94523, USA.

BRANDEWYNE Rebecca, b. 1955, USA. Full-time Writer. *Publications:* No Gentle Love, 1980; Forever My Love, 1982; Love, Cherish Me, 1983; Rose of Rapture, 1984; And Gold Was Ours, 1984; The Outlaw Hearts, 1986; Desire in Disguise, 1987; Passion Moon Rising, 1988; Upon a Moon-Dark Moor, 1988. *Address:* PO Box 780036, Wichita, KS 67206, USA.

BRANDIS Marianne. *See:* **BRENDER A BRANDIS Marianne.**

BRANDON (Oscar) Henry, b. 1916, United Kingdom. Journalist. *Appointments:* Joined paper, 1939, War Correspondent, North Africa and Western Europe, 1943-45, Paris Correspondent, 1945-46, Roving Diplomatic Correspondent, 1947-49, Washington Correspondent, 1950-, Associate Editor, Chief American Correspondent, retired 1983, The Sunday Times newspaper, London; Syndicated Columnist for Washington Star, 1979-81; Syndicated Columnist for New York Times News Service, 1983-. *Publications:* As We Are, 1961; In the Red, 1966; Conversations with Henry Brandon, 1966; The Anatomy of Error, 1970; Retreat of American Power, 1973; Special Relationships, 1989, (Biography); In Search of a New World Order, 1992. *Honour:* CBE 1985. *Address:* 3604 Winfield Lane NW, Washington DC 20007, USA.

BRANDON Joe. *See:* **DAVIS Robert Prunier.**

BRANDON Sheila. *See:* **RAYNER Claire.**

BRANFIELD John Charles, b. 19 Jan 1931, Burrow Bridge, Somerset, England. Writer; Teacher. m. Kathleen Elizabeth Peplow, 2 sons, 2 daughters. *Education:* MA, Queen's College, Cambridge; MEd, University of Exeter. *Publications include:* Nancekuke, 1972; Sugar Mouse, 1973; The Fox in Winter, 1980; Thin Ice, 1983; The Falklands Summer, 1987; The Day I Shot My Dad, 1989; Lanhydrock Days, 1991. *Literary Agent:* A P Watt Ltd, 20 John Street, London WC1N 2DR. *Address:* Mingoose Villa, Mingoose, Mount Hawke, Truro, Cornwall TR4 8BX, England.

BRANIGAN Keith, b. 15 Apr 1940, Slough, England. University Lecturer (Archaeology). m. Kuabrat Sivadith, 20 June 1965, 1 son, 2 daughters. *Education:* BA (Hons) 1st Class Archaeology & Ancient History 1963, PhD 1966, University of Birmingham. *Publications:* Roman Britain, 1980; Archaeology Explained, 1988; The Foundations of Palatial Crete, 1970; The Tombs of Mesara, 1970; Aegean Metalwork of the Early & Middle Bronze Age, 1974; The Catuvellauni, 1986; Gatcome: A Roman Villa Estate, 1977; Hellas, 1980; The Roman Villa in Southwest England, 1977; Prehistoric Britain, 1975; Verulamium & The Roman Chilterns, 1973; Latimer, 1971. *Contributions to:* Over 100 papers in journals. *Honour:* Elected Fellow, Society of Antiquaries, 1970. *Memberships:* The Prehistoric Society (Vice President, 1984-86); The Society for Promotion of Roman Studies. *Address:* Department of Archaeology & Prehistory, University of Sheffield, Sheffield S10 2TN, England.

BRASHER Christopher William, b. 21 Aug 1928, Guyana. Journalist. m. Shirley Bloomer, 28 Aug 1959, 1 son, 2 daughters. *Education:* MA, St John's College, Cambridge. *Appointments:* Columnist, The Observer, 1961-92; Chairman, Berghans Ltd, The Brasher Boot Co Ltd and The London Marathon Ltd. *Publications:* The Red Snows with Sir John Hunt, 1960; Sportsman of Our Time, 1962; A Dairy of the XVIIIth Olympiad, 1964; Mexico, 1968; Munich, 1972; (ed) The London Marathon: The First Ten Years, 1991. *Contributor to:* numerous professional journals and magazines. *Honours:* Sportswriter of the Year, 1968, 1976; National Medal of Honour, Finland. 1975. *Address:* The Navigator's House, River Lane, Richmond, Surrey, TW10 7AG, England.

BRAWNE Michael, b. 1925, United Kingdom. Architect; Professor Emeritus of Architecture. *Publications:* The New Museum: Architecture and Display, 1965; University Planning and Design: A Symposium (editor), 1967; Libraries: Architecture and Equipment, 1970; The Museum Interior: Temporary and Permanent Display Techniques, 1982; Arup Associates: The Biography of an Architectural Practice, 1983; Museum fur Kunsthandwerk: Architecture in Detail, 1992; Kimbell Art Museum: Architecture in Detail, 1992; From Idea to Building: issues in Architecture. *Address:* Michael Brawne and Associates, 28 College Road, Bath BA1 5RR, England.

BRAY John Jefferson, b. 16 Sept 1912, Adelaide, Australia. Retired Chief Justice. *Education:* Sevenhill Primary School 1922-24, St Peter's College, Adelaide, 1925-28; University of Adelaide, 1929-32; LLB (Ord) 1932, LLB (Hons) 1933, LLD 1937, University of Adelaide. *Publications:* Satura: Selected Poetry and Prose, 1988; Poems 1962; Poems 1961-1971, 1972; Poems, 1972-1979, 1979; The Bay of Salamis and Other Poems, 1986; The Emperor's Doorkeeper (Occasional Addresses) 1988; Seventy Seven (poems) 1990. *Contributor to:* Adelaide Review; Festscrifts. *Honours:* Companion of the Order of Australia, 1979; South Australian Non-Fiction Award (Satura) 1990. *Memberships:* English Association; Friendly St Poets

(Adelaide); Law Society of South Australia (honorary); University of Adelaide Club; Chief Justice of South Australia 1967-78; Chancellor, University of Adelaide, 1968-82. *Address:* 39 Hurtle Square, Adelaide, SA., Australia 5000.

BRAYFIELD Celia Frances, b. 21 Aug 1945, Ealing, England. Writer. 1 daughter. *Education:* St. Paul's Girls' School; Universitaire de Grenoble. *Appointments:* TV Critic, The Evening Standard, 1974-82; The Times, 1984-89; London Daily News, 1987; The Sunday Telegraph, 1989. *Publications:* The Body Show Book, 1981; Glitter, The Truth About Fame, 1985; Pearls, 1987; The Prince, 1990. *Contributions to:* various journals, magazines & newspapers. *Literary Agent:* Andrew Henson, John Johnson Agency. *Address:* c/o John Johnson Agency, Clerkenwell House, Clerkenwell Green, London EC4 ROHJ, England.

BREARS Peter Charles David, b. 30 Aug 1944. Museum Director. *Education:* Dip AD, Leeds College of Art. *Publications:* English Country Pottery, 1971; The Gentlewoman's Kitchen, 1984; Yorkshire Probate Inventories, 1972; Horse Brasses, 1980; Traditional Food in Yorkshire, 1987; Northcountry Folk Art, 1989; Of Curiosities & Rare Things, 1989; Treasures for the People, 1989; Collector's Book of English Country Pottery, 1974; Images of Leeds, 1992; Leeds Describ'd, 1993. *Contributions to:* Connoiseur; Folk Life; Post Medieval Archaeology. *Memberships:* Fellow, Museums Association; Fellow, Society of Antiquities; Chairman, Leeds Symposium on Food History; Secretary, Society for Folklife Studies. *Address:* City Museum, Calverley Street, Leeds LS1 3AA, England.

BREBNER Philip Alan, b. 14 Oct 1955. Author. m. Maria Joao Ramos, 22 July 1983, 1 daughter. *Education:* BSc, Dundee University, 1978; PhD, Glasgow University, 1982. *Publications:* A Country of Vanished Dreams; Toward Mecca. *Contributions to:* Building Law; Policy & Design in The Arab World; Travel Articles. *Memberships:* Society of Authors; PEN; Oporto Cricket & Lawn Tennis Club. *Literary Agent:* Charles Walker at Peters Fraser & Dunlop. *Address:* Rua Dr Melo Leote 97, 4100 Porto, Portugal.

BRECHER Michael, b. 14 Mar 1925, Montreal, Quebec, Canada. Political Science Educator. m. Eva Danon, 7 Dec 1950, 3 children. *Education:* BA, McGill University1946; MA 1948, PhD 1953, Yale University. *Appointments:* Member, Faculty, McGill University, Montreal 1952-; Professor of Political Science, McGill University 1963-; Visiting Professor, University of Chicago 1963, Hebrew University, Jerusalem, 1970-75, University of California, Berkeley, 1979, Stanford University 1980. *Publications:* The Struggle for Kashmir, 1953; Nehru: A Political Biography, 1959; The New States of Asia, 1963; Succession in India, 1966; India and World Politics, 1968; Political Leadership in India, 1969; The Foreign Policy System of Israel, 1972; Decisions in Israel's Foreign Policy, 1975; Studies in Crisis Behavior, 1979; Decisions in Crisis, 1980; Crisis and Change in World Politics, 1986; Crises in the 20th Century: Vol 1, Handbook of International Crises, Vol 2 Handbook of Foreign Policy Crises 1988; Crisis, Conflict and Instability, 1989. *Contributor to:* Over 70 articles in field to professional journals. *Honours include:* Canada Council and Social Science and Humanities Research Council of Canada, research grantee 1960, 65, 69-70, 75-76, 80-87, 90-92; Killam Awards, Canada Council, 1970-74, 1976-79; Watamull Prize, American Historical Association, 1960; Woodrow Wilson Foundation Award, American Political Science Association, 1973; Fieldhouse Award, McGill University, 1986; Fellow, Royal Society of Canada. *Memberships:* Several professional organisations. *Address:* McGill University, 855 Sherbrooke Street W, Montreal, PQ, Canada H3A 2T7.

BREINBURG Petronella (Alexandrina), b. 1927, Netherlands. Children's Writer; Teacher. *Appointments:* Part-time English Teacher, Bexley Education Authority, 1974-; Storyteller and Lecturer, various libraries, London. *Publications:* Legends of Surinam, 1971; Ballad of a Swan, poetry, 1972; Shawn Goes to School, 1973; Doctor Sean, 1973; My Brother Sean, 1974; Paleface and Me, 1974; Tinker and Me, 1975; Sean's Red Bike, 1975; Us Boys of Westcroft, 1975; Sally-Ann's Umbrella, 1975; What Happened at Rita's Party, 1976; Tiger, Paleface and Me, 1976; Sally-Ann in the Snow, 1977; A Girl, A Frog, and a Petticoat, 1978; Sally-Ann's Skateboard, 1979. *Address:* 7 Tuam Road, Plumstead Common, London SE18 2QX, England.

BRELIS Matthew, b. 30 Aug 1957, Boston, Massachusetts, USA. Journalist. *Education:* Graduated, Vassar College, 1980. *Appointments:* Journalist, Washington Star, Reporter, Pittsburgh Press, 1981-. *Honours:* Pulitzer Prize for collaboration with Andrew Schneider on fourteen articles that probed the Federal Aviation Administration's screening of airline pilots for substance abuse and other medical problems, leading to important reforms in testing procedures, 1987; Keystone Press and Roy W Howard Newspaper awards, 1987. *Address:* Pittsburgh Press, Box 566, Pittsburgh, PA 15230, USA.

BRENDER A BRANDIS Marianne, (Marianne Brandis), b. 5 Oct 1938, Netherlands. Writer. *Education:* BA, 1960, MA, 1964, McMaster University, Hamilton, Ontario, Canada. *Publications:* This Spring's Sowing, 1970; A Sense of Dust, 1972; The Tinderbox, 1982; The Quarter-Pie Window, 1985; The Sign of the Scales, 1990; Special Nests, 1990; Fire Ship, 1992. *Contributions to:* Article to Canadian Children's Literature, 1987. *Honours:* Young Adult Canadian Book Award, Saskatchewan Library Association, 1986; National Chapter IODE Book Award, 1986; Bilson Award, Historical Fiction for Young People, 1991. *Membership:* Writers Union of Canada. *Address:* 10 Lamport Ave, Apt 206, Toronto, Ontario, Canada M4W 1S6.

BRENDON Piers George Rundle, b. 21 Dec 1940, Stratton, Cornwall, England. Writer. m. Vyvyen Davis, 1968, 2 sons. *Education:* MA, PhD, Magdelene College, Cambridge. *Publications:* Hurrell Froude and the Oxford Movement, 1974; Hawker of Morwenstow, 1975; Eminent Edwardians, 1979; The Life and Death of the Press Barons, 1982; Winston Churchill, A Brief Life, 1984; Our Own Dear Queen, 1985; Ike : The Life and Times of Dwight D Eisenhower, 1986. *Contributor include:* Reviews for many papers and journals including: Times; Observer; The Mail on Sunday. *Literary Agent:* Curtis Brown Ltd. *Address:* 4B Millington Road, Cambridge CB3 9HP, England.

BRENNAN Joseph Payne, b. 20 Dec 1918, Bridgeport, Connecticut, USA. Library Assistant (Retired). m. 24 Oct 1970. *Publications include:* Heart of Earth, poems, 1950; Nine Horrors and A Dream, 1958; The Wind of Time, poems, 1962; Nightmare Need, poems, 1964; Stories of Darkness and Dread, 1973; 60 Selected Poems, 1985; The Borders Just Beyond, 1986. Total, 18 books. *Contributions to:* Esquire; American Scholar; Commonwealth; University Review; Yale Literary Magazine; New York Times; Alfred Hitchcock's Mystery Magazine; Weird Tales; Georgia Review; Southern Poetry Review. *Honours:* Leonora Speyer Award, Poetry Society of America, 1961; Clark Ashton Smith Poetry Award, 1978; Life Achievement Award, World Fantasy Convention, 1982. *Literary Agent:* Kirby McCauley Ltd, 432 Park Avenue South, Suite 1509, New York Ny 10016, USA. *Address:* 26 Fowler Street, New Haven, CT 06515, USA.

BRENNAN Patricia Winifred, (Patricia Daly; Anne Rodway), b. Shaftesbury, Dorset, England. Writer. m. (1) Denis William Reed, 31 Dec 1947, (2) Peter Brennan, 19 Sept 1960. *Education:* Bristol University; University of London, 1967. *Appointments:* Production Editor, Pitmans Publishing, 1946-48. *Publications:* Penguin Parade; Writing Today; Albion; Poems: PEN; The Iron Dominion; Arts Council New Poetry; Women Writing.

Contributions to: Kimber Anthologies of Ghost Stories; After Midnight Stories; In My Fathers House; The day Trip; Hesperios; Narcissus; Night Driver; Institute of Jewish Affairs; Patterns of Prejudice; Art & Sexual Taboo; Encounter; our family Doctors; Swedish Veekojournalen. *Memberships:* Society of Authors; PEN; Royal Society of Arts; British Federation of Graduate Women; Richmond & Hampton Association; Bath Association. *Address:* Iford House, 30 Newbridge Road, Bath BA1 3JZ, England.

BRENT Iris. *See:* **BANCROFT Iris.**

BRENTON Howard, b. 1942, United Kingdom. Playwright; Poet. *Appointments:* Resident Dramatist, Royal Court Theatre, London, 1972- 73; Resident Writer, University of Warwick, 1978-79. *Publications:* Notes from a Psychotic Journal and Other Poems, 1969; Revenge, 1969; Scott of the Antartic (or what God didn't see) 1970; Christie in Love and Other Plays, 1970; Lay By (co-author), 1972; Plays for Public Places, 1972; Hitler Daries 1972; Brassneck (with David Hare), 1973; Magnificence, 1973; Weapons of Happiness, 1976; The Paradise Run, television play, 1976; Epsom Downs, 1977; Sore Throats, with Sonnets of Love and Opposition, 1979; The Life of Galileo (adaptor), 1980; The Romans in Britain, 1980; Plays for the Poor Theatre, 1980; Thirteenth Night, and A Short Sharp Shock, 1981; Danton's Death (adaptor), 1982; The Genius, 1983; Desert of Lies, television play, 1983; Sleeping Policemen (with Tunde Ikoli), 1984; Bloody Poetry, 1984; Pravda (with David Hare), 1985; Dead Head, TV series, 1987; Greenland, 1988; H.I.D. (Hess Is Dead) 1989; Iranian Night, (with Tariq Ali) 1989; Diving for Pearls, a novel, 1989; Moscow Gold (with Tariq Ali), 1990. *Literary Agent:* Margaret Ramsey Ltd, England. *Address:* c/o Margaret Ramsey Ltd, 14a Godwin's Court, London WC2N 4LL, England.

BRETNOR Reginald, (Grendel Briarton), b. 30 July 1911, Vladivostok, Siberia. Writer. m. (1) Helen Harding, deceased, 1967, (2) Rosalie Leveille, 1969. *Appointments:* Writer, Office of War Information (US) later OIICA, 1943-47. *Publications:* Decisive Warfare, A Study in Military Theory, 1969, 1986; (Fiction) Schimmelhorn's Gold, 1986; Gilpin's Space, 1986; A Killing in Swords, 1978; (Story Collection) The Schimmelhorn File, 1979; Translator, Moncrif's Cats, Les Chats by Francois-Augustin Paradis de Moncrif, 1961; Editor, various books including; Modern Science Fiction, Its Meaning and Its Future, 1953, 1979; Science Fiction, Today and Tomorrow, 1974; The Craft of Science Fiction, 1976; The Future at War, anthology: I Thor's Hammer, 1979; II, The Spear of Mars, 1980; III, Orion's Sword, 1980; Works of Reginald Bretnor, (bibliography), 1988. *Contributions to:* various journals and magazines. *Honour:* Eaton Award (science fiction criticism), 1988. *Memberships:* Science Fiction Writers of America; Writers Guild of America; National Rifle Association; Military Conflict Institute. *Literary Agent:* Owlswick Literary Agency, Philadelphia, USA; Visual Media, All Talent Agency, Pasadena, California, USA. *Address:* PO Box 1481, Medford, OR 97501, USA.

BRETT Jan Churchill, b. 1 Dec 1949, Bryn Mawr, Pennsylvania, USA. Illustrator; Writer. m. Joseph Hearne, 18 Aug 1980, 1 daughter. *Education:* Colby Junior College, 1968-69; Boston Museum School, 1970. *Publications:* Author and Illustrator: Fritz and the Beautiful Horses, 1981; Good Luck Sneakers, 1981; Annie and the Wild Animals, 1985; Goldilocks and the Three Bears, 1987; Illustrator: Wood and Crossings, 1978; Inside a Sand Castle, 1979; Secret Clocks, 1979; St. Patrick's Day in the Morning, 1980; Some Birds Have Funny Names, 1981; I Can Fly, 1981; Young Melvin and Bulger, 1981; In the Castle of Cats, 1981; Some Plants Have Funny Names, 1983; Valentine Bears, 1983; Where Are All the Kittens, 1984; Cabbage Patch Kids, The Great Rescue, 1984; Old Devil is Waiting, 1985; Mother's Day Mice, 1986; The Twelve Days of Christmas, 1986; Scary, Scary Halloween, 1986; Noelle of the Nutcracker, 1986; Look at the Kittens, 1987; The Enchanted Book, 1987. *Contributions to:* Cricket

Magazine. *Honours:* Best of Year, Parent's Choice Magazine, 1981; Best of Year for 1983 and 1984 Sunrise Calendar, Gene Shalit NBC Television, 1983, 1984; Ambassador of Honor, English Speaking Union of the United States, 1983; Outstanding Science Trade Book for Children, National Science Teachers Association, 1984; Children's Book Award, University of Nebraska, 1984; Top Ten Children's Book of the Year, Redbook Magazine, 1985; Booklist Magazine Editor's Choice, American Library Association, 1986. *Membership:* Society of Children's Book Writers. *Address:* 132 Pleasant Street, Norwell, MA 02061, USA.

BRETT John Michael. *See:* **TRIPP Miles Barton.**

BRETT Mary Elizabeth, (Molly Brett), b. United Kingdom. Freelance Artist and Writer. *Publications:* The Japanese Garden; Story of a Toy Car; Drummer Boy; Duckling; Mr Turkey Runs Away; Puppy Schooldays; Tom Tit Moves House; Follow Me Round the Farm; Master Bunny the Baker's Boy; Adventures of Plush and Tatty; A Surprise for Dumpy; The Untidy Little Hedgehog; Robin Finds Christmas; The Forgotten Bear; Two in a Tent; Flip Flop's Secret; Paddy Gets into Mischief; Teddy Flies Away; Midget and the Pet Shop, 1969; Jiggy's Treasure Hunt, 1973; The Party That Grew, 1976; Jumble Bears, 1977; The Molly Brett Picture Book, 1978; An Alphabet by Molly Brett, 1980; The Runaway Fairy, 1982; Good-Night Time Tales, 1982; Plush and Tatty on the Beach, 1987; The Magic Spectacles, 1987. *Address:* Chimes Cottage, Horsell Vale, Woking, Surrey, England.

BRETT Michael. *See:* **TRIPP Miles Barton.**

BRETT Molly. *See:* **BRETT Mary Elizabeth.**

BRETT Raymond Laurence, b. 1917, United Kingdom. Emeritus Professor. *Appointments:* Lecturer in English, University of Bristol, 1946-52; G F Grant Professor of English, 1952-82, Dean, Faculty of Arts, 1960- 62, Emeritus Professor, 1982-, University of Hull; General Editor, Writers and Their Background Series. *Publications:* The Third Earl of Shaftesbury, 1952; George Crabbe, 1956, Revised Edition, 1968; Reason and Imagination, 1960; Lyrical Ballads by Wordsworth and Coleridge, 1798-1805 (edited with A R Jones), 3rd Edition, 1968, 4th Edition, 1991; An Introduction to English Studies, 1965; Poems of Faith and Doubt (editor), 1965; Fancy and Imagination, 1969; S T Coleridge (editor), 1971; William Hazlitt, 1977; Andrew Marvell Tercentenary Essays (editor), 1979; Barclay Fox's Journal (editor), 1979; Coleridge, Writers and Their Work series, 1980. *Address:* 19 Mill Walk, Cottingham, North Humberside HU16 4RP, England.

BRETT Simon Anthony Lee, b. 28 Oct 1945, Surrey, England. Writer. m. Lucy Victoria McLaren, 27 Nov 1971, 2 sons, 1 daughter. *Education:* BA Hons English (1st Class), Wadham College, Oxford, 1964-67. *Appointment:* Chairman, The Crime Writers' Association, 1986-87. *Publications:* 15 Charles Paris Crime Novels, 1975-93; 4 Mrs Pargeter Crime Novels, 1986-1992; Editor, Faber Books of Useful Verse, Parodies, Diaries; A Shock To The System, 1984; Dead Romantic, 1985; The Booker Book, 1989; How To Be A Little Sod, 1992; After Henry (Radio and TV Series), 1985-92. *Honours:* Best Radio Feature, Writers' Guild, 1973; Outstanding Radio Programme, Broadcasting Press Guild, 1987. *Memberships:* Crime Writers' Association; Detection Club; PEN; Writers' Guild; Society of Authors. *Literary Agent:* Michael Motley. *Address:* Frith House, Burpham, Arundel, West Sussex BN18 9RR, England.

BRETUO A. *See:* **ASSENSOH Akwasi Bretuo.**

BREWER Derek Stanley, b. 13 July 1923, Cardiff, Wales. Academic; Emeritus Professor. m. Lucie Elisabeth Hoole, 17 Aug 1951, 3 sons, 2 daughters.

Education: Magdalen College, Oxford, 1941-42, 1945-48; BA (Oxon), 1948; MA (Oxon), 1948; PhD, Birmingham University, 1956; LittD, Cambridge University, 1980. *Appointments:* Master, Emmanueal College, Cambridge, 1977-90; Editor, The Cambridge Review, 1981-86. *Publications:* Chaucer, 1953; Proteus, 1958; (ed) The Parlement of Foulys, 1960; Chaucer: The Critical Heritage, 1978; Chaucer and his World, 1978, reprinted, 1992; Symbolic Stories, 1980, reprinted, 1988; English Gothic Literature, 1983; Chaucer: an Introduction, 1984; Books and articles on Chaucer, Malory and other authors, mediaeval to nineteenth century. *Contributions to:* About 100 articles of various kinds to many learned and other journals. *Honours:* Seatonian Prize, Cambridge, 1969, 1972, 1979 (jointly), 1980 (jointly), 1983, 1986, 1988, 1992; Matthew Arnold Essay Prize, Oxford, 1948; Honorary LLD: Keio University, 1982; Harvard, 1984; Honorary DLitt, Birmingham, 1985; DUniv: York, 1985; Sorbonne, 1988; Williams College, 1988; Liege, 1990. *Memberships:* Chaucer Society, Past President; English Association, Past President; Fellow, Society of Antiquaries; Honorary Member, Japan Academy; Corresponding Fellow, Medieval Academy of America. *Address:* Emmanuel College, Cambridge, England.

BREWSTER Robin. *See:* **STAPLES Reginald Thomas.**

BREWSTER Townsend Tyler, b. 23 July 1924, Glen Cove, New York, USA. Playwright; Librettist; Lyricist; Poet; Translator; Critic. *Education:* BA, Queens College, 1947; MA, Columbia University, 1962. *Appointments include:* Lecturer, Theatre Department, City College, NY, 1969-73; Translator, adapter, continuity writer, NBC Television Opera, 1950- 51; Copywriter, Hicks & Greist, 1959-61. *Publications include:* Translations: Bernard Dadie's Monsieur Thogo-gnini, 1976; Maxime N'Debeka's Equatorium, 1987; Various others commissioned & published by Ubu Repertory Theatre. Also: Choreography of Love, opera libretto, broadcast 1947; Libretto, The Tower, Santa Fe Opera, 1957; 2 radio lectures, Copenhagen, Denmark, 1972. Plays produced include: Little Girl, Big Town, revue, 1953; Please Don't Cruy and Say "No", 1972; Though It's Been Said Many Times, Many Ways, 1976; The Girl Beneath the Tulip Tree, 1977; Black-Belt Bertram, 1979; Arthur Ashe & I, 1979; The Liar, translation, Corneille, 1984. *Honours include:* Playwrights fellowship, National Theatre Conference, 1947; Story Magazine Playwriting Award, 1968; MCTV Playwright-in-Residence, University of Denver, 1969; Louise Bogan Memorial Prize, poetry, 1975; Grant, National Endowment for the Arts, 1977; Jonathan Swift Award, satire, 1979; Various scholarships. *Memberships include:* ASCAP; Vice president, Harlem Performance Centre; Board, Harlem Culture Council, Centre for Contemporary Opera; Consultant, Apollo Opera & Drama Company; International Brecht Society. *Address:* 171-29 103 Road, Jamaica, New York 11433, USA.

BREZHNEV Dennis. *See:* **BARNETT Paul le Page.**

BRIARTON Grendel. *See:* **BRETNOR Reginald.**

BRICKLEBANK Peter Noel, b. 19 Oct 1955, Leeds, England. Writer. *Education:* BA, Communication Studies (Hons), Sheffield Polytechnic, 1977; MA, Literature, City College of New York, USA, 1985. *Contributions to:* Fiction to: The American Voice; Carolina Quarterly; Confrontation; Kansas Quarterly; Mid-American Review; Webster Review; Writers' Forum; The Crescent Review; Descant; Alaska Quarterly Review; Queens' Quarterly, Canada; Others; Non-fiction to: The American Book Review; another Chicago magazine; Minnesota Review; Others. *Honours:* Bertram D Wolfe Memorial Creative Writing Award, City University of New York, 1985; Nomination, Pushcart Prize, 1989; Fellowship in Fiction, New York Foundation for the Arts, 1990. *Address:* 1803 Riverside Drive 2J, New York, NY 10034, USA.

BRICKNER Richard P, b. 14 May 1933, New York City. USA. Writer; Teacher. *Education:* BA, Columbia College, 1957. *Publications:* My Second Twenty Years; Tickets; The Broken Year; Bringing Down the House; After She Left. *Contributions to:* NY Times Book Review. *Honours:* National Foundation for the Arts; Guggenheim Fellowship in Fiction. *Literary Agent:* Joy Harris. *Address:* c/o Joy Harris, 888 Seventh Avenue, New York, NY 10106, USA.

BRIDGEMAN Harriet (Victoria) (Lucy) (Viscountess), b. 30 Mar 1942. Director, The Bridgeman Art Library; Author. *Education:* MA, Trinity College, Dublin. *Publications:* The Masters, Executive Editor, 1965-68; Discovering Antiques, Editor 1970-71; The British Eccentric, 1974; An Encyclopaedia of Victoriana, 1975; Society Scandals, 1976; Beside the Seaside, 1976; Needlework : An Illustrated History, 1978; A Guide to Gardens of Europe, 1979; The Last Word, 1983. *Literary Agent:* Abner Stein. *Address:* 19 Chepstow Road, London W2 5BP, England.

BRIDGEMAN Richard. *See:* **DAVIES Leslie Purnell.**

BRIDGES Ben. *See:* **WHITEHEAD David Henry.**

BRIDWELL Norman Ray, b. 1928, USA. Children's Writer; Freelance Artist. *Publications:* Clifford the Big Red Dog, 1962; Zany Zoo, 1963; Bird in the Hat, 1964; Clifford Gets a Job, 1965; The Witch Next Door, 1965; Clifford Takes a Trip, 1966; Clifford's Halloween, 1966; A Tiny Family, 1968; The Country Cat, 1969; What Do They Do When It Rains, 1969; Clifford's Tricks, 1969; How To Care for Your Monster, 1970; The Witch's Christmas, 1970; Monster Jokes and Riddles, 1972; Clifford the Small Red Puppy, 1972; The Witch's Vacation, 1973; Merton the Monkey Mouse, 1973; The Dog Frog Book, 1973; Clifford's Riddles, 1974; Monster Holidays, 1974; Clifford's Good Deeds, 1974; Ghost Charlie, 1974; Boy on the Ceiling, 1976; The Witch's Catalog, 1976; The Big Water Fight, 1977; Clifford at the Circus, 1977; Kangaroo Stew, 1978; The Witch Grows Up, 1979; Clifford Goes to Hollywood, 1980; Clifford's ABC's, 1983; Clifford's Story Hour, 1983; Clifford's Family, 1984; Clifford's Kitten, 1984; Clifford's Christmas, 1984; Clifford's Grouchy Neighbors, 1985; Clifford's Pals, 1985; Count on Clifford, 1985; Clifford's Manners, 1987; Clifford's Birthday Party, 1988; Fun With Clifford, 1989; Clifford's Puppy Days, 1989; Where Is Clifford?; Clifford's Happy Days, 1990; Clifford, We Love You!, 1991; Clifford's Bath Time, 1991; Clifford's Bed Time, 1991; Clifford's Animal Noises, 1991; Clifford's Peek-A-Boo, 1991; The Witch Goes To School, 1992; Clifford Counts Bubbles, 1992; Clifford's Noisy Day, 1992; Clifford's Thanksgiving Visit, 1993. *Honour:* Jeremiah Ludington Memorial Award, 1991. *Address:* Box 869, Edgartown, MA 02539, USA.

BRIEN Alan b. 12 Mar 1925. Novelist; Journalist. m. (1) Pamela Mary Jones, 1947, 3 daughters, (2) Nancy Newbold Ryan, 1 son, 1 daughter, 1961, (3) Jill Sheila Tweedie, 1973. *Education:* BA, English Literature, Jesus College, Oxford. *Appointments:* Associate Editor, Mini-Cinema, 1950-52; Courier, 1952-53; Film Critic, Columnist, Truth, 1953-54; TV Critic, Observer, 1954-55; Film Critic, 1954-56, New York Correspondent, 1956-58, Evening Standard; Drama Critic, Features Editor, Spectator, 1958-61; Columnist, Sunday Daily Mail, 1958-62, Sunday Dispatch 1962-63; Political Columnist, Sunday Pictorial, 1963-64; Drama Critic, Sunday Telegraph, 1964-67; Columnist: Spectator, 1963-65; New Statesman, 1966-72, Punch 1972-84; Diarist, 1967-75; Film Critic 1976-84, Sunday Times. *Publications:* Domes of Fortune, 1979; Lenin the Novel, 1986; Heaven's Will (novel), 1989; And When Rome Falls (novel), 1991. *Contributions to:* various professional journals. *Address:* 14 Falkland Road, London NW5, England.

BRIERLEY David, b. 30 July 1936, Durban, South Africa. Author. m. Caroline Gordon Walker, 23 Apr.

1960, 1 daughter. *Education:* BA, Honours, Oxon. *Publications:* Cold War, 1979; Blood Group O, 1980; Big Bear, Little Bear, 1981; Shooting Star, 1983; Czechmate, 1984; Skorpion's Death, 1985; Snowline, 1986; One Lives, One Dies, 1987. *Literary Agent:* James Hale. *Address:* La Vieille Ferme, 24170 St-Germain-de-Belvès, France.

BRIGGS Asa (Baron), b. 7 May 1921, Keighley, Yorkshire, England. m. Susan Anne Banwell, 1955, 2 sons, 2 daughters. *Education:* 1st Class History Tripos, Parts I and II, Sidney Sussex College, Cambridge, 1941; BSc, 1st Class (Economics), London, 1941; Gerstenberg Studentship in Economics, London, 1941. *Publications:* Victorian People, 1954; The Age of Improvement, 1959. History of Broadcasting in the United Kingdom, 4 volumes, 1961-79; Victorian Cities, 1963; A Social History of England, 1983; Victorian Things, 1988; *Honours:* Life Peerage, 1976; Marconi Medal for Communications History, 1975; Medaille de Vermeil de la Formation, Fondation de l'Academie d'Architecture, 1979; 15 Honorary Degrees. *Memberships:* Fellow, British Academy; American Academy of Arts and Sciences; President, Social History Society. *Address:* The Caprons, Keere Street, Lewes, BN7 1TY, England.

BRIGGS Freda, b. 1 Dec 1930, Huddersfield, England. Associate Professor. m. Kenneth Briggs, 24 Dec 1952, 1 son, 1 daughter, dec. *Education:* Associate of the College of Preceptors, 1968; Advanced studies in Education, 1973; BEd, 1975; University of Sheffield, MA, 1978. *Appointments:* Lecturer, Sheffield, 1970; Derbyshire, 1971-76; Director, of Early Childhood Education, State College of Victoria, Coburg, Australia, 1976-80; Foundation Dean, De Lissa Institute of Early Childhood & Family Studies, Hartley College of Advanced Education, 1980-83; Principal Lecturer, South Australian College of Advanced Education, 1984-90. *Publications:* Teaching Children in the First Three Years of School; Why My Child? Keep Children Safe; Child Sexual Abuse - Confronting the Problem; Developing Personal Safety Skills in Children with Disabilities; Children and Families in Australia. *Contributions to:* Early Child Developement and Care; Australian Journal of Early Childhood; NZCER/ACER Set; Child Abuse and Neglect - The International Journal; British Journal of Social Work; Child Abuse Review; Education Today; Australian Police; Pivot; Australian Journal of Teaching Practice; Australian Society. *Honours:* Fellow of the College of Preceptors; Creswick Foundation Scholar. *Memberships:* International Society of Prevention of Child Abuse and Neglect; National Association of Prevention of Child Abuse and Neglect; British Association for the Study and Prevention of Child Abuse and Neglect; Education Adviser on the Overseas Project Advisory Committee Save the Children Fund - Australia; United Kingdom Coalition on Disability and Abuse. *Address:* University of South Australia, Lorne Avenue, Magill, South Australia 5072, Australia.

BRIGGS Raymond Redvers, b. 18 Jan 1934, Wimbledon, London, England. Illustrator; Writer; Cartoonist. m. Jean T. Clark, 1963 (dec.1973). *Education:* Wimbledon School of Art; Slade School of Fine Art, London. NDD; DFA; FSIAD. Freelance illustrator, 1957-; Children's author, 1961-. *Publications:* The Strange House, 1963; Midnight Adventure, 1961; Sledges to the Rescue, 1963; Ring-a-Ring o'Roses, 1962; The White Land, 1963; Fee Fi Fo Fum, 1964; The Mother Goose Treasury, 1966; Jim & the Beanstalk, 1970; The Fairy Tale Treasury, 1975; Fungus the Bogeyman, 1977; The Snowman, 1978; Gentleman Jim, 1980; When the Wind Blows 1982, stage & radio versions 1983; The Tinpot Foreign General & the Old Iron Woman, 1984; Unlucky Wally, 1987; Unlucky Wally, Twenty Years On, 1989; The Man, 1992. *Honours:* Awards including: Kate Greenaway Medal, 1966, 1973; BAFTA Award (British Academy of Film & Television Arts). *Address:* Weston, Underhill Lane, Westmeston, near Hassocks, Sussex, BN6 8XG, England.

BRILEY John, b. 1925, USA. Screenwriter; Novelist. *Appointments:* Staff Writer, MGM, 1960-64; Freelance Screenwriter, Trevone Productions Inc, Los Angeles, California, 1965-. *Publications:* Invasion Quartet (with J T Storey), screenplay; Postman's Knock (with J T Storey), screenplay; Children of the Damned, screenplay; Seven Bob a Buck, play; Pope Joan, screenplay; The Traitors, novel, UK Edition How Sleep the Brave, 1969; So Who Needs Men, play; The Last Dance, novel, 1978; That Lucky Touch, screenplay; The Medusa Touch, screenplay; Eagle's Wing, screenplay; Enigma, screenplay; Gandhi, screenplay; Marie, screenplay. *Memberships:* Executive Committee, Writers Guild of Great Britain, 1978-. *Address:* 2686 Basil Lane, Los Angeles, CA 90077, USA.

BRIN David, b. 1950, USA. Science Fiction Writer. *Publications:* Sundiver, 1980; Startide Rising, 1983; The Practice Effect, 1984; The Postman, 1985. *Memberships:* Secretary, Science Fiction Writers of America. *Address:* 5081 Baxter Street, San Diego, CA 92117, USA.

BRINGHURST Robert, b. 16 Oct 1946, Los Angeles, California, USA. Poet. *Education:* BA, Comparative Literature, Indiana University, Bloomington, 1973; MFA, University of British Columbia, Vancouver, Canada, 1975. *Appointments:* General Editor, Kanchenjunga Poetry Series, 1973- 79; Visiting Lecturer, Department of Creative Writing, 1975-77, Lecturer, 1979-80, Department of English, University of British Columbia, Vancouver, Reviews Editor, Canadian Fiction Magazine, 1974-75; Adjunct Lecturer, Simon Fraser University, Burnaby, British Columbia, 1983-84; Contributing Editor, Fine Print: A Review for the Arts of the Book, 1985-90. *Publications:* Poetry: The Shipwright's Log, 1972; Cadastre, 1973; Deuteronomy, 1974; Eight Objects, 1975; Bergschrund, 1975; Jacob Singing, 1977; The Stonecutter's Horses, 1979; Tzuhalen's Mountain, 1982; The Beauty of the Weapons: Selected Poems 1972-82; Tending the Fire, 1985; The Blue Roofs of Japan, 1986; Pieces of Map, Pieces of Music, 1987; Conversations with a Toad, 1987; History and criticism: Visions: Contemporary Art (with Geoffrey James, Russell Keziere, Doris Shadbolt), 1983; Ocean, Paper, Stone, 1984; Shovels, Shoes and the Slow Rotation of Letters, 1986; Part of the Land, Part of the Water: A History of the Yukon Indians (with Catharine McClellan et al), 1987; The Black Canoe: Bill Reid Reid and the Spirit of Haida Gwaii, 1991; The Elements of Typographic Style, 1992; The Raven Steals the Light (with Bill Reid), narrative prose, 1984, 2nd Edition, 1988, French Edition, 1989; Poems in anthologies. *Honours:* Macmillan Prize for Poetry, 1975; Canada Council Grants, 1975-76, 1977, 1980-81, 1983, 1984-85, 1986-87; 1993-94; Ontario Arts Council Literary Grant, 1982; Alcuin Society Design Award, 1984, 1985; Canadian Broacasting Corporation Poetry Prize, 1985; Guggenheim Fellowship, 1987-88; Canada Council/ Scottish Arts Council Canada/Scotland Exchange Fellowship, 1989-90. *Memberships:* Writers Union of Canada, National Council 1985-87, Chairman, Committee on Social Responsibility of the Artist, 1988-90; Sierra Club; Greenpeace; Other environmental organisations. *Address:* PO Box 280, Bowen Island, British Columbia, Canada VON 1G0.

BRINK Andre Philippus, b. 29 May 1935, Vrede, South Africa. Professor. *Education:* DLitt, Rhodes University; DLitt (honoris causa) University of the Witwatersrand. *Publications:* Lobola vir die Lewe, 1962; File on a Diplomat, 1966; Mapmakers (essays), 1983; Looking on Darkness, 1974; An Instant in The Wind, 1976; Rumours of Rain, 1978; A Dry White Season, 1979; A Chain of Voices, 1982; The Wall of the Plague, 1984; The Ambassador, 1985; A Land Apart, 1986; States of Emergency, 1988; An Act of Terror, 1991; The First Life of Adamastor, 1993; On the Contrary, 1993. *Contributions to:* World Literature Today; Theatre Quarterly; Standpunte. *Honours:* Reina Prinsen Geerligs Prize, 1964; CNA Award, 1965, 1978, 1982; Academy Prize for Prose Translation, 1970; Martin Luther King Memorial Prize, 1980; Prix Medicis Etranger, 1980;

Chevalier de la Legion d'Honneur, 1982; Commandeur de l'Ordre des Arts et des Lettres, 1992. *Address:* University of Cape Town, Randebosch, South Africa.

BRINKLEY Alan, b. 2 June 1949, Washington, District of Columbia, USA. Historian. m. Evangeline Morphos, 3 June 1989. *Education:* AB, Princeton University, 1971; PhD, Harvard University, 1979. *Appointments:* Assistant Professor of History, Massachusetts Institute of Technology, Boston, 1978-82; Dunwalke Associate Professor of American History, Harvard University, 1982-88; Professor of History, City University of New York Graduate School, 1988-91; Professor of History, Columbia University, New York City, 1991-. *Publications:* The Unfinished Nation: A Concise History of The American People, 1993; Voices of Protest: Huey Long, Father Coughlin, and the Great Depression, 1982; America in the Twentieth Century, 1982; American History: A Survey, 1990. *Honours:* National Book Award for History, 1983; Guggenheim Fellowship, 1984-85; Woodrow Wilson Center Fellowship, 1985; National Humanities Center Fellowship, 1988-89. *Memberships:* Executive Board, Society of American Historians; Executive Board, Organization of American Historians. *Address:* 15 West 81st Street, New York, NY 10024, USA.

BRINNIN John Malcolm, b. 13 Sept 1916, Halifax, Canada. Teacher; Author. *Education:* BA, University of Michigan; Harvard University. *Appointments include:* Director, Poetry Centre, New York City, 1949-57; Instructor, English, Vassar College, 1942-47; Associate Professor, English, University of Connecticut, 1951-62; Emeritus Professor of English, Boston University. *Publications:* Dylan Thomas in America, 1955; The Third Rose, Gertrude Stein & Her World, 1958; Selected Poems of John Malcolm Brinnin, 1964; The Sway of the Grand Saloon: A Social History of the North Atlantic, 1971; Sextet: T.S. Eliot & Truman Capote & Others, 1981. *Honours:* Award, National Institute of Arts & Letters, 1968; Centennial Medal, Distinction in Literature, Michigan University; Gold Medal, Poetry Society of America. *Membership:* National Institute of Arts & Letters. *Address:* King Caesar Road, Duxbury, MA 02332, USA.

BRINSMEAD H F. *See:* **BRINSMEAD HUNGERFORD Hesba Fay.**

BRINSMEAD Hesba. *See:* **BRINSMEAD HUNGERFORD Hesba Fay.**

BRINSMEAD HUNGERFORD Hesba Fay (Hesba Brinsmead, H F Brinsmead), b. 15 Mar 1922, Australia. Writer. div. *Education:* Blackfriars Correspondance School, 1929-34; Avandale Teachers Training College, 1940-42. *Publications:* Pastures of the Blue Crane; Seasons of the Briar; Bent of the City; Isle of the Sea Hose; Who Call From Afar?; Others inc. Under the Silkwood; The Wind Harp; The Sand Forest. *Contributions to:* NSW School Magazine; Womens Weekly; Teachers Journal; Victorian School Paper; A Handfull of Ghosts. *Honours:* Book of the Year; Mary Gilmore Award; Elizabethian award; German Childresn Book of the Year. *Memberships:* Australian Society of Authors. *Address:* Shanava Road, Terrana, NSW, Australia.

BRINTON Alexander. *See:* **BATTIN B W.**

BRISCO P A. *See:* **MATTHEWS Patricia Anne.**

BRISCO Patty. *See:* **MATTHEWS Patricia Anne.**

BRISKIN Jacqueline, b. 1927, London, England. Novelist; Short Story Writer. *Publications:* California Generation, 1970; Afterlove, 1974; Rich Friends, 1976; Paloverde, 1978; The Onyx, 1982; Everything and More, 1983; Too Much Too Soon, 1985; Dreams Are Not Enough, 1987; The Naked Heart, 1989; The Other Side of Love, 1991. *Memberships:* PEN; Author's Guild. *Address:* Los Angeles, California, USA.

BRISKIN Mae Seidman, b. 20 Oct 1924, Brooklyn, New York, USA. Writer. m. Herbert B Briskin, 1 Dec 1946, 2 sons, 1 daughter. *Education:* BA magna cum laude, Brooklyn College, 1944; MA, Columbia University, 1946. *Publications:* A Boy Like Astrid's Mother, Stories, 1988; The Tree Still Stands, 1991. *Contributions to:* Numerous. *Honours:* Best American Short Stories, 1976; PEN Syndicated Fiction Awards, 1985, 1986, 1987, 1988; Award for collection of short fiction, PEN International-USA West, 1989. *Membership:* PEN. *Literary Agent:* Ellen Levine. *Address:* 3604 Arbutus Drive, Palo Alto, CA 94303, USA.

BRISTER Commodore Webster, b. 15 Jan 1926, Alexandria, LA, USA. Theological Educator. m. Gloria Virginia Nugent, 28 Mar 1946, 1 son. *Education include:* Louisiana College, Pineville, LA, BA, 1947; New Orleans Baptist Seminary, BD, 1952; M Div, 1973; Southwestern Baptist Seminary, ThD, 1957; PhD, 1974. *Appointments include:* Distinguished Professor, Pastoral Ministry, Southwestern Baptist Theological Seminary, 1957. *Publications:* Pastoral Care in the Church; People Who Care; Dealing With Doubt; Its Tough Growing Up; Life Under Pressure: Dealing with Stress in Marriage; The Promise of Counseling; Take care; Becoming You; Beginning Your Ministry; Caring for the Caregivers. *Contributions to:* Holman Study Bible; Pastoral Psychology Home Life; The Baptist Program; Southwestern Journal Theology; The Baptist Student; Home Missions; Church Administration; Royal Service. *Honours:* Fellow in Economics, Louisiana State University; Fellow, Association of Theological Schools; Research fellow in Psychiatry; UT Southwestern Medical School. *Memberships:* Baptist World Alliance Commission on Church Leadership; Association for Clinical Pastoral Education; Society for Pastoral Theology; Assocation of Couples for Marriage Enrichment. *Address:* Southwestern Baptist Theological Seminary, PO BOX 22036, Fort Worth, TX 76122, USA.

BRISTOW Robert O'Neil, b. 17 Nov 1926, St Louis, Missouri, USA. Author. m. Gaylon Walker, 23 Dec 1950, 2 sons, 2 daughters. *Education:* BA Journalism 1951, MA Journalism 1965, University of Oklahoma. *Appointment:* Writer-in-Residence, Winthrop College, South Carolina, 1961-87. *Publications:* Time For Glory, 1968; Night Season, 1970; A Faraway Drummer, 1973; Laughter In Darkness, 1974. *Contributions to:* Approximately 200 short stories to magazines and journals. *Honours:* Award for Literary Excellence, University of Oklahoma, 1969; Friends of American Writers Award, 1974. *Address:* 613 1/2 Charlotte Avenue, Rock Hill, SC 29730, USA.

BRITAIN Dan. *See:* **PENDLETON Donald.**

BRITAIN Ian Michael, b. 30 Aug 1948, Bombay, India. Historian. *Education:* BA, 1972; MA, 1976; D Phil, 1980. *Appointments:* Co Editor, Webbers Magazine, 1989-. *Publication:* Fabianism & Culture. *Contributions to:* Studio International; Victorian Studies; History Today; Historical Studies. *Membership:* Australian Historical Association. *Address:* 5 Tyson Street, Richmond, Victoria 3121, Australia.

BRITTAN Samuel, b. 29 Dec 1933, London, England. Journalist. *Education:* 1st Class Honours, Economics, Jesus College, Cambridge; Research Fellow, Nuffield College, 1973-74. *Literary Appointments:* Various posts, 1955-61, Principal Economic Commentator, 1966-, Assistant Editor, 1978-, Financial Times, London; Economics Editor, The Observer, 1961-64. *Publications include:* Steering the Economy, 3rd Edition, 1971; Left or Right - The Bogus Dilemma, 1968; The Price of Economic Freedom: A Guide to Flexible Rates, 1970; Is There and Economic Consensus?, 1973; Capitalism and the Permissive Society, 1973; Second Thoughts on

Full Employment Policy, 1975; The Delusion of Incomes Policy (with Peter Lilley), 1977; The Economic Consequences of Democracy, 1977; How British is the British Sickness?, 1978; How to End the 'Monetarist' Controversy, 1981; Role and Limits of Government: Essays in Political Economy, 1983; Jobs, Pay Unions and The Ownership of Capital, 1984; Two Cheers for Self-Interest, 1985. *Honours:* Senior Wincott Award for Financial Journalists, 1971; Elected Visiting Fellow, Nuffield College, 1974; George Orwell Prize for Political Journalism, 1981; Honorary DLitt, Heriot-Watt University, 1985; Member, Peacock Committee on the Finance of the BBC, 1985-86; Légion D'Honneur, 1993. *Address:* The Financial Times, Number One, Southwark Bridge, London SE1 9HL, England.

BROCH Harald Beyer, b. 17 May 1944, Oslo, Norway. 1 son, 1 daughter. *Education:* PhD, Bergen, 1974; Doctor Phiosophy, Bergen, 1990. *Publications:* Growing Up Agreeably; Woodland Trappers. *Contributions to:* Some 50 articles, Anthropological Journals. *Memberships:* The Norwegian Non Fiction Writers & Translators Assocation. *Address:* Department of Social Anthropology, PO Box 1091 Blindern, N-0317 Oslo 3, Norway.

BROCK Edwin, b. 1927, United Kingdom. Writer; Poet. *Appointments:* Editorial Assistant, Stonhill and Gillis, London, 1947- 51; Poetry Editor, Ambit magazine, London, 1960-; Advertising Writer, Mather and Crowther, London, 1959-63; Advertising Writer, J Walter Thompson, London, 1963-64; Advertising Writer, Masius Wynne-Williams, London, 1964; Creative Group Head, S H Benson, London, 1964-72; Freelance Writer, Ogilvy Benson and Mather, London, 1972-. Retired from Advertising, 1988. *Publications:* An Attempt at Exorcism, 1959; Night Duty on Eleven Beat, radio play, 1960; A Family Affair: Two Sonnet Sequences, 1960; The Little White God, novel, 1962, televised, 1964; With Love from Judas, 1963; Penguin Modern Poets 8 (with Geoffrey Hill and Stevie Smith), 1966; Fred's Primer: A Little Girl's Guide to the World Around Her, 1969; A Cold Day at the Zoo, 1970; Invisibility is the Art of Survival: Selected Poems, 1972; The Portraits and the Poses, 1973; Paroxisms, 1974; I Never Saw It Lit, 1974; The Blocked Heart, 1975; Song of Battery Hen, Selected Poems 1959-75, 1977; Here, Now, Always, autobiography, 1977; The River and the Train, 1979; Five Ways to Kill a Man, (New & Selected Poems), 1990. *Address:* The Granary, Lower Tharston, Norfolk NR15 2YN, England.

BROCK Rose. *See:* **HANSEN Joseph.**

BROCK William Ranulf, b. 16 May 1916, Farnham, Surrey, England. University Teacher (retired). m. Constance Helen Brown, 8 July 1950, 1 son, 1 daughter. *Education:* BA 1937, MA 1945, PhD 1941, Trinity College, Cambridge. *Appointments:* Fellow of Selwyn College, Cambridge; Professor of Modern History, University of Glasgow, 1967-81. *Publications:* Lord Liverpool and Liberal Toryism, 1941; Character of American History, 1960; An American Crisis, 1963; Conflict and Transformation: USA 1844-77, 1973; USA 1739-1870 (Sources of History), 1975; Parties and Political Conscience (USA 1840- 52), 1979; Evolution of American Democracy, 1979; Scotus Americanus (Scotland and America, 15th C), 1981; Investigation and Responsibility (State Agencies in USA), 1984; Welfare, Democracy and the New Deal, 1988. *Memberships:* Fellow of the British Academy; Fellow, Royal Historical Society; British Association of American Studies (Founder member, Committee 1954-64); Organization of American Historians. *Address:* 49 Barton Road, Cambridge CB3 9LG, England.

BROCKHOFF Stefan. *See:* **PLANT Richard.**

BRODERICK Damien Francis, b. 22 Apr 1944. Writer. *Education:* BA, Monash University, Australia, 1966; PhD, Deakin University, 1990. *Literary Appointments:* Writing Fellowships, Literature Board, Australia Council, 1980, 1984, 1990; Writer-in-Residence, Deakin University, 1986. *Publications:* A Man Returned (short stories), 1965; The Dark Between the Stars (Stories), 1991; Novels: The Dreaming Dragons, 1980; The Judas Mandala, 1982, revised 1990; Transmitters, 1984; The Black Grail, 1986; Striped Holes, 1988; The Sea's Furthest End, 1993; Valencies (with Rory Barnes), 1983; The Zeitgeist Machine (edited), 1977; Strange Attractors (edited), 1985; Matilda At the Speed of Light (edited), 1988. *Contributions to:* Melbourne Age, Australian; Australian Book Reivew; New York Review, SF; Foundation; Age Monthly Review; Australian Science Fiction Review. *Honours:* Ditmar, Australian Science Fiction Achievement Award for The Dreaming Dragons 1981, Transmitters 1985 and Striped Holes, 1989; Runner-up John Campbell Memorial Award, 1980. *Address:* 23 Hutchinson St, Brunswick East, VIC 3057, Australia.

BRODEUR Paul, b. 16 May 1931, Boston, Massachusetts, USA, Writer, div, 1 son, 1 daughter. *Education:* BA, English, Harvard College, 1953. *Appointments:* Lecturer, Columbia University Graduate School of Journalism, 1969-80; Lecturer, Boston University School of Public Communication, 1978-79; Lecturer, University of California at San Diego, 1989. *Publications:* The Sick Fox, 1963; The Stunt man, 1970; Expendable Americans, 1974; Outrageous Misconduct, 1985; The Zapping of America, 1977; Downstream Atheneum, 1972; Currents of Death, 1989; Asbestos and Enzymes, 1972; Restitution, 1985. *Contributor to:* Staff Writer, The New Yorker, 1958-; Contributor of dozens of articles. *Honours:* Sidney Hillman Prize, 1973; Columbia University National Magazine Award, 1973; American Association for the Advancement of Science Award, 1976; Guggenheim Fellowship, 1976-77; Alicia Patterson Foundation Fellowship, 1978; American Bar Association Certificate of Merit, 1983; American Association of Trial Lawyers Public Service Award, 1986p; Global 500 Honour Roll, United Nations Environment Programme, 1989. *Literary Agent:* Sandra Dijkstra, 1155 Camino Del Man, Del Man, CA 92041, USA. *Address:* c/o The New Yorker, 20 West 43rd Street, New York, NY 10036, USA.

BRODIE Malcolm, b. 27 Sept 1926, Glasgow, Scotland. Journalist. m. Margaret Elizabeth Stevenson, 14 Sept 1949, 3 sons. *Appointments:* Staff, Belfast Telegraph, 1943; Sports Editor, 1951-1991. *Publications:* History of Irish FA, 1980; Story of Glentoran, 1982; Official History of Linfield, 1986; Irish Soccer, 1962; Best - Anatomy of a Star, 1974, Co-author; Glenavon 100 Years, 1989. *Contributions to:* Northern Ireland Sports Correspondent, The Daily Telegraph, Sunday Telegraph, News of the World, Associated Press. *Honours:* MBE, 1978; Northern Ireland Rothmans Sportswriter of the Year, 1980; Highly Commended, British Sports Journalism Awards, 1982, 1986; Sports Writers Association and Sports Council Doug Gardner award for outstanding service to British sports journalism. *Membership:* National Union of Journalists. *Address:* 3 Rochester Drive, Cregagh, Belfast, Northern Ireland BT6 9JX.

BRODKEY Harold, b. 1930, USA. Short Story Writer. *Appointments:* Associate Professor of English, Cornell University, Ithaca, New York, 1977-78, 1979, 1981. *Publications:* First Love and Other Sorrows, 1958; Women and Angels, 1985; Stories In An Almost Classical Mode, 1988; The Abundant Dreamer, 1989; The Runaway Soul, 1991. *Contributions to:* New Yorker, Esquire, Vanity Fair, Paris Review, Partisan Review. *Honours:* Prix d Rome, American Academy, 1959-60; National Magazine Award, 1974; Brandeis University Award, 1975; O'Henry First Prize, 1975, 1976; Guggenheim Fellow, 1987; National Endowment Arts Grantee, 1984-85; Present Tense Magazine Award (fiction), 1989. *Membership:* PEN American. *Literary Agent:* Andrew Wylie, Wylie, Aitken & Stone. *Address:* c/o Andrew Wylie, Wylie, Aitken & Stone, 250 W 57th Street, Suite 2106, New York, NY 10107, USA.

BRODSKY Iosif Alexsandrovich, b. 24 May 1940, Leningrad, USSR. Russian-Jewish Poet. *Education:* Secondary school. Began writing poetry, 1955; Sentenced, hard labour, for 'social parasitism' 1964; Sentence commuted, 1965; Refused visa to attend Poetry International, London, and Festival of Two Worlds, Spoleto, 1969; Involuntary exile in USA after brief stays in Vienna & London; Appeared at Poetry International, 1972. Poet in residence, University of Michigan, USA 1972-73, 1974-, Queen's College, New York 1973-74. *Publications:* A Christmas Ballad, 1962; Elegy for John Donne, 1963; Isaac & Abraham, 1963; New Stanzas to Augusta, 1964; Einem alten Architekten in Rom, 1964; Verses on the Death of T.S. Eliot, 1965; Verse & Poems, New York 1965, French & German translations 1966; English translation, John Donne & Other Poems, 1967; Song Without Music, 1969; A Stop in the Desert; Verse & Poems, 1970; Selected Poems, (Penguin), 1973; A Part of Speech, 1980; Less Than One, 1981; To Urania, 1988; Watermark, 1992. *Address:* Farrer, Straus & Giroux Inc, 19 Union Square West, New York, NY 10003, USA.

BROIDA Helen, b. 28 May 1916, St Louis, Missouri, USA. Speech Pathologist. divorced, 2 daughters. *Education:* BS, Speech Pathology, Washington University, St Louis, 1938; MS, Speech Pathology 1959, PhD Speech Pathology 1962, University of Southern California. *Publication:* Coping With Stroke, 1979. *Contributions to:* Archives of Physical Medicine and Rehabilitation. *Membership:* Life Member, American Speech, Language & Hearing Association. *Address:* 3241-2B San Amadeo, Laguna Hills, CA 92653, USA.

BROME Vincent, Author. *Publications:* Anthology, 1936; Clement Attlee, 1947; H.G. Wells, 1951; Aneurin Bevan, 1953; The Last Surrender, 1954; The Way Back, 1956; Six Studies in Quarrelling, 1958; Sometimes at Night, 1959; Frank Harris, 1959; Acquaintance with Grief, 1961; We Have Come a long Way, 1962; The Problem of Progress, 1963; Love in our Time, 1964; Four Realist Nvelists, 1964; The International Brigades, 1965; The World of Luke Jympson, 1966; Freud and His Ealry Circle, 1967; The Surgeon, 1967; Diary of a Revolution, 1968; The Revolution, 1969; The Imaginary Crime, 1969; Confessions of a Writer, 1970; The Brain Operators, 1970; Private Prosecutions, 1971; Reverse Your Verdict, 1971; London Consequences, 1972; The Embassy, 1972; The Day of Destruction, 1975; The Happy Hostage, 1976; Jung - Man and Myth, 1978; Havelock Ellis - Philosopher of Sex, 1981; Ernest Jones: Freud's alter ego, 1983; The Day of the Fifth Moon, 1984; J.B.Priestly, 1988. *Contributions to:* The Times; Sunday Times; Observer; Manchester Guardian; New Statesman; New Society; Encounter; Spectator; Times Literary Supplement. *Address:* 45 Great Ormond Street, London WC1, England.

BROMIGE David Mansfield, b. 22 Oct 1933, London, England. University Profesor. m. Ceelia Belle, 3 Jan 1981, 1 son, 1 daughter. *Education:* BA (Hons), English, University of British Columbia, Canada, 1962; MA, English 1964, ABD 1969, University of California, Berkeley, USA. *Appointments:* Editor, Critis' Page, Ubyssey, Vancouver, Canada, 1958- 62; Editor, Raven, University of British Columbia, 1960-62; Poetry Editor, Northwest Review, 1962-64; Editor, R C Lion, Berkeley, USA, 1966-68; Editor, Open Reading, Cotati, 1970-76; Contributing Editor, Avec, Penngrove, 1987-; Contributing Editor, Kaimana, Honolulu, 1989-; Director, Public Poetry Center, Sonoma State University, 1970-92. *Publications:* Desire, 1988; Tight Corners, 1974; My Poetry, 1980; Men, Women & Vehicles, 1990; Tiny Courts, 1991; They Ate, 1992; The Harbor-Master of Hong Kong, 1993; Birds of the West, 1973; The Ends of the Earth, 1968; Threads, 1971; 3 Stories, 1973; Out of My Hands, 1974; Credences of Winter, 1975; Spells & Blessings, 1974; P-E-A-C-E, 1981; You See, 1986; Red Hats, 1986. *Contributions include:* Caterpillar; Sulfur; Boxcar; This. *Honours:* Poet Laureate, University of California (all campuses), 1965; Writers Fellowships, Canada Council, 1976-77 and National Endowment for the Arts, 1980-81; Western States Book Award for Poetry, 1988. *Memberships:* Rimers' Club: Secretary, University of California, Berkeley 1966-68, President, Sonoma State University, 1970-76; New Langton Arts, SF, 1982-. *Address:* 461 High Street, Sebastopol, CA 95472, USA.

BRONISLAWSKI Jerzy-Stanislaw Kudas, b. 7 May 1930, Lodz, Poland. Writer. m. Zebina Sobczynska, 18 Dec 1968, 1 son, 1 daughter. *Education:* MSc, Faculty of Law, 1970; PhD, Institute of Political Sciences, 1972, Adam Mickiewicz University. *Literary Appointments:* Editor: Iskry, Warsaw, 1967-74; Mon, Warsaw, 1969-74; Maw, Warsaw, 1974- 84; OPZZ, Warsaw, 1985-86; Pojezzierze, Olsztyn, 1987-; Gantaleba - Tbilisi/Georgien. *Publications:* Sabres and Usurers, 1970; The Espionage, Intelligence, Paragraphs, 1974; Life without Safeguard, 1975; The Master of Empty House, 1978; Without Scruples, 1979; Mazurian Saga, 1980; Duel, 1972; Mr Bailey's Mistake, 1970; The Anatomy of Treason, 1971; The Invisible in the Crowd, 1967, 1968, 1975; Before They Come at Daybreak, 1969, 1970, 1973; The Alienateds, 1972; The Falste Prophetes, 1981, 1984; The Furtively Observed Land, 1987; Polish Dialoque, 1990; 52 reports, 1 adaptation for film and 3 for television. *Contributions to:* Kultura; Zeszyty Historyczne; Zycie Literackie; Profile; Za Wolnosc i Lud; Wprost/Poznań. *Honours:* Rafal Urban Award, 1977; Zycie Literackie Award, 1978; Polityka Award, 1983; J Iwaszkiewicz Award, 1990; Polityka Award, 1992. *Memberships:* ZLP, Polish Writers Association; ZAIKS, Societe des Auteurs. *Address:* ul Powsinska 70 m. 48, 02-903 Warsaw,Poland.

BRONK William, b. 1918, USA. Poet; Essayist. *Publications:* Light and Dark, 1956; The World, The Worldless, 1964; The Empty Hands, 1969; That Tantalus, 1971; To Praise the Music, 1972; Utterances, 1972; Looking as It, 1973; The New World, essays, 1974; A Partial Glossary: Two Essays, 1974; Silence and Metaphor, 1975; The Stance, 1975; My Father Photographed with Friends and Other Pictures, 1976; The Meantime, 1976; Finding Losses, 1976; Twelve Losses Found, 1976; That Beauty Still, 1978; The Force of Desire, 1979; Six Duplicities, 1980; The Brother in Elysium, essays, 1980; Life Supports: New and Collected Poems, 1981; Light in a Dark Sky, 1982; Vectors and Smoothable Curves, collected essays, 1983; Careless Love and Its Apostrophes, 1985; Manifest, and Furthermore, 1987; Death Is The Place, 1989; Living Instead, 1991. *Address:* 57 Pearl Street, Hudson Falls, NY 12839, USA.

BROOKE Michael Zachary, b. 5 Nov 1921, Cambridge, England. Author; Consultant. m. Hilda Gillatt, 25 July 1953, 2 sons, 1 daughter. *Education:* BA, History, 1st Class Honours, 1943; MA, University of Cambridge, 1945; MA, 1964, PhD, 1969, University of Manchester. *Publications:* Frederic Le Play: Engineer and Social Scientist, 1970; The Strategy of Multinational Enterprise, co-author, 1970, 2nd edition, 1978; The Multinational Company in Europe, co-author, 1972; A Bibliography of International Business, co-author, 1977; The International Firm, co-author, 1977; International Corporate Planning, co-author, 1979; International Financial Management Handbook, co-author, 2 volumes, 1983; Centralization and Autonomy, 1984; Selling Management Service Contracts in International Business, 1985; International Travel and Tourism Forecasts, co-author, 1985; International Management, 1986; South Pennine Escort, 1987; Handbook of International Trade, co-author, 1988; Profits from Abroad, 1988 (co-author); International Business Studies (co-author), 1991. *Contributions to:* Numerous professional journals. *Honour:* Fellow, Academy of International Business, 1982. *Memberships:* Society of Authors, Chairman, Authors North, 1978-80; Independent Publishers' Guild (Chairman North West Region, 1989-91); The Circumnavigator's Club, 1991. *Address:* 21 Barnfield, Urmston, Manchester M31 1EW, England.

BROOKE-LITTLE John Philip, b. 6 Apr 1927, London, England. Norroy & Ulster King of Arms. m. Mary Lee Pierce, 30 Apr 1960, 3 sons, 1 daughter. *Education:* MA (Hons) Modern History, New College, Oxford University. *Appointments:* Honorary Editor, The Coat of Arms, 1950-; Editor, Dod's Peerage and Dod's Parliamentary Companion, 1953-58. *Publications:* Boutell's Heraldry (Edited), 1970-1983; Knights of the Middle Ages, 1966; Kings and Queens of Great Britain (with Anne Taute & Don Pottinger), 1969; Beasts in Heraldry, 1974; The British Monarchy in Colour, 1976; Royal Arms Beasts & Badges, 1977; Royal Ceremonies of State, 1979. *Contributions to:* Many magazines and journals. *Honours:* CVO (Commander of the Royal Victorian Order); Knight of Justice, Most Venerable Order of St John of Jerusalem; Knight Grand Cross of Grace and Devotion, Order of Malta. *Memberships:* President, English Language Literary Trust; Fellow, Society of Antiquaries of London; Fellow, The Heraldry Society; Fellow, Society of Genealogists; Honorary Fellow, Institute of Heraldic & Genealogical Studies. *Address:* Heyford House, Lower Heyford, Bicester, Oxon OX6 3NZ, England.

BROOKER Jewel Fay Spears, b. 13 June 1940, Jenkins, Kentucky, USA. Professor; Scholar. m. Hampton Ralph Brooker, 21 Dec 1962, 1 son, 1 daughter. *Education:* Stetson University, 1962; MA, University of Florida, 1964; PhD, University of South Florida, 1976. *Appointments:* University of Tampa, Lecturer, 1966-71, 1975; University of South Florida, Lecturer, 1972, 1974-75, 1978-80; Yale University, Postdoctoral Fellow, 1980-81; Eckerd College, Professor, 1981-; Columbia University, Visiting Professor, 1988; Doshisha University, Visiting Professor, 1992-93. *Publications:* Approaches to Teaching T S Eliots Poetry & Plays; Reading The Waste Land; The Placing of T S Eliot; Mastery and Escape: T S Eliot and the Dialectic of Modernism. *Contributions to:* 35 Articles, The Southern Review; Centennial Review; South Atlantic Review; Modern Philology; ELH; Massachusetts Review. *Honours:* Teaching Excellence & Campus Leadership Award; Knight Foundation; Wilbur Foundation; National Endowment for Humanities; Southern Regional Educational Board; Missouri Arts Council, Grant; Florida Endowment for the Humantities. *Memberships include:* Association for Christianity & Literature; T S Eliot Society; Modern Language Association; National Council of Teachers of English; South Atlantic Modern Language Association. *Address:* Letters Collegium, Eckerd College, 4200 54th Avenue South, St Petersburg, FL 33711, USA.

BROOKNER Anita, b. 16 July 1928, London, England. Art Historian. *Publications:* Jean-Baptiste Grevze, 1972; Genius of the Future, 1971; Jacques-Louis David, 1980; A Start in Life, 1982; Providence, 1982; Look at Me, 1983; Hotel Du Lac, 1984; Family and Friends, 1985; A Misalliance, 1986; A Friend from England, 1987; Latecomers, 1989 Lewis Percy, 1989; A Closed Eye, 1990; Fraud, 1991. *Contributions to:* Times Literary Supplement; LRB; Burlington Magazine; Spectator. *Honour:* Booker Prize, 1984. *Literary Agent:* A M Heath, London, WC2. *Address:* 68 Elm Park Gardens, London SW10, England.

BROOKS Andree Nicole Aelion, b. 2 Feb 1937, London, England. Journalist; Author; Lecturer; Columnist. m. Ronald J Brooks, div 19 Aug 1959, 1 son, 1 daughter. *Education:* Queens College, London, 1952; Journalism Certificate, 1958. *Appointments include:* Adjunct Professor, Fairfiled University, 1982-87; Associate Fellow, Yale University, 1989-. *Contributions to:* Over 3000 Articles, 1959-; Contributing Columnist, New York Times, 1978-. *Honours include:* Best Non Fiction Book of the Year for 1990, from National Federation of Press Women for book, Children of Fast Track Parents; Journalism Awards, Connecticut Society of Architects; National Federation of Press Women; Women in Communications; American Jewish Committee. *Literary agent:* Suzanne Gluck, ICM. *Address:* 15 Hitchcock Road, Westport, CT 06880, USA.

BROOKS George E. Jr, b. 1933, USA. Professor of History. *Appointments:* Member, Editorial Advisory Board, International Journal of African Historical Studies, 1968-; Member, Editorial Advisory Board, Liberian Studies Journal, 1968-77. *Publications:* New England Merchants in Africa: A History Through Documents, 1802-1865 (edited with N R Bennett), 1965; Yankee Traders, Old Coasters and Africa Middlemen: A History of American Legitimate Trade with West Africa in the Nineteenth Century, 1970; The Kru Mariner in the Nineteenth Century: An Historical Compendium, 1972; Themes in African and World History, 1983; Landlords and Strangers: Ecology, Sociaty and Trade in Western Africa, 1993. *Address:* Department of History, Indiana University, Bloomington, IN 47405, USA.

BROOKS Jeremy, b. 1926, United Kingdom. Novelist; Playwright; Reviewer. *Appointments:* Feature Writer, Pictorial Press, London, 1950- 52; Literary Agent, Christy & Moore, London, 1952-53; Fiction and General Reviewer, The Guardian, 1958-60; Play Reader, BBC Television, London, 1959-60; Drama Critic, New Statesman, 1961-62; Literary Manager, 1962-69, Play Adviser, 1969-, Royal Shakespeare Co, Stratford-upon-Avon and London; Reviewer, Sunday Times, 1962-. *Publications:* The Water Carnival, 1957; Jampot Smith, 1960; Henry's War, 1962; Smith, As Hero, 1965; The Magic Perambulator, 1965; I'll Fight You, 1966; A Value, 1976; Doing The Voices, 1985. *Address:* 12 Bartholomew Road, London NW5, England.

BROOKS Mel, b. 1926, Brooklyn, USA. Writer; Director; Actor. m. (1) Florence Baum, 2 sons, 1 daughter, (2) Anne Bancroft, 1964, 1 son. *Publications:* TV Script Writer for Series: Your Show of Shows, 1950-54; Caesar's Hour, 1954-57; Get Smart, 1965-70; Films: (cartoon) The Critic, 1963; Writer, Director: The Producers, 1968; Young Frankenstein, 1974; Writer, Director, Actor, The Twelve Chairs, 1970; Blazing Saddles, 1973; Silent Movie, 1976; Writer, Director, Actor, Producer: High Anxiety, 1977; History of the World Part 1, 1981; Actor, Producer, To Be Or Not To Be, 1983; Writer, Director, Producer, Actor, Spaceballs, 1987; Actor, Producer, Director, Life Stinks, 1991. *Address:* c/o Twentieth Century Fox Film Corporation, Box 900, Beverly Hills, CA 90213, USA.

BROOKS Richard, b. 1912, USA. Film Writer and Director. *Films:* Co-Scriptwriter: Sin Town, Men of Texas, 1942; The White Savage, Cobra Women, My Best Gal, Don Winslow of the Coast Guard, 1943; Swell Guy, The Killers, 1946; Brute Force, 1947; To the Victor, Key Largo, The Naked City, 1948; Storm Warning, Any Number Can Play, 1949; Mystery Street, 1950; Scriptwriter and Director: Crisis, 1950; The Light Touch, 1951; Deadline USA, 1952; Battle Circus, Take the High Ground (director only), 1953; The Flame and the Flesh (director only), The Last Time I Saw Paris (co-screenwriter), 1954; The Blackboard Jungle, 1955; The Last Hunt, The Catered Affair (director only), 1956; Something of Value, 1957; The Brothers Karamazov (co-screenwriter), Cat on a Hot Tin Roof (co-screenwriter), 1958; Elmer Gantry, 1960; Sweet Bird of Youth, 1961; Lord Jim, 1965; The Professionals, 1966; In Cold Blood, 1967; The Happy Ending, 1969; Dollars (The Heist, in UK) (co- screenwriter), 1971; Bite the Bullet, 1975; Looking for Mr Goodbar, 1977; Wrong Is Right (also producer), 1982; The Man with the Deadly Lens. *Publications:* Brick Foxhole, novel, 1946; Boiling Point, 1948; The Producer, novel, 1951. *Honour:* Academy Award for Screenplay, for Elmer Gantry, 1960. *Address:* c/o Directors Guild, 7950 Sunset Boulevard, Hollywood, CA 90046, USA.

BROOKS-GUNN Jeanne, b. 9 Dec 1946. Psychologist. m. Robert W Gunn, 1970 *Education:* BA, Conn Colleg, 1969; Ed M, Harvard University, 1970; PhD, University Pa, 1975. *Appointments include:* Associate Director, Institute for the Study of Exceptional Children, Educational Testing Service, Princeton, NJ, 1977-82; Assistant Professor of Pediatrics, Columbia University, 1978-85; Senior Research Scientist,

Director, of Adolescent Study Program, St Lukes Rossevelt Hospital Center, NYC, 1983-; Adjunct Professor, University of Pa, 1985-91; Visiting Scholar, Russell Sage Foundation, 1989-90; Director, Center for the Study of Parents & Their Children, Columbia University, 1991; Virginia & Leonard Marx Professor of Child Development, Teachers College, Columbia University; Professor of Pediatrics, College of Physoans and Surgeons, Columbia University, 1992-. *Publications:* He And She; How Children Develop Their Sex Role Identity; Social Cognition and the Acquisition of Self; Girls at Puberty; Women in Midlife; The Study of Maturational Timing Effects in Adolescence; Adolescent Mothers in Later Life; The Encyclopedia of Adolescence; The Emergence of Depression & Depressive Symptoms During Adolescence; Escape From Poverty: What Makes a Difference for Children. *Contributions to:* Numerous Articles, Son Child Developement; Social Psychology. *Memberships:* Society for Research in Child Development; AAAS; President, Society for Research in Adolescence;National Academy of Science Committees on (Preventing Aids, Child Abuse, Neglect, and Poverty). *Address:* Province Line Road, Hopewell, NJ 08525, USA.

BROPHY Brigid, b. 12 June 1929, London, England. Writer. m. Sir Michael Levey q.v., 12 June 1954, 1 daughter. *Education:* St. Hugh's College, Oxford. *Literary Appointments:* Vice-Chairman, British Copyright Council, 1976-80. *Publications include:* Hackenfeller's Ape, 1953; The King of a Rainy Country, 1956; Black Ship to Hell, 1962; Flesh, 1962; The Finishing Touch, 1963; The Snow Ball, 1964; Mozart the Dramatist, 1964; Don't Never Forget, 1966; Fifty Works of English Literature We Could Do Without, with Michael Levey and Charles Osborne, 1967; Black and White: A Portrait of Aubrey Beardsley, 1968; In Transit, 1969; Prancing Novelist, 1973; The Adventures of God in his Search for the Black Girl and Other Fables, 1973; Pussy Owl, 1976; Beardsley and His World, 1976; Palace Without Chairs, 1978; The Prince and the Wild Geese, 1983; A Guide to Public Lending Right, 1983; Baroque-N-Roll, 1987; Reads, 1989. Plays Include: The Burglar, 1967; The Waste Disposal Unit, Radio, 1968. *Contributions to:* London Review of Books; Times Literary Supplement. *Honours:* Cheltenham Literary Festival, 1st Prize, first novel, 1954; London Magazine Prize for Prose, 1962. *Membership:* Executive Council 1975-78, Writers Guild of Great Britain; London Magazine Prize for Prose, 1962. *Literary Agent:* Giles Gordon, Sheil and Associates. *Address:* Fir Close, 2 Westgate, Louth, Lincolnshire, LN11 9YH, England.

BROSSARD Chandler, (Daniel Harper), b. 1922, USA. Writer; Former Journalist/Editor. *Appointments:* Reporter, Washington Post, Washington, District of Columbia, 1940-42; Writer, The New Yorker, New York City, 1942-43; Senior Editor, Time magazine, New York City, 1944; Executive Editor, American Mercury, New York City, 1950-51; Senior Editor, Look magazine, New York City, 1956-67; Associate Professor, Old Westbury College, Oyster Bay, Long Island, New York, 1968-70. *Publications:* Who Walk in Darkness, 1952; The Bold Saboteurs, 1953; The Wrong Turn (as Daniel Harper), 1954; All Passion Spent, also as Episode with Erika, 1954; The Scene Before You: A New Approach to American Culture (editor), 1955; Harry the Magician, play, 1961; The Double View, 1961; Some Dreams Aren't Real, play, 1962; The Man with Ideas, play, 1962; The Insane World of Adolf Hitler, 1967; The Spanish Scene, 1968; Wake Up, We're Almost There, 1971; Did Christ Make Love, 1973; Raging Joys, Sublime Violation, 1981. *Address:* 251 West 89th Street, New York, NY 10024, USA.

BROTHER Antoninus. *See:* EVERSON William Oliver.

BROUGHTON John Renata, b. 19 Mar 1947, Hastings, New Zealand. University Lecturer in Maori Health. *Education:* BSc, Massey University, 1971; Bachelor of Dental Surgery, Otago University, 1977. *Publications:* A Time Journal for Halley's Comet,

children's book, 1985; Te Hokinga Mai (The Return Home), stage play, 1990; Te Hara (The Sin), stage play, 1990; Nga Puke (The Hills), stage play, 1990; Nga Mahi Ora, TV documetary on health career for young Maori people, 1990; Michael James Manaia, stage play, 1991; Maraq, stage play, 1992. *Contribution to:* Everything you wanted to know about mouthguards, to Te Hau Ora Sports Journal. *Honour:* Dominion Sunday Times Bruce Mason Playwright Award, 1990. *Memberships:* PEN New Zealand; Chairman, Araiteuru Marae Council Inc; Foundation Member, Maori Health Workforce Development Group, Department of Health; Otago Branch, New Zealand Dental Association, Committee Member 1979-84. *Literary Agent:* Playmarket, PO Box 9767, Wellington, New Zealand. *Address:* Te Maraenui, 176 Queen Street, Dunedin, New Zealand.

BROWN Anthony Eugene Sr, b. 22 July 1937, Rocky Mount, North Carolina, USA. Writer. 3 sons. *Education:* BA, University of South Carolina, 1960; MA, 1962; PhD, Vanderbilt University, 1971. *Appointments:* Fellow, American Philosophical Society, 1971; Senior Fellow, American Society of Learned Scholars, 1972-73. *Publications:* Boswellian Studies; Edinburgh. *Contributions to:* Various Items in Local Newspapers. *Memberships:* American Aociety for Eighteenth Century Studies; Eighteenth Century Scottish Studies Society; Ashville Downtown City Club. *Literary Agent:* Edinburgh University Press. *Address:* PO Box 10, Webster, NC 28788, USA.

BROWN Archibald Haworth, b. 1938, United Kingdom. University Professor. *Publications:* Soviet Politics and Political Science, 1974; The Soviet Union since the Fall of Khrushchev (edited with M Kaser), 1975, 2nd Edition, 1978; Political Culture and Political Change in Communist States (edited with Jack Gray), 1977, 2nd Edition, 1979; Authority, Power and Policy in the USSR (edited with T H Rigby and P Reddaway), 1980; The Cambridge Encyclopaedia of Russia and the Soviet Union (co-editor), 1982; Soviet Policy for the 1980s (edited with M Kaser), 1982; Political Culture and Communist Studies (editor), 1984; Political Leadership in the Soviet Union (editor), 1989; The Soviet Union: A Biographical Dictionary (editor), 1990; New Thinking in Soviet Politics (editor), 1992; The Gorbachev Factor in Soviet Politics, 1993. *Contributions to:* Various Papers in Academic Journals and Symposia. *Honour:* Elected Fellow of the British Academy, 1991. *Address:* St Antony's College, Oxford OX2 6JF, England.

BROWN Dale W., b. 1926, USA. Professor of Christian Theology. *Publications:* In Christ Jesus: The Significance of Jesus as the Christ, 1965; Four Words for the World, 1968; So I Send You, 1969; Brethren and Pacifism, 1970; The Christian Revolutionary, 1971; Flamed by the Spirit, 1978; Understanding Pietism, 1978; What About the Russians, 1984; Biblical Pacifism, 1986. *Address:* Bethany Theological Seminary, Butterfield and Meyers Road, Oak Brook, IL 60521, USA.

BROWN Diana, b. 8 Aug 1928, Twickenham, England. Author; Librarian. m. Ralph Herman Brown, 31 Dec 1964, 2 daughters. *Education:* MLS, 1976, MA, Instructional Technology, 1977, San Jose State University. *Publications:* The Blue Dragon, 1988; The Hand of a Woman, 1984; The Sandalwood Fan, 1983; Come Be My Love, 1982; The Emerald Necklace, 1980; St Martin's Summer, 1981; A Debt of Honour, 1981. *Contributions to:* San Jose Mercury News; Fresno Bee; Good Housekeeping. *Honour:* Hand of a Woman, named outstanding title, American Library Association Booklist, 1984. *Memberships:* Authors Guild; Phi Kappa Phi. *Agent:* International Creative Management. *Address:* 1612 Knollwood Avenue, San Jose, CA 95125, USA.

BROWN George McKay, b. 17 Oct 1921, Stromness, Orkney, Scotland. Writer. *Education:* Newbattle Abbey College, 1951-52; MA, Edinburgh University, 1956-60. *Publications:* Fisherman with Ploughs, poems, 1971; The Wreck of the Archangel, poems, 1989; Greenvoe, novel, 1972; Magnus, novel, 1973; The Golden Bird, two novellas, 1987; Portrait of Orkney, 1988; The Masked Fisherman, 1989; The Sea Kings Daughter, 1991; The Loom of Light, play, 1987. *Contributions to:* Scotsman; Glasgow Herald; Guardian; New Statesman; Tablet. *Honours:* OBE, 1974; LLD, Dundee University, 1973; D.Litt. Glasgow University, 1985. *Membership:* FRSL. *Address:* 3 Mayburn Court, Stromness, Orkney KW16 3DH, Scotland.

BROWN Helen Gurley, b. 18 Feb 1922, Green Forest, Arkansas, USA. Author; Editor. m. David Brown, 1959. *Education:* Texas State College for Women, Woodbury College. *Appointments include:* Executive Secretary, Music corporation of America, 1942-45; William Morris Agency, 1945-47; Copywriter, Foote Cone & Belding Advertising Agency, Los Angeles, 1948-58; Advertisement Writer, Account Executive, Kenyon & Eckhard Advertising Agency, Hollywood, 1958-62; Editor in Chief, Cosmopolitan Magazine, 1965-. *Publications:* Sex and the Single Girl, 1962; Sex and the Office, 1965; Outrageous Opinions, 1966; Helen Gurley Brown's Single Girl's Cook Book, 1969; Sex and the New Single Girl, 1971; Having it All, 1982. *Honours:* Francis Holm Achievement Award, 1956-59; University of Southern California School of Journalism, 1971; Special award for Editorial Leadership, 1972; establishment of Helen Gurley Brown Research Professorship, Northwestern University, 1985. *Memberships:* various professional organisations including: AFTRA; Authors League of America; American Society of Magazine Editors. *Address:* 1 West 81st Street, New York, NY 10024, USA.

BROWN Jamie, b. 1945, Canada. Author. *Appointments:* Consultant, National Film Board of Canada, 1974-77; Lecturer in Creative Writing, Concordia University, Montreal, 1979-85. *Publications:* The Lively Spirits of Provence, non-fiction, 1974; Stepping Stones, fiction, 1975; So Free We Seem, fiction, 1976; Shrewsbury, fiction, 1977; The War Is Over, screenplay, 1979; Superbike (for children), 1980; Toby McTeague, screenplay, 1986; Keeping Track (also co-producer), screenplay, 1986. *Address:* 174 Beacon Hill, Beaconsfield, Quebec, Canada H9W 1T6.

BROWN John Russell, b. 15 Sept 1923, Bristol, England. Writer; Teacher; Theatre Director. m. Hilary Sue Baker, 5 Apr 1961, 1 son, 2 daughters. *Education:* BA, 1949 B Litt 1951, Oxford University; PhD, University of Birmingham 1960. *Literary Appointments:* Member of Drama Panel of the Arts Council of Great Britain, 1978-82, Chairman 1980-82, and Member of the Arts Council. *Publications:* Shakespeare and His Comedies, 1957, 1962; Shakespeare's Plays in Performance, 1966, 1969; Effective Theatre, 1969; Shakespeare's Dramatic Style, 1970; Theatre Language, 1972; Free Shakespeare, 1974, 1978; Discovering Shakespeare, 1981; Shakespeare and His Theatre, 1982; A Short Guide to Modern British Drama, 1983; Shakescences, 1992. *Contributor to:* General Editor, Theatre Production Studies (Routledge 1981 -). *Address:* Court Lodge, Hooe, Battle, Sussex TN33 9HJ, England.

BROWN Judith K, b. 31 Oct 1930, Professor of Anthropology, 1 son, 1 daughter. *Education:* Cornell University, BS, 1952; Harvard Graduate School of Education, MEd, 1954; University London, Certificate in Child Development, 1955; Harvard Graduate School of Education, Ed D, 1962; Bunting Institute of Radcliffe College, 1967-69; Institute for Research on Women & Gender, Stanford University, 1989. *Publications:* In Her Prime: New Views of Middle Aged Women; Sanctions And Sanctury: Culture Perspectives on the Beating of Wives; In Her Prime: A New View of Middle Aged Women. *Contributions to:* Numerous Book Reviews; Chapters in Collections & Journal Articles. *Honours:* Grant From National Institute on Aging. *Memberships:* American Anthropological Association; American Assocation of University Professors; Society for Psychological Anteropolopy. *Address:* Department of Sciology & Anthropology, Oakland University, Rochester, MI 48309, USA.

BROWN Marjorie Clair, b. 8 Apr 1923, Manly, New South Wales, Australia. Retired Excl Management Secretary; Writer. 1 daughter. *Publications:* Discarded Heart; More than Yesterday; That Man. *Contributions to:* Nation; Looking forward; BBW Aust; Writers News; Childrens History Project; Swan on the Swamp. *Memberships:* Faw Macarthur Region. *Address:* 15 Tallawarra Road, Leumeah, New South Wales 2560, Australia.

BROWN Richard E, b. 11 Feb 1946, Kansas City, USA. English Professor. *Education:* Stanford University, AB, 1968; Cornell University, PhD, 1972. *Publications:* Chesters Last Stand. *Contributions to:* Fields: Restoration & 18th Drama; Irish Literature; English Romanticism. *Address:* Department of English, University of Nevada, Reno, NE 89557, USA.

BROWN Rita Mae, b. 28 Nov 1944. *Education:* Broward Junior College, 1965; New York University, BA, 1968; School of the Visual Arts, 1968; Institute for Policy Studies, PhD, 1976. *Appointments:* Writer in Residence, Womens Writers Center, Cazenovia College, 1977-78;Review Translations, Attic Greek & Latin, 1978-; President, American Artists Inc. *Publications include:* Rest In Pieces; Wish You Were Here; Starting From Scratch: A Different Kind of Writers Manual; Six of One; In Her Day; The Hand That Cradles the Rock; Songs to a Handsome Women; Hrotsvitha: Six Medieval Latin Plays; The Plain Brown Rapper. *Contributions to:* Vogue Magazine; Various Anthologies inc: Sisterhood is Powerful; The New Women; Women: The New Voice; Book Reviews. *Honours include:* Nominated Emmy for Best Mini Series, The Long Hot Summer; Writers Guild of America Award for Best Variety Show on Television; Outstanding Yound Women of America. *Address:* c/o American Artists Inc, PO Box 4671, Charlottesville, VA 22905, USA.

BROWN Robert Douglas, b. 17 Aug 1919, Trealaw. Journalist; Publisher. m. Elsie Mary Warner, 17 Aug 1940, 1 son, 2 daughters. *Education:* BA, Open University, 1986. *Appointments:* Political Staff, News Chronicle, 1951-60; Managing Director, Anglia Echo Newspapers, 1964-80. *Publications:* The Battle of Crichel Down; The Survival of the Printed Word; The Port of London; East Anglia: The War Years. *Memberships:* Fellow of PEN; Former Member, Former President, 1976-78, Media Society. *Address:* Lower Green, Stoke By Clare, Sudbury, Suffolk, England.

BROWN Stewart, b. 14 Mar 1951, Lymington, England. University Lecturer. m. Priscilla M Brant, 1977, 1 son, 1 daughter. *Education:* BA, Falmouth School of art; MA, University of Sussex; PhD, University of Wales. *Publications:* Lugards Bridge; The Art of Derek Walcott; Zinder; Caribbean Poetry Now; Voiceprint; Caribbean New Wave; Heinemann Book of Caribbean Poetry; African Writers: A Readers Guide. *Honours:* Eric Gregory Award; South west Arts Literature Award; Elected Member Welsh Academy. *Address:* Centre of West African Studies, University of Birmingham, Edgbaston, Birmingham B15 2T4, England.

BROWN Terence, b. 1944, Republic of Ireland. Associate Professor of English. *Appointments:* Lecturer, 1968-81, Fellow, 1976-, Associate Professor of English, 1981-, Trinity College, Dublin. *Publications:* Time Was Away: The World of Louis MacNeice (edited with Alec Reid), 1974; Louis MacNeice: Sceptical Vision, 1975; Northern Voices: Poets from Northern Ulster, 1975; The Irish Short Story (edited with Patrick Rafroidi), 1979; Ireland: A Social and Cultural History 1922-79, 1981; 1985, Ireland's Literature: Selected Essays, 1988; Tradition and Influence in Anglo-Irish Poetry, (edited with Nicolas Greve), 1989. *Address:* Department of English, Trinity College, Dublin 2, Republic of Ireland.

BROWN Theodore M., b. 1925, USA. Professor of History of Art. *Publications:* The Work of G Rietveld, Architect, 1958; Introduction to Louisville Architecture,

1960; Old Louisville (with M M Bridwell), 1961; Margaret Bourke-White, Photojournalist, 1972. *Address:* History of Art Department, Goldwin Smith 35, Cornell University, Ithaca, NY 14853, USA.

BROWNE Michael Joseph Dennis, b. 28 May 1940, Walton-on-Thames, England. Teacher. m. Lisa Furlong McLean, 18 July 1981, 1 son, 2 daughters. *Education:* BA, Hull University, 1962; MA, University of Iowa, 1967. *Publications:* The Wife of Winter, London 1970, New York 1970; Sun Exercises, 1976; The Sun Fetcher, 1978; Smoke from the Fires, 1985; Over a dozen libretti, music by David Lord, Stephen Paulus, John Foley SJ. *Contributor to:* Tri-quarterly, The Iowa Review; Virginia Quarterly Review; American Poetry Review; Prairie Schooner. *Honours:* NEA 1977; Bush fellowship, 1983. *Memberships:* American PEN; Poetry Society of America. *Address:* 2111E 22nd Street, Minneapolis, MN 55404, USA.

BROWNING Robert, b. 15 Jan 1914, Glasgow, Scotland. Emeritus Professor. *Education:* MA, University of Glasgow, 1931-35; MA, Balliol College, Oxford. *Appointments:* Editorial Board, Past and Present, 1960-78; Reviews Editor, Journal of Hellenic Studies, 1964-74. *Publications:* Studies in Byzantine History, Literature and Education, 1977; History, Language and Literacy in the Byzantine World, 1989; Medieval and Modern Greek, 1969, revised 1983; Justinian and Theodora, 1971, revised 1987; The Emperor Julian, 1976; Byzantium and Bulgaria, 1975; The Byzantine Empire, 1980, revised edition, 1992; Editor: The Greek World: Classical, Byzantine and Modern, 1985. *Contributions to:* Learned journals in many countries. *Honours:* Fellow, British Academy, 1978; Corresponding member, Academy of Athens, 1982; Hon DLitt, Birmingham, 1980; Hon Doctor, University of Athens, 1988; Gold Medal, Excellence in Hellenic Studies, The Alexander S Onassis Center, New York University, 1990. *Membership:* President, Society for the Promotion of Hellenic Studies, 1974-77. *Address:* 17 Belsize Park Gardens, London NW3 4JG, England.

BROWNING Sterry. *See:* **GRIBBLE Leonard (Reginald).**

BROWNING Vivenne, (Elaine Vivienne Browning Baly), b. 1 Dec 1922, Sydney, Australia. Writer; Lecturer; Broadcaster Radio & TV. m. W F Baly, 21 Aug 1954, 1 son, 3 daughters. *Education:* Hazlehurst College, Melbourn Australia. *Appointments:* S/Sgt Intelligence Corps ATS, 1942- 46; Civil Resettlement of Repatriated Prisoners of War, 1945-46; Met Police, CID, London, 1946-50; Board of Directors, International Browning Society, Baylor University. *Publications:* My Browning Family Album; The Uncommon Medium; BBC Radio; From Stores Detective to Private Eye; Living in Addis Ababa; TV Wednesday Magazine Addis Ababa; Lord Haw-Haw. *Contributions to:* Magazines: The Real Identity of Pauline; From Russia with Love & Plain Speaking. *Memberships:* Browning Society; New Barnet Literary & Debating Society; Boston Browning Society; Arthur Machen Society; Intelligence Corps Comrades Association; Metropolitan Police Association; Friend of the Royal Academy of Arts; Sadlers Wells Royal Ballet; Australian Film Society; Keats-Shelley Association; Royal Society of Literature, Society of Authors; PEN. *Address:* 14 Oakhurst Avenue, East Barnet, Herts EN4 8DL, England.

BROWNJOHN Alan Charles, (John Berrington), b. 1931, United Kingdom. Poet. *Appointments:* Senior Lecturer in English, Battersea College of Education (now Polytechnic of the South Bank), London, 1965-79; Member, Arts Council Literature Panel, 1968-72; Poetry Critic: New Statesman, London, 1968- 76; Encounter, 1978-80. *Publications:* Verse: Travellers Alone, 1954; The Railings, 1961; The Lions' Mouths, 1967; Oswin's Word, libretto for children, 1967; Woman Reading Aloud, 1969; Being a Garoon, 1969; Sandgrains on a Tray, 1969; Penguin Modern Poets 14 (with Michael Hamburger and Charles Tomlinson), 1969; A Day by Indirections, 1969; Brownjohn's Beasts, 1970; Synopsis, 1970; Frateretto Calling, 1970; Transformation Scene, 1971; An Equivalent, 1971; Warrior's Career, 1972; She Made of It, 1974; A Song of Good Life, 1975; A Night in the Gazebo, 1980; Collected Poems 1952-1983; The Old Flea-Pit, 1987; Other: To Clear the River (as John Berrington), 1964; First I Say This: A Selection of Poems for Reading Aloud (editor), 1969; New Poems 1970-71 (edited with Seamus Heaney and Jon Stallworthy), 1971; The Little Red Bus Book, 1972; Philip Larkin, 1975; New Poetry 3 (edited with Maureen Duffy), 1977; New Year Poetry Supplement (editor), 1982; Torquato Tasso, by Goethe, translation, 1985; Meet and Write (with Sandy Brownjohn), I, II and III, 1985-87; The Way You Tell Them (novel), 1990; The Observation Car (poems), 1990; (ed., with K.W.Gransden), The Gregory Anthology, 1987-1990. *Memberships:* Poetry Society, London, Chairman 1982-88; Chairman, Literature Panel, Greater London Arts Association, 1973-77. *Literary Agent:* Rosica Colin Ltd, London, England. *Address:* 2 Belsize Park, London NW3, England.

BROWNJOHN John Nevil Maxwell, b. Rickmansworth, England. Literary Translator; Screenwriter. *Education:* MA, Lincoln College, Oxford. *Publications:* Night of The Generals, 1962; Memories of Teilhard de Chardin, 1964; Klemperer Recollections, 1964; Brothers in Arms, 1965; Goya, 1965; Rodin, 1967; The Interpreter, 1967; Alexander the Great, 1968; The Poisoned Stream, 1969; The Human Animal, 1971; Hero in the Tower, 1972; Strength through Joy, 1973; Madam Kitty, 1973; A Time for Truth, 1974; The Boat, 1974; A Direct Flight to Allah, 1975; The Manipulation Game, The Night of the Long Knives, 1976; The Hittites, 1977; Willy Brandt Memoirs, 1978; Canaris, 1979; Life with the Enemy, 1979; A German Love Story, 1980; Richard Wagner, 1983; The Middle Kingdom, 1983; Solo Run, 1984; Momo, 1985; The Last Spring in Paris, 1985; Invisible Walls, 1986; Mirror in the Mirror, 1986; The Battle of Wagram, 1987; Assassin, 1987; Daddy, 1989; The Marquis of Bolibar, 1989; Eunuchs for Heaven, 1990; Little Apple, 1990; Jaguar, 1990; siberian Transfer, 1992; The Swedish Cavalier, 1992; Turlupin, 1993. Screen credits: Tess (with Roman Polanski), 1979; The Boat, 1981; Pirates, 1986; The Name of the Rose, 1986; The Bear, 1989; Bitter Moon (with Roman Polanski), 1992. *Honours:* Schlegel Tieck Special Award, 1979; US Pen Prize, 1981. *Memberships:* Past Chairman, Translators Association; Society of Authors. *Address:* The Vine House, Nether Compton, Sherborne, Dorset, DT9 4QA, England.

BROWNLOW Kevin, b. 1938, United Kingdom. Author; Film Director; Former Film Editor. *Publications:* The Parade's Gone By..., 1968; How It Happened Here, 1968; Adventures with D W Griffith, by Karl Brown (editor), 1973; Hollywood: The Pioneers, 1979; The War, The West, and the Wilderness, 1979; Napoleon: Abel Gance's Classic Film, 1983; Behind the Mask of Innocence, 1990. *Address:* c/o Photoplay, 21 Princess Road, London NW1 8JR, England.

BROXON Mildred Downey, (Sigfriour Skaldaspillir), b. 1944, USA. Freelance Writer; Former Psychiatric Nurse. *Publications:* A Witch's Welcome (as Sigfriour Skaldaspillir), 1979; The Demon of Scattery (with Poul Anderson), 1979; Too Long a Sacrifice, 1981; Too Long a Sacrifice, 1984. *Memberships:* Science Fiction Writers of America, Vice-President 1976-78. *Literary Agent:* Sharon Jarvis and Co, USA. *Address:* c/o Sharon Jarvis and Co, 260 Willard Avenue, Staten Island, NY 10314, USA.

BRUCE George, b. 10 Mar 1909, Fraserburgh, Aberdeenshire, Scotland. Writer; Lecturer; Broadcaster. m. Elizabeth Duncan, 25 Jul 1935, 1 son, 1 daughter. *Education:* MA, First Class Honours in English Language and Literature, Aberdeen University, 1932. *Appointments:* BBC Producer with special responsibility for Arts Programmes, mainly literature, 1956-70; First Fellow in Creative Writing, Glasgow University, 1971-73; Prescott College, Arizona (Spring Quarter 1974);

Lectures at US Colleges, Washington and Lee University, 1975; Visiting Professor, College of Wooster, 1976-77; Extra-mural lectures at Glasgow University and Edinburgh University, 1970-80, Scottish-Australia Writing Fellow, 1982. *Publications include:* Sea Talk, (poems) 1944; Landscapes and Figures (poems) 1968; Collected Poems 1940-70; Anne Redpath - a monograph of the Scottish painter, 1975; Some Practical Good - The Cockburn Association, 1875-1975, a history of a hundred years planning in Edinburgh, 1975; Festival in the North, an account of the Edinburgh Festival, 1947-75, 1975; Perspectives, Poems 1970-86, 1986; The Land Out There - A Land Anthology, edited by George Brice with Frank Rennie, 1991. *Contributor to:* A Book of Scottish Verse; The Oxford Book of Scottish Verse; Modern Scottish Poetry; The Penguin Book of Scottish Verse; Scottish Love Poems. *Honours:* Scottish Arts Council Award for Landscapes and Figures, 1967; Scottish Arts Council Award for Collected Poems, 1971; Honorary Doctor of Letters, College of Wooster, 1977; OBE 1984. *Memberships:* Honorary President of the Scottish Poetry Library; Honorary Member, The Cockburn Association; Saltire Society, formerly Vice-Chairman of the Council. *Address:* 25, Warriston Crescent, Edinburgh EH3 5LB, Scotland.

BRUCE Lennart, b. 21 Feb 1919, Stockholm, Sweden. Writer. m. Sonja Wiegandt, 22 July 1960, 1 son, 1 daughter. *Education:* University studies. *Publications:* Agenda (on the works of Wilhelm Ekelund), 1976; Sannsaga, 1982; The Broker, 1983; The Second Light (on the works of Wilhelm Ekelund), 1986; Utan synbar anledning, 1988; Forskingringen, 1989; En Nasares Gang, 1993. *Contributions to:* Over 100 poems, articles to US and Swedish literary magazines. *Honours:* Swedish Academy Award, 1977, 1988. *Memberships:* PEM American Center, New York; Swedish Writers Union, Stockholm. *Address:* 31 Los Cerros Pl, Walnut Creek, CA 94598, USA.

BRUCHAC Joseph, b. 1942, USA. Author; Poet; Journalist. *Appointments:* Editor, Greenfield Review, Greenfield Center, New York, 1970-; Director, Greenfield Review Literary Center, 1981-. *Publications:* Indian Mountain & Other Poems, 1971; Words from the House of the Dead: Prison Writings from Soledad (co-editor), 1972; The Poetry of Pop, 1973; The Last Stop (editor), 1974; Flow, 1975; The Road to Black Mountain, 1976; Aftermath: Poems in English from Africa, Asia and the Caribbean (co-editor), 1977; The Earth Is a Drum, 1977; Entering Onondaga, 1978; The Dreams of Jesse Brown, 1978; The Next World: Poems by 32 Third World Americans (editor), 1978; There Are No Trees in the Prison, 1978; Stone Giants and Flying Heads: More Iroquois Folk Tales, 1978; Mu'undu Wi Go: Mohegan Poems, 1978; The Good Message of Handsome Lake, 1979; Ancestry, 1980; How to Start and Sustain a Literary Magazine, 1980; Translator's Son, 1981; Songs from this Earth on Turtle's Back, verse, 1983; Remembering the Dawn and Other Poems, verse, 1983; The Light From Another Country (editor), verse, 1984; Breaking Silence, verse, 1984; The Wind Eagle and Other Abenaki Stories, 1985; Iroquois Stories, 1985; Walking with My Sons and Other Poems, 1985; Tracking, 1986; Near the Mountains: Selected Poems, 1987; Survival This Way: Interviews with American Indian Poets, 1987; Turtle Meat and Other Stories, 1992; Dawn Land, novel, 1993; Hoop Snakes, Hide-Behinds and Sidehill Winders, Adirondack Tall Tales, 1991; Flying with The Eagle, Racing The Great Bear and other Native American Stories, 1993; Raven Tells Stories, an Anthology of Alaskan Native Writing (editor), 1991. *Membership:*Board Member, National Association for the Preservation and Perpetuation of Storytelling. *Literary Agent:* Barbara Kouts, PO Box 558, Bellport, NY 11713, USA. *Address:* c/o The Greenfield Review, Greenfield Center, NY 12833, USA.

BRUCKSTEIN Ludovic, b. 27 July 1920, Mukacevo, Czechoslovakia, Author; Playwright; Journalist. m. Charlotte Czig, 29 Oct. 1947, (deceased 1983), 1 son. *Education:* Graduate in Commerical Studies, 1938; Literature and Literary Criticism, Bucharest, Romania,

1952. *Appointments:* Lecturer Theatre and Cinemat Arts Institute; Editor, Literary Monthly Magazine, The Romanian Life, 1952-53; Director, Professor of Theatre Arts and History, Theatre Art School, 1955-70; Secretary, Drama Department, Writers Union of Romania, 1953-54. *Publications:* Night Shift, play, 1949; The Greenwald Family, play, 1953; Generation of the Wilderness, play, 1956; Sleepless Night, 1957; Panopticum, 1969; The Confession, 1973; Yaacov Magif's Destiny, 1975; The Tinfoil Hallo, 1979; As in Heaven, so on Earth, 1981; The Return of Christopher Columbis, play, 1957; An Unfinished Trial, play, 1962; The Unexpected Guest, play, 1959; Three Histories, 1977; May be Happiness, 1985. *Contributions To:* Gazeta Literara; Luceafaril Tribuna; Korunk; Ufunk; Numerous other magazines and journals. *Honours:* Recipient of numerous literary awards and citations in Romania; Brickman Prize for Literature, Israel, 1976; Sion Prize for Literature, Israel, 1977; Creation Prize, World Sionist Organisations and Jewish Agency, Israel, 1986. *Memberships:* Writers Union of Romania, Secretary, Dramaturgical Department; Chamber of Writers Union of Israel; President, Union of Israeli Writers in Romanian Language; Yiddish Writers Association in Israel; President, Committee for Culture and Arts in Maramuresh, Romania; Member, Chairman, Various cultural literary and Art Associations. *Literary Agent:* Panopticum, Tel-Aviv, Israel. *Address:* PO Box 37151, Tel-Aviv, 61370, Israel.

BRUDER Judith, b. 6 Nov 1934, USA. Writer. m. Frank Bruder, 28 Feb 1960, 1 son, 1 daughter. *Education:* BA, Wellesley College, 1956; MA, C W Post Center, Long Island University, 1973. *Publications:* Going to Jerusalem, 1979; Convergence, 1993. *Literary Agent:* Charlote Sheedy. *Address:* 132 Wagon Road, Roslyn Heights, NY 11577, USA.

BRUIN John. *See:* **BRUTUS Dennis Vincent.**

BRULOTTE Gaetan, b. 8 Apr 1945, Levis, Canada. Writer. *Education:* BA, Education, 1966, BA, French, 1969, MA, French, 1972, Laval University; Diplome Ecole Normal Superior, Laval University, 1971; PhD, French Literature, Sorbonne, Paris, France, 1978. *Appointments:* Professor, French Literature, Trois-Rivieres College, 1970-82; Université du Quebec, 1980-81, 1989-90; University of New Mexico, USA, 1981-84, 1993; University of California, 1982, University of South Florida, 1984-; Director, Book Reviews, Le Nouvelliste, 1980-82. *Publications:* L'Emprise, novel, 1979; Le Surveillant, short stories, 1982; Le Client, play, 1983; Aspects du Texte Erotique, 1978; L'Imaginaire Et L'Ecriture, 1972; Le Dechet in Le Colloque De Tanger, 1976; Ce Qui Nous Tient, short stories, 1988; Plages, 1987; Double Exposure, 1988; The Secret Voice, 1990. *Contributions to:* PoéFique, France; L'Arc, France; Etudes Litteraires, Canada; The Comparatist, USA; Liberte, Canada; Breves, France; Revue De Louisiane, USA; Revue Des Sciences Humaines, France. *Honours:* Prix Robert Cliche, 1979; Prix Adrienne Choquette, 1981; Prix France Quebec, 1983; Grand Prize of CBC Radio Drama, 1983; Literary prize of Trois Rivieres, 1989; 2nd finalist Goncourt prize, 1989, France; 4 other literary awards, 20 grants. *Memberships:* Fellow, WLA; UNEQ; Mauricies Writers' Society, Past President; PEN; Canadian Writers' Society, Past Director; ADELF, France; International Council on Francophone Studies; Modern Language Association; International Comparative Literature Association; AATF; SARDEC; ACFAS. *Address:* 82 Rue Des Casernes, Trois Rivieres, Quebec, Canada, G9A 1X2.

BRUMARU Emil, b. 1 Jan 1939, Bahmutea, Romania. Physician. m. Tamara Pintilie, 4 Feb 1980, 1 son. *Education:* Faculty of General Medicine. *Appointments:* Physician, Dolhasch, 1963-75; Unemployed, 1975-1983; Corrector, Half Norm, Literary Discussions Review, 1983-90; Vice Chief Editor, 1990-. *Publications:* Lyrics; Detective Arthur; Hospitable Julien; Naive Songs; The Wardrobe In Love; Farewell to Robinson Crusoe; The Ruin of a Samovar. *Contributions to:* Literary Reviews inc, Echinox; Steaua;

Vatra. *Honours:* Eminescu Festival Prize; The Writers Union Prize for Poetry. *Memberships:* Writers Union of Romania; Bucharest Association; PEN; Civil Alliance. *Address:* Str Cuza Voda Nr 6, APt 14, Iassy, 6600 Romania.

BRUNDENELL Carmel. *See:* **BERMINGHAM Carmel Mary.**

BRUNNER John Kilian Houston, (John Loxmith, Trevor Staines, Keith Woodcott), b. 24 Sept 1934, Preston Crowmarsh, Oxfordshire, England. Author; Company Director. m. Marjorie Rosamond Sauer, 12 July 1958, deceased 1986. *Publications include:* Age of Miracles, 1973; A Hastily Thrown-Together Bit of Zork, 1974; Interstellar Empire, 1976; The Book of John Brunner, 1976; Foreign Constellations, 1979; Players At The Game of People, 1980; The Infinitive Of Go, 1980; Manshape, 1982; The Crucible of Time, 1983; The Great Steamboat Race, 1983; The Tides Of Time, 1984; The Compleat Traveller In Black, 1986; The Shift Key, 1987; The Days of March, 1988; Children Of The Thunder, 1989; Victims Of The Nova, 1989; The Best of John Brunner, 1988. *Contributions to:* Numerous periodicals. *Honours include:* Hugo Award, 1968; British Fantasy Award; British Science Fiction Award (twice); Bronze Porgie Award; Prix Apollo (France); Grand Prix du Festival de l'Insolite (France). *Memberships:* Past Joint President, European Science Fiction Society; Science Fiction Writers of America; World SF; Writers Guild; Society of Authors; Past Chairman, British Science Fiction Association; Past Vice President, Science Fiction Foundation. *Literary Agent:* A M Heath & Co. *Address:* c/o A M Heath & Co, 79 St Martins Lane, London WC2N 4AA, England.

BRUNSE Niels Henning, b. 24 Aug 1949, Silkeborg, Denmark. Translator; Writer. m. Galina Ivashkina, 18 Mar 1977, div. *Education:* University of Copenhagen & Moscow. *Appointments:* Co Editor, Literary & Cultural Magazine, Hug, 1974-76; Co Editor, Political Bi weekly, Politisk Revy, 1978-82; Reviews of Books, Theatre and Film, Daily Newspaper, Information, 1982-; Editor, Danish Writers Association Journal, 1983-85. *Publications:* Everyday Moscow; History Never Stops; But Where Does It Actually Go?; Commonplaces; The Richest Person in the World; 125 translations, including: 9 plays by Shakespeare (from English); Complete Short Stories by Heinrich v. Kleist (from German); The Aesthetics of Resistance by Peter Weiss (from German); Petersburg by Andrei Bely (from Russian). *Contributions to:* Numerous. *Honours:* Honorary Award of Danish Translators Association; Life Long Grant Danish State Art Foundation; Columbia University Thornton Niven Wilder Award. *Memberships:* Danish Writers association; Danish PEN; Danish Dramatists Association. *Address:* Aalandsgade 26, DK 2300 Copenhagen S, Denmark.

BRUNSKILL Ronald William, b. 1929, United Kingdom. Hon. Fellow in Architecture. *Publications:* Illustrated Handbook of Vernacular Architecture, 1970, 3rd Edition, 1987; Vernacular Architecture of the Lake Counties, 1974; English Brickwork (with Alec Clifton-Taylor), 1978; Traditional Buildings of Britain, 1981, 2nd edition, 1992; Houses, 1982; Traditional Farm Buildings of Britain, 1982, 2nd Edition, 1987; Timber Buildings of Britain, 1985; Brick Building in Britain, 1990. *Honour:* OBE, 1990. *Memberships:* FSA, 1975. *Address:* School of Architecture, University of Manchester, Manchester M13 9PL, England.

BRUSEWITZ Gunnar (Kurt), b. 7 Oct 1924, Stockholm, Sweden. Author; Artist. m. Ingrid Andersson, 21 Oct 1946, 2 daughters. *Education:* Royal Academy of Art; Ph.dr HC. *Publications include:* Arstidsbockerna 1-IV, Jakt, 1967, (enl., americ., finn., dan., editions); Bjornjagare och Fjarilsmalare, 1968; Stockholm-Staden pa Landet, 1969; Skissbok, 1970; Sjo, 1970; Nature in Gambia, 1971; Skog, 1974; Lang Var, 1977; Strandspegling, 1979; Wings & Seasons, 1980; Arktisk Sommar, 1981; Den Nojsamma

Nyttigheten, 1982; Solvarvets Tecken, 1983; Sveriges Natur: En Resa i Tid och Rum, 1984; Guldörnen och duvorna (The birds of Strindberg). *Contributions to:* Stockholms Tidningen; Svenska Dagbladet; Various other Swedish magazines & publications; Biography, B. Christoffersson: G. Brusewitz - antecknare, 1988. *Honours include:* Stockholm City Presentation Prize, 1970; Dag Hammarskjold Medal, 1975; Die goldne Blume von Rheydf, Düsseldorf, 1989; Honorary DPhil, University of Stockholm, 1982. *Memberships include:* Publicistklubben; PEN; Swedish section, World Wildlife Fund; Royal Society of Science, Uppsala. *Literary Agent:* Wahlstrom & Widstrand forlag, Stockholm. *Address:* Lisinge, 762 93 Rimbo, Sweden.

BRUTON Eric (Moore), b. 1915, United Kingdom. Author; Company Director. *Appointments:* Managing Director, NAG Press Ltd, Colchester, 1963-; Managing Director, Diamond Boutique Ltd, 1965-80; Chairman, Things and Ideas Ltd, 1970-78. *Publications:* True Book about Clocks, 1957; Death in Ten Point Bold, 1957; Die, Darling, Die, 1959; Violent Brothers, 1960; True Book about Diamonds, 1961; The Hold Out, 1961; King Diamond, 1961; The Devil's Pawn, 1962; Automation, 1962; Dictionary of Clocks and Watches, 1962; The Laughing Policeman, 1963; The Longcase Clock, 1964, 2nd Edition, 1978; The Finsbury Mob, 1964; The Smithfield Slayer, 1964; The Wicked Saint, 1965; The Fire Bug, 1967; Clocks and Watches 1400-1900, 1967; Clocks and Watches, 1968; Diamonds, 1970, 2nd Edition, 1977; Antique Clocks and Clock Collecting, 1974; The History of Clocks, 1978; The Wetherby Collection of Clocks, 1980; Legendary Gems, 1984. *Memberships:* Council Member, Gemmological Association of Great Britain, 1972-91; Council Member, British Horological Institute, 1955-62; Committee Member, Crime Writers Association, 1959-62. *Address:* Pond House, Great Bentley, Colchester CO7 8QG, England.

BRUTUS Dennis Vincent, (John Bruin), b. 28 Nov 1924, Salisbury, Southern Rhodesia (now Harare, Zimbabwe). Professor of English & African Literature. m. May Jaggers, 14 May 1950, 4 sons, 4 daughters. *Education:* BA, Fort Hare University, South Africa, 1944-47; Part LLB, University of Witwatersrand, South Africa, 1962-63. *Appointments include:* Editorial Boards and Advisory Boards: Africa Today (Denver), Black Lines (Pittsburgh), National Writers Union, American Poetry Center. *Publications include:* Sirens, Knuckles, Boots, 1963; Letters to Martha, 1968; Poems from Algiers, 1979; Thoughts Abroad (John Bruin), 1970; A Simple Lust, 1972; Strains, 1975; China Poems, 1975; Stubborn Hope, 1978, 1983; Salutes and Censures, 1982; Airs & Tributs, 1989; Still the Sirens, forthcoming. *Contributions to:* Various anthologies, collections and journals. *Honours include:* Mbari Prize, Poetry in Africa, 1963; First Recipient, Outstanding Teacher Award, Institute for Policy Studies, 1987; Fellow, African Academy of Arts, 1989; Honorary degrees, Worcester State College & University of Massachusetts, Amherst, Northeastern University, Boston, USA. *Memberships:* 1st President, African Literature Association; Vice President, Union of Writers of the African People; Modern Language Association, President South African Non- Racial Olympic Committee, (SAN.ROC). *Address:* 3812 Bates Street, Bates Hill Apts No 311, Pittsburgh, PA 15213, USA.

BRYANS Robin. *See:* **HARBINSON-BRYANS Robert.**

BRYANT Dorothy (Mae), b. 1930, USA. Writer; Publisher. *Appointments:* English Teacher, San Francisco Public Schools, California, 1953-56; English Teacher, Lick-Wilmerding High School, 1956-61; Instructor in English, San Francisco State University, 1962; Instructor in English, Golden Gate College, San Francisco, 1963; Instructor in English and Creative Writing, Contra College, San Pable, California, 1964-76; Publisher, Ata Books, 1978-90. *Publications:* The Comforter, 1971, retitled The Kin of Ata Are Waiting For You, 1976; Ella Prince's Journal, 1972; Miss

Giardino, 1978; Writing a Novel, non-fiction, 1979; The Garden of Eros, 1979; Prisoners, 1980; Killing Wonder, 1981; A Day in San Francisco, 1983; Myths to Lie By, 1984; Confessions of Madame Psyche, 1986; The Test, 1991. *Address:* 1928 Stuart Street, Berkeley, CA 94703, USA.

BRYANT Joseph Allen Jr, b. 1919, USA. Professor of English. *Appointments:* Professor, Chairman of English, University of North Carolina, Greensboro, 1961-68; Professor, Chairman of English, Syracuse University, Syracuse, New York, 1968-71; Professor of English, University of Kentucky, Lexington, 1973-90. *Publications:* Hippolyta's View: Some Christian Aspects of Shakespeare's Plays, 1961; Shakespeare: Romeo and Juliet (editor), 1964; Eudora Welty, 1968; The Compassionate Satirist: Ben Jonson and His Imperfect World, 1972; Understanding Randall Jarrell, 1986; Shakespeare and the Uses of Comedy, 1986. *Address:* 713 Old Dobbin Road, Lexington, KY 40502, USA.

BRYANT Robert Harry, b. 1 Sept 1925, Nokesville, Virginia, USA. Emeritus Professor of Constructive Theology, United Theological Seminary. m. Emily Christine Rentsch, 11 Aug 1951, dec., 2 sons, 1 daughter. *Education:* BA, College of William and Mary, 1946; MDiv magna cum laude, Yale University Divinity School, 1949; Fulbright Scholar, Heidelberg University, Federal Republic of Germany, 1954-55; PhD, Yale University, 1956; Strasbourg University, France, 1966-67. *Appointments:* Visiting Assistant Professor, Vanderbilt University, 1953-54; Visiting Professor, St John's University, Collegeville, Minnesota, 1972; Visiting Professor, Adam's College, Federal Seminary, South Africa, 1973-74. *Publications:* The Bible's Authority for Today, 1968; Contributor to Oecumenica, Center for Ecumenical Studies, Strasbourg, 1967. *Contributions to:* Kairos and Logos, Tillich's Theology, 1984; Albert Camus, to Religion in Life; The Bible's Relevance Today, to Interpretation; Liberation Theology in Latin America, to Theological Markings; Christologies of Bonhoeffer and Pittenger Compared, to Theological Markings. *Honours:* Algernon Sydney Sullivan Award, Phi Beta Kappa; Danforth Fellow, Universities of Chicago and Minnesota, 1960; Grantee, Eli Lilly Fund, 1960; Association of Theological Schools Grants, 1985, 1990. *Memberships:* Phi Beta Kappa; American Academy of Religion; American Theological Society, Midwestern Section; Dietrich Bonhoeffer Society. *Address:* Apt 413, 4300 West River Parkway, Minneapolis, MN 55406, USA.

BUCHAN Tom (Thomas Buchanan Buchan), b. 1931, Scotland. Writer; Poet; Former Educator. *Appointments:* Teacher, Denny High School, Stirlingshire, 1953-56; Lecturer in English, University of Madras, India, 1957-58; Warden, Community House, Glasgow, Scotland, 1958-59; Teacher, Irvine Royal Academy, 1963-65; Senior Lecturer in English and Drama, Clydebank Technical College, Glasggow, 1967-70; Currently Partner: Poni Press, Edinburgh; Offshore Theatre Co, Edinburgh; Arts Projects, Edinburgh. *Publications:* Ikons, 1958; Dolphins at Cochin, 1969; Makes You Feel Great, novel, 1971; Exorcism, 1972; Poems 1969-1971, 1972; Forwards, 1978. *Address:* Scoraig, Dundonnell, Wester Ross IV23 2RE, Scotland.

BUCHANAN Colin Ogilvie, b. 9 Aug 1934, Croydon, Surrey, England. Church of England Clerk in Holy Orders (Bishop). m. Diana Stephenie Gregory, 14 June 1963, 2 daughters. *Education:* BA 1959, MA 1962, Lincoln College, Oxford; Tyndale Hall, Bristol, 1959-61; D. D. (Lambeth), 1993. *Appointments:* Honorary Assistant Bishop, Diocese of Rochester, 1989-; Vicar of St Mark's, Gillingham, Kent, 1991. *Publications include:* Editor: Modern Anglican Liturgies 1958-1968, 1968; Further Anglican Liturgies 1968-1975, 1975; Latest Anglican Liturgies 1976-1984, 1985; Modern Anglican Ordination Rites, 1987; The Bishop in Liturgey, 1988; Joint Editor with others: Growing into Union, 1970; Anglican Worship Today: Collins Illustrated Guide to the Alternative Service Book, 1980; Reforming Infant Baptism, 1990; Author: Open to Others, 1992; Infant Baptism and the Gospel, 1993. *Contributions:* Editor: News of Liturgy, published monthly since 1975. *Membership:* Vice-President, Electoral Reform Society; Member, House of Bishops of the General Syrod of the Church of England, 1990-. *Address:* St Mark's Vicarage, 173 Canterbury Street, Gillingham, Kent, ME7 5UA, England.

BUCHANAN (Eileen) Marie (Duell), (Claire Curzon, Rhona Petrie), b. 1922, United Kingdom. Author. *Publications:* Mystery novels, as Rhona Petrie: Death in Deakins Wood, 1963; Murder by Precedent, 1964; Running Deep, 1964; Dead Loss, 1966; Foreign Bodies, 1967; MacLurg Goes West, 1968; Despatch of a Dove, 1969; Come Hell and High Water: Eleven Short Stories, 1970; Thorne in the Flesh, 1971; Novels, as Marie Buchanan: Greenshards, US Edition Animal, 1972; An Unofficial Death, 1973; The Dark Backward, 1975; Morgana, 1977; The Countess of Sedgwick, 1980; As Clare Curzon: A Leaven of Malice, 1979; Special Occasions, 1981; I Give You Five Days, 1983; Masks and Faces, 1984.

BUCHWALD Art, b. 20 Oct 1925, New York, USA. Journalist; Author; Playwright. m. Ann McGarry, 1952, 1 son, 2 daughters. *Education:* University of Southern California, Los Angeles. *Appointments:* Columnist, Herald Tribune, Paris, 1948-62; Syndicated columnist to 550 newspapers throughout the world, 1952-. *Publications:* Paris After Dark; Art Buchwald's Paris; I Chose Caviar; More Caviar; A Gift from the Boys; Don't Forget to Write; How Much is That in Dollars? 1961; Is It Safe to DrinK the Water? 1962; I Chose Capitol Punishment, 1963; And Then I Told the President, 1965; Son of the Great Society, 1967; Have I Ever Lied to You? 1968; Oh, To Be A Swinger, 1970; Getting High in Government Circles, 1971; I Never Danced at the White House, 1973; I Am Not A Crook, 1974; Washington is Leaking, 1976; Down the Seine & Up the Potomac, 1977; The Buchwald Stops Here, 1978; Laid Back in Washington with Art Buchwald, 1981; While Reagan Slept, 1983; You CAN Fool All of the People All of the Time, 1985; I Think I Don't Remember, 1987; Who's Rose Garden is it Anyway, 1989; Lighten Up, George, 1991. *Honours:* Prix de la Bonne Humeur; Pulitzer Prize, outstanding commentary, 1982. *Membership:* American Academy of Arts and Letters. *Address:* 2000 Pennsylvania Avenue NW, Washington DC 20006, USA.

BUCKAWAY Catherine M, b. 7 July 1919, North Battleford, Saskatchewan, Canada. Poet. m. 1 Apr 1941, 2 daughters. *Education:* Bronze Medal & Bar; Silver Medal & Bar; Instructors Certificate; Dale Carnegie Course. *Publications:* Blue Windows; Riding Into Morning; The Silver Cuckoo; Alfred the Dragon Who Lost His Flame; Strangely The Bords Have Come Air 17; The Lavender Nightingale Charlotte; Dinosaurs Have Feelings Too. *Contributions to:* 3334 Published Poems. *Honours:* Canada Council Grant; Sask Arts Grant. *Memberships:* League of Canadian Poets; CANSCAIP; Writers Guild. *Address:* Porteous Lodge, 833 Ave P North, Saskatoon, Saskatchewan, 57L 2W5, Canada.

BUCKERIDGE Anthony Malcolm, b. 20 June 1912. Writer. m. (1) Sylvia Brown, 1936, (2) Eileen Norah Selby, 25 Feb 1972, 2 sons, 1 daughter. *Education:* University College, London, 1932-35. *Publications:* The Jennings series of children's books comprising 24 titles 1950-1991; The Rex Milligan series, 4 titles 1953-56; A Funny Thing Happened, 1953. Musicals: It Happened in Hamelin, 1980; Jennings A-Bounding, 1979; The Cardboard Conspiracy, 1985. *Memberships:* The Society of Authors; Writers' Guild of Great Britain; British Actors' Equity. *Literary Agent:* L R Associates, Aylesbury. *Address:* East Crink, Barcombe Mills, Lewes, Sussex BN8 5BL, England.

BUCKINGHAM Nancy. *See:* SAWYER John and SAWYER Nancy.

BUCKMAN Repha Joan Glenn, b. 18 Aug 1942, St Paul, Kansas, USA. Artist-in-Education; Artistic Director. m. 16 Jan 1960, divorced 1978, 3 sons. *Education:* BA, Southwestern College, 1970; MA, Fort Hays State Union, 1978 *Appointments:* Artist in Education: Documentary Research Writer, 1982-84, Poet, 1984, 1986-87, 1987-88. *Publications:* Repha, 1987; Critter Crossin, 1978; Cleaving the Surface, 1980; Puppetry Language, and the Special Child : Discovering Alternate Language (chapter); Repha, The Record, 1978; The Teacher's Edition, 1986, Editor; Kate's Taming of The Cook's Book, Editor, 1983; 1983-84, 1984-85 Literary Calendars, Editor; 13 locks Imagination Game, 1987. *Contributions to:* Odessa Poetry Review; Kansas English; Kansas Eng.; Women Writers in Kansas; Cottonwood Review. *Honours:* Outstanding Young Woman in America, 1977; Rocky Mountains Poetry Society Honorable Mention, 1980; Director/AKT Competition, 5 awards, 1983. *Memberships include:* Bob Woodley Foundation, Drama Editor; Tri-Crown Press, President; Kansas Writers Association, Board Member; Kansas Authors Club; Association of Kansas Theatres. *Address:* Box 175, Sterling, KS 67579, USA.

BUCZACKI Stefan Tadeusz, b. 16 Oct 1945, Derby, England. Writer; Broadcaster. m. Beverley Ann Charman, 8 Aug 1970, 2 sons. *Education:* BSc, 1st Class Honours Botany, Southampton University; DPhil, forestry, Oxford University. *Publications:* Collins' Guide to Pests, Diseases & Disorders of Garden Plants, 1981, shorter version 1983; Collins' Gem Guide to Mushrooms & Toadstools, 1982; Zoosporic Plant Pathogens, 1983; Beat Garden Pests & Diseases, 1985; Gardeners' Questions Answered, 1985; Ground Rules for Gardeners, 1986; 3 Men in a Garden, 1986; Creating a Victorian Flower Garden, 1988; Beginners Guide to Gardening, 1988; Garden Warfare, 1988; New Generation Guide to the Fungi of Britain and Europe, 1989; A Garden for all Seasons, 1990; Understanding Your Garden, 1990; The Essential Gardener, 1991; Dr Stefan Buczacki's Gardening Hints, 1992; The Plant Care Manual, 1992. *Contributions to:* Times; Financial Times; Country Life; Sunday Telegraph; Guardian; The Gardener; Geographical Magazine; Countryman; House & Garden; Numerous other journals & magazines. Also 70 scientific papers to major professional journals. *Memberships:* Fellow, Institute of Biology; Fellow, Institute of Horticulture; Associate, Royal Photographic Society; Fellow, Linnean Society. *Literary Agent:* Barbara Levy. *Address:* c/o Barbara Levy, Literary Agent, 21 Kelly Street, London NW1 8PG, England.

BUDDEE Paul Edgar, b. 12 Mar 1913, Western Australia. Author; Retired School Principal; Lecturer. m. Elizabeth Vere Bremner, 12 Jan 1944. 1 son, 1 daughter. *Publications:* Fate Of The Artful Dodger, 1984; The Escape Of The Fenians, 1972; The Escape Of John O'Reilly, 1973; Stand To And Other War Poems, 1943; The Osca and Olga Trilogy, 1943-47; The Unwilling Adventurers, 1967, 1989; The Mystery of Moma Island, 1969; The Air Patrol Series (4 books), 1972; The Ann Rankin Series (4 books), 1972; The Peter Devlin Series (4 books), 1972; The Call Of The Sky, 1978. *Contributions to:* State and Australian major papers, magazines and journals. *Honours:* Grants from Australia Commonwealth Literary Board, 1977, 1978, 1984; Western Australian Citizen of the Year Award, 1977; OAM, 1989. *Memberships:* Western Australia Fellowship of Writers, Past President 1947-49, Honorary Life Member; Trustee, Perth PEN Centre; Australia Society of Authors. *Address:* 11 The Parapet, Willetton, WA 6155, Australia.

BUDRYS Algis, b. 1931, Lithuania. Science Fiction Writer; Editor. *Appointments:* Assistant Editor, Gnome Press, New York City, 1952; Assistant Editor, Galaxy magazine, New York City, 1953; On staff, Royal Publications, New York City, 1958-61; Editor-in-Chief, Regency Books, Evanston, Illinois, 1961-63; Editorial Director, Playboy Press, Chicago, Illinois, 1963-65; Magazine Manager, Woodall Publishers, 1973-74; President, Unifont Co, Evanston, 1974-. *Publications:* False Night, 1953, as Some Will Not Die, 1961; Man of Earth, 1955; Who, 1958; The Falling Torch, 1959; The Unexpected Dimension, 1960, Rogue Moon, 1960; The Furious Future, 1964; The Iron Thorn, 1968; Michaelmas, 1977; Blood and Burning, 1978; The Life Machine, 1979; Benchmarks: Galaxy Bookshelf, 1985. *Address:* 824 Seward Street, Evanston, IL 60202, USA.

BUDZISZEWSKI J, b. 19 Apr 1952, USA. Political & Ethical Philosophy. m. Sandra Hall, 4 Sept 1971, 2 daughters. *Education:* BA, University of South Florida, 1975; MA, University of Florida, 1977; PhD, Yale University, 1981. *Publications:* The Resurrection of Nature; The Nearest Coast of Darkness; True Tolerence. *Contributions to:* NOMOS; Journal of Politics; Public Affairs Quarterly; Public Choice; Social Theory and Practice; International Journal of Public Administration. *Memberships:* American Political Science Association; National Association of Scholars. *Address:* Department of Government, University of Texas, Austin, TX 78712, USA.

BUELL Frederick Henderson, b. 17 Nov 1942, Bryn Mawr, Pennsylvania, USA. Professor; Poet. m. 30 Oct 1982, 1 son. *Education:* BA, Yale University, 1964; PhD, Cornell University, 1970. *Publications:* Theseus & Other Poems, 1971; W.H. Auden as a Social Poet, 1973; Full Summer, 1978; Forthcoming, From the Postwar to The Postnational. *Contributions include:* Poetry; Hudson Review; Minnesota Review; Little Magazine; Articles to: Iowa Review; Cornell Review; Boundary 2. *Honours:* Poets Prize, Academy of American Poets, 1969; NEA Fellowship, 1972. *Address:* 72 Amity Road, Warwick, NY 10990, USA.

BUERO-VALLEJO Antonio b. 29 Sept 1916, Guadalajara, Spain. Playwright. m. Victoria Rodriguez, 5 Mar 1959, 2 sons. *Education:* Bachelor's Degree, 1932; Fine Arts Studies, 1934-36. *Publications:* In the Burning Darkness, 1950; Concert at St Ovide, 1962; The Basement Window, 1967; The Sleep of Reason, 1970; The Foundation, 1974; Lazarus in the Labyrinth, 1986; Near Music, 1989; Also: Story of a Stairway, 1949; The Words in the Sand, 1949; The Dream Weaver, 1952; The Awaited Sign, 1952; Almost a Fairy Tale, 1953; Dawn 1953; Irene or the Treasure, 1954; Today's a Holiday, 1957; The Cards Face Down, 1957; A Dreamer for a People, 1958; The Ladies in Waiting, 1960; Adventure in Gray, 1963; The Double Case History of Dr Valmy, 1968; Alligator, 1981; Secret Dialogue, 1984. *Contributions to:* Various journals. *Honours include:* Miguel de Cervantes Prize, 1986; Pablo Iglesias Prize, 1986; National Theatre Prize, 1957, 1958, 1959, 1980; Mayte Prize, 1974; El Espectador y la Critica Prize, 1967, 1970, 1974, 1976, 1976, 1977, 1981, 1984, 1986; Fundacion March Prize, 1959; Lope de Vega Prize, 1949. *Memberships:* Real Academia Espanola; Hispanic Society of America; Ateneo de Madrid; MLA; Circulo de Bellas Artes, Madrid; Fellow, American Association of Teachers of Spanish and Portuguese; Society of Spanish and Spanish-American Studies; Modern Language Association of America; Honorary Councilor, Sociedad General de Autores de Espana, 1987. *Literary Agent:* Sociedad General de Autores de Espana. *Address:* General Diaz Porlier 36, Madrid 28001, Spain.

BUISSERET David Joseph, b. 18 Dec 1934, Isle of Wight, England. History Teacher; Researcher. m. Patricia Connolly, 9 Sept 1961, 3 sons, 2 daughters. *Education:* Corpus Christi College, Cambridge, BA, 1958; PhD, 1961. *Appointments:* University of the West Indies, 1964-80; The Newberry Library, Chicago, 1980-. *Publications:* Sully; Port Royal, Jamaica; Historic Architecture of the Caribbean; Henry IV; Historic Illinois from the Air. *Honours:* Premiere Medaille, Institute of France; Centennial Medal, Institute of Jamaica; J B Jackson Prize. *Address:* The Newberry Library, 60 West Walton Street, Chicago, IL 60610, USA.

BUKOWCZYK John Joseph, b. 16 June 1950, Perth, New Jersey, USA. Historian. *Education:* BA, Northwestern University, 1972; MA, Harvard University,

1973; PhD, 1980. *Appointments:* Visiting Assistant Professor, Connecticut College, New London, USA, 1979-80; Assistant Professor, Wayne State University, Detroit, 1980-86; Associate Professor, 1986-92; Professor, 1992-. *Publications:* And My Children Did Not Know Me: A History of the Polish American's; Detroit Images. *Contributions to:* Articles in Labor History; Journal of American Ethnic History; International Labor & Working Class History; Polish American Studies. *Honours:* Rev Joseph P Swastek Prize; Richard C McCormick Prize for Scholarly Publication; Oskar Halecki Award. *Memberships:* Polish American Historical Association; Immigration History Society; Social Science History Association. *Address:* Department of History, 3094 Faculty/Administration Building, Wayne State University, Detroit, MI 48202, USA.

BUKOWSKI Charles, b. 1920, USA, Writer, Novels, Short stories, Poetry, Autobiography, Memoirs, Personal. Former Editor, Harlequin, Wheeler, Texas, later Los Angeles, California, and Laugh Literary, and Man the Humping Guns, both Los Angeles; Former Columnist, Notes of a Dirty Old Man, Open City, Los Angeles, later Los Angeles Free Press. *Publications include:* To Kiss the Worms Goodnight, 1966; The Girls, 1966; The Flower Lover, 1966; All the Assholes in the World and Mine, 1966; 2 by Bukowski, 1967; The Curtains Are Waving, 1967; At Terror Street and Agony Way, 1968; Notes of a Dirty Old Man, 1969; If We Take...1969; The Days Run Away Like Wild Horses over the Hills, 1969; (with Philip Lamantia and Harold Norse), Penguin Modern Poets 13, 1969; Another Academy, 1970; Fire Station, 1970; Post Office (novel), 1971; Erections, Ejaculations, Exhibitions and General Tales of Ordinary Madness, 1972; Mockingbird Wish Me Luck, 1972; Me and Your Sometimes Love Poems, 1972; South of No North (short stories), 1973; While the Music Played, 1973; Life and Death in the Charity Ward (short stories), 1974; Factotum: A Novel, 1975; Burning in Water, Drowning in Flames, Poems, 1977; Love Is a Dog from Hell (poetry), 1977; Women (novel), 1978; You Kissed Lilly, 1978; Shakespeare Never Did This, 1979; Dangling in the Tournefortia, 1981; Ham on Rye, 1982; Play the Piano Drunk Like a Percussion Instrument until the Fingers Begin the Bleed a Bit, 1982; The Most Beautiful Woman in Town, 1983; Bring Me Your Love, 1983; Hot Water Music, 1983; There's No Business, 1984; War All the Time, Poems, 1981-84, 1984. *Address:* PO Box 32, San Pedro, CA 90731, USA.

BULL Angela Mary, b. 28 Sept 1936, Halifax, Yorkshire, England. Writer. m. Rev. Martin Wells Bull, 15 Sept 1962, 1 son, 1 daughter. *Education:* Badminton School, Bristol; MA, Hons, English Language and Literature, Edinburgh University; St Hugh's College, Oxford University. *Publications include:* Child of Ebenezer, 1973; The Machine Breakers, 1980; Anne Frank, 1984; Noel Streatfeild, 1984; Up The Attic Stairs, 1989; The Friend With a Secret, 1965. *Honours:* Runner-Up for The Guardian Award, 1974; The Other Award, 1980. *Literary Agent:* Gina Pollinger, 222 Old Brompton Road, London SW5 0BZ. *Address:* The Vicarage, Hall Bank Drive, Bingley, West Yorkshire BD16 4BZ, England.

BULLA Clyde Robert, b. 1914. USA, Writer, Novels, Short stories, Children's fiction, Translations. *Appointments:* Farmer until 1943; Linotype Operator and Columnist, Tri-County News, King City, Missouri, 1943- 49. *Publications include:* A Tree is a Plant, 1960; Three-Dollar Mule, 1960; The Sugar Pear Tree, 1961; Benito, 1961; What Makes a Shadow? 1962; The Ring and the Fire: Stories from Wagner's Niebelung Operas, 1962; Viking Adventure, 1963; Indian Hill, 1963; St Valentine's Day, 1965; More Stories of Favorite Operas, 1965; Lincoln's Birthday, 1966; White Bird, 1966; Washington's Birthday, 1967; Flowerpot Gardens, 1967; Stories of Gilbert and Sullivan Operas, 1968; The Ghost of Windy Hill, 1968; Mika's Apple Tree: A Story of Finland, 1968; The Moon Singer, 1969; New Boy in Dublin: A Story of Ireland, 1969; Jonah and the Great Fish, 1970; Joseph the Dreamer, 1971; Pocahontas and the Strangers, 1971; (trans), Noah and the Rainbow, by Max Bollinger, 1972; Open the Door and See All the People, 1972; Dexter 1973; The Wish at the Top, 1974; Shoeshine Girl, 1975; Marco Moonlight, 1976; The Beast of Lorr, 1977; (with Michael Syson), Conquista! 1978; Lst Look, 1979; The Stubborn Old Woman, 1980; My Friend the Monster, 1980; Daniel's Duck, 1980; A Lion to Guard Us, 1981; Almost a Hero, 1981; Dandelion Hill, 1982; Poor Boy, Rich Boy, 1982; Charlie's House, 1983; The Cardboard Crown, 1984; A Grain of Wheat, 1985; The Chalk Box Kid, 1987; Singing Sam, 1989; The Christmas Coat, 1989. *Address:* 1230 Las Flores Drive, Los Angeles, CA 90041, USA.

BULLOCK Kenneth (Ken), b. 26 July 1929, Liverpool, England. Canadian Citizen, 1951-66, Australian Citizen 1966-. Writing Consultant. m. Elizabeth Bullock (Mooney), 1979, 2 sons, 2 daughters, (former marriage). *Education:* Dip Comm, 1961; Royal Canadian Naval College, HMCS, Victoria, British Columbia, (RCN-RAN, 1950-72). *Literary Appointments:* British Mercantile Marine, 1946-49; Prime Minister's Department, Office of Information, Port Moresby, Papus New Guinea, 1980-93; Publications, Writer, Editor; Teacher, English; Journalist Counsellor; External tutor, Creative Writing, James Cook University, 1984-93. *Publications:* Emergency, 1979; Family Guide to Beach and Water Safety, 1980; Silly Billy Learns a Lesson, 1981; Papua New Guinea (with James Siers), 1981; Water Proofing Your Child, 1982; Pelandok, 1986; Port Pirie The Friendly City, 1988. *Contributions to:* Papua New Guinea: Post Courier; National Times; AUstralia; Adelaide Advertiser, Queensland; Sunshine Coast Daily. *Honours:* CD; Canadian Military Service Decoration, 1963; Citizen of the Year, 1984, Port Pirie (South Australia) for Historical Research, 1984-88, and Creation of City's History. *Memberships:* Fellowship of Australian Writers (South Australian Branch), Federal Secretary, 1978-79, President (former), 1984-85; Australian Society of Authors. *Address:* 63 Buderim Garden Village, Mooloolaba Road, Buderim, Queensland 4556, Australia.

BULLOUGH Robert V Jr, b. 12 Feb 1949, Salt Lake City, Utah, USA. Professor of Educational Studies. m. 18 June 1976, 3 sons, 1 daughter. *Education:* University of Illinois, 1980; PhD, Ohio State University, 1976; BS, MED University of Utah. *Appointments:* Various Editorial Boards of Professional Journals. *Publications:* Enering as a Teacher; First Year Teacher; The Forgotten Dream of Am Public Education; Human Interests in The Curriculum; Democracy in Education. *Contributions to:* Numerous Publications in Professional Journals. *Honours:* Phi Beta Kappa; Phi Kappa Phi. *Memberships:* Phi Beta Kappa; Phi Kappa Phi; Phi Deta Kappa; Professors of Curriculum; American Educational Research Association; American Association of Colleges of Teachers Education. *Address:* 413 4th Avenue, Salt Lake City, UT 84103, USA.

BULMER Henry Kenneth, (Alan Burt Akers, Ken Blake, Kenneth Bulmer, Ernest Corley, Arthur Frazier, Kenneth Johns, Philip Kent, Bruno Krauss, Neil Langholm, Karl Maras, Charles R Pike, Andrew Quiller, Richard Silver, Tully Zetford), b. 14 Jan 1921, London, England, Author, m. Pamela Buckmaster, 7 Mar 1953, 2 daughters, 1 son. *Appointment:* Editor, New Writings in SF, 1972-79. *Publications:* Dray Prescot Saga as by Alan Burt Akers and Dray Prescot, 1972- ; FOX series as by Adam Hardy, 1972-77; Sea Wolf Series as by Bruno Kraus and Kenneth Bulmer, 1978-82; City Under the Sea, 1957; Strike Force Falklands as by Adam Hardy, 1984-86; The Ulcer Culture, 1969; The Odan Trilogy as by Manning Norvil, 1977-80; Roller Coaster World, 1972. *Contributions to:* New Worlds; Authentic; Nebula; Mag of Fantasy and SF; Infinity; Science Fantasy; Universe. *Literary Agent:* Carnell Literary Agency. *Address:* 5/20 Frant Road, Tunbridge Wells, Kent TN2 5SN, England.

BULMER Kenneth. *See:* **BULMER Henry Kenneth.**

BULPIN Thomas Victor, b. 1918, South Africa. Writer; Publisher. *Appointments:* Writer and Publisher, Books of South Africa (Pty) Ltd and T V Bulpin Ltd, Cape Town, 1946-. *Publications:* Lost Trails on the Low Veld, 1950; Shaka's Country, 1952; To the Shores of Natal, 1953; The Golden Republic, 1953; The Ivory Trail, 1954; Storm Over the Transvaal, 1955; Lost Trails of the Transvaal, 1956; Islands in a Forgotten Sea, 1958; Trail of the Copper King, 1959; The White Whirlwind, 1961; The Hunter is Death, 1962; To the Banks of the Zambezi, 1965; Natal and the Zulu Country, 1966; Low Veld Trails, 1968; The Great Trek, 1969; Discovering South Africa, 1970; Treasury of Travel Series, 1973-74; Southern Africa Land of Beauty and Splendour, 1976; Illustrated Guide to Southern Africa, 1978; Scenic Wonders of Southern Africa, 1985. *Address:* PO Box 1516, Cape Town, South Africa.

BUNCH Charlotte, (Charlotte Bunch-Weeks), b. 13 Oct 1944, West Jefferson, North Carolina. USA. Director, Center for Women's Global Leadership; Rutgers University; Writer. m. James L Weeks, 25 Mar 1967 (div 1971). *Education:* Attended University of California, Berkeley, 1965; BA (magna cum laude) Duke University 1966: Attended, Institute for Policy Studies, 1967-68. *Appointments:* University Christian Movement, New York, Co-Founder and National President 1966-67, consultant to Experimental Education Groups on fifty college campuses, 1967-68; Case Western Reserve University, Cleveland, Ohio, Member of Campus Ministry Staff, 1968-69; Institute for Policy Studies, Washington DC, Visiting Fellow, 1969-70, Resident Fellow 1971-75, Tenured Fellow, 1975-77; Public Resource Center, Washington DC, Founder and Co-Director, 1977-79; Interfem Consultants, New York City, Founder and Director and Consultant to various organizations, 1979-87; Douglass College, Rutgers University, New Brunswick, New Jersey, Laurie New Jersey chair in women's studies, 1987-89. Numerous guest lecturing appointments. *Publications:* Under name Charlotte Bunch-Weeks: The New Women, 1971; Passionate Politics: Feminist Theory in Action-Essays 1968-86, 1987; Editor of many books. *Contributor to:* numerous volumes, author or co-author of pamphlets on feminist topics; Numerous Feminist, Gay and Christian periodicals; Co-founder and editor of The Furies 1972-73 and Quest: A Feminist Quarterly, 1974-81; Editor of special editions of Motive and Off Our Backs. *Honours:* Community service awards from Lambda Legal Defense Fund 1982 and National Lesbian and Gay Health Foundation, 1986. *Memberships:* Member of editorial board of Motive, 1967-73; Numerous professional memberships. *Address:* Center for Women's Global Leadership, PO Box. 270, Douglass College, Rutgers University, New Brunswick, NJ 08903, USA.

BUNCH-WEEKS Charlotte. *See:* **BUNCH Charlotte.**

BUNGAY Stephen Francis, b. 2 Sept 1954, Kent, England. Management Consultant. m. Atalanta Armstrong Beaumont, 31 Oct 1987, 1 son. *Education:* MA, Oxford, 1972-76; D Phil, Oxford, 1976-81. *Publications:* Beauty & Truth. *Address:* The Boston Consulting Group Ltd, Devonshire House, Mayfair Place, London W1X 5FH, England.

BUNSHICHI Miyauchi, b. 1 Dec 1908, Kagoshima, Japan. Professor Emeritus. m. 1 Apr 1935, 3 sons, 2 daughters. *Education:* Department of English Language and Literature, Hiroshima Normal College, 1930; Litterarum Doctor. *Appointments:* Professor of English Language and Literature, 1955-74, Professor Emeritus, 1974-, Kagoshima University. *Publications:* Shakespeare's First Step Abroad, 1972; Immortal Longings: The Structure of Shakespeare's Antony and Cleopatra, 1978; Shakespeare's Structural Poetics, 1979; In and Out of Old Sites, 1985. *Contributions:* Tragicality of Dialogue, 1950; Whether an Artificer or not: a Plea for Shakespeare, 1951; Shakespeare's Drifting Soliloquy, 1953; Desire Named Utopia, 1984. *Memberships:* International John Steinbeck Society; Renaissance Institute of Japan; Japan Society of

Shakespeare. *Address:* 201 Cosmo- Kamifukuoka, 57-910 Fujma Kawagoe Shi, Saitama Ken, 356 Japan.

BURACK Sylvia Kamerman, b. 16 Dec 1916, Hartford, Connecticut, USA. Editor; Publisher. m. Abraham S Burack, 28 Nov 1940 (deceased). 3 daughters. *Education:* BA magna cum laude, Smith College, 1938. *Literary Appointments:* Editor and Publisher, The Writer Magazine; The Writer, Inc; Plays, The Drama Magazine for Young People and Plays, Inc, 1978-. *Publications:* Editor numerous collections of plays for young people including: Little Plays for Little Players, 1952; Blue Ribbon Plays for Girls, 1955; Blue Ribbon Plays for Graduation, 1957; Children's Plays from Favourite Stories, 1957; A Treasury of Christmas Plays, 1958; 50 Plays for Junior Actors, 1966; 50 Plays for Holidays, 1969; Dramatized Folk Tales of the World, 1971; On Stage for Christmas, 1978; Christmas Play Favorites for Young People, 1982; Holidays Plays Round the Year, 1983; Plays of Black Americans, 1987. Edited adult books including: Writing the Short Short Story, 1942; Book Reviewing, 1978; Writing and Selling Fillers, Light Verse and Short Humor, 1982; Writing and Selling the Romance Novel, 1983; Writing Mystery and Crime Fiction, 1985; Plays of Black Americans, 1988; The Big Book of Christmas Plays, 1988; The Big Book of Comedies, 1989; The Writer's Handbook, 1989-90. *Honours:* Honorary Degree, Doctor of Letters, Boston University, 1985; Distinguished Service Award, Brookline (Massachusetts) Rotary Club, 1973; Brookline High School Library named in her honour - The Sylvia K Burack Library; Freedoms Foundation Award, 1988. *Memberships:* National Book Critics Circle; Friends of the Libraries of Boston University; Director 1979-, President, 1981-83, Phi Beta Kappa; PEN American Centre. *Address:* 72 Penniman Road, Brookline, MA 02146, USA.

BURCH Claire R, b. 19 Feb 1925, New York, USA. Writer; Filmmaker. m. Bradley Burch, 24 Apr 1944, 1 son, (dec), 3 daughters. *Education:* BA, Washington Square College, 1947. *Publications:* Stranger in the Family, 1972; You Be the Mother Follies; Solid Gold Illusion, 9 books of images; Goodbye My Coney Island Baby; Notes of a Survivor; Shredded Millions; Winter Bargains; Homeless In The Nineties - collection of poetry, paintings and photographs, 64-93; 7 Plays; The Day a Thousand People Went to Jail, non-fiction. *Contributions to:* Life Magazine; McCalls; Redbook; Saturday Review; Good Housekeeping; Arts and Sciences; New York Times Book Review; Literary Journals and Quarterlies. *Honours:* 2 Carnegie Awards, 1978, 1979; Grants from California Arts Council, 1991, 1992; First Prize Historical documentary James Balwin, East Bay Media Center, People's Choice Alfonia and Entering Oakland, PCTV, prize Oracle Rising, East Bay Media Center Festival, 1992. *Memberships:* Poetry Society of America; Writer's Guild. *Literary Agent:* Regent Press, Oakland, California. *Address:* Art and Education Media, inc, 2747 Regent Street, Berkeley, CA 94705, USA.

BURCHFIELD Robert William, b. 27 Jan 1923, Wanganui, New Zealand. Lexicographer; Grammarian. m. (1) Ethel May Yates, 2 July 1949, Palmerston North, New Zealand. 1 son, 2 daughters. divorced 1976, (2) Elizabeth Austen Knight, 5 Nov. 1976, London. *Education:* MA, Victoria University of Wellington, 1948; BA 1951, MA 1955, Magdalen College, Oxford, England. *Appointments:* Lecturer, English, Christ Church, Oxford, 1953-57; Editor, A Supplement to the Oxford English Dictionary, 1957-86. *Publications:* A Supplement to the Oxford English Dictionary, Volume I 1972, II 1976, III 1982, IV 1986; The Spoken Word, 1981; The English Language, 1985; The New Zealand Pocket Oxford Dictionary, 1986; Studies in Lexicography, 1987; Unlocking the English Language, 1989; Points of View, 1992. *Contributions include:* The Sunday Times, Encounter; Transactions Philological Society. *Honours:* CBE 1975; Hon DLitt, Liverpool, 1978; Hon DLit, Wellington, New Zealand, 1983; Freedom of City of Wanganui, 1986. *Membership:* Early English Text Society, Secretary 1955-62, Council, 1968-80,

Athenaeum. *Address:* 14 The Green, Sutton Courtenay, Oxon, OX14 4AE, England.

BURCHILL Julie, b. July 1960, Bristol, England. Journalist; Writer. *Publications include:* The Boy Looked at Johnny; Love It or Shoo It; Damaged Gods; Girls On Film; Ambition. *Contributor to:* The Mail on Sunday; Tatler; Elle; The Face; Cosmopolitan. *Honour:* Ambition, Bestseller in UK. *Address:* c/o Bodley Head.

BURFIELD Eva. *See:* **EBBETT Frances Eva.**

BURFORD Ephraim John, b. 15 July 1905, London England. Author. *Publications:* Royal St James; Wits Wenchers & Wantons; London, Synfull Cite; A Pleasant Collection of Bawdy Ballads; Bawds & Lodgings; The Queen of the Bawds; The Orrible Synne; A History of the Clink; The Bridles to Burnings - A Social History of Female Punishments (with Sandra Shulman), 1992; The Bishop's Brothels, 1993. *Address:* 111 Addison House, Grove End Road, London NW8 9EJ, England.

BURG Dale, b. 27 Apr 1942, New York, USA. Writer. m. Richard Nusser, 4 Oct 1981, 1 son. *Education:* AB, cum laude, Brown University, 1962; MA, Cornell University, 1964. *Publications:* Mary Ellen's Help Yourself Diet Plan, 1984; Great Carmen Miranda Look Alike Contest, 1984; How to Stop the One You Love from Drinking, co-author, 1986; What's Stopped Happening to Me?, 1990; Clean House, 1993. *Contributions To:* Columnist Star Magazine, 1983-; Family Circle, 1984-88; Columnist; Woman's Day, 1988-; Columnist, New Woman Magazine, 1991-; Harper's Bazaar, Cosmopolitan. *Memberships:* American Society Journalists and Authors; Writers Guild. *Address:* 130 West 57 Street, New York, NY 10019, USA.

BURGESS Anthony, b. 25 Feb 1917, Manchester, England. Author. m. Llewela Isherwood Jones, 23 Jan 1942 (dec. 1968). m. Liliana Macellari, 1968. *Education:* BA (Hons) Manchester University, 1940. *Literary Appointments:* Lecturer, schoolmaster, 1946-54; Education Officer, Malaya and Borneo, 1954-59; Disting. Prof. CCNY, 1972-73. *Publications:* The Right to an Answer, 1961; Devil of a State, 1962; The Wanting Seed, 1963; A Clockwork Orange, 1963; Honey for the Bears, 1964; Nothing Like the Sun, 1964; The Long Day Wanes, 1965; Language Made Plain, 1965; Re Joyce, 1965; The Doctor is Sick, 1965; Tremor of Intent, 1966; The Novel Now, 1967; Enderby, 1968; Urgent Copy, 1969; Shakespeare, 1970; MF, 1971; Cyrano de Bergerac - a version for the modern stage, 1971; Oedipus the King, 1972; Napoleon Symphony, 1974; The Clockwork Testament, 1974; Moses, 1976; A Long Trip to Teatime, 1976; Beard's Roman Women, 1976; ABBA ABBA, 1977; Nineteen Eighty-Five, 1978; World, 1978; Hemingway and His Man of Nazareth, 1980; Earthly Powers, 1980; On Going to Bed, 1982; This Man and Music, 1982; The End of the World News, 1982; Enderby Outside, 1984; Enderby's Dark Lady, 1984; The Clockwork Testament, 1984; The Kingdom of the Wicked, 1985; The Devil's Mode, 1989; You've Had Your Time (autobiog), 1990; Mozart and the Wolf Gang, 1991. *Honour:* Visiting Fellow, Princeton University, 1970-71. *Address:* 44 Rue Grimaldi, Monte Carlo 98000, Monaco.

BURGIN Richard Weston, b. 30 June 1947, Boston, USA. Teacher; Writer; Editor. m. Linda K Harris, 7 Sept 1991, 1 step daughter. *Education:* BA, Brandeis University, 1968; MA, Columbia University, 1969; M Phil, Columbia University, 1981. *Appointments:* New York Arts Journal, Founding Editor, 1976-83; Critic at Large, Globe Magazine, 1973-74; Boulevard, Founding Editor, 1986-. *Publications:* Conversations with Jorge Luis Borges; Conversations with Isaac Bashevis Singer; Man Without Memory; Private Fame; The Man With Missing Parts. *Contributions to:* Partisan Review; Triquarterly; Shenandoah; Southwest Review; Transatlantic Review; The New York Times Book Review;

Chicago Review; Hudson Review; Mississippi Review. *Honours:* Pushcart Prize. *Memberships:* National Book Critics Circle, YMHA. *Literary Agent:* Kim Witherspoon. *Address:* PO Box 30386, Philadelphia, PA 19103, USA.

BURKE James, b. 22 Dec 1936, Londonderry, Northern Ireland. Writer, Broadcaster. m. Madeline Hamilton, 27 Jan 1967. *Education:* MA, English Literature, Jesus College, Oxford, 1961. *Publications:* Tomorrow's World I, 1971; Tomorrow's World II, 1972; Connections, UK, 1978, USA, 1979, Foreign, 1980; The Day The Universe Changed, UK, 1985, USA, 1986, Foreign, 1987; Editor, Weidenfeld and Nicholson Encyclopaedia of World Art, 1964; Editor, Zanichelli Italian-English Dictionary, 1965. *Contributions to:* Various Publications including: Daily Mail; Listener; Vogue; Vanity Fair; Punch; TV Times; Radio Times. *Honours:* Gold Medal, 1971, Silver Medal, 1972, Royal Television Society; Edgar Dale Award for screen writing, USA, 1986. *Memberships:* Royal Institution; Savile Club. *Literary Agent:* Jonathan Clowes Limited. *Address:* c/o Jonathan Clowes Limited, 22 Prince Albert Road, London, NW1 7ST, England.

BURKE James Lee, b. 5 Dec 1936, Houston, Texas, USA. Novelist. m. 22 Jan 1960, 1 son, 3 daughters. *Education:* BA, MA, University of Missouri. *Publications:* A Stained White Radiance; A Morning for Flamingos; Black Cherry Blues; Heavens Prisoners; The Neon Rain; The Lost Get Back Boogie; The Convict; Two for Texas; Lay Down My Sword And Shield; To The Bright And Shining Sun; Half of Paradise. *Contributions to:* Atlantic Monthly; Southern Review; Antioch Review; Best American Short Stories; New England Review; Epoch; Kenyon Review; Cimmaron Review; New Stories From The South. *Honours:* Breadloaf Fellowship; National Endowment to the Arts Awards; Pulitzer Prize Nomination; Guggenheim Fellowship; Edgar Allen Poe Award. *Memberships:* Amnesty International. *Literary Agent:* Philip G Spitzer. *Address:* 11100 Grant Creek, Missoula, MT 59802, USA.

BURKE John Frederick (Jonathan Burke, Harriet Esmond, Jonathan George, Joanna Jones, Robert Miall, Sara Morris, Martin Sands), b. 8 Mar 1922, Rye, Sussex, England, Author. m. (1) Joan Morris, 13 Sept 1940, 5 daughters, (2) Jean Williams, 29 June 1963, 2 sons. *Appointments:* Production Manager, Museum Press; Editorial Manager, Paul Hamlyn Books for Pleasure Group; European Story Editor, 20th century Fox productions. *Publications:* Swift Summer, 1949; A Illustrated History of England, 1974, revised 1985; Musical Landscapes, 1983; Illustrated Dictionary of Music, 1988; A Traveller's History of Scotland, 1990; Dr Caspian trilogy, 1976, 1977, 1978; Author of over 120 titles, including film and television novelisations such as Look back in Anger, The Angry Silence, A Hard Day's Night, The Bill. *Contributions to:* The Bookseller; Country Life; Denmark. *Honours:* Atlantic Award in Literature, Rockefeller Foundation, 1948-49. *Memberships:* Society of Authors; The Danish Club, London. *Literary Agent:* David Higham Associates. *Address:* 5 Castle Gardens, Kirkcudbright, Dumfires and Galloway, DG6 4JE, Scotland.

BURKE Jonathan. *See:* **BURKE John Frederick.**

BURKE Shifty. *See:* **BENTON Peggie.**

BURKHOLZ Herbert Laurence, b. 9 Dec 1932, New York City, New York, USA. Author. m. Susan Blaine, 1 Nov 1961, 2 sons. *Education:* BA, New York University, 1951. *Appointments:* Writer-in-Residence, college of William and Mary, Virginia, 1975. *Publications:* Sister Bear, 1969; Spy, 1969; The Spanish Soldier, 1973; Mulligan's Seed, 1975; The Death Freak, 1978; The Sleeping Spy, 1983; The Snow Gods, 1985; The Sensitives, 1987; Strange Bedfellows, 1988; Brain Damage, 1992; Writer-in-Residence, 1992. *Contributions to:* The New York Times Magazine; Town and Country; Playboy; Penthouse; Longevity; Others.

Honours: Distinguished Scholar of the Commonwealth of Virginia, 1976. *Literary Agent:* Georges Borchardt Inc, New York, USA. *Address:* c/o Georges Borchardt Inc, 136 East 57th St, New York City, NY 10022, USA.

BURKIN Mary, b. 8 Sept 1949, Kansas City, USA. Actress; Writer. *Education:* BA, University of Southern California, 1970; MA, California State University, Long Beach, 1978. *Appointments:* Artistic Director, Women in Theatre, Playwright's Workshop, 1983-86. *Publications:* Plays: I Lift My Lamp; Susan B. Anthony; The Road Show; Love and Friendship; A Sable Song (co-author). *Honours:* Dramalogue Award for Playwriting, 1981; Outstanding Achievement in Production, 1984, Artistic Merit, 1985, Women in Theatre. *Memberships:* Dramatist's Guild of America; Women in Film; Actors' Equity. *Address:* PO Box 176, Altadena, CA 91001, USA.

BURLEIGH Michael Christopher Bennet, b. 3 Apr 1955, London, England. Lecturer. m. Linden Mary Brownbridge, 11 Nov 1990. *Education:* University College, London, 1977; PhD, 1982. *Publications:* The Racial State: Germany; Germany Turns Eastwards; Prussian Society And The German Order. *Contributions to:* TLS; Ethnic & Racial Studies; Social History of Medicine: History Today; Journal of Contemporay History; AHR; EHR; European History Quarterly. *Memberships:* Fellow of the Royal Historical Society. *Literary Agent:* Ann McDiarmid, Curtis Brown Ltd. *Address:* Department of International History, London School of Economics & Political Science, Houghton Street, London, WC2A 12AE, England.

BURLEY Kathleen M, b. 17 Jan 1942, Minot, North Dakota, USA. Training; Finance. m. Henry R. Burley, 27 Dec 1966. *Education:* BSc., Music, Education, Minot State University, 1963; MA, Arizona State University, 1966; MBA, University of Phoenix, 1984. *Publications include:* Looking Back, Book One, 1987; Who You Are, Where You Are, 1988; Poetry in the following collections: Scratchings to a Flea, 1987; Chasing Rainbows, Volume II, 1987; Hearts on Fire, Volume III, 1986; Best New Poets of 1986, 1986; Words of Praise, Volume II, 1986; American Poetry Anthology, 1985, 1986; Ashes to Ashes, Volume IV, 1985. *Honour:* One of Best New Poets of 1986, American Poetry Association. *Memberships;* American Society of Training and Development; Los Angeles Chapter, National Society of Presentation & Instruction; National Association for Female Executives. *Address:* BCD Enterprises, 1251 W. Sepulveda Blvd., No. 170, Torrance, CA 90502, USA.

BURLEY William John, b. 1 Aug 1914, Falmouth, Cornwall, England, Retired Teacher, Muriel Wolsey, 10 Apr 1938, 2 sons. *Education:* Honours Graduate in Zoology, Balliol College, Oxford University, 1950-53. *Publications:* Wycliffe and the Beales, 1983; Wycliffe and the Four Jacks, 1985; Wycliffe and the Quiet Virgin, 1986; Wycliffe and the Windsor Blue, 1987; Wycliffe and the Tangled Web, 1988; Wycliffe and the Cycle of Death, 1989; A Taste of Power, 1966; Three-toed Pussy, 1968; Death in Willow pattern, 1969; To Kill a Cat, 1970; Guilt Edged, 1971; Death in a Salubrious Place, 1973; Death in Stanley Street, 1974; Wycliffe and the Pea-Green Boat, 1975; Wycliffe and the Schoolgirls, 1976; The Schoolmaster, 1977; Wycliffe and the Scapegoat, 1978; The Sixth Day, 1978; Charles and Elizabeth, 1979; Wycliffe in Paul's Court, 1980; The House of Care, 1981; Wycliffe's Wild Goose Chase, 1982; Wycliffe and a Dead Flautist, 1991; Wycliffe and the Last Rites, 1992; Wycliffe and the Dunes Mystery. *Memberships:* Author's Copyright and Lending Society; Crime Writers Association; South West Writers. *Literary Agent:* Victor Gollancz. *Address:* St Patrick's, Holywell, Newquay, Cornwall TR8 5PT, England.

BURN Andrew Robert, b. 25 Sept 1902, Kynnersley, Salop, England. m. 31 Dec 1938. *Education:* Uppingham School; BA, 1st Class Hons) 1925, MA, 1928, Christ Church, Oxford; D Litt (Oxon), FSA. *Publications include:* Minoans, Philistines & Greeks 1400-900 BC, 1930; Romans in Britain: Anthology of Inscriptions, 1932, revised 1969; Modern Greeks, 1942; Pericles & Athens, 1948; Agricola & Roman Britain, 1953; Lyric Age of Greece, 1960; Persia & the Greeks, 1962; Traveller's History of Greece, 1965, reprinted as Pelican History of Greece, 1966, revised 1978; Warring States of Greece, 1968; Living Past of Greece (with Mary W Burn), 1980, UK and USA, 2nd edition, Persia & The Greeks to 449 BC (with postscript by D M Lewis), 1984. *Contributions to:* Chapter, Persia & the Greeks 546-334 BC, in volume II, Cambridge History of Iran, 1984; Articles in various journals. *Honours include:* Various academic prizes, including Charles Oldham Prize, 1924, Cromer Greek Prize (open to British Empire), 1926, and Arnold Historical Essay Prize (Oxford), 1927; Silver Cross of Phoenix, Greece; Fellow, Society of Antiquaries, London, 1981; Doctor of Letters, University of Oxford, 1982. *Address:* 23 Ritchie Court, 380 Banbury Road, Oxford OX2 7PW, England.

BURN Gordon, b. 16 Jan 1948, Newcastle upon Tyne, England. Writer. *Education:* BA, Sociology, University of London, 1969. *Publications:* Somebody's Husband, Somebody's Son: The Story of Peter Sutcliffe, 1984; Pocket Money, 1986; Alma Cogan: A Novel, 1991. *Contributions to:* Numerous, including The Sunday Times Magazine 1971-; the Telegraph Magazine; The Face; The Independent. *Literary Agent:* Gillon Aitken and Stone, 29 Fernshaw Road, London SW10 0TG. *Address:* c/o Gillon Aitken and Stone, 29 Fernshaw Road, London SW10 0TG, England.

BURN Michael Clive, b. 11 Dec 1912, London, England. Writer. m. Mary Walter, 27 Mar 1947. *Education:* Winchester, 1926-31; Open Scholar, New College, Oxford, 1931; Diploma in Social Sciences (Oxford) while POW, Colditz, 1944. *Appointments:* Staff, The Times, 1938-39; Correspondent, Vienna, Budapest, Belgrade, 1947-49. *Publications:* Yes Farewell, 1946; The Modern Everyman, 1947; Childhood at Oriol, 1951; The Midnight Diary, 1952; The Flying Castle, 1954; Mr Lyward's Answer, 1956; The Trouble with Jake, 1957, The Debatable Land, 1970; Out on a Limb, 1973; Open Day and Night, 1978; Mary and Richard, 1988. *Contributions to:* Articles and poems to: Encounter; Guardian; Times Literary Supplement. *Honours:* Keats Poetry First Prize, 1973. *Membership:* Society of Authors. *Address:* Beudy Gwyn, Minffordd, Gwynedd, N Wales.

BURNET James William Alexander (Alastair), Sir b. 12 July 1928, Sheffield, Yorkshire, England. Journalist. m. Maureen Sinclair, 1958. *Education:* Worcester College, Oxford. *Appointments:* Sub-Editor, Leader Writer, Glasgow Herald, 1951-58; Leader Writer, The Economist, 1958-62; Political Editor, Independent TV News, 1963-64, rejoined ITN 1976-, Director 1981-, Associate Editor, 1982-; Editor, The Economist 1965-74; Editor, Daily Express, 1974-76; Director, The Times, 1982-. *Publications:* The Time of Our Lives (with Willie Landels), 1981; The Queen Mother, 1985. *Contributions include:* TV Current Affairs Programmes, This Week, Panorama, News at Ten. *Honours:* Richard Dimbleby Award, BAFTA, 1966, 1970, 1979; Judges Award, RTS, 1981; Knighthood, 1984. *Address:* 43 Hornton Court, Campden Hill Road, London W8 7NT, England.

BURNETT Al. *See:* **BURNETT-LEYS Alan Arbuthnott.**

BURNETT John, b. 20 Dec 1925, Nottingham, England. Professor of Social History. *Education:* BA 1946, MA 1950, LLB 1951, Cambridge University; PhD, London University 1958. *Publications:* Plenty & Want - A Social History of Diet in England from 1815 to the Present Day, 1966; Plenty & Want, 1968, 3rd ed. Routledge, 1989; A History of the Cost of Living, 1969; The Challenge of the 19th Century, 1970; Useful Toil - Autobiographies of Working People from the 1820's to the 1920's, published as The Annals of Labour; A Social History of Housing from 1815 to the Present Day;

The Autobiography of the Working Class; Bibliography. 3 vols. (eas. John Burnett, David Vincent, David Maynell), 1984-9. *Contributions to:* History Today; Business History; Economic History Review; British Journal of Sociology. *Address:* Faculty of Social Sciences, Brunel University, Uxbridge, Middlesex, England.

BURNETT-LEYS Alan Arbuthnott (Al Burnett), b. 10 Jan 1924, Natal, South Africa. Author; Screenwriter. m. 4 July 1960 (widower), 2 daughters. *Education:* BSc, Glasgow University, Scotland, 1952; DLitt, University of California, Los Angeles, USA, 1959. *Literary Appointments:* Scenario Writer, MGM, 1954-59; Scenario Writer, Fox, 1960-63; Editor, Sphere International (Australia), 1981-84; Managing Editor, Able Publications Co Ltd, 1984-; Freelance Screenwriter since leaving Hollywood; Managing Editor, Able Publications and Co (UK), Able Productions Pty Ltd (Australia). *Publications:* Water Wings (Flying boats, amphibians and seaplanes), 1953; 8 feature films; Over 150 telefilm series episodes. *Contributions to:* Flight International; Rotor and Wing; Yachting Monthly; Motor Boat; Various travel and technical publications, USA, UK, Australia. *Honour:* Croix de Guerre. *Memberships:* Aviation/Space Writers Association; Australian Writers Guild; The Writers Guild of Great Britain; Fellow, Institute of Scientific and Technical Communicators; Associate, Royal Aeronautical Society; Pilot Member, Aircraft Owners and Pilots Association; Institute of Petroleum; RNVR Officers Association. *Literary Agent:* ATP, 32 Kings Road, West Perth, Western Australia 6005. *Address:* Norwood House, Seafield Place, Cullen, Buckie, AB5 2TE, Scotland.

BURNHAM Sophy, b. 12 Dec. 1936, Baltimore, Maryland, USA. Writer. *Education:* BA, Smith College, 1958. *Publications:* The Art Crowd, 1973; Editor, Threat to Licensed Nuclear Facilities, 1975; Landed Gentry, 1978; Buccaneer, 1977; The Dogwalker, 1979; A Book of Angels, 1990. Plays: Penelope, 1976; The Witch's Tale, 1978; The Study, 1979; etc. Films: The Smithsonian's Whale, 1963; The Leaf Thieves. *Contributions to:* Magazines: Town & Country; Esquire; New York Times; New Woman. *Honours:* Best magazine feature, National Steeplechase & Hunt Association, 1974; Best Children's Radio Play, National Association of Community Broadcasters, 1980; Award of Excellence, Communications Arts magazine, 1980; 1st prize, Women's Theatre Award, Seattle, Washington, 1981; Public Humanities Award, D.C.Community Humanities Council, 1988. *Memberships include:* Authors Guild; Washington Independent Writers; Daughter, Mark Twain Society. *Literary Agent:* Ann Edelstein, 510 N 110th St. New York City 10025, USA. *Address:* 1405 31st Street NW, Washington, DC 20007, USA.

BURNINGHAM John (Mackintosh), b. 1936, United Kingdom. Free-Lance Author, Designer. *Publications:* Borka: The Adventures of a Goose with No Feathers, 1963; Trubloff: The Mouse Who Wanted to Play the Balalaika, 1964; ABC, 1964; Chitty Chitty Bang Bang (illustrator), 1964; Humbert, Mister Firkin and the Lord Mayor of London, 1965; Cannonball Simp, 1966; Birdland: Wall Frieze, 1966; Lionland: Wall Frieze, 1966; Storyland: Wall Frieze, 1966; Harquin: The Fox Who Went Down to the Valley, 1967; Jungleland; Wall Frieze, 1968; Wonderland: Wall Frieze, 1968; The Extraordinary Tug-of-War, 1968; Seasons, 1969; Mr Gumpy's Outing, 1970; Around the World: Two Wall Friezes, 1972; Around the World in Eighty Days, 1972; Little Book series: The Baby, The Rabbit, The School, The Snow, 1974; Mr Gumpy's Motor Car, 1974; Little Book series: The Blanket, The Cupboard, The Dog, The Friend, 1975; Come Away from the Water, Shirley, 1977; Time to Get Out of the Bath, Shirley, 1978; Would You Rather, 1978; The Shopping Basket, 1980; Avocado Baby, 1982; The Wind In The Willows (illustrator), 1985; John Burningham's Number Play Series; Granpa, 1984; First Words, 1984; Play and Learn Book: abc, 123, Opposites, Colours, 1985; Where's Julius, 1986; John Patrick Norman McHennessy - The Boy Who Was Always Late, 1987; Rhymetime: A Good Job, The Car Ride, 1988;

Rhyme: Animal Chatter, A Grand Band, 1989; Oi! Get Off Our Train, 1989; Aldo, 1991; England, 1992; Films: Cannonball Ship, 1967; Granpa, 1989. *Address:* c/o Jonathan Cape Ltd, 20 Vauxhall Bridge Road, London, SW1V 2FA, England.

BURNS Alan, b. 29 Dec 1929, London, England. Author; Professor of English. m. (1) Carol Lynn, 1954, (2) Jean Illien, 1980, 1 son, 2 daughters. *Appointments:* Henfield Writing Fellow, University of East Anglia, 1971; C Day Lewis Writing Fellow, Woodberry Down School, London, 1973; Arts Council Writing Fellow, City Literary Institute, London, 1976-77; Professor, English, University of Minnesota, USA, 1977-; Writer in Residence, Associated Colleges of the Twin Cities, Minneapolis St Paul, 1980; Bush Foundation of Minnesota Writing Fellow, 1984-85. *Publications include;* Buster, 1961; Europe After the Rain, 1965; Celebrations, 1967; Babel, 1969; Dreamerika!, 1972; The Angry Brigade, 1973; The Day Daddy Died, 1981; Revolutions of the Night, 1986; Play: Palach, 1970; To Deprive and Corrupt, 1972; The Imagination on Trial, 1981. *Contributions to:* Kenyon Review, 1967; Books & Bookmen; New Statesman; Minnesota Daily, 1981, 1982; Times Higher Educaiton Supplement, 1982. *Honours:* Arts Council Maintenance Grant, 1967; Arts Council Bursaries, 1969, 1973. *Membership:* Poets & Writers, New York. *Literary Agent:* Deborah Rogers, London W11. *Address:* English Dept., University of Minnesota, Lind Hall, Church Street S E, Minneapolis, MN 55455, USA.

BURNS George (Nathan Birnbaum), b. 1896, USA. Comedian. m. Gracie Allen. *Career:* TV shows: Burns and Allen Show, 1950-58; George Burns Show, 1959-60; Wendy and Me, 1964; Films include: The Big Broadcast, 1932; International House, 1932; Love in Bloom, 1933; Many Happy Returns, 1939; Honolulu, 1939; The Sunshine Boys, 1975; Oh God, 1977; Going in Style, 1979; Just You and Me, Kid, 1979; Oh God, You Devil, 1984. *Publications:* I Love Her, That's Why, 1955; Living It Up, or They Still Love Me in Altoona, 1976; How to Live to Be One Hundred or More, 1983; Dear George: Dr Burns' Prescription for Happiness, 1986. *Honours:* Academy Award for Best Supporting Actor, The Sunshine Boys, 1975. *Address:* c/o Putnam, 200 Madison Avenue, New York, NY 10016, USA.

BURNS James MacGregor, b. 1918, USA. Professor of Political Science; Author. *Publications:* Congress on Trial: The Legislative Process and the Administrative State, 1949; Government by the People: The Dynamics of American National Government (with Jack Walter Peltason), 1952; Government of the People: The Dynamics of American State and Local Government (with Peltason), 1952; Government by the People: The Dynamics of American National State and Local Government (with Peltason), revision of 2 previous books, 1954, 12th Edition (with Peltason and E Cronin), 1984; Roosevelt: The Lion and the Fox, 1956; Functions and Policies of American Government (edited with Peltason), 1958, 3rd Edition, 1967; John Kennedy: A Political Profile, 1960; The Deadlock of Democracy: Four-Party Politics in America, 1963; Dialogues in Americanism (co-author), 1964; Presidential Government: The Crucible of Leadership, 1966; Our American Government Today (co-author), 1966; Lyndon Baines Johnson: To Heal and to Build (editor), 1968; Roosevelt: The Soldier of Freedom, 1970; Uncommon Sense, 1973; Leadership, 1978; The Vineyard of Liberty, 1982; The Power to Lead, 1984; The Workshop of Democracy, 1985. *Honours:* Recipient, Pulitzer Prize and National Book Award. *Address:* Department of Political Science, Williams College, Williamstown, MA 01267, USA.

BURNS Jim, b. 1936, United Kingdom. Writer; Poet; Editor. *Appointments:* Editor, Move magazine, Preston, Lancs, 1964-68; Editor, Palantir, Preston, 1976-. *Publications:* Some Poems, 1965; Some More Poems, 1966; My Sad Story and Other Poems, 1967; Cells: Prose Pieces, 1967; Saloon Bar: 3 Jim Burns Stories, 1967; The Store of Things, 1967; Types: Prose Pieces and Poems, 1970; A Single Flower, 1972; Leben in Preston, 1973; Easter in Stockport, 1976; Fred Engels in Woolworths, 1975; Playing It Cool, 1976; The Goldfish Speaks from Beyond the Grave, 1976; Catullus in Preston, 1979; Aristotle's Grill, 1979; Notes from a Greasy Spoon, 1980; Internal Memorandum, 1982. *Contributions to:* The Tribune, London, 1964-. *Address:* 7 Ryelands Crescent, Larches Estate, Preston, Lancs, England.

BURNS Rex Raul Stephen Sehler, b. 13 June 1935, San Diego, California, USA. University Teacher; Writer. m. Terry Fostvedt, 10 Apr 1987, 5 sons, 2 daughters. *Education:* AB Stanford University 1958; MA 1963, PhD 1965, University of Minnesota. *Literary Appointments:* Regional Editor, Per Se, 1966-68; Editor, People and Policy, 1976-79; Staff Book Reviewer, Kansas City Star, 1966-68; Staff Book Reviewer, Denver Post, 1982- 86; Mystery Book Columnist, Rocky Mountain News, 1989- . *Publications:* The Alvarez Journal, 1975; Success in America: The Yeoman Dream and the Industrial Revolution, 1976; The Farnsworth Score, 1977; Speak for the Dead, 1978; Angle of Attack, 1979; The Avenging Angel, 1983; Strip Search, 1984; Ground Money, 1986; Suicide Season, 1987; The Killing Zone, 1988; Parts Unknown, 1990; Crime Classics; The Detective Story From Poe to the Present (Ed.), 1990; Body Guard, 1991; Endangered Species, 1993. *Contributions to:* Rocky Mountain Social Sciences Journal; Texas Studies in Literature and Language; American Literary Realism; Colloquium on Crime; The Writer. *Honours:* Fulbright Lecturer, Thessaloniki, Greece, 1969-70; Edgar Allen Poe Award: Best First Mystery, 1976; Fulbright Lecturer, Buenos Aires, Argentina, 1976; Chancellor's Achievement Award, 1982; President's Teaching Scholar Award, 1990. *Memberships:* Colorado Authors' League, President 1980-81; Regional Vice-President, Mystery Writers of America, 1977-79; PEN; Private-Eye Writers of America; International Association of Crime Writers. *Literary Agent:* Carl D Brandt, 1501 Broadway, New York City 10036, USA. *Address;* 1017 Vivian Circle, Boulder, CO 80303, USA.

BURNSHAW Stanley, b. 20 June 1906, New York, USA. Writer. m. Lydia Powsner (dec.), 1942, 1 daughter. *Education:* BA, University of Pittsburgh, 1925; MA, Cornell University, 1933. *Publications include:* The Poem Itself, 1960, revised ed. 1989; The Seamless Web, 1970; In the Terrified Radiance, (poems) 1974; Robert Frost Himself, hardcover, 1986, paperback, 1989; A Stanley Burnshaw Reader, intoduction by Denis Donoghue, 1990. *Contributions to:* Poetry; Atlantic Monthly; Sewanee Review; NY Times Book Review; Saturday Review of Literature; Agenda, (issued Special Stanley Burnshaw Issue, 1983-84). *Honours:* National Institute of Arts and Letters, NY, Creative Writing (cash award), 1971; Honorary Doctorate of Humane Letters, Hebrew Union College, Cincinnati, 1983. *Address:* 250 West 89th Street, New Yor, NY 10024, USA.

BURRINGTON Ernest, b. 13 Dec 1926. Editor; Assistant Publisher; Managing Director. m. Nancy Crossley, 1950, 1 son, 1 daughter. *Appointments:* Reporter, Oldham Chronicle, 1941-43; Army Service, 1943-47; Reporter, Sub-editor, Oldham Chronicle, 1947-49; Sub Editor, Bristol Evening World, 1950; Daily Herald, Sub Editor Manchester, 1950, Night Editor, 1955, London Night Editor, 1957; IPC Sun Night Editor, 1964; Assistant Editor, 1965, Assistant Editor & Night Editor, News International Sun, 1969; Deputy Night Editor, Daily Mirror, 1970; Deputy Editor, Sunday People, 1971; Editor, The People, 1985-88, 89-90; Deputy Chairman and Assistant Publisher, 1988; Deputy Chairman and Managing Director, 1990. *Memberships:* Foreign Press Association, International Press Institute Executive. *Address:* c/o The People, Orbit House, New Fetter Lane, London EC4A 1AR, England.

BURROUGHS William S(eward), b. 1914, USA. Author; Former Journalist, Private Detective and Bartender. *Publications:* Junk (as William Lee), 1953, reissued under real name Junkie, 1964; The Naked Lunch, 1959; The Exterminator, poetry, 1960; The Soft Machine, 1961; The Ticket That Exploded, 1962; Dead Fingers Talk, 1963; The Yage Letters (with Allen Ginsberg), 1963; Towers Open Fire, screenplay, 1963; Nova Express, 1964; Time, poetry, 1965; APO-33: A Metabolic Regulator; A Report on the Synthesis of the Amorphine Formula, 1968; The Third Mind, essays, 1970; The Job: Interviews with William Burroughs, by Daniel Odier,1970; The Last Words of Dutch Schultz, play, 1970, novel, 1975; Who's Who (with A Balch), screenplay, 1970; The Wild Boys: A Book of the Dead, 1971; Exterminator!, novel, 1973; White Subway, 1974; Port of Saints, 1975; Ah Pook is Here, 1979; Cities of the Red Night, 1981; Blade Runner, screenplay, 1980; The Book of Breething, 1980; Letters to Allen Ginsberg 1953-57, letters, 1980; The Place of Dead Roads, 1983; The Burroughs File, 1984; The Adding Machine, 1984; Queer, 1985; The Cat Inside, novella, 1986; The Western Lands, novel, 1987; Interzone, 1989; Ghost of Chance, novella, 1991. *Honour:* Commandeur de l'Ordre des Arts et des Lettres of France, 1984. *Memberships:* The Authors Guild; PEN International; Dept of Literature, The American Academy and Institute of Arts and Letters. *Address:* c/o Andrew Wylie Agency, 250 West 57th Street, New York, NY 10107, USA.

BURROW J(ohn) A(nthony), b. 1932, United Kingdom. Professor of English. *Appointments:* Fellow, Jesus College, Oxford University, 1961-75; Winterstoke Professor of English, University of Bristol, 1976-. *Publications:* A Reading of Sir Gawain and the Green Knight, 1965; Geoffrey Chaucer: A Critical Anthology (editor), 1969; Ricardian Poetry: Chaucer, Gower, Langland, and the Gawain Poet, 1971; Sir Gawain and the Green Knight (editor), 1972; English Verse 1300-1500 (editor), 1977; Medieval Writers and Their Work, 1982; Essays on Medieval Literature, 1984; The Ages of Man, 1986; A Book of Middle English (co-editor), 1992; Langland's Fictions, 1993. *Address:* 9 The Polygon, Clifton, Bristol, England.

BURROWAY Janet Gay, b. 1936, Phoenix, AZ, USA. McKenzie Professor of English. m. (1) Walter Eysselinck, 1961, (div), 2 sons, (2) William Dean Humphries, (div 1981). *Education:* University of Arizona, 1954-55; AB cum laude, Barnard College, 1958; BA, Hons, 1960; MA, 1965, Cambridge University, England; Yale School of Drama, 1960-61. *Appointments:* Instuctor, Lecturer, Professor in English; Mackenzie Professor of English 1989. *Publications include:* Descend Again, 1960; But to the Season, 1961; Eyes, 1966; The Buzzards, 1970; The Giant Jam Sandwich, 1972; Raw Silk, 1977; Material Goods, (poems), 1980; Writing fiction, 1982; Opening Nights, 1985; Cutting Stone, 1992; Poetry: The Rivals, 1954; Abade, 1959; James's Park, 1961; A Few Particulars, 1966; Nuns at Birth, 1970; Separation, 1975; Mother Hood, 1983; Maternal Line, 1985; This is, 1987. *Contributions to:* New Statesman; MS Magazine; Florida Review; Apalachee Quarterly; Yearbook of American Poetry; and many other articles in other journals and magazines. *Honours include:* Various scholarships; Elizabeth Janeway Prize for Prose Writing; Barnard Phi Beta Kappa; Barnard Memorial Prize for Drama; Mount Holyoke Intercollegiate Poetry Prize; Woodrow Wilson Fellowship; Harvard-Yale Henry Fellowship; RCA/NBC Special Fellow in Playwriting, Yale School of Drama; AMOCO Award for Excellence in Teaching, Florida; Florida Fine Arts Council Creative Writing Grant; First Prize, Florida Poetry Contest; First Prize New Letters Novella Contest. *Address:* 240 De Soto Street, Tallahassee, FL 32303, USA.

BURSTEIN Chaya M, b. 9 Oct 1923, USA. m. Murray Burstein, 7 Apr 1946, 1 son, 2 daughters. *Education:* BA, Hofstra University, 1970; MA, Suny Stony Brook, 1984. *Publications:* The Jewish Kids Catalog; Kids Catalog of Israel; A First Jewish Holiday Cook Book; The Mystery of the Coins; Joseph & Annas Time Capsule; Rifka Grows Up; Hanukkah Cat; The Hebrew Prophets. *Contributions to:* Reform Judaism Magazine. *Honours:* National Jewish Book Council Award; NJBC Award. *Address:* 29 Audley Circle, Plainview, NY 11803, USA.

BURTON Anthony George Graham, b. 24 Dec. 1934, Thornaby, England. Writer; Broadcaster. m. 28 Mar. 1959, 2 sons, 1 daughter. *Education:* St James's Grammar School, Knaresborough, Yorkshire. *Publications:* A Programmed Guide to Office Warfare, 1969; The Jones Report, 1970; The Canal Builders, 1972, 2nd Edition, 1981, 3rd edition, 1993; The Reluctant Musketeer, 1973; Canals in Colour, 1974; Remains of a Revolution, 1975; The Master Idol, 1975; Josiah Wedgwood, 1976; Canal (with Derek Pratt), 1976; The Navigators, 1976; The Miners, 1976; Back Door Britain, 1977; Industrial Archaeological Sites of Britain, 1977; A Place to Stand, 1977; The Green Bag Travellers (with Pip Burton), 1978; The Past At Work, 1980; The Rainhill Story, 1980; The Past Afloat, 1982; The Changing River, 1982; The Shell Book of Curious Britain, 1982; The National Trust Guide To Our Industrial Past, 1983; The Waterways of Britain, 1983; The Rise and Fall of King Cotton, 1984; Walking The Line, 1985; Wilderness Britain, 1985; Britain's Light Railways (with John Morgan), 1985; The Shell Book of Undiscovered Britain and Ireland, 1986; Landscape Detective (with John May), 1986; Britain Revisited, 1986; Opening Time, 1987; Steaming Through Britain, 1987; Walk the South Downs, 1988; Walking Through History, 1988; The Great Days of the Canals, 1989; The Yorkshire Dales and York, 1989; Cityscapes, 1990; Astonishing Britain, 1990; Slow Roads, 1991; The Railway Builders, 1992; Canal Maina, 1993; The Grand Union Canal Walk, 1993. *Literary Agent:* Murray Pollinger. *Address:* 25 Cowper Road, Redland, Bristol, BS6 6NZ, England.

BURTON Gabrielle B, b. 21 Feb 1939, USA. Freelance Writer. m. Roger V Burton, 18 Aug 1962, 5 daughters. *Education:* BA, Marygrove College, Detroit, Michigan, US. *Publications:* Heartbreak Hotel; I'm Running Away from Home But I'm Not Allowed to Cross the Street. *Contributions to:* Numerous Essays & Reviews; NY Times Features Syndicate; The Washington Post; Family Circle Magazine; Buffalo News; Spree. *Honours:* Maxwell Perkins Prize; Great Lakes Colleges Association New Writers Award. *Memberships:* National Writers Union. *Literary Agent:* Mildred Marmur. *Address:* 211 Le Brun Road, Eggertsville, NY 14226, USA.

BURTON Hester b. 6 Dec 1913, Beccles, Suffolk. Author. m. R W B Burton, 7 Aug 1937, 3 daughters. *Education:* Honours Degree in English Literature, Oxford University, 1932-36. *Publications:* Castors Away, 1962; Time of Trial, 1963; No Beat of Drum, 1966; In Spite of All Terror, 1968; Thomas, 1969; The Henchmans at Home, 1970; Barbara Bodichon, 1949 (biography); 11 other children's books. *Honour:* Carnegie Medal for the Best Children's Book, 1963. *Membership:* Society of Authors. *Address:* Mill House, Mill End, Kidlington, Oxford OX5 2EG, England.

BURTON Iris Grace, b. 7 Mar 1940, London, England. Editorial Director, G & J of the UK Publications. m. Joseph Lucas, 1 son, 1 daughter. *Education:* Roan Girls' Grammar School, Greenwich, City of London College. *Publications:* Editor, Woman's Own 1980-86; Editor, Prima, 1986-87; Editor, Best 1987-88; Editor in Chief, Let's Cook 1990-; Assistant Editor, TV Times 1978-80. *Address:* G & J of the UK, Portland House, Stag Place, London SW1E 5AU, England.

BURTON John (Wear), b. 1915, Australia. University Educator; Writer. *Publications:* The Alternative: An Examination of Western Policies in S E Asia, 1954; Peace Theory, 1962; International Relations: A General Theory, 1965; Nonalignment (editor, contributor), 1966; Systems, States, Diplomacy, Rules, 1968; Conflict and Communication, 1969; World Society, 1972; Deviance, Terrorism and War, 1979; Global Conflict, 1984. *Honours:* Research Fellowship and Rockefeller Grant, Australian National University, 1960-63. *Address:* c/o Wheatsheaf Books, 16 Ship Street, Brighton BN1 1AD, England.

BURTON John Andrew, b. 2 Apr 1944, London,

England. Writer; Wildlife Consultant. m. Viven Gledhill, 1 Nov 1980. *Publications:* Over 20 books including: The Naturalist in London, 1975; Nature in the City, 1976; Owls of the World (editor), 1976; Field Guide to Amphibians and Reptiles of Europe, 1978; Gem Guide to Animals, 1980; Gem Guide to Zoo Animals, 1984; Collins Guide to Rare Mammals of the World, 1987. *Contributions to:* New Scientist; Vole; Oryx. *Memberships:* Fellow, Linnean Society of London; Executive Secretary, Fauna and Flora Preservation Society, 1975-87; Royal Geographical Society; British Ornithologists Union. *Literary Agent:* Murray Pollinger.

BUSBEE Shirlee, b. 1941, USA. Author. *Publications:* Gypsy Lady, 1977; Lady Vixen, 1980; While Passion Sleeps, 1983; Deceive Not My Heart, 1984; The Tiger Lily, 1985; Spanish Rose, 1986. *Address:* c/o Avon Books, 105 Madison Avenue, New York, NY 10016, USA.

BUSBY F.M., b. 11 Mar 1921, Indianapolis, Indiana, USA. Communications Engineer (retired); Freelance Author. m. Elinor Doub, 28 Apr 1954, 1 daughter. *Education:* BSc. Physics, Mathematics, 1946; BSc. Electrical Engineering, 1947, Washington State University. *Publications include:* Rissa Kerguelen, 1977; All These Earths, 1978; The Demu Triology, 1980; The Breeds of Man, 1988; Zelde M'tana, 1980; Star Rebel, 1984; Rebel's Quest, 1985; The Alien Debt, 1984; Rebels' Seed, 1986; Getting Home, (short stories), 1987; The Breeds of Man, 1988; Slow Freight, 1991; The Singularity Project, 1993; The Island of Tomorrow, 1994. *Contributions to:* Over 40 short stories to magazines and multi-author collections. *Honours:* Three short stories included in Best of Year anthologies; one in Best of New Dimensions. *Memberships:* Science Fiction and Fantasy Writers of America, Vice President 1974-76. *Literary Agent:* Donald Maass Agency, NYC, USA. *Address:* 2852 14th Avenue West, Seattle, WA 98119, USA.

BUSBY Roger (Charles), b. 1941, United Kingdom. Writer; Public Relations Officer. *Appointments:* Journalist, Caters New Agency, Birmingham, 1959-66; Journalist, Birmingham Evening Mail, 1966-73; Head of Public Relations, Devon & Cornwall Police, 1973-. *Publications:* Main Line Kill (with Gerald Holtham), 1968; Robbery Blue, 1969; The Frighteners, 1970; Deadlock, 1971; A Reasonable Man, 1972; Pattern of Violence, 1973; New Face in Hell, 1976; Garvey's Code, 1978; Fading Blue, 1984; The Hunter, 1986; Snow Man, 1987; Crackshot, 1990. *Memberships:* Crime Writers' Association; Institute of Public Relations; National Union of Journalists. *Address:* Sunnymoor, Bridford, nr Exeter, Devon, England.

BUSCH Frederick, b. 1 Aug 1941. Writer. m. Judith Burroughs, 29 Nov 1963, 2 sons. *Education:* AB, Muhlenberg College, 1962; MA, Columbia University, 1967; LittD, Muhlenberg, 1981. *Appointments:* Fairchild Professor of Literature, Colgate University, 1986. *Publications:* The Mutual Friend, 1978; Hardwater Country, stories, 1979; Rounds, 1979; Too Late American Boyhood Blues, stories, 1984; Invisible Mending, 1984; Sometimes I Live in the Country, 1986; Absent Friends, stories, 1989; Harry and Catherine, 1990; Closing Arguments, 1991; Long Way From Home, 1993. *Contributions to:* New Yorker; Harper's; Esquire; Others. *Honours:* National Endowment for the Arts Fellow, 1976; Guggenheim Fellow, 1981; Ingram Merrill Fellow, 1982; Award in Fictin, American Academy and Institute of Arts and Letters, 1986; Jewish Book Award for Fiction, 1986; PEN-Malamud Award for Achievement in the Short Story, 1991. *Memberships:* PEN, America; Authors Guild; Writers Guild. *Literary Agent:* Elaine Markson, 44 Greenwich Ave, New York, NY 10011, USA. *Address:* RR1, Box 31A, Sherburne, NY 13460, USA.

BUSH Duncan, b. 6 Apr 1946, Cardiff, Wales. Poet; Writer. m. Annette Jane Weaver, 4 June 1981, 2 sons. *Education:* BA, (Honours), English & European

Literature, Warwick University, 1978; Exchange Scholarship, Duke University, USA, 1976-77; D.Phil., Research in English Literature, Wadham College, Oxford, 1978-81. *Appointments:* Lecturer, Director, The Word Workshop, Gwent College of Higher Education, 1984-; Writing Tutor, various Bodies. *Publications:* The Genre of Silence, 1988; Salt, 1985; Aquarium, 1983; Black Faces Red Mouths, 1986; Nostos, 1980; Editor, On Censorship, 1985. *Contributions to:* Numerous journals and magazines. *Honours:* Eric Gregory Award for Poetry, 1978; Barbara Campion Memorial Award for Poetry, 1982; Welsh Arts Council Prize for Poetry, 1984, 1986; etc. *Memberships:* Welsh Academy; Vice Chairman, Welsh Union of Writers, 1982-86. *Address:* 1 Kemps Covert, St Donats Castle, Llantwit Major, South Glamorgan CF6 9WF, Wales.

BUSH Ronald, b. 16 June 1946. Professor of English. m. Marilyn Wolin, 14 Dec 1969, 1 son. *Education:* BA, University of Pennsylvania, 1968; BA, Cambridge University, 1970; PhD, Princeton University, 1974. *Appointments:* Assistant Professor, 1974-79, Associate Professor, 1979- 82, Harvard University; Associate Professor, 1982-85, Professor, 1985-, California Institute of Technology, Pasadena. *Publications:* The Genesis of Ezra Pound's Cantos, 1976; T S Eliot: A Study of Character and Style, 1983; T S Eliot: The Modernist in History (editor), 1991; Prehistories of the Future: Modernism, Primitivism, Politics (editor), forthcoming. *Contributions to:* The Southern Review; American Literary History; Text; JEGP; Criticism; Yeats: An Annual; The Wallace Stevens Journal; The James Joyce Quarterly; Others. *Honours:* National Endowment for the Humanities Fellowships, 1977-78; 1992-93. *Membership:* Modern Language Association Executive Committee, Division of 20th-Century English Literature. *Address:* Division of Humanities, 101-40, Caltech, Pasadena, CA 91125, USA.

BUSH Susan Ensign Hilles, b. 8 Sept 1933, New Haven, Connecticut, USA. Art Historian. m. Jeffrey (formerly Geoffrey) Bush, 25 Feb 1956, (div 1990) 3 sons. *Education:* AB magna cum laude, 1955, AM, 1957, Radcliffe College; PhD, Harvard University, 1968. *Appointments:* Lecturer in Oriental Art, University of Massachusetts, Boston, 1969-75; Visiting Assistant Professor, Columbia University, New York, 1974; Instructor in Oriental Art, Harvard University Extension Programme, 1975-76, 1979-89; Visiting Associate Professor, University of Michigan, 1989; Brian Mawr College, 1991. *Publications:* The Chinese Literati on Painting: Su Shih (1037-1101) to Tung Ch'i-ch'ang (1555-1636), 1971, 2nd Edition, 1978; Theories of the Arts in China (editor with Christian Murck), 1983; Early Chinese Texts on Painting (editor with Hsio-yen Shih), 1985. *Contributions to:* Scholarly articles on 4th to 6th century Chinese decorative motifs and 12th and 13th century painting in North China, journals including Archives of Asian Art, Artibus Asiae, Boston Museum Bulletin, Bulletin of the National Palace Museum, Oriental Art, Ars Orientalis. *Honours:* History and Literature Sophomore Prize, Radcliffe College, 1953; Phi Beta Kappa, 1955; Bunting (Radcliffe) Institute Fellowship, 1976-77; Grant for research in Chinese Civilisation, American Council of Learned Societies, 1976-77, 1977-78. *Memberships:* Past Assistant Secretary and Treasurer, Rdacliffe Chapter, Phi Beta Kappa, Iota of Massachusetts, current Chairman, Committee on Undergraduate Eligibility; College Art Association of America; Association for Asian Studies; Women's Travel Club of Boston. *Address:* 147 Mt Auburn Street, Cambridge, MA 02138, USA.

BUSHELL Agnes Barr, b. 25 Mar 1949, New York City, USA. Writer; Teacher. m. James Bushell, 20 Jan 1968, 1 son, 1 daughter. *Education:* University of Chicago, 1966-68; University of South Maine, BA, 1978. *Appointments:* Book Review, Maine Progessive, 1990-92. *Publications:* Local Deities; Shadowdance; Death By Crystal. *Memberships:* National Writers Union. *Literary Agent:* Edite Kroll. *Address:* 18 Exeter Street, Portland, ME, 04102, USA.

BUTLER Dorothy. *See:* **BUTLER Muriel Dorothy.**

BUTLER Frederick Guy, b. 21 Jan 1918, Cradock, Cape Province, South Africa. Professor of English; Author. m. Jean Murray Satchwell, 10 Dec. 1940. 3 sons, 1 daughter. *Education:* BA 1938, MA 1939, Rhodes University, South Africa; BA 1947, MA 1951, Oxford University, England. *Publications:* Poetry: Stranger To Europe, 1952, with additional poems, 1960; South of the Zambezi, 1966; Selected Poems, 1975, 1989; Song and Ballads, 1978; Pilgrimage To Dias Cross, 1987. Autobiography: Karoo Morning (1918- 35), 1977; Bursting World (1936-45), 1983; A Local Habitation, 1945-1990; Plays: The Dam, 1953; The Dove Returns, 1956; Cape Charade, 1968; Take Root or Die, 1970; Richard Gush of Salem, 1982; Demea, 1990. Editor: A Book of SA Verse, 1959; A New Book of SA Verse (with Chris Mann), 1979; Out of the African Ark (with David Butler), 1988; The Magic Tree (with Jeff Opland), 1989. History: When Boys were Men, 1969; The 1820 Settlers, 1974. Novel: A Rackety Colt, 1989. Short Stories: Tales of the Old Karoo, 1989.; South Africa: Landshapes, Landscapes, Manscapes (with Herman Potgieter), 1990. *Contributions to:* Literary and academic journals. *Honours include:* Cape Tercentenary Foundation Literature Award, 1953; CNA. prize for Literature, 1976; English Academy of SA Gold medal for contributions to English, 1989; Recipient of honorary degrees from Universities of Natal, (1970), Witwatersrand, (1984) and South Africa, (1989); Lady Usher Award for Literature, 1992. *Memberships:* Shakespeare Society of SA (Hon Life President); English Academy of SA (Honorary Life President). *Address:* High Corner, 122 High Street, Grahamstown, South Africa.

BUTLER Gwendoline (Williams), (Jennie Melville), b., United Kingdom. Author. *Publications:* Receipt for Murder, 1956; Dead in a Row, 1957; The Dull Dead, 1958; The Murdering Kind, 1958; The Interloper, 1959; Death Lives Next Door, US Edition Dine and Be Dead, 1960; Make Me a Murdered, 1961; Series of books featuring John Coffin: Coffin on the Water; Coffin in Oxford, 1962; Coffin for Baby, 1963; Coffin Waiting, 1963; Coffin in Malta, 1964; A Nameless Coffin, 1966; Coffin Following, 1968; Coffin's Dark Number, 1969; A Coffin from the Past, 1970; A Coffin for Pandora, 1973, US Edition Olivia, 1974; A Coffin for the Canary, US Edition Sarsen Place, 1974; The Vesey Inheritance, 1975; Brides of Friedberg, US Edition Meadowsweet, 1977; The Red Staircase, 1979; Albion Walk, 1982, UK Paperback Cavalcade, 1984; As Jennie Melville: Come Home and Be Killed, 1962; Burning Is a Substitute for Loving, 1963; Murderers' Houses, 1964; There Lies Your Love, 1965; Nell Alone, 1966; A Different Kind of Summer, 1967; The Hunter in the Shadows, 1969; A New Kind of Killer, An Old Kind of Death, 1970, US Edition A New Kind of Killer, 1971; Ironwood, 1972; Nun's Castle, 1973; Raven's Forge, 1975; Dragon's Eye, 1976; Axwater, US Edition Tarot's Tower, 1978; Murder Has a Pretty Face, 1981; The Painted Castle, 1982; The Hand of Glass, 1983; A series of Charmian Daniel's novels beginng with Windsor Red, 1985. *Literary Agent:* Vanessa Holt. *Address:* c/o Vanessa Holt Ass, 59 Crescent Rd, Leigh-on-Sea, Essex, SS9 2PF, England.

BUTLER Joseph T, b. 25 Jan. 1932, Winchester, Virginia, USA. Curator. *Education:* BS, University of Maryland, 1954; MA, Ohio University, 1955; MA, University of Delaware, 1957. *Publications:* American Antiques 1800-1900, A Collector's History and Guide, 1965; Candleholders in America, 1650-1900, 1967; American Furniture, 1973; Sleepy Hollow Restorations, A Cross Section of the Collection, 1983; A Field Guide to American Antique Furniture, 1985, 1986; The Family Collections at Van Cortlandt Manor, 1967. *Contributions to:* Antiques; Antiques Journal; Art & Antiques; The Connoisseur; The Rushlight; Early American Life; Encyclopedia Americana; Encyclopedia Britannica; Encyclopedia of World Biography; House Beautiful. *Honour:* Winterthur Fellow, University of Delaware. *Address:* 222 Martling Avenue, Tarrytown, NY 10591, USA.

BUTLER Marilyn (Speers), b. 1937, United Kingdom. Professor of English Literature. *Appointments:* Current Affairs Producer, BBC, 1960- 63; Research Fellow, St Hilda's College, Oxford, 1970-73; Fellow and Tutor, St Hugh's College, and Lecturer in English Literature, Oxford University, 1973- 86; King Edward VII Professor of English, Cambridge University, 1986-. *Publications:* Maria Edgeworth: A Literary Biography, 1972; Jane Austen and the War of Ideas, 1975; Peacock Displayed: A Satirist in His Context, 1979; Romantics, Rebels, and Reactionaries: English Literature and Its Background 1760-1830, 1981; Burke, Paine, Godwin and the Revolution Controversy (editor), 1984; Collected Works of Mary Wollstonecraft (edited with J Todd), 1989; Maria Edgeworth, Castle Rachrent and Ennui, 1992. *Memberships:* FRSL; FRSA. *Address:* King's College, Cambridge, England.

BUTLER Muriel Dorothy (Dorothy Butler), b. 24 Apr 1925, Auckland, New Zealand. Teacher; Bookseller; Author. m. Roy Edward Butler, 11 Jan 1947, 2 sons, 6 daughters. *Education:* BA, University of Auckland, 1940; Diploma in Education, 1976. *Publications:* Gushla And Her Books; Babies Need Books; Five to Eight; Come Back Ginger; A Bundle of Birds; Others inc. My Brown Bear Barney; Higgledy Piggledy Hobbledy Hoy; Good Morning Mrs Martin; Reading Begins At Home; I Will Build You A House. *Honours:* The Eleanor Faijeon Award; The May Hill Arbuthnot Honor Lectureship; American Library Citation; Childrens Literature Association of New Zealand Honor Award; The Margaret Mahy Lecture Award; Awarded OBE, New Years Honors List, 1993. *Memberships:* PEN; Childrens Literature Association; Reading Association, NZ; Childresn Book Foundation of NZ. *Literary Agent:* Richards Literary Agency. *Address:* The Old House, Karekare, Auckland West, New Zealand.

BUTLER Nathan. *See:* **SOHL Gerald A.**

BUTLER Octavia E., b. 1947, USA. Science Fiction Writer. *Publications:* Pattermaster, 1976; Mind of My Mind, 1977; Survivor, 1978; Kindred, 1979; Wild Seed, 1980; Clay's Ark, 1984. *Address:* PO Box 6604, Los Angeles, CA 90055, USA.

BUTLER Richard. *See:* **ALLBURY Theo Edward Le Bouthillier.**

BUTLER Richard, b. 1925, United Kingdom. Novelist; Playwright; Television Actor. *Publications:* Fingernail Beach, 1964; South of Hell's Gates, 1967; More Dangerous Than the Moon, 1968; The Doll, teleplay, 1970; Sharkbait, 1970; Jakt i Morker, 1971; I Sista Sekunden, 1972; The Buffalo Hook, 1974; The Men That God Forgot, 1975; And Wretches Hang, 1977; Lift-Off at Satan, 1978. *Address:* c/o St Martin's Press, 175 Fifth Avenue, New York, NY 10010, USA.

BUTLIN Martin, (Richard Fletcher), b. 1929, United Kingdom. Art Consultant. *Appointments:* Assistant Keeper, 1955-67, Keeper of the Historic British Collection, 1967-1989, Tate Gallery, London. *Publications:* Catalogue of the Works of William Blake in the Tate Gallery, 1957, Revised Editions, 1971 and 1990; Samuel Palmer's Sketch Book of 1824, 1962; Turner Watercolours, 1962; Turner (with John Rothenstein), 1965; Tate Gallery Catalogues: Modern British Paintings, Drawings and Sculpture (co-author), 1964; William Blake, 1966; The Blake-Varley Sketchbook of 1819, 1969; Turner 1775-1851 (with A Wilton and John Gage), exhibition catalogue London, 1974; The Paintings of J M W Turner (with Evelyn Joll), 1977, 2nd Edition, 1984; William Blake, exhibition catalogue, 1978; The Paintings and Drawings of William Blake, 1981; Turner at Petworth, (co-author), 1989; William Blake in the Collection of the National Gallery of Victoria, (co-author), 1989; William Blake, exhibition catalogue, (co-author), Tokyo, 1990. *Honours:* Fellow of the British Academy, 1984; CBE, 1990. *Address:* 74c Eccleston Square, London SW1V 1PJ, England.

BUTLIN Ron, b. 17 Nov 1949, Edinburgh, Scotland. Writer. *Education:* MA, Dip CEAD, Edinburgh University. *Appointments:* Writer-in-Residence, Edinburgh University, 1983, 1985; Scottish-Canadian Writing Fellow, 1984; Writer-in-Residence, Midlothian Region, 1990-91. *Publications:* Creatures Tamed by Cruelty, 1979; The Exquisite Instrument, 1982; The Tilting Room, 1984; Ragtime in Unfamiliar Bars, poetry, 1985; Sound of My Voice, novel, 1987. *Contributions to:* The Scotsman. *Honours:* Writing Bursary, 1977, 1987, 1990, Book Awards, 1982, 1984, 1985, Scottish Arts Council; Poetry Book Society Recommendation, 1985. *Literary Agent:* Giles Gordon. *Address:* 9 Moncrieff Terrace, Edinburgh EH9 1NB, Scotland.

BUTORA Martin, b. 7 Oct 1944, Bratislava, Czechoslovakia. Sociologist. m. Zora Butorova, 18 Aug 1978, 3 sons, 1 daughter. *Education:* Graduated, Philosophy, Sociology minor, 1976, PhD, Sociology, 1980, Comenius University, Bratislava; Senior Lecturer (Associate Professor), Dozent, Sociology, Charles University, Prague, 1992. *Appointments:* Editor-in-Chief, Editor: Echo, Reflex, student newspaper, Kulturny Zivot, Bratislava, 1966-69. *Publications:* Fiction: Lahkym perom, 1987; Posolene v Azii, 1990; Skok a kuk, 1990; Non-fiction: Mne sa to nemoze stat, sociological chapters on alcoholism, 1989; Prekrocit svuj stin, Self-help groups in health care, 1991; From the Velvet Revolution to the Velvet Divorce?, 1993. *Contributions to:* Slovenske Pohlady; Kulyturny Zivot; Romboid; Fragment K; Lettre Internationale, Journal of Democracy, Europäische Rundschau. *Honours:* Slovensky Spisovatel Publishing House, 1988; Osveta Publishing House, 1990; Slovak Literary Fund Prize, 1991. *Memberships:* Obec spisovatelov Slovenska; PEN-Club Bratislava; International Sociological Association; Masarykova sociologicka spolecnost. *Literary Agent:* LITA, Bratislava, Slovakia. *Address:* Lubinska 6, 811 03 Bratislava, Slovakia.

BUTTER Peter Herbert, b. 7 Apr 1921, Coldstream, Scotland. University Professor. m. Bridget Younger, 30 Aug 1958, 1 son, 2 daughters. *Education:* MA, 1st class honours, English, Balliol College, Oxford, 1948. *Publications:* Shelleys Idols Of The Cave, 1954; Francis Thompson, 1961; Edwin Muir, 1962; Edwin Muir: Man And Poet, 1966; Editor: Shelley's Alastor, Prometheus Unbound and Other Poems, 1971; Selected Letters of Edwin Muir, 1974; Selected Poems of William Blake, 1982; The Truth of Imgaination: Some Uncollected Essays and Reviews of Edwin Muir, 1988; (ed) Complete Poems, Edwin Muir, 1992. *Contributions to:* Akros; Lines Review; Modern Language Review; Review of English Literature; Review of English Studies. *Membership:* International Association of University Professors of English, Secretary-Treasurer, 1962-71. *Address:* Ashfield, Prieston Road, Bridge of Weir, Renfrewshire PA11 3AW, Scotland.

BUTTERS Dorothy Gilman. *See:* **GILMAN Dorothy.**

BUTTERWORTH Neil, b. 4 Sept 1934, London, England. Writer. m. Anna Barnes, 23 Apr 1960, 3 daughters. *Education:* Nottingham University, BA, MA; London University; Guildhall School of Music. *Appointments:* Lecturer, Kingston College of Technology, 1960-68; Head of Music Department, Napier Polytechnic, 1968-87. *Publications:* Music of Aaron Copland; Dictionary of American Composers; Ralph Vaughan Williams; Neglected Music; Haydn; Dvorak; English For Business & Professional Students; 400 Aural Exercises. *Contributions to:* Times Educational Supplement; Classical Music; Classic CD; Library Review; Sunday Standard; Sunday Times; Musical Opinion; Opera. *Honours:* Conducting Prize; Fellow London College of Music; Winston Churchill Travelling Fellowship. *Memberships:* Performing Rights Society; Incorporated Society of Musicians; Scottish Society of Composers. *Address:* The White House, Inveresk, Musselburgh, Midlothian EH21 7TG, Scotland.

BUXTON Anne (Arundel), (Anne Maybury,

Katherine Troy). British. Writer of Historical/Romance/ Gothic novels. *Publications include:* Goodbye, My Love, 1952; The Music of Our House, 1952; Her Name Is Eve, 1953; The Heart Is Never Fair, 1954; Prelude to Louise, 1954; Follow Your Hearts, 1955; The Other Juliet, 1955; Forbidden, 1956; Dear Lost Love, 1957; Beloved Enemy, 1957; The Stars Cannot Tell, 1958; My Love Has A Secret, 1958; The Gay of Heart, 1959; The Rebel Heart, 1959; Shadow Of A Stranger, 1960; Bridge To The Moon, 1960; Stay Until Tomorrow, 1961; (as Katherine Troy), Someone Waiting, 1961, (US as Anne Maybury, 1966); (as Katherine Troy), Whisper in the Dark, 1961, (US as Anne Maybury, 1966); The Night My Enemy, 1962; I am Gabriella!, 1962 (as Gabriella, 1979); Green Fire, 1963; (as Katherine Troy), Enchanter's Nightshade, 1963 (US as Anne Maybury, The Winds of Night, 1967); My Dearest Elizabeth (US as The Brides of Bellenmore), 1964; (as Katherine Troy), Falcon's Shadow, 1964, (US as Anne Maybury, 1967); Pavilion at Monkswood, 1965; Jessica, 1965; (as Katherine Troy), The House of Fand, 1966, (US as Anne Maybury); The Moonlit Door, 1967; (as Katherine Troy), The Night of the Enchantress, 1967; The Minerva Stone, 1968; (as Katherine Troy), Farramonde, 1968; (as Katherine Troy), Storm Over Roseheath (US as Roseheath), 1969; Ride a White Dolphin, 1971; The Terracotta Palace, 1971; Walk in Paradise Garden, 1972; The Midnight Dancers, 1973; Jessamy Court, 1974; The Jewelled Daughter, 1976; Dark Star, 1977; Radiance, 1979; Invitation to Alannah, 1983. *Memberships:* Vice-President, Society of Women Journalists and Romantic Novelists Association. *Address:* c/o A M Heath, 40-42 William IV Street, London WC2N 4DD, England.

BUXTON John, b. 16 Dec 1912, Bramhall, Cheshire, England. Emeritus Fellow of New College, Oxford. m. Marjorie Lockley, 12 Apr 1939, deceased 1977. *Education:* MA, New College, Oxford, 1935. *Appointments:* Fellow, New College, Oxford, 1949; Reader, English Literature, University of Oxford, 1972; General Editor, Oxford History of English Literature, 1972. *Publications:* Such Liberty, 1944; Atropos & Other Poems, 1946; Island of Skomer, 1950, with R.M. Lockley; The Redstart, 1950; Editor, Poems of Michael Drayton, 1953; Sir Philip Sidney & The English Renaissance, 1954; Editor, Poems of Charles Cotton, 1958; Elizabethan Taste, 1963; Twelve Poems, 1966; A Tradition of Poetry, 1967; Byron & Shelley, 1968; The Grecian Taste, 1978; New College, Oxford 1379-1979, with P. Williams, 1979; The Birds of Wiltshire, 1981; Editor, Walton & Cotton: The Compleat Angler, 1982. *Contributions to:* Country Life; Times Literary Supplement; Apollo; RES; MLR; Etc; Encyclopaedia Britannica; Collins Encyclopaedia. *Honours:* Atlantic Award in English Literature, 1946. *Memberships:* Fellow, Society of Antiquaries. *Address:* The Grove, East Tytherton, Chippenham, Wiltshire, England.

BUZO Alexander John, b. 23 July 1944, Sydney, Australia. Playwright; Author. m. Merelyn Johnson, 21 Dec 1968, daughters. *Education:* BA, University of NSW, 1966. *Appointments:* Resident Dramatist, Melbourne Theatre Company, 1972-73; Writer in Residence, James Cook University, 1985; University of Wollongong, 1989. *Publications include:* Tavtology, 1980; Meet the New Class, 1981; The Search for Harry Allway, 1985; Glancing Blows, 1987; The Young Persons Guide to the Theatre and almost Everything Else, 1988; Plays: Norm and Amed, 1967; Rooted, 1968; The Front Room Boys, 1969; The Roy Murphy Show, 1970; Tom, 1972; Big River, 1980; Stingray, 1987; Shellcove Road, 1989; The Longest Game (with Jamie Grant), 1990; Prue Flies North, 1991; Macquarie, (play), 1993. *Contributions to:* The Australian Way; The Independent Monthly; Readers Digest; Playboy; Northern Herald; Pacific Islands Monthly; New Straits Times. *Honour:* Gold Medal, Australian Literature Society, 1972. *Memberships:* Centre for Australian Language and Literature Studies, University of New England, Patron; Australian Writers Guild, Management Committee 1972-73, 1984-85. *Literary Agent:* Curtis Brown Ltd. *Address:* 14 Rawson Avenue, Bondi Junction, Sydney, NSW 2022, Australia.

BYARS Betsy (Cromer), b. 1928, USA. Children's Fiction Writer. *Publications:* Clementine, 1962; The Dancing Camel, 1965; Rama, The Gypsy Cat, 1966; The Groober, 1967; The Midnight Fox, 1968; Trouble River, 1969; The Summer of the Swans, 1970; Go and Hush the Baby, 1971; The House of Wings, 1972; The 18th Emergency, 1973; The Winged Colt of Casa Mia, 1973; After the Goat Man, 1974; The Lace Snail, 1975; The T V Kid, 1976; The Pinballs, 1977; The Cartoonist, 1978; Goodbye, Chicken Little, 1979; Night Swimmers, 1980; The Animal, The Vegetable, and John D Jones, 1981; The Two Thousand Pound Goldfish, 1981; The Cybil War, 1982; The Glory Girl, 1983; The Computer Nut, 1984; Cracker Jackson, 1985; Sugar and Other Stories, 1987. *Address:* 4 Riverpoint, Clemson, SC 29631, USA.

BYATT Antonia Susan, b. 24 Aug 1936. Author. m. (1) Ian C.R. Byatt, 1959, divorced 1969, 1 son (dec), 1 daughter, (2) Peter J. Duffy, 1969, 2 daughters. *Education:* Newnham College, Cambridge; Bryn Mawr College, Pennsylvania, USA, Somerville College, Oxford. *Appointments:* Extra Mural Lecturer, University of London, 1962-71; Lecturer, Literature, Central School of Art and Design, 1965-69; Lecturer in English, University College, London, 1972-81; Senior Lecturer 1981-83; Associate, Newnham College, Cambridge, 1977-1982; Broadcaster, Reviewer and Judge of Literary Prizes. *Publications:* Shadow of a Sun, 1964; Degrees of Freedom, 1965; The Game, 1967; Wordsworth and Coleridge in their Time, 1970; Iris Murdoch, 1976; The Virgin in the Garden, 1978; Still Life, 1985; Sugar and Other Stories, 1987; Unruly Times, 1989, (Non Fiction); Possession, 1989; Passions of the Mind, 1991; Angels and Insects, 1992. *Honours:* FRSL; Hon D.Litt, Bradford, 1987, Durham, 1991, York, 1991, Nottingham, 1992; Macmillan Silver Pen Award for Still Life; Winner, Booker Prize for Possession, 1990; CBE. *Memberships:* Chairman, Society of Authors, 1986-88; Kingman Committee on English, 1987-88. *Address:* 37 Rusholme Road, London, SW15, England.

BYLINSKY Gene Michael, b. 30 Dec 1930, Belgrade, Yugoslavia. Science Writer. m. Gwen Gallegos, 14 Aug 1955, 1 son, 1 daughter. *Education:* BA, Journalism, Louisiana State University, USA, 1955. *Literary Appointments:* Staff writer, Wall Street Journal, 1957-61; Science writer, National Observer 1961-62, Newhouse Newspapers 1962-66; Editorial board, Fortune Magzine, 1966-. *Publications include:* Life in Darwin's Universe, 1981; High Tech Window on the Future (Story of Silicon Valley), 1985; The Innovation Millionaires, 1976; Mood Control, 1978. *Contributions to:* New York Times Sunday Magazine, Sunday Book Review; New Republic; American Legion Magazine; Saturday Evening Post; Omni; Science Digest; Science Year; etc. *Honours include:* Albert Lasker Award, medical journalism, 1970; Deadline Award, Sigma Delta Chi, 1970; Gold Medal, American Chemical Society, 1973; Science writing award, American Medical Association, 1975; Claude Bernard Award, National Association for Medical Research, 1975; Journalism award, University of Missouri, 1985. *Membership:* National Association of Science Writers. *Literary Agent:* Diane Cleaver, Diane Cleaver Inc, 55 Fifth Avenue, New York, NY 10003. *Address:* c/o Fortune Magazine, Time & Life Building, Rockefeller Centre, New York, NY 10020, USA.

BYRD Odell Richard, Jr, b. 22 Sept 1944, Richmond, Virginia, USA. Educator; Writer. *Education:* AA, BA, New York University, Albany, 1978. *Publications:* A Voice Within, 1979; Love Poems, 1980; Richmond Virginia: A City of Monuments & Statues, 1990; Black History of Richmond: Concise & Condense; Black History of Richmond: 19600-1900. *Contributions to:* New Renaissance; New World Anthology; Black Books Bulletin; International Black Writer. *Honours:* Outstanding Contribution to Literature, 1981; Fellow, International Academy of Poets, 1981; Human Service Club Award, 1989; Golden Poet Award, 1989, 1990. *Address:* PO Box 25455, Richmond, VA 23260, USA.

BYRNE Gavin Francis, b. 2 Aug 1928, Melbourne,

Australia. Mathematical Physicist; Writer. m. Mary Inverarity, 27 Sept 1958, div, 4 sons. *Education:* Xavier College, Melbourne, 1940-46; BS, Melbourne University, 1947-52. *Publication:* How To Stuff Up A Small Business. *Contributions to:* Various inc, Journal of Remote Sensing; Remote Sensing of Environment. *Memberships:* Royal Society of Arts. *Address:* 15A Faunce Crescent, O'Connor Act 2601, Australia.

BYRNE John, b. 6 Jan 1940, Paisley, Renfrewshire, Scotland. Writer. m. Alice Simpson, 1964, 1 son 1 daughter. *Education:* St Mirin's Academy and Glasgow School of Art, 1958-63. *Appointments:* Graphic Designer, Scottish Television, Glasgow, 1964-66; Designer, A F Stoddard, carpet manufacturers, Elderslie 1966-68; Writer-in-residence, Borderline Theatre, Irvine, Ayrshire, 1978-79 and Duncan of Jordanstone College, Dundee, 1981; Associate Director, Haymarket Theatre, Leicester 1984- 85; Theatrical set and costume designer. *Publications:* Plays include: The Slab Boys Trilogy (originally called Paisley Patterns) London, Penguin, 1987 - The Slab Boys (produced Edinburgh and London 1978, Louisville 1979, New York 1980), Cuttin' a Rug (as The Lovliest Night of the Year, produced Edinburgh 1979, revised version, as Threads, produced London, 1980, as Cuttin' a Rug, produced London, 1982, Still Life (produced Edinburgh 1982); Normal Service (produced London 1979); Hooray for Hollywood (produced Louisville, 1980); The London Cuckolds, adaptation of the play by Edward Ravenscroft (produced Leicester and London, 1985). Radio and Television plays. *Honour:* Evening Standard award, 1978. *Literary Agent:* Margaret Ramsey Ltd, London. *Address:* 3 Castle Brae, Newport-on-Tay, Fife, Scotland.

BYRNE John Keyes. *See:* **LEONARD Hugh.**

BYRNE Malcolm M, b. 30 Aug 1955, Newport, Rhode Island, USA, Research Director; Writer. m. Leila J Afzal, 1 Aug 1987, 1 son. *Education:* Tufts University, BA, 1977; Johns Hopkins University, MA, 1986. *Publications:* The Chronology: The Documented Day by Day Account of the Secret Military Assistance to Iran and the Contras; The Iran Contra Affair: The Making of a Scandal; A Pattern of Deceit: The Iran contra Affair. *Contributions to:* Dissent; The Nation; The Washington Monthly. *Address:* c/o The National Security Archive, 1755 Massachusetts Avenue, NW Suite 500, Washington DC 20036, USA.

C

CABANIS Jose, b. 24 Mar 1922. Writer. 1 son, 1 daughter. *Education:* University de Toulouse. *Publications:* Novels: L'age ingrat, 1952; Juliette Bonviolle, 1954; Les mariages de raison, 1958; Le bonheur du jour, 1961; Les cartes du temps, 1962; Les jeux de la nuit, 1964; La Bataille de Toulouse, 1966; Les jardins de la nuit, 1973; un essai sur Marcel Journandeau, 1960; Plaisir et lectures, 1964; Plaisir et Lectures II, 1968; Des jardins en Espagne, 1969; Le sacre de Napoleon, 1970; Charles X roi ultra, 1972; Saint-Simon l'Admirable, 1975; Les profondes annes, 1976; Michelet, le pretre et la femme, 1978; Petit entracte a la guerre, 1981; Lacordaire et quelques autres, 1983. *Honours:* Prix des Critiques, 1961; Prix des Libraires, 1962; Prix Theophraste Renaudot, 1966; Prix des Ambassadeurs, 1972; Grand Prix de la Critique, 1975. *Address:* 5 rue Darquie, 31000 Toulouse, France.

CADDEL Richard Ivo, b. 13 July 1949, Bedford, England. Librarian. m. Ann Barker, 31 Aug 1971, 1 son, 1 daughter. *Education:* BA, Music, English, History, Newcastle University, 1971; Postgraduate Librarianship, Newcastle Polytechnic, 1971-72; ALA Charter, 1974. *Appointments:* Staff, Durham University Library, 1972-; Founder, Pig Press, 1973; Organiser, Morden Tower readings, 1974-75; Founder, Colpitts Poetry readings, 1975; Organiser, Basil Bunting celebration, Newcastle, 1986; Secretary, Basil Bunting Poetry Archive, 1987-; Director, Basil Bunting Poetry Centre, 1989-, Durham University. *Publications:* Sweet Cicely: New and Selected Poems, 1983; Uncertain Time, poetry, 1990; Editor: 26 New British Poets (editor), 1991; Basil Bunting: Uncollected Poems (editor), 1991. *Contributions to:* Poems and criticism to numerous magazines and periodicals including: Atlantic Review; Lycanthrope Quarterly; Kite; Other Poetry; Poesie Europe; Zen News; Durham University Journal; Journal of the John Clare Society; Library Review; Literary Review; Sagetrieb. *Honours:* Northern Arts Writers Awards, 1985, 1988, 1990; Fund for Poetry Award, 1992. *Address:* 7 Cross View Terrace, Neville's Cross, Durham DH1 4JY, England.

CADE Robin. *See:* NICOLE Christopher Robin.

CADLE Farris William, b. 12 Aug 1952, Millen, USA. Land Surveyor; Title Abstractor. *Education:* BSFR University of Georgia, 1974; San Diego State University. *Publications:* Georgia Land Surveying History & Law University of Georgia Press. *Memberships:* American Mensa; Clean Coast, Environmental Organization. *Address:* 317 West Pine Street, Swainsboro, GA 30401, USA.

CADOGAN Mary (Rose), b. 1928, United Kingdom. Writer; Foundation Secretary; Governor, Educational Centre. *Appointments:* Secretary, Krishnamurti Writings Inc, London, 1958-68; Secretary, The Krishnamurti Foundation, Beckenham, Kent, 1968-; Governor, Brockwood Park Education Centre, Bramdean, Hants, 1968-. *Publications:* The Greyfriars Characters (with John Wernham), 1976; You're a Brick, Angela: A New Look at Girls' Fiction from 1839 to 1975, (with Patricia Craig), 1976; Women and Children First: The Fiction of Two World Wars (with Patricia Craig), 1978; Charles Hamilton Schoolgirls' Album (with John Wernham), 1978; The Lady Investigates: Women Detectives and Spies in Fiction (with Patricia Craig), 1981; The Morcove Companion (with Tommy Keen), 1981; From Wharton Lodge to Linton Hall: The Charles Hamilton Christmas Companion (with Tommy Keen), 1984; Richmal Crompton: The Woman Behind William, 1986. *Address:* 46 Overbury Avenue, Beckenham, Kent BR3 2PY, England.

CADY Jack, b. 20 Mar 1932, Columbus, Ohio, USA. Writer. *Education:* BSc, University of Louisville, Louisville, Kentucky. *Appointments:* University of Washington, 1968-73; Knox College, 1973-74; Clarion College, 1974; University of Alaska SE, 1977-78; University of Washington Extension, 1978-; Pacific Lutheran University, 1984. *Publications:* The Burning, 1972; Tattoo, 1978; The Well, 1982; The Jonah Watch, 1982; Singleton, 1982; McDowell's Ghost, 1983; The Man Who Could Make Things Vanish, 1984; The Night We Buried Road Dog, 1992; The Sons of Noah and Other Stories, 1992; Inagehi, 1993. *Contributions to:* Seattle Post Intelligencer; Daily News; OMNI; Pulphouse; Glimmer Train; Chariton Review; Anthologies: Final Shaows and Prime Evil. *Honours:* Atlantic Monthly First Award, 1965; National Literary Anthology Award, 1970; Iowa Prize for short Fiction, 1972; Washington State Governor's Award, 1972; Washington Distinguished Writer Award, 1978; National Endowment for The Arts Fellowship, 1992. *Memberships:* PEN International; Authors Guild; Society of Professional Journalists. *Literary Agent:* Clyde Taylor, Curtis Brown Ltd, NY, USA. *Address:* Box 872, Port Townsend, WA 98368, USA.

CAHILL Mike. *See:* NOLAN William Francis.

CAIDIN Martin Karl von Strasser, b. 14 Sept 1927, New York, New York, USA. Author; Commercial, Professional Pilot; Teacher, Lecturer; Telekinetics Researcher, Instructor; Bionics Development; Radio, TV Broadcaster and War Correspondent; Stunt Pilot and Actor. m. Dee Dee Autry Caidin. *Education:* Graduated High School and College, 1948; A-2 Advanced Course with US Air Force; Atomic-Biological-Chemical Warfare advanced courses completed US Army and US Air Force; Maritime School with US Coast Guard; Advanced Flight Training (heavy equipment); Astronautics OJT Air Force Missile Test Center; Parapsychology at Santa Fe College. *Publications:* Nearly 200 books including: Cyborg (Six Million Dollar Man; Bionic Woman), 1972; Marooned, 1964; Samurai, 1955; Saga of Iron Annie, 1978; Hydrospace, 1959; The Messiah Stone, 1988. *Contributions to:* Thousands of articles, short fiction, newspaper stories. *Honours include:* James Strebig Memorial Award (aviation/space writing) several 1958-; Master Aviator and Pioneer Aviator awarded by Silver Wings, 1987. *Memberships:* Aviation/Space Writers Association; Science Fiction Writers; Authors' Guild; Authors' League; Knight of Mark Twain; Silver Wings; Ten-Ton Club; Valiant Air Command; Confederate Air Force. *Address:* 13416 University Station, Gainesville, FL 32604, USA.

CAILLOU Alan, (Alan Lyle-Smythe) b. 1914, British Writer - Novels, Short stories, Mystery, Crime, Suspense, Plays, Screenplays, Autobiography, Memoirs, Personal. Actor and writer in California 1957- (in Canada 1952-57). *Appointments:* Commissioner for the Reserved Areas Police in Ethiopia and Somalia, 1945-47; Guide/interpreter, hunter and trapper in Africa, 1947-52. *Publications:* (with Arnold M Walter and Frank Chappell), The Shakespeare Festival: A Short History of Canada's First Shakespeare Festival 1949-54, 1954; The World is Six Feet Square (autobiography), 1954; Rogue's Gambit (mystery novel), 1955; Alien Virus (mystery novel), 1957 (in US as Cairo Cabal, 1974); The Mindanao Pearl (mystery novel), 1959; The Plotters (mystery novel), 1960; The Walls of Jolo (novel), 1960; Rampage (novel), 1961; Field of Woman (novel), 1963; The Hot Sun of Africa (novel), 1964; Marseilles (mystery novel), 1964; A Journey to Orassia (mystery novel), 1965; Who'll Buy My Evil? (mystery novel), 1966; Khartoum (novelization of screenplay), 1966; Charge of the Light Brigade (novel), 1968; Bichu the Jaguar (novel), 1969; Assault on Kolchak (mystery novel), 1969; Assault on Loveless (mystery novel), 1969; Assault on Ming (mystery novel), 1970; The Cheetahs (novel), 1970; The Dead Sea Submarine (mystery novel), 1971; Terror in Rio (mystery novel), 1971; Congo War-Cry, (mystery novel), 1971; Afghan Onslaught (mystery novel), 1971; Assault on Fellawi (mystery novel), 1972; Assault on Agathon (mystery novel), 1972; Swamp War (mystery novel), 1973; Death Charge (mystery novel), 1973; The Garonsky Missile (mystery novel), 1973; Sheba Slept Here (autobiography), 1973; South from Khartoum: The Story of Emin Pasha, 1974; Assault on Aimata (mystery novel), 1975; Diamonds Wild (mystery novel), 1979; Joshua's People, 1982; The House on Curzon Street,

1983; The Prophetess, 1984; A Woman of Quality, 1984. *Address:* 55 Grasshopper Lane, Sedona, AZ 86366, USA.

CAIN Geoffrey. *See:* **WALKER Robert Wayne.**

CAINE Mark. *See:* **MASCHLER Thomas Michael.**

CAIRNCROSS Alexander Kirkland (Sir), b. 11 Feb 1911, Lesmahagow, Scotland. Economist. m. Mary Frances Glynn, 29 May 1943, 3 sons, 2 daughters. *Education:* MA 1933, University of Glasgow, Scotland; PhD, University of Cambridge, England, 1936. *Publications:* Introduction to Economics, 1944 (6 editions); Home and Foreign Investment 1870-1913, 1953; Factors in Economic Development, 1962; Snatches (poems), 1980; Sterling in Decline (with Barry Eichengreen), 1983; Years of Recovery, 1985; Economics and Economic Policy, 1986; The Price of War, 1986; The Economic Section (with Nita Watts), 1989; Planning in Wartime, 1991; Good-by Great Britain (with K Burk), 1992; The Legacy of the Golden Age (ed with F Cairncross), 1992. *Contributions to:* Numerous journals. *Memberships:* President 1971, British Association for Advancement of Science & Technology; Past President & Vice President, Royal Economic Society, Scottish Economic Society. *Address:* 14 Staverton Road, Oxford OX2 6XJ, England.

CAIRNCROSS Frances Anne, b. 30 Aug 1944, Otley, Yorkshire, England. Journalist. m. Hamish McRae, 10 Oct 1971, 2 daughters. *Education:* Honours Degree in Modern History, Oxford University, 1962-65; MA Economics, Brown University, Providence, Rhode Island, USA, 1965-66. *Appointments:* Staff, The Times, 1967-69; Staff, The Banker, 1969; Staff, The Observer, 1969-71; Economics Correspondence, The Guardian, 1971-81; Women's Editor, The Guardian, 1981-84; Britain Editor, The Economist, 1984-. *Publications:* Capital City (with Hamish McRae), 1971; The Second Great Crash, 1973; The Guardian Guide to the Economy, 1981; Changing Perceptions of Economic Policy, 1981; Second Guardian Guide to the Economy, 1983; Guide to the Economy, 1987; Costing the Earth, 1991. *Address:* 6 Canonbury Lane, London, N1 2AP, England.

CALAIS Jean. *See:* **RODEFER Stephen.**

CALDECOTT Moyra b. 1 June 1927, Author. m. Oliver Zerffi Stratford Caldecott, 5 Apr 1951, 2 sons 1 daughter. *Education:* BA, English Literature, Philosophy, 1947; BA Hons, English Literature, 1948; MA, English Literature, 1949, Natal University, Pietermaritzburg, South Africa. *Publications:* Guardians of the Tall Stones, 1977, 1986, 1987; The Silver Vortex, 1987; Women in Celtic Myth, 1988; Egyptian Triology: Daughter of Amun; Son of the Sun; Daughter of Ra, 1989-90; Crystal Legends 1990; Etheldreda 1987.

CALDER Angus, b. 5 Feb 1942, Sutton, Surrey, England. University Teacher. m. (1) Jennifer Daiches, 1 Oct 1963, 2 sons, 2 daughters, (2) Catherine Kyle, 21 Dec 1987, 1 son. *Education:* MA, English Literature, King's College, Cambridge, 1963; D Phil, Social Studies, University of Sussex, 1968. *Appointments:* Lecturer in Literature, University of Nairobi, 1968-71; Staff Tutor (Reader) in Arts, Open University in Scotland 1979-93; Visiting Professor of English, University of Zimbabwe, 1992; Joint Convener, Festival of East African Writing, Nairobi, 1971; Convener, Scottish Poetry Library, 1983-88; Convener, Commonwealth Writers Conference, Edinburgh, 1986; Convener, Writing Together, Glasgow, 1990. *Publications:* The People's War, 1969; Revolutionary Empire, 1981; Russia Discovered 1976; Byron 1987; T S Eliot, 1987; The Myth of the Blitz, 1991. *Contributions to:* Editor, Journal of Commonwealth Literature, 1981-87; articles and reviews in Cencrastus, London Review of Books, New Statesman, Scotland on Sunday. *Honours:* John Llewellyn Rhys Memorial Prize, 1970; Scottish Arts Council Book Award, 1981. *Memberships:* Society of

Authors; Scottish PEN. *Literary Agent:* Peters, Fraser and Dunlop. *Address:* 15 Leven Terrace, Edinburgh EH3 9LW, Scotland.

CALDER Nigel David Ritchie, b. 2 Dec 1931. Writer. m. Elisabeth Palmer, 12 May 1954, 2 sons, 3 daughters. *Education:* Sydney Sussex College, Cambridge University, 1954. *Appointments:* Physicist, Mullard Research Laboratories, 1954-56; Editorial Staff, New Scientist, 1956-62; Editor, New Scientist, 1962-66; Science Editor 1960-62, Editor, 1962-66, Science Correspondent, New Statesman; Chairman, Association of British Science Writers, 1962-65. *Publications:* Electricity Grows Up, 1958; Robots, 1958; Radio Astronomy, 1958; Editor, The World in 1984, 1965; The Environment Game, 1967; Editor, Unless Peace Comes, 1968; Technopolis: Social Control of the Uses of Science, 1969; Living Tomorrow, 1970; Editor, Nature in the Round: A Guide to Environmental Science, 1973; Timescale, 1983; 1984 and After, 1983; The English Channel, 1986; The Green Machines, 1986; Books of Own TV Programmes; The Violent Universe, 1969; The Mind of Man, 1970; The Restless Earth, 1972; The Life Game, 1973; The Weather Machine, 1974; The Human Conspiracy, 1975-76; The Key to the Universe, 1977; Spaceships of the Mind (TV Series), 1978; Einstein's Universe, 1979; Nuclear Nightmare, 1979; The Comet is Coming!, 1980; Scientific Europe, 1990; Giotto to the Comets, 1992. *Contributions to:* many and various magazines and journals in UK, Japan, USA, and Europe. *Honours:* UNESCO Kalinga Prize, 1972; AAAS, Honorary Fellow, 1986. *Memberships:* Writers' Guild; International PEN; US Authors' Guild; Vice-President, Cruising Association; Athenaeum. *Literary Agent:* Lizzie Calder. *Address:* 8 The Chase, Furnace Green, Crawley, West Sussex RH10 6HW, England.

CALDERWOOD James Lee, b. 1930, American. *Appointments:* Instructor, Michigan State University, East Lansing, 1961-63; Assistant Professor, University of California, Los Angeles, 1963-66; Professor of English 1966-, Associate Dean of Humanities 1974-, University of California, Irvine. *Publications:* Forms of Poetry (co-ed), Perspectives on Poetry (co-ed), Perspectives on Fiction (co-ed), Perspectives on Drama (co-ed), 1968; Forms of Drama (co-ed), Essays in Shakespearean Criticism (co-ed), 1969; Love's Labour's Lost, by Shakespeare, 1970; Shakespearean Metadrama, 1971; Forms of Prose Fiction (co-ed), Forms of Tragedy (co-ed), 1972; Metadrama in Shakespeare's Henriad, 1979; To Be or Not to Be, 1983; If It Were Done: Tragic Action in Macbeth, 1986; Shakespeare and the Denial of Death, 1987; The Properties of Othello, 1989; A Midsummer Night's Dream, 1992. *Address:* 1323 Terrace Way, Laguna Beach, CA 92651, USA.

CALHOUN Charles William, b. 24 Feb 1948, South Bend, Indiana, USA. Historian. m. Mary Bankhead Foord, 29 Aug 1972. *Education:* Yale University, BA, 1970; Columbia University, MA, 1972; M Phil, 1974; PhD, 1977. *Appointments:* Editorial Board, Hayes Historical Journal, 1987- 93. *Publications:* Gilded Age Cato: The Life of Walter Q Gresham; Biographical Directory of the Indiana General Assembly. *Contributions to:* Articles & Book Reviews; American Historical Review; Journal of American History; The Historian; Diplomatic History; Pacific Review; Presidential Studies Quarterly; Indiana Magazine of History. *Honours:* John Addison Porter 3rd Prize; National Endowment for the Humanities Fellow. *Memberships:* Society for Historian of the Gilded Age & Progressive Age; American Hisorical Association; Society for Historians of American Foreign Relations; Phi Alpha Theta. *Address:* Department of History, East Carolina University, Greenville, NC 27858, USA.

CALHOUN Craig Jackson, b. 16 June 1952, Watseka, Illinois, USA. *Education:* BA, University of Southern California, 1972; MA, Columbia University, 1974; MA, 1975; D Phil, Oxford University, 1980. *Appointments include:* Research Associate, Columbia University, 1973-74; Visiting Research Associate, University of Khartoum, Sudan, 1983; Visiting Lecturer, Univserity of Oslo, 1991; Research fellow, Research

Governing Board, Center for Psychosocial Studies, Chicago, Illinois, 1991-. *Publications:* The Anthropological Study of Education: The Question of Class Struggle; Structures of Power & Constraint; Beijing Spring. *Contributions to:* Numerous Articles & Chapters; Review Essays; Translations. *Honours:* National Merit Scholar; W K Kellogg National Fellowship; Reynolds Fund Award; W R Kenan Fellowship; Order of the Golden Fleece, Honorary Member; P & R Hettleman Faculty Fellowship. *Memberships:* American Anthropoligical Association; Royal Anthropological Institute; British Sociological Association; Southern Sociological Society; Social History Society; International Sociological Association; International studies Association; Assocaition of International Education Administrators; Society for the Study of Social Problems. *Address:* Office of International Programs, University of North Carolina, Chapel Hill, NC 27599, USA.

CALHOUN Wes. *See:* **SADLER Geoffrey Willis.**

CALIFANO Joseph A Jr, b. 1931, American. *Appointments:* Admitted to New York Bar, 1955; US Naval Reserve, 1955-58; With Law Firm of Dewey, Ballantine, Bushby, Palmer and Wood, NYC, 1958-61; Special Assistant to General Counsel, Department of Defense, 1961-62; General Counsel, Department of the Army, 1963-64; Special Assistant to the Secretary and Deputy Secretary of Defense, 1964-65, and to President Lyndon Johnson, 1965-69; Member of the firm of Arnold and Porter, 1969-71; Partner, Williams, Conolly and Califano, 1971-76; United States Secretary of Health, Education and Welfare, 1977-79; Partner, Dewey Ballantine, 1983-, WA. *Publications:* The Student Revolution: A Global Confrontation, 1969; A Presidential Nation, 1975; Media and the Law (with H Simons), 1976; The Media and Business (with H Simons), 1978; Governing America: An Insider's Report from the White House and the Cabinet, Report on Drug Abuse and Alcoholism, 1982; America's Health Care Revolution: Who Lives? Who Dies? Who Pays?, 1986. *Address:* 1775 Pennsylvania Avenue NW, Washington DC 20006, USA.

CALINESCU Matei, b. 15 June 1934, Bucharest, Romania. Professor of Comparative Literature. m. Adriana Gane, 29 Apr 1963, 1 son, 1 daughter. *Education:* IL Caragiale Lycee, 1947-52; Baccalaureate, University of Bucharest, 1952-57; Doctorate, University of Cluj, 1968-72. *Appointments:* Literary Editor, Gazeta Literara, 1958-62; Assistant Professor, Associate Professor, Comparative Literature, University of Bucharest, 1963-73; Associate Professor, Full Professor, Indiana University, Bloomington, IN 47405, 1973. *Publications:* Five Faces of Modernity; Rereading postmodernism; Rereading. *Contributions to:* Yearbook of Comparative Literature; Clio; Stanford French Review; Journal of Religion; World Literature Today; Problems of Communism. *Honour:* Guggenheim Fellowship. *Memberships:* American Comparative Literature Association; American Romanian Academy. *Address:* 1028 East Wylie Street, Bloomington, IN 47401, USA.

CALLAHAN Steven P, b. 6 Feb 1952, USA. Author; Illustrator. *Education:* BA, Philosophy, Psychology, Syracuse University, 1974. *Appointments:* Cont. Editor: Sail Magazine 1982-84, Sailor Magazine, 1984-85. *Publications:* Adrift, 76 Days Lost at Sea, 1986. *Contributions include:* Sail; Sailor; Cruising World; Sailing; Multihull; NE Offshore; Yankee; High Technology; New York Times; Ultrasport; International Wildlife; Yachting World; Yachts & Yachting. *Honours:* Salon Du Libre Maritime, France, 1986; Dolphin Book Club Main Selection, 1986; Best Books for Young Adults, American Library Association, 1986. *Membership:* Society of Naval Architects & Marine Engineers. *Address:* Box 277 RFD 2, Ellsworth, ME 04605, USA.

CALLAS Theo. *See:* **MCCARTHY Shaun.**

CALLICOTT J Baird. *See:* **CALLICOTT John Baird.**

CALLICOTT John Baird (J Baird Callicott), b. 9 May 1941, Memphis, USA. College Professor. m. (1) Ann Nelson Archer, div, 1 son, (2) Frances Moore Lappe, div. *Education:* BA, Rhodes Collge; MA, PhD, Syracuse University. *Publications:* In Defense of the Land Ethic; Nature in Asian Traditions of Thought; Companion to a Sand County Almanac; The River of the Mother of God and Other Essays; Clothed in Fur & Other Tales. *Contributions to:* more than 50, Journals & Book Chapters. Honours: Wisconsin Libraries Association, Distinguished Achievement Award. *Memberships:* American Philosophical Association; Society for Conservation Biology; International Society for Environmental Ethics. *Address:* Department of Philosophy, University of Wiscousin, SP Stevens Point, WI 54481, USA.

CALLISON Brian (Richard), b. 1934, British. *Appointments:* Deck Officer, British Merchant Navy, 1951-54; Managing Director, Construction Company, 1956-63; General Manager, Entertainment Centre, 1963-67; Freelance Writer, 1967-. *Publications:* A Flock of Ships, 1970; A Plague of Sailors, 1971; Dawn Attack, 1972; A Web of Salvage, 1973; Trapp's War, 1974; A Ship is Dying, 1976; A Frenzy of Merchantmen, 1977; The Judas Ship, 1978; Trapp's Peace, 1979; The Auriga Madness, 1980; The Sextant, 1981; Spearfish, 1982; Bone Collectors, 1984; Thunder of Crude, 1986; Trapp and World War Three, 1988; The Trojan Hearse, 1990. *Membership:* Royal Institute of Navigation (M.R.I.N). *Literary Agent:* Harper Collins. *Address:* c/o Harper Collins Publishers, 77-85 Fulham Palace Road, Hammersmith, London W6 8JB, England.

CALLOW Philip, b. 1924, British. *Publications:* The Hosanna Man, 1956; Common People, 1958; Native Ground, 1959; Pledge for the Earth, 1960; The Honeymooners, 1960; Turning Point, 1961; Clipped Wings, 1963; The Real Life, 1964; In My Own Land, 1965; Going to the Moon, 1968; The Bliss Body, 1969; Flesh of Morning, The Lamb, 1971; Bare Wires, Yours, 1972; Son and Lover: The Yound D H Lawrence, 1975; The Story of My Desire, 1976; Janine, 1977; The Subway to New York, 1979; Cave Light, 1981; Woman with a Poet, 1983; New York Insomnia, 1984. *Address:* Little Thatch, Haselbury, Nr Crewkerne, Somerset, England.

CALLOWAY Colin Gordon, b. 10 Feb 1953, Yorkshire, England. Historian; Author. m. Marcia Bezanson, 28 Dec 1980. *Education:* BA, 1974; PhD, 1978. *Publications:* Western Abenakis of Vermont; Dawnland Encounters; Crown & Calumet; New Directions in American Indian History; The Abenaki; Indians of the Northeast; North Country Captives. *Contributions to:* American Indian Quarterly; Vermont History; Western Historical Quarterly; Historical New Hampshire; Montana; Annals of Wyoming; N Dakota History; The Historian; Journal of American Studies. *Honours:* Various Research Awards, Teaching Awards & Fellowships. *Memberships:* American Society for Ethnohistory. *Address:* Bellows Falls, VT 05101, USA.

CALLUM Myles, b. 4 Apr 1934, Lynn, Massachusetts, USA. Editor; Writer. m. Suzanne Connellis, 22 Apr 1967 (div.1974), 2 daughters. *Education:* University of Connecticut, 1951-53; New York University, 1958-61. *Appointments:* Leisure Magazine, 1959-60; Good Housekeeping, 1961-70; Managing editor, Better Homes & Gardens, 1970-75; Associate editor 1977-86, senior editor 1986-, TV Guide. *Publications:* Body Building & Self Defence, 1962; Body Talk, 1972. *Contributions include:* Journals as listed, also: Boys Life; Going Places, travel; Dare; Leisure. *Memberships:* National Association of Science Writers, inactive; Mensa; US Chess Federation. *Literary Agent:* Nancy Love, NYC. *Address:* 291 Poplar Avenue, Q592, Devon, PA 19333, USA.

CALLWOOD June, b. 2 June 1924, Chatham, Canada. Writer. m. Trent Frayne, 13 May 1944, 2 sons, 2 daughters. *Literary Appointments:* Reporter, Brantford

Expositor, 1941; Toronto Globe & Mail 1942; Freelance journalist 1945-; Columnist, Globe and Mail 1983-89; Judge, Governor General's Non-fiction Award, 1984-86, National Newspaper Awards, 1976-83, National Magazine Awards,1977, 1988-90, Stephen Leacock Award, 1977-80. *Publications:* 27 books including: Twelve Weeks in Spring, 1986; Emotions, 1986; Portrait of Canada 1981; The Sleepwalker 1990; Jim: A Life with AIDS, 1988; Emma 1984; Emotions, 1986; Twelve Weeks in Spring, 1986. *Honours:* City of Toronto Award of Merit, 1974; Member, Order of Canada, 1978; Canadian News Hall of Fame, 1984; Officer, Order of Canada, 1986; Windsor Press Club Quill Award, 1987; Order of Ontario 1989; Udo Award 1989; Lifetime Achievement Award, Toronto Arts Foundation, 1991; Margaret Lawrence Letterss, 1993; Thirteen honorary degrees. *Memberships:* Founding Member, The Writers' Union of Canada, Chair 1979; Founding Member, The Canadian Centre PEN President 1989; Founding Member, Writers' Development Trust, Vice-President, 1978; Toronto Arts Council, Director 1985-89; Canada Council Writing and Publishing Advisory Committee, 1989-92; Founding Member, Canadian Magazine Awards Foundation, Director 1981-83. *Address:* 21 Hillcroft Drive, Islington, Ontario, Canada M9B 4X4.

CALMAN Mel, b. 19 May 1931, London, England. Free-lance cartoonist. m. (1) Pat McNeill, 1957 (divorced) 2 daughters; (2) Karen Usborne (divorced 1982). *Education:* National Diploma in Design, St Martin's School of Art; Art Teachers' Diploma, Goldsmiths College, London. *Appointments:* Cartoonist, Daily Express, London, England, 1957-63; Cartoonist for Tonight Programme, British Broadcasting Corporation, London, 1963-64; Cartoonist, Sunday Telegraph, London, 1964-65; Cartoonist, Observer, London, 1965-66; Free-lance Cartoonist for magazines and newspapers, 1966-; Designer of book jackets and advertising campaigns; Illustrator for books; founder of Cartoon Gallery, 1970; producer of animated cartoon The Arrow and syndicated feature Men and Women, 1976-82. *Publications:* Bed-Sit, 1963; Boxes, 1964; The Penguin Calman, 1968; Contributor, B S Johnson, editor, The Evacuees, 1968; My God, 1970; This Pestered Isle, 1973; Calman at the Movies, 1990; Merry England Plc, 1990; Calman at the Royal Opera House, 1990. *Contributions to:* B S Johnson, editor, All Bull: The National Servicemen, 1973; The New Penguin Calman, 1977; DR Calman's Dictionary of Psychoanalysis, 1979; But It's My Turn to Leave You, 1980; How About a Little Quarrel Before Bed? 1981; Help! and Other Ruminations, 1982; Calman Revisited, 1983; The Big Novel (radio play; first broadcast by British Broadcasting Corporation) 1983; It's Only You That's Incompatible, 1984; What Else Do You Do? Sketches From a Cartoonist's Life (Biography) 1986; Sweet Tooth (radio play) first broadcast by British Broadcasting Corporation, 1987; Through the Telephone Directory, 1962; Calman and Women, 1967; Couples 1972. *Memberships:* Alliance Graphique Internationale; Royal Society of Art (Fellow); Society of Industrial Artists (Fellow); Society of Artists and Designers (Fellow); Garrick Club. *Address:* 44 Museum Street, London WC1A 1LY, England.

CALMENSON Stephanie Lyn, b. Brooklyn, New York, USA. Writer. *Education:* BA, Brooklyn College; MA, New York University. *Publications:* Never Take a Pig to Lunch, anthology, 1982; One Little Monkey, 1982, 4th edition 1983, produced by BBC TV, 1984; My Book of the Seasons, 1982; Where Will the Animals Stay?, 1983; That's not Fair!, 1983; Where is Grandma Potamus?, 1983; The Birthday Hat : A Grandma Potamus Story, 1983; The Kindergarten Book, 1983; Barney's Sand Castle, 1983; Bambi and the Butterfly, 1983; Ten Furry Monsters, 1984; The Afterschool Book, 1984; All Aboard the Goodnight Train, 1984; Waggleby of Fraggle Rock, 1985; Ten Items or Less, 1985; Happy Birthday Buddy Blue, 1985; The Laugh Book, anthology with Joanna Cole, 1986; Gobo and the Prize from Outer Space, 1986; The Sesame Street ABC Book, 1986; The Sesame Street Book of First Times, 1986; Little Duck's Moving Day, 1986; The Little Bunny, 1986; Who Said Moo?, 1987; Beginning Sounds Workbook, 1987; The Read-Aloud Treasury, anthology with Joanna Cole, 1987; Tiger's Bedtime, 1987; One Red Shoe (The Other One's Blue!), 1987; Spaghetti Manners, 1987; The Giggle Book, 1987; Fido, 1987; Where's Rufus, 1988; Little Duck and the New Baby, 1988; The Children's Aesop, 1988; The Read-Aloud Treasury with Joanna Cole, 1988; No Stage Fright for Me, 1988; Where is Grandma Rabbit?, 1988; 101 Turkey jokes, 1988; Ho! Ho! Ho! Christmas Jokes and Riddles, 1988; What Am I? Very First Riddles, 1989; The Principal's New Clothes, 1989; Come To My Party; Many others. *Contributor to:* numerous journals & magazines. *Memberships include:* Mystery Writers of America; Society of Childrens Book Writers; Authors Guild.

CALVERT Mary. *See:* **DANBY Mary.**

CALVERT Patricia Joyce b. 22 July 1931, Great Falls, Montana, USA, Editor; Proofreader. m. George J Calvert, 27 Jan 1951, 2 daughters. *Education:* BA, Summa Cum Laude, Winona State University, 1976. *Publications:* The Snowbird, 1980; The Stone Pony, 1982; The Hour of the Wolf, 1983; Hadder MacColl, 1985; Yesterday's daughter, 1986; Stranger, You and I, 1987; When Morning Comes, 1989. *Contributor to:* Highlights for Children; Junior Life; The Adventurer; American Farmer; The Friend; Capper's Weekly; Grit; The Writer Magazine; Farmland News; The War Cry. *Honours:* Society of Children's Book Writers, Work-in-Progress Award, 1978; American Library Society, Best Book Award, 1980, 1987; Woman in the Arts Award, YWCA, 1981; Friends of American Writers Award, 1981; Society of Midland Authors, 1981. *Memberships:* Society of Children's Book Writers; Children's Reading Round Table; Minnesota Reading Association; International Reading Association. *Literary Agent:* Chaire M Smith. *Address:* Foxwood Farm, RR2, Box 91, Chatfield, MN 55923, USA.

CALVERT Peter Anthony Richard, b. 19 Nov 1936, Islandmagee, County Antrim, Northern Ireland. University Professor. m. Susan Ann Milbank, 1987. *Education:* Campbell College, Belfast; Queens' College, Cambridge; BA, 1960, MA, PhD, 1964, Cambridge; AM, University of Michigan, Ann Arbor, USA, 1961. *Appointments:* Lecturer in Politics, 1964-71, Senior Lecturer, 1971-74, Reader in Politics, 1974-83, Professor of Comparative and International Politics, 1984-, University of Southampton. *Publications:* The Mexican Revolution, 1910-1914, 1968; A Study of Revolution, 1970; The Falklands Crisis, 1982; The Concept of Class, 1982; Politics Power and Revolution, 1983; Guatemala, 1985; The Foreign Policy of New States, 1986; Argentina: Political Culture and Instability (with Susan Calvert), 1989; Revolution and Counter-Revolution, 1990; Editor: The Process of Political Succession, 1987; The Central American Security System, 1988. *Contributions to:* International Affairs; Political Studies; The World Today. *Memberships:* Fellow, Royal Historical Society, 1972. *Address:* Department of Politics, University of Southampton, Southampton SO9 5NH, England.

CALVIN Henry. *See:* **HANLEY Clifford.**

CALVOCORESSI Peter (John Ambrose), b. 1912, British. Author. *Appointments:* Called to the Bar, 1934; Wing Commander, trial of Major War Criminals, Nuremberg, 1945-46; Member of Staff 1949-54, and of Council, 1955-72, Royal Institute of International Affairs; Director, Chatto and Windus Limited and The Hogarth Press Limited, publishers, London 1954-65; Reader, part-time, in International Relations, University of Sussex, Brighton, 1965-71; Editorial Director 1972-73, Publisher and Chief Executive 1973-76, Penguin Books Limited, London; Member of the Council, Institute for Strategic Studies, 1961-71; Chairman, The Africa Bureau, 1963-71; Chairman, London Library, 1970-73; Chairman, Open University Education Enterprises, 1979-. *Publications:* Nuremburg: The Facts, the Law and the Consequences, 1947; Survey of International Affairs, 5 volumes, 1947-54; Middle East Crisis (with

G Wint), 1957; South Africa and World Opinion, 1961; World Order and New States, 1962; World Politics since 1945, 1968, 1975; Total War (with G Wint), 1972; The British Experience 1945-1975, 1978; Top Secret Ultra, 1980; Independent Africa and the World, 1985; A Time for Peace, 1987; Who's Who in the Bible, 1987; Resilient Europe - 1870-2000, 1991. *Address:* 1 Queen's Parade, Bath BA1 2NJ, England.

CAMERON Deborah, b. 10 Nov 1958, Glasgow, Scotland. Lecturer; Writer. *Education:* BA, Hons, University of Newcastle upon Tyne, 1980; M Litt, Oxford University, 1985. *Appointments:* Lecturer at Roehampton Institute of Higher Education, Digby Stuart College, London, 1983-; Visiting Professor at College of William and Mary, 1988-90; Worked as teacher of English as a foreign language; Active in British women's movement for more than ten years. *Publications:* Feminism and Linguistic Theory, 1985; (with T J Taylor), Analysing Conversation, 1987; (with Elizabeth Frazer), The Lust to Kill, 1987; Editor: The Feminist Critique of Language, 1990; Editor with Jennifer Coates: Women in Their Speech Communities, 1989. *Contributions to:* Articles and reviews to magazines and newspapers, including Language and Communication, City Limits and Cosmopolitan. *Address:* Digby Stuart College, Roehampton Lane, London SW15 5PH, England.

CAMERON Donald. *See:* **HARBINSON-BRYANS Robert.**

CAMERON Dy. *See:* **COOK Dorothy Mary.**

CAMERON Eleanor, b. 23 Mar 1912, Canada. Writer m. Ian Stuart Cameron, 24 June 1934, 1 son. *Education:* 2 years at University of California, Los Angeles. *Literary Appointment:* Editorial Board, Cricket (magazine for children) 1973-. *Publications include:* Children's Novels: The Wonderful Flight to the Mushroom Planet, 1954; A Room Made of Windows, 1971; The Court of the Stone Children, 1973; Julia and the Hand of God, 1977; Julia's Magic, 1984; That Julia Redfern, 1982; For Young Adults: To the Green Mountains, 1975; The Private Worlds of Julia Redfern, 1988; Essays for Adults: The Green and Burning Tree: On the Writing and the Enjoyment of Children's Books, 1969. *Contributions to:* Various publications. *Honours:* Distinguished Contribution to Children's Literature Annual Award, 1965, Southern California Council on Literature for Children and Young People; Commonwealth Award, 1969 for The Green and Burning Tree; Boston Globe Horn Book Award 1971 for A Room Made of Windows; National Book Award 1973 for The Court of the Stone Children; The Kerlan Award, University of Minnesota 1985. *Memberships include:* The Authors League; Children's Literature, New England; Children's Literature Association. *Address:* E P Dutton Children's Books, 375 Hudson Street, New York, NY 10014, USA.

CAMERON Ian. *See:* **PAYNE Donald Gordon.**

CAMERON Lorna. *See:* **FRASER Anthea Mary.**

CAMERON Silver Donald, b. 21 June 1937, Toronto, Ontario, Canada. Author. m. (1) Catherine Ann Cahoon, 21 Aug 1959, 3 sons, 1 daughter, (2) Lulu Terrio, 17 May 1980, 1 son. *Education:* BA, University of British Columbia, 1959; MA, University of California, 1962; PhD, University of London, 1967. *Appointments:* Associate Professor of English, University of New Brunswick, 1968-71; Freelance Writer, 1971-; Writer-in-Residence: University College of Cape Breton, 1978-80; University of Prince Edward Island, 1985-86; Nova Scotia College of Art and Design, 1987-88; Founding Executive Director, Centre Bras d'Or, Baddeck, Nova Scotia; President, Novara Software; Owner, Paper Tiger Enterprises Ltd, editorial and consulting services. *Publications:* Faces of Leacock, 1967; Conversations with Canadian Novelists, 1973; The Education of Everett Richardson, 1977; Seasons in the Rain, essays, 1978; Dragon Lady, 1980, paperback, 1981; The Baitchopper,

children's novel, 1982; Schooner: Bluenose and Bluenose II, 1984; Outhouses of the West, 1988; Wind, Whales and Whisky: A Cape Breton Voyage, 1991; Lifetime: A Treasury of Uncommon Wisdoms (co-author), 1992; Once Upon a Schooner: An Offshore Voyage in Bluenose II, 1992; Iceboats to Super Ferries: An Illustrated History of Marine Atlantic (co-author); Numerous articles, radio drama, short stories, television scripts and stage plays including The Prophet at Tantramar, 1988. *Honours:* Several ACTRA Award nominations for radio drama; 4 National Magazine Awards; Best Short Film, Canadian Film Celebration; Nominated, Prix Italia for Radio Drama, 1980; City of Dartmouth Book Award, 1992; Atlantic Provinces Booksellers Choice Award, 1992. *Memberships:* Writers Union, Canada, Vice-Chairman; Periodical Writers Association, Canada; ACTRA; Writers Federation, Nova Scotia. *Address:* D'Escousse, Nova Scotia, Canada B0E 1K0.

CAMERON WATT Donald, b. 1928, British. *Appointments:* Assistant Lecturer in Political History 1954-56, Lecturer in International History 1956-62, Senior Lecturer 1962-66, Reader 1966-72, Professor of International History 1972-81, Stevenson Professor of International History 1981-, University of London; Secretary and Chairman, Association of Contemporary Historians, 1966-89; Assistant Editor, Documents on German Foreign Policy 1918-1945, 1951-54, 1957-59; Editor, Survey of International Affairs, 1962-71; Chairman, Greenwich Forum, 1974-84. *Publications:* Britain and the Suez Canal, 1956; Documents on the Suez Crisis (ed), 1957; Britain Looks to Germany, Personalities and Policies: Studies in the Formulation of British Foreign Policy in the Twentieth Century, 1965, 1970; Survey of International Affairs, 1961, 1962, 1963, 1969, 1973; Documents on International Affairs 1961 (ed), 1966; Studies in International History (ed with K Bourne), A History of the World in the Twentieth Century (with F Spencer and N Brown), 1967; Contemporary History in Europe (ed), 1969; Hitler's Mein Kampf (ed), 1970, 1992; Current British Foreign Policy 1970 (ed with J B Mayall), 1971; Current British Foreign Policy 1971 (ed with J B Mayall), Documents on International Affairs 1963 (ed with J B Mayall), 1973; Too Serious a Business: European Armies and the Approach of the Second World War, 1975, 1992; Succeeding John Bull: America in Britain's Place 1900-1975, 1983; How War Came: The Immediate Origins of the Second World War, 1989; Argentina Between the Great Powers (ed with Guido Di Tella), 1990. *Honour:* Fellow of the British Academy, DLitt (Oxon). *Address:* C/o London School of Economics and Political Science, Houghton Street, London WC2A 2AE, England.

CAMPBELL Alistair Te Ariki, b. 25 June 1925, Rarotonga. Writer. m. (1) Fleur Adcock, 1952, (2) Meg Andersen, 1958, 3 sons, 2 daughters. *Education:* BA, Victoria University of Wellington, New Zealand, 1953; Teaching Diploma, Wellington Teachers College, 1954. *Appointments:* Editor, School Publications, 1955-72; Senior Editor, New Zealand Council for Educational Research, 1972-87. *Publications include:* Mine Eyes Dazzle, verse, 1950; Wild Honey, verse, 1964; Kapiti: Selected Poems, 1972; Collected Poems, 1981; Stone Rain: The Polynesian Strain, verse, 1992; Island to Island, autobiography, 1984; The Frigate Bird, novel, 1989; Sidewinder, novel, 1991; Tia, novel, 1993. *Contributions to:* New Zealand Listener; Landfall; Comment; Poetry New Zealand; Poetry Australia. *Honours:* Gold Medal for TV documentary Island of Spirits, La Spezia International Film Festival, 1974; New Zealand Book Award for Poetry, Collected Poems, 1982. *Memberships:* President, President of Honour, PEN International, New Zealand Centre; Patron, Poetry Society, Wellington, New Zealand. *Address:* 4 Rawhiti Road, Pukerua Bay, Wellington, New Zealand.

CAMPBELL Donald, b. 1940, British. *Appointments:* Writer-in-Residence, Edinburgh Department, 1974-77; Director, Lothian Young Writers Project, 1978-79; Writer-in-Residence, Royal Lyceum Theatre, 1981-82. *Publications:* Poems, 1971; Rhymes 'n Reasons, 1972;

Murals: Poems in Scots, 1974; The Jesuit, 1976; Somerville the Soldier, 1978; The Widows of Clyth, Blether, 1979; A Brighter Sunshine, 1983. *Address:* 85 Spottiswoode Street, Edinburgh EH9 1BZ, Scotland.

CAMPBELL Ewing, b. 26 Dec 1946, Alice, Texas, USA. Novelist. *Education:* BBA, Northern Texas State University (now University of Northern Texas), 1968; MA, University of Southern Mississippi, 1972; PhD, Oklahoma State University, 1980. *Appointments:* Lecturer, 1981-82, Visiting Scholar, 1992, University of Texas; Lecturer, Oklahoma State University, 1982-83; Instructor, Wharton College, 1983-84; Assistant Professor, 1984-89, Associate Professor, 1990, Texas A&M University, College Station; Fulbright Lecturer, National University of Cordoba, Argentina, 1989. *Publications:* Weave It Like Nightfall, 1977; The Way of Sequestered Places, 1982; The Rincon Triptych, 1984; Piranesi's Dream: Stories, 1986; Raymond Carver: A Study of the Short Fiction, 1992. *Contributions to:* The Bezoar, to London Magazine; Sister Love, to New England Review; Sen- Sen, to New England Review; Conveniences, to Kenyon Review. *Honours:* Fulbright Fellow, 1989; Fiction Fellowship, National Endowment for the Arts, 1990; Dobie-Paisano Ralph Johnston Memorial Fellowship, 1992. *Address:* English Department, Texas A&M University, College Station, TX 77843, USA.

CAMPBELL Ian, b. 25 Aug 1942, Lausanne, Switzerland. Reader, English, University of Edinburgh. *Education:* MA, Aberdeen, 1964; PhD, Edinburgh, 1970. *Appointments:* Member, English Literature Dept., University of Edinburgh, 1967-; Guest Appointments, Guelph, Duke, UCLA; British Council Appointments, France, Germany. *Publications:* Co-Editor, McLellan's Jamie The Saxt; Editor: Carlyle's Reminiscences & Selected Essays, Critical Essays in Nineteenth Century Scottish Fiction; Thomas Carlyle Letters, 15 volumes, 1970-87; Carlyle, 1974, 1975, 1978; Nineteenth Century Scottish Fiction: Critical Essays, 1978; Thomas and Jane, 1980; Kailyard, 1981; Lewis Grassic Gibbon, 1986; Spartacus, 1987. *Contributions to:* Numerous papers to learned journals. *Honour:* British Academy Research Fellowship, 1980. *Memberships:* President, Carlyle Society; Past President Scottish Association for the Speaking of Verse; Council Member, Association for Scottish Literary Studies. *Address:* Dept. of English, University of Edinburgh, David Hume Tower, George Square, Edinburgh EH8 9JX, Scotland.

CAMPBELL James, b. 5 June 1951, Glasgow, Scotland. Writer. *Education:* Edinburgh University, MA. *Appointments:* Editor, New Edinburgh Review, 1978-82. *Publications:* Talking at the Gates: A Life of James Baldwin; Gate Fever; Invisible Country; The New Edinburgh Review Anthology; The Panther Book of Scottish Short Stories. *Contributions to:* Numerous newspapers & journals including: London Magazine; London Review of Books; New Statesman; The Nation. *Literary agent:* Antony Harwood, Curtis Brown. *Address:* c/o TLS, Priory House, St Johns Lane, London EC1, England.

CAMPBELL John Malcolm b. 2 Sept 1947, London, England. Writer. m. Alison McCracken, 5 Aug 1972, 1 son, 1 daughter. *Education:* Charterhouse, 1960-65; MA (Hons) 1970, PhD, 1975, University of Edinburgh. *Publications:* Lloyd George: The Goat in the Wilderness, 1977; F E Smith, First Earl of Birkenhead, 1983; Roy Jenkins: A Biography, 1983; Nye Bevan and the Mirage of British Socialism, 1987; The Experience of World War II (editor), 1989; Series Editor, Makers of the Twentieth Century, 1990-. *Contributions to:* Regular Book Reviews for The Times since 1984; Times Literary Supplement, New Statesman, London Review of Books, *Honour:* Yorkshire Post, Best First Book Award (Second Prize), 1977. *Memberships:* Society of Authors; Trollope Society. *Literary Agent:* Bruce Hunter, David Higham Associates. *Address:* 35 Ladbroke Square, London W11 3NB, England.

CAMPBELL Judith, (Anthony Grant), b. 1914, British. *Appointments:* Journalist; Broadcaster. *Publications:* Family Pony, 1962; The Queen Rides, 1965; Horses in the Sun, 1966; Police Horse, 1967; Pony Events, World of Horses, 1969; Horses and Ponies, World of Ponies, Anne - Portrait of a Princess, 1970; Family on Horseback (with N Toyne), Princess Anne and Her Horses, Elizabeth and Philip, 1972; The Champions, 1973; Royalty on Horseback, 1974; The World of the Horse, 1975; Eventing, Anne and Mark, 1976; Your own Pony Club, Queen Elizabeth II, 1979; The Mutant (as A Grant), Charles A Prince of His Time, 1980; The Royal Partners, 1982; Royal Horses, 1983; Ponies, People & Palaces, autobiography; Freddy & The Fiddler, co-author & illustrator Oliver Marland.*Address:* c/o A M Heath Limited, 79 St Martin's Lane, London WC2N 4AA, England.

CAMPBELL Karen. *See:* BEATY Betty.

CAMPBELL Martin Crafts, (Marty), b. 24 June 1946, Oakland, California, USA. Writer. *Education:* BA, Biochemistry, University of Chicago, 1968; MA, Teaching, Northwestern University, Evanston, Illinois, 1972. *Appointments:* Featured Performer, Poetry, extensively, USA and St Croix, 1976-; Publisher, Mar Crafts, 1981-; Editor, SENYA and Companion to Senya, 1989; Editor, Collage Two, St Croix Anthology of Poetry, 1991; Editor, Poetry Corner, weekly in Caribbean Impressions, 1991-. *Publications:* Chapters of Pomes, Mesh Up, 1981; Croix These Tears, 1982; Dreem, 1982; Church, 1985; Saint Sea, 1986; Companion to Senya, 1989. *Contributions to:* Hammers, Chicago, 1989-; Collage One, Two, and Three, St Croix, 1990, 1991, 1993; Caribbean Writer, 1990, 1991; VERVE; Lilliput Review. *Honours:* 1st Place, Caribbean Poetry Contest, BBC, London, 1981; 1st Place, Adult, Black History Month Poetry Contest, Department of Education and Public Libraries, St Croix, 1987. *Memberships:* Poet, Writer, Performance Poet and Writer, Poets and Writers, New York; Collage Group, Christiansted, St Croix; Finmen Ocean Swimmers; St Croix Basketball Association; Courtyard Players; Island Center for the Performing Arts. *Address:* Box 2565, Frederiksted, VI 00841, USA.

CAMPBELL Ramsey, b. 4 Jan 1946, Liverpool, England. Writer; Film Reviewer. m. Jenny Chandler, 1 Jan 1971, 1 daughter, 1 son. *Education:* Ryebank Private School, Liverpool 1953-57; Saint Edward's College, Liverpool, 1957-62. *Literary Appointments:* Fulltime writer 1973-; Film Reviewer for BBC Radio Merseyside, 1969-. *Publications:* Novels: The Doll Who Ate His Mother, 1976, (definitive edition, 1985); The Face That Must Die, 1979, (definitive edition, 1983); The Parasite, 1980; The Nameless, 1981, (definitive edition, 1985); Incarnate, 1983; The Claw, 1983, (US - Night of the Claw); Obsession, 1985; The Hungary Moon, 1986; The Influence, 1988; Ancient Images, 1989; Midnight Sun, 1990; The Count of Eleven, 1991; The Long Lost, 1993. Short Stories: The Inhabitant of the Lake and Less Welcome Tenants, 1964; Demons by Daylight, 1973; The Height of the Scream, 1976; Dark Companions, 1982; Cold Print, 1985; Black Wine (with Charles L Grant), 1986; Night Visions 3 (with Clive Barker and Lisa Tuttle), 1986; Scared Stiff, 1987; Dark Feasts: The World of Ramsey Campbell, 1987; Waking Nightmares, 1991; Alone With The Horrors, 1993; Strange Things and Stranger Places, 1993. Novella: Needing Ghosts, 1990. *Contributions to:*Anthologies including: Superhorror, 1976; New Terrors, 1980; New Tales of the Cthulhu Mythos, 1980; Fine Frights: Stories That Scared Me, 1988; Uncanny Banquet, 1992. *Honours:* The Chimney - World Fantasy Award, Best Short Story, 1978; In The Bag - British Fantasy Award, Best Short Story, 1978; The Parasite - British Fantasy Award, Best Novel, 1980; Mackintosh Willy - World Fantasy Award, Best Novel, 1980; Incarnate - British Fantasy Award, Best Novel, 1985; The Hungry Moon - British Fantasy Award, Best Novel, 1988; The Influence - British Fantasy Award, Best Novel, 1989; Ancient Images - Bram Stoker Award, 1989; Midnight Sun - British Fantasy Award, Best Novel, 1991; Best New Horror (co-edited with

Stephen Jones) - British Fantasy Award and World Fantasy Award, Best Anthology or Collection, 1991. *Membership:* President, British Fantasy Society; Society of Fontastic Films. *Literary Agent:* Carol Smith (UK) Kirby McCauley (US) Ralph Vicinanza (foreign). *Address:* 31 Penkett Road, Wallasey L45 7QE, Merseyside, England.

CAMPBELL Stewart James, (S J Campbell), b. 30 June 1944, Aberdeen, Scotland. Associate Professor of Physics. m. Iris Anne Evans, 27 July 1968, 1 son, 1 daughter. *Education:* BSc (Hons), Aberdeen University, 1966; MSc, Salford University, 1969; PhD, Monash University, 1974. *Publications:* Proceedings of the International Conference on the Applications of the Mössbauer Effect (co-editor), 1988; Mössbauer Spectroscopy Applied to Inorganic Chemistry, Chapter 4, 1989; In Press, Mössbauer Spectroscopy Applied to Materials and Magnetism, Chapter 7, 1993. *Contributions to:* Over 130 Scientific/Research publications, International Journals of Science. *Memberships:* Fellow, Institute of Physics; Fellow, Australian Institute of Physics, Chairman ACT Branch, 1993; Chartered Physicist. *Address:* Department of Physics, University College, University of New South Wales (Australian Defence Force Academy), Canberra, ACT 2600, Australia.

CAMPION Joan Berengaria, (Betty Anne Arner), b. 14 Apr 1940, Weissport, PA, USA. Freelance Writer; Editor; Historian. *Education:* Cedar Crest College, Allentown, PA, BA, 1961; Western State College, Gunnison, 1962-63. *Publications:* In The Lion's Mouth: Gisi Fleischmann and the Jewish Fight for Survival; Saturday Night on the South Side; Mahoning: Memories of a Lost Valley; Smokestacks and Black Diamonds: A History of Carbon County. *Contributions to:* Numerous magazines and newpapers. *Honours:* Fellowship, Memorial Foundation for Jewish Culture; Publication Grant Dokumentationszentrum, Vienna, Austria. *Memberships:* International Womens Writing Guild; Founder, South Bethleham Historical Society. *Address:* 1270 E Blakeslee Boulevard, Lehighton, PA 18235, USA.

CAMPS Arnulf. *See:* **CAMPS Petrus Henricus Johannes.**

CAMPS Petrus Henricus Johannes Maria (Arnulf Camps), b. 1 Feb 1925, Eindhoven, Netherlands. Emeritus Professor. *Education:* B Th University Nijmegen, 1951; DD University Fribourg, 1957. *Appointments include:* Professor, Karachi Pakistan, 1957-61; Mission Sec, Netherlands, 1961-63; Ordinary Professor, University Nijmegen, 1963-90; Consultor, Dialogue Vatican, 1964-79; Board of Directors, World Conf. Religion & Peace, 1979-; Board of Directors, Institute Missiol & Ecumenics, 1981-91. *Publications:* Partners in Dialogue; The Sanskrit Grammer & Manuscripts of the Father Heinrich Roth; Jerome Xavier S J and the Muslims of the mogul Empire; Trilogy on Theology of Religions; Het Derde Oog, Van een Theologie in Azië naar een aziatische Theologie. *Contributions to:* The Identity of Europe & Cultural Plurality; Studies in Interreligious Dialogue; For My Bibliography See, Popular Religion, ed by J Van Nieuwenhove, 1991. *Honours:* Night of the Order of the Dutch Lion. *Address:* Helmkruidstraat 35, NL 6602, CZ Wijchen, Netherlands.

CAMPTON David, b. 1924. British, Playwright; Writer of children's fiction. *Appointments:* Clerk, City of Leicester Education Department, 1941-49 and East Midlands Gas Board, Leicester, 1949-56; Professional actor and director, 1959-. *Publications include:* On Stage: Containing Seventeen Sketches and One Monologue, 1964; Resting Place, 1964; The Manipulator, 1964; Split Down the Middle, 1965; Little Brother, Little Sister and Out of the Flying Pan, 1966; Two Leaves and a Stalk, 1967; Angel Unwilling, 1967; More Sketches, 1967; Ladies Night: Four Plays for Women, 1967; The Right Place, 1969; Laughter and Fear, 9 One-Act Plays, 1969; On Stage Again: Containing Fourteen Sketches and Two Monologues,

1969; The Life and Death of Almost Everybody, 1970; Now and Then, 1970; Timesneeze, 1970; Gulliver in Lilliput (reader) 1970; Gulliver in the Land of Giants (reader) 1970; The Wooden Horse of Troy (reader) 1970; Jonah, 1971; The Cagebirds, 1971; Us and Them, 1972; Carmilla, 1972; Come Back Tomorrow, 1972; In Committee, 1972; Three Gothic Plays, 1973; Modern Aesop (reader), 1976; One Possessed, 1977; The Do-It-Yourself Frankenstein Outfit, 1978; What Are You Doing Here? 1978; Zodiac, 1978; After Midnight: Before Dawn, 1978; Parcel, 1979; Everybody's Friend, 1979; Pieces of Campton, 1979; Who Calls? 1980; Attitudes, 1980; Freedom Log, 1980; Dark Wings, 1981; Look - Sea, 1981; Great Whales, 1981; Who's a Hero, Then? 1981; But Not Here, 1984; Dead and Alive, 1983; Mrs Meadowsweet, 1986; Singing in the Wilderness, 1986; Our Branch in Brussels, 1986; Cards, Cups and Crystal Ball, 1986; The Vampyre (children's book) 1986; Can You Hear The Music, 1988; The Winter of 1917, 1989; Smile, 1990; Becoming a Playwright, 1992. *Contributions to:* Amateur Stage; Writers News; Drama; Whispers. *Memberships:* Writers Guild of Great Britain; Society of Authors. *Literary Agent:* ACTAC (Theatical & Cinematic) Ltd, Wilts, England. *Address:* 35 Liberty Road, Glenfield, Leicester LE3 8JF, England.

CANAWAY Bill. *See:* **CANAWAY W H.**

CANAWAY W H, (Bill Canaway, William Hamilton, Hermes), b. 1925, British. *Appointments:* Teacher in various education establishments, 1949-62. *Publications:* A Creel of Willow, 1957; A Snowdon Stream (The Gwyrfai) and How to Fish It, The Ring-Givers, 1958; The Seal, 1959; Sammy Going South (in US as Find the Boy), Horse on Fire, 1961; The Hunter and the Horns, 1962; My Feet upon a Rock, 1963; Crows in a Green Tree, The Ipcress File (with J Doran), 1965; The Grey Seas of Jutland, 1966; The Mules of Borgo San Marco, 1967; A Moral Obligation, 1969; A Declaration of Independence, Roll Me Over, 1971; Rendezvous in Black, 1972; Harry Doing Good, 1973; Glory of the Sea, 1975; The Willow-Pattern War, 1976; The Solid Gold Buddha, 1979; Love of Life, The Race for Number One, 1984; The Helmet and the Cross, 1986. *Address:* 42 Main Street, Repton, Derbyshire, England.

CANNON Bettie, b. 13 Nov 1922, Detroit, Michigan, USA. Writer. m. Charles Joseph Cannon, 22 July 1944, 1 son, 3 daughters. *Education:* Attended Michigan State University 1940-42 and Oakland University 1972-74. *Appointments:* Writer; Vice President, Secretary, Cannon Engineering and Equipment Co, Troy, Michigan, 1957-87; Writer 1967-; Conference co-ordinator, Oakland University, 1970-74; Member of Board of Directors, Readings for the Blind, Southfield, Michigan. *Publications:* All About Franklin: From Pioneer to Preservation, 1980; A Bellsong for Sarah Raines (young adult novel), 1987; Begin The World Again (young adult novel) 1991. *Contributions to:* Articles and stories to periodicals. *Honour* Award of Merit from Historical Society of Michigan, (All About Franklin), 1980. *Memberships:* Authors Guild; Society of Children's Book Authors; Detroit Women Writers, President 1975-77. *Address:* Charles Scribner's Sons, 866 Third Avenue, New York, NY 10022, USA.

CANNON Curt. *See:* **LOMBINO Salvatore A.**

CANNON Geoffrey John, b. 12 Apr 1940, Witham, Essex, England. Writer. m. (1) Antonia Mole, 1961, divorced. (2) Caroline Walker, 1987, (dec), 2 sons, 1 daughter. *Education:* BA, Philosophy and Psychology, Balliol College, Oxford, 1958-61. *Publications:* Dieting Makes You Fat (co-author), 1983; The Food Scandal (co-author), 1984; Additives: Your Complete Survival Guide (contributor), 1986; Fat To Fit, 1986; The Politics of Food, 1987; The Good Fight, 1988; The Safe Food Handbook (contributor), 1990; Healthy Eating: The Experts Agree, 1990; Superbug (co- author), 1991. *Contributions to:* Most leading British newspapers. *Honour:* Cantor Lecturer, Royal Society of Arts, 1988. *Memberships:* Secretary, Guild of Food Writers, 1988-

91; Secretary, Caroline Walker Trust; Secretary, London Road Runners; Nutrition Society. *Literary Agent:* Deborah Rogers. *Address:* 6 Aldridge Road Villas, London W11 1BP, England.

CANNON Steve, b. 10 Apr 1935, New Orleans, Louisiana, USA. Writer; Educator; Publisher. 2 sons, 4 daughters. *Education:* BA, History, University of Nebraska, 1954. *Appointments:* Professor of Humanities, Medgar Evers College, 1971-92. *Publications:* Groove, Bang and Jive Around, 1968, 1971; Introduction to Rouzing the Rubble, 1991; Plays: The Set Up, 1992; Chump Change, 1992. *Contributions to:* Excerpts from novel Looney Tunes under Deep Blue Moon, to Gathering of the Tribes, 1991, Pean Sensible, 1992. *Membership:* PEN, New York Chapter. *Address:* 285 East Third St, New York, NY 10009, USA.

CANTALUPO Charles, b. 17 Oct 1951, Orange, New Jersey, USA, Assistant Professor of English; Writer. m. Catherine Musello, 21 Aug 1976 (died 1983) 1 son. *Education:* Attended University of Kent at Canterbury, 1971-72, BA, Washington University, 1973; MA 1978, PhD 1980, Rutgers University, New Brunswick. *Appointments:* Teaching Assistant 1973-76, Instructor in English, 1977-79, Rutgers University, New Brunswick; Instructor 1980, Assistant Professor of English 1981, Pennsylvania State University, University Park, Pennsylvania, affiliated to a number of organisations at Pennsylvania State University; Director and Chairman of Catherine M Cantalupo Scholarship Foundation at Rutgers University 1984-; Eucharistic Minister at Pottsville/Warne Hospital Clinic, Pottsville, Pennsylvania. *Publications:* (Contributor), Seabury in Memorium: A Bicentennial Anthology, 1983; The Art of Hope (poetry), 1983; (Contributor), John H Morgan editor, Fleet Street Poet: A Memorial Anthology to Samuel Johnson, 1984; On Common Ground: An Anthology of Poems, 1985; (Contributor), Thomas N Corns editor, The Literature of Controversy, 1986; (Contributing editor), Contemporary Authors, Volume 120 Gale, 1987. *Contributions to:* Other edited volumes, encyclopaedias, periodicals. *Honours:* American Academy of Poets Prize 1976 for The Death of Colin Clout; Faculty Organization Teaching Award, 1985-86, Student Government Association Faculty Student Service Award, 1987-88. *Memberships:* Various professional memberships. *Address:* Department of English, Pennsylvania State University, Schuylkill Campus, Schuylkill Haven, PA 17972, USA.

CAPLAN Coren, b. 25 Aug 1944, Federal Republic of Germany. Writer. Academic. 1 daughter. *Education:* PhD, 1984. *Publications:* Seiltanz, poetry collection, 1984. *Contributions to:* Poetry and short stories in literary journals, anthologies and books in Germany and Australia. *Honours:* Short Story Award, International Association of German Speaking Media, 1977; Short Story and Poetry Award, Australian National Competition, Swan Writers and Authors Group, 1987. *Memberships:* PEN, Australia; Australian Poets Union; Australian Society of Authors. *Address:* 12 Bowman Park Estate, New England Highway, Armidale, NSW 2350, Australia.

CAPLAN Paula Joan, b. 7 July 1947. Full Professor. *Education:* AB, Harvard University, 1969; MA, Duke University, 1971; PhD, 1973; Internship, John Umstead Hsopital, North Carolina Memorial Hospital. *Appointments include:* Postdoctoral Fellow, The Hospital for Sick Children, 1974-76; Assistant Professor, Ontario Institute for Studies in Education, 1980-81; Lecturer, University of Toronto, 1979-; Head, Educations Centre for Womens Studies in Education, 1984-85; Full Professor, Ontario Institute for Studies in Education, 1987-. *Publications:* Books inc. Thinking Critically About Research on Sex & Gender (co-authored with Jeremy B Caplan); Lifting a Ton of Feathers: A Woman's Guide to Surviving in the Academic Waves; The Myth of Women's Masochism; Between Women: Lowering the Barriers; Barriers Between Women. *Contributions to:* Numerous Chapters, Monographs, Refereed Journals. *Honours:* Nominated for First Toronto Womens Health

Award; YWCA Women of Distinction Award. *Memberships:* Fellow of American Orthopsychiatric Association and of Canadian Psychological Association; Harvard Radcliffe Club of Toronto. *Address:* Department of Applied Psychology, Ontario Institute for Studies in Education, 252 Bloor Street West, Toronto, Ontario, Canada M5S 1V6.

CAPUTI Jane Elizabeth, b. 27 Oct 1953, Brooklyn, New York. USA. Professor. *Education:* Boston College, BA, 1974; Simmons College, MLS, 1977; Bowling Green State University, PhD, 1982. *Publications:* The Age of Sex Crime; Websters First New Intergalatic Wickedary of the English Language; Gossips, Gorgons and Crones: The Fates of the Earth, 1993. *Contributions to:* MS; Feminist Studies; Womens Studies; Joural of Popular Film & Television; Journal of American Culture. *Honours:* Emily Toth Award. *Address:* Dept of American Studies, Univ of New Mexico, Albuquerque, NM 87131, USA.

CAPUTO Philip Joseph, b. 10 June 1941, USA. Novelist. m. 21 June 1969, 2 sons. *Education:* BA, English, Loyola University, 1964. *Publications:* A Rumor of War, 1972; Horn of Africa, 1980; Del Corso's Gallery, 1983; Indian Country, 1987. *Contributions to:* New York Times; Washington Post; Chicago Tribune; Esquire; Playboy. *Honours:* Pulitzer Prize (Shared), 1972; Sidney Hillman Foundation Award, 1977; Finalist, American Book Award, 1980. *Memberships:* PEN; Authors Guild; national Writer's Union; Writer's Guild of America. *Agent:* Aaron M. Priest. *Address:* c/o Aaron Priest Literary Agency, USA.

CARAS Roger Andrew, (Roger Sarac), b. 24 May 1928, Massachusetts, USA. Author; Television Correspondent. m. Jill Langdon Barclay, 5 Sept 1954, 1 son, 1 daughter. *Education:* BA, Northeastern University, Western Reserve University, University of Southern California. *Appointments:* Adjunct professor, English, Southampton College. Adjunct Professor of Animal Ecology, School of Vet. Med., Univ of Penn. *Major Publications include:* Antarctica: Land of Frozen Time, 1962; Dangerous to Man, 1964; Wings of Gold, 1965; The Custer Wolf, Last Chance on Earth, 1966; North American Mammals, 1967; Source of the Thunder, 1970; Private Lives of Animals, Venomous Animals of the World, 1974; A Zoo in Your Room, Sockeye, 1975; The Forest, Yankee, 1979; The Roger Caras Dog Book, 1980; Celebration of Dogs, 1982; The Endless Migration, Mara Simba, 1985; Celebration of Cats, 1986; Roger Caras Treasury of Great Cat Stories, editor; Roger Caras Treasury of Great Dog Stories, editor; Animals in Their Places, 1987. Board of Overseers, School of Vet. Med., Univ of Penn. A Cat Is Listening, 1989; Roger Caras Treasury of Great; Horse Stories, 1990, (Editor); A Dog Is Watching, 1992; Thistle Hill Regulars, 1993. *Contributions to:* Audubon; New York Times; Ladies Home Journal; National Wildlife; Science Digest; National Observer; Financial Times; Family Health; Physicians World; Family Circle; Numerous other journals. *Honours include:* Honorary degrees from: Rio Grande College; University of Pennsylvania; State University of New York; Numerous awards, television writing & reporting, humane work; Fellow, Royal Society of Arts. *Memberships:* Outdoor Writers Association of America; Dog Writers Association. *Literary Agent:* Perry Knowlton, c/o Curtis Brown Ltd, 10 Astor Place, New York, NY 10003, USA. *Address:* Thistle Hill Farm, 21108 Slab Bridge Road, Freeland, MD 21053, USA.

CARD Orson Scott, b. 1951, American. *Appointments:* Volunteer Mormon Missionary in Brazil, 1971-73; Operated Repertory Theatre, Provo, UT, 1974-75; Proofreader 1974, Editor 1974-76, Brigham Young University Press, Provo; Editor, Ensign Magazine, Salt Lake City, 1976-78 and Compute Books, Greensboro, NC, 1983. *Publications:* Listen Mom and Dad, Hot Sleep, Capitol, 1978; A Planet Called Treason, 1979; Songmaster, 1980; Unaccompanied Sonata and Other Stories, Saintspeak, Dragons of Darkness, 1981; Ainge, 1982; Hart's Hope, Dragons of Light (ed), The Worthing Chronicle, 1983; Compute's Guide to IBM PCjr Sound and Graphics, A Woman of Destiny, 1984; Ender's Game, 1985. *Address:* 546 Lindley Road, Greensboro, NC 27410, USA.

CAREW Jan (Rynveld), b. 1925, Guyanese. *Appointments:* Lecturer in Race Relations, University of London Extra-Mural Department, 1953-57; Writer and Editor, BBC Overseas Service, London, 1954-65; Editor, African Review, Ghana, 1965-66; CBC Broadcaster, Toronto, 1966-69; Senior Fellow, Council of Humanities and Lecturer, Department of Afro-American Studies, Princeton University, 1969-72; Professor, Department of African-American Studies, Northwestern University, Evanston, IL, 1972-87, now Emeritus; Visiting Clarence J Robinson Professor of Caribbean Literature and History, George Mason University, 1989-91; Visiting Professor of International Studies, Illinois Wesleyan University, 1992-93; Co-Chairman, Third World Energy Institute, 1978-85; Co-founder Africa Network, 1981-; Chairman, Caribbean Society for Culture and Science, 1979-. *Publications:* Streets of Eternity, 1952; Black Midas (in US as A Touch of Midas), The Wild Coast, 1958; The Last Barbarian, 1961; Green Winter, 1964; University of Hunger, 1966; The Third Gift, 1975; The Origins of Racism and Resistance in the Americas, Rape of the Sun-people, 1976; Children of the Sun, 1980; Sea Drums in My Blood, 1981; Grenada: The Hour Will Strike Again, 1985; Fulcrums of Change, 1987. *Membership:* Co-chairman, Africa Network, 1981-. *Address:* Department of African-American Studies, Northwestern University, Evanston, IL 60208, USA.

CAREY John, b. 5 Apr 1934, London, England. University Professor. m. Gillian Booth, 13 Aug 1960, 2 sons. *Education:* Lambe Open Scholar 1954-57, BA Class I 1957, DPhil 1960, St John's College, Oxford. *Publications:* Milton, 1969; The Violent Effigy: A Study of Dickens' Imagination, 1973; Thackeray, Prodigal Genius, 1977; John Donne: Life, Mind and Art, 1981; Original Copy: Selected Reviews and Journalism, 1987; The Faber Book of Reportage, 1989; (ed) 'Donne' 1990; The Intellectuals and the Masses, 1992. *Contributions to:* Principal Book Reviewer, Sunday Times, London, 1977-. *Honour:* Fellow, Royal Society of Literature. *Membership:* Council, Royal Society of Literature. *Literary Agent:* Xandra Hardie, London. *Address:* Merton College, Oxford OX1 4SD, England.

CAREY Peter Philip, b. 7 May 1943, Bacchus Marsh, Australia. Novelist. m. Alison Summers, 16 Mar 1985. 2 sons. *Education:* Doctor of Letters (honoris causa), University of Queensland, 1989. *Appointment:* Writer-in-Residence, New York University, 1990. *Publications:* The Fat Man in History, 1974, in UK 1980; War Crimes, 1979. Bliss, 1981; Illywhacker, 1985; Oscar & Lucinda, 1989; Until the End of the World (with Wim Wenders), 1990; The Tax Inspector, 1991. *Honours:* NSW Premier's Literary Award (twice); Miles Franklin Award (twice); National Book Council Award (three); The Age Book of the Year Award; The Victorian Premier's Literary Award; The Booker Prize. *Membership:* Fellow, Royal Society of Literature. Resident: New York. *Literary Agent:* Deborah Rogers, Rogers, Coleridge & White Ltd. *Address:* c/o Deborah Rogers, Rogers, Coleridge & White Ltd, 20 Powis Mews, London W11 1JN, England.

CARFAX Catherine. *See:* **FAIRBURN Eleanor M.**

CARKEET David Corydon, b. 15 Nov 1946, Sonora, California, USA. Writer. m. Barbara Lubin, 16 Aug 1975, 3 daughters. *Education:* AB, University of California, 1968; MA, University of Wisconsin, 1970; PhD, Indiana University, 1973. *Publications:* The Full Catastrophe; I Been There Before; The Greatest Slump of All Time; Double Negative. *Honours:* O Henry Award. *Literary Agent:* Barney M Karpfinger. *Address:* 23 Ridgemoor Drive, St Louis, MO 63105, USA.

CARLEON A. *See:* **SKINNER June O'Grady.**

CARLINO Lewis John, b. 1932, American. *Publications:* The Brick and the Rose: A Collage for Voices, 1957; Junk Yard, 1959; Used Car for Sale, 1959; Objective Case, Mr Flanner's Ocean, Piece and Precise, Two Short Plays: Sarah and the Sax and High Sun, 1962; Cages: Snowangel and Epiphany, Telemachus Clay: A Collage of Voices, 1963; Doubletalk: Sarah and the Sax and The Dirty Old Man, 1964; The Exercise, 1967; The Brotherhood, 1968; The Mechanic, 1972. *Membership:* Actors Studio Playwrights Unit, NY. *Address:* c/o Dramatists Play Service, 440 Park Avenue South, New York, NY 10016, USA.

CARLISLE D M. *See:* **COOK Dorothy Mary.**

CARLO Schaerf, b. 2 May 1935, Rome, Italy. Physics Professor. m. Mirella Casini, 26 June 1960, 2 sons. *Publications include:* Editor: Phtonuclear Reactions, 1977; Perspectives of Fundamental Physics, 1979; Eletron and Pion Interactions with Nuclei at Intermediate Energies, 1980; Intermedite Energy Nuclear Physics, 1982, 1984, 1986, 1989, 1990. *Honours:* Grant, Fulbright University of Rochester, 1955-56. *Memberships:* National Committes for Physical Sciences and for Physical Research, CNR, Rome; Board of Directors, INFN, Rome. *Address:* American and Italian Physical Societies; Department of Physics, II University of Rome Tor Vergata, Via Della Ricera Scientifica 1, 00133 Rome, Italy.

CARMEN Ira Harris, b. 3 Dec 1934, Boston, USA. Political Scientist; University Professor. m. Sandra Vineberg, 6 Sept 1958, 2 daughters. *Education:* BA, University of New Hampshire, 1957; MA, University of Michigan, 1959; PhD, 1964. *Appointments:* Professor of Political Science, University of Illinois, Urbana, 1968-. *Publications:* Cloning and the Constitution; Power & Balance; Movies, Censorship, and the Law. *Contributions to:* Michigan Law Review; Virginia Law Review; Journal of Politics; Science; Political Behaviour; American Journal of Human Genetics. *Honours:* Phi Beta Kappa; Visiting Scholar, Yale Law School; George Bush's Inaugural Educators Advisory Committee; Recombinant DNA Advisory Committee. *Memberships:* American Political Science Association; American Association for the Advancement of Science; American Society of Law & Medicine. *Address:* Department of Political Science, University of Illinois, Urbana, IL 61801, USA.

CARMICHAEL Fred Walker, b. 1924, American. *Appointments:* Producer, with Patricia Carmichael, of Caravan Theatre Incorporated, Summer Theatre, Dorset Playhouse, VT, 1949-76. *Publications:* Florence Unlimited, 1952; He's Having a Baby, 1953; She Sickness, More Than Meets the Eye, 1954; Inside Lester, 1955; The Night is My Enemy, Four For the Money, 1956; Petey's Choice, 1958; The Pen is Deadlier, Divorce Granted, 1959; Luxury Cruise, 1960; Green Room Blues, 1961; Exit the Body, 1962; The Robin Hood Caper, 1963; Dream World, 1964; Any Number Can Die, Dear Millie, 1965; The Best Laid Plans, 1966; Double in Diamonds, 1967; All The Better To Kill You With, So Nice Not to See You, 1968; Land of Promise, A Pack of Rascals, The Turning Point, 1969; Victoria's House, 1970; Ten Nights in a Bar Room, 1970; Surprise!, 1971; Done to Death, 1972; Mixed Doubles, There's a Fly in my Soap, 1973; Who Needs a Waltz, 1974; Hey, Naked Lady, 1975; Last of the Class, 1976; Whatever Happened to Mrs Kong, Foiled by an Innocent Maid, 1977; Don't Step on My Footprint, 1978; Exit Who?, The Three Million Dollar Lunch, 1982; Out of Sight...Out of Murder, P is for Perfect, 1983.

CARMICHAEL Jack B, b. 31 Jan 1938, Ravenswood, USA. Writer; Consultant. m. Julie Ann Carmichael, 2 Oct 1981, 4 daughters. *Education:* Bachelor of Arts, Ohio Wesleyan University, 1959; Doctor of Philosophy, Michigan State University, 1964; Post-doctoral, University of Oregon, 1966-67. *Appointments:* Editor, Publisher, Dynamics Press, Mason, Michigan, USA. *Publications:* A New Slain Knight; Black Knight; Tales of the Cousin; Memoirs of the Great Gorgeous; Industrial Water Use & Treatment Practice. *Contributions to:* Magazines & Journals; Over 30 Articles; 45 Offical Reports. *Honours:* The American Poetry Association Awarded Grandpa Outstanding Achievement; 3 Poems, Finalists in 1990 Juried Competition of the Florida Literary Foundation; Merit Awards for A Song to Heidi. *Memberships:* The Academy of American Poets; The International Organization for Chemistry in Development. *Address:* Dynamics Press, 519 South Rogers Street, Mason, MI 48854, USA.

CARMICHAEL Joel, b. 1915, American. *Appointments:* Editor, Weizmann Letters and Papers, 1968-71, Midstream magazine, NYC, 1975-87, 1990- . *Publications:* The Russian Revolution 1917: A Personal Record (ed and trans), 1955; Anna Karenina by Tolstoy (trans), The Death of Jesus, 1962; An Illustrated History of Russia, 1963; Karl Marx: The Passionate Logician, 1964; A Short History of the Russian Revolution, 1965; A Cultural History of Russia, 1966; The Shaping of the Arabs, 1967; Trotsky, 1975; Stalin's Masterpiece, 1976; St Paul's Timetable (German), 1982; The Birth of Christianity: Reality and Myth, 1989; The Satanizing of The Jews, 1992. *Address:* 302 West 86th Street, New York, NY 10024, USA.

CAROL Bill J. *See:* **KNOTT William Cecil.**

CARPENTER Allan, b. 11 May 1917, Waterloo, Iowa, USA. Author; Publisher. *Education:* BA, University of Northern Iowa. *Publications:* Between Two Rivers, 1938; Hi, Neighbor, 1942; Your Guide to Successful Singing, 1945; Popular Mechanics Home Handyman, 16 volumes, 1961; Enchantment of America, 52 volumes, 1962-65; Enchantment of Latin America, 20 volumes, 1965-68; Enchantment of Africa, 39 volumes, 1968-72; New Enchantment of America, 52 volumes, 1972-79; All About the USA, 7 volumes, 1983-86; Encyclopedia of the Regions of the US, 5 volumes, 1986- ; Great Generals, 4 volumes, 1987-88; Facts About the Cities, 1990. *Contributions to:* Monthly to Popular Mechanics and Science Digest, 1945-62; Most major magazines including Reader's Digest, 1945-62. *Memberships:* Literati Member, The Arts Club of Chicago. *Literary Agent:* Carolyn Kuhn. *Address:* Suite 4602, 175 East Delaware Place, Chicago, IL 60611, USA.

CARPENTER Bogdana Maria Magdalena Chetkowska, b. 2 June 1941, Czestochowa, Poland. Professor. m. John Randell Carpenter, 15 Apr 1963, 1 son, 1 daughter. *Education:* Warsaw University, 1963; PhD, University of California, 1974. *Appointments:* Assistant Professor, University of Washington, Seattle, 1974-83; University of Michigan, 1983-; Assistant Professor, 1983-84; Associate Professor, 1985-91; Professor, 1991-. *Publications:* The Poetic Avant Garde in Poland; Monumenta Polonica: The First Four Centuries of Polish Poetry; Translations, Selected Poems of Zbigniew Herbert; Report from the Besieged City and Other Poems; Still Life with a Bridle. *Contributions to:* Articles & Reviews, World Literature Today; Translation Review; the Malahat Review; Slavic & East European Journal; The Polish Review; Cross Currents. *Honours include:* Witter Bynner Poetry Translation Prize; American Council for Polish Culture First Prize. *Memberships:* PEN Club; AAASS; AATSEEL. *Address:* Department of Slavic Languages & Literature, University of Michigan, 3040 MLB, Ann Arbor, MI 48109, USA.

CARPENTER Humphrey (William Bouverie), b. 1946, British. Author; Broadcaster; Musician. *Appointments:* Staff Producer, BBC, 1968-74; Freelance Broadcaster and Reviewer. *Publications:* A Thames Companion (with M Prichard), 1975; J R R Tolkien, The Joshers, 1977; The Inklings: C S Lewis, J R R Tolkien, Charles Williams and Their Friends, 1978; The Captain Hook Affair, 1979; Jesus, 1980; W H Auden, The Letters of J R R Tolkien (ed with C Tolkien), 1981; Mr Majeika, The Oxford Companion to Children's Literature (with M Prichard), 1984; O U D S: A Centenary History of the Oxford University Dramatic Society, Secret Gardens: A Study of the Golden Age of Children's Literature, 1985; Mr Majeika and the Music Teacher, 1986; Mr Majeika and the Haunted Hotel, 1987; A Serious Character: The Life of Ezra Pound, 1988; The Brideshead Generation, 1989; Benjamin Britten, (biography), 1992. *Address:* 6 Fardon Road, Oxford OX2 6R6, England.

CARPENTER Lucas, b. 23 Apr 1947, Elberton, Georgia, USA. Professor. m. Judith Leidner, 2 Sept 1972, 1 daughter. *Education:* BS, English, College of Charleston, 1968; MA, English, University of North Carolina at Chapel Hill, 1973; PhD, English, State University of New York, Stony Brook, 1982. *Appointments:* Instructor, SUNY at Stony Brook, 1973-78; Instructor - Assistant Professor - Associate Professor, Suffolk College, 1978-85; Associate Professor, Oxford College of Emory University, 1985- . *Publications:* A Year for the Spider (poetry) 1972; Editor: Selected Poetry of John Gould Fletcher, 1988, Selected Essays of John Gould Fletcher, 1989; John Gould Fletcher and Southern Modernism, 1990. *Contributions to:* Poetry, critical essays and short fiction in over 35 journals, magazines and newspapers. *Membership:* Poetry Society of America. *Address:* English Department, Oxford College of Emory University, Oxford, GA 30267, USA.

CARR Glyn. *See:* **STYLES Frank Showell.**

CARR Margaret, (Martin Carroll, Carole Kerr), b. 1935. British. Writer of novels, short stories, mystery, crime, suspense, historical, Romance, Gothic. Local government secretary, retired. *Publications:* (as Martin Caroll), Begotten Murder (mystery novel), 1967; Spring into Love (novel), 1967; (as Martin Carroll), Blood Vengeance (mystery novel), 1968; (as Martin Carroll), Dead Trouble (mystery novel), 1968; (as Martin Caroll), Goodbye Is Forever (mystery novel), 1968; (as Martin Caroll), Too Beautiful to Die (mystery novel), 1969; (as Martin Caroll), Bait (mystery novel), 1970; (as Martin Caroll), Miranda Said Murder (mystery novel), 1970; (as Martin Carroll), Hear No Evil (mystery novel), 1971; Tread Warily at Midnight (mystery novel), 1971; Sitting Duck (mystery novel), 1972; Who's The Target (mystery novel), 1974; Wait for the Wake (mystery novel), 1974; Too Close for Comfort (mystery novel), 1974; (as Carole Kerr), Not for Sale (novel), 1975; (as Carole Kerr), Shadow of the Hunter (novel), 1975; (as Carole Kerr), A Time to Surrender (novel), 1975; Blood Will Out (mystery novel), 1975; Blindman's Buff (mystery novel), 1976; Out of the Past (mystery novel), 1976; (as Margaret Carr), Dare the Devil (novel), 1976, Sharendel (novel), 1976; Twin Tragedy (mystery novel), 1977; (as Carole Kerr), Love All Start (novel), 1977; (as Carole Kerr), Lamb to the Slaughter (novel), 1978; The Witch of Wykham (mystery novel), 1978; (as Carole Kerr), An Innocent Abroad (novel), 1979; Daggers Drawn, 1980; (as Carole Kerr), When Dreams Come True (romance), 1980, Stolen Heart, 1981; (as Belle Jackson), In the Dark of the Day (fantasy thriller), 1988, Valdez's Lady (romance), 1989; (as Margaret Carr), Deadly Pursuit, (mystery), 1991, Dark Intruder, (mystery), 1991. *Address:* Waverley, Wavering Lane, Gillingham, Dorset, England.

CARR Pat Moore, b. 13 Mar 1932, Grass Creek, Wyoming, USA. Writer; Professor. m. (1) Jack Esslinger, 4 June 1955, div. 1970, (2) Duane Carr, 26 Mar 1972, 1 son, 3 daughters. *Education:* BA, MA, Rice University; PhD, Tulane University. *Publications:* Bernard Shaw, 1976; The Grass Creek Chronicle, 1976, 1992; The Women in the Mirror, 1977; Mimbres Mythology, 1979, 1988, 1990; Night of the Luminaries, 1985; Sonahchi, 1988. *Contributions to:* Stories and articles to: Southern Review; Yale Review; Best American Short Stories; Kansas Qaurterly; Arizona Quarterly; Modern Fiction Studies; Modern Drama; Western Humanities Review; Oxford Magazine; Seattle Review; Women Writing; Puerto del Sol; Florida Review; Cedar Rock; Others. *Honours:* Phi Beta Kappa, 1955; South and West Fiction Award, 1969; Library of Congress Marc IV, 1970; National Endowment for the Humanities, 1973; Iowa

Fiction Award, 1977; Short Story Award, Texas Institute of Letters, 1978; Green Mountain Fiction Award, 1985; First Stage Drama Award, 1991. *Memberships:* Poets and Writers; International Women Writers Guild. *Literary Agent:* Barbara Kouts. *Address:* Department of English, Western Kentucky University, Bowling Green, KY 42101, USA.

CARR Robert. *See:* **ROBERTS Irene.**

CARR Roger Vaughan, b. 6 Nov 1937, Melbourne, Australia. Author. m. Patricia Adele Butler, 14 Apr 1971, 3 sons, 1 daughter. *Publications:* Surfie, 1966; 31 children's novels including Firestorm!, 1985; Piano Bay, 1991; Nipper and The Gold Turkey, 1991. *Contributions to:* Bulletin, Sydney; Pony Magazine & Annual, UK; Weekly Times; Victorian Education Department school magazines. *Honours:* Grant, Commonwealth Literary Fund, 1965; 2-year Writing Fellowship, Australia Council, 1973-75. *Membership:* Australian Writers Guild. *Address:* 69 Outer Crs., Brighton, Victoria, 3186, Australia.

CARR Terry, (Norman Edwards), b. 1937, America. Freelance writer, Editor; Lecturer since 1971. *Appointments:* Assoc. Editor Scott Meredith Literary Agency, NYC, 1962-64; Editor Ace Books, NYC, 1964-71; Editor SFWA Bulletin, 1867-68; Founder, Science Fiction Writers of America Forum, 1967-68. *Publications:* Warlord of Kor, 1963, (as Norman Edwards with Ted White), 1963; Invasion from 2500, (ed. with Donald A Wollheim), 1964; World's Best Science Fiction, 1965-71, 7 vols, 1965-71, first 4 vols. as World's Best Science Fiction: First (to fourth) Series, 1970; (ed.) Science Fiction for People Who Hate Science Fiction, 1966; (ed.) New World's of Fantasy 1-3, 3 vols. 1967-71, Vol. 1 in UK as Step Outside Your Mind, 1969; (ed.) The Others, 1968; (ed.) Universe 1-13, 13 vols, 1971-83; (ed.) The Best Science Fiction of the Year 1-13, 1972-84; (ed.) This Side of Infinity, 1971; (ed.) An Exaltation of Stars, 1973; (ed.) Into the Unknown, 1973; (ed.) World's Near and Far, 1974; (ed.) Creatures from Beyond, 1975; (ed.) The Ides of Tomorrow, (juvenile)), 1976; (ed.) Planets of Wonder: A Treasury of Space Opera (juvenile), 1976; The Light at the End of the Universe, (short stories), 1976; Cirque, 1977; (ed.) To Follow a Star (juvenile), 1977; (ed.) The Infinite Arena (juvenile), 1977; (ed.) Classic Science Fiction: The First Golden Age, 1978; (ed.) The Year's Finest Fantasy 1-V, 1978-84; (ed.) The Best Science Fiction Novellas of the Year 1-2, 2 vols, 1979-80; (ed.) Beyond Reality, 1979; (ed.) Dream's Edge: Science Fiction about the Future of the Planet Earth, 1980; (ed.) The Best from Universe, 1984.

CARRIER Warren, b. 1918, American. *Appointments:* Associate Dean, Rutgers University, New Brunswick, NJ, 1968-69; Dean, California State University, San Diego, 1969-72; Vice-President, University of Bridgeport, CT, 1972-75; Chancellor, University of Wisconsin, Platteville, 1975-82; Chancellor Emeritus, 1982-; Founder and former Editor, Quarterly Review of Literature. *Publications:* City Stopped in Time (trans), 1949; The Hunt, 1952; The Cost of Love, 1953; Reading Modern Poetry (ed with Paul Engle), 1955, revised edition, 1968; Bay of the Damned, 1957; Toward Montebello, 1966; Leave Your Sugar for the Cold Morning, 1978; Guide to World Literature (ed), 1980; Literature from the World (ed with Bonnie Neumann), 1981; The Diver, 1985; Death of a Chancellor, 1986; An Honorable Spy, 1992; Murder at the Strawberry Festival, 1993. *Address:* 69 Colony Park Circle, Galveston, TX 77551, USA.

CARRINGTON-WINDO Tristam, b. 25 Apr 1955, Eastbourne, England. Writer; Translator. m. Katrin M Kohl, 15 Sept 1984, 1 daughter. *Education:* BSc, London; Dip Trans, Institute of Linguistics; Diploma in Translation, MA, Polytechnic of Central London. *Publications:* Deutsches Business-Magazin; German Means Business. *Memberships:* Institute of Translation and Interpreting; Society of Authors; Translators Association; Institute of Linguists. *Address:* 124 Headley Way, Headington, Oxford OX3 7SY, England.

CARROLL Martin. *See:* **CARR Margaret.**

CARROLL Mary. *See:* **SANFORD Annette Schorre.**

CARROLL Paul, b. 1927, American. *Appointments:* Poetry Editor, Chicago Review, 1957-59; Editor, Big Table Magazine, 1959-61, Big Table Books, Follett Publishing Company, 1966-71; Visiting Professor of English, University of Iowa, IA, 1966-67; Professor of English, University of Illinois, 1968-. *Publications:* Edward Dahlberg Reader (ed), 1966; Odes, The Poem in Its Skin, The Young American Poets, 1968; The Luke Poets, 1971; New and Selected Poems, 1978; The Garden of Earthly Delights, 1986; Poems, 1987. *Address:* 1682 North Ada Street, Chicago, IL 60622, USA.

CARROLL Raymond, b. 10 Aug 1924, Brooklyn, New York, New York, USA. Writer. m. Anne Starck, 1954 (div 1979), 1 son, 1 daughter. *Education:* BA, Hamilton College, 1948; Graduate study at Johns Hopkins School of Advanced International Studies 1949-51. *Appointments:* Owner, Cadmus Book Store, Washington DC, 1953-55; Designer of Promotional Material, Translator from Spanish and Newspaper Columnist, Editors Press Service, New York, 1955-61; Associate Editor 1961-69, General Editor 1969-81, also Chief, United Nations Bureau, Newsweek, New York City; Freelance writer 1981-. *Publications:* Juvenile publications: Anwar Sadat 1982; The Palestine Question 1983; The Caribbean Issues in US Relations, 1984; The Future of the United Nations, 1985. *Contributions to:* Family Encyclopaedia of American History, 1975; The Story of America, 1975; America's Fascinating Indian Heritage, 1978; Consumer Advisor: An Action Guide to Your Rights, 1984. Funk and Wagnalls New Encyclopaedia Yearbook. *Memberships:* English-speaking Union; Amnesty International. *Address:* New York, USA.

CARRUTHERS Peter Michael, b. 16 June 1952, Manila. Philosopher. m. Susan Levi, 21 Oct 1978, 2 sons. *Education:* University of Leeds, 1971-77; Calliol College, Oxford, 1977-79. *Appointments:* Lecturer, University of St Andrews, 1979-81; Lecturer, Queens University of Belfast, 1981-83; Lecturer, University of Essex, 1985-91; Visiting Professor, University of Michigan, 1989-90; Senior Lecturer, University of Sheffield, 1991-92; Professor, University of Sheffield, 1992-. *Publications:* Introducing Persons; Tractarian Semantics; The Metaphysics of the Tractatus; Human Knowledge and Human Nature; The Animals Issue. *Contributions to:* Philosophical Quarterly; MIND; Journal of Philosophy; Synthese. *Membership:* Aristotelian Society. *Address:* Department of Philosophy, University of Sheffield, Sheffield, S10 2TN, England.

CARSWELL John Patrick, b. 1918, British. *Appointments:* Served with Treasury, 1960-64; Assistant Under Secretary of State, Department of Education and Science, 1964-74; Secretary, University Grants Committee, 1974-78; Secretary, British Academy, 1978-83, London. *Publications:* Marvellous Campaigns of Baron Munchausen (ed), 1946; The Prospector: The Life of Rudolf Erich Raspe (in US as The Romantic Rogue), 1950; The Old Cause: Four Biographical Studies in Whiggism, 1954; The South Sea Bubble, 1960, revised and enlarged, 1993; The Civil Servant and His World, 1966; The Descent on England, 1969; From Revolution to Revolution: English Society 1688-1776, 1973; Lives and Letters, 1978; The Exile, 1983; The State and the Universities in Britain 1966-1978, 1985; The Porcupine: The Life of Algernon Sidney, 1989; The Saving of Kenwood and the Northern Heights, 1992. *Address:* 5 Prince Arthur Road, London NW3, England.

CARTANO Tony, b. 27 July 1944, Bayonne, France. Author; Editor. m. Francoise Perrin, 10 Nov 1966, 1 son, 1 daughter. *Education:* Licence-es-Lettres, 1964, Diplome d'Etudes superieures, 1965, University of Paris. *Appointments:* Currently: Editorial Director of Editions Belfond in Paris. *Publications include:* Novels: Bocanegra (After the Conquest) 1984; Blackbird, 1980; Le Bel Arturo, 1989; Le Souffle de Satan, 1991; Le singe hurleur, 1978; Schmutz, 1987; Malcolm Lowry, an essay, 1979; La sourde oreille, novella, 1982; Travel Book: American Boulevard, 1992. *Honours:* Blackbird and Bocanegra have been nominated for the Prix Goncourt; Chevalier dans l'Ordre des Arts et Lettres. *Literary Agents:* La Nouvelle Agence, 7 rue de Corneille, 75006, Paris; A M Heath, London. *Address:* 157, Boulevard Davout, 75020 Paris, France.

CARTENS Jan, b. 25 May 1929, Roosendaal, Netherlands. Writer. *Publications:* Dat meisje uit Munchen, 1975; De thuiskomst, 1976; Vroege herfst, 1978; Een Roomsche Jeugd, 1980; De verleiding, 1983; Maagdenbruiloft, 1987; Het verraad van Nausikaa, 1989; Een indringer, 1990. *Address:* Markenland 15, 4871 AM, Etten-Leur, Netherlands.

CARTER Angela, b. 1940. Author; Reviewer. *Education:* Bristol University; Fellow in Creative Writing, Sheffield University, 1976-78. *Publications:* Screenplay (jointly), The Company of Wolves, 1984; Fiction, Novels: Shadow Dance, 1966; The Magic Toyshop, 1967; Several Perceptions, 1968; Heroes & Villains, 1969; Miss Z, the Dark Young Lady, 1970; Love, 1971; The Infernal Desire Machines of Doctor Hoffman, 1972; The Passion of New Eve, 1977; Nights at the Circus, 1984; Short Stories: Fireworks : 9 Profane Pieces, 1974; The Bloody Chamber and Other Stories, 1979; Black Venus, 1985; Comic and Curious Cats, 1979; Moonshadow, 1982; Sleeping Beauty and other Favourite Fairy Tales, (jointly), 1983; Non-fiction: The Sadeian Woman : An Exercise in Cultural History, 1979; Nothing Sacred : Sacred Writings, 1982; Come into these Yellow Sands and Other Plays for Radio, 1985; Wise Children, 1991; (ed) The Virago Book of Fairy Stories, 1990; (ed) Wayward Girls and Wicked Women, 1986; (contrib) The Virago Book of Ghost Stories, 1987. *Contributions to:* New Society. *Honours:* John Llewellyn Rhys Prize, 1967; Somerset Maugham Award, 1968; James Tait Black Memorial Prize (jointly)), 1984. *Address:* c/o Virago Press Ltd., 41 William IV Street, London WC2N 4DB, England.

CARTER Ashley. *See:* WHITTINGTON Harry.

CARTER Bruce. *See:* HOUGH Richard Alexander.

CARTER Francis William, b. 4 July 1938, Wednesfield, Staffs, England. m. Krystyna Stephania Tomaszewska, 3 June 1977. *Education:* BA, Sheffield, MA, PhD, London, D Nat Sc, Prague; D Phil, Cracow. *Publications:* Dubrovnik: A Classic City State; An Historical Geography of the Balkans; Trade and Urban Development in Poland; Environmental Problems in Eastern Europe. *Contributions to:* Over 100 Articles. *Honour:* Croatian Academy of USA. *Memberships:* Institute of British Geographers; Royal Geographical Society; Royal Asiatic Society; PEN. *Address:* Department of Social Sciences, School of Slavonic & East European Studies, University of London, Malet Street, London WC1E 7HU, England.

CARTER Harold Burnell, b. 3 Jan 1910, Mosmna, Sydney, NSW. Scientific Civil Servant, 1939-70. m. Mary Brandon Jones, 21 Sept 1940, 3 sons. *Education:* University of Sydney, BVSc, 1933. *Appointments:* Walter & Eliza Hall Fellow, University of Sydney, 1936-39; Honorary Fellow, University of Leeds, 1962-70; Director, Banks Archive Project, British Museum, 1989-. *Publications:* His Majestys Spanish Flock; The Sheep and Wool Correspondence of Sir Joseph Banks; Sir Joseph Banks: A Guide to Biographical and Bibliographical Sources; Sire Joseph Banks 1743-1820. *Contributions to:* Australian and British Scientific Journals; Bulletin; British Museum; Historical Series.

Honours: American Philosophical Society History of Science Grants; Royal Society History of Science Grants; British Academy Major Awards. *Memberships:* Royal Society of Edinburgh; FLS; FIBiol. *Address:* Yeo Bank, Congresbury, Nr Bristol, Co Avon, BS19 5JA, England.

CARTER Mary Arkley, b. Oregon, USA. Novelist; Professor. 2 sons. *Education:* University of Oregon; Pitzer College, Claremont, California. *Appointments Include:* Director, Creative Writing Programme, University of Arizona, 1981-; Lecturer in Fiction, graduate programme, Boston University, 1980-81, 1978-79, 1971-72; Various other university posts. *Publications:* A Fortune in Dimes, 1963; The Minutes of the Night, 1965; La Maestra, 1973; A Member of the Family, 1974; Tell Me My Name, 1975. Numerous short stories, reviews, articles, column. *Contributions include:* New York Times; Holiday Magazine; Vanity Fair; Kenyon Review; Boston A.D.Review; column, Connexions. *Honours:* Fellow, MacDowell 1973-80, Virginia Centre for Creative Arts 1972-73, Ossabaw Foundation 1973, Fondation Karolyi, France 1973-74, 1977; Fellowship grant, National Endowment for the Arts, 1986. *Memberships:* PEN; Authors Guild; Directors Committee, Associated Writing Programmes. *Literary Agent:* Brandt & Brandt, New York. *Address:* 169 Fentiman Road, London SW8 1YJ, England.

CARTER Nick. *See:* AVALLONE Michael.

CARTER Nick. *See:* LYNDS Dennis.

CARTER Nick. *See:* SMITH Martin Cruz.

CARTER Nick. *See:* WALLMAN Jeffrey M.

CARTER Peter, b. 1929, British. *Appointments:* Apprentice in the Building Trade, 1942-49; Teacher in Birmingham. *Publications:* The Black Lamp, 1973; The Gates of Paradise, 1974; Madatan, 1975; Mao, 1976; Under Goliath, 1977; The Sentinels, 1980; Children of the Book, 1982; Bury the Dead, 1986. *Address:* c/o Oxford University Press, Walton Street, Oxford OX2 6DP, England.

CARTER Walter Horace. b. 20 Jan 1921, Albemarle, North Carolina, USA. Newspaper Publisher; Author; Magazine Writer. m. (1) Lucille Miller Carter, (dec); (2) Brenda C Strickland, 29 Oct 1983, Tabor City, NC. 1 son, 2 daughters. *Education:* AB Journalism, University of North Carolina. *Publications:* Land That I Love, 1978; Creatures and Chronicles from Cross Creek, 1980; Wild and Wonderful Santer-Cooper Country, 1982; Nature's Masterpiece, A Homosassa, 1984; Return to Cross Creek, 1985; Virus of Fear, 1991. *Contributions to:* Various magazines; over 1000 stories published. *Honours:* Pulitzer Prize for Meritorious Public Service, 1953; Sidney Hillman Award, One of Ten Most Outstanding Young Men in America, 1954. *Memberships:* Director of Outdoor Writers Association of America; President, Florida Outdoor Writers Association, 1981-83; President, Southeastern Outdoor Press Association, 1984-85. *Address:* 101 Crescent Street, Tabor City, NC 28463, USA and Rt 3, Box 139A, Hawthorne, FL 32640, USA.

CARTLAND Dame Barbara. *See:* MCCORQUODALE Barbara Hamilton.

CARUS Marianne, b. 16 June 1928, Germany. Editor-in-Chief; Publisher. m. Milton Blouke Carus, 3 Mar 1951, 1 son, 2 daughters. *Education:* Abitur, Gymnasium Gummersbach, 1948; Masters equivalent, Freiburg University; Additional studies, Sorbonne, Paris, France, and University of Chicago, USA *Appointments:* Editor-in-chief, Publisher, Cricket and Ladybug Magazines. *Publication:* Editor, compiler, with Clifton Fadiman, Cricket's Choice, 1974. *Contributions to:* Children's Literature in Education, volume II, 1980. *Memberships:* ALSC Division, ALA; Director, ALSC

Board, 1982-85; Magazine Publishers Association; Children's Reading Roundtable, Chicago; Society of Children's Book Writers; Friends of CCBC; VP, IBBY. *Address:* Cricket Magazine, PO Box 300, Peru, Illinois 61354, USA.

CARY Jud. *See:* TUBB E C.

CARY Lorene Emily, b. 29 Nov 1956, Philadephia, USA. Writer. m. R C Smith, 27 Aug 1983, 1 daughter, 1 stepson. *Education:* University of Pennsylvania, BA, MA, 1978; University of Sussex, MA, 1980. *Appointments:* Apprentice Writer, Time, 1980; Associate Editor, TV Guide, 1980-82; Contributing Editor, Newsweek Magazine, 1991. *Publication:* Black Ice. *Honour:* Doctorate of Letters, Colby College. *Memberships:* Authors Guild; Association of Black Journalists. *Literary Agent:* Jane Dystel, Acton & Dystel Inc. *Address:* c/o Alfred A Knopf, 201 East 50th Street, New York, NY 10022, USA.

CARY Richard, b. 1909, American. *Appointments:* Professor of English 1952-75, Curator of Rare Books and Manuscripts 1958-75, Editor, Colby Library Quarterly 1959-75, Director, Colby College Press 1959-75, Colby College, Waterville, ME. *Publications:* The Genteel Circle: Bayard Taylor and His New York Friends, 1952; Sarah Orne Jewett Letters, (ed), 1956, revised edition, 1967; Sarah Orne Jewett, 1962; Deephaven and Other Stories by Sarah Orne Jewett (ed), 1966; Mary N Murfree, 1967; Edwin Arlington Robinson's Letters to Edith Brower (ed), Thomas Hardy: The Return of the Native (ed), 1968; Thomas Hardy: The Mayor of Casterbridge (ed), Appreciation of Edwin Arlington Robinson (ed), 1969; The Uncollected Short Stories of Sarah Orne Jewett (ed), 1971; Appreciation of Sarah Orne Jewett (ed), 1973; Early Reception of Edwin Arlington Robinson (author and ed), 1974; Uncollected Poems of Edwin Arlington Robinson (ed), 1975. *Address:* 31 Highland Avenue, Waterville, ME 04901, USA.

CASEY John D, b. 18 Jan 1939, Worcester, Massachusetts, USA. Writer; Professor of English. M. Rosamund Pinchot Pittman, 26 June 1982, 4 daughters. *Education:* BA, Harvard College, 1962; LLB, Harvard Law School, 1965; MFA, University of Iowa, 1967. *Appointments:* Professor, English, University of Virginia, Charlottesville, 1972-; Residency, American Academy in Rome, 1990-91; Strauss Living, American Academy of Arts and Letters, 1992-97. *Publications:* An American Romance, 1977; Testimony and Demeanor, 1979; Spartina, 1989. *Contributions to:* Stories, articles, reviews, 1968-, to: The New Yorker; New York Times Book Review; Esquire; Harper's; Washington Post Book World; Others. *Honours:* Runner-up, Ernest Hemingway Award, 1978; Guggenheim Fellowship, 1979-80; Friends of American Writers Award, 1980; National Endowment for the Arts Fellowship, 1983; National Book Award, 1989; Ingram-Merril Fellowship, 1990. *Memberships:* PEN; National Writers Union. *Literary Agent:* Michael Carlisle, William Morris Agency. *Address:* Department of English, University of Virginia, Charlottesville, VA 22903, USA.

CASINADER Niranjan Robert, b. 24 Dec 1955, London, England. Secondary Teacher. m. Christine Lynette Dunner, 18 Apr 1981, 2 sons. *Education:* BA (Hons), University of Melbourne, 1978; Dip Ed, Melbourne State College, 1979; MEd, Monash University, 1990. *Publications:* The Faces of Development; Geography at Work. *Contributions to:* Interaction; The New Global Geography: Resource Materials of the 26th Annual Confernce. *Memberships:* Geography Teachers Association of Victoria; Australian Geography Teachers Association. *Address:* 63 Beauford Street, Huntingdale, Victoria 3166, Australia.

CASS Joan E(velyn), British. *Appointment:* Former Lecturer in Child Development, Institute of Education, University of London. *Publications:* The Cat Thief, 1961; The Cat Show, 1962; Blossom Finds a House, 1963; The Canal Trip, 1966; Literature and the Young Child, 1967; The Cats Go to Market, 1969; The Cats and the Cat Thieves, Aloysious the Redundant Engine, The Dragon Who Was Too Hot, The Significance of Children's Play (in US as Helping Children Grow Through Play), Chang and the Robber, 1971; The Dragon Who Grew, The Witch of Witchery Wood, 1973; The Role of the Teacher in the Nursery School, Hubert Hippo, Milly Mouse, 1975; Baby Bear's Bath, Milly Mouse's Measles, The Witch and the Naughty Princesses, 1976; Alexander's Magic Quilt, 1978; The Witch's Lost Spell Book, 1980; The Four Surprises, 1981; Trouble Among the Witches, 1983; The Persistent Mouse, 1984; The Witches School, Six Mice Too Many, 1985. *Address:* c/o Abelard-Schuman Limited, 14-18 High Holborn, London WC1V 6BX, England.

CASS Zoe. *See:* LOW Lois.

CASSELLS Cyrus Curtis, b. 16 May 1957, Dover, Delaware, USA. Poet; Teacher; Translator. *Education:* BA, Communications, Stanford University, 1979. *Publications:* The Mud Actor, 1982; Down from the Houses of Magic. *Contributions to:* Southern Review; Callaloo; Translation; The Seneca Review; Quilt; Sequoi. *Honours:* Academy of American Poets Prize, 1979; National Poetry Series Winner, 1982; Bay Area Book Reviewers Association Award Nominee, 1983; Callaloo Creative Writing Award, Poetry, 1983; Massachusetts Artists Foundation Fellowship, 1985; NEA Fellowship, 1986. *Memberships:* PEN; Poetry Society of America; Writers League of Boston, Board Member; North American Catalan Society. *Address:* c/o 1142 E. Ave J-1, Lancaster, CA 93535, USA.

CASSIDY Frederic Gomes, b. 10 Oct 1907. Professor of English Language and Literature; Lexicographer. m. Helene Lucile Monod, 26 Dec 1931, 3 sons, 1 daughter. *Education:* BA magna cum laude, 1930, MA, 1932, Oberlin College; PhD, University of Michigan, 1938. *Appointments:* Chief Editor, Dictionary of American Regional English, 1975-. *Publications:* The Place-Names of Dane County, Wisconsin, 1947; A Method for Collecting Dialect, 1953; Development of Modern English (with Stuart Robertson), 1954; Jamaica Talk, 1961, 2nd Edition, 1971; Dictionary of Jamaican English (with R B Le Page), 1967, Revised Edition, 1980; Bright's Old English Grammar and Reader (with Richard N Ringler), 1971; Dictionary of American Regional English, Vol 1, 1985, Vol II, 1991, further volumes in preparation. *Contributions to:* English Journal; American Spech; Zeitschrift fur deutsche Linguistik; Computers and the Humanities; Journal of English Linguistics; Various other publications. *Honours:* University Fellow, University of Michigan, 1933-35; Fulbright Research Fellow to Jamaica, 1951-52, 1958-59; 1st Visiting Fellow, University College of the West Indies, 1958-59; Musgrave Silver Medal, 1962, Centenary Medal, 1980, Musgrave Gold Medal, 1983, Institute of Jamaica; LittD: Memorial University of Newfoundland, 1982; Indiana State University, Terre Haute, 1983; University of the West Indies, Jamaica, 1984; University of Michigan, Ann Arbor, 1986; HumD, Oberlin College, Ohio, 1983; SNACS Distinguished Service Award, 1986. *Memberships:* American Dialect Society, Past President; Society for Caribbean Linguistics; American Name Society, Past President. *Address:* 207 N Spooner St, Madison, WI, USA.

CASSILL Ronald Verlin, (Owen Aherne, Jesse Webster), b. Iowa, USA. Author. m. Kay, 2 sons, 1 daughter. *Education:* BA, University of Iowa, 1939; MA 1947. *Appointments:* Teacher, Writers Workshop, University of Iowa, 1948-52, 1960-66; Professor, Brown University, 1966-83; Reviewer for New York Times. *Publications:* Eagle on the Coin, 1950; Clem Anderson, 1961; Pretty Leslie, 1963; The President, 1964; The Father, 1965; The Happy Marriage, 1966; LaVie Passionnee of Rodney Buckthorne, 1968; In An Iron Time, 1969; Doctor Cobb's Game, 1970; The Goss Women, 1974; Hoyt's Child, 1976; Editor, Norton Anthology of short Fiction, 1977; Labors of Love, 1980; Flame, 1980; After Goliath, 1985; several short stories.

Contributions to: Atlantic Monthly; Esquire; Holiday; Saturday Evening Post; Horizon. *Honours:* Atlantic First Prize, Atlantic Monthly, 1947; Rockefeller Grant Fiction Writing, 1954; O Henry Prize Stories, 1956; Third Prize, Guggenheim Grant Fiction Writing, 1968. *Memberships:* Associated Writing Programmes, (Organize: President 3 years); Phi Beta Kappa. *Address:* 22 Boylston Avenue, Providence, RI 02906, USA.

CASTANEDA Omar S, b. 6 Sept 1954, Guatemala, Professor. m. (1) 11 Aug 1984, (2) 26 Feb 1992, 1 son, 1 daughter. *Education:* BA, Indiana University, 1980; MFA, 1983. *Publications:* Among the Volcanoes, Dutton; Cunuman; New Visions: Fiction by Florida Writers; Abuela's Weave; Sudden & Uncommon Acts. *Contributions to:* Over 40 inc. Kenyon Review; Caliban; Mid-American Review; Left Bank; Latin American Literary Review; Nuestro; Special Report: Fiction; Fiver Fingers Review. *Honours:* Fulbright Research Award; Critchfield Award; Florida Arts Council Award. *Memberships:* AWP; SCBW; Modern Language Association. *Literary Agent:* JET Literary Associates. *Address:* Department of English, MS 9055 Western Washington University, Bellingham, WA 98225, USA.

CASTEDO Elena, b. 1 Sept 1937, Barcelona, Spain. Writer. m. A Denny Elleman, 15 Apr 1973, 2 sons, 1 daughter. *Education:* University of Chile, 1966; University of California, 1968; Harvard University, 1976. *Appointments include:* Teacher, English College, Santiago, Chile, 1954; Mascimiento Institute, Santiago, Chile, 1966-67; Teaching Fellow, Harvard University, 1969-72; Lecturer, American University, Washington, 1976-77; Editor, Inter American Review, 1987-80. *Publications:* El Paraiso; Paradise; Iquana Dreams; The Sound of Writing; Others inc. El Teatro Chileno de Mediados del Sigioxx; Diario. *Contributions to:* Numerous inc. Linden Lane Magazine; Phoebe Magazine; The Human story; Americas Magazine. *Honours:* UCLA Masters Award; Simon Bolivar Medal; Several Fellowship; Phoebe Award; Nominated 1990 National Book Award; Nominated Spains 1990 Cervantas Prize. *Memberships:* PEN; Authors Guild; Modern Language Association; Washington Independent Writers Association; Poets & Writers; Bruno Schultz International Literary Prize. *Literary agents:* Elaine Markson, US. Carmen Balcells, Spain. *Address:* c/o Accent Media, 36 Lancaster St, Cambridge, MA 02140, USA.

CASTELLIN Philippe, b. 26 June 1948, Isle sur Sorgnes, Vaucluse, France. Fisherman. 3 sons. *Education:* Agrege de Philosophie, ENS, Ulm; Docteur de Lettres, University of Paris-Sorbonne. *Appointments:* Publisher, Director of Docks. *Publications:* Il Disinganno, essay, 1985; Rene Char, Traces, essay, 1988; Projets de Constitution pour la Corse, essay, 1989; Paesine, poems, 1989; Livre, poem, 1990; Vers la poesie totale, essay-translation, 1992; HPS, poem, 1992. *Contributions to:* Tam Tam; Lotta Poetica; Texture Press; Others. *Honours:* Charge de Mission, Homage to Rene Char, Festival d'Avignon, 1990; Expert Manager, Exhibition of Poetry and Painting, Marseille, Vieille Charite. *Membership:* Societe des Gens de Lettres, Paris. *Address:* c/o Akenaton Doc(k)s, 20 Rue Bonaparte, F-20000 Ajaccio, France.

CASTLE Barbara Anne, b. 6 Oct 1910, Chesterfield, England. Journalist; Author. m. Edward Cyril Castle, 1944. *Education:* St Hughs College, Oxford. *Appointments:* Elected to St Pancras Borough Council, 1937; Member, Metropolitan Water Board, 1940-43; Editor, Town and County Councillor, 1936-40; Administrative Officer, Ministry of Food, 1941-44; Housing Correspondent and Affairs Advisor, Daily Mirror, 1944-45; Labour Member, Blackburn, 1945-79; Member, National Executive Committee of the Labour Party, 1950-79; Vice Chairman, Labour Pary, 1957-58; Chairman, Labour Party, 1958-59; Minister of Overseas Development, 1964-65; Privy Counsellor, 1964; Minister of Transport, 1965-68; First Secretary of State for Employment and Productivity, 1968-70; Secretary of State for Social Services, 1974-76; Member,

European Parliament for Greater Manchester North, 1979-84; Member, European Parliament for Greater Manchester West, 1984-89; Leader, British Labour Party, European Parliament, 1979-85; Vice-Chairman, Socialist Group, European Parliament, 1979-86. *Publications:* Castle Diaries 1964-70, 1984; Sylvia & Christabel Pankhurst, 1987; Castle Diaries 1964-76, 1990. *Honours include:* Honorary Fellow of: St Hugh's College, Oxford, 1966; Bradford and Ilkley Community College, 1985; UMIST, 1991; Humberside Polytechnic, 1991; York University, 1992. Honorary Doctor of: Technology, Bradford University, 1968; Technology, Lougborough, 1969; Laws, Lancaster University, 1991. Cross of Order of Merit Federal Republic of Germany, 1990; Created Life Peer as Baroness Castle of Blackburn, ·1990. *Literary Agent:* David Higham Associates Ltd. *Address:* c/o House of Lords, London SW1A 0PW, England.

CASTLE Charles, b. 1939, British. *Appointments:* Production Assistant, Film Instructor, Producer, BBC Television; Former Production Manager, MGM Television. *Publications:* I Start Running; The Keys on the Street; This Was Richard Tauber, 1970, biography with D N Tauber, 1971; Noel, 1972; This is Noel Coward, 1973; Farewell to Woburn: The Duke and Duchess of Bedford Leave Home, 1974; Raging Star: Biography of Joan Crawford, Model Girl, 1977; Belle Otero: The Last Great Courtesan, 1981; The Folies Bergere, 1982; Oliver Messel, 1983. *Address:* Ewhurst Green, Nr Robertsbridge, Sussex, England.

CASTLEDEN Rodney, b. 23 Mar 1945, Worthing, Sussex, England. Head of Humanities. m. Sarah Dee, 29 July 1987. *Education:* BA, MA, Hertford College, Oxford, 1964-67; DipEd, Oxford University, 1967-68; MSc, 1970-78. *Publications:* The Stonehenge People; The Wilmington Giant; The Knossos Labyrinth; Minoans; Book of British Dates; Classic Landforms of the Sussex Coast; Neolithic Britain; The Making of Stonhenge. *Contributions to:* The Origin of Chalk Dry Valleys; A General Theory of Fluvial Valley Development. *Memberships:* FGS; FRGS; The Quarternary Research Association. *Address:* 15 Knepp Close, Brighton, Sussex, BN2 4LD, England.

CASTO Robert Clayton, b. 31 May 1932. Associate Professor, English Literature. *Education:* BA, Yale University, USA, 1954; MA, 1965; MFA, University of Iowa, 1966; MLitt, Oxford University, England, 1968. *Appointments include:* Assistant Professor, English, State University College, New York, 1968-70; Assistant Professor, 1970-74, Associate Professor, 1974-, York University, Toronto, Canada. *Publications:* A Strange and Fitful Land, 1959; The Arrivals, 1980. *Contributions include:* Numerous anthologies, USA, and periodicals including: Yale Review; VA Quarterly Review; Literary Review; Commonwealth; Beloit Poetry Journal; The Lyric; Chelsea; Yankee; Poet Lore; De Kalb Literary Arts Journal. *Honours:* Recorded work for the Archives of the Library of Congress, 1961; 1st Prize, Academy of American Poets Competition, 1965. *Memberships:* Poetry Society of America; Poets and Writers Inc NYC; Elizabethan Club, Yale University. *Address:* 67 Forman Avenue, Toronto, Ontario M4S 2R4, Canada.

CATANACH J N, b. USA. Writer. *Publications:* White Is the Color of Death, 1988; Briceprice, 1989; The Last Rite of Hugo T, 1992. *Address:* Box 310, Lenox Hill Station, New York, NY 10021, USA.

CATANZARITI John, b. 1 June 1942, USA. Historian. m. 1965, 1 son, 1 daughter. *Education:* Queens College, New York, BA, 1964; MA, 1973. *Appointments include:* Lecturer, Queens College, NY, 1965-67; The Papers of Robert Morris: Editorial Assistant, 1968-70; Associate Editor, 1970-80; Co Editor, 1980-81; Editor, 1981-86; Senior Research Historian and Editor, The Papers of Thomas Jefferson, Princeton University, 1987-. *Publications:* The Papers of Robert Morris; The Papers of Thomas Jefferson. *Contributions to:* Wall Street Journal; Journal of

Commercial Bank Lending; American Writers Before 1800; Prologue: Quarterly of the National Archives; Proceedings of the Massachusetts Historical Society. *Memberships:* Massachusetts Historical Society; Institute of Early American History & Culture; Association for Documentary Editing. *Address:* The Papers of Thomas Jefferson, Princeton University Library, Princeton, NJ 08544, USA.

CATHCART Helen, Author; Biographer. *Publications:* Her Majesty, 1962; The Queen Mother, 1965; The Married Life of the Queen, 1970; Anne and the Princesses Royal, 1973; Princess Margaret, 1974; Prince Charles, 1976; The Queen in Her Circle, 1977; The Queen Mother Herself, 1979; The Queen Herself, 1981; The Queen Mother - 50 Years a Queen, 1986; The Queen and Prince Philip, 40 Happy Years, 1987; Anne, Princess Royal, 1988; Charles, Man of Destiny, 1988. *Contributions to:* Several journals including the Strand. *Membership:* Society of Authors. *Literary Agent:* Rupert Crew Limited. *Address:* 1a King's Mews, London WC1N 2JA, England.

CATHERWOOD (Sir) (Henry) Frederick (Ross), b. 1925, British. *Appointments:* Chief Executive, Richard Costain Ltd, 1955-60; Assistant Managing Director, 1960-62 and Managing Director, 1962-64, British Aluminium Co. Ltd; Chief Industrial Adviser, Dept. of Economic Affairs, 1964-66; Director General National Economic Development Council, 1966-71; Managing Director, John Laing & Son Ltd, 1971-74; Chairman, British Overseas Trade Board, 1975-79. *Publications:* The Christian in Industrial Society, 1964; Britain with the Brakes Off, 1966; The Christian Citizen, 1969; A Better Way, 1976; First Things First, 1979; God's Time, God's Money, 1987; Pro Europe? 1991; David: Poet, Soldier, King, 1993. *Honour:* Kt, 1971. *Memberships:* European Parliament since 1979. *Address:* Sutton Hall, Balsham, Cambridgeshire, England.

CATUDAL Honore (Marc), b. 17 Oct. 1944, Washington, District of Columbia, USA. Professor of Politics. m. Carol Robinson, 25 July 1987. 3 sons, 4 daughters. *Education:* Zertifikat, FU of Berlin, 1968; BA, Utica College of Syracuse University, 1969; MIS 1970, PhD 1973, School of International Service, American University. *Publications:* Steinstucken: A Study in Cold War Politics, 1971; The Diplomacy of the Quadripartite Agreement on Berlin, 1977; A Balance Sheet of the Quadripartite Agreement on Berlin, 1978; The Exclave Problem of Western Europe, 1979; Kennedy and the Berlin Wall Crisis, 1980; Nuclear Deterrence: Does it Deter, 1985; Soviet Nuclear Strategy from Stalin to Gorbachev, 1988. *Contributions to:* Utia College News; Department of State Newsletter; St John's Magazine. *Honours:* Presented with Berlin Bear, Mayor Heinrich Albertz, 1965; Invited to participate in Scholar-Diplomat Seminar, US State Department, 1974; Invited to Seminar with West German President, Gustav Heinemann, 1975; Interviewed on All Things Considered, National Public Radio, 1976. *Address:* Department of Government, St John's University, Collegeville, MN 56321, USA.

CAULDWELL Frank. *See:* **KING Francis Henry.**

CAUTE (John) David, (John Salisbury), b. 1936, British. *Appointments:* Fellow, All Souls College, Oxford, 1959-65; Visiting Professor New York and Columbia Universities, 1966-67; Reader in Social and Political Theory, Brunel University, 1967-70; Regents Lecturer, University of California, 1974; Literary and Arts Editor, New Statesman, London, 1979-80; Co-Chairman, Writers Guild of Great Britain, 1981-82. *Publications:* At Fever Pitch, 1959; Comrade Jacob, 1961; Communism and the French Intellectuals 1914-1960, 1964; The Decline of the West, The Left in Europe since 1789, 1966; Essential Writings of Karl Marx (ed), 1967; The Demonstration, 1969; Fanon, 1970; The Occupation, 1971; The Illusion, 1971; The Fellow-Travellers, 1973 (revised 1988); Collisions: Essays and Reviews, Cuba Yes?, 1974; The Great Fear: the Anti-Communist Purge under Truman and Eisenhower, 1978; The K-Factor, Under the Skin: The Death of White Rhodesia, 1983; The Espionage of the Saints, News from Nowhere, 1986; Sixty-Eight: the Year of the Barricades, 1988; Veronica or The Two Nations, 1989; The Women's Hour, 1991. Radio plays: The Demonstration, 1971; Fallout, 1972; The Zimbabwe Tapes, 1983; Henry and the Dogs, 1986; Sanctions, 1988. *Address:* 41 Westcroft Square, London W6 0TA, England.

CAVENDISH Richard, b. 1930, British. *Appointments:* Editor, Partworks Division, B P C Publishing Limited, London, 1967-72; Editor, Out of Town magazine, 1983-. *Publications:* Nymph and Shepherds, 1959; The Balancing Act, 1960; On the Rocks, 1963; The Black Arts, 1967; Man, Myth and Magic (ed and co-author), 1970-72; Encyclopedia of the Unexplained (ed and co-author), 1974; The Powers of Evil, The Tarot, 1975; A History of Magic,Visions of Heaven and Hell, 1977; King Arthur and the Grail, 1978; Mythology (ed and co-author), 1980; Legends of the World, 1982; Prehistoric England, 1983. *Address:* 19 Campion Road, London SW15, England.

CAWS Mary Ann, b. 1933, American. Writer on Art and Literature, Translator. *Appointments:* Faculty member, Barnard College, Columbia University, New York City, 1962-63 and Sarah Lawrence College, Bronxville, New York, 1963; Assistant Professor, 1966-70, Associate Professor, 1970-72, Professor 1972-83, Distinguished Professor of Romance Languages and Comparative Literature, 1972-, Hunter College and Graduate Center, City University of New York; Distinguished Professor of English, French, and Comparative Literature, Graduate Center, City University of New York, 1986; Co-Director, Henri Peyre Institute for the Humanities, 1981-; Co-Editor, Dada/ Surrealism, University of Iowa; Director, Le Siecle eclate, Paris; Member, Editorial Boards, French Review, Diacritics, New York Literary Forum; Modern Fiction Studios PMLA. *Publications:* Surrealism and the Literary Imagination, 1966; The Poetry of Dada and Surrealism, 1970; Andre Breton, 1971; The Inner Theatre of Recent French Poetry, 1972; (editor and translator), Approximate Man and Other Writings of Tristan Tzara, 1974; (editor), About French Poetry from Dada to Tel Quel, 1975; The Presence of Rene Char, 1976; (translator and editor), Selected Poems of Rene Char, 1976; The Surrealist Voice of Robert Desnos, 1977; Rene Char, 1977; La Main de Pierre Reverdy, 1979; (co-translator-editor), Roof Slates and Other Poems of Pierre Reverdy, 1981; (editor), Stephen Mallarme: Selected Poetry and Prose, 1981; A Metapoetics of the Passage, 1981; (editor), St John Perse, Selected Poems, 1982; L'Oeuvre Filante de Rene Cher, 1983; (editor), Writing in a Modern Temper, 1984; Reading Frames in Modern Fiction, 1985; (editor), Textual Analysis: Some Readers Reading, 1986; (translator), Mad Love (of Andre Breton), 1988; The Art of Interference, 1990; Women of Bloomsbury, 1990; (co-translator), Communicating Vessels (of Andre Breton), 1990; (editor and translator), Selected Poems of Rene Char, 1991; Chief Editor, Harper, Collins World Reader, 1993; Forthcoming: Robert Motherwell: What Art Holds; Co-Editor, Ecritures de Femmes. *Memberships:* Vice-President, 1982-83, President, 1983-84, Modern Language Association; President, 1985, Academy of Literary Studies; Vice President, 1986-88, President, 1988-90, American Comparative Literature Association. *Address:* 140 E 81st Street, Apt 11D, New York, NY 10028, USA.

CAWTHORNE Nigel, b. 27 Mar 1951, England. Writer. 1 son. *Education:* BSc (Hons), Physics, University College London. *Publications:* The Bamboo Gage; The Sixties Source Book; The Loving Touch. *Contributions to:* Over 150 contributions to UK and US publications. *Address:* 36D Boswell Street, London WC1N 3BT, England.

CAYTON Andrew Robert Lee, b. 9 May 1954, Cincinnati, Ohio, USA. Historian. m. Mary Alice Kupiec, 23 Aug 1975. 2 daughters. *Education:* BA, University of Virginia, 1976; MA 1977, PhD 1981, Brown University. *Publications:* The Frontier Republic: Ideology and Politics in The Ohio Country 1780-1825, 1986; The Midwest and The Nation: Rethinking The History of An American Region, 1990. *Contributions to:* Scholarly articles in: The William and Mary Quarterly; The Journal of the Early Republic; The Historian; Ohio History. *Honours:* Phi Beta Kappa, 1976; Ohioana Book Award for History, 1987. *Memberships:* American Historical Association; Organization of American Historians; Society for Historians of the Early American Republic; Ohio Historical Society; Indiana Historical Society. *Address:* Department of History, Miami University, Oxford, OH 45056, USA.

CEADEL Martin Eric, b. 28 Jan 1948, Cambridge, England. University Teacher. m. Deborah Stockton, 27 July 1974, 2 sons, 1 daughter. *Education:* BA, Corpus Christi College, Oxford, 1969; MA, DPhil 1977. *Publications:* Pacifism in Britain 1914-1945: The Defining of a Faith; Thinking About Peace & War. *Contributions to:* Numerous Academic Journals. *Address:* New College, Oxford, OX1 3BN, England.

CEDERING Siv, b. 5 Feb 1939, Sweden. Writer; Artist. m. David Swickard, 11 Sept 1983, 1 son, 2 daughters. *Publications:* Mother Is, poetry, 1975; The Juggler, poetry, 1977; The Blue Horse, and Other Night Poems, 1979; Leken i grishuset, novel, 1980; Oxen, novel, 1981; Letters from the Floating World, Selected and New Poems, 1984; Mannen i odebyn, 1989; Author, illustrator: Cup of Cold Water, poems: Grisen som ville bli ren, for children, 1983; Polis, polis, potatisgris, for children, 1985; Grisen som ville bli julskinka, for children, 1986; Grisen far till Paris, for children, 1987; Chapbooks; Several translations. *Contributions to:* Harper's; Ms; New Republic; Paris Review; Partisan Review; New York Times; Georgia Review; Fiction International; Shenandoah; Confrontation; Numerour other literary magazines; Over 80 anthologies and textbooks. *Honours:* Best Books of the Year, 1980; New York Foundation Fellowship, 1985, 1992. *Memberships:* Board Member, PSA; Poets and Writers; American PEN; Consultant to Board, CCLM. *Literary Agent:* Diana Finch, Ellen Levine Agency. *Address:* Box 800, Amagansett, NY 11930, USA.

CEGIELKA Francis Anthony, b. 16 Mar 1908, Grabow, Poland. Roman Catholic Priest in the Society of the Catholic Apostolate. *Education:* Collegium Marianum 1921-27, Wadowice (Krakow); Pontifical Gregorian University, Rome, Italy, 1927-31; Ordained Priest 1931; Doctorate in Theology (STD) 1931. *Appointments:* Teacher, Minor Seminary of the Society of the Catholic Apostolate, Chelmno, Poland, 1932-34; Teacher, Major Seminary, SAC, Wadowice, Poland, 1934-36; Rector, Polish Catholic Mission, Paris, France, 1937-47; Prisoner of German Gestapo, held in 9 prisons and 2 concentration camps, 1940-45; Rector, Polish Catholic Mission, Paris, France, 1945-48; Sent to the USA by his Superior General to conduct retreat work; Professor, Felician College, Lodi, New Jersey, 1967-70; Professor, Holy Family College, Philadelphia, USA, 1970-76. *Publications include:* Reparatory Mysticism of Nazareth, 1951; Holy Mass School of Religious Life, 1953; Life on Rocks (among the Natives of the Union of South Africa), 1957; Spiritual Theology for Novices, 1961; Segregavit nos Dominus, 1963; Three Hearts - Meditations, 1963, second volume 1964; Nazareth Spirituality, 1966; All Things New - Radical reform of religious life, 1969; Handbook of Ecclesiology and Christology, 1971; Toward a New Spring of Humankind, 1987; also publications in Polish. *Honours:* Legion d'Honneur - Chevalier, French Government, 1945; Nominated as an outstanding Educator of America, 1972 and 1974. *Memberships:* American Association of University Professors; Polish Institute of Arts and Sciences in America. *Address:* 3452 Niagara Falls Boulevard, PO Box 563, North Tonawanda, NY 14120, USA.

CHADWICK Geoffrey, (Geoffrey Wall), b. 10 July 1950, Cheshire, England. University Lecturer. 3 sons, 1 daughter. *Education:* BA, University of Sussex, 1972; BPhil, St Edmund Hall, Oxford, 1975. *Publications:* Madame Bovary, translated from the French, 1992. *Contributions to:* Literature and History; Cambridge Quarterly. *Memberships:* Society of Authors; Association of University Teachers; Translators Association. *Address:* Department of English, University of York, Heslington, York YO1 5DD, England.

CHADWICK (William) Owen, b. 20 May 1916, Bromley, Kent, England. Historian. m. Ruth Hallward, 28 Dec 1949. 2 sons, 2 daughters. *Education:* BA, 1939, St. John's College, Cambridge. *Publications:* John Cassian, 1950 revised edition, 1968; The Founding of Cuddesdon, 1954; From Bossuet to Newman, 1957, 2nd edition 1987; Western Asceticism, 1958; Creighton on Luther, 1959; Mackenzie's Grave, 1959; Victorian Miniature, 1960, 2nd edition 1991; The Mind of the Oxford Movement, 1960; From Uniformity to Unity 1662-1962 (with G. Nuttall), 1962; Westcott and the University, 1962; The Reformation, 1964; The Victorian Church, vol 1, 1966, 3rd edition, 1972; vol II, 1970, 2nd edition, 1972; Acton and Gladstone, 1976; The Secularization of the European Mind, 1977; Catholicism and History, 1978; The Popes and European Revolution, 1981; The Oxford History of the Christian Church (editor with brother Henry Chadwick), 1981; Newman, 1983; Hensley Henson: A Study in the Friction Between Church and State, 1983; Britain and the Vatican in the Second World War, 1986; Michael Ramsey, 1990, 2nd edition, 1991; The Spirit of the Oxford Movement: Tractarian Essays, 1990; The Christian Church in the Cold War, 1992. *Contributions to:* Times (London); New Statesman; Spectator; Manchester Guardian; Sunday Times; Observer; History and Ecclesiastical History journals - Essays in honour of, in G. Best and D. Beates (editors). *Honours:* Order of Merit, 1983; KBE, 1982; Wolfson Prize for History (for The Popes and European Revolution), 1981. *Memberships:* Fellow, British Academy; Fellow, Royal Historical Society. *Address:* 67 Grantchester Street, Cambridge CB3 9H2, England.

CHADWICK Whitney, b. 28 July 1943, New York, USA. Art Historian. m. Robert A Bechtle, 6 Nov 1982. *Education:* BA, Middlebury College, 1965; MA, The Pennsylvania State University, 1968; PhD, 1975. *Publications:* Women, Art & Society; Women Artists and the Surrealist Movement; Myth in Surrealist Paiting. *Contributions to:* Art in America; Artforum; The Art Bulletin; Art International; Womens Art Journal. *Membership:* College Art Association of America. *Literary Agent:* Elaine Markson. *Address:* 871 DeHaro Street, San Francisco, CA 94107, USA.

CHAGALL David, b. 22 Nov 1930, Philadelphia, Pennsylvania, USA. Author; Journalist. m. Juneau Joan Alsin, 15 Nov 1957. *Education:* Swarthmore College, 1948-49; BA, Pennsylvania State University, 1952; Licence (postgraduate), Sorbonne, University of Paris, France, 1954. *Appointments:* Associate Editor, IEE Journal, UK, 1960-61; Investigative Reporter, national magazines, USA, 1975-; Editor, Publisher, Inside Campaigning, 1984; Contributing Editor, Los Angeles Magazine, 1986-89. *Publications:* The Century God Slept, novel, 1963; Diary of a Deaf Mute, novel, 1971; The Spieler for the Holy Spirit, novel, 1972; The New Kingmakers, nonfiction, 1981; The Sunshine Road, nonfiction, 1988. *Contributions to:* TV Guide; Time/Life; Family Weekly; Los Angeles Magazine; California Business; Valley Magazine; Inside Campaigning; New West. *Honours:* Carnegie Award, 1964; Poetry Prize, University of Wisconsin, 1971; Nominee, fiction, National Book Award, 1972; Nominee, Pulitzer Prize in Letters, 1973; Health Journalism Award, 1980; Honorary Member, Mark Twain Society, 1981; Presidential Achievement Award, 1982. *Memberships include:* Authors Guild; National Society For The Book; Academy of Political and Social Science; American Academy of Political Science. *Literary Agent:* Jay Garon, 415 Central Park West, 17th Floor, New York, NY 10025, USA. *Address:* PO Box 85, Agoura Hills, CA 91301, USA.

CHAGNON Napoleon Alphonseau, b. 27 Aug 1938, Michigan, USA. Anthropologist. m. Carlene Faye Badgero, 19 July 1960, 1 son, 1 daughter. *Education:* BA, University of Michigan, 1961; MA, 1963; PhD, 1966. *Appointments:* Assistant Professor, University of Michigan, 1966; Professor, Pennsylvania State University, 1972; Professor, Northwestern University, 1980; Professor, University of California, Santa Barbara, 1984-. *Publications:* Yanomamo: The Fierce People; Studing the Yanomamo; Evolutionary Biology and Human Social Behaviour: An Anthropological Perspective; Toward the PhD for Dogs; Films. The Feast; Magical Death; The Ax Fight; A Man Called Bee; The Yanomamo Myth of Naro. *Contributions to:* Numerous inc. National Geographic; Natural History; The Sciences; Ranger Rick; Geo; Dozens of Scientific Journals. *Honours include:* Two Blue Ribbons; Two Red Ribbons; Golden Buccranium; Cine Golden Eagle Award. *Memberships:* American Anthropological Association; Aurrent Anthropoligy; American association for the Advancement of science; Psychological Cinema Register; Ethology & Sociobiology. *Address:* 405 Calle Granada, Santa Barbara, CA 93105, USA.

CHALFONT Alun Arthur Gwynne Jones (Baron), b. 1919, British. *Appointments:* Served as Regular Officer in the British Army, 1939-61; Defence Correspondent, the Times, 1961-64; Minister of State, Foreign and Commonwealth Office, 1964-70; Representative to the Council of the Western European Union, 1969-70; Foreign Office Correspondent, New Statesman, 1970-71; Chairman, UN Association, 1972-73; Director, IBM UK Limited and Lazard Brothers Limited; President, Nottingham Building Society; Chairman, All Party Defence Group, House of Lords, 1980-. *Publications:* The Sword and the Spirit, 1963; The Great Commanders, 1973; Montgomery of Alamein, 1976; Waterloo (ed), 1979; Star Wars: Suicide or Survival, 1985; Defense of the Realm, 1987; By God's Will - a portrait of the Sultan of Burnei, 1991. *Contributions to:* The Times, National and Professional Journals. *Address:* House of Lords, London SW1A 0PW, England.

CHALKER Jack L(aurence), b. 1944, American. *Appointments:* Founder-Director, Mirage Press, Baltimore, 1961-; English, History and Geography Teacher, Baltimore Public High Schools, 1966-78. *Publications:* The New H P Lovecraft Bibliography, 1962, as The Revised H P Lovecraft Bibliography (with Mark Owings), 1973; In Memoriam Clark Ashton Smith (ed), 1963; Mirage on Lovecraft (ed), 1964; The Index to the Science-Fantasy Publishers (with Mark Owings), 1966, as Index to the SF Publishers, 1979; The Necronmicon: A Study (with Mark Owings), 1967; An Informal Biography of Scrooge McDuck, 1974; A Jungle of Stars, 1976; Midnight in the Well of Souls, 1977; Dancers in the Afterglow, The Web of the Chosen, Exiles at the Well of Souls, Quest for the Well of Souls, 1978; A War of Shadows, And the Devil Will Drag You Under, Dancers in the Afterglow, 1979; Twilight at the Well of Souls, The Devil's Voyage, 1980; Lilith: A Snake in the Grass, 1981; Cerberus: A Wolf in the Fold, The Identity Matrix, 1982; Medusa: A Tiger by the Tail, Four Lords of the Diamond, 1983; The River of Dancing Gods, Spirits of Flux and Anchor, Empires of Flux and Anchor, 1984; Masters of Flux and Achor, Downtiming the Night Side, Vengeance of the Dancing Gods, The Messiah Choice, The Birth of Flux and Anchor, 1985; Children of Flux and Anchor, 1986.

CHALLIS Chris, b. 11 Feb 1952, Essex, England. Writer; Lecturer. *Education:* BA, Leicester University, 1973; MA, 1974; PhD, 1979. *Appointments:* ACGB Writer in Residence, Northampton, 1982-83; Four BBC Radio Stations, 1985; Doncaster Libraries, 1987; WIR Featherstone Library, 1987; WIR Co Durham, 1989-90; WIR West Norfolk, 1991-92. *Publications:* Quest for Kerouac; Highfields Landscape; William of Cloudeslee; The Wild Thing Went From Side to Side; Four Stout Shoes; Jack Kerouac, Charles Bukowski And Me; A Little Earth For Charity; Ten Plays; Common Ground; A Sense of Place; Wordscan. *Contributions:* Numerous. *Honours:* Nanda Award; Ema Travel Bursary; Ema Writers Bursary; Judge for Literary Comps; Heinemann Fiction Award, finalist. *Membership:* Writers Guild. *Address:* 67 Prospect Hill, Leicester, LE5 3RT, England.

CHALMERS Mary Eileen, b. 16 Mar 1927, Camden, New Jersey, USA. Author; Artist (Children's Books). *Education:* Diploma, College of Art, 1945-48; Barnes Foundation, 1948-49. *Publications:* A Christmas Story, 1956; Throw A Kiss, Harry, 1958; Take A Nap, Harry, 1964; Come To The Doctor, Harry, 1981; 6 Dogs, 23 Cats, 45 Mice and 116 Spiders, 1986; Easter Parade, 1988. *Address:* 4Q Laurel Hill Rd, Greenbelt, MD 20770, USA.

CHALON Jon. *See:* **CHALONER John.**

CHALONER John, (Jon Chalon), British. *Publications:* Three for the Road, 1954; Eager Beaver, 1965; The Flying Steamroller (as J Chalon), The House Next Door (as J Chalon), 1967; Sir Lance-a-little and the Knights of the Kitchen Table (as J Chalon), 1971; The Voyage of the Floating Bedstead (as J Chalon), 1972; The Green Bus (as J Chalon), 1973; Family Hold Back, 1975; The Dustman's Holiday (as J Chalon), 1976; To the Manner Born, 1978; The Great Balloon Adventure (as J Chalon), Bottom Line, 1984; Will O' The Wheels and Speedy Sue (as Jon Chalon), 1990; Occupational Hazard, 1991. *Honour:* Verbundesdienstkreuz 1st Kt for services Anglo-German relationships, 1990. *Address:* 4 Warwick Square, London SW1, England.

CHAMBERS Aidan, (Malcolm Blackin), b. 27 Dec 1934, Chester-le-Street, County Durham, England, Author; Publisher. m. Nancy Harris Lockwood, 30 Mar 1968. *Education:* Borough Road College, Isleworth; London University. *Publications:* The reluctant Reader, 1969; Introducing Books to Children, 1973, 1983; Breaktime, 1978; Seal Secret, children's novel, 1980; The Dream Cage, play, 1981; Dance on My Grave, 1982; The Present Takers, children's novel, 1983; Booktalk, 1985; Now I Know, 1987; The Reading Environment, 1991; The Toll Bridge, 1992. *Contributions to:* Numerous magazines and journals. *Honours:* Children's Literature Award for Outstanding Criticism, 1978; Eleanor Farjeon Award, 1982; Silver Pencil, Netherlands, 1985, 1986. *Membership:* Society of Authors. *Literary Agent:* Pat White, Coleridge Rogers and White. *Address:* Lockwood, Station Road, Woodchester, Stroud, Gloucestershire GL5 5EQ, England.

CHAMBERS Catherine E. *See:* **JOHNSTON Norma.**

CHAMBERS Kate. *See:* **JOHNSTON Norma.**

CHAMBERS Marjorie Elizabeth, b. 15 May 1938, Northern Ireland. University Lecturer. m. Cyril Weir Chambers, 30 June 1969, 1 son. *Education:* BA (Hons), English, French, 1961-62, MA, 1968, Trinity College, Dublin; Sorbonne, Paris, 1961-62; PGCE. Goldsmiths College, London, 1964; Intermediate Certificate, Greek Institute, 1978; Advanced Level Certificate, Modern Greek, University of Thessalonika, 1981. *Appointments:* Currently Lecturer, Modern Greek Language and Literature, Queen's University, Belfast. *Publications:* Translation: Farewell by Yannis Ritsos and Introduction, Modern Greek Studies Yearbook, 1991; Translations: The Charioteer; My Sister's Song. The March of the Ocean (Yannis Ritsos), 1987-88; (George Vafopoulos), 1989-90; Poems from collection: The Big Night and the Window, Songs of Resurrection, The Offering, The Sequel; Translation of Nikiforos Vrettakos: Chorus, collection of poems, also poems from collection Gift in Abeyance, 1991-92. *Honours:* British Council Grants, research on Yannis Ritsos, 1987, research on Nikiforos Vrettakos, 1990. *Memberships:* Translators Association, Society of Authors; ITI; Directory of Translators and Interpreters; Northern Ireland Representative, Examiner in Modern Greek, Greek Institute, London; Standing

Committee on Modern Greek in Universities. *Address:* 3 The Esplanade, Holywood, Co Down BT18 9JG, Northern Ireland.

CHAMBERS R(aymond) (John), b. 1917, Australian. *Appointments:* Senior Lecturer 1953-55, Associate Professor 1955-59, Professor of Accounting 1960-82, now Emeritus, University of Sydney; Editor, Abacus, 1964- 74. *Publications:* Financial Management, 1947, 2nd revised edition, 1967; Function and Design of Company Annual Reports, 1955; Accounting and Action, 1957, revised edition, 1964; The Accounting Frontier (ed with L Goldberg and R L Mathews), 1965; Accounting, Evaluation and Economic Behavior, 1966; Accounting Finance and Management, 1969; Securities and Obscurities, 1973; Price Variation and Inflation Accounting, 1980. *Address:* Department of Accounting, University of Sydney, Sydney, NSW 2006, Australia.

CHAMPION Larry Stephen, b. 27 Apr 1932, Shelby, North Carolina, USA. University Professor of English. m. Nancy Ann Blanchard, 22 Dec 1956, 1 son, 2 daughters. *Education:* BA cum laude, Davidson College, 1954; MA, University of Virginia, 1955; PhD, University of North Carolina, 1961. *Publications include:* Evolution of Shakespeare's Comedy; Essential Shakespeare; King Lear, Annotated Bibliography; Shakespeare's Tragic Perspective; Perspective in Shakespeare's English Histories; Tragic Patterns in Jacobean & Caroline Drama; Thomas Dekker & Traditions of English Drama; Editor: Quick Springs of Sense: Essays on 18th Century Literature; The Noise of Threatening Drum: Dramatic Strategy and Political Ideology in Shakespeare and the English Chronicle Plays. *Contributions to:* Numerous scholarly journals. *Honours include:* Academy of Outstanding Teachers, 1966; Member 1975-, Chairman 1976-78, SAMLA Studies Awards Committee, Member 1971-, President 1974, South Atlantic Association of Departments of English; Triangle University Advisory Board, National Humanities Centre, 1977; James E.Savage Lecturer in Renaissance, University of Mississippi, 1984; Alumni Distinguishd Professor, 1987. *Memberships include:* Malone Society; Renaissance English Text Society; Phi Beta Kappa; Phi Kappa Phi; American & International Shakespeare Associations; Renaissance Society of America; Modern Language Association. *Address:* Department of English, Box 8105, North Carolina State University, Raleigh, NC 27695, USA.

CHAMPLIN Charles Davenport, b. 23 Mar 1926, USA. Writer. m. Margaret Frances Derby, 11 Sept 1948, 2 sons, 4 daughters. *Education:* AB Harvard College, 1948. *Appointments:* Writer-Correspondent, Life Magazine, 1948-60, Time Magazine, 1960-65; Arts Editor, Los Angeles Times, 1965-; Principal Film Critic, 1967-80; Critic at Large 1980-; Adjunct Assistant Professor, University of Southern California School of Cinema-Television 1984-; TV Host. *Publications:* Back There Where the Past Was, 1989; The Flicks 1978, revised and enlarged as The Movies Grow Up, 1981. *Contributions to:* Various magazines. *Honours:* Order of Arts and Letters, French 1977. *Memberships:* National Society of Film Critics; National Book Critics Circle; National Society of Journalists; Los Angeles Film Critics Association. *Literary Agent:* Ned Brown, Malibu, California, USA. *Address:* Los Angeles Times, Los Angeles, CA 90053, USA.

CHAN Stephen, b. 11 May 1949, New Zealand. Director of University of Kent, London Centre of International Relations; Research Professor, University of Zambia; Former International Civil Servant, Commonwealth Secretariat. *Education:* BA, University of Auckland, 1972; MA, 1975; MA, London University Kings College, 1977; PhD, University of Kent, Canterbury, 1992. *Publications:* Kaunda And Southern Africa; Crimson Rain; Exporting Apartheid; Songs of the Maori King; Arden's Summer; Total of Eight Scholarly Books & Five Volumes of Poetry. *Honours:* LittD, World Academy of Arts And Culture. *Memberships:* PEN; Chief Technical Adviser, British Students Karate Federation; Various African Karate Unions. *Address:* Darwin College, University of Kent, Canterbury, CT2 7NY, England.

CHANCE Stephen. *See:* **TURNER Philip.**

CHANCELLOR Alexander Surtees, b. 4 Jan. 1940, Ware, Hertfordshire, England. Journalist. m. Susanna Elizabeth Debenham, 1964, 2 daughters. *Education:* Trinity Hall, Cambridge. *Appointments:* Reuters News Agency, 1964-74, Chief Correspondent, Italy 1968-73; ITV News, 1974-75; Editor, The Spectator, 1975-84; Assistant Editor, Sunday Telegraph, 1984- ; Editor, Time and Tide, 1984-86; Dep Editor, Sunday Telegraph, 1986; Editor, The Independent Magazine, 1988-92. *Address:* c/o The Independent, 40 City Road, London, EC1Y 2DB, England.

CHANDLER David (Geoffrey), b. 1934, British. *Appointments:* British Army Officer, 1957-60; Lecturer, Department of Modern Subjects 1960-64, Senior Lecturer, Department of Military History 1964-69, Deputy-Head, Department of War Studies 1969-80, Head, Department of War Studies 1980-94, Royal Military Academy Sandhurst, Camberley, Surrey; President Emeritus, British Military History Commission, 1967-86; President Emeritus, 1986-; Mershon Visiting Professor, Ohio State University, Columbus, 1969-70; Vice-President, International Commission of Military History, 1975-; Northern Visiting Professor, VMI, 1988; Editor, David Chandler's Newsletter on the Age of Napoleon, 1987-89; Military Affairs Visiting Professor, Quantico, 1991; DLitt by Oxford University, 1991. *Publications:* A Traveller's Guide to the Battlefields of Europe (ed), 2 volumes, 1965; The Campaigns of Napoleon, 1966; Two Soldiers of Marlborough's Wars: Captain Robert Parker and the Count of Merode Westerloo (ed and trans), 1968; Marlborough as Military Commander, 1973; The Art of Warfare on Land, Napoleon, 1974; The Art of Warfare in the Age of Marlborough, 1976; Dictionary of the Napoleonic Wars, 1979; Waterloo: The Hundred Days, Atlas of Military Strategy, 1980; A Journal of Marlborough's Wars, by Private J M Deane (ed), 1984; Sedgemoor: An Account on Anthology, 1985; Napoleon's Marshals (ed), 1987; Napoleon's Military Maxims (ed), 1987; Austerlitz 1805, 1990; Great Battles of the British Army (ed), 1991; RMA Sandhurst - 250 Years, 1991; Jena - 1806, 1993. *Address:* Hindford, Monteagle Lane, Yateley, Camberley, Surrey, England.

CHANDLER Frank. *See:* **GILMAN George G.**

CHANDLER Mark. *See:* **SHARKEY Jack.**

CHANDLER Otis, b. 23 Nov 1927, Los Angeles, USA. Newspaper Executive. m. (1) Marilyn Chandler, 1951, divorced 1981, (2) Bettina Whitaker, 1981, 3 sons, 2 daughters. *Education:* Stanford University. *Appointments:* Trainee, Times Mirror Co., 1953, Assistant to President (assigned to Mirror News), 1957, Marketing Manager, Los Angeles Times, 1958-60, Publisher, Los Angeles Times, 1960-80; Publisher, Chief Executive Officer, 1978-80; Vice Chairman, Times Mirror Co., 1968-80, Chairman, Editor in Chief, 1981-85, Chairman, Executive Committee, 1986-. *Address:* Times Mirror Square, Los Angeles, CA 90053, USA.

CHANEY Edward Paul De Gruyter, b. 11 Apr 1951. Historian. m. Lisa Maria Jacka, 2 daughters. *Education:* BA, Reading University; M Phil, PhD, London University. *Publications:* The Grand Tour & the Great Rebellion; Florence: A Travellers Companion; Oxford, China and Haly; England and the Continental Renaissance; Journal of Anglo Italian Studies; English Architecture: Public and Public. *Contributions to:* TLS; Country Life; Apollo; English Historical Review; Burlington Magazine; Journal of Anglo Italian Studies. Honour: Laurea Di Dottore. *Literary Agent:* Gabriele Pantucci. *Address:* 40 Southfield Road, Oxford, OX4 1NZ, England.

CHANG David Wenwei, b. 1 Juy 1929, China. Professor. m. Alice G Tan, 11 Aug 1962, 2 sons. *Education:* Tamkang University, 1950-52; Diploma, Rhodes College, 1953-55; BA, University of Minnesota, 1955-57; MA, University of Illinois, 1957-60; PhD, University of Illinois, 1960. *Appointments:* Instructor, University of Wisconsin, Oshkoch, 1960-62; Assistant Professor, 1962-64; Associate Professor, 1964-67; Full Professor, 1968-; Fulbright Professor, People's University of China, Beijing. *Publications:* China Under Deng Xiaoping; Zhou Enlai And Deng Xiaoping; Chinese Communities and Political Developement in Southeast Asia; Sun Yat Sen's Doctine and the Future of China. *Publications:* China's Search for a New Political Typology for Systemic Integration; On Tang Tsou's Middle Course Theory in Post Mao Reform. *Honours:* Rosebush Professor in Political Science. *Memberships:* Chinese Social Scientist Association; American Political Science Association; Association of South East Asian Studies; Mid West Association of Asian Studies. *Address:* Department of Political Science, University of Wisconsin Oshkosh, WI 54901, USA.

CHAPLIN Jenny, (Tracie Telfer, Wendy Wentworth), b. 22 Dec 1928, Glasgow, Scotland. Head Mistress; Editor; Publisher. m. J mcDonald Chaplin, 21 Apr 1951, 1 daughter. *Education:* Jordanhill Collefe of Education, 1946-49. *Appointments:* Editor, Founder, Publisher, Internationl, The Writers Rostrum, 1984-. *Publications:* A Glasgow Childhood; A Glasgow Fair; A Glasgow Hogmonay; one Editors Life; The Puzzle of Parkinsons Disease; Thoughts on Writing. *Contributions to:* Numerous inc. Writers News; Sharpen Your Writing Skills; Self publishing Feature; Article of D C Thomson; You Too Can Be An Editor; The Scotsman Newspaper; Thought for Today; Life on the Lean Side; The Scots Magazine. *Address:* The Writers Rostrum, 14 Ardbeg Road, Rothesay, Bute PA20 0NJ, Scotland.

CHAPMAN Elizabeth, b. 5 Jan 1919, Writer. m. Frank Chapman, 22 Nov 1941, 3 sons. *Education:* Barnsley High School for Girls; College of Technology, Barnsley, England, 1938-39. *Publications:* Marmaduke The Lorry, 1953; Marmaduke and Joe, 1954; Riding with Marmaduke, 1957; Merry Marmaduke, 1957; Marmaduke and His Friends, 1958; Marmaduke and the Elephant, 1959; Marmaduke and the Lambs, 1960; Marmaduke Goes to France, 1961; Marmaduke Goes to Holland, 1963; Marmaduke Goes To America, 1965; Marmaduke Goes to Italy, 1970; Marmaduke Goes to Spain, 1978; Marmaduke Goes to Switzerland, 1977; Marmaduke Goes to Morocco, 1979; Marmaduke Goes to Scotland, 1986; Marmaduke Goes to Wales, 1982; Marmaduke Goes to Ireland, 1987. *Contributions to:* Sunny Stories. *Address:* 88 Grange Gardens, Pinner, Middlesex HA5 5QF, England.

CHAPMAN Ivan Douglas, b. 14 Feb 1919, Werris Creek, New South Wales, Australia. Journalist; Military Historian. m. Moira Helen Menzies, 12 Sept 1953, 3 daughters. *Education:* Sydney Technical College, 1946-47. *Appointments:* Journalist, ABC News, Radio, 1947-52, TV, 1956-76; BBC News, Radio, 1952-54; TV, 1954-56, 1973-74; SBS News, Radio, 1979- 80. *Publications:* Details Enclosed; Iven G Mackay; Private Eddie Leonski; Tokyo Calling. *Contributions to:* Australian Dictionary of Biography; Australian Encyclopaedia; Weekend Australian; The Bulletin; British History Illustrated; Time Life Books. *Memberships:* Australian Society of Authors; National Press Club Canberra; Journalists Club Sydney; Ex PoW Association of Australia. *Address:* c/o Australian Society of Authors, PO Box 1566, Strawberry Hills, NSW 2012, Australia.

CHAPMAN Jean, b. 30 Oct 1929, England. Writer. m. Lionel Alan Chapman, 24 Mar 1951, 1 son, 2 daughters. *Education:* BA, Open University, 1989. *Appointments:* Creative Writing Tutor, 5 community colleges. *Publications:* The Unreasoning Earth, 1981; Tangled Dynasty, 1984; Forbidden Path, 1986; Savage Legacy, 1987; The Bell Makers, 1990; Fortune's Woman, 1992; Wide range of short stories. *Honours:* Short-listed, Romantic Novel of the Year, 1981; Short-listed, Kathleen Fidler Award, Book Trust of Scotland for Children's Literature, 1990. *Memberships:* Society of Authors; Committee Member, Romantic Novelists Association. *Literary Agent:* Jane Judd. *Address:* 3 Arnesby Lane, Peatling Magna, Leicester LE8 3UN, England.

CHAPMAN Richard Arnold, b. 15 Aug 1937, Bexleyheath, Kent, England. University Professor. *Education:* BA, University of Leicester, 1961; MA, Carleton University, 1962; PhD, University of Leicester, 1966; D Litt, 1989. *Publications:* Decision Making; The Higher Civil Service in Britain; Leadership in the British Civil Service; Ethics in the British Civil Service; The Art of Darkness; Several Other Publications. *Contributions to:* Public Policy and Administration; Review of Politics; International Review of Administrative Sciences; International Review of History and Political Science. *Memberships:* Joint University Council; Political Studies Association. *Address:* University of Durham, Department of Politics, 48 Old Elvet, Durham DH1 3LZ, England.

CHAPMAN Stanley David, b. 1935, British. *Appointments:* Lecturer 1968-73, Pasold Reader in Business History 1973-, Professor of Business History 1993-, University of Nottingham; Editor, Textile History bi-annual. *Publications:* The Early Factory Masters, 1967; The Beginnings of Industrial Britain (co-author), 1970; The History of Working Class Housing (ed), 1971; The Cotton Industry in the Industrial Revolution, 1972; Jesse Boot of Boot's the Chemists, 1974; The Devon Cloth Industry in the Eighteenth Century, 1978; Stanton and Staveley: A Business History, European Textile Printers in the 18th Century (co-author), 1981; The Rise of Merchant Banking, 1984; Merchant Enterprise in Britain from the Industrial Revolution to World War I, 1992. *Address:* Birchlea, Beetham Close, Bingham, Notts NG13 8ED, England.

CHAPMAN Walker. *See:* **SILVERBERG Robert.**

CHAPPELL Fred, b. 28 May 1936. Teacher. m. Susan Nichols, 22 July 1959, 1 son. *Education:* Duke University, BA, 1961; MA, 1963. *Publications:* I Am One Of You Forever; Midquest; Brighten The Corner Where You are; More Shapes Than One; The Fred Chappell Reader. *Contributions to:* Numerous. *Honours:* Award in Literature; Sire Walter Raleigh Prize; Bollingen Prize in Poetry. *Memberships include:* Southern Writers Fellowship. *Literary Agent:* Rhoda Weyr. *Address:* 305 Kensington Road, Greensboro, NC 27403, USA.

CHAPPELL Mollie, British. *Publications:* Little Tom Sparrow, Tusker Tales, Rhodesian Adventure, 1950; The Gentle Giant, The House on the Kopje, 1951; The Sugar and Spice, St Simon Square, 1952; The Fortunes of Frick, 1953; Cat with No Fiddle, 1954; The Mystery of the Silver Circle, Kit and the Mystery Man, 1955; The Widow Jones, 1956; Endearing Young Charms, 1957; Bachelor Heaven, 1958; A Wreath of Holly, 1959; One Little Room, 1960; A Lesson in Loving, The Measure of Love, 1961; Caroline, 1962; Come by Chance, 1963; The Garden Room, 1964; The Ladies of Lark, 1965; Bright Promise, 1966; Bid Me Live, Since Summer, 1967; The Wind in the Green Trees, 1969; The Hasting Day, 1970; Summer Story, Valley of Lilacs, 1972; Family Portrait, Cressy, 1973; Five Farthings, A Letter from Lydia, 1974; Sefton's Wife, 1975; In Search of Mr Rochester, 1976; Loving Heart, Country Air, 1977; The Romantic Widow, Wintersweet, 1978; Serena, 1980; Dearest Neighbour, 1981; Cousin Amelia, 1982; Springtime for Sophie, The Yellow Straw Hat, 1983; Stepping Stones, The Family at Redburn, 1985. *Address:* c/o Curtis Brown Limited, 162-168 Regent Street, London W1R 5TA, England.

CHAPPLE John Alfred Victor, b. 1928, British. *Appointments:* Assistant University College, 1953-55; Research Assistant, Yale University, New Haven CT, 1955-58; Assistant Lecturer, Aberdeen University,

1958-59; Assistant Lecturer 1959-61, Lecturer 1961-67, Senior Lecturer 1967-71, Manchester University; Professor of English, Hull University, 1971-92, Emeritus Professor, 1992-; Visiting Fellow, Corpus Christi College, Cambridge, 1992. *Publications:* The Letters of Mrs Gaskell (ed with A Pollard), 1966; Documentary and Imaginative Literature 1880-1920, 1970; Dryden's Earl of Shaftesbury, 1973; Elizabeth Gaskell: A Portrait in Letters (with J G Sharps), 1980; Science and Literature in the Nineteenth Century, 1986. *Memberships:* The Brontë Society; Chairman, The Gaskell Society; International Association of University Professors of English. *Address:* 173 Newland Park, Hull, HU5 2DX, Yorkshire, England.

CHARBONNEAU Louis (Henry), (Carter Travis Young), b. 1924. American, Writer of Mystery, Crime, Suspense, Westerns, Adventure, Science fiction, Fantasy. *Appointments:* Instructor in English, University of Detroit, 1948-52; Copywriter, Mercury Advertising Agency, Los Angeles, 1952-56; Staff writer, Los Angeles Times, 1956-71; Freelance writer, 1971-74; Editor, Security World Publishing Co, Los Angeles, 1974-79. *Publications:* No Place on Earth (science fiction), 1958; Night of Violence, 1959, in UK as The Trapped Ones, 1960; Nor All Your Tears, 1959, in UK as The Time of Desire, 1960; Corpus Earthling (science fiction), 1960; (as Carter Travis Young), The Wild Breed, in UK as The Sudden Gun, 1960; (as Carter Travis Young), The Savage Plain, 1961; (as Carter Travis Young), Shadow of a Gun, 1962; The Sentinel Stars (science fiction), 1964; (as Carter Travis Young), The Bitter Iron, 1964; (as Carter Travis Young), Long Boots, Hard Boots, 1965; Psychedelic-40 (science fiction), 1965, in UK, as The Specials, 1967; Way Out, 1966; Down to Earth (science fiction); in UK as Antic Earth, 1967; (as Carter Travis Young), Why Did They Kill Charlie? 1967; The Sensitives (science fiction), 1968; Down from the Mountain, 1969; And Hope to Die, 1970; (as Carter Travis Young), Winchester Quarantine, 1970; Barrier World (science fiction), 1970; (as Carter Travis Young), The Pocket Hunters, 1972; (as Carter Travis Young), Winter of the Coup, 1972; (as Carter Travis Young), The Captive, 1973; (as Carter Travis Young), Guns of Darkness, 1974; (as Carter Travis Young), Blaine's Law, 1974; From a Dark Place, 1974; Embryo (novelization of SF screenplay), 1976; (as Carter Travis Young), Red Grass, 1976; Intruder, 1979; The Lair, 1979; (as Carter Travis Young), Winter Drift, 1980; The Brea File, 1983. *Address:* c/o Scott Meredith Literary Agency, 845 Third Avenue, New York, NY 10022, USA.

CHARD Dorothy Doreen (Judy), b. 8 May 1916, Tuffley, Gloucestershire, England. Author; Freelance Journalist, Broadcaster. m. Maurice Noel Chard, 26 July 1941. *Appointments:* Editor, Devon Life Magazine, 4 years; Tutor, Creative Writing, Devon County Council & WEA; Director of Studies with David and Charles Correspondence College, now Writers College, Northumbria; Critic for Second Opinion on short stories for South West Arts, 1991; Broadcaster, BBC and Local Radio. *Publications:* Through the Green Woods, 1974; The Weeping and the Laughter, 1975; Encounter in Berlin, 1976; The Uncertain Heart, 1977; The Other Side of Sorrow, 1978; In the Heart of Love, 1979; Out of the Shadow, 1980; All Passion Spent, 1981; Seven Lonely Years, 1982; The Darkening Skies, 1982; When the Journey's Over, 1983; Haunted by the Past, 1984; Sweet Love Remembered, 1985; Where the Dream Begins, 1985; Rendevous with Love, 1986; Hold Me in Your Heart, 1987; Live with Fear, 1987; Wings of the Morning, 1987; A Time to Love, 1987, also on Audio Cassette; For Love's Sake, To Be So Loved; Enchantment; Person Unknown; Appointment with Danger, 1988-91; Seven local books on Devon, The Devon Guide; Traditional Cooking. *Contributions include:* Magazines, National & Local Newspapers, Heritage Magazine; Regular Broadcaster with BBC and Commercial Radio. *Address:* Morley Farm, Highweek, Newton Abbot, Devon TQ12 6NA, England.

CHARLES Nicholas. *See:* **KUSKIN Karla Seidman.**

CHARLES Searle F, b. 1923, American. *Appointments:* Assistant Dean for Instruction, Flint Community Junior College, 1956-62; Dean of College 1962-66, President 1966-69, Eastern Connecticut State College; Executive Director, Board of Trustees, Regional Community Colleges, Hartford, CT, 1970-. *Publications:* Minister of Relief: Harry L Hopkins and the Depression, 1963, 1974; Balancing State and Local Control (ed), 1978.

CHARLIER Roger Henri, (Henry Rochard), b. 10 Nov 1921, Antwerp, Belgium. University Professor. m. Patricia Mary Simonet, 17 June 1958, 1 son, 1 daughter. *Education:* PhD, Erlangen, 1947; LittD, 1956, ScD, 1958, Paris; Lic Sci, 1945, Lic Pol Sci, 1941, Brussels; B Sci geol, 1942, B Sci Geogr, 1943, Liege. *Appointments:* Contributing Editor, Hexagon, 1962; Consulting Editor, Ocean Abstracts, 1965; Consultant Editor, Foreign Language Quarterly, 1956. *Publications:* I Was a Male War Bride, 1948; For the Love of Kate, 1962; Marine Science and Technology, 1970; Marine Resources, 1968; Tidal Energy, 1982; Ocean Energies, 1990; Pensees, 1965; The World Around Us, 1966; The Physical Environment, 1964. *Contributions to:* Over 600 Literary, Political and Scientific articles in magazines and journals. *Honours:* Prize Francois Franck, 1939; National Academy of Arts Sciences and Fine Letters, France, 1973; Knight Order of Leopold Belgium, 1973; Knight of the Order of Academic Palms, France, 1973; Grand Medal of Arts Letters and Sciences, France, 1971; Presidential Award, 1980; Publication Award, University Foundation, Belgium, 1989. *Memberships:* Geological Society of America; American Association Advancement of Science; New Jersey Academy of Science, President, 1957-59. *Literary Agent:* Hollywood; New York. *Address:* 4055 North Keystone Avenue, Chicago, IL 60641, USA.

CHARLIP Remy, b. 1929, American. *Appointments:* Choreographer, London Contemporary Dance Theatre, 1972-76; Choreographer, Scottish Theatre Ballet, 1973, Welsh Dance Theatre, 1974; Director, Remy Charlip Dance Company, NY, 1977-; Director, The All Star International Dance Company. *Publications:* Dress Up and Let's Have a Party, 1956; Where Is Everybody?, 1957; It Looks Like Snow, 1962, 1982; Fortunately, 1964; Mother Mother I Feel Sick Send for the Doctor Quick Quick Quick (with Burton Supree), 1966; I Love You, 1967, 1981; Arm in Arm, Harlequin and the Gift of Many Colors (with Burton Supree), 1973; The Tree Angel (with Judith Martin); Jumping Beans (with Judith Martin); Handtalk: An ABC of Finger Spelling and Sign Language (with Mary Beth), 1974; Thirteen (with J Joyner), Hooray for Me, 1975; Arm in Arm, 1980; I Love You, 1981; It Looks Like Snow, 1982; First Remy Charlip Reader, 1986; Handtalk Birthday: A Number and Storybook in Sign Language (with Mary Beth), 1987. *Address:* 60 East 7th Street, New York, NY 10003, USA.

CHARNAS Suzy McKee, b. 1939, American. *Appointments:* Formerly English and History Teacher for the Peace Corporations in Nigeria; Teacher, New Lincoln School; Worker for Community Mental Health Organisation, NYC; Freelance Writer, 1969-; Judge, James Tiptree Award, first year, 1991. *Publications:* Walk to the End of the World, 1974; Motherlines, 1979; The Vampire Tapestry, 1980; The Bronze King, 1985; Dorothea Dreams, 1986; The Silver Glove, 1988; THe Golden Thread, 1989; The Kingdom of Kevin Malone, 1993; Stage Play - Vampire Dreams performed (premier), Magic Theatre, San Francisco, 1990. *Address:* 520 Cedar North East, Albuquerque, NM 87106, USA.

CHARTERS Samuel Barclay, b. 1 Aug 1929, Pittsburgh, Pennsylvania, USA. Writer; Music Producer. m. Ann Danberg, 19 Mar 1959, 1 son, 2 daughters. *Education:* AB, University of California. *Publications:* The Country Blues, 1959; The Poetry of the Blues, 1963; The Roots of the Blues, 1981; Mr Jabi and Mr Smythe, 1983; Jelly Roll Morton's Last Night, 1984; Louisiana Black, 1987; Elvis Presley Calls his Mother, 1992; A Country Year (Memoir), 1992; Several collections of poetry; I Love, Biography; Jazz, The New York Scene, Music History; Translations from the Swedish of Tomas

Transtromer, Bo Carpelan and Edith Sodergran. *Contributions to:* Numerous. *Honours:* Deems Taylor Award for Excellence in Writing on Music, 1984; Artur Lundqvist Translation Award, 1984. *Address:* c/o Gazell Music, Box 20055, S-16102 Bromma, Sweden.

CHARYN Jerome, b. 1937, USA. Author; Educator. *Appointments:* English Teacher, High School of Music and Art, and School of Performing Arts, New York City, 1962-64; Assistant Professor of English, Stanford University, California, 1965-68; Professor of English, Herbert Lehman College, City University of New York, 1968-80; Founding Editor, The Dutton Review, New York City, 1970; Lecturer in Creative Writing, Princeton University, New Jersey, 1980-86. *Publications:* Once Upon a Droshky, 1964; On the Darkening Green, 1965; The Man Who Grew Younger and Other Stories, 1967; Going to Jerusalem, 1967; American Scrapbook, 1969; The Single Voice: An Anthology of Contemporary Fiction (editor), 1969; The Troubled Vision (editor), 1970; Eisenhower, My Eisenhower, 1971; The Tar Baby, 1973; Blue Eyes, 1975; The Education of Patrick Silver, 1976; Marilyn the Wild, 1976; The Franklin Scare, 1977; Secret Isaac, 1978; The Seventh Babe, 1979; The Catfish Man, 1980; Darlin' Bill, 1980; Panna Maria, 1982; Pinocchio's Nose, 1983; The Isaac Quartet, 1984; War Cries Over Avenue C, 1985, Metropolis, 1986; Paradise Man, 1987; Movieland, 1989; The Good Policeman, 1990; Elsinore, 1991; Marias' Girls, 1992. *Memberships:* American PEN; Mystery Writers of America; International Association of Crime Writers, Executive Board of all three. *Literary Agent:* George Borchardt. *Address:* 302 West 12th Street, Apt 10-c , New York NY 10014, USA.

CHASE Elaine Raco, b. 31 Aug 1949, Schenectady, USA. Author. m. Gary Dale Chase, 26 Oct 1969, 1 son, 1 daughter. *Publications:* Rules of the Game, 1980; Tender Yearnings, 1981; A Dream Come True, 1982; Double Occupancy, 1982; Designing Woman, 1982; No Easy Way Out, 1983; Video Vixen, 1983; Calculated Risk, 1983; Best Laid Plans, 1983; Special Delivery, 1984, Lady Be Bad, 1984; Dangerous Places, 1987; Dare the Devil, 1987; Dark Corners, 1988; Rough Edges; Best of Elaine Raco Chase, Vol 1, 1991, Vol 2 and Vol 3, 1992, Vol 4, 1993. *Contributions to:* Love's Leading Ladies and How to Write a Romance (Kathryn Falk), Lovelines (Rosemary Guiley), So You Want a TV Career, Fine Art of Murder. *Honours;* Walden Book Award, 1985; Top Romantic Suspense Series Award (Rave Reviews), 1987-88. *Memberships:* Romance Writers of America, Sisters in Crime National, Publicity Chair. *Literary Agent:* Denise Marcil Agency. *Address:* 4333 Majestic Lane, Fairfax, VA 22033-3538, USA.

CHASE Isabel. *See:* **DE GUISE Elizabeth (Mary Teresa).**

CHATTERTON-NEWMAN Roger (Holmes), b. 17 Mar 1949, Haslemere, Surrey, England. Author. *Appointments:* Editorial Staff, Haymarket Publishing, 1970-88. *Publications include:* A Hampshire Parish, 1976; Brian Boru, King of Ireland, 1983; Murtagh & The Vikings, 1986; Betwixt Petersfield and Midhurst, 1991; Edward Bruce: A Medieval Tragedy, 1992; Polo at Cowdray (with Derek Russell-Stoneham), 1992. *Contributor to:* Hampshire Magazine; Cricket World; Horse and Hound; The Countryman; Gardeners Chronicle. *Address:* Rose Cottage, Rake, West Sussex GU33 7JA, England.

CHAWLA Jasbir, b. 20 June 1953, Etawah, India. Government Servant. m. Ravinder Kaur, 15 Oct 1980, 2 daughters, 1 son. *Education:* Diploma, Russian, 1974; BTech, Metallurgical Engineering, 1975, MBA, 1990; Diploma, French, 1991. *Appointments:* Member, Editorial Panel, Ispat- Vikas, 1984. *Publications:* Chernobyl, 1989; Roti Ki Gandh, 1990; Halafnama, 1991; Eh Nahin Awaz Khalistan Ki, 1991; Niche Wali Chitkhani, 1992; Punjab: Dararen Aurdalal, 1992; Janta Jaan Gayi, 1992. *Contributions to:* Dharmyng; Saptahik Hindustan; Pahal; Other literary Hindi, Bengali, Panjabi

and English magazines; Journal of Institution of Engineers; Avishkar; Ispat Vikas; Other technical journals; Regular programmes with all India Radio and Doordarshan Centres in India. *Honours:* Award, Central Hindi Directorate, 1991; Diploma, Excellence for Poetry, International Section, Scottish International Open Poetry Competition. *Memberships:* Authors Guild of India; PEN; Indian Institute of Metals; Institution of Engineers. *Address:* 247 Defence Colony, Jalandhar City 144001, India.

CHEE R. *See:* **WELLER Archie Irving Kirkwood.**

CHELES Luciano, b. 7 Sept 1948, Cairo, Egypt. University Lecturer. *Education:* BA, Reading University, 1973; PGCE, Cardiff University, 1974; M Phil, Essex University, 1980; PhD, Lancaster University, 1992. *Publications:* The Studiolo of Urbino: An Iconographic Investigation; Neo-Fascism in Europe. *Contributions to:* Women in Italy; Atlante di Schifanoia; Le Muse E Il Principe; Mots; Art Pouvoir Et Affichage; Artension. *Memberships:* Society for Italian Studies; Society for Renaissance Studies; Istituto di Studi Rinascimentali; Association for the Study of Modern Italy. *Address:* Department of Modern Languages, Italian Studies, Lonsdale College, Lancaster University, Lancaster LA1 4YN, England.

CHELLAPPAN Kasiviswanathan, b. 11 Apr 1936, Pagneri, India. Professor of English. *Education:* MA, English, Annamalai, 1958; Diploma, Teaching of English, Manchester, 1965; PhD, Madurai, 1975. *Appointments:* Editor, Tamil Language Section, Dakshina, Sahitya Akademi of India Annual, 1990. *Publications:* Shakespeare and Ilango as Tragedians, 1985; Towards Creative Unity: Tagore, Bharathi and T S Eliot, Bharathi, the Visionary Humanist, 1988; Translations: History of the Growth and Tamil in Freedom Movement, 1979; History of the Freedom Movement in Tamil, 1988; Kuraloviyom, 1990; In Tamil: Enkenku Kaninum Sakthi, 1981; Ilakkiyathil Pazham Pudumaiyum, Puthup Pazhmaiyum, 1986; Oppival Tamil, 1987. *Contributions to:* 60 articles to New Helicon, Indian Literature, New Comparison, and others; 10 articles to: The Hinustan Times; The Hindu; Others. *Honours:* Best University Teacher Award, 1985; Honoured for services to Tamil, Tamil Nadu Government, 1988; Silver Jubilee Fellowship, Regional Institute of English, 1988. *Memberships:* International Comparative Literature Association; British Comparative Literature Association; Vice-President, Indian National Comparative Literature Association; International Shakespeare Association; All India English Teachers Association. *Address:* Department of English, Bharathidasan University, Trichy 620 024, Tamil Nadu, India.

CHELTON John. *See:* **DURST Paul.**

CHENG Tsu-yu, b. 18 Mar 1916, China. Professor (Senior Research Fellow). m. Ting Kwee Choo, 1944, 1 son. *Education:* Diploma of Rhetoric, Institute of Language Teaching of Waseda University, Tokyo, Japan, 1964-65. *Appointments:* Visiting Professor, The Graduate Division of Literature, Waseda University, Tokyo, Japan, 1964-65; Full Professor, The Daito Bunka University, Tokyo, Japan, 1978-80; Visiting Professor, Amoy University, 1986-. Senior Research Fellow, The Institute of Chinese Studies, The Chinese University of Hong Kong, Hong Kong, 1984-; Visiting Professor, Peking University, 1992-. *Publications include:* Poetry and Poetics of Lu Xun (Hong Kong 1951); Criticism of the Works of Huang Zunxian (Hong Kong 1959); Tokyo Lectures (Singapore 1963); Evolution of Chinese Rhetoric (Tokyo 1965); Sinological Research in Japan (Hong Kong 1972); The History of Chinese Rhetoric (Shanghai 1984, Taipei 1990. *Contributions to:* Journal of the Peking University; Journal of the Fudan University (Shanghai); Journal of the Waseda University, Tokyo, Japan; Journal of the South Seas Society, Singapore. *Honours:* Advisory Professor at Fudan University (Shanghai) 1986-; Advisor, South China Rhetorical

Society (Shanghai) 1986-; Honorary Councillor, China Rhetorical Society, Peking, 1987. *Memberships:* China Society, Singapore; Member, Councillor, Hon Secretary, Editor (1949-62), South Seas Society. *Address:* Institute of Chinese Studies, The Chinese University of Hong Kong, Shatin, NT. Hong Kong.

CHERCHES Peter, b. 8 Mar 1956, Brooklyn, New York, USA. *Education:* MFA, 1981. *Publications:* Condensed Book; Between A Dream And A Cup of Coffee. *Contributions to:* Harper's; Fiction International; Transatlantic Review; The Big Book of New American Humor. *Honours:* NY Foundation for the Arts Fellowship. *Address:* 195 Garfield Place, Brooklyn, NY 11215, USA.

CHERNAK Judith Esterson, (Judy Chernak), b. 15 Jan 1936, Baltimore, MD. Writer; Composer; Pianist; Singer; Audio Materials Producer; Owner & President. m. Theodore N Chernak, 9 June 1954, 2 sons, 2 daughters *Education:* Peabody Institute, 1952; Baltimore Hebrew College, 1952; Towson State University. *Appointments:* Administrator, Producer, Home Start Program for Baltimore Board of Jewish Education, 1982-83. *Publications:* Five Stories From The Aleph-Bet Story Book (cassette); K'tonton in Israel Read-Along Book & Cassette Series; Editor: The Complete Jewish Wedding Planner; The Mysterious Chanukah Candles; The Miraculous Matzah Balls; Combat Communications; Getting What's Yours; Grenada Eyewitnesses; Poetry in Baltimore Evening Sun. *Memberships:* National League of American Pen Women; Baltimore Writers Alliance. *Literary Agent:* S J Clark. *Address:* Judy Chernak Productions, 3114 Hatton Road, Pikesville, MD 21208, USA.

CHERNOFF Maxine, b. 24 Feb 1952, Chicago, IL, USA. Writer; Professor; Editor. m. Paul Hoover, 5 Oct 1974, 2 sons, 1 daughter. *Education:* BA, MA, University of Illinois. *Appointments:* Creative Writing Instructor, Columbia College, Chicago, 1979-85; Associate Professor of Communications, 1980-; Adjunct Associate Professor, School of The Art Institute of Chicago, 1988-. *Publications:* Plain Grief; Bop; Leap Year Day: New & Selected Poems; New Faces of 1952. *Contributions to:* The Paris Review; New Directious; Partisan Review; Sulfur; Caliban; Triquarterly; Mississippi Review; New York Times Book Review. *Honours:* Illinois Arts Council Literary Fellowship; Carl Sandburg Award; Friends of American Writers Fiction Award; LSU Southern Review Short Fiction Award. *Memberships:* Poetry Center, School of The Art Institute; MLA; CCLP; AWP. *Literary Agent:* Amanda Urban. *Address:* 2920 W Pratt, Chicago, IL, 60645, USA.

CHERRY Carolyn Janice, (C J Cherryh), b. 1 Sept 1942, St Louis, Missouri, USA. Writer. *Education:* BA Oklahoma University, 1964; MA, Classics, Johns Hopkins University, Baltimore, Maryland, 1965. *Publications include:* Downbelow Station, 1981; Cyteen, 1989; The Faded Sun, 1976; Rusalka, 1989; 40,000 in Gehenna, 1983; Cuckoo's Egg, 1985; The Paladin, 1988; Rimrunners, 1989; Chernevog, 1990. *Honours:* John Campbell Award, 1977; Hugo Award, Short Story 1979; Hugo Award, Novel, 1982 and 1989. *Memberships:* Science Fiction Writers Association (Secretary); National Space Society (Board of Advisors). *Literary Agent:* Curtis Brown Ltd, New York City, New York, USA.

CHERRY Gordon Emanuel, b. 6 Feb 1931, Barnsley, England. Town Planning Consultant; Professor Eneritus. m. Margaret Mary London Cox, 8 June 1957, 1 son, 2 daughters. *Education:* BA, London, 1953; DSc, Heriotwatt, 1984. *Publications:* Town PLanning In Its Social Context; Urban Change And Planning; The Evolution of British Town Planning; Environmental Planning; The Politics of Town Planning; Cities and Plans *Contributions to:* Planning Perspectives; Studies in History, Planning and the Environment. *Memberships:* Royal Town Planning Institute; Royal Isntitute of Chartered Surveyors; Royal Society of Arts. *Address:*

Quaker Ridge, 66 Meriden Road, Hampton In Arden, Solihull, West Midlands, BG2 0BT, England.

CHERRY Kelly, Writer; Professor, Bascom Professor of English, 1993-. m. Jonathan B Silver, 23 Dec 1966, div. 1969. *Education:* Du Pont Fellow, Philosophy, University of Virginia, 1961-63; MFA, University of North Carolina, 1967. *Appointments include:* Elected, Board of Directors, Associated Writing Programs; Member, Discipline Advisory Committee, Fulbright Awards. *Publications:* Fiction: Sick and Full of Burning, 1974; Augusta Played, 1979; Conversion, 1979; In the Wink of an Eye, 1983; The Lost Traveller's Dream, 1984; My Life and Dr Joyce Brothers, 1990; Poetry: Lovers and Agnostics, 1975; Relativity, 1977; Songs for a Soviet Composer, 1980; Natural Theology, 1988; Benjamin John, 1993; God's Loud Hand, 1993; The Exiled Heart, non-fiction, 1991; Octavia (Seneca), translation, forthcoming. *Contributions to:* Atlantic; Commentary; Ms; Esquire; New Literary History; American Scholar; Virginia Quarterly Review; Southern Review; Mademoiselle; Redbook; Others. *Honours include:* Best American Short Stories, 1972; Pushcart Prize, 1977; National Endowment for the Arts Fellowship, 1979; Wisconsin Arts Board Fellowships, 1984, 1989; Hanes Poetry Prize, Fellowship of Southern Writers, 1989; Arts America Speaker Award, 1992. *Address:* English Department, University of Wisconsin, Madison, WI 53706, USA.

CHERRYH C J. *See:* **CHERRY Carolyn Janice.**

CHESHER Kim, b. 1955, United Kingdom. Children's Fiction Writer. *Appointments:* Editorial Trainee, Hamish Hamilton Children's Books, London, 1975-76; Plays Assistant, Evans Bros, London, 1978-81. *Publications:* The Fifth Quarter, 1976; Cuthbert series, 5 vols, 1976-82; The Carnford Inheritance, 1977; The Finn Bequest, 1978. *Address:* c/o Hamish Hamilton Ltd, 57-59 Long Acre, London WC2E 9JZ, England.

CHESTER Tessa Rose, b. 19 Oct 1950, Stanmore, Middlesex, England. Museum Curator. m. (1) Richard James Overy, 18 Apr 1969, 1 son, 2 daughters. (2) Ronald Albert Chester, 8 Aug 1980. *Education:* North London Collegiate School, 1957-68; Harrow Art College, 1968-69; Polytechnic of North London, BA, 1977-81. *Appointments:* Curator of Childrens Books, Bethnal Green Museum of Childhood, London, 1984-. *Publications:* A History of Childrens Book Illustration; Childrens Books Research; Sources of Information About Childrens Books. *Contributions to:* Times Educational Supplement; Phaedrus; International Review of Childrens Literature & Librarianship; Galleries; The Library; Signal; Country Life. *Memberships:* Childrens Books History Society; Beatrix Potter Society; Poetry Society; British Haiku Society; William Morris Society; Library Association; World Foundation of Successful Women. *Address:* Bethnal Green Museum of Childhood, Cambridge Heath Road, London E2 9PA, England.

CHILDS Bette, (Bette Paul), b. 9 June 1935, Yorkshire, England. Writer; Teacher. *Education:* Froebel Diploma, 1956; LGSM, Drama, 1960; BEd Hons, 1983. *Publications:* Ladlass, 1991; Unlucky Lucky, 1991; Becca's Race, 1992; Step This Way; Doone House Mystery. *Contributions to:* Stories to Playday Magazine; Occasional articles to Times Educational Supplement; Regular articles to Report, 1988-90; Regular column, Sheffield Telegraph, 1989-92. *Memberships:* Founder, Higham Writers; Friend of Arvon Foundation; Society of Authors; East Midland Arts Literary Register. *Literary Agent:* Lesley Hadcroft, Laurence Pollinger. *Address:* Higham House, Higham, Alfreton, Derbyshire DE 55 6EM, England.

CHILDS David Haslam, b. 25 Sept 1933, Bolton, England. University Professor. m. 13 June 1964, 2 sons. *Education:* BSc (Econ) London University, 1956; British Council Scholarship, Hamburg University, 1956-57;

PhD, London University, 1962. *Appointments:* Editor, PASGAS - Politics and Society in Germany, Austria and Switzerland, 1988-92. *Publications include:* GDR Moscow's German Ally (2nd edition 1988); Britain since 1945 (3rd edition 1992); Germany since 1918 (2nd edition 1980); Marx and the Marxists, 1973; East Germany, 1969; East Germany to the 1990s (1987); West Germany Politics and Society (2nd edition 1981); Germany on the Road to Unity, 1990; Germany in the 20th Century, 1991. *Contributions to:* Contemporary Review; Current History; Journal of Contemporary History; THES; TLS; TES; Guardian; Independent; Daily Telegraph; World Today and books. *Honours:* Fellow of the Royal Society of Arts (RSA). *Memberships:* Association for the Study of German Politics, Chairman 1981-86, Secretary 1986-88, Committee 1981-; Anglo-German Association, Executive Committee 1987-; Member: AUT; German History Society; European Movement; Member: BASSEES - British Association of Soviet, Slavonic and East European Studies. *Address:* Department of Politics, University of Nottingham, Nottingham NG7 2RD, England.

CHILVER Peter, b. 1933, United Kingdom. Educator. *Appointments:* Teacher, Inner London Education Authority, 1964-68; Senior Lecturer in Drama, Thomas Huxley College, London, 1968-77; Head of English Department, Langdon School, London, 1977-. *Publications:* Improvised Drama, 1967; Talking: Discussion, Improvement and Debate in Schools, 1968; Stories for Improvisation, 1969; Producing the Play, 1974; Teaching Improvised Drama, 1978; Learning and Language in the Classroom (with G Gould), 1982; In the Picture series, 1985; English Coursework for GCSE, 1987. *Contributions to:* Perspectives on Small Group Learning, 1990. *Address:* 27 Cavendish Gardens, Barking, Essex, England.

CHINERY Michael, b. 1938, United Kingdom. Author. *Publications:* Pictorial Dictionary of the Animal World, 1966; Human Kind (with Michael Gabb), 1966; The World of Plants (with Michael Gabb), 1966; Patterns of Living (with David Larkin), 1966; The Life of Animals with Backbones (with Michael Gabb), 1966; The Life of Animals without Backbones (with Michael Gabb), 1966; Breeding and Growing, 1966; Pictorial Dictionary of the Plant World, 1967; Visual Biology, 1968; Purnell's Concise Encyclopedia of Nature, 1971; Animal Communities, 1972; Animals in the Zoo, 1973; Field Guide to the Insects of Britain and Northern Europe, 1973; Life in the Zoo, 1976; The Natural History of the Garden, 1977; The Family Naturalist, 1977; Nature All Around, 1978; Discovering Animals, 1978; Killers of the Wild, 1979; Garden Birds (with Maurice Pledger), 1979; Collins Gem Guide to Butterflies and Moths, 1981; The Natural History of Britain and Europe, 1982; Collins Guide to the Insects of Britain and Western Europe, 1986; Garden Creepy Crawlies, 1986; The Living Garden, 1986; Collins Gem Guide to Insects, 1986; Exploring the Countryside, 1987; Butterflies and Day-flying Moths of Britain and Europe, 1989; All About Baby Animals, 1989; Countryside Handbook, 1990; Shark; Butterfly; Ant; Spider; Snake; Frog (six children's books, with photographs by Barry Watts), 1991; All About Wild Animals, 1991; Explore the World of Insects, 1991; Wild World of Animals: Rainforests, 1991; Wild World of Animals: Oceans, 1991; Wild World of Animals: Deserts, 1991; Wild World of Animals: Grassland and Prairies, 1991; The Kingfisher Natural History of Britain and Europe, 1992; Wild World of Animals: Seashores, 1992; Wild World of Animals: Forests 1992; Wild World of Animals: Polar Lands, 1992; Wild World of Animals: Lakes and Rivers, 1992. *Address:* Mousehole, Mill Road, Hundon, Suffolk CO10 8EG, England.

CHISSELL Joan Olive, b. 22 May 1919, Cromer, Norfolk, England. Musicologist. *Education:* ARCM; GRSM, Royal College of Music, 1937-42. *Appointments:* Piano teacher, Junior Department, Royal College of Music, 1942-53; Lecturer in Music for Extra-Mural Departments Oxford and London Universities, 1942-48; Assistant Music Critic, The Times, 1948-79; Reviewer, The Gramophone, 1968-; Broadcaster, BBC, 1943-; Jury Member at International Piano Competitions in Milan, Leeds, Zwickau, Budapest, Sydney and Dublin. *Publications:* Robert Schumann, 1948; Chopin, 1965; Schumann's Piano Music, 1972; Brahms, 1977; Clara Schumann: A Dedicated Spirit, 1983. *Contributions to:* A Companion to the Concerto, 1988, and numerous journals and magazines. *Honour:* Awarded Robert Schumann Prize by City of Zwickau, 1991. *Memberships:* The Critics Circle; RCM Union; Royal Life Boat Society. *Literary Agent:* David Higham Associates. *Address:* Flat D, 7 Abbey Road, St John's Wood, London NW8 9AA, England.

CHITHAM Edward Harry Gordon, b. 16 May 1932, Harborne, Birmingham, England. Education Consultant. m. Mary Patricia Tilley, 29 Dec 1962, 1 son 2 daughters. *Education:* BA, MA (Classics), Jesus College, Cambridge, 1952-55; PGCE, University of Birmingham, 1955-56; MA, English, University of Warwick, 1973-77 part-time; PhD, University of Sheffield, 1978- 83. *Publications:* Ghost in the Water, 1972; The Black Country, 1973; The Poems of Anne Brontë, 1979; Brontë Facts and Brontë Problems (with T J Winnifrith), 1983; Selected Brontë Poems (with T J Winnifrith), 1985; The Brontës' Irish Background, 1986; A Life of Emily Brontë, 1987; Charlotte and Emily Brontë (Macmillans Literary Lives, with T J Winnifrith) 1989; A Life of Anne Brontë, 1991. *Contributions to:* Byron Journal, Gaskell Society Journal, ISIS Magazine. *Memberships:* Brontë Society; Gaskell Society; Joint Association of Classics Teachers. *Address:* 11 Victoria Road, Harborne, Birmingham B17 0AG, England.

CHITNIS Anand Chidamber, b. 4 Apr 1942, Birmingham, England. Principal. m. Bernice Anne, 4 July 1970, 2 sons, 1 daughter. *Education:* Stonyhurst College, Lancashire, 1949-60; University of Birmingham, BA, 1960-63; University of Kansas, MA, 1963-65; University of Edinburgh, PhD, 1965-68. *Publications:* The Scottish Enlightenment: A Social History; Early Victorian English Society. *Contributions to:* Anuals of Science; Enlightenment Essays; Medical History; Studies in Voltaire and the Eighteenth Century. *Honours:* Fellowship of the Royal Historical Society. *Memberships:* Catholic Union of Great Britain; British Society for 18th Century studies; Eighteenth Century Scottish Studies Society. *Literary Agent:* David Higham Associates. *Address:* LSU College of Higher Education, The Avenue, Southampton, SO9 5HB, England.

CHITTOCK John Dudley, b. 29 May 1928. Writer; producer. m. Joyce Kate Winter, 23 Aug 1947. South West Essex Technical College. *Appointments:* Executive Editor, Focal Press, 1954-58; Part-time Editor, Industrial Screen, 1962-63; Film and Video Columnist, Financial Times, 1963-87; Founder/Publisher, Screen Digest 1971-, Editor 1971-74; Inaugural Editor of Vision (British Academy of Film and Television Arts), 1976; Founder/Publisher, Training Digest 1978-87; Consultant Editor, Television - Journal of the Royal Television Society 1978-82. *Publications:* Executive editor, Focal Encyclopedia of Photography, 1956; Images of Britain, 1986; Film and Effect, 1967; Executive Editor, An International Directory of Stock shot Libraries, 1969; Editor, A Long Look at Short Films, 1967; How to Produce Magnetic Sound for Films, 1962. *Honours:* Hood Medal of Royal Photographic Society, 1973; Presidential Award of the Incorporated Institute of Professional Photography, 1983; Video Writer of the Year Award, 1983; Queen's Silver Jubilee Medal, 1977; Officer of the Order of the British Empire, 1982. *Memberships:* Fellow, Royal Photographic Society; Fellow, British Kinematograph, Sound and Television Society, 1976; Fellow, Royal Television Society, 1983; Fellow, Royal Society of Arts, 1985. *Address:* 37 Gower Street, London WC1E 6HH, England.

CHITTY Susan, b. 18 Aug 1929. Freelance Writer, Lecturer and Journalist. *Publications:* The Diary of a Fashion Model, 1958; Editor, The Intelligent Woman's Guide to Good Taste, 1958; White Huntress, 1963; My Life and Horses, 1966; The Woman Who Wrote Black Beauty, 1971; The Beast and the Monk: A Life of Charles

Kingsley, 1975; On Next to Nothing (with Thomas Hinde), 1975; Charles Kingsley's Landscape, 1976; (with Thomas Hinde), The Great Donkey Walk, 1977; The Young Rider, 1979; Gwen John, 1981; Now To My Mother, 1985; Edward Lear, 1988; Davies of Antonia White (editor), 1991, 1992. *Address;* Bow Cottage, West Hoathly, Sussex, RH19 4QF, England.

CHITTY Thomas Willes, Sir, (Thomas Hinde) b. 1926. Author. *Publications:* Mr. Nicholas, 1952; Happy as Larry, 1957; For the Good of the Company, 1961; A Place Like Home, 1962; The Cage, 1962; Spain: A Personal Anthology, 1963; Ninety Double Martinis, 1963; The Day the Call Came, 1964; Games of Chance: The Interviewer and the Investigator, 1965; The Village, 1966; High, 1968; Bird, 1970; Generally a Virgin, 1972; Agent, 1974; Our Father, 1975; On Next to Nothing (with Susan Hinde), 1975; The Great Donkey Walk (with Susan Chitty), 1977; The Cottage Book, 1979; Sir Henry and Sons: A Memoir, 1981; Daymare, 1981; Field Guide to the Country Parson, 1983; Stately Gardens of Britain, 1983; Forests of Britain, 1985; Capability Brown: biography, Courtiers, 1986; Tales from the Pump Room, 1988; Imps of Promise, 1990; Looking-Glass Letters, 1991; Paths of Progress, 1993. *Address:* Bow Cottage, West Hoathly, Sussex, RH19 4QF, England.

CHIU Hungdah, b. 1936. Chinese. Writer on History, International relations/Current affairs, Law. Professor of Law. *Appointments:* Associate Professor of International Law, National Taiwan University, 1965-66; Research Associate in Law, Harvard Law School, Cambridge, Massachusetts, USA, 1966-70 and 1972-74; Professor of Law, National Chengchi University, Taipei, Taiwan, 1970-72; Associate Professor 1974-77, Professor of Law 1977-, University of Maryland School of Law, Baltimore, Maryland, USA; Editor-in-Chief, Chinese Yearbook of International Law and Affairs, vols 1-11, 1981-93. *Publications:* The Capacity of International Organization to Conclude Treaties, 1966; (ed with D M Johnston), Agreements of the People's Republic of China, 1949-67: A Calendar, 1968; The People's Republic of China and the Law of Treaties, 1972; (contributor and editor with S C Leng), Law in Chinese Foreign Policy, 1972; (editor and contributor), China and the Question of Taiwan: Documents and Analysis, 1973; (with Jerome Alan Cohen), People's China and International Law: A Documentary Study, 2 vols, 1974; (editor with D Simon), Legal Aspects of US-Republic of China Trade and Investment, 1977; (ed) Normalizing Relations with the People's Republic of China: Problems, Analysis and Socuments, 1978; (editor and contributor), China and the Taiwan Issue, 1979; (editor with K Murphy), The Chinese Connection and Normalization, 1980; Agreements of the People's Republic of China: A Calendar of Events, 1966-80, 1981; (editor with R Downen), Multi-System Nations and International Law, 1981; (contributor and editor with S C Leng), China, 70 Years After the 1911 Hsin-hai Revolution, 1984; (with S C Leng), Criminal Justice in Post-Mao China, 1985; (co-editor), The Future of Hong Kong: Towards 1997 and Beyond, 1987; (with Gary Knight), International Law of the Sea: Cases, Documents and Readings, 1991. *Address:* University of Maryland School of Law, 500 West Baltimore Street, Baltimore, MD 21201, USA.

CHODES John Jay, b. 23 Feb 1939, New York City, New York, USA. Writer. *Education:* Commercial Photographer Certificate, Germain School of Photography. *Appointments:* Technical Advisor to Dustin Hoffman in Paramount Pictures film Marathon Man. *Publications:* The Myth of America's Military Power, 1972; Corbitt, 1973; Bruce Jenner, 1977; Chapter, Work and Employment in Liberal Democratic Societies, 1990; Plays: Avenue A Anthology, 1969; Molineaux, 1979; Frederick Two, 1985; The Longboat, 1987. *Contributions to:* Articles on education, politics or social issues in: The New York Times; New York City Tribune; Reason; The Freeman; The Pragmatist; Chronicles. *Honours:* Journalistic Excellence Award for Corbitt Sports Biography, Road Runners Club of America, 1974; Outstanding Service Award, Libertarian

Party of New York, 1988. *Memberships:* Dramatists Guild; Professors World Peace Academy; Road Runners Club of New York; Vice-Chairman, Libertarian Party of New York. *Literary Agent:* Charles Rywick. *Address:* 411 East 10th Street 22-G, New York, NY 10009, USA.

CHOI Jin Young, b. 29 Mar 1937, Korea. University Professor. m. Kim Jung Ju, 4 Sept 1963, 1 son, 2 daughters. *Education:* BA, College of Liberal Arts, Seoul National University, 1959; MA, University of North Carolina, 1963; PhD, Seoul National University, 1984. *Appointments:* Columnist, Korea Herald, 1985-91. *Publications:* Theodore Dreiser; Sister Carrie; The English Novel; One Womans Way; A Study of Theodore Dreiser; The Wind and the River; Nickel Mountain; With God In Russia, Lord of the Files. *Memberships:* PEN; English Language & Literature Association of Korea; The Hawthorne Society of Korea; The International Steinbeck Society; The Korean Society of Modern British & American Fiction. *Address:* 95 503 Banpa Apts, Sucho Ku, Seoul, Korea 137-049.

CHON Kuttikhat Purushothaman, b. 7 May 1932, India. Government Servant. m. Mythily Chon, 27 Apr 1963, 1 son, 2 daughters. *Education:* Graduate, Philosophy; Diploma, Office Management; Diploma, Materials Management. *Publications:* Remedy the Frauds in Hinduism, 1991; Nair's Mother Pulayi, 1992; Cherumi That of Ezhava, 1992; Simplifying the Alphabetical system in Malayalam; Simplifying the Alphabetical system in Hindi. *Contributions:* On Indology. *Membership:* PEN. *Literary Agent:* Bharatiya Vidhya Bhavan. *Address:* Kuttikhat House, Peringottukara, Trichur, Kerala, India.

CHOPRA Nirmal Tej Singh, b. 1 Apr 1929, India. Publisher. m. Kuldip Kaur, 31 Dec 1953, 2 sons, 1 daughter. *Education:* BA, English, Economics. *Appointments:* Formerly Editor, Society of Singapore Writers Newsletter; Currently: Editor, Singapore Book Publishers Association Newspaper, 1990-; Managing Director, Chopmen Publishers, Singapore. *Publications:* English Revision Papers for School Certificate, 1962; The Pictorial History Textbook (co-author), 1963; English Revision Papers for Secondary School Entrance, 1967; Examination Guide to Shakespeare's Macbeth, 1974; A Revision Course in Shakespeare's Julius Caesar, 1979. *Contributions to:* Articles to: Literary Magazine of Society of Singapore Writers; Singapore Book World. *Memberships:* Former Honorary Secretary, Society of Singapore Writers; Founder Member, President, Singapore Book Publishers Association; Founder Member, former President, Honorary Secretary, Honorary Treasurer, National Book Development Council of Singapore; Rotary Club of Singapore, Director of Community Service. *Address:* Chopmen Publishers, 865 Mountbatten Road, Suite 05-28, Katong Shopping Centre, Singapore 1543.

CHOUKRI Mohamed, b. 25 Mar 1935, Beni Chiker, Morocco. Writer. *Education:* Teacher; Classical Education. *Publications:* Al Hobs Al Hafi, 1973; Jean Genet in Tangier, 1973; Majnoun Al Ouarde, 1978; Tennessee Williamsm in Tangier, 1979; A; Suk Al Dahili, 1985; Al Haima, 1985; Zemen Al Akhtaa, 1992; Translations into 12 languages. *Contributions to:* Al Adab, Beirut; A; Aqlam, Iraq; Al Alam, Morocco; Harper's, USA; Transatlantic, UK; Antheus, USA; Liberation Al Itihade Al Ichtiraki, Morocco; Many others. *Membership:* Moroccan Writers Association. *Literary Agent:* Roberto de Hollanda, Bonn, Germany. *Address:* BP 179, Tanger, Morocco.

CHOYCE Lesley, b. 21 Mar 1951, Riverside, New Jersey, USA. Novelist; Editor; Professor. m. Terry Paul, 19 Aug 1974, 2 daughters. *Education:* BA, Rutgers; MA, Montclair; MA, CUNY. *Appointments:* Editor, Pottersfield Portfolio, 1979-83; Editor, Pottersfield Press, 1979- ; Professor, Dalhousie University, 1986-. *Publications:* The Second Season of Jonas MacPherson; Magnificent Obessions; Avalanche of Ocean; Wavewatch; The End of Ice; Numerous Other Publications. *Contributions to:*

MacLeans; Harrowsmith; Canadian Literature; Fiddlehead. *Honours:* Canadian Science Fiction & Fantasy award; Novel Writers, Nova Scotia Literary Competition; Pierian Spring Editors Award; St John Award of Merit; The Stephen Leacock Award; Dartmouth Book Award; Event Magazine, Creative Nonfiction Competition. *Memberships:* Writers Union of Canada; Writers Federation of Nova Scotia; CANSCAIP; Literary Press Group. *Address:* RR2 Porters Lake, Nova Scotia, Canada B0J 2SO.

CHRIST Henry I, b. 1915, USA. Former Teacher; Writer. *Appointments:* Teacher, 1936-46; Chairman of English, Andrew Jackson High School, St Albans, New York, 1947-70. *Publications:* Winning Words, 1948, 3rd Edition, 1967; Odyssey of Homer (adaptor), 1948, 2nd Edition, 1968; Myths and Folklores, 1952, 2nd Edition, 1968; Modern English in Action 7-12, 1965, 1968, 1975, 1978, 1982; Modern Short Biographies, 1970; Language and Literature, 1972; Short World Biographies, 1973; The World of Sports, 2 vols, 1975, 1977; The Challenge of Sports, 1978; Going Places, 1980; Globe American Biographies, 1987; Globe World Biographies, 1987; English for the College Boards, 1987; Building Power in Writing, 1992; Building Power in Reading; English for the College Boards, Revised Edition, 1992; Greek Tragedies, 1993. *Address:* PO Box 361062, Melbourne, FL 32936, USA.

CHRISTIAN Carol Cathay, b. 15 Nov 1923, Peking, China. Freelance Writer and Editor. m. John Christian, 23 June 1945, 3 sons, 1 daughter. *Education:* BA, magna cum laude, Smith College, Northampton, Massachusetts, USA, 1944. *Publications:* Into Strange Country, 1958; God and One Redhead, Mary Slessor of Calabar, biography with G Plummer, 1970; editor of In The Spirit of Truth, a reader in the work of Frank Lake, 1991; EFL Readers: Great People of Our Time, 1973; More People of Our Time, 1978; Johnny Ring, 1975; (with Diana Christian) Famous Women of the 20th Century, 1982; Save the Goldfish, 1988, and others. *Memberships:* Society of Authors; Clinical Theology Association. *Address:* 22 Pitfold Avenue, Shottermill, Haslemere, Surrey GU27 1PN, England.

CHRISTIAN John. *See:* **DIXON Roger.**

CHRISTIAN Mary Blount, b. 1933. USA, Writer of children's fiction. *Appointments:* Instructor of Creative Writing, Rice University, Continuing Studies; Lecturer; Co-founder, Associated Authors of Children's Literature, Houston, Texas; Correspondence School Teacher; Book Reviewer, The Houston Chronicle; Creator and Moderator, Children's Bookshelf, PBS-TV. *Publications:* The Stitch in Time Solution, 1978; Il a du Flair, Babylas! 1978; The Lucky Man, 1979; The Devil Take You, Barnabas Beane! 1980; Christmas Reflections, 1980; Anna and the Strangers, 1981; Doggone Mystery, 1980; Two Ton Secret, 1981; The Ventriloquist, 1982; The Firebug Mystery, 1982; (co-author), Bible Heroes, Kings and Prophets, 1982; The Green Thumb Thief, 1982; April Fool, 1982; The Double Double Cross, 1982; Sebastian Super Sleuth and the Hair of the Dog Mystery, 1982; Deadline for Danger, 1982; Grandfathers: God's Gift to Children, 1982; Grandmothers: God's Gift to Children, 1982; Just Once, 1982; Microcomputers, 1983; Sebastian (Super Sleuth), and the Bone to Pick Mystery, 1983, 1986; Sebastian (Super Sleuth), and the Crummy Yummies Caper, 1983, 1985; Swamp Monsters, 1983; The Museum Mystery, 1983; Sebastian (Super Sleuth), and the Santa Claus Caper, 1984; Sebastian (Super Sleuth), and the Secret of the Skewered Skier, 1984; Deadman in Catfish Bay, 1985; Everybody Else Is, 1985; Go West, Swamp Monsters! 1985; Growin' Pains, 1985; Mystery at Camp Triumph, 1985; The Mysterious Case Case, 1985; The Toady and Dr Miracle, 1985; Sebastian (Super Sleuth), and the Clumsy Cowboy, 1985; Penrod's Pants, 1986; Sebastian (Super Sleuth), and Purloined Sirloin, 1986; Singin' Somebody Else's Song, 1986. *Address:* 1108 Danbury Road, Houston, TX 77055, USA.

CHRISTIAN Roy Cloberry, b. 8 Oct 1914, Riddings, Derbyshire, England. Lecturer. m. Mary Elizabeth Mansfield, 20 Apr 1940, 1 daughter. *Publications:* Derbyshire, 1978; Nottinghamshire, 1974; The Peak District, 1976; Vanishing Britain, 1977; Old English Customs, 1966; Ghosts and Legends, 1972; Red Guide - Derbyshire, 1989; Nature and Lovers Companion, (editor), 1972. *Contributions to:* Country Life; Derbyshire Life and Countryside. *Honour:* MBE, June 1976. *Memberships:* Derby Writers Guild, Vice President; Derby Civic Society, Chairman, Vice President; Derbyshire Historic Buildings Trust. *Literary Agent:* David Higham Associates. *Address:* 53 Littleover Lane, Littleover, Derby DE23 6JH, England.

CHRISTIE Ian Ralph, b. 11 May 1919, Preston, Lancashire, England, Retired University Teacher. *Education:* Robert Herbert prize, 1947, BA, 1948, MA, 1948, Magdalen College, Oxford. *Appointments:* War service, RAF, Britain, West Africa and India, 1940-46. *Appointments:* Assistant Lecturer in History, University College London, 1948; Lecturer, 1951, Reader, 1960; Professor of Modern British History, 1966-79; Dean of Arts, 1971-73; Chairman, History Department, 1975-79; Astor Professor of British History, 1979-84; Professor Emeritus and Honorary Research Fellow, 1984-. *Publications:* The End of North's Ministry 1780-1782, 1958; Wilkes, Wyvill and Reform, 1962; Crisis of Empire, 1966; The Correspondence of Jeremy Bentham, (Editor), volume 3, 1971; Empire or Independence 1760-1776, (Co-author B W Labaree), 1976; Bibliography of British History, 1789-1851, (Co-author Lucy M Brown), 1977; Wars and Revolutions, Britain 1760-1815, 1982; Stress and Stability in Late 18th Century Britain, 1984; The Benthams In Russia 1780-1791, 1993. *Contributions to:* Various journals. *Honour:* Elected Fellow, The British Academy, 1977. *Memberships:* Royal Historical Society, Joint Literary Director, 1964-70, Member of Council, 1970-74; Editorial Board, History of Parliament Trust, 1973-. *Address:* 10 Green Lane, Croxley Green, Hertfordshire WD3 3HR, England.

CHRISTIE-MURRAY David Hugh Arthur, b. 12 July 1913, London, England, Retired Schoolmaster. m. (1) Ena Louise Elisabeth Mumford, 11 July 1942, (2) Sheila Mary Blackmore (Watson), 15 Apr 1972, 1 son, 3 daughters, 2 stepdaughters. *Education:* Diploma in Journalism, University College, University of London, 1932-34; BA, 1942, MA, 1945, General Ordination Examination, 1942, St Peter's Hall, Oxford University and Wyclif Hall, Oxford. *Publications:* Beckenham Heraldry, 1954; Armorial Bearings of British Schools, series, 1956-66; collected edition, 1966; Illustrated Children's Bible, 1974, 1993; A History of Heresy, 1976, 1989; Voices From the Gods, 1978; My First Prayer Book, 1981, 1985; Reincarnation: Ancient Beliefs and Modern Evidence, Norwegian Edition 1989, Spanish Edition 1991; The Practical Astrologer, 1990. *Contributions to:* Times Literary and Educational Supplements; The Armorial; Christian Parapsychologist; Journal of the Society for Psychical Research; Light. *Literary Agent:* Watson Little Limited. *Address:* Imber Court Cottage, Orchard Lane, East Molesey, Surrey KT8 0BN, England.

CHRISTOPHER Matthew (Matt) F (Frederic Martin), b. 16 Aug 1917, Pennsylvania, USA, Writer. m. Catherine (Cay) M Krupa, 13 July 1940, 3 sons, 1 daughter. *Publications:* The Lucky Baseball Bat, 1954, 1991; Catcher With A Glass Arm, 1964; The Year Mom Won the Pennant; The Kid Who Only Hit Homers; Dirt Bike Runaway; The Dog That Pitched A No-Hitter, 1989; Diamond Champs; The Hit-Away Kid; The Fox Steals Home; Skateboard Tough, 1991. *Contributions to:* Approximately about 275 stories and articles in magazines including: The Atlantic Advocate; The Christian Science Monitor; Catholic Boy; Treasure Chest. *Honour:* Boys' Clubs of America Junior Book Award Certificate for Basketball Sparkplug, 1957. *Membership:* Society of Children's Book Writers. *Address:* 1830 Townes Court, Rock Hill, SC 29730, USA.

CHRISTOPHERSEN Paul (Hans), b. 1911, Denmark. Emeritus Professor. *Appointments:* Professor of English, University of Copenhagen, 1946-48; Professor of English, University of Ibadan, Nigeria, 1948-54; Professor of English, University of Oslo, Norway, 1954-68; Reader in English, 1969-74, Professor, 1974-77, Emeritus Professor, 1977-, New University of Ulster, Northern Ireland; Professor of English, University of Qatar, 1977-81. *Publications:* The Articles, 1939; A Modern English Grammar (with O Jespersen), vol 6, 1942; To Start You Talking (with H Krabbe), 1948; Bilingualism, 1949; The Ballad of Sir Aldingar, 1952; An English Phonetics Course, 1956; Some Thoughts on the Study of English as a Foreign Language, 1957; An Advanced English Grammar (with A Sandved), 1969; Second-Language Learning, 1973; Tina, by Herman Bang, translation, 1984. *Address:* 1 Corfe Close, Cambridge CB2 2QA, England.

CHURCH Avery Grenfell, b. 21 Feb 1937, North Wilkesboro, North Carolina, USA. Educator; Scientist; Poet. m. Dora Ann Creed, 5 Oct 1991. *Education:* University of North Carolina, Chapel Hill; BA cum laude, Baylor University, 1962; MA, University of Colorado, Boulder, 1965. *Publications:* Poetry: Rainbows of the Mind, 1982; Patterns of Thought, 1986; Poems in Anthology on World Brotherhood and Peace; Dakota: Plains and Fancy, Dan River Anthology; New Dawn Poetry; Yearbook of Modern Poetry; others. *Contributions to:* American Bard; Bardic Echoes; Hoosier Challenger; Orphic Lute; Parnassus Literary Journal; Pasque Petals; San Fernando Poetry Journal; Several others. *Honours:* Poet of the Year Award, National Poetry Publishers Association, 1976; Lloyd Frank Merrell Award, Bardic Echoes, 1977; Fellow, International Academy of Poets, 1981; Poet Laureate of the Month, Centro Studi e Scambi Internazionali Accademia Leonardo da Vinci, July 1981; Honorary Doctorate in Anthropology, World University, 1981; Poets Hall of Fame, Parnassus Literary Journal, 1982; International Cultural Diploma of Honor, American Biographical Institute, 1988; September Prize, Pasque Petals, 1989. *Memberships:* Poetry Society of America; Past Vice-Chairman of Anthropology, Past Vice-President, Former Executive Committee Member, Alabama Academy of Science; Fellow, American Anthropological Association; Honorary Member, Editorial Advisory Board, American Biographical Institute, 1980-83. *Address:* 2749 Park Oak Drive, Clemmons, North Carolina 27012, USA.

CHURCH Robert, b. 20 July 1932, London, England. Author. m. Dorothy June Bourton, 15 Apr 1953, 2 daughters. *Education:* Beaufoy College, London, 1946-48. *Appointments:* Served Army 1950-52; Metropolitan Police, 1952-78; Probation Service, 1978-88. *Publications:* Murder in East Anglia, 1987; Accidents of Murder, 1989; More Murder in East Anglia, 1990. *Contributions to:* Miscellaneous magazines. *Memberships:* The Society of Authors; Crime Writers Association; Society of Civil Service Authors. *Address:* Woodside, 7 Crome Walk, Gunton Park, Lowestoft, Suffolk NR32 4NF, England.

CHURCHILL Elizabeth. *See:* HOUGH Richard Alexander.

CIMINO Michael, b. 1949, USA. Screenplay and Film Writer; Film Director. *Publications:* Silent Running, 1972; Magnum Force, 1973; Thunderbolt and Lightfoot (writer, director), 1974; The Deer Hunter (writer, producer, director), 1978; Heaven's Gate (writer, director), 1980. *Honours:* 5 Academy Awards, Japenese Academy Award for Deer Hunter, 1979; 1 Academy nomination for Thunderbolt and Lightfoot, 1974; 2 Academy Award nominations for Heaven's Gate, 1980; Golden Globe nomination for Year of The Dragon, 1986; BFA, MFA, Magna Com Laude, Yale University. *Memberships:* Directors Guild of America; Writers Guild of America; Yale Club. *Address:* c/o Jeff Berg, I.C.M, 8899 Beverly Blvd, Beverly Hills, CA 90048, USA.

CIPOLLA Carlo M, b. 1922, Italy. Economic Historian.
Appointments: Professor Emeritus, University of California, Berkeley and at the Scuola Normale Superiore, Pisa, Italy. *Publications:* Studi di Storia della moneta, 1948; Money, Prices and Civilization, 1956; Storia dell'economia italiana (editor), 1959; The Economic History of World Population, 1962; Guns and Sails, 1965; Clocks and Culture, 1967; Literacy and Development, 1969; The Economic Decline of Empires (editor), 1970; The Fontana Economic History of Europe (editor), 1970; Cristofano and the Plague, 1973; Before the Industrial Revolution, 1976; Public Health and the Medical Profession in the Renaissance, 1976; Chi ruppe i rastelli a Monte Lupo, 1977; I pidocchi e il Granduca, 1979; Fighting the Plague in 17th Century Italy, 1981; The Monetary Policy of Fourteenth Century Florence, 1982; La moneta a Firenze nel Cinquecento, 1987; Allegro ma non troppo, 1988; Between History and Economics: An Introduction to Economic History, 1991; Miasmas and Disease, 1992; Il burocrate e il marinaio, 1992. *Address:* Via Montebello Battaglia 4, Pavia, Italy.

CIVASAQUI Jose (Shibasaki Sosuke), b. 12 Jan 1916, Saitama-ken. Lecturer; Translator; Poet. m. 18 Sept 1940, 2 sons, 1 daughter. *Education:* HHD, World University, Tucson, USA, 1977. *Appointments:* President, Poetry Society of Japan, 1987; Managing Director, Japan League of Poets, 1972; Japan Guild of Authors and Composers, 1973; President, 1983-85, Honorary President, 1985-, United Poets Laureate International, USA; Deputy Director General, Asia, IBC, 1987. *Publications:* In His Bosom, 1950; In Thy Grace, 1971; Doshin Shien, Translation of A Child's Garden of Verses, 1973; Beyond Seeing, 1977; Living Water, 1984; Invitation to the World of Haiku, 1985; Numerous songs both original and translations. *Contributions to:* Japan Times, 1947-48; Mainichi, 1949-50, 1954-55; Study of Current English, 1960-61, 1965-68. *Honours:* Excellence in Poetry, 3rd World Congress of Poets, 1976; International Poet Laureate, 8th World Congress of Poets, 1985; Knight Commander, Royal Knights of Justice, England, 1986; Premio Speciale, Pelle di Luna, Italy, 1985; Premio Internazional "San Valentino d'Oro", Italia, 1989; Senator, International Parliament for Safety & Peace, 1989; Medal for Peace, Albert Einstein International Academy Foundation, 1990; D.Lit.Hon, Albert Einstein International Academy Foundation, 1991. *Memberships:* Poetry Society of Japan; United Poets Laureate International; PEN, Tokyo. *Address:* Honcho 2-12-11, Ikebukuro, Toshima-ku, Tokyo 170, Japan.

CIXOUS Helene, b. 5 June 1937, Oran, Algeria. Professor of English Literature; Writer. m. 1955, divorced 1964, 1 son, 1 daughter. *Education:* Received Agregation d'Anglais, 1959 and Docteur es Lettres, 1968. *Appointments:* Assistant, University of Bordeaux, France, 1962-65; Master Assistant, University of Paris (Sorbonne) Paris, France, 1965-67; Master of Conference, University of Paris X, Nanterre, France, 1967-68; University of Paris VIII (Vincennes at St Denis), St Denis, France, helped found the university's experimental branch at St Denis, 1968, Professor of English Literature, 1968-, founder and director of Centre de Techerches en Etudes Feminines, 1974-. Visiting professor and lecturer to many universities in the USA, Austria, Canada, Denmark, England, Spain and Holland. *Publications include:* Le Livre de Promethea (fiction), 1983, translation by Betsy Wing, published by University of Nebraska Press, Entre l'ecriture (essays), 1986, translation by Deborah W Carpenter, Sarah Cornell and Susan Sellers, 1988. Author of manifesto, La Rire de la Meduse; Co-founder of Revue de Theorie d'Analyse Litteraire: Poetique, 1969; Manna (ed Catherine McGillivray), 1993; The Ladder of Writing, 1993. Work represented in anthologies. Eight plays. *Contributions to:* Member of Editorial Board: Poetique, Signs, New Literary History. *Honours:* Prix Medicis, 1969 for Dedans; Chevalier Croix Dusud, 1988; Doctor of Laws, Queen's University, Kinston, Canada; Doctor of Laws, University of Edmonton, Alberta, Canada; Doctor honoris causa, University of York, England; Corresponding member, European Academy of Arts, Sciences and Humanities. *Address:* Universite de Paris VIII, 2 rue de la Liberte, 93526 St Denis, France.

CIZMAR Paula L, b. 30 Aug 1949, Youngstown, Ohio, USA. Playwright; Screenwriter. *Education:* Ohio University, 1967-71. *Publications:* Plays: Candy & Shelley Go To the Desert, 1988; The Death of a Miner, 1983; The Girl Room, 1979; many plays produced. *Contributions to:* Mother Jones; The Chronicle of Higher Education; Lilith; Detroit Free Press; others. *Honours include:* Susan Smith Blackburn Literary Prize, Runner Up, 1981; Jerome Foundation Commission/Fellowship, 1981; NEA Fellowship, 1982; Rockefeller Foundation, International Residency, Bellagio, Italy, 1983. *Memberships:* Dramatists Guild; Writers Guild of America; League of Professional Theatre Women. *Agent:* Lynn Pleshette, Pleshette-Green Agency. *Address:* c/o 2700 N Beachwood Drive, Los Angeles, CA 90068, USA.

CLADPOLE Jim. *See:* **RICHARDS James (Sir).**

CLANCY Joseph Patrick Thomas, b. 8 Mar 1928, New York City, USA. College Teacher. m. Gertrude Wiegand, 31 July 1948, 4 sons, 4 daughters. *Education:* BA, 1947, MA 1949, PhD 1957, Fordham University. *Appointments:* Faculty, 1948-, Professor, English Literature & Theatre Arts, 1962-, Marymount Manhattan College. *Publications:* The Odes and Epodes of Horace, 1960; Medieval Welsh Lyrics, 1965; The Earliest Welsh Poems, 1970; Pendragon: Arthur and His Britain, 1971; Twentieth Century Welsh Poems, 1982; Gwyn Thomas: Living a Life, 1982; The Significance of Flesh: Poems 1950-1983, 1984; The Plays of Saunders Lewis, 4 volumes, 1985-86; Bobi Jones: Selected Poems, 1987. *Contributions include:* Poetry Wales; Planet; Anglo Welsh Review; Book News from Wales; Manhattan Poetry Review; Epoch; College English; America. *Honours:* American Philosophical Society Fellowships, 1963, 1968; National Translation Center Fellowship, 1968; Welsh Arts Council: Literature Award, 1971, Major Bursary, 1972; National Endowment for the Arts Translation Fellowship, 1983; St David's Society of New York Annual Award, 1986. *Memberships:* American Literary Translators Association; Dramatists Guild; Yr Academi Gymreig; Eastern States Celtic Association, President 1987-89; St David's Society of New York. *Address:* 1549 Benson St, New York City, NY 10461, USA.

CLANCY Laurence James b. 2 Dec 1942, Melbourne, Australia. Senior Lecturer. Divorced, 2 sons. *Education:* BA (Hons) Melbourne University, 1964; MA, 1973, La Trobe University. *Publications include:* A Collapsible Man (novel), 1975; The Wife Specialist (short stories), 1978; Xavier Herber, 1981; Perfect Love (novel), 1983; The Novels of Vladimir Nabokov, 1984; City to City (short stories), 1989. *Contributions to:* Regular contributor, reviewer to many Australian journals and newspapers. *Honours:* Co-winner of National Book Council Award for A Collapsible Man, 1975; Winner of Australian Natives Association Award for Perfect Love, 1983. *Membership:* Past President, PEN International (Melbourne Centre). *Literary Agent:* Curtis Brown (Australia) Pty Ltd. *Address:* 227 Westgarth Street, Northcote, Victoria 3070, Australia.

CLARE Elizabeth. *See:* **COOK Dorothy Mary.**

CLARE Ellen. *See:* **SINCLAIR Olga Ellen.**

CLARE Helen. *See:* **BLAIR Pauline Hunter.**

CLARESON Thomas Dean, b. 26 Aug. 1926, Austin, USA. College Teacher; Writer; Editor. m. Alice Jane Super, 23 Dec. 1954, 1 son. *Education:* BA, University of Minnesota, 1948; MA, Indiana University, 1949; PhD, University of Pennsylvania, 1956. *Appointments:* Editor, Extrapolatin, 1959-90; Editorial Board: Victorian Poetry, 1960-84, Journal of Popular Culture, 1970-. *Publications;* SF: The Other Side of Realism, 1971; SF Criticism: An Annotated Bibliography, 1972; A Spectrum of Worlds, Anthology, 1972; Voices for the Future, 3 volumes, 1976, 1979, 1984; Many Futures, Many Worlds, 1977; Robert Silverberg: An Annotated Bibliography, 1983; Robert Silverberg: Critical Evaluation, 1983; Science Fiction in America 1870s-1930s: An Annotated Bibliography, 1984; Some Kind of Paradise: The Emergence of American Science Fiction, 1985; Frederick Pohl, 1987; Contemporary Understanding American Science Fiction, 1990. *Contributions to:* Anatomy of Wonder; Science Fiction Reference Book; Journal of Popular Culture; Princeton University Library Journal; American Literary Realism. *Honours:* SFRA Pilgrim Award, 1977; Ohioana Library Association Citation, 1985; Eaton Award, 1987. *Memberships include:* President, Science Fiction Research Association, 1970-76; President, College English Association of Ohio, 1975-76; Executive Committee, MLA Group on Popular Culture, 1979-84; CEAO; American Studies Association. *Address:* 2223 Friar Tuck Circle, Wooster, OH 44691, USA.

CLARK Brian Robert, b. 3 June 1932. Playwright. m. (1) Margaret Paling, 1961, 2 sons, (2) Anita Modak, 1983, 1 stepson, 1 stepdaughter, (3) Cherry Potter, 1990. *Education:* Central School of Speech and Drama, London; BA, Honours English, Nottingham University. *Appointments:* Teacher, 1955-61, 1964-68; Staff Tutor, Drama, University of Hull, 1968-72; Since 1971 Author, 30 TV plays; Founder, Amber Lane Press, 1978; Group Theatre. *Publications:* TV plays include: Whose Life Is It Anyway?; The Saturday Party; TV Series: Telford's Change; Late Starter; Stage Plays: Whose Life is It Anyway?; Can You Hear Me At the Back?, 1978; Kipling, 1985, (London & New York); The Petition, also in London, 1986; Campions Interview: Post Mortem; The Petition, NY, 1986; Hopping to Byzantum, with Kathy Levin, Germany 1990, Sydney, 1991. *Address:* c/o Judy Daish Associates, 83 Eastbourne Mews, London W2 6LQ, England.

CLARK Bruce (Budge), b. 1918, USA. Professor Emeritus. *Appointments:* Currently Emeritus Professor of English, Emeritus Dean, College of the Humanities, Brigham Young University, Provo, Utah. *Publications:* The Longer Carmel Narrative Poems of Robinson Jeffers, 1947; The English Sonnet Sequence 1850 to 1900, 1951; The Spectrum of Faith in Victorian Literature, 1962; The Challenge of Teaching, 1964; Out of the Best Books: A Critical Anthology of Literature, 5 vols, 1964-69; Wisdom and Beauty Through Literature, 1966; Oscar Wilde: A Study in Genius and Tragedy, 1970; Romanticism Through Modern Eyes, 1970; Brigham Young on Education, 1970; Rochard Evans Quote Book, 1971; Idealists in Revolt: An Introduction to English Romanticism, 1975; Favorite Selections from Out of the Best Books, 1979; Great Short Stories for Discussion and Delight, 1980; The Brigham Young University, College of Humanities, 1965-1981, 3 vols, 1985; My Brother Richard L. (editor), 1985. *Address:* 365 East 1655 Street, Orem, UT 84058, USA.

CLARK Curt. *See:* **WESTLAKE Donald E.**

CLARK David. *See:* **HARDCASTLE Michael.**

CLARK David Ridgley, b. 1920, USA. Emeritus Professor of English. *Appointments:* Assistant Professor, 1958, Associate Professor, 1958-65, Professor, 1965-85, Chairman, Department of English, 1975-76, Emeritus Professor, 1985-, University of Massachusetts, Amherst; Visiting Professor, Chairman, Department of English, St Mary's College, Notre Dame, Indiana, 1985-87; Visiting Professor, Williams College, Williamstown, Massachusetts, 1989-90. *Publications:* A Curious Quire, poetry (with G S Koehler, L O Barron, R G Tucker), 1962, 2nd Edition, 1967; W B Yeats and the Theatre of Desolate Reality, 1965, Revised and Expanded Edition, (with Rosalind Clark), 1993; Irish Renaissance (edited with R Skelton), 1965; Dry Tree, poetry, 1966; Reading Poetry (with F B Millett and A W Hoffman), 1968; Riders to the Sea (editor), 1970; Studies in The Bridge (editor), 1970; A Tower of Polished Black Stones: Early Versions of The Shadowy Waters (edited with G P Mayhew), 1971; Druid Craft: The

Writing of The Shadowy Waters (edited with M J Sidnell and G P Mayhew), 1971; Twentieth Century Interpretations of Murder in the Cathedral (editor), 1971; Lyric Resonance: Glosses on Some Poems of Yeats, Frost, Crane,.Cummings and Others, essays, 1972; That Black Day: The Manuscripts of Crazy Jane on the Day of Judgment, 1980; Critical Essays on Hart Crane (editor), 1982; Yeats at Songs and Choruses, 1983; W B Yeats: The Writing of Sophocles' King Oedipus (edited with James McGuire), 1987. *Contributions to:* The Poet and the Actress: An Unpublished Dialogue by W B Yeats (edited), The Irish National Theatre: An Uncollected Address by W B Yeats (edited), to Yeats Annual No 8, 1990; Gaelic Poets and Yeats's Middle and Late Songs, to Yeats: An Annual of Critical and Textual Studies, 1990. *Memberships:* Modern Language Association of America; American Conference for Irish Studies; Canadian Association for Irish Studies; International Association for the Support of Anglo-Irish Literature; The Yeats Association, Dublin. *Address:* 159 Glendale Road, Amherst, MA 01002, USA.

CLARK Douglas (Malcolm Jackson), (Peter Hosier, James Ditton), b. 1919, United Kingdom. Author; Pharmaceutical Company Executive (retired). *Publications:* Suez Touchdown: A Soldier's Tale, 1964; Nobody's Perfect, 1969; Death after Evensong, 1969; Deadly Pattern, 1970; Sweet Poison, 1970; Sick to Death, 1971; The Miracle Makers, non-mystery novel (as Peter Hosier), 1971; You're Fairly Welcome (as James Ditton), 1973; The Bigger They Are (as James Ditton), 1973; Escapemanship (as James Ditton), 1975; Premedicated Murder, 1975; Dread and Water, 1976; Table d'Hote, 1977; The Gimmel Flask, 1972; The Libertines, 1978; Hheberden's Seat, 1979; Poacher's Bag, 1980; Golden Rain, 1980; Roast Eggs, 1981; The Longest Pleasure, 1981; Shelf Life, 1982; Doone Walk, 1982; Vicious Circle, 1983; The Monday Theory, 1983; Bouquet Garni, 1984; Dead Letter, 1984; Performance, 1985; Jewelled Eye, 1985; Storm Centre, 1986; The Big Grouse, 1986; Plain Sailing, 1987; Bitter Water, 1990. *Address:* c/o Vanessa Holt Associate Ltd, 59 Crescent Road, Leigh-on-Sea, Essex SS9 2PF, England.

CLARK Eleanor, b. 6 July 1913, Los Angeles, California, USA. Author. m. Robert Penn Warren, 7 Dec 1952, 1 son, 1 daughter. *Education:* BA, Vassar College. *Publications:* Fiction: Bitter Box, 1946; Baldur's Gate; Dr Heart: A Novella and Other Stories, 1974; Gloria Mundi; Camping Out, 1986; Non-fiction: Rome and a Villa, 1952, New and Expanded Edition, 1975, 1992; Oysters of Locmariaquer, 1964, 1992; Eyes etc: A Memoir, 1977; Tamrart: 13 Days in the Sahara, 1982. *Contributions to:* Partisan Review; The Nation; The New Republic; Kenyon Review; Southern Review; Atlantic Monthly. *Honours:* Guggenheim Fellowship, 1947-48; 1959-60; National Book Award, 1965. *Memberships:* National Institute of Arts and Letters; Board Member, Corporation of Yaddo. *Address:* 2495 Redding Road, Fairfield, CT 06430, USA.

CLARK Eric, b. 29 July 1937, Birmingham, England, Author; Journalist. m. Marcelle Bernstein, 12 Apr 1972, 1 son, 2 daughters. *Appointments:* Staff of various newspapers including, Daily Mail, The Guardian, The Observer until 1972; Full-time Author, 1972-. *Publications:* The Want Makers (Inside the Hidden World of Advertising), 1988; Chinese Burn, 1984, China Run, USA edition, 1984; Send in the Lions, 1981; The Sleeper, 1979; Black Gambit, 1978; Corps Diplomatique, 1973, USA Edition, Diplomat, 1973; Len Deighton's London Dossier, (Part-author), 1967; Everybody's Guide to Survival, 1969. *Contributions to:* The Observer; Sunday Times; Daily Mail; Daily Telegraph; Washington Post; Melbourne Age. *Memberships:* Society of Authors; Fellow, UK Centre International PEN; Crime Writers Association. *Literary Agent:* Jonathan Clowes, Iron Bridge House, Bridge Approach, London NW1 8BD. *Address:* c/o Child and Company, 1 Fleet Street, London EC4Y 1BD, England.

CLARK John Pepper, (J P Clark Bekederemo), b. 6 Apr 1935, Kiagbobo, Nigeria. Writer. m. Ebun Odutola

Clark, 1 son, 3 daughters. *Education:* Warri Government College, Ughelli, 1948-54; University of Ibadan 1955-60, BA (hons) English, 1960 and graduate study (Institute of African Studies fellowship), 1963-64; Princeton University, New Jersey (Parvin Fellowship). *Appointments:* Information Officer, Government of Nigeria, 1960-61; Head of Features and Editorial Writer, Lagos Daily Express, 1961-62; Research Fellow, 1964-66 and Professor of African Literature 1966-85, University of Lagos; Founding editor, Horn magazine, Ibadan; co-editor, Black Orpheus, Lagos, 1968-. *Publications:* Plays include: The Raft (broadcast 1966; produced New York, 1978), Included in Three Plays 1964; Ozidi, Ibadan, London and New York, Oxford University Press, 1966; The Bikoroa Plays (as J P Clark Bekederemo), includes The Boat, The Return Home, Full Circle, (produced Lagos, 1981), Oxford, Oxford University Press, 1985. Screenplay: The Ozidi of Atazi; Radio Play: The Raft, 1966; Verse and other publications. *Membership:* Founding member, Society of Nigerian Authors. *Literary Agent:* Andrew Best, Curtis Brown, London. *Address:* c/o Andrew Best, Curtis Brown, 162-168 Regent Street, London W1R 5TB, England.

CLARK John Richard, b. 2 Oct 1930, Philadelphia, Pennsylvania, USA, Professor of English. m. Dr Anna Lydia Motto, 7 November 1959, 1 son, 1 daughter. *Education:* BA, Pennsylvania State University, 1952; MA, Columbia University, 1956; PhD, University of Michigan, Ann Arbor, 1965. *Appointments:* Member, Editorial Board, Studies in Contemporary Satire, journal, 1978-. *Publications:* Form and Frenzy in Sweift's Tale of a Tub, 1970; Satire, That Blasted Art, (Editor), 1973; Senecan Tragedy, 1988; Seneca: A Critical Bibliography 1900-1980, 1989; The Modern Satiric Grotesque and its Traditions, 1991; Essays on Seneca, 1993. *Contributions to:* Guest Editor, Satire Issue, Seventeenth century News, 1975; Guest editor, Satire Issue, Thalia, 1982; American Notes and Queries; Centennial Review; Classical Philology; College English; Explicator; Journal of Popular Culture; Mosaic; Novel; Philological Quarterly; Renaissance Drama; Rheinisches Museum; Studies in Contemporary Satire; Studies in Philology; Thought; Transactions of the American Philological Association. *Honours:* Rackham Fellowship, University of Michigan, 1962-63, Summer, 1963; Invited Resident, Institute for Advanced Study, Princeton, Summers, 1979, 1980. *Memberships:* Modern Language Association, South Atlantic Modern Language Association, American Philological Association, Classical Association of the Middle West and South, College English Association. *Address:* Department of English, University of South Florida, Tampa, FL 33620, USA.

CLARK Jonathan Charles Douglas, b. 28 Feb 1951, London, England, Historian. *Education:* BA, 1972, PhD, 1981, Cambridge University. *Appointments:* Research Fellow, Peterhouse, Cambridge, 1977; Research Fellow, The Leverhulme Trust, 1983; Fellow, All Souls College, Oxford, 1986. *Publications:* The Dynamics of Change, 1982; English Society 1688-1832, 1985; Revolution and Rebellion, 1986; The Memoirs of James, 2nd Earl Waldegrave, 1988; Ideas and Politics in Modern Britain, 1990; The Language of Liberty, 1993. *Contributions to:* Revolution and Counter-Revolution, 1990; Christianity and Conservatism, 1990; Articles in learned journals; Features and book reviews in: The Times; Sunday Times; Sunday Telegraph; Independent on Sunday; Evening Standard; The Spectator. *Memberships:* Fellow, Royal Historical Society; American Historical Association; North American Conferencce on British Studies; British Society for Eighteenth Century Studies; British Association for American Studies. *Literary Agent:* Michael Shaw, Curtis Brown. *Address:* All Souls College, Oxford OX1 4AL, England.

CLARK LaVerne Harrell, b. 6 June 1929, Smithville, Texas, USA. Writer; Photographer; Lecturer. m. L D Clark, 15 Sept 1951. *Education:* BA, Journalism, Texas Woman's University, 1950; Creative Writing courses, Columbia University, 1951-54; MA, English, 1962, MFA, Creative Writing, 1992, University of Arizona.

Appointments: Reporter, Librarian, Fort Worth Press, Fort Worth, Texas, 1950-51; Sales and Advertising Department, Columbia University Press, 1951-53; Assistant, Promotion-News Department, Episcopal Diocese, New York City, 1958-59; Founding Director, 1962-66, Photographer, 1966-, Poetry Center, University of Arizona, Tucson. *Publications:* They Sang for Horses, 1966, 3rd print, 1984; The Face of Poetry, 1976, 1979; Focus 101, 1979; Revisiting the Plains Indians Country of Mari Sandoz, 1979; The Deadly Swarm and Other Stories, 1985, 1987; The Restoration, novel, in progress. *Contributions to:* Pembroke; Vanderbilt Review; The Pawn Review; Sands; Journal of Popular Culture; Arizona Quarterly; Arizona and the West; St Andrews Review; Others. *Memberships:* American Philosophical Society Grant, 1967-69; 1st Place, University of Chicago Folklore Prize, 1967; Non-Fiction Award, Biennial Letters Contest, National League of American Pen Women, 1968; Distinguished Alumna Award, Texas Woman's University, 1973; 9 Biennial Awards, stories, articles, novelettes, slide presentations, National League of American Pen Women; Julian Ocean Literary Prize, 1984; Finalist, Short Fiction Spur Award, Western Writers of America; Downs Fiction, Short Story, University of Arizona, 1986. *Memberships:* PEN, New York Center; PEN West; National League of American Pen Women; Western Writers of America; Society of Southwestern Authors; Honorary Board, Mari Sandoz Heritage Society, Chadron College, Nebraska; Westerners International; Women In Communication (Theta Sigma Phi); Kappa Alpha Mu; Golden Key Honor Society. *Address:* 4690 N Campbell No C, Tucson, AZ 85718, USA.

CLARK Marcelle Ruth, (Marcelle Bernstein), b. 14 June 1945, Manchester, England. Writer; Journalist. m. Eric Clark, 12 Apr 1972, 2 daughters, 1 son. *Appointments:* Staff, The Guardian, Daily Mirror, Observer. *Publications:* Nuns, Documentary, 1976; Sadie, Fiction: 1983; Salka, 1986; Lili, 1988; Body And Soul, 1991; Body And Soul also major 6-part ITV Drama series. *Contributions to:* Numerous US & UK Magazines. *Honours:* Arts Council Best First, Novel, 1983; Arts Council Bursary, 1986; Helene Heroys Award, 1988.*Membership:* Society of Authors. *Literary Agent:* Caradoc King, A P Watt. *Address:* AP Watt, 20 John Street, London WC1N 2DR, England.

CLARK Marie Catherine Audrey, (Catherine Clifton Clark, Audrey Curling), b. London, England. Writer. m. Clifton Clark, 16 Feb. 1938. *Publications:* (Novels) The Running Tide, 1963; Sparrow's Yard, 1964; (Historical Novels) The Echoing Silence, 1967; Castle for Comedy, 1970; The Sapphire and the Pearl, 1970; Cry of the Heart, 1971; A Quarter of the Moon, 1972; Shadows on the Grass, 1973; Enthusiasts in Love, 1975; Publisher: Hurst and Blackett; The Lamps in the House (as Catherine Clifton Clark), 1990; The Saturday Treat, 1993; (Biography) The Young Thackeray (Max Parrish), 1966. *Contributions to:* Home & Gardens; Womens Own; Woman; Woman's Realm; The Lady. *Honours:* Theodora Roscoe Award, 1978; 1st Prize, Wandsworth All London Literary Competition, 1982. *Memberships:* Society of Authors; Institute of Journalists; Romantic Novelists Association; Society of Women Writers and Journalists (Council Member). *Address:* 35 Hadley Gardens, Chiswick, London W4 4NU, England.

CLARK Mary Higgins, b. 24 Dec 1929, New York City, USA. Writer. m. Waren F Clark, 26 Dec 1949, 2 sons, 3 daughters. *Education:* BA Philosophy, Fordham University; Honorary Doctorate, Villanora University, 1983, Rider College, 1986. *Publications include:* Where Are the Children 1975; A Stranger is Watching, 1978; the Cradle Will Fall, 1980; A Cry in the Night, 1982; Stillwatch, 1984; Weep No More My Lady, 1987; While My Pretty One Sleeps, 1989; The Anastasia Syndrome and Other Stories, 1989. *Contributions include:* Ladies Home Journal; Women's Day; Saturday Evening Post. *Honours include:* Grand Prix de Litteratae Policcere, 1980. *Memberships:* Mystery Writers of America, President 1987; PEN; American Society of Journalists and Authors; National Arts Club. *Agent:* Eugene Winick,

McIntosh & Otis. *Address:* 15 Werimas Brook Road, Saddle River, NJ 07458, USA.

CLARK Patricia Denise, (Claire Lorrimer, Patricia Robins, Susan Patrick), b. 1921. British. Writer of Historical/Romance/Gothic, Children's fiction, Poetry. Sub-Editor, Woman's Illustrated magazine, London 1938-40. *Publications include:* As Claire Lorrimer: A Voice in the Dark, 1967; The Shadow Falls, 1974; Relentless Storm, 1975; The Secret of Quarry House, 1976; Mavreen, 1976; Tamarisk, 1978; Chantal, 1980; The Garden (a cameo), 1980; The Chatelaine, 1981; The Wilderling, 1982; Last Year's Nightingale, 1984; Frost in the Sun, 1986; House of Tomorrow (biography), 1987; Ortolans, 1990; The Spinning Wheel, 1991; Variations (short stories), 1991; The Silver Link, 1993. As Patricia Robins: To the Stars, 1944; See No Evil, 1945; Three Loves, 1949; Awake My Heart, 1950; Beneath the Moon, 1951; Leave My Heart Alone, 1951; The Fair Deal, 1952; Heart's Desire, 1953; So This Is Love, 1953; Heaven in Our Hearts, 1954; One Who Cares, 1954; Love Cannot Die, 1955; The Foolish Heart, 1956; Give All to Love, 1956; Where Duty Lies, 1957; He Is Mine, 1957; Love Must Wait, 1958; Lonely Quest, 1959; Lady Chatterley's Daughter, 1961; The Last Chance, 1961; The Long Wait, 1962; The Runaways, 1962; Seven Loves, 1962; With All My Love, 1963; The Constant Heart, 1964; Second Love, 1964; The Night is Thine, 1964; There Is But One, 1965; No More Loving, 1965; Topaz Island, 1965; Love Me Tomorrow, 1966; The Uncertain Joy, 1966; The Man Behind the Mask, 1967; Forbidden, 1967; Sapphire in the Sand, 1968; Return to Love, 1968; Laugh on Friday, 1969; No Stone Unturned, 1969; Cinnabar House, 1970; Under the Sky, 1970; The Crimson Tapestry, 1972; Play Fair with Love, 1972; None But He, 1973. Others: The Adventure of the Three Baby Bunnies (juvenile), 1934; Seven Days Leave (verse), 1943; Tree Fairies (juvenile), 1945; Sea Magic (juvenile), 1946; The Heart of a Rose (juvenile), 1941; 100 Reward (juvenile), 1966. *Address:* Chiswell Barn, Marsh Green, Edenbridge, Kent TN8 5AP, England.

CLARK Robert Phillips, b. 3 Dec 1921, Randolph, Vermont, USA. Newspaper Editor and Consultant. m. Jeanne Orr Rice, 14 Dec 1949, 2 daughters. *Education:* AB, English, Tufts University, 1942; MA, Journalism, University of Missouri, 1948; Nieman Fellow in Journalism 1960-61, Harvard University. *Appointments:* Reporter, Owensboro, Kentucky, Messenger-Inquirer, 1948-49; Reporter/Science Writer, Louisville, Kentucky, Courier-Journal, 1949-62, Washington Correspondent 1958; Managing Editor, Louisville, Kentucky, Times, 1962-71; Executive Editor, Courier-Journal and Times, 1971-79; Editor, Florida Times-Union and Jacksonville Journal, 1979-82; Vice President, News, Harte-Hanks Newspapers, 1983-86; News/Editorial Consultant, 1987-. *Publications include:* Success Stories: What 28 Newspapers Are Doing to Gain and Retain Readers, 1988; Keys to Success: Strategies for Newspaper Marketing in the 90s, 1989. *Contributions to:* Numerous articles in Bulletin of the American Society of Newspaper Editors, Quill (publication of the Society of Professional Journalists), Nieman Reports, Editor and Publisher Magazine. *Honours:* Four times Pulitzer Prize juror, latest 1988, 1989; Distinguished Visiting Professor, Baylor University, 1990-92; Distinguished Visiting Professor, Slippery Rock University, 1990; Numerous speeches and lectures to journalistic and educational organizations. *Memberships:* American Society of Newspaper Editors, President 1985-86; Associated Press Managing Editors Association, President 1974-75; International Press Institute, Director, American Committee, 1981-87; Society of Professional Journalists, Sigma Delta Chi; Association for Education in Journalism and Mass Communication. *Address:* 3506 Elm Knoll, San Antonio, TX 78230, USA.

CLARKE Anna, b. 28 Apr 1919, Cape Town, South Africa. Author. *Education:* Schools in Cape Town, Montreal, Oxford. BSc, Economics, University of London, 1945; BA, Open University, 1971-75; MA, University of Sussex, 1975. *Appointments:* Private Secretary, Victor Gollancz Publishers, 1947-50; Private Secretary, Eyre and Spottiswoode, Publishers, 1951-53; Administrative Secretary, British Association for American Studies, London 1956-63. *Publications include:* The Poisoned Web, 1979; Poison Parsley, 1979; Last Voyage, 1980; Game, Set and Danger, 1981; Desire to Kill, 1982; We the Bereaved, 1982; Soon She Must Die, 1983; Paula Glenning stories: Last Judgement, 1985; Cabin 3033, 1986; The Mystery Lady, 1986; Last Seen in London, 1987; Murder in Writing, 1988; The Whitelands Affair, 1989. *Contributions to:* Short stories in Ellery Queen Mystery Magazine, New York. *Literary Agent:* Wendy Lipkind, New York. *Address:* c/o Wendy Lipkind, 165 East 66 Street, New York, NY 10021, USA.

CLARKE Arthur C (Charles), b. 16 Dec 1917, Minehead, England. Author. m. Marilyn Mayfield, 1953, div. 1964. *Education:* BSc, 1st Class Honours, King's College, London, 1946-48. *Appointments:* Auditor, HM Exchequer and Audit Department, 1936-41; Royal Air Force, 1941-46; Originated Communication Satellites, Wireless World, 1945; Lunar Massdriver, Journal of the British Interplanetary Society, 1950; Assistant Editor, Science Abstracts, Institution of Electronic Engineers, 1949-50; Diver, Great Barrier Reef and Indian Ocean, 1954-; Lecturer, USA, 1957-70; Played Leonard Woolf in film, Beddegama, 1979. Vikram Sarabhai Professor, Physical Research Laboratory, Ahmedabad, 1980; Writer and Host, Television series, Arthur C Clarke's Mysterious World, Yorkshire Television, 1980, and World of Strange Powers, 1984; Host, The Communications Revolution, NVC Television Series, 1983; Delivered Nehru Memorial Lecture, New Delhi, India, 1986; Chancellor, International Space University, 1989-; Chancellor, University of Moratuwa, Sri Lanka, 1979-. *Publications include:* Author of over 70 books including: Against the Fall of Night; The City and the Stars; The Deep Range; A Fall of Moondust; Glide Path; The Lion of Comarre; The Other Side of the Sky; Prelude to Space; Rendezvous with Rama; The Songs of Distant Earth; Tales from the White Hart; Tales of Ten Worlds; The Wind from the Sun; 2001: A Space Odyssey; 2010: Odyssey Two; Ascent to Orbit; The Coast of Coral; The Exploration of Space; Interplanetary Flight; The Promise of Space; Report on Planet Three; Voice Across the Sea; Voices from the Sky; The Young Traveller in Space, 1984; Spring; The Ghost from the Green Banks, 1990; The Garden of Rama, 1991; Beyond the Night, 1991. *Contributions to:* Over 500 articles and short stories. *Honours include:* Recipient of numerous honours and awards including: Honorary DSc, Beaver College, Pennsylvannia, 1971; Honorary DSc, University of Moratuwa, 1979; International Fantasy Award, 1952; Kalinga Prize, 1961; SF Writers of America Grand Master, 1986; CBE, 1989. *Memberships:* Fellow, Royal Astronomical Society; Fellow, International Science Writers Association; American Association for the Advancement of Science; British Astronomical Association; Association of British Science Writers; Society of Authors; Vice President, H G Wells Society. *Literary Agent:* c/o David Higham Associates, 5 Lower John Street, Golden Square, London W1R 3PE. *Address:* 25 Barnes Place, Colombo 7, Sri Lanka.

CLARKE Austin Ardinel Chesterfield, b. 26 July 1934, Barbados, West Indies. Author. m. 14 Sept. 1957, 2 daughters. *Education:* Trinity College, University of Toronto, Canada. *Appointments:* Hoyt Fellow, Yale University, 1968; Margaret Bundy Scott Professor of Literature, 1970; Jacob Ziskind Professor Literature, Brandeis University, 1970; Fellow, School of Letters, Indiana, 1969. *Publications:* The Meeting Point, 1967; Storm of Fortune, 1972; The Biggor Light, 1973; When he Was Young & Free He Used to Wear Silks, 1972; The Prime Minister, 1977; Growing Up Stupid Under the Union Jack, 1980; When Women Rule, 1985; Nine Men Who Laughed, 1986; Proud Empires, 1986. *Contributions to:* Tamarack Review, Canada; Canadian Literature; Chelsea, USA. *Honours:* President's Medal, 1965; Canada Council Awards, 1968, 1972; Casa de las Americas Literary Prize, 1980; Arts Council Award, Ontario, 1985. *Membership:* Arts & Letters Club. *Literary Agent:* Harold Ober Associates, USA; David

Higham, UK. *Address:* 62 McGill Street, Toronto M5B 1H2, Canada.

CLARKE Brenda (Margaret Lilian) (Brenda Honeyman, Kate Sedley), b. 1926, United Kingdom. Author. *Publications:* Richard By Grace of God, 1968; The Kingmaker, 1969; Richard and Elizabeth, 1970; Harry the King, 1971; Brother Bedford, 1972; Good Duke Humphrey, 1973; The King's Minions, 1974; The Queen and Mortimer, 1974; Edward, The Warrior, 1975; All the King's Sons, 1975; The Golden Griffin, 1976; At the King's Court, 1976; The King's Tale, 1977; MacBeth, King of Scots, 1977; Emma, The Queen, 1978; The Glass Island, 1978; The Lofty Banners, 1979; Harold of the English, 1979; The Far Morning, 1982; All Through the Day, 1983; A Rose in May, 1984; Three Women, 1985; Winter Landscape, 1986; Under Heaven, 1988; An Equal Chance, 1989; Sisters and Lovers, 1990; Beyond The World, 1991, as Brenda Clarke; Death and The Chapman, 1992, as Kate Sedley. *Literary Agent:* David Grossman Literary Agency, London. *Address:* 25 Torridge Road, Keynsham, Bristol BS18 1QQ, England.

CLARKE Hugh Vincent, b. 27 Nov 1919, Brisbane, Australia. Journalist; Author. m. Mary Patricia Ryan, 6 June 1961. *Education:* St Josephs College, Brisbane. *Appointments:* Director of Information & Publicity, Department of Territories; Director of Information and PR, Department of Aboriginal Affairs. *Publications:* The Tub; Breakout; To Sydney by Stealth; The Long Arm; Fire one; The Broke and the Broken; Last Stop Nagasaki; Twilight Liberation; A Life for Every Sleeper; Prisoners of War; When the Balloon Went Up. *Contributions to:* Australian Writes; Australians at War; The Bulletin; Canberra Times; Australasion Past. *Memberships:* Australian Society to Authors; National Press Club. *Address:* 14 Chermside Street, Deakin, Canberra 2600, Australia.

CLARKE Joan Lorraine, b. 23 Aug 1920, Sydney, Australia, Author; Freelance Editor. m. R G Clarke, 1946, div, 1 son. *Education:* Diploma, Secretarial College, 1938. *Appointments:* Editor, The Australian Author, 1977-81; Editor, Australian Society of Authors, Writers Handbook 2nd edition, 1980. *Publications:* The Tracks We Travel: Australian Short Stories, 1953; Girl Fridays in Revolt, (Co-author), 1969; Max Herz, Surgeon Extraordinary, 1976; Contributing Author, Australian Political Milestone, 1976; Gold, (Co-author), 1981; The Doctor Who Dared, 1982; Just Us, 1988. *Contributions to:* Sydney Morning Herald; Australian Women's Weekly; Flair; Pol; The Australian Author; Overland; Radio talks and features for the Australian Broadcasting Commission and commercial radio. *Honours:* Co-recipient, Woman of the Year Award, 1969; Senior Literary Fellowship, 1978. *Memberships:* Fellowship of Australian Writers, Vice President, 1953; Australian Society of Authors, Committee of Management, 1963, 1968-69, 1978, 1981, Treasurer, 1966-67; International PEN, Sydney Centre, Treasurer, 1971-76, Vice President, 1987-89; Society of Women Writers, 1976-88; Society of Editors; Sydney Secretaries Forum, President, 1971. *Address:* 42/114 Spit Road, Mosman, NSW 2088, Australia.

CLARKE Mary, b. 23 Aug 1923, London, England. Editor; Writer. *Literary Appointments:* Editor, The Dancing Times, London. *Publications:* The Sadler's Wells Ballet: A History and an Appreciation, 1955; Six Great Dancers, 1957; Dancers of Mercury; The Story of Ballet Rambert, 1962; Ballet: An Illustrated History (with Clement Crisp), 1973, 1992; recent Books with Clement Crisp: Design for Ballet; Making A Ballet; Dancer: Men in Dance; Ballerina; History of Dance. *Contributions to:* Encyclopeadia Britannica; The Guardian; Dance Magazine, New York; Dance News, New York; The Observer; Sunday Times. *Honours:* 2nd Prize, Café Royal Literary Prize for Best Book on Theatre, 1955; Queen Elizabeth II Award, Royal Academy of Dancing, 1990; Knight, Order of Dannebrog (Danish), 1992. *Membership:* Gautier Club. *Address:* 54 Ripplevale Grove, London, N1 1HT, England.

CLARKE Pauline. *See:* **BLAIR Pauline Hunter.**

CLARKSON Ewan, b. 1929, United Kingdom. Children's Writer. *Publications:* Break for Freedom, US Edition Syla the Mink, 1967; Halic, The Story of a Grey Seal, 1970; The Running of the Deer, 1972; In the Shadow of the Falcon, 1973; Wolf Country, a Wilderness Pilgrimage, 1975; The Badgers of Summercombe, 1977; The Many Forked Branch, 1980; Wolves, 1980; Reindeer, 1981; Eagles, 1981; Beavers, 1981; In the Wake of the Storm, novel, 1984; Ice Trek, 1986. *Address:* Moss Rose Cottage, Preston, Kingsteignton, Newton Abbot, Devon, England.

CLARKSON J F. *See:* **TUBB E C.**

CLARY Sydney Ann, b. 13 Feb 1948, Auburn, Alabama, USA. Writer. m. Bishop D Clary, 26 Sept 1967, 2 daughters. *Education:* Palm Beach Community College, 2 years. *Publications:* Double Solitaire; Devil and the Duchess; Eye of the Storm; A Touch of Passion; Her Golden Eyes; Fire in the Night; With a Little Spice; Southern Comfort; This Wildfire Magic. *Contributions to:* Numerous articles to Romantic Times; Articles to Romance Writers of America Magazine. *Honours:* Reviewers Choice Finalist, 1983, 1984, 1987, 1990; Gold Medallion Finalist, Romance Writers of America, 1988; Reviewers Choice Best All Around Series Author, 1989-90. *Memberships:* Charter Member, Romance Writers of America; National Writers Club; Florida and Orange County Chapters, Romance Writers of America. *Literary Agent:* Maureen Walters, Curtis Brown Ltd, USA. *Address:* c/o Curtis Brown Ltd, 10 Astor Place, New York, NY 10013, USA.

CLAUSEN Christopher John, b. 14 May 1942, Richmond, Virginia, USA. Writer. m. Nancy Tunstal Palmer, 3 Aug 1976. *Education:* BA, Earlham College, 1964; MA, University of Chicago, 1965; PhD, Queen's University, 1972. *Appointments:* English Department, University of Hawaii, 1965-66; Concord College, 1966-68; Virginia Tech, 1973-85; Professor, Pennsylvania State University, 1985-. *Publications:* The Place of Poetry; The Moral Imagination. *Contributions to:* Numerous Essays; Articles; Poems; Reviews; American & British Magazines. *Honours:* Canada Council Doctoral Fellow; Djerassi Foundation Writer in Residence. *Memberships:* AAUP; NAS. *Address:* Department of English, Pennsylvania State University, University Park, PA 16802, USA.

CLAVELL James, Author; Screenwriter; Film Director & Producer. m. 1953, 2 daughters. *Publications:* Screenwriter: The Fly, 1958; Watussi, 1958; The Great Escape, 1960; Satan Bug, 1962; 633 Squadron, 1963; Director, Where's Jack, 1968; Writer, Producer, Director: Five Gates to Hell, 1959; Walk Like a dragon, 1960; To Sir With Love, 1966; Last Valley, 1969; Author of: Children's Story ... But Not for Children, 1982; King Rat, 1962; Tai-pan, 1966; Shogun, 1976; Noble House 1980; Thrump-O-Moto, 1985; Whirlwind, 1986. *Honours:* Emmy; Peabody; Critics; Golden Globe; Golden Eiger (Austria), 1972. *Address:* c/o Foreign Rights Inc, 136 E 57th Street, New York, NY 10022, USA.

CLAYPOOL MINER Jane, b. 22 Apr 1933, McAllen, Texas, USA. Writer. m. (1) Dennis A. Shelley, 1952 (dec. 1953), 1 daughter; (2) Richard Yale Miner, 1962 (dec. 1965). *Education:* BA, Art Education, California State University, Long Beach; Graduate work, University of California, Los Angeles. *Publications include:* 60 books for teenagers including: Alcohol & You, 1980; Dreams Can Come True, 1981; Joanna, 1985; History of Workers, 1986; Corey, 1987. *Contributions to:* Numerous feature articles, local & national publications; Weekly Column, Real Estate. *Honour:* Member of Year, Society of Children's Book Writers. *Memberships:* Society of Children's Book Writers; American Society of Authors & Journalists; National Arts Club; National Board of Realtors. *Address:* 2883 Lone Jack Road, Olivenhain, California 92024, USA.

CLAYTON Bess. *See:* **LOCKE Robert Howard.**

CLAYTON Jay. *See:* **CLAYTON John B IV.**

CLAYTON John B IV (Jay Clayton), b. 11 July 1951, Dallas, Texas, USA. Professor. m. Ellen Wright Clayton, 19 June 1982, 2 sons. *Education:* AB, Yale University, 1974; PhD, University of Virginia, 1979. *Appointments:* Associate Professor, Vanderbilt University. *Publications:* Romantic Vision and the Novel, 1987; Influence and Intertextuality in Literary History (co-editor), 1991; The Pleasures of Babel: Contemporary American Literature and Theory, 1993. *Contributions to:* Southern Review; Southwest Review; Critical Inquiry; American Literary History; ELH; Contemporary Literature; Denver Quarterly; Kansas Quarterly; Nineteenth-Century Literature. *Honours:* Fellow, American Council of Learned Societies, 1981-82; Fellow, Robert Penn Warren Center for the Humanities, 1988-90; Robert A Partlow Prize for Romantic Vision and the Novel, 1988. *Membership:* Second Vice President, Society of the Study of Narrative Literature; Trustee, Dickens Society. *Address:* Department of English, Vanderbilt University, Nashville, TN 37235, USA.

CLAYTON John J, b. 5 Jan 1935, New York City, New York, USA. Writer; Professor of Literature and Creative Writing. 3 sons, 1 daughter. *Education:* BA (Honours), Columbia College, 1956; MA, Modern Literature, New York University, 1959; PhD, Indiana University, 1966. *Publications:* What Are Friends For, novel, 1979; Bodies of the Rich, stories, 1984; Criticism: Saul Bellow: In Defense of Man, 1968, 1979; Gestures of Healing, 1991. *Contributions to:* Esquire; Playboy; Virginia Quarterly Review; Agni; Ploughshares; Tri-Quarterly; Massachusetts Review; Others. *Literary Agent:* Ellen Levine. *Address:* English Department, University of Massachusetts, Amherst, MA 01002, USA.

CLAYTON Peter Arthur, b. 27 Apr 1937, London, England. Publishing Consultant; Archaeological Lecturer. m. Janet Frances Manning, 5 Sept 1964, 2 sons. *Education:* School of Librarianship; NW Polytechnic, London, 1958; Institute of Archaeology, London University, 1958-62; University College, London, 1968-72. *Appointments:* Librarian, 1953-67; Archaeological Editor, Thames & Hudson, 1963-73; Humanities Publisher, Longmans, 1973; Managing Editor, British Museums Publications, 1971-79; Publications Director, BA Seaby, 1980-87; Writer, Lecturer, 1987-. *Publications:* The Rediscovery of Ancient Egypt; Archaeological Sites of Britain; Seven Wonders of the Ancient World; Treasures of Ancient Rome; Companion to Roman Britain; Great Figures of Mythology; Gods and Symbols of Ancient Egypt. *Contributions to:* Journal of Egyptian Archaeology; Numismatic Chronicle; Coin & Medal Bulletin; Minerva. *Honours:* FRNS; FLA; FSA; Honorary Member, Institute of Archaeology, London University. *Memberships:* Society of Antiquaries; Library Association; Egypt Eaploration Society; Royal Numismatic Society; Society for Promotion of Roman Studies; British Museums Society; T E Lawrence Society; Museum Association. *Address:* 41 Cardy Road, Boxmoor, Hemel Hempstead, Herts, HP1 1RL, England.

CLEALL Charles, b. 1 June 1927, Heston, Middlesex, England. Writer. m. Mary Turner, 25 July 1953, 2 daughters. *Education:* Trinity College of Music, London, GTCL; LRAM; ARCO; Jordanhill College of Education, BMus; FRCO; MA, University College of North Wales. *Appointments include:* Intructor, Lieut, Royal Navy Command, 1946-48; Professor, Solo-Singing and Voice Production, TCL, 1949-52; Choral Scholar, Westminster Abbey, 1949-52; Conductor, Morley College Orchestra, 1950-52; BBC Music Assistant, Midland Region, 1954-55; Lecturer in Music, The Froebel Institute, Roehampton, 1967-68; Editor, Journal of The Ernest George White Society, 1983-87. *Publications:* Voice Production in Choral Technique, 1955, revised 1970; The Selection and Training of Mixed Choirs in Churches, 1960; Sixty Songs from Sankey, 1960, revised 1966;

John Merbecke's Music for the Congregation at Holy Communion, 1963; Music and Holiness, 1964; Plainsong for Pleasure, 1969; Authentic Chanting, 1969; A Guide to Vanity Fair, 1982; Walking Round the Church of St James' the Great, Stonehaven, 1993. *Honours:* Limpus Fellowship Prizeman of The Royal College of Organists, 1953; International Composition Prizeman of the Cathedral of St John The Devine, New York, 1954. *Memberships:* The Ernest George White Society, Trustee and Member of Council; Incorporated Association of Organists; Incorporated Society of Musicians, Warden, Education Section, 1971-72; Methodist Church Music Society, Scottish Commissioner; Royal College of Organists. *Address:* 10 Carronhall, Stonehaven, Aberdeen AB3 2HF, Scotland.

CLEARE John Silvey, b. 2 May 1936, London, England, Photographer; Writer. m. (1), (2) Jo Jackson, 12 May 1980, 1 daughter. *Education:* Wycliffe College, 1945-54; Guildford School of Photography, 1957-60. *Appointments:* Joint Editor, Mountain Life magazine, 1973-75; Editorial Board, Climber and Rambler magazine, 1975-85. *Publications:* Trekking- Great Walks of the World, 1988; John Cleare's 50 Best Hill Walks in Britain, 1988; World Guide to Mountains, 1979; Mountains, 1975; Rock Climbers in Action in Snowdonia, 1966; Sea-Cliff Climbing in Britain, 1973; Mountaineering, 1980; Scrambles Among The Alps, 1986. *Contributions to:* Times; Sunday Times; Independent; Observer; World; Country Living; Boat International; Intercontinental; Alpine Journal; High; Climber; Great Outdoors. *Honours:* 35mm prize, Trento Film Festival, for film The Climber, (as Cameraman), 1971. *Memberships:* Outdoor Writers Guild, Committee, 1989- 90; British Association of Picture Libraries, Committee, 1989-90; Alpine Club, Committee, 1968-70, 1983-86; Alpine Ski Club, Committee, 1988-; Himalayan Club; Climbers Club. *Address:* Hill Cottage, Fonthill Gifford, Salisbury, Wiltshire SP3 6QW, England.

CLEARY Beverly Atlee, b. 12 Apr 1916, McMinnville, Oregon, USA. Writer of children's books. m. Clarence T Cleary, 6 Oct 1940, 1 son, 1 daughter. *Education:* BA, University of California, Berkeley, 1938; BA, Librarianship, University of Washington, 1939. *Publications include:* Henry Huggins, 1950; Fifteen, 1956; The Mouse and the Motorcycle, 1965; Ramona The Pest, 1968; Dear Mr Henshaw, 1983; A Girl From Yamhill: A Memoir, 1988. *Contribution to:* The Horn Book Magazine. *Honours:* Laura Ingalls Wilder Award, ALA, 1975; Newbery Honor Books, ALA, 1978, 1982; Newbery Award, ALA, 1984; Christopher Award, Catholic Livary Association, 1984; Everychild Award, Children's Book Council, 1985. *Membership:* Authors League of America. *Address:* Morrow Junior Books, 1350 Avenue of the Americas, New York, NY 10019, USA.

CLEARY Jon (Stephen), b. 1917. Writer of Novels/ Short stories/Screenplays. *Appointments:* Journalist, Australian News and Information Bureau, London 1948-49 and New York City 1949- 51. *Publications:* The Small Glories (short stories) 1945; You Can't See Round Corners, 1947; The Long Shadow, 1949; Just Let Me Be, 1950; The Sundowners, 1952, screenplay 1961; The Climate of Courage (in US as Naked in the Night) 1954; Justin Bayard, 1955; The Green Helmet, 1957, screenplay 1960; Back of Sunset, 1959; (with H Watt) The Siege of Pinchgut (screenplay) 1959; North from Thursday, 1960; The Country of Marriage, 1961; Forest of the Night, 1962; Pillar of Salt (short stories), 1963; A Flight of Chariots, 1964; The Fall of an Eagle, 1965; The Pulse of Danger, 1966; The High Commissioner, 1967; The Long Pursuit, 1968; Season of Doubt, 1969; Remember Jack Hoxie, 1970; Helga's Webb, 1971; The Liberators (in UK as Mask of the Andes), 1971; The Ninth Marquess (in UK as Man's Estate) 1972; Ransom, 1973; Peter's Pence, 1974; Sidecar Boys (screenplay) 1974; The Safe House, 1975; A Sound of Lightning, 1976; High Road to China, 1977; Vortex, 1977; The Beaufort Sisters, 1979; A Very Private War, 1980; The Golden Sabre, 1981; The Faraway Drums, 1981; Spearfield's Daughter, 1982; The Phoenix Tree, 1984;

The City of Fading Light, 1985; Dragons at the Party, 1987; Now and Then, Amen, 1988; Babylon South, 1989; Murder Song, 1990; Pride's Harvest, 1991; Dark Summer, 1992; Bleak Spring, 1993. *Honours:* 2nd Prizewinner, Sydney Herald Novel Contest, 1946; Best Australian Novel 1950, Australian Literature Society; Regional Winner, NY Herald Tribune Short Story Contest, 1950; Edgar Winner, US Crime Writers, 1974. *Memberships:* Society of Authors; Writers Guild. *Address:* c/o Harper Collins, 77-85 Fulham Palace Road, London W6 8JB, England.

CLEESE John (Marwood), b. 1939, United Kingdom. Actor; Frequent stage, TV and film appearances. *Publications:* Monty Python Books (contributor); Families and How to Survive Them (with Robin Skynner), 1983; The Complete Fawlty Towers, 1989; Life and How To Survive It (with Robin Skynner), 1993. *Honour:* Hon. LLD, St Andrews. *Address:* c/o David Wilkinson, 115 Hazlebury Road, London, SW6 2LX, England.

CLEEVE Brian Talbot, b. 22 Nov 1921, Thorpe Bay, Essex, England. Author. Journalist. m. Veronica McAdie, 24 Sept 1945, 2 daughters. *Education:* BA, University of South Africa, 1954; PhD, University of Ireland, Dublin, 1956. *Publications:* Cry of Morning, 1970; Sara, 1975; House on the Rock, 1980; The Fourth Mary, 1982; Biographical Dictionary of Irish Writers, 1985; A Woman of Fortune, 1993. *Contributions to:* Numerous short stories, various magazines. *Honours:* Award, Mystery Writers of America, 1965 (short story, Foxer); Knight of Mark Twain, 1972-73. *Literary Agent:* Elaine Markson, 44 Greenwich Avenue, NY, USA. *Address:* 60 Heytesbury Lane, Ballsbridge, Dublin 4, Ireland.

CLEMENT Hal. *See:* **STUBBS Harry Clement.**

CLEMENT Richard (Dick), b. 5 Sept. 1937. Writer; Director; Producer. m. (1) Jennifer Sheppard, divorced 1981, 3 sons, 1 daughter, (2) Nancy Campbell, 1 daughter. *Publications:* Co-Writer with Ian La Frenais, TV: The Likely Lads, 1964-66; Whatever Happened to the Likely Lads, 1972-73; Porridge, 1974-76; Thick as Thieves, 1974; Going Straight, 1978; Auf Wiedershen Pet, 1984; Freddie and Max 1990; Stretch, Over the Rainbow, 1993. Films: The Jokers, 1967; Otley, 1968; Hannibal Brooks, 1968; Villain, 1971; Prisoner of Zenda, 1977; Porridge, 1979; Water, 1984; Vice Versa, 1988; The Committments, 1991; Stage: Billy, 1974; Anyone for Denis? (director), 1981. *Honour:* Jointly, Peter Seller's Award, 1991. *Address:* 9700 Yoakum Drive, Beverly Hills, CA 90210, USA.

CLEMO Jack. *See:* **CLEMO Reginald John.**

CLEMO Reginald John, (Jack Clemo), b. 11 Mar 1916, St Austell, Cornwall, England, Literature. m. Ruth Grace Peaty, 26 Oct 1968. *Publications:* Wilding Craft, 1948, paperback, 1983; Confession of a Rebel, 1949, paperback, 1988; The Invading Gospel, 1958, paperback, 1972, 1986; The Map of Clay, 1961; The Shadowed Bed, 1986; Selected Poems, 1988; Cactus on Carmel, 1967; The Echoing Tip, 1971; Broad Autumn, 1975; A Different Drummer, 1986; The Bouncing Hills, 1983; Banner Poems, 1989. *Contributions to:* Acumen; Christian Woman; Cornish Banner; Dorset Year Book; Orbis; Outposts; Poetry Ireland; South-west Review; Westwords. *Honours:* Atlantic Award in Literature, 1948; Arts Council Festival Poetry Prize, 1951; Civil List Pension, 1961; Cornish Gorsedd Bardship, 1970; Honorary D.Litt degree, Exeter University, 1981. *Memberships:* Honorary Member, West Country Writers' Association; Honorary member, Arts Centre Group. *Address:* 24 Southlands Road, Rodwell, Weymouth, Dorset DT4 9LQ, England.

CLERK David. *See:* **HARDCASTLE Michael.**

CLEVELAND John. *See:* **MCELFRESH (Elizabeth) Adeline.**

CLEVELAND-PECK Patricia, b. 17 Feb 1939, Maidstone, England. Writer. m. W D Cleveland Peck, 20 Feb 1963, 2 sons, 1 daughter. *Education:* Sorbonne, Trinity College, Dublin, MA, 1967. *Publications:* The String Family; The Cello and The Nightingale; Evasion Tango; Many Children Books. *Contributions to:* Guardian; Observer; Homes & Gardens; Country Home Interiors; Traditional Homes. *Memberships:* PEN; Society of Authors. *Address:* Harelands, Ashurst Wood, Grinstead, Sussex RH19 3SL, England.

CLIFFORD Derek Plint, b. 1917, United Kingdom. Author. *Publications:* Mad Pelynt and the Bullet, 1940; The Perracotts, 1948; Geraniums, 1953; Pelargoniums Including the Popular Geranium, 1958, 2nd Edition, 1970; A History of Garden Design, 1962, 2nd Edition, 1966; Watercolours of the Norwich School, 1967; Art and Understanding, 1968; John Crome (co-author), 1968; The Paintings of Philip de Laszlo, 1969; Collecting English Watercolours, 1970, 2nd Edition, 1976; To Catch a Fox, 1982; The Affair of the Forest, 1982. *Address:* c/o Springwood Books, The Avenue, Ascot SL5 7LY, England.

CLIFT Patricia Elizabeth, (Pat Studdy-Clift), b. 30 July 1926, Sydney, New South Wales, Australia. Writer; Illustrator. m. James William Clift, 5 Aug 1948, 4 sons. *Appointments:* Intercultural Conference, University of Technology, Sydney, 1993; Australian Stockmans Hall of Fame, Longreach, 1993. *Publications:* Only Our Gloves on; The Many Faces of the Tweed I, II; Bush Justice; Darwin Dilemmas. *Contributions to:* Country Life; Chinchilla News. *Memberships:* Country Women Association; Graziers Association Beaudesert; Oral History Association. *Literary Agent:* Peter Bridge Hesperian Press, PO Box 317 Victoria Park 6100. *Address:* 75 McLeod Street, Condong, NSW 2484, Australia.

CLIFTON CLARK Catherine. *See:* **CLARK Marie Catherine Audrey.**

CLINTON Dorothy Louise Randle, b. 6 Apr 1925, Des Moines, Iowa, USA. Writer. m. Moses S Clinton, 6 June 1950, 1 son. *Education:* Bachelor of Fine Arts, Drake University, 1949. *Publications:* The Only Opaque Light (poem), in Golden Voices Past and Present, 1989; Memory Lapse (poem), in Lyrical Treasures Classic and Modern, 1983; Ascending Line (poem), bought by Carousel Quarterly, 1978; The Look and the See (poem), bought by Carousel Quarterly, 1979; Snobbery in Nuance, published in Magic of the Muse, 1978; Black Dignity in Marsh & Haunting Could Be Love, published in Publisher's Choice: Selected Poets of the New Era by American Poetry Association; Our Plant Of Walking Tabloids, published in Perception Vol II; Weed, Weed The Word Jungle, published in Vol I of Perceptions; You Don't Hear The Echo, You Don't Knoe, Best Poets of 1991; Blind Transfer, three act play; Stop The Itch Without A Bitch. *Honours:* Clover Award for A Cruise, 1974; Clove Award for Clouds, 1975; Editor's Choice Award for The Crucial Must But How and for The Only Opaque Light from the National Library of Poetry, 1989; Editor's Choice Award for Judicial Red Alert; The National Library of Poetry, A Question of Balance Contest for It's Not Always Red; 2 Accomplishment of Merit, Creative Arts & Science Enterprises, one of the poems was called Temporary Symphony. *Membership:* The International Society of Poets. *Address:* 1530 Maple, Des Moines, IA 50316, USA.

CLINTON Jeff. *See:* **BICKHAM Jack Miles.**

CLIVE William. *See:* **BASSETT Ronald Leslie.**

CLOSE Francis Edwin (Frank Close), b. 24 July 1945, Peterborough, England. Physicist. m. Gillian Boyce, 22 Mar 1969, 2 daughters. *Education:* BSc, St Andrews University, 1967; D Phil, Oxford University, 1970. *Publications:* Too Hot To Handle; End; The Particle Explosion; The Cosmic Onion; Introduction to Quarks and Partons. *Contributions to:* Over 200 Scientific Papers; Articles on Rhysics & Cosmology in Nature; New Scientist; BBC World Service. *Honours:* Royal Copus Cience Book Prize. *Memberships:* Fellow of Institute of Physics; British Association. *Literary Agent:* Sheila Watson. *Address:* Rutherford Appleton Lab, Chilton, Didcot, Oxon OX11 1QX, England.

CLOSE Frank. *See:* **CLOSE Francis Edwin.**

CLOUDSLEY-THOMPSON John Leonard, b. 23 May 1921, Murree, India. Professor of Zoology. m. Jessie Anne Cloudsley, 1944. 3 sons. *Education:* MA, PhD, Pembroke College, Cambridge; DSc, London, 1960. *Publications include:* Spiders, Scorpions, Centipedes and Mites, 1958, 2nd edition 1968; Insects and History, 1976; Tooth and Claw, 1980; Rhythmic Activity in Animal Physiology and Behaviour, 1961; The Desert, 1977; Evolution and Adaptation of Terrestrial Arthropods, 1988; Guide to Woodlands, 1985; Evolution and Adaptation of Terestrial Arthropals, 1988; Erophysiology of Desert Arthropods and Reptiles, 1991; (novel), Nile Quest, 1992; many other books including 11 children's books. *Contributions to:* Encyclopaedia Britannica; Encyclopedia Americana. *Honours:* Honorary DSc, Khartoum, 1981; Silver Jubilee Gold Medal, Foundation for Environmental Conservation (Best Paper Award, 1989). *Address:* Department of Biology, (Medawar Building), University College, University of London, Gower Street, London WC1E 6BT, England.

CLOUGH Brenda Wang, b. 13 Nov 1955, Washington, DC, USA. Writer. m. Lawrence A. Clough, 21 May 1977, 1 daughter. *Education:* BA, English, Carnegie-Mellon University, 1977. *Appointments:* Circulation Department, United Chapters of Phi Beta Kappa, Washington, DC; Associate Editor, Research Institute of America, Washington Office. *Publications:* Novels: The Crystal Crown, 1984; The Dragon of Mishbil, 1985; The Realm Beneath, 1986; The Name of the Sun, 1988. *Membership:* Science Fiction Writers of America. *Address:* 1941 Barton Hill Road, Reston, VA 22091, USA.

CLOUSE Robert Gordon, b. 26 Aug 1931, Mansfield, Ohio, USA, Professor of History; Christian Minister. m. Bonnidell Barrows Clouse, 17 June 1955. *Education:* BA, Bryan College, 1954; BD, Grace Theological Seminary, 1957; MA, 1960, PhD, 1963, University of Iowa. *Appointments:* Visiting Scholar, Folger-Shakespeare Library, 1963-75; Visiting Scholar, Clark Library, UCLA, 1988; Visiting Scholar, Newberry Library, 1976; Visiting Scholar, Lilly Library, 1974; Professor of history, Indiana State University, 1963-. *Publications:* Women in Ministry, Four Views, 1989; Meaning of the Millennium, Four Views, 1977; The Church in an Age of Orthodoxy and Enlightenment, 1980; Wealth and Poverty, Four Views, 1984; War, Four Christian Views, 1985. *Contributions to:* Second Opinion; Regnum, Religio et Ratio; The Journal of Interdisciplinary History; Sixteenth Century Journal. *Honours:* ISU Research Creativity Award, 1986; Grant, National Endowment for the Humanities, 1983; Award, Institute for Research in the Humanities, 1964. *Memberships:* Conference on Faith and History, Director, 1968-; Central Renaissance Conference, President, 1968, 1988; American Historical Association; American Society of Church History; Sixteenth Century Studies Conference; National Fellowship of Garce Brethren Ministers. *Address:* 2122 South 21st Street, Terre Haute, IN 47802, USA.

CLUSTER Dick. *See:* **CLUSTER Richard Bruce.**

CLUSTER Richard Bruce (Dick Cluster), b. 17 Jan 1947, Baltimore, Maryland, USA. Writer. 1 son. *Education:* BA, Harvard University, 1968; Venceremos Brigade, Aguacate, Cuba, 1970; Auto Mechanics Certificate, Newton Massachusetts High School, 1971. *Publications:* They Should Have Served That Cup of

Coffee, 1979; Shrinking Dollars, Vanishing Jobs, 1980; Return to Sender, 1988; Repulse Monkey, 1989; Obligations of the Bone, 1992. *Literary Agents:* Gina Maccoby, New York, USA (US rights); Gregory and Radice, London, England (European rights). *Address:* 33 Jackson St, Cambridge, MA 02140, USA.

CLUTTERBUCK Richard Lewis, b. 22 Nov 1917, London, England. Security Consultant. m. Angela Muriel Barford, 15 May 1948. 3 sons. *Education:* MA, Mechanical Sciences, Cambridge University, 1939; PhD, Politics, London University, 1971. *Publications:* Living With Terrorism, 1975; Guerrillas & Terrorists, 1980; Britain In Agony, 1980; The Media & Political Violence, 1983; Industrial Conflict & Democracy, 1984; Conflict & Violence in Singapore & Malaysia, 1985; Kidnap Hijack & Extortion, 1987; Terrorism Drugs & Crime in Europe After 1992, 1990; Terrorism & Guerrilla Warfare: Forecasts & Remedies, 1990. *Contributions to:* Magazines and journals in UK and USA. *Address:* Department of Politics, University of Exeter, Exeter EX4 4RJ, England.

COATES Ken, b. 16 Sept 1930, Leek. Member European Parliament; Chairman, Human Rights Sub-Committee of European Parliament. m. Tamara Tura, 21 Aug 1969, 3 sons, 3 daughters. *Education:* BA, Nottingham University, 1959. *Publications:* Industrial Democracy in Great Britain (w Tony Topham); Poverty: The Forgotten Englishmen (w Bill Silburn); The Crises of British Socialism; Essays in Industrial Democracy; The New Unionism (w Tony Topham); Beyond Wage Slavery; The Shop Stewards' Guide to the Bullock Report (w Tony Topham); Democracy in the Labour Party; The Case of Nikolai Bukharin; Work-ins. Sit ins and Industrial Democracy; Trade Unions in Britain (w Tony Topham); Heresies; The Most Dangerous Decade; Trade Unions and Politics (w Tony Topham); Think Globally, Act Locally; The Making of the Transport & General Workers Union (w Tony Topham). *Memberships:* Bertrand Russell Peace Foundation. *Address:* Bertrand Russell House, Gamble Street, Nottingham, NG7 4ET, England.

COATES Sheila. *See:* **HOLLAND Sheila.**

COBB Vicki, b. 19 Aug 1938, Brooklyn, New York, USA. Writer. Divorced, 2 sons. *Education:* BA, Barnard College, 1958; MA, Columbia University. *Publications include:* Science Experiments You Can Eat 1972; Lots of Rot, 1981; How to Really Fool Yourself: Illusions for All Your Senses, 1981; The Secret Life of School Supplies: A Science Experiment Book, 1981; Bet You Can't! Science Impossibilities to Fool You, 1981; Fuzz Does It, 1982; Gobs of Goo, 1983; The Monsters Who Died, 1983; Chemically Active!, 1985; Inspector Bodyguard, 1986; The Science Safari Series; The Imagine Living Here Series. *Contributions to:* numerous professional journals. *Honours:* Children's Science Book Award, New York Academy of Sciences, 1981; Washington Irving Children's Book Choice Award, 1984; Eva L Gordon Award, 1985; commended by COPUS and the London Science Museum, 1989. *Memberships:* Authors' Guild; ASJA; Society of Children's Book Writers; National Writers Union. *Literary Agent:* Christine Tomasino, RLR Associates Ltd. *Address:* 302 Pondside Drive, White Plains, NY 10607, USA.

COBBETT Richard. *See:* **PLUCKROSE Henry Arthur.**

COBBING Bob, b. 1920, British, Poet. *Appointments:* Coordinator, Association of Little Presses, 1971-92; Co-editor, Poetry and Little Press Information, 1980-92. *Publications include:* Bill Jubobe: selected Poems 1942-75, 1976; Cygnet Ring: Collected Poems 1, 1977; A Movie Book, 1978; Two-Leaf Book, 1978; (with Peter Mayer), Concerning Concrete Poetry, 1978; Found: Sound, 1978; Principles of Movement, 1978; Meet Bournemouth, 1978; Fugitive Poem No X, 1978; Game and Set, 1978; Ginetics, 1978; ABC/Wan de Tree: Collected Poems 2, 1978; Sensations of the Retina,

1978; A Peal in Air: Collected Poems 3, 1978; Fiveways, 1978; Niagara, 1978; Grin, 1979; (with Jeremy Adler), A Short History of London, 1979; The Kollekted Kris Kringle: Collected Poems 4, 1979; Pattern of Performance, 1979; The Sacred Mushroom, 1980; (with Jeremy Adler), Notes from the Correspondence, 1980; Voicings, 1980; (Soma), Light Song, 1981; Serial Ten (Portraits), 1981; Four Letter Poems, 2 series, 1981; Sound of Jade, 1982; In Line, 1982; Baker's Dozen, 1982; Lightsong Two, 1983; Bob Cobbing's Girlie Poems, Collected Poems 5, 1983; Sockless in Sandals: Collected Poems 6, 1985; Vowels and Consequences, Collected Poems 7, 1985; Lame, Limping, Mangled, Marred and Mutilated: Collected Poems 9, 1986; Metamorphosis, 1986; Variations on a Theme, 1986; Astound and Risible: Collected Poems 8, 1987; Processual, Collected Poems 10, 1987; Entitled: Entitled: Collected Poems 11, 1987; Improvisation is a Dirty Word: Collected Poems 12, 1990; Bob Jubile: Selected Poems 1944-90, 1990; Resonanzas, 1991; Grogram, 1991; Fuerteventura, 1992. *Address:* 89A Petherton Road, London N5 2QT, England.

COBURN Andrew, b. 1 May 1932, Exeter, New Hampshire, USA. *Education:* Suffolk University, Boston, 1954-58. *Publications:* Novels: The Trespassers, 1974; The Babysitter, 1979; Off Duty, 1980; Company Secrets, 1982; Widow's Walk, 1984; Sweetheart, 1985; Love Nest, 1987; Goldilocks, 1989; No Way Home, 1992. *Contributions to:* Transatlantic Magazine. *Honour:* Honorary DLitt, Merrimack College, USA, 1986. *Literary Agent:* Smith/Skolnik, 23 East 10th Street No 712, New York, NY 10003, USA. *Address:* 3 Farrwood Drive, Andover, MA 01810, USA.

COCHRAN Jeff. *See:* **DURST Paul.**

COCKCROFT John, b. 8 Feb 1917, Townsville, Australia. Author; Beef Cattle Producer. m. Joy Kirkness, 27 Oct 1947, 2 sons, 1 daughter. *Publications:* Isles of 5th Pacific; Polynesian Isles; Melanesian Isles; Indonesia Timor; Singapore, Malaysia; The Philipiines; India. *Contributions to:* Womens Weekly; Sydney Morning Herald; Daily Telegraph; Qantas Inflight Magazine. *Honours:* TV Logie Award. *Memberships:* Royal Geographical Society; Australian Authors Society; Gosford Amateur Swimming Association; Z Special Forces Association. *Address:* Glencona, Quirindi, NSW 2343, Australia.

COCKETT Mary, b. 1915. British Children's fiction and non-fiction. *Appointments:* Editor, National Institute of Industrial Psychology, 1943-48 and International Congress of Mental Health, 1948-49. *Publications include:* The Marvellous Stick (reader), 1972; The Joppy Stories: Joppy Crawling and Joppy on His Feet; Joppy Steps Out and Caught on a Tree Stump; Joppy in a Bucket and the Moving Cot, 3 vols, 1972; Boat Girl, 1972; Bells in Our Lives, 1973; Treasure, 1973; The Rainbow Walk (reader), 1973; An Armful of Sparrows (reader), 1973; As Big as the Ark, 1974; Look at the Little One, 1974; Dolls and Puppets, 1974; Walls, 1974; He Cannot Really Read (reader), 1974; Snake in the Camp, 1975; Tower Raven, 1975; Backyard Bird Hospital, 1975; The Story of Cars, 1976; The Magician (reader), 1976; Fly High, Magpie, (reader), 1976; Missing (reader), 1978; The Drowning Valley, 1978; The Birthday, 1979; Ladybird at the Zoo, Monster in the River, Pig at the Market, 3 picture books, 1979; The Christmas Tree, 1979; Money to Spend (reader), 1980; The Bell (reader), 1980; Witch of Candlewick, 1980; Enough is Enough, 1980; The Kneeling Knight, 1981; Shadow at Applegarth, 1981; Hoo-Ming's Discovery, 1982; The Cat and the Castle, 1982; The School Donkey, 1982; At the Tower (reader), 1984; Crab Apples (reader), 1984; Strange Hill, 1984; Tracker, 1984; Paper Boys (reader), 1984; Better Than a Party, 1985; Zoo Ticket, 1985; Rescue at the Zoo, 1986; Winning All the Way, 1987; Kate of Candlewick, 1987; The Day of the Squirrels, 1987; A Place of His Own, 1987; Mystery on the Farm, 1988; Bridesmaids, 1989. *Address:* 24 Benville Avenue, Bristol BS9 2RX, England.

CODE Keith Patrick, b. 3 Jan 1945, Pittsburgh, Pennsylvania, USA. Writer. m. 1 May 1976, 1 son. *Education:* Akron Art Institute, 1963. *Publications:* A Twist of the Wrist, 1983; The Soft Science of Road Racing Motorcycles, 1986; A Twist of the Wrist, Vol II, 1993. *Contributions to:* Articles to: Road Racing World; American Road Racing; Cycle World; Motorcylist Magazine. *Honours:* Citizen of the Year, Los Angeles Police Department, 1986; Addressed Society of Automotive Engineers, 1987; Awards of Merit, Motorcycle Safety Foundation, 1990, 1992; Motorcyclist of the Year, Motorcyclist Magazine, 1990. *Address:* c/o California Superbike School, PO Box 3107, Hollywood, CA 90078, USA.

CODRESCU Andrei, b. 20 Dec 1946, Romania. Writer. m. Alice Henderon, 12 Sept 1969, 2 sons. *Education:* Gh Lazar Lyceum, Sibiu, Romania, 1964. *Appointments:* Professor, Louisiana State University, 1986. *Publications:* The Hole in the Flag; Belligerence; The Disappearance of the Outside; Raised by Puppets; License to Carry a Gun; Life & Times of an Involuntary Genius; In Americas Shoes; Comrde Past & Mr Present; Monsieur Teste in America; A Craving for Swan. *Contributions to:* Numerous Journals inc, Harpers; The New York Times; The Paris Review; New American Writing; New Directions. Honours: Big Table Younger Poets Award; National Endowment for the Arts; Towson University Prize for Literature; Pushcart Prize; General Electric CCLM Poetry Prize. *Memberships:* MLA; PEN; Authors League. *Literary Agent:* Jonathon Lazear Inc. *Address:* English Department, LSU, Baton Rouge, LA 70803, USA.

CODY James. *See:* **ROHRBACH Peter Thomas.**

CODY Stetson. *See:* **GRIBBLE Leonard (Reginald).**

COE Jonathan, b. 19 Aug 1961, Birmingham, England. Novelist. m. Janine McKeown, 28 Jan 1989. *Education:* Trinity College, Cambridge, 1980-83; Warwick University, 1983-86. *Publications:* The Accidental Woman; A Touch of Love; The Dwarves of Death; Humphrey Bogart: Take It And Like It. *Contributions to:* Guardian; London Review Of Books; Wire; Spectator; Gegenwart. *Literary Agent:* Tony Peake, Peake Associates. *Address:* c/o Peake Associates, 18 Grafton Crescent, London NW1 8SL, England.

COE Richard N(elson Caslon), b. 1923, United Kingdom. Professor of French and Comparative Literature. *Appointments:* Lecturer, University of Leeds, 1950-62; Senior Lecturer, University of Queensland, Australia, 1962-63; Reader, 1963-66, Personal Professor of French, 1969-72, University of Melbourne; Reader, 1966-69, Professor of French, 1972-79, University of Warwick, Coventry, England; Fellow, Australian Academy of the Humanities, 1970-; Professor of French and Comparative Literature, University of California, Davis, USA, 1979-; Member, Editorial Board: Australian Journal of French Studies, 1964-; Comparison, 1975-83; New Comparison, 1985-. *Publications:* Stendhal's Life of Rossini, translation, 1956; Stendhal's Rome, Naples and Florence in 1826, translation, 1959; Morelly: Ein Rationalist auf dem Wege zum Sozialismus, 1961; Ionesco, 1961, edited, 1969; Robert Pinget's No Answer, translation, 1961; Beckett, 1964; Crocodile, by Kornyei Chukovsky (adaptor), 1964; Doctor Concoctor, by Kornyei Chukovsky (adaptor), 1967; The Vision of Jean Genet, 1968; The Theater of Jean Genet: A Casebook (editor), 1970; Eugene Ionesco: A Study of His Theatre, with (translation) The Niece-Wife, by Ionesco, 1971; Stendhal's Lives of Haydn, Mozart and Metastasio (translator and editor), 1972; When the Grass Was Taller, 1984. *Address:* 307 Balboa Avenue, Davis, CA 95616, USA.

COE Tucker. *See:* **WESTLAKE Donald E.**

COEN Ethan, b. 1958, Minneapolis, Minnesota. Writer and Producer of Motion Pictures. m. Hilary, Dec 1985. *Education:* Studied Philosophy at Princeton University. *Appointments:* Statistical Typist at Macy's Department Store, New York, 1979-80. Writer and producer of Motion Pictures 1980-. *Publications:* Screenplays: With brother, Joel Coen, Blood Simple, Circle Releasing Corporation, 1984; With J Coen and Sam Raimi, The XYZ Murders, Embassy unreleased, limited release as Crimewave, Columbia 1986; With J Coen, Raising Arizona, Twentieth Century Fox, 1987; With J Coen, Miller's Crossing, 1990. *Honour:* Grand Jury Prize from the United States Film Festival, 1984 for Blood Simple. *Address:* c/o Leading Artists, 445 North Bedford Drive, Penthouse, Beverly Hills, CA 90210, USA.

COEN Joel, b. 1955, Minneapolis, Minnesota. Divorced. *Education:* Studied filmmaking at New York University. *Appointments:* Writer and Director of Motion Pictures, 1980-; Production Assistant and Assistant Editor of low-budget horror films, including The Evil Dead in the late 1970s and early 1980s. *Publications:* Screenplays: With brother Ethan Coen: and director, Blood Simple, Circle Releasing Corporation, 1984; With E Coen and Sam Raimi, The XYZ Murders, Embassy unreleased, limited release as Crimewave, Columbia, 1986; With E Coen and director, Raising Arizona, Twentieth Century-Fox, 1987; with E Coen, Miller's Crossing, 1990. *Honours:* Grand Jury Prize from the United states Film Festival 1984 for Blood Simple; Independent Spirit Award for best director from Independent Film Project/West, 1986 for Blood Simple. *Address:* c/o Leading Artists, 445 North Bedford Drive, Penthouse, Beverly Hills, CA 90210, USA.

COERR Eleanor Beatrice, (Eleanor Hicks, Eleanor Page), b. 1922, USA. Writer. *Appointments:* Reporter, Editor, Edmonton Journal, Canada, 1944-49; Editor, Illustrator, syndicated weekly column, Manila Times, Philippines, 1958-61; Contract Writer for USIS in Taiwan, 1960-62, Voice of American Special English Division, Washington, DC, 1963-65; Librarian, David Library, Bethesda, Maryland, 1971-72. *Publications:* Children's non-fiction as Eleanor Hicks: Circus Day in Japan, 1953, 2nd Edition, 1968; The Mystery of the Golden Cat, 1968, 2nd Edition, 1973; Twenty-Five Dragons, 1971; Biography of a Giant Panda, 1975; The Mixed-Up Mystery Smell, 1975; The Biography of Jane Goodall, 1976; Biography of a Red Kangaroo, 1976; Sadako and the Thousand Paper Cranes, 1977; Waza at Windy Gulch, 1977; Gigi, A Whale Borrowed for Science and Returned to Sea, 1980; The Big Balloon Race, 1980; The Bell Ringer and the Pirates, 1983; The Josefina Story Quilt, 1986; Lady with a Torch, 1986.

COERS Donald Vernon, b. 2 June 1941, San Marcos, Texas, USA. University Professor. m. 30 Dec 1966, 1 son, 1 daughter. *Education:* BA, 1963, MA, 1969, University of Texas, Austin; PhD, Texas A&M University, 1974. *Appointments:* Professor of English, Sam Houston State University, 1969-; Associate Editor, The Texas Review, 1979-. *Publications:* John Steinbeck as Propagandist: The Moon Is Down Goes to War, 1991. *Honours:* The Elizabeth Agee Prize in American Literature, 1990. *Address:* 3799 Summer Lane, Huntsville, TX 77340, USA.

COETZEE John M, b. 9 Feb 1940. Writer; Professor. 1 son, 1 daughter. *Education:* MA, University of Cape Town; PhD, University of Texas, USA. *Appointments:* Assistant Professor, English, State University of New York, Buffalo, 1968-71; Lecturer, English, University of Cape Town, 1972-82; Butler Professor of English, State University of New York, Buffalo, 1984, 1986; Hinkley Professor of English, Johns Hopkins University, 1986, 1989; Visiting Ptofessor, English, Harvard University, 1991. *Publications:* Dusklands, 1974; In the Heart of the Country, 1977; Waiting for the Barbarians, 1980; Life and times of Michael K, 1983; Foe, 1986; White Writing, 1988; Age of Iron, 1990; Doubling the Point, 1992. *Contributions to:* essays in various journals. *Honours:* CNA Literary Award, 1977, 1980; James Tait Black Prize, 1980; Geoffrey Faber Award, 1980; CNA Literary Award, 1983; Booker McConnell Prize, 1983;

Prix Femina Etranger, 1985; Jerusalem Prize, 1987; Sunday Express Award, 1990. *Address:* PO Box 92, Rondebosch, Cape Province 7700, South Africa.

COFFEY Brian. *See:* **KOONTZ Dean R.**

COFFMAN Virginia (Edith), (Victor Cross, Virginia Du Vaul, Virginia C Du Vaul, Jeanne Duval, Anne Stanfield), b. 1914, America. Author, Historic/Romance/Gothic. *Appointments:* Film Reviewer, Oakland Tribune, California, 1933-40; Secretary and Writer various film and TV Studios, Hollywood, California, 1944-56; Secretary and Office Manager, Chick Bennett Inc, realtors, Reno, Nev, 1956-66. *Publications include:* The Evil at Queens Priory, 1973; Survivor of Darkness, 1973; The House at Sandalwood, 1974; Hyde Place, 1974; The Ice Forest, 1975; Veronique, 1975; Marsanne, 1976; The Alpine Coach, 1976; Careen, 1977; Enemy of Love, 1977; Fire Dawn, 1977; The Gaynor Women, 1978; Looking-Glass, 1979; Dinah Faire, 1979; (as Jeanne Duval), The Lady Serena, 1979; (as Jeanne Duval), The Ravishers, 1980; Pacific Cavalcade, 1980; (as Anne Stanfield), The Golden Marguerite, 1981; The Lombard Cavalcade, 1982; Dynasty of Desire, 1982; The Lombard Heiress, 1983; Dynasty of Dreams, 1984; The Orchid Tree, 1984; Dark Winds, 1985.

COGGESHALL Rosanne H, b. 15 May 1946, Florence, South Carolina, USA. Teacher. *Education:* BA, 1968, MA, 1970, Hollins College; MA, Johns Hopkins University, 1969; PhD, University of North Carolina, Chapel Hill, 1978. *Appointments:* Graduate Assistant, University of North Carolina, Chapel Hill, 1973-78; Assistant Professor, English, Hollins College, 1978-85; Department of Continuing Education, Duke University, 1988-92. *Publications:* Hymn for Drum, 1978; Traffic, with Ghosts, 1984. *Contributions to:* Southern Review; Epoch; Iowa Review; South Carolina Review; Carolina Quarterly; New Orleans Review; Southern Poetry Review; Antimis; Crescent Review; Hampden Sq Review. *Honours:* Phi Beta Kappa, 1968. *Literary Agent:* Gina Maccoby. *Address:* PO Box 255, Fincastle, VA 24090, USA.

COGGINS Paul E, b. 21 May 1951, Hugo, Oklahoma, USA. Attorney. m. Regina T Montoya, 6 June 1976. 1 daughter. *Education:* BA, summa cum laude, Yale University, 1973; MA (First Class Honours), 1975, Diploma of Law 1976, Oxford University, England; JD, summa cum laude, Harvard University, USA, 1978. *Publications:* The Lady is the Tiger, 1987; Out of Bounds (co-author), 1992 . *Contributions to:* Numerous articles for Dallas Morning News; Texas Observer. *Honour:* Dallas Literary Lion, 1987. *Memberships:* Harvard Club; American Bar Association; Yale Club; Dallas Bar Association; The Texas Lyceum. *Literary Agent:* Jan Miller, c/o Dupree & Miller, Dallas, Texas, USA. *Address:* 3302 Oakhurst Street, Dallas, TX 75214, USA.

COGSWELL Fred(erick William), b. 1917, Canada. Professor of English; Author; Poet; Translator. *Appointments:* Assistant Professor, 1952-57, Associate Professor, 1957-61, Professor of English, 1961-, University of New Brunswick, Fredericton; Editor: Fiddlehead magazine, Fredericton, 1952- 66; Humanities Association Bulletin, Fredericton, 1967-72. *Publications:* The Stunted Strong, 1955; The Haloed Tree, 1956; Testament of Cresseid, 1957; Descent from Eden, 1959; Lost Dimensions, 1960; A Canadian Anthology (editor), 1960; Five New Brunswick Poets (editor, contributor), 1962; The Arts in New Brunswick (edited with R Tweedie and S W MacNutt, contributor), 1966; The Enchanted Land: Canadian Poetry for Young Readers, 1967; Star-People, 1968; Immortal Plowman, 1969; In Praise of Chastity, 1970; One Hundred Poems of Modern Quebec (translator), 1970; A Second Hundred Poems of Modern Quebec, 1971; The Chains of Liliput, 1971; The House Without a Door, 1973; Confrontation, by G Lapointe (translator), 1973; Light Bird of Life, 1974; The Poetry of Modern Quebec (editor), 1977; Against Perspective, 1979; A Long Apprenticeship: Collected

Poems, 1980; Selected Poems, 1983; Pearls, 1983; Meditations, 1986; The Edge to Life, 1987; The Best Notes Merge, 1988; Black and White Tapestry, 1989; Unfinished Dreams Contemporary Poetry of Acadie, (Editor and Translator with Jo-Ann Elder), 1990. *Address:* Camp A6, Site 6, RR 4, Fredericton, New Brunswick, Canada E3B 4X5.

COHAN Anthony Robert (Tony), b. 28 Dec 1939, New York City, New York, USA. Writer. m. 1 June 1974, 1 daughter. *Education:* BA, University of California, 1961. *Publications:* Nine Ships, 1975; Canary, 1981; The Flame, 1983; Opium, 1984. *Honour:* Notable Book of the Year, New York Times Book Review, 1981. *Memberships:* Authors Guild; PEN. *Literary Agent:* Don Congdon, USA; Anthony Sheil, UK. *Address:* P O Box 480277, Los Angeles, CA 90048, USA.

COHEN Daniel (E), b. 1936, USA. Children's non-fiction; Film; Supernatural/Occult. Writer for Science Digest magazine, New York 1969- (Managing Editor 1960-69). *Publications include:* Young adult books: Southern Fried Rat and Other Gruesome Tales, 1983; Monster Dinosaur, 1983; The Restless dead, 1983; (with Susan Cohen), The Kid's Guide to Home Computers, 1983; (with S Cohen), Teenage Stress, 1984; Hiram Bingham and the Dream of Gold, 1984; Masters of Horror, 1984; (with S Cohen), The Kid's Guide to Home Video, 1984; America's Very Own Ghosts, 1985; Henry Stanley and the Quest for the Source of the Nile, 1985; (with S Cohen), Rock Video Superstars, 1985; (with S Cohen), Wrestling Superstars, 1985; (with S Cohen) Wrestling Superstars, 1985 vol II, 1986; (with S Cohen), Heroes of the Challenger, 1986; (with S Cohen), A Six-Pack and a Fake ID, 1986. Other works: Myths of the Space Age, 1967; Mysterious Places, 1969; A Modern Look at Museums, 1970; Masters of the Occult, 1971; Voodoo Devils, and the New Invisible World, 1972; The Far Side of Consciousness, 1974; Biorhythms in Your Life, 1976; Close Encounters with God, 1979; The Great Airship Mystery, 1981; Re: Thinking, 1982; The Encyclopedia of Monsters, 1983; The Encyclopedia of Ghosts, 1984; Musicals, 1984; Horror Movies, 1984; (with S Cohen), Screen Goddesses, 1984; The Encyclopedia of the Strange, 1985; (with S Cohen), Hollywood Hunks and Heroes, 1985; (with S Cohen),The Encyclopedia of Movie Stars, 1986; (with S Cohen), A History of the Oscars, 1986; When Someone You Know is Gay, (with S Cohen), 1988; Zoos, (with S Cohen), 1992; Where to Find Dinosaurs Today, 1992 (with S Cohen); Ghosts of War, 1989; Phantom Animals, 1990; Railway Ghosts and Highway Horrors, 1991; What Kind of Dog is That, 1989 (with S Cohen). *Membership:* Author's Guild. *Literary Agent:* Henry Morrison Inc. *Address:* 24, Elizabeth Street, Port Jervis, NY 12771, USA.

COHEN Jack Sidney, b. 6 Sept 1938, London, England. Professor. m. Naomi Ruth Silverstein. *Education:* BSc, Queen Mary College, London University; PhD, St Catherines College, Cambridge University. *Publications:* A Century of DNA; Magnetic Resonance in Biology; Noninvasive Probes of Tissue Metabolism; Oligodeoxynucleatides. *Contributions to:* About 200 Papers in Scientific Journals. *Memberships:* American Chemical Society; Biophysical Society; American Society of Biochemistry and Molecular Biology; Society of Magnetic Resonance in Medicine. *Address:* Georgetown University Medical Center, Cancer Pharmacology Section, 4 Research Court, Room 331, Rockville, MD 20850, USA.

COHEN Janet (Neel), b. 4 July 1940, Oxford, England. Merchant Banker. m. James Lionel Cohen, 18 Dec. 1971. 2 sons, 1 daughter. *Education:* Honours Degree (2:1), Law, Newnham College, Cambridge, 1962; Solicitor, 1965. *Publications:* as Janet Neel: Death's Bright Angel, 1988; Death On Site, 1989; Death Of A Partner, 1991; as Janet Cohen: The Highest Bidder, 1992. *Honour:* John Creasey Prize for Best First Thriller by an Unpublished Author, 1988. *Memberships:* Society of Authors; Crime Writers Association; Solicitor, Admitted 1965; Women in Management Forum. *Literary*

Agent: Anthony Goff, David Higham Associates. *Address:* 50 Blenheim Terrace, London NW8 0EH, England.

COHEN Leonard, b. 1934, Canada. Novellist/Short Story Writer; Playwright/Screenplay Writer; Poet; Songwriter/Lyricist; Professional Composer and Singer. *Publications:* Let Us Compare Mythologies, 1956; The Spice-Box of Earth, 1961; The Favourite Game, novel, 1963; Flowers for Hitler, 1964; Parasites of Heaven, 1966; Beautiful Losers, novel, 1966; Selected Poems, 1956-68, 1968; Leonard Cohen's Song Book, 1969; The Energy of Slaves, 1972; The Next Step, play, 1972; Sisters of Mercy: A Journey to the Words and Music of Leonard Cohen, 1973; Death of a Lady's Man, 1979; Two Views, poetry, 1980; Book of Mercy, poetry, 1984. *Literary Agent:* McClelland and Stewart Ltd, Canada. *Address:* McClelland and Stewart Ltd, 25 Hollinger Road, Toronto, Ontario, Canada M4B 3G2.

COHEN Marion Deutsche, b. 2 Jan 1943, Perth, New Jersey, USA. Writer. m. Jeffrey M Cohen, 9 Aug 1964, 3 sons, 2 daughters. *Education:* BA, New York University, 1964; MA, Wesleyan University, 1966; PhD, 1970. *Publications:* An Ambitious Sort of Grief; She Was Born She Died; The Sitting Down Hug; Counting To Zero; The Weirdest Is The Sphere; The Shadow of an Angel; A Garden Flower; These Covers to Crawl Under; Tuesday Nights; Mother Poet; The Limits of Miracles. *Contributions to:* American Poetry Review; Plain Brown Wrappen; Opposom Hollen Tarot; Mothering; Famous Last Words. *Memberships:* Poets & Writers; Eminist Writers Guild; Sigma Xi; Phi Beta Kappa; American Mathematical Society. *Address:* 2203 Spruce Street, Phila, PA 19103, USA.

COHEN Matt(hew), b. Canada, 1942. Novelist; Short Story Writer; Poet; Translator; Former Teacher. *Publications:* Korsoniloff, 1969; Johnny Crackle Sings, 1971; Columbus and the Fat Lady and Other Stories, 1972; Too Bad Galahad, short stories, 1972; The Disinherited, 1974; Peach Melba, poetry, 1975; The Colours of War, 1978; Night Flights: Stories New and Selected, 1978; The Sweet Second Summer of Kitty Malone, 1979; Flowers of Darkness, 1981; The Expatriate: Collected Short Stories, 1982; Cafe Le Dog, short stories, 1983; The Spanish Doctor, novel, 1984; Nadine, novel, 1986; Living On Water, stories, 1988; Emotional Arithmetic, novel, 1990. *Membership:* Chairman, The Writer's Union of Canada, 1985-86. *Literary Agent:* Bella Pomer Agency, Canada. *Address:* Bella Pomer Agency, 22 Shallmar Blvd., PH2, Toronto, Ontario, Canada M5N 2Z8.

COHEN Maxwell QC, b. 1910, Canada. Lawyer; Emeritus Professor of Law, McGill University, Scholar in Residence, University of Ottawa. *Education:* LLM; LLD. *Publications:* Dominion and Provincial Relations, 1945; Law and Politics in Space, 1964; Nuclear Weapons and the Law, 1987; many published professional and academic articles. *Honours:* O.C.; Q.C.*Memberships:* Canadian Bar Association, Chairman, International and Constitutional Law Section, 1964-71; President, Quebec Advisory Council on the Administration of Justice, 1972-74; Chairman, Intern. Joint Commission (1974-79); Judge ad hoc International Court of Justice, 1982-85. *Address:* Suite 1404, 200 Rideau Terrace, Ottawa, Ontario, Canada K1M 0Z3.

COHEN Michael Joseph, b. 29 Apr 1940, London, England. Professor of History. *Education:* BA, History, 1969; PhD, Politics, 1971. *Appointments:* Professor, Bar Ilan University, Lecturer, 1972; Senior Lecturer, 1976; Professor, 1981. *Publications:* Palestine & The Great Powers; Churchill & The Jews; Truman & Israel; The Origins & Evolution of the Arab Zionist Conflict; Palestine: Retreat From The Mandate. *Contributions to:* Middle Eastern Studies; The Historical Journal; Studies in Zionism; Jerusalem Quarterly; The Jerusalem Post; Modern Judaism; Jewish Social Studies; Asian & African Studies. *Memberships:* The American Historical Association. *Address:* Department of General History, Bar Ilan University, Ramat Gan, Israel 52100.

COHEN Morton Norton (John Moreton), b. 27 Feb 1921, Calgary, Canada. Professor; Lecturer; Author. *Education:* AB, Tufts University, 1949; MA, Columbia University. 1950; PhD, 1958. *Appointments Include:* Professor Emeritus, City University of New York, 1981-; Deputy Executive Officer, PhD Programme in English, CUNY, 1976-78, 1979-80; Tutor to Professor, City College of CUNY, 1952-81, Member of Doctoral Faculty, 1964-81. *Publications:* The Selected Letters of Lewis Carroll, (Editor), 1982, 2nd edition, 1990; Lewis Carroll: Interviews and Recollections, 1989; Lewis Carroll and Alice 1832-1982, 1982; The Letters of Lewis Carroll, (Editor), 2 volumes, 1979; Lewis Carroll's Photographs of Nude Children, 1978, republished as Lewis Carroll, Photographer of Children: Four Nude Studies, 1979; The Russian Journal II, 1979; Lewis Carroll and the Kitchins, 1980; Rudyard Kipling to Rider Haggard: The Record of a Friendship, 1965, 1968; A Brief Guide to Better Writing, (Co-author); 1960; Rider Haggard: His Life and Works, 1960, 2nd revised edition, 1968. *Contributions to:* Articles, chapters, introductions and book reviews in numerous magazines, journals, papers and books including: The Times; New York Times Book Review; Independent; Kipling Journal; Dalhousie review; Jabberwocky; Illustrated London News' Sydney Morning Herald; Columbia Library Columns; Manuscripts; Sunday Telegraph Magazine; Harper's. *Honours include:* Research Grant, National Endowment for the Humanities, 1974-75; Fulbright Fellowships, 1954-55, 1974-75; Guggenheim Fellowship, 1966-67; Guggenheim Foundation Publication Grant, 1979. *Address:* 72 Barrow Street, Apartment 3-N, New York, NY 10014, USA.

COHEN Peter Sachary, b. 1931, USA. Children's Fiction Writer; Playwright; Screenplay Writer; University Educator. *Publications:* The Muskie Hook, 1969; The Bull in the Forest, 1969; Morena, 1970; Foal Creek, 1972; Authorized Autumn Charts of the Upper Red Canoe River Country, 1972; Bee, 1975; The Cannon in the Park, play, 1975; Deadly Game at Stony Creek, 1978; Calm Horse, Wild Night, 1982; The Great Red River Raft, 1984. *Address:* Rt 1, Alta Vista, KS 66834, USA.

COHEN Stephen F, b. 25 Nov 1938, Indianapolis, Indiana, USA. Professor; Writer; Television Commentator. *Education:* BS, 1960, MA 1962, Indiana University; PhD, Columbia University, 1969. *Publications:* Bukhatin and the Bolshevik Revolution, 1973; An End to Silence, 1982; Rethinking the Soviet Experience, 1985; Sovieticus, 1985; The Soviet Union Since Stalin, 1980; Voices of Glasnost: Interviews with Gorbachev's Reformers, 1989. *Contributions to:* Numerous journals. *Honours:* Bukharin and the Bolshevik Revolution, Nominated for National Book Award, 1974; Newspaper Guild Page One Award for Column Writing (Sovieticus), 1985. *Memberships:* AAASS; APSA; Council on Foreign Relations. *Address:* Dept. of Politics, Princeton University, Princeton, NJ 08544, USA.

COHEN Susan (Elizabeth St Clair), b. 1938, USA. Author; Social Worker. m. Daniel Cohen. *Publications:* Gothic novels (as Elizabeth St Clair): Stonehaven, 1974; The Singing Harp, 1975; Secret of the Locket, 1975; Provenance House, 1976; Mansion in Miniature, 1977; Dewitt Manor, 1977; The Jeweled Secret, 1978; Mysteries (as Elizabeth St Clair): Murder in the Act, 1978; Sandcastle Murder, 1979; Trek or Treat, 1980; Sealed with a Kiss, 1981; With Daniel Cohen: The Kids' Guide to Home Computers, 1983; The Kids' Guide to Home Video, 1984; Teenage Stress, 1984; Screen Goddesses, 1984; Rock Video Superstars, 1985; Wrestling Superstars, vol I, 1985, vol II, 1986; Hollywood Hunks and Heroes, 1985; Heroes of the Challenger, 1986; A Six-Pack and a Fake ID, 1986; The Encyclopedia of Movie Stars, 1986; A History of the Oscars, 1986; When Someone You Know is Gay, 1988; What Kind of Dog is That, 1989; Zoos, 1992; Where to Find Dinosaurs Today, 1992; Sole author: The Liberated Couple, 1971, as Liberated Marriage, 1973. *Address:* 24 Elizabeth Street, Port Jervis, NY 12771, USA.

COHN Jack Magnus, b. 20 Dec 1926, Swan Hill, Australia. Company Director. m. Zena Johnson, 6 Apr 1953, 1 son, 3 daughters. *Education:* University of Melbourne, 1949; Australian Diploma of Food Technology, 1951; The Australian Institute of Management, 1967. *Publications:* Log of the PS Gem; 115 Years of Service; Tablets of Memory. *Contributions to:* Various. *Honours:* JP, A Justice of the Peace for the state of Victoria; Alexander Henderson Award. *Memberships:* Fellowship of Australiam Writers; Royal Victorian Association of Honorary Justices; Rotary International; Probus Club of Frankston. *Address:* 57 Bellbird Road, Mount Eliza, Victoria 3930, Australia.

COHN Ruby, b. 1922, USA. University Professor. *Appointments:* Professor Emeritus of Comparative Drama, University of California, Davis. *Publications:* Samuel Beckett: The Comic Gamut, 1962; Currents in Contemporary Drama, 1969; Dialogue in American Drama, 1971; Back to Beckett, 1973; Modern Shakespeare Offshoots, 1976; Just Play: Beckett's Theatre, 1980; New American Dramatists, 1982, & 1991 (revised); Samuel Beckett Disjecta (editor), 1983; From Desire to Godot, 1987; Retreats from Realism in Recent English Drama, 1990. *Address:* Department of Dramatic Art, University of California, Davis, CA 95616, USA.

COHN Samuel Kline, b. 13 Apr 1949. History. *Education:* Union College, BA, 1971; University of Wisconsin, MA, 1972; Harvard University, PhD, 1978. *Appointments:* Harvard University, Teacher, 1976-78; Weslayan University, 1978-79; Branders University, Assistance Professor, 1979-; Associate Professor, 1985-; Professor, 1988-; Visiting Professor, Brown University, 1990. *Publications:* The Laboring Classes in Renaissance Florence; Death And Propetry in Siena: Strategies For The After Life; The Cult of Remembrance And The Black Death: Six Cities in Central Italy. *Honours:* The Marraro Award for the Best Book. *Memberships:* American Historical Association; The Society for Italian Historical Studies. *Address:* History Department, Branders University, Waltham, MA 02254, USA.

COLBECK Maurice, b. 21 Sept 1925, Batley, Yorkshire, England. Journalist. m. Brenda Barrowclough, 25 Mar 1950, 1 son, 1 daughter. *Literary Appointments:* Reporter, Sub-Editor, Various Yorkshire Newspapers; Assistant Editor, E J Arnold and Son Limited; Editor, Yorkshire Life, 1956-. *Publications:* White God's Fury; Four Against Crime; Jungle Rivals; Mosquitoes; Sister Kenny of the Outback; How to be a Family Man (with William Geldart), 1970; Yorkshire, 1976; Yorkshire Historymakers, 1976; Queer Fold, 1977; Yorkshire Laughter, 1978; Yorkshire: The Dales, 1979; Queer Goings On, 1973; Yorkshire Moorlands, 1983; The Calendar Year (Editor), 1983; Village Yorkshire, 1987. *Memberships:* Society of Authors; Institute of Journalists. *Address:* Yorkshire Life, Lensett House, 45 Boroughgate, Otley, LS21 1AG, England.

COLBORN Nigel, b. 20 Feb 1944, England. Journalist; TV Presenter; Author; Gardener. m. Rosamund F M Hewlett, 10 Nov 1972, 2 sons, 2 daughters. *Education:* King's School, Ely, Cambs. UK; BSc, Cornell University, USA. *Publications:* This Gardening Business (Humour) 1989; Leisurely Gardening (Gardening) 1989; The Classic Horticulturist (Garden History) 1987; Family Piles (Humour) 1990; The Container Garden (Conran Octopus), 1990. *Contributions to:* Gardening and rural press, including New York Times, Country Life, Homes and Gardens, Hortus, The Garden; BBC Gardeners' World Magazine. *Memberships:* Society of Authors; Royal Horticultural Society, Member of Standing Committee; Hardy Plant Society; Alpine Garden Society. *Literary Agent:* Laurence Pollinger (Juliet Burton) 18, Maddox Street,

London. *Address:* Careby Manor, Careby, Stamford, Lincolnshire PE9 4EA, England.

COLDWELL Joan, b. 3 Nov 1936, Huddersfield, England. Professor of English. *Education:* BA, Honours, 1958; MA, Distinction, 1960, University of London; PhD, Harvard University, 1967. *Appointments:* Professor English, McMaster University, 1972-. *Contributions to:* Oxford Companion to Canadian Literature, 1983; Articles in Canadian Literature; Journal of Canadian Fiction; Keats-Shelley Memorial Bulletin; Shakespeare Quarterly; English Studies in Canada; Canadian Journal of Irish Studies; Atlantis. *Honours:* Social Sciences and Humanities Research Council of Canada Leave Fellowship, 1969, 1977, 1984. *Memberships:* International Shakespeare Association; Shakespeare Association of America; Charles Lamb Society; Secretary-Treasurer, 1976-77, Canadian Association for Irish Studies.

COLE Adrian Christopher Synnot, b. 22 July 1949, Plymouth, England. Local Government Officer; Author. m. 25 May 1977, 1 son, 1 daughter. *Publications:* The Dream Lords, 1975; Madness Emerging, 1976; Paths in Darkness, 1977; Wargods of Ludorbis, 1981; The Lucifer Experiment, 1981; Moorstones, 1982; The Sleep of Giants, 1984; A Place Among the Fallen, 1986; Throne of Fools, 1987; The King of Light & Shadows, 1988; The Gods in Anger, 1988; Mother of Storms, 1989; Thief of Dreams, 1989; Warlord of Heaven, 1990; Labyrinth of Worlds, 1990. *Contributions to:* Numerous magazines & journals. *Membership:* British Fantasy Society. *Literary Agent:* Abner Stein. *Address:* The Old Forge, 35 Meddon Street, Bideford, Devon EX39 2EF, England.

COLE Barry, b. 13 Nov 1936. Writer. m. Rita Linihan, 1959, 3 daughters. *Literary Appointments:* Northern Arts Fellow in Literature, Universities of Durham and Newcastle-upon-Tyne, England, 1970-72. *Publications:* Blood Ties, 1967; Ulysses in the Town of Coloured Glass, 1968; A Run Across The Island, 1968; Moon Search, 1968; Joseph Winter's Patronage, 1969; The Search for Rita, 1970; The Visitors, 1970; The Giver, 1971; Vanessa in the City, 1971; Pathetic Fallacies, 1973; The Rehousing of Scaffardi; Dedications, 1977; The Edge of the Common, 1989. *Contributions To:* Numerous Publications including: New Statesman; Spectator; The Listener; Times Educational Supplement; Times Higher Educational Supplement; Critical Review; New Yorker; Tribune; London Magazine; Transatlantic Review; The Observer; The Guardian. *Address:* 68 Myddelton Square, London, EC1R 1XP, England.

COLE Jackson. *See:* GERMAUO Peter B.

COLE John Morrison, b. 23 Nov 1927, Belfast, Northern Ireland. Journalist; Broadcaster. m. Margaret Isobel Williamson, 4 Sept 1956, 4 sons. *Education:* External degree, English Honours, London University, 1952. *Publications:* The Poor of the Earth, 1976; The Thatcher Years, 1987. *Contributions to:* Various books, British & Irish politics. Also: Guardian, 1956-75; Observer, 1975-81; Listener, political column, 1982-. *Membership:* Athenaeum Club. *Address:* c/o BBC Office, House of Commons, Westminster, London, SW1A 0AA, England.

COLE William, American, b. 1919. Children's non-fiction writer, Humour, Satire, Book Reviewer for Saturday Review. *Publications:* (ed with M Rosenberg), The Best Cartoons from Punch, 1952; (ed) The Best Humour from Punch, 1953; (ed with F Robinson), Women Are Wonderful: A Cartoon History, 1954; (ed) Humorous Poetry for Children, 1955; (co-ed) The Poetry-Drawing Book, 1956; (ed) Story Poems Old and New, 1957; (ed) I Went to the Animal Fair, 1958; (ed) The Fireside Book of Humorous Poetry, 1959; (ed) Poems of Magic and Spells, 1960; (ed) Poems for Seasons and Celebrations, 1961; (ed) Folk Songs of England, Ireland, Scotland and Wales, 1961; (ed with J Colmore), New

York in Photographs, 1961; (ed with J Colmore), The Second Poetry-Drawing Book, 1962; (ed) The Most of A J Liebling, 1963; (ed) Erotic poetry, 1963; (ed) The Birds and the Beasts Were There, 1963; A Car-Hater's Handbook, 1963; Frances Face-Maker, 1963; (ed) Beastly Boys and Ghastly Girls, 1964; (ed) A Big Bowl of Punch, 1964; (ed) A Book of Love Poems, 1965; What's Good for a Six-Year-Old? 1965; (ed) Oh What Nonsense! 1966; Uncoupled Couplets: A Game of Rhymes, 1966; (ed with M Thaler), The Classic Cartoons, 1966; (ed) The Sea, Ships, and Sailors, 1967; (ed) D H Lawrence Poems Selected for Young People, 1967; (ed) Poems of W S Gilbert, 1967; (ed) Eight Lines and Under, 1967; (ed) A Case pf the Giggles, 1967; (ed) Man's Funniest friend, 1967; What's Good for a Four-Year-Old? 1967; What's Good for a Five-Year-Old? 1968; (ed) Poems of Thomas Hood, 1968; (ed) A Book of Nature Poems, 1969; (ed) Pith and Vinegar, 1969; That Pest, Jonathan, 1970; Aunt Bella's Umbrella, 1970; (ed) Oh How Silly! 1970; (ed) The Poet's Tales, 1971; (ed) Poetry Brief, 1971; (ed) Pick Me Up, 1971; (ed) Oh! That's Ridiculous! 1972; (ed) Poems from Ireland, 1972; (ed)...And Be Merry! 1972; What's Good for a Three-Year-Old? 1972; (ed) Poems One Line and Longer, 1973; A Boy Named Mary Jane: Nonsense Verses, 1975; Knock, Knock: The Most Ever, 1976; Knock Knocks You've Never Heard Before, 1977; An Arkful of Animals, 1978; Oh, Such Foolishness, 1978; I'm Mad at You, 1978; Dinosaurs and Beasts of Yore, 1979; The Poetry of Horses, 1979; Good Dog Poems, 1980; Poem Stew, 1981. *Address:* 201 West 54th Street, New York, NY 10019, USA.

COLEGATE Isabel Diana, b. 10 Sept 1931. Novelist. m. Michael Briggs, 12 Sept 1953. 2 sons, 1 daughter. *Appointment:* Literary Agent, Anthony Blond (London) Ltd, 1952-57. *Publications:* The Blackmailer, 1958; A Man of Power, 1960; The Great Occasion, 1962; Statues in a Garden, 1964; Orlando King, 1968; Orlando at the Brazen Threshold, 1971; Agatha, 1973; News from the City of the Sun, 1979; The Shooting Party, 1980 (filmed 1985); A Glimpse of Sion's Glory, 1985; Deceits of Time, 1988; The Summer of the Royal Visit, 1991. *Honours:* Fellow, Royal Society of Literature, 1981; W H Smith Literary Award, 1981; Honorary MA, University of Bath, 1988. *Membership:* Author's Society. *Literary Agent:* Peters Fraser & Dunlop.

COLEMAN Jane Candia. See: **COLEMAN Jane Winthrop.**

COLEMAN Jane Winthrop (Jane Candia Coleman), b. 9 Jan 1939, Pittsburgh, PA, USA. Writer. m. (1) Bernard D Coleman, div 1989, (2) Glenn G Boyer, 1989, 2 sons. *Education:* University of Pittsburgh, BA, 1961. *Appointments:* Lecturer, University of Pittsburgh, 1981; Writer in Residence, Carlow College, Pittsburgh, 1980-85; Director Womens Creative Writing Center, Carlow College, 1985-86. *Publications:* Stories From Mesa Country; No Roof But Sky; Deep In His Heart JR Is Laughing At Us; Discovering Eve. *Contributions to:* The Christian Science Monitor; Horseman; Puerto Del Sol; South Dakota Review; The pennsylvania Review; Yankee; The Aqassiz Review; Snowy Eqret. *Honours:* Pennsylvania Council on the Arts, Writing Grant; Western Heritage Award, Poetry, Short Fiction. *Memberships:* Western Writers of America; The Authors Guild; PEN. *Literary Agent:* Susan Craw Ford. *Address:* PO Box 40, Rodeo, NM 88056, USA.

COLEMAN Robert Gordon, b. 17 July 1922, Beechworth, Victoria, Australia. Journalist; Author. m. Lilian Gill, 4 June 1949, 1 daughter. *Appointments:* Working Journalist, 1940-86; Reporter, Feature Writer, Cadet Counsellor, Columnist, Leader Writer, Freelance Journalist, Author, 1986-. *Publications:* Above Renown; The Pyjama Girl; (ed) Reporting for Work; Seasons in the Sun. *Honours:* Australian Automobile Association National Journalism Award; Highly Commended, Graham Perkin Award for Journalist of the Year. *Memberships:* Melbourne University Board of Studies in Journalism; Australian Journalists Association.

Address: 34 Folkstone Crescent, Beaumaris, Victoria 3193, Australia.

COLEMAN Terry, b. 13 Feb 1931, Bournemouth, England. Reporter and Author. *Education:* LLB, London University. *Appointments:* Reporter, Poole Herald; Editor, Savoir Faire; Sub-Editor, Sunday Mercury; Sub-Editor, The Birmingham Post; Reporter, Arts Correspondent and then Chief Feature Writer, The Guardian 1961-74; Special Writer, Daily Mail 1974-76; Special Correspondent, The Guardian, 1976-89; Associate Editor, The Independent, 1989-91. *Publications:* The Railway Navvies, 1965; Providence and Mr. Hardy (with Lois Deacon) 1966; The Only True History, 1969; Passage to America 1971; The Liners 1976; Southern Cross, 1979; The Scented Brawl, 1979; Thanksgiving 1981; Movers and Shakers 1987; Thatcher's Britain, 1987. *Honours:* Yorkshire Post Prize, Best First Book of Year, 1965; Feature Writer of the Year, British Press Awards, 1982; Journalist of the Year, Granada Awards 1988. *Literary Agent:* Peters, Fraser, Dunlop. *Address:* c/o A D Peters, The Chambers, Chelsea Harbour, London SW10 0XF, England.

COLERIDGE Nicholas David, b. 4 Mar 1957, London, England. Journalist; Author. m. Georgia Elizabeth Metcalfe, 22 July 1989, 2 sons. *Education:* Trinity College, Cambridge; Eton College. *Literary Appointments:* Editor, Harpers & Queen Magazine, 1986-89; Managing Director, Conde Nast Publications, 1992-, Editorial Director, 1989-91. *Publications:* Tunnel Vision, 1981; Around the World in 78 Days, 1984; Shooting Stars, 1984; The Fashion Conspiracy, 1988; How I Met My Wife and Other Stories, 1991; Paper Tigers, 1993. *Contributions to:* Harpers & Queen; Spectator; Sunday Telegraph; Tatler; Evening Standard (1982-85); GQ; Vanity Fair. *Honour:* Young Journalist of the Year, 1983. *Literary Agent:* Leslie Gardner. *Address:* 24 Chepstow Crescent, London W11 3EB, England.

COLES Donald Langdon, b. 12 Apr 1928, Woodstock, Ontario, Canada. Professor. m. 28 Dec 1958, 1 son, 1 daughter. *Education:* BA, Victoria College; MA, University of Toronto; MA, Cantab, 1954. *Appointments:* Fiction Editor, The Canadian Forum, 1975-76; Poetry Editor, May Studio, Banff Centre for the Fine Arts, 1984-93; Director, Creative Writing Programme, York University, 1979-85. *Publications:* Sometimes All Over, 1975; Anniversaries, 1979; The Prinzhorn Collection, 1982; Landslides, 1986; Poetry books: K. in Love, 1987; Little Bird, 1991; Forests of the Medieval World, 1993. *Contributions to:* Saturday Night; Canadian Forum; London Review of Books; Poetry (Chicago); Globe and Mail; Arc; Ariel. *Honours:* Poetry Gold Medal; National Magazine Awards, 1986; CBC Literary Competition, 1980. *Literary Agent:* Lee Davis Creal, Lucinda Vardey Agency, Toronto. *Address:* 122 Glenview Avenue, Toronto, Ontario, Canada M4R 1P8.

COLES Robert, b. 12 Oct 1929. Physician; Teacher; Writer. m. Jane Hallowell Coles. 3 sons. *Education:* AB, English, Harvard College, 1950; MD, College of Physicians & Surgeons, Columbia University, 1954; Internship, University of Chicago Clinics, 1954-55; Psychiatric Residency, Massachusetts General Hospital, 1955-56; Psychiatric Residency, McLean Hospital, 1956-57. *Appointments:* Contributing Editor: The New Republic, 1966-; American Poetry Review, 1972-; Aperture, 1974-;. Literature & Medicine, 1981-; New Oxford Review, 1981-. *Publications:* Children of Crisis (5 volumes), 1967, 1972, 1978; The Moral Life of Children, 1986; The Political Life of Children, 1986; The Old Ones of New Mexico, 1973; the Middle Americans, 1970; The Call of Stories: Teaching and the Moral Imagination, 1989; Harvard Diary, 1988; Simone Weil, 1987; Dorothy Day, 1987; Walker Percy, 1978; William Carlos Williams, 1975; Flannery O'Connor's South, 1980; The Geography of Faith, 1971. *Contributions to:* The Atlantic Monthly; The New Yorker; New York Times Book Review. *Honours:* Atlantic Grant, 1966; Weatherford Prize, 1973; Lillian Smith Award, 1973; McAlpin Medal, 1972; Pulitzer Prize, 1973; MacArthur

Prize, 1981. *Address:* 81 Carr Road, Concord, MA 01742, USA.

COLLIER Catrin. *See:* **WATKINS Karen Christina.**

COLLIER Jane. *See:* **COLLIER Zena.**

COLLIER Peter (Anthony), b. 1939, USA. Writer; Editor. *Appointments:* Professor, Department of English, University of California, Berkeley, 1963-67; Executive Editor, Ramparts magazine, San Francisco, California, 1967-72; Consulting Editor, California Magazine, 1981-. *Publications:* Justice Denied (editor), 1971; When Shall They Rest, 1973; The Rockefellers: An American Dynasty, 1976; Downriver, novel, 1978; The Kennedys: An American Drama (with David Horowitz), 1984. *Address:* 12294 Willow Valley Road, Nevada City, CA 95959, USA.

COLLIER Richard Hughesdon b. 8 Mar 1924, London, England. Author m. Patricia Eveline Russell, 24 July 1953. *Education:* Whitgift School, Croydon, England. *Appointments:* Associate Editor, Phoenix Magazine for the Forces, SE Asia, 1945-46; Editor, Town and Country Magazine, 1946-48; Features Staff, Daily Mail, 1948-49. *Publications:* Ten Thousand Eyes, 1958; The Sands of Dunkirk, 1961; The General Next to God, 1965; Eagle Day, 1966; Duce! 1971; Bridge Acrosss the Sky, 1978; The City That Wouldn't Die, 1959; 1940: The World in Flames, 1979; 1941:Armageddon, 1981; The War That Stalin Won, 1983; The Rainbow People, 1984; The Warcos, 1989; The Few (co-author), 1989; D-Day: 6 June 1944, 1992. *Contributions to:* Reader's Digest; Holiday; The Times. *Honour:* Knight of Mark Twain, 1972. *Memberships:* Author's Guild of America; Author's League of America; Royal Horticultural Society; Society for Theatre Research. *Literary Agent:* Curtis Brown. *Address:* c/o Curtis Brown and John Farquharson, 162/168 Regent Street, London W1R 5TB, England.

COLLIER Zena (Jane Collier), b. 21 Jan 1926, London, England. Writer. m. Thomas M Hampson, 30 Dec 1969, 2 sons (1 dec) by previous marriage. *Appointments:* Writer in Residence, Just Buffalo, 1984-; Writer in Residence, Southern Tier Library System, Corning NY, 1985-; Niagara Erie Writers, Buffalo, NY, 1986; Teacher, Writers Workshop, Nazareth College, Rochester, NY. *Publications:* Novels: A Cooler Climate, 1990; Ghost Note, 1992. Children's books: First Flight; The Year of the Dream; Shutterbug; A Tangled Web; Next Time I'll Know; Seven For The People - Public Interest Groups At Work. *Contributions to:* Southern Humanities Review; Southwest Review; Prairie Schooner; McCalls; Alfred Hitchcocks Mystery Magazine; Literary Review; New Letters; Upstate; Ford Times. *Honours:* Hoepfner Prize; Gold cited on Honor Roll of Best American Short Stories; Resident Fellow at Yaddo, MacDowell, Virginia Centre for the Creative Arts, Alfred University Summer Place. *Memberships:* Authors Guild; Writers & Books; Poets & Writers; National Writers Union. *Literary Agent:* Harvey Klinger. *Address:* 83 Berkeley Street, Rochester, NY 14607, USA.

COLLINGS Michael Robert, b. 28 Oct 1947, Rupert ID, USA. Professor. m. Judith Lynn Reeve, 21 Dec 1973, 2 sons, 2 daughters. *Education:* AA, Bakersfield College, 1967; BA, Whitter College, 1969; MA, University of California, 1973; PhD, University of California, 1977. *Publications:* A Season of Calm Weather; Stephen King As Richard Bachman; The Many Facets of Stephen King; The Shorter Works of Stephen King; The Films of Stephen King; The Stephen King Phenomenon; Piers Anthony; Naked to the Sun; Dark Transformations; In The Image of God. *Contributions to:* Christinity & Literature; Cuyahoga Review; Extrapolation; Expressionists; The Leading Edge; Dialogue; Sunstone; Zarahemla; Wasatch Review; Star Line; Poet; New Era; California State Poetry Journal. *Honours:* Triton College Salute to the arts; Williams Contest, Winner; Rhysling Nominee; Nebula Recommendation; California State Poetry Contest, 1st Place; Best Writer, SPWAO. *Memberships:* Science Fiction Research Association; Science Fiction Poetry Association. *Address:* 1089 Sheffield Place, Thousand Oaks, CA 91360-5353, USA.

COLLINS Hunt. *See:* **LOMBINO Salvatore A.**

COLLINS Jackie, b. United Kingdom. Novelist; Short Story Writer. *Publications:* The World is Full of Married Men, 1968; The Stud, 1969; Sunday Simmons and Charlie Brick, 1971, as Sinners, 1981; Lovehead, 1974, as The Love Killers, 1977; The World is Full of Divorced Women, 1975; Lovers and Gamblers, 1977; The Bitch, 1979; Chances, 1981; Hollywood Wives, 1983; Lucky, 1985; Hollywood Husbands, 1986; Rock Star, 1988; Lady Boss, 1990; American Star, 1993. *Address:* c/o Simon and Schuster, 1230 Avenue of the Americas, New York, NY 10020, USA.

COLLINS James Lee (Jim), b. 30 Dec 1945, Beloit, Wisconsin, USA. Author; Editor. m. Joan Hertel, 27 Dec 1974, 2 sons. *Appointments:* Contributing Editor, Encyclopedia USA, 1982-. *Publications:* Western Writers Handbook, 1987; Sonny, 1987; Spencer's Revenge, 1987; Mister Henry, 1986; The Big Fifty, 1986; The Brass Boy, 1987; Sunsets, 1983; Gone to Texas, 1984; Comanche Trail, 1984; War Clouds, 1984; Riding Shotgun, 1985; Orphans Preferred, 1985; Campaigning, 1985. *Contributions to:* The Blue & The Gray; Writers Digest Magazine. *Memberships:* National Writers Club; Western Writers of America; Colorado Authors League. *Literary Agent:* Ray Peekner. *Address:* c/o NWC, 194500 S. Havana St, Suite 620, Aurora, CO 80014, USA.

COLLINS Larry, b. 1929, USA. Author. *Appointments:* Correspondent, UPI, Paris, Rome and Beirut, 1957-59; Middle East Correspondent, Newsweek magazine, Beirut, Lebanon, 1959-61; Bureau Chief, Newsweek magazine, Paris, France, 1961-65. *Publications:* Is Paris Burning (with D Lapierre), 1965; Or I'll Dress You in Mourning (with D Lapierre), 1968; O Jerusalem (with D Lapierre), 1972; Freedom at Midnight (with D Lapierre), 1975; The Fifth Horseman, novel (with D Lapierre), 1980; Fall from Grace, 1985; Maze, 1989. *Address:* c/o Simon and Schuster, 1230 Avenue of the Americas, New York, NY 10020, USA.

COLLINS Max Allan, b. 3 Mar 1948, Muscatine, Iowa, USA, Writer. m. Barbara Jane Mull, 1 June 1968, 1 son. *Education:* AA, Muscatine Community College, 1966-68; BA, 1970, MFA, 1972, University of Iowa. *Appointments:* Instructor of English and Literature, Muscatine Community College, 1971-77; Professor of Creative Writing, University of Iowa Summer Writing Programme (Mystery Fiction), 1989-; Workshop Leader (Fiction), Mississippi Valley Writers Conference, Augustana College, Rock Island, Illinois, 1973-. *Publications:* True Detective, 1983; True Crime, 1984; The Million-Dollar Wound, 1986; Neon Mirage, 1988; The Dark City, 1987; A Shroud for Aquarius, 1985; Author of 6 novels in the Nolan Series including, Bait Money, 1973; Author of 5 novels in the Quarry Series including Primary Target, 1987; 4 additional Mallory mysteries; 3 additional Eliot Ness novels. *Contributions to:* Writer of Comic Strip, Dick Tracy, 1977-93; Movie critic for Mystery Scene Magazine, 1985-; Writer and Co-creator of Ms Tree Comic Book, 1983-; Numerous short stories and articles. *Honours:* Inkpot Award for Outstanding Achievement in Comic Arts, 1982; Private Eye Writers of America Shamus for Best Novel of 1983 and 1991; Distinguished Alumnus Award, Muscatine Community College, 1984; Edgar Allan Poe Special Award for Critical/Biographical Work, Mystery Writers of America, 1985. *Memberships:* Mystery Writers of America; Private Eye Writers of America; American Crime Writers League. *Literary Agent:* Dominick Abel, 146 W 82nd No 1B, New York, NY 10024, USA. *Address:* 301 Fairview Avenue, Muscatine, IA 52761, USA.

COLLINS M C. *See:* **PASZKOWSKI Kazimierz Jan.**

COLLINS Michael. *See:* **LYNDS Dennis.**

COLLINS Philip Arthur William, b. 1923, United Kingdom. *Appointments:* Warden, Vaughan College, 1954-62, Senior Lecturer, 1962-64, Professor of English, 1964-82, University of Leicester; Member, Board of Directors, The National Theatre, 1976-82. *Publications:* James Boswell, 1956; English Christmas (editor), 1956; Dickens and Crime, 1962; Dickens and Education, 1963; The Impress of the Moving Age, 1965; Thomas Cooper the Chartist: Byron and the Poets of the Poor, 1969; A Dickens Bibliography, 1970; Dickens: A Christmas Carol: The Public Reading Version, 1971; Bleak House: A Commentary, 1971; Dickens: The Critical Heritage (editor), 1971; Reading Aloud: A Victorian Metier, 1972; Charles Dickens: The Public Readings (editor), 1975; Charles Dickens: David Copperfield, 1977; Charles Dickens: Hard Times (editor), 1978; Dickens: Interviews and Recollections (editor), 1981; Thackeray: Interviews and Recollections (editor), 1982; Tennyson, Poet of Lincolnshire, 1985; The Annotated Dickens (edited with Edward Giuliano), 1986. *Contributions to:* Encyclopaedia Britannica; Listener; Times Literary Supplement. *Address:* 26 Knighton Drive, Leicester LE2 3HB, England.

COLLINS Timothy Maurice, (Mit Snilloc), b. 18 June 1957, Brisbane, Australia. Writer; Author; Tutor. m. Anastacia Messinis, 25 Nov 1982, 1 son. *Education:* Villanova College, Senior Certificate. *Appointments:* External Tutor, James Cook University Institute of Modern Language, 1991-; Writer in Residence, Ferny Hills School, 1991; Brisbane Boys Grammar School and Girls Grammar School, 1992; Ipswich Girls Grammar School, 1993; Emerald Writers Week, 1992. *Publications:* My Poetry; The Poetic Totem; Australasian Anthology of New Poets; Five Dollar Freedom Essential Poetry Anthology; Harold Kesteven Poetry Prize Anthology. *Contributions to:* All Main Literary Journals, Magazines & Newspapers. *Honours:* Northern Territory Government Literary Award; Denis Butler Memorial Poetry Award; This Brittle Bastion Poetry Award. *Memberships:* Queensland Poets Association; International PEN; Australian Society of Authors; National Book Council; Queensland Writers Centre; Fellowship of Australian Writers. *Address:* PO Box 328 Annerley 4103, Queensland, Australia.

COLLINSON Laurence (Henry), b. 1925, United Kingdom. Novelist; Short Story Writer; Playwright; Screenplay Writer; Poet; Columnist. *Appointments:* Teacher, English and Mathematics, 1956-61, Editor, The Educational Magazine, 1961-64, Victoria Education Department, Australia; Sub-Editor, International Publishing Corporation, London, England, 1965-73; Columnist, Quorum journal, 1973-. *Publications:* Friday Night at the Schrammers' 1949; No Sugar for George, 1949; Poet's Dozen, 1952; The Moods of Love, 1957; A Slice of Birthday Cake, 1963; Who is Wheeling Grandma, 1967; The Wangaratta Bunyip, 1970; Cupid's Crescent, 1973; Thinking Straight, 1975; Hovering Narcissus, 1977; One Penny for Israel, 1978.

COLLINSON Roger (Alfred), b. 1936, United Kingdom. Children's Fiction Writer; Schoolteacher. *Publications:* A Boat and Bax, 1967; Butch and Bax, 1970; Four Eyes, 1976; Get Lavinia Goodbody, 1983; Paper Flags and Penny Ices, 1984; Hanky-Panky, 1986. *Address:* 231 Carlton Avenue, Westcliff-on-Sea, Essex SS0 0QD, England.

COLLIS Louise Edith, b. 29 Jan 1925, Burma. Writer. *Education:* BA History, Reading University, England, 1945. *Publications:* Without a Voice, 1951; A Year Passed, 1952; After the Holiday, 1954; The Angel's Name, 1955; Seven in the Tower, 1958; The Apprentice Saint, 1964; Soldier in Paradise, 1965; The Great Flood, 1966; A Private View of Stanley Spencer, 1972; Maurice Collis Diaries (Editor), 1976; Impetuous Heart, the story

of Ethel Smyth, 1984. *Contributions to:* Books and Bookmen; Connoisseur; Art and Artists; Arts Review; Collectors Guide; Art and Antiques; and others. *Memberships:* Society of Authors; International Association of Art Critics. *Address:* 65 Cornwall Gardens, London, SW7, England.

COLLOMS Brenda, (Brenda Cross, Brenda Hughes), b. 1919, United Kingdom. Writer. *Appointments:* Editor, The Film Star Diary, Cramp Publishers, London, 1948-63. *Publications:* Happy Ever After (as Brenda Cross), 1947; The Film Hamlet (as Brenda Cross), 1948; New Guinea Folk Tales (as Brenda Hughes), 1959; Folk Tales from Chile (as Brenda Hughes), 1962; Certificate History, Books 1-4: Britain and Europe, 1966-70; Israel, 1971; The Mayflower Pilgrims, 1973; Charles Kingsley, 1975; Victorian Country Parsons, 1977; Victorian Visionaries, 1982; The Making of "Tottie" Fox. *Address:* 123A Gloucester Avenue, London NW1 8LB, England.

COLMAN E Adrian M, b. 1930, Scotland. Professor Emeritus. *Appointments:* Lecturer in English, 1962-70, Senior Lecturer, 1970-74, Associate Professor, 1974-78, University of Sydney, New South Wales; Research Associate, The Shakespeare Institute, University of Birmingham, England, 1968- 69; Professor of English, University of Tasmania, Hobart, 1978-90; Chairman of Board, Australian Theatre for Young People, 1975-78. *Publications:* Shakespeare's Julius Caesar, 1965; The Structure of Shakespeare's Antony and Cleopatra, 1971; The Dramatic Use of Bawdy in Shakespeare, 1974; Poems of Sir Walter Raleigh (editor), 1977; King Lear (editor), 1982; Henry IV Part I (editor), 1987; Romeo and Juliet (editor), 1993. *Address:* Department of English, University of Tasmania, Box 252C, GPO, Hobart, Tasmania 7001, Australia.

COLMAN John Edward, b. 8 Mar 1923, Philadelphia, PA, USA. Roman Catholic Priest and Educator. *Education:* AB, St. Josephs College; University of Notre Dame; Mary Immaculate Seminary; University of Pennsylvania; Johns Hopkins University; MA; PhD, St. Vincents Seminary, Philadelphia. *Publications:* The Master Teachers and the Art of Teaching, 1967; editor several books. *Contributions to:* Various professional journals, including School and Society; The Catholic Library World; The Educational Forum. *Honours:* Pi Mu Epsilon, National Honorary Mathematics Fraternity, 1966; Salute to Amazing Priest-Educator, The Torch, 1964; Man of the Pulpit, New York Sunday Times, 1961; Received Pen used by President Lyndon Johnson, for assistance in passing Higher Education Act, 1965. *Memberships:* National Council of University Research Adminstrators, Executive Committee; International Platform Association; Phi Delta Kappa; American Cancer Society, Board of Directors. *Address:* St. Johns University, Jamaica, NY 11439, USA.

COLMER John Anthony, b. 1921, United Kingdom. Professor of English. *Appointments:* Lecturer, Senior Lecturer, University of Khartoum, Sudan, 1949-59; Senior Lecturer, 1961-64, Reader, 1964, Professor of English, 1964-86, University of Adelaide, South Australia; Visiting Professor, National University of Singapore, 1989-90. *Publications:* Coleridge: Critic of Society, 1959; Coleridge: Selected Poems (editor), 1965; Shakespeare: Henry IV, Part I (co-editor), 1965; Approaches to the Novel (editor), 1966; E M Forster: A Passage to India, 1967; New Choice (co-editor), 1967; Mainly Modern (co-editor), 1969; E M Forster: The Personal Voice, 1975; Coleridge: On the Constitution of the Church and State (editor), 1976; Riders in the Chariot: Patrick White, 1978; Coleridge to Catch-22: Images of Society, 1978; Pattern and Voice (co-editor), 1981; Through Australian Eyes, 1984; Patrick White, 1984; The Penguin Book of Australian Autobiography (co-editor), 1987; Australian Autobiography: the Personal Quest, 1989. *Address:* 4 Everard Street, Glen Osmond, South Australia 5064, Australia.

COLOMBO Furio Marco, b. 1 Jan 1931, Chatillon,

Italy. Journalist; Writer. m. Alice Oxman, 16 Aug 1969, 1 daughter. *Education:* Law Degree, University of Turin. *Appointments:* Editor, Communicazione Visiva University of Bologna, 1970-77; Communicazioni di Massa Milan, 1979-84; Sanpaolo Chair, International Journalism, Graduate School of Journalism, Columbia Univ., 1991. *Major Publications include:* Nuovo Teatro Americano, 1963; L'America di Kennedy, 1964; Le Donne Matte, 1964; Il Prigioniero della Torre Velasca, Racconti, 1965; with many others. Latest Publications include: Cosa Faro da Grande, 1986 Giovanni Verga, in European Writers, Essay, 1985; Carriera: Vale Una Vita, Rizzoli, 1989; Il Destino Del Libro E Altri Destini, Bollati, 1990; Il Terzo Dopoguerra, Rizzoli, 1990; Scene Da Una Vittoria, Leonardo, 1991; Oer Israele, Rizzoli, 1991; La Citta Profona, Feltrinelli, 1991. *Contributions to:* Various journals including: LI Mondo, Rome; L'Expresso, Rome; Ulisse, Rome. Il Caffe, Rome; Bianco e Nero, Rome; Il Menabo, Turin; Revista di Estrtica, University of Turin; L'Editore, Turin; New York Review of Books; Enciclopedia Garzanti; Atlante Geografico De Agostini; Enciclopedia Europea Garzanti, 1980; Political Science Quarterly; L'Europeo, 1990-91; Panorama, 1991; La Stampa, 1972. *Honours:* Trumbull Lecturer, Yale University, USA, 1964; Chair, Italian Culture, University of California, Berkeley, 1975; Tevere Prize for Literature, Rome, 1986; Amalfi Prizew ffor Best TV Documentary; Capri Prize for Journalism; Board Director, Agnelli Foundation, Turin, 1991; Board Director, La Stampa Newspaper, Turin, 1991. *Memberships include:* Scientific Committee, Pio Manzu International Research Centre; Secretary, Friends of Palazzo Grassi Committee, Venice; Board of Visitors, Columbia University, New York. *Address:* Fiat USA, Inc, 375 Park Avenue, Suite 2703, New York, NY 10152, USA.

COLOMBO John Robert, b. 24 Mar 1936, Kitchener, Ontario, Canada. Author; Editor; Communications Consultant. m. Ruth, 3 children. *Publications:* Author, compiler or translator of 82 separate books, Quote books, reference books, humour and lore, compilations. Titles include: The Poets of Canada, 1978; Colombo's Names and Nicknames, 1979; Colombo's Hollywood, 1979; Poems of the Inuit, 1981; Colombo's Canadiana Quiz Book, 1983; Great Moments in Canadian History, 1984; We Stand on Guard, co-author, 1985; 1001 Questions About Canada, 1986; Colombo's New Canadian Quotations, 1987; The Dictionary of Canadian Quotations, 1991; Walt Whitman's Canada, 1992; The Little Blue Book of UFO's, 1993; The Canadian Global Almanac, 1993; Editor of over 100 books for Canadian publishing houses, 1960-80; Columnist. *Contributions to:* Canadian Encyclopaedia; Oxford Companion to Canadian Literature; Various journals, radio programmes. *Honours include:* Guest, Writers' Unions, USSR, Romania, Bulgaria; 1st Writer in Residence, Mohawk College, 1979-80; Certificate of Merit, Ontario Library Association; Best Paperback of the Year, Periodical Distributors of Canada, 1976; Centennial Medal, Esteemed Knight of Mark Twain; Order of Cyril and Methodius, 1st Class; Literary Prize, Philips Informations Systems, 1985. *Address:* 42 Dell Park Avenue, Toronto, Ontario, Canada M6B 2T6.

COLP Ralph Jr, b. 12 Oct 1924, New York, USA. Psychiatrist. m. Charlotte Rappaport, 22 Nov 1956, 2 daughters. *Education:* BA, Columbia University, 1945; MD, 1948; Mass Mental Health, Specialised Training in Psychiatry, 1957-59. *Publications:* To Be An Invalid; Recollection of Charles Darwin (forthcoming). *Contributions to:* Many inc. ISIS. *Memberships:* American Association History of Medicine. *Address:* 301 East 79th Street, Apt 12A, New York, NY 10021, USA.

COLQUHOUN Keith, b. 5 Aug 1933, London, England. Novelist; Journalist. 3 sons, 3 daughters. *Appointments:* Asian Affairs Writer, The Economist, 1980-. *Publications:* The Money Tree, 1958; Point of Stress, 1960; The Sugar Coating, 1973; St Petersburg Rainbow, 1975; Goebbels and Gladys, 1981; Filthy Rich, 1982; Kiss of Life, 1983; Foreign Wars, 1985; Mad Dog,

1992. *Address:* 8 Meadow Lane, West Mersea, Essex, England.

COLT Clem. *See:* **NYE Nelson.**

COLT Zandra. *See:* **STEVENSON Florence.**

COLTON James. *See:* **HANSEN Joseph.**

COLVIN Howard Montagu, b. 15 Oct 1919, Sidcup, Kent, England, Historian. m. Christina Edgeworth Butler, 16 Aug 1943, 2 sons. *Education:* BA, University College, London, 1940; MA Oxford University, 1948. *Publications:* A Biographical Dictionary of British Architects 1600-1840, 1978; Unbuilt Oxford, 1983; Calke Abbey, Derbyshire, 1985; The History of the King's Works, (General Editor and Part Author), 6 volumes, 1963-82; The White Canons in England, 1951; A History of Deddington, 1963; Catalogue of Architectural Drawings in Worcester College Library, 1964; The Canterbury Quadrangle: St John's College Oxford, 1988; (With J S G Simmons), All Souls: An Oxford College and its Buildings, 1989; Architecture and the After-Life, 1991. *Contributions to:* Architectural Review; Archaeological Journal; Country Life. *Honours:* Sir Banister Fletcher Prize, Authors' Club, 1957; Alice Davis Hitchcock Medallion, Society of Architectural Historians of Great Britain, 1959, 1981; CBE, 1964; Wolfson Literary Award for History, 1978; Honorary D Univ, York, 1978; CVO, 1983. *Memberships:* Fellow, British Academy; Fellow, Society of Antiquaries of London; Honorary fellow, Society of Antiquaries of Scotland; Honorary Fellow, Royal Institute of British Architects; Society of Architectural Historians of Great Britain, President, 1979-81; Fellow, Royal Historical Society. *Address:* 50 Plantation Road, Oxford OX2 6JE, England.

COLWELL Maxwell Gordon, b. 10 Oct 1926, Brompton, South Australia. Author. m. Betty Joy Holthouse, 27 Nov 1948, 2 sons. *Appointments:* Journalist, The Young Australian, 1960-62. *Publications:* Half Days and Patched pants; Full Days and Pressed Pants; Glorious Days and Khaki Pants; Whaling Aroung Australia; Voyages of Matthew Flinders; The Journey of Birke Wills; Others in. Big Rivers; Lights Vision the City of Adelaide. *Contributions to:* The Bulletin. *Honours:* Australian Council Literature Board Senior Fellowship. *Memberships:* Australian Society of Authors. *Address:* 102 8th Avenue Joslin, South Australia 5070, Australia.

COMAROFF John L, b. 1 Jan 1945, Cape Town, South Africa. Professor. m. Jean Rakoff, 15 Jan 1967, 1 son, 1 daughter. *Education:* BA, University of Cape Town, 1966; PhD, University of London, 1973. *Appointments:* Lecturer, University of Manchester, 1972-78; Professor, University of Chicago, 1987; Director, Ecole des Hautes Studies in Sciences Socials, Paris, 1988; Senior Research Fellow, American Bar Foundation, 1991; Chairman, University of Chicago, 1991. *Publications:* Of Revalation and Revolution: Christinaty & Colonisalism in South Africa; Rules & Process; African Context; The Diary of Sol T plaatje; An African At Mafekinn; Essays on African Marriage in Southern Africa. *Contributions to:* American Ethnologist; Journal of Southern African studies; Journal of Historical Sociology; Man; Journal of African Law; Thnos; Economy & Society. *Memberships:* Association of Political & Legal Anthropology; Association of Social Anthropologist; American Anthropological Association; Royal Anthropological Institute. *Address:* University of Chicago, Department of Anthropology, 1126 E 59th Street, Chicago, IL 60637, USA.

COMFORT Alex(ander), b. 1920. Physician; Poet; Novelist. *Appointments:* Consultant Psychiatrist, Brentwood Veterans Hospital, Los Angeles, California, USA 1973-89; Lecturer in Psychiatry, Stanford University, California, 1974-81; Fellow, Institute for Higher Studies, Santa Barbara, California, 1975-80;

Professor of Pathology, University of California School of Medicine, Irvine, 1976-79; and Adjunct Professor, University of California at Los Angeles, 1979-. House Physician, London Hospital, 1944; Resident Medical Officer, Royal Waterloo Hospital, 1944-45; Lecturer in Physiology, 1945-51; Honorary Research Associate, Department of Zoology, 1951-73, Director of Medical Research Council Group on the Biology of Ageing, 1966-70, and Director of Research in Gerontology, 1970-73, University College, London. *Publications include:* The Silver River, 1936; The Power House, 1945; On This Side Nothing (novel), 1949; The Right Thing to Do, Together with the Wrong Thing to Do, 1949; Authority and Delinquency in the Modern State: A Criminal Approach to the Problem of Power, 1950; Sexual Behaviour in Society, 1950, as Sex in Society, 1963; And All But He Departed (poetry), 1951; Delinquency (lecture), 1951; Art and Social Responsibility, 1952; A Giant's Strength (novel), 1952; The Biology of Senescence, 1953, as Ageing: The Biology of Senescence, 1964, 1979; Darwin and the Naked Lady: Discursive Essays on Biology and Art, 1961; Come Out to Play (novel), 1964; (translation), The Koka Shastra, 1964; The Nature of Human Nature, 1965, in UK as Nature and Human Nature, 1966; The Anxiety Makers: Some Curious Preoccupations of the Medical Profession, 1967; (ed) History of Erotic Art, vol I 1969; What Rough Beast? and What is a Doctor? (lectures), 1971; The Joy of Sex: A Gourmet's Guide to Love Making, 1973; More Joy: Sequel to The Joy of Sex, 1974; A Good Age, 1976; (ed) Sexual Consequences of Disability, 1978; Tetrarch (novel), 1978; Poems for Jane, 1978; I and That 1979; A Practise of Geriatric Psychiatry, 1979; (with Jane Comfort), The Facts of Love: Living, Loving and Growing Up (juvenile), 1979; Reality and Empathy, 1984; Imperial Patient (novel), 1987; The Philosophers (novel), 1989; Science, Religion and Scientism (Conway Mem Lecture), 1990; The New Joy of Sex, 1991. *Address:* 2 Fitzwarren House, Hornsey Lane, N6 5LX, England.

COMFORT Nicholas Alfred Fenner, b. 4 Aug 1946, London, England. Journalist. m. (1) 1970, dissolved 1988, 1 son, 1 daughter, (2) Corinne Reed, 1990. *Education:* MA, History, (Exhibitioner), Trinity College, Cambridge, 1968. *Appointments:* Morning Telegraph, Sheffield, 1968-74, Daily Telegraph, 1974-89 (Washington 1976-78, Political Staff, 1978-87 Leader Writer, 1987-89); Political Editor, the Independent on Sunday, 1989-90; Political Editor, The European, 190-92; Political Editor, Daily Record, 1992-. *Publications:* Mid-Suffolk Light Railway, 1986; The Tunnel - The Channel and Beyond, Contributor, 1987; Brewer's Political Dictionary, 1993; The Lost City of Dunwich, forthcoming. *Contributions to:* Numerous political, transport and other journals. *Membership:* Fellow, Royal Geographical Society. *Address:* 20 Avenue Road, London N6 5DW, England.

COMINI Alessandra, b. 1934, USA. University Distinguished Professor of Art History. *Publications:* Schiele in Prison, 1974; Egon Schiele's Portraits, 1975; Gustav Klimt, 1975; Egon Schiele, 1976; The Fantastic Art of Vienna, 1978; The Changing Image of Beethoven, 1987; co-author, World Impressionism, 1990. *Address:* Department of Art History, Southern Methodist University, Dallas, TX 75275, USA.

COMPTON David Guy (Guy Compton, Frances Lynch), b. 1930. Mystery/Crime/Suspense, Historical/Romance/Gothic. Science fiction/Fantasy. *Appointments:* Worked as stage electrician, furniture maker, salesman, docker and postman. Editor, Reader's Digest Condensed Books, London 1969-81. *Publications:* Too Many Murderers, 1962; (as Guy Compton), Medium for Murder, 1963; (as Guy Compton), Dead on Cue, 1964; (as Guy Compton), Disguise for a Dead Gentleman, 1964; (as Guy Compton), High Tide for a Hanging, 1965; The Quality of Mercy, 1965, 1970; Farewell Earth's Bliss, 1966; The Silent Multitude, 1966; (as Guy Compton), And Murder Came Too, 1966; Synthajoy, 1968; The Palace, 1969; The Electric Crocodile (in US as The Steel Crocodile), 1970;

Chronocules, 1970, in UK as Hot Wireless Sets, Aspirin Tablets, The Sandpaper Sides of Used Matchboxes and Something That Might Have Been Castor Oil, 1971; The Missionaries, 1972; The Unsleeping Eye, 1973, in UK as The Continuous Katherine Mortenhoe, 1974; (as Frances Lynch), Twice Ten Thousand Miles, 1974, as Candle at Midnight, 1977; (as Frances Lynch), The Fine and Handsome Captain, 1975; (as Frances Lynch), Stranger at the Wedding, 1977; (as Frances Lynch), A Dangerous Magic, 1978; A Usual Lunacy, 1978; Windows, 1979; (as Frances Lynch), In the House of Dark Music, 1979; Ascendancies 1980; Scudder's Game, 1985; Ragnarok, (with John Gibbin), 1991; Nomansland, 1993. *Address:* c/o Murrary Pollinger, 222 Old Brompton Road, London, SW5 0BZ.

COMPTON Guy. *See:* **COMPTON David Guy.**

CONDON Richard, b. 18 Mar 1915, New York City, New York, USA. Writer. m. Evelyn Rose Hunt, 14 Jan 1938, 2 daughters. *Publications:* The Horse Stories, children's record albums, 1947; Men of Distinction, play, 1953; Novels: The Oldest Confession, 1958; The Manchurian Candidate, 1959; Some Angry Angel, 1960; A Talent for Loving, 1961; An Infinity of Mirrors, 1964; Any God Will Do, 1966; The Ecstasy Business, 1967; Mile High, 1969; Vertical Smile, 1971; Arigato, 1972; And Then We Moved to Rossenarra, 1973; The Mexican Stove, 1973; Winter Kills, 1974; The Star Spangled Crunch, 1974; Money is Love, 1975; The Whisper of the Axe, 1976; The Abandoned Woman, 1977; Bandicoot, 1978; Death of a Politician, 1978; The Entwining, 1980; Prizzi's Honor, 1982; A Trembling Upon Rome, 1983; Prizzi's Family, 1986; Screenplays: Prizzi's Honour (with Janet Roach), 1984; Arigato, 1985; Prizzi's Glory, 1988. *Contributions to:* Over 100, USA and UK publications. *Honours:* Chevalier, La Confrerie du Tastevin, 1968; Commanderie de Bontemps, 1969; Chevalier, Chaine des Rotisseurs, 1976; Best Screenplay Award, Writers Guild of America, 1986; Best Screenplay Award, British Academy of Film and TV, 1986. *Literary Agent:* Harold Matson Co, 276 Fifth Avenue, New York, NY 10001, USA. *Address:* 3436 Asbury Avenue, Dallas, TX 75205, USA.

CONDRY William Moreton, b. 1 Mar 1918, Birmingham, England. Writer. m. Penny Bailey, 17 Apr 1946.*Education:*BA, 1939; DipEd, 1940, Birmingham University; BA (hons.French), London, 1945; MA, Wales, 1951. *Publications:* The Snowdonia National Park, 1966; Exploring Wales, 1970; Pathway to the Wild, 1975; Woodlands, 1974; The Natural History of Wales, 1981; Snowdonia, 1987; Thoreau, 1954; Birds and Wild Africa, 1967; World of a Mountain, 1977; The National Trust - Wales, 1991. *Contributions to:* Many articles in Country Life, and other magazines. *Honour:* MSc. (Honoris causa), University of Wales, 1980. *Address:* Ynys Edwin, Eglwysfach, Machynlleth, Powys SY20 8TA, Wales.

CONE Molly Zelda, b. 3 Oct 1918, Tacoma, Washington, USA. Writer. m. Gerald J Cone, 9 Sept 1939, 1 son, 2 daughters. *Education:* University of Washington 1936-38. *Publications include:* For children: Mishmash; Mishmash and the Substitute Teacher; Mishmash and the Sauerkraut Mystery; Mishmash and the Venus Flytrap; Mishmash and the Big Fat Problem. Biographies: Hurry Henrietta, 1966; Leonard Bernstein, 1970; The Ringling Brothers 1971. Non-fiction includes: Stories of Jewish Symbols, 1963; Who Knows Ten, 1965; The Jewish Sabbath, 1966; The Jewish New Year 1966; Purim 1967; The Mystery of Being Jewish, 1989. Play: John Bunyan and His Blue Ox, 1966. *Honours include:* Neveh Shalom Centennial Award for Literary Contribution toward the Education of Jewish Children, 1970; Governor's Festival of Arts, Certificate of Recognition, 1970 (State of Washington); Washington Press Women First Place Award, 1970 for Juvenile Book: Simon; National Federation of Press Women Award, 1970 for Simon; Washington Press Women Second Place Award, 1971 for Juvenile Book: You Can't Make Me If I Don't Want To; Washington Press Women Sugar Plum Award, 1972, Field of

Communications; The Shirley Kravitz Children's Book Award, 1973, The Association of Jewish Libraries; Washington Press Women First Place Award, 1974, Juvenile Book: Dance Around the Fire. *Memberships:*)Authors League of America; Seattle Free Lances. *Literary Agent:* McIntosh and Otis, Inc, 310 Madison Avenue, New York, NY 10017, USA. *Address:* 8003, Sand Point Way NE B-24, Seattle, WA 98115, USA.

CONEY Michael Greatrex, b. 28 Sept 1932, Writer, m. Daphne, 14 May 1957, 1 son, 1 daughter. *Education:* King Edwards School, Birmingham, England, 1949. *Publications include:* King of the Scepter'd Isle; Mirror Image, 1972; Syzygy, 1973; Friends Come in Boxes, 1973; The Hero of Downways, 1973; Winter's Children, 1974; Monitor Found in Orbit, 1974; The Jaws that Bite, The Claws that catch, 1975; Hello Summer, Goodbye, 1976; Charisma, 1975; Brontomek!, 1976; The Ultimate Jungle, 1979; Neptune's Children, 1981; Cat karina, 1982; The Celestial Steam Locomotive, 1983; Gods of the Greataway, 1984; Fang, the Gnome, 1988; No Place for a Sealion; A Tomcat Called Sabrina; A Judge of Men, 1969; Whatever Became of the McGowans?, 1971; The Snow Princess, 1971; Susanna! Susanna!, 1971; The Bridge on the Scraw, 1973; The Hook, the Eye and the Whip, 1974; The Hollow Where, 1975; Trading Post, 1976; Just an Old-Fashioned War Story, 1977; Penny on a Skyhorse, 1979; The Byrds, 1983. *Honour:* Best British Novel (BSFAA Award) for Brontomek!, 1976. *Memberships:* Science Fiction Writers of America; Writers Union of Canada; Institute of Chartered Accountants. *Literary Agent:* E J Carnell Agency, UK; Virginia Kidd, USA. *Address:* 2082 Neptune Road RR3, Sidney, British Columbia, Canada V8L 3X9.

CONFORD Ellen, b. 1942, American. *Publications:* Impossible Possum, 1971; Why Can't I Be William?, 1972; Dreams of Victory, Felicia the Critic, 1973; The Luck of Pokey Bloom, Me and the Terrible Two, 1974; Just the Thing for Geraldine, Dear Lovey Hart I Am Desperate, 1975; The Alfred G Graebner Memorial High School Handbook of Rules and Regulations, 1976; And This Is Laura, 1977; Eugene the Brave, Hail Hail Camp Timberwood, 1978; Anything for a Friend, We Interrupt This Semester for an Important Bulletin, 1979; The Revenge of the Incredible Dr Rancid and His Youthful Assistant Jeffrey, 1980; Seven Days to a Brand-New Me, 1981; To All My Fans with Love from Sylvie, 1982; Lenny Kandell Smart Aleck, If This is Love I'll Take Spaghetti, 1983; You Never Can Tell, 1984; Strictly for Laughs, Why Me?, 1985. *Address:* 26 Strathmore Road, Great Neck, NY 11023, USA.

CONGER Jay, b. 29 July 1952, Washington, DC, USA. Professor. *Education:* BA, Dartmouth College, 1974; MBA, University of Virginia, 1977; DBA, Harvard University, 1985. *Publications:* Learning to Lead; The Charismatic Leader; Charismatic Leadership. *Contributions to:* Numerous. *Membership:* Academy of Management. *Address:* Faculty of Managment, McGill University, 1001 Sherbrooke Street West, Montreal, Quebec, Canada H3A 1G5.

CONLON Kathleen. *See:* **LLOYD Kathleen Annie.**

CONN Stewart, b. 1936, British. *Appointments:* Radio Producer, BBC, Glasgow, 1962-77; Head of Radio Drama, BBC Edinburgh, 1977-92; Literary Adviser, Edinburgh Royal Lyceum Theatre, 1972-75. *Publications:* Thunder in the Air: Poems, The Chinese Tower, Poems, 1967; Stoats in the Sunlight: Poems (in US as Ambush and Other Poems), 1968; The Burning, 1971; In Transit, An Ear to the Ground, Poems, 1972; PEN New Poems 1973-74 (Editor), 1974, Thistlewood, 1975; The Aquarium, The Man in the Green Muffler, I Didn't Always Live Here, 1976; Under the Ice, Poems, 1978; Play Donkey, 1980; In the Kibble Palace, new & selected poems: 1987; The Luncheon of the Boating Party, poems, 1992. *Contributions to:* Poetry, Chicago; The Observer, London; 12 More Modern Scottish Poets, 1986; The Best of Scottish Poetry, 1989; The Faber Book of Twentieth-Century Scottish Poetry, 1992; Six Poetes

Ecossais, 1992. *Honours:* EC Gregory Award,1964; Scottish Arts Council awards & poetry prize, 1968, 1978, 1992. *Membership:* Knight of Mark Twain. *Address:* 1 Fettes Row, Edinburgh EH3 6SF, Scotland.

CONNELL Brian Reginald, b. 12 Apr 1916, London, England. Author; Journalist; Broadcaster. m. Esmee Jean Mackenzie, 27 Nov 1944. *Education:* Brighton Grammar School, 1927-33; Madrid University 1933-36; Berlin University, 1936-37. *Appointments:* Reuters 1940-43; Daily Mail 1946- 50; News Chronicle 1950-55; ITN 1955-86; Chairman, Connell Literary Enterprises/Partner Connell Editors, 1960-. *Publications:* Regina v Palmerston, 1962; Return of the Tiger, 1960; The Plains of Abraham, 1959; Watcher on the Rhine, 1957; Knight Errant, 1955; Manifest Destiny, 1953; Portrait of a Whig Peer, 1957; The War in the Peninsula, 1973; The Siege of Quebec, 1976; America in the Making, 1977; Editor and compiler of ten autobiographies. *Contributions to:* European Review; The Economist; The Times 1975-83. *Honours:* Producers Guild Award, 1963; Cannes Festival International Award, 1965. *Memberships:* The Pilgrims; National Union of Journalists; Reform Club; Lansdowne Club. *Address:* B2 Marine Gate, Marine Drive, Brighton, Sussex BN2 5TQ, England.

CONNELL Maureen. *See:* **GUILLERMAN Maureen Therese.**

CONNOLLY Peter, b. 8 May 1935, Surbiton, Surrey, England. *Publications:* The Roman Army, 1975; The Greek Armies, 1977; Hannibal and the Enemies of Rome, 1978; Pompeii, 1979; Greece and Rome at war, 1981; Living in the Time of Jesus of Nazareth, 1983; The Legend of Odysseus, 1986; Tiberius Claudius Maximus The Cavalryman, 1988; Tiberius Claudius Maximus The Legionary, 1988; Warfare in the Ancient World, (Co-author), 1989; The Roman Fort, 1991. *Contributions to:* Numerous articles on Roman military equipment. *Honours:* Honorary Fellow, Institute of Archaeology, University College, London, 1985; Fellow, Society of Antiquaries, London, 1985; Winner, Senior Information Book Award, Times Educational Supplement for The Legend of Odysseus, 1987. *Memberships:* Society of Authors; Society for Promotion of Roman Studies; Society for Promotion of Hellenic Studies. *Address:* 22 Spring Street, Spalding, Lincolnshire PE11 2XW, England.

CONNOLLY Ray, British. Writer. *Publications:* A Girl Who Came to Stay: That'll Be the Day, 1973; Stardust, 1974; Trick or Treat?, James Dean: The First American Teenager, 1975; Newsdeath, 1978; A Sunday Kind of Woman, Honky Tonk Heroes, 1980; John Lennon 1940-1980, The Sun Place, 1981; Stardust Memories (ed), 1983; Forever Young, 1984; Lytton's Diary, 1985; Defrosting The Fridge, 1988; Perfect Scoundrels, 1989; Sunday Morning, 1992. *Contributions to:* Columnist for London Evening Standard, 1967-1973, 1983-1984; The Times, 1989-90. *Honours:* Stardust, Best Original British Screenplay, 1974, Writers Guild of Great Britain. *Literary Agent:* Gill Coleridge, Rogers, Coleridge and White, London. *Address:* c/o Rogers, Coleridge and White, 20 Powis Mews, London, W11 1JN, England.

CONNOR Tony, b. 16 Mar 1930, Manchester, Lancashire, England. Author; Playwright. m. Frances Foad, 22 July 1961. *Education:* Schools in Manchester, left school at fourteen; Night classes in painting at Regional College of Art, Manchester; Extra mural course in Modern Literature, Manchester University; non-graduate MA, Manchester University. *Appointments:* Early career in textile design; Army service as tank driver in the Fifth Royal Inniskilling Dragoon Guards; Part-time teacher of textile design and life drawing at Salford School of Art; Appointed full-time teacher of Liberal Studies at Bolton Technical College, 1961; Writer-in-residence, Amherst College, USA, 1967; Writer-in-residence, Wesleyan University, Connecticut, 1968; two years in England, unemployed and part-time teaching job at Bolton Technical College; Professor of English,

Wesleyan University, USA, 1971-; Visiting Playwright, Oxford Playhouse, England, 1974-75. *Publications:* Books: With Love Somehow, 1962; Lodgers, 1965; 12 Secret Poems, 1965; Kon in Springtime, 1968; In the Happy Valley, 1971; Then Memoirs of Uncle Harry, 1974; Seven Last Poems from the Memoirs of Uncle Harry, 1974; Billy's Wonderful Kettle, 1974; City of Strangers, 1975; To a Friend, Who Asked for a Poem, 1975; Twelve Villanelles, 1977; Spirits of the Place, 1986; New and Selected Poems, Athens: University of Georgia Press, 1982; London, Anvil Press, 1982; Play productions: Billy's Wonderful Kettle, Manchester, 1970; I Am Real and So Are You, Manchester, 1971; The Last of the Feinsteins, London 1972; A Couple with a Cat, London, 1972; Otto's Interview, London, 1973; Dr Crankenheim's Mixed-Up Monster, Oxford, Oxford Playhouse, 1974; David's Violin, New York, 1976.

CONNORS Bruton. *See:* **ROHEN Edwards.**

CONOLEY Gillian Flavia, b. 29 Mar 1955, Austin, Texas, USA. Writer; Professor. m. 22 Mar 1986. *Education:* BFA, Journalism, Southern Methodist Univesity, 1977; MFA, Creative Writing, University of Massachusetts, 1983. *Appointments:* Staff, Dallas Morning News, 1978- 80; Instructor, University of New Orleans, 1984-87; Visiting Lecturer, Tulane University, 1984-87; Artist In Residence, Eastern Washington University, 1987- ; Editor, Willow Springs, 1987-. *Publications:* Woman Speaking Inside Film Noir, 1984; Some Gangster Pain, 1987; Tall Stranger. *Contributions to:* American Poetry Review; Ironwood; North American Review. *Honours:* Fellowship, MacDowell Colony, 1984; Academy of American Poets Prize, 1984; Honourable Mention, Great Lakes College Association Award for a First Book of Poems, 1987. *Memberships:* Associated Writing Programmes; MLA. *Address:* Eastern Washington University, English Dept. M5-25, Pattison Hall, Cheney, WA 99004, USA.

CONOT Robert E, b. 1929, American. *Appointments:* Journalist, 1952-58; Television Writer, 1958-60; Special Consultant, National Advisory Commission on Civil Disorders, 1967-68; Senior Lecturer, University of South Carolina School of Journalism, 1983-. *Publications:* Ministers of Vengeance, 1964; Rivers of Blood, Years of Darkness, 1967; Commission on Civil Disorders, 1968; American Odyssey, 1974; Urban Poverty in Historical Perspective: The Case of the United States, 1975; A Steak of Luck: The Life and Legend of Thomas Alva Edison, 1979; Justice at Nuremburg, 1983; The Nuremburg Gift, 1986.

CONQUEST (George) Robert (Acworth), b. 15 July 1917, Malvern, Worcestershire, England. Writer. m. (1) Joan Watkins, 2 sons, (4) Elizabeth Neece, 1 Dec 1979. *Education:* Winchester College, 1931-35; University of Grenoble, France, 1935-36; Magdalen College, Oxford, 1936-39; MA (Oxon), 1972, DLitt (Oxon), 1975. *Appointments:* Visiting Poet, University of Buffalo, USA, 1959-60; Literary Editor, The Spectator, 1962-63. *Publications:* Poems, 1955; A World of Difference, 1955; Power and Policy in the USSR, 1961; Between Mars and Venus, 1962; The Egyptologists (with Kingsley Amis), 1965; The Great Terror, 1968 (The Great Terror, A Reassessment, 1990); Arias from a Love Opera, 1969; The Nation Killers, 1970; Lenin, 1972; Kolyma, 1978; Forays, 1979; The Abomination of Moab, 1979; We and They, 1980; Inside Stalin's Secret Police, 1985; The Harvest of Sorrow, 1986; New and Collected Poems, 1988; Tyrants and Typewriters, 1989; Stalin: Breaker of Nations, 1991. *Contributions to:* London Magazine; TLS, Analog Science Fiction; Soviet Studies; Neva, Leningrad; Novy Mir, Moscow; Poetry, Chicago; The New Republic; The Spectator. *Honour:* CBE, 1955. *Memberships:* Fellow, Royal Society of Literature; Travellers Club; Fellow, British Interplanetary Society; Society for the Promotion of Roman Studies; American Association for the Advancement of Slavic Studies. *Literary Agent:* Curtis Brown. *Address:* 52 Peter Coutts Circle, Stanford, CA 94305, USA.

CONRAN Anthony, b. 1931, British. *Appointments:* Research Fellow and Tutor, University College of North Wales, 1957-. *Publications:* Formal Poems, 1960; Metamorphoses, 1961; Icons (opus 6), Asymptotes (opus 7), A String o Blethers (opus 8), Sequence of the Blue Flower, The Mountain, For the Marriage of Gerald and Linda, 1963; Stelae and Other Poems, 1965; Guernica, 1966; Collected Poems: volume I (1951-58), 1966, volume II (1959- 61), 1966; volume III (1962-66), 1967; volume IV (1967), 1968; The Penguin Book of Welsh Verse (ed and translator), 1967; Claim, Claim, Claim: A Book of Poems, 1969; Spirit Level, 1974; Poems 1951-67, 1974; Life Fund, On to the Fields of Praise: Essays on the English Poets of Wales, 1979; The Cost of Strangeness: Essays on the English Poets of Wales, 1982; Welsh Verse (trans), 1987. *Address:* 1 Frondirion, Glanrafon, Bangor, Carnavanshire, Wales.

CONRAN Shirley (Ida), b. 1932, British. *Appointments:* Founder and Co-Owner, Conran Fabrics Limited, 1957; Editorial Adviser, Sidgwick and Jackson Limited; Home Editor, Daily Mail, 1962; Women's Editor 1964, Women's Editor, Observer Magazine, 1969-70; Women's Editor, Daily Mail 1968; Design and Promotion Consultant, Westinghouse Kitchens, 1969; Columnist, Vanity Fair Magazine, 1970-71; Life and Styles Editor, Over 21 Magazine, 1972; Handled publicity for Women in Media campaigns, 1972-74. *Publications:* Printed Textile Design for Studio Publication, 1956; Superwoman, 1975; Superwoman Yearbook, 1976; Superwoman 2 (in US as Superwoman in Action), 1977; Futures: How to Survive Life after Thirty (with E Sidney), 1979; Lace, 1982; The Magic Garden, 1983; Lace 2, 1984; Savages, 1987; Down with Superwoman, 1990; The Amazing Umbrella Shop, 1990; Crimson, 1992. *Address:* Monaco.

CONROY John, b. 29 Mar 1951, Chicago, Illinois, USA. Writer. m. Colette Davison, May 1986. *Education:* BA, English Literature, University of Illinois, 1973. *Appointments:* Senior Editor, Chicago Magazine, 1974-76; Staff Writer, Chicago Reader, 1978-. *Publications:* Belfast Diary: War as a Way of Life, 1987, UK Edition as War as a Way of Life, A Belfast Diary, 1988. *Contributions to:* Foreign Correspondent, articles from Belfast, Bonn, Athens and Beirut to: New York Times; Boston Globe; Boston Phoenix; Chicago Daily News; Chicago Sun-Times; Chicago Tribune; Atlanta Constitution; Dallas Morning News; San Diego Union; Village Voice; Others; Freelance articles to: Chicago Magazine; Chicago Reader; Washington Post; Geo; Mother Jones; Granta. *Honours:* Peter Lisagor Award for Exemplary Journalism, Society of Professional Journalists, Chicago Chapter, 1977, 1991; Clarion Award, Magazine Series Division, Women in Communications, 1978; National Award for Magazine Writing, Society of Professional Journalists, 1978; Alicia Patterson Fellowship, Alicia Patterson Foundation, 1980; Best Nonfiction Book of 1987: Society of Midland Authors Award, Carl Sandburg Award, Friends of Literature Award; Research and Writing Grants: John D and Catherine T Macarthur Foundation and J Roderick MacArthur Foundation, 1990; 2nd Place, John Bartlow Martin Award for Public Interest Magazine Journalism, 1991. *Literary Agent:* Wendy Weil, Wendy Weil Agency, New York, NY, USA. *Address:* c/o Chicago Reader, 11 E Illinois Street, Chicago, IL 60611, USA.

CONSTABLE Trevor James, b. 17 Sept 1925, Wellington, New Zealand. Radio Electronics Officer. m. Gloria Garcia, 14 Sep. 1983, 1 daughter. *Education:* Rongotai College, Wellington, 1936-42. *Appointments:* Staff Writer, National Commercial Broadcasting Service, Wellington, 1942-44; Staff Writer, International Broadcasting Company, Vancouver, Canada, 1950-52; US Correspondent, New Zealand Weekly News, 1958-68; Freelance Magazine Writer, USA, 1960-70. *Publications:* Blond Knight of Germany, 1970, Fighter Aces of the USA, 1977, Fighter Aces of the Luftwaffe, 1978, Horrido!, 1968, Fighter Aces, 1966, all with Colonel Raymond F. Toliver, USAF; Hidden Heroes, 1971; The Cosmic Pulse of Life, 1978; Fighter General, The Life of Adolf Galland, with, Raymond Toliver, 1988.

Contributions *to:* Numerous military and aviation articles. *Honour:* Aviation/Space Writers Book of the Year Award, 1978. *Memberships:* Aviation/Space Writers Association; National Maritime Historical Society; American Radio Association. *Address:* 3726 Bluff Place, San Pedro, CA 90731, USA.

CONSTANT Clinton, b. 20 Mar 1912, Nelson, British Columbia, Canada. US Citizen. Chemical Engineer; Author. *Education:* BSc, Alberta University, 1935; Doctorate, Western Reserve University, USA, 1941; Registered Professional Engineer. *Publications:* The War of the Universe, 1931; The Martian Menace, 1934; O and M Manual for Industrial Waste Treatment Plant, 1975. *Contributions to:* Numerous Technical publications and reports on Astronomy, Chemistry and Rocketry. *Memberships include:* American Chemical Society; Royal Astronomical Society, Canada; American Water Works Association; Fellow, New York Academy of Science; American Astronomical Society; Fellow, American Institute of Chemical Engineers; Fellow, American Institute of Chemists; Fellow, American Association for the Advancement of Science; Associate Fellow, American Institute Aeronautics and Astronautics; National Society of Professional Engineers, Air Pollution Control Association, Water Pollution Control Federation, Astronomical Society of the Pacific. *Address:* PO Box 2529, Victorville, CA 92393, USA.

CONWAY David, b. 29 Jan 1939, Aberystwyth, Wales. Principal Director, European Patent Office. *Education:* BA 1961, MA 1963, University of London. *Publications:* Magic: An Occult Primer, 1972, new edition 1988; The Magic of Herbs, 1973; Secret Wisdom, 1984. *Address:* Franziskanerst 18/II, 8000 Munich 80, Germany.

CONWAY Peter. *See:* **MILKOMANE George Alexis Milkomanovich.**

CONWAY Troy. *See:* **AVALLONE Michael.**

COOK Christopher Piers, b. 20 June 1945, Leicester, England. Writer; Historian. *Education:* BA (1st class honours) History 1967, MA 1970, Cambridge University; DPhil, Modern History, Oxford University, 1974. *Appointment:* Editor, Pears Cyclopaedia, 1976-. *Publications:* Sources in British Political History, 6 volumes, 1975-84; A Short History of the Liberal Party 1900-92, 1993; The Slump (with John Stevenson), 1976; Dictionary of Historical Terms, 2nd edition, 1989; Longman Handbook of Modern British History 1714-1987, 1988; Longman Handbook of Modern European History 1763-1991, 1992; World Political Almanac, 1989. *Contributions to:* The Guardian; Times Literary Supplement; THES. *Honour:* Fellow, Royal Historical Society, 1977. *Literary Agent:* Clarissa Rushdie, A P Watt & Co, 20 John Street, London WC1. *Address:* c/o Pears Cyclopaedia, Pelham Books, 27 Wrights Lane, Kensington, London W8 5TZ, England.

COOK David, b. 1940, British. *Appointments:* Professional actor, 1961-; Writer-in-Residence, St Martin's College, Lancaster, 1982-83. *Publications:* Albert's Memorial, 1972; Happy Endings, 1974; Walter, 1978; Winter Doves, 1979; Sunrising, 1983; Missing Persons, 1986; Crying Out Loud, 1988; Walter and June, 1989; Second Best, 1991. *Honours:* E M Forster Award, 1977; Hawthorn Prize, 1978; Southern Arts Fiction Prize, 1984; Arthur Welton Scholarship, 1991; Oddfellows Social Concern Award, 1992. *Membership:* Society of Authors. *Literary Agents:* Elaine Greene Ltd. *Address:* 7 Sydney Place, London SW7 3NL, England.

COOK Don, b. 1920, American. *Appointments:* European Diplomatic Correspondence, New York Herald Tribune, Washington, London, Bonn, Paris 1943-65, Los Angeles Times 1965-. *Publications:* Floodtide in Europe, 1965; The War Lords: Eisenhower, 1976; Ten Men and History, 1981; Charles De Gaulle: A Biography, 1984.

Address: 73 Avenue des Champs-Elysees, Paris 75008, France.

COOK Dorothy Mary, (Dy Cameron, D M Carlisle, Elizabeth Clare). British. *Publications:* as D Y Cameron: Chasing Shadows, 1962; Out of the Storm, Strange Byways, 1963; The Unreasonable Heart, The Searching Heart, 1964; The Loving Cup, 1965; Love Unfolding, A Land of Stars (as E Clare), 1966; A Puzzled Heart, Sunlight Through the Mist (as E Clare), 1967; The Enchanted Way, In Spring Time (both as E Clare), 1968; Conflicting Tides, Enchanting Adventure, A Song to the Sun (as E Clare), 1969; Moonlight and March Roses, A Royal Occasion (as E Clare), 1970; Magic of Springtime, 1971; Sunlit Waterways 1972, (both as B Clare); Night Scented Air, Althea's Falcon (as D M Carlisle), Glade in the Woods (as E Clare), 1974; Scent of Jasmin, 1975; Down by the Willows (as E Clare), 1977; Music in the Wind, 1978; Jenny's Searching Heart, 1979; The Delightful Valley (as E Clare), 1980; A Touch of Spring, By the Golden Waters (as E Clare), 1981; as D M Carlisle: The Secret of the Chateau, 1981; Straws in the Wind, 1983; The Harvest is Sure, 1985; Harvest Issue, 1986. *Address:* c/o Hale, 45-47 Clerkenwell Green, London EC1R OHT, England.

COOK Glen, b. 9 July 1944, New York City, New York, USA. Auto Assembler; Writer. m. 14 June 1971, 3 sons. *Publications:* The Tower of Fear, 1989; The Dragon Never Sleeps, 1988; The Garrett Files (series), 1987-; Passage At Arms, 1985; A Matter of Time, 1985; The Black Company (series), 1984-89. *Contributions to:* Numerous magazines, journals. *Literary Agent:* Scott Meredith, Inc, 845 Third Avenue, New York, NY 10022, USA. *Address:* c/o Scott Meredith, Inc, 845 Third Avenue, New York, NY 10022, USA.

COOK Lila. *See:* **AFRICANO Lillian.**

COOK Lyn. *See:* **WADDELL Evelyn Margaret.**

COOK Michael, b. 1933, Canadian. *Appointments:* Specialist in Drama 1967-70, Lecturer 1970-74, Assistant Professor 1974-78, Associate Professor of English 1978-, Memorial University, St John's Newfoundland; Film and Drama Critic, Evening Telegram, St John's, 1967-82; Member, Editorial Board, Canadian Theatre Review, Downsview, Ontario, 1973-; Artistic Director, Newfoundland Summer Festival of the Arts, 1970-74; Director, Newfoundland Arts and Culture Centre Productions, 1971-74; One-time host of weekly television review Our Man Friday, CBC St John's: Originator and Writer for TV series Up at Ours, 1980-82; Governor, Canadian Conference on the Arts, Ottawa, 1975-79; Vice-Chairman , Guild of Canadian Playwrights, 1979; Chairman, Playwrights Canada, 1982-83; Founding Member, Newfoundland Arts Council, 1980-82. *Publications:* The Head Guts and Soundbone Dance, 1974; Jacob's Wake, 1975; Not as a Dream, Tiln and Other Plays, 1976; Three Plays, Terese's Creed, 1977; The Gayden Chronicles, 1979; The Island of Fire, 1980; The Terrible Journey of Frederick Dunglass, 1982; The Fisherman's Revenge, 1985. *Address:* 43 Shrewsbury Street, Stratford, Ontario N5A 2V4, Canada.

COOK Norman Edgar, CBE, b. 4 Mar. 1920. Writer, Chief book critic, Liverpool Daily Post, 1980-90. m. Mildred Warburton, 1942, 3 sons. *Appointments:* Ministry of Information, 1943-45; Editor, Northwich Guardian, 1945-47; Liverpool Daily Post, 1947-49; Information Officer, Air Ministry, 1949-53; Night News Editor, Daily Post, 1953-55, Deputy News Editor, 1955-59, London Editor, 1959-72, Executive News Editor,1972-77, Liverpool Daily Post and Echo; Editor, Liverpool Daily Post, 1978-79; Retired, Sept 1979; Chief Book Critic, Liverpool Daily Post, 1980-1991. *Publications:* Numerous articles and reviews. *Honours:* CBE, 1980. *Address:* 7 Trinity Gardens, Southport, Lancashire PR8 1AU, England.

COOK Peter Edward, b. 17 Nov 1937. Writer; Entertainer. m. (1) Wendy Snowden, 1964, 2 daughters, (2) Judy Huxtable, 1973. *Education:* Radley College, Pembroke College, Cambridge. *Publications:* Appeared In and Co-Author of Revues: Pieces of Eight, 1958; One Over the Eight, 1959; Beyond the Fringe, London and New York, 1959-64; Behind the Fridge, Australia & London, 1971-72; Good Evening USA, 1973-75; TV Series Not Only but Also (with Dudley Moore), 1965-71; Revolver, 1978; Films Include: The Wrong Box, 1965; Bedazzled, 1967; A Dandy in Aspic, 1969; Monte Carlo or Bust, 1969; The Bed Sitting Room, 970; The Rise and Rise of Michael Rimmer, 1971; The Hound of the Baskervilles, 1978; Derek and Clive 1980; Yellowbeard, 1983; Supergirl, 1984; Whoops Apocalypse, 1987; Mr Jolly Lives Next Door, 1987; (Book) Dud and Pete: The Dagenham Dialogues, 1971. *Contributions to:* various humorous and satirical periodicals. *Address:* c/o Wright and Webb, Syvett and Sons, 10 Soho Square, London W1, England.

COOK Petronelle Marguerite Mary, b. 16 May 1925, Plymouth, Devon, England. Writer; Teacher. m. Philip R. Cook, 20 July 1949, 2 sons, 1 daughter. *Education:* BA(Hons), 1946, Diploma in Prehistoric Archaeology and Anthropology, 1947, MA, 1950, Oxford University. *Publications:* As Margot Arnold: The Officers' Woman, 1972; The Villa on the Palatine, 1975; Marie, 1979; Exit Actors, Dying, 1980, 1988; The Cape Cod Caper, 1980, 1988; Death of a Voodoo Doll, 1981, 1989; Zadok's Treasure, 1981, 1989; Affairs of State, 1981; Love Among the Allies, 1982; Lament for a Lady Laird, 1982, 1990; Death on the Dragon's Tongue, 1982, 1990; Desperate Measures, 1983; Sinister Purposes, 1985; The Menehune Murders, 1989; Toby's Folly, 1990. *Contributions to:* Numerous short stories. *Honours:* Elected President, Oxford University Archaeological Society, 1945; Fiction Prize, National Writers Club, 1983. *Memberships:* National Writers Club of America; New England Historic and Genealogical Society. *Address:* 619 High Street, Bethlehem, PA 18018, USA.

COOK Robert William Arthur, (Robin Cook, Derek Raymond), b. 1931, United Kingdom. Author. *Publications:* The Crust on Its Uppers, 1962; Bombe Surprise, 1963; The Legacy of the Stiff Upper Lip, 1966; Private Parts and Public Places, 1967; A State of Denmark, 1970; Tenants of Dirt Street, 1971; Le soleil qui s'eteint, 1983; He Died with His Eyes Open (as Derek Raymond), 1984; The Devil's Home on Leave (as Derek Raymond), 1985; How the Dead Live, 1986; Nightmare in the Street, 1987; Harmful Intent, 1989. *Address:* Toby Eady Associates, 7 Gledhow Gardens, London SW5 0BL, England.

COOK Robin. *See:* **COOK Robert William Arthur.**

COOKE (Alfred) Alistair, b. 20 Nov 1908, England. Writer; Broadcaster. m. (1) Ruth Emerson, 1934, (2) Jane White Hawkes, 1 son, 1 daughter. *Education:* Jesus College, Cambridge; Yale and Harvard Universities. *Appointments:* Film Critic, BBC 1934-37; London Correspondent, National Broadcasting Co., 1936-37; Special Correspondent, American Affairs, The Times, 1938-41; Commentator, American Affairs, BBC 1938-; American Feature Writer, Daily Herald, 1941-44; UN Correspondent, Manchester Guardian (now The Guardian), 1945-48; Chief Correspondent, USA, The Guardian, 1948-72. *Publications:* Garbo and the Night Watchmen, Editor, 1937; Douglas Fairbanks, 1940; A Generation on Trial: USA v Alger Hiss, 1950; One Man's America (English Title, Letters from America), 1952; Christmas Eve, 1952; A Commencement Address, 1954; The Vintage Mencken, Editor, 1955; Around the World in Fifty Years, 1966; Talk About America, 1968; Alistair Cooke's America, 1973; Six Men, 1977; The Americans: Fifty Letters from America on Our Life and Times, 1979; Above London, (with Robert Cameron), Masterpieces, 1982; The Patent Has The Floor, 1986; America Observed, 1988. *Honours:* Peabody Award, 1952, 1972; Writers Guild Award for Best Documentary, 1972; Dimbleby Award, 1973; 4 Emmy Awards, 1973;

Benjamin Franklin Award, 1973; Hon. KBE, 1973; Hon. LLD, Edinburgh, Manchester; Hon. Litt.D. St Andrews, 1975; Hon Litt.D, Cambridge University, 1988. *Address:* 1150 Fifth Avenue, New York, NY 10128, USA.

COOKSON Catherine (Ann), (Catherine Fawcett, Catherine Marchant), b. 1906, British, Writer of historical/romance/Gothic, children's fiction, autobiography/memoirs/personal. *Publications include:* Mary Ann and Bill, 1967; Katie Mulholland, 1967; The Round Tower, 1968; Joe and the Gladiator (juvenile) 1968; The Glass Virgin, 1969; The Nice Bloke, 1969, in US as The Husband, 1976; Our Kate: An Autobiography, 1969, 1982; The Invitation, 1970; The Nipper (juvenile) 1970; The Dwelling Place, 1971; Feathers in the Fire, 1971; Pure as the Lily, 1972; Blue Baccy (juvenile) 1972; The Mallen Girl, 1973; The Mallen Streak, 1973; The Mallen Lot (in UK as The Mallen Litter) 1974; (trilogy) in vol as The Mallen Novels, 1979; Our John Willy (juvenile) 1974; The Invisible Cord, 1975; The Gambling Man, 1975; (as Catherine Marchant) Miss Martha Mary Crawford, 1975; The Tide of Life, 1976; (as Catherine Marchant) The Slow Awakening, 1976; Mrs. Flannagan's Trumpet (juvenile) 1976; Go Tell It to Mrs Golightly (juvenile) 1977; The Girl, 1977; The Cinder Path, 1978; The Man Who Cried, 1979; Tilly Trotter (in US as Tilly) 1980; Tilly Trotter Ed (in US as Tilly Wed) 1981; Lanky Jones (juvenile) 1981; Tilly Trotter Widowed (in US as Tilly Alone) 1982; The Whip, 1982; Nancy Nutall and the Mongrel (juvenile) 1982; Hamilton, 1983; The Black Velvet Gown, 1984; Goodbye Hamilton, 1984; A Dinner of Herbs, 1985; Harold, 1985; The Moth, 1985; Bill Bailey, 1985; Catherine Cookson Country, 1986; The Parson's Daughter, 1987; Bill Bailey's Lot, 1987; The Cultured Handmaiden, 1988; Bill Bailey's Daughter, 1988; Let Me Make Myself Plain, 1988; The Harrogate Secret, 1989; The Black Candle, 1989; The Wingless Bird, 1990; The Gillivors, 1990; My Beloved Son, 1991; The Rag Nymph, 1991; The House of Women, 1992; The Maltese Angel, 1992; The Year of the Virgins, 1993. *Honours:* OBE, 1985; Hon. D. Litt, 1991; DBE, 1993. *Address:* c/o Anthony Sheil Associates, 43 Doughty Street, London, WC1N 2LF, England.

COOLIDGE Clark, b. 1939, USA. Dramatist; Poet. *Appointments:* Editor, Joglar Magazine, Providence, Rhode Island, 1964-66. *Publications:* Flag Flutter and US Electric, 1966; Poems, 1967; Ing, 1969; Space, 1970; To Obtain the Value of the Cake Measure from Zero (with T Veitch), play, 1970; The So, 1971; Moroccan Variations, 1971; Clark Coolidge Issue of Big Sky, 1972; Suite V, 1973; The Maintains, 1974; Polaroid, 1975; Quartz Hearts, 1978; Own Face, 1978; Smithsonian Deposition and Subject to a Film (co-author), 1980; American Ones, 1981; Research, 1982. *Address:* c/o Tombouctou Books, PO Box 265, Bolinas, CA 94924, USA.

COOMBS Patricia, b. 23 July 1926, Los Angeles, California, USA, Author; Illustrator of Childrens' books, m. L James Fox, 13 July 1951, 2 daughters. *Education:* BA, 1947, MA, 1950, University of Washington. *Publications:* Dorrie and the Blue Witch, 1964; Dorrie and the Haunted House, 1970; Dorrie and the Goblin, 1972; Mouse Cafe, 1972; Molly Mullett, 1975; The Magic Pot, 1977; Dorrie and the Screebit Ghost, 1979; The Magician McTree, 1984; Dorrie and the Pin Witch, 1989; Dorrie and the Haunted Schoolhouse, 1992. *Contributions to:* Partisan Review; The Hudson Review; Poetry. *Honours:* Dorries Magic, New York Times Ten Best Books of the Year, 1963; Dorrie and the Haunted House, Child Study Association, Childrens Books of the Year, 1970; Mouse Café, New York Times 10 Best Illustrated Books of the Year. *Membership:* Authors Guild Incorporated. *Literary Agent:* Dorothy Markinko, McIntosh and Otis, New York, USA; Gerald Pollinger, Laurence Pollinger Limited, London, England. *Address:* 178 Oswegatchie Road, Waterford, CT 06385, USA.

COONEY Raymond George Alfred, (Ray Cooney), b. 30 May 1932, London, England. Actor; Writer; Director. m. Linda Dixon, 8 Dec 1962, 2 sons.

Publications: (Plays): It Runs in the Family, 1987; Two into One, 1985; Run for your Wife, 1984; (With John Chapman): There Goes the Bride, 1974, Not Now Darling, 1967, Move Over Mrs Markham, 1969, My Giddy Aunt, 1968; (With Tony Hilton): One for the Pot, 1961; Stand By Your Bedouin, 1966; Why Not Stay for Breakfast, (with Gene Stone, 1970); Wife Begins at Forty, with Arne Sultan & Earl Barrett, 1986; Chase Me Comrad, 1964; Charlie Girl, (with Hugh & Margaret Williams), 1965; It Runs in the Family, 1989; Out of Order, 1990. *Memberships:* Dramatists Club. *Agent:* H Udwin. *Address:* The Playhouse, Northumberland Ave, London WC2N 5DE, England.

COONTZ Stephanie, b. 31 Aug 1944, Seattle, WA, USA. Professor. 1 son. *Education:* BA, University of California, 1966; MA, University of Washington, 1970. *Appointments:* Faculty Member,The Evergreen State College, Olympia, WA, 1975-; Lecturer, WA Commission for the Humanities, 1989- 91; Visiting Scholar, The National Faculty, 1990-. *Publications:* The Way We Never Were: American Families and The Nostalgia Trap; The Social Origins of Private Life: A History of American Families; Womens Work, Mens Property: On The Origins of Gender And Class. *Honours:* Woodrow Wilson Fellow; WA Govenors Writers Award. *Memberships:* Organization of American Historians; American Studies Association; American Historical Association. *Literary Agent:* Sydelle Kramer, Francis Goldin Agency. *Address:* 3127 Seminar Building, The Evergreen State College, Olympia, WA 98505, USA.

COOPER Brenda Clare, (Clare Cooper), b. 21 Jan 1935, Falmouth, Cornwall, England. Nurse. m. Bill Cooper, 6 Apr 1953, 2 sons, 1 daughter. *Publications:* Davids Ghost; The Black Horn; Earthchange; Ashar of Qarius; The Skyrifters; Andrews and the Gargoyle; A Wizard Called Jones; kings of The Montain; Children of the Camps; The settlement on Planet B; Miracles and Rubies. *Honour:* Runner Up Tir Na Nog Award. *Memberships:* PEN; Society of Authors; Welsh Academy. *Literary Agent:* Jennifer Luithlen. *Address:* Tyrhibin Newydd, Newport, Dyfed, SA42 ONT, Wales.

COOPER Bryan, b. 6 Feb 1932, Paris, France. Editor; Author. m. Judith Williams, 7 Apr 1979, 2 sons, 2 daughters (by previous marriage). *Appointments:* Reporter Kentish Times 1948-50; Feature writer Flying Review magazine 1950-52; Sub-editor Exchange Telegraph 1953-54; Public relations executive British Petroleum in London, 1954-58 and New York 1958-64; Editor and Publisher, Petroleum Economist, the International Energy Journal, 1975-89; Energy Writer and Consultant for JLW Energy Research Ltd, Cyprus, 1990-. *Publications:* North Sea Oil - The Great Gamble, 1966; The Ironclads of Cambrai, 1967; Battle of the Torpedo Boats, 1970; The Buccaneers, 1970; PT Boats, 1970; Alaska - The Last Frontier, 1972; Tank Battles of World War 1, 1973; Fighter, 1973; Bomber, 1974; Stones of Evil, (novel), 1974; The E Boat Threat, 1976; The Wildcatters, (novel), 1976; The Adventure of North Sea Oil, 1982. *Contributions to:* The Times; Financial Times; numerous magazines; Scriptwriter, over 100 Radio and TV and Film Scripts. *Memberships:* Writers Guild of Great Britain; Garrick; London Press Club. *Literary Agent:* Shelia Watson, Watson, Little Ltd, 12 Egbert Street, London, NW1 8LJ, England. *Address:* 4 Oldlands Hall, Herons Ghyll, Uckfield, East Sussex TN22 3DA England.

COOPER Clare. See: COOPER Brenda Clare.

COOPER Colin Symons, (Daniel Benson), b. 5 July 1926, Birkenhead, England. Journalist; Editor. m. Maureen Elizabeth Goodwin, 6 Sept 1966. 2 sons. *Appointments:* Features Editor, Guitar Magazine, 1972-73; News Editor 1982-84, General Editor 1984-, Classical Guitar. *Publications:* The Thunder and Lightning Man, 1968; Outcrop, 1969; Dargason, 1977; The Epping Pyramid, 1978; The Argyll Killings, 1980. *Contributions to:* Times Literary Supplement; Times Education Supplement; The Guardian; The Independent;

Gendai Guitar (Tokyo); Asta Journal (USA). *Membership:* Writers' Guild of Great Britain. *Literary Agent:* Bruce Hunter. *Address:* 25 Warner Road, London N8 7HB, England.

COOPER Derek MacDonald, b. 25 May 1925. Author; Broadcaster; Journalist. m. Janet Marian Feaster, 1953, 1 son, 1 daughter. *Education:* University College, Cardiff, Wales; Wadham College, Oxford; MA(hons) Oxon. *Literary Appointments:* Columist: The Listener; The Guardian; Observer Magazine; World Medicine; Scottish Field; Sunday Standard; Homes and Gardens; Saga Magazine; Women's Journal. *Publications:* The Bad Food Guide, 1967; Skye, 1970, 2nd Edition, 1977; The Beverage Report, 1970; The Gullibility Gap, 1974; Hebridean Connection, 1977; Guide to the Whiskies of Scotland, 1978; Road to the Isles, 1979; Enjoying Scotch (with Dione Pattullo), 1980; Wine With Food, 1982, 2nd Edition, 1986; The Whisky Roads of Scotland (with Fay Godwin), 1982; The Century Companion to Whiskies, 1983; Skye Remembered, 1983; The World of Cooking, 1983; The Road to Mingulay, 1985; The Gunge File, 1986; A Taste of Scotch, 1989; Television programmes. *Contributions to:* In Britain; Signature; Taste; A La Carte; The West Highland Free Press. *Honours:* Glenfiddich Trophy as Wine and Food Writer, 1973, 1980; Scottish Arts Council Award, 1980; Broadcaster of the Year, 1984; House of Fraser Press Award, 1984. *Membership:* Founder Member, 1st Chairman, Guild of Food Writers. *Address:* Seafield House, Portree, Isle of Skye, Scotland.

COOPER Dominic (Xavier), b. 1944, United Kingdom. Writer. *Publications:* The Dead of Winter, 1975; Sunrise, 1977; Men at Axlir, 1978; The Horn Fellow, 1987. *Honour:* Somerset Maugham Award, 1976. *Address:* c/o John Johnson Ltd., Clerkenwell House, 45/47 Clerkenwell Green, London EC1R OHT, England.

COOPER Edger S. See: HOEPPNER Iona Ruth.

COOPER Helen, b. 6 Feb 1947, Nottingham, England. University Lecturer. m. M G Cooper, 18 July 1970, 2 daughters. *Education:* BA, New Hall, Cambridge, 1968; MA, PhD, 1972. *Appointments:* English Editor, Medium Ævum, 1989. *Publications:* The Oxford Guides to Chaucer: The Canterbury Tales; The structure of the Canterbury Tales; Pastoral: Medieval into Renaissance; Great Grand Mother Goose. *Contributions to:* Numerous. *Address:* University College, Oxford, OX1 4BH, England.

COOPER Jean Campbell b. 27 Nov 1905, Chefoo, North China. Author; Lecturer. m. Commander V M Cooper DSO, OBE, RN, 21 June 1945. *Education:* Various boarding schools in China, Australia and England. LLA Hons, 1st Class, Moral Philosophy, St Andrew's University, 1930. *Publications:* Taoism, the Way of the Mystic, 1972; An Illustrated Encyclopaedia of Traditional Symbols, 1978; Yin and Yang, the Harmony of Opposites, 1981; Symbolism, The Universal Language, 1982; Fairy Tales, Allegories of the Inner Life, 1983; Chinese Alchemy, 1984; Aquarian Dictionary of Festivals, 1990. *Contributions to:* Articles, translations, reviews for Studies in Comparative Religion. *Memberships:* English PEN; Life Member, Royal Commonwealth Society; Justice of the Peace. *Address:* Bobbin Mill, Ulpha, Broughton-in-Furness, Cumbria LA20 6DU, England.

COOPER Jilly (Sallitt), b. 1937, United Kingdom. Writer; Journalist. *Appointments:* Reporter, Middlesex Independent newspaper, Brentford, 1957-59; Columnist, The Sunday Times, 1969-85; Columnist, The Mail on Sunday, 1985-; Various other positions including Copywriter and Publishers Reader. *Publications:* How to Stay Married, 1969; How to Survive from Nine to Five, 1970; Jolly Super, 1971; Men and Super Men, 1972; Jolly Super Too, 1973; Women and Super Women, 1974; Jolly Superlative, 1975; Emily, romance novel, 1975; Super Men and Super Women, omnibus, 1976; Bella, romance novel, 1976; Harriet, romance novel, 1976; Octavia, romance novel, 1977; Work and Wedlock, omnibus, 1977; Superjilly, 1977; Imogen, romance novel, 1978; Prudence, romance novel, 1978; Class: A View from Middle England, 1979; Supercooper, 1980; Little Mabel series, juvenile, 4 vols, 1980-85; Violets and Vinegar: An Anthology of Women's Writings and Savings (edited with Tom Hartman), 1980; The British in Love (editor), 1980; Love and Other Heartaches, 1981; Jolly Marsupial, 1982; Animals in War, 1983; The Common Years, 1984; Leo and Jilly Cooper on Rugby, 1984; Riders, 1985; Hotfoot to Zabriskie Point, 1985; Leo and Jilly Cooper on Cricket, 1985; Horse Mania, 1986; How to Survive Christmas, 1986; Turn Right at The Spotted Dog, 1987; Rivals, 1988; Angels Rush In, 1990; Polo, 1991; The Man Who Made Husbands Jealous, 1993. *Address:* c/o Desmond Elliott, 15-17 King Street, St Jame's, London SW1, England.

COOPER Kenneth Hardy, b. Physician; Author. *Appointments:* Developed Fitness Regime for US Air Force Training Astronauts; Established The Cooper Aerobics Center in Dallas; 13yrs US Air Force, 1957-70. *Publications include:* Aerobics; The New Aerobics; The Aerobics Way: New Data on the Worlds Most Popular Exercise Program; The Aerobics Program for Total Well-Being: Exercise, Diet, Emotional Balance; Running Without Fear: How to Reduce the Risk of Heart Attack & Sudden Death During Aerobic Exercise; The New Aerobics for Women; Overcoming Hypertension; Kid Fitness: A Complete Shape Up Program from Birth Through High School. *Contributions to:* Numerous. *Honours:* Presidential Citation; Inducted into Oklahoma Hall of Fame; Lifetime Achievment Award; Religious Heritage of America, Churchman of the Year Award. *Memberships:* American Medical Association; Texas Medical Association; Dallas County Medical Society; American Running and Fitness Association; Association for Fitness in Business; American College of Sports Medicine; American Geriatrics Society. *Address:* The Cooper Aerobics Center, 12200 Preston Road, Dallas, TX 75230, USA.

COOPER M E. *See:* **WAGNER Sharon Blythe.**

COOPER Richard Newell, b. 14 June 1934, Seattle, USA. Economist; Educator. m. Ann L. Hollick, 1 Jan 1982, 1 son, 1 daughter. *Education:* AB, Oberlin College, 1956; MSC, London School of Economics, England, 1958; PhD, Harvard University, 1962. *Publications:* The Economics of Interdependence, 1968; A World Re-Ordered, 1973; Economic Policy in an Interdependent World, 1986; The International Monetary System, 1987; Economic Stabilization and Debt in Developing Countries, 1992. *Contributions to:* The New Republic; The New York Times; The Washington Post; Journal for Political Economy; Quarterly Journal of Economics, and others. *Honours:* Phi Beta Kappa, 1955; Marshall Scholarship, 1956; Elected Fellow, American Academy of Arts and Sciences, 1974; LLD, Oberlin College, 1958. *Memberships:* Council on Foreign Relations; American Economic Association. *Address:* 1737 Cambridge St, Cambridge, MA 02138, USA.

COOPER Susan, b. 23 May 1935, Burnham, Buckinghamshire, England. Writer. m. Nicholas J Grant, 1963, (div 1982), 1 son, 1 daughter. *Education:* MA, Somerville College, Oxford, 1953-56. *Publications:* Over Sea, Under Stone, 1965; The Dark is Rising, 1973; Greenwitch, 1974; The Grey King, 1975; Silver on the Tree, 1977; Seaward, 1983. Mandrake, 1964; Dawn of Fear, 1970; J B Priestley: Portrait of an Author, 1970; Behind the Golden Curtain: A View of the USA, 1968; Jethro and the Jumbie, 1979; The Silver Cow, 1983; The Selkie Girl, 1986. *Contributions to:* Many magazines and journals. *Honours:* Boston Globe-Horn Book Award, 1973; Newbery Medal, 1976; Welsh Arts Council Tir Nan og Award, 1976, 1978; Humanitas Award, 1985; Christopher Medal, 1985; Hugo Award, 1984; Writers Guild of America Award, 1984, 1988. *Memberships:* Society of Authors; Authors' Guild; Writers' Guild of America. *Literary Agent:* ICM, New York, (Sam Cohn), USA.

COOPER William. *See:* **HOFF Harry Summerfield.**

COOPER COHEN Sharleen, b. 11 June 1940, Los Angeles, California, USA. Author. m. Martin L Cohen, 27 Aug 1972, 2 daughters. *Education:* University of California, Berkeley, 1957-58; University of California, Los Angeles, 1958-60; Los Angeles Valley Film School, 1976-78. *Publications:* The Day after Tomorrow, 1979; Regina's Song, 1980; The Ladies of Beverly Hills, 1983; Marital Affairs, 1985; Love, Sex and Money, 1988; Lives of Value, 1991. *Contributions to:* Serialisation of novel, Good Housekeeping, 1990; Santa Barbara Writers Conference, 1978; National Gaucher Foundation Newsletter. *Honours:* Honourable Mention, Santa Barbara Writers Conference, 1978; Beverly Hills Hadassah; Women of Achievement, 1989. *Memberships:* PEN; Authors Guild; Writers Guild of America; National Gaucher Foundation, Board of Directors, Los Angeles Founder and Director; Executive Committee, Women of Distinction, United Jewish Appeal; California State Commission on Humanities. *Literary Agent:* Elaine Markson Literary Agency, New York City, USA. *Address:* 16170 Clear Valley Place, Encino, CA 91436, USA.

COOVER Robert, b. 1932, USA. Author. *Appointments:* Writer-in-Residence, Brown University, Providence, Rhode Island, 1979-. *Publications:* The Origin of the Brunists, 1966; The Universal Baseball Association, Inc, J Henry Waugh, Prop, 1968; Pricksongs and Descants, short stories, 1969; A Theological Position, plays, 1972; The Public Burning, 1977; Hair o' the Chine, 1979; After Lazarus, 1980; Charlie in the House of Rue, 1980; A Political Fable, 1980; Spanking the Maid, 1982; In Bed One Night and Other Brief Encounters, 1982; Gerald's Party, 1986; Aesop's Forest, 1986; A Night at the Movies, short fictions, 1987; Whatever Happened to Gloomy Gus of the Chicago Bears, 1987; Pinocchio in Venice, 1991. *Honours:* William Faulkner Award, 1966; Rockefellar Foundation Fellowship, 1969; Guggenheim Foundation Fellowship, 1971, 1974; 3 Obie awards for The Kid, 1973; American Academy of Arts and Letters Award, 1976; National Endowment of the Arts Award, 1985; REA Award for the Short Story, 1987. *Memberships:* PEN; American Academy & Institute of Arts & Letters. *Literary Agent:* Georges Borchardt, USA. *Address:* c/o Georges Borchardt, 136 East 57th Street, New York, NY 10022, USA.

COPE Jack Robert Knox, b. 3 June 1913, Mooi River, Natal, Writer; Poet. m. Lesley de Villiers, 4 June 1942, 2 sons. *Education:* DLitt, Rhodes University, 1981. *Appointment:* Co-founder and Editor, South African Literary magazine, Contrast, 1960-80. *Publications include:* The Rain Maker, 1971; The Tame Ox; Lyrics and Diatribes, 1948; Penguin Book of South African Verse, (Editor); The Student of Zend, 1972; Selected Poems of Ingrid Jonker, co-translator,1968, revised 1988; The Adversary Within; Radio broadcasts, stage and TV adaptations. *Contributions to:* New Yorker; Harpers; Esquire; reporter; Short Story International; John Bull; Mademoiselle; Paris Review; Argosy; London Magazine; Leading South African magazines and school textbooks. *Honours:* British Council Award, 1960; Carnegie Fellowship USA, 1966; CNA Prize, Argus prize and Gold Medallist for Literature, Veld Trust Prize, 1971; DLitt, Rhodes. *Literary Agent:* Shelley Power. *Address:* 21 Bearton Road, Hitchin, Hertfordshire SG5 1UB, England.

COPELAND Ann. *See:* **FURTWANGLER Virginia Anne.**

CORBEN Beverly Byrd Balkum, b. 6 Aug 1926. Artist/Writer; Educator (retired). m. Dr Herbert Charles Corben, Professor Emeritus, University of Toronto, 25 Oct 1957, 1 son, 2 daughters. *Education:* AA, Santa

Monica College, 1950; BA (with honours) University of California, Los Angeles, 1960; MA, Case Western Reserve University, 1972. *Appointments:* Editorial Associate, Technical Public Relations, The Ramo-Wooldridge Corporation (now TRW Inc) 1954-57; Teaching Assistant, Case Western Reserve University, 1971; Teaching Assistant 1972-73, Director of Writing Laboratory, 1973-82 (on leave 1978-80), Scarborough College, University of Toronto; Visiting Scholar, Harvey Mudd College, 1978-80; Scholar-in-Residence (Humanities) 1982-88; Volunteer Literary appointments: Chairman, Pascagoula Women's Club May Day 1990 and May Day 1991 (Statewide) Poetry Contests; Creative Writing Director, the Pascagoula Senior Citizens Centre, 1990-. *Publications:* On Death and Other Reasons for Living (poems), Cleveland State University Poetry Centre, 1972. *Contributor to:* Poetic Justice; The Texas Review, Voices International; Prophetic Voices and other Journals. *Honours:* Cleveland State University Honorary Alumna, 1971; Two President's Awards, 1990, Loving Cup for September, Mississippi Poetry Society, Inc, South; Christmas Poem Award, Writers Unlimited, Jan 1990; Certificates of Merit, Florida State Writing Competition, 1989; More than 50 awards for poetry and fiction nationwide since 1989; Mississippi Poetry Society , South Poet of the Year, 1990; Missisppi, Poet of the Year Statewide, 1991. *Memberships:* Member of Mississippi Poetry Society, 3rd Vice President, 1990-91; Poetry Society of Tennessee; Gulf Coast Writers Association; Writers Unlimited, president, 1991, 1992. *Address:* 4304 O'Leary Street, Pascagoula, MS 39581, USA.

CORD Barry. *See:* **GERMANO Peter B.**

CORDELL Alexander, b. 9 Sept 1914, Ceylon. Author. m. 20 Mar 1937, 1 daughter. *Education:* Partly at Marist Brothers College, Tientsin, N China. *Publications include:* Welsh Trilogy: (Rape of the Fair Country, The Hosts of Rebecca, Song of the Earth); Race of the Tiger; This Proud and Savage Land; Land of my Fathers; The Fire People; This Sweet and Bitter Earth; If You Believe the Soldiers; A Thought of Honour; The Bright Cantonese; Tales from Tiger Bay; The Sinews of Love; To Slay the Dreamer; The Dream and the Destiny; Rogue's March; Peerless Jim; Tunnel Tigers; Requiem for a Patriot; Moll; Beloved Exile. For children: Irish Trilogy: (The White Cockade; Witch's Sabbath; The Healing Blade); The Traitor Within; Sea Urchin. *Address:* The Conifers, Railway Road, Rhossdu, Wrexham, Clwyd, Wales.

COREN Alan, b. 27 June 1938, London, England. Editor of Punch. m. Anne Kasriel, 14 Oct 1963, 1 son, 1 daughter. *Education:* BA, 1st Class Honours, Wadham College, Oxford, 1961; Harkness Fellowship, Yale, USA, 1961-62, Berkeley, USA, 1962-63. *Appointments:* Assistant Editor, 1963-67, Literary Editor, 1967-69, Deputy Editor, 1969-77, Editor, 1978-87, Punch Magazine; Editor, The Listener, 1988-89. *Publications:* The Dog It Was That Died, 1965; All Except the Bastard, 1969; The Sanity Inspector, 1974; The Collected Bulletins of Idi Amin, 1974; Golfing for Cats, 1975; The Further Bulletins of Idi Amin, 1975; The Rhinestone As Big as the Ritz, 1977; The Peanut Papers, 1978; The Lady from Stalingrad Mansions, 1979; Issues for Men, 1980; The Cricklewood Diet, 1982; Bumf, 1984; Something for the Weekend, 1986; Bin Ends, 1987; 12 novels for children (The Arthur Books, 1979-82); The Penguin Book of Modern Humour, Editor, 1983; Seems Like Old Times, 1989, (Autobiography); More Like Old Times, 1990; A Year in Cricklewood, 1991 *Contributions include:* Punch; Atlantic Monthly; Tatler; Harpers; Playboy; London Review of Books; The Listener; Sunday Times; Observer; Daily Mail; The Times; The Telegraph; Vogue; Nova; Era; New York Times; Evening Standard. *Honour:* Editor of the Year, British Society of Magazine Editors, 1986. *Address:* c/o Robson Books, 5 Clipstone Street, London WC1, England.

COREN Victoria Elizabeth, b. 18 Aug 1972, London, England. Student; Journalist. *Education:* St Johns College, Oxford. *Appointments:* Daily Telegraph

Columnist, 1987-90. *Publication:* Love 16. *Contributions to:* Daily & Sunday Telegraph; Evening Standard; Harpers Queen; Tatler; Country Living; The Bookseller; Today; The Indy. *Membership:* Oxford Union Society. *Literary Agent:* Jacqueline Korn, David Higham Associates. *Address:* 26 Ranulf Road, London NW2 2DG, England.

CORIOLANUS. *See:* **MCMILLAN James.**

CORK Richard Graham, b. 25 Mar 1947, Eastbourne, England. Art Critic. m. Vena Jackson, Mar 1970, 2 sons, 2 daughters. *Education:* Kingswood School, Bath, 1960-64; Trinity Hall, Cambridge, 1965-69. *Appointments:* Art Critic, Evening Standard, 1969-77, 1980-83; Editor, Studio International, 1975-79; Art Critic, The Listener, 1984-90; Slade Professor of Fine Art, Cambridge, 1989-90; Art Critic, The Times, 1991-; Henry Moore Senior Research Fellow at the Courtauld Institute, London, 1992-. *Publications:* Vorticism & Abstract in the First Machine Age; The Social Role of Art; Art Beyond the Gallery in Early 20th Century England; David Bomberg; Architects Choice. *Contributions to:* The Burlington Magazine; Apollo; Artforum; Art in America; New Statesman; The Independent Magazine. *Honours:* John Llewelyn Rhys Memorial Prize; Sir Banister Fletcher Award. *Memberships:* South Bank Board Visual Art Panel; British Council Visual Art Committee; Public Art Development Trust; Contemporary Art Society Trustees. *Address:* 24 Milman Road, London NW6 6EG, England.

CORLETT William, b. 1938, United Kingdom. Children's Author; Dramatist; Repertory and Television Actor. *Publications:* The Gentle Avalanche, 1962; Another Round, 1962; Return Ticket, 19562; The Scallop Shell, 1963; Flight of a Lone Sparrow, 1965; Dead Set at Dream Boy, 1965; The Scourging of Matthew Barrow, 1965; Tinker's Curse, 1968; We Never Went to Cheddar Gorge, 1968; The Story Teller, 1969; The Illusionist, 1969; National Trust, 1970; The Deliverance of Fanny Blaydon, 1971; A Memory of Two Loves, 1972; Conversations in the Dark, 1972; The Gate of Eden, 1974; The Land Beyond, 1975; The Ideal Tale, 1975; The Once and Forever Christmas (with John Moore), 1975; Return to the Gate, 1975; Mr Oddy, 1975; The Orsini Emeralds, 1975; Emmerdale Farm series, 1975-77; Orlando the Marmalade Cat Buys a Cottage, adaption of story by Kathleen Hale, 1975; The Dark Side of the Moon, 1976; Orlando's Camping Holiday, adaptation of story by Kathleen Hale, 1976; Paper Lads, 1978-79; Question series (The Question of Religion, The Christ Story, The Hindu Sound, The Judaic Law, The Buddha Way, The Islamic Space), 1978-79; Kids series, 1979; Going Back, 1979; The Gate of Eden, 1980; Barriers series, 1980; Agatha Christie Hour, adaptation of 4 short stories, 1982; The Machine Gunners, adaptation of Robert Westall book, 1982; Dearly Beloved, 1983; Bloxworth Blue, 1984; Return to the Gate, 1986. *Address:* Cottesbrook, Great Bardfield, nr Braintree, Essex, England.

CORLEY Ernest. *See:* **BULMER Henry Kenneth.**

CORMAN Avery, b. 28 Nov 1935, New York City, USA. Writer (Novelist). m. Judith Lishinsky, 5 Nov 1967, 2 sons. *Education:* BS, New York University, 1952. *Publications:* Oh, God!, 1971; Kramer Vs Kramer, 1977; The Bust-Out King, 1977; The Old Neighborhood, 1980; Fifty, 1987; Prized Possessions, 1991. *Memberships:* PEN American Center; The Writers' Guild of America. *Literary Agent:* Morton L Janklow, Janklow & Nesbit Associates. *Address:* c/o Janklow & Nesbit Associates, 598 Madison Avenue, New York City, NY 10022, USA.

CORMAN Cid (Sidney Corman), b. 1924, USA. Poet. *Appointments:* Poetry Broadcaster, WMEX, Boston, Massachusetts, 1949-51; Editor, Origin magazine and Origin Press, Kyoto, Japan, 1951-. *Publications:* Subluna, 1945; Thanksgiving Eclogue, 1954; The Precisions, 1955; The Responses, 1956; Stances and

Distances, 1957; The Marches, 1957; A Table in Provence, 1958; The Descent from Daimonji, 1959; Clocked Stone, 1959; For Sure, 1959; Cool Melon, by Basjo, translation, 1959; Cool Gong, translation, 1959; For Instance, 1959; For Good, 1961; Sun Rock Man, 1962; Selected Frogs, by Shimpoo Kusano (translated with Kamike Susumu), 1963; In Good Time, 1964; In No Time, 1964; All in All, 1965; Nonce, 1965; For You, 1966; For Granted, 1966; At: Bottom, 1966; Stead, 1966; Words for Each Other, 1967; Back Roads to Far Towns, by Basho, translation, 1967; Frogs and Others: Poems, by Shimpoo Kusano (translated with Kamike Susumu), 1968; & Without End, 1968; No Less, 1968; Hearth, 1968; No More, 1969; Plight, 1969; Nigh, 1969; Livingdying, 1970; Of the Breath of, 1970; For Keeps, 1970; For Now, 1971; Things, by Francis Ponge, translation, 1971; Out and Out, 1972; Be Quest, 1972; A Language Without Words, 1973; So Far, 1973; The Gist of Origin: An Anthology (editor), 1973; Leaves of Hypnos, by Rene Char, translation, 1973; Poems: Thanks to Zukerkandi, 1973; Breathing, 1973; Breathings, by Phillippe Jaccottet, translation, 1974; O/1, 1974; Once and For All, 1976; Auspices, 1978; At Their Word: Essays on the Arts of Language, 2 vols, 1977-78; Aegis: Selected Poems 1970-1980, 1983. *Honour:* Lenore Marshall Poetry Prize for O/1. *Address:* c/o Black Sparrow Press, Box 3993, Santa Barbara, CA 93130, USA.

CORMANY Michael Eugene, b. 8 Jan 1951, Aurora, IL, USA. Laborer. *Publications:* Skin Deep Is Fatal; Rich or Dead; Polaroid Man; Red Winter; Lost Daughter. *Honours:* Best First novel; BOMC Mysterious Book Club. *Memberships:* Mystery Writers of America; Private Eye Writers of America. *Literary Agent:* George Ziegler. *Address:* 1050 N Farnsworth 315, Aurora, IL 60505, USA.

CORMIER Robert, b. 1925, USA. Writer. *Appointments:* Writer, Radio WTAG, Worcester, Massachusetts, 1946-48; Reporter and Columnist: Worcester Telegram and Gazette, 1948-55; Fitchburg Sentinel and Enterprise, Massachusetts, 1955-78. *Publications:* For Adults: Now and at the Hour, 1960; A Little Raw on Monday Morning, 1963; Take Me Where the Good Times Are, 1965. For Young Adults: The Chocolate War, 1974; I Am the Cheese, 1977; After the First Death, 1979; Eight Plus One, 1980; The Bumblebee Flies Anyway, 1983; Beyond the Chocolate War, 1985; Fade, 1988; Other Bells For Us to Ring, 1990; We All Fall Down, 1991; I Have Words To Spend, 1991; Tunes For Bears To Dance To, 1992. *Honours:* Alan Award by National Council of Teachers of English, 1982; Margaret Edwards Award by American Library Association, School Library Journal. *Address:* 1177 Main Street, Leominster, MA 01453, USA.

CORN Alfred, b. 14 Aug 1943, Bainbridge, Georgia, USA. Poet. m. Ann Jones, 1967 (divorced 1971). *Education:* Emory University, Atlanta, 1961-65, BA, French, 1965; Columbia University, New York (Woodrow Wilson Fellow; Faculty Fellow) 1965-67, MA 1967; Fulbright Fellow, Paris, 1967-68. *Appointments:* Preceptor, Columbia University, 1968-70; Associate Editor, University Review, New York, 1970; staff writer, DaCapo Press, New York, 1971-72; Assistant Professor, 1978 and Visiting Lecturer, 1980-81, Connecticut College, New London; Visiting Lecturer, Yale University, New Haven, Connecticut, 1977, 1978, 1979, Columbia University 1983, 1985 and City University of New York, 1983, 1985. *Publications:* Verse: All Roads at Once, 1976; A Call in the Midst of the Crowd, 1978; The Various Light, 1980; Notes from a Child of Paradise, 1984. *Honours:* Ingram Merrill Fellowship, 1974; George Dillon Prize, 1975; Oscar Blumenthal Prize, 1977 and Levinson Prize 1982 (Poetry, Chicago); Davidson Prize, 1982; American Academy Award 1983.

CORNISH Sam(uel James), b. 1935, USA. Children's Fiction Writer; Poetry; Consultant (Elementary School Teaching). *Appointments:* Formerly Editor, Chicory, Enoch Pratt Library publications, Baltimore, Maryland; Currently Editor, Mimeo magazine.

Publications: In This Corner: Sam Cornish and Verses, 1961; People Under the Window, 1962; Generations, 1964; Angles, 1965; Winters 1968; Chicory: Young Voices from the Black Ghetto (edited with L W Dixon), 1969; The Living Underground: An Anthology of Contemporary American Poetry (edited with H. Fox), 1969; Your Hand in Mine, 1970; Generations: Poem, 1971; Streets, 1973; Sometimes: Ten Poems, 1973; Grandmother's Pictures, children's fiction, 1974; Sam's World, 1978. *Address:* c/o Bookstore Press, Box 191, RFDI, Freeport, ME 04032, USA.

CORNWELL David John Moore (John Le Carre), b. 19 Oct 1931. Writer. m. (1) Alison Ann Veronica Sharp, 1954, divorced 1971, 3 sons, (2) Valerie Jane Eustace, 1972, 1 son. *Education:* Berne University; Lincoln College, Oxford. *Appointments:* Teacher, Eton College, 1956-58; Foreign Service, 1959-64. *Publications:* Call for the Dead, 1961 (filmed as The Deadly Affair, 1967); Murder of Quality, 1962; The Spy Who Came in From the Cold, 1963; The Looking Glass War, 1965; A Small Town in Germany, 1968; The Naive and Sentimental Lover, 1971; Tinker, Tailor, Soldier, Spy, 1974; The Honourable Schoolboy, 1977; Smiley's People, 1979; The Quest for Carla (collected edition of previous 3 titles), 1982; The Little Drummer Girl, 1983; A Perfect Spy, 1986; The Russia House, 1989; The Secret Pilgrim, 1991. *Honours:* Somerset Maugham Award, 1963; James Tait Black Award, 1977; Premio Malaparte, 1987; Hon. Fellow, Lincoln College, Oxford. *Address:* David Higham Associates, 5-8 Lower John Street, Golden Square, London W1R 4HA, England.

CORNWELL Judy Valerie, b. 22 Feb 1940, London, England. Actress; Author. m. John Kelsall Parry, 18 Dec 1960, 1 son. *Education:* Convent of Mercy, Queensland. *Publications:* Cow and Cow Parsley; Fishcakes at the Ritz; Seventh Sunrise. *Contributions to:* Occasional Articles. *Memberships:* Society of Authors; PEN; Magistrates Association JP Equity. *Literary Agent:* Andrew Hewson, John Johnson Limited. *Address:* c/o Andrew Hewson, John Johnson Ltd, Clerkenwell House, 45/47 Clerkenwell Green, London EC1R OHT, England.

CORREN Grace. *See:* HOSKINS Robert.

CORREY Lee. *See:* STINE George Harry.

CORRIGAN Robert W(illoughby). b. 1927, American. Theatre; Translations. *Appointments:* Andrew Mellon Professor and Head of the Department of Drama, Carnegie Institute of Technology, Pittsburgh, 1961-64; Professor of Dramatic Literature, 1964-68 and Dean of School of Arts, 1965-68, New York University, New York City; Director, Critics' Programme for National Endowment for the Humanities, 1967-68; President, California Institute of the Arts, Valencia, 1968-74; Dean of School of Fine Arts, University of Wisconsin, Milwaukee, 1974-; Chairman of the Board, SPACE for Innovative Development, New York City. *Publications:* (ed)The New Theatre of Europe, vol 1, 1962; (trans with M D Dirks), Appia's Music and the Art of the Theatre, 1962; (trans) Chekhov: Six Plays, 1962; The Theatre in the Twentieth Century, 1963; (ed)The New Theatre of Europe, vol II, 1964; (ed with J L Rosenberg), The Art of the Theatre, 1964; (ed with J L Rosenberg), The Context and Craft of Drama, 1964; The Modern Theatre, 1964; (ed)New American Plays, vol 1, 1965; (ed)Comedy: Meaning and Form, 1965, 1981; (ed)Tragedy: Vision and Form, 1965, 1981; (ed)Laurel British Drama: 20th Century, 1965; (ed)Laurel British Drama: 19th Century, 1967; (ed)Masterpieces of the Modern Theatre, 9 vols, 1967; (ed)The New Theatre of Europe, vol III, 1968; Arthur Miller, 1969; (ed with G Loney) Comedy: A Critical Anthology, 1971, 1980; (ed with G Loney) Tragedy: A Critical Anthology, 1971, 1980; (ed with G Loney) The Forms of Drama, 1972; The Theatre in Search of a Fix, 1973; The World of the Theatre. 1979; The Making of Theatre: From Drama to Performance, 1980; The World of Theatre, 1979; The Making of Theatre: From Drama to Performance, 1980. *Address:* 1037 E Ogden Avenue, Milwaukee, WI 53202, USA.

CORSON Richard, b. 27 Dec, Genoa, Illinois, USA. Teacher; Writer. *Education:* BA, De Pauw University, 1939, Phi Beta Kappa; MA, Louisiana State University, 1941. *Publications:* Stage Makeup, 1942, 1960, 1967, 1975, 1981, 1986, 1989; Fashions in Hair, The First 5,000 Years, 1965, 1971, 1980; Fashions in Makeup, From Ancient to Modern Times, 1972, 1981, 1989 (also published in Japanese); Fashions in Eyeglasses, 1967, 1980 (also published in Japanese). *Contributions to:* Problems in Makeup in Players Magazine, 1943-45 (monthly).

CORY Desmond. *See:* **MCCARTHY Shaun.**

COSGRAVE Patrick, b. 28 Sept 1941. Writer. m. (1) Ruth Dudley Edwards, 1965, divorced, (2) Norma Alice Green, 1974, divorced, 1 daughter, (3) Shirley Ward, 1981. *Education:* BA, MA, University College, NUI, Dublin; PhD, University of Cambridge. *Appointments:* London Editor, radio Telefis Eireann, 1968-69; Conservative Research Dept., 1969-71; Political Editor, The Spectator, 1971-75; Features Editor, Telegraph Magazine, 1974-76; Special Advisor to Rt. Hon. Mrs Margaret Thatcher, 1975-79; Managing Editor, Quartet Crime (Quartet Books), 1979-81. *Publications:* The Public Poetry of Robert Lowell, 1969; Churchill at War: Alone, 1974; Cheyney's Law, (novel), 1976; Margaret Thatcher: a Tory and her Party, 1978, 2nd edition as Margaret Thatcher: Prime Minister, 1979; The Three Colonels (novel), 1979; R.A. Butler: an English Life, 1981; Adventure of State (novel), 1984; Thatcher: the First Term, 1985; Carrington: A Life and a Policy, 1985; The Lives of Enoch Powell, 1989; The Strange Death of Socialist Britain, 1992. *Contributions to:* various journals and magazines. *Address:* 21 Thornton Road, London SW12 0JX, England.

COSSI Olga, b. St Helena, Napa Valley. Freelance Writer. *Appointments:* Staff Correspondent & Columnist, Regional Newspapers. *Publications:* Robin Deer; Fire Mate; Gus the Bus; The Wonderful Wonderfull Donkey; Orlanda and the Contest of Thieves; The Magic Box; Adventure on the Graveyard of the Wrecks; The Great Getaway (Parent's Read Aloud Book Club selection); Harp Seals; Think Pink; Fresh Water. *Honours:* New York Public Library's Books for the Teen Age List; Most Outstanding Childrens Science Trade Book; Books included in Sonoma County Museum's Cover to Cover 1992-93 exhibit now on a travelling tour. *Memberships:* California Society of Children's Book Writers. *Address:* 800 H Avenue, Colorado, CA 92118, USA.

COTES Peter, b. 19 Mar 1912. Author; Lecturer; Theatrical Producer. m. Joan Miller, 19 May 1948 (dec 1988). *Education:* Italia Conti Stage School. *Appointments:* Lecturer in Drama, Rose Bruford College; Adjudicator and Public Speaker. *Publications:* No Star Nonense, 1949; The Little Fellow, (Co-author Thelma Niklaus), 1951); Handbook for the Amateur Theatre, 1957; George Robey, 1972; JP: The Man Called Mitch, 1976; Elvira Barney, 1977; World Circue, (Co-author R Croft-Cooke), 1978; Performing (Album of the) Arts, 1980; Dickie: The Story of Dickie Henderson, 1988; Sincerely Yours, 1989; Thinking Aloud, 1993. *Contributions to:* Daily Telegraph; Guardian; The Independent; the Times; The Field; The Stage; Plays and Players; Irish Times; The Spectator. *Honours:* Fellow, Royal Society of Arts; Knight of Mark Twain. *Memberships:* Savage Club; Our Society; Press Club. *Literary Agent:* Jeffrey Simmons. *Address:* 7 Hill Lawn Court, Chipping Norton, Oxon OX7 5ME, England.

COTTERILL Kenneth Matthew, b. 17 Sept 1950, Sheffield, England. Playwright. m. Marilyn Bokiagon, 6 Oct 1984, 1 son. *Education:* BA, University of Queensland, 1980; Queensland University of Technology, 1981. *Publications:* Re Electing Roger;

Richard the Thirds Revenge; Perfect Murder; Rhinocerus Hides. *Contributions to:* Australian Jewish Democrat; British Soccer Week; Flashing Blade; International Association of Agricultural Information Specialists, Quarterly Bulletin. *Honours:* Australias Bicentennial Award. *Memberships:* Australian Society of Authors; Playlab. *Address:* 44 Martin Avenue, Mareeba, Queensland, Australia.

COTTON John, b. 7 Mar 1925, Hackney, London. m. Peggy Midson, 27 Dec 1948, 2 sons. *Education:* BA, Hons, English, London University. *Literary Appointments:* Editor, Priapus, a magazine of poetry and art, 1962-72; Editor, The Private Library, a book collectors' journal, 1969-79; Advisory Editor, Contemporary Poets of the English Language. *Publications:* Old Movies and other poems, 1971; Kilroy Was Here, 1975; Daybook, 1983; The Storyville Portraits, 1984; The Crystal Zoo, 1984; Oh Those Happy Feet, 1986; The Poetry File, 1989; Two by Two (with Fred Sedgwick) 1990; Here's Looking At You Kid, 1992. *Contributions to:* Sunday Observer; Poetry Chicago; Times Literary Supplementary; Encounter; The New Review; Outposts; Ambit. *Honours:* Arts Council Publication Award, 1971; Deputy Lieutenant of the County of Hertfordshire, 1989. *Memberships:* Poetry Society, Chairman 1972-74 and 1977, Treasurer 1986-89. *Address:* 37 Lombard Drive, Berkhamstead, Hertfordshire HP4 2LQ, England.

COUFOUDAKIS Van, b. 27 May 1938, Athens, Greece. Professor; Associate Vice Chancellor. m. Marion Mason, 26 Dec 1964, 1 daughter. *Education:* BA, American University of Beirut, 1962; MPA, University of Michigan, 1964; PhD, 1972. *Appointments:* Lecturer, Indiana, Purdue University, Fort Wayne, 1967-72; Assistant Professor, 1972-77; Associate Professor, 1977-85; Professor, 1985-; Associate Vice Chancellor, 1986-; Director, Indiana University, Center For Global Studies, 1981-87. *Publications:* Superpower Strategy in the Persian Gulf and the Eastern Mediterranean; Athens: Foundation for Mediterranean Studies; Essays on the Cyprus Conflict, New York: Pella. *Contributions to:* Over 50 Articles, Book Chapters. *Honours:* Hon, Consul, Republic of Cyprus. *Memberships:* Modern Greek Studies Association; International Studies Association. *Address:* Office Of the Vice Chancellor for Academic Affairs, Indiana University Purdue University, Fort Wayne, IL 46805, USA.

COULSON Juanita Ruth, b. 12 Feb 1933, Anderson, Indiana, USA, Freelance Writer. m. Robert Stratton Coulson, 21 Aug 1954, 1 son. *Education:* BS, 1954 MA, 1961, Ball State University. *Publications:* The Scent of Magic, anthology in Tales of the Witch World (edited by Andre Norton); Crisis on Cheiron, 1967; The Singing Stones, 1968; Door into Terror, 1972; Dark Priestess, 1976; Space Trap, 1976; Web of Wizardry, 1978; The Death God's Citadel, 1980; Tomorrow's Heritage, 1981, 1989; Outward Bound, 1982, 1989; Legacy of Earth, 1989; The Past of Forever, 1989; Starsister, 1990. *Contributions to:* Magazine of Fantasy and Science Fiction; Fantastic Science Fiction and Fantasy Stories; Goldman Fantasy Foliant III. *Honours:* Hugo, Best Amateur Publication, Co-winner, World Science Fiction Convention, London, 1965. *Memberships:* Past member, Science Fiction Writers of America. *Literary Agent:* James Allen, 538 E Harford Street, Milford, PA 18337, USA. *Address:* 2677 W 500 N, Hartford City, IN 47348, USA.

COULSON Robert Stratton, b. 12 May 1928, Sullivan, IN, USA. Writer. m. 21 Aug 1954, 1 son. *Publications:* Charles Fort Never Mentioned Wombats, 1977; But What of Earth?, 1976; To Renew The Ages, 1976; The Invisibility Affair, 1967; Gates of the Universe, 1975; High Spy, 1987; The Mind-Twisters Affair, 1967; Now You See It/Him/Them, 1975; Nightmare Universe, 1985. *Contributions to:* Dictionary of Literary Biography; Fantasy Empire; Amazing Stories; Official Price Guide to Science Fiction and Fantasy Collectibles; Paper Collectors Marketplace; Viking-Penguin Science Fiction Encyclopedia; Reviews: Comic Buyers Guide.

Memberships: Science Fiction Writers of America; SFWA Forum, Co-editor, 1971-72, Secretary 1972-74. *Literary Agent:* James Allen. *Address:* 2677W-500N, Hartford City, IN 47348, USA.

COULTER Harris Livermore, b. 8 Oct 1932, Baltimore, Maryland, USA. Writer; Translator; Interpreter. m. Catherine Nebolsine, 10 Jan 1960, 2 sons, 2 daughters. *Education:* BA, Yale University, 1954; PhD, Department of Political Science, Columbia University, 1969. *Publications:* Divided Legacy: A History of the Schism in Medical Thought, Volume I: The Patterns Emerge, 1975, Volume II: The Origins of Modern Western Medicine, 1977, Volume III: Homeopathy and the American Medical Association, 1973, 1981, Volume IV: The Bacteriological Era: 1870-1990; Homeopathic Science and Modern Medicine, 1981; DPT: A Shot in the Dark (with Barbara Fisher), 1985; Vaccination, Social Violence, and Criminality, 1990; The Controlled Clinical Trial: An Analysis, 1991. *Honours:* Hahnemann Prize, Societe Royale Belge d' Homoeopathie, 1985; La Medalla d'Or del Centenari, Academia Medico- Homeopatica de Barcelona, 1990. *Membership:* American Institute of Homeopathy. *Address:* Center for Empirical Medicine, 4221 45th Street NW, Washington, DC 20016, USA.

COULTER Stephen, (James Mayo), b. 1914, United Kingdom. Author. *Appointments:* Reporter, home counties, England; Joined Reuters as Parliamentary Staff Correspondent, 1937; Staff Correspondent for Kemsley Newspapers, in Paris, 1945-65. *Publications:* Mystery novels as Stephen Coulter: The Loved Enemy, 1962; Threshold, 1964; Offshore, 1965; A Stranger Called the Blues, US Edition Players in a Dark Game, 1968, UK Paperback Death in the Sun, 1970; Embassy, 1969; An Account to Render, 1970; The Soyuz Affair, 1977; Mystery novels as James Mayo: The Quickness of the Hand, 1952; Rebound, 1961; A Season of Nerves, 1962; Hammerhead, 1964; Let Sleeping Girls Lie, 1965; Shamelady, 1966; Once in a Lifetime, US Edition Sergeant Death, 1968; The Man Above Suspicion, 1969; Asking for It, 1971; Other novels as Stephen Coulter: Damned Shall Be Desire: The Loves of Guy de Maupassant, 1958; The Devil Inside: A Novel of Dosteovsky's Life, 1960; Other: The Chateau, 1974. *Address:* c/o Grafton Books, 8 Grafton Street, London W1X 3LA, England.

COULTON James. *See:* **HANSEN Joseph.**

COUPER John Mill, b. 7 Sept 1914, Dundee, Scotland. University Lecturer in English Literature. m. Katharine Boyd, 17 July 1940, 2 sons, 1 daughter. *Education:* MA 1936, PhD 1948, Aberdeen University. *Appointments include:* Lecturer, University of Queensland, Australia, 1951-54; Headmaster, Knox Grammer School, 1954-55; Lecturer, University of New South Wals, 1958-67; Senior Lecturer, Associate Professor, Macquarie University, 1968-78. *Publications:* Poetry: The Book of Bligh, 1969; East of Living, 1967; In From The Sea, 1974; The Lee Shore, 1979; Canterbury Folk, 1984; Australian Poetry, editor, 1973. Novels, published UK & USA: The Thundering Good Today, 1970; Looking for a Wave, 1973. *Honour:* Moomba Prize, for The Book of Bligh, 1970. *Membership:* Australian Society of Authors. *Address:* 9 Dudley Street, Asquith, NSW 2077, Australia.

COURLANDER Harold, b. 18 Sept 1908, Indianapolis, USA. Author. *Education:* BA, University of Michigan, 1931; Postgraduate Work, Columbia University, 1939-50. *Publications include:* Haiti Singing, 1939; Kantchil's Lime Pit, 1960; The Hat Shaking Dance, 1957; The Drum and the Hoe, 1960; The King's Drum, 1962; Negro Folk Music USA, 1963; People of the Short Blue Corn, 1970; The Fourth World of the Hopis, 1971; Tales of Yoruba Gods and Heroes, 1973; A Treasury of African Folklore, 1975; A Treasury of Afro-American Folklore, 1976; The Crest and the Hide, 1982; The Heart of the Ngoni, 1982; Hopi Voices, 1982; Novels: The Caballero, 1940; The Big Old World of Richard Creeks,

1962; The African, 1967; The Son of the Leopard, 1974; The Mesa of Flowers, 1977; The Master of the Forge, 1985; Compiler, Editor, and Annotator, Big Falling Snow, 1978; Novels: The Bordeaux Narrative, 1990. *Contributions to:* Musical Quarterly; Journal of Negro History; African Arts; Phylon; The American Scholar; Michigan Alumnus; Negro History Bulletin; Resound; Saturday Review; Tomorrow; Bulletin du Bureau National d'Ethnologie; Village Voice; Ethnic Folkways Library; Chronicle, the Quarterly Magazine of the Historical Society of Michigan. *Honours:* John Simon Gugenheim Fellowships, 1948, 1955; Various awards & academic grants in aid; University of Michigan Outstanding Achievement Award, 1984. *Address:* 5512 Brite Drive, Bethesda, MD 20817, USA.

COURTER Gay, b. 1 Oct 1944, Pittsburgh, PA, USA. Writer; Film maker. m. Philip Courter, 18 Aug 1968, 2 sons. *Education:* AB Drama, Film Antioch College, Ohio, 1966. *Publications:* The Bean Sprout Book, 1974; The Midwife, 1981; River of Dreams, 1984; Code Ezra, 1986; Flowers in the Blood, 1990; The Midwife's Advice, 1992. *Contributions to:* Parents; Womens Day; Publishers Weekly, and others. *Memberships:* Authors Guild; Writers Guild of America East; Guardian Ad Litem; International Childbirth Association. *Literary Agent:* Donald Cutler, Bookmark: The Literary Agency. *Address:* 121 NW Crystal Street, Crystal River, FL 34428, USA.

COURTNEY Nicholas Piers, b. 20 Dec 1944, England. Author. m. Vanessa Hardwicke, London, 1980. *Education:* ARICS; MRAC, Royal Agricultural College, Cirencester. *Publications:* Shopping & Cooking in Europe, 1980; The Tiger, Symbol of Freedom, 1981; Diana, Princess of Wales, 1982; Royal Children, 1982; Prince Andrew, 1983; Sporting Royals, 1983; Diana, Princess of Fashion, 1984; Queen Elizabeth, The Queen Mother, 1984; The Very Best of British, 1985; In Society, The Brideshead Era, 1986; Princess Anne, 1986; Luxury Shopping in London, 1987; Sisters in Law, 1988; A A Stratford Kinshall, 1989; The Man, 1990; Windsor Castle, 1991. *Contributions to:* Times; Redbook. *Memberships:* Brooks's; Hurlingham PEN Club. *Literary Agent:* Sonia Land, Shell Land, 43 Doughty Street, London WC1N 2LF, England. *Address:* 9 Kempson Road, London, SW6 4PX, England.

COVARRUBIAS ORTIZ Miguel, b. 27 Feb 1940, Monterrey, Mexico. Writer; Professor. m. Silvia Mijares, 18 Mar 1967, 2 daughters. *Education:* Licenciado en letras, 1973, Maestria en letras espanolas, (pasantia), 1987, Universidad Autonoma de Nuevo Leon, Monterrey. *Appointments:* Coordinator, Department of Literature, Escuela de Verano, University of Nuevo Leon, 1970; Director, Centre for Literary and Linguistic Research, 1976- 79, Coordinator, Creative Writing Workshop, 1981-, Universidad Autonoma de Nuevo Leon, Monterrey. *Publications:* La raiz ausente, 1962; Custodia de silencios, 1965, 1982; Minusculario, 1966; Poetry: El poeta, 1969; El segundo, 1977, 1981, 1988; Pandora, 1987; Essays: Papeleria, 1970; Olavide o Sade, 1975; Nueva papeleria, 1978; Editor: Desde el Cerro de la silla, research, 1992. *Contributions to:* Vide universitaria, 1960-66; Apolodionis, 1959-67; Trabajo y cultura, 1967; Gaceta (Office of Foreign Affairs, Mexico), 1967-68; Suplemento Cultural de El Porvenir, 1968-71, 1982- 90; Calendario de Ramon Lopez Velarde (Office of Public Education, Mexico), 1971; Deslinde, 1982-. *Honours:* 2nd Place, Stgory, Xalapa Arts Festival, 1962; Arts Prize, Literature, Universidad Autonoma de Nuevo Leon, 1989. *Membership:* Sociedad General de Escritores de Mexico. *Address:* Kant 2801, Contry-La Silla, Guadalupe, N L, Mexico 67170.

COVILLE Bruce Farrington, b. 16 May 1950, Syracuse, New York, USA. Writer. Separated, 2 sons, 1 daughter. *Education:* Duke University 1968-69, State University of New York at Binghamton, 1969-72, State University College at Oswego, 1973, BA, Elementary Education. *Appointments:* Teacher 1974-81, specializing in gifted education for last three years. Left teaching for a career in publishing. *Publications include:*

Books include: Sarah's Unicorn, 1979; The Monster's Ring, 1982; Sarah and the Dragon, 1984; Operation Sherlock, 1986; Ghost in the Third Row, 1987; My Teacher is an Alien, 1989; Herds of Thunder, Manes of Gold, 1989. Plays: Faculty Room 1988; It's Midnight 1983; Out of the Blue 1982; The Dragonslayers 1981. *Contributions to:* Editor, Seniority Magazine, 1983-84. *Honours:* Second place winner of the Colorado Children's Book Award, 1984 - Sarah's Unicorn; Winner, South Carolina Children's Choice Award, 1984-85, Nominated for Children's Choice Awards in Arizona, Indiana and Iowa - The Monster's Ring. IRA Children's Choice List for 1985 - Sarah and the Dragon; IRA Children's Choice List for 1987 - Operation Sherlock; Nominated for Young Hoosier Book Award, Ghost in the Third Row. *Memberships:* Society of Children's Book Writers; Science Fiction Writers of America; Dramatists' Guild. *Address:* 14 East 11th Street, New York, NY 10003, USA.

COWAN Henry Jacob, b. 21 Aug 1919. Professor Emeritus of Architectural Science. *Education:* BSc., MSc., Manchester University, England; PhD, D.Eng., Sheffield University; M.Arch., Sydney University, Australia. *Appointments:* Editor, Architectural Science Review, 1958-; Editor, Vestes, 1966-78. *Publications include:* The Design of Reinforced Concrete, 1963, 5th edition, 1988; An Historical Outline of Architectural Science, 1966, 2nd edition, 1977; Architectural Structures, 1971, 3rd edition, 1980; Dictionary of Architectural Science, 1973, 2nd edition, 1985; The Master Builders, 1977, 2nd edition 1985 (Russian translation, 1982, also Science and Buildings, 1982); Science and Building, 1978; Building Science Laboratory Manual, 1978; Solar Energy Applications in the Design of Buildings, 1980; Structural Systems, 1981; Environmental Systems, 1983; Predictive Methods for the Energy Conserving Design of Buildings, 1983; Energy Conservation in the Design of Multi Storey Buildings, 1984; Encyclopedia of Building Technology, 1987; The Science and Technology of Building Materials, 1988; Handbook of Architectural Technology, 1991; A Contridiction In Terms, 1993. *Contributions to:* various journals. *Honours:* Recipient, Chapman Medal, Institution of Engineers, Australia, 1956; Honorary Fellowship, Royal Australian Institute of Architects, 1980; Officer, Order of Australia, 1984; Honorary Doctorate, Architecture, University of Sydney, 1987. *Memberships:* Fellow, Royal Society of Arts; American Society of Civil Engineers; Institution of Structural Engineers; Institution of Engineers Australia. *Address:* 57/6 Hale Road, Mosman, NSW 2088, Australia.

COWAN Peter, b. 1914, Australia. Academic; Author. *Appointments:* Senior English Master, Scotch College, Swanbourne, Western Australia, 1950-62; Member of Faculty, 1962-79, Research Fellow, Department of English, 1979-, University of Western Australia, Nedlands. *Publications:* Drift Stories, 1944; The Unploughed Land: Stories, 1959; Summer, 1964; Short Story Landscape: The Modern Short Story (editor), 1964; The Empty Street: Stories, 1965; Seed, 1966; Spectrum One to Three (co-editor), 1970-79; Today: Contemporary Short Stories (editor), 1971; The Tins and Other Stories, 1973; A Faithful Picture: Letters of Eliza and Thomas Brown, Swan River Colony 1841-1851 (editor), 1977; A Unique Position: A Biography of Edith Dircksey Cowan, 1978; Westerly 21 (editor), 1978; Mobiles, stories, 1979; Perspectives One (editor), short fiction, 1985; A Window in Mrs X's Place, short stories, 1986; The Color of the Sky, novel, 1986; Voices, short fiction, 1988; Maitland Brown: A View of Nineteenth Century Western Australia (biography), 1988; The Hills of Apollo Bay, novel, 1989; Impressions: West Coast Fiction 1829-1988, (editor), 1989; Western Australian Writing: A Bibliography, co-ed, 1990. *Address:* English Department, University of Western Australia, Nedlands, WA 6009, Australia.

COWANNA Betty. *See:* **HARRISON Elizabeth C.**

COWASJEE Saros, b. 12 July 1931, Secundrabad, India. Professor of English. *Education:* MA, Agra University, 1955; PhD, University of Leeds, England.

Appointments: Assistant Editor, Times of India Press, Bombay, 1961-63; Teaching, 1963-, Professor, English, 1971-, University of Regina, Regina, Canada; General Editor, Literature of the Raj series, Arnold Publishers, New Delhi, 1984-. *Publications:* Sean O'Casey: The Man Behind the Plays, 1963; Sean O'Casey, 1966; Stories and Sketches, 1970; Goodbye to Elsa, novel, 1974; So Many Freedoms; A Study of the Major Fiction of Mulk Raj Anand, 1977; The Last of the Maharajas, screenplay, 1980; Suffer Little Children, novel, 1982; Studies in Indian and Anglo-Indian Fiction, 1993; Others; Editor, several fiction anthologies including: Stories from the Raj, 1982; More Stories from the Raj and After, 1986; Women Writers of the Raj, 1990. *Contributions to:* Encounter; A Review of English Literature; Journal of Commonwealth Literature; The Literary Criterion; World Literature Written in English; Literature East and West; International Fiction Review; Journal of Canadian Fiction. *Honours:* J N Tata Scholarship, 1957-69; Canada Council and SSHRC Leave Fellowships, 1968-69, 1974-75, 1978-79, 1986-87. *Memberships:* Cambridge Society; Writers Union of Canada; Authors Guild of India; Association of Commonwealth Literature and Language Studies. *Address:* Department of English, University of Regina, Regina, Saskatchewan, Canada S4S 0A2.

COWDREY Herbert Edward John, b. 29 Nov 1926, Basingstoke, Hants, England. University Teacher. m. Judith Watson Davis, 14 July 1959, 1 son, 2 daughters. *Education:* BA, Oxford University, 1949; MA, 1951. *Appointments:* Chaplain & Tutor, St Stephen's House, Oxford, 1952-56; Fellow, St Edmund Hall, Oxford, 1956-. *Publications:* The Cluniacs and the Gregorian Reform; The Epistolae Vagantes of Pope Gregory VIII; Two Studies in Cluniac History; The Age of Abbot Desiderius; Popes, Monks and Crusaders. *Contributions to:* Many Articles. *Honour:* Fellow of the British Academy. *Memberships:* Royal Historical Society; Henry Bradshaw Society. *Address:* 30 Oxford Road, Old Marston, Oxford, OX3 0PQ, England.

COWEN Frances, (Eleanor Hyde), b. 1915, British. Writer of mystery/crime/suspense, historical/ romance/Gothic, children's fiction. *Appointment:* Assistant Secretary, Royal Literary Fund, London, 1955-66. *Publications:* juvenile publications include: Mystery at the Walled House, 1951; The Little Countess, 1954; The Riddle of the Rocks, 1956; Clover Cottage, 1958; The Secret of Grange Farm, 1961; The Secret of the Loch, 1963; mystery and romance novels for adults include: The Unforgiving Moment, 1971; (as Eleanor Hyde), Tudo Maid, 1972; (as Eleanor Hyde), Tudor Masquerade, 1972; (as Eleanor Hyde), Tudor Mayhem, 1973; The Curse of the Clodaghs, 1973; Shadow of Theale, 1974; The Village of Fear, 1974; (as Eleanor Hyde), Tudor Mystery, 1974; The Secret of Weir House, 1975; The Dangerous Child, 1975; The Haunting of Helen Farley, 1976; The Medusa Connection, 1976; Sinister Melody, 1976; (as Eleanor Hyde), Tudor Myth, 1976; The Silent Pool, 1977; The Lost One, 1977; (as Eleanor Hyde), Tudor Mausoleum, 1977; (as Eleanor Hyde), Tudor Murder, 1977; Gateway to Nowhere, 1978; The House Without a Heart, 1978; (as Eleanor Hyde), Tudor Mansion, 1978; (as Eleanor Hyde), Tudor Malice, 1979; (as Eleanor Hyde), The Princess Passes, 1979; House of Larne, 1980; Wait for Night, 1980; The Elusive Lover, 1981; Sunrise at Even, 1982.

COWIE Leonard Wallace, b. 10 May 1919, Brighton, England. Clerk in Holy Orders. m. Evelyn Elizabeth Trafford, 9 Aug 1949, 1 son. *Education:* BA, 1941; MA, 1946, Pembroke College, Oxford; PhD, University of London, 1954. *Publications:* Seventeenth-Century Europe, 1960; The March of the Cross, 1962; Eighteenth-Century Europe, 1963; Hanoverian England, 1967; The Reformation, 1968; Martin Luther, 1969; Sixteenth-Century Europe, 1977; Life in Britain, 1980; Years of Nationalism, (with R. Wolfson), 1985; The French Revolution, 1987; Lord Nelson: A Bibliography, 1990; William Wilberforce: A Bibliography, 1992. *Contributions to:* History To-Day; History; Church Times. *Memberships:* Royal Historical Society, Fellow; The

Athenaeum. *Address:* 38 Stratton Road, Merton Park, London SW19 3JG.

COWLES Ernest John Robert (Uncle Jack), b. 22 July 1903, Stutton, Ipswich, England. m. 6 June 1936. *Publications:* Past Present Future; Why Am I There? Looking Forward; The Unknown Dimension. *Contributions to:* Various. *Honours:* Highly Recommended Henry Lawson Festival. *Memberships:* Australian Society of Authors; National Book Council. *Address:* 9 Hutchinson Street, Geraldton, Western Australia, Australia.

COWLES Fleur, b. USA. Painter and Writer. *Appointments:* Associate Editor, Look magazine, USA, 1949-55; Founder, Editor, Flair Magazine, USA, 1950-51; Editor, Flairbook, USA, 1952. *Publications:* Bloody Precedent, 1951; The Case of Salvador Dali, 1959; The Hidden World of Hadhramoutt, 1964; I Can Tell It Now, 1965; Treasures of the British Museum, 1966; Tiger Flower, 1969; Lion and Blue, 1974; Friends and Memories, 1975; Romany Free, 1977; The Love of Tiger Flower, 1980; All Too True, 1980; The Flower Game, 1983; Flowers, 1985; People as Animals, 1985; To Be a Unicorn, An Artist's Journey, 1986; The Life & Times of the Rose, 1991. *Address:* A5 Albany, Piccadilly, London W1, England.

COWLEY Joseph Gilbert, b. 9 Oct 1923, Yonkers, New York, USA. Writer. m. Ruth Muriel Wilson, 28 Feb 1948, 2 sons, 2 daughters. *Education:* BA, Columbia College, 1947; MA, Columbia University, 1948. *Publications:* The Executive Strategist, 1969; The Chrysanthemum Garden, 1981. *Contributions to:* Short stories to: Prairie Schooner; New Story; The Maryland Review; Ohio Short Fiction; Other literary journals. *Literary Agent:* Agnes Birnbaum, Bleecker Street Associates. *Address:* 96 Mound St, Lebanon, OH 45036, USA.

COX Charles Brian, b. 1928, United Kingdom. Professor of English Literature. *Appointments:* Lecturer, Senior Lecturer, University of Hull, 1954-66; Co-Editor, Critical Quarterly, 1959-; Professor of English Literature, University of Manchester, 1966-; Director, Manchester Poetry Centre, 1971-; Pro-Vice Chancellor, Manchester University, 1987-91. *Publications:* The Free Spirit, 1963; Modern Poetry (with A E Dyson), 1963; Conrad's Nostromo, 1964; The Practical Criticism of Poetry (with A E Dyson), 1965; Poems of This Century (edited with A E Dyson), 1968; Word in the Desert (edited with A E Dyson), 1968; The Waste Land: A Casebook (edited with A P Hinchliffe), 1968; The Black Papers on Education (edited with A E Dyson), 1971; The Twentieth Century Mind (edited with A E Dyson), 3 vols, 1972; Conrad: Youth, Heart of Darkness, and The End of the Tether (editor), 1974; Joseph Conrad: The Modern Imagination, 1974; Black Paper 1975 (edited with R Boyson), 1975; Black Paper 1977 (edited with R Boyson), 1977; Conrad, 1977; Every Common Sight, verse, 1981; Two Headed Monster, verse, 1985; Cox on Cox: AN English Curriculum for the 1990's, 1991; The Great Betrayal: Autobiog, 1992. *Honour* CBE, 1990. *Address:* 20 Park Gates Drive, Cheadle Hulme, Stockport, SK8 7DF, England.

COX David Dundas, b. 20 June 1933, Goondiwindi. Graphic Artist; Author. m. Elizabeth Beath, 21 Feb 1976, 1 son, 2 daughters. *Education:* St Martin's School of Art, London, England. *Appointments:* Head Artist, The Courier Mail, Brisbane. *Publications:* Tin Lizzie and Little Nell, 1982; Bossyboots, 1985; Ayu and the Perfect Moon, 1984; Spice and Magic, collaboration with Betty Beath, 1983; Miss Bunkle's Umbrella, 1981; (Music Drama for Children) Abigail and the Rainmaker, 1976; Abigail and the Bush Ranger, 1976; The Raja Who Married an Angel, 1981; Frances, 1983; all with Betty Beath. *Contributions to:* Art Reviews; Childrens Book Reviews. *Honours:* Walkeley Award (Illustration), 1978; Highly Commended Children's Book of the Year Awards, 1983, 1985. *Memberships:* Australian Society of Authors; Opera for Youth, USA; Greek Community of

St George, Queensland; Playlab, Queensland. *Address:* 8 St James St, Highgate Hill, Queensland 4101, Australia.

COX Geoffrey Sandford, (Sir), b. 7 Apr 1910. Writer; Broadcaster. m. Cecily Barbara Talbot, 25 May 1935, 2 sons, 2 daughters. *Education:* MA, New Zealand, 1931; BA, Oxon, 1934. *Appointments:* Reporter, News Chronicle, London, 1935; War Correspondent, Spain, 1936; Foreign Correspondent, Daily Express, 1937-40; Political Correspondent, 1945-54; Assistant Editor, 1954-56, News Chronicle; Editor Independent TV News, 1956-58; Deputy Chairman, Yorkshire TV, 1968-71; Chairman Tyne Tees RTV, 1972-74; LBC, 1977-81. *Publications:* Defence of Madrid, 1937; Race for Trieste, 1977; See it Happen, 1983; A Tale of Two Battles, 1987; Countdown to War, 1988. *Honours:* MBE, 1945; CBE, 1959; Knighted, 1966; Silver Medal Royal TV Society, 1968; Gold Medal Royal TV Society, 1978; BAFTA Award, 1962. *Address:* Garrick Club, London WC2, England.

COX Richard, b. 8 Mar 1931, Winchester, England. m. 1963, 2 sons, 1 daughter. *Education:* Stowe School; Honours degree in English, St Catherine's College, Oxford. *Publications include:* Sam 7, 1976; Operation Sealion, 1974 (paperback 1978); Auction, 1978; Auction, 1978; KGB Directive, 1981; Ground Zero, 1985; An Agent of Influence, 1988; Park Plaza, 1991. *Contributions include:* The Daily Telegraph (Staff Correspondent 1966-72), Travel & Leisure, Traveller, Orient Express Magazine. *Honour:* Territorial Decoration, 1966. *Membership:* Army and Navy Club. *Literary Agent:* William Morris Agency, New York. *Address:* PO Box 88, Alderney, Channel Islands.

COX Roger L(insay), b. 23 Mar 1931, Manson, Iowa, USA. Univeristy Professor. m. Joan Rae Damerow, 5 Aug 1951, 2 sons, 2 daughters. *Education:* BA, Morningside College, Sioux City, 1951; MA, University of California, 1952; The Sorbonne, Paris, 1054-55; University of Florence, 1955-56; PhD, Columbia University, NY, 1961. *Appointments:* Instructor, Bates college, Lewiston, 1958-61; Assistant, Associate Professor, DePauw University, Greencastle, Ind, 1961-71; Associate Professor, Professor, University of Delaware, 1971-. *Publications:* Between Earth and Heaven; Shakespeares Comic Changes. *Contributions to:* Yale Review; Soundings LVII; Canadian Slavonic Papers. *Honours:* American Council of Learned Societies; Andrew Mellon Postdoctoral Fellow. *Memberships:* North American Dostoevsky Society. *Address:* 404 Vassar Drive, Newark, DE 19711, USA.

COX William Trevor (William Trevor), b. 24 May 1928, Co. Cork, Ireland. Author. m. Jane Ryan, 1952, 2 sons. *Education:* Trinity College, Dublin. *Publications:* The Old Boys, 1964; The Boarding House, 1965; The Love Department, 1966; The Day We Got Drunk on Cake, 1967; Mrs Eckdorf in O'Neill's Hotel, 1968; Miss Gomez and the Brethren, 1969; The Ballroom of Romance, 1970; Elizabeth Alone, 1972; Angels at the Ritz, 1973; The Children of Dynmouth, 1977; Lovers of Their Time, 1979; Other People's Worlds, 1980; Beyond the Pale, 1981; Fools of Fortune, 1983; A Writer's Ireland: Landscape in Literature, 1984; The News from Ireland, 1986; Nights at the Alexandra, 1987; Family Sins & other stories, 1989; The Silence in the Garden, 1989; The Oxford Book of Irish Short Stories, 1989; Family Sins and Other Stories, 1989; Two Lives, 1991; Juliet's Stories, 1992. *Honours:* Hawthornden Prize, 1965; Royal Society of Literature Prize, 1978; Whitbread Prize for Fiction, 1978; Allied Irish Banks Award for Services to Literature, 1978; Whitbread Prize, 1983; Hon DLitt, Exeter, 1984, Dublin, 1986, Queens's University, Belfast, 1989. *Address:* c/o A D Peters, 5th Floor, The Chambers, Chelsea Harbour, London SW10, England.

COX-JOHNSON Ann. *See:* SAUNDERS Ann Loreille Cox.

COXE Louis (Osborne), b. 1918, USA. Professor of English; Poet; Playwright. *Education:* Briggs-Copeland Fellow, Harvard University, Cambridge, Massachusetts, 1948-49. *Appointments:* Assistant Professor, Associate Professor, University of Minnesota, Minneapolis, 1959-55; Professor, 1955-56, Pierce Professor of English, 1956-, Bowdoin College, Brunswick, Maine, 1956-; Fulbright Lecturer, Trinity College, Dublin, Republic of Ireland, 1959-60. *Publications:* The Sea Faring and Other Poems, 1947; Billy Budd, UK Edition The Good Sailor (with R Chapman), play, 1951; The General, play, 1954; The Witchfinders, play, 1955; The Second Man and Other Poems, 1955; The Wilderness and Other Poems, 1958; The Middle Passage, 1960; Edwin Arlington Robinson, 1962; Chaucer (editor), 1963; The Last Hero and Other Poems, 1965; Nikal Seyn, Decoration Day: A Poem and a Play, 1966; Edwin Arlington Robinson: The Life of Poetry, 1969; Enabling Acts: Selected Essays, 1976; Passage: Selected Poems 1943-1978, 1979. *Address:* Department of English, Bowdoin College, Brunswick, ME 04011, USA.

COYNE P J. *See:* **MASTERS Hilary Thomas.**

CRAFT Robert, b. 1923, USA. Orchestral Conductor; Author. *Publications:* Le Musiche religiose di Igor Stravinsky con il catalogo analitico completo di tutte le sue opere di Craft, Piovesan, Vlad (with A Piovesan and R Vlad), 1957; Conversations with Igor Stravinsky, 4 vols, 1959; Memories and Commentaries, 1960; Expositions and Developments, 1962; Dialogues and a Diary, 1963; Table Talk, 1965; Themes and Episodes, 1966; Bravo Stravinsky (with A Newman), 1967; Retrospectives and Conclusions, 1969; Stravinsky: The Chronicle of a Friendship 1948-71, 1972; Prejudices in Disguise, 1974; Current Convictions: Views and Reviews, 1977; Stravinsky: Selected Correspondence (editor), 3 vols, 1981-85; A Stravinsky Scrapbook, 1984; Present Perspectives: Critical Writings, 1985. *Address:* c/o Alfred A Knopf Inc, 201 East 50th Street, New York, NY 10022, USA.

CRAGGS Robert S (Jack Creek, Luke Lanside), b. 6 Apr 1920, Manitoba, Canada. Freelance Writer. *Publications:* Trees for Shade and Beauty, 1961; Sir Adams Archibald, 1967; Ghostwriting for the Mail Order Trade, 1968; Writer Without a By-Line, 1968; Organic Gardening for Profit, 1990. *Contributions to:* Hundreds of articles, shortstories, cartoon gags to Canadian and US publications; Columnist for various publications. *Memberships:* National Writers Club, Aurora, Colorado; Friends of Merril collection, Toronto. *Address:* 25 McMillan Ave, West Hill, Ontario, Canada M1E 4B4.

CRAIG Alisa. *See:* **MACLEOD Charlotte.**

CRAIG Jasmine. *See:* **CRESSWELL Jasmine Rosemary.**

CRAIG Jonathan. *See:* **POSNER Richard.**

CRAIG Malcolm McDearmid, b. 1 July 1937, South Shields, County Durham, England. Publisher/Writer. m. Jill Christine Hampson, 31 Jan 1965, 1 son, 2 daughters. *Education:* BSc Econ (Hons), Dip Cam; Sloan Fellow, London Graduate School of Business. *Literary Appointments:* Editor, Stockmarket Confidential; Editor, Finance Confidential; Editor and Publisher, Craig's Investment Letter; Craig's Confidential Finance Letter. *Publications:* The Sterling Money Markets, 1975; Successful Investment, 1977; Investing to Survive the 80's, 1979, 80; Invisible Britain, 1981; Making Money Out of Gold, 1982; Making Money Out of Shares, 1983; Successful Investment Strategy, 1984, 2nd edition 1987. *Contributions to:* All UK national and leading provincial press, specialist investment and financial publications; BBC Radio; BBC TV. *Literary Agent:* Dasha Shankman, Ed Victor Literary Agency. *Address:* 15 Dukes Ride, Gerrards Cross, Buckinghamshire, England.

CRAIG Patricia, b. 16 Jan 1948, Belfast, Ireland. Writer; Critic; Anthologist. *Education:* Belfast; London. *Publications:* Oxford Book of English Defective Stories; Pengain Book of British Comic Stories; You're A Brick Angela; Women and Children First; The Lady Investigates: Women Detective. *Contributions to:* The Twice Lit Supp; London Review of Books; Observer; Independent; Sunday Times; New York Times; New York Review of Books; Guardian; Irish Times; Literary review. *Literary Agent:* Peters, Fraser & Dunlip. *Address:* c/o Peter, Fraser & Dunlop, Fifth Floor, The Chambers, Chelsea Harbour, Pots Road, London SW10 0XF, England.

CRAIK Elizabeth Mary, b. 25 Jan 1939. University Teacher. m. Alexander Craik, 15 July 1964, 1 son, 1 daughter. *Education:* MA, University of St Andrews, 1960; M Litt, University of Cambridge, 1965. *Appointments:* University of Birmingham 1963-64; University of St Andrews, 1964-. *Publications* The Dorian Aegean; Marriage And Propetry; Euripiotes Phoenician Women; Owls to Athens. *Contributions to:* Scholarly Journals; Many Articles & Reviews. *Address:* Department of Greek, University of St Andrews KY16 9AL, Scotland.

CRAIK Thomas Wallace, b. 17 Apr 1927, Warrington, England. Professor of English (Emeritus 1989). m. Wendy Ann Sowter, 25 Aug 1955 (div 1975), 1 son. *Education:* Boteler Grammar School, Warrington, 1937-45; BA, English Tripos: Part 1 1947, Part 2 1948; MA 1952; PhD 1952, Christ's College, Cambridge. *Appointments:* Assistant Lecturer in English 1953, Lecturer 1954-65, University of Leicester; Lecturer in English 1965-67, Senior Lecturer 1967-73, University of Aberdeen; Professor of English, University of Dundee, 1973-77; Professor of English 1977 until retirement in 1989, University of Durham, now Professor Emeritus. *Publications include:* The Tudor Interlude, 1958; The Comic Tales of Chaucer, 1964; (ed) Marlowe, The Jew of Malta, 1966; (ed) Shakespeare, Twelfth Night 1975; (ed) Beaumont and Fletcher, The Maid's Tragedy, 1988; (ed) Shakespeare, The Merry Wives of Windsor, 1989. *Contributions to:* Articles in Modern Language Review, Review of English Studies, Scrutiny, Notes and Queries, Stratford-upon-Avon Studies, Renaissance Drama. *Membership:* International Shakespeare Association. *Address:* 58 Albert Street, Western Hill, Durham City DH1 4RJ, England.

CRAIK Wendy Ann, b. 7 Feb 1934, London, England. Professor of English. m. Thomas Wallace Craik, 25 Aug 1955, (div 1975), 1 son. *Education:* BA, English, London University, 1953; PhD, Leicester University, 1963. *Publications:* Jane Austen: The Six Novels, 1965; The Bronte Novels, 1968; Jane Austen in Her Time, 1971; Elizabeth Gaskell & the 19th Century Novel, 1975. *Contributions to:* Review of English Studies; Notes & Queries; Times Higher Educational Supplement; Gaskell Society Journal. *Memberships:* Association for Scottish Literary Studies; Bronte Society; Elizabeth Gaskell Society. *Address:* Middle East Technical University, 06531 Ankara, Turkey.

CRANE Richard Arthur, b. 4 Dec 1944, York, England. Writer. m. Faynia Williams, 5 Sept 1975, 2 sons, 2 step-daughters. *Education:* BA Hons, Classics/English, 1966; MA, 1971, Jesus College, Cambridge. *Appointments:* Fellow in Theatre, University of Bradford, 1972-74; Resident Dramatist, National Theatre, 1974-75; Fellow in Creative Writing, University of Leicester, 1976; Literary Manager, Royal Court Theatre, 1978-79; Associate Director, Brighton Theatre, 1980-85; Dramaturg, Tron Theatre Glasgow, 1983-84; Visiting Writers Fellowship, University of East Anglia, 1988. *Publications include:* Thunder, 1976; Gunslinger, 1979; Stage Plays: The Tenant, 1971; Crippen, 1971; Decent Things, 1972; Secrets, 1975; The Quest, 1974; Clownmaker, 1975; Venus and Superkid, 1975; Bloody Neighbours, 1975; Satan's Ball, 1977; Gogol, 1979; Vanity, 1980; Brothers Karamazov, 1981; The Possessed, 1985; Mutiny!, (with David Essex), 1985; Soldier Soldier (with Tony Parker) 1986; Envy (with

Donald Swann) 1986; Pushkin, 1987; Red Magic, 1988; Rolling the Stone, 1989; Phaedra (with Michael Glenny) 1990; TV Plays: Rottingdea, 1980; The Possessers, 1985; Radio Plays: Gogol, 1980; Decent Things, 1984. *Contributions to:* The Edinburgh Fringe; The Guardian. *Honours:* Edinburgh Fringe First Awards, 1973, 1974, 1975, 1977, 1980, 1986, 1987, 1988, 1989. *Literary Agent:* Margaret Ramsay. *Address:* 14A Goodwins Court, St. Martins Lane, London WC2 N4LL, England.

CRANSTON Maurice William, b. 8 May 1920, London, England. Professor. m. Maximiliana, 11 Nov 1958, 2 sons. *Education:* University of London, St Catherines College, Oxford, BA, 1948; MA, 1951; European University Institute, Florence, 1978-81. *Appointments:* Teacher, London School of Economics, 1959-85; Vice Chairman, English Centre of International PEN, 1965-69; Registrar, Royal Literary Fund, 1974-79. *Publications include:* Jean Jacques; The Noble Savage; John Locke; Freedom; Political Dialogues; What are Human Rights? *Contributions to:* The London Magazine; Encounter; History of European Ideas; The American Spectator *Honours include:* Commandeur de L'Ordre des Palmes Academiques, Paris; Hon Fellow, St Catherines College; LSE. *Memberships:* International PEN; Society of Authors; Authors Guild of USA. *Literary Agent:* Peters, Fraser & Dunlop. *Address:* 1A Kent Terrace, London NW1 4RP, England.

CRAWFORD Linda, b. 2 Aug 1938, Detroit, Michigan, USA. Writer. *Education:* BA, 1960, MA, 1961, University of Michigan. *Publications:* In a Class by Herself, 1976; Something to Make Us Happy, 1978; Vanishing Acts, 1981; Ghost of a Chance, 1985. *Membership:* PEN. *Literary Agent:* Charlotte Sheedy. *Address:* 131 Prince St, New York, NY 10012, USA.

CRAWFORD Robert. See: RAE Hugh Crauford.

CRAWFORD Thomas, b. 6 July 1920. University Teacher. m. Jean Ronnie Macbribe, 19 Aug 1946, 1 son, 1 daughter. *Education:* MA, 1944; MA, 1953. *Appointments:* Lecturer, Auckland, 1953; Associate Professor, Auckland, 1962; Senior Lecturer, Aberdeen, 1967; Reader, 1973. *Publications:* Burus: A Study of the Prews n Songs; Scott; Love, Labour and Liberty; Society and the Lyric; Boswell, Burbub and the French Revolution. *Contributions:* Scottish Studies; Studies in Scottish Literature; Scottish Literary Journal; Review of English studies; Modern Language Review. *Memberships:* Association for Scottish Literary Studies. *Address:* Department of English, University of Aberdeen, Old Aberdeen AB9 2UB, Scotland.

CRAWLEY Anthony Francis (Tony Crawley), b. 26 Mar 1938, Farnham, Surrey, England. Freelance Journalist. m. (1) Jeannette Wild, 1967, (2) Nicole Michelet, 26 Feb 1970, 1 son, 1 daughter. *Publications:* The Films of Sophia Loren; Bébé, The Films of Brigitte Bardot; Screen Dreams; The Steven Spielberg Story; Entre Deux Censures; Film Quotes. *Contributions to:* Paris Match; Premiere; Photoplay; Variety; Screen International; Nouvel Observateur; Panorama; Cinephage; Starburst; Starfix; Sunday Telegraph Magazine. *Address:* 6 Alleć Claude Monet, 78160 Marly-le-Roi, France.

CRAWLEY Tony. See: CRAWLEY Anthony Francis.

CRAY Roberta. See: EMERSON Ru.

CREASEY Jeanne. See: WILLIAMS Jeanne.

CRECY Jeanne. See: WILLIAMS Jeanne.

CREEK Jack. See: CRAGGS Robert S.

CREELEY Robert White, b. 21 May 1926, Arlington, Massachusetts, USA. Writer; Professor of English. m.

(1) Ann McKinnon, 1946, divorced 1955, 2 sons, 1 daughter, (2) Bobbie Louise Hall, 1957, divorced 1976, 4 daughters (3) Penelope Highton, 1977, 1 son, 1 daughter. *Education:* BA, Black Mountain College, 1954; MA, University of New Mexico, 1960. *Appointments:* Lecturer, Black Mountain College, 1954-55, University of British Columbia, 1962-63; Professor, 1967-78, David Gray Professor, Poetry & Letters, 1978-89, State University of New York at Buffalo; Advisory Editor: American Book Review, 1983-; Sagetrieb, 1983-; New York Quarterly, 1984-; Samuel P. Capen Professor of Poetry and the Humanities, 1989; Director, Poetics Program, 1991-92. *Publications:* Poetry: For Love, Poems 1950-60, 1962; Words, 1967; Pieces, 1969; A Day Book, 1972; Selected Poems, 1976; Hello, 1978; Later, 1979; Mirrors, 1983; Collected Poems, 1945-75, 1983; Memory Gardens, 1986; Windows, 1990; Selected Poems, rev, 1991; Prose: The Island, 1963; The Gold Diggers, 1965; Mabel: A Story, 1976; The Collected Prose, 1984; Criticism: A Quick Graph, 1970; Was That A Real Poem & Other Essays, 1979; Collected Essays, 1989; Autobiography, 1990; Editor, with Donald M. Allen, New American Story, 1965, The New Writing in the USA, 1967; Editor, Selected Writings of Charles Olson, 1967; Whitman: Selected Poems, 1973; Editor, The Essential Burns, 1989; Charles Olson, Selected Poems, 1993. *Honours include:* Guggenheim fellow, 1964, 1971; Rockefeller Grantee, 1965; Shelley Memorial award, Poetry Society of America, 1981 NEA, 1982; DAAD, Berlin Artists Programme Grantee, 1983, 1987; Leone d'Oro Premio speziale, 1984; Frost Medal, Poetry Society of America, 1987; Distinguished Fulbright Award: Bicentennial Chair of American Studies, University of Helsinki, 1988; SUNY Distinguished Professor, 1989; Walt Whitman Citation, State Poet of New York, 1989-91. *Memberships:* American Academy and Institute of Arts and Letters, 1987; PEN American Center. *Address:* 64 Amherst St., Buffalo, NY 14207, USA.

CREGAN David (Appleton Quartus), b. 30 Sept 1931, United Kingdom. m. Ailsa Mary Wynne Willson, 1960, 3 sons, 1 daughter. Author; Dramatist. *Education:* BA, English Tripos, Cambridge University. *Appointments:* Worked with Cambridge Footlights, 1953, 1954, The Royal Court Theatre Studio, London, 1964, 1968, Midlands Arts Centre, Birmingham, 1971; Head of English Department, Palm Beach Private School, Palm Beach, Florida, USA, 1955-57; Assistant English Master, Burnage Boys Grammar School, Manchester, England, 1957; Assistant English Master, Head of Drama Department, 1958-62, Part-time Drama Teacher, 1962-67, Hatfield School, Hatfield, Herts; Conducted 3-week studio, Royal Shakespeare Company Memorial Theatre, Stratford-upon-Avon, 1971. *Publications:* Ronald Rossiter, novel, 1959; Miniatures, 1965; Transcending, and The Dancers, 1966; Three Men for Colverton, 1966; The Houses by the Green, 1968; How We Held the Square: A Play for Children, 1973; The Land of Palms and Other Plays, 1973; Poor Tom and Tina, 1976; Play Nine, 1980; Sleeping Beauty, 1984; Red Riding Hood, 1985; Jack and the Beanstalk, 1987. *Memberships:* Drama Panel, West Midlands Arts Association, 1972-75. *Address:* 76 Wood Close, Hatfield, Herts, England.

CRESKOFF Ellen Ann Hood, b. 3 Oct 1943, Philadelphia, USA. Translator and Information Analyst. m. Stephen M Creskoff, 11 Aug 1963, 2 sons. *Education:* BA, magna cum laude, Chemistry, University of Pennsylvania 1964; Equivalent of Masters: Courses in Biochemistry, Psychology, Scientific and Medical Russian, French and Computer Science. *Appointments:* Chemist, National Cancer Institute, NIH, Bethesda, Maryland, 1964-68; Translator, College of Physicians, Medical Documentation Service, 1972-74; Editor/Translator/Abstractor, Biosciences Information Service of Biological Abstracts (BIOSIS), 1978-86; Freelance Translator, Abstractor, Indexer, 1968-. *Publications:* Co-author: Isolation and characterization of rat liver mitochondrial DNA, Journal of Molecular Biology, 1970; Co-author: Macroion interactions involving components of the cytochrome system V. Reduction of cytochrome c by synthetic polysaccharides, Journal of Biological

Chemistry, 1967; Co-author, Reduction-like effect of carbohydrates on cytochrome c, Science, 1965; Regular contributor to Delaware Valley Translators Association Newsletter, 1979-, Editor 1982-83; Author, English On-Line Glossaries in Translation, ATA Chronicle, May 1986; Author, Nida Proposes New Classification, ATA Chronicle, June 1990; Translation of Soviet text on Neurophysiology, 1973; Translation of Soviet text on Origin of Life by Oparin, 1969. *Honour:* Phi Beta Kappa. *Memberships:* Board of Delaware Valley Translators Association, President 1985-90; Accredited by American Translators Association (Russian to English); Board of Hebrew Immigrant Aid Society; Phi Beta Kappa. *Address:* 2101 Walnut Street 201, Philadelphia, PA 19103, USA.

CRESSWELL Helen (Mrs Brian Rowe), b. July 1934. Freelance Author. m. Brian Rowe, 1962, 2 daughters. *Education:* BA, English, Honours, King's College, London. *Publications:* TV Series: Lizzie Dripping, 1973-75; Jumbo Spencer, 1976; The Bagthorpe Saga, 1980; The Haunted School, 1987; The Secret World of Polly Flint, 1987; Moondial, 1988; Five Children and It, 1990; The Return of the Psammead, 1993; numerous TV Plays. Books: Sonya-by-the-Shire, 1961; Jumbo Spencer, 1963; The White Sea Horse, 1964; Pietro and the Mule, 1965; Jumbo Back to Nature, 1965; Where the Wind Blows, 1966; Jumbo Afloat, 1966; The Piemakers, 1967; A Tide for the Captain, 1967; The Signposters, 1968; The Sea Piper, 1968; The Barge Children, 1968; The Nightwatchman, 1969; A Game of Catch, 1969; A Gift from Winklesea, 1969; The Outlanders, 1970; The Wilkses, 1970; The Bird Fancier, 1971; At The Stroke of Midnight, 1971; The Beachcombers, 1972; Lizzie Dripping, 1972; Thee Bongleweed, 1972; Lizzie Dripping Again, 1974; Butterfly Chase, 1975; The Winter of the Birds, 1975; My Aunt Polly, 1979; My Aunt Polly By the Sea, 1980; Dear Shrink, 1982; The Secret World of Polly Flint, 1982; Ellie and the Hagwitch, 1984; The Bagthorpe Saga: pt. 1, Ordinary Jack, 1977, pt. 2 Absolute Zero, 1978, pt. 3 Bagthorpes Unlimited, 1978, pt. 4 Bagthorpes v the World, 1979, pt. 5 Bagthorpes Abroad, 1984, pt. 6 Bagthorpes Haunted, 1985, pt. 7 Bagthorpes Liberated, 1988; Time Out, 1987; Whodunnit, 1987; Moondial, 1987; Two Hoots, 1988; The Story of Grace Darling, 1988; Dragon Ride, 1988; Trouble, 1988; Rosie and the Boredom Eater, 1989; Whatever Happened in Winklesea?, 1989; Meet Posy Bates, 1990; Hokey Pokey Did it!, 1990; Posy Bates Again, 1991; Lizzie Dripping and The Witch, 1991; Posy Bates and the Bag Lady, 1992; The Bagthorpe Triangle, 1992; The Return of the Psammead, 1992; (ed) The Puffin Book of Funny Stories, 1992; The Watchers, 1993. *Literary Agent:* A M Heath, London. *Address:* Old Church Farm, Eakring, Newark, Notts. NG22 0DA, England.

CRESSWELL Jasmine Rosemary (Jasmine Craig), b. 14 Jan 1941, Wales. Writer. m. Malcolm Candlish, 15 Apr 1963, 1 son, 3 daughters. *Education:* BA, Melbourne University; BA, Honours, Macquarie University; MA, Case Western Reserve University. *Publications:* more than 30 novels, including: The Abducted Heiress, 1976; Stormy Reunion, 1981; Under Cover of Night, 1984; Traitor's Heir, 1984; Hunter's Prey, 1986; Chase the Past, 1987; The Devil's Envoy, 1988. *Honours:* Colorado Romance Writer of the Year, 1986; 1987; Top Hand Award for Best Original Paperback published by Colorado Author. *Memberships:* President, Colorado Authors' League; Editor, Writers of America; Authors' Guild of America. *Agent:* Curtis Brown, New York. *Address:* c/o Maureen Walters, 10 Astor Place, New York, NY 10003, USA.

CREW Gary David, b. 23 Sept 1947, Brisbane, Queensland, Australia. Lecturer; Writer. m. Christine Joy Crew, 4 Apr 1970, 1 son, 2 daughters. *Education:* MA, English (Post-Colonial), University of Queensland. *Appointments:* Lecturer, Queensland University of Technology, 1987-. *Publications:* Inner Circle, 1986; The House of Tomorrow, 1988; Strange Objects, 1991; No Such Country, 1992; Tracks, 1992; Lucy's Bay, 1992. *Honours:* For Strange Objects: Australian Children's

Book of the Year, New South Wales Premier's Award and The Alan Marshall Prize, 1991. *Membership:* Australian Society of Authors. *Address:* Green Mansions, 66 Picnic St, Enoggera, Queensland 4051, Australia.

CREW Louie, b. 1936, USA. Educator. *Appointments:* Master of English and Bible, Darlington School, Rome, Georgia, 1959-62; Master of English and Sacred Studies, St Andrew's School, Middletown, Delaware, 1962-65; Instructor of English, Penge Secondary Modern School, London, England, 1965-66; Instructor of English, University of Alabama, Tuscaloosa, USA, 1966-70; Director, Independent Study in England for Experiment in International Living, 1970-71; Professor of English, Claflin College, Orangeburg, South Carolina, 1971-73; Associate Professor of English, Fort Valley State College, Georgia, 1973-79; Founder, Integrity, International Ministry of Lesbian and Gay Anglicans, 1974-; Member of Board, Journal of Homosexuality, 1978-; Associate Professor of English, University of Wisconsin, Stevens Point, 1979-84; Director, Writing Programme, Chinese University of Hong Kong, 1984-. *Publications:* Sunspots, poetry, 1976; The Gay Academic, essays, 1978. *Address:* PO Box 754, Stevens Point-on-the-Wisconsin, WI 54481, USA.

CREWE Candida Annabel, b. 6 June 1964, London, England. Writer; Novelist. *Publications:* Focus; Romantic Hero; Accommodating Molly; Mad About Bees. *Contributions to:* Times; Telegraph; Spectator; Observer; Independent; Guardian; Tatler; Harpers & Queen; The Standard. *Honours:* Winner, Catherine Pakenham Award for Journalism. *Memberships:* PEN; The Groucho CLub. *Literary Agent:* Antony Harwood. *Address:* c/o Curtis Brown, 162-168 Regent Street, London W1R 5TB, England.

CREWS Judson, b. 1917, USA. Poet. *Appointments:* Publisher, Motive Press and Este Es Press, Texas and New Mexico, 1946-66; Printer, Taos Star, El Crepusculo and Taos News, New Mexico, 1948-66. *Publications:* Psalms for a Late Season, 1942; The Southern Temper, 1946; No is the Night, 1949; Come Curse to the Moon, 1952; The Anatomy of Proserpine, 1955; Patrocinio Barela: Taos Wood Carver (with M Tolbert and W B Anderson), 1955, Revised Edition, 1962; The Wrath Wrenched Splendor or Love, 1956; The Heart in Naked Hunger, 1958; To Wed Beneath the Sun, 1958; A Sheaf of Christmas Verse: The Ogres Who Were His Henchman, 1958; Inwade to Briney Garth, 1960; The Feel of the Sun and Air upon Her Body, 1960; A Unicorn When Needs Be, 1963; Hermes Past the Hour, 1963; Selected Poems, 1964; You, Mark Antony, Navigator upon the Nile, 1964; Angels Fall, They Are Towers, 1965; Three on a Match (with W B Anderson and C Farallon), 1966; The Stones of Konarak, 1966; Nations and Peoples, 1976; Nolo Contendere, 1978; The Noose, 1980; If I, 1981; The Clock of Moss, 1983.

CRIBB Phillip James, b. 12 Mar 1946, Sussex, England. Botanist. *Education:* MA; PhD. *Publications:* Manual of Cultivated Orchid Species; The Genus Paphiopedium; The Genus Cymbidium; The Genis Pleione; Mountain Flower of Southern Tanzania. *Contributions to:* Numerous. *Address:* The Herbarium, Royal Botanic Gardens, Kew, Surrey TW9 3AB, England.

CRICHTON Michael, (John Michael, Jeffrey Hudson, John Lange), b. 23 Oct 1942, Chicago, Illinois, USA. Film Director; Author. *Education:* AB summa cum laude 1964, MD 1969, Harvard University; Cambridge University, UK, 1965; Postdoctoral Fellow, Salk Institute for Biological Siences, California, 1969-70. *Publications include:* The Andromeda Strain, 1969; The Terminal Man, 1972; The Great Train Robbery, 1975; Congo, 1980; Sphere, 1987; Five Patients, 1970; Eaters of the Dead, 1976; Jasper Johns, 1977; Electronic Life, 1983; Travels, 1988. *Honours:* Edgar Awards, Mystery Writers of America, 1968, 1979. *Memberships:* Authors Guild; Writers Guild of America; Directors Guild; Academy of

Motion Picture Arts & Sciences. *Literary Agent:* Lynn Nesbit, ICM, 40 West 57th Street, New York, NY 10025.

CRICHTON Ronald Henry, b. 28 Dec 1913, Scarborough, England. Writer; Music Critic. *Education:* Radley College, 1927-31; Christ Church, Oxford, 1932-36. *Appointments:* Programme Organizer, Anglo French Art & Travel Society, London, 1937-39; Army Service, 1940-46; British Council, Greece, Belgium, West Germany, London, 1946-67; Music Critic, Financial Times, 1967; Freelance , 1979; Governing Body, British Institute of Recorded Sound, 1973-77; Arts Council, Sub Committees, Dance Theatre, 1973- 76; Opera, 1976-80. *Publications:* A Dictionary of Modern Ballet; Manuel de Falla: A Descriptive Catalogue of His Works; Falla: BBC Music Guide; The memoirs of Ethel Smyth. *Contributions to:* The New Grove Dictionary of Music & Musicians. *Memberships:* Reform Club; Critics Club; Society of Authors. *Address:* c/o David Higham Associates Ltd, 5-8 Lower John Street, London W1R 4HA, England.

CRICK Donald Herbert, b. 16 July 1916, Sydney, Australia, m. 24 Dec 1943, 1 daughter. *Publications:* Novels: Bikini Girl, 1963; Martin Place, 1964; Period of Adjustment, 1966; A Different Drummer, 1972; The Moon to Play With, 1981; Screenplays: The Veronica, 1983; A Different Drummer, 1985; The Moon to Play With, 1987. *Contributions to:* Sydney Morning Herald; The Australian; Overland; The Australian Author. *Honours:* Mary Gilmore Centenary Award, Novel, 1966; Rigby Anniversary Award, Novel, 1980; Awgie Screenplay Award, 1983-85. *Memberships:* Australian Society of Authors, Board of Management. *Literary Agent:* Richard Deutch, Sydney. *Address:* 1/1 Elamang Avenue, Kirribilli, NSW 2061, Australia.

CRIDDLE Joan D, b. 9 Dec 1935, Deweyville, Utah, USA. Author; Lecturer; Homemaker. m. Dr Richard S Criddle, 1 June, 1956, 1 son, 4 daughters. *Education:* Utah State University, 1954-55; AA, Sacramento City College, 1978; California State University, Sacramento, 1979. *Publication:* To Destroy You Is No Loss: The Odyssey of a Cambodian Family, 1987; Bamboo & Butterflies: from Refugee to Citizen, 1992. *Honour:* Educator's Award, Delta Kappa Gamma Society International awarded Honorable Mention for 1988. *Address:* 1375 Estates Drive, CA 95620, USA.

CRISCUOLO Anthony Thomas (Tony Crisp), b. 10 May 1937, Amersham, Bucks, England. Photographer; Nurse; Driver; Journalist; Plumber; Writer; Therapist. 4 sons, 1 daughter. *Publications:* Yoga and Relaxation, 1970; Do You Dream? 1971; Yield, 1974; Yoga and Childbirth, 1975; The Instant Dream Book, 1984; Mind and Movement, 1987; Dream Dictionary, 1989; Liberating The Body, 1992. *Contributions to:* Dream columnist for Daily Mail, 1982-84; She; Over 21; Cosmopolitan; I to I; Yoga and Health; Energy and Character; Bio-Energy (Japan); Best; LBC Dream Therapist (Broadcasting Radio); Teletext's Dream Interpreter (TV Channel 4). *Address:* Ashram, King Street, Combe Martin, Devon EX34 0AG, England.

CRISP Tony. *See:* CRISCUOLO Anthony Thomas.

CRISTOFER Michael. *See:* PROCASSION Michael.

CRITCHFIELD Richard, b. 1931, USA. Freelance Writer. *Appointments:* Reporter, Cedar Valley Daily Times, 1955-56; Washington Correspondent, Salt Lake City Desert News, 1957-58; Acting Assistant Professor, University of Nagpur, India, 1960-62; Asia and National Correspondent, 1963-72, White House Correspondent, 1968-69, The Washington Star. *Publications:* The Indian Reporters Guide, 1962; Lore and Legend of Nepal (editor and illustrator), 1962; The Long Charade: Political Subversion in the Vietnam War, 1968; The Golden Bowl Be Broken, 1974; Shahat, 1978; Villages, 1981; Those Days: An American Album, 1986. *Contributions to:* The Christian Science Monitor; The New York Times; Los Angeles Times; Wall Street Journal; Reader's Digest; The Economist, London. *Address:* c/o Peggy Ann Trimble, 4532 Airlie Way, Annandale, VA 22003, USA.

CRITCHLEY Julian Michael Gordon, b. 8 Dec 1930, Chelsea, England. 1 son, 3 daughters. *Education:* MA, Pembroke College, Oxford. *Appointment:* Editor, Town Magazine, 1966. *Publications:* Collective Security, 1974; Warning & Response, 1978; The North Atlantic Alliance & the Soviet Union, 1987; Westminster Blues, 1985; Britain: a View from Westminster Editor, 1986; Heseltine: the Unauthorised Biography, 1987; Palace of Varieties, 1989; Hung Parliament, 1991; Floating Voter, 1992; Some of Us, 1992. *Contributions to:* The Conservative Opportunity, 1966, The Complete Imbiber, 1956; The Illustrated Counties of England, 1984; Sunday Times; Times; Daily Telegraph; The Sun; Observer. *Honours:* Political Journalist of the Year, 1985. *Memberships:* Various professional organisations. *Literary Agent:* Curtis Brown. *Address:* 44 Mill Street, Ludlow SX81 1BB, England.

CRITTENDEN Toya Cynthia, b. 19 Dec 1958, River Rouge, Michigan, USA. Poetic Author. *Education:* Speech Pathology, English Literature, Wayne State Unviersity, Detroit, Michigan, 1977-80. *Publications:* World of Poetry Anthology, 1987; Poem, publshed in Insight magazine, 1988. *Honours:* Award Merit Certificate, 1985, 1986, 1987; Golden Poet Award, 1986, 1987; Silver Poet Award, 1989, World of Poetry. *Memberships:* International Platform Association; The American Biographical Association. *Address:* 4060 Pasadena, Detroit, MI 48238, USA.

CROCOMBE Ronald Gordon, b. 8 Oct 1929, Auckland, New Zealand. m. Marjorie Tuainekore Crocombe, 7 Apr 1959, 3 sons 1 daughter. *Education:* BA, Victoria University, 1955; PhD, Australian National University, 1961. *Appointments:* Director, Institute of Pacific Studies, University of the South Pacific, 1976-85; Chairman of Judges, Asia/Pacific Region, Commonwealth Writers Prize, 1987, 1988. *Publications include:* The South Pacific, 1973, 1978, 1983, 1987, 1989, (revised editions); The Pacific Way, 1976 (reprinted many times); Land Tenure in the Pacific, 1971, 1977 Revised edition 1987; Foreign Forces in Pacific Politics, 1983, 1985; Land Tenure in the Cook Islands, 1963, 1971; Pacific Universities, 1988. *Contributions to:* numerous professional and academic journals. *Memberships:* South Pacific Social Sciences Association, Past President; Pacific History Association, Past President; South Pacific Creative Arts Society. *Address:* Box 309, Rarotonga, Cook Islands.

CROFT Julian Charles Basset, b. 31 May 1941, NSW, Australia. University Lecturer. m. (1) Loretta De Plevitz, 23 Oct 1967, (2) Caroline Ruming, 1 son. *Education:* Ba, University of NSW, 1961; Ma, University of Newcastle, NSW, 1967. *Appointments:* Lecturer, University of Sierra Leone, 1968-70; Lecturer, University of New England, 1970-. *Publications:* T H Jones; Breakfast in Shanghai; Their Solitary Way; Confessions of a Corin Thian; The Life & Opinions of Tom Collins. *Memberships:* Association for the Study of Australian Literature. *Address:* Department of English, University of New England, Armidale, Australia 2351.

CROLL Carolyn, b. 20 May 1945, South Dakota, USA. Childrens Book Author, Illustrator. *Education:* BFA, Philadelphia College of Art, 1967. *Publications:* The Three Brothers; The Little Snowgirl; Too Many Babas; The Man Who Painted Flowers. *Honours:* The Federation of Childrens Book Groups, The Pick of the Year; The Drexel Citation. *Address:* 1420 Locust St 22H, Phila, PA 19102, USA.

CROMIE Stanley. *See:* SIMMONS J S A.

CROMWELL Elsie. *See:* LEE Elsie.

CRONE Alla Marguerite, b. 22 Dec 1923, Harbin, Manchuria. Writer. m. Richard I. Crone, 27 Mar 1946, 2 sons. *Education:* San Francisco Conservatory of Music, 1953-57. *Publications:* Novels: East Lies the Sun, 1982; Winds over Manchuria, 1983; North of the Moon, 1984; Legacy of Amber, 1985. *Contributions to:* Christian Science Monitor; Michigan Quarterly Review. *Honours:* Gold Medal West Coast Review of Books, 1982; Finalist, Gold Medallion Romance Writers, 1983; 2nd Prize, National League of American Penwomen, 1984; Best Book on Russia, Romantic Times, New York, 1985. *Memberships:* Authors Guild; Romance Writers of America; President, 1981, California Writers Club, Redwood Branch. *Address:* Santa Rosa, CA 95405, USA.

CRONIN Vincent Archibald Patrick, b. 24 May 1924. Author. m. Chantal, 1949, 2 sons, 3 daughters. *Education:* Trinity College, Oxford. *Publications:* The Golden Honeycombe, 1954; The Wise Man from the West, 1955; The Last Migration, 1957; A Pear to India, 1959; The Letter after Z, 1960; Louis XIV, 1964; Four Women in Pursuit of an Ideal, 1965; The Florentine Renaissance, 1967; The Flowering of the Renaissance, 1970; Napoleon, 1971; Louis and Antoinette, 1974; translator, Giscard d'Estaing, Towards a New Democracy, 1977; Catherine Empress of all the Russias, 1978; The View from Planet Earth, 1981; Paris on the Eve, 1989. *Address:* Brion, Dragey, 50530 Sarfilly, France.

CROOK Joseph Mordaunt, b. 27 Feb 1937, London, England. Professor of Architectural History, London University; formerly Slade Professor and Waynflete Lecturer, Oxford University. m. Susan Mayor, 9 July 1975. *Education:* Wimbledon College; BA, 1st Class, Modern History, 1958, D Phil 1961, Brasenose College, Oxford. *Literary Appointment:* Editor, Architectural History, 1967-75. *Publications:* The Dilemma of Style: Architectural Ideas from the Picturesque to the Post Modern, 1987; The Greek Revival, 1972; William Burges and the High Victorian Dream, 1981; The British Museum, 1971. Co-author: The History of the King's Works, vols 5 and 6, 1973- 76. *Contributions to:* Times Literary Supplement; Country Life; Architectural Review; Architectural History. *Honours:* Fellow, Society of Antiquaries, 1973; Fellow, British Academy, 1987; Public Orator, London University, 1987-90. *Memberships:* Council, British Academy, 1988-; Historic Buildings Council for England, 1974-80. *Address:* 55 Gloucester Avenue, London NW1 7BA, England.

CROSLAND Margaret McQueen, b. Bridgnorth, Shropshire, England. Writer; Translator. *Education:* BA, London University. *Publications:* Madame Colette, 1954; Jean Cocteau, 1955; Louise of Stolberg, 1962; Colette: The Difficulty of Loving, 1973; Raymond Radiguet, 1976; Women of Iron and Velvet, 1976; Beyond the Lighthouse, 1981; Piaf, 1985; The Passionate Philosopher, A de Sade Reader, 1991; Simone de Beauvoir, 1992; (ed) Cocteau's World, 1971; many translations. *Honours:* Prix Bourgogne, France, 1975; Enid McLeod Literary Award, 1992. *Membership:* Society of Authors. *Address:* The Long Croft, Upper Hartfield, Sussex, England.

CROSS Anthony Glenn, b. 21 Oct 1936, Nottingham, England. Educator. m. Margaret Elson, 11 Aug 1960, 2 daughters. *Education:* MA, 1964, PhD, 1966, Cambridge University; MA, Harvard University, USA, 1961; LittD, University of East Anglia, 1981. *Appointments:* Editor, Newsletter, Study Group 18th Century Russia, 1973-; Review Editor, Journal European Studies, 1971-; Chairman, British Academic Committee for Cooperation with Russia, 1981-; Currently, Professor of Slavonic Studies. *Publications:* N M Karamzin, 1971; Russian Under Western Eyes, 1971; Russian Literature in Age of Catherine the Great, 1976; Russians in 18th Century Britain, 1981; The Russian Theme in English Literature, 1985; Anglo-Russia, 1993; Engraved in the Memory, 1993. *Contributions to:* professional journals. *Honours:* Frank Knox Fellow, Harvard University, 1960-61; Visiting Fellow, University of Illinois, Urbana, 1969-70, All Souls College, Oxford, 1978-79; Fellow of British

Academy, 1989. *Memberships:* British University Association Slavists, President 1982-84. *Address:* Department of Slavonic Studies, University of Cambridge, Sidgwick Avenue, Cambridge, CB3 9DA, England.

CROSS (Alan) Beverley, b. 13 Apr 1931, England. Dramatist. m. Dame Maggie Smith, 1975. *Education:* Balliol College, Oxford, 1952-54. *Publications include:* Plays: One More River, 1956; Boeing-Boeing, 1962; Miranda, 1987. Musicals: Half A Sixpence, 1962; Jorrocks, 1965; Hans Andersen, 1972. Opera Libretti: Mines of Sulphur, 1966; The Rising of the Moon, 1972. Screenplays: Jason and the Argonauts; Genghis Khan; Half A Sixpence; Clash of the Titans. *Membership:* Garrick Club. *Literary Agent:* Curtis Brown. *Address:* c/o Curtis Brown, 162 Regent Street, London, W1R 5TA, England.

CROSS Brenda. *See:* **COLLOMS Brenda.**

CROSS Gillian Clare, b. 24 Dec 1945, London, England. Writer. m. Martin Cross, 10 May 1967, 2 sons, 2 daughters. *Education:* BA (Hons) Class I, Somerville College, Oxford, 1965-69; DPhil, University of Sussex, 1970-73. *Publications:* The Runaway, 1979; The Iron Way, 1979; Revolt At Ratcliffe's Rags, 1980; Save Our School, 1981; A Whisper Of Lace, 1981; The Demom Headmaster, 1982; The Dark Behind The Curtain, 1982; The Mintyglo Kid, 1983; Born Of The Sun, 1983; On The Edge, 1984; The Prime Minister's Brain, 1985; Swimathon, 1986; Chartbreak, 1986; Roscoe's Leap, 1987; A Map Of Nowhere, 1988; Rescuing Gloria, 1989; The Monster From Underground, 1990; Twin and Super-Twin, 1990; Wolf, 1990; Gobbo The Great, 1991; Rent-A-Genius, 1991; The Great Elephant, 1992. *Honours:* Wolf, Carnegie Medal, 1990; The Great Elephant Chase, Whitbread Children's Novel Award and Smarties Prize, 1992. *Membership:* Society of Authors. *Address:* The Gate House, 39 Main Street, Wolston, Coventry CV8 3HH, England.

CROSS Victor. *See:* **COFFMAN Virginia (Edith).**

CROSSLEY-HOLLAND Kevin John William, b. 7 Feb 1941, Buckinghamshire, England. Author; Broadcaster; Teacher. m. (1) 2 sons. (2) Gillian Cook, 2 daughters. *Education:* MA, Oxford. *Appointments include:* Editor, Macmillan, 1962-69; Editorial Director, Victor Gollancz, 1972-77; Endowed Chair in Humanities and Fine Arts, St Thomas University, Minnesota, 1991-. *Publications:* Poetry: The Rain-Giver, 1972; The Dream-House, 1976; Time's Oriel, 1983; Waterslain, 1986; The Painting-Room, 1988; New and Selected Poems, 1991. For Children: Havelok the Dane, 1964; King Horn, 1965; The Green Children, 1966; The Callow Pit Coffer, 1968; Wordhoard (w Jill Paton Walsh), 1969; Storm and Other Old English Riddles, 1970; The Pedlar of Swaffham, 1971; The Sea Stranger, 1973; The Fire-Brother, 1974; Green Blades Rising, 1975; The Earth-Father, 1976; The Wildman, 1976; The Dead Moon, 1982; Beowulf, 1982; The Mabinogion (w Gwyn Thomas), 1984; Axe-Age, Wolf-Age, 1985; Storm, 1985; The Fox and the Cat (w Susanne Lugert), 1985; British Folk Tales, 1987; Wulf, 1988; The Quest for Olwen (w Gwyn Thomas), 1988; Piper and Pooka, 1988; Small Tooth Dog, 1988; Boo!, 1988; Dathera Dad, 1989; Under the Sun and Over the Moon (w Ian Penney), 1989; Sleeping Nanna, 1989; Sea Tongue, 1991; Tales From Europe, 1991; Long Tom and The Dead Hand, 1992; Taliesin (w Gwyn Thomas), 1992. Travel: Pieces of Land, 1972. Mythology: The Norse Myths, 1980. History: The Stones Remain (w Andrew Rafferty), 1989. Translations from Old English: The Battle of Maldon (w Bruce Mitchell), 1965; Beowulf (w Bruce Mitchell), 1968; The Exeter Book Riddles, 1978; The Illustrated Beowulf, 1987; The Anglo-Saxon Elegies, 1988. Edited: Running to Paradise, 1967; Winter's Tales for Children 3, 1967; Winter's Tales 14, 1968; New Poetry 2 (w Patricia Beer), 1976; The Faber Book of Northern Legends, 1977; The Faber Book of Northern Folk-Tales, 1980; The Anglo-Saxon World, 1982; The Riddle Book, 1982; Folk-Tales of the British Isles, 1985;

The Oxford Book of Travel Verse, 1986; Northern Lights, 1987; Medieval Lovers, 1988; Medieval Gardens, 1990; Peter Grimes by George Crabbe, 1990. Opera: The Green Children (w Nicola LeFanu), 1990. Contributions to: Numerous magazines and journals. Honours: Arts Council Award, Best Book for Young Children, The Green Children, 1966; Poetry Book Society Choice, 1976; Carnegie Medal, Storm, 1985; Poetry Book Society Recommendation, 1986. Literary Agent: Rogers, Coleridge and White. Address: The Old Vicarage, Walsham-le-Willows, Bury St Edmunds, Suffolk, England.

CROUCH David, b. 20 July 1948, Richmond, England. Academic Lecturer; Researcher; Writer. m. Elisabeth Darlaston, 1 son, 1 daughter. Education: Reading University, BSc, MSc; Polytechnic of Central London. Appointments: Television, Channel Four, Earth Wind & Fire. Publication: The Allotment: Landscape & Culture. Contributions to: Continuities in Popular Culture (book); Landscape and Culture (book); Country Living; Ideas & Production; Journal of Rural Studies; Landscape USA; Landscape Research. Honour: Angel Literary Award. Memberships: Institute of British geographers; Popular Culture Association (USA); Leisure Studies Association; Landscape Research Institute. Address: Anglia University, Cambridge and Chelmsford, England.

CROUCH Marcus, b. 12 Feb 1913, Tottenham, Middlesex, England, Chartered Librarian. m. Olive King, 13 Apr 1955, 1 son. Education: BA, Queen Mary College, London University, 1931-34. Appointment: Deputy County Librarian, Kent County Library. Publications: Treasure Seeker and Borrowers, 1962; The Nesbit Tradition, 1972; Kent, 1966; Essex, 1969; The Home Counties, 1975; Canterbury, 1970; Victorian and Edwardian Kent, 1974; Britain in Trust, 1963; Fingerprints of History, 1968; The Ivory City, 1980; The Whole World Story Book, 1985; Ivan, 1989; Kentish Books Kentish Writers, 1989. Contributions to: Times Literary Supplement; Times Educational Supplement; Junior Bookshelf; School Librarian. Memberships: Society of Authors; Library Association, Fellow; LA Youth Library Section, Chairman; School Library Association, Chairman, Kent Branch. Address: Ty'n Llidiart, Pentrecelyn, Ruthin, Clwyd, Wales.

CROWE John. See: **LYNDS Dennis**.

CROWLEY Shauna Mary, b. 22 Aug 1960, Townsville, Queensland, Australia. Writer; Producer. m. Chris Roache, 18 Apr 1992. Education: Swinburne University; Australian Institute of Radio and Television; The Australian Film, Television and Radio School. Publications: The Screen Test Handbook. Memberships: Australian Writers Guild; Australian Film Institute. Address: PO Box 220, Alexandria, NSW 2015, Australia.

CROWN David Allan, b. 13 Sept 1928, Long Beach, New York, USA. Forensic Consultant; Educator. m. Maria Braml, 14 Feb 1954, 1 son, 1 daughter. Education: BS, Union College, Schenectady, New York, 1948; MCrim, 1960, DCrim, 1969, University of California, Berkeley. Appointments: Book Review Editor, 1976-80, Associate Editor, 1980-85, Journal of Forensic Sciences. Publications: The Forensic Examiniation of Paints and Pigments, 1969; Forensic Science (co-author), 1981; Legal Medicine 1985 (co-author), 1985. Contributions to: Journal of Criminal Law, Criminology and Police Science; Journal of Forensic Science; Kriminalistik; Journal of the Forensic Science Society; Security Management. Memberships: President, American Academy of Forensic Sciences, 1974-75; President, American Society of Questioned Documents Examiners, 1980-82. Address: 3103 Jessie Court, Fairfax, VA 22030, USA.

CROZIER Brian Rossiter, b. 4 Aug 1918. Writer; Journalist. m. Mary Lillian Samuel, 1940, 1 son, 3 daughters. Education: Peterborough College, Harrow;

Trinity College of Music, London. Appointments: Music & Art Critic, London, 1936-39; Reporter, Sub-Editor, Stoke-on-Trent, Stockport, London, 1940-41; Aeronautical Inspection 1941-43; Sub-Editor, Reuters, 1943-44, News Chronicle 1944-48, Sub-Editor and Writer, Sydney Morning Herald, Australia, 1948-51; Correspondent, Reuters-AAP 1951-52; Features Editor, Straits Times, Singapore, 1952-53; Leader Writer, Correspondent, The Economist, 1954-64; BBC Commentator, English French and Spanish overseas services, 1954-65; Chairman, Forum World Features, 1965-74; Editor, Conflict Studies, 1970-75; Co-Founder, Director, Institute for the Study of Conflict, 1970-79; Consultant, 1979-; Columnist, National Review, New York, 1978-; Now!, London 1980-81, The Times, 1982-84. Publications: The Rebels, 1960; The Morning After, 1963; Neo-Colonialism, 1964; South East Asia in Turmoil, 1965-66-68; The Struggle for the Third World, 1966; Franco, 1967; The Masters of Power, 1969; The Future of Communist Power (in USA: Since Stalin), 1970; De Gaulle, Volume I, 1973, Volume II, 1974; A Theory of Conflict, 1974; The Man Who Lost China, 1977; Strategy of Survival, 1978; The Minimum State, 1979; Franco: Crepusculo de un hombre,(Spanish orig), 1980; The Price of Peace, 1980; Socialism Explained, co-author, 1984; This War Called Peace, co-author, 1984; The Andropov Deception, novel, as John Rossiter, 1984.(under own name, New York, 1986); Socialism: Dream and Reality, 1987; The Gorbachev Phenomenon, 1990; Communism: Why prolong its death thrones?, 1990. Contributions to: Numerous journals. Address: Kulm House, Dollis Avenue, Finchley, London N3 1DA, England.

CROZIER Lorna Jean, b. 24 May 1948, Swift Current, Saskatchewan, Canada. Writer; Teacher. Education: BA, Hons., 1969, Pofessional A Teaching Certificate, 1970, University of Saskatchewan; MA, University of Alberta, 1980. Appointment: Special Lecturer, University of Saskatchewan, 1986-89. Publications: Inside Is the Sky, 1976; Crows Black Joy: Humans and Other Beasts, 1980; No Longer Two People (with Patrick Lane Turnstone); The Weather, 1983; The Garden Going On Without Us, 1985. Contributions include: Ariel; Athanos; Event; Grain; Saturday Night; South Dakota Review; Prism International; Fiddlehead; Canadian Forum. Honours: University of Alberta Creative Writing Scholarship, 1978-79; Department of Culture and Youth Poetry Manuscript Award; Saskatchewan Writers; Guild Poetry Manuscript Award, 1983, 1986; Governor General Awards Nominee, 1986. Memberships: Saskatchewan Writers Guild, Vice President, President, Colony Committee; The League of Canadian Poets, Saskatchewan Representative, Chairman of Membership Committee. Address: 1005 13 St, East, Saskatoon, Saskatchewan, S7H 0B8, Canada.

CRUMP Barry (John), b. 1935, New Zealand. Author; Hunter; Goldminer; Radio Announcer. Publications: A Good Keen Man, 1961; Hang on a Minute Mate, 1962; One of Us, 1963; Two in One, 1964; There and Back, 1965; Gulf, 1966; Scrapwagon, 1966; The Odd Spot of Bother, 1967; No Reference Intended, 1968; Warm Beer, short stories, 1969; A Good Keen Girl, 1970; Bastards I Have Met, 1971; Fred, 1972; The Best of Barry Crump, 1974; Shorty, 1980; Puha Road, 1981. Address: PO Box 1424, Auckland, New Zealand.

CRYSTAL David, b. 1941, British. Writer of children's non-fiction, Linguistics/language, medicine/health, speech/rhetoric. Professorial Fellow, University College of North Wales, Bangor, 1985-, Editor, Child Language Teaching and Therapy 1985- and Linguistics Abstracts 1985-; Consultant Editor, English Today 1986-. Appointments: Assistant Lecturer, University College of North Wales, 1963-65; Lecturer and Reader, 1965-75, and Professor of Linguistic Science, 1976-85, University of Reading. Publications include: Child Language, Learning and Linguistics, 1976; Working with LARSP, 1979; Eric Partridge: In His Own Words, 1980; A First Dictionary of Linguistics and Phonetics, 1980; Introduction to Language Pathology, 1980; Clinical

Linguistics, 1981; Directions in Applied Linguistics, 1981; Linguistic Controversies, 1981; Profiling Linguistic Disability, 1982; Linguistic Encounters with Language Handicap, 1984; Language Handicap in Children, 1984; Who Cares about English Usage? 1984; Listen to Your Child, 1986; (ed with W Bolton), The English Language, 1987; Cambridge Encyclopaedia of Language, 1987; Rediscover Grammar, 1988; The English Language, 1988; children's non-fiction: (with J Bevington), Skylarks, 1975; (with John Foster), Heat, Light, Sounds, Roads, Railways, Canals, Monasteries, Manors, Catles, Money, Parliament, Newspapers, The Romans, The Greeks, The Ancient Egyptians, Air, Food, Volcanoes, Deserts, Electricity, Motorcycles, Computers, Horses and Ponies, The Normans, The Vikings, The Celts, The Anglo-Saxons, The Stone Age, Fishing, 29 vols, 1979-85; Pilgrimage, 1988; Language A-Z, 1991; Nineties Knowledge, 1992; Am Encyclopeadia Dictionary of Language and Languages, 1992; The Cambridge Encyclopeadia (ed), 1990; The Cambridge Concise Encyclopeadia (ed), 1992. *Address:* Akaroa, Gors Avenue, Holyhead, Angelsey, Gwynedd, LL65 1RG, Wales.

CSAK Gyula, b. 12 Jan 1930, Nyiregyhaza. Writer. m. Eva forras, 16 Nov 1967, 1 son. *Education:* University of Eotvos Lorand, 1960. *Appointments:* Secretary to the Hungarian Writers Association, 1974- 84;Head of the Information And Cultural Centre, New Delhi, 1984-87. *Publications:* Melytengeri Aramlas; Ember a Kovon; Alomzug; A tolvaj es a Birak; Glemba; Ket Karacsony Kozott; Bontjak a Kemenceket; A Szikfold Sohaja; A Parasztsido. *Contributions to:* Kortars; UJ Iras; Elet es Irodalom. *Honours:* Jozsef Attila Prize; Szot Prize. *Memberships:* Hungarian Writers Association; PEN. *Address:* Mozsar, u6, 1066 Budapest, Hungary.

CSANDA Endre, b. 14 Mar 1923, Nagyvarad, Hungary. Professor of Neurology. 2 daughters. *Education:* Medical degree, 1947, PhD, 1962, Budapest, 1947; SBE: Neurology, 1951; General Surgery, 1954; Neurosurgery, 1959; Psychiatry, 1974. *Appointments:* Neuropsychiatric Department, University Medical School, 1947-50; Neurosurgical Institute, 1956-59; Neuropsychiatric and Neurosurgical Department, 1959-61; Neuropsychiatric Department, University Medical School, Szeged, 1971-75; Professor, Chairman, Semmelweis University Medical School, Institute of Neurology, Budapest, 1975-. *Publications:* Cerebral Oedema as a Consequence of Experimental Cervical Lymphatic Blockage, 1968; Radiation Brain Edema, 1980; Central Nervous System and Lymphatic System, 1983; Adjuvant Drugs in the Treatment of ON-OFF Phenomena in Parkinson's Disease; Some possible histo-pathological correlates of dementia in Parkinsonian patients, 1990. *Contributions to:* 172 publications or chapters in medical journals and books; Senior author in 105. *Honours:* Kivalo Award, Finnish Neurological Society, 1985; Apaczai Csere Janos Award, 1986; Honorary Member, Austrian, Czechoslovakian and Polish Neurological Societies. *Memberships:* President, Hungarian Society for Neurology and Psychiatry; Vice-President, European Federation of Neurological Societies; Past Vice-President, World Federation of Neurology; Past Vice-President, Paneuropean Neurological Society. *Address:* Balassa u 6, 1083 Budapest, Hungary.

CSERES Tibor, b. 1 Apr 1915, Gyergyoremete, Tras, Hungary. Writer. m. Nora Ulkey, 15 Nov 1944, 1 daughter. *Education:* University of Economics, Kolozsvar. *Publications:* Cold Days, 1964; Players and Lovers, 1970; I, Lajos Kossuth, 1980; Pass of Foksany, 1985; Battles of Vizamua, 1988; Vendeta in Backa, 1991. *Honours:* Kossuth Prize, 1975; Order of Flag, Hungarian Republic, 1990. *Memberships:* President, Hungaria Writers Association, 1986-89; President, Hungarian Writers Chamber; Hungarian Academy of Literature and Arts. *Address:* Orlo 14, 1026 Budapest II, Hungary.

CUDDON John Anthony Bowden, b. 2 June 1928, Southsea, England. Writer; Teacher. m. Anna-Clare Dale, 17 May 1975, 1 son, 2 daughters. *Education:* Douai School, 1939-46; Brasenose College, Oxford, 1949-55, MA, BLitt. *Publications:* The Owl's Watchsong (travel), 1960; A Multitude of Sins (novel), 1961; Testament of Iscariot (novel), 1962; Jugoslavia (travel), 1968; Dictionary of Literary Terms, 1977; Dictionary of Sport and Games, 1981; Acts of Darkness (novel), 1963; The Six Wounds (novel), 1964; The Bride of Battersea (novel), 1967; Penguin Book of Ghost Stories, 1984; Penguin Book of Horror Stories, 1984; Penguin Dictionary of Literary Terms and Literary Theory, 1992. *Contributions to:* British daily and weekly papers and various journals. *Membership:* MCC. *Address:* 43, Alderbrook Road, London SW12, England.

CULLEN BROWN Joanna, b 5 Sept 1930, Tianjin, China. Writer. m. Bernard H V Brown, 19 June 1954, 1 son, 2 daughters. *Education:* Walthamstow Hall, Sevenoaks, Kent, 1937-48; St Hildas College, Oxford, BA Hons, 1948-51, MA, 1955; University of Cambridge, CertEd, 1951-52. *Publications:* A Journey into Thomas Hardys Poetry; Figures in a Wessex Landscape; Let Me Enjoy the Earth. *Contributions to:* The Countryman; Country Quest; The Lady; Vogue. *Honours:* A S M Studentship; Essay Prizes, Council for Education in World Citizenship; PEN Club. *Memberships:* Thomas Hardy Society. *Address:* c/o Allison & Busby, 5 The Lodge, Richmond Way, London W12 8LW, England.

CULME John, b. 3 May 1946, London, England. *Publications:* The Directory of Gold & Silversmiths, Jewellers & Allied Traders 1838-1914; Nineteenth Century Silver; The Jewels of the Duchess of Windsor; Antique Silver & Silver Collecting. *Contributions to:* The Connoisseur; Sothebys Preview; The Antique Collector. *Memberships:* The Silver Society. *Address:* Sothebys, 34/35 New Bond Street, London, W1A 2AA, England.

CULVER Timothy J. *See:* **WESTLAKE Donald E.**

CUMMING Peter E, b. 23 Mar 1951, Brampton, Ontario, Canada. Writer; Teacher. m. Mary Shelleen Nelson, 14 Oct 1970. *Education:* BA, English Literature, 1972; Diploma in Education, 1976; MA, English Literature, 1992. *Appointments:* Resident Artist in Drama, Wilfrid Laurier University, 1972-73; Executive Director, Atlantic Publishers Association, 1984-85. *Publications:* Snowdreams, 1982; Ti-Jean, 1983; A Horse Called Farmer, 1984; Mogul and Me, 1989; Out on the Ice in the Middle of the Bay, 1993. *Contributions to:* Contributing editor, Quill and Quire, 1982-84. *Honours:* 1st Prize, Children's Prose, 1980, 1st Prize, Adult Fiction, 1981, Writers Federation of Nova Scotia; Toronto Board of Education Canada Day Playwriting Competition, 1981; Our Choice, Children's Book Centre, 1984, 1989; Hilroy Award for Innovative Teaching, 1990. *Memberships:* Playwrights Union of Canada; Writers Union of Canada; Canadian Society of Children's Authors, Illustrators, and Performers; Association of Canadian College and University Teachers of English. *Address:* 201 Front St, Stratford, Ontario, Canada N5A 4H8.

CUMMINS Walter (Merrill), b. 6 Feb 1936, USA. Professor of English. m. Alison Cunningham, 14 Feb 1981, 2 daughters. *Education:* Rutgers University, BA, 1957; University of Iowa, MA, 1962; MFA, 1962; PhD, 1965. *Appointments:* Editor in Chief, The Literary Review, 1984-; Editorial Committee, Fairleigh Dickinson University Press, 1984-. *Publications:* Where We Live; Witness; A Stranger to the Deed; Into Temptation. *Contributions to:* Virginia Quarterly Review; Kansas Quarterly; West Branch; Other Voices; South Carolina Review. *Honours:* New Jersey State Council, Arts Fellowship. *Address:* Fairleigh Dickinson University, Madison, NJ 07940, USA.

CUNLIFFE Barrington Windsor, b. 10 Dec 1939, Portsmouth, England. University Teacher. m. Margaret Herdman, 5 Jan 1979. 1 son, 1 daughter. *Education:* BA 1962, MA 1962, PhD 1966, LittD 1977, Cambridge

University. *Appointments:* Editorial Boards: Oxford Journal of Archaeology, World Archaeology. Series Editor for: Longmans, Routledge, Cambridge University Press. *Publications:* Iron Age Communities in Britain, 1974, 2nd edition 1978; Rome and Her Empire, 1978; The Celtic World, 1979; Danebury: Anatomy of an Iron Age Hillfort, 1983; The City of Bath, 1986; Greeks Romans and Barbarians, 1988; Roman Bath Discovered, 2nd edition 1984; Heywood Sumners Wessex, 1985. *Contributions to:* Times Literary Supplement; Encounter; Good Book Review. *Honours:* Fellow, The British Academy, 1979; Honorary Doctrates: University of Bath, University of Sussex. *Literary Agent:* Curtis Brown, 162-8 Regent Street, London. *Address:* Institute of Archaeology, 36 Beaumont Street, Oxford, England.

CURL James Stevens, b. 26 Mar 1937, Belfast, Northern Ireland. Professor of Architectural History, Department Architecture, De Montfort University, Leicester; Architect; Historian. m. (1) Eileen Elizabeth Blackstock, 1 Jan 1960. divorced 1986. 2 daughters, (2) Stanistawa Dorota Iwaniec, 1993. *Education:* Queen's University, Belfast and School of Architecture, 1954-58; DiplArch, Oxford School of Architecture, 1961-63; Oxford Department of Land Use Studies, 1963-67; PhD, University College, London, 1978-81; DipTP; MRTPI; RIBA; ARIAS; FSA; FSAScot. *Publications:* The Victorian Celebration of Death, 1972; City of London Pubs, 1973; A Celebration of Death, 1980; The Egyptian Revival, 1982; The Life and Work of Henry Roberts (1803-76), Architect, 1983; The Londonderry Plantation 1609-1914, 1986; English Architecture: an Illustrated Glossary, 1987; Victorian Architecture, 1990; The Art and Architecture of Freemasonry, 1991; Classical Architecture, 1992; Encyclopaedia of Architectural Terms, 1992; Georgian Architecture, 1993. *Contributions to:* Connaissance des Arts; Country Life; Royal Society of Arts Journal; Architects' Journal; Bauwelt; The World of Interiors; The Literary Review. *Honours:* Sir Charles Lanyon Prize, 1956 and 1958; Ulster Arts Club Prize, 1958; Stevens Prize for Thesis, 1963; Baroque Prize, 1962; British Academy Research Awards, 1982 and 1983; Society of Antiquaries of London Research Award, 1980, 1981. *Address:* 2 The Coach House, Burley-on-the-Hill, Rutland LE15 7SU, England.

CURLING Audrey. *See:* **CLARK Marie Catherine Audrey.**

CURLING Bryan William Richard (Bill), b. 15 Nov 1911, Bitterne, Hampshire, England. Retired Racing Journalist; Author. m. Elizabeth Mary Bonham, 1 June 1939, 3 sons, 1 daughter. *Education:* Eton College, 1924-30. *Appointments:* Journalist, Southern Echo, Southampton, 1931- 34; Journalist, 1934-1939, including Racing Correspondent (pen-name Julius), 1936-39, Yorkshire Post; Racing Correspondent (pen-name Hotspur), Daily Telegraph, 1946-65; PRO to the Jockey Club, 1965-69. *Publications:* British Racecourses,1951; The Captain (biography of Royal trainer Captain Sir Cecil Boyd Rochfort), 1970; The Grand National (with Clive Graham), 1972; Derby Double, the story of racehorse trainer Arthur Budgett, 1977; All The Queen's Horses, 1978; Royal Champion, the Story of Steeplechasing's First Lady, 1980; The Sea Pigeon Story, 1982. *Contributions to:* The European Racehorse. *Memberships:* The Naval Club, London; Bembridge Sailing Club, Bembridge, Isle of Wight. *Literary Agent:* Andrew Hewson of John Johnson, 45 Clerkenwell Green, London EC1R OHT, England. *Address:* 1 Fullerton Manor, Andover, Hants SP11 7LA, England.

CURNOW Thomas Allen Monro, b. 17 June 1911, Timaru, New Zealand. Author. m. (1) Elizabeth Jaumaud Le Cren, 1936, 2 sons, 1 daughter, (2) Jenifer Mary Tole, 1965. *Education:* BA, 1934, LittD, 1965, Universities of Canterbury and Auckland. *Appointments:* Staff, The Press, 1935-48; News Chronicle, London, 1949; Associate Professor, University of Auckland, 1967-76. *Publications:* 17 Volumes of Poems; 1 plays; 1 Criticism; Editor, Anthologies including: Penguin book

of New Zealand Verse; Poetry Titles include: Not in Narrow Seas, 1939; Island and Time, 1941; Sailing or Drowning, 1943; At Dead low Water, 1949; A Small Room with Large Windows, 1962; Trees, Effgies Moving Objects, 1972; Collected Poems, 1933-73, 1974; An Incorrigible Music, 1979; You Will know When you Get There, 1982; The Loop in Lone Kauri Road, 1986; Continuum, New & Later Poems, 1988; Selected Poems, 1940-1989, 1990. Plays include: The Axe, 1949; The Duke's Miracle, 1968. *Contributions to:* Encounter; London Magazine; London Review of Books; Partisan Review; Times Literary Supplement; Islands; Landfall. *Honours:* New Zealand Book Award for Poetry, 5 times, 1958-83; Katherine Mansfield Memorial Fellowship, 1983; LittD, 1975; CBE 1986; Dillons Commonwealth (overall) Poetry Prize, 1989; The Queen's Gold Medal for Poetry, 1989; Cholmondeley Award, 1992. *Agent:* Curtis Brown. *Address:* 62 Tohunga Crescent, Parnell, Auckland 1, New Zealand.

CURRAN Colleen, b. 23 Aug 1954, Montreal, Canada. Playwright. *Education:* BA, Hons, English, Loyola College, Concordia University, 1976; Teaching Certificate, McGill University, 1981. *Appointment:* Playwright in residence, Centaur Theatre, Montreal, 1984-85. *Publications:* Major plays produced: El Clavidista, 1 act, Mayor's Council on the Arts, Burlington, 1982; Another Labor Day, 1 act, Montreal, 1984; Cake-Walk, comedy, Blyth Festival, 1984; Maisonneuve, drama series for CBC Radio, 1984; Nuclear Hollywood, performance piece-play, Playwrights' Workshop, Montreal, 1985; Moose County, comedy Blyth Festival, 1985; Uluru, drama, CBC Radio; Miss Balmoral of the Bayview, Blyth Festival, 1987; Spooks, A haunting comedy, 1987; Cake-Walk in Four New Comedies, 1987; Triple-Play, 3 one-acts: El Clavadista, A Sort of Holiday, Amelia Earhart Was Not A Spy, 1990; Sacred Hearts, play, Alberta Theatre, Projects newplay Rites 1989; adapted CBC Radio Morningside, 1991; Radio Plays, CBC Radio Vanashing Point: Kiss The Bride Goodbye; Lisdoonvarna; A Natural Death (Adaptation); Keeping Up With The Smythe-Joneses; Mariana of the Universe (Adaptation); for A.T.P. 'Shorts' First Night; Stopping by Woods; Parental Guidance; Whale Watch, premiere 1989 Solar Stage; Senetta Boynton Talent, comedy, Blyth Festival, 1991; Ceili House, comedy Blythe Festival, 1993; (Ed) Escape Acts: Seven Canadian One Acts, 1992; work included in The Perfect Piece; You're Making A Canadian Comedy. *Contributions to:* Theatre Writer, Montreal Review and Montreal Calendar; Writer; Loyola News, 1972-76; Book Reviewer, The Gazette, 1985; Travel Writer Contributor, The Gazette, 1993. *Honours:* Honourable Mention, Ottawa Little Theatre Playwrighting Competition, 1982; Dorothy White Playwrighting Award, Ottawa Little Theatre Playwrighting competition, 1983; Best New Play, Quebec Drama Festival, 1984; Expo '86 'Shorts' Competition; Gabriel Radio Award, Texas, 1991. *Memberships:* Board Member, Playwrights Workshop, Montreal; ACTRA; Playwrights Union of Canada (Editorial Board Chair, National Council 1991-92); Co-Artistic Director Triumvirate Theatre Company, Montreal, 1992-. *Literary Agent:* Patricia Ney, Christopher Banks and Associates. *Address:* 148 Abbott Avenue, Montreal, Quebec, Canada H3Z 2J9.

CURRY Avon. *See:* **BOWDEN Jean.**

CURRY Glen David, b. 15 Dec 1948, Kimball, West Virginia, USA. College Professor. m. Janet Bonham, 14 July 1988. *Education:* BS, University of Southern Mississippi, 1969; MA, University of Mississippi, 1973; PhD, Sociology, University of Chicago, 1976. *Publications:* Sunshine Patriots: Punishment and the Vietnam Offender, 1985. *Contributions to:* Gang Homicide and Delinquency, to Criminology, 1988; Effectiveness of Gang Strategies, to Huff's Gangs in America, 1990; Gang Involvement and Delinquency (with Irving A Spergel), to Journal of Research on Crime and Delinquency, 1992; 7 others. *Memberships:* American Sociological Association; President-Elect Marxist Section; Vice-President Elect, West Virginia

Sociological Association; American Society of Criminology; National Staff Member, Vietnam Veterans Against the War. *Address:* 908 Garrison Avenue, Morgantown, WV 26505, USA.

CURRY Jane Louise, b. 24 Sept 1932, USA. Writer. *Education:* Pennsylvania State University 1950-51; BA, Indiana University of Pennsylvania, 1954; University of California, Los Angeles, 1957-59; London University, 1961-62; 1965-66; AM, 1962; PhD, 1969, Stanford University. *Appointments:* Teaching Assistant, 1959-61, 1963-65; Acting Instructor, 1967-68; Instructor, 1983-84; Lecturer, 1987, Stanford University, English Department; Free-lance Lecturer, Consultant on Children's Books, 1970-. *Publications include:* The Housenapper, (also published as Mindy's Mysterious Miniature and The Mysterious Shrinking House), 1970; Beneath the Hill, 1967; The Sleepers, 1968; The Change-Child, 1969; The Day Breakers, 1970; The Ice Ghosts Mystery, 1972; The Lost Farm, 1974; Poor Tom's Ghost, 1977; The Great Flood Mystery, 1985; The Lotus Cup, 1986; Me, Myself and I, 1986; Little Little Sister, 1989; What The Dickens!, 1991; The Christmas Knight, 1993. *Contributions to:* Medium Aevum. *Honours:* Fulbright Grant, 1961-62; Stanford Leverhulme Fellowship, 1965-66; Southern California Council on Literature for Children Book Award, 1971; Special Award, 1979; Ohioana Book Award, 1978, 1987. *Memberships:* The Authors Guild; International Arthurian Society; Southern California Council on Literature for Children and Young People. *Address:* McElderry Books, Macmillan Children's Book Group, 866 Third Avenue, New York, NY 10022, USA.

CURRY Mary Earle Lowry, b. 13 May 1917, Seneca, South Carolina, USA. Writer. m. Reverend Peden Gene Curry, 25 Dec 1941, 1 son, 1 daughter. *Education:* Seneca High School; Furman University, 1944-45. *Publications:* Looking Up, 1949; Looking Within 1961, 1980; Hymn: Church in the Heart of the City, 1973. *Contributions to:* Numerous anthologies and journals including: Yearbook of Modern Poetry; Poets of America; Poetic Voice of America; We, the People; Poetry Digest; Poetry Anthology of Verse; International Anthology on World Brotherhood and Peace; The Greenville News; Inman Times. *Honour:* World Award for Culture, Centro Studi e Ricerche Delle Nazioni, Italy, 1985. *Memberships:* Aux Rotary, Charleston, South Carolina, 1972-74; Centro Studi Scambi International Roma; United Methodist Church Women's Organizations; United Methodist Church Ministers' Wives Clubs, President 1973-74, Charleston; Community clubs. *Address:* 345 Curry Drive, Seneca, SC 29678, USA.

CURRY Richard Orr b. 26 Jan 1931, USA. Professor of History. m. 11 Feb 1968, 2 sons, 2 daughters. *Education:* BA, 1952; MA, 1956, Marshall University; PhD, University of Pennsylvania, 1961; Post Doctoral Fellow, Harvard University, 1965-66. *Publications include:* The Shaping of America, 1972; Conspiracy: The Fear of Subversion in American History, 1972; Radicalism, Racism and Party Realignment: The Border States During Reconstruction, 1973; The Abolitionists, 1985; Freedom at Risk: Secrecy, Censorship and Repression in the 1980's, 1988; An Uncertain Future: Thought Control and Repression During The Reagan-Bush Era, 1992. *Contributions to:* Journal of Southern History; Civil War History; Mid-America; Journal of the Early Republic; Ohio History, and others. *Honours:* Award of Merit, American Association of State and Local History, 1971; Senior Fulbright Lecturer, 1981; von Mises Postdoctoral Fellow, 1982-83; Distinguished Alumnus Award, 1986; H L Mencken Award, 1989; Outstanding Book Award, 1989. *Memberships include:* Organization of American Historians; Society for the Historians of the Early Republic; American Historical Association; Fulbright Association. *Address:* 106 Windham St, Willmantic, CT 06226, USA.

CURTEIS Ian Bayley, b. 1 May 1935, London, England. Playwright. m. (1) Joan Macdonald, 1964 (dissolved) 2 sons; (2) Joanna Trollope, 1985, 2 stepdaughters. *Appointments:* Director and actor in theatres all over Great Britain; BBC tv script reader 1956-63; BBC and ATV staff director (drama) 1963-67; Chairman, Committee on Censorship, Writers' Guild of Great Britain 1981-85. *Creative Works:* Television plays: Beethoven, Sir Alexander Fleming (BBC's entry at 1973 Prague Festival); Mr Rolls and Mr Royce; Long Voyage Out of War (trilogy); The Folly; The Haunting; Second Ti9me Round; A Distinct Chill; The Portland Millions; Philby, Burgess and Maclean (British entry 1978 Monte Carlo Festival, BAFTA nomination); Hess; The Atom Spies; Churchill and the Generals (BAFTA nomination, Grand Prize, Best Programme of 1980, NY International Film and TV Festival); Suez 1956 (BAFTA nomination); Miss Morrison's Ghosts (British entry 1982 Monte Carlo Festival; nomination US EMMY); The Mitford Girls; BB and Joe (trilogy); Lost Empires (adapted from J B Priestley); The Trials of Lady Sackville; Eureka (1st Euroserial, simultaneously shown in UK, West Germany, Austria, Switzerland, Italy and France); The Nightmare Years; Also originated and wrote numerous popular drama series; film screenplays: Andre Malraux's La Condition humaine, 1982; Graham Greene's The Man Within,. 1983; Tom Paine (for Sir Richard Attenborough) 1983; play: A Personal Affair, Globe 1982. Publications: plays: Long Voyage Out of War (trilogy), 1971; Churchill and the Generals, 1979; Suez 1956, 1980; The Falklands Play, 1987. *Memberships:* Royal Society of Literature; Writers' Guild of Great Britain; Garrick Club. *Address:* The Mill House, Coln St Aldwyns, Cirencester, Glos. GL7 5AJ, England.

CURTEIS Joanna (Caroline Harvey, Joanna Trollope), b. 9 Dec. 1943, Gloucestershire, England. Writer. m. Ian Curteis, 12 Apr. 1985, 2 step-sons, 2 daughters. *Education:* MA, English Language & Literature, Oxford University. *Publications:* 8 Historical Novels; 1 Historical Survey; 6 Modern Novel; Best Known Historical Novels: Eliza Stanhope, 1978; Mistaken Virtues, 1979; Leaves from the Valley, 1980; The City of Gems, 1981; The Steps of the Sun, 1983; The Taverners Place, 1986; The Choir, 1988; A Village Affair, 1989; Historical/Biography, Britannia's Daughters, 1983; The Choir, 1988; A Village Affair, 1989; A Passionate Man, 1990; The Rector's Wife, 1991; The Men and the Girls, 1992; A Spanish Lover, 1992. *Contributions To:* Books reviews for Books Magazine; Daily Telegraph; Channel Four; Evening Standard. Introductions to reprints of Anthony Trollope; articles for Harpers and Queen, Options. *Honours:* Romantic Historical Novel of the Year, with Parson Harding's Daughter, 1980. *Memberships:* PEN; Trollope Society, Committee; Society of Authors. *Literary Agent:* Pat Kavanagh of A.D. Peters.

CURTIS Anthony Samuel, b. 12 Mar 1926, London, England. Journalist. m. Sarah, 3 Oct 1960, 3 sons. *Education:* Midhurst Grammar School, 1940-44; BA (Inter MA) 1st Class Hons, English, Chancellor's Prize for an English Essay, Oxford University, Merton College, 1948-50; US Harkness Fellowship in Journalism, 1958-59. *Literary Appointments:* Deputy Editor, Times Literary Supplement), 1959-60; Literary Editor, Sunday Telegraph, 1960-70; Literary Editor, Financial Times, 1970-90. *Publications:* The Pattern of Maugham, 1974; Somerset Maugham: The Critical Heritage (with John Whitehead), 1987. *Contributions to:* Times Literary Supplement; Financial Times; BBC Radio 3 and 4. *Honour:* Fellow, Royal Society of Arts. *Memberships:* Treasurer, Royal Literary Fund; Trustee, Society of Authors Pension Fund; Garrick Club; Travellers; Beefsteak. *Literary Agent:* A M Heath. *Address:* 9 Essex Villas, London W8 7BP, England.

CURTIS Jack, b. 4 Jan 1922, Lincoln Center, Kansas, USA. Writer. m. LaVonn Renaas, 7 Sept 1949, 3 sons, 1 daughter. *Education:* US University, CA, Fresno, BA, 1941. *Publications:* The Kloochman; Banjo; Eagles Over Big Sur; Red Knife Valley; The Sheriff Kill; Texas Rules; Jury on Smoky Hill; Blood Cut; Paradise Valley; Poetry inc. Cool Of A Kansas; Arctic Circle. *Contributions to:* Various. *Memberships:* Western Writers of America. *Literary Agent:* Ben Kemsler. *Address:* Apple Pie Ranch Hwy 1, Big Sur, CA 93920, USA.

CURTIS Sharon, (Laura London), b. 6 Mar 1951, Dahran, Saudi Arabia. Writer. m. Thomas Dale Curtis, 1970, 2 children. *Education:* University of Wisconsin-Madison. *Publications:* A Heart Too Proud; The Bad Baron's Daughter, 1978; Moonlight Mist, 1979; Love's a Stage, 1980; The Gypsy Heiress, 1981; The Windflower, 1984; Sunshine and Shadow, 1986; Keepsake, 1987, (all with Thomas Dale Curtis).

CURTIS Susannah. *See:* UPSHALL Helen Ruby.

CURTIS Thomas Dale, b. 11 Nov 1952, Antigo, Wisconsin, USA. Writer. m. Sharon, 1970, 2 children. *Education:* Attended University of Wisconsin - Madison. *Career:* Writer; Worked as a professional musician and actor. *Publications:* Romance novels with wife, Sharon Curtis, under joint pseudonym Laura London: A Heart Too Proud, 1978; The Bad Baron's Daughter, 1978; Moonlight Mist, 1979; Love's a Stage, 1980; The Gypsy Heiress, 1981; The Windflower, 1984; Under name Tom Curtis, with Sharon Curtis, Sunshine and Shadow, 1986; Keepsake, 1987.

CURTIS Wade. *See:* POURNELLE Jerry (Eugene).

CURZON Claire. *See:* BUCHANAN Elllen Marie (Duell).

CURZON Lucia. *See:* STEVENSON Florence.

CURZON-BROWN Daniel, b. Litchfield, Illinois, USA. Writer; Professor. 1 son. *Education:* PhB, University of Detroit, 1960; MA, Kent State University, 1971; PhD, Wayne State University, 1969. *Appointments:* Currently Bay Area Theatre Critics Circle, San Francisco, California. *Publications:* Something You Do in the Dark, 1971; The Revolt of the Parents, 1978; Human Warmth and Other Stories, 1981; The Joyful Blue Book of Gay Etiquette, 1982; The World Can Break Your Heart, 1984; Curzon in Love, 1988. *Contributions to:* Colorado Quarterly; North American Review. *Membership:* American Association of Composers, Authors and Publishers. *Literary Agent:* Jeffrey Simmons, London, England. *Address:* 416 Dorado Terrace, San Francisco, CA 94112, USA.

CUSHMAN Dan, b. 1909, USA. Freelance Writer; Journalist; Former Mining Prospector, Assayer and Geologist. *Publications:* Montana, Here I Be, 1950; Badlands Justice, 1951; Naked Ebony, 1951; Jewel of the Java Sea, 1951; The Ripper from Rawhide, 1952; Savage Interlude, 1952; Stay Away, Joe, 1953; Timberjack, 1953; Jungle She, 1953; The Fabulous Finn, 1954; Tongking, 1954; Port Orient, 1955; The Fastest Gun, 1955; The Old Copper Collar, 1957; The Silver Mountain, 1957; Tall Wyoming, 1957; The Forbidden Land, 1958; Goodbye, Old Dry, 1959, Paperback Edition The Con Man, 1960; The Half-Caste, 1960; Brothers in Kickapoo, 1962, UK Edition Boomtown, US Paperback On the Make, 1963; 4 for Texas, novelisation of screenplay, 1963; The Grand and the Glorious, 1963; Opium Flower, 1963; North Fork to Hell, 1964; The Great North Trail: America's Route of the Ages, non-fiction, 1966; The Long Riders, 1967; Cow Country Cook Book, non-fiction, 1967; Montana: The Gold Frontier, non-fiction, 1975; The Muskrat Farm, 1977; Rusty Iron, 1984. *Address;* Box 2054, Great Falls, MT 69403, USA.

CUSSLER Clive (Eric), b. 15 July 1931, USA. Author. m. Barbara Knight, 28 Aug 1955. 3 children. *Appointments:* Served in USAF, 1950-54; Owner, Bestgen & Cussler Advertising, Newport Beach, California, 1961-65; Creative Director, Darcy Advertising, Hollywood, California, 1965-67; Advertising Director, Aquatic Marine Corporation, New Port Beach, 1967-69; Vice-President, Creative Director of Broadcast, Mefford, Wolff & Weir Advertising, Denver, Colorado, 1970-. *Publications:* The Mediterranean Caper, 1973; Iceberg, 1975; Raise the Titanic, 1976; Vixen O-Three, 1978; Night Probe, 1981; Pacific Vortex, 1982; Deep Six, 1984; Cyclops, 1986, Treasure, 1988, Dragon, 1990; Shara, 1992. *Honours:* Recipient numerous advt. awards; Fellow Explorers Club (Lowell Thomas Explorers award). *Memberships:* Royal Geog. Soc; Chairman, National Underwater & Marine Agency.

CUTLER David Wales, b. 14 Sept 1956 Manhattan, KS, USA. Writer; Editor; Publishing & Communications Consultant. m. Laurie Alderman, 30 July 1984, 2 d. *Education:* Carleton College, BA, 1978; University of Virginia, MA, 1979. *Appointments:* Publishing Director, Cultural Alliance of Greater Washington, 1981-82; Communications Manager, Washington Convention & Visitors Association, 1983-84; President, David Cutler & Associates, 1984-92; Managing Director, Novis Communications Group, 1993-. *Publications:* Literary Washington: A Complete Guide to the Literary Life in the Nation's Capital. *Contributions to:* Numerous articles in local & national magazines. *Memberships:* Washington Independent Writers; Momus Society; Judeo-Christian Society for the Promulgation of Holiday Cheer. *Address:* 2960 Chain Bridge Road (110), Oakton, VA 22124, USA.

CZERKAWSKA Catherine Lucy, b. 3 Dec 1950, Leeds, England. Full Time Writer. m. Alan Lees, 10 Oct 1985, 1 son. *Education:* MA, Edinburgh University, 1972; MA, Leeds University, 1974. *Appointments:* Community Writer, 1979-80; Creative Writing Tutor. *Publications:* The Golden Apple; Shadow of the Stone; A Book of Men. *Honours:* SAC Grant & New Writing Award; Pye award for Best Play; Scottish Arts Council Major Bursary. *Memberships:* Writers Guild; Society of Authors; PEN. *Literary Agent:* Peters Fraser & Dunlop. *Address:* c/o Peters Fraser & Dunlop, The Chambers, Lots Road, Chelsea Harbour, London SW10 0XF.

CZIGANY Lorant Gyorgy, b. 3 June 1935, Hungary. m. Magda Salacz, 28 Sept 1957, 1 daughter. *Education:* University of Szeged, 1954-56; University of Oxford, 1957-58; University of London, BA, 1958-60; PhD, 1960-64. *Appointments:* Szepsi Csombor Literary Circle, 1965-88; Editor, Atelier Hongrois, Paris, 1974; Minister, Plenipotentiary for Cultural Affairs, 1990-92. *Publications:* The Oxford History of Hungarian Literature; The Reception of Hungarian Literature in Victorian England; The Origins of state Control of Hungarian Literature; The Bela Ivanyi Grunwald Collection of Hungarica. *Contributions to:* The Times; BBC Overseas Service; Outside Contributor. *Memberships:* Szepsi Csombor Literary Circle; International Association of Hungarian Studies. *Address:* 15 Temple Fortune Lane, London NW11 7UB, England.

D

D'ALFONSO Antonio, b. 6 Aug 1953, Publisher; Writer. m. 8 Sept 1990. *Education:* BA; MSc. *Publications:* Julia; Panick Love; Avril ov L'Anti-passion; L'Amour Panique; L'Autre Rivage; The Other Shore; Black Tongue; Queror; La Chanson du Shaman à Sedna. *Contributions to:* The Gazette. *Memberships:* Various. *Literary Agent:* Guernica Editions. *Address:* PO Box 633, Station N DG, Montreal, Canada H4A 3R1.

DA SILVA Leon. *See:* **WALLMAN Jeffrey M** .

DABYDEEN Cyril, b. 15 Oct 1945, Guyana. Writer. m. 6 June 1989, 1 daughter. *Education:* Lakehead University, 1973; Queens University, Ontario, 1974; Master of Public Administration, 1975. *Appointments:* League of Canadian Poets. *Publications:* Distances, 1977; Goatsong, 1977; This Planet Earth, 1980; Still Close to the Island, 1980; (ed) A Shapely Fire: Changing the Literary Landscape, 1987; Islands Lovelier than a Vision, 1988; The Wizard Swami, 1989; Dark Swirl, 1989; Jogging In Havana, 1992; (ed) Another Way to Dance: Asian-Canadian Poetry, 1992. *Contributions to:* The Canadian Forum; The Canadian Fiction Magazine; The Fiddlehead; The Dalhousie Review; Quarry; Grain; Waves; The Antigonish Review; Canadian Author & Bookman; The Toronto South Asian Review; Journal of South Asian Literature; Kunapipi; Wascana Review; The Literary Review; The Globe & Mail; Kyk-over-al; The Caribbean Quarterly. *Honours:* Sandback Parker Gold Medal; A J Seymour Lyric Poetry Prize; Poet Laureate of Ottawa. *Memberships:* Canadian Association of Commonwealth Language & Literature Studies. *Address:* 106 Blackburn, Ottawa, Canada, KIN 8A7.

DABYDEEN David, b. 9 Dec 1956, Writer; Academic. *Education:* Cambridge University, BA, 1974-78; London University, PhD, 1978-82. *Appointments:* Literature Panel, Arts Council of Great Britain, 1985- 89. *Publications:* The Intended; Slave Song; Coolie Odyssey; Hogarths Blacks; Hogarth, Walpole And Commercial Britain. *Contributions to:* New Statesman; Guardian. *Honours:* Sir Authur Quiller Couch Prize; Commonwealth Poetry Prize. *Literary Agent:* Xandra Hardie. *Address:* c/o Centre for Caribbean Studies, University of Warwick, Coventry CV4 7AL, England.

DAFTARY Farhad, b. 23 Dec 1938, Brussels, Belgium. Academic. m. Fereshteh Kashanchi, Feb 1980, 1 daughter. *Education:* BA, The American University, 1962; MA, 1964; MA, University of California, 1966; PhD, 1971. *Appointments:* Lecturer, Tehran University, 1972-73; Lecturer, National University, Tehran, 1973-74; Professor, The Institute of Ismaili Studies, London, 1988-. *Publications:* The Ismailis: Their History & Doctrines; The Assassin Legends; A Short History of the Ismailis; Essays in Ismaili History & Thought. *Contributions to:* Islamic Culture; Arabica; Iran; Studia Islamica; Encyclopaedia Iranica; Encyclopaedia of Islam. *Memberships:* American Oriental Society; British Institute of Persian Studies; British Society for Middle Eastern Studies; Society for Iranian Studies. *Address:* 77 Hamilton Terrace, London NW8, England.

DAHL Arlene, b. 11 Aug 1928, USA. Actress; Author; Designer. m. Marc A Rosen, 30 July 1984, 2 sons, 1 daughter. *Education:* University of Minnesota; Minneapolis College of Music. *Publications:* 17 books on Beauty, Health, Fashion and Astrology including: Always Ask a Man, 1965; Your Beautyscope (series of 12), 1968, revised 1978; Arlene Dahls' Secrets of Haircare, 1970; Arlene Dahl's Secrets of Skin Care, 1972; Beyond Beauty, 1980; Lovescopes, 1983; Internationally Syndicated Beauty Column, Lets Be Beautiful, Chicago Tribune/New York News Syndicate, 1950-1970. *Contributions to:* Girl Talk; Woman's World; Good Housekeeping; Woman's Own, (England); Family Circle; Parade; The Best (Europe); Jupiter Magazine; Soap Opera Digest; Arlene Dahl's Lucky Stars, Globe Communications, 1988-90; Arlene Dahl's Astrological Forecast, 1990-93, 1994 in progress. *Honours:* Award: Love's Leading Astrologer (Romantic Times book convention 1985). *Memberships:* Academy of Motion Picture Arts & Sciences, (New York Screening Committee); Academy of Television Arts & Sciences, (Board of Governors); IPA. *Literary Agent:* Mitch Douglas, ICM, New York. *Address:* PO Box 116, Sparkill, New York, NY 10976, USA.

DAICHES David, b. 2 Sept 1912, Sunderland, England. Emeritus Professor; Writer. m. Isobel Janet Mackay, 28 July 1937, 1 son, 2 daughters. *Education:* MA, Edinburgh University, 1934; D.Phil, Oxford, 1939; Honorary Degrees: Brown University; University Sorbonne; Edinburgh University; Sussex University; Glasgow University; Stirling University; Bologna University; Guelph University. *Appointments:* Fellow Balliol College, Oxford, 1936-37; Assistant Professor English, University of Chicago, 1939-43; Professor, Cornell University, 1946-51; University Lecturer, Cambridge 1951-61; Fellow Jesus College, Cambridge, 1957-62; Professor, University of Sussex, 1961-77; Director, Institute Advanced Studies, University of Edinburgh, 1980-86. *Publications include:* A Critical History of English Literature, 1960; Two Worlds, 1956; The Novel and the Modern World, 1960; Robert Burns, 1950; The Paradox of Scottish Culture, 1964; God and the Poets, 1984; Edinburgh: A Travellers Companion, 1986; A Wee Drum, 1990. *Honours:* FRSL, 1957; Scottish Arts Council Book Award, 1973; FRSE, 1980; Scottish Book of the Year Award, 1984; CBE, 1991. *Memberships:* Association for Scottish Literary Studies, Honorary President; Saltire Society, President, Honorary President; Modern Language Society of America, Honorary Member. *Literary Agent:* David Higham Associates. *Address:* 12 Rothesay Place, Edinburgh EH3 7SQ, Scotland.

DAISY Vivienne. *See:* **KENYON Bruce Guy.**

DALE Celia Marjorie, b. London. Author; Literary Consultant. m. Guy Ramsey, 30 Oct 1938, 1 son. *Publications:* 14 novels including: A Helping Hand; Act of Love; A Dark Corner; The Innocent Party; Helping with Inquiries; A Personal Call (short stories); Sheeps Clothing. *Memberships:* Crime Writers' Association. *Literary Agent:* Curtis Brown, London. *Address:* 25 Nuffield Lodge, 22 Shepherds Hill, London N6 5UZ, England.

DALE Margaret Jessy, (Margaret J Miller), b. 27 Aug 1911, Edinburgh, Scotland. Writer. m. Clunie Rutherford Dale, 3 Sept 1938, divorced 1954, 1 son, 2 daughters. *Education:* 2nd Class Honours BA, English Language and Literature, Lady Margaret Hall, Oxford, 1933. *Literary Appointments:* Scenario Writer, Associated Screen News, Montreal, Canada, 1935-36; Assistant Editor, Shell Magazine, London 1937-39. *Publications:* The Queen's Music, 1961; The Powers of the Sapphire, 1962; The Far Castles, 1978; Emily, A Life of Emily Brontë, 1969; Knights, Beasts and Wonders, 1969; Mouse Tails, 1967; The Fearsome Road, 1975; The Fearsome Island, 1975; The Fearsome Tide, 1976. *Contributions to:* 200 scripts for Schools Broadcasting; The Times; Times Literary Supplement; Scottish Field; The Scots Magazine; Scotland's Magazine. *Memberships:* PEN; National Book League. *Literary Agent:* John Johnson. *Address:* 26 Grey's Hill, Henley, Oxon RG9 1SJ, England.

DALE Peter John, b. 21 Aug 1938, England. Writer. m. Pauline Strouvelle, 29 June 1963, 1 son, 1 daughter. *Education:* BA (Hons) English, Oxford University, 1963. *Literary Appointment:* Co-Editor, Agenda, 1972-. *Publications include:* Selected Poems François Villon (Verse translation) 1978-88; One Another Sonnet Sequence, 1978; Poems of Jules Laforgue (Verse translation), 1988; Mortal Fire: Selected Poems, 1976; Narrow Straits (Verse translation) 19th Century French, 1985; Too Much of Water (Poems 1978-82) 1983; The Divine Comedy (Targa rima version), 1993. *Contributions to:* Agenda; Chronicles (USA); Outposts;

Acumen; Le Courrier (Brussels). *Honour:* 1970 Arts Council Bursary. *Membership:* Society of Authors. *Address:* 5, Cranbourne Court, Albert Bridge Road, London SW11 4PE, England.

DALESKI H M, b. 1926. Professor of English. *Appointments:* Assistant Lecturer to Associate Professor, 1958-76, Professor of English 1976-, Chairman, Department of English, 1968-70, 1984-85, Provost, School of Overseas Students, 1973-76, Hebrew University, Jerusalem. *Publications:* The Forked Flame: A Study of D H Lawrence, 1965; Dickens and the Art of Analogy, 1970; Jospeh Conrad: The Way of Dispossession, 1977; The Divided Heroine: A Recurrent Pattern in Six English Novels, 1984; Unities: Studies in the English Novel, 1985. *Membership:* President, The Dickens Society, 1985. *Address:* Department of English, The Hebrew University, Jerusalem, Israel.

DALEY Brian Charles, (Jack McKinney), b. 22 Dec 1947, Englewood, New Jersey, USA. Writer. *Education:* Bachelor's degree (Communications), Jersey City State College, 1974. *Publications:* The Doomfarers of Coramonde, 1977; The Starfollowers of Coramonde, 1979; The Han Solo Trilogy, 1979-1980; A Tapestry of Magics; The Alacrity Fitzhugh & Hobart Floyt Trilogy, 1985-1986; The Robotyech Series (1-18) (with Janes Luceno) under pseudonym Jack McKinney, 1987-89; Novelization: Tron, 1982; Radio serial adpations: Star Wards, The Empire Stricks Back. TV Scripts: Galaxy Rangers. *Membership:* Science Fiction Writers of America. *Address:* c/o Ballantine del Rey Books, 201c 50th Street, New York City, NY 10022, USA.

DALEY Robert (Blake), b. 1930. America, Photographer; Writer. *Appointments:* Publicity Director, New York Giants, 1953-58; Foreign and War Correspondent in Europe and North Africa, New York Times, 1959-64; Deputy Commissioner, New York Police Department, 1971-72; Photographs exhibited at Baltimore Museum, Art Institute of Chicago and New York Gallery of Modern Art, 1968-69. *Publications:* The World Beneath the City, 1959; Cars at Speed 1961; The Bizarre World of European Sports, 1963; The Cruel sport, 1963; The Swords of Spain, 1965; The Whole Truth, 1967; Only a Game, 1967; A Priest and a Girl, 1969; A Star in the Family, 1971; Target Blue, 1973; Strong Wine Red as Blood, 1974; To Kill a Cop, 1976; Treasure, 1977; The Fast One, 1978; Prince of the City, 1979; An American Saga, 1980; Year of the Dragon, 1981; The Dangerous Edge, 1983.

DALLAS Ruth. *See:* MUMFORD Ruth.

DALLY Ann Gwendolen, (Mrs Egerton), b. 29 Mar 1926, London, England. Medical Practitioner (Psychiatry) m. (1) Peter Dally, 1950, 3 sons, (1 dec), 2 daughters, (2) Philip Egerton, 1979. *Edcuation:* BA, 1946; MA, 1950, Somerville College, Oxford; MB, BS, 1953; DObst, RCOG, 1955,. St. Thomas's Hospital, London. *Publications include:* Inventing Motherhood, 1982; A Doctors Story, 1990; Mothers: Their Power and Influence, 1975; Women Under The Knife, 1991. *Contributions to:* numerous articles in journals and magazines. *Memberships:* Royal Society of Medicine, Fellow; Association of Independent Doctors, President; Action Needed Now, President. *Literary Agent:* Jane Hall Literary Agency. *Address:* 13 Devonshire Place, London W1N 1PB, England.

DALMAS John, b. 3 Sept 1926, Chicago, Illinois, USA. Author. m. Gail Hill, 15 Sept 1954, 1 son, 1 daughter. *Education:* BSc, Michigan State College, 1954; Master of Forestry, University of Minnesota, 1955; PhD, Colorado State Univerity, 1967. *Publications:* 18 Science Fiction Novels: The Yngling, 1969, 1971, 1977, 1984, 1987; The Varkaus Conspiracy, 1983, 1987; Touch the Stars: Emergence, with Carl Martin, 1983; Homecoming, 1984; The Scroll of Man, 1985; Fanglith, 1985, 1987; The Reality Matrix, 1986; The Walkaway Clause, 1986; The Regiment,

1987, 1989; The Playmasters (w Rodney Martin), 1987; Return to Fanglith, 1987; The Lantern of God, 1987; The General's President, 1988; The Lizard War, 1989; The White Regiment, 1990; The Kalif's War, 1991; The Yngling and the Circle of Power, 1992; The Orc Wars (collection), 1992; The Regiments of War, 1993. *Contributions to:* various journals and magazines including: Analog; Saint Magazine; 1985 Annual World's Best SF; Science Fiction Yearbook, 1985; Far Frontiers III, IV, V, VI; Magazine of Fantasy & Science Fiction. *Honours:* Xi Sigma Pi, Forestry Honorary Society, 1953; Phi Kappa Phi, Scholastic Honorary Society, 1954; Sigma Xi, Scientific Research Society, 1963. *Memberships:* Science Fiction Writers of America; Vasa Order of America. *Address:* West 1425 Glass Street, Spokane, WA 99205, USA.

DALTON Annie, b. 18 Jan 1948, Weymouth, England. Writer. div, 1 son, 2 daughters. *Education:* Upper 2nd, English and American Literature, University of Warwick, 1967-70. *Publications:* Nightmaze; The After Dark Princess; The Real Tilly Beany; The Alpha Box; Swan Sister; The Witch Rose; Demon Spawn; Out of the Ordinary; Naming the Dark, 1992. *Honours:* East Midlands Arts Bursary, 1987; Winner, Nottingham Oak Children's Book Award, 1991; Commended for Carnegie, 1992. *Literary Agent:* Elizabeth Stevens, Curtis Brown. *Address:* 13 Selbourne Street, Loughborough, Leics LE11 1BS, England.

DALTON Pricilla. *See:* AVALLONE Michael.

DALY Christopher, b. 7 July 1954, Boston, Massachusetts, USA. England Correspondent for the Washington Post; Free-lance magazine writer. m. Anne K Fishel, 1982; 2 sons. *Education:* BA, magna cum laude, Harvard University, 1976; MA, University of North Carolina at Chapel Hill, 1982. *Appointments:* Writer and Editor, Associated Press, New York, 1976-80; State House Reporter 1982-87, State House Bureau Chief, 1987-89, Associated Press, Boston. *Publications:* With Jacqueline D Hall, Bob Korstad, Lu Ann Jones and others, Like a Family: The Making of a Southern Cotton Mill World, 1987; Author of a magazine column on politics, under a pseudonym. *Honours:* Shared Merle Curti Prize from Organization of American Historians, 1988 for Like a Family. *Memberships:* Wire Service Guild, American Federation of Labor-Congress of Industrial Organizations, Penultimate Society. *Address:* Associated Press, 184 High Street, Boston, MA 02110, USA.

DALY Maureen (Maureen Daly McGivern), Journalist; Writer. *Appointments:* Police Reporter and Columnist, Chicago Tribune, 1946-48; Associate Editor, Ladies' Home Journal, Philadelphia, 1948-54; Editorial Consultant, Saturday Evening Post, Philadelphia, 1960-69. *Publications:* Seventeenth Summer, 1942; Smarter and Smoother: A Handbook on How to Be That Way, 1944; The Perfect Hostess: Complete Etiquette and Entertainment for the Home, 1948; (ed)My Favorite Stories, 1948; (ed) Profile of Youth, 1951; What's Your PQ (Personality Quotient)? 1952; Twelve Around the World, 1957; (as Maureen Daly McGivern with William P McGivern) Mention My Name in Mombasa: The Unscheduled Adventures of and American Family Abroad, 1958; Patrick series, 4 vols, 1959-63; Spanish Roundabout, 1960; Moroccan Roundabout, 1961; Sixteen and Other Stories, 1961; The Ginger Horse, 1964; (ed) My Favorite Mystery Stories, 1966; The Small War of Sergeant Donkey, 1966; Rosie: The Dancing Elephant, 1967; (ed) My Favorite Suspense Stories, 1968; (with William McGivern) The Seeing, 1981; Acts of Love, 1986; Promises to Keep, 1987. *Contributions to:* The Desert Sun. *Memberships:* Authors' League; Writers Guild of America; West; Society of Professional Journalists; Mystery Writers of America. *Address:* 73-305 Ironwood Street, Palm Desert, CA 92260, USA.

DALY Niki, b. 13 June 1946, Cape Town, South Africa. Writer; Illustrator; Editor. m. 7 July 1973, 2 sons. *Education:* Diploma in Art and Design, 1969, Cape Town

Technikon. *Literary Appointments:* Publisher; Head of Songololo Books (A division of David Philip Publishers, Cape Town). *Publications include:* Not So Fast Songololo; Charlie's House; The Little Girl Who Lived Down the Road; Vim the Rag Mouse; Story Time Series for Walker Books; Joseph's Other Red Sock. *Honours:* The Little Girl Who Lived Down the Road - 1978 Provisional Booksellers/British Arts Council Award; Not So Fast Songololo, 1986, USA Parents Choice Award and 1987 (SA) Katrien Harries Award. *Literary Agent:* Laura Cecil. *Address:* 36 Strubens Road, Mowbray, 7700 Cape Town, South Africa.

DALY Patricia. *See:* **BRENNAN Patricia Winifred.**

DALY MCGIVERN Maureen. *See:* **DALY Maureen.**

DANA Robert (Patrick), b. 1929, America. Professor of English; Poet. *Appointments:* Joined Faculty 1953, Professor of English 1968-, Cornell College, Mount Vernon, Iowa, USA; Contributing Editor, American Poetry Review 1971-, New Letters 1980-; Editor, Hillside Press, 1957-67 and North American Review 1964-68, Mount Vernon, Iowa. *Publications:* My Glass Brother and Other Poems, 1957; The Dark Flags of Waking, 1964; Journeys from the Skin: A Poem in Two Parts, 1966; Some Versions of Silence: Poems, 1967; The Power of the Visible, 1971; In a Fugitive Season, 1980; What the Stones Know, 1984; Blood Harvest, 1986; Against the Grain: Interviews with Maverick American Publishers, 1986; Starting Out for the Difficult World, 1987; What I Think I Know: New & Selected Poems, 1990. *Address:* Department of English, Cornell College, Mount Vernon, IA 52314, USA.

DANBY Mary, (Mary Calvert, Simon Reed, Andy Stevens), b. 1941. Writer; Consultant Editor. *Appointments:* Television Production Assistant, 1962-69; Fiction Editor, Fontana Books, London 1969-72; Consultant Editor, Armada Books, London, 1973-. *Publications:* as Mary Danby: (ed) Fontana Books of Great Horror Stories, 5-15, 1970-82; (with D Dickens), The Armada Quiz and Puzzle Book, 1-8, 1970-80; (ed) The Armada Ghost Book, 3-14, 1970-82; (ed) The Armada Book of Fun, 1-3, 1971-75; A Single Girl, 1972; (ed) The Armada Book of Cartoons, 1-3 1972-77; Fun on Wheels, 1973; (ed) Frighteners 1-2, 1974-76; The Best of Friends, 1975; (ed) The Armada Book of Christmas Fun, 1975; (ed) The Armada Book of Limericks, 1-2, 1977-78; (ed) 65 Great Tales of the Supernatural, 1979; (ed) The Awful (Even More Awful, Most Awful), Joke Book, 3 vols 1979-84; (with Jane Allen), Hello to Ponies, 1979; (with Jane Allen), Hello to Riding, 1980; (ed) The Armada Funny Story Book, 1980; (with C Bostock-Smith), Metal Mickey's Boogie Book, 1981; (ed) 65 Great Tales of Horror (and Terror), 2 vols 1981-82; (ed) The Funniest Fun Book, 1984; (ed) The Batty Book and Cartoon Book, 2 vols, 1985-86; How Trivial Can You Get? 1986; as Mary Calvert: Turnip Tom and Big Fat Rosie, 1972; The Big Fat Rosie Storybook, 1977; as Andy Stevens: (with E Sticklee), World of Stars, 1980; as Simon Reed: (with D Dickens) Quick Quiz, 1981. *Address:* Noakes Hill Cottage, Ashampstead, Berks. RH8 8RY, England.

DANCE Stanley, b. 1910, Britain. Reviewer. *Appointments:* Reviewer, Jazz Journal, London 1948-93, The Saturday Review, New York City, 1962-72, and Music Journal, New York City, 1962-79; Reviewer, Jazz Times, Washington, DC, 1980-. *Publications:* (ed)Jazz Era, 1961; (with D Wells), The Night People, 1971; The World of Duke Ellington, 1970; The World of Swing, 1974; The World of Earl Hines, 1977; (with M Ellington), Duke Ellington in Person, 1978; The World of Count Basie, 1980; (with Charlie Barnet), Those Swinging Years, 1984. *Address:* 1745 Bittersweet Hill, Vista, CA 92084, USA.

DANE Mark. *See:* **AVALLONE Michael.**

DANIEL Colin. *See:* **WINDSOR Patricia.**

DANIEL Wayne Wendell, b. 14 Feb 1929, Georgia, USA. m. Mary Yarbrough, 2 June 1956, 1 son, 2 daughters. *Education:* BS, University of Georgia, 1951; MPH, University of North Carolina, 1959; PhD, University of Oklahoma, 1965. *Publications:* Business Statistics; Biostatistics; Applied Nonparametric Statistics; Essentials of Business Statistics; Introductory Statistics with Applications; Pickin On Peachtree; A History of Country Music in Atlanta. *Contributions to:* More than 100 Articles. *Memberships:* American Statistical Association; American public Health Association. *Address:* 2943 Appling Drive, Chamblee, GA 30341, USA.

DANIELS Dorothy, (Danielle Dorsett, Angela Gray, Cynthia Kavanaugh, Helaine Ross, Suzanne Somers, Geraldine Thayer, Helen Gray Weston), b. 1 July 1915, Waterbury, USA. Writer. m. 7 Oct. 1937. *Publications include:* numerous Romantic Fiction books, most recent being: The Magic Ring, 1978; Purple and the Gold, 1978; Yesterday's Evil, 1980; Veil of Treachery, 1980; Legend of Death, 1980; Valley of Shadows, 1980 Monte Carlo, 1981; Saratoga, 1981; Sisters of Valcour, 1981; For Love and Valcous, 1983; Crisis at Valcour, 1985. *Honours:* National Honorary Member, National League of American Pen Women. *Memberships:* Authors' Guild; National League of American Pen Women; Ventura Country Writers'. *Literary Agent:* Richard Curtis Asosciates, New York, USA. *Address:* 6107 Village 6, Camarillo, CA 93010, USA.

DANIELS Mary, b. 1937, America. Feature Writer and Columnist. *Appointment:* Feature Writer and Columnist, Chicago Tribune, 1969-. *Publications:* Morris: An Intimate Biography: The Nine Lives of Morris the Cat, 1974; Cat Astrology, 1976; Dressage For The New Age, (with Dominique Barbier), 1990; (ed) Robert Vaura's Classic Book of Horses, 1992. *Address:* Chicago Tribune, 435 N Michigan Avenue, Chicago, IL 60611, USA.

DANIELS Max. *See:* **GELLIS Roberta Leach.**

DANIELS Molly Ann, (Shouri Daniels), b. 2 July 1932, Kerala, India. Writer; Teacher; Editor. 1 son, 1 daughter. *Education includes:* PhD, University of Chicago's Committee on Social Thought, 1986. *Appointments* Director, The Clothesline School of Writing, Chicago, Illinois, 1984-. *Publications:* Fiction: The Yellow Fish, 1966; The Salt Doll, 1978; The City of Children, 1986; The Prophetic Novel: A Study of A Passage to India, criticism, 1990; The Clotheslines Review, 4 issues of anthology of fiction (editor), 1986-90; Father Gander Rhymes and Other Poems (editor), 1990; The Clothesline Review Manual for Writers, textbook. *Contributions to:* Indian PEN; Quest; Femina; The Chicago Review; Primavera; The Carleton Miscellany; Tri-Quarterly; Journal of Literary Studies; The Saul Bellow Journal. *Honours:* Fulbright-Smith Mundt, 1961-62; Illinois Arts Council Fiction, 1978; Illinois Arts Council Criticism, 1982; Syndicated Fiction Award, PEN. *Membership:* Midwest Authors. *Literary agent:* Jane Jordan Browne. *Address:* The Clothesline School of Writing, Department of Continuing Education, University of Chicago, 5835 S Kimbark, Chicago, IL 60637, USA.

DANIELS Norman. *See:* **LEE Elsie.**

DANIELS Olga. *See:* **SINCLAIR Olga Ellen.**

DANIELS Shouri. *See:* **DANIELS Molly Ann.**

DANKOVA Jana. *See:* **TANSKA Natalie.**

DANN Colin Michael, b. 10 Mar 1943, Richmond, Surrey. Author. m. Janet Elizabeth Stratton, 4 June, 1977. *Education:* Shene County Grammar School. *Publications:* The Animals of Farthing Wood, 1979; In the Grip of Winter, 1981; Fox's Feud, 1982; The Fox

Cub Bold, 1983; The Seige of White Deer Park, 1985; The Ram of Sweetriver, 1986; King of the Vagabonds, 1987; The Beach Dogs, 1988; The Flight from Farthing Wood, 1988; Just Nuffin, 1989; In the Path of the Storm, 1989; A Great Escape, 1990; A Legacy of Ghosts, 1991; The City Cats, 1991; Battle for the Park, 1992. *Honour:* Arts Council National Award for Children's Literature, 1980. *Memberships:* Society of Authors. *Address:* The Old Forge, Whatlington, Battle, East Sussex, England.

DANN Jack, b. 15 Feb 1945, Johnson City, USA. Author. m. Jeanne Van Buren Dann, *Education:* BA, State Univerity of New York, Binghamton, 1968. *Publications:* Wandering Stars, editor, 1974; Novels: Starhiker, 1977; Time Tipping, 1980 (Coll); Junction, 1981; The Man Who Melted, 1984; In the Field of Fire, Editor with wife, 1987; The Work of Jack Dann, by Jeffrey M Elliot. *Contributions to:* New Dimensions; Orbit; New Worlds; Asimov's Science Fiction Magazine; Fiction Writers Handbook; many others. *Honours:* Nebula Award Finalist, 1973, 1975, 1978, 1979, 1981, (in 2 categories) 1983, 1984, 1985; Esteemed Knight (Hon. Member), Mark Twain Society, 1975-; British Science Fiction Association Award Finalist, 1979; World Fantasy Award Finalist, 1981, 1984, 1987; Winner (with Gardner Dozois) Gilgamesh Award, 1986, (Spanish Language Award). *Memberships:* Judge, Nebula Award Rules Committee, 1980;Science Fiction Writers of America; Authors Guild; World Future Society. *Literary Agent:* John Schaffner Agency, New York. *Address:* 825 Front Street, Binghamton, NY 13905, USA.

DARBY Catherine. *See:* PETERS Maureen.

DARBY (Henry) Clifford, Sir, b. 7 Feb 1909, Resolven, West Glamorgan, Wales. Emeritus Professor of Geography. m. Eva Constance Thomson, 26 Dec 1941. 2 daughters. *Education:* BA 1928, PhD 1931, MA 1932, St Catharine's College, Cambridge. *Literary Appointments:* Lecturer in Geography, 1931-45, Professor of Geography, 1966-76, University of Cambridge; Fellow, King's College, Cambridge, 1932-45, 1966-81; Professor of Geography, University of Liverpool, 1945-49; Professor of Geography, University College London, 1949-66. *Publications:* An Historical Geography of England, Editor; The Medieval Fenland; The Draining of the Fens; The Changing Fenland; A New Historical Geography of England, Editor; The Domesday Geography of England, 7 volumes, Editor and Contributor; The University Atlas, (with Harold Fullard); The New Cambridge Modern History Atlas (with Harold Fullard). *Contributions to:* Geography Journal; Econ History Review; Journal of Historical Geography. *Honours:* OBE, 1946; CBE 1978; Kt, 1988; Honorary Doctorates: Chicago, 1967; Liverpool, 1968; Durham, 1970; Hull, 1975; Ulster, 1977; Wales, 1979; London, 1987; Victoria Medal, Royal Geographical Society, 1963; Daly Medal, American Geographical Society, 1963; Honours Award, Association of American Geographers, 1977. *Memberships:* FBA, 1967. *Address:* 60 Storey's Way, Cambridge CB3 0DX, England.

DARBY John, b. 18 Nov 1940, Belfast, Northern Ireland. University Professor. m. Marie, 13 Apr 1966, 2 sons. *Education:* BA, Honours, Modern History, 1962; HDipEd, 1970; DPhil, Ulster, 1985. *Appointments:* Editorial Board, International Journal of Group Tensions; Editorial Committee, Cahier du Centre Irelandaises, Paris, 1982. *Publications:* Conflict in Northern Ireland, 1976; Violence and Social Services in Northern Ireland, 1978; Northern Ireland: Background to the Conflict, 1983; Dressed to Kill: Cartoonists and Northern Irish Conflict, 1983; Intimidation and the Control of Conflict in Northern Ireland, 1986; Political Violence: Ireland in a Comparative Perspective, 1990. *Address:* 17 Lever Road, Portstewart, Co. Derry, Northern Ireland.

DARCY Clare, b. America. Writer of Historical/ Romance/Gothic Books. *Publications:* Georgina, 1971; Cecily, or A Young Lady of Quality, 1972; Lydia, or Love in Town, 1973; Victoire, 1974; Allegra, 1975; Lady Pamela, 1975; Regina, 1976; Elyza, 1976; Cressida,

1977; Eugenia, 1977; Gwendolen, 1978; Rolande, 1978; Letty, 1980; Caroline and Julia, 1982. *Address:* c/o Walker & Co, 720 Fifth Avenue, New York, NY 10019, USA.

DARDIS Thomas A, b. 19 Aug 1926, New York, New York, USA, Writer; Teacher. *Education:* BA 1949; MA, 1952; PhD, 1980. *Publications:* Some Time in the Sun, 1976; Keaton, 1979; Harold Lloyd, 1983; The Thirsty Muse, 1989; Keaton, The Man Who Wouldn't Lie Down, 1989. *Contributions to:* American Film; Journal of Popular Film and Television; Resources for American Literary Study. *Membership:* PEN. *Literary Agent:* George Borichardt.

DARKE Marjorie Sheila, b. 25 Jan 1929. Writer. m. 1952, 2 sons, 1 daughter. *Education:* Worcester Grammar School for Girls, 1938-47; Leicester College of Art, 1947-50; Central School of Art, London, 1950-1951; Diploma in Textile Design/Printing, 1949. *Publications:* For young adults: Ride the Iron Horse, 1973; The Star Trap, 1974; A Question of Courage, 1975; The First of Midnight, 1977; A Long Way to Go, 1978; Comeback, 1981, (trilogy); Tom Post's Private Eye, 1982; Messages and Other Shivery Tales, 1984; A Rose From Blighty, 1990. For Beginner Readers: Mike's Bike, 1974; What Can I Do, 1975; The Big Brass Band, 1976; My Uncle Charlie, 1977; Carnival Day, 1979. For young children: Kipper's Turn, 1976; Kipper Skips, 1979; Imp, 1985; The Rainbow Sandwich, 1989; Night Windows, 1990; Emma's Monster, 1992. *Honours:* Runner-Up, Guardian Award for Children's Books, 1978, for The First of Midnight. *Memberships:* Society of Authors, Committee Member, Children's Writers Group, 1980-1983; International PEN. *Literary Agent:* Rogers, Coleridge and White Ltd. *Address:* c/o Rogers, Coleridge and White, 20 Powis Mews, London W11 1JN, England.

DARNTON John (Townsend), b. 20 Nov 1941, New York, USA. Metropolitan Editor, New York Times. m. Nina Lieberman, 21 Aug 1966, 1 son, 2 daughters. *Education:* Attended University of Paris IV, Sorbonne and Alliance Francaise, Paris, 1960-61; BA, University of Wisconsin, 1966. *Appointments:* New York Times, New York: Copy Boy, News Clerk and News Assistant, 1966-68; City Reporter 1968-69; Connecticut Correspondent 1969-70; Chief Suburban Correspondent, 1970-71; Night Rewriter 1971-72; Reporter for New York City fiscal crisis, 1972-75; Correspondent in Lagos, Nigeria 1976-77 and Nairobi, Kenya 1977-79; Bureau Chief in Warsaw, Poland, 1979-82 and Madrid, Spain, 1982-84I Deputy Foreign Editor 1984-86; Metropolitan Editor, 1987-; Correspondent and narrator for film, Spain: Ten Years After; Member Board of Directors, New York State Associated Press; News Editor/Weekends, New York Times, 1991-. *Publications:* A Day in the Life of Spain; Contributor to Assignment America; A Collection of Outstanding Writing from the New York Times and About Men: Reflections on the Male Experience. *Contributor to:* Periodicals including Readers Digest. *Honours:* George Polk Award from Long Island University 1979 and 1982 for foreign reporting; Pulitzer Prize in International Reporting from Columbia University Graduate School of Journalism, 1982 for Dispatches from Poland. *Membership:* Ferris Professor, Princeton University, 1991-92. *Address:* New York Times, City Desk, 229 West 43rd Street, New York, New York, NY 10036, USA.

DARROLL Sally. *See:* ODGERS Sally Patricia Farrell.

DARVI. *See:* PLATE Andrea Margolis.

DARVILL Timothy Charles, b. 22 Dec 1957, Cheltenham, England. Archeologist. *Education:* BA, 1979; PhD, 1983. *Appointments:* Reviews Editor, Transactions Bristol & Gloucestershire Archaeological Society, 1985-90. *Publications:* Prehistoric Britain; Ancient Monuments in the Contryside; The Archaeology of the Uplands; Prehistoric Gloucestershire; Glovebox

Guide to Ancient Britain; New Approaches to our Past; Megalithnic Chambered Tombs of the Cotswold Severn Region. *Contributions to:* 40 Articles to Journals. *Memberships:* Institute of Field Archaeologists, Chairman 1989-91; Fellow of the Society of Antiquaries of London; Society of Antiquaries of Scotland; Council of the National Trust, 1988. *Address:* Department of Conservation Science, Bournemouth Polytechnic, Fern Barrow, Poole, Dorset, England.

DARWISH Ahmed Adel Abed EL-Moneim, (Adel Darwish), b. 8 Dec 1945, Alexandria. Writer; Journalist. m. Elizabeth Catherine Margaret, 6 Apr 1976, div, 1 son, 1 daughter. *Education:* BSc, Ludda. *Appointments:* Writer, Reporter, 1967-76; play Wright, Theatre Producer, 1976-81; Writer, Journalist, 1981-86; Writer, Reporter, 1986-. *Publications:* Unholy Babylon: The Secret History of Saddam's War; Between the Quill and the Sword: The Political Background to the Rushdie Affair; The Muslim Brotherhood and British Secret Diplomacy; Security in the Gulf: Chances of Iraqi Defences; Strategy for the 1990's in the Middle East. *Contributions to:* The Sunday Telegraph; The Economist; The Independent; The Evening Standard; Index on Censorship; Defence and Foreign Affairs; American Arab Affairs; Foreign Report. *Memberships:* National Union of Journalists; The Writers Guild. *Literary Agent:* Dianne Coles. *Address:* 42 Greenwood Road, London E8 1AB, England.

DASENBROCK Reed Way, b. 18 Sept 1953, Detroit, Michigan, USA. Professor. m. 26 July 1982, 1 son. *Education:* BA, McGill University, 1974; B Phil, Oxford University, 1977; MA, Johns Hopkins University, 1980; PhD, 1982. *Publications:* The Literary Vorticism of Ezra Pound and T S Eliot; Imitating the Italains: Wyatt, Spenser, Synge, Pound, Joyce; Interviews with Writers of the Post Colonial World. *Memberships:* Modern Language Association. *Address:* Department of English, New Mexico State University, Las Cruces, NM 88003, USA.

DASGUPTA Sukamal, b. India. Economist; Poet. *Education:* MA, Economics, Allahabad University, 1939. *Appointments:* Lyricist, All India Radio and Doordarshan (Indian Television). *Publications:* Books of verse: Gadadhar, Life of Sri Ramakrishnan, for children, 1958; Ma Mani, Life of Sarada Devi, wife of Sri Rama Krishna, verse, 1958; Biliti Chhara, Bengali translation of English nursery rhymes, 1960; Saradiya, Chhara, for children, 1962; Chhara Dilam chhariye, for children, 1964; Chharate Ramayan, for children, 1967; K Khelar Chhara, for children, 1969; Bigyaner Chhara, book of elementary science in verse for children; Jagrata Bharat, sonmgs, 1978; Purba Negh, book of verse, 1980; Satabdir Aovan, songs, 1985; Bania Bina, songs and poems, 1991; Arati Ajan, songs; 2 unpublished dance dramas. *Contributions to:* Magazines and journals for children and adults including: Sishusathi; Mauchak; Ramdhanu; Nabakoli; Sandesh. *Honours:* Prize, Certificate, Critics Council of India, 1982; Bhubaneswari Padak (medal), Sisha Sahitya Parishad, Bengal, 1985. *Memberships:* Past Secretary, Sishu Sahitya Parishad; Executive Council, PEN. *Address:* E-161 Ramgarh, Calcutta 700 047, India.

DASSANOWSKY-HARRIS Robert von, b. 28 Jan 1956, New York, USA. Writer; Editor; Educator. *Education:* BA, American Academy of Dramatic Arts, 1985; MA, 1988; PhD, 1992; University of California, Los Angeles. *Appointments:* Founding Editor, Rohwedder, 1986-; Contributing Editor, Osiris, 1991-; Rampike, 1991-; PEN Center Magazine, 1992-; Television Writer, The Disney Channel, USA; Assistant Professor of German, University of California, 1992-93; University of Colorado, Colorado Springs, 1993-. *Publications:* Telegrams from the Metropole, Poems; Numerous Play Productions and readings. *Contributions to:* American Book Review; Films in Review; Starlog; East European Quarterly; Germanic Review; Modern Austrian Literature; Germanic Notes; Manhattan Review; Jacaranda Review; Poeesie Europe (Ger); Log (Austraia); Caracteres (France); PEN International (UK). *Honours:* Accademico Honoris Causa; Accademia

Culturale d'Europe; BHTG/Julie Harris Playwright Award. *Memberships:* Board of Directors, PEN USA/West, 1992-; Dramatists Guild; Poets & Writers; Paneuropa Union. *Address:* 4346 Matilija Avenue 27, Sherman Oaks, CA, 91423, USA.

DATHORNE O(scar) R(onald), b. 1934, Britain. Professor of English, Writer, Poet. *Appointments:* Associate Professor, Ahmadu Bello University, Zaria, 1959-63 and University of Ibadan, 1963-66, Nigeria; UNESCO Consultant to the Government of Sierra Leone, 1967-68; Professor of English, Njala University College, University of Sierra Leone, 1968-69; Professor of African Literature, Howard University, 1970; Professor of Afro-American Literature, University of Wisconsin, Madison, 1970-71; Professor of English and Black Literature, Ohio State University, Columbus, 1971-74; Professor of English, Florida International University, 1974-75; Professor of English and Black Literature, Ohio State University, 1975-77; Professor of English, University of Miami, Coral Gables, Florida, 1977-. *Publications:* Dumplings in the Soup (novel), 1963; The Scholar Man (novel), 1964; (ed) Caribbean Narrative, 1965; (ed) Caribbean Verse, 1967; (ed with W Feuser), Africa in Prose, 1969; The Black Mind, 1975; African Literature in the Twentieth Century, 1976; Dark Ancestor, 1981; Dele's Child, 1985. *Address:* Department of English, University of Miami, Coral Gables, FL 33124, USA.

DAUNTON Martin James, b. 7 Feb 1949, Cardiff. University Professor. m. Claire Gobbi, 7 Jan 1984. *Education:* BA, University of Nottingham, 1970; PhD, University of Kent, 1974. *Appointments:* Lecturer, University of Durham, 1973-79; Lecturer, University College of London, 1979-85; Reader, 1985-89; Professor, 1989-. *Publications:* Coal Metropolis: Cardiff; House and Home in the Victorian City, 1850- 1914; Royal Mail: The Post Office Since 1840; A Property Owing Democracy?. *Contributions to:* Economic History Review; Past & Present; Business History; Historical Research; Journal of Urban History. *Memberships:* Royal Historical Society. *Address:* Department of History, University College London, Gower Street, London WC1E 6BT, England.

DAVEY Frank(land Wilmot), b. 1940, Canada. University Professor, Writer, Poet. *Appointments:* Lecturer 1963-66 and Assistant Professor 1967-69, Royal Roads Military College, Victoria; Writer-in-Residence, Sir George Williams University, Montreal, 1969-70; Editor, Tish magazine, Vancouver, 1961-63 and Open Letter magazine, Toronto, 1965-82; Co-ordinator of Creative Writing Program 1976-79, Associate Professor, Professor 1970-, Chairman, Department of English, 1985-, York University, Toronto; General Editor, Quebec Translations series 1973-; Member of the Editorial Board, Coach House Press, Toronto, 1975-; General Editor, New Canadian Citicism series, Talonbooks, Vancouver, 1977-. *Publications:* D-Day and After, 1962; City of the Gulls and Sea, 1964; Bridge Force, 1965; The Scarred Hull, 1966; Four Myths for Sam Perry, 1970; Weeds, 1970; Five Readings of Olson's Maximus (criticism), 1970; Earle Birney (criticism), 1971; Griffon, 1972; King of Swords, 1972; L'An Trentiesme: Selected Poems, 1961-70, 1972; Areana 1973; The Clallam or, Old Glory in Juan de Fuca, 1973; From There to Here: A Guide to English Canadian Literature since 1960, 1974; (ed) Tish 1-19, 1975; (ed) Mrs Dukes' Million, by Wyndham Lewis, 1977; War Poems, 1979; The Arches: Selected Poems, 1980; Louis Dudek and Raymond Souster (criticism), 1981; The Contemporary Canadian Long Poem, 1981; Capitalistic Affection! 1982; Surviving the Paraphrase, 1983; Edward and Patricia, 1984; Margaret Atwood: A Feminist Poetics, 1984; The Louis Riel Organ and Piano Company, 1985. *Address:* 133 Calumet College, York University, Downsview, Ontario, Canada M35 1P3.

DAVEY Peter John, b. 28 Feb 1940, Cleckheaton, England. Architect; Editor; Critic. m. 21 Sept 1968, 2 sons. *Education:* B Arch, Edinburgh University, 1967-68. *Appointments:* Editor, Architectural Review, 1981.

Publication: Arts and Crafts Architecture. Contributions to: Numerous Architectural Journals. *Honor:* Knight, Order of White Rose of Finland. *Memberships:* Royal Institute of British Architects. *Address:* 44 Hungerford Road, London, England.

DAVEY Thomas A, b. 2 Jan 1954, Philadelphia, Pennsylvania. Adult and child psychologist; Writer. *Education:* BA, Duke University, 1976; EdD, Harvard University, 1984. *Appointments:* Teaching Fellow, Harvard University, Cambridge, Massachusetts; Conducts Private Practice in Adult and Child Psychology, Cambridge. *Publications:* A Generation Divided: German Children and the Berlin Wall, 1987. *Contributions to:* Articles and reviews to magazines and newspapers, including New Republic, Boston Review, Los Angeles Times Bookreviewer and New Age Journal. *Honours:* Grants from German Academic Exchange Service, 1981-82 and 1988; Lyndhurst Foundation Prize, 1985, for pursuit of writing and research interests. *Memberships:* American Psychological Association; Massachusetts Psychological Association. *Address:* Boston, Massachusetts, USA.

DAVIDSON Basil Risbridger, b. 9 Nov 1914, Bristol, England. Writer. m. Marion Young, 7 July 1943, 3 sons. *Publications include:* Old Africa Rediscovered, 1959; The African Slave Trade, 1961; The Africans, 1969; Africa in Modern History, 1978; The Rapids, 1956; Special Operations Europe, 1980; The Fortunate Isles, 1989; African Civilisation Revisited, 1991; The Black Man's Burden: Africa and The Curse of the Nation - State, 1992. *Honours:* Military Cross, British Army; Bronze Star, US Army; Ansfield Woolf Award, 1959; D.Letters (hc), University of Ibadan, 1975; University of Dars-Salaam, 1985; DUniv (hc), Open University of Great Britain, 1980; University of Edinburgh, 1981; Agnelli Visiting Professor, University of Tuscin, 1990. *Address:* Old Cider Mill, North Wootton, Somerset BA4 4HA, England.

DAVIDSON Lionel (David Line), b. 31 Mar 1922, Hull, England. Author. *Publications:* The Night of Wenceslas, 1960; The Rose of Tibet, 1962; A Long Way to Shiloh, 1966; Making Good Again, 1968; Smith's Gazelle, 1971; The Sun Chemist, 1976; The Chelsea Murders, 1978; Under Plum Lake, 1980; Run for Your Life, 1966; Mike & Me, 1974; Screaming High, 1985. *Honours:* Most Promising First Novel Award, Authors CLub, 1961; Gold Dagger CWA, 1961, 1967, 1979. *Literary Agent:* Curtis Brown. *Address:* c/o Curtis Brown, 162-168 Regent Street, London W1R 5TA, England.

DAVIDSON Michael, b.1944, America. Research Historian, Associate Professor, Writer, Poet. *Appointments:* Lecturer, San Diego State University, 1973-76; Research Historian 1975-; Assistant Professor 1976-81, Associate Professor 1981-, University of California, San Diego. *Publications:* Exchanges, 1972; Two Views of Pears, 1973; The Mutabilities and the Foul Papers, 1976; Summer Letters, 1976; Grillwork, 1980; Discovering Motion, 1980; The Prose of Fact, 1981; The Landing of Rochambeau, 1985.

DAVIDSON Mildred, b. 1935, Britain. Senior Lecturer in English; Writer. *Appointments:* Lecturer, Baghdad University, 1964-65; Lecturer and Senior Lecturer in English, Hendon College of Technology, 1966-73; Senior Lecturer in English, Middlesex Polytechnic, 1973-. *Publications:* The Poetry in the Pity, 1972; The Last Griffin, 1974; Dragons and More, 1976; Link of Three, 1980. *Address:* c/o Chatto and Windus, 20 Vauxhall Bridge Road, London, SW1V 2SA, England.

DAVIDSON Ralph P, b. 17 Aug. 1927, Santa Fe, New Mexico, UsA. Magazine Publisher. m. Jeanne Skidmore, 1951, div, 2 sons. *Education:* Stanford University. *Appointments:* with CIA, 1952-54; Advertising Salesman, Life Magazine, 1954-56; European Advertising Director, 1956-62, Time Magazine, London; European Advertising Director, Time-Life International, London, 1964; Managing Director, Time International, New York, 1967-; Assistant Publisher, Time, 1968, Associate Publisher, 1969, Publisher 1972-78; Chairman, Board, Time Inc., 1972-. *Address:* Time Inc., Time & Life Building, Rockefeller Centre, New York, NY 10020, USA.

DAVIDSON William H, b. 25 Sept 1951, New Mexico. Professor. m. Anneke Rozendaal, 16 June 1973, 3 sons. *Education:* Harvard College, AB, 1973; Harvard Business School, MA, 1975; Harvard University, DBA, 1979. *Publications:* 2020 Vision; The Amazing Race; US Competitiueness. *Contributions to:* Numerous. *Honours:* Academy of International Business Dissentation award; Fortune Magazine, Best Business Book of the Year. *Memberships:* Academy of International Business. *Literary Agent:* Rafoel Sagalyn. *Address:* 26 Sea Cove Drive, Rancho Palos Verdes, CA 90274, USA.

DAVIE Donald Alfred, b. 17 July 1922, Barnsley, Yorkshire, England. Academic; Literary Critic. m. Doreen John, 1945, 2 sons, 1 daughter. *Education:* St Catharine's College, Cambridge. *Appointments include:* Lecturer, University of Cambridge, 1958-64, Fellow, Gonville and Caius College, Cambridge, 1959-64; Professor, Literature, 1964-68, Pro-Vice- Chancellor, 1965-68, University of Essex; Professor, English, Stanford University, USA, 1968-74; Olive H. Palmer Professor in the Humanities, 1974-78; Clark Lecturer, Trinity College, Cambridge, 1976; Andrew W. Mellon Professor, Humanities, Vanderbilt University, 1978-88. *Publications:* Poetry: Brides of Reason, 1955; A Winter Talent, 1957; The Forests of Lituania, 1959; A Sequence for Francis Parkman, 1961; Events and Wisdoms, 1964; Essex Poems, 1969; Six Epistles to Eva Hese, 1970; Collected Poems, 1972; The Shires, 1975; In the Stopping Train, 1977; Collected Poems 1972-83, 1983; Literary Criticism: Purity of Diction in English Verse, 1952; Articulate Energy, 1957; The Heyday of Sir Walter Scott, 1961; Ezra Pound : Poet as Sculptor, 1965; Thomas Hardy and British Poetry, 1972; Pound, 1976; The Poet in Imaginary Museum (essays), 1978; A Gathered Church : the Literature of the English Dissenting Interest 1700-1930, 1978; Dissentient Voice : Enlightenment and Christian Dissent, 1982; Czeslaw Milosz & The Insufficiency of Lyric, 1986; Anthologies: The Late Augustans, 1958, with Angela Livingstone; Modern Judgement : Pasternak, 1969; Augustan Lyric, 1974; The New Oxford Book of Christian Verse, 1981. *Honours:* Recipient, numerous honours and awards; FBA, 1986. *Address;* 4 High Street, Silverton, Exeter, EX5 4JB, England.

DAVIE Elspeth, b. 1919, Kilmarnock, Scotland. Teacher; Author. m. George Elder Davie. *Education:* DA, Edinburgh College of Art. *Publications:* Novels: Providing, 1965; Creating a Scene, 1971, 1984; Climbers ona Stair, 1978. Short Stories: The Spark and Other Stories, 1968, 1984; The High Tide Talker and Other Stories, 1976; The Night of the Funny Hats, 1980; A Traveller's Room, 1985; Coming to Light, 1989. *Honours:* Scottish Arts Council grants 1971, 1977 and 1979; Katherine Mansfield Prize from English Centre of International PEN, 1978 for short story The High Tide Talker.

DAVIE-MARTIN Hugh. *See:* **MCCUTCHEON Hugh.**

DAVIES Andrew (Wynford), b. 1936, Britain. Lecturer, Writer; Playwright. *Appointments:* Teacher, St Clement Danes Grammar School, 1958-61 and Woodberry Down School, 1961-63, both in London; Lecturer, Coventry College of Education and University of Warwick, Coventry, 1963-. *Publications:* plays: Marmalade Atkins in Space, 1982; also radio and television plays for children and numerous radio plays for adults. Children's fiction: The Fantastic Feats of Doctor Boox, 1972; Conrad's War, 1978; Marmalade and Rufus, 1979, as Marmalade Atkins' Dreadful Deeds, 1982; Marmalade Atkins in Space, 1982; Educating Marmalade, 1983; Danger! Marmalade at Work, 1984; Alfonso Bonzo, 1986; Poonam's Pets, 1990; Fiction Includes: Getting Hurt, 1989; Dirty Foxes, 1990; B. Monkey, 1992. *Address:* c/o Leinon, Unna & Durbridge, 24 Pottery Lane, London W11 4LZ, England.

DAVIES (Edward) Hunter, b. 7 Jan 1936, Renfrew, Scotland. Writer. m. 11 June 1960, 1 son, 2 daughters. *Education:* University College, Durham, England; BA, DipEd. *Publications:* 40 Books including: Here We Go Round the Mulberry Bush, 1965; The Beatles, 1968, 2nd Edition, 1985; The Glory Game, 1972, 2nd Edition, 1985; A Walk Along the Wall, 1974, 2nd Edition, 1986; A Walk Around the Lakes, 1979; Flossie Teacake's Fur Coat, 1982; Stars, 1989; Fit for the Sixth, 1989; In Search of Columbus, 1991. *Contributions to:* Sunday Times, 1960-84; Punch, 1979-89; Independent, London, 1990-. *Literary Agent:* Giles Gordon. *Address:* 11 Boscastle Road, London, NW5, England.

DAVIES James Atterbury, b. 25 Feb 1939, Llandeilo Dyfed, Wales. University Lecturer. m. Jennifer Hicks, 1 Jan 1966, 1 son, 1 daughter. *Education:* BA, 1965; PhD, 1969. *Appointments:* Senior Lecturer, University College of Swansea, 1990-. *Publications:* John Forster: A Literary Life; The Textual Life of Dickens's Characters; Leslie Norris; Dylan Thomas's Places. *Contributions to:* RES; DUJ; DSA; NWR. *Memberships:* University of Wales Association for the Study of Welsh Writing in English. *Address:* Department of English, University of Swansea, Singleton Park, Swansea, SA2 8PP, Wales.

DAVIES Leslie Purnell (Leo Berne, Robert Blake, Richard Bridgeman, Morgan Evans, Ian Jefferson, Lawrence Peters, Thomas Philips, G K Thomas, Leslie Vardre, Rowland Welch), b. 1914, British, Writer. *Appointments:* Former subpostmaster, optician and tabocconist; Cuurently writer of novels, short stories, mystery/crime/suspense. *Publications:* The Paper Dolls, 1964; Man Out of Nowhere (in US as Who is Lewis Pinder?), 1965; The Artificial Man 1965; Psychogeist, 1966; The Lampton Dreamers, 1966; (in UK as Leslie Vardre) Tell It to the Dead (in US as The Reluctant Medium), 1966; Twilight Journey, 1967; (in UK as Leslie Vardre)The Namelees Ones (in US as A Grave Matter), 1967; The Alien, 1968; Dimension A, 1969; Stranger in Town, 1969; Genesis Two, 1969; The White Room, 1969; Adventure Holidays Ltd, 1970; The Shadow Before, 1970; Give Me Back Myself, 1971; The Silver Man, 1972; What Did I Do Tomorrow? 1972; Assignment Abacus, 1975; Possession, 1976; The Land of Leys, 1979; Morning Walk, 1983. *Address:* Apt K-1, Edificio Alondra, El Botanico, Puerto de la Cruz, Tenerife, Canary Islands.

DAVIES Pauline (Pauline Fisk), b. 27 Sept 1948, London, England. Writer. m. David Davies, 12 Feb 1972, 2 sons, 3 daughters. *Publications:* Midnight Blue, 1990; Telling the Sea, 1992. *Contributions to:* Homes and Gerdens, 1989. *Honours:* For Midnight Blue: Smarties Grand Prix Prize, 1990; Shortlisted, Whitbread Award. *Membership:* Society of Authors. *Literary agents:* Cecily Ware Agency; Comstock Smith Agency. *Address:* c/o Cecily Ware, 19c John Spencer Square, Canonbury, London, N1 2L3, England.

DAVIES Peter Joseph, b. 15 May 1937, Terang, Vic, Australia. Physician, Writer. m. Clare Lougman, 21 Dec 1960, 1 daughter. *Education:* MB, 1961; MRACP, 1968; FRACP, 1974; MRCP, 1970; MD, 1991. *Publications:* Mozart In Person: His Character & Press; Mozarts Health in 1790; Bicentenary Collection; Sadie. *Contributions to:* The Musical Times. *Memberships:* The Royal Australian College of Physicians; The Gastro Enterological Society of Australia; The Royal Society of Medicine. *Literary Agent:* The Greenwood Press. *Address:* 220 Springvale Road, Glen Wavbeles, Vic 3150, Australia.

DAVIES Piers Anthony David, b. 1941, New Zealand. Barrister and Solicitor; Scriptwriter; Poet. *Appointments:* Barrister and Solicitor, Jordans, Auckland, New Zealand (qualified 1965). Chairperson, Short Film Fund of NZ Film Commission, 1987-91. *Publications:* East and Other Gong Songs, 1967; (with Peter Weir), Life and Flight of Rev Buck Shotte (screenplay), 1969; Day Trip from Mount Meru, 1969; (with Peter Weir), Homesdale (screenplay), 1971; (with Peter Weir), The Cars That Ate Paris (screenplay), 1973; Diaspora, 1974; Bourgeois Homage to Dada, 1974; (ed) Central Almanac, 1974; Skin Deep (screenplay), 1978; R V Huckleberry Finn (video documentary), 1979; Olaf's Coast (documentary), 1982; Jetsam, 1984; The Lamb of God (screenplay), 1985. *Address:* 16 Crocus Place, Remuera, Auckland 5, New Zealand.

DAVIES Robertson (Samuel Marchbanks), b. 1913, Canada. Emeritus Professor, Writer; Playwright. *Appointments:* Actor and Teacher, Old Vic Theatre Company, London, 1938-40; Literary Editor, Saturday Night, 1940-42; Editor 1942-58 and Publisher 1958-68, Peterborough Examiner; Professor of English and Master of Massey College, University of Toronto, Ontario, 1963-81, now Emeritus Professor. *Publications:* Shakespeare's Boy Actors, 1939; Shakespeare for Young Players, 1942; The Diary of Samuel Marchbanks, 1947; The Table Talk of Samuel Marchbanks, 1949; Eros at Breakfast and Other Plays, 1949; Fortune My Foe (play), 1949; At My Heart's Core (play), 1950; Tempest Tost (novel), 1951; A Masque of Aesop (play), 1952; (with Tyrone Guthrie), Renown at Stratford, 1953; (with Tyrone Guthrie), Twice Have the Trumpets Sounded, 1954; A Jig for the Gypsy (play), 1954; Leaven of Malice (novel), 1954; (with Tyrone Guthrie), Thrice the Brinded Cat Hath Mew'd, 1955; A Mixture of Frailties (novel), 1958; A Voice from the Attic, 1960; The Personal Art, 1961; A Masque of Mr Punch (play), 1963; Samuel Marchbanks' Almanack, 1967; Stephen Leacock, 1970; Feast of Stephen (anthology), 1970; Fifth Business (novel), 1970; Hunting Stuart and Other Plays, 1972; The Manticore (novel), 1972; World of Wonders (novel), 1975; Question Time (play), 1975; One Half of Robertson Davies, 1977; The Enthusiasms of Robertson Davies, 1979; Robertson Davies: The Well-Tempered Critic, 1981; The Rebel Angels (novel), 1981; High Spirits: A Collection of Ghost Stories, 1982; The Mirror of Nature (lectures), 1983; What's Bred in the Bone (novel), 1985; The Papers of Samuel Marchbanks, 1985; The Lyre of Orpheus (novel), 1988; Murther & Walking Spirits (novel), 1991. *Honours include:* Lorne Pierce medal, Royal Society of Canada, 1961; Companion of the Order of Canada, 1972; Lifetime Achievement Award, Toronto Arts Awards, 1986; Molson Prize in the Arts, Canada Council, 1988; 19 Honorary degrees in Canada, 3 in USA and DLitt from Trinity College, Dublin and from Oxford. *Literary Agent:* Curtis Brown Ltd, Ten Astor Place, New York, NY 10003, USA. *Address:* Massey College, 4 Devonshire Place, Toronto, Ontario, Canada M5S 2E1.

DAVIES Sumiko, b. 21 Sept 1942, Tokyo, Japan. Illustrator and Writer. m. Derek Davies, 7 Jan 1967, 1 son, 1 daughter. *Education:* Kuwazawa Design Institute, Diploma in Design and Illustration, 1966. *Appointments:* Free-lance illustrator, Art Director of Marklin Advertising Agency in Thailand, 1966-67; Work exhibited at Pinky Gallery, Tokyo, Japan, 1979 and Museum of Modern Art, Oxford, England, 1984. *Publications include:* Self-Illustrated Books under name Sumiko: Hans Andersen's Fairy Tales 1979, 1980; My Baby Brother Ned, 1984; My School, 1983; A Kiss on the Nose, 1984; My Holiday 1987; Peter and Cat, 1989. *Membership:* Foreign Correspondents Club of Hong Kong. *Address:* 7C Scenic Villas, Victoria Road, Pokfulam, Hong Kong.

DAVIES William Thomas Pennar, b. 12 Nov 1911, Aberpennar (Mountain Ash), Glamorgan, Wales. m. Rosemarie Wolff, 26 June 1943, 4 sons, 1 daughter. *Education:* University of Wales, Cardiff, 1929-34; Balliol College, Oxford, 1934-36; Yale University, USA, 1936-38; Mansfield College, Oxford, 1940-43. BA (Wales),

1932; BLitt (Oxon), 1938; PhD (Yale), 1943. *Publications include:* Cudd fy Meiau, diary, 1957; Anadl o'r Uchelder, novel, 1958; Yr Efrydd o lyn Cynon, poems, 1961; Caregl Nwyf, short stories, 1966; Meibion Darogan, novel, 1968; Llais y Durtur, short stories, 1985. Also: Cinio'r Cythraul, poems, 1946; Naw Wfft, poems, 1957; Rhwng Chwedl a Chredo, studies, 1966; Y Tlws yn y Lotws, poems, 1971; Y Brenin Alltud, studies; Yr Awen Almaeneg, anthology, German verse in Welsh translation, 1984; Llef, poems, 1987. *Contributions to:* Articles, reviews, studies, various periodicals, published separately. *Honours:* Commonwealth Fund Fellow, 1936-38; Fellow, University of Wales, 1938-40; Welsh Academy Prize, 1968; Fellow Honoris Causa, University of Wales, Cardiff, 1986; Honorary DD, ibid, 1987; Honorary Fellow, Yr Academi Gymreig (Welsh Academy), 1989. *Membership:* Undeb Awduron Cymru. *Address:* 10 Heol Grosvenor, Sgeti, Abertawe (Swansea), Wales SA2 0SP.

DAVIS Alan R, b. 30 June 1950, New Orleans, LA, USA. Writer; Professor. m. Catherine Culloden, 4 July 1981, 1 son, 1 daughter. *Education:* BA, University of Louisiana, 1973; MA, 1975; PhD, University of Denver, 1981. *Appointments:* Loyola University, 1980-81; University of North Carolina, 1981-85; Moorhead State University, 1985-; Chair of English, Director of creative Writing; Editor, American Fiction, 1987-. *Publications:* Rumors From The Lost World; American Fiction. *Contributions to:* The New York Times Book Review; San Francisco Chronicle; Cleveland Plain Dealer; Chicago Sun Times; Hudson Review; Kansas Quarterly. *Honours:* Breadloaf Scholarship; State Arts Board Fellow; Minnesota Voices Winner. *Memberships:* National Book Critics Circle; Associated Writing Programs. *Literary Agent:* Nat Sobel. *Address:* PO Box 229, MSU, Moorhead, MN 56563, USA.

DAVIS Burke, b. 1913, America. Writer, Historian, Biographer. *Appointments:* Editor, Feature Writer and Sports Editor, Charlotte News, North Carolina, 1937-47; Reporter, Baltimore Evening Sun, Maryland, 1947-52; Reporter, Greensboro News, North Carolina, 1951-60; Writer and Historian, Colonial Williamsburg, Virginia, 1960-78. *Publications:* Whisper My Name, 1949; The Ragged Ones, 1951; Yorktown, 1952; They Called Him Stonewall, 1954; Gray Fox, 1956; Roberta E Lee, 1956; Jeb Stuart, The Last Cavalier, 1957; To Appomattox, 1959; Our Incredible Civil War, 1960; Marine! 1961; The Cowpens-Guilford Courthouse Campaign, 1962; America's First Army, 1962; Appomattox: Closing Struggle of the Civil War, 1963; The Summer Land, 1965; (co-author), Rebel Raider, 1966; The Billy Mitchell Affair, 1967; A Williamsburg Galaxy, 1967; (co-author), The World of Currier & Ives, 1968; Get Yamamoto, 1969; Yorktown: The Winning of American Independence, 1969; Billy Mitchell Story, 1969; The Campaign that Won America: Yorktown, 1970; Heroes of the American Revolution, 1971; Jamestown, 1971; Thomas Jefferson's Virginia, 1971; Amelia Earhart, 1972; Biography of a Leaf, 1972; Three for Revolution, 1975; Biography of a Kingsnake, 1975; George Washington and the American Revolution, 1975; Newer and Better Organic Gardening, 1976; Biography of a Fish Hawk, 1976; Black Heroes of the American Revolution, 1976; Old Hickory: A Life of Andrew Jackson, 1977; Mr. Lincoln's Whiskers, 1978; Sherman's March 1980; The Long Surrender, 1985; The Southern Railway, 1985; War Bird: The Life and Times of Elliott White Springs, 1986. *Address:* Rt 1 Box 66, Meadows of Dan, VA 24120, USA.

DAVIS Christopher, b. 23 Oct 1928, Philadelphia, PA, USA. Writer; Teacher. m. Sonia Fogg, 6 June 1953, 4 daughters. *Education:* BA, University of Pennsylvania, 1955. *Appointments:* Pennsylvania Council on The Arts, 1981-86. *Publications:* Lost Summer; A kind of Darkness; A Peep into The 20th Century; Suicide Note; Waiting For It; The Producer; Dog Horse Rat; First Family; Belmarch; Ishmael; The Sun in Mid Career. *Contributions to:* Esquire; Argosy; Der Monat; Travel & Leisure; Holiday; The New York Times; La Times; The Pennsylvania Gazette; Saturday Evening Post. *Honours:*

O'Henry Prize Story; Best Magazine Articles; National Book Award; Nominee, American Academy & Institute of Arts & Letters Career Award. *Memberships:* Pen; Authors Guild. *Literary Agent:* Curtis Brown. *Address:* Curtis Brown, 10 Astor Place, New York City, NY 10003, USA.

DAVIS David Brion, b.1927, America. University Professor; Writer. *Appointments:* Ernest I White Professor of History, Cornell University, Ithaca, New York, 1963-69; Harold Vyvyan Harmsworth Professor, Oxford University, 1969-70; Chair in American Civilization, Ecole des Hautes Etudes en Sciences Sociales, Paris, 1980-81; Professor and Farnum Professor, 1969- 78,Sterling Professor of History, 1978-, Yale University, New Haven, Connecticut. *Publications:* Homicide in American Fiction, 1957; (ed)Ante-Bellum Reform, 1967; The Problem of Slavery in Western Culture, 1967; The Slave Power Conspiracy and the Paranoid Style, 1969; (ed)The Fear of Conspiracy, 1971; The Problem of Slavery in the Age of Revolution, 1975; (co-author), The Great Republic, 1977, 1980, 1992; (ed) Antebellum American Culture, 1979; Slavery and Human Progress, 1984; From Homicide to Slavery: Studies in American Culture, 1986; Revolutions: Reflections on American Equality and Foreign Liberations, 1990. *Address:* Department of History, Yale University, New Haven, CT 06520, USA.

DAVIS Dorothy Salisbury, b. 26 Apr 1916, Chicago, Illinois, USA. Writer. *Education:* AB, Barat College, Lake Forest, Illinois. *Publications:* A Gentle Murderer, 1951; Men of No Property, 1956; The Evening of the Good Samaritan, 1961; Enemy and Brother, 1967; Where the Dark Streets Go, 1969; The Little Brothers, 1974; A Death in the Life, 1976; Scarlet Night, 1980; Lullaby of Murder, 1984; Tales for a Stormy Night, 1985; The Habit of Fear, 1987. *Contributions to:* New Republic. *Honours:* Grand Master's Award, Mystery Writers of America, 1985; Lifetime Achievement Award, Bouchereon XX, 1989. *Memberships:* President, Executive Vice President, Mystery Writers of America; Crime Writers Association, UK; Authors' Guild. *Literary Agent:* McIntosh and Otis. *Address:* Palisades, NY 10964, USA.

DAVIS Gordon. *See:* **HUNT E(verette) Howard.**

DAVIS Jack Leonard, b. 11 Mar 1917, Perth, Western Australia. Writer. m. Madelon Jantine Wilkens, 12 Dec 1987, 1 daughter. *Appointment:* Writer-in-Residence, Murdoch University, 1982. *Publications:* The First Born & other poems, 1968; No Sugar, play, 1986; Jagardoo- poems from Aboriginal Australia, 1978; John Pat and other Poems, 1988; The Dreamers & Kullark, plays, 1983; Burungin (Smell the Wind), play, 1989; Honey Spat, 1986; Plays from Black Australia, 1989. *Contributions to:* Identity. *Honours:* Human Rights Award, 1987; BHP Award, 1988; Advance Australia, 1987; Awgie, 1986; Australian Artists Creative Fellowship, 1989; Honorary degrees: DLitt, Murdoch University; DLitt, University of Western Australia. *Memberships:* Australian Writers Guild; PEN International (Life Member); Aboriginal Writers Oral Literature & Dramatists Association, Chairman. *Address:* 3 Little Howard Street, Fremantle, Western Australia, Australia.

DAVIS Jon Edward, b. 28 Oct 1952, New Haven, Connecticut, USA. Author. m. Terry Layton, 8 Jan 1978, 1 daughter. *Education:* BA, English, 1984, MFA, Creative Writing, 1985, University of Montana. *Appointments:* Writing Programme Co-ordinator, Fine Arts Work Centre, Provincetown, 1987-. *Publications:* West of New England, 1983; Dangerous Amusements, 1987; *Contributions to:* Poetry; Georgia Review; Missouri Review; Stand; Malahat Review. *Honours:* Academy of American Poets Prize, 1985; NEA Fellowship, 1986; Fine Arts Work Centre, Provincetown Creative Writing Fellowship, 1986-87. *Memberships:* Academy of American Poets; Poets & Writers Inc; Associated Writing

Programmes. *Address:* Fine Arts Work Centre, Box 565, Provincetown, MA 02657, USA.

DAVIS Margaret Thomson, b. Bathgate, West Lothian, Scotland. Novelist. Divorced, 1 son. *Education:* Albert Secondary School. *Publications include:* The Breadmakers Saga; A Very Civilized Man; The Prisoner; Rag Woman, Rich Woman; Daughters and Mothers; Wounds of War. *Contributions to:* 200 short stories to women's magazines in Britain and overseas and also to newspapers. *Memberships:* Committee Member of PEN; Committee Mmember of Society of Authors (Scottish branch); Committee Mmember, Swanwick Writers School; Honorary President, Strathkelvin Writers Club; Member, Strathclyde Writers Group; Scottish Labour History Society; Member, Great Britain-USSR Friendship Society. *Literary Agent:* Heather Jeeves, London. *Address:* c/o Heather Jeeves, 15 Campden Hill Square, London W8 7JY, England.

DAVIS Nathaniel, b. 12 Apr 1925, Boston, MA, USA. Professor. m. Elizabeth Kirkbride Creese, 24 Nov 1956, 2 sons, 2 daughters. *Education:* AB, Brown University, 1944; MA, The Fletcher School of Law and Diplomacy, 1947; PhD, 1960; LLD, Brown University, 1970. *Appointments:* Apprentice Seaman, 1943-44; Ensign, Lt, USNR, 1944-46; Teacher, Tufts College, 1947; Centro Venezolano Americano, 1961; Howard University, 1962-68; Salve Regina College, Newport, 1981-82; US Naval War College, 1977-83; Harvey Mudd College, 1983-. *Publications:* The Last Two Years of Salvador Allende; Ambassadors in Foreign Policy; Eqaity and Equal Security in Soviet Foreign Policy. *Contributions to:* New York Times Magazine; The Washington Post; Foreign Affairs; the Foreign Service Journal; The Department of State Newsletter; The Los Angels Times; San Diego Union Magazine; Journal of Religious Thought; Naval War College Review. *Memberships:* National Book Critics Circle; American Association for the Advancement of Slavic Studies; American Foreign Service Association; Council on Foreign Relations; American Historical Association; The Academy of Political Science. *Address:* 1783 Longwood Avenue, Claremont, CA 91711, USA.

DAVIS Neil. *See:* DAVIS T(homas) Neil.

DAVIS Robert Prunier, (Joe Brandon), b. 1929, America. Writer; Playwright. *Publications:* Day of the Painter (screenplay), 1961; Apes on a Tissue-Paper Bridge, 1963; Good-bye, Bates McGee, 1967; The Dingle War, 1968; (as Joe Brandon), Cock-A-doodle-Dew, 1972; (as Joe Brandon), Paradise in Flames; The Pilot, 1976; Cate Five, 1977; The Divorce, 1980; Control Tower, 1981.

DAVIS T N. *See:* DAVIS T(homas) Neil.

DAVIS T(homas) Neil, (Neil Davis, T N Davis) b. 1 Feb 1932, Greeley, Colorado, USA. Geophysicist. m. 10 June 1951, 1 son, 2 daughters. *Education:* BS, University of Alaska, 1955; MS, University of Technology, 1957; PhD, University of Alaska, 1961. *Appointments:* Editor, Alaska Science Forum, 1976-82; Director, University Alaska Press, 1982-86; Member, Editorial Board, 1986-. *Publications:* The Aurora Watchers Hand Book; Alaska Science Niggets; Energy, Alaska. *Contributions to:* Journal of Geophysical Research; Planetary and Space Science. *Honours:* Professor Emeritus. *Memberships:* American association for the Advancement of Science; Arctic Division; Committee on Council Affairs. *Address:* 375 Miller Hill Road, Fairbanks, AK 99709, USA.

DAVIS William, b. 6 Mar 1933. Author; Publisher; Broadcaster. m. Sylvette Jouclas, 1967. *Appointments:* Staff, Financial Times, 1954-59; Editor, Investor's Guide, 1959-60; City Editor, Evening Standard, 1960-65 (with one years break as City Editor, Sunday Express); Financial Editor, The Guardian, 1965-68;; Editor, Punch, 1968-77; Editor, Publisher, High Life, 1973- ; Chairman,

Headway Publications, 1977- ; Editorial Director, Executive World, 1980- , Moneycare, 1983- ; Presenter, Money Programme, BBC TV, 1967-69; English Tourist Board, 1990-; Premier Publication Showing since 1992. *Publications:* Three Years Hard Labour: the Road to Devaluation, 1968; Merger Mania, 1970; Money Talks, 1972; Have Expenses Will Travel, 1975; It's No Sin to be Rich, 1976; Editor, The Best of Everything, 1980; Money in the 1980's, 1981; The Rich: A Study of the Species, 1982; Fantasy: A Practical Guide to Escapism, 1984; The Corporate Infighter's Handbook, 1984; Editor, The World's Best Business Hotels, 1985; Children of the Rich, 1989, (Non-Fiction). *Address:* British Tourist Authority, Thames Tower, Black's Road, London W6 9EL, England.

DAVIS-GOFF Annabel Claire, b. 19 Feb 1942. Writer. M. Mike Nichols, 1976, div. 1987, 1 son, 1 daughter. *Publications:* Night Tennis, 1978; Tail Spin, 1980; Walled Gardens, 1989. *Literary Agent:* Owen Laster, William Morris Agency, New York, USA. *Address:* 1 West 67th Street, New York, NY 10023, USA.

DAVISON Geoffrey Joseph, b. 10 Aug 1927, Newcastle-upon-Tyne, England. m. Marlene Margaret Wilson, 15 Sept 1956, 2 sons. *Education:* Qualifications: TD (Territorial Decoration); FRICS (Fellow of the Royal Institution of Chartered Surveyors). *Publications:* The Spy Who Swopped Shoes, 1967; Nest of Spies, 1968; The Chessboard Spies, 1969; The Fallen Eagles, 1970; The Honorable Assassins, 1971; Spy Puppets, 1973; The Berlin Spy Trap, 1974; No Name on Their Graves, 1978; The Bloody Legionnaires, 1981. *Address:* 95 Cheviot View, Ponteland, Newcastle-upon-Tyne NE20 9BH, England.

DAWE Donald Bruce, b. 15 Feb 1930, Geelong, Australia. Teacher. m. Gloria Desley Blain, 27 Jan 1964, 2 sons, 2 daughters. *Education:* BA, 1969; MA, 1975; PhD, 1980, Queensland; LittB, UNE, 1973. *Appointment:* Writer-in-Residence, University of Queensland 1984. *Publications:* No Fixed Address, 1962; A Need of Similar Name, 1965; An Eye for a Tooth, 1968; Beyond the Subdivisions, 1969; Condolences of the Season: Selected Poems, 1971; Just a Dugong at Twilight, 1975; Sometimes Gladness: Collected Poems, 1987; Over Here, Harv! and Other Stories, 1983; Towards Sunrise, 1986; This Side of Silence, 1990; Bruce Dawe: Essays and Opinions, 1990; Sometimes Gladness: Collected Poems, 1954-1992. *Contributions to:* Journals and magazines. *Honours:* Myer Poetry Prize, 1966, 1969; Ampol Arts Award for Creative Literature, 1967; Dame Mary Gilmore Medal of Australian Literary Society, 1973; Grace Leven Poetry Prize, 1978; Braille Book of the Year, 1979; Patrick White Literary Award, 1980; Christopher Brennan Award, 1984; Inaugral Institute Award for Excellence in Teaching, 1987; Paul Harris Fellow of Rotary International; Order of Australia (AO), 1992. *Memberships:* Centre for Australian Studies in Literature, Associate Member; Australian Association for Teaching English, Honorary Life Member; Victorian Association for Teaching of English, Honorary Life Member. *Address:* 30 Cumming Street, Toowoomba, Queensland 4350, Australia.

DAWSON Elizabeth. *See:* GEACH Christine.

DAWSON Jennifer, (Jenny Sargesson, Jenny Hinton), b. 23 Jan 1929, Hertfordshire, England. m. Michael Hinton, 2 Apr 1964. *Education:* St Annes College, Oxford; University College, London. *Publications:* The Ha-Ha, 1961; Fowlers Square, 1962; The Cold Country, 1965; Strawberry Boy, 1976; Hospital Wedding, 1978; A Field of Scarlet Poppies, 1979; The Upstairs People, 1988; Judasland, 1989; The Queen of Trent, (with W. Mitchell), 1962; As Jenny Sargesson: The Flying Gardens, 1993. *Poems in:* Ambit. *Honours:* James Tait Black Award, 1961; Cheltenham Festival Award, 1962; Fawcett Society Fiction Award, 1990. *Address:* 6 Fisher's Lane, Charlbury, Oxon OX7 3RX, England.

DAWSON Jill Dianne, b. 1962. Writer; Editor. 1 son. *Education:* BA, American Studies, University of Nottingham, 1980-83. *Appointments:* Writer in Residence, Doncaster; Fareham College, Hampshire; Tutor of Creative Writing, Au Pair, Yoga Teacher, Market Researcher, Freelance Writer. *Publications:* Virago Book of Wicked Verse; In The Gold of Flesh; Virago New Poets; The Gregory Anthology. *Contributions to:* She; Slow Dancer; Ambit; Envoi; Spectrum; Writing Women; Tears in the Fence; Aurora; Spare Rib; Everywoman; Distaff. *Honours:* Hackney Poetry Competition; Runner Up KQBX Experimental Poetry Competition; Runner Up Dragon Heart Poetry; Major Eric Gregory Award. *Address:* 12 Danby House, Frampton Park Estate, London E9 7RD, England.

DAY Edward Crocker, b. 7 May 1932, Boston, MA, USA. Writer. m. (1) Caroline Foster, 1960, (2) Joanna Butts, 8 July 1988, 2 sons. *Education:* AB, Harvard College, 1953. *Publication:* John Tabor's Ride. *Contributions to:* Boating Magazine; Nor Westing Magazine; Woodwork Magazine. *Honours:* Reading Magic Award; International reading Association, 30 Best. *Memberships:* Council for the Advancement & Support of Education. *Literary Agent:* Harvey Klinger Inc. *Address:* 12 Jay Street, Montpelier, VT 05602, USA.

DAY John Robert, b. 1917, Britain. Transportation Manager, London Transport Collection of Historical Vehicles; Writer. *Appointments:* Assistant Editor, The Railway Gazette, 1954-57; Senior Assistant to Press Officer, 1964-74, Head, Technical Press Section, 1957-64, Transportation Manager, 1974-, London Transport Collection of Historical Vehicles. *Publications:* (with B G Wilson), Unusual Railways, 1957; (with B K Cooper), Railway Locomotives, 1960; More Unusual Railways, 1960; Railways of Southern Africa, 1962; Railways Under the Ground, 1963; The Story of London's Underground, 1963; Railways of Northern Africa, 1964; (with P Duff and M Hill), Transport Today and Tomorrow, 1967; Trains, 1969; The Story of the Victoria Line, 1969; The Last Drop, 1971; The Story of the London Bus, 1973; London's Trams and Trollybuses, 1977; Engines, 1980; Source Book of Underground Railways (London Transport), 2 vols, 1980-82.

DAY Robin (Sir), b. 24 Oct 1923, London, England. TV and Radio Journalist. m. Katherine Mary Ainslie, 1965, div 1986, 2 sons. *Education:* Oxford University. *Appointments:* President, Oxford Union, 1950; Called to the Bar, 1952; BBC Radio Journalist, 1954-55; Independent TV News Newscaster & Political Correspondent, 1955-59; BBC TV Political Interviewer and Reporter, 1959-89; BBC Radio World at One Presenter, 1979-. *Publications:* Television - A personal Report, 1961; The Case for Televising Parliament, 1968; Troubled Reflections of a TV Journalist, 1970; Day by Day, 1975; Grand Inquisitor, 1989, (Autobiography); But With Respect, political interviews, 1993. *Honours:* Richard Dimbleby Award, 1974; Broadcasting Press Guild Award (for Question Time), 1980; Kt, 1981; RTS Judges Award for 30 years TV Journalism, 1985; HonLLD, Exeter, 1986 and Keele, 1988; HonDU, Essex, 1988; Hon Bencher Middle Temple, 1990. *Memberships:* Phillimore Committee on Law of Contempt, 1971-74; Chairman, Hansard Society for Parliamentary Government, 1981-83. *Address:* c/o Capron Productions, Gardiner House, Broomhill Road, London SW18 4JQ, England.

DAY Stacey Biswas, b. 31 Dec 1927, London, England, Physician; Educator. m. Ivana Podvalova 23 Oct 1973, 2 sons. *Education:* MD, Dublin, Republic of Ireland, 1955; PhD, McGill University, Canada, 1964; DSc, Cincinnati, USA, 1970. *Appointments:* Formerly Editor-in-Chief, Biosciences Communications and Health Communications; Consulting Editor, Plenum Publishing Corporation; Raven Press; Van Nostrand Reinhold; Karger, Basel; Academic Press; University of Minnesota; Editorial Board, Stress Medicine. *Publications:* Health Communications, 1978; Cancer, Stress and Death, 2nd Edition, 1986; Life Stress, 1982; American Lines, 1968; Rosalita, 1968; East of the Navel,

poems from Easter Island, 1978; Hagakure-Spirit of Bushido (Japanese & English), 1993; Author of over 30 edited medical and scientific books; 15 books of literary titles including verse history and essays; Consultant Editor, Dictionary of Scientific Biography. *Contributions to:* Numerous articles, 1955-93; Regular radio and television presentations, USA, Nigeria, Kenya, India. *Honours:* Various Medical Distinctions and Communications (USA) Awards; WHO Medal, 1987. *Memberships:* Various National and International Societies. *Address:* 6 Lomond Avenue, Spring Valley, NY 10977, USA.

DAYDI-TOLSON Santiago, b. 30 Apr 1943, Chile. College Professor. 1 son. *Education:* Language and Literature: Licenciado en Filsofia Educacion, University Catolica de Valparaiso, Chile, 1968; Doctor of Philosophy, University of Kansas, 1973. *Appointments:* Assistant Professor, 1968-69; Visiting Lecturer, University of Kansas, 1969-70; Instructor, 1970-72; Assistant Professor, Fordham University, 1973-77; University of Virginia, 1977-84; Director Spanish Speaking Outrech Institute, University of Wisconsin Milwaukee, 1984-87; Associate Professor, 1984-90; Chairman, 1987-90; Full Professor, 1990-. *Publications:* El ultimo viaje de Gabriela Mistral; Five Poets of Aztlan; Voces y Ecos En La Poesia De Jose Angel Valente The Post Civil War Spanish Social Poets; Vicents Aleixandre: A critical Appraisal. *Contributions to:* Numerous inc, Journal of Spanish Studies. *Honours include:* Woodrow Wilson Dissertation Fellowship; NEH Travel to Collection Grant; American Philosophical Society Grant. *Memberships include:* Modern Language Association of America; American Association of Teachers of Spanish & Portuguese; Asociacion Infernacional De Hispanistas. *Address:* Department of Spanish And Portuguese, University of Wisconsin Milwaukee, Milwaukee, WI 53201, USA.

DE ARAUGO Sarah Therese (Tess), b. 26 May 1930. Lismore, Victoria, Australia. Writer. m. Maurice De Arauge, 11 Apr 1950, 2 sons, 2 daughters. *Education:* Notre Dame de Sion College, Warragal, Victoria. *Publications:* You Are What You Make Yourself To Be, 1980, Revised Edition, 1989; The Kurnai of Gippsland, 1985. *Contributions to:* Biographies to Encyclopaedia of Aboriginal Australia; Echo of Aboriginal Past, to Weekly Times, 1983; Memories of the Murray River People, to This Australia, 1984-85; Aboriginal Australians and Their Descendants, to Annals Journal, 1990; Articles to newspapers; Biographies to Australian Dictionary of Evangelical Biography. *Honours:* New South Wales Premier's Award for Australian Literature, 1985; Banjo Award, Australian Literature, National Book Council, 1985; Fellowship, 1987, Writer's Grant, 1989, Australian Literature Board; Short Story Award, PEN International, Australia, 1991. *Memberships:* Australian Society of Authors; Fellowship of Australian Writers; Royal Historical Society of Victoria; Women Writers of Australia; Nepean Historical Society. *Address:* 19 Grenville Grove, Rosebud West, Victoria 3940, Australia.

DE BELSER Raymond Charles Maria (Ward Ruyslinck), b. 17 June 1929, Antwerp, Belgium, Retired Librarian, m. (1) 1 son, (2) Monika Macken, 18 Dec 1992. *Publications:* De ontaarde slapers, 1957, as The deadbeats, 1968; Wierook en tranen, 1958; Het dal van Hinnom, 1961; Het reservaat, 1964, as The reservation, 1978; Golden Ophelia, 1966, 1975; De heksenkring, 1972; Het ganzenbord, 1974; Wurgtechnieken, 1980; Leegstaande huizen, 1983; De uilen van Minerva, 1985; Stille waters, 1987; Ijlings naar nergens, 1989. *Contributions to:* Records of travel, papers on literature and plastic arts to various Belgian and Dutch magazines and journals. *Honours:* Ark Prize for Free Speech, 1960; Flemish Reader Award, 1964; Prize for Literature of the Flemish Provinces, 1967; Europalia Prize for Literature, 1980. *Membership:* Royal Flemish Academy of Language and Literature, Ex- Chairman. *Address:* Potaardestraat 25, 1860 Meise, Belgium.

DE BERNIERE-SMART Louis Henry Piers (Louis

de Bernières), b. 8 Dec 1954, Woolwich, London, England. Novelist. *Education:* Bradfield College, Berkshire; Manchester University, BA; Leicester Polytechnic and University of London (MA). *Publications:* The War of Don Emmanuels Nether Parts; Senior Vivo & The Coea Lord; The Troublesome Offspring of Cardinal Guzman. *Contributions to:* Second Thoughts and Granta. *Honours:* Commonwealth Writers Prize, 1991, 1992; Best of Young British Novelists, 1993. *Memberships:* PEN. *Literary Agent:* William Morris Agency UK Ltd. *Address:* c/o William Morris Agency, 31/32 Soho Square, London W1V 5DG, England.

DE BERNIÈRES Louis. *See:* **DE BERNIERE-SMART Louis Henry Piers.**

DE BLASIS Celeste Ninette, b. 8 May 1946, California, USA. Writer. *Education:* Wellesley College, 1964-65; Oregon State University, 1965-66; BA, cum laude, English, Pomona State College, 1968. *Publications:* The Night Child, 1975; Suffer a Sea Change, 1976; The Proud Breed, 1978; The Tiger's Woman, 1981; Wild Swan, 1984; Swan's Chance, 1985; A Season of Swans, 1989; Graveyard Peaches: A California Memoir, 1991. *Contributions to:* Writers Digest. *Memberships:* Authors Guild; Novelists Inc; Nature Conservancy; California State Library Foundation. *Literary Agent:* Jane Berkey, Jane Rotrosen Agency. *Address:* c/o Jane Rotrosen Agency, 318 East 51st Street, New York, NY 10022, USA.

DE BLIEU Martha Onuferko, b. 15 Jan 1954, Philadelphia, Pennsylvania, USA. Editor; Journalist. m. Kenneth A. De Blieu, 11 Sept 1976, 1 daughter. *Education:* BA, Journalism, Temple University, 1975. *Literary Appointments:* Editor, New Student Handbook, Temple University 1974, Temple News 1975; Reporter, Hunterdon County Democrat 1975-77, Delaware Valley News 1975-77; Editor, NJEA Reporter 1977-83, NJEA Review 1983-present. *Contributions to:* NJEA Review; NJEA Reporter; Hunterdon County Democrat; Delaware Valley News. *Honours:* Best photo, Keystone Press Association, 1976; Best Feature 1983, Feature Writing Award 1986, State Education Editors; Best series 1985, best editorial 1985, 1987, Edpress. *Memberships:* Secretary/Treasurer, State Education Editors; Educational Press Association (Edpress); New Jersey Press Association. *Address:* 180 West State Street, PO Box 1211, Trenton, NJ 08607, USA.

DE BONO Edward (Francis Charles), b. 1933, British. Assistant Director of Research; Writer. *Appointments:* Assistant Director of Research, Department of Investigative Medicine, University of Cambridge, 1964- ; Director, Cognitive Research Trust. *Publications:* The Five Day Course in Thinking, 1967; The Use of Lateral Thinking (in US as New Think), 1967; The Mechanism of Mind, 1969; Lateral Thinking: A Textbook of Creativity (in US as Lateral Thinking: Step By Step Creativity) 1972; (ed)Technology Today, 1972; Lateral Thinking for Management, 1972; The Dog Exercising Machine, 1972; Po: Beyond Yes and No, 1972; Children Solve Problems, 1973; Practical Thinking, 1973; The Case of the Disappearing Elephant, 1974; (ed), Eureka! History of Inventions, 1974; The Greatest Thinkers, 1976; The Happiness Purpose, 1972; Opportunities: A Handbook of Business Opportunity Search, 1978; Future Positive, 1979; Atlas of Management Thinking, 1981; DeBono's Course in Thinking, 1982; Tactics: The Art and Science of Success, 1984; Conflicts: A Better Way to Resolve Them, 1985; Six Thinking Hats, 1985; Masterthinker's Handbook, 1985; I am Right, You are Wrong, 1989; Six Action Shoes, 1991; Sur/Petition, 1992; Serious Creativity, 1992; Teach Your Child to Think, 1992. *Address:* 12 Albany, Piccadilly, London W1V 9RR, England.

DE CAMP L(yon) Sprague, b. 27 Nov 1907, New York City, New York, USA. Writer. m. Catherine Adelaide Crook, 12 Aug 1939, 2 sons. *Education:* BA, Aeronautical Engineering, California Institute of Technology, 1930; MA, Engineering, Economics,

Stevens Institute of Technology, 1933. *Publications:* Fiction: Lest Darkness Fall, 1939; Rogue Queen, 1951; Non-fiction: The Ancient Engineers, 1963; The Great Monkey Trial, 1968; Heroes and Hobgoblins, verse, 1981; About 125 other books including fiction (mostly science fiction and fantasy), historical novels, non-fiction in science, history, biography, juvenile, textbooks, others. *Contributions to:* About 425 stories and articles to periodicals, anthologies, symposia; Also many poems, book reviews, other fugitive pieces. *Honours:* International Fantasy Award for Non-Fiction, 1953; Athenaeum of Philadelphia Award for Fiction, 1959; Pat Terry Award, 1973; Grandmaster Fantasy Award, 1976; Nebula Award, Science Fiction Writers of America, 1978; World Fantasy Conference Award, 1984. *Memberships:* Authors Club, New York, Past Vice-President; Philadelphia Science Fiction Society; Authors Guild; Science Fiction and Fantasy Writers of America; Trap Door Spiders; Smithsonian Associates; Dallas Museum of Natural History; Audubon Society; Dallas Paleontological Society; University Museum, University of Pennsylvania; History of Science Society; Society for the History of Technology. *Literary Agent:* Eleanor Wood, Spectrum Literary Agency, 111 8th Av 1501, New York, NY 10011, USA. *Address:* 3453 Hearst Castle Way, Plano, TX 75025, USA.

DE CARLO Andrea, b. 11 Dec 1952, Milano, Italy. Novelist. 1 daughter. *Publications:* Treno Di Panna; Uccetti Da Gabbia & DA voliera; Macno; Yucatan; Due Di Due; Tecniche Di Seduzione. *Honours:* Premio Giouanni Comisso; Premio le Elea; Premio Societa Dei Lettori. *Address:* Via Fumagalli 7, 20143 Milano, Italy.

DE CRESCENTIS James, b. 29 May 1948, Rochester, New York, USA. Poet; Visual Artist; English Instructor. *Education:* BA, English, State University of New York, Geneseo, 1971; MFA, Creative Writing, Bowling Green State University, 1984. *Appointments:* Alternative Literature Programmes in the Schools (ALPS/NY State), 1985, 1986, 1987. *Publications:* Poetry Chapbooks: The Space Out Back, 1975; Last Minute Notes About Deep Terror, 1984; Poetry Broadside: Pockets of Light, 1981. *Contributions include:* The Experimentalist; Cloud Chamber; La Huerta; Ragged Oaks; Clifton Magazine; New Letters; Greenfield Review. *Honours:* Mary E. Thomas Award, Poetry, State University of New York, Geneseo, 1971; Devine Award, Poetry, Bowling Green State University; Theodore Enslin Jude, Summer, 1984. *Membership:* Poets and Writers Inc. *Address:* Boston, MA, USA.

DE CRESPIGNY (Richard) Rafe (Champion), b. 1936, Australia. University Reader in Chinese; Writer. *Appointments:* Lecturer 1964-70, Senior Lecturer 1970-73, Reader in Chinese 1973-, Australian National University, Canberra; Master of University House, 1991- . *Publications:* The Biography of Sun Chien, 1966; (with H H Dubs), Official Titles of the Former Han Dynasty, 1967; The Last of the Han, 1969; The Records of the Three Kingdoms, 1970; China: The Land and Its People, 1971; China This Century: A History of Modern China, 1975; Portents of Protest, 1976; Northern Frontier, 1984; Emperor Huan and Emperor Ling, 1989; Generals of the South, 1990; China This Century (2nd ed), 1992. *Address:* 5 Rous Crescent, Forrest, ACT 2603, Australia.

DE GRUCHY John Wesley, b. 18 Mar 1939, Pretoria, South Africa. Professor. m. Isobel Dunstan, 2 sons, 1 daughter. *Education:* BA, Rhodes University, 1959; BD, 1961; M Th Summa Cum Laude, 1964; DD, University of South Africa, 1972. *Appointments:* Head of Department Religious Studies, 1981-82, 1990-1992; Deputy Dean, Faculty of Social Science & Hummanities, 1984-86; Acting Dean, 1986-87; Deputy Dean, 1988-89; Member UCT General Purpose Committee, 1986-87; Academic Planning Committee, 1987-89; University Research Committee, 1990-; University of Cape Town, 1991-. *Publications:* The Church Struggle in South Africa; Apartheid is a Heresy; Bonhoeffer and South Africa: Theology in Dialogue; Cry Justice; Dietrich Bonhoeffer: Witness to Jesus Christ; Liberating Reformed Theology. *Contributions to:* Journal of

Theology for Southern Africa. *Memberships:* Theological Society of Southern Africa; International Bonhoeffer Society for Archive & Research; HSRC Dicipline Oriented Main Committee for Theology. *Address:* 10 Vredenburg Avenue, Rosebank 7700, South Africa.

DE GUISE Elizabeth (Mary Teresa), (Isobel Chase, Elizabeth Hunter), b. 1934, Nairobi, Kenya. *Education:* Attended Open University. *Appointments:* Landholder in Kent, England, 1952-58; English teacher to Arabic students in Folkestone, England, 1958-62; Writer 1960-. *Publications include:* Romance novels under name Elizabeth Hunter include: Fountains of Paradise, 1983; London Pride, 1983; Shared Destiny, 1983; A Silver Nutmeg, 1983; Kiss of the Rising Sun, 1984; Rain on the Wind, 1984; Song of Surrender, 1984; A Tower of Strength, 1984; A Time to Wed, 1984; Loving Relations, 1984; Eye of the Wind, 1985; Legend of the Sun, 1985; The Painted Veil, 1986; The Tides of Love, 1988. Romance novels under pseudonym Isobel Chace include: The House of Scissors, 1972; The Dragon's cave, 1972; The Edge of Beyond, 1973; A Man of Kent, 1973; The Elban Adventure, 1974; The Cornish Hearth, 1975; A Canopy of Rose Leaves, 1976; The Clouded Veil, 1976; The Desert Castle, 1976; Singing in the Wilderness, 1976; The Whistling Thorn, 1977; The Mouth of Truth, 1977; Second Best Wife, 1978; Undesirable Wife, 1978. Historical novels under name Elizabeth de Guise: Dance of the Peacocks, 1988; Flight of the Dragonfly, 90; Came Forth the Sun, 1991; Bridge of Sighs, 92. *Contributions to:* Women & Home; Woman's Weekly. *Memberships:* Campaign for Nuclear Disarmament; Pax Christi; Romantic Novelists Association. *Literary Agent:* June Hall Literary Agents Ltd, 504 The Chambers, Chelsea Harbour, London SW10 0XF. *Address:* 113 Nun Street, St Davids, Haverfordwest, Dyfed SA62 6BP, Wales.

DE JONGE Alex, b. 1938, Britain. University Fellow and Tutor; Writer. *Appointments:* Fellow and Tutor, New College, Oxford, 1965-. *Publications:* (with others), Nineteenth Century Russian Literature, 1973; Nightmare Culture, Lautreamont and Les Chants de Maldoror, 1973; Dostoevsky and the Age of Intensity, 1975; Prince of Clouds: A Biography of Baudelaire, 1976; The Weimar Chronicle A Prelude to History, 1977; Napoleon's Last Will and Testament, 1977; Fire and Water: A Life of Peter the Great, 1979; The Life and Times of Grigorii Rasputin, 1982; Stalin and the Shaping of the Soviet Union, 1986.

DE LANGE Nicholas, b. 7 Aug 1944, Nottingham, England. Scholar; Translator. *Education:* Christ Church, Oxford, 1962-70; MA, 1969; DPhil, 1970. *Publications:* Apocrypha, 1978; Atlas of the Jewish World, 1984; Judaism, 1986; Many literary translations incl: My Michael (Amos Oz); Black Box (Amos Oz), 1990. *Contributions to:* Contributing editor, Tel Aviv Review. *Honours:* George Webber Prize for Translation, 1990. *Memberships:* Society of Authors; Committee Member, Translators Association; Fellow, Wolfson College, Cambridge; British Association of Jewish Studies, Past President. *Address:* The Divinity School, St John's St, Cambridge CB2 1TW, England.

DE LINT Charles (Henri Diederick Hoefsmit), b. 22 Dec 1951, Bussum, Netherlands, immigrated to Canada 1952, naturalized citizen 1961. Owner and Editor of Triskell Press; Writer. m. MaryAnn Harris, 15 Sept 1980. *Education:* Attended Aylmer and Philemen Wright High Schools. *Appointments:* Worked in various clerical and construction positions 1967-71, and as retail clerk and manager of record stores, 1971-83; Writer in Ottawa, Ontario, 1983-; Owner and editor of Triskell Press. *Publications include:* The Fair in Emain Macha, 1990; Drink Down The Moon, 1990; Ghostwood, 1990; Angel of Darkness, 1990; (Contributor), The Annual Review of Fantasy and Science Fiction, 1988; The Valley of Thunder, Philip Jose Farmer's The Dungeon: Book Three, 1988; The Hidden City, Philip Jose Farmer's The Dungeon: Book Five, 1988; The Fair in Emain Macha, 1990; Drink Down the Moon: A Novel of Urban Faerie, 1990; Ghostwood, 1990; Angel of Darkness, 1990; The

Dreaming Place, 1992; The Little Country, 1991; Ghosts of Wind and Shadow, 1991; Uncle Dobbin's Parrot Fair, 1991; Death Leaves an Echo, 1991; Hedgework and Guessery, 1991; Our Lady of the Harbour, 1991; Paperjack, 1991; The Harp of The Grey Rose, 1991; Mulengro: A Romany Tale; Yarrow: An Autumn Tale; Ascian in Rose; Spiritwalk, 1992; Merlin Dreams in The Mondream Wood, 1992; From A Whisper to a Scream, 1992; Dreams Underfoot: The Newford Collection, 1993. *Contributions to:* Poetry included in anthologies; Columns in horror and science fiction magazines; periodicals. *Honours:* William L Crawford Award for best new fantasy author from International Association for the Fantastic in the Arts, 1984; Canadian SF/Fantasy Award (Casper), nominations, 1986 for Mulengro and 1987 for Yarrow; Casper Award for best work in English, 1988 for Jack the Giant-Killer; Readercon Small Press Award for Best Short Work for The Drowned Man's Reel, 1989; juror for William L Crawford Award; Canadian Science Fiction/Fantasy Award, World Fantasy Award, Theodore Sturgeon Memorial Short Fiction Award, Horror Writers of America Award and Nebula Award; World Fantasy Award Nominations include: Best Novel for The Little Country, Best Novella for Our Lady of the Harbour, Best Short Story for Pity the Monsters, The Conjure Man, 1992. *Memberships:* Science Fiction Writers of America; Vice-President, Horror Writers of America, 1992-93; Small Press Writers and Artists Organization; Theodore Sturgeon Memorial Short Fiction Award Committee. *Literary Agent:* Richard Curtis Associates, Inc, New York. *Address:* P O Box 9480, Ottawa, Ontario, Canada K1G 3V2.

DE MILLE Richard, b. 12 Feb 1922, CA, USA. Writer. m. Margaret Agnes Belgrano, 7 Aug 1955, 2 sons. *Education:* PhD, Psychology, University of Southern California, 1961. *Publications:* The Don Juan Papers, 1990; Castanedas Journey, 1976; Put Your Mother on the Ceiling, 1973. *Contributions to:* Numerous journals and magazines. *Membership:* The Authors Guild. *Address:* 960 Lilac Drive, Montecito, CA 93108, USA.

DE MIOMANDRE Marguerite Maria Julia Ghislaine, b. 11 June 1925. Belgium. Doctor. m. Emmanuel de Miomandre, 25 Apr 1962. *Education:* Lycee de Forest, 1941; Brussels University, 1949. *Publications:* Short Stories in Audace; L'ecole des Anobs; Performed Play, Enamourcomme à la Guerre; 5 plays. *Contributions to:* Audace; Les Caliers de la Bilogue; Femmes d'Aujourd'hui. *Honours:* Grand prize de la Nouvelle de l'Academic Litte; Menthe ou Cassis, 1992. *Memberships:* Pen CLub; AEB. *Address:* 151 Avenue Moliere, 1060 Brussels, Belgium.

DE PAZZI Ellen Eugenia, b. 7 Apr 1915, Elcador, Iowa, USA. Artist; Poet. m. 17 Aug 1940, 2 sons. *Education:* Indiana University, 1935-38; Atelier Caterina Baratolli in portraiture, Rio de janrieo, Brazil, 1949-52; Fine Arts Degree, Suffolk Community College, 1988. *Contributions to:* Poetry and short stories to: Tap Roots magazine and annuals, 1973-90; Poetry Anthology, 1974-75; Soundwaves, 1985-90; East End QArts Poetry Corner, 1987-88; Westhampton Chronicle; Col9or and Rhyme. *Honours:* DAR Essay prize for history of Frontier Days, 1934; Poetry Prize, Soundwaves, 1985-87;I Poetry Bi-annual, for Floodtide and Wildwind. *Memberships:* Tap Roots for Poets and Writers, 1972-90; Soundwaves, Editorial Staff, 1984-80; Southbay Poetry Association, 1987-88; Westhampton Writers Festival, 1986-90; Hampton Centre Gallery Incorporated, Director, 1975-90; South Fork Craftsmen's Guild, Publicity Officer, 1970-88. *Address:* 5126 Bur Oak Circle, PO Box 31226, Raleigh, NC 27622, USA.

DE PRE Jean-Anne. *See:* **AVALLONE Michael.**

DE QUIROS Beltran. *See:* **ROMEU Jorge Luis.**

DE REGNIERS Beatrice Schenk (Tamara Kitt), b. 1914, America. Writer; Poet; Playwright. *Appointments:*

Director of Educational Materials, American Heart Association, New York City, 1949-61; Editor, Lucky Book Club, Scholastic, Inc, New York City, 1961-81. *Publications:* The Giant Story, 1953; A Little House of Your Own, 1954; What Can You Do With a Shoe? 1955; Was It a Good Trade? 1956; A Child's Book of Dreams, 1957; Something Special, 1958; Cats Cats Cats Cats Cats, 1958; The Snow Party, 1959, 1989; What Happens Next? 1959; The Shadow Book, 1960; Who Likes the Sun? 1961; The Little Book, (illustrated by the Author) 1961, reissued as Going for a Walk, 1982, reissued 1993 with new illustrations by Robert Knox; (as Tamara Kitt), The Adventures of Silly Billy, 1961; (as Tamara Kitt), The Surprising Pets of Billy Brown, 1962; (as Tamara Kitt), Billy Brown: The Baby Sitter, 1962; (as Tamara Kitt), The Boy Who Fooled The Giant, 1963; The Little Girl and Her Mother, 1963; May I Bring a Friend? 1964; The Abraham Lincoln Joke Book, 1965; David and Goliath, 1965; How Joe the Bear and Sam the Mouse Got Together, 1965, 1990; Penny, 1966, 1987; Circus, 1966; The Giant Book, 1966; (as Tamara Kitt), A Special Birthday Party for Someone Very Special, 1966; (as Tamara Kitt), Sam and the Impossible Thing, 1967; The Day Everybody Cried, 1967; Willy O'Dwyer Jumped in the Fire, 1968; (as Tamara Kitt), Jake, 1968; Catch a Little Fox, 1969; Poems Children Will Sit Still For, 1969; The Boy, the Rat and the Butterfly, 1971; Red Riding Hood Retold in Verse for Boys and Girls to Read Themselves, 1972; It Does Not Say Meow and Other Animal Riddle Rhymes, 1972; The Enchanted Forest 1974; Little Sister and the Month Brothers, 1976; A Bunch of Poems and Verses, 1977; Laura's Story, 1979; Everyone Is Good for Something, 1979, playscripts and lyrics for musical based on book, 1990; Picture Book Theater, 1982; Waiting for Mama, 1984; So many Cats, 1985; This Big Cat and Other Cats I've Known, 1985; Jack and the Beanstalk Retold in Verse, 1985; A Week in the Life of Best Friends and Other Poems of Friendship, 1986; Jack The Giant Killer Retold in Verse and Other Useful Information about Giants, 1987; The Way I Feel ....Sometimes, 1988; Sing a Song of Popcorn, Every Child's Book of Poems (co-editor), 1988. *Memberships:*Authors Guild; Dramatists Guild; PEN; Society of Children's Book writers & illustrators. *Address:* 180 West 58th Street, New York, NY 10019, USA.

DE ROO Anne (Louise), b. 1931, New Zealand. Children's Fiction Writer. *Appointments:* Library Assistant, Dunedin Public Library, 1956; Assistant Librarian, Dunedin Teachers' College, 1957-59; Governess, Part-time Gardener, Shropshire, England, 1962-68; Part-time Secretary, Hertfordshire, England, 1969-73. *Publications:* The Gold Dog, 1969; Moa Valley, 1969; Boy and the Sea Beast, 1971; Cinnamon and Nutmeg, 1972; Mick's Country Cousins, 1974; Scrub Fire, 1977; Traveller, 1979; Because of Rosie, 1980; Jacky Nobody, 1984; Friend Troll, Friend Taniwha, 1986; The Bat's nest, 1986. *Address:* 38 Joseph Street, Palmerston North, New Zealand.

DE VERE Jane. *See:* **WATSON Julia.**

DE WAELE Michele, (Michele Morhange), b. 5 Nov 1943, Ghent, Belgium. m. 1 son, 2 daughters. *Education:* College in Ghent. *Publications:* Le Jardinier de la Solitude; Le Piège; Fausse Note. *Memberships:* Society des Gens de Lettres. *Address:* De Heide 9, B-9831 Deurle, Belgium.

DE-WEESE Gene Thomas Eugene (Jean De-Weese, Thomas Stratton, Victoria Thomas), b. 1934. Romance/Gothic, Science Fiction/Fantasy, Children's fiction, Crafts. *Appointments:* Electronics Technician, Delco Radio, Kokomo, Indiana, 1954-59; Technical Writer, Delco Electronics, Milwaukee, 1959-74. *Publications:* (As Thomas Stratton, with Robert Coulson), The Invisibility Affair: Man from UNCLE No 11, 1967; The Mind-Twisters Affair: Man from UNCLE No 12, 1967; (with Robert Coulson), Now You See It/Him/Them... 1975; (with Gini Rogowski), Making American Folk Art Dolls, 1975; (as Jean DeWeese), The Reimann Curse, 1975, expanded version as A Different

Darkness, 1982; (as Jean DeWeese), The Carnelian Cat, 1975; (as Jean DeWeese), The Moonstone Spirit, 1975; (as Jean DeWeese), the Doll With Opal Eyes, 1976; (as Jean DeWeese), Cave of the Moaning Wind, 1976; (as Jean DeWeese), Web of Guilt, 1976; Jeremy Case, 1976; (with Robert Coulson), Charles Fort Never Mentioned Wombats, 1977; (as Jean DeWeese), Nightmare in Pewter, 1978; Major Corby and the Unidentified Flapping Object (juvenile), 1979; The Wanting Factor, 1980; The Adventures of a Two-Minute Werewolf (juvenile), 1983; (as Jean DeWeese), Hour of the Cat, 1980; Nightmares From Space (juvenile), 1981; (as Jean DeWeese), the Backhoe Gothic, 1981; Something Answered, 1983; Computers in Entertainment and the Arts (juvenile non-fiction), 1984; Black Suits from outer Space (juvenile science fiction), 1985; (as Victoria Thomas, with Connie Kugi), Ginger's Wish, 1987; (with Robert Coulson), Nightmare Universe, 1985; The Dandelion Caper (juvenile science fiction), 1986; The Calvin Nullifier (juvenile science fiction), 1987; Chain of Attack (Star Trek No 32), 1987; The Peacekeepers, 1988, (Star Trek: Next Generation No 2); The Final Nexus, 1988, (Star Trek No 43); Whatever Became of Aunt Margaret?, (juvnenile science fiction), 1990; Renegade (Star Trek No54), 1991. *Address:* 2718 N Prospect, Milwaukee, WI 53211, USA.

DEAR Nick, b. 11 June 1955, Portsmouth, England. Playwright. Partner: Penny Downie, 2 sons. *Education:* BA, Hons, European Literature, University of Essex, 1977. *Appointments:* Playwright-in-Residence, Essex University, 1985; Playwright-in-Residence, Royal Exchange Theatre, 1987-88. *Publications:* The Art of Success, 1986; In the Ruins, 1989; A Family Affair (after Ostrovsky), 1988; The Last Days of Don Juan (after Tirso), 1990; Le Bourgeois Gentilhomme (after Molièro), 1992; Temptation, 1984; Pure Science, 1986; Food of Love, 1988; Several plays for Radio; Films: The Monkey Parade, 1983; The Ranter, 1988. *Honours:* John Whiting Award, 1987; Olivier Award nominations, 1987, 1988. *Membership:* Writers' Guild of Great Britain. *Literary Agent:* Rosica Colin Ltd. *Address:* c/o Rosica Colin Ltd, 1, Clareville Grove Mews, London SW7 5AH, England.

DEARDEN James Shackley, b. 9 Aug 1931, Barrow-in-Furness, England. Curator; Printer. *Publications include:* The Professor; Arthur Severn's Memoir of Ruskin, 1967; A Short History of Brantwood, 1967; Iteriad by John Ruskin, (editor), 1969; Facets of Ruskin, 1970; Ruskin and Coniston, (with K G Thorne), 1971; Turners Isle of Wight Sketch Book, 1979; John Ruskin, 1981; John Ruskins's Le Alpi, 3 eds, 1989-90; John Ruskins Camberwell, 1990; A Tour to the Lakes in Cumberland, John Ruskin's Diary for 1830, (editor), 1990; John Ruskin and Victorian Art, 1993. *Contributions to:* Book Collector; Connoisseur; Apollo; Burlington; Bulletin of John Rylands Lib.; Country Life; Ruskin Newsletter, (editor); Ruskin Research Series, (general editor); Journal of Pre-Rephaehte Studies (editorial advisory board). *Memberships:* Bibliographical Society; Ruskin Association, Secretary and Treasurer; Turner Society; Companion of the Guild of St. George; Isle of Wight Foot Beagles, Chairman and Past Master. *Address:* 4 Woodlands, Foreland Road, Bembridge, Isle of Wight, England.

DEDERER John Morgan, b. 14 Jan 1951, Ft Mende, Maryland, USA. Historian. m. Melissa G Wetterborg, 22 Jan 1977, 1 son, 2 daughters. *Education:* BA, 1980, MA, 1982, University of South Florida, Tampa; PhD, University of Alabama, Tuscaloosa, 1988; Olin Postdoctoral Fellow, Yale University, 1988-89. *Appointments:* Editor, Southern Historian, 1984- 87. *Publications:* Making Bricks Without Straw, 1983; War in America to 1775: Before Yankee Doodle, 1990. *Contributions to:* Essays to: Military Affairs, 1983, 1986; A Guide to Sources in US Military History, Supplements II and III, 1986, 1992. *Memberships:* American Historical Association; Organization of American Historians; Society of Military Historians; Southern Historical Association; Life Member, Disabled American Veterans. *Literary Agent:* Gerard McCauley Agency,Inc. *Address:* 20 Shady Hill Road, Fairfield, CT 06430, USA.

DEFORD Frank, b. 16 Dec 1938, Baltimore, Maryland, USA. Writer; Editor. m. Carol Penner, 28 Aug 1965, 1 son, 2 daughters. *Education:* BA, Princeton University, 1962. *Appointments:* Writer, Sports Illustrated, 1962-89; Commentator, Cable News Network, 1980-86; Commentator, National Public Radio, 1980-89; Commentator, NBC, 1986-89; Editor-in-Chief, The National, 1989-1991. *Publications:* Five Strides On The Banked Track, 1969; Cut 'N' Run, 1971; There She Is, 1972; The Owner, 1974; Big Bill Tilden: The Triumphs & The Tragedy, 1977; Everybody's All-American, 1981; Alex: The Life Of A Child, 1982; Spy In The Deuce Cort, 1987; World's Tallest Midget, 1988; Casey On The Loose, 1989. *Contributions to:* Numerous magazines; Contributing editor, Vanity Fair, 1993-. *Honours:* Christopher Award, 1982; US Sportswriter Of The Year, 1982, 1984-88; Emmy Award, 1988; University of Missouri Journalism Award, 1987; US Magazine Writer of the Year Award (Washington Journalism Review), 1987-88; Ronald Reagan Award for Sports Journalism, 1987; Best Sportswriter, 1992 (American Journalism Review). *Literary Agent:* Sterling Lord, Sterling Lord Literistic, New York, USA. *Address:* Box 1109, Greens Farms, CT 06436, USA.

DEFORD Sara Whitcraft, b. 9 Nov 1916, Youngstown, Ohio, USA. Professor. *Education:* BA 1936, MA 1938, Mount Holyoke College; PhD, Yale Universty, 1942. *Appointments include:* College English teacher, 1942-81. *Publications include:* Return to Eden, 1940; Lectures on Modern American Poetry, 1957; City of Love, 1958; The Pearl, 1966; Lectures on Paradise Lost, I & II, 1970; Short Love Poems of John Donne, 1971; Forms of Verse, with Clarinda Lott, 1971. Poetry includes: Japanese Scroll Painting, 1969; Account in Gold, 1969; The Circle, 1969; High Wire Act, 1972; The Bridge, 1974; Plastic, 1974; Island Paradise, 1974; Magnolia, 1976; Lily of the Valley, 1976. *Contributions include:* Numerous professional journals & magazines including: Poetry & Music; College Verse; Mount Holyoke Monthly; Poetry World; Westminster Magazine; Christian Science Monitor; Catholic World; Friends Journal; Arizona Quarterly. *Honours:* Sigma Theta Chi Alumnae Poetry Prize, 1935; Albert Stanburrough Cook Prize, 1941; Eugene Saxton Memorial Fellowship, 1947; Fulbright Professor, Japan, 1954-55, 1961-62. *Membership:* Poetry Society of America. *Address:* 1961 South Josephine, no.302, Denver, Colorado 80210, USA.

DEIGHTON Len, b. 1929, British. Writer. *Publications:* The Ipcress File, 1962; Horse Under Water, 1963; Funeral in Berlin, 1964; Action Cook Book: Len Deighton's Guide to Eating (in US as Cookstrip Cook Book), 1965; Ou est le Garlic: or Len Deighton's French Cook Book, 1965, revised edition as Basic French Cooking, 1978; The Billion Dollar Brain, 1966; An Expensive Place to Die, 1967; (ed), London Dossier, 1967; Only When I Larf, 1968; (compiled by Victor and Margaret Pettit), Len Deighton's Continental Dossier: A Collection of Cultural Culinary, Historical, Spooky, Grim and Preposterous Facts, 1968; Bomber, 1970; Declarations of War (stories), 1971; Close-Up, 1972; Spy Story, 1974; Yesterday's Spy, 1975; Twinkle, Twinkle, Little Spy, 1976; Fighter: The True Story of the Battle of Britain, 1977; SS-GB, 1978; (with Arnold Schwartzman), Airshipwreck, 1978; Blitzkrieg: From the Rise of Hitler to the Fall of Dunkirk, 1979; Battle of Britain, 1980; XPD 1981; Goodbye Mickey Mouse, 1982; Berlin Game, 1983; Mexico Set, 1984; London Match, 1985; Spy Hook, 1988; Spy Line, 1989; Spy Sinker, 1990; ABC of French Food, 1989; Basic French Cookery Course, 1990; MAMista, 1991; City of Gold, 1992. *Address:* c/o Jonathan Clowes Ltd, 10 Iron Bridge House, Bridge Approach, London NW1 8BD, England.

DEIMER Lorena Ruth, b. 11 Jan 1926, Thermopolis, Wyoming, USA. Freelance Writer. m. (1) 1946, (2) Marshall F Deimer, 21 Feb 1971, 1 son, 1 daughter. *Education:* High School Casper, Junior College; International Aurora Community College. *Publications:* Book: Magnolia Blossoms; Other books in preparation: Roots of Evil; Murder in Church; Elisia. Poetry: Golden Voices Past and Present, 1989; World Treasury of Great Poems, 1989; Great Poems of the Western World, vol 11, 1989; Today's Poets, 1989; Misty and Me, 1991; The Write Technique, 1991. *Contributions to:* McCall's; Ladies Home Journal; Colorado Old Times, 1980-82; Colorado Genealogical; The Denver Post; The Senior Beacon; The Keyboard & Pen Denver Metro Chapter of the National Writers Club; Aurora Community College newspaper, The National Writers Club Denver Merto Newspaper 1988-89. *Honours include:* Golden Poet Award, 1987, 1988, 1989. *Memberships:* The National Writers Club; The Fictional Group, Denver Chapter, The Genealogical Club; Baptist Youth Fellowship Group, President 1944. *Literary Agent:* James Lee Young, National Writers Club. *Address:* 1164 Macon Street, Aurora, CO 80010, USA.

DEJEVSKY Nikolai James, b. 22 Sept 1945, Hanau, Germany. Publishing Consultant. m. Mary Peake, 13 Sept 1975. *Education:* BA, Cornell University, USA, 1968; MA, University of Pennsylvania, USA, 1971; DPhil, Christ Church, University of Oxford, UK, 1977. *Appointments include:* Assistant Editor, Clio Press Ltd, Oxford, 1977-80; Publishing Manager, Pergamon Press Ltd, Oxford, 1980-82; Publisher, Professional Publishing Ltd, London, 1982-84; Editorial Director, Gower Publishing Ltd, Aldershot, 1984-85; Publisher, Longman Group Ltd, Harlow, 1985-88. *Publications:* Cultural Atlas of Russia and the Soviet Union, 1989. *Contributions to:* California Slavic Studies; Cambridge Encyclopaedia of Archaeology; Medieval Scandinavia; Solanus; Modern Encyclopaedia of Russian & Soviet History; Year's Work in Modern Language Studies. *Address:* 37 Ulysses Road, West Hampstead, London NW6 1ED, England.

DEKKER Carl. *See:* **LYNDS Dennis.**

DEKKER George, b. 1934, America. Professor of English; Writer. *Appointments:* Lecturer, University College, Swansea, Wales, 1962-64; Lecturer 1964-66, Senior Lecturer 1966-70, Reader in Literature, 1970-72, University of Essex, Colchester; Associate Professor 1972-74, Professor of English, 1974-, Joseph S Atha, Professor of Humanities, 1988-, Stanford University, California, USA. *Publications:* Sailing After Knowledge: The Cantos of Ezra Pound, 1963; James Fenimore Cooper: The Novelist, 1967; (ed with Larry Johnston), The American Democrat, by James Fenimore Cooper, 1969; (ed with John McWilliams), James Fenimore Cooper: The Critical Heritage, 1973; Coleridge and the Literature of Sensibility, 1978; (ed) Donald Davie and the Responsibilities of Literature, 1984; The American Historical Romance, 1987. *Address:* Department of English, Stanford University, Stanford, CA 94305, USA.

DEKKER Rudolf Michel, b. 6 June 1951, Amsterdam, Netherlands. m. Florence Wilhelmina Johanna Koorn, 2 May 1985, 1 daughter. *Education:* University of Amsterdam, 1969-76. *Appointments:* Lecturer, Erasmus University Rotterdam, 1981-. *Publications:* Holland in Beroering. Oproeren in de 17de en 18de eeuw; The Tradition of Female Transvestism in Early Modern Europe; De Bredasche Heldinne; Arenout van Overbeke, Anecdota Sive Historiae Jocosae. *Contributions to:* Theory and Society; History of European Ideas; Women And Politics in the Age of the Democratic Revolution. *Memberships:* Maatschappy der Vederlandse Letterkunde; Nederlands Historisch Genootschap. *Address:* Westerhout Straat 28, 2012JS Haarlem, Netherlands.

DEL MAR Norman, b. 31 July 1919, London, England. Orchestral Conductor. m. Pauline Mann, 24 Jan 1947, 2 sons. *Education:* Royal College of Music. *Publications:* Richard Strauss, 3 volumes, 1962-72, 1986; Anatomy of the Orchestra, 1981; Mahler's Sixth Symphony - A Study, 1980; Companion to the Orchestra, 1987; Conducting Beethoven, 1992. *Honours:* CBE, 1975; Hon. D.Litt., Sussex, 1977. *Literary Agent:* David Higham Associates. *Address:* Clarion/

Seven Muses, 47 Whitehall Park, London N19 3TW, England.

DEL REY Lester, b. 2 June 1915, Minnesota, USA. Author; Editor. m. Judy-Lynn Benjamin, 21 Mar 1971. *Education:* GeoGeorge Washington University, 1931-33. *Appointments:* Fantasy Editor, Ballatine Books, 1975. *Publications:* Nerves, 1956; And Some Were Human, 1949; The Eleventh Commandement, 1962; Police Your Planet, 1975; The Early del Rey, 1975; Pstalemate, 1971; about 20 novels for teenagers; 5 science-fact book; 20 Miscellaneous books as Editor; Works on photography, space, gem-stones. *Contributions to:* Numerous articles and stories in professional journals and magazines. *Honours:* Boys Club of America, Junior Book Award, 1952; Guest of Honour, World Science Fiction Convention, 1967. *Memberships:* Authors Guild; Society of Illustrators. *Literary Agent:* Scott Meredith Literary Agency Inc., New York, USA. *Address:* 310 East 46th St, New York, NY 10017, USA.

DELAHAYE Michael John, b. 6 Apr 1946, Romsey, Hampshire, England. Author; Journalist; Broadcaster. m. Ann Chovy, 19 Jan 1980, 1 daughter. *Education:* BA Honours, English, Van Mildert College, University of Durham, 1968. *Appointments include:* Reporter, BBC TV News & Current Affairs, 1969-79. *Publications:* The Sale of Lot 236, 1981; The Third Day (in USA, On The Third Day), 1984; Stalking-Horse, 1987. *Contributions to:* Numerous magazines & journals. *Literary Agents:* David Higham Associates, London; Harold Ober Associates, New York. *Address:* c/o David Higham Associates, 6-8 Lower John Street, London, W1R 4HA, England.

DELANEY Denis. *See:* **GREEN Peter Morris.**

DELANEY Shelagh, b. 1939, Salford, Lancashire, England. Playwright. 1 daughter. *Publications:* Plays: A Taste of Honey, 1958; The Lion in Love, 1960; Films: A Taste of Honey; The White Bus, 1966; Charlie Bubbles, 1968; Dance with a Stranger, 1985; TV Plays: St Martin's Summer, 1974; Find Me First, 1979; TV Series: The House that Jack Built, 1977 (stage adaptation, New York, 1979); Radio Plays: So Does the Nightingale, 1980; Don't Worry About Matilda, 1983; Sweetly Sings the Donkey, 1963. *Honours:* Charles Henry Foyle New Play Award, Arts Council Bursary, New York Drama Critics Award, A Taste of Honey; British Film Academy Award, Robert Flaherty Award, A Taste of Honey, 1961; Prix Film Jeunesse Etranger, Cannes, 1985. *Address:* c/o Tessa Sayle, 11 Jubilee Place, London SW3 3TE, England.

DELANO Anthony, b. 1930, Britain. Writer. *Appointments:* Rome Correspondent, 1956-60, Paris Correspondent 1960-63, American Correspondent 1963-70, London Diary Editor, 1970-74, Roving Correspondent, 1970-74, Chief American Correspondent 1974-78, Managing Editor, 1978-84, Daily Mirror, London; Director, New Media, London 1984-; Senior Lecturer University of Queensland, 1989-1992; Visiting Professor, London College of Printing, 1993. *Publications:* Breathless Diversions (novel), 1975; Slip-Up (documentary), 1977; Manacled Mormon, 1978. *Address:* 4 Moscow Mansions, 224 Cromwell Road, London SW5 0SP, England.

DELANY Samuel R(ay), b. 1942. Science fiction/Fantasy. *Publications:* The Jewels of Aptor, 1962, unabridged edition 1968; The Fall of the Towers, vol I, Captives of the Flames, 1963, as Out of the Dead City, 1968, vol II, The Towers of Toron, 1964, vol III, City of a Thousand Suns, 1965; The Ballad of Beta-2, 1965; Empire Star, 1966; Babel-17, 1966; The Einstein Intersection, 1967; Nova, 1968; Driftglass: Ten Tales of Speculative Fiction, 1971; Dhalgren, 1975; Triton, 1976; The Jewel-Hinged Jaw: Notes on the Language of Science Fiction, 1977; The American Shore, 1978; Empire, 1978; (ed) Nebula Award Winners

13, 1979; Distant Stars, 1981; Stars in My Pocket Like Grains of Sand, 1984; Starboard Wine: More Notes on the Language of Science Fiction, 1984; The Splendour and Misery of Bodies, 1985; Flight from Neveryon, 1985. *Address:* c/o Bantam Books, 666 Fifth Avenue, New York, NY 10019, USA.

DELBANCO Nicholas Franklin, b. 27 Aug 1942, London, England. Writer. m. Elena Carter Greenhouse, 12 Sept 1970, 2 daughters. *Education:* BA, History & Literature, Harvard College, 1963; MA, English, Comparative Literature, Columbia University, 1966. *Appointments:* Member, Language & Literature Division, Bennington College, 1966-85; Director, Bennington Writing Workshops, 1977-; Visiting Professor, Iowa Writers Programme, University of Iowa, 1979; Adjunct Professor, School of the Arts, Columbia University, 1979; Visiting Artist in Residence, Trinity College, 1980; Visiting Professor, Williams College, 1982; Professor, English, Skidmore College, 1984-85; Professor, English, Director, MFA Programme, University of Michigan, 1985-. *Publications:* The Martlet's Tale, 1966; Grasse 3/23/66, 1968; Consider Sappho Burning, 1969; News, 1970; In the Middle Distance, 1971; Fathering, 1973; Small Rain, 1975; Possession, 1977; Sherbrookes, 1978; Stillness, 1980; Group Portrait : Conrad Crane Ford James & Wells, 1982; About My Table and Other Stories, 1983; The Beaux Arts Trio: A Portrait, 1985; Running in Place: Scenes from the South of France, 1989; The Writers' Trade, and Other Stories, 1990. *Contributions to:* Atlantic Monthly; Esquire; New York Times Book Review; New Republic; others. *Honours include:* NEA Creative Writing Fellowships, 1973, 1982; Guggenheim Fellowship, 1979. *Memberships:* Authors League; Authors Guild; Signet Society; Phi Beta Kappa; New York State Writers Institute; PEN. *Address:* c/o Dept. of English, University of Michigan, 7601 Haven Hall, Ann Arbor, MI 48109, USA.

DELDERFIELD Eric Raymond, b. 4 May 1909, London, England. Author; Journalist. m. 1934, 1 daughter. *Appointment:* Director, David & Charles Publishers 1962-67. *Publications:* Lynmouth Flood Disaster, 1953, reprinted 14 times; British Inn Signs and Their Stories, 1965, 1984; West Country Houses and Their Families, 3 vols., 1968, 1970, 1973; Kings and Queens of England, 1966, 1970, 1981; True Animal Stories, 4 vols. 1970-73; Cotswold Villages and Churches, 1961, 1985; Exmoor Wanderings; King and Queens' Colour, 1990; numerous guides on areas of Britian. *Contributions to:* Devon Life; This England; and others. *Address:* 51 Ashleigh Road, Exmouth, Devon, EX8 2JY, England.

DELEHANTY Randolph, b. 5 July 1944, Memphis, Tennessee, USA. Writer; Lecturer; Art Curator . *Education:* Georgetown University, BA, 1966; University of Chicago, MA, 1968; Harvard University, MA, 1969; PhD, 1992. *Publications:* In The Victorian Style; San Francisco: The Ultimate Guide; Preserving The West; California: A Guidebook; San Francisco: Walks And Tours in the Golden Gate City; New Orleans: Elegance and Decadence, 1993. *Address:* Curator, The Roger Houston Ogden Collection of Southern Art, 460 Broadway Street, New Orleans, Louisiana 70118, USA.

DELGADO James P, b. 11 Jan 1958, San Jose, California, USA. Historian; Museum Director, Vancouver. m. Mary Jean Bremmer, 7 Oct 1978, 1 son, 1 daughter. *Education:* BA magna cum laude, American History, San Francisco State University, 1981; MA, Maritime History, Underwater Research, East Carolina University, Greenville, North Carolina, 1985. *Appointments:* Assistant to Regional Historian, Western Region (Hawaii, Guam, American Samoa, California, Arizona), 1978-79; Chief Historian, Golden Gate National Recreation Area, San Francisco, California, 1979-86; Chief Maritime Historian, National Park Service, Washington, 1987-91; Executive Director, Vancouver Maritime Museum, Canada, 1991-. *Publications:* Alcatraz Island: The Story Behind the Scenery, 1985; The Log of the Apollo: Joseph Perkins

Beach's Log of the Voyage of the Ship Apollo from New York to San Francisco, 1849 (editor), 1986; Shipwrecks at the Golden Gate (with Stephen A Haller), 1989; To California By Sea: A Maritime History of the California Gold Rush, 1990; National Parks of America, 1990; Pearl Harbor Recalled; New Images of the Day of Infamy (with Tom Freeman), 1991; Great American Ships (with J Candace Clifford), 1991; Alcatraz Island, 1991; Dauntless St Roch: The Mounties' Arctic Schooner, 1992; Shipwrecks of the Northern Shore, forthcoming; Ghost Fleet of the Atomic Age: The Sunken Ships of Bikini Atoll, forthcoming. *Contributions to:* Professional and popular journals including: The Pacific Historian; The Book Club of California Quarterly; The Point Reyes Historian; The Public Historian; American History Illustrated; CRM Bulletin. *Memberships:* Society for Historical Archaeology; California Historical Society; Canadian Nautical Research Society; National Maritime Historical Society; Canadian Representative, International Committee of Monuments, and Sites, Committee on the International Underwater Heritage; Trustee, Council of American Maritime Museums. *Address:* 4204 West 10th Avenue, Vancouver, British Columbia, Canada V6R 2H4.

DELL Belinda. *See:* **BOWDEN Jean.**

DELVIN David George, b. 28 Jan 1939. Doctor; TV Broadcaster; Writer. *Education:* MB.BS, BS., LRCP, MRCS, King's College Hospital, University of London; D.Obst., RCOG; DCH; Dip.Ven.; FPA Cert; MRCGP. *Appointments include:* Associate Editor, New English Encyclopaedia; Consultant Editor, General Practitioner; Contributing Editor, SHE. *Publications:* The Home Doctor; The Book of Love; You and Your Back; A Patient's Guide to Operations'; Your Good Health; The SHE Guide to Family Health; Common Childhood Illnesses; Taking the Pill; How to Improve Your Sex Life; Dear Doc; Carefree Love; An A-Z of Your Child's Health. *Contributions include:* World Medicine, Dr Jekyll Columnist, 1972-82; Columnist, SHE, Weekend, Titbits, Mother & Baby. *Honours:* Medical Journalists' Association Award of Special Merit, 1974, jointly 1975; American Medical Writers' Asociation Best Book Award, 1976; Medaille de la Ville de Paris, Echelon Argent, 1983; Consumer Columnist of the Year, 1986. *Memberships include:* Vice Chairman, Medical Journalists' Association; GMC; Royal Society Medicine; BMA. *Literary Agent:* A P Watt. *Address:* c/o Coutts Ltd, 440 Strand, London WC2R 0QS, England.

DEMARIA Robert, b. 28 Sept 1928, New York City, New York, USA. Writer; Professor. m. (1) Maddalena Buzeo, (2) Ellen Hope Meyer, 3 sons, 1 daughter. *Education:* BA, 1948, MA, 1949, PhD, 1959, Columbia University. *Appointments:* Professor, English, University of Oregon, 1949-52; Professor, English, Hofstra University, 1952-61; Associate Dean, New School for Social Research, New York City, 1961-64; Professor, English, Dowling College, 1965-; Editor, Publisher, The Mediterranean Review, 1969-73. *Publications:* Carnival of Angels, 1961; Clodia, 1965; Don Juan in Lourdes, 1966; The Satyr, 1972; The Decline and Fall of America, 1973; To Be a King, 1976; Sons and Brothers, 1985. *Contributions to:* Antaeus; California Quarterly; Southwest Review; Cimarron Review; Beloit Fiction Journal; New Letters; Florida Review. *Memberships:* Authors Guild; PEN American Center. *Literary Agent:* Diane Cleaver, 55 Fifth Ave, New York, NY 10003, USA. *Address:* 106 Vineyard Place, Port Jefferson, NY 11777, USA.

DEMARIS Ovid. *See:* **DESMARIS Ovide E.**

DEMASSA Jessie G., b. Aliquippa, Pennsylvania, USA. Freelance Writer. 3 sons. *Education:* BS, Journalism, Temple University, Philadelphia, Pennsylvania; MA, Librarianship, San Jose State University, San Jose, California; Postgraduate studies, University of Oklahoma, Norman, and University of Southern California, Los Angeles (Administrative credential). *Publications:* Unfinished Business, mystery-

suspense novel, in progress. *Contributions to:* Short stories, Decade of Short Stories and Family Weekly; Articles, Collier's, Sports Afield, The Woman, Today's Woman, Read, other national publications. *Membership:* National Writers Club. *Address:* 9951 Garrett Circle, Huntington Beach, CA 92646, USA.

DEMBSKI Stephen Michael, b. 13 Dec 1949, Boston, Massachusetts, USA. Composer; University Professor. m. Sonja Sullivan, 9 July 1988. *Education:* BA, Anticch College, 1973; MA, SUNY, Stony Brook, 1975; MFA, Princeton University, 1977; PhD, 1980. *Appointments:* Associate Professor, University of Wisconsin, 1982-; Board of Directors, League of Composers/ISCM, US Chapter, 1977-; CRI, 1984-; NY New Music Ensembly, 1982-; Board of Governors, American Composers Alliance, 1988-90. *Publications:* Milton Babbitt: Words About Music; Compositions inc. Alba; Alta; Of Mere Being; String Quartet. *Honours:* Composer Fellowship Grant; National Endowment of the Arts; American Academy and Institute of arts and Letters, Lieberson Award; NYSCA Commission Grant; George A and Eliza Gardener Howard Foundation Fellowship; Segualazioue, Premio Musicale Citta di Trieste. *Memberships:* ASCAP, American Music Center. *Address:* 96 Perry Street, Apartment B-22, New York, NY 10014, USA.

DEMETILLO Ricaredo, b. 1920, Philippines. Professor of Humanities; Writer. *Appointments:* Assistant Professor 1959-70, Chairman, Department of Humaniities 1961-62, Associate Professor 1970-75, Professor of Humanities, University of the Philippines, Diliman, Quezon City, Philippines. *Publications:* No Certian Weather: A Collection of Poetry, 1956; La Via: A Spiritual Journey, 1958; Daedalus and Other Poems, 1961; Barter in Panay (poetry), 1961; The Authentic Voice of Poetry, 1962; Masks and Signature (poetry), 1968; The Scare-Crow Christ (poetry), 1973; The Heart of Emptiness is Black (play), 1973; The City and the Thread of Light (poetry), 1974; Lazarus, Troubadour (poetry), 1974; The Genesis of a Troubled Vision (novel), 1976; Major and Monor Keys (criticism), 1986; First and Last Fruits (poetry), 1989. *Address:* 38, Balacan Street, West Avenue, Quezon City, Philippines.

DEMPSTER Nigel Richard Patton, b. 1 Nov 1941. Editorial Executive. m. (1) Emma de Bendern, 1971, (div 1974), (2) Lady Camilla Godolphin Osborne, 1978, 1 daughter. *Appointments:* Broker, Lloyds of London, 1958-59; Stock Exchange, 1959-60; PR Account Executive, Earl of Kimberley Associates, 1960-63; Journalist, Daily Express, 1963-71; Columnist, Daily Mail, 1971-; London Correspondent, Status Magazine, USA, 1965-66. *Publications:* H.R.H The Princess Margaret - A Life Unfulfilled, (Biography), 1981; Heiress - The Story of Christina Onassis, 1989; Nigel Dempster's Address Book (Biography), 1991. *Contributions to:* Queen Magazine; Columnist (Grovel) Private Eye Magazine, 1969-85; Broadcaster with ABC, USA and CBC, Canada, 1970- and with TV am 1983- *Address:* c/o Daily Mail, Northcliffe House, 2 Derry Street, London W8 5TT, England.

DENGLER Sandy, b. 8 June 1939. Writer. m. William F Dengler, 11 Jan 1963, 2 daughters. *Education:* Sidney High School, 1957; BSc, Bowling Green State University, Ohio, 1961; MSc, Arizona State University, 1967. *Publications include:* Fanny Crosby, 1985; Florence Nightingale, 1988; Susanna Wesley, 1987; John Bunyan, 1986; D L Moody, 1987; Romance Novels, Juvenile Historical Fiction including: Barn Social, 1978; Yosemite's Marvellous Creatures, 1979; Summer of the Wild Pig, 1979; Melon Hound, 1980; Horse Who Loved Picnics, 1980; Mystery at McGehan Ranch, 1982; Chain Five Mystery, 1984; Summer Snow, 1984; Winterspring, 1985; This Rolling Land, 1986; Jungle Gold, 1987; Code of Honour, 1988; Power of Pinjarra, 1989; Taste of Victory, 1989; East of Outback, 1990; Death valley, 1993; Cat killer, 1993; Dublin Crossing, 1993. *Contributions to:* Numerous articles in journals and magazines. *Honours:* Writer of the Year, Warm Beach, 1986; Golden Medallion, Romance Writers of

America, 1987. *Address:* 112 Tanoma Woods, Ashford, WA 98304, USA.

DENISOFF R Serge, b. 1939, America. Professor of Sociology; Editor; Writer. *Appointments:* Assistant Professor, California State University, Los Angeles, 1969-70; Associate Professor, then Professor of Sociology, Bowling Green State University, Ohio, 1970-; Editor, Popular Music and Society. *Publications:* (compiler), Protest Songs of War and Peace: A Bibliography and Discography, 1970; Great Day Coming: Folk Music and the American Left, 1971; (with Gary B Rush), Social and Political Movements, 1971; (contributing editor with Richard A Peterson), The Sounds of Social Change: The Uses of Music in Contemporary Society, 1972; (contributing editor), Sociology: Theories in Conflict, 1972; (editor with Charles H McCaghy), Deviance, Criminality and Conflict: The Sociology of Criminality and Non-Conformity, 1973; (contributuing editor with M Levine and O Callahan), Theories and Paradigms of Contemporary Sociology, 1974; (ed) The Sociology of Dissent, 1974; Solid Gold: The Popular Record Industry, 1975; (with R Wahrman), An Introduction to Sociology, 1975, 3rd ed 1982; Sing a Song of Social Significance, 1983; Waylon: A Biography, 1983; Tarnished Gold: The Record Industry Revisited, 1986; Inside MTV, 1988; Risky Business: Rock and the Film Industry, 1992 (with William Romanoski). *Address:* 7 Valley View Drive, Bowling Green, OH 43402, USA.

DENISON Edward Fulton, b. 18 Dec 1915, Omaha, Nebraska, USA. Economist. m. Elsie Lightbown, 14 June 1941, 1 son, 1 daughter. *Education:* AB, Oberlin College, 1936; MA 1938, PhD 1941, Brown University; Graduate, National War College, 1951. *Appointments:* Instructor, Brown University, 1940-41; Economist, US Department of Commerce, 1941-48; Assistant Director, Office of Business Economics, US Department of Commerce, 1949-56; Economist, Associate Director, Committee for Economic Development, 1956-62; Senior Fellow, 1962-78, Senior Fellow Emeritus 1978-, The Brookings Institution; Associate Director, Bureau of Economic Analysis, US Department of Commerce, 1979-82. *Publications include:* The Sources of Economic Growth in the United States and the Alternatives Before Us, 1962; Why Growth Rates Differ: Post War Experience in Nine Western Countries, 1967; Accounting for United States Economic Growth, 1929-69, 1974; Accounting for Slower Economic Growth: The United States in the 1970s, 1979; Trends in American Economic Growth 1929-82, 1985; Estimates of Productivity Change by Industry: an Evaluation and an Alternative, 1989; How Japan's Economy Grew So Fast (with William K Chung), 1976. *Contributions to:* American Economic Review; Survey of Current Business; Journal of Political Economy; Review of Income and Wealth; Review of Economics and Statistics. *Honours:* W S Woytinsky Lectureship Award from University of Michigan, 1967; Fellow, American Statistical Association, 1960; Fellow, American Economic Association, 1985; Shiskin Award from Washington Statistical Society, 1982. *Memberships:* National Academy of Sciences; American Academy of Arts and Sciences; American Economic Association (Vice-President 1978); International Association for Research in Income and Wealth; Conference on Research in Income and Wealth (Former Chairman). *Address:* Brookings Institution, 1775 Massachusetts Avenue NW, Washington, DC 20036, USA.

DENKER Henry, b. 1912, America. Writer; Playwright. *Appointment:* Member, Council of the Dramatists' Guild, 1970-73. *Publications:* I'll Be Right Home, Ma, 1947; My Son, The Lawyer, 1949; Salome: Princess of Galilee, 1951; The First Easter, 1951; Time Limit! (play), 1957; A Far Country (play), 1961; A Case of Libel (play), 1963; What Did We Do Wrong? (play), 1967; The Director, 1970; The Kingmaker, 1972; A Place for the Mighty, 1974; The Physicians, 1975; The Experiment, 1976; The Headhunters (play), 1976; The Starmaker, 1977; The Scofield Diagnosis, 1977; The Second Time Around (play), 1977; The Actress, 1978;

Error of Judgement, 1979; Horowitz and Mrs Washington, 1979, as play, 1980; The Warfield Syndrome, 1981; Outrage, 1982, as play, 1983, as film, 1985; The Healers, 1983; Kincaid, 1984; Robert, My Son, 1985; Judge Spence Dissents, 1986; The Choice, 1987. *Address:* 241, Central Park W, New York, NY 10024, USA.

DENMARK Harrison. *See:* **ZELAZNY Roger.**

DENNING Alfred Thompson Lord, b. 1899, Britain. Lawyer; Former Master of the Rolls. *Career:* Called to the Bar 1923; King's Counsel, 1938; Judge of the High Court of Justice, 1944; a Lord Justice of Appeal, 1948-57; a Lord of Appeal in Ordinary, 1957-62; Master of the Rolls 1962-82. *Publications:* (joint editor), Smith's Leading Cases, 1929; (joint editor), Bullen and Leake's Precedents, 1935; Freedom under the Law (Hamlyn Lectures), 1949; The Changing Law, 1953; The Road to Justice, 1955; The Discipline of Law, 1979; The Due Process of Law, 1980; The Family Story, 1981; What Next in the Law, 1982; The Closing Chapter, 1983; Landmarks in the Law, 1984; Leaves from My Library, 1986. *Address:* The Lawn, Whitchurch, Hants, England.

DENNING Mark. *See:* **STEVENSON John.**

DENNIS-JONES Harold (Paul Hamilton, Dennis Hessing), b. 2 Dec 1915, Port-Louis, Maritius. Journalist; Author; Photographer. 2 daughters. *Education:* Open Scholar in Classics, St. Johns College, Oxford, 1934-38; First Class Honours in Classical Honour Moderations; Second Class Lt Hum. *Appointments:* Kensley Newspapers 1945- 47; Travel Correspondent, Geographical Magazine, 1947-56; London Correspondent, Het Geillustreerde Pers, Amsterdam, 1947-52; UK Editor, Guide Kleber, Paris, 1963-72. *Publications include:* Fifty-three guide books titles/editions, covering all Europe, Morocco, Israel; Verse translations from Greek, French, Spanish, Romanian; Three language learning titles, French, Spanish, Italian. *Contributions to:* Most UK Newspapers; many magazines in UK; newspapers and magazines in Europe, USA, etc; Radio and TV Broadcasts. *Memberships:* British Society of Authors; British Guild of Travel Writers; Federation Internationale des Journalistes et Evivains du Tourisme; International Council for Traditional Music; Great Britain/ East Europe Centre. *Address:* 38 Broadwater Down 14, Tunbridge Wells, Kent TN2 5NX, England.

DENNY Robert Robinson, b. 18 Dec 1920, USA. Writer. m. Susan Hight, 3 Oct 1954, 2 sons, 2 daughters. *Education:* George Washington University; Pennsylvania State College. *Publications:* Aces; Night Run. *Contributions to:* Military History Quarterly; Parable; Washington Post. *Literary Agent:* Jay Caron, NYC. *Address:* 4611 Overbrook Road, Bethesda, MD 20816, USA.

DENOO Joris, b. 6 July 1953, Torhout, Belgium. Author; Teacher. m. Lut Vandemeulebroecke, 23 July 1976, 1 son, 2 daughters. *Education:* Graduate, German Philology, Louvain, 1975; Aggregation PHO, 1976; Specialised in Dutch, Comparative Literature, Poetry. *Appointments:* Freelance Reporter, Book Reviewer, Flemish journals, 1986-. *Publications:* Repelsteel in Bourgondie, novel, 1986; De Bende van de Beeldewaar, story for children, 1986; Binnenscheepvaart, poetry, 1988; Staat van Medewerking, poetry, 1988; Een Paar Kinderen, Graag, story for children, 1992; Voltooid Verwarmde Tijd, poetry, 1992; Taal Is een Aardig Ding, essay, 1993; Verkeerde Lieveheer, novel, 1993. *Contributions to:* Many Flemish and Dutch magazines and journals including: Revisor; Hollands Maandblad; Maatstaf; Brakke Hond. *Honours:* Vlaamse Klub Prize, Brussels, 1979; Premies West-Vlaanderen, 1983,1991; Prijs Tielt Boekenstad, 1992. *Honours:* SABAM, Belgium; Commission Taal en Letterkunde, Province of West Flanders, Bruges. *Literary Agent:* Lut

Vandemeulebroecke. *Address:* Oude leperseweg 85, B-8501 Heule, Belgium.

DENSLOW Sharon Kay, (Sharon Phillips Denslow), b. 25 Aug 1947, Murray, Kentucky, USA. Librarian; Writer. m. Leroy A Denslow, 13 June 1969, 2 daughters. *Education:* BS, English, Journalism, Murray State University, 1969. *Publications:* Night Owls, 1990; At Taylor's Place, 1990; Riding with Aunt Lucy, 1991; Hazel's Circle, 1992; Bus Riders, 1993. *Contributions to:* Grandad's Watermelon, to Country Living magazine, 1990. *Honours:* 1st Place Award for Night Owls, Friends of American Writers, Chicago, 1991. *Address:* 130 Villanova, Elyria, OH 44035, USA.

DENSLOW Sharon Phillips. *See:* **DENSLOW Sharon Kay.**

DENVER Drake C. *See:* **NYE Nelson.**

DENVER Lee. *See:* **GRIBBLE Leonard (Reginald).**

DEPAOLA Tomie, b. 15 Sept 1934, Meriden, Connecticut, USA. Children's Book Artist; Author. *Education:* BFA, Pratt Institute, 1956; MFA, California College of Arts & Crafts, 1969; Doctoral Equivalency, Lone Mountain College, 1970. *Publications:* 200 books from 1964-1992 including: Strega Nona, 1975; The Clown of God, 1978; The Legend Of The Bluebonnet, 1983; Tomie de Paola's Mother Goose, 1985; The Art Lesson, 1989; Tomie de Paola's Book of Bible Stories, 1990; Jingle, The Christmas Clown, 1992. *Honours:* Caldecott Honor Book, American Library Association, 1976; Regina Medal, Catholic Library Association, 1983; Doctor of Letters, honoris causa, Colby-Sawyer College, 1985; American Nominee in Illustration for Hans Christian Andersen Award, International Board of Books for Young People, 1990. *Memberships:* Authors Guild; Society of Children's Book Writers. *Address:* G P Putnam's Sons, Putnam & Grosset Book Group, 200 Madison Avenue, New York City, NY 10016, USA.

DERFLER (Arnold) Leslie, b. 1933, United States of America. Writer (History). *Appointments:* Faculty, Carnegie Mellon University, Pittsburgh, 1962-68; Faculty, University of Massachusetts, Amherst, 1968-69; Professor of History, Florida Atlantic University, Boca Raton, 1969-. *Publications:* The Dreyfus Affair: Tragedy of Errors, 1963; The Third French Republic 1870-1940, 1966; Socialism since Marx, 1973; Alexandre Millerand: The Socialist Years, 1977; Hindi, 1977; President and Parliament: A Short History of the French Presidency, 1984; An Age of Conflict: Readings in 20th Century European History, 1990; Paul Lafargue and the Founding of French Marxism, 1991. *Address:* Department of History, Florida Atlantic University, Boca Raton, FL 33431, USA.

DERR Mark, b. 20 Jan 1950, Baltimore, MD, USA. Writer. m. Gina L Maranto, 11 Sept 1982. *Education:* AB, Johns Hopkins University, 1972; MA, 1973. *Publications:* Some Kind of Paradise; Over Florida; The Frontiersman: The Real Life and Many Legends of Davy Crockett. *Contributions to:* The Atlantic; Andubon. *Literary Agent:* Barney Karpfinger, The Karpfinger Agency, New York, USA. *Address:* 4245 Sheridan Avenue, Miami Beach, FL 33140, USA.

DERRY John Wesley, b. 1933. Writer (History, Biography). *Publications:* William Pitt, 1962; Reaction and Reform, 1963, 3rd edition, 1970; The Regency Crisis and the Whigs, 1963; Parliamentary Reform, 1966; The Radical Tradition, 1967; Political Parties, 1968; Cobbett's England, 1968; Charles James Fox, 1972; Castlereagh, 1976; English Politics and the American Revolution, 1976; Politics in the Age of Fox, Pitt and Liverpool, 1990; Charles, Earl Grey, 1992. *Address:* Department of History, University of Newcastle upon Tyne, Newcastle, NE1 7RU, England.

DERY Mark Alexander, b. 24 Dec 1959, Writer (Essayist, Journalist). m. Margot Mifflin, 20 June 1992. *Publications:* Cyberculture: Road Warriors, Console Cowboys and the Silicon Underground, 1994; Articles in The Utne Reader, underground anthologies including Semiotext(e), 1992, college textbooks including State of the Art: Issues in Contemporary Communications, 1992, academic publications including Present Tense, 1992. *Contributions to:* The New York Times; Elle; Interview; New York; The Philadelphia Inquirer; The Chicago Tribune; The International Herald Tribune; Notes From the Underground monthly music column, to Keyboard and Guitar Player; Guerrilla Semiotics quarterly cultural criticism column, to Mondo 2000; Liner notes for laserdiscs of Cyberpunk and Dr Strangelove. *Literary Agent:* Linda Chester Literary Agency, New York, New York, USA. *Address:* 503 Clinton St 2, Brooklyn, NY 11231, USA.

DESAI Anita, b. 24 June 1937, Mussoorie, India, Writer. m. Ashvin Desai, 13 Dec 1958, 2 sons, 2 daughters. *Education:* BA, Honours, Miranda House, University of Delhi. *Appointments:* Member of Advisory Board for English, Sahitya Akademi, India, 1975-80; Member, Royal Society of Literature, England, 1978-. *Publications:* Cry, The Peacock; Voices in the City; Fire on the Mountain; Clear Light of Day; In Custody; Baumgartner's Bombay; Where Shall We Go This Summer?; Bye Bye Blackbird; The Peacock Garden; Cat on a Houseboat; The Village by the Sea; Games at Twilight. *Contributions to:* Writers' Workshop; Quest; Illustrated Weekly of India; The London Magazine; The Literary Review; New York Times Book Review; Washington Post Book World. *Honours:* Winifred Holtby Award, Royal Society of Literature, 1978; Sahitya Akademi Award for English, 1978; Federation of Indian Publishers Award, 1978; The Padma Shri Award, India, 1989; Hadassah Magazine Award, 1989; Guardian Prize for Children's Fiction, 1983, filmed 1992. *Memberships:* Royal Society of Literature; Sahitya Akademi of India; PEN. *Literary Agent:* Deborah Rogers, c/o Rogers, Coleridge and White Limited. *Address:* c/o Rogers, Coleridge and White Limited, 20 Powis Mews, London W11 1JN, England.

DESAI Chitra Ushakant, b. 22 Dec 1926, Bandra, Bombay, India. Social Counsellor. m. Shri Ushakant Shashikant Desai, 27 July 1947, 1 son, 1 daughter. *Education:* Benares Hindu University, 1946; Nirmala Niketan, Bombay, 1958; Bombay University, 1988. *Appointments:* PEN, All India Centre, 1948, 1951. *Publications:* I Fought For My Countrys Freedom; Bapu: My Mother; Sage of sevagram; The Flute of Reed. *Contributions to:* Book Reviews to Pen Monthly; Articles Gujarati. *Memberships:* Poets And Playrights, Editors, Essayists, Novelist; The Indian Council for Mental Health & Human Relations; Satark. *Address:* 12/C, Maheshwari Mansion, 34 Nepean Sea Road, Bombay 400 026, India.

DESCHOEMAEKER Frans, b. 8 Sept 1954, Belgium. m. Myriam Blyau. *Education:* Institute for Psychical and Social Training, Kortryk, 1973-74. *Appointments:* Editor, Literary Magazine, Diogines, 1984-. *Publications:* Stroomafwaarts; In de Spiegelzalen van de Hefst; De Onderhuidse Lach van de Landjonker; Beginselen van Archcologie. *Contributions to:* The Genesis of a Poem; The Splendid Regions Behind Words; Bottas Glance, about poetry and Archaeology. *Honours:* Poetry Prize Flemish Club Brussels; Poetry Prize of West Flanders; Nominated Hughes C Pernath Prize; Critical Lexicon of Dutch Literature. *Address:* Vontstraat 69, 9700 Oudenaarde, Belgium.

DESCOMBES Vincent, b. 4 Dec 1943, Paris, France. Professor. m. Yasuko Ohno, 1981, 1 daughter. *Education:* Agregation de Philosophie, 1967; PhD, 1970. *Publications:* Modern French Philosophy; Objects of All Sorts; Proust: Philosophy of the Novel; The Barometer of Reason. *Contributions to:* Critique. *Address:* 66 Avenue de la Republique, 75011 Paris, France.

DESJARLAIS John Joseph, b. 19 Mar 1953, Germany. Writer. m. Virginia Louise Wolff, 26 Aug 1978. *Education:* BA, University of Wisconsin Madison, 1976; MA, Columbia University, 1984. *Appointments:* Assistant Editor, Student Leadership Journal, 1992-. *Publications:* The Throne of Tara; Relics; Habakkuk; Beyond Human Control; Its Our Destiny; WorldView Boutique; God Is Building A City. *Contributions to:* University Magazine; Student Leadership Journal; STAFF. *Honours:* Gold Medal, International Multi Image Festival; Christianity Today Readers Choice Award nominee. *Memberships:* Association for Educational Communcations & Technology. *Literary Agent:* Donald Brandenburgh, Brandenburgh & Associates. *Address:* PO Box 7895, Madison, WI 53707, USA.

DESMARAIS Ovide E, (Ovid Demaris), b. 1919, American. Writer. *Publications:* mystery novels: Ride the Gold Mare, 1956; The Hoods Take Over, 1957; The Long Night, 1957; The Lusting Drive, 1958; The Slasher, 1959; The Enforcer, 1960; The Extortioners, 1960; The Gold-Plated Sewer, 1960; Candyleg, 1961 (as Machine Gun McCanin, 1970); The Parasite, 1963; The Organization, 1965 (as The Contract, 1907); The Overlord, 1972; other - Lucky Luciano, 1960; The Lindbergh Kidnapping Case, 1961; The Dillinger Story, 1961; (with Edward Reid), The Green Felt Jungle, 1963; (with Garry Wills), Jack Ruby, 1968; Captive City; Chicago in Chains, 1969; America the Violent, 1970; Poso del Mundo: Inside the Mexican-American Border, 1970; Dirty Business: The Corporate-Political Money-Power Game, 1974; The Director: An Oral Biography of J Edgar Hoover, 1975; Brothers in Blood: The International Terrorist Network, 1977; My Story (by Judith Exner as told to Demaris), 1977; The Lost Mafioso: The Treacherous World of Jimmy Fratianno, 1981; The Vegas Legacy, 1983.

DETHIER Vincent G(aston), b. 1915, American. *Appointments:* Associate Professor 1947-51, Professor of Biology 1951-58, Johns Hopkins University, Baltimore, MD; Professor of Biology and Psychology, University of Pennsylvania, Philadelphia, 1957-68; Professor of Biology, Princeton University, NJ, 1968-75; Professor of Zoology, University of Massachusetts, Amherst, 1975-. *Publications:* Chemical Insect Attractants and Repellents, 1947; Animal Behavior (co-author), 1961; To Know a Fly, 1962; The Physiology of Insect Senses, 1963; Fairweather Duck, 1970, Biological Principles and Processes, 1971; Buy Me a Volcano, 1972; The Hungry Fly: A Physiological Analysis, 1975; Man's Plague, 1976; The Ant Heap, 1979; The World of the Tent Makers: The Natural History of Tent Caterpillars, 1980; Newberry: The Life and Times of a Maine Clam, 1981; The Ecology of a Summer House, 1984; Ten Masses, 1988. *Address:* Department of Zoology, University of Massachusetts, Amherst, MA 01003, USA.

DEUTSCH Andre, b. 15 Nov 1917. Publisher. *Education:* Budapest, Vienna & Zurich. *Appointments:* Nicholson & Watson, 1942; Independent Publisher under imprint Allan Wingate (Publrs.) Ltd., 1945; formed Andre Deutsch Ltd., 1951, Chairman & Managing Director 1951-84, Co-Chairman and Co-Managing Director, 1984-89, President, 1989-91; Founder, African University Press, Lagos, 1962, East Africa Publishing House, Nairobi, 1964. *Honour:* CBE, 1989.

DEVERELL Rex Johnson, b. 17 July 1941, Toronto, Canada. Playwright. m. Rita Joyce Shelton, 24 May 1967, 1 son. *Education:* BA, 1963; BD, 1966; STM, 1967. *Appointments:* Resident Playwright, Globe Theatre, Regina, 1975-. *Publications:* Boiler Room Suite, 1978; Drift, 1981; Black Powder, 1981; Superwheel, 1979; 3 Plays for Children; Various other plays, TV and Radio Scripts; Anthology, Deverell of the Globe, Opera Libretti: Boiler Room Suite; Land. *Contributions include:* Canadian Theatre Review; Canadian Childrens Literature; Canadian Drama; Prairie Fire; Grain. *Honours:* McMaster University Honour Society, 1963; Ohio State Award, 1974; Canadian Authors Association Medal, 1978; Major Armstrong Award, 1986.

Memberships: Saskatchewan Writers Guild; Playwrights Union of Canada; Saskatchewan Playwrights Centre; Amnesty International. *Address:* 36 Dentonia Park Avenue, Toronto, Ont, M4C 1WY, Canada.

DEVEREUX Eve. *See:* **BARNETT Paul le Page.**

DEVINE Thomas Martin, b. 30 July 1945, Motherwell, Scotland. m. Catherine Mary Lynas, 6 July 1971, 2 sons, 3 daughters. *Education:* BA, University of Strathclyde, 1968; PhD, 1971; D Litt, 1991; Fellow of the Royal Society of Edinburgh, 1992. *Appointments:* Assistant Lecturer, 1969-71; Lecturer, Senior Lecturer, 1971-83; Reader, 1983-88; Professor, 1988; Dean of Faculty of Arts and Social Studies, 1993. *Publications:* The Tobacco Lords; Ireland & Scotland 1700-1850; The Great Highland Famine; People & Society in Scotland; Farm Servants & Labour in Lowland Scotland; Irish Immigrants and Scottish Society in the Eighteenth and Nineteenth Centuries; Scottish Emigration & Scottish Society; Clanship to Crofters' War: The Social Tranformation of the Scottish Highlands; The Transformation of Rural Scotland: Agrarian & Social Change 1680-1815. *Contributions to:* Times Literary Supplemnt; Times Higher Education Supplement; Economic History Review; Social History; Scottish Historical Review; History Today; Scottish Economic & Social History. *Honours:* Senior Hume Brown Prize; Saltire Prize. *Memberships:* Economic & Social History Society of Scotland; Scottish Catholic Historical Association; Royal Society; Royal Historical Society. *Address:* Department of History, University of Strathclyde, McCance Building, 16 Richmond Street, Glasgow, Scotland.

DEWEY Donald William, b. 30 Sept 1933, Honolulu, Hawaii, USA. Magazine Editor and Publisher; Author. m. Sally Rae Ryan, 7 Aug 1961, 1 son, 1 daughter. *Education:* Pomona College, 1953-55. *Appointments:* Editor, Publisher, R/C Modeler Magazine, Sierra Madre, California, 1963-; President, Board Chairman, R/C Modeler Corporation, Sierra Madre, 1963-; Editor, Publisher, Freshwater And Marine Aquarium magazine, 1978-. *Publications:* Radio Control From The Ground Up, 1970; Flight Training Course, 1973; For What It's Worth, Volume 1, 1973; For What It's Worth, Volume 2, 1975. *Contributions to:* Numerous journals and magazines, 1951-. *Memberships:* Sustaining Member, Republican National Committee; Charter Member, National Congressional Club; Republican Presidential Task Force; US Senatorial Club; Presidential Trust; American Radio Relay League; National Amateur Radio Association; International Platform Association; Theodore Roosevelt Association; National Tax Limitation Committee; Associate, Methodist Hospital of Southern California; California Historical Society; Sierra Madre Historical Society; National Trust For Historic Preservation; Smithsonian Institute; Greater Los Angeles Zoo Association; American Indian Heritage Foundation; Los Angeles County Arboretum Association; National Miniature Pylon Racing Association; American Life League; Oceanic Society; International Oceanographic Foundation; Federation of American Aquarium Societies; American Philatelic Society; American Topical Association; APS Writers Unit 30; American First Day Cover Society; United Postal Stationery Society; Confederate Stamp Alliance; American Air Mail Society; Bureau Issues Association; American Revenue Association; Canal Zone Study Group; Precancel Stamp Society; Pet Industry Joint Advisory Council; International Betta Congress; National Fisheries Association; Goldfish Society of America. *Address:* 410 West Montecito Avenue, Sierra Madre, CA 91024, USA.

DEWEY Jennifer Owings, b. 2 Oct 1941, Chicago, Illinois, USA. Writer; Illustrator. div., 1 daughter. *Education:* University of New Mexico, 1960-63; Rhode Island School of Design. *Publications:* CLEM, The Story Of A Raven, 1986; At The Edge Of The Pond, 1987; Birds of Antarctica, The Adelie Penguin, 1989; Birds of Antarctica, The Wandering Albatross, 1989; Can You

Find Me, A Book About Animal Camouflage, 1989; About 12 illustrated books including: The Sagebrush Ocean; Birds of the Great Basin; Wilderness Sojourn, 1988. *Contributions:* Stories to Highlights for Children, 1989. *Honours:* New York Academy of Science Award for illustration for The Secret Language of Snow; Bookbuilders West, and Bookbuilders East, for illustration and design in At The Edge Of The Pond; Bookbuilders West for illustrations in Idle Weeds. *Memberships:* San Francisco Society of Illustrators; American Society of Scientific Illustrators; President, Founder, The No Poets Society. *Address:* 607 Old Taos Highway, Santa Fe, NM 87501, USA.

DEWHIRST Ian, b. 17 Oct 1936, Keighley, West Yorkshire, England. Librarian. *Education:* BA Hons, 1958. *Publications:* Yorkshire Through the Years, 1975; The Story of a Nobody, 1980; You Don't Remember Bananas, 1985; A History of Keighley, 1974; Gleamings from Victorian Yorkshire, 1972; Gleanings from Edwardian Yorkshire, 1975. *Contributions to:* Yorkshire Ridings Magazine; Lancashire Magazine; The Dalesman; Cumbria; Pennine Magazine; Transactions of the Yorkshire Dialect Society. *Memberships:* The Bronte Society; Yorkshire Dialect Society, Hon Secretary, 1964-74; Associate of Library Association. *Address:* 14 Raglan Avenue, Fell Lane, Keighley, West Yorkshire BD22 6BJ, England.

DEWHURST Eileen Mary, b. 27 May 1929, Liverpool, England. Author. Divorced. *Education:* BA (Hons) English Language and Literature, St Anne's College, Oxford, 1951; MA, Oxford, 1958. *Publications:* Crime Novels: Death Came Smiling, 1975; After the Ball, 1976; Curtain Fall, 1977; Drink This, 1980; Trio in Three Flats, 1981; Whoever I am, 1982; The House that Jack Built, 1983; There Was a Little Girl, 1984; Playing Safe, 1985; A Private Prosecution, 1986; A Nice Little Business, 1987; The Sleeper, 1988; Dear Mr Right, 1990; The Innocence of Guilt, 1991; Death in Candie Gardens, 1992. *Contributions to:* Various newspapers and journals. *Memberships:* Crime Writers Association; The Society of Authors. *Literary Agent:* Gregory and Radice, London. *Address:* c/o Gregory and Radice, Riverside Studios, Crisp Road, Hammersmith, London W6 9RL, England.

DEWHURST Keith, b. 1931, British. *Appointments:* Sports Writer, Evening Chronicle, 1955-59; Granada Television Presenter, 1968-69; Arts Columnist, The Guardian, 1969-72; BBC2 Television Presenter, 1972; Writer-in-Residence, Western Australia APA Perth, 1984. *Publications:* Lark Rise to Candleford, 1980; Captain of the Sands, 1981; Don Quixote, 1982; McSullivan's Beach, 1985; Black Snow, 1992. *Address:* c/o Alexandra Cann Representation, 337 Fulham Road, London SW10 9TW, England.

DEWLEN Al, b. 1921, American. Freelance writer and lecturer. *Appointments:* Reporter, Daily News, Amarillo, 1946-47; City Editor, Amarillo Times, 1947-51; Night Editor, United Press, Dallas, 1951-52. *Publications:* The Night of the Tiger, 1956, in paperback as Ride Beyond Vengeance, 1966; The Bone Pickers, 1958, in paperback as The Golden Touch, 1959; Twilight of Honor, 1961; Servants of Corruption, 1971; Next of Kin, 1977; The Session, 1981. *Address:* 7720 Croftwood Drive, Austin, TX 78749, USA.

DEXTER Colin, b. 29 Sept 1930, Stamford, Lincolnshire, England. Educational Administrator. *Education:* Christ's College, Cambridge; MA (Cantab); MA (Oxon). *Publications:* Last Bus to Woodstock, 1975; Last Seen Wearing, 1976; The Silent World of Nicholas Quinn, 1977; Service of All the Dead, 1979; The Dead of Jericho, 1981; The Riddle of the Third Mile, 1983; The Secret of Annexe 3, 1986; The Wench is Dead, 1989; The Jewel That Was Ours, 1991; The Way Through the Woods, 1992. *Honours:* Recipient, Silver Dagger 1979 and 1981 and Gold Dagger 1989 and 1992 Crime Writers Association. *Memberships:* Crime Writers Association; Detection Club. *Address:* 456 Banbury Road, Oxford OX2 7RG, England.

DI CESARE Mario A, b. 1928, USA. *Appointments:* Instructor, 1959-61; Assistant Professor, 1961-64; Associate Professor, 1964-68; Master of Newing College, Harpur, College, 1967-68; Chairman, English Department, 1968-73; Professor, 1968-89; Distinguished Professor, 1989-. *Publications:* Vidas Christiad And Vergilian Epic; The Book of Good Love; Bibliotheca Vidiana: Critical Biblography of Marco Girolamo Vida; The Altar and the City; A Reading of Vergil's Aeneid; A Concordance to the Complete Writings of George Herbert; Poetry and Prophecy; George Herbert and the Seventeenth Century Religious poets; A Concordance to the Nondramatic Poems of Ben Jonson; The Bodleian Manuscript of George Herbert's the Temple; Milton in Italy; Reconsidering the Renaissance. *Contributions to:* Journal of the American Academy of Religion; English Literary Renaissance; Yearbook of English Studies; The Chaucer Review; Mediavalia. *Honours:* Samuel S Fels Fellow; Guggenheim Fellow; Robert Frost Library Fellow; National Endowment for the Humanities Senior Fellow. *Memberships:* Renaissance Society of America; Center for International Scholarly Exchange; Renaissance English Text Society. *Address:* Tamarack Wood, 1936 Cafferty Hill Road, Owego, NY 13760, USA.

DIAMAN Nickolas Antony, b. 1 Nov 1936, San Francisco, USA. Novelist; Videomaker. *Education:* University of Southerm California, 1958. *Publications:* Castro Street Memories; Reunion; Second Crossing; The Fourth Wall; Ed Dean is Queer. *Memberships:* Gay/Lesbian Organization of Videomakers. *Address:* c/o Persons Press, Box 14022, San Francisco, CA 94114, USA.

DIBBA Ebou, b. 10 Aug 1943, The Gambia. Assistant Diector, Head of Sector. m. Tonia May, 1973, 1 son, 2 daughters. *Education:* University College, Cardiff, 1963-67. *Publications:* Chaff on the Wind; Fafa; The African Child; Olu and the Smugglers; The Marriage of Anansewa; Cheddo; Alhaji. *Contributions to:* The Independent Newspaper, west Africa; The London Magazine. *Address:* Stable House, Castle Hill, Bletchingley, Surrey RH1 4LB, England.

DICK Bernard F, b. 25 Nov 1935, Scranton, Pennsylvania, USA. University Professor. m. Katherine M Restaino, 31 July 1965. *Education:* BA, Classics and Literature, University of Scranton, 1957; MA, Classics, 1960; PhD, Classics, 1962, Fordham University. *Publications:* The Hellenism of Mary Renault, 1972; The Apostate Angel: A Critical Study of Gore Vidal, 1974; Billy Wilder, 1980; Hellman in Hollywood, 1982; Joseph L Mankiewicz, 1983; The Star-Spangled Screen, 1985; William Golding, revised edition 1987; Radical Innocence: A Critical Study of the Hollywood Ten, 1989; Anatomy of Film, 2nd edition 1990. *Contributor to:* Wall Street Journal; College English; Comparative Literature; World Literature Today; Modern Drama; Sewanee Review. *Honour:* 1985: Choice Magazine award for one of the year's outstanding scholarly books for The Star-Spangled Screen. *Membership:* Modern Language Association. *Address:* 580 Wyndham Road, Teaneck, NJ 07666, USA.

DICK Kay, b. 1915, British. Writer. *Appointments:* Many appointments in publishing including: Editor, The Windmill series and other anthologies. *Publications:* By the lake, 1949; Young Man, 1951; An Affair of Love, 1953; Solitaire, 1958; Pierrot, 1960; Sunday, 1962; Bizarre and Arabesque: Selections from Edgar Allen Poe (ed), 1967; Ivy and Stevie, 1971; Writers at Work (ed), 1972; Friends and Friendship, 1974; They, 1977; The Shelf, 1984. *Honour:* Literature Prize for They in 1977. *Address:* Flat 5, 9 Arundel Terrace, Brighton, Sussex BN2 1GA, England.

DICKENS Eric Anthony, b. 29 Jan 1953, Dewsbury, Yorkshire, England. Translator. *Education:* BA, University of East Anglia, 1975; PGCE, University of Leicester, 1977. *Publications:* Jan Mårtenson, Drottningholm; Lars & Annika Bäckström; Jaan Kräss,

The Peeter Mirk Stories. *Contributions to:* Index on Censorship; Stand; Swedish Book Review; PEN International; Swedish Books; Horisont; Ny Tid; Sirp. *Memberships:* Pen; Translators Association; SELTA; AITI. *Literary Agent:* Ann Christine Danielsson, Karlstad, Sweden. *Address:* Karekiet 1, 1261 RL Blaricum, Netherlands.

DICKEY Angela Renée, b. 19 July 1957, Rome, GA, USA. Diplomat; Freelance Writer. *Education:* BA, Berry College, GA, 1979; MSc, Georgetown University, 1981; Post-graduate work, University of Florida, 1983- 84. *Appointments:* Editorial Assistant, African Studies Review, 1983- 84; Editor, Harcourt Brace Javanovich, Orlando, 1984-86; Reporter, Editor, The Orlando Sentinel, 1986-88; Founding Editor, Pencil Press Quarterly. *Contributions to:* Orlando Sentinel; Florida Magazine; Pencil Press Quarterly; and others. *Address:* US Embassy Novakchott, BP 222, Navakchott, Mauritania (RIM).

DICKEY James Lafayette III, b. 2 Feb 1923, Atlanta, GA, USA. Poet; Novelist. m. (1) Maxine Syerson (dec), 1948; (2) Deborah Dodson, 1976, 2 sons, 1 daughter. *Education:* BA, 1949; MA, 1950, Vanderbilt University, Nashville. *Appointments:* Poetry Consultant to Library of Congress, 1966-68; First Carolina Professor and Poet-in-Residence, University of South Carolina, Columbia, 1968-. *Publications include:* Buckdancer's Choice, (verse), 1965; James Dickey: Poems, 1957-1967; Babel to Byzantium: Poets and Poetry Now, 1968; Deliverance, 1970; Falling, May Day Sermon and Other Poems, 1981; Alnilam, 1987; Drowning with Others, 1962; Jericho: The South Beheld, 1974; Wayfarer, 1988. *Honours:* Vachel Lindsay Award, 1959; Longview Foundation Award, 1960; Guggenheim Fellowship, 1962; National Book Award, 1965; Melville Cane Award, 1965; Prix Medicis, 1971; Levinson Prize, 1981; Yale Series of Younger Poets judge, 1989-90. *Memberships:* American Academy of Arts and Letters; American Institute of Arts and Letters; American Academy of Arts and Sciences; Fellowship of Southern Writers; Writers Guild of America. *Literary Agent:* Theron Raines, Raines and Raines, New York, NY. *Address:* 4620 Lelia's Court, Columbia, SC 29206, USA.

DICKEY William, b. 1928, American. *Appointments:* Instructor, Cornell University, Ithaca, NY, 1956-59; Assistant Professor, Denison University, Granville, OH, 1960-62; Professor of English and Creative Writing 1962-, Chairman, Creative Writing Department 1974-77, San Francisco State University, CA; Emeritus Professor, 1991-. *Publications:* Of the Festivity, 1959; Interpreter's House, 1964; Rivers of the Pacific Northwest, 1969; More Under Saturn, 1971; The Rainbow Grocery, 1978; Sacrifice Consenting, 1981; Six Philosophical Songs, Joy, 1983; Brief Lives, 1985; The King of the Golden River, 1986; Metamorphoses, 1991; Night Journey, 1992. *Memberships:* PEN American Center; Phi Beta Kappa; Modern Language Association. *Address:* Department of Creative Writing, San Francisco State University, 1600 Holloway, San Francisco, CA 94132, USA.

DICKINSON Donald Percy, b. 28 Dec 1947, Prince Albert, Canada. Writer; Teacher. m. Chellie Eaton, 1 May 1970, 2 sons, 1 daughter. *Education:* MFA, University of Brtosh Columbia, 1979; BA, University of Saskatchewan, 1973. *Appointments:* Fiction Editor, Prisim International, 1977-79. *Publications:* Fighting the Upstream; Blue Husbands; The Crew. *Contributions to:* Best Canadian Short Fiction; Words We Call Home; The New Writers. *Honours:* Bankson Award; Governor General of Canada Award Nominee; Ethel Wilson Fiction Prize. *Memberships:* Writers Union of Canada. *Address:* 554 Victoria Street, Lillooet, British Columbia, Canada V0K 1V0.

DICKINSON Harry Thomas, b. 9 Mar 1939, Gateshead, England. University Professor. m. Jennifer Elizabeth Galtry, 26 Aug 1961, 1 son, 1 daughter. *Education:* BA Hons, 1960; DipEd, 1961; MA, 1963, Durham University; PhD, Newcastle University, 1968; DLitt, Edinburgh University, 1986. *Publications:* Correspondence of Sir James Clavering, 1967; Bolingbroke, 1970; Walpole and the Whig Supremacy, 1973; Politics and Literature in the 18th Century, 1974; Liberty and Property, 1977; The Political Works of Thomas Spence, 1982; British Radicalism and the French Revolution, 1985; Caricatures and the Constitution, 1987; Britain and the French Revolution, 1989; Editor of History, 1993-. *Contributions to:* English Historical Review; Transactions of Royal History Society; Journal of British Studies; Huntington Library Quarterly; and others. *Honours:* Earl Grey Fellow, Newcastle University, 1964-66; Fulbright Fellow, 1973; Huntington Library Fellow, 1973; Folger Shakespeare Library Senior Fellow, 1973; Churchill Fellow, 1980; Leverhulme Award, 1987; Ahmanson Fellow UCLA, 1987; Anstey Memorial Lecturer, Kent University, 1989. *Memberships:* Royal Historical Society, Council Member 1986-90; Vice-President, 1991-95; Historical Association, Council Member 1984-. *Address:* 44 Viewforth Terrace, Edinburgh EH10 4LJ, Scotland.

DICKINSON Margaret. *See:* MUGGESON Margaret Elizabeth.

DICKINSON Patric (Thomas), b. 26 Dec 1914. Poet; Playwright; Freelance Broadcaster. m. Sheila Dunbar Shannon, 1945, 1 son, 1 daughter. *Education:* St Catharine's College, Cambridge (Crabtree Exhibitioner). *Appointments:* Assistant Schoolmaster, 1936-39; Artists Rifles, 1939- 40; BBC 1942-48; Acting Poetry Editor, 1945-48; sometime Gresham Professor, in Rhetoric, City University. *Publications:* Translations: Aristophanes Against War, 1957; The Aeneid of Vergil, 1960; Aristophanes, volumes I and II, 1970; Play: A Durable Fire, 1962; Autobiography, The Good Minute, 1965; Poetry: The Seven Days of Jericho, 1944; Soldiers Verse, 1945; Theseus and the Minotaur, Play and Poems, 1946; Stone in the Midst, play and poems, 1949; Editor, Byron (selection), 1949; A Round of Golf Courses (prose), 1951; The Sailing Race, 1952; The Scale of Things, 1955; Editor with Sheila Shannon: Poems to Remember, 1958; Poets's Choice : An Anthology of English Poetry from Spenser to the Present Day, 1967; The World I See, 1960; This Cold Universe, 1964; Editor, C. Day Lewis, Selections from his Poetry, 1967; Selected Poems, 1968; More Than Time, 1970; A Wintering Tree, 1973; The Bearing Beast, 1976; Our Living John, 1979; Poems from Rye, 1980; Winter Hostages, 1980; Editor, Introduction, Selected Poems Henry Newbolt, 1981; A Rift in Time, 1982; To Go Hidden, 1984; A Sun Dog, (poems) 1988; Two into One, 1989; Not Hereafter, 1991. *Address:* 38 Church Square, Rye, East Sussex, England.

DICKINSON Peter Malcolm (The Honourable), b. 16 Dec 1927, Livingstone, Zambia. Author. m. Mary Rose Barnard, 26 Apr 1953, (dec 1988), 2 daughters, 2 sons. *Education:* Scholar, Eton College; Exhibitioner, Kings College, Cambridge; 2ndly Robin McKinley, 3 Jan 1992; BA (Cantab), 1951. *Appointments:* Various editorial posts, Punch, 1952-69; Chairman, Management Committee, Society of Authors, 1978-80. *Publications:* Children's novels: The Weathermonger, 1968; Heartease, 1969; The Devil's Children, 1970 (trilogy republished as The Changes, 1970); Emma Tupper's Diary, 1970; The Dancing Bear, 1972; The Dancing Bear, 1972; The Gift, 1973; The Iron Lion, 1973; Chance Luck and Destiny, 1975; The Blue Hawk, 1976; Annerton Pit, 1977; Hepzibah, 1978; Tulku, 1979; The Flight of Dragons, 1979; City of Gold, 1980; The Seventh Raven, 1981; Healer, 1983; Giant Cold, 1984; Editor: Hundreds and Hundreds, 1984; A Box of Nothing, 1985; Eva, 1988; Merlin Dreams, 1988; AK, 1990; A Bone from a Dry Sea, 1992; TV Series: Mandog; Adults novels: Skin Deep, 1968; A Pride of Heroes, 1969; The Seals, 1970; Sleep and His Brother, 1971; The Lizard in the Cup, 1972; The Green Gene, 1973; The Poison Oracle, 1974; The Lively Dead, 1975; King and Joker, 1976; Walking Dead, 1977; One Foot in the Grave, 1979; A Summer in the Twenties, 1981; The Last Houseparty, 1982; Hindsight, 1983; Death of a Unicorn, 1984; Tefuga, 1986; Perfect Gallows, 1988; Skeleton-in-

Waiting, 1989; Play Dead, 1991. *Contributions to:* Regular verse to Punch, 1952-69. *Honours:* Golden Dagger, Crime Writers Association, 1968, 1969; Guardian Award, 1976; Carnegie Medal, 1979, 1980; Whitbread Prize, 1979; Various awards, USA. *Memberships:* Society of Authors, Chairman 1978-80; Crime Writers Association; Detection Club; PEN. *Literary Agent:* A P Watt Ltd, 20 John Street, London WC1N 2DL, England. *Address:* 61a Ormiston Grove, London W5S12 OJP, England.

DICKSON Donald Richard, b. 19 Aug 1951, Biloxi, Mississippi, USA. Assistant Professor of English. m. Jayn Pollan Dickson, 1 May 1990, 1 daughter. *Education:* BA, University of Connecticut, 1973; AM, 1976, PhD, 1981, University of Illinois. *Appointments:* Assistant Professor of English, 1981-87, Associate Professor of English, 1987-, Texas A&M University, College Station; Gastprofessor, Institut fur Anglistik, Universitat ErlangenNuremberg, Germany, 1992-93. *Publications:* The Fountain of Living Waters: The Typology of the Waters of Life in Herbert, Vaughan and Traherne, 1987; Contributing Editor, vol VI, Variorum Edition of the Poetry of John Donne: Anniversaries and Episedes and Obsequies; Essays on various 17th century writers. *Honours:* National Endowment for the Humanities Summer Institute, 1983; Faculty Research Grant, Texas A&M University, 1988; Alexander von Humboldt Fellowship, 1992-93. *Memberships:* Modern Language Association; Renaissance Society of America; Milton Society; South Central Modern Language Association; South Central Renaissance Conference, Executive Director 1983-92. *Address:* Department of English, Texas A&M University, College Station, TX 77843, USA.

DICKSON Gordon (Rupert), b. 1923, American. *Publications:* Alien From Archturus, Mankind on the Run, 1956; Earthman's Burden (with Poul Anderson), 1957; Secret Under the Sea, Time to Teleport, The Genetic General, Delusion World, 1960; Spacial Delivery, Naked to the Stars, 1961; Necromancer, 1962; Secret Under Antarctica, 1963; Secret Under the Carribean, 1964; Space Winners, The Alien Way, Mission to Universe, 1965; Planet Run, Soldier Ask Not, The Space Swimmers, 1967; None But Man, Spacepaw, Wolfing, 1969; Hour of the Horde, Danger - Human (also known as The Book of Gordon R Dickson), Mutants, 1970; Sleepwalker's World, The Tactics of Mistake, 1971; The Outposter, The Pritcher Mass, 1972; The Star Road, Alien Art, The R-Master, 1973; Gremlins Go Home! (with Ben Bova), Ancient My Enemy, 1974; Three to Dorsai, Combat SF (ed), Star Prince Charlie (with P Anderson), 1975; The Lifeship (with Harry Harrison), The Dragon and the George, 1976; Time Storm, 1977; Nebula Award Stories Twelve (ed), The Far Call, Home from the Shore, 1978; Spirit of Dorsai, Masters of Everon, 1979; Lost Dorsai, 1980; In Iron Years, Love Not Human, 1981; The Space Swimmers, The Outposter, 1982; The Pritcher Mass, 1983. *Address:* PO Box 1569, Twin Cities Airport, MN 55111, USA.

DICKSON Mora Agnes, b. 1918, British. Self employed author and artist. *Publications:* New Nigerians, 1960; Baghdad and Beyond, 1961; A Season in Sarawak, 1962; A World Elsewhere, 1964; Israeli Interlude, 1966; Count Us In, 1968; Longhouse in Sarawak, 1971; Beloved Partner, 1974; A Chance to Serve (ed), The Inseparable Grief, 1977; Assignment in Asia, 1979; The Powerful Bond, 1980; The Aunts, 1981; Teacher Extraordinary, 1986; Nannie, 1988. *Address:* 19 Blenheim Road, London W4, England.

DIEHL Digby Robert, b. 14 Nov 1940, Boonton, New Jersey, USA. Journalist. m. Kay Beyer, 6 June 1981, 1 daughter. *Education:* AB, American Studies, (Henry Rutgers Scholar), Rutgers University, 1962; MA, Theatre Arts, UCLA, 1966, Postgraduate, 1969-. *Appointments:* Editor, Learning Centre Inc, Princeton, 1962-64; Director, Research Creative Playthings, Los Angeles, 1964-66; Editor, Coast Magazine, Los Angeles, 1966-68, Show Magazine, Los Angeles, 1968-69; Book Editor, Los Angeles Times, 1969-78; Vice President, Editor in Chief, Harry N. Abrams, Inc., New York City, 1978-80; Book Editor, Los Angeles Herald Examiner, 1981-86; Movie Critic, Entertainment Editor Station KCBS TV, Los Angeles, 1986-87; Book Critic; Playboy Magazine; Modern Maturity, IBM/Prodigy, 1987-. *Publications:* Supertalk : Extraordinary Conversations, 1974; Front Page, 1981. *Contributions to:* various journals and magazines. *Honours:* Jurist National Book Awards, 1972; Jurist (Ch) International Imitation Hemingway Competition, 1978-; Jurist, American Book Awards, 1981-85. *Memberships include:* American Society Journalists and Authors; AAUP; Phi Beta Kappa; Phi Sigma Delta; PEN International, USA West. *Address:* 788 So Lake Ave, Pasadena, CA 91106, USA.

DIETRICH Robert. See: HUNT E(verette) Howard.

DIGBY Joan (Hildreth), b. 16 Nov 1942, New York, USA. Professor of English and Director of Honors Program and Merit Fellowship; Writer. m. 1. William Howard Owen, 26 Nov 1965 (divorced), 2. John Michael Digby, 3 Mar 1979. *Education:* BA, summa cum laude, 1963, PhD 1969, New York University; MA, University of Delaware, 1965. *Appointments:* Assistant Professor 1969-73, Associate Professor 1973-77, Professor of English and Director of Honors Program and Merit Fellowship, 1977-, Long Island University, C W Post Campus, Brookville, New York. *Publications:* A Sound of Feathers (prose poems) collage illustrations by husband, John Digby, 1982; (with husband, John Digby), The Collage Handbook, 1985; (Editor with Bob Brier), Permutations: Readings in Science and Literature, 1985; (Editor with husband, John Digby), Food for Thought, 1987; (Editor with husband, John Digby), Inspired By Drink, 1988; Two Presses (nonfiction), 1988; (with husband, John Digby), The Wood Engravings of John de Pol, 1988. *Honours:* Excellence in Teaching Award from New York State Council of English Teachers, 1987. *Memberships:* American Society for Eighteenth Century Studies, National Collegiate Honors Council; Phi Beta Kappa. *Address:* 30 Kellogg Street, Oyster Bay, NY 11771, USA.

DIGBY John (Michael), b. 18 Jan 1938, London, England. immigrated to United States 1978. m. (1) Erica Susan Christine Berwick-Stephens, 1963 (div) 1 son; (2) Joan Hildreth Weiss, 3 Mar 1979. *Education:* Attended school in London, England. *Career:* Collagist and poet. *Publications:* The Structure of Biofocal Distance (poems), 1974; Sailing Away From Night (poems and collages), 1978; To Amuse a Shrinking Sun (poems and collages), 1985; (with wife, Joan Digby), The Collage Handbook, 1985; Miss Liberty (collages), 1986; Incantation (poems and collages), 1987; (editor with wife, Joan Digby), Food for Thought, 1987; (editor with wife, Joan Digby), Inspired By Drink, 1988; (with wife, Joan Digby), The Wood Engravings of John de Pol, 1988; A Parliament of Owls (poems and collages), 1989. *Address:* 30 Kellogg Street, Oyster Bay, NY 11771, USA.

DIKEMAN May, b. 8 Sept 1923, Baldwin, Long Island, USA. Writer. m. Norman Hoss, 12 Sept 1946, 1 son, 2 daughters. *Education:* Vassar, BA, 1945-49. *Publications:* The Pike; The Angelica; The Devil We Know. *Contributions to:* The Atlantic Monthly; Harpers Magazine. *Honours:* Atlantic First; Ingram Merrill; Best American Stories. *Memberships:* PEN. *Address:* 70 Irving Place 4C, New York, NY 10003, USA.

DILLARD R(ichard) H(enry) W(ilde), b. 1937, American. *Appointments:* Instructor in English, University of Virginia, Charlottesville, 1961-64; Contribution Editor, The Hollins Critic, 1966-77; Assistant Professor 1964-68, Associate Professor 1968-74, Chairman of Graduate Program in Contemporary Literature and Creative Writing, 1971-, Professor in English, 1974-, Hollins College, VA; Vice President, The Film Journal, NYC, 1973-. *Publications:* The Day I Stopped Dreaming about Barbara Steele and Other Poems, Frankenstein Meets the Space Monster (with G Garrett and J Rodenbeck), 1966; The Experience of America: A Book of Readings (ed with L D Rubin), 1969; News of the Nile, The Sounder Few: Essays from The Hollins Critic (ed with G Garrett and J R Moore), 1971; After Borges, 1972; The Book of Changes, 1974; Horror Films, 1976; The Greeting: New and Selected Poems, 1981; The First Man on the Sun, 1983; Understanding George Garrett, 1988. *Address:* Box 9671, Hollins College, VA 24020, USA.

DILLINGHAM William Byron, b. 7 Mar 1930, Atlanta, Georgia, USA. Writer and Teacher. m. Elizabeth Joiner, 3 July 1952, 1 son, 2 daughters. *Education:* BA 1955, MA 1956, Emory University; PhD, University of Pennsylvania, 1961. *Appointments:* Emory University 1956-58, 1959-, Instructor, Assistant Professor, Associate Professor, Professor, Charles Howard Candler Professor of American Literature; Editorial Boards: Nineteenth- Century Literature, Frank Norris Society Journal, South Atlantic Bulletin. *Publications:* Books: Melville's Later Novels, 1986; Melville's Short Fiction, 1853-1856, 1977; An Artist in the Rigging: The Early Work of Herman Melville, 1972; Frank Norris: Instinct and Art, 1969; Humor of the Old Southwest, 1965 (revised edition 1974); Practical English Handbook, 9th Edition, 1992. *Contributions to:* Many articles and reviews in such journals as Nineteenth Century Literature; American Literature; Philological Quarterly; College English; English Studies. *Honours:* Fulbright Award, 1964-65; National Endowment for the Humanities Fellow, 1978-79; Guggenheim Fellow, 1982-83; Phi Beta Kappa; Scholar-Teacher of the Year, Emory University, ODK. *Memberships:* Melville Society (former President); Whitman Society; South Atlantic Modern Language Association; Modern Language Association of America; Frank Norris Society. *Address:* 1416 Vistaleaf Drive, Decatur, GA 30033, USA.

DILLON Ellis, b. 1920. Irish, Writer of Novels/Short stories, Children's fiction, Plays/Screenplays. *Appointments:* Lecturer in creative writing, Trinity College, Dublin, 1971-72; Writer in Residence, University College, Dublin, 1988. *Publications:* An Choill Bheo (The Live Forest), 1948; Midsummer Magic, 1950; Oscar agus an Coiste Sen Easog (Oscar and the Six-Weasel Coach), 1952; The Lost Island, 1952; Death at Crane's Court, 1953; The San Sebastian, 1953; Sent to His Account, 1954; Ceol ne Coille (The Song of the Forest), 1955; The House on the Shore, 1955; The Wild Little House, 1955; Death in the Quadrangle, 1956; The Island of Horses, 1956; Plover Hill, 1957; The Bitter Glass, 1958; Aunt Bedelia's Cats, 1958; The Singing Cave, 1959; Manna (radio play), 1960; The Head of the Family, 1960; King Big-Ears, 1961; A Pony and a Trap, 1962; The Cat's Opera, 1963; The Coriander, 1963; A Family of Foxes, 1964; Bold John Henebry, 1965; The Sea Wall, 1965; The Lion Cub, 1966; The Road to Dunmore, 1966; A Page of History (play), 1966; The Cruise of the Santa Maria, 1967; The Key, 1967; Two Stories: The Road to Dunmore and The Key, 1968; The Seals, 1968; Under the Orange Grove, 1968; A Herd of Deer, 1969; The Wise Man on the Mountain, 1969; The Voyage of Mael Duin, 1969; The King's Room, 1970; The Five Hundred, 1972; Across the Bitter Sea, 1973; Living in Imperial Rome (in US as Rome under the Emperors), 1975; (ed) The Hamish Hamilton Book of Wise Animals, 1975; The Shadow of Vesuvius, 1977; Blood Relations, 1977; The Cats' Opera (play), 1981; Wild Geese, 1981; Inside Ireland, 1982; Down in the World, 1983; Citizen Burke, 1984; (ed) The Lucky Bag, 1984; The Horse Fancier, 1985; The Seekers, 1986; The Interloper, 1987; The Islands of Ghost, 1989; Children of Bach, 1992. *Address:* 7 Templemore Avenue, Dublin 6, Ireland.

DILLON Millicent Gerson, b. 24 May 1925. Writer. m. Murray Lesser, 1 June 1948, 2 daughters. *Education:* BA, Hunter College, 1944; MA, San Francisco State University, 1966. *Publications:* Baby Perpetua and Other Stories, 1971; The One in the Bach is Medea, novel, 1973; A Little Original Sin: The Life and Work of Jane Bowles, 1981; After Egypt, 1990; The Dance of the Mothers, novel, 1991. *Contributions to:* Southwest Review; Witness; Threepenny Review. *Honours:* 5 O

Henry Short Story Awards; Best American Short Stories, 1992; Guggenheim Fellowship; Fellowship from the National Endowment for the Humanities. *Memberships:* PEN; Authors Guild. *Literary Agent:* Renee Golden. *Address:* 72 6th Avenue, San Francisco, CA 94118, USA.

DIMBLEBY David, b. 28 Oct 1938, London, England. Broadcaster; Newspaper Proprietor. m. Josceline Gaskell, 1967, 1 son, 2 daughters. *Education:* Christ Church Oxford; Universities of Paris and Perugia. *Appointments:* News Reporter, BBC Bristol, 1960-61; Presenter, Interviewer, various scientific, religious and political programmes, BBC TV 1961-63; Foreign affairs, Film Reporter and Director, 1964-65; Special Correspondent, CBS News, 1966; Reporter, Panorama, BBC TV, 1967-69, Presenter 1974-77, 1980-81; Presenter, 24 Hours, BBC TV 1969-72; Dimbleby Talk In, 1972-74; People and Power, 1982; General Election Results Programmes, BBC 1979, 1983; Presenter, This Week, Next Week, BBC TV, 1985-87; Managing Director, Dimbleby Newspaper Group, 1966-86; Chairman, 1986-; Reporter, The White Tribe of Africa, BBC TV, 1979. *Publication:* An Ocean Apart (with David Reynolds), 1988. *Honours:* Supreme Documentary Award, 1979; Emmy Ward, 1991; Golden Nymph Award, 1991. *Address:* 14 King Street, Richmond, Surrey TW9 1NF, England.

DIMBLEBY Jonathan, b. 31 July 1944. Freelance Broadcaster; Journalist; Author. m. Bel Mooney, 1968, 1 son, 1 daughter. *Education:* BA, Honours, Philosophy, University College, London. *Appointments:* TV and Radio Reporter, BBC Bristol, 1969-70; BBC Radio, World at One, 1970-71; for Thames TV: This Week, 1972-78; TV Eye, 1979; Jonathan Dimbleby in South America, 1979; for Yorkshire TV: series, Jonathan Dimbleby in Evidence: The Police, 1980; The Bomb, 1980; The Eagle and the Bear, 1981; The Cold War Games, 1982; The American Dream, 1984; Four Years On - The Bomb, 1984; First Tuesday (Associate Editor, Presenter), 1982-86; TV AM: Jonathan Dimbleby on Sunday (Presenter/Editor), 1986-; Thames Television: (Presenter/Reporter) This Week, 1986-88, Series Editor, Witness, documentary series, 1986-; BBC Radio 4, Chairman, Any Questions, 1987-; BBC 1: On the Record, 1988-; Radio 4: Any Answers, 1988-; Election Call, BBC1 & Radio 4, 1992. *Publications:* Richard Dimbleby, 1975; The Palestinians, 1979. *Memberships:* Richard Dimbleby Cancer Fund; Board, International Broadcasting Trust; VSO; etc; Trustee, National Aids Trust; President of CPRE, 1992-. *Address:* c/o David Higham Associates Ltd., 5 Lower John Street, London W1R 4HA, England.

DIMBLEBY Josceline Rose, b. 1 Feb 1943, Oxford, England. m. 20 Jan 1967, 1 son, 2 daughters. *Appointments:* Contributor, Daily Mail, 1976-78; Cookery Editor, Sunday Telegraph, 1982-; Regular Contributor to Country Homes and Interiors, 1986-. *Publications:* A Taste of Dreams, 1976; Party Pieces, 1977; Cooking for Christmas, 1978; Josceline Dimbleby's Book of Puddings, Deserts & Savouries, 1979; Cooking With Herbs & Spices, 1979; Curries & Oriental Cookery, 1980; Salads for All Seasons, 1981; Festive Food, 1982; Marvellous Meals with Mince, 1982; Sweet Dreams, 1983; The Josceline Dimbleby Collection, 1984; First Impressions, 1984; Main Attractions, 1985; A Traveller's Tastes, 1986; The Josceline Dimbleby Christmas Book, 1987; The Josceline Dimbleby Book of Entertaining, 1988; The Essential Josceline Dimbleby, 1989; The Cook's Companion, 1991. *Contributions to:* Numerous magazines; Various Television Programmes. *Honour:* Andre Simon Memorial Award, 1979. *Literary Agent:* Curtis Brown. *Address:* 14 King Street, Richmond, Surrey, TW9 1NF, England.

DIMEN Muriel Vera (Dimen-Schein M V), b. 24 Sept 1942, Bronx, New York USA. Psychoanalyst; Writer; Anthropologist. *Education:* BA, Barnard College, New York City, 1964; MA, 1966, PhD, 1970, Columbia University, New York City; Certificate in Psychoanalysis,

New York University, 1983. *Appointments:* Consulting Editor, Feminist Studies, 1979-89; Book Review Editor, Psychoanalytic Dialogues, 1990-. *Publications:* Regional Variation in Modern Greece and Cyprus (co-edited with E Friedl), 1976; The Anthropological Imagination, 1977; Surviving Sexual Contradictions, 1986. *Contributions to:* Many articles on psychoanalysis, social theory and criticisms, feminism, gender and sexuality, the ethnography of Greece, to scholarly and popular press. *Honours:* President's Fellow, Columbia University, 1965-66; Fellow, New York Institute for the Humanities, New York University, 1990-. *Literary Agent:* Charlotte Sheedy. *Address:* 3 East 10th Street, New York, NY 10003, USA.

DIMEN-SCHEIN M V. *See:* **DIMEN Muriel Vera.**

DIMITROFF Pashanko, b. 22 Mar 1924, Stanimaka, Bulgaria. Journalist. m. Margaret Greenwood, 18 July 1959, 2 sons. *Education:* Law, University of Sofia, 1943-46; Music, Cello, Academy of Music, Sofia, 1943; Doctor of Law, Faculte de Droit, Paris, France, 1959. *Publications:* Boris III of Bulgaria, 1986; The Silent Bulgarians, in Bulgarians, 1991. *Address:* 50 Aberdare Gardens, London NW6 3QA, England.

DIMONT Penelope. *See:* **MORTIMER Penelope (Ruth).**

DIMOV Alexandre. *See:* **SAVITSKI Dmitri.**

DINAN Carolyn, b. England. Writer and Illustrator. *Education:* Attended Chelsea School of Art; Graduate study at Royal College of Art. *Career:* Writer and illustrator; Visiting lecturer in illustration, Chelsea School of Art, London, England. *Publications:* Self-illustrated Children's Books: The Lunch Box, 1983; Skipper and Sam, 1984; Say Cheese! 1985, 1986; Ada and the Magic Basket, 1987; Born Lucky, 1987. Illustrator of numerous books, most recent: Gene Kemp editor, Ducks and Dragons, Poems for Children, 1980; Gene Kemp, The Clock Tower Ghost, 1981; Catherine Cookson, Nancy Nutall and the Mongrel, 1982; June Counsel, 1984; Martin Waddell, Owl and Billy, 1986; Dorothy Edwards, Robert Goes to Fetch a Sister, 1986. *Address:* Chelsea School of Art, Manresa Road, London SW3 6LS, England.

DINNERSTEIN Leonard, b. 1934, United States of America. Writer (History). *Appointments:* Instructor, New York Institute of Technology, New York City, 1960-65; Assistant Professor, Fairleigh Dickinson University, Teaneck New Jersey, 1967-70; Associate Professor, 1970-72, Professor of American History, University of Arizona, Tucson, 1972-. *Publications:* The Leo Frank Case, 1968; The Aliens (with F.C. Jaher), 1970, as Uncertain Americans, 1977; American Vistas (with K.T.Jackson), 1971, 6th edition 1991; Antisemitism in the United States, 1971; Jews in the South (with M.D. Palsson, 1973; Decisions and Revisions (with J. Christie), 1975; Ethnic Americans: A History of Immigration and Assimilation (with D.M. Reimers), 1975, 3rd Edition 1988; Natives and Strangers (with R.L. Nichols and D.M. Reimers), 1979, 2nd edition 1990; America and the Survivors of the Holocaust, 1982; Uneasy at Home, 1987. *Address:* 5821 East 7th Street, Tucson, AZ 85711, USA.

DIORIO Mary Ann Lucia, (Lucia St John), b. 11 Nov 1945, Norristown, Pennsylvania, USA. Freelance Writer; Businesswoman. m. Dominic A Diorio, 25 Oct 1969, 2 daughters. *Education:* BA, Immaculata College, 1967; MA, Middlebury College, 1968; M Phil, University of Kansas, 1974; PhD, 1977. *Publications:* Selling Yourself On You; Balancing Your Budget God's Way; Dating Etiquette for Christian Teens; From Feminism to Freedom. *Contributions to:* The Saturday Evening Post; The Atlantic City Press; Human Events; Decision; Christian Parenting; Pentecostal Evangel; Moody Magazine. *Honours:* Poetry Award; AMY Writing Award; Short Story Contest, National Writers Club, 5th Place.

Memberships: Lambda Lota Tau; The New Jersey Society of Christian Writers, Founder and Director; National Writers Club; Society of Childrens Book Writers. *Address:* PO Box 748, Millville, NJ 08332, USA.

DISCH Thomas Michael (Leonie Hargrave, Dobbin Thorpe), b. 1940, American. Writer of novels/short stories, science fiction/fantasy, poetry, songs, lyrics and libretti, literature. Freelance writer and lecturer, 1964-. Theatre critic, The Nation magazine, New York City, Formerly, draftsman and copywriter. *Publications include:* The Prisoner, 1969; (with Marilyn Hacker and Charles Platt), Highway Sandwiches 9poetry) 1970; The Right Way to Figure Plumbing (poetry), 1971; (ed) The Ruins of Earth: An Anthology of the Immediate Future, 1971: 334 1972; (ed) Bad Moon Rising, 1973; Getting into Death (short stories), 1973; (ed) The New Improved Sun: An Anthology of Utopian Science Fiction, 1975; (as Leonie Hargrave), Clara Reeve, 1975; (ed with Charles Naylor), New Constellations, 1976; (ed with Charles Naylor), Strangeness, 1977; On Wings of Song, 1979; Triplicity (omnibus), 1980; Fundamental Disch (short stories), 1980; (with CharlesNaylor), Neighboring Lives (historical novel), 1981; ABCDEFGHIJKLMNOPQRSTUVWXYZ (poetry), 1981; Orders of the Retina (poetry), 1982; Burn This (poetry), 1982; The Man Who Had No Idea (short stories), 1982; Frankenstein (libretto for opera by Gregory Sandow), 1982; Ringtime, 1983; The Businessman: A Tale of Terror, 1984; Torturing Mr. Amberwell, 1985; The Brave Little Toaster (children's Book), 1986; Amnesia (computer-interactive novel), 1986. *Address:* 31 Union Square W No 11E, New York, NY 10003, USA.

DITTMERS Manuel, b. 15 Apr 1961, Berlin, Germany. Author; Economist. *Education:* LSH-Holzminder; Studio School, Cambridge; Mander Portmann Woodward, London; Eurocentre Paris; University of Nice; University of Lille; University of Buckingham; BA, MEd, US International University; MSc, London School of Economics. *Appointments:* Founder of World Wide Peace, 1984; Founder of World Wide Peace Animal Rights, 1987; Responsible for: Middle East Peace Plan, 1986-1991; Amazons and Jahara World Park Project, 1987; Mediterranean Environmental Fund, 1987; World Citizen Passport, 1988. *Publications:* Charter of World-Wide Peace, 1984; The Green Party in West Germany, 1986; World and Environment, 1989; Impressions of Fuerteventura, 1990; European Poems, 1990. *Honours:* FRSA, 1990. *Memberships:* PEN; British Institute of Management; Phi Delta Kappa; Fellow, Institute of Directors; Convocation of University of London; Chairman of Board of World-Wide-Peace; Royal Ocean Racing Club; Silverstone Racing Club. *Address:* World-Wide-Peace, PO Box 55-10-42, 2000 Hamburg 55, Germany.

DITTON James. *See:* **CLARK Douglas.**

DIVINE Robert A(lexander), b. 1929, United States of America. Writer (History). *Appointments:* Instructor, 1954-57, Assistant Professor, 1957-61, Associate Professor, 1961-63, Professor of History, 1963- 80, George W. Littlefield Professor in American History, 1981-, University of Texas, Austin, USA; Fellow, Institute for Advanced Study in Behavioral Sciences, Stanford, California, 1962-63. *Publications:* American Immigration Policy, 1924-52, 1957; American Foreign Policy, 1960; The Illusion of Neutrality, 1962; The Reluctant Belligerent, 1965, 1979; Second Chance, 1967; The Age of Insecurity, 1968; Twentieth Century America (with J.A. Garraty), 1968; Roosevelt and World War II, 1969; Causes and Consequeces of World War II, 1969; American Foreign Policy since 1945, 1969; The Cuban Missile Crisis, 1971, 1988; Foreign Policy and US Presidential Elections 1940-1960, 2 vols, 1974; Since 1945, 1975, 1979, 1985; Blowing on the Wind, 1978; Eisenhower and the Cold War, 1981; Exploring the Johnson Years, 1981; America: Past and Present (with T.H. Breen, G.M. Frederickson and R.H. Williams), 1984, 1987, 1991; The Johnson Years: Volume Two, 1987; The Sputnik Challenge, 1993. *Address:*

Department of History, University of Texas, Austin, TX 78712, USA.

DIVINSKY Nathan J, b. 29 Oct 1925, Winnipeg, Canada. Mathematician. 3 daughters. *Education:* BSc, University of Manitoba, 1946; SM, 1947, PhD, 1950, University of Chicago, USA. *Appointments:* Editor, Canadian Chess Chat, 1959-74. *Publications:* Around the Chess World in 80 Years, 1963; Rings and Radicals, 1965; Linear Algebra, 1970; Warriors of the Mind (with R Keene), 1988; Chess Encyclopedia, 1990. *Memberships:* Life Master, ACBL (Bridge League); President, Commonwealth Chess Association; Canada's Representative to FIDE (World Chess Federation). *Address:* 5689 McMaster Road, Vancouver, British Columbia, Canada V6T 1K1.

DIVOK Mario J, b. 22 Sept 1944, Benus, Czechoslovakia. Real Estate Broker; Author. m. Eva Pytlova, 1990, 1 daughter. *Publications:* The Relations, 1975; The Voice, 1975; The Wind of Changes, 1978; Equinox, 1978; The Collection, 1978; I Walk the Earth, 1980; The Blind Man, 1980; Looking for the Road to the Earth, 1983; The Birthday, 1984; Forbidden Island Complete Works : Two, 1986; Selected Work, 1993; MPA, Cal. State University. *Honours include:* Schlossar Award for Play, Switzerland, 1980; Potpourri International Award, London, 1980; Winner, One-Act Play Competition, One Way Theatre, San Francisco, 1980; Orange County poetry Contest, Laguna Poets, 1981; World of Poetry, 1990. *Literary Agent:* Martin Littlefield. *Address:* 5 Misty Meadow, Irvine, CA 92715, USA.

DIXON Dougal, b. 1947. Author; Freelance Writer. *Appointments:* Researcher, Editor, Mitchell-Beazley Limited, 1973-78, Blandford Press, 1978-80; Part-time Tutor in Earth Sciences, Open University, 1976-78; Chairman, Bournemouth Science Fiction and Fantasy Group, 1981-82; Freelance Writer, 1980-. *Publications:* Doomsday Planet (comic strip), 1980; After Man: A Zoology for the Future, 1981; Discovering Earth Sciences, 1982; Science World: Geology, 1982; Science World: Geography, 1983; Picture Atlas: Mountains, 1984; Picture Atlas: Forests, 1984; Picture Atlas: Deserts, 1984; Find Out about Prehistoric Reptiles, 1984; Find Out about Jungles, 1984; The Age of Dinosauras (with Jane Burton), 1984; Nature Detective Series: Minerals, Rocks, and Fossils, 1984; Time Machine 7: Ice Age Explorer, 1985; Secrets of the Earth, 1986; Find Out about Dinosaurs, 1986. *Address:* c/o Hamlyn, 69 London Road, Twickenham, Middlesex, TW1 3SB, England.

DIXON Larry, b. Tulsa, Oklahoma, USA. Writer; Artist. m. Mercedes Lackey, 14 Dec 1990. *Publications:* Arrows of the Queen, 1987; Arrow's Flight, 1987; Arrow's Fall, 1988; Oathbound (Vows and Honor Book One), 1988; Oathbreakers (Vows and Honor Book Two(, 1989; Magic's Pawn (The Last Herald- Mage Book One), 1989; Reap the Whirlwind, 1989; Magic's Promise (The Last Herald-Mage Book Two), 1990; Knight of Ghosts and Shadows (with Ellen Guon), 1990; Magic's Price (The Last Herald-Mage Book Three), 1990; By the Sword, 1991; Winds of Fate, 1991; The Elvenbane (with Andre Norton), 1991; Sacred Ground; Diane Tregarde Investigations: Burning Water, 1989; Children of the Night, 1990, Jinx High, 1991; Triangle Park; Arcanum 101; Serrated Edge series: Born to Run (with Larry Dixon), 1992; Wheels of Fire (with Mark Shepherd), 1992; When the Bough Breaks (with Holly Lisle), 1992; The Mage- Wars; The Black Gryphon (with Larry Dixon); The Eric Banyon books: Summoned to Tourney (with Ellen Guon); Beyond World's End (with Ellen Guon); The Mage-Wind Books: Winds of Change, 1992; Winds of Fury, 1993; The Bardic Voices series: The Lark and the Wren, 1992; The Robin and the Kestrel; The Eagle and the Nightingale; Numerous short stories, novelettes and novellas. *Honours:* Arrows of the Queen selected for Best Books of 1987 for Young Adults, American Library Association. *Membership:* Science Fiction and Fantasy Writers of America. *Address:* PO Box 8309, Tulsa, OK 74101, USA.

DIXON Norman Frank, b. 19 May 1922, Cheam, London, England. Psychologist. *Education:* BA 1st Class, 1953, PhD, 1956, Reading University; DSc, University of London, 1981. *Publications:* Subliminal perception: the Nature of a Controversy, 1971; Psychology of Military Incompetence, 1976; Preconscious Processing, 1981; Our Own Worst Enemy, 1987. *Contributions to:* 50 papers to academic journals in psychology including: British Journal of Psychology; Journal of Nervous and Mental Disease, USA. *Honours:* MBE (Military), 1944; Carpenter Medal for Research, University of London, 1981; Honorary PhD, Lund University, Sweden, 1984. *Membership:* Fellow, British Psychological Society. *Address:* Department of Psychology, University College, Gower Street, London WC1, England.

DIXON Roger, (John Christian, Charles Lewis), b. 1930. Author; Playwright. *Publications:* Over 50 Radio/ Television Plays and Series. Novels: Noah II, 1970; Christ on Trial, 1973; The Messiah, 1974; Five Gates to Annegeddon (as John Christian), 1975; The Cain Factor (as Charles Lewis), 1975; Going to Jerusalem, 1977; Georgiana, 1984; Return to Nebo, 1991. Musical: The Commander of New York (with Phil Medley and Basil Bova), 1987. *Address:* Badgers, Warren Lane, Cross-in-Hand, Heathfield, Sussex, England.

DIXON Stephen, b. 6 June 1936, New York City, New York, USA. Fiction Writer; University Teacher. m. Anne Frydman, 17 Jan 1982, 2 daughters. *Education:* BA, City College of New York, 1958. *Publications:* No Relief, 1976; Work, 1977; Too Late, 1978; Quite Contrary, 1979; 14 Stories, 1980; Movies, 1983; Time to Go, 1984; Fall and Rise, 1985; Garbage, 1988; Love and Will, 1989; The Play and Other Stories, 1989; All Gone, 1990; Friends, 1990; Frog, 1991; Moon, 1993. *Contributions to:* 350 short stories to magazines and journals including: Atlantic; Harper's; Esquire; Playboy; Paris Review; Triquarterly; Western Humanities Review; Ambit; Bananas; Boulevard; Glitter Train. *Honours:* Stegner Fiction Fellowship, Stanford, 1964-65; National Education Association, fiction, 1974-75, 1990-91; American Academy- Institute of Arts and Letters Award in Literature, 1983; John Train Prize, Paris Review, 1984; John Simon Guggenheim Fellowship, 1985-86; Finalist in Fiction for Frog, NBA, 1991; Finalist for Fiction for Frog, PEN Faulkner Prize, 1992. *Literary Agent:* Kim Witherspoon, 130 W 57th Street 15C, New York, NY 10019, USA. *Address:* Writing Seminars, Gilman 135, Johns Hopkins University, Baltimore, MD 21218, USA.

DJERASSI Carl, b. 29 Oct 1923, Vienna, Austria. University Professor; Chemist; Writer. m. Diane Wood Middlebrook, 20 June 1985, 1 son. *Education:* AB summa cum laude, Kenyon College, 1942; PhD, University of Wisconsin, 1945. *Publications:* Optical Rotatory Dispersion, 1959; Steroid Reactions, 1963; Mass Spectrometry of Organic Compounds (with H Budzikiewicz and D H Williams), 1967; The Politics of Contraception, 1979; The Futurist and Other Stories, 1988; Steroids Made It Possible, 1990; Cantor's Dilemma, 1989, 1991 (novel); The Clock Runs Backward, poetry, 1991; The Pill, Pygmy Chimps, and Degas' Horse, 1992 (autobiography); Bourbaki Gambit, 1993 (novel in German). *Contributions to:* Kenyon Review; Southern Review; Grand Street; New Letters; Exquisite Corpse; Michigan Quarterly Review; South Dakota Review; Frank; Midwest Quarterly. *Honours:* National Medal of Science, 1973; Perkin Medal, 1975; Wolf Prize in Chemistry, 1978; National Medal of Technology, 1991; Priestley Medal, 1992; Honorary doctorates: National University of Mexico, 1953; Kenyon College, 1958; Worcester Polytechnic Institute, 1972; Wayne State University, 1974; Columbia University, 1975; Uppsala University, 1977; Coe College, 1978; University of Geneva, 1978; University of Ghent, 1985; University of Manitoba, 1985; Adelphi University, 1993. *Memberships:* Modern Languages Association; National Academy of Sciences; American Academy of Arts and Sciences; Royal Swedish Academy of Sciences; Leopoldina; Bulgarian Academy of Sciences; Honorary Member, Royal Society of Chemistry. *Literary Agents:* Michael Carlisle, William Morries Agency, Inc, 1350

Avenue of the Americas, New York, NY 10019, USA; Andrew Nurnberg Associates, 45-47 Clerkenwell Green, London EC1R OHT, England. *Address:* Department of Chemistry, Stanford University, Stanford, CA 94305, USA.

DOBAI Peter, b. 12 Aug 1944, Budapest, Hungary. Writer. m. (1) Donatella Failoni, 1972, (2) Maria MATE, 1992. *Education:* Sailor, Mate, 1963-65; Teacher's Diploma, Philosophy, Italian, Faculty of Humanities, Budapest, 1970. *Appointments:* Scriptwriter, Dramaturgist, Assistant Director, Mafilm, 1970. *Publications:* Film scripts: Punitive Expedition, 1971; Csontvary, the Painter, 1979; Mephisto, 1980; Colonel Redl, 1983; Hanussen, the Prophet, 1984; Consciousness, 1987; Rembrandt van Rijn (Life and Works), 1992; Books of poetry: Kilovaglas egy öszi erödböl, 1973; Egy arc modosulasai, 1976; Lying on the Back, 1978; Pitfalls of Eden, 1985; Selected poems, 1989; Novels: Csontmolnarok, 1974; Belonging Life, 1975; Avalanche, 1980; Wilderness, 1982; A birodalom ezredese, 1985; Arch, 1988; Fly-Wheel, 1989; Short story collections: Fatek a szobakkal, 1976; Chess-board with two Figures, 1978; 1964-Island, diary, 1977; Archaic torso, scripts, essays, 1983. *Contributions to:* Essays, articles and reviews to magazines and journals. *Honours:* Jozsef Attila Prize, 1976; Several awards, Hungarian Literary Foundation and Minister of Culture; Best Filmscript for Mephisto, Cannes Film Festival, 1981; Balazs Bela Prize for scripts, 1990. *Memberships:* Executive Board, Hungarian Writers Association, Leading Member, Prose Committee; Chamber of Writers; Hungarian Academy of Artists; Hungarian PEN Club; Association of Hungarian Film and Television Artists; Professional Feature Film Advisory Board; Hungarian Seamen's Association. *Address:* Kozraktar u 12 B, 1093 Budapest, Hungary.

DOBBS Gregory Allan, b. 9 Oct 1946, San Francisco, California, USA. Journalist (Correspondent, ABC News). m. Carol Lynn Walker, 25 Nov 1973, 2 sons. *Education:* BA, University of California, Berkeley, 1968; MSc, Journalism (MSJ), Northwestern University, 1969. *Honours:* Distinguished service award, Society of Professional Journalists (Sigma Delta Chi), 1980; National News Emmy, National Academy of TV Arts & Sciences, 1981; Nomination, ibid, 1984; National News Emmy and National Headliners Award for ABC News documentary, Burning Question: The Poisoning of America. *Memberships:* Society of Professional Journalists, Sigma Delta Chi. *Address:* c/o ABC News, 2460 West 26th Avenue, Denver, Colorado, USA.

DOBEREINER Peter Arthur Bertram, b. 3 Nov 1925, England. Golf Correspondent; Author. m. Betty Evelyn Jacob, 20 Jan 1951, 2 sons, 2 daughters. *Education:* Lincoln College, Oxford. *Appointments:* East Essex Gazette, Oxford Times, News Chronicle, Daily Express, Daily Mail, The Guardian,1949-65; The Observer, 1965-. *Publications:* Book of Golf Disasters, 1983; The Game with a Hole in It, 1970, 1973; The Glorious World of Golf, 1973; The World of Golf, 1982; Arnold Palmers Complete Book of Putting, 1986; Golf Rules Explained, 1980; Down the 19th Fairway, 1982; Tony Jacklins Golf Secrets, 1982; Stroke, Hole or Match, 1976; The Golfers, 1982; The 50 Greatest Pot-War Golfers, 1985; Preferred Lies, 1987. *Contributions to:* Numerous journals and magazines. *Honours:* Screen Writers Guild Award, 1962; MacGregor Writing Awards, 1977; Donald Ross Award, 1985; Irish Golf Fellowship Awad, 1987. *Memberships:* West Kent Golf Club; Bally Bunion, Ireland; Honorary Member, American Society of Golf Course Architects. *Address:* Chelsfield Hill House, Pratts Bottom, Nr. Orpington, Kent BR6 7SL, England.

DOBSON Andrew Nicholas Howard, b. 15 Apr 1957, Doncaster, England. Politics Lecturer. *Education:* BA 1st Class, Politics, Reading University, 1979; DPhil Politics, Oxford University, 1983. *Appointments:* Editorial Board, Environmental Values, 1991-; Editorial Board, Environmental Politics, 1991-. *Publications:* Introduction to the Politics and Philosophy of José Ortega y Gasset, 1989; Green Political Thought, 1990; The Green Reader, 1991; The Politics of Nature: Explorations in Green Political Theory (edited with Paul Lucardie); Jean-Paul Satre and the Politcs of Reason: A Theory of History. *Contributions to:* Numerous articles and book reviews to magazines and journals. *Honours:* Spanish Government Scholar, 1983-84; ESRC Postdoctoral Fellow, 1984-87. *Address:* Politics Department, Keele University, Keele, Staffs ST5 5BG, England.

DOBSON Julia Lissant (Julia Tugendhat), b. 1941, British. *Publications:* The Children of Charles I, 1975; The Smallest Man in England, 1977; Mountbatten Sailor Hero, Children of the Tower, 1978; They Were at Waterloo, 1979; The Ivory Poachers: A Crisp Twins Adventure, The Tomb Robbers, 1981; The Wreck Finders, The Animal Rescuers, 1982; Danger In The Magic Kingdom, 1983; The Chinese Puzzle, 1984; As Julia Tugendhat: What Teenagers Can Tell Us About Divorce and Step Families, 1990; The Adoption Triangle, 1992. *Address:* 35 Westbourne Park Road, London W2, England.

DOBSON Sue (Susan Angela), b. 31 Jan 1946, Maidstone, Kent, England. Magazine Editor. *Education:* Dip HE; BA Hons. *Literary Appointment:* Editor, Woman and Home. *Publication:* The Wedding Day Book, 1981, 1984, revised 1989. *Contributions to:* Femina; Fair Lady; Wedding Day; Successful Slimming; Woman and Home. *Address:* Editor, Woman and Home, IPC Magazines, Kings Reach Tower, Stamford Street, London SE1 9LS, England.

DOCHERTY John. *See:* **SILLS-DOCHERTY Jonathan John.**

DOCTOROW Edgar Lawrence, . 6 Sept 1931, New York, New York, USA. Writer. m. Helen Setzer, 20 Aug 1954, 1 son, 2 daughters. *Education:* AB, Kenyon College, 1952; Graduate study, Columbia University, 1952-53. *Appointments:* Script reader, Columbia Pictures, 1956-59; Senior Editor, New American Library, 1960-64; Editor-in-Chief, Dial Press, 1964-69; Publisher 1969; writer-in-Residence, University of Californiam Irvine, 1969-70; Member of Faculty, Sarah Lawrence College, 1971-78; Creative Writing Fellow, Yale School of Drama, 1974-75; Visiting Senior Fellow, Council on the Humanities, Princeton University, 1980; Glucksman Professor of American and English Letters, New York University, 1987-. *Publications:* Welcome to Hard Times, 1960; Big As Life, 1966; The Book of Daniel, 1971; Ragtime, 1975; (play) Drinks Before Dinner 1979; Loon Lake, 1980; Lives of the Poets, 1984; World's Fair, 1985; Billy Bathgate, 1989; *Honours:* Guggenheim Fellowship, 1973; Arts and Letters Award, American Academy and National Institute for Arts and Letters for Ragtime 1976; National Book Critics Circle Award for Ragtime 1976 and for Billy Bathgate, 1989; National Book Award for World's Fair, 1985; PEN/Faulkner Award for Billy Bathgate, 1990; Howells Medal, American Academy and Institute of Arts and Letters for Most Distinguished Work of Fiction in Five Years for Billy Bathgate, 1990. *Memberships:* PEN, American Center; Writers Guild of America; Authors Guild; Century Association. *Literary Agent:* Arlene Donovan, ICM, 40 West 57th Street, New York, NY 10022, USA. *Address:* c/o Random House, 201 East 50th Street, New York, NY 10019, USA.

DODSON Daniel B, b. 21 Mar 1918, Portland, Oregon, USA. Professor of English, (retired). *Education:* BA, Reed College, 1941; MA, 1947; PhD, 1952, Columbia University. *Publications:* The Man Who Ran Away, 1960; Scala Dei, 1962; On A Darkling Plain, 1964; Looking for Zo, 1976; Dancers in the Dark, 1978; The Dance of Love, 1958; The Last Command, 1989; Malcolm Lowry, (literary study), 1958. *Contributions to:* Short stories in Esquire Story; various scholarly journals. *Literary Agent:* Harold Ober, New York, USA. *Address:* Place Jean Aicard, Sollies Ville, 83210 Sollies Pont, France.

DODWELL Charles Reginald, b. 3 Feb 1922, Cheltenham, England. Professor Emeritus. m. Sheila Juliet Fletcher, 5 Dec 1942, 1 son, 1 daughter. *Education:* Gonville and Caius College, Cambridge, 1940-41, 1945-46; MA, 1946; PhD, 1953; LittD, 1970. *Appointments:* Research Fellow, Gonville and Caius College, Cambridge, 1950-51; Senior Research Fellow, Warburg Institute, 1950-53; Librarian, Lambeth Palace, London, 1953-58; Fellow, Lecturer, Librarian, Trinity College, Cambridge, 1958-66; Pilkington Professor, History of Art, Director, Whitworth Art Gallery, Manchester University, 1966-89. *Publications:* Canterbury School of Illumination, 1954; Lambeth Palace, 1958; The Great Lambeth Bible, 1959; Theophilus de Diversus Artibus, 1961; Reichenau Reconsidered, 1965; Painting in Europe 800- 1200, 1971; Anglo-Saxon Art, 1982; Pictorial Arts of the West 800-1200, 1993. *Contributions to:* Burlington Magazine; Gazette de Beaux Arts; Enciclopedia Italiena; Congres Scientifique du 13 Centenaire l'Archologie; Others. *Memberships:* Fellow, British Academy; Fellow, Royal Historical Society; Fellow, Society of Antiquaries. *Address:* The Yews, 37 South Road, Taunton, Somerset, TA1 3DU, England.

DOHERTY Berlie, b. 6 Nov 1943, Liverpool, England. Novelist; Playwright; Poet. m. Gerard Doherty, 17 Dec 1966, 1 son, 2 daughters, (div 1993). *Education:* BA Hons, English, Durham University, 1964; Post-Graduate Certificate in Social Studies, 1965, Liverpool University, 1965; Post-Graduate Certificate of Education, Sheffield University, 1976. *Appointments:* Member, Literature Panel, Yorkshire Arts Association, 1986-87; Chairperson, Arvon Foundation, Lumb Bank, 1988-; Deputy Chairperson, National Association of Writers in Education, 1988. *Publications:* Requiem, novel, 1991; Children's books: How Green You Are, 1982; The Making of Fingers Finnigan, 1983; White Peak Farm, 1984; Granny Was A Buffer Girl, 1986; Children of Winter, 1986; Tilly Mint Tales, 1986; Tilly Mint and the Dodo, 1987; Paddiwak and Cosy, 1988; Tough Luck, 1988; Dear Nobody, 1991. *Contributions to:* Numerous reviews, some articles to The Times Educational Supplement; Reviews, articles to Yorkshire Art Scene. *Honours:* For Granny Was A Buffer Girl: Carnegie Medal, 1987; Boston Globe Horn Honor, 1987; Burnley Children's Book of the Year Award, 1987; Bronze Award for White Peak Farm, International Film and Television, 1988; Dear Nobody; Carnegie Medal, 1991; Snowy, 1992; Walking on Air, 1993; Street Child, 1993. *Memberships:* Arvon Foundation, National Literature Initiative Committee; Writers of Great Britain. *Literary Agent:* Gina Pollinger (Murray Pollinger). *Address:* 222 Old Brompton Road, London, England.

DOLL Mary Aswell, b. 4 Jun 1940, New York City, New York, USA. Professor of English. m. William Elder Doll Jr, 25 June 1966, 1 son. *Education:* BA, Connecticut College, New London, 1962; MA, Johns Hopkins University, Baltimore, Maryland, 1970; PhD, Syracuse University, Syracuse, New York, 1980. *Appointments:* Assistant Professor, State University of New York, Oswego, 1978-84; Lecturer, University of Redlands, California, 1985-88; Assistant Professor, Loyola University, 1988; Visiting Assistant Professor, Tulane University, 1988; Associate Professor, Our Lady of Holy Cross College, 1989-. *Publications:* Rites of Story: The Old Man at Play, 1987; Beckett and Myth: An Archetypal Approach, 1988; In the Shadow of the Giant: Thomas Wolfe, 1988; Walking and Rocking, 1989; Joseph Cambell and The Power of Wilderness, 1992; Stoppard's Theatre of Unknowing, 1993. *Contributions to:* The Temple Symbol in Scripture, to Soundings, 1987; The Demeter Myth in Beckett, to Journal of Beckett Studies, 1988. *Honours:* In the Shadow selected as 1 of Choice's Outstanding Books, 1989; Sears-Roebuck Teaching Excellence Award. *Memberships:* Modern Language Association; Board of Directors, Thomas Wolfe Society; American Academy of English. *Address:* 69 Belle Grove, Destrehan, LA 70047, USA.

DOLLE Raymond Francis, b. 22 May 1952, Westfield, Massachusetts, USA. div, 2 sons. *Education:* BA, North Adams State College, 1978; MA, The Pennsylvania State Univserity, 1981; PhD, 1985. *Appointments:* Assistant Professor, Indiana State University, 1986-90; Associate Professor, 1990-. *Publication:* Anne Bradstreet: A Reference Guide. *Contributions to:* The Beacon Handbook; The Heath Anthology of American Literature; Early American Literature & Culture; Annual Bibliography of English Language & Literature; Encyclopedia of American Literature; Journal of Environmental Health; College Literature; Seventeenth-Century News; Midwestern Folklore; Black American Literature Forum; Indiana Englsh; Shakespeare Quarterly. *Memberships:* Modern Language Association; Indian College English Association. *Address:* 1144 Hulman Street, Terre Haute, IN 47802, USA.

DOLMETSCH Carl Richard, b. 5 July 1924, USA. University Professor; Writer. m. Joan Downing, 7 Feb 1948, 2 sons. *Education:* BA, 1948; MA, 1959; PhD, University of Chicago, 1957. *Appointments:* Music Columnist, The Virginia Gazette, 1973-; Advisory Editor, Eighteenth Century Life, 1977-; Staff Contributor, Oper Canada, 1978-. *Publications:* The Smart Set: A History & Anthology; Our Famous Guest: Mark Twain in Vienna; The poems of Charles Hansford. *Contributions to:* Musical America; Opera Magazine; Orpheus; American Record Guide; The Mark Twain Journal. *Memberships:* Music Critics Association. *Address:* 108 Hermitage Road, Williamsburg, VA 23188, USA.

DOMINIQUE Meg. *See:* **SANFORD Annette Schorre.**

DONALDS Gordon. *See:* **SHIRREFFS Gordon Donald.**

DONALDSON Frances, b. 13 Jan 1907. Writer. m. J G S Donaldson, 20 Feb 1935, 1 son 2 daughters. *Publications:* Edward VIII, 1974; Evelyn Waugh: Portrayal of a Country Neighbour, 1967; P G Wodehouse, 1982; The Marconi Scandal, 1962; Freddy Lonsdale, 1957; The British Council: The first fifty years, 1984; Child of the Twenties, 1959. *Honour:* Wolfson Prize, 1974. *Membership:* Fellow, Royal Society of Literature. *Literary Agent:* A D Peters. *Address:* 17 Edna Street, London SW11 3DP, England.

DONALDSON Gordon, b. 1913. Writer (History). *Appointments:* Assistant Keeper, Scottish Record Office, 1938-47; Lecturer, 1947-55, Reader, 1955-63, Professor, 1963-79, Emeritus Professor of Scottish History and Palaeography, University of Edinburgh, 1979-. *Publications:* The Making of the Scottish Prayer Book 1637, 1954; The Register of the Privy Seal of Scotland, Vols. V-VIII, 1957-82; Shetland Life under Earl Patrick, 1958; Scotland: Church and Nation Through Sixteen Centuries, 1960, 1972; The Scottish Reformation, 1960, 1972; Scotland: James V to James VII, 1965, 1978; The Scots Overseas, 1966; Northwards by Sea, 1966, 1978; Scottish Kings, 1967, 1977; Memoirs of Sir James Melville, 1969; The First Trial of Mary, Queen of Scots, 1969; Scottish Historical Documents, 1970; Who's Who in Scottish History, 1974; Mary, Queen of Scots, 1974; Scotland: The Shaping of a Nation, 1974, 1980; Dictionary of Scottish History, 1977; All the Queen's Men, 1983; Isles of Home, 1983; Scottish Church History, 1985; The Faith of the Scots, 1990; A Northern Commonwealth, Scotland and Norway, 1990. *Honour:* CBE, 1988. *Address:* 6 Pan Ha' Dysart, Fife, KY1 2TL, Scotland.

DONALDSON Stephen Reeder (Reed Stephens), b. 13 May 1947, Cleveland, Ohio, USA. Writer. m. Stephanie Boutz, 1 son, 1 daughter. *Education:* BA, English, Wooster College, 1968; MA, Kent State University, 1971. *Appointment:* Associate instructor, Ghost Ranch Writers Workshops, 1973-77. *Publications:* Lord Foul's Bane, 1977; The Illearth War, 1977; The Power That Preserves, 1977; The Wounded Land, 1980; The One Tree, 1982; White Gold Wielder,

1983; Daughter of Regals, 1984; The Mirror of her Dreams, 1986; (as Reed Stephens), The Man Who Killed his Brother, 1980; The Man Who Risked his Partner, 1984. *Honours:* Best Novel, British Fantasy Society, 1979; Best New Writer, John W.Campbell, 1979. *Literary Agent:* Howard Morhaim. *Address:* c/o Del Rey/Ballantine, 201 East 50th Street, New York, NY 10022, USA.

DONKIN Nance (Clare), b. 1915, Australia. Children's Fiction Writer; Journalist. *Appointments:* Journalist, Daily Mercury, Maitland, Morning Herald, Newcastle; President, Children's Book Council, Victoria, 1968- 76. *Publications:* Araluen Adventures, 1946; No Medals for Meg, 1947; Julie Stands By, 1948; Blue Ribbon Beth, 1951; The Australian Children's Annual, 1963; Sheep, 1967; Sugar, 1967; An Emancipist, 1968; A Currency Lass, 1969; House by the Water, 1969; An Orphan, 1970; Johnny Neptune, 1971; The Cool Man, 1973; A Friend for Petros, 1974; Margaret Catchpole, 1974; Patchwork Grandmother, 1975; Green Christmas, 1976; Yellowgum Girl, 1976; A Handful of Ghosts, 1976; The Best of the Bunch, 1978; The Maidens of Pefka, 1979; Nini, 1979; Stranger and Friend, 1983; We of the Never Never Retold for Children, 1983; Two at Sulivan Bay, 1985; Blackout, 1987; A Family Affair, 1988; The Women Were There, 1988; Always A Lady, 1990. *Honours:* AM, Member of Order Australia, 1986; Alice Award, Society Women Writers, Australia, 1990 for Distinguished Contribution to Australian Literature. *Memberships:* FAW, (Fellowship Australian Writers); ASA, (Australian Society of Authors); Society of Women Writers of Australia; Royal Historical Society; Children's Book Council; Gallery Society; National Trust; Melbourne Theatre Company. *Address:* 8/8 Mooltan Avenue, Balaclava, Victoria 3183, Australia.

DONLEAVY James Patrick, b. 1926, Brooklyn, New York. Author; Playwright. *Publications:* The Ginger Man, 1955, Paris, France, UK edition 1956; The Ginger Man (play), 1959 (in United Kingdom as What They Did in Dublin, with the Ginger Man, 1961); Fairy Tales of New York (play), 1961; A Singular Man, 1963; A Singular Man (play), 1965; Meet My Maker the Mad Molecule (short stories), 1964; The Saddest Summer of Samuel S., 1966; The Beastly Beatitudes of Balthazar B., 1968; The Onion Eaters, 1971; The Collected Plays of J.P. Donleavy, 1972; A Fairy Tale of New York, 1973; The Unexpurgated Code: A Compete Manual of Survival and Manners, 1975; The Destinies of Darcy Dancer, Gentleman, 1977; Shultz, 1979; Leila, 1983; De Alfonce Tennis, 1984; J P Donleavy's Ireland, 1986; Are You Listening Rabbi Low, 1987; A Singular Country, 1989; That Darcy That Dancer That Gentleman, 1990; The History of The Ginger Man. *Contributions to:* Journals, including The Observer, The Times (London), New York Times, Guardian and Punch. *Address:* Levington Park, Mullinger, Co. Westmeath, Republic of Ireland.

DONNE Maxim. *See:* **DUKE Madelaine Elizabeth.**

DONOGHUE Denis, b. 1928, Ireland. Writer (Literature). *Publications:* The Third Voice: Modern British and American Verse Drama, 1959; Connoisseurs of Chaos: Ideas of Order in Modern American Literature, 1965; An Honoured Guest: New Essays on W. B. Yeats (with J.R. Mulryne), 1965; Swift Revisited, 1968; The Ordinary Universe: Soundings in Modern Literature, 1968; Jonathan Swift: A Critical Introduction, 1969; Emily Dickinson, 1969; William Butler Yeats, 1971; Jonathan Swift: A Critical Anthology, 1971; Memoirs, by W.B. Yeats, 1973; Thieves of Fire, 1973; The Sovereign Ghost: Studies in Imagination, 1976; Ferocious Alphabets, 1981; The Ants Without Mystery, 1983. *Address:* Department of English, New York University, New York, NY 10003, USA.

DONOUGHUE Bernard (Baron), b. 1934. *Appointments:* Editorial Staff, The Economist, London, 1959-60; Senior Research Officer, Political and Economic Planning (PEP), London, 1960-63; Senior Lecturer, Politics, London School of Economics, 1963-74; Senior Policy Adviser to the Prime Minister, 1974-79; Director, Economist Intelligence Unit, London, 1979-81; Assistant Editor, The Times, London, 1981-82; Head of Research, Kleinworth Grieveson and Company, 1982- . *Publications:* Oxford Poetry, 1956; British Politics and the American Revolution, 1963; Co-Author, The People into Parliament, 1964; Co-Author, Herbert Morrison: Portrait of a Politician, 1973; Prime Minister, 1987. *Address:* 71 Ebury Mews West, London, SW1W 9QA W5.

DONOVAN John, (Hugh Hennessey), b. 1919, United States of America. Author; Freelance Public Relations Consultant. *Publications:* Eichmann, Man of Slaughter, 1960; Red Machete, 1963; Not For Eternity (novel), 1971; International Businessman's Travel Guide, 1972; U.S. and Soviet Policy in the Middle East, vol 1, 1972, vol II, 1974; There's Money in Your House, 1976; Bitter Sweet Temptation, 1980.

DOR Moshe, b. 9 Dec 1932, Tel Aviv, Israel. Poet; Journalist. m. Ziona Dor, 29 Mar 1955, 2 sons. *Education:* Hebrew University of Jerusalem, 1949-52; BA, Political Science, University of Tel Aviv, 1956. *Appointments:* Counsellor for Cultural Affairs, Embassy of Israel, London, England, 1975-77; Distinguished Writer-in-Residence, American University, Washington, District of Columbia, USA, 1987; President, Israel PEN Centre, 1988-90. *Publications:* From the Outset, 1984; On Top of the Cliff (in Hebrew), 1986; Crossing the River, 1989; From the Outset (selected poems in Dutch translation), 1989; Crossing the River (selected poems in English translation), 1989; Some 20 other books of poetry, children's verse, literary essays, interviews with writers. *Honours:* Honourable Citation, International Hans Christian Andersen Prize for Children's Literature, 1975; Holon Prize for Literature, 1981; Prime Minister's Award for Creative Writing, 1986; Bialik Prize for Literature, 1987. *Memberships:* Association of Hebrew Writers, Israel; National Federation of Israel Journalists; Isreal PEN Centre. *Address:* 11 Brodetsky Street, Tel Aviv, Israel 69051.

DORLAND Henry. *See:* **ASH Brian.**

DORMAN Michael L, b. 9 Oct 1932, New York City, USA. Writer. m. Jeanne Darrin O'Brien, 25 June 1955, 2 daughters. *Education:* BS, Journalism, New York University 1953. *Appointments:* Correspondent, The New York Times 1952-53; Reporter and Editor, The Houston Press 1953-58; Reporter and Editor, Newsday (Long Island, New York), 1959-64; Freelance writer 1965-. *Publications include:* We Shall Overcome, 1964; Payoff: The Role of Organized Crime in American Politics, 1972; King of the Courtroom, 1969; The Secret Service Story, 1967; The Making of a Slum, 1972; The George Wallace Myth, 1976; The Second Man, 1969; Under 21, 1970; Politics and Protest, 1974; Witch Hunt, 1976; Detectives of the Sky, 1976; Vesco: The Infernal Money-Making Machine, 1975; Dirty Politics, 1979; Blood and Revenge, 1991. *Contributor to:* Publications such as The New York Times Magazine; Playboy; New York Magazine. *Honours:* James Fenimore Cooper Prize for best critical article on American press, New York University, 1953; Houston (Texas) Press Club award for best news story of 1953 (coverage of Hurricane Audrey in Louisiana); New York State Bar Association press award, 1984. *Membership:* Authors League of America; Authors Guild. *Literary Agent:* Philippa Brophy, Sterling Lord Literistic Inc, New York. *Address:* 7 Lauren Avenue South, Dix Hills, NY 11746, USA.

DORN Ed(ward Merton), American, b. 1929. Poetry, Anthropology/Ethnology, Literature, Translations. *Appointments:* Member, English Department, University of Colorado, Boulder 1977-; Visiting Professor of American Literature 1965-68 and Member of English Department, 1974-75, University of Essex, Wivenhoe, UK; Visiting Professor, University of Kansas, Lawrence, 1968-69. *Publications include:* Geography 1965; The Shoshoneans: The People of the Basin-Plateau, 1966;

The North Atlantic Turbine, 1967; (translation with G Brotherston), Our Word: Guerrilla Poems from Latin America, 1968; Gunslinger Book I, 1968; Gunslinger Book II, 1969; Gunslinger Books I and II, 1969; Twenty-Four Love Songs, 1969; (translation with G Brotherston), Tree Between the Tow Walls, by Jose Emilio Pacheco, 1969; The Midwest is that Space Between the Buffalo Statlet and the Lawrence Eldridge, 1969; The Cosmology of Finding Your Spot, 1969; Songs: Set Two, A Short Count, 1970; Spectrum Breakdown: A Microbook, 1971; A Poem Called Alexander Hamilton, 1971; The Cycle, 1971; Some Business Recently Transacted in the White World (short stories), 1971; The Hamadryas Baboon at the Lincoln Park Zoo, 1972; Gunslinger Book III: The Winterbook Prologue to the Great Book IV Kornerstone, 1972; Recollections of Gran Apacheria, 1973; Gunslinger, Books I, II, III, IV, 1975; Collected Poems of Edward Dorn, 1975; (with Jennifer Dunbar), Manchester Squarer (poetry), 1975; (translation with Gordon Brotherston), Selected Poems by Vallejo, 1976; Hello La Jolla (poetry), 1978; Views, Interviews, 2 vols, 1978; Selected Poems, 1978; (translation), Images of the New World, 1979; Yellow Lola, 1981. Address: 1035 Mapleton, Colorado 80302, USA.

DORNBERG John Robert, b. 22 Aug 1931, Efurt, Germany. Journalist; Writer. Education: University of Denver, Denver, Colorado, USa 1949- 52. Appointments: Harry Shubart Co Public Relations, Denver 1952-54; US Military Service 1954-56; The Overseas Weekly, Frankfurt, Germany, Managing Editor, 1956-63; Newsweek Magazine, Correspondent, Bureau Chief, Bonn, Vienna, Moscow, Munich 1963-73; Freelance journalist/writer based in Munich 1973-. Publications: Munich 1923 - The Story of Hitler's First Grab for Power, 1982; Brezhnev - The Masks of Power, 1973; The New Tsars - Russia Under Stalin's Heirs, 1972; The Other Germany, 1968; Schizophrenic Germany, 1961; Penguin Travel Guide, Germany 1991 (author and consulting editor), 1990; Eastern Europe - The Communist Kaleidoscope, 1980. Contributions to: Reader's Digest; National Geographic Traveller; ARTnews; Connoisseur; Travel and Leisure; The Smithsonian; Institutional Investor; Business Month; New York Times; Washington Post. Memberships: Foreign Press Association, Germany (Bonn); Overseas Press Club, New York. Literary Agent: Sterling Lord Literistic Inc, New York. Address: Kreiller Str 3, D-8000 Munich 80, Germany.

DORNER Marjorie, b. 21 Jan 1942, Luxemburg, Wisconsin, USA. University Professor. 2 daughters. Education: BA, English, St Norbert College, 1964; MA, English, Marquette University, 1965; PhD, English, Purdue University, 1971. Appointments: Professr of English Literature, Winona State University, Winona, Minnesota, 1971-. Publications: Nightmare, 1987; Family Closets, 1989; Freeze Frame, 1990; Winter Roads, Summer Fields, 1992; Blood Kin, 1992. Contributions to: Mass for the Dead, to Great River Review, 1981; Accessory, to Cottonwood Review, 1982; Lee Ann's Little Killing, to Fall Out, 1983; Winter Roads, to Mississippi Valley Review, 1984- 85; Pin Money, to Primavera, 1985; Changeling, to New Renaissance, 1988. Honours: Minnesota Book Award for Best Mystery, for Freeze Frame, 1991. Literary Agent: Judith Weber, Sobel Weber Associates, New York, NYC, USA. Address: 777 West Broadway, Winona, MN 55987, USA.

DORSETT Danielle. See: DANIELS Dorothy.

DOSS Margot P(atterson), b. 1922, United States of America. Writer. Appointments: Performer and Outdoor Editor, KPIX-TV Evening Magazine, 1977-83; Columnist, San Francisco Chronicle, 1961-. Publications: San Francisco at Your Feet, 1964, 3rd edition, 1980; Walks for Children in San Francisco, 1970; Bay Area at Your Feet, 1970, 3rd edition, 1986; Golden Gate Park at Your Feet, 1970, 1978; Paths of Gold, 1974; There, There, 1978; A Walker's Yearbook, 1984. Address: 1331 Greenwich Street, San Francisco, CA 94109, USA.

DOTSON Robert Charles, b. 3 Oct 1946, St Louis, Missouri, USA. Network Correspondent. m. 1 July 1972, 1 daughter. Education: BS, Journalism & Political Science, Kansas University, 1968; MS, TV, Syracuse University, 1969. Publication: In Pursuit of the American Dream, 1985. Honours: Still Got life to Go, 1972, Smoke and Steel, 1973 - Emmy Nominations; Through the Looking Glass Darkly, 1974 - Emmy Award, DuPont Columbia Journalism Award, Robert F Kennedy Award; The Urban Reservation, 1975 - RFK Award; 'NBC Nightly News with Tom Brokaw', 'Today', and 'Prime Time Saturday with Tom Snyder' - Emmy, DuPont-Columbia, Robert F Kennedy, Silver Medals from International Film and TV Festival of NY and the International Film Festival of Mountains, Trento, Italy; National Headliners Award, Gabriel, Media Access, Wilbur, Ohio State University, TV of Merit Award-DAR, Clarion; Women in Communications, Epilepsy Foundation and the Sprague Memorial for Lifetime Achievement from the National Press Photographers Association. Memberships; Sigma Delta Chi; Writers Guild of America; National Academy of Television Arts and Sciences; National Press Photographers Association; Faculty Affiliate, Colorado State University, Ft Collins. Agent: Paul Millman, White Plains, New York 10601, USA. Address: NBC News, 100 Colony Square, Suite 1140, Atlanta, GA 30361, USA.

DOUBTFIRE Dianne (Joan), b. 1918. Author; Creative Writer. Appointments: Lecturer, Creative Writing, Isle of Wight County Council Adult Education, 1965-85; Lecturer, Creative Writing, University of Surrey, 1986-. Publications: Lust for Innocence, 1960; Reason for Violence, 1961; Kick a Tin Can, 1964; The Flesh Is Strong, 1966; Behind the Screen, 1969; Escape on Monday, 1970; This Jim, 1974; Girl in Cotton Wool, 1975; A Girl Called Rosemary, 1977; Sky Girl, 1978; The Craft of Novel-Writing, 1978; Girl in a Gondola, 1980; Sky Lovers, 1981; Teach Yourself Creative Writing, 1983; The Wrong Face, 1985; Overcoming Shyness, 1988; Getting Along With People, 1990. Address: April Cottage, Beech Hill, Headley Down, Hampshire, GU35 8EQ, England.

DOUGALL Robert Neill, b. 27 Nov 1913, Croydon, England. BBC TV Newscaster, Retired; Writer. m. N A Byam, 7 June 1947, 1 son, 1 stepdaughter. Education: Whitgift School, 1923-31. Publications: In and Out of the Box, 1973; A Celebration of Birds, 1978; Now for the Good News 1976; British Birds, 1983; Birdwatch Round Britain, 1985; Basil Ede's Birds, text by Robert Dougall, published by Severn House and Van Nostrand Reinhold Co, New York; Years Ahead, 1984. Contributions to: Newspapers and magazines including: Sunday Telegraph Magazine; Spectator; Daily Mail; High Life. Honour: MBE 1965. Memberships: Royal Society for Literature, 1975-83; Garrick Club; President, Royal Society for the Protection of Birds, 1970-75. Literary Agent: Curtis Brown. Address: Box Bush, Walberswick, Nr Southwold, Suffolk IP18 6UL, England.

DOUGLAS Amanda Hart. See: WALLMAN Jeffrey M.

DOUGLAS Ellen. See: HAXTON Josephine Ayres.

DOUGLAS R M. See: MASON Douglas Rankine.

DOVE Rita, b. 28 Aug 1952, Akron, Ohio, USA. Author; Educator. m. Fred Viebahn, 1 daughter. Education: BA summa cum laude, Miami University, Ohio, 1973; Modern European literature, University of Tubingen, Germany, 1974-75; MFA, University of Iowa, 1977. Appointments: Professor of English/Creative Writing, Arizona State University, 1981-89; Professor of English/Creative Writing, University of Virginia, 1989-; Poetry panellist, National Endowment for the Arts (chairperson 1985), 1984-86; Editorial board, National Forum, 1984-; Associate editor, Callaloo 1986-, Advisory editor, Gettysburg Review 1987-; TriQuarterly 1988-. Publications: The Yellow House on the Corner,

1980; Museum, 1983; Fifth Sunday, short stories, 1985; Thomas & Beulah, 1986. Chapbooks: 10 Poems, 1977; The Only Dark Spot in the Sky, 1980; Mandolin, 1982; Grace Notes, 1989. *Contributions to:* Numerous magazines & journals. *Honours:* Creative Writing Grant, National Endowment for the Arts, 1978; Portia Pitman Fellowship, Tuskegee Institute, 1982; Guggenheim Fellowship, 1983; Lavan Younger Poet Award, Academy of American Poets, 1986; Pulitzer Prize, poetry, 1987; General Electric Foundation Award, poetry, 1987; Ohio Governor's Award, 1988; Honorary Doctor of Letters, Miami University, 1988; Mellon Senior Fellow, National Humanities Center, 1988-89; Creative Writing Grant, National Endowment of the Arts, 1989; Honorary Doctor of Humane Letters, Knox College, 1989; Fellow, Center for Advanced Studies, University of Virginia, 1989-. *Memberships:* President 1986-87, Board Member, Associated Writing Program; PEN Club, American Centre. *Address:* Department of English, Wilson Hall, University of Virginia, Charlottesville, VA 22903, USA.

DOVER Kenneth James, b. 11 Mar 1920, Croydon, England. Retired, formerly President of College. m. Audrey Ruth Latimer, 17 Mar 1947, 1 son, 1 daughter. *Education:* BA, MA 1946, Balliol College and Merton College, Oxford; DLitt, Oxford, 1974. *Publications:* Greek Popular Morality in The Time of Plato & Aristotle, 1974; Greek Homosexuality, 1978; Aristophanic Comedy, 1972; Lysias and The Corpus Lysiacum, 1968; Collected Papers, 1987, 1988; Various commentaries on Greek Texts. *Contributions to:* Many articles and reviews in classical journals. *Honour:* Knighthood, 1977. *Memberships:* President, British Academy, 1978-81; President, Hellenic Society, 1971-74; President, Classical Association 1975. *Address:* 49 Hepburn Gardens, St Andrews, Fife KY16 9LS, Scotland.

DOVRING Karin Elsa Ingeborg, b. 5 Dec 1919, Stenstorp, Sweden. American Citizen. Journalist; Author; Communication Analyst. m. Folke Ossiannilsson Dovring, 30 May 1943. *Education:* Fil.Mag., 1942, Fil.Dr., 1951, Lund University; Fil.Lic., Gothenburg University, 1947. *Appointments:* Journalist, Swedish Newspapers and Magazines, 1945-60; Foreign Correspondent, Switzerland, France, Germany, Italy, 1953-60; Editor, Journal of Communication, 1965-70; Writer, Illinois Alliance to Prevent Nuclear War, 1982-; Writer, American Newspapers, 1976-. *Publications:* Road of Propaganda, 1959; Songs of Zion, 1-2, 1951; Land Reform as a Propaganda theme, 3rd edition 1965; Frontiers of Communication, 1975; No Parking This Side of Heaven, 1982; The Optional Society, 1972; Harold Dwight Lasswell : His Communication With A Future, second printing 1988; If the Bombs Fall....A World of its Own, 1982; Forked Tongue? Body-snatched English in Political Communications, 1990, Heart in Escrow (novel), 1990. *Contributions to:* Numerous professional journals. *Honours include:* Visiting Professor, Vatican's University for International Studies, Rome, 1956-58. *Membership include:* President, Scandinavian Linguists, 1945-46; National Society of Communications; President, Gerd Literary Society, Sweden, 1938; International Studies Association. *Literary Agent:* Barbara Bauer Literary Agency, New Jersey, USA. *Address:* 613 West Vermont Avenue, Urbana, IL 61801, USA.

DOWNER Lesley. *See:* **DOWNER Lesley Ann.**

DOWNER Lesley Ann (Lesley Downer), b. 9 May 1949, London, England. Writer; Journalist; Broadcaster. *Education:* St Anne's College, Oxford, 1968- 71; BA (Hons), MA, English Language and Literature, Oxford University. MA, Area Studies, South Asia, School of Oriental and African Studies, University of London, 1974. *Publications:* Step-by-Step Japanese Cooking, 1986; Japanese Vegetarian Cookery, 1986; Economist Business Travellers' Guide to Japan (consultant editor, co-author), 1986, 1989; On the Narrow Road to the Deep North, 1989; A Taste of Japan, 1991. *Contributions to:* Independent; Times; Financial Times; Observer; Sunday Times; Correspondent magazine; Sunday Telegraph magazine; Vogue. *Honours:* Glenfiddich Food Book of the Year, 1986. *Memberships:* Guild of Food Writers; Society of Authors; Japan Society; Groucho Club. *Literary Agent:* Gill Coleridge. *Address:* 40 Beresford Road, London N5 2HZ, England.

DOWNES David Anthony, b. 17 Aug 1927, Victor, Colo, USA. Professor of English. m. Audrey Romaine Ernst, 7 Sept 1949, 1 son, 3 daughters. *Education:* BA cum laude, Regis College, 1949; MA, Marquette College, 1950; PhD, University of Washington, 1956. *Appointments:* Instructor in English, Gonzaga University, 1950-53; Assistant Professor, Professor of English; Chairman of Department, Seattle University, 1953-68; Professor of English, Dean of Humanities and Fine Arts, 1968-72; Director of Educational Development Projects, 1972-; Director of Humanities Programme, 1972-74, California State University; Director of Graduate English Studies, 1975-78, California State University, Chico. *Publications include:* Gerard Maley Hopkins: A Study of his Ignation Spirit, 1959; Victorian Portraits: Hopkins and Pater, 1965; The Temper of Victorian Belief: Studies in Victorian Religious Fiction; Pater, Kinglsey and Newman, 1972; Ruskin's Landscape of Beatitude, 1984; The Great Sacrifice: Studies in Hopkins, 1983; Hopkins' Sanctifying Imagination, 1985; The Ignatian Personality of Gerard Manely Hopkins, 1990; Chapters in: Hopkins, The Man and the City, 1988; The Fine Delight: Centenary Essays, 1989; Gerard Manley Hopkins: New Essays, 1989; Critical Essays on Gerard Manley Hopkins, 1990. *Contributions to:* Thought; Victorian Poetry; Hopkins Quarterly; Studies in the Imagination; Ultimate Reality; Member of Editorial Board, Hopkins Quarterly; University Journal, Editor, 1974-77. *Honours:* Western Gear Foundation Publication Grant, 1960; Seattle University Research Grants, 1961, 1962, 1967; Publication Grant, 1967; Chico State College, (now California State University), Foundation Research Grant, 1969; Andrew Mellon Grant for Summer Seminar, Stanford University, 1982; Senior Scholar International Hopkins Association; Professional Achievement Award, 1984; Exceptional Merit Award for Scholarship, 1984, 1988, 1990. *Address:* 1076 San Ramon Drive, Chicago, CA 95926, USA.

DOWNES (John) Kerry, b. 1930. Writer (Architecture, Art). *Appointments:* Lecturer, 1966-71, Reader, 1971-78, Professor, History of Art, 1978-, University of Reading; Librarian, Barber Institute of Fine Arts, University of Birmingham, 1958-66. *Publications:* Hawksmoor, 1959, 1979; English Baroque Architecture, 1966; Christopher Wren, 1971; Vanbrugh, 1977; The Georgian Cities of Britain, 1979; Rubens, 1980; The Architecture of Wren, 1982. *Memberships:* Library Staff, Coutauld Institute of Art, London, 1954-58; Royal Commision on Historical Monuments (England), 1981-. *Address:* Department of History of Art, Reading University, Reading, Berkshire, RG1 5AQ, England.

DOWNES Mary Raby (Jayne Noble), b. 31 May 1920, Calcutta, India. Writer. m. (1) Henry May Poade Ashby, 25 Nov 1942, dec, (2) Eric Mytton Downes, 28 Dec 1963, dec, 2 daughters. *Education:* Oxford and Cambridge School Certificate, 1938; Countryside Conservation 2-year course, Department of Continuing Education, University of Oxford, 1990-91. *Appointments:* Currently Village Correspondent, Andover Midweek Advertiser. *Publications:* Loving is Living, 1965; Out of Evil, novel, 1975; Emma's Family Pony, Delight, 1992. *Contributions to:* Two Worlds; Psychic News; London Calling; Resurgence; Light; Prediction; Game Research; Poem to Scottish Forestry and other publications; Poem to Arrival Press Anthology, 1992. *Honours:* 1st Prize, national newspaper's competition writing about The Best Day of My Holiday. *Memberships:* PEN; The Society of Authors; The College of Psychic Studies, The National Federation of Spiritual Healers; BHS, Dressage Group, Danebury Riding Club; Overseas League: Formerly: Council member of, Beauty Without Cruelty; The Poetry Society; Mike Shields Poetry

Society. *Address:* Wheat Cottage, Barton Stacey, Winchester, Hants SO21 3RS, England.

DOWNEY Laura. *See:* **JACOBS Barbara.**

DOWNIE Freda Christina, b. 20 Oct 1929, London, England. m. David Charles James Turner, 27 Mar 1957. *Education:* A Stranger Here, 1977; Plainsong, 1981; Even the Flowers, 1989; Night Music, 1974; Night Sucks Me In, 1976; Man Dancing With The Moon, 1979; A Sensation, 1975; A Berkhamsted Three, (Co-authors Fred Sedgewick and John Cotton), 1978. *Address:* 32 Kings Road, Berkhamsted, Hertfordshire HP4 3BD, England.

DOWNIE Leonard, b. 1 May 1942, Cleveland, Ohio, USA. Newspaper Editor; Author. m. (1) Barbara Lindsey, 1960, (div 1971), (2) Geraldine Rebach, 1971, 3 sons, 1 daughter. *Education:* MA, Ohio State University. *Appointments:* Reporter, Editor, 1964-74, Metropolitan Editor 1974-79, London Correspondent, 1979-82, National Editor 1982-84, Managing Editor, 1984-91, Executive Editor, 1991-, Washington Post. *Publications:* Justice Denied, 1971; Mortgage on America, 1974; The New Muckrakers, 1976. *Address:* Washington Post, 1150 15th Street NW, Washington, DC 20071, USA.

DOWNIE Mary Alice Dawe (nee Hunter), b. 12 Feb 1934, USA. Writer. m. John Downie, 27 June 1959, 3 daughters. *Education:* BA (hons), English Language & Literature, Trinity College, University of Toronto. *Appointments:* Book Review Editor, Kingston Whig-Standard, 1973-78. *Publications:* The Wind Has Wings; Poems from Canada, with Barbara Robertson, 1968; Seared Sarah, 1974; Dragon on Parade, 1974; The Last Ship, 1980; Jenny Greenteeth, 1981; A Proper Acadian, with George Rawlyk, 1982; The Wicked Fairy-Wife, 1983; Alison's Ghosts, with John Downie, 1984; Stones and Cones, with Jillian Gilliland, 1984; Stories: Four Short Stories, 1973; La Belle et la Laide, 1978; Chapters from Honor Bound reprinted in Inside Outside and Measure Me Sky, 1979; Stories from the Witch of the North, reprinted in Storytellers Rendezvous, 1980; Crossroads 1, 1979 and Out and About, 1981; The Window of Dreams: New Canadian Writing for Children, 1986; The Well-Filled Cupboard, with Barbara Robertson, 1987; How the Devil Got his Cat, 1988; The Buffalo Boy and the Weaver Girl, 1989; Doctor Dwarf & Other Poems for Children, 1990; Cathal the Giant-Killer and the Dun Shaggy Filly, 1991. *Contributions to:* Hornbook Magazine; Pittsburgh Press; Kingston Whig-Standard; Ottawa Citizen; Globe and Mail; United Church Observer; OWL Magazine; Chicadee; Crackers. *Memberships:* Writers Union of Canada; PEN. *Address:* 190 Union Street, Kingston, Ontario, Canada K7L 2P6.

DOWNING Angela, b. 28 Sept 1933, Liverpool, England. Full Professor of English. m. Enrique Hidalgo, 22 Aug 1959, 2 sons, 3 daughters. *Education:* BA, Modern Languages, University of Oxford, 1956; MA University of Oxford, 1962; Licenciatura in English Philology, 1973, PhD, 1976, Universidad Complutense de Madrid. *Appointments:* Currently Full Professor of English, Universidad Complutense, Madrid, Spain; Editor, Estudios Ingleses de la Universidad Complutense, 1991. *Publications:* La metáfora gramatical de M A K Halliday y su motivación funcional en el discurso, 1991; An alternative approach to Theme: a systemic functional perspective, 1991; A University Course in English Grammar (with Philip Locke), 1992. *Contributions to:* Articles on English language, discourse and stylistics to specialised journals, UK, USA, Spain. *Honours:* Mary Ewart Scholar, Somerville College, University of Oxford, 1952-55. *Memberships:* European Society for the Study of English; Sociedad Espanola de Linguistica; Asociacion Espanola de Lingüística Aplicada; Asociación Espanola de Estudios Ingleses Medievales; International Association of University Professors of English. *Address:* Arascues 43 (ant 65), 28023 Madrid, Spain.

DOWNS Donald Alexander, b. 2 Dec 1948, Toronto, Ontario, Canada. Assistant Professor. m. Susan Yeager Downs, 30 Jan 1971, 1 son, 1 daughter. *Education:* BA, Cornell University, 1971; MA, University of Illinois, 1974; PhD, University of California, Berkeley, 1983. *Appointment:* Assistant Professor, Political Science, University of Wisconsin, Madison. *Publication:* Nazis in Skokie : Freedom Community & The First Amendment, 1985; The New Politics of Pornography and the Forms of Democracy, forthcoming, 1988. *Contributions to:* Professional Journals, Newspapers and Magazines. *Honours:* American Political Science Association's Edward S. Corwin Award, 1984; Anisfield-Wolf Book Award in Race Relations, for Nazis in Skokie, 1986. *Memberships:* American Political Science Association; Amnesty International; Southern Poverty Association. *Address:* 4429 Waite Lane, Madison, W1 53711, USA.

DOWNS Robert Conrad Smith, b. 23 Nov 1937, Chicago, IL, USA. Professor of English. m. Barbara Lewry, 6 Sept 1968, 2 daughters. *Education:* AB, Harvard University, 1960; MFA, University of Iowa, 1965. *Appointments:* University of Arizona, 1973-80; Pennsylvania State University, 1980-. *Publications:* Peoples, 1973; Going Gently, 1975; Country Dying, 1976; White Mama, 1980; Living Together, 1983; White Mama (film scriptt for CBS Wednesday Night Movie). *Honours:* Fellow, John Simon Guggenheim Foundation, 1979-80; NAACP Image Award (screenplay for White Mama). *Literary Agent:* Don Congdon Associates Inc., 156 Fifth Avenue, New York, NY 10010. *Address:* 764 West Hamilton Avenue, State College, PA 16801, USA.

DOYLE Richard, b. 1948. Author. *Publications:* Deluge, 1976; Imperial 109, 1978; Havana Special, 1982; Pacific Clipper, 1987. *Address:* c/o Arlington Books, 15 King Street, London, SW1, England.

DOYRAN Turhan, b. 20 June 1926, Ankara, Turkey. Poet; Writer; Photographer. m. Madeleine Doyran, 17 Aug 1953. 1 daughter. *Education:* Diploma of Filmology, University of Ankara, Grenoble, Paris (Sorbonne), 1957; Ansaldi Academy Theatre, 1953; National Conservatory of Arts and Trades, Paris, 1958; Institut of Advanced International Studies, Paris, 1953. *Publications:* Plays-Theatre: The Promise, 1946; The Offense, 1947; La Premeditation, 1961; Maree Haute, 1965; Le Mobile, 1967; Les Rois Demeurent, 1984. Poetry: Siirler, 1955; Sehir, 1959; Partir, 1962; Gecilmez, 1962; Le Jour, 1962; Il Faut Bien, 1962; Comme Autrefois, 1964; Je ne suis pas de Bologne, 1967; The Tree, 1967; The Way, 1975; The Mirror, 1975; Photo-Graphies, 1980; The Rain, 1986. *Contributions to:* Magazines and journals in France, Turkey, Belgium, Italy, Egypt, Switzerland, England, USA. *Honours:* Prize for Photography, Cannes, 1958; Prize Academy Leonardo da Vinci, Poetry, 1964; Prize Comite Europeen Arts et Culture, 1985; Named Artist of Year Plastic Arts, Turkey, 1987. *Memberships:* Academy Leonardo da Vinci, Rome; Centro Studi et Scambi Internationale, Rome; International High Committee for World Culture and Arts; President, Commission International d'Art Photographique. *Address:* 8 rue du Cambodge, 75020 Paris, France.

DOZOIS Gardner, b. 1947, United States of America. Writer. *Appointments:* Reader, Dell and Award Publishers, Galaxy, If, Worlds of Fantasy, Worlds of Tomorrow, 1970-73; Co-Founder and Associate Editor, Isaac Asimov's Science Fiction Magazine, 1976-77. *Publictions:* A Day in the Life, 1972; Beyond the Golden Age; Nightmare Blue (with Geo Alec Effinger), 1975; Future Power (with Jack Dann), 1976; Another World (juvenile), 1977; The Visible Man (short stories), 1977; The Fiction of James Tiptree, Jr., 1977; Best Science Fiction Stories of the Year 6-9, 4 vols, 1977-80; Strangers, 1978; Aliens! (with Jack Dann), 1980; The Year's Best science Fiction (with Jim Frenkel), 1984. *Address:* 401 Quince Street, Philadelphia, PA 19147, USA.

DR A. *See:* **ASIMOV Isaacs.**

DRABBLE Margaret, b. 1939. Author. *Education:* Newnham College, Cambridge. *Publications:* A Summer Bird-Cage, 1963; The Garrick Year, 1964; The Millstone, 1965; Wordsworth, 1966; Jerusalem the Golden, 1967; The Waterfall, 1969; A Touch of Love (screenplay), 1969; The Needle's Eye, 1972; Arnold Bennett, 1974; The Realms of Gold, 1975; The Ice Age, 1977; For Queen and Country (juvenile), 1978; A Writer's Britain, 1979; The Middle Ground, 1980; The Oxford Companion to English Literature, 1985; The Radiant Way, 1987; A Natural Curiosity, 1989; Safe as Houses, 1989; The Gates of Ivory, 1991. *Honours:* CBE, 1980. *Address:* c/o A.D. Peters, Fifth Floor, The Chambers, Chelsea Harbour, Lots Road, London, SW10 UXF, England.

DRACHE Daniel Aaron, b. 9 Oct 1941, Toronto, Ontario, Canada. Professor of Political Science. m. Marilyn Lambert, 10 Sept 1985, 1 daughter. *Education:* BA, University of Toronto, 1963; MA, Political Science, Queen's University, Kingston, Ontario. *Publications:* TheNew Era of Global Competition:State Policy and Market Power (edited with M Gertler), 1991; Work Without Illusions: A Diagnosis of What Ails Labour (with H J Glasbeek), 1992; Negotiating with a Sovereign Quebec (edited with R Perin), 1992. *Honours:* Atkinson Leave Fellowship, 1987; AAHRCC Award, 1991. *Address:* Department of Political Science, Atkinson College, York University, 4700 Keele Street, North York, Canada M3J 1P3.

DRACKETT Philip Arthur (Phil), (Paul King), b. 25 Dec.1922, Finchley, Middlesex, UK. Writer; Broadcaster. m. Joan Isobel Davies, 19 June 1948. *Education:* Woodhouse School, 1934-39; Junior County Award, Cambridge University; General Schools, London University. *Appointments:* With: News Chronicle; Press Association; Puck Publications; Royal Automobile Club. *Publications include:* You & Your Car, 1957; Great Moments in Motoring, 1958; Automobiles Work Like this, 1958; Like Father, Like Son, 1969; Rally of the Forests, 1970; The Classic Mercedes-Benz, 1984; Flashing Blades, 1988; Also: Inns & Harbours of North Norfolk; Brabham, Story of a Racing Team; Story of RAC International Rally; Encyclopaedia of the Motor Car; Fighting Days; They Call It Courage, The Story of the Segrave Trophy, 1990; Benetton & Ford, A Racing Partnership, 1991. *Contributions include:* Autoworld; Toyota Today; Yours; Choice; Saga; Ice Hockey World; Mayfair; Sport & Leisure; Titbits; Today; Many Newspapers. *Memberships include:* Sports Writers Association; Former committee member, Guild of Motoring Writers; British Ice Hockey Writers Association. *Address:* 9 Victoria Road, Mundesley, Norfolk NR11 8JG, England.

DRAGONWAGON Crescent, b. 25 Nov 1952, Manhattan, New York, USA. Freelance Writer. m. Ned Shank, 20 Oct 1978, Eureka Springs, Arkansas. *Publications:* Always, Always, 1984; The Year It Rained, 1985, also in Danish and Swedish; The Dairy Hollow House Cookbook, 1986; Half a Moon and One Whole Star, 1986, also in British editions; Alligator Arrived with Apples: A Thanksgiving Potluck Alphabet, 1987; Margaret Zeigler, 1988; This is the Bread I Baked for Ned, 1988; Home Place, 1990; The Itch Book, 1990; Winter Holding Spring, 1990; Dairy Hollow House Soup & Bread, A Country Inn Cookbook, 1992; Annie Flies the Birthday Bike, 1993. *Contributions to:* Ms Magazine; McCall's; Ladies Home Journal; Cosmopolitan; New York Times Book Review; Lear's. *Honours:* Wind Rose, Outstanding Science Trade Books for Children, 1976; To Take a Dare, American Library Association Best Book, 1982; Always, Always, Social Sciences Book of the Year, 1984; I Hate My Brother Harry, Childrens Choice Nominee, Georgia and Colorado, 1985; Half a Moon and One Whole Star, Coretta Scott King Award, 1987; Winner, Porter Fund Prize for Literary Excellence, 1991; Dairy Hollow House Soup & Bread, Nominee, Julia Child, IACP Cookbook Award, James Beard Cookbook Award, 1992-1993; Home Place: winner 1990, Golden Kite Award; Winner, Cuffie, Publisher's Weekly Bookseller's Award; The National Conference of Christians and Jews Recommended Reading List for Children and Young Adults, 1990-1991; Notable, 1990 Children's Trade Books on the Field of Social Studies; Winter Holding Spring, Notable 1990 Children's Trade Books on the Field of Social Studies; William Allen White Children's Book Award Master Listm 1992-1993; New York State Charlotte Award Nominee. *Memberships:* Authors Guild; Society of Childrens Book Writers. *Literary Agent:* Edite Kroll. *Address:* Route 4, Box 1, Eureka Springs, AR 72632, USA.

DRAKE Albert Dee, b. 26 Mar 1935, Portland, Oregon, USA. Professor; Writer. div., 1 son, 2 daughters. *Education:* Portland State College, 1956-59; BA, English, 1962, MFA, English, 1966, University of Oregon. *Appointments:* Research Assistant, 1965, Teaching Assistant, 1965-66, English Department, University of Oregon; Assistant Professor, 1966-70, Associate Professor, 1970-79, Professor, 1979-, Department of English, Michigan State University, East Lansing. *Publications:* Michigan Signatures (edited), 1968; Riding Bike, 1973; Roadsalt, 1975; Returning to Oregon, 1975; The Postcard Mysteries, 1976; Tillamook Burn, 1977; In the Time of Surveys, 1978; One Summer, 1979; Garage, 1980; Beyond the Pavement, 1981; The Big Little GTO Book, 1982; Street Was Fun in '51, 1982; I Remember the Day James Dean Died, 1983; Homesick, 1988; Herding Goats, 1989. *Contributions to:* Over 350 magazines and periodicals including: Redbook; Best American Short Stories; Epoch; December; Northwest Review; Pebble; Arts in Society; Fiction International; Shenandoah; Rod Action; etc. *Honours:* 1st, Ernest Haycox Fiction Award, 1962; 1st Prize, Writer's Digest Fiction Contest, 1979; Grants for Fiction, National Endowment for the Arts, 1974-75, 1983-84; Grant for Fiction, Michigan Council for the Arts, 1982. *Address:* Department of English, Michigan State University, East Lansing, MI 48824, USA.

DRAKE Charles D, b. 1924. Writer. *Publications:* Law of Partnership, 1972, 1976; Labour Law, 2nd edition, 1973, 3rd edition, 1981; The Employment Acts 1974-1980 (with B. Bercusson), 1981; Law of Health and Safety at Work (with F. Wright), 1982; Trade Union Acts, 1985. *Address:* 4 North Lane, Leeds, LS8 2QJ, West Yorkshire, England.

DRAKE Walter Raymond, b. 2 Jan 1913, Middlesbrough, Yorkshire. Retired Surveyor, HM Customs & Excise. m. Marjorie Cawthorne, 24 June 1944. *Publications:* Gods or Spacemen?, 1964; Gods and Spacemen in the Ancient East, 1968; Gods and Spacemen in the Ancient West, 1974; Gods and Spacemen of the Ancient Past, 1975; Gods and Spacemen Throughout History, 1975; Gods and Spacemen in Greece and Rome, 1976; Gods and Spacemen in Ancient Israel, 1976; Messengers from the Stars, 1977; Cosmic Continents, 1986. *Contributions include:* Flying Saucer Review; Flying Saucer Search; Beyond Science; UFO Nachrichten. *Honours:* Doctorate in Sacred Philosophy, World University, Tucson, 1985; member, L'Academie Europeenne Des Sciences Des Arts et Des Letrtres, 1986. *Memberships:* Society of Authors; Sunderland Rotary Club. *Address:* 2 Peareth Grove, Roker, Sunderland, England.

DRAPER Alfred Ernest, b. 26 Oct 1924. Author m. Barbara Pilcher, 31 Mar 1951, 2 sons. *Education:* North West London Polytechnic. *Publications include:* Swansong for a Rare Bird, 1969; The Death Penalty, 1972 (made into French TV film); Smoke Without Fire, 1974; The Prince of Wales, 1975; The Story of the Goons, 1976; Operation Fish, 1978; Amritsar, 1979; Grey Seal, 1981; Grey Seal: The restless Waves, 1983, The Raging of the Deep, 1985, Storm over Singapore, 1986, The Con Man, 1987; Dawns Like Thunder, 1987; The Great Avenging Day, 1989; A Crimson Splendour, 1991; Operation Midas, 1993. *Contributions to:* Numerous articles for many national newspapers and magazines. *Honour:* Runner-up 1969 in Macmillan/Panther First Crime Novel Competition for Swansong for a Rare Bird. *Memberships:* Society of Authors; Life Member of NUJ. *Literary Agent:* Juri Gabriel. *Address:* 31 Oakridge Avenue, Radlett, Herts WD7 8EW, England.

DRAPER Ronald Philip, b. 3 Oct 1928, Regius Chalmers Professor of English. m. Irene Margaret Aldridge, 19 June 1950, 3 daughters. *Education:* BA, 1950; PhD, 1953. *Publications:* D H Lawrence, 1964, 3rd edition, 1984; D H Lawrence, The Critical Heritage, (Editor), 1970; Lyric Tragedy, 1985; The Winter's Tale, Text and Performance, 1985; The Literature of Region and Nation, (Editor), 1989; Hardy, The Tragic Novels, (Editor) 1975, 6th edition, 1985; George Eliot, The Mill on the Floss and Silas Marner, (Editor), 1977; Tragedy, Developments in Criticism, (Editor), 1980; Hardy, Three Pastoral Novels, (Editor), 1987; An Anotated Critical Bibliography of Thomas Hardy, (Co-author M Ray), 1989; The Epic, Developments in Criticism, (Editor), 1990. *Contributor to:* Articles and reviews: Critical Quarterly; Essays in Criticism; Etudes Anglaises; English Studies; Journal of D H Lawrence Society; MLR; New Literary History; Notes and Queries; Revue des Langues Vivantes; Review of English Studies; Shakespeare Quarterly; Studies in Short Fiction; Thomas Hardy Annual; Thomas Hardy Journal. *Membership:* International Association of University Professors of English. *Address:* 50 Queen's Road, Aberdeen AB1 6YE, Scotland.

DRAULANS Dirk J E, b. 4 May 1956, Turnhout, Belgium. Journalist. 1 daughter. *Education:* Doctor in Science, 1983. *Publications:* Paarse Dijen; Gele Modder; De Schaduw Van Saddam; Welkom In De Hel. *Contributions to:* Knack Magazine. *Address:* Tervurenlaan 153, B-1150 Brussels, Belgium.

DRECKI Zbigniew Bogdan, b. 20 Nov 1922, Warsaw, Poland. Artist. m. Cynthia Josephine Scott, 22 Feb 1961. *Education:* Humanistic Gymnasium (High School), Warsaw, 1928-39; Art Diploma, Darmstadt Academy of Art, Federal Republic of Germany, 1952. *Publications:* Freedom and Justice Spring from the Ashes of Auschwitz, 1992, Polish version in Auschwitz Museum. *Contributions to:* Polish medical journals; British and US newspapers. *Memberships:* Life Member, West Country Writers Association; Association of Little Presses. *Literary Agent:* Self. *Address:* Winterhaven, 23 Albion Street, Exmouth, Devon EX8 1JJ, England.

DRENNAN William D, b. 12 Feb 1935, New York City, New York, USA. Writer; Editor; Literary Firm Executive. m. Christina Lavery, 18 Mar 1978, 1 son, 1 daughter. *Education:* BA, St John's University, New York City, 1956; St John's University School of Law, New York City, 1956-57. *Appointments:* Copy Editor, Doubleday and Company, New York City, New York, 1961-67; Chief Copy Editor, L W Singer Company, New York City, 1967-68; Associate Acquisitions and Planning Editor, American Management Association, New York City, 1968-70; Editor, Praeger Publishers, New York City, 1970-72; Consulting Editor, New York City, 1972-80; President, Editorial Director, Drennan Communications, Weston, Connecticut, 1980-. *Publications:* The Fourth Strike: Hiring and Training the Disadvantaged (editor), 1970. *Contributions to:* Take the Local to the Midnight Sun, to Qantas Airways Inflight, 1978. *Memberships:* National Association of Book Editors, 1967-70, Member-at-Large 1969-70. *Address:* 6 Valley Forge Lane, Weston, CT 06883, USA.

DRENNEN Marcia Simonton, b. 19 July 1915, Columbus, Ohio, USA. Writer; Editor. m. Everett Drennen, 21 Jan 1939, 1 son. *Education:* BA, English, Ohio State University, 1936; Graduate: Columbia University Adult Education, 1958, New School for Social Research Adult Education, 1964, 1986. *Appointments:* Staff, Memphis Press-Scimitar, 1941-46; Staff, United Press International, 1946-50; Staff, NBC Television News, 1950-56; Senior Editor, Reader's Digest Condensed Books, 1958-80. *Publications:* American Poetry Association anthology, 1985; Poetry Showcase, 1986; Best of New Poets, 1986; Art of Poetry Anthology,

1984. *Contributions To:* Plains Poetry Journal; Poetry Press; Scimitar and Song; The Lyric; International Poetry Review. *Honours:* 1st Prize, 1985, 5th Prize, 1985, Grant, 1987, American Poetry Association; Honourable Mention, Writer's Digest, 1986. *Memberships:* Browning Dramatic Society; Chi Delta Phi, President; Overseas Press Club of America. *Address:* 11 West 9th Street, New York, NY 10011, USA.

DREXLER Rosalyn, (Julia Sorel), b. 1926, United States of America. Author; Playwright; Painter; Sculptor; Singer. *Publications:* With Others: I Am the Beautiful Stranger (novel), 1965; The Line of Least Existence and Other Plays, 1967; The Investigation, and Hot Buttered Roll, 1969; One or Another (novel), 1970; The Bed Was Full, 1972; Skywriting, 1968; To Smithereens (novel), 1972; She Who Was He, 1973; The Cosmopolitan Girl (novel), 1975; Unwed Widow (novel as Julia Sorel), 1975; Dawn (novelization), 1976; Rocky (novelization), 1976; Alex (novelization), 1977; See How She Runs (novelization), 1978; Forever Is Sometimes Temporary When Tomorrow Rolls Around, 1979; Starburn (novel), 1979; Bad Guy, 1982; Transients Welcome (plays), 1984. *Address:* c/o Georges Borchardt Inc., 136 E. 57th Street, New York, NY 10022, USA.

DREZE Jean, b. 22 Jan 1959, Leuven, Belgium. Development Economist. *Education:* BA (Hons), Mathematical Economics, University of Essex, England, 1979; PhD, Economics, Indian Statistical Institute, New Delhi, India, 1983. *Publications:* Books: Hunger and Public Action (with Amartye Sen), 1989; The Political Economy of Hunger (edited with Amartya Sen), 1990; No 1, Clapham Road: The Diary of a Squat, 1990; The Political Economy of Hunger (with Amartya Sen), 1990; Articles: The Theory of Cost-Benefit Analysis (with Nicholas Stern), 1987; Famine Prevention in India, 1990. *Contributions to:* Policy Reform, Shadow Prices and Market Prices, to Journal of Public Economics, 1990; Hunger and Poverty in Iraq, 1991, to World Development, 1992. *Literary Agent:* Oxford University Press. *Address:* London School of Economics, Houghton St, London WC2A 2AE, England.

DRISCOLL Peter, b. 1942. Writer; Journalist. *Appointments:* Reporter, Rand Daily Mail, Johannesburg, South Africa, 1959-67; Sub-Editor, Scriptwriter, ITV News, London, 1969-73. *Publications:* The White Lie Assignment, 1971; The Wilby Conspiracy, 1972; In Connection with Kilshaw, 1974; The Barboza Credentials, 1976; Pangolin, 1979; Heritage, 1982; Spearhead, 1987; Secrets of State, 1991. *Address:* c/o David Higham Associates, 5-8 Lower John Street, London, W1R 4HA, England.

DRIVER Charles Jonathan (Jonty), b. 19 Aug 1939, South Africa. Headmaster. m. Ann Elizabeth Hoogewerf, 8 June 1967, 2 sons, 1 daughter. *Education:* BA, BEd, University of Cape Town, 1958-62; MPhil, Trinity College, Oxford University, England, 1965-67. *Appointments:* Literature Panel, 1975-77, Chairman, 1977, Lincolnshire and Humberside Arts; Literary Panel, Arts Council, 1975-77. *Publications:* Elegy for a Revolutionary, 1968; Send War in Our Time, O Lord, 1970; Death of Fathers, 1972; A Messiah of the Last Days, 1974; Patrick Duncan, 1980; Hong Kong Portraits, 1985; I Live Here Now, 1979; Occasional Light, (Co-author Jack Cope), 1979; Patrick Duncan, (Biog), 1980. *Contributions to:* Numerous magazines and journals. *Honour:* FRSA. *Memberships:* Headmasters Conference. *Literary Agent:* Andrew Hewson, John Johnson Authors' Agents. *Address:* The Master's Lodge, Wellington College, Crowthorne, Berkshire RG11 7PU, England.

DRIVER Paul William, b. 14 Aug 1954, Manchester, England. Music Critic; Writer. *Education:* Oxford University, 1972-79; MA (Hons), 1979. *Appointments:* Music Critic, The Boston Globe, 1983-84; Music Critic, Sunday Times, 1985-; Member, Editorial Board, The Contemporary Music Review. *Publications:* A Diversity of Creatures (editor), 1987; Music and Text (editor),

1989. *Contributions to:* Sunday Times; Financial Times; Tempo; Numerous others. *Membership:* Critics Circle. *Address:* 15 Victoria Road, London NW6 6SX, England.

DROBOT Eve Joanna, b. 7 Feb 1951, Cracow, Poland. Journalist; Author. m. Jack Kapica, 9 Apr 1983, 1 daughter. *Education:* Baccalaureat, Universite d'Aix-Marseille, Aix-en-Provence, France, 1971; BA magna cum laude, Tufts University, Medford, Massachusetts, USA, 1973. *Appointments:* Columnist, The Globe and Mail, 1980-82, 1990-; Contributing Editor, Saturday Night Magazine, 1988-; Toronto Correspondent, L'Actualite Magazine, 1989-. *Publications:* Words for Sale (co-editor), 1979, 1983, 1989; Class Acts, 1982, 1984; Zen and Now, 1985; Amazing Investigations: Money, 1987, 1988; Chicken Soup and Other Nostrums, 1987. *Contributions to:* Hundreds including book reviews, to magazines and journals. *Honours:* Gold Medal, Canadian National Magazine Award, 1989; Canadian Authors Award, 1989. *Membership:* International PEN. *Address:* 17 Simpson Ave, Toronto, Ontario, Canada M4K 1A1.

DROSTE Flip G, (Frits van Noord), b. 4 July 1928, Arnhem, Netherlands. Professor. m. Nanja Koster, 30 Dec 1952, 1 son, 1 daughter. *Education:* Doctor of Phil, 1956. *Publications:* Roosjes Thuiskomst; Het Bittere Gelijk Van de Dageraad; Schuldgevoelens En Andere Liefdesverhalen; Scientific Books & Papers. *Memberships:* Editor of Linguistics; Louvain Contributions to Language. *Address:* Losbergenlaan 13, B-3010 Kessel 10, Belgium.

DROWER George, b. 21 July 1954, London, England. Feature Writer. *Education:* BA (Hons), Politics & Government, City of London Polytechnic, 1979; MA, Area Studies, University of London, 1980; PhD, London School of Economics, 1989. *Publications:* Neil Kinnock: The Path to Leadership, 1984; Britain's Dependent Territories: A Fistful of Islands, 1992. *Contributions to:* The Times; The Sunday Times; Financial Times; Independent Mail on Sunday; Sun; House and Garden; Traditional Homes. *Honours:* University of London Central Research Fund Travelling Scholarship to Hong Kong; London School of Economics Director's Fund Scholarship. *Membership:* Inner Temple Rowing Club. *Literary Agent:* Serafina Clarke, 98 Tunis Road, London W12, England. *Address:* 480A, Church Road, Northolt, Middx, UB5 5AU, England.

DRUCKER Henry Mathew, b. 29 Apr 1942, New Jersey, USA. University Development Director. m. Nancy Livia Newman, 29 Mar 1975. *Education:* BA, Philosophy, Allegheny College, Pennsylvania, 1964; PhD, Political Philosophy, London School of Economics, 1967. *Publications:* Doctrine and Ethos in the Labour Party, 1979; Developments in British Politics (Series) Editor, 1983 and following; Breakaway: The Scottish Labour Party, 1978; The Politics of Nationalism and Devolution (with Gorden Brown); The Scottish Government Yearbook (Series from 1978-88). *Membership:* Reform Club. *Address:* Campaign for Oxford, University of Oxford, University Offices, Wellington Square, Oxford OX1 2JD, England.

DRUKS Herbert, b. 1 Apr 1937, Vienna, Austria. Professor. m. 21 Aug 1985, 1 son, 1 daughter. *Education:* BA, City College of New York, USA, 1958; MA, Rutgers University, 1959; PhD, New York University, 1964. *Appointments:* Professor History, Brooklyn College, CUNY; Faculty History and Political Science, The School of Visual Arts; Associate Editor, East Europe magazine, 1972-75; Editor, R Hecht Papers, published by Garland, New York, 1991. *Publications:* Truman and the Russians, 1967, 2nd Edition, 1981; The Failure to Rescue, 1977; The US and Israel, 1979; From Truman through Johnson; A Documentary History 1945-68. *Contributions to:* American Historical Association; Journal of Thought; Midstream; Journal of Church and State; Journal of American History. *Honours:* Founders Day Award, New York University; Fellowship, Haifa University, 1987, 1988-89.

Memberships: American Historical Association; Professional Staff Conference. *Literary Agent:* Louis Phillips, New York City, USA. *Address:* POB 309, Forest Hills, NY 11375, USA.

DRUMMOND Ivor. *See:* **LONGRIGG Roger Erskine.**

DRUMMOND June, b. 15 Nov 1923, Durban, South Africa. Author. *Education:* BA, English, University of Cape Town. *Publications include:* Junta 1989; The Trojan Mule, 1982; The Bluestocking, 1985; The Unsuitable Miss Pelham, 1990; The Patriots, 1979; Slowly the Poison, 1975. *Memberships:* Writers Circle (Durban), of South Africa; Soroptimist International (Durban); Democratic Party of South Africa. *Address:* 24 Miller Grove, Durban 4001, South Africa.

DRUMMOND Violet Hilda. *See:* **SWETENHAM Violet Hilda.**

DRUMMOND Walter. *See:* **SILVERBERG Robert.**

DRURY Allen Stuart, b. 2 Sept 1918, Houston, Texas, USA. Writer. *Education:* BA, Stanford University. *Appointments:* Editor, Tulare Bee, 1940-41; County Editor, Bakersfield Californian, 1942; Senate Staff, United Press, 1943-45; Freelance Correspondent, Washington DC, 1946-47; National Editor, Pathfinder Magazine, 1947-52; National Staff, Washington Evening Star, 1952-54; Senate Staff, New York Times, 1954-59. *Publications:* Advise and Consent, 1959; A Shade of Difference, 1962; A Senate Journal, 1963; That Summer, 1965; Three Kids in a Cart, 1965; Capable of Honor, 1966; A Very Strange Society, 1967; Preserve and Protect, 1968; The Throne of Saturn, 1971; Courage and Hesitation, 1972; Come Nineveh, Come Tyre, 1973; The Promise of Joy, 1975; A God Against the Gods, 1976; Return to Thebes, 1977; Anna Hastings, 1977; Mark Coffin, U.S.S., 1979; Egypt; The Eternal Smile, 1980; The Hill of Summer, 1981; Decision, 1983; The Roads of Earth, 1984; Pentagon, 1986; Toward What Bright Glory? 1990. *Contributions to:* Readers Digest, 1959-62. *Honours:* National Editorial Award, Sigma Delta Chi, 1942; Pulitzer Prize for novel Advise and Consent, 1960. *Memberships:* Authors Guild; Sigma Delta Chi; University and Cosmos, Washington DC; Bohemian, San Francisco. *Literary Agency:* Lantz-Harris Agency. *Address:* c/o Lantz-Harris Agency, 888 Seventh Avenue, New York, NY 10106, USA.

DRYDEN Pamela. *See:* **JOHNSTON Norma.**

DRYSDALE Helena Claire, b. 6 May 1960, London, England. Writer. m. Richard Pomeroy, 21 May 1987, 1 daughter. *Education:* Charterhouse, 1975-1977; Trinity College, Cambridge, 1978-82; BA Hons, History, Art History, Cambridge. *Publications:* Alone through China and Tibet, 1986; Dancing with the Dead, 1991. *Contributions to:* Vogue; Marie Claire; The Independent; The Independent on Sunday; Harpers and Queen; Cosmopolitan; World. *Honours:* Exhibitioner, Trinity College. *Memberships:* PEN Club; Society of Authors; Royal Geographical Society; Globetrotters Club. *Literary Agent:* A P Watt. *Address:* 22 Stockwell Park Road, London SW9 0A7, England.

DU BOULAY Shirley, b. 4 Mar 1933, London, England. m. John Francis Xavier Harriott, 15 Sept 1979. *Education:* Royal College of Music, 1952. *Appointments:* British Broadcasting Corporation, 1954-78; Music Studio Manager, 1957-61; Radio Producer, Woman's Hour, 1962-67; Television Producer, 1967-78; Freelance Film And Radio Producer, Writer, 1978-1982. *Publications:* Dame Cicely Saunders: Founder of the Modern Hospice Movement; The Gardeners; The Changing Face of Death; Tutu: Voice of the Voiceless; The World Walks; Teresa of Avila, 1991. *Address:* 180 Woodstock Road, Oxford, OX2 7NG.

DU VAUL Virginia. *See:* **COFFMAN Virginia (Edith).**

DU VAUL Virginia C. *See:* **COFFMAN Virginia (Edith).**

DUBERMAN Martin Bauml, b. 6 Aug 1930, New York City, USA. Professor of History; Writer. *Education:* BA, Yale University, 1952; MA, Harvard University, 1953; PhD, Harvard University, 1957. *Publications:* Charles Francis Adams, 1963; In White America, 1964; The Antislavery Vanguard, (ed), 1965; James Russell Lowell, 1966; The Uncompleted Past, 1970; The Memory Bank, 1970; Black Mountain, 1972; Male Armor, 1974; Visions of Kerouac, 1977; About Time : Exploring the Gay Past, 1986; Hidden From History: Reclaiming the Gay and Lesbian Past; Paul Robeson, 1989; Mother Earth: An Epic Drama of Emma Goldman's Life, 1991; Cures: A Gay Man's Odyssey, 1991; 5 Tonewall, 1993. *Contributions include:* New York Times; New Republic; Partisan Review; Harpers; Atlantic Monthly; New York Review; Native; Christopher Street; Radical History Review; Village Voice; Signs; Journal of Homosexuality; Show. *Honours:* The Vernon Rice Drama Desk Award, 1965; The Bancroft Prize, 1964; Finalist, National Book Award, 1966; Special Award for Contributions to Literature, from The American Academy of Arts and Sciences, 1972; Manhattan Borough President's Gold Medal in Literature, 1988; George Freedley Prize, 1990. *Literary Agent:* Frances Goldin. *Address:* History Department, Lehman College, CUNY, Bedford Park Blvd W, Bronx, NY 10468, USA.

DUBERSTEIN Larry, b. 18 May 1944, New York City, New York, USA. Writer; Cabinetmaker. 3 daughters. *Education:* BA, Wesleyan University, 1966; MA, Harvard University, 1971. *Publications:* Nobody's Jaw, 1979; The Marriage Hearse, 1983; Carnovsky's Retreat, 1988; Postcards from Paris, 1991; Eccentric Circles, 1992. *Contributions to:* Articles, essays, reviews to: The Saturday Review; The Boston Review; The National; The Phoenix; New York Times; Book Review; Others. *Address:* Box 609, Cambridge, MA 02139, USA.

DUBIE Norman (Evans Jr.), b. 1945, United States of America. Poet. *Appointments:* Teaching Assistant, 1969-71, Lecturer, 1971-74, Creative Writing, Univerity of Iowa, Iowa City; Assistant Professor, Ohio University, Athens, 1974-75; Writer-in-Residence, 1975-76, Director of the Gradual Writing Program, 1976-77, Professor of English, 1980-, Arizona State University, Tempe. *Publications:* The Horsechair Sofa, 1969; Alehouse Sonnets, 1971; The Prayers of the North American Martyrs, 1975; Popham of the New Song and Other Poems, 1975; In the Dead of the Night, 1975; The Illustrations, 1977; A Thousand Little Things and Other Poems, 1978; Odalisque in White, 1978; The City of the Olesha Fruit, 1979; The Everlastings, 1980; The Selected and New Poems, 1983; The Springhouse, 1986. *Address:* Department of English, Arizona State University, Tempe, AZ 85281, USA.

DUBIE William, b. 24 July 1953, Salem, Massachusetts, USA. Writer; Editor. m. Jo-Ann Trudel, 6 June 1987. *Education:* BA, English, Salem State College, 1977; AA, Liberal Arts, 1981, AA, General Studies, 1984, North Shore Community College; BS, University of the State of New York, 1989; MA, Candidate, Media Studies, New School of Social Research. *Literary Appointment:* Editor, Synapse, an electronic literary magazine to premier in autumn 1990. *Publications:* Closing the Moviehouse (poems), 1981; The Birdhouse Cathedral (poems), 1990. *Contributions to:* Poems and articles in more than 90 small press, university and literary magazines. *Honours:* Chapbook Competition winner for Closing the Moviehouse, 1981; First Prize, Spring Concourse, American Collegiate Press, 1983; Sparrowgrass Poetry Forum, 1990. *Membership:* Society of Technical Communications. *Address:* 150A Ayer Road, Shirley, MA 01464, USA.

DUBINSKY Rostislav, b. 23 Nov 1923, Kiev, Ukraine. Musician (Violinist); Professor of Music. m. Luba Edlina, 22 Oct 1951. *Education:* Diploma, Concert Violinist, Chamber Musician, Teacher, Moscow State Conservatory. *Publication:* Stormy Applause, 1989. *Address:* 305 Lookout Lane, Bloomington, IN 47401, USA.

DUBOIS M. *See:* **KENT Arthur.**

DUBUS Andre III, b. 11 Sept 1959, Oceanside, California, USA. Writer; Teacher. m. Fontaine Dollas Dubus, 25 June 1989. *Education:* AA, Bradford College, Bradford, Massachusetts, 1979; BA, Sociology, University of Texas, Austin. *Appointments:* Part-time Professor of Creative Writing, Emerson College, Boston, Massachusetts. *Publications:* Forky, short story, 1984; Last Dance, short story, 1985; The Cage Keeper, novella, 1988; The Cage Keeper and Other Stories, 1989, soft cover edition, 1990; In the Quiet, short story, 1992; Bluesman, novel, 1993; Tracks & Ties, essay, Epoch Magazine, 1993; novel excerpt in Image, 1993. *Contributions to:* Playboy magazine; Yankee magazine; The Crescent Review; Crazyhorse Quarterly; America magazine; The Los Angeles Times Book Review. *Honours:* National Magazine Award in Fiction, 1985; Breadloaf Scholarship, 1986. *Membership:* Authors Guild. *Literary Agent:* Philip Spitzer, 50 Talmago Farm Lane, East Hampton, NY 11937, USA. *Address:* 16 Summit Place, Newburyport, MA 01950, USA.

DUCKWORTH Marilyn, b. 10 Nov 1935, Auckland, New Zealand. Writer. m. (1) Harry Duckworth, 28 May 1955, (2) Ian Macfarlane, 2 Oct 1964, (3) Dan Donovan, 9 Dec 1974, (4) John Batstone, 8 June 1985, 4 daughters. *Publications:* A Gap in the Spectrum, 1959; The Matchbox House, 1960; A Barbarous Tongue, 1963; Over the Fence Is Out, 1969; Disorderly Conduct, 1984; Married Alive, 1985; Rest for the Wicked, 1986; Pulling Faces, 1987; A Message from Harpo, 1989; Explosions on the Sun, 1989; Unlawful Entry, 1992. *Contributions to:* Stories to: Landfall; New Zealand Listener; Critical Quarterly; Islands; Others. *Honours:* New Zealand Literary Fund Scholarship in Letters, 1961, 1972; Katherine Mansfield Fellowship, 1980; New Zealand Book Award for Fiction, 1985; Shortlisted, Wattie Book of the Year Award, 1985; OBE for services to literature, 1987; Fulbright Visiting Writers Fellowship, 1987; Australia-New Zealand Writers Exchange Fellowship, 1989; Victoria University of Wellington Writers Fellowship, 1990. *Membership:* PEN. *Literary Agent:* Dinah Wiener, London, England. *Address:* 46 Roxburgh Street, Wellington, New Zealand.

DUDLEY Helen. *See:* **HOPE-SIMPSON Jacynth.**

DUFFIELD Robert McGregor, b. 16 Aug 1935, Adelaide, Australia. Journalist. m. 22 Nov 1958, 2 daughters, 1 son. *Appointments:* Various editorships and editorial executive positions around Australia, including Foreign Editor, The Australian, 1967-74; Editorial consultancies to various publications; Part-time Lecturer, Journalism, WA Institute of Technology, 1978-79; Full-time Lecturer, WA Institute of Technology (now Curtin University), 1980-83. *Publications:* Rogue Bull - The Story of Lang Hancock, King of the Pilbara, 1980; For the Love of Words (booklet), 1985; Hundreds of Thousands of Words in Newspaper Stories, Leading Articles, Columns & Commentaries; Broadcast Commentaries for various radio and TV stations. *Contributions to:* The Bulletin; The Australian; The Age; Sydney Morning Herald; Sunday Telegraph (Sydney). *Honours:* Australia Council Literary Grant; 4 gold Citations, United Nations Peace Prize; Australian Journalists Association Gold Honour Badge, 1981. *Memberships:* Australian Journalists Association, Federal Vice President, 1977-80; Founded his own company, Media Extra, 1986. *Address:* Unit 7, 6 Minora Place, Rivervale, WA 6103, Australia.

DUFFY Carol Ann, b. 23 Dec 1955, Glasgow, Scotland. Poet. *Education:* BA, Honours, Philosophy,

University of Liverpool, 1977. *Publications include:* Standing Female Nude, 1985; Selling Manhattan, 1987. Also Fleshweathercock, Fifth Last Song, Thrown Voices (limited edition poetry); 3 stage plays; 2 radio plays. *Contributions To:* Numerous magazines and journals. *Honours:* C. Day Lewis Fellowship, 1983; Eric Gregory Award, 1985; Book Award, Scottish Arts Council, 1986. *Literary Agent:* Liz Graham. *Address:* c/o Liz Graham, 4 Camp View, London, SW19 4VL, England.

DUFFY Maureen Patricia, b. 21 Oct 1933, Worthing, Sussex, England. Author. *Education:* BA(hons) English, King's College, University of London, 1956. *Publications include:* That's How It Was, 1962; The Microcosm, 1966; Wounds, 1969; Love Child, 1971; The Venus Touch, 1971; The Erotic World of Faery, 1972; I Want to Go to Moscow, 1973; Capital, 1975; The Passionate Shepherdess, 1977; Housespy, 1978; Poetry: Lyrics for the Dog Hour, 1968; Evesong, 1975; Memorials of the Quick and the Dead, 1979; Plays: Rites, 1969; A Nightingale in Bloomsbury Square, 1974; Visual Art; Prop Art Exhibition (with Brigid Brophyl), 1969; Gorsaga, 1981; Londoners, 1983; Change, 1987; A Thousand Capricious Chances, 1989; Poetry: Collected Poems, 1985; Illuminations (novel) 1991; Ocean's Razor (novel), 1993. *Contributions to:* New Statesman. *Memberships:* Co-Founder, Writers' Action Group; President Writers' Guild of Great Britain; Chair, Authors Licensing and Collecting Society; British Copywright Council. *Literary Agent:* Jonathan Clowes Ltd, 88D Iron Bridge House, Bridge Approach, London, NW1, England. *Address:* 18 Fabian Road, London, SW6 7TZ, England.

DUGAN Alan, b. 1923, United States of America. Poet. *Appointments:* Faculty, Sarah Lawrence College, Bronxville, New York, 1967-71; Staff Member for Poetry, Fine Arts Work Center, Provincetown, Massachusetts, 1971-. *Publications:* General Prothalamion in Populous Times, 1961; Poems, 1961; Poems 2, 1963; Poems 3, 1967; Collected Poems, 1969; Poems 4, 1974; Sequence, 1976; Collected Poems 1961-1983, 1983. *Address:* Box 97, Truro, MA 02666, USA.

DUKE Madelaine (Elizabeth), (Maxim Donne, Alex Duncan), b. 1925. Author. *Publications:* Novels: Azael and the Children, 1958; No Margin or Error, 1959; A City Built to Music, 1960; Ride the Brooding Wind, 1961; Thirty Pieces of Nickel, 1962; The Soverign Lords, 1963; Sobaka, 1965; The Lethal Innocents, 1968; Because of Fear in the Night, 1973; Novels as Alex Duncan: It's a Vet's Life, 1961; The Vet Has Nine Lives, 1962; Vets in the Belfry, 1964; Vet Among the Pigeons, 1977; Vets in Congress, 1978; Vet in the Manger, 1978; Vet in a State, 1979; Vet on Vacation, 1979; To Be a Country Doctor, 1980; God and the Doctor, 1981; The Diary of a Country Doctor, 1982; The Doctor's Affairs All Told, 1983; The Women's Specialist, 1988; Mystery novels: Claret, Sandwiches and Sin, 1964; This Business of Bomfog, 1967; Death of a Holy Murderer, 1975; Death at the Wedding, 1976; The Bormann Receipt, 1977; Death of a Dandie Dimmont, 1978; Flashpoint, 1982; Others: The Secret Mission, 1954; Slipstream: The Story of Anthony Duke, 1955; No Passport: The Story of Jan Felix, 1957; Beyond the Pillars of Hercules: A Spanish Journey, 1957; The Secret People (juvenile), 1967; The Sugar Cube Trap (juvenile), 1989; Once In Austria, 1987. *Address:* c/o Mondial Books Limited, Norman Alexander and Co., 5th Floor, Grosvenor Gardens House, 35/37 Grosvenor Gardens, London SW1 0BS, England.

DUKE Will. *See:* **GAULT William Campbell.**

DUKORE Bernard Frank, b. 11 July 1931, USA. Professor. m. Barbara, 1 son, 2 daughters. *Education:* BA, 1952; MA, 1953; PhD, 1957. *Appointments:* Professor, University of Hawaii; City University of New York; Stanford University; California State University at LA; University of Southern California; Currently University Distinguished Professor of Theatre Arts and Humanities, VPI&SU. *Publications include:* Bernard Shaw, Director, 1971; Bernard Shaw, Playwright, 1973; Dramatic Theory and Criticism, 1974; Collected Screenplays of

Bernard Shaw, 1980; Where Laughter Stops: Pinter's Tragicomedy, 1976; The Theatre of Peter Barnes, 1981; Harold Pinter, 1982; Money and Politics in Ibsen, Shaw and Brecht, 1980; Alan Atckbourns A Casebook, 1991. *Contributions to:* Modern Drama; Theatre Journal; The World and I; New York Times Book Review; Twentieth Century Literature; Essays in Theatre; Tulane Drama Review. *Honours:* Guggenheim Fellowship 1969-70; Fellow, American Theatre Association, 1975; NEH Fellowship 1976-77, 1984- 85; Fulbright Research Fellowship, 1991-92; Visiting Fellowship, Humanitites Research Centre of the Australian National University 1979; University Distinguished Professor of Theatre Arts and Humanities, 1985-. *Memberships:* Association for Theatre in Higher Education; Ibsen Society of America. *Address:* Theatre Arts Department, VPI&SU, Blacksburg, VA 24061, USA.

DUMAS Claudine. *See:* **MALZBERG Barry Norman.**

DUNANT Peter. *See:* **DUNANT Sarah.**

DUNANT Sarah, b. 8 Aug 1950. Writer; Broadcaster. Partner of Ian David Willox, 2 daughters. *Education:* Newnham College, Cambridge, 1969-72; BA, 2: I, History, Cambridge University, 1972. *Publications:* As Peter Dunant: Exterminating Angels (co-author), 1983; Intensive Care (co-author), 1986; As Sarah Dunant: Snow Storms in a Hot Climate, 1988; Birth Marks, 1991; Fatlands, 1993. *Contributions to:* Various London magazines; The Listener; The Guardian, occasionally. *Honours:* Shortlisted for Crime Writers Golden Dagger, 1987, 1991. *Literary Agent:* Gillon Aitken, Aitken and Stone, London, England. *Address:* c/o Gillon Aitken, 29 Fernshaw Road, London SW10 0TG, England.

DUNBAR Andrea, b. 22 May 1961, Bradford, Yorkshire. Playwright. 1 son, 2 daughters. *Education:* Educated at Buttershaw Comprehensive School, Bradford. *Publications:* Plays: The Arbor (produced London, 1980; New York, 1983), London, Pluto Press, 1980; Rite, Sue and Bob Too (produced London 1982), London, Methuen, 1982; Shirley (produced London, 1986). Screenplay: Rite, Sue and Bob Too, 1987. *Honours:* George Devine Award 1981. *Address:* 7 Edge End Gardens, Buttershaw, Bradford, West Yorkshire BD6 2BB, England.

DUNBAR Maxwell (John), b. 1914, Canada. Science Writer. *Appointments:* Arctic Explorer, 1935-58; Canadian Consul, Greenland, 1941-46; Professor of Oceanography, Institute of Oceanography, McGill University, Montreal. *Publications:* Marine Distributions, 1963; Ecological Development in Polar Regions, 1968; Environment and Good Sense, 1971; Polar Oceans, 1977; Marine Production Mechanisms, 1979. *Contributions to:* 150 papers in scientific journals. *Honours:* Arctic Science Awards, 1986, 87, 88; Order of Canada, 1990; Honorary DSc, University of Copenhagen, 1991. *Memberships:* Fellow, AAAS; Linnean Society, London; Fellow, Royal Society of Canada. *Address:* 488 Strathcona Avenue, Montreal, Quebec H3Y 2X1, Canada.

DUNCAN Alex. *See:* **DUKE Madelaine Elizabeth.**

DUNCAN Sandy Frances Mary, b. 24 Jan 1942, Vancouver, British Columbia, Canada. Writer. m. Norman James Duncan, 10 May 1963, 2 daughters. *Education:* BA, English & Psychology 1962, MA, Clinical Psychology 1963, University of British Columbia. *Publications:* Cariboo Runaway, 1976; Kap-Sung Ferris, 1977; The Toothpaste Genie, 1981; Dragon Hunt, 1981; Finding Home, 1982; Pattern Makers, 1989; Listen to Me, Grace Kelly, 1990. *Contributions to:* Anthologies: New West Coast, 1977; Common Ground, 1980; Canadian Short Fiction, Volume 2, 1982; Baker's Dozen, 1984; Vancouver Short Stories, 1985. *Honours:* Awards: Children's Book Centre, 1982, 1983; Greater Vancouver Library Federation, 1982, 1983; Surrey Book of the Year,

1983. *Memberships:* British Columbia-Yukon representative 1980-81, National Council 1985-86, Writers Union of Canada; Founding Chair 1980-82, Federation of BC Writers; PEN International; Canadian Association of Childrens Authors & Illustrators. *Address:* c/o Writers Union of Canada, 24 Ryerson Avenue, Toronto, Ontario, Canada M5T 2P3.

DUNCAN Lois, b. 28 Apr 1934, Philadelphia, Pennsylvania, USA. Writer. m. Donald W Arquette, 15 July 1965, 2 sons, 3 daughters. *Publications:* 10 Children's Books; 20 Young Adult Novels; 2 Adult Novels; 3 Non-fiction books including: Ransom, 1966; A Gift of Magic, 1971; I Know What You Did Last Summer, 1973; Down a Dark Hall, 1974; Summer of Fear, 1976; Killing Mr Griffin, 1978; Daughters of Eve, 1979; Stranger with My Face, 1981; Chapters: My Growth as a Writer, 1982; The Third Eye, 1984; Locked in Time, 1985; Horses of Dreamland, 1986; The Twisted Window, 1987; Songs From Dreamland, 1989; The Birthday Moon, 1989; Don't Look Behind You, 1989. *Address:* 1112 Dakota NE, Albuquerque, NM 87110, USA.

DUNCAN Paul Edwin, b. 20 Aug 1959, Cape Town, South Africa. Writer; Journalist. *Education:* University of Edinburgh, 1978-84; MA (Hons), History of Art. *Appointments:* London Correspondent, Casa Vogue, 1989-92; Writer, Researcher, The Royal Fine Art Commission, England, 1991-. *Publications:* Scandal, Georgian London in Decay (co-author), 1986; Insight Guide Tuscany (contributor), 1989; Discovering the Hilltowns of Italy, 1991; AA Tour Guide Italy, 1991; Sicily, A Traveller's Companion, 1992; The Traditional Architecture of Rural Italy, 1993; The Art of Living in London, forthcoming. *Contributions to:* Italian Vogue; Vogue Glamour; Casa Vogue; GQ; The World of Interiors; The Independent; Sunday Times; Evening Standard; Harpers and Queen; Architect's Journal; Elle; Elle Decoration; L'Uomo Vogue; Country Life. *Memberships:* Architectural Association. *Literary Agent:* Anne Engel. *Address:* 10 The Woodlands Mansions, Clapham Common North Side, London SW4 0RJ, England.

DUNHAM William Wade, b. 8 Dec 1947, Pittsburgh, Pennsylvania, USA. Professor of Mathematics. m. Penelope Higgins, 26 Sept 1970, 2 sons. *Education:* BS, University of Pittsburgh, 1969; MS, 1970, PhD, 1974, The Ohio State University. *Publication:* Journey through Genius: The Great Theorems of Mathematics, 1990. *Contributions to:* Number of articles on history of mathematics to journals including: The American Mathematical Monthly; Mathematics Magazine; The College Mathematics Journal; Mathematics Teacher. *Honours:* Phi Beta Kappa, 1968; M M Culver Award, University of Pittburgh, 1969; Master Teacher Award, Hanover College, 1981; Director, NEH Summer Seminars on Great Theorems, 1988, 1990, 1992; Humanities Achievement Award for Scholarship, Indiana Humanities Council, 1991; George Pólya Award, Mathematical Association of America, 1993; Truman Koehler Professor of Mathematics, Muhlenberg College, 1992-. *Memberships:* Mathematical Association of America; National Council of Teachers of Mathematics; Civil War Roundtable (US). *Address:* Department of Mathematics. Muhlenberg College, Allentown, PA 18104, USA.

DUNKERLEY James, b. 15 Aug 1953, England. University Professor. *Education:* BA, Modern History, University of York, 1974; MPhil, Latin American Studies, 1977, DPhil, 1979, University of Oxford. *Publications:* The Long War. Dictatorship and Revolution in El Salvador, 1982; Rebellion in the Veins. Political Struggle in Bolivia, 1984; Los Origenes del Poder Militar en Bolivia, 1987; Power in the Isthmus. A History of Central America, 1988; Political Suicide in Latin America, 1992. *Address:* Department of Political Studies, Queen Mary and Westfield College, Mile End Road, London E1 4NS, England.

DUNKLEY Christopher, b. 22 Jan 1944,

Scarborough, Yorkshire, England. Critic; Broadcaster. m. Carolyn Elizabeth Lyons, 18 Feb 1967, 1 son, 1 daughter. *Education:* Haberdasher's Aske's 1955-62, expelled. *Appointments include:* Mass media correspondent, Television critic, The Times, 1968-73; Television critic, Financial Times, 1973-; Presenter, Feedback, BBC Radio 4, 1986-. *Publications:* Television Today and Tomorrow: Wall to Wall Dallas? 1985. *Contributions to:* Telegraph Magazine; Listener; Sunday Times; Stills; Television World; Electronic Media. *Honours:* Critic of the Year, British Press Awards, 1976, 1986; Broadcast Journalist of the Year, 1989 & Judges Award, 1990, TV-AM Awards. *Membership:* Commodore, Theta Club. *Address:* 38 Leverton Street, London NW5 2PG, England.

DUNLAP Leslie W, b. 1911, United States of America. Writer; Librarian. *Appointments:* Associate Director, University of Illinois Libraries, 1951-58; Dean of Library Administration, 1970-82, Emeritus, 1982-, University of Iowa, Iowa City. *Publications:* Letter of Willis Gaylord Clark and Lewis Gaylord Clark, 1940; American Historical Societies, 1944; Readings in Library History, 1972; The Wallace Papers: An Index, 1975; The Publication of American Historical Manuscripts, 1976; Your Affectionate Husband, J.F. Culver, 1978; Our Vice-Presidents and Second Ladies, 1988. *Membership:* National Commision on Library and Information Sciences, 1970-74.

DUNLOP Richard, b. 1921, United States of America. Writer. *Publications:* The Mississippi River, 1956; St. Louis, 1957; Burma, 1958; The Young David (novel), 1959; Rand McNally Vacation Guide, 1964; Doctors of the American Frontier, 1965; Texaco Touring Atlas, 1968; Texaco Touring Atlas (with E. Snyder), 1970; Great Trails of the West, 1971; Outdoor Recreation Guide, 1974; Backpacking and Outdoor Guide, 1977, 1978; Wheels West, 1977; Behind Japanese Lines: With the OSS in Burma, 1979; Donovan: America's Master Spy, 1982. *Honours:* Midland Authors' Best Biography Award for Donovan: America's Master Spy, 1982. *Memberships:* President, Society of American Travel Writers, 1971; Society of Midland Authors, 1980. *Address:* 1115 Mayfair Road, Arlington Heights, IL 60004, USA.

DUNLOP Storm Richard, b. 5 Oct 1942, Hillingdon, Middlesex, England. Author; Translator. *Education:* Private Tuition. *Publications:* Amateur Astronomy; Astronomy: A Step By Step Guide to the Night Sky; Weather Forecasting; Atlas of the Night Sky. *Memberships:* Society of Authors; Translators Association; Royal Astronomical Society; Royal Meteorological Soceity; British Astronomical Association. *Address:* 140 Stocks Lane, East Wittering, Chichester, West Sussex, PO20 8NT, England.

DUNMORE Spencer, b. 16 Dec 1928, London, England. Advertising Executive. m. Jeanne Plant, 23 Oct 1970, 1 daughter. *Publications:* Bomb Run, 1971; Tower of Strength aka Last Hill, 1973; Collision, 1974; Final Approach, 1976; Means of Escape, 1978; Ace, 1982; The Sound of Wings, 1984; No Holds Barred, 1987. *Honour:* Arts Council Award, 1983. *Literary Agent:* Lucinda Vardey, Toronto. *Address:* 44 Ravenscliffe Avenue, Hamilton, Ontario, Canada L8P 3M4.

DUNN Douglas Eaglesham, b. 23 Oct 1942, Inchinnan, Scotland. Writer. m. Lesley Jane Bathgate, 10 Aug 1985, 1 son, 1 daughetr. *Education:* BA, University of Hull, England. *Literary Appointments:* Writer-in- Residence: University of Hull, 1974-75; University of Dundee, Scotland, 1981- 82; Duncan of Jordanstone College of Art, Dundee District Library, 1986-88; Honorary Visiting Professor, University of Dundee, 1987-89; Fellow in Creative Writing, University of St Andrews, 1989-91; Professor in English, University of St Andrews, 1991-. *Publications:* Terry Street, 1969; The Happier Life, 1972; Love or Nothing, 1974; Barbarians, 1979; St. Kilda's Parliament, 1981; Elegies,

1985; Secret Villages, 1985; Selected Poems, 1986; Northlight, 1988; New and Selected Poems (USA), 1989; Poll Tax: The Fiscal Fake, 1990; Andromache, 1990; Scotland, An Anthology, 1991; Faber Book of 20th Century Scottish Poetry, 1992. *Contributions to:* New Yorker; Punch; Times Literary Supplement; Glasgow Herald. *Honours:* Fellow, Royal Society of Literature, 1981; Honorary LLD, University of Dundee, 1987; Hon Fellow, Humberside College, 1987; Whitbread Book of the Year Award, 1985. *Memberships:* Scottish PEN; Society of Authors; Literature Committee, Scottish Arts Council, 1991-; Scottish Arts Council, 1992. *Literary Agent:* Peters, Fraser and Dunlop, 5th Floor, The Chambers, Chelsea Harbour, Lots Road, London SW10 0XF, England. *Address:* Dept of English, The University, St Andrews, Fife, Scotland.

DUNN Nell (Mary), b. 1936, London. Writer. m. Jeremy Sandford, 1956, 3 children. *Publications:* Plays: Steaming (produced London, 1981; Stamford, Connecticut and New York, 1982), Ambergate, Derbyshire, 1981; New York, Limelight, 1984; Sketches in Variety Night (produced London, 1982); I Want, with Adrian Henri, adaptation of their own novel (produced Liverpool, 1983; London 1986). Screenplay: Poor Cow, with Ken Loach, 1967; Television Play: Up the Junction, from her own stories, 1965; Novels: Poor Cow, London, New York, 1967; The Incurable, London, New York, 1971; I Want, with Adrian Henri, London, 1972; Tear His Head Off His Shoulders, London, 1974; New York, 1975; The Only Child: A Simple Story of Heaven and Hell, London, 1978; Short Stories: Up the Junction, London, 1963; Philadelphia, Lippincott, 1966. *Honours:* Rhys Memorial Prize for Fiction, 1964; Susan Blackburn Prize, 1981; Evening Standard Award, 1982; Society of West End Theatres Award, 1982. *Literary Agent:* Curtis Brown, London. *Address:* 10 Bell Lane, Twickenham, Middlesex, England.

DUNNETT Dorothy (Dorothy Halliday), b. 25 Aug 1923, Dunfermline, Scotland. Novelist; Portrait Painter. m. Alastair M.Dunnett, 17 Sept 1946, 2 sons. *Publications include:*The Game of Kings, 1961, 7th edition 1986; Queen's Play, 1964, 8th edition 1986; The Disorderly Knights, 1966, 8th edition 1987; Dolly & the Singing Bird (also The Photogenic Soprano), 1968, 4th edition 1984; Pawn in Frankincense, 1969, 8th edition 1987; Dolly & the Cookie Bird (also Murder in the Round), 1970, 4th edition 1985; The Ringed Castle, 1971 8th edition 1987; Dolly & the Doctor Bird (also Match for a Murderer), 1971, 4th edition 1985; Checkmate, 1975, 8th edition 1987; King Hereafter, 1982, 3rd edition 1983; Dolly & the Bird of Paradise, 1983, 4th edition 1985; Niccolo Rising, 1986, 4th edition 1987; The Spring of the Ram, 1987, 2 editions; Scottish Short Stories, 1973; Dolly and the Starry Bird, 1973, 4th edition 1986; Dolly and the Nanny Bird, 1976, 4th edition 1985; The Scottish Highlands, (with Alastair M Dunnett and David Paterson), 1988; Moroccan Traffic, 1991; Race of Scorpions, 1990; Scales of Gold, 1991; The Unicorn Hunt, 1991. *Honour:* OBE, 1992; Award, Scottish Arts Council, 1976; Fellow, Royal Society of Arts; Trustee, National Library of Scotland; Board Member, Edinburgh Book Festival. *Literary Agent:* Curtis Brown. *Address:* 87 Colinton Road, Edinburgh EH10 5DF, Scotland.

DUNNING Lawrence, b. 8 Aug 1931, Kansas City, Missouri, USA. Writer; Editor. *Education:* BS, Southern Methodist University, Dallas, Texas. *Appointments:* Instructor, University of Denver, 1980-83; Instructor, University of Colorado at Denver, 1984-86. *Publications:* Neutron Two is Critical, 1977; Keller's Bomb, 1978; Taking Liberty, 1980. *Contributions to:* Denver Post. *Honours:* Short Story Listed in Best American Short Stories, 1971; Top Hand Award for Best Short Story, Colorado Authors League, 1979. *Memberships:* Authors Guild Incorporated; Colorado Authors League; MENSA. *Literary Agent:* Peter Livingston. *Address:* c/o Peter Livingston, 143 Collier Street, Toronto, Ontario, Canada, M4W 1M2.

DUPUY Arnold C, b. 22 May 1962, Fort Belvoir,

Virginia, USA. Military Historian. 1 son. *Education:* George Mason University, 1988; Matriculating, George Mason University. *Publications:* How to Defeat Saddam Hussein (co-author), 1991; Contributing author: The Encyclopedia of Military History: From 3500 BC to the Present, 1986; The Harper Encyclopedia of Military Biography, 1992; International Military and Defense Encyclopedia, 1993. *Contributions to:* Understanding Was from Historical Perspective (co-author), to Marine Corps Gazette. *Address:* 7342 Lee Highway 201, Falls Church, VA 22046, USA.

DUPUY T(revor) N(evitt), b. 1916. History, Military/ Defence. *Appointments:* President and Executive Director and Member of the Board, Historical Evaluation and Research Organization, Washington DC 1962-; President, Data Memory Systems Inc 1983-. Colonel, US Army 1938-58; Professor of Military Science and Tactics, Harvard University, Massachusetts, 1952-56; Director, Ohio State University, Military History Course, 1956-57; with International Studies Division, Institute of Defence Analyses, 1960-62. *Publications include:* Civil War Naval Actions, 1961; Military History of World War II, 19 vols, 1962-65; Compact History of the Revolutionary War, 1963; (ed co-author) Holidays 1965; Military History of World War I, 12 vols, 1967; The Battle of Austerlitz, 1968; Modern Libraries for Modern Colleges: Research Strategies for Design and Development, 1968; Ferment in College Libraries; The Impact of Information Technology, 1968; Military History of the Chinese Civil War, 1969; Military Lives Series, 12 vols, 1969-70; (co-author) Encyclopedia of Military History, 1970, 1977; (co-author) Revolutionary War Land Battles, 1970; (co-author) Revolutionary Way Naval Battles, 1970; (ed and co-author) Almanac of World Military Power, 1970, 1972, 1974, 1978; (co-ed) Documentary History of Arms Control and Disarmament, 1973; (co-author) People and Events of the American Revolution, 1974; (co-author) Outline History of the American Revolution, 1975; A Genius of War: The German Army and General Staff, 1977; Numbers, Predictions and War, 1978; Elusive Victory: The Arab- Israeli Wars, 1947-1974, 1978; The Evolution of Weapons and Warfare, 1980; (co-author) Great Battles on the Eastern Front, 1982; Options of Command, 1984; (with Paul Martell) Flawed Victory: The 1982 War in Lebanon, 1986. *Address:* 8316 Arlington Boulevard, Fairfax, VA 22031, USA.

DURACK Mary, b. 20 Feb 1913, Adelaide, South Australia. Writer. m. Horace Clive Miller, 1938, dec 1980, 2 sons, 4 daughters. *Education:* Loreto Convent, Perth. *Publications:* All-About, 1935; Chunuma, 1936; Son of Djaro, 1938; the Way of the Whirlwind, 1941; Piccaninnies, 1943; The Magic Trumpet, 1944; Keep him my Country, 1955; Kings in Grass Castles, 1959; To Ride a Fine Horse, 1963; The Courteous Savage, 1964; Yagan of the Bibbulmun, 1976; Kookanoo & Kangaroo, 1963; An Australian Settler, 1964; A Pastoral Emigrant, 1964; The Rock and the Sand, 1969; To be Heirs Forever, 1976; Tjakamarra - Boy between Two Worlds, 1977; Swan River Saga, 1975; Sons in the Saddle, 1983; Plays: The Ship of Dreams; Author, numerous scripts for Australian broadcasting Commission, Drama Department; Libretto for Opera, Dalgerie, 1966. *Honours:* OBE, 1966; Commonwealth Literary Grant, 1973, 1977; Hon.D.Litt., University of Western Australia, 1978; DBE, 1978; Australian Resarch Grant, 1980, 1984-85; Emeritus Fellowship, Literary Board, Australia Council, 1983-86, 1987-. *Memberships:* Numerous professional organisations including: Fellowship of Australian Writers, President, WA Branch, 1958-63; Australian Society of Authors; National Trust; Royal Western Historical Society; Patron, Australian Society of Women Writers, Presented with the Alice Award, 1982; Foundation Fellow, Curtin University of Technology, Perth, WA, 1987; Patron & Director, Stockman's Hall of Fame & Outback Heritage Centre; Member of W.A. Branch; AC, 1989; Patron, Friends of the Battye Library, 1989. *Address:* 12 Bellevue Avenue, Nedlands, 6009, WA, Australia.

DURANTI Francesca. *See:* **ROSSI Maria Francesca.**

DURBAND Alan, b. 1927. Writer (Literature, Theatre). *Publications:* English Workshop Books 1-3, 1959; New Directions: Five One-Act Plays in the Modern Idiom, 1961; Contemporary English Books 1-2, 1962; Shorter Contemporary English, 1964; New English Books 1-4, 1966; Playbill 1-3, 1969; Second Playbill 1-3, 1973; Prompt 1-3, 1975; Wordplays 1-2, 1982; Shakespeare Made Easy (12 plays), 1984-89. *Address:* Ty-Nant, Llansilin, Near Oswestry, Salop, SY10 7QQ, England.

DURBRIDGE Francis Henry (Paul Temple), b. 25 Nov 1912. Playwright; Author. m. Norah Elizabeth Lawley, 1940, 2 sons. *Education:* Birmingham University. *Publications:* Radio Plays Include: Promotion, 1933; Created Character of Paul Temple; Entered TV with The Broken Horseshoe, 1952 (the first adult TV serial); other serials followed: Portrait of Alison, 1954; My Friend Charles, 1955; The Other Man, 1956; The Scarf, 1960; The World of Tim Frazer (Executive Producer), 1960-61; Melissa, 1962; Bat Out of Hell, 1964; Stupid Like a Fox, 1971; The Doll, 1976; Breakaway, 1980; Films Include: 2 for Korda and Romulus, 1954-57; Stage Plays: Suddenly at Home, 1971; The Gentle Hook, 1974; Murder with Love, 1976; House Guest, 1980; Nightcap, 1983; Murder Diary, 1986; The Small Hours, 1989; Sweet Revenge, 1991; Side Effects. *Contributions to:* various journals, newspapers and magazines. *Literary Agent:* Lemon Unna and Durbridge Ltd. *Address:* c/o Lemon Unna and Durbridge Ltd, 24 Pottery Lane, Holland Park, London W11 4LZ, England.

DURCAN Paul, b. 16 Oct 1944, Dublin, Ireland. Poet. *Education:* BA. *Publications:* Endsville, 1967; O Westport in the Light of Asia Minor, 1975; Teresa's Bar, 1976; Sam's Cross, 1978; Jesus, Break His Fall, 1980; Ark of the North, 1982; The Selected Paul Durcan, 1982, 85; Jumping the Train Tracks With Angela, 1983; The Berlin Wall Cafe, 1985; Going Home to Russia, 1987; In The Land of Punt, 1988; Jesus and Anglela, 1988. *Contributions to:* Irish Press; Irish Times; Hibernia; Magill; Cyphers; Honest Ulsterman; Gorey Detail; Cork Examiner; Aquarius. *Honours:* Patrick Kavanagh Poetry Award, 1974; Arts Council of Ireland Bursary for Creative Writing, 1976, 1980-81; Poetry Book Society Choice for the Berlin Wall Cafe, 1985; The Irish American Cultural Institute Poetry Award, 1989. *Membership:* Aosdána. *Address:* 14 Cambridge Avenue, Ringsend, Dublin 4, Republic of Ireland.

DURGNAT Raymond Eric (O O Green), b. 1 Sept 1932, London, England. Writer; Lecturer. *Education:* BA Hons, English Literature, Pembroke College, Cambridge, 1957; MA, 1970. *Appointment:* Staff Writer, British Picture Coporation, Elstree Studios, 1957-60. *Publications include:* Durgnat on Film, 1976; Strange Case of Alfred Hitchcock, 1973; Luis Bunuel, 1988; A Mirror for England, 1973; Michael Powell and the English Genius, 1991; The Crazy Mirror; Films and Feelings. *Contributions to:* British Journal of Aesthetics. *Membership:* British Society of Aesthetics. *Literary Agent:* MBA, Campbell Thompson MacLaughlin. *Address:* 84 Saint Thomas's Road, London N4 2QW, England.

DURKIN Barbara Rae Wernecke, b. 13 Jan 1944, Baltimore, Maryland, USA. Writer. m. William J Durkin, 20 May 1973, 2 sons. *Education:* AA, Essex Community College, 1964; BS, English, Towson State University, 1966; Graduate studies, English, the Humanities, Morgan State University and Johns Hopkins University, Baltimore, Maryland. *Publications:* Oh, You Dundalk Girls, Can't You Dance the Polka, 1984. *Honours:* Best of 1984 list, American Library Association, 1984. *Membership:* International Women's Writing Guild. *Literary Agent:* Robin Rue, Anita Diamant Agency, New York City, New York, USA. *Address:* 531 Phillips Road, Webster, NY 14580, USA.

DURMUSH Fatma, b. 28 July 1959, Cyprus. Businesswoman. *Education:* Open University credit, 1984; Diploma in Writing, 1987; Certificate in Poetry, 1991; A level Turkish, 1992. *Contributions to:* Short story to She; 4 short stories to More; Article to London Calling; 17 poems to Gunaydin; Poem to Kibris; Poem to Postasi; Playlet to Open Univesrity; Short extract from unpublished novel. *Address:* 129 New Cross Road, London SE14, England.

DURRELL Gerald Malcolm, b. 7 Jan 1925, Jamshedpur, India. Zoologist; Author. m. Lee McGeorge, 24 May 1979. *Education:* Educated by private tutors, with special emphasis on natural history. *Career:* Student Keeper, Zoological Society of London's Whipsnade Park, 1945; Embarked on career of financing, organizing and leading zoological collecting expeditions to lesser known parts of the world, 1946; Created own zoological park in Jersey, Channel Islands, 1959. In 1963, as Founder and Honorary Director, he formed the Jersey Wildlife Preservation Trust, which took over the park. Established Wildlife Preservation Trust International in the USA 1973; Wildlife Preservation Trust Canada founded 1985. The Trust now has 20,000 members all over the world, publishes regular newsletters, an annual report and a journal called The Dodo. *Publications include:* My Family and Other Animals, 1956; Birds, Beasts and Relatives, 1969; Garden of the Gods, 1978; The Amateur Naturalist (with Lee Durrell) 1982; How to Shoot an Amateur Naturalist, 1984; Durrell in Russia, 1986; The Fantastic Flying Journay, 1987; The Fantastic Dinosaur Adventure, 1989; Marrying Off Mother, 1990; The Ark's Anniversary, 1990; The Aye-aye and I, 1992. Films for Television include: The Edge of Extinction, 1980; Ark on the Move (13 part series), 1981; The Amateur Naturalist (13 programmes), 1983; Durrell in Russia (13 programmes), 1986; Ourselves and Other Animals (13 part series), 1987. *Honours:* OBE 1982: LHD (Hon) Yale University, 1977; DSc (Hon) Durham, 1988; DSc (Hon) Canterbury 1989. *Literary Agent:* Anthea Morton-Saner, Curtis Brown, 161-168 Regent Street, London. *Address:* Les Augres Manor, Trinity, Jersey, Channel Islands.

DURST Paul (Paul Bannon, John Chelton, Jeff Cochran, John Shane), b. 1921, United States of America. Writer. *Appointments:* Editorial Writer, Newscaster, St. Joseph News-Press, 1946-48; Advertising Supervisor, Southwestern Bell Telephone Company, Kansas City and St. Louis, 1948-50; Advertising Manager, Crofts Engineering, Bradford, 1958-60; J.G. Graves, Mail Order Firm, Sheffield, 1960-62. *Publications:* Die, Damn You!, 1952; Bloody River, 1953; Trail Herd North, 1953; Guns of Circle 8 (as Jeff Cochran), 1954; Along the Yermo Rim (as John Shane), 1954; My Deadly Angel (crime as John Chelton), 1955; Showdown, 1955; Justice, 1956; Kid From Canadian, 1956; Praire Reckoning, 1956; Sundown in Sundance (as John Shane), 1956; Six-Gun Thursday (as John Shane), 1956; Gunsmoke Dawn (as John Shane), 1957; John Law, Keep Out, 1957; Ambush at North Platte, 1957; The River Flows West, 1957; They Want Me Dead (crime as Peter Bannon), 1958; If I Should Die (crime as Peter Bannon), 1958; Kansas Guns, 1958; Dead Man's Range, 1958; The Gun Doctor, 1959; Johnny Nation, 1960; Whisper Murder Softly (crime as Peter Bannon), 1963; Backlash (crime), 1967; Badge of Infamy (crime), 1968; Intended Treason: What Really Happened in the Gunpowder Plot, 1970; A Roomful of Shadows (autobiography), 1975; The Florentine Table (crime), 1980; Paradiso County (crime), 1985. *Address:* The Keep, West Wall, Presteigne, Powys, LD8 2BY, Wales.

DUSEK Dusan, b. 4 Jan 1946, Czechslovakia. Writer. m. Nadja Vrabelova, 22 Sept 1973. *Education:* Magister, University of Komensky, Bratislava, 1970. *Appointments:* Editor, Smena daily, 1970-71; Editor, Tip sports magazine, 1972-73; Editor, Kamarat magazine for young, 1973-78; Freelance Writer, 1978-. *Publications include:* The Roof of the House, 1972; The Carriage Beside the Heart, 1982; The Calendar, 1983; The Thimble, 1985; Merciful Time, 1992; Books for young people including: The Oldest of All Sparrows, 1976; The True Story of Paco, 1980; The Grandma on the Ladder, 1986. *Contributions to:* Slovenske pohl'ady;

Romboid; Kulturny zivot. *Honours:* Honour List IBBY, 1988. *Memberships:* Obec spisovatel'ov Slovenska; Slovak Centre PEN. *Address:*Dusan Dusek, Stare zahrady 10, 821 05 Bratislava, Slovakia.

DUTTON Geoffrey Piers Henry, b. 2 Aug 1922, Anlaby, South Australia. Writer. m. (1) Ninette Trott, 1944, 2 sons, 1 daughter, (2) Robin Lucas, 1985. *Education:* University of Adelaide; BA, Magdalen College, Oxford, 1949. *Appointments:* Co-Editor, Australian Letters, 1957-68, Australian Book Review, 1961-70; Editor, The Bulletin Literary Supplement, 1980-85, The Australian Literary Magazine, 1985-88; Editorial Director, Sun Books Ltd., 1965-83. *Publications:* Nightflight and Sunrise, 1945; The Hero as Murderer, 1967; Andy, 1968; Walt Whitman:Patrick White, 1961; Findings & Keepings, 1970; Queen Emma of the South Seas, 1976; Patterns of Australia, 1978; White on Black, 1978; Snow on the Saltbush, 1984; The Innovators, 1986; Kenneth Slessor, 1991; Flying Low, 1992. *Contributions to:* Numerous journals and magazines and broadcasting services. *Honour:* Officer, Order of Australia, 1976. *Literary Agent:* Curtis Brown. *Address:* c/o Curtis Brown, PO Box 19, Paddington, NSW 2021, Australia.

DUVAL Jeanne. *See:* **COFFMAN Virginia (Edith).**

DWYER K R. *See:* **KOONTZ Dean R.**

DYER Geoff, b. 5 June 1958, Cheltenham, Gloucestershire, England. Writer; Critic. *Education:* BA (Hons), English, Corpus Christi College, Oxford, 1980. *Publications:* The Colour of Memory, 1989; But Beautiful, 1991; Ways of Telling: The Work of John Berger, 1986. *Literary Agent:* Xandra Hardie and Toby Eady. *Address:* 4 Crownstone Ct, Crownstone Rd, London SW2 1LS, England.

DYER James Frederick, b. 23 Feb 1934, Luton, England. Archaeological Writer. *Education:* MA, Leicester University, 1964. *Publications:* Southern England, An Archaeological Guide, 1973; Penguin Guide to Prehistoric England and Wales, 1981; Discovering Archaeology in England and Wales, 1985; Ancient Britain, 1990. *Contributions to:* Bedfordshire Magazine; Illustrated London News; Archaeological Journal. *Memberships:* Society of Authors; Royal Archaeological Institute; Society of Antiquaries. *Address:* 6 Rogate Road, Luton, Bedfordshire LU2 8HR, England.

DYMOKE Juliet, b. 28 June 1919, Enfield, England. Writer. m. Hugo de Schanschieff, 9 May 1942, 1 son, 1 daughter. *Publications:* The White Cockade, 1979; Ride to Glencoe, 1989; The Cloisterman, 1969; March to Corunna, 1985; A King of Warfare, 1981; Plantagenet Series, 6 books 1978-80; The Queens Diamond, 1985; Norman Triology 1970-74; A Border Knight, 1987; Aboard the Mary Rose, 1985; Two Flags for France, 1986; Portrait of Jenny, 1990; Hollanders House, 1991; Cry of The Peacock, 1992. *Contribution to:* Lady. *Membership:* Romantic Novelists Association. *Literary Agent:* Jane Conway-Gordon, 1 Old Compton Street, London W1. *Address:* Heronswood, Chapel Lane, Forest Row, East Sussex RH18 5BS, England.

DYSON Anthony Edward, b. 1928. Writer (Literature). *Appointments:* Lecturer, English, University College of North Wales, Bangor, 1955-63; Co-Editor, Critical Quarterly, 1959-; Co-Founder, Director, Critical Quarterly Society, 1960-84; Visiting Professor, Concordia University, Montreal, Canada, 1967, 1969; General Editor, Macmillan Casebooks, England, 1968-; Visiting Professor, University of Connecticut, USA, 1976; Director, Norwich Tapes Ltd, England, 1979-; Honorary Fellow, former Reader in English, University of East Anglia, Norwich. *Publications:* Modern Poetry (with C B Cox), 1963; The Crazy Fabric: Essays in Irony, 1965; The Practical Criticism of Poetry, 1965; Modern Judgements on Dickens, 1968; Word in the Desert (with

C B Cox), 1968; Casebook on Bleak House, 1969; Black Papers on Education, 3 vols, 1969-70; The Inimitable Dickens, 1970; Between Two Worlds: Aspects of Literary Form, 1972; Twentieth Century Mind, 3 vols (with C B Cox), 1972; English Poetry: Select Bibliographical Guides, 1973; English Novel: Select Bibliographical Guides, 1974; Casebook on Paradise Lost (with Julian Lovelock), 1974; Masterful Images: Metaphysicals to Romantics (with Julian Lovelock), 1975; Education and Democracy (with Julian Lovelock), 1975; Yeats, Eliot and R S Thomas: Riding the Echo, 1981; Poetry Criticism and Practice, 1986; Thom Gunn, Ted Hughes and R S Thomas, 1990. *Contributions to:* Over 100 articles in world of English Criticism to various US, UK and European Community journals; 8 teaching tapes. *Address:* c/o Lloyds Bank, 3 Sidney Street, Cambridge CB2 3HQ, England.

DYSON Freeman (John), b. 1923, United States of America. Writer. *Publications:* Disturbing the Universe (autobiography), 1979; Weapons and Hope, 1984; Origins of Life, 1986; Infinite in All Directions, 1988; From Eros to Gaia, 1992. *Honour:* Recipient of National Book Critics Circle Award for Non-fiction, 1984. *Address:* 105 Battle Road Circle, Princeton, NJ 08540, USA.

DZVONIK Michal, b. 28 Dec 1923, Lastomir, CS. Writer; Historian. m. (1) Stromkova, 2 June 1948, (2) Kopcanova, 1 Apr 1972, 1 son, 2 daughters. *Education:* University Prague; Doctor of Philosophy; Associate Professor. *Publications:* Scenes of a Fire; Tetanus; Ducats in Naphtaline; Jealousy; Blind Cave; The First Sorrow; Relativity Law. *Contributions to:* Word of a Defendant; Literary Criticism as a Lawsuit. *Honours:* Award of Publishing Company. *Memberships:* Club of Independent Writers. *Address:* Nejedlého 1, 84102 Bratislava, Slovakia.

E

EAGLETON Terence Francis, b. 22 Feb 1943, Salford, England. University Teacher. 2 sons. *Education:* MA, Trinity College, 1964; PhD, Jesus College, Cambridge, 1967. *Appointments:* Poetry Book Society Selector, 1972-74; Sinclair Prize Judge, 1984. *Publications:* Criticism and Ideology, 1976; Literary Theory: An Introduction, 1983; The Ideology of the Aesthetic, 1990; Marzism and Literary Criticism, 1976; The Rape of Clarissa, 1985; The Function of Criticism, 1984; Walter Benjamin, 1981; William Shakespeare, 1986; Against the Grain, 1986; Saint Oscar, a play, 1989. *Contribution to:* Observer; Times Literary Supplement; New York Times Book Reivew; New Statesman; New Left Review. *Honour:* Irish Sunday Tribune Arts Award, 1990. *Literary Agent:* Elaine Steel. *Address:* St Catherine's College, Oxford, England.

EARLY Gerald, b. 21 Apr 1952, Philadelphia, Pennsylvania, USA. Professor of English and Afro-American Studies. m. Ida Haynes, 27 Aug 1977, 2 daughters. *Education:* BA cum laude, English, University of Pennsylvania, 1974; MA, English, 1980, PhD, English, 1982, Cornell University. *Publications:* Tuxedo Junction: Essays on American Culture, 1990; My Soul's High Song, 1991. *Contributions to:* Essays and reviews to: Salmagundi; The Antioch Review; Cottonwood; The Kenyon Review; American Studies; The Forest Park Review; Antaeus; The Massachusetts Review; The Iowa Review; The New York Times Book Review; Others; Poetry to: The American Poetry Review; Northwest Review; Tar River Poetry; Raccoon; Seneca Review; Obsidian II; Black American Literature Forum; Others. *Honours:* Cornell University: 1st Year Minority Graduate Fellowship, 1977; Summer Fellowship, Summer Tuition Grant, 1978-80; Creative and Performing Arts Council Creative Writing Award, 1978; 2nd Place, 1979, 3rd Place, 1981, Arthur Lynn Andrews Prize for Short Stories; Dissertation Research Award, 1980; Graduate Fellowship and Research Assistantship, 1981; Josephine de Karman Graduate Fellowship, 1981; Washington University Faculty Summer Research Fellowship, 1984; University of Kansas Minority Postdoctoral Fellowship, 1985-87; The Passing of Jazz's Old Guard selected for publication, Ticknor and Early, 1985; The Whiting Foundation Writer's Award, 1988; CCLM-General Electric Foundation Award for Younger Writers, 1988; Her Picture in the Papers: Remembering Some Black Women, selected as Notable Essay, Ticknow and Gerald Early, 1989. *Address:* Washington University, Campus Box 1109, One Brookings Drive, St Louis, MO 63130, USA.

EASTAUGH Kenneth, b. 1929. Writer. *Appointments:* Television Critic, 1965-67, Show Business Writer, 1967-70, Daily Mirror, London; Chief Show Business Writer, The Sun, London, 1970-73; TV Columnist, The Times, London, 1977; Chief Show Business Executive, Daily Star, London, 1978-83; Film Critic, Prima Magazine, Music Critic, Classical Music Weekly, 1976-. *Publications:* The Event (television play), 1968; Better Than a Man (television play), 1970; Dapple Downs (radio serial), 1973-74; Awkward Cuss (play), 1976; Havergal Brian: The Making of a Composer (biography), 1976; Coronation Street (TV series), 1977-78; The Carry On Book (Cinema), 1978; Havergal Who? (TV Documentary), 1980; Mr Love (novel, screenplay), 1986; Dallas (TV serial), 1989. *Address:* David Higham Associates, 5/8 Lower John Street, Golden Square, London W1R 4HA, England.

EASTHOPE Antony Kelynge Revington, b. 14 Apr 1939, Portsmouth, England. Lecturer. m. Diane Garside, 1 Feb 1972, 1 son, 2 daughters. *Education:* Christ's College, Cambridge, 1958-64; BA, 1961; MA, 1965; MLitt, 1967. *Appointments:* Brown University, Rhode Island, USA, 1964- 66; Warwick University, England, 1967-68; Manchester Polytechnic, 1969-. *Publications:* Poetry as Discourse, 1983; What a Man's Gotta Do, 1986; British Post-Structuralism, 1988; Poetry and Phantasy, 1989; Literary into Cultural Studies, 1991. *Contributions to:* Numerous magazines and journals.

Honours: Charter Fellow, Wolfson College, Oxford, 1985-86; Visiting Fellow, University of Virginia, Centre for Literary and Cultural Change, 1990. *Address:* 27 Victoria Avenue, Didsbury, Manchester M20 8QX, England.

EASTON Robert Olney, b. 4 July 1915, San Francisco, CA. Writer. m. Jane Faust, 24 Sept 1940, 4 daughters. *Education:* Stanford University, 1933-34; SB, Harvard University, 1938; MA, University of California, Santa Barbara, 1960. *Publications:* The Happy Man, 1943; Lord of Beasts, (co-author), 1961; The Book of the American West, (co-author), 1963; The Hearing, 1964; Californian Condor, (co-author), 1964; Max Brand, 1970; Black Tide, 1972; This Promised Land, 1982; China Caravans, 1982; Life and Work, (co-author), 1988; Power and Glory, 1989; co-author, Love and War, 1991. *Contributions to:* various magazines. *Literary Agent:* Jon Tuska. *Address:* 2222 Las Canons Road, Santa Barbara, CA 93105, USA.

EATON Charles Edward, b. 1915, America. Writer. *Publications:* The Bright Plain, 1942; Write Mr From Rio, 1959; The Shadow of the Swimmer, 1951; The Greenhouse in the Garden, 1956; Countermoves, 1963; The Edge of the Knife, 1970; Karl Knathss, 1971; The Girl from Ipanema, 1972; Karl Knaths: Five Decades of Painting, 1973; The Man in the Green Chair, 1977; The Case of the Missing Photographs, 1978; Colophon of the Rover, 1980; The Thing King, 1983; The Work of the Wrench, 1985; New and Selected Poems, 1942-87, 1987.

EATON John P, b. 27 May, 1926. Hospital Admissions Officer. *Education:* AB, Lafayette College, Easton, Pennsylvania, USA, 1948. *Publications:* Written with Charles A Haas: Titanic: Triumph and Tragedy, 1986; Titanic: Destination Disaster, 1987; Falling Star, 1990. *Contributions to:* Consultant on the subject of Titanic to numerous nationally-published magazines and newspapers; consultant and guest on many radio and television programmes in America, Canada and England. *Memberships:* Titanic International (co-founder, Historian); Titanic Historical Society (former member) (Co-founder, Historian 1963-88). *Address:* 53 Downing Street, New York, NY 10014, USA.

EATON Trevor Michael William, b. 26 Mar 1934, Harrow, London, England. Professional Performer of Chaucer's Tales. m. Beryl Elizabeth Rose Conley, 29 Sept 1958, 2 sons, 2 daughters. *Education:* New College, Oxford University, 1955-58; MA, English Language and Literature, Oxford; MA, Applied Linguistics, University of Kent, Canterbury, 1988. *Appointments:* Section Convenor, Linguistics and Literature Section, Linguistics Association of Great Britain; Founder, International Association of Literary Semantics, 1992. *Publications:* The Semantics of Language, 1966; Theoretical Semics, 1972; Editor: Essays in Literary Semantics (editor), 1978; Poetries: Their Media and Ends (A I Richards); Commercial recordings: Chaucer's The Canterbury Tales, recited on 18 audio cassettes in Middle English, 1986-93. *Contributions to:* Linguistics; Cahier Roumains d'Etudes Littéraires; Style; Educational Studies. *Honours:* Founder, Editor, Journal of Literary Semantics, 1972-. *Memberships:* International Association of Literary Semantics; International PEN; Linguistics Association of Great Britain; PALA. *Address:* Honeywood Cottage, 35 Seaton Avenue, Hythe, Kent CT21 5HH, England.

EBBETT Eve. *See:* EBBETT Frances Eva.

EBBETT Frances Eva (Eva Burfield, Eve Ebbett), b. 6 June 1925, Wellingborough, England. Author. m. Trevor George Ebbett, 22 Oct 1949, 1 daughter. *Publications:* AS Eve Ebbett: In True Colonial Fashion, 1977; Victoria's Daughters, 1981; When The Boys Were Away, 1984; Give Them Swing Bands, 1969; To The Garden Alone, 1970. As Eva Burfield: Yellow Kowhai, 1957; A Chair To Sit On, 1958; The Long Winter, 1964;

After Midnight, 1965; Out Of Yesterday, 1965; The White Prison, 1966; The New Mrs Rainier, 1967; The Last Day of Summer, 1968. *Contributions to:* Short stories New Zealand, Australia, England, France, Italy, Holland, Norway, Sweden and Denmark. *Address:* 908 Sylvan Road, Hastings, New Zealand.

EBEJER Francis, b. 28 Aug 1925, Malta. Novelist and Playwright (English and Maltese). m. Jane Couch, 5 Sept 1947 (sep 1957), 2 sons (1 dec), 1 daughter. *Education:* Matriculated, Malta Lyceum, 1939; Fulbright Grant, USA, 1961-62. *Appointments:* English-Italian Interpreter with British 8th Army Tripolitania, 1943-44; Member, Radio and TV Drama Panel, various periods; Occasional Drama and Literature Lecturer. *Publications:* A Wreath of Maltese Innocents, London, 1958, Malta, 1981; Evil of the King Cockroach, London, 1960, Malta, 1968; In the Eye of the Sun, London, 1969; Requiem for the Malta Fascist, 1980-; Come Again in Spring, New York, 1980; Leap of Malta Dolphins, New York, 1982; Plays: Over 40 in Maltese, 7 vols, 1950-85; 11 in English, 3 vols, 1950-85; Vacances d'Ete, France, 1985; Vacanze d'Estate, Italy, 1988; For Rozina A Husband, book of 16 short stories. *Contributions to:* Various, including poetry, essays, to Maltese publications, 1940s-; Short story, Foot-Feet, to PEN Broadsheet; 12 short stories to Short Story, New York, 1980-; 5 short stories for BBC; 3 short stories in Italian translation, to Delta Focus; 1-act play in Polish translation, to Dialog and on Polish TV; Play on WDR Cologne; 4 stories on Radio Free Berlin, Sachsen Radio Leipzig and Radio Basle. *Honours:* Cheyney Award for Drama, 1964; Malta Literary Award, 4 times, 1972-; Phoenicia Trophy Award for Culture, 1982; Médaille d'Honneur de la Ville d'Avignon, France, 1986. Maltese Academy of Letters, Council Member 1984-88; Honorary President, Malta Literary Society; Fellow, English PEN; Associate Member, French Academy of Vaucluse, Provence. *Address:* Apt 3, Nivea Court, Swieqi Valley, Swieqi, Malta STJ 05.

EBEL Suzanne (Suzanne Goodwin, Cecily Shelbourne), Writer - Historical, Romance, Travel. *Publications:* Love, the Magician, 1956; Journey from Yesterday, 1963; The Half-Enchanted, 1964; The Love Campaign, 1965; The Dangerous Winter, 1965; A Perfect Stranger, 1966; A Name in Lights, 1968; A Most Auspicious Star, 1968; Somersault, 1971; Portrait of Jill, 1972; Dear Kate, 1972; To Seek a Star, 1973; The Family Feeling, 1973; Girl by the Sea, 1974; Music in Winter, 1975; A Grove of Olives, 1976; River Voices, 1976; The Double Rainbow, 1977; A Rose in Heather, 1978; Julia's Sister, 1982; The Provencal Summer, 1982; House of Nightingales, 1986; The Clover Field, 1987. As Suzanne Goodwin: The Winter Spring, 1978 (USA - Stage of Love, as Cecily Shelbourne, 1978); The Winter Sisters, 1980; Emerald, 1980; Floodtide, 1983; Sisters, 1985; Cousins, 1986; Daughters, 1987; Lovers, 1988; To Love a Hero, 1989; A Change of Season, 1990; The Rising Storm, 1992; While The Music Lasts, 1993. Non-fiction: Explore the Cotswold by Bicycle (with Doreen Impey), 1973; London's Riverside, From Hampton Court in the West to Greenwich Palace in the East (with Doreen Impey), 1975. *Address:* 52A Digby Mansions, Hammersmith Bridge Road, London W6 9DF, England.

EBERSOHN Wessel (Schalk), b. 1940, South Africa. Author; Writer. *Appointments:* Technician, Department of Posts and Telecommunications, Pretoria, 1956-62; Technician, Gowlett Alpha, Johannesburg, 1962-69; Technician, Department of Posts of Telecommunications, Durban, 1970-79; Freelance Writer, 1979-. *Publications:* A Lonely Place to Die (mystery novel), 1979; The Centurion (mystery novel), 1979; Store Up the Anger (novel), 1981; Divide the Night (mystery novel), 1981; Klara's Visitors (novel), 1987. *Address:* 491 Long Avenue, Ferndale 2194, Transvaal, South Africa.

EBERT Alan, b. 1935, United States of America. Author. *Publications:* The Homosexals, 1977; Every Body is Beautiful (with Ron Fletcher), 1978; Intimacies, 1979; Traditions (novel), 1981; The Long Way Home (novel), 1984; Marriages (novel), 1987. *Address:* 353 W. 56th Street, New York, NY 10019, USA.

EBERT Tibor, b. 14 Oct 1926, Bratislava, Czechoslovakia. Writer; Poet; Dramatist. m. Eva Gati, 11 Feb 1968, 1 daughter. *Education:* BA, Music, Ferenc Liszt Academy of Music, 1952; Law, Philosophy, Literature studies, Departments of Law and Philosophy, Eotvos Lorand University, Budapest, 1951-53. *Appointments:* Dramaturg, Jozsef Attila theatre, Budapest, Hungary, 1984-85; Editor-in-Chief, Agora Publishers, Budapest, 1989-92; Editor, Hirvivo literary magazine, 1990-92. *Publications:* Mikrodramak, 1971; Rosarium, 1987; Kobayashi, 1989; Legenda egy fuvoszenekarrol, 1990; Job konyve, 1991; Several plays performed on stage including: Les Escaliers; Musique de Chambre; Demosthenes; Esterhazy. *Contributions to:* Numerous short stories, poems, dramas and essays to several leading Hungarian literary journals and magazines. *Honours:* Honorary Member, Franco-Hungarian Society, 1980-; Bartok Prize; 1987; Commemorative Medal, City of Pozsony-Pressburg-Bratislava, 1991. *Membership:* PEN Club. *Literary Agent:* Artisjus Budapest, Hungary. *Address:* Csevi u 15c, 1025 Budapest, Hungary.

ECHESKE. *See:* **KRISHASWAMY Iyenger H S.**

ECKARDT Arthur Roy, b. 1918, United States of America. Writer, Philosophy, Theology, Religion. *Appointments:* Editor, Journal of the American Academy of Religion, 1961-69. Professor of Religion Studies Emeritus, Lehigh University; Visiting Scholar, Centre for Hebrew Studies, University of Oxford, 1982-88; Senior Associate Fellow, 1990. *Publications:* Christianity and the Children of Israel, 1948; The Surge of Piety in America, 1958; Elder and Younger Brothers, 1967, 1973; The Theologian at Work, 1968; Encounter with Israel (with Alice Eckardt), 1970; Your People, My People, 1974; Long Night's Journey into Day (with Alice Eckardt), 1982, rev. ed. 1988; Jews and Christians, 1986; For Righteousness' Sake, 1987; Black-Woman-Jew, 1989; Reclaiming the Jesus of History, 1992; Sitting in the Earth and Laughing, 1992; Collecting Myself (ed Alice L Eckardt), 1993. *Address:* 6011 Beverley Hill Road, Coopersburg, PA 18036, USA.

ECO Umberto, b. 5 Jan 1932, Alessandria, Italy. Writer. m. Renate Ramge, 24 Sept 1962, 1 son, 1 daughter. *Education:* PhD, University of Turin, 1954. *Publications:* Diario minimo, 1963, revised edition, 1976; Appunti per una semiologia delle communicazioni visive, 1967; La definizione dell'arte (The Definition of Art), 1968; Le forme del contenuto, 1971; I pampini bugiardi, 1972; Editor, Estetica e teoria dell'informazione, 1972; Storia di una rivoluzione mai esistita l'esperimento Vaduz, 1976; Dalla periferia dell'impero, 1976; Come si fa una tesi di laurea, 1977; Perche continuiamo a fare e a insegnare arte?, 1979; Sette anni di desiderio, 1983; in English: A Theory of Semiotics, 1976; The Role of the Reader: Explorations in the Semotics of Texts, 1979; Semotics and the Philosophy of Language, 1984; Sign of the Three: Dupin, Holmes, Pierce, 1984; The Name of the Rose; Fouccult's Pendulum, 1989. *Contributions to:* Numerous Encyclopedias including Enciclopedia Filosofica and Encyclopedic Dictionary of Semotics; Essays, Reviews to numerous periodicals including Espresso, Corriere della Sera, Times Literary Supplement, Revue Internationale de Sciences Sociales, Nouvelle Revue Francaise. *Honours:* Premio Stega and Premio Anghiari, 1981 (for Il nome della rosa); Named Honorary Citizen of Monte Cerignon, Italy, 1982; Prize for Best Foreign Novel, 1982 (for french Version of Il nome della rosa); Los Angeles Times Fiction Prize Nomination for The Name of the Rose. *Memberships:* Secretary General, 1972-79, Vice President, 1979-, International Association for Semiotic Studies; Honorary Trustee, James Joyce Foundation. *Address:* Via Melzi d'Eril 23, 20154 Milano, Italy.

EDDINGS David, b. 1931, Washington, USA. Science Fiction Writer. *Education:* BA, University of Washington. *Appointments include:* Teacher, college-level English. *Publications:* High Hunt, adventure story; Belgariad series: Pawn of Prophecy; Queen of Sorcery; Magician's Gambit; Castle of Wizardry; Enchanters' End Game; Mallorean series: Guardians of The West; King of The Murgos; Demon Lord of Karanda; Sorceress of Darshiva, 1989; The Diamond Throne; The Seeress of Kell.

EDELMAN Bernard L, b. 14 Dec 1946, Brooklyn, New York, USA. Editor; Consultant. m. Ellen M. Leary, 31 May 1985. *Education:* BA, Brooklyn College, 1968; MA, John Jay College of Criminal Justice, 1983. *Publication:* Dear America: Letters Home from Vietnam (editor), 1988. *Contributions to:* Dear America excerpted in several publications including Time magazine; Articles to: Police magazine; Daily News Sunday magazine; Others. *Honours:* Documentary film based on Dear America received 2 Emmy Awards, numerous film festival citations and critical acclaim. *Literary Agent:* Phillipa Brophy, Sterling Lord Literistic. *Address:* Mount Joy Road, Finesville, NJ 08865, USA.

EDGAR David, b. 26 Feb 1948, Birmingham, England. Playwright. *Education:* Oundle School, Northampton, 1961-65; BA, Hons, Drama, Manchester University, 1969. *Appointments:* Reporter, Bradford Telegraph and Argus, Yorkshire, 1969-72; Yorkshire Arts Association Fellow, Leeds Polytechnic, 1972-73; Resident Playwright, Birmingham Repertory Theatre, 1985-; Lecturer in Playwriting, Birmingham University, 1974-78; Literary Consultant, Royal Shakespeare Company, 1984-8; Honorary Senior Research Fellow, University of Birmingham, 1988-, Honorary Professor, 1992-. *Publications:* The Second Time as Farce, 1988; Edgar Shorts (Blood Sports with Ball Boys, Baby Love, The National Theatre, The Midas Connection), 1990. Plays include: The Life and Adventures of Nicholas Nickleby, adaptation of the novel by Dickens (produced London, 1980, New York, 1981) New York, Dramatists Play Service, 2 vols 1982; Maydays (produced London, 1983) London, 1983, revised edition 1984; Entertaining Strangers: A A Play for Dorchester (produced Dorchester, Dorset, 1985; revised version produced, London 1987). London, 1986; That Summer (produced London, 1987) London, 1987; Plays I (includes The Jail Diary of Albie Sachs, Mary Barnes, Saigon Rose, O Fair Jerusalem, Destiny) London, Methuen, 1987; Heartlanders, (with Stephen Bill and Anne Devlin), 1989; The Shape of the Table, (produced London), 1990; Dr Jekeyll and Mr Hyde, 1991. Screenplay: Lady Jane, 1986; Radio Plays: Ecclesiastes, 1977; A Movie Starring Me, 1991. Television plays: The Eagle Has Landed, 1973; Sanctuary from his play Gangsters, 1973; I Know What I Meant, 1974; The Midas Connection, 1975; Censors, with Hugh Whitemore and Robert Muller, 1975; Vote For Them, (with Neil Grant), 1989; Buying a Landslide, 1992. *Honours:* John Whiting Award, 1976; Bicentennial Exchange Fellowship, 1978; Society of West End Theatre award, 1980; New York Drama Critics Circle award, 1982; Tony award, 1982. *Literary Agent:* Michael Imison Playwrights, London. *Address:* c/o Michael Imison Playwrights, 28 Almeida Street, London N1 1TD, England.

EDINGER Catarina Tereza, b. 30 July 1944, Sao Paulo, SP, Brazil. Professor. m. Robert Edinger, 18 June 1978, 1 son. *Education:* BA, 1965, MA, 1970, PhD, 1973, Faculdade de Filosofia, Letras e Ciencias Humanas, University of Sao Paulo; Fulbright-Fletcher Fellowship, Tufts University, 1976-77. *Appointments:* Professor of English, University of Sao Paulo, SP, 1967-77; Mackenzie University, Sao Paulo, 1966-74; William Paterson College, New Jersey, USA, 1985-. *Publications:* Book: A Metáfora e o Fenômeno Amoroso nos Poemas Ingleses de Fernando Pessoa, 1982; The Sun vs Ice-Cream and Chocolate: The Works of Wallace Stevens and Fernando Pessoa (essay in 'The Man Who Never Was: Essays on Fernando Pessoa', 1982; Translation: Senhora - Profile Of A Woman by José de Alencar, (forthcoming). *Contributions to:* Machismo

and Androgyny in Mid-Nineteenth-Century Brazilian and American Novels, to Comparative Literature Studies, 1990; Dona Flor in Two Cultures, to Literature and Film Quarterly, 1991; Hawthorne and Alencar Romancing the Marble, to Brasil-Brazil. *Memberships:* Modern Language Association of America; American Comparative Literature Association; American Translators Association. *Address:* 60 Old Crown Road, Old Tappan, NJ 07675, USA.

EDMOND Lauris Dorothy, b. 2 Apr. 1924. Dannevirke, New Zealand. Writer; Editor; University Tutor. m. 16 May 1945, 1 son, 5 daughters. *Education:* Teaching Diploma, 1943; Speech Therapy Diploma, 1944; BA, Waikato University, 1966; MA 1st Class Honours, Victoria University, Wellington, 1971. *Literary Appointments:* Katherine Mansfield Memorial Fellowship, 1981; Writer-in-Residence, Deakin University, Melbourne, Victoria, Australia, 1985; Writer's Fellowship, Victoria University, Wellington, 1987. *Publications:* Poetry: In Middle Air, 1975; The Pear Tree, 1977; Salt from the North, 1980; Wellington Letter, 1980; Catching It, 1983; Selected Poems, 1984; Seasons and Creatures, 1986; New and Selected Poems, 1991; Summer Near the Arctic Circle, 1988; High Country Weather (novel), 1983; The Mountain Cycle of 4 Plays for Radio, 1981; Between Night and Morning (stage play), 1981; Autobiography, Hot October, 1989; Bonfires in the Rain, 1991;; The Quick World, 1992. *Contributions to:* Womens Fiction; PN Review; Stand; Planet; The Honest Ulsterman; Verse; Numbers; Poetry Now, UK; Meanjin Westerly; Overland, Australia; Landfall, New Zealand; Poetry New Zealand; The New Zealand Listener; Islands. *Honours:* Best First Book, PEN New Zealand Centre, 1975; Commonwealth Poetry Prize, 1985; O.B.E. for Service to Poetry and Literature, 1986; Lilian Ida Smith Award for Poetry, (PEN.NZ), 1987; Hon DLitt Massey University, 1988. *Memberships:* PEN (President 1979-80); Wellington Poetry Society. *Address:* 22 Grass Street, Oriental Bay, Wellington, New Zealand.

EDMUNDSON Bruce, b. 20 June 1952, Edmonton, Alberta, Canada. Writer. *Education:* BFA, University of Victoria, 1982; MFA, University of British Columbia, 1986. *Appointments:* Writer. Worked as a tree planter and carnival worker. *Publications:* Two Voices (stories) 1987; Scriptwriter for Canadian Broadcasting Corporation. *Memberships:* Amnesty International; Greenpeace; British Columbia Federation of Writers. *Address:* 1240 South Dyke Road, New Westminster, British Columbia, Canada V3M 5A2.

EDRIC Robert (Gary Armitage), b 14 Apr 1956, Sheffield, England. Writer. m. 12 Aug 1978. *Education:* BA, 1st Class Honours, PhD, Hull University. *Publications;* Winter Garden, 1985; A New Ice Age, 1986; A Season of Peace, 1985; Across the Autumn Grass, 1986. *Contributions to:* London Magazine; Stand; Critical Quarterly; PEN; New Fiction II; Proof. *Honours:* James Tait Black Memorial Award, 1985; Trask Award, 1985. *Literary Agent:* A Harwood, Aitken & Stone Ltd. *Address:* The Lindens, Atwick Road, Hornsea, N. Humberside, England.

EDSON J T, b. 17 Feb. 1928, Worksop, Nottinghamshire, England. Author. div, 2 sons, 1 daughter. *Publications include:* Trail Boss, 1961; Ole Devil Hardin series; Civil War series; Floating Outfit series; Waco series; Calamity Jane series; Waxahachie Smith series; Alvin Dustine Cap Fog series; Rockabye County series; Bunduki series. Over 120 titles. *Contributions to:* Victor Boys Paper Boys World in early career. *Honours:* 2nd Prize, Brown Watson Literary Competition (Western Section), 1960; approx. 24,000,000 copies of Books sold worldwide. *Membership:* Western Writers of America. *Literary Agent:* Joanna Marston, Rosica Colin Ltd, 1 Clareville Grove Mews, London, SW7, England. *Address:* P O Box 13, Melton Mowbray, Leicestershire, England.

EDSON Russell, b. 1935, American. Writer, Poet,

Playwright. *Publications:* Appearances: Fables and Drawings, 1961; A Stone is Nobody's: Fables and Drawings, 1961; The Boundry, 1964; The Very Thing That Happens: Fables and Drawings, 1964; The Brain Kitchen: Writings and Woodcuts, 1965; What a Man Can See, 1969; The Childhood of an Equestrian, 1973; The Clam Theater, 1973; The Falling Sickness (plays), 1975; The Intuitive Journey, 1976; The Reason Why the Closet-Man Is Never Sad, 1977; With Sincerest Regrets, 1980; Wuck Wuck Wuck! 1984; Gulping's Recital (novel), 1984; The Wounded Breakfast, 1985; The Song Of Percival Peacock (novel), 1992. *Honours:* Guggenheim Fellowship, 1974; NEA, 1981, 1992; Whiting Writers' Award, 1989. *Address:* 149 Weed Avenue, Stamford, CT 06902, USA.

EDWARDS Anne, b. 1927, America. Writer. *Appointments:* Member of Council 1978-81, President 1981-85, The Authors Guild. *Publications:* (adaptor), A Child's Bible, 1967; The Survivors, 1968; Miklos Alexandrovitch Is Missing, (in UK as Alexandrovitch Is Missing), 1969; Shadow of a Lion, 1970; The Hesitant Heart, 1974; Judy Garland: A Biography, 1974; (with Stephen Citron), The Inn and Us (reminiscences), 1975; Child of Night (in UK as Ravenwings), 1975; P T Barnum (juvenile), 1976; The Great Houdini (juvenile), 1977; Vivien Leigh: A Biography, 1977; Sonya: The Life of the Countess Tolstoy, 1981; The Road to Tara: The Life of Margaret Mitchell, 1983; Matriarch Queen Mary and the House of Windsor, 1984; A Remarkable Woman: Katherine Hepburn, 1985; Early Reagan: The Rise to Power, 1986; The DeMilles: An American Dynasty, 1987; American Princess: A Biography of Shirley Temple, 1988; Royal Sisters: Queen Elizabeth and Princess Margaret, 1990; Wallis - The Novel, 1991; The Grimaldis of Monaco: Centuries of Scandals, Years of Grace, 1992. *Address:* c/o International Creative Management, Inc, 40 W 57th Street, New York, NY 10019, USA.

EDWARDS F E. *See:* NOLAN William Francis.

EDWARDS June. *See:* BHATIA Jamunadevi.

EDWARDS Norman. *See:* CARR Terry.

EDWARDS Page Lawrence Jr, b. 15 Jan 1941. Archivist. m. Diana Selser, 26 Aug 1986, 2 sons, 2 daughters. *Education:* BA, Stanford University, 1963; MFA, University of Iowa, 1974; MLS, Simmons College, 1982. *Appointments:* Staff, Breadloaf Writers' Conference, 1982-84; Writer-in-Residence, Flagler College, St Augustine, Florida, 1985-. *Publications:* Mules that Angels Ride, 1972; Touring, 1974; Staking Claims, 1976; Peggy Salte, 1984; Scarface Joe, 1985; The Lake, 1986; American Girl, 1990. *Contributions to:* Redbook; Woman's World; Bananas; Iowa Review. *Literary Agent:* Amanda Urban, ICM. *Address:* c/o Marion Boyars Ltd, 26 East 33rd Street, New York, NY 10016, USA.

EDWARDS Philip Walter, b. 7 Feb 1923, Cumbria, England, Professor of English Literature. m. Sheila Mary Wilkes, 8 May 1952, 3 sons, 1 daughter. *Education:* BA, 1942, MA, 1946, PhD, 1960, University of Birmingham. *Appointments:* Lecturer, University of Birmingham, 1946-60; Professor of English Literature, Trinity College, Dublin, Republic of Ireland, 1960-66; Professor of Literature, University of Essex, 1966-74; Professor of English Literature, University of Liverpool, 1974-90. *Publications:* Sir Walter Ralegh, 1953; Kyd, The Spanish Tragedy. (Editor), 1959; Shakespeare and the Confines of Art, 1968; Massinger, Plays and Poems, (Co-editor C Gibson), 1976; Threshold of a Nation, 1979; Hamlet, (Editor), 1985; Shakespeare's Pericles, (Editor), 1976; Last Voyages, 1988. *Membership:* Fellow, The British Academy, 1986-. *Address:* High Gillinggrove, Gillinggate, Kendal, Cumbria LA9 4JB, England.

EDWARDS Rowan (Judith), b. 19 Nov 1945. India. Writer; Former Teacher in Adult Education. m. Martin Brian Edwards, 18 Dec 1965, 1 son, 1 daughter. *Education:* BA (Hons), English, King's College, University of London, 1966; Certificate in Teaching English to Adult Immigrants (Royal Society of Arts), 1976. *Appointments:* Personal Assistant to Labour Member of Parliament and Junior Minister; Teacher, English as a Second Language, Adult Literacy, Inner London Education Authority; Freelance Editor, London, West Country; Freelance Writer (Novelist, Journalist); Examiner, A-Level Literature; Creative Writing Tutoring (contributed Romantic Fiction section to postal tuition course); Adjudicating, local competitions; Assessing in SS for South West Arts. *Publications:* 15 romantic novels, 1983-; trans into 15 languages in paperback; also large print and audio-cassette editions. *Contributions:* Short stories to magazines; articles to: Guardian; Bristol Evening Post; Birmingham Post; Travel, local and other specialist magazines. *Honours:* Bristol Poetry Competition, 1988; ORBIS Rhyme International Competition, 1989; 1st Prize for radio play, 6 Counties Festival, South West Arts, 1989; . *Memberships:* Society of Authors; Romantic Novelists Association; Society of Freelance Editors and Proofreaders. *Address:* 2 Highbury Hall, 22 Highbury Road, Weston-super-Mare BS23 2DN, England.

EDWARDS Ted (Brian), b. 25 Apr 1939, Leigh, Lancashire, England. Explorer; Author; Teacher; Song Writer. *Education:* BEd, Honours, Art & Drama, Manchester Polytehnic, 1975-79. *Publications:* A Slutchy Brew, 1971; Beyond the Last Oasis,1985; Fight the Wild Island, 1986; Beyond the Last Oasis, Film BBC TV, 1983; The Empty Quarter, BBC Radio 4 Programme, 1984. *Contributions to:* Expedition Year Book, 1983 1984, 1985; Readers Digest, 1986; other journals and magazines. *Memberships:* FRGS; PRS; MCPS; BASCA; BAEA. *Literary Agent:* Watson Little Ltd, London. *Address:* The Garret, 6 Westminster Road, Eccles, Manchester M30 9HF, England.

EFFINGER George Alec, b. 1947, America. Writer of novels, short stories, science fiction/fantasy. *Appointment:* Teacher of Science Fiction Course, Tulane University, New Orleans, 1973-74. *Publications:* What Entropy Means to Me, 1972; Relatives, 1973; Mixed Feelings (short stories), 1974; (with G Dozois), Nightmare Blue, 1975; Irrational Numbers (short stories), 1976; Those Gentle Voices, 1976; Felicia, 1976; Death in Florence, 1978, as Utopia Three, 1980; Dirty Tricks (short stories), 1978; Heroics, 1979; The Wolves of Memory, 1981; Idle Pleasures (short stories), 1983; The Nick of Time, 1986; The Birds of Time, 1986; When Gravity Falls, 1987. *Address:* Box 15183, New Orleans, LA 70175, USA.

EGLETON Clive Frederick William (Patrick Blake, John Tarrant), b. 25 Nov 1927. Author; Retired Army Officer; Retired Civil Servant. m. Joan Evelyn Lane, 9 Apr 1949, 2 sons. *Education:* Graduate, Staff College, Camberley, 1957. *Publications include:* Seven Days to a Killing, 1988; The October Plot, 1985; The Winter Touch, 1982; Backfire, 1979; Picture of the Year, 1987; Gone Missing, 1988; A Conflict of Interests, 1984. *Memberships:* Crime Writers Association. *Literary Agent:* Anthony Geff, David Higham Associated Ltd. *Address:* Dolphin House, Beach House Lane, Bembridge, Isle of Wight PO35 5TA, England.

EHRENBERG Miriam Colbert, hb. 6 Mar 1930, New York City, New York, USA. Psychologist. m. Otto Ehrenberg, 20 Sept 1956, 2 daughters. *Education:* BA, Queens College; MA, City University of New York; PhD, New School for Social Research, New York. *Publications:* The Psychotherapy Maze, 1977, 2nd Edition, 1986; Optimum Brain Power, 1985; The Intimate Circle, 1988. *Membership:* American Psychological Association. *Literary Agent:* Writers House. *Address:* 118 Riverside Drive, New York, New York, NY 10024, USA.

EHRLICH Eugene, b. 1922, America. University Faculty Member; Writer. *Appointments:* Associated with Department of English, Columbia University, New York

City, 1948-. *Publications:* How to Study Better, 1960, 1976; (with D Murphy), The Art of Technical Writing, 1962; (with D Murphy) Researching and Writing Term Papers and Reports, 1964; (with D Murphy and D Pace), College Developmental Reading, 1966; (with D Murphy), Basic Grammar for Writing, 1970; (with D Murphy), Concise Index to English, 1974; Basic Vocabulary Builder, 1975; English Grammar, 1976; Punctuation, Capiptalization and Spelling, 1977; (with others), Oxford American Dictionary, 1980; (with Gorton Carruth), The Oxford Illustrated Literary Guide to the United States, 1982; Speak for Success, 1984; Amo, Amas, Amat & More, 1985; The Bantam Concise Handbook of English, 1986. *Address:* 15 Park Road, Scarsdale, NY 10583, USA.

EHRLICH Paul, b. 1932, America. Professor of Population Studies; Writer. *Appointments:* Assistant Professor and Associate Professor 1959-66, Professor 1966-76, Bing Professor of Population Studies, 1976-, Stanford University, California; Advisor in Biological Sciences, 1966-75, Editor in Population in Biology, 1966-, McGraw Hill Book Co, New York City; President 1969-70, currently Honorary President 1970-, Zero Population Growth. Member, National Academy of Sciences; Fellow, American Academy of Arts and Sciences; Member, American Philosophical Society, 1991. *Publications:* How to Know the Butterflies, 1961; Process of Evolution, 1963, 1964; Principles of Modern Biology, 1968; Population Bomb, 1968; Population, Resources, Environment Issues in Human Ecology, 1970; How to Be a Survivor, 1971; The Bomb, 1977; Ecoscience: Population, Resources, Enviroment, 1977; Golden Door: International Migration, Mexico and the United States, 1980; Extinction, 1981; (with others), The Cold and the Dark: The World After Nuclear War, 1984; The Machinery of Nature, 1986; Earth, 1987; The Science of Ecology, 1987, (with others), Birders Handbook, 1988; Population Explosion, 1990; Healing the Planet, 1991; Birds in Jeopardy, 1992. *Address:* Department of Biological Sciences, Stanford University, Stanford, CA 94305, USA.

EHRLICHMAN John, b. 20 Mar 1925, Tacoma, Washington, USA. Writer. 4 sons, 2 daughters. *Education:* AB, 1945; JD, 1951. *Publications:* The Company (Washington Behind Closed Doors), 1976; The Whole Truth, 1978; Witness to Power, 1980; The China Card, 1986; Sketches & Notes, 1987; An Indispensable Guide to Santa Fe, 1987; The Rigby File, 1990. *Contributions include:* Newsweek, Time, New York Magazine; Travel & Leisure; Parade. *Literary Agent:* Morton L Janklow & Associates. *Address:* 795 Hammond Dr, 1607, Atlanta, GA 30328, USA.

EIBEL Deborah, b. 25 June 1940, Montreal, Canada. Poet. *Education:* BA, McGill University, 1960; AM, Radcliffe College, 1962; MA, The Johns Hopkins University, 1971. *Publications:* Kayak Sickness, 1972; Streets Too Narrow for Parades, 1985; Making Fun of Travellers, 1992. *Contributions to:* Canadian Literature; The Malahet Review; Moosehead Anthology; Canadian Woman Studies. *Honours:* Chester McNaghten Award, 1959; Arthur Davison Ficke Sonnet Award of the Poetry Society of America, 1965; Canada Council Arts Bursary 'B'. *Memberships:* The League of Canadian Poets; The Poetry Society of America. *Address:* 6657 Wilderton Avenue, Montreal, Quebec, Canada, H3S 2L8.

EICHENBAUM Luise Ronni, b. 22 July 1952, New York, USA. Psychotherapist; Lecturer; Writer. m. Jeremy Pikser, 1 daughter, 1 son. *Education:* BA, highest honours, City University of New York, 1973; MSW, State University of New York at Stony Brook, 1975. *Appointments:* Women's Therapy Centre, London, England, co-founder and co-director, psychotherapist and lecturer, 1976-80; co-founder and co-director, Women's Therapy Centre Institute, New York, New York, psychotherapist and lecturer, 1980-. *Publications:* Understanding Women: A Feminist Pychoanalytic Approach, 1983; What Do Women Want: Exploring the Myth of Dependency, 1983; Between Women: Love, Envy and Competition in Women's Friendships, 1989.

Memberships: Co-Founder of the Women's Therapy Centre, London, England; Co-Founder of the Women's Therapy Centre Institute, New York, USA. *Literary Agent:* Ellen Levine. *Address:* 80 E 11th Street, New York, NY 10003, USA.

EIGNER Larry (Laurence Joel), b. 1927, America. Writer; Poet. *Publications:* (some are broadsides): From the Sustaining Air, 1953, augmented ed 1967; Look at the Park, 1958; On My Eyes: Poems, 1960; Murder Talk: The Reception: Suggestions for a Play; Five Poems, Bed Never Self Made, 1964; The Music, The Rooms, 1965; The Memory of Yeats, Blake, DHL, 1965; Six Poems, 1967; Another Time in Fragments, 1967; The-/Towards Autumn, 1967; Air the Trees, 1967; The Breath of Once Live Things, In the Field With Poe, 1968; A Line That May Be Cut, 1968; Valleys, Branches, 1969; Flat and Round, 1969, 1980; Over and Over, Ends, As the Wind May Sound, 1970; Poem Nov 1968, 1970; Circuits: A Microbook, 1970; Looks Like Nothing, The Shadow Through Air, 1972; What You Hear, 1972; Selected Poems, 1972; Words Touching Ground Under, 1972; Shape Shadow Elements Move, 1973; Things Stirring Together or Far Away, 1974; Anything on Its Side, 1974; No Radio, 1974; My God the Proverbial, 1975; Suddenly It Gets Light and Dark in the Streets: Poems, 1961-74, 1975; The Music Variety, 1976; The World and Its Streets, Places, 1977; Watching How or Why, 1977; Cloud, Invisible Air, 1978; Flagpole Riding, 1978; Running Around, 1978; Heat Simmers Cold, 1978; Time, Details of a Tree, 1979; Country-Harbour-Arouond (prose) 1978; Earth Birds, 1981; Now There's-a-Morning-Holk of the Sky, 1981; Waters-Places-A Time, 1983; Areas, Lights, Heights (essays, reviews, letters), 1989; A Count of Some Things, 1991. *Address:* 2338 McGee Avenue, Berkeley, CA 94703, USA.

EINARSSON Sveinn, b. 18 Sept 1934, Reykjavík, Iceland. Writer; Theatre & TV Director; Councellor of Culture. m. Thóra Kristjánsdóttir, 17 Oct 1964, 1 daughter. *Education:* Fil kand, Stockholm, 1958; Fil lic, Theatre, 1964. *Appointments:* Member, Jury, Nordic Price in Literature, 1985-90; Vice President, International Theatre Institute, 1979-81; Pres Poetry Committee, Council of Europe, 1987-90; Member Board, European Cultural Centre of Delphi, 1990-. *Publications:* Gabriella in Portugal (children's book), 1984. Several Plays including: Egg of Life, 1984; I'm Gold and Treasures, 1985; Búkolla (children's play), 1991. Books on the Theatre: Theatre by the Lake, 1972; My 9 Years Down There, 1987, Icelandic Theatre, vol 1, 1991. *Honours:* Children's Book of the Year, 1985; Clara Lachmann-Price, 1990. *Memberships:* Icelandic Writer's Union, Pres, Union of Icel Playwrights, 1986-89, Pres Icelandic Theatre Union, 1972-89. *Literary Agent:* Almenna Bókafélagio, Reykjavík. *Address:* Tarnargata 26, 101 Reykjavík, Iceland.

EINZIG Barbara Ellen, b. 31 May 1951, Michigan, USA. Poet; Fiction Writer. m. 20 Mar 1985, 1 daughter. *Education:* BA, High Honours, Literature, University of California, San Diego, 1972. *Publications:* Color, 1976; Disappearing Work, 1979; Robinson Crusoe: A New Fiction, 1983; Life Moves Outside, 1987; Editor, Special Dreamworks Issue of New Wilderness Letter, 1981, Associate Editor, 1977-85. *Contributions to:* Various journals and magazines. *Honours:* Chancellors Prize, Literature, UC San Diego 1972; Granted MacDowell Colony Residency, 1984; Visiting Scholar, Tisch School of the Arts, 1984-87; Writer in Residence, Rockland Centre for the Arts, 1987. *Memberships:* Director, Water Street Arts Centre Poetry Series, 1974-75; Participant, Poetry in the Schools Programme, California, 1981-83. *Address:* 21 Bay Street, Piermont, NY 10968, USA.

EIRE Carlos M N, b. 23 Nov 1950, Havana, Cuba. Professor. m. Jane Vanderlyn Ulrich, 6 Jan 1984, 1 son, 1 daughter. *Education:* BA, Loyola University of Chicago, USA, 1973; MA, 1974, MPhil, 1976, PhD, 1979, Yale University. *Publications:* War Against the Idols: The Reformation of Worship from Erasmus to Calvin, 1986; Attitudes toward Death and the Afterlife in Sixteenth Century Spain, in progress. *Contributions* *to:* Sixteenth Century Journal; Archive for Reformation History; Church History; Journal of Ecclesiastical History; Journal of Religion; Religious Studies Review. *Address:* Department of Religious Studies, Cocke Hall, University of Virginia, Charlottesville, VA 22903, USA.

EISELE Robert H, b. 9 June 1948, Writer. *Education:* BA, 1971; MFA, 1974; UCLA, USA, 1971. *Appointments:* Playwrighting Fellow, Actor, American Conservatory Theatre, 1975-76; Associate Professor, Theatre Arts, Rio Hondo College, California, 1976-87. *Publications:* Plays: Animals are Passing from our Lives. Productions: A Dark Night of the Soul; A Garden in Los Angeles; Goats; The Green Room. Film: Breach of Contract, 1982. TV: Murder of Einstein, aired on PBS, 1981; Ordinary Hero & Schedule One (episodes of Cagney and Lacey), aired on CBS; 4 episodes of Crime Story, aired on NBC; Suspicion of Innocence; Shadow Play, The Rehearsal, No Place Like Home, Day of the Covenant, The Visitation, Starfire, Prisoners of Conscience, (episodes of The Equalizer, aired on CBS); Last Light, Film to be aired on Showtime. *Honours include:* Samuel Goldwyn Writing Awards, 1973; Oscar Hammerstein Playwriting Fellowship, 1973-74; Donald Davis Dramatic Writing Awards, 1974; American Conservatory Theatre Playwriting Fellowship, 1975-76; 1st Prize, Theatre Arts Corporation Playwriting Contest, 1979; Humanitas Award, 1986. *Memberships:* Writers' Guild of America; Dramatists Guild; Actors Equity Association; Academy of TV Arts & Sciences. *Address:* Ken Shearman & Associates, 9507 Santa Monica Blvd, No. 212, Beverly Hills, CA 90210, USA.

EISENBORG Deborah b. 20 Nov 1945, Chicago, Illinois, USA. Writer. *Publications:* Transactions in a Foreign Currency; Under The 82nd Airborne; Pastorale. *Honours:* O'Henry Story Award; John Simon Guggenheim Fellowship; Mrs Giles Whiting Award; Friends of American Writers Award; Ingram Merril Foundation Award; Award in Literature from the American Academy of Arts and Letters. *Literary Agent:* Lynn Nesbit. *Address:* c/o Lynn Nesbit, Jarklow & Nesbit Associates, 598 Madison Avenue, New York, NY 10022, USA.

EISS Harry Edwin, b. 17 May 1950, Minneapolis, Minnesota, USA. Associate Professor. m. Betty Jean Palm, 1 Sept 1978, 3 sons, 2 daughters. *Education:* BA, Humanities, BA, English, University of Minnesota, 1976; MS, Continuing Studies, Mankato State University, 1977; PhD, English, University of North Dakota, 1982. *Publications:* A Dictionary of Language Games, Puzzles, and Amusements, 1986; A Dictionary of Mathematical Games, Puzzles, and Amusements, 1987; Annotated Bibliography of Books about War and Peace for Young People, 1989. *Memberships:* Advisor, Sigma Tau Delta; Area Chair, Popular Culture Association; President, Michigan College English Association. *Address:* 18521 English Rd, Manchester, MI 48158, USA.

EKINS Paul Whitfield, b. 24 July 1950, Djakarta, Indonesia. Economist. m. Susan Anne Lofthouse, 24 Sept 1979, 1 son. *Education:* BSc, Engineering, Imperial College, London, 1971; MSc, Economics, Birkbeck College, London, 1988; MPhil, Peace Studies, University of Bradford, 1990. *Publications:* The Living Economy: A New Economics in the Making (editor), 1986; A New World Order, 1992; Wealth Beyond Measure (with Mayer Hillman and Robert Hutchison), 1992; Real-Life Economics (edited with Manfred Max-Neef), 1992. *Contributions to:* The Ecologist; Journal of Environmental Conservation; Development; International Environmental Affairs; Integrated Environmental Management; Service and Public Policy; Resurgence. *Memberships:* European Association of Evolutionary Political Economy; International Society for Ecological Economics; Society for the Advancement of Socio-economics; Society for International Development. *Address:* 42 Warriner Gardens, London SW11 4DU, England.

EKLUND Gordon, b. 24 July 1945, Seattle, Washington, USA. Writer. 1 daughter. *Publications:* The Eclipse of Dawn, 1971; Beyond the Resurrection, 1973; All Times Possible, 1974; If the Stars Are Gods, 1976; Find the Changeling, 1980; The Garden of Winter, 1980; A Trace of Dreams, 1972; Serving in Time, 1975; Falling Toward Forever, 1975; The Dance of the Apocalypse, 1976; The Grayspace Beast, 1976. *Contributions to:* Analog; Galazy; If Science Fiction; Fantasy & Science Fiction; Universe; New Dimensions; Amazing Stories; Fantastic. *Honour:* Nebula Award, 1975. *Membership:* Science Fiction Writers of America. *Literary Agent:* Martha Millard. *Address:* 6305 East D Street Tacoma, WA 98404, USA.

EKSTROM Margareta, b. 23 Apr 1930, Stockholm, Sweden. Writer Translator. (Virginia Woolf, Era Figes et alt). 1 son, 1 daughter. *Education:* Stockholm University, BA, 1956. *Publications:* Afternoon in St Petersburg; On Nature at Stora Skuggan; The Foreign Country of Love; Under the Empty Sky; Seperate Fortunes; Screens. *Contributions to:* Literary Critic Expressen; Columnist Skona Hem; Dagens Nyheter. *Honours:* Albert Bonniers Foundation; The Swedish Academy; The Swedish Academy Hirseh Foundation. *Memberships:* Swedish PEN; Swedish Institute. *Address:* Store Skuggans v 23, 11542 Stockholm, Sweden.

EKWENSI Cyprian, b. 26 Sept 1921, Minna, Nigeria. Pharmacist; Author. *Education:* Government College, ibadam; Achimota College, Ghana; School of Forestry, Ibadan; Chelsea School of Pharacy, Univerity of London; Iowa University. *Appointments include:* Lecturer, Igbobi College, Lagos, 1947-49; Lecturer, Pharmacy, Lagos, 1949-56; Pharmacist, Nigerian Medical Service, 1956; Head, Features, Nigerian Broadcasting Corporation, 1956-61; Director of Information, Federal Ministry of Information, Lagos, 1961-66; Director, Informations Services, Enugu, 1966; Managing Director, Star Printing and Publishing Co. Ltd, 1975-79; Niger Eagle Press, 1981-. *Publications:* When Love Whispers, Ikolo the Wrestler, 1947; The Leopard's Claw, 1950; People of the City, 1954; Passport of Mallam Ilia; The Drummer Boy, 1960; Jagua Nana, 1961; Burning Grass; An African Night's Entertainment; Yaba Round about Murder, 1962; Beautiful Feathers 1963; Great Elephant Bird; Rainmaker, 1965; Lokotown Juju Rock; Trouble in Form VI; Iska; Boa Suitor, 1966; Coal Camp Boy, 1973; Samankew in the Strange Forest, 1974; Samankwe and The Highway Robbers; Restless City; Christmas Gold, 1975; Survive the Peace, 1976; Divided We Stand, 1980; Motherless Baby, 1980; Jaguanana's Daughter, 1986; For a Roll of Parchment, 1986. *Address* 12, Hillview Crescent, Independence Layout, PO Box 317 Enugu, Nigeria.

ELDER Michael Aiken, b. 30 Apr 1931, London, England. Actor; Author. m. Sheila Donald, 2 Apr 1953, 2 sons. *Education:* Royal Academy of Dramatic Art, 1948-51. *Appointments:* Editor, The Scottish Life-Boat, 1971-83. *Publications:* The Alien Earth; Nowhere on earth; The Perfumed Planet; Oil-Seeker; The Walls of Jericho; Take the High Road, 4 novels based on the TV Series); 18 other novels; Radio & TV Scripts. *Memberships:* Writers Guild. *Literary Agent:* Yvonne Heather, Film Link. *Address:* 20 Zetland Place, Edinburgh EH5 3LY, Scotland.

ELDRIDGE Colin Clifford, b. 16 May 1942, University Lecturer. m. Ruth Margaret Evans, 3 Aug 1970, 1 daughter. *Education:* BA, 1963, PhD 1966, Nottingham University. *Publications:* England's Mission: The Imperial Idea in the Age of Gladstone and Disraeli, 1973; Victorian Imperialism, 1978; (Ed) British Imperialism in the Nineteenth Century, 1984; (Ed) From Rebellion to Patriation: Britain and Canada in the Nineteenth and Twentieth Centuries, 1989; (Ed) Essays in Honour of C D Chandaman, 1980; (Ed) Empire, Politics and Popular Culture, 1989. *Contributions to:* Various learned journals. *Honour:* Fellow, Royal Historical Society. *Memberships:* Historical Association; Association of History Teachers in Wales; British

Association of Canadian Studies; British Australian Studies Association. *Address:* Tanerdy, Ciliau Aeron, Lampeter, Dyfed SA48 8DL, Wales.

ELEGANT Robert Sampson, b. 7 Mar 1928, New York City, USA. Author; Journalist; Novelist. m. Moira Clarissa Brady, 16 Apr 1956, 1 son, 1 daughter. *Education:* AB, University of Pennsylvania, 1946; Japanese, Army Language School, 1947-48; Diploma, Chinese, Yale University, 1948; MA Chinese & Japanese Studies 1950, MS Journalism 1951, Columbia University. *Appointments include:* War, Southeast Asia correspondent, various agencies/associations, 1951-61; Central European Bureau, Newsweek, 1962-64; Others, Los Angeles Times/Washington Post News Service, 1965-70; Foreign Affairs Columnist, 1970-76; Speaker, lecturer, 1964-; Independent author & journalist, 1977-. *Publications include:* Books (non-fiction): China's Red Masters, 1951; The Dragon's Seed, 1959; The centre of the World, 1961; Mao's Great Revolution, 1971; Mao v. Chiang: The Battle for China, 1972; The Seeking, 1969; The Great Cities: Hong Kong, 1977; Pacific Destiny, 1990. (Fiction) A Kind of Treason, 1966; Dynasty, 1977; Manchu, 1980; Mandarin, 1983; White Sun, Red Star (US title, From A Far Land), 1987; Bianca, 1992. *Contributions to:* Numerous articles; New York Times Encounter (travel). *Honours Include:* Pulitzer Fellow 1951-52, Ford Foundation 1954-55; Edgar Allen Poe Award, Mystery Writers of America, 1967; Sigma Delta Chi Award, foreign reporting, 1967; Various other awards, recognitions, honorary societies; Senior Fellow, American Enterprise Institute for Public Policy, 1977-78; Fellow, Institute for Advance Study, Berlin, 1993-94. *Memberships:* Authors League of America; Past president, Hong Kong Foreign Correspondents Club. *Literary Agent:* Robert I Ducas, 350 Hudson Street, New York, USA. *Address:* The Manor House, Middle Green nr Langley, Buckinghamshire SL3 6BS, England.

ELFYN Menna, b. 1 Jan 1951, Glanaman, Wales. Materials Writer for NFER. m. 2 Sept 1974, 1 son, 1 daughter. *Education:* BA, Honours Welsh Literature, Univerity College, Swansea; Diploma, Education, University College, Aberystwyth. *Appointments:* Welsh Arts Council Bursary, 1981-; Writing Fellow, st David's University College, Lampeter Tutor, Creative Workshops, Extra Mural Dept. University College, Wales, Aberystwyth. *Publications:* Mwyara, 1976; Stafelloedd Aros, 1978; Tror Haul Arno, 1981; Hel Dail Gwyrdd, 1985, Editor; Mynd Lawr ir Nefuedd, 1986; Glasnos, co- editor, 1987; Fel y hed y Fran, 1986. *Contributions to:* various Welsh journals and English articles for Planet and Radical Wales. *Honours:* Welsh Arts Council Prize, Best Volume of Verse at Eisteddfod, 1977; Member, Welsh Academy, 1984. *Address:* Cartrefle, Penrhiw-Llan, Llandysul, Dyfed SA44 5NU, Wales.

ELISH Dan, b. 22 Sept 1960, Washington, DC. USA. Writer. *Education:* BA, Middlebury College, 1983. *Publications:* The Worldwide Dessert Contest; Jason and the Baseball Bear; The Great Squirrel Uprising. *Contributions to:* Sports Illustrated for Kids; 3.2.1 Contest. *Honours:* National arts Club, Scholar; The Bread Loaf Writers Conference. *Literary Agent:* Fran Liebouritz, Writers House. *Address:* 251 West 97th Street 2H, New York, NY 10025, USA.

ELISHA Ron, b. 19 Dec 1951, Jerusalem. Medical Practitioner; Playwright. m. Bertha Rita Rubin, 6 Dec 1981, 1 son. *Education:* BMed, BSurg, Melbourne University, 1975. *Publications:* In Duty Bound, 1983; Two, 1985; Einstein, 1986; The Levine Comedy, 1987; Pax Americana, 1988; Safe House, 1989; Esterhaz, 1990. *Contributions to:* Business Review Weekly; The Age; Vogue Australia; Australian Book Review; Centre Stage Magazine; Melbourne Jewish Chronicle. *Honours:* Best Stage Play, 1982, Major Award, 1982, for Einstein, Best Stage Play, 1984, for Two, Australian Writers' Guild; Gold Award, Best Screenplay, Houston International Film Festival, 1990; Best Television Feature, Australian Writers' Guild Award, 1992.

Memberships: Australian Writers' Guild; International PEN; Fellowship of Australian Writers. *Address:* 4 Bruce Ct, Elsternwick, VIC 3185, Australia.

ELIZABETH Von S. *See:* **FREEMAN Gillian.**

ELIZUR Yoel (Joel), b. 25 Feb 1952, Israel. Clinical Psychologist. m. sther Friedman, 2 Apr 1974, 1 son, 1 daughter. *Education:* BA, Psychology, 1973; MA, Clinical Psychology, 1976; PhD, Clinical Psychology, 1980. *Appointments:* Currently: Department of Psychology, Hebrew University of Jerusalem; Director, Medical Psychology Centre, Kibbutz Family Clinics, Tel Aviv. *Publications:* Institutionalizing Madness, 1989. *Contributions to:* Professional journals in psychology and psychiatry. *Honours:* Fulbright Fellowship, 1986-87. *Membership:* Israel Psychological Association, Chairman of Medical Psychology Section 1988-91. *Address:* PO Box 153, Mevasseret Zion, 90805 Israel.

ELKIN Stanley (Lawrence), b. 1930, America. Writer; Playwright. *Appointments:* Visiting Lecturer, Smith College, Northampton, Massachusetts, 1964-65; Joined Faculty of Washington University, St Louis in 1960, Professor of English 1968-. *Publications:* Boswell 1964; Criers and Kibitzers Kibitzers and Criers (short stories) 1966; A Bad Man 1967; The Six-Year-Old Man (filmscript) 1969; (ed)Stories from the Sixties, 1971; The Dick Gibson Show, 1971; The Making of Ashenden, 1972; Searchers and Seizures, 1973, 1974; Eligible Men (short stories), 1974; The Franchiser, 1976; The Living End, 1979; Stanley Elkin's Greatest Hits, 1980; George Mills, 1982; The Magic Kingdom, 1985. *Address:* Department of English, Washington University, St Louis, MO 63130, USA.

ELKINS Aaron J, b. 24 July 1935, Brooklyn, New York, USA. Lecturer; Writer. m. 1. Toby Siev, 1959, (div) 1972, 2 sons; 2. Charlotte Trangmar, 1972. *Education:* BA, Hunter College (now City University of New York), 1956; Graduate study at University of Wisconsin-Madison, 1957-59; MA, University of Arizona, 1960; MA, California State University, Los Angeles, 1962; EdD, University of California, Berkeley, 1976. *Appointments:* Personnel Analyst, Government of Los Angeles County, California, 1960-66; Training Director, Government of Orange County, California, 1966-69; Instructor in Anthropology and Business, Santa Ana College, Santa Ana, Califronia, 1969-70; Management Consultant, Ernst and Whinney, Chicago, Illinois, 1970-71; Director of Management Development, Government of Contra Costa County, California, 1971-76; Lecturer in Anthropology, Psychology and Business, University of Maryland at College Park, European Division, 1976-78; Management Analyst, US Office of Personnel Management, San Francisco, California, 1979-80; Director of Management Development, Government of Contra Costa County, 1980-83; Lecturer in Business, University of Maryland at College Park, European Division, 1984-85; Writer 1984-; Lecturer at California State University, Hayward and Fullerton, and at Golden Gate University, Member of Clallam County Civil Service Commission, 1987-. *Publications:* Fellowship of Fear, 1982; The Dark Place, 1983; Murder in the Queen's Armes, 1985; A Deceptive Clarity, 1987; Old Bones, 1987; Curses! in press. *Honour:* Edgar Allan Poe Award for best mystery novel from Mystery Writers of America 1988, for Old Bones. *Memberships:* Authors Guild; Mystery Writers of America. *Literary Agent:* Karpfinger Agency, New York. *Address:* c/o Karpfinger Agency, 500 Fifth Avenue, Suite 2800, New York, NY 10110, USA.

ELLERBECK Rosemary Anne L'Estrange (Anna L'Estrange, Nicola Thorne, Katherine Yorke), b. England. Writer. *Education:* BSc, Sociology, London School of Economics. *Appointments include:* Former publishers reader & editor. *Publications:* Numerous historical, contemporary & gothic novels. Titles include: Inclination to Murder, 1965; The Girls, as N. Thorne, 1967; Bridie Climbing, as NT, 1969; In Love, as NT, 1973; Hammersleigh, 1976; Rose, Rose Where Are You?, 1977; Return to Wuthering Heights, as

A.L'Estrange, 1978; A Woman Like Us, as NT, 1979; Perfect Wife & Mother, as NT, 1980; Daughters of the House, as NT, 1981; Where the Rivers Meet, as NT, 1982; Affairs of Love, as NT, 1983; A Woman's Place, as KY, 1983; Pair Bond, as KY, 1984; Never Such Innocence, as NT, 1985; Askham Chronicles 1898-1967, 4 titles as NT, 1985-87; Champagne, as NT, 1988. Also: The Enchantress 1979, Falcon Gold 1980, Lady of the Lakes 1981, as K.Yorke, reissued in 1 volume as The Enchantress Saga, as N.Thorne, 1985. *Membership:* PEN. *Literary Agent:* Richard Scott Simon Ltd. *Address:* 96 Townshend Court, Mackennal Street, London NW8 6LD, England.

ELLIOTT Janice, b. 14 Oct 1931, Derby, England. Novelist. *Education:* BA, St Anne's College, Oxford. *Publications:* Cave With Echoes, 1962; The Somnambulists, 1964; The Godmother, 1966; The Buttercup Chain, 1967; The Singing Head, 1968; Angels Falling, 1969; The Kindling, 1970; A State of Peace, 1971; Private Life, 1972; Heaven on Earth, 1975; A Loving Eye, 1977; The Honey Tree, 1978; Summer People, 1979; Secret Places, 1981; The Country of her Dreams, 1982; Magic, 1983; The Italian Lesson, 1985; Dr Gruber's Daughter, 1986; The Sadness of Witches, 1987; Life on the Nile, 1989; Necessary Rites, 1990; The Noise from the Zoo, 1991; City of Gates, 1992. Children's Books: The Birthday Unicorn, 1970; Alexander in the Land of Mog, 1973; The Incompetent Dragon, 1982; The King Awakes, 1987; Life On the Nile, 1989; The Empty Throne, (Children's Book), 1988. *Contributions to:* Numerous magazines & newspapers, short story collections. *Honour:* Southern Arts Award for Literature, 1981. *Memberships:* FRSL, PEN; Society of Authors. *Literary Agent:* Richard Scott Simon. *Address:* c/o Hodder & Stoughton, 47 Bedford Square, London WC1B 3DP, England.

ELLIOTT Lawrence, b. 18 Jan 1924, New York City, USA. Writer. m. (2) Gisele Suzanne Kayser, 19 July 1969, 1 son, 3 daughters, previous marriage. *Education:* BSS, City College of New York, 1950. *Literary Appointments:* Associate editor, Coronet Magazine, 1948-54; Freelance; Staff writer 1961-70, roving editor 1970-, Reader's Digest. *Publications:* A Little Girl's Gift, 1963; George Washington Carver, 1966; On the Edge of Nowhere, with James Huntington, 1966; Journey to Washington, with Senator D. Inouye, 1967; Legacy of Tom Dooley, 1969; I Will Be Called John, biography, Pope John XXIII, 1973; The Long Hunter: Life of Daniel Boone, 1976; Little Flower: Life & Times of Fiorello La Guardia, 1983. *Contributions to:* Numerous articles, Reader's Digest & other magazines & newspapers. *Honours:* Freedoms Foundation Medal, 1950; Alaska Press Club Award, best book, 1966; German Jugendbuchpreis, biography, 1970. *Memberships:* Overseas Press Club of America; Anglo-American Press Club, Paris; Authors Guild; Vice President, American International School, Luxembourg; Lotos Club. *Address:* c/o Reader's Digest, 54 rue de Varenne, 75007 Paris, France.

ELLIS Alice Thomas. *See:* **HAYCRAFT Anna Margaret.**

ELLIS Bret Easton, b. 7 Mar 1964, California, USA. Writer. *Education:* BA, Bennington College, Vermont, 1986. *Publications:* Less Than Zero, 1985; The Rules of Attraction, 1987. *Contributions to:* Rolling Stone; Vanity Fair; Elle; Wall Street Journal; Bennington Review. *Membership:* Authors Guild. *Literary Agent:* Amanda Urban, with ICM. *Address:* c/o Amanda Urban, ICM, 40 West 57th Street, New York, NY 10019, USA.

ELLIS Ella Thorp, b. 14 July 1928, Los Angeles, California, USA. Novelist. m. Leo H. Ellis, 17 Dec 1949, 3 sons. *Education:* BA, English, University of California, Los Angeles, 1967; MA, English, San Francisco State University, 1975. *Publications include:* Roam The Wild Country, 1967; Riptide, 1969; Celebrate the Morning, 1972; Halleluyah, 1974; Hugo and The Princess Nena, 1983; Where the Road Ends. *Contributions to:*

Mademoiselle. *Honours:* ALA Honor Books, 1967, 1969, 1972. *Memberships:* Authors Guild; Society of Childrens Book Writers; California Writers' Club; Sierra Club; ACLU; Opera International. *Literary Agent:* Julie Fallowfield, McIntosh and Otis. *Address:* 1438 Grizzly Peak, Berkeley, CA 94708, USA.

ELLIS Mark Karl b. 1 Aug 1945, Mussoorie, India. Training Consultant; Author. m. Printha Jane, 30 Aug 1969, 2 sons. *Education:* MA, Cambridge University. *Publications:* Novels: Bannerman; Adoration of the Hanged Man; Fatal Charade; Survivors Beyond Babel; Co-author: Nelson Counterpoint Series; Nelson Skill of Reading Series; Longman Business Skills Series; Professional English; The Economist: An English Language Series; Giving Presentations; Teaching Business English. *Literary Agent:* Deborah Rogers. *Address:* 39 St Martins, Marlborough, Wiltshire SN8 1AS, England.

ELLIS Richard J, b. 27 Nov 1960, USA. Assistant Professor. m. Juli Takenaka, 18 July 1987, 1 daughter. *Education:* BA with highest honours, University of Califorina, Santa Cruz, 1982; MA, Political Science, 1984, PhD, Politics, 1989, University of California, Berkeley. *Appointments:* Visiting Lecturer, University of California, Santa Cruz, 1989; Assistant Professor, Willamette University, Salem, Oregon, 1990-. *Publications:* Dilemmas of Presidential Leadership (co-author), 1989; Cultural Theory (co-author), 1990; American Political Cultures, 1993. *Contributions to:* Comparative Studies in Society and History; The Journal of Behavioral Economics; Presidential Studies Quarterly; Political Parties and Elections in the United States: An Encyclopedia; Journal of Theoretical Politics; Studies in American Political Development; Routledge Encyclopedia of Government and Politics; Society; Review of Politics; Polity; Western Political Quarterly. *Honours:* Regents Fellowship, University of California, 1983-85; I G S Harris Fellowship, 1986-88; Lyned and Harry Bradley Fellowship, 1986-88; Summer Stipend, National Endowment for the Humanities, 1991. *Address:* Willamette University, Salem, OR 97301, USA.

ELLIS Royston (Richard Tresillian), b. 10 Feb 1941, Pinner, Middlesex, England. Author; Travel Writer. 1 son. *Appointments:* Freelance Poet, Travel Writer, 1957-61; Assistant Editor, Jersey News & Features Agency, 1961-63; Associate Editor, Canary Islands Sun, Las Palmas, 1963-66; Editor, The Educator, Director, Dominica Broadcasting Service & Reuter/Cana Correspondent, Dominica, 1974-76; Managing Editor, Wordsman Features Agency, 1977-86; Editorial Consultant, Explore Sri Lanka, Colombo, 1990-. *Publications:* Author, 30 books including: Jiving to Gyp, 1959; The Cherry Boy, 1966; The Flesh Merchants, 1966; The Rush at the End, 1967; The Bondmaster Series, 1977-83; The Fleshtrader Series, 1984-85; The Bloodheart Series, 1986-88; Rave, 1960; The Rainbow Walking Stick, 1961; The Mattress Flowers, 1963; Burn Up, 1963; Drifting with Cliff Richard; The Shadows By Themselves; The Big Beat Scene; Rebel; Giselle, 1987; Guide To Mauritius, 1988; India By Rail, 1989; Sri Lanka By Rail, 1994. *Contributions to:* The Times, The Guardian, The Sunday Times, Daily & Sunday Telegraphs, Business Traveller Asia/Pacific and airline and hotel magazines in Asia. *Honours:* Honorary Dukedom of the Caribbean Island Realm of Redonda for services to Literature, 1961; Winner, Dominica National Poetry Awards, 1967, 1971. *Memberships:* Life Fellow, Royal Commonwealth Society; Life Member, Institute of Rail Transport, India. *Literary Agent:* Artellus Ltd., London, England. *Address:* Royal Cottage, Bentota, Sri Lanka.

ELLIS Wesley. *See:* **WALLMAN Jeffrey M.**

ELLISON Harlan Jay, b. 27 May 1934, Cleveland, Ohio, USA. Author. m. (1) Charlotte Stein, 1956, div. 1959, (2) Billie Joyce Sanders, 1961, div. 1962, (3) Lory Patrick, 1965, div. 1965, (4) Lori Horwitz, 1976, div. 1977, (5) Susan Toth, Sept 1986. *Education:* Ohio State

University, 1953-55. *Appointments:* Publisher, Editor, Rogue Magazine, Chicago, Illinois, 1959-60; Editor, Regency Books, Chicago, 1960-61; Editor, Dangerous Visions, 1967; Editor, Again, Dangerous Vision, 1972; TV Scriptwriter, 1962-; Book Critic, Los Angeles Times, 1969-82; Instructor, Clarion Writer's Workshop, Michigan State University, 1969-77, 1984; Editorial Commentator, Canadian Broadcasting Co, 1972-78; Editorial Commentator, USA Network's Sci-Fi Channel, 1993-; Film writer, 1964-; President, Kilimanjaro Corporation, 1979-. *Publications:* 58 books including: Web of the City, 1958; The Sound of a Scythe, 1960; Spider Kiss, 1961; Paingod, 1965; I Have No Mouth & I Must Scream, 1967; Partners in Wonder, 1971; Deathbird Stories, 1975; The Fantasies of Harlan Ellison, 1979; All the Lies That Are My Life, 1980; Stalking the Nightmare, 1982; Demon with a Glass Hand, 1986; Night and the Enemy, 1987; The Essential Ellison, 1987; Angry Candy, 1988; Harlan Ellison's Watching, 1989; Run for the Stars, 1991; Non-fiction and essay collections; 4 books on juvenile delinquency. *Contributions to:* Weekly columns to Los Angeles Free Press; Los Angeles Weekly. *Honours:* Numerous including: Most Outstanding Scripts Award, Writers Guild of America, 1965, 1967, 1974, 1986; 9 Hugo Awards, 1965-86; Nebula Awards, 1965, 1969, 1977; British Fantasy Award, 1978; American Mystery Award, 1987; Certificate of Merit, Trieste Film Festival, 1970; George Melies Award, Cinematic Achievement, 1972, 1973; Edgar Allan Poe Award, 1974, 1988; Bram Stoker Award, 1988, 1990; Major works in American Literature Award, 1988; World Fantasy Award, Best Short Story Collection, 1989; Inclusion in Best American Short Stories: 1993. *Memberships:* Writers Guild of America, West Council 1971-72, 1985-87; Science Fiction Writers of America, Vice-President 1965-66; Cleveland Science Fiction Society, Founder 1950. *Address:* 3484 Coy Drive, Sherman Oaks, CA 91423, USA.

ELLISON Virginia Howell (Virginia Tier Howell, Leong Gor Yun, Mary A Mapes, Virginia T H Mussey, V H Soskin), b. 1910, America. Writer for children and adults. *Appointments:* Part Owner and Editor, Howell, Soskin Publications, Inc, New York City 1940-48; Editor, Crown Publishers Inc and Lothrop Lee & Shephard Co, 1948-55; Director of Publications and Promotion, CWU National Council of Churches, New York City, 1961-64; *Publications:* (as Virginia T H Mussey), The Exploits of George Washington, 1933; (with Y K Chun as Leong Gor Yun), Chinatown Inside Out, 1936; (as Virginia Howell), Falla, A President's Dog, 1941; (as Mary A Mapes), Fun With Your Child, 1943; (as Mary A Mapes), Surprise! 1944; (as Virginia Howell), Who Likes The Dark, 1945; (as Virginia Howell), Training Pants, 1946; The Pooh Cook Book, 1969; The Pooh Party Book, 1971; The Pooh Get Well Book, 1973, all as Virginia H Ellison; inventor: Patent No. 4, 811, 747 on March 14. 1989 to Virginia H Reis (Mrs M J.). *Address:* 92 Mather Road, Stamford, CT 06903, USA.

ELMAN Richard, b. 23 Apr 1934, Brooklyn, New York, USA, Writer. m. Alice Neufeld, 9 Apr 1978, 2 daughters. *Education:* BA, Honours, Syracuse University, 1955; MA, Stanford University, 1957. *Appointments:* Lecturer, Literature, Bennington College, 1967-68; Adjunct Professor, Creative Writing, Columbia University, 1968-74; Lecturer, Sarah Lawrence College, 1971; Visiting Professor, University of Pennsylvania, 1980-82; Visiting Professor, SUNY Stony Brook, 1983; Visiting Professor, University of Arizona, Tucson, 1985; Hopwood Professor, (Visiting), University of Michigan, Ann Arbor, 1988; Abrams Professor, Notre Dame University, 1990. *Publications include:* Tar Beach, 1991; Disco Frito, 1988; Cocktails At Somoza's, 1981; An Education In Blood, 1970; The Reckoning, 1969; Lilo's Diary, 1968; The Breadfruit Lotteries, 1980; The 28th Day of Elul, 1967; The Poorhouse State, 1966; The Menu Cypher, 1983; Taxi Driver, 1976; Homage to Fats Navarro, 1975. *Contributions to:* Reviewer, New York Times; Newsday; National Public Radio; The Nation; Geo; Atlantic; New Republic; Antaeus; LA Daily News; Wall Street Journal; Peace News; Midstream; Partisan Review. *Honours:* PEN Syndicated Short Story Writers, 3 times; NEA Fiction, 1971; CAPS Fiction, 1974. *Memberships:* PEN;

Author's Guild; National Yiddish Book Centre. *Address:* PO Box 216, Stony Brook, New York, NY 11790, USA.

ELMORE James B, b. 13 Apr 1949, Buffalo, New York, USA; School Administration; Counselling; Music. m. Lorraine J Corbin, 1 Apr 1978, 2 sons, 1 daughter. *Education:* BA, 1971; MSc, Education, 1972; School Social Studies, 1972; School Counsellor, 1974; Certified Rehabilitaion Counsellor, 1977; School Administration, 1987. *Publications:* A Dream's Fantasy, 1978; The Legacy, 1978; A Special Child, 1980; Lorri, 1980; Jason, David and Kristen, 1980; A Thinker's Treatise, 1981; Essence, 1981; At the Point of a Dream, 1982; Wake Up, 1982; Look at Kristen, 1982; Remembrances, 1983; Canandaigua, 1985; Will There Be a Time, 1985; Armageddon: The Raging War, 1985; A New Tomorrow, 1987. *Contributions to:* Magic Aura Magazine; Buffalo Evening News; Rochester Art Scene Quarterly; The Chord; Niagara Gazette. *Honours:* United Nations Citation, 1981; Niagara Falls Chamber of Commerce, Certificate of Appreciation, 1981. *Memberships:* Various writing and music societies and professional organisations. *Address:* Elmore Enterprises, 1200 Doebler Drive, North Tonawanda, NY 14120, USA.

ELMSLIE Kenward Gray, b. 27 Apr 1929, New York City, New York, USA. Poet; Librettist; Talespinner; Performer. *Education:* BA, Harvard University, Cambridge, Massachusetts, 1950. *Publications:* Motor Disturbance, 1971; Circus Nerves, 1971; The Grass Harp, musical play, 1972; The Orchid Stories, 1973; The Seagull, a libretto, 1974; Tropicalism, 1975; 26 Bars (drawings by Donna Dennis), 1987; City Junket, 1987; Sung Sex (drawings by Joe Brainard), 1989. *Contributions to:* The Partisan Review; Paris Review; The Oxford Literary Review; Art & Literature; Big Sky; New American Writing; Locus Solus; Conjunctions; Oblek. *Honour:* Frank O'Hara Poetry Award, 1971. *Membership:* American Society of Composers, Authors and Publishers. *Address:* Box 38, Calais, VT 05648, USA.

ELPHINSTONE Francis. *See:* **POWELL-SMITH Vincent.**

ELRICK George Seefurth, b. 7 Oct 1921, Evanston, Illinois, USA. Writer; Editor; Publisher. m. Marilyn Jean Whaton, 11 Jan 1947, 2 sons. *Education:* BS, Northwestern University, 1943. *Publications include:* Exciting Africa, 1965; Exotic Asia, 1965; Australia and Oceania, 1965; North America, 1966; The Bubble Gum Kind, 1967; Adventure in Alaska, 1967; Night of Terror, 1968; The Shabby Sheik, 1968; The Cheetah Caper, 1969; The Yellow Moth, 1970; Mission Possible: The Zenolta Lak Story, 1970; The Joyce Murff Story, 1971; The Emmett Stovel Story, 1972; The Dog Who Could Talk Business, 1972; Lassie and the Sasquatch, 1975; Spiderman Zaps Mr Zodiac, 1976; The Collected Works of Buck Rogers in the 25th Century, with Robert Dille, 1977; The Science Fiction Handbook, 1978; You Can Negotiate Anything, with Herb Cohen, 1980; Hearts and Dollars: How to Beat the High Cost of Falling in and out of Love, 1983; A History of the Solomon Islands, 1946. *Contributions to:* Editorial director, abstract Publishing, Illinois; Field Correspondent, Stars and Strips, World War II; Former Editor, Holida Inn Magazine and United Airlines Magazine. *Honour:* Contemporary Authors. *Memberships:* Dickens Fellowship; Cakes and Ale Bookseller Club; Science Fiction Research Association; Past Editorial Board Member, Classic Press Incorporated. *Literary Agent:* Carol DeChant. *Address:* 2136 Fir Street, Glenview, IL 60025, USA.

ELSEN Albert Edward, b. 1927, America. Professor of Art History. *Appointments:* Professor of Art History, Stanford University, California since 1968. Assistant Professor of Art History, Carleton College, Northfield, Minn., 1952-58; Professor of Art History, Indiana University, Bloomington, 1958-68. *Publications:* Rodin's Gates of Hell, 1960; Purposes of Art, 1962; 4th edition, 1981; Rodin, 1963; (ed.) Auguste Rodin: Readings on His Life and Work, 1965; The Partial Figure in Modern Sculpture: From Rodin to 1969, 1969; Seymour Lipton,

1970; (with K. Varnedoe), Rodin Drawings, 1972; The Sculpture of Henri Matisse, 1972; Paul Jenkins, 1973; (with S. McGough and S Wander), Rodin and Balzac, 1973; Pioneers of Modern Sculpture, 1973; rev. edition as origins of Modern Sculpture: Pioneers and Premises, 1974; Modern European Sculpture, 1918-45, 1979; In Rodin's Studio, 1980; (with J.H. Merryman), Law, Ethics and the Visual Art, 2 vols., 1979, 2nd edition 1987; Rodin's Thinker and the Dilemmas od Modern Public Sculpture, 1985.

ELSOM John Edward, b. 31 Oct 1934, Leigh-on-Sea, Essex, England. Author; Journalist; Broadcaster; University Lecturer. m. Sally Mays, 3 Dec 1956, 2 sons. *Education:* BA, Hons Cantab, 1956; PhD, City University, London, 1991. *Appointments:* Script Advisor, Paramount Pictures, 1960-68; Theatre Critic, London Magazine, 1963-68; The Listener, 1972-82; Correspondent, Contemporary Review, 1978-88; Lecturer/Course Leader, Arts Criticism, Department of Arts Policy and Management, City University, London, 1986. *Publications:* Theatre Outside London, 1969; Erotic Theatre, 1972; Post-War British Theatre, 1976; The History of the National Theatre, (with Nicholas Tomalin), 1978; Is Shakespeare Still our Contemporary?, (Edited), 1989; Cold War Theatre, 1992; Post-War British Theatre Criticism, 1981; Change and Choice, 1978; The Shaping of Experience, 1986; Forthcoming Plays published: How I Coped, 1969; Malone Dies, (adapted from Samuel Beckett for Max Wall, Edinburgh International Festival, 1984; The Man of the Future Is Dead, 1986. *Contributions to:* The Observer; The Mail on Sunday; Encounter; Times Literary Supplement; The World and I; Sunday Telegraph; Plays International; Plays and Players; San Diego Union. *Memberships:* Liberal Party of Great Britains Arts and Broadcasting Committee, Chair 1978-88; International Association of Theatre Critics, President, 1985-92. *Address:* Stella Maris, Angelsea Road, Kingston-upon-Thames, Surrey KT1 2EW, England.

ELSTOB Peter, b. 1915, British. Writer. *Appointments:* Vice President, International PEN 1982-, Press Officer 1970-74, Secretary- General 1974-82; Director, Archive Press Ltd, 1965-; Director, Arts Theatre Club, London, 1946-54; Director, Trade Winds Films, 1958-62. *Publications:* Spanish Prisoner, 1938; (co-author) The Flight of the Small World, 1959; Warriors for the Working Day, 1960; The Armed Rehearsal, 1964; Bastogne, The Road Block, 1968; The Battle of Reichswald, 1970; Hitler's Last Offensive, 1971; (ed) A Register of the Regiments and Corps of the British Army, 1972; Condor Legion, 1973; (ed)The Survival of Literature, 1979; Scoundrel, 1986. *Memberships:* Vice-President, English PEN; Secretary-General, 1974-82, International Vice-President, 1982, International PEN; Writers Guild; Society of Authors. *Address:* Burley Lawn House, Burley Lawn, Hampshire BH24 4AR, England.

ELSY Mary, b. Great Britain. Freelance Travel Journalist; Writer. *Education:* Teaching Diploma, Oakley Training College for Teachers, Cheltenham, England, 1945. *Appointments:* Teacher, 1946-51; Realist Film Unit, 1953-55; Editorial Assistant, Children's Encyclopedia, 1959-62; Editorial Assistant, British Publishing Corporation, 1963; Editorial Assistant, Evans Bros, 1965-66; Children's Book Editor, Abelard-Schuman, 1967-68. *Publications:* Travels in Belgium and Luxembourg, 1966; Brittany and Normandy, 1972; Travels in Brittany, 1988; Travels in Normandy, 1988; Travels in Alsace and Lorraine, 1989; Travels in Burgundy, 1989. *Contributions to:* Daily Telegraph; Sunday Telegraph; Observer; Irish Times; Universe; Woman's Journal; In Britain; Illustrated London News; Travel; Ham and High; Camping and Walking; My Family; Voyager; Family Life. *Memberships:* PEN International; Society of Authors; Institute of Journalists; British Guild of Travel Writers; R Overseas League; Camden History Society. *Address:* 519c Finchley Road, London NW3 7BB, England.

ELTIS Walter, b. 23 May 1933, Warnsdorf, Czechoslovakia. Economist. m. Shelagh Mary Owen, 5 Sept 1959, 1 son, 2 daughters. *Education:* Emmanuel College, Cambridge; BA 1st Class Honours, Economics, Cambridge University; MA, Nuffield College, Oxford, 1960; DLitt, Oxford University, 1990. *Appointments:* Fellow, Tutor, Economics, 1963- 88, Emeritus Fellow, 1988-, Exeter College, Oxford, England; Director General, National Economic Development Office, London, 1988-92, Chief Economic Adviser to the President of the Board of Trade, 1992-; Visiting Professor of Economics, University of Reading, 1992-. *Publications:* Growth and Distribution, 1973; Britain's Economic Problem: Too Few Producers (with Robert Bacon), 1976; The Classical Theory of Economic Growth, 1984; Keynes and Economic Policy (edited with P J N Sinclair), 1988; Classical Economics, Public Expenditure and Growth, 1993. *Contributions to:* Many to economic journals and bank reviews. *Honours:* Adam Smith Prize, Cambridge University. *Memberships:* Reform Club; Political Economy Club. *Address:* Danesway, Jarn Way, Boars Hill, Oxford OX1 5JF, England.

ELTON Ben, b. 1959. Writer, Comedian. *Career:* Writer of television series including The Young Ones, Blackadder, Happy Families, Filthy Rich and Catflap; Writer for British comedians including Rowan Atkinson, Rik Mayall, Lenny Henry, French and Saunders and Adrian Edmondson. Highly successful stand-up commedian - Host of British television comedy showcase, Friday Night Live; Co-writer and presenter of 30 episodes of South of Watford, documentary series on London art and entertainment, 1984-85. *Publications:* Regular columnist on The Daily Mirror, 1986 and 1987; Bachelor Boys (The Young Ones Book), best selling book in UK in 1984 selling three quarter of a million copies. Also topped best seller lists in Australia; Stark, 1989; Gridlock, 1992. Recordings: The Young Ones single, an old Lionel Bart number with gags by Ben Elton, 1986, sold over half a million copies; Album Motormouth was top selling UK comedy album of 1987; 2 Plays: Gasping, 1990; Silly Cow, 1991. *Honours:* The Young Ones - British Academy Award for best comedy show of 1984; Blackadder - British Academy Award for best comedy show of 1987 and also won The ACE Award for best comedy of 1987 after its airing on American Cable Television. Friday Night Live was British Independent Television's Light Entertainment entry to the Montreux Television Festival in 1986. South of Watford won awards at Chicago Film Festival, The New York Festival of Film and Television and the San Francisco Film and Television Festival and was selected for the prestigious Input Festival held in Granada, Spain in 1987. *Address:* c/o Phil McIntyre, 15 Riversway, Navigation Way, Preston, Lancs PR2 2YP, England.

ELTON Geoffrey Rudolph, b. 17 Aug 1921, Tuebingen, Germany, Historian. m. Sheila Lambert, 31 Aug 1952. *Education:* BA, 1943, PhD, 1949, London; LittD, Cambridge, 1960. *Appointments:* Assistant in History, University of Glasgow, 1948-49; Assistant Lecturer, 1949-53, Lecturer, 1954-63, Reader in Tudor Studies, 1963-67, Professor of Constitutional History, 1967-83, Regius Professor of Modern History, 1983-88, Cambridge University. *Publications include:* The Tudor Revolution in Government, 1953; England Under the Tudors, 1955; Policy and Police, 1972; Reform and Reformation, 1976; F W Maitland, 1984; The Parliament of England 1559-1581, 1986; The Tudor Constitution, 1960; Reformation Europe, 1963; The Practice of History, 1967; Which Road to the Past, 1984; The Parliament of England, 1559-1981, 1986; Return to Essentials, 1991; The English, 1992. *Contributions to:* Collected in Studies in Tudor and Stuart Politics and Government, 4 volumes, 1973, 1982, 1992. *Honour:* Knighted, 1986. *Memberships:* Fellow, The British Academy, 1967, Publications Secretary, 1981-90; Fellow, Royal Historical Society, 1954, President, 1972-76; President, Selden Society, 1982-84; President, Ecclesiastical History Society, 1983-84. *Address:* Clare College, Cambridge CB2 1TL, England.

ELYTIS Odysseus, b. 2 Nov. 1911, Heracleion, Crete, Greece. Poet; Essayist. *Education:* Universities of Athens and Paris. *Publications:* Clepsydras of the Unknown, 1937; Sporades, 1938; Orientations, 1940; Sun the First, 1943; An Heroic and Funeral Chant for the Lieutenant Lost in Albania, 1946; To Axion Esti - It is Worthy, 1959; Six Plus One Remorses for the Sky, 1960; The Light Tree and the Fourteenth Beauty, 1972; The Sovereign Sun, 1972; The Trillso of Love, 1973; The Monogram, 1973; The Painter Theophilos, 1973; Steppoems, 1974; Offering My cards to Sight, 1974; Second Writing, 1976; The Magic of Papadiamentis, 1976; Signalbook, 1977; Maria Nefeli, 1978; Selected Poems, 1981; Three Poems, 1982; Journal of an Unseen April, 1984; Saphfo, 1984; The Mariner, 1985. *Honours include:* Drhc, Phil, Thessaloniki, 1975; Drhc, Paris, 1980; Hon DLitt, London, 1981; Nobel Prize for Literature, 1979; Benson Silver Medal (RSL), 1981. *Memberships:* National Theatre Administrative Council; Counsultative Committee, Greek National Tourist Organisation on the Athens Festival. *Address:* 23 Skoufa Street, Athens, Greece.

EMECHETA Buchi, b. 21 July 1944, Lagos, Nigeria, Writer; Visiting Professor; Lecturer. m. S Onwordi, 7 May 1960, 2 sons, 3 daughters. *Education:* BSc, Honours, Sociology, London University, 1974. *Appointments:* Professorial-Senior Research fellow, University of Calabar, Nigeria; Visiting Professor to many American Universities including Yale, Harvard, UCLA, temple, Brown, 1982-87; Fellow, University of London, England, 1986-. *Publications:* Second Class Citizen, 1975; The Bride Price, 1976; The Slave Girl, 1977; Joys of Motherhood, 1979; Rape of Shavi, 1987; Gwendolen, 1989; In the Ditch, 1972; Double Yoke, 1982; Destination Biafra, 1982; Head Above Water, 1987; Naura Power, 1981; A Land of Marriage, 1983; Gwendoline, 1989; Numerous children's books of essays. *Contributions to:* New Staesman; New Society; New International; Sunday Times Magazine. *Honours:* One of Best Young British Writers, 1983; Jack Campbell New Statesman Award, 1979; Best Black British Writer, 1978. *Memberships:* PEN International, Women's Committee. *Literary Agent:* Collins Publishers. *Address:* Collins Publishers, 8 Grafton Street, London W1X 3LA, England.

EMERSON Ru, b. 15 Dec 1944, Monterey, California, USA. Writer. *Education:* University of Montana, 1963-66. *Publications:* Princess of Flames, 1986; To the Haunted Mountains, 1987; In the Caves of Exile, 1988; On the Seas of Destiny, 1989; Spell Bound, 1990; Two-Edged Choice, novella in collection of 4 women fantasy writers entitled Spellsingers, 1989; Novelization (at invitation) of TV series Beauty and the Beast (3 episodes, 2nd book in series); Trilogy: Night Threads, 1990, 1991 and 1992; The Bard's Tale: Fortress of Frost and Fire (with Mercedes Lackey), 1993; Night-Threads: The Craft of Light (first vlume of a new trilogy in that world), 1993. As Robert Cray: The Sword and the Lion, 1993. *Contributions to:* Short story: A Golden Net for Silver Fishes, Argos Magazine; The Werewolf's Gift, Werewolves (a collection); Ali Achmed and The City of Illusion in Arabesques II, 1989; A Spell for Brass Buttons, The Crafters, Book One, 1991; Ironsides and Cottonsed Oil, The Crafters, Book Two, 1992; Of Women and Honor, Tales of Talislanta, 1992. *Honours:* Year's Best Fantasy, 1989, St Martin's Press for A Golden Net for Silver Fishes and Honorary mention for Werewolf's Gift. *Membership:* Science Fiction Writers' of America. *Literary Agent:* Richard Curtis Associates, New York, New York, USA. *Address:* 2600 Reuben Boise, Dallas, OR 97338, USA.

EMERY Edwin, b. 14 May 1914, California, USA. Professor; Author. m. Mary M McNevin, 28 Dec 1935, 1 son, 2 daughters. *Education:* BA, 1935, PhD, 1943, University of California. *Appointments:* Reporter, San Francisco Examiner, 1935; Editor, California Monthly, 1936-43; Staff, United Press, 1943-45; Faculty, University of Minnesota, 1945-. *Publications:* The Press and America, 1954, 7th edition, 1992; Introduction to Mass Communications, 1960, 11th edition, 1993; America's Front Page News, 1971; History of the American Newspaper Publishers Association, 1950; Highlights in the History of the American Press, 1954; Maincurrents in Mass Communication, 1985; Perspectives on Mass Communication, 1982; Reporting and Writing the News, 1983; Reporting the News, 1959; The Story of America as Reported by Its Newspapers 1690-1965, 1965. *Contributions include:* Editor, Journalism Quaterly, 1964-73; Gazette; Editor & Publisher; Media Asia; Annals of American Academy of Political & Social Science. *Honours:* Sigma Delta Chi Journalism Research award, 1950, 1954; Guggenheim Fellowship, 1959-60; Bieyer Award, 1980; Distinguished Scholar, National Academy of Science, 1985; Kobre Research Award, 1992. *Memberships include:* President, Association for Education in Journalism; Phi Beta Kappa; Kappa Tau Alpha; Society of Professional Journalists; international Press Institute. *Address:* 2524 Seabury Ave, Minneapolis, MN 55406, USA.

EMERY John Cameron, b. 19 Feb 1947, Cairns, Australia. Writer. m. Audrey Joan Rau, 18 July 1969, Canberra, 1 son, 1 daughter. *Education:* BA, Library Studies, South Australia Institute of Technology. *Appointments include:* Chairman, Writers Week, Adelaide Festival of Arts, 1984; Features editor, Lowdown Performing Arts Magazine, Australia/Canada. *Publications:* Summer Ends Now, 1980; The Sky People, 1984. *Contributions to:* Numerous magazines & journals, Australia, UK, USA, Kiev. *Honours:* National Short Story of Year, Australia, 1974; Awgie Award, Best Childrens TV Adaptation, 1984. *Memberships:* Australian Society of Authors; Executive 1979-84, Australian Writers Guild. *Literary Agent:* Goodman Associates, 500 West End Avenue, New York, NY 10024, USA. *Address:* 59 Sparks Terrace, Rostrevor, South Australia 5073, Australia.

EMMERICH Andre, b. 11 Oct 1924, Frankfurt, Germany, Art Dealer; Author. m. Constance Marantz, 25 Aug 1958, 3 sons. *Education:* Dalton School, Amsterdam, The Netherlands; Amsterdamschlyceum, Amsterdam; Kew Forest School, New York, USA; BA, Oberlin College, USA, 1944; Graduate Studies, New School for Social Research and New York University. *Publications:* Art Before Columbus, 1963; Sweat of the Sun and Tears of the Moon: Gold and Silver in Pre-Columbian Art, 1965. *Contributions to:* Many articles on Pre-Columbian art and other subjects for: Natural History; Americas; Travel and Camera; Art in America; American Heritage; Arts; Archaeology; Apollo; Art and Antiques; House and Garden.*Memberships:* Art Dealers of America, President, 1972-74, 1991-; American Association of Dealers in Ancient, Oriental and Primitive Art, Board of Directors, 1985-; President's Council, Memorial Sloan-Kettering Cancer Centre; Trustee, Visiting Committee, Allen Memorial Art Museum, Oberlin College, Ohio; President's Council, New School for Social Research, New York, 1988-; The Gallatin Art Program Advisory Council, New York University, 1989-; Century Association; Quaker Hill Club, Pawling, New York. *Address:* Andre Emmerich Gallery, 41 East 57th Street, New York, NY 10022, USA.

ENDERSBY Clive Paul, b. 9 Dec 1944, Edinburgh, Scotland. Author; Screenwriter. m. Nanci Rossov, 18 May 1986. *Publications:* Read All About It, 1981; Journey Through the Stars, (Novel serialised by Nelson Canada in School Readers - Zoom Shots), 1982, Flip Flops, 1983; Ripple Effects, 1984; Time Spinners, 1984; Star Flights, 1984; Sky Striders, 1985; Alice, The Wizard of Oz, 1983; Young King Arthur, the Adventures of Robin Hood, 1983; Snow White, 1983; Special Things; over 200 produced TV Scripts. *Honours:* TV Scripts have won: Silver Medal, new York Film Festival, 1981, Bronze Medal, 1983; Award of Merit, International Reading Association, 1981; ACT Awards, 1982, 1984; Award of Excellence, AMTEC, 1981; Bronze Medal, Columbu Ohio Awards, 1982. *Memberships:* Canadian Society of Children's Authors, Illustrators & Performers; Writers Guild of America; Playwrights Union of Canada; Alliance of Canadian Cinema, TV and Radio Artists; Performing Rights Organisation of Canada; British Actors Equity Association; Canadian Actors Equity Association.

Address: 23 Corley Avenue, Toronto, Ontario, Canada, M43 1T8.

ENGEL Diana (neé Reilly), b. 25 Aug 1947, New York, USA. Writer; Illustrator. m. 23 Aug 1969, 2 daughters. *Education:* Boston University, BFA, 1968; Pratt Institute, MFA, 1975. *Publications:* Josephina The Great Collector; Josephina Hates Her Name; The Little Lump of Clay; Gino Badino; Eleanor, Arthur & Claire; Fishing; The Shelf Paper Jungle. *Memberships:* Society of Childrens Book Writers. *Literary Agent:* Susan Schulman, 454 West 44th Street, NYC, 10036, USA. *Address:* 245 West 104th Street, New York, NY 10025, USA.

ENGEL Matthew Lewis, b. 11 June 1951, Northampton, England. Journalist. *Education:* BA, Economics, Manchester, 1972. *Literary Appointments:* Northampton Chronicle & Echo, 1972-75; Reuters, 1977-79; The Guardian, 1979-; Cricket correspondent, ibid, 1983-87; Future writer and columnist, 1987-. *Publications:* Ashes '85, 1985; Editor, Guardian Book of Cricket, 1986; Sportswriter's Eye, 1989; Sportspages Almanac, 1989. *Honour:* Sports Writer of the Year, 'What the Papers Say', 1985. *Literary Agent:* Richard Scott Simon Ltd. *Address:* 39 York Rise, London NW5, England.

ENGELS John (David), b. 1931, America. Poet, Professor of English. *Appointments:* Assistant Professor 1962-70, Professor of English 1970-, St Michael's College, Winooski Park, Vermont; Secretary 1971- 72, Trustee 1971-75, Vermont Council on the Arts. *Publications:* (with Norbert Engels), Writing Techniques, 1962; (with Norbert Engels), Experience and Imagination, 1965; The Homer Mitchell Place (verse), 1968; (ed) The Merrill Guide to Wuilliam Carlos Williams, 1969; (ed) The Merrill Checklist of William Carlos Williams, 1969; (ed) The Merrill Studies in Paterson, 1971; Signals from the Safety Coffin (verse), 1975; Vivaldi in Early Fall (collection), 1981; The Seasons in Vermont (verse), 1982; Weather-Fear: New and Selected Poems, 1958- 1982, 1983. *Address:* Department of English, St Michael's College, Winooski Park, VT 05404, USA.

ENGLE-PAANANEN Eloise, b. 12 Apr 1923, Seattle, USA. Writer. m. Lauri A Paananen, 1 Oct 1973, 1 son, 1 daughter. *Education:* BA, Foreign Affairs, George Washington University, 1947. *Appointments:* Guam News Columnist, Editor, Paradise of the Pacific. *Publications:* The Winter War 1939-40, 1973; Man in Flight, 1979; America's Maritime Heritage, 1975; The House that Half Jack Built, 1971; Medic, 1969; Earthquake: Alaska's Great Disaster, 1966; The America I Love, 1986; The Baltimore One-Day Trip Book, 1985; The Finns in North America, of Cabbages & The King, 1984. *Contributions include:* The World & I; Washington Times; Washington Post; Flying; Marine Corps Gazette. *Honours:* CINDY Award for film More than Shelter; Best Book Award, National Federation of Press Women; Best Book Award, Virginia Press Women (twice). *Memberships:* Society of Woman Geographers, former National Secretary; American Society of Journalists & Authors, former Regional Chairperson. *Address:* 6348 Cross Woods Drive, Falls Church, VA 22044, USA.

ENGLISH David, Sir, b. 26 May 1931. Editor. m. Irene Mainwood, 1954, 1 son, 2 daughters. *Appointments:* Daily Mirror, 1951-53; Feature Editor, Daily Sketch, 1956; Foreign Correspondent: Sunday Dispatch, 1959, Daily Express, 1960; Washington Correspondent, Express, 1961-63 Chief American Correspondent, Express, 1963-65; Foreign Editor, Express, 1965-67; Associate Editor, Express, 1967-69; Editor, Daily Sketch, 1969-72. *Publication:* Divided They Stand (a British View of the 1968 American Presidential Election), 1969. *Honours:* Knighted, 1982. *Memberships:* Board, Association of British Editors, 1985-. *Address:* Daily Mail, London EC4Y 0JA, England.

ENGLISH Isobel, b. 9 June 1925, London, England. Fiction Writer. m. Neville Braybrooke, 5 Dec 1953, 1 daughter. *Publications:* Novels: The Key That Rusts, 1954; Every Eye, 1956; Four Voices, 1960; Life After All, 1975; Meeting Point, play, 1978. *Contributions to:* Harper's; New Statesman; The Tablet; New Yorker. *Honour:* Katherine Mansfield Prize, 1975. *Membership:* PEN. *Address:* 10 Gardnor Road, London NW3 1HA, England.

ENRIGHT Dennis Joseph, b. 11 Mar 1920, Leamington, Warwickshire, England, Writer. m. Madeleine Harders, 3 Nov 1949, 1 daughter. *Education:* BA, Honours, Cambridge, 1949; MA, 1946; D Litt, University of Alexandria, Egypt, 1949. *Appointments:* Teacher of English Literature in Egypt, Japan, Berlin, Bangkok and Singapore, 1947-70; Co-editor, Encounter, 1970-72; Director, Chatto and Windus publishers, 1974-82. *Publications:* Academic Year, 1955; Memoirs of a Mendicant Professor, 1969; (editor) The Oxford Book of Death, 1983; A Mania for Sentences, 1983; The Alluring Problem, 1986; Collected Poems 1987, 1987; Fields of Vision, 1988; The Faber Book of Fevers and Frets, 1989; The Oxford Book of Friendship, (Editor with David Rawlinson), 1991; The Way of the Cat, 1992; Old Men and Comets, 1993. *Contributions to:* Scrutiny; TLS; Encounter; Observer; Listener; London Magazine; New York Review of Books. *Honours:* Cholmondeley Award, 1974; Queen's Gold Medal for Poetry, 1981; Honorary DLett, University of Warwick, 1982; Honorary Doctor University, University of Surrey, 1985. *Membership:* Fellow, Royal Society of Literature. *Literary Agent:* Watson, Little Limited. *Address:* 35a Viewfield Road, London SW18 5JD, England.

ENYEART James L, b. 1943, America. Photographer; Adjunct Professor; Writer. *Appointments:* Charter Director, Albrecht Gallery of Art, St Joseph, Missouri, 1967-68; Curator of Photography, University of Kansas Museum of Art, 1969-76; Executive Director, Friends of Photography, Carmal, California, 1976-77; National Conference Chairman, 1976, and Member of the Board of Directors, 1978-82, Nations Society for Photographic Education; Director, Center for Creative Photography and Adjunct Professor of Artm, University of Arizona, Tucson, 1977-89; Director, George Eastman House, 1989-. *Publications:* Karsh (catalogue), 1970; Kansas Landscape (catalogue), 1971; Invisible in America (catalogue), 1973; Language of Light (catalogue), 1974; No Mountains in the Way (catalogue), 1975; (ed) Kansas Album, 1977; Francis Bruguiere, 1977; George Fiske, Yosemite Photographer, 1980; Photography of the Fifties: An American Perspective, 1980; (ed), Heinecken 1980; W Eugene Smith; Master of the Photographic Essay, 1981; Jerry Uelsmann: Twenty-Five years, a Retrospective, 1982; Aaron Siskind: Terrors and Pleasures, 1931-1980, 1982; (with R D Monroe and Philip Stoker), Three Classic American Photographs: Texts and Contexts, 1982; (with others), Edward Weston Omnibus, 1984; Edward Weston's California Landscapes, 1984; Judy Dater: Twenty Years, 1986; Andreas Feininger: A Retrospective, 1986; (co-ed) Henry Holmes Smith: Collected Writings 1935-1985, 1986. *Address:* George Eastman House: 900 East Avenue, Rochester, NY 14607, USA.

EÖRSI István, b. 16 June 1931, Budapest, Hungary. Writer. m. 3 times div, 2 sons, 1 daughter. *Education:* Eötvös Loránd University, 1949-53. *Publications:* Prison Memoirs; A kihallgatás; Nine plays; Selected Poems; Several Others. *Contributions to:* Many Journals. *Honours:* József Attila Prize; Preis der Frankfurter Autorenstifung. *Memberships:* Hungarian Writers Union; Hungarian PEN Club. *Literary Agent:* Aritsjus, Budaest, Verleg der Autoren, Frankfurt. *Address:* Belgrád rkp 27, H 1056 Budapest, Hungary.

EPP Margaret Agnes, b. 1 Aug 1913, Waldheim, Saskatchewan, Canada. Writer. *Publications:* More than 30 books including: But God Hath Chosen, biography, 1963; A Fountain Sealed, novel, 1965, reissued 1982; Walk in My Woods, autobiography, 1967, reissued with update, 1990; This Mountain is Mine, biography, 1969, reissued 1990; Into All The World, travel, 1973; Tulpencasse, 1978; Chariots in the Smoke, novel, 1990. *Contributions to:* Numerous magazines and journals. *Address:* Box 178, Waldheim, Saskatchewan, Canada SOK 4R0.

EPSTEIN Ann Wharton. *See:* **WHARTON Annabel J.**

EPSTEIN Charlotte, b. 1921, America. Professor Emeritus; Writer. *Appointments:* Professor Emeritus, Temple University, Philadelphia, 1985-, Assistant Professor of Human Relations and Staff Associate of the Greenfield Center for Human Relations, 1957-61, Associate Professor of Curriculum and Instruction 1966-69, Professor of Curriculum and Instruction and Adjunct Proprietor of Nursing, 1969-74, Professor of Elementary education, 1974-85. *Publications:* Intergroup Relations for Police Officers, 1961; Intergroup Relations for the Classroom Teacher, 1968; Affective Subjects in the Classroom: Exploring Race, Sex and Drugs, 1972; Effective Interaction in Contemporary Nursing, 1974; Nursing the Dying Patient, 1975; Learning to Carer for the Aged, 1977; Classroom Management and Teaching: Persistent Problems and Rational Solutions, 1979; Introduction to the Human Services, 1981; The Nurse Leader: Philosophy and Practice, 1982; Special Children in Regular Classrooms: Mainstreaming Skills for Teachers, 1984; Murder in China (mystery novel) 1986. *Address:* Professor of Elementary Education Emeritus, Temple University, Philadelphia, PA 19122, USA.

EPSTEIN Lawrence Jeffrey, b. New York City, New York, USA. College Professor. m. Sharon Selib, 16 June 1973, 1 son, 3 daughters. *Education:* BA, 1967, MA, 1968, PhD, 1976, State University of New York, Albany. *Appointments:* Professor of English, Suffolk Community College, 1974-. *Publications:* Samuel Goldwyn, 1981; Zion's Call, 1984; A Treasury of Jewish Anecdotes, 1989; The Theory and Prictice of Welcoming Converts to Judaism, 1992; A Treasury of Jewish Inspirational Stories, 1993. *Contributions to:* Over 100 articles in Jewish studies to magazines and journals. *Address:* 533 College Road, Selden, NY 11784, USA.

EPSTEIN Seymour (Sy), b. 2 Dec 1917, New York, New York, USA, Writer; Retired Professor. m. Miriam Kligman, 5 May 1956, 2 sons. *Education:* College, 2 years. *Appointment:* Guggenheim Fellow, 1965. *Publications:* Leah, 1964; Pillar of Salt, 1960; Caught in That Music, 1967; Looking for Fred Schmidt, 1973; The Dream Museum, 1971; A pecial Destiny, 1986; September Faces, 1987; Light, 1989. *Contributions to:* Stories in: Esquire; Harper's; Antioch Review; Redbook; Articles in: The Denver Quarterly; New University Quarterly. *Honours:* Edward Lewis Wallant Memorial Award, for novel, Leah, 1965; Leah reprinted in Gems of Jewish Literature, 1987; Best Short Stories of 1962. *Memberships:* PEN; Author's Guild. *Literary Agent:* Danadio and Ashworth Incorporated. *Address:* 750 Kappock St, Apt 608, Riverdale, Bronx, NY 10463, USA.

ERHARD Tom, b. 1923, America. Writer; Playwright; Professor of Drama. *Appointments:* Information Director, Albuquerque Public Schools, New Mexico, 1953-57; Assistant Director for Press and Radio, National Education Association, Washington, DC, 1957-58; Professor of Drama, New Mexico State University, Las Cruces, 1960-. *Publications:* For the Love of Pete, 1954; The High White Star, 1957; Rocket in His Pocket, 1960, 1964; The Electronovac Gasser, 1963; A Wild Fight for Spring, 1966; In Search of Leaders, 1967; Stress and Campus Response, 1968; The Agony and Promise, 1969; The Cataclysmic Loves of Cooper and Looper and Their Friend Who Was Squashed by a Moving Van, 1969; The Troubled Campus, 1970; Lynn Riggs: Southwestern Playwright, 1970; The New Decade, 1971; 900 Plays: A Synopsis - History of American Theatre, 1978; Pomp and Circumstances, 1982; I Saved a Winter Just for You, 1984; A Merry Medieval Christmas, 1985; Laughing Once More, 1986.

Address: 2110 Rosedale Drive, Las Cruces, NM 88005, USA.

ERICKSON Donna Mary Hacking, b. 7 May 1940, Tremonton, Utah, USA. Writer; Poet; Entertainer. m. Royle Dee Erickson, 21 Aug 1958, 3 sons, 8 daughters. *Education:* Utah State University, 1962; Institute of Children's Literature, 1987; Writer's Digest School, 1987. *Appointments:* Instructor, Poetry Workshops, 1987. *Publications:* Book of Poetry, 1988. *Contributor To:* Rexburg Standard-Journal; Ensign; Country People Magazine. *Honours:* 3rd Place, Local Poetry Contest, 1968; 1st Place, Idaho Writers League Serious Poetry, Open Title, 1986; Golden Poet of the Year, 1985, 1986, 1987. *Memberships:* Idaho Writers League. *Address:* 533 East 900 South, Rexburg, Idaho 83440, USA.

ERICKSON Peter Brown, b. 11 Aug 1945, Worcester, Massachusetts, USA. Literary Critic; Librarian. m. Tay Gavin, 30 June 1968, 2 sons, 1 daughter. *Education:* BA, Amherst College, 1967; Centre for Contemporary Cultural Studies, University of Birmingham, England, 1967-68; PhD, University of California at Santa Cruz, 1975; MSLS, Simmons College, 1984. *Appointments:* Assistant Professor, Williams College, 1976-81; Visiting Assistant Professor, Wesleyan University, 1982-83; Research Librarian, Clark Art Institute, 1985-. *Publications:* Patriarchal Structures in Shakespeare's Drama, 1985; Skakespeare's Rough Magic: Renaissance Essays in Honor of C L Barber, 1985; Rewriting Shakespeare, Rewriting Ourselves, 1991; Shakespeare's Comedies, in series on Feminist Readings of Shakespeare, 1994. *Contributions to:* 16 essays in books and journals on Shakespeare and on contemporary African-American literature; 25 book and theatre reviews. *Honours:* Phi Beta Kappa, 1967; Amherst Memorial Fellowship, 1967-68; Kent Fellowship, Wesleyan University, 1981-82. *Memberships:* Shakespeare Association of America; Renaissance Society of America; Modern Language Association. *Address:* Clark Art Institute, PO Box 8, Williamstown, MA 01267, USA.

ERICKSON Stephen (Steve) Michael, b. 20 Apr 1950, Santa Monica, CA, USA. Novelist. *Education:* BA, 1972, Master of Journalism, 1973, University of California at Los Angeles. *Appointments:* Arts Editor, LA Weekly, 1989-1991. *Publications:* Days Between Stations, 1985; Rubicon Beach, 1986; Tours of the Black Clock, 1989; Leap Year, 1989; Arc d'X, 1993. *Contributions to:* New York Times, Esquire, Rolling Stone, LA Style, LA Weekly. *Honours:* Samuel Goldwyn Award, 1972; National Endowment for the Arts Fellowship, 1987. *Literary Agent:* Melanie Jackson. *Address:* c/o Melanie Jackson, 250 West 57th Street, Suite 1119, New York 10107, USA.

ERIKSEN Jens-Martin, b. 23 Feb 1955, Aalborg, Denmark. Writer. *Education:* Cand Phil, Scandinavian Letters. *Publications:* Nani, French and Swedish Editions, 1985; Jim og Jag, 1989; Den Hvide Vaeg, 1990; De Uforsonlige, 1992. *Honours:* Several grants, National Endowment for the Arts; Benzon Prize; Leo Estvad Prize. *Memberships:* Danish Association of Poets and Novelists; PEN. *Literary Agent:* Leonhardt Literary Agency, Copenhagen, Denmark; E W Cruse, Paris, France. *Address:* Norrebrogade 48, 4 tv, 2200 Copenhagen N, Denmark.

ERLICH Gloria C, b. Baltimore, Maryland, USA. Writer. m. Philip Erlich, 1 son, 1 daughter. *Education:* BA, Goucher College; MA, Stanford University; PhD, Princeton University, 1977. *Publications:* Family Themes and Hawthorne's Fiction, 1984; The Sexual Education of Edith Wharton, 1992. *Contributions to:* 10 articles to scholarly journals including: 19th-Century Fiction; Women's Studies; Literature and Psychology. *Honours:* Phi Beta Kappa; Prize for Independent Scholars, Modern Language Association, 1985; Fellowship, American Council of Learned Societies, 1988-89. *Memberships:* Modern Language Association; President, Nathaniel Hawthorne Society; Board, Edith

Wharton Society. *Address:* 41 Littlebrook Rd, Princeton, NJ 08540, USA.

ERSKINE Barbara, b. 10 Aug 1944, Nottingham, England. Writer. m., 2 sons. *Education:* MA (Hons), Edinburgh University, 1967. *Publications:* Lady of Hay, 1986; Kingdom of Shadows, 1988; Encounters, 1990; Child of the Phoenix, 1992. *Contributions to:* Numerous short stories to magazines and journals. *Membership:* Society of Authors. *Literary Agent:* Blake Friedmann, London, England. *Address:* c/o Blake Friedmann, 37-41 Gower Street, London WC1E 6HH, England.

ERSKINE Rosalind. *See:* **LONGRIGG Roger Erskine.**

ESCANDELL Noemi, b. 27 Sept 1936, Havana, Cuba. Poet; Educator. *Education:* Bachiller en Letras, Institute de segunda Ensenanza de la Vibora, 1955; BA, Queens college, NY, 1968; MA, 1971, PhD, 1976, Harvard University, USA. *Publications:* Cuadros; Ciclos; Palabras. *Contributions to:* Letras Femeninas; Third Woman; Dialogue; Peregrine; El Gato Tuerto; Plaza; El Comercio; Verbena. *Honours:* Residencies, Millay Colony for the Arts, 1983, 1990. *Memberships:* Modern Language Association; Massachusetts Foreign Language Association; American Association of Teachers of Spanish & Portuguese; Feministas Vnidas. *Address:* Department of Foreign Languages and Literatures, Westfield State College, Westfield, MA 01086, USA.

ESLER Anthony James, b. 20 Feb 1934, New London, Connecticut, USA. Novelist; Historian. m. (1) Carol Clemeau, 17 June 1961, div 1988, 2 sons. (2) Cam Walker, 24 July 1992. *Education:* BA, University of Arizona, 1956; MA, Duke University, 1958; PhD, 1961. *Publications:* The Human Venture; The Western World; Forbidden City; Bastion; Aspiring Mind of Elizabethan Younger Generation; Others include: Freebooters; Babylon; Bombs, Beards and Barricades; Generations in History; Conflict of Generations in Modern History; Generation Gap in Society and History. *Contributions to:* American Historical Review; Journal of Social History; English Literary History; Journal of Contemporary History; Journal of Political and Military Sociology. *Honours:* Fulbright Postdoctoral Fellowship; American Council of Learned Societies Fellowship. *Memberships:* Authors Guild; American Historical Association; World History Association. *Literary Agent:* Scott Meredith. *Address:* 1523 Jamestown Road, Williamsburg, VA 23185, USA.

ESMOND Harriet. *See:* **BURKE John Frederick.**

ESSER Robin Charles, b. 6 May 1935. Editor. m.(1) Irene Shirley Clough, 1959 (dec), 2 sons, 2 daughters, (2) Tui France, 1981, 1 son. *Education:* BA, Honours, MA, Wadham College, Oxford. *Appointments:* Edited, Oxford University Newspaper, Cherwell, 1954; Commissioned, King's Own Yorkshire Light Infantry, 1956; Freelance Reporter, 1957-60; Staff Reporter, 1960, Editor, William Hickey Column, 1963, Features Editor, 1965, New York Bureau, 1969, Northern Editor, 1970, Executive Editor, 1985, Daily Express; Editor, Sunday Express, 1986-; Group Editorial Consultant, Express Newspapers, 1989-90 *Publications:* The Hot Potato, 1969; The Paper Chase, 1971. *Address:* 35 Elthiron Road, London SW6 4EW, England.

ESSEX Harry J, b. 1915, America. Writer, Novels/short stories, Plays and Screenplays. *Appointment:* Teacher, Script Writing. *Publications:* Something for Nothing, 1937; Dragnet, 1947; He Walked by Night, 1948; (with F Niblo Jr, G W George and R B Altman), Bodyguard, 1948; (with Leonard Lee and R H Andrews), Wyoming Mail, 1950; (with F Rosenwald), Undercover Girl, 1950; The Killer That Stalked New York, 1951; The Fat Man, 1951; (with R Bradbury), It Came from Outer Space, 1953; Devil's Canyon, 1953; I Put My Right Foot In, (novel), 1954; The Creature from the Black Lagoon, 1954; (with R Hill), Raw Edge, 1956 (with R

Smith), The Lonely Man, 1957; Neighborhood Affair, 1960; One for the Dame, 1965; (with W H Right, A Weiss and T Jennings), The Sons of Katie Elder, 1965; Man and Boy, 1971; Fatty, 1974; Marina, 1981; Terror in the Skies, (for television), 1986.

ESSOP Ahmed, b. 1 Sept 1931, Dabhel, India. m. 17 Apr 1960, 1 son, 3 daughters. *Education:* BA Hons, English, University of South Africa, 1964. *Publications:* The Hajii and Other Stories, 1978; The Visitation, 1980; The Emperor, 1984; Noorjehan and Other Stories, 1990. *Honours:* Olive Schyeiner Award, English Academy of Southern Africa, 1979. *Literary Agent:* Ravan Press. *Address:* P.O. Box 1747, Lenasia 1820, Johannesburg, South Africa.

ESTLEMAN Loren D, b. 15 Sept 1952, Ann Arbor, Michigan, USA. Writer. *Education:* BA, English Literature/Journalism, Eastern Michigan University, 1974. *Publications:* Novels include: The Oklahoma Punk, 1976; The Hider, 1978; Sherlock Holmes vs Dracula, 1978; The High Rocks, 1979; Dr Jekyll and Mr Holmes, 1979; Stamping Ground, 1980; Motor City Blue, 1980; Aces & Eights, 1981; Angel Eyes, 1981; The Wolfer, 1981; Murdock's Law, 1982; The Midnight Man, 1982; Mister St John, 1983; This Old Bill, 1984; Kill Zone, 1984; Sugartown, 1984; Roses are Dead, 1985; Gun Man, 1985; Every Brilliant Eye, 1986; Any Man's Death, 1986; Lady Yesterday, 1987; Downriver, 1988; Bloody Season, 1988; Silent Thunder, 1989; Peeper, 1989; Sweet Women Lie, 1990; Whiskey River, 1990; Sudden Country, 1991; Motown, 1991; King of the Corner, 1992. Non-fiction: The Wister Trace, 1987. *Contributions include:* numerous professional journals including: Baker Street Journal; Mystery. *Honours include:* WWA Golden Spur Award, 1987; Michigan Arts Foundation Award, 1987; WWA Stirrup Award, 1983; WWA Golden Spur Award, 1981; Nominee, American Book Award, for The High Rocks, 1980; Nominee, Pulitzer Prize for This Old Bill, 1984. *Literary Agent:* Ray Peekner Literary Agency. *Address:* 5695 Walsh Road, Whitmore Lake, MI 48189, USA.

ESTORIL Jean. *See:* **ALLAN Mabel Esther.**

ETCHEMENDY Nancy Howell, b. 19 Feb 1952, Reno, Nevada, USA. Writer; Graphic Designer. m. 14 Apr 1973, 1 son. *Education:* BA, University of Nevada, Reno, 1974. *Publications:* The Watchers of Space, 1980; Stranger from the Stars, 1983; The Crystal City, 1985. *Contributions include:* Fantasy & Science Fiction; Shadows 8; Twilight Zone. *Memberships:* Science Fiction Writers of America; Society of Children's Book Writers; Western Art Directors Club. *Address:* 410 French Court, Menlo Park, CA 94025, USA.

ETZIONI-HALEVY Eva, b. 21 Mar 1934, Vienna, Austria. Political Sociologist. m. Zvi Halevy, 2 sons, 1 daughter. *Education include:* PhD, Tel-Aviv University, 1971. *Appointments:* Currently Professor, Bar-Ilan University, Ramat Gan, Israel. *Publications:* Social Change, 1981; Bureaucracy and Democracy, 1985; The Knowledge Elite and the Failure of Prophecy, 1985; National Broadcasting Under Siege, 1987; Fragile Democracy, 1989; The Elite Connection, 1992. *Contributions to:* Numerous magazines and journals. *Honours:* Fellow, Academy of the Social Sciences in Australia. *Address:* Department of Sociology, Bar-Ilan University, Ramat Gan, 52900 Israel.

EULO Ken, b. 17 Nov 1939, Newark, New Jersey, USA. Writer. Married, 1 son. *Education:* Attended University of Heidelberg, 1961- 64. *Appointments:* Playwright, director, novelist. Director of Playwrights Forum and O'Neill Playwrights; Artistic director of Courtyard Playhouse, New York; Member of Actors Studio Playwriting Workshop; Staff writer for Paramount 1988-. *Publications include:* Plays include: Bang?, 1969; Zarf, I Love You, 1969; SRO, 1970; Puritan Night, 1971; Billy Hofer and the Quarterback Sneak, 1971; Black Jesus, 1972; The Elevator, 1972; 48 Spring Street,

1973, published in Off-Broadway Theatre Collection, Volume 1, 1977; Final Exams, 1975; The Frankenstein Affair, 1979; Say Hello to Daddy, 1979; Novels: Bloodstone, 1982; The Brownstone, 1982; The Deathstone, 1982; Nocturnal, 1983; The Ghost of Veronica, 1985; House of Caine, 1988; Script writer for television. *Contributions to:* Magazines and newspapers including Back Stage, Janus, New York Post, New York Times, Off-Off Broadway, Show Business and Village Voice. *Honours:* Prize from O'Neill Summer Conference, 1971 for SRO; Grant from Howard P Foster Memorial Fund, 1972; Fellowship from Arken Industries and J & L Tanner, 1973-74; Winner of Children's Theatre Contest sponsored by Children's Theatre of Richmond, 1974 for Aladdin. *Memberships:* Italian Playwrights of America - The Forum; Writers Guild of America; Dramatists Guild. *Literary Agent:* Mitch Douglas, International Creative Management, New York. *Address:* 14633 Valley Vista Boulevard, Sherman Oaks, CA 91403, USA.

EVANS Alan (Alan Stoker), b. 2 Oct 1930, Sunderland, UK. Civil Servant. m. Irene Evans, 30 Apr 1960, 2 sons. *Education:* Grammar school. *Publications:* Thunder at Dawn, 1978; Ship of Force, 1979; Dauntless, 1980; Seek Out & Destroy, 1982; Deed of Glory, 1984; Audacity, 1985; Eagle at Taranto, 1987; End of the Running, 1966; Mantrap, 1967; Bannon, 1968; Vicious Circle, 1970; The Big Deal, 1971; Night Action, 1989; Orphans of the Storm, 1990. Also various books for children, short stories. *Contributions to:* Various newspapers & magazines. *Memberships:* Crime Writers Association; Society of Authors. *Literary Agent:* Murray Pollinger. *Address:* 9 Dale Road, Walton-on-Thames, Surrey KT12 2PY, UK.

EVANS Craig Alan, b. 21 Jan 1952, Ontario, California, USA. Professor of Biblical Literature. m. Virginia Anne McKee, 22 June 1974, 2 daughters. *Education:* BA, Claremont McKenna College, 1974; MDiv, Western Seminary, 1977; MA, 1980, PhD, 1983, Claremont Graduate School. *Publications:* Early Jewish and Christian Exegesis, 1987; To See And Not Perceive, 1989; Life of Jesus Research, 1989; Luke, 1990. *Contributions to:* The Colossian Mystics, to Biblica, 1982; Paul and the Hermeneutics of 'True Prophecy' to Biblica, 1984; Jesus' Action in the Temple: Cleansing or Portent of Destruction?, to Catholic Biblical Quarterly, 1989. *Memberships:* Institute for Biblical Research; Society of Biblical Literature; Society of New Testament Studies. *Address:* Trinity Western University, 7600 Glover Road, Langley, British Columbia, Canada V3A 6H4.

EVANS Gillian Rosemary, b. 26 Oct 1944, Birmingham, England. *Education:* St Annes College, Oxford, BA, 1966; MA, 1970; PhD, 1974; D Litt, 1983; Litt D, 1983. *Appointments:* Associated with Queen Annes School, Caversham, Berkshire, 1967-72; University of Reading, Berkshire, 1972-78; Department of Theology, University of Bristol, 1978-80; Lecturer, Cambridge University, Cambridge, 1980-; Research Reader, Theology for British Academy, 1986-88. *Publications:* Old Arts and New Theology; Problems of Authority in the Reformation Debates; Authority in the Church; Anselm and Talking About God; Others include: A Concordance to the Works of St Anselm; Augustine on Evil. *Memberships:* Royal Historial Society. *Address:* Faculty of History, Cambridge University, Cambridge, England.

EVANS Grose, b. 1916, America. Writer. *Appointments:* Professorial Lecturer in Art History, 1953-61, Adjunct Professor 1973-90, George Washington University; Curator, National Gallery of Art, Washington, DC, 1946-73. *Publications:* Benjamin West and the Taste of his Time, 1959; Vincent Van Gogh, 1968. *Address:* 2308 Glasgow Road, Alexandria, VA 22307, USA.

EVANS Harold Matthew, b. 28 June 1928, England. Editor; Writer. m. 21 Aug 1981, 2 sons, 2 daughters.

Education: Durham University, 1949-52; Chicago University, 1956; MA, Durham University, 1962. *Appointments:* Editor, Northern Echo, 1961-65; Editor, Sunday Times, 1967-81; Editor, The Times, 1981-82; Editor in Chief, Atlantic Monthly Press, 1984-86; Editorial Director, US News and World Report, Editor-in-Chief, Conde Nast Traveler, 1986-. *Publications:* Good Times, Bad Times, 1983; Pictures on a Page, 1978; Newsmans English, 1971; Newspaper Design, 1973; Newspaper Headlines, 1974; Newspaper Typography, 1974; Co-Author, We Learned to Ski, Suffer the Children, Eye-Witness, Front Page History. *Contributions to:* numerous including: Punch; Harpers; US News and World Report; Encyclopaedia Britannica. *Honours:* Journalist of the Year, British Press Awards, 1967; Editor of the Year, British Press Awards, 1973; Hood Medal, Royal Photographic Society, 1981; Honorary Doctorate, University of Stirling, 1981; Editor of the Year, (Granada), 1982. *Memberships:* International Press Institute; Garrick Club, London; Century, New York. *Literary Agent:* Michael Sissons, A D Peters, London; Mortimer Janklow, New York. *Address:* c/o Condé Nast's Traveler Magazine, 360 Madison Avenue, New York, NY 10017, USA.

EVANS John David Gemmill, b. 27 Aug 1942, London, England. University Professor. m. Rosemary Ellis, 14 Sept 1974. *Education:* Queens' College, Cambridge, 1960-67; BA Class I, 1963, MA, 1967; Sidney Sussex College, Cambridge, 1963-69; PhD, 1969. *Publications:* Aristotle's Concept of Dialectic, 1977; Truth and Proof, 1979; Aristotle, 1987; Moral Philosophy and Contemporary Problems, 1987. *Contributions to:* Philosophy; Philosophical Quarterly; Philosophical Books; Contemporary German Philosophy; Annales; Philosophical Studies; Irish Philosophical Journal; Others. *Memberships:* Royal Irish Academy; Royal Institute of Philosophy; International Federation of Philosophical Societies; Aristotelian Society; British Society for the History of Philosophy. *Address:* Philosophy Department, Queen's University, Belfast BT7 1NN, Northern Ireland.

EVANS Julia (Polly Hobson), b. 1913, Britain. Writer of mystery/crime/suspense and children's fiction. *Publications:* All as Polly Hobson: Brought Up in Bloomsbury, 1959; The Mystery House, 1963; Murder Won't Out, 1964; Titty's Dead (USA as A Terrible Thing Happened to Miss Dupont), 1968; The Three Graces, 1970; Henry Bada-Bada (with J Rendel), 1971; Venus and Her Prey, 1975; Sarah's Story, 1983. *Address:* 21 The Close, Chequens Park, Wye, Ashford, Kent, England.

EVANS Max, b. 1925, America. Writer; Painter. *Appointments:* Vice President, Taos Minerals Inc, 1955-58 and President, Solar Metals Inc, 1957-59, both in Taos, New Mexico. *Publications:* Southwest Wind (short stories), 1958; Long John Dunn of Taos, 1959; The Rounders, 1960; The Hi Lo Country, 1961; Three Short Novels: The Great Wedding, The One-Eyed Sky, My Pardner, 1963; The Mountain of Gold, 1965; Shadow of Thunder, 1969; Bobby Jack Smith, You Dirty Coward! 1974; The White Shadow, 1977; Three West: Conversations with Vardis Fisher, Max Evans, Michael Straight, 1970; Sam Peckinpah, Master of Violence, 1972; Xavier's Folly and Other Stories, 1984; Super Bull and Other True Escapades, 1985. *Address:* 1111 Ridgecrest Drive SE, Albuquerque, NM 87108, USA.

EVANS Morgan. *See:* **DAVIS Leslie Purnell.**

EVANS Stuart (Hugh Tracey), b. 20 Oct 1934, Swansea, Wales. Writer. m. Kathleen Bridget Treacy, 31 Dec 1960 (dec 1993). *Education:* MA, Honours, English Language & Literature, Diploma, Education, Jesus College, Oxford. *Publications:* The Windmill Sequence: Centres of Ritual, 1978; Occupational Debris, 1979; Temporary Hearths, 1982; Houses on he Site, 1984; Seasonal Tribal Feasts, 1987; Meritocrats, 1974; The Gardens of the Casino, 1976; The Caves of Alienation, 1977; The Function of the Fool, poems, 1977; Imaginary Gardens with Real Toads, poems, 1972.

Contributions to: Reviewer for The Times, The Independent. *Honours:* Newdigate Prize for English Verse, 1955; Welsh Arts Council Prize, 1978. *Memberships:* Yr Academi Cymreig; Marylebone Cricket Club. *Address:* 9 Abbey Park Road, Grimsby DN32 0HJ, England.

EVANS Tabor. *See:* **KNOTT William Cecil.**

EVELING (Harry) Stanley, b. 1925, Britain. Playwright; Screenwriter. *Appointments:* Teaching Fellow, Edinburgh University, Assistant Lecturer, Department of Logic and Metaphysics, King's College, Aberdeen University 1955-57; Lecturer, Department of Philosophy, University College of Wales, Aberystwyth, 1957-60. *Publications:* Poems, 1956; The Lunatic, The Secret Sportsman and the Woman Next Door and Viberations, 1970; The Baldchites and The Strange Case of Martin Richter, 1970; Come and Be Killed and Dear Janet Rosenberg, Dear Mr Kooning, 1971; The Total Theatre (non-fiction) 1972; Mister, in A Decade's Drama, 1980; The Buglar Boy and His Swish Friend, 1983. *Address:* 30 Comely Bank, Edinburgh EH4 1AS, Scotland.

EVELYN John Michael (Michael Underwood), b. 2 June 1916, Worthing, Sussex, England. Retired Lawyer; Writer. *Education:* MA, Oxford University; Barrister at Law. *Publications:* 45 Crime Novels written under the name of Michael Underwood, 1954-90; The Seeds of Murder, 1991; Guilty Conscience, 1992. *Honour:* CB, 1976. *Memberships:* Detection Club; Chairman, Crime Writers Association, 1964-65. *Literary Agent:* A M Heath & Company Ltd. *Address:* 100 Ashdown, Eaton Road, Hove, Sussex, BN3 3AR, England.

EVERETT Peter, b. 1931, Britain. Writer; Playwright; Screenwriter. *Publications:* A Day of Dwarfs, 1962; The Instrument, 1962; Negatives, 1964; The Fetch, 1966; The Last of the Long-Haired Boys (screenplay), 1971; Visions of Heydrich, 1979; A Death in Ireland, 1981. *Address:* c/o Little Brown, 34 Beacon Street, Boston, MA 02106, USA.

EVERS Larry (Lawrence Joseph), b. 15 Aug 1946, Grand Island, Nebraska, USA. Professor of English. m. Barbara Zion Erygutis, 20 Dec 1982, 1 son, 1 daughter. *Education:* BA, 1968, MA, 1969, PhD, 1972, University of Nebraska, Lincoln, Postdoctoral Fellow, University of Chicago, 1973-74. *Appointments:* Assistant Professor, English, 1974-86, Full Professor, English, 1986, University of Arizona, Tucson. *Publications:* Words and Place: Native Literature from the American Southwest, 1979; The South Corner of Time, 1980; With Felipe S Molina: Yaqui Deer Songs-Maso Burikam, 1987; Woi Bwikam-Coyote Songs, 1990; Hiakim: The Yaqui Homeland, 1992. *Honours:* National Endowment for the Arts Fellowship, 1972-73; 1st Place, The Chicago Folklore Prize, 1987; Burlington Foundation Award, 1992. *Memberships:* Modern Language Association; Commission on the Literatures and Languages of America, 1984-87. *Address:* 273 N Main Avenue, Tucson, AZ 85701, USA.

EVERSON William Oliver, (Brother Antoninus), b. 10 Sept 1912, Sacramento, California, USA. Poet. m. (1) Edna Poulson, 1938 (div 1948); (2) Mary Fabilli, 1948 (div 1960); (3) Susanna Rickson, 1969, 1 stepson. *Education:* Fresno State College, California, 1931, 1934-35; Conscientious objector during World War II, with the Civilian Public Service 1943-46. *Appointments:* Worked for the Civilian Conservation Corps, 1933-34; Co- Founder, Untied Press, Wadport, Oregon; Staff member, University of California Press, Berkeley, 1947-49; Member of the Catholic Worker Movement, 1950-51; Dominican lay brother (Brother Antoninus), 1951-69; Poet-in-Residence, Kresge College, University of California, Santa Cruz, 1971-82. *Publications include:* Verse as William Everson includes: Blame It on the Jet Stream! 1978; The Masks of Drought, 1980; Eastward the Armies: Selected Poems 1935-42 That Present the

Poet's Pacifist Position Through the Second World War, edited by Les Ferriss, 1980; Renegade Christmas, 1984. Verse as Brother Antoninus includes: The Vision of Felicity, 1966; The Rose of Solitude (collection) 1967; The Achievement pf Brother Antoninus: A Comprehensive Selection of His Poems with a Critical Introduction, by Qilliam Stafford, 1967; A Canticle to the Waterbirds, 1968; The City Does Not Die, 1969; The Last Crusade, 1969; Who Is She That Looketh Forth as the Morning, 1972. Recording: Savagery of Love, 1968. Author or editor of other works. *Honours:* Guggenheim fellowship, 1949; Shelley Memorial Award 1978; National Endowment for the Arts grant, 1982. *Address:* 312 Swanton Road, Davenport, CA 95017, USA.

EWART Gavin Buchanan, b. 4 Feb 1916, London, England, Freelance Writer. m. Margaret Adelaide Bennett, 24 Mar 1956, 1 son, 1 daughter. *Education:* Wellington College, 1929-33; Christ' s College, Cambridge, 1934-37; Exhibitioner, 1936; BA, 1937; MA, 1942. *Appointments:* Literary Editor, The Granta, 1936-37; Production Manager, Editions Poetry London, 1946. *Publications:* The Collected Ewart 1933-1980; The Gavin Ewart Show, 1971; The Penguin Book of Light Verse, (Editor), 1980; The Complete Little Ones of Gavin Ewart, 1986; Pleasures of the Flesh, 1966; Penultimate Poems, 1989; The Learned Hippopotamus, Caterpillar Stew, (for children); Selected Poems 1933-1988 (USA), 1988; Collected Poems, 1980-1990, 1991; Like It Or Not, 1992; Last Poems, 1992. *Contributor to:* Times Literary Supplement; New Statesman; Encounter; London Magazine; Ambit; The Listener; New Verse; Poetry London; New Directions. *Honours:* Colmondeley Award for Poetry, 1971; Travelling Scholarship, 1978. *Memberships:* The Royal Society of Literature; The Poetry Society, Chairman, 1978; PEN International; Society of Authors. *Address:* 57 Kenilworth Court, Lower Richmond Road, London SW15 1EN, England.

EXTON Clive, b. 11 Apr 1930. Scriptwriter; Playwright. m. (1) Patricia Fletcher Ferguson, 1951, (div 1957), 2 daughters, (2) Margaret Josephine Reid, 1 son, 2 daughters. *Education:* Christ's Hospital. *Publications:* TV Plays: No Fixed Abode, 1959; The Silk Purse; Where I Live; Some Talk of Alexander; Hold My Hand, Soldier; I'll Have You to Remember; The Big Eat; The Trial of Doctor Fancy; Land of My Dreams; The Close Prisoner; The Bone Yard; Are You Ready for the Music; The Rainbirds; Killers (series); Stigma; Henry Intervenes; The Crezz (series); Dick Barton - Special Agent (series); Dramatizations of Ruth Rendell's 'Wexford' novels for TVS; Dramatizations of Agatha Christie's 'Poirot' short stories for LWT. Stage Plays: Have You Any Dirty Washing, Mother Dear?; Twixt; Murder is Easy (from Agatha Christie novel); Jeeves and the Last of the Woosters (from characters created by P G Wodehouse. Films: Night Must Fall; Isadora; Entertaining Mr Sloane; Ten Rillington Place; Running Scared; Doomwatch; The House in Nightmare Park; The Awakening. Dramatization of works of P G Wodehouse under the title, Jeeves and Wooster, for Granada TV (Writers' Guild Award, 1992). *Publications:* No Fixed Abode (in Six Granada Plays Anthology), 1960; Have You Any Dirty Washing, Mother Dear? (in Plays of the Year, volume 37), 1970. *Address:* c/o Rochell Stevens & Co, 2 Terret's Place, London N1 1QZ, England.

EYEN Tom, b. 14 Aug 1941, Cambridge, Ohio, USA. Playwright. m. Lisa Giradeux, 1963, 3 sons. *Education:* BA, English, Ohio State University, Columbus, 1961; American Academy of Dramatic Arts, New York, 1961-62. *Career:* Taught drama for Metropolitan Television Arts, New York, 1962; also worked as a publicity agent. Founded Theatre of the Eye (affiliated with the La Mama group), New York, 1967; Director, sometimes under pseudonym of Jerome Eyen or Roger Short, Jr; director and writer, Theatre of Big Dreams, 1982-83. *Publications:* Plays include: Women Behind Bars (produced New York, 1974, London 1977) New York and London, French, 1975; Dirtiest Show II, music by Henry Krieger (produced New York, 1975); The Neon Woman (produced New York, 1978); Independence Day, in Holidays (produced Louisville, 1979); Dreamgirls, music by Henry Krieger (produced New York, 1981). Television plays: Mary Hartman, Mary Hartman series, 1976-77; Milliken Show, 1977-78; Bette Midler TV Special, 1977; Melody of the Glittering Parrot, 1980. *Honours:* Rockefeller grant, 1967; Guggenheim fellowship, 1970; Tony award 1982; NAACP award 1982. *Literary Agent:* Bridget Aschenberg, International Creative Management, New York. *Address:* c/o Bridget Aschenberg, International Creative Management, 40 West 57th Street, New York, NY 10019, USA.

EYRE Annette. *See:* **WORBOYS Annette Isobel.**

EYRE Peter Gervaise Joseph, b. 11 Mar 1942, New York City, New York, USA. Actor. *Education:* Downside Abbey, Stratton-on-the-Fosse, Bath, England, 1954-59. *Publication:* Adaptation of the play Siblings (Klaus Mann), 1992. *Contributions to:* Vogue; Tatler; Harpers and Queen; Vanity Fair; The Spectator; The Literary Review; Financial Times. *Memberships:* Royal Automobile Club; The Groucho Club. *Literary Agent:* Antony Harwood, c/o Curtis Brown. *Address:* c/o ICM, Oxford House, 76 Oxford Street, London W1R 1RB, England.

EYSENCK Hans, b. 4 Mar 1916, Psychologist, 4 sons, 1 daughter. *Education:* BA, 1958, PhD, 1940. DSc, 1964, University of London. *Appointments:* Reader in Psychology, 1950; Professor of Psychology, 1955-83; Professor Emeritus, 1983-. *Publications include:* Dimensions in Personality, 1947; Psychology of Politics, 1954; The Biological Basis of Personality, 1967; Smoking, Health and Personality, 1965; The Inequality of Man, 1973; Genes, Culture and Personality, (Co-authors L Eaves and N Martin), 1989. *Memberships:* President, International Society for the Study of Individual Differences; Fellow, British Psychological Society; American Psychological Association; German Psychological Society. *Address:* 10 Dorchester Drive, London SE24, England.

F

FABEND Firth Haring, b. 12 Aug 1937, Tappen, New York, USA. Writer; Historian. m. E Carl Fabend, 12 Feb 1966, 2 daughters. *Education:* BA, Barnard College, 1959; PhD, New York University, 1988. *Publications:* As Firth Haring: The Best of Intentions, 1968; Three Women, 1972; A Perfect Stranger, 1973; The Woman Who Went Away, 1981; Greek Revival, 1985; As Firth Haring Fabend: A Dutch Family in the Middle Colonies, 1660-1800. *Honours:* Ms Award, New York State Historical Association, 1989; Hendricks Prize, 1989. *Literary Agent:* Roberta Pryor. *Address:* Upper Montclair, NJ 07043, USA.

FÁBRI Peter, b. 21 Dec 1953, Budapest, Hungary. Writer; Poet; Lyricist. m. (1) 1 son, (2) Kriszta Kovats, 7 June 1986, 1 daughter. *Education:* History of Fine Arts and Aesthetics, Eotvos Lorand University, Budapest, 1973-78. *Publications:* Folytatasos Regeny, novel, 1981; Az Elvarazsolt Hangok, tales, 1986; Napfordulo, poems, 1987; Bameszkodasaim Konyve, stories, 1991; Kolumbusz, Az Orult Spanyol, rock opera text, 1992; Books of poems; Lyrics for Hungarian singers' LPs; Books and lyrics for musicals. *Contributions to:* Articles to about a dozen Hungarian papers and monthlies, 1973-89. *Honours:* Emerton Prize, Best Lyricist of Year, Hungarian Radio, 1990. *Memberships:* Zenesz Kor (Circle of Musicians); Hungarian PEN Clb. *Address:* Rippl Ronai u 27, 1068 Budapest, Hungary.

FACOS James Francis, b. 28 July 1924, Lawrence, Massachusetts, USA. Professor. m. 1 Dec 1956, 1 son, 2 daughters. *Education:* AB, Bates College, 1949; MA, Florida State University, 1958. *Publications:* The Legacy, 1967; A Day of Genesis, 1969; The Silver Lady, 1972; Silver Wood, 1977, One Daring Fling, 1978; Morning's Come Singing, 1981; Sara Varn (one act play), 1988. Also: Fugitives' Fair, 1985; Crumpet, 1985. *Honours:* Bates Prize, 1949; Alden Award, drama, 1956; Walter Peach Award, poetry, 1962; Corinne Davis Award, poetry, 1970; Honorary Doctor of Humane Letters Degree, Norwich University, 1989. *Membership:* New England Poetry Club. *Address:* 333 Elm Street, Montpelier, Vermont 05602, USA.

FAGAN Brian Murray, b. 1936, American (b. British). *Appointments:* Keeper of Prehistory, Livingstone Museum, Zambia, 1959- 65; Former Director, Bantu Studies Project, British Institute in Eastern Africa; Visiting Associate Professor, University of Illinois, 1965-66; Associate Professor 1967-69, Professor of Anthropology 1969-, University of California, Santa Barbara. *Publications:* Victoria Falls Handbook (ed), 1964; Southern Africa During the Iron Age, A Short History of Zambia (ed), 1966, 1968; Iron Age Cultures in Zambia (with S G H Daniels and D W Phillipson), volume I, 1967, volume II, 1969; The Hunter-Gatherers of Gwisho (with F Van Noten), 1971; In the Beginning, 1972, 7th edition, 1991; People of the Earth, 1974, 7th ed. 1992; The Rape of the Nile, 1975; Elusive Treasure, 1977; Quest for the Past, Archaeology: A Brief Introduction, 1978, 4th ed. 1991; Return to Babylon, 1979; The Aztecs, Clash of Cultures, 1984; Adventures in Archaeology, Bareboating, Anchoring, 1985; The Great Journey, 1987; The Journey from Eden, 1990; Ancient North America, 1991; Kingdoms of Jade, Kingdoms of Gold, 1991. *Address:* Department of Anthropology, University of California, Santa Barbara, CA 93106, USA.

FAIERS Christopher Fordham, b. 28 June 1948, Hamilton, Ontario, Canada. Library Assistant. *Education:* AA, Miami-Dade Community College. *Literary Appointments:* Founder, publisher, Unfinished Monument Press; Founder, Main Street Library Poetry Series (6 years, 125 poets). *Publications include:* Collections: Cricket Formations, Haiku, 1969; Dominion Day in Jail, 1978; Unacknowledged Legislator, 1981; White Rasta in Wintertime, 1982; Island Women, 1983; 5 Minutes Ago They Dropped the Bomb, 1984; Foot Through the Ceiling, 1986. Editor: Unfinished Anthology, volume 1, 1984. *Contributions include:* Anthologies & textbooks including: Poems for Sale in the Street, 1979; Canadian Haiku Anthology, 1979; Modern English Haiku, 1981; Toronto Collection, 1984; Other Channels, 1984; Anti-War Poems, 1984; Also: Alchemist; Alive; Canadian Book Review Annual 1983; Haiku Highlights; Poetry Toronto; Various readings, broadcasts. *Honour:* 1st recipient, Milton Acorn Memorial People's Poetry Award, 1987. *Memberships:* Haiku Society of Canada; Founding Member, Canadian Poetry Association. *Address:* c/o Unfinished Monument Press, Box 67, Station H, Toronto, Ontario, Canada M4C 5H7.

FAINLIGHT Ruth b. 2 May 1931, New York City, USA. Writer. m. Alan Sillitoe, 19 Nov 1959, 1 son, 1 daughter. *Education:* Primary and Secondary schools in New York City and London, England; Colleges of Arts and Crafts, Birmingham and Brighton, England. *Appointments:* Poet in Residence, Vanderbilt University, Nashville, Tennessee, USA, Spring semesters 1985 and 1990. *Publications:* Poetry collections: Cages, 1966, USA, 1967; To See the Matter Clearly, 1968, USA, 1969; Poems (with Ted Hughes and Alan Sillitoe), 1971; The Region's Violence, 1973; Another Full Moon, 1976; Sibyls and Others, 1980; Climates, 1983; Fifteen to Infinity 1983, USA 1986; Selected Poems, 1987; The Knot, 1990; This Time of Year, forthcoming; Short Stories: Daylife and Nightlife, (book), 1971; Dr Clock's Last Case, forthcoming; Book of translations of poems, Marine Rose, 1988; Translation of play, All Citizens Are Soldiers, 1969. *Contributions to:* Critical Quarterly, Encounter, English, Hudson Review, Lettre Internationale, London Magazine, London Review of Books, The New Yorker, Poetry, Threepenny Review, TLS, Yale Review. *Memberships:* PEN, Writers in Prison Committee. *Address:* 14, Ladbroke Terrace, London W11 3PG, England.

FAIRBAIRNS Zoe Ann, b. 20 Dec 1948, United Kingdom. Writer. *Education:* MA, Honours, University of St Andrews, Scotland, 1972. *Appointments:* C Day Lewis Fellowship, Rutherford School, London, 1977-78; Writer-in-Residence, Deakin University, Australia, 1983; Writer-in-Residence, Sunderland Polytechnic, 1983-85. *Publications:* Live as Family, 1968; Down, 1969; Benefits, 1979; Stand We At Last, 1983; Here Today, 1984; Closing, 1987; Dady's Girls, 1991. *Contributions to:* New Scientist; The Guardian; Women's Studies International Quarterly; Spare Rib; Arts Express. *Honour:* Fawcett Book Prize, 1985. *Membership:* Writer's Guild. *Literary Agent:* A M Heath. *Address:* c/o A M Heath, 79 St Martins Lane, London WC2N 4AA, England.

FAIRBANKS Douglas Elton Jr, b. 9 Dec 1909, New York City, New York, USA. Actor; Producer; Captain, USNR (Ret'd); Writer; Artist; Corporation Director. m. (1) Joan Crawford, June 1929, (2) Mary Lee Epling, 22 Apr 1939, (3) Vera Shelton, 30 May 1991. 3 daughters. *Education:* Pasadena Polytechnic; Harvard; Military School, Los Angeles; Hon DFA, Westminster College, Senior Churchill Fellow; 1966; Visiting Fellow, St Cross College, Hon. MA Oxford University; MA (Oxon), 1971; Hon LLD, Denver University, 1974; Fellow, Boston University Libraries, 1978. *Publications:* Salad Days, (author), 1988; A Hell of A War, (author), 1993; Author of screen plays, articles, acted in over 80 films, 12 plays, 35 TV plays, political essays, short stories. *Honours:* Silver Star, Combat Legion of Merit (Once or Twice), with attachment for Valor, USA; Croix de Guerre with Palm, Comdr. Legion d'Honneur (Twice. Once Military, Once Civil), France; Distinguished Service Cross, UK; War Cross for Military Valor, Italy; Order of the British Empire; Knight, Order of St John of Jerusalem; Officer, Legion of Honour; Knight Commander, Order of George I, Greece; Commander, Order of Orange-Nassau, Netherlands; Commander, Knight Commander, Order of Merit; Star of Italian Solidarity; Knight Chile; Officer, Comdr. Order of the Southern Cross, Brazil; Officer, Order of the Crown, Belgium; National Medal, USSR Campaign Decoration for Murmansk (Russia), Convoys; & Honorary Citizen, Korea; Gold Medal of Honour, VFW,

1966; Armed Forces Award, 1972; American Image Award, 1976; Award, Contribution to the Arts, Unviersity of Notre Dame, 1971; Award, Contribution to World Understanding & Peace, World Affairs Council, Philadelphia, 1978; Award, international artistic achievement, New School for Social Research, 1978; National Humanitarian Award, NCCJ, 1979; National Brotherhood Award, Salvation Army, 1980; Annual National Veterans' Day Award, 1981. *Memberships include:* British-American Alumni Association, President 1950; American Friends of the Order of St John of Jerusalem, Deputy Chancellor (USA), 1970-; Association des Anciens Combatants, France, 1950; White's Club, London; RAC; Travellers'; Paris; Brook, Knicerbocker, Century, New York City. *Address:* Inverness Corporation, 545 Madison Avenue, New York, NY 10022, USA.

FAIRBURN Eleanor M, (Catherine Carfax, Emma Gayle, Elena Lyons), b. 23 Feb 1928, Republic of Ireland. Author. m. Brian Fairburn, 1 daughter. *Appointments:* Past Member, Literary Panel for Northern Arts; Tutor, Practical Writing, University of Leeds Adult Education Centre. *Publications:* The Golden Hive, 1966; Crowned Ermine, 1968; The Green Popinjays, 1962, 1968; A Silence with Voices, 1969, 1971; The Rose in Spring, 1971, 1972, 1973; White Rose, Dark Summer, 1972, 1973; The Rose At Harvest End, 1975, 1976; Winter's Rose, 1976; House of the Chestnut Trees, 1977; The Haunting of Abbotsgarth, 1980, 1982; A Scent of Lilacs, 1982. The White Seahorse, 1964, 1970, 1985; To Die a Little, 1972, 1973, 1979, 1986; The Sleeping Salamander 1973, 1981, 1986; The Semper Inheritance, 1972-75, 1987; Cousin Caroline, 1981, 1987; Frenchman's Harvest, 1982, 1987. *Contributions to:* Brief Biography of Lady Mary for Diver, 1983, and of Nurse Edith Cavell for This England, 1985, and of Mary Horneck-Glyn, 1987. *Memberships;* Middlesbrough Writers Group. *Address:* 27 Minsterley Drive, Acklam, Middlesbrough, Cleveland TS5 8QU, England.

FAIRE Zabrina. *See:* **STEVENSON Florence.**

FAIRFAX John, b. 9 Nov 1930, London, England. Writer. 2 sons. *Publications:* Poems: The Fifth Horseman Of The Apocalypse, 1969; Adrift On The Star Brow Of Taliesin, 1974; Bone Harvest Done, 1980; Wild Children, 1985. The Way To Write (with John Moat), 1981; Creative Writing, 1989; Double Image, 1971; Spindrift LP, 1981. 100 Pems, 1992; Co-Founder: The Arvon Foundation.. *Contributions to:* Most major literary magazines. *Literary Agent:* A D Peters. *Address:* The Thatched Cottage, Eling, Hermitage, Newbury, Berkshire RG16 9XR, England.

FAIRLEY John Alexander, b. Liverpool, England. Author; Television Producer. 3 daughters. *Education:* The Queen's College, Oxford; MA (Oxon). *Appointments include:* Formerly Lieutenant, Royal Naval Volunteer Reserve. *Publications:* The Coup, 1975; The Monocled Mutineer (with Wn Allison), 1976; Great Racehorses in Art, 1984; Racing in Art, 1991; With S Welfare: Arthur C Clarke's World of Strange Powers, 1983; Chronicles of the Strange and Mysterious, 1987; Arthur C Clarke's Mysterious World; A Cabinet of Curiosities; A Century of Mysteries, 1993. *Contributions to:* The Field; Countryweek.

FAIRWEATHER Digby (Richard John Charles), b. 25 Apr 1946, Rochford, Essex, England. Jazz Musician. *Education:* ALA (Librarianship), Ealing Technical College, 1968; Self-taught in Jazz, professional Jazz musician 1977-. *Publications:* How to Play Trumpet, 1985; Jazz: the essential companion, 1987; Major contributor to New Grove Dictionary of Jazz, 1988; Short story in: B-flat, bebop and scat (Quartet c 1986) (titled The killers of '59); Chapter in Blackwell Guide to Recorded Jazz, 1991. *Contributions to:* Numerous journals including: Jazz Journal International; Melody Maker; The Jazz Rag. *Address:* 41 Cobham Road, Westcliff-on-Sea, Essex SSO 8EG, England.

FALCK Colin, b. 14 July 1934, London. University Teacher. 1 daughter. *Education:* BA, 1957, MA 1986, University of Oxford; PhD 1988, University of London. *Appointments:* Associate Editor, The Review, 1962-72; Poetry Editor, The New Review, 1974-78; Associatee Professor, York college, pennsylvania, 1989-. *Publications:* Backwards into the Smoke, 1973; In This Dark Light, 1978; ed. with Ian Hamilton, Poems Since 1900, 1975; ed. Robinson Jeffers: Selected Poems, 1987; Myth, Truth and Literature, 1989; ed. Edna ST Vincent Millay: Selected Poems, 1991; Memrobilia, 1992. *Contributions to:* Many literary and philosophical journals in the UK and the USA. *Address:* 20 Thurlow Road, London NW3 5PP, England.

FALCO Edward, *Education:* SUNY, New Paltz, BS, 1971; Syracuse University, MA, 1979. *Publications include:* Books, Plato at Scratch Daniels & Other Stories; Winter in Florida; Concert in the Park of Culture; Numerous Poems; Several Essays & Plays. *Contributions to:* Virginia Quarterly Review; New Virginia Review; Blue Light Red Light; River Styx; St Andrews Review; Shenandoah; Gettysburg Review; The Missouri Review; North Dakota Review; Sou Wester; Greensboro Review; Georgia Review; The Heights; Kansas Quarterly; Akros Review; Alaska Quarterly Review; Madison Review; Southern Humanities Review; Contraband. *Honours:* Virginia Commission for the Arts, Project Grant; Hampden Sydney playwriting Award; Walter E Dakin Fellowship; National Poetry Series Finalist; The Governors Screenwriting Award; St Andrews Review's Mishima Prize; Emily Clark Balch Prize. *Address:* 1450 Thomas Lane, Blacksburg, VA 24060, USA.

FALCONER James. *See:* **KIRKUP James.**

FALKIRK Richard. *See:* **LAMBERT Derek.**

FALKUS Hugh Edward Lance, b. 15 May 1917. Naturalist; Independent Writer; Film Director; Broadcaster. *Publications:* Films for Cinema include: Drake's England, 1950; Shark Island, 1952; TV Films Include: Salmo - The Leaper; (with Niko Tinbergen), Signals for Survival; Highland Story : The Gull Watchers; The Signreaders; The Beachcombers; The Riddle of the Rook; Tender Trap; Self-portrait of a Happy Man; Sea Trout Fishing, 1962, 2nd edition 1975, revised 2nd edition 1981; The Stolen Years, 1965, 2nd edition 1979; (with Niko Tinbergen), Signals for Survival, 1970; (with Fred Buller), Freshwater Fishing, 1975, new editon 1978, revised edition 1988; (Jointly), Successful Angling, 1977; Nature Detective, 1978, revised 2nd edition 1987; (with Joan Kerr), From Sydney Cove to Duntroon, 1982; Master of Cape Horn, 1982; Salmon Fishing, 1984; The Sea Trout, 1987. *Honours:* Italia Prize, 1969; Blue Ribbon, New York Film Festival, 1971; Venice Film Festival, 1972; Royal Geographical Society Cherry Kearton Medal and Award, 1982. *Address* Cragg Cottage, Near Ravenglass, Cumbria CA18 1RT, England.

FALLACI Oriana, b. 29 June 1930, Florence, Italy. Author. *Education:* Liceo Classico Galileo, Galilei; Faculty Medicine, University of Florence, 1946-48. *Appointments:* Editor, Special Correspondent, Europeo magazine, Milan, 1958-77; Currently Special Correspondent, Corriere della Sera, Milan. *Publications:* The Egotists, 1965; Penelope at War, novel, 1966; If the Sun Dies, 1967; Nothing and So Be It, 1972; Interview with History, 1976; Letter to a Child Never Born, novel, 1977; A Man, novel, 1979; Insciallah, 1990. *Contributions to:* Collaborated with major publications throughout world including: Look; Life; Washington Post; New York Times; London Times; Corriere della Sera; Europeo; Der Spiegel; L'Express. *Honours:* St Vincent Award for Journalism, 1971, 1973; Bancarella Award for Nothing and So Be It (onon- fiction on Vietnam war), 1972; Honorary LittD, Columbia College, Chicago, 1977; 2 Viareggio Prize Awards for A Man, 1979; Hemingway Prize for Literature and Super Bancarella Prize, for Insciallah, 1991. *Address:* c/o RCS Rizzoli Corp, 31 West 57th Street, New York, NY 10019, USA.

FALLON Ivan Gregory, b. 26 June 1944. Deputy Editor. m. Susan Mary Lurring, 1 son, 2 daughters. *Education:* St Peter's College, Wexford, 1952-62; BBS, Trinity College, Dublin, 1966. *Appointments:* Irish Times, 1964-66; Thomson Provincial Newspapers, 1966-67; Daily Mirror, 1967-68; Sunday Telegraph, 1968-70; Deputy City Editor, Sunday Express, 1970-71; Sunday Telegraph, 1971-84; Deputy Editor, Sunday Times, 1984-. *Publications:* DeLorean ; the Rise and Fall of a Dream Maker, (with James L. Srodes), 1983; Takeovers (with James L Srodes), 1987; The Brothers - The Rise of Saatchi and Saatchi, 1988; Billionaire: The Life and Times of Sir James Goldsmith, 1991. *Memberships include:* Council of Governors, United Medical and Dental Schools of Guy's and St Thomas's Hospitals, 1985-; Trustee, Project Trust, 1984-; Generation Trust, Guy's Hospital; President, Trinity College, Dublin, Business Alumni, London Chapter, Fellow of The Royal Society of Arts, 1989; Beefsteak and RAC. *Literary Agent:* Vivienne Schuster, Curtis Brown. *Address:* Clare Cottage, Mill Street, East Malling, Kent ME19 6BU, England.

FALLON Martin. See: PATTERSON Harry.

FALLOWELL Duncan Richard, b. 26 Sept 1948, Harrow, Middlesex, England. Writer. *Education:* 2nd Class Hons, Modern History, Magdalen College, Oxford. *Publications:* Drug Tales, 1979; April Ashley's Odyssey, 1982; Satyrday, 1986; The Underbelly, 1987; To Noto, 1989. *Contributions to:* Various, worldwide. *Literary agent:* Aitken and Stone, 29 Fernshaw Road, London SW10, England. *Address:* 44 Leamington Road Villas, London W11 1HT, England.

FANTHORPE Robert Lionel, b. 9 Feb 1935, Dereham, Norfolk, England. Priest (Anglican); Author; Tutor. m. Patricia Alice Tooke, 7 Sept 1957, 2 daughters. *Education:* Teaching Certificate; BA (Hons); FIMgt; FCP; Anglican Ordination Certificate. *Publications include:* The Black Lion, 1979; The Holy Grail Revealed, 1982; Life of St Francis, 1988; Thoughts and Prayers For Troubled Times, 1989; God In All Things, 1988; Birds and Animals Of The Bible, 1990; Thoughts and Prayers For Lonely Times, 1990; The First Christmas, 1990. *Contributions to:* Purnell's History of World War I. *Honours:* Electrical development Association Diploma for Public Speaking, 1958; Membership, The Welsh Academy, 1989. *Memberships:* MENSA, Past President, Norwich Science Fiction Society; Past President, Cardiff Science Fiction Society. *Address:* Rivendell, 48 Claude Road, Roath, Cardiff, Wales.

FANTHORPE Ursula Askham, b. 22 July 1929, Kent, England. Writer. *Education:* BA, MA, Oxford University. *Literary Appointments:* Writer in Residence, St Martin's College, Lancaster, 1983-85; Northern Arts Literary Fellow, Universities of Durham and Newcastle, 1987. *Publications:* Side Effects, 1978; Standing To, 1982; Voices Off, 1984; Selected Poems, 1986; A Watching Brief, 1987; Neck Verse, 1992. *Contributions to:* Poems: Times Literary Supplement; Encounter; Outposts; Firebird; Bananas; South West Review; Quarto; Tribune; Country Life; Use of English; Poetry Review; Poetry Book Society Supplement; Writing Women; Spectator; BBC. *Honours:* Travelling Scholarship, The Society of Authors, 1983; Hawthornden Scholarship, 1987. *Memberships:* Fellow, Royal Society of Literature; PEN. *Address:* Culverhay House, Wotton-under-Edge, Gloucestershire GL12 7LS, England.

FARAH Nuruddin, b. 24 Nov 1945, Baidoa, Somalia. Writer. m Amina Mama, 24 July 1992, 1 son from previous marriage. *Education:* Panjab University, 1966-70; Institute of Education, University of London, 1974-75; Essex University, Colchester, 1975-1976. *Appointments:* Writer-in-Residence, Dept of English, University of Jos, Nigeria, 1981-83; Writer-in-Residence, Dept of English, University of Minnesota, 1989; Professor, Makerere University, Kampala, Uganda, 1989-91; Writer-in-Residence, Dept of English, Brown University, Providence, 1991. *Publications:* From

a Crooked Rib, 1970; A Naked Needle, 1976; Sweet and Sour Milk, 1979; Sardines, 1981; Close Sesame, 1983; Maps, 1986; Gifts, 1993. *Contributions to:* TLS; The Guardian; New African; Transition Magazine. *Honours:* English-Speaking Literary Award, Sweet and Sour Milk, 1980; DAAD (German) Prize, 1990; Tucholsky (Swedish) Award for Literary Exiles, 1991. *Membership:* Union of Writers of the African Peoples. *Literary Agent:* Curtis Brown. *Address:* c/o Curtis Brown, 162-168 Regent Street, London W1R 5TB, England.

FARBER Donald C, b. Nebraska, USA. Attorney. m. Ann Eis, 1 son, 1 daughter. *Education:* BA, Law, 1948, JD, 1950, University of Nebraska. *Appointments:* Attorney (Theatrical Practice), of Counsel to Tanner Propp Farber, New York City; General Editor, Entertainment Industry Contracts - Negotiating And Drafting Guide, for Matthew Bender and Company Inc. *Publications:* From Option to Opening; Producing on Broadway; Actor's Guide: What You Should Know About The Contracts You Sign; Producing, Financing and Distributing Film; Producing Theatre: A Comprehensive Legal And Business Guide; Theatre vol (author), Entertainment Industry Contracts - Negotiating And Drafting Guide, 1986, on Faculty of New School for Social Research. *Address:* c/o Tanner Propp Farber, 99 Park Avenue, New York, NY 10016, USA.

FARELY Alison. See: POLAND Dorothy Elizabeth Haywood.

FARIAS Victor, b. 4 May 1940, Santiago, Chile. Philosopher. m. Teresa Zurita, 31 Dec 1960, 1 son, 2 daughters. *Education:* Philosophy, Universidad Catolica, Chile, 1957-60; Dr Phil, Philosophy and History of Religions, University of Freiburg, Federal Republic of Germany, 1967; Dr Habilitation, Free University, Berlin, 1985. *Appointments:* La Estética de la Agresión: Diálogo de J L Borges-E Junger, Madrid, 1986. *Publications:* Sein und Gegenstand (F Brentanos Ontology), 1967; Los Manuscritos de Melquìades, 1981; Heidegger et le Nazisme, La Grasse, 1987, Paris, 1989, also editions, Netherlands, Italy, Brazil, USA, Japan, Spain, Portugal, Germany. *Honours:* Heidegger et le Nazisme selected as 1 of the Most Important Books of the Decade, Lire, Paris, 1990; Lógica, Lecciones de verano de Martin Heidegger (1934) en el legado de Helene Weiss, 1991; La Metafisica del Arrabal; El tamano de mi esperanza: un libro desconocido de Jorge Luis Borges, 1992. *Address:* Freie Universitat, Rudesheimerstr 54-56, 1000 Berlin 49, Germany.

FARLEY Carol, b. 20 Dec 1936, Ludington, Michigan, USA. Children's Book Writer. m. 21 June 1954, 1 son, 3 daughters. *Education:* Western Michigan University, 1956; BA, Michigan State University, 1980; MA, Children's Literature, Central Michigan University, 1983. *Publications:* The Garden is Doing Fine, 1976; Mystery of the Fog Man, 1974; Mystery in the Ravine, 1976; Mystery of the Melted Diamonds, 1985; Case of the Vanishing Villain, 1986; Case of the Lost Look Alike, 1988. *Contributions to:* The Writer; Society of Children's Book Writers' Bulletin; Cricket. *Honours:* Best Book of Year, Child Study Association, 1976; Golden Kite Award, Excellence in Writing, Society of Children's Book Writers, 1976; Best Juvenile Book by Mid-West Writer, Friends of the Writer, 1978; IRA/CBC Children's Choice Book, 1987. *Memberships:* Mystery Writers of Amrica; Authors Guild; Children's Book Guild; Society of Childrens Book Writers; Chicago Chidrens Reading Round Table. *Address:* 8574 W. Higgins Lk. Rd., Roscommon, MI 48653, USA.

FARMER David Hugh, b. 30 Jan 1923, Ealing, London, England. University Lecturer and Reader. m. Pauline Ann Widgery, 1966, 2 sons. *Education:* Linacre College, Oxford; BLitt (Oxon). *Appointments:* Lecturer in Medieval History, 1967-77, Reader, 1977-88, Reading University. *Publications:* Life of St Hugh of Lincoln, 1961, 2nd Edition, 1985; The Monk of Farne, 1962; The Rule of St Benedict, 1968; The Oxford Dictionary of Saints, 1978, 3rd Edition 1992; Benedict's

Disciples, 1980; The Age of Bede, 1983, 2nd Edition, 1988; St Hugh of Lincoln, 1985; Bede's Ecclesiastical History, 1990. *Contributions to:* Dictionnaire d'Histoire Ecclesiastique; New Catholic Encyclopedia; Bibliotheca Sanctorum; Lexikon der Christlichen Ikonographie; Studia Monastica; Studia Anselmiana; Journal of Ecclesiastical History; The Tablet; Others. *Honours:* FSA, 1962; FRHistS, 1967. *Address:* 26 Swanston Field, Whitchurch, Reading, Berks RG8 7HP, England.

FARMER James, b. 12 Jan 1920, Marshall, Texas, USA. Distinguished Visiting Professor. 2 daughters. *Education:* BS, Wiley College, 1938; BD, Howard University, 1941. *Publications:* Freedom When, Random House; Lay Bare the Heart, Arbor House. *Contributions to:* Over 100 Articles. *Membership:* Fund for Open Society. *Address:* 3805 Guinea Station Road, Fredericksburg, VA 22401, USA.

FARMER Penelope, b. 1939, British. *Appointment:* Teacher, London, 1961-63. *Publications:* The China People, 1960; The Summer Birds, 1962; The Magic Stone, 1964; Saturday Shillings, The Seagull, 1965; Emma in Winter, 1966; Charlotte Sometimes, 1969; The Dragonfly Summer, Daedalus and Icarus, Serpent's Teeth: The Story of Cadmus, 1971; A Castle of Bone, 1972; William and Mary, Heracles, August the Fourth, 1974; Year King, The Coal Train, 1977; Beginnings: Creation Myths of the World, 1978; The Runaway Train, 1980; Standing in the Shadow, 1984; Eve: Her Story, 1985; Away from Home, 1987. *Address:* 39 Mount Ararat Road, Richmond, Surrey, England.

FARR Diana (Diana Pullein Thompson), b. Surrey, England. Author. *Publications:* Over 30 books, titles include: I Wanted a Pony, 1946; The Boy & the Donkey, 1958; The Secret Dog, 1959; Bindi Must Go, 1962; Ponies in the Valley, 1976; Ponies on the Trail, 1978; Gilbert Cannan: Georgian Prodigy, 1978; Ponies in Peril, 1979; Cassidy in Danger, 1979; Five at Ten, 1985; Choosing, 1988. Many books in foreign editions. *Contributions include:* Daily Telegraph; Pony; Bookseller; Author; Good Housekeeping. *Memberships:* Founder Member, Children's Writers Group; PEN; Society of Authors. *Address:* 35 Esmond Road, Chiswick, London W4 1JG, England.

FARRANT Trevor, b. South Australia. Writer. m. 1965, 2 sons. *Education:* BA, Honours, University of Adelaide, 1966. *Publications:* Winter Grass, 1969; The Laugh-in Scripts, 1972; The Best of Norman Gunston, 1976; The Pirate Movie, 1982; HooRoo Saves the Whale, 1985. *Contributions to:* Founding Contributor, Matilda, 1985. *Honours:* Australian Film & TV Arts & Sciences Awards, 1977, 1978, 1980; Australian Writers Guild Award, 1981. *Memberships:* Writers Guild of America, West; Australian Writers Guild. *Literary Agent:* Philip Gerlach, Woolloomooloo, New South Wales. *Address:* 46 Monmouth Road, South Australia 5041, Australia.

FARRELL David. *See:* **SMITH Frederick E.**

FARRELL Pamela Barnard, b. 11 Oct 1943, Mt. Holly, New Jersey, USA. Writer; Teacher. m. Joseph Donald Farrell, 1 Sept 1968. *Education:* BA, English, Radford College, 1965; MS, English, Radford University, 1975; MA, Writing, Northeastern University, 1988. *Appointments:* Editor, The Grapevine, Northeastern University Writing Program Newsletter, 1986-90; Editorial Board, Computors and Composition, 1987-90; The Writing Center Journal, 1988-; Poetry Teacher/Consultant, Geraldine R. Dodge Foundation, 1986-. *Publications:* Waking Dreams, (poetry collection), 1989; The High School Writing Center: Establishing and Maintaining One, 1989; Poetry, in American Poetry Anthology, 1986; poems in several anthologies and collections, 1985-91; Waking Dreams II, 1990; National Directory of Writing Centres, 1992. *Contributions to:* Writing with a Word Processor in a Writing Center, 1985; Collaboration: Science Research Writing, 1986; Writer, Peer, Tutor and Computer: A Unique

Relationship, 1987; Footprints: Paterson Literary Review, 1990. *Honours:* Dishonorable Mention, Bulwer Lytton Contest, 1984; Woodrow Wilson National Fellowship Foundation Fellow, 1985; Golden Poet Award, 1986; Invitation to present IFTE Conference, 1986-90; Caldwell Chair of Composition, The McCallie School, 1991-. *Memberships:* Modern Language Association; National Writing Center Association, President; Assembly of Computer in English, Treasurer; NCTE. *Address:* The McCallie School, 2850 McCallie Avenue, Chattanooga, TN 37404, USA.

FARRINGTON David Philip, b. 7 Mar 1944, Ormskirk, Lancashire, England. Psychologist; Criminologist. m. Sally Chamberlain, 30 July 1966, 3 daughters. *Education:* BA, Psychology, 1966, MA, Psychology, 1970, PhD, Psychology, 1970, Cambridge University. *Publications:* Who Becomes Delinquent (with D J West), 1973; The Delinquent Way of Life (with D J West), 1977; Psychology, Law and Legal Processes (with K Hawkins and S Lloyd-Bostock), 1979; Behaviour Modification with Offenders (with G B Trasler), 1979; Abnormal Offenders, Delinquency and the Criminal Justice System (with J Gunn), 1982; Prediction in Criminology (with R Tarling), 1985; Reactions to Crime (with J Gunn), 1985; Aggression and Dangerousness (with J Gunn), 1985; Understanding and Controlling Crime (with L E Ohlin and J Q Wilson), 1986; Human Development and Criminal Behaviour (with L E Ohlin and M Tonry), 1991. *Contributions to:* Over 130 articles to journals. *Honours:* Sellin-Glueck Award for International Contributions to Criminology, American Society of Criminology, 1984. *Memberships:* British Society of Criminology, President 1990-93; British Psychological Society, Chairman of Division of Criminological and Legal Psychology 1983-85. *Address:* Institute of Criminology, 7 West Road, Cambridge CB3 9DT, England.

FARROW James S. *See:* **TUBB E C.**

FARSON Daniel Negley, b. 8 Jan 1927, Longon, England; Writer; Journalist; Photographer. *Education:* BA, Pembroke College, Cambridge. *Appointments:* Stars & Stripes; Panorama, founded & edited; Youngest Lobby Correspondent, House of Commons Central Press; Television Interviewer; Photographer. *Publications:* Jack the Ripper, 1972; The Man Who Wrote Dracula, 1975; Henry, Biograph of Henry Williamson, 1982; Soho in the Fifties, 1987; Sacred Monsters, 1988; Escapades, 1989; Gallery, 1990; With Gilbert & George in Moscow, 1991; Lime House Days, 1991; The Gilded Gutter Life of Francis Bacon, 1993; A Dry Ship To The Mountains, 1993; Deviser of Art Quiz (Channel 4 TV), Gallery; The Collins Independent Guide to Turkey. *Contributions to:* Mail on Sunday; Sunday Today; Daily Telegraph. *Memberships:* The Academy Society; Society of Authors; The London Library. *Literary Agent:* Bill Hamilton, A M Heath, 79 St Martin's Lane, London WC2, England. *Address:* 129 Irsha Street, Appledore, North Devon, England.

FAST Jonathan (David), b. 1948, American. Independent Composer and Writer. *Publications:* The Secrets of Synchronicity, 1977; Mortal Gods, 1978; The Inner Circle, 1979; The Beast, 1980; The Golden Fire: A Novel of Ancient India, 1986; The Jade Stalk: A Novel of Tang China, 1988.

FAST Julius, b. 17 April 1919. Writer. m. 8 June 1946, 1 son, 2 daughters. *Education:* BS, New York University, 1940. *Publications:* Fiction: Watchful at Night, 1945; The Bright Face of Danger, 1946; Walk in Shadow, 1947; A Model for Murder, 1956; Street of Fear, 1958; The League of Grey-Eyed Women, 1969; Body Language, 1970; What Should We Do About Davey, 1988; Non-fiction including: The Beatles, 1968; The Incompatibility of Men and Women, 1971; The Pleasure Book, 1975; Bisexual Living, 1975; Creative Coping, 1976; Psyching Up, 1978; Talking Between the Lines, 1979; Body Politics, 1980; Body Language of Sex, Power, Aggression, 1983; Sexual Chemistry, 1983; Ladies' Man, 1985; Omega 3, 1987; Subtext, 1991.

Honours: Edgar Allan Poe Award for Best First Mystery, 1945. *Literary Agent:* Bob Markel. *Address:* 45 East 85th St, New York, NY 10028, USA.

FATCHEN Maxwell Edgar, b. 3 Aug 1920, Adelaide, South Australia. Author. m. Jean Wohlers, 15 May 1942, 2 sons, 1 daughter. *Appointments:* Journalist and Feature Writer, Adelaide News, 1946-55; Special Writer 1955 and 1981-84, Literary Editor 1971-81, The Advertiser. *Publications:* The River Kings, 1966; Conquest of the River, 1970; The Spirit Wind, 1973; Chase Through the Night, 1977; The Time Wave, 1978; Songs for My Dog, 1980; Closer to the Stars, 1981; Wry Rhymes, 1983; A Paddock of Poems, 1987; A Pocketful of Rhymes, 1987; A Country Christmas, 1990. *Contributions to:* Denver Post, USA; Sydney Sun; Regional South Australian Histories. *Honours:* Commendation 1967, Runner-up 1974, Australian Children's Book of the Year; Awarded, Member of the Order of Australia, 1980; Honour Award, 1988; Advance Australia Award for Literature (SA), 1991. *Memberships:* Australian Society of Authors; Australian Fellowship of Writers; South Australian Writers Centre; Australian Journalists Association. *Literary Agent:* John Johnson, Clerkenwell House, 45/47 Clerkenwell Green, London EC1R OHT, England. *Address:* 15 Jane Street (Box 6), Smithfield, South Australia, Australia 5114.

FAULK Odie B, b. 26 Aug 1933, Professor of History. m. 22 Aug 1959, 1 son, 1 daughter. *Education:* BS 1958, MA 1960, PhD 1962, Texas Tech University. *Appointments:* Teaching appointments: Texas A & M 1962; University of Arizona 1963; Oklahoma State University, 1968; Northeastern State University (Oklahoma) 1980. *Publications:* Over fifty publications authored, co-authored or edited including Land of Many Frontiers: A History of the American Southwest, 1968; The Geronimo Campaign, 1969; North America Divided; the War with Mexico, 1972; Tombstone: Myth and Reality, 1973; Crimson Desert: Indian Wars of the Southwest, 1975; Dodge City: The Most Western Town of All, 1977. *Contributions to:* More than 100 major academic journals of history. *Honours:* Fellow, Texas State Historical Association, 1965; Best Non-Fiction Book of the Year (North America Divided), National Cowley Hall of Fame, 1972; Best Non-Fiction Book of Year (Tombstone: Myth and Reality), Southwestern Border Library Association, 1973. *Memberships:* Board of Directors, Westerners International; Oklahoma Historical Society, Board of Directors; Texas State Historical Association. *Address:* 5008 Sturbridge Temple, TX 76502, USA.

FAULKNER Howard John, b. 14 July 1945, Ames, Iowa, USA. Professor of English. *Education:* BA, University of Northern Iowa, 1966; MA, 1968, PhD, 1973, University of Oklahoma. *Appointments:* Department of English, Washburn University, Topeka, Kansas, 1972-; Fulbright Professor of American Literature, Universitet Kiril i Metodij, Skopje, Macedonia, 1979-80; Visiting Professor, University of Metz, Metz, France, 1987-88. *Publications:* Selected Correspondence of Karl A Menninger, 1919-1945 (edited with Virginia Pruitt), 1989. *Contributions to:* James Weldon Johnson's Portrait of the Artist as Invisible Man, to CLA Journal; Text as Pretext in Turn of the Screw, to Studies in Short Fiction; Numerous other contributions on African-American and American literature. *Honours:* National Endowment for the Humanities Fellow, School of Criticism and Theory, 1977; Fulbright Professorship, 1987. *Memberships:* Midwest Modern Language Association; College Language Association. *Address:* Department of English, Washburn University, Topeka, KS 66621, USA.

FAULKNOR (Chauncey) Cliff(ord Vernon), b. 1913, Canadian. *Appointment:* Associate Editor, Country Guide Magazine, Winnipeg, Manitoba, 1954-75. *Publications:* The White Calf, 1965; The White Peril, The Romance of Beef, 1966; The In-Betweener, 1967; The Smoke Horse, 1968; West to Cattle Country, 1975; Pen and Plow, 1976; Turn Him Loose, 1977; Alberta Hereford Heritage, 1981; Johnny Eagleclaw, 1982.

Membership: The Writers Union of Canada. *Address:* 403-80 Point McKay Crescent NW, Calgary, Alberta, Canada T3B 4W4.

FAWCETT Catherine. *See:* **COOKSON Catherine.**

FAWDRY Marguerite, b. 14 May 1912, England. Writer. m. Kenneth Fawdry, 28 Mar 1942, 1 son. *Education:* Licence-es-Lettres, Lille University, France, 1935. *Publications:* Chinese Childhood, 1977; English Dolls and Toys, 1979; The Book of Samplers, 1980; British Tin Toys, 1990; Rocking Horses, 1992. *Address:* 10 Colville Place, London W1P 1HN, England.

FAWKES Richard Brian, b. 31 July 1944, Camberley, Surrey. Writer; Film Director. m. Cherry Elizabeth Cole, 17 Apr 1971, 2 sons. *Education:* BA, Honours, St David's University College, 1967. *Publications:* The Last Corner of Arabia, with Michael Darlow, 1976; Fighting for a Laugh, 1978; Dion Boucicault - A Biography, 1979; Notes from a Low Singer, with Michael Langdon, 1982; Welsh National Opera, 1986; Plays for TV, Radio and Stage; Documentary Film Scripts; Book and Lyrics for Musical, The Misfortunes of Elphin, 1988. *Contributions to:* Classical Music; Sunday Times; Observer; She; Music and Musicians; various other journals & magazines. *Honour:* West Midlands Arts Association Bursary, 1978. *Memberships:* Society of Authors; ACTT; Society for Theatre Research. *Literary Agent:* David Higham. *Address:* 5-8 Lower John Street, Golden Square, London W1R 4HA, England.

FAYER Steve, b. 11 Mar 1935, Brooklyn, New York, USA. Writer. *Education:* BA, honours in English Literature, University of Pennsylvania, 1956. *Appointments:* Series Writer, Eyes On The Prize I, 6 1-hour documentaries for Public Broadcasting Service, 1987; Series Writer, Eyes On The Prize II, 8 1-hour documentaries for Public Broadcasting Service, 1990; Series Writer, The Great Depression, 8 1-hour documentaries for Public Broadcasting Service, 1993. *Publications:* Voices of Freedom, 1990. *Honours:* Emmy Award, National Academy of Television Arts and Sciences, 1987. *Membership:* International Documentary Association, Los Angeles, California. *Address:* 189A Bay State Road, Boston, MA 02215, USA.

FEDERMAN Raymond, b. 15 May 1928, Paris, France. Novelist; Poet. m. Erica Hubscher, 14 Sept 1960, 1 daughter. *Education:* BA, Columbia University, USA, 1957; MA, 1958, PhD, 1963, University of California, Los Angeles. *Appointments:* Honorary Trustee, Samuel Beckett Society, 1979. *Publications:* Novels: Double or Nothing, 1971; Amer Eldorado, 1974; Take It or Leave It, 1976; The Voice in the Closet, 1979; The Twofold Vibration, 1982; Smiles on Washington Square, 1985; To Whom It May Concern, 1990; Criticism: Journey to Chaos, 1965; Samuel Beckett, 1970; Among the Beasts, poetry, 1967; Surfiction, essays, 1976. *Contributions to:* Paris Review; Partisan Review; Chicago Review; The Quarterly; Mississippi Review; Fiction International; Substance; Caliban. *Honours:* Guggenheim Fellowship, 1967; Frances Steloff Fiction Prize, 1971; The American Book Award for Smiles on Washington Square, 1986; Distinguished Faculty Professor, State University of New York, 1990. *Memberships:* PEN American Center; Board of Editors, Fiction Collective. *Literary Agent:* Erica Hubscher Federman. *Address:* 46 Four Seasons West, Eggertsville, NY 14226, USA.

FEIFFER Jules, b. 26 Jan 1929, New York, USA. Cartoonist; Writer. m. Judith Sheftel, 1961, 1 daughter. *Education:* Art Students League; Pratt Institute. *Appointments:* Assistant to Cartoonist Will Eisner, 1946-51; Cartoonist, Author, syndicated Sunday page, Clifford, engaged in various jobs, 1953-56; contributing cartoonist, Village Voice, New York City, 1956-; cartoons published weekly in: The Observer (London), 1958-66, 1972-82, regularly in Playboy Magazine; Cartoons nationally syndicated in USA, 1959-. *Publications:*

Books: Sick, Sick, Sick, 1959; Passionella and other Stories, 1960; The Explainers, 1961; Boy, Girl, Boy, Girl, 1962; Hold Me!, 1962; Harry, The Rat With Women (novel), 1963; Feiffer's Album, 1963; The Unexpurgated Memoirs of Bernard Mergendeiler, 1965; The Great Comic Book Heroes, 1967; Feiffer's Marriage Manual, 1967; Pictures at a Prosecution, 1971; Ackroyd (novel), 1978; Tantrum, 1980; Jules Feiffer's America : From Eisenhower to Reagan, 1982; Marriage is an Invasion of Privacy, 1984; Feiffer's Children, 1986; Plays: Crawling Arnold, 1961; Little Murders, 1966; God Bless, 1968; The White House Murder Case, 1970; Feiffer on Nixon : The Cartoon Presidency, 1974; Knock Knock, 1975; Grown Ups, 1981; A Think Piece 1982; Feiffer's America, 1985; Screenplays; Little Murders 1971; Carnal Knowledge, 1971; Popeye, 1980. Honours: Academy Award for Animated Cartoon,Munro, 1961; Special George Polk MemOrlal Award, 1962. Membership: Sponser, National Committee for Sane Nuclear Policy. Address: c/o Universal Press Syndicate, 4400 Johnson Drive, Fairway, KS 66205, USA.

FEIKEMA Feike. See: **MANFRED Frederick Feikema.**

FEINBERG Barry Vincent, b. 26 Dec 1938, South Africa. Writer; Designer; Film-Maker. Education: Slade School of Art, London, 1964-65. Appointments: Editor to Bertrand Russell, The Bertrand Russell Estate, 1966-75; Director of Research, Information & Publications, International Defence & Aid Fund for Southern Africa, London, 1977-87. Publications: Editor, Dear Bertrand Russell, 1969; Editor, Collected Stories of Russell, 1972; Co-Author, Bertrand Russell's America Volume 1, 1973, Volume 2, 1984; Editor, Poets to the People, 1974, expanded, 1980. Contributions to: numerous professional journals. Honours: Director, several prize winning documentary films. Address: 6 Carlton Mansions, 73 Chichele Road, London NW2, England.

FEINBERG David B, b. 25 Nov 1956, Massachusetts, USA. Writer. Education: SB, Mathematics, Massachusetts Institute of Technology, 1977; MA, Linguistics, New York University, 1982. Publications: Eighty-Sixed, 1989; Spontaneous Combustion, 1991. Contributions to: Tribe; Outweek; The Advocate; NYQ-QUU; The New York Times Book Review; Diseased Pariah News; Mandate; Torso. Honours: Lambda Literary Award for Best Gay Male Novel, 1989; Best Fiction, American Library Association Gay and Lesbian Caucus, 1989; Selected by New York Public Library for Books to Remember, 1989. Membership: Act Up, New York. Literary Agent: Norman Laurila. Address: 410 West 23rd Street, 2B, New York, NY 10011, USA.

FEINBERG Joan Miriam, (Joan Schuchman), b. 13 Oct 1934, Far Rockaway, New York, USA. Freelance Writer. m. Arnold I Feinberg, 4 Oct 1986, 2 sons. Education: Brooklyn College, 1952-54; BA, 1970, University of Minnesota. Publications: Astrology: Science or Hoax, 1978; Help for Your Hyperactive Child, 1978; Two Places to Sleep, 1979; Broken Dreams, 1992. Contributions to: Carolrhoda Publishing Company; Pamphlet Publications; The Daimandis Corporation; The Institute for Research; Today's Family; Conquest Magazine; Horoscope Guide: World Book and Travel; New York Times Syndicate; International Travel News. Honours: Writer's Digest Article Writing Contests: Depression: The Living Death Disease, 1987, The Diet That Calms Hyperactive Children, 1987. Memberships: Conservatory of American Letters; Women in Communication; Florida Freelance Writers Association; International Women's Writers' Guild. Address: 4725 Excelsior Blvd Suite 300, Minneapolis, MN 55416, USA.

FEINBERG Leonard, b. 26 Aug 1914, Vitebsk, Russia. Professor. m. Lilian Okner, 26 Nov 1938, 1 daughter. Education: BS, 1937, MA, 1938, PhD, 1946, University of Illinois. Appointments: Instructor in English, University of Illinois, 1938; Assistant Professor, 1946, Associate Professor, 1950, Professor of English, 1957, Iowa State University. Publications: The Satirist,

1963; Introduction to Satire, 1967; Asian Laughter, 1971; The Secret of Humor, 1978. Contributions to: Atlantic; College English; Satire Newsletter. Honours: Fulbright Lecturer, University of Ceylon, 1957-58; Wilton Park Fellow, 1972; Named Distinguished Professor, Iowa State University, 1973. Address: 2404 Loring Street, San Diego, CA 92109, USA.

FEINSTEIN (Allan) David, b. 22 Dec 1946, Brooklyn, New York, USA. Psychologist. m. Donna Eden, 7 Oct 1984. Education: BA, Whittier College, 1968; MA, US International University, 1970; PhD, Union Institute, 1973. Publications: Personal Mythology, 1988; Rituals for Living and Dying, 1990; Serenade at the Doorway, album, 1991. Contributions to: Common Boundary; Magical Blend; Psychotherapy; American Journal of Orthopsychiatry; American Journal of Hypnosis. Honours: William James Award, 1968. Memberships: American Psychological Association; Association for Humanistic Psychology. Address: 777 East Main Street, Ashland, OR 97520, USA.

FEINSTEIN Elaine, b. 1930, British. Appointments: Editorial Staff Member, Cambridge University Press, 1960-62; Lecturer in English, Bishop's Stortford College, 1963-66; Assistant Lecturer in Literature, University of Essex, Wivenhoe, 1967-70. Publications: In a Green Eye, 1966; Selected Poems of John Clare (ed), 1968; The Circle, 1970; The Selected Poems of Marina Tsvetayeva (trans), The Magic Apple Tree, 1971; At the Edge, The Amberstone Exit, Matters of Chance, 1972; The Celebrants and Other Poems, The Glass Alembic (in US as The Crystal Garden), 1973; The Children of the Rose, 1974; The Ecstasy of Miriam Garner, 1976; Some Unease and Angels, 1977; The Shadow Master, Three Russian Poets (trans), 1978; New Stories 4 (ed with Fay Weldon), 1979; The Silent Areas, The Feast of Euridice, 1980; The Survivors, 1982; The Border, 1984; Bessie Smith, 1985; A Captive Lion: The Life of Marina Tsvetayeva, 1987. Address: c/o Hutchinson Publishing Group Limited, 62-65 Chandos Place, London WC2N 4NW, England.

FEKETE John, b. 7 Aug 1946, Budapest, Hungary. Professor of English and Cultural Studies. Education: BA with honours, English Literature, 1968, MA, English Literature, 1969, McGill University; PhD, Cambridge University, 1973. Appointments: Visiting Assistant Professor, English, McGill University, Montreal, Quebec, Canada, 1973-74; Associate Editor, Telos, 1974-84; Visiting Assistant Professor, Humanities, York University, Toronto, Ontario, 1975-76; Assistant Professor, 1976-78, Associate Professor, 1978-84, Professor, English, Cultural Studies, 1984-, Trent University, Peterborough, Ontario. Publications: The Critical Twilight: Explorations in the Ideology of Anglo-American Literary Theory From Eliot to McLuhan, 1978; The Structural Allegory: Reconstructive Encounters With the New French Thought, 1984; Life After Postmodernism: Essays on Culture and Value, 1987. Contributions to: Editorial contributor to: Canadian Journal of Political and Social Theory; Canadian Journal of Communications; Science-Fiction Studies. Honours: Grants and Fellowships, Social Sciences and Humanities Research Council of Canada, 1979, 1984, 1988, 1991-94; Distinguished Faculty Research Award, Trent University, 1990. Memberships: Association of Canadian College and University Teachers of English; Modern Language Association; Science Fiction Research Association; Canadian Association of University Teachers, Board of Directors 1979-81; Federation des Associations de Professeurs des Universites du Quenec, Comite de la liberte universitaire 1981-84; Board of Directors, Canadian Images Film Festival, 1982-84; Board of Directors, Trent Institute for the Study of Popular Culture, 1987-90. Address: 181 Wallis Drive, Peterborough, Ontario, Canada K9J 6C4.

FELD Karen Irma, b. 23 Aug 1947, Washington, District of Columbia, USA. Columnist; Journalist; Public Speaker. Education: University of Pittsburgh, 1965-67; BA, American University, 1969. Appointments: Columnist, Reporter, Roll Call Newspaper, Washington,

1969-74; Publicist, Twentieth Century Fox, Los Angeles, 1974-75; Freelance Writer, Broadcaster, 1970-; Correspondent, People Magazine, Washington, 1980-85; Broadcaster, Voice of America, 1984; Columnist, Contributing Editor, Capitol Hill magazine, Washington, 1980-89; Columnist, Washington Times, 1986- 87; Universal Press Syndicate, 1988-89; Creators Syndicate, 1989-. *Publication:* Contributor to: Readings in Brain Injury, 1984. *Contributions to:* Poeple; Money; Time; Vogue; Los Angeles Times Syndicate; American Politics; Family Circle. *Honours:* National Federation Press Women's Excellence in Journalism Awards, 1984-89; Capital Press Women's Excellence in Journalism, 1984-90. *Memberships:* National Federation Press Women; Women in Communications; Capital Press Women (Vice President 1985-); American Society of Journalists and Authors. *Address:* 1698 32nd Street, Washington, DC 20007, USA.

FELD Werner J, b. 1910, American. *Appointments:* Professor and Chairman, Department of Political Science, University of New Orleans, LA; President, Dixie Speciality Company Incorporated, 1948-61. *Publications:* Reunification and West German-Soviet Relations, 1963; The Court of the European Communities: New Dimension in International Adjudication, 1964; The European Common Market and the World, 1967; Transnational Business Collaboration among Common Market Countries, 1970; Nongovernmental Forces and World Politics: A Study of Business, Labor and Political Groups, 1972; The European Community in World Affairs: Economic Power and Political Influence, 1976; Domestic Political Realities and European Unification: A Study of Mass Publics and Elites in the European Community Countries, 1977; The Foreign Policies of West European Socialist Parties, 1978; International Relations: A Transnational Approach, 1979; Multinational Corporations and UN Policies, 1980, Comparative Regional Systems (editor and contributor), Western Europe's Global Reach (ed), 1980; West Germany and the European Community, NATO and the Atlantic Defense: Perceptions and Illusions, 1981; International Organizations: A Comparative Appriach, American Foreign Policy: Aspirations and Reality, 1983; Congress and National Defense, 1985; Europe in the Balance (co-author), 1986; Arms Control and the Atlantic Community, 1987. *Address:* 3743 Blue Merion Court, Colorado Springs, CO 80906, USA.

FELDER David Wellington, b. 25 Apr 1992, Providence, Rhode Island, USA. Professor. m. Judith R Platt, 7 July 1977. *Education:* BA, Boston University, 1967; NA, Wayne State University, 1969; MA, Florida State University, 1979; PhD, 1979. *Publications:* How to Work for Peace; Best Investment: Land In A Loving Community. *Contributions to:* Jounral of Social Philosophy; Journal of Special Education; The Philosophy Forum. *Honours:* Visiting Scholar, Boston University; Visiting Scholar, New York University. *Memberships:* North American Society for Social Philosophy; American Philosophical Association; Society for Business Ethics; Hobbes Society; Institute for Advanced Philosophical Research. *Address:* 9601 30 Miccosukee Road, Tallahassee, FL 32308, USA.

FELDMAN Alan Grad, b. 16 Mar 1945, New York City, New York, USA. Writer; Teacher. m. Nanette Hass, 22 Oct 1972, 1 son, 1 daughter. *Education:* AB, Columbia College, 1966; MA, Columbia University, 1969; PhD, State University of New York, Buffalo, 1973. *Publications:* The Household, 1966; The Happy Genius, 1978; Frank O'Hara, 1978; The Personals, 1982; Lucy Mastermind, 1985; Anniversary, 1992. *Contributions to:* New Yorker; The Atlantic; Kenyon Review; Mississippi Review; Ploughshares; North American Review; Threepenny Review; Boston Review; Tendril; College English. *Honours:* Award for Best Short Story in a College Literary Magazine, Saturday Review-National Student Association, 1965; Elliston Book Award for Best Book of Poems by a Small Press in US, for The Happy Genius, 1978. *Address:* 399 Belknap Rd, Framingham, MA 01701, USA.

FELDMAN Gerald D, b. 24 Apr 1937, New York City, USA. Historian. m. Norma von Ragenfeld, 30 Nov 1983, 1 son, 1 daughter (by first marriage). *Education:* BA, Columbia College, 1958, MA, 1959, PhD 1964, Harvard University (all degrees in History). *Appointments:* Assistant Professor 1963-68, Associate Professor 1968-70, Professor 1970-, University of California, Berkeley; Currently member of editorial boards or advisory boards for Geschichte und Gesellschaft, German Yearbook on Business History and Contemporary European History. *Publications include:* Books: Army, Industry and Labor in Germany, 1914-1918, 1966; Iron and Steel in the German Inflation, 1916-1923, 1977; with Heidrun Homburg, Industrie und Inflation, 1977; Vom Weltkrieg zur Weltwirtschaftskrise, 1984; with Irmgard Steinisch, Indistrie und Gewerkschaften 1918-1924. (with Klaus Tenfelde), Workers, Owners and Politics in Coal Mining, An International Comparison of Industrial Relations, 1990; The Great Disorder: Politics, Economics and Society in the German Inflation, 1914-1923, 1993. Also edited collections of documents and papers, articles and review essays. *Honours include:* Appointed to Historisches Kolleg Munich for 1982-83; Stephen Allen Kaplan Memorial Lecture at the University of Pennsylvania 1984; Invited Guest, Rockefeller Center at Bellagio, Sept 1987; Appointed to the Wissenschaftskolleg (Institute for Advanced Study) Berlin for 1987-88; Appointed to Woodrow Wilson Center, 1991-92. *Memberships include:* Corresponding member, Historische Kommission zu Berlin, 1980-; Chairman, Conference Group for Central European History of the AHA, 1990; Executive Committee, Friends of the German Historical Institute in Washington, 1990-91. *Address:* Department of History, University of California, Berkeley, CA 94720, USA.

FELDMAN Paula R, b. 4 July 1948, Washington, District of Columbia, USA. University Professor; Writer. m. Robert H Stuart, 28 Jan 1989. *Education:* BA, Bucknell University, 1970; MA, 1971, PhD, 1974, Northwestern University. *Appointments:* Assistant Professor, English, 1974-79, Associate Professor, English, 1979-89, Professor, English, 1989-, Director, Graduate Studies in English, 1991-, University of South Carolina, Columbia. *Publications:* The Microcomputer and Business Writing (with David Byrd and Phyllis Fleishel), 1986; The Journals of Mary Shelley (with Diana Scott-Kilvert), 2 vols, 1987; The Wordworthy Computer: Classroom and Research Applications in Language and Literature (with Buford Norman), 1987. *Contributions to:* Articles in: Studies in English Literature; Papers of the Bibliographical Society of America; Modern Language Association's Approaches to Teaching Shelley's Frankenstein volume. *Memberships:* Modern Language Association of America; South Atlantic Modern Language Association; The Byron Society. *Address:* Department of English, University of South Carolina, Columbia, SC 29208, USA.

FELDMAN Ruth (Wasby), b. 21 May 1911, USA. Poet; Translator. m. Moses D Feldman (dec). *Education:* BA, Wellesley College, 1931; Workshops, Boston University, Radcliffe Institute. *Publications include:* Books: The Ambition of Ghosts, poetry, 1979; Poesie di Ruth Feldman, poetry, 1981; To Whom it May Concern, poetry, 1986; (Co-editor, translator), Collected Poems of Lucio Piccolo, 1973; Selected poems of Andrea Zanzotto, 1975; Shema, 1976; Italian Poetry Today, 1979; The Dawn Is Always New, 1980; The Hands of the South, 1980; The Dry Air of the Fire, 1981; Collected poems of Primo Levi, 1988. Sole translator: Moments of Reprieve, 1986; Liber Fulguralis: Poems by Margherita Guidacci, 1986. *Contributions to:* Anthologies: New York Times Book of Verse; Anthology of Magazine Verse; Voices Within the Ark; Peter Kaplan's Book; Sotheby's Poetry Competition Prize Anthology; Poesia della Metamorfosi; Poetry Society of America Diamond Anthology; Penguin Book of Women Poets; Barnstone Book of Women Poets; Gates to the New City; In the Pink; Editor's Choice II. Numerous literary magazines & reviews. *Honours include:* Devil's Advocate Award, 1972; Monthly awards, 1 annual award, Poetry Society of America; Prize, Sotherby's

International Poetry Competition, 1982; Co-winner John Florio, 1976; Cire-Sabaudia, 1983. *Memberships:* Poetry Society of America; New Zealand Poetry Club; American Literary Translators Association; PEN.

FELICE Cynthia, b. 10 Oct. 1942, Chicago, Illinois, USA. Writer; Technical Manager. m. Robert E. Felice Sr, 23 Dec. 1961, 2 sons. *Publications:* Godsfire, 1978; The Sunbound, 1981; Eclipses, 1983; Downtime, 1985; Double Nocturne, 1986; Water Witch, with Connie Willis, 1982; Light Riad, with Connie Willis, 1988. Many novels (translated) published in Holland, Germany, Japan. *Contributions to:* Fiction, non-fiction: Omni; The Writer; Galileo; Various anthologies. *Honours:* Finalist, Campbell Award nomination 1979; Outstanding paper, Society for Technical Communication, 1983. *Memberships:* Science Fiction Writers Association; Society for Technical Communications. *Literary Agent:* Richard Curtis. *Address:* 5025 Park Vista Boulevard, Colorado Springs, CO 80918, USA.

FELLOWS Malcolm Stuart, b. 1924, British. *Appointments:* Justice of the Peace, 1973-; Editor, Laurel and Hardy Magazine; Former Chairman; Education Committee. *Publications:* The Truth About Helen, 1961; Shame in Summer, 1964; Projects for School, Eight Plays (ed), 1965; Behind the Wheel, Come Fly with Me, Red Lion Plays (ed), 1968; Home Movies, 1973; Success, 1976. *Membership:* Executive Council, Writers' Guild of Great Britain. *Address:* Denham, 42 Queens Walk, Kinsgbury, London NW9 8ER, England.

FENNARIO David, b. Montreal, 1947. Playwright. m. Elizabeth Fennario, 1976, 1 child. *Education:* Dawson College, Montreal 1969-71. *Career:* Playwright-in-residence, Centaur Theatre, Montreal, 1973-; Co-founder, Cultural Workers Association. *Publications:* Plays: On the Job (produced Montreal 1975), Vancouver, Talonbooks, 1976; Nothing to Lose (produced Montreal 1976), Vancouver, Talonbooks, 1977; Toronto (produced Montreal 1978); Without a Parachute, adaptation of his own book produced Toronto, 1978; Balconville (produced Montreal 1979; Bath and London 1981), Vancouver, Talonbooks, 1980; Changes, adaptation of his journal Without a Parachute (produced Ottawa, 1980); Moving (produced Montreal, 1983); Blue Mondays, poems by Daniel Adams, Verdun, Quebec, Black Rock Creations, 1984. *Honours:* Canada Council grant, 1973; Chalmers award, 1979. *Address:* c/o Centaur Theatre Compny, 453 St Francois Xavier Street, Montreal, Quebec H2Y 2T1, Canada.

FENNELLY Tony (Antonia), b. 25 Nov 1945, Orange, New Jersey, USA. Author. m. James Richard Catoire, 27 Dec 1972. *Education:* BA, Drama, & Communications, University of New Orleans, 1976. *Publications:* The Glory Hole Murders, 1985; The Closet Hanging, 1987; Kiss Yourself Goodbye, 1989; Der Hippie In Der Wand (Germany, 1992. *Honours:* Edgar Allan Poe Special Award, Mystery Writers of America, 1986. *Memberships:* Mystery Writers of America; Authors Guild; International Association of Crime Writers. *Address:* 921 Clouet St., New Orleans, LA 70117, USA.

FENNER Carol. See: **WILLIAMS Carol Elizabeth.**

FENNER James R. See: **TUBB E C.**

FENTON Edward, b. 1917, USA. Author. *Appointments:* Staff Member, Print Department, Metropolitan Museum of Art, New York City, 1950-55. *Publications:* Soldiers and Strangers: Poems, 1945; The Double Darkness, 1945; Us and the Duchess, 1947; Aleko's Island, 1948; Hidden Trapezes, 1950 Nine Lives, or, The Celebrated Cat of Beacon Hill, 1951; The Golden Doors, UK Edition Mystery in Florence, 1957; Once Upon a Saturday, 1958; Fierce John, 1959; The Nine Questions, 1959; The Phantom of Walkaway Hill, 1961; An Island for a Pelican, 1963; The Riddle of the Red Whale, 1966; The Big Yellow Baloon, 1967; A Matter of Miracles, 1967; Petro's War, by Alki Zei, translation,

1968; Penny Candy, 1970; Anne of a Thousand Days, novel, 1970; Duffy's Rocks, 1974; The Sound of the Dragon's Feet, translation, 1979; The Refugee Summer, 1982. *Address:* 24 Evrou Street, Athens 610, Greece.

FENTON James Martin, b. 25 Apr 1949. Writer. *Education:* MA, Magdalen College, Oxford; FRSL, 1983. *Appointments:* Assistant Literary Editor, 1971, Editorial Assistant, 1972, New Statesman; Freelance Correspondent, Indo-China, 1973-75; Political Columnist, New Statesman, 1976- 78; German Correspondent, The Guardian, 1978-79; Theatre Critic, Sunday Times, 1979-84; Chief Book Reviewer, The Times, 1984-86; Far East Correspondent, The Independent, 1986-88. *Publications:* Our Western Furniture, 1968; Terminal Moraine, 1972; A Vacant Possession, 1978; A German Requiem, 1980; Dead Soldiers, 1981; The Memory of War, 1982; Translations: Rigoletto, 1982; You Were Marvellous, 1983; Editor, The Original Michael Frayn, 1983; Children in Exile, 1984; Poems 1968-83, 1985; Translation, Simon Boccanegra, 1985; The Fall of Saigon, In Granta 15, 1985; The Snap Revolution in Granta, 1986; Partingtime Hall (with John Fuller), 1987; All the Wrong Places, adrift in the Poltics of Asia, 1989. *Address:* c/o A D Peters & Co Ltd, 10 Buckingham Street, London WC2N 6BU, England.

FENWICK Ian (Graham Keith), b. 1941, United Kingdom. Educator; College Dean. *Publications:* The Comprehensive School, 1944-1970, 1976; The Government of Education, 1981. *Address:* Christchurch College, Canterbury, Kent, England.

FERDINANDY György (Georges), b. 11 Oct 1935, Budapest, Hungary. Professor. m. (1) Colette Peyrethon, 27 May 1958, (2) Maria Teresa Reyes- Cortes, 3 Jan 1981, 3 sons, 1 daughter. *Education:* Doctorate in Literature, University of Strasbourg, France, 1969. *Appointments:* Freelance Literary Critic, Radio Free Europe, 1977-86; Professor, University of Puerto Rico, Cayey, Puerto Rico. *Publications:* In French: L'ile sous l'eau, 1960; Famine au Paradis, 1962; Le seul jour de l'année, 1967; Itinéraires, 1973; Chica, Claudine, Cali, 1973; L'oeuvre hispanoaméricaine de Zs Remenyik, 1975; Fantomes magnétiques, 1979; Youri, 1983; Hors jeu, 1986; Mémoires d'un exil terminé, 1992; In Hungarian: Látószeméeknek, 1962; Tizenhárom Töredék, 1964; Futószalagon, 1965; Nemezio Gonzalez, 1970; Valenciánál a tenger, 1975; Mammuttemetö, 1982; A Mosoly Albuma, 1982; Az elveszett gyermek, 1984; A Vadak Útján, 1986; Szerecsenségem története, 1988; Furcsa, idegen szerelem, 1990; Üzenöfüzet, 1991; Szomorü Szigetek, 1992; Afrancia uölegény, 1993; Saldo a medio camino, Spanish translation, 1976. *Contributions to:* Le Monde; NRF; Europe; Élet és Irodalom; Kortárs; Üj Hold; Magyar Naplo. *Honours:* Del Duca Prix, 1961; St Exupéry Literary Award, 1964. *Memberships:* Société des Gens de Lettres, France; Hungarian Writers Association; International PEN Club. *Address:* Joaquin Lopez Lopez 1056, Sta Rita, Rio Piedras, PR 00925, USA.

FERGUS Jan, b. 5 Apr 1943, Bronxville, New York, USA. Professor of English. *Education:* BA, Stanford University, 1964; PhD, City University of New York, 1975. *Appointments:* Adjunct Lecturer, Brooklyn College, New York, 1971-76; Le High University, 1976- ; Visiting Professor, New York University, 1985-86. *Publications:* Jane Austen and the Didactic Novel, 1983; Jane Austen: A Literary Life, 1991. *Contributions to:* Several articles on 18C reading public to: PBSA; SECC; Elsewhere. *Honours:* Phi Beta Kappa, 1963; Woodrow Wilson Fellow, 1964; National Endowment for the Humanities Fellow, 1989. *Memberships:* American Society for 18C Studies, Book Review Editor, Eighteenth Century Studies, 1992-95; Jane Austen Society, UK; Jane Austen Society of North America. *Address:* 79 West Goepp Street, Bethlehem, PA 18018, USA.

FERGUSON Joseph Francis, b. 11 Feb 1952, Yonkers, New York, USA. Public Relations; Journalist;

Critic; Author. m. Janice Robinson, 30 July 1986, 1 son. *Education:* BA, SUNY, New Paltz, 1979; MS, Pace University (not completed). *Publications:* Night Image; Duecy and Detour; Priorities; Autumn Road Kill; Autumn Poem; Sky and Stream at Sunset; End of Daylight in a Car Mirror; The Atlar; Jazz; New Orleans; the Glory; Another Damn Dream Poem; Grave Dreams; View From the Graveyard Shift. *Contributions to:* Hundreds of News and feature Articles, Wide Variety of Local, National & International Publi. *Honours:* 1990 World of poetry Golden Poet; American Poetry Association Contest, Honorable Mention; Finalist, San Diego Poets Press. *Address:* 26 Bank Street, Cold Spring, NY 10516, USA.

FERGUSON Robert Thomas, b. 2 June 1948, Stoke-on-Trent, England. Writer. m. 3 Apr 1987. *Education:* BA Hons, Scandinavian Studies, University College, London, 1980. *Publications:* Enigma - The Life of Knut Hamsun, 1987; Henry Miller - A Life, 1991; As contributor: Best Radio Drama, 1984; Best Radio Drama, 1986. *Honours:* BBC-Methuen Giles Cooper Award for Best Radio Drama, 1984, 1986; J G Robertson Prize, for Enigma, 1985-87. *Literary Agent:* Scott Ferris Associates Ltd, PO Box 317, 15 Gledhow Gardens, London SW5 0AY, England. *Address:* Steinspranget 7, 1156 Oslo 11, Norway.

FERGUSON William Rotch, b. 14 Feb 1943, Fall River, Massachusetts, USA. Author; Foreign Languages Educator. m. Nancy King, 23 Nov 1983. *Education:* BA, 1965, MA, 1970, PhD, 1975, Harvard University. *Publications:* Dream Reader, poems, 1973; La Versificacion Imitativa en Fernando de Herrera, scholarly, 1981; Freedom and Other Fictions, stories, 1984. *Contributions to:* Paris Review; Harper's; Insula; Massachusetts Review; Mississippi Review; Canto; Malahat Review; Reviewer; New York Times Book Review. *Membership:* Modern Language Association. *Address:* Foreign Languages Department, Clark University, 950 Main St, Worcester, MA 01610, USA.

FERLINGHETTI Lawrence, b. 24 Mar 1919, Yonkers, New York, USA. Writer. m. 1951, 1 son, 1 daughter. *Education:* MA, Columbia University; University of Paris. *Publications include:* Poems: Pictures of the Gone World; A Coney Island of the Mind; Starting from San Francisco; The Secret Meaning of Things; Tyrannus Nix?; Back Roads to Far Places; Open Eye, Open Heart; Landscapes of Living and Dying, 1979; Endless Life: Selected Poems, 1981; Over All the Obscene Boundaries, 1984; Plays: Unfair Arguments with Existence; Routines; Her (novel); Love in the Days of Rage (E.P. Dutton), (novel), 1988; The Mexican Night (travel journal); We Are We Now?, 1976; Literary San Francisco : A Pictorial History from the Beginnings to the Present (with Nancy J. Peters), 1980; Leaves of Life : Drawings from the Model, 1983; Editor, City Lights Books; translations; film- scripts; phonograph records, painter, paintings. *Address:* c/o City Lights Bookstore, 261, Columbus Avenue, San Francisco, CA 94133, USA.

FERLITA Ernest Charles, b. 1 Dec 1927, Tampa, Florida, USA. Jesuit Priest; Educator; Playwright. *Education:* BS, Spring Hill College, 1950; STL, St Louis University, 1964; DFA, Yale University, 1969. *Publications:* The Theatre of Pilgrimage, 1971; Film Odyssey (Co- author), 1976; The Way of The River, 1977; The Parables of Lina Wertmuller (Co-author), 1977; Religion in Film (Contributor), 1982; Gospel Journey, 1983; The Mask of Hiroshima in Best Short Plays, 1989; The Uttermost Mark, 1990. *Honours:* Play Awards: 1st Prize Christian Theatre Artists Guild, 1971; American Radio Scriptwriting Contest, 1985; Miller Award, 1986. *Memberships:* Dramatists Guild; Theatre in Higher Education; International Hopkins Society. *Address:* Loyola University, New Orleans, LA 70118, USA.

FERNANDEZ-ARMESTO Felipe Fermin Ricardo, b. 6 Dec 1950, London, England. Historian. m. Lesley Patricia Hook, 16 July 1977, 2 sons. *Education:* Magdalen College, Oxford, 1969-72; 1st Class Hons, Modern History, 1972, MA, 1976, DPhil, 1977, Oxford University. *Appointments:* Journalist, The Diplomatist, 1972-74. *Publications:* The Canary Islands after the Conquest, 1982; Before Columbus, 1987; The Spanish Armada, 1988; Barcelona, 1991; The Times Atlas of World Exploration (general editor), 1991; Columbus, 1991; Edward Gibbon's Atlas of the World, 1992; Others. *Contributions to:* English Historical Review; History; History Today; Anuarto de Estudios Atlanticos; Other English and Spanish historical periodicals; The Sunday Times Magazine; Others. *Honours:* Arnold Modern History Prize, 1971; Leverhulme Research Fellowship, 1981; Commendation, Library Association, 1992. *Memberships:* Council, Hakluyt Society; Society of Authors; PEN; Library Committee, The Athenaeum; Fellow, Royal Historical Society; Historical Association; Association of Hispanists. *Literary Agent:* Serafina Clarke. *Address:* River View, Headington Hill, Oxford OX3 0BT, England.

FERRARI Ronald Leslie, b. 3 Feb 1930, Romford, Essex, England. Electrical Engineer. m. Judith Wainwright, 5 Sept 1959, 1 son, 3 daughters. *Education:* BSc (London); DIC, Imperial College, London; MA (Cambridge). *Appointments:* Lecturer, Engineering, Cambridge University, 1965; Fellow, Trinity College, Cambridge, 1966. *Publications:* Problems in Physical Electronics (edited with A K Jonscher), 1973; Introduction to Electomagnetic Fields, 1975; Finite Elements for Electrical Engineers (with P P Silvester), 1983, 2nd Edition, 1990. *Contributions to:* As Editor, Special Issue of IEE Proceedings, Part A, Electromagnetism, in Vol 135, 1988. *Membership:* Institution of Electrical Engineers (MIEE). *Address:* Trinity College, Cambridge CB2 1TQ, England.

FERRARO Bernadette A., b. 19 Apr 1952, USA. Biomedical Writer. *Education:* BA, Zoology, Rutgers University, 1974; University of Medicine and Dentistry, New Jersey, 1977. *Appointments:* Staff, Magazine, Sol '70, 1969-700; Writer, Il Lettere, 1972-73. *Publications:* (Poetry) Peace, 1972; Journey, 1973; Butterfly 1986; Multiple Primary Malignancies of Larynx and Lung : Detection By Cytology, 1981, abstracted 1982; Wrote videoscript entitled: 'Room for Us All', 1986; Vincent Van Gough, Did He Suffer from Immotile Celia Syndrome?, 1987. *Contributions to:* numerous journals and magazines including: Respiration; International Synopses periodical; The Sciences. *Honours:* Golden Poet Award, 1986; Board of Directors of Nargis Dutt Memorial Foundation, 1986-87; Nominated for position of Executive Committee-At-Large, Nargis Dutt Memorial Foundation, 1987; Judge, Biology & Environmental Sciences Category, 49th Annual School Science Fair, New York City, 1987; Recipient, Grand Ambassador of Achievement, USA Representative, American Biographical Institute, 1987; Fellow International Biographical Association, 1987. *Memberships:* American Film Institute, 1976-; American Society of Cytology, 1978; American Society Clinical Pathologists, 1978; New York Academy of Sciences, 1985; American Association for the Advancement of Science, 1985-; Nargis Dutt Memorial Foundation, 1985-. *Address:* 77 Povershon Road, Nutley, NJ 07110, USA.

FERRERI Marco, b. 11 May 1928, Milan, Italy. Screenwriter and director of motion pictures. m. Jacqueline. *Education:* Studied veterinary medicine in mid-1940s. *Career:* Screenwriter and director of motion pictures, Worked as liquor salesman and advertising agent in late 1940s; founder and promoter of filmed periodical, Documento Mensile, 1950-51; actor and production assistant in Italian film industry in early 1950s; optical instruments salesperson in Spain 1954. *Creative Works:* Screenplays and director - Films include: (with Rafael Azcona, El cochecito (The Wheelchair), 1960; (with Jean-Claude Carriere), Liza 1972, also released abroad as La Cagna; (with Azcona), La Grande Bouffe (The Big Feast), 1973, also released abroad as Blow-out; (with Azcona), Touochez pas la Femme blanche, 1974; L'ultima donna Productions Jacques Roltfeld/Flaminia Produzioni 1976, released in US as The Last Woman, 1976; Co-author, Bye Bye Monkey, 1978; Chiedo asilo (My Asylum), Gaumont,

1979; (with Sergio Amidei and Anthony Foutz), Tales of Ordinary Madness, 1983; (with Piera Degli Esposti and Dacia Maraini), Storia di Piera, 1983, released in USA as The Story of Piera, 1983; (with Esposti and Maraini), Il futuro e donna (The Future is Woman), 1984; (with Didier Kaminka and Enrico Oldoini), I Love You, 1988. *Honours:* International Film Critics Award from Venice Film Festival 1960 for El cochecito; International Critics Award from Cannes Film Festival 1973 for La Grande Bouffe. *Address:* Piazza Mattei 10, Rome, Italy.

FERRIS Monk. *See:* **SHARKEY Jack.**

FERRIS Paul, b. 1929, United Kingdom. Freelance Writer. *Publications:* A Changed Man, 1958; The City, 1960; Then We Fall, 1960; The Church of England, 1962; A Family Affair, 1963; The Doctors, 1965; The Destroyer, 1965; The Nameless Abortion in Britain Today, 1966; The Dam, 1967; Men and Money: Financial Europe Today, US Edition The Money Men of Europe, 1968; The House of Northcliffe, 1971; The New Militants: Crisis in the Trade Unions, 1972; Very Personal Problems. 1973; The Cure, 1974; The Detective, US Edition High Places, 1976; Dylan Thomas, 1977; Talk to Me about England, 1979; Richard Burton, 1981; A Distant Country, 1983; Gentlemen of Fortune, US Edition The Master Bankers, 1984; Collected Letters of Dylan Thomas (editor), 1985; Children of Dust, 1988; Sir Huge the life of Huw Wheldon, 1990; Sex and the British: A 20th Century History, 1993; Catlin, 1993; TV plays: The Revivalist, 1975; Dylan, 1978; Nye, 1982; The Extremist, 1983; The Fasting Girl, 1984. *Literary Agent:* Curtis Brown Ltd, England. *Address:* c/o Curtis Brown Ltd, 162-168 Regent Street, London W1R 5TA, England.

FERRISS Lucy, b. 14 Jan 1954, St Louis, Missouri, USA. Novelist. m. Mark P. Couzens, 19 May 1984, New York. *Education:* BA, Pomona College; MA, San Francisco State University; Ph.D, Tufts University. *Appointments:* Writer in Residence, Phillips Exeter Academy; Teaching Fellow, Harvard University; Lecturer, Tufts University. *Publications;* One Step Closer, Anthology, 1976; Philip's Girl, 1985; The Gated River, 1986. *Contributions to:* Pequod; Transfer; Marilyn; Seven Stars; New England Review; San Francisco Chronicle Magazine; Southern Review; Sewanee Review, Massachusetts Review, New York Times Magazine. *Honours:* Alliance Francaise Deuxieme Prix, 1970; Dole prize, 1975; Women's Commission Writing Prize, 1975; Redbook Short Fiction Finalist, 1979; Bennett Fellowship, 1979; Yaddo Fellowship, 1983; MacDowell Fellowship, 1986, 1987. *Literary Agent:* Catherine Ward. *Address:* 72 Standish St, Cambridge, MA 02138, USA.

FERRON Madeleine, b. 24 July 1922, Louisville, Canada. Writer. m. Robert Cliche, 22 Sept 1945, 2 sons, 1 daughter. *Education:* Université de Montréal, 1944; Université Laval, Québec City, 1960. *Appointments:* Freelance Writer, 1973-75; Revue France, Québec, 1977-78; L'Actualité, 1977; Châtelaine, 1980; Critère, 1981; Liberté, 1981; Possibles, 1982-87. *Publications:* Coeur de Sucre; La Fin des Loups Garous; Le Baron Ecarlate; Le Chemin des Dames; Histoires Edifiantes; Sur Le Chemin Craig; Un Singulier Amour; Le Grand Theatre. *Contributions to:* Several. *Honours:* Prix du Magazine Châtelaine; Grand Prix Littéraire de Montréal Finalist; Prix France Québec, Finalist; Prix des Editions la Presse; Ordre national du Québec. *Memberships:* Fondation Robert-Chiche pour la protection du patrimoine des Beaucerons. *Address:* 1130 de La Tour, Québec, Canada G1R 2W7.

FIACC Padraic b. 1924, Ireland. Author; Poet. *Publications:* By the Black Stream, 1969; Odour of Blood, 1973; The Wearing of the Black (editor), 1974; Nights in the Bad Place, 1977; Selected Poems, 1979; Missa Terriblis. *Address:* 43 Farmley Park, Glengormley, Newtownabbey, Co Antrim, Northern Ireland.

FICKERT Kurt Jon, b. 19 Dec 1920, Pausa, Germany, Professor. m. Madlyn Barbara Janda, 6 Aug 1946, 2 sons, 1 daughter. *Education:* BA, Hofstra University, 1941; MA, 1947, PhD, 1952, New York University, USA. *Appointment:* President, Ohio Poetry Day Association, 1968-70. *Publications:* Kafka's Doubles, 1979; Franz Kafka: Life, Work and Criticism, 1984 Hermann Hesse's Quest, 1978; Neither Left Nor Right, 1987; To Heaven and Back: The New Morality in the Plays of Duerrenmatt; Signs and Portents: Myth in Wolfgang Borchert's Work; Johnson: Ansichten, Einsichten, Aussichten, (Contributor), 1989. *Contributions to:* Articles in magazines and journals including: International Fiction Review; The German Quarterly; Monatshefte; Modern Fiction Studies; Journal of Modern Literature. *Memberships:* Phi Beta Kappa; American Association of Teachers of German; Wolfgang Borchert Gesellschaft. *Address:* 33 South Kensington Place, Springfield, OH 45504, USA.

FIELD D M. *See:* **GRANT Neil David Mountfield.**

FIELD Edward, b. 7 June 1924, Brooklyn, New York, USA. Writer. *Education:* New York University (no degree), 1946-48. *Appointments:* Guggenheim Fellow, 1963; Fellow, American Academy of Rome, 1980. *Publications:* Stand Up, Friend, With Me, 1963; Variety Photoplays, 1967; A Full Heart, 1977; A Geography of Poets, editor, 1979; Village (as Bruce Elliott); New and Selected Poems, 1987; Counting Myself Lucky, 1992; The Office (as Bruce Elliott); Eskimo Songs & Stories, 1973; (ed) Head of a Sad Angel: Stories 1953-1966, 1990. *Contributions to:* New Yorker; New York Review of Books; Partisan Review; Evergreen Review; Botteghe Oscure; Harper's; Kenyon Review; The Listener. *Honours:* Lamont Award, 1963; Shelley Memorial Award, 1978. *Membership:* Authors Guild. *Address:* 463 West Street, A323, New York, NY 10014, USA.

FIELD Stanley, b. 20 May 1911, Ukraine. Writer; Professor. m. Joyce Stillman, 7 Dec 1935, 1 son, 1 daughter. *Education:* BA, Brooklyn College, 1934. *Appointments:* Writer, National Broadcasting Co, New York City, 1934-40; Script Writer, Radio and TV Programme, US Department of Defense, 1942-75; Adjunct Professor, Creative Writing, The American University, Washington, District of Columbia, 1952-77; Instructor, Creative Writing, Mt Vernon College. *Publications:* Television and Radio Writing, 1959; Guide to Scholarships, 1967; Bible Stories, 1967; Broadcast Writers Handbook, 1974; The Mini-Documentary, 1975; The Freelancer, 1984. *Contributions to:* Short stories and poetry to: Virginia Country; Adventure; War Cry; Writers Journal; Green's; Omega Chronicles; Minnesota Ink; A Loving Voice; Wellspring; Cats; Articles to: Photo; Stag; Woman's Life; Live; Washington Star; Home Life; New York Alive; Poets and Writers; Women's Household; Friar. *Honours:* YMCA International Script Award, 1945; Fund for the Republic Award, 1952; Freedoms Foundation, 1953, 1954; Writers Digest Fiction Award, 1972; Writers Journal Fiction Award, 1986; Literary Lights Fiction Award, 1988; Wellspring Fiction Award, 1991. *Memberships:* The Authors Guild; Poets and Fiction Writers; International Society of Dramatists; San Diego Writers Guild; Broadcast Education Association; Associated Writing Programmes. *Literary Agent:* West Coast Literary Associates. *Address:* 5196 Middleton Rd, San Diego, CA 92109, USA.

FIELDER Mildred, b. 14 Jan 1913, Quinn, South Dakota, USA. Author. m. Ronald G. Fielder, 17 Sept 1932, 2 sons. *Education:* Huron College, 1930-31; University of Colorado, 1946. *Publications:* Wandering Foot in the West, 1955; Railroads of the Black Hills, 1960; Wild Bill and Deadwood, 1965; Treasure of Homestake Gold, 1970; Guide to Black Hills Ghost Mines, 1972; Chinese in the Black Hills, 1972; Potato Creek Johnny, 1973; Hiking Trails in the Black Hills, 1973; Wild Bill Hickok Gun Man, 1974; Theodore Roosevelt in Dakota Territory, 1974; Deadwood Dick and the Dime Novels, 1974; Sioux Indian Leaders, 1975; Plant Medicine and Folklore, 1975; Lost Gold, 1978;

Poker Alice, 1978; Silver is the Fortune, 1978; Preacher Smith of Deadwood, 1981; Fielder's Herbal Helper, 1982; The Legend of Lame Johnny Creek, 1982; Wild Fruits, 1983; Captain Jack Crawford, 1983; Invitation to Fans, 1988. *Contributions to:* Numerous historical articles and many poems, USA and Canada; 7 prose anthologies; 11 poetry anthologies. *Honours:* 3 Literary Awards; Certificate of Recognition, South Dakota Historical Society, 1975; Sweepstakes Award, National League of American Pen Women, 1976; Distinguished Service Award, National League of American Pen Women, 1980; Total Awards to date 425, of which 56 were national. *Memberships:* Life Member, Society of American Historians; South Dakota Poetry Society, 1955-65 (Regional Vice-President); South Dakota Historical Society; National League of American Pen Women, National Historian 1962, National Auditor 1968-70, several National Chairmanships, Book Review Editor, Endowment Fund, in Focus Column for Pen Women Magazine; NLAPW National Letters Board, 1987-88. *Address:* 264 San Jacinto Drive, Los Osos, CA 93402, USA.

FIELDING Raymond Edwin, b. 3 Jan 1931, Brockton, Massachusetts, USA. Author; University Professor and Administrator. m. Carole Louise Behrens, 7 Oct 1963. *Education:* BA, Theatre Arts, 1953, MA, Theatre Arts, 1956, University of California, Los Angeles; PhD, Communication, University of Southern California, 1961. *Appointments:* Associate 1957-61, Assistant Professor, 1961-65, Associate Professor, 1965, University of California, Los Angeles; Associate Professor, University of Iowa, 1965-69; Professor, School of Communication, Temple University, 1969-78; Director and Professor, School of Communication, University of Houston, 1978-90; Dean, School of Motion Picture, Television and Recording Arts, Florida State University, 1990-. *Publications:* The Technique of Special Effects Cinematography, 1965, 1985; The American Newsreel, 1980; The March of Time 1935-51, 1978; A Technological History of Motion Pictures and Television, 1967. Motion Picture/Television Writer: Eyewitness to Yesterday, Walt Disney Productions, 1978; Yesterday's Witness, PBS Television Network, 1979; The Honorable Mountain, CBS Television Network, Hoffberg Productions, 1954-55. *Contributions to:* Numerous articles in Smithsonian Journal of History, Journal of Film and Video, Cinema Journal, Historical Journal of Film, Radio and Television; American Archivist; American Cinematographer; Journal of Broadcasting; Quarterly of Film, Radio and Television and Journal of Society of Motion Picture and Television Engineers. *Honours:* First Prize, Lion of St Marc, 13th International Exposition of Books on Cinema and Television, Venice International Film Festival, 1968; Elected Fellow of the Society of Motion Picture and Television Engineers, 1976; Elected Active Member of the Academy of Motion Picture Arts and Sciences, 1981. *Memberships:* Member and Past President, 1972-74, Society of Cinema Studies; Member and Past President, 1967-68, Awarded Eastman Kodak Gold Medal of the Society of Mation Picture & Television Engineers, 1991; University Film and Video Association; Trustee and Past President, 1985-88, University Film and Video Foundation; Member and Past Vice President for Education, 1978-79, Society of Motion Picture and Television Engineers; Academy of Motion Picture Arts and Sciences. *Address:* School of Motion Picture, Television and Recording Arts, Florida State University, Tallahassee, FL 32306, USA.

FIENNES Ranulph Twisleton-Wykeham (Sir), b. 7 Mar 1944, England. Travel Writer; Explorer. m. 9 Sept 1971. *Education:* Eton College, 1956-59; DSc (Hon), Loughborough College. *Publications:* Talent or Trouble, 1972; Icefall in Norway, 1973; The Headless Valley, 1974; Where Soldiers Fear to Tread, 1975; Hell on Ice, 1977; To the Ends of the Earth, 1983; Bothie - The Polar Dog, 1985; Living Dangerously, 1987; The Feather Men, 1991. *Contributions to:* The Geographical Magazine (UK); The National Geographical Magazine (US); The Smithsonian; Observer Colour Supplement; Sunday Times. *Honours:* Founders Medal, Royal Geographical Society; Gold Medal, Explorers Club of New York; Polar Medal, awarded by H.M. The Queen, 1987. *Memberships:* Antarctic Club; Fellow, Royal Geographical Society; The Arctic Club. *Literary Agent:* George Greenfield, John Farquharson Ltd.

FIFIELD Christopher, b. 4 Sept 1945, Croydon, England. Musician. m. Judith Weyman, 28 Oct 1972. *Education:* ARCO, 1967; MusB (Hons), 1968; GRSM, 1969; ARMCM, 1969. *Publications:* Max Bruch: His Life and Works, 1988; Wagner in Performance, 1992; Hans Richter, 1993. *Contributions to:* Musical Times; Strad; Classical Music, Music and Letters. *Address:* Coach House, 38 Wrights Rd, London SE25 6RY, England.

FIGES Eva, b. 15 Apr 1932, Berlin, Germany. Writer. 1 son, 1 daughter. *Education:* BA, Honours, English Language & Literature, University of London, 1953. *Publications:* Patriarchal Attitudes, 1970; Winter Journey, 1967; Waking, 1981; Light, 1983; The Seven Ages, 1986; Nelly's Version, 1977; B, 1972; Little Eden, 1978; Sex & Subterfuge, 1982; Ghosts, 1988; The Tree of Knowledge, 1990; The Tenancy, 1993. *Honours:* Guardian Fiction Prize, 1967. *Memberships:* Writers Guild of Great Britain, Chairperson, 1986-87; PEN. *Literary Agent:* Rogers, Coleridge & White Ltd. *Address:* 24 Fitzjohns Avenue, London NW3 5NB, England.

FILTZER Donald, b. 8 Jan 1948, Baltimore, USA. m. Frances (Sacks) Filtzer, 1 son. *Education:* Wesleyan University, Middletown, Conn., USA; BA, (cum laude), 1969; PhD, University of Glasgow, 1976. *Appointments:* Research Fellow of Centre for Russian and East European studies, University of Birmingham, Birmingham, England, 1978-. *Publications:* The Crisis of Soviet Industrialization, (editor and author of Introduction), 1979; A History of Economic Thought, (editor and translator), 1979; Soviet Workers and Stalinist Industrialization: The Formation of Modern Soviet Production Relations, 1928-41; Research on the position of the Soviet work force during the Khrushchev period and the impact of de-Stalinization on Soviet production relations. *Contributions to:* The Times Literary Supplement, 1987.

FINALE Frank Louis, b. 10 Mar 1942, Brooklyn, New York, USA. Educator. m. Barbara Long, 20 Oct 1973. 3 sons. *Education:* BS, Education, Ohio State University, 1964; MA, Human Development, Fairleigh Dickinson University, 1976. *Appointment:* Editor-in-Chief, Without Halos, helped found 1983, 1985-. *Publications:* Poems included in anthologies: Life on the Line, 1992; A Loving Voice, 1993; A Celebration of Cats (Ed Jean Burden), 1974; Anthology of Magazine Verse, 1985, 1986-88; Blood to Remember, 1990; Movie Works, 1991; Peace Is Our Profession, 1981; Dear Winter (Ed Marie Harris), 1984. *Contributions to:* The Christian Science Monitor; Pig Iron; Georgia Review; New York Quarterly; Kansas Quarterly; The New Renaissance; Negative Capability; Blue Unicorn; Poetry NOW; Poet Lore; Plains Poetry Journal; Visions; Coast. *Membership:* Founding Member, Ocean County Poets Collective, 1983. *Address:* 921 Riverside Drive, Pine Beach, NJ 08741, USA.

FINCH Peter, b. 6 Mar 1947, Cardiff, Wales. Bookshop Manager for Welsh Arts Council; Creative writing tutor, experimenter, literary entrepreneur. m. 2 sons, 1 daughter. *Literary Appointments:* Treasurer, Association of Little Presses; Former executive member, Poetry Society, and Yr Academy Cymreig; Former editor, Second Aeon (journal). *Publications include:* Wanted, 1967; Pieces of the Universe, 1968; How to Learn Welsh, 1977; Between 35 & 42, short stories, 1982; Some Music & A Little War, 1984; How to Publish Your Poetry, 1985; Reds in the Bed, 1986; Selected Poems, 1987; How to Publish Yourself, 1988; Selected Poems, 1987; Poems for Ghosts, 1991; Make, 1990; The Cheng Man Ch'ing Variations, 1991; Also: Cycle of the Suns; Beyond the Silence; An Alteration in the Way I Breathe; Edge of Tomorrow; End of the Vision; Antarktika; Trowch Eich Radio 'mlaen; Connecting Tubes; O Poems; Blues & Heartbreakers; Blats; Big Band Dance Music; Dances Interdites; Visual Texts 1970-1980; Editor, Green Horse.

Contributions include: Most major magazines & journals including: PN Review; Ambit; Poetry Review; Stand; Poetry Wales; Planet. *Address:* 19 Southminster Road, Roath, Cardiff, Wales.

FINCH Matthew. *See:* FINK Merton.

FINCH Merton. *See:* FINK Merton.

FINCKE Gary W, b. 7 July 1945, Pittsburgh, Pennsylvania, USA. College Educator; Writer. m. Elizabeth Locker, 17 Aug 1968, 2 sons, 1 daughter. *Education:* BA, Thiel College, 1967; MA, Miami University, 1969; PhD, Kent State University, 1974. *Appointments:* Writing Program Director, Susquehanna University, 1980-. *Publications:* Inventing Angels; For Keepsies; The Double Negatives of the Living; Plant Voices; The Public Talk of Death; The Days of Uncertain Health; Handing the Self Back; The Coat in the Heart; Breath. *Contributions to:* Harpers; The Paris Review; Poetry; Yankee; The Georgia Review; The Quarterly; Kenyon Review; Missouri Review; The Gettysburg Review; Poetry Northwest. *Honours:* Poetry/Fiction Fellowships; PEN Syndicated Fiction Prize; Bess Hokin Prize. *Memberships:* Poetry Society of America; Associated Writers Programs; Poets and Writers. *Address:* 3 Melody Lane, Selinsgrove, PA 17870, USA.

FINDLEY Timothy Irving Frederick, b. 30 Oct 1930, Toronto, Canada. Writer. *Appointments include:* Playwright-in-residence, National Arts Centre, Ottawa, 1974-75; Writer-in-residence, University of Toronto 1970-80, Trent University 1984, University of Winnipeg 1985. *Publications include:* Last of the Crazy People, 1967; Butterfly Plague, 1969; Can You See Me Yet?, play, 1977; The Wars, 1977; Famous Last Words, 1981; Dinner Along the Amazon, collected stories, 1984; Not Wanted on the Voyage, 1984; The Telling of Lies, 1986; Stones (short fiction), 1988. *Honours include:* Armstrong Award, radio, 1971; ACTRA Award, TV documentary, Canada, 1975; Toronto Book Award, 1977; Governor General's Award, fiction, 1977; Anik Award, TV, Canada, 1980; Honorary DLitt, Trent University, 1982, University of Guelph 1984; Author of Year, Periodical Distributors of Canada 1983, Canadian Booksellers Association 1984; Novel of Year, Canadian Authors Association, 1985; Officer, Order of Canada, 1986; Trillium Award, 1989; Edger Award, (Mystery Writes of America), 1989. *Memberships:* Association of Canadian TV & Radio Artists (ACTRA); Past Chairman, Writers Union of Canada; Past Chairman, English Canadian Centre, PEN International. *Literary Agent:* Colbert Agency. *Address:* c/o The Colbert Agency, 303 Davenport Road, Toronto, Ontario, Canada M5R 1K5.

FINE Anne, b. 7 Dec 1947, Leicester, England. Writer. m. Kit Fine, 3 Aug 1968, 2 daughters. *Education:* BA Hons, History/Politics, University of Warwick. *Publications include:* Novels: The Killjoy, 1986; Taking the Devils Advice, 1990; For Older Children: Round Behind the Ice House, 1981; The Granny Project, 1983; Madame Doubtfire (on cassettee), 1987; Goggle-Eyes, 1989; The Book of the Banshee, 1991; Flour Babies, 1992; For Middle Children: A Sudden Swirl of Icy Wind, 1990; A Sudden Glow of Gold, 1991; Anneli the Art Hater, 1986; Crummy Mummy and Me, 1988; A Pack of Liars, 1988; The Angel of Nitshill Road, 1991; The Chicken Gave it to Me, 1992; For Younger Children: The Worst Child I Ever Had, 1991; The Same Old Story Every Year, 1992; The Haunting of Pip Parker, 1992; Picture Book: Poor Monty, 1991. *Honours:* Smarties Prize, 1990; Library Association Carnegie Medal, 1990; Guardian Children's Literature Award, 1990; Publishing News, Children's Author of the year, 1990. *Membership:* Society of Authors. *Literary agent:* Murray Pollinger, *Address;* 222 Old Brompton Road, London SW5 OB2, England.

FINER Samuel (Edward), b. 1915, United Kingdom. Emeritus Professor of Politics, Oxford University. *Publications:* A Primer of Public Administration, 1950;

The Life and Times of Sir Edwin Chadwick, 1952; Local Government in England and Wales (with Sir J Maud), 1953; Anonymous Empire: A Study of the Lobby in Britain, 1958, 2nd Edition, 1966; Private Industry and Political Power, 1958; Backbench Opinion in the House of Commons 1955-59 (with D Bartholomew and H Berrington), 1961; The Man on Horseback: The Role of the Military in Politics, 1962, 2nd Edition, 1976; Sieves: What Is the Third Estate (editor), 1963; Pareto; Sociological Writings (editor), 1966; Comparative Government, 1970; Adversary Politics and Electoral Reform, 1975; Five Constitutions, 1979; The Changing British Party Systems, 1980; The British Party System, 1986. *Address:* All Souls College, Oxford, OX1 4AL, England.

FINK Merton, (Matthew Finch, Merton Finch), b. 17 Nov 1921, Liverpool, England. Author. m. (1) 15 Mar 1953, 1 son, 1 daughter, (2) 24 Nov 1981. *Education:* School of Military Engineers, 1942; School of Military Intelligence, 1943; LDS, Liverpool University, 1947-52. *Publications:* 17 Books: 14 novels, 2 historical, 1 technical; Dentist in the Chair, 1953, filmed 1956; Teething Troubles, 1954; The Third Set, 1955; Hang Your Hat on a Pension, 1956; The Empire Builder, 1957; Snakes and Ladders, 1958; Solo Fiddle, 1959; The Beauty Bazaar, 1960; Matchbreakers, 1961; Five Are The Symbols, 1962; Jones Is A Rainbow, 1963; Succobus, 1964; Chew The Over, 1965; Eye With Mascara, 1966; Eye Spy, 1967; Simon Bar Cochba, 1971; A Fox Called Flavus, 1973; Open Wide, 1976. *Contributions to:* Dental Practice, monthly, 1964-. *Honour:* Richard Edwards Scholar, 1950. *Memberships:* Civil Service Writers; Deputy Chairman, Bath Literary Society; British Dental Association; Admiralty Rifle Club; Chairman Service Committee, Bath British Legion; Police Interpreters for German; Committee, Bath Arts Association. *Literary Agent:* Laurence Pollinger Limited. *Address:* 27 Harbutts, Bathampton, Bath, BA2 6TA, England.

FINKEL Donald, b. 21 Oct 1929, New York, USA. Poet. m. Constance Urdang, 14 Aug 1956, 1 son, 2 daughters. *Education:* B, Philosophy, 1952, MA English, 1953, Columbia University. *Appointment:* Poet in Residence, Washington University, 1964-. *Publications:* The Clothing's New Emperor, 1959; Simeon, 1964; A Joyful Noise, 1966; Answer Back, 1968; The Garbage Wars, 1970; Adequate Earth, 1972; A Mote in Heaven's Eye, 1975; Endurance and Going Under, 1978; What Manner of Beast, 1981; The Detachable Man, 1984; Selected Shorter Poems, 1987; The Wake of the Electron, 1987. *Contributions to:* numerous journals and magazines. *Honours:* Phi Beta Kappa, 1953; Helen Bullis Award, 1964; Guggenheim Fellowship, 1967; Nomination, National Book Award, 1970; Ingram Merrill Foundation Grant, 1972; NEA Grant, 1973; Theodore Roethke Memorial Award, 1974; Morton Dauwen Zabel Award, 1980; Nomination, National Book Critics Circle Award, 1975, 1981. *Address:* 6943 Columbia Pl, St Louis, MO 63130, USA.

FINLAY Ian Hamilton, b. 1925, British. Writer of short stories; poetry; Publisher, Wild Hawthorn Press, Dunsyre, Lanarkshire (formerly in Edinburgh and Easter Ross), 1961-. *Publications include:* Tea-Leaves and Fishes, 1966; Ocean Stripe Series 4, 1966; 4 Sails, 1966; Headlines, Eavelines, 1967; Stonechats, 1967; Ocean Stripe Series 5, 1967; Canal Game, 1967; The Collected Coaltown of Challenge Tri-kai, 1968; Air Letters, 1968; The Blue and the Brown Poems, 1968; 3/3's 1969; A Boatyard, 1969; Lanes, 1969; Wave, 1969; Rhymes for Lemons, 1970; Fishing News, 1970; 30 Signature to Silver Catches, 1971; Poems to Hear and See, 1971; A Sailor's Calendar, 1971; The Olsen Exerpts, 1971; A Memory of Summer, 1971; From An Island Garden, 1971; Evening/Sail 2, 1971; The weed Boat Masters Ticket, Preliminary Text (Part Two) 1971; Sail/Sundial, 1972; Jibs, 1972; Honey by the Water, 1973; Butterflies, 1973; A Family, 1973; Exercise X, 1974; So Youo Want to Be a Panzer Leader, 1975; Airs-Waters-Graces, 1975; The Wild Hawthorn Wonder Book of Boats, 1975; A Master of Hankies, 1975; The Axis,

1975; Trombone Carrier, 1975; Homage to Watteau, 1975; Three Sundials, 1975; Imitations, Variations, Reflections, Copies, 1976; The Wild Hawthorn Art Test, 1977; Heroic Emblems, 1977; The Boy's Alphabet Book, 1977; The Wartime Garden, 1977; Trailblazers, 1978; Homage to Poussin, 1978; Peterhead Fragments, 1979; SS 1979; Dzaezl, 1979; Woods and Seas, 1979; Two Billows, 1979; Romances, Emblems, Enigmas, 1981; Developments, 1982. *Address:* Stoneypath, Dunsyre, Lanarkshire, Scotland.

FINLAY Roger Anthony Peter, b. 24 Jan 1952, London, England. Author; Bookseller. m. Lorna Anne Smith, 5 Oct 1984. *Education:* Hertford College, Oxford, 1970-73; BA 1st Class, 1973, MA, 1977, Oxford University; Peterhouse, Cambridge, 1973-77; PhD, Cambridge University, 1977. *Appointments:* Research Fellow, University of Lancaster, 1977-80; Librarian, John Rylands Library, Manchester, 1980-87; Principal, Barlow Moor Books, Manchester, 1987-. *Publications:* Population and Metropolis: The Demography of London 1580-1650, 1981; London 1500-1750: The Making of the Metropolis (edited with A L Brier), 1986; Japenese translation, Sanrei Shobo, Tokyo, 1992. *Contributions to:* Past and Present; Population Studies; Journal of Family History; Annales de Demographie Historique, Paris; Others; Also many reviews and short contributions. *Honours:* Herbertson Memorial Prize, University of Oxford, 1973. *Address:* 29 Churchwood Road, Didsbury, Manchester M20 0TZ, England.

FINLAY William. *See:* **MACKAY James Alexander.**

FINLEY Michael Craig, b. 7 Apr 1950, Flint, Michigan, USA. Editor. m. Rachel M Frazin, 25 July 1980, 1 daughter. *Education:* BA, University of Minnesota. *Publications:* The Movie Under the Blindfold, 1978; Home Trees, 1978; Water Hills, 1984. *Contributor To:* Paris Review; Rolling Stone. *Honour:* Pushcart Prize, 1984. *Memberships:* Wisconsin Arts Board Evaluations Panel, (literature); Poets & Writers Inc. *Address:* 2320 E Bradford Avenue 2, Milwaukee, WI 53211, USA.

FINN Ralph Leslie,b. 17 Jan 1912, London, England. Advertising Creative Head; Lecturer; Tutor. m. Freda Nathanson, 15 June 1936, 1 son, 1 daughter. *Education:* B.Ed; Dips Psychology; Oxford; University of London; Advertising MIPA; Dip, CAM; Dr.Lit, 1966. *Publications include:* He Said Whats Blue, 1944; Down Oxford Street, 1947; No Tears in Aldgate, 1973; Spring in Aldgate, 1975; Time Remembered, 1988; Grief Forgotton, 1989. *Contributions to:* leading newspapers and journals. *Honours:* World Award Short Story, 1945; One of Worlds Six Best Creative Men, 1957. *Membership:* Institute of Journalists. *Address:* 7 Red Lodge, Red Road, Elstree, Hertfordshire WD6 4SN, England.

FINNERAN Richard J(ohn), b. 1943, USA. Professor of English. *Appointments:* Instructor, University of Florida, 1967-68; Instructor, New York University, 1968-70; Assistant Professor, 1970-74, Associate Professor, 1974-77, Professor of English, 1977-, Newcomb College, Tulane University; Editor, Yeats Annual, 1982-. *Publications:* John Sherman and Dhoya by W B Yeats (editor), 1969; William Butler Yeats: The Byzantium Poems (editor), 1970; The Prose Fiction of W B Yeats: The Search for Those Simple Forms, 1973; Letters of James Stephens (editor), 1974; Anglo-Irish Literature: A Review of Research (editor), 1976; The Correspondence of Robert Bridges and W B Yeats (editor), 1977; Letters to W B Yeats (edited with George Mills Harper and William M Murphy), 1977; Recent Research in Anglo-Irish Writers (editor), 1982; Editing Yeats's Poems, 1983; The Poems of W B Yeats (editor), 1983; Critical Essays on W B Yeats, 1986. *Address:* 89 Versailles Boulevard, New Orleans, LA 70125, USA.

FINNEY Mark. *See:* **MUIR Kenneth Arthur.**

FINNIGAN Joan, b. 23 Nov 1925, Ottawa, Canada. Writer. m. Charles Grant, 23 May 1949, 2 sons, 1 daughter. *Education;* BA, Queens University, 1967. *Publications include:* Screenplay: The Best Damn Fiddler from Calabodie to Kaladar, 1982; CBC Radio Scripts, Songs for the Bible Belt, May Day Rounds, Children of the Shadows, There's No Good time Left - None at All, 1976; Poetry: Through the Glass, Darkly, 1963; A Dream of Lilies, 1965; Entrance to the Greenhouse, 1968; It Was Warm and Sunny When We Set Out, 1970; In the Brown Cottage on Loughborough Lake, 1970; Living Together, 1976; A Reminder of a Familiar Faces, 1978; This Series Has Been Discontinued, 1980; Poetry: The Watershed Collection, 1988; Wintering Over, 1992. *Contributions to:* numerous journals and magazines. *Honours:* Various honours and awards. *Address:* Hartington, Ontario KOH 1WO, Canada.

FINSTAD Suzanne, b. 14 Sept 1955, Minneapolis, Minnesota, USA. Author; Attorney (non-practising). *Education:* University of Texas, Austin, 1973-74; BA, French, University of Houston, 1976; University of Grenoble, France, 1979; JD, Bates College of Law, 1980; London School of Economics, 1980. *Publications:* Heir Not Apparent, 1984; Ulterior Motives, 1987; Sleeping with the Devil, 1991; Biography of Queen Noor of Jordan, in progress. *Contributions to:* Cover profile of Queen Noor for European Travel and Life; Fame; Penthouse; Mademoiselle; Cosmopolitan; Good Housekeeping; Marie Claire (British edition). *Honours:* American Jurisprudence Award in Criminal Law, Bancroft-Whitney Publishing Co, 1979; Order of the Barons, 1980; Frank Wardlaw for a first work of literary excellence, for Heir Not Apparent. *Membership:* State Bar of Texas. *Literary Agent:* Joel Gotler, Los Angeles, USA. *Address:* c/o Joel Gotler, 9000 Sunset Boulevard, Los Angeles, CA, USA.

FINUCANE Ronald C, b. 10 Aug 1939, Los Angeles, California, USA. University Professor. *Education:* BA, University of Nevada, 1967; MA, 1968, PhD, 1972, Stanford University; Matriculated, Wadham College, Oxford, England, 1970. *Appointments:* General Editor, (New) History of Europe, 7 vols, Blackwell, UK, 1991-. *Publications:* Miracles and Pilgrims: Popular Beliefs in Medieval England, 1977; Soldiers of the Faith: Crusaders and Moslems at War, 1983; Appearances of the Dead: A Cultural History, 1984; Contributions to: History of Christianity, 1977; Encyclopedia of Religion, 1987. *Contributions to:* Several to: Journal of Ecclesiastical History; Speculum; Church History; Psychiatry; History; Journal of Medieval History; Religious Studies Review. *Honours:* Leverhulme Fellowship, Oxford University; Various awards and grants, National Endowment for the Humanities and American Council of Learned Societies, 1980s-1990s. *Memberships:* Phi Kappa Phi; Phi Alpha Theta. *Address:* Department of History, Oakland University, Rochester, MI 48309, USA.

FISCHER Lynn Helen b. 2 June 1943, Red Wing, Minnesota, USA. Author; Inventor. *Education:* Approximately 4 years college, Doctor of Genius Degree, 1986. *Appointments:* Author, Editor, Publisher, Genius Newsletter, 1990-. *Publications include:* The 1, 2, 4 Theory: A Synthesis, 1971; Sexual Equations of Electricity, Magnetism & Gravitation, 1971; Human Sexual Evolution, 1971; Middle Concept Theory, 1972; A Revised Meaning of Paradox, 1972; Unitary Theory, 1973; An Introduction To Circular or Fischerian Geometry, 1976; Two, Four, Eight Theory, 1976; Fischer's Brief Dictionary of Sound Meanings, 1977; Introducing the Magnetic Sleeve: A Novel Sexual Organ, 1983; The Expansion of Duality, 1984; The Inger POems, 1985; Letters of the Poet Lynn, 1987; Country Wit/ The Inger Poems & Early Poems; Mathematical Philosophy Of The Poet Lynn/The Mathematics of Poetry on cassette, 1987; The Inventions & Essays, 1988 on cassette; Cave Man Talk & Other Essays, 1989, on cassette; Inventions and Essays, 1988; Cave Man Talk, 1990; Circular Geometry, 1990; The Four Inventions, 1990; A Story of Creation: The Expansion of Dualism, 1990; The Early Poems by Musical Lynn, 1990; The Musical Lynn Song Lyrics, 1991; The Musical Lynn Essays, Vol. 1, 1992; Caveman Talk, 1992; The Three

In One Ring and The Magnetic Woman, 1992; Apple Skies, 1993. *Memberships:* NAFE; National Association for Female Executives. *Address:* Apt 1108, 1415 E 22nd Street, Minneapolis, MN 55404, USA.

FISCHER Tibor, b. 15 June 1959, Stockport, England. *Contributions to:* Under the Frog; Polygon; Edinburgh. *Honours:* Betty Trask Award; Best of Young British Novelists, 1993. *Address:* Polygon, 22 George Square, Edinburgh, EH8 9LF, Scotland.

FISCHER-FABIAN Siegfried, b. 22 Sept 1922, Bad Elmen, Germany. Author. m. Ursula Pauling, 1950, 2 sons. *Education:* German, History, History of Art, Dramatic Art, Humboldt University and Free University, Berlin; Graduated, Free University, Berlin; Dr phil. *Appointments:* Journalist, Collaborator with the press and radio; Theatre Critic, Schweizer Monatshefte, BV. *Publications:* Mit Eva fing d Liebe an, E Kulturgesch d Liebe u Ehe, 11 stories, 1958, 1964; Venus m Herz u Kopfchen, E Liebeserklarung an d Berlinerin, 1959; Mussen Berliner so sein...?, E Bekenntnis in Portraits, 1960; Hurra, wir bauen uns e Haus!, D Gesch e bundesdt Baufamilie, 1962, 1965; Liebe im Schnee, Fast e Tatsachenbericht, 1965, 1968; Das Ratsel in Dir, D Welt d Triebe, Traume u Komplexe, 1966; Deutschland kann lachen..., V Bayern, Berlinern, Sachsen u a Germanen, 1966; Traum ist rings d Welt, E Bericht ub d Liebe gr Dichte, 1967; Europa kann lachen, V Englandern, Franzosen, Schweizern, Russen u a Europiden, 1972; Geliebte Tyrannen, E Brevier f alle Katzenfreunde u solche, d es werden wollen, 1973; Berlin-Evergreen, Bild e Stadt in 16 Portraits, 1973; Aphrodite ist an allem schuld, 1974; D Ersten Deutschen, D Bericht ub d ratselhafte Volk d Germanen, 1975; D deutschen Casaren - Triumph u Tragodie d Kaiser d Mittelalters, 1977; Preussens Gloria, D Aufstieg eines Staates, 1979; Preussens Krieg u Frieden, D Weg ins dt Reich, 1981; Vergesst d Lachen Nicht, D Humor d Deutschen, 1982; Herrliche Zeiten, D Deutschen u ihr Kaiserreich, 1983; D Jungste Tag, D Deutschen im spaten Mittelalter, 1985; Die Macht des Gewissens (Von Sokrates bis Sophie Scholl), 1987; Um Gott und Gold (Columbus entdeckt eine neue Welt), 1991; Columbus, Lebensbilder (Bildband), 1991; F.C. Piepenburg, SEIN WEG, 1982; W.Ch. Schmitt, Die Auflagenmillonäre, 1988. *Contributions to:* Festschrifts: Prinz Louis Ferdinand, 1982; D Fischer-Dieskau, 1985. *Honours:* Christophorus Prize, 1988. *Address:* Sonnenhof, 8137 Aufkirchen, Starnberger See, Germany.

FISH Stanley, b. 19 Apr 1938, Providence, Rhode Island, USA. Professor of English & Law. m. 7 Aug 1982, 1 daughter. *Education:* BA, University of Pennsylvania, 1959; MA 1960, PhD 1962, Yale University. *Appointments include:* Full Professor, English, University of California, Berkeley, 1962-74; William Kenan Jr Professor, Humanities, Johns Hopkins University, 1974-85; Chairman and Arts and Science Distinguished Professor of English, Professor of Law, Duke University. *Publications include:* John Skelton's Poetry, 1965; Surprised by Sin: The Reader in Paradise Lost, 1967; Self-Consuming Artifacts, 1972; Living Temple: George Herbert and Catechizing, 1978; Is There a Text in This Class?, 1980; Doing What Comes Naturally, 1989. *Contributions to:* Various scholarly journals including Times Literary Supplement, Yale Review. *Honours:* ACLS Fellowship, 1966; Guggenheim Fellowship, 1969-70; Humanities Research Professorship, UC Berkeley, 1966, 1970; 2nd place, Explicator Prize, 1968; Nomination, National Book Award, 1972. *Memberships:* Past President, Milton Society of America; American Academy of Arts & Sciences. *Address:* Department of English, Allen Building, Duke University, Durham, North Carolina 27706, USA.

FISHER Allen, b. 1 Nov 1944, Norbury, Surrey, England. Painter; Poet; Art Historian. *Education:* BA (Hons), University of London; MA, University of Essex. *Publications:* Over 80 books including: Place Book One, 1974; Brixton Fractals, 1985; Unpolished Mirrors, 1985; Stepping Out, 1989; Future Exiles, 1991. *Contributions*

to: Numerous contributions to various magazines and journals. *Honours:* Co-winner, Alice Hunt- Bartlett Award, 1975. *Address:* 14 Hopton Road, Hereford HR1 1BE, England.

FISHER Leonard Everett, b. 24 June 1924, New York City, USA. Artist; Author. m. Margery Meskin, 21 Dec 1952, 1 son, 2 daughters. *Education:* BFA 1949, MFA 1950, Yale University. *Appointment:* President of Westport (CT) Public Library Board of Trustees, 1986-89. *Publications include:* 75 books written and illustrated including: Non Fiction: Colonial Americans, 19 volumes, 1964-76; Ellis Island, 1986; Look Around, 1987; The Tower of London, 1987; Galileo, 1992; Tracks Across America, 1992; Stars and Stripes, 1993; Fiction: Death of Evening Star, 1972; Across the Sea from Galway, 1975; Sailboat Lost, 1991; Cyclops, 1991; Illustrator of morethan 250 books for young readers. *Contributions to:* Five Owls, USA; National Council Teachers of English, USA; Magpies, Australia; North Light, USA; Cricket, USA; Voice of the Narrator. *Honours:* Pulitzer Art Award, 1950; Premio Grafico, Fiera di Bologna, 1968; Medallion, University of Southern Mississippi, 1979; Christopher Medal, 1980; National Jewish Book Award, 1981; Children's Book Guild Parents Choice Award, 1989; Washington Post-Washington Children's Book Guild Non Fiction Award, 1989; Regina Medal, Catholic Library Association, 1991; Kerlan Award, University of Minnesota, 1991. *Memberships:* Authors Guild; Society of Children's Book Writers and Illustrators; Society of Illustrators. *Literary Agent:* William B R Reiss, John Hawkins & Associates, New York, USA. *Address:* 7 Twin Bridge Acres Road, Westport, CT 06880, USA.

FISHER Nigel (Sir), b. 14 July 1913, Cosham, Hants, England. Retired. m. (1) Lady Gloria Vaughan, 1935, (2) Patricia Smiles, 1 son, 1 daughter. *Education:* Eton College; BA 1934, MA 1939, Trinity College, Cambridge. *Publications:* Biographies: Iain Macleod 1973, Harold Macmillan 1982, The Tory Leaders 1977. *Honours:* MC 1944; Kt 1974. *Memberships:* Society of Authors; MCC; Boodles. *Address:* 45 Exeter House, Putney Heath, London SW15 3SX, England.

FISHER Roy, b. 11 June 1930, Birmingham, England. Poet; Musician. *Education:* BA 1951, MA 1970, Birmingham University. *Literary Appointments include:* Various committees. *Publications include:* City, 1961; The Ship's Orchestra, 1967; Collected Poems 1968, 1969; Matrix, 1971; The Thing about Joe Sullivan, 1978; Poems 1955-80, 1980; A Furnace, 1986; Poems 1955-87; 1988. Also: Interiors, 1966; The Memorial Fountain, 1968; Metmorphoses, 1971; The Cut Pages, 1971, 1986; Also, 1973; The Left-Handed Punch, 1987. *Contributions to:* Numerous journals & magazines. *Honours:* Andrew Kelus Prize, 1979; Cholmondeley Award, 1981. *Memberships:* Society of Authors; Musicians Union. *Address:* Four Ways, Earl Sterndale, Buxton, Derbyshire SK17 0EP, England.

FISHLOCK Trevor, b. 21 Feb 1941, Hereford, England. Journalist; Author. m. Penelope Symon, 1978. *Appointments:* Portsmouth Evening News, 1957-62; Freelance News Agency Reporter, 1962-68; The Times, Wales and West England Staff Correspondent, 1968-78; The Times South Asia Correspondent, 1980-83; The Times New York Correspondent, 1983-86; Roving Foreign Correspondent, The Daily Telegraph, 1986-89; Moscow Correspondent, 1989-91; Roving Foreign Correspondent, The Sunday Telegraph, 1991-. *Publications:* Wales & The Welsh, 1972; Talking of Wales, 1975; Americans & Nothing Else, 1980; India File, 1983; The State of America, 1986; Discovering Britain - Wales, 1975; Indira Gandhi (For Children), 1986; Out of Red Darkness, 1992. *Honours:* David Holden Award for Foreign Reporting, British Press Awards, 1983; International Reporter of the Year, British Press Awards, 1986. *Memberships:* Council for Welsh Language, 1973-77; Fellow, World Press Institute; Society of Authors. *Address:* The Sunday Telegraph, Peterborough Court At South Quay, 181 Marsh Wall, London E14 9SR, England.

FISHMAN Charles (Munro), b. 10 July 1942, Oceanside, New York, USA. Educator; Writer. m. 25 June 1967. 2 daughters. *Education:* BA English 1964, MA English 1965, Hofstra; Doctor of Arts, State University of New York, Albany, 1982; Permanent Certification, Secondary Education, New York, 1965. *Appointments:* Poet-in-Residence 1970, Director Visiting Writers Program 1979, Director Programs in the Arts 1987, State University of New York, Farmingdale. *Publications:* Aurora, 1974; Mortal Companions, 1977; Warm-Blooded Animals, 1977; Index to Women's Magazines & Presses, 1977; The Death Mazurka, 1987; Catlives (with Marina Roscher), 1991; Zoom, 1990; Blood To Remember: American Poets On The Holocaust, 1991; As The Sun Goes Down In Fire, 1992. *Contributions to:* Prism International; Poetry Canada Review; Cyphers (Ireland). *Honours:* Gertrude B Claytor Memorial Award, Poetry Society of America, 1987; Distinguished Service Professorship, State University of New York, 1989; Fellow of the Society for Values in Higher Education, 1990. *Memberships:* American PEN; Poetry Society of America; Long Island Poetry Collective, Co-founder, 1973; ALPS; Poets & Writers. *Address:* Knapp Hall, SUNY Farmingdale, Farmingdale, NY 11735, USA.

FISK Nicholas, b. 14 Oct 1923, London, England. Author. m. Dorothy Antoinette Richold, 29 Oct 1948, 2 sons, 2 daughters. *Education:* Ardingly College, Susses; Mainly self-educated through books and talented people. *Appointments:* Book Editor, Odhams, 1949; Copywriter, Stuart Advertising Agency, then other agencies, also Creative Director; Founder, Director, Publisher, Icon Books; Freelance creative partnership with Donald Onbridge, Mayfair; Creative Consultant to Lund Humphries, 1965-79; Currently full-time Author. *Publications:* Trillions, 1971; Grinny, 1973, sequel You remember me, 1983; A rag, a bone and a hank of hair, 1980; Snatched, 1983; Backlash, 1988; Sweets from a stranger, short stories, 1989; Some 40 titles in all, mostly science fiction for intelligent older children; Some book illustrations. *Contributions to:* Numerous and varied. *Membership:* Savile Club. *Literary Agent:* Laura Cecil. *Address:* 59 Elstree Road, Bushey Heath, Herts WD2 3QX, England.

FISK Pauline. *See:* **DAVIES Pauline.**

FISKE Sharon. *See:* **HILL Pamela.**

FISKE Tarleton. *See:* **BLOCH Robert.**

FITTER Richard Sidney Richmond, b. 1 Mar 1913. Author; naturalist. m. Alice Mary Stewart Park, 1938, 2 sons, 1 daughter. *Publications:* London's Natural History, 1945; London's Birds, 1949; Pocket Guide to British Birds, 1952; Pocket Guide to Nests and Eggs, 1954; (with David McClintock), Pocket Guide to Wild Flowers, 1956; The Ark in Our Midst, 1959; Six Great Naturalists, 1959; Guide to Bird Watching, 1963; Wildlife in Britain, 1963; Britain's Wildlife : Rarities and Introductions, 1966; (with Maisie Fitter), Penguin Dictionary of Natural History, 1967; Vanishing Wild Animals of the World, 1968; Finding Wild Flowers, 1972; (with H Heinzel & J Parslow), Birds of Britain and Europe, with North Africa and the Middle East, 1972; (with A Fitter and M Blamey), Flowers of Britain and Northern Europe, 1974; The Penitent Butchers, 1979; (with M Blamey), Handguide to the Wild Flowers of Britain and Northern Europe, 1979, Gem Guide to Wild Flowers, 1980; (with N Arlott and A Fitter), The Complete Guide to British Wildlife, 1981; Editor, with Eric Robinson, John Clare's Birds, 1982; (with A Fitter and J Wilkinson), Collins Guide to the Countryside, 1984; (with A Fitter and A Farrer), Grasses, Sedges, Rushes and Ferns of Britain and Northern Europe, 1984; Editor, The Wildlife of the Thames Counties, 1985; Wildlife for Man: How and Why we should conserve our Species, 1986; (with Richard Manuel), Field Guide to the Freshwater Life of Britain and North-West Europe, 1986; (with A Fitter), Collins Guide to the Countryside in Winter, 1988. *Address:* Drifts, Chinnor Hill, Oxon OX9 4BS, England.

FITZGERALD Ellen. *See:* **STEVENSON Florence.**

FITZGERALD Julia. *See:* **WATSON Julia.**

FITZGERALD Maureen Elizabeth, b. 24 Dec 1920, Mumbles, Glamorgan, Wales. Journalist. *Education:* Pensionnat des Servites, Brussels, Belgium; BSc, Economics, University College, London, 1946-49. *Appointments:* Associate Editor, Local Government Chronicle, 1952-62; Editor, Local Government Chronicle, 1963-73; Director, 1968-77; Managing Editor, 1973-77; Editorial Adviser, 1978-80; Consultant and Profile Writer, 1981-85; Profile Writer, 1985-88. *Publication:* The Story of a Parish, 1990. *Contributions to:* Local Government Chronicle; District Council Review; Rating and Valuation; Chamber's Encyclopaedia, Review of the Year; Local Government Review. *Honour:* MBE, 1979. *Memberships:* Society of Women Writers and Journalists; Institute of Journalists; Associate Member, United Oxford and Cambridge University Club. *Address:* 5 Buckingham Court, Chestnut Lane, Amersham, Buckinghamshire HP6 6EL, England.

FITZGERALD Penelope Mary, b. 17 Dec 1916, Lincoln, England. Teacher; Writer. m. Desmond Fitzgerald, 1942, 1 son, 2 daughters. *Education:* BA, Somerville College, Oxford. *Appointments:* English Tutor, Westminster Tutors, London, 1965-. *Publications:* Biography, Edmund Burne-Jones, 1975; The Knox Brothers, 1977; Charlotte Mew and her Friends, 1984; Novels: The Golden Child, 1978; The Bookshop, 1978; Offshore 1979; Human Voices, 1980; At Freddies, 1982; Innocence, 1986; Editor, William Morris's unpublished Novel on Blue Paper, 1982; The Beginning of Spring, 1989; The Gate of Angels, 1990. *Honour:* The Booker McConnell Prize for Fiction, 1979; Fellow, Royal Society of Literature. *Address:* c/o Harper Collins (Publishers), 77-85 Fulham Palace Road, London W6 8JB, England.

FITZHARDINGE Joan Margaret, (Joan Phipson), b. 1912, Australia. Freelance Writer; Grazier. *Publications:* Good Luck to the Rider, 1953; Six and Silver, 1954; It Happened One Summer, 1957; The Boundary Riders, 1962; The Family Conspiracy, 1962; Threat to the Barkers, 1963; Birkin, 1965; The Crew of the Merlin, US Edition Cross Currents, 1966; A Lamb in the Family, 1966; Peter and Butch, 1969; The Haunted Night, 1970; Bass and Bill Martin, 1972; The Way Home, 1973; Polly's Tiger, 1973; Helping Horse, US Edition Horse with Eight Hands, 1974; Bennelong, 1975; The Cats, 1976; Fly into Danger, 1977, Australian Edition The Bird Smugglers, 1979; Hide till Daytime, 1977; Keep Calm, US Edition When the City Stopped, 1978; No Escape, US Edition Fly Free, 1979; Mr Pringle and the Prince, 1979; a Tide Flowing, 1981; The Watcher in the Gardens, 1982; Beryl the Rainmaker, 1984; The Grannie Season, 1985; Dinko, 1985; Hit and Run, 1985; Bianca, 1988. *Address:* Wongalong, Mandurama, NSW 2792, Australia.

FITZSIMMONS Thomas, b. 21 Oct 1926, Lowell, Massachusetts, USA. Poet; Educator. m. Karen Hargreaves, 2 sons. *Education:* Fresno State College, 1947-49; Sorbonne, Institut de Science Politique, Paris, France, 1949-50; BA, Stanford University, 1951; MA Honours, Columbia University, 1952. *Appointments include:* Writer, Editor, New Republic magazine, Washington DC, 1952-55; Faculty 1961-, Professor of English 1966-, Oakland University, Michigan. Visiting lecturer/professor, various Japanese Universities. *Publications:* Books of Poetry: This Time This Place, 1969; Morningdew, 1970; Downinside, 1970; Meditation Seeds, 1970; Mooning, 1971; With the Water: Selected Poems 1969-70, 1972; Playseeds, 1973; Big Huge, 1975; House of my Friend, 1977; Trip Poems, 1978; Great Hawaiian Conquest, 1979; Nine Seas & Eight Mountains, 1981; Rocking Mirror Daybreak, 1983; Japan Personally, 1985. Translations: Ghazals of Ghalib, 1971; Japanese Poetry Now, 1972; A String Around Autumn, 1982. Editor: A Play of Mirrors: Eight Major Poets of Modern Japan, 1986; Muscle and Machine Dream, 1986. Series editor: Asian Poetry in

Translation; Prspectives on the Arts of Asia. *Honours:* Awards, poetry 1967, work with Japanese poets 1982, National Endowment for the Arts; Fulbright Lecturer, 1962-64, 1967-68, 1988-89; Award, Michigan Council for the Arts, 1986. *Address:* c/o Department of English, Oakland University, Rochester, Michigan 48063, USA.

FJELDE Rolf (Gerhard), b. 1926, American. *Appointments:* Founding Editor, Yale Poetry Review, 1945-49 and Poetry New York, 1949-51; Instructor 1954-58, Assistant Professor 1958-64, Associate Professor 1964-69, Professor of English and Drama 1969-, Pratt Institute, Brooklyn, NY; Teacher of Drama History, Academic Faculty, Juilliard School, NYC, 1973-83; President, Ibsen Society of America, 1979-; Editor, Ibsen News and Comment, 1979-85. *Publications:* Washington, 1955; The Imaged Word, 1962; Peer Gynt, by Ibsen (trans), 1964, 1980; Four Major Plays, by Ibsen (trans), volume I, 1965, volume II, 1970; Ibsen: A Collection of Critical Essays (ed), 1965; Washington, 1966; The Rope Walk, 1967; Rafferty One by One, 1975; Complete Major Prose Plays, by Ibsen (trans), 1978; The Bellini Look, 1982. *Address:* 261 Chatterton Parkway, White Plains, NY 10606, USA.

FLAM Jack Donald, b. 2 Apr 1940, USA. Writer; Professor. m. Bonnie Burnham, 7 Oct 1977, 1 daughter. *Education:* BA, Rutgers University, 1961; MA, Columbia University, 1963; PhD, New York University, 1969. *Appointments:* Art Critic, The Wall Street Journal, 1984-. *Publications:* Matisse on Art; Zoltan Gorency; Robert Motherwell; Matisse: The Man and His Art; Motherwell; Bread & Butter. *Contributions to:* New York Review of Books; Arts; Art News; Art Journal; Art in America; Art International Artforum. *Honours:* Guggenheim Fellow; NEA Fellow; Nawfactuvers Hauover AA World First Prize; Charles Rufus Morey Award. *Memberships:* PEN; International Association of Art Critics. *Literary Agent:* Georges Borchardt. *Address:* c/o Georges Borchardt Inc, 136 East 57th Street, New York, NY 10022, USA.

FLANAGAN Mary, b. 20 May 1943. USA. Writer. *Education:* Bachalor of Arts, Brandeis University. *Publications:* Bad Girls; Trust; Rose Reasen. *Contributions to:* The Guardian; The Observer; The New Statesman; The Sunday Times; The Evening Standard. *Memberships:* PEN; Society of Authors; The Authors Guild. *Address:* Hackney, London, England.

FLANAGAN Patrick Joseph, b. 1940, Irish. *Appointments:* Assistant Lecturer, Department of Civil Engineering, University College, Dublin, 1965-70; Research Officer, An Foras Forbartha, National Planning Institute, 1970-. *Publications:* The Cavan and Leitrim Railway, 1966; Dublin's Buses (co-author), 1968; Transport in Ireland 1880-1910, 1969; The Ballinamore and Ballyconnell Canal, 1972; The National Survey of Irish Rivers: A Report (and Second Report) on Water Quality (with P F Toner), 2 volumes, 1972-74. *Address:* 33 Fortfield Park, Dublin 6, Ireland.

FLANNAGAN Roy Catesby, b. 2 Dec 1938, Richmond, Virginia, USA. Professor; Editor. m. Anne Villers, 30 Dec 1984, 2 sons, 3 daughters. *Education:* BA, Washington, Lee University; MA, PhD, University of Virginia. *Publications:* Paradise Lost; Comus Contexts; Electronic Milton. *Contributions to:* Milton Quarterly. *Honours:* Folger Shakespeare Library Fellow; Fulbright Travel Award; Ohio University Baker Award. *Memberships:* Milton Society of America; Modern Language Association; Renaissance Society of America; Renaissance English Text Society. *Address:* 43 Briarwood Drive, Athens, OH 45701, USA.

FLEET Kenneth George, b. 12 Sept 1929, Cheshire, England. Journalist. m. (Alice) Brenda Wilkinson, 28 Mar 1953, 3 sons, 1 daughter. *Education:* BSc., Economics, London School of Economics. *Appointments:* Journal of Commerce, Liverpool, 1950-52; Sunday Times, 1955-56; Deputy City Editor, Birmingham Post, 1956-58; Deputy Financial Editor, Guardian, 1958-63; Deputy City Editor, 1963, City Editor, 1966-77, Daily Telegraph; City Editor, Sunday Telegraph 1963-66; Editor, Business News, 1977-78, Sunday Times; City Editor, Sunday Express, 1978-82; City Editor-in-Chief, Express Newspapers plc, 1982-85; Executive Editor, Finance and Industry, The Times, 1983-87. *Honour:* Wincott Award, 1974. *Memberships:* Director: TUS Entertainment Plc, 1990-1993; Director, Young Vic, 1976-83; Chairman, Chichester Festival Theatre, 1985-; Governor, London Schools of Economics, 1989-. *Address:* c/o 20 Farrington Road, London, EC1M 3NH, England.

FLEISCHMAN (Albert) Sid(ney), b. 1920, American. *Appointments:* Magician in vaudeville and night clubs, 1938-41; Reporter, San Diego Daily Journal, 1949-50; Associate Editor, Point Magazine, San Diego, 1950-51. *Publications:* The Straw Donkey Case, 1948; Murder's No Accident, 1949; Shanghai Flame, 1951; Look Behind You, Lady (in UK as Chinese Crimson), 1952; Danger in Paradise, 1953; Counterspy Express, Malay Woman (in UK as Malayan Manhunt), 1954; Blood Alley, 1955; Good-bye My Lady, 1956; Lafayette Escadrille, 1958; Yellowleg, 1960; The Deadly Companions, 1961; Mr Mysterious and Company, 1962; By The Great Horn Spoon!, 1963, retitled as Bullwhip Griffin, 1967; The Ghost in the Noonday Sun, 1965; McBroom series, 9 volumes, 1966-80; Chancy and the Grand Rascal, 1966; Longbeard the Wizard, 1970; Jingo Django, 1971; The Wooden Cat Man, 1972; The Ghost on a Saturday Night, 1974; Mr Mysterious's Secret of Magic (in UK as Secrets of Magic), 1975; Me and the Man on the Moon-Eyed Horse, 1977; Humbug Mountain, 1978; The Hey Hey Man, 1979; The Case of the Cackling Ghost (Princess Tomorrow, Flying Clock, Secret Message), 4 volumes, 1981; The Case of the 264-Pound Burglar, 1982; McGroom's Almanac, 1984; The Whipping Boy, 1986. *Address:* 305 Tenth Street, Santa Monica, CA 90402, USA.

FLEISHMAN Avrom, b. 1933, American. *Appointments:* Instructor, Columbia University, 1958-59 and Hofstra University, Hempstead, 1960-63; Assistant Professor, University of Minnesota, Minneapolis, 1963-66 and Michigan State University, East Lansing, 1966-67; Associate Professor 1968-70; Professor of English 1970-, Johns Hopkins University, Baltimore, MD. *Publications:* A Reading of Mansfield Park: An Essay In Critical Synthesis, Conrad's Politics: Community and Anarchy in the Fiction of Joseph Conrad, 1967; The English Historical Novel: Walter Scott to Virginia Woolf, 1971; Virginia Woolf: A Critical Reading, 1975; Fiction and the Ways of Knowing: Essays on British Novels, 1978; Figures of Autobiography: The Language of Self Writing in Victorian and Modern England, 1983. *Address:* English Department, Johns Hopkins University, Baltimore, MD 21218, USA.

FLEISHMAN Lazar, b. 15 May 1944. Professor. m. Irene Strelnikova, 12 Mar 1972, (div), 1 son, 1 daughter. *Education:* Latvian State University, 1961-66. *Publications:* Boris Pasternak: The Poet and His Politics; Boris Pasternak v Tridtsatye gody; Boris Pasternak v duadtsatye gody; Russkii Berlin. *Contributions to:* Stanford Slavic Studies; Slavica Hierosolymitana; Russian Literature; Izvestiia Akademii Nank SSSR: Seriia Literary; Iazyka; Druzhla Narodoc. *Honours:* The Pew Foundation Grant; The Guggenheim Foundation Fellowship. *Memberships:* American Association for the Advancement of Slavic Studies. *Address:* Department of Slavic Languages and Literature, Stanford University, Stanford, CA 94305, USA.

FLEMING Laurence William Howie b. 8 Sept 1929, Shillong, Assam, India. Author; Artist; Landscape Designer. *Education:* The New School, Darjeeling, India, 1941-44; Repton School, Derbyshire, 1945-47; Royal Air Force, 1947-49; St Catharine's College, Cambridge, 1949-52, BA. 1952; MA 1956. *Publications:* The English Garden (with Alan Gore), 1979; The One Hour Garden (illustrated by the author), 1985; Old English Villages (with Ann Gore), 1986; Novel: A Diet of Crumbs, 1959. *Contributions to:* Brazil Journal, 1970: A Great Brazilian (Roberto Burle Marx), Royal Horticultural Society's

Journal, 1972; Gardens of Burle Marx Interiors, 1982; Villandry. *Memberships:* International PEN, 1960; The Writers' Guild; The Anglo-Brazilian Society. *Address:* c/o Lloyds Bank plc, 112 Kensington High Street, London W8 4SN, England.

FLEMMONS Jerry, b. 14 Jan 1936, Stephenville, Texas, USA. Journalist; Author. div, 1 son. *Education:* AA, Tarleton State University, 1957; BSc 1959, MSc 1965, East Texas State University. *Publications include:* Amon: Life of Amon G.Carter of Texas, 1978; Texas, 1980, revised 1986; Plowboys, Cowboys & Slanted Pigs, 1984; O Dammit!, play, 1985. Also: Fodor's Caribbean Guide, author/editor, 1979. *Contributions to:* Numerous magazines, national & international. *Honours include:* Runner-up, Best US Travel Story 1987, winner 1986, Best Newspaper Article on US Travel 1985, Society of American Travel Writers, Lowell Thomas Foundation, University of Missouri School of Journalism; Henry Bradshaw Award, Best Travel Journalism, 1987; 1st runner-up, Grand National prize, Best Travel journalism in America, 1985; 1st recipient, Governor's Award, contributions to Texas tourism, 1985; Pulitzer Prize nomination, 1983. *Memberships* Board member 1968-78, Society of American Travel Writers. *Address:* 3716 Bryce Avenue, Fort Worth, TX 76107, USA.

FLESHER Dale Lee, b. 27 June 1945, Muncie, Indiana, USA. Professor of Accountancy. m. Tonya Kay Maloney, 6 June 1970, 1 son. *Education:* Diploma, Albany High School, Albany, Indiana, 1963; BA, 1967, MA, 1968, Ball State University, Muncie, Indiana; CPA, State of Indiana, 1969; PhD, University of Cincinnati, Cincinnati, Ohio, 1975. *Publications:* Operations Auditing in Hospitals, 1976; Accounting for Advertsing Assets, 1978; Accounting for Mid-Management, 1980; Tax Tactics for Small Business, 1980; Independent Auditors Guide to Operational Auditing, 1982; CMA Examination Review, 1984, 1987, 1990; An Operational Audit of the Purchasing Function, 1985; Introduction to Financial Accounting, 1986; Operational Auditing for the 1990's, 1990; The IIA - 50 Years of Progress Through Sharing, 1991; The Third Quarter Century of the American Accounting Association, 1991. *Contributions to:* Over 230 articles to 86 magazines including: Organic Gardening; Journal of Accountancy; The Accounting Review; Taxation for Accountants; The Internal Auditor; The CPA Journal; Management Accounting; Journal of Mississippi History; Accounting Organizations and Society; Bank-Note Reporter; North Carolina Wildlife; Hoosier Outdoors. *Honours:* Burlington Norther Faculty Achievement Award, 1987; Leon Radde Award, Outstanding Educator in North America, 1990. *Memberships:* Academy of Accounting Historians, President 1988; American Institute of CPAs; National Association of Accountants; American Accounting Association; Mississippi Society of CPAs; Mississippi Historical Society; Institute of Internal Auditors; American Taxation Association; Association of Government Accountants. *Address:* School of Accountancy, University of Mississippi, University, MS 38677, USA.

FLETCHER Colin Robert, b. 20 Sept 1937, Salford, Lancashire, England. University Lecturer. m. Pamela Jones, 21 July 1962, 3 sons. *Education:* MA, New College, Oxford, 1958-61; M Phil, Kings College, London, 1963-66; PhD, University of Wales, 1969. *Publications include:* The structure of Unique Fastorisation Rings; G H Hardy: Applied Mathematrician. *Contributions to:* Several Journals. *Memberships:* London Mathematical Society; British Society for the History of Mathematics. *Address:* Department of Mathematics, University of Wales, Aberystwyth, Dyeed, SY23 3BZ, Wales.

FLETCHER David. *See:* **BARBER Dulan Friar.**

FLETCHER Richard. *See:* **BUTLIN Martin.**

FLETCHER John Walter James, (Jonathan Fune),

b. 23 June 1937, Barking. England. University Teacher. m. Beryl Sibley Connop, 14 Sept 1961, 2 sons, 1 daughter. *Education:* BA, University of Cambridge, 1959; MA, 1963; M Phil, University of Toulouse, 1961; PhD, 1964. *Publications:* The Novels of Samuel Beckett; Samuel Beckett's Art; Claude Simon and Fiction Now; Novel and Reader; Alain Robbe Grillet; New Directions in Literature; Samuel Beckett: His Works and His Critics. *Contributions to:* Spectator; New Statesman; Numerous Academic Journals. *Honours:* Scott Moncrieff Translation Prize. *Memberships:* Society of Authors; Translators Association; Society for the Study of French History; Assocation for the Study of Modern and Contemporary France; Association of University Teachers. *Address:* School of Modern Languages and European History, University of East Anglia, Norwich NR4 7TJ, England.

FLETT Ethel Snelson, (Essie Summers), b. 24 July 1912, Christchurch, New Zealand. Novelist. m. Rev. William Nugent Flett, 18 May 1940, 1 son, 1 daughter. *Publications include:* Author of 53 published works including: New Zealand Inheritance, 1957; The Essie Summers Story, 1974. *Contributions to:* Australian Woman's Mirror; New Zealand Mirror; New Zealand Home Journal; New Zealand Womens Weekly; New Zealand Dairy Exporter; Womans Weekly, UK, Serials; Columnist, Timaru Herald; Good Housekeeping, UK; Scots Magazine; numerous newspapers. *Address:* Jesmond Cottage, 32a Tom Parker Avenue, Napier, New Zealand.

FLEXNER Stuart Berg, b. 22 Mar 1928, Jacksonville, USA. Editor; Writer. m. Doris L. Hurcamb, 12 Nov 1967, 1 son, 1 daughter. *Education:* BA, 1948, MA, 1949, University of Louisville; Advanced Graduate Study, Cornell University. *Appointments:* Executive Editor, Verlen Books, 1952-57; President, Jugetas, SA, Mexico City, 1958-64; Senior Editor, then Divisional Vice President, then Editor in Chief, Reference Dept., Random House Inc., 1964-72, 1981-. *Publications include:* The Dictionary of American Slang, 1960; How to Increase Your Word Power, 1968; I Hear America Talking, 1976; Listening to America, 1982; The Family Word Finder, 1977; The Oxford American Dictionary, 1980; Editor in Chief, Random House Dictionary of the English Language, The Random House College Dictionary. *Contributions to:* Professional journals. *Memberships:* Authors Guild of America; PEN; Modern Language Association; National Council of Teachers of English; American Historical Association. *Address:* 19C Weavers' Hill, Greenwich, CT 06831, USA.

FLINN Eugene Christopher, b. 17 July 1924, Jersey City, New Jersey, USA. Writer; College Professor. m. Patrica Pean, 5 June 1971, 4 sons, 4 daughters. *Education:* BS, Seton Hall University, 1949; MA, St John's University, 1950; PhD, 1954. *Appointments:* Literary Advisor, Olympia Dukakis's TV Film. *Publications:* The Literary Guide to the United States; Telling the School Story; Never Mind Whos on First. *Contributions to:* Numerous inc. Life; Good Housekeeping. *Honours:* Winner, National Poetry Contest; Winner, Short Story Contest. *Address:* PO Box 2, Gillette, NJ 07933, USA.

FLORA James Royer, b. 25 Jan 1914, Bellefontaine, Ohio, USA. Artist and Writer. m. Jane Sue Sinnickson, 1 Mar 1941, 2 sons, 3 daughters. *Education:* Cincinnati Art Academy, 1934-39, Urbana University, 1931- 33. *Publications:* The Fabulous Firework Family, 1955; The Day The Cow Sneezed, 1957; Leopold, The See-Through Crumbpicker, 1961; My Friend Charlie, 1964, The Great Green Turkey Creek Monster, 1976; Grandpa's Ghost Stories, 1978. *Honours:* Recipient of numerous awards. *Membership:* Art Clubs.*Address:* 7 St James Place, Rowayton, CT, 06853, USA.

FLORA Joseph Martin, b. 9 Feb 1934, Toledo, Ohio, USA. Educator; Professor. m. 30 Jan 1959. 4 sons. *Education:* BA 1956, MA 1957, PhD 1962, University of Michigan. *Publications:* Hemingway's Nick Adams,

1982; Ernest Hemingway: The Art of the Short Fiction, 1989; Vardis Fisher, 1965; William Ernest Henley, 1970; Frederick Manfred, 1974. Co-editor: Southern Writers: A Biographical Dictionary; Fifty Southern Writers Before 1900, 1987; Fifty Southern Writers After 1900, 1987; Editor, The English Short Story 1880-1945, 1985. *Contributions to:* Studies in Short Fiction; Dialogue. *Honours:* Phi Beta Kappa, 1956; Mayflower Award, North Carolina Literary and Historical Association, 1982; Distinguished PhD Alumnus, Horace H Rackham School of Graduate Studies, University of Michigan, 1988. *Memberships:* Western Literature Association (Executive Council 1979- 81, 1984-86, Vice President 1990, President, 1992; Society for the Study of Southern Literature (Executive Council 1984-86); Hemingway Society; Thomas Wolfe Society. *Address:* 505 Caswell Road, Chapel Hill, NC 27514, USA.

FLOREN Lee, (Brett Austin, Lisa Franchon, Claudia Hall, Wade Hamilton, Matt Harding, Matthew Whitman Harding, Felix Lee Horton, Stuart Jason, Grace Lang, Marguerite Nelson, Lew Smith, Maria Sandra Sterling, Lee Thomas, Len Turner, Will Watson, Dave Wilson), b. 1910, USA. Author. *Publications:* Over 300 novels including most recently: Gambler with a Gun, 1971; Wyoming Showdown, 1972; The Bloodskinners, 1972; War Drum (as Maria Sandra Sterling), 1973; Trail to High Pine, 1974; Long Knife and Musket (as Felix Lee Horton), 1974; Muskets on the Mississippi (as Matthew Whitman), 1974; Valley of Death (as Stuart Jason), 1974; Deadly Doctor (as Stuart Jason), 1974; Boothill Riders, 1979; Renegade Gambler, 1979; Gun Chore, 1979; High Border Riders, 1979; Powdersmoke Attorney, 1979; Edge of Gunsmoke (as Matt Harding), 1979; Nedra (as Grace Lang), 1979; Mercy Nurse (as Marguerite Nelson), 1979; Rope the Wild Wind, 1980; The Bushwhackers, 1980; High Trail to Gunsmoke, 1980; Hard Rock Nurse (as Marguerite Nelson), 1980; Smoky River, 1980; Ride Against the Rifles (as Wade Hamilton), 1980; The High Gun, 1980; North to Powder River, 1981; Cowthief Clanton, 1982; Renegade Rifles, 1983; Buckskin Challenge, 1983; Boothill Brand, 1984; Gun Quick, 1985; West of Barbwire, 1985; Wyoming Gun Law, 1985; The Gringo (as Lee Thomas), 1985; Fighting Ramrod, 1986; Bring Bullets, Texan, 1986; The Tall Texan, 1986; Others as Brett Austin, Claudia Hall, Lew Smith, Len Turner, Will Watson and Dave Wilson. *Address:* c/o Hale, 45-47 Clerkenwell Green, London EC1R OHT, England.

FLORENCE Ronald, b. 1942, American. History. *Appointments:* Associate Professor of History, State University of New York, Coll. at Purchase, since 1971. Research Fellow, Joint Center for Urban Studies, MIT and Harvard University, Cambridge, Mass., 1965-66; Professor of History, Sarah Lawrence College, Bronxville, New York, 1968-71. *Publications:* Fritz: The Story of a Political Assassin, 1971; Marx's Daughters, 1975; Zeppelin, 1982; The Gypsy Man, 1985; The Optimum Sailboat, 1987.

FLOURNOY Don Michael, b. 20 Oct 1937, Lufkin, Texas, USA. University Professor. m. Mary Anne Boone, 27 July 1963, 1 son, 1 daughter. *Education:* BA, Southern Methodist University, 1959; University of London, 1962; MS, Boston University, 1963; MA, PhD, University of Texas, 1964-65. *Appointments:* Assistant Director, Case Institute of Technology, 1965-66; Assistant Dean, Case Western Reserve University, 1965-69; Associate Dean, University of New York, 1969-71; Dean, Ohio University, 1971-81; Director, Center for International Studies, 1981-84; Director, Institute for Telcommunications Studies, 1984-. *Publications:* CNN World Report; Content Analysis of Indonesian Newspapers; The Rationing of American Higher Education; The New Teachers. *Contributions to:* Journalism Quarterly; Commdev News; Journal of Development Communications; Satellite Communications; Gazette; The Athens Messenger; Electronic Media. *Address:* Institute for Telecommunications Studies, Ohio University, Athens, OH 45701, USA.

FLYNN David. *See:* **FLYNN John David.**

FLYNN Jackson. *See:* **SHIRREFFS Gordon Donald.**

FLYNN John David, (David Flynn), b. 4 Apr 1948, USA. Writer; Teacher; Editor. div, 1 daughter. *Education:* BA, BJ, University of Missouri, 1971; MA, University of Denver, 1972; MA, Boston University, 1980; PhD, University of Nebraska, 1984. *Appointments:* Teacher, Tennessee State University, 1988-89; Artist in Residence, Williamson County Public Schools, 1988; University of Hawaii, 1989-91; Tokai International College, 1992-93; Fiction Editor, Manor, 1990-91. *Contributions to:* 50 plus Poems & Stories; The Salmon; Panurge; StoryQuarterly; Confrontation. *Honours:* Millay Colony for the arts; The Tyrone Guthrie Centre; The Israeli Center for the arts; Wurlitser Fellowship. *Memberships:* Hawaii Literary Arts Council; Associated Writing Programs. *Address:* 2241 Kapiolani Blvd, Honalulu, HI 96826, USA.

FLYNN Robert (Lopez), b. 1932, American. *Appointments:* Assistant Professor, Baulor University, Waco TX, 1959-63; Professpr and Novelist-in-Residence, Trinity University, San Antonio, 1963-. *Publications:* North to Yesterday, 1967; In the House of the Lord, 1969; The Sounds of Rescue, The Signs of Hope, 1970; Seasonal Rain and Other Stories, 1986; Wanderer Springs, 1987; A Personal War in Vietnam, 1989; When I Was Just Your Age, 1992. *Address:* 101 Cliffside Drive, San Antonio, Texass 78231, USA.

FLYNT Candace, b. 12 Mar 1947, Greensboro, North Caroline, USA. Author. m. John Franklin Kime, 29 Jan 1992, 1 son. *Education:* BA, Greensboro College, 1969; MFA, University of NC, 1974. *Publications:* Mother Love; Sins of Omission; Chasing Dad. *Memberships:* Authors Guild; PEN. *Literary Agent:* Rhoda A Weyr. *Address:* c/o Rhoda A Weyr, 151 Bergen Street, Brooklyn, NY 11217, USA.

FOGARASSY Helen Catherine, b. 30 Oct 1949, Gyula, Hungary. Writer. m. Karl Stanley Matlin, 26 Aug 1972, div. *Education:* Indiana University. *Publications:* Novel. Mix Bender. *Contributions to:* Queens Quarterly; Home Planet News; Innisfree; Portland Monthly; EOTU; Gypsy; Echoes. *Memberships:* The Authors Guild; Poets & Writers; International Women's Writing Guild; The Small Press Center. *Literary Agent:* Maximilian Becker. *Address:* 58 West 36 Street, 2A, New York, NY 10018, USA.

FOLDENYI F Laszlo, b. 19 Apr 1952, Debrecen, Hungary. Essayist. m. Marianne Bara, 1978, 2 daughters. *Education:* PhD, 1978. *Publications:* Melancholy; Caspar David Friedrich; The Glance of the Medusa; On The Other Shore; In The Abyss of the Soul: Goyas Saturn; The age of Daniel Defoe; The Young Lukacs; In The Trap of Dramaturgy: The Restoration drama. *Honours:* Mikes Literary Prize; Prize of the Hungarian Writers Association. *Memberships:* Hungarian Writers Association; PEN. *Literary Agent:* Matthes & Seitz Verlag GmbH, 8000 Munchen 19, Hubnerstr 11. *Address:* Aladar u 24, 1016 Budapest, Hungary.

FOLDESSY Edward Patrick, b. 20 Sept 1941, NY, USA. Writer. m. Andrea I Vescia, 21 Aug 1965, 2 daughters. *Education:* BS, Iona College, 1963. *Appointments:* Assistant on national news desk and for What's News 1963-64, News Assistant for columns Bond Markets and Financing Business 1964-68, Reporter and Special Writer 1966-, Author of column Credit Markets 1980, Wall Street Journal, NY. *Publications:* Crime and Business (Co-author), 1968; News Systems (Editor). *Address:* Allendale, NJ, USA.

FOLEY (Mary) Louise Munro, b. 1933, American (b. Canadian). *Appointments:* Columnist, News-Argus, Goldsboro, NC, 1971-73; Editor of Publications, Institute for Human Service Management, California State University, Sacramento, 1975-80. *Publications:* The Caper Club, 1969; No Talking, Sammy's Sister, A Job for Joey, 1970; Somebody Stole Second, 1972; Stand Close to the Door (ed), 1976; Tackle 22, 1978; Women in Skilled Labor (ed), 1980; The Train of Terror, 1982; The Sinister Studies of KESP-TV, 1983, The Lost Tribe, 1983; The Mystery of the Highland Crest, 1984; The Mystery of Echo Lodge, Danger at Anchor Mine, 1985; The Mardi Gras Mystery, 1987; Mystery of the Sacre Stones, 1988; Australia! Find the Flying Foxes, 1988; The Cobra Connection, 1990; Ghost Train, 1991. *Memberships:* Authors Guild; California Writers Club; National League of American Pen Women. *Literary Agent:* Ruth Cohen Inc. *Address:* 5010 Jennings Way, Sacramento, CA 95819, USA.

FOLEY Johanna Mary, (Jo), b. 8 Dec. 1945. Editor, Observer Magazine. m. Desmond Francis Conor, 1973. *Education:* BA, Joint Honours English & Drama, Manchester University, 1968. *Appointments:* Woman's Editor, Walsall Observer, 1968; Reporter, Birmingham Post, 1970; English Teacher, Monkwick Secondary Modern School, Colchester, and More House School, London, 1972-73; Deputy Beauty Editor, Woman's Own, 1973; launched and edited magazine, Successful Slimming, 1976; Senior Assistant Editor, Woman's Own, 1978; Woman's Editor, The Sun, 1980; Editor, Woman, 1982; Executive Editor, Features, The Times, 1984-85; Managing Editor, The Mirror, 1985-86; Editor, Observer Magazine, 1986-. *Publication:* The Pick of Woman's Own Diets, 1979. *Honours:* Editor of the Year, British Society of Magazine Editors, 1983. *Address:* The Observer, 8 St Andrew's Hill, London EC4V 5JA, England.

FOLKE Will. *See:* **BLOCH Robert.**

FOLLETT Ken, b. 5 June 1949, Cardiff, Wales. Author. m. (1) 5 Jan 1968, (2) 8 Nov 1985. 1 son, 1 daughter. *Education:* BA Honours, University College, London; Apprenticeship, Journalism. *Publications include:* Eye of the Needle, 1978; Triple, 1979; The Key to Rebecca, 1980; The Man from St Petersburg, 1982; On Wings of Eagles, 1983; Lie Down With Lions, 1986. Also: The Modigliani Scandal, 1976; The Shakeout, 1975; The Bear Raid, 1976; Secret of Kellerman's Studio, 1976; The Power Twins & the Worm Puzzle, 1976; Paper Money, 1977; The Pillars of the Earth, 1989; Various screenplays. *Contributions to:* Book reviews, essays, New York Times & other publications. *Honour:* Edgar Award, Best Novel, Mystery Writers of America, 1979. *Memberships:* Mystery Writers of America; Crime Writers Association, UK; National Union of Journalists, UK; Writers Guild, USA. *Literary Agent:* Writers House Inc, 21 West 26th Street, New York, NY 10010, USA. *Address:* PO Box 708, London SW10 0DH, England.

FOON Dennis, b. 18 Nov 1951, Detroit, USA. Playwright; screen Writer. 1 daughter. *Appointments:* Instructor of Playwrighting, University of BC, 1974-79; Playwright, Young Peoples Theatre, Toronto, 1983- 84; Co Founder, Artistic Director, Green Thumb Theatre for Young People, Vancouver, 1975-88; Consultant, Sesame Street Canada, 1988-. *Publications:* Mirror Game; New Canadian Kid & Invisible Kids; Skin & Liars; The Short Tree and the Bird That Could Not Sing; Am I The Only One?; The Hunchback of Notre Dame; Trummi Kaput; New Canadian Kid; The Windigo; Heracles; Raft Baby; The Last Days of Pual Bunyan. *Honours:* Scott Newman Award; AYA Award; Chalmers Award; British Theatre Award; Jesse Award; CBC Literary Award; Hopwood Award; Writers Digest Award. *Memberships:* WGC; PUC; CAPAC; ACTRA; Equity. *Address:* 647 E 12th Avenue, Vancouver, BC, Canada VJT 2H7.

FOOT Michael Mackintosh, Rt. Hon. b. 23 July 1913. Journalist; Politician. m. Jill Craigie, 1949. *Education:* Wadham College, Oxford. *Appointment:* Assistant Editor, 1937-38, Joint Editor, 1948-52, Editor, 1952-59, Managing Director, 1952-74, Tribune; Staff member, Evening Standard, 1938, Acting Editor, 1942-

44; Political Columnist, Daily Herald, 1944-64; MP. *Publications include:* Armistice 1918-1939, 1940; Trial of Mussolini, 1943; Brendan and Beverley, 1944; part author, Guilty Men, 1940 and Who Are the Patriots?, 1949; Still at Large, 1950; Full Speed Ahead, 1950; The Pen and the Sword, 1957; Parliament in Danger, 1959; Aneurin Bevan Volume I, 1962, Volume II, 1973; Harold Wilson : A Pictorial Biography, 1964; Debts of Honour, 1980; Another Heart and Other Pulses, 1984; Loyalists and Loners, 1986; The Politics of Paradise, 1988. *Honours:* Hon. Fellow, Wadham College, 1969; Hon. Member, NUJ, 1985; Hon. D.Litt., University of Wales, 1985. *Address:* 308 Gray's Inn Road, London WC1X 8DY, England.

FOOT Michael Richard Daniell, b. 1919, British. *Appointments:* Professor of Modern History, Manchester University, 1967-73. *Publications:* Gladstone and Liberalism (with J L Hammond), 1952; British Foreign Policy since 1898, 1956; Men in Uniform, 1961; SOE in France, 1966, 1968; Gladstone Diaries (ed), volumes I and II: 1825-1839, 1968, volumes, III and IV: 1840-55, (with H C G Matthew), 1975; (ed) War and Society, 1973; Resistance, 1976, 1978; Six Faces of Courage, 1978; M19 (with J M Langley), 1979; SOE: An Outline History, 1984, 1990; (Ed)Holland at war against Hitler, 1990; Art and War, 1990; *Address:* 45 Countess Road, London NW5 2XH, England.

FOOT Paul Mackintosh, b. 8 Nov 1937. Writer; Journalist. m. 3 sons. *Appointments:* Editor, Isis, 1961; President, Oxford Union, 1961; TUC Delegate, National Union of Journalists, 1967, 1971; Contested (Socialist Workers Party) Birmingham, Stechford, March 1977; Editor, Socialist Worker, 1974-75; Journalist, Daily Mirror, 1979-. *Publications:* Immigration and Race in British Politics, 1965; The Politics of Harold Wilson, 1968; The Rise of Enoch Powell, 1969; Who Killed Hanratty?, 1971; Why You Should Be a Socialist, 1977; Red Shelley, 1981; The Helen Smith Story, 1983; Murder at the Farm, 1986; Who Framed Colin Wallace, 1989. *Honours:* Journalist of the Year, Granada, 1972; Campaigning Journalist of the Year, British Press Awards, 1980. *Address:* c/o The Daily Mirror, Holborn Circus, London EC1, England.

FOOTE (Albert) Horton (Jr), b. 14 Mar 1916, Wharton, Texas, USA. Playwright. m. Lillian Vallish, 1945, 2 daughters, 2 sons. *Education:* Educated at Pasadena Playhouse Theatre, California 1933-35, Tamara Daykarhanova Theatre School, New York, 1937-39. *Career:* Actor with American Actors Theatre, New York, 1939-42; Theatre Workshop Director and Producer, King-Smith School of Creative Arts, 1944-45 and Manager, Productions Inc, 1945-48, both Washington DC. *Publications:* Plays include: The Road to the Graveyard (produced New York, 1985); Blind Date (produced New York, 1986) New York, Dramatists Play Service, 1986; Lily Dale (produced New York, 1986); The Widow Claire (produced New York, 1986); Courtship, Valentine's Day 1918, New York, Grove Press, 1987. Screenplays: Storm Fear, 1955; To Kill a Mockingbird, 1962; Baby, The Rain Must Fall, 1964; Hurry Sundown, with Thomas Ryan, 1966; Tomorrow, 1972; Tender Mercies, 1983; 1918, 1984; The Trip to Bountiful, 1985; On Valentine's Day 1985; Courtship, 1986. Novel: The Chase, New York, Reinhart, 1956; Many television plays. *Honours:* Oscar, for screenplay, 1963, 1983; D Litt, Austin College, Sherman, Texas, 1987, Drew University, Madison, New Jersey, 1987. *Literary Agency:* Lucy Kroll Agency, New York. *Address:* c/o Lucy Kroll Agency, 390 West End Avenue, New York, NY 10024, USA.

FOOTE Geoffrey, b. 4 Sept 1950, Oswestry, England. Lecturer. m. Rowena Elizabeth Andrea Jewen, 19 Dec 1987, 2 sons. *Education:* University of Lancaster, 1969-72; University of Bristol, 1973-75; College University of Oxford, 1986-90. *Publications:* The Labour Partys Political Thought: A History; A Chronology of British Politics 1945-87. *Memberships:* F K History Society. *Address:* Department of Humanities, Teessive Polytechnic, Middlesbrough, Cleveland, England.

FOOTMAN Robert, b. 26 Apr 1916, Oakland, California, USA. Writer. m. (1) Ella Hedrick, 21 June 1937, divorced 1951, (2) Margaret Cunha, 26 Sept 1952, dec 1987, 3 sons, 1 daughter. *Education:* BA, Yale University, 1937. *Appointments:* Instructor in English, Middlebury College, Middlebury, Vermont, 1937-38; Instructor in English, Marot Junior College, Thompson, Connecticut, 1938-41; Worked for advertising agencies, including McCann Erickson, 1946-54, Guild Bascom Bonfigli, 1954-59, D'Arcy, 1959-66, Foote Cone Belding, 1966-70, Honig-Cooper, 1970-72, and M Arnold 1972-78; free-lance writer, 1978-. *Publications:* Novels: Once a Spy, 1978; Always a Spy, 1986; China Spy, 1987. *Membership:* California Tennis Club. *Literary Agent:* Bonnie Nadell, Frederick Hill Associates, 2237 Union Street, San Francisco, CA 94123, USA. *Address:* 465 Boynton, Berkeley, CA 94707, USA.

FORBES Bryan, b. 22 July 1926, Stratford, London, England. Film Executive; Director; Screenwriter. m. Nanette Newman, 1955, 2 daughter. *Education:* West Ham Secondary School; Royal Academy Dramatic Art. *Publications:* Truth Lies Sleeping (short stories), 1951; The Distant Laughter (novel), 1972; Notes for a Life, autobiography, 1974; The Slipper and the Rose, 1976; Ned's Girl, biography of Dame Edith Evans. 1977; International Velvet (novel), 1978; Familiar Strangers (novel, US title Stranger), 1979; The Despicable Race - A History of the British Acting Tradition, 1980; The Rewrite Man (novel), 1983; The Endless Game, 1986; A Song at Twlight (novel), 1989; A Divided Life (autobiography), 1992. *Honours:* Best Screenplay awards for: The Angry Silence, Only Two Can Play; Edgar award for Seance on a Wet Afternoon; UN Award for The L Shaped room; many Film Festival Prizes; Hon DL London, 1987. *Memberships include:* President, Beatrix Potter Society, 1982-, President National Youth Theatre, 1984-; Writers Guild of GB. *Address:* c/o The Bookshop, Virginia Water, Surrey, England.

FORBES Colin, British. *Publications:* Tramp in Armour, 1969; The Heights of Zervos, 1970; The Palermo Ambush, 1972; Target Five, 1973; Year of the Golden Ape, 1974; The Stone Leopard, 1975; Avalanche Express, 1977; The Stockholm Syndicate, 1981; Double Jeopardy, 1982; The Leader and the Damned, 1983; Terminal, 1984; Cover Story, 1985; The Janus Man, 1987; Deadlock 1988; The Greek Key, 1989; Shockwave, 1990; Whirlpool, 1991; Cross of Fire, 1992; By Stealth, 1993. *Address:* c/o Elaine Greene Limited, 37 Goldhawk Road, London W12 8QQ, England.

FORBES Daniel. *See:* **KENYON Michael.**

FORBES DeLoris Stanton, (Stanton Forbes, Forbes Rydell, Tobias Wells), b. 29 July 1923. Writer. m. William James Forbes, 29 Oct 1948, 2 sons, 1 daughter. *Appointments:* Associate Editor, Wellesley Townsman, Wellesley, Mass., 1960- 72. *Publications:* Over 40 mystery novels, including, Annalisa, 1959; Grieve the Past, 1963; Of Graves, Worms and Epitaphs, 1988; Don't Die on Me, Billie Jean, 1987. *Contributions to:* several magazines. *Honours:*Scroll for Grieve for the Past; Best Mystery of the Year, 1963; Best short stories included Quetzalcoatl, 1967. *Membership:* Mystery Writers of America. *Address:* Sanford, Florida 32771, USA.

FORBES Stanton. *See:* **FORBES DeLoris Stanton.**

FORD Brian John, b. 13 May 1939, Corsham, Wiltshire, England, Chartered Research Biologist; Author and Broadcaster; m. Janice May Smith, 2 sons, 2 daughters, 2 foster-children. *Education:* Biology, Cardiff University. *Publications:* Radio and Television Programmes: Science Now; Where Are You Taking Us?; It's Your Line; Food for Thought; Heart Attack; Computer Challenge, game show; Editor: Science Diary; Science and Technical Authors' Newsletter; Biology History; Books include: Microbiology and Food, 1970; Nonscience, 1971; Revealing Lens, 1973; Microbe Power, 1976; Patterns of Sex, 1978; Cult of the Expert, 1982; Single Lens, 1985; Leeuwenhoek Legacy, 1991; Image of Science, 1992; First Encyclopeadia of Science, 1993; Co-author, The Cardiff Book, 1971; Viral Pollution of the Environment, 1983; Walking in Britain, 1988; Sex and Health, 1989. *Contributions to:* The Times; Guardian; New Scientist; Nature; Microscopy; Private Eye; Daily Telegraph; British Medical Journal. *Memberships:* Former Chairman of Nutrition, Royal Society of Health; Former member, Council of the National Book League; Past President, European Union of Science Journalists' Associations; Former Chairman, Science and Technical Writers, Society of Authors, London; Former Head of Entertainments, Savage Club, London; Fellow, Member of, Court of Governors, Cardiff University; Fellow, and Chairman of History Committee, Insitute of Biology; Fellow, Member of Council, and Surveyor of Scientific Instruments, Linnean Society. *Address:* Rothay House, Mayfield Road, Eastrea, Cambridgeshire PE7 2AY, England.

FORD David. *See:* **GILMAN George G.**

FORD George H(arry), b. 1914, American. *Appointments:* Professor of English, University of Rochester, NY, 1958-; Member, American Academy of Arts and Science, 1980-; President, International Society for the Study of Time, 1981-84. *Publications:* Keats and the Victorians, 1944; Dickens and His Readers, 1955; Thackeray, Vanity Fair (ed), Dickens' David Copperfield (ed), 1958; Double Measure: The Novels of D H Lawrence, 1965; The Dickens Critics (ed with L Lane), 1966; Dickens' Hard Times (co-ed), 1970; The Norton Anthology of English Literature (co-ed), 1974; Selected Poems of John Keats (ed); Dickens' Bleak House (ed), Victorian Fiction: A Second Guide to Research (ed), The Making of a Secret Agent, 1978. *Address:* Department of English, University of Rochester, Rochester, NY 14627, USA.

FORD Jesse Hill, b. 28 Dec 1928, Troy, Alabama, USA. Author. m. Lillian Shelton Pellettieri, 15 Nov 1975, 2 sons, 2 daughters. *Education:* BA Classics, Vanderbilt University, 1947-51; MA, University of Florida, 1953-55; Post-graduate, University of Oslo, Norway, 1961-62. *Appointments:* Staff, The Tennessean, 1950-51; Associated Press, 1953-55; Guest Editorialist, USA Today, 1986-; Writer-in-Residence, Drama, Vanderbilt University, 1987-. *Publications:* The Liberation of Lord Byron Jones, 1965; Mountains of Gilead, 1961; The Feast of St. Barnabas, 1969; The Raider, 1975; Fishes, Birds and Sons of Men, short stories, 1967; Mr. Potter and His Bank, 1976; The Conversion of Buster Drumwright, play, 1960, musical, 1982. *Contributions include:* Short fiction in Playboy; Esquire; Atlantic; Paris review; Travel essays in major magazines and newspapers. *Honours:* Best Story, Atlantic First, The Atlantic Monthly, 1959; Atlantic Grant, 1959; O Henry Prize Collection Stories, 1961, 1966, 1967; Best detective stories, 1972-76; Edgar Allen Poe Prize Best Storey for The Jail, 1976; Guggenheim Fellow, fiction, 1966; Visiting Fellow, Fiction, centre for Advanced Study, Middletown, Connecticut, 1965. *Memberships:* Overseas Press Club of New York; Writers Guild of American, West. *Literary Agent:* Harold Ober Associates, New York City, USA. *Address:* Box 43, Bellevue, TN 37221, USA.

FORD Kirk. *See:* **SPENCE William John Duncan.**

FORD Logan. *See:* **NEWTON Dwight Bennett.**

FORD Peter, b. 3 June 1936, Harpenden, Hertfordshire, England. Author; Editorial Consultant. div., 2 sons, 1 daughter. *Education:* St George's School, Harpenden, 1948-52. *Appointments:* Editor, Cassell, 1958-61; Senior Copy Editor, Penguin Books, 1961-64; Senior Editor, Thomas Nelson, 1964-70. *Publications:* The Fool on the Hill (with the late Max Wall), 1975; Scientists and Inventors (with Anthony Feldman), 1979; The True History of the Elephant Man (with the late

Dr Michael Howell), 1980, Revised Editions, 1983, 1992; Medical Mysteries (with the late Dr Michael Howell), 1985, retitled The Ghost Disease (paperback), The Beetle of Aphrodite (USA); The Picture Buyer's Handbook (with John Fisher), 1988; A Collector's Guide to Teddy bears, 1990; Rings and Curtains: Family and Personal Memoirs (with Albert Whiteley (Jack Le White)), 1992. *Memberships:* Society of Authors; Society of Freelance Editors and Proofreaders; Folklore Society; Academy. *Literary Agent:* David Grossman, 110-114 Clerkenwell Road, London EC1M 5SA, England. *Address:* 42 Friars Street, Sudbury, Suffolk CO10 6AG, England.

FOREST Dial. *See:* **GAULT William Campbell.**

FORKER Charles Rush, b. 11 Mar 1927, Pittsburgh, Pennsylvania, USA. Professor of English. *Education:* Bowdoin College, AB, 1951; Merton College, BA, 1953; MA, 1955; Harvard University, PhD, 1957. *Appointments include:* Resident Tutor, Kirkland House, Harvard University, 1955-57; Instructor, University of Wisconsin, 1957-59; Assistant Professor, Indiana University, 1959-64; Associate Professor, Ind University, 1964-68; Professor, Ind University, 1968-92; Professor, Emeritus Ind University, 1992-. *Publications:* The Cardinal; Henry V: An Annotated Biblegraphy; Skull Beneath the Skin; Fancy's Images; Edward II. *Contibutions to:* Shakespeare Quarterly; Shakespeare Studies; Medieval and Renaissance Drama. *Honours:* Phi Beta Kappa; Fulbright Fellowship to ENgland; Shakespeare Prize; ACLS Grant; NEH Senior Research Fellow. *Memberships:* Guild of Scholars of the Episcopal Church; Shakespeare Society of America; International Shakespeare Society; Malone Society; Marlowe Society. *Address:* 1219 East Maxwell Lane, Bloomington, IN 47401, USA.

FORREST Leon, b. 1937, American. *Appointments:* Editor of Community Newspaper, 1965-69; Associate Editor 1969-72 and Managing Editor 1972-73, Muhammad Speaks (Black Muslim newspaper); Associate Professor 1973- 84, Professor 1984-, Chairman of the Department of African-American Studies 1985-, Northwestern University, Evanston. *Publications:* There Is a Tree More Ancient Than Eden, 1973; The Bloodworth Orphans, 1977; Two Wings to Veil My Face, 1984. *Address:* Department of African-American Studies, Northwestern University, Arthur Andersen Hall, 2003 Sheridan Road, Evanston, IL 60201, USA.

FORREST Richard Stockton, b. 8 May 1932, Orange, New Jersey, USA. Writer. m. 11 May 1955. 3 sons, 3 daughters. *Education:* Dramatic Workshop, NYC 1950; University of South Carolina, 1953-54. *Publications:* Who Killed Mr Garland's Mistress? 1974; A Child's Garden of Death, 1975; The Wizard of Death, 1977; Death Through the Looking Glass, 1978; The Death in the Willows, 1979; The Killing Edge, 1980; Death at Yew Corner, 1981; Death Under the Lilacs, 1985; Lark's Song, 1986. Under the name of Stockton Woods: The Laughing Man, 1980; Game Bet, 1981; The Man Who Heard Too Much, 1983. Death on the Mississippi, 1989. *Contributions to:* Many short stories to numerous magazines. *Honour:* Special Edgar Allen Poe Award, by MWA, 1976. *Membership:* Mystery Writers of America. *Literary Agent:* Phyllis Westberg, Harold Ober Associates, New York City. *Address:* Box 724, Old Saybrook, CT 06475, USA.

FORRESTER Duncan Baillie, b. 10 Nov 1933, Scotland. Theological Educator. m. Margaret R McDonald, 9 June 1964, 1 son, 1 daughter. *Education:* Madras College, St Andrews; University of St Andrews; University of Chicago; University of Edinburgh; University of Sussex. *Publications:* Caste and Christianity; Christianity and the Future of Welfare; Theology and Politics; Beliefs, Values and Policies; Encounter with God; Studies in the History of Worship in Scotland; Theology and Practice. *Memberships:* Society for Study of Theology; Society for Study of Christian Ethics. *Address:* 25 Kingsburgh Road, Edinburgh EH12 6DZ, Scotland.

FORSHAY-LUNSFORD Cin, b. 2 May 1965, New York, USA. Author; Lecturer. *Education:* Currently attending, Queens College, Flushing, New York. *Publications:* Walk Through Cold Fire, 1985; Saint Agnes Sends the Golden Boy, in Anthology Visions, 1987. *Contributions To:* Top of the News. *Honours:* 2nd Annual Delacorte Press Prize for Outstanding First Young Adult Novel, 1985. *Address:* 2929 Longbeach Road, Apt.A, Oceanside, NY 11572, USA.

FORSTER Margaret, b. 25 May 1938, Carlisle, Cumberland, England. Writer. m. Hunter Davies, 11 June 1960, 1 son, 2 daughters. *Education:* BA, Modern History, Sommerville College, Oxford (Scholar), 1960. *Appointments:* Teacher, Barnsbury Girls' School, London, 1961-63; Chief Non-fiction Reviewer, London Evening Standard, 1977-80. *Publications:* Lady's Maid, 1989; The Battle for Christobel, 1991; 13 novels; 3 non-fiction books. *Memberships:* Fellow, Royal Society of literature, 1975. *Literary Agent:* Tessa Sayle, 11 Jubilee Place, London. *Address:* 11 Boscastle Road, London NW5, England.

FORSYTH Frederick, b. 1938, British. *Appointment:* Former staff member, BBC, London. *Publications:* The Biafra Story, 1969; Day of the Jackal, 1971; The Odessa File, 1972; The Dogs of War, 1974; The Shepherd, 1975; The Devil's Alternative, 1979; No Comebacks: Collected Short Stories, 1982; The Fourth Protocol, 1984; The Negotiator, 1990. *Literary Agent:* Curtis Brown. *Address:* c/o Curtis Brown, 162-168 Regent Street, London W1R 5TB, England.

FORSYTH Michael Graham de Jong, b. 26 Nov 1951, Tynemouth, England. Architect. m. Vera Papaxanthou, 18 Sept 1975, 1 son, 2 daughters. *Education:* University of Liverpool, BArch, 1975; University of Bristol, PhD, 1984; Rome Scholarship, 1975. *Appointments:* University of Bristol, Lecturer, 1979-84; Research Fellow, 1984-89. *Publications:* Buildings for Music: The Architect, The Musician and the Listener, from the Seventeenth Century to the Present Day; Auditoria: Designing for the Performing Arts. *Contributions to:* Architect's Journal; Classical Music; Architecture d'Aujourd'hui; Theatre Crafts. *Honours:* Rome Scholarship; The American Society of Authors, 19th Annual ASCAP Deems Taylor Award; Vern Oliver Knudsen Distinguished Lecturer. *Memberships:* Royal Institute of British Architects; ARCUK; Selection Board, British School at Rome; Bath Preservation Trust; Renovations Committee; Chelsea Arts Club. *Address:* 26 Great Pulteney Street, Bath, BA2 4BU, England.

FORTINI BROWM Patricia Ann, b. 16 Nov 1936, Oakland, CA, USA. University Professor; Art Historian. m (1) Peter Claus Meyer, May 1957, div 1978, (2) Peter Robert Lamont Bown, Aug 1980, div 1989, 2 sons. *Education:* University of California, Berkeley, AB, 1959; MA, 1978; PhD, 1983. *Appointments:* Princeton University, Assistant Professor, 1983-89; Associate Professor, 1989-; Andrew W Mellon Professor, 1991-. *Publication:* Venetian Narrative Painting in the age of Carpaccio. *Contributions to:* Art History; Christian Science; Monitor Book Review; Burlington Magazine; Renaessance Quarterly; Biography. *Honours:* Premio Salotto Veneto. *Memberships:* Renaissance Society of America; American academy in Rome, College Art Association. *Address:* Department of At and Archaeology, Princeton University, Princeton, NJ 08544, USA.

FOSKETT Daphne, b. 23 Dec 1911, Kimpton, Hampshire, England. Author. m. The Rev Reginald Foskett, 7 Apr 1937, late Bishop of Penrith and Holoure, FRSA 1976; RMS 1986, 2 daughters. *Education:* Private school in Sussex, 1921-27. *Publications:* Dictionary of British Portrait Miniatures (2 vols) 1972; British Portrait

Miniatures, 1963; Samuel Cooper, 1974; John Smart, 1964; John Harden of Brathy Hall, 1974; Collecting Miniatures, 1979; Miniatures, Dictionary and Guide, 1987; Scottish Arts Council Catalogue, 1965 and 1974. *Contributions to:* Apollo; Antique Collector; Antique Collectors Guide; The Connoiseur. *Honours:* FRSA, 1976; Theta Sigma Phi, 1964; Commendation for McColvin Medal, 1972. *Membership:* Royal Overseas League. *Address:* Flat 55, Riverside Drive, Solihull, West Midlands B91 3HR, England.

FOSTER Donald Wayne, b. 22 June 1950, Chicago, USA. m. Gwen Bell Foster, 29 Dec 1974, 2 sons. *Education:* BA, Wheaton College, 1972; MA, University of California, 1983; PjD, 1985. *Appointments:* Visiting Lecturer, UCSB, 1984-85; Assistant Professor, Vassar College, 1986-90; Associate Professor, 1990-; Jean Webster Chair of Dramatic Literature, 1991- *Publications:* Eleg, by W S: A Study in Attribution; Womens Works: An Anthology of British Literature. *Contributions to:* The Bible and Narrative Tradition; Privileging Gendes in Early Modern England; Philosophy & Literature; PMLA; Shakespeare Quarterly; ELR; TLS. *Honours:* William Ritey Parker Prize; Delaware Shakespeare Prize. *Memberships:* MLA; Shakespeare Association of America; Renaissance English Text Society; AAUP. *Address:* Box 388, Vassar College, Poughkeepsie, NY 12601, USA.

FOSTER George. *See:* HASWELL C J D.

FOSTER Iris. *See:* POSNER Richard.

FOSTER James Anthony, (Tony Foster), b. 3 Aug 1932, Winnipeg, Canada. m. 10 Oct 1964, 1 son, 2 daughters. *Education:* University of Brunswick, 1950. *Appointments include:* Royal Canadian Air Force, 1950; US Army 10th Special Forces Group, 1952-53; Itinerant Crop Duster Pilot, 1954; Bush Pilot for Sask, 1957-58; Chief Pilot, 1959; Real Estate Development in Caribbean, 1968; MGm & Wm, 1976. *Publications:* Zig Zag to Armageddon; The Bush Pilots; By Pass; The Money Burn; Heart of Oak; Sea Wings; meeting of Generals; Muskets to Missiles; Rue Du Bac; For Love And Glory; Ransom for A God; The Sound and the Silence; Swan Song. *Contributions to:* Numerous TV Movies, Documentaries and Series Scripts. *Memberships:* Writers Union of Canada; Canadian Authors Association; PEN; Writers Guild of America. *Address:* 67 Briarwood Crescent, Halifax, NS, Canada B3M 1P2.

FOSTER Linda Nemec, b. 29 May 1950, Garfield Heights, Ohio, USA. Poet; Teacher of Creative Writing. m. Anthony Jesse Foster, 26 Oct 1974, Maple Heights, Ohio, USA. 1 son, 1 daughter. *Education:* BA, Aquinas College, Grand Rapids, Michigan; MFA, Creative Writing, Goddard College, Plainfield, Vermont. *Literary Appointments:* Board Member, Cranbrook Writers Guild, Birmingham, Michigan; Creative Writers in Schools Programme, Michigan Council for the Arts, Detroit; Board Member, Mecosta County Council for the Humanities, Big Rapids, Michigan. *Publications:* A History of the Body, chapbook of prose poems, 1986; Manhattan Poetry Review; The Penn Review; American Poetry Anthology; Negative Capability; Anthology of Contemporary Michigan Poetry. *Contributions to:* Poetry Now; Nimrod; Tendril; Invisible City; Chowder Review; Midwest Poetry Review; Another Chicago Magazine; Croton Review; The Alchemist; University of Windsor Review, Canada; Sierra Madre Review; Room and others. *Honours:* Poetry manuscript nominated for Anne Sexton Prize, 1979; 2 poems nominated for Pushcart Prize, 1982; Poetry Grant, Michigan Council for the Arts, 1983-84; Prizewinner, Croton Review poetry competition, 1985; Grand Prize, American Poetry Association contest, 1986. *Memberships:* Detroit Women Writers; Poetry Society of America; Academy of American Poets. *Address:* 427 W Pere Marquette, Big Rapids, MI 49307, USA.

FOSTER Paul, b. 15 Oct 1931, Pennsgrove, New Jersey, USA. Writer. *Education:* BA, Rutgers University; LLB, New York University Law School. *Publications:* 25 books of plays including: Tom Paine, 1971, 1975, 1978; Madonna in the Orchard, 1971, 1974; Satyricon, 1972; Elizabeth I, 1972, 1974, 1978; Marcus Brutus, 1976; Silver Queen Saloon, 1976, 1978; Mellon & the National Art Gallery, 1980; A Kiss Is Just A Kiss, 1984; 3 Mystery Comedies, 1985; The Dark & Mr Stone, 1985. Translation: Odon von Horvath's Faith, Hope & Charity, 1987. Films: Smile, 1980; Cop & the Anthem, 1982; When You're Smiling, 1983; Cinderella, 1984; Home Port, 1984. *Contributions to:* Off-Off Broadway Book, 1972; Best American Plays of Modern Theatre, 1975; New Stages magazine. *Honours:* Rockefeller Foundation Fellowship, 1967; British Arts Council Award, 1973; J.S. Guggenheim Fellowship, 1974; Theatre Heute Award, 1977. *Memberships:* Dramatists Guild; Society of Composers & Dramatic Authors, France; Players Club, NYC. *Address:* 44 W 10 Street, New York, NY 10011, USA.

FOSTER Raymond, b. 21 June 1931, England. Forester; Gardener; Writer; Painter. *Publications:* The Woodland Garden; Trees & Shrubs in Garden Design; Rock Garden & Alpine Plants; The Garden in Autumn & Winter; Rare, Exotic & Difficult plants; Giardini Rocciosi; Overlook Guide to Growing Rare & Exotic Plants. *Membership:* Subud Writers International. *Address:* 8 Yew Tree Grove, Highley, Bridgnorth, Shropshire, WV16 6DG, England.

FOSTER Simon. *See:* GLEN Duncan Munro.

FOSTER Tony. *See:* FOSTER James Anthony.

FOUGERE Jean, b. 5 May 1914, St Amand, Cher, France. Writer. *Publications include:* Novels: La Pouponniere, 1948; La Cour des Miracles, 1955; La Vie de Chateau, 1958; Les Petits Messieurs, 1963; Nos Tantes d'Avallon, 1968; Les Passagers, 1975; Destinee City, 1983; Short stories: Un Cadeau Utile, 1953; La Belle Femme, 1971; Essays: Voulez-vous Voyager Avec Moi? 1957; Les Nouveaux Bovides, 1966; Lettre Ouverte a un Satyre, 1969; Un Carnet Du Jour, 1989, novels; Le Faiseur Dor, 1989, short stories. *Contributions to:* Le Figaro; les Nouvelles Litteraires. *Honours:* Grand Prix de la Nouvelle, Academie Francaise, 1972; Chevalier Legion d'Honneur. *Membership:* Former Vice President, Society of Men of Letters. *Address:* 22 Quai de Bethune, 75004 Paris, France.

FOWLER Alastair (David Shaw), b. 1930, British. *Appointments:* Junior Research Fellow, Queen's College, 1955-59; Fellow and Tutor in English, Brasenose College, 1962-71, Oxford; Regius Professor of Rhetoric and English Literature, 1971-, now Emeritus, University of Edinburgh; Professor of English, University of Virginia, 1990. *Publications:* Richard Will's De Re Poetica (trans and ed), 1958; Spenser and the Numbers of Time, 1964; C S Lewis's Spenser's Images of Life (ed), 1967; The Poems of John Milton (ed with John Carey), 1968; Triumphal Forms, 1970; Silent Poetry (ed), 1970; Topics in Criticism (ed with I C Butler), Seventeen, 1971; Conceitful Thought, 1975; Catacomb Suburb, 1976; Spenser, 1978; From the Domain of Armheim, Kinds of Literature, 1982; A History of English Literature, 1987; The New Oxford Book of Seventeenth-Century Verse, 1991; The Country House Poem, 1993. *Address:* Department of English, David Hume Tower, University of Edinburgh, George Square, Edingburgh EH8 9JX, Scotland.

FOWLER Christopher Robert, b. 26 Mar 1953, London, England. Writer. *Publications:* Roofworld; Rune; City Jitters I & II; Red Bride; Sharper Knives; The Bureau of Lost Souls; Darkest Day; How To Impersonate Famous people; The Ultimate Party Book; Spanky; Menz Insana. *Memberships:* PEN; Writers Guild. *Literary Agent:* Serafina Clarke. *Address:* 19 Greek Street, London W1, England.

FOWLER Don D, b. 1936, American. *Appointments:* Assistant Professor 1964-67, Associate Research Professor 1968-72, Research Professor of Anthropology 1972-78, Mamie Kleberg Professor of Anthropology and Historic Preservation, 1978-, University of Nevada, Reno; Research Associate, Smithsonian Institution, WA, 1970-; President, Society for American Archaeology, 1985-87. *Publications:* Down the Colorado: John Wesley Powell's Diary of the First Trip Through the Grand Canyon (ed), 1969; Photographed All the Best Scenery: Jack Hiller's Diary of the Powell Expedition (ed), In a Sacred Manner We Live - Edward S Curtis's Photographs of North American Indians, 1972; The Western Photographs of Jack Hillers, 1989. *Address:* Historic Preservation Program, University of Nevada, Reno, NV 89557-0111, USA.

FOWLER Marian Elizabeth, b. 15 Oct 1929, Newmarket, Ontario, Canada. Writer. m. Dr Rodney Singleton Fowler, 19 Sept 1953, Toronto, divorced 1977. 1 son, 1 daughter. *Education:* BA Hons, English, 1951; MA, English, 1965; PhD English, 1970, University of Toronto. *Publications:* The Embroidered Tent, Five Gentlewomen in Early Canada, 1982; Redney: A Life of Sara Jeannette Duncan, 1983; Below the Peacock Fan: First Ladies of the Raj, 1987; Blenheim: Biography of a Palace, 1989. *Contributions to:* English Studies in Canada; University of Toronto Quarterly; Dalhousie Review; Ontario History; Dictionary of Canadian Biography; Oxford Companion to Canadian Literature; New Canadian Encyclopaedia. *Honours:* Governor-General's Gold Medal in English, 1951; Canadian Biography Award, 1979. *Memberships:* International PEN; Writers' Union of Canada. *Literary Agent:* Vardey and Brunton. *Address:* Kilmara, RR2, Lisle, Ontario, Canada, L0M 1M0.

FOWLER Richard Hindle, b. 13 May 1910, Melbourne, Victoria, Australia. Retired Science Museum Director. m. Dorothy Isabel Nicholson, 17 Apr 1937, dec, 1 son, 1 daughter. *Education:* University of Melbourne 1927-30. *Publications:* Robert Burns; False Foundations of British History (editor). *Contributions to:* Various. *Memberships:* Museums Association of Australia; Australian Institute of Agricultural Science; Robert Burns Club of Melbourne inc; Astronomical Society of Victoria. *Address:* 8 Kelvin Grove, Ashburton, Victoria 3147, Australia.

FOX Geoffrey Edmund, b. 3 Apr 1941, Chicago, USA. Writer; Sociologist; Translator. m. (1) Sylvia Herrora, 8 Aug 1966, (2) Mirtha Quintanales, 15 June 1975, (3) Susana Torre, 5 Oct 1979, 2 sons. *Education:* BA, Harvard, 1963; Northwestern University, PhD, 1975. *Appointments:* Editor, Hispanic Monitor, 1983-84; Guest Editor, NACLA Report on the Americas, 1989, 1991. *Publications:* Hispanic National (in progress); Welcome to My Contri; The Land and People of Argentina; The Land and People of Venezuela; Working Class Emigres from Cuba. *Contributions to:* New York Times; The Nation; Village Voice; Yellow Silk; Fiction International; Central Park. *Memberships:* Authors Guild; National Writers Union; Latin American Studies Association. *Literary Agent:* Colleen Mohyde. *Address:* 14 East 4th Street 812, New York, NY 10012, USA.

FOX Levi, b. 1914, United Kingdom. Author. *Appointments:* Director and Secretary, Shakespeare Birthplace Trust, 1945-89; Director Emeritus of the Trust, 1990; General Editor, Dugdale Society, 1945-80. *Publications:* Leicester Abbey, 1938; Administration of the Honor of Leicester in the Fourteenth Century, 1940; Leicester Castle, 1943; Leicester Forest (with P Russell), 1945; Coventry's Heritage, 1946; Stratford-upon-Avon, 1949; Shakespeare's Town, 1949; Oxford, 1951; Shakespeare's Stratford-upon-Avon, 1951; Shakespeare's Country, 1953; The Borough Town of Stratford-upon-Avon, 1953; English Historical Scholarship in the 16th and 17th Centuries (editor), 1956; Shakespeare's Town and Country, 1959, 2nd Edition, 1976; 3rd Edition, 1990; Stratford-upon-Avon: An Appreciation, 1963, 2nd Edition, 1976; The 1964 Shakespeare Anniversary Book, 1964; Celebrating Shakespeare, 1965; Correspondence of the Reverend Joseph Greene, 1965; A Country Grammar School, 1967; The Shakespeare Book, 1969; Shakespeare's Sonnets (editor), 1970; Shakespeare's England, 1972; In Honour of Shakespeare, 1972, 2nd Edition, 1982; The Shakespeare Treasury, compiler, 1972; The Stratford-upon-Avon Shakespeare Anthology, compiler, 1975; Stratford: Past and Present, 1975; Shakespeare's Flowers, 1978, 2nd Edition, 1990; Shakespeare's Birds, 1978; The Shakespeare Centre, 1982; Shakespeare in Medallic Art, 1982; Shakespeare's Magic, 1982; The Early History of King Edward VI School, Stratford-upon-Avon, 1984; Coventry Constables' Presentments, 1986; Historic Stratford-upon-Avon, 1986; Shakespeare's Town and Country, 1986, 1990; Minutes and Accounts of the Corporation of Stratford-upon-Avon (1592-96), 1990. *Address:* The Shakespeare Centre, Stratford-upon-Avon, CV37 6QW, England.

FOX Mem, b. 5 Mar 1946, Australia. College Lecturer. m. Malcolm, 2 Jan 1969, 1 son. *Education;* BA, Flinder University, 1978; B.Ed., Sturt College, 1979; Graduate Diploma, Underdale College, 1981. *Publications:* Possum Magi, 1983; Wilfrid Gordon McDonald Partridge, 1984; A Cat Called Kite, 1985; Zoo-Looking, 1986; Hattie and the Fox, 1986; Sail Away, 1986; How to Teach Drama to Infants, 1984; Arabella, 1986; Just Like That, 1986; A Bedtime Story, 1987; The Straight Line Wonder, 1987. *Contributions to:* Language Arts. *Honours:* New South Wales Premier's Literary Award, Best Children's Book, 1984; Koala First Prize, 1987. *Memberships:* Australian Society of Authors; Australian Children's Book Council. *Literary Agent:* Caroline Lurie, Victoria Australia. *Address:* 40 Melton St., Blackwood, South Australia 5051, Australia.

FOX Paula, b. 22 Apr 1923, New York, New York, USA, Novelist. m. (2) Martin Greenberg, 9 June 1963, 2 sons. *Appointments:* State University of New York, 1974; University of Pennsylvania, 1980-85; New York University, 1989. *Publications:* Desperate Characters, 1970; The Slave Dancer, 1974; One-Eyed Cat, 1984; A Servant's Tale, 1983; How Many Miles to Babylon, 1967; The Village by the Sea, 1989; The Western Coast, 1972; The Widow's Children, 1976; The God of Nightmares, 1990. *Honours:* Guggenheim Fellow, 1972; American Academy of Arts and Letters, 1972; NEA Award, 1973; Brandeis Fiction Citation, 1984; Newbery Medal, 1974; Hans Christian Andersen Medal, 1983; American Book Award, 1980; Rockefeller Foundation Residency Fellow, 1985; Newbery Honour Medal, 1986. *Membership:* PEN. *Literary Agent* Robert Lescher. *Address:* c/o Robert Lescher, 67 Irving Place, New York, NY 10003, USA.

FOX Robert R, b. 2 Feb 1943, Brooklyn, USA. Literature Program Coordinator. m. Susan, 1 son, 1 daughter. *Education:* BA, Brooklyn College, 1967; MA, Ohio University, Athens, 1970. *Publications:* Destiny News; TLAR & CODPOL; A Fable. *Contributions to:* Fiction International; Pig Iron; Pulpsmith; American Book Review. *Honours:* Citation, Ohioana Library Association; PEN Syndicated Fiction Award; Nelson Algren Short Fiction Award. *Memberships:* Associated Writing Program; Modern Language Association. *Address:* c/o The Ohio Council, 727 East Main Street, Columbus, OH 43205, USA.

FOXALL Raymond, b. 26 Mar 1916, Irlam, Lancashire, UK. Author; Journalist. m. Audrey Pamela Owen, 25 Jan 1940, 2 daughters. *Education:* Manchester College of Commerce. *Appointments include:* Staff appointments with: Warrington Guardian, Lancashire; Daily Mirror, Manchester & London; Press Association, London; Sunday Express, London; Daily Telegraph, London, 1936-52; Feature writer, Sunday Express, Manchester, 1958-73. Also author, full-time 1973-. *Publications include:* Squire Errant, historical novel, 1968; The Little Ferret, historical novel, 1968; John McCormack, biography, 1963; The Amateur Commandos, non-fiction, 1980; The Guinea-Pigs, non-fiction, 1983; The Dark Forest, historical novel, 1972. Novels: Here Lies the Shadow, 1957; Song for a Prince,

1959; The Devil's Smile, 1960; The Wicked Lord, 1962; Brandy for the Parson, 1970; The Last Jacobite, 1975; Society of the Dispossessed, 1976; The Noble Pirate, 1978. *Contributions To:* Perthshire Advertiser, Scottish & Universal Newspapers, weekly columnist 1973-. *Memberships:* Society of Authors; National Union of Journalists. *Literary Agent:* David Bolt Associates, 12 Heath Drive, Send, Woking, Surrey GU23 7EO, UK. *Address:* The Old Crossings House, Balgowan, by Tibbermore, Perthshire PH1 1QW, Scotland, UK.

FRAGOLA Anthony, b. 22 June 1943, Syracuse, New York, USA. Professor. 1 son, 2 daughters. *Education:* BA, Columbia University, 1966; MA, University of North Carolina, 1974; Master, Professional Writing, University of Southern California, 1985. *Publications:* 2 stories by BBC World Service Short Story Series; Author, Adaptor, number of films. *Contributions include:* Encounter & The Cornhill; Lectures pour tous, France; Dewan Sastra, Malaysia; Chariton Review; St Andrews Review; Sudia Mystica; Greensboro Review. *Honours:* UNICO National Fiction Award, 1975; Greensboro Review Fiction award, 1976; Excellence Summer Fellowship, 1978; Recipient, other honours and awards. *Memberships:* Associated Writing Programme; Poets & Writers; University Film and Video Association. *Literary Agent:* Mary Jack Wald Agency. *Address:* 301 Woodlawn Ave, Greensboro, NC 27401, USA.

FRAILE Medardo, b. 21 Mar. 1925, Madrid, Spain. Emeritus Professor in Spanish. *Education:* DPh, DLitt, University of Madrid, 1968. *Publications:* Cuentos con Algun Amor, 1954; A La Luz Cambian las Cosas, 1959; Cuentos de Verdad, 1964; Descubridor de Nada y Otros Cuentos, 1970; Con Los Dias Contados, 1972; Hacia una Generacion Sin Critica, 1972; La Penultima Inglaterra, 1973; Poesia y Teatro Espanoles Contemporaneos, 1974; Ejemplario, 1979; Autobiografia, 1986; Cuento Espanol de Posguerra, 1986; El gallo puesto en hora, 1987; Entre parentesis, 1988; Santa Engracia, numero dos o tres, 1989; Teatro Espanol en un Acto, 1989; El rey y el pais con granos, 1991; Cuentos Completos, 1991; Claudina y lo, cacos, 1992. *Contributions to:* Numerous including: Cuadernos de Agora, Sub- Editor, Drama Critic, 1957-64; Abside; Revista de Occidente, Caravelle; Clavileno; Cuadermos Hispano-Americanos. *Honours include:* Critics Book of the Year, 1965; Hucha de Oro Prize, 1971; Research Grant, Carnegie Trust for Universities of Scotland, 1975. *Memberships:* General Society of Spanish Authors; Working Community of Book Writers, Spain; Association of University Teachers; College of Doctors of Philosophy and Letters, Officer; Membre Correspondant de L'Academie Europeenne des Sciences, des Arts et des Lettres, Paris. *Address:* 24 Etive Crescent, Bishopbriggs, Glasgow G64 1ES, Scotland.

FRAME Janet, b. 1924, New Zealand. Author. *Publications:* The Lagoon Stories, 1951; Revised Edition The Lagoon and Other Stories, 1961; Owls Do Cry, 1957; Faces in the Water, 1961; The Edge of the Alphabet, 1961; Scented Gardens for the Blind, 1963; The Reservoir Stories and Sketches, and Snowman, Snowman: Fables and Fantasies, 1963; The Adaptable Man, 1965; A State of Siege, 1966; The Reservoir and Other Stories, 1966; The Pocket Mirror: Poems, 1967; The Rainbirds, US Edition Yellow Flowers in the Antipodean Room, 1968; Mona Minim and the Small of the Sun, 1969; Intensive Care, 1970; Daughter Buffalo, 1972; Living in the Maniototo, 1979; To the Island, autobiography, 1982; An Angel at My Table, autobiography, 1984; You Are Now Entering the Human Heart, short stories, 1984; The Envoy from the Mirror City, autobiography, 1985. *Address:* 276 Glenfield Road, Auckland 10, New Zealand.

FRANCHON Lisa. *See:* **FLOREN Lee.**

FRANCIS Clare, b. 17 Apr 1946, Surrey, England. Writer. 1 son. *Education:* Economics Degree, University College, London. *Publications:* Come Hell or High Water,

1977; Come Wind or Weather, 1978; The Commanding Sea, 1981; Night Sky, 1983; Red Crystal, 1985; Wolf Winter, 1987; Requiem, 1991; Deceit, 1993. *Honours:* Member, Order of British Empire (MBE); Honorary Fellow, University College, London. *Membership:* Society of Authors. *Literary Agent:* John Johnson. *Address:* c/o John Johnson, Clerkenwell House, 45-47 Clerkenwell Green, London EC1R OHT, England.

FRANCIS Dick. *See:* **FRANCIS Richard Stanley.**

FRANCIS Philip. *See:* **LOCKYER Roger Walter.**

FRANCIS Richard Stanley (Dick Francis), b. 31 Oct 1920, Pembrokeshire, South Wales. Ex Steeplechase Jockey; Author. m. Mary Margaret Brenchley, 21 June 1947, 2 sons. *Appointments:* Racing Correspondent, London Sunday Express, 1957-63. *Publications:* Dead Cert, 1962; Nerve, 1964; For Kicks, 1965; Odds Against, 1965; Flying Finish, 1966; Blood Sport, 1967; Forfeit, 1968; Enquiry, 1969; Rat Race, 1970; Bonecrack, 1971; Smokescreen, 1972; Slay-Ride, 1973; Knock Down, 1974; High Stakes, 1975; In the Frame, 1976; Risk, 1977; Trial Run, 1978; Whip Hand, 1979; Reflex, 1980; Twice Shy, 1981; Banker, 1982; The Danger, 1983; Proof, 1984; Break In, 1985; Bolt, 1986; Hot Money, 1987; The Edge, 1988; Straight, 1989; Longshot, 1990; Comeback, 1991; Driving Force, 1992; Autobiography, The Sport of Queens, 1957; Biography, Lester, 1986. *Contributions to:* Sunday Express; Daily Express; Sunday Times; Daily Mail; New York Times; Washington Post; The Age, Melbourne; Horse & Hound; Sports Illustrated; Classic. *Honours:* OBE, 1954; MWA's Edgar Allen Poe Best Novel Award, Forfeit, 1970, Whip Hand, 1981; CWA's Gold Dagger Award, For Kicks, 1966, Whip Hand, 1980; Honorary LHD, Tufts University, MA, USA, 1991. *Memberships:* Crime Writers Association, Chairman, 1965-66; Mystery Writers of America; Society of Authors; Racecourse Association. *Literary Agent:* Andrew Hewson, John Johnson Agency, London. *Address:* c/o John Johnson Agency, 45/47 Clerkenwell Green, London EC1R OHT, England.

FRANCK Thomas Martin, b. 1931, USA. Professor of Law; Author. *Publications:* Race and Nationalism, 1960; The Role of the United Nations in the Congo (co-author), 1963; African Law (co-author), 1963; East African Unity Through Law, 1964; Comparative Constitutional Process, 1968; The Structure of Impartiality, 1968; A Free Trade Association (co-author), 1968; Why Federations Fail (co-author), 1968; Word Politics: Verbal Strategy among the Superpowers (co-author), 1971; Secrecy and Foreign Policy (co-editor), 1974; Resignation in Protest (co-author), 1975; Control of Sea Resources by Semi- Autonomous States, 1975; Foreign Policy by Congress (co- author), 1979; United States Foreign Relations Law, vols I-III, (co-author), 1981; The Tethered Presidency, 1981; Human Rights in Third World Perspective, 3 vols, 1982; United States Foreign Relations Law, vols IV-V (co-author), 1984; Nation Against Nation, 1985; Judging the World Court, 1986; Foreign Relations and National Security Law (co-author), 1987; The Power of Legitimacy Among Nations, 1990. *Address:* 15 Charlton Street, New York, NY 10014, USA.

FRANGOPOULOS Theophilos D, b. 15 June 1923, Athens, Greece. Retired University Professor. m. Katy Tsitsekli, 14 Dec 1947, 2 sons. *Education:* Athens University of Law, LLD, 1947; University of Surrey, 1967; Boston University, 1978; Queens College, NY, 1979-81; University Berlin, 1986. *Appointments:* Secretary General, PEN Club, 1974-89; Treasurer, 1991-; Secretary General, international Theatre Institute, 1975-82; Member, State Literary Price Awards Committee, 1983-85; Columnist Newspapers. *Publications:* Collected Poems; Battle Before the Walls; Fortitude; The Critique of the Critic. *Contributions to:* Over 60 Magazines, Newspapers. *Honours:* Over 10 Awards. *Memberships include:* Panhellenic Cultural Soceity; Parnassos Society. *Address:* Skoufa 32, Athens 106-73, Greece.

FRANK Elizabeth, b. 14 Sept 1945. Los Angeles, California, USA. Writer; Teacher. m. Howard Buchwald, 3 Aug 1984, 1 daughter. *Education:* Attended Bennington College, 1963-65; BA 1867, MA 1969, PhD 1973, University of California, Berkeley. *Appointments:* Writer, Teacher of English literature at various institutions, including Mills College, 1971-73, Williams College 1973-75, University of California, Irvine, 1975-76, Temple University, 1976-77 and Bard College 1982-. Story editor for Connaught Films, 1979-82. *Publications:* Jackson Pollock, 1984; Louise Bogan: A Portrait, 1985. *Contributions to:* Periodicals including Art in America, Nation, New York Times Book Review and Artnews. *Honours:* Pulitzer Prize for biography and nomination for best biography from National Book Critics Circle, both 1986, both for Louise Bogan: A Portrait. *Literary Agent:* Joy Harris, Lantz Office, 888 7th Avenue, New York, NY 10106, USA. *Address:* Department of English, Bard College, Annandale on Hudson, NY 12504, USA.

FRANK Joseph Nathaniel, b. 6 Oct 1918, New York, New York, USA. Professor Emeritus of Comparative Literature. m. Marguerite J Straus, 11 May 1953. 2 daughters. *Education:* Studied, New York University, 1937-38, University of Wisconsin, 1941-42, University of Paris, 1950-51; PhD University of Chicago, 1960. *Literary Appointments include:* Editor, Bureau of National Affairs, Washington, 1942-50; Lecturer, Department of English, Princeton University; Associate Professor, Rutgers University, 1961-66; Professor of Comparative Literature, 1966-85, Director of Christain Gauss Seminars, 1966-83, Princeton University; Visiting Member, Institute for Advanced Study, 1984-87; Professor of Slavic & Comparative Literature, Stanford University. *Publications:* The Widening Gyre, Crisis and Mastery in Modern Literature, 1963; F M Dostoevsky: The Seeds of Revolt, 1821-1849, 1976; F M Dostoevsky: The Years of Ordeal, 1850-1859, 1983. Editor, A Primer of Ignorance, 1967; Dostoevsky: The Stir of Liberation, 1860-1865, 1986; Coeditor, Selected Letters of Fyodor Dostoevsky, 1987; Through The Russian Prisions; 1989. *Contributions to:* The Southern Review; The Sewanee Review; The Hudson Review; The Partisan Review; Art News; Critique; The Chicago Review; The Minnesota Review; The Russian Review; Le Contradt Social; Commentary; Encounter; New York Review, and others. Contributions to various books, numerous book reviews and translations. *Honours include:* Fulbright Scholar, 1950-51; Rockefeller Fellow, 1952-53, 53-54; Guggenheim Fellow, 1956-57, 1975-76; Award, National Institute of Arts and Letters, 1958; Fellow, American Academy of Arts and Sciences, 1969; Research Grants: American Council of Learned Societies, 1964-65, 1967-68, 1970-71; James Russell Howell Prize, 1977; Christian Gass Award, 1977;Rockefeller Foundation, 1979-80, 1983-84; National Book Critics Circle Award, 1984; James Russell Howell Prize, 1986. *Address:* Department of Comparative Literature, 326 East Pyne, Princeton University, Princeton, NJ 08544, USA.

FRANKEL Ellen, b. 22 May 1951, NYC, USA. Editor; Writer; Story Teller. m. Herbert Levine, 3 Aug 1975, 1 son, 1 daughter. *Education:* BA, University of Michigan, 1973; PhD, Princeton University, 1978. *Appointments:* Editor in Chief, Jewish Publication Society, 1991-. *Publications:* Choosing To Be Chosen, Ktav; The Classic Tales: 4000 Years of Jewish Lore; The Encyclopedia of Jewish Symbols; George Washington and the Constitution. *Contributions to:* Judaism; Jewish Spectator; Moment; Jewish Monthly; Shefer Magazine. *Memberships:* Association of Jewish Studies; Phi Beta Kappa. *Address:* 6670 Lincoln Drive, Philadelphia, PA 19119, USA.

FRANKEL Max, b. 3 Apr 1930, Gera, Germany. Journalist. m. Tobia Brown, 1956, 2 sons, 1 daughter. *Education:* MA, Columbia University, New York, USA. *Appointments:* Staff, 1952-, Chief Washington Correspondent 1968-72, Sunday Editor, 1973-76, Editorial Pages Editor, 1977- 86, Executive Editor, 1986-, New York Times. *Honour:* Pulitzer Prize for International Reporting, 1973. *Address:* The New York Times, 229 West 43rd Street, New York, NY 10036, USA.

FRANKLAND (Anthony) Noble, b. 4 July 1922, Ravenstonedale, England, Historian; Biographer. m. (1) Diana Madeline Fovargue Tavernor, 28 Feb 1944, dec 1981, 1 son, 1 daughter, (2) Sarah Katharine Davies, 7 May 1982. *Education:* Open Scholar, MA, 1948, DPhil, 1951, Trinity College, Oxford. *Appointments:* Official British Military Historian, 1951-60; Deputy Director of Studies, Royal Institute of International Affairs, 1956-60; Director, Imperial War Museum, 1960-82. *Publications:* Crown of Tragedy: Nicholas II, 1960; The Strategic Air Offensive Against Germany, (Co-author), 4 volumes, 1961; The Bombing Offensive Against Germany: Outlines and Perspectives, 1965; Bomber Offensive: The Devastation of Europe, 1970; Prince Henry Duke of Gloucester, 1980; Witness of a Century, Prince Arthur Duke of Connaught 1850-1942, 1993; Encyclopedia of Twentieth Century Warfare, (General Editor and Contributor), 1989; Editor of 3 Volumes, Documents of International Affairs, 1955, 1956, 1957; The Politics and Strategy of the Second World War, (Joint Editor), 9 volumes; The Manual of Air Force Law, (Contributor), 1956; Decisive battles of the Twentieth century, Land Sea and Air, (Contributor), 1976. *Contributions to:* Encyclopedia Britannica; TLS; Times; Daily Telegraph; Observer; Military journals. *Honours:* DFC, 1944; CBE, 1976; CB, 1983. *Address:* Thames House, Eynsham, Witney, Oxford OX8 1DA, England.

FRANKLIN Alexander John, b. 13 July 1921, Stratford-upon-Avon, England, Lecturer; Writer. m. Pamela Mary Hardy, 19 Feb 1944, 1 son, 2 daughters. *Education:* Eastbourne Training College; Central School of Speech and Drama, London. *Appointments:* Principal Scriptwriter and Script Editor, You in the 70s, ILEA TV, 1970-75. *Publications:* Seven Miracle Plays, 1963; Ways, (Co-author P Franklin), 1973; About 30 television scripts for ITV and ILEA TV, 3 film scripts and 1 opera libretto. *Contributions to:* The Use of English; Speech and Drama; Good Housekeeping; The Times; Gambit. *Membership:* The Writers' Guild of Great Britain. *Address:* 23 Abinger Place, Lewes, East Sussex BN7 2QA, England.

FRANKLIN Harry, b. 1906, United Kingdom. Author. *Appointments:* Director, Information and Broadcasting Service, 1941-51, Minister of Education and Social Services, 1954-59, Government of Northern Rhodesia. *Publications:* Ignorance is No Defence, 1940; Unholy Wedlock; Crash, 1968; Don't Go to Ceuta, 1970; The Flag Wagger, 1972. *Address:* Warren House, Warren Lane, Froxfield, Petersfield, Hants, England.

FRANKLIN John Hope, b 2 Jan 1915, Rentiesville, Oklahoma, USA. Writer; University Professor. m. Aurelia E. Whittington, 1940, 1 son. *Education:* AM, Fisk University; PhD, Harvard University. *Appointments Include:* Various Teaching positions, 1936-64; Professor, American History, 1964-82, Chairman, History, 1967-70, John Matthews Manly Distinguished Sevice Professor, 1969-, University of Chicago; Visiting Professor, various Universities. *Publications:* Free Negro in North Carolina, 1943; From Slavery to Freedom: A History of Negro Americans, (6th ed), 1987; Militant South, 1956; Reconstruction After the Civil War, 1961; The Emancipation Proclamation, 1963; Land of the Free (with others), 1966; Illustrated History of Black Americans, 1970; A Southern Odyssey, 1976; Racial Equality in America, 1976; George Washington Williams: A Biography, 1985; Editor, Civil War Diary of James T Ayers, 1947, A Fool's Errand (by Albion tourgee), 1961, Army Life in a Black Regiment (by Thomas Higginson), 1962, Color and Race, 1968, Reminiscences of an Active Life (by John R Lynch), 1970. *Honours:* Numerous honorary degrees; Edward Austin Fellow, 1937-38, Rosenwald Fellow, 1937-39, Guggenheim Fellow, 1950-51, 1973-74, President's Fellow, Brown Univesity, 1952-53, Centre for Advanced Study in Behavioural Science, 1973-74; Senior Mellon Fellow, National Humanities Centre, 1980-; etc. *Memberships:* Various professional organisations including: American Philosophical Society; Association for Study of Negro Life and History; American Association of University Professors. *Address:* 208 Pineview Road, Durham, NC 27707, USA.

FRANKLIN Jimmie Lewis, b. 10 Apr 1939, Moscow, USA. Professor. m. 1961, 1 child. *Education:* BA, Jackson State College, 1961; MA 1964, PhD 1968, University of Oklahoma. *Appointments:* Assistant Professor of History, University of Wisconsin, Stevens Point, 1966-69; Assistant Professor of History, University of Washington, Seattle, 1969-70; Associate Profesor of History, Eastern Illinois University, Charleston, 1970-; Visiting Professor at American Studies Center, Hyderabad, India, 1970. *Publications:* Born Sober: A History of Prohibition in Oklahoma 1907-1959, 1971; The Blacks in Oklahoma, 1980; Journey Toward Hope: A History of Blacks in Oklahoma, 1982. *Memberships:* Organization of American Historians; Association for the Study of Negro Life and History; Southern Historical Association. *Address:* Department of History, Eastern Illinois University, Charleston, IL 61920, USA.

FRANTZ Douglas, b. 29 Sept 1949, North Manchester, Indiana, USA. m. Catherine Ann Collins, 15 Oct 1983, 1 son, 2 daughters. *Education:* BA, DePauw University, 1971; MS, Columbia University, 1975. *Appointments:* City Editor, Albuquerque Tribune, Albuquerque, New Mexico, 1975-78; Reporter, Chicago Tribune, Chicago, Illinois, 1978-87; Reporter, Los Angeles Times, Los Angeles, California, 1987-. *Publications:* Levine & Co: The Story of Wall Street's Insider Trading Scandal, 1987. *Contributions to:* Various magazines, including Esquire. *Honours:* Sigma Delta Chi Award, 1985 for financial reporting; Associated Press-Illinois Award, 1986 and Raymond Clapper Award, 1987. both for investigative reporting; Business Week named Levine & Co one of the best books in 1987. *Literary Agent:* Dominick Abel, New York. *Address:* c/o Dominick Abel, 498 West End Avenue, New York, NY 10024, USA.

FRANTZ Joe B, b. 1917, USA. Professor of History, University of Texas. *Publications:* Gail Borden: Dairyman to a Nation, 1951; The American Cowboy: Myth or Reality (with Choate), 1955; An Honest Preface and Other Essays (editor), 1959; 6000 Miles of Fence (edited with Duke), 1961; Readings in American History (co-editor); The Heroes of Texas (co-author), 1964; Turner, Bolton and Webb: Three Historians of the American Frontier (co- author), 1965; LBJ: 37 Years of Public Service, 1973; Texas, 1976; Aspects of the American West. *Memberships:* Advisory Board, National Park Service; Phi Alpha Theta, President 1962-64; Southwestern Social Science Association, President 1963-64; President, Texas Institute of Letters, 1967-69. *Address:* 4301 Edgemond Avenue, Austin, TX 78731, USA.

FRANZKE Andreas, b. 27 Sept 1938, Breslau. Professor of Art History. m. Irmela Franzke, 1969, 1 son, 1 daughter. *Education:* University Marburg, Heidelberg, PhD, 1969. *Appointments:* Assistant Professor, 1969; Lecturer, 1972; Professor, 1980; Head of Art History Department, 1982; President of Academy of Fine Arts, Karlsruhe, 1988. *Publications:* Jean Dubuffet; Antoni Tàpies; Christian Boltannski; Georg Baselitz; Jean Dubuffet; Antoni Tapies; Skulpturen & Objekte. *Contributions to:* Pantheon; Das Kunstwerk; Tema Celeste; DV. *Address:* AM Rueppurrer Schloss 3A, 7500 Karlsruhe 51, Germany.

FRASER Anthea Mary, (Lorna Cameron, Vanessa Graham), b. Blundellsands, Lancashire, England, Author. m. Ian Mackintosh Fraser, 22 Mar 1956, 2 daughters. *Publications:* Laura Possessed, 1974, 1989; Home Through the Dark, 1974; Whistler's Lane, 1975; Breath of brimstone, 1977, 1978; Presence of Mind, 1978; Island-in-Waiting, 1979; The Stone, 1980; A Shroud for Delilah, 1984; A Necessary End, 1985; Pretty Maids All In A Row, 1986; Death Speaks Softly, 1987;

The Nine Bright Shiners, 1987; Six Proud Walkers, 1988; The April Rainers, 1989; Symbols at Your Door, 1990; The Lily-White Boys, 1991; Three, Three, The Rivals, 1992; Author of 9 romantic/suspense novels under pseudonyms of Vanessa Graham and Lorna Cameron. *Contributions to:* Woman; Woman's Realm; Woman's Own; Woman's Weekly; Homes and Gardens; Rio; Cosmopolitan; Various magazines worldwide. *Memberships:* Secretary, Crime Writers' Association; Society of Women Writers and Journalists. *Literary Agent:* Laurence Pollinger Limited. *Address:* c/o Laurence Pollinger Limited, 18 Maddox Street, Mayfair, London W1R 0EU, England.

FRASER Antonia (Lady), b. 27 Aug 1932, London, England. Author. m. (1) Hugh Fraser, 1956, (div 1977), 3 sons, 3 daughters, (2) Harold Pinter, 1980. *Education:* Ma, Lady Margaret Hall, Oxford. *Publications:* King Arthur, 1954; Robin Hood, 1955; Dolls, 1963; History of Toys, 1966; Mary Queen of Scot, 1973; Cromwell : Our Chief of Men, 1973; King James VI and I, 1974; Scottish Love Poems, A Personal Anthology, 1974; Kings and Queens of England, editor, 1975; Love Letters, anthology, 1976; Quiet as a Nun, 1977; The Wild Island, 1978; King Charles II, 1979; Heroes and Heroines, Editor, 1980; A Splash of Red, 1981; Cool Repentance, 1982; Oxford in verse, Editor, 1982; The Weaker Vessel, 1984; Oxford Blood, 1985; The Warrior Queens, 1989; TV adaptations Quiet as a Nun, 1978, Jemima Shore Investigates, 1983; TV Plays: Charades, 1977; Mister Clay, 1985. *Honours:* James Tait Black Memorial Prize; Wolfson History Prize; Hon DLitt, Hull, 1986. *Memberships:* Committee, English PEN, 1979-; Crimewriters Association. *Address:* c/o Curtis Brown Ltd, 1 Craven Hill, London W2 3EP, England.

FRASER George MacDonald, b. 1925, United Kingdom. Author; Journalist. *Appointments:* Deputy Editor, Glasgow Herald newspaper, 1964-69. *Publications:* Flashman, 1969; Royal Flash, 1970, screenplay, 1975; The General Danced at Dawn, 1970; Flash for Freedom, 1971; Steel Bonnets, 1971; Flashman at the Charge, 1973; The Three Musketeers, screenplay, 1973; The Four Musketeers, screenplay, 1974; McAuslan in the Rough, 1974; Flashman in the Great Game, 1975; The Prince and the Pauper, screenplay, 1976; Flashman's Lady, 1977; Mr American, 1980; Flashman and the Redskins, 1982; Octopussy, screenplay, 1983; The Pyrates, 1983; Flashman and the Dragon, 1985; Casanova, TV screenplay, 1987; The Hollywood History of the World, 1988; The Sheikh and the Dustbin, 1988; The Return of the Musketeers, screenplay, 1989; Flashman and the Mountain of the Light, 1990. *Address:* Baldrine, Isle of Man, United Kingdom.

FRASER Jane. *See:* **PILCHER Rosamunde.**

FRASER Sylvia Lois, b. 8 Mar 1935, Hamilton, Ontario, Canada. Author; Novelist. *Education:* BA, University of Western Ontario, 1957. *Appointments:* Guest Lecturer at Banff Centre, 1973-79, 1985, 1987, 1988; Writer in Residence, University of Western Ontario, 1980; Arts Advisory Panel to Canada Council, 1978-81; Member Canadian Cultural Delegation to China, 1985; Instructor, University of New Brunswick, 1986. *Publications:* The Book of Strange; My Fathers House; Berlin Solstice; The Candy Factory; Pandora; A Casual Affair; The Emperors Virgin. *Contributions to:* Feature Writer, Toronto Star Weekly Magazine. *Honours:* Womens Press Club Award; Presidents Medal for Canadian Journalism; Canadian Authors Association Non Fiction Book Award. *Memberships:* Writers Development Trust; PEN; ACTRA. *Literary Agent:* Sterling Lord Literistic, 1 Madison Avenue, New York, 10010. *Address:* 701 Kins Street West 302, Toronto, Canada M5V 2W7.

FRATTI Mario, b. 5 July 1927, L'Aquila, Italy, came to US 1963, naturalized 1974. Playwright; Educator. 3 children. *Education:* PhD, Ca Foscari University, 1951. *Appointments:* Teacher 1964-65; Faculty, Columbia

University, 1965-66; Adelphi College, 1964-65; Faculty, Hofstra University, 1973-74; Professor of Literature, New School, Hunter College, New York City, 1967-; Drama Critic: Paese 1963-, Progresso 1963-, Ridotto 1963-, Ora Zero 1963-. *Publications:* Books: Eleonora Duse-Victim, 1981; Nine 1982; Biography of Fratti, 1982; AIDS, 1987; VCR 1988. Plays: Cage-Suicide, 1964, Academy-Return, 1967, Mafia, 1971, Races, 1972, Bridge, 1971, Eleven Plays in Spanish, 1977, Refrigerators, 1977. *Honours:* Awards for plays and musicals. *Memberships:* Drama Desk; American Theatre Critics; Outer Critics Circle, Vice-President. *Address:* Hunter College, 695 Park Avenue, New York, NY 10021, USA.

FRAYN Michael, b. 1933, London, England. Author; Journalist. *Education:* BA, Emmanuel College, Cambridge University. *Publications:* Novels: The Tin Men, 1966; The Russian Interpreter, 1967; Towards the End of the Morning, 1969; A Very Private Life, 1968; Sweet Dreams, 1973; Philosophy: Constructions, 1974; Plays: The Two of Us, 1970; Alphabetical Order and Donkeys Years, 1977; Clouds, 1977; Make and Break, 1980; Noises Off, 1982; Benefactors, 1984; Translations:- Chekhov: The Cherry Orchard, 1978; Tolstoy: The Fruits of Enlightenment, 1979; Chekhov: Three Sisters, 1983, Wild Honey, 1984; The Seagull, 1987; Balmoral, 1987; Uncle Vanya, 1989; The Sneeze, 1989; The Trick of It (novel), 1989; A Landing on the Sun (novel), 1991; Now You Know (novel), 1992; Stage Productions Include: Make and Break, Lyric, Hammersmith, 1980, Haymarket, 1980; Noises Off, Lyric, Hammersmith, 1982, Savoy, 1982, Brooks, Atkinson, New York, 1983; Three Sisters, Royal Exchange, Manchester, 1985; Benefactors, Uncle Vanya, Vandeville, 1988; The Sneeze, Aldwych, 1988; Vandeville 1984; Brooks Atkinson, New York, 1985; TV: Making Faces (6 plays for Eleanor Bron), 1975; Jerusalem, 1984; Screenplay: Clockwise, 1986. *Honours:* Somerset Maugham Award, 1966; Hawthornden Prize, 1967; National Press Award, 1970; 3 SWET/Olivier Awards; 4 Evening Standard Drama Awards; Sunday Express Book of the Year Award, 1991. *Memberships:* FRSL; Hon Fellow, Emmanuel College, Cambridge. *Literary Agent:* Elaine Green Limited; Plays: Fraser and Dunlop (Scripts) Ltd. *Address:* c/o Elaine Greene Limited, 31 Newington Green, London N16 9PU, England.

FRAZE Candida (Merrill), b. 25 Mar 1945, American. m. Peter Moskovitz, 25 Aug 1967, 2 children. *Education:* BA, Swarthmore College, 1967; Columbia University, 1968-69; George Washington University, 1969-71. *Appointments:* Urban planner, 1971-73; Writer 1980-. *Publications:* Renifleur's Daughter (novel), 1987. A further novel in progress. *Contributions to:* Poetry to magazines, including Poet Lore and Centennial. *Memberships:* Watershed Foundation; Poetry Committee, Folger Library; Authors Guild. *Literary Agent:* John Ware, 392 Central Park W, New York, NY 10025, USA. *Address:* Washington, DC.

FRAZER Lance William, b. 19 Aug 1954, Ann Arbor, Michigan, USA. Freelance Writer. m. Celia Burki, 24 July 1976, 1 son. *Education:* BA, University of Santa Clara, 1976. *Appointments:* Correspondent, Space World Magazine; Correspondent, Ad Astra Magazine; reporter, The Business Journal; Correspondent, Trials Digest Magazine. *Contributions to:* Ad Astra; Arizona Highways; Barrister; Diversion; Mens Fitness; Pacific Discovery; Student Lawyer; Space World; The New Physician; Trials Digest; US Air; The Washington Times. *Honours:* Society of National Associated Publications, Award Magazine Feature Writing. *Memberships:* American Society of Journalists and Authors; National Writers Club; Society of Professional Journalists. *Address:* 209 Gareffa Way, Santa Rosa, CA 95401, USA.

FRAZIER Arthur. *See:* BULMER Henry Kenneth.

FRAZIER Pamela. *See:* STEVENSON Florence.

FREBURGER William Joseph, b. 6 Oct 1940, Baltimore, Maryland, USA. Editor; Author. m. Mary Elizabrth Algeo, 23 Feb 1979, Missouri. 1 son. *Education:* BA, 1962, St Mary's Seminary, Baltimore, Maryland; STL, 1966, Gregorian University, Rome, Italy. *Appointments:* Editor, Celebration: A Creative Worship Service, 1978-; Editor, Eucharistic Minister, 1984-87; Editor, The Caring Community, 1985-87. *Publications:* Repent and Believe, 1972; This Is the Word Of the Lord, 1974; Eucharistic Prayers for Children, 1976; The Forgiving Christ, 1977; Liturgy: Work of the People, 1984; Birthday Blessings, 1985. *Contributions to:* Numerous Theological Journals including: National Catholic Reporter. *Address:* 11211 Monticello Avenue, Silverspring, MD 20902, USA.

FREEBORN Richard Harry, b. 19 Oct 1926, South Wales. University Professor (Retired). m. Anne Davis, 14 Feb 1954, 1 son 3 daughters. *Education:* MA, PhD, Brasenose College, Oxford University. *Appointments:* Emeritus Professor of Russian Literature, University of London. *Publications:* Turgenev, The Novelist's Novelist: A Study 1960; Two Ways of Life, 1962; The Emigration of Sergey Ivanovich, 1962; A Short History of Modern Russia, 1966; Turgenev: Sketches from a Hunter's Album, 1967; Turgenev: Home of the Gentry, 1970; The Rise of the Russian Novel, 1973; Turgenev: Rudin 1975; Russian Roulette 1979; The Ratzian Revolutionary, novel, 1982, p/b 1985; Turgenev: Love and Death, 1983; The Russian Crucifix, 1987; Turgenev: First Love and Other Stories, 1989; Ideology in Russian Literature (ed) 1990; Turgenev: Sketches from a Hunter's Album (ed), 1990; Turgenev: Fathers and Sons, 1991; Turgenev: A Month in the Country, 1991; Chekhov, The Steppe and other stories (ed), 1991; Goncharov, Oblomov (ed), 1992. *Honour:* D Lit, University of London, 1984. *Membership:* Crime Writers Association. *Literary Agent:* Jon Thurley. *Address:* 24 Park Road, Surbiton, Surrey KT5 8QD, England.

FREEDLAND Michael Rodney, b. 18 Dec 1934, London, England. Biographer; Journalist; Broadcaster. m. Sara Hockerman, 3 July 1960, 1 son, 2 daughters. *Education:* Luton Grammar School, 1946-51. *Appointments:* Local Papers; Daily Sketch, London; Freelance Journalist, 1961-. *Publications:* 23 Biographies, mainly of show business personalities; new Study of Jewish Communities of Eastern Europe; Own BBC Twice-weekly radio programme. *Address:* 35 Hartfield Avenue, Elstree, Herfordshire, WD6 3JB, England.

FREELING Nicolas, b. 3 Mar 1927, London, England, Fiction Writer. m. Cornelia Termes, 1954, 4 sons, 1 daughter. *Publications include:* Author of 30 fiction books most recent including, The Pretty How Town, 1992; You Who Know, 1993. *Contributions to:* Occasional essays and travel articles. *Honours:* Crimewriters Gold Dagger, London, 1963; Grand Prix de Roman Policier, Paris, 1965; Edgar Allan Poe Prize, New York, 1966. *Literary Agent:* Curtis Brown, London and New York. *Address:* 67130 Grandfontaine, France.

FREEMAN Anne Hobson, b. 19 Mar 1934, Richmond, Virginia, USA. Fiction Writer; Essayist. m. George Clemon Freeman, 6 Dec 1958, 2 sons, 1 daughter. *Education:* AB, Bryn Mawr College, 1956; MA, University of Virginia, 1973. *Appointments:* Reporter, International News Service, Russia & Eastern Europe, 1957; Editor, Member's Bulletin, Virginia Museum of Fine Arts, 1958-63; Lecturer, English, University of Virginia, 1973-88. *Publication:* The Style of a Law Firm: Eight Gentlemen from Virginia, 1990. *Contributions to:* Hugh, in Virginia Quarterly Review, 1985; The Girl Who Was No Kin to the Marshalls, in Best American Short Stories, 1982; Miss Julia and the Hurricane, in Mademoiselle Prize Stories, 1951-75; articles and stories in various journals and magazines. *Honours:* M. Carey Thomas Essay Prize; Mademoiselle Fiction Contest Prize, 1956; Best American Short Stories, 1982; Emily Clark Balch Prize for Fiction, 1985. *Memberships include:* Virginia Writer's Club; Ellen Glasgow Society; Virginia Foundation for the Humanities and Public

Policy; Virginia Historical Society, Board, 1986-. *Literary Agent:* Virginia Barber. *Address* 10, Paxton Road, Richmond, VA 23226, USA.

FREEMAN David Edgar, b. 7 Jan 1945, Toronto, Canada. *Education:* McMaster University, BA, 1966-71. *Appointments:* CREEPS in Montreal, Toronto, Washington, New York. *Publications:* Battering Ram; Creeps; Youre Gonna be Alright; Flytrap. *Contributions to:* Star Weekly; Macleans Magazine; The Silhouette; Stage Voices; The Gazette. *Honours:* Chalmers Award for Best Canadian Play; New York Drama Desk Award; Prize for Creeps. *Literary Agent:* Agence Goodwin. *Address:* B39 Sherbrooke Estate, Suite, Montreal, Quebec, Canada H2L 1K6.

FREEMAN Gillian, (Von S Elizabeth, Elizabeth Von S), b. 5 Dec 1929, London, England. Writer. m. Edward Thorpe, 12 Sept 1955, 2 daughters. *Education:* BA, Honours, University of Reading, 1951. *Publications:* The Liberty Man, 1955; The Leather Boys, 1961; The Alabaster Egg, 1970; An Easter Egg Hunt, 1981; The Undergrowth of Literature, 1969; The Schoolgirl Ethic : The Life and Work of Angela Brazil, 1976; Fall of Innocence, 1956; Jack would be a Gentleman, 1959; The Campaign, 1963; The Leader, 1965; The Marriage Machine, 1975; Nazi Lady, 1979; The Story of Albert Einstein, 1960; An Easter Egg Hunt, 1981; As Elaine Jackson, Lovechild, 1984; Ballet Genius (with Edward Thorpe), 1988; Termination Rock, 1989. *Contributions to:* numerous journals & magazines; many original screenplays & adaptions; Ballet scenarios for Kenneth Macmillans' Mayerling and Isadora. *Memberships:* Writers Guild of Great Britain, Film Committee, Literature Panel, Arts Council. *Literary Agent:* Richard Scott Simon. *Address:* c/o Richard Scott Simon, 48 Doughty Street, London WC1N 2LP, England.

FREEMAN John, Rt. Hon. b. 19 Feb 1915. Journalist; Diplomatist; Businessman. m. (1) Elizabeth Johnston, 1938, (div 1948), (2) Margaret Kerr 1948, dec 1957, (3) Catherine Dove, 1962, (div 1976), (4) Judith Mitchell, 1976, 2 sons, 3 daughters, 1 adopted daughter. *Education:* Brasenose College, Oxford. *Appointment:* Advertising Consultant, 1937-40; active service, North Africa, Italy and North-West Europe, 1940-45; MP, Labour, Watford 1945-55; Financial Secretary to War Office, 1946-47; Under Secretary of State for War, 1947-48; Parliamentary Secretary to Ministry of Supply, 1948- 51; Deputy Editor, New Statesman, 1958-61, Editor 1961-65; British High Commissioner in India, 1965-68; Ambassador to USA, 1969-71; Chairman, London Weekend TV, 1971-84, CEO, 1971-76; Chairman and CEO, LWT Holdings, 1977-84; Visiting Professor, Intrnational Relations, Univerity of California, Davis, 1985-90. *Honours:* Gold Medal, Royal Television Society, 1981; Trustee, Reuters, 1984-.

FREEMAN Sarah Caroline, b. 12 Dec 1940, Newcastle, Staffs, England. Writer. m. Michael Robert Freeman, 12 June 1965, 1 son, 1 daughter. *Education:* Somerville College, Oxford, 1958-61. *Appointments:* Junior Editor, Penguin Books, 1961-64; Sub Editor Harpers Bazaar, 1964-67; Managing Editor, Wine & Food, 1969-70; Arts Editor, Harpers & Queen, 1970-73. *Publications:* Isabella and Sam: The Story of Mrs Beeton; Mutton and Oysters: The Victorians and their Food; The Student Cookbook; The Student Vegetarian Cookbook; The Piccolo Picture Cookbook; Forthcoming: The Student Pasta Cookbook. *Contributions to:* Harpers Bazaar; Harpers & Queen; The Guardian; Observer. *Memberships:* Mary Somerville Art Trust; Contemporary Art Society. *Literary Agent:* SheiLland Associates Limited. *Address:* 47 Onslow Gardens, London N10 3JY, England.

FREEMAN Simon David, b. 16 Aug 1952, Windsor, England. Journalist. *Education:* Worcester College, Oxford, 1971-74. *Publications:* Whiz Kids Guide to Football; Sport Behind the Iron Curtain; Conspiracy of silence. *Literary Agent:* Rogers, Coleridge & White,

Powis Mews, London W11. *Address:* 2 Norburn Street, London W10 6EQ, England.

FREEMAN-GRENVILLE Greville Stewart Parker, b. 1918, United Kingdom. Historian; Honorary Fellow, University of York. *Publications:* The Medieval History of the Coast of Tanganyika, 1962; The East African Coast: Select Documents (editor and translator), 1962, 2nd Edition, 1975; The Muslim and Christian Calendars, 1963, 2nd Edition, 1977; The French at Kilwa Island, 1965; Chronology of African History, 1973; Chronology of World History, 1975, 1978; A Modern Atlas of African History, 1976; The Queen's Lineage, 1977; Atlas of British History, 1979; The Mombasa Rising Against the Portuguese 1631, 1980; The Beauty of Cairo, 1981; Buzurg ibn Shahriyar: The Book of Wonders of India (c 953) (editor and translator), 1982; Emily Said-Ruete: Memoirs of An Arabian Princess (1888) (editor), 1982, 1993; The Beauty of Jerusalem and the Holy Places of the Gospels, 1982, 2nd edition, 1987; The Stations of the Cross, 1982; The Beauty of Rome, 1988; The Swahili Coast; Islam Christianity and Commerce in Eastern Africa, 1988; A New Atlas for African History, 1991; Historical Atlas of the Middle East, 1993. *Address:* North View House, Sheriff Hutton, York YO6 1PT, England.

FREEMANTLE Brian Harry, b. 10 June 1936, Southampton, England. Author. m. Maureen Hazel Tipney, 8 Dec 1956, 3 daughters. *Publications:* 33 books in total, 9 books in Charlie Muffin series, including, Comrade Charlie, 1989; KGB, 1983; Cia, 1984. *Contributions to:* Articles on espionage in London Daily Mail. *Honours:* Nominated Mystery Writer of America, 1987; Edgar Allan Foe Award. *Membership:* Mystery Writers of America. *Literary Agent:* Jonathan Clowes Ltd. *Address:* 4 Great Minster Street, Winchester, Hampshire SO23 9HA, England.

FREESE Mathias Balogh, b. 23 July 1940, USA. Teacher; Psychotherapist; Writer. m. 15 Feb 1970, 1 son, 2 daughters. *Education:* BA, Queens College, 1962; MS, 1966; MSW, SUNY, 1978. *Publications:* Short Story Writer. *Contributions to:* Showcase the Stony Brook Magazine of Fiction; Taboo Magazine; Pig Iron Press; Jewish Currents. *Honours:* Listed in Distinguished Short Stories of 1974; Awardee John Warkentin Essay Contest. *Address:* 9050 Union Turnpike, Glendale, NY 11385, USA.

FREILICHER Melvyn, b. 8 Nov 1946, New York City, University Lecturer; Writer. *Education:* Brandeis University, 1968; University of California, San Diego, 1972. *Appointments:* Lecturer, Writing Programme, University of California, San Diego, 1979-. *Publications:* Contemporary American Fiction. *Contributions to:* numerous professional journals. *Honours include:* National Endowment for the Arts Awards; Pushcart Prize, 1979. *Memberships include:* President, United Artists Coalition of San Diego; President, Foundation for New Literature; National Writers Union. *Address:* 4641 Park Blvd, San Diego, CA 92116, USA.

FREMLIN Celia, b. 1914, United Kingdom. Author. *Publications:* The Seven Chairs of Chelsea, 1940; The Hours Before Dawn, 1958; Seven Lean Years, 1961; Uncle Paul: The Trouble-Makers, 1963; The Jealous One, 1965; Prisoner's Base, 1967; Possession, 1969; Don't Go to Sleep in the Dark, 1970; Appointments with Yesterday, 1972; By Horror Haunted, 1974; The Long Shadow, 1975; The Spider Orchid, 1977; With No Crowing, 1980; The Parasite Person, 1982; A Lovely Way to Die and Other Stories, 1984. *Address:* 50 South Hill Park, London NW3, England.

FRENCH Alfred, b. 12 July 1916. University Lecturer; Writer. m. Alleeta Ruge Garson, 10 May 1980, 1 son. *Education:* BA, 1938; MA, 1946, Selwyn College, Cambridge, England. *Appointment:* Lecturer, Reader in Classics, University of Adelaide, Australia. *Publications:* The Growth of the Athenian Economy, 1964; The Poets of Prague, 1969; Czech Poetry Vol 1, 1973; Czech Writers and Politics, 1984; A Book of Czech Verse, 1958; The Athenian Half-Century, 1971; The Poet's Lamp, 1986. *Contributions to:* Journal of Hellenic Studies; Historia; Slavic Review; Greece and Rome; Ceska Literature; Mnemosyne; Antichthon, and others. *Memberships:* Australian Language and Literary Association; SVU; Australian Academy of Humanities, Council 1982- 84; Australian Society for Classical Studies, President 1986-87. *Address:* 27 Woodfield Avenue, Fullarton, SA 5063, Australia.

FRENCH David, b. 1939, Canada. Playwright. *Publications:* Leaving Home, 1972; Of the Fields, Lately, 1973; One Crack Out, 1976; The Seagull, by Anton Chekov, translation, 1978; Jitters, 1980; Salt-Water Moon, 1985. *Address:* c/o Tarragon Theatre, 30 Bridgman Avenue, Toronto, Onatrio, Canada M5R 1X3.

FRENCH Fiona, b. 1944, United Kingdom. Children's Fiction Writer; Illustrator. *Publications:* Jack of Hearts, 1970; Huni, 1971; The Blue Bird, 1972; King Tree, 1973; City of Gold, 1975; Aio the Rainmaker, 1975; Matteo, 1976; Hunt the Thimble, 1978; Oscar Wilde's Star Child, 1979; The Princess and the Musician, 1981; John Barley Corn, 1982; Future Story, 1983; Fat Cat, 1984; Going to Squintums, 1985; Maid of the Wood, 1985; Snow White in New York, 1986; Song of the Nightingale, 1986; Cinderella, 1987. Rise Shine!, 1989. The Magic Vase, 1990. *Address:* Flat B, 70 Colney Hatch Lane, London N10 1EA, England.

FRENCH Paul. *See:* **ASIMOV Isaac.**

FRENCH Philip (Neville), b. 1933, United Kingdom. Radio Producer; Film Critic. *Appointments:* Senior Talks and Documentary Producer, BBC Radio, London, 1959-1990; Film Critic, The Observer, London, 1978-. *Publications:* The Age of Austerity 1945-51 (co-editor), 1963; The Novelist as Innovator (editor), 1966; The Movie Moguls, 1969; Westerns, 1974, 2nd Edition, 1977; Three Honest Men: Portraits of Edmund Wilson, F R Leavis, and Lionel Trilling, 1980; The Third Dimension: Voices from Radio 3 (editor), 1983; (ed) Malle on Malle, 1992. *Conbtributions to:* Numerous articles and essays in magazines, newspapers and anthologies. *Address:* 62 Dartmouth Park Road, London NW5 1SN, England.

FRENCH Warren Graham, b. 26 Jan 1922, Philadelphia, Pennsylvania, USA. Retired College Professor. *Education:* BA, University of Pennsylvania, Philadelphia, USA, 1943; MA 1948, PhD, American Literature 1954, University of Texas. *Publications:* John Steinbeck, 1961, revised 1974; Frank Norris, 1962; J D Salinger, 1963; The Social Novel at the End of an Era, 1966; Jack Kerouac, 1986; J D Salinger, Revisited, 1988; The San Francisco Poetry Renaissance 1955-1960, 1991; Editor: The South in Film, 1981; The Thirties, 1967; The Forties, 1969; The Fifties, 1971; The Twenties, 1975. *Contributions to:* Numerous American Academic Journals. *Honour:* DHL, Ohio University, 1985. *Memberships:* President, International John Steinbeck Society; Editorial Board, American Literature; Modern Language Association of America; American Studies Association; Western American Literature Association. *Address:* 23 Beechwood Road, Uplands, Swansea, West Glamorgan, SA2 0HL Wales.

FREWER Glyn Mervyn Louis, (Mervyn Lewis), b. 4 Sept 1931, Oxford, England. m. Lorna Townsend, 2 sons, 1 daughter. *Education:* St Catherines College, Oxford, 1952-55. *Appointments:* Advertising Agency Associate Director; Proprietor Antiquarian/Secondhand Bookshop. *Publications:* The Hitch Hikers (BBC Radio Play); Adventure in Forgotten Valley; Adventure in the Barren Lands; The Last of the Wispies; Death of Gold; The Token of Elkin; Crossroad; The Square Peg; The Raid; The Trackers; Tyto: the Odyssey of an Owl; Bryn of Brockle Hanger; Fox; The Call of the Raven; also scripts for children's TV series, industrial films and others.

Contributions to: Birds; Imagery. *Honours:* Junior Literary Guild of America Choice; Freeman of the City of Oxford. *Literary Agent:* Watson, Little Ltd. *Address:* Fairfield Cottage, Brook End, Chadlington, Oxon OX7 3NF, England.

FREWER Louis Benson, b. 15 Jan 1906, Oxford, England. Retired University Librarian; Writer; Editor; Translator. m. Dorothy Ada Poulter, 28 June 1929, 2 sons. *Education:* MA, St Catherine's College, Oxford, 1927. *Appointments:* Senior Assistant Librarian, Bodleian Library, 1921-71; Superintendent, Rhodes House Library, Oxford (Department of Bodleian) 1930-71. *Publications:* British Editor, International Bibliography of Historical Sciences, 1937-; Translator: Frederic Masson: Napoleon at St Helena, 1815-1821, 1949; Pictorial Guide to Oxford, City and University, 1960; Manuscript Collections in Rhodes House Library, Oxford, 1970; Manuscript Collections of Africana in Rhodes House Library, Oxford, 1971; Rhodes House Library, Its Function and Resources, 1956; Editor, St Catherine's Year 1928-78; Editor, The Oxford Freeman, 1970-; Africana, a Select Bibliography of Books published between 1961-71, 1972. *Memberships:* Comite International des Sciences Historiques; Standing Conference on Library Materials on Africa; Standing Conference of African University Librarians; MCC. *Address:* 58 Sunderland Avenue, Oxford OX2 8DU, England.

FRIEDBERG Maurice, b. 1929, USA. Professor of Slavic Languages and Literatures. *Appointments:* Associate Professor of Russian, Chairman of Russian Division, Hunter College, City University of New York, 1955-65; Fulbright Visiting Professor of Russian Literature, Hebrew University, Jerusalem, Israel, 1965-66; Professor of Slavic Languages and Literatures, 1966-75, Director, Russian and East European Institute, 1967-71, Indiana University, Bloomington; Professor of Slavic Languages and Literatures, Department Head, University of Illinois, Urbana, 1975-; Directeur d'Etudes Associe, Ecole des Hautes Etudes en Sciences Sociales, Paris, France, 1984-85. *Publications:* Russian Classics in Soviet Jackets, 1962; A Bilingual Edition of Russian Short Stories, vol II (edited and translated with R A Maguire), 1965, 1966; The Jew in Post Stalin Soviet Literature, 1970; Encyclopedia Judaica (editor and co-author), 16 vols, 1971-72; The Young Lenin, by Leon Trotsky (editor), 1972; A Decade of Euphoria: Western Literature in Post-Stalin Russia, 1977; Russian Culture in the 1980's, 1985; (edited with Heyward Isham), Soviet Society under Gorbachev, 1987; (edited with Marianna Tax Choldin), The Red Pencil, 1989; How Things Were Done In Odessa, 1991. *Honours include:* Two Guggenheims; NEH. *Address:* 3001 Meadowbrook Court, Champaign, IL 61821, USA.

FRIEDEN Bernard J, b. 1930, USA. Professor of Urban Planning. *Appointments:* Editor, Journal of the American Institute of Planners, 1962-65; Director MIT-Harvard Joint Center for Urban Studies, 1971-75; Chairman, MIT Faculty, 1987-89. *Publications:* The Future of Old Neighbourhoods, 1964; Urban Planning and Social Policy (edited with R Morris), 1968; Shaping an Urban Future (edited with W Nash), 1969; The Politics of Neglect (with M Kaplan), 1975, 2nd Edition, 1977; Managing Human Services (edited with W Anderson and M Murphy), 1977; The Environmental Protection Hustle, 1979; Downtown, Inc. (with L Sagalyn), 1989. *Address:* 245 Highland Avenue, West Newton, MA 02165, USA.

FRIEDMAN Alan Howard, b. 4 Jan 1928, New York City, USA. Writer. m. (1) Lenore Ann Helman, 1 Aug 1950, divorced, 1 son, (2) Kate Miller Gilbert, 30 Oct 1977, 1 son. *Education:* BA, Harvard College, 1949; MA, Columbia University, 1950; PhD, University of California, Berkeley, 1964. *Publications:* The Turn of the Novel, 1966; Hermaphrodeity: The Autobiography of a Poet (novel, National Book Award Nominee), 1972. *Contributions To:* (Stories) Hudson Review; Mademoiselle; Partisan Review; New American Review; Paris Review; Fiction International; Kansas Quarterly;

Denver Quarterly; Other Voices; Raritan; Formations; Articles, Chapters and Reviews; The Stream of Conscience, Hudson Review, Winter, 1964-65; The Other Lawrence, Partisan Review No 2, 1970; The Novel, The Twentieth Century Mind, edited by C.B. Cox and A.E. Dyson, 1972; Reviews in New York Times Book Review; The Little Magazine. (Poems) Partisan Review; Raritan; Denver Quarterly; Another Chicago Magazine. *Honours:* D.H. Lawrence Fellowship, 1974; National Endowment in the Arts Award, 1975; Pen Syndicated Fiction Award, 1987; Illinois Arts Council Award, 1992. *Memberships:* American PEN; Executive Board, PEN Midwest. *Literary Agent:* Lynn Nesbit, New YorK City. *Address:* 2406 Park Place, Evanston, IL 60201, USA.

FRIEDMAN Bruce Jay, b. 1930, USA. Writer. *Appointments:* Editorial Director, Magazine Management Co, Publishers, New York City, 1953-64. *Publications:* Stern, 1962; Far from the City of Class and Other Stories, 1963; A Mother's Kisses, 1964; Black Humor (editor), 1965; 23 Pat O'Brian Movies, 1966; Black Angels, 1966; Scuba Duba: A Tense Comedy, 1967; Steambath, play, 1970; The Dick, 1970; About Harry Towns, 1975; The Lonely Guy's Book of Life, 1979; Let's Hear It for a Beautiful Guy, 1984; Tokyo Woes, 1985; The Current Climate, 1989. *Address:* PO Box 746, Water Mill, NY 11976, USA.

FRIEDMAN Eve Rosemary, (Rosemary Friedman, Robert Tibber, Rosemary Tibber), b. 5 Feb 1929, London, England. Writer. m. Dennis Friedman, 2 Feb 1949, 4 daughters. *Education:* Queen's College, Harley Street, London; Law faculty, University College, London University. *Publications:* An Eligible Man, 1989; To Live in Peace, 1987, A Second Wife, 1986; Rose of Jericho, 1984; A Loving Mistress, 1983; Proofs of Affection, 1982; The Long Hot Summer, 1980; The Life Situation, 1977; Juvenile: Aristide, Aristide in Paris 1987; as Robert Tibber: Practice Makes Perfect, 1969; The General Practice 1967; The Commonplace Day, 1964; The Fraternity 1963; Patients of a saint 1961; We All Fall Down, 1960; Love on My List 1959; No White Coat 1957; For Euston Films: Shrinks; For London Weekend Television: An Eligible Man (6 part series); BBC Film, Paris Summer, 1992; Play, Visitor From Seil, 1993. *Contributor to:* Reviewer: Times Literary Supplement; Articles: The Guardian; The Sunday Times. *Memberships:* Fellow, PEN; Council and Management Committee Member, Society of Authors. *Address:* 2 St Katharine's Precinct, Regent's Park, London NW1 4HH, England.

FRIEDMAN Rosemary. *See:* **FRIEDMAN Eve Rosemary.**

FRIEDMAN Joshua M, b. 22 Dec 1941, American. Journalist. *Appointments:* Statehouse Bureau Chief, New York Post, 1972; Philadelphia Inquirer, reporting on mishap in 1979 at the Three Mile Island Nuclear Power plant in Pennsylvania; Soho Weekly News as Editor in Chief, 1980; Bureau Chief for Newsday, 1982; International Reporting of Coverage of African famine, 1985. *Honours:* Pulitzer Prize, 1985; Thomas L. Stokes Award from the Washington Journalism Center and a Page One Award from the New York Newspaper Guild.

FRIEDMAN Milton, b. 31 July 1912, Brooklyn, New York, USA. Economist. m. Rose Director, 25 June 1938. 1 son, 1 daughter. *Education:* BA, Rutgers University, 1932; AM, University of Chicago, 1933; PhD, Columbia University, 1946. *Appointments:* Board of Editors: American Economic Review, 1951-53; Econometrica, 1957-69; Columnist 1966-84, Contributing Editor 1974-84, Newsweek; Advisory Board, Journal of Money, Credit and Banking, 1968-. *Publications:* Income From Independent Professional Practice (with Simon Kuznets), 1946; Sampling Inspection (with H A Freeman etc), 1948; Essays in Positive Economics, 1953; A Theory of the Consumption Function, 1957; A Program for Monetary Stability, 1960; Capitalism and Freedom, 1962; A Monetary History of the United States (with A J Schwartz), 1963; Dollars and Deficits, 1968;

Monetary Statistics of the United States (with A J Schwartz), 1970; Price Theory, 1976; Free To Choose (Rose Friedman), 1980; Tyranny Of The Status Quo (Rose Friedman), 1984; Money Mischief, 1992. *Contributions to:* Numerous magazines and journals. *Honours:* John Bates Clark Medallist, American Economics Association, 1951; Chicagoan of the Year, Chicago Press Club, 1972; Educator of the Year, Chicago Jewish United Fund, 1973; Nobel Prize for Economic Science, 1976; Tuck Media Award for Economic Understanding, 1980; National Medal of Science, 1988; Presidential Medal of Freedom, 1988; Numerous honorary degrees. *Address:* Hoover Institution, Stanford, CA 94305, USA.

FRIEDMAN Yona, b. 5 June 1923, Budapest, Hungary. Architect; Sociologist. m. Denise Charvein, 1960, 2 daughters. *Education:* Architect, 1949. *Appointments:* University Professor, 1960-74; Coordinator, Communication Centre, United Nations University. *Publications:* L'Architecture Mobile, Paris; Utopies Realisables; Vers Une Architecture Scientifique; L'Architecture De Survie; Better Life in Cities; L'Univers Erratique, Presses Universitaires de France, 1993. *Contributions to:* Several Hundred Articles. *Honours:* Great Award Golden Lion of Venice Film Festival; Great Award of Berlin Academy; Grand Prize of the Prime Minister of Japan; United Nations' Habitat Scroll of Honour, 1992. *Memberships:* Royal academy of the Hague; World Academy of Arts & Science; World Federation of Future Studies; Societe Des Gens De Letters. *Address:* 33 Bd Garibaldi, 75015, Paris, France.

FRIEL Brian, b. 9 Jan 1929. Writer. m. Anne Morrison, 1954, 1 son, 4 daughter. *Education:* St Columb's College, Derry; St Patrick's College, Maynooth; St Joseph's Training College, Belfast. *Appointments:* Taught in various schools, 1950-60; Writer, 1960- . *Publications:* Collected Stories: The Saucer of Larks, 1962; The Gold in the Sea, 1966; Plays: Philadelphia Here I Come!, 1965; The Loves of Cass McGuire, 1967; Lovers, 1968; The Mundy Scheme, 1969; Crystal and Fox, 1970; The Gentle Island, 1971; The Freedom of the City, 1973; Volunteers, 1975; Living Quarters, 1976; Aristocrats, 1979; Faith Healer, 1979; Translations, 1981; Three Sisters, translation, 1981; The Communication Cord, 1983; Fathers and Sons, 1987; Making History, 1988; Dancing at Lughnara, 1990. *Honours:* Honorary DLitt, NUI, 1983; Ewart Biggs Memorial Prize, British Theatre Association Award. *Address:* Drumaweir House, Greencastle, Co. Donegal, Ireland.

FRINETIUS Karl. *See:* **BABINECZ Friedrich Karl.**

FRITH David Edward John, b. 16 Mar 1937, London, England. Cricket-Writer. m. 11 May 1957, 2 sons, 1 daughter. *Education:* Canterbury High School, Sydney, 1949-53. *Appointments:* Editor, The Cricketer, 1973-78; Editor, Wisden Cricket Monthly, 1979-. *Publications:* England v Australia Pictorial History, 1977; The Fast Men, 1975; The Slow Men, 1984; The Golden Age of Cricket 1890-1914, 1978; The Archie Jackson Story, 1974; A.E. Stoddart Biography, 1970; Pageant of Cricket, 1987; The Ashes '77, 1977; The Ashes '79, 1979; Runs in the Family, 1969; Cricket's Golden Summer, 1985; Jeff Thomson Biography, 1980; England v Australia Test Match Records, 1986; Cricket Gallery, editor, 1976; By His Own Hand, 1991. *Contributions to:* Australian Cricket; Cricket Society Journal; Cricketer, Australia; Sportsworld, India; Observer Colour Supplement; Benefit Booklets. *Honours:* Cricket Society Jubilee Literary Award, 1970, 1987; Cricket Writer of the Year, Wombwell Cricket-Lovers Society, 1984; British Magazine Sportswriter of the Year, 1988. *Memberships:* Committee Member, Cricket Writers Club, 1977-; Cricket Society; Association of Cricket Statisticians. *Address:* 6 Beech Lane, Guildford, Surrey, GU2 5ES, England.

FRITZ Jean, b.16 Nov 1915, Hankow, China. Writer. m. Michael Fritz, 1 Nov 1941, 1 son, 1 daughter.

Education: BA, Wheaton College, Norton, Massachusetts, 1937. *Publications:* The Cabin Faced West, 1957; And Then What Happened, Paul Revere, 1973; Stonewall, 1979; Homesick: My Own Story, 1982; The Double Life of Pocahontas, 1983; The Great Little Madison, 1989; Bully for You, Teddy Roosevelt, 1991. *Contributions to:* The New Yorker, Redbook, The New York Times, The Washington Post, Seventeen, The Horn Book, Children's Literature in Education. *Honours:* Doctor of Literature, Washington and Jefferson College, 1982; Doctor of Letters, Wheaton College 1987; American Book Award, 1982; Newbery Honor Book, 1982; Regina Medal 1985; Christopher Award, 1982; Boston Globe/Horn Book Award 1980, 1984, 1990; Laura Ingalls Wilder Award, 1986. *Membership:* Authors Guild. *Literary Agent:* Gina Maccoby. *Address:* 50 Bellewood Avenue, Dobbs Ferry, NY 10522, USA.

FRITZ Walter Helmut, b. 26 Aug 1929. Writer. *Education:* Literature & Philosophy, University of Heidelberg. *Publications:* Achtsam sein, 1956; Veranderte Jahre, 1963; Umwege, 1964; Zwischenbemerkungen, 1965; Abweichung, 1965; Die Zuverlassigkeit der Unruhe, 1966; Bemerkungen zu einer Gegend, 1969; Die Verwechslung, 1970; Aus der Nahe, 1972; Die Beschaffenheit solcher Tage, 1972; Bevor uns Horen und Sehen Vergeht, 1975; Schwierige Uberfahrt, 1976; Auch Jet und morgen, 1979; Gesammelte Gedichte, 1979; Wunschtraum alptraum, 1981; Werkzeuge der Freiheit, 1983; Cornelias Traum und andere Aufzeichnungen, 1985; Immer einfacher, immer schwieriger, 1987; Zeit des Sehens, 1989. *Contributions include:* Neue Rundschau; Neue Deutsche Hefte; frankfurter Hefte; Jahresring; Ensemble. *Honours:* Literature Prize, City of Karlsruhe, 1960; Prize, Bavarian Academy of Fine Arts, 1962; heine-Taler, Lyrik Prize, 1966; Prize, Culture circle, Federation of German Industry, 1971; Stuttgarter Literaturpreis, 1986. *Memberships:* German Academy for Speech & Poetry; Academy for Sciences & Literature; Bavarian Academy of fine Arts; PEN; Union of German Writers. *Address:* Kolbergerstr 2a, 75 Karlsruhe 1, Germany.

FROHBIETER-MUELLER Jo, b. 5 June 1934, Evansville, Indiana, USA. Writer. m. W P Mueller, 1 son, 1 daughter. *Education:* BA, University of Evansville, 1956; MA, Indiana University, 1962. *Publications:* Your Home Business Can Make Dollars and Sense; Stay Home and Mind Your Own Business; Practical Stained Glass Craft; Growing Your Own Mushrooms; The Business of Writers. *Contributions to:* Over 700 Articles. *Honours:* Member, Academy of Arts & Sciences. *Memberships:* Ohio Valley Writers Guild. *Address:* 2357 Trail Drive, Evansville, IN 47711, USA.

FROMMER Harvey, b. 10 Oct 1937, Brooklyn, New York, USA. Professor; Author. m. Myrna Katz, 23 Jan 1960, 2 sons, 1 daughter. *Education:* BS Journalism; MA English; PhD Communications, New York University. *Appointments:* Professor, Writing, Speech, New York City Technical College, City University of New York, 1970-; Visiting Professor of Liberal Studies, Dartmouth College, Hanover, New Hampshire, 1992; Reviewer for: Yankees Magazine, Library Journal, Choice, Kliatt Paperback Book Guide, Dodger Blue. Lectures & Appearances: Hundreds of Radio, TV, Community Organizations dates. *Publications include:* A Baseball Century, 1976; A Sailing Primer, 1978; The Martial Arts Book, 1978; Sports Lingo, 1979, 1983; Sports Roots, 1979; The Great American Soccer Book, 1980; New York City Baseball 1947-57, 1980, 1985, 1992; The Sports Date Book, 1981; Basketball My Way, Nancy Lieberman, 1982; Rickey and Robinson, 1982; Baseball's Greatest Rivalry, 1982, 1984; Sports Genes, 1982; Baseball's Greatest Records, 1983; Jackie Robinson, 1984; Baseball's Hall of Fame, 1985; Baseball's Greatest Managers, 1985; Red on Red, 1987; The Autobiography of Red Holzman, 1987; City Tech: The First Forty Years, 1986; Olympic Controversies, 1987; Throwing Heat: The Autobiography of Nolan Ryan, 1989; 150th Anniversary Baseball Album, 1988; Primitive Baseball - The National Pastime in the Gilded Age, 1988; Growing Up At Bat: 50 Years of Little League

Baseball, 1989; Running Tough: The Autobiography of Tony Dorsett, 1989, 1992; It Happened in the Catskills (with Myrna Katz Frommer): An Oral History of the Catskill Resorts, 1990; Behind the Lines: The Autobiography of Don Strock, 1991; Holzman On Hoops, 1991; Shoeless Joe and Ragtime Baseball, 1992; It Happened in Brooklyn (with Myrna Katz Frommer), 1993; Redbook Magazine, (supplement), 1989; Reviewer: Redbird Review. *Contributions to:* Numerous professional journals and magazines. *Honours include:* Selected as Guest Curator and Executive Producer of Stars of David Jews in Sports, 1991; Official Guest, Mexican Government to tour nation to write about Mexican Sports, Summer, 1983; Salute to Scholars Award, City University of New York, 1984; As A Result of Nationwide Search chosen to be Editor and Chief Author of Games of the XXIIIrd Olympiad, Los Angeles 1984 Commemorative Book; Official Guest, Government of Mexico to tour nation and write about its culture, 1983; Official Guest, Government of England to tour and write about its culture, 1986; Official Guest, Government of Finland to tour nation and write about Finnish Culture, 1987; Official Guest, Government of Jamaica to tour nation & write about its culture, 1987; Official Guest, Government of Greece to tour nation and write about its culture, 1988. *Literary Agent:* Don Congdon, New York City. *Address:* 791 Oakleigh Road, North Woodmere, NY 11581, USA.

FROST David Paradine, Sir, b. 7 Apr 1939, Beccles, Suffolk, England. TV Personality; Writer. m. (1) Lynne Frederick, 1981, divorced, 1982, (2) Lady Carina Fitzalan Howard, 1983, 2 sons. *Education:* Gonville and Caius College, Cambridge. *Publications:* That Was The Week That Was; How To Live Under Labour; Talking With Frost; To England with Love (with Antony Jay); The Americans; Whitlam and Frost; I Gave Them a Sword; I Could Have Kicked Myself, 1982; Who Wants to Be a Millionaire?, 1983; The Mid-Atlantic Companian, (jointly), 1986; The Rich Tide, (jointly), 1986; The World's Shortest Books, 1987; TV Programme: Through The Keyhole. *Honours:* Golden Rose Award, Montreux, 1967; OBE; Richard Dimbleby Award, 1967; Emmy Award, 1970, 1971; Religious Heritage of America Award, 1970; Albert Einstein Award, 1971. *Address:* David Paradine Ltd, 115-123 Bayham Street, London NW1 0AG, England.

FROST Jason. *See:* **OBSTFELD Raymond.**

FROST Peter Kip, b. 1936, USA. Professor of History. *Publications:* The Bakumatsu Currency Crisis, 1970; The Golden Age of China and Japan, 1971; China and Japan in the Modern World, 1973. *Address:* Williams College, Williamstown, MA 01267, USA.

FROY Herald. *See:* **WATERHOUSE Keith.**

FRUMKES Lewis Burke, b. Brooklyn, New York City, USA. *Education:* Trinity College, 1957; Columbia University, 1959; Pace University, 1960; New York University, BA, 1962. *Appointments include:* Instructor, Marymount Manhattan College, 1986; Visiting Professor, 1989; Distinguished Visiting Lecturer, 1991-92; Visiting Professor, Harvard Summer School, 1988-1991; Freelance Writer. *Publications:* Meta-Punctuation: When a comma isn't enough; Manhattan Cocktail; Name Crazy; The Mensa Think Smart Book; How to Raise Your I Q By Eating Gifted Children. *Contributions to:* NY times; Harpers; Punch; Readers Digest; Travel & Leisure; Child; Cosmopolitan; Glamour; Family Circle; McCalls; Playbill; Penthouse; Psychology Today; Redbook; Town & Country. *Memberships:* ASJA; Pen; Poets & Writers; National Association of Science Writers; Mensa; Society of American Magicians. *Address:* One Gracie Terrace, New York, NY 10028, USA.

FRUMKIN Gene, b. 29 Jan 1928, New York City, USA. Poet; Professor. University of New Mexico. m. Lydia Samuels, 3 July 1955, 1 son, I daughter. *Education:* BA, English, University of California, Los

Angeles. *Appointments include:* Editor, Coastlines Literary Magazine, 1958-62; Guest edltor, New Mexico Quarterly, 1969; Co-editor, Indian Rio Grande: Recent Poems from 3 Cultures, anthology, 1977; Co-editor, San Marcos Review, 1978-83. *Publications:* Hawk & the Lizard, 1963; Orange Tree, 1965; Rainbow-Walker, 1969; Dostoevsky & Other Nature Poems, 1972; Locust Cry: Poems 1958-65, 1973; Mystic Writing-Pad, 1977; Clouds & Red Earth, 1982; Lover's Quarrel With America, 1985; Sweetness in the Air, 1987. *Contributions include:* Paris Review; Prairie Schooner; Yankee; Conjunctions; Sulfur; PoEtry; Saturday Review; Nation; Evergreen Review; Dacotah Territory; Malahat Review; Minnesota Review. *Honours:* Visiting professor, modern literature, SUNY Buffalo, 1975; 1st prize, poetry, Yankee magazine, 1979; Visiting Exchange Professor, University of Hawaii, 1980-81, 1984-85. *Memberships:* Past President, Rio Grande Writers Association; Hawaii Literary Arts Council. *Address:* 3721 Mesa Verde NE, Albuquerque, New Mexico 87110, USA.

FRY Christopher, b. 18 Dec 1907. Dramatist. m. Phyllis Marjorie Hart, 1936, (dec 1987), 1 son. *Education:* Bedford Modern School; Actor at Citizen House, Bath, 1927. *Publications:* The Boy With a Cart, 1939; The Firstborn, 1946; A Phoenix Too Frequent, 1946; The Lady's Not for Burning, 1949; Thor, with Angels, 1949; Venus Observed, 1950, revised, 1992; Translation: Ring Round the Moon, 1950; A Sleep of Prisoners, 1951; The Dark is Light Enough, 1954; The Lark, 1955; Tiger at The Gates, 1955; Duel of Angels, 1958; Curtmantle, 1961; Judith, 1962; A Yard of Sun, 1970; Peer Gynt, 1970; Television Plays: The Brontes at Haworth, 1973; Sister Dora, 1977; The Best of Enemies, 1977; Cyrano de Bergerac, 1975 (translation); Can You Find Me: A Family History, 1978; Editor and Introduction Charlie Hammond's Sketch Book, 1980; Selected Plays, 1985; Genius, Talent and Failure, 1986 (Adam Lecture); One Thing More of Caedmon Construed, 1987; Looking for a Language (Lecture); Films: The Queen is Crowned, 1953; The Beggar's Opera, 1953; Ben Hur, 1958; Barabbas, 1960; The Bible: In The Beginning, 1962. *Honours:* FRSL; Honorary Fellow, Manchester Metropolitan University, 1988; D.Litt, Lambeth, 1988; Queen's Gold Medal for Poetry, 1962. *Membership:* Garrick Club. *Address:* The Toft, East Dean, Chichester, West Sussex PO18 0JA, England.

FRY Howard Tyrrell, b. 15 Sept 1919, Clydach, Swansea, Wales. Retired University Professor. m. Georgiana Alipio, 25 Apr 1981. *Education:* Pembroke College, Cambridge, 1938-39, 1946-48; Madingley Hall, Cambridge, 1963-67. *Publications:* Alexander Dalrymple and the Expension of British Trade; A History of the Moutain Province. *Contributions to:* Asian Pacific Quarterly; Historical studies; Journal & pacific History; New Zealand Journal of history; Philippine Studies. *Honours:* Bartle Frere Award; National Library of Australia Research Fellowship. *Memberships:* The Society of Quthors. *Address:* Kiln Bank, Horton, Swansea SA3 1LQ, Wales.

FRY Paul Harrison, b. 28 Oct 1944, New York, USA. Professor. m. Brigitte Peucker, 24 Aug 1974, 1 son. *Education:* BA, University of California, 1965; PhD, Harvard University, 1973. *Appointments:* Assistant Professor, Yale University, 1972; Associate Professor, 1979; Professor, 1983; William Lampson Professor, 1993. *Publications:* The Poet's Calling in the English Ode; The Reach of Criticism; William Empson: Prophet Against Sacrifice. *Contributions to:* Numerous Articles. *Honours:* Melville Caine Award; Best Essay Award. *Memberships:* Modern Language Association. *Address:* 509 Boston Post Road, Madison, CT 06443, USA.

FRYE Roland Mushat, b. 3 July 1921, Birmingham, Alabama, USA. Literary and Theological Scholar. m. Jean Elbert Steiner, 11 Jan 1947, 1 son. *Education:* AB, 1943, PhD 1952, Princeton University (Special student in theology, Princeton Theological Seminary 1950-52). *Appointments:* Emory University 1952-61; Folger Shakespeare Library, 1961-65; University of

Pennsylvania 1965-83; Emeritus Professor 1983-; National Phi Beta Kappa Visiting Scholar, 1985-86; L P Stone Foundation Lecturer, Princeton Theological Seminary 1959; Center of Theological Inquiry, Princeton, New Jersey, Chairman. *Publications include:* God, Man and Satan: Patterns of Christian Thought and Life, 1960; Shakespeare and Christian Doctrine, 1963; Shakespeare's Life and Times: A Pictorial Record, 1967; Milton's Imagery and the Visual Arts: Iconographic Tradition in the Epic Poems, 1978; Is God a Creationist? The Religious Case Against Creation-Science, 1983; The Renaissance Hamlet: Issues and Responses in 1600, 1984. *Contributions to:* The Dissidence of Dissent and the Origins of Religious Freedom in America: John Milton and the Puritans, in Proceedings of the American Philosophical Society, 1989. Numerous other articles and reviews in learned journals, literary and theological. *Honours:* John Frederick Lewis Prize, 1979 from American Philosophical Society and James Holly Hanford Award 1979 from Milton Society of America, both for Milton's Imagery and the Visual Arts; Henry Allen Moe Prize from American Philosophical Society for most distinguished 1988 paper in humanities (on nature of Shakespeare's permanence). *Memberships:* Renaissance Society of America, President 1984-95; Milton Society of America, President 1977-78; American Philosophical Society, Secretary; American Academy of Arts and Sciences; Cosmos Club of Washington DC. *Address:* 226 West Valley Road, Strafford-Wayne, PA 19087, USA.

FRYER Jonathan, b. 5 June 1950, Manchester, England. Writer; Broadcaster. *Education:* Diplome D' Etudes Francaises, Universite de Poitiers (France), 1967; BA Hons (Chinese with Japanese), University of Oxford, 1973; MA, University of Oxford, 1980. *Appointment:* Visiting Lecturer, School of Journalism, University of Nairobi, Kenya, 1976. *Publications:* The Great Wall of China, 1975; Isherwood, 1977; Brussels as Seen by Naif Artists (with Rona Dobson), 1979; Food For Thought, 1981; George Fox and the Children of the Light, 1991; Eye of the Camera, 1993; Numerous political pamphlets, mainly on Third World themes. *Contributions to:* The Economist; The Tablet; The European. *Membership:* Member of Executive, English PEN. *Literary Agent:* Jennifer Kavanagh, 39 Camden Park Road, London NW1 9AX, England. *Address:* 140 Bow Common Lane, London E3 4BH, England.

FUCHS Vivian Ernest (Sir), b. 11 Feb 1980, Freshwater, Isle of Wight. Geologist. m. (1) Joyce Connell, 6 Sept 1933 (dec 1990), 1 son, 2 daughters, (2) Eleanor Honnywill, 8 Aug 1991. *Education:* BA 1929, MA 1935, PhD 1936. *Publications:* The Crossing of Antarctica (with Hillary), 1958; Antarctic Adventure, 1959; Forces of Nature (editor), 1977; Of Ice and Men, 1982; A Time to Speak, 1990. *Honour:* Kt, 1958. *Memberships:* FRS, 1974; FRGS, Vice President 1961, President 1982-84; British Association for the Advancement of Science, President 1972; International Giaciological Society, President 1963-66. *Address:* 106 Barton Road, Cambridge CB3 9LH, England.

FUENTES Carlos, b. 11 Nov 1928, Panama City, Republic of Panama. Writer; Mexican Ambassador to France; University Professor. m. Sylvia Lemus, 24 Jan 1973, 1 son, 2 daughters. *Education:* Law School, National University of Mexico; Institute de Hautes Etudes Internationales, Geneva, Switzerland. *Appointments include:* Simon Bolivar Professor, Cambridge, UK; Robert F. Kennedy Professor, Harvard, USA; Teaching positions, Columbia, Princeton, Dartmouth College, Washington University, George Mason University, USA; Numerous lectures, European & North American universities; Lecturer, El Colegio Nacional, Mexico; Mexican Ambassador to France, 1975-77. *Publications:* La Region Mas Transparente, 1958; La Muerte de Artemio Cruz, 1962; Cambio de Piel, 1967; Terra Nostra, 1975; Gringo Viejo, 1985; Cristobal Nonato, 1987. Also: Las Buenas Conciencias, 1959; Aura, 1962; Cantar de Ciegos, 1965; Zona Sagrada, 1967; Una Familia Lejana, 1980; Agua Quemada, 1983; Myself with Others, essays, 1987;

Orchids in the Moonlight, play, 1987; The Campaign, novel, 1991; The Buried Mirror, essay, 1992. *Contributions to:* New York Times; Guardian; Le Monde; Nouvel Observateur; Washington Post; El Pais; etc. *Honours include:* Biblioteca Breva Prize, Barcelona, 1967; Romulo Gallegos Prize, Caracas, 1975; Honorary doctorates, Harvard University 1983, Cambridge University 1987, Essex University, 1987; National Prize for Literature, Mexico, 1984; Miguel de Cervantes Prize for Literature, Madrid, 1988; HDLL - Miami University, Georgetown University and Warwick University, 1992. *Memberships:* American Academy of Arts & Sciences; Trustee, New York Public Library. *Literary Agent:* Carl Brandt, Brandt & Brandt, 1501 Broadway, New York, NY 10036, USA.

FUGARD Athol Harold, b. 11 June 1932, Middelburg Cape, South Africa. Playwright. m. Sheila Meiring, 22 Sept 1956, 1 daughter. *Appointments:* Playwright; Director; Actor. *Publications:* Three Port Elizabeth Plays, 1974; Statements, three Plays, co-author, 1974; Sizwi Banzzi is Dead, and The Island, Co-author, 1976; Dimetos and Two Early Plays, 1977; Boesman and Lena and Other Plays, 1978; Tsotsi, (novel), 1980; A Lesson from Aloes, 1981; Master Harold and the Boys, 1982; The Road to Mecca, 1985; Notebooks 1960-1977, 1983; (Film Scripts), The Guest, 1977; Marigolds in August, 1981; My Children! My Africa!, 1990. *Honours:* Numerous Prizes and Honorary Doctorates including: New York Drama Critics Circle Award for Best Play, 1980-81 Season; Evening Standard Award, Best Play of the Year, 1984. *Memberships:* Fellow, Royal Society of Literature; Fellow, Royal Society of Literature; Member, American Academy of Arts and Science. *Address:* Po Box 5090 Walmer, Port Elizabeth 6065, South Africa.

FUGARD Sheila Mary, b. 25 Feb 1932, Birmingham, England. Novelist; Poet. m. Athol Fugard, 22 Sept 1956, 1 daughter. *Education:* University of Cape Town, 1952. *Publications:* A Revolutionary Women; The Castaways; Rife of Passage; Threshold; Mythic Things. *Honours:* South African Literary Award; CHA Literary Award; The Olive Schrelhee Prize. *Literary Agent:* Susan Bergholz, 340 West 72th Street, New York, NY 10023, USA. *Address:* PO Box 5090, Walmer, Port Elizabeth 6065, South Africa.

FUKS Ladislav, b. 24 Sept 1923, Prague, Czechoslovakia. Writer. *Education:* Charles University, Prague, 1949. *Appointments:* Author of Merit. *Publications:* Mr Theodor Mundstock; Variation for Violin String; Cremator 1st Edition; mice of Natalia Mooshaber; The Deads on the Ball. *Contibutions to:* Czechoslovak Awards of the Year for Literature. *Memberships:* Czech Writers Union; Bernard Bolzan Foundation; Czech Pen Club; Society of Franz Kafka. *Literary Agent:* Ivana Mazalova, Dilia, Polska 1, 120 00 Prague 2, Czechoslovakia. *Address:* Narodni obrany 15, 160 00 Praha 6, Czechoslovakia.

FULLER Jean Violet Overton, b. 7 Mar 1915, Iver Heath, Bucks. Author. *Eductation:* Brighton High School, 1927-31; Royal Academy of Dramatic Art, 1931-32; BA Honours, English, University of London, 1944; University College of London, 1948-50. *Publications include:* Sickert and the Ripper Crimes, 1990; Dericourt The Chequered Spy, 1989; The Comte de Saint-Germain, 1988; Blavatsky And Her Teachers, 1988; Cats and Other Immortals, 1992. *Honours:* Writers Manifold Poems of the Decade, 1968. *Membership:* Society of Authors. *Address:* Fuller D'Arch Smith Ltd, 37b New Cavendish Street, London, England.

FULLER John L, b. 1 Jan 1937, Ashford, Kent, England. Fellow, Magdalen College, Oxford. m. Cicely Prudence Martin, 20 July 1960, 3 daughters. *Education:* New College, Oxford, 1957-62; BA, BLitt, MA. *Publications include:* 12 collections of poetry, criticism, children's books, 4 novels. Titles include: The Illusionists, 1980; Flying to Nowhere, 1983; Selected Poems 1954-82, 1985; Adventures of Speedfall, 1985;

Partingtime Hall, with James Fenton, 1987; The Burning Boys, 1989; Look Twice, 1991; The Machanical Body, 1991. *Honours:* Geoffrey Faber Memorial Prize, 1974; Southern Arts Prize, 1980; Whitbread Prize, 1983; Shortlisted, Booker Prize, 1983; Fellow, Royal Society of Literature. *Literary Agent:* Peters, Fraser & Dunlop. *Address:* 4 Benson Place, Oxford OX2 6QH, England.

FULLERTON Alexander Fergus, b. 20 Sept 1924, Saxmundham, Suffolk, England, Writer, m. Priscilla Mary Edelston, 10 May 1956, 3 sons. *Education:* Royal Naval College, Dartmouth, 1938-41; Cambridge University, School of Slavonic Studies, 1947. *Appointments:* Sales manager, Wm Heinemann, 1959-61; Editorial Director, Peter Davies Limited, 1961-64; General Manager, Arrow Books, 1964-67. *Publications:* Surface!, 1953; A Wren Called Smith, 1957; The White Men Sang, 1958; The Everard Series of Naval Novels: The Blooding of the Guns, 1976; Sixty Minutes for St George, 1977; Patrol to the Golden Horn, 1978; Storm Force to Narvik, 1979; Last Lift from Crete, 1980; All the Drowning Seas, 1981; A Share of Honour, 1982; The Torch Bearers, 1983, The Gatecrashers, 1984; Special deliverance, 1986; Special Dynamic, 1987; Special Deception, 1988; Bloody Sunset, 1991; Look at the Wolves, 1992; Love For An Enemy, 1993. *Literary Agent:* John Johnson Limited. *Address:* C/O John Johnson Limited, 45 Clerkenwell Green, London EC1R OHT, England.

FULTON Robin, b. 6 May 1937, Arran, Scotland. Writer. *Education:* MA, Hons., 1959, PhD, 1972, Edinburgh; LittD. *Appointments:* Editor Literary Quarterly Lines Review, 1967-76. *Publications:* Poetry: Instances, 1967; Inventories, 1969; The Spaces Between the Stones, 1971; The Man with the Surbahar, 1971; Tree-Lines, 1974; Music and Flight, 1975; Between Flights, 1976; Places to Stay In, 1978; Following a Mirror, 1980; Selected Poems, 1963-78, 1980; Fields of Focus, 1982; Coming Down to Earth and Spring is Soon, 1990; Criticism: Contemporary Scottish Poetry : Individuals and Contexts, 1974; The Way the Words Are Taken, Selected Essays, 1989; Editorial: Trio; New Poets from Edinburgh, 1971; Iain Crichton Smith : Selected Poems, 1955-80, 1982; Robert Garioch : The Complete Poetical Works with Notes, 1983; Robert Garioch : A Garioch Miscellany, Selected Prose and Letters, 1986; Translations: An Italian Quartet, 1966; Blok's Twelve, 1968; Five Swedish Poets, 1972; Lars Gustafsson, Selected Poems, 1972; Gunnar Harding, They Killed Sitting Bull and Other Poems, 1973; Tomas Tranströmer, Citoyens, 1974; Tomas Tranströmer, Selected Poems, 1974, expanded 1980; Osten Sjöstrand, The Hidden Music & Other Poems, 1975; expanded and with others, Toward the Solitary Star: Selected Poetry and Prose, 1988; Werner Aspenström 37 Poems, 1976; Tomas Tranströmer, Baltics, 1980; Johannes Edfelt, Family Tree, 1981; Werner Aspenström, The Blue Whale and Other Prose Pieces, 1981; Kjell Espmark, Bela Bartok Against The Third Reich and Other Poems, 1985; Olav Hauge, Don't Give Me the Whole Truth and other Poems, 1985; Tomas Tranströmer, Collected Poems, 1987; Stig Dagerman, German Autumn, 1988; Par Lagerkvist, Guest of Reality, 1989; Preparations for Clight, and other Swedish Stories, 1990; Four Swedish Poets (Kjell Espmark, Lennart Sjögren, Eva Ström & Tomas Tranströmer), 1990; Olav Hauge, Selected Poems, 1990; Hermann Starheimsæter, Stone-Shadows, 1991. *Contributions to:* various journals and magazines. *Honours include:* Gregory Award, 1967; Writers Fellowship, Edinburgh University, 1969; Scottish Arts Council Writers Bursary, 1972; Arthur Lundqvist Award for translations from Swedish, 1977; Swedish Academy Award, 1978. *Address:* Postboks 467, N 4001, Stavanger, Norway.

FUNE Jonathan. *See:* FLETCHER John Walter James.

FURIA Philip George, b. 15 Nov 1943, Pittsburgh, Pennsylvania, USA. Professor. m. Karen Johnson, 19 Mar 1966, 2 sons. *Education:* BA, Oberlin College, 1965; MA, University of Chicago, 1966; MFA, University of

Iowa, 1970; PhD, 1970. *Appointments:* Professor, University of Minnesota, 1970-. *Publications:* The Poets of Tin Pan Alley: A History of America's Great Lyricists; Pounds Cantos Declassified. *Contributions to:* PMLA; American Literature. *Honours:* Fulbright Professorship; Bush Sabbatical Grant. *Literary Agent:* The Lazear Agency, Minneapolis, Minnesota. *Address:* 4209 Dupont Avenue South, Minneapolis, MN 55409, USA.

FURTWANGLER Virginia Anne, (Ann Copeland), b. 16 Dec 1932, Hartford, Connecticut, USA. Fiction Writer; Teacher. m. Albert Furtwangler, 17 Aug 1968, 2 sons. *Education:* BA, College of New Rochelle, 1954; MA, Catholic University of America, 1959; PhD, Cornell University, Kent, 1970. *Appointments:* Writer in Residence, CoOllege of Idaho, 1980; Linfield College, 1980-81; University of Idaho, 1982, 1986; Bemidji, 1987; Wichita State University, 1988; Mt Allison Univrsity, 1990; St Marys University, 1993. *Publications:* At Peace; The Back Room; Earthen Vessels; The Golden Thread; The Back Room. *Contributions to:* The Fiddlehead; Matrix; Turnstile; CFM; Southwest Review; The New Quarterly; Wild east; University of Windsor Review; Best American Short Stories; Best canadian Stories. *Honours:* Kent Fellowship; Contributor Prize, CFM; Canada Council Grant; NEA Writing Fellowship; Arts award; Finalist Governor Generals Award; Ingram Merrill Award; Judge, Smith First Novel Competition. *Memberships:* Authors Guild; writers Union of Canada; International Womens Writing Guild; AWP; NB Writers Federation. *Address:* PO 1450, Sackville, NB, Canada EOA 3CO.

G

GAAN Margaret, b. 1914, Shanghai, China. Writer. *Appointments:* Executive Secretary, China Mercantile Co, Shanghai, 1940-49; Programme Officer, 1950-65, Chief of the Asia Desk, 1966-68 and Deputy Regional Director for East Asia and Pakistan, 1969-74, United Nations Children's Fund, now retired. *Publications:* Last Moments of a World (autobiography), 1978; Little Sister (novel) 1983; Red Barbarian (novel), 1984; White Poppy (novel), 1985; Blue Mountain (novel), 1987. *Address:* 3325 Northrop Avenue, Sacramento, CA 95864, USA.

GABBARD Gregory N, b. 4 Oct 1941, USA. Teacher. *Education:* BS, MIT, 1962; MA, University of Texas, 1964; PhD, 1968. *Appointments:* Assistant Professor, University of Nevada, 1969-74. *Publications:* A Mask for Beowulf; Knights Errand; Dragon Raid; Tiger Web. *Contributions to:* Years Best Horror Stories; Beloit Poetry Journal; Poetry Northwest; Literary Review; Counter/ Measures; Song; light Year; Texas Quarterly; Hellas; Michigan Quarterly Review. *Honours:* John Masefield Award. *Address:* 602 Cannon, New Boston, TX 75570, USA.

GADDIS William, b. 1922, America. Writer. *Publications:* The Recognitions, 1955; J R 1975; Carpenter's Gothic, 1985. *Address:* c/o Candida Donadio Literary Agency, 231 W 22nd Street, New York, NY 10011, USA.

GADGIL Gangadhar, b. Bombay, India. Writer; Economic Adviser. m. Vasanti, 12 Dec 1948, 1 son, 2 daughters. *Education:* MA, Bombay University, 1944. *Appointments:* Honarary Professor, University of Bombay. *Publications:* Durdamya; Bandoo; crazy Bombay; Women & Other Stories; Kadu and God. *Contributions to:* Satyakatha; Hans; Kirloskar; Yugawani; Illustrated Weekly of India; Times of India; Indian Express; Economic Times; Quest; Marg; Evergreen Review; American review; Western Humanities Review; Quadrant. *Honours:* RS Jog Award; N C Kelkar Award; State Award Sat Samudra Palikade; State Award Ole Unha; State Award Talavatale Chandane; Abhiruchi Award; President, All India Marathi Literary Conference, 1981; Vice President, Sahitya Akademi, 1988-93; President, Marathi Sahitya Mahamandal, 1987; President, Mumbai Marathi Sahitya Sangh; Vice President, Mumbai Marathi Grantha Sangrahalay; Invited to inaugurate, Marathi Drama Conference, Deliver Presidential addresses/ lectures and inaugural addresses at various public functions, seminars; President, Mumbai Grahak Panchayat, (Bombay Consumers' Organisation). *Memberships:* Mumbai Marathi Sahitya Sangh; Mumbai Marathi Granth Sangrahalay; Asiatic Society of Bombay; Vidarbha Sahitya Sangh, Marathwada Sahitya Parishad, Maharashtra Sahitya Parishad and Indian PEN. *Address:* 4 Abhang, Sahitya Sahawas, Bandra, Bombay 400051, India.

GAGE Wilson. *See:* **STEELE Mary Quintard Govan.**

GAGLIANO Frank, b. 1931, America. Playwright; Screenwriter; Novelist; Professor of Playwriting. *Appointments:* Playwright-in-Residence, Royal Shakespeare Co, London, 1967-69; Assistant Professor of Drama, Playwright-in-Residence and Director of Contemporary Playwright's Center, Florida State University, Tallahassee 1969-73; Lecturer in Playwrighting and Director of the Conkie Workshop for Playwrights, University of Texas, Austin, 1973-75; Distinguished Visiting Professor, University of Rhode Island, 1975; Benedum Professor of Theatre, West Virginia University, 1976-; Artistic Director, Carnegie Mellon, 'Showcase of New Plays', 1986-. *Publications:* The City Scene (2 plays), 1966; Night of the Dunce, 1967; Father Uxbridge Wants to Marry, 1968; The Hide-and-Seek Odyssey of Madeleine Gimple, 1970; Big Sur, 1970; The Prince of Peasantmania, 1970; The Private Eye of Hiram Bodoni (TV play), 1971; Quasimodo (musical), 1971; Anywhere the Wind Blows (musical),

1972; In the Voodoo Parlour of Marie Laveau, 1974; The Comedia World of Lafcadio Beau, 1974; The Resurrection of Jackie Cramer (musical), 1974; Congo Square (musical), 1975, revised, 1989; The Total Immersion of Madelaine Favorini, 1981; San Ysidro (dramatic cantata), 1985; From The Bodoni County Songbook Anthology, Book 1, 1986, musical version, 1989; Anton's Leap (Novel). 1987. *Address:* c/o Gilbert Parker, William Morris Agency, 1350 Avenue of the Americas, New York, NY 10019, USA.

GAIL. *See:* **KATZ Bobbi.**

GAINES Donna, b. 21 Mar 1951, Brooklyn, New York, USA. Sociologist; Journalist. *Education:* BA, State University of NY; MSW, Adelphi University; PhD, State University of NY. *Appointments:* Editorial Board, Verstehen, 1984. *Publications:* Teenage Wasteland: Suburdias Dead End Kids. *Contributions to:* Village Voice; Newsday; Spin. *Honours:* Levenstein Fellowship. *Memberships:* Authors Guild; National Writers Union; American Sociological association; Eastern Sociological Society. *Literary Agent:* Charlotte Sheedy. *Address:* Institute for Social Analysis, State University of NY, Stony Brook, NY 11794, USA.

GAINHAM Sarah. *See:* **AMES Sarah Rachel.**

GALBRAITH James Kenneth, b. 29 Jan 1952, Boston, USA. Professor. m. Lucy Ferguson, 28 July 1979, div, 1 son, 1 daughter. *Education:* Harvard College, AB, 1974; University of Cambridge, 1974-75; Yale University, MA, 1976; M Phill, 1977; PhD, 1981. *Appointments:* Professor, LBJ School of Public Affairs, The University of Texas at Austin, 1985. *Publications:* Balancing Acts; The Economic Problem; Macroeconomics. *Contributions to:* Numerous. *Honours:* Marshall Scholar, University of Cambridge. *Memberships:* American Economic Association; Association for Public Policy Analysis and Management. *Address:* LBJ School of Public Affairs, University of Texas at Austin, Austin, TX 78713, USA.

GALICIAN Mary-Lou, b. 5 Apr 1946, New Bedford, Massachusetts, USA. University Professor of Broadcasting. *Education:* BA magna cum laude, English, Journalism, Long Island University, 1966, MS Broadcasting, Syracuse University, 1969; EdD, Higher Education, Memphis State University, 1978; Clinical Residency, UTCHS. *Literary Appointments:* Byline Writer, Standard Times, Massachusetts, 1961-66; Syndicated Feature Writer, Franklin Fisher Enterprises, 1964; Series Writer, Witch Is It?, WCMU-TV, 1969; Communication Consultant, 1976-80; Creator, Presenter, FUN-dynamics!, 1978-. *Publications include:* No Miracles Here, 1967; Witch Is It? (TV series), 1969; FUN-dynamics!, Fun-notes, 1982; The American Dream and the Media Nightmare: Good News and Bad News on Television (research article series), 1985-; The Coming Victory (editor), 1980; Numerous byline newspaper columns, TV scripts; Numerous copyrights for lyrics and music. *Contributions to:* Journalism Quarterly; Southwestern Mass Communication Journal; Journalism Educator; NAB Radio Active; ARC International Newsletter; Communications Visions; Many Others. *Honours:* Conolly College Scholar in Journalism, Long Island University, 1963-66; Fellowship in Broadcasting, Syracuse University, 1966-67; Women of the Year, Outstanding Americans Foundation, 1968; Numerous grants for scholarly research and publication, Arizona State University, 1983-87; Certificate of Outstanding Scholarly Achievement, Southwest Education Council for Journalism/Mass Communication, 1985; Outstanding Advisor, Women in Communications Inc, 1986. *Memberships:* National Board of Directors, Farwest Region Vice President, Women in Communications Inc; Board Member, Newsletter Editor, American Association of University Women; Committees/Chairs, numerous communication related organisations. *Address:* Walter Cronkite School of Journalism, Arizona State University, Tempe, AZ 85287, USA.

GALINDO P. *See:* **HINOJOSA-SMITH R Roland.**

GALIOTO Salvatore, b. 6 June 1925, Italy. Professor of Humanities (retired); Poet. m. Nancy Morris, 8 July 1978, 1 son. *Education:* BA, University of New Mexico, Albuquerque, USA, 1952; MA, Denver University, Denver, Colorado, 1955; John Hay Fellow, Yale University, New Haven, Connecticut, 1959-60; Catskill Area Project Fellow, Columbia University, New York City, 1961-62; Mediaeval and Renaissance Doctoral Programme, University of New Haven. *Appointments:* Member, Judging Jury for Poetry, ASLA Premio Internazionale di Poesia, Sicily, 1986. *Publications:* The Humanities: Classical Athens, Renaissance Florence and Contemporary New York, 1970; Bibliographic Materials on Indian Culture, 1972; Let Us Be Modern, collection of poems in English and Italian, 1985; INAGO Newsletter, collection of poems, 1988; Many poems in Snow Summits in the Sun, anthology of poems, edited by Blair H Allen, 1989; Is Anybody Listening, collections of poems in English, 1990; Flap Your Wings, collection of poems in English, 1992; Rosebushes and the Poor, collection of poems in Italian, 1993. *Contributions to:* New York Times; Cleaveland Plain Dealer; Herald Tribune; Library Journal; Contro Campo; Alla Bottega; Quaderi dell' ASLA; The Poet; California State Quarterly; Agni Review; Manna Prose Poetry; San Fernando Poetry Journal; Prophetic Voices; American Atheist; Midwest Poetry Review; Italian Correspondent for Italian American Heritage Foundation of San Jose, CA; Feelings of PA. *Honours:* Purple Heart and Bronze Star, 1944; John Hay Fellowship, 1958-59; Asian Studies Fellow, 1965-66; The Mole of Turino, 1st Prize for Foreign Writer, 1984; Chapbook Competition, 1985, 1st Prize, Chapbook Competition, 1986, The Poet; 1st Prize for Poetry, Gli Etrusci, Italy, 1985; 3rd Prize for Poetry, ASLA, Italy; Trofeo delle Nazioni for Poetry, Italy; Gold Medal for Let Us Be Modern, Istituto Carlo Capodieci, 1987; Selected by newsletter INAGO as Poet for 1989. *Memberships:* L I Historians Society; The Asian Society;, ASLA, Sicily; California State Poetry Society, San Francisco; Poets and Writers of America, New York City; Representative in Italy for International Society of Poets. *Address:* Via Bruno Buozzi, 15 Montecatini Terme, 51016 (Pistoia) Italy.

GALL Henderson Alexander (Sandy), b. 1 Oct 1927, Penang, Malaysia. Television Journalist. m. Aug 1958, 1 son, 3 daughters. *Education:* MA, 1952, Hon. LLD, 1981, Aberdeen University, Scotland. *Publications:* Gold Scoop, 1977; Chasing the Dragon, 1981; Don't Worry about the Money Now, 1983; Behind Russian Lines: An Afghan Journal, 1983; Afghanistan: Agony of a Nation, 1988; Salang, 1989; George Adamson: Lord of The Lions, 1991. *Honours:* Sitara-i-Pakistan, 1986; Lawrence of Arabia Medal, 1987; Rector, Aberdeen University, 1978-81; CBE, 1988. *Agent:* Peters, Fraser Dunlop, 503/4 The Chambers, Chelsea Harbour, London SW10 0XF, England.

GALL Sally Moore, b. 28 July 1941, New York, USA. Librettist. m. Wm. Einar Gall, 8 Dec 1967. *Education:* BA, cum Laude, 1963, Harvard; MA, 1971, Phd, 1976, New York University. *Appointments:* Poetry editor, Free Inquiry, 1981-84; Founding Editor, Eidos/The International Prosody Bulletin, 1984-88. *Publications:* The Modern Poetic Sequence: The Genius of Modern Poetry, co-author, 1983, pbk 1986; Ramon Guthrie's Maximum Security Ward: An American Classic, 1984; Editor, Maximum Security Ward and Other Poems, 1984; versification editor, Poetry in English: An Anthology, 1987. *Contributions to:* reference books, professional journals, and literary magazines. *Honours:* Penfield Fellow, New York University, 1973-74; Academy of American Poets Award, (NYU), 1975; Key Pin and Scroll Award, New York University, 1976; Explicator Literary Foundation Award, (co-winner) 1984. *Memberships:* Dramatists Guild; Lyrica; Modern Language Association; National Opera Association; Opera for Youth, Poets and Writers; Various wildlife societies and community music groups. *Address:* 29 Bayard Lane, Suffern, NY 10901, USA.

GALLAGHER Tess, b. 21 July 1943, USA. Poet; Writer. m. Raymond Carver, 17 June 1988. *Appointments:* Teacher,St Lawrence University, 1975-76; Kirkland College, 1976-77; University of Montana, 1978-79; University of Arizona, 1979-80; Syracuse University, 1980-90; Presently, advising on Film, Short Cuts, based on 9 short stories by Raymond Carver. *Publications:* Moon Crossing Bridge; Portable Kisses; The Lover of Horses; A Concert of Tenses; Amplitude; Under Stars; Carver Country. *Honours:* Cohen award; Maxine Cushing Gray Foundation Award; Guardian Fiction Award; First Lois & Willard Mackay Chair Holder, Poetry & Fiction; Literary Lion; NY State Arts Grant; Washington State Governors Award; Chancellers Award; Guggenheim Fellowship; NEA Fellowship. *Memberships:* PEN; AWP. *Literary Agent:* Amanda Urbam, ICM. *Address:* c/o Graywolf Press, 2402 University Avenue, Suite 203, St Paul, MN 55114, USA.

GALLAHER Art Jr, b. 1925, America. Emeritus. Professor of Anthropology and Chancellor. Writer. *Appointments:* Assistant to Associate Professor, Department of Sociology and Anthropology, University of Houston, 1956-62; University of Nebraska, 1962-63; Professor of Anthropology, 1963-,Deputy Director, Center for Developmental Change, 1966-70, Chairman, Department of Anthropology, 1970-72, Dean of College of Arts and Sciences, 1972-80, Chancellor 1981-89, University of Kentucky, Lexington. *Publications:* Plainville Fifteen Years Later, 1961; (ed)Perspectives in Developmental Change, 1968; (ed with Harland Padfield) The Dying Community, 1980. *Address:* 3167 Roxburg Drive West, Lexington, KY 40503-3439, USA.

GALLAHER John G, b. 28 Dec 1928, St Louis, USA. Professor. m. C Maia Hofacker, 2 June 1956, 1 son, 2 daughters. *Education:* BA, Washington University, 1954; MA, St Louis University, 1957; PhD, 1960. *Publications:* The Iton Marshal, A Biography of Louis N Davout; The Students of Paris and the Revolution of 1848; Napoleans Irish Legion. *Contributions to:* French Historical Studies; Military Affairs; The Irish Sword. *Memberships:* Society for French Historical Studies. *Address:* History Department, Southern Illinois, University of Edwardsville, Edwardsville, IL 62026, USA.

GALLANT Roy Arthur, b. 17 Apr 1924, ME, USA. Author; Teacher. m. Kathryn Dale, 1952, 2 sons. *Education:* BA, Bowdoin College, 1948; MS, 1949; Doctoral Work, 1953-79, Columbia University. *Appointments:* Editor-in-Chief, The Natural History Press, 1962-65; Editorial Director, Aldus Books, London, 1959-62; Author-in-Residence, Doubleday, 1957-59; Managing Editor, Scholastic Teachers Magazine, 1954-57. *Publications include:* Our Universe, 1986; Private Lives of the Stars, 1986; Rainbows, Mirages and Sundogs, 1987; Before the Sun Dies, 1989; Ancient Indians, 1989; The Peopling of Planet Earth, 1990; Earth's Vanishing Forests, 1991; A Young Person's Guide to Science, 1993. *Contributions to:* Science-86; Sky and Telescope; Book of Knowledge; Nature and Science; Senior Scholastic; American Biology Teacher; Science World, and others. *Honours:* Thomas Alvu Edison Foundation National Mass Media Award, 1959; Geographic Society of Chicago Publication Award, 1980; National Science Teachers Association Award, 1982-87; Distinguished Acheivement Award, University of Southern Maine, 1981; Childrens Book Council Award, 1987. *Memberships:* American Pen; Authors Guild; American Association for the Advancement of Science; New York Academy of Sciences; Center for the Study of the First Americans; Royal Astronomical Society, Fellow. *Address:* P.O. Box 228, Beaver Mountain Lake, Rengeley, Maine 04990, USA.

GALLENKAMP Charles, b. 13 Apr 1930, Dallas, Texas, USA. Author. *Education:* University of Texas; University of New Mexico, BA. *Publications:* Jovenile Books inc. The pueblo Indians in Story, Song, and Dance; The Mystery of the Ancient Maya; Books inc. Maya: The Riddle and Rediscovery of a Lost Civilization; Maya: Treasures of an Ancient Civilization. *Contributions to:* New Mexico Magazine; Natural History; Toronto Star

Weekly; Dance Magazine; Desert Magazine; Canadian Geographical Journal; Archaeologia. *Literary Agent:* The Young Agency. *Address:* 29 Grace Court, Brooklyn Heights, NY 11201, USA.

GALLIE Duncan Ian Dunbar, b. 16 Feb 1946, Guildford, England. Sociologist; Offical Fellow, Nuffield College, Oxford. m. Martine Josephine, 17 July 1971, 2 daughters. *Education:* Magdalen College, Oxford, 1964- 67; London school of Economics, MSc, 1967-69; St Anthonys College, Oxford, D Phil, 1969-71. *Appointments:* Lecturer, University of Essex, 1973-79; Reader, University of Warwick, 1979-85; Official Fellow, Nuffield College, 1985-. *Publications:* Social Inequality and Class Radicalism in France & Britain; Employment in Britain; In Search of the New Working Class; New Approaches to Economic Life. *Contributions to:* Work Employment and Society; European Journal of Sociology. *Honours:* American Sociological Association, Distinguished Contribution to Scholarship Award. *Memberships:* International Sociological Association; British Sociological Association. *Address:* 149 Leam Terrace, Leamington Spa, Warwickshire, CU31 1DE, England.

GALLINER Peter, b. 19 Sept 1920, Berlin, Germany. British Publisher. m. (1) Edith Marquerite Goldsmidt, 1948, 1 daughter, (2) Helga Stenschke, 1990. *Education:* Berlin & London. *Appointments:* Worked for Reuters, London, 1944-47; Foreign Man, Financial Times, London, 1947-60; Chairman of Board, Managing Director, Illstein Publishing Group, Berlin, 1960-64; Vice Chairman, Managing Director, British Printing Corporation, 1965-70; International Publishing Consultant, 1965-67 and 1970-75; Chairman, Peter Galliner Associates, 1970; Director, Interanation Press Institute, 1975-. *Honours:* Order of Merit, 1st Class, 1961 (GFR); Ecomienda, Orden de Isabel la Catolica, Spain, 1982; Commander's Cross of the Order of Merit, 1990, (GFR). *Address:* Untere Zaune 9, 8001 Zurich, Switzerland.

GALLOWAY David Darryl, b. 5 May 1937, Memphis, USA. Journalist; Novelist; Professor; Art consultant. m. Sally Lee Gantt, 1959, dec, 1 son. *Education:* BA, Harvard College, 1959; PhD, State University of New York, 1962. *Appointments:* Lecturer, State University of New York, 1962-64; Lecturer, University of Sussex, 1964-67; Chair of American Studies, University of Hamburg, 1967-68; Associate Professor, Case Western Reserve University, 1968-72; Chair of American Studies, Ruhr University, Germany, 1972-. *Publications:* The Absurd Hero; Lamaar Ransom; Calamus; Artware; A Family Album; Tamsen; The Selected Writings of Edgar Allan Poe; Melody Jones. *Contributions to:* International Herald Tribune; Art in America; Art News. *Memberships:* Royal Society of arts; The Harvard Club. *Address:* Band Str. 13, 56 Wuppertal 2, Germany.

GALLOWAY Priscilla, (Anne Peebles), b. 22 July 1930, Montreal, Quebec, Canada. Author. m. Bev Galloway 17 Sept 1949, div, 2 sons, 1 daughter. *Education:* BA, Queens University, 1951; MA, University of Toronto, 1958; PhD, 1977. *Appointments:* Scholar in residence, Queens University, 1978; Writer in Residence, Cobalt Haileybury, New Liskeard, 1987- 88. *Publications:* What's Wrong with High School English?; Timely and Timesless; When You Were Little And I Was Big; Good Times, Bad times, Mummy & Me; Seal Is Lost. *Contributions to:* Northward Journal; Waves; Forum 8; Chatelaine; Women in Leadership News; Tri Town Writers Anthology; Art Council News; Show & Tell; Indirections; English Quarterly. *Honours:* ssa OOTeacher of the Year; Marty Memorial Award. *Memberships:* writers Union of Canada; Canadian Society of Childrens Authors, Illustrators and Performers; Ontario Council of Teachers of English; Canadian Council of Teachers of English. *Address:* 12 Didrickson Drive, North York, Ontario, Canada M2P 1J6.

GALLUN Raymond Zinke, b. 22 Mar 1911, Beaver Dam, Wisconsin, USA, Technical Writer. m. (1) Frieda Talmey, 26 Dec 1959, dec 1974, (2) Bertha Erickson, 25 Feb 1977, dec 1989, 1 stepdaughter. *Education:* University of Wisconsin-Madison, 1929-30. *Publications include:* People Minus X, 1957; The Eden Cycle, 1974; The Best of Raymond Z Gallun, 1977; Sky Climber, 1982; Bioblast, 1985; Star Climber, autobiography, 1990. *Contributions to:* Science Wonder Stories; Air Wonder Stories; Astounding Stories; Colliers Magazine; The Best of Science Fiction; Adventures in Time and Space. *Honours:* Hall of Fame Award, Sealon 37th World Science Fiction Convention, Brighton, England, 1979; Lifetime Achievement Award, I-CON IV, New York State University Campus, Stony Brook, 1985. *Literary Agent:* Forest J Ackerman. *Address:* 110-20 The Avenue, Forest Hills, NY 11375, USA.

GALTON Raymond Percy, b. 17 July 1930. Author; Scriptwriter. m. Tonia Phillips, 1956, 1 son, 2 daughters. *Publications:* TV - With Alan Simpson: Hancock's Half Hour, 1954-61; Comedy Playhouse, 1962-63; Steptoe and Son, 1962-74; Galton-Simpson Comedy, 1969; Clochermerle, 1971; Casanova '74, 1974; Dawson's Weekly, 1975; The Galton and Simpson Playhouse, 1976-77; with Johnny Speight: Tea Ladies, 1979; Spooner's Patch, 1979-80; with John Antrobus: Room at the Bottom, 1986; Films with Alan Simpson: The Rebel, 1960; The Bargee, 1963; The Wrong Arm of the Law, 1963; The Spy with a Cold Nose, 1966; Loot, 1969; Steptoe and Son, 1971; Steptoe and Son Ride Again, 1973; Den Siste Fleksnes, 1974; Die Skraphandlerne, 1975; Theatre with Alan Simpson: Way Out in Piccadilly, 1969; the Wind in the Sassfras Trees, 1968; Albert och Herbert, 1981; Fleksnes, 1983; Mordet pa Skolgatan 15, 1984; with John Antrobus: When Did You Last See Your Trousers?, 1986; (Books) with Alan Simpson: Hancock, 1961; Steptoe and Son, 1963; The Reunion and Other Plays, 1966; Hancock Scripts, 1974; The Best of Hancock, 1986. *Address:* The Ivy House, Hampton Court, Middlesex, England.

GALWAY Robert Connington. *See:* **McCUTCHAN Philip Donald.**

GAMBLE Andrew Michael, b. 1947, Britain. University Professor; Writer. *Appointments:* Reader 1982-86, Professor 1986-, University of Sheffield. *Publications:* (with P Walton), From Alienation to Surplus Value, 1972; The Conservative Nation, 1974; (with P Walton), Capitalism in Crisis: Inflation and the State, 1976; An Introduction to Modern Social and Political Thoought, 1981; Britain in Decline, 1981; (with S A Walkland), The British Party System and Economic Policy, 1945-83, 1984. *Address:* Department of Politics, University of Sheffield, Sheffield S10 2TN, England.

GAMBLE Eddy Edward Hill, b. 12 May 1943, Morristown, TN, USA. Editorial Cartoonist. m. Saundra Lancaster, 28 June 1964. *Education:* University of South Florida, BA, 1970; Graduate School, University of Tennessee, 1971. *Publications:* A Cartoon History of Reagan Years, 1988; A Peek at the Great Society. *Contributions to:* Newsweek; Time; US News & World Report; People Magazine; Business Week; Newsweek Japan; Veja; Panorma. *Honours:* George Washington Freedom Foundation Award; United State Industrial Councils Dragonslayer Award. *Memberships:* National Cartoonist Society; Americain Editorial Cartoonists Association. *Address:* The Florida Times Union, One Riverside Avenue, Jacksonville, FL 32202, USA.

GAMBONE Philip Arthur, b. 21 July 1948, Melrose, MA, USA. Teacher; Writer. *Education:* AB, Harvard, 1970; MA, Episcopal Divinity School, 1970. *Publications:* The Language We USe Up Here and Other Stories. Contributions to: Hometowns: Gay Men Write About Where They Belong; A Member of the Family. *Honours:* MacDowell Colony Fellow; Lambda Literary Award, nominee. Membership: PEN. *Address:* 47 Waldeck Street, Dorchester, MA 02124, USA.

GANDLEY Kenneth Royce, (Oliver Jacks, Kenneth

Royce), b. 11 Dec 1920, Croydon, Surrey, England. Novelist. m. Stella Parker, 16 Mar 1946. *Publications:* My Turn to Die, 1958; The Soft Footed Moor, 1959; The Long Corridor, 1960; No Paradise, 1961; The Night Seekers, 1962; The Angry Island, 1963; The Day the Wind Dropped, 1964; Bones in the Sand, 1967; A Peck of Salt, 1968; A Single To Hong Kong, 1969; The XYY Man (also adapted for TV), 1970; The Concrete Boot, (also adapted for TV), 1971; The Miniatures Frame (also adapted for TV), 1972; Spider Underground, 1973; Trapspider, 1974; Man on a Short Leash, 1974; The Woodcutter Operation (also adapted for TV), 1975; Bustillo, 1976; Assassination Day, 1976; Autumn Heroes 1977; The Satan Touch (also adapted for TV), 1978; The Third Arm, 1980; 10,000 Days, 1981; Channel Assault, 1982; The Stalin Account, 1983; The Crypto Man, 1984; The Mosley Receipt, 1985; Breakout, 1986; No Way Back, 1987; The President is Dead, 1988; Fall-Out, 1989; Exchange of Doves, 1990; Limbo, 1992; Remote Control, 1993. *Memberships:* Society of Authors; Crime Writers Association. *Literary Agent:* David Higham Associates. *Address:* 3 Abbotts Close, Abbotts Ann, Andover, Hants SP11 7NP, England.

GANN Lewis Henry, b. 1924, America. Senior Fellow; Curator, the Western European Collection; Writer. *Appointments:* Senior Fellow, Hoover Institute, Stanford University, California, 1964-; Member, Editorial Board, Intercollegiate Review. *Publications:* The Birth of a Plural Society: The Development of Northern Rhodesia under the British South Africa Company, 1894-1914, 1958; (with P Duignan), White Settlers in tropical Africa, 1962; A History of Northern Rhodesia: Early Days to 1953, 1964; (with M Gelfand), Huggins of Rhodesia: The Man and His Country, 1964; A History of Southern Rhodesia: Early Days to 1934, 1965; (with P Duignan), Burden of Empire: An Appraisal of Western Colonialism in Africa South of the Sahara, 1967; Central Africa: The Former British States, 1971; Guerillas in History, 1971; (with P Duignan), Africa and the World at Large: An Introduction to the History of the Sub-Saharan Africa from Antiquity to 1840, 1972; (with P Duignan), Colonialism in Africa 1870-1960, 5 vols, 1969-73; (with P Duignan), The Rulers of German Africa, 1884-1914, 1977; (with P Duignan), The Rulers of British Africa 1870-1914, 1978; (with P Duignan), South Africa: War, Revolution or Peace, 1978; (with P Duignan), The Rulers of Belgian Africa 1884-1914, 1979; (with P Duignan), Why South Africa Will Survive, 1981; (with T Henriksen), The Struggle for Zimbabwe, 1981; (with P Duignan), The US and Africa: A History, 1984; (with P Duignan), The Hispanics in the US, 1986; (with P Duignan), Hope for South Africa, 1991; (with P Duignan), The Rebirth of the West, The Americanization of the Democratic World, 1945-1958, 1992. *Address:* Hoover Institute, Stanford University, Stanford, CA 94305, USA.

GANNON Francis Xavier. b. 30 Aug 1952, Camden, New Jersey, USA. Writer. m. 2 Apr 1976, 1 s, 2 d. *Education:* BA, University of Georgia, 1974; MA, 1976. *Appointments:* National Endowment For the Humanities Fellow, 1986. *Publications:* Yo Poe; Vanna Karenina. *Contributions to:* New Yorker; Atlantic; Harpers; Gentlemans Quarterly. *Honours:* Magna Cum Laude. *Memberships:* Authors Guild. *Literary Agent:* International Creative Management. *Address:* Demorest, Georgia, USA.

GANSLER Jacques S, b. 21 Nov 1934, Newark, NJ, USA. Economist; Engineer. m. Leah M Calabro, 17 Apr 1982, 1 s, 2 d. *Education:* Yale University, BE, 1956; Northeastern University, MS, 1959; New School for Social Research, MA, 1972; American University, PhD, 1978. *Appointments:* Adjunct Professor, University of Virginia, 1982-84; Visiting Scholar, Kennedy School of Government, Harvard University, 1984-. *Publications:* The Defense Industry; Affording Defense. *Contributions to:* Harvard Bus Review; International Security; Washington Post; Issues in Science and Technology. *Literary Agent:* MIT Press. *Address:* 8442 Clover Leaf Drive, McLean VA, 22102, USA.

GANT Jonathan. *See:* **ADAMS Clifton.**

GARAFOLA Lynn, b. 12 Dec 1946, New York City, USA. Dance Critic; Historian. m. Eric Foher, 1 May 1980, 1 d. *Education:* AB, Bannard College, 1968; PhD, City University of New York, 1985. *Appointments:* Editor, Studies in Dance History, 1990-. *Publications:* Diaghilevs Ballets Russes; Andre Levinson on Dance: Writings from Paris in the Twenties. *Contributions to:* Dance Magazine; Ballet Review; The Dancing Times; Dance Research Journal Rasitan; The Nation; The Womens Review of Books; The times Literary Supplement. *Honour:* Torre de lo Bueno Prize. *Memberships:* Society of Dance History Scholars; Dance Critics Association. *Address:* 606 West 116th Street, New York, NY 10027, USA.

GARB Solomon, b. 1920, America. Associate Clinical Professor of Medicine; Writer. *Appointments:* Research fellow in Pharmacology, 1949- 50, Instructor in Pharmacology 1950-53, Assistant Professor of Clinical Pharmacology, 1953-56, and Assistant Professor of Pharmacology, 1956-57, Cornell University Medical College; Associate Professor of Pharmacology, Albany Medical College, 1957-61; Associate Professor of Pharmacology 1961-66, Professor of Pharmacology and Associate Professor of Community Health, 1966- 70, University of Missouri Medical School; Scientific Director, American Medical Center, Denver, 1970-80; Associate Clinical Professor of Medicine, University of Colorado Medical Center, 1974-. *Publications:* Laboratory Tests in Common Use, 1956, 6th edition 1976; Essentials of Therapeutic Nutrition, 1958; (with B Chrim), Pharmacology and Patient Care, 1962, 3rd edition 1970; (with E Eng), Disaster Handbook, 1964, 1969; A Cure for Cancer - A National Goal, 1968; Clinical Guide to Undesirable Drug Interactions, 1971, 1974; Abbreviations and Acronyms in Medicine and Nursing, 1976. *Address:* 6401 West Colfax Avenue, Lakewood, CO 80214, USA.

GARBER Joseph Rene, b. 16 Aug 1943, USA. Management Consultant. *Education:* Stanford Graduate Schoo of Business, 1982. *Publication:* Rascal Money. *Contributions to:* A Very Large Number. *Memberships:* Authors Guild; Various Corporate Directorships. *Address:* Woodside, CA 94062, USA.

GARCIA-PENA Roberto, b. 1910. Journalist. *Education:* University of Chile. *Appointments:* Reporter, El Tiempo, 929; Private Secretary to Minister of Government, 1930; Secretary, Colombian Embassy, Peru, 1934; Chile 1935, Charge d'affaires, 1937; Secretary-General, Ministry of Foreign Affairs, 1938; Editor, El Tiempo, 1939-81. *Honours:* Best Journalist Award, 1977; Gold Medal, 1978. *Membership:* Council of Directors, International American Press Society. *Address:* Avenida Jimenez 6-77, Apdo. Aereo 3633, Bogota, DE, Columbia.

GARDAM Jane Mary, b. 11 July 1928, Yorkshire, England. Writer. m. 20 Apr 1954, 2 sons, 1 daughter. *Education:* BA, London University, 1950. *Publications:* A Few Fair Days; A Long Way from Verona; The Summer After the Funeral; God on the Rocks; Bilgewater; Black Faces White Faces; Crusoes Daughter; Short Stories, adaptations for TV and film: The Sidmouth Letters; The Pangs of Love; The Hollow Land; Showing the Flag, 1989; Childrens Books: Bridget & William; Kit; Kit in Boots; Swans; Through the Dolls' House Door. *Contributions include:* Guardian; London Review of Books; Books & Bookmen; Daily Telegraph. *Honours:* David Higham's Award, 1978; Winifred Holtby award, 1978; Whitbread Award, 1983; Katherine Mansfield Award, 1984. *Memberships:* Committee of English Centre of International PEN; Arts Club; University Womens Club. *Literary Agent:* David Higham. *Address:* c/o Hamish Hamilton, 27 Wrights Lane, London W8 5TZ, England.

GARDAPHE Frederico Luigi, b. Sept 1952, Chicago.

Professor. m. 18 Sept 1982, 1 son, 1 daughter. *Education:* Fenwick Prep, 1970; Triton Junior College, 1972; University of Wisconsin, BS, 1976; University of Chicago, AM, 1972; University of Illinois, PhD, 1993. *Appointments:* Professor, Columbia College, 1983; Arts Editor, Era Noi, 1987-; Editor, Voices in Italian Americana, 1990. *Publications:* From the Margin; Italian American Ways; New Chicago Stories; Italian Ethnics. *Contributions to:* Melus; Misure Critiche; Italica; Italian Canadiana; Romance Languages Annual; Haymarket; Almanacco; Fra Noi; il caffe. *Honours:* Irene Kogan Award; Memorial Fellowship; Illinois Arts Council Fellowship; Unico National Writers Contest, 2nd Place. *Memberships:* National Writers Union; American PEN; Modern Language Association; American Italian Historical Association; The Society for the Study of Multi Ethnic Literature of the US; Am Association of Italian Studies. *Address:* Department of English, Columbia College, 600 S Michiigan Avenue, Chicago, IL 60605, USA.

GARDEN Bruce. *See:* **MacKAY James Alexander**

GARDEN Nancy, b. 15 May 1938, Boston, Massachusetts, USA. Writer; Editor; Teacher. *Education:* BFA, Columbia University School of Dramatic Art, 1961; MA, Teachers College, Columbia University, 1962. *Appointments:* Actress, Lighting Designer, 1954-64; Teacher of Speech and Dramatics, 1961-64; Editor, educational materials, textbooks, 1964-76; Teacher of Writing, Adult Education, 1974; Correspondence School, 1974-. *Publications:* What Happened in Marston, 1971; The Loners, 1972; Maria's Mountain, 1981; Fours Crossing, 1981; Annie on My Mind, 1982; Favourite Tales from Grimm, 1982; Watersmeet, 1983; Prisoner of Vampires, 1984; Peace, O River, 1986; The Door Between, 1987; Lark in the Morning, 1991; Monster Hunter series: Case No 1: Mystery of the Night Raiders, 1987; Case No 2: Mystery of the Midnight Menace, 1988; Case No 3: Mystery of the Secret Marks, 1989; Non- fiction: Berlin: City Split in Two, 1971; Vampires, 1973; Werewolves, 1973; Witches, 1975; Devils and Demons, 1976; Fun with Forecasting Weather, 1977; The Kids' Code and Cipher Book, 1981. *Contributions to:* The New York Kid's Book, 1979; Occasional book reviews to various publications. *Honours:* Annie on My Mind listed as 1 of Best Books of the 1980s, 1989, and 1 of Best of the Best for 1870-1983, American Library Association. *Memberships:* Society of Children's Book Writers; Former Member, Authors Guild. *Literary Agent:* Dorothy Markinko, McIntosh and Otis Inc, USA. *Address:* c/o McIntosh and Otis Inc, 310 Madison Avenue, New York, NY 10017, USA.

GARDNER Colin Raymond, b. 15 Oct 1952, Isleworth, Middlesex, England. Writer. *Education:* MA, St Johns College, Cambridge, 1979; MA, University of California, Los Angles, 1977; BA, St Johns College, Cambridge, 1975. *Appointments:* Managing Editor: Synapse International Electronic Music Magazine, 1977-79; Arts Editor, The Reader, 1985-88; Editor, Visions Art Quarterly, 1988-90. *Contributions to:* ArtForum International; Tema Celeste; Flash Art International; Art Space; Art Issues; Artweek; Los Angeles Times; Los Angeles Herald Examiner. *Memberships:* National Writers Union; College Art Association. *Literary Agent:* The Rose Group. *Address:* 1015 N Edinburgh Av 2, West Hollywood, CA 90046, USA.

GARDNER John (Edmund), b. 1926, Britain. Writer. *Appointments:* Theatre Critic and Arts Editor, Stratford-upon-Avon Herald, 1959-65. *Publications:* Spin the Bottle (autobiography), 1964; The Liquidator, 1964; The Undstrike, 1965; Amber Nine, 1966; Madrigal 1967; Hideaway (stories), 1968; A Complete State of Death, 1969; Founder Member, 1969; The Censor, 1969; Traitor's Exit, 1970; The Airline Pirates (in US as Air Apparent), 1970; Every Night's a Bullfight, (in US as Every Night's a Festival), 1971; The Assassination File (stories), 1974; The Corner Men, 1974; The Return of Moriaty, 1974; A Killer for a Song, 1975; The Revenge of Moriarty, 1975; To Run a Little Faster, 1976; The werewolf Trace, 1977; The Dancing Dodo, 1978; The Nostradamus Traitor, 1979; The Garden of Weapons, 1980; License Renewed, 1981; For Special Services, 1982; The Quiet Dogs, 1982; Icebreaker, 1983; Flemingo, 1983; Role of Honour, 1984; The Secret Generations, 1985.

GARDONS S S. *See:* **SNODGRASS W D.**

GAREBIAN Keith Stephen, b. 15 July 1943, Bombay, India. Teacher. m. Caryl Taugher, 23 Dec 1972, div, 1 s. *Education:* B Ed, 1964; BA, 1966; MA, 1971; PhD, 1973. *Publications:* Hugh Hood; William Hutt: A Theatre Portrait; A Well-Bred Muse: Selected Theatre Writings; Shaw & Newton; Explorations of Shavian Theatre; Leon Rooke and His Works; Hugh Hood and His Works; The Making of 'My Fair Lady'; The Making of 'Gypsy'. *Contributions to:* The Oxford Companion to Canadaian Literature; The Oxford Companion to Canadian Theatre; Das Moderne English Kanadische Drama; The Bumper Book; Carry on Bumping; The Montreal Story Tellers. *Address:* 2001 Bonnymede Drive, 150 Mississauga, Ontario, Canada L5J 4H8.

GARFIELD Leon, b. 14 July 1921. Author. m. Vivien Dolores Alcock, 1948, 1 daughter. *Publications:* Jack Holborn, 1964; Devil in the Fog, 1966; Smith, 1967; Black Jack, 1968 (filmed 1979); Mister Corbett's Ghost and Other Stories, 1969; The Boy and the Monkey, 1969; The Drummer Boy, 1970; The Strange Affair of Adelaide Harris, 1971; The Ghost Downstairs, 1972; The Captain's Watch, 1972; Lucifer Wilkins, 1973; Baker's Dozen, 1973; The Sound of Coaches, 1974; The Prisoners of September, 1975; The Pleasure Garden, 1976; The Booklovers, 1976; The House of Hanover, 1976; The Lamplighter's Funeral, 1976; Mirror Mirror, 1976; Moss and Blister, 1976; The Cloak, 1976; The Valentine, 1977; Labour in Vain, 1977; The Fool, 1977; Rosy Starling, 1977; The Dumb Cake, 1977; Tom Titmarsh's Devil, 1977; The Filthy Beast, 1977; The Enemy, 1977; The Confidence Man, 1978; Bostock & Harris, 1978; John Diamond, 1980; The Mystery of Edwin Drood, 1980; Fair's Fair, 1981; The House of Cards, 1982; King Nimrod's Tower, 1982; The Apprentices, 1982; The Writing on the Wall, 1983; The King in the Garden, 1984; The Wedding Ghost, 1984; Guilt and Gingerbread, 1984; Shakespeare Stories, 1985; The December Rose, 1986; The Empty Sleeve, 1988; Blewcoat Boy, 1988; The Saracen Maid, 1991; Shakespeare: The Animated Tales, 1992; with Edward Blishen : The God Beneath the Sea, 1970; The Golden Shadow, 1973; with David Proctor: Child O'War, 1972. *Honours:* Prix de la Fondation de France, 1984; Swedish Golden Cat, 1985; FRSL, 1985; Guardian award for children's fiction; Whitbread award; Carnegie Medal. *Address:* c/o John Johnson, Ltd., Clerkenwell House, 45/47 Clerkenwell Green, London EC1R 0HT, England.

GARFINKEL Patricia Gail, b. 15 Feb 1938, New York City, USA. Writer. 2 sons. *Education:* BA, New York University. *Publications:* Ram's Horn, 1980 (poems); From The Red Eye of Jupiter, 1990. *Contributions to:* numerous publications and anthologies including; Hollin's Critic; Seattle Review; Cedar Book; Washington Magazine; Black Box, City Lights Anthology, 1976; Anthology of Magazine Verse/Yearbook of American Poetry, 1980; Poet Upstairs Anthology; Miller Cabin Anthology, 1984; Montpelier Culture Arts Centre Anthology, 1984; Snow Summits in the Sun Anthology, 1985. *Honours:* Poetry in Public Places Award for New York State, 1977; Lip Service, Poetry Competition, 1st prize winner, 1990; Washington Writers Publishing House, Book Competition Winner, 1990. *Memberships:* Poets and Writers Inc; Writer' Centre, Glen Echo, Maryland; Academy of American Poets; elected to Board of Poetry Committee of the Greater Washington, DC Area. *Address:* 2031 Approach Lane, Reston, VA 22091, USA.

GARFITT Roger b.12 Apr 1944. Poet and Prose Writer. *Education:* BA, Hons, Merton College, Oxford,

1968. *Literary Appointments:* Arts Council Poet in Residence, University College of North Wales, Bangor, 1975-77; Editor, Poetry Review 1978-81; Arts Council Poet in Residence, Sunderland Polytechnic, 1978-80; Member, Literature Panel of Arts Council of Great Britain, 1986-90. *Publications:* Poetry: Caught on Blue, 1970; West of Elm, Carcanet, 1974; The Broken Road, Northern House, 1982; Rowlstone Haiku, Five Seasons, 1982; Given Ground, 1989. *Contributor to:* Prose in Granta 27 and 29, 1989. *Honours:* Guinness International Poetry Prize, 1973; Gregory Award, 1974. *Literary Agent:* Jane Turnbull. *Address:* c/o Jane Turnbull, 13 Wendell Road, London W12 9RS, England.

GARLICK Helen Patricia, b. 21 Apr 1958, Doncaster, England. Writer; Solicitor; Appears on TV and Radio. m. Richard Howard, 1 daughter. *Education:* LLB Class 2i (Hons), University of Bristol, 1979; Solicitor of Supreme Court, 1983. *Publications:* The Good Marriage, 1990; The Separation Survival Handbook, 1989; The Which? Good Divorce Guide, 1992; Penguin Guide to the Law, 1992. *Contributions to:* The Independent; The Guardian; various magazines. *Memberships:* Chair of National Council for One Parent Families; Family Law Adviser to Consumers Association. *Address:* c/o Carolyn Brunton, Studio 8, 125 Moore Park Road, London SW6 4PS, England.

GARLINSKI Jozef, b. 1913, Polish. Writer. *Appointments:* Chairman, Executive Committee, Polish Home Army Circle, London 1954-65; Cultural Vice-Chairman, Polish Cultural and Social Centre, London 1970-79; Chairman, Union of Polish Writers Abroad, 1975-. *Publications:* Dramat i Opatrznosc, 1961; Matki i zony, 1962; Ziemia (novel), 1964; Miedzy Londynem i Warszawa, 1966; Poland SOE and the Allies, 1969; Fighting Auschwitz, 1975; Hitler's Last Weapons, 1978; Intercept: Secrets of the Enigma War, 1979; The Swiss Corridor, 1981; Polska w Drugiej Wojnie Swaiatowej, 1982; Poland in the Second World War, 1985; Szwajcarski Kryterz, 1987, Niezapomniane lata, 1987. *Address:* 94 Ramillies Road, London W4 1JA, England.

GARNER Alan, b. 17 Oct 1934, Cheshire, England. Author. m. (1) Ann Cook, 1956, (div), 1 son, 2 daughters; (2) Griselda Greaves, 1972, 1 son, 1 daughter. *Education:* Magdalen College, Oxford, 1955-56. *Publications:* The Weirdstone of Brisingamen, 1960; The Moon of Gomrath, 1963; Elidor, 1965; Holly from the Bongs, 1966; The Owl Service, 1967; The Book of Goblins, 1969; Red Shift, 1973; The Guizer, 1975; The Stone Book Quartet, 1976-78; Fairy Tales of Gold, 1979; The Lad of the Gad, 1980; British Fairy Tales, 1984; A Bag of Moonshine, 1986; Jack and the Beanstalk, 1992. *Honours:* Carnegie Medal, 1967; Guardian Award, 1968; Gold Plaque, Chicago International Film Festival, 1981. *Membership:* Portico Library, Manchester. *Literary Agent:* David Higham Associates Limited. *Address:* Blackden, Holmes Chapel, Crewe, Cheshire, CW4 8BY, England.

GARNER Helen, b. 1942, Geelong, Victoria, Australia. Freelance Journalist; Author; Film Scriptwriter. *Education:* University of Melbourne. *Publications:* Monkey Grip, 1977; Honour and Other People's Children, 1980; The Children's Bach, 1984; Postcards from Surfers, 1985. *Honours:* National Book Council Award, 1978; South Australian Premier's Literary Award, 1985; New South Wales Premier's Literary Award, 1986. *Address:* Melbourne, Victoria, Australia.

GARNER William Vivian Nigel, b. 14 Dec 1944, Bendigo, Australia. Writer. m. (1) Helen Garner, 1968, (div), 1 daughter, (2) Susan Gore, 1979, 1 son, 1 daughter. *Education:* BA, Honours, Melbourne University, 1966. *Appointment:* Script Editor, ABC, 1982-85. *Publications:* One Summer Again, Screenplay, 1985; Pokerface, Screenplay, 1986; Cake, Play, 1986; Winner Take All, Screenplay, 1982; The Second Rater, Play, 1977; Domestic Contradictions, Radio Play, 1976. *Contributions to:* Numerous journals & magazines.

Honours: Australian Writers' Guild (Awgie) for Original Work for Television, 1985. *Membership:* Australian Writers Guild. *Literary Agent:* John Timlin. *Address:* 51 Robe St, St Kilda, Victoria 3182, Australia.

GARNER William, Writer. *Education:* BSc Hons, University of Birmingham, England. *Publications:* 13 novels between 1965-90: The Morpurgo Trilogy; Think Big, Think Dirty, 1982; Rats' Alley, 1984; Zones of Silence, 1986; Paper Chase, 1988; Sleeping Dogs, 1990; In-depth newspaper feature articles especially for Daily Telegraph Weekend Magazine. *Contributions to:* Numerous magazines and journals. *Membership:* Writers' Guild of Great Britain. *Literary Agent:* Elaine Green Limited. *Address:* c/o Elaine Green Ltd, 372 Goldhawk Road, London W12 8QQ, England.

GARNETT Eve C R, b. Upper Wick, Worcestershire, England. Author; Illustrator. *Education:* Scholarship, Royal Academy Schools - School of Painting; (Creswick Prize and Silver Medal). *Publications:* With Illustrations: The Family From One End Street, 1937; Is It Well With the Child, with Foreward by Walter de la Mare, 1938; In and Out and Roundabout : Stories of a Little Town, 1948; A book of the Seasons : An Anthology, 1952; Further Adventures of the Family from One End Street, 1956; Holiday at The Dew Drop Inn, 1962; To Greenlands Icy Mountains: The Story of Hans Egede, Explorer, Coloniser, Missionary, with Foreward by Professor N E Bloch-Hoell, University of Oslo, Norway, 1968; Lost and Found, 4 stories, 1974; Illustrations to Penguin R L Stevenson's A Child's Garden of Verses, 1948; First Affections: Some Autobiographical Chapters of Early Childhood, 1982. *Contributions to:* various journals. *Honour:* Carnegie Gold Medal, 1938. *Memberships:* PEN; Society of Authors. *Address:* c/o Lloyd's Bank Limited, 29-31 Grosvenor Gardens, London SW1W 0BU, England.

GARNETT Richard (Duncan Carey), b. 1923, Britain. Writer; Publisher; Translator. *Appointments:* Production Manager, 1951-59, Director 1954-66, Rupert Hart-Davis Ltd; Director, Adlard Coles Ltd, 1963-66; Editor 1966-82, Director 1972-82, Macmillan, London; Director, Macmillan Publishers, 1982-87. *Publications:* (ed) Goldsmith: Selected Works, 1950; (trans) Robert Gruss: The Art of the Aqualung, 1955; The Silver Kingdom (in US as The Undersea Treasure), 1956; (trans) Bernard Heuvelmans: On the Track of Unknown Animals, 1958; The White Dragon, 1963; Jack of Dover, 1966; (trans) Bernard Heuvelmans: In the Wake of the Sea-Serpents, 1968; (ed with Reggie Grenfell), Joyce, 1980; Constance Garnett, A Heroic Life, 1991. *Literary Agent:* A P Watt Ltd, 20 John Street, London WC1N 2DR, England. *Address:* Hilton Hall, Hilton, Huntingdon, Cambridgeshire PE18 9NE, England.

GARRARD Timothy Francis, b. 28 Apr 1943, Peterborough, England. Historian; Lawyer. *Education:* BA, Oxford, 1964; MA, University of Ghana, 1980; PhD, UCLA Los Angeles, 1986; Barrister at Law, Lincoln's Inn, 1965; Solicitor and Advocate of the Supreme Court of Ghana, 1976. *Publications:* Akan Weights and the Gold Trade; Akan Transformations: Problems in Ghanaian Art History; Gold of Africa; Frafra Brass Casting; Benin Metal casting Technology; A Royal Bronze Ornament from the Mali Empire. *Contributions to:* Journal of African History; African Arts; Iowa Studies in African Art. *Honour:* Initiate of the Senufo Poro Society. *Memberships:* Honourable Society of Lincoln's Inn; Ghana Bar Association; African Studies Association. *Address:* 21 Richmond Road, Malvern, Worcs, WR14 1NE, England.

GARRETT George (Palmer, Jr), b. 11 June, 1929, Orlando, Florida, USA. Writer. m. Susan Parrish Jackson, 1952, 2 sons, 1 daughter. *Education:* Sewanee Military Academy; Graduated, The Hill School, 1947; Princeton University, New Jersey, 1947-48, 1949-52, BA, 1952, MA 1956; Columbia University, New York, 1948-49; Served in the United States Army Field Artillery, 1952-55. *Appointments:* Assistant Professor,

Wesleyan University, Middletown, Connecticut, 1957-60; Visiting Lecturer, Rice University, Houston, 1961-62; Associate Professor, University of Virginia, Charlottesville, 1962-67; Writer-in-Residence, Princeton University, 1964-65; Professor of English, Hollins College, Virginia, 1967-71; Professor of English and Writer-in-Residence, University of South Carolina, Columbia, 1971-73; Senior Fellow, Council of the Humanities, Princeton University, 1974-77; Adjunct Professor, Columbia University, 1977-78; Writer-in-Residence, Bennington College, Vermont, 1979 and University of Michigan, Ann Arbor, 1979- 84; Hoyns Professor of English, University of Virginia, Charlottesville, 1984- ; President, Associated Writing Programs 1971-73; United States Poetry Editor, Transatlantic Review, Rome (later London), 1958-71; Contemporary Poetry Series Editor, University of North Carolina Press, Chapel Hill, 1962-68; Co-editor, Hollins Critic, Virginia, 1965-71; Contributing Editor, Contempora, Atlanta, 1971-; Assistant Editor, Film Journal. Hollins College, Virginia, 1972-; Co-editor, Worksheet, Columbia, South Carolina, 1981-; Editor with Brendan Galvin, Poultry: A Magazine of Voice, Truro, Massachusetts. *Publications:* Novels include: In the Briar Patch, 1961; Cold Ground Was My Bed Last Night, 1964; A Wreath for Garibaldi and Other Stories, 1969; The Magic Striptease, 1973; To Recollect a Cloud of Ghosts: Christmas in England, 1979; Plays: Sir Slolb and the Princess: A Play for Children, 1962; Garden Spot, 1962; Screenplays: The Young Lovers, 1964; The Playground, 1965; Frankenstein Meets the Space Monster, with R H W Dillard and John Rodenbeck, 1966; Verse includes: For a Bitter Season and Selected Poems, 1967; Welcome to the Medicine Show: Postcards, Flashcards, Snapshots, 1978; Love's Shining Child: A Miscellany of Poems and Verses, 1981; The Collected Poems of George Garrett, 1984; Fiction: King of The Mountain, 1958; The Finished Man, 1959; Which Ones Are The Enemy, 1961; Do, Lord, Remember Me, 1965; Death Of The Fox, 1971; The Siccession, 1984; An Evening Performance, 1985; Poison Pen, 1986; Entered From The Sun, 1990; Whistling in the Dark, 1992; The Sorrows of Fat City, 1992. James Jones, 1984 and many edited volumes. *Honours:* Sewanee Review, Fellowship, 1958; American Academy in Rome Fellowship, 1958; Ford Grant for drama, 1960; National Endowment for the Arts Grant, 1967; Contempora Award, 1971; Guggenheim Fellowship, for Fiction, 1974; T.S. Eliot Award, 1990; Pen, Malamud Award, 1991. *Memberships:* Vice Chancelor, Fellowship of Southern Writers. *Literary Agent:* Jane Gelfman/John Farquharson Ltd, 250 W, 57th Street, NYC 10, USA. *Address:* 1853 Fendall Avenue, Charlottesville, VA 22903, USA.

GARRETT Leslie, b. 5 July 1932, Philadelphia, Pennsylvania. USA. Writer. m. (1) Jean Collier, 16 June 1951, (2) Linda Kerby, 18 Mar 1973, 1 daughter. *Appointments:* Director, Fiction Writers Workshop, Knoxville, 1983-84. *Publications:* The Beasts; In The Country of Desire. *Contributions to:* New World Writing; Nugget; Escapade; Evergreen Review; Four Quarters; Karamu; Climax; Confrontation; Gallery Magazine; Phoenix; The Crescent Review. *Honours:* The Maxwell Perkins Commemorative Novel Award; Art Alliance Award; The Alex Halery Literary Fellowship award. *Literary Agent:* The Loretta Barret Literary Agency. *Address:* 1531 Forest Avenue, Knoxville TN 37916, USA.

GARRETT Richard, b. 15 Jan 1920, London, England. Author; Journalist. m. Margaret Anne Selves, 20 Aug 1945, 2 sons, 1 daughter. *Education:* Bradfield College. *Publications include:* Fast and Furious - the Story of the World Championship of Drivers, 1968; Cross Channel, 1972; Scharnhorst and Gneisenau - The Elusive Sisters, 1978; The Raiders, 1980; POW, 1981; Atlantic Disaster - The Titanic and Other Victims, 1986; Flight Into Mystery, 1986; Voyage Into Mystery, 1987; Great Escapes of World War II, 1989; Sky High, 1991; The Final Betrayal - The Armistice 1918 ... And Afterwards, 1990. Biographies of Generals Gordon, Wolfe and Clive. *Contributions to:* Was Freelance editor of periodical published by Shell for over 30 years;

Sometime broadcaster of talks on Radio 2's John Dunn Show; Latterly regular contributor to County Magazine until its demise in late 1989. *Membership:* Society of Authors. *Literary Agent:* Watson, Little Ltd, 12 Egbert Street, London NW1 8LJ. *Address:* The White Cottage, 27A Broadwater Down, Tunbridge Wells, Kent TN2 5NL, England.

GARRISON Daniel H, b. 24 Dec 1937, Hamilton, New York, USA. Professor. m. Tina Tinkham, 30 May 1992, 1 daughter. *Education:* AB, Harvard, 1959; MA, University of North Carolina, 1963; PhD, University of Calif, 1968. *Publications:* Mild Frenzy; The Language of Virgil; Whos Who in Wodehouse; The Students Catullur; Horace Epoles and Odes. *Contributions to:* 19th century Fiction; Arion 3; Medical History. *Memberships:* American Philological Association. *Address:* 1228 Simpson Street, Evanston, IL 60201, USA.

GARRISON Omar V, b. 2 June 1913, Author. m. Virginia Leah Herrick, 11 Sept 1952. *Education:* PhD, 1938. *Publications:* Balboa Conquistador (biography) 1971; Tantra (philosophy) 1964; Secret World of Interpol (non-fiction) 1977; Howard Hughes in Las Vegas (non-fiction) 1970; Spy Government (non-fiction) 1967; Playing Dirty (non-fiction) 1980; Hidden Story of Scientology (non-fiction) 1974; Lost Gems of Secret Knowledge (non- fiction) 1973; The Baby That Laughed All Night (novel) 1989. *Membership:* Authors Guild. *Address:* 10 99 Cedar Knolls South, Cedar City, UT 84720, USA.

GARROW David J, b. 11 May 1953, New Bedford, Massachusetts, USA, Author; Professor. m. Susan Foster Newcomer, 18 Dec 1984. *Education:* BA, magna cum laude, Wesleyan University, 1975; MA 1978, PhD, 1981, Duke University. *Appointments:* Senior Fellow, The Twentieth Century Fund, 1991-; Visiting Distinguished Professor, The Cooper Union, 1992-. *Publications:* Bearing the cross, 1986; The FBI and Martin Luther King Jr, 1981; Protest at Selma, 1978; Editor, The Montgomery Bus Boycott and the Women Who Started It, 1987; Liberty Sexuality, 1993. *Contributions to:* New York Times; Washington Post; Dissent; The Journal of American History; Constitutional Commentary. *Honours:* Pulitzer Prize in Biography, 1987; Robert F Kennedy Book Award, 1987; Gustavus Myers Human Rights Book Award, 1987. *Memberships:* Authors' Guild; Phi Beta Kappa. *Literary Agent:* Jane Cushman, JCA Literary Agency, New York. *Address:* 200 Cabrini Boulevard PH9, New York, NY 10033, USA.

GARSIDE Jack Clifford, (Willian K Wells), b. 4 Oct 1924, Montreal, Canada. Consultant; Author; Lecturer. m. Mary Wyness Mason, 2 Sept 1944, 2 sons. *Education:* University of Toronto; Sir George Williams University, Montreal; Princeton University, New Jersey, USA. *Appointments:* Creative Writing Instructor (voluntary), Venice Library, Florida, 1986-90. *Publications:* As William K Wells: Chaos, 1986, As Jack Hild: Sakhalin Breakout, 1986; Alaska Deception, 1986; As Nick Carter: East of Hell, 1986; Pressure Point, 1987; Lethal Prey, 1987; Afghan Intercept, 1987; Sukhumi Destruction, 1987; Black Sea Blood Bath, 1987; Sanction to Slaughter, 1988; Deep Sea Death, 1988; Singapore Sling, 1988; Arctic Abduction, 1989; As Don Pendleton, Desert Strike, 1988. *Contributions to:* Columnist, Friends of the Library, Venice, Florida. *Membership:* Mystery Writers of America. *Literary Agent:* Don Cong Don Associates Inc, New York. *Address:* Coleman Lake, West Guildford, Ontario, Canada K0M 2S0.

GARTNER Chloe Maria, b. 21 Mar 1916, Troy, Kansas, USA. Writer. m. Peter Godfrey Trimble, 22 Jan 1942, San Francisco, California, (div 1957). 1 daughter. *Education:* University of California; Mesa College, Grand Junction Colorado; College Marin, Kentfield, California. *Publications:* The Infidels, 1960; Drums of Khartoum, 1967, 2nd edition, 1968; German translation, Die Trommein von Khartoum, 1970; Die Longe Sommer, 1970; Woman From The Glen, 1973; Mistress of the

Highlands, 1976; Anne Bonney, 1977; The Image and the Dream, 1980, UK, 1986; Still Falls the Rain, 1983; Greenleaf, UK, 1987; Lower Than The Angels, 1989. *Contributions include:* Cosmopolitan; Good Housekeeping. *Honours include:* Silver Medal, Commonwealth Club of California for, The Infidels, 1960. *Memberships include:* Authors' Guild. *Literary Agents:* John Hawkins & Associates, New York City; Murray Pollinger, London. *Address:* John Hawkins & Associates, Suite 1600, 71 West 23rd Street, New York, NY 10010, USA.

GARTON ASH Timothy John, b. 12 July 1955, England. Writer; Fellow of St Antonys College. m. Danuta Maria, 1982, 2 s. *Education:* Sherborne, Oxford. *Appointments:* Editorial Writer, The Times, 1984-86; Foreign Editor, The Spectator, 1984-90; Columnist, The Independent, 1988-91; Fellow, St Antonys College, Oxford, 1990-. *Publications:* We The People; The Uses of Adversity; The Polish Revolution. *Contributions to:* New York Review of Books; The Spectator; The Independent; Granta. *Honours:* Somerset Mangham Award; David Watt Memorial Prize; Prix Européen de Essai. *Address:* St Antonys College, Oxford OX2 6JF, England.

GASCHE Rodolphe, b. 7 Aug 1938, Mondorf, Luxembourg. Professor of Comparative Literature. m. Bronislawa Karst, 2 Oct 1979, 1 d. *Education:* Magister Artium, Freie Universitat Berlin, 1972; PhD, 1976. *Appointments:* The Johns Hopkins University, 1974-78; State University of New York at Buffalo, 1978. *Publications:* Die Hybride Wissenschaft; System und Metaphorik in der Philosophie vou Georges Bataille; The Tain of the Mirror. *Contributions to:* MLN; Boundary 2; Diacritics; Studies in Romanticism; Revista di Estetica; Oxford Literary Review; Studies in 20th Century Literature; French Yale Studies; The Journal of Philosophy. *Honours:* ACLS Fellowship; Eugenio Donato Professor of Comparative Literature. *Memberships:* MLA; IAPL; SPEP. *Address:* Program in Comparative Literature, 638 Clemens Hall, SUNY at Buffalo, Buffalo, NY 14260, USA.

GASCOIGNE Bamber, b. 24 Jan 1935. Author; Broadcaster; Publisher. m. Christina Ditchburn, 1965. *Education:* Scholar, Eton; Scholar, Magdalene College, Cambridge; Commonwealth Fund Fellow, Yale, 1958-59. *Appointments:* Theatre Critic, Spectator, 1961-63, Observer, 1963- 64; Co-Editor, Theatre Notebook, 1968-74; Founder, Saint Helena Press, 1977; Chairman, Ackermann Publishing, 1981-85. *Publications:* Twentieth Century Drama, 1962; World Theatre, 1968; The Great Moghuls (with photographs by Christina Gascoigne), 1971; Murgatreud's Empire, 1972; The Heyday, 1973; The Treasures and Dynasties of China, (photographs by Christina Gascoigne), 1973; Ticker Khan, 1974; The Christians, (photographs by Christina Gascoigne), 1977; Images of Richmond, 1978; Images of Twickenham, 1981; (Illustrated by Christina Gascoigne), Why the Rope went Tight, 1981; Fearless Freddy's Magic Wish, 1982; Fearless Freddy's Sunken Treasure, 1982; Quest for the Golden Hare, 1983; Cod Streuth, 1986; How to Identify Prints, 1986; Encyclopedia of Britain, 1993; TV Presenter: University Challenge, 1962-87; Connoisseur, 1988-89; Presenter and author of documentary series: The Christians, 1977; Victorian Values, 1987; Man and Music, 1987-89; The Great Moghuls, 1990; Brother Felix and the Virgin Saint, 1992. *Address:* Saint Helena Terrace, Richmond, Surrey TW9 1NR, England.

GASCOIGNE John, b. 20 Jan 1951. Historian. m. Kathleen May Bock, 6 Apr 1980, 1 s, 1 d. *Education:* BA, Sydney University, 1969- 72; MA, Princeton University, 1973-74; PhD, Cambridge University, 1974-79. *Appointments:* Lecturer, Department of History, University of Papua, 1977-78; Tutor, University of NSW, 1980-84; Lecturer, 1984-89; Senior Lecturer, 1989-. *Publication:* Cambridge in the Age of the Enlightenment. *Contributions to:* Historical Journal; Social Studies of Science; History Science in Context. *Honours:* Joint Winner, Australian Historical Association Hancock Prize. *Address:* School of History, University of New South Wales, Kensington NSW 2033, Australia.

GASCOYNE David Emery, b. 10 Oct 1916, Harrow, Middlesex, England. Writer/Poet. m. Judy Tyler Lewis, May 1975, 4 stepchildren. *Education:* Salisbury Cathedral Choir School, 1924-30; Regent Street Polytechnic Secondary, 1930-32. *Publications include:* Collected Poems 1965, Collected Poems 1988; A Short Survey of Surrealism 1936, USA 1982; Night Thoughts, 1956, USA 1958; Collected Verse Translations, 1970; Paris Journal 1937-39, 1978; Journal 1936-37, 1980; The Collected Journals 1936-42, 1990. *Contributions to:* New Verse; The Criterion; Partisan Review; New Writing; Adam International; Horizon; Poetry Nation Review; Cahiers du Sud; Nouvelle Revue Francaise; Europe; Botteghe Oscure; Temenos; Times Literary Supplement; The Independent. *Honours:* Atlantic Award 1946/47; Primo Biella - Poesia europea, 1982. *Memberships:* Fellow, Royal Literary Society; Committee World Organization of Poets (Luxembourg); Committee Biennales Internationales de Poesie (Belgium). *Literary Agent:* Alan Clodd, 22 Huntington Road, London N2 9DU. *Address:* 48 Oxford Street, Northwood, Cowes, Isle of Wight PO31 8PT, England.

GASH Jonathan, (Graham Gaunt), b. 30 Sept 1933, Bolton, Lancashire, England. Doctor of Medicine. 3 daughters. *Education:* Graduated Faculty of Medicine, London University, 1958; Royal Colleges of Surgeons and Physicians, London, England; Pathologist, specialist in infectious diseases. *Publications:* The Judas Pair, 1976; Adapted for BBC TV series Lovejoy: Gold from Gemini, 1977, The Grail Tree, 1978, Firefly Gadroon, 1979, The Gondola Scam, 1980, The Vatican Rip, 1981, The Tartan Ringers, 1982, The Sleepers of Erin, 1983, Moonspender, 1984, Pearlhanger, 1985, Spend Game, 1986; Jade Woman, 1987; The Very Last Gambado, 1989; Writing as Graham Gaunt: The Incomer, 1980. *Honour:* John Creasey Award (Best First Crime Novel) of Crime Writers' Association of UK, 1976. *Membership:* Visiting Professor, Royal Society of Medicine Foundation. *Literary Agent:* Desmond Elliott, London. *Address:* c/o Desmond Elliott, 38 Bury Street, St James's, London SW1Y 6QU.

GASKELL Jane, b. 7 July 1941, Lancashire, England. Writer. *Appointments:* Feature Writer, Daily Express, 1961-65; Daily Sketch, 1965-71; Daily Mail, 1971-84. *Publications:* Atlan Books, including The Serpent, (fantasy books), 1961 onwards; Strange Evil, 1957; King's Daughter, 1958; All Neat in Black Stockings, 1964, (filmed 1966); A Sweet Sweet Summer, 1970; Attic Summer; The Shiny Narrow Grin; The Fabulous Heroine; Summer Coming; Some Summer Lands, 1977; Sun Bubble, 1990. *Honour:* Somerset Maugham Award, 1970. *Literary Agent:* Michael Sharland. *Address:* Sharland Organisation, 9 Marlborough Crescent, Bedford Park, London W4 1HE, England.

GASKIN Catherine Marjella, b. 2 Apr 1929, Co. Louth, Dundalk, Republic of Ireland. Novelist. m. Sol Cornberg, 1 Dec 1955. *Education:* Holy Cross College, Sydney, Australia. *Appointments:* Freelance Writer, 1946-. *Publications:* This Other Eden, 1946; With Every Year, 1947; Dust in Sunlight, 1950; All Else is Folly, 1951; Daughter of the House, 1952; Sara Dane, 1955; Blake's Reach, 1958; Corporation Wife, 1960; I Know My Love, 1962; The Tilsit Inheritance, 1963; The File on Devlin, 1965; Edge of Glass, 1967; Fiona, 1970; A Falcon for a Queen, 1972; The Property of a Gentleman, 1974; The Lynmara Legacy, 1975; The Summer of the Spanish Woman, 1977; Family Affairs, 1980; Promises, 1982; The Ambassador's Women, 1985; The Charmed Circle, 1988. *Memberships:* Society of Authors; Author's Guild of America. *Address:* White Rigg, East Ballaterson, Maughold, Isle of Man, England.

GASKIN John Charles Addison, b. 4 Apr 1936, Hitchin, England. Philosopher. m. 20 May 1972, 1 s, 1 d. *Education:* Oxford University, MA, 1956-60. *Publications:* The Quest for Eternity; Humes Philosophy of religion; Varieties of Unbelief. *Contributions to:* Philosophy; Ratio; Hibbert Journal; Hermathene; Icarus; Hume Studies; ET Al. *Address:* Trinity College, Dublin 2, Republic of Ireland.

GASS William Howard, b. 30 July 1924, Fargo, North Dakota, USA. Professor. m. (1) Mary Pat O'Kelly, 1952, 2 sons, 2 daughters. (2) Mary Henderson, 1969, 1 daughter. *Education:* AB, Kenyon College, 1947; PhD, Cornell University, 1954; D Litt, Purdue University, 1985. *Appointments:* Director, International Writers Center, 1991-. *Publications:* Omensetters Luck; In The Heart of the Heart of the Country; Fiction and the Figures of Life; On Being Blue; Habitations of the World; Willie Masters lonesome Wife; The World Within the Word. *Contributions to:* NY Review of Books; NY Times Book Review; Times Literary Supplement; New Republic; Harpers; The NAtion; Esquire; Yale Review; Salmagundi; Iowa Review; River Styx; New Yorker; New American Review. *Honours:* Rockerfellow; Guggenheim; National Institute of Arts & Letters Prize; Gold Medal for Literature; National Book Critics Circle Award. *Memberships:* PEN; National Institute for Arts & Letters, Arts & Science; American Philosophical Association; American Academy & Institute of Arts & Letters. *Literary Agent:* Lynn Nesbit. *Address:* International Writers Center, Washington University, St Louis, MO 63130, USA.

GATCH Milton McCormick, b. 22 Nov 1932. Educator; Librarian. m. Ione G White, 25 Aug 1956, 1 son, 2 daughters. *Education:* AB, Haverford College, 1953; BD, Episcopal Divinity School, 1960; PhD, Yale University, 1963. *Publications:* Preaching and Theology in Anglo-Saxon England, 1977; Loyalties and Traditions: Man and His World in Old English Literature, 1971; Death: Meaning and Mortality in Christian Thought and Contemporary Culture, 1969. *Contributions to:* Anglo-Saxon England; Tradition; Church History and other learned journals. *Honours include:* Quatercentenary Visiting Fellow, Emmanual College, Cambridge, 1991. *Memberships:* Medieval Academy of America (delegate to American Council of Learned Societies); International Society of Anglo-Saxonists; Grolier Club, New York; Century Association, New York; Fellow, Society of Antiquaries, London. *Address:* Union Theological Seminary, 3041 Broadway, New York, NY 10027, USA.

GATES Henry Louis Jr, b. 16 Sept 1950. Professor of English; Writer. *Education:* BA. Summa cum laude, History, Yale University, 1973; MA English Language and Literature, 1974, PhD, English Language and Literature, 1979, Clare College, University of Cambridge. *Appointments:* Lecturer, English and Afro-American Studies, Director of Undergraduate Studies, 1976-79, Assistant Professor of English and Afro-American Studies, 1979-84, Associate Professor, English and Afro-American Studies, 1984-85, Yale University; Professor of English, Comparative Literature and Africana Studies, 1985-88, W E B DuBois Professor of Literature, 1988-90, Cornell University; John Spencer Bassett Professor of English, Duke University, 1990-. Numerous editorial appointments. *Publications include:* Books: Figures in Black: Words, Signs and the Racial Self, 1987; The Signifying Monkey: Towards A Theory of Afro-American Literary Criticism, 1988. Editor of many books including: Their Eyes Were Watching God, introduction by Mary Helen Washington, 1989; Jonah's Gourd Vine, introduction by Rita Dove, 1990. Tell My Horse, introduction by Ishmael Reed, 1990; Mules and Men, introduction by Arnold Rampersad, 1990; Voodoo Gods of Haiti, introduction by Ishmael Reed, 1990; Reading Black, Reading Feminist, 1990. *Contributions to:* Numerous essays, articles and book reviews. *Honours include:* American Book Award, 1989; Anisfield- Wolf Book Award for Race Relations, 1989; Candle Award, Morehouse College, 1989; Honorable Mention, John Hope Franklin Prize, American Studies Association, 1988; Zora Neal Hurston Society Award for Cultural Scholarship, 1986; Yale Afro-American Cultural Center Faculty Prize, 1983. *Memberships include:* Council on Foreign Relations; Union of Writers of the African Peoples; African Roundtable; African

Literature Association. *Address:* Department of English, Allen Building, Duke University, Durham, NC 27706, USA.

GATHORNE-HARDY Jonathan, b. 15 May 1933, Edinburgh, Scotland. Author. m. (1) Sabrina Tennant, 1962, 1 son, 1 daughter. (2) Nicolette Sinclair Loutit, 12 Sept. 1985. *Education:* BA, Arts, Trinity College, Cambridge, 1954-57. *Publications:* One Foot in the Clouds, novel, 1961; Chameleon, novel, 1967; The Office, novel, 1970; The Rise & Fall of the British Nanny, 1972, new editions, 1985-93; The Public School Phenomenon, 1977; Love, Sex, Marriage & Divorce, 1981; Doctors, 1983; The Centre of the Universe is 18 Baedeker Strasse, short stories, 1985; The City Beneath the Skin, novel, 1986; The Interior Castle - A Life of Gerald Brenan, biography, 1992; 7 novels for children. *Contributions to:* Numerous magazines and journals. *Literary Agents:* Curtis Brown. For children's books: Laura Cecil. *Address:* 31 Blacksmith's Yard, Binham, Fakenham, Norfolk NR21 0AL, England

GATTEY Charles Neilson, b. 3 Sept 1921, London, England. Author; Playwright; Lecturer. *Education:* London University. *Publications include:* Queens of Song, 1979 (opera); They Saw Tomorrow 1977 (Paranormal); Prophecy and Prediction in the 20th Century, 1989; The Incredible Mrs Van Der Eist (biography) 1972; Foie Gras and Trumpets (foreword by Dame Kiri Te Kanawa) 1984; Books: The Elephant that Swallowed a Nightingale, 1981 (opera); Peacocks on the Podium, 1982 (music); Excess in Food, Drink and Sex, 1987; TV Play: The White Falcon, 1955; Film: The Love Lottery, starring David Niven, 1954. *Memberships:* Society of Civil Service Authors, President since 1980; The Garrick. *Address:* 15 St Lawrence Drive, Pinner, Middlesex HA5 2RL, England.

GAULDIE Enid Elizabeth, b. 1928, Britain. Writer on Architecture, Business/Trade/Industry, Country life/Rural societies. *Publications:* (ed)The Dundee Textile Industry from the Papers of Peter Carmichael of Arthurstone, 1969; (co-author) Dundee and its Textile Industry, 1850-1914, 1969; Cruel Habitations: A History of Working Class Housing, 1780-1918, 1974; The Scottish Country Miller, 1980; The Quarries and the Fens, 1981; One Artful and Ambitious Individual, 1989. *Address:* Waterside, Invergowrie, Dundee, Scotland.

GAULT William Campbell, (Will Duke, Dial Forest, Roney Scott), b. 1910, America. Writer of mystery, crime, suspense and children's fiction. Full-time writer since 1939. *Publications:* Mystery novels: Don't Cry For Me, 1952; The Bloody Bokhara, 1952, in UK as the Bloodstained Bokhara, 1953; The Canvas Coffin, 1953; Blood on the Boards, 1953; Run, Killer, Run, 1954; Ring Around Rosa, 1955 (in US paperback, Murder in the Raw, 1956); Square in the Middle, 1956; Day of the Ram, 1956; (as Will Duke) Fair Prey, 1956; The Convertible Hearse, 1957; The Atom and Eve, 1958; End of a Call Girl, 1958, in UK as Don't Call Tonight, 1959; The Wayward Widow, 1959; Come Die With Me, 1959; Million Dollar Tramp, 1960; The Hundred Dollar Girl, 1961; Vein of Violence, 1961; County Kill, 1962; Dead Hero, 1963; The Bad Samaritan, 1982; The Cana Diversion, 1982; The Chicano War, 1984; children;'s fiction: Thunder Road, 1952; Mr Fullback, 1953; Gallant Colt, 1954; Mr. Quarterback, 1955; Speedway Challenge, 1956; Bruce Benedict, Halfback, 1957; Dim Thunder, 1958; Rough Road to Glory, 1958; Drag Strip, 1959; Dirt Track Summer, 1961; Through the Line, 1961; Road-Race Rookie, 1962; Two-Wheeled Thunder, 1962; Little Big Foot, 1963; Wheels of Fortune: Four Racing Stories, 1963; The Checkered Flag, 1964; The Karters, 1965; The Long Green, 1965; Sunday's Dust, 1966; Backfield Challenge, 1967; The Lonely Mound, 1967; The Oval Playground, 1968; Stubborn Sam, 1969; Quarterback Gamble, 1970; The Last Lap, 1972; Trouble at Second, 1973; Gasoline Cowboy, 1974; Wild Willie, Wide Receiver, 1974; The Black Stick, 1975; Underground Skipper, 1975; Showboat in the Backcourt, 1976; Cut-Rate Quarterback, 1977; Thin Ice 1978; Sunday Cycles, 1979; Superbowl Bound, 1980; Death in Donegal Bay, 1984; The Dead Seed, 1985. *Address:* 482 Vaquero Lane, Santa Barbara, CA 93111, USA.

GAUNT Graham. *See:* **GASH Jonathan.**

GAVAC Donna B, b. 16 Sept, 1926, Oregon, USA. Educator; Writer. m. Stanley Gavac, 8 June 1979, 2 sons, 2 stepsons, 1 step daughter. *Education:* BA, History, George Fox College, 1949; MA, History, University of Michigan, 1949; PhD, Education Administration, University of Portland, 1960. *Appointments:* Editor, George Fox College, Crescent, 1947; Associate Editor, Northwest Sundial, 1956-59; Abstractor, Clio Press, 1960-65; Academic Dean, University of Alaska, 1970s; Researcher/Writer, Western Wordcraft, 1985- *Publications include:* Teaching of High School Social Studies (co-author) 1962; TV series, Homemaker in History, KLOR-TV 1957-58; Sources of Educational Controversy (book) 1960; Poems in American Poetry Anthology; Many Voices, Many Lands; Select Poets of the New Era, 1988-90; Co-presenter: Employment Workshop, Bad Kissingtonm Germany, 1983. *Contributions to:* Historical Abstracts; His Magazine; America, History and Life; Northwest Sundial; Crescent; Alaska Women; Research in Education. *Honours:* 1947 National Collegiate Press Award; 1961 Gresham Lecturer, Renaissance Institute; 1962-63 (1 year) Ford Foundation Grant; 1975 (3 months) Danforth Grant; 1977-78 (6 months) University of Alaska Research and Travel Grant; 1989 Poetry Award, US and Canada Poetry Center, California. *Memberships:* National Writers' Club; Northwest Association of Community and Junior Colleges, Vice-President and Treasurer; Anchorage Civic Opera, Director and Board Secretary; Northwest Association of Schools and Colleges, Trustee and Commissioner; Director, Alaska Press Women, 1991; National Federation of Press Women. *Address:* Western Wordcraft, PO Box 220707, Anchorage, Alaska 99522, USA.

GAVASKAR Sunil, b. 10 July 1949, Bombay, India. Business. m. Mehrotra Marshniel, 23 Sept 1974, 1 s. *Education:* Bachelor of Arts, Bombay University. *Publications:* Sunny Days; Idols; Runs n Ruins; One Day Wonders. *Contributions to:* Times of India; Hindustan Times; The Hindu; The Statesman; India Todai; The Telegraph; Khales Times; Gulf News. *Memberships:* Cricket Club of India. *Address:* E6 Everest, Tardeo, Bombay 400034, India.

GAVIN Catherine, b. Aberdeen, Scotland. Author. m. John Ashcraft, 1948. *Education:* MA, PhD, University of Aberdeen, Scotland; Sorbonne, Paris, France. *Publications:* Madeleine, 1957; The Cactus and The Crown, 1962; The Fortress, 1964; The Moon Into Blood, 1966; The Devil in Harbour, 1968; The House Of War, 1970; Give Me The Daggers, 1972; The Snow Mountain, 1973; Traitors' Gate, 1976; None Dare Call It Treason, 1978; How Sleep The Brave, 1980; The Sunset Dream, 1983; A Light Woman, 1986; The Glory Road, 1987; A Dawn of Splendour, 1989; The French Fortune, 1991. *Contributions to:* Time magazine; Kemsley newspapers; Daily Express. *Honours:* University Medal of Honour, Helsinki, 1970; Honorary DLitt, University of Aberdeen, 1986. *Literary Agent:* Scott Ferris Associates, London, England. *Address:* 1201 California Street, San Francisco, CA 94109, USA.

GAVIN Thomas Michael, b. 1 Feb 1941, Newport, News, Virginia USA. Professor. m. Susan Holahan, 5 July 1991, 2 daughters. *Education:* BA, MA, The University of Toledo. *Appointments:* Delta College, University Center, Michigan, 1972-75; Middlebury College, Middlebury, Vermont, 1975-80; University of Rochester, NY, 1980-. *Publications:* Forthcoming, Breathing Water; Kingkill; The Last Film of Emile Vico; 'The Truth Beyond Facts'. *Contributions to:* The Georgia Review; TriQuarterly. *Honours:* National Endowment for the Arts Fellowship; Andrew W Mellon Fellowship; Nominated Pushcart Prize; Best of the Small Prasses. *Literary Agent:* Georges Borchardt. *Address:* English Department, The University of Rochester, Rochester, NY 14627, USA.

GAY Kathlyn Ruth, b. 4 Mar 1930, Zion, Illinois, USA. Author. m. Arthur L Gay, 28 Aug 1948. 2 sons, 1 daughter. *Education:* Northern Illinois University, 1947-50. *Publications:* Author of 50 books including: Silent Killers: Radon & Other Hazards, 1988; Ozone, 1989; Greenhouse Effect, 1987; The Rainbow Effect: Interracial Families, 1987; Changing Families, 1988; Bigotry, 1989; Ozone, 1989; Adoption & Foster Care, 1989; Water Pollution, 1990; They Don't Wash Their Socks (sports superstitions), 1990; Adoption & Foster Care, 1990; The World Around Us: Indiana (social study textbook), 1990; Discovery Reader Booklets (3) The Science Connection, 1990; Collier's Encyclopedia & Book of Knowledge entries, 1990; Air Pollution, 1991; Garbage and Recycling, 1991; Day Care, 1992; Church and State, 1992; Global Garbage, 1992; Caution: This May Be An Advertisement, 1992; Caretakers of the Earth, 1993; The Right to Die, 1993; Breast Implants: Making the Right Choices, 1993; Pregnancy: Public and Private Dilemmas, 1993; Rainforests of the World, 1993. *Contributions to:* Family Weekly; The Rotarian; Dynamic Years; Kiwanis Magazine; Friends; Chicago Tribune; Sunday Magazine; Tampa Tribune; Indianapolis Mothly; Better Homes & Gardens. *Honours:* Silent Killers: Radon & Other Hazards; and Acid Rain both chosen Best Science Books for Children, National Science Teachers Association; Crisis in Education chosen, Outstanding book on Education, National Education Association; Science of Ancient Greece, Best Children's Science Book List, 1988. *Memberships:* Authors Guild; Society of Children's Book Writers; Childrens Reading Round Table of Chicago. *Address:* 1711 East Beardsley Avenue, Elkhart, IN 46514, USA.

GAY Marilyn Fanelli Martin, b. 16 July 1925, San Francisco, California, USA. Television Show Hostess; Producer; Writer. m. Melvin Raymond Gay, 3 May 1963. *Education:* University of California, Berkeley, 1943-46; University of Oregon, Eugene, 1946. *Publications:* Teleplays, ABC Network's Telephone Time series; Passing Parade films, Hal Roach Studios; Major stars appeared in the dramatic anthology series. By-lined feature writer. *Contributions to:* General Practice (editor), medical journal; Los Angles Times, features. *Honours:* Hall of Fame, Personalities of America; Tape recorded interviews with last 9 US Presidents & 8 1st ladies, over 2800 leaders, all fields. *Memberships:* Past member, Academy of Television Arts & Sciences; Founding member, Writers Guild of America West; National Federation of Press Women; Alpha Delta Pi Alumnae Association. *Address:* 1990 Ginger Street, No. 101, Oxnard, CA 93030, USA.

GAY Peter (Jack), b. 20 June 1923, Berlin, Germany. Writer. m. Ruth Slotkin, 30 May 1959, 3 stepdaughters. *Education:* AB, University of Denver, 1946; MA, 1947, PhD, 1951, Columbia University; Psychoanalytic Training, Western New England Institute for Psychoanalysis, 1976-83. *Publications:* The Dilemma of Democratic Socialism: Eduard Bernstein's Challenge to Marx, 1952; The Question of Jean Jacques Rousseau, 1954; Voltaire's Politics: The Poet as Realist, 1959; Voltaire: Philosophical Dictionary, 1962; Voltaire: Candide, 1963; The Party of Humanity: Essays in the French Enlightenment, 1964; John Locke on Education, 1964; The Enlightenment: An Interpretation, Vol I: The Rise of Modern Paganism, 1966; Vol II: The Science of Freedom, 1969; A Loss of Mastery: Puritan Historians in Colonial America, 1966; Weimar Culture: The Outsider as Insider, 1968; Deism: An Anthology, 1968; Columbia History of the World, (with John A Garraty), 1972; Modern Europe, (with R K Webb), 2 vols, 1973; The Enlightenment: A Comprehensive Anthology, 1973, revised edition, 1985; Style in History, 1974; Art and Act: On Causes in History - Manet, Gropius, Mondrian, 1976; The Bourgeois Experience, Victoria to Freud, Vol I, Education of the Senses, 1984, Vol II, The Tender Passion, 1986; Freud: A Life for Our Time, 1989. *Honours Include:* Frederic G. Melcher Book Award, 1967; National Book Award, 1967 (both for The

Enlightenment: An Interpretation, Volume I: The Rise of Modern Paganism); Guggenheim Fellow, 1967-68, 1977-78; Los Angeles Times Book Prize nomination, 1984 for The Bourgeois Experience: Victoria to Freud, Volume I: Education of the Senses, Amsterdam Prize for History, 1990. *Memberships:* American Historical Association; Phi Beta Kappa. *Address:* 105 Blue Trail, Hamden, CT 06518, USA.

GAYLE Emma. *See:* **FAIRBURN Eleanor M.**

GE Wujue, b. 12 Sept 1937, Wen Zhou, Zhe Jiang, China. Writer. m. Zhao Baotsing, 1 Feb 1962, 1 daughter. *Education:* Chinese Language & Literature Department, Beijing University, graduated 1959. *Literary Appointments:* Vice Chairman: Ningxia Literature & Art Federation, Chinese Writers Association. *Publications:* The Story of Summer, 1982; Ma Long's Call, 1980; Melody of the Banquet, 1982; She & Her Girl Friends, 1983; Four Days in Their Lives, 1985; That Strange Feeling, 1987. *Contributions to:* People's Literature; October. *Honours:* More than 10 awards for novels, reportages, TV plays including: October Prize for Literature, 1982; Novel Circles Prize for Works, 1984; Prize for Excellent Plays of Chinese TV Drama, 1985; People's Literature Prize, Readers Most Favourite Work, 1986. *Memberships:* Chinese Writers Association; Ningxia Calligraphers Association; Chinese Journalists Society. *Address:* Ningxia Literature & Art Federation, Yingchuan, Ningxia, People's Republic of China.

GEACH Christine, (Elizabeth Dawson, Anne Lowing, Christine Wilson), b. 22 Nov 1930, Plymouth, England. m. Kenneth Russel Geach, 17 July 1954, 1 daughter. *Education:* Qualified Radiographer, Plymouth School of Radiography, 1954 *Publications:* Author of various romances. *Membership:* Romantic Novelists Association. *Literary Agent:* Sam Walker Literary Agency, Bedford. *Address:* 6 Seaview Drive, Wembury, Plymouth, Devon, England.

GEBAUER Phyllis Feltskog, b. 17 Oct 1928, Chicago, II, USA. Writer. m. Frederick A Gebauer, 2 Dec 1950. *Education:* MA, University of Houston, 1966; BS, Northwestern University, Evanston, II, 1950; UCLA, UCSD, Universidad Nacional Autonoma de Mexico. *Appointments:* Staff, Santa Barbara Writers Conference, 1980-; Instructor, UCLA Extension, 1989-; Staff, So. Cal Writers Conference, 1989-. *Publication:* Novel: The Pagan Blessing. *Contributions to:* Stories and Articles: The Final Murder of Monica Marlowe; The Cottage; Lemuria II; The Canine Manifesto; Criticism; The Art of Give & Take; A Writers LA. *Honours:* 1st Prize, Fiction, Santa Barbara City College Extension; Honorable Mention non Fiction. *Memberships:* International PEN; Mystery Writers of America. *Literary Agent:* Bobbe Siegel, New York. *Address:* 515 W Scenic Drive, Monrovia, CA 91016, USA.

GEBLER Ernest, b. 1915, Irish. Writer of novels and short stories; Playwright; Screenwriter. *Publications:* He Had My Heart Scalded, 1946; The Plymouth Adventure: The Voyage of the Mayflower, 1949; A Week in the Country; The Love Investigator; The Old Man and the Girl; Girl with Green Eyes (screenplay) 1962; Day of Freedom (screenplay) 1968; Call Me Daddy (TV play) 1968, (US Emmy); Hoffman (play) 1976; Cry for Help (play) 1976; A Civilized Life (novel) 1979; Not the End of the World (novel) 1985. *Address:* 92 Coliemore Road, Dalkey Dublin, Ireland.

GEDDES Diana Elizabeth Campbell, b. 3 May 1947, Woburn, England. Journalist. *Education:* BA, Honours, Barnard College, Columbia University, USA, 1969. *Appointments:* The Scotsman, Edinburgh, 1970-73; The Economist, 1973-74; The Times, (Education Correspondent, Paris Correspondent), 1984-87; Paris Correspondent for The Spectator, Sunday Correspondent and European Times, 1988-; Freelance Journalist, 1988-. *Membership:* President, Anglo-American Press Association, Paris, 1988. *Address:* 29 Rue de Grenelle, Paris 75007, France.

GEDDES Gary, b. 1940, Canadian. Writer. *Appointments:* Professor of English, Concordia University, Montreal, since 1979, (Visiting Associate Professor, 1978-79). General Editor, Studies in Canadian Literature series. Visiting Assistant Professor, Trent University, Peterborough, Ont., 1968-69; Lecturer Carleton University, Ottawa, 1971-72 and University of Victoria, B.C. 1972-74; Writer-in-Residence, 1976-77 and Visiting Associate Professor, 1977-78, University of Alberta, Edmonton. *Publications:* 20th Century Poetry and Poets, 1969, 3rd Edition 1985; (ed. with Phyllis Bruce), 15 Canadian Poets, 1970, 3rd ed. 1988; Poems, 1970; Rivers Inlet (verse), 1972; Snakeroot (verse), 1973; Letter of the Master of Horse (verse), 1973; (ed.) Skookum Wawa: Writings of the Canadian Northwest, 1975; (ed.) the Inner Ear: An Anthology of New Canadian Poets, 1983; The Terracotta Army (verse), 1984; (co-trans), I Didn't Notice the Mountain Growing Dark, 1985; Changes of State (verse), 1986; (ed.) Vancouver: Soul of a City, 1986; The Unsettling of the West (stories), 1986; Hong Kong (verse), 1987.

GEDDES Paul, b. England. Writer. 2 daughters. *Publications:* The High Game, 1968; A November Wind, 1970; The Ottawa Allegation, 1973; Hangman, 1977; A State of Corruption, 1985; Goliath, 1986; A Special Kind of Nightmare, 1988; A Green Bag Affair, 1993. Address: c/o Sinclair-Stevenson, Michelin House, 81 Fulham Road, London SW3 6RB, England.

GEE Maurice Gough, b. 22 Aug 1931, Whakatane, New Zealand. Writer. *Education:* MA, University of Auckland, 1954. *Appointments:* Robert Burns Fellow, University of Otago, 1964; Writing Fellow, Victoria University of Wellington, 1989; Katherine Morsfield Fellow, Menton, France, 1992. *Publications:* Novels: Plumb, 1978; Meg, 1981; Sole Survivor, 1983; Prowlers 1987; The Burning Boy, 1990; Going West, 1993; Collected Stories 1986; Seven novels for children. *Honours:* New Zealand Book Award, 1976, 1979, 1981, 1991; New Zealand Book of the Year Award, 1979; James Tait Black Memorial Prize, 1979; Hon D Litt, Victoria University of Wellington, 1987. *Memberships:* PEN (New Zealand Centre), National Vice-President, PEN, 1990-. *Literary Agent:* Richards Literary Agency, Auckland. *Address:* 41, Chelmsford Street, Ngaio, Wellington, New Zealand.

GEE Shirley, b. 25 Apr 1932, London, England, Playwright. m. Donald Gee, 30 Jan 1965, 2 sons. *Education:* Webber-Douglas Academy of Music and Drama. *Publications:* Plays on radio, TV and Stage; Stones, 1974; Typhoid Mary, 1979; Never in My Lifetime, 1983; Long Live the Babe, 1985; Awsk for the Moon, 1986; Warrior, 1989; Bedrock, 1982; Moonshine, 1977; Flights, 1984; Against the Wind, 1988; Adaptations: The Vet's daughter; Men on White Horses; The Forsyte Saga (Co-adapted); Children's poems, stories and songs. *Honours:* Radio Times Drama Bursary Award, 1974; Giles Cooper Award, 1979; Pye Award, 1979; Jury's Special Commendation Prix Italia, 1979; Giles Cooper Award, 1983; Sony Award, 1983; Samuel Beckett Award, 1984; Susan Smith Blackburn Prize, 1985. *Memberships:* Broadcasting Committee, Society of Authors, 1983-85; Theatre Committee/Women's Committee, Writers Guild, 1986-88. *Literary Agent:* John Rush, David Higham Associates. *Address:* c/o David Higham Associates, 5-8 Lower John Street, Golden Square, London W1R FHA, England.

GEEHR Richard Stockwell, b. 6 May 1938, New Brunswick, New Jersey, USA. Professor. m. Gerda Kalchschmid, 9 Sept 1961. *Education:* BA, Middlebury College, 1956-60; MA, Columbia University, 1963-65; PhD, University of Mass, Amhurst, 1967-73. *Publications:* Karl Lueger Major of Fin De Siècle Vienna. *Contributions to:* Austrian History Yearbook; Oswald Meughiu; Hans Eibl. *Honours:* Fulbright Fellow; National Endowment for the Humanities Fellow; Beutley College

Teacher of the Year; Advisor of the Year; Research Scholar of the Year. *Memberships:* International Robert Musil Gesellschaft. *Address:* 143 Willow Street, Acton, MA 0720, USA.

GEISMAR Ludwig Leo, b. 1921, America. Professor of Social Work and Sociology; Writer. *Appointments:* Co-ordinator of Social Research, Ministry of Social Welfare, Israel, 1954-56; Research Director, Family Centered Project, St Paul, Minnesota, 1956-59; Associate Professor 1959-62, Professor of Social Work and Sociology and Director of Social Work Research Center, Graduate School of Social Work and Department of Sociology, Rutgers University, New Brunswick, New Jersey, 1963-. *Publications:* (with M A LaSorte), Understanding the Multi-Problem Family: A Conceptual Analysis and Exploration in Early Identification, 1964; (with J Krisberg), The Forgotten Neighborhood: Site of an Early Skirmish in the War on Poverty, 1967; Preventive Intervention in Social Work, 1969; Family and Community Functioning, 1971, 1980; (with Lagay, Wolock Gerhart and Fink), Early Supports for Family Life, 1972; 555 Families: A Social Psychological Study of Young Families in Transition, 1973; (with S Geismar), Families in an Urban Mold, 1979; (edited with M Dinerman), A Quarter Century of Social Work Education, 1984; (with K Wood), Family and Delinquency: Resocializing the Young Offender, 1986; (with K Wood), Families at Risk, 1989; The Family Functioning Scale: A Guide to Research and Practise, (with M Camasso), 1993. *Address:* 347 Valentine Street, Highland Park, NJ 08904, USA.

GEIST Harold, b. 22 July 1916, Pittsburgh, Pennsylvania, USA. Clinical Psychologist. *Education:* AB, Cornell University, Ithaca, New York, 1936; MA, Columbia University, New York City, 1937; PhD, Stanford University, Palo Alto, California, 1951. *Publications:* Tennis Psychology, 1981; A Child Goes to the Hospital, 1964; Emotion Aspects of Heart Disease, 1982; From Eminently Disadvantaged to Eminence, 1980; The Etiology of Idiopathic Epilepsy, 1962; The Psychological Aspects of Diabetes, 1965; The Psychological Aspects of Rheum Arthritis, 1967; The Psychological Aspects of the Aging Process, 1968; Bahian Adventure (novel) 1982; Migraine, 1983; Manual for Retirement Counsellors, 1988; To Russia With Love (novel) 1990; Commonalities in Psychosomatic Medicine, 1991. *Contributions to:* 75 articles in magazines and journals. *Honour:* Honorary Doctor of Letters, University of London, 1991. *Memberships:* Authors Guild of America; Life Member: American Psychological Association; American Association for the Advancement of Science; American Personnel and Guidance Association; International Council of Psychologists; Authors Guild. *Address:* 2255 Hearst Avenue, Berkeley, CA 94709, USA.

GELBART Larry, b. 25 Feb 1928, Chicago, Illinois, USA. Writer. m. Pat Marshall, 25 Nov 1956, 3 sons, 2 daughters. *Publications:* Co-author: Musical Comedy, A Funny Thing Happened on the Way to the Forum, 1963; Screenplay: Tootsie, 1984; Play: Mastergate, 1989; Author: Musical, City of Angels, 1989; Screenplay: The Wrong Box; Screenplay: Oh, God; Screenplay: Movie, Movie; Developed and wrote for TV: MASH (series); Barbarians at the Gate, 1993. *Honours:* Edgar Allan Poe Award for Oh God in 1978 and for City of Angels, 1990; Honorary Doctor of Letters, Union College, 1986; Outer Critics Circle Awards, for Contributions to Comedy 1980 and for Best Musical (City of Angels), 1990; Drama Desk Award for Outstanding Broadway Musical (City of Angels), 1990; New York Drama Critics Circle Award for Best New Musical (City of Angels), 1990; Antoinette Perry Awards for Best Book of a Musical: A Funny Thing Happened on the Way to the Forum, 1963, City of Angels, 1990. *Memberships:* Dramatists Guild; PEN; ASCAP; Authors League; Writers Guild of America, West. *Address:* 9255 Sunset Boulevard, Suite 404, Los Angeles, CA 90069, USA.

GELINAS Gratien, b. 8 Dec. 1909, Canada. Actor; Playwright; producer. m. (1) Simone Lalonde, 1935, dec 1967, 4 sons, 1 daughter, (2) Huguette Oligny, 1973. *Appointments:* Accountant, La Sauvegarde Insurance Co., 1929-37; casual radio and stage performances including creation of character of 'Fridolin' in series of monologues; Wrote, Starred in TV serial Les quat'fers en l'air, 1954-55; Fridolinades (revue), 1956. *Publications:* series of ten topical revues starring 'Fridolin'; Tit- Coq (play), 1949; Bousille et les justes, 1959; Le diable a quatre (satirical revue), 1964; hier les enfants dansaient, 1966; Films: La Dame aux Camelias, 1942; Tit-Coq. *Honours:* Grand Prix, Dramatists Society, 1949; Film of Year Award, Tit-Coq, 1953; Honoray LL.D., Saskatchwan, 1966, McGill, 1968, New Brunswick, 1969, Trent, 1970, Mount Allinson, 1973; Victor Morin Prize, 1967. *Memberships:* President, Canada Theatre Institute, 1959- 60; Founding Member, National Theatre School of Canada, 1960; Royal Society of Canada; Chairman, Canada Film Development Corporation, 1969-78; other professional organisations. *Address:* 316 Girouard Street, Box 207, OKA, Quebec JON 1EO, Canada.

GELLES-COLE Sandi, (Samantha Phillips), b. 25 Aug 1949, Chicago, III, USA. Editor; Writer. m. (1) Dennis Cole, 10 June 1972, (2) Gary Koopman, 28 April 1988. *Education:* Bachelor of Arts, Northeastern University, Boston. *Appointments:* Senior Acquisitions Editor, 1978-83; President, Literary Enterprises, 1983-. *Publications:* Secret & Desire; Mothers & Daughters; Unchartered Loves, 1984; Wanted Man; Letita Baldrige's Complete Guide to Executive Manners, 1985. *Contributions to:* Suburban Horse Woman; Horse Digest. *Literary Agent:* Helen Rees. *Address:* 320 & 42 411, New York, NY 10017, USA.

GELLIS Roberta Leah, (Max Daniels, Priscilla Hamilton, Leah Jacobs), b. 27 Sept 1927, Brooklyn, New York, USA. Author. m. Charles Gellis, 14 Apr 1947. 1 son. *Education:* BA, Hunter College, 1947; MS, Brooklyn Polytechnic Institute, 1952. *Appointments:* Copy Editor, McGraw Hill Book Company, 1953-55; Freelance Editor, 1955-. *Publications:* Bond of Blood, 1965; Knight's Honor, 1964; The Dragon and the Rose, 1977; The Sword and the Swan, 1977; The Rope Dancer, 1986; Masques of Gold, 1987. (Series) The Roselynde Chronicles: Roselynde, 1978, Alinor 1978, Joanna 1979, Gilliane 1980, Rhiannon 1982, Sybelle 1983. The Royal Dynasty Series: Siren Song 1980, Winter Song 1982, Fire Song 1984, A Silver Mirror 1989. Tales of Jernaeve: Tapestry of Dreams 1985, Fires of Winter 1986. The Napoleonic Era: The English Heiress 1980, The Cornish Heiress 1981, The Kent Heiress 1982, Fortune's Bride 1983, A Woman's Estate 1984. As Max Daniels: The Space Guardian, 1978; Offworld 1979. *Honours include:* Romantic Times Award, 1982; West Coast Review of Books, Silver Medal Porgy 1983, Gold Medal Porgy 1984; Romantic Times Reviewer's Award, 1988; Affaire de Coeur, Golden Pen Award, 1990. *Memberships:* Authors League; Pen and Brush; Romance Writers of America; Science Fiction Writers of America; Novelists Inc. *Address:* P O Box 483, Roslyn Heights, NY 11577, USA.

GELPI Albert, b. 1931, America. Coe Professor of American Literature; Writer. *Appointments:* Assistant Professor, Harvard University, Cambridge, Massachusetts, USA, 1962-68; Associate Professor, 1968- 74, Professor 1974-78, Coe Professor of American Literature, 1978-, Stanford University, California. *Publications:* Emily Dickinson: The Mild of the Poet, 1965; The Poet in America, 1950 to Present, 1973; (ed with Barbara Charlesworth Gelpi), The Poetry of Adrienne Rich, 1975; The Tenth Muse: The Psyche of the American Poet, 1975; (ed)Wallace Stevens: The Poetics of Modernism, 1986; A Coherent Splendor: The American Poetic Renaissance 1910-1950, 1987; (ed with Barbara Charlesworth Gelpi), Adrienne Rich's Poetry and Prose, 1993; (ed with Denise Levertov) Selected Criticism, 1993; (ed with intro) The Blood of the Poetry: Selected Poems of William Everson, 1993. *Address:* Department of English, Stanford University, Stanford, CA 94305, USA.

GENSLER Kinereth Dushkin, b. 17 Sept 1922, New York City, New York, USA. Poet; Teacher. Widow, 2 sons, 1 daughter. *Education:* BA, University of Chicago, 1943; MA, Columbia University, 1946. *Appointments:* Editor, Alice James Books, 1976-90. *Publications:* Threesome Poems, 1976; The Poetry Connection (co-author), 1978; Without Roof, 1981; Book chapters: Dream Poems in Broad Daylight, 1975; Poetry and the Impossible, 1988; Poems in anthologies: Best Poems of 1975. *Contributions to:* Andover Review; Florida Review; Green House; Massachusetts Review; New Renaissance; New York Times; Ploughshares; Poetry; Poetry Northwest; Poets On; Prairie Schooner; Radcliffe Quarterly, including Making of a Cooperative Feminist Press, 1988; Sequoia; Shenandoah; Slant; Sojourner; Virginia Quarterly Review; Women/Poems; Yankee; Yarrow. *Honours:* Members Award, Poetry Society of America, 1969; Power Dalton Award, New England Poetry Club, 1971; Borestone Mountain Award, 1973; Residency, Ragdale, 1981; Residency, MacDowell Colony, 1982, 1983. *Memberships:* Academy of American Poets; Alice James Cooperative Society; New England Poetry Club; Poetry Society of America. *Address:* 45 Gale Road, Belmont, MA 02148, USA.

GENTLE Mary Rosalyn, b. 29 Mar 1956, Sussex, England. Writer. *Education:* BA, English, Politics, Geography, 1985; MA. 17th Century Studies, 1988. *Literary Appointments:* Chairperson of Milford SF Writers Convention, 1989; Guest of Honour, Chronoclasm Convention, Derby, 1990. *Publications:* Golden Witchbreed, 1983; A Hawk in Silver, 1977; Ancient Light, 1987; Scholars and Soldiers, 1989; Rats and Gargoyles, 1990; The Architecture of Desire, 1991; Grunts!, 1992; Co edited, the Midnight Rose/Penguin Books anthologies: The Weerde bOOk 1, 1992; Villains!, 1992; The Weerde Book 2, The Book of the Ancients, 1993. *Contributions to:* Review Column, Interzone. *Memberships:* Society of Authors; British Science Fiction Association; SWFA. *Literary Agent:* Maggie Noach, The Maggie Noach Literary Agency, 21 Redan Street, London W14 0AB. *Address:* 37 Beane Avenue, Stevenage, Herts, SG2 7DL, England.

GENTRY Robert Bryan, b. 21 July 1936, Knoxville, Tennessee, USA. Writer; Educator. m. Mary Sue Koeppel, 31 May 1980, 2 sons. *Education:* Graduate Work, University of New Hampshire, 1977; Graduate Work, University of Georgia, 1968-72; MA, University of Tennessee, 1964-66; US Army Language School, 1959; BS, University of Tennessee, 1954-58. *Appointments:* College Historian, Florida Community College, 1988-91; Editor, Riverside-Avondale Historic Preservation Publication, 1975-76; Professor of Humanities, Florida Community College, 1972-. *Publications:* A College Tells Its Story: An Oral History of Florida Community College at Jacksonville, 1963-1991, 1991; The Rise of the Hump House, novel, 1976. *Contributions to:* A Diarist's Journal; Kalliope: A Journal of Women's Art; Teaching English in the Two-Year College. *Honours:* Professor of the Year, Florida Community College, 1985; Prize Winner, Quest for Peace Writing Contest, University of California, 1988; Nominated, National Pushcart Award. *Memberships:* Community College Humanities Association; US English. *Address:* 3879 Oldfield Trail, Jacksonville, FL 32223, USA.

GEORGE Barbara. *See:* **KATZ Bobbi**.

GEORGE Emily. *See:* **KATZ Bobbi**.

GEORGE Elizabeth. Author. *Publications:* Detective novels: A Great Deliverance; Payment in Blood; Payment Defence, 1990; For The Sake of Elena, 1992. *Honour:* Grand Prix de Literature Policiere, 1990. *Address:* Huntington Beach, California, USA.

GEORGE Jean Craighead, b. 21 July 1919, Washington, DC, USA. Author; Illustrator. m. John L. George, 28 Jan 1944, (div 1963), 2 sons, 1 daughter. *Education:* BA, Pennsylvania State University. *Appointments:* Roving Editor, Reader's Digest, 1965-84; Washington Post, Reporter, 1940-46. *Publications:* My Side of the Mountain, 1959; Summer of the Falcon, 1962; The Thirteen Moons, 1967-1969; Julie of the Wolves, 1972; Going to the Sun, 1976; Wounded Wolf, 1978; The American Walk Book, 1978; River Rats, 1979; The Grizzly Bear with the Golden Ears, 1982; The Cry of the Crow, 1982; Journey Inward, 1982; Talking Earth, 1983; How to Talk to Your Animals, 1985; Water Sky, 1987; One Day in the Woods, 1988; Shark Beneath the Reef, 1989; Musical: One Day in the Woods, 1989; On the Far Side of the Mountain, 1990; One Day in a Tropical Rain Forest, 1990. *Contributions to:* 50 articles in Readers Digest, National Wildlife. *Honours:* Newbery Medal, 1973; Newbery Honor Book, 1960; The Kerlan Award, 1982; De Grumman Award, 1985; Jungbuch Prize, 1974; World Book Award, 1971; Claremont Colleges Award, 1969; Penn State Woman of the Year, 1968. *Literary Agent:* Curtis Brown Ltd. *Address:* 20 William St., Chappaqua, NY 10514, USA.

GEORGE Jonathan. *See:* **BURKE John Fredrick**.

GEORGE Kathleen Elizabeth, b. 7 July 1943, Johnstown, Pennsylvania, USA. Professor. *Education:* BA, 1964; MA, 1966; phD, 1975; MFA, 1988. *Appointments:* Associate Professor, University of Pittsburgh Theatre Department. *Publications:* Rhythm in Drama. *Contributions to:* Cineaaon Review; Great Stream; Gulf Stream; Alaska Quarterly; West Branch. *Honours:* Louise Laititia Mill Writing Award; Best American Short Story; Finalist, pirates Alley contest. *Memberships:* Poets & Writers; Association for Theatre in Higher Education. *Literary Agent:* Kit Ward. *Address:* 167 CL, University of Pittsburgh, Pittsburgh, PA 15260, USA.

GEORGEOGLOU Nitsa-Athina, b. 4 Sept 1922, Athens, Greece. Author. m. 9 Nov 1947, 2 sons. *Education:* Graduate: Greek Gymasium, 1938, Superior Studies, French Institute of Athens. *Publications include:* 21 novels, 5 books of essays, 1 historical book including: The Wrath of the Earth, 1978; Tom, Tommy and Co., 1971; Vravron, before the Christian Era, 1980; Chronicle of Thyateira, 1981; Seas Afire, 1984; SOS Danger!, 1986; Once in Missolonghi, 1971; The Secret Society, 1973; A Ship Called Hope, 1975; Enterprise Archemides, 1977; Toto is My Guest, 1977; Waves and Islands, 1978; Up the Hill, 1979; The Horse Farm, 1981; The Golden Coin, 1982; Saturn Calling, 1984; On Foreign Land, 1985; The Will of Youth, 1987; Uranus Calling, 1987; Walking Through the Centuries, 1987. *Contributions to:* Numerous journals and magazines. *Honours include:* Award, Woman's Literary Committee of Athens, 1969, 1970, 1971, 1979, 1980, 1981, 1985; Award Circle of Greek Childrens Book Authors, 1970, 1977, 1978; Hans Christian Anderson Honour List, 1982. *Memberships include:* National Society of Greek Authors; Greek IBBY; Vice President, Greek Union, International Soroptimist; Hestia Cultural Club. *Address:* 83 Plastira Street, 171 21 Nea Smirni, Athens, Greece.

GERGELY Agnes, b. 5 Oct 1933, Endrod, Hungary. Writer. *Education:* University of Liberal Arts, Budapest, MA 1957; PhD, 1979. *Appointments:* Teacher, 1957-63; Producer, Radio Budapest, 1963-71; writer, 1971-74; Editor, 1974-77; Head of Third World Literature Column, 1977-88; Freelance Writer, 1988-; University Lecturer, 1992-. *Publications include:* Cobalt Country; Shadow City; The Interpreter; The Chicago Version; Stations of the Cross. *Contributions to:* Contemporary; Life & Letters; Great World; By the Tisza; Present Day; Pompeii. *Honours:* Attila Jozsef Prize; Tibor Dery Award; Honorary Fellow of University of Iowa. *Memberships:* Hungarian Writers Union; Hungarian Creative Artists Foundation; Hungarian PEN Club; Hungarian Journalists National Union. *Literary Agent:* Hungrian Copyright Agency, ARTISJUS. *Address:* Pannonia u 64/B, 1133 Budapest, Hungary.

GERMAIN Jean-Claude, b. 18 June 1939, Montreal, Canada. Author; Director; Actor. *Education:* College Sainte, University de Montreal. *Appointments:* Anchorman, Faut Voirca, Weekly Television Show; Anchorman, Daily Radio Chronic, CBF Bonjour. *Publications:* Les Hauts et les Bas d'la Vie d'one Diva; Un Pays dont la devise est je M'oublie; Les Faux; L'Ecole des reues; A canadian Play. *Contributions to:* Le Quebec Litteraire; L'Illettre; MacLean Magazine; Jeu and Canadian Theatre Review. *Honours:* prix Victor Morin; Le Salon du Livre de Montreal; Conseil des Arts du Canada. *Memberships:* Centre d'essai des auteurs dramatiques; L'Association Des Directeurs de Theatre; L'Ecole National de Theatre Du Canada. *Literary Agent:* Agence Goodwin, 839 Est, Rue Sherbrooke, H2L 1K6. *Address:* 839 Est, Rue Sherbrooke, MH, PQ, Canada H2L 1K6.

GERMAN William, b. 4 Jan 1919, Brooklyn, New York, USA. Newspaper Editor. m. Gertrude Pasenkoff, 12 Oct 1940, 2 sons, 1 daughter. *Education:* BA, Brooklyn College, 1939; MS, Columbia University, 1940. *Appointments:* San Francisco Chronicle, Reporter, 1940-43; US Army, 1943-45; Chief Copy Desk, 1945-49; News Editor, 1950-60; Executive News Editor, 1960-77; Executive Editor, 1982-. *Contributions to:* Chronicle Reader; KQED Newspaper. *Honours:* Nieman Fellow; Juror, Pulitzer Prize. *Memberships:* American Society of Newspaper Editors; Associated press Managing Editors; World Affairs Council; Commonwealth Club of California. *Address:* San Francisco Chronicle, 901 Mission Street, San Francisco, CA 94103, USA.

GERMANO Peter B, (Jack Bertin, Jackson Cole, Barry Cord, Jim Kane, Jack Slade), b. 1913, USA. Freelance Writer. *Publications:* Trail Boss from Texas, 1948; The Gunsmoke Trail, 1951; Shadow Valley, 1951; Mesquite Johnny, 1952; Trail to Sundown, 1953; Cain Basin, 1954; The Sagebrush Kid, 1954; Boss of Barbed Wire, 1955; Dry Range, 1955, UK Edition The Rustlers of Dry Range, 1956; The Guns of Hammer, 1956; The Gunshy Kid, 1957; Sheriff of Big Hat, 1957; Savage Valley, 1957; The Prodigal Gun, 1957; Concho Valley, 1958; Gun-Proddy Hombre, 1958; The Iron Trail Killers, 1959; Starlight Range, 1959; The Third Rider, 1959; Six Bullets Left, 1959; War in Peaceful Valley, 1959; Maverick Gun, 1959; Last Chance at Devil's Canyon, 1959; Gunman's Choice (as Jim Kane), 1960; Renegade Rancher (as Jim Kane), 1961; Two Guns to Avalon, 1962; The Masked Gun, 1963; Spanish Gold (as Jim Kane), 1963; Tangled Trails (as Jim Kane), 1963; Lost Canyon (as Jim Kane), 1964; Red River Sheriff (as Jim Kane), 1965; Last Stage to Gomorrah, 1966; A Ranger Called Solitary, 1966; Rendezvous at Bitter Wells (as Jim Kane), 1966; Canyon Showdown, 1967; Gallows Ghost, 1967; The Long Wire, 1968; Trouble in Peaceful Valley, 1968; The Interplanetary Adventurers, (as Jack Bertin), science fiction, 1970; Texas Warrior (as Jim Kane), 1971; The Coffin Fillers, 1972; Brassado Hill, 1972; Desert Knights, 1973; The Running Iron Samaritans, 1973; Hell in Paradise Valley, 1978; Gun Junction, 1979; Deadly Amigos: Two Graves for a Gunman, 1979.

GERONTIUS. *See:* **HATAR Victor Gyozo George John.**

GERRISH Brian Albert, b. 14 Aug 1931, London, England. University Professor. *Education:* BA, 1952, MA, 1956, Queens' College, Cambridge; Exit Certificate, Westminster College, Cambridge, 1955; STM, Union Theological Seminary, New York, USa, 1956; PhD, Columbia University, 1958. *Appointments:* Editor, Journal of Religion, 1972-85; John Nuveen Professor, Divinity School, University of Chicago, Illinois. *Publications:* Grace and Reason : A Study in the Theology of Luther, 1962; Tradition and the Modern World : Reformed Theology in the Nineteenth Century, 1978; The Old Protestantism and the New : Essays on the Reformation Heritage, 1982; A Prince of the Church : Schleiermacher and the Beginnings of Modern Theology, 1984; Grace and Gratitude: The Eucharistic Theology of John Calvin, 1993; Continuing the

Reformation: Essays on Modern Religious Thoughts, 1993; Editor, The Faith of Christendom, A Source Book of Creeds and Confessions, 1963; Reformers in Profile, 1967; Reformatio Perennis : Essays on Calvin and the Reformation in Honor of Ford Lewis Battles, 1981. *Contributions to:* Various professional journals. *Honours:* Guggenheim Fellowship, 1970; NEH Fellowship, 1980; DD, HC, University of St Andrews, Scotland, 1984; Festschrift (essays dedicated to B A Gerrish), Mary Potter Engel and Walter E Wyman, Jr., eds, Revisioning the Past: Prospects in Historical Theology, 1992. *Memberships:* Fellow, American Academy of Arts & Sciences; President, American Theological Society, (Mid-west division), 1973-74; President, American Society of Church History, 1979; many other professional organisations. *Address:* Swift Hall 301, University of Chicago, 1025 East 58th Street, Chicago, USA.

GERROLD David, b. 1944, American. Writer of science fiction and fantasy. Computer Columnist. *Appointments:* Computer Columnist, CIT Profiles, 1984- ; Columnist, Starlos and Galileo mags; Story editor, Land of the Lost TV series, 1974; Freelance writer and science fiction short stories, screenplays and Tv plays. *Publications:* (with Larry Niven), The Flying Sorcerers, 1971; (ed with Stephen Goldin), Protostars 1971; (ed)Generation, 1972; Space Skimmer, 1972; Yesterday's Children, 1972; When Harlie Was One, 1972; With a Finger in My I (short stories), 1972; Battle for the Planet of the Apes (novelization of screenplay), 1973; The Man Who Folded Himself, 1973; The Trouble with Tribbles, 1973; The World of Star Trek, 1973; (ed with Stephen Goldin), Science Fiction Emphasis 1, 1974; (ed with Stephen Goldin), Alternities, 1974; (ed with Stephen Goldin), Ascents of Wonder, 1977; Deathbeast, 1978; The Galactic Whirlpool, 1980; The war Against the Chtorr: A Matter for Man, 1983; A Day for Damnation, 1984; When Harlie Was One, 1987; When Harlie Was Two, 1987. *Address:* Box 1190, Hollywood, CA 90028, USA.

GERWIN Donald, b. 1937, America. Professor, Business Administration and Systems and Computer Engineering, Writer. *Appointments:* Assistant Professor 1967-70, Associate Professor 1970-75, Professor 1975-89, School of Business Administration, University of Wisconsin, Milwaukee; Professor, School of Business, 1989-91; Professor, School of Business and Department of Systems and Computer Engineering, Carleton University, 1991-. *Publications:* Budgeting Public Funds: The Decision Process in an Urban School District, 1969; (ed)The Employment of Teachers: Some Analytical Views, 1974; Management of Advanced Manufacturing Technology, 1992. *Address:* School of Business, Carleton University, Ottawa, Canada K1S 5B6.

GEVE Thomas, b. 1929, Germany. Engineer. m. 1963, 1 son, 2 daughters. *Education:* National Diploma of Building, 1950; BSC, 1957. *Publications:* Youth in Chains; Guns and Barbed Wire. *Literary Agent:* M J Wald, New York, USA. *Address:* PO Box 4727, Haifa, Israel.

GEYER Georgie Anne, b. 2 Apr 1935, Chicago, Illinois, USA. Syndicated Columnist; Author; Foreign Correspondent; Speaker; Educator. *Education:* BS, Journalism, Northwestern University, 1956; Fulbright Scholarship, University of Vienna, Australia, 1956-57. *Appointments include:* Chicago Daily News, 1959-75; Syndicated columnist, Los Angeles Times Syndicate 1975-80, Washington Star 1980-81, Universal Press Syndicate 1980-. *Publications:* Books: New Latins, 1970; New 100 Years' War, 1972; Young Russians, 1976; Buying the Night Flight, 1983. Chapters in: Responsibilities of Journalism, 1984; Beyond Reagan; Politics of Upheaval, 1986. *Contributions to:* Thrice-weekly column, Domestic/Foreign Affairs, approximately 120 leading newspapers in USA & Latin America. Also articles, various magazines including: Saturday Review; Atlantic; New Republic; Progressive; Nation; People; Lincoln Review; etc. *Honours include:*

Awards & Prizes: Chicago Newspaper Guild, 1962; Overseas Press Club, 1967; Northwestern University, 1968; National Council for Jewish Women, 1971; Columbia University, 1971; Who's Who in America, 1971; Newsweek Magazine; Illinois State, 1975. Memberships include: Cosmos Club; Council on Foreign Relations, New York; International Institute for Strategic Studies, UK; Women in Communications; Midland Authors; Womens Institute for Freedom of Press; National Press Club. Address: The Plaza, 800 25th Street NW, Washington DC 20037, USA.

GHALEM Nadia, b. 26 June 1941, Oran, Algeria. Journalist. Education: Studied, Psychology & Literature. Appointments: Montreal Book Exhibition, 1981; Quebec Book Exhibition, 1981; Assembly of French Speaking Authors; Jack Kerouac Assembly, 1987. Publications: Les Jardins de Cristal, 1981; L'oiseau de Fer, 1981; Exil, 1980. Contributions to: Dimension Sciences et Technologie; Le Devoir; Chatelaine; L'Actualite; etc. Honours: Grant, Canadian Arts Council, 1983; Finalist, Grand Prix Guerin for Literature. Memberships: Union of Quebec Authors; Professional Federation of Journalists of Quebec; Quebec Press Council; Union des Artistes Federation. Literary Agent: M. Jeau Beaudet (Trois Rivieres). Address: 3495 Ave. Van Horne, Montreal, Quebec, H3S 1R7, Canada.

GHISELIN Brewster, b. 13 June 1903, Webster Green, Missouri, USA. Writer; Poet. m. Olive F Franks, 1929, 2 sons. Education: AB, University of California, Los Angeles, 1927; MA, University of California, Berkeley, 1928, Graduate studies 1931-33; Oxford University, 1928-29. Appointments: Instructor in English, University of Utah, Salt Lake City, 1929-31; Assistant in English, University of California, Berkeley, 1931- 33; Instructor 1934-38, Lecturer 1938-39, Assistant Professor, 1939-46, Associate Professor, 1946-50, Director of Writers' Conference, 1947-66, Professor of English, 1950-71, Distinguished Research Professor, 1967-68 and Professor Emeritus 1971-, University of Utah; Poetry Editor 1937-46 and Associate Editor, 1946-49, Rocky Mountain Review, later Western Review, Salt Lake City and Lawrence, Kansas. Publications: Verse: Against the Circle, 1946; The Nets, 1955; Images and Impressions, with Edward Lueders and Clarice Short, 1969; Country of the Minotaur, 1970; Let There Be Light, 1976; Light, 1978; Windrose: Poems 1929-1979, 1980; The dreamers, 1981; Flame, 1991. Other works: Writing, 1959; (ed)The Creative Process: A Symposium, 1952. Honours: Ford Fellowship, 1952; Ben and Abby Grey Foundation Award, 1965; American Academy Award, 1970; Oscar Blumenthal Prize, 1973; Levinson Prize 1978 (Poetry Chicago); William Carlos Williams Award, 1981; Utah Arts Council Governor's Award, 1982. Address: Department of English, University of Utah, Salt Lake City, UT 84112, USA.

GHOSE Zulfikar, b. 1935, Pakistan. Author; Poet. Appointments Include: Cricket Correspondent, The Observer, London, 1960-65; Teacher London, 1963-69. Publications: Statement Against Corpes (with B.S. Johnson), 1964; The Loss of India (verse), 1964; Confessions of a native- Alien, 1965; The Contradictions (novel), 1966; The Murder of Aziz Khan (novel), 1967; Jets from Orange (verse), 1967; The Incredible Brazilian Book 1 (novel), 1972; The Violent West (verse), 1972; Penguin Modern Poets 25 (with Gavin Ewart and B.S. Johnson), 1974; Crump's Terms (novel), 1975; The Beautiful Empire (novel), 1975; Hamlet, Prufrock and Language, 1978; A Different World (novel), 1978; Hulme's Investigations Into the Bogart Script (novel), 1981; A New History of Torments (novel), 1982; The Fiction of Reality (criticism), 1983; Don Bueno (novel), 1983; A Memory of Asia (poetry), 1984; Figures of Enchantment (novel), 1986; Selected Poems, 1991; The Art of Creating Fiction, (Criticism) 1991; The Triple Mirror of the Self (novel) 1992; Shakespeare's Mortal Knowledge, (criticism), 1993. Literary Agent: Aitken & Stone, London; Wylie, Aitken & Stone, New York. Address: Department of English, University of Texas, Austin, TX 78712, USA.

GHOSH Ajit Kumar, b. 1 Jan 1919, Shaistanager, Noakhali, India (now Bangladesh). Professor. m. Belarani Ghosh, 20 Apr 1940, 2 sons. Educatin: Matriculation, 1st Division, 1934; BA, Honours in English, 2nd class, 1938; MA, Bengali, 2nd class, 1940; PhD, 1959; D Litt, 1969. Appointments: Lecturer in Bengali: M M College, Jessore, 1941-47; Surendranath College, Calcutta, 1947-63; Lecturer, Reader, then Professor, 1963-91, Dean, Faculty of Arts, Head, Department of Bengali, 1970-83, Rabindra Bharati University; Editor, Encyclopaedia of Indian Literature; Editor, Modern Indian Literature. Publications: Bangla Nataker Itihas (History of Bengali Drama); Banga Sahitye Hasyaraser Dhara (Humour in Bengali Literature); Saratchandrer Jibani-O-Sahitya Viehar (Life and Literary Arts of Saratchandra Chatterjee); Bangla Natyabhinayer Itihar (History of Stage Acting in Bengal); Nataker Katha (Principles of Drama); Natyatattva Parichay (Theory of Drama); Jibansilpi Saratchandra (Saratchandra: the Artist of Life); Thakurbarir Abhinay (History of Acting in Jorasanko Tagore family); Edited many famous writers' works. Contributions to: Over 50 scholarly articles to various magazines and journals. Honours: Appointed Dwijendralal Roy Reader, Rammohan Roy Lecturer, Dineschandra Sen Lecturer, Calcutta University; President, Literary Conferences; Participant, national seminars; Invited by International Congress of Human Sciences, Tokyo and Kyoto, 1983. Memberships: President, Bangiya Sahitya Parishad; Bangla Akademi; Natya Akademi; Senate, Calcutta University; Court, Rabindra Bharati University; President, Calcutta Film Circle; President, Natya Vicharak Samiti; Nominated Member to select Authors, Nobel Prize Committee. Address: AE 510, Salt Lake, Calcutta 700064, India.

GHOSH Oroon Kumar, b. 22 Aug 1917, Culcutta, India. Civil Servant. m. Rekha Majurndar, 29 June 1943, 1 daughter. Education: Bachelor of Science, Rangoon University, 1938; Delhi University, 1953. Appointments: Editorial Director, Minerva Associates, 1976-90. Publications include: Tales from the Indian Classics; The Dance of Shiva and Other Tales From India; Science, Society and Philosphy; Convergence of Civilizations; How India Won Freedom. Contributions to: Radical Humanist; World History Bulletin; Jijnasa. Memberships: PEN; Royal Asiatic Society; International Society for the Comparative Study of Civilizations; World History Association. Address: CD 6 Sector I, Salt Lake, Calcutta 700064, India.

GIANAKARIS Constantine John, b. 1934, United States of America. Writer. Appointments include: Co-Founder, Comparative Drama Quarterly, 1966-90. Publications: Antony and Cleopatra, 1969; Plutarch, 1970; Author, Peter Shaffer, 1992; Editor, Peter Shaffer: A Casebook, 1991; Author, Editor, Foundations of Drama, 1974; co-editor, Drama in the Middle Ages, 1984; co-editor, Drama in the Twentieth Century, 1985; co-editor, Drama in the Renaissance, 1985. Contributions to: Theater Week, mag; Opera News, mag; Theater/Music reviewer for Kalamazoo Gazatte, daily. Address: Department of English, Western Michigan University, Kalamazoo, MI 49008, USA.

GIBB Lee. See: WATERHOUSE Keith.

GIBBS Alonzo Lawrence, b. 17 Feb 1915, Brooklyn, New York, USA. Engineer; Writer. m. (1) Iris H. Ebisch, 17 June 1939, dec. April 1983, 1 son, (2) Priscilla Moss, 1986. Education: Hofstra University, 1938; Certificate in Aircraft Structural Layout, Columbia University, 1941. Appointments: Poetry Reviewer, Voices magazine, 1953-64; President, Kinsman Publications, 1961-64; Editor, Kinsman Literary Quarterly; Contributing Editor, Long Island Forum, 1964-. Publications include: Weather-House, 1959; The Fields Breathe Sweet, 1963; Monhegan, 1963; The Least Likely One, 1964; Dolphin Off Hippo, libretto, 1965; A Man's Calling, 1966; By a Sea-Coal Fire, 1969; Drift South, 1969; One More Day, 1971; Sir Urian's Letters Home, 1974; The Rumble of Time thru Town, 1980; Harking Back, 1983; In the Weir of the Marshes, 1990. Contributions to: Poetry and criticism to Voices magazine, 1953-64; Long Island Forum; Essays to Christian Science Monitor. *Honours:* Section Chief Engineer, Grumman Aerospace Corporation, Bethpage, New York, 1965-73. *Membership:* Authors Guild. *Literary Agent:* Curtis Brown. *Address:* HC 60, Box 20, Waldoboro, ME 04572, USA.

GIBBS Angelina, b. 20 July 1957, England. Freelance Writer; Editor; Proofreader. m. Christopher Richard Gibbs, 19 Oct 1985, 1 son. *Education:* BSc, University of Bradford, 1979. *Appointments:* Researcher, Writer, Which? Magazine, 1979-82; Freelance Writer, Editor, Proofreader, 1982-. *Publications:* A Patient's Guide to the National Health Service; Understanding Mental Health. *Contributions to:* Which? Magazine; Upton St Leonards Parish Appraisal. *Memberships:* British Psychological Society; Society of Freelance Editors & Proofreaders. *Address:* White Gates, Old Way, Upton St Leonards, Gloucester GL4 8AF, England.

GIBBS Barbara. *See:* **GOLFFING Barbara Francesca.**

GIBSON Charles E(dmund), b. 1916. Writer (Children's Fiction, History). *Publications:* The Story of the Ship, 1948; The Secret Tunnel, 1948; Wandering Beauties, 1960; The Clash of Fleets, 1961; Knots and Splices, 1962; Plain Sailing, 1963; Daring Prows, 1963; Be Your Own Weatherman, 1963; The Two Olafs of Norway: With a Cross on Their Shields, 1964; The Ship With Five Names, 1965; Knots and Splices, 1979; Death of a Phantom Raider, 1987. *Literary Agent:* A.M. Heath & Co Ltd. *Address:* 59 Victoria Road, Shoreham-by-Sea, Sussex, England.

GIBSON Josephine. *See:* **JOSLIN Sesyle.**

GIBSON Miles, b. 10 Feb 1947, England. Writer. *Education:* Somerford Secondary Modern. *Publications:* Novels: The Sandman, 1984; Dancing with Mermaids, 1985; Vinegar Soup 1987; Kingdom Swann 1990. *Literary Agent:* Jonathan Clowes. *Address:* c/o Jonathan Clowes Ltd, Iron Bridge House, Bridge Approach, London NW1 8BD, England.

GIBSON Morgan, b. 6 June 1929, Cleveland, Ohio, USA. Poet; Writer; Professor. m. (1) Barbara Gibson, 1950, div 1972, 2 daughters, (2) Keiko Matsui, 1978, 1 son. *Education:* BA, Oberlin College, 1950; MA, University of Iowa, 1952; PhD, 1959. *Publications:* Revolutionary Rexvoth: Poet of East West Wisdom; Tantic Poetry of Kukai; Amoung Buddhas in Japan; The Great Brook Book; Speaking of Light. *Memberships:* PEN; Academy of American Poets; Poetry Society of America; Buddhist Peace Fellowship. *Address:* Department of English, Japan Womens University, 2-8-1 Mejiro Jai, Boukyo Ku, Toyko 112 Japan.

GIBSON Roger Fletcher, b. 21 Feb 1944, St Louis, MO, USA. Professor of Philosophy. m. Sharon Haverinen, 23 Mar 1984, 1 daughter. *Education:* BA, Northeast Missouri State University, 1971; MA, University of Mo Columbia, 1973; PhD, 1977. *Publications:* The Philosophy of W V Quine; Enlightened Empiricism; Perspectives on Quine. *Contributions to:* Erkenntnis; Synthese; Ethics; Metaphilosophy; Dialectica; Philosophical Psychology; The Philosophical Review. *Honours:* NEH Fellowship. *Memberships:* Americal Philosophical Association. *Address:* Department of Philosophy, Box 1073, Washington University, One Brookings Drive, St Louis MO 63130, USA.

GIBSON Walter Samuel, b. 1932. USA. Writer. *Publications:* Hieronymus Bosch: The Paintings of Cornells Engerbrechsz; Bruegel; Hieronymus Bosch; An Annotated Bibliography; Mirror of the Earth: The World Landscape in Sixteenth Century Flemish Painting. *Address:* Department of Art History and Art, Mather House, Case Western Reserve University, Cleveland, OH 44106, USA.

GIBSON William (Ford), b. 1948, United States of America. Author. *Publications:* Neuromancer, 1984; Count Zero, 1985; Burning Chrome, 1986; Mona Lisa Overdrive, 1987. *Address:* 2630 W. 7th Avenue, Vancouver, British Columbia, Canada V6K 1Z1.

GIDLEY Charles b. 21 Aug 1938, Bristol, England. m. (1) Felicity Bull, 1962, div 1992, 1 son, 1 daughter. (2) Susan Keeble, Artiste, 1993. *Education:* University College School, Hampstead; Royal Naval College, Dartmouth. *Publications include:* Novels: The River Running By; The Raging of the Sea; The Believer; Armada; The Fighting Spirit; The Crying of the Wind. *Contributions to:* Blackwoods Magazine; The Naval Review. *Memberships:* PEN International. *Literary Agent:* A M Heath. *Address:* Winchester, England.

GIFFORD Barry Colby, b. 18 Oct 1946, Illinois, USA, Writer. m. Mary Lou Nelson, 23 Oct 1970, 1 son, 1 daughter. *Publications:* Jack's Book, (Co-author), biography, 1978; Port Tropique, 1980; Landscape with Traveler, 1980; The The Neighborhood of Baseball, 1981; Devil Thumbs a Ride, 1988; Ghosts No Horse Can Carry, 1989; Wild at Heart, 1990; Sailor's Holiday, 1991; Night People, 1992. *Contributions to:* Punch; Esquire; Rolling Stone. *Honours:* PEN Maxwell Perkins Award, 1983; National Endowment for the Arts Fellowship, 1982; PEN Syndicated Fiction Award, 1987; American Library Association Notable Book Award, 1978, 1988. *Literary Agent:* Peter Ginsberg, President, Curtis Brown Limited, 10 Astor Place, New York, NY 10003, USA. *Address:* 833 Bancroft Way, Berkeley, CA 94710, USA.

GIFFORD Denis, b. 26 Dec 1927, London, England. Author and cartoonist. Divorced, 1 daughter. *Education:* St Bartholomew's Sydenham 1931-39; Dulwich College 1939-44. *Appointment:* Art Assistant, Reynolds News, 1944-45. *Publications include:* British Film Catalogue 1895-1980; British Comic Catalogue 1874-1974; Pictorial History of Horror Movies, 1973; International Book of Comics, 1984; Golden Age of Radio, 1985; Encyclopaedia of Comic Characters 1987; Best of Eagle Annual 1951-59, 1989; Comic Art of Charlie Chaplin, 1989; The American Comic Book Catalogue, 1990; Books and Plays in Films, 1991. *Contributions include:* TV Times, Radio Times, Guardian, Times, Observer, Sunday Times, Independent, Collectors Fayre, Book Collector. *Memberships include:* Association of Comics Enthusiasts (founder); Society of Strip Illustration (co-founder); Edgar Wallace Society; Old Bill Society; Savers of Television and Radio Shows (founder); 1940 Society. *Address:* 80 Silverdale, Sydenham, London SE26 4SJ, England.

GIGGAL Kenneth, (Angus Ross), b. 19 Mar 1927, Dewsbury, Yorkshire, England. *Publications include:* The Manchester Thing, 1970; The Huddersfield Job, 1971; The London Assignment, 1972; The Dunfermline Affair, 1973; The Bradford Business, 1974; The Amsterdam Diversion, 1974; The Leeds Fiasco, 1975; The Edinburgh Exercise, 1975; The Ampurias Exchange, 1976; The Aberdeen Conundrum, 1977; The Congleton Lark, 1979; The Hamburg Switch, 1980; A Bad April, 1980; The Menwith Tangle, 1982; The Darlington Jaunt, 1983; The Luxembourg Run, 1985; Doom Indigo, 1986; The Tyneside Ultimatum, 1988; Classic Sailing Ships, 1988; The Greenham Plot, 1989; The Leipzig Manuscript, 1990; The Last One, 1992; John Worsley's War, 1992. Scripts and Films for TV. *Contributions to:* Many magazines, national and international. *Honour:* Truth Prize for Fiction, 1954. *Memberships:* The Savage Club; The Arms and Armour Society; The Writers Guild of Great Britain; The Crime Writer's Association. *Literary Agent:* Andrew Mann Ltd. *Address:* The Old Granary, Bishop Monkton, Near Harrogate, N Yorkshire, England.

GIL David Georg, b. 16 Mar 1924, Vienna, Austria,

Professor of Social Policy; Author. m. Eva Breslauer, 2 Aug 1947, 2 sons. *Education:* DSW, 1963, MSW, 1958, University of Pennsylvania; BA, 1957, Diploma in Social Work, School of Social Work, 1953, Hebrew University, Jerusalem, Israel; Certificate in Psychotherapy with Children, Israeli Society for Child Psychiatry, 1952. *Appointments:* Member, Editorial Boards: American Journal of Orthopsychiatry, Journal of Sociology and Social Welfare; Social Development Issues; Humanity and Society; Evaluation and the Health Professions; Children and Youth Services Review; Victimology; Journal of International and Comparative Social Welfare; Journal of Progressive Human Services; Journal of Teaching in Social Work; Journal of Social Service Research; Changing Work; Child Welfare; Our Generation. *Publications:* Violence Against Children, 1970; Unravelling Social Policy, 1973, 1976, 1981, 1990, 1992; The Challenge of Social Equality, 1976; Beyond the Jungle, 1979; Child Abuse and Violence, editor, 1979; Toward Social and Economic Justice, (Co-Editor Eva A Gil), 1985; The Future of Work, (Co-editor Eva A Gil), 1987. *Contributions to:* Over 50 articles in professional journals, book chapters and book reviews. *Honours:* Study awards, United Nations, 1953-54; Research Grants, US Department of Health Education and Welfare, 1965-73; Foundation Grants, 1984-87. *Memberships:* Association for Humanist Sociology, President, 1981; National Association of Social Workers, delegate assembly, 1987-90; American Orthopsychiatric Association, Fellow; Board of Director, 1990-93. *Address:* Heller Graduate School, Brandeis University, Waltham, MA 02254, USA.

GILB Dagoberto G, b. 31 July 1950, Los Angeles, Calfornia, USA. Writer. m. Rebeca Santos, 1978, 2 sons. *Education:* BA, MA, University of California. *Appointments:* Visiting Writer, University of Texas, 1988-89; Visiting Writer, University of Arizona, 1992-93. *Publications:* Winners on the Pass Line; The Magic Blood; The Last Known Residence of Michey Nuez. *Honours:* James D Phelan Award; Dobie Paisano Fellowship; National Endowment for the arts Creative Writing Fellowship. *Memberships:* Texas Institute of Letters. Address: PO Box 31001, El Paso, TX 79931, USA.

GILBERT Anna, b. 1 May 1916, England. Teacher; Writer. m. Jack Lazarus, 3 Apr 1956. *Education:* BA, Hons, English Language and Literature, 1937, MA 1945, Durham University. *Publications:* Images of Rose, 1973; The Look of Innocence 1975; A Family Likeness 1977; Remembering Louise, 1978; The Leavetaking, 1979; Flowers for Lilian, 1980; Miss Bede is Staying, 1982; The Long Shadow, 1984; A Walk in the Wood, 1989; The Wedding Guest, 1993. *Contributions to:* Good Housekeeping; Woman; BBC Woman's Hour. *Honour:* Romantic Novelists' Major Award 1976 for The Look of Innocence. *Literary Agent:* Watson Little Ltd, 12 Egbert Street, London NW1 8LJ, England.

GILBERT Bentley Brinkerhoff, b. 1924, United States of America. Writer (History). *Publications:* The Evolution of National Insurance in Great Britain, 1966; Britain since 1918, 1967; British Social Policy, 1914-1939, 1971; The Heart of the Empire, 1973; David Lloyd George: A Political Life, vol 1, The Architect of Change, 1987; David Lloyd George: A Political Life, Vol 2; The Organiser of Victory, 1992. *Address:* 830-D Forest Avenue, Evanston, IL 60202, USA.

GILBERT Douglas L, b. 1925, United States of America. Writer, (Agriculture/Forestry, Environmental Science/Ecology, Zoology). *Publications:* Economics, Ecology and Biology of the Black Bear in Colorado, 1953; Forester's Handbook, 1957; A Contribution Toward the Bibliography of the Black Bear (with R Tigner), 1960; Field Wildlife Studies in Colorado, 1961; Public Relations and Communications in Wildlife Management, 1962; Public Relations and Communications in Natural Resource Management, 1964; Field Wildlife Studies in Colorado (with D R Smith), 1967; Proceedings of Third Annual Short Course in Game and Fish Management, 1967; Natural Resources and Public Relations, 1971;

Forestry and Natural Resources Professions, 1973; Big Game Management and Ecology, 1978; Public Relations for Natural Resources Personnel (with J R Fazio), 1981. *Address:* 1205 Ellis Street, Fort Collins, CO 80521, USA.

GILBERT Harriett Sarah, b. 25 Aug 1948, London, England, Writer. *Education:* Diploma, Rose Bruford College of Speech and Drama, 1966-69. *Appointments:* Co-Books Editor, City Limits magazine, 1981-83; Deputy Literary editor, 1983-86, Literary Editor, 1986-88, New Statesman. *Publications:* The Riding Mistress, 1983; Hotels with Empty Rooms, 1973; A Women's History of Sex, 1987; An Offence Against the Persons, 1974; Tide Race, 1977; I Know Where I've Been, 1972; Running Away, 1979. *Contributions to:* Time Out; City Limites; New Statesman; Guardian; BBC; Australian Broadcasting Corporation; Washington Post. *Memberships:* Writers Guild of Great Britain, Ex-chair, Women's Committee. *Literary Agent:* Richard Scott Simon. *Address:* 2 Oaktree Court, Valmar Road, London SE5 9NH, England.

GILBERT Ilsa, b. 27 Apr 1933, Brooklyn, New York, USA. Poet; Playwright; Librettist; Lyricist. *Education:* University of Michigan, 1951-52; BA, Brooklyn College, 1955. *Appointments include:* Editor, copywriter, creative director, various companies, 1955-68; Freelance copywriter, Vantage Press, 1962-79. *Publications include:* Survivors & Other New York Poems, 1985; Pardon the Prisoner, mini-play, 1976; Rooms to Let Live, poems, publication pending. Also: 45 productions, staged readings, various one-act plays, verse plays, musicals, concert pieces for theatre, mainly Off-Off Broadway, New York City. Titles include: A Dialogue Between Didey Warbucks & Mama Vaseline, 1969; The Dead Dentist, 1968; The Bundle Man, 1967; Little Onion Annie, 1971; The Black Carousel, (later called Berlin Blues), 1977; Travellers, 1977; Watering Holes & Garden Paths, 1983; The First Word, 1987; Opera: The Bundle Man, 1993. *Contributions to:* Numerous magazines, countrywide. *Honours include:* Honourable mention, Atlantic Monthly Nationwide College Poetry Contest 1955, Best Subjective Poem published in Poet Lore 1968; Guest poet/playwright, Proscenium, Cable TV, 1973; Writers Colony residencies, Dorset, Vermont, 1982, 1986, 1987; etc. *Memberships:* Pentangle Literary Society; Womens Salon; PEN American Centre; Poets & Writers; Dramatists Guild; Authors League of America. *Literary Agent:* Claudia Menza. *Address:* 203 Bleecker Street, Apt 9, New York, NY10012, USA.

GILBERT Jack, b. 17 Feb 1925, Pittsburgh, Pennsylvania, USA. Writer. *Education:* BA, University of Pittsburgh, 1954; MA, San Francisco State University, 1962. *Literary Appointments:* University of California, Berkeley, 1958-59; Faculty at: San Francisco State, 1962-63, 1965-67, 1971; Syracuse University, 1982-83; University of San Francisco, 1985; Chair of Creative Writing, University of Alabama, Tuscalousa, 1986. Professor at Kyoto University, Tokyo,Japan, 1974-75. *Publications:* Poems: Views of Jeopardy, 1962; Monolithos, 1982; Kochan, 1984. *Contributions to:* The New Yorker; The American Poetry Review; Kenyon; Poetry, Chicago; The Atlantic Monthly; The Nation; Ironwood; The Iowa Review; Encounter, England; The Quarterly. *Honours:* Winner, Yale Younger Poets Award, 1962; Guggenheim Fellowship, 1964; Nominated for the Pulitzer Prize in 1962 and 1982; National Endowment of the Arts Award, 1974; American Poetry Review's first prize, 1983; Stanley Kunitz Prize, 1983. *Address:* 919 Oak Street, New Port Richey, Florida 33552, USA.

GILBERT John Raphael, b. 1926. Writer (Natural History, Travel, Translations). *Publications:* Modern World Book of Animals, 1947; Cats, Cats, Cats, 1961; Famous Jewish Lives, 1970; Myths of Ancient Rome, 1970; Pirates and Buccaneers, 1971, 1975; Highwaymen and Outlaws, 1971; Charting the Vast Pacific, 1971; National Costumes of the World, 1972; World of Wildlife, 1972-74; Miracles of Nature, 1975; Knights of the Crusades, 1978; Vikings, 1978; Prehistoric Man, 1978; Leonardo da Vinci, 1978; La

Scala, 1979; Dinosaurs Discovered, 1980; Macdonald Guide to Trees, 1983; Macdonald Encyclopedia of House Plants, 1986; Theory and Use of Colour, 1986; Macdonald Encyclopedia of Roses, 1987; Gardens of Britain, 1987; Macdonald Encyclopedia of Butterflies and Moths, 1988; Trekking in the USA, 1989; Macdonald Encyclopedia of Orchids, 1989; Macdonald Encyclopedia of Bulbs, 1989; Trekking in Europe, 1990; Macdonald Encyclopedia of Herbs and Spices, 1990; Macdonald Encyclopedia of Bonsai, 1990; Macdonald Encyclopedia of Amphibians and Reptiles, 1990. *Address:* 28 Lyndale Avenue, London, NW2, England.

GILBERT Martin, b. 25 Oct 1936, London, England. Historian; Official Biographer of Sir Winston Churchill, 1968-. *Education:* BA, MA Oxford University, Magdalen, St Antony's & Merton (Fellow 1962-), Colleges, Oxford. *Publications include:* The Appeasers, with Richard Gott, 1963; The European Powers 1900-45, 1966; Historical Atlases on recent History, British and American History & many aspects of Jewish History; Winston S Churchill, volume III 1914-1916, 1971 (2 pt companion Volume 1973), volume IV, 1917-1922, 1975 (3 part companion volume 1977), volume V, 1922-1939, 1976 (3 part companion volume 1979-80), volume VI, 1939-1941, 1983, (Companion volume September 1939 and May 1940, 1993), volume VII, 1941-1945, 1986, volume VIII, 1945-1965, 1988; Exile & Return, The Emergence of Jewish Statehood, 1978; Children's Illustrated Bible Atlas, 1979; Auschwitz & The Allies, 1980; Churchill's Wilderness Years, 1981; The Holocaust Atlas, 1984; Jerusalem, Rebirth of a City, 1985; The Holocaust, the Jewish Tragedy, 1986; Shcharansky, Portrait of a Hero, 1986; Second World War, 1988; Churchill, A Life, 1990; Forthcoming, In Search of Churchill; several publications translated into other languages. *Contributions to:* The Guardian; Sunday Times; Observer; TV Times; Jerusalem Post; New York Review of Books. *Membership:* FRSL. *Literary Agent:* A P Watt. *Address:* Merton College, Oxford University, Oxford, England.

GILBERT Michael, b. 1912. Author; Solicitor. *Publications:* Close Quarters, 1947; They Never Looked Inside, 1948; The Doors Open, 1949; Smallbone Deceased, 1950; Death has Deep Roots, 1951; Death in Captivity, 1952; Fear to Tread, 1953; Sky High, 1955; Be Shot for Sixpence, 1956; The Tichborn Claimant, 1957; Blood and Judgement, 1958; After the Fine Weather, 1963; The Crack in the Teacup, 1965; The Dust and the Heat, 1967; Game Without Rules (stories), 1967; The Etruscan Net, 1969; The Body of a Girl, 1972; The Ninety Second Tiger, 1973; Amateur in Violence (stories), 1973; Flash Point, 1975; The Night of the Twelfth, 1976; Petrella at Q (stories), 1977; The Empty House, 1978; Death of a Favourite Girl (in United States of America as The Killing of Katie Steelstock), 1980; Mr. Calder and Mr. Behrens (stories), 1982; The Final Throw (in United States of America as End-Game), 1982; The Black Seraphim, 1983; The Long Journey Home, 1985; The Oxford Book of Legal Anecdotes, 1986; Trouble, 1987; Paint Gold & Blood, 1989; Anything for a Quiet Life, 1991; Prep School, an anthology, 1991. *Memberships:* Garrick Club; HAC, Crime Writers Association, 1953. *Address:* Luddesdown Old Rectory, Gravesend, Kent, DA13 0XE, England.

GILBERT Robert Andrew, b. 6 Oct 1942, Bristol, England. Antiquarian Bookseller. m. Patricia Kathleen Linnell, 20 June 1970, 3 sons, 2 daughters. *Education:* BA (Hons), Philosophy and Psychology, University of Bristol, 1961-64. *Publications:* The Golden Dawn: Twilight of the Magicians, 1983; A E Waite: Magician of Many Parts, 1987; The Golden Dawn Companion, 1986; A E Waite, a bibliography, 1983; The Treasure of Montsegur (with W N Birks), 1987; The Oxford Book of English Ghost Stories (Editor with M A Cox), 1986; Elements of Mysticism, 1991; Victorian Ghost Stories, an Oxford Anthology, (Editor with M A Cox), 1991; World Freemasonry, an Illustrated History, 1992; Freemasonry: a Celebration of the Craft, 1992; Casting the First Stone, 1993. *Contributions to:* Ars Quatuor Coronatorum; Avallaunius; Christian Parapsychologist; Gnosis; Hermetic Journal; Cauda Pavonis; Yeats

Annual. *Memberships:* Advisor, Arthur Machen Society; Society of Authors; Antiquarian Booksellers Association; Societas Rosicruciana in Anglia (Librarian). *Address:* 4 Julius Road, Bishopston, Bristol BS7 8EU, England.

GILDERSLEEVE Thomas, b. 1927 United States of America. Writer. *Publications:* co-author, System Design for Computer Applications, 1963; Design of Sequential File Systems, 1971; Decision Tables and Their Practical Application in Data Processing, 1971; Data Processing Project Management, 1974; 1985; Successful Data Processing System Analysis, 1978. *Address:* 56 Witch Lane, Rowayton, CT 06853, USA.

GILES Frank Thomas Robertson, b. 31 July 1919. Retired Editor, Writer. m. Lady Katharine Sackville, 29 June 1946, 1 son, 2 daughters. *Education:* Wellington College; Brasenose College, Oxford (Open Scholar in History) MA 1946. *Appointments:* Assistant Correspondent of The Times in Paris1947-50; Chief Correspondent of The Times in Rome, 1950-53; Chief Correspondent of The Times in Paris, 1953-61; Foreign Editor of The Sunday Times 1961-77; Deputy Editor of The Sunday Times, 1967-81; Editor of The Sunday Times, 1981-83. *Publications:* A Prince of Journalists - Life and Times of Henri de Blowitz, 1962; Sundry Times (autobiography), 1986; The Locust Years, story of Fourth French Republic, 1991; 40 Years On (editor), a record of the Anglo-German Königwinter Conferences, 1990. *Contributions to:* DNB, Obituary Notices in The Times, Independent, Sunday Times. Book reviews in various publications. *Honour:* Winner of Franco-British Society's Prize for Contribution to Franco-British Understanding. *Memberships:* Brooks's Club, London; Beefsteak Club, London. *Address:* 42, Blomfield Road, London W9 2PF, England.

GILES Kris. *See:* **NEILSON Helen Berniece.**

GILL Anton, b. 22 Oct 1948, Essex, England. Writer. m. Nicola Susan Browne, 6 Nov 1982. *Education:* Clare College, Cambridge, 1967- 70. *Publications:* The Journey Back From Hell; Berlin to Bucharest; City of the Horizon; City of Dreams; A Dance Between Flames; City of the Dead; An Honourable Defeat. *Honours:* HH Wingate Award. *Literary Agent:* Mark Lucas, PFD Group Limited. *Address:* c/o Mark Lucas, PFD Group Ltd, 5 The Chambers, Chelsea Harbour, SW10 0XF, England.

GILL David (Lawrence William), b. 1934. Poet. *Publications:* Men Without Evenings, 1966; The Pagoda and Other Poems, 1969; Peaches and Apercus, 1974; In the Eye of the Storm, 1976; The Upkeep of the Castle, 1978; One Potato, Two Potato (with Dorothy Clancy), 1985. *Address:* 32 Boyn Hill Road, Maidenhead, Berks, England.

GILL Jerry Henry, b. 7 Feb 1933, Lynden, Washington, USA. College Teacher. m. M Sorri, 3 Sept 1982. *Education:* BA, Westmont College, 1956; MA, University of Washington, 1957; MDiv, New York Theological Seminary, 1960; PhD, Duke University, 1966. *Publications:* Mediated Transcendence, 1989; Post-Modern Epistemology (with M Sorri), 1989; Enduring Questions (with M Rader), 1990; Faith in Dialogue, 1985; On Knowing God, 1981; Wittgenstein and Metaphor, 1980; Essays on Kerkegaard?, 1969; Possibility of Religious Knowledge, 1971; Philosophy Today, Volumes 1, 2, 3, 1968, 1969, 1970. *Contributions to:* Theology Today; Soundings; International Philosophical Quarterly; Mind; Philosophy and Phenomenological Research; Journal of Aesthetics. *Honour:* Danforth Teacher Grant, 1964-66. *Address:* College of St Rose, 432 Western Avenue, Albany, NY 12203, USA.

GILL Stephen Matthew, b. 25 June 1932, Sialkot, Panjab, India. Writer. m. Sarala, 1 son, 2 daughters. *Education:* Panjab University, BA, 1956; Agra University, MA, 1963; University of Ottawa, 1967-70; Oxford University, 1971. *Appointments:* Teacher, India,

Ethiopia, Canada; Editor, Canadaian World Federalist, 1971-73, 1977-79; Editor, Writers Lifeline, 1982-; President, Vesta Publications Ltd, 1974-90. *Publications include:* Simon and the Snow King; The Blessing of A Bird; Tales From Canada for Children Everywhere; English Grammar for Beginners; Six Symbolist, Plays of Yeats; Anti War Poems; Seaway Valley Poets; Poets of the Capital; Songs for Harmony; Shrine of Social Demons; The Flowers of Thirst, Love poems; Life's Vagaries, short stories; The Loyalist City, novel; Immigrant, novel; Scientific Romances of H G Wells, critical study; Discovery of Bangladesh, history; Sketches of India,, illust. essays about India. *Honours:* Ontario Graduate Fellowship; Honorable Doctorate in Literature; Volunteer Service Award; Honorary Life Membership from Texas State Poetry Society, 1991; Pegasus International poetry for Peace Award, 1991; Certificate of Appreciation, Asian Canada Biological Centre, 1992; A Laurel Leaf, 13th World Congress of Poets, 1992; Honorable mention, third place, 53rd Annual International Poetry Contest, 1993. *Memberships:* PEN; World Federalists of Canada. *Address:* PO Box 32, Cornwall, Ontario, Canada K6H 5R9.

GILLEN Lucy. *See:* **STRATTON Rebecca.**

GILLESPIE Robert B, b. 31 Dec 1917, Brooklyn, New York, USA. Writer. m. Marianna Albert, 26 June 1957, (dec), 1 daughter. *Education:* Brooklyn College, 1935-37; St John's Law School, 1937-40, LLB. *Publications:* Murder Mysteries: The Crossword Mystery, 1979; Print-Out, 1983; Heads You Lose, 1985; Empress of Coney Island, 1986; The Hell's Kitchen Connections, 1987; The Last of the Honeywells, 1988; Little Sally Does It Again, 1982; Deathstorm, 1990; Many crossword books. *Contributions to:* St John's Law Review; Discovery 6. *Memberships:* Authors Guild; Mystery Writers of America. *Literary Agent:* Albert Zuckerman, Writers House, New York City. *Address:* 226 Bay Street, Douglaston, NY 11363, USA.

GILLETT Charlie, b. 1942. Writer (Music). *Appointments include:* Production Assistant, BBC-TV, 1971-72; Co-Director, Oval Records, Radio Presenter, 1972-. *Publications:* All In The Game (sport), 1970; The Sound of the City: The Rise of Rock and Roll, 1970, 1983; Rock File, 5 vols, 1972-78; Making Tracks: The Story of Atlantic Records, 1974. *Address:* 11 Liston Road, London, SW4 0DG, England.

GILLETT Margaret, b. 1930, Canada. Author. *Publications:* A History of Education: Thought and Practice, 1966; co-author, The Laurel and the Poppy (novel), 1968; Readings in the History of Education, 1969; co- editor, Foundation Studies in Education: Justifications and New Directions, 1973; Educational Technology: Toward Demystification, 1973; We Walked Very Warily: A History of Women at McGill, 1981; A Fair Shake: Autobiographical Essays by McGill Women, 1984; Dear Grace: A Romance of History, 1986. *Address:* 35 Bruce Street, Westmount, Quebec, H3Y 2E1, Canada.

GILLETTE. *See:* **SHAW Bynum G.**

GILLIATT Penelope, b. London, England. UK Citizen. Author; Film Critic. m. (1) Professor R.W. Gilliatt, (div), (2) John Osborne, 1963, (div), 1 daughter. *Education:* Queen's College, University of London; Bennington College, Vermont, USA; FRSL. *Appointments:* Film Critic, The Observer, 1961-67, Theatre Critic 1965; The New Yorker, Guest Film Critic, 1967, Contracted fiction writer, 1967-, Regular Film Critic, 1968-79. *Publications:* Novels: One by One, 1965; A State of Change, 1968; The Cutting Edge 1979; Mortal Matters, 1983; A Woman of Singular Occupation, 1988; Short Stories: What's It Like Out?, 1968 (Come Back if It Doesn't Get Better, USA, 1967); Nobody's Business, 1972; Penguin Modern Short Stories, 1970; Splendid Lives, 1977; Quotations From Other Lives, 1983; They

Sleep Without Dreaming, 1985; 22 stories, 1986; Lingo, 1990; Plays, Films: Property, 1970; Sunday Bloody Sunday (screenplay), 1971 (reprint with new essay by author 1986); Cliff Dwellers, 1981; Property, 1983; Nobody's Business, 1983; But When All's Said and Done, 1985; TV Plays; Living on the Box, The Flight Fund, 1974; In the Unlikely Event of Emergency, 1979; non-fiction: Unholy Fools; Film and Theatre, 1972; Jean Renoir, Essays, Conversations, Reviews, 1975; Jacques Tati, 1976; Three Quarter Face, 1980; To Wit, 1990; Beach of Aurora, opera libretto commissioned by English National Opera Co., 1973-83; Profiles of Jean Renoir, John Huston, Woody Allen, Jean-Luc Godard, Diane Keaton, John Cleese, Jonathan Miller, Katharine Hepburn and many others. *Honours:* Awards for Fiction, American Academy, National Institute of Arts and Letters 1972; Awards for Screenplay, Sunday Bloody Sunday, Oscar nomination, Best Original Screenplay, Winner Best Original Screenplay. *Memberships include:* Writers Guild of America, Writers Guild of England, National Society of Film Critics (New York), New York Film Critics Society. *Address:* c/o The New Yorker, 25 West 43rd Street, New York, NY 10036, USA.

GILLIE Christopher, b. 1914. Writer. *Publications:* Character in English Literature, 1965; Longman's Companion to English Literature, 1972; Jane Austen: A Preface Book, 1974; English Literature 1900- 1939, 1975; E.M. Forster: A Preface Book,1983. *Address:* Trinity Hall, Cambridge, England.

GILLON Adam, b. 1921. Author; Emeritus Professor. *Appointments:* Professor of English, Head of Department, Acadia University, Nova Scotia, Canada, 1957-62; Faculty Member, 1962-, currently Emeritus Professor of English and Comparative Literature, State University of New York, New Paltz, USA; Editor, Polish Series, Twayne Publishers Inc, 1963- 72; Regional Editor, Conradiana, 1968-72; Editor, Joseph Conrad Today, 1975; Member, Editorial Board, Institute for Textual Studies, Texas Technical University, Lubbock. *Publications:* Joseph Conrad, radio play, 1959; The Bet, radio play, 1969; The Eternal Solitary: A Study of Joseph Conrad, 1960, 2nd Edition, 1966; A Cup of Fury, novel, 1962; Selected Poems and Translations, 1962; Introduction to Modern Polish Literature (editor, translator, contributor), 1964, 2nd Edition, 1982; In the Manner of Haiku: Seven Aspects of Man, 1967, 2nd Edition, 1970; The Dancing Socrates and Other Poems, by Julian Tuwim (editor and translator), 1968; Poems of the Ghetto: A Testament of Lost Men (editor, translator, contributor), 1969; The Solitary, radio play, 1969; Daily New and Old: Poems in the Manner of Haiku, 1971; Strange Mutations: In the Manner of Haiku, 1973; Joseph Conrad: Commemorative Essays (editor), 1975; Summer Morn...Winter Weather: Poems 'Twixt Haiku and Senryu, 1975; Conrad and Shakespeare and Other Essays, 1976; Joseph Conrad, 1982; The Withered Leaf: A Medley of Haiku and Senryu, 1982; The Conspirators, screenplay (co-author), 1985; Jared, novel, 1986; Dark Country, screenplay, 1989; Under Wester Eyes, screenplay, 1989; The Bet , screenplay, 1990; From Russia with Hope, screenplay, 1990; Joseph Conrad: Comparative Essays, 1993. *Memberships:* Polish Institute of Arts and Sciences, 1954; Modern Language Association, 1955; President, Joseph Conrad Society of America, 1975-. *Address:* Lake Illyria, 490 Rt 299 West, New Paltz, NY 12561, USA.

GILMAN Dorothy, (Dorothy Gilman Butters), b. 1923, United States of America. Author; Children's Writer. *Publications:* Novels: The Unexpected Mrs. Pollifax, 1966 (in United Kingdom as Mrs. Pollifax, Spy, 1971); Uncertain Voyage, 1967; The Amazing Mrs. Pollifax, 1970; The Elusive Mrs. Pollifax, 1971; A Palm for Mrs. Pollifax, 1973; A Nun in the Closet, 1975 (in United Kingdom as A Nun in the Cupboard, 1976); The Clairvoyant Countess, 1975; Mrs. Pollifax on Safari, 1977; A New Kind of Country (non-mystery novel), 1978; The Tightrope Walker, 1979; For Children: Enchanted Caravan, 1949; Carnival Gypsy, 1950; Ragamuffin Alley, 1951; The Calico Year, 1953; Four-Party Line, 1954; Papa Dolphin's Table, 1955; Girl in Bucksin, 1956;

Heartbreak Street, 1958; Witch's Silver, 1959; Masquerade, 1961; Ten Leagues to Boston Town, 1962; The Bells of Freedom, 1963; Mrs. Pollifax on the China Station, 1983; The Maze in the Heart of the Castle, 1983; Mrs. Pollifax and the Hongkong Buddha, 1985.

GILMAN George G, (Frank Chandler, David Ford, Terry Harknett, William M James, Charles R Pike, James Russell, William Terry, b. 1936, British, Writer of mystery/crime/suspense, westerns/adventure, travel/exploration/adventure. Freelance writer since 1972. *Appointments:* Copyboy, Reuters, 1952; Clerk, Newspaper Features Ltd, 1952-54; Typist, Reuters, Comtelburo, 1956-57; publicity assistant, 20th-Century Fox, 1957-58; Editor, Newspaper Features Ltd, 1958-61; Reporter and Features Editor, National Newsagent, 1961-72, all London. *Publications include:* Edge series include: Arapaho Revenge, 1983; The Blind Side, 1983; House on the Range, 1983; The Godforsaken, 1982; Edge Meets Steele No 3 Double Action, 1984; The Moving Cage, 1984; School for Slaughter, 1985; Revenge Ride, 1985; Shadow of the Gallows, 1985; A Time for Killing, 1986; Brutal Border, 1986; Hitting Paydirt, 1986; Backshot, 1987; Uneasy Riders. 1987; Adam Steele series includes: Canyon of Death, 1985; High Stakes, 1985; Rough Justice 1985; The Sunset Ride, 1986; The Killing Strain, 1986; The Big Gunfight, 1987; The Hunted 1987; Code of the West, 1987; The Undertaker series includes: Three Graves to a Showdown, 1982; Back from the Dead, 1982; Death in the Desert, 1982. As William Terry: Red Sun (novelization of screenplay), 1972. As Frank Chandler: A Fistful of Dollars (novelization of screenplpay), 1972. As Charles R Pike: Jubal Cade series, The Killing Trail, 1974; Double Cross, 1974; The Hungry Gun, 1975. As William M James: Apache series - The First Death, 1974; Duel to the Death, 1974; Fort Treachery, 1975. As Terry Harknett: The Caribbean, 1972. As James Russell: The Balearic Islands, 1972. As David Ford: Cyprus, 1973; ghostwriter: The Hero by Peter Haining, 1973; The Savage and Doomsday Island, both by Alex Peters, 1979. *Address:* Spring Acre, Springhead Road, Uplyme, Lyme Regis, Dorset DT7 3RS, England.

GILMAN Richard, b. 1925, USA. Professor of Drama. *Appointments:* Professor of Drama, Yale University, New Haven, Connecticut, 1967-. *Publications:* The Confusion of Realms, 1969; Common and Uncommon Masks, 1970; The Making of Modern Drama, 1974; Decadence, 1979; Faith, Sex, Mystery, autobiography, 1987. *Honours:* George Jean Nathan Award for Drama Critism, 1970-71; Morton Dauwen Zable Award, American Academy, 1979. *Memberships:* PEN, New York, President 1981-83, Vice-President 1983-85. *Address:* 329 W 108th Street 5-D, New York, NY 10025, USA.

GILMORE Clarence Percy, b. 8 Feb 1926, Baton Rouge, Louisiana, USA. Writer; Editor. m. (2) Elaine Oliver, 1985. 1 son, 1 daughter, previous marriage. *Education:* Louisiana State University, 1942-44, 1946-48. *Appointments include:* Reporter, various radio, TV stations, 1948-56; Freelance Magazine Writer, 1956-; Science Editor, Metromedia TV, 1974-84; Editor-in-Chief, Times Mirror Magazines, New York City, 1971-; Consultant in Field. *Honours:* Claude Bernard Science Journalism Award, 1969; Howard W. Blakeslee Award, American Heart Association, 1969; Special commendations, Medical Journalism, American Medical Association, 1969, 1970; Science Writing Award, Physics & Astronomy, American Institute of Physics, 1970; Science Writing Award, American Association for Advancement of Science, 1980. *Memberships:* National Association of Science Writers; American Association for Advancement of Science. *Address:* 19725 Creekround Avenue, Baton Rouge, LA 70817, USA.

GILMOUR Robin, b. 17 June 1943, Hamilton, Scotland. Reader. m. Elizabeth Simpson, 29 Dec 1969, 2 sons, 2 daughters. *Education:* Loretto School, 1956-61; St Johns College, Cambridge, MA, 1961-64; Edinburgh University, PhD, 1964-69. *Appointments:* Lecturer, University of Ulster, 1969-73; Lecturer,

University of Aberdeen, 1973; Senior Lecturer, 1984; Reader, 1990. *Publications:* The Idea of the Gentleman in the Victorian Novel; The Novel in the Victorian Age. *Contributions to:* The Gradgrind School, Victorian Studies; Memory in David Copperfield, Dickesian. *Address:* 9 Brighton Place, Aberdeen, AB1 6RT, Scotland.

GILROY Frank D(aniel), b. 13 Oct 1925, New York City, USA. Writer. m. Ruth Dorothy Gaydos, 1954, 3 sons. *Education:* BA, magna Cum laude, Dartmouth College, Hanover, New Hampshire, 1950; Yale University School of Drama, New Haven, Connecticut, 1950-51. Served in United States Army 1943-46. *Publications:* Plays include: Who'll Save the Plowboy?, 1962; The Subject Was Roses, 1964; That Summer - That Fall, 1966; The Only Game in Town, 1969, (all produced in New York); The Next Contestant (produced New York, 1978) New York, French, 1979; Dreams of Glory (produced New York 1979) New York, French, 1980; Last Licks (produced New York, 1979 as The Housekeeper produced Brighton and London, 1982); Real to Reel (produced New York, 1987); Match Point, 1990; A Way With Words, 1919. Screenplays include: The Fastest Gun Alive, 1956; The Gallant Hours (with Bierne Lay), 1960; The Subject Was Roses, 1968; The Only Game in Town, 1969; Desperate Characters, 1971; From Noon till Three, 1976; Once in Paris, 1978; The Gig, 1985; The Luckiest Man in the World, 1989; Television Plays include: Nero Wolfe, from the novel The Doorbell Rang by Rex Stout, 1979; Burke's Law series; plays for US Steel Hour, Omnibus, Kraft Theater, Studio One, Lux Video Theatre and Playhouse 90, 1952-. Novels: Private, New York, Harcourt Brace, 1970; From Noon til Three; The Possibly True and Certainly Tragic Story of an Outlaw and a Lady Whose Love Knew No Bounds, New York, Doubleday, 1973; as For Want of a Horse, London, Coronet, 1975; Little Ego (childrens book with Ruth Gilroy), 1970. *Honours:* Obie Award, 1962; Outer Circle Award, 1964; Pulitzer Prize, 1965; New York Drama Critics Circle Award, 1965; Berlin Film Festival Silver Bear, 1971; D Litt, Dartmouth College, 1966. *Memberships:* Council Member 1964-, President 1969-71, Dramatists Guild, New York. *Address:* c/o Dramatists Guild, 234 West 44th Street, New York, NY 10036, USA.

GILSON Estelle, b. 16 June 1926, New York City, New York, USA. Writer. m. Saul B Gilson, 21 Dec 1950, 2 sons. *Education:* Brooklyn College, AB, 1946; Col,umbia University, MSSW, 1949. *Appointments:* Teacher College of Mt St Vincent Seton seminars. *Publications:* Translations: Poetry of Gabriel Preil; Stories and Recollections of Umberto Saba. *Contributions to:* Columbia Magazine; Present Tense; Congress Monthly. *Honours:* Silver Medal, Best Article of the Year; italo Calvino Award for Translating; PEN American Center Renato Poggioll Award for Translating. *Memberships:* Poets & Writers; National Association of Social Workers; American Society of Journalists & Authors. *Address:* 7 Sigms Place, Bronx, NY 10471, USA.

GINDIN James Jack, b. 23 May 1926, Newark, New Jersey, USA. Professor of English. m. Joan Phyllis Frimel, 14 July 1955. 1 son, 1 daughter. *Education:* BA, Yale University, 1949; MA 1950, PhD 1954, Cornell University. *Literary Appointments:* Checker, New Yorker Magazine, 1954- 55. *Publications:* John Galsworthy's Life and Art, 1987; Postwar British Fiction, 1962; Harvest of A Quiet Eye: The Novel of Compassion, 1971; The English Climate: An Excursion into The Life of John Galsworthy, 1979; William Golding, 1988; British Fiction of the 1930's; The Dispiriting Decade, 1992. *Contributions to:* Frequent articles on 19th and 20th Century Fiction, British and American, journals and magazines. *Honour:* University of Michigan Press Prize for John Galsworthy's Life and Art, 1988. *Membership:* MLA. *Address:* 1615 Shadford Road, Ann Arbor, MI 48104, USA.

GINSBERG Allen, b. 3 June 1926, Newark, New Jersey, USA. Poet; School Director. *Education:* Paterson

High School, New Jersey; BA, Columbia University, 1948; Served inMilitary Sea Transport Srevice. *Career:* Book reviewer, Newsweek, 1950; Market Researcher, New York and San Francisco, 1951-53; Freelance writer; Participant in many poetry readings and demonstrations; Director, Committee on Poetry Foundation, New York, 1971-; Director, Kerouac School of Poetics, Naropa Institute, Boulder, Colorado. *Publications include:* Verse includes: Poems All Over the Place: Mostly Seventies, 1978; Mostly Sitting Haiku, 1978, revised edition 1979; Careless Love: Two Rhymes, 1978; Straight Hearts' Delight: Love Poems and Selected Letters 1947-80 with Peter Orlovsky, edited by Winston Leyland, 1980; Plutonian Ode: Poems 1977-1980, 1982; Collected Poems, 1947-1980, 1984. Recordings: Howl and Other poems, Fantasy-Galaxy, 1959; Kaddish, Atlantic Verbum, 1966; William Blake's Songs of Innocence and Experience Tuned by Allen Ginsberg, 1969; First Blues, Folkways, 1982. Kaddish (produced New York, 1972). *Honours:* Guggenheim Fellowship, 1969; National Endowment for the Arts grant, 1966; American Academy grant, 1969; National Book Award 1974; National Arts Club Gold Medal, 1979; Los Angeles Times Award, 1982. *Membership:* American Academy, 1973. *Address:* PO Box 582, Stuyvesant Station, New York, NY 10009, USA.

GINSBURG Mirra, b. Bobruisk, USSR. Translator; Editor; Author. *Appointments:* Translation Juries, NBA, 1974, ABA, 1982, PEN, 1984. *Publications include:* Editor and Translator: The Fatal Eggs and Other Soviet satire, 1965, 1968, 1987, 1993; The Dragon: Fifteen Stories by Yevgeny Zamyatin, 1966, 5th edition, 1976; A Soviet Heretic Essays by Yevgeny Zamyatin, 1970, 1975, 1992; We, 1972, 1983; Mikhail Bulgakov: Heart of a Dog, 1968, 1982, 1987; Flight and Bliss, two plays, 1985; The Life of Monsieur de Moliere, 1972, 1986, 1988; The Master and Margarita, 1967, 1987; Andrey Platonov: The Foundation Pit, 1975; Yury Tynyanov: Lieutenant Kije and Young Vitushishnikov, 1991, 1992; Children's Books: The Master of the Winds, Folk Tales from Siberia, 1970; The kaha Bird, Tales from Central Asia, 1971; The Lazies, Folk Tales from Russia, 1973; The Twelve Clever Brothers and Other Fools, Tales from Russia, 1979; 25 picture books translated, adapted, written, 1969- 89. *Honours:* National Translation centre Grant, 1967; Lewiss Carroll Shelf Award, 1972; Guggenheim Fellowship, 1975-76; Honour List of Austrian National Award for Books for Children, 1985. *Memberships:* PEN; Dramatists Guild; American Association of Literary Translators; Authors Guild. *Address:* 150 West 96th Street, Apt 9-G, New York, NY 10025, USA.

GINZBERG Eli, b. 1911. American; Writer; Director; Consultant. *Appointments:* Governor, Hebrew University of Jerusalem, 1953-59; Chairman, National Manpower Advisory Committee, 1962-74; Chairman, National Commission for Manpower Policy (since 1978, National Commission for Employment Policy), 1974-81; Emeritus A Barton Hepburn Professor of Economics and Special Lecturer, 1979- (A Barton Hepburn Professor 1967-79); Director, The Eisenhower Center for the Conservation of Human Resources, Columbia University, New York City, 1950-; Consultant to US Departments of State, Defence, Labour, Health, Education and Welfare. *Publications include:* The Middle-Class Negro in the White Man's World, 1967; Manpower Agenda for America, 1968; Men, Money and Medicine, 1969; Urban Health Services: The Case of New York, 1970; Career Guidance, 1971; Manpower for Development Perspectives on Five Continents, 1971; Manpower Advice for Government, 1972; New York Is Very Much Alive, 1973; (ed)Corporate Lib: Women's Challenge to Management, 1973; The Manpower Connection: Education and Work, 1975; The Human Economy, 1976; The Limits of Health Reform: The Search for Realism, 1977; Regionalization and Health Policy, 1977; Health Manpower and Health Policy, 1978; Good Jobs, Bad Jobs, No Jobs, 1979; Employing the Unemployed, 1980; The School-Work Nexus, 1980; Tell Me About Your School, 1980; American Jews: The Building of a Voluntary Community (in Hebrew) 1980; Home Health Care: Its Role in the Changing Service

Market, 1984; The Coming Physician Surplus: In Search of Policy, 1984; Beyond Human Scale: The Large Corporation at Risk, 1985; Local Health Policy in Action, 1985; Technology and Employment, 1986; American Medicine: The Power Shift, 1985; The US Health Care System: A Look to the 1990s (editor), 1985; From Physician Shortage to Patient Shortage: The Uncertain Future of Medical Practice (editor), 1986; From Health Dollars to Health Services: New York City 1965-1985, 1986; Medicine and Society: Clinical Decisions and Societal Values (editor), 1987; Young People at Risk: Is Prevention Possible?, 1988; The Financing of Biomedical Research, 1989; Public & Professional Attitudes Toward AIDS Patients (editor), 1989; The Medical Triangle, 1990; Health Services Research: Key to Health Policy (editor), 1991; The Skeptical Economist, 1987; My Brother's Keeper, 1989; The Eye Illusion, 1993; Health Reform: Dilemmas and Choices, 1993; The Economics of Medical Educationn, 1993. *Address:* 525 Uris, Columbia University, New York, NY 10027, USA.

GIROUX Joye, b. 31 May 1930. Teacher. *Education:* BA, Ctrl. Michigan University, 1952; University of Michigan; Michigan State University; Wayne State University; Ctrl. Michigan University. *Appointments include:* Teacher, South Lake Schools, St Clair Shores, 1954-56, 1962-66; Teacher, Big Rapids Public Schools, 1969-87. *Publications:* A Grain of Sand, No More, 1976; Where Lies the Dream, 1976; Four Women..Getting On With It, with others, 1977; The Whispering of Leaves, 1978; Draw Me a Morning or Two, 1978; Dust I Cannot Hold, 1978; Whispers Lost in Thunder, 1980; Survivor, 1981; And Who's To Pay Your Passage, 1984; Sunlight I Cannot Capture, 1987. *Contributions to:* Various anthologies including: Poetry of Our Time; Notable American Poets; The Lark and the Dawn; Journal of Contemporary Poets; Forty Salutes to Michigan Poets; American Poetry Fellowship Society Bi-Centennial Anthology; Convergence 1980; Golden Song, 1985; Ezra Pound Memorial Anthology, 1985; Access to Literature (a college literature text), 1981. Poetry in various journals including: Bardic Echoes; Peninsula Poets; Driftwood E; Gusto; Woods Runner; Adventures in Poetry; American Poet; Jeans's Journal; Wayside Quarterly; Wayside Poetry Quarterly; Wayside Poetry Forum; Kansas Quarterly. *Honour:* 1st Prize, NFSPS Massachusetts Contest, 1989. *Memberships:* President 1980-84, Poetry Society of Michigan; North Carolina Poetry Society. *Address:* 3408 Oak Trail Drive, Clayton, NC 27520, USA.

GJERTSEN Derek, b. 13 Oct 1933, Grimsby, England. University Lecturer. m. 26 June 1967, 1 son, 2 daughters. *Education:* Leeds University, 1955-58; Queens College, Oxford, 1958-60. *Publications:* The Classics of Science; The Newton Handbook; Science and Philosophy. *Address:* 1 Ash Grove, Formby, Mereyside L37 2DT, England.

GLADSTONE Arthur M, b. 22 Sept 1921, New York, USA. Writer. m. Helen Worth, Andover, New Jersey, 1980. *Education:* BA, Chemistry; MS, Chemistry, New York University. *Publications include:* The Honourable Miss Clarendon, 1975; The Poor Relation, 1978; My Lord Rakehell, 1977; Bow Street Gentleman, 1977; Bow Street Brangle, 1977; The Young Lady from Alton-St-Pancras, 1977; Miss Letty, 1977; That Savage Yankee Squire!, 1978; Lord Dedringham's Divorce, 1978; The Honourable Miss Clarendon, 1978; The Courtship of Colonel Crowne, 1978; The Awakening of Lord Dalby, 1979; Dilemma in Duet, 1980; Byway to Love, 1980; Meg Miller, 1981; Lord Orlando's Protegee, 1981; The Plight of Pamela Pollworth, 1982; Dilemma in Duet, 1982; Byway to Love, 1982; A Keeper for Lord Linford, 1982. *Memberships:* Authors League; Virginia Writers Club; Entomological Society of America. *Address:* 1701 Owensville Road, Charlottesville, VA 22901, USA.

GLAISTER Lesley Gillian, b. 4 Oct 1956, Wellinborough, Northamptonshire, England. Writer. 3 sons. *Education:* University of Sheffield, MA. *Publications:* Honour Thy Father; Trick or Treat; Digging to Australia. *Honours:* Somerset Maucham award; Betty Trask Award. *Address:* 80 Wayland Road, Sheffield, S11 8YE, England.

GLANTZ Kalman, b. 13 Oct 1937, NYC, USA. Psychotherapist. m. Lorraine Fine, 13 Apr 1986, 1 son. *Education:* Hebrew University, BA, 1955-58; La Sorbonne, Paris, 1958-62; Union Institute, PhD, 1985-87. *Publications:* Exiles from Eden; Staying Human in the organisation. *Contributions to:* Journal of Sex and Marital Therapy; American Journal of Psychotherapy; The Psychotherapy Bulletin; Contributions to Three Books; Several Book Reviews. *Memberships:* American Psychological Association. *Literary Agent:* Candice Fuhrman. *Address:* 49 Granite Street, Cambridge, MA 02139, USA.

GLANVILLE Brian Lester, Author, Journalist. m. Elizabeth Pamela De Boer, 19 Mar 1959, 2 sons 2 daughters. *Education:* Charterhouse, England, 1958-62. *Appointments:* Literary Adviser to the Bodley Head, 1958-62. *Publications include:* The Relucant Dictator, 1952; Henry Sows the Wind, 1954; Along the Arno, 1956; The Bankrupts, 1958; After Rome Africa, 1959; A Bad Streak, 1961; Diamond, 1962; The Director's Wife 1963; The King of Hackney Marshes, 1965; The Olmypian, 1969; A Cry of Crickets, 1970; The Thing He Loves, 1973; The Catacomb, 1988. *Contributions to:* Sunday Times (as football correspondent and sports columnist), 1958-; New Statesman; Spectator and others. *Honour:* Thomas Y. Coward Award, New York, 1969. *Address:* 160 Holland Park Avenue, London W11 4UH, England.

GLASKIN G(erald) M(arcus), (Neville Jackson), b. 1923, Australian. Writer. *Appointments:* Partner, Lyall & Evatt, Stockbrokers, Singapore, 1951-59. President Fellowship of Australian Writers in Western Australia, 1968-69. *Publications:* A World of Our Town, 1955; A Minor Portrait, 1957; A Change of Mind, 1959; A Lion in the Sun, 1960; A Waltz Through the Hills, 1961; The Land That Sleeps, 1961; The Beach of Passionate Love, 1961; A Small Selection, 1962; Flight to Landfall, 1963; O Love, O Loneliness, 1964; No End to the Way (as Neville Jackson), 1965; The Man Who Didn't Count, 1965; Turn on the Heat, (play), 1967; The Road to Nowhere, 1967; A Bird in My Hands, 1967; Windows of the Mind, 1974; Two Women: Turn on the Heat and The Eaves of Night, 1975; Worlds Within, 1976; A Door to Eternity, 1979; One Way to Wonderland, 1984.

GLAZE Andrew, b. 1920, USA. Writer. *Appointments:* Press Officer, British Tourist Authority, New York City, 1958-82. *Publications:* Lines, 1964; Damned Ugly Children, 1966; Miss Pete, play, 1966; Kleinholf Demonstrates Tonight, play, 1971; Masque of Surgery, 1974; The Trash Dragon of Shensi, 1978; I Am the Jefferson County Courthouse, 1980; A City, 1982; Uneasy Lies, (play), 1983; Earth That Sings: The Poetry of Andrew Glaze, 1985. *Address:* 803 Ninth Avenue, New York, NY 10019, USA.

GLAZEBROOK Philip Kirkland, b. 3 Apr 1937, London, England. Writer. m. Clare Rosemary Gemmell, 5 Oct 1968, 2 sons, 2 daughters. *Education:* MA, Trinity College, Cambridge. *Publications:* Try Pleasure, 1968; The Eye of the Beholder, 1975; Byzantine Honeymoon, 1978; Journey to Kars, 1985; Captain Vinegar's Commission, 1988; The Walled Garden, 1989; The Gate at the End of the World, 1989; Journey to Khiva, 1992. *Contributions to:* The Spectator; Sunday Times; New York Times; Washington Post; Daily Telegraph. *Literary Agent:* Richard Scott Simon. *Address:* Strode Manor, Bridport, Dorset, England.

GLEASNER Diana, b. 26 Apr 1936, New Brunswick, New Jersey, USA. Writer. m. G William Gleasner, 12 July 1958, 1 son, 1 daughter. *Education:* BA, cum laude, Ohio Wesleyan University, 1958; MA, University of Buffalo (now State University of New York at Buffalo), 1964. *Publications:* The Plaid Mouse, 1966; Pete Polar Bear's Trip Down the Erie Canal, 1970; Women in Swimming, 1975; Women in Track and Field, 1977; Hawaiian Gardens, 1978; Kauai Traveler's Guide, 1978; Oahu Traveler's Guide, 1978; Big Island Traveler's Guide, 1978; Maui Traveler's Guide, 1978; Breakthrough: Women in Writing, 1980; Illustrated Dictionary of Surfing, Swimming and Diving, 1980; Sea Islands of the South, 1980; Rock Climbing, 1980; Callaway Gardens, 1981; Inventions that Changed Our Lives: Dynamite, 1982; Inventions That Changed Our Lives: The Movies, 1983; Breakthrough: Women in Science, 1983; Charlotte: A Touch of Gold, 1983; Woodloch Pines-An American Dream, 1984; Windsurfing, 1985; Lake Norman-Our Inland Sea, 1986; Florida Off The Beaten Path, 1986; Governor's Island-From the Beginning, 1988; RVing America's Backroads-Florida, 1989; Touring by Bus at Home and Abroad, 1989. *Contributions to:* Numerous magazines and newspapers. *Memberships:* American Society of Journalists and Authors; Society of American Travel Writers; Travel Journalists Guild. *Address:* 7994 Holly Court, Denver, NC 28037, USA.

GLECKNER Robert F(rancis), b. 1925, USA. Professor of English. *Appointments:* Instructor in English, Johns Hopkins University, Baltimore, Maryland, 1949-51; Editor, Research Studies Institute, Maxwell Air Force Base, Alabama, 1951-52; Instructor in English: University of Cincinnati, Ohio, 1952-54; University of Wisconsin, Madison, 1954-57; Assistant Professor and Associate Professor of English, Wayne State University, Detroit, Michigan, 1957-62; Professor of English, 1962-78, Chairman, Department of English, 1962-66, Associate Dean, College of Letters and Science, 1966-68, Dean, College of Humanities, 1968-75, University of California, Riverside; Advisory Editor: Criticism, 1962-; , Blake Studies, 1970-; Studies in Romanticism, 1977-; Professor of English, 1978-, Acting Chairman of Department, 1983, Duke University, Durham, North Carolina; Advisory Editor, Romanticism Past and Present, (now Nineteenth-Century Contexts), 1980-; The Byron Journal, 1990. *Publications:* The Piper and the Bard: A Study of William Blake, 1957; Romanticism: Points of View (edited with G E Enscoe), 1962, Revised Edition (sole editor), 1970, 3rd Edition, 1975; Selected Writings of William Blake (editor), 1967, 2nd Edition, 1970; Byron and the Ruins of Paradise, 1967, 2nd Edition, 1982; Complete Poetical Works of Lord Byron (editor), 1975; Blake's Prelude: Poetical Sketches, 1982; Blake and Spenser, 1985; Approaches to the Teaching of Blake's Songs, 1989; Critical Essays on Lord Byron (editor), 1991. *Honours:* Poetry Society of America Award, for The Piper and the Bard, 1957; Elected, Faculty Research Lecturer, University of California, Riverside, 1973; Keats-Shelley Association of America Distinguished Scholar Award, 1991; Mellon Research Fellowship, Huntington Library, San Marino, California, 1987, 1991. *Memberships:* The Byron Society; Keats-Shelley Association of America. *Address:* English Department, Duke University, Durham, NC 27708, USA.

GLEN Duncan Munro, (Simon Foster, Ronald Eadie Munro), b. 11 Jan 1933, Lanarkshire, Scotland. Retired Professor; Writer. m. Margaret Eadie, 4 Jan 1958, 1 son, 1 daughter. *Publications:* Hugh MacDiarmid and the Scottish Renaissance, 1964; Editor, Selected Essays of Hugh MacDiarmid, 1969; In Appearances: A Sequence of Poems, 1971; The Individual and the Twentieth Century Scottish Literary Tradition, 1971; Mr & Mrs J L Stoddard at Home, poems, 1975; Buits and Wellies : A Sequence of Poems, 1976; Gaitherings, poems, 1977; Realities, poems, 1980; On Midsummer Even in Merriest of Nights?, 1981; The Turn of the Earth: Sequence of Poems, 1985; The Autobiography of a Poet, 1986; Tales to Be Told, 1987; (Ed) European Poetry in Scotland, 1990; Poetry of the Scots, 1991; Selected Poems, 1965-1990, 1991; Hugh MacDiamed: Out of Langholm and Into the World, 1992. *Contributions to:* Numerous journals and magazines. *Honours:* Special Prize, Services to Scottish Literature, Scottish Arts Council, 1975. *Membership:* Fellow, Chartered Society of Designers. *Address:* 18 Warrender Park Terrace, Edinburgh EH9 1EF, Scotland.

GLENDINNING Victoria, b. 23 Apr 1937, Sheffield, England. Author; Journalist. m. (1) O.N.V. Glendinning, 1958, 4 sons, (2) Terence de Vere White, 1981. *Education:* BA, Honours, Modern Languages, Somerville College, Oxford, 1959; Diploma, Social Administration, 1969. *Appointments:* Editorial Assistant, Times Literary Supplement, 1970-74. *Publications:* A Suppressed Cry, Life & Death of a Quaker Daughter, 1969; Elizabeth Bowen : Portrait of a Writer, 1977; Edith Sitwell : A Unicorn Among Lions, 1981; Vita : the Life of V. Sackville West, 1983; Rebecca West: A Life, 1987; The Grown-ups, 1989; Hertfordshire, 1989. *Contributions to:* various journals, newspapers & magazines. *Honours:* Duff Cooper Memorial Award & James Tait Black Prize, for Edith Sitwell, 1981; Whitbread Award, for Vita, 1983; Whitbread Award, Trollope, 1992. *Memberships:* Fellow, Royal Society of Literature; PEN. *Literary Agent:* David Higham Associates. *Address:* c/o David Higham Associates, 5/8 Lower John Street, Golden Square, London W1, England.

GLENDOWLER Rose. *See:* **HARRIS Marion Rose.**

GLOAG Julian, b. 2 July 1930, London, England. Novelist. 1 son, 1 daughter. *Education:* Exhibition, BA, 1953, MA 1959, Magdalene College, Cambridge. *Publications:* Our Mother's House, 1963; A Sentence of Life, 1966; Maundy, 1969; A Woman of Character, 1973; Sleeping Dogs Lie, 1980; Lost and Found, 1981; Blood for Blood, 1985; Only Yesterday, 1986; Love as a Foreign Language, 1991; Forthcoming: Ultimate Help. Teleplays: Only Yesterday, 1986; The Dark Room, 1988. *Memberships:* Fellow, Royal Society of Literature; Authors Guild. *Literary Agent:* Georges Borchardt Inc., New York, USA; MBA, London; Michelle Lapautre, Paris. *Address:* c/o Michelle Lapautre, 6 rue Jean Carriès, 75007, Paris, France.

GLOVACH Linda R, b. 24 June 1947, Rockville Centre, Long Island, New York, USA. Author; Illustrator; Fine Artist. *Education:* Farmingdale University, Long Island, 1965-66; College of Design, Los Angeles Art Centre, 1966-67; Art Students League, New York City, 1968-71. *Publications include:* Hey, Wait for Me, I'm Amelia, 1971; The Cat & the Collector, 1972; The Little Witch's Black Magic Cookbook, 1972; The Little Witch's Disguise Book, 1972; Let's Make a Deal, 1975; The Little Witch's Christmas Book, 1975; The Little Witch's Halloween Book, 1975; The Little Witch's Birthday Book, 1982; The Little Spring Holiday Book, 1983; The Little Witch's Cat Book, 1985; The Little Witch's Dinosaur Book, 1985; The Little Witch's Toy Book, 1986; The Little Witch's Summertime Book, 1987. *Contributions to:* Cricket Magazine. *Memberships:* Authors Guild; Society of Illustrators, NYC; Humane Society of the US. *Literary Agent:* Barbara Lucas, Lucas & Evans, New York City. *Address:* 233 8th Avenue, Sea Cliff, Long Island, NY 11759, USA.

GLOVER Judith, b. 31 Mar 1943, Wolverhampton, England. Author 2 daughters. *Education:* Wolverhampton High School for Girls, 1954-59; Aston Polytechnic 1960. *Publications:* Drink Your Own Garden (non-fiction) 1979; The Sussex Quartet: The Stallion Man, 1982, Sisters and Brothers, 1984, To Everything a Season, 1986 and Birds in a Gilded Cage, 1987; The Imagination of the Heart, 1989; Tiger Lilies, 1991; Mirabelle, 1992. *Literary Agent:* Artellus. *Address:* c/o Artellus Ltd, 30 Dorset House, Gloucester Place, London NW1 5AD, England.

GLÜCK Louise, b. 22 Apr 1943, New York, USA, Author; Poet. m. John Dranow, 1 Jan 1977, 1 son. *Education:* Attended, Sarah Lawrence College; Columbia University. *Publications:* Firstborn, 1968, 1981; The House on Marshland, 1975; Descending Figure, 1980; The Triumph of Archilles, 1985; Ararat, 1990; The Wild Iris, 1992. *Honours:* NEA Fellowship, 1969-70, 1979-80, 1988-89; Guggenheim Fellowship, 1975-76, 1987-88; American Academy iof Arts and Letters Award in Literature, 1981; National Book Critics Circle Award, 1985; Melville Cane Award, 1985; Sara Teasdale Memorial Prize, 1986; Phi Beta Kappa Poet, Harvard Commencement, 1990; Bobbitt National Prize for Poetry, 1992; W M Carlos Williams Award, 1993. *Address:* Creamery Road, Plainfield, NJ 05667, USA.

GLUT Don(ald) F, (Johnny Jason, Mick Rogers), b. 1944, USA. Author. *Appointments:* Musician/Singer, Actor, Bookstore Clerk, Assistant Copywriter, 1965-71; Contributing Editor, Castle of Frankenstein, 1969-71; Associate Editor, Monsters of the Movies magazine, Marvel Comic Group, 1974-; Creator, many comic strip characters including Tragg, Simbar, Dagar, Durak, Dr Spektor and Baron Tibor. *Publications:* Frankenstein Lives Again, novels, 1971; Terror of Frankenstein, and sequels, 1971; The Great Movie Serials: Their Sound and Fury (with Jim Harmon), 1972; True Vampires of History, 1972; The Dinosaur Dictionary, 1972, Revised Edition The New Dinosaur Dictionary, 1982; The Frankenstein Legend: A Tribute to Mary Shelley and Boris Karloff, 1973; The Comic-Book Book (contributor), 1973; Bugged, science fiction, 1974; The Dracula Book, 1974; Spawn, novel, 1976; Classic Movie Monsters, 1978; The Empire Strikes Back, novel, 1980; The Dinosaur Scrapbook, 1980; Dinosaurs, Mammoths, and Cavemen: The Art of Charles R Knight (with Sylvia Massey), 1982; The Frankenstein Catalog, 1984. *Address).* 2805 Keystone Street, Burbank, CA 91504, USA.

GLUYAS Constance, b. 1920, United Kingdom. Author. *Publications:* The King's Brat, 1972; Born to Be King, 1974; My Lady Benbrook, 1975; Brief Is the Glory, 1975; The House on Twyford Street, 1976; My Lord Foxe, 1976; Savage Eden, 1976; Rogue's Mistress, 1977; Woman of Fury, 1978; Flame of the South, 1979; Madame Tudor, 1979; Lord Sin, 1980; The Passionate Savage, 1980; The Bridge to Yesterday, 1981; Brandy Kane, 1985. *Address:* c/o Teresa Kralik, New American Library, 1633 Broadway, New York, NY 10019, USA.

GLYN JONES Kenneth, b. 13 Nov 1915, New Tredegar, Wales. Air Navigator. m. Brenda Margaret Thomas, 8 June 1969. *Education:* RAF Staff Navigation School, 1944; Civil Aviation Flight Navigator's Licence, 1946. *Publications:* 2 Science Survey Broadcasts on BBC, 1950; Messier's Nebulae and Star Clusters, 1968; The Search for the Nebulae, 1975; The Webb Society Deep Sky Observer's Handbook (Editor), 7 volumes, 1979-87. *Contributions to:* The Aeroplane; Sky and Telescope; British Astronomical Association Journal; Journal for the History of Astronomy. *Memberships:* Fellow, Royal Astronomical Society, 1969-; President, The Webb Society, 1967-. *Address:* Wild Rose, Church Road, Winkfield, Windsor, Berkshire SL4 4SF, England.

GLYNN Jenifer Muriel, b. 5 Nov 1929, London, England. m. Ian Michael Glynn, 9 Dec 1958, 1 son, 2 daughters. *Education:* St Pauls Girls School, 1941-48; Newnham College, Cambridge, BA, 1948-51. *Publications:* Prince of Publishers. *Address:* Daylesford, Conduit Head Road, Cambridge CB3 0EY, England.

GODARD Barbara, b. 24 Dec 1941, Toronto, Canada. Professor; Translator; Critic; Editor. 1 son. *Education:* BA, University of Toronto, 1964; MA, University de Montreal, 1967; Doct. University de Bordeaux, 1971. *Appointments:* Lecturer, University de Montreal, 1964-67; University de Paris, 1968-70; Assistant Professor, York University, 1971; Associate Proffesor, 1981-. *Publications:* Talking about Ourselves; Bibliography of Feminist Criticism; Audrey Thomas: Her Life and Work; Gynocritics/Gynocritiques. *Contributions to:* (Ed) Tessera; Open Letter. *Honour:* Gabrielle Roy Prize. *Memberships:* PEN International; Association of Canadian plus Quebec Literatures; Association Canadian University Professors of English. *Address:* English Department, York University, 4700 Keele Street, North York, Ontario, Canada M3J 1P3.

GODBER John (Harry), b. 15 May 1956, Upton, Yorkshire, England. Writer. *Education:* Minsthorpe High

School, South Elmsall, Yorkshire; Bretton Hall College, West Bretton, Yorkshire, 1974-78; Certificate of Education, 1977, BEd (honours) 1978; MA, Theatre Leeds University, 1979; Graduate Studies 1979-83. *Appointments:* Teacher, Minsthorpe High School, 1981-83; Artistic Director, Hull truck theatre company, 1984-. *Publications:* Plays include: A Clockwork Orange, adaptation of the novel by Anthony Burgess (produced Edinburgh 1980, London 1984); Cry Wolf (produced Rotherham, Yorkshire, 1981); Blood, Sweat and Tears (produced Hull and London 1986); The Ritz (televised 1987; as Putting on the Ritz, produced Leicester 1987); Teechers (produced Edinburgh and London 1987. Television plays: series scripts for Grange Hill 1981-83, Brookside 1983-84 and Crown Court 1983; The Rainbow Coloured Disco Dancer, from work by C P Taylor, 1984; The Ritz series, 1987; The Continental, 1987. Director of all his own plays; Imagine by Stephen Jeffreys, Hedda Gabler by Ibsen and The Dock by Phil Woods, Hull, 1987. *Honours:* Edinburgh Festival Award 1981, 1982, 1984; Olivier Award, 1984; Los Angeles Drama Critics Circle Award, 1986. *Address:* Hull Truck, Spring Street Theatre, Spring Street, Hull, Yorkshire HU2 8RW, England.

GODDARD Hazel Idella Firth, b. 12 Dec 1911, Jordan Ferry, Novia Scotia, Canada. School Teacher; Secretary; Nurse/Aid. m. Roland Bernard N Goddard, 8 July 1930, 1 son. *Education:* Business School, Canada. *Publications:* Prisms in Print, 1966; Hazel Bough, 1972; Chestnuts and Autumn Leaves, 1980; Scattered Stars, 1984; My Loyalist Years. *Contributions To:* Canadian Poets and Friends; Amber; Marsh and Magpie; Harbour Lights; Prophetic Voices; Our World's Best Beloved Poems; The Poet; Parnassus; Quickenings; Poet's Study Club; Haiku Column in Mainichi Daily News, Tokyo, Japan; White Wall Review . *Honours:* 6 Honourable Mentions, World of Poetry and Golden Poet Award; Honourable Mention, Kentucky State Contest, 1985; 1st Prize, Golden Poet Award; 1st Prize, Haiku and 2nd Prize Sonnet, International Poetry Contest, Canadian Authors Association, 1985; 3rd place, 1986, Writer's Digest, 7th place, 1987, with Poetry, 2nd prize for Triolet, 1988, World Order of Narrative Poets, 2nd finalist & sold haiku to Midwest Poetry Review, 4th prize World of Poetry, 1987. Published in Channels, Carrousal, & Psychopoetica, Dept. Psychology, University of Hull, England. Also in Back Home In Kentucky, Voices International; 55 out of 100 list, Writer's Digest, 1989; 7 Awards, Kentucky State Annual Poetry Contest; Honorable Mention, National Library of Poetry, USA; 3 Honorable Mentions, National Federation of State Poetry, USA; 2 Honorable Mentions, Chapparral Poetry Society, California, USA. *Memberships:* Canadian Authors Association; Scotian Pen Guild, President, Editor; Canadian Authors Association, N.S. Poetry Society; Poet's Study Club, Terre Haute, Indiana, USA; Contributing member to Academy of American Poets; Kentucky State Poetry Society, Poetry Society of Tennessee, CHANNELS (Christian League of America). *Address:* 404 40 Rose Street, Dartmouth, Nova Scotia, Canada B3A 2T6.

GODDEN (Margaret) Rumer, b. 1907. British, Novels/Short stories, Children's fiction, Poetry, Autobiography/Memoirs/Personal, Documentaries/Reportage, Translations. *Publications include:* The Greengage Summer (novel) 1958; Candy Floss (juvenile) 1960; Miss Happiness and Miss Flower (juvenile) 1961; China Court: The Hours of a Country House (novel) 1961; St Jerome and the Lion (juvenile poetry), 1961; (translation) Prayers from the Ark (poetry), by Carmen de Gasztold, 1962; Little Plum (juvenile) 1963; The Battle of the Villa Fiorita (novel) 1963; Home is the Sailor (juvenile) 1964; (trans) The Creatures' Choir (poetry) by Carmen de Gasztold, 1965, in US as The Beasts' Choir, 1967; (with Jon Godden), Two under the Indian Sun (autobiography), 1966; (ed) Round the Day, Round the Year, The World Around: Poetry Programmes for Classroom or Library, 6 vols, 1966-67; Swans and Turtles: Stories (in US as Gone: A Thread of Stories) 1968; (ed) A Letter to the World: Poems for Young Readers by Emily Dickinson, 1968; (ed) Mrs Manders' Cookbook by Olga Manders, 1968; The Kitchen Madonna (juvenile) 1969; Operation Sippack (juvenile) 1969; In This House of Brede (novel) 1969; (ed) The Raphael Bible, 1970; The Tale of Tales: The Beatrix Potter Ballet, 1971; (with Jon Godden) Shiva's Pigeons: An Experience of India (autobiography) 1972; The Old Woman Who Lived in a Vinegar Bottle (juvenile) 1972; The Diddakoi (juvenile) 1972; Mr McFadden's Hallowe'en (juvenile), 1975; The Peacock Spring (novel) 1975; The Rocking Horse Secret (juvenile), 1977; The Butterfly Lions: The Story of the Pekingese in History, Legend and Art, 1977; A Kindle of Kittens (juvenile) 1978; Five for Sorrow, Ten for Joy, (novel) 1979; Gulbadan: Portrait of a Rose Princess at the Mughal Court, 1981; The Dragon of Og (juvenile) 1981; The Dark Horse (novel) 1981; Thursday's Children, 1984; A House With Four Rooms, 1989; Caromandel Sea Change, 1991; Listen to the Nightingale (juvenile) 1992. *Address:* Ardnacloich, Moniaive, Thornhill Dumfriesshire D63 4HZ, Scotland.

GODFREY Ellen Rachel, b. 15 Sept 1942, Chicago, Illinois, USA. Company President; Author. m. William David Godfrey, 25 Aug 1963, 1 son, 1 daughter. *Publications:* Georgia Disappeared; Murder Behind Locked Doors; By Reason of Doubt; Murder Among the Well to Do; the Case of the Cold Murderer; Common or Garden Murderer. *Honours:* Special Award; Edgar Allan poe Award. *Memberships:* Canadian Crime Writers Association; Women in Crime association; BC Trade Development Corporation; Vancouver Island Advanced Technology centre; The University of Victoria Coop Council; The Premier Advisory Council on Science & Technology. *Literary Agent:* Lucinda Vardey Agency, Toronto, Canada. *Address:* 4252 Commerce Circle, Victoria, British Columbia, Canada V8Z 4M2.

GODFREY John M, b. 7 July 1945, Massena, New York, USA. Poet. *Education:* AB, Princeton University, 1967. *Publications:* Dabble: Poems 1966-1980, 1982; Where the Weather Suits My Clothes, 1984; Midnight on Your Left (The Figures), 1988; 26 Poems (Adventures in Poetry), 1971; Three Poems (Bouwerie Editions), 1973; Music of the Curbs (Adventures in Poetry), 1976. *Contributions to:* Mother; Paris Review; United Artists; MagCity; Big Sky; ZZZZZ; The World; Oink!; Broadway: An Anthology of Poets and Painters. *Honours:* Poetry Fellow of the General Electric Foundation/Coordinating Council of Literary Magazines, 1984. *Address:* 437 E 12th Street, Apt 32, New York, NY 10009, USA.

GODFREY Martyn N, b. 17 Apr 1949, Birmingham, England. immigrated to Canada, naturalized citizen. Writer. m. Carolyn Boswell, 1973 (div 1985), 2 children. *Education:* BA, Hons, 1973, BEd 1974, University of Toronto. *Appointments:* Teacher, elementary schools in Kitchener and Waterloo, Ontario, 1974-77, Mississauga, Ontario, 1977-80 and Assumption, Alberta, 1980-82; junior high school teacher in Edson, Alberta 1983-85; Writer 1985-. *Publications include:* For Children: The Last War 1986; It Isn't Easy Being Ms Teeny-Wonderful, 1987; Wild Night, 1987; More Than Weird, 1987; Rebel Yell, 1987; It Seemed Like a Good Idea at the Time, 1987; Baseball Crazy, 1987; Sweat Hog, 1988; Send In Ms Teeny-Wonderful, 1988; In the Time of the Monsters, 1988. *Honours:* Award for Best Children's Short Story from Canadian Authors Association, 1985 and Award for Best Children's book from University of Lethbridge, 1987, both for Here She Is, Ms Teeny-Wonderful. *Memberships:* Writers Union of Canada; Canadian Authors Association; Canadian Society of Children's Authors, Illustrators and Performers; Writers Guild of Alberta, Vice-President, 1986, President 1987. *Literary Agent:* Joanne Killock. *Address:* c/o Killock & Associates, 11017-80 Avenue, Edmonton, Alberta, Canada T66 OR2.

GODFREY Peter, b. 8 Sept 1917. Journalist; Author. m. Naomi Cowan, 3 July 1941, 2 sons. *Education:* BA, Witwaterand University; University of South Africa. *Appointments:* Professional journalist, 1933; Editor, Drum, London, 1962; London Times, 1970; Freelance Writer, 1980. *Publications:* Death Under the Table; Four

O'Clock Noon; Various Radio, TV Stage Scripts; Over 2000 Short Stories & Articles. *Contributions to:* The Criminologist. *Honours:* Ellery Queen Short Story Awards. *Memberships:* Crime Writers Association; Mystery Writers of America; NUJ. *Address:* 3 Ribblesdale, Roman Road, Dorking, Surrey RH4 3EX, England.

GODKIN Celia Marilyn, b. 15 Apr 1948, London, England. Teacher; Illustrator; Childrens Author; Biologist. *Education:* BSc, London University, 1969; MSc, University of Toronto, 1983; AOCA, Ontario College of Art, 1983. *Publications:* Wolf Island; Ladybug Garden. *Contributions to:* Bulletin of Marine Science; Canadian Journal of Fisheries and Aquatic Science; Environmental Biology of Fishes; Guild of Natural Science Illustrators Newsletter. *Honours:* Best Information Book Award. *Memberships:* Guild of Natural Science Illutrators. *Address:* Division of Biomedical Communications, University of Toronto, 256 McCaul Street, Toronto, Ontario, Canada M5T 1W5.

GODMAN Arthur, b. 10 Oct 1916, Educationalist, m. Jean Barr Morton, 24 June 1950, 2 sons, 1 daughter. *Education:* BSc, 1937, BSc, 1938, Honours, Chemistry, University College, London, England; Dip Ed, Institute of Education, London, 1939; Malay Government Exam Standards, 1948. *Appointments:* Colonial Education Service, 1946-63; Educational Consultant, Longman Group, 1966-77; Honorary Fellow, University of Kent, 1978-; Research Fellow, Department of SE Asian Studies, 1978-. *Publications:* Dictionary of Scientific Usuage, (Co-author E M F Payne), 1979; Illustrated Science Dictionary, 1981; Illustrated Dictionary of Chemistry, 1981; Illustrated Thesaurus of Computer Sciences, 1984; Health Science for the Tropics, 1962; Chemistry: ANEW Certificate Approach, (Co-author S T Bajah), 1969; Human and Social Biology, 1973; Energy Supply, 1990. *Contributions to:* Babel, 1990; paper read at SOAS, 1988. *Memberships:* Society of Authors; Royal Society of Chemistry, C Chem; Royal Asiatic Society. *Address:* Sondes House, Patrixbourne, Canterbury, Kent CT4 5DD, England.

GODWIN Peter Christopher, b. 4 Dec 1957, Zimbabwe. Journalist. *Education:* MA, Cambridge University. *Literary Appointments:* East European Correspondent, 1984-86, Africa Correspondent, 1986-, Sunday Times. *Publications:* Articles on Africa especially South Africa and Eastern Europe. *Contributions to:* Sunday Times; Sunday Times Magazine; Wall Street Journal; Illustrated London News; Economist. *Honour:* Commended, British Press Awards, 1984. *Membership:* Foreign Correspondents Association. *Address:* The Sunday Times, Foreign Department, 1 Pennington Street, London E1, England.

GOEDICKE Patricia, b. 21 June 1931, Boston, USA. Poet. m. Leonard Wallace Robinson, 3 June 1971. *Education:* BA, Middlebury College, 1953; MA, Ohio University, 1965. *Appointments:* Editorial Secretary, Harcourt Brace & World Inc., 1953-54; Editorial Assistant, T. Y. Crowell Co. 1955-56; Lecturer, English, Ohio University, 1963-68; Lecturer, English, Hunter College, 1969-71; Associate Professor, creative Writing, Institute Allende, 1972-79; Visiting Writer in Residence, Kalamazoo College, 1977; Guest Faculty Writing Programme, Sarah Lawrence College, 1980; Visiting Poet in Residence, 1981-82, 1982-83, Associate Professor, Creative Writing, 1983-, University of Montana; Professor, Creative Writing, University of Montana, 1990-. *Publications:* Between Oceans, 1968; For the Four Corners, 1976; The Trail That Turns On Itself, 1978; The Dog That Was Barking Yesterday, 1980; Crossing The Same River, 1980; The King of Childhood, 1984; The Wind of Our Going, 1985; Listen Love, 1986; The Tonques We Speak, 1989; Paul Bunyan's Bearskin, 1991. *Contributions to:* New Yorker; Hudson Review; Poetry; The Nation; The American Poetry Review; Ploughshares; Paris Review; Iowa Review; Kenyon Review; New Letters; Missouri Review; Virginia Quarterly Review; Poetry Northwest; Tar River Review; North American Review. *Honours:* CLM prize, 1976;

NEA Creative Writing Fellowship, 1976; William Carlos Williams Prize, 1977; Pushcart Prize II Anthology, 1977-78; Carolyn Kizer Poetry Prize, 1987; Strousse Award, Prairie Schooner, 1987; Hohenberg Award, The Memphis State Review, 1987; Special Commendation in Arvon International Poetry Competition, 1987; Honorable Mention in Vibale Award, Hubbub, 1987; The Tongues We Speak named a Notable Book of the Year, by New York Times, 1990; The Edward Stanley Award from Prairie Schooner, 1993; Artist's Residency at the Rockefeller Foundation's Bellagio Study and Conference Center, Lake Como, Italy, 1993. *Memberships:* PEN; Poetry Society of America, etc. *Address:* 310 McLeod, Missoula, MT 59801, USA.

GOFF James Rudolph Jr, b. 9 Jan 1957, Goldsboro, NC. Historian; Writer. m. Connie, 22 Dec 1978, 1 son, 1 daughter. *Education:* BA, Wake Forest University, 1978; M Div, Duke University, 1981; PhD, University of Arkansas, 1987. *Appointments:* Teaching Assistant, University of Arkansas, 1982-86; Lecturer, Appalachian State University, 1986-87; Instructor, 1987-88; Lecturer, 1988-89; Assistant Professor, 1989-. *Publications:* Fields White Unto Harvest. *Contributions to:* Christianity Today; Kansas History; Ozark Historical Review; Pentecostals From The Inside Out. *Honours:* Faculty award; Phi Theta Kappa; Gordon H McNeil Award; Charles Oxford Scholar. *Memberships:* American Historical Association; Organization of American Historians; Society for Pentecostal Studies; Southern Historical Association. *Address:* Department of History, Appalachian State University, Boone, NC 28608, USA.

GOGGIN Dan, b. 31 May 1943, Alma, Michigan, USA. Writer; Composer; Playwright; Stage Director. *Education:* Attended Manhattan School of Music and University of Michigan. *Career:* Singer; Composer; Playwright; Stage Director. Performed as lead singer for the musical Luther first produced on Broadway at St James Theater, New York in 1963; Toured for five years with the folk singing duo The Saxons; Creator with Marilyn Farina of Nunsense greeting cards. *Publications:* Writer and Director, Nunsense (musical), first produced Off-Broadway at Cherry Lane Theater, New York City, 1985. *Contributions to:* of musical scores for Broadway and off-Broadway productions including Hark, Legend and Seven and for revues Because We're Decadent and Something for Everybody's Mother. *Honours:* Best Musical, Best Book and Best Music Awards from the Outer Critics Circle, 1986 All for Nunsense. *Membership:* Dramatists Guild. *Literary Agent:* Mitch Douglas, International Creative Management, New York. *Address:* c/o Mitch Douglas, International Creative Management, 40 West 57th Street, New York, NY 10019, USA.

GOKANI Pushkar Haridas, (Bhikkhoo Sudama, Gopu), b. 23 June 1931, Dwarka, India. m. Jayshree P Mithaiwala, 19 Jan 1955, 2 sons, 1 daughter. *Education:* BE, 1953; First Aid, 1946. *Appointments include:* Vice President, Trustee Gujarat Itihas Parishad, 1969-77; Astrological Conference, Kutch Bhuj, 1985-; Research Editor, Sanesh, 1983-. *Publications:* Manvina Man, (6 editions 1979-93); Man Teva Manvi; Sarva-Priya Mulla Nasrudin; Gurdjief ni Jeevankali; Numerous Others, 20 Nos. *Contributions to:* Gujarati Magazine; Spiritual Psychology; Gujarat Sama Char. *Honours:* Best Astrological Writer Award; Best Writer Shield. *Memberships:* PEN; Gujarat Itihas Partshad; Lions Club; Municipal Dwarka; Lohana Maha Jan; Indian Roads Congress. *Literary Agent:* Stringer to Times of India. *Address:* Near Brahmkund, Dwarka 361335, India.

GOLĄB Marcin Marian, b. 9 Nov 1926, Wadowice, Poland. Physician. m. Maria Nowak, 23 Sept 1953, 1 daughter. *Education:* Medical Academy, Cracow, 1953; Degree in Internal Medicine, 1967. *Appointments:* Articles for Magazines, 1956-57; Author of Screenplay, Actor, 1956-. *Publications:* Young Cracow; We Are Writing Our Cracow; Scattered Stars to Orthodox Churches; Pieces; Birds are Crying. *Contributions to:* Zycie Literackie; Podhalanka; Pismo Literackie; Lektura;

Gazeta Krakowska. *Honours:* Zakopane, Festiwal Ziem Gorskich; Zakopane. *Memberships:* Society of Polish Writers. *Address:* ul Lobzowska 57/65, 31-139 Krakow, Poland.

GOLD Ivan, b. 12 May 1932, NYC. USA. Writer. m. Vera Cochran, 22 Oct 1968, 1 son. *Education:* BA, Columbia College, NYC, 1953; MA, University of London. *Appointments:* Writer in Residence, Austin peay State University, 1991; Writer in Residence, University of Massachusetts, Boston, 1992. *Publications:* Nickel Misenies; Sick Friends; Sams in a Dry Season. *Literary Agent:* Many Yost Associates. *Address:* c/o Many Yost Associates, 59 E 54, New York City, NY 10022, USA.

GOLDBERG Barbara June, b. 26 Apr 1943, Wilmington, USA. Writer; Poet; Editor. m. (1) J Peter Kiers, 1963 div 1970, (2) Charles Goldberg, 1971, div 1990, 2 sons. *Education:* BA, Mount Holyoke College, 1963; MA, Yeshiva University, 1969; MEd, Columbia University, 1971; MFA, American University, 1985. *Appointments:* Director of the Editorial Board, The World Works publishers, 1987-; Executive Editor, Poet Lore, 1990-. *Publications:* Berta Broad Foot and Pepin the Short; Cautionary Tales; The Stones Remember. *Contributions to:* The American Scholar; Antioch Review; New England Review; Bread Loaf Quarterly. *Honours:* Work in Progress Grant; National Endowment for the arts Fellowship; Armand G Erpf Award; Writter Bynner Foundation Award. *Memberships:* Poetry Society of America, Poets & Writers; Poetry Committee of the Greater Washington Area. *Address:* 6623 Fairfax Road, Chevy Chase, MD 20815, USA.

GOLDBERG Hillel, b. 10 Jan 1946, Denver, Colorado, USA. Writer; Rabbi. m. Elaine Silberstein, 19 May 1969, 1 son, 1 daughter. *Education:* BA, Yeshiva University, 1969; MA, 1972, PhD, 1978, Brandeis University; Rabbinical Ordination, Chief Rabbi of Israel, 1976. *Appointments:* Co-Publisher, Co-Editor, Tempo, 1964; Intermountain Jewish News, Senior Editor, Editor, Literary Supplement, 1966-; Editor, Pulse, 1968-69; Editorial Board, Tradition, 1978-. *Publications:* Israel Salanter: Text, Structure, Idea, The Ethics and Theology of an Early Psychologist of the Unconscious, 1982; Living Musar: The Face of Torah of Rabbi Yisrael Salanter and His Disciples, 1987; The Fire Within: The Living Heritage of the Musar Movement, 1987; Between Berlin and Slobadka: Jewish Transition Figures from Eastern Europe, 1989. *Contributions to:* various journals and newspapers. *Honours:* Academic Book of the Year Citation, Choice, 1982; Rockower Award for Distinguished Editorial Writing, 1983, 1984, 1986, 1987; Rockower Award for Distinguished News Reportage, 1988. *Memberships:* Literary Guild; Corresponding Secretary, American Jewish Press Association. *Address:* 1275 Sherman St, Denver, CO 80203, USA.

GOLDBERG Lester, b. 3 Feb 1924, Brooklyn, New York, USA; Real Estate; Writer. m. Dorothy Weinstein, June 1947, 1 son, 3 daughters. *Education:* BS, City College (now City University of New York), 1946. *Career:* Worked in Real Estate, affiliated with the State Division of Housing, 1988-; Writer. *Publications:* One More River (stories) 1978; In Siberia It Is Very Cold (novel), 1987. Work represented in anthologies, including Best American Short Stories, edited by Martha Foley, 1974-77 and O Henry Prize Stories edited by William Abrahams, 1979. *Contributions to:* More than 60 stories to magazines, including Cimarron Review; Sou'Wester; Mid-American Review; Kansas Quarterly; National Jewish Monthly and Transatlantic Review. *Honours:* Fellow, National Endowment for the Arts, 1979; Grants from New Jersey Arts Council, 1982 and 1986; Award from International PEN Syndicated Fiction Project, 1984 for short story Hardware. *Memberships:* Poets and Writers; Metropolitan Association of Housing and Redevelopment Officials. *Address:* 18 Woods Hole Road, Cranford, NJ 07016, USA.

GOLDEN Mark, b. 6 Aug 1948, Winnipeg, Canada

. Professor. m. Monica Becker, 1 son. *Education:* BA, University of Toronto, 1970; MA, 1976; PhD, 1981. *Publications:* Children and Childhood in Classical Athens. *Address:* Department of Classics, University of Winnipeg, Winnipeg, Monitoba, Canada R3B 2E9.

GOLDIN Barbara Diamond, b. 4 Oct 1946, NYC, USA. Teacher; Writer. m. Alan Goldin, Mar 1968, (div 1991), 1 son, 1 daughter. *Education:* BA, University of Chicago. *Publications:* Just Enough Is Plenty; The Worlds Birthday; A Childs Book of Midrash; Cakes and Miracles; Fire; The Magician's Visit. *Contributions to:* Cricket Highlights; Jack & Jill; Childlife; Shofan Magazine. *Honours:* National Jewish Book Award; Anne Izand Storytellers Choice Award; Sydney Taylor Picture book Award. *Memberships:* Society of Childrens Book Writers. *Literary Agent:* Virginia Knowlton. *Address:* P O Box 981, Northampton, MA 01061, USA.

GOLDIN Stephen, b. 1947, USA. Freelance Writer. *Appointments:* Editor: Jaundice Press, Van Nuys, California, 1973-74; San Francisco Ball, 1973-74; Science Fiction Writers of America Bulletin, 1975-77; Currently Director, Merrimont House Creative Consultations. *Publications:* Protostars (edited with David Gerrold), 1971; The Alien Condition (editor), 1973; Science Fiction Emphasis 1 (edited with David Gerrold), 1974; Alternities (edited with David Gerrold), 1974; Herds, 1975; Caravan, 1975; Scavenger Hunt, 1975; Finish Line, 1976; Imperial Stars, 1976; Strangler's Moon, 1976; The Clockwork Traitor, 1976; Assault on the Gods, 1977; Getaway World, 1977; Ascents of Wonder (edited with David Gerrold), 1977; Mindfight, 1978; Appointment at Bloodstar, UK Edition The Bloodstar Conspiracy, 1978; The Purity Plot, 1978; Trek to Madworld, 1979; The Eternity Brigade, 1980; A World Called Solitude, 1981; And Not Make Dreams Your Master, 1981; Planet of Treachery, 1982; The Business of Being a Writer (with Kathleen Sky), non-fiction, 1982; Eclipsing Binaries, 1984; The Omicron Invasion, 1984; Revolt of the Galaxy, 1985. *Address:* 389 Florin Road, No 22, Sacramento, CA 95831, USA.

GOLDING William (Gerald), b. 19 Sept 1911. Author. m. Ann, 1939, 1 son, 1 daughter. *Education:* MA, Brasenose College, Oxford, 1961. *Publications:* Lord of the Flies, 1954 (filmed 1963); The Inheritors, 1955; Pincher Martin, 1956; Brass Butterfly (play), 1958; Free Fall, 1959; The Spire, 1964; The Hot Gates (essays), 1965; The Pyramid, 1967; The Scorpion God, 1971; Darkness Visible, 1979; Rites of Passage, 1980; A Moving Target (essays), 1982; The Paper Men, 1984; An Egyptian Journal (Travel), 1985; Close Quarters, 1987; Fire Down Below, 1989. *Honours:* Hon. Fellow, Brasenose College, Oxford, 1966; Hon. DLitt: Sussex, 1970, Kent 1974, Warwick 1981, Oxford 1983, Sorbonne, 1983; James Tait Black Memorial Prize, 1980; Booker McConnell Prize, 1980; Hon. LLD, Bristol 1984; Nobel Prize for Literature, 1983. *Address:* c/o Faber and Faber, 3 Queen Square, London WC1N 3AU, England.

GOLDMAN Arnold (Melvyn), b. 19 July 1936, Lynn, Massachusetts, USA. Academic. m. Dorothy Joan Shelton, 22 Mar 1963, 2 sons. *Education:* AB, Harvard University 1957; AM 1959, PhD 1964, Yale University. *Literary Appointments:* Advisory Editor, James Joyce Quarterly; Advisory Editor, James Joyce Studies: an annual; Associate Editor, Journal of American Studies 1977-83; senior Enterprise Adviser & Co-ordinator of Academic Staff Development & Training, University of Kent. *Publications:* The Joyce Paradox 1966; Fitzgerald's Tender is the Night (edition) 1982; Dickens' American Notes (with J S Whitley) edition 1972; Faulkner's Absalom, Absalom!. 1971; The Profile Joyce, 1968. *Contributions to:* Journal of Modern Literature; James Joyce Literary Supplement; Journal of American Studies; James Joyce Quarterly; Times higher Education Supplement; Yearbook of English Studies; Encounter etc. *Honours:* Fulbright Fellow, 1957-58; Honorary Woodrow Wilson Fellow, 1957-58; Honorary Professor of American Studies, University of Kent at Canterbury, 1985-. *Memberships:* British Association for American

Studies; Modern Languages Association of America; Society for Research in Higher Education; Standing Council on Educational Development. *Address:* 8 St Stephen's Hill, Canterbury, Kent CT2 7AX, England.

GOLDMAN James, b. 30 June 1927, Chicago, Illinois, USA, brother of writer William Goldman. Writer. m. (1) Marie McKeon, 1962 (div 1973) 1 daughter, 1 son; (2) Barbara Deren, 1975. *Education:* PhB 1947, MA 1950, University of Chicago; Columbia University, New York, 1950-52; Served in United States Army 1952-54. *Publications:* Plays include: A Family Affair, with William Goldman, music by John Kander (produced New York, 1962); The Lion in Winter (produced New York 1966) New York, Random House and London, French, 1966; Follies, music and lyrics by Stephen Sondheim (produced New York, 1971) revised version produced Manchester, 1985, London 1987) New York, Random House, 1971; Robin and Marian (screenplay). New York, Bantam, 1976. Screenplays: The Lion in Winter, 1968; They Might Be Giants, 1970; Nicholas and Alexandra, 1971; Robin and Marian, 1976; White Nights, with Eric Hughes, 1985. Television Plays: Evening Primrose, music by Stephen Sondheim, 1966; Anna Karenina, from the novel by Tolstoy, 1985; TV: Oliver Twist, 1983. Novels: Waldorf, New York, Random House, 1965; London, Joseph 1966; The Man From Greek and Roman, New York, Random House 1974; London, Hutchinson, 1975; Myself as Witness, New York, Random House, 1979; London, Hamish Hamilton, 1980; Fulton County, 1989. *Honours:* Oscar 1969; Writers Guild of America West award, 1969; Oliver Award, Best Musical, Follies; Evening Standard, Best Musical, Follies; British Writers Guild, Lion in Winter. *Memberships:* Council Member, Dramatists Guild, 1966-; Council Member, Authors League of America, 1967-. *Literary Agent:* Owen Laster. *Address:* c/o William Morris Agency, 1350 Avenue of the Americas, New York, NY 10019, USA.

GOLDMAN Louis, b. 8 June 1925, Germany. Photographer. m. Leak Ildiko, 30 Mar 1970, 1 son, 2 daughters. *Education:* Montpellier, France. *Publications:* Lights, Camera Action; A Week in Hagars world; Turkey, A Week in Samils World; The Burning Bush. *Contributions to:* Numerous. *Memberships:* International Photographers. *Address:* 40 Waterside Plaza, New York, NY 10010, USA.

GOLDMAN Paul H J b. 3 Apr 1950, London, England. Museum Curator; Art Historian. m. Corinna Maroulis, 11 July 1987. *Education:* BA Hons, English, London University 1971; Postgraduate Diploma in Art Gallery and Museum Studies (Dip AGMS) University of Manchester, 1972; Diploma of the Museums Association in Art (AMA) obtained by examination, 1978. *Publications:* Looking at Prints, Drawings and Watercolours, 1988; Sporting Life, An Anthology of British Sporting Prints, 1983; Looking at Drawings, 1979; Looking at Prints, 1981. *Contributions to:* Connoisseur; Antique Collector; British Library Journal; Antique; Antiquarian Book Monthly Review; Print Quarterly; Art Bulletin of Tasmania. *Honours:* Elected Fellow of the Royal Society of Arts, 1989 (FRSA); Elected Fellow of the Museums Association (FMA), 1990. *Memberships:* Society of Authors; Museums Association. *Address:* c/o Department of Prints and Drawings, British Museum, London WC1, England.

GOLDREIN Iain Saville, b. 10 Aug 1952, Crosby, Liverpool, England. Barrister. m. Margaret de Haas, 18 May 1980, 1 son, 1 daughter. *Education:* Pembroke College, Cambridge. *Appointments:* Visiting Professor, Sir Jack Jacob Chair of Litigation, Nottingham Law School. *Publications:* Personal Injury Litigation Practice & Precedents, 1985; Ship Sale and Purchase Law and Technique, 1985; Commercial Litigation Pre- Emptive Remedies, 1987 (2nd edition 1991); Butterworths Personal Injury Litigation Service, 1988; Pleadings: Principles and Practice (with Sir Jack Jacob), 1990; Bullen, Leake & Jacob, Precedents of Pleadings, 1990. *Contributions to:* Law Society Gazette; New Law Journal; Solicitors Journal, Insurance at Re-insurance

Research Group. *Memberships:* Middle Temple; Inner Temple; Northern Circuit; Associate of the Chartered Institute of Arbitrators; British Academy of Experts; British Insurance Law Association; Committee of the International Litigation Practitioners Forum; International Union of Lawyers. *Address:* J Harcourt Buildings, Temple, London EC4Y 9DA, England.

GOLDSBERRY Steven, b. 22 Apr 1949, St Paul, USA. English Professor; Writer. m. 17 Dec 1975, 1 son, 1 daughters. *Education:* MA, 9173; MFA, 1978; PhD, University of Iowa, 1979. *Appointments:* English Professor, University of Hawaii, 1975-. *Publications:* Maui the Demigod; Over Hawaii; The Craft of Hawaiian Lauhala Weaving. *Contributions to:* Honolulu Magazine; Honolulu; Aloaa; American Poetry Review; The New Yorker. *Honours:* Michener Fellowship; Cades Award. *Literary Agent:* Tim Schaffner, 6625 N Casas, Adobias, Tueson, Ariz, USA 85704. *Address:* 1733 Douaghho Road, Honolulu, HI 96822, USA.

GOLDSMITH Edward Rene David, b. 8 Nov 1928. Author; Publisher; Editor. m. (1) Gillian Marion Pretty, 1953, 1 son, 2 daughters, (2) Katherine Victoria James, 1981, 2 sons. *Education:* MA, Magdalen College, Oxford. *Appointments:* Publisher, Editor, The Ecologist, 1970-; Adjunct Associate Professor, University of Michigan, 1975; Visiting Professor, Sangamon State University, 1984. *Publications:* Editor, Can Britain Survive?, 1971; (with R. Allen) A Blueprint for Survival, 1972; The Future of an Affluent Society: the Case of Canada, (report for Env. Canada), 1976; The Stable Society, 1977; (Ed with J.M. Brunetti) La Medecine a la Question, 1981; The Social and Environmental Effects of Large Dams, volume 1 (with N. Hildyard), 1984, volume II (editor with N. Hildyard), 1986; Green Britain or Industrial Wasteland? (with N. Hildyard), 1986; The Earth Report (ed. with N. Hildyard), 1988; The Great U-Turn, 1988. *Address:* Whitehay, Withiel, Bodmin, Cornwall, England.

GOLDSTEIN Robert Justin, b. 28 Mar 1947, Albany, NY, USA. College Professor. *Education:* BA, University of illinois, 1969; MA, University of Chicago, 1971; PhD, 1976. *Appointments:* Research & Administrative Assistant, University of Illinois, 1972-73; Lecturer, San Diego State University, 1974-76; Assistant, Associate, Full Professor, Oakland University, Rochester, Michigan 1976-. *Publications:* Political Repression in Modern America; Political Repression in Nineteenth Century Europe; Political Censorship of the Press and the Arts in Nineteenth Century Europe; Censorship of Political Caricature in Nineteenth Century France; Limits in the Land of the Free. *Contributions to:* French History; Art Journal; Print Collectors Newsletter; International Handbook of Human Rights; Human Rights Quarterly. *Honours:* Phi Beta Kappa; Phi Eta Sigma; Phi Kappa Phi; Oakland University Summer Research Fellowship; Research Grant; Marian Wilson Award; American Association for the Advancement of Science Award. *Address:* Department of Political Science, Oakland University, Rochester, MI 48309, USA.

GOLFFING Barbara Francesca, (Barbara Gibbs), b. 23 Sept 1912, Los Angeles, USA. Housewife; Writer. m. Francis Golffing, 2 Feb 1942, 1 daughter. *Education:* BA, Stanford University, 1934; MA, UCLA, 1935. *Publications:* The Well; The Green Chapel; Poems Written in Berlin; The Meeting Place of the Colors. *Contributions to:* The New Republic; The Southern Review; Poetry; Hudson Review; The New Yorker; Yankee. *Honours:* James Phelan Fellowship; The Oscar Blumenthal prize; Guggenheim Fellowship. *Address:* 272 Middle Hancock Road, Peterborough, NH 03458, USA.

GOLFFING Francis, b. 20 Nov 1910, Vienne. Retired University Professor. m. Barbara Gibbs, 2 Feb 1941, 1 son. *Education:* University of Berlin. *Appointments:* Instructor, Utah State University, 1945; Queens College, NY, 1946; Bennington College, 1948-68; Franklin Pierce College, NH, 1968-74. *Publications:* Nietzsche, Birth of Tragedy and Genealogy of Morals; Collected Poems;

Possibility. *Contributions to:* Stand; Encounter; Commentary; The Nation; The Kenyon Review. *Honours:* Ingram Merritt Foundation Award; Oscar Williams & Gene Derwood Award. *Address:* 272 Middle Hancock Road, Peterborough, NH 03458, USA.

GOMERY Douglas, Professor. *Education:* BS, cum laude, Lehigh University, Bethlehem, Pennsylvania, USA, 1967; MA, Economics, 1970, PhD, Communication, 1975, University of Wisconsin-Madison. *Appointments:* Instructor, Assistant Professor, Associate Professor, Department Mass Communication, 1974-81, Visiting Professor, Department of Communication Arts, 1977, University of Wisconsin-Madison; Visiting Professor, Division of Radio-Television-Film, School of Speech, Northwestern University, 1981; Visiting Professor, Division of Broadcasting and Film, department of Communication and Theatre Arts, University of Iowa, 1982; Visiting Professor, University of Utrecht (Netherlands), 1990; Associate Professor, 1981-86, Professor, 1987-92, Department of Communication Arts and Theatre, University of Maryland; Professor, College of Journalism, University of Maryland, 1992. *Publications:* The Art of Moving Shadows, 1989; American Media: The Wilson Quarterly Reader, 1989; The Will Hays Papers, 1987; The Hollywood Studio System, 1986; Film History: Theory and Practice, 1985; High Sierra: Screenply and Analysis, 1979; Movie History: A Survey, 1990; Shared Pleasures, 1992; The Future of News, 1992. *Contributions to:* More than 300 articles, reviews and papers in professional magazines and journals. *Honours include:* Phi Beta Kappa; Beta Gamma Sigma; Phi Kappa Phi; Graduate Research Award, 1985, Fellow, Centre for Arts and Humanities, 1988, University of Maryland. *Memberships include:* Board of Trustees, American Film Institute, 1986-88; Society for Cinema Studies Task Force on Moving Images Archives Policy, 1987-89. *Address:* 4817 Drummond Avenue, Chevy Chase, MD 20815, USA.

GOMEZ Christine, b. 24 Apr 1947, Madras, India. Teacher. m. Patrick Gomez, 21 Oct 1970, 1 son. *Education:* BSc, 1966; MA, 1968; PhD, 1982. *Appointments:* Board of Studies, Bharathidasan University, 1982-84; Ad Hoc Committee, Mother Theresa Womens University, 1984-85; Board of Studies, Bharathi Dasan University, 1984-87. *Publications:* The Alienated Figure in Drama; Fire Blossoms; The Treasure Hunt; Favourite Stories; Lamplight and Shadows; Love's Triumph; Deiva Dharisanam; Stations of the Cross; Yatra. *Contributions to:* Hamlet Studies; Indian Journal of Shakespeare Studies. *Honours:* First Prize, All India Play Writing Competition. *Memberships:* PEN; Indian Society for Commonwealth Studies; Indian Association of Literary Critics and Theorists; ASRC. *Address:* Vilma, C91 North East Extension, Thillainagar, Tiruchy 620 018 India.

GONCZ Arpad, b. 10 Feb 1922, Budapest, Hungary. President, Republic of Hungary. m. Zsuzsanna Maria Gonter, 2 sons, 2 daughters. *Education:* Pazmany Peter University, 1938-44; University of Agricultural Sciences, 1952-66. *Appointments:* Editor, Nemzedek, 1947- 48. *Publications:* Hungarian Medea; Men of God; Iron Bars; Balance; A Pessimistic Comedy; Persephone; Encounters; Homecoming. *Contributions to:* Regularly in Hungarian Literary Magazines. *Honours:* Jozsef Attila Award; Wheatland Prize; Premio Mediterraneo. *Memberships:* Hungarian Writers Association; Hungarian Writers Union; Hungarian PEN Club. *Literary Agent:* Artisjus, Agency for Literature and Theatre. *Address:* Parliament, Kossuth ter 1-3, Budapest V, 1055 Hungary.

GONDOSCH Linda, b. 25 Oct 1944, Hinton, WV, USA. Author. m. Werner Gondosch, 4 Sept 1965, 1 son, 3 daughters. *Education:* BS, 1966; MA, 1986. *Publications:* Who Needs A Bratty Brother?; The Witches of Hopper Street; Who's Afraid of Haggerty House; The Monsters of Marble Avenue; Brutus The Wonder Poodle; The Best Bet Gazette. *Honours:* Kentucky Bluegrass Childrens Choice Award. *Memberships:* Society of Childrens Bookwriters. *Address:* 1020 Fairview Drive, Lawrenceburg, IN 47025, USA.

GONZÁLEZ César Augusto, (González-Trujillo),b. 17 Jan 1931, Los Angeles, CA, USA. College Professor. m. Bette L Beattie, 30 Aug 1969. *Education:* BA, Gonzaga University, 1951; MA, Gonzaga University, 1954; Santa Clara, Calif, 1961; Los Angeles, CA, 1962-65. *Publications:* Rudolfo A Anaya: Focus on Criticism; Unwinding the Silence; Fragmentos de Barro: University of Santa Clara, Masters in Sacred Theology, Licentiate in Sacred Theology, Pieces of Clay; Fragmentos de Barro: The First Seven Years. *Contributions to:* Literary Criticism In Journals; The Bilingual Review; Blue Mesa Review; Maize; Imagine San Diego Writers Monthly; Chiricu. *Honours:* Fellow, Fulbright Hays; Fellow, NEH; Com SVC Award; Outstanding Teacher; Outstanding Teacher & Scholar, 1993 National Institute for Staff Organizational Development (NISOD) Excellence in Teaching Award. *Memberships:* Poets and Writers; Asociacion Internacional de Hispanistas; Contemporary Authors; American Federation of Teachers; National Association of Chicano Studies. *Address:* San Diego Mesa College, 7250 Mesa College Drive, San Diego, CA 92111, USA.

GONZALEZ-CRUSSI Frank, b. 4 Oct 1936, Mexico City, Mexico. Professor. m. (1) Ana Luz, (div) 2 sons, 1 daughter, (2) Wei Hsueh, 7 Oct 1978. *Education:* BA 1954, MD 1961, Universidad Nacional Autonoma de Mexico. *Appointments:* Intern, Penrose Hospital, Colorado Springs, 1962; Resident in Pathology, St Lawrence Hospital, Lansing, MI, Shands Teaching Hospital, University of Florida, Gainesville, FL, 1963-67; Assistant Professor of Pathology, Queens University, Kingston, Ontario, 1967-73; Associate Professor of Pathology, Indiana University-Purdue University at Indianapolis, 1973-78; Professor of Pathology, Northwestern University, Chicago, IL, 1978-; Head of laboratories at Children's Memorial Hospital, Chicago. *Publications:* Notes of an Anatomist, 1985; Three Forms of Sudden Death; Other Relections on the Grandeur and Misery of the Body, 1986; On the Nature of Things Erotic; 1988; Extragonadal Teratomas; Wilm's Tumor and Related Renal Neoplasms of Childhood. *Contributions to:* Numerous specialized medical journals. *Honours:* Best Nonfiction award from the Society of Midland Authors, 1985. *Memberships:* International Academy of Pathology; Society for Pediatric Pathology; American Society of Clinical Pathologists; Royal College of Physicians and Surgeons of Canada; Chicago Pathology Society; Authors Guild; Society of Midland Authors. *Address:* 2626 North Lakeview Avenue, Chicago, IL 60614, USA.

GONZÁLEZ-TRUJILLO. *See:* **GONZÁLEZ César Augusto.**

GOOCH John, b. 25 Aug 1945, Weston Favell. Professor. m. Catherine Ann Staley. *Education:* BA (First Class Honours) 1966, PhD 1969, King's College, London. *Appointments:* Secretary of the Navy Senior Research Fellow, US Naval War College, Newport, Rhode Island, 1985- 86; Reader in History, University of Lancaster, England, 1986-87; Visiting Professor, Yale University, 1988; Professor, International History, University of Leeds, 1991-. *Publications:* The Plans of War: The General Staff and British Military Strategy c. 1900-1916, 1974; Armies in Europe, 1980; The Prospect of War: Studies in British Defence Policy 1847-1942, 1981; Strategy and the Social Sciences, 1981; Politicians and Defence: Studies in the Formulation of British Defence Policy (with Ian F W Beckett), Military Deception and Strategic Surprise, Soldatie e Borghesi nell' Europa moderna, 1982; Army State and Social in Italy 1870-1915, 1989; Military Misfortunes, (with Eliot A Cohen) 1990; Decisive Campaignes of the Second World War, 1990. *Contributions to:* History Journals. *Memberships:* Fellow, Royal Historical Society; Chairman, Army Records Society; Vice President, Royal Historical Society. *Honours:* Premio internazionale di cultura from Citta di Anghiari, 1983. *Address:* c/o

School of History, University of Leeds, Leeds LS2 9JT, England.

GOOCH Stanley Alfred, b. 13 June 1932, London, England. m. Ruth Senior, 1 Apr 1961. *Education:* BA (Hons), Modern Languages King's College 1955, BSc (Hons) Psychology, Birkbeck College 1962, London; Diploma in Education, Institute of Education, London, 1957. *Publications:* Four Years On, 1966; Total Man, 1972; The Neanderthal Question, 1977; The Paranormal, 1978; Guardians of The Ancient Wisdom, 1979; Creatures From Inner Space, 1984; Cities of Dreams, 1989; Personality and Evolution, 1973; The Double Helix of The Mind, 1980; The Secret Life of Humans, 1981; The Child With Asthma, 1986; Cities of Dreams, 1989. *Contributions to:* New Scientist; New Society; British Journal of Psychology; British Journal of Social & Clinical Psychology; British Journal of Educational Psychology; International Journal of Human Development. *Honours:* Royal Literary Fund Award, 1984 and 1987. *Literary Agent:* David Bolt, David Bolt Associates, England. *Address:* c/o David Bolt, David Bolt Associates, 12 Heath Drive, Send, Surrey GU23 7EP, England.

GOOCH Steve, b. 1945, United Kingdom. Playwright. *Appointments:* Assistant Editor, Plays and Players magazine, London, 1972-73; Resident Dramatist: Half Moon Theatre, London, 1973-74; Greenwich Theatre, London, 1974-75; Solent People's Theatre, Southampton, 1982; Theatre Venture, London, 1983-84; Warehouse Theatre, Croydon, 1986-87; Gate Theatre, Notting Hill, 1990-91. *Publications:* Big Wolf, translation, 1972; The Mother, translation, 1973; Female Transport, 1974; The Motor Show (with Paul Thompson), 1974; Will Wat, If Not, What Will, 1975; Wolf Biermann's Poems and Ballads, translation, 1977; The Women Pirates, 1978; Wallraff: The Undesirable Journalist, translation, 1978; Fast One, 1982; Landmark, 1982; All Together Now, 1984; Taking Liberties, 1984; Mr Fun, 1986; Writing A Play, 1988; Lulu and The Marquis of Keith, 1990; MASSA, 1989. *Literary Agent:* Margaret Ramsay Ltd, England. *Address:* c/o Margaret Ramsay Ltd, 14a Goodwins Court, St Martin's Lane, London WC2N 4LL, England.

GOODE James Arthur, b. 22 Jan 1924. Editor. *Education:* AB, Wabash College, 1949. *Appointments:* Editor, Earth, 1969-71; Correspondent, Life, 1952-61; Executive Editor, Play Girl, 1976; Play Boy, 1975; Editorial Director, Pent House, 1972-81; Editor, National Times, 1991-2. *Publications:* The Making of the Misfits; Wiretap. *Contributions to:* Numerous. *Address:* 6215 Mulholland Highway, Los Angeles, CA 90068, USA.

GOODFIELD June, b. 1 June 1927, Stratford-on-Avon, England. Author; Clarence J Robinson Professor. *Education:* BSc (Honours) Zoology, University of London, 1949; PhD, History and Philosophy of Science, University of Leeds, 1959. *Publications:* From the Face of the Earth; An Imagined World; Playing God; The Siege of Cancer; Courier to Peking (a novel); A Chance to Live; The Planned Miracle, 1991. *Contributions to:* London Review of Books; Nature; Scientific American; The American Scholar; Science. *Memberships:* PEN Club; English Speaking Union; President, United Nations Association (Lodnon), 1986-87. *Literary Agent:* Hilary Rubinstein, A P Watt Ltd, London. *Address:* The Manor House, Alfriston, East Sussex BN26 5SY, England.

GOODHEART Eugene, b. 26 June 1931, New York, USA. Professor. m. Joan Bamberger, 1 son, 1 daughter. *Education:* BA 1953, PhD English 1961, Columbia University; MA English, University of Virginia, 1954. *Publications:* Pieces of Resistance, 1987; Skeptic Disposition in Contemporary Criticism, 1984; The Failure of Criticism. 1978; Cultural and The Radical Conscience, 1973; The Cult of The Ego, 1968; The Utopian Vision of D H Lawrence, 1963; Desire and its Discontents, 1991. *Contributions to:* Partisan Review; Salmagundi; Yale Review; New Literary History; Critical Inquiry; London Review of Books. *Honours:* ACLS, 1965-

66; Guggenheim, 1970-71; NEH, 1980-81; Numerous other Fellowships. *Membership:* PEN. *Address:* Dept of English, Brandeis University, Waltham, MA 02254, USA.

GOODMAN Joan Elizabeth, b. 18 June, 1950, Fairfield, Conn., USA. m. Keith A. Goldsmith, 12 Sept 1987. Writer; Artists. *Education:* L'Accademia de Belle Arti, Rome, Italy, 1969-70; Pratt Institute, B.F.A., 1973. *Appointments:* Village Voice, New York, N.Y., type specker, 1968-69; Hallmark Cards, Kansas City, Mo., greeting card artist, 1974-76; free-lance writer and illustrator, 1976-. *Publications:* Self-illustrated Children's Books: Teddy Bear, Teddy Bear, 1979; Bear and His Book, 1982; Right's Animal Farm, 1983; Amanda's First Day at School, 1985; The Secret Life of Walter Kitty, 1986; Good Night, Pippin, 1986; The Bunnies' Get Well Soup, 1987; Edward Hopper's Great Find, 1987; Hillary Squeak's Dreadful Dragon, 1987; The Bear's New Baby, 1988; Time for Bed, 1989. Illustrator: The Gingerbread Boy, 1979; The Grape Jelly Mystery, 1979; The Teddy Bear's Picnic, 1979; Johnny Appleseed, 1980; Yummy, Yummy, 1981; Hocus Pocus, Magic Show! 1981; The Case of the Missing Rattles, 1982; Easter Parade, 1985; The Cat Who Wanted to Fly, 1986.

GOODMAN Jonathan, b. 1933, United Kingdom. Author; Publisher; Editor. *Appointments:* Theatre Director and Television Producer, various companies, United Kingdom, 1951-64; Director, Anbar Publications Ltd, London, 1967-; General Editor, Celebrated Trials Series, David & Charles (Publishers) Ltd, Newton Abbott, Devon, 1972-. *Publications:* Matinee Idylls, poetry, 1954; Instead of Murder, novel, 1961; Criminal Tendencies, novel, 1964; Hello Cruel World Goodbye, novel, 1964; The Killing of Julia Wallace, 1969; Bloody Versicles, 1971; Posts-Mortem, 1971; Trial of Ian Brady and Myra Hindley (editor), 1973; Trial of Ruth Ellis (editor), 1975; The Burning of Evelyn Foster, 1977; The Last Sentence, novel, 1978; The Stabbing of George Harry Storrs, 1982; Pleasure of Murder, 1983; Railway Murders, 1984; Who-He, 1984; Seaside Murders, 1985; The Crippen File (editor), 1985; The Underworld (with I Will), 1985; Christmas Murders (editor), 1986; The Moors Murders, 1986; Acts of Murder, 1986; Murder in High Places, 1986; The Slaying of Joseph Bowne Elwell, 1987. *Address:* 43 Ealing Village, London W5 2LZ, England.

GOODMAN Mark, b. 5 May, 1939, Dallas, Texas, USA. Writer; Author. m. (1) Sherida Shepherd, 14 Sept 1968 (div 1972), 1 daughter; m. (2) Esther Nichol, 19 Dec 1981, 1 child. *Education:* BA, Cornell University, 1961. *Appointments:* Bartender in San Francisco, California., Fort Lauderdale and Hyannis, Mass., 1961-63; United Press International, New York, reporter, 1965-66; Times Magazine, New York City, film critic, 1967-72; writer, 1972. *Publications:* Hurrah for the Next Man Who Dies, (novel), 1985; Author of Final Tribute, column in New Times. Silent Dreams, 1990. *Contributions to:* Esquire, Gentlemen's Quarterly, New York Times Sunday Magazine, Playboy, Reader's Digest and Time. *Honours:* U.S. Army in Europe award, 1964 for 'Outstanding Journalism'.

GOODRICH Norma Lorre, b. 10 May 1917, Huntington, Vermont, USA. Professor. m. Jan 1953, 1 son. *Education:* BS, University of Vermont, 1938; Université de Grenoble, 1939; Université de Paris, 1946-53; PhD, Columbia University, 1965. *Appointments:* Encyclopedia Articles for the Grolier Corp, and Princeton University Press, 1953-70; Columbia University Press, 1965-70; Newspaper Articles Throughout, US, 1938-59; Author Franklin Watts Publishers, 1982-; Harper Collins, 1986-. *Publications:* Medieval Myths; Ancient Myths; King Arthur; Merlin; Guinevere; Priestesses; Jean Giono, A Study of Themes; The Doctor and Maria Theresa; The Ways of Love, The Holy Grail. *Contributions to:* 50- 60 Scholarly Articles, Etudes Rabelaisiennes; Revue de Littérature Comparée; Romanic Review; French Review. *Honours:* Prize & Medal, Vermont Historical Society; Wallace Award; Citizenship Medal;

Martha Washington Medal. *Memberships:* J P Morgan Library; South Bay Scottish Society; Authors Guild; American Association of University Women; Alumni Association of the University of Vermont Libraries; Dante Society of Harvard University; Arthurian Society of Longtown Cumbria; American Association of University Women; National Organization of Women; Metropolitan Opera Society; Friends of the Upland Library; Friends of the Claremont Library. *Literary Agent:* Mr Harold Schmidt. *Address:* 620 Diablo Drive, Claremont, CA 91711, USA.

GOODRICK-CLARKE Nicholas, b. 15 Jan 1953, Lincoln, England. Author; Historian. m. Clare Radene Badham, 11 May 1985. *Education:* Lancing College, 1966-70; Jagdschloss Glienicke, Berlin, 1971; University of Bristol, 1971-74; University of Oxford, 1975-78. *Appointments:* Editor, Essential Readings, 1983-; Director, IKON Productions Ltd, 1988-. *Publications:* The Occult Roots of Nazism; Paracelsus; The Enchanted City; Unholy Relics. *Contributions to:* Durham University Journal; Theosophical History; Images of War; Decadence and Innovation. *Memberships:* The Society of Authors; The Scientific & Medical Network; Keston College. *Address:* Manor Farm House, Manor Road, Wantage OX12 8NE, England.

GOODWIN Suzanne. See: EBEL Suzanne.

GOODWIN Trevor Noel, b. 25 Dec 1927, Fowey, Cornwall, England. Writer. Critic. m. Anne Mason Myers, 23 Nov 1963, 1 stepson. *Education:* BA, London. *Appointments:* Assistant Music Critic, News Chronicle, 1952-54; Manchester Guardian, 1954-55; Music & Dance Critic, Daily Express, 1956-78; Associate Editor, Dance & Dancers, 1958-; Executive Editor, Music & Muscians, 1963-71; London Dance Critic, International Herald Tribune, 1963-71; International Herald Tribune, Paris, 1978-83; London Correspondent, Opera News, New York, 1980-91; Overseas News Editor, Opera, 1985-91, now member of Editorial Board; planned And Presented Numerous Radio Programmes. *Publications:* London Symphony, Portrait of an Orchestra; A Ballet for Scotland; A Knight at the Opera; Royal Opera and Royal Ballet Yearbooks; Area Editor, Writer, New Grove Dictionary of Music & Musicians; a Portrait of the Royal Ballet. *Contributions to:* Encyclopeaedia Britannica; Encyclopaedia of Opera; Britannica Books of the Year; Cambridge Encyclopaedia of Russia and the Soviet Union; New Oxford Companion to Music; Pipers Enzyklopadie des Musiktheaters; New Grove Dictionary of Opera. *Memberships include:* Arts Council of Great Britain; Drama And Dance Advisory Committee. *Address:* 76 Skeena Hill, London SW18 5PN, England.

GOONERATNE Malini Yasmine, b. 22 Dec 1935, Colombo, Sri Lanka, University Professor of English. m. Dr Brendon Gooneratne, 31 Dec 1962, 1 son, 1 daughter. *Education:* BA, 1st class Honours, Ceylon, 1959; PhD, English Literature, Cambridge University, England, 1962; DLitt, English and Cmmonwealth Literature, Macquarie University, Australia, 1981. *Appointments include:* Editor, Koinonia, 1957; Editor, Thunapaha, 1958; editor, New Ceylon Writing, 1971-; Editor, Journal of South Asian Literature, Michigan State University, 1976; Judge, Commonwealth Poetry Prize, 1985; Director, Macquarie University Post-Colonial Literatures and Language Research Centre, 1988-; National Co-ordinator, Australian Government Commonwealth Visiting Fellowship, 1989; Patron, Jane Austen Society of Australia, 1990-; Vice-President, Federation INternationale des Langues et Litteratures Modernes (FILLM), 1990; Visiting Professor of English, University of Michigan, USA, Edith Cowan University, Western Australia, 1991; External Advisor, Dept of English, University of the South Pacific, 1993. *Publications include:* Jane Austen, 1970; Relative Merits, 1986; Alexander Pope, 1976; Silence, Exile and Cunning. The Fiction of Ruth Prawer Jhabvala, 1983; Word, Bird, Motif, 53 Poems, 1971; Jane Austen: Sense and Sensibility, 1980; The Lizard's Cry and Other Poems, 1972; Diverse Inheritance, A Personal Perspective on Commonwealth Literature, 1980; English Literature in Ceylon 1815-1878: The Development of an Anglo-Ceylonese Literature, 1968; Stories From Sri Lanka, (Editor), 1979; Poems From India, Sri Lanka, Malaysia and Singapore, (Editor) 1979; A Change of Skies (novel) 1991; Celebrations & Departures, Poems, 1991; 6000 Ft Death Dive, Poems, 1981. *Contributions to:* Literary, critical and bibliographical articles in numerous magazines and journals including: ACLALS Bulletin; Australian Library Journal; Cambridge Historical Journal; Journal of Commonwealth Literature, SPAN. *Honours include:* Macquarie University Research Grants, 1981, 1985, 1989, 1992; Australian Research Council Grant, 1991. International Rotary Foundation Travel Grant, 1987; Australia Council Literature Board Travel Grant, 1989; National Swiss Foundation for Scientific Research Travel Grant, 1989; Order of Australia, 1990; Eleanor Dark Writers Fellowship, 1991. *Memberships include:* Australian Society of Authors; 1st Convenor, Macquarie Unit for the Study of the New Literatures in English; Jane Austen Society of Australia, Patron; International Association of University Professors of English (IAUPE); South Pacific Branch of the Assoc for Commonwealth Literature & Language Studies (SPACLALS); Fulbright Association (NSW); South Asian Studies Association of Australia (SASA). *Address:* Post-Colonial Literatures and Language Research Centre, School of English & Linguistics, Macquarie University, North Ryde, NSW 2109, Australia.

GOONETILLEKE Devapriya Chitra Ranjan Alwis, b. 9 Oct 1938, Colombo. Professor of English. m. Chitranganie Lalitha Dalpatad, 23 Nov 1967, 2 sons. *Education:* BA, 1961; PhD, 1970. *Appointments:* Regional Representative, The Journal of Commonwealth Literature, 1978; Associate Editor, Journal of South Asian Literature, 1980; National Editor, The Routledge Encyclopaedia of Commonwealth Literature, 1990; Advisor, Contemporry Novelists, 1990; Advisor, Reference Guilde to Short Fiction, 1992. *Publications:* Developing Countries in British Fiction; Images of the Raj; Joseph Conrad: Beyond Culture and Background; The Penguin New Writing in Sri Lanka; Between Cultures: Essays on Literature, Language & Education. *Contributions to:* 46 Articles. *Honours:* Commonwealth Scholar; Foundation Visiting Fellow, Clare Hall; Henry Charles Chapman Visiting Fellow. *Memberships:* International Chairperson, the Association for Commonwealth Literature and Language Studies; American Studies Association. *Address:* No. 1 Kandewatta Road, Nugegoda, Sri Lanka.

GOPALACHAR Aalavandar. (Aalavandaar), b. 1 July 1929, Nanjangud Tq, Karnataka. m. 3 sons, 2 daughters. *Appointments:* Kannada Language, Novels & Short Stories, Weekly and Monthly Kannada Magazines. *Publications:* Naadini; Punya Purushartha; Mannu Masana; Tumbida Baduky; Baalondu Nandana; Yeru Peru; Sanjaya Mogilu; Gangaalahari; Sethu Bandhana; Baalina Sanjeyali; Raaja Drohini; Veera Pungava; Rohini Chandra; Jeevana Chakra Bharamana; Bandhamukthi; Jeeva Vahini; 32 novels in total; Short Stories: Kallu Sakkare Kolliro; Allola Kallola. *Contributions to:* Numerous. *Honours:* Jnana Jyothi Kala Sangha, Rajajinagar, Bangalore, Yagnananarayana Deekshit Smaraka Memory Award; Award for best Novelist, Short Story Writer by Tarangaranga Associates of Davangere, Chitradurga District, 1984. *Memberships:* Kannada Sahithya Parishat; Kannada Lekhakara Sangha; Shankara Bhashkara Magazine; Poets International Organisation, Bangalore. *Literary Agent:* T S Subramaniyam. *Address:* 261/1 Byrappa Block, 2nd Main, Thyagarajanagar, Bangalore 28, Bangalore 560028.

GOPU. See: GOKANI Pushkar Haridas.

GORAK Jan, b. 12 Oct 1952, Black. Professor of English. m. Irene Elizabeth Mannion, 12 Dec 1983. *Appointments:* Lecturer, Senior Lecturer, University of the Witwatersrand, Johannesburg, 1984-88; Associate, Full Professor, University, Denver. *Publications:* The

Making of the Modern Canon; The Alien Mind of Raymond Williams; God the Artist; Critic of Crisis. *Contributions to:* Denver Quarterly; English Studies in Africa; Theatre Journal; Cambridge History of Literary Criticism, forthcoming. *Honours:* Thomas Pringle Prize. *Memberships:* International Association for the study of Anglo Irish Literature; Modern Language Association; Society for Theatre Research. *Address:* Department of English, University of Denver, Denver, Co 80208, USA.

GORDEY Michel, b. 17 Feb 1913, Berlin, Germany. Journalist; Writer. m. Beverly Bronstein, 1950, 1 son, 1 daughter. *Education:* Law Faculty, Sorbonne and Ecole des Sciences Politiques, Paris. *Appointmeents:* Lawyer, Paris 1933-37; French Army, 1937-40; US Office of War Information, French Editor, Voice of America, 1941-45, Chief Editor, 1944-45; US Correspondent, Paris-presse, 1945; US and UN Correspondent, agence France-Presse, New York & Washington, 1945-46; Roving Foreign and Diplomatic Correspondent, France-Soir, Paris, 1945-56, Chief Foreign Correspondent, 1956- 73; assignments to USSR, USA, Germany, Far East (China, Japan), and most Summit Meetings from 1954-1976; Roving Foreign and Diplomatic Correspondent, L'Express, Paris, 1973-77; Special Correspondent, Europe, Newsday, New York, 1977-. *Publication:* Visa pour Moscou, 1951 *Contributions to:* Numerous journals and magazines. *Honours:* Several journalistic Awards. *Address:* 16 rue de Savoie, 75006 Paris, France.

GORDIMER Nadine, b. 20 Nov 1923. Writer. m. Reinhold Cassirer, 1954, 1 son, 1 daughter. *Publications:* The Soft Voice of the Serpent; The Lying Days, 1953; Six Feet of the Country, 1956; A World of Strangers, 1958; Friday's Footprint, 1960; Occasion for Loving, 1963; Not for Publication, 1965; The Late Bourgeois World, 1966; A Guest of Honour, 1970; Livingstone's Companions, 1972; The Black Interpreters (literary criticism), 1973; The Conservationist, 1974; Selected Stories, 1975; Some Monday for Sure, 1976; Burger's Daughter, 1979; A Soldier's Embrace, 1980; July's People, 1981; Something Out There, 1984; Six Feet of Country, 1986; A Sport of Nature, 1987; The Essential Gesture (essays), 1988; Non-fiction: On The Mines (photographs, David Goldblatt); Lifetimes: Under Apartheid (excerpts from W G's novels and stories, photographs, David Goldblatt). *Contributions to:* Co-Editor, South African Writing Today, 1967. *Honours:* W.H. Smith Literary Award 1961; Thomas Pringle Award, 1969; James Tait Black Memorial Prize, 1971; Booker Prize (co-winner), 1974; Grand Aigle d'Or Prize, France, 1975; Scottish Arts Council Neil M. Gun Fellowship, 1981; Modern Language Association Award, USA, 1981; Premio Malaparte, Italy, 1985; Nobel Prize for Literature, 1991; Sachs Prize, Germany, 1985; Bennett Award, USA, 1987; Hon. member American Academy of Arts & Sciences; Hon. Fellow Modern Language Association (USA); Fellow Royal Society of Literature; Patron Congress of South African Writers. *Memberships:* Vice President, International PEN; Hon. Member, American Academy, Institute of Arts and Letters. *Address:* 7 Frere Road, Parktown, Johannesburg 2193, South Africa.

GORDON David M, b. 4 May 1944, Washington, DC, USA. Economist. m. Dinna R Gordon, 7 Sept 1967. *Education:* BA, Harvard College, 1965; PhD, 1971. *Publications:* After the Waste Land; Beyond the Waste Land; Segmented Work, Divided Workers; Problems in Political Economy; Theories of Poverty & Under Employment. *Contributions to:* Nation; Atlantic; NY Times. *Honours:* C Wright Mills Award; GrigglInheim Fellowship. *Memberships:* Signet Society; American Economics Association; Union of Radical Political Economics; National Writers Union. *Address:* 317 E 10th Street, New York, NY 10009, USA.

GORDON Diana. *See:* **ANDREWS Lucilla.**

GORDON Donald. *See:* **PAYNE Donald Graham.**

GORDON Donald Ramsay, b. 14 Sept 1929, Toronto, Canada. Writer. m. Helen E. Currie, 21 Dec 1952, 3 sons. *Education:* BA (Hons), Political Science and Economics, Queen's University, Kingston, Ontario, 1953; MA, Political Economy, University of Toronto, 1955; Predoctoral studies in Political Science, London School of Economic and Political Science, England, 1956-63. *Appointments:* Writer, Filing Editor, The Canadian Press, Toronto, Montreal, Edmonton, 1955; Assistant Editor, The Financial Post, Toronto, 1955-57; European Correspondent, Canadian Broadcasting Corporation, London, England, 1957-63; Assistant/ Associate Professor of Political Science, University of Calgary, Alta, 1963-66; Assistant/Associate Professor of Political Science, University of Waterloo, Ontario, 1966-75; Self-employed Writer, Consultant, Waterloo, London, Ontario, Toronto, Ottawa, 1975-81; Chief Writer, The Image Corporation, Waterloo, 1983-. *Publications:* Language, Logic and the Mass Media, 1966; The New Literacy, 1971; The Media, in Read Canadian, 1972; Fineswine, 1984; The Rock Candy Bandits, 1984; S.P.E.E.D., 1984; The Prosperian Papers, Vol 1 The Rock Candy Bandits, 1989; The Choice, 1990. *Contributions to:* Canadian Commentator; Canadian Forum; Saturday Night; Macleans; The Globe and Mail; The Financial Post; The Times; Everybody's Magazine; The Guardian; The Spectator; New Statesman and Nation; Canadian Dimension; The Toronto Star; Hamilton Spectator; The World Today (RIIA); CIIA; Radio and TV reports, documentaries. *Honours:* Ford Foundation Communications Fellowship, 1954; Open Fellowship, University of Toronto, 1955; Travel and Research Award, International Institute of Education, 1962-63; Canada Council Research Award, 1969. *Memberships:* Canadian Authors Association; Writers Union of Canada; Alliance of Canadian Cinema, Television and Radio Artists; Canadian Society of Children's Authors, Illustrators and Performers. *Literary Agent:* Morris Talent Management, 33 Nasmith Avenue, Toronto, Ontario Canada M5A 3J2. *Address:* 134 Iroquois Place, Waterloo, Ontario, Canada N2L 2S5.

GORDON Gaelyn Mary, b. 26 Nov 1939, Hawela, New Zealand. Writer. m. Peter Gordon, 16 May 1964, 1 son, 1 daughter. *Education:* BA, University of NZ, 1961; LTCL, 1961. *Appointments:* Frank Sargeson Fellow, 1992. *Publications:* Above Suspicion; Prudence M Muggendge, Damp Rat; Stonelight; Strained Relations; Several Things Are Alive & Well & Living in Alfed Browns Head; Tales from Another Home; Mindfire; Duckat; Tripswitch; Last Summer. *Contributions to:* Landfall; NZ Listener. *Honours:* Cheysa Bursary; QE11 Literary Grant. *Memberships:* childrens Book Founder; NZ Book Council; PEN; New Zealand Writers Guild. *Literary Agent:* Michael Gifkins. *Address:* PO Box 15-235, Dinsdale, Hamilton, New Zealand.

GORDON Giles Alexander Esme, b. 23 May 1940, Edinburgh, Scotland. Lecturer; Literary Agent; Writer; Theatre Critic. m. (1) Margaret Gordon (dec), 2 sons, 1 daughter, (2) Maggie McKernan, 1 daughter. *Education:* Edinburgh Academy. *Appointments:* Advertising Manager, Secker & Warburg; Editor, Hutchinson & Co, & Penguin Books; Editorial Director, Victor Gollancz Ltd; Member, Literature Panel, Arts Council of Great Britain; Chairman, Society of Young Publishers; Lecturer, Creative Writing, Tufts University, USA; Lectuer, Theatre Critism, Hollins College, USA; Secretary/Fellow, Royal Society of Literature, 1991; Council Member, RSL, 1992-. *Publications:* Two & Two Make One, 1966; Two Elegies, 1968; Pictures from an Exhibition, 1970; The Umbrella Man, 1971; Twelve Poems for Callum, 1972; About a Marriage, 1972; Girl With Red Hair, 1974; Farewell Fond Dreams, 1975; Beyond the Words, Editor, 1975; 100 Scenes from Married Life, 1976; Members of the Jury, Editor with Dulan Barber, 1976; Enemies, 1977, Ambroses Vision, 1980, Modern Short Stories, 1940-1980, Editor, 1982; Best Short Stories, 1986, 1987, 1988, 1989, 1990, 1991, 1992, 1993 co-editor with David Hughes; Short Stories from 1900-1985, Editor, 1988; The Twentieth Century Short Story in English, 1989; Aren't We Due a Royalty Statement, 1993. *Contributions to:* Theatre Critic, Spectator, 1983-84; Deputy Theatre Critic, Punch,

1985-87; Reviewer of Plays, Observer, Plays & Players, Editor, Drama Magazine; articles in various journals, magazines & newspapers including, The Times, Bookseller; etc; Theatre Critic, London Daily News, 1987; Sunday Time, Private Eye, Evening Standard, Forte. *Memberships:* Society of Authors; Garrick Club, PEN. *Address:* 9 St Ann's Garden's, London, NW5, England.

GORDON Ian Alistair, b. 30 July 1908, Edinburgh, Scotland. Professor of English, Emeritus. m. Mary Ann Fullarton, 1936. 1 son, 3 daughters. *Education:* MA 1930, 1932, PhD 1936, University of Edinburgh. *Appointments:* Chairman, New Zealand Literary Fund, -1973; Columnist, New Zealand Listener, 1975-88. *Publications:* The Movement of English Prose, 1966; Katherine Mansfield, 1954; Undiscovered Country, 1974; John Galt, 1972; A Word in Your Ear, 1980; John Skelton, 1943; Consulting Editor, Collins English Dictionaries, 1981-; The Urewera Notebook, 1986. *Contributions to:* Times Literary Supplement; Times Education Supplement; New Zealand Listener; Poetry Chicago; Review of English Studies; Modern Language Review; Landfall; New Scientists. *Honours:* Honorary LLD, Bristol University, 1948; Honorary DLitt, University of New Zealand, 1961; Honorary Doctorate, University of Stirling, 1975; CBE, 1971; Visiting Professor: London 1954, Edinburgh 1962, 1974, Fiji 1972, Leeds 1975; Lectured in USA, France, Belgium, Holland. *Address:* 10 Hukanui Crescent, Herne Bay, Auckland, New Zealand.

GORDON Jane. *See:* **LEE Elsie.**

GORDON John Fraser, b. 1916, United Kingdom. Managing Director; Writer. *Appointments:* Managing Director, Dongora Mill Co Ltd, London, and J F Gordon (London) Ltd, 1963-. *Publications:* Staffordshire Bull Terrier Handbook, Bull Terrier Handbook, Bulldog Handbook, Dandie Dinmont Terrier Handbook, 1952-59; Staffordshire Bull Terriers, 1964; Miniature Schnauzers, 1966; Spaniel Owner's Encyclopedia, 1967; Staffordshire Bull Terrier Owner's Encyclopedia, 1967; The Beagle Guide, 1968; The Miniature Schnauzer Guide, 1968; All About the Boxer, 1970; The Staffordshire Bull Terrier, 1970; All About the Cocker Spaniel, 1971; The Pug, 1973; The Irish Wolfhound; The Borzoi; Some Rare and Unusual Breeds; The Bull Terrier; The Bulldog; The Dandie Dinmont Terrier; The German Shepherd, 1978; The Pyrenean Mountain Dog, 1978; The Alaskan Malamute, 1979; Schnauzers, 1982; All About the Staffordshire Bull Terrier, 1984; All About the Cairn Terrier, 1987. *Honours:* Freeman of the City of Lonndon and Member of the Guild of Freemen, 1938; Horticultural Hybridist of Fuchsia Gordon's China Rose, 1953. *Membership:* Society of Authors. *Address:* 13 Maypole Drive, Chigwell Row, Essex IG7 6DE, England.

GORDON John William, b. 19 Nov 1925, Jarrow-on-Tyne, England. Writer. m. Sylvia Young, 9 Jan 1954. 1 son, 1 daughter. *Publications:* The Giant Under The Snow, 1968, sequel, Ride The Wind, 1989; The House On The Brink, 1970; The Ghost On The Hill, 1976; The Waterfall Box, 1978; The Spitfire Grave, 1979; The Edge Of The World, 1983; Catch Your Death, 1984; The Quelling Eye, 1986; The Grasshopper, 1987; Secret Corridor, 1990; Blood Brothers, 1991; Ordinary Seaman, autobiography, 1992; The Burning Baby, 1992. *Contribution to:* Beginnings (Signal 1989). *Literary Agent:* AP Watt, London, England. *Address:* 99 George Borrow Road, Norwich NR4 7HU, England.

GORDON Keith. *See:* **BAILEY Gordon.**

GORDON Mary (Catherine), b. 1949, USA. Author. *Appointments:* English Teacher, Dutchess Community College, Poughkeepsie, New York, 1974- 78. *Publications:* Final Payments, 1978; The Company of Women, 1981; Men and Angels, 1985; The Other Side. *Literary Agent:* Peter Matson, USA. *Address:* c/o Peter Matson, 32 West 40th Street, New York, NY 10023, USA.

GORDON Rex. *See:* **HOUGH Stanley Bennett.**

GORDON Sheila, b. 22 Jan 1927, Johannesburg, South Africa. Writer. m. Harley Gordon, 7 July 1947, 2 sons, 1 daughter. *Education:* BA, University of the Witwatersrand, Johannesburg. *Publications:* Unfinished Business; A Modest Harmony; A Monster in the Mailbox; Waiting for the Rain; The Middle of Somewhere. *Contributions to:* New York Times; Antaeus Quarterly. *Honours:* Jane Addams Award. *Memberships:* PEN; Authors Guild. *Literary Agent:* Elaine Markson. *Address:* c/o Elain Markson Literary Agency, 44 Greenwich Avenue, New York, NY 10011, USA.

GORDON Stewart. *See:* **SHIRREFFS Gordon Donald.**

GOREKAR Nizamuddin Sharafuddin, b. 12 Aug 1921, Bhiwandi. Professor. m. Haseena, 11 Jan 1953, 1 son. *Education:* BA, 1942; MA, 1944; PhD, 1968; D Litt, 1973. *Appointments include:* Sophia College for Women, St Xavcer's College, 1944-; Director, A J URDU Research Institute, 1975-; Principal, KME Societys Womens College, 1988-91. *Publications:* Glimpses of Urdu Literature; Urdu Marathi Shabdakosha; Nawa e Wagt; Indo Iran Relations; Tutiyan e Hind; Adab; Amuzgar e Farsi & Armughane Farsi; Talimul Arabiyah & Faraidul Adab; (Ed) Nawa-e-Adali, a bi-annual Research Journal, 1976. *Contributions to:* Indo Iranica; Sabras; Indica; Shair; Tehzibul Akhlaq; Nawa e Adab; Indian Magazine. *Honours include:* President of Indias Certifiacte of Honor in Literature. *Memberships:* Indian Institute of Public Administration; Heres Society of History and Culture;; Asiatic Society of Bombay; Rotary Club and Giants Group of Kelyan; All India Oriental Conference's Arabic-Persian Section, Islamic Studies Section., West Asian Studies and South East Asian Section, Natural and International Seminars and Symposia, various places; Expert, Selection Committees by Public Service Commissions, State Level and Central Level at Delhi. *Address:* Bait Ush Sharaf, Bunder Road, Kalyan, MS 421301, India.

GORES Joe, b. 25 Dec 1931, Rochester, Minnesota, USA. Writer; Novelist; Screenwriter. m. Dori Corfitzen, 16 May 1976. 1 son, 1 daughter. *Education:* BA, University of Notre Dame, 1953; MA, Stanford University, 1961. *Appointments:* Story Editor, B.L. Stryker Mystery Movie Series, ABC-TV, 1988-89. *Publications:* Hammett, 1975; Interface, 1974; Come Morning, 1986; Wolf Time, 1989; A Time of Predators, 1969; Dead Skip, 1972; Final Notice, 1973; Gone, No Forwarding, 1978; Marine Salvage (non fiction), 1971; 32 Cadillacs, awaiting publication; Mostly Murder, short story collection, 1992; Dead Man, 1993. *Contributions to:* Numerous magazines and anthologies; 8 film scripts; 25 hours of television drama. *Honours:* MWA Edgar, Best First Novel, 1969; MWA Edgar, Best Short Story, 1969; MWA Edgar, Best Episodic TV Drama, 1975; The Maltese Falcon Society of Japan, Falcon, 1986. *Memberships:* Mystery Writers of America, President 1986; International Association of Crime Writers; Crime Writers Association. *Literary Agent:* Henry Morrison, Henry Morrison Inc, P O Box 235, Bedford Hills, NY 10507, USA. *Address:* P O Box 446, Fairfax, CA 94978, USA.

GORGEY Gabor, b. 22 Nov 1929, Budapest, Hungary. Writer. m. 1954-1984, 1 daughter. *Education:* Maturity Examination, 1948; Study of Phil, 1948-49; Theology, 1954-55. *Appointments:* Dramaturgist of Pannonia Film, 1964-72; Art Director, National Theatre of Szeged, Hungary, 1982-88; Columnist of the Daily Magyar Nemet, 1959-. *Publications:* One Pistol for Five; Encounter with a Half a Dog; Second Half of a Half a Dog; Anatomy of a Supper; The Hunting Carpet; Book of Temptations; Heads for Ferdinand; Revenge of the

Diva; There Was Sometime a Hungary. *Honours:* Robert Graves Prize; Jozsef Attila Prize; Pro Arte. *Memberships:* PEN; International Theatre Institute; ITI. *Literary Agent:* Artisjus, Budapest 1054, Vorosmarty ter 1. *Address:* Jozsa B.U. 32, Budapest 1125, Hungary.

GORMAN Brian. *See:* **GORMAN Clem.**

GORMAN Clem, (Brian Gorman), b. 18 Oct 1942, Perth, Western Australia. Writer m. Sarah Dent 1967 (div 1986). *Education:* Louis School, Perth, 1955-56; Aquinas College, Perth 1957-60; Ba, Dip Ed, University of Sydney, 1963-67; Diploma in Arts Administration, Polytechnic of Central London, 1975. *Career:* Freelance Stage Manager and Theatre Administrator, Sydney, 1967-68; Founder, Australian Free Theatre Group; Co-founder, Masque Theatre Magazine, 1968; Lived in London 1970-79, Deputy Administrator, Round House Trust, London 1975-76; Administrator, Moving Being dance company, Cardiff, 1976-77; Administrator, Australian National Playwrights Conference, Sydney, 1982; Lecturer in Playwriting, Victorian College of the Arts, Melbourne, 1984 and Adelaide University 1985; Training Officer, Australian Book Publishers Association, Sydney, 1986; Freelance journalist 1966-. *Publications:* Plays include: A Fortunate Life, adaptation of the autobiography of A B Facey (produced Melbourne 1984); The Journey Home (for children, produced Adelaide, 1985); A Face from the Street (produced Canberra, 1985); The Last Night-Club, Montmorency, Victoria, Yackandandah, 1985. Screenplay: The Swans Away (documentary) 1986 and other publications. *Honours:* Australia Council Literature Board Grant, 1980 and fellowship 1981. *Literary Agent:* Anthony Williams, POtts Point, New South Wales, Australia. *Address:* 505/3 Greenknowe Avenue, Potts Point, NSW 2011, Australia.

GORMAN Ed, b. 29 Nov 1941, Cedar Rapids. Writer. m. Carol Maxwell, 2 Jan 1982, 1 son. *Education:* Coe College, 1962-66. *Publications:* Night Kills; The Autumn Dead; The Night Remembers; Prisoners Collection of Short Stories; A Cry of Shadows. *Contributions to:* Redbook; Ellery Queen; Mayayneof Poetry. *Literary Agent:* Dominick Abel, 146 West 82nd Street, New York, NY 10024. *Address:* 3601 Skylark Lane, Cedar Rapids, IA 52403, USA.

GORMAN Ginny. *See:* **ZACHARY Hugh.**

GOSLING Paula Louise, b. 12 Oct 1939, Detroit, Michigan, USA. Author. m. Christopher Gosling, 20 July 1968, 2 daughters, div, (2) John Anthony Hare, 17 Sept. 1981. *Education:* BA, Wayne State University. *Publications:* Running Duck, (Fair Game-USA), 1978; Zero Trap, 1979; Loser's Blues (Solo Blues - USA), 1980; Woman in Red, 1983; Monkey Puzzle, 1985; The Wychford Murders, 1986; Hoodwink, 1988; Backlash, 1989; As Ainslie Skinner: Mind's Eye, (The Harrowing-USA), 1980; Death Penalties, 1991; The Body in Blackwater Bay, 1992. *Contributions to:* Various Womens Magazines. *Honours:* John Creasey Award, 1978; Gold Dagger Award, 1986. *Memberships:* Society of Authors; Crime Writers' Association, Deputy Chairman, 1987, Chairman, 1988. *Literary Agent:* Lady Elaine Greene. *Address:* c/o Elaine Greene Ltd., 31 Newington Green, London N16 9PU, England.

GOSSOP Michael, b. 2 June 1948, Chesterfield, England. Psychologist. *Education:* BA, University College of Cardiff, 1969; PhD, 1972. *Appointments:* Head of Research, Drug Dependence Clinical Research and Treatment Unit, National Addiction Centre, London, 1972-. *Publications:* Living With Drugs; Theories of Neurosis; Relapse and Addictive Behaviour; Preventing & Controlling Drug Abuse. *Contributions to:* Times Literary Supplement; Observer; British Medical Journal; Lancet. *Memberships:* Fellow British Psychological Society. *Address:* National Addiction Centre, London SE5 8AF, England.

GOTFRYD Bernard, b. 25 May 1924, Poland. m. 22 Mar 1952, 1 son. *Publications:* Anton The Dove Fancier and Other Tales Of The Holocaust; Translations: Dutch, Italian, Swedish. *Contributions to:* Midstream; Jewish Monthly; Forward; Literary Cavalcade. *Honours:* Christopher Award; Pen American Martha Albrand Award; Nominated for New Visions. *Memberships:* PEN. *Literary Agent:* Julian Bach. *Address:* 46 Wendover Road, Forest Hills, NY 11375, USA.

GOTLIEB Phyllis (Fay), b. 1926, Canada. Author. *Publications:* Within the Zodiac, 1964; Sunburst, novel, 1964; Why Should I Have All the Grief, novel, 1969; Ordinary, Moving, 1969; Garden Varieties, 1972; Doctor Umlaut's Earthly Kingdom, 1974; O Master Caliban, novel, 1976; The Works, poetry, 1978; A Judgement of Dragons, novel, 1980; Emperor Swords Pentacles, novel, 1982; Son of the Morning and Other Stories, short stories, 1983; The Kingdom of the Cats, novel, 1985. *Address:* 29 Ridgevale Drive, Toronto, Ontario, Canada M6A 1K9.

GOTTLIEB Alma, b. 10 July 1954, Queens, NY, USA. Cultural Anthropologist. m. Philip Graham, 7 Aug 1977, 1 son. *Education:* BA, Sarah Lawrence College, 1975; MA, University of Virginia, 1978; PhD, 1983. *Publications:* Blood Magic; Under the Kapok Tree; Parallel Worlds; Beng English Dictionary. *Contributions to:* Man; Africa; American Ethnologist; Anthropology Today; Dialectical Anthropology. *Honours:* One of Ten best Books in Anthropology; Fellowships from National Endowment for the Humanities. *Memberships:* American Anthropological Association; Royal Anthropological Institute of Great Britain & Ireland; International African Institute; MANSA. *Literary Agent:* Geri Thoma. *Address:* Department of Anthropology, 109 Davenport Hall, 607S Mathews Avenue, University of Illinois, Urbana, IL 61801, USA.

GOTTSCHALL Edward Maurice, b. 28 Dec 1915, NYC, USA. Graphic Arts Company Executive. m. (1) Lee Beatrice Natale, 6 Feb 1943, 1 son, (2) Alice J Wise, 1985. *Education:* BS, CCNY 1937; MS, Columbia University, 1938. *Appointments include:* Managing Editor, Graphic Arts Production Yearbook, 1937-51; Editor Art Direction, 1952-69; Senior Editor, Popular Merchandising Co, 1964-67; Editorial Director, Advt Trade Publs, 1967-69; Vice Chairman, International Typeface Corporation, 1986-; Editor, 1981-90. *Publications:* Commerical Art As A Business; Graphic Communication '80s; Typographic Communications Today; Advertising Directions. *Contributions to:* Graphic Arts Manual; Contemporary Masterworks. *Address:* 63 Highland Ave, Eastchester, NY 10707, USA.

GOUDGE Eileen, b. 4 July 1950. Writer m. Albert J Zuckerman, 28 Apr 1985, 1 son, 1 daughter. *Education:* 1 year San Diego State University; California State Vocational Teaching Degree, 1976. *Publication:* Garden of Lies, 1989; Such Devoted Sisters, 1992. *Contributions to:* Good Housekeeping; McCall's; Highlights for Children; National Geographic; San Francisco Chronicle. *Literary Agent:* Albert J Zuckerman, Writers House. *Address:* 234 W 22 Street, New York, NY 10011, USA.

GOULD James L, b. 31 July 1945, Tulsa, Oklahoma, USA. Professor. m. Carol Holly Grant, 6 June 1970, 1 son, 1 daughter. *Education:* BS, California Institute of Technology, 1970; PhD Rockafellow University, 1975. *Publications:* Biological Science; Sexual Selection; Ethology; The Honey Bee; Life At The Edge. *Contributions to:* More than 100 Articles inc. Science Nature; Harpers; Scientific American; The science; Animal Behaviour. *Address:* Department of Ecology & Evolutionary Biology, Princeton University, Princeton, NJ 08544, USA.

GOULDEN Joseph C, b. 23 May 1934, Marshall, Texas, USA. Writer. m. Leslie Cantrell Smith, 23 June 1979, 2 sons by previous marriage. *Education:*

University of Texas, 1952-56. *Appointment:* Staff Writer, Dallas (TX) Morning News, Philadelphia Inquirer, 1958-68. *Publications:* The Curtis Caper, 1965; Monopoly, 1968; Truth is the First Casualty, 1969; The Money Givers, 1971; The Superlawyers, 1972; Meany: The Unchallenged Strong Man of America Labor, a biography of Geo Meany, the AFL - CIO president; The Benchwarmers, 1974; Editor, Mencken's Last Campaign, 1976; The Best Years, 1976; The Million Dollar Lawyers, 1978; Korea: Untold Story of War, 1982; Labor's Last Angry Man: A biography of public workers union president, Jerry Wurf; The Death Merchant, 1984; There Are Alligators in Our Sewers, with Paul Dickson, 1984; Dictionary of Espionage, (as Henry S A Becket), 1986; Fit to Print: A M Rosenthal and His Times. *Contributions to:* over 200 magazine articles. *Honours:* National Magazine Award, 1969; Carr P Collins Award, 1976; Distinguished Alumnus Award, University of Texas Communications College, 1987. *Memberships:* Co-Founder, Washington Independent Writers; Texas Institute of Letters; PEN; Association of Former Intelligence Officers; H.L. Mencken Society. *Literary Agent:* Brandt & Brandt, New York. *Address:* 1534, 29th Street NW, Washington. DC 20007, USA.

GOVER (John) Robert, (O Govi), b. 1929, USA. Author. *Appointments:* Reporter, newspapers in Pennsylvania and Maryland, until 1961. *Publications:* One Hundred Dollar Misunderstanding, 1962; The Maniac Responsible, 1963; Here Goes Kitten, 1964; Poorboy at the Party, 1966; J C Saves, 1968; The Portable Walter: From the Poetry and Prose of Walter Lowenfels (editor), 1968; Luke Small Tells All, 1973; Going for Mr Big, 1973; Tomorrow Now Occurs Again (as O Govi), 1975; Getting Pretty on the Table (as O Govi), 1975; Bring Me the Head of Rona Barrett, stories, 1981. *Address:* General Delivery, Carpinteria, CA 93013, USA.

GOVI O. *See:* **GOVER (John) Robert.**

GOWAR Michael Robert, (Mick Gowar), b. 27 Nov 1951, England. Writer; Performer. 1 daughter. *Education:* BA, Anglia polytechnic, 1974; Kingston Polytechnic, 1975. *Appointments:* Coordinator, Cambridge Poetry Festival, 1981; Various Regional Arts Boards; Many Single visits and Short Residencies in Schools. *Publications:* Third Time Lucky; So Far So Good; Live Album; A Hard Days Work; Brenda The Do It Yourself Brownie; Caroline Columbus Walker. *Memberships:* Cambridge Poetry Festival Society. *Literary Agent:* Murray Pollinger. *Address:* c/o Murray Pollinger, 222 Old Brampton Road, London, SW5, England.

GRABES Herbert, b. 8 June 1936, Professor. m. Hannelore Koch, 2 Mar 1962, 2 sons, 1 daughter. *Education:* University of Cologne, 1963; University of Mannheim, 1969. *Publications:* Der Begriff Des A Priori in Nicolai Hartmann; Fictitious Biographies; The Mutable Glass; Fiktion, Imitiation, Asthetik; Das Engusche Pamphlet I. *Contributions to:* 47 Longer Articles in Various German Literary Periodicals. *Memberships:* Nabokov Society; Deutsche Shakespeare; Gesellschaft Fur Englische Romantik. *Address:* Sonnenstr 37, 6301 Biebertal 1, Germany.

GRACE Peter J, b. 25 May 1913, Manhasset, NY. m. Margaret Fennelly, 24 May 1941. *Education:* BA, Yale University, 1936. *Appointments include:* Member of Staff 1936-42, Secretary 1942-43, Member of Board of Directors 1943, Chief Executive Officer 1945-1990, Chairman and Chief Executive Officer 1990-, W.R. Grace & Co, Fl; Member, Board of Directors of Canonie Environmental Services Corp; Office Warehouse, Inc; Milliken & Company, Omnicare, Inc; Restaurant Enterprises Group Inc; Roto-Rooter, Inc; Stone & Webster, Inc; Director Emeritus, Ingersoll-Rand Company; Chairman of the Board of Director of Chemed Corp, and Del Taco Restaurants, Inc; Chairman of the Board, Chief Executive Officer and Director of Grace Energy Corp; Chairman of President Reagan's Private Sector Survey on Cost Control in the Federal Government (Grace Commission) 1982-84. *Publication:* Burning Money: The Waste of Your Tax Dollars, 1984. *Honours:* Recipient of numerous honours and awards for professional services. *Memberships include:* Everglades Club; The Links; Lotos Club; President, Member of Board of Counsellors, American Association of the Sovereign Military Order of Malta. *Address:* c/o W R Grace and Company, One Town Center Rd, Boca Raton, FL 33486, USA.

GRAEF Roger Arthur, b. 18 Apr 1936, New York, New York, USA, Writer; Television producer; Filmmaker. m. Susan Mary Richards, 20 Nov 1985, 1 son, 1 daughter. *Education:* BA, Honours, Harvard University; Actors Studio's, New York City. *Appointment:* Consultant to Collins Publishers, 1982-88. *Publications:* Talking Blues, 1989; Living Dangerously, 1993; Over 100 films and television programmes for British and International Television. *Contributions to:* Media columns, The Times; The Telegraph; Sunday Telegraph; The Observer; The Guardian; The Independent; The Independent on Sunday; Sunday Times; The Listener; New Society. *Honours:* Winner, Royal Television Society Award, 1979; British Academy of Television and Film Arts, (BAFTA) 1982; European Television Magazines Award. *Membership:* Writers' Guild. *Literary Agent:* Rogers, Coleridge and White. *Address:* 72 Westbourne Park Villas, London W2, England.

GRAFF Henry Franklin, b. 1921, USA. Historian; Professor Emeritus of History. *Publications:* Bluejackets with Perry in Japan, 1952; The Modern Researcher (with J Barzun), 1957, 5th Edition, 1992; American Themes (with C Lord), 1963; Thomas Jefferson, 1968; The Free and the Brave, 1967, 4th Edition, 1980; American Imperialism and the Philippine Insurrection (editor), 1969; The Tuesday Cabinet: Deliberation and Decision on Peace and War under Lyndon B Johnson, 1970; The Adventure of the American People (with J A Krout), 3rd Edition, 1973; The Grand Experiment (with P J Bohannan), vol I, The Call of Freedom, vol II, The Promise of Democracy, 1978; This Great Nation, 1983; The Presidents: A Reference History, 1984; America: The Glorious Republic, 1985, 2nd Edition, 1990. *Address:* 47 Andrea Lane, Scarsdale, NY 10583, USA.

GRAFTON David, b. 13 Nov 1930, Brockport, New York, USA. *Appointments:* Contact US (performing arts management company), Chicago, Ill, President, 1971-82; Triad Consulting Services, Chicago, Consultant, 1982-; Lecturer on Cole Porter and the Cafe Society. *Publications:* Red Hot and Rich - An Oral History of Cole Porter, 1987. *Contributions to:* Various journals. *Honour:* The Friends of Literature Award, 1988. *Memberships:* Authors Guild. *Address:* 707 Waveland Avenue, Apartment 404, Chicago, IL 60613, USA.

GRAHAM Ada, b. 1931, USA. Author. *Appointments:* Vice-Chairman, Maine State Commission on the Arts, 1975-80; Board Member, New England Foundation for the Arts, 1977-80; Developer, Writer, Audubon Adventures, National Audubon Society, 1984-. *Publications:* The Great American Shopping Cart (with Frank Graham), 1969; Wildlife Rescue (with Frank Graham), 1970; Puffin Island (with Frank Graham), 1971; The Mystery of the Everglades, 1972; Dooryard Garden, 1974; Let's Discover the Winter Woods, 1974; Let's Discover the Floor of the Forest, 1974; Let's Discover Changes Everywhere, 1974; Let's Discover Birds in Our World, 1974; The Careless Animal, 1974; The Milkweed and Its World of Animals (with F Graham), 1976; Foxtails, Ferns and Fishscales: A Handbook of Art and Nature Projects, 1976; Whale Watch, 1978; Bug Hunters, 1978; Coyote Song, 1978; Falcon Flight, 1978; Audubon Readers, (with F Graham), 6 vols, 1978-81; Alligators (with F Graham), 1979; Careers in Conservation (with F Graham), 1980; Birds of the Northern Seas (with F Graham), 1980; Bears, 1981; The Changing Desert (with F Graham), 1981; Jacob and the Owl (with F Graham), 1981; Three Million Mice (with F Graham), 1981; Six Little Chickadees, 1982; Busy Bugs (with F Graham), 1983; The Big Stretch (with

F Graham), 1985; We Watch Squirrels (with F Graham), 1985. *Honours:* First Prize, Annual Children's Science Book Award, New York Academy of Sciences, 1986; Eva L. Gordon Award of The American Nature Study Soicety, 1989. *Membership:* Board of Directors, Maine Family Planning Association, 1973-80. *Address:* Milbridge, ME 04658, USA.

GRAHAM Charles S. *See:* **TUBB E C.**

GRAHAM Donald Edward, b. 22 Apr 1945, Baltimore, Maryland, USA. Newspaper Publisher. m. Mary L. Wissler, 1967, 1 son, 3 daughters. *Education:* BA, Harvard University. *Appointments:* Joined Washington Post, 1971, Assistant Managing Editor/ Sports, 1974-75, Assistant General Manager, 1975-76, Executive Vice-President and General Manager, 1976-79, Publisher, 1979-; formerly Reporter and Writer for Newsweek. *Address:* The Washington Post, 1150 15th Street NW, Washington, DC 20071, USA.

GRAHAM Frank Jr, b. 1925, USA. Author; Editor. *Appointments:* Field Editor, Audubon magazine, 1968-. *Publications:* It Takes Heart (with M Allen), 1959; Disaster by Default, 1966; The Great American Shopping Cart (with Ada Graham), 1969; Since Silent Spring, 1970; Wildlife Rescue (with A Graham), 1970; Puffin Island (with A Graham), 1971; Man's Dominion, 1971; The Mystery of the Everglades (with A Graham), 1972; Where the Place Called Morning Lies, 1973; Audubon Primers (with A Graham), 4 vols, 1974; The Careless Animal (with A Graham), 1975; Gulls: A Social History, 1975; Potomac: The Nation's River, 1976; The Milkweed and Its World of Animals (with A Graham), 1976; The Adirondack Park: A Political History, 1978; Audubon Readers (with A Graham), 6 vols, 1978-81; Careers in Conservation (with A Graham), 1980; Birds of the Northern Seas (with A Graham), 1981; A Farewell to Heroes, 1981; The Changing Desert (with A Graham), 1981; Jacob and Owl (with A Graham), 1981; Three Million Mice (with A Graham), 1981; Busy Bugs (with A Graham), 1983; The Dragon Hunters, 1984; The Big Stretch (with A Graham), 1985; We Watch Squirrels (with A Graham), 1985; The Audubon Ark, 1990. *Address:* Milbridge, ME 04658, USA.

GRAHAM Henry, b. 1 Dec 1930, Liverpool, England. Lecturer. *Education:* Liverpool College of Art, 1950-52. *Appointments:* Poetry Editor, Literary Magazine, Ambit, London, 1969-90. *Publications:* Good Luck To You Kafka/You'll Need It Boss, 1969; Soup City Zoo, 1969; Passport to Earth, 1971; Poker in Paradise Lost, 1977; Europe After Rain, 1981; Bomb, 1985; The Very Fragrant Death of Paul Gauguin, 1987; Jardin Gobe Avions, 1991. *Contributions to:* Ambit; Transatlantic Review; Prism International; Evergreen Review; Numerous anthologies worldwide. *Honours:* Arts Council Literature Awards, 1969, 1971, 1975. *Address:* Flat 5, 23 Marmion Road, Liverpool, L17 8TT, England.

GRAHAM James. *See:* **PATTERSON Harry.**

GRAHAM Vanessa. *See:* **FRASER Anthea Mary.**

GRAHAM Victor Ernest, b. 1920, Canada. Emeritus Professor. *Appointments:* Professor of French, University of Alberta, Calgary, 1948-58; Professor of French, 1958- (currently Emeritus Professor), Chairman, Graduate Department of French, 1965-67, Associate Dean, School of Graduate Studies, 1967-69, Vice-Principal, University College, 1969-70, University of Toronto. *Publications:* Phildippe Desportes: Cartels et Masquarades (editor), 1958; Desportes: Les Amours de Diana, vols 1 and 2 (editor), 1959; Desportes: Les Amours d'Hippolyte (editor), 1960; Desportes: Les Elegies (editor), 1961; Desportes: Cleonice, Dernieres Amours (editor), 1962; Representative French Poetry (editor), 1962; Desportes: Diverses Amours (editor), 1963; Sixteenth French Poetry (editor), 1964; André Chamson: Le Chiffre de nos jours (editor), 1965; The Imagery of Proust, 1966; Pernette du Guillet: Rimes (editor), 1968; Estienne Jodelle: Le Recueil des inscriptions 1558 (with W McAllister Johnson), 1972; The Paris Entries of Charles IX and Elisabeth of Austria 1571 (with W McAllister Johnson), 1974; Bibliographies des études sur Marcel Proust et son oeuvre, 1976; The Royal Tour of France by Charles IX and Catherine de Medici: Festivals and Entries 1564-66 (with W McAllister Johnson), 1979. *Address:* French Department, University College, University of Toronto, Toronto, Ontario, Canada M5S 1A1.

GRAHAM Winston Mawdsley, b. Victoria Park, Manchester. m. Jean Mary Williamson, 1939, 1 son, 1 daughter. *Publications:* Books translated into 17 languages: some early novels (designedly out of print) and: Night Journey, 1941 (revised edition 1966); The Merciless Ladies, 1944 (revised edition 1979); The Forgotton Story, 1945 (ITV production 1983); Ross Poldark, 1945; Demelza, 1946; Take My Life, 1947 (filmed 1947); Cordelia, 1949; Night Without Stars, 1950 (filmed 1950); Jeremy Poldark, 1950; Fortune is a Woman, 1953 (filmed 1956); Warleggan, 1953; The Little Walls, 1955; The Sleeping Partner, 1956 (filmed 1958); Greek Fire, 1957; The Tumbled House, 1959; Marnie, 1961 (filmed 1963); The Grove of Eagles, 1963; After the Act, 1965; The Walking Stick, 1967, (filmed 1970); The Spanish Armadas, 1972; The Black Moon, 1973; Woman in the Mirror, 1975; The Four Swans, 1976; The Angry Tide, 1977; The Stranger from the Sea, 1981; The Millers Dance, 1982; Poldark's Cornwall, 1983; The Loving Cup, 1984; The Green Flash, 1986; Cameo, 1988; The Twisted Sword, 1990; Stephanie, 1992; BBC TV Series Poldark (the first 4 Poldark novels), 1975- 76, second series (the next 3 Poldark novels), 1977; Circumstantial Evidence, play, 1979. *Honours:* OBE, 1983; FRSL. *Address:* Abbotswood House, Buxted, East Sussex, TN22 4PB, England.

GRAHAM-YOOLL Andrew Michael, b. 5 Jan 1944, Buenos Aires, Argentina. Journalist; Writer. m. 17 Jan 1966, 1 son, 2 daughters. *Appointments include:* News Editor & Political Columnist, Buenos Aires Herald, 1966-76; Freelance Writer, San Francisco Chronicle, 1967-70, & 1976, Baltimore Sun, 1967-69, & 1976, The Miami Herald, 1969, Kansas City Star, 1969-73, New York Times, 1970, Newsweek, 1970, others; Broadcaster, BBC World Service, London, 1976; Occasional News Commentary, London Broadcasting Company; Sub Editor, Foreign News, Daily Telegraph, London, 1976-77; Foreign Correspondent, The Guardian, London, 1977-84; Editor, Writers News, London, 1983-85; Deputy Editor, 1984-85, Editor, 1985-88, South Magazine, London; Editor, Index on Censorship, 1989-93; senior Visiting Fellow, Queen Mary and Westfield College, London, 1990-. *Publications:* The Press in Argentina, 1973-78, 1979; Portrait of an Exile, 1981; The Forgotten Colony, 1981; Small Wars You May Have Missed (in South America), 1983; A State of Fear, 1986; Argentina, Peron to Videla 1955-1976, 1989; Point of Arrival, 1992; Short Stories: The Date Might Be Forgotten, 1967; The Premonition, 1968; Twenty Pages of Garcia, 1974; Money Cures Melancholy, 1974; Sirens, 1980; After The Despots, 1991; Poetry in Spanish. *Honours:* Poetry Prize, El Vidente Ciego Magazine Rosario, Argentina, 1975; British Council Visitorship to Britain, 1976; Nicholas Tomalin Memorial Award for Journalists, 1977. *Memberships:* PEN; Press Officer, 1979-87; Writers Guild of Great Britain, Executive Council, 1983; Argentine Writers Society; Anglo-Argentine society, Committee Member, 1989-1990; The Royal Literary Fund, Life Member, 1987; Association of British Editors, Member of the Board, 1990-93; Arts Council Literature Touring Panel, 1992-. *Address:* 10 Rothwerwick Road, London NW11 7DA, England.

GRANADOS Paul. *See:* **KENT Arthur.**

GRANDOWER Elissa. *See:* **WAUGH Hilary Baldwin.**

GRANGE Peter. *See:* **NICOLE Christopher Robin.**

GRANT Anthony. See: CAMPBELL Judith.

GRANT Charles L, b. 1942, USA. Freelance Writer; Former Teacher. *Appointments:* English Teacher: Toms River High School, New Jersey, 1964-70; Chester High School, New Jersey, 1970-72; Mmt Olive High School, New Jersey, 1972-73; English and History Teacher, Roxbury High School, New Jersey, 1974-75. *Publications:* The Shadow of Alpha, science fiction novel, 1976; The Curse, 1976; The Hour of the Oxrun Dead, 1977; Writing and Selling Science Fiction (editor), 1977; Ascension, science fiction novel, 1977; The Ravens of the Moon, science fiction novel, 1978; The Sound of Midnight, 1978; Shadows 1-9 (editor), 9 vols, 1978-86; Nightmares (editor), 1979; The Last Call of Mourning, 1979; Legion, science fiction novel, 1979; Tales from the Nightside, 1981; Glow of Candles and Other Stories, 1981; Nightmare Seasons, science fiction novel, 1982; Night Songs, science fiction novel, 1984; The Tea Party, 1985; The Pet, 1986; The Orchard, 1986; Something Stirs, 1992.

GRANT David. See: THOMAS Craig.

GRANT Ellen Catherine Gardner, b. 29 Sept 1934, Scotland. Medical Practitioner. m. David Norman Grant, 12 Sept 1959. 1 son, 2 daughters. *Education:* MB ChB (Commend), St Andrews University, 1958; DRCOG, London, England, 1959. *Publications:* The Bitter Pill, 1985, 1986; L'Aer Pillule (France), 1988; Den Bitre Pillen (Norway), 1987; De Bitre Pille (Denmark), 1986; De Bittere Pil (Holland), 1986; Chapters in: Smoking and Migraine, 1981; Biological Aspects of Schizophrenia and Addiction, 1982. *Contributions to:* Lancet; British Medical Journal; Clinical Oncology; The Ecologist; Journal of Obstetrics & Gynaecology of the British Commonwealth; Headache; International Journal of Environmental Studies; Nutrition & Health. *Memberships:* British Society for Nutritional Medicine; British Society for Allergy & Environmental Medicine; Foresight (Association for the Promotion of Preconception Care); The Dyslexia Institute. *Literary Agent:* Deborah Rodgers. *Address:* 20 Coombe Ridings, Kingston-upon-Thames, Surrey KT2 7JU, England.

GRANT John. See: BARNETT Paul le Page.

GRANT Landon. See: GRIBBLE Leonard (Reginald).

GRANT Maxwell. See: LYNDS Dennis.

GRANT Michael, b. 21 Nov. 1914, London, England. Writer; Former University Professor & Vice Chancellor. m. Rut Anne Sophie Beskow, 2 Aug. 1944, 2 sons. *Education:* BA, MA, Litt.D, Trinity College, Cambridge. *Publications include:* From Imperium to Auctoritas, 1946; Roman Imperial Money, 1954; The World of Rome, 1960; Myths of the Greeks & Romans, 1962; The Civilizations of Europe, 1965; The Climax of Rome, 1968; The Ancient Mediterranean, 1969; Julius Caesar, 1969; The Ancient Historians, 1970; The Roman Forum, 1970; Herod the Great, 1971; The Jews in the Roman World, 1973; Cleopatra, 1972; the Fall of the Roman Empire, 1976; Greek and Latin Authors 800BC - AD 1000, 1980; The Dawn of the Middle Ages, 1981; From Alexander to Cleopatra, 1982, reprinted as The Hellemstic Greeks, 1990; History of Ancient Israel, 1984; The Roman Emperors, 31BC - AD476, 1985; A Guide to the Ancient World, 1986; The Rise of the Greeks, 1987; The Classical Greeks, 1989; The Visible Past, 1990; Short History of Classical Civilizatiion (Founder of the Western World in USA) 1991; Greeks and Romans: A Social History (A Social History of Greece and Rome in USA), 1992; Readings in the Classical Historians, 1992. *Contributions to:* Various journals. *Honours:* OBE, 1946; CBE, 1958; Honorary Litt.D. Dublin, 1961; Honorary LLD, Belfast, 1967; Gold Medal, Education, Sudan, 1977; Premio del Mediterraneo Mazara del Vallo, 1983; Premio Latina, 1986; Premio Internazionale delle Muse (Florence), 1989. *Memberships:* President, Medallist, Honorary Fellow, Royal Numismatic Society; Huntingdon Medalist, American Numismatic Society; President, Virgil Society; President, Classical Association. *Address:* Le Pitturacce, Gattaiola, 55050 Lucca, Italy.

GRANT Neil David Mountfield, (David Mountfield, D M Field and Gail Trenton), b. 9 June 1938, England. Writer. m. Vera Steiner, 23 Sept 1979. 2 daughters. *Education:* MA (Hons), St Johns College, Cambridge, 1958-61. *Publications include:* Children's History of Britain, 1977; Greek and Roman Erotica, 1982; A History of Polar Exploration, 1974; A History of African Exploration, 1976; American Folktales & Legends, 1988; The White Bear (fiction), 1983; Neil Grant's Book of Spies & Spying, 1975; London's Villages, 1990. *Membership:* Royal Geographical Society. *Literary Agent:* Laurence Pollinger. *Address:* 2 Avenue Road, Teddington, Middlesex TW11 0BT, England.

GRANT Nicholas. See: NICOLE Christopher Robin.

GRANT Roderick, b. 1941, United Kingdom. Author. *Appointments:* Sub Editor, Weekly Scotsman, 1965-67. *Publications:* Adventure in My Veins, 1968; Seek Out the Guilty, 1969; Where No Angels Dwell, 1969; Gorbals Doctor, 1970; The Dark Horizon (with Alexander Highlands), 1971; The Lone Voyage of Betty Mouat, 1973; The Stalking of Adrian Lawford, 1974; The Clutch of Caution, 1975, 2nd Edition, 1985; The 51st Highland Division at War, 1976; Strathalder: A Highland Estate, 1978 (2nd Edition, with illustrations, 1989); A Savage Freedom, 1978; The Great Canal, 1978; A Private Vendetta, 1978; But Not in Anger (with C Cole), 1979; Clap Hands for the Singing Molecatcher, 1989. *Address:* 3 Back Lane Cottages, Bucks Horn Oak, Farnham, Surrey, England.

GRATUS Jack, b. 1935, United Kingdom. Writer; Educator. *Appointments:* Organising Tutor, Creative Writing Course, Glamorgan Summer School, South Wales, 1968-77; Tutor in charge of Non-Fiction Writing, City Literary Institute, London, 1974-. *Publications:* A Man in His Position, 1968; The Victims, 1969; Mister Landlord Appel, 1971; Night Hair Child (with T Preston), 1971; The Great White Lie: History of the Anti-Slave Trade Campaign, 1973; The False Messiahs, 1976; The Joburgers, 1979; The Redneck Rebel, 1980. *Memberships:* Executive Councillor, Writers' Guild of Great Britain, 1978-. *Address:* 17 Cunnington Street, London W4 5ER, England.

GRAU Shirley Ann, b. 8 July 1930, New Orleans, USA. Writer. m. James Feibleman, 4 Aug 1955, 2 sons. 2 daughters. *Education:* BA, Tulane University, New Orleans. *Publications:* The Black Prince, 1955; The Hard Blue Sky, 1958; The House on Coleseum Street, 1961; The Keepers of the House, 1964; The Condor Passes, 1971; The Wind Shifting West, 1973; Evidence of Love, 1977; Nine Women, 1985. *Contributor To:* New Yorker; Saturday Evening Post; etc. *Honour:* Pulitzer Prize for Fiction, 1965. *Agent:* Brandt and Brandt, New York City. *Address:* 210 Baronne Street, Suite 1120, New Orleans, LA 70112, USA.

GRAVER Elizabeth, b. 2 July 1964, Los Angeles, CA, USA. Writer; Teacher. *Education:* Wesleyan University, BA, 1986; Washington University, MFA, 1990; Cornett University, MA, 1992. *Publication:* Have You seen Me? *Contributions to:* Best American Short Stories; Story; Southern Review; Antaeus; Seventeen; Southwest Review. *Honours:* Fulbright Fellowship; Drue Heinz Literature Prize; National Endowment for the Arts Fellowship; Writers Exchange Winner. *Memberships:* Phi Beta Kappa. *Literary Agent:* Richard Parks, *Address:* c/o Richard Parks Agency, 138 E 16th Street 58, New York, NY 10003, USA.

GRAVER Lawrence Stanley, b. 6 Dec 1931, New York, New York, USA. Professor of English. m. Suzanne Levy Graver, 28 Jan 1960, 2 daughters. *Education:* BA, City College of New York, 1954; PhD, University of

California, Berkeley, 1961. *Appointments:* Assistant Professor, University of California at Los Angeles, 1961-64; Associate Professor, 1964-71, Professor, 1971-, Williams College, 1964-. *Publications:* Conrad's Short Fiction, 1968; Carson McCullers, 1969; Beckett: The Critical Heritage, 1979; Mastering the Film, 1974; Beckett: Waiting for Godot, 1989. *Contributions to:* New York Times Book Review; Saturday Review; New Republic; New Leader; 19th century Fiction. *Membership:* Modern Language Association. *Address:* Department of English, Williams College, Williamstown, MA 01267, USA.

GRAVER Suzanne, b. 17 Aug 1936, New York City, New York, USA. Professor; Dean of the Faculty. m. Lawrence Graver, 28 Jan 1960, 2 daughters. *Education:* Queens College, BA, 1954-57; University of California, MA, 1958-60; University of Massachusetts, PhD, 1972-76. *Appointments include:* Teacher, Berkeley High school, 1960-61; Berskshire Community College, Asst Professor, 1966-72; Empire State College, SUNY, 1978; Williams College, 1978-93, Professor, 1991. *Publications:* George Eliot & Community: A Study in Social Theory and Fictional Form; Mill, Middlemarch and Marriage, (in Portraits of Marriage in Literature); In Progress, Thinking Woman: A Victorian Debate. *Contributions to:* Dickens Quarterly; Studies in the Novel; Approaches to Teaching Middlemarch; Victorian Periodicals Review, New Republic, Modern Philology, Victorian Studies. *Honours:* Phi Beta Kappa; Summa Cum Laude; Teaching Assistantship; University Fellowship; Robert B Partlow Prize; American Council of Learned Societies Fellowships, 1985-86; National Endowment for the Humanities Fellowship; National Humanities Center Fellowship. *Memberships include:* Bronfman Committee; Jewish Religious Center Advisory Committee; Womens Studies Advisory Committee; Advisory committee on Writing; Northeast Modern Language Association. *Address:* Hopkins Hall, Williams College, PO Box 141, Williamstown, MA 01267, USA.

GRAVINA Maria Estefania, b. 12 Dec 1939, Uruguay. Teacher; Writer. m. Washington Lopez, 10 Feb 1966, 3 daughters. *Education:* College of Arts Literature, 1960-65; Alliance Francaise, 1959. *Appointments:* Latinoamerican Young Writers, 1982; Latinomericans Writers, 1982; Uneac Congress Cuba, 1988. *Publications:* Lazaro Vuela Rojo; Que Diga Quincho; La Leche De Las Piedras. *Contributions to:* Numerous Magazines & Supplements. *Honours:* Premio Casa de las Americas; Premio Instituto de las Comarcas; Honours in Cuadernos De Marcha. *Memberships:* Cultural Group; Ramon Masini. *Literary Agent:* Ada lernadez Chagas. *Address:* Libertad 2879 Apt 1, Montrevideo, Uruguay.

GRAY Alasdair, b. 28 Dec 1934, Glasgow, Scotland. 1 son. *Education:* Diploma, Glasgow Art School, 1957, Awarded Bellohouston Travelling Scholarship. *Appointments:* Part time art teacher 1958-62; Theatrical scene painter 1962-63, Free-lance playwright and painter 1963-75, Artist-recorder, People's Palace (local history museum) 1977, Writer in residence, University of Glasgow, 1977-79, Free-lance painter and maker of books 1979-. *Publications:* Lanark: a novel 1981, revised 1985; Unlikely Stories, 1983, revised 1984; 1982 Janine, a novel, 1984, revised 1985; The Fall of Kelvin Walker: A Fable of the Sixties; Lean Tales (with James Kelman and Agnes Owens), 1985; Saltire Self-Portrait 4, 1988; Old Negatives, four verse sequences; McGrotty and Ludmilla, or The Harbinger Report: A Romance of the Eighties, 1989. *Contributions to:* Periodicals including Chapman and The Edinburgh Review. *Honours:* Three grants from Scottish Arts Council, between 1968 and 1981; Saltire Society, 1982; Cheltenham Literary Festival, 1983; Scottish branch of PEN, 1986; Whitbread Award, Poor Things, 1992. *Memberships:* Society of Authors; Scottish Society of Playwrights; Glasgow Print Workshop; Various organizations supporting coal miners and nuclear disarmament. *Literary Agent:* Xandra Hardie. *Address:* 18 Park Walk, London SW10 0AQ, England.

GRAY Alice Wirth, b. 29 Apr 1934, Chicago, Illinois,

USA. Writer. m. Ralph Gareth Gray, 16 July 1954, 2 daughters. *Education:* BA, University of California, 1958; MA, 1960. *Publication:* What The Poor Eat. *Contributions to:* The Atlantic; The American Scholar; Poetry; Breakfast Without Meat; The Little Magazine; Helicon None; Primavera; Sequoia. *Honours:* Illinois Arts Council Literary award; Gordon Barber Memorial Award; Duncan Lawrie Award. *Memberships:* Poetry Society of America; California Writers Club. *Literary Agent:* Martha Casselman, Calistoga, CA. *Address:* 1001 Merced Street, Berkeley, CA 94707, USA.

GRAY Angela. *See:* **DANIELS Dorothy.**

GRAY Caroline. *See:* **NICOLE Christopher Robin.**

GRAY Dorothy Randall, b. Davisboro, GA, USA. Executive Director. m. Ronald K Gray. *Education:* BS, City College. *Appointments:* Poet in Residence, Hunter College, 1989; Skidmore, Writing Facilitator, 1990-92; Columbia University, Writing Consultant, 1991; Anges Scott College, Writing Facilitator, 1992. *Publications:* Gaptooth Girlfriends; Muse Blues; The Passion Collection; a Rock Against The Wind; Glowchold; 360 Degrees of Blackness; Women Writing. *Contributions to:* The New York Times; Blacks On Black; The paper. *Memberships:* Internation Womens Writers Guild; Poets & Writers; Associated Writing Programs. *Address:* 162 Underhill Avenue, Brooklyn, NY 11231, USA.

GRAY Douglas b. 17 Feb 1930, Melbourne. University Teacher. m. 3 Sept 1959, 1 son. *Education:* MA, Victoria University of Wellington, New Zealand, 1952; BA, 1956; MA, 1960, Merton College, Oxford. *Publications:* Oxford Book of Late Medieval Verse and Prose, 1985; Robert Henryson, 1979; Themes and Images in the Medieval English Religious Lyric, 1972; articles in medieval literature. *Honour:* FBA, 1989. *Memberships:* President, Society for Study of Medieval Languages and Literatures, 1982-86; Council, Early English Text Society. *Address:* Lady Margaret Hall, Oxford OX2 6QA, England.

GRAY Dulcie Winifred, b. 20 Nov 1920. m. 29 Apr 1939, Michael Denison. *Publications:* Murder on the Stairs, 1957; Baby Face, 1959; For Richer for Richer, 1970; Ride on Tiger, 1975; Butterflies on my Mind, 1978; Dark Calypso, 1979; The Glanvill Women, 1982; Mirror Image, 1987; Looking Forward, Looking Back, autobiography, 1991. *Contributions to:* Daily Express; Evening Standard; Womans Own; Vogue. *Honours:* Queens Silver Jubliee Medal, 1977; The Times Educational Supplelement Senior Information Award, 1978; CBE, 1983. *Memberships:* Society of Authors; Royal Society of Arts, Fellow; Linnean Society; British Actors Equity. *Literary Agent:* Douglas Rae, *Address:* 28 Charing Cross Road, London WC2, England.

GRAY Francine du Plessix, b. 1930, USA. Author. *Appointments:* Reporter, United Press International, New York City, 1952-54; Assistant Editor, Realites magazine, Paris, France, 1954-55; Book Editor, Art in America, New York City, 1962-64; Visiting Professor: City University of New York, 1975; Yale University, New Haven Connecticut, 1981; Columbia University, New York City, 1983; Ferris Professor, Princeton University, New Jersey, 1986. *Publications:* Divine Disobedience: Profiles in Catholic Radicalism, 1970; Hawaii: The Sugar-Coated Fortress, 1972; Lovers and Tyrants, 1976; World Without End, 1981; October Blood, 1985; Adam and Eve and the City, 1987; Soviet Women; Walking the Tightrope, 1991. *Literary Agent:* Georges Borchardt Inc, USA. *Address:* c/o Georges Borchardt Inc, 145 East 57nd Street, New York, NY 10022, USA.

GRAY Marianne Claire, b. 1947, Cape Town, South Africa. Journalist; Biographer. *Education:* University Aix Marseille, 1965-66; Cambridge Polytechnic, 1967; BA, UNISA, 1972. *Appointments:* Reporter, Argus Group South Africa, 1968-70; Reporter, Cape Times, 1970-73; Editor, Athens News 1974; Syndication Assistant,

South African National Mags London, 1975-77; Freelance Journalist, 1977-. *Publications:* Depardieu; Freelance Alternative; The Other Arf; Working from Home; Thoughts About Architecture. *Contributions to:* Cosmopolitan; Arena Options; Empire Company; The Face; Radio Times; New Women; Womens Journal. *Memberships:* Women in Publishing; Critics Circle; Women in Film International. *Literary Agent:* Blake Friedmann. *Address:* 32 Eburne Road, London, N7 6AU, England.

GRAY (John) Richard, b. 1929, United Kingdom. Professor Emeritus of African History, University of London. *Appointments:* Editor, Journal of African History, 1968-71. *Publications:* The Two Nations: Aspects of the Development of Race Relations in the Rhodesias and Nyasaland, 1960; A History of the Southern Sudan, 1839-1889, 1961; Materials for West African History in Italian Archives (with D Chambers), 1965; Pre-Colonial African Trade (edited with D Birmingham), 1970; Cambridge History of Africa, vol IV (editor), 1975; Christianity in Independent Africa (edited with E Fasholé-Luke and others), 1978; Black Christians & White Missionaries, 1990. *Membership:* Britain-Zimbabwe Society, Chairman 1981-85. *Address:* 39 Rotherwick Road, London NW11 7DD, England.

GRAY Richard Butler, b. 29 May 1922, Ft. Atkinson, Wisconsin, USA. Professor Emeritus of Political Science. *Education:* BA, Hispanic Studies, University of Wisconsin, 1947; MA, International Relations, Fletcher School of Law and Diplomacy, 1949; Diploma, Cuban Politics, University of Havana, 1957; PhD, Political Science, University of Wisconsin, 1957. *Publications:* José Martí, Cuban Patriot, 1962; International Security Systems, Concepts and Models of World Order, (editor), 1969; Security in a World of Change, Readings and Notes in International Relations, (edited with Lee W. Farnsworth), 1969; Latin America and the United States in the 1970's, (editor), 1971; A Dictionary of Political Science, (contributor), 1964; Handbook of World History, (contributor), 1967; An Encyclopedia of Latin America, (contributor), 1975; World Encyclopedia of Peace, (contributor), 1986. *Contributions to:* The Americas; Hispanic American Historical Review; Inter-American Review of Bibliography; Journal of Developing Areas; Journal of Inter-American Studies; Journal of Southeastern Latin American Studies. *Honours:* Sigma Delta Pi, 1943; Pi Gamma MU, 1958; Pi Sigma Alpha, 1959; Pi Gamma Mu National Merit Award, 1981; Award Premio Periodístico José Martí, 1966. *Memberships:* Honorary Member, Dobro Slovo, 1985; Southeastern Conference of Latin American Studies, President 1974-75; Southern Political Science Association. *Address:* 1502 Mitchell Avenue, Tallahassee, FL 32303, USA.

GRAY Simon John Halliday, b. 21 Oct 1936, Hayling Island, Hants, England. Playwright. m. Beryl Mary Kevern, 1966, 1 son, 1 daughter. *Education:* BA, Honours, Cambridge. *Publications:* Novels: (As Hamish Reade), Colmain; Simple People; Little Portia; A Comeback for Stark; TV Plays: Sleeping Dog; Death of a Teddy Bear; Pig in a Poke; Man in a Side- Car; Two Sundays; Plaintiffs and Defendants; After Pilkington; Quatermaine's Terms; Stage Plays: Wise Child, 1967; Dutch Uncle, 1969; Spoiled, 1971; Butley, 1971; Otherwise Engaged; Dog Days, 1976; Molly, 1977; The Rear Column, 1978; Close of Play, 1979; Stage Struck, 1979; Quartermaine's Terms, 1981; The Common Pursuit, 1984; Melon, 1987; Non-fiction: An Unnatural Pursuit & Other Pieces, 1985; How's That For Telling 'Em, Fat Lady?, 1988. *Honours:* Writers' Guild Award; Evening Standard Best Play Award, 1971; Evening Standard & Plays & Players Best Play Awards, 1975. *Memberships:* Fellow, Royal Society of Literature; Dramatists Society. *Literary Agent:* Judy Daish Associates. *Address:* c/o Judy Daish Associates, 83 Eastbourne Mews, London W2 6LQ, England.

GRAY Spalding, b. 5 June 1941, Providence, Rhode Island, USA. Playwright. *Education:* Fryeburg Academy, Maine; BA, Emerson College, Boston, 1965. *Career:*

Actor in summer stock, Cape Cod, Massachusetts and in Saratoga, New York, 1965-67; with Performance Group, New York, 1969-75; founder, with Elizabeth LeCompte, the Wooster Group, New York, 1975. *Publications:* Plays include: Travels Through New England (produced Cambridge, Massachusetts, 1984); Rivkala's Ring, adaptation of a story by Chekhov in Orchards, (produced Urbana, Illinois, 1985; New York, 1986) New York, Knopf, 1986; Terrors of Pleasure: The House (produced Cambridge, Massachusetts, 1985, New York, 1986, London 1987) Included in Sex and Death at the Age 14, 1986; Sex and Death at the Age 14, New York, Random House, 1986; aygmented edition, including Swimming to Cambodia, parts 1 and 2, as Swimming to Cambodia: The Collected Works, London, Pan, 1987. Screenplay: Swimming to Cambodia, 1987; Television Play: Bedtime Story with Renee Shafransky, 1987. *Honours:* National Endowment for the Arts Fellowship, 1977; Rockefeller Grant, 1980; Guggenheim Fellowship, 1985; Obie Award, 1985. *Literary Agent:* Suzanne Gluck, International Creative Management, New York. *Address:* c/o The Wooster Group, Box 654, Canal Street Station, New York, NY 10013, USA.

GRAY Tony (George Hugh), b. 1922, Irish. Writer. *Appointments:* Former Features Editor, Daily Mirror, London. *Publications:* Starting from Tomorrow, 1965; The Real Professionals, 1966; Gone the Time, 1967; The Irish Answer, 1967; (adaptor) Interlude, 1968; (with L. Villa) The Record Breakers, 1970; The Last Laugh, 1972; The Orange Order, 1972; Psalms and Slaughter, 1972; (with C. McBride) The White Lions of Timbavati, 1977; (with T. Murphy) Some of My Best Friends Are Animals, 1979; (with C. McBride) Operation White Lion, 1981; The Irish Times Book of the 20th Century, 1985; The Road to Success: Alfred McAlpine, 1935-85, 1987.

GREAVES Margaret, b. 1914, United Kingdom. Lecturer in English (retired). Children's Fiction Writer. *Appointments:* Principal Lecturer in English, 1946-70; Head of Department, 1960-70, St Mary's College of Education, Cheltenham. *Publications:* The Blazon of Honour, 1964; Regency Patron, 1966; Gallery, 1968; Gallimaufry, 1971; The Dagger and the Bird, 1971; The Grandmother Stone, US Edition Stone of Terror, 1972; Little Jacko, 1973; The Gryphon Quest, 1974; Curfew, 1975; Nothing Ever Happens on Sundays, 1976; The Night of the Goat, 1976; A Net to Catch the Wind, 1979; The Abbottsbury Ring, 1979; Charlie and Emma series, 5 vols, 1980-87; Cat's Magic, 1980; The Snake Whistle, 1980; Once There Were No Pandas, 1985; Nicky's Knitting Grannary, 1986; The Mouse of Nibbling Village, 1986; Hetty Pegler, 1987; Mouse Mischief, 1989; Juniper's Journey, 1990; Magic from the Ground, 1990; Henry's Wild Morning, 1990. *Address:* 8 Greenways, Winchcombe GL54 5LG, England.

GREBER Judith, (Gillian Roberts), b. 27 July 1939, Philadelphia, Pennsylvania, USA. Writer. m. Robert Martin Greber, 23 Dec 1962, 2 sons. *Education:* University of Pennsylvania, BS, 1961; MA. *Publications:* Caught Dead in Philadelphia; Philly Stakes; I'd Rather Be in Philadelphia; With Friends Like These; Easy Answers; the Silent Partner; Mendocino; As Good as It Gets. *Contributions to:* Sisters in Crime. Elley Queen. *Honours:* World Mystery Conventions Anthony. *Memberships:* Authors Guild; Mystery Writers of America. *Literary Agent:* Jean V Naggar. *Address:* PO Box 423, Tiburon, CA 94920, USA.

GREEN Andrew M(alcolm), b. 1927, British. *Appointments:* Development Chemist, Thermionic Products, London, 1948-52; Sale Executive, Thorn Electrical Industries, London, 1952-57; Sales Office Manager, Crypto, London, 1957-59; Publicity Manager, Stanley-Bridges, London, 1959-63; Press Relations Officer, Industrial and Trade Fairs, London, 1963-65; Editor, Trade and Technical Press, Morden, Surrey, 1965-68; Managing Editor, Perry Press Productions, London, 1968-72; Founder, Ealing Psychical Research Society and Co-founder, National Federation of Psychical Research Societies, 1951. *Publications:*

Mysteries of Surrey, 1972, 1973; Ghost Hunting, 1973, 1976; Our Haunted Kingdom, 1973, 3rd Ed. 1975; Mysteries of Sussex, 1973; Mysteries of London, 1973; Haunted Houses, 1975, 3rd Ed. 1985; Ghosts of the South East, 1976, 1981; Phantom Ladies, 1977; Ghosts of Tunbridge Wells, 1978; The Ghostly Army, 1979; Ghosts of Today, 1980.

GREEN Benjamin, b. 17 July 1956, San Bernardino, CA, USA. Writer. *Education:* BA, Humboldt State Universtiy, Arcata, 1985. *Publications:* The Field Notes of a Madman; The Lost Coast; From a Greyhound Bus; Monologs From The Realm of Silence. *Honours:* Ucross Fellow. *Address:* 3415 Patricks Point Drive 3, Trinidad, CA 95570, USA.

GREEN Benny, b. 9 Dec 1927. Freelance Writer. m. Antoinette Kanal, 1962, 3 sons, 1 daughter. *Appointments:* Saxophonist, 1947-60; Jazz Critic, Observer, 1958-77; Literary Critic, Spectator, 1970-; Film Critic, Punch, 1972-77; TV Critic, 1977-. *Publications:* Books and Lyrics: Boots with Strawberry Jam, 1968; Co-Deviser, Cole, 1974; Oh Mr Porter, 1977; D.D. Lambeth, 1985; (Books) The Reluctant Art, 1962; Blame it on my Youth, 1967; 58 Minutes to London, 1969; Drums in my Ears, 1973; I've Lost My Little Willie, 1976; Swingtime in Tottenham, 1976; Editor, Cricket Addict's Archive, 1977; Shaw's Champions, 1978; Fred Astaire, 1979; Editor, Wisden Anthology, volume 1 1864-1900, 1979, volume 11 1900-1940, 1980, volume 111, 1940-63, 1982, volume 1V 1963-82, 1983; P.G. Wodehouse : a Literary Biography, 1981; Wisden Book of Obituaries, 1986; A History of Cricket, 1988; Let's Pace the Music, 1989. *Address:* c/o BBC Broadcasting House, Portland Place, London W1, England.

GREEN Clifford, b. 6 Dec 1934, Melbourne, Victoria, Australia. Author; Screenwriter. m. Judith Irene Painter, 16 May 1959, 1 son, 3 daughters. *Education:* Primary Teachers Certificate, Toorak Teachers' College, 1959. *Publications:* Marion, 1974; The Incredible Steam-Driven Adventures of Riverboat Bill, 1975; Picnic at Hanging Rock : A Film, 1975; Break of Day, 1976; The Sun is Up, 1978; Four Scripts, 1978; Burn the Butterflies, 1979; Lawson's Mates, 1980; The Further Adventures of Riverboat Bill, 1981; Plays for Kids, 1981; Cop Out!, 1983; Riverboat Bill Steams Again, 1985; Boy Soldiers, 1990. *Honours:* Australian Writers Guild Awards, 1973, 1974, 1976, 1978, 1979; Television Society of Australia Awards, 1974, 1976, 1978, 1980; Variety Club of Australia Award, 1978; Australian Writers Guild Awards, 1990-92. *Memberships:* Australian Society of Authors; Australian Writers Guild, former Vice-President. *Address:* c/o Rick Raftor Management, PO Box 445, Paddington, NSW 2021, Australia.

GREEN Dorothy, (Dorothy Auchterlonie), b. 1915, United Kingdom. University Lecturer (retired). Poet. m. H. M. Green. *Appointments:* Teacher, 1933-38; Journalist, Sydney Daily Telegraph, New South Wales, Australia, 1941; News Editor, Australian Broadcasting Commission, Brisbane, 1942-44; Teacher, then Co-Principal, Presbyterian Girls' College, Warwick, Queensland, 1955-60; Lecturer in English, Monash University, Melbourne, 1960-63; Senior Lecturer in English and Australian Literature, Australian National University, Canberra, 1964-72; Lecturer in English, 1977-80, Honorary Visiting Fellow, 1980-, Royal Military College, Duntroon, Canberra. *Publications:* Kaleidoscope (as Dorothy Auchterlonie), verse, 1940; Fourteen Minutes (with H M Green), 1950; The Dolphin (as Dorothy Auchterlonie), verse, 1967; Australian Poetry (editor), 1968; Ulysses Bound: A Study of Henry Richardson and Her Fiction, 1973, 2nd Edition, 1986; The Music of Love, essays, 1985; Something to Someone (as Dorothy Auchterlonie), verse, 1984; A History of Australian Literature 1789-1950, 2 vols, 1985. *Address:* 18 Waller Crescent, Campbell, ACT 2601, Australia.

GREEN Hannah. *See:* **GREENBURG Joanne.**

GREEN Jonathon, b. 20 Apr 1948, Kidderminster, Worcs, England. Writer; Broadcaster. 2 sons. *Education:* Brasenose College, Oxford, BA, 1966-69. *Publications:* Dictionary of Contemporary Slang; Dictionary of Contemporary Quotations; Dictionary of Jargon; Days in the Life; Them; Others inc. Famous Last Words. *Contributions to:* GQ; Daily Telegraph. *Literary Agent:* Curtis Brown. *Address:* c/o Curtis Brown, 162-68 Regent Street, London W1R 5TB, England.

GREEN John F, b. 5 June 1943, Saskatoon, Saskatchewan, Canada. Teacher. m. Maureen Anne Horne, 1 Feb 1969, 3 sons, 1 daughter. *Education:* Ryerson Institute, 1964-67; Teacher's certificate, Red River Community College, 1976. *Appointments:* Professor, Arts & Sciences, Durham College, Oshawa, Ontario, 1976-; Writer and producer for western Canadian broadcasting companies. *Publications:* There are Trolls, The Bargain, 1974; The House on Geoffrey Street, 1981; The Gadfly, 1983; There's a Dragon in My Closet, 1986; Alice and The Birthday Giant, 1989; Junk-Pile Jennifer, 1991; The House That Max Built, 1991. *Honour:* Canadian Children's Book Centre Gold Seal Award for Alice and The Birthday Giant, Awarded 1990. *Literary Agent:* Denise Anderson, Sholastic Publishers, 123 Newkirk Road, Richmond Hill, Ontario, Canada, L4C 365. *Address:* 966 Adelaide Street East, No 70 Oshawa, Ontario, Canada L1K 1L2.

GREEN Martin (Burgess), b. 1927, United Kingdom. Professor of English. Writer. *Appointments:* Instructor, Wellesley College, Massachusetts, USA, 1957-61; Lecturer, Birmingham University, England, 1965-68; Professor of English, Tufts University, Medford, Massachusetts, 1968-. *Publications:* Mirror for Anglo-Saxons, 1960; Reappraisals, 1965; Science and the Shabby Curate of Poetry, 1965; The Problem of Boston 16; Yeat's Blessings on von Hugel, 1968; Cities of Light and Sons of the Morning, 1972; The von Richthofen Sisters, 1974; Children of the Sun, 1975; The Earth Again Redeemed, novel, 1976; Transatlantic Patterns, 1977; The Challenge of the Mahatmas, 1978; Dreams of Adventure, Deeds of Empire, 1979; The Old English Elegies, 1983; Tolstoy and Gandhi, 1983; The Great American Adventure, 1984; Mountains of Truth, 1986; The Triumph of Pierrot (with J Swan), 1986. *Address:* 8 Boylston Terrace, Medford, MA 02144, USA.

GREEN Michael Frederick, b. 2 Jan 1927, Leicester, England, Writer. *Education:* BA, Honours, Open University. *Publications:* The Art of Coarse Rugby, 1960; The Art of Coarse Sailing, 1962; The Art of Coarse Acting, 1964; The Art of Coarse Golf, 1967; The Art of Coarse Moving, 1969 (TV Serial 1977); The Art of Coarse Drinking, 1973; Squire Haggard's Journal, 1976, television series, 1990; Tonight Josephine, 1981; The Art of Coarse Sex, 1981; Don't Swing from the Balcony Romeo, 1983; The Art of Coarse Office Life, 1985; The Boy Who Shot Down an Airship, (credited twice), 1988; The Boy Who Shot Down An Airship, 1988; Nobody Hurt in Small Earthquake, 1990. *Memberships:* Society of Authors; Equity; National Union of Journalists. *Literary Agent:* Anthony Sheil Associates. *Address:* 78 Sandall Road, Ealing, London W5 1JB, England.

GREEN Peter Morris, (Denis Delaney), b. 22 Dec 1924, London, England. Professor; Writer; Translator. m. (1) Lalage Isobel Pulvertaft, 28 July 1951, (div), 2 sons, 1 daughter, (2) Carin Margreta Christensen, 18 July 1975. *Education:* BA, 1st Class Honours, 1950, MA, 1954, PhD, 1954, Trinity College, Cambridge. *Appointments:* Literary Adviser, The Bodley Head, 1958; General Editor, Hodder and Stoughton, 1959-63; Member, Book Society Selection Committee, 1959-62; Professor of Classics, University of Texas, Austin, 1972-; Dougherty Centennial Professor, Classical Studies, 1982-. *Publications include:* Kenneth Grahame: A Biography, 1958; Essays in Antiquity, 1960; The Laughter of Aphrodite, 1965; The Shadow of the Parthenon, 1972; Armada from Athens, 1970;

Alexander of Macedon, 356-323 BC a Historical Biography, 1974; Classical Bearings, 1989; Alexander to Actium: the Historical Evolution of the Hellenistic Age, 1990; Ovid: The Erotic Poems, 1982; The Year of Salamis, 480-479 BC, 1971. *Contributions include:* Times Literary Supplement; New York Review of Books; Grand Street; Southern Humanities Review. *Honours:* Heinemann Award for Literature, 1957; Senior Fellow, National Endowment for the Humanities, 1983-84. *Memberships:* Royal Society of Literature, Fellow, 1957, Council, 1959-63; Classical Association; Hellenic Society; many other professional organisations. *Literary Agent:* David Higham Associates, UK; Harold Ober Inc., USA. *Address:* Dept. of Classics, University of Texas, Austin, TX 78712, USA.

GREEN O O. *See:* **DURGNAT Raymond Eric.**

GREEN Sharon, b. 6 July 1942, Brooklyn, New York, USA. Novelist. Divorced, 3 sons. *Education:* BA, New York University, 1963. *Publications:* The Warrior Within, 1982; The Crystals of Mida, 1982; The Warrior Enchained, 1983; An Oath to Mida, 1983; The Warrior Rearmed, 1984; Chosen of Mida, 1984; Mind Guest, 1984; The Will of the Gods, 1985; Gateway to Xanadu, 1985; To Battle The Gods, 1986; The Warrior Challenged, 1986; The Rebel Prince, 1987; The Far Side of Forever, 1987; Lady Blade, Lord Fighter, 1987; The Warrior Victorious, 1988; Mists of the Ages, 1988; Dawn Song, 1988. *Contributions to:* various journals and magazines. *Memberships:* Science Fiction Writers of America; The Planetary Society. *Literary Agent:* Richard Curtis, New York, USA. *Address:* c/o Richard Curtis Associates, Inc, 164 E. 64th Street, New York, NY 10021, USA.

GREEN Timothy (S), b. 1936, United Kingdom. Writer. *Appointments:* London Correspondent, Horizon, and American Heritage, 1959-62; London Correspondent, Life, 1962-64; Editor, Illustrated London News, 1964-66. *Publications:* The World of God, 1968; The Smugglers, 1969; Restless Spirit, UK Edition The Adventurers, 1970; The Universal Eye, 1972; World of Gold Today, 1973; How to Buy Gold, 1975; The Smuggling Business, 1977; The World of Diamonds, 1981; The New World of Gold, 1982, 2nd Edition, 1985; The Prospect for Gold, 1987. *Literary Agent:* A D Peters and Co, England. *Address:* c/o A D Peters & Co, 10 Buckingham Street, London WC2N 6BU, England.

GREEN Vivian Hubert Howard, b. 18 Nov 1915. Honorary Fellow, Lincoln College, Oxford. *Education:* BA 1937, BD 1941, Cambridge University; DD (Oxford and Cambridge) 1957. *Publications include:* Renaissance and Reformation, 1952; Oxford Common Room, 1957; The Young Mr Wesley, 1961; Religion at Oxford and Cambridge, 1964; The Commonwealth of Lincoln College 1427-1977, 1979; Love in a Cool Climate: the Letters of Mark Pattison and Meta Bradley, 1985. *Honours:* Thireswall Prize and Medal, Cambridge University, 1940. *Membership:* Fellow of the Royal Historical Society. *Address:* Calendars, Sheep Street, Burford, Oxford OX8 4LS, England.

GREENBAUM Sidney, b. 31 Dec 1929, London, England. *Education:* BA Honours, 1951, MA, 1953, Postgraduate Certificate in Education, 1954, BA, Honours, 1957, PhD, 1967, London University. *Appointments:* Visiting Assistant Professor, University of Oregon, USA, 1968-69; Associate Professor, University of Wisconsin, Milwaukee, 1969-72; Visiting Professor, Hebrew University, 1972-73; Professor, University of Wisconsin-Milwaukee, 1972-83; Quain Professor of English Language and Literature, University College London, England, 1983-90; Director of Survey of Englisg Usage, University College, London, 1983-; Visiting Professor, University College, London, 1991-. *Publications include:* Studies in English Adverbial Usage, 1969; Verb-Intensifier Collocations in English, 1970; Elicitation Experiments in English, (Co-author), 1970; A Grammar of Contemporary English, (Co-author), 1972; A University Grammar of English, (Co-author), 1973; A Comprehensive Grammar of the English Language, (Co- author), 1985; Good English and the Grammarian, 1988; The Longman Guide to English Usage, (Co-author), 1988; A College Grammar of English, 1989; A Student's Grammar of the English Language, (Co-author), 1990; An Introduction to English Grammar, 1991; The Oxford Companion to the English Language (Association Editor), 1992. *Contributions to:* About 50 articles in magazines and journals. *Honours:* 1st prize for A Comprehensive Grammar of the Engish language, Duke of Edinburgh Language award, 1986; Honorary DHum, University of Wisconsin-Milwaukee, 1989. *Memberships:* International Association of University Professors of English; Linguistic Society of America; Linguistic Association of Great Britain; Reform Club. *Address:* 73 Highfield Avenue, London NW11 9UB, England.

GREENBERG Alvin David, b. 10 May 1932. Author; Teacher. *Educaiton:* BA, MA, University of Cincinnati, USA; PhD, University of Washington. *Appointments:* University of Kentucky, 1963-65; Professor, English, Macalester College, St Paul, 1965-. *Publications:* The Metaphysical Giraffe, 1968; Going Nowhere, 1971; House of the Would-Be Gardener, 1972; Dark Lands, 1973; Metaform, 1975; The Invention of the West, 1976; In Direction, 1978; The Discovery of America and Other Tales, 1980; And Yet, 1981; Delta Q, 1983; The Man in the Cardboard Mask, 1985; Heavy Wings (poetry), 1988; Why We Live With Animals, (poetry). *Contributions to:* American Review; Antioch Review; Ploughshares; Poetry North West; American Poetry Review; Mississippi Review; Georgia Review; Gettysburg Review; Ohio Review. *Honours:* Bush Foundation Artist Fellowships, 1976, 1980; NEA Fellowship, 1972, 1992; Short Fiction Award, Associated Writing Programmes, 1982. *Address:* Dept. of English, Macalester College, St Paul, MN 55105, USA.

GREENBERG Joanne, (Hannah Green), b. 24 Sept 1932, Brooklyn, New York, USA. Author; Teacher. m. Albert Greenberg, 4 Sept 1955, 2 sons. *Education:* BA, American University. *Publications:* The King's Persons, 1963; I Never Promised You A Rose Garden, 1964; The Monday Voices, 1965; Summering: A Book of Short Stories, 1966; In This Sign, 1970; Rites of Passage, 1972; Founder's Praise, 1976; High Crimes and Misdeamours, 1979; A Season of Delight, 1981; The Far Side of Victory, 1983; Simple Gifts, 1986; Age of Consent, 1987; Of Such Small Differences, 1988. *Contributions to:* Articles, reviews, short stories to numerous periodicals including: Hudson Review; Virginia Quarterly; Chatelaine; Saturday Review. *Honours:* Harry and Ethel Daroff Memorial Fiction Award, 1963; William and Janice Epstein Fiction Award, 1964; Marcus L Kenner Award, 1971; Christopher Book Award, 1971; Freida Fromm Reichman Memorial Award, 1971; Honorary Doctorates from: Western Maryland College, 1977; Gallaudet College, 1979; University of Colorado, 1987; Rocky Mountain Women's Institute Award, 1983. *Memberships:* Authors Guild; PEN; Colorado Authors League; National Association of the Deaf; Ladies Tuesday Skiing and Terrorist Society. *Literary Agent:* Lois Wallace. *Address:* 29221 Rainbow Hill Road, Golden, CO 80401, USA.

GREENBERGER Evelyn Barish. *See:* **BARISH Evelyn.**

GREENBERGER Howard, b. 4 Sept 1924, New York City, USA. Writer. *Education:* BBA, City College of New York; Postgraduate theatre studies, Columbia University. *Appointments include:* TV & radio producer, 1955-65. *Publications:* Shadow on the Moon, play, 1944; Gay Masquerade, musical, 1945; Birthday of Eternity, 1946; The End of the Circle, play, 1948; Turning Points, radio series; Once Upon a Tune, TV series, 1950; Inside Times Square, TV series, 1955; A Celebration for Emily, TV play, 1968; Our Play on the Future Has No Name, musical, with Robert Rheinhold, 1970; Everything's the Same, Only Different, musical, 1971; The Off-Broadway Experience, history, 1971; Bogey's Baby, biography, 1976; Grow With Me, play, with R Rheingold, 1980;

Getting Your Foot in the Door, book, (with Dr Kenneth S L Brownlie). *Contributions to:* Book Digest. *Address:* 404 East 55th Street, New York, NY 10022, USA.

GREENE A C, b. 4 Nov 1923, Texas, USA. Professor; Historian; Author. m. Judy Dalton, 20 Jan 1990, 3 sons, 1 daughter. *Education:* BA, Abilene Christian University. *Appointments:* Critic in Residence, University of North Texas; Co-Director, Center for Texas Studies, University of North Texas. *Publications:* A Personal Country, 1969; The Santa Claus Bank Robbery, non-fiction, 1972; The Last Captive, 1972; Dallas: The Deciding Years, 1972; The Highland Park Woman, fiction, 1984; Taking Heart, 1990. *Contributions to:* Atlantic; McCalls; Southwestern History Quarterly; New York Times Book Review. *Honours:* National Conference of Christians and Jews, 1964; Dobie-Paisano Fellow, 1968; Fellow, Texas State History Association, 1990. *Memberships:* Texas Institute of Letters, President 1969-71, Fellow 1981-; Writers Guild of America, West; PEN International. *Literary Agent:* Jan Miller, 5518 Dyer, Dallas TX 75206, USA. *Address:* 4359 Shirley Drive, Dallas, TX 75229, USA.

GREENE Constance C(larke), b. 1924, USA. Writer. *Publications:* A Girl Called Al, 1969; Leo the Lioness, 1970; Good Luck Bogie Hat, 1971; Unmaking of Rabbit, 1972; Isabelle the Itch, 1973; The Ears of Louis, 1974; I Know You, Al, 1975; Beat the Turtle Drum, 1976; Getting Nowhere, 1977; I and Sproggy, 1978; Your Old Pal, Al, 1979; Dotty's Suitcase, 1980; Double-Dare O'Toole, 1981; A(lexandra) the Great, 1982; Ask Anybody, 1983; Isabelle Shows Her Stuff, 1984; Star Shine, 1985; Other Plans, for adults, 1985; Just Plain Al, 1986; The Love Letters of J Timothy Owen, 1986. *Address:* c/o Viking Press Inc, 40 W 23rd Street, New York, NY 10010, USA.

GREENE Jenny, b. 9 Feb 1937. Freelance Writer. m. John Gilbert, 1971, (div 1987). *Education:* BA, Trinity College, Dublin; Dip. d'Etudes Francaises, University of Montpellier, France. *Appointments:* Researcher, Campbell-Johnson Ltd., 1963-64; Account Executive, Central News, 1964-65; Account Executive, Pemberton Advertising, 1965-66; Publicity Executive, Revlon, 1966-71; Beauty Editor, Woman's Own, 1971-75; Features Writer, Theatre Critic, Manchester Evening News, 1975-77; Assistant Editor, Woman's Own, 1977-78; Editor, Home and Gardens, 1978-86, A La Carte, 1984-85; Editor, Country Life, 1986-.92 *Contributions to:* National Press. *Address:* National Westminster Bank, March, Cambridgeshire, England.

GREENE Jonathan (Edward), b. 1943, USA. Editor; Poet. *Appointments:* Founding Editor, Director, Gnomon Press, Frankfort, Kentucky, 1965-; Editor, Kentucky Renaissance, 1976. *Publications:* The Reckoning, 1966; Instance, 1968; The Lapidary, 1969; A 17th Century Garner, 1969; An Unspoken Complaint, 1970; The Poor in Church, by Arthur Rimbaud, translation, 1973; Scaling the Walls, 1974; Glossary of the Everyday, 1974; Peripatetics, 1978; Jonathan Williams: A 50th Birthday Celebration (editor), 1979; Once a Kingdom Again, 1979; Quiet Goods, 1980; Idylls, 1983; Small Change for the Long Haul, 1984; Trickster Tales, 1985. *Address:* PO Box 475, Frankfort, KY 40602, USA.

GREENER Michael John, b. 28 Nov 1931, Barry, Wales, Chartered Accountant Company Director. m. May 1964, (div 1972), 1 son. *Education:* BA, University of South Wales and Monmouthshire, 1949-53; Articled, Deloitte Plender Griffiths, Cardiff, 1949-57; Qualified as Chartered Accountant, 1957; FCA, 1967; BA Open University, 1991. *Publications:* Between the Lines of the Balance Sheet, 1968, revised 1980; Penguin Dictionary of Commerce, 1970, revised 1980, revised and reissued as Penguin Business Dictionary, 1987; Problems for Discussion in Mercantile Law, 1970; The Red Bus, 1973. *Contributions to:* 60 articles in business and professional journals. *Membership:* Fellow, Institute of Chartered Accountants, 1967. *Address:* 33 Glan Hafren, The Knap, Barry, South Glamorgan CF6 8TA, Wales.

GREENFIELD Harry Isaac, b. 8 Sept 1922, NYC, USA. Professor. m. Gladys Frohlinger, 23 June 1943, 2 sons, 1 daughter. *Education:* Bacheler of Scoial Science, City College NY, 1942; Master of Arts, 1948; PhD, Columbus University, 1959. *PublicationsL:* Manpower and Growth of Producer Services; Allied Health Manpower; Hospital Efficiency & Public Policy; Accountability in Health Facilities; Principal Editor of Theory for Economic Efficiency. *Address:* 11205 Watermill Lane, Wheaton, Maryland 20902, USA.

GREENHILL Basil Jack, b. 26 Feb 1920, Great Britain, Author; Company Director. m. Ann Giffard, 2 June 1961, 2 sons. *Education:* BA, 1946, PhD, 1980, University of Bristol. *Publications:* The Merchant Schooners, 1951, 1968, 1978, 1988; The British Assault on Finland, (Co-author Ann Giffard), 1988; The Grain Races, (Co-author John Hickman), 1986; Westcountrymen in Prince Edward's Isle, 1967, 1975, (Co-author Ann Giffard), 1991; The Evolution of the Wooden Ship, 1988; The Last Tall Ships, 1978, 1990; The Archaeology of the Boat, 1976; The Life and Death of the Sailing Ship, 1980; The British Seafarer, 1980; The Herzojin Cecilie, 1991; (Joint Editor), The Maritime History of Devon, 1993. *Contributions to:* The Times; The Observer; Radio Times; The Listener; Country Life; Daily Telegraph; Christian Science Monitor; Guardian; Antiquity; Classic Boat; Wooden Boat. *Honours:* CMG, 1967; CB, 1981; Knight Commander of the White Rose of Finland, 1980; Award of Merit, American Association for State and Local History, 1968. *Memberships:* Vice President, Society for Nautical Research; Honorary Member, the Arts Club, London. *Address:* West Boetheric Farmhouse, St Dominic, Saltash, Cornwall PL12 6SZ, England.

GREENLAND Colin, b. 17 May 1954, Dover, Kent, England. Freelance Writer. *Education:* MA, 1978, D.Phil, 1981, Pembroke College, Oxford. *Appointments:* Writer-in-Residence, NE London Polytechnic, 1980-82. *Publications:* The Entropy Exhibition, 1983; Daybreak on a Different Mountain, 1984; The Hour of the Thin Ox, 1987; with Roger and Martyn Dean: Magnetic Storm, 1984; with Paul Kerton: The Freelance Writer's Handbook, 1986; Co-Editor, Interzone: The First Anthology, 1985, Storm Warnings, 1987; Other Voices, 1988; Stories in Other Edens II, 1988; Zenith, 1989; Take Back Plenty, 1990; Michael Moorcock: Death Is No Obstacle, 1992. *Contributions to:* Book Reviews etc for Foundation: The Review of Science Fiction; Times Literary Supplement; New Statesman; British Book News; City Limits; Time Out; Sunday Times; The Face; Zenith 2: The Best in New British S F, 1990; More Tales From The Forbidden Planet, 1990; Journal Wired, 1990; Temps, 1991; Final Shadows, 1991; The Weerds, 1992; In Dreams, 1992; R.E.M. 1992; Eurotemps, 1992. *Honour:* Eaton Award for Science Fiction Criticism, 1985; Arthur C Clarke Award and BSFA Award, Best SF Novel, 1992; Eastercon Award, 1992. *Memberships:* Chair, Milford S.F. Writers' Conference, 1986; Council Member, Science Fiction Foundation, 1989-. *Literary Agent:* Maggie Noach, 21 Redan Street, London W14 0AB. *Address:* 2A Ortygia House, 6 Lower Road, Harrow, Middlesex, HA2 0DA, England.

GREENLEAF Stephen (Howell), b. 1942, USA. Attorney; Novelist (Mystery, Crime, Suspense). *Education:* JD; Bar Admissions: California, 1968; Iowa, 1977. *Publications:* Grave Error, 1979; Death Bed, 1980; State's Evidence, 1982; Fatal Obsession, 1983; The Ditto List, 1985; Beyond Blame, 1986; Toll Call, 1987. *Address:* c/o Esther Newberg, ICM, 40 W 57th Street, New York, NY 10019, USA.

GREENLEAF William, b. USA. Science Fiction Writer. *Publications:* Time Jumper, 1981; The Tartarus Incident, 1983; The Pandora Stone, 1984; Starjacked, 1987. *Address:* c/o Ace Books, 220 Madison Avenue, New York, NY 10016, USA.

GREENOAK Francesca Lavinia, b. 6 Sept 1946, Derbyshire, England. Writer. m. 21 Jan 1981, 1 son, 1 daughter. *Education:* University of Essex. *Appointments:* Editor: Harraps; Penguin Education. *Publications:* God's Acre; All the Birds of the Air; Forgotten Fruit; Gilbert White Journals; Glorious Gardens; Fruit and vegetables Gardens, Editor. *Contributions to:* The Times, Gardening Correspondent; Garden Editor, Good Housekeeping; Sunday Times; BBC Wildlife; She Magazine; Times Literary Supplement. *Membership:* Society of Authors. *Address:* 4 Wood Row, Wigginton, Tring, Hertfordshire HP23 6HS, England.

GREENSTEIN George, b. 28 Sept 1940, Williams Bay, Wisconsin, USA. Astrophysicist; Writer. m. Barbara Kunharlt, 25 Sept 1980, 3 daughters. *Education:* BS, Stanford University, 1962; PhD, Yale University, 1968. *Publications:* Frozen Star; The Symbiotic Universe. *Contributions to:* Numerous Technical and Non Technical Magazines. *Honours:* Phi Beta Kappa; American Institute of Physics, Science Writing Award. *Memberships:* The Authors Guild; American Astronomical Society; International Astronomical Union; PEN. *Literary Agent:* Raines and Raines, NYC. *Address:* Department of Astronomy, Amherst College, Amherst, MA 01002, USA.

GREENWOOD Duncan, b. 30 Aug 1919, Bradford, Yorkshire, England, chartered Civil Engineer. m. Joyce Black, 24 Feb 1949, 3 sons. *Education:* BSc; AMICE. *Publications:* Plays: Cat Among the Pigeons, 1957; Strike Happy, 1960; Murder Delayed, 1961; No Time For Fig Leaves, (Co-author Robert King), 1966; Surprise Package, (Co-author Derek Parkes), 1975; Murder By The Book, (Co-author Robert King), 1982; Waiting For Yesterday, 1985. *Literary Agent:* Samuel French. *Address:* 58 High View, Pinner, Middlesex HA5 3PB, England.

GREENWOOD Edward Alister. *See:* **GREENWOOD Ted.**

GREENWOOD Ted (Edward Alister Greenwood), b. 1930, Australia. Children's Fiction Writer; Former Lecturer in Art Education. *Publications:* Obstreperous, 1969; Alfred, 1970; V I P: Very Important Plant, 1971; Joseph and Lulu and the Prindiville House Pigeons, 1972; Terry's Brrrmmm GT, 1974; The Pochetto Coat, 1978; Ginnie, 1979; Curious Eddie, 1979; The Boy Who Saw God, 1980; Everlasting Circle, 1081; Flora's Treasures, 1982; Marley and Friends, 1983; Warts and All (with S Fennessy), 1984; Ship Rock, 1985; I Don't Want To Know (with Fennessy), 1986; Windows, 1989; Uncle Theo is a Number Nine, 1990. *Address:* 50 Hilton Road, Ferny Creek, Victoria 3786, Australia.

GREER Anne. *See:* **JACOBS Barbara.**

GREER Germaine, (Rose Blight), b. 29 Jan 1939. Writer; Broadcaster. *Education:* BA, Hon., University of Melbourne, 1959; MA, Hon. Sydney University, 1962; PhD, Cambridge University, 1967. *Appointments:* Senior Tutor in English, Sydney University, 1963-64; Assistant Lecturer, Lecturer in English, University of Warwick, 1967-72; Visiting Professor, Graduate Faculty of Modern Letters, University of Tulsa, 1979; Professor of Modern Letters, University of Tulsa, 1980-83; Founder-Director, Tulsa Centre for Study of Woman's Literature; Editor, Tulsa Studies in Women's Literature, 1981; Director, Stump Cross Books, 1988-; Lecturer, Unofficial Fellow, Newnham College, Cambridge, 1989-. *Publications:* The Female Eunuch, 1969; Foreword to Autobiography of Anna Kollontain, 1970; Introduction to Stonehill ed. of Goblin Market, 1971; The Revolting Garden, (as Rose Blight), 1971; The Obstacle Race: The Fortunes of Women Painters and Their Work, 1979; Sex and Destiny: The Politics of Human Fertility, 1984; Women and Power in Cuba - Women a World Report, 1985; Shakespeare, 1986; The Madwoman Underclothes, 1986; Daddy, We Hardly Knew You, 1989; Co-Editor, Kissing the Rod: An Anthology of Seventeenth Century Women's Verse, 1989; (editor) The Uncollected Verse of Aphra Behn, 1989; The Change: Women, Ageing and the Menopause, 1991. *Contributions to:* Columnist, Sunday Times, 1971-73; Esquire; Harper; Playboy; The Listener; The Spectator. *Honour:* Playboy Journalist of the Year, 1973. *Literary Agent:* Aitken & Stone Ltd. *Address:* c/o Gillon Aitken, Aitken and Stone Ltd., 29 Fernshaw Road, London SW10 OTG, England.

GREGG Pauline, b. United Kingdom. Historian. *Publications:* Social and Economic History of Britain from 1760 to the Present Day, 1950, 8th Revised Edition, 1981; The Chain of History, 1958; Freeborn John: A Biography of John Lilburne, 1961; The Welfare State, 1963; Modern Britain, 1967; A Social and Economic History of England from the Black Death to the Industrial Revolution, 1975; King Charles the First, 1981. *Address:* c/o Dent, 33 Welbeck Street, London W1, England.

GREGORY John. *See:* **HOSKINS Robert.**

GREGORY Richard L, b. 1923, United Kingdom. Emeritus Professor of Neuropsychology. *Publications:* Eye and Brain, 1966, 3rd Edition, 1977; The Intelligent Eye, 1970; Illusions in Nature and Art (edited with E H Gombrich), 1973; Concepts and Mechanisms of Perception, 1974; Mind in Science, 1981; Odd Perceptions, 1986; Oxford Companion to the Mind, 1987; Evolution of the Eye and Visual System, Vol 2 of Vision and Visual Dysfunction, 1991. *Honour:* CBE, 1989; FRS 1992. *Address:* University of Bristol, Department of Psychology, 8 Woodland Road, Bristol BS8 1TN, England.

GREGORY Stephan. *See:* **PENDLETON Donald.**

GRENDEL Lajos, b. 6 Apr 1948, Levice, CSFR. Writer. m. Agota Sebök, 6 July 1974, 1 son, 1 daughter. *Education:* University Komens Keho. *Appointments:* Editor, Publishing House, Medech Brehsleva; Editor in Chief, Lit Monthly, Kalligram, Chairman, Publishinh House, Kalligram, 1992. *Publications:* Elesloveszet; Attetelek; Borondok Tartalma; Theszevz es a Pekete Ozvegy; Einstein Harangjai; Galeri; Hutlenek. *Contributions to:* Hungarian & Slovak Magazines. *Honours:* Dery Prize; Jozsef Attila Prize; Cryslal Vilenica. *Memberships:* Union of Hungarian Writers. *Address:* Vazovova 15, 81107 Bratislava, CSFR.

GRENNAN Eamon, b. 13 Nov 1941, Dublin, Ireland. Teacher. 1 son, 2 daughters. *Education:* BA, University College Dublin, 1963; MA, 1964; PhD, Harvard University, 1972. *Publications:* wildly for Days; What Light There Is; What Light There Is and Other Poems; As If It matters. *Contributions to:* Ireland & America; Poetry Ireland; Irish Times; The New Yorker; Poetry; The Nation. *Honour:* NEA Award. *Address:* Box 352 Vassar College, Poughkeepsie, NY 12601, USA.

GRENVILLE John A. S., b. 1928, United Kingdom. Professor of Modern History. *Publications:* The Coming of the Europeans (with Joan Fuller), 1962; Lord Salisbury and Foreign Policy, 1964; Politics Strategy and American Diplomacy 1873-1917 (with G B Young), 1966; The Munich Crisis (with Nicholas Pronay), film, 1968; The End of Illusions, from Munich to Dunkirk (with N Pronay), film, 1970; The Major International Treaties, 1914-1973: A History and Guide with Texts, 1974, Revised Edition in 2 vols, 1987; Europe Reshaped 1948-1878, 1976 and subesquent editions; Film as Evidence: Tomorrow the World, film, 1977; World History of the Twentieth Century, vol I 1900- 1945, 1980. *Address:* School of History, University of Birmingham, PO Box 363, Birmingham B15 2TT, England.

GRESS Esther, Editor. *Literary Appointments:* Editor, Encyclopedia Vor Tids Konversations Leksikon Supplement, 1948; Mentor, 1949; Dansk Rim-Ordbog, 1950; Newspaper Berlingske Tidende, 1950-;

Publications of Det Berlingske Officin A/S including Radiolytteren, Landet, Det Danske Magasin and Berlingske Aftenavis; Radio, film and theatre columnist; Pictor Editor. *Publications:* Skal, 1974; Liv, 1977; Villevejenivejen, 1979; Det Sker-maske, 1982; Det gik, 1983; Raise, with English poems, 1984; Let Us, with poems in 17 languages, 1985, and 1987; Det Sker - maske II, 1985; Raise with English and Indian poems, (Telegu), 1989, Grow with English poems, 1989, Poems in 21 languages; Poems set to music. *Contributions to:* Anthologies, papers and magazines including: Lyrikarbogen, 1974 and 1977; Citabogen, 1977 and 1979; Spejlinger, 1977; Digte 80, 1980; Lyrikcafe, 1980; Frederiksborg Amts Avis; Berlingske Tidende; Berlingske Aftenavis; Politiken; Kristeligdt Dagblad; Svenska Dagbladet; Jul i Nordsjoellaid; Nauncer; English poems in magazines in United Kongdom, USA, Italy, Switzerland, Austria, Korea, Portugal Thailand and India. *Honours include:* Awards in USA, Italy, and India. Academy Consul for Denmark, Accademia d'Europa, Naples, 1982; Guest of Honour, New York Poetry Forum, 1983; Grand Dame in Knight of Malta, 1984; Doctor of Literature, Honorary, 1984; Co-Founder and International Regent of International Poets Academy, India, 1985; Poet Laureate, 1987; The Bugler, Lachian Art Letters Campbell, California, 1987; Chinese Home Education Promotion Association, Taiwan, 1987; Grand Medal of World Culture, Milano, 1988; Dr Amado Yuzon's Medal for Exemplary Services for World Brotherhood & Peace, Rome, 1988; Grand Prix Méditerranée Étoiles d'Europe Trofeo Italia, Naples, 1989; Regional Coordinator for Europe in World Congress of Poets, 1989. *Memberships include:* World Poetry Society Intercontinental; United Poets Laureate International; Danish Authors Association; Accademia Internazionale di Lettere; Arti Virgiglio-Mantegna; Accademia Internazionale Leonardo da Vinci; New York Poetry Forum, Inc; National Federation of States Poetry Societies Inc; Danish Press Historic Association; Accademia d'Europa; International Academy of Poets; Danish Publicistklub; Fellow, IBC; The World Literary Academy, Cambridge; Danish Press Staff Association. *Address:* Ny Strandvej 27, 3050 Humlebaek, Denmark.

GRESSER Seymour Gerald, b. 9 May 1926, Baltimore, Maryland, USA, Sculptor; Writer. m. (1) 1 July 1950, (2) 9 July 1976, div, 3 sons, 1 daughter. *Education:* BS, 1949, MA, 1972, Maryland University; Stone Carving, Institute of Contemporary Arts, Washington DC 1949-52. *Appointments:* Sculptor Residency, Mt Rushmore, South Dakota, 1980; Colgate University, 1989; Yale University, 1969. *Publications:* Stone Elegies, 1955; Coming of Atom, 1957; Poems from Mexico, 1964; Voyages, 1969; A Garland for Stephen, 1971; A Departure for Sons, 1973; Fragments and Others, 1982; Hagar and Her Elders, 1989. *Contributor To:* Numerous literary quarterlies worldwide including: Gargoyle Magazine, Washington DC. *Address:* 1015 Ruatan Street, Silver Spring, MD 20903, USA.

GREX Leo. *See:* **GRIBBLE Leonard (Reginald).**

GREY Anthony Keith, b. 5 July 1938, Norwich, England. Author. m. Shirley McGuinn, 4 April 1970. 2 daughters. *Appointments:* Journalist, Eastern Daily Press, 1960-64; Foreign Correspondent, Reuters, East Berlin and Prague, 1965-67, Peking, 1967-69. *Publications:* Hostage in Peking, 1970; Saigon, 1982; A Man Alone, 1971; Some Put Their Trust in Chariots, 1973; The Bulgarian Exclusive, 1976; The Chinese Assassin, 1978; The Prime Minister was a Spy, 1983; Peking, 1988; The Naked Angels, 1990; The Bangkok Secret, 1990. Himself (radio play); Contributor of short stories and feature articles to various publications. *Honours:* O.B.E., 1969; U.K. Journalist of the Year, 1970. *Memberships:* Society of Authors; Royal Institute of International Affairs. *Literary Agent:* Michael Sissons.*Address:*A.D. Peters & Co. Ltd., 5th Floor, The Chambers, Chelsea Harbour, Lots Road, London SW10 OXF, England.

GREY Belinda. *See:* **PETERS Maureen.**

GREY Brenda. *See:* **MacKINLAY Leila Antoinette Sterling.**

GREY Charles. *See:* **TUBB E C.**

GREY Ian, b. 5 May 1918, Wellington, New Zealand. Author; Editor. *Education:* LLB University of Sydney, Australia. *Major Publications:* Peter the Great, 1960; Catherine the Great, 1961; Ivan the Terrible, 1964; The First Fifty Years: Soviet Russia 1917-67; The Romanovs: Rise & Fall of the Dynasty, 1970; A History of Russia, 1970; Boris Godunov, 1973; Stalin: Man of History, 1979; Parliamentarians, The History of the Commonwealth Parliamentary Association 1911-1985, 1986. *Literary Agent:* John Farquharson Ltd. *Address:* 10 Alwyn Avenue, Chiswick, London W4, England.

GREY Louis. *See:* **GRIBBLE Leonard (Reginald).**

GRIBBLE Leonard (Reginald), (Sterry Browning, Stetson Cody, Lee Denver, Landon Grant, Leo Grex, Louis Grey, Piers Marlowe, Dexter Muir, Bruce Sanders), b. 1908. British, Full-time writer of Mystery/Crime/Suspense, Western/Adventure. *Publications include:* Mystery novels include: (as Leo Grex), Terror Wears a Smile, 1962; (as Leo Grex), The Brass Knuckle, 1964; Heads You Die, 1964; The Violent Dark, 1965; Strip-Tease Macabre, 1967; (as Leo Grex), Violent Keepsake, 1967; A Diplomat Dies, 1969; (as Leo Grex), The Hard Kill, 1969; Alias the Victim, 1971; (as Leo Grex), Kill Now - Pay Later, 1971; Programmed for Death, 1973; (as Leo Grex), Die- as in Murder, 1974; You Can't Die Tomorrow, 1975; The Cardinal's Diamonds, 1976; (as Leo Grex), Death Throws No Shadow, 1976; Midsummer Slay Ride, 1976; The Deadly Professionals, 1976; Compelled to Kill, 1977; Crime on Her Hands, 1977; The Dead End Killers, 1978; (as Leo Grex), Mix Me a Murder, 1978; Death Needs No Alibi, 1979; Dead End in Mayfair, 1981; The Dead Don't Scream, 1983; (as Leo Grex), Hot Ice, 1983; Western novels as Landon Grant: Rustler's Gulch, 1935; Wyoming Deadline, 1939; Texas Buckeroo, 1948; Ramrod of the Bar X, 1949; Scar Valley Bandit, 1951; The Rawhide Kid, 1951; Gunsmoke Canyon, 1952; Outlaws of Silver Spur, 1953; Marshall of Mustang, 1954; Thunder Valley Deadline, 1956; western novels as Lee Denver: Cheyenne Jones, Maverick Marshal, 1977; Cheyenne's Sixgun Justice, 1980; Cheyenne's Trail to Perdition, 1982; Cheuenne's Two-Gun Shoot-Out, 1983; Cheyenne at Dull-Knife Pass, 1982; Others works include: They Conspired to Kill, 1975; (as Leo Grex), Murder Stranger Than Fiction, 1975; Famous Mysteries of Detection, 1976; Famous Mysteries of Modern Times, 1976; (as Leo Grex), Detection Stranger Than Fiction, 1977; Crimes Stranger Than Fiction, 1981; Notorious Killer in the Night, 1983; Mysteries Behind Notorious Crimes, 1984; Notorious Crimes, 1985; Such Lethal Ladies, 1985. *Address:* Chandons, Firsdown Close, High Salvington, Worthing, Sussex, €ngland.

GRIDBAN Volsted. *See:* **TUBB E C.**

GRIER Eldon (Brockwill), b. 1917, Canada. Painter; Poet. *Publications:* A Morning from Scraps, 1955; Poems, 1956; The Ring of Ice, 1957; Manzanillo and Other Poems, 1958; A Friction of Lights, 1963; Pictures on the Skin, 1967; Selected Poems 1955-1970, 1971; The Assassination of Colour, 1978. *Address:* 6221 St George's Place, West Vancouver, British Columbia, Canada V7W 1YC.

GRIFFIN Keith B(roadwell), b. 1938, United Kingdom. Economist; Professor and Chair, Department of Economics, University of California, Riverside. *Publications:* Underdevelopment in Spanish America, 1969; Planning Development (with John Enos), 1970; Financing Development in Latin America (editor), 1971; Growth and Inequality in Pakistan (edited with A R Khan), 1972; The Political Economy of Agrarian Change, 1974; Land Concentration and Rural Poverty, 1976; International Inequality and National Poverty, 1978; The

Transition to Egalitarian Development (with J James), 1981; Growth and Equality in Rural China (with A Saith), 1981; Institutional Reform and Economic Development in the Chinese Countryside (editor), 1984; World Hunger and the World Economy, 1987; Alternative Strategies for Economic Development, 1989; Human Development and the Internatumal Development Strategy for the 1990s (edited with J Knight), 1990; (Ed), The Economy of Ethiopia, 1992. *Address:* Department of Economic, University of California, Riverside, CA 92521, USA.

GRIFFIN Russell M., b. 1943, USA. Professor of English; Science Fiction Writer. *Appointments:* English Teacher, Proctor Academy, Andover, New Hampshire, 1965-67; Professor of English, University of Bridgeport, Bridgeport, Connecticut, 1970-. *Publications:* Makeshift God, 1979; Century's End, 1981; The Blind Man and the Elephant, 1982; The Timeservers, 1985.

GRIFFITH Arthur Leonard, b. 1920, England. Retired Minister of Religion. *Publications:* The Roman Letter Today, 1959; God and His People, 1960; Beneath the Cross of Jesus, 1961; What is a Christian, 1962; Barriers to Christian Belief, 1962; A Pilgrimage to the Holy Land, 1962; The Eternal Legacy, 1963; Pathways to Happiness, 1964; God's Time and Ours, 1964; The Crucial Encounter, 1965; This is Living, 1966; God is Man's Experience, 1968; Illusions of Our Culture, 1969; The Need to Preach, 1971; Hang on to the Lord's Prayer, 1973; We Have This Ministry, 1973; Ephesians: A Positive Affirmation, 1975; Gospel Characters, 1976; Reactions to God, 1979; Take Hold of the Treasure, 1981; From Sunday To Sunday, 1987. *Address:* 71 Old Mill Road, 105, Etobicoke, Ontario, M8X 1G9, Canada.

GRIFFITH Bill. *See:* **GRIFFITH William Henry Jackson.**

GRIFFITH Thomas, b. 30 Dec 1915, Tacoma, Washington, USA. Writer; Editor. m. Caroline Coffman, 1937. *Education:* University of Washington. *Appointments:* Reporter, then Assistant City Editor, Seattle Times, Seattle, Washington, 1936-41; Nieman Fellow, Harvard, 1942; Contributing Editor, then Associate Editor, 1943-46, Senior Editor 1946, National Affairs Editor 1949-51, Foreign Editor 1951-60, Assistant Managing Editor, 1960-63, Time Magazine; Senior Staff Editor, all Time Inc. Publications, 1963-67; Editor, Life Magazine, 1968-73; Press Columnist, Time Magazine, 1973-; Staff Contributor, Fortune Magazine; Columnist, Atlantic Monthly, 1974-81; Newswatch Columnist, Time Magazine, 1976-1987. *Publications:* The Waist-High Culture, 1958; How True - A Skeptic's Guide to Believing the News, 1974. *Address:* 25 East End Ave, New York, NY 10028, USA.

GRIFFITH William Henry Jackson, (Bill Griffith), b. 20 Jan 1944, Brooklyn, NY, USA. Cartoonist. m. 18 Nov 1980. *Education:* Pratt Institute Art School. *Publications:* Zippy Quarterly; From A To Zippy; Pinheads Progress; Kingpin; Zippy Stories; Get Me A Table Without Flies, Harry; Nation of Pinheads; Pointed Behavior; Pindemonium; Are We Having Fun Yet; *Contributions to:* National Lampoon; Village Voice; Over 200 Newspapers. *Honour:* Harvard Lampoon. *Memberships:* Writers Guild; National Cartoonists Society. *Literary Agent:* Paul Yamamoto, Favored Artists Agency, Los Angeles. *Address:* PO Box 460154, San Francisco, CA 94146, USA.

GRIFFITHS Bryn(lyn David), b. 1933, United Kingdom. Poet. *Publications:* The Mask of Pity, 1966; The Stones Remember, 1967; Welsh Voices (editor), 1967; Scars, 1969; The Survivors, 1971; Beasthoods, 1972; Starboard Green, 1973; The Dark Convoys: Sea Poems, 1974; Love Poems, 1980. *Address:* 65 Gwili Terrace, Mayhill, Swansea, Wales.

GRIFFITHS Helen, (Helen Santos), b. 8 May 1939, London, England. Writer. *Publications:* Horse in the Clouds, 1957; Wild & Free, 1958; Moonlight, 1959; Africano, 1960; The Wild Heart, 1962; The Greyhound, 1963; Wild Horse of Santander (award), 1965; Dark Swallows, 1965; Leon, 1966; Stallion of the Sands, 1967; Moshie Cat, 1968; Patch, 1969; Federico, 1970; Russian Blue, 1973; Just a Dog, 1974; Witch Fear (award), 1975; Pablo, 1976; Kershaw Dogs, 1978; The Last Summer, 1979; Blackface Stallion, 1980; Dancing Horses, 1981; Hari's Pigeon, 1982; Rafa's Dog, 1983; Jesus, As Told By Mark, 1983; Dog at the Window, 1984. Also, as Helen Santos: Caleb's Lamb 1984, If Only 1987; Scripture Union. *Honours:* Daughter of Mark Twain, 1966; Highly Commended, Carnegie Medal Award, 1966; Silver Pencil Award, best children's book, Netherlands, 1978. *Address:* 9 Ashley Terrace, Bath, Avon BA1 3JZ, England.

GRIFFITHS Linda, b. 7 Oct 1956, Montreal, Canada. Writer; Actor. *Education:* Dawson College. *Publications:* The Book of Jessica; Maggie & Pierre; The Darling Family; OD on Paradise. *Contributions to:* Poety; Anthology; Barbed Lyres; Praire Womens Jounral of Pregnancy Loss. *Honours:* Dora Mauor Moore Award; Governor Generals Award. *Memberships:* Theatre Passe Muraille. *Literary Agent:* Patty Ney. *Address:* c/o Patty Ney, Chris Banks & Associates, 219 Dufferin Street, 305, Toronto, Ontario, Canada.

GRIFFITHS Trevor, b. 4 Apr 1935, Manchester, Lancashire, England. Playwright. m. (1) Janice Elaine Stansfield 1960 (dec 1977), 1 son, 2 daughters, (2) Gillian Cliff, 1992. *Education:* St Bede's College, Manchester 1945-52; BA, English, Manchester University, 1955. *Appointments:* Teacher of English, Oldham, Lancashire, 1957-61; Lecturer in Liberal Studies, Stockport Technical College, Cheshire, 1962-65; Further Education Officer, BBC Leeds, 1965-72; Co-editor, Labour's Northern Voice, 1962-65 and series editor for Workers Northern Publishing Society. *Publications:* Plays include: Apricots (produced London 1971), and Thermidor, London, 1978, (prod. Edinburgh 1971); Lay By, with others (produced Edinburgh and London, 1971), London, 1972; Sam, Sam (produced London 1972; revised version produced London, 1978), Published in Plays and Players (London), April 1972; The Party (produced London 1973; revised version produced 1974), London, 1974; Occupations, 1980; All Good Men and Absolute Begginers, (both produced BBC TV, 1974), London, 1977; Comedians, 1976; Through the Night, (produced BBC TV, 1975), London, 1977; Bill Brand, (produced Thames TV), 1976; The Cherry Orchard, London 1989; Deeds (with others), 1978; Sons and Lovers, (version for TV, produced BBC TV 1981), Nottingham, 1982; Country, (produced BBC TV 1981), London, 1981; Reds, 1981; Oi for England, 1982; The Last Place on Earth, (produced Central TV 1985), published as Judgment Over the Dead, 1986; Real Dreams (produced Williamstown, 1984, also director); London, 1986, 1987; Fatherland, (film released 1986), London, 1987; Collected plays for Television, 1988; Piano London, 1990; The Gulf Between Us, (produced Leeds, 1992, also director; published London, 1992). *Honour:* BAFTA Award for screenplay, 1982. *Literary Agent:* c/o Peters Fraser and Dunlop Group Ltd, London. *Address:* c/o Peters Fraser and Dunlop Group Ltd, 503/4 The Chambers, Chelsea Harbour, Lots Road, London, SW10 0XF, England.

GRIFFITHS ORMHAUG Ella, b. 22 Mar 1926, Oslo, Norway. Author; Copywriter; Radio Reporter; Journalist; Columnist; Translator. *Education:* Oslo University; Conservatory of Music, Oslo; Mass Media Studies, American University, Salzburg Seminar in American Studies, Salzburg, Austria; Certificate, proficiency, English, University of Cambridge; Film/Video Seminar, Norwegian Film Industries. *Publications:* Some 25 adult books including the police procedurals: The Water Widow; Unkown Partner; Murder on Page 3; Five to Twelve; 12 Children's and Youth Novels including: Pia, Kim and tiny, 1979; Tiny and Bombastus, the Cat, 1981; Tiny and Pepper, the Tortoise, 1983; Fiddle Diddle Grasshopper and other Fairytales, 1984; Thursday, January 32, (science fiction), 1985; Short Stories in The John Creasey Crime Collections, 1980, 1983, 1984,

1986; several of her works are published in Sweden, Denmark, Finland, UK, USA and Unknown Partner in USSR, 1986-87. *Honours include:* US Information Agency (Washington) Award for Meritorious Service, 1962; Department of State AID—USIA (Washington) Outstanding Services Award, 1977. *Literary Agent:* Ulla Lohren, Nordic Countries; Laurence Pollinger Limited, London. *Address:* Kirkeveien 99a, 1344 Haslum, Norway.

GRIGG John (Edward Poynder), b. 15 Apr 1924. Writer. m. Patricia, 1958, 2 sons. *Education:* Exhibitioner, MA Modern History, Gladstone Memorial Prize, New College, Oxford. *Appointments:* Grenadier Guards, 1943-45; Editor, National and English Review, 1954-60; Columnist, The Guardian, 1960-70. *Publications:* Two Anglican Essays, 1958; The Young Lloyd George, 1973; Lloyd George : the People's Champion, 1978, 1943; The Victory That Never Was, 1980; Nancy Astor: Portrait of a Pioneer, 1980; Lloyd George: From Peace to War 1912-1916, 1985. *Contributions to:* various books of essays, magazines and journals. *Honours:* Whitbread Award, 1978; Wolfson Literary Prize, 1985. *Memberships:* Chairman, the London Library, 1985-91; President, Blackheath Society; Vice Chairman, Greenwich Festival Trustees; FRSL. *Address:* 32 Dartmouth Row, London SE10, England.

GRIGGS Terry Jean, b. 20 Dec 1951, Ontario, Canada. Writer. m. David Burr, 17 Nov 1978, 1 son. *Education:* University of Western Ontario, BA, 1972-75; MA, 1977-79. *Publications:* Quickening; Harrier; The New Press Anthology; The Macmillan Anthology; Street Songs; The New Story Writers. *Contributions to:* The Malahat Review; The Canadian Forum; The New Quarterly; Room of Ones Own; Brick and What. *Honours:* Short List, Governor General's Award; Journey Prize Anthology. *Address:* 27 Garfield Avenue, London, Ontario, Canada N6C 2B4.

GRIMM Barbara Lockett, (Cherry Wilder), b. 3 Sept 1930, Auckland, New Zealand. Science Fiction & Fantasy Writer. m. Horst Grimm, 1963, 2 daughters. *Education:* BA, Canterbury University College, Christchurch, NZ, 1952. *Publications include:* Novels: The Luck of Brin's Five, 1977, The Nearest Fire, 1979, The Tapestry Warrior's, 1982 (Torin Trilogy); Second Nature, 1982; A Princess of the Chameln, 1983, Yorath the Wolf, 1984, The Summer's King, 1985 (Rulers of Hylor Trilogy); Cruel Designs, 1988. *Contributions:* Short stories: Various anthologies; Journals including Meanjin (Australia), Prism International (Canada), Omni, Galileo, Issac Asimov's SF Magazine, Interzone (UK). Reviews: Sydney Morning Herald; The Australian, 1965-75; Various science fiction journals, UK & Australia. *Honours:* Literary Grants, Australia Council, 1973, 1975; Ditmar, Australian Science Fiction Award, 1978. *Memberships:* Women Writers of Australia; Science Fiction Writers of America; British Science Fiction Association; Science Fiction Club of Germany. *Literary Agents:* Virginia Kidd, 538 East Harford, Milford, PA 18337, USA; Maggie Noach, 21 Redan Street, London W14 0AB, UK; Thomas Schlück, Hinter der Worth 12, 3008 Garbsen 9, Germany. *Address:* 19 Egelsbacherstrasse, 6070 Langen/Hesseh, Germany.

GRIMM-RICHARDSON Anna Louise, b. 2 Mar 1927, Menlo, Washington, USA. Writer; Photographer. m. Alfred Joseph Richardson, 9 Mar 1951, 2 sons, 1 daughter. *Education:* Broadway Edison Business College, 1947; Clark College, 1966; Florida State University, 1972-75. *Appointments include:* Consultant, Star & Herald, 1980-81; Editor, Gatun Key, 1981-82; Editor, publisher, Tiptoe Publishing, 1985-. *Publications:* Hits & Mrs, column, 1957-65; Of Shoes & Ships, column, 1970-83; Pearls, book of cartoons, 1986; Writer & Illustrator, How Good Are Your Interpersonal Relations, 1987; Also Illustrator, Blueprint to Better Eating, 1962; Something Fishy at Panama Canal, 1986. *Contributions to:* Numerous magazines, journals, newspapers, North, South & Central America. *Honours:* Prizes, local essay contests, 1943, 1945; 1st prize,

National IAM Auxilliary Contest, 1959; Honourable Mention, Poetry Contest, Writers Digest, 1977; Honorary DD, Universal Life Church University. *Memberships:* Former Secretary/President, Crossroads Writers of Panama; Crossroads Writers International; Adviser 1986-, Wakiakum-Pacific Writers Association. *Address:* 12 Km East of 101 at Wilderness, PO Box 206-W, Naselle, Washington 98638, USA.

GRODEN Michael Lewis, b. 30 May 1947. Professor. *Education:* Dartmouth College, BA, 1969; Princeton University, MA, 1972; PhD, 1975. *Publications:* Ulysses in Progress; The James Joyce Archive; James Joyces Manuscripts. *Contributions to:* Twentieth Century Literature 21; Modern British Literature; A Companion to Joyce Studies; James Joyce Quarterly. *Memberships:* Modern Language Association of America; Canadian College & University Teachers of English. *Address:* 229 Emery Street E, London, Ontario, Canada N6C 2E3.

GROFE Ferde Jr. (Ferdinand Rudolph von Grofe, Jr), b. 3 July 1930, Englewood, New Jersey, USA. Writer; Film Director and Producer; Aviator; Poet. m. Constanze Gomez, 13 Nov 1965. *Education:* 1 Year, Maren Elwood College, Los Angles, 1949. *Appointments include:* Production Associate, Columbia Pictures, 1956-57; Judge, Aviation Writers Association, 1977-78; International Film Festival, Huesca, Spain, 1981; President, Chief Executive Officer, Ferde Grofe Films Inc, Aviation A V Library, 1975-. *Productions:* The Steel Claw, 1959; Samar, 1960; From Hell to Borneo, 1963; Guerrillas in Pink Lace, 1963; Warkill, 1967; The Walls of Hell, 1964; Soul of a Fortress, 1962; Sentimental Journey, 1976; (All these are writing credits with most also including directorial/producer credit). *Contributions to:* Philippine Free Press; American Cinematographer; Various film and trade journals. *Honours:* Awards, Miquelde de Plata, Bilbao Film Festival, Spain, 1963, Philippine National Film Festival, 1964, Week of the Asian Film, Frankfurt, 1964; Aviation Writers Association, 1977, 1978. *Memberships include:* various committees, Aviation Writers Association, Academy of Motion Picture Arts and Sciences; National Press Club; Writers Guild of America; AOPA-EAA. *Address:* 3100 Airport Avenue, Santa Monica, CA 90405, USA.

GRONBECK Bruce Elliot, b. 9 Mar 1941, Bertha, Minnesota, USA. Professor. m. Wendy Gilbert, 28 Sept 1968, 2 sons, 1 daughter. *Education:* BA, summa cum laude, 1963; MA 1966; PhD, 1970; DHL honoris causa, 1991. *Publications:* Principles and Types of Speech Communication, 1990; Principles of Speech Communication, 1992; Media, Consciousness and Culture, ed, 1991; Spheres of Argument, ed, 1989; Writing Television Criticism, 1984. *Contributions to:* Quarterly Journal of Speech; Presidential Studies Quarterly; Critical Studies in Mass Communication; Comtemporary Psychology; Philosophy and Rhetoric; Vichiana; The American Scholar; Association for Communication Administration Newsletter; Spectra; Vital Speeches of the Day. *Honours:* Research Fellow, London Centre for the Study of Communication and Culture; SCA Golden Anniversary Monograph Award, 1982; NEH Research Grant, 1990-92; Fulbright, 1992; DHL, 1991. *Memberships:* Speech Communication Association, President, 1994; University Society for the Study of Rhetoric; Rhetoric Society of America; Central States Speech Association, President, 1978; Centre for the Study of the Presidency. *Address:* 1017 Bowery Street, Iowa City, IA 52240, USA.

GROSS John Jacob, b. 12 Mar 1935, London, England. Author; Editor; Publisher. m. Miriam, May 1965, 1 son, 1 daughter. *Education:* Wadham College, Oxford. *Appointments:* Editor, Victor Gollancz Ltd., 1956-58; Lecturer, Queen Mary College, University of London, 1959-62; Fellow, King's College, Cambridge, 1962-65; Assistant Editor, Encounter, 1963- 65; Literary Editor, New Statesman, 1972-73; Editor, Times Literary Supplement, 1974-81; Literary Editor, Spectator, 1983-; Journalist, New York Times, 1983-; Director, Times Newspapers Holdings Ltd (formerly Times Newspapers Ltd), 1982; Editorial Consultant, The

Weidenfield Publishing Group, 1982. *Publications:* The Rise and Fall of the Man of Letters, 1969; James Joyce, 1971; Editor, The Oxford Book of Aphorisms, 1983. *Memberships include:* Trustee, National Portrait Gallery, 1977-84; Fellow, Queen Mary College, 1987. *Address:* 24A St Petersburgh Place, London W2, England.

GROSS Natan, b. 16 Nov 1919, Poland. Film Director; Poet; Translator; Journalist. m. Shulamit Lifszyc, 1 son, 1 daughter. *Education:* Dip. Film Directing, Polish Film Institute, 1946. *Publications include:* Selection of new Hebrew Poetry, 1947; Song of Israel, 1948; What is left of it all.., 1971; Holocaust in Hebrew Poetry, (anthology), 1974; Songs of Holocaust and Rebellion, 1975; Crumbs of Youth, 1976; Children in the Ghetto, (with Sarah Nishmith), 1978; This was the Hebrews School in Krakow, (editor), Who Are You Mr Grymek?, 1989; History of Jewish Film in Poland, 1989; History of Hebrew Film, (with Jacob Gross), 1991. *Contributions to:* Arts Lexicon; Polish Jews Art and Culture, Photo Album; and many other professional journals and magazines. *Honours:* Ben-Dor Prize, Davar Newspaper, 1960; Jugenspreis, Film Fesitval Berlin, 1964; Israeli and International Film Fesitval Awards; Leon Lustig Prize, 1986; IUPA Award, 1988; Israel, Film Academy Award, 1991. *Memberships include:* Israeli Film Union, Secretary 1951-71; Film Critics Sec.; Film and TV Directors Guild of Israel; Israel Journalists Association; Israel Federation of Writers Union. *Address:* 14 Herzog Street, Givatayim 53586, Israel.

GROVE Fred(erick Herridge), b. 1913, USA. Author; Former Journalist. *Appointments:* Reporter, Sports Editor, Daily Citizen, Cushing, Oklahoma, 1937-40; Reporter, Morning News, Shawnee, Oklahoma, 1940-42; Sports Editor, Star, Harlingen, Texas, 1942; Reporter, 1943-44, Managing Editor, 1944-45 Morning News and Star, Shawnee; On copy desk, Times and Daily Oklahoma, Oklahoma City, 1946-47; Senior Assistant, University of Oklahoma Public Relations Officer, 1947-53; Part-time Instructor of Journalism, University of Oklahoma, 1964-68; Director of Public Information, Oklahoma Educational Television Authority, Norman, 1969-74. *Publications:* Flame of the Osage, 1958; Sun Dance, 1958; No Bugles, No Glory, 1959; Comanche Captives, 1961; The Land Seekers, 1963; Buffalo Spring, 1967; The Buffalo Runners, 1968; War Journey, 1971; The Child Stealers, 1973; Warrior Road, 1974; Drums Without Warriors, 1976; The Great Horse Race, 1977; Bush Track, 1978; The Running Horses, 1980; Phantom Warrior, 1981; Match Race, 1982; A Far Trumpet, 1985; Search for the Breed, 1986; Deception Trail, 1988; Bitter Trumpet, 1989; Trail of Roguues, 1993. *Address:* PO Box 1248, Silver City, NM 88062, USA.

GRUENWALD George Henry, b. 23 Apr 1922, Chicago, Illinois, USA. Writer; Management Consultant. m. Corrine Rae Linn, 16 Aug 1947, 1 son, 1 daughter. *Education:* Evanston Academy of Fine Arts, 1937-38; Chicago Academy of Fine Arts, 1938-39; Grinnell College, 1940-41; Medill School of Journalism, Northwestern University, 1941-43, 1945-47, Bachelor of Science. *Literary Appointments:* Public Relations Writer, Mediterranean Allied Tactical Air Force. 1943-44; Feature Writer. Mediterranean Allied Air Force, 1943-44; Editor, 12th Air Force daily Morning Mission and Sunday Weekly Mission newspapers, 1944-45; Contributor, The Stars and Stripes newspaper, 1944; Night Editor, The Daily Northwestern newspaper, 1946; Editor-in-Chief, The Purple Parrot Magazine, 1946-47; Editor-in-Chief, The UARCO Barker Magazine, 1947-49; Editor-in-Chief, The Willys-Overland Motors (now Chrysler) Salesbuilder Magazine, 1949-51; Editor-in-Chief, Hudson Family Magazine, 1955-56; Editor-in-Chief, Oldsmobile Rocket Circle (General Motors) Magazine, 1956-65; Expert columnist, Marketing News, publication of American Marketing Association, 1988-. *Publications include:* New Product Development - What Really Works, 1985; New Product Development, 1986, 1988, 1991; New Products - Seven Steps to Success, video, 1988; New Product Development, video, 1989; New Product Checklists - System Workbook, 1991; New Product Development, Responding to Market Demmand, 1992. *Contributions to:* Contributing feature writer: Advertising Age, 1972, 1981, 1984; New Product Development newsletter, 1984, 1986, 1987; Feature writer, Intrapreneurial Excellence, American Management Association publication, 1986. Other writings: Training films for the automobile industry, 1949-51; television commercials, 1951-84; Corporate communications, 1953-84. *Honours include:* Hermes Award, 1963, Educational Television Awards 1969, 1971, 1986; Journalism Feature award, Society of Professional Journalists, San Diego chapter, 1990. *Memberships include:* President, Northwestern University chapter, National Society of Professional Journalists, 1946-47; Director, Executive Committee, Public Broadcasting Service, 1978-86, Director 1988-; Trustee, Chicago Public Television, 1969-78; Chairman, President, Chief Executive, Twin Cities Public Television, 1972-84; Vice-Chairman, Minnesota Public Radio, 1974-75; Board Member, San Diego Public TV/ Radio; Trustee, The Linus Pauling Institute of Science and Medicine, 1984-92; Director, The American Institute of Wine and Food, 1985-91; Management Committee, American Association of Advertising Agencies 1976-84; Society of Professional Journalists, 1989-. *Address:* P O Box 1696, 5012 El Acebo del Norte, Rancho Santa Fe, CA 92067, USA.

GRUFFYDD Peter, b. 12 Apr 1935. Writer; Poet. m. Susan Soar, 28 Dec 1974, 3 sons, 1 daughter (1 son 1 daughter by previous marriage). *Education:* BA, Honours, University of Wales, Bangor. *Publications:* Triad, 1963; The Shivering Seed, 1972; Anthologies: Anglo Welsh Poetry, 1984; Glas-Nos, 1987; On Censorship, 1985; Welsh Voices, 1967; The Lilting House, 1970; Poems, 1969; Poems, 1972; etc. *Contributions to:* Sunday Observer; Western Mail; Critical Quarterly; Poetry Wales; Transatlantic Review; Anglo-Welsh Review; Planet; The Golden Blade; The London Welshman; Decal; Mabon; Bread Loaf Quarterly; etc. *Honours include:* Eric Gregory Trust, 1963; 2nd, Young Poets Competition, Welsh Arts Council, 1969; Welsh Arts Council, 1969, 1970; The Arts Council of Great Britain, 1972. *Memberships:* Yr Academi Gymraeg; Welsh Union of Writers. *Address:* 21 Beech Road, Norton, Stourbridge West Midlands, DY8 2AS, England.

GRUFFYDD Robert Geraint, b. 9 June 1928. Director, University of Wales for Advanced Welsh and Celtic Studies. m. Eluned Roberts, 1 Oct 1953, 2 sons, 1 daughter. *Education:* BA, UCNW, Bangor, Wales; DPhil, Jesus College, Oxford. *Appointments:* Assistant Editor, University of Wales Dictionary of the Welsh Language, 1953-55; Lecturer on Welsh UCNW, 1955-70; Professor of Welsh, UCW, Aberystwyth, 1970-80; Librarian, National Library of Wales, Abeerystwyth, 1980-85. *Publications:* Editor: Cerddi '73, 1973, Meistri'r Ianrifoedd, 1973, Bardos, 1982, Cerddi Saunders Lewis, 1986; Gair ar Waith, 1988. *Honours:* FBA, 1991. *Memberships:* Chairman, Welsh Books Council, 1980-85; Chairman, Welsh Language Section, Welsh Academy, 1986-90; President, Cambrian Archaeological Association, 1991-92; Honorable Society of Cymmrodorion (Co-Editor of Transactions, 1989-). *Address:* Eirianfa, Caradog Road, Aberystwyth, Dyfed SY23 2JY, Wales.

GRUMBACH Doris, b. 1918, USA. Writer; Former Professor of English; Radio Critic; Bookstore owner. *Appointments:* Title-Writer, MGM, 1940; Associate Editor, Architectural Forum, 1941; Professor of English, College of St Rose, Albany, New York, 1952-70; Literary Editor, New Republic, 1973-75; Columnist, Saturday Review, 1975-76; Professor of English, American University, Washington, District of Columbia, 1976-85; Columnist, New York Times Book Review, 1977-80. *Publications:* The Spoil of the Flowers, 1962; The Short Throat, the Tender Mouth, 1964; The Company She Kept, biography of Mary McCarthy, 1967; Chamber Music, 1979; The Missing Person, 1981; The Ladies, 1984; The Magician's Girl, 1987; Coming Into the End of the Zone, 1992; Extra Innings, 1993. *Address:* Sargentville, Maime o4673, USA.

GRUMLEY Michael, b. 1941, USA. Author. *Publications:* Atlantis: The Auto-biography of a Search (with R Ferro), 1970; There Are Giants in the Earth, 1974; Hard Corps, 1977; After Midnight, 1978; Life Drawing, novel, 1988.

GRUNFELD Frederic V, b. 1929, USA. Writer; Magazine Editor. *Appointments:* Radio Commentator, WQXR, New York City, 1950-55; Cultural Correspondent, Reporter Magazine, 1958-67; Consulting Editor, 1964- 70, Editor, 1970, Queen Magazine; Roving Editor, Horizon Magazine, 1967-77; Connoisseur magazine, 1982. *Publications:* Music and Recordings, 1955; The Art and Times of the Guitar, 1970; The Hitler File, 1974; Music, 1974; Berlin (The Great Cities), 1976; Prophets Without Honour, 1970; Vienna, 1981; Wayfarers of the Thai Forest: The Akha, 1982; The Kings of France, The Princes of Germany, The Spanish Kings, 3 vols, 1983-84. *Address:* Son Rullan, Deya, Mallorca, Spain.

GRUNBAUM Adolf, b. 15 May 1923, Cologne, Germany. Educator. m. Thelma Braverman, 26 June 1943, 1 daughter. *Education:* BA, Wesleyan University, 1943; MS, 1948, PhD, 1951, Yale University. *Publications:* Philosophical Problems of Space and Time, 1963, Russian translation, 1969, 2nd enlarged edition, 1973; Modern Science and Zeno's Paradoxes, 1967, British Edition, 1968; Geometry and Chonometry in Philosophical Perspective, 1968; The Foundations of a Psychoanalysis: A Philosophical Critique, 1984. *Contributions to:* British Journal for the Philosophy of Science; Erkenntis; Journal of Philosophy; American Philosophical Quarterly; Psychoanalysis and Contemporary Thought; Free Inquiry, among others. *Honours:* President, American Philosophical Association, Eastern Division, 1982-83; Gifford Lectures, University of St Andrews, Scotland, 1985; Werner Heisenberg Lecturer, Bavarian Academy of Science, Munich, 1965; Senior US Scientist Award, Alexander von Humboldt Foundation, Germany, 1985. *Memberships:* Fellow, American Academy for the Advancement of Science; American Academy of Arts and Sciences; Laureate Academy of Humanism. *Address:* 2510 Cathedral of Learning, University of Pittsburgh, PA 15260, USA.

GUARE John, b. 1938, USA. Dramatist. *Publications:* The Loveliest Afternoon of the Year, and Something I'll Tell You Tuesday, 1968; Muzeeka, and Other Plays, 1969; Kissing Sweet, and A Day for Surprises, 1970; Taking Off (with Milos Forman), screenplay, 1970; Two Gentlemen of Verona, (with Mel Shapiro), adaptation, 1973; Marco Polo Sings and Solo, 1977; The Landscape of the Body, 1978; The House of Blue Leaves, 1979; Bosoms and Neglect, 1980; Three Exposures, 1982; Lydie Breeze, 1982; Gardenia, 1982. *Literary Agent:* Dramatists Play Service, USA. *Address:* c/o Dramatists Play Service, 440 Park Avenue S, New York, NY 10016, USA.

GUEST Henry Bayly (Harry), b. 6 Oct 1932, Penarth, Glamorgan, Wales, Schoolmaster. m. Lynn Doremus Dunbar, 28 Dec 1963, 1 son, 1 daughter. *Education:* BA, Trinity Hall, Cambridge, 1951-54; DES, Sorbonne, 1954- 55. *Publications:* Arrangements, 1968; The Cutting-Room, 1970; A House Against the Night, 1976; Days, 1978; The Distance, The Shadows, 1981; Lost and Found, 1983; Post-War Japanese Poetry, editor and translator, 1972; The Emperor of Outer Space, radio play, broadcast 1976, published 1983. *Contributions to:* Agenda; Ambit; Atlantic Review; Outposts; Pacific Quarterly; Poetry Australia; Poetry Review; Times Educational Supplement. *Memberships:* General Council, Poetry Society, 1972-75. *Address:* 1 Alexandra Terrace, Exeter, Devon EX4 6SY, England.

GUEST Lynn Doremus, b. 6 Oct 1939, Missouri, USA. Writer. m. Harry Guest, 28 Dec 1963, 1 son, 1 daughter. *Education:* BA, Sarah Lawrence College, Edinburgh University. *Publications:* Post-War Japanese Poetry, 1972; (novels): Children of Hachiman, 1980; Yedo, 1985. *Honour:* Georgette Heyer Historical Novel Prize for Children of Hachiman, 1980. *Address:* 1 Alexandra Terrace, Exeter, Devon EX4 6SY, England.

GUGLIELMO Dolores, b. 29 Aug 1928, Corona, Long Island, New York, United States of America; Writer (Poetry). *Education:* BA English, St John's University, Jamaica, New York, 1983; currently working on Master's Degree in English. *Publications:* Premier Poets: Down By the Beach, 1985-86; Christ Was a Hod Carrier, 1987-88; Poet International: Autumn 1986; Sea Shells, 1987; Woman at Window, 1987; Jazz Man, 1987; A Prayer for Tolerance, 1988; Love's Prayer, 1988; Wild Horses, 1989; The Tolling, 1989; The Sitters, 1989; Alma Mater, 1989; Conversations, 1989; Tree By Side of Road, 1989; Old Dog, 1990; Brownstone Window Box, 1990; Hi-Rise Spring Song, 1992; Daylight Savings Time, 1992; City Street, 1991; The Station Master, 1992; Forthcoming Poet International: Dead of Night, 1992; Beginnings, 1993. *Contributions to:* World Poetry, Wroxton Abbey 1993, (Poetic Symphony 1987 (Summer Nights); A Galaxy of Verse; Midwest Poetry Review; Soundings East; Poems of The Century; Reflections; Images; American Poetry Anthology; River Run; Drum Magazine; Ripples. *Honours:* Winner, International Poetry Contest, Seven Magazine, 1967; Poetry Recital on David Frost Show, 1970; The Writers Club Award Excellence in Poetry, 1992; Queen's College, English Honours Award. *Memberships:* World Poetry Society; Fine Arts Society, Mishawaka, Indianna; The Writers Club. *Address:* 43-44 Kissena Boulevard, Flushing, NY 11355, USA.

GUILES Fred Lawrence, b. 1922, USA. Author. *Publications:* Norma Jean: The Life of Marilyn Monroe, 1969; Marion Davies, 1973; Hanging on in Paradise, 1975; Tyrone Power: The Last Idol, 1979; Stan: The Life of Stand Laurel, 1981; Jane Fonda: The Actress in Her Time, 1982; Legend: The Life and Death of Marilyn Monroe, 1984; Loner At The Ball, 1989.

GUILLERMIN Maureen Therese, (Maureen Connell), b. 3 Aug 1931, Nairobi, Kenya. Writer. m. John Guillermin, 20 July 1956, 1 daughter. *Education:* Loreto Convent, Kenya. *Publication:* Mary Lacey. *Contributions to:* The New Yorker; Book Reviewer for Los Angeles Herald; Angeles Times. *Honours:* Macdowell Fellowship; Honors, The London Academy of Music & Dramatic Art. *Memberships:* PEN West; Authors Guild. *Literary Agent:* Georges Borchardt Inc, New York. *Address:* 29805 Cuthbert Road, Malibu, CA 90265, USA.

GUNN James Edwin, b. 12 July 1923, Kansas City, USA. Professor; Writer. m. Jane Frances Anderson, 6 Feb 1947, 2 sons. *Education:* BS, Journalism, 1947, MA, English, 1951, University of Kansas, USA. *Appointments:* Assistant instructor, 1950-51, 1955, Instructor, English, 1958-70, Lecturer, English, 1970-74, Professor, 1974-, University of Kansas. *Publications:* Star Bridge, (Co-author Jack Williamson), 1955; The Joy Makers, 1961; The Immortals, 1962; The Listeners, 1972; Kampus, 1977; The Dreamers, 1981; Alternate Worlds: The Illustrated History of Science Fiction, 1975; Isaac Asimov: The Foundations of Science Fiction, 1982; The Road to Science Fiction, (Editor), Numbers 1-4 1977, 1979, 1979, 1982; Crisis!, 1986; (Ed) The New Encyclopedia of Science Fiction, 1988; The Best of Astounding: Classic Short Novels fro the Golden Age of Science Fiction, 1992; Forthcoming: The Road to Science Fiction Number 5: The British Way. *Contributions to:* Over 80 science fiction stories and over 100 articles in magazines and journals, many reprinted in Australia, England, France, Germany, Greece, Hungary, Italy, Japan, the Netherlands, Poland, Romania, Scandinavia, South America, Spain, Russia, Ukraine and Yugoslavia. *Honours:* Byron Caldwell Smith Prize, 1971; SFRA Pilgrim Award, 1976; Hugo Awards,

1976, 1983; President, Science Fiction Writers of America, 1971-72; President, Science Fiction Research Association, 1980-82; Edward Grier Award, 1989; Eaton Award, for Lifetime Achievement, 1992. *Memberships:* Science Fiction Research Association, President, 1980-82; Science Fiction Writers of America, President, 1971-72; Authors Guild. *Literary Agent:* Dorris Halsey; Maggie Noach. *Address:* 2215 Orchard Lane, Lawrence, KS 66049, USA.

GUNN Steven John, 1 daughter. *Appointments:* Fellow, Tutor, Modern History, Merton College, Oxford, 1989-. *Publications:* Charles Brandon Duke of Suffolk; Cardinal Wolsey: Church, State and Art. *Membership:* Royal Historical Society. *Address:* Merton College, Oxford OX1 4JD, England.

GUNN Thom(son William), b. 29 Aug 1929, Gravesend, England. Poet. *Education:* Trinity College, Cambridge. *Appointments:* Taught English, 1958-66, Lecturer, English, 1977-, Senior Lecturer, 1988-, University of California, Berkeley, USA. *Publications:* Fighting Terms, 1954; The Sense of Movement, 1957; My Sad Captains, 1961; Positives (with Ander Gunn), 1966; Touch, 1967; Moly, 1971; Jack Straw's Castle, 1976; Selected Poems, 1979; The Passages of Joy, 1982; The Occasions of Poetry (prose), 1982 (expanded edition 1985); The Man with Night Sweats, Faber, 1992; Collected Poems, 1993 Shelf Life (prose), 1993. *Honours:* Levinson Prize, 1955; Somerset Maugham Prize, 1959; Grants, National Institute of Arts and Letters, 1964; Rockefeller Foundation, 1966, Guggenheim Foundation, 1972; Lila Wallace/Reader's Digest Fund Award, 1991; Forward Poetry Prize, 1992. *Address:* 1216 Cole Street, San Francisco, CA 94117, USA.

GUNSTON Bill. *See:* **GUNSTON William Tudor.**

GUNSTON William Tudor (Bill Gunston), b. 1 Mar 1927, London, England. Author. m. Margaret Anne, 10 Oct 1964, 2 daughters. *Education:* Pinner County School 1938-45; University College, Durham, 1945-46; RAF pilot 1946-48; City University, London 1948-51. *Literary Appointments:* Editorial staff, Flight, 1951-55; Technical Editor, Flight, 1955-64; Technology Editor, Science Journal, 1964-70; Freelance author 1970-; Director, So Few Ltd. *Publications:* Total of 311 hardback titles including: Aircraft of the Soviet Union, 1983; Jane's Aerospace Dictionary, 1980, 1986, 1988; Encyclopaedia of World Aero Engines, 1986, 1989; Avionics, 1990; Airbus, 1988; Encyclopaedia of Aircraft Armament, 1987; Giants of the Sky, 1991; Faster Than Sound, 1992; World Encyclopedia of Aircraft Manufacturers, 1993. *Contributions to:* 188 periodicals, 18 partworks and 75 video scripts. *Honours:* FRAeS. *Address:* High Beech, Kingsley Green, Haslemere, Surrey GU27 3LL, England.

GUNTRUM Suzanne Simmons, (Suzanne Simms), b. 29 Aug 1946, Storm Lake, Iowa, USA. Writer. m. Robert Ray Guntrum, 9 Sept 1967, 1 son. *Education:* BA, English Literature, 1967, Pennsylvania State University. *Publications:* Made in Heaven, 1988; The Genuine Article, 1987; Christmas in April, 1986; (As Suzanne Simms): Moment of Truth, 1986; Nothing Ventured, 1986; Dream within a Dream, 1984; Only This Night, 1984; So Sweet a Madness, 1983; All the Night Long, 1983; A Wild Sweet Magic, 1983; Of Passion Born, 1982; Moment in Time, 1982; 8 other books. *Contributions to:* Numerous Regional magazines. *Honour:* Silhouette Desire of the Year, 1982-83. *Memberships:* Romance Writers of America; Authors Guild; Mensa. *Agent:* Curtis Brown Ltd, New York, USA. *Address:* 5245 Willowview Road, Racine, WI 53402, USA.

GURNEY A(lbert) R(amsdell) Jr, b. 1 Nov 1930, Buffalo, New York, USA. Professor of Literature; Writer. m. Mary Goodyear, 1957, 2 sons, 2 daughters. *Education:* St Paul's School, New Hampshire, 1944-48;

BA, Williams College, Williamstown, Massachusetts, 1952; MFA, Yale University School of Drama, 1958. Served in US Naval Reserve 1952-55. *Career:* Member of Faculty 1960-, Professor of Literature 1970-, Massachusetts Institute of Technology, Cambridge. *Publications:* Plays include: The Dining Room (produced New York, 1982; London 1983); London, French 1982; included in Four Plays 1985; Four Plays, New York, Avon, 1985; The Perfect Party (produced New York 1986; London 1987) New York, Dramatists Play Service, 1986; Another Antigone (produced San Diego, 1986; New York, 1987); Sweet Sue (produced Williamstown, Massachusetts, 1986; New York 1987). Screenplay: The House of Mirth, 1972; Television Play: O Youth and Beauty, from a story by John Cheever, 1979. Novels: The Gospel According to Joe, 1974; Entertaining Strangers, New York 1977, London 1979; The Snow Ball, 1985. *Honours:* Drama Desk Award, 1971; Rockerfeller grant, 1977; National Endowment for the Arts award, 1982; DDL, Williams College, 1984. *Literary Agent:* Gilbert Parker, William Morris Agency, New York. *Address:* 74 Wellers Bridge Road, Roxbury, CT 06783, USA.

GURR Andrew, b. 23 Dec 1936, Leicester, England. University Teacher. m. Elizabeth Gordon, 1 July 1961, 3 sons. *Education:* BA 1957, MA 1958, University of Auckland, New Zealand; PhD, University of Cambridge, 1963. *Appointments:* Lecturer, Leeds University, 1962; Professor of University of Nairobi, 1969; Professor, University of Reading, 1976-. *Publications:* The Shakespeare Stage 1574-1642, 1970, 1980, 1992; Writers in Exile, 1982; Katherine Mansfield, 1982; Playgoing in Shakespeare's London, 1987; Studying Shakespeare, 1988; Rebuilding Shakespeare's Globe, 1989; ed: Shakespeare, Richard II, Henry V,; ed: Beaumont and Fletcher, Philaster, The Maid's Tragedy, Knight of the Burning Pestle. *Contributions to:* Articles in magazines and journals on Shakespeare and Elizabethan Drama and on Commonwealth Literature. *Memberships:* International Shakespeare Association; Association of Commonwealth Literature and Language Studies; Society for Theatre Research; Malone Society. *Address:* English Department, University of Reading, P O Box 218, Reading, Berks. RG6 2AA, England.

GURT Elisabeth, b. 18 May 1917, Vienna, Austria. Freelance Writer. *Education:* Examination as School Teacher; Studies of languages. *Publications:* Author of over 40 novels, childrens books & short stories including: Eine Frau fur drei Tage, 1942; Es gehort dir nichts, 1947; Bis dass der Tod euch scheidet, 1953, 1979; Ein Stern namens Julia, 1955; Kein Mann fur alle Tage, 1961, 1975; Verzaubert von Tuju, 1980; Vierzig Jahre und ein Sommer, 1981; Denkst du noch an Korfu?, 1982; Hinter Weissen Turen, 1984; Manchmaltraumich von Venedig, 1986; Komm Doch Mitnach ischia, 1987; Young Peoples Novels: Vor uns das Leben; Wolken im Sommer; Du bist kein Kind mehr, Gundula, 1982; Erwachsen wirst du ober Nacht, 1984; Short Stories; Wunsche sind Wie Sommerwolken; Flammen im Schnee; Die Stunde zwischen act und neun; Immer werde ich dich lieben. *Contributions to:* various journals and magazines. *Honour:* Silver Honorary Award of Merit, Republic of Austria, 1981. *Memberships:* Austrian Writers Association; Der Ereis; Austrian Womens Club; Association of Female Writers & Artists; Landtmannkreis. *Address:* Schaumburger Gasse 16, A-1040 Vienna, Austria.

GUTHRIE Alan. *See:* **TUBB E C.**

GUTMAN Roy W, b. 5 Mar 1944, New York, USA. Reporter. m. ELizabeth Dribben, 1 daughter. *Education:* BA Haverford College, 1966; MSc, London School of Economics, 1968. *Appointments:* Belgrade Bureau Chief, Reuters, 1973-75; State Department, Reuters, 1976-80; National Security Reporter, Newsday, 1981-89; European Bureau Chief Newsday, 1990-. *Publications:* Banana Diplomacy, 1987, 1988. *Contributions to:* Foreign Policy; Foreign Service Journal. *Honours:* Pulitzer Prize for International Reporting, 1993; Polk Prize for International Reporting,

1993; Selden Ring Prize for Investigative Reporting, 1993; Heywood Brown Prize, 1993; Special Human Rights in Media Award, International League for Human Rights, (USA), 1992. *Memberships:* Overseas Writers Club, Washington DC, Past President. *Address:* c/o Newsday Foreign Desk, Pinelawn Drive, Melville, NY 11747, USA.

GUTTMANN Allen, b. 1932, USA. Professor of English and American Studies. *Appointments:* Professor of English and American Studies, Amherst College, Amherst, Massachusetts, 1959-. *Publications:* The Wound in the Heart: America and the Spanish Civil War, 1962; The Conservative Tradition in America, 1967; The Jewish Writer in America, 1971; From Ritual to Record: The Nature of Modern Sports, 1978; Life of George Washington, by Washington Irving (co-editor), 5 vols, 1981; The Games Must Go On: Avery Brundage and the Olympic Movement, 1984; Sports Spectators, 1986.

GUY Rosa, b. 9 Jan 1928, Trinidad, West Indies. Professor; Writer-in-Residence. *Appointment:* Writer-in-Residence, Michigan Technical University. *Publications:* The Friends, 1973; Edith Jackson, 1978; Ruby, 1976; The Disappearance, 1979; A Measure of Time, 1983; New Guys Around the Block, 1983; My Love, My Love; The Ups and Downs of Carl Davis III; Bird At My Window, 1966, 1989; Pee Wee and Big Dog, 1984; I Heard a Bird Sing, 1986. *Contributions to:* New York Times Sunday Magazine; Red Book; Cosmopolitan. *Honours:* The Other Award, England; Best of the Best, New York Times. *Memberships:* Harlem Writers Guild, President; PEN. *Literary Agent:* Ellen Levine. *Address:* 20 West 72nd Street, New York, NY 10023, USA.

GÝARFÁS Endre, b. 6 May 1936, Szeged, Hungary. Poet; Novelist; Playwright. m. Edit Kincses, 7 Dec 1963, 1 son. *Education:* Hungarian- English Literature, Elte University of Budapest, 1961. *Appointments:* Editor, Publisher Europa, 1960-63; Editor, Hung Television, 1964-66. *Publications:* Partkozelben, poems, 1964; Pazarlo Skotok, travel book, 1970; Apaczai, novel, 1978; Varazslasok, poems, 1984; Hosszu Utnak Pora, novel, 1988; Zsuzsanna Kertje, novel, 1989; Zoldag-Parittya, poems, 1990; Cowboyok, Aranyasok, Csavargok, Folk Poetry of North America, 1992. *Honours:* Gold Medal for Children's Literature, 1976. *Memberships:* PEN Club of Hungary; Union of Hungarian Writers. *Literary Agent:* Artisjus, Budapest. *Address:* I Attila ut 133, Budapest 1012, Hungary.

GYLLENSTEN Lars Johan Wictor, b. 12 Nov 1921, Stockholm, Sweden. Former Professor of Histology; Author. *Education:* MD. *Publications include:* Camera obscura (poetry with T Greitz), 1946; Moderna myter (miscellany), 1949; Barnabok (novel), 1952; Senilia (novel), 1956; Sokratsdod (novel), 1960; Desperados (short stories), 1962; Juvenilia (novel), 1965; Palatseti parken (novel), 1970; Ur min offentliga sektor (essays), 1971; Grottan i oknen (novel), 1973; I skuggan av Don Juan (novel), 1975; Baklangesminnen (novel), 1978; Skuggans aterkomst (novel), 1985; Sju vise mastare om karlek (short stories), 1986; Just sa ellen kareske det (short stories), 1989. *Honours include:* Lilla Nobelpriset, 1972; Pilot Prize, 1986. *Memberships:* Swedish Academy; Royal Swedish Academy of Sciences. *Address:* Karlavagen 121, 115 26 Stockholm, Sweden.

GYORE Balazs, b. 8 May 1951, Hungary. Writer. m. Adrienn Scheer, 25 Sept 1980, 1 daughter. *Education:* Eotvos Lorand University in Budapest, 1971-76; Studies Hungarian and Russian. *Publications:* The Hand of Humble Abbot Paphnutius, 1982 (poems); I Can Safely Asleep on the 91 Bus, 1989, (novel). *Contributions to:* Ujhold; Liget; Elet es Irodalom. *Memberships:* Association of Hungarian Writers; Hungarian Pen Club. *Address:* Bartok B 52, 1111 Budapest, Hungary.

H

HAAKANA Anna-Liisa, b. 30 Jan 1937, Rovaniemi, Finland. Author. m. Veikko Olavi Haakana, 24 Feb 1963. 1 son, 1 daughter. *Education:* Literature studies, University of Tampere. *Publications include:* 3 children's books, 1978-84; 4 books for young people, Ykä All Alone, 1980; Top Girl, 1981; A Flower, Nevertheless, 1983; The Black Sheep of the Family, 1986; The Love of an Ugly Girl, 1989. *Honours:* National Award for Literature, 1981; Anni Swan Medal, 1982; H C Andersen's Certificate of Honour, 1982; Church's Award for Literature, 1982; Arvid Lydecken Award, 1984. *Memberships:* Association of Finnish Writers for Children & Youth; Finnish Society of Authors. *Literary Agent:* Werner Söderström Oy/Gummerus Oy. *Address:* 99600 Sodankylä, Finland.

HAAS Carolyn Buhai, b. 1 Jan 1926, Chicago, USA. Author; Publisher; Consultant. m. Robert Green Haas, 29 June 1947, 2 sons, 3 daughters. *Education:* BEd., Smith College, 1947. *Appointments:* Co-Founder, Parents As Resource, 1968-81; President, CBH Publishing Inc., 1979-. *Publications:* Co-Author: I Saw a Purple Cow, 1972; A Pumpkin in a Pear Tree, 1976; Children are Children, 1978; Bakyard Vacation, 1980; Purple Cow to the Rescue, 1982; Fun and Learning, 1982; Recipes for Fun Series, 1979-85; Author: The Big Fun Book, 1980; Look at Me, Activities for Babies and Toddlers, 1985. *Contributions include:* Parents' Magazine; McCalls; Day Care & Early Education; My Own Magazine; CRRT Newsletter; Family Lesiure. *Memberships include:* Childrens Reading Roundtable; The Writer; Society of Childrens Book Writers; International Reading Association; Phi Delta Kappa; President, Friends of the Glencoe Public Library; American Library Association. *Literary Agent:* Curtis Brown Ltd., New York City. *Address:* 400 E. Ohio Street No 2302, Chicago, IL 60611, USA.

HABECK Fritz, b. 8 Sept 1916, Neulengbach. Writer. m. Gerda Vilsmeier, 1951, 2 sons, 2 daughter. *Education:* Univeristy of Vienna. *Publications:* Novels: Der Scholar vom linken Gaigen, 1941; Der Tanz der sieben Teufel, 1950; Das Boot kommt nach Mitternacht, 1951; Das zerbrochene Dreieck, 1953; Ronan Gobain, 1956; Der Ritt auf dem Tiger, 1958; Der Kampf um die Barbacane, 1960; Die Stadt der grauen Gesichter, 1961; Der verliebt Oesterreicher, 1961; Der einaugige Reiter, 1963; In eigenem Auftrag (Selections), 1963; Der Piber 1965; Die Insel Oer den Wolken, 1965; Konig Artus, 1965; Aufstand der Salzknechte, 1967; Salzburg-Spiegel, 1967; Marianne und der wilde Mann, 1968; Francois Villon, 1969; Doktor Faustus, 1970; Johannes Gutenberg, 1971; Schwarzer Hund im goldenen Feld, 1973; Der schwarze Mantel meines Vaters, 1976; Wind von Sudost, 1979; Der Gobelin, 1982; Der General und die Distel, 1985; Plays: Swei und zwei ist vier, 1948; Baiser mit Schlag, 1950; Marschall Ney, 1954. *Honours:* Goehe Award City of Vienna; Ciety Prize of Vienna; Austrian State Prize; Handel-Mazzetti Prize; Vienna Children's Book Prize, 1960, 1961, 1963, 1967, 1970, 1973; State Children's Book Prize, 1963, 1967; Wildgans Prize of Austrian Industry, 1964; Stifter prize, 1973; Prize City of Vienna. *Memberships:* PEN, President, Austrian Centre, 1978. *Address:* Grillparzerstrasse 6, A- 2500 Baden, Austria.

HABGOOD John Stapylton (Archbishop of York), b. 23 June 1927, England. m. Rosalie Mary Ann Boston, 7 June 1961, 2 sons, 2 daughters. *Education:* MA, PhD, King's College, Cambridge; Cuddesdon College, Oxford. *Publications:* Religion and Science, 1964; A Working Faith: Essays and Addresses on Science, Medicine and Ethics, 1980; Church and Nation in a Secular Age, 1983; Confessions of a Conservative Liberal, 1988. *Contributions include:* many symposia including Soundings, 1962; numerous essays and reviews in: Journal of Physiology; Nature; New Scientist; Theology; Expository Times; Frontier; Journal of Theological Studies; Crucible; Times Supplements. *Honours:* Hon.DD, Durham, 1975, Cambridge, 1984; Hon.DD, Aberdeen, 1988, Huron 1990; Hull 1991; Hon. Fellow, King's College, Cambridge, 1985. *Address:* Bishopthorpe, York YO2 1QE, England.

HACKER Marilyn, b. 27 Nov 1942, New York, USA. Writer; Editor; Critic; Teacher. 1 daughter. *Education:* BA, Washington Square College, New York University, 1963. *Appointments:* Jenny McKean Moore Fellow in Writing, George Washington University, 1976-77; Writer-in-Residence, American Studies Institute, Columbia University, 1988; George Elliston Poet-in-Residence, University of Cincinnati, 1988; Distinguished Writer in Residence, The American University, 1989. *Publications:* Presentation Piece, 1974; Separations, 1976; Taking Notice, 1980; Assumptions, 1985; Love, Death and the Changing of the Seasons, 1986, 1987; Going Back to the River, 1990; The Hang-Glider's Daughter, 1990; Forthcoming: New and Selected Poems; Editor, The Kenyon Review;. *Contributions to:* The Nation; Grand Street; The Paris Review; Boulevard; The Women's Review of Books; Ambit. *Honours:* Lamont Poetry Selection, Academy of American Poets, 1973; National Book Award, 1975; Guggenheim Fellowship, 1980; Lambda Literary Award, 1991. *Memberships:* PEN; The Authors' Guild; Poetry Society of America. *Literary Agent:* Frances Collin. *Address:* The Kenyon Review, Kenyon College, Gambier, OH 43022, USA.

HACKETT Dennis William, Journalist; Publishing & Communications Consultant; Executive Editor; TV Critic. m. (1) Agnes Mary Collins, 1953, 2 sons, 1 daughter, (2) Jacqueline Margaret Totterdell, 1974, 1 daughter. *Appointments:* Sheffield Telegraph, 1945-47, 1949-54; Daily Herald, 1954; Odhams Press, 1954; Deputy Editor, Illustrated, 1955-58; Daily Express, 1958-60; Daily Mail, 1960; Art Editor, Observer, 1961-62; Deputy Editor, 1962, Editor 1964-65, Queen; Editor, Nova, 1965-60; Publisher, Twentieth Century Magazine, 1965-72; Editorial Director, George Newnes Ltd., 1966-60; Director, IPC newspapers, 1969-71; Associate Editor, Daily Express, 1973-74; TV Critic, The Times, 1981-85; Editorial Consultant, You, The Mail on Sunday Magazine, 1982-86; TV Critic, New Scientist, 1983-, The Tablet, 1984-; Executive Editor, Today, 1986, Editor-in-Chief, Today, 1987; Editor-in-Chief, The Observer Magazine, 1987-88. *Publications:* The History of the Future : Bemrose Corporation, 1826-1976, 1976; The Big Idea : the Story of Ford in Europe, 1978. *Memberships:* Chairman, Design and Art Directors' Association, 1967-68. *Address:* 4 East Heath Road, London NW3 1BN, England.

HACKETT John Winthrop, General Sir, b. 5 Nov 1910, Perth, Australia. Soldier; Academic; Author. m. Margaret Frena, 21 Mar 1942, 1 daughter (dec), 2 adopted stepdaughters. *Education:* MA, B.Litt, New College, Oxford, 1929-33. *Appointments:* Commissioned 8th King's Royal Hussars, 1931; Service before, through, after World War II; Deputy Chief General Staff, Commander in Chief, British Army of the Rhine; Commander, Northern Army Group, NATO; Principal, University of London, King's College, 1968-75; President, UK English Association; President, UK Classical Association; Fellow, Royal Society of Literature; Visiting Professor, Classics, King's College London, 1977-. *Publications include:* I Was a Stranger, 1977; The Third World War (jointly), 1978; The Untold Story, 1982; The Profession of Arms, 1983; Warfare in the Ancient World (ed), 1989; Chapters and forewords in a number of books. *Contributions include:* Articles, reviews, lectures. *Honours include:* MBE, 1938; MC, 1941; DSO, 1942, Bar, 1945; CBE, 1953; CB, 1958; KCB, 1962; GCB, 1967; Honorary Degrees: LLD Queen's University, Belfast, 1967, University of Western Australia, 1963, Exeter University, 1977, Buckingham University, 1987; Honorary Fellow, St George's College, Perth, New College Oxford, 1972; Fellow, King's College, London. *Memberships:* Principal: Council of International Institute of Strategic Studies, 1968-77; Lord Chancellor's Committee on the Reform of the law of Contempt of Court, 1971-74; Disciplinary Committee, Senate of the Inns of Court and Bar, 1972-83. *Literary Agent:* David Higham Associates, London. *Address:*

Coberley Mill, Cheltenham, Gloucestershire GL53 9NH, England.

HACKNEY Rod. *See:* **HACKNEY Roderick Peter.**

HACKNEY Roderick Peter, (Rod Hackney), b. 3 Mar 1942, Liverpool, England. Architect and Developer. m. Christine Thornton, 1 son. *Education:* John Bright's Grammar School, Llandudno; BA Arch, 1967, MA 1969, PhD, 1973, Manchester University. *Appointments:* Editorial Board, UIA International Architect, 1983; Editorial Consultant, World Architecture Review, China, 1992. *Publications:* The Good, the Bad and the Ugly, 1990; Highfield Hall: A community project, 1974. *Contributions to:* Various British and international journals and newspapers. *Honours:* Hon DLitt, Keel University, 1989. *Memberships:* Royal Institute of British Architects, past President and Council Member; International Union of Architects, past President, Bureau and Council Member; Honorary Fellow, National Archt. Institutes of USA, Canada, India, Mexico and The Philippines and Hon member, Spain; National Historical Building and Crafts Institute, Member of Council; Chartered Institute of Building. *Address:* St Peter's House, Windmill Street, Macclesfield, Cheshire SK11 7HS, England.

HADLEY Leila (E B), b. 1929, USA. Writer. *Appointments:* Associate Editor, Diplomat Magazine, 1965-67; Associate Editor, Saturday Evening Post, 1967-68. *Publications:* Give Me the World, 1958; How to Travel with Children in Europe, 1964; Manners for Young People (co-author), 1964; Fielding's Guide to Traveling with Children in Europe, 1972, 2nd Edition, 1974; Traveling with Children in the USA, 1977; Tibet: 20 Years after the Chinese Takeover, 1979; Fielding's Europe with Children, 1984.

HAGAR Judith. *See:* **POLLEY Judith Anne.**

HAGER Thomas A, b. 18 Apr 1953, Portland, Oregon, USA. Writer; Editor. m. Lauren Kessler, 7 July, 1985, 2 sons. *Education:* BS Biology, 1975; MS Microbiology and Immunology, 1979; MS Journalism, 1981. *Appointments:* Correspondent, American Health Magazine, 1984-88; Editor: LC Magazine, 1983-87; Old Oregon Magazine, 1985-92; Oregon Quarterly Magazine, 1993-. *Publication:* Aging Well, 1989. *Contributions to:* American Health; Reader's Digest; Self Journal of the American Medical Association; Medical Tribune; Medical Post; Cardio. *Honours:* Council for the Advancement and Support of Education National Award for Magazine Special issue, 1988; Magazine Publishing, 1990; Magazine Feature Writing, 1993. *Literary Agent:* Nat Sobel. *Address:* 84898 S Willamette St, Eugene, OR 97405, USA.

HAGERMAN Edward Hayes, b. 18 May 1939, New Brunswick, Canada. Professor of History. *Education:* BA, University of New Brunswick, 1961; MA, 1963, PhD 1965, Duke University. *Publications:* The American Civil War and the Origins of Modern Warfare, 1988. *Honours:* Moncado Prize of the American Military Institute, 1980. *Memberships:* Fellow, Interuniversity Seminar on Armed Forces and Society. *Address:* Department of History, Atkinson College, York University, Toronto, Canada M3J 1P3.

HAGON Priscilla. *See:* **ALLAN Mabel Esther.**

HAIBLUM Isidore, b. 1935, USA. Freelance Writer; Former Interviewer, Scriptwriter and Folk-Singers' Agent. *Publications:* The Tsaddik of the Seven Wonders, 1971; The Return, 1973; Transfer to Yesterday, 1973; The Wilk Are Among Us, 1975; Interworld, 1977; Nightmare Express, 1979; Outerworld, 1979; Faster Than a Speeding Bullet: An Informal History of Radio's Golden Age, (with Stuart Silver), 1980; The Mutants Are Coming, 1984; The Identity Plunderers, 1984; The Hand of Ganz, 1985; Murder in Yiddish, 1988.

Contributions to: Book reviews. *Address:* 160 West 77th Street, New York, NY 10024, USA.

HAIGH Christopher, b. 28 Aug 1944, Birkenhead, England. Lecturer. 2 daughters. *Education:* BA, Cambridge University, 1966; PhD, Victoria University of Manchester, 1969. *Appointments:* Lecturer in history, Victoria University of Manchester, 1969-79; Lecturer in Modern History, Oxford University, Christ Church, Oxford, 1979-. *Publications:* The Last Days of the Lancashire Monasteries, 1969; Reformation and Resistance in Tudor Lancashire, 1975; The Cambridge Historical Encyclopedia of Great Britain and Ireland, 1984; The Reign of Elizabeth I, 1985; The English Reformation Revised, 1987; Elizabeth I: A Profile in Power, 1988; English Reformations: Religion, Politics and Society under the Tudors, 1993. *Membership:* Fellow, Royal Historical Society; The Church of England and Its People, 1559-1642, forthcoming. *Address:* c/o Christ Church, Oxford University, Oxford OX1 1DP, England.

HAIGH Jack, b. 21 Feb 1910, West Hartlepool, England. Journalist. m. Josephine Agnes Mary McLoughlin, 7 July 1949, London. *Appointments:* Script Writer, The Rascals, official soldiers' concert party for Palestine, 1939-41; Editor, Jerusalem Services Magazine, 1941-42; Staff, The Racing Calendar, 1956-68; Sports Sub Editor, The Daily Sketch, 1968-71; The Daily Mirror, 1971-72; The Daily Mail, 1972-84; Proprietor, Greenfriar Press. *Publications:* Theory of Genius, 1972; Constellation of Genius, 1982; Phillimore: The Postcard Art of R P Phillimore, 1985; Psychology of Genius, 1991. *Contributions to:* 30 Children's Radio plays broadcasts from Jerusalem, 1941-44; Special Feature Programme introduced by Prince Peter of Greece & Denmark, 1944; 116 Radio Programmes broadcast, Forces Broadcasting Service, 1945-47. *Memberships:* Honorary Secretary, Freelance Specialist Panel, Institute of Journalists, 1951-53, 1964-72. *Address:* 28 Manville Road, London SW17 8JN, England.

HAIGHT Mary Ellen Jordan, b. 22 Apr 1927, Los Angeles, California, USA. Writer. m. Raymond L Haight Jr, 20 Dec 1948, 4 sons. *Education:* BA, 1971; MA 1973; PhD 1976. *Publications:* Walks in Gertrude Stein's Paris, 1988; Paris Portraits: Renoir to Chanel, 1991; Walks in Picassa's Barcelona, 1992. *Address:* 2782 Bush Street, San Francisco, CA 94115, USA.

HAILEY Elizabeth Forsythe, b. 31 Aug 1938, Dallas, Texas, USA. Novelist. m. Oliver Hailey, 25 June 1960, 2 daughters. *Education:* BA, Hollins College, Virginia, 1960; Diplome d'Etudes (Mention Tres Bien), Sorbonne, Paris, France, 1959. *Publications:* Novels: A Woman of Independent Means, 1978; Life Sentences, 1982; Joanna's Husband and David's Wife, 1986; Hoem Free, 1991; Her Work (Anthology of Stories by Texas Women); New Growth (Anthology). *Literary Agent:* Molly Friedrich, The Aaron M Priest Literary Agency, New York, USA. *Address:* 11747 Canton Place, Studio City, CA 91604, USA.

HAILSHAM OF ST MARYLEBONE, Quintin McGarel (Hogg), Baron, b. 9 Oct 1907, London, England; Law; Politics. m. Mary Evelyn Martin, 18 Apr 1944, dec 1978, 2 sons, 3 daughters. *Education:* 1st Class Honour Moderatous, 1928, 1st Class Literae Humaniores, 1930, Fellow, All Souls, 1931, Oxford University; Barrister at Law, 1932; QC, 1953; Bencher, 1956, Lincoln's Inn. *Publications:* The Law of Arbitration, 1935; The Left was Never Right, 1945; The Case for Conservatism, 1947, 1959; The Devils Own Song and Other Verses, 1968; The Door Wherein I Went, 1975; The Dilemma of Democracy, 1978; A Sparrow's Flight, 1990; On The Constitution, 1992. *Contributions to:* numerous articles in journals and magazines. *Honours include:* Honorary Degrees: DCL, Oxford, 1974; LLD, Cambridge; Knight of the Garter, 1988. *Memberships:* Royal Society of Arts; Royal Institute of Arbitrators. *Literary Agent:* Curtis Brown Limited. *Address:* The

Corner House, Heath View Gardens, London SW15 3SZ, England.

HAINES John Meade, b. 29 June 1924, Norfolk, Virginia, USA, Poet; Essayist; Teacher, 1 stepson, 3 stepdaughters. *Education:* American University, 1948-49; Hans Hofmann School of Fine Art, New York City, 1950-52. *Appointments:* Writer in Residence, University of Alaska, 1972-73; Visiting Professor, University of Washington, 1974; Visiting Lecturer, University of Montana, 1974-75; Visiting Writer, Djerassi Foundation, 1984; Visiting Writer, Montalvo Centre, 1986; Visiting Lecturer, UC Santa cruz, 1986; Writer in Residence, Ucross Foundation, 1987; visiting Writer, The Loft, 1987; Visiting Professor, Ohio University, 1989-90; Visiting Writer, George Washington University, Washington DC, 1991-92. *Publications:* The Stars, The Snow, The Fire, 1989; News From the Glacier, 1982; Living Off the Country, 1981; The Stone Harp, 1971; Winter News, 1966; New Poems 1980-88, 1990' Stories We Listened To, 1986; Other Days, 1982; OPf Traps and Snares, 1983; Cicada, 1977; In A Dusty Light, 1977; Meditation On a Skull Carved in Crystal, 1989; Rain Country, 1990. *Contributions to:* Poems, critical and general essays including: Hudson Review; Ohio Review; New Virginia Review; Gettysburg Review; Northwest Review; AWP Chronicle; TriQuarterly; Graywolf Annual; New England/Breadloaf Quarterly; ZYZZYVA; Pushcart Annual. *Honours:* Guggenheim Fellowship, 1965-66, 1984-85; NEA Fellowship, 1967-68; Amy Lowell Scholarship, 1976-77; Alaska State Council on the Arts Fellowship, 1979-80; Honorary Doctor of Letters, University of Alaska, 1983; Western States Arts Federation Award, 1990; Elliston Fellow in Poetry, University of Cincinnati, 1992; Lenore Marshall, Nation Award for New poems, 1991; Winner, The Poets Prize for New Poems, 1992; Chair of Excellence in the Arts, Austin Peay State University, Clarksville, Tennessee, 1993. *Memberships:* Poetry Society of America; Academy of American Poets; PEN American Centre; Wilderness Society; Sierra Club; Alaska Conservation Society; Natural Resources Defence Council. *Address:* English Department, Ellis Hall, Ohio University, Athens, OH 45701, USA.

HAINES Joseph Thomas William, b. 29 Jan 1928, London, England. Journalist. m. 20 Aug 1955. *Appointments include:* Sub-editor, Outram Group, 1953; Parliamentary correspondent, The Bulletin, 1955; Political correspondent, ibid 1959, Scottish Daily Mail 1960, Sun 1964-68; Press Secretary to Prime Minister, 1969-70, 1974-76; Chief Leader Writer 1978, Assistant Editor 1984, Daily Mirror; Group Political Editor 1984, Director 1985-, Mirror Group Newspapers; Director, Scottish Daily Record and Sunday Mail Ltd., 1985. *Publications include:* Politics of Power, 1977; Co-author, Malice in Wonderland, 1986; Maxwell, 1988. *Address:* 1 South Frith, London Road, Southborough, Tunbridge Wells, Kent, England.

HAINES Pamela Mary, b. 4 Nov 1929, Harrogate, England, Writer. m. Anthony Haines, 24 June 1955, 2 sons, 3 daughters. *Education:* Honours degree, English Literature, Newnham College, Cambridge University, 1949-52. *Publications:* Tea at Gunters, 1974; A Kind of War, 1976; Men on White Horses, 1978; The Kissing Gate, 1981; The Diamond Waterfall, 1984; The Golden Lion, 1986; Daughter of the Northern Fields, 1987. *Honours:* Spectator New Writing Prize, 1971; Yorkshire Arts Young Writers Award, 1975. *Memberships:* Society of Authors; PEN, Committee, 1981-86; Royal Commonwealth Institute; Academy Club. *Literary Agent:* Peters Fraser Dunlop, London SW10. *Address:* 57 Middle Lane, London N8 8PE, England.

HAINING Peter Alexander, b. 1940, British, Novels/ Short stories, Supernatural/Occult topics. *Appointments:* Editorial Director, New English Library, publishers, London 1970-73. *Publications:* (ed) The Dream Machines: An Illustrated History of Ballooning, 1973; (ed) The Magic Valley Travellers, 1974; (ed) The Monster Makers, 1974; (ed) The Hashish Club, 1974; (ed) The Sherlock Holmes Scrapbook, 1974; The Hero (novel) 1974; The Witchcraft Papers, 1974; Ghosts: An Illustrated History, 1974; (ed) The Fantastics Pulps, 1975; (ed) The Ghost's Companion, 1975; (ed) An Illustrated History of Witchcraft, 1975; The Ancient Mysteries Reader, 1975; (ed) Black Magis Omnibus, 1976; The Great English Earthquake, 1976; The Complete Birdman, 1976; (ed) Weird tales, 1976; (ed) First Book (and Second) of Unknown Tales of Horror, 1977-78; The Monster Trap, 1977; (ed) Deadly Nightshade, 1977; Spring Heeled Jack, 1977; The Restless Bones, 1978; (ed) The Shilling Shockers, 1978; Movable Books, 1979; Superstitions, 1979; (ed) M R James Book of the Supernatural, 1979; The Leprechaun's Kingdom, 1979; The Man Who Was Frankenstein, 1980; Sweeney Todd, 1980; (ed) The Edgar Allan Poe (and Gaston Leroux) Bedside Companion, 2 vols, 1980; Buried Passions, 1980; (ed) The Final Adventures of Sherlock Holmes, 1981; (ed) The Best Short Stories of Rider Haggard, 1981; (ed) Dead of Night, 1981; Dictionary of Ghosts, 1981; (ed) Greasepaint and Ghosts, 1982; Where the Nightmares Are, 1983; Raquel Welch, 1984; Spitfire Log, 1985; Restless Bones and Other Mysteries, 1985; The Savage, 1986; Race for Mars, 1986; The Television Sherlock Holmes, 1986; (ed) Charlie Chaplin: A Centenary Celebration, 1989; The Day War Broke Out, 1989; (ed) Hook, Line and Laughter, 1989; (ed) Bob Hope: Thanks for the Memory, 1989; (ed) W Heath Robinson: Meals on Wheels, 1989; Spitfire Summer, 1990; (ed) The Legend of Garbo, 1990; (ed) Midnight Tales, 1990; Agatha Christie: Murder In Four Acts - A Centenary Celebration, 1990; (ed) The Best Supernatural Tales of Wilkie Collins, 1990; (ed) Laughter Before Wicket: The Second Innings, 1990. *Address:* Peyton House. Boxford, Suffolk. England.

HAKIM Seymour (Sy), b. 23 Jan 1933, New York City, USA. Poet; Writer; Artist; Educator. m. Odetta Roverso, 18 Aug 1970. *Education:* AB, Eastern New Mexico University, 1954; MA, New York University, 1960; Postgraduate work, various universities. *Appointments include:* Consultant editor, Poet Gallery Press, New York, 1970; Editor, Overseas Teacher, 1977. *Publications:* The Sacred Family, 1970; Manhattan Goodbye, poems, 1970; Under Moon, 1971; Museum of the Mind, 1971; Wine Theorem, 1972; Substituting Memories, 1976; Iris Elegy, 1979; Balancing Act, 1981; Birth of a Poet, 1985; Eleanor, Goodbye, 1988. *Contributions to:* Overseas Eductor; California State Poetry Quarterly; American Writing; Dan River Anthology; It's On My Wall; Older Eyes. *Honours:* exhibits with accompanying writings: 1970, 1973, 1982-83, 1985; Art works in public collections in various countries, prints in collections in Taiwan, Korea and Japan. *Memberships:* Association of Poets and Writers; National Photo Instructors Association; Italo-Brittanica Association, 1972-80. *Address:* Via Chiesanuova No. 1, 36023 Longare, VI 36023, Italy.

HALDEMAN Joe William, b. 9 June 1943, Oklahoma City, USA. Novelist. m. Mary Gay Potter, 21 Aug 1965. *Education:* BS, Physics & Astronomy, University of Maryland, 1967; MFA, English, University of Iowa, 1975. *Appointment:* Associate Professor, writing programme, Massachusetts Institute of Technology, 1983-. *Publications:* War Year, 1972; Cosmic Laughter, editor, 1974; The Forever War, 1975; Mindbridge, 1976; Planet of Judgment, 1977; All My Sins Remembered, 1977; Study War No More, editor, 1977; Infinite Dreams, 1978; World Without End, 1979; Worlds, 1981; (co-author) There Is No Darkness, 1983; Worlds Apart, 1983; (ed) Nebula Awards 17, 1983; Dealing In Futures, 1985; Tool of the Trade, 1987; (co-ed) Body Armour 2000, 1986; (co-ed) Supertanks, 1987; (co-ed) Starfighters, 1988; The Long Habit of Living (called Buying Time in the US), 1989; The Hemingway Hoax, 1990; Worlds Enough and Time, 1992. *Honours:* Purple Heart, US Army, 1969; Hugo Award, 1976, 1977-91; Nebula Award, 1975, 1992; Rhysling Award, 1984; 1990. *Memberships:* Offices, Science Fiction Writers of America; Authors Guild; Poets & Writers Inc; National Space Institute; Writers Guild. *Literary Agent:* Kirby

McCauley. *Address:* 5412 NW 14th Avenue, Gainesville, FL 32605, USA.

HALE John, b. 1926, United Kingdom. Freelance Writer (Fiction and Plays) and Director. *Appointments:* Founder, Artistic Director, Lincoln Theatre, 1955-58; Artistic Director, Arts Theatre, Ipswich, 1958-59; Artistic Director, Bristol Old Vic, 1959-61; Member, Board of Governors, Associate Artistic Director, Greenwich Theatre, London, 1963-71. *Publications:* Kissed the Girls and Made Them Cry, 1963; The Grudge Fight, 1964; A Fool at the Feast, 1966; The Paradise Man, 1969; The Fort, 1973; The Love School, 1974; Lovers and Heretics, 1976; The Whistle Blower, 1984. *Literary Agent:* Harvey Unna and Stephen Durbridge Ltd, England.

HALE Keith, b. 3 July 1955, Little Rock, AR. Writer. *Education:* BSE, University of Texas at Austin, 1980. *Appointments:* Schoolteacher, Austin, Texas, 1981-82; Publicity Office, University of Texas, Performing Arts Centre, 1982-84; Editor, English Language Book Editors, Amsterdam, Holland, 1984; Editor, Arkansas Writers' Project, Little Rock, 1984-86-87; Copy Editor, Arkansas Gazette, Little Rock, 1987-. *Publications:* Clicking Beat on the Brink of Nada, 1983; Cody, 1987.

HALEY Gail E(inhart), b. 1939, USA. Children's Fiction Writer. *Publications:* My Kingdom for a Dragon, 1962; The Wonderful Magical World of Marguerite, 1964; Round Stories about Things That Live on Land and in Water, 1966; Round Stories about Things That Grow, 1966; Round Stories about Our World, 1966; A Story, A Story: An African Tale, Retold, 1970; Noah's Ark, 1971; Jack Jouett's Ride, 1973; The Abominable Swamp Man, 1975; The Post Office Cat, 1976; Go Away, Stay Away, 1977; Costumes for Plays and Playing, 1977; The Green Man, 1980; Birdsong, 1984. *Address:* c/o A P Watt, 26-28 Bedford Row, London WC1R 4HL, England.

HALEY Kenneth Harold Dobson, b. 19 Apr 1920, Historian. m. Iris Houghton, 22 Mar 1948, 1 son, 2 daughters. *Education:* MA; BLitt, Balliol College, 1938-40, 1945-47. *Publications:* William of Orange and the English Opposition 1672-74, 1953; The First Earl of Shaftesbury, 1968; The Dutch in the Seventeenth Century, 1972; Politics in the Reign od Charles II, 1985; An English Diplomat in the Low Countries: Sir William Temple and John de Witt, 1986; The British and the Dutch, 1988. *Contributions to:* Articles to various historical journals. *Honour:* FBA, 1987. *Address:* 15 Haugh Lane, Sheffield S11 9SA, England.

HALL Angus, b. 1932, United Kingdom. Author; Editor. *Appointments:* Film and Theatre Critic, London Daily Sketch, 1958-61; Editor, IPC Publishers, London, 1971-; Editor, BPC Publishers, London, 1972-. *Publications:* London in Smoky Region, 1962; High-Bouncing Lover, 1966; Live Like a Hero, 1967; Come-uppance of Arthur Hearne, 1967; Qualtrough, 1968; Late Boy Wonder, 1969; Devilday, 1970; To Play the Devil, 1971; Scars of Dracula, 1971; Long Way to Fall, 1971; On the Run, 1974; Signs of Things to Come: A History of Divination, 1975; Monsters and Mythic Beasts, 1976; Strange Cults, 1977; The Rigoletto Murder, 1978; Selt-Destruct, 1985. *Address:* 96 High Street, Old Town, Hastings, Sussex, England.

HALL Carl William, b. 16 Nov 1924, Tiffin, Ohio, USA. Engineer and Educator. m. Mildred E Wagner, 5 Sept 1949, 1 daughter. *Education:* BS, BAE summa cum laude, Ohio State University, 1948; MME, University Delaware, 1950; PhD, Michigan State University, 1952; Certificate, SMG, JFK School of Government, Harvard University, 1983. *Publications:* Agricultural Engineers Handbook, 1961; Biomass handbook, 1988; Encyclopaedia of Food Engineering, 1971, 1986; Dictionary of Drying, 1979; Food and Natural Resources, 1984, author, 26 books. *Contributions to:* 34 books, 175 articles in technical journals and 250 articles in general

interest non-technical media; Founding Editor, and Editor Emeritus of Drying Technology: An International Journal; Regular column in Drying Technology. *Honours:* Max Eyth Medal, 1979; Massey-Ferguson Gold Medal, 1976; Cyrus Hall McCormick Gold Medal, 1984. *Memberships:* National Academy of Engineers; National Society of Professional Engineers. International Club of Washington. *Address:* 2454 N Rockingham St, Arlington, VA 22207, USA.

HALL Claudia. *See:* FLOREN Lee.

HALL Evan. *See:* HALLERAN Eugene Edward.

HALL Gimone, b. 30 Apr 1940, Highland Park, Illinois, USA. Novelist. m. Lawrence C Hall, 13 July 1963, 2 sons, 1 daughter. *Education:* BA, University of Texas. *Publications include:* Raptures' Mistress, 1979; Rules of the Heart, 1983; Fury's Sun, Passion's Moon, 1980; The Kiss flower, 1985; The Jasmine Veil, 1987; Ecstasy's Empire, 1981. *Contributions to:* Fiction in Red Book, Good Housekeeping, Woman's Own. *Honour:* Best Romantic Fiction of the Year, West Coast Review of Weeks, 1980. *Literary Agent:* Donald MacCampbell. *Address:* Million Wishes Farm, P O Box 485, Ottsville, PA 18942, USA.

HALL Hugh Gaston, b. 7 Nov 1931, Jackson, Mississippi, USA. Emeritus Reader, University of Warwick. m. Gillian Gladys Lund, 16 July 1955, 1 son, 2 daughters. *Education:* BA Millsaps College, 1952; Diplome pour l'Enseignement, University of Toulouse, 1953; MA Oxon, 1959; PhD Yale, 1959. *Appointments:* Yale University, 1958-60; University of Glasgow, Lecturer, 1960-64; University of California, Berkeley, Art Professor, 1963; Monash University, Senior Lecturer, 1965; University of Warwick, Senior Lecturer, 1966-74; Reader, 1974-89; City University of New York, Professor of Romance Language, 1970-72. *Publications:* Moliere: Tartuffe, 1960; Quadruped Octaves, 1983; Comedy in Context, 1984; Alphabet Aviary, 1987; Richelieu's Desmarets and the Century of Louis XIV, 1990; Moliere's Le Bourgeois Gentilhomme, 1990. *Contributions:* Numerous professional humanities journals and reference books. *Address:* 18 Abbey End, Kenilworth, Warwick, England.

HALL James Byron, b. 21 July 1918, Midland, Ohio, USA. Writer; Professor. m. Elizabeth Cushman, 14 Feb 1946, 1 son, 4 daughters. *Education:* Miami University, Ohio, 1938-39; University of Hawaii, 1938-40; BA 1947, MA 1948, PhD 1953, State University of Iowa. *Appointments include:* Writer-in-residence, various universities; Faculty 1958-68, Professor 1960-68, Director, Writing Centre 1965-68, University of California, Irvine; Provost 1968-75, Emeritus 1983-, University of California, Santa Cruz. *Publications include:* Not By The Door, 1954; The Short Story, 1955, 1957; Racers to the Sun, 1960; Us He Devours, 1964; Realm of Fiction, 1965, 1977; Modern Culture & Arts, 1967, 1975; Mayo Sergeant, 1967; The Hunt Within, 1973; Short Hall, stories, 1981; Squall Line, 1989. *Contributions to:* Stories, poetry, various anthologies; Literary archive, Miami University, Oxford, Ohio. *Honours include:* Numerous prizes & awards, poetry & fiction; Rockefeller grantee, 1955; James B. Hall Gallery named, University of California Regents, 1985; James B. Hall Travelling Fellowships founded, University of California Santa Cruz, 1985. *Memberships include:* American Association of University Professors; Past Local President, National Writers Union. *Literary Agent:* Gerard McCauley Agency, PO Box AE, Katona, NY. *Address:* 1670 East 27th Avenue, Eugene, OR 97403, USA.

HALL Jane Anna, b. 4 Apr 1959, New London, Connecticut, USA. Writer; Model. *Education:* Professional Model, Barbizon School, 1976; Diploma, Westbrook High School, 1977. *Appointments:* Freelance Poet/Writer, 1986-; Poetry reading, Congregational Church Broadbrook, Aug 1988; Participant, group poetry reading and display, Westbrook Public Library, Westbrook, Connecticut, Apr 1989; Founder, Editor, Poetry in Your Mailbox Newsletter, 1989-. *Publications:* Cedar and Lace, 1986; Satin and Pinstripe, 1987; Fireworks and Diamonds, 1988; Stars and Daffodils, 1989; Sun Rises and Stone Walls, 1990; Mountains and Meadows, 1991; (chapbook) Moonlight and Waterlilles, 1993. *Contributions to:* Poems published in The Bell Bouy; Expressions I and II; Connecticut River Review; Connecticut Chapter of Romance Writers of America Newsletter; Contributing editor, Match Book Magazine, 1993. *Honours:* 2nd Prize for Post Dawn Enchantment, Connecticut Poetry Society Contest, 1983; 2nd Prize for Polar Bear Frolic, Connecticut Poetry Society Contest, 1986; Honourable Mention for In Your Arms, World of Poetry Contest, 1988; Certificate of Merit for Distinguished Service to the Community, 1989; Certificate of World Leadership, 1989. *Memberships:* Romance Writers of America; Connecticut Chapter, Romance Writers of America; Connecticut Poetry Society; President, World Poetry Chairman, Old Saybrook Chapter, Connecticut Poetry Society; Former Member, Board of Christian Education and International Platform Association. *Address:* PO Box 629, Westbrook, CT 06498, USA.

HALL Jay, b. 18 Oct 1932, Houston, Texas, USA. Social Psychologist. 1 son, 2 daughters. *Education:* BA 1959, MA 1961, PhD 1963, Psychology, University of Texas. *Publications:* Ponderables: Essays on Managerial Choice-Past and Future, 1982; The Competence Connection: A Blueprint for excellence, 1988; Models for Management: The Structure of Competence, 1988; The Executive Trap, 1992. Numerous articles and psychological tests. *Memberships:* American Psychological Association; AAAS; Sigma Xi; New York Academy of Science. *Address:* 1755 Woodstead Court, The Woodlands, TX 77380, USA.

HALL Leslie (Leslie Hall Pinder), b. 21 Sept 1948. Barrister and Solicitor. *Education:* BA, Dalhousie University, 1968; LLB, University of British Columbia, 1977. *Appointments:* Barrister and Solicitor, Vancouver, British Columbia, 1978-. *Publications:* Under the House, 1986; Selbie, 1989. *Memberships:* Law Society of British Columbia; British Columbia Federation of Writers; Authors League of America; Authors Guild. *Address:* 3569 West 12th Avenue, Vancouver, British Columbia, Canada V6R 2N3.

HALL Oakley Maxwell, (Jason Manor), b. 1 July 1920, San Diego, California, USA. Author; Professor. m. Barbara Edinger, 28 June 1945. 1 son, 3 daughters. *Education:* BA, University of California, Berkeley, 1943; MFA, University of Iowa, 1950. *Appointments:* Director, Programs in Writing, University of California, Irvine, 1969-89; Director, Squaw Valley Community of Writers, 1969-. *Publications:* So Many Doors, 1950; Corpus of Joe Bailey, 1953; Mardios Beach, 1955; Warlock, 1958; The Downhill Racers, 1962; The Pleasure Garden, 1962; A Game for Eagles, 1970; Report From Beau Harbor, 1971; The Adelita, 1975; The Badlands, 1978; Lullaby, 1982; The Children of the Sun, 1983; The Coming of the Kid, 1985; Apaches, 1986; The Art and Craft of Novel Writing, 1989. As O M Hall: Murder City, 1949. As Jason Manor: Too Dead to Run, 1953; The Red Jaguar, 1954; The Pawns of Fear, 1955; The Tramplers, 1956. *Honours:* Nomination for Pulitzer Prize, 1953; Commonwealth Club of California Silver Medal, 1954; Western Writers of America Golden Spur Award, 1984; Cowboy Hall of Fame Wrangler Award, 1989. *Literary Agent:* Don Congdon Associates, New York, USA. *Address:* Department of English, University of California, Irvine, CA 92717, USA.

HALL Peter (Geoffrey), b. 1932, United Kingdom. Professor of Geography; Professor of City and Regional Planning. *Publications:* The Industries of London, 1962; London 2000, 1963, Revised Edition, 1969; Labour's New Frontiers (editor), 1964; Land Values (editor), 1965; The World Cities, 1966, 3rd Edition, 1984; Von Thunen's Isolated State (editor), 1966; An Advanced Geography of North-West Europe (co-author), 1967; Theory and Practice of Regional Planning, 1970; Containment of Urban England: Urban and Metropolitan Growth Processes or Megalopolis Denied (co-author), 1973; Containment of Urban England: The Planning System: Objectives, Operations, Impacts (co-author), 1973; Planning and Urban Growth: An Anglo-American Comparison (with M Clawson), 1973; Urban and Regional Planning: An Introduction, 1974, 2nd Edition, 1982; Europe 2000, 1977; Great Planning Disasters, 1980; Growth Centres in the European Urban System, 1980; Transport and Public Policy Planning (edited with D Banister), 1980; The Inner City in Context (editor), 1981; Silicon Landscapes (editor), 1985; Can Rail Save the City (co-author), 1985; High-Tech America (co-author), 1986; Western Sunrise (co-author), 1987; The Carrier Wave (co-author), 1988; Cities of Tomorrow, 1988; London 2001, 1989; The Rise of the Gunbelt, 1991; Technology of the World, 1993. *Address:* The Bartlett School of Planning, University College London, Wates House, 22 Gordon Street, London WC1H 0QB.

HALL Rand, b. 17 July 1945, New Jersey, USA. Writer; Editor; Publisher - Shadowood Publications. 1 son, 1 daughter. *Education:* Hofstra University, New York; New York University Agricultural & Technical Institute, Farmingdale, NY; St Petersburg Jr College, St Petersburg, Florida, USA. *Publications:* Voices in the Night, Clies Press McNarron & Morgan, editors, 1984; The Alternative Papers, Temple University Press, 1984; Lavenderblue, Shadowood Publications, 1988. *Contributions to:* Poetry, essays in: Sinister Wisdom; Common Lives; Feminary; Oblisk. *Honour:* World of Poetry, Silver Poet Award, 1986. *Memberships:* Womonwrites (Registrar - Southeastern Lesbian Writers Conf. 1981-89); National Board for Certification - CDT; Tampa Bay Business Guild. *Address:* 7134 5th Avene N, St Petersburg, FL 33710, USA.

HALL Redd. *See:* **HALLUM Rosemary.**

HALL Rodney, b. 18 Nov 1935, Solihull, England. Writer. m. Bet MacPhail, 3 daughters. *Education:* BA, Queensland University, Australia. *Appointments:* Poetry Editor, The Australian, 1967-78; Creative Arts Fellow, Australian National University, 1968-69. *Publications:* (Poetry), Penniless Till Doomsday, 1962; Selected Poems, 1975; Black Bagatelles, 1978; (Novels) The Ship on the Coin, 1972; A Place Among People, 1975, 2nd edition 1984; Just Relations, 1982, 4th edition, 1985; Kisses of the Enemy, 1987. *Contributions to:* Hundreds of poems and several short stories in, Australian Literary Magazines, Newspapers, Journals; Book Reviews, The Australian; Sydney Morning Herald; The Bulletin. *Honours:* Grace Leven Prize for Poetry, 1973; Australia Council, Senior Fellowships, 1973, 1976, 1983, 1985; Miles Franklin Award, for Novel, 1982. *Address:* PO Box 7, Bermagui South, NSW 2547, Australia.

HALL Roger Leighton, b. 17 Jan 1939, Woodford Wells, Essex, England. Writer. m. Dianne Sturm, 20 Jan 1968, 1 son, 1 daughter. *Education:* BA, 1966; MA, 1968, Victoria University, Wellington, New Zealand; Diploma of Teaching. *Publications:* Plays: Glide Time, 1976; Middle Age Spread, 1977; State of the Play, 1978; Prisoners of Mother England, 1979; The Rose, 1981; Hot Water, 1982; Fifty-Fifty, 1982; Multiple Choice, 1984; Dream of Sussex Downs, 1986; The Hansard Show, 1986; The Share Club; 1987; After the Crash, 1988; Conjugal Rites, 1990; Musicals with Philip Norman & A K Grant; many plays for TV, Radio, and for children; TV: Conjugal Rites, Granada UK, 1993. *Honours:* Robert Burns Fellow, Otago University, 1977, 1978; Fulbright Travel Award, 1982; QSO, 1987; Turnovsky Award Outstanding Contribution to the Arts, 1987. *Memberships:* PEN; NZ Scriptwriters Guild. *Literary Agent:* Playmarket, Box 9767, Wellington, New Zealand; The Casarotto Company Ltd, 60-66 Wardour Street, London W1V 3HP, England. *Address:* English Department, University of Otago, P.O. Box 56, Dunedin, New Zealand.

HALL Trevor Henry, b. 28 May 1910. Writer;

Historian; Lecturer. m. (1) Dorothy, 1937, (dec 1973), 1 son, 1 daughter, (2) Marguerite, 1977, 1 step-son, 1 step-daughter. *Education:* MA, Perrott Student, Trinity College, Cambridge; FSA 1978. *Publications:* The Testament of R W Hull, 1945; (with E J Dingwall and K M Goldney), The Haunting of Borley Rectory: A Critical Survey of the Evidence, 1956; A Bibliography of Books on Conjuring in English from 1580 to 1850, 1957; (with E J Dingwall) Four Modern Ghosts, 1958; The Spiritualists: The Story of William Crookes and Florence Cook, 1962; The Strange Case of Edmund Gurney, 1964; The Mystery of the Leeds Library, 1965; New Light on Old Ghosts, 1965; (with J L Campbell) Strange Things, 1968; Sherlock Holmes: Ten Literary Studies, 1969; Mathematical Recreations, 1633: An Exercise in 17th Century Bibliography, 1970; The Late Mr Sherlock Holmes, 1971; Old Conjuring Books: a bibliographical and historical study, 1972; The Card Magic of Edward G Brown, 1973; The Early Years of the Huddersfield Building Society, 1974; A New Era, 1974; The Winder Sale of Old Conjuring Books, 1975; (with Percy H Muir) Some Printers and Publishers of Conjuring Books and Other Ephemera 1800-1850, 1976; The Leeds Library, 1977; Sherlock Holmes and his Creator, 1978; Search for Harry Price, 1978; The Strange Story of Ada Goodrich Freer, 1979; Dorothy L Sayers: Nine Literary Studies, 1980; Twelve Friends, 1981; The Leeds Library: a checklist of publications relating to its history from 1768 to 1977, 1983; Daniel Home: a Victorian Enigma, 1984. *Memberships:* Numerous professional and civic organisations. *Address:* The Lodge, Selby, North Yorkshire, YO8 0PW, England.

HALL Willis, b. 6 Apr 1929. Writer. m. Valerie Shute, 1973, 1 son (3 sons by previous marriages). *Publications include:* TV Plays: The Villa Maroc; They Don't Open Men's Boutiques; Song at Twilight; The Road to 1984; TV Series: The Fuzz, 1977; The Danedyke Mystery, 1979; Stan's Last Game, 1983; The Bright Side, 1985; The Return of the Antelope, 1986; (with Keith Waterhouse), The Upper Crusts, 1973; Billy Liar, 1974; Worzel Gummidge, 1979 (adapted as stage musical, 1981); Books: (with Michael Parkinson) The A-Z of Soccer, 1970; Football Report, 1973; Football Classified, 1974; My Sporting Life, Football Final, 1975; Childrens Books: The Royal Astrologer, 1960; The Gentle Knight, 1967; The Incredible Kidnapping, 1975; The Summer of the Dinosaur, 1977; The Last Vampire, 1982; The Inflatable Shop, 1984; The Return of the Antelope, 1985; Dragon Days, 1986; The Antelope Company Ashore, Spooky Rhymes, The Antelope Company at Large, 1987; Doctor Jekyll and Mr Hollins, 1988; The Vampire's Holiday, 1992; The Vampire's Revenge, 1993. Plays: The Long and the Short and the Tall, 1959; A Glimpse of the Sea, 1969; Kidnapped at Christmas, 1975; Walk on Walk On, 1975; Stag Night, 1976; Christmas Crackers, 1976; A Right Christmas Caper, 1977; (with Keith Waterhouse): Billy Liar, 1960; Celebration 1961; All Things Bright and Beautiful, 1962; England Our England, 1962; Squat Betty and The Sponge Room, 1963; Say Who You Are, 1965; Whoops a Daisy, 1968; Children's Day, 1969; Who's Who, 1972; Saturday, Sunday, Monday (adaptation from de Filippo), 1973; Filumena (adaptation from de Filippo), 1977; Musicals: (with Keith Waterhouse) The Card, 1973; (with Denis King): Treasure Island, 1985; The Wind in the Willows (adaptation from A A Milne), 1985; (with John Cooper) The Water Babies (adaptation from Charles Kingsley), 1987; Jane Eyre, adaptation from Charlotte Brontë, 1992 . *Address:* c/o Alexander Cann Representation, 337 Fulham Road, London SW10 9TW, England.

HALLAHAN William H(enry), b. USA. Author. *Publications:* The Dead of Winter, 1972; The Ross Forgery, 1973; The Search for Joseph Tully, 1974; Catch Me, Kill Me, 1977; Keeper of the Children, 1978; The Trade, 1981; The Monk, 1983. *Address:* c/o William Morrow Inc, Madison Avenue, New York, NY 10016, USA.

HALLER Bill. *See:* BECHKO Peggy Anne.

HALLERAN Eugene Edward, (Evan Hall), b. 28 Feb 1905, Wildwood, New Jersey, USA. Retired Teacher. m. 23 Mar 1929 (widower), 1 son. *Education:* AB, Bucknell University, 1927; EdM, Rutgers University. *Publications include:* No Range is Free, 1944; Prairie Guns, 1944; Outposts of Vengeance, 1945; 13 Toy Pistols, novel, 1945; Shadow of the Badlands, 1946; Double Cross Trail, 1946; Outlaw Guns, 1947; Outlaw Trail, 1947 (UK, The Outlaw, 1952); Rustlers Canyon, 1948; High Prairie, 1950; Smoky Range, 1951; Gunsmoke Valley, 1952; Straw Boss, 1952; Colorado Creek, 1953; Winter Ambush, 1954; Blazing Border, 1955; Logan, 1956; Devils's Canyon, 1956; Wagon Captain, 1956; Spanish Ridge, 1957; Shadow of the Big Horn, 1960; Dark Raiders, 1960; Warbonnet Creek, 1960; Convention Queen, novel, 1960; Blood Brand (UK, Gringo Gun), 1961; Crimson Desert, 1962; Far Land, 1963; Indian Fighter, 1964; Summer of the Sioux, 1965; High Iron, 1965; Red River Country, 1966; Pistoleros, 1967; Outlaws of Empty Poke, 1969; Cimarron Thunder, 1970. *Honour:* Spur Award, Best Western, 1964. *Address:* 2600 SE Ocean, Apt. JJ-12, Stuart, FL 33494, USA.

HALLIDAY Dorothy. *See:* DUNNETT Dorothy.

HALLIGAN Marion Mildred, b. 16 Apr 1940, Newcastle, Australia. Writer; Reviewer; Schoolteacher. m. Graham Halligan, 8 June 1963, 1 son, 1 daughter. *Education:* BA, Honours, 1961, DipEd, 1962, University of New South Wales. *Appointments:* Literature Board Granst, 1981, 1987; Chairperson of Australian National Word Festival, 1987. *Publications:* Self Possession, novel, 1987; The Living Hothouse, short stories, 1988. *Contributions to:* over 40 short stories in magazines in Australia & overseas. *Honours:* Patricia Hackett Prize, 1985; A M Butterlay-F Earle Hooper Award, 1986; Commended, Canberra Times Short Story Competition. *Memberships:* Australian Society of Authors, Canberra Representative; Seven Writers; Australian Symposium of Astronomy. *Literary Agent:* Curtis Brown. *Address:* 6 Caldwell Street, Hackett, ACT 2602, Australia.

HALLIN Emily W, b. Ark, USA. Writer. m. Clark Ossell Hallin, 16 Aug 1952, 2 sons, 1 daughter. *Education:* AB, University of Missouri, 1948. *Appointments:* Editor, Publicist, United Aircraft Corp. Chance Vought Division, 1948-52. *Publications:* Wild White Wings, 1962; Follow the Honey Bird, 1964; Moya and the Flamingoes, 1966; Blossom Valley Series, (19 books), 1980-88; Wanted: Tony Roston, 1988; A Dark Horse, 1989; Queen Bee, 1989; The Meg and Stanley Series, (3 books), 1990. *Contributions to:* Various children's magazines, journals. *Memberships:* Mystery Writers of America; California Writers Club; Society of Childrens Book Writers. *Literary Agent:* Ruth Cohen *Address:* 1350 Castro Way, Monterey, CA 93940, USA.

HALLMUNDSSON Hallberg, b. 29 Oct 1930, Iceland. Poet; Translator; Editor. m. May Newman, 29 July 1960. *Education Includes:* BA, University of Iceland, 1954; University of Barcelona, 1955-56; New York University 1961 *Appointments:* columnist, Frjals Thjod, 1954-60; Stringer, Newsweek, 1960; Assistant, Associate Senior Editor, Encyclopedia International, 1961-76; Senior Editor, American Annual, 1977-78; Senior Editor, Funk & Wagnalls New Encyclopedia, 1979-82; Production Copy Editor, Business Week, 1984- . *Publications:* Anthology of Scandinavian Literature, 1966; Poetry; Haustmal, 1968; Neikvaeda, 1977; Spjaldvisur, 1985; Thraetubók, 1990; Spjaldvisur, 1991; Skyggnur, 1993; Short Stories, Eg kalla mig Ofeig, 1970; Icelandic Folk and Fairy Tales, with May Hallmundsson, 1987; Translator, various books. *Contributions include:* Americana Annual; Icelandic Canadian; Iceland Review. *Honours include:* 1st prize, short story contest, Reykjavik, 1953; 1st prize, Translation of Norwegian Poetry, Minneapolis, 1966; Grant, Translation Centre, New York, 1975; Grant, Government of Iceland, 1976-79; Grant, American Scandinavian Society, 1991. *Memberships:* Writers Union of Iceland; American Literary Translators Association; Reykjavik Drama Critics' Society, Treasurer 1957-59. *Address:* 30 Fifth Avenue, New York, NY 10011, USA.

HALLS Geraldine. *See:* **JAY Geraldine Mary.**

HALLUM Rosemary, b. 2 Oct, Oakland, California, USA. Writer. *Education:* BA, UC Berkeley; MA, San Jose State University; PhD Walden University; General Elementary and Secondary Teaching Credentials. *Publications:* Action Reading Kit Series, 1973-77; I like to Read Series, 1982; 29 Children's Records including Mother Goose Favourites, Fingerplay Fun and Fingerplays & Footplays, 1971-91; Multicultural Folktales, filmstrip set, 1977; Beginnings, 1982, (book). *Contributions to:* Contributing Editor, Iron man, Muscular Development, Muscle Mag, Fitness Plus and Muscle Training Illustrated, 1982-. Former Columnist for Teacher Magazine; Contributor to Several Magazines including Walking, Grand Slam, Black Beat, Childhood Education, Flex. *Honours:* Best of the Year, Filmstrip Award in Language Arts, Previews Magazine; National Educational Film Festival Finalist Award. *Memberships:* International Society of Food Wine andtravel Writers; California Writers Club; National Writers Club. *Literary Agent:* Florence Feiler. *Address:* 1021 Otis Drive, Alameda, CA 94501, USA.

HALPERIN Irving, b. 17 Jan 1922, New York, USA. Professor of English and Creative Writing. 2 sons, 1 daughter. *Education:* BA 1947; MA 1950; PhD 1957. *Publications:* Messengers from the Dead; Literature of the Holocaust, 1970; Here I am: A Jew in today's Germany, 1971; The Jewish Catastrophe in Europe, 1966. *Contributions to:* Christian Century, Commonwealth, Prairie Schooner, College English, English Journal, Massachusetts Review, Saturday Review, The Nation, The Chronicle of Higher Education, Phi Delta Kappa, New England Review, Midstream, University of Kansas City Review, The Louisville Review, Kansas Quarterly. *Honours:* National Curriculum Research Institute of the American Association of Jewish Education, 1965; National Foundation for Jewish Culture, 1966. *Memberships:* Associated Writing Programme, Poets and Writers; PEN Centre of America. *Address:* 148 Meadowbrook Avenue, San Francisco, CA 94132, USA.

HALPERIN Mark W, b. 19 Feb 1940, New York City, USA. Professor of English; Writer. m. Barbara Scot, 1 son. *Education:* BA Physics, Bard College, 1960; MFA Poetry, University of Iowa, 1966. *Publications:* Backroads, 1976; A Place Made Fast, 1982; The Measure of Islands, 1990. *Contributions to:* Poetry, Iowa Review, Shenandorn, Senica, Seattle Review. *Honours:* Glasscock Award, Undergrad Poetry, 1960; US Award, International Poetry Forum, 1976. *Address:* Rt 4 Box 279A Ellensburg, WA 98926, USA.

HAM Wayne Albert, b. 1938, USA. Author. *Publications:* Enriching Your New Testament Studies, 1965; Man's Living Religion, 1965; Faith and the Arts, 1968; The Call to Covenant, 1969; Publish Glad Tidings, 1970; The First Century Church, 1971; Where Faith and World Meet, 1972; Listening for God's Voice, 1973; On the Growing Edge, 1973; Yesterday's Horizons, 1975; More Than Burnt Offerings, 1978; My Million Faces, 1985. *Address:* PO Box 1059, Independence, MO 64051, USA.

HAMBRICK-STOWE Charles Edwin, b. 4 Feb 1948, Worcester, Massachusetts, USA. m. Elizabeth Anne Hambrick-Stowe, 11 Sept 1971, 2 sons, 1 daughter. *Education:* BA, Hamilton College, 1970; MA and MDiv, Pacific School of Religion, 1973; PhD, Boston University Graduate School, 1980. *Appointments:* Religion Columnist, Evening Sun Newspaper, Carrol County, Maryland, 1982-85. *Publications:* The Practice of Piety: Puritan Devotional Disciplines in 17th C New England, 1982; Early New England Meditative Poetry: Anne Bradstreet and Edward Taylor, 1988; Theology and Identity: Traditions Movements and Issues in the United Church of Christ, 1990; A Living Theological Heritage: American Beginnings, 1994; Massachusetts Militia Companies and Officers of the Lexington Alarm, 1976; charles G Finney and The Spirit of American

Evangelicalism, forthcoming. *Contributions to:* Christian Century, Japan Christian Quarterly, Lutheran Quarterly, Bulletin of the Congregational Library, Journal of Presbyterian Church History; Book chapters: Encyclopaedia of Religion in America; Encyclopaedia of the Reformed Faith; Dictionary of Christianity in America. *Honours:* Jamestown Prize for Early American History, 1980. *Memberships:* American Historical Association; American Society of Church History; AMerican Academy of Religion; Cliosophic Society (Lancaster, PA). *Address:* 1101 Davis Drive, Lancaster, PA 17603, USA.

HAMILTON Charles, b. 1913, USA. Author; President, Hamilton Galleries, New York City. *Publications:* Cry of the Thunderbird: The American Indian's Own Story, 1950; Men of the Underworld: The Professional Criminal's Own Story, 1952; Braddock's Defeat, 1959; Collecting Autographs and Manuscripts, 1961; Lincoln in Photographs (with L Ostendorf), 1963; The Robot That Helped to Make a President, 1965; Scribblers and Scoundrels, 1968; Big Name Hunting (with D Hamilton), 1973; Collecting Autographs and Manuscripts, 1974; The Book of Autographs, 1978; The Signature of America, 1979; Great Forgers and Famous Fakes, 1980; Auction Madness, 1981; American Autographs, 1983; Leaders of the Third Reich, 1984; In Search of Shakespeare, 1985. *Address:* c/o Harvard University Press, 79 Garden Street, Cambridge, MA 02138, USA.

HAMILTON Donald B, b. 24 Mar 1916, Uppsala, Sweden, Writer. m. Kathleen Stick, 12 Sept 1941, (dec. Oct 1989), 2 sons, 2 daughters. *Education:* BS, University of Chicago, USA, 1938. *Publications:* Author of 25 novels featuring agent Matt Helm, 1960-89; The Big Country, 1958; Author of 4 other western novels, 1954-60 and 5 mystery novels, 1947-56; On Guns and Hunting, 1970; Cruises with Kathleen, 1980. *Contributions to:* Articles on photography, guns and hunting, yachting and writing. *Honour:* WWA Spur, 1967. *Memberships:* Authors Guild; Mystery Writers of America; Western Writers of America; Outdoor Writer's Association of America. *Literary Agent:* Brandt and Brandt. *Address:* PO Box 1045, Santa Fe, NM 87504, USA.

HAMILTON Eleanor, b. 6 Oct 1909, Portland, Oregon, USA. Marriage Counsellor; Sex Therapist. m. A E Hamilton, 11 Aug 1932, 1 son, 3 daughters. *Education:* AB, University of Oregon, 1930; MA, Teachers College, Colombia University, 1939; PhD, Columbia University, 1955. *Publications:* Partners in Love, 1969; Sex before Marraige; Sex with Love: A guide for young People, 1979; Pleasure Anxiety, 1983; Love and Sex in old Age, in progress. *Contributions to:* Modern Bride Magazine; Living and Loving; Science; and several newspapers. *Honours:* American Library Award, 1979; Woman of the Year, Society for Scientific Study of Sex. *Memberships:* AFTRA; American Association of Marriage and Family Therapists; Social Scientific Study of Sex; American Society of Sex Education Counsellors and Therapists. *Address:* 60E Robert Drive, P O Box 765, Inverness, CA 99937, USA.

HAMILTON John Maxwell, b. 28 Mar 1947, Evanston, Illinois, USA. Journalist; Lecturer. m. Regina N, 19 Aug 1975, 1 son. *Education:* BA, Journalism, Marquette University, 1969; MS, Journalism, Boston University, 1974; PhD, American Civilization, George Washington University, 1983. *Appointments:* The Milwaukee Journal, 1967-69; Marine Corps, 1969-73; Freelance Writer, ABC Radio Correspondent, 1973-78; Agency for International Development (political appointee), 1979-81; House Foreign Affairs Committee, 1981-83; World Bank, 1983-84 and 1988-1992; Society of Professional Journalists, 1985-87; Visiting Professor, Journalism, Northwestern University, 1985-87; Director, Manship School of Mass Communication, Louisiana State University. *Publications:* Main Street America and the Third World, 1986, revised, enlarged edition, 1988; Edgar Snow: A Biography, 1988; Entangling Alliances, 1990. *Contributions include:*

Numerous book chaprters in: The Nonproliferation Predicament; From Parachialism to Globalism; Numerous newspapers and magazines including: Christian Science Monitor; New York Times; Washington Post; Boston Globe. *Honours:* Ford Foundation, Germon Marshall Fund, Carnegie Corporation and Benton Foundation Grants, 1985-88; Frank Luther Mott Journalism Research Award, (for Snow biography), 1989; By-line Award, Marguette University, 1993. *Memberships:* Society of Professional Journalists; Society of International Developement; Director, Board of Directors, Center for Foreign Journalists. *Literary Agent:* Peter Shepherd, Harold Ober Associates. *Address:* 567 LSU Avenue, Baton Rouge, LA 70808, USA.

HAMILTON Julia. *See:* **WATSON Julia.**

HAMILTON Kenneth (Morrison), b. 1917, Canada. Professor of Religious Studies; Former Minister of Religion. *Publications:* The Protestant Way, 1956; The System and the Gospel: A Critique of Paul Tillich, 1963; Revolt Against Heaven, 1965; God Is Dead: The Anatomy of a Slogan, 1966; In Search of Contemporary Man, 1967; J D Salinger: A Critical Essay, 1967; John Updike: A Critical Essay (with A Hamilton), 1967; What's New In Religion, 1968; Life in One's Stride: A Short Study in Dietrich Bonhoeffer, 1968; The Promise of Kierkegaard, 1969; The Elements of John Updike (with A Hamilton), 1970; Words and the Word, 1971; To Turn from Idols, 1973; To Be a Man - To Be a Woman (with A Hamilton), 1975; Condemned to Life: The World of Samuel Beckett (with A Hamilton), 1976. *Address:* 246 Harvard Avenue, Winnipeg, Manitoba, Canada R3M 0K7.

HAMILTON Mollie. *See:* **KAYE Mary Margaret.**

HAMILTON Morse, b. 16 Aug 1943, Detroit, Michigan, USA. Teacher. m. Sharon Saros, 20 Aug 1966, Detroit. 3 daughters. *Education:* BA, University of Michigan, 1967; MA 1968, PhD 1974, Columbia University. *Publications:* Children's Books: My Name is Emily, 1979; Big Sisters Are Bad Witches, 1980; Who's Afraid of the Dark? 1983; How Do You Do, Mr Birdsteps? 1983; Effie's House (novel), 1990; Little Sister For Sale, 1992. *Honours:* Hopwood Award, 1967; Woodrow Wilson Dissertation Fellow, 1971; George Bennett Memorial Fellow, 1973. *Address:* c/o English Department, tufts University, Medford, MA 02155, USA.

HAMILTON Paul. *See:* **DENNIS-JONES Harold.**

HAMILTON Priscilla. *See:* **GELLIS Roberta Leach.**

HAMILTON Wade. *See:* **FLOREN Lee.**

HAMILTON William. *See:* **CANAWAY W H.**

HAMLYN Paul Bertrand, b. 12 Feb 1926, Berlin, Germany Publisher. m. (1) Eileen Margaret Watson, 1952, divorced 1969, (2) Helen Guest, 1970, 1 son, 1 daughter. *Appointments:* Founder, Hamlyn Publishing Group; Formed Books for Pleasure, 1949; Prints for Pleasure, 1960; Records for Pleasure; Golden Pleasure Books, 1961; Music for Pleasure (EMI), 1965; Paul Hamlyn Group acquired by IPC, 1964; joined IPC Board with special responsibility for all book publishing activities; acquired Butterworth and Co., 1968; Director, IPC 1965-70, Chairman, IPC Books, 1965-70; Joint Managing Director, News International Ltd., 1970-71; Founder, Chairman, Octopus Publishing Group, 1971-; Chairman, Octopus Books Ltd., 1971-, Mandarin Publishers, Hong Kong, 1971-; Co-founder (with David Frost), and Director, Sundial Publications, 1973-; Co-founder (with Doubleday & Co., New York), and Director, Octopus Books International BV, Netherlands, 1973-; Director, News America, Tigerprint Ltd., News International, etc.; TV AM, 1981-83; Co-Chairman, Conran Octopus Ltd., 1983-; Chairman, Heinemann Group of Publishers Ltd., 1985-, Hamlyn Publishing Group, 1986-; Board Director International Plc, Chairman, Reed International Books, 1987-; Chancellor of Thames Valley University, 1993-; Chairman, Book Club Associates, 1993; Director, Reed Elsevier PLC, 1993-. *Honours:* University of Keele, 1988; University of Wariwck, 1991. *Address:* Michelin House, 81 Fulham Road, London SW3 6RB, England.

HAMMER Reuven, b. 30 June 1933, Syracuse, New York, USA. Rabbi; Professor. m. Rahel Chibnik, 13 June 1954, 2 sons, 3 daughters. *Education:* BA, Yeshiva University, 1953; MHL, Rabbi; DHL, Jewish Theological Seminary, 1958, 1968; PhD Communicative Disorders, Northwestern , 1974. *Publications:* The Other Child in Jewish Education, 1974; Sifre Deuteronomy, 1988; The Classical Midrash, 1993. *Contributions to:* Jewish Quarterly Review; Proceedings of the American Academy of Jewish Studies; Hebrew Union College Annual; Judaism; Conservative Judaism; Midstream. *Honours:* Jewish Book Council Award, 1988. *Membership:* Rabbinical Assembly of Israel - President. *Address:* 31 Adam Street, Jerusalem, Israel.

HAMMICK Georgina, b. 24 May 1939, Hampshire, England. m. 24 Oct 1961, 1 son, 2 daughters. *Education:* Educated boarding schools, England and Kenya, Studied Fine Art at Academie Julian, Paris, 1956-57; Salisbury Art School, 1957-59. *Publications:* People for Lunch, 1987; A Poetry Quintet (poems) 1976; Spoilt, short stories, 1992; editor, The Virago Book of Love and Loss, 1992. *Contributor to:* Critical Quarterly; The Listener; Woman's Journal; Fiction Magazine etc. *Membership:* The Writers' Guild. *Literary Agent:* Rachel Calder, Tessa Sayle Agency. *Address:* Bridgewalk House, Brixton Deverill, Warminster, Wiltshire BA12 7EJ, England.

HAMMOND Jane. *See:* **POLAND Dorothy Elizabeth Haywood.**

HAMMOND Ralph. *See:* **HAMMOND-INNES Ralph.**

HAMMOND Susan Montgomery, (Sue McCauley), b. 1 Dec 1941, New Zealand. Writer. m. Pat Hammond, 1979, 1 son, 1 daughter. *Appointments:* Writer in Residence, University of Auckland, 1986; University of Canterbury, 1993. *Publications:* Other Halves; Then Again; Bad Music. *Contributions to:* Numerous. *Honours:* Wattie Book of the Year Award; NZ Book Award; Mobil Award. *Memberships:* PEN. *Literary Agent:* Glenys Bean. *Address:* 59 Lawrence Street, Christchurch, New Zealand.

HAMMOND-INNES Ralph, (Ralph Hammond, Hammond Innes), b. 15 July 1913, Horsham, Sussex, England. Author. m. Dorothy Mary Lang, 21 Aug 1937 (dec 3 Feb 1989). *Education:* Feltonfleet and Cranbrook School. *Publications include:* Wreckers Must Breathe, 1940; The Trojan Horse, 1940; Attack Alarm, 1941; Dead and Alive, 1946; The Lonely Skier, 1947; The Killer Mine, 1947; Maddon's Rock, 1948; The Blue Ice, 1948; The White South (Book Society Choice) 1949; The Angry Mountain, 1950; Air Bridge, 1951; Campbell's Kingdom (Book Society Choice) 1952; The Strange Land, 1954; The Mary Deare (chosen by Literary Guild of America, Book Society Choice) 1956; The Land God Gave to Cain, 1958; Harvest of Journeys (Book Society Choice) 1959; The Doomed Oasis (chosen by Literary Guild of America, Book Society Choice) 1960; Atlantic Fury (Book Society Choice) 1962; Scandinavia, 1963; The Strode Venturer, 1965; Sea and Islands, (Book Society Choice) 1967; The Conquistadors (Book of the Month and Literary Guild) 1969; Levkas Man, 1971; Golden Soak, 1973; North star, 1974; The Big Footprints, 1977; The Last Voyage (Cook), 1978; Solomons Seal, 1980; The Black Tide, 1982; High Stand, 1985; Hammond Innes's East Anglia, 1986; Medusa, 1988; Isvik, 1991; Target Antartica, 1993. *Contributions to:* Fiction and travel articles in numerous journals. *Honours:* CBE 1978; Hon D Litt, Bristol University, 1985. *Memberships:* PEN; Society of

Authors. *Literary Agent:* Curtis Brown. *Address:* Ayres End, Kersey, Suffolk IP7 6EB, England.

HAMPSHIRE Susan, b. 12 May 1942. m. 1981. 1 son, 1 daughter dec. *Education:* Hampshire School, Knightsbridge. *Publications:* Susan's Story, 1981; The Maternal Instinct, 1984; Lucy Jane at the Ballet, 1985; Lucy Jane on Television, 1989; Trouble Free Gardening, 1989; Every Letter Counts, 1990; Lucy Jane and the Dancing Competition, 1991; Easy Gardening, 1992; Lucy Jane and the Russian Ballet, 1993. *Honours:* HonD, London University, 1984; Hon DLitt, St Andrew's University, 1986. *Memberships:* Royal Society of Authors. *Address:* c/o Chatto & Linnit Ltd, Prince of Wales Theatre, Coventry Street, London W1V 7FE, England.

HAMPSON Anne British. Writer of Historical/Romance/Gothic fiction. *Appointments:* Currently full-time writer; formerly cafe owner, sewing factory worker and teacher. *Publications include:* The Black Eagle, 1973; Dear Plutocrat, 1973; After Sundown, 1974; Stars over Sarawak, 1974; Fetters of Hate, 1974; Pride and Power, 1974; The Way of a Tyrant, 1974; Moon Without Stars, 1974; Not Far from Heaven, 1974; Two of a Kind, 1974; Autumn Twilight, 1975; Flame of Fate, 1975; Jonty in Love, 1975; Reap the Whirlwind, 1975; South of Capricorn, 1975; Sunset Cloud, 1976; Song of the Waves, 1976; Dangerous Friendship, 1976; Satan and the Nymph, 1976; A Man to be Feared, 1976; Isle at the Rainbow's End, 1976; Hills of Kalamata, 1976; Fire Meets Fire, 1976; Dear Benefactor, 1976; Call of the Outback, 1976; Call of the Veld, 1977; Harbour of Love, 1977; The Shadow Between, 1977; Sweet is the Web, 1977; Moon Dragon, 1978; To Tame a Vixen, 1978; Master of Forrestmead, 1978; Under Moonglow, 1978; For Love of a Pagan, 1978; Leaf in the Storm, 1978; Above Rubies, 1978; Fly Beyond the Sunset, 1978; Isle of Desire, 1978; South of the Moon, 1979; Bride for a Night, 1979; Chateau in the Palms, 1979; Coolibah Creek, 1979; A Rose for Lucifer, 1979; Temple of Dawn, 1979; Call of the Heathen, 1980; The Laird of Locharrun, 1980; Pagan Lover, 1980; The Dawn Steals Softly, 1980; Stormy Masquerade, 1980; Second Tomorrow, 1980; Man of the Outback, 1980; Where Eagles Nest, 1980; Payment in Full, 1980; Beloved Vagabond, 1981; Man Without a Heart, 1981; Shadow of Apollo, 1981; Love So Rare, 1983. *Address:* c/o Mills and Boon Ltd, 15-16 Brooks Mews, London W1A 1DR, England.

HAMPSON Norman, b. 8 Apr 1922, Leyland, Lancashire, England. Retired University Professor. m. Jacqueline Gardin, 22 Apr, 1948, 2 daughters. *Education:* Manchester Grammar School, 1932-40; University College Oxford, 1940-41, 1945-47. *Publications:* La Marine de L'an II, 1959; A Social History of the French Revolution, 1963; The Enlightenment, 1968; The Life and Opinions of Maximilien Robespierre, 1974; Will and Circumstance, 1983; Prelude to Terror, 1988; The First European Revolution, 1963; A Concise History of the French Revolution, 1975; Danton, 1978. *Contributions to:* Numerous journals and magazines. *Honour:* D Litt (Edinburgh) 1989. *Memberships:* Fellow of the British Academy; Fellow of the Royal Historical Society. *Address:* 305, Hull Road, York YO1 3LB, England.

HAMPTON Angeline Agnes, (A A Kelly), b. 28 Feb 1924, London, England. Writer. m. George Hughan Hampton, 31 Dec 1944, 1 son, 3 daughters. *Education:* BA (Ext) English Honours, University of London, 1965; Les- L, 1969, D.Es-L, 1973, University of Geneva, Switzerland. *Publications:* Liam O'Flaherty the Storyteller, 1976; Mary Lavin Quiet Rebel, 1980; Joseph Campbell, 1879-1944, Poet and Nationalist, 1988; Editor, The Pillars of the House, 1987; Editor, The Letters of Liam O'Flaherty (forthcoming). *Contributions to:* English Studies; Comparative Education; Eire, Ireland; Hibernia; Linen Hall Review; Geneva News and International Report; Christian. *Honours:* British Academy Grant, 1987. *Memberships:* International Association for the Study of Anglo-Irish Literature; Society of Authors; PEN International. *Literary Agent:*

Gregory & Radice, London. *Address:* Gate Cottage, Pilley Green, Lymington, Hampshire SO41 5QQ, England.

HAMPTON Christopher (James), b. 26 Jan 1946, Fayal, The Azores. Playwright. m. Laura de Holesch, 1971, 2 daughters. *Education:* Educated at schools in Aden and Alexandria, Egypt; Lancing College, Sussex 1959-63; BA, Modern Languages (French and German) 1968, MA, New College, Oxford. *Career:* Resident dramatist, Royal Court Theatre, London, 1968-70. *Publications include:* A Night of the Day of the Imprisoned Writer, with Ronald Harwood (produced London 1981); The Portage to San Cristobal of A H, adaptation of the novel by George Steiner (produced London and Hartford, Connecticut, 1982). London, Faber, 1983. Tales from Hollywood (produced Los Angeles, 1982; London 1983) London, Faber, 1983; Tartuffe; or, The Imposter, adaptation of the play by Moliere (produced London 1983) London, Faber, 1984; Les Liaisons Dangereuses, adaptation of the novel by Choderlos de Laclos (produced Stratford on Avon, 1985; London 1986; New York, 1987) London, Faber, 1985. Screenplays include: Beyond the Limit (The Honorary Consul) 1983; The Good Father, 1986; Various radio and television plays. *Literary Agent:* Margaret Ramsay Ltd, London. *Address:* 2 Kensington Park Gardens, London W11, England.

HAMPTON Christopher (Martin), b. 1929, United Kingdom. Author; Educator. *Appointments:* Teacher of English, Director of Studies, Shenker Institute, Rome, Italy, 1962-66; Lecturer in English, Davies' School of English, London, England, 1966-68; Lecturer in English, Polytechnic of Central London, 1968-; Poetry Adviser, Globe Playhouse Trust, 1972-. *Publications:* The Fantastic Brother, translation, 1961; Island of the Southern Sun, 1962; A Group Anthology (co-author), 1963; The Etruscans and the Survival of Etruria, US Edition The Etruscan Survival, 1969; Poems for Shakespeare (editor), 1972; An Exile's Italy, 1972; Poems for Shakespeare (editor), 1978; A Cornered Freedom, 1980; Socialism in a Crippled World, 1981; The Penguin Radical Reader, 1983. *Memberships:* Poetry Society, London, Council Member 1969-75. *Address:* c/o Penguin, 27 Wright's Lane, London W8 5TZ, England.

HAN Suyin, b. 12 Sept 1917, Sinyang Honan Province, China. Novelist; Medical Doctor. *Education:* Yenching University, Beijing, China; Brussels University, Belgium; London University, Royal Free Hospital, London. *Publications:* A Many Splendoured Thing, 1952; The Mountain is Young, 1958; The Crippled Tree, 1965; My House Has Two Doors, 1980; Till Morning Comes, 1982; A Share of Loving, 1987; Lhassa The Open City, 1977; The Enchantress, 1985; Wind in the Tower; Les Cent Fleurs; Chinese Painting Today; La Chine Aux Mille Visages (Photography); Chine Terre, Eau et Hommes (Photography); Han Suyin's China, 1987; Film Scripts: Man's Fate; The Marvellous Mongolian; Cast the Same Shadow, 1963. *Contributions include:* New York Times; Life Holiday; New Yorker; Medical Journals. *Honours:* Bancaralla Prize, Italy, 1956; McGill Beatty prize, Canada, 1968; Nutting Prize, Canada, 1980; Woman Reader Prize, Italy, 1983. *Address:* c/o Jonathan Cape, 32 Bedford Square, London WC1, England.

HANAMOTO Kingo, b. 21 Mar 1936, Japan. University Professor. m. Shizue Saitoh, 5 Jan 1962, 1 son, 1 daughter. *Education:* BA, 1959, MA 1962, PhD, 1965, Waseda University. *Appointments:* Lecturer, Rissho Women's Junior College, 1965; Assistant Professor, 1975, Professor, 1982, Waseda University. *Publications:* A Thematic Study of William Faulkner, 1970. *Contributions to:* Jinbun-Ronshu. *Memberships:* The Japan Society of English Usage and Style; The Japan Association of College English Teachers; The English Linguistic Society of Japan. *Address:* 1108 Kami- Kodanaka, Nakahara-ku, Kawasaki City 211, Japan.

HANBURY-TENISON Robin, b. 1936, United

Kingdom. Writer; Farmer. *Publications:* The Rough and the Smooth, exploration, 1969; A Question of Survival for the Indians of Brazil, 1973; A Pattern of Peoples: A Journey Among the Tribes of the Outer Indonesian Islands, 1975; Mulu: The Rain Forest, 1980; The Aborigines of the Amazon Rain Forest: The Yanomami, 1982; Worlds Apart autobiography, 1984; White Horses over France, 1985; A Ride Along the Great Wall, 1987; Fragile Eden: A Ride Through New Zealand, 1989; Spanish Pilgrimage: a Canter to St James, 1990; The Oxford Book of Exploration, 1993. *Honours:* OBE, 1981; DRE, 1992. *Memberships:* President, Survival International, 1969-; Council Member, Royal Geographical Society, 1968-82; Gold Medallist, Royal Geographical Society, 1979; Vice President, Royal Geographical Society, 1982-86. *Address:* Cabilla Manor, Cardinham, Bodmin, Cornwall PL30 4DW, England.

HANCOCK Beryl Lynette (Lyn), b. 5 Jan 1938, East Fremantle, Australia. Writer; Photographer; Lecturer; Teacher. *Education:* MA (Comm), BEd., Simon Fraser University, Canada; LRAM, England; LTCL, England; LSDA, Australia. *Publications:* There's a Seal in My Sleeping Bag; The Mighty Mackenzie; There's a Raccoon in My Parka; Love Affair with a Cougar; An Ape Came out of my Hatbox; Vanderhoof - A History; Tell Me, Grandmother; Northwest Territories: Canada's Last Frontier; Looking for the Wild; Alaska Highway: Road to Adventure, 1988. *Contributions include:* Canadian Geographic; BC Outdoors; Northwest Explorer; Above and Beyond; Toronto Star; West Australian; Pacific Yachting; Nature Canada; Up Here. *Honours:* Pacific Northwest Booksellers' Award, 1972; Francis Kortright Conservation Award for Excellence in Outdoor Writing, 1978, 1987; American Express Travel Writing Award, Canada. *Memberships:* Writers' Union of Canada (TWUC); Outdoor Writers of Canada; Friends of the Sea Otter; The Periodical Writers Association of Canada (PWAC); Canadian Nature Federation (CNF). *Literary Agent:* The Bukowsky Agency, Toronto. *Address:* 2457 Baker View Road, Mill Bay, British Columbia, Canada V0R 2P0.

HANCOCK Geoffrey White, b. 14 Apr 1946, New Westminster, Canada. Writer; Literary journalist. m. Gay Allison, 6 Aug 1983, Toronto. 1 daughter. *Education:* BFA 1973, MFA 1975, University of British Columbia. *Literary Appointments:* Editor in chief, Canadian Fiction magazine, 1975; Consulting editor, Canadian Author and Bookman, 1978; Fiction editor, Cross-Canada Writers Quarterly, 1980; Literary Consultant, CBC Radio, 1980. *Publications:* Magic Realism, 1980; Illusion: fables, fantasies and metafictions, 1983; Metavisions, 1983; Shoes and Shit: Stories for Pedestrians, 1984; Published in Canada, 1990; Invisible Fictions: Contemporary Stories from Quebec, 1987; Moving Off the Map: From Story to Fiction, 1986; Canadian Writers at Work: Interviews, 1987; Fast Travelling, 1990; Singularities, 1990. *Contributions to:* Toronto Star; Writer's Quarterly; Canadian Author and Bookman; Books in Canada; Canadian Forum. *Honour:* Fiona Mee Award for Literary Journalism, 1979. *Memberships:* Periodical Writers of Canada; Director, Canadian Magazine Publishers Association. *Address:* c/o Canadian Fiction Magazine, Box No 946 Station F, Toronto, Ontario M4Y 2N9, Canada.

HANCOCK SCHOBER Lyn, b. 5 Jan 1938, Western Australia. Writer; Photographer; Lecturer. m. (2) Frank Schober, 14 Sept 1991. *Publications include:* There's a Seal in my Sleeping Bag; Looking for the Wild; Love Affair with a Cougar; There's a Racoon in my Parka; Canada's Outback, Northwest Territories, Canada's Outback, 1993. *Address:* Box 244, Fort Simpson, Northwest Territories, Canada X0E 0N0.

HANDLEY Graham Roderick, b. 1926, British, Writer. *Appointments:* Head of English Department, Borehamwood Grammar School, Hertfordshire, 1957-62, and Hatfield School, Hertfordshire, 1962-67; Senior Lecturer, 1967-76 and Principal Lecturer in English, 1967-80, College of All Saints, Tottenham, London; Research Officer in English, Birbeck College, University of London, 1981-83. *Publications include:* An Informal History of the College of All Saints, 1978; Dickens' Little Dorrit, 1979; (with Stanley King) O'Casey's Shadow of a Gunman and The Plough and the Stars, 1980; (with Stanley King)Graham Greene's The Quiet American, 1980; (with Barbara handley)Wilkie Collins' The Woman in White, 1980; (ed)Short Stories on Sport, 1980; The Metaphysical Poets, 1981; (ed)Wuthering Heights, 1982; (ed)Daniel Deronda, by George Eliot, 1984; Thackeray's Vanity Fair, 1985; Harper Lee's To Kill a Mockingbird, 1985; (ed)The Mill on the Floss by George Eliot, 1985; Shakespeare's Macbeth, 1985; Shakespeare's Twelfth Night, 1985; George Eliot's Silas Marner, 1985; George Eliot's Middlemarch, 1985; Shakespeare's As You Like It, 1985; Hardy's Tess of the D'Urbervilles, 1986; Wycherley's The Country Wife, 1986; Chaucer's The Pardoner's Tale, 1986; Trollope's Barchester Towers, 1987; Hartley's The Go-Between, 1987; Hardy's The Woodlanders, 1987; Fielding's Tome Jones, 1987. *Address:* Glasgow Stud Farmhouse, Crews Hill, Enfield, Middlesex, England.

HANKIN Cherry Anne, b. 30 Sept 1937, Nelson, New Zealand. University Professor. m. John Charles Garrett, 18 May 1981. *Education:* MA, University of New Zealand, 1959; Ph.D, University of California, Berkeley, 1971. *Appointments:* The University of Canterbury, Christchurch, New Zealand, 1971-; Chief Fiction Judge, New Zealand Department of Internal Affairs Literary Awards, 1975; Judge, Katherine Mansfield Centennial Award, 1988. *Publications:* Katherine Mansfield and her Confessional Stories; The Letters of John Middleton Murry to Katherine Mansfield; Letters Between John Middleton Murry and Katherine Mansfield; Critical Essays on the New Zealand Novel; Life in a Young Colony: Selections from Early New Zealand Writing; Critical Essays on the New Zealand Short Story. *Contributions to:* Language as Theme in Janet Frame's, Owls Do Cry; New Zealand Women Writers: their attitudes to the Criticism of New Zealand Fiction; Fantasy and the Sense of an Ending in the Work of Katherine Mansfield. *Honours:* Advanced Graduate Travelling Fellowship in English, University of California, Berkeley, 1969. *Memberships:* NZ Institute of International Affairs, committee member; Board of Trustees, Christchurch Theatre Trust. *Address:* 5 Stratford Street, Christchurch 1, New Zealand.

HANKINSON Alan, b. 25 May 1926, Gatley, Cheshire, England. Freelance Writer. m. Roberta Lorna Gibson, 15 Dec 1951, div. 1985, 1 son. *Education:* Bolton School, 1936-43; MA History, Magdalen College, Oxford, 1949. *Publications:* The First Tigers, 1972; Camera on the Crags, 1975; The Mountain Men, 1977; Man of Wars, 1982; The Blue Box, 1983; The Regatta Men, 1988; A Century on the Crags, 1988; Coleridge Walks the Fells, 1991. *Contributions to:* Cumbria Life. *Honours:* BP Arts Journalism, runner up, 1991; Portico Prize, 1991; Cumbria Book of the Year, 1992. *Address:* 30 Skiddaw Street Keswick, Cumbria CA12 4BY, England.

HANKLA Cathy, b. 20 Mar 1958, Richlands, Virginia, USA. Professor. *Education:* MA, Hollins College, 1980; BA, Hollins College, 1982. *Appointments:* Hollins College, 1982-; Lecturer, Theatre Arts, 1982-83; Lecturer, English, 1983-86; Assistant Professor, 1986-; Associate Professor, 1993-; Washington & Lee University, 1989-91. *Publications:* A Blue Moon in Poor Water; Afterimages; Learning the Mother Tongue; Phenomena. *Contributions to:* College English; The World and I; Chicago Tribune Magazine. *Honours:* PEN Syndicated Fiction Prize. *Memberships:* Authors Guild; Associated Writing Program; Academy of American Poets; PEN America. *Address:* Box 9673, Hollins College, VA 24020, USA.

HANKLA (Bonnie) Susan, b. 22 Sept 1951, Roanoke, Virginia, USA. Writer; Teacher; Poet-in-the-Schools. m. Jack Glover, 22 Apr 1981. *Education:* BA, Hollins College; MA, Creative Writing, Brown University. *Appointments:* Fellow, Virginia Centre for the Creative Arts Sweet Briar, 1985. *Publications:* Mistral for Daddy and Van Gogh, 1976; I Am Running Home, 1979; Co-Editor, Sermons in Paint, 1985. *Contributions to:* Permanent Press; Artemis; Boys and Girls Grow Up; The Burning Deck Anthology; Film Journal; Gargoyle; Hollins Critic; Intro 5; Laurel Review; New Virginia Review; Open Places; Poetry Northwest; Richmond Arts Magazine; Richmond Quarterly Review; Southern Poetry Review; Fiction: Commonwealth; Michigan Quarterly Review; American Signatures. *Honours:* Nancy Thorpe Memorial Prize for Poetry, Hollins College, 1973; Finalist, Virginia Prize for Fiction, 1985; Finalist, Virginia Prize for Fiction, 1987. *Address:* 1109 West Avenue, Richmond, VA 23220, USA.

HANLEY Clifford, (Henry Calvin), b. 28 Oct 1922, Glasgow, Scotland. Writer. m. Anna Clark, 10 Jan 1948, 1 son, 2 daughters. *Education:* Eastbank Academy, Glasgow. *Appointment:* Professor of Creative Writing, York University, Toronto, 1979. *Publications include:* Dancing in the Streets, 1958; The Taste of Too Much, 1960; Nothing But the Best, 1964; Prissy, 1978; The Scots, 1980; Another Street Another dance, 1983. *Contributions to:* Numerous articles in magazines and journals. *Honour:* Hollywood Oscar for best foreign documentary, Seawards the Great Ships, of which Mr Hanley wrote the commentary, 1960. *Memberships:* Ours Club, Glasgow, President; PEN, Scottish President, 1975. *Address:* 36 Munro Road, Glasgow, Scotland.

HANLEY Gerald (Anthony), b. 1916, Ireland. Author; Playwright. *Publications:* Monsoon Victory, 1946; The Consul at Sunset, 1951; The Year of the Lion, 1954; Drinkers of Darkness, 1955; Without Love, 1957; The Journey Homeward, 1961; Gilligan's Last Elephant, 1962; A Voice from the Top (radio play), 1962; Gandhi (screenplay), 1964; The Blue Max (screenplay), 1966; See You in Yasukuni, 1970; Warriors and Strangers (travel), 1971; Noble Descents, 1982. *Address:* c/o Gillon Aitken, 17 S. Eaton Place, London, SW1W 9ER, England.

HANNAH Barry, b. 1942, United States of America. Author. *Appointments include:* Writer-in-Residence, Middlebury College, Vermont, 1974-75; Writer for Director Robert Altman, Hollywood, 1980; Writer-in-Residence, University of Iowa, Iowa City, 1981, University of Mississippi, Oxford, 1982, 1984, 1985, University of Montana, Missoula, 1982-83. *Publications:* Geronimo Rex (novel), 1972; Nightwatchmen (novel), 1973; Airships (short stories), 1978; Ray (novel), 1981; Black Butterfly (short stories), 1982; The Tennis Handsome (novel), 1983; Power and Light (novel), 1983; Captain Maximus (short stories), 1985.

HANNON Brian Owens, b. 20 Apr 1959, Florida, USA. Administrative Co-Ordinator of Contemporary Arts Center. *Education:* BA, Florida State University, 1982; MA, Creative Writing, University of Southern Mississippi, 1984. *Appointments:* Served, Advisory Panel, Louisiana Division of the Arts, Literature Panel, 1987. *Publication:* The Deep End of Dogtown, 1986. *Honours:* Story Dogs in Texas, nominated, Pushcart Prize XII, Best of the Small Presses. *Memberships:* President, Tallahassee Writer's Guild, 1982; Associated Writing Programmes. *Address:* 1231 Decatur St, 3rd Floor, New Orleans, LA 70116, USA.

HANNON Ezra. *See:* **LOMBINO Salvatore A.**

HANSEN Ann Natalie, b. 15 Sept 1927, Newark, Ohio, USA. Historian. *Education:* BA, College of St Mary of the Springs, 1948; MA, Ohio State University, 1950; BLitt, Somerville College, Oxford University, 1963.. *Appointments:* Editor, Martha Kinney Cooper Ohioana Library Association, 1951-53; Staff, The Columbus Dispatch, 1954-58. *Publications:* Westward the Winds : Being Some of the Main Currents of Life in Ohio 1788-1873, 1974; So You're Going Abroad, How to Do It, 1984; The English Origins of the "Mary & John" Passengers, 1985; The Dorchester Group: Puritanism

and Revolution, 1987; Etienne Francois Duc de Choseul, New Catholic Encyclopedia. *Contributions to:* American Neptune; New England Quarterly; Wisconsin Magazine of History; Timeline; Silver Magazine. *Honours:* Honourable Mention, Lyrics, National League of American Pen Women, 1976; Recipient, First Distinguished Alumni Award, Ohio Dominican College (formerly College of St Mary of the Springs), 1981. *Memberships:* National League of American Pen Women, Past President, Columbus Branch; English Speaking Union, Past President Columbus Branch. *Address:* 2341 Brixton Road, Columbus, OH 43221, USA.

HANSEN Joseph, (Rose Brock, James Colton, James Coulton), b. 1923, United States of America. Author. *Publications:* Lost on Twilight Road (as James Colton), 1964; Strange Marriage (as James Colton), 1965; The Corrupter and Other Stories (as James Colton), 1968; Known Homosexual (as James Colton), 1968 (as Stranger to Himself, 1978 and Pretty Boy Dead, 1984); Cocksure (as James Colton), 1969; Hang-Up (as James Colton), 1969; Gard (as James Colton), 1969; Fadeout (mystery), 1970; Tarn House (as Rose Brock), 1971; The Outward Side (as James Colton), 1971; Todd (as James Colton), 1971; Death Claims (mystery), 1973; Longleaf (as Rose Brock), 1974; Troublemaker (mystery), 1975; One Foot in the Boat (verse), 1977; The Man Everybody Was Afraid of (mystery), 1978; Skinflick (mystery), 1979; The Dog and Other Stories, 1979; A Smile in His Lifetime (novel), 1981; Gravedigger (mystery), 1982; Backtrack (mystery), 1982; Job's Year (novel), 1983; Brandsetter and Others (short stories), 1984; Steps Going Down (mystery), 1985; The Little Dog Laughed, 1986; Early Graves, 1987; Bohannon's Book (five mysteries), 1988; Obedience (mystery), 1988; The Boy Who Was Buried This Morning (mystery), 1990; A Country of Old Men (mystery), 1991. *Address:* 2638 Cullen Street, Los Angeles, CA 90034, USA.

HANSON Joan, b. 1938, United States of America. Children's Writer. *Publications:* The Monster's Nose Was Cold, 1971; Alfred Snood, 1972; I Don't Like Timmy, 1972; Synonyms, 1972; Antonyms, 1972; Homographs, 1972; More Synonyms, 1973; More Antonyms, 1973; More Homonyms, 1973; Homographic Homophones, 1973; I Won't Be Afraid, 1974; I'm Going to Run Away, 1976; Still More Homonyms, 1976; Sound Words, 1976; Similes, 1976; Plurals, 1979; More Sound Words, 1979; More Similes, 1979; Possessives, 1979; The Cat's Out of the Bag, 1986. *Address:* 15707 Afton Hills, Afton, MN 55001, USA.

HANSON William Stewart, b. 22 Jan 1950, Doncaster, Yorkshire, England. University Lecturer; Archaeologist. m. Lesley Macinnes. *Education:* BA Ancient History/Archaeology, 1972, PhD Archaeology, 1982, Manchester. *Publications:* Rome's North-West Frontier: The Antonine Wall, 1983; Agricola and the Conquest of the North, 1987; Scottish Archaeology: New Perceptions (co-ed), 1991. *Contributions to:* Major academic archaeological and antiquarian journals. *Memberships:* President, Council for Scottish Archaeology; Fellow, Societies of Antiquaries of London and Scotland; Executive Committee, Council for British Archaeology. *Address:* 4 Victoria Road, Stirling, Scotland.

HARAN Maeve Olivia, b. 12 Apr 1950, England. Writer. m. Alexander Graham, 2 daughters. *Education:* BA, Oxford University, 1969- 72. *Appointments:* Journalist, Television Producer, Executive, London Weekend Television. *Publications:* Having It All; Scences From The Sex War. *Contributions to:* She; New Woman; Womans Own. *Literary Agent:* Carole Blake, Blake Friedmann Limited. *Address:* c/o Blake Friedmann Limited, 37-41 Gower Street, London WC1E 6HH, England.

HARASYMIW Bohdan, b. 30 Aug 1936, Saskatchewan, Canada. Professor. m. Elaine Louise Verchomin, 14 May 1966. 1 son, 1 daughter. *Education:*

BA 1962; MA 1965; PhD 1970. *Publication:* Political Elite Recruitment in the Soviet Union, 1984. *Contributions to:* Canadian Journal of Political Science, Canadian Slavonic Press. *Memberships:* Canadian Association of Slavists, Secretary, Treasurer, 1975-78, President, 1980-81; American Association for the Advancement of Slavic Studies; American Political Science Association. *Address:* 4616- 148 Street, Edmonton, Alberta, Canada T6H 5N5.

HARBINSON Robert. *See:* **HARBINSON-BRYANS Robert.**

HARBINSON William Allen, b. 9 Sept 1941, Belfast, Northern Ireland. Writer. m. Ursula Elizabeth Mayer, 3 Nov 1969, 1 son, 1 daughter. *Education:* Belfast College of Technology, 1956-57; Liverpool College of Building, 1958-61. *Publications:* Genesis; Inception; Revelation; Otherworld; The Lodestone; Dream Maker; The Light of Eden; None But The Damned; Knock; Strykers Kingdom; Elvis Presley: An Illustrated Biography; Charles Bronson; George C Scott; Evita Peron. *Contributions to:* Books & Bookmen; The Lady; 19; Lookout; The Unexplained; Disc; Goldmine; Club International; Mayfair. *Memberships:* PEN; Society of Authors; Institute of Journalists; British Film Institute. *Literary Agent:* MBA, London; Writers House, New York. *Address:* 44 Rosebery Road, Muswell Hill, London N10 2LJ, England.

HARBINSON-BRYANS Robert, (Robin Bryans, Donald Cameron, Robert Harbinson), b. 1928, United Kingdom. Author. *Publications:* Gateway to the Khyber, 1959; Madeira, 1959; Summer Saga, 1960; No Surrender (as Robert Harbinson), 1960; Song of Erne (as R Harbinson), 1960; Up Spake the Cabin Boy (as R Harbinson), 1961; Danish Episode, 1961; Tattoo Lily (as R Harbinson), 1962; Fanfare for Brazil, 1962; The Protuge (as R Harbinson), 1963; The Azores, 1963; Ulster, 1964; Lucio, 1964; Malta and Gozo, 1966; The Field of Sighing (as Donald Cameron), 1966; Trinidad and Tobago, 1967; Faber Best True Adventure Stories (editor), 1967; Sons of El Dorado, 1968; Crete, 1969; Songs Out Of Oriel (as R Harbinson); The Dust Has Never Settled, 1992; Let The Petals Fall, 1993. *Address:* 58 Argyle Road, London W13 8AA, England.

HARBOTTLE Michael Neale, b. 7 Feb 1917, Littlehampton, Sussex, England. Army. m. (1) 1 Aug 1940, divorced 1 son, 1 daughter. (2) Eirwen Helen Simonds, 5 Aug 1972. *Publications:* The Impartial Soldier, 1970; Blue Berets, 1971; Kanves of Diamonds, 1976; The Thin Blue Line (co-author), 1974; The Peace Keppers Handbook (Collaborator), 1978; Ten Questions Answered, 1983; Reflections on Security in the Nuclear Age, 1988; What is Proper Soldiering, 1991. *Contributions to:* Building & Social Housing Foundation; Columbia University Press; Princeton University Press; Massachusetts Institute of Technology Press. *Honour:* OBE, 1960. *Address:* 9 West Street, Chipping Norton, Oxon OX7 5LH, England.

HARBURY Colin, b. 21 Dec 1922. Retired University Teacher (Professor of Economics). *Education:* BCom, London School of Economics; PhD, Wales. *Publications:* 7 books including First Principles of Economics (with R G Lipsey), 1988; Introduction to UK Economy (with R G Lipsey), 4th edition, 1993; Descriptive Economics (7th edition) 1987-; Intro to Economic Behaviour, 1986; Workbook in Introduction to Economics, 4th edition, 1986; Income and Wealth Inequality in Britain, 1980. *Contributions to:* Economic Journal; Journal Beh Economics; Oxford Economic Papers et alia. *Membership:* RES. *Address:* Bridge House, The Street, Pakenham, Suffolk IP31 2JU.

HARCOURT Geoffrey Colin, b. 27 June 1931, Australia. University Teacher. m. Joan Margaret Bartrop, 30 July 1955, 2 sons, 2 daughters. *Education:* B Com (Hons) 1954, M Com 1956, University of Melbourne; PhD, 1960, Litt D, Cambridge University,

1988. *Publications include:* Some Cambridge Controversies in the Theory of Capital, 1972, Italian edition 1973, Polish edition 1975, Spanish edition 1975, Japanese edition 1980; The Social Science Imperialists, Selected Essays G C Harcourt, Edited by Prue Kerr, 1982; Controversies in Political Economy, Selected Essays by G C Harcourt, Edited by O F Hamouda, 1986; (With R H Parker and G Whittington eds., Readings in the Concept and Measurement of Income, 2nd edition 1986; (Ed) Keynes and his Contemporaries. The Sixth and Centennial Keynes Seminar held in the University of Kent at Canterbury 1983, 1985; (Ed) The Microeconomic Foundations of Macroeconomics, 1977; On Political Economists and Modern Political Economy, Selected Essays of G C Harcourt, edited by Claudio Sardoni, 1992; Post-Keynesian Essays in Biography, Portraits of Twentieth Century Political Economists, 1993. *Contributor to:* Over 100 articles in learned journals and/or chapters in books. *Honours:* Fellow of the Academy of the Social Sciences in Australia (FASSA), 1971; Professor Emeritus, University of Adelaide, 1988; Reader in the History of Economic Theory, Cambridge University, 1990; President, Jesus College, Cambridge 1988-89, 1990-92. *Memberships:* Royal Economic Society, Council Member 1990; Economic Society of Australia and New Zealand, President 1974-77. *Address:* Jesus College, Cambridge CB5 8BL, England.

HARCOURT Palma, Author. *Publications:* Climate for Conspiracy, 1974; A Fair Exchange, 1975; Dance for Diplomats, 1976; At High Risk, 1977; Agents of Influence, 1978; A Sleep of Spies, 1979; Tomorrow's Treason, 1980; A Turn of Traitors, 1981; The Twisted Tree, 1982; Shadows of Doubt, 1983; The Distant Stranger, 1984; A Cloud of Doves, 1985; A Matter of Conscience, 1986; Limited Options, 1987; Clash of Loyalties, 1988; Cover for a Traitor, 1989; Double Deceit, 1990; The Reluctant Defector, 1991; Cue for Conspiracy, 1992; Bitter Betrayal, 1993. *Address:* c/o Murray Pollinger, Literary Agent, 222 Old Brompton Road, London SW5 0BZ.

HARDCASTLE Michael, (David Clerk), b. 6 Feb 1933, Huddersfield, England, Author. m. Barbara Ellis Shepherd, 30 Aug 1979, 4 daughters. *Appointment:* Literary Editor, Bristol Evening Post, 1960-65. *Publications:* Author of over 100 children's books, 1966-; One Kick, 1986; James and the TV Star, 1986; Mascot, 1987; Quake, 1988; The Green Machine, 1989; Walking the Goldfish, 1990; Penalty, 1990; Advantage Miss Jackson, 1991; Dog Bites Goalie, 1993. *Contributions to:* Numerous articles in magazines and journals. *Honour:* MBE, 1988. *Memberships:* Federation of Children's Book Groups, National Chair, 1989-90, Vice Chair, 1988-89, Newsletter Editor, 1985-89; Society of Authors. *Address:* 17 Molescroft Park, Beverley, East Yorkshire HU17 7EB, England.

HARDEN Blaine, b. 4 Apr 1952, Washington State, USA. Journalist. *Education:* BA Philosophy and Political Science, Gonzaga University, Spokane, WA, 1974; MA Journalism, Syracuse University, NY, 1976. *Appointments:* East Europe Correspondent, Washington Post, 1989-93; Africa Correspondent, Washington Post, 19885-89. *Publications:* Africa: Dispatches from a fragile continent, 1990. *Contributions to:* Washington Post. *Honours:* Livingston Award for Young Journalists, 1986; America Society for Newspaper Editors, Feature Writing, 1987; Pen's Martha Albrand Citation for First Book of non-fiction, 1991; Ernie Pyle Award for Human Interest Reporting, 1993. *Literary Agent:* Raphael Sagalyn. *Address:* c/o Foreign Desk, The Washington Post, 1150 15th St NW, Washington DC 20071, USA.

HARDIE Katherine Melissa (Melissa Hardie), b. 20 Apr 1939, Houston, Texas, USA. Writer; Publisher; Collector. m. (1) J W Woelfel, 1958, diss 1967, 2 daughters; (2) M C Hardie, 1974, diss 1984; (3) Philip Graham Budden, 8 Jan 1986. *Education:* BA English Language and Literature, Boston University, 1961; SRN, St Thomas Hospital, UK, 1969; PhD, Social Sciences, Nursing Sciences, Edinburgh University, 1980. *Appointments:* Publisher, The Patten Press, 1981-;

Director, The Jamieson Library of Women's History, 1986-. *Publications:* Understanding Ageing, Facing Common Family Problems, 1978; Nursing Auxiliaries in Health Care, 1978; In time and Place Lamorna: Life of E Lamorna Kerr, 1990; A Mere Interlude, Some Literary Visitors to Lyonnesse, 1992 (ed); Chapters in books such as Patterns in Western Civilisation, 1991. *Contributions to:* Social Work Today; Nursing Times; Nursing Mirror; Health and Social Services Journal. *Honours:* Winston Churchill Travelling Fellow, 1975. *Memberships:* Council of Management, Thomas Hardy Society; West Country Writers Association; Private Libraries Association. *Address:* The Old Post Office, Newmill, Penzance, Cornwall TR20 4XN, England.

HARDIE Melissa. *See:* **HARDIE Katherine Melissa.**

HARDIN Clement. *See:* **NEWTON Dwight Bennett.**

HARDING Christopher Philip, b. 4 Aug 1944, Somerset, England. Test Author. *Education:* SFPE, 1977; DPhE, 1978; FIBA, 1985; AAABI, 1986; MCC, 1988; PhD, 1988, World University; KtMSS, 1989. *Publications include:* Poetry published in: A First Anthology: 2200 Years under Capricorn, 1988; Of Penchants and Passions Terrors and Tears; American Poetry Anthology, 1989. *Honours:* Kay Award, ABI Research Association, 1986; Biography of the Year Award, 1987, 1988-89; Member of the Year Award, OMEGA Society. *Memberships:* International Society for Philosophical Enquiry; Mega Society; Omega Society; American Library Association; Classification Society of North America; The Psychometric Society; ABI Research Association. *Address:* PO Box 5271, Rockhampton Mail Centre, North Rockhampton, Queensland 4702, Australia.

HARDING Cole. *See:* **KRAUZER Steven M.**

HARDING George. *See:* **RAUBENHEIMER George H.**

HARDING Karl Gunnar, b. 11 June 1940, Sundsvalla, Sweden. Poet; Translator; Critic; Editor. m. Ann Charlotte Jending, September 1966, 1 son, 3 daughters. *Education:* BA, University of Uppsala, 1967. *Appointments:* Editor, FIB: Lyrikklabb and magazine, Lyrikvannen, 1971- 74; Poetry Critic, Expressen, daily paper, 1970-88; Editor, Artes Magazine, 1989. *Publications:* Blommor til James Dean, 1969; Ballander, 1975; Starnberger See, 1977; Stjarndykaren, 1987; Mitt Vinterland 1991; Vortex, 1990; Kreol, 1991. *Contributions to:* Evergrgreen Review; Ambit. *Honours:* Lifetime Scholarship, Swedish Writer's Union; Several Poetry Prizes. *Memberships:* Vice President, Swedish PEN, 1975-78; Swedish Writer's Union; Swedish Bunk Johnson Society. *Address:* Vasterled 206, S-16142, Bromma, Sweden.

HARDING Lee (John), b. 1937, Australia. Writer (Science Fiction, Children's Fiction. *Appointments:* Freelance Writer, SF Novels, Short Stories, Radio Plays; Freelance Photographer, 1953-70. *Publications:* The Fallen Spacemen (juvenile), 1973, 1980; A World of Shadows, 1975; Future Sanctuary, 1976; The Children of Atlantis (juvenile), 1976; The Frozen Sky (juvenile), 1976; Return to Tomorrow (juvenile), 1976; Beyond Tomorrow: An Anthology of Modern Science Fiction, 1976; The Altered I: An Encounter with Science Fiction, 1976, 1978; The Weeping Sky, 1977; Rooms of Paradise, 1978; Displaced Person (in United States of America as Misplaced Persons), 1979; The Web of Time (juvenile), 1979; Waiting for the End of the World (juvenile), 1983; Born a Number: Autobiography, 1986.

HARDING Matt. *See:* **FLOREN Lee.**

HARDING Matthew Whitman. *See:* **FLOREN Lee.**

HARDWICK Mollie, (Mary Atkinson), British. Writer; Author. *Appointments:*Announcer, 1943-46; Producer and Script Editor, Drama Department. *Publications include:* (with Michael Hardwick), The Sherlock Holmes Companion, 1962; (with M Hardwick), The Man Who Was Sherlock Holmes, 1964; (with M Hardwick), Four Sherlock Holmes Plays, 1964; (with M Hardwick), The Charles Dickens Companion, 1965; (compiler), Stories from Dickens, 1967; (with M Hardwick), Alfred Deller: A Singularity of Voice, 1968, 1980; (with M Hardwick), Writers' Houses, 1968; Emma, Lady Hamilton, 1969; (with M Hardwick), Dickens's England, 1970; (with M Hardwick), Plays from Dickens, 1970; Mrs Dizzy, 1972; (with M Hardwick), The Charles Dickens Encyclopedia, 1973; Upstairs, Downstairs: Sarah's Story, 1973; (with M Hardwick), Four More Sherlock Holmes Plays, 1973; Upstairs, Downstairs: The Years of Change, 1974; (with M Hardwick), The Bernard Shaw Companion, 1974; (with M Hardwick), The Charles Dickens Quiz Book, 1974; Upstairs, Downstairs: Mrs Bridges' Story, 1975; Upstairs, Downstairs: The War to End Wars, 1975; (with M Hardwick), The Upstairs, Downstairs Omnibus, 1975; World of Upstairs, Downstairs, 1976; Beauty's Daughter, 1976; The Duchess of Duke Street: The Golden Years, 1976; (with M Hardwick), The Turning, 1977; Charlie Is My Darling, 1977; The Atkinson Heritage, 1978; The Atkinson Heritage: Sisters in Love, 1979; Thomas and Sarah, 1979; Lovers Meeting, 1979; Willowood, 1980; The Atkinson Heritage: Dove's Nest, 1980; Juliet Bravo 1, 1980; Juliet Bravo 2, 1980; The Shakespeare Girl, 1983; By the Sword Divided, 1983; The Merrymaid, 1984; Girl With a Crystal Dove, 1985; Malice Domestic, 1986; Parson's Pleasure, 1987.

HARDY Barbara (Gladys), Writer (Literature); Lecturer. *Appointments:* Emeritus Professor, University of London, Bilkbeck College; Honorary Professor, University College of Wales, Swansea. *Publications:* The Novels of George Eliot: A Study in Form, 1959; Wuthering Heights, 1963; The Appropriate Form: An Essay on the Novel, 1964; Jane Eyre, 1964; Middlemarch: Critical Approaches to the Novel, 1967; Daniel Deronda, by George Eliot (ed), 1967; Charles Dickens: The Later Novels, 1968; Critical Essays on George Eliot, 1970; The Moral Art of Dickens, 1970; The Exposure of Luxury: Radical Themes in Thackeray, 1972; The Trumpet Major, by Thomas Hardy (ed), 1974; Tellers and Listeners: The Narrative Imagination, 1975; A Laodicean, by Hardy (ed), 1975; A Reading of Jane Austen, 1976; The Advantage of Lyric: Essays on Feeling in Poetry, 1976; Particularities: Readings in George Eliot, 1983; Forms of Feeling in Victorian Fiction, 1985; Narrators and Novelists, 1989. *Memberships:* Hon Member, MLA; Fellow, Welsh Academy; Vice-President, George Eliot Fellowship, Thomas Hardy Society. *Address:* Birkbeck College, Malet Street, London, WC1E 7HX, England.

HARDY John Philips, b. 1933, Australia. Writer (Literature). *Publications:* Johnson, Boswell and Their Circle: Essays Presented to Lawrence Fitzroy Powell (edited with others), 1965; The Political Writings of Dr. Johnson: A Selection, 1968; The History of Rasselas, Prince of Abissinia, 1968; Reinterpretations: Essays on Poems by Milton, Pope and Johnson, 1971; Johnson's Lives of the Poets: A Selection, 1971; Samuel Johnson: A Critical Study, 1979; co-editor, The Classical Temper in Western Europe, 1983; Jane Austen's Heroines: Intimacy in Human Relationships, 1984.

HARDY Laura. *See:* **HOLLAND Sheila.**

HARE David, b. 1947. Playwright. *Appointments Include:* Literary Manager, 1969-70, Resident Dramatist, 1970-71, Royal Court Theatre, London; Resident Dramatist, Nottingham Playhouse, 1973; Associate Director, National Theatre, 1984-. *Publications:* Slag, 1970; Lay By (with Others), 1971; The Great Exhibition, 1972; Brassneck (With Howard Brenton), 1974; Knuckle, 1974, 1978; Teeth 'n' Smiles, 1976; Fanshen, 1976; Licking Hitler, 1978; Plenty, 1978; Dreams of Leaving, 1980; Saigon, 1981; A Map of the World, 1982; The History Plays, 1984; Wetherby (screenplay), 1985; Pravda (with Howard Brenton), 1985; The Asian Plays, 1986; The Bay at Nice, 1986; Paris By Night (Screenplay), 1988; The Secret Rapture, 1988; Strapless (Screenplay), 1990; Racing Demon, 1990; Writing Lefthanded (collected essays), 1991; The Early Plays, 1991. *Address:* c/o Margaret Ramsay Ltd, 14a Goodwins Ct, St Martins Lane, London WC2.

HARFIELD Alan, b. 12 Dec 1926, Gosport, Hampshire, England. Freelance Author. m. June Bowler, 6 June 1966, 1 daughter. *Publications include:* A History of the Village of Chilmark, 1961; The Royal Brunei Malay Regiment, English and Malay, 1977; Headdress and Badges of the Royal Signals, 1982; British & Indian Armies in the East Indies, 1984; Blandford and the Military, 1984; Fort Canning Cemetary, 1981; Christian Cemeteries and Memorials in Malacca, 1984; Bencoolen - the Christian Cemetery and the Fort Marlborough Monuments, 1986; Christian Cemeteries of Penang and Perak, 1987; Early Cemeteries in Singapore, 1988; Pigeon to Packhorse, 1989; British and Indian Armies on the China Coast 1785-1985, 1990; Indian Army of the Empress 1861-1903, 1990. *Contributions to:* Crown Imperial; Hamilton's Medal Journal Despatch; The Military Chest; Military Historical Society Journal; Society for Army Research. *Honours:* Fellow, Royal Historical Society; Fellow, Company of Military Historians (of USA, Class of '89); Military, British Empire Medal, 1953; Most Blessed Order of the Setia Negara Brunei 3rd Class. *Memberships:* Society for Army Research; Royal Asiatic Society; Company of Military Historians; The Military Historical Society, Hon Editor 1978-90. *Address:* Plum Tree Cottage, Royston Place, Barton-on-Sea, Hampshire BH25 7AJ, England.

HARGITAI Peter, b. 28 Jan 1947, Budapest, Hungary. Writer. m. Dianne Kress, 24 July 1967, 1 son, 1 daughter. *Education:* MFA, University of Massachusetts, 1988. *Appointments:* Lecturer in English; University of Miami, 1980-85, University of Massachusetts, 1987-88; Professor and Writing Specialist, Florida International University, 1990-. *Publications:* Perched on Nothings Branch, 1986; Budapest to Bellevue, 1989; Budapesttol New Yorkig es tovabb ..., 1991; Magyat Taler, 1989; Farum: Ten Poets of the Western Reserve, 1976; Fodois Budget Zion, 1991. *Contributions to:* North Atlantic Review; Colorado Quarterly; Nimrod; College English; California Quarterly; Spirit; Prarie Schooner; Poetry East; Cornfield Review; Blue Unicorn. *Honours:* Academy of American Poets Translation Award, 1988; Fulbright Grant, 1988; Florida Arts Council Fellowship, 1990. *Memberships:* PEN International; Literary Network, New York. *Address:* Katalin Katai, Artisjus, Budapest, Hungary.

HARGRAVE Leonie. *See:* **DISCH Thomas Michael.**

HARI KUMAR Kanekal Nettakallappa, b. 11 Feb 1952, Bangalore, India. Editor in Chief, Deccan Heraly and Prajavani. m. Parul Shah, 12 Oct 1986, 1 son. *Education:* BA Hons, Economics, 1972; MA, History, 1975. *Contributions to:* Reports, editorials, articles in newspapers and magazines on current affairs with special reference to Indian politics and society. *Honours:* Karnataka State Rajyotsava Award for Journalism, 1985. *Memberships:* President, Karnataka Press Academy, Bangalore; Trustee, Research Institute for Newspaper Development Press Inst of India, Madras; Executive Committee, Editors Guild of India, New Delhi. *Address:* 66 Mahata Gandhi Road, Bangalore 560001, India.

HARING Firth. *See:* **FABEND Firth Haring.**

HARIS Petros. *See:* **MARMARIADES Yannis.**

HARKEY Ira Brown Jr, b. 1918, United States of America. Writer. *Appointments:* Reporter, Rewriter, Magazine Writer, New Orleans Times - Picayune, 1940-49, 1946-49; Editor, Pascagoula, Mississippi Chronicle,

1949-66. *Publications:* The Smell of Burning Crosses, 1967; Pioneer Bush Pilot: The Story of Noel Wien, 1974; Alton Ochsner (co-author), 1990. *Honour:* Pulitzer Prize for Distinguished Editorial Writing, 1963. *Address:* HCR 5, Box 574-540, Kerrville, TX 78028, USA.

HARKNETT Terry. *See:* **GILMAN George G.**

HARLAN Elizabeth, b. 11 Nov 1945, New York City, USA. Writer. m. Leonard Harlan, 27 Aug 1969, New York City. 2 sons. *Education:* BA, Barnard College, 1967; MPhil, Yale Graduate School, 1971; MFA, Columbia University, 1987. *Publications:* Footfalls, novel, 1982; Watershed, 1986. *Contributions to:* New York Times; Harpers. *Literary Agent:* Rosalie Siegel. *Address:* Windmill Farm, Cranbury, NJ 08512, USA.

HARLE Elizabeth. *See:* **ROBERTS Irene.**

HARLEMAN Ann, b. 28 Oct 1945, Youngstown, Ohio, USA. Writer; Educator. m. Bruce A Rosenberg, 20 June 1981. 1 daughter. *Education:* BA English Literature, Rutgers University, 1967; PhD Linguistics, Princeton University, 1972; MFA Creative Writing, Brown University, 1988. *Literary Appointments:* Assistant Professor of English, Rutgers University, 1973-74; Assistant Professor of English, 1974-79, Associate Professor of English, 1979-84, University of Washington; Visiting Professor of Rhetoric, Massachusetts Institute of Technology, 1984-86; Visiting Scholar, Programme in American Civilization, Brown University, 1986-. *Publications:* Graphic Representation of Models in Linguistic Theory, 1976; Ian Fleming: A Critical Biography, with Bruce A Rosenberg; Women's Stories, a translation of Zhenskije Rasskazy by Ruth Zernova, with Sam Driver. *Contributions to:* Numerous magazines and journals. *Honours:* Numerous awards and honours including: Guggenheim Fellowship, 1976; Fulbright Fellowship, 1980; Winner, Raymond Carver Contest, 1986; Runner-up, Nelson Algren Competition, Chicago Tribune, 1987; Finalist, PEN/Algren Competition, 1987 and 1988; Macdowell Colony Fellow, 1988; National Endowment for the Humanities (NEH) Fellowship, 1989; Rhode Island State Council on the Arts Fellowship, 1990; Rockefeller Foundation Grant; Winner, Iowa Short Fiction Prize, 1993. *Memberships:* Modern Language Association, Chair, General Linguistics Executive Committee; Linguistic Society of America; Poets & Writers Inc; American Literary Translators Association. *Address:* 55 Summit Avenue, Providence, RI 02906, USA.

HARLOW Robert Grant, b. 19 Nov 1923, Prince Rupert, BC, Canada. div, 4 daughters. *Education:* BA, University of BC, 1948; MFA, University of Iowa, 1950. *Appointments:* Head, Department of Creative Writing, University of BC, 1965-77; Professor, 1977-88; Emeritus, 1988-. *Publications:* Scann; Making Arrangements; Paul Nolan; Felice; The Saxophone Winter. *Contributions to:* Numerous Canadian Magazines & Newspapers. *Honours:* Canada Council Special Grant; Canada Special Senior Grant. *Membership:* Writers Union of Canada. *Literary Agent:* Linda McKnight. C9 Bluffway RR1, Mayne, BC, Canada V0N 2J0.

HARMON Maurice, b. 1930, Ireland. Associate Professor. *Appointments:* Teaching Fellow, Research Assistant, Harvard University, Cambridge, Massachusetts, USA, 1955-58; Instructor, Department of English, Lewis and Clark College, Portland, Oregon, 1958-61; Assistant Professor, Department of English, University of Notre Dame, Indiana, 1961-64; Lecturer in English, 1964-76, Associate Professor of Anglo-Irish Literature and Drama, 1976-, Professor Emeretus, 1990, University College, Dublin, Republic of Ireland; Editor, University Review, 1964-68; Editor, Irish University Review, 1970-. *Publications:* Sean O'Faolain: A Critical Introduction, 1967, 2nd Edition, 1985; Modern Irish Literature, 1967; Fenians and Fenianism (editor), essays, 1968; The Celtic Master (editor), essays, 1969; King Lear, by Shakespeare (editor), 1970; Romeo and Juliet, by Shakespeare (editor), 1970; J M Synge Centenary Papers 1971 (editor), 1971; King Richard II, by Shakespeare (editor), 1971; Coriolanus, by Shakespeare (editor), 1972; The Poetry of Thomas Kinsella, 1974; The Irish Novel in Our Times (edited with Patrick Rafroidi), 1976; Select Bibliography for the Study of Anglo-Irish Literature and Its Background, 1976; Richard Murphy: Poet of Two Traditions (editor), 1978; Irish Poetry after Yeats: Seven Poets (editor), 1979; Image and Illusion: Anglo-Irish Literature and Its Contexts (editor), 1979; A Short History of Anglo-Irish Literature from Its Origins to the Present (with Roger McHugh), 1982; The Irish Writer and the City (editor), 1985; James Joyce: the Centennial Symposium (with Morris Beja et al), 1986; Austin Clarke, A Critical Introduction, 1989. *Memberships:* Executive Committee, American Committee for Irish Studies; Vice-President, Royal Irish Academy; Chairman, International Association for the Study of Anglo-Irish Literature, 1979-82; President Irish National Committee, UNILEF, 1980-90. *Address:* 20 Sycamore Road, Mount Merrion, Blackrock, Co Dublin, Ireland.

HARMS Valerie, b. 17 July 1940, Chicago, Illinois, USA. Writer. m. Laurence Sheehan, 12 Jan 1962, div, 1 son, 1 daughter. *Education:* Smith College, 1962. *Publications:* The Inner Lover; Trying to Get to You; Celebration With Anais Nin; Unmasking; Frolics Dance; Stars In My Sky. *Contributions to:* Humanic Arts; Audubon Activist; Westport News; Pilgrimage; Anais Journal; MBI Inc; School Library Journal; Profiles; Womens Dairies; County Magazine; Connecticut Woman; New Age; Book Forum; Parents Choice; Womanspirit; Chrysalis; Ms Magazine; Camera 35; Harpers Magazine; New York Times; Mens Journal; Advocate. *Honours:* Un Award. *Memberships:* PEN; Authors Guild. *Address:* 10 Hyde Ridge, Weston, CT 06883, USA.

HARNESS Charles L(eonard), b. 1915, United States of America. Writer (Science Fiction/Fantasy, Earth Sciences, Marketing). *Publications:* Marketing Magnesite and Allied Products (with Nan C Jensen), 1943; Mining and Marketing of Barite (with F.M. Barsigian), 1946; Flight into Yesterday, 1953 (as The Paradox of Men, 1955, in United Kingdom with Dome Around America, 1964); The Rose (short stories), 1966; The Ring of Ritornel, 1968; Wolfhead, 1978; The Catalyst, 1980; Firebird, 1981; The Venetian Court, 1984; Redworld, 1986. *Address:* 6705 White Gate Road, Clarksville, MD 21029, USA.

HARONITIS G. Vassilios, b. 24 Aug 1933, Anogia Rethimnon, Greece. Teacher. m. Klio Koutoulaki, 26 Apr 1965, 1 son, 1 daughter. *Education:* Diploma, Pedagogical Academy of Heraklion, 1954; Univerity of Athens, 1964. *Appointment:* Spokesman, 6th Inernational Cretological Congress. *Publications:* I Kriti ton Thrilon, 1986; Drosostalides 1975; Kalimera stin Anixi, 1977; Ola gia ti Lefteria, 1980; Titivismata, 1975; Haroumenes Strofes, 1960; To Pedi mou ki Ego, 1979; Asterakia, 1978; Parthenios Peridis, 1966; Theatrikes Scholikes Parastasis, 1978; Nicon, 1978. *Contributions to:* Kretan Estia; We; Amalthia; Intellectual Deletion. *Honours:* Award, Group of Women Writers; 1st Laudation, Circle of Greek Childrens Books; 1st Award Greek Association of the Journalists and Writers of Tourism. *Memberships:* Literary Association of Hania Chrysostomos; Union of Intellectual Creators of Hania; Historical and Cultural Association of Crete; Teachers Association of Hania; Christian Union of Teachers. *Address:* Parodos Meletiou Piga 5, 73100 Hania, Crete, Greece.

HARPER Daniel. *See:* BROSSARD Chandler.

HARPER George Mills, b. 1914, United States of America. Writer (Literature). *Publications:* The Neoplatonism of William Blake, 1961; Selected Writings of Thomas Taylor the Platonist, 1969; Yeat's Golden Dawn, 1974; The Mingling of Heaven and Earth: Yeat's Theory of Theatre, 1975; Yeats and the Occult, 1976; Letters to W.B. Yeats, 2 vols, 1977; A Critical Edition of Yeat's A Vision, 1978; W.B. Yeats and W.T. Horton, 1980; The Making of Yeats A Vision, 1987. *Address:* Department of English, Florida State University, Tallahasse, FL 32306, USA.

HARPER Marjory-Ann Denoon, b. 6 Apr 1956, Blackpool, Lancashire, England. University Lecturer. m. Andrew J Shere, 22 Aug 1991. *Education:* MA Hons History, 1978, PhD, 1984, University of Aberdeen. *Publications:* Emigration from N E Scotland: Willing Exiles, 1988; Emigration from NE Scotland: Beyond the Broad Atlantic, 1988. *Contributions to:* History Today; British Journal of Canadian Studies; Northern Scotland; Southwestern Historical Quarterly; Aberdeen Leopard; The Weekend Scotsman; The Glasgow Herald; The Highlander. *Memberships:* Fellow, Royal Historical Society; British Association of Canadian Studies. *Address:* Department of History, University of Aberdeen, Old Aberdeen AB9 2UB, Scotland.

HARPER Michael S(teven), b. 1938, United States of America. Poet. *Publications:* Dear John, Dear Coltrance, 1970; History is Your Own Heartbeat, 1971; Photographs: Negatives: History as Apple Tree, 1972; Song: I Want a Witness, 1972; Debridement, 1973; Nightmare Begins Responsibility, 1974; Heartblow: Black Veils, 1974; Images of Kin: New and Selected Poems, 1977; Chant of Saints: A Gathering of Afro-American Literature, Art and Scholarship (with Robert B. Stepto), 1979; The Collected Poems of Sterling A. Brown, 1980; Rhode Island: Eight Poems, 1981; Healing Song for the Inner Ear, 1986. *Address:* Box 1852, Brown University, Providence, RI 02912, USA.

HARPER Stephen, b. 15 Sept 1924, Newport, Monmouthshire, England. Journalist. *Publications:* Novels: A Necessary End, 1975; Mirror Image, 1976; Live Till Tomorrow, 1977; Non-Fiction: Last Sunset, 1978; Miracle of Deliverance, 1985, 1987. *Membership:* Society of Authors. *Address:* Green Dene Lodge, Greene Dene, East Horsley, Surrey, England.

HARRINGTON Alan Stewart, b. 16 Jan 1919, Newton, Massachusetts, USA. Writer. m. (1) Virginia Hannah Luba Petrova, 28 Nov 1941; (2) Margaret Young, 18 Jan 1968; 2 sons, 1 daughter. *Education:* AB, English Literature, Harvard University, 1939. *Appointments:* Adjunct Lecturer, Creative Writing Programme, University of Arizona 1983-92; Lecturer in Creative Writing, University of Arizona Extended University, 1990-92. *Publications:* The Revelations of Dr Modesto; Life in the Crystal Palace, 1959; The Secret Swinger, 1966; The Immortalist, 1969; Psychopaths... , 1972; Love and Evil: From a Probation Officers Casebook, 1974; Paridise I, 1978; The White Rainbow, 1981. *Contributions to:* Harper's Atlantic; Saturday Review; The Nation; The New Republic; Playboy; Penthouse; The Chicago Review. *Memberships:* PEN: Author's Guild. President, *Address:* 2831 North Orlando Avenue, Tucson, AZ 85712, USA.

HARRIS Aurand, b. 1915, USA. Dramatist; Educator. *Appointments:* Drama Teacher, Gary Public Schools, Indiana, 1939-41; Head, Drama Department, William Woods College, Fulton, Missouri, 1942-45; Drama Teacher, Grace Church School, New York City, 1946-77; Teacher of Playwrighting and Directing: University of Texas, Austin, 1977-87, University of Kansas City, 1979, California State University, Northridge, 1981, Purdue University, Indiana University, Indianapolis, 1985; University of Hawaii, 1989; New York University, 1990. Summer theatre work: Cape May, New Jersey, 1946, Bennington, Vermont, 1947, Peaks Island, Maine, 1948, Harwich, Massachusetts, 1963-86, Cleveland Play House, Ohio, 1984-87; Akron Children's Theatre, Ohio, 1986-87. *Publications:* Plays for children: Pinocchio and the Fire-Eater, 1949; Once upon a Clothesline, 1944; The Doughnut Hole, 1947; The Moon Makes Three, 1947; Seven League Boots, 1947; Circus

Days, 1948, Revised Edition Circus in the Wind, 1960; Pinocchio and the Indians, 1949; Simple Simon: or Simon Big-Ears, 1952; Buffalo Bill, 1953; We Were Young That Year, 1954; The Plain Princess, 1954; The Flying Prince, 1958, 1985; Junket (No Dogs Allowed), 1959; The Brave Little Tailor, 1960; Pocahontas, 1961; Androcles and the Lion, 1964; Rags to Riches, 1965; The Comical Tragedy or Tragical Comedy of Punch and Judy, 1969; Just So Stories, 1971; Ming Lee and the Magic Tree, 1971; Steal Away Home, 1972; Peck's Bad Boy, 1973; Robin Goodfellow, 1974; Yankee Doodle, 1975; Star Spangled Minstrel, 1975; Six Plays for Children, 1977; A Toby Show, 1978; Plays Children Love: An Anthology (co-editor), 1979; The Arkansaw(sic) Bear, 1980; The Magician's Nephew, 1984; Ride a Blue Horse, 1986; Huck Finn's Story, 1988; Plays Children Love, Vol. 2: An Anthology, 1988; Monkey Magic, 1990. Adult plays: Ladies of the Mop, 1945; Madam Ada, 1948; And Never Been Kissed, 1950; Romancers, adaptations, 1978; Short Plays of Theatre Classics, an Anthology, 1991. *Address:* c/o Anchorage Press, Box 8067, New Orleans, LA 70182, USA.

HARRIS Christie Lucy, b. 21 Nov 1907, New Jersey, USA. Writer. m. Thomas A Harris, 13 Feb 1932, 3 sons, 2 daughters. *Education:* BC Teachers Diploma, 1924. *Publications to:* 19 Books inc. Once Upon A Totem; Ravens Cry; Secret in the Stlalakum Wild; Mouse Woman and the Vanished Princesses; The Trouble with Princesses; You Have to draw the Line Somewhere. *Contributions to:* Canadian Broadcasting Corporation; Juvenile Musical Fantasies; Adult Plays & Humour Sketches; Womens Talk; School Broadcasts; Adventure Serial for Children. *Honours include:* CACL Medal, Book of the Year for Children; BC Library Commissions Award; Vicky Metcalf Award; Canada Council Childrens Literature Prize; Order of Canada. *Memberships;* Writers Union of Canada; BC Federation of Writers; CANSCAIP. *Address:* 430 Arnold Avenue, Victoria, BC, Canada V8S 3M2.

HARRIS Christopher. *See:* FRY Christopher.

HARRIS Francis Charlton, b.25 Sept 1957, Brooklyn, New York, USA. *Education:* Master's of Education in Management, Cambridge College, Massachussets, USA, 1992. *Publications:* A Hard Road to Glory The History of the African: American Athlete, 1988, 1993. *Honours:* Contemporary Authors, Volume 130, 1990. *Memberships:* National Black MBA Association. *Address:* 140-35 Burden Crescent, Apt No. 207, Briarwood, NY 11435, USA.

HARRIS Frida Elizabeth Ruth, (Elizabeth Windrush), b. 4 June 1924, London, England. Teacher; Lecturer. *Education:* Teachers Certificate, 1966; FCP, 1970. *Publications:* Voyage to Freedom; Through the Fear Barrier; Out of Bondage, 1993. *Contributions to:* Hampshire County; Cotswold Life; The Lady. *Memberships:* The Society of Authors; society of Women Writers & Journalists; Fellowship of Christian Writers; West Country Writers Association. *Address:* 31 Western Avenue, Barton On Sea, New Milton, Hants, BH25 7PY, England.

HARRIS Harold, b. 20 Jan 1915, London, England. Publisher; Freelance Editor. m. Josephine Byford, 2 Apr 1941. *Education:* St Paul's School, London, 1928-32. *Appointments:* Literary Editor, London Evening Standard, 1957-62; Editorial Director, Hutchinson Publishing Group, 1962-80. *Contributions to:* Book reviews, articles, short stories in various newspapers and magazines. *Memberships:* Fellow, English Centre of International PEN; Society of Bookmen; Groucho Club. *Address:* 17 Brendon House, 3 Nottingham Place, London W1M 3FN, England.

HARRIS Jana N, b. 21 Sept 1947. Writer. m. Mark Allen Bothwell. *Education:* BS, University of Oregon, 1969; MA, San Francisco State University, 1972. *Appointments:* Poet-in-Residence, Alameda County Neighborhood Arts; Instructor, California Poetry in Schools; Instructor, Creative Writing, Modesto Junior College, California; Instructor, Creative Writing, New York University, 1980; Director, Writers in Performance, Manhatten Theatre Club, New York, 1981; Instructor, Creative Writing, University of Washington, 1986-. Pacific Luteran University, 1988. *Publications include:* This House that Rocks with Every Truck on the Road, 1976; Pin Money, 1977; The Clackamas, 1980; Alaska, novel, 1980; Who's That Pushy Bitch, 1981; Running Scared, 1981; Manhatten as a Second Language, 1982; The Sourlands, Poems by Jana Harris (Ontario Review Press, Princeton, NJ), 1989; Oh How Can I Keep On Singing, Voices of Pioneer Women, Poems, 1993. *Contributions to:* US Congressional Record; New Letters; Berkeley Monthly; Berkeley Poetry Review; Sunbury; Black Maria; Napa College Catalogue; East Bay Review; Performing Arts; San Francisco Bay Guardian; Room; Beatitudes. *Honours:* Berkeley Civic Arts Commemoration Grant 1974; Washington State Arts Council Fellowship, 1993. *Memberships:* Poets & Writers Incorporated; Poets & Writers, New Jersey; Feminist Writers Guild; Associated Writing Programs; Women's Salon; New Jersey State Arts Council, 1982; PEN; Associated Writing Programs; Poetry Society of America; National Book Critics Club. *Address:* 32814 120th St SE, Sultan, WA 98294, USA.

HARRIS Jocelyn Margaret, b. 10 Sept 1939, Dunedin, New Zealand. University Teacher. 1 son, 1 daughter. *Education:* MA (Otago), 1961; PhD (London), 1969. *Publications:* Editor, Samuel Richardson, Sir Charles Grandison, 1972; Samuel Richardson, 1987, 1989; Jane Austen's Art of Memory, 1989. *Contributions to:* Studies in Bibliography, Bulletin of Research in the Humanities, British Journal of 18th Century Studies, 18th Century Fiction. *Memberships:* President, Australian and South Pacific 18th Century Society, 1984-90. *Address:* English Department, University of Otago, Box 56, Dunedin, New Zealand.

HARRIS Kenneth, b. 11 Nov 1919. Journalist; Author; Business Executive. m. (1) Doris Young-Smith, 1949, (dec 1970). (2) Jocelyn Rymer, 1987. *Education:* Wadham College, Oxford. *Appointments:* War Service, R.A., 1940-45; Washington Correspondent, 1950-53, Associate Editor, 1976-, Director 1978, The Observer; Radio and TV work (mainly for BBC), 1957-; Chairman, George Outram Ltd., The Observer Group, 1981-. *Publications:* Travelling Tongues : Debating Across America, 1949; About Britain, 1967, Conversations, 1968; Life of Attlee, 1982; The Wildcatter: The Life of Robert O. Anderson; David Owen, 1987; Thatcher, 1988. *Address:* The Observer, Chelsea Bridge House, Queenstown Road, London, SW8, England.

HARRIS Larry Mark. *See:* HARRIS Laurence Mark.

HARRIS Laurence Mark, (Alfred Blake, Andrew Blake, Larry Mark Harris, Laurence M Janifer, Barbara Wilson), b. 1933, American, Writer of Crime; Suspense; Historical; Romance; Gothic; Science fiction; Fantasy. Professional comedian, 1957-; Editor, Scott-Meredeth, 1985-. *Appointments:* Pianist and arranger, New York City, 1950-59; Editor, Scott Meredith Literary Agency, New York City, 1952-57; Editor and art director, detective and science fiction magazines, 1953-57; Carnival fire-eater, 1960-69. *Publications include:* Slave Planet (science fiction), 1963; The Impossibles (as Mark Phillips), 1963; Supermind (as Mark Phillips), 1963; Faithful for 8 Hours (as Alfred Blake), 1963; Sex Swinger (as Andrew Blake), 1963; Love Hostess (as Andrew Blake), 1963; The Wonder War (science fiction), 1964; The Pleasure We Know (as Barbara Wilson), 1964; You Sane Men (science fiction), 1964, as Bloodworld, 1968; The Velvet Embrace (as Barbara Wilson), 1965; The Woman Without a Name, 1966; (ed), Master's Choice, 1966, as 18 Great Science Fiction Stories, 1971; The Final Fear, 1967; You Can't Escape, 1967; A Piece of Martin Cann (science fiction), 1968; (with S J Treibich), Target: Terra (science fiction), 1968; Impossible? (SF short fiction), 1968; (with S J Treibich), The High Sex (science fiction), 1969; (with S J Treibich), The Wagered

World (science fiction), 1969; (ghostwriter), Tracer! by Ed Goldfader, 1970; Power (science fiction), 1974; Survivor (science fiction), 1977; Knave in Hand, 1979; Reel, 1983. *Address:* c/o Doubleday, 245 Park Avenue, New York, NY 10167, USA.

HARRIS Lavina. *See:* **JOHNSTONE Norma.**

HARRIS Leonard R, b. 16 Oct 1922, New York City, USA. Newspaper Publishing Company Executive. m. Barbara Fox, 1949, 1 daughter. *Education:* Cornell University, 1939-42; BA, McGill University, 1947. *Appointments include:* Former Promotion Director, Editorial Board, Prentice Hall Inc; New Products Director, Bantam Books; Officer, Book Club Guild, Channel Press Inc; Consultant, new projects, NY Times; Vice President Editorial, Vice President Corporate Development, Encyclopaedia Britannica, Chicago, 1967-69; Executive Vice President, World Publishing Company, 1969-73; Director Projects Subsidiaries 1973-77, Director Corporate Development 1977-80, Director Corporate Relations & Public Affairs 1980-, New York Times. *Contributions to:* Numerous magazines. *Memberships include:* President, Jesse Owens Foundation; Boards, Encyclopaedia Britannica, NY Convention & Visitors Bureau, NYC Better Business Bureau. *Address:* 300 Central Park West, New York, NY 10024, USA.

HARRIS Marilyn, b. 1931, United States of America. Author. *Publications:* King's Ex (short stories), 1967; In the Midst of Earth, 1969; The Peppersalt Land (juvenile), 1970; The Runaway's Diary (juvenile), 1971; Hatter Fox, 1973; The Conjurers, 1974; Bledding Sorrow (romance), 1976; Eden series (romance): This Other Eden, 1977, The Prince of Eden, 1978, The Eden Passion, 1979, The Woman of Eden, 1980, Eden Rising, 1982; The Last Great Love, 1982; The Portent, 1982; The Diviner, 1984; Warrick, 1985. *Address:* 1846 Rolling Hills, Norman, OK 73069, USA.

HARRIS Marion Rose, b. 12 July 1925, Cardiff, South Wales. Author. m. Kenneth Mackenzie Harris, 23 Aug 1943. 2 sons, 1 daughter. *Appointments:* Freelance, 1953-63; Editor/Owner, Regional Feature Service, 1964-74; Editorial Controller, W Foulsham & Co Ltd, 1974-82; Authorship, 1982-. *Publications:* Soldiers' Wives, 1986; Officers Ladies, 1987; Nesta, 1988; Amelda, 1989; The Queen's Windsor, 1985; Captain of Her Heart, 1976; Just a Handsome Stranger, 1983; Sighing for the Moon (as Rose Glendowler), 1991; To Love and Love Again (as Rose Young), 1993. *Memberships:* Society of Authors; Romantic Novelists Association; The Welsh Academy. *Literary Agent:* International Scripts, 1 Norland Square, Holland Park, London W1 4PX, England. *Address:* Walpole Cottage, Long Drive, Burnham, Slough SL1 8AJ, England.

HARRIS Philip Robert, b. 1926, USA. Writer Administration/Management, Education. *Appointments Include:* Co- Author, Insight Series, Harcourt Brace Jovanovitch, New York City, 1957-65; Co-Author, Challenge Series, St. Paul Publishers, Allahabad, India, 1963. *Publications:* Regents Study Guide to State Scholarships, 1949, 1965; Offical Guide to Catholic Educational Institutions, 1959; co-author, It's Your Future, 1964; Impact (textbook), 1965; Organizational Dynamics, 1973; Effective Management of Change, 1976; Improving Management Communication Skills (with D Harris), 1978; Managing Cultural Differences (with R Moran), 1979, 1987, 1991; Innovations in Global Consultation (with G Malin), 1980; Managing Cultural Synergy (with R T Moran), 1982; New Worlds, New Ways, New Management, 1983; Global Strategies for Human Resource Development, 1984; Innovations in Global Consultation, 1984; Management in Transition, 1985; High Performance Leadership, 1987; Human Enterprise in Space, 1989; co-editor, Managing Cultural Differences Series, 1991-3; Editorial board, European Business Review, 1990-; co-author, Transcultural Leadership, (with G M Simons & C Vazquez) 1993; author, Human Enterprise in Space, 1992; co-author, Multicultural Management (with F

Elashmarie), 1993; Developing Global Organisations (with R T Moran and W G Stripp), 1993. *Address:* 2702 Costebelle Drive, La Jolla, CA 92037, USA.

HARRIS Rosemary (Jeanne), b. 1923. Author. *Appointments:* Formerly Picture Restorer, Reader for Metro-Goldwyn-Mayer, 1951-52; Children's Book Reviewer, The Times, London, 1970-73. *Publications:* The Summer-House (romance), 1956; Voyage to Cythera (romance), 1958; Venus with Sparrows (romance), 1961; All My Enemies (romance), 1967; The Nice Girl's Story (romance), 1968 (in United States of America as Nor Evil Dreams, 1974); The Moon in the Cloud, 1968; A Wicked Pack of Cards (romance), 1969; The Shadow on the Sun, 1970; The Seal-Singing, 1971; The Child in the Bamboo Grove, 1972; The Bright and Morning Star, 1972; The King's White Elephant, 1973; The Double Snare (romance), 1974; The Lotus and the Grail: Legends from East to West (abridged edition in United States of America as Sea Magic and Other Stories of Enchantment), 1974; The Flying Ship, 1975; The Little Dog of Fo, 1976; Three Candles for the Dark (romance), 1976; I Want to Be a Fish, 1977; A Quest for Orion, 1978; Beauty and the Beast (folklore), 1979; Green Finger House, 1980; Tower of the Stars, 1980; The Enchanted Horse, 1981; Janni's Stork, 1981; Zed, 1982; Summers of the Wild Rose, 1987; Editor, Poetry Anthology, Love and the Merry-Go-Round, 1988; Ticket to Freedom, 1991. *Honour:* Awarded Library Association Carnegie Medal for The Moon in the Cloud. *Address:* c/o A.P. Watt Limited, 20 John Street, London WC1N 2DR, England.

HARRIS Sheldon H, b. 1928, United States of America. Writer. *Publications:* Paul Cuffe: Black America and the African Return, 1972; Intervention: President Johnson's Decision to Intervene in Vietnam, 1972; The Prohibition Era: A Study of Law and Private Moralty, 1974; Blues Who's Who, 1979; I Remember (with Clyde Berhardt), 1986. *Address:* 17144 Nanette Street, Granada Hills, CA 91344, USA.

HARRIS William M, b. 20 Oct 1941, Richmond, Virginia, USA. College Professor. 3 daughters. *Education:* BSc Physics, Howard University, 1964; Master of Urban Planning, 1972, PhD Urban Planning, 1974, University of Washington. *Appointments:* Western Washington State University, 1973; Portland State , 1974-76; Adjunct, Virginia State University, 1979-85; Visiting, Cornell University, 1986; University of Virginia, 1976-92. *Publications:* Black Community Development, 1976; Perspectives of Black Studies, 1977; The Chesapeake Bay: A Black Perspective, 1982; Black Congretational Economic Development, 1985; A Conceptual Scheme for Analysis of the Social Planning Process, 1987; Race and Ethical Issues in the Academy, 1992; Mortgage Disclosure and Redlining in Central Virginia, 1992; What Else to look for when Choosing a College, 1990; Black Community Development in Charlotessville, 1982. *Contributions to:* Business and Professional Ethics Journal; College Digest; Thoughtlines; Urban League Review; Western Journal of Black Studies; Northwest Journal of African and Black American Studies; Journal of the National Technical Association; Housing and Society Journal; Negro Educational Review; Planning Magazine. *Honours:* NDEA Fellow, University of Washington, 1992-94; Visiting Associate, Battelle Seattle Research Centre, 1970-74; Danforth Associate, 1980; Ethics and Professions Workshop, 1989. *Memberships:* Association for the Study of Afro-American Life and History; American Planning Association; National Council for Black Studies. *Address:* Department of Urban and Environmental Planning, School of Architecture, Campbell Hall, University of Virginia, Charlottesville, VA 22903, USA.

HARRIS (Theodore) Wilson, b. 24 Mar 1921, New Amsterdam, British Guiana, Poet; Novelist. m. (1) Cecily Carew, 1945; (2) Margaret Whitaker, 1959. *Education:* Queen's College, Georgetown. *Appointments:* Government Surveyor in 1940's and Senior Surveyor, 1955-58, Government of British Guiana; moved to london in 1959; Visiting Lecturer, State University of New York, Buffalo, 1970; Writer-in-Residence, University of West Indies, Kingston, Jamaica; Scarborough College, University of Toronto, 1970, University of Newcastle, New South Wales, 1979; Commonwealth Fellow in Caribbean Literature, Leeds University, Yorkshire, 1971; Visiting Professor, University of Texas, Austin, 1972 and 1981-82, University of Mysore 1978, Yale University, New Haven, Connecticut, 1979; Regents Lecturer, University of California, Santa Cruz, 1983; Delegate to the National Identity Conference, Brisbane, 1968; to Unesco Symposium on Caribbean Literature, Cuba, 1968. *Publications include:* Verse: Fetish, 1951; The Well and the Land, 1952; Eternity to Season, 1954, revised edition 1979; Novels include: The Guyana Quartet, 1960-63; Tumatumari, 1968; Black Marsden, 1972; Companions of the Day and Night, 1975; Da Silva da Silva's Cultivated Wilderness, and Genesis of the Clowns, 1977; The Tree of the Sun, 1978; The Angel at the Gate, 1982; The Carnival Trilogy, 1985-90; Resurrection at Sorrow Hill, 1993-. Short stories and other publications. *Honours:* Arts Council grant, 1968, 1970; Guggenheim Fellowship 1973; Henfield Writing Fellowship, 1974; Southern Arts Writing Felowship, 1976; Premio Mundello Cinque Continenti, 1992; Mondello Prize, Five Continents, 1992. *Address:* c/o Faber and Faber Ltd, 3, Queen Square, London WC1N 3AU, England.

HARRISON Edward Hardy (Ted), b. 28 Aug 1926, Wingate, Co. Durham, England. Artist; Writer. m. Robina McNicol, 12 Nov 1960, 1 son. *Education:* Hartlepool College of Art, 1943-45, 1948-50; National Diploma, Design, Kings College, Newcastle-upon-Tyne, 1951; B.Ed, University of Alberta, Canada, 1977. *Publications:* Children of the Yukon, 1977; The Last Horizon, 1980; A Northern Alphabet, 1982; The Cremation of Sam McGee, by R. W. Service, Illustrator, 1986; The Blue Raven, Story for Television, 1987. *Honours:* Best Childrens Book, A Child Study Association of Canada, 1977; Choice Book, Childrens' Book Centre, Toronto, 1978; Ibby - Certificate of Honour for Illustration, 1984. *Memberships:* Writers Union of Canada; The Order of Canada; PEN, Canada. *Literary Agent:* Wingate Arts Ltd., 30-12th Avenue E, Whitehorse, Yukon, Canada Y1A 4J6. *Address:* 30-12th Avenue E. Whitehorse, Yukon Territory, Canada, Y1A 4J6.

HARRISON Elizabeth C, (Betty Cowanna, Elizabeth Headley), b. 24 June 1909, Camden, New Jersey. Author. m. (1) Edward Headley, 5 Aug 1940, (dec 1952), 1 son, (2) George Russell Harrison, 9 Mar 1957. *Education:* AB, 1929. *Publications include:* All juvenile or young adult books: Puppy Stakes, 1943; The Black Spaniel Mystery, 1945; Secret Passage, 1946; Going on Sixteen, 1946, Spurs for Suzanna, 1947; A Girl Can Dream, 1948; Paintbox Summer, 1949; Spring Comes Riding, 1950; Two's Company, 1951; Lasso Your Heart, 1952; Love, Laurie, 1953; Six on Easy Street, 1954; The Boy Next Door, 1956; Angel on Skis, 1957; Stars in Her Eyes, 1958; The Scarlet Sail, 1959; Accent on April, 1960; A Touch of Magic, 1961; Fancy Free, 1961; The First Book of Wildflowers, 1961; A Breath of Fresh Air, 1966; The First Book of Fiji, 1969; The First Book of Morocco, 1970; Mystery on Safari, 1971; Around the World Today Series; Connie Blair Mystery Series; The Surfer and the City Girl, 1981; Stamp Twice for Murder, 1981; Wanted: A Girl for the Horses, 1984; Romance on Trial, 1984; Banner Year, 1987. *Honours:* Honorary Phi Beta Kappa, Douglas College, 1935; Hall of Distinguished Alumni, Rutgers University, 1990. *Address:* 45 Pasture Lane, Bryn Mawr, PA 19010, USA.

HARRISON Elizabeth Fancourt, b. 12 Jan 1921, Watford, Hertfordshire, England. Author. *Publications include:* Coffee at Dobree's, 1965; The Physicians, 1966; The Revelston Affair, 1967; Corridors of Healing, 1968; Emergency Call, 1970; Accident Call, 1971; Ambulance Call, 1972; Surgeon's Call, 1973; On Call, 1974; Hospital Call, 1975; Dangerous Call, 1976; To Mend A Heart, 1977; Young Dr Goddard, 1978; A Doctor Called Caroline, 1979; A Surgeon Called Amanda, 1982; A Surgeon's Life, 1983; Marrying A Doctor, 1984;

Surgeon's Affair, 1985; A Surgeon at St Mark's, 1986; The Surgeon She Married, 1988. Paperback editions, throughout world. *Honours:* Runner-up 1970, short-listed 1971, 1972, 1973, major award, Romantic Novelists Association. *Memberships:* Editor, Overseas Secretary, Chest & Heart Association, 1947-72; Society of Authors; Vice-President, Romantic Novelists Association. *Literary Agent:* Mary Irvine. *Address:* 71 Wingfield Road, Kingston-on-Thames, Surrey KT2 5LR, England.

HARRISON Graham John, b. 5 Feb 1943, Lichfield, England. Lecturer. m. Sheila Gillen, 4 Jan 1988. *Education:* Erlangen University, 1965-66; Manchester University, BA, 1967; Leeds University, BA, 1971. *Appointments:* Freelance Translator, 1982-90. *Publications:* Balthasar Theo Drama; Balthasar Truth is Symphonic; Balthasar Prayer; Ratzinger The Feast of Faith; Brunner Our Christ; Brunner the Tyranny of Hate; Goetz to Live is to Think. *Memberships:* Society of Authors; German History Society; Irish Slavists Association. *Address:* Glendoon Cottage, Gortnacorrib, Letterkenny, County Donegal, Ireland.

HARRISON Jim, b. 1937, United States of America. Author; Poet. *Publications:* Plain Song, 1965; Locations, 1968; Walking, 1969; Outlyers and Ghazals, 1971; Wolf (novel), 1971; A Good Day to Die (novel), 1973; Letters to Yesenin, 1973; Farmer (novel), 1976; Legends of the fall (novel), 1979; Warlock (novel), 1981; New and Selected Poems, 1982; Natural World (with Diana Guest), 1983; Sundog (novel), 1984. *Address:* Box 120a, Lake Leelanau, MI 49653, USA.

HARRISON Kenneth (Cecil), b. 1915. Writer (Librarianship). *Appointments:* Chief Librarian, Hyde, 1939-47, Hove, 1947-50, Eastbourne, 1950-55, Hendon, 1958-61; City Librarian, Westminster, 1960-81; Editor, Library World, 1961-71; Advisory Editor, Libri, 1972-; President, Library Association, 1973-; President, 1972-75, Consultant Librarian, 1983-, Commonwealth Library Association. *Publications:* First Steps in Librarianship, 1950, 5th edition, 1980; Libraries in Scandinavia, 1961, 1969; Public Libraries Today, 1963; The Library and the Community, 1963, 3rd edition, 1976; Facts at Your Fingertips: Everyman's Guide to Reference Books, 1964; British Public Library Buildings, 1966; Libraries in Britain, 1969; Public Relations for Librarians, 1973, 1982; Prospects for British Librarianship, 1976; Public Library Policy, 1981. *Address:* 50 West Hill Way, London, N20 8QS, England.

HARRISON M(ichael) John, b. 1945. Writer (Science Fiction/Fantasy). *Appointments:* Literary Editor and Reviewer, New Worlds Magazine. *Publications:* The Committed Men, 1971; The Pastel City, 1971; The Centauri Device, 1974; The Machine in Shaft Ten and Other Stories, 1975; A Storm of Wings, 1980; In Viriconium, 1982; The Floating Gods, 1983; The Ice Monkey and Other Stories, 1983; Viriconium Nights, 1984; Climbed, 1989. *Address:* c/o Anthony Sheil Associates, 43 Doughty Street, London, WC1N 2LF, England.

HARRISON Philip Lewis, b. 30 Nov 1945, Lynn, Massachusetts, USA. Writer. m. Margaret Anne Taylor, 19 Aug 1977, 1 son, 1 daughter. *Education:* BSc, Brooklyn College, 1969. *Appointments:* Associate Editor, ASHRAE, New York City, 1967-69; Associate Editor, Railway Age, New York City, 1969-71; Associate Editor, Reader's Digest, New York City, 1971-72; Assistant Director, Worcester (Massachusetts) Science Centre Planetarium 1972-74; Associate Engineer/ Motion Pictures, Goodyear Aerospace, Arizona, 1974-76; Freelance writer, 1976-; Vice-President, Director of Marketing, H W & E Inc (Phoenix), 1991-. *Publications include:* Official Evan Mecham Joke Book, 1987; Ghost writer: Enjoying the Riches of Retirement, 1987; Ghost writer: Managing Mobile Home Parks, 1990; Ghost writer: The Property Management Business Handbook, 1990. *Contributions to:* Hundreds of articles for local, regional, national and international journals specializing in science and technology, business and economics. *Honours:* Gold Pen, PHX Gazette, 1986; Award of Excellence, IABC-Phoenix, 1986, 1988, 1989, 1991; Award of Merit, IABC Phoenix, 1990, 1992. *Memberships:* Publishing Editor, 1985-90, Editorial Consultant, 1990-93, Media and Public Relations Committee, 1991-92, Make-A-Wish Foundation; Arizona Museum of Science and Technology, 1989-93. *Address:* 3370 W Grandview Road, Phoenix, AZ 85023, USA.

HARRISON Raymond Vincent, b. 26 Oct 1928, Chorley, Lancashire, England. Inspector of Taxes; Financial Consultant. m. 7 Apr 1977. *Education:* Ormskirk Grammar School, 1939-47; BA, Hons, 1952, MA, 1954, Magdalene College, Cambridge. *Publications:* French Ordinary Murder, UK 1983, USA 1984; Death of an Honourable Member, UK 1984, USA 1985; Deathwatch, UK 1985, USA 1986; Death of a Dancing Lady, UK 1985, USA 1986; Counterfeit of Murder, UK 1986, USA 1987; A Season for Death, UK 1987, USA 1987; Harvest of Death, UK 1988, USA 1988; Tincture of Death, UK 1989, USA 1990; Sphere of Death, UK 1990, USA 1990; Patently Murder, UK 1991, USA 1992; Akin to Murder, UK 1992; Murder in Petticoat Square, UK 1993. *Address:* Forthill, Kinsale, Co Cork, Eire.

HARRISON Sarah, b. 1946. Author. *Appointment:* Journalist, IPC Magazines, London, 1969-72. *Publications:* The Flowers of the Field (novel), 1980; In Granny's garden (children's book), 1980; A Flower That's Free (novel), 1984; Hot Breath (novel), 1985; Laura from Lark Rise series (children's books), 4 vols, 1986; An Imperfect Lady (novel), 1987; Cold Feet (novel), 1989. *Address:* 17 Station Road, Steeple Morden, Royston, Hertfordshire, England.

HARRISON Sue. *See:* **HARRISON Sue Ann McHaney.**

HARRISON Sue Ann McHaney, (Sue Harrison), b. 29 Aug 1950, Lansing, Michigan, USA. Novelist. m. Neil Douglas Harrison, 22 Aug 1969, 1 son, 2 daughters (1 dec). *Education:* BA English, 1971. *Publications:* Mother Earth Father Sky, 1990; My Sister the Moon, 1992. *Literary Agent:* Rhoda Weyr. *Address:* PO Box 6, 18 Mile Road, Pickford, MI 49774, USA.

HARRISON Tony, b. 1937, England. *Publications:* Earthworks, 1964; Aikin Mata, (Co-author J Simmons), play, 1965; Newcastle Is Peru, 1969; The Loiners, 1970; Voortrekker, 1972; The Misanthrope, 1973; Poems of Palladas of Alexandria, (Editor and translator), 1973; Phaedra Britannica, play, 1975; Bow Down, music theatre, 1977; The Passion, play, 1977; The Bartered Bride, libretto, 1978; The School of Eloquence, poems, 1978; Oresteia, adaptation, 1981; Continuous, 1981; A Kumquat for John Keats, 1981; US Martial, 1981; Selected Poems, 1984, revised 1985; The Fire Gap, 1985; Dramatic Verse 1973-1985, 1985; The Mysteries, 1985; Theatre Works 1973-1985, 1986; The Trackers of Oxyrhynchus, 1990; A Cold Coming: Gulf War Poems, 1991; The Common Chorus, 1992; The Gaze of the Gorgon, 1992; Square Rounds, 1992; Black Daisies for the Bride, 1993. *Honour:* Whitbread Award, 1992. *Address:* c/o Peters, Fraser & Dunlop, The Chambers, Chelsea Harbour, Lots Road, SW10 0XF, England.

HARRISON Whit. *See:* **WHITTINGTON Harry.**

HARSENT David, b. 9 Dec 1942, Devonshire, England. Writer. m. (1) (Div), 2 sons, 1 daughter. m. (2) 1 daughter. *Appointments:* Bookseller in Aylesbury, then worked for the publishers Eyre Methuen, Arrow Books and Deutsch, all London; ran his own imprint, Enigma; Fiction Critic, Times Literary Supplement, London 1965-73 and Poetry Critic, Spectator, London 1970-73, now full-time writer. *Publications:* Verse: Tonight's Lover, 1968; A Violent Country, 1969; Ashridge, 1970; After Dark, 1973; Truce, 1973; Dreams

of the Dead, 1977; Mister Punch, 1984; Selected Poems, 1989. Novel: From an Inland Sea, 1985; Editor: New Poetry 7, 1981; Poetry Book Society Supplement, 1983; Savremena Britanska Poezija: selection of British & Irish poetry made for Writers' Union, Sarajevo (selection & introduction by David Harsent, translations by Mario Susko), 1988; Storybook Hero (limited edition), 1992; News From the Front, 1993. *Honours:* Eric Gregory Award, 1967; Cheltenham Festival prize, 1968; Arts Council Bursary, 1969, 1984; Faber Memorial Award, 1978; Society of Authors Travel Fellowship, 1989. *Address:* c/o Oxford University Press, Walton Street, Oxford OX2 6DP, England.

HART Benjamin, b. 18 Feb 1958, NY. Writer. *Education:* BA, Dartmouth College, 1982. *Appointments:* Political Analyst, Heritage Foundation (public policy research group), WA, 1983-. *Publication:* Poisoned Ivy, 1984. *Contributions to:* Articles to newspapers and magazines including National Review; Policy Review; Detroit News; Washington Post; USA Today.

HART John, b. 18 June 1948, Berkeley, California, USA. Writer. *Education:* AB, Princeton University, 1970. *Publications include:* Walking Softly in the Wilderness; the Climbers, poems; San Francisco's Wilderness Next Door; The New Book of California Tomorrow; Hiking the Great Basin; Hiking the Bigfoot Country. Booklength reports for various organizations, titles include: Endangered Harvest; Eroding Choices/Emerging Issues; California 2000; Democracy in the Space Age. *Contributions include:* Numerous publications, including: Sierra; Outside; Cry California; Poetry Letter; Interim; Southern Poetry Review; Works. *Honours include:* James D. Phelan Award, poetry, 1970; Merit award, California chapter, American Institute of Planners, 1972. Organizational awards: Outstanding Planning Programme Award, American Planning Association, 1982; Conservation Community Award, Natural Resources Council of America, 1987. *Memberships:* Secretary, Lawrence Hart Institute for Study of Excellence in Poetry; American Alpine Club; Sierra Club; Wilderness Society. *Address:* Box 556, San Anselmo, CA 94960, USA.

HART-DAVIS Duff, b. 1936. Author. *Appointments:* Feature Writer, 1972-76, Literary Editor, 1976-77, Assistant Editor, 1977-78, Sunday Telegraph, London; Country Columnist, Independent, 1986-. *Publications:* The Megacull, 1968; The Gold of St. Matthew (in United States of America as The Gold Trackers), 1968; Spider in the Morning, 1972; Ascension: The Story of a South Atlantic Island, 1972; Peter Fleming (biography), 1974; Monarchs of the Glen, 1978; The Heights of Rimring, 1980; Fighter Pilot (with C. Strong), 1981; Level Five, 1982; Fire Falcon, 1984; The Man-Eater of Jassapur, 1985; Hitler's Games, 1986; Armada, 1988; The House the Berrys Built, 1990; Horses at War, 1991; Country Matters, 1991; Wildings: The Secret Garden of Eileen Soper, 1992; Further Country Matters, 1993. *Address:* Owlpen Farm, Uley, Dursley, Gloucestershire, England.

HART-DAVIS Rupert (Charles) Sir, b. 28 Aug 1907. Author; Editor; Former Publisher. m. (1) Peggy Ashcroft, 1929, (div), (2) Catherine Comfort Borden-Turner, 1933, (div), (3) Winifred Ruth, 1964, (dec 1967), (4) June Clifford, 1968. 2 sons, 1 daughter. *Education:* Eton; Balliol College, Oxford; Student, Old Vic, 1927-28; DLitt Reading University, 1964; DLitt Durham University, 1981. *Appointments:* Actor, Lyric Theatre, Hammersmith, 1928-29; Office Boy, William Heinemann Ltd., 1929-31; Manager, book Society, 1932; Director, Jonathan Cape Ltd., 1933-40; Served in Coldstream Guards, 1940-45; Founder, Rupert Hart-Davis Ltd., 1946, Director 1946-64; Vice President, Committee of the London Library, 1971-, Chairman 1957-69. *Publications:* Hugh Walpole, a Biography, 1952; The Arms of Time, a memoir, 1979; Editor: the Essential Neville Cardus, 1949; E.V. Lucas: Cricket all his Life, 1950; George Moore: Letters to Lady Cunard, 1957; The Letters of Oscar Wilde, 1962; Max Beerbohm: Letters to Reggie Turner, 1964; Max Beerbohm: More

Theatres, 1969; Max Beerbohm: Last Theatres, 1970; Max Beerbohm: A Peep into the Past, 1972; A Catalogue of the Caricatures of Max Beerbohm, 1972; The Autobiography of Arthur Ransome, 1976; William Plomer: Elecric Delights, 1978; The Lyttelton Hart-Davis Letters, volume 1, 1978, volume II, 1979, volume III, 1981, volume IV, 1982, volume V, 1983, volume VI, 1984; Selected Letters of Oscar Wilde, 1979; Two Men of Letters, 1979; Siegfried Sassoon Diaries: 1920- 1922, 1981, 1915-1918, 1983, 1923-25, 1985; The War Poems of Siegried Sassoon, 1983; A Beggar in Purple: Commonplace Book, 1983; More Letters of Oscar Wilde, 1985; Siegfried Sassoon: letters to Max Beerbohm, 1988; Letters of Max Berrbohm, 1982-1956, 1989; The Power of Chance, 1991. *Address:* The Old Rectory, Marske-in-Swaledale, Richmond, North Yorkshire, DL11 7NA, England.

HARTCUP Adeline, b. 26 Apr 1918, Isle of Wight, England. Writer. m. John Hartcup, 11 Feb 1950, 2 sons. *Education:* MA, Oxon, Classics and English Literature. *Appointments:* Editorial Staff, Times Educational Supplement; Honorary Press Officer, Kent Voluntary Service Council. *Publications:* Angelica, 1954; Morning Faces, 1963; Below Stairs in the Great Country Houses, 1980; Children of the Great Country Houses, 1982; Love and Marriage in the Great Country Houses, 1984; Spello: Life Today in Ancient Umbria, 1985. *Contributions to:* Times Educational Supplement; Harpers; Queen; Times Higher Educational Supplement; etc. *Address:* Swanton Court, Sevington, Ashford, Kent, TN24 0LL, England.

HARTE Marjorie. See: McEVOY Marjorie.

HARTFELD Hermann, b.14 Nov 1942, Yagodnoye, USSR. Pastor; Instructor; Author. m. 16 July 1970. *Education:* English Language, University of London, 1978-7; MMin, Winnipeg Theological Seminary, 1980-81; MDiv, Mennonite Brethren Biblical Seminary, 1981-83; DTheol, Facultatis Theological Reformatorie Brussels, 1985-87; PhD, Pacific Western University, 1988-89. *Publications include:* Faith Despite KGB, 1976; Irina, Wuppertal: Brockhaus, 1980; Faith Despite KGB; Evangelistische Strategie; Homosexualitat in Kontext von Bible, Theologie und Seelsroge. *Contributions to:* Fresno-Winnipeg; Sword and Trowel; Christian Herald; Transormation. *Honours:* Gold Medallion Award, Evangelical Christian Publishers Association, 1981; Plaque of Recognition, Alliance for Democracy and Morality, Manila, Philippines, 1989. *Literary Agent:* Winfried Bluth. *Address:* Freiherr-vom-Stein Str 30, 4132 Kamp-Lintfort, Germany.

HARTILL Rosemary Jane, b. 11 Aug 1949, Oswestry, England. Writer; Broadcaster. *Education:* BA Hons, English, University of Bristol, 1970. *Appointments:* Presenter of BBC World Service's Meridian Books Programme, 1990-92; Presenter of Writers Revealed (Radio 4, 18 part, BBC Series); and Immortal Diamonds (Radio 4, 12 part, Series on Poets). *Publications:* Writers Revealed, 1989; In Perspective, 1988; Wild Animals, 1976; Emily Brontë: Poems (editor), 1973. *Honours:* Nominated for Sony Award Best Arts Radio Feature, 1990. *Membership* National Union of Journalists. *Literary Agent:* Sue Freathy, Curtis Brown/John Farquharson. *Address:* Old Post Office, 24 Eglingham Village, Alnwick, Northumberland NE66 2TX, England.

HARTLAND Michael, b. 1941, Cornwall, England. Writer. m. 1975, 2 daughters. *Education:* Christs College, Cambridge, 1960-63. *Appointments:* British Diplomatic Service, 1963-78; United Nations, 1978-83; Full-time Writer, 1983-; Regular Book Reviewer and Feature Writer: The Sunday Times, The Times, Today, Western Morning News; Resident Thriller Critic The Times, 1989-90; Chairman, Wade Hartland Films Limited; Radio and television include: Sonja's Report, (ITV Channel 3), 1990; Masterspy, interviews with Oleg Gordievsky (BBC Radio 4), 1991. *Publications:* Down Among The Dead men; Seven Steps to Treason (dramatzed for BBC Radio 4, 1990); The Third Betrayal; Frontier of Fear; The Year of the Scorpion (adapted as

feature film, 1993).*Honours:* Fellow of the Royal Society of Arts; Hon Fellow, University of Exeter; South West Arts Literary Award. *Memberships:* Crime Writers Association; Mystery Writers of America; Society of Authors. *Address:* Cotte Barton, Branscombe, Devon, EX12 3BH, England.

HARTLE Mary Jean McCoy, b. 21 Jan 1938, Montrose, South Dakota, USA. Secretary; Housewife. m. Kenneth A. Hartle, 28 Dec 1957, 3 sons, 1 daughter. *Education:* Office Procedures, 1978, Medical Secretary Course, 1984-85, Writers Seminar, Oct 1986, Sioux Falls Community College, South Dakota. *Publications:* Humboldt Centennial Book - The Pioneers, 1989; Book on handicapped children and poetry book, in progress; Poems in anthologies: Spring's Rebirth, 1986; The Challenger Crew, 1987; A Doll Is A Special One, 1988; Liberty - The Spirit of America, 1988; Our Lady Liberty (as Mary J McCoy), 1988; Life's Keepsakes, 1988; Work and Prayer, 1989; Apple Orchard Memories, 1989; The Party Line, 1989; The Founding of the Constitution - To Our Modern Day (Phillip Morris Writers Competition entry), 1986. *Contributions to:* South Dakota Pasque Petals; Phillip Morris Magazine; Montrose Herald; Humboldt Journal. *Honours:* Honourable Mention, Golden Poet Award, Silver Poet Award for Our Lady Liberty and Liberty - The Spirit of America, Great American Poetry Anthology, 1988; Golden Poet, World of Poetry, 1991. *Memberships:* South Dakota State Poetry Society; Pasque Petals; National Federation of State Poetry Societies; Former Member, Officers Wives Clubs: Randolph AF Base, San Antonio, Texas, Reese AF Base, Texas, Moody AF Base, Georgia, Ramstein AF Base, West Germany; Past Secretary, Past Treasurer, Catholic Daughters of Americas; Sioux Vocational Auxiliary for the Handicapped; St Ann's Altar Society, *Address:* 412 S Jefferson, Humboldt, SD 57035, USA.

HARTLEY Jean, b. 27 Apr 1933, Hull, England. English Lecturer. m. Aug 1953, 2 daughters. *Education:* BA Hons, English Language and Literature, 1972; MA Victorian Thought and Literature, 1973. *Appointments:* Joint Founder and Proprietor, Listen Magazine, 1954; The Marvell Press, 1955 and Listen Records. *Publications:* Philip Larkin, The Marvell Press and Me, 1989. *Contributions to:* Bete Noire, short stories and articles. *Literary Agent:* A M Heath & Co Ltd. *Address:* 82 Victoria Avenue, Hull HU5 3DS, England.

HARTMAN Geoffrey H, b. 1929 Germany. Writer. *Publications:* The Unmediated Vision: A Interpretation of Wordsworth, Hopkins, Rilke and Valery, 1954; Andre Malraux, 1960; Wordsworth's Poetry 1787-1814, 1964; Hopkins: A Collection of Critical Essays, 1966; Beyond Formalism: Literary Essays 1958-1970, 1970; Selected Poetry and Prose of William Wordsworth, 1970; New Perspectives on Coleridge and Wordsworth, 1972; Romanticism: Vistas, Instances, Continuities, 1973; The Fate of Reading and Other Essays, 1975; Criticism in the Wilderness, 1980; Saving the Text, 1981; Easy Pieces, 1985; Midrash and Literature, 1986; Bitburg in Moral and Political Perspective, 1986; The Unremarkable Wordsworth, 1987. *Address:* 260 Everit Street, New Haven, CT 06511, USA.

HARTMAN Jan, b. 23 May 1936, Stockholm, Sweden. Writer-Dramatist. m. 9 June 1960, 2 daughters. *Education:* Phillips Andover Academy, 1956; BA, Harvard College, 1960. *Literary Appointments:* Resident Playwright, The Theatre of The Living Arts, Philadelphia, 1964-65; Instructor in Theatre, 1969; Teacher of Political Theatre, 1975; New School; Contributing Editor, Religious Theatre Magazine; Director, Founder: Playwrights Theatre Project, Circle in the Square, 1967-69, and Eleventh Hour Productions 1977; Resident Playwright, Theatre St. Clements, 1977-78; Visiting Professor, Syracuse University, Fall Semester, 1985-86; Resident Playwright, Co-artistic Director, The Performance Theatre Centre; Professor of Dramatic Writing and Shakespeare, New York University, 1981-. *Publications:* Television: Felling Good; Alfred Running Wild; The Long Conversation; A Memory of Autumn; The Survivor; Alexander, 1963-75; Board

For Freedom; With All Deliberate Speed; Song of Myself 1976; Fellow The North Star; Hewitt's Just Different; The Great Wallendas, 1977-78; His First Love; Second Sight, 1978-79; The Herman Graebe Story; The Late Great Me; Ethics In The Professions; The Maimie Papers, 1979-80; A Lasting Love, 1980-81; Killing The Goose; Stix and Stones; The Next War, 1982-83; The Manor and The Estate, 1983-84; The Campbells; Muir: Earth, Planet, Universe, 1984-85; Pigeon Feathers, 1985-86; The Presidents; Ganesh; The Story of Mother Teresa of Calcutta; A Winter Visitor; The James Family, 1986-87; The Last Weapon; Les Egare's, 1987-88. Theatre Productions: Samuel Hoopes Reading From His Own Works 1963; The Shadow of The Valley, 1964; Legend of Daniel Boone, 1986; Antique Masks, 1966; Freeman, Freeman; Final Solutions, 1968; Fragment of A Last Judgment, 1967; The American War Crimes Trial, 1973; Flight 981, 1977; Abelard and Heloise; To The Ninth Circle, 1983; K, 1987. Feature Films - Screenplays: Prior to 1983: Hail to the Chief; The Kastner Affair; Emily; The Cursed Medallion; Jelly Roll; The Bauhaus, 1982-83. Publications: Samuel Hoopes Reading From His Own Works, 1978; Political Theatre, An Anthology; Elements of Film Writing; Joshua; The Shadow of The Valley; 4 Contemporary Religious Plays; Flatboatment; Every Year A St Carnival. Contributions to: Articles in The Dramatists Guild Quarterly. Honours: Many Awards and Fellowships given in recognition of work commissioned. Memberships include: PEN; Writers Guild of America; Eugene O'Neill memorial Theatre Foundation; American National Theatre and Academy; Dramatists Guild; Chairman Committee On Censorship WGA, East. Address: c/o Robert A. Freeman Dramatic Agency Inc., 1501 Broadway, Suite 2310, New York, NY 10036, USA.

HARTMANN Michael John, b. 1944. Author; Playwright. Publications: Pepper in a Milkshake (play), 1966; Feather in a Battered Cap (play), 1972; Game for Vultures, 1975; Leap for the Sun, 1976; Shadow of the Leopard, 1978; Days of Thunder, 1980; Web of Dragons, 1987. Address: P.O. Box 19, Harare, Zimbabwe.

HARTMANN Betsy. See: **HARTMANN Elizabeth.**

HARTMANN Elizabeth, (Betsy Hartmann), b. 20 July 1951, Princeton, NJ. Lecturer; Writer. m. James Kenneth Boyce, 17 Nov 1976, 2 sons. Education: BA (magna cum laude), Yale University, 1974. Appointments: Project Manager at Economic Development Bureau, New Haven, CT; Visiting Lecturer in Economics at Yale University; Public speaker on issues of international development and reproductive rights; Fellow of Institute for Food and Development Policy, 1978-79; Writer, 1980-. Publications: Needless Hunger: Voices From a Bangladesh Village (with James Boyce), 1979; A Quiet Violence: View From a Bangladesh Village (with James Boyce), 1983; Food, Saris and Sterilization: Population Control in Bangladesh (with Hilary Standing), 1985; Reproductive Rights and Wrongs: The Global Politics of Population Control and Contraceptive Choice, 1987. Contributions to: Magazines and newspapers in the United States and abroad, including Nation, New Internationalist, South. Honours: Howland Fellowship, 1974. Memberships: Women's Global Network on Reproductive Rights; Bangladesh International Action Group; National Women's Health Network; National Writers Union; New England Women and Development Group.

HARTNETT David William, b. 4 Sept 1952, London, England. Writer. m. Margaret R N Thomas, 26 Aug 1976, 1 son, 1 daughter. Education: Scholarship to read English Language and Literature at Exeter College, Oxford, 1971, First Class Honour Moderations 1973, First Class BA in English Language and Literature, 1975, MA 1981, D Phil 1987. Literary Appointment: Editor (with Michael O'Neill and Gareth Reeves) of the literary magazine Poetry Durham (founded 1982). Publications: Collections of poetry: A Signalled Love, 1985; House of Moon 1988; Dark Ages, 1992. Contributor to: Reviews in Times Literary Supplement. Honour: Winner of the 1989 Times Literary Supplement/Cheltenham Festival

Poetry Competition. Address: c/o Secker & Warburg, Michelin House, 81 Fulham Road, London SW3 6RB, England.

HARTSHORNE Charles, b. 5 June 1897, Kittanning, USA. University Professor; Writer. m. Dorothy E. Cooper, 22 Dec 1928, 1 daughter. Education: BA, 1921, MA 1922, PhD 1923, Harvard; Postdoctoral Study in Europe, 1923-25. Appointments: Consulting Editor, Journal of Philosophy & Phenomenological Research, many years; Contributor to many Encyclopedias including Britannica, and Encyclopedia of Religion. Publications: The Divine Relativity, 1947; Philosophers Speak of God, with W. Reese, 1953; The Logic of Perfection, 1962; Creative Synthesis and Philosophic Method, 1970; Insights and Oversights of Great Thinkers, 1983; Omnipotence & Other Theological Mistakes, 1984; The Philosophy and Psychology of Sensation, 1934; Beyond Humanism : Essays in the New Philosophy of Nature, 1937; Anselm's Discovery, 1965; A Natural Theology for Our Time, 1967; Creativity in American Philosophy, 1984; Wisdom as Moderation, 1987. Contributor to: over 400 articles & reviews in journals and magazines. Honours: Lecomte du Nouy Award, 1963; Honorary Degrees: Haverford, 1967; Emory University 1969; Episcopal Seminary of the Southwest, 1977; Leuven, Belgium, 1978; Terry Lecturer, Yale, 1947; Fulbright Lecturer, Australia & Japan; Chosen as Principal Subject for a volume of the Library of living Philosophers, 1986. Memberships: many professional organisations, has been President of five. Address: 724 Sparks Ave., Austin, TX 78705, USA.

HARTSTON William Roland, b. 1947. Writer. Appointments Include: Chess Columnist, The Mail on Sunday. Publications: The King's Indian Defence (with L Barden and R. Keene), 1969, 1973; The Benoni, 1969, 1973; The Grunfeld Defence, 1971, 1973; Karpov-Korchnoi (with R Keene), 1974; The Best Games of C H O'D Alexander (with H Golombek), 1975; How to Cheat at Chess, 1976; The Battle of Baguio City, 1978; Soft Pawn, 1979; The Penguin Book of Chess Openings, 1980; Play Chess 1 and 2, 2 vols, 1980-81; London (with S Reuben), 1980; The Master Game Book Two (with J James), 1981; Karpov v Korchnoi, 1981; The Psychology of Chess (with P C Wason), 1983; The Ultimate Irrelevant Encyclopaedia (with J Dawson), 1984; Teach Yourself Chess, 1985; Kings of Chess, 1985; Chess: The Making of a Musical, 1986. Address: 48 Sotheby Road, London N5 2UR, England.

HARUF Alan Kent, b. 24 Feb 1943. Writer. m. Ginger Koom, 11 Dec 1967, 3 daughters. Education: Nebraska Wesleyan University, BA, 1965; Iowa University, MFA, 1973. Appointments: Assistant Professor, Southern Illinois University. Publications: Where You Once Belonged; The Tie That Binds. Contributions to: Best American Short Stories. Honours: Special Citation from PEN; Whiting Writers Award. Literary Agent: Sterling Lord Literistic Inc. Address: Department of English, SIUC, Carbondale, IL 62901, USA.

HARVEY Anne Berenice, b. 27 Apr 1933, London, England. Actress; Freelance Writer; Editor. m. Alan Harvey, 13 Apr 1957, 1 son, 1 daughter. Education: Guildhall School of Music & Drama, 1950-54; AGSM; LGSM. Publications: A Present for Nellie, 1981; Poets in Hand, Editor, 1985; Of Caterpillars, Cats & Cattle, Editor, 1987; In Time of War: War Poetry, Editor, 1987; Something I Remember, Selection of Eleanor Farjeon Poetry, Editor, 1987; A Picnic of Poetry, Editor, 1988; The Language of Love, Editor, 1989; Six of the Best, Editor, 1989; Faces in a Crowd, Editor, 1990; Headlines from the Jungle, Editor with Virginia McKenna, 1990; Occasions, Editor, 1990; Shades of Green, Editor, 1991; Elected Friends, (Poems for & About Edward Thomas), Editor, 1991; Scenes for 2 books, Solo, and Take Two; numerous radio scripts. Contributions to: various journals and magazines. Memberships: Poetry Society; Edward Thomas Fellowship; Childrens Books History Society; British Federation of Music Festivals, Board Member. Honour: Winner of the Signal Poetry Award for Shaes of Green. *Address:* 37 St Stephen's Road, Ealing, London W13 8HJ, England.

HARVEY Brett, b. 28 Apr 1936, NY. Writer. 1 son, 1 daughter. *Appointments:* Drama and Literature Director, WBAI-FM, 1971-74; Publicity and Promotion Director, The Feminist Press, Old Westbury, 1974-80, NY; Free-lance journalist, book critic and children's book author, 1980-. *Publications:* My Prairie Year, 1986; Immigrant Girl, 1987; Cassie's Journey, Various Gifts: Brooklyn Fiction, 1988; My Prairie Christmas, 1990; The Fifties: A Women's Oral History, 1993. *Contributions to:* Articles in periodicals, including Village Voice, New York Times Book Review, Psychology Today, Voice Literary Supplement, Mirabella, Mother Jones, Mademoiselle. *Honours:* My Prairie Year was named a notable children's book by the American Library Association, Philadelphia Children's Reading Round Table, 1986; Named to the William Allen White Award Master List, 1988-89; Golden Sower Award nomination from Nebraska Library Association, 1988. *Memberships:* Authors Guild; National Writers' Union; Vice-president, National Executive Board. *Address:* 305 8th Avenue, Brooklyn, NY 11215, USA.

HARVEY John Barton, b. 21 Dec 1938, London, England. Writer. *Education:* Goldsmith College, University of London; Hatfield Polytechnic; University of Nottingham. *Publications:* What about it, Sharon, 1979; Ghosts of a Chance (collected poems), 1992; Taking the Long Road Home (poetry), 1989; Lonely Hearts, 1989; Rough Treatment, 1990; Cutting Edge, 1991; Off minor, 1992; Wasted Years, 1993; Numerous Scripts for Radio & Television. *Literary Agent:* Blake Friedmann. *Address:* 37-41 Gower Street, London WC1E 6HH, England.

HARVEY John Robert, b. 25 June 1942, Bishops Stortford, Hertfordshire, England. University Lecturer, Cambridge English Faculty. m. Julietta Chloe Papadopoulou, 1968, 1 daughter. *Education:* BA, Honours Class 1, English 1964, MA 1967, PhD 1969, University of Cambridge. *Appointments:* Editor, Cambridge Quarterly 1978-86. *Publications:* Victorian Novelists and Their Illustrators, 1970; The Plate Shop, novel, 1979; Coup d'Etat, novel, 1985; The Legend of Captain Space, novel, 1990. *Contributions to:* London Review of Books; Sunday Times; Sunday Telegraph; Listener; Encounter; Cambridge Quarterly; Essays in Criticism. *Honour:* David Higham Prize, 1979. *Agent:* Curtis Brown. *Address:* Emmanuel College, Cambridge, England.

HARVEY Lynne. *See:* ROTH Eleanor.

HARVEY (Charles) Nigel, (Hugh Willoughby), b. 8 Aug 1916, Oxford, England. Civil Servant (Retired); Honorary Librarian, Royal Agricultural Society. m. 4 Apr 1950, 2 sons. *Education:* BA, History, Oxford University, 1938; Associate, Chartered Land Agents Society, 1950. *Publications include:* Story of Farm Buildings, 1953; The Farming Kingdom, 1955; Ditches, Dykes & Deep Drainage, 1956; History of Farm Buildings in England & Wales, 1970, 1984; Old Farm Buildings, 1975, 3rd edition 1987; Fields, Hedges & Ditches, 1976; Discovering British Farm Livestock, 1979; Industrial Archaeology of Farming in England & Wales, 1980; Trees, Woods & Forests, 1981; Historic Farm Buildings Study: Sources of Information, 1986; Editor, Agricultural Research Centres, World Directory, 1983; Redundant Farm Buildings - Present Liabilities, Future Assets, 1993. Also: Amid the Alien Corn, as Hugh Willoughby, USA 1958. *Contributions to:* Agriculture; Country Life; Farmer & Stockbreeder; Farmers Weekly; New Statesman. *Honour:* Honorary member, Royal Agricultural Society, 1986-. *Memberships include:* Chairman, Historic Farm Buildings Group. *Address:* 41 Corringham Road, Golders Green, London NW11 7BS, England.

HARWOOD David, b. 14 May 1938, Ruislip,

Middlesex, England; Marketing Officer; Freelance Writer. m. Freida Finnie, 29 June 1968, 2 sons. *Education:* Graduate Cum Laude, St George's School, Newport, Rhode Island, USA, 1956-57; BA, Honours, University of Exeter, Devon, England, 1957-60; Cert Ed, Newton Park College, Bath, 1973-74. *Appointments:* Editor, The Arrow Books, The Scout Association, London, 1973; Editor, The Cub Scout Annual, World International, Manchester, 1977-89; Marketing Office, Filton College, Bristol, England. *Publications:* Scouts in Action, 1963; Scouts on Safari, 1965; Scouts Indeed, 1967; Alert to Danger!, 1969; International Cub Scout Book, 1980; The Scout Handbook, 1967; Exploring Your Neighbourhood and How to Read Maps, 1970; Cub Scouts, 1970; Scouts, 1971; Extension Activities Handbook, 1972; Learnabout Camping, 1977; Car Games, 1978; Butterflies, 1990. *Contributions to:* Scouting; The Guide; Cub Scout Annual; Scout Annual; Beaver Annual. *Address:* 4 Prospect Close, Frampton Cotterell, Bristol, BS17 2DQ, England.

HARWOOD Gwen(doline Nessie nee Foster). b. 8 June 1920, Taringa, Queensland. Writer. m. Frank William Harwood, 1945, 3 sons, 1 daughter. *Education:* Brisbane Girls' Grammar School. *Career:* Formerly organist, All Saints' Church, Brisbane; secretary to a Consultant Physician, Hobart, Tasmania 1964-73. *Publications:* Verse: Poems, 1963; Poems, Volume Two, 1968; Selected Poems, 1975; The Lion's Bride, 1981. Plays: The Fall of the House of Usher, music by Larry Sitsky (produced Hobart, 1965); Commentaries on Living, music by James Penberthy (produced Perth, 1972); Lenz, music by Larry Sitsky, adaptation of the story by Georg Buchner (produced Sydney, 1974); Sea Changes, music by Ian Cugley (Produced Hobart) 1974; Fiery Tales, music by Larry Sitsky (produced Adelaide 1976). Radio play: Voices in Limbo, music by Larry Sitsky, 1983. *Honours:* Meanjin Prize, 1958, 1959; Commonwealth Literary Fund Grant, 1973; Grace Leven Prize, 1976; Robert Frost Award, 1977; Patrick White Award, 1978. *Address:* Halcyon, Kettering, Tasmania 7155, Australia.

HARWOOD Lee, b. 1939. Poet; Translator. *Publications:* Verse: Title Illegible, 1965; The Man with Blue Eyes, 1966; The White Room, 1968; The Beautiful Atlas, 1969; Landscapes, 1969; The Sinking Colony, 1970; Penguin Modern Poets 19 (with John Ashbery and Tom Raworth), 1971; The First Poem, 1971; New Year, 1971; Captain Harwood's Log of Stern Statements and Stout Sayings, 1973; Freighters, 1975; H.M.S. Little Fox, 1976; Boston - Brighton, 1977; Old Bosham Bird Watch and Other Stories, 1977, 1978; Wish You Were Here (with A. Lopez), 1979; All the Wrong Notes, 1981; Faded Ribbons, 1982; Wine Tales (with Richard Caddel), 1984; Crossing the Frozen River: Selected Poems 1965-1980, 1984; Monster Masks, 1986; translations of the works of Tristan Tzara: A Poem Sequence, 1969, revised edition as Cosmic Realities Vanilla Tobacco Drawings, 1975; Destroyed Days, 1971; Selected Poems, 1975. *Address:* c/o 9 Highfield Road, Chertsey, Surrey, England.

HARWOOD Ronald, b. 1934, Cape Town, South Africa. Writer. *Publications include:* Novels: All the Same Shadows; The Guilt Merchants; The Girl in Melanie Klein; Articles of Faith; The Genoa Ferry; Cesar and Augusta; and a selection of short stories, One, Interior, Day, - adventures in the film trade. Biography: Sir Donald Wolfit, CBE. Plays include: Country Matters; A Family; The Ordeal of Gilbert Pinfold (from Evelyn Waugh); The Dresser; After the Lions, 1982; Tramway Road, 1984; Another Time, 1989; Reflected Glory, 1992. Films: One Day in the Life of Ivan Denisovich; Operation Daybreak; The Dresser. Television: Mandela; Breakthrough at Reykjavik; Countdown to War, 1989. *Memberships:* President, English PEN, 1990. *Address:* 83 Eastbourne Views, London W2 6LQ, England.

HASHMI (Aurangzeb) Alamgir, b. 15 Nov 1951, Lahore, Pakistan. Professor; Editor; Broadcaster. 2 sons, 1 daughter. *Education:* MA, 1972; MA, 1977; Litt D, 1984. *Appointments:* Assistant Editor, The Ravi, 1970-

71; Faculty Adviser, Folio, 1973-74; Editor, broadcaster, English Magazine, 1973-74; Foreign Editor, Explorations, 1978-88; Corresponding Editor, Associate Editor, Helix, 1978-85; Correspondent, Regional Representative, The Journal of Commonwealth Literature, 1979-; Staff Reviewer, World Literature Today, 1981-; Editorial Adviser, Kunapipi, 1981-; Member, Editorial Board, Poetry Europe, 1982. *Publications:* The Oath and Amen; America Is a Punjabi Word; An Old Chair; Pakistani Literature; My Second in Kentucky; This Time in Lahore; Commonwealth Literature; Ezra Pound in Melbourne; Neither This Time/ Nor That Place; The Worlds of Muslim Imagination; The Commonwealth, Comparative Literature and the World; Inland and Other Poems; The Poems of Alamgir Hashmi; Sun and Moon and Other Poems. *Contributions to:* Chelsea; Seneca Review; Westerly; Poetry Australia; Contemporary Review; Pen International; Poetry Review; Edinburgh Review; Asiaweek; Landfall; Journal of South Asian Literature; Paris Voices; Chicago Review; New Letters; Modern Asian Studies; Journal of Modern Literature; Critical Survey's; The International Fiction Review; World Literature Written in English. *Honours:* All Pakistan Universities Creative Writing Contest, 1 st Prize; The Patras Bokhari Award; The Academic Roll of Honor. *Memberships:* Standing International Conference Committee on English in South Asia. *Address:* c/o Indus Books, PO Box 2905, Islamabad GPO, Pakistan.

HASKINS James, b. 19 Sept 1941, Alabama, USA. Professor; Writer. *Education:* BA, Georgetown University, 1960; BA, Alabama State University, 1962; MA, University of New Mexico, 1963. *Publications include:* The Cotton Club, 1977, 2nd edition 1984; Diary of a Harlem Schoolteacher, 1969; Resistance: Profiles in Nonviolence, 1970; The War and the Protest: Vietnam, 1970; Jokes from Black Folks, 1973; Sreet Gangs, Yesterday and Today, 1974; Witchcraft, Mysticism & Magic in the Black World, 1974; Jobs in Business and Office, 1974; The Picture Life of Malcolm X, 1975; Dr J: A Biography of Julius Erving, 1975; A New Kind of Joy: The Story of the Special Olympics, 1976; Pele: A Biography, 1976; The Life and Death of Martin Luther King, Jr, 1977; Barbara Jordan, 1977; Voodoo & Hoodo: Their Tradition and Craft, 1978; Scott Joplin: The Man Who Made Ragtime, 1978; The New Americans Vietnamese Boat People, 1980; Werewolves, 1981; The New Americans: Cuban Boat People, 1982; Sugar Ray Leonard, 1982; Black Theatre in America, 1982; Lena Horne, 1983; Bricktop, with Bricktop, 1983; About Michael Jackson, 1985; Breakdancing, 1985; Ella Fitzgerald: A Life Through Jazz, several languages, 1992; I Have a Dream: The Life of Martin Luther King, Jr. 1992; The March on Washington, 1992; Diana Ross: Star Supreme, 1985; Queen of the Blues: A Biography of Dinah Washington, 1987; Black Music In America, 1987. *Contributions to:* numerous journals, magazines & newspapers. *Honours:* Recipient, many honours & awards. *Memberships:* Authors Guild; National Book Critics Circle, 1975-79. *Address:* 325 West End Avenue, 7D, New York, NY 10023, USA.

HASLAM Gerald William, b. 18 Mar 1937, Bakersfield, California, USA. Writer; Educator. m. Janice E. Pettichord, 1 July 1961, 3 sons, 2 daughters. *Education:* BA, 1963, MA, 1965, San Francisco State University; PhD, Union Graduate School, 1980. *Appointments:* Associate Editor, ETC: A Review of General Sementics, 1967-69; Editor, Ecolit, 1971-73; General Editor, Western American, 1973-76; Columnist, California English, 1987-; Columnist, Califronia English, 1987-1993; Columnist, San Francisco, 1992-. *Publications:* Snapshots, 1985; Okies, 1973; The Wages of Sin, 1980; Voices of a Place, 1987; Hawk Flights, 1983; Masks, 1976; The Man Who Cultivated Fire, 1987; Forgotten Pages of American Literature, Editor, 1970; Western Writing, Editor, 1974; California Heartland, Editor, with James D. Houston, 1978; Coming of Age in California, 1990; That Constant Coyote, 1990; The Other California, 1990; Many Californias, Editor, 1992; The Great Central Valley: California's Heartland, 1993. *Contributions to:* The Nation; California Magazine; Pacific Discovery. *Honours:*

Arizona Quarterly Award, 1969; Honourable Mention, Joseph Henry Jackson Award, 1971; Bernard Ashton Raborg Award, 1985; Creative Writing Fellowship (California Arts Council), 1989; Josephine Miles Award (from PEN), 1990. *Memberships:* Western Literature Association, Past President; MELUS, Founding Member; various other professional organisations. *Address:* Box 969, Penngrove, CA 94951, USA.

HASLIP Joan, b. 27 Feb 1912. Author. *Appointments:* Sub-Editor, London Mercury, 1929-39; Broadcast and contributed articles to BBC; Lectured for British Council, Italy and Middle East. *Publications:* (several translated): Out of Focus, 1931; Grandfather Steps, 1932 (USA 1933); Lady Hester Stanhope, 1934; Parnell, 1936, (USA 1937); Portrait of Pamela, 1940; Lucrezia Borgia, 1953 (USA 1954); The Sultan, Life of Abdul Hamid, 1958, reprinted 1973; The Lonely Empress, a Life of Elizabeth of Austria, 1965 (translated into 10 languages); Imperial Adventurer, 1971; Catherine the Great, 1976; The Emperor and the Actress, 1982; Marie Antoinette, 1987 (translated into 10 languages); Madame Du Barry, 1991. *Contributions to:* various magazines and journals. *Honours:* Book of Month Choice, USA, 1972. *Address:* 8 Via Piana, Bellosguardo, 50124 Florence, Italy.

HASSEL R Chris Jr, b. 16 Nov 1939, Richmond, Virginia, USA. Professor of English. m. Sedley Hotchkiss, 16 June 1962, 2 sons. *Education:* BA, University of Richmond, 1961; MA, University of North Carolina, 1962; PhD, Emory University, 1968. *Appointments:* Instructor in English, Mercer University, 1962-65; Professor of English, Vanderbilt University, 1968 *Publications:* Faith and Folly in Shakespeare's Romantic Comedies, 1980; Ranaissance Drama and the English Church Year, 1979; Songs of Death, 1987; Context and Charisma: The Sher-Alexander Richard 3 SQ, 1985; Military Oratory in Richard 3, SQ, 1984; Love Versus Charity in Love's Labour's Lost Shakespeare Studies; Donne... and the New Astronomy MP, 1971; Shakespeare's Comic Epilogues, Shakespeare Jahrbuch, 1970. *Contributions to:* Vanderbilt Review; Anglican Theological Review; Cithara. *Honours:* Phi Beta kappa; Omicron Delta Kappa; Woodrow Wilson Fellow; Folger Summer Fellow; ACLS and American Philosophical Society Research Grants. *Memberships:* Modern Language Association; Shakespeare Association of America; Christianity and Literature; Malone Society. *Address:* Box 129-B, Vanderbilt University, Nashville, TN 37235, USA.

HASTINGS Max Macdonald, b. 28 Dec 1945, London, England. Author; Broadcaster; Journalist. m. Patricia Edmondson, 27 May 1972, 2 sons, 1 daughter. *Education:* Exhibitioner, University College, Oxford, 1964-65; Fellow, World Press Institute, St Paul, Minnesota, USA, 1967-68. *Appointments:* Researcher, BBC TV, 1963-64; Reporter, London Evening Standard 1965-67, BBC TV Current Affairs 1970-73; Editor, Evening Standard Londoner's Diary, 1976-77; Columnist, Daily Express 1981-83, Sunday Times 1985-86; Editor, Daily Telegraph, 1986-. *Publications:* The Fire This Time, 1968; Ulster 1969: The Struggle for Civil Rights in Northern Ireland, 1970; Montrose: The King's Champion, 1977; Yoni: The Hero of Entebbe, 1979; Bomber Command, 1979; The Battle of Britain (with Lee Deighton), 1980; Das Reich, 1981; Battle for the Falklands, with Simon Jenkins, 1983; Overlord: D-Day & the Battle for Normandy, 1984; Oxford Book of Military Anecdotes, editor, 1985; Victory in Europe, 1985; The Korean War, 1987; Outside Days, 1989. *Honours:* Somerset Maugham Prize, non-fiction, 1979; Yorkshire Post Book of the Year, 1983, 1984; British Press Awards, Journalist of the Year, 1982 (cited 1973, 1980); Granada TV Reporter of the Year, 1982; Editor of the Year, 1988. *Literary Agent:* The Peters Fraser and Dunlop Group Ltd. *Address:* c/o The Daily Telegraph, 1 Canada Square, London E14 5DT, England.

HASTINGS Michael, b. 2 Sept 1938. Playwright. m. Victoria Hardie, 1975, 2 sons, 1 daughter by previous marriage. *Education:* Various South London Schools; Bespoke tailoring apprenticeship, London, 1953-56;

FRGS. *Publications:* Plays: Don't Destroy Me, 1956; Yes and After, 1957; The World's Baby, 1962; Lee Harvey Oswald : a Far Mean Streak of Indepence Brought on by Negleck' 1966; The Cutting of the Cloth, 1969; The Silence of Saint-Just, 1971; For the West (Uganda), 1977; Gloo Joo, 1978; Full Frontal, 1979; Carnival war a Go Hot, 1980; Midnite at the Starlite, 1980; Moliere's The Miser (adaptation), 1982; Tom and Viv, 1984; The Emperor (with Jonathan Miller) 1987; Novels: The Game, 1957; The Frauds, 1960; Tussy is Me, 1968; The Nightcomers, 1971; And in the Forest the Indians, 1975; Poems: Love me Lambeth, 1959; Stories: Bart's Mornings and Other Tales of Modern Brazil, 1975; Criticism: Rupert Brooke, The Handsomest Young Man in England, 1967; Sir Richard Burton, a biography, 1978; Films and TV: For the West (Congo), 1963; Blue as his Eyes the Tin Helmet he Wore, 1966; The Search for the Nile, 1972; The Nightcomers, 1972; Auntie Kathleen's Old Clothes, 1977; Murder Rap, 1980; Midnight at the Starlight, 1980; Michael Hastings in Brixton, 1980; Stars of the Roller State Disco, 1984; The Emperor (Michael Hastings/Jonathan Miller - Miller co-wrote and directed) 1988; Three Political Plays, with introductory essay, (Penguin Books), 1990. *Address:* 2 Helix Gardens, Brixton Hill, London, SW2, England.

HASWELL Chetwynd John Drake, (George Foster, Jock Haswell), b. 18 July 1919, Penn, Buckinghamshire, England, Soldier; Author. m. Charlotte Annette Petter, 25 Oct 1947, 2 sons, 1 daughter. *Education:* Winchester College, 1933-37; Royal Military College, Sandhurst, 1938-39. *Appointments:* Soldier, 1939-60; Appointed Author, Service Intelligence, Intelligence Centre, Ashford, 1966-84. *Publications:* (Under the name of Jock Haswell) Indian File, 1960; Soldier on Loan, 1961; The First Respectable Spy, 1967; The Queen's Royal Regiment, 1967; James II, Soldier and Sailor, 1972; Citizen Armies, 1973; British Military Intelligence, 1973; The British Army, 1975; The Battle for Empire, 1976; The Ardent Queen, 1976; Spies and Spymasters, 1977; The Intelligence and Deception of the D Day Landings, 1979; The Tangled Web, 1985; Spies and Spying, 1986. *Memberships:* Regimental Historian for the Queen's Regiment. *Address:* The Grey House, Lyminge, Folkestone, Kent CT18 8ED, England.

HASWELL Jock. *See:* **HASWELL Chetwynd John Drake.**

HATAR Victor Gyozo George John, b. 13 Nov 1914, Gyoma, Hungary. Architect. m. Piroska Pragai, 21 Sept 1958. *Education:* Architecture Degree, Budapest University, 1938. *Appointments:* BBC World Service, Hungarian Section, Literary Editor; theatrical, literary and art criticism. *Publications:* Heliane, 1947; Pepito et Pepita, 1963; Anibel, 1969; Archie Dumbarton, 1977; Golgheloghi I-IX, 1976; Cosmic Uncern, 1980; Antisumma, 1983; Julian, 1985; Hajszalhid, 1970; Lelekharangjatek, 1986; Az eg Csarnokai, 1987; Filozofiai Zarlatok, 1992. *Contributions to:* Rainbow; Uj Latohatar; Irodalmi; Ujsag; Kortars; Holmi. *Honours:* Star Order Distinction decorated with the Golden Wreath of Hungarian Republic, 1989; State Literary Kossuth Prize, 1991. *Memberships:* Fellow, English Pen. *Literary Agent:* Artisjus, Budapest, Vorosmarty ter 1, Hungary. *Address:* Hongriuscule, 12 Edge Hill, London SW19 4LP, England.

HATCHER Robin Lee, b. 10 May 1951, Payette, Idaho, USA. Novelist. m. Jerrold W. Neu, 6 May 1989, 2 daughters. *Education:* General High School Diploma, 1969. *Publications:* Stormy Surrender, 1984; Heart's Landing, 1984; Thorn of Love, 1985; Passion's Gamble, 1986; Heart Storm, 1986; Pirate's Lady, 1987; Gemfire, 1988; The Wager, 1989; Dream Tide, 1990; Promised Sunrise, 1990; Promise Me Spring, 1991; Rugged Splendor (as Robin Leigh), 1991; The Hawk and the Heather, 1992; Devlin's Promise, 1992; Midnight Rose, 1992; A Frontier Christmas, 1992; The Magic, 1993; Where The Heart Is, 1993. *Contributions to:* Assembling Your Press Kit, to Fiction Writers Magazine, 1987; Full Time Writer, to Affaire de Coeur, 1988; The Stuff that Dreams are made of, to Romantic Times Magazine, 1989; Go the Distance, to Romance Writers Report, 1990; Have We Learned So Much We've Lost The Passion, to Romance Writer's Report, 1992. *Honours:* Writer of the Year, Idaho Writers League, 1983; Vignette Award, Boise Chapter, Idaho Writers League, 1983, 1984, 1986; Storyteller of the Year, Romantic Times Reviewer's Choice Award, 1990; Favorite Author of 1991, Affaire de Coeur Magazine; RITA Award Finalist, Romance Writers of America, 1992. *Memberships:* Romance Writers of America, Region IV Advisor, Board of Directors 1989-91; Romance Writers of America Southern Idaho Chapter, Chapter Advisor 1989, Chapter Vice President 1986; Novelists Inc; Boise Chapter, Idaho Writers League, Chapter President 1985, 1986; President, Romance Writers of America, 1992-94; Coeur du Bois Chapter RWA, President 1991-1992; Th Authors Guild. *Literary Agent:* Natasha Kern. *Address:* PO Box 4722, Boise, ID 83711, USA.

HATHAWAY Michael Jerry, b. 20 Sept 1961, El Paso, Texas, USA. Typesetter. *Appointments:* Chairman, Poetry Rendezvous (Great Bend, Ks.), 1988-89. *Publications:* Shadows of Myself, 1980; Puddle of Stars, 1984; Founder & Editor, The Kindred Spirit, 1982-; Inconspicuous, 1988; Excerpt, 1989; Come Winter and Other Poems, 1989. *Contributions include:* New Voices; WOP; APA; Explorer; Baltimore Vegetarian; Manna; Wheels; Alchemist Review; Cat Fancy. *Honours:* Featured Editor: The Forum for Universal Spokesmen, 1987; Featured Poet, Keith Publications Newsletter, 1987; 1st place, Jubilee Press contest, 1987; Judge, various poetry contests. *Memberships:* Forthwriters (Treasurer), 1985. *Address:* Rt 2, Box 111, St John, KS 67576, USA.

HATTENDORF John Brewster, b. 22 Dec 1941, Hinsdale, Illinois, USA. Naval and Maritime Historian. m. Berit Sundell, 15 Apr 1978, 3 daughters. *Education:* AB Kenyon College, 1964; AM Brown University, 1971; DPhil, University of Oxford, 1979. *Appointments:* Serving Officer, US Navy, 1964-1973; Professor, Military History, National University of Singapore, 1981-83; Ernest J King Professor of Maritime History, US Naval War College, 1984-. *Publications:* The Writings of Stephen B Luc, 1975; On His Majesty's Service, 1983; Sailors and Scholars, 1984; England in the War of the Spanish Succession, 1987; Maritime Strategy and the Balance of Power, 1989; The Limitations of Military Power, 1990; A Bibliography of the Works of A T Mahan, 1986; Mahan on Naval Strategy, 1991; The Influence of History on Mahan, 1991; Co-editor, British Naval Documents, 1993. *Contributions to:* Naval War College Review; International History Review; US Naval Institute Proceedings. *Memberships:* Fellow, Royal Historical Society, UK; Corresponding member: Royal Swedish Society of Naval Sciences; Society for Nautical Research; Academie du Var, France . *Address:* 28 John Street, Newport, RI 02840, USA.

HATTERSLEY Roy (Sydney George), b. 1932, British. *Appointments:* Journalist and Health Service Executive, 1956-64; Member of City Council, Sheffield, 1957-65; Labour Member of Parliament (UK) for Sparkbrook Division of Birmingham 1964-, Parliamentary Private Secretary, Minister of Pensions and National Insurance 1964-67, Parliamentary Secretary, Ministry of Labour 1967-68, Department of Employment and Productivity 1968-69, Minister of Defence for Administration 1969-70, Labour Party Spokesman on Defence 1972, and on Education 1972-74, Minister of State, Foreign and Commonwealth Office 1974-76, Secretary of State for Prices and Consumer Protection 1976-79, Opposition Spokesman on Home Affairs 1980-83, and on Treasury Affairs 1983-, Deputy Leader of the Labour Party 1983-; Director, Campaign for a European Political Community, 1966-67; Columnist for the Guardian, 1981-, and Punch, 1982-. *Publications:* Nelson: A Biography, 1974; Goodbye to Yorkshire, 1976; Politics Apart, 1982; A Yorkshire Boyhood, Press Gang, 1983; Endpiece Revisited, 1984; Choose Freedom, 1987; Economic Priorities for a Labour Government, 1987; The Maker's Work (novel), 1991;

In That Quiet Earth, 1991. *Address:* House of Commons, London SW1A DAA, England.

HAUCK Dennis William, b. 8 Apr 1945, Hammond, Indiana, USA. Writer. *Education:* Indiana University, 1963-66; University of Vienna, Austria, 1969-72. *Appointments:* Editor: Infor Services Inc, 1973-76; Countrywide Publications, NY, 1976-79; Writer, Odenberg Group Inc, Sacramento, 1983-91; Columnist: Today's Supervisor, Sacramento, 1991-; The Long Island Journal, Long Beach, NY, 1977-78. *Publications:* The UFO Handbook, 1974; Ufology, 1975; The Secret of the Emerald Tablet, 1991; The Haunted Places Guidebook, 1991; William Shatner: A Biography, 1992; Jewish Alchemy, 1992. *Contributions to:* Suttertown News, Sacramento Magazine, Highway Patrol Magazine, The City, San Francisco Magazine; Articles in Sign of the Times, Poet, In the Company of Poets, Journal of Occult Studies, Approche, Accept, Omega Magazine. *Honours:* Appeared in and wrote script for theatrical release, Mysteries of the Gods, 1976. *Memberships:* Author's Guild; National Writers Union; Society for Technical Communicatin; California Writers Club. *Literary Agent:* Michael Larsen, Elizabeth Pomada, San Francisco. *Address:* P O 22201, Sacremanto, CA 95822, USA.

HAUGAARD Erik Christian, b. 13 Apr 1923, Copenhagen, Denmark. Author. m. (1) Myrna Seld, 23 Dec 1949, deceased 1981. (2) Masako Taira, 27 July 1986. 1 son, 1 daughter. *Publications include:* The Little Fishes, 1967; Orphas Of The Wind, 1969; The Untold Tale, 1972; Translated all Hans Christian Andersen's Fairy Tales, 1973; Chase Me Catch Nobody, 1980; Leif The Unlucky, 1982; The Samurai's Tale, 1984; Princess Horrid, 1990; The Boy and The Samurai, 1991. *Honours:* Herald Tribune Award; Boston Globe-Horn Book Award; Jane Addams Award; Danish Cultural Ministry Award; 1988 Phoenix Award. *Memberships:* The Authors Guild; The Society of Authors; British PEN; Danish Author's Union. *Literary Agent:* McIntosh and Otis Inc, 310 Madison Avenue, New York, USA. *Address:* Toad Hall, Ballydehob, West Cork, Ireland.

HAUGEN Einar Ingvald, b. 19 Apr 1906, Sioux City, Iowa, USA. m. 18 June 1932, 2 daughters. *Education:* BA 1928; PhD, 1931. *Appointments:* University of Wisconsin, 1931; Harvard University, 1964. *Publications include:* Fire and Ice, (translated), 1970; First Grammatical Treatise, 1972; The Scandinavian Languages, 1976; The Ecology of Language, 1977; The Land of the Free, 1978; Scandinavian Structures, 1982; Oppdalsmolet, 1982; Ole E Rolvaag, 1983; Han Ola og han Per, 1984; Blessings of Babel, 1987; Immigrant Indealist, 1989; Ole Bull: Romantisk musiker og kosmopolitisk Nordmann, 1992 (co-author); Studies by Einar Haugen, 1971; Studies for Einar Haugen, 1972; Linguistics in North America: Current Trends in Linguistics, 1971; Die Skandinavisches Sprachen, 1984. *Honours:* Fulbright Award, 1951; See Studies for Einar Haugen, 1972; Ellis Island Medal of Honour, 1990. *Memberships:* Linguistic Society of America, President; Ygdras il Literary Society, Madison, Wisconsin; American Scandinavian Foundation, New York. *Address:* 45 Larch Circle, Belmont, MA 02178, USA.

HAUGEN Paal-Helge, b. 26 Apr 1945, Valle, Norway. Author. *Education:* Studied medicine, film and theatre, Norway and USA. *Appointments:* Chairman, Board of Literary Advisors, Society of Norwegian Writers, 1984-88; Chairman, International Pegasus Prize Committee, 1988. *Publications:* Poetry: Pa botnen av ein mork sommar, 1967; Sangbok 1969; Det synlege menneske, 1975; Fram i lyset, tydeleg, 1978; Steingjerde, 1979; Spor, Selected and new poems, 1981; I dette huset, 1984; Det overvintra lyset, 1985; Anne, novel, 1968; Herr Tidemann reiser, 1980, Childrens book. Inga anna tid, ingen annan stad, stage play, 1986; Horisont (poems, with lithographies by Kjell Nupen), 1986; Verden open, selected poems, 1988; Vårfuglen, Children's book, 1989; translations in German: Das überwinterte Licht, Münster, 1988; Anne, Münster, 1989. *Contributions to:* Various professional journals; Plays for radio, television and stage. *Honours include:* Literary Prize, Norwegian

Cultural Council, 1968; The English edition of Steingjerde (Stone Fences, University of Missouri Press), translated by Roger Greenwald and William Mishler awarded The American Translators Association's Richard Wilbur Prize, 1986; The Dobloug Prize of the Swedish Academy, 1987. *Memberships:* Society of Norwegian Writers; Society of Norwegian Playwrights; Society of Norwegian Translators. *Literary Agent:* Kirsten Lier, Cappelen, Kirkegt.15, 0153 Oslo 1. *Address:* Skrefjellv 5, 4645 Nodeland, Norway.

HAUPTMAN William (Thornton), b. 26 Nov 1942, Wichita Falls, Texas, USA. Playwright. m. (1) Barbara Barbat, 1968 (div 1977), 1 daughter; (2) Marjorie Endreich, 1985, 1 son. *Education:* Graduated, Wichita Falls Senior High School, 1961; BFA, Drama, 1966, University of Texas, Austin; MFA, Playwriting, Yale University School of Drama, New Haven Connecticut, 1973. *Publications:* Plays include: Hear (produced NYC, 1974) New York, Samuel French, 1977; Domino Courts/Comanche Cafe (produced NYC, 1975) New York, Samuel French, 1977; New York, Performing Arts Journal Publications, 1980; Big River, music and lyrics by Roger Miller, adaptation of the novel Adventures of Huckleberry Finn by Mark Twain (produced Cambridge, Massachusetts, 1984; New York, 1985). New York, Grove Press, 1986. Gillette (produced Cambridge Massachusetts, 1985; revised version produced La Jola, California, 1986). New York, Samuel French, 1989. Television Play: A House Divided series (3 episodes) 1981; Fiction: Good Rockin' Tonight and Other Stories, New York, Bantam, 1988; The Storm Season, Bantam, 1992. *Honours:* CBS grant, 1976; National Endowment for the Arts grant, 1977; Obie award, 1977; Guggenheim grant, 1978; Boston Theatre Critics Circle award, 1984; Tony award, 1985; Drama-Logue award, 1986; Jesse Jones Award (best work of fiction), Texas Institute of Letters, 1989. *Literary Agent:* Gloria Loomis, Watkins-Loomis, NYC. *Address:* 240 Warren Street. Apartment E, Brooklyn, NY 11201, USA.

HAUTZIG Esther, (Esther Rudomin), b. 1930, American. *Publications:* Let's Cook Without Cooking (as E Rudomin), 1955; Let's Make Presents, 1961; Redecorating Your Room for Practically Nothing, 1967; The Endless Steppe, In the Park, 1968; At Home, 1969; In School, 1971; Let's Make More Presents, 1973; Cool Cooking, 1974; I L Peretz: The Case Against the Wind and Other Stories (trans and adaptor), 1975; Life with Working Parents, 1976; A Gift for Mama, 1981; Holiday Treats, 1983; I L Peretz: The Seven Good Years and Other Stories (trans and adaptor), 1984; Make It Special, 1986; Christmas Goodies, 1989; Remember Who You Are, 1990; On The Air, 1991; Riches, 1992. *Address:* 505 West End Avenue, New York, NY 10024, USA.

HAVEL Václav, b. 5 Oct 1936, Prague, Czechoslovakia. President of the Czech and Slovak Federal Republic; Playwright; Essayist. m. Olga Haviova Splichalova, 1964. *Education:* Faculty of Economy 1955-57 (unfinished); Drama Department, Academy of Arts, Prague, 1966. *Appointments:* Chemical laboratory worker, 1951-55; Stage technician, ABC Theatre, Prague, 1959-60; Dramaturgist, ''Na Zabradli'' Theatre, Prague, 1960-68; Freelance work 1969-74; Workman in Trutnov Brewery, 1974; Freelance work 1975-89; President of the Czech and Slovak Federal Republic since 29th December, 1989; 'Sentenced: for damaging concerns of republic to 14 months conditionally, 1977, to four and a half years for subversion of the republic, imprisoned October 1979 (released for health reasons April 1984), sentenced to 8 months for participating in demonstration in January 1989 (in prison Jan-May 1989). *Creative Works include:* Plays: Zahradni slavnost (The Garden Party) 1963; Vyrozumeni (The Memorandum), 1965; Ztiizena moznost soustredeni (The Increased Difficulty of Concentration) 1968; Zebracka opera (The Beggars Opera) 1972; Audience, 1975; Vernisaz (Private View) 1975; Horsky hotel (A Hotel in the Hills) 1976; Protest, 1979; Chyba (Mistake) 1983; Largo Desolato, 1984; Pokouseni (Temptation) 1985; Asanace (Slum Clearance) 1987; Essays: A Letter to Dr Husak, 1977; Power of Powerless, 1978; Politics and Conscience, 1984; Six about Culture, 1984; Thriller, 1984; An Anatomy of a Reticence, 1985; A Word about Words, 1989; Books: Anticodes (Antikody) 1964; Letters to Olga (Dopisy Olze) 1983; Disturbing the Peace (Dalkovy vyslech) 1989; Summer Meditations, 1992. *Honours:* Obie Prizes, 1968, 1970; Austrian State Prize for European Literature, 1969; Erasmus Prize, 1986; Olof Palme Prize, 1989; Peace Prize from German Bookselllers, 1989; Simon Bolivar Prize, UNESCO, 1990; Beyond War Prize, 1990. *Memberships:* Chairman, Young Writers in the Czechoslovak Writers Association, 1965; Co-Founder of Charter 77 (Human rights group) and one of the first three spokespersons (also spokesperson of CH 77 in 1978, 1989); Co-foudner of committee for the Defense of the Unjustly Prosecuted (VONS); Member, Czechoslovak Helsinki Committee; Member, Czech Pen Club; Co-founder and leading person of Civic Forum (Obcanske forum) 1977. *Address:* Rasinovo nabrezi 78, 12000 Prague 2, Czechoslovakia.

HAVIL Anthony. *See:* **PHILIPP Elliot Elias.**

HAWK Alex. *See:* **KELTON Elmer Stephen.**

HAWKES Jacquetta, b. 5 Aug 1910, Cambridge, England. Author; Archaeologist. m. (1) Christopher Hawkes, 1933, 1 son (div. 1953), (2) J. B. Priestley, 1953. *Education:* MA, Newnham College, Cambridge, 1951. Research & Excavation, UK, Eire, France, Palestine, 1931-40. *Literary Appointments:* John Danz Visiting Professor, University of Washington, USA, 1971; Governor, British Film Institute, 1950-55; Member, UNESCO Cultural Advisory Committee, 1966-79; Life Trustee, Shakespeare Birthplace Trust, 1985-. *Publications include:* A Land, 1951; Guide to Prehistoric & Roman Monuments in England & Wales, 1951; Man on Earth, 1954; The Dawn of the Gods, 1968; The First Great Civilizations, 1973; Mortimer Wheeler: Adventurer in Archaeology, 1982; Shell Guide to British Archaeology, 1986; Also poetry, plays, fiction. *Contributions to:* Many leading journals & national periodicals. *Honours:* OBE, 1952; 100 Kemsley Award (A Land), 1951; Honorary DLitt, Warwick University, 1986. *Memberships:* Society of Authors; PEN; Fellow, Society of Antiquaries, 1940-; Antiquity Trustee; CPRE, Warwickshire, President. *Literary Agent:* A. D. Peters. *Address:* Littlecote, Leysbourne, Chipping Campden, Gloucestershire GL55 6HL, England.

HAWKES John, b. 17 Aug 1925, Stamford, Connecticut, USA. Writer; Profesor Emeritus of English. m. Sophie Parks Goode Tazewell, 5 Sept 1947. 3 sons, 1 daughter. *Education:* AB, Harvard University, 1949. *Publications:* Novels: The Cannibal, 1949; The Lime Twig, 1961; Second Skin, 1964; The Blood Oranges, 1971; Adventures in the Alaskan Skin Trade, 1985; Whistlejacket, 1988; The Beetle Leg, 1951; The Goose on the Grave and The Owl, 1954; Death, Sleep and the Traveler, 1974; Travesty, 1976; The Passion Artist, 1979; Virgine: Her Two Lives, 1983. *Honours:* Guggenheim Fellowship, 1962; Award in Literature, American Academy of Arts and Letters, 1962; Ford Fellowship for Drama, 1964; Rockefeller Fellowship, 1968; Le Prix du Meilleur Livre Etranger, 1973; Prix Medicis Etranger, 1986; Lannon Foundation Award in Literature, 1990. *Memberships:* American Academy of Arts and Letters. *Literary Agent:* Lynn Nesbit, Janklow & Nesbit Associates, 598 Madison, NYC 10022. *Address:* 18 Everett Avenue, Providence, RI 02906, USA.

HAWKESWORTH John, b. 1920, London, England. Film & TV Producer, & Writer. *Education:* BA, Oxford University. *Publications:* Film and TV Scripts: Tiger Bay; The Conan Doyle Series; The Million Pound Bank Note, adaptation; The Elusive Pimpernel; The Goldrobbers; Upstairs, Downstairs, TV Series 1-5; Novels: Upstairs: Secrets of an Edwardian Household, 1972; Upstairs, Downstairs in My Lady's Chamber, 1973; The Duchess of Duke Street, 2 TV Series; Danger UXB; Creator and Scriptwriter (TV): The Flame Trees of Thika; The Tale of Beatrix Potter; By the Sword Divided, 2 series; Oscar;

Campion; Chelworth; The Adventures of Sherlock Holmes; The Sign of Four; Mrs Arris Goes To Paris. *Literary Agent:* Casarotto Co Limited. *Address:* Fishponds House, Knossington, Oakham, Leics, LE15 8LX, England.

HAWKING Stephen William, b. 8 Jan 1942, Oxford, England. British Physicist; Educator; Editor; Author. *Publications:* The Large Scale Structure of Space-time (co-author), 1973; Is the End in Sight for Theoretical Physics? An Inaugural Lecture, 1980; Superspace and Supergravity: Proceedings of the Nuffield Workshop (co-editor), 1981; The Very Early Universe: Proceedings of the Nuffield Workshop, 1983; Three Hundred Years of Gravitation, 1987; A Brief History of Time: From the Big Bang to Black Holes, 1988. *Honours:* Pius XI Gold Medal from the Pontifical Academy of Sciences, 1975; Dannie Heineman Prize for Mathematical Physics from the American Physical Society and the American Institute of Physics, 1976; Royal Astronomical Society Gold Medal, 1985; Paul Dirac Medal and Prize from the Institute of Physics, 1987. *Address:* 5 West Road, Cambridge, England.

HAWKINS Aileen Daisy Doreen, b. 24 Feb 1916, Dorchester, England. Housewife. m. Edgar Hawkins, 16 Oct 1943, dec 1990. *Education:* Dorset County School. *Publications:* A Patchwork Book of Poems, 1974; Peace, 1984; The World of Verse, 1971; Poetry International, 1971; World Poets, 1971; Author of 3,275 poetic works. *Contributions to:* Sensibility Magazine; The Dorset Year Book; Poetry Now Magazine. *Memberships:* West Country Writers Association. *Address:* Craigaras, Wavering Lane, Gillingham, Dorset SP8 4NR, England.

HAWKINS Angus Brian, b. 12 Apr 1953, Portsmouth, England. Historian. m. Esther Armstrong, 20 May 1980, 2 daughters. *Education:* BA Hons, Reading University, 1975; PhD, London School of Economics, 1980. *Publications:* Parliament Party and the Art of Politics in Britain, 1987; Victorian Britain: An Encyclopaedia, 1989. *Contributions to:* English Historical Review, Parliamentary History, Journal of British Studies, Victorian Studies. *Honours:* McCann Award, 1972; Gladstone Memorial Prize, 1978. *Memberships:* Reform Club. *Address:* Rewley House, University of Oxford, 1 Wellington Square, Oxford, England.

HAWORTH-BOOTH Mark, b. 20 Aug 1944, Westow, Yorks, England. m. Rosemary Joanna Miles, 19 July 1979, 2 daughters. *Education:* English Tripos, parts I & II, Cambridge University, 1963-66; Postgraduate Diploma in Fine Art, Edinburgh University, 1967-69. *Publications:* E McKnight Kauffer: A Designer and his Public, 1979; The Golden Age of British Photography, 1839-1900, 1983; Bill Brandt's Literary Britain, 1984; Photography Now, 1989; Camille Silvy: River Scene, France, 1992. *Contributions to:* Times Literary Supplement; London Magazine; The Spectator; New Statesman; Aperture. *Honours:* Hood Medal, 1988; Sudek Medal, 1989. *Address:* Victoria & Albert Museum, London SW7 2RL, England.

HAWTHORNE Susan, b. 30 Nov 1951, Wagga Wagga, New South Wales, Australia. Writer; Publisher. *Education:* DipT, 1972, MA (prelim), 1981, University of Melbourne; BA Hons, La Trobe University, 1976. *Appointments:* Coordinator, New Moods Women Writers' Festival, 1985; Editor, Commissioning Editor, Penguin Books Australia, 1987-91; Chair, Australian Feminist Book Fortnight Management Committee, 1989-91; Chair, 6th International Feminist Book Fair, 1992-1994; Publisher, Spinifex Press, 1991-. *Publications:* The Falling Woman, 1992; The Language in my Tongue, 1993; The Spinifex Book of Women's Answers, 1991; The Spinifex Quiz Book, 1993; Co-editor: Angels of Power, 1991, Moments of Desire, 1989, The Exploding Franipani, 1990; Editor, Difference, 1985. *Contributions to:* Australia: Meanjin, Fine Line, Mattoid, Outrider; UK: Slow Dancer; USA: Sinister Wisdom; NSWA Journal; Women's Studies International Forum; Canada: Tessera; Germany:

Beitrage. *Honours:* Florence James Pandora Award for Outstanding Contribution to Women's Publishing, 1989; Barbara Ramsden Award for Editing, 1988; Australian Feminist Fortnight Favourite, 1991; Pandora New Venture Award, 1991. *Memberships:* PEN; Australian Society of Authors; Fellowship of Australian Writers; Women in Publishing. *Address:* c/o Spinifex Press, 504 Queensbury Street, North Melbourne, Victoria 3051, Australia.

HAXTON Josephine Aynes, (Ellen Douglas), b. 12 July 1921, USA. Novelist; Teacher. m. Kenneth Haxton, 12 Jan 1945, 3 sons. *Education:* BA, University of Mississippi. *Appointments:* Writier in residence, University of Virginia, 1984-; Writer in Residence, University of Mississippi, 1985-91. *Publications:* Cant Quit You Baby; A Lifetime Burning; The Rock Cried Out; Apostle of Light; A Family's Affairs; Where The Dreams Cross; Black Claud; White Cloud; The Magic Carpet. *Honours:* NEA Fellowship; National Book Award, finalist; Fellowship of Southern Writers Award. *Literary Agent:* RLR Associates, 7 West 51st Street, NYC. *Address:* 1600 Pine Street, Jackson, MS 39202, USA.

HAY Elizabeth Jean, b. 15 Aug 1936, Ajmer, India. m. Geoffrey P Smith, 23 Feb 1960, 1 son, 1 daughter. *Education:* St George's School, Edinburgh; MA (Hons) History, University of Edinburgh. *Publications:* Sambo Sahib, 1981; Sayonara Sambo, 1992. *Address:* 12 Highbury Terrace, London N5 1UP, England.

HAYASHI Tetsumaro, b. 22 Mar 1929, Sakaide, Japan. University Professor. m. Akiko Sakuratani, 14 Apr 1960, 1 son. *Education:* University of Okayama, BA, 1953; University of Florida, 1957; Kent State University, 1959, 1968. *Appointments:* Editor in Chief, Steinbeck Quarterly; Steinbeck Monograph Series; Steinbeck Essay series; President International John Steinbeck Society. *Publications:* A Study to Steinbecks Major Work; Steinbecks Literary Dimension; John Steinbeck on Writing. *Contributions to:* Southern Humanities Review; Literature; East & West; Shakespear Quarterly; Steinbeck Quarterly. *Honours:* Outstanding Research Award; Outstanding Service Award; Outstanding Lifelong Achievement Award. *Memberships:* International sTeinbeck Society; Modern Language Association; Shakespeare Society of Japan; Shakespeare Association of America; Steinbeck Society of Japan. *Address:* English Department, Ball State University, Muncie, IN 47306, USA.

HAYCRAFT Anna. *See:* **HAYCRAFT Anna Margaret.**

HAYCRAFT Anna Margaret, (Alice Thomas Ellis, Anna Haycraft, Brenda O'Casey), Writer. *Appointment:* Director, Duckworth, publishers, London. Columnist (Home Life), The Spectator, London, also The Universe, The Catholic Herald. *Publications:* Natural Baby Food: A Cookery Book (as Brenda O'Casey) 1977; The Sin Eater (novel) 1977; Darling You Shouldn't Have Gone to So Much Trouble (cookery) (as Anna Haycraft with Caroline Blackwood) 1980; The Birds of the Air (novel) 1980; The 27th Kingdom (novel) 1982; (ed) Mrs Donald by Mary Keene, 1983; The Other Side of the Fire (novel) 1983; Unexplained Laughter (novel) 1985; Home Life (collected columns from the Spectator), 1986; Secrets of Strangers (with Tom Pitt Aikens) (psychiatry), 1986; The Clothes in the Wardrobe (novel), 1987; More Home Life (collection) 1987; The Skeleton in the Cupboard (novel) 1988; Home Life III (collection), 1988; The Loss of the Good Authority (with Tom Pitt Aikens), (psychiatry), 1989; Wales: An Anthology, 1989; The Fly in the Ointment (novel), 1989; Home Life IV (collection), 1989; The Inn at the Edge of the World (novle), 1990; A Welsh Childhood (autobiography), 1990; Pillars of Gold, 1992. *Address:* 22 Gloucester Crescent, London NW1 7DY, England.

HAYCRAFT Howard, b. 24 July 1905, Publisher; Author. *Education:* University of Minnesota.

Appointments: H.W. Wilson Co., New York, 1929-, Vice President 1940-52, President 1953-67, Chairman, Board of Directors, 1967-. *Publications:* As Author, Editor or Joint Editor: Authors Today and Yesterday, 1933; Junior Book of Authors, 1934; Boys' Sherlock Holmes, 1936; Boys' Book of Great Detective Stories, 1938; American Authors, 1600-1900, 1938; Boys' Second Book of Great Detective Stores, 1940; Murder for Pleasure: The Life and Times of the Detective Story, 1941; Crime Club Encore, 1942; Twentieth Century Authors, 1942; Art of the Mystery Story, 1946; Fourteen Great Detective Stories, 1949; British Authors Before 1800, 1952; Treasury of Great Mysteries, 1957; Ten Great Mysteries, 1959; Five Spy Novels, 1962; Books for the Blind: A Postcript and an Appreciation, 1965. *Honours:* Campbell Medal and Citation, American Library Association, 1966; Centennial Citation, 1976. *Memberships:* President, Committee, Employment of the Handicapped, 1963-74; Mystery Writers of America Club, President 1963. *Address:* 950 University Avenue, Bronx, NY 10452, USA.

HAYDEN Dolores, b. 15 Mar 1945, New York, USA. Professor; Author. m. Peter Marris, 18 May 1975, 1 daughter. *Education:* BA, Mount Holyoke College, 1966; Dipl. English Studies, Girton College, Cambridge, 1967; M.Arch, Harvard Graduate School of Design, 1972. *Publications:* Seven American Utopias, 1976; The Grand Domestic Revolution, 1981; Redesigning the American Dream, 1984; Co-Author, The Power of Place, 1986. *Contributions to:* Poetry in numerous journals including: Electrum; Poets On; Witness; Manhattan Poetry Review. *Honours:* NEH Fellowship, 1976; NEA, 1980; Guggenheim, 1981; Rockefeller, 1981; ACLS/Ford, 1988. *Memberships:* Poetry Society of America; American Planning Association; American Studies Association; Society of Architectural Historians. *Literary Agent:* Elaine Markson Associates, New York City. *Address:* Graduate School of Architecture & Urban Planning, UCLA, Los Angeles, CA 90024, USA.

HAYDEN Donald E, b. 1915, American. *Appointments:* Instructor, Syracuse University, NY, 1937-42; Head of English, Westbrook Junior College, Portland, ME, 1942-47; Assistant Professor of English 1947-56, Professor 1956-85, Dean of Liberal Arts 1956-70, Professor Emeritus of English 1985-, University of Tulsa, OK. *Publications:* After Conflict, Quiet - A Study of Wordsworth, 1951; A Semantics Workbook (with E P Alworth), 1956; Classics in Semantics (ed), 1965; Classics in Linguistics (co-author), His Firm Estate (ed), 1967; Classics in Composition (ed), 1969; Introspection - The Artist Looks at Himself, 1971; Literary Studies: The Poetic Process, 1978; Wordsworth's Walking Tour of 1790, 1983; Wordsworth's Travels in Scotland (Wales and Ireland, Europe), 3 volumes, 1985-88. *Address:* 3626 South Birmingham Avenue, Tulsa, OK 74105, USA.

HAYDEN Eric William, b. 23 Oct 1919, St Albans, Hertfordshire, England, Minister of Religion; Architectural Illustrator. m. Marjorie Lapworth, 13 Nov 1948, 1 son (dec), 1 daughter. *Education:* BA, 1952, MA, 1956, Dunelm; DD, ABI, Kansas, USA, 1970; MSAI, United Kingdom, 1970. *Publications:* History of Spurgeon's Tabernacle, 1962, 1971, 1992; Searchlight on Spurgeon, 1973; Letting the Lion Loose - Spurgeon and the Bible, 1984; Preaching Through the Bible, Volume 1, 1964, Volume 2, 1966; Sermon Outlines, 6 volumes, 1974-80; Joshua Thomas, 1976; Spurgeon on Revival, 1962; God's Answer for Fear, 1985; Pressure, 1987; People Like Us, 1989. *Contributions to:* Christian Herald; Moody Monthly; Baptist Times. *Honour:* Honorary Paramount Chief of Gio tribe, Liberia. *Address:* 7 Nanfan and Dobyn Place, Newent, Gloucestershire GL18 1TF, England.

HAYLOCK John Mervyn, b. 22 Sept 1918, Bournemouth, England. Writer. *Education:* Diplome francais, Institut de Touraine, Tours, France, 1937; Certificat d'Immatriculation, Grenoble University, France, 1938; Pembroke College, Cambridge, England, 1938-40, 1946-47; BA Hons, 1940; MA Hons, 1946.

Publications: New Babylon, A Portrait of Iraq (with Desmond Stewart), 1956; See You Again, 1963; It's All Your Fault, 1964; Choice and Other Stories, 1979; One Hot Summer in Kyoto, 1980; Tokyo Sketch Book, 1980; Japanese Excursions, 1981; Japanese Memories, 1987; Romance Trip and Other Stories, 1988; A Touch of the Orient, 1990; Uneasy Relations, 1993; Translation from French of Philippe Jullian's Flight into Egypt, 1970. *Contributions to:* Regularly to Blackwoods Magazine (1975-80); London Magazine; Short Story International, New York; The Japan Times; Winter's Tales. *Membership:* Oriental Club, London. *Literary Agent:* Rivens Scott, 15 Gledhow Gardens, London SW5 0AY, England. *Address:* 5 Powis Grove, Brighton BN1 3HF, England.

HAYMAN Carole, b. 16 Dec 1944, Kent, England. Actress; Director; Writer. m. Max Stafford Clark, div. *Education:* BA, Hons, Leeds University. *Publications:* All The Best Kim Grafton; Ladies of Wizors Futura; The Refuge TV Series; How The Vote Was Won; Rides, Series 1 & Series 2, BBC 1 Drama. *Contributions to:* The Guardian; Just 17. *Memberships:* PEN. *Literary Agent:* Judy Daish.

HAYMAN David, b. 7 Jan 1927, New York, USA. University Professor. m. Loni Goldschmidt, 28 June 1951, 2 daughters. *Education:* BA, New York University, 1948; Doctorat d'Universite de Paris, 1955. *Appointments:* Instructor of English, 1955-57, Assistant Professor, 1957-58, Associate Professor, 1958-65, University of Texas; Professor of English and Comparative Literature, University of Iowa, 1965-73; Professor of Comparative Literature, University of Wisconsin, 1973-; Evjue-Baslom Professor, 1990-. *Publications:* Joyce et Mallarme, 1956; A First Draft Version of Finnegans Wake, 1963; Configuration Critique de Jamees Joyce (ed) 1965; Ulysses: The Mechanics of Meaning, 1970; Form in Ficiton (with Eric Rabkin), 1974; The James Joyce Archive (ed 25 Finnegans Wake vols) 1978; Philippe Sollers: Writing and the Experience of Limits (ed and co-translator), 1980; Re-forming the Narrative, 1987; The Wake in Transit, 1990; James Joyce's Ulysses: Critical Essays (ed with Clive Hart) 1974; In the Wake of the Wake (ed) 1978. *Contributions to:* Novel, PMLA, ELH, Comparative Literature Studies, James Joyce Quarterly, Joyce Studies Annual, Art Forum, Art and Antiques, Poétique, Tel Quel, Tri Quarterly, Orbis Litterarum, Quimera, Diario 16, Contemporary Literature; Beckett Studies; Change; Contemporary Literature; ELH; Espiral; Etudes Anglaises; Europe; European Joyce Studies; Iowa Review; James Joyce Literary Supplement; Joyce Studies Annual; Ligua y Stile; La Revue des Lettres Modernes; The Review of Contemporary Fiction; substance; Texas Studies in English; Texas Quarterly. *Honours:* Guggenheim Fellowship 1958-59; National Endowment for the Humanities, 1979-80; Harry Levin Prize (American Comparative Literature Association) 1989. *Memberships:* MLA; ACLA. *Address:* 2913 Columbia Road, Madison, WI 53705, USA.

HAYMAN Ronald, b. 1932, British. *Appointment:* Assistant Producer, Northampton Repertory Company, 1962-63. *Publications:* Harold Pinter, Samuel Beckett, John Osborne, John Arden, 1968; Robert Bolt, John Whiting, Collected Plays of John Whiting (ed) 2 volumes, Techniques of Acting, 1969; The Art of the Dramatist and Other Pieces (ed), Arthur Miller, Tolstoy, Arnold Wesker, 1970; John Gielgud, Edward Albee, 1971; Eugène Ionesco, 1972; Playback, 1973; The Set-Up, Playback 2, 1974; The First Thrust, The German Theatre (ed), 1975; The Novel Today 1967-75, 1976; My Cambridge (ed), Tom Stoppard, How to Read a Play, Artaud and After, 1977; De Sade, 1978; Theatre and Anti-Theatre, British Theatre since 1955: A Reassessment, 1979; Nietzsche: A Critical Life, 1980; K: A Biography of Kafka, 1981; Brecht: A Biography, 1983; Fassbinder: Film Maker, Brecht: The Plays, 1984; Günter Grass, Secrets: Boyhood in a Jewish Hotel 1932-54, 1985; Writing Against: A Biography of Sartre, 1986; Proust; A Biography, 1990; The Death and Life of Sylvia

Platle, 1991. *Address:* 64 Canonbury Road, London N1 2DQ, England.

HAYS Donald Slaven, b. 14 Feb 1947, Jacksonville, Florida, USA. Teacher and Professor of Literature and Writing. m. Patricia Chambers Hays, 27 Sept 1968, 1 son. *Education:* BA English, Southern Arkansas University, 1969; MFA, Creative Writing, University of Arkansas, 1984. *Publications:* The Dixie Association, 1984; The Hangman's Children, 1989; Editor - Stories: Contemporary Southern Short Fiction, 1989. *Honours:* Nominated for PEN/Faulkner Award for Fiction, 1985. *Memberships:* PEN America; Associate Writing Programmes. *Literary Agent:* Marcy Posner of the William Morris Agency, New York, USA. *Address:* 441 East Sutton, Fayetteville, AR 72701, USA.

HAYTER Alethea Catharine, b. 1911, Cairo, Egypt. Former British Council Representative and Cultural Attache. *Education:* MA, University of Oxford. *Publications:* Mrs Browning: A Poet's Work and Its Setting, 1962; A Sultry Month: Scenes of London Literary Life in 1846, 1965; Elizabeth Barrett Browning, 1965; Opium and the Romantic Imagination, 1968; Horatio's Version, 1972; A Voyage in Vain, 1973; Fitzgerald to His Friends: Selected Letters of Edward Fitzgerald, 1979; Portrait of a Friendship, Drawn From New Letters of James Russell Lonell to Sybella Lady Lyttelton 1881-1891, 1990. *Contributions to:* Oxford Companion to English Literature; Sunday Times; Times Literary Supplement; New Statesman; History Today; Ariel; London Review of Books; The Longman Encyclopaedia. *Honours:* W. H. Heinemann Prize, RSL for Mrs Browning : A Poet's Work and Its Setting; Rose Mary Crawshay Prize, British Academy, for Opium and the Romantic Imagination; OBE. *Memberships:* FRSL; Society of Authors, Committee of Management, 1975-79; PEN. *Address:* 22 Aldebert Terrace, London SW8 1BJ, England.

HAYWARD Lana Janes, b. 9 Oct 1943, Ft Worth, Texas, USA. Writer. m. John Edward Hayward, 1 Dec 1961, 1 daughter. *Education:* English and Psychology, University of Texas, San Antonio, 1981-86. *Publications:* Of Hobos and Rainbows, 1992; House Cleaning, 1992; Cat's in Cradle, 1992; Ink on the Trees, 1987; Son of Man, 1987; Nickels and Dimes, 1985; Clean, 1992. *Contributions to:* Denver Post; Air Force Times; Colorado Woman's News; San Antonio Light; Alamagordo Daily News; Aurora Sentinel; Lowry Airman; Journal of University of Texas. *Honours:* 3rd Place, National League of American Pen Women, 1992; National Writers Club Award, 1992; Denver Woman's Press Club Award, 1990. *Memberships:* National Writers Club; President, Denver Chapter, 1992. *Address:* Aurora, CO 80013, USA.

HAZARD Jack. *See:* **BOOTH Edwin.**

HAZLETON Lesley, b. 20 Sept 1945, Reading, England. Writer. *Education:* BA, Hons, Psychology, Manchester University, England, 1963-66; MA, Psychology, Hebrew University of Jerusalem, Israel, 1970-72. *Literary Appointment:* Visiting Professor, Penn State University, USA. *Publications:* England, Bloody England, 1989; Jerusalem, Jerusalem, 1986; In Defence of Depression, 1984; Where Mountains Roar, 1980; Israeli Women, 1978. *Contributor to:* New York Times; Harper's; Tikkun; The Nation; New York Review of Books; Vanity Fair and many others; Automotive columnist for Fame and Lear's magazines. *Memberships:* PEN American Center; IMPA (International Motor Press Association). *Literary Agent:* Watkins-Loomis Inc. *Address:* c/o Watkins-Loomis Inc, 150 East 35, New York, NY 10016, USA.

HAZO Samuel (John), b. 1928, American. *Appointments:* joined Faculty 1955, Dean, College of Arts and Science 1961-66, Professor of English 1965-, Duquesne University, Pittsburgh; Director, International Forum, 1966-. *Publications:* Discovery and

Other Poems, 1959; The Quiet Wars, 1962; Hart Crane: An Introduction and Interpretation, 1963, as Smithereened Apart: A Critique of Hart Crane, 1978; The Christian Intellectual: Studies in the Relation of Catholicism to the Human Sciences (ed), 1963; A Selection of Contemporary Religious Poetry (ed), 1963; Listen with the Eye, 1964; My Sons in God: Selected and New Poems, 1965; Blood Rights, 1968; The Blood of Adonis (with Ali Ahmed Said), 1971; Twelve Poems (with George Nama), Seascript: A Mediterranean Logbook, Once for the Last Bandit: New and Previous Poems, 1972; Quartered, 1974; Inscripts, 1975; The Very Fall of the Sun, 1978; To Paris, 1981; The Wanton Summer Air, 1982; Thank a Bored Angel, 1983; The Feast of Icarus, 1984; The Color of Reluctance, The Pittsburgh that Starts Within You, 1986; Silence Spoken Here, 1988; STILLS, 1989; The Restis Prose, 1989; Lebanon, 1990; Picks, 1990; The Past Won's Stay Behind You, 1993. *Address:* 785 Somerville Drive, Pittsburgh, PA 15243, USA.

HAZZARD Shirley, b. 30 Jan 1931, Sydney, Australia. Writer. m. Francis Steegmuller, 22 Dec 1963. *Publications:* Novels: The Transit of Venus, 1980; The Evening of The Holiday, 1966; The Bay of Noon, 1970. Stories: Cliffs of Fall, 1963; People in Glass Houses, 1967. History: Defeat of An Ideal, 1973; Countenance of Truth, 1990. *Contributions to:* The New Yorker; Times Literary Supplement. *Honours:* Award in Literature, National Institute of Arts and Letters, USA, 1966; Guggenheim Fellow, 1974; First prize, O Henry Short Story Awards, 1976; National Book Critics Circle Award for Fiction, 1981. *Membership:* Trustee, New York Society Library. *Literary Agents:* McIntosh & Otis, 310 Madison Avenue, New York, NY 10017, USA and A M Heath, London, England. *Address:* 200 East 66th Street, New York, NY 10021, USA.

HEADLEY Elizabeth. *See:* **HARRISON Elizabeth C.**

HEADLEY John Miles, b. 23 Oct 1929, New York, USA. Educator; Historian. m. Anne Renouf, 27 July 1965, div. *Education:* BA Princeton University, 1951; MA, 1952, PhD, 1960, Yale University. *Publications:* Luther's View of Church History, 1963; The Emperor and his Chancellor, 1983; Co-author, San Carlo Borromeo: Catholic Reform and Ecclesiastical Politics, 1988; Editor, Responsio ad Lutherum, Complete works of St Thomas More, 1969. *Contributions to:* Several journals and magazines including Journal of the History of Ideas. *Honours:* Selma V Forkosch Prize, 1988. *Memberships:* American Society for Reformation Research, Pres, 1978-80; Renaissance Society of America. *Address:* Department of History, University of North Carolina, Chapel Hill, NC 27599, USA.

HEALD Timothy Villiers, (David Lancaster), b. 28 Jan 1944, Dorset, England, Writer. m. Alison Martina Leslie, 30 Mar 1968, 2 sons, 2 daughters. *Education:* MA, Honours, Balliol College, Oxford, 1962-65. *Appointments:* Chairman, Crime Writers Association, 1987-88; International Co-ordinator, Writers in Prison Committee, PEN, 1986-89; Council of Management, Society of Authors, 1988-91. *Publications Include:* Unbecoming Habits; HRH The Man Who Would Be King; The Character of Cricket; Networks; Class Distinctions; Murder at Moosejaw; Blue Blood Will Out; Deadline; Let Sleeping Dogs Die; Masterstoke; Red Herrings; Brought to Book; Business Unusual; The Rigby File (Editor); Its a Dog's Life; Making of Space 1999; John Steed (The Authorised Biography) volume 1; The Newest London Spy (Editor); By Appointments: 150 Years of the Royal Warrant and Its Holders; My Lord's (Editor). *Contributions to:* Numerous magazines and journals; Editor, Sixth Form Opinion; U. *Memberships:* PEN Detection Club; Society of Authors; Crime Writers Association; MCC; Hampton Court Royal Tennis Court. *Literary Agent:* Anthony Harwood, c/o Aitken and Stone. *Address:* 305 Sheen Road, Richmond, Surrey TW10 5AW, England.

HEALEY Denis (Winston), b. 1917, British.

Appointments: Member, Labour Party National Executive Committee; Secretary, Labour Party International Department, 1946-52; Member of Council, Royal Institute of International Affairs, London, 1948-60; Member of the Executive Fabian Society, 1954-61; Member of the Council, Institute of Strategic Studies, 1958- 61; MP for SE Leeds, 1952-55; Labour MP for Leeds East, 1955-1992; Secretary of State for Defence, 1964-70; Shadow Foreign Secretary, 1970-74, 1980; Chancellor of the Exchequer, 1974-79; Baron Healy of Riddlesden, 1992. *Publications:* The Curtain Falls, 1951; New Fabian Essays, 1952; Neutralism, 1955; Fabian International Essays, 1956; A Neutral Belt in Europe, 1958; NATO and American Security, 1959; The Race Against the H Bomb, 1960; Labour Britain and the World, 1963; Managing the Economy, 1979; Healey's Eye, 1980; Labour and World Society, 1985; Beyond Nuclear Deterrence, 1986; The Time of My Life, 1989; (essays) When Shrimps Learn to Whistle, 1990; My Secret Planet, 1992. *Address:* House of Commons, London SW1A 0AA, England.

HEANEY Seamus, b. 13 Apr 1939, Northern Ireland. Author; Poet. m. Marie Devlin, 1965, 2 sons, 1 daughter. *Education:* Queen's University of Belfast. *Appointments:* Lecturer St Joseph's College, Belfast, 1963-66, Queen's University, Belfast, 1966-72; Freelance Writer, 1972-75; Lecturer, Carysfort College, 1975-81; Senior Visiting Lecturer, Harvard University, 1982-; Boylston Professor, Rhetoric and Oratory, 1984-. *Publications:* Poetry: Death of a Naturalist, 1966; Door into the Dark, 1969; Wintering Out, 1972; North, 1975; Field Work, 1979; Sweeney Astray, 1984; Station Island, 1984; The Haw Lantern, 1987; Prose: Preoccupations, 1980; New Selected Poems, 1966-1987, 1990; Seeing Things, 1991; Sweeney's Flight, 1992 (with photographs by Rachel Giese). *Honours:* W. H. Smith Prize, 1975; Bennet Award, 1982. *Address:* c/o Faber and Faber, 3 Queen Square, London WC1N 3AU, England.

HEARLE Kevin James, b. 17 Mar 1958. Poet; Scholar. m. Elizabeth Henderson, 26 Nov 1983. *Education:* AB English, (dist), Stanford , 1980; MFA English, University of Iowa, 1983; MA, Literature, University of California, Santa Cruz, 1991; PhD Literature, University of California, Santa Cruz, 1991. *Appointments:* Poetry Co-Editor, Quarry West, 1988-91; Assistant, National Endowment for the Humanities Summer Institutes on Literary Translation, 1988-89; Lecturer in English, San Jose State University, 1992; Lecturer in American Literature, University of California, Santa Cruz, 1993. *Publications:* Each Thing We Know Is Changed Because We Know It, 1994; (Dissertation), Regions of Discourse: Steinbeck, Cather, Jewett and the Pastoral Tradition of American Regionalism, 1991. *Contributions to:* Yale Review, Georgia Review, University of Windsor Review, American Literature, Quarterly West, New Orleans Review, Poetry Flash, Steinbeck Newsletter; Western American Literature, Steinbeck Quarterly. *Honours:* Finalist: National Poetry Series, Yale Series of Younger Poets, both 1992. *Memberships:* American Literary Translator's Association; Modern Language Association; Western Literature Association; Robinson Jeffers Association, Steinbeck Society. *Address:* 860 Campus Drive No 101, Daly City, CA 94015, USA.

HEARNE John, (John Morris), b. 1926, Jamaican. *Appointments:* Teacher in London and Jamaica, 1950-59; Resident Tutor, Department of Extra-Mural Studies 1962-67, Head of Creative Arts Centre 1968-92, University of West Indies, Kingston. *Publications:* Voices Under the Window, 1955; Stranger at the Gate, 1956; The Faces of Love (in US as The Eye of the Storm), 1957; Autumn Equinox, 1959; Land of the Living, 1961; Fever Grass (with Morris Gargill as John Morris), 1969; The Candywine Development (with Morris Cargill as John Morris), 1970; The Sure Salvation, 1981. *Address:* PO Box 335, Kinston 8, Jamaica.

HEARON Shelby, b. 18 Jan 1931, Kentucky, USA. Writer. m. (1) Robert Hearon Jr, 15 June 1953; (2) Billy Joe Lucas, 19 Apr 1981, 1 son, 1 daughter. *Education:*

BA, University of Texas at Austin, 1953. *Appointments:* Writer in Residence: Ohio Wesleyan University, 1989, The University of California at Irvine, 1987; Writing Tutorial, The 92nd St Y Poetry Centre, Manhattan, 1986-92; Writer in Residence: Clark University, 1985, Wichita State University, 1984; Visiting Writer, Associate Professor, The University of Houston, 1981; Visiting Lecturer, University of Texas at Austin, 1978-80; Professor, University of Illinois Chicago, 1993; Professor, Colgate University, 1993. *Publications:* Armadillo in the Grass, 1968; The Second Dune, 1973; Hannah's House, 1975; Now and Another Time, 1976; A Prince of a Fellow, 1978; Painted Dresses, 1981; Afternoon of a Faun, 1983; Group Therapy, 1984; A Small Town, 1985; Five Hundred Scorpions, 1987; Owning Jolene, 1989; Hug Dancing, 1991; Friends for Life, 1993. *Honours include:* American Academy and Institute of Arts and Letters Literature Prize, 1990; Ingram Merrill Grant, 1987; National Endowment for the Arts Fiction Fellowship, 1983; John Simon Guggenheim Memorial Fellowship for Fiction, 1982. *Memberships:* PEN American Centre; Authors League and Authors Guild; Associated Writing Programmes; Poets and Writers; Women in Communications; Texas Institute of Letters. *Literary Agent:* Wendy Weil; Lecture Agent: Bill Thomson. *Address:* 5 Church Street, North White Plains NY 10603, USA.

HEATER Derek Benjamin, b. 28 Nov 1931, Sydenham, England. Writer. m. Gwyneth Mary Owen, 12 Mar 1982, 1 son, 1 daughter. *Education:* BA, Honours, History, University College London, 1950-53; Postgraduate Certificate in Education, Institute of Education, University of London, 1953- 54. *Appointments:* Editor, Teaching Politics, 1973-79; British member, Editorial Board, International Journal of Political Education, 1977-84; Co-editor, with Bernard Crick, Political Realities Series, 1974-93. *Publications:* Political Ideas in the Modern World, 1960; Contemporary Political Ideas, 1974; Essays on Political Education, (Co-author Bernard Crick), 1977; Our World This Century, 1982; Our World Today, 1985; World Affairs, (Co-author Gwyneth Owen), 1972; World Studies, 1980; Peace Through Education, 1984; Reform and Revolution, 1987; Refugees, 1988; Case Studies in Twentieth-Century World History, 1988; Citizenship: The Civic Ideal in World Histroy, Politics and Education, 1990; The Idea of European Unity, 1992. *Contributions to:* Over 70 articles in learned journals, educational press and contributions to symposia; Approximately 100 entries for encyclopaedias. *Honour:* Children's Book of the Year Award for Refugees, 1988. *Membership:* Founder-Chairman, The Politics Association, 1969-73. *Address:* 3 The Rotyngs, Rottingdean, Brighton BN2 7DX, England.

HEATH Edward (Richard George), Sir, Rt. Hon., b. 1916, Broadstairs, Kent, England. Member of Parliament, Old Bexley & Sidcup; Former Prime Minister, UK and Leader of the Conservative Party. *Education:* Balliol College, Oxford University. *Publications include:* One Nation: A Tory Approach to Social Problems, co-author, 1950; Old World; New Horizons, 1970; Sailing - A Course of My Life, 1975; Music - A Joy for Life, 1976; Travels - People and Places in My Life, 1977; Carols - The Joy of Christmas, 1977. *Honours include:* MBE, 1946; Honorary Degrees: Oxford; Bradford; Westminster College, Salt Lake City, Utah, USA; Paris-Sorbonne, France; Kent University, England, 1985; Visiting Chubb Fellow, Yale University and Montgomery Fellow, Dartmouth College, USA; Lecturer several universities; Guest conductor, various orchestras; Numerous yachting trophies; KG, 1992. *Memberships include:* Past Chairman and Gala Concert Conductor, London Symphony Orchestra Trust; President and Past Tour Conductor, European Economic Community Youth Orchestera; Independent Commission on International Development Issues. *Address:* c/o House of Commons, Westminster, London SW1A 0AA, England.

HEATH Roy A K, b. 1926, Guyanese. *Appointments:* Teacher in London, 1959-; Barrister, 1964-.

Publications: A Man Come Home, 1974; The Murderer, 1978; From the Heat of the Day, 1979; One Generation, 1980; Genetha, 1981; Kwaku, 1982; Orealla, 1984.

HEATHCOTT Mary. *See:* **KEEGAN Mary.**

HEATH-STUBBS John (Francis Alexander), b. 1918. Poet. *Education:* Worcester College for the Blind; Queen's College, Oxford. *Appointments:* English Tutor, 1944-45; Editorial Assistant, Hutchinsons, 1945-46; Gregory Fellow, Poetry, University of Leeds, 1952-55; Visiting Professor English, University of Alexandria, 1955-58, University of Michigan, 1960-61; Lecturer, English Literature, College of St Mark and St John, Chelsea, 1963-73; President, Poetry Society, 1992. *Publications:* Poetry: Wounded Thammuz, 1942; Beauty and the Beast, 1943; The Divided Ways, 1946; The Swarming of the Bees, 1950; A Charm Against the Toothache, 1954; The Triumph of the Muse, 1958; The Blue Fly in his Head, 1962; Selected Poems, 1965; Satires and Epigrams, 1968; Artorius, 1973; A Parliament of Birds, 1975; The Watchman's Flute, 1978; Birds Reconvened, 1980; Buzz Buzz, 1981; Naming of the Best, 1982; The Immolation of Aleph, 1985; Cats Parnassus, 1987; Time Pieces, 1988; Partridge in a Pear Tree, 1988; Ninefold of Charms, 1989; The Parson's Cat, 1991; Collected Poems, 1990; Drama: Helen in Egypt, 1958; Criticism: The Darkling Plain, 1950; Charles Williams, 1955; The Pastoral, 1969; The Ode, 1969; The Verse Satire, 1969; Translations: Hafir of Shiraz, 1952; The Rubiyyat of Omar Khayyam (both with Peter Avery), 1979; Leopardi : Selected Prose and Poetry (with Iris Origo), 1960; the Poems of Anyte with Carol A. Whiteside), 1974; Editor, Selected Poems of Jonathan Swift, 1948; of Tennyson; of Alexander Pope, 1964; In The Shadows, (with David Gray), 1991. *Honours:* Queen's Gold Medal for Poetry, 1973; OBE, 1989. *Address:* 22 Artesian Road, London, W2, England.

HEBALD Carol, b. 6 July 1934, New York City, USA. Writer. *Education:* MFA, University of Iowa, 1971; BA, City College of City University of New York, 1969. *Publications:* Three Blind Mice and Clara Kleinschmidt, (novel), 1989; Martha, (play), 1991. *Contributions to:* Antioch Review; Massachusetts Review; The Humanist; New Letters; Confrontation; North American Review; New York Tribune. *Honours:* McGraw Hill Nomination; Editor's Book Award Pushcart Prize, 1987; PEN American Fund, 1985, 1986; Seaton Award for Poems. *Memberships:* PEN American Centre; Authors Guild of American; Poet and Writers Inc; Phi Beta Kappa. *Address:* 463 West Street No 353, New York, NY 10014, USA.

HEBBLETHWAITE Peter, (Robert Myddleton), b. 30 Sept, Ashton-under-Lyne, England. Writer; Journalist. m. Margaret Speaight, 21 July 1974, 2 sons, 1 daughter. *Education:* MA, 1st Class Honours, Oxford, 1958; Licentiate in Theology, Heythrop College, 1964. *Appointments:* Literary Editor of the Month, then Editor, 1965-73; Lecturer, French, Wadham College, Oxford, 1976-79; Vatican Affairs Writer, The National Catholic Reporter, Kansas City. *Publications:* The Runaway Church, 1975; Christian-Marxist Dialogue, 1977; The Year of Three Popes, 1978; Introducing John Paul II, the Populist Pope, 1982; John XXIII, Pope of the Council, 1984; In the Vatican, 1985; Synod Extraordinary, 1986; Paul VI, The First Modern Pope, 1993. *Contributions to:* Sunday Times; Times Literary Supplement; The Spectator; The Guardian; The Tablet. *Honours:* Christopher Award, 1985. *Memberships:* Catholic Theological Association of Great Britain; National Union of Journalists. *Agent:* Sheila Watson. *Address:* 45 Marston St., Oxford, OX4 1JU, England.

HEBEBER Thomas, b. 13 Nov 1947, Offenbach, Germany. Professor; Political Scince, East Asia and China, University of Trier. m. Jing Wang, 24 Aug 1979, 1 son, 1 daughter. *Education:* University of Heidelberg, 1973; Doctor's Degree, University of Bremen; Qualifications for Professorship, 1989. *Publications:* etal. Corruption in China, 1991; The Functions of the

Individual Sector in China for Labour market and urban development, 1989; Xiandaihua: The modernization process of China, 1990; Nationalitics Policy and Development Policy in China's Minority Areas, 1984; China and its National Minorities: Autonomy or Assimilation, 1989; Editor: Ethnic Minorities in China: Tradition and Transformation, Problems and Strategies in German-Chinese Trade, 1992; Economic Reform in China, 1985; China on its way to the year 2000, 1989; China's Economic Policy after Mao, 1989. *Contributions to:* Various magazines, and journals. *Honours:* Honorary Professor, University of Economics and Finance, Gausu Province, China. *Memberships:* German Associations of Asian Studies, Political Science, Ethnology and Mongolian Studies. *Address:* Pommernstr. 19, 5500 Trier, Germany.

HECHT Anthony Evan, b. 16 Jan 1923, New York, USA. Poet; Professor of English. m. (1) Patricia Harris, 1954, (div 1961), 2 sons, (2) Helen d'Alessandro, 1971, 1 son. *Education:* Bard College; MA, Columbia University. *Appointments:* Teacher, Kenyon college, 1947-48, State University, Iowa, 1948-49, New York University, 1949-56, Smith College, 1956-59; Associate Professor, English, Bard College, 1961-67; Faculty, 1967, John H. Deane Professor, Rhetoric and Poetry, 1968, University of Rochester; Hurst Professor, Washington University, 1971; Professor Graduate School, Georgetown University, 1987-. *Publications:* Poetry: A Summoning of Stones, 1954; The Seven Deadly Sins, 1958; A Bestiary, 1960; The Hard Hours, 1968; Million of Strange Shadows, 1977; Jiggery Pokery (co-author and co-editor), 1967;Seven Against Thebes (translated with Helen Bacon), 1973; The Venetian Vespers, 1979; Obbligati : Essays in Criticism, 1986. *Honours:* Guggenheim Fellow, 1954, 1959; Ford Foundation Fellow, 1967; Rockefeller Foundation Fellow, 1967; Fellow, Academy of American Poets, Chancellor 1971-; Prix de Rome, 1950; Brandeis University Creative Arts Award, 1965; Pulitzer Prize, 1968; Bollingen Prize, 1983; Eugenio Montale Prize for Poetry, 1985. *Memberships:* Trustee, American Academy, Rome; National Institute of Arts and Letters; American Academy of Arts and Science. *Address:* 4256 Nebraska Avenue NW, Washington, DC 20016, USA.

HECKELMANN Charles N, b. 24 Oct 1913, Brooklyn, New York, USA. Book Publisher (Retired); Author. m. 17 Apr 1937, 1 son, 1 daughter. *Education:* BA maxima cum laude, University of Notre Dame, 1934. *Appointments include:* Various editorial, administrative positions with: Cupples & Leon Company, 1937-41; Popular Library, 1941-58; Monarch Books, 1958-65; David McKay Company, 1965-68; Cowles Book Company, 1968-71; Hawthorn Books, 1971-75; National Enquirer, 1975-78. *Publications include:* Trumpets in the Dawn, 1958; Guns of Arizona, 1949; Rawhider, 1952; Bullet Law, 1955; Big Valley, 1966; Writing Fiction for Profit, 1968; Return to Arapahoe, 1980; Wagons to Wind River, 1982. Also: Vengeance Trail, 1944; Lawless Range, 1945; Six-Gun Outcast, 1946; Deputy Marshall, 1947 (also filmed); Let the Guns Roar, 1950. *Contributions to:* 200 short stories, novels, newsletter, various magazines. *Honours:* Valedictorian, senior class, Meyers Burse Award, University of Notre Dame. *Memberships:* Past president, Catholic Writers Guild, Western Writers of America; Life Member, National Cowboy Hall of Fame. *Address:* 10634 Green Trail Drive South, Boynton Beach, Florida 33436, USA.

HECKLER Jonellen, b. 28 Oct 1943, Pittsburgh, Pennsylvania, USA. Writer. m. Lou Heckler, 17 Aug 1968, 1 son. *Education:* BA English Literature, University of Pittsburgh, 1965. *Publications:* Safekeeping, 1983; A Fragile Peace, 1986; White Lies, 1989; Circumstances Unknown, 1993. *Contributions to:* Numerous poems and short stories in Ladies Home Journal magazine between 1975-83. *Memberships:* The Authors Guild. *Literary Agent:* Janklow & Nesbit Associates. *Address:* 5562 Pernod Drive SW, Ft Myers, FL 33919, USA.

HECKSCHER William S(ebastian) b. 14 Dec 1904,

Hamburg, Germany. Professor of Art History; Painter; Freelance Writer. m. Roxanne Sanossian, 15 Feb 1973, 3 daughters. *Education:* Palaeography, Corpus Christi College, Oxford, England; New York University; PhD, Hamburg University, 1936; Diploma in Teaching. *Appointments:* Linguistic Intelligence Work, Canadian Government; Professor of German Language and Literature: Carleton College, Ottawa, Ontario, Canada, Universities of Saskatchewan and Mantioba; Art Histroy Teacher (especially mediaeval art): State University of Iowa, Utrecht University (keeper of 2 libraries); Duke University (founder and director Museum of Art); member Advisory Council to the Minister of Education, the Netherlands. *Publications include:* Sixtvs IIII aeneas Statvas restitvendas censvit, 1955; Rembrandt's Anatomy of Dr. Tulp, 1956; Art and Literature, 1986; The Human Form in Contemprary Art, 1971. *Contributions to:* over 100 articles to literature and art history journals. *Honours:* Hon. Doctorate, McGill University; Carey Award (Society of Indexers), 1987; Bronze Medal, Collège de France, Paris, 1981. *Memberships include:* Fellow, Royal Society of Art; National Gallery Washington DC; six times Member of the Princeton Institute for Advanced Study; Consultant Rare Books, Princeton University Library. *Address:* 32 Wilton Street, Princeton, NJ 08540, USA.

HEDIN Mary Ann, b. 3 Aug 1929, Minneapolis, Minnesota, USA. Professor. m. Roger Willard Hedin, 3 sons, 1 daughter. *Education:* BS, University of Minnesota; MA, University of California. *Appointments:* Fellow, Yaddo, 1974; Writer in Residence Robinson Jeffers Tor House Foundation, 1984-85. *Publications:* Fly Away Home, 1980; Direction, 1983. *Contributions to:* McCalls; Red Book; Southwest Review; South Dakota Review; Descant; O Henry Prize Short Stories; Best American Short Stories; Poems in: Shenandoah; South; Perspective World Order. *Honours:* John H McGinnis Memorial Award, 1979; Iowa School of Letters Award for Short Fiction, 1979. *Memberships:* Authors Guild; PEN; American Poetry Society. *Address:* 182 Oak Avenue, San Anselmo, CA 94960, USA.

HEDLEY Annie. *See:* **HUNT Fay Ann.**

HEFFERNAN Thomas (Carroll), b. 19 Aug 1939, Hyannis, USA. Lecturer. m. Nancy E Iler, 15 July 1972, (div 1978). *Education:* AB, Boston College, 1961; MA, English Literature, University of Manchester, England, 1963; Universita per-Stranieri, Perugia, Italy, Summer, 1965. *Appointments:* Poet in the Schools, North Carolina Department of Public Instruction, Raleigh, 1973-77; Visiting Artist, Poetry, North Carolina Department of Community Colleges, 1977-81; Visiting Artist, Poetry, South Carolina Arts Commission, 1981-82. *Publications:* Mobiles, 1973; A Poem Is A Smile You Can Hear, Editor, 1976; A Narrative of Jeremy Bentham, 1978; The Liam Poems, 1981; City Renewing Itself, 1983. *Contributions to:* various journals and magazines. *Honours:* Recipient, various honours and awards including: NEA Literary Fellowship, 1977; Gordon Barber Memorial Award, Poetry Society of America, 1977; Mainichi Award Tokyo, 1985; JAL/Mainichi Culture Seminar Haiku Award, 1986. *Memberships include:* Poetry Society of America; Academy of American Poets; North Carolina Writers Conference; Modern Language Association. *Address:* Univesity of Maryland, Asian Division Box 100, APO San Francisco, CA 96328, USA.

HEFFRON Dorris M, b. 18 Oct 1944, Canada. Novelist. m. D L Gauer, 29 Oct 1980, 1 son, 3 daughters. *Education:* BA, MA. *Appointments:* Tutor, Lecturer, Oxford University, 1970-80; Tutor, The Open University, 1972-78. *Publications:* A Nice Fire and Some Moonpenies; Crusty Crossed; Rain and I; The Saving Note. *Contributions to:* Queens Quarterly. *Honours:* Canada Council Arts Grant. *Memberships:* Authors Society; Writers Union of Canada; PEN. *Literary Agent:* Sheila Watson, Watson Little Limited. *Address:* 202 Riverside Drive, Toronto, Ontario, Canada. M6S 4A9.

HEGI Ursula Johanna, b. 23 May, 1946, West Germany. Writer and Professor. 2 sons. *Education:* BA, 1978, MA, 1979, UNH. *Appointment:* Currently: Associate Professor of English, Eastern Washington University. *Publications:* Intrusions, 1981; Unearned Pleasures and Other Stories, 1988; Floating in My Mother's Palm, 1990. *Contributions to:* Los Angeles Times Book Review. *Honours:* PEN Syndicated Fiction - four years; NEA 1990; Artist Trust, 1988. *Literary Agent:* Gail Hochman, Brandt and Brandt. *Address:* Eastern Washington University, Cheney, WA 99004, USA.

HEIDE Florence Parry, b. 1919. America, Writer of children's fiction. *Appointments:* Currently fulltime writer. Formerly worked for RKO and in public relations and advertising, New York; former public relations director, Pittsburgh Playhouse. *Publications include:* God and Mr (non-fiction), 1975; You and Me (non-fiction), 1975; (with Roxanne Heide), Mystery of the Vanishing Visitor, 1975; (with Roxanne Heide), Mystery of the Bewitched Bookmobile, 1975; When the Sad One Comes to Stay, 1975; Growing Anyway Up, 1976; (with Roxanne Heide), Mystery of the Lonely Lantern, 1976; (with Roxanne Heide), Mystery at Keyhole Carnival, 1977; (with Roxanne Heide), Brillstone Break-In, 1977; (with Roxanne Heide), Mystery of the Midnight Message, 1977; (with Sylvia W Van Clief), Fables You Shouldn't Pay Any Attention To, 1978; Banana Twist, 1978; Secret Dreamer, Secret Dreams, 1978; (with Roxanne Heide), Feat at Brillstone, 1978; (with Roxanne Heide), Mystery at Southport Cinema, 1978; (with Roxanne Heide), I Love Every-People, 1978; Changes (non-fiction), 1978; Who taught Me? Was It You, God? (non-fiction), 1978; By the Time You Count to Ten (non-fiction), 1979; (with Roxanne Heide), Face at the Brillstone Window, 1979; (with Roxanne Heide), Mystery of the Mummy's Mask, 1979; (with Roxanne Heide), Body in the Brillstone Garage, 1980; (with Roxanne Heide), Mystery of the Forgotten Island, 1980; (with Roxanne Heide), A Monster Is Coming! A Monster Is Coming! 1980; (with Roxanne Heide), Black Magic at Brillstone, 1981; Treehorn's Treasure, 1981; Time's Up! 1982; The Problem with Pulcifer, 1982; The Wendy Puzzle, 1982; (with Roxanne Heide), Time Bomb at Brillstone, 1982; (with Roxanne Heide), Mystery On Danger Road, 1983; Banana Blitz, 1983; Treehorn's Wish, 1984; Time Flies, 1984; Tales for the Perfect Child, 1985; The Day of Ahmed's Secret (with Judith Heide Gilliland), 1990. *Address:* 6910 Third Avenue, Kenosha, WI 53143, USA.

HEIDELBERGER Michael, b. 9 Aug 1947, Karlsruhe, Germany. University Professor. m. Nicole Jeannet, 16 Sept 1978, 1 son, 1 daughter. *Education:* PhD, Philosophy, History of Science, University of Munich, 1978; Habilitation, Philosophy of Science, University of Goettingen, 1989. *Publications:* Co-editor: The Probabilistic Revolution, 1987; Natur und Erfahrung, 1981; Die innere Seite der Natur: Gustav Theodor Fechners Missenschaftlich, a study on G T Fechner (1801-87). Many articles in professional journals, editions of anthologies. *Contributions to:* Studies in history and philosophy of science; Erkennthis; Philosophia Naturalis; British Journal for the Philosophy of Science; Corpus. *Honours:* Best New PSP Book in Social and Behavioural Sciences, Professional and Scholarly Division, Association of American Publishers, 1987. *Memberships:* Philosophy of Science Association; History of Scence Association; Allgemeine Gesellschaft fuer Philosophie in Deutschland; Gesellschaft fuer Wissenschaftsgeschichte; Gesellschaft fuer Analytische Philosophie. *Address:* Philosophisches Seminar, Universitaet Freiburg, 7800 Freiburg, Germany.

HEIGERT Hans A, b. 21 Mar 1925, Mainz, Germany. Journalist. m. Hildegard Straub, 1951, 3 sons, 2 daughters. *Education:* PhD., Universities of Stuttgart, Heidelberg and Oklahoma. *Appointments:* Journalist, Newspapers, Radio and TV, 1950-; Chief Editor, Suddeutsche Zeitung, 1970-85. *Publications:* Statten der Jugend, 1958; Sehnsucht nach der Nation, 1966; Deutschlands falsche Traume, 1968. *Honours:* Winner,

Theodor Heuss Preis, 1969; Bayersicher Verdienstorden, 1974; Bundesverdienstrkreuz, 1979. *Membership:* Presidium Goethe Institute, Munich, 1984-93. *Address:* Eichenstr. 12, 8034 Unterpfaffenhofen/Oberbayern, Germany.

HEILMAN Joan Rattner, b. New York, USA. Freelance Writer. m. 12 Aug 1956, 1 son, 2 daughters. *Education:* BA, Smith College. *Publications:* Unbelievably Good Deals andd Great Adventures That You Absolutely Can't Get Unless You're Over 50, 1988, 1989; Estrogen: The Facts Can Change Your Life, 1991; Ford Models, Crash Course in Looking Great, 1985; Bluebird Rescue, 1992; Having a Cesarean Baby, 1978, 1984; Controlling Diabetes The Easy Way, 1984; The Story of Weight Watches, 1972. *Contributions to:* Numerous major magazines; Contributing editor and a Newspaper Syndicate. *Honour:* Children's Book of the Year, Child Study Book Committee, 1983. *Memberships:* Active Times, Travel Smart, Elke Magazine, American Society of Journalists and Authors; Authors Guild. *Address:* 812 Stuart Avenue, Mamaroneck, NY 10543, USA.

HEIM Alice Winifred, b. 19 Apr 1913, London, England, psychologist. *Education:* BA, 1934, MA, 1938, PhD, 1939, Newnham College, Cambridge. *Publications:* The Appraisal of Intelligence, 1954; Intelligence and Personality, 1970; Psychological Testing, 1975; Teaching and Learning in Higher Education, 1976; Barking Up the Right Tree, 1980; Thicker than Water?, 1983; Understanding Your Dog's Behaviour, 1984; Where Did I Put My Spectacles?, 1990. Nine Psychological Tests, 1955-78. *Contributions to:* Personnel Management; New Universities Quarterly; The Best of Health. *Honours:* Smith-Mundt Fulbright Fellowship, 1951-52; Fellow, British Psychological Society, 1956-; President, Scientists' Lunch Club, 1970-73; President, Psychology Section, British Association for the Advancement of Science, 1977-78. *Membership:* Society of Authors. *Address:* 8 Bateman Street, Cambridge CB2 1NB, England.

HEINERMAN John, b. 3 Dec 1946, Salt Lake City, Utah, USA. Medical Anthropologist; Author; Lecturer. *Education:* Bachelor's and Master's degrees, Union University, Los Angeles; PhD, Ying Ming University, Taipei, Taiwan. *Appointments:* Director, Anthropological Research Center, Salt Lake City, Utah, 1976-; Editor, The Herb Report international newsletter, 1982-86. *Publications:* Science of Herbal Medicine, 1979; Mormon Corporate Empire, 1986; Heinerman's Encyclopedia of Fruits, Vegetables and Herbs, 1988; Spiritual Wisdom of The Native American, 1989; The Herbal Pharmacy, 1989; People in Space, 1990; How To Double The Power of Your Immune System, 1991; Health Secrets From The Ancient World; Treasures in the Earth - Hidden Records of Ancient Empires, 1992; Bible Nutrition & Medicine, 1992; plus 23 other books. *Contributions to:* The Herbalist magazine; Let's Live magazine; East West Journal; Whole Life Magazine; Herbs; The Vitamin Supplement; Language Origins; Society Newsletter; The Herb Report; Vegetarian Times; Anthropological Reports. *Honours:* Chairman of Scientific Papers Session, 2nd International Congress on Traditional Asian Medicine, Surabaya, Indonesia, 1984; Chairman of Scientific Papers Session, 5th International Symposium on Medicinal Plant Research, Airlangga University, Surabaya, 1986; The Matthew and Jason Fountaine Agape Award for Humanitarian Service, 1990. *Memberships:* Society for Medical Anthropology; American Anthropological Association; American Association for the Advancement of Science; International Association for the Study of Traditional Asian Medicine. *Address:* Anthropological Research Center, PO Box 11471, Salt Lake City, UT 84147, USA.

HELD Peter. *See:* **VANCE John Holbrook.**

HELDRETH Leonard Guy, b. 8 Apr 1939, Shinnston, West Virginia, USA. University Professor and Department Head. m. Lillian R Marks, 18 June 1964,

2 sons. *Education:* BS, 1962, MA, English, 1964, West Virginia University; PhD, English, University of Illinois, 1973. *Appointments:* Abstractor/Editor, National Council of Teachers of English/ERIC Clearing House, 1968-70; Instructor, Department of English, then Assistant Professor, 1973-76, Associate Professor, 1976-81, Professor, 1981-, Department Head, 1988-91, 1992-, Interim Dean, College of Arts & Science, 1991-92, Northern Michigan University; Film Reviewer, WNMU-FM Radio, Marquette, Michigan; Video Reviewer, Marquette Monthly newspaper, 1987-. *Publications:* Book chapters: in Search of the Ultimate Weapon: The Fighting Machine in Science Fiction Novels and Films, 1982; Ascending the Depths: Wordsworth on Mt Snowdon, 1982; Clockwork Reels: Mechanical Environments in Science Fiction Films, 1983; The Ultimate Horror: The Image of the Dead Child in King's Stories and Novels. 1985; Close Encounters of the Carnal Kind; Sex with Aliens in Science Fiction, 1986; The Beast Withing: Sexuality and Mwetamorphosis in Horror Films, 1986; Viewing The Body: Stephen King's Portrait of the Artist as Survivor, 1987; The Dead Child as Fantasy in Albee's Plays, 1988; From Reality to Fantasy in Albee's The Zoo Story, 1988-89; Fantasy in Forster's Short Fiction, 1990; The Supernatural Short Fiction of Henry James, 1990; The Cutting Edges of Blade Runner. *Contributions to:* Video Views to Marquette Monthly; 12 articles or features, Marquette Monthly, Journal of the Fantastic in the Arts, Fantasy Review, CEA Critic. *Honour:* Distinguished Faculty Award, Northern Michigan University, 1987. *Memberships:* Secretary, International Association for the Fantastic in the Arts; Popular Culture Association; Science Fiction Research Association; Popular Culture in the South; Secretary/Treasurer, Michigan Association of Departments of English; Board Member, Michigan Council for the Humanities. *Address:* 367 East Hewitt Avenue, Marquette, MI 49855, USA.

HELLER Joseph, b. 1 May 1923, Brooklyn, USA. Writer. m. (1) Shirley Held, 1945, 1 son, 1 daughter, (2) Valerie Humphries, 1987. *Education:* New York University; Columbia University; University of Oxford; MA. *Appointments:* Instructor, Pennsylvania State University, 1950-52; Advertisement Writer, Time Magazine, 1952-56, Look Magazine, 1956-58; promotion Manager, McCall's Magazine, 1958-61; Former Teacher of Writing, Yale University, University of Pennsylvania, City University, New York. *Publications:* Novels: Catch 22, 1961; Something Happened, 1974; Good as Gold, 1979; God Knows, 1984; Poetics, 1987; Plays: We Bombed in New Haven, 1968; Clevinger's Trial, 1974; No Laughing Matter (with Speed Vogel), 1985. *Honours:* National Institute of Arts and Letters Grant for Literature, 1963; Prix Medicis Etranger, 1985. *Address:* c/o General Publishing Co., Po Box 429, Dayton, OH 45449, USA.

HELLER Marlene Ann,b. 31 Aug 1953, Brooklyn, New York, USA. Freelance Writer; Editor; Personal Poet. m. Gary Robert Heller, 27 July 1985, 1 son, 1 daughter. *Education:*BA, Monmouth College, 1975. *Appointments:* Associate Editor, Craft Model & Hobby Industry Magazine, 1975; Production Editor, Bell Labs, 1976; Marketing Editor, Gifts & Decorative Accessories Magazine, 1977-80; Business Correspondent, North Brunswick Post, 1987. *Contributions to:* Model Retailer; Home Fashions-Textiles; Retail Week; Flowers; Stringer, Princeton Packet Newspapers. *Memberships:* National Writers Club; Writers Data Bank.

HELLER Ruth. *See:* HELLER GROSS Ruth Myrtle.

HELLER GROSS Ruth Myrtle, (Ruth Heller), b. 2 Apr 1923, Winnipeg, Canada. m. (1) Henry David Heller, 21 Dec 1951; (2) Richard Philip Gross, 121 Feb 1987, 2 sons. *Education:* BA Fine Arts, University of California, 1946; California College of Arts and Crafts, 1963-65. *Publications:* Chickens Are'nt the Only Ones, 1981; The Reason for a Flower, 1983; A Cache of Jewels, 1987; Kites Sail High, 1988; Many Luscious Lollipops, 1989; Animals Born Alive and Well, 1982; Plants that Never Ever Bloom, 1984; How to Hide a Butterfly, How to Hide a Polar Bear, How to Hide an Octopus, 1984; How to Hide a Crocodile, How to Hide a Grey Tree Frog, How to Hide Whip Pool Will, 1986; Merry Go Round, 1990; Up Up and Away, 1991. *Honours:* Chickens Aren't The Only Ones won a honorable mention from the New York Academy of Science, 1983. *Address:* 150 Lombard St, San Francisco, CA 94111, USA.

HELLIKER Adam Andrew Alexander, b. 13 Sept 1958, Nocton, Lincolnshire, England. Journalist. *Appointments:* Staff, Western Times Co Ltd, 1978-81; Staff, 1981-, Deputy Editor, 1986-, Daily Mail. *Publications:* The Debrett Season, 1981. *Contributions to:* Country Life; Harpers & Queen; Majesty; Tatler; Working Woman, Motoring Editor, 1986; Woman's Own; Spectator. *Memberships:* Fellow, Royal Geogrpahical Society; Royal Automobile Club; Carlton Club; Fellow, Royal Society of Arts. *Address:* 1 Sandilands Road, London SW6, England.

HELLYER Jill, b. 17 Apr 1925, Writer. m. 21 Aug 1948, div, 2 sons, 1 daughter. *Appointment:* Foundation Executive Secretary, Australian Society of Authors. *Publications:* The Exile, 1969; Not Enough Savages, 1975; Song of the Humpback Whales, 1981. *Contributions to:* Sydney Morning Herald; The Age; The Australian; Overland; Southerly; Meanjin; Westerly; New Poetry. *Honours:* Grenfell Henry Lawson Award, 1963; Poetry Magazine Award, 1965. *Membership:* Australian Society of Authors. *Address:* 25 Berowra Road, Mt Colah, New South Wales 2079, Australia.

HELMINEN Jussi, b. 7 Oct 1947, Turku, Finland. Dramatist; Theatre Director. m. Tellervo Helminen, 1973, 3 sons. *Education:* Finnish Theatre Academy. *Publications:* Up to the Stage! 1989; Plays: The Drugstory, 1972; Hello World, 1973; The Numskulls, 1975; Yellowcloth, 1985; Mutjo, 1987; 'Try With Water' answered the firechief, 1977; Cortex, 1990; TV Plays: Mother Gets Married, 1973; Bigboy and the Boot, 1975; Hands, 1975; Mother's Difficult Age, 1983; Reflection, 1984; Smiley, 1984; Impossibles, 1986. *Honours:* Finnish State Drama Award, 1971, 1972; TV (Eurovision) Prix Jeunesse in Munich, 1974; TV (Intervision) Prix Donau Bratislava, 1975; Tampere Theatre Summer Award, 1972, 1973. *Membership:* Finnish Dramatists Union. *Agent:* Finnish Dramatists Union. *Address:* TTT, PI 139, 33201 Tampere, Finland.

HELMKER Judith A, b. 1940, United States of America. Writer. *Publications:* The Organization and Administration of High School Girl's Athletic Association, 1968; A Manual of Snowmobling, 1971, 1975; All Terrain Vehicles, 1974; The Autobiography of Pain, 1976; The Complete Guide to Aerobic Exercise, 1986.

HELPRIN Mark, b. 1947, United States of America. Author. *Publications:* A Dove of the East and Other Stories, 1975; Refiner's Fire, 1977; Ellis Island and Other Stories, 1980; Winter's Tale, 1983. *Address:* c/o Julian Bach Literary Agency, 747 Third Avenue, New York, NY 10017, USA.

HELWIG David (Gordon), b. 1938, Canada. Author; Poet. *Publications:* Figures in a Landscape, 1967; A Time in Winter (play), 1967; The Sign of Gunman, 1969; The Streets of Summer (short stories), 1969; The Day Before Tomorrow (novel), 1971; Fourteen Stories High: Best Canadian Stories of 71 (with T. Marshall), 1971; The Best Name of Silence, 1972; A Book about Billie, 1972, 72, 73 and 74 (with J. Harcourt); New Canadian Stories, 3 vols, 1972-74; The Glass Knight (novel), 1976; The Human Elements, 1978; A Book of the Hours (poetry), 1979; Jennifer (novel), 1979; The King's Evil (novel), 1981; It Is Always Summer (novel), 1982; The Rain Falls Like Rain (verse), 1982; Catchpenny Poems, 1983; A Sound Like Laughter (novel), 1983; The Only Son (novel), 1984; The Bishop, 1986; A Postcard from Rome (novel), 1988; Old Wars (novel) 1989; The Hundred Old Names (verse) 1988; Of Desire (novel) 1990. *Address:* 106 Montreal Street, Kingston, Ontario, Canada K7K 3E8.

HELYAR Jane Penelope Josephine (Josephine Poole), b. 12 Feb 1933, London, England. Writer. m. (1) T R Poole, 1956, (2) V J H Helyar, 1975, 1 son, 5 daughters. *Major Publications:* A Dream in the House, 1961; Moon Eyes, 1965; The Lilywhite Boys, 1967B; Catch as Catch Can, 1969; Yokeham, 1970; Billy Buck, 1972; Touch & Go, 1976; When Fishes Flew, 1978; The Open Grave, The Forbidden Room, (remedial readers), 1979; Hannah Chance, 1980; Diamond Jack, 1983; The Country Dairy Companion (to accompany Central TV series), 1983; Three for Luck, 1985; Wildlife Tales, 1986; The Loving Ghosts, 1988; Angel, 1989; This Is Me Speaking, 1990; Paul Loves Amy Loves Christo, 1992; Puss in Boots, 1988; The Sleeping Beauty, 1989; Snow White, 1990; TV Scripts: The Harbourer, 1975; The Sabbatical, The Breakdown, Miss Constantine (all 1981); Ring a Ring a Rosie, With Love, Belinda, The Wit to Woo, (all 1983) in West Country Stories Series: Fox, Buzzard, Dartmoor Pony, (all 1984), in Three in the Wild Series. *Literary Agent:* Gina Pollinger. *Address:* Poundisford Lodge, Poundisford, Taunton, Somerset TA3 7AE, England.

HEMINGWAY Maggie, b. 17 Mar 1946, Orford, England. Writer. *Education:* MA, Edinburgh. *Publications:* The Bridge, 1986; Stop House Blues, 1988; The Postmen's House, 1990. *Honours:* The Royal Society of Literature Winifred Holtby Ward, 1980. *Memberships:* PEN. *Literary Agent:* Curtis Brown. *Address:* c/o Curtis Brown, 162- 168 Regent Street, London W1V 5TB, England.

HEMLEY Robin, b. 28 May 1958, New York City, USA. Associate Professor of English. m. Beverly Bertling Hemley, 18 July 1987, 1 daughter. *Education:* BA, Comparative Literature, Indiana University, 1980; MFA, University of Iowa, 1982; Associate Professor of English, University of North Carolina at Charlotte, 1986-. *Appointments:* Associate Professor of English, University of North Carolina at Charlotte, 1986-. *Publications:* The Last Studebaker, 1992; All you can Eat, 1988, 1989, The Mouse Town, 1987; Stadt Der Maus, 1992; Tabehodai (translation of A You Can Eat, Hakusui-sha, Tokyo, Japan, 1990). *Contributions to:* Pushcard Prize Anthology XV; North American Review; Story; 20 Under 30: Best Stories by America's New Young Writers. *Honours:* Illinois Arts Council Fellowship, 1983, 1984; Walter Rumsey Marvin Award for Fiction, Ohioana Library Association, 1984; Word Beat Press Book Award, 1986; North Carolina Arts Council Fellowship, 1988; Story Magazine Humour Competition, 1991; PEN Syndicated Fiction Award, 1991. *Memberships:* PEN; Poets and Writers; National Book Critics Circle; Associated Writers Program; North Carolina Writers' Network. *Literary Agent:* Elizabeth Grossman, Sterling Lord Literistic. *Address:* 2021 Thomas Avenue, Charlotte, NC 28205, USA.

HEMMING John Henry, b. 5 Jan 1935, Vancouver, Canada. Author; Publisher. m. Sukie Babington-Smith, 1979, 1 son, 1 daughter. *Education:* McGill and Oxford Universities; MA; D.Litt. *Appointments:* Director, Secretary, Royal Geographical Society, 1975-; Joint Chairman, Hemming Publishing Ltd., 1976-; Chair, Brintex Ltd., Newman Books Ltd; Explorations in Peru and Brazil, 1960, 1961, 1971, 1972, 1986-87. *Publications:* The Conquest of the Incas, 1970; Tribes of the Amazon Basin in Brazil (with others), 1973; Red Gold: The Conquest of the Brazilian Indians, 1978; The Search for El Dorado, 1978; Machu Picchu, 1982; Monuments of the Incas, 1983; Change in the Amazon Basin, 2 volumes (Editor), 1985; Amazon Frontier: The Defeat of the Brazilian Indians, 1987; Maracá, 1988; Roraima: Brazil's Northern Most Frontier, 1990. *Honours:* Pitman Literary Prize, 1970; Founder's Medal, Royal Geographical Society, 1971; Christopher Award, USA, 1971; Orden de Merito, Peru, 1987; Mungo Park Medal, Royal Scottish Geographical Society, 1988; Hon DLitt, University of Warwick, 1989, University of Stirling,

1991. *Address:* Hemming Publishing Ltd., 32 Vauxhall Bridge Road, London SW1V 2SS, England.

HENDERSON Kathy Caecilia, b. 22 Apr 1949, Oxford, England. Writer; Illustrator; Editor. 2 sons, 1 daughter. *Education:* BA Hons, English Language and Literature, Oxford, 1969. *Publications:* My Song is My Own, 1979; Sam and the Big Machines, 1985; 15 Ways to go to Bed, 1986; Series, Where does it come from? Water, 1986; Sweater, 1986; Lego, 1986, Banana, 1986, Bread, 1987, Letter, 1987; Sam and the Box, 1987; The Babysitter, 1988; Don't Interrupt!, 1988; The Baby's Book of Babies, 1988; 15 Ways to get Dressed, 1989; Sam, Lizzie and the Bonfire, 1989; Baby Knows Best, 1991; Annie and the Birds, 1991; Second Time Charley, 1991; In the middle of the Night, 1992; Pappy Mashy, 1992; Annie and the Tiger, 1992; Jim's Winter 1992; *Honours:* 15 Ways to go to Bed, Shortlisted for the Smarties Prize, 1986; Sam and the Big Machines, Selected by Parents magazine for its Best Books for Babies, 1987; Selected for the Book Trust's Childrens Books of the Year, 1987, 1989, 1990, 1993. *Address:* Muswell Hill, London N10 3UN, England.

HENDERSON Laurence, b. 1928. Author. *Publications:* With Intent, 1968; Sitting Target, 1970; Cage Until Tame, 1972; Major Enquiry, 1977; The Patriot Game, 1985; The Final Glass, 1990. *Address:* 57 Crown Hill, Rayleigh, Essex, England.

HENDERSON Maurice Brian, b. 1 Jan 1961, Philadelphia, Pennsylvania, USA. Professional Writer; Teacher. *Education:* BBA, Adelphi University, New York, 1983; New York Institute of Technology,1984. *Appointments include:* Associate Editor, Umoja national news magazine, 1983-85; Theatre Critic, Scoop USA newspaper. *Publications include:* When I Stopped To Think, 1983; Images, 1984; When the Walls Come Tumbling Down, 1986; Voices Around Me, 1987; A Collectors Item, 1987. Also various plays: Ghettoland; No Where to Run; Color Me Black. Nationally syndicated column. *Contributions to:* Black American; Norfolk Journal; Final Call; Scoop USA; Black Masks. *Honours include:* Langston Hughes Award, 1983; Black Arts Award, 1984; Alpha Phi Alpha Literary Award, 1985. *Membership:* NYC Critics Association. *Literary Agent:* New Arts Productions. *Address:* 2340 Tasker Street, Philadelphia, Pennsylvania 19145, USA.

HENDERSON Nicholas, b. 1 Apr 1919, London, England. Diplomat; Author; Company Director. m. 19 Dec 1951, 1 daughter. *Education:* Stowe School; MA Hon DCL, Hertford College, Oxford. *Publications:* Prince Eugen, 1964; The Birth of NATO, 1982; The Private Office, 1984; Channels and Tunnels, 1986. *Contributions to:* History Today; Country Life; Daily and weekly press. *Memberships:* Literary Society. *Address:* 6 Fairholt Street, London SW7 1EG, England.

HENDERSON Richard, b. 20 Oct 1924, Baltimore, Maryland, USA. Commercial Artist; Writer. m. Sarah L Symington, 28 June 1947, 1 son, 1 daughter. *Publications include:* First Sail for Skipper, 1960; Hand, Reef and Steer, 1965; Dangerous Voyages of Capt William Andrews (ed), 1966; Sail and Power, 1967; The Racing-Cruiser, 1970; Encyclopedia of Sailing, (Co-author), 1971; Sea Sense, 1972; The Cruisers Compendium, 1973; Singlehanded Sailing, 1976; Better Sailing, 1977; Choice Yacht Design, 1979; Philip L Rhodes and His Yacht Designs, 1981; 53 Boats You can Build, 1985; John G Alden and His yacht Designs, (Co-author Robert Carrick), 1983; Heavy Weather Guide, (Co-author William J Kotsch), 1984; Understanding Rigs and Rigging, 1985; Sailing at Night, 1987; Sailing in Windy Weather, 1987; East to the Azores, 1978. *Contributions to:* Yachting; Telltale Compass; Rudder; Cruising World; Ocean Navigator; Yachting Monthly; Motor Boating and Sailing. *Memberships:* American Boat and Yacht Council, Seaworthiness Technical Committee; Cruising Club of America; Ocean Cruising Club; Slocum Society. *Address:* Box 185, Gibson Island, MD 21056, USA.

HENDERSON-HOWAT Gerald. *See:* **HOWAT Gerald Malcolm David.**

HENDON Donald W, b. USA. University Professor; Author. *Education:* MBA, University of California, Berkeley; BBA, PhD, University of Texas Austin. *Appointments:* Professor, Marketing, University of North Alabama; President, Business Consultants International; Adviser to firms in USA and Worldwide. *Publications:* Author, 335 separate works including: Battling for Profits, How to Negotiate Worldwide, World Class Negotiating, Classic Failures in Product Marketing; 4 monographs; 50 journal articles. *Contributions to:* numerous journals and magazines including: Journal of Marketing; Journal of Applied Psychology; Business Horizons; 8 journals in the UK, Singapore, Hong Kong, Mexico, Philippines, Peru, and 5 in Australia. *Memberships:* 16 professional associations including: Academy of International Business; Academy of Management; MENSA; American Marketing Association. *Address:* Dept. of Marketing, University of North Alabama, Florence, TN 35632, USA.

HENDRICKS Kathleen, b. 28 July 1939, Salem, Virginia, USA. Author. m. Robert F. Hendricks, 26 Apr 1958, 1 son, 1 daughter. *Education:* National Business College, 1957-58; Writer's Institute of America, 1968-70. *Publications:* Man's Zeal, 1986; Freedom, 1986; To Bob, My Love, 1987; Coming of Age, 1987; Clan-Destined, 1987; Destiny, 1987. *Contributions to:* Columnist, Solon, Iowa Newspaper; Organization Reporter, Iowa City; Contributor, numerous articles to professional journals. *Honours:* Honourable Mention: Lyrical Iowa, 1987, World of Poetry, 1987; Golden Poet Award, World of Poetry, 1987. *Memberships:* Chairperson, numerous community and national Charities in Virginia, Michigan and Iowa; Active, Community activities and Improvement Plans. *Address:* 261 Hillcrest Court, Central City, IA 52214, USA.

HENDRIKS A(rthur) L(emiere), b. 1922, Jamaica. Poet; Freelance Writer. *Publications:* The Independence Anthology of Jamaican Literature (with C. Lindo), 1962; On This Mountain and Other Poems, 1965; These Green Islands, 1971; Muet, 1971; Madonna of the Unknown Nation, 1974; The Islanders and Other Poems, 1983; Archie and the Princess and the Everythingest Horse (for children), 1983; The Naked Ghost and Other Poems, 1984; Great Families of Jamaica, 1984; To Speak Slowly: Selected Poems, 1986. *Address:* Box 265, Constant Spring, Kingston 8, Jamaica.

HENDRY Diana, Writer. *Education:* BA, University of Bristol; M Litt. *Appointments include:* Part Time English Teacher, Clifton College, 1984-87; Part Time Lecturer, Bristol Polytechnic, 1987-; WEA, Modern Poets Course, 1987-; Tutor, Open University, 1991-92. *Publications:* Midnight Pirate; Fiona Finds Her Tongue; Hettys First Fling; The Not Anywhere House; The Rainbow Watchers; The Carey Street Cat; Christmas in Exeter Street; Sam Sticks and Delilah; A Camel Called April; Double Vision; A Moment for Joe; Harvey Angell; Kid Kibble. *Contributions to:* Bananas Magazine; The Guardian; TES; THEs; Poetry Review. *Honours:* Stroud International Poetry Competition, 1st Prize; Runner Up, Manchester Open Poetry Competition; 3rd Prize, Peterloo Poetry Competition; Whitbread Award; 5th Prize, Cardiff International Poetry. *Memberships:* Society of Authors. *Address:* 52 York Road, Montpelier, Bristol, BS6 5QF, England.

HENDRY Joy McLaggan b. 3 Feb 1953, Perth, Scotland. Writer; Broadcaster. m. Ian Montgomery, 25 July 1986. *Education:* MA, Honours, Edinburgh University, 1970-76; Diploma in Education, Moray House College, Edinburgh University, 1976-77. *Appointments:* Editor, Chapman Magazine; General Editor, Scottish Critics Series, Edinburgh University Press; Director, Chapman Publications; Radio critic, Scotsman newspaper. *Publications:* (Editor) Poems and Pictures by Wendy Wood, 1985; Critical Essays on Sorley MacLean, (Co-editor Raymond J Ross), 1986;

Critical Essays on Norman MacCaig, (Co-editor Raymond Ross), 1991; The Land for the People, (Co-editor Irene Tait); Sang down wi' a Sang, Play on Perth poet William Soutar, Produced at Perth Theatre, 1990. *Contributions to:* Cencrastus; Oxford Poetry; Agenda; Lallans; Scottish Literary Journal; The Scots Magazine; The Scotsman; Glasgow Herald; Scotland on Sunday; Der Spiegel; Poetry Ireland; BBC Scotland, Radio 3, Radio 4 and STV. *Memberships:* Scottish PEN; Deputy Convener, Scottish Poetry Library; Ex-convener, Committee for the Advancement of Scottish Literature in Schools; Committee Member, Advisory Council for the Arts in Scotland; NUJ; Member, Scottish Arts Council Drama Committee, 1991-. *Address:* 4 Broughton Place, Edinburgh EH1 3RX, Scotland.

HENDRY Thomas, b. 1929, Canada. Author; Playwright. *Appointments Include:* Editor, The Stage in Canada, Toronto, 1965-69; Literary Manager, Stratford Festival, Ontario, 1969, 1970. *Publications:* 15 Miles of Broken Glass, 1968, 1972; The Canadians (on English-Canadian theatre), 1967; That Boy-Call Him Back, 1972; You Smell Good To Me and Seance, 1972; The Missionary Position, 1972; Grave Diggers of 1942 (musical - with S. Jack), 1973; Lady Byron Vindicated, 1976; Naked at the Opera, 1976; Farr Away (novel), 1978; Cultural Capital: The Care and Feeding of Toronto's Artistic Assets, 1983. *Address:* 34 Elgin Avenue, Toronto, Ontario, Canada M5R 1G6.

HENES Donna, b. 19 Sept 1945, Cleveland, Ohio, USA. Urban Shamam; Writer; Educator; Photographer. *Education:* BS, 1970, MS, 1971, City College of New York. *Publications:* Dressing our Wounds in Warm Clothes, 1982; Noting the Process of Noting the Process, 1977. *Contributions to:* Bimonthly column for Free Spirit Magazine and Syndicated in the US and Canada: Celestially Auspicious Occasions: Seasons, Cycles and Celebrations. *Honours:* Fellow, Creative Non Fiction, NY Foundation for the Arts. *Memberships:* Poets and Writers; International Centre for Celebration, Co-Founder and Board Member; International Friends of Transformative Art; Healing Through the Arts. *Literary Agent:* Donale Lehr. *Address:* Old PS 9 279 Sterling Place, Exotic Brooklyn, NY 11238, USA.

HENISSART Paul, b. 1923, United States of America. Author. *Appointments:* Correspondent, Bureau Chief, Radio Free Europe, 1961- 63; Writer, ABC, New York City, 1964-65; Correspondent, Voice of America, Washington, DC, 1965-66; European Correspondent, Mutual Broadcasting System, New York City, 1966-73. *Publications:* Wolves in the City: The Death of French Algeria, 1971; Narrow Exit, 1974; The Winter Spy (in United Kingdom as Winter Quarry), 1976; Margin of Error, 1980. *Address:* c/o William Morris Agency, 1350 Avenue of the Americas, New York, NY 10019, USA.

HENLEY Elizabeth Becker, b. 8 May 1952, Jackson, Mississippi, USA. Playwright. *Education:* BFA, Southern Methodist University. *Publications:* Crimes of the Heart, 1981; The Wake of Jamey Foster, 1982; Am I Blue, 1982; The Miss Firecracker Contest, 1984; The Lucky Spot, 1987; The Debutante Ball, 1988. *Honours:* Pulitzer Prize for Drama, 1981; New York Drama Critics Circle Best Play Award, 1981; George Oppenheimer/Newsday Playwriting Award, 1981. *Address:* c/o Gilbert Parker, The William Morris Agency, 1350 Avenue of the Americas, New York, NY 10019, USA.

HENNESSEY Hugh. *See:* **DONOVAN John.**

HENNESSY Peter John, b. 28 Mar 1947, London, England. Author; Professor; Journalist; Broadcaster. m. Enid Mary Candler, 14 June 1969, 2 daughters. *Education:* BA 1969, PhD 1990, Cambridge; London School of Economics, 1969-71; Harvard, Kennedy Memorial Scholar, 1971-72. *Appointments:* Times Higher Education Supplement, 1972-74; The Times, 1974-76; Lobby Correspondent, Financial Times, 1976; Whitehall Correspondent, The Times, 1976-82; The

Economist, 1982; Leader Writer, The Times, 1982-84; Columnist, New Statesman, 1986-87; Columnist, The Independent, 1987-91; Professor of Contemporary History, Queen Mary and Westfield College, University of London, 1992-. *Publications:* Never Again: Britain, 1945-51, Duff Cooper Prize, 1993; Whitehall, 1989; Cabinet, 1986; Sources close to the Prime Minister, 1984, co-author: States of Emergency, 1983, co-author: What the Papers Never Said, 1985. *Contributions to:* Columnist, Director Magazine, 1990-. *Literary Agent:* Giles Gordon, Shieland Associates. *Address:* Department of History, Queen Mary and Westfield Colege, Mile End Road, London E14 N5O.

HENNING Ann Margareta Maria (Viscountess Jocelyn), b. 5 Aug 1948, Goteborg. Author; Translator. m. Viscount Jocelyn, 13 Feb 1986, 1 son. *Education:* BA, Lund University, Sweden, 1975. *Publications:* The Connemara Whirlwind, 1990; The Connemara Stallion, 1991; Modern Astrology, 1985. *Contributions to:* Vogue Magazine. *Memberships:* Translators Association; Society of Authors; SWEA; SELTA. *Address:* 4 The Boltons, London SW10 9TB, England.

HENRY Desmond Paul, b. 5 July 1921, Almondbury, Yorks, England. Philosopher; Artist. m. Louise H J Bayen, 19 May 1945, 3 daughters. *Education:* BA Hons, Philosophy, University of Leeds, 1949; PhD, University of Manchester, 1960. *Appointments:* Philosophy Teacher, University of Manchester, 1949-82; Visiting Professor: Brown University, 1966; University of Pennsylvania, 1970. *Publications:* The Logic of St Anselm, 1967; Medieval Logic and Metaphysics, 1972; Commentary on De Grammatico, 1974; That Most Subtle Queston, 1984; Medieval Mereology, 1991; The De Grammiatco of St Anselm, 1964; Teaching and Study Companion, 1977. *Contributions to:* The Proslogion Proofs, 1955; St Anselm's Nonsense, 1963 and dozens of others. *Memberships:* Societe Internationale pour L'Etude de la Philosophie Medievale; Past President, Manchester Mediaeval Society. *Address:* 4 Burford Drive, Whalley Range, Manchester M16 8FJ, England.

HENSHAW James Ene, b. 29 Aug 1924, Calabar, Nigeria. Medical Practitioner. m. Caroline Womadi, 15 Feb 1958, 5 sons, 3 daughters. *Education:* Christ the King College, Onitsha, Nigeria, 1938-41; MB,BCh, BAO(NUI), University College, Dublin, Ireland, 1949; TDD, Cardiff, Wales, 1954. *Literary Appointments:* Editor, Eastern Nigeria Medical Circular, special publication, Nigerian Independence, 1960-61. Chairman, Cultural Centre Board, Cross River State, Nigeria, 1975-78. *Publications:* This Is Our Chance: Plays from West Africa, London, 1957; Children of the Goddess, 1964; Medicine for Love, London, 1964; Dinner for Promotion, London, 1967; Enough is Enough, Nigeria, 1976; A Song to Mary Charles, Irish Sister of Charity, Nigeria, 1985. *Contributions to:* Medical journals, West Africa, UK. *Honours:* Henry Carr Memorial Cup, 1st prize, playwriting, All Nigeria Festival of Arts, 1952; Knight, Order of St Gregory, (Pope Paul VI), 1965; Officer, Order of Niger, for medical services & contributions to literature, 1978. *Memberships include:* Association of Nigerian Authors; Nigerian Medical Association; Nigerian Medical Council, 1970-72. *Address:* Itiaba House, 4 Calabar Road, Calabar, Nigeria.

HENSTELL Bruce Michael, b. 3 Oct 1945, Los Angeles, California, USA. Writer; Producer. m. 4 Aug 1983, 1 son. *Education:* Ba University of California, Berkeley; MA University of Michigan; MLS, University of California, Los Angeles. *Appointments:* Freelance Writer, 1967-; Film Writer, 1972-; Writer, Producer: KCBS TV, 1981-86, Los Angeles History Project, KCTV, 1989, 1990; Chief Librarian, Curator of Photographic Collections, California Historical Society, 1979-80; Director of Research, LA Daily News Project, UCLA University Research Library, 1981-82. *Publications:* American Film Criticism, 1967; Los Angeles: An illustrated History, 1981; Sunshine and Wealth: Los Angeles in the 20s and 30s, 1985; The Home Front: Los Angeles in the 1940s. *Contributions to:* Los Angeles

Times; Los Angeles Magazine; New York Times; Westways. *Honours:* Southern California Radio and TV News Editors Golden Mike, 1981; Academy of Television Arts and Sciences Emmy Nominations, 1982, 1983, 1984, 1989; Academy of Television Emmy, 1984. Silver Medal, NY International Film and Video Festival, 1984. WAVE Award, 1991; Southern California Cable Association Diamond Award. *Memberships:* Society of Los Angeles Chronologers (past President). *Literary Agent:* Mitchell Hamilburg. *Address:* Santa Monica, CA 90405, USA.

HERALD Kathleen. *See:* PEYTON Kathleen Wendy.

HERBERT Brian Patrick, b. 29 June 1947, Seattle USA. Author. *Education:* BA, Sociology, University of California at Berkeley, 1968. *Publications:* Songs of Muad' Dib (Editor), 1992; The Race for God, 1990; Memorymakers, (Co-author Marie Landis), 1990; The Notebooks of Dune, (Editor), 1988; Prisoners of Arionn, 1987; Man of Two Worlds, (Co-author Frank Herbert), 1986; Sudanna, Sudanna, 1985; The Garbage Chronicles, 1984; Sidney's Comet, 1983; Incredible Insurance Claims, 1982; Classic Comebacks, 1981. *Honours:* Guest of Honour, Dragon Con SF-Fantasy Convention, 1987. *Memberships:* Science Fiction Writers of America; National Writers Club; L-5 Society. *Literary Agent:* Curtis Brown Limited, New York City. *Address:* PO Box 3381, Bellevue, WA 98009, USA.

HERBERT Ivor, b. 1925. Author; Journalist; Scriptwriter. *Appointments:* Travel Editor, Racing Editor, The Mail on Sunday, 1982-. *Publications:* Eastern Windows, 1953; Point to Point, 1964; Arkle: The Story of a Champion, 1966, 1975; The Great St Trinian's Train Robbery, screenplay, 1966; The Queen Mother's Horses, 1967; The Winter Kings, co author, 1968, enlarged, 1989; The Way to the Top, 1969; Night of the Blue Demands, play, co-author, 1971; Over Our Dead Bodies, 1972; The Diamond Diggers, 1972; Scarlet Feaver, co-author, 1972; Winter's Tale, 1974; Red Rum: Story of a Horse of Courage, 1974; Television scripts: Hyperion: THe Millionaire Horse, Odds Against?, The Queens Horses; The Filly, novel, 1977; Six at the Top, 1977; Classic Touch, TV documentary, 1985; Spot the Winner, 1978, updated, 1990; Longacre, 1978; Horse Racing, 1980; Vincent O'Brien's Great Horses, co-author, 1984; Revolting Behaviour, 1987; Herbert's Travels, 1987; Reflections on Racing, co-author, 1990; Riding Through My Life (with HRH The Princess Royal), 1991; Partner in: Equus Productions Ltd (video) and Bradenham Wines. *Address:* c/o David Higham Associates Ltd, 5-8 Lower John Street, London W1R 4HA, England.

HERBERT James (John), b. 1943. Author. *Publications:* The Rats, 1974; The Fog, 1975; The Survivor, 1976; Fluke, 1977; The Spear, 1978; Lair, 1979; The Dark, 1980; The Jonah, 1981; Shrine, 1983; Domain, 1984; Moon, 1985; The Magic Cottage, 1986; Sepulchre, 1987; Haunted, 1988; Creed, 1990; Portent, 1992. *Address:* c/o Bruce Hunter, David Higham Associates, 5-8 Lower John Street, London, W1R 4HA, England.

HERBERT Sandra, b. 10 Apr 1942, Chicago, Illinois, USA. m. 4 June 1966, 2 daughters. *Education:* BA Interdisciplinary Studies, Wittenberg University; MA 1965, PhD 1968, History of Ideas, Brandeis University. *Publications:* Books: Charles Darwin's Notebooks, 1836-1844: Geology Transmutation of Species, Metaphysical Enquiries, 1987; The Red Notebook of Charles Darwin, 1980. *Contributions to:* British Journal of the History of Science; The Darwinian Heritage; Journal Hist. Biology; Ann. Science; Scientific American; Charles Darwin: A centennial Commemorative. *Memberships:* History of Science Society, Council, 1977-79, 1982-84, Chair, Programme Committee for Annual Meeeing, 1978, Nominating Committee, 1986, Visiting Historians of Science Programme, 1988; Darwin Letters Project US Advisory Board; American Historiacal Association; American Association of University Professors. *Address:*

605 South Carolina Avenue SE, Washington, DC 20003, USA.

HERBERT Zbigniew, b. 29 Oct 1924, Lvov, Poland. Poet; Essayist; Playwright. *Education:* Cracow, Torun and Warsaw Universities. *Appointments:* Co-Editor, Tworczosc, 1955-65, Poezja, 1965-68; Professor, Modern European Literature California State College, Los Angeles, 1970. *Publications:* Poetry Includes: Struna swiatla (A String of Light), 1956; Hermes pies i gwiazda (Hermes, A Dog and a Star), 1957; Studium przedmiotu (The Study of an Object), 1961; Napis (The Inscription), 1969; Wiersze Zebrane (Collected Verse), 1971; Pan Cogito (Mr Cogito), 1974; Selected Poems (in English and German); Wybor wierszy, 1983; Radio plays and Drama Include: Dramaty (Dramas), 1970; Inny pokoj (The Other Room); Jaskinia filozofow (Cove of Philosophers); Lalek, Rekonstrukcja Poety, 1973; Essays; etc. *Honours:* Alfred Jurzykowski Foundation award, New York; Lenau International Prize for European Literature Vienna, 1965; Knight's Cross, Order Polonia Restituta, 1974. *Membership:* Polish Writers Association. *Address:* ul. Promenady 21m 4, 00-778 Warsaw, Poland.

HERD Shirley Mae Deal, b. 13 Sept 1935, Wichita, Kansas, USA. Author; Book Reviewer; Publisher. Divorced, 2 sons. *Education:* BSc., Spanish Education, University of Kansas, 1957. *Publications:* The Cruising Cook, 1977; Easy Spanish for the Traveler, 1982; Blimey, Limey! Wha'd He Say?, 1983; Seawoman's Handbook, 1989. *Contributor to:* Over 500 magazines & newspaper articles. *Honours:* 1st Place, 1979, 1980, National Federation of Presswomen. *Memberships:* Boating Writers International; Writers and Editors Guild; Book Publicists; National Federation of Press Women; Outdoor Writers Association. *Address:* 1629 Guizot St., San Diego, CA 92107, USA.

HEREN Louis Philip, b. 6 Feb 1919, London, England. Journalist; Author. m. Patricia Cecilia O'Regan, 2 June 1948, 1 son, 3 daughters. *Education:* St George's School, London. *Publications:* New American Commonwealth, 1968; No Hail, No Farewell, 1970; Growing Up Poor in London, 1973; The Story of America, 1976; Growing Up on the Times, 1978; Alas, Alas For England, 1981; Power of the Press? 1985; Memories of Times Past, 1988. *Contributions to:* UK and USA newspapers and magazines. *Honour:* John F Kennedy Memorial Award, 1968. *Memberships:* Fellow, Royal Society of Literature; Garrick Club. *Literary Agent:* David Higham Associates. *Address:* Fleet House, Vale of Health, London NW3 1AZ, England.

HERMES. See: CANAWAY W H.

HERMODSSON Elisabet, b. 20 Sept 1927, Gothenburg. Writer; Artist; Songwriter. m. (1) Ingemar Olsson, 1951; (2) Olof Hellstrom, 1956; 2 daughters. *Publications include:* Poem-things, 1966; Human landscape unfairly, 1968; Rite and Revolution, 1968; Swedish soul-life, 1970; Culture at the bottom, 1971; Voices in the human landscape, 1971; What Shall We Do With The Summer, Comrades?, (Songs), 1973; Disa Nilsons Songs, 1974; Through The Red Waist Coat Of The Ground 75; Visional Turning Point, 1975; Words in human time, 1979; Wake up with a summer soul, 1979; Make Yourself Visible, 1980; Discourses meanwhile, 1983; Stones, shards, layers of Earth, 1985; Creation Betrayed, 1986; Streams of Mist, 1990; Cration betrayed, 1988; Only Fools and Dreamers, 1992 (songs); The Dumb in the Word, 1993. *Contributions to:* Journals, magazines, and the editor of several anthologies. *Memberships:* PEN Club. *Address:* Ostra Agatan 67, 75322 Uppsala, Sweden.

HERR Pamela (Staley), b. 24 July 1939, Cambridge, MA. Writer. 2 daughters. *Education:* BA, (magna cum laude), Harvard University, 1961; MA, George Washington University, 1971. *Appointments:* Writer and Editor, Field Educational Publications 1973, Editor,

Sullivan Associates 1973- 74, Palo Alto, CA; Project Manager, Sanford Associates, Educational Development Corporation, Menlo Park, 1974-76; Managing Editor, American West, Cupertino, CA, 1976-79; Historian and Writer, 1980-. *Publications:* The Women Who Made the West (Contributor), 1980; Jessie Benton Fremont: A Biography, 1987; Selected Letters of Jessie Benton Fremont (with Mary Lee Spence), 1993. *Contributions to:* Articles and reviews to magazines and newspapers, including Californians; American West; California History; Western Historical Quarterly. *Memberships:* Coalition for Western Women's History; Western Writers of America; Western History Association; Western Association of Women Historians; Phi Beta Kappa. *Honours:* Grant from National Historical Publications and Records Commission, 1987-90; Western Writers of America Spur Award for best Western nonfiction book, 1987, for Jessie Benton Fremont: A Biography. *Address:* 2300 Hanover Street, Palo Alto, CA 94306, USA.

HERRIOT James. See: WIGHT J A.

HERSEY John Richard, b. 17 June 1914, Tientsin, China. Writer. m. (1) Frances Ann Cannon, 1940, divorced 1958, (2) Barbara Day Kaufman, 1958, 3 sons, 2 daughters. *Education:* BA, Yale University; Clare College, Cambridge England. *Appointments include:* Editor, Time, 1937-42; War and Foreign Correspondent, Time, Life, New Yorker, 1942-46; Master, Pierson College, 1965-70, Fellow, 1965-, Lecturer, 1971-75, Visiting Professor, 1976-77, Adjunct Professor, 1977-84, Adjunct Professor Emeritus, 1984-, Yale University. *Publications:* Men on Bataan, 1942; Into the Valley, 1943; A Bell for Adano, 1944; Hiroshima, 1946; The Wall, 1950; The Marmot Drive, 1953; A Single Pebble, 1956; The War Lover, 1959; The Child Buyer, 1960; Here to Stay, 1962; White Lotus, 1965; Too Far to Walk, 1966; Under the Eye of the Storm, 1967; The Algiers Motel Incident, 1968; Letter to the Alumni, 1970; The Conspiracy, 1972; The Writers' Craft, 1974; My Petition for More Space, 1974; The President, 1975; The Walnut Door, 1977; Aspects of the Presidency, 1980; The Call, 1985; Blues, 1987; Life Sketches, 1989; Fling and Other Stories, 1990. *Honours:* Recipient, numerous honours and awards including Honorary Degrees; Pulitzer Prize for Fiction, 1945; Sidney Hillman Foundation Award, 1951; Howland Medal, Yale, 1952. *Memberships include:* American Academy Arts and Letters, Secretary 1961-75, Chancellor, 1981-84; National Institute of Arts and Letters; Authors Guild; Authors League, Vice-president, 1949-55, President, 1975-80; American Academy of Arts and Sciences; Honorary Fellow, Clare College, Cambridge University, 1967. *Address:* 719 Windsor Lane, Key West, FL 33040, USA.

HERSH Burton David, b. 18 Sept 1933, Chicago, Illinois, USA. Author; Biographer. m. Ellen Eiseman, 3 Aug 1957. 1 son, 1 daughter. *Education:* BA, magna cum laude, Harvard College, 1955; Fulbright Scholar, 1955-56. *Publications:* The Ski People, 1968; The Education of Edward Kennedy, 1972; The Mellon Family, 1978; The Old Boys, 1992. *Contributions to:* Many major American magazines including: Holiday; Esquire; The Washingtonian, etc. *Honours:* History and Literature Prize, Harvard College, 1954; Bowdoin Prize, Harvard College, 1955; Senior Phi Beta Kappa, Harvard College, 1955; Book Find Selection, 1972; Book-of-the-Month Club Selection, 1978. *Memberships:* Authors Guild; American Society of Journalists and Authors; PEN. *Literary Agent:* Jonathan Matson, harold Matson Company, Inc, 276 Fifth Avenue, New York, NY 10001, USA. *Address:* PO Box 433, Bradford, New Hampshire 03221, USA.

HERTZBERG Hendrik, b.23 July 1943, New York, USA. Journalist. *Education:* AB, Harvard College, 1965. *Appointments:* Correspondent, Newsweek, 1966; Staff Writer, The New Yorker, 1969-77; Speechwriter, The White House, 1977-81; Various positions including editor, contributing editor, senior editor, The New Republic, 1981-1992; Executive Editor, The New Yorker, 1992-. *Publications:* One Million, 1970, 1993;

Candidates, 1988 (co-author), 1988. *Contributions to:* Time; The New Republic; New Yorker; New York Review of Books; Esquire; Dissent; New York Times; Washington Post; Los Angeles Times. *Honours:* National magazine Award, 1991, 1992. *Memberships:* Council on Foreign Relations; National Press Club; Overseas Press Club. *Literary Agent:* Esther Newberry, ICM. *Address:* The New Yorker, 20 W 43rd Street, New York, NY 10036, USA.

HESS Jovak Van. *See:* **HOEPPNER Iona Ruth.**

HESSAYON David Gerald, b. 13 Feb 1928, Manchester, England. Author; Publisher. m. Joan Parker Gray, 2 Apr 1951,, 2 daughters. *Education:* BSC, Leeds University, 1950; PhD, Manchester University, 1954; Hon Doctorate of Science, 1990. *Publications:* The House Plant Expert, 1980; The Tree and Shrub Expert, 1983; The Flower Expert, 1984; The Garden Expert, 1986; The Bedding Plant Expert, 1991; The Rose Expert, 1988; The Lawn Expert, 1982; The Armchair Book of the Garden, 1983; The Vegetable Expert, 1985; The Indoor Plant Spotter, 1985; The Home Expert, 1987; The Fruit Expert, 1990; Be you Own Greenhouse Expert, 1990; The New House Plant Expert, 1991; The Garden DIY Expert, 1992; The Rock & Water Garden Expert, 1993. *Honours:* Lifetime Achievement Trophy, National British Book Awards, 1992; Gold Veitch Momorial Medal, Royal Horticultural Society, 1992. *Memberships:* Chairman, Expert Publications Ltd, Hessayon Books Ltd, PBI Publications; Director, Orion Publishing Group; Member: Royal Society of Arts, Society of Authors. *Address:* Hilgay, Mill Lane, Broxbourne, Herts EN10 7AX, England.

HESSAYON Joan Parker, b. 21 Jan 1932, Louisville, Kentucky, USA. Author. m. David Hessayon, 2 Apr 1951, 2 daughters. *Publications:* All Kinds of Courage, 1983; For All Good Men, 1984; Little Maid All Unwary, 1985; Sylbilla, 1986; Thorsby, 1987; Lady from St Louis, 1989; Belle's Daughter, 1990; Roxanne's War, 1991; House on Pine Street, 1992. *Memberships:* Vice Chairman, The Society of Women Writers and Journalists; The Romantic Novelists Association, former Council member. *Address:* Hilgay, Mill Lane, Broxbourne, Herts EN10 7AX, England.

HESSING Dennis. *See:* **DENNIS-JONES Harold.**

HESTER William, b. 6 June 1933, Detroit, Michigan, USA. Author; Lyricist. div., 1 daughter. *Education:* Brown University, 1951-52; University of Detroit, 1956; BA, Mesa College, 1970; MA certificate, Special Studies, UCLA/NYU; currently PhD candidate. *Literary Appointments:* Staff, Warner Brothers Pictures, 1961-62; Creative staff, Sierra Productions, 1962-65; Staff, Playboy Magazine, 1966-68; Associate director, Vance Publications, 1970-73. *Publications:* Please Don't Die In My House, 1965; Selections, 1967; Running Off, 1970; Not the Right Season, 1984; Another Town, 1984; Still Not the Right Season, 1985; Our Place, 1986; Sleeping Neighbours, 1986, 1992; Tyranny/2000, 1988. Also music. *Contributions to:* Pulpsmith; Confrontation; Amelia; Easy Riders; The Poet; Playboy; Witness; Golf Magazine; Fortune News; Wind. *Honours include:* EMMY nominee, 1974; Eisner Fellowship, 1984; 1st & 2nd awards, fiction & non-fiction, PEN American Centre, 1985, 1986; Various awards, American Song Festival. *Memberships:* Authors Guild; Conservatory of American Letters; Broadcast Music Inc (lyricist): ASCAP (publisher). *Literary Agents:* Al Hart, Fox Chase Agency, Public Ledger Building, Philadelphia, PA 19106, USA. *Address:* c/o James McDonald Inc, 1130-20th St, 5, Santa Monica, CA 90403, USA.

HETHERINGTON (Hector) Alastair, b. 31 Oct 1919, Llanishen, Galmorganshire, Wales. Journalist. m. (1) Helen Miranda Oliver, 1957, (div 1978), 2 sons, 2 daughter, (2) Sheila Cameron, 1979. *Education:* MA, Corpus Christi College, Oxford. *Appointments:* Staff, Glasgow Herald, 1946-50; Joined Manchester Guardian, 1950, Foreign Editor 1953, Editor 1956-75,

Director, Guardian Newspapers Ltd., 1967-75; with BBC, 1975-80, Controller BBC Scotland 1975-78, Manager, BBC Highland 1979-80; Research Professor, Stirling University, 1982-88, Emeritus since 1988. *Publications:* Guardian Years, 1981; News, Newspapers and Television, 1985; Perthshire in Trust, 1988; News in the Regions, 1989; Highlands and Islands, a generation of progress, 1990; Cameras in the Commons, 1990; Inside BBC Scotland, 1975-1980, 1982. *Address:* High Corrie, Isle of Arran, KA27 8GB, Scotland.

HETHERINGTON Norriss Swigart, b. 30 Jan 1942, Berkeley, CA. Professor. m. Edith Wiley White, 10 Dec 1966, 1 son, 1 daughter. *Education:* BA 1963, MA 1965, MA 1967, University of California, Berkeley; PhD, Indiana University - Bloomington, 1970. *Appointments:* Lecturer in Physics and Astonomy, Agnes Scott College, Decatur, GA, 1967- 68; Assistant Professor of Mathematics and Science, York University, Toronto, Ontario, 1970-72; Administrative Specialist in History Office, National Aeronautics and Space Administration, WA, 1972; Assistant Professor of History, University of Kansas, Lawrence, 1972-76; Chairman of Program in History and Philosophy of Science, 1973-74; Assistant Professor of Science, Technology and Society, Razi University, Sanandaj, Iran, 1976-77; Visiting Scholar, Cambridge University, Cambridge, England, 1977-78; Associate Professor of History of Science, Oklahoma University, Norman, 1981; Research Associate at Office for History of Science and Technology, University of California, Berkeley, 1981-. *Publications:* Ancient Astronomy and Civilization, 1987; Science and Objectivity: Episodes in the History of Astronomy, 1988. *Contributions to:* Magazines and newspapers, including Journal of the History of Ideas; Annals of Science; Middle East Journal; Journal of Portfolio Management; Bay Area Business; American Scientist; Nature; Science. *Honours:* Robert H Goddard Historical Essay Award from National Space Club, 1974; Fellow of National Endowment for the Humanities 1974-75 and 1990-91; American Historical Association 1986-87, National Science Foundation 1988; Dudley Award, 1984, 1988 and 1990. *Memberships:* International Astronomical Union; Berkeley Science Historians (chief financial officer, 1984-); Sigma Xi. *Address:* 1742 Spruce, Apartment 201, Berkeley, CA 94709, USA.

HEWETT Dorothy (Coade), b. 1923, Australia. Author; Playwright; Poet. *Appointments include:* Advertising Copywriter, Sydney, 1956-58; Poetry Editor, Westerly Magazine, Perth, 1972-73; Editorial Committee, Overland Magazine, Melbourne, 1970-; Writer in Residence, Monash University, Melbourne, 1975; Editor, Director, Big Smoke Books, Review Editor, Poetry, Sydney, 1975-. *Publications:* Bobbin' Up (novel), 1959; What about the Poeple (poetry with Merv Lilly), 1962; The Australians have a Word for It (stories), 1964; The Old Man Comes Rolling Home, 1968; Windmill Country (poetry), 1968; The Hidden Journey (poetry), 1969; Late Night Bulletin (poetry), 1970; The Chapel Perilous; or, The Perilous Adventures of Sally Bonner, 1971; Sandgropers: A Western Australian Anthology, 1973; Rapunzel in Suburbia (poetry), 1975; Miss Hewett's Shenanigans, 1975; Bon-Bons and Roses for Dolly, and The tatty Hollow Story, 1976; Greenhouse (poetry), 1979; The Man from Mukinupin (play), 1979; Susannah's Dreaming, and The Golden Oldies (plays), 1981; Joan, 1984; Golden Valley, Song of the Seals, 1985. *Address:* 49 Jersey Road, Woollahra, NSW 2025, Australia.

HEWISON William Shearer, b. 5 Nov 1916, Banbury Oxon, England. Journalist. m. Agnes Hall Ramsay, 8 July 1949. *Education:* Banbury Grammar School. *Publications:* This Great Harbour - Scapa Flow, 1985, second Ed, 1990; Kirkwall Official Guide, 1951; Orkney Official Guide, several editions since 1960. *Contributions to:* Orkney Micellany of Orkney Record and Antiquarian Society; Kirkwall and St Ola Section of the Third Statistical Account of Scotland. *Address:* Newark, Weyland Bay, Kirkwall, Orkney, Scotland.

HEWITT Geof, b. 1943, United States of America.

Poet. *Appointments include:* Assistant Editor, Epoch Magazine, Ithaca, New York, 1964-66; Editor in Chief, The Trojan Horse Magazine, Ithaca, New York, 1965-66; Founding Editor, The Kumquat Press, Montclair, New York, 1966-; Contributing Editor, Cornell Alumni News, Ithaca, New York, 1970-. *Publications:* Poem and Other Poems, 1966; Waking Up Still Pickled, 1967; Quickly Aging Here: Some Poets of the 1970s, 1969; Selected Poems of Alfred Starr Hamilton, 1969; Living in Whales: Stories and Poems from Vermont Public Schools, 1972; Stone Soup, 1974; I Think They'll Lay My Egg Tomorrow, 1976. *Address:* Calais, VT 05648, USA.

HEYDEN Haye van der, b. 20 Feb 1957. Actor; Singer; Writer; Director. *Education:* Gymnasium; Dutch Literature, State University, Utrecht. *Publications:* For Queen and Country; Three Girls, Three Boys; The Woman and the Stranger; 10-15 Theatre shows and various TV programmes; Director, TV and Theatre, mostly musical comedy. *Honours:* Literary prize for Three Girls, Three Boys and The Woman and the Stranger. *Address:* Bosboom Toussaintstr, 25 I, 1054 AM Amsterdam, The Netherlands.

HEYEN William H, b. 1 Nov 1940, New York, USA. Professor. m. Hannelore Greiner, 1962, 2 children. *Education:* BS.Ed., SUNY College, Brockport, 1961; MA, 1963, PhD, 1967, English, Ohio University. *Publications:* Depth of Field, 1970; A Profile of Theodore Roethke, Editor, 1971; Noise in the Trees : Poems and a Memoir, 1974; American Poets in 1976, Editor, 1976; The Swastika Poems, 1977; Long Island Lights, 1979; The City Parables, 1980; Lord Dragonfly : Five Sequences, 1981; Erika : Poems of the Holocaust, 1984; The Generation of 2000 : Contemporary American Poets, Editor, 1984; Vic Holyfield and the Class of 1957 : A Romance, 1986; the Chestnut Rain : A Poem, 1986. *Contributions to:* numerous journals and magazines. *Honours:* Borestone Mountain Poetry Prize, 1965; Senior Fulbright Lectureship, 1971-72; NEA Fellowship, 1973-74; Ontario Review Poetry Prize, 1977; Guggenheim Fellowship, 1977-78; Outstanding Alumni Award, SUNY College, 1977; Invited to Write & Deliver, Official Poem, City of Rochester's Bicentennial, 1984; NEA Fellowship, 1984-85; New York Foundation for the Arts Poetry Fellowship, 1984-85. *Address:* 142 Frazier Street, Brockport, NY 14420, USA.

HEYERDAHL Thor, b. 6 Oct 1914. Author; Anthropologist. m. (1) Liv Coucheron Torp, 1936, (dec 1969), 2 sons, (2) Yvonne Dedekam-Simonsen, 1949, 3 daughters. *Education:* University of Oslo, 1933-36. *Appointments Include:* Organised and Led, Kon-Tiki expedition, 1947; made crossing from Safi, Morocco to West Indies in papyrus boat, RAII, 1970. *Publications:* Paa Jakt efter Paradiset, 1938; The Kon-Tiki Expedition, 1948; American Indians in the Pacific : the theory behind the Kon-Tiki Expedition, 1952; (with A. Skjolsvold) Archaeological Evidence of pre-Spanish Visits to the Galapagos Islands, 1956; Aku-Aku : the Secrets of Easter Island, 1961, volume II Miscellaneous Papers, 1965; Navel of the World (Chapter XIV) in Vanished Civilizations, 1963; Indianer und Alt-Asiaten im Pazifik : Das Abenteuer einer heorie, 1965 (Vienna); Sea Routes to Polynesia, 1968; The Ra Expeditions, 1970; Chapters in Quest for America, 1971; Fatu-Hiva Back to Nature, 1974; Art of Easter Island, 1975; Zwischen den Kontinenten, 1975; Early Man and the Ocean, 1978; The Tigris Expedition, 1980; The Mystery of the Maldives, 1986; Easter Island, 1990. *Contributions to:* Numerous professional journals. *Honours:* Recipient, numerous honours and awards including: Royal Gold Medal, Royal Geographical Society, London, 1964; Commander with Star, Order of St Olav, Norway, 1970; Order of Merit, Egypt, 1971; Grand Officer, Royal Alaouites Order, Morocco, 1971; Hon. Citizen, Larvik, Norway, 1971; International Pahlavi Environment Prize, UN, 1978; Order of Golden Ark, Netherlands, 1980; etc. *Address:* Kan-Tiki Museum, Oslo, Norway.

HEYLIN Clinton Manson, b. 8 Apr 1960, Urmston, England. Writer. *Education:* BA Hons, History, University

of London, 1978-81; MA History, University of Sussex, 1982-83. *Publications:* Dylan: Behind the Shades, 1991; The Penguin Book of Rock and Roll Writing, 1992; From the Velvets to the Voidoids, 1993; Rise/Fall, 1989; Stolen Moments, 1988; Form and Substance: Gypsy Love Songs and Sad Refrains, 1989. *Contributions to:* Q; Goldmine; Record Collector; Music Collector; Spiral Scratch; Dirty Linen; The Telegraph. *Address:* 203 Northenden Road, Sale, Cheshire M33 2JB, England.

HEYWOOD Colin Michael, b. 4 Oct 1947. University Lecturer. m. Olena Kaye, 1 June 1972, 1 son, 1 daughter. *Education:* Magdalen College School, Oxford, 1959-65; BA Hons History, 1969, PhD History, 1973, University of Reading. *Publications:* Childhood in 19th Century France, 1988; The Development of the French Economy 1750-1914, 1992. *Contributions to:* History; Economic History Review; Journal of European Economic History; European History Quarterly; French History. *Memberships:* Society for the Study of French History, Committee; Economic History Society. *Address:* Department of History, University of Nottingham, Nottingham RG7 2RD, England.

HIAT Elchik. *See:* **MENKE Katz.**

HIBBERD Jack, b. 1940, Australia. Playwright. *Publications:* White with Wire Wheels, 1967; Dimboola: A Wedding Reception Play, 1969; A Stretch of the Imagination, 1971; Three Popular Plays, 1976; The Overcoat, Sin, 1981; Squibs, 1984; A Country Quinella, 1984; Captain Midnight V.C., 1984. *Address:* 27 Scenic Drive, Victoria 3934, Australia.

HIBBERT Alun James, b. 22 Apr 1949, Builth Wells, Wales. Playwright. m. Laurel Christie Hampton, 4 July 1970, 2 daughters. *Education:* BA, Honours, Russian Studies, McGill University, 1978. *Publications:* Playing the Fool, 1983; October's Soldiers, 1980; A Majority of Two. *Honours:* Finalist, Best New Canadian Play, Clifford E. Lee Award, 1979; Nominee, Outstanding New Play, Dora Mavor Moore Awards, 1980. *Memberships:* Playwrights Union of Canada; Playrights Workshop Montreal, Past President. *Address:* 115 King's Rd, Pte. Claire, Quebec H9R 4H5, Canada.

HIBBERT Christopher, b. 5 Mar 1924, Author, m. Susan Piggford, 1948, 2 sons, 1 daughter. *Education:* MA, Oriel College, Oxford. *Appointments:* Served in Italy, 1944-45; Captain, London Irish Rifles; Partner, firm of land agents, auctioneers and surveyors, 1948-59. *Publications include:* The Road to Tyburn, 1957; King Mob, 1958; Wolfe at Quebec, 1959; The Destruction of Lord Raglan, 1961; Corunna, 1961; Benito Mussolini, 1962; The Battle of Arnhem, 1962; The Roots of Evil, 1963; The Court at Windsor, 1964; Agincourt, 1964; The Wheatley Diary, (Editor), 1964; Garibaldi and His Enemies, 1965; The Making of Charles Dickens, 1967; Waterloo: Napoleon's Last Campaign, (Editor), 1967; An American in Regency England: The Journal of Louis Simond, (Editor), 1968; Charles I, 1968; The Grand Tour, 1969; London: Biography of a City, 1969; The Search for King Arthur, 1970; Anzio: The Bid for Rome, 1970; The Dragon Wakes: China and the West, 1793-1911, 1970; The Personal History of Samuel Johnson, 1971; George IV, Prince of Wales 1762-1811, 1972; George IV, Regent and King 1812-1830, 1973; The Rise and Fall of the House of Medici, 1974; Edward VII: A Portrait, 1976; The Great Mutiny: Rome 1857, 1978; The French Revolution, 1981; Africa Explored: Europeans in the Dark Continent, 1769-1889, 1982; Queen Victoria in Her Letters and Journals, 1984; Rome: The Biography of a City, 1985; The English: A Social History, 1987; Venice: Biography of a City, 1988; The Encyclopaedia of Oxford, (Editor), 1988; Redcoats and Rebels: The War for America 1760-1781, 1990; The Virgin Queen: The Personal History of Elizabeth I, 1990; Captain Gronow: His Reminiscences of Regency and Victoiran Life (ed), 1991; Cavaliers and Roundheads: The English at War 1642-1649, 1993; Florence: Biography of a City, 1993. *Honours:* Heinemann Award for Literature, 1962; McColvin Medal, 1989. *Address:* c/o David Higham

Associates, 5-8 Lower John Street, Golden Square, London W1R 4HA, England.

HICKMAN Tracy Raye, b. 26 Nov 1955, Salt Lake City, UT. m. Laura Curtis, 17 June 1977, 2 sons, 2 daughters. *Appointments:* Projectionist, Mann Theatres 1974-78, Assistant Director of KBYU-TV 1976-77, Theatre Manager in Provo and Logan 1978-81, UT; Game Designer, TSR Incorporated, Lake Geneva, WI, 1981-86; Consultant, 1986-; Missionary in Java and Indonesia. *Publications:* Dragons of Autumn Twilight, 1984; Dragons of Winter Night, Dragons of Spring Dawning, 1985; Time of the Twins, War of the Twins, Test of the Twins, Magic of Krynn, 1986; Kender Gnomes and Gully Dwarves, Love and War, 1987 (all with Margaret Weis); Forging the Darksword, Doom in the Darksword, Triumph of the Darksword, 1988; Rose of the Prophet, 1989; Dragonwing, 1990; Elvenstar. *Address:* 453 Forest Highlands, Flagstaff, AZ 86001, USA.

HICKS Eleanor. *See:* **COERR Eleanor Beatrice.**

HIGDON Hal, b. 1931, United States of America. Writer. *Appointments:* Assistant Editor, The Kiwanis Magazine, 1957-59. *Publications:* The Union vs. Dr. Mudd, 1964; Heroes of the Olympics, 1965; Pro Football USA, 1967; The Horse That Played Center Field, 1967; The Business Healers, 1968; Stars of the Tennis Courts, 1969; 30 Days in May, 1969; The Electronic Olympics, 1969; On the Run from Dogs and People, 1969; Finding the Goove, 1973; Find the Key man, 1974; The Last Series, 1974; Six Seconds to Glory, 1974; The Crime of the Century, 1976; Summer of Triumph, 1977; Fitness after Forty, 1977; Beginner's Running Guide, 1978; Runner's Cookbook, 1979; Johnny Rutherford, 1980; The Marathoners, 1980; The Team That Played in the Space Bowl, 1981; The Masters Running Guide, 1990; Run Fast, 1992; Marathon: The Ultimate Training and Racing Guide, 1993; Falconara: A Family Odyssey, 1993. *Address:* 2815 Lake Shore Drive, Michigan City, IN 46360, USA.

HIGGINBOTHAM Prieur Jay, b. 16 July 1937, Pascagoula, Mississippi, USA. Archivist. m. Louisa Martin, 27 June 1970, 2 sons, 1 daughter. *Education:* BA, University of Mississippi; Graduate study, City College of New York, American University Washington DC. *Publications:* Discovering Russia, 1989; Autumn in Petrishchevo, 1987; Fast Train Russia, 1983; Old Mobile, 1977; Voyage to Dauphin Island, 1974; Brother Holyfield, 1972; Fort Maurepas, 1968. *Contributions to:* Library Journal; Alabama Review; Foreign Literature; Literaturnaya Gazeta; Louisiana Studies; Encyclopaedia Britannica; Dictionary of Louisiana Biography. *Honours:* Louisiana Historical Association, 1978; Alabama Library Association Award, 1978; Gilbert Chinard Prize, 1978; Mississippi Historical Society Award, 1979; Elizabeth Gould Award, 1981. *Memberships:* Authors League of America; National Geographic Society; Franklin Society. *Literary Agent:* Brandt & Brandt, New York. *Address:* 60 North Monterey Street, Mobile, Alabama 36604, USA.

HIGGINS George V(incent), b. 13 Nov 1939, Brockton, Massachussets, United States of America. Writer; Journalist. m. (1) Elizabeth Mulkerin, 4 Sept 1965 (div) 1 son, 1 daughter; (2) Loretta Lucas Cubberley, 23 Aug. 1979. *Education:* BA, 1961, JD, 1967, Boston College; MA, Stanford University, 1965. *Appointments:* Reporter, Journal and Evening Bulletin, Providence, Rhode Island, 1962-63; Newsman, Boston, Massachussets, 1964; Writer, Instructor in Law Enforcement Programs, Northeastern University, Boston, 1969-71; Consultant, National Institute of Law Enforcement and Criminal Justice, Washington DC, 1970-71. *Publications:* The Friends of Eddie Coyle, 1972; The Digger's Game, 1973; Cogan's Trade, 1974; A City on a Hill, 1975; The Judgement of Deke Hunter, 1976; Dreamland, 1977; A Year or So with Edgar, 1979; Kennedy for the Defense, 1980; The Rat on Fire, 1981; The Patriot Game, 1982; A Choice of Enemies, 1984;

Penance for Jerry Kennedy, 1985; Imposters, 1986; Wonderful Years, Wonderful Years, 1989; Trust, 1989. *Contributions to:* Columnist, Boston Herald American, 1977-79; Author of Magazine Criticism Column, Boston Globe, 1979-85; Biweekly Television Column, Wall Street Journal, 1984-; Contributor of Essays and Short Fiction to Journals and Magazine including Arizona Quarterly, Cimarron Review, Esquire, Atlantic, Playboy, GQ, New Republic, Newsweek. *Honours:* The Friends of Eddie Coyle, chosen as one of the top twenty postwar American novels by Book Marketing Council, 1985. *Membership:* Writer Guild of America. *Address:* 15 Brush Hill Lane, Milton, MA 02186, USA.

HIGGINS Jack. *See:* **PATTERSON Harry.**

HIGGINS John Dalby, b. 7 Jan 1934, Hong Kong. Editorial Executive. m. Linda Christmas, 3 Sept 1977. *Education:* MA, Worcester College, Oxford, 1957. *Appointment:* Literary/Arts Editor, Financial Times, 1966-69; Arts Editor, The Times, 1970-88; Chief Opera Critic/Obituaries Editor, The Times, 1988-. *Publications:* Don Giovanni - The Making of an Opera, 1977; Glyndebourne - A Celebration, Editor, 1984; Travels in the Balkans, 1969; British Theatre Design, (contributor) 1978-88. *Honours:* Chevalier des Arts et des Lettres; Ehrenkreuz fur Kunst und Wissenschaft, Austria; Goldenes Verdienstzeichnis. *Membership:* Royal Literary Fund, Committee, 1970-. *Address:* The Times, London, England.

HIGGINS Richard C (Dick), b. 15 Mar 1938, Cambridge, England. Writer. m. 30 Jan 1960, 2 daughters. *Education:* BS, English, Columbia University, 1960; Manhattan School of Printing. *Publications:* 38 books including: (most recent) Intermedia, 1985; Poems, Plain and Fancy, 1986; Pattern Poems: Guide to an Unknown Literature, 1987; Fluxus: Theory and Reception, 1986; 5 Hear-Plays, 1987; On the Composition of Images, Signs and Ideas, 1987. *Contributions to:* Numerous journals and magazines including: Fluxshoe; The Beat Scene; WIN Magazine; West Coast Poetry Review. *Honours:* Grants for pattern poetry projects, Purchase College Foundation, 1984-6, 1988-; Bill C Davis Drama Award for The Journey, 1988; New York State Council on the Arts: Collaborations Grant from Visual Arts Program to build The Hanging Gardens of Lexington at Art Awareness in Lexington, NY, 1989-; Pollck Krasher Grant in Painting, 1993; Recipient various other awards. *Address:* PO Box 27 Barrytown, NY 12507, USA.

HIGHAM Robin (David Stewart), b. 20 June 1925, London, England. Professor of History. m. Barbara Jane Davies, 5 Aug 1950, 3 daughters. *Education:* AB, cum laude, Harvard, 1950; MA, Claremont Graduate School, 1953; PhD, Harvard University, 1957. *Appointments:* Editor, Military Affairs; Editor, Aerospace Historian; Editor, Journal of the West; President, Sunflower University Press. *Publications include:* Britain's Imperial Air Routes, 1960; The British Rigid Airship, 1961, 1982; Armed Forces in Peacetime, 1963; The Military Intellectuals in Britain, 1966; Air Power: A Concise History, 1973, 1984; The Diary of a Disaster, 1986. *Contributions to:* American Neptune; Balkan Studies; Business History Review; Airpower Historian; Military Affairs; Naval War College Review. *Honours:* Aviation and Space Writers' Award, 1973; History Book Club Selection, 1973; Samuel Eliot Morison Prize, American Military Institute, 1986-87. *Memberships:* Publications Committee, Conference of British Studies; Editorial Advisory Board, Technology and Culture. *Literary Agent:* Bruce Hunter, David Higham; Claire Smith, Harold Ober. *Address:* 2961, Nevada Street, Manhattan KS 66502, USA.

HIGHLAND Dora. *See:* **AVALLONE Michael.**

HIGHLAND Monica. *See:* **SEE Carolyn.**

HIGHSMITH (Mary) Patricia, (Claire Morgan), b. 19

Jan 1921, Fort Worth, Texas, USA. *Education:* BA, Barnard College, 1942. *Publications:* Author, numerous books including Ripley Under Water, 1992. *Honours:* Recipient, Grand Prix de Litterature Policiere, 1957; Crime Writers Association Silver Dagger, 1964; Le Prix Litteraire (Deauville), 1987. *Agent:* Digenes Verlag. *Address:* c/o Diogenes Verlag, Sprecherstrasse 8, CH 8032, Zurich, Switzerland.

HIGHWATER Jamake, Educator; Author; Arts Critic. *Appointments include:* Lecturer, primal culture, various Universities, USA & Canada, 1970-; Founding Member 1980-87, Indian Art Foundation, Santa Fe; Various offices, New York State Council on Arts, 1981-83, Cultural Council, American Indian Community House, NYC 1976-78; National Advisory Board of: Visions Magazine, American Poetry Center, Pew Fellowships in the Arts, Mary Anderson Art Center; General Director of two major arts festivals: The Native Arts Festival, Houston, 1986; Festiva; Mythos, Philadelphia, 1991. *Publications include:* Indian America: Cultural & Travel Guide, 1975; Song from the Earth: American Indian Painting, 1976; Ritual of the Wind: North American Indian Ceremonies, Music & Dances, 1977; Many Smokes, Many Moons, 1978; Journey to the Sky: Stephens & Catherwood's Rediscovery of the Maya World, novel, 1978; Sweet Grass Lives On: Masterpieces of American Indian Painting, 2 volumes, 1978-80; 50 Contemporary North American Indian Artists, 1980; Primal Mind: Vision & Reality in Indian America, 1981. Novels: Anpao, American Indian Odyssey, 1977; The Sun, He Dies: End of the Aztec World, 1980; Eyes of Darkness, 1986; Legend Days, Ceremony of Innocence, 1986; I Wear the Morning Star, 1986; Native Land, 1986; Shadow Show, 1987; Myth and Sexuality, 1990; The World of 1492, 1992; Kill Hole, 1992; Songs for the Seasons, 1993; Dark Legend, 1993; The Language of Vision, forthcoming. Also numerous TV programmes, etc. *Honours include:* Anisfield-Wolf Award, race relations, 1980; Jane Addams Peace Book Award, 1978; Virginia McCormick Scully Literary Award, 1982; Newbury Honour Award, 1978; Best book for young adults, American Library Association, 1978, 1980; National Educational Film Festival, Best Film of the Year, 1984; American Film Festival, Finalist, 1984. *Memberships include:* Authors Guild; Dramatists Guild; Authors League; PEN. *Address:* Suite 202, 1201 Larrabee Street, Los Angeles, CA 90060, USA.

HIGNETT Sean, b.18 Sept 1934, Birkenhead, England. Writer. m. Josephine Lewington, 17 Sept 1957, 1 son, 1 daughter. *Education:* MA (Oxon), Dip. Stat (Oxon. *Publications:* A Picture to Hang on the Wall, 1966; Brett, 1984; A Cut Loaf, 1971; The Crezz, 1974. *Contributions to:* Numerous magazines and journals. *Honour:* D H Lawrence Fellow, University of New Mexico, 1970. *Address:* Brunstane House, Edinburgh EH15 2NQ, Scotland.

HILDICK Edmund Wallace, (Wallace Hildick), b. 29 Dec 1925, Bradford, England. Author. m. Doris Clayton, 9 Dec 1950. *Appointments:* Visiting critic and associate Editor, Kenyon Review, Gambier, Ohio, USA, 1966-67. *Publications:* The Boy at the Window, 1960; Jim Starling Series, 1958- 63; Birdy Jones Series, 1969-74; McGurk Series, 1974-90; *Contributions to:* Various journals. *Memberships:* Authors Guild, USA; Society of Authors, England. *Honours:* Tom Gallon Short Story Award, 1957; Edgar Allan Poe Special Award, 1979; Best Translated Works Award (Japan), 1979. *Address:* c/o Coutts and Co., 440 Strand, London WC2R 0QS, England.

HILDICK Wallace. See: HILDICK Edmund Wallace.

HILL (John Edward) Christopher, (K E Holme), b. 1912. Writer (History). *Publications:* The English Revolution 1640, 1940; As K.E. Holme: Two Commonwealths, 1945; Lenin and the Russian Revolution, 1947; The Good Old Cause (with E. Dell), 1949; Economic Problems of the Church, 1956; Puritanism and Revolution, 1958; The Century of Revolution, 1961; Society and Puritanism, 1964; Intellectual Origins of the English Revolution, 1965; Reformation to Industrial Revolution, 1967; God's Englishman, 1970; Antichrist in Seventeenth Century England, 1971; The World Turned Upside Down, 1972; The Law of Freedom and Other Writings by Gerrard Winstanley, 1973; Change and Continuity in Seventeenth Century England, 1975; Milton and the English Revolution, 1978; Some Intellectual Consequences of the English Revolution, 1980; The Experience of Defeat, 1983; Writing and Revolution, 1985; Religion and Politics in 17th Century England, 1986; People and Ideas in 17th Century England, 1986; A Turbulent 5 Editions & Factives People: John Bunyan and his Church, 1988; A Nation of Change and Novelty, 1990; The English Bible and The 17th Century Revolution, 1993. *Address:* Woodway House, Sibford Ferris, Oxon, England.

HILL Donna Marie, b. Salt Lake City, Utah, USA. Author; Artist; Librarian. *Education:* BA George Washington University, 1948; Masters in Library Science, Columbia University, 1952. *Publications:* Joseph Smith: The First Mormon, 1977; First Your Penny, 1985; Murder Uptown, 1992; Third Book of Junior Authors, 1972; Eerie Animals: Seven Stories, 1983; Mr Peeknuff's Tiny People, 1981; The Picture File: A Manual and Curriculum-Related Subject Heading List, 1975, 1978; Ms Glee Was Waiting, 1978. *Honours:* Certificate of Distinction, Alumni Association Central High School, 1984; Lolabel Hall Scholarship, 1988, Ruth Mack Havens, 1991, Delta Kappa Gamma Soc Int. *Memberships:* Women's National Book Association, Membership Chair, New York City Chapter, 1990-1993. *Literary Agent:* Kidde Hoyt and Picard. *Address:* 530 East 23rd Street, Apt 6B, NY 10010, USA.

HILL Douglas Arthur, (Martin Hillman), b. 6 Apr 1935, Canada. Author. m. Gail Robinson, 8 Apr 1958, div, 1975, son. *Education:* BA Hons, University of Saskatchewan, Canada, 1957. *Appointments:* Literary Editor, Tribune, London, 1971-84. *Publications:* Adult non-fiction: Supernatural, 1965; The Opening of the Canadian West, 1967; John Keats, 1969; The Scots to Canada, 1972; Fortune Telling: A Guide, 1978; Children's fiction: Galactic Warlord, 1980; The Huntsman, 1982; Exiles of Colsec, 1984; The Last Legionary Quartet, 1985; Blade of the Poisoner, 1987; Moon Monsters, 1984; Penelope's Pendant, 1990; The Unicorn Dream, 1992; Adult Fiction: The Lightless Dome, 1993. *Honours:* Parents' Choice Award, USA, 87. *Memberships:* Society of Authors, UK: Children's Book Circle. *Literary Agent:* Sheila Watson of Watson, Little Ltd, London. *Address:* 3 Hillfield Avenue, London N8 7DU, England.

HILL Elizabeth Starr, b. 4 Nov 1925, USA. Author. m. Russell Gibson Hill, 28 May 1949, 1 son, 1 daughter. *Publications:* The Wonderful Visit to Miss Liberty, 1961; The Window Tulip, 1967; Evan's Corner, 1967; Master Mike and the Miracle Maid, 1967; Pardon My Fangs, 1968; Bells: A Book to Begin On, 1970; Ever After Island, 1977; Fangs Aren't Everything, 1985; When Christmas Comes, (Viking Penguin), 1989. *Contributions to:* New Yorker; Reader's Digest; Harper's; Seventeen; Cricket. *Honours:* Evans Corner, 1967, American Library Association Notable Book for Children; Ever After Island, 1977, Junior Literary Guild Selection; When Christmas Comes, Junior Library Guild selection. *Literary Agent:* Harold Ober. *Address:* c/o Harold Ober Associates Inc., 40 East 49th Street, New York, NY 10017, USA.

HILL Errol Gaston, b. 5 Aug 1921, Trinidad, West Indies. College Professor Emeritus. m. Grace Lucille Eunice Hope, 11 Aug 1956, 1 son, 3 daughters. *Education:* Graduate Diploma, Royal Academy of Dramatic Art, London, England, 1951; Diploma in Dramatic Art with distinction, London University, 1951; BA summa cum laude, 1962, MFA, Playwriting, 1962, DFA, Theatre History, 1966, Yale University, USA. *Publications:* Man Better Man: a musical comedy, 1964, reprinted, 1985; The Trinidad Carnival, 1972; The Theatre of Black Americans, 1980, reprinted, 1987;

Shakespeare in Sable: A History of Black Shakespearean Actors, 1984; The Jamaican Stage, 1655-1900, 1992; Editor: Caribbean Plays, vol 1, 1958, vol 2 1965; A Time and a Season: 8 Caribbean Plays, 1976; Plays for Today, 1985; Black Heroes: Seven Plays, 1989. *Contributions to:* McGraw Encyclopedia of World Drama, 1984; Theatre Journal; Theatre History Studies; American Literature Forum; Caribbean Quarterly; Cambridge Guide to World Theatre; Others. *Honours:* British Council Scholarship, 1949-51; Rockefeller Foundation Fellowship, 1958-60, 1965; Theatre Guild of America Fellowship, 1961; Visiting Scholar, Bellagio Center, 1978 and 1991; Guggenheim Foundation Fellowship, 1985-86; Barnard Hewitt Award for Theatre History, 1985; Fulbright Fellowship, 1988. *Memberships include:* Executive Committee, American Society for Theatre Research; Executive Committee, American Theatre and Drama Society; Association of Commonwealth Language and Literature Studies; Phi Beta Kappa, President of Alpha of New Hampshire 1982-85; International Federation for Theatre Research. *Literary Agent:* Lucy Kroll Agency, New York City, USA. *Address:* 3 Haskins Road, Hanover, NH 03755, USA.

HILL Jane, b. 17 Oct 1950, Seneca, South Carolina, USA. Teacher; Editor; Writer. m. Robert W Hill, 16 Aug 1980, 1 daughter. *Education:* BA 1972, MA 1978, Clemson University; PhD, University of Illinois, 1985. *Appointments:* Associate Editor, Peachtree Publishers, 1986-88; Senior Editor, Longstreet Press, 1988-91; Director, Kennesaw Summer Writers Workshop, 1988-1992; Assistant Professor, West Georgia College, 1992-. *Publications:* Gail Godwin, 1992; Editor: Street Songs: New Voices in Fiction, 1990; Our Mutual Room: Modern Literary Portarits of the Opposite Sex, 1987; An American Christmas: A Sampler of Contemporary Stories and Poems, 1986; You Haven't to Deserve: A Gift to the Homeless/Fiction by 21 Writers, 1991; Author, Cobb County: At the Heart of Change, 1991. *Contributions to:* Numerous stories, poems, essays and reviews since 1978. *Honours:* Frank O'Connor Prize for Fiction, 1989; Syvenna Foundation Fellow, 1991; Monticello Fellowship for Female Writers, 1992. *Memberships:* Modern Language Association. *Address:* 1419 Arden Drive, Marietta, GA 30060, USA.

HILL Niki, b. 19 June 1938, Belfast, Northern Ireland. Journalist. m. Ian Hill, 6 Oct 1961, 2 daughters. *Education:* BSc (Econ), Queen's University, Belfast. *Appointments:* Food & Consumer Freelance; Feature writer, Belfast Telegraph, 1977; Woman's editor, News letter, Belfast, 1978-. *Publications include:* Culinary Tales, 1973. *Contributions to:* Assorted journals, newspapers; BBC TV & Radio; Ulster TV. *Honours:* Glenfiddich Award, Excellence in food writing, 1973, 1974; Argos Consumer Award, 1977. *Literary Agent:* Patricia Robertson, 87 Caledonian Road, London N1. *Address:* 19 Windsor Park, Belfast BT9 6FR, Northern Ireland.

HILL Pamela, (Sharon Fiske), b. 26 Nov 1920, Nairobi, Kenya. Writer. *Publications:* 54 Books including: Flaming Janet, 1954; The Devil Of Aske, 1972; The Malvie Inheritance, 1973; The Green Salamander, 1974; Homage To A Rose, 1979; Fire Opal, 1980; This Rough Beginning, 1981; The House Of Cray, 1982; Duchess Cain, 1983; The Goveness, 1985; My Lady Glamis, 1981; Venables, 1988; The Sutburys, 1987; The Brocker, 1991; The Sword and the Flame, 1991; Mercer, 1992; The Silver Runaways, 1992; O Madcap Duchess, forthcoming; The Parson's Children, forthcoming. *Contributions to:* Argosy; Chambers' Journal. *Memberships:* Society of Authors; Author's Club. *Address:* 89A Winchester Street, Pimlico, London SW1V 4NU, England.

HILL Reginald (Charles), (Dick Morland, Patrick Ruell, Charles Underhill), b. 1936. Author; Playwright. *Publications:* A Clubbable Woman, 1970; Fell of Dark, 1971; As Patrick Ruell: The Castle of the Demon, 1971; An Advancement of Learning, 1972; A Fairly Dangerous Thing, 1972; As Patrick Ruell: Red Christmas, 1972; An Affair of Honour (play), 1972; Ruling Passion, 1973;

As Dick Morland: Heart Clock, 1973; A Very Good Hater, 1974; As Dick Morland: Albion! Albion!, 1974; As Patrick Ruell: Death Takes the Low Road, 1974; An April Shroud, 1975; As Patrick Ruell: Urn Burial, 1976; Another Death in Venice, 1976; As Charles Underhill: Captain Fantom, 1978; A Pinch of Snuff, 1978; As Charles Underhill: The Forging of Fantom, 1979; Pascoe's Ghost (stories), 1979; A Killing Kindness, 1980; The Spy's Wife, 1980; Who Guards a Prince, 1981; Traitor's Blood, 1983; Deadheads, 1983; Exit Lines, 1984; No Man's Land, 1984; As Patrick Ruell: The Long Kill, 1986; Child's Play, 1987; As Patrick Ruell: Death of a Dormouse, 1987; The Collaborators, 1987; There are no Ghosts in the Soviet Union, 1987; Under World, 1988; As Patrick Ruell: Dream of Darkness, 1989; Bones and Silence, 1990; One Small Step (Novella), 1990; As Patrick Ruell: The Only Game, 1991; Recalled to Life, 1992; Blood Sympathy, 1993. *Address:* Oakbank, Broad Oak, Ravenglass, Cumbria, England.

HILL Susan Elizabeth, b. 5 Feb 1942. Novelist; Playwright. m. Stanley W. Wells, 3 daughters (1 dec). *Education:* BA, Honours, English, King's College, University of London, 1963. *Appointments:* Literary Critic, various journals, 1963-; numerous plays for BBC, 1970-. *Publications:* The Enclosure, 1961; Do Me a Favour, 1963; Gentleman and Ladies, 1969; A Change for the Better, 1969; I'm the King of the Castle, 1970; The Albatross, 1971; Strange Meeting, 1971; The Bird of Night, 1972; A Bit of Singing and Dancing, 1973; In the Springtime of the Year, 1974; The Cold Country and Othe Plays for Radio, 1975; Editor, The Distracted Preacher and Other Stories by Thomas Hardy, 1979; The Magic Apple Tree, 1982; The Woman in Black : a Ghost Story, 1983; Editor, Ghost Stories, 1983, People, an Anthology, 1983; One Night at a Time (for children), 1984; Through the Kitchen Window, 1984; Through the Garden Gate, 1986; Mother's Magic (for children), 1986; Play: The Ramshackle Company, 1981; Shakespeare Country, 1987; The Lighting of the Lamps - Essays & Previews, 1987; Lanterns Across the Snow, 1987; The Spirit of the Cotswolds, 1988; Can it be True? (for children), 1988. *Membership:* FRSL, 1972. *Address:* Midsummer Cottage, Church Lane, Beckley, Oxon, England.

HILLARD Darla, b. 7 July 1946, Illinois, USA. *Publications:* Vanishing Tracks: Four years Among the Snow Leopards of Nepal, 1989. *Contributions to:* National Geographic, 1986; French Geographic, 1988; Airone, 1987. *Address:* International Snow Leopard Trust, 4649 Sunnyside Avenue North, Seattle, WA 98103, USA.

HILLARY Edmund (Percival) (Sir), b. 1919, New Zealand. Writer. *Appointments:* New Zealand High Commissioner in India, 1984-; Conducted Many Expeditions including reaching summit of Mount Everest, 1953. *Publications:* High Adventure, 1955; East of Everest (with G. Lowe), 1956; The Crossing of Antarctica (with V. Fuchs), 1958; No Latitude for Error, 1961; High in the Thin Cold Air (with D.Doig), 1963; School House in the Clouds, 1965; Nothing Venture, Nothing Win, 1975; From the Ocean to the Sky, 1979; Two Generations, 1983. *Address:* 278a Remuera Road, Auckland 5, New Zealand.

HILLERT Margaret, b. 22 Jan 1920. Teacher. *Education:* RN, University of Michigan School of Nursing, USA; AB, Wayne University College of Education. *Appointments include:* Registered Nurse, 3 years; Primary Teacher, 34 years. *Publications:* Farther Than Far, 1969; I Like to Live in the City, 1970; Who Comes to Your House, 1973; Come Play With Me, 1975; The Sleepytime Book, 1975; What Is It? 1978; I'm Special...So Are You! 1979; Action Verse for the Primary Classroom, 1980; Doing Things, 1980; Let's Take a Break, 1981; Rabbits and Rainbows, 1985; 55 juvenile books, 12 in, Dear Dragon Series; various translations into Swedish, Danish, German, Portuguese. Poetry: Seasons, Holidays, Anytime, 1987; Dandelions and Daydreams, 1987; Lightning Bugs and Lullabies (poetry), 1988; God's Big Book, 1988; Guess, Guess, 1988; The

Birth of Jesus, 1988; Jesus Grows Up, 1988; Sing A Song of Christmas (poetry), 1989. *Contributions to:* Numerous literary magazines & journals; numerous anthologies. *Honours include:* Various 1st Prizes; TV Interview, Channel 7, WXYZ Detroit, 1979; Annual Award of Children's Reading Round Table of Chicago, 1991. *Memberships:* Detroit Women Writers; Poetry Society of Michigan; International League of Children's Poets; Society of Children's Book Writers; Emily Dickinson Society. *Address:* 31262 Huntley Square East, Birmingham, MI 48025, USA.

HILLIS Rick L, b. 3 Feb 1956, Canada. Writer. m. Patricia Appelgren, 29 Aug 1988, 1 son, 1 daughter. *Education:* BED, University of Saskatchewan, 1979; MFA, University of Iowa, 1974. *Appointments:* Stegner Fellow, Stanford University, 1988-90; Jones Lecturer in Fiction, Stanford, 1990-92; Chesterfield Film Writer's Fellowship, 1991-92. *Publications:* Limbo River, 1990; The Blue Machines of Night, 1988. *Honours:* Drue Heinz Literature Prize, 1990; Commonwealth Club of California, silver medal, 1990. *Memberships:* PEN; ACTRA. *Address:* 499A Thompson Avenue, Mountain View, CA 94040, USA.

HILLMAN Barry Leslie, b. 18 Aug 1945, London. Local Government Officer. *Education:* Trinity High School, Northampton. *Publications:* Poetry: Endymion Rampant (Juvenilia) 1964; These Little Songs, 1979; Full-length published plays: Happy Returns, 1970; Two Can Play at That Game, 1973; Six for the Charleston, 1974; The Queen and the Axe, 1976; Castle on the Rocks, 1980; Three's a Crowd; One-Act plays: Partly Furnished, 1971; Roly-Poly, 1973; The Dispossessed, 1974; Face the Music, 1975; The Guests, 1978; A Few Minor Dischords with Robert G Newton, 1979; ....Never the Blushing Bride, 1980; The Establishment of Arles, 1981; Beyond Necessity, 1982; Collections: Odds & Sods, 1977; Bibs & Bobs with Robert G Newton, 1975. *Honours:* Partly Furnished, joint winner of the O Z Whitehead Award, Dublin Theatre Festival, 1971; Prof. Production, Eblana Theatre, Dublin, 1971; Leicester Haymarket, 1979; The Amazing Dancing Bear, Runner-up Bristol Old Vic/Harris Trust New Play Awards, 1980; Amateur Premiere, The Questors Theatre, Ealing, 1981; Professional Premiere, Leeds Playhouse, 1984. *Membership:* TWU. *Literary Agent:* Bill Ellis, A & B, Jermyn Street, London. *Address:* Lynry, 48 Louise Road, Northampton NN1 3RR, England.

HILLMAN Ellis Simon, b. 17 Nov 1928, London, England. University Lecturer. m. Louise, 10 Dec 1967, 1 son. *Education:* University College School, 1942-46; RAF Instruction in Ground Wireless, 1947-49; Chelsea College of Advanced Technology, 1971. *Appointments:* Local Government Correspondent, the Tribune, 1963-67; Editorial Advisory Board, Underground Services, 1975-79; Editorial Board, Colson News, 1986-. *Publications:* London under London, 1985; Essays in Local Government Enterprise, editor, 1964-67; Earthquake in London, 1967; Editor, The Built Environment, 1984. *Contributions to:* Underground Services; Architect and Surveyor; Architect's Journal; Structural Survey; The Environmentalist; Municipal Journal. *Honours:* ssa 00The London Visitors and Convention Bureau Best Known Book, 1985; National Book League Prize, 1986. *Memberships:* Council Science Fiction Foundation; Honorary President and Founder, Lewis Carroll Society, 1969-; LCC, GLC, ILEA; Barnet Council. *Address:* 29 Haslemere Avenue, Hendon NW4 2PU, England.

HILLMAN Martin. *See:* **HILL Douglas Arthur.**

HILLS C A R. *See:* **HILLS Charles Albert Reis.**

HILLS Charles Albert Reis, b. 21 Aug 1955, London, England; Report Writer BBC Monitoring. *Publications:* The Facist Dictatorships, 1979; The Hitler File, 1980; World Trade, 1981; Modern Industry, 1982; Growing up in the 1950s, 1983; The Second World War, 1985;

The Destruction of Pompeii and Herculaneum, 1987. *Contributions to:* The Guardian; The Daily Telegraph; Encounter; Books; Jennings Magazine; The Lady. *Memberships:* English Centre PEN. *Address:* 3 Lucas House, Albion Avenue, London SW8 2AD, England.

HILTON Margot Pamela, b. 18 Aug 1947, London, England. Arts Administrator; Writer; Journalist. m. Graeme Blundell, 3 Oct 1979, 1 son, 1 daughter. *Education:* BA, English, Honours, 1971, MA, Drama & Theatre Arts, 1972, Leeds University, England. *Appointments:* Drama Adviser, Victorian Ministry for the Arts, 1974-79; Storyliner & Scriptwriter with Grundy Organisation, 1980; Executive Officer, Australian Society of Authors, 1981-84; Playwright in Residence, Australian National Playwrights Conference, 1983; Executive Secretary, Victorian Premier's Inaugural Literary Awards, 1984-85; Publicity Manager, Angus & Robertson Publishers, 1985-87. *Publications:* (Performer Plays): Potiphar's Wife, 1979, 1980, 1981; Marmalade File, 1983; Squealing Pips, 1983; Books: Women on Men, 1987; Potiphar's Wife, 1987. *Contributions to:* Theatre Australia; Playboy; New Review; Australian Author; Bulletin; Architecture Australia; National Times; Times on Sunday; Sydney Morning Herald; Sun-Herald. *Agent:* Hickson Assocs. *Address:* 84 Surrey Street, Potts Point, NSW 2011, Australia.

HILTON Suzanne McLean, b. 3 Sept 1922, Pittsburgh, Pennsylvania, USA. Writer. m. Warren Mitchell Hilton, 15 June 1946, 1 son, 1 daughter. *Education:* BA, Beaver College, 1945. *Appointments:* Editor, Bulletin of Old York Road Historical Society, 1976-1992; Associate Editor, Montgomery County History, 1983; Editor, Bulletin of Historical Society of Montgomery County, 1987-1989. *Publications:* 18 books including: How Do They Get Rid of It?, 1970; How Do They Cope with It?, 1970; Beat It, Burn It and Drown It, 1974; The Way It Was - 1876, 1975; Who Do You Think You Are?, 1976; Yesterday's People, 1976; Here Today & Gone Tomorrow, 1978; Faster than a Horse: Moving West with Engine Power, 1983; Montgomery County, The Second Hundred Years, 1983; The World of Young Tom Jefferson, 1986; The World of Young George Washington, 1986; The World of Young Herbert Hoover, 1987; The World of Young Andrew Jackson, 1988; A Capital Capitol City, 1991. *Contributions to:* historical journals. *Honours:* Legion of Honour, Chapel of the Four Chaplains, 1978; Award for Excellence in Non Fiction, Drexel University, 1979; Golden Spur, Western Writers of America, 1980; Gold Disc, Beaver College, 1981. *Memberships:* Society of Children's Book Writers and Illustrators; Philadelphia Childrens Reading Round Table. *Address:* 3320-108th St NW, Gig Harbour, A 98332, USA.

HINDE Wendy, b. 1919. Writer (Biography). *Appointments:* Editorial Staff, The Economist, London, 1950-71; Editor, International Affairs, Royal Institute of International Affairs, London, 1971-79. *Publications:* George Canning, 1973; Castlereagh, 1981; Richard Cobden, 1987; Catholic Emancipation, 1991. *Address:* 8 Chedworth Street, Cambridge, CB3 9JF, England.

HINDIN Nathan. *See:* **BLOCH Robert.**

HINDLE Timothy Simon, b. 7 June 1946, Cleveleys, Lancashire England. Journalist. m. Ellian Lea Aciman, 11 June 1975, 1 son, 1 daughter. *Education:* MA, Worcester College, Oxford, 1967. *Appointments:* Financial Times, 1977-80; The Economist, 1980-, World Business Editor, 1986, Finance Editor, 1984. *Publication:* The Pocket Banker, 1984. *Address:* 22 Royal Crescent, London W11, England.

HINE Daryl, b. 1936, Canada. Author; Playwright; Poet. *Publications:* Five Poems, 1955; The Carnal and the Crane, 1957; The Devil's Picture Book: Poems, 1960; The Prince of Darkness and Co (novel), 1961; Heroics: Five Poems,1961; Polish Subtitles: Impressions of a

Journey, 1962; The Wooden Horse: Poems, 1965; Minutes: Poems, 1968; The Death of Seneca (play), 1968; The Homeric Hymns and the Battle of the Frogs and the Mice, 1972; Resident Alien: Poems, 1975; In and Out: Poems, 1975; Daylight Saving: Poems, 1978; The Poetry Anthology 1912-1977, 1978; Selected Poems, 1981; Theocritus: Idylls and Epigrams, 1982; Academic Festival Overtures, 1985. *Address:* 2740 Ridge Avenue, Evanston, IL 60201, USA.

HINES Barry Melvin, b. 30 June 1939, Barnsley, Yorkshire, England. Writer. (div), 1 son, 1 daughter. *Education:* Ecclesfield Grammar School, 1950-71; Loughborough College of Education, 1958-60, 1962-63. *Literary Appointments:* Yorkshire Arts Association Fellow In Creative Writing, Sheffield University 1972-74; East Midlands Arts Association Fellow In Creative Writing, Matlock College of High Education, 1975-77; Arts Council of Great Britain Fellow In Creative Writing, Sheffield City Polytechnic, 1982-84. *Publications:* Novels: The Blinder, 1966; A Kestrel For A Knave, 1968; First Signs, 1972; The GameKeeper, 1975; The Price of Coal, 1979; Looks and Smiles, 1981; Unfinished Business, 1983. TV and Film: Billy's Last Stand, 1970; Two Men From Derby, 1976; Speech Day, 1973; The Price of Coal, 1977; The GameKeeper, 1979; A Question of Leadership (with Ken Loach), 1981; Threads, 1984; Kes, 1970; Looks and Smiles, 1981; Shooting Stars, 1990; Born Kicking, 1992. *Honours:* Fellow Royal Society of Literature, 1977; BAFTA Best Single Drama (Threads), 1984; Press Guild, Best Single Drama (Threads), 1984; Honorary Fellow, Sheffield City Polytechnic, 1985. *Memberships:* Royal Society of Literature; Hoyland Common Working Men's Club; Writer's Guild of Great Britain. *Literary Agent:* Sheila Lemon, Lemon and Durbridge Ltd, 24 Pottery Lane, London, W11 4LZ, England and Curtis Brown, 162-168 Regent Street, Holland Park, London, W1R 5TA, England. *Address:* 323 Fulwood Road, Sheffield, S10 3BJ, England.

HINES Donald Merrill, b. 23 Jan 1931, Minnesota, USA. Writer; Publisher. m. Linda Marie Arnold, 10 June 1961, 3 sons. *Education:* BS English and Speech Arts, Lewis and Clark College, Portland, Oregon, 1953; MAT English and Education, Reed College, Portland, 1960; PhD Folklore and American Studies, Indiana University, 1969. *Appointments:* Associate Professor, Departments of English: Washington State University, 1968-77; College of Education, King Saud University, Saudi Arabia, 1982-90; Blue Mountain Community College, Pendleton, OR, 1990-91. *Publications:* Ghost Voices, Yakima Indian Myths, Legends, Humor and Hunting Stories, 1992; Tales of the Okanogans, 1976; Cultural History of the Inland Pacific Northwest Frontier, 1976; Frontier Folksay: Proverbial Lore of the Inland Pacific Northwest Frontier, 1977; Tales of the Nez Perce, 1984; The Forgotten Tribes, Oral Tales of the Tenino and Adjacent Mid-Columbia River Indian Nations, 1991. *Contributions to:* Southern Folklore Quarterly; Western Review; Pennsylvania Folklife; American Speech; Journal of Folklore Institute; The Folklore Historian. *Honours:* Ford Foundation Fellowship, Indiana University, 1965; Third Prize, Chicago Folklore Contest, University of Chicago, 1970. *Memberships:* American Folklore Society. *Address:* 3623- 219th Place SE, Issaquah, WA 98027, USA.

HINGAMIRE Buddanna (Buddappa), b. 4 Sept 1933, India. Translator. m. 1964, 1 son, 2 daughter. *Education:* BA, 1958, MA Russian, Karnatak University; MA, 1961, PhD, 1967, Poona University. *Publications:* Shabda Rakta Mamsa; Haddugala Haddu; Hosakavya Hosa Dikku, 1976; Teerpu and Other Plays; Ahalye; Neelanjane and Other Plays; Editor, Ilidu Ba Ta; Poetry of Dr Karki D.S.; Translations: Russian Modern Poems; Taras Shevchenko-Some Poems; Poems of Pushkin; Gipsies (a play based on Pushkin's narrative Poem 'Tsiganni'; Byelorussian Poems; Kelasadake (drama); Yuddha mattu Prema (drama); The Poetry of Avetik Issakian. *Contributions to:* various journals and magazines. *Honours:* Sahitya Akademi Award, 1976; Golden Jubilee Award, Mysore University, 1978; Soviet

Land Nehru Award, 1980. *Memberships:* Advisory Board, Kannada Central Sahitya Akademi, New Delhi; Managing Committee, Vidyavardhak Sangh-Dharwad. *Address:* Attikolla Road 3, Malmaddi, Dharwad 580007, India.

HINOJOSA-SMITH R Roland, b. 21 Jan 1929, Mercedes, Texas, USA. English Professor; Writer. m. Patricia Sorensen, 1 Sept 1963, 1 son, 2 daughters. *Education:* BS, University of Texas at Austin, 1953; Highlands University, New Mexico, 1963; PhD, University of Illinois, 1969. *Appointments:* University of Minnesota, 1977-81; University of Texas, 1981-. *Publications:* The Valley, 1983; Klail City, 1986; Dear Rafe, 1985; Partners in Crime, 1987; Korean Love Songs, 1978; Rites and Witnesses, 1984; Estampas del Valle, 1973; Klail City y sus alrededores, 1976; Claros varones de Belken, 1987; Becky and her Friends, 1989. *Contributions to:* Texas Monthly; Southwest Airlines Spirit; Latin American Review Magazine; Southwest Review. *Honours:* Best Novel, 1973, 1976, 1981; Qinto Sol Prize; Case de Las Americas Prize; Best Writing in the Humanities Prize, 1981; Alumnus of the University of Illinois, 1989. *Memberships:* Modern Language Association; Board of Directors, Texas Committee on the Humanities. *Address:* Department of English, University of Texas, Austin, TX 78712, USA.

HINTON Jenny. *See:* **DAWSON Jennifer.**

HIPPOPOTAMUS Eugene H. *See:* **KRAUS Robert.**

HIRO Dilip, Writer. *Education:* MS, State University of Virginia, USA, 1962. *Publications:* Lebanon, Fire and Embers: A History of The Lebanese Civil War, 1993; Black British, White British: A History of Race Relations in Britain, 1992; Desert Shield To Desert Storm: The Second Gulf War, 1992; The Longest War: The Iran-Iraq Military Conflict, 1989; Islamic Fundamentalism, 1988; Iran Under the Ayatollahs, 1985; Inside the Middle East, 1982; Inside India Today, 1976; Black British, White British, 1971; Three Plays, 1987; Iran: The Revolution Within, 1988; Interior, Exchange, Exterior, 1980; Apply, Apply, No Reply, play, 1978' Clean Break, play, 1978; The Untouchables of India, 1975; To Anchor A Cloud, 1972; A Triangular View, 1969. *Contributions to:* Washington Post; Wall Street Journal; Los Angeles Times; Boston Globe; Sunday Times; Observer; Guardian; New Statesman and Society; Nation; Atlantic Community Journal; Middle East Report; Toronto Star; Times Literary Supplement. *Honours:* Silver Hugo, Chicago Film Festival to A Private Enterprise, British Feature Film co-scripted by him, 1975. *Memberships:* Middle Studies Association of North America; Centre for Iranian Research and Analysis. *Literary Agent:* David Higham Associates, London. *Address:* 31 Waldegrave Road, Ealing, London W5 3HT, England.

HIRSCHHORN Clive Errol, b. 20 Feb 1940, Johannesburg, South Africa. Critic. *Education:* BA, University of Witwatersrand, Johannesburg, South Africa. *Publications:* Gene Kelly - a biography, 1974; Films of James Mason, 1976; The Warner Bros' Story, 1978; The Hollywood Musical, 1981; The Universal Story, 1983; The Columbia Story, 1989. *Contributions to:* Film and Theatre Critic of the London Sunday Express, 1966-. *Literary Agent:* Tony Peake. *Address:* 42a South Audley Street, Mayfair, London W1, England.

HIRSCHMAN Jack, b. 1933, American, Poet; Translator; Painter and collage maker. *Appointments:* Instructor, Dartmouth College, Hanover, New Hampshire, 1959-61; Assistant Professor, University of California, Los Angeles, 1961-66. *Publications:* Fragments, 1952; A Correspondence of Americans, 1960; Two, 1963; Interchange, 1964; Kline Sky, 1965; (ed)Artaud Anthology, 1965; Yod, 1966; London Seen Directly, 1967; Wasn't It Like This in the Woodcut, 1967; William Blake, 1967; (with Asa Benveniste) A Word in Your Season, 1967; Ltd. Interchangeable in Eternity: Poems of Jackruthdavidcelia Hirschman, 1967;

Jerusalem: A Three Part Poem, 1968; Aleph, Benoni and Zaddik, 1968; Jerusalem, Ltd, 1968; Shekinah, 1969; Broadside Golem, 1969; Black Alephs: Poems, 1960-68, 1969; NHR, 1970; Scintilla, 1970; (trans with V Erlich) Electric Iron by Vladimir Mayakovsky, 1970; Soledeth, 1971; DT, 1971; The Burning of Los Angeles, 1971; HNYC, 1971; (trans) Love Is a Tree, by Antonin Artaud, 1972; (trans) A Rainbow for the Christian West, by Rene Depestre, 1972; Les Vidanges, 1972; The R of the Ari's Raziel, 1972; Adamnan, 1972; (trans) The Exiled Angel by Luisa Pasamanik, 1973; (trans) Igitur by Stephane Mallarme, 1973; (trans) Wail for the Arab Beggars of the Casbah, by Ait Djafer, 1973; Aur Sea, 1973; Cantillations, 1973; Djackson, 1974; Cockroach Street, 1975; The Cool Boyetz Cycle, 1975; Kashtaninyah Segodnyah, 1976; Lyripol, 1976; The Arcanes of Le Comte de St Germain, 1977; The Jonestown Arcane, 1979; The Cagliostro Arcane, 1981; The David Arcane, 1982; Kallatumba, 1984; The Necessary Is, 1984. Address: PO Box 26517, San Francisco, CA 94126, USA.

HIRST Paul Quentin, b. 1946. Writer (Sociology). Publications: Durkheim, Bernard and Epistemology, 1975; Pre-Capitalist Modes of Production (with B. Hindess), 1975; Social Evolution and Sociological Categories, 1976; Mode of Production and Social Formations (with B. Hindess), 1977; Marx's Capital and Capitalism Today, 2 vols, 1977-78; Social Relations and Human Attributes (with P. Woolley), 1982; Marxism and Historical Writing, 1985; Law, Socialism and Democracy, 1986; After Thatcher, 1989; Representative Democracy and its Limits, 1990. Address: Department of Politics and Sociology, Birkbeck College, University of London, Malet Street, London, WC1, England.

HISSEY Jane Elizabeth, b. 1 Sept 1952, Norwich, Norfolk, England. Author; Illustrator. m. Ivan James Hissey, 1 Aug 1979, 2 sons, 1 daughter. Education: Art Foundation Course, Great Yarmouth College of Art and Design, 1970; BA Illustration and Design, 1974, Art Teachers Certificate, 1975, Brighton Polytechnic. Publications: Old Bear, 1986; Little Bears Trousers, 1987; Little Bear Lost, 1989; Jolly Tall, 1990; Jolly Snow, 1991; Old Bear Tales, 1991; Old Bear and His Friends, 1991; Little Bears Day, 1992; Little Bears Bedtime, 1992. Address: c/o Hutchinson Childrens Books, Random Century House, Vauxhall Bridge Rd, London SW1V 2SA, England.

HIVNOR Robert, b. 19 May 1916, Zanesville, Ohio, USA. Playwright; Teacher. m. Mary Otis, Aug 1947, 2 sons, 1 daughter. Education: AB, Akron University, 1936; MFA, Yale University, 1946; Graduate studies, Columbia University. Appointments: Teacher, University of Minnesota, Reed College, Bard College. Publications: Too Many Thumbs, a play 1949; The Ticklish Acrobat, play, 1956; The Assault upon Charles Sumner, play 1966; Love Reconciled to War, 1968, 1973; A Son is Always Leaving Home, short play, 1970; Apostle/ Genius/God, excerpt from play, Bostonia, 1990; Radio plays and sketches. Contributions to: Partisan Review; The Noble Savage, 1961; Bostonia, 1990. Honours: University of Iowa Fellowship, 1951; Rockefeller Grant, 1968. Address: 420, East 84th Street, New York, NY 10028, USA.

HJORTSBERG William Reinhold, b. 23 Feb 1941, New York City, USA. Author. Education: BA, Dartmouth College, 1962; Postgrad, Yale Drama School, 1962-63; Stanford University, 1967-68. Publications: ALP, 1969; Gray Matters, 1971; Symbiography, 1973; Toro! Toro! Toro!, 1974; Falling Angel, 1978; Tales and Fables, 1985; Films, Thunder and Lightning, 1977, Legend, 1986, Georgia Peaches (Co-author), 1980. Contributions to: Various journals, magazines and newspapers. Honours: Wallace Stegner Fellowship, 1967-68; Playboy Editorial Award, 1971, 1978; National Endowment for the Arts Grant, 1976. Memberships: Authors Guild, Writers Guild of America, West. Literary Agent: Robert Dattila, Phoenix Literary Agent. Address: Main Boulder Route, McLeod, MT, USA 59052.

HOBAN Russell Conwell, b. 4 Feb 1925, Lansdale, USA. Author. m. (1) Lillian Aberman, 1944, (div 1975), 1 son, 3 daughters, (2) Gundula Ahl, 1975, 3 sons. Education: Philadelphia Museum School of Industrial Art. Publications: Novels: The Mouse and His Child, 1967; The Lion of Boaz-Jachin and Jachin-Boaz, 1973; Kleinzeit, 1974; Turtle Diary, 1975; Riddley Walker, 1980; Pilgermann, 1983; 51 children's picture books and 2 books of verse for children, 1959-; Text for The Carrier Frequency (theatre piece, Impact Theatre Co-operative), 1984; Stage version of Riddley Walker (Manchester Royal Exchange Theatre Co), 1986; various essays and pieces for Granta and The Fiction Magazine. Honours: Whitbread Prize for How Tom Beat Captain Najork and His Hired Sportsmen, 1974; John W. Campbell Memorial Award and Australian Science Fiction Achievement Award for Riddley Walker, 1983. Address: David Higham Associates Ltd., 5-8 Lower John Street, Golden Square, London W1R 4HA, England.

HOBBS Anne Stevenson. Museum Curator, Victoria and Albert Museum; Frederick Warne Curator of Children's Literature. Education: BA, 1964; MA Hons 1967, Newnham College, Cambridge. Publications: Fables: 500 years of illustration and Text, 1986; Beatrix Potter: The V & A Collection, 1985; Beatrix Potter, 1866-1943: The Artist and her World, 1987; Beatrix Potter's Art, 1990; A Victorian Naturalist: Beatrix Potter's Drawings in the Armitt Collection, 1992. Contributions to: Beatrix Potters Writings: Some Literary and Linguistic Influences a major article in Beatrix Potter Studies III, 1989. Honours: Committee, Beatrix Potter Society. Memberships: Children's Books History Society; European String Teacher's Association; Lewis Carroll Society; Arthur Rackham Society. Address: c/o Archive of Art and Design, 23 Blythe Road, London W14 O9F, England.

HOBFOLL Stevan E, b. 25 Sept 1951, Chicago, Illinois, USA. Professor of Psychology. m. Ivonne H Hobfoll, 18 May 1977, 2 sons, 1 daughter. Education: London Kings College, 1971-72; BS Psychology, University of Illinois, 1973; MA 1975, Phd 1977, Psychology, University of South Florida. Publications: The Ecology of Stress, 1988; Stress, Social Support and Women, 1986; War-Related Stress, 1991; Conservation of Resources, 1989. Contributions to: Over 60 journal articles and 25 book chapters; Editor: Anxiety, Stress and Coping: An International Journal, 1992-. Honours: Ecology of Stress judged significant contribution to learning and understanding by Encyclopaedia Britannica 1989 yearbook; Peer recognition award for work with HIV/AIDS on Ohio's racial and ethinic communities, 1990. Memberships: Fellow, American Psychological Association; Society for Test Anxiety Research; International Society for the Study of Personal Relationships. Address: Applied Psychology Centre, 106 Kent Hall, Kent State University, OH 44242, USA.

HOBHOUSE Hermione, b. 1934. Urban Historian and Writer, since 1983 General Editor, Survey of London, RCHME. Appointments include: Researcher, Scriptwriter, Associated-Rediffusion Television, 1956-58; Researcher, Scriptwriter, Granada Television, 1958-63; General Editor, Survey of London, 1983-. Publications: The Ward of Cheap in the City of London: A Short History, 1963; Thomas Cubitt: Master Builder, 1971; Lost London, 1971; History of Regent Street, 1975; Oxford and Cambridge, 1980; Prince Albert: His Life and Work, 1983; (Ed) Southern Kensington, Earl's Court, 1986. Honour: MBE, 1981. Address: 61 Dunstan's Road, London, W6 8RE, England.

HOBHOUSE Penelope. See: MALINS Penelope.

HOBSBAUM Philip Dennis, b. 29 June 1932, Writer; University Professor. m. Rosemary Phillips, 20 July 1976. Education: BA, 1955, MA 1961, Downing College, Cambridge; LRAM, Royal Academy of Music, 1956; PhD, University of Sheffield, 1968. Appointments: Lecturer in English, Queen's University, Belfast, Northern Ireland, 1962-66; Lecturer in English Literature, 1966-72,

Senior Lecturer, 1972-79, Reader, 1979-85, Titular Professor, 1985-, Glasgow University, Scotland. *Publications:* A Reader's Guide to Charles Dickens, 1972, 1982, 1989; Essentials of Literary Critism, 1982, 1989; A Reader's Guide to D H Lawrence, 1981, 1989; A Theory of Communication, 1970; Tradition and Experiment in English Poetry, 1979; A Reader's Guide to Robert Lowell, 1988; The Place's Fault and Other Poems, 1964; In Retreat and Other Poems, 1966; Coming Out Fighting: Poems, 1969; Women and Animals: Poems, 1972. *Contributions to:* Times Literary Supplement; Spectator; Listener; Poetry Review; Outposts; The Hudson Review; Encounter; Modern Language Review. *Memberships:* Chairman, Sheffield University Arts Society, 1960-61; Scottish Association for Literary Studies; BBC Club; Association of University Teachers. *Address:* c/o Department of English Literature, University of Glasgow, Glasgow G20 6BS, Scotland.

HOBSON Fred Colby Jr, b. 23 Apr 1943, Winston-Salem, NC, USA. Professor Literature; Writer. m. 17 June 1967, (div.), 1 daughter. *Education:* AB, English, University of North Carolina, 1965; MA, History, Duke University, 1967; PhD, English, University of North Carolina, 1972. *Appointments:* Professor of English, University of Alabama, 1972-86; Professor English and Co-editor, Southern Review, Louisiana State University, 1986-89; Professor of English and Co-editor, Southern Literary Journal, University of North Carolina. *Publications:* Tell About the South: The Southern Rage to Explain, 1984; Serpent in Eden: H.L. Mencken and the South, 1974; South-Watching: Selected Essays of Gerald W. Johnson, (editor), 1984; Literature at the Barricades: The American Writer in the 1930's, (co-editor), 1983; The Southern Writer in the Post-Modern World, 1990. *Contributions to:* Virginia Quarterly Review; Sewanee Review; Kenyon Review; New York Times Book Review; Commonweal; American Literature; Times Literary Supplement. *Honours:* National Endowment Humanities Fellow, 1976-77; Jules F. Landry Award, 1984; Lillian Smith Award, 1984; shared Pulitzer Prize (Journalism) for Meritorious Public Service, 1970; National humanities Cnter Fellow, 1991-92. *Memberships:* South Atlantic Modern Language Association; Society for the Study of Southern Literature. *Address:* Department of English, University of North Carolina, Chapel Hill, NC 27514, USA.

HOBSON Mary, b. 1926, British. *Publications:* This Place Is a Madhouse, 1980; Oh Lily, 1981; Poor Tom, 1982. *Address:* 63 Horniman Drive, Forest Hill, London SE23, England.

HOBSON Polly. *See:* EVANS Julia.

HOCH Edward D, b. 22 Feb 1930, Rochester, New York, USA, Author. m. Patricia A McMahon, 5 June 1957. *Education:* University of Rochester, 1947-49. *Publications:* The Thefts of Nick velvet, 1978; The Quests of Simon Ark, 1984; Leopold's Way, 1985; The Night My Friend, 1991; The Shattered Raven, 1969; The Transvection Machine, 1971; The Spy and the Thief, 1971; Best Detective Stories of the Year, (Editor), 1976-81; Year's Best Mystery and Suspense Stories, (Editor), 1982-93; All But Impossible, (Editor), 1981. *Contributions to:* Over 800 stories in mystery magazines and anthologies, including a story in every issue of Ellery Queen's Mystery Magazine, 1973-. *Honours:* Mystery Writers of America Edgar Award for best short story, The Oblong Room, 1967; Edgar Nominee for The Most Dangerous Man, 1980. *Memberships:* President, Mystery Writers of America, 1982- 83; Author's Guild; Crime Writers Association, England; Science Fiction Writers of America. *Literary Agent:* Larry Sternig, 742 Robertison Street, Milwaukee, WI. *Address:* 2941 Lake Avenue, Rochester, NY 14612, USA.

HOCHHUTH Rolf, b. 1 Apr 1931. Playwright. m. 3 sons. *Appointments:* Former Publisher's Reader; Resident Municipal Playwright, Basel, 1963. *Publications:* Plays: The Representative, 1962; The Employer, 1965; The Soldiers, 1966; Anatomy of Revolution, 1969; The Guerillas, 1970; The Midwife, 1972; Lysistrata and the NATO, 1973; A German Love Story (novel), 1980; Judith, 1984. *Membership:* PEN, Germany. *Address;* PO Box 661, 4002 Basel, Switzerland.

HOCHMAN Sandra, b. 1936, American. *Appointment:* Actress. *Publications:* Voyage Home: Poems, 1960; Manhattan Pastures, 1963; The World of Gunter Grass, The Vaudeville Marriage: Poems, Love Poems, 1966; Love Letters from Asia: Poems, 1968; Earthworks: Poems 1960-70, Walking Papers, The Magic Convention, 1971; Year of the Woman, 1973; Futures: New Poems, 1974; Happiness Is Too Much Trouble, 1976; Explosion of Loneliness, Endangered Species, 1977; Streams: Life-Secrets for Writing Poems and Songs, 1978; Jogging, 1979; Playing Tahoe.

HOCHSCHILD Adam, b. 5 Oct 1942, New York City, USA. Writer. m. Arlie Russell, 26 June 1965, 2 sons. *Education:* AB cum laude, Harvard University, 1963. *Appointments include:* Reporter, San Francisco Chronicle, 1965-66; Editor & writer, Ramparts magazine, 1966-68, 1973-74; Commentator, National Public Radio 1982-83, Public Interest Radio 1987-88; Co-founder, editor, now writer, Mother Jones magazine, 1974-; Regents Lecturer, University of California at Santa Cruz, 1987; Lecturer, Graduate School of Journalism, University of California at Berkeley, 1992. *Publications include:* Half the Way Home: A Memoir of Father & Son, 1986; The Mirror at Midnight: A South African Journey, 1990. *Contributions to:* Harpers; New York Times; Los Angeles Times; The Washington Post; Progressive; Village Voice; Mother Jones. *Honours:* Certificate of Excellence, Overseas Press Club of America, 1981; Bryant Spann Award, Eugene V. Debs Foundation, 1984; 'Notable Book of Year' American Library Association/New York Times Book Review, 1986; Thomas More Storke International Journalism Award, from the World Affairs Council of Northern California, 1987. *Memberships:* National Writers Union; Media Alliance; National Book Critics Circle; Overseas Press Club. *Literary Agent:* Georges Borchardt Inc, NYC. *Address:* 84 Seward St, San Francisco, CA 94114, USA.

HOCKING Mary (Eunice), b. 1921, British. *Appointment:* Local Government Officer, 1946-70. *Publications:* The Winter City, 1961; Visitors to the Crescent, 1962; The Sparrow, 1964; The Young Spaniard, 1965; Ask No Question, 1967; A Time of War, 1968; Checkmate, 1969; The Hopeful Traveller, 1970; The Climbing Frame, 1971; Family Circle, 1972; Daniel Come to Judgement, 1974; The Bright Day, 1975; The Mind Has Mountains, 1976; Look Stranger, 1979; He Who Plays the King, 1980; March House, 1981; Good Daughters, 1984; Indifferent Heroes, 1985; Welcome Strangers, 1986; An Irrelevant Woman, 1987; A Particular Place, 1989; Letters from Constance, 1991; The Very Dead of Winter, 1993. *Address:* 3 Church Row, Lewes, Sussex, England.

HODDER-WILLIAMS Christopher, b. 25 Aug 1926, London. Author; Composer. m. Deirdre Matthew, November 1967, 1 son, 1 daughter. *Education:* Eton College. *Publications include:* Chain Reaction; Fistful of Digits; The Main Experiment; The Chromosome Game; The Higher They Fly. TV plays including: The Ship That Couldn't Stop. *Contributions to:* Journals including, Computer Weekly and Melody Maker. *Honour:* Award for The Higher They Fly. *Membership:* National Book League. *Address:* 19 Erpingham Road, Putney, London SW15 1BE, England.

HODGE Jane Aiken, b. 4 Dec 1917, Author. m. Alan Hodge, 3 Jan 1949, 2 daughters. *Education:* BA, Somerville College, Oxford, 1935-38; AM, Radcliffe College, Cambridge, Massachusetts, USA, 1938-39. *Publications:* Leading Lady, 1990; First Night, 1989; Polonaise, 1987; Secret Island, 1985; The Private World of Georgette Heyer, 1984; The Lost Garden, 1982; Last Act, 1979; One Way to Venice, 1975; Savannah

Purchase, 1971; The Double Life of Jane Austen, 1972; Greek Wedding, 1970; The Adventurers, 1966; Maulever Hall, 1964; and others. *Contributor to:* Various short stories reviews in History Today, Sunday Telegraph and Evening Standard. *Membership:* Lewes Monday Literary Club, Secretary, 1972. *Literary Agent:* David Higham Associates. *Address:* 23 Eastport Lane, Lewes, East Sussex BN7 1TL, England.

HODGE Paul William, b. 8 Nov 1934, Seattle, Washington, USA. Astronomer. m. Ann Uran, 14 June 1962, 2 sons, 1 daughter. *Education:* BS, Yale University, 1956; PhD, Harvard University, 1960. *Appointment:* Editor, Astronomical Journal, 1984-. *Publications:* Concepts of the Universe, 1969; Revolution in Astronomy, 1970; Contemporary Astronomy, 1979; Interplanetary Dust, 1981; Atlas of the Andromeda Galaxy, 1981; Galaxies, 1986; Solar System Astrophysics; Atlas of the Small Magellanic Cloud; Atlas of the Large Magellanic Cloud. *Contributions to:* 300 technical articles to astronomical journals. *Honours:* Beckwith Prize in Astronomy, 1956; Bart Bok Prize in Astronomy, 1962; Award for Best Physical Science Book for Galaxies, 1986. *Memberships:* American Astronomical Society; Vice President, Astronomical Society of the Pacific, Board of Directors, Vice President. *Address:* Astronomy, FM-20, University of Washington, Seattle, WA 98195, USA.

HODGINS Jack Stanley, b. 3 Oct 1938, Vancouver Island, Canada. Novelist; Teacher. m. Dianne Child, 17 Dec 1960, 2 sons, 1 daughter. *Education:* BEd, University of British Columbia. *Publications:* Spit Delaney's Island, 1976; The Invention of the World, 1977; The Resurrection of Joseph Bourne, 1979; The HOnorary Patron, 1987; Innocent Cities, 1990; Over Forty in Broken Hill, 1992. *Honours:* Gibson First Novel Award, 1978; Governor General's Award for Fiction, 1980; Canada- Australia Literature Prize, 1986; Commonwealth Literature Prize, 1988. *Memberships:* PEN; The Writers Union of Canada. *Literary Agent:* Bela Power Agency. *Address:* c/o, Bela Power Agency. 22 Shallmon Blvd, Toronto, Canada.

HOEPPNER Iona Ruth, (C C Arndt, Edgar S Cooper, Jovak Von Hess, Ruth Snider), b. 17 Aug 1939, Denver, Colorado, USA. Financial Advisor; Author. m. Richard A Hoeppner, 14 Dec 1975, 4 sons, 6 daughters. *Appointments:* Editor in Chief, Highlighter Inc, 1985-88; Reporter, Columnist, Haxton Heraly, 1986-88; Editor, Columnist: Write Now, 1986-89, Moneyline, 1990-. *Publications:* The Gypo's Guide to Making it on 18 Wheels, 1984; Incorporate yourself for Under $20!, 1985; Highway to Nowhere, 1986; Just me, 1985; WAter, 1986; How to Really get Started in Business, 1986; The COmplete Guide to RVs 1987; The Executive Syndrome, 1987; Private Stock issues Can Make you Rich, 1987; The Complete RV Handbook, 1988; The Teacher's Guide to Rural Education, 1988; The Administrator's Guide to Rural Education, 1988. *Contributions to:* Model Railroader; Writer Now; Haxton herald; Moneyline. *Memberships:* National Writer's Club; National Platform Association; Rocky Mt Biological Lab. *Address:* 32360 Big Springs Road, Yoder, CO 80864, USA.

HOERR John Peter III, b. 12 Dec 1930, Pennsylvania, USA. Writer. m. Joanne Lillig, 24 Nov 1960, 2 sons. *Education:* AB, Penn State University, 1953. *Appointments:* Reporter, United Press International, 1956-57, 1958-60; The Daily Tribune, Royal Oak, Mich. 1957-58; Reporter, Business Week, 1960-63, 1964-69; Labour Editor, Senior Writer, Business Week, 1975-91; Reporter and Commentator, WQED-TV, public television, Pittsburgh, 1969-74. *Publications:* And the Wolf Finally Came: The Decline of the American Steel Industry, 1988; Co-author, The Reindustrialization of America, 1981. *Contributions to:* The ATlantic; The American Prospect; Pittsburgh Magazine; Harvard Business Review. *Honours:* Richard A Lester Award, Princeton University, Outstanding Book in industrial relations and labour economics, 1988; Page One Award, Best Labour Story, Magazine, 1985, 1988, New York

Newspaper Guild. *Memberships:* National Writers Union; Industrial Relations Research Association. *Address:* 12 Parker Lane, Teaneck, NJ 07666, USA.

HOFF Harry Summerfield, (William Cooper), b. 1910. Novelist. m. Joyce Barbara Harris, 1951, 2 daughters. *Education:* Christ's College, Cambridge. *Appointments:* Assistant Commissioner, Civil Service Commission, 1945-58; Personnel Consultant to: UKAEA, 1958-72; CEGB, 1958-72; Commission of European Communities, 1972-73; Assistant Director, Civil Service Selection Board, 1973-75; Member, Board of Crown agents, 1975-77; Personnel Advisor, Millbank Technical Services, 1975-77; Adjunct Professor, English Literature, Syracuse University, London Centre, 1977-90. *Publications:* (as H.S. Hoff) Trina, 1934; Rhea, 1935; Lisa, 1937; Three Marriages, 1946; (as William Cooper) Scenes from Provincial Life, 1950; The Struggles of Albert Woods, 1952; The Ever Interesting Topic, 1953; Disquiet and Peace, 1956; Young People, 1958; C.P. Show, 1959; Prince Genji, (a play), 1960; Scenes from Married Life, 1961; Memoirs of a New Man, 1966; You Want the Right Frame of Reference, 1971; Shall We Ever Know?, 1971; Love on the Coast, 1973; You're Not Alone, 1976; Scenes from Metropolitan Life, 1982; Scenes from Later Life, 1983; From Early Life, 1990; Immortality At Any Price, 1991. *Memberships:* Fellow, Royal Society of Literature; Council of RSL, 1987-91; Member, English Centre of International PEN, 1950-, twice Member of Executive, Vice-President, 1991-. *Literary Agent:* Gillon Aitken, Aitken & Stone, 29 Fernshaw Road, London SW10 0TC, England. *Address:* 22 Kenilworth Court, Lower Richmond Road, London SW15 1EW, England.

HOFFMAN Alice, b. 1952, American. *Appointment:* Freelance Writer. *Publications:* Property Of, 1977; The Drowning Season, 1979; Angel Landing, 1980; White Horses, 1982; Fortune's Daughter, 1985. *Address:* c/o Putnam, 200 Madison Avenue, New York, NY 10016, USA.

HOFFMAN Daniel, b. 3 Apr 1923, New York City, USA. Professor of English; Writer. m. Elizabeth McFarland, 1948, 2 children. *Education:* AB 1947, MA 1949, PhD 1956, Columbia University, New York. *Appointments:* Instructor in English, Columbia University, 1952-56; Visiting Professor, University of Dijon, 1956-57; Assistant Professor 1957-60, Associate Professor 1960-65 and Professor of English, 1965-66, Swarthmore College, Pennsylvania. Professor of English 1966-, Poet-in-Residence 1978-, Felix E Schelling Professor of English, University of Pennsylvania, Philadelphia; Visiting Professor, King's College London, 1991-92. *Publications:* Verse includes: An Armada of Thirty Whales, 1954; Striking the Stones, 1968; Broken Laws, 1970; Corgi Modern Poets in Focus 4, with others, 1971; The Center of Attention, 1974; Able Was I Ere I Saw Elba: Selected Poems 1954-1974, 1977; Brotherly Love, 1981; Hang-Gliding from Helicon, 1988. Author or editor of various other publications. *Honours:* New York YMHA Poetry Center Introduction Award, 1951; Yale Series of Younger Poets Award, 1954; Ansley Prize, 1957; American Council of Learned Societies Fellowship, 1962 & 1966; Columbia University Medal for Excellence, 1964; American Academy grant 1967; Ingram Merrill Foundation Grant, 1971; National Endowment for the Humanities Fellowship, 1975; Hungarian PEN Medal, 1980; Guggenheim Fellowship, 1983; Paterson Poetry Prize, 1989; Chancellor, Academy of American Poets, 1972-; Consultant in Poetry of The Library of Congress, 1973-74. *Address:* Department of English, University of Pennsylvania, Philadelphia. PA 19104, USA.

HOFFMAN Gloria Levy, b. 8 Feb 1933, Norfolk, Virginia, USA. Author. m. 18 Sept 1954, widowed, 1982, 3 sons, 1 deceased, 1 daughter. *Education:* BA, Speech, University of Wisconsin, 1954. *Appointments:* Editor, The Norah, 1964; Editor, O Magazine, 1972; Editor, The Scope, TM, 1977. *Publications:* We Who Learn to Live with Hate, 1968; The Auntie-Biotics, 1971; Grief is Not a Thief, 1983; I Belong to Me!, 1984; I Belong to Me!,

1986. *Contributions to:* Squires Publications; Kansas City Times; Kansas City Star; Brandeis Bulletin; The Sun. *Honours:* Quill and Scroll, 1952; various other honours and awards. *Memberships:* Barn Players, Vice President, Promotion; Menorah Medical Centre, Board, Publication/Promotion; Brandeis University Women, Vice President, Board, Publication/Promotion. *Literary Agent:* Richard Leiter and Jeffrey Katz. *Address:* Creative Concepts in Communications Ltd., 1250 West 63rd Street, Kansas City, MO 64113, USA.

HOFFMAN Lee, (Georgia York), b. 1932, American. *Appointments:* Formerly in Printing Production; Assistant Editor, Infinity and Science Fiction Adventures, both 1956-58; Freelance Writer 1965-. *Publications:* Gunfight at Laramie, The Legend of Blackjack Sam, 1966; Bred to Kill, The Valdez Horses, Telepower, 1967; Dead Man's Gold, The Yarborough Brand, 1968; Wild Riders, Loco, Return to Broken Crossing, West of Cheyenne, 1969; Always the Black Knight, 1970; The Caves of Karst, Change Song, 1972; Wiley's Move, The Truth about the Cannonball Kid, 1975; Fox, Nothing but a Drifter, Trouble Valley, 1976; The Sheriff of Jack Hollow, 1977; The Land Killer, 1978; Savage Key (as Georgia York), 1979; Savannah Grey (as Georgia York), 1981; In and Out of the Quandry, 1982; Savage Conquest (as Georgia York), 1983. *Address:* 3290 Sunrise Trail N W, Port Charlotte, FL 33952, USA.

HOFFMAN Mary Margaret Lassiter, b. 20 Apr 1945, Eastleigh, Hants, England. Writer and Journalist. m. Stephen James Barber, 22 Dec 1972, 3 daughters. *Education:* James Allen's Girl's School, Dulwich; BA, 1967, MA 1973, Newnham College, Cambridge; Postgraduate Diploma, General Linguistics, University College London, 1970. *Appointments:* Children's Books Award: Judge on Other Award Panel, 1981-87; Judge, Ibby Hans Anderson Award British Panel, three times; research Associate, University of Exeter. *Publications:* 50 Children's books, including: Amazing Grace, 1991; Beware, Princess, 1983; Dracula's Daughter, 1988; Nancy No-Size, 1988; My Grandma has Black hair, 1989. 16 non-fiction titles in the series Animals in the Wild. *Contributions to:* Daily Telegraph, Guardian, Independent, Sunday Times, Specialist Children's Book Press. *Memberships:* Society of Authors Hornsey Library Campaign (Chair); Co-ordinator and Founder, CENTRAL (Children's Education Needs Teaching Resources and Libraries; NUJ; IBBY. *Literary Agent:* Pat White, Rogers Coleridge & White. *Address:* c/o Rogers Coleridge & White, 20 Powis Mews, London W11 1JN, England.

HOFFMAN William M, b. 12 Apr 1939, New York City, USA. Writer. *Education:* BA, cum laude, City College of New York. *Publications:* As Is, 1985; Gay Plays (Editor), 1977; New American Plays 2,3,4, Editor, 1968, 1970, 1971. *Contributions to:* Numerous journals and magazines. *Honours:* Obie, 1985; Drama Desk, 1985; Tony Nomination, 1985. *Memberships:* ASCAP; Writers Guild of America; Dramatists Guild; PEN; Circle Repertory Company. *Literary Agent:* Mitch Douglas, ICM, New York. *Address:* c/o Mitch Douglas, ICM, 40 W 57th St., New York, NY 10019, USA.

HOFFMANN Ann Marie, b. 6 May 1930, Abingdon, Berks, UK. Author and Researcher. *Education:* Tunbridge Wells County Grammar School, 1940-46; St Godric's College, London, 1947-48. *Appointments:* Various, publishing/international conference organising, London, 1948-51, 1962-66; United Nations, Geneva, Paris, The hauge, 1952-58; PA to Author, Robert Henriques, 1959-61; Principal, Author's Research Services, 1966-87. *Publications:* Research For Writers, 1975, 1979, 1986, 1992; Majorca, 1978; Lives of the Tudors, 1977; Bocking Deanery, 1976; The Dutch: How they Live and Work, 1971, 1973. *Memberships:* Society of Authors; PEN: Society of Women Writers and Journalists; Society of Sussex Authors. *Address:* Baixada del Rei 8, Carretera de las Cuevas, 07580 Capdepera, Mallorca, Spain.

HOFFMANN Donald, b. 24 June 1933, Illinois, USA. Architectural Critic; Historian. m. Theresa McGrath, 12 Apr 1958, 4 sons, 1 daughter. *Education:* University of Chicago; University of Kansas City. *Appointments:* General Assignment Reporter 1956-65, Art Critic 1965-90, Kansas City Star; Assistant Editor, Journal of the Society of Architectural Historians, 1970-72. *Publications:* The Meanings of Architecture: Buildings and Writings by John Wellborn Root (ed), 1967; The Architecture of John Wellborn Root, 1973; Frank Lloyd Wright's Fallingwater, 1978 (2nd edit, 1993); Frank Lloyd Wright's Robie House, 1984; Frank Lloyd Wright: Architecture and Nature, 1986; Frank Lloyd Wright's Hollyhock House, 1992. *Honours:* Fellow, National Endowment for the Humanities, 1970-71; Fellow, National Endowment for the Arts, 1974; Graham Foundation Grant, 1981. *Membership:* Life Member, The Art Institute of Chicago. *Address:* 6441 Holmes St, Kansas City, MO 64131-1110, USA.

HOFMAN David, b. 26 Sept 1908, Poona, India. Author and Publisher. 1 son, 1 daughter. *Appointments:* Editor, New World Order, 1937-39; Editor, the Bahii World, 1963-88; Founder, George Ronald Publishers, 1948. *Publications:* The Renewal of Civilization, 1946; God and His Messengers; George Townshend, 1983; A Commentary on the Wise Testament of Abdul'haba, 1950; Baha v Uah, The Prince of Peace, A Protrait, 1992; Essays, poems, and editorials. *Memberships:* Publishers Association, 1948. *Address:* The Bivvy, Heyford Road, Steeple Aston, Bicester, Oxon, OX6 3SH, England.

HOFMANN Michael, b. 1957, Germany. Freelance Writer; Poet. *Publications:* Nights in the Iron Hotel, 1983; Acrimony, 1986; KS in Lakeland: New and Selected Poems, 1990. *Address:* c/o Faber and Faber, 3 Queen Square, London WC1N 3AU, England.

HOGAN Desmond, b. 10 Dec 1950, Ballinasloe, Republic of Ireland, Teacher; Writer. *Education:* BA, 1972, MA, 1973, University College, Dublin. *Appointment:* Strode Fellow, University of Alabama, 1989. *Publications:* A Link with the River, 1989; A Curious Street, 1984; The Ikon Maker, 1976; The Leaves on Grey, 1980; A New Shirt, 1986. *Honours:* Hennessy Award, 1971; Rooney Prize, 1977; John Llewellyn Memorial Prize, 1980; Irish Post Award, 1985; Strode Fellow, University of Alabama, 1989. *Literary Agent:* Deborah Rogers. *Address:* Basement, 6 Stanstead Grove, London SE6, England.

HOGAN James P(atrick), b. 1941, United Kingdom. Full-time Writer; Former Electronics Engineer and Sales Executive. *Publications:* Inherit the Stars, 1977; The Genesis Machine, 1977; The Gentle Giants of Ganymede, 1978; The Two Faces of Tomorrow, 1979; Thrice upon a time, 1980; Giants' Star, 1981; Voyage from Yesteryear, 1982; Lode of the Lifemaker, 1983; The Proteus Operation, 1985; Minds, Machines and No-Nuke Neanderthals, short stories, 1986.

HOGAN Kathleen Margaret, (Kay Hogan), b. 13 Feb 1935, Bronx, New York, USA. Writer; Lab Technician; Housewife. m. James P Hogan, 4 sons, 1 daughter. *Education:* High School Graduate, 1952. *Publications:* The El Train, 1982; The Silent Men, 1984; Widow Women, 1985; Little Green Girl, 1986; Of Saints and Other Things, 1992; The Women Wore Black, 1993. *Contributions to:* Descant; Long Pond Review; Journal of Irisl Literature; North Country Anthology; Catholic Girls Anthology; Glens Falls Review. *Honours:* 3rd Place in Writing Contest, Crandell Library, 1980; Parnassus Award for Fiction, 1981. *Memberships:* Poets and Writers. *Address:* 154 East Avenue, Saratoga Springs, NY 12866, USA.

HOGAN Kay. *See:* **HOGAN Kathleen Margaret.**

HOGAN Robert (Goode), b. 1930, USA. Professor of English. *Appointments:* Publisher, Proscenium Press, 1964-; Professor of English, University of Delaware,

Newark, 1970-; Editor, Journal of Irish Literature, 1972-; Editor, George Spelvin's Theatre Book, 1978-85. *Publications:* Experiments of Sean O'Casey, 1960; Feathers from the Green Crow, 1962; Drama: The Major Genres (edited with S Molin), 1962; Arthur Miller, 1964; Independence of Elmer Rice, 1965; Joseph Holloway's Abbey Theatre (edited with M J O'Neill), 1967; The Plain Style (with H Bogart), 1967; After the Irish Renaissance, 1967; Seven Irish Plays (editor), 1967; Joseph Holloway's Irish Theatre (edited with M J O'Neill), 3 vols, 1968-70; Dion Boucicault, 1969; The Fan Club, 1969; Betty and the Beast, 1969; Lost Plays of the Irish Renaissance (with J Kilroy), 1970; Crows of Mephistopheles (editor), 1970; Towards a National Theatre (editor), 1970; Eimar O'Duffy, 1972; Mervyn Wall, 1972; Conor Cruise O'Brien (with E Young-Bruehl), 1974; A History of the Modern Irish Drama, vol I, The Irish Literary Theatre (with J Kilroy), 1975, vol II, Laying the Foundation (with J Kilroy), 1976, vol III, The Abbey Theatre 1905-09 (with J Kilroy), 1978, vol IV, The Rise of the Realists 1910-1915 (with R Burnham and D P Poteet), 1979, vol V, The Art of the Amateur 1916-1920 (with R Burnham), 1984, Vol V1, The Years of O'Casey (with R Burnham), 1992; The Dictionary of Irish Literature (editor), 1979; Since O'Casey, 1983; The Plays of Frances Sheridan (edited with J C Beasley), 1984; Guarini's The Faithful Shepherd, translated by Thomas Sheridan (edited and completed with E. Nickerson), 1990; Murder At The Abbey (with J Douglas), 1993. *Address:* PO Box 361, Newark, DE 19711, USA.

HOGGARD James Martin, b. 21 June 1941, Wichita Falls, Texas, USA. Professor of English. m. Lynn Taylor, 23 May 1976, 1 son, 1 daughter. *Education:* BA, Southern Methodist University; MA, University of Kansas. *Appointments:* Newspaper Reporter; University Professor, English. *Publications;* Eyesigns, 1977; Trotter Ross, 1981; The Shaper Poems, 1983; Elevator Man, 1983; Two Gulls, One Hawk, 1983; Breaking an Indelicate Statue, 1986; The Art of Dying (translations), 1988; Love Breaks (translations), 1991. *Contributions to:* Beyond Baroque; Blackbird Circle; Descant; Alembic; Cedar Rock; Kansas Quarterly; Mississippi Review; Partisan Review; Poet & Critic; Poet; Poet Lore; Southern Poetry Review; Southwest Review; The Smith; Karamu Latin American Literary Review; Ohio Review; Mundus Artium; Texas Observer. *Honours:* David Russell Poetry Award, 1963; Fine Arts Festival Award, Midwestern University, 1968; Hart Crane and Alice Crane Williams Memorial Award, 1969. *Memberships:* Texas Institute of Letters; Texas Association of Creative Writing Teachers; American Literary Translators Association. *Address:* 111 Pembroke Lane, Wichita Falls, TX 76301, USA.

HOGGART Simon David, b. 26 May 1946. United States Corespondent, The Observer, 1985-89; Political Editor, 1992-. m. Alyson Clare Corner, 1983, 1 son, 1 daughter. *Education:* MA, King's College, Cambridge. *Appointments:* Reporter, 1968-71, The Guardian, Northern Ireland Correspondent, 1971-73, Political Correspondent, 1973-81; Feature Writer, 1981-85, The Observer; Political Columnist, Punch, 1979-85. *Publications:* The Pact (with Alistair Michie), 1978; Michael Foot: a Portrait (with David Leigh), 1981; On the House, 1981; Back on the House, 1982; House of III Fame, 1985; America, A Users Guide, 1990. *Contributions to:* New Society; Presenter, BBC Forth Column. *Honours:* David Holden Award for Resident Foreign Correspondent, British Press Awards, 1987. *Literary Agent:* Curtis Brown, London. *Address:* The Observer, Chelsea Bridge House, Queenstown Road, London SW8 4NN, England.

HOGWOOD Christopher Jarvis Haley. b. 10 Sept 1941. Musicologist; Writer; Editor and Broadcaster. *Education:* MA, Pembroke College, Cambridge. *Appointments:* Editor of books and music. *Publications:* Music at Court, 1977; The Trio Sonata, 1979; Haydn's Visits to England, 1980; Music in the 18th Century England, (co-editor), 1983; Handel, 1984. Holmes Life of Mozart, (editor), 1991. *Honours:* Honorary Professor of Music, 1986-90, Honorary DMus, University of Keele,

1991. Honorary Fellow, Jesus College, Cambridge, 1989; FRSA, 1982; Freeman, Company of Musicians, 1989; Walter Cobbett Medal, Company of Musicians, 1986. *Address:* 10 Brookside, Cambridge CB2 1JE, England.

HOLBROOK David Kenneth, b. 9 Jan 1923, Norwich, England. Author; Emeritus Fellow, Downing College, Cambridge. m. 23 Apr 1949, 2 sons, 2 daughters. *Education:* MA, Honours, Cantab, 1945; Exhibitioner, Downing College, Cambridge, 1941-42, 1945-47. *Appointments:* Fellow, King's College, Cambridge, 1961-65; Writer in Residence, Dartington Hall, 1972-73; Fellow, director of English Studies, Downing College, 1981-88; Senior Leverhulme Research Fellow, 1965; Leverhulme Emeritus Research Fellow, 1988-90. *Publications:* English for the Rejected, 1964; Flesh Wounds, 1966; A Play of Passion, 1978; Selected Poems, 1980; Nothing Larger Than Life, 1987; English for Maturity, 1961; Imaginings, 1961; Against the Cruel Frost, 1963; Object Relations, 1967; Old World New World, 1969; Chance of a Lifetime, 1978; The Secret Places, 1964; The Exploring Word, 1967; Children's Writing, 1967; English in Australia Now, 1972; English for Meaning, 1980; Education & Philosophical Anthropology, 1987; Evolution and the Humanities, 1987; The Novel and Authenticity, 1987; Images of Woman in Literature, 1990; Edith Wharton and the Unsatisfactory Man, 1991; Where D D H Laurence Was Wrong About Women, 1992; Charles Dicken's and the Image of Women, 1993; A Little Athens, 1990; Jennifer, 1991; Even If They Fail, 1992. *Contributions to:* Numerous professional journals. *Memberships:* Society of Authors; Editorial Board, Universities Quarterly, 1972-87. *Address:* Denmore Lodge, Brunswick Gardens, Cambridge CB5 8DQ, England.

HOLBROOK Jack. *See:* **VANCE John Holbrook.**

HOLBROOK John. *See:* **VANCE John Holbrook.**

HOLDEN Joan, b. 18 Jan 1939, Berkeley, California, USA. Playwright. m. (1) Arthur Holden, 1958 (divorced), (2) Daniel Chumley, 1968, 3 daughters. *Education:* BA, Reed College, Portland, Oregon, 1960; MA, University of California, Berkeley, 1964. *Career:* Waitress, Claremont Hotel, Berkeley, 1960-62; copywriter, Librairie Larousse, Paris 1964-66; Research Assistant, University of California, Berkeley, 1966-67; Playwright 1967-, Publicist 1967-69, Business Manager 1978-79, San Francisco Mime Troupe; Editor, Pacific News Service, 1973-75; Instructor in Playwriting, University of California, Davis, 1975, 1977, 1979, 1983, 1985, 1987. *Publications include:* Americans; or, Last Tango in Huahuatenango, with Daniel Chumley (produced Dayton, Ohio, and London 1981; New York 1982); Factwino Meets the Moral Majority, with others (produced San Francisco, 1981; New York, 1982). Published in West Coast Plays 15-16 (Berkeley, California) Spring 1983; Factwino vs Armaggedonman (produced San Francisco, 1982). Published in West Coast Plays 15-16 (Berkeley, California) Spring 1983; Steeltown, music by Bruce Barthol (produced San Francisco, 1984; New York 1985); 1985, with others (produced San Francisco, 1985; Spain/36, music by Bruce Barthol (produced Los Angeles, 1986); The Mozamgola Caper, with others (produced San Francisco, 1986). *Honours:* Obie Award, 1973; Rockefeller Grant, 1985. *Address:* San Francisco Mime Troupe, 855 Treat Street, San Francisco, CA 94110, USA.

HOLDEN William Melville, b. 25 Apr 1923, Richmond, California, USA, Writer. m. (1) Bertha Audrey Jones, 26 Jan 1956 (div), (2) Patricia E Mayer, 24 Nov 1974, 4 daughters. *Education:* AB, economics, 1950, Postgraduate study in Philosophy, 1951, New York University. *Appointments:* Newspaper reporter, northern California newspapers including San Francisco Examiner, 1953-62. *Publications:* Sacramento, Excursions Into Its History and Natural World, 1988. *Contributions to:* Saturday Evening Post; Popular

Science; Science News; Oceans; Boats; Rudder; Westways; American Legion; Southwest; Sacramento. *Honours:* Award for Sacramento Book, Sacramento County Historical Society, 1988; Merit Award in Regional History, California Historical Society, 1989. *Memberships:* California Writers Club; Vice President, Sacramento County Historical Society. *Literary Agent:* Florence Feiler, 1524 Sunset Plaza Drive, Los Angeles, CA 90069, USA. *Address:* PO Box 2384, Fair Oaks, CA 95628, USA.

HOLDSTOCK Robert, b. 1948, United Kingdom. Freelance Writer. *Publications:* Eye among the Blind, 1976; Earthwind, 1977; Necromancer, 1978; Octopus Encyclopaedia of Science Fiction (editor), 1978; Stars of Albion (edited with Christopher Priest), anthology, 1979; Alien Landscapes (with Malcolm Edwards), non-fiction, 1979; Tour of the Universe (with Malcolm Edwards), non-fiction, 1980; Where Time Winds Blow, 1981; In the Valley of the Statues, stories, 1982; Realms of Fantasy (with Malcolm Edwards), non-fiction, 1983; Lost Realms (with Malcolm Edwards), non-fiction, 1984; Mythago Wood, 1984; Bulman, 1984; The Emerald Forest, novelisation of screenplay, 1985; One of Our Pigeons Is Missing, 1985; The Labyrinth, 1987; Other Edens (edited with Christopher Evans), 1987; Lavondyss, 1988. *Address:* 54 Raleigh Road, London N8, England.

HOLEMAN Marilyn Batey, b. 20 Feb 1938, Gainesville, Florida, USA. Freelance Writer; Technical Writer; Homemaker. m. James Lynn Holeman, 6 June 1957. 1 son, 1 daughter. *Education:* Institute of Children's Literature, 1977; University of Florida, 1956; University of Maryland, 1964; Athen's State College, 1985; BA, University of Alabama, Huntsville, 1991. *Appointments:* Staff Writer, The Exponent 1981, Technical Writer/Editor, Center for High Technology Management and Economic Research, summer 1987, University of Alabama in Huntsville; Technical Writer/Editor and Vice President, Holeman Scientific Corporation, 1990-. *Contributions to:* Plane & Pilot; The Shepherd's Din; Shadows, University of Alabama in Huntsville's Literary publication. *Memberships:* Huntsville Literary Association; Fiction Writer's Group. *Address:* Holeman Scientific Corporation, 600 Boulevard South, Suite 104E, Huntsville, AL 35802, USA.

HOLLAND Cecelia (Anastasia), b. 1943, USA. Author. *Publications:* The Firedrake, 1966; Rakosy, 1967; Kings in Winter, 1968; Until the Sun Falls, 1969; Ghost on the Steppe, 1969; The King's Road, 1970; Cold Iron, 1970; Antichrist, 1970; Wonder of the World, 1970; The Earl, 1971; The Death of Attila, 1973; The Great Maria, 1975; Floating Worlds, 1976; Two Ravens, 1977; The Earl, 1979; Home Ground, 1981; The Sea Beggars, 1982; The Belt of Gold, 1984; Pillar of Sky, 1985. *Address:* c/o Knopf, 201 East 50th Street, New York, NY 10022, USA.

HOLLAND Elizabeth Anne, b. 1928, United Kingdom. Writer. *Appointments:* Currently Director: Survey of Old Bath; New Tolkien Newsletter; The Road. *Publications:* A Separate Person, 1962; The House in the North, 1963; The House by the Sea, 1965; The Adding Up, 1968; J R R Tolkien: The Shores of Middle-Earth (with R Giddings), 1981. *Address:* 16 Prior Park Buildings, Bath, Avon BA2 4NP, England.

HOLLAND Gail Bernice, b. 13 Apr 1940, London, England. Writer. m. Peter Holland, 1 daughter. *Appointments:* Staff Writer, Modern Women 1957-59, Staff Writer, Home 1959-61, London, England; Staff Writer, Sears-Golick Fabrics, Montreal, Quebec, Canada, 1962; Staff Writer, Gumps 1963-65, Staff Writer, Joseph Magnin 1965-67, San Francisco, CA; Free-lance writer, 1967-69; Staff Writer Peninsula Living, Palo Alto, 1969; Free-lance writer, 1969-74; Staff Writer, Cinema Financial of America Incorporated 1974, Staff Writer, San Francisco Examiner 1975-78, San Francisco, CA; Free-lance writer, 1978-.

Publications: Weekend Guide to San Francisco, 1972; For Sasha With Love: An Alzheimer's Crusade, 1985. *Contributions to:* Magazines and newspapers, including Mademoiselle; Saturday Review; Science Digest; California Living; Harley Davidson; Family; Women's Sports; San Francisco Magazine. *Honours:* Merit from Valley Writers Council, 1969; Top award from Sigma Delta Chi and California State Bar, 1972, for outstanding achievement by an editorial worker in reporting and interpreting the administration of justice in California. *Address:* PO Box 370971, Montara, CA 94037, USA.

HOLLAND Isabelle, (Francesca Hunt), b. 1920, USA. Author. *Appointments:* Publicity Director, Lippincott, Dell, and Putnam publishing companies, New York City, 1960-68. *Publications:* Cecily, 1967; Amanda's Choice, 1970; The Man Without a Face, 1972; The Mystery of Castle Renaldi (as Francesca Hunt), 1972; Heads You Win, Tails I Lose, 1973; Kilgaren, romance, 1974; Trelawny, romance, UK Edition Trelawny's Fell, 1976; Moncrieff, romance, 1975, UK Edition The Standish Place, 1976; Of Love and Death and Other Journeys, 1975; Journey for Three, 1975; Darcourt, romance, 1976; Grenelle, romance, 1976; Alan and the Animal Kingdom, 1977; Hitchhike, 1977; The de Maury Papers, romance, 1977; Dinah and the Green Fat Kingdom, 1978; Ask No Questions, 1978; Tower Abbey, romance, 1978; The Marchington Inheritance, romance, 1979; Counterpoint, romance, 1980; Now Is Not Too Late, 1980; Summer of My First Love, 1981; The Lost Madonna, romance, 1981; A House Named Peaceable, 1982; Abbie's God Book, 1982; Perdita, 1983; God, Mrs Musket and Aunt Dot, 1983; The Empty House, 1983; Kevin's Hut, 1984; Green Andrew Green, 1984; A Death at St Anselm's, 1984; Flight of the Archangel, 1985; The Island, 1985; Jennie Kiss'd Me, 1985; Love Scorned, 1986; Henry and Grudge, 1986. *Address:* c/o JCA, 242 West 27th Street, New York, NY 10010, USA.

HOLLAND Kel. *See:* **WHITTINGTON Harry.**

HOLLAND Norman N, b. 1927, USA. Professor. *Appointments:* Instructor to Associate Professor, Massachusetts Institute of Technology, Cambridge, 1955-66; Professor, 1966-79, Chairman of English Department, 1966-68, McNulty Professor, 1979-83, State University of New York, Buffalo; Milbauer Professor, University of Florida, Gainesville, 1983-. *Publications:* The First Modern Comedies, 1959, 2nd Edition, 1967; The Shakespearean Imagination, 1964, 2nd Edition, 1968; Psychoanalysis and Shakespeare, 1966, 2nd Edition, 1975; The Dynamics of Literary Response, 1968, 2nd Edition 1989; Poems in Persons, 1973, 2nd Edition 1989; 5 Readers Reading, 1975; Laughing, 1982; The I, 1985; The Brain of Robert Frost, 1988; Holland's Guide to Psychoanalytic Psychology and Literature-and-Psychology, 1990; The Critical I, 1992. *Literary Agent:* Sterling Lord Literistics. *Address:* Department of English, University of Florida, Gainesville, FL 32611, USA.

HOLLAND Sheila, (Sheila Coates, Laura Hardy, Charlotte Lamb, Sheila Lancaster), b. 1937. British, Historical/Romance/Gothic. *Appointments:* Secretary, Bank of England, London 1954-56 and BBC, London, 1956-58. *Publications include:* as Sheila Holland: The Masque, 1979; The Merchant's Daughter, 1980; Miss Charlotte's Fancy, 1980; Secrets to Keep, 1980; Secrets, 1984; as Sheila Coates: A Crown Usurped, 1972; The Queen's Letter, 1973; The Flight of the Swan, 1973; The Bells of the City, 1975; as Charlotte Lamb: Call Back yesterday, 1978; Desert Barbarian, 1978; Disturbing Stranger, 1978; Autumn Conquest, 1978; The Long Surrender, 1978; The Cruel Flame, 1978; Duel of Desire, 1978; The Devil's Arms, 1978; Pagan Encounter, 1978; Forbidden Fire, 1979; The Silent Trap, 1979; Dark Dominion, 1979; Fever 1979; Dark Master, 1979; Temptation, 1979; Twist of Fate, 1979; Possession 1979; Love Is a Frenzy, 1979; Frustration, 1979; Sensation, 1979; Compulsion, 1980; Crescendo 1980; Stranger in the Night, 1980; Storm Centre, 1980; Seduction 1980; Savage Surrender 1980; A Frozen Fire, 1980; Man's World, 1980; Night Music, 1980;

Obsession, 1980; Retribution, 1981; Illusion, 1981; Heartbreaker, 1981; Desire 1981; Dangerous 1981; Abduction 1981; A Violation, 1983; as Sheila Lancaster: Dark Sweet Wanton, 1979; The Tilthammer, 1980; Mistress of Fortune, 1982; as Laura Hardy: Burning Memories, 1981; Playing with Fire, 1981; Dream Master, 1982; Tears and Red Roses, 1982. *Address:* Applegate, Post St Mary, Isle of Man, England.

HOLLAND Tom, b. 11 July 1947, Poughkeepsie, NY, USA. Screenwriter. *Education:* BA (summa cum laude) 1970, JD 1973, University of California, Los Angeles. *Appointments:* Actor in plays and motion pictures, director of plays, and director of motion pictures, including Fright Night, 1985. *Publications:* The Beast Within, 1981; Psycho II, 1983; Class of 1984, Scream for Help, Cloak and Dagger, 1984; Fright Night, 1985. *Membership:* Phi Beta Kappa. *Honours:* Nominated for Edgar Allan Poe Award from Mystery Writers of America for Psycho II. *Address:* c/o Columbia Pictures, Producers Eight, Room 247, Burbank, CA 91505, USA.

HOLLANDER Paul, b. 3 Oct 1932, Budapest, Hungary. Professor. m. Mina Harrison, 1977, 1 daughter. *Education:* BA LSE, 1959; MA University of Illinois, 1960; MA 1962, PhD 1963, Princeton University, all in Sociology. *Publications:* Editor, American and Soviet Society, 1969; Soviet and American Society: A Comparison, 1973, 1978; Many Faces of Socialism, 1984; Survival of the Adversary Culture, 1988; Political Pilgrims, 1981, 1983, 1990; Anti-Americanism, 1992; Decline and Discontent, 1992. *Contributions to:* Commentary; Encounter; Partisan; Review; Policy Review; American Sociological Review; Problems of Commumist; Society; Wall Street Journal; New York Times. *Honours:* Guggenheim Fellowship, 1973-74; Ford Foundation Fellow, 1963; Visiting Scholar, Hoover Institute, summers of 1985, 1986 and spring 1993. *Memberships:* National Association of Scholars, Advisory Panel. *Address:* 35 Vernon Street, Northampton, MA 01060, USA.

HOLLANDS Roy Derrick, b. 20 July 1924, Canterbury, Kent, England. Writer of Mathematics Books. m. Sarah Carroll, 14 Apr 1945, 1 daughter. *Education:* BSc, Southampton, 1951; MA, Exeter University, 1969; MSc, Newcastle University, 1980; Certificate of Education, 1952; Advanced Certificate of Education, 1964. *Literary Appointments:* Advisor to Longman, Blackwell, CUP, Ginn, Macmillan etc 1967-. *Publications include:* Headway Maths (Series for less-able secondary pupils) 1979; Ginn Mathematics (primary series) 1983; Let's Solve Problems, 1986; SMP 7-13, 1973; Primary Mathematics for Nigeria, 1979. Author and co-author of nearly 200 books. Primary Maths series for UK, Egypt, Nigeria, Cameroon, Caribbean. Lesotho, Uganda. *Contributions to:* Over 100 articles in the main mathematical journals. *Honour:* Fellow of College of Preceptors, 1979; Mensa Chess Champion, 1992. *Memberships:* Past Vice-Chairman, Education Committee, Chairman of Educational Writers Group, 1991-, Society of Authors; Mensa; Past member AMA, Mathematics Society. *Address:* 6 Wyde Feld, Chawkmare Coppice, Aldwick, Bognor Regis, West Sussex PO21 3DH, England.

HOLLANEK Adam Michal Franciszek, b. 4 Oct 1922, Lwow, Poland. Writer; Journalist. m. Anna Eva Owsianka, 24 Dec 1970, 1 son, 2 daughters (1 child from 1st marriage). *Publications:* About 40 books including: (Fiction) Plaza w Europie, 1967; Bandyci i Policjanci, 1982; Ksiezna z Florencji, 1988; Topless, 1988; (Science Fiction) Katastrofa na Sloncu Antarktydy, 1958; Zbrodnia wielkiego czlowieka, 1960; Muzyka dla was, chlopcy, 1975; Ukochany z ksiezyca, 1979; Jeszcze troche pozyc, 1980; Olsnienie, 1982; Kochac bez skory, 1983; (Poetry) Pokuty, 1986; (Non-fiction) Niewidzialne armie kapituluja, 1954; Sprzedam smierc, 1961; Skora jaszczurcza, 1965; Lewooki cyklop, 1966; etc. *Contributions to:* Numerous papers and magazines. *Honours:* Polish Academy of Sciences Award, 1978; Prix Europeenne de Science Fiction, 1986; Special W-SF President's Award, 1987. *Memberships:* ZAIKS; World

Science Fiction Professional Association, President, Polish Section, 1983-85; Societe Europeenne de Science Fiction, General Secretary, 1987-. *Literary Agent:* Authors Agency, Warsaw, Hipoteczna 2. *Address:* Warsaw, Poland.

HOLLES Robert, b. 11 Oct 1926. Author; Playwright. m. Philippa Elmer, 12 July 1952, 2 sons, 1 daughter. *Appointments:* Former Member, Broadcasting Commission, Society of Authors; Artist in Residence, Central State University of Oklahoma, USA, 1981-82. *Publications:* Novels: Now Thrive the Armourers, 1952; The Bribe Scorners, 1956; Captain Cat, 1960; The Siege of Battersea 1962; Religion and Davey Peach, 1964; The Nature of the Beast 1965; Spawn, 1978; I'll Walk Beside You, 1979; Sunblight, 1981; Humour: The Guide to Real Village Cricket, 1983; The Guide to Real Subversive Soldiering, 1985; Screenplay: Guns at Batasi, 1965; some 30 plays in TV series such as: Armchair Theatre; Play for Today etc. *Contributions to:* various magazines and journals. *Literary Agent:* David Higham Associates. *Address:* Ware House, Stebbing, Essex, England.

HOLLIMAN Mary Constance, b. 28 Jan 1930, Bethlehem, Pennsylvania, USA. Editor; Writer. m. Rhodes Burns Holliman, 17 Dec 1950, 2 sons, divorced 1980. *Education:* BA, Howard College, Birmingham, 1951; MA, University of Miami, Florida, 1953. *Appointments:* Editor, Howard College Crimson, 1950-51; Reporter, Tooele Daily News, Utah, 1953-55; Insturctor and Assistant Professor, English Department, Radford College, Radford, Virginia, 1965-70; English Teacher, Blacksburg High School, Blacksburg, Virginia, 1964-65; part-time Instructor, English Department, Florida State University, Tallahassee, Florida, 1958-61; Managing Editor, Journal of the Mineralogical Society of America, 1972-75; Communicator Sea Grant at Virginia Tech, 1975-79; Director, Information & Awareness, National Sea Grant College Programme, 1979-81; University Research Editor, Virginia Tech, Blacksburg, 1981-; President, Pocahontas Press Inc. (Publishers), 1984-. *Publications:* Index to Volumes 51-60, The American Mineralogist, 1966-75, Edited 1976; Environmental Impact in Antarctica, Editor, 1978; Endangered & Threatened Plants & Animals of Virginia, Editor, 1980; Seafood Processing Pest Management, editor, 1983; A Teacher's Story : An Autobiography, Editor, 1985; Sea Grant Biennial Report, 1977-79 (author & editor), 1980; Quarter-Acre of Heartache, by Claude Clayton Smith, editor, 1985; We Thought at Least the Roof Would Fall, by Leslie Mellichamp, Editor, 1987; From Lions to Lincoln - The Life of Dan French, by Fran Hartman, Editor, 1987; The Legend of Natural Tunnel, by Clare Talton Fugate, Editor, 1985. *Contributions to:* various journals and magazines. *Honours:* numerous awards. *Memberships:* Virginia Press Women; National Federation of Press Women; American Association of University Women; Society for Scholarly Publishing. *Address:* 2805 Wellesley Court, Blacksburg, VA 24060, USA.

HOLLINGDALE Reginald John, b. 1930, British. *Appointment:* Sub-Editor, The Guardian newspaper, London, 1968-1991. *Publications:* Thus Spoke Zarathustra, by Nietzsche (trans), 1961, 1969; One Summer on Majorca, by Marielis Hoberg (trans), 1961; The Voyage to Africa, by Hoberg (trans), 1964; Nietzsche: The Man and His Philosophy, 1965; Western Philosophy: An Introduction, 1966, 1979; The Will to Power, by Nietzsche (trans with Walter Kaufmann), On the Genealogy of Morals, by Nietzsche (trans with Kaufmann), 1967; Twilight of the Idols and the Anti-Christ, by Nietzsche (trans), 1968; Essays and Aphorisms of Schopenhauer (trans and ed), 1970; Elective Affinities, by Goethe (trans), Thomas Mann: A Critical Study, 1971; Beyond Good and Evil, by Nietzsche (trans), Nietzsche, 1973; Tangram, by Joost Eeffers (trans), 1976; A Nietzsche Reader (ed and trans), 1977; Ecce Homo by Nietzsche (trans), 1979; Otto Dix, by Fritz Loeffler (trans), 1981; Daybreak, by Nietzsche (trans), Tales of Hoffmann (ed and trans), 1982; Untimely Meditations, by Nietzsche (trans), 1983; Dithyrambs of

Dionysus, by Nietzsche (ed and trans), 1984; Before the Storm, by Fontane (ed and trans), 1985; Human, All Too Human, by Nietzsche (trans), 1987; Between Literature and Science, by Wolf Lepenies (trans), 1988; Aphorisms of Lichtenberg (trans and ed), 1990; The Rise of Neo-Kantianism by Klaus Christian Köhnke (trans), 1991. *Honour:* Visiting Fellow, Trinity College, Melbourne, 1991. *Membership:* Hon President, B Nietzsche Society. *Address:* 32 Warrington Crescent, London W9 1EL, England.

HOLLINGSWORTH Margaret, b. 1940, Canadian (born British). *Appointments:* Journalist, Librarian and Teacher in England, 1960-68; Librarian, Fort William Public Library, Ontario, 1968-72; Freelance Writer, 1972-; Assistant Professor, David Thompson University Centre, Nelson BC, 1981- 83. *Publications:* Dance for My Father, 1976; Alli Alli Oh, 1979; Mother Country, 1980; Bushed and Operators, Ever Loving, 1981; Islands, 1983; Willful Acts, 1985.

HOLLIS Carolyn Sloan, b. 15 Apr 1937, London, England. Freelance Journalist and children's author. m. David Hollis, 15 May 1961, 2 sons. *Education:* Harrogate College; Tutorial Schools in Newcastle and Guildford. *Appointments:* Editorial Secretary, Features Assistant, Queen Magazine, 1956-60; Press Officer, Yvonne Arnaud Theatre, Guildford, 1976-80. *Publications:* The Sea Child, 1987; Victoria and the Crowded Pocket, 1973; Helen Keller, 1984; Don't Go near the Water, 1988; Shakespeare Theatre Cat; Carter is a Painter's Cat, 1971; Th Penguin and the Vacuum Cleaner, 1974; Sam Snake, 1975; Mr Cogg and his Computer, 1979; Further Inventions of Mr Cogg, 1981; Skewer's Garden, 1983; Mr Cogg and the Exploding Easter Eggs, 1984; The Friendly Robot, 1986; An Elephant for Muthu, 1986; T- Boy's Weekend, 1988; The Mall Series, 4 books, 1989; Nine Lives, 1991; Working Dogs, 1991; Working Elephants, 1991; Working Horses, 1992. *Contributions to:* Features contributed to Daily Telegraph, Sunday Telegraph and Radio Times. *Memberships:* Society of Authors; New Playwrights Trust. *Literary Agent:* Murray Pollinger. *Address:* 7 Dapdune Road, Guildford, Surrey GU1 4NY, England.

HOLLO Anselm (Paul Alexis), b. 1934. Finland, Poetry, Translations. *Career:* Programme Assistant and Co-ordinator, BBC, London, 1958-66; Visiting Lecturer, 1968-69, Lecturer in English and Music, 1970-71, and Head, Translation Workshop, 1971-72, University of Iowa, Iowa City; Poetry Editor, Iowa Review, Iowa City, 1971-72; Associate and Visiting Professor, Bowling Green University, Ohio, 1972-73; Poet-in-Residence, Hobart and William Smith College, Geneva, New York, 1973-74; Write-in-Residence, Sweet Briar College, Virginia, 1978-80; Associate Professor, Writing & Poetics, The Naropa Institute, Boulder, Co, 1989-. *Publications include:* Message, 1970; (ed and trans), The Twelve and Other Poems by Aicksandr Blok, 1971; (with Jack Marshall and Sam Hamod), Surviving in America, 1972; Sensation 27, 1972; Some Worlds, 1974; Lingering Tangos, 1976; Sojourner Microcosms: New and Selected Poems 1959-1977, 1977; Heavy Jars, 1977; Curious Data, 1978; (ed and trans with Gunnar Harding), Recent Swedish Poetry in Translation, 1979; With Ruth in Mind, 1979; Finite Continued, 1980; No Complaints, 1983; (ed and trans), Pentti Saarikoski: Poems, 1958-80, 1984; Pick Up the House, 1986; Egon Schiele: The Poems, 1988; Peter Stephan Jungk: Franz Werfel: The Story of a Life, 1990; Outlying Districts: New Poems, 1990; Near Miss Haiku, 1990; Space Baltic: the science fiction poems 1962-1987, 1991; Paavo Haavikko: Selected Poems 1949-1989, 1991; Blue Ceiling (a poem), 1992; Jaan Kross: The Czar's Madman (a novel), 1993; High Beam: 12 Poems, 1993; West Is Left on the Map (a poem sequence), 1993. *Address:* 3336 14th Street, Boulder, Colorado 80804, USA.

HOLLOWAY David Richard, b. 3 June 1924. Literary Editor. m. Sylvia Eileen, (Sally), Gray, 1952, 2 sons, 1 daughter. *Education:* Birbeck College, London; Magdalen College, Oxford. *Appointments:* Reporter, Middlesex County Times, 1940-41; Daily sketch, 1941-42; Daily Mirror, 1949; News Chronicle: Reporter and Leader Writer, 1950-53; Assistant Literary editor, Novel Reviewer, 1953-58; Book Page Editor, 1958-60; Deputy Literary editor, 1960-68, Literary Editor, 1968-88, The Daily Telegraph. *Publications:* John Galsworthy, 1968; Lewis and Clark and the Crossing of America, 1971; Derby Day, 1975; Playing the Empire, 1979; Nothing So Became Them .... (with Michael Geare), 1987; Editor, Telegraph Year 1-3, 1977-79. *Contributions to:* Folio Magazine and Book Trade Journals. *Memberships:* Committee of Royal Literary Fund, 1976-, Registrar, 1981-. *Literary Agent:* Scott Ferris. *Address:* 95 Lonsdale Road, London SW13 9DA, England.

HOLLOWAY Glenna Rose, b. 7 Feb. 1928, Nashville, Tennessee, USA. Silversmith; Enamelist. m. Robert Wesley Holloway. *Contributions to:* Western Humanities Review; Georgia Review; Poet Lore; Christian Science Monitor; Modern Maturity; Manhattan Review; Orbis; Voices International; Poetry International; Northwest Magazine; The Lyric; Connecticut River Review; McCall's; Louisiana Literature; Saturday Review; Chicago Tribune; Illinois Magazine; Miami Magazine; Chimera Connections; Crazy Quilt Quarterly; Independent Review; Light Year 87; Icon; Christian Single; Conerstone; America; The New Renaissance; Shorelines; Moody Monthly; Chicago Sun Times; Anhinga Press; The Formalist; The Retired Officer; Amelia; Hammers; Wisconsin Review; Pikestaff Forum; Ariel; many other journals and magazines. *Honours include:* Dellbrook-Shenendoah, 1979; Firsts: National Federation of State Poetry Societies, 1978-91; World Order of Narrative and Formalist Poets 1980-91; National League of American Pen Women 'Best of Best', 1987 and 1990; Sterling Pegasus Grand Prize, 1982, 1983; Georgia State Poetry Society, 1982-86 & 1991; Poetry Society of Virginia, Beach Poets; Poetry Society of West Virginia; Bright Horizons; American Pen Women Biennial, 1987; Best of Best, Chicago Poets Club, 1984, 1987, 1988, 1989, 1991; Hart Crane Memorial, Kent State, 1987; numerous others. *Memberships include:* National League of American Penwomen; Poetry Societies of America; National Federation of State Poetry Societies; President, Poetry Society of Illinois; Ragdale Foundation Fellow, 1988. *Address:* 913 East Bailey Road, Naperville, IL 60565, USA.

HOLLOWAY John, b. 1920, Croydon, Surrey, England. University Professor, Modern English (retired); Author. *Education:* MA, DPhil, New College, All Souls College, Oxford; DLitt, University of Aberdeen; LittD, University of Cambridge. *Publications include:* The Victorian Sage, 1953; The Minute (verse) 1956; The Fugue (verse) 1960; The Landfallers (verse) 1962; The Story of the Night, 1962; Wood and Windfall (verse) 1964; The Lion Hunt, 1964; Blake, The Lyric Poetry, 1968; New Poems (verse) 1970; Planet of Winds, 1977 (verse); The Proud Knowledge, 1977; Narrative and Structure, 1979; The Slumber of Apollo, 1983; The Oxford Book of Local Verses, 1987. *Contributions to:* Hudson Review; Burlington Magazine; London Magazine; Encounter; Art International; Essays in Criticism; Critical Inquiry; Kenyon Review; P N Review; Landfall (NZ). *Membership:* FRSL, 1956; B.R.O.N.Z.S. *Address:* Queens' College, Cambridge, England.

HOLLOWAY Nigel Robert, b. 16 Nov 1953, London, England. Journalist. m. Stella Danker, 8 Sept 1959, 1 daughter. *Education:* BA Magdalen College, Oxford. *Appointments:* Business Editor; Far Eastern Economic Review; Hong Kong. *Publications:* Unequal Equities, (co-author) 1990; Japan in Asia, (editor) 1991. *Address:* c/o FEER, GPO Box 160, Hong Kong.

HOLM Peter Rowde, b. 5 Apr 1931, Oslo, Norway. Writer. m. 28 Sept 1954, 1 son, 1 daughter. *Education:* Graduate, St Gallen; Certificate of Proficiency in English, Cambridge, England, 1955. *Publications:* 22 books of poetry; Literary reviews, articles on arms control; 2 books on East-West tension and the arms race; 1 anthology, translated into 12 languages. *Contributions To:* Numerous Norwegian, Swedish and Danish Journals and Periodicals; many articles on international security problems. *Honours:* Sarpsborg Literary Prize, 1957; Mads Wiel Nygaards Prize, 1962; Dagbladets Poetry Prize, 1964; Norwegian Cultural Council Prize, 1966; Literary Critics Prize, 1966; Riksmals Prize, 1977; Oslo City Prize, 1983. *Memberships:* Norwegian Union of Authors; de Niderton; The Johnson Society. *Literary Agent:* Aschehoug, Oslo. *Address:* Ostre Holmensvingen 4, 0387 Oslo 3, Norway.

HOLMAN Robert, b. 1936, British. *Appointments:* Child Care Officer, Hertfordshire County Council, 1962-64; Lecturer in Social Work, University of Birmingham, 1964-72; Senior Lecturer in Social Administration, University of Glasgow, 1972-74; Professor of Social Administration, University of Bath, 1974-76; Leader of Southdown Community Project, 1976-86. *Publications:* Trading in Children, 1973; Social Welfare in Modern Britain (ed with E Butterworth), 1975; Inequality in Child Care, 1976; Poverty, 1978; Kids at the Door, 1981; Resourceful Friends, 1983; More Than a Friend (as B Laken), 1984; Putting Families First, 1988; Good Old George: the Life of George Lansbury, 1990. *Address:* Flat 2/1, 18 Finlarig Street, Easterhouse, Glasgow G34, Scotland.

HOLME K E. *See:* **HILL (John Edwards) Christopher.**

HOLMES B J. *See:* **HOLMES Bryan John.**

HOLMES Bryan John, (B J Holmes; Ethan Wall), b. 18 May 1939, Birmingham, England. Lecturer. m. 1962, 2 sons. *Education:* BA Hons, University of Keele, 1968. *Publications:* The Avenging Four, 1978; Hazard, 1979; Blood, Sweat and Gold, 1980; Gunfall, 1980; A Noose for Yanqui, 1981; Shard, 1982; Bad times at Backwheel, 1982; On the Spin of a Dollar, 1983; Guns of the Reaper, 1983; Another Day, 1984; Dark Rider, 1987; I Rode with Wyatt, 1989; Dollars for the Reaper, 1990; A Legend Called Shatterhand, 1990; Loco, 1991; Shatterhand and the People, 1992; The Last Days of Billy Patch, 1992; Blood on the Reaper, 1992; All Trials Lead to Dodge, 1993; Montana Hit, 1993. *Contributions to:* Miscellaneous short stories in magazines, scholarly articles in academic and professional journals. *Address:* c/o Robert Hale Ltd, Clerkenwell Green, London EC1R OHT, England.

HOLMES Charlotte Amalie, b. 26 Apr 1956, Georgia, USa. University Professor. m. James Brasfield, 7 Mar 1983, 1 son. *Education:* MFA Writing, Columbia University, 1977; BA English, Louisiana State University, 1980. *Appointments:* Editorial Assistant, Paris Review, 1979; ASsociate and Managing Editor, The Ecco Press, 1980; Instructor, Western Carolina University, 1984; Assistant Professor, Pennsylvania Stae University, 1987. *Publications:* Gifts and other Stories, 1993. *Contributions to:* The Antioch Review; Carolina Quarterly; Epoch; Grand Street; The New Yorker The Southern Review; Story Magazine. *Honours:* Stegner Fellowship, Stanford University, 1982; Bread Loaf Writer's Conference National Arts Club Scholarship, 1990; North Carolina Arts Council Grant, 1986; Pennsylvania Council on the Arts Fellowshp, 1988; Pennsylvania Council on the Arts Fellowship, 1993; Poets & Writers, Inc, Writers Exchange Award, 1993. *Memberships:* Associated Writing Programs. *Literary Agent:* Neil Olson, Donadio & Ashworth Inc. *Address:* Department of English, Pennsylvania State University, University Park PA 16802, USA.

HOLMES Geoffrey Shorter, b. 17 July 1928, Sheffield, England. Emeritus Professor of History. m. Ella Scott, 16 Sept 1955, 1 son, 1 daughter. *Education:* Pembroke College, Oxford, 1945-48, 1950-51; BA (Oxon), 1948; MA (Oxon), 1952; BLitt (Oxon), 1952; DLitt (Oxon), 1978. *Publications:* British Politics in the Age of Anne, 1967, Revised Edition, 1987; The Divided Society (with W A Speck), 1967; Britain after the Glorious Revolution (editor, co-author), 1969; The Trial of Doctor Sacheverell, 1973; The Prime Ministers (co-author), 1974; The Electorate and the National Will in

the First Age of Party, 1976; The Whig Ascendency (co-author), 1981; Augustan England: Professions, State and Society 1680-1730, 1982; The London Diaries of William Nicolson, Bishop of Carlisle 1702-1718 (edited with Clyve Jones), 1985; Politics, Religion and Society in England 1679-1742, 1986; Stuart England (co-author), 1986; The Making of a Great Power: Late Stuart and Early Georgian Britain 1660-1722, 1993; The Age of Oligarchy: Pre-industrial Britain 1722-1783, 1993; General Editor, Longman's Foundations of Modern Britain series, 1983-93. *Contributions to:* History; English Historical Review; Bulletin of the Institute of Historical Research; The Times; Times Literary Supplement; Transactions of the Royal Historical Society; British Journal for the History of Science; Parliamentary History; Proceedings of the British Academy. *Honour:* Fellow, British Academy, 1983. *Membership:* Fellow, Royal Historical Society, Vice-President 1985-89. *Literary Agent:* London Management. *Address:* Tatham Lodge, Burton-in-Lonsdale, Carnforth, Lancs LA6 3LF, England.

HOLMES John. *See:* **SOUSTER Raymond.**

HOLMES John, b. 12 May 1913, Bishopton, Renfrewshire, Scotland, Farmer; Dog Breeder/Trainer. m. Kathleen Mary Trevethick, 6 Dec 1955. *Education:* Edinburgh and East of Scotland College of Agriculture, 1929-30. *Publications:* The Family Dog, 1957, 13 editions; The Farmers Dog, 1960, 13 editions; The Obedient Dog, 1975, 6 editions; Looking After Your Dog, (Co-author Mary Holmes), 1985; The Complete Australian Cattle Dog (Co-author Mary Holmes), 1993. *Contributions to:* The Kennel Gazette; Dog World; Our Dogs; The Field; Carriage Driving; Horse and Hound; Pedigree Digest. *Memberships:* Society of Authors; British Actors Equity Association; UK Registry of Canine Behaviourists. *Address:* Formakin Farm, Cranborne, Dorset BH21 5QY, England.

HOLMES Marjorie Rose, b. Storm Lake, Iowa, USA. Author. m. (1) Lynn Mighell, 9 Apr 1932, 1 son, 2 daughters, (2) George Schmieler, 4 July 1981. *Publications:* World by the Tail, 1943; Ten O'Clock Scholar, 1946; Saturday Night, 1959; Cherry Blossom Princess, 1960; Follow Your Dream, 1961; Love is a Hopscotch Thing, 1963; Senior Trip, 1962; Love and Laughter, 1967; I've Got to Talk to Somebody, God, 1969; Writing the Creative Article, 1969; Who Am I, God? 1969; To Treasure Our Days, 1971; Two from Galilee, 1972; Nobody Else Will Listen, 1973; You and I and Yesterday, 1973; As Tall as My Heart, 1974; How Can I Find You God?, 1975; Beauty in Your Own back Yard, 1976; Hold Me Up a little Longer, Lord, 1977; Lord, Let Me Love, 1978; God and Vitamins, 1980; To Help You Through the Hurting, 1983; Three from Galilee, 1985; Secrets of Health, Energy and Staying Young, 1987; The Messiah, 1987; At Christmas the Heart Goes Home, 1991; The Inspirational Writings of Marjorie Holmes, 1991; Gifts Freely Given, 1992; Second Wife, Second Life!, 1993; Writing Articles From the Heart, 1993. *Contributions to:* numerous journals and magazines. *Address:* 8681 Cobb Road, Lake Jackson Hills, Manassas, VA 22110, USA.

HOLMES Raymond. *See:* **SOUSTER Raymond.**

HOLMES Richard, 5 Nov 1945, London, England. British Poet; Biographer. *Publications:* One for Sorrow, Two for Joy, 1970; Shelley: The Pursuit, 1975; Inside the Tower, 1977; Shelley on Love: An Anthology, 1980; Coleridge, 1982; Footsteps: Adventures of a Romantic Biographer, 1985; Coleridge: early visions, 1989; Dr Johnson and Me Savage, 1992. *Honours:* Somerset Maugham Award, 1974, for Shelley: The Pursuit; Whitbread Book of the Year Prize, 1989. *Address:* c/o Hodden & Stoughton, 47 Bedford Square, London WC1B 3DP, England.

HOLMES Sherlock S, b. 25 Oct 1962, Massachusetts, USA. Author; Freelance Journalist;

Indexer. *Education:* Ordained Minister, 1983; Emergency Medical Technician Certificate, 1980; Doctor of Divinity, 1983; Certificate of Journalism Arts, 1991. *Appointments:* Assistant News Director, Radio Station WNEB, 1982; Staff Editor, Writer, RCMA Journal, 1990; Staff Column Editor; Journalist, NESN Magazine, 1990; Corresponding Journalist, CNS News International, 1991. *Publications:* Many News Pieces with Associated Press Wire Service, 1981-; Modern Maturity magazine, 1991, 1992; Personality Profile of an Assasin, co-author, 1991; Various Medical Journal Articles, 1991; RCMA Journal, monthly columnist, 1991-; NESN Magazine, two monthly columns, 1991-; American History Illustrated, magazine aticle, 1991; Various brochures, manuals, handouts, speeches; Hundred of news stories while employed as Assistant News Director for radio station. *Contributions to:* RCMA Journal; NESN Magazine; Modern Maturity; Sword of th Lord; CGT Newsletter; New England Journal of Medicine; Journal of America Medical Association. *Honours:* Hon Doctor of Psychology; McGraw Hill Highest Honours Achievement Award, 1991; NESN Editor's Award, 1991; Worcester County news Broadcaster Excellence Award, 1983. *Memberships:* San Francisco Literary Society, Founding Member and Past President; National Writers Union, Local Steering Committee; American medical Writers Association; American Society of Indexers; National Writers Club. *Address:* POB 3, Worcester, MA 01613, USA.

HOLMES Stewart Quentin, b. 25 Dec 1929, London, England. Journalist; Actor. *Education:* Hendon College; Kings Lynn Technical Institute; Hong Kong University. *Appointments:* Telephone Reporter, Reuters Ltd, 1952-58; Reporter, Chief Film and Drama Critic, Harrow Observer, 1958-61; Sub-Editor, Diary Writer, Hendon Times, 1961-63; Reporter, The Daily Telegraph, 1963-66; Sub-Editor, Exchange Telegraph, 1966-68; Script Writer, British Movietone News, 1968-70; Press Officer, Decimal Currency Board, 1970; correspondent to BBC and numerous British papers, in Persia, Hong Kong, Tokyo, Hawaii; Freelance for journals, magazines, 1970-89. *Publications:* Odes and Ends, 1985; Once Upon a Rhyme, 1986; London Correspondent, International Press Bureau, USA; London Life columnist, Union Jack Newspaper, California; and other UK publications. *Memberships:* Poetry Society; Chartered Institute of Journalists; Foreign Press Association; British Actors Equity; British MENSA. *Address:* 146 Clarence Gate Gardens, Baker Street, London NW1 6AN, England.

HOLROYD Michael, b. 27 Aug 1935, London, England. Author. m. Margaret Drabble, 1982. *Appointments:* Chairman, Society of Authors, 1973-74, National Book League (Book Trust), 1976-78; Chairman, Arts Council Literature Panel, 1992-; President, English Centre of PEN, 1985-88. *Publications:* Hugh Kingsmill, 1964; Lytton Strachey, 1967-68; Unreceived Opinions, 1973; Augustus John, 1974-75; Bernard Shaw: The Search for Love, 1988; The Pursuit of Power, 1989; (Bernard Shaw): The Lure of Fantasy, 1991; The Last Laugh, 1992. *Honour:* CBE, 1989. *Literary Agent:* A P Watt. *Address:* c/o A P Watt Ltd, 20 John Street, London WC1N 2DL, England.

HOLSTI Ole Rudolf, b. 7 Aug 1933, Geneva, Switzerland, Professor; Researcher. m. Ann Wood, 20 Sept 1953, 1 son, 1 daughter. *Education:* BA, 1954, PhD, 1962, Stanford University, USA; MAT, Wesleyan University, 1956. *Appointments include:* Professor, Department of Political Science, University of California, 1978-79; George V Allen Professor, 1974-, Chairman, 1978-83, Department of Political Science, Duke University. *Publications:* Content Analysis: A Handbook with Application for the Study of International Crisis, 1963; Enemies in Politics, 1967; Content Analysis for the Social Sciences and Humanities, 1969; The Analysis of Communication Content: Developments in Scientific Theories and Computer Techniques, (Co-author), 1969; Crisis Escalation War, 1972; Unity and Disintegration in International Alliances: Comparative Studies, 1973, reprinted 1985; Change in the International System, 1980; American Leadership in World Affairs: The Breakdown of Consensus, (Co-author James N Rosenau), 1984. *Contributions to:* Numerous articles and chapters in numerous magazines, journals and books including: Journal of Conflict Resolution; Components of Defense Policy; International Politics and Foreign Policy; Behavioural Science; International Social Science Journal; American Political Science Review; Journal of Politcs, International Studies Quarterly, American Review of Politics. *Honours include:* National Science Foundation Research Grant, 1983-85, 1988-90; Nevitt Sanford Award for Distinguished Contributions to Political Psychology, International Society of Political Psychology, 1988; Howard Johnson Distinguished Teaching Aard, 1990; Pew Faculty Fellowship, 1990. *Memberships include:* International Studies Association, President, 1979-80, Communications Committee, 1987-89; Advisory Board, University Press of America, 1976-; Contributing Editor, Running Journal, 1985-. *Address:* 608 Croom Court, Chapel Hill, NC 27514, USA.

HOLT Bertha Marian, b. 5 Feb 1904. Founder of Holt International Children's Services. m. Harry Holt, 31 Dec 1927, 5 sons, 8 daughters. *Education:* BS, with certificate as Registered Nurse, University of Iowa, 1925. *Publications:* Seed from the East, 1956; Outstretched Arms, 1972; Created for God's GLory, 1980; Bring My Sons from Afar, 1986. *Honours:* Honorary Doctor of Humane Letters, Linfield College, Oregon, 1977; Alumni Distinguished Achievement Award, University of Iowa, 1977; Plaque of Recognition, Associated Catholic Charities, Baltimore, MD, 1981; Presidential Award for Social Welfare, Manila, Philippines, 1981; Governor Sloan of Kentucky declared September 7 1983 as Grandma Bertha Holt Day; Plaque of Honour, Hannibal La Grange College, 1984; Steward of Life Award, Right to Life Organization, Eugene, Oregon, 1984; Father Clement De Muth Service to Children Award from OURS Inc, 1987. *Memberships:* Board, Holt International Children's Services. *Address:* International Children's Services, PO Box 2880, Eugene, OR 97402, USA.

HOLT George. *See:* TUBB E C.

HOLT Wilma Geraldene, b. 6 Oct 1937, England. Food Writer. m. Maurice Holt, 26 Dec 1959, 1 son, 1 daughter. *Education:* Art. *Publications:* French Country Kitchen; Recipes From A French Herb Garden; The Gourmet Garden; A Cup Of Tea; Complete Book of Herbs. *Contributions to:* Homes and Gardens; Independent. *Honours:* The Booksellers Most Outstanding Column Prize; Prix Seb du Livre de Cuisine. *Memberships:* Founder Trustee, Jane Grigson Trust Library; Guild of Food Writers; Society of Authors. *Literary Agent:* A P Watt Limited. *Address:* c/o A P Watt Limited, 20 John Street, London, WC1N 2DL, England.

HOLUB Miroslav, b. 13 Sept 1923, Pilsen, Czechoslovakia. Scientific worker; Writer. m. Jitka Langrova, 6 July 1969. 2 sons, 1 daughter. *Education:* MD, Charles University, Prague, 1953; PhD, Czechoslovak Academy of Science, 1958; Dr of Humanities and Letters, h.c., Oberlin College, Oberlin, Ohio, USA, 1985. *Appointments:* Scientist; Member, editorial boards of literary magazines. *Publications:* Poetry: Selected Poems, 1967; Notes of a Clay Pigeon, 1977; Interferon or on the Theater, 1982; Vanishing Lung Syndrome, 1990; Essays: The Dimension of the Present Moment, 1990; Jingle Bell Principle, 1992. *Contributions to:* Most European and many US magazines, newspapers. *Honours:* Publishers Awards 1963, 1965, 1967, 1969, 1987; J E Purkynje Medal for Achievements in Biological Sciences, 1988; G. Theiner Award, 1991. *Memberships:* Vice President, Czech PEN, 1988; European Society for the Promotion of Poetry, President 1989-90; Pangea, President, 1992-; Czechoslovak Writers Union, Central Committee 1963-69; Community of Czech Writers, 1989-; Bavarian Academy of arts, 1972-. *Literary Agent:* Dilia, Prague. *Address:* Svepomocna 107 Hrncire, CS 149 00 Prague 4, Czechoslovakia.

HOLYER Erna Maria, b. 15 Mar 1925, Germany, Author; Freelance Writer. m. Gene Wallace Holyer, 24 Aug 1957. *Education:* AA, San Jose Evening College, 1964; College of San Mateo, San Jose State University, University of Cruz, 1965-74; Creative writing instruction under Louise Boggess, Duane Newcomb and Norma Youngberg, 1959-68; Lifetime California Teaching Credential in Creative Writing and Journalism, 1971; Doctor of Literature, World University, 1984; Diploma, Writing to Sell Fiction, Writer's Digest School, 1987. *Appointments:* Instructor, creative and nonfiction writing, San Jose Metropolitan Adult Education, 1968- ; Seminar Leader, Writer's Connection. *Publications:* Reservoir Road Adventure, 1982; Sigi's Fire Helmet, 1975; The Southern sea Otter, 1975; Shoes for Daniel, 1974; Lone Brown Gull, 1971; Song of Courage, 1970; At The Forest's Edge, 1969; A Cow for Hansel, 1967; Steve's Night of Silence, 1966; Rescue at Sunrise, 1965. *Contributions to:* Reader's Digest; Encyclopaedia Britannica; Advent Verlag Zurich. *Honours include:* Lefoli Award for Excellence in Adult Education Instruction, Adult education Senate, 1972; Women of Achievement Honour Certificate, San Jose Mercury News, 1973-75; IBC Medal of Congress, 1988, 1989. *Memberships:* California Writers Club; American Federation of Teachers; World University Roundtable; American Biographical Institute Research Association. *Address:* 1314 Rimrock Drive, San Jose, CA 95120, USA.

HOMBERGER Eric (Ross), b. 1942, American. *Appointment:* Lecturer in American Literature, University of East Anglia, Norwich, 1970-; Reader in American Literature, 1988; Visiting Professor of American Literature, University of New Hampshire, 1991-92. *Publications:* The Cambridge Mind: Ninety Years of the Cambridge Review 1879-1969 (ed with William Janeway and Simon Schama), 1970; Ezra Pound: The Critical Heritage (ed), 1972; The Art of the Real: Poetry in England and America since 1939, 1977; The Second World War in Fiction (ed with H Klein and J Flower), 1984; American Writers and Radical Politics 1900-1939: Equivocal Commitments, John le Carre, 1986; The Troubled Face of Biography (ed with J Charmley), 1987; John Reed, 1990; John Reed and the Russian Revolution: Uncollected Articles, Letters, Speeches on Russia, 1917-1920 (ed with John Biggart, 1992). *Address:* 74 Clarendon Road, Norwich NR2 2PN, England.

HOME William Douglas, b. 3 June 1912. Playwright. m. Rachel Brand, 26 July 1951, 1 son, 3 daughters. *Education:* Eton College; Oxford University; 4th Degree in History. *Publications:* Half Term Report, autobiography, 1954; Mr Home Pronounced Hume, autobiography, 1979; Sins of Commission, 1985; Letters to Parents, 1939-45 War; Old Men Remember, 1991; Plays include: The Chiltern Hundreds; Now Barrabas; The Reluctant Debutante; The Secretary Bird; Lloyd George Knew My Father; The Kingfisher Master of Arts; The Dame of Sark, 1974; Portraits, 1987; A Christmas Truce, 1989. *Honour:* ITV Writer of the Year (Playwright), 1973. *Memberships:* The Literary Society; Traveller's Club; Beefsteak Club; Garrick Club. *Literary Agent:* Eric Glass. *Address:* Derry House, Kilmeston, near Alresford, Hampshire SO24 0NR, England.

HOMES A M, b. Washington DC, USA. Writer. *Education:* MFA, University of Iowa, 1988; BA, Sarah Lawrence College, 1985. *Appointments:* Creative Writing Lecturer: New York University, 1988, Columbia University, 1991-. *Publications:* In a Country of Mothers, 1993; The Safety of Objects, 1990; Jack, 1989; Film scripts: Hi I'm Bob, and, Boonie Ted and Me. *Contributions to:* Art Forum, Bomb, Christopher Street, Mirabella, Cosmpoilitan, UK, Der Alttag, Between Co D; The Village Voice; The Quarterly; Story; New York Woman; Newspaper Reviews for: The Washington Post, Miami Herald, Boston Globe, Philadelphia Inquirer. *Honours:* Helfield Transatlantic Review Award, 1988; James Michener Fellowship, 1988-89; New York Foundation Arts Fellowship, 1988; Helena Rubenstein Fellowship, Whitney Museum of Art, 1988.

Memberships: PEN. *Literary Agent:* Wylie, Aiken & Stone, 250 West 57th Street, New York, NY 10107, USA.

HONAN Park, b. 1928. *Appointments:* Dumptruck driver in Oregon Lumber Mills, 1950's; Professor of English and American Literature, University of Leeds, 1984-; British Editor, Novel: A Forum on Fiction; Co-editor, Ohio and Baylor presses' Browning Edition. *Publications:* Browning's Characters: A Study in Poetic Technique, 1961; Shelley (ed), 1963; Bulwer Lytton's Falkland (ed), 1967; The Complete Works of Robert Browning (co-ed), 9 volumes, 1969-; The Book, The Ring and The Poet: A Biography of Robert Browning (co-author), 1975; Matthew Arnold: A Life, 1981; Jane Austen: Her Life, 1987; The Beats: An Anthology of 'Beat' Writing (ed), 1987; Authors' Lives: On Literary Biography and the Arts of Language, 1990. *Literary Agent:* Gerald J Pollinger. *Address:* School of English, University of Leeds, Leeds, LS2 9JT, England.

HONAN William Holmes, b. 11 May 1930, New York City, USA. Journalist. m. Nancy Burton, 22 June 1975, 2 sons, 1 daughter. *Education:* BA, Oberlin College, 1952; MA, University of Virginia, 1955. *Appointments:* Editor, The Villager, New York, 1957-60; Assistant Editor, New Yorker Magazine, 1960-64; Freelance Writer, national magazines, 1964-68; Associate Editor, Newsweek, New York City, 1969; Assistant Editor, New York Times Magazine, 1969-70; Travel Editor, 1970-72, 1973-74, Arts & Leisure Editor, 1974-82, Culture Editor, 1982-88, Chief Cultural Correspondent, 1988- , New York Times; Managing Editor, Saturday Review, 1972-73. *Publications:* Greenwich Village Guide, 1959; Ted Kennedy: Profile of a Survivor, 1972; Bywater: The Man Who Invented the Pacific War, British edition, 1990; Visions of Infamy: The Untold Story of How Journalist Hector C Bywater Devised the Plans that Led to Pearl Harbor, 1991; Fire When Ready, Gridley! - Great Naval Stories from Manila Bay to Vietnam, editor, 1992; pamplet, Another LaGúardia, 1960; also numerous articles. *Contributions to:* Numerous national magazines. *Literary Agent:* Roslyn Tarq, Roslyn Tarq Literary Agency. *Address:* c/o New York Times, 229 West 43rd Street, New York City, NY 10036, USA.

HONDERICH John Allen, b. 6 July 1946, Toronto, Canada. m. Katherine Govier, 27 Feb 1981, 1 son. *Education:* BA Political Science, LLB, both from University of Toronto. *Publications:* Arctic Imperative. *Contributions to:* Toronto Star. *Address:* One Yonge St, Toronto, Ontario, Canada M5E 1E6.

HONE Joseph, b. 25 Feb 1937, London, England. Writer; Broadcaster. m. Jacqueline Mary Yeend, 5 Mar 1963, 1 son, 1 daughter. *Education:* Kilkenny College; Sandford Park School, Dublin; St Columba's College, Dublin. *Publications:* The Flowers of the Forest (fiction) 1982; Children of the Country (travel) 1986; Duck Soup in the Black Sea (travel) 1988; Summer Hill (fiction) 1990. *Contributions to:* Radio and TV critic in The Listener 1975-80; Book reviews for TLS, Spectator. *Membership:* Upton House Cricket Club. *Literary Agent:* Gillon Aitken, Aitken and Stone Ltd. *Address:* Aitken and Stone Ltd, 29 Fernshaw Road, London SW10, England.

HONEYCOMBE Gordon, b. 27 Sept 1936, Karachi, India. Writer; TV Presenter; Actor. *Education:* The Edinburgh Academy, 1946-55; University College, Oxford, 1957-61 MA (Hons) English, Oxford. *Publications:* Fiction: Neither the Sea Nor the Sand, 1969; Dragon under the Hill, 1972; The Edge of Heaven, 1981; The Redemption (play) 1964; Non-Fiction: Adam's Tale, 1974; Red Watch, 1976; Nagasaki, 1945, 1981; Royal Wedding, 1981; The Murders of the Black Museum, 1982; The Year of the Princess, 1982; Selfridges, 1984; TV-am's Official Celebration of the Royal Wedding, 1986; More Murders of the Black Museum, 1993; Documentary Novels: Red Watch, 1976; Siren Song, 1992. TV Plays: The Golden Vision, 1968; Time and Again, 1974; The Thirteenth Day of Christmas,

1986. Stage Plays: The Miracles 1960; The Princess and the Goblins (musical) 1976; Paradise Lost (dramatisation) 1976; Waltz of My Heart (musical) 1980; Lancelot and Guinevere (dramatisation) 1980; Royal Galas: God Save the Queen! 1977; A King Shall have a Kingdom, 1977. Radio: Paradise Lost, 1975; Lancelot and Guinevere, 1976. *Membership:* Society of Authors. *Literary Agent:* Dianne Coles Agency, c/o Dianne Coles Agency, The Old Forge House, Sulgrave, Banbury, OX17 2RP, England. *Address:* c/o Peters, Fraser and Dunlop, The Chambers, Chelsea Harbour, Lots Road, London SW10 OXF, England.

HONEYMAN Brenda. *See:* **CLARKE Brenda.**

HONIG Edwin, b. 3 Sept 1919, New York City, USA. Poet; Playwright; Author. m. (1) Charlotte Gilchrist, 1940 (died 1963); (2) Margot S Dennes, 1963 (div 1978); 2 sons. *Education:* Educated in public schools, New York; BA 1941, MA 1947, University of Wisconsin, Madison; Served in the US Army 1943-46. *Appointments:* Library Assistant, Library of Congress, Washington DC, 1941-42; Instructor in English, Purdue University, Lafayette, Indiana, 1942-43; New York University and Illinois Institute of Technology, Chicago, 1946-47; University of New Mexico, Albuquerque, 1947-49 and Claremont College, California, Summer 1949; Instructor 1949-52 and Briggs Copeland Assistant Professor 1952-57, Harvard University, Cambridge Massachusetts; Associate Professor 1957-60, Professor of English 1960-, Professor of Comparative Literature, 1962-, Brown University, Providence, Rhode Island; Visiting Professor, University of California, Davis, 1964-65; Mellon Professor, Boston University, 1977; Poetry Editor, New Mexico Quarterly, Albuquerque, 1948-52; Director, Rhode Island Poetry in the Schools Program 1968-72. *Publications include:* Verse includes: At Sixes, 1974; Selected Poems 1955-1976, 1979; Interrupted Praise: New and Selected Poems, 1983; Gifts of Light, 1983. Plays: Cervantes: Eight Interludes, adaptations by Honig, 1964; Calisto and Melibea (produced Stanford, California, 1966) published 1972, opera version (produced Davis, California 1979); Ends of the World and Other Plays, 1983. Radio Play: Life is a Dream, 1970 (UK). *Honours:* Guggenheim Fellowship 1948, 1962; Saturday Review prize, 1957; New England Poetry Club Golden Rose, 1961; Bollingen grant, for translation, 1962; American Academy grant, 1966; Amy Lowell Travelling Fellowship, 1968; National Endowment for the Arts grants, 1975, 1977; MA, Brown University, 1958. *Address:* Box 1852, Brown University, Providence, RI 02912, USA.

HOOD Ann, b. 9 Dec 1956, Rhode Island, USA. Writer. *Education:* BA, University of Rhode Island, 1978; MA, New York University, 1985. *Publications:* Somewhere Off The Coast of Maine; Waiting to Canish; Three Legged Horse; Something Blue; Places To Stay The Night. *Contributions to:* Glamour; Cosmoolitan; Mademoiselle; New Women; Redbook; Seventeen; Washington Post. *Memberships:* PEN; Authors Guild. *Literary Agent:* Gail Hochman.

HOOD Hugh, b. 30 Apr 1928, Toronto, Canada. Writer; Teacher. m. Noreen Mallory, 22 Apr 1957, 2 sons. *Education:* BA, 1050, MA 1052, PhD, 1955, University of Toronto. *Appointments:* Professor Titulaire, Department of English Studies, University of Montreal, 1961-. *Publications:* The Swing in the Garden, 1975; Black and White Keys, 1982; Be Sure to Close Your Eyes, 1993; Flying a Red Kite, 1962; You'll Catch Your Death, 1992. *Honours:* City of Totonto Literary Award, 1975; SQPELL Literary Award, 1988; Officer of the Order of Canada, 1988. *Memberships:* The Arts and Letters CLub of Toronto. *Address:* 4242 Hampton Avenue, Montreal, Quebec, Canada H4A 2K9.

HOOKER Jeremy, b. 23 Mar 1941, Warsash, Hampshire. College Lecturer. *Education:* BA 1963, MA 1965, Southampton University. *Appointments:* Arts Council Creative Writing Fellow, Winchester School of Art, 1981-83. *Publications include:* Soliloquies of a Chalk Giant, 1974; Solent Shore, 1978; Poetry of Place, 1982; A View from the Source: Selected Poems, 1982; The Presence of the Past, 1987; Master of the Leaping Figures, 1987. *Contributions to:* Anglo-Welsh Review; New Welsh Review; PN Review; Planet; The Green Book; Poetry Wales. *Honour:* Welsh Arts Council Literature Prize for Soliloquies of a Chalk Giant, 1975. *Memberships:* Academi Gymreig - English Language Section; Powys Society; Richard Jefferies Society. *Address:* Old School House, 7 Sunnyside, Frome, Somerset BA11 1LD, England.

HOOPES Lyn Littlefield, b. 14 July 1953, New York City, USA. Writer. m. Claude B Hoopes, 20 May 1978, 1 son. *Education:* AB, English Literature, Stanford University, 1975. *Appointments:* Editorial Assistant Harper & Row, 1975-77; Assistant Editor, Atlantic Monthly Press, 1977-80; Editor, Childrens Books, Houghton Mifflin Co., 1980-82. *Publications:* Childrens Books: Nana, 1981; When I Was Little, 1983; Daddy's Coming Home, 1984; Mommy, Daddy, Me, 1988; Half a Button, 1989; Wing-a-Ding! , 1990; My Own Home, 1991; Forthcoming: The Unbeatable Bread. *Contributions to:* Childrens Book Reviewer: Christian Science Monitor, Parents' Choice. *Honour:* Nana, Children's Choice, Children's Book Council. *Address:* 91 Piney Point Road, Marion, MA 02738, USA.

HOORENS Vera Margariet, b. 31 Aug 1963, Wevelgem, Belgium. Assistant Professor in Psychology. *Education:* License, Psychology, 1986, Doctorate, 1990, KU, Leuven. *Publications:* De Eekhoornval, 1993; Het Asgrauwe Licht, 1991; Antigua (radio play), 1990. *Contributions to:* European Journal of Social Psychology; Social Cognition. *Memberships:* European Association of Experimental Social Psychology; Associate Van Sociaal Psychologische Onderzoekers. *Address:* Sectie Sociale & Organisatie Psychologie, RUG Groye Kruissyr 2/1, 9712 TS Groningen, Netherlands.

HOOVER Dwight, b. 15 Sept 1926, Oskaloosa, Iowa, USA, College Professor. m. Janet Holmes, 20 July 1983, 3 daughters. *Education:* BA, William Penn College, 1948; MA, Haverford College, 1949; PhD, University of Iowa, 1953. *Appointments:* Co-editor, Conspectus on History, 1972-82; Member, Editorial Advisory Board, Indiana Magazine of History, 1978-82; Associate Editor, Social Change Newsletter, 1986-; Associate Editor, Historical Journal of Film, Radio and Television, 1986-89. *Publications:* The Red and the Black, 1976; A Pictorial History of Indiana, 1980; Magic Middletown, 1986; Understanding Negro History, 1968; Henry James Sr and the Religion of Community, 1969; Cities, 1976; A Teacher's Guide to American Urban History, 1971. *Contributions to:* Changing View of Community Studies: Middletown as a Case Study, 1989; The Return of the Narrative, 1989; The Sporting Live in Middletown, 1990; The Long Ordeal of Modernization Theory, 1987; censorship or Bad Judgement, 1987; The Diverging Paths of American Urban History, 1968. *Memberships:* American Historical Association; Organization of American Historians; American Studies Association; American Association of University Professors; Indiana Association of Historians. *Address:* 705 N Forest, Muncie, IN 47304, USA.

HOOVER Helen Mary, (Jennifer Price), b. 5 Apr 1935, Stark County, Ohio, USA. Writer. *Publications:* Children of Morrow, 1973; The Lion's Cub, 1974; Treasures of Morrow, 1976; The Delikon, 1977; The Rains of Eridan, 1977; The Lost Star, 1979; Return to Earth,, 1980; The Time of Darkness, 1980; Another Heaven, Another Earth, 1981; The Bell Tree, 1982; The Shepherd Moon, 1984; Orvis, 1987; The Dawn Palace, 1988; Away Is A Strange Place To Be, 1989. *Contributions to:* Language Arts; Top of the News; Journal of American Library Association. *Honours:* Best Book List, for Another Heaven, Another Earth, American Library Association, 1981; Ohioana Award, 1982; Award, Outstanding Contribution to Children's Literature, Central Missouri State University, 1984; Parents Choice Award (Orvis), 1987, and (The Dawn Palace), 1988; Library of Congress Best Book of 1988;

American Library Association, Best Y.A. Book of 1988. *Membership:* Authors Guild. *Address:* c/o Viking Penguin Children's Books, 40 West 23rd Street, New York City, NY 10010, USA.

HOOVER Kenneth R, b. 15 Sept 1940, Marshalltown, Iowa, USA. University Professor, Chair. *Education:* BSc Government, Beloit College, 1962; MSc 1965, PhD 1970, Political Science, University of Wisconsin, Madison. *Publications:* Conservative Capitalism in Britain and the US: A Critical Appraisal, 1989; The Elements of Social Scientific Thinking, 5th ed, 1992; Ideology and Political Life, 2nd ed, 1993; A Politics of Identity, 1975. *Contributions to:* Routledge Encyclopaedia of Government and Politics; Comparative Studies in Society and History: An International Quarterly. *Honours:* Senior Fellow, Centre for 20th Century Studies, University of Wisconsin, Milwaukee, 1988; Visiting Fellow, University of Southampton Centre for International Policy Studies, 1987-90. *Memberships:* International Political Science Association; International Society of Political Psychology; American and Midwest Political Science Associations. *Address:* Department of Political Science, Western Washington University, Bellingham, WA 98225, USA.

HOOVER Paul, b. 30 Apr 1946, Harrisonburg, Virginia, USA. Writer and Teacher. m. Maxine Chernoff, 5 Oct 1974, 2 sons, 1 daughter. *Education:* BA cum laude, Manchester College, 1968; MA, University of Illinois, 1973. *Appointments:* Poet in Residence, Columbia College, 1974-; Editor, New American Writing (journal). *Publications:* Saigon, Illinois, 1988; Editor, Postmodern American Poetry, 1993; Poetry: The Novel, 1990; Idea, 1987. *Contributions to:* The Paris Review; The New Yorker; Partisan Review; Sulfur; New Directions and others. *Honours:* NEA Fellowship in Poetry, 1980; GE Foundation Award for Younger Writers, 1984; Carl Sandburg Award for Poetry, 1987. *Memberships:* The Poetry Centre at Museum of Comtemporary Art, Chicago, 1974-88; President of Org, 1977-80; MLA; Associated Writing Programmes. *Literary Agent:* Irene Skolnick of Curtis Brown. *Address:* 2920 W Pratt, Chicago, IL 60645, USA.

HOPCRAFT Arthur Edward, b. 29 Nov 1932, Essex, England. Writer. *Appointments:* Staff, The Daily Mirror, 1956-59, The Guardian 1959-64. *Publications include:* Born to Hunger, 1968; The Football Man, 1968; The Great Apple Raid, 1970; Mid-Century Men, 1982; Major TV Dramatisations, & original screenplays 1971-92 include: Tinker, Tailor, Soldier, Spy; Hard Times; Bleak House; A Perfect Spy; The Nearly Man; The Reporters; Jingle Bells; Baa Baa Blacksheep; The Mosedale Horseshoe; A Tale of Two Cities; Hostage; and others. *Contributions to:* The Observer; Sunday Times Magazine; Nova; New Statesman; The Listener. *Honours:* Broadcasting Press Guild TV Award, Best Single Play, 1974, Best Drama Series, 1977. British Academy of Film and TV Arts Writers Award, 1985. *Memberships:* Writers Guild of Great Britain. *Literary Agent:* A P Watt Ltd. *Address:* c/o 20 John Street, London WC1N 2DL, England.

HOPE Christopher David Tully, b. 26 Feb. 1944, Johannesburg, South Africa. Writer. m. Eleanor Marilyn Margaret Klein, 1967, 2 sons. *Education:* BA, Natal University, 1969; MA, University of Witwatersrand, 1972. *Publications:* (Fiction) A Separate Development, 1981; Private Parts & Other Tales, 1982; Kruger's Alp, 1984; The Hottentot Room, 1986; Black Swan, 1987; My Chocolate Redeemer, 1989. (Non-fiction) White Boy Running, 1988; Moscow! Moscow! 1990; Serenity House, 1992. (Poetry) Cape Drives, 1974; In the Country of the Black Pig, 1981; Englishmen, 1985; (For Children) The King, The Cat and the Fiddle, with Yehudi Menuhin, 1983; The Dragon Wore Pink, 1985. *Contributions include:* Times Literary Supplement; London Magazine; Les Temps Modernes. *Honours:* Cholmondely Award, 1974; David Higham Prize for Fiction, 1981; International PEN Award, 1983; Whitbread Prize for Fiction, 1985; FRSL. *Memberships:* Society of Authors. *Literary Agent:* Deborah Rogers, Rogers, Coleridge &

White Ltd. *Address:* c/o Deborah Rogers, Rogers, Coleridge & White Ltd., 20 Powis Mews, London W11 1JN, England.

HOPE Ronald, b. 1921, British. *Appointments:* Fellow, Brasenose College, Oxford, 1945-47; Director, Seafarers Education Service, London, 1947-76; Director, The Marine Society, 1976-86. *Publications:* Spare Time at Sea, 1954, revised edition 1974; Economic Geography, 1956, 5th edition 1969; Dick Small in the Half-Deck, Ships, 1958; The British Shipping Industry, 1959; The Harrap Book of Sea Verse (ed), 1960; The Shoregoer's Guide to World Ports, 1963; Seamen and the Sea (ed), 1965; Introduction to the Merchant Navy, 1965, 4th edition 1973; Retirement from the Sea (ed), 1967; In Cabined Ships at Sea, 1969; Voices from the Sea (ed), 1977; John Masefield: The Sea Poems (ed), 1978; Twenty Singing Seamen (ed), 1979; The Merchant Navy, 1980; The Seaman's World (ed), 1982; Sea Pie (ed), 1984; A New History of British Shipping, 1990. *Address:* Kilmadock House, Doune FK16 6AA, Scotland.

HOPE-SIMPSON Jacynth (Ann), (Helen Dudley), b. 1930, British. *Publications:* Anne Young, Swimmer, 1959; The Stranger in the Train, 1960; The Bishop of Kenelminster, Young Netball Player, 1961; The Man Who Came Back, Danger on the Line, The Bishop's Picture, 1962; The Unravished Bride, 1963; The Witch's Cave, The Ninepenny, 1964; Hamish Hamilton Book of Myths and Legends, The Ice Fair, 1965; The High Toby, The Edge of the World, Hamish Hamilton Book of Witches, 1966; Escape to the Castle, 1967; The Unknown Island, 1968; They Sailed from Plymouth, 1970; Elizabeth I, Tales in School (ed), 1971; The Gunner's Boy, 1973; Save Tarranmoor!, 1974; Always on the Move, The Hijacked Hovercraft, 1975; Black Madonna, Vote for Victoria, 1976; The Making of the Machine Age, 1978; The Hooded Falcon (as Helen Dudley), 1979; Island of Perfumes, 1985; Cottage Dreams, 1986. *Address:* Franchise Cottage, Newtown, Milborne Port Sherborne, Dorset, England.

HOPKINS Antony, b. 1921, British. Composer; Conductor. *Appointment:* Former Professor, Royal College of Music, London; Presenter, Talking about Music, BBC, 1955-90. *Publications:* Talking about Symphonies, 1961; Talking about Concertos, 1964; Music All Around Me, 1967; Music Face to Face (with A Previn), Talking about Sonatas, 1971; Downbeat Guide, 1977; Understanding Music, 1979; The Nine Symphonies of Beethoven, 1980; Songs for Swinging Golfers, 1981; Sounds of Music, Beating Time (autobiography), 1982; Musicamusings, Pathway to Music, 1983; The Concertgoer's Companion, volume I, 1984, volume II, 1985; Exploring Music, 1991. *Address:* Woodyard, Ashridge, Berkhamsted, Hertfordshire, England.

HOPKINS Harry, b. 26 Mar 1913, Preston, Lancashire, England. Journalist; Author. m. Endla Kustlov, 26 Jan 1948. *Education:* BA, Merton College, Oxford, 1935. *Appointments:* Assistant Editor, Birmingham Gazette, 1936-38; Diplomatic Correspondent, Manchester Evening News, 1946-47; Feature Writer, John Bull magazine, 1947-60. *Publications:* New World Arising: A Journey through the New Nations of SE Asia, 1952; England is Rich, 1957; The New Look: A Social History, 1963; Egypt the Crucible, 1969; The Numbers Game, 1972; The Strange Death of Private White, 1977; The Long Affray, 1985. *Memberships:* National Union of Journalists; Society of Authors. *Address:* 61 Clifton Hill, St John's Wood, London NW8 0JN, England.

HOPKINS Lee Bennett, b. 1938. America, Novels/Short stories; Children's fiction. Poetry. Children's non-fiction. Freelance writer and educational consultant. *Publications include:* (ed) Beat the Drum! Independence Day Has Come, 1977; (ed) A-Haunting We Will Go, 1977; (ed) Monsters, Ghoulies and Creepy Creatures, 1977; (ed) Witching Time, 1977; Poetry to Hear, Read, Write and Love, 1978; (ed) To Look at Any Time, 1978; (ed) Merrily Comes Our Harvest In, 1978; (ed) Kits, Cats, Lions and Tigers, 1978; (ed) Go to Bed, 1979; Wonder Wheels (novel) 1979; (ed) Merely Players, 1979; (ed) Easter Buds Are Springing, 1979; (ed) My Mane Catches the Wind: Poems About Horses, 1979; (ed) Pups, Dogs, Foxes and Wolves, 1979; (ed) Elves, Fairies and Gnomes: A Book of Poems, 1980; The Best of Book Bonanza, 1980; (ed) Moments, Poems about the Seasons, 1980; (ed) By Myself, 1980; (ed) Morning, Noon and Nightime, Too! 1980; Mama and Her Boys (novel) 1981; (ed) An God Bless Me, Prayers, Lullabies and Dream-Poems, 1982; (ed) Circus! Circus! 1982; (ed) Rainbows Are Made: Poems By Carl Sandburg, 1982; (ed) The Sky Is Full of Song, 1983; (ed) A Song in Stone, 1981; (ed) A Dog's Life, 1983; (ed) Crickets and Bullfrogs and Whispers of Thunder: Poems by harry Behn, 1984; (ed) Surprises: An I can read Book, 1984; (ed) Creatures, 1985; (ed) Munching: Poems About Food and Eating, 1985; (ed) Love and Kisses, 1984; (ed) Best Friends, 1986; (ed) The Sea Is Calling Me, 1986; (ed) Dinosaurs 1987; (ed) Click, Rumble, Roar, Poems about Machines, 1987; (ed) More Surprises, 1987. Address: Kemey's Cove (3-7), Scarborough, NY 10510, USA.

HOPKINSON David Hugh, b. 9 June 1930. Chief Night Editor. Appointments: Entered Journalism, Huddersfield Examiner, 1950; Yorkshire Observer, 1954; Yorkshire Evening News, 1954; Evening Chronicle, Manchester, 1956; Chief Sub-Editor, Sunday Graphic, London, 1957; Assistant Editor, Evening Chronicle, Newcastle upon Tyne, 1959; Chief Assistant Editor, Sunday Graphic, 1960; Deputy Editor, Sheffield Telegraph, 1961; Editor, 1962-64; Editor, The Birmingham Post, 1964-73; Director, Birmingham Post & Mail Ltd., 1967-80; Editor, Birmingham Evening Mail, 1974-79; Editor in Chief, Evening Mail Series, 1975-79, Birmingham Post and Evening Mail, 1979-80; Assistant to Editor, The Times, Chief Night Editor, The Times, 1982-. Honour: National Press Award, Journalist of the Year, 1963.

HOPPE Arthur Watterson, b. 23 Apr 1925, Honolulu, USA, Journalist. m. Gloria Nichols, 27 Apr 1946, 1 son, 3 daughters. Education: AB, cum laude, Harvard, 1949. Publications: The Love Everybody Crusade, 1960; Dreamboat, 1962; The Perfect Solution to Absolutely Everything, 1968; Mr Nixon and My Other Problems, 1971; Miss Lollipop and the Doom Machine, 1973; The Tiddling Tennis Theorum, 1977; The Marital Arts, 1985. Contributions to: Esquire; The New Yorker; The Atlantic Monthly. Literary Agent: Don Congdon. Address: The San Francisco Chronicle, 901 Mission Street, San Francisco, CA 94103, USA.

HORABIN Roshan Erica Faith, b. 9 May 1923, Bombay, India. m. Ivan Samuel Horabin, 20 July 1945, 3 daughters. Education: Home Office Diploma (Criminal Law, Social Studies), 1967; Cropwood Fellowship, Institute of Criminology, 1976. Publication: Problems of Asians in Peral Institution. Contributions to: Home Office Magazines ISTD; CJM. Memberships: PEN; Howard League; ISTD; Prison Reform Trust; Prisoners Abroad; Princes Trust. Address: Jasmine College, 69 Seckford Street, Woodbridge, Suffolk IP12 4LZ, England.

HORNE Alistair Allan, b. 9 Nov 1925. Author; Journalist; Lecturer. m. (1) Renira Margaret Hawkins, (diss 1982), 3 daughters. (2) The Hon Mrs Sheelin Eccles, Dec 1987. Education: MA, Jesus College, Cambridge. Appointments: Foreign Correspondent, Daily Telegraph, 1952- 55; Official Biographer of Prime Minister Harold Macmillan, 1979. Publications: Back into Power, 1955; The Land is Bright, 1958; Canada and the Canadians, 1961; The Price of Glory: Verdun 1916, 1962; The Fall of Paris: The Siege and The Commune 1870-71, 1965; To Lose a Battle: France 1940, 1969; Death of a Generation, 1970; The Terrible Year: The Paris Commune, 1971; Small Earthquake in Chile, 1972; A Savage War of Peace: Algeria 1952-62, 1977; Napoleon, Master of Europe 1805-1807, 1979; The French Army and Politics 1870-1970, 1984; Macmillan, the Official Biography, Volume I - 1988, Volume II - 1989; A Bunddle

from Britain, 1993. Contributions to: Various periodicals. Honours: Hawthornden Prize, 1963; Yorkshire Post Book of Year Prize, 1978; Wolfson Literary Award, 1978; Enid Macleod Prize, 1985; CBE, 1992; Chevalier Legion d'Honneur, 1993; LittD (Cambridge). Membership: Fellow, Royal Society of Literature. Address: The Old Vicarage, Turville, near Henley-on-Thames, Oxon RGG 6QU, England.

HORNE Donald Richmond, b. 26 Dec 1921, Sydney, Australia. Author; Lecturer; Professor Emeritus, University of NSW. m. 22 Mar 1960, 1 son, 1 daughter. Education: Sydney University, Canberra University College, 1944-45. Appointments: Editor, The Observer, 1958-61, The Bulletin, 1961-62, 1967-72, Quadrant, 1963-66; Contributing Editor, Newsweek International, 1973-76; Chancellor, University of Canberra, 1992-. Publications: The Lucky Country, 1964; The Permit, 1965; The Education of Young Donald, 1967; God is an Englishman, 1969; But What if There are No Pelicans, 1971; Money Madus, 1976; Death of the Lucky Country, 1976; His Excellency's Pleasure, 1977; Right Way Don't Go Back, 1978; In Search of Billy Hughes, 1979; Time of Hope, 1980; The Great Museum, 1984; Confessions of a New Boy, 1985; Story of the Australian People, 1985; The Public Culture, 1986; Portrait of an Optimist, 1988; Ideas for a Nation, 1989; The Intelligent Tourist, 1993. Contributions to: numerous professional journals. Honours: AO, 1982; Honorary DLitt, University of New South Wales, 1986. Memberships: Chairman, Australia Council, 1985-; President, Australian Society of Authors, 1984-85; Chairman, Copyright Agency Ltd., 1983-84. Address: 53 Grosvenor St, Woollahra, Sydney 2025, Australia.

HOROVITZ Michael, b. 1935, British. Appointment: Editor and Publisher, New Departures International Review, 1959-; Founder, Co-ordinator and Torchbearer, Poetry Olympics Festivals, 1980-. Publications: Europa (trans), 1961; Alan Davie, 1963; Declaration, 1963; Strangers: Poems, 1965; Poetry for the People: An Essay in Bop Prosody, 1966; Bank Holiday: A New Testament for the Love Generation, 1967; Children of Albion (ed), 1969; The Wolverhampton Wanderer: An Epic of Football, Fate and Fun, 1970; Love Poems, 1971; A Contemplation, 1978; Growing Up: Selected Poems and Pictures 1951-1979, The Egghead Republic (trans), 1979; Poetry Olympics Anthology (ed), 3 volumes, 1980-83; A Celebration of and for Frances Horovitz, 1984; Midsummer Morning Jog Log, 1986; Bop Paintings, Collages and Drawings, 1989; Grandchildren of Albion (ed), 1992. Address: New Departures, Mullions, Bisley, Stroud, Gloucestershire GL6 7BU, England.

HOROWITZ Donald Leonard, b. 27 June 1939, New York City, New York, USA. Professor. m. Judith Anne Present, 4 Sept 1960, 2 sons, 1 daughter. Education: AB, 1959, LLB, 1961, Syracuse University; LLM, 1962, AM, 1965, PhD, 1968, Harvard University. Appointments include: Charles S Murphy Professor of Law and Professor of Political Science, Duke University, Durham, North Carolina, 1980-. Publications: The Courts and Social Policy, 1977; The Jurocracy, 1977; Coup Theories and Officers' Motives, 1980; Ethnic Groups in Conflict, 1985; A Democratic South Africa, 1991. Contributions to: Articles to: Le Monde; The New Republic; Commentary; The Washington Post; The New Leader; The Los Angeles Times; The Wall Street Journal; Also to scholarly journals including: World Politics; Comparative Politics; Policy Sciences; Third World Quarterly. Memberships: American Bar Association; American Political Science Association. Address: Duke University, School of Law, Durham, NC 27706, USA.

HOROWITZ Irving Louis, b. 25 Sept 1929, Harlem, New York, USA. Social Scientist; Publisher. m. Mary Ellen Curtis, 9 Oct 1979. Education: BSS, City University of New York, 1951; MA, Columbia University, 1952; PhD, Buenos Aires University, 1957; Post-doctoral research in Philosophy, Brandeis University. Appointments: Social Science Editor, Oxford University Press, 1965-73; Editor-in-Chief, Society, 1962-90; President, Transaction Publishers, 1966-90; Senior

Editor, Book Research Quarterly, 1984-; Senior Editor, Academic Questions, 1988-. *Publications:* Three Worlds of Development, 1965, 1972; Beyond Empire & Revolution, 1982; The War Game, 1963; Foundations of Political Sociology, 1972; Radicalism and Revolt Against Reason, 1961; Ideology and Utopia in The United States, 1976; Communicating Ideas, 1986, 1991; Daydreams and Nightmares: Reflections of a Harlem Childhood, autobiography, 1990; Delivered The Bacardi Lectures for 1992, published under the title: The Conscience of Worms and the Cowadice of Lions. *Contributions to:* Encounter; Atlantic; Partisan Review; Antioch Review; New Society; Present Tense; Washington Quarterly; Society; Academic Questions; Commentary; Spectator; Queen's Quarterly. *Honours:* Carnegie Peace Foundation for War and Peace in Contemporary Social Theory and Philosophy, 1957; St Peter's Centennial Medallion for Foundations of Political Sociology; National Jewish Book Award (autobiography), 1991. *Memberships:* Society for Scholarly Publishers; Association of American Publishers; National Association of Scholars; American Association for the Advancement of Science, Fellow, 1980. *Address:* 1247 State Road (Route 206), Blawenburg Road/Rocky Hill Intersection, Princeton, NJ 08540, USA.

HORSFORD Howard C, b. 26 Nov 1921, Montezuma, Iowa, USA. *Education:* BA magna cum laude, Ripon College, 1943; University of Iowa, 1947; MA, 1951, PhD, 1952, Princeton University. *Appointments:* Instructor, Assistant Professor, Princeton University, 1951-60; Assistant to Full Professor, Rochester University, 1960-87; Bread Loaf, School of English, 1980, 1961, 1963, 1964. *Publications:* Melville's Journal of a Voyage to Europe and the Levant, 1856-57, 1955; Melvilles Journals, 1989; Editor: An Oxford Anthology of English Poetry, 1956, The Southern Mandarins: Letters of Caroline Gordon to Sally Wood, 1984. *Contributions to:* Irving, Hawthorne, Melville, Crane, C Gordon, Faulkner. *Honours:* Phi Beta Kappa, 1955; Bicentennial Preceptor, Princeton University, 1957-60. *Memberships:* Melville Society, President, 1957. *Address:* Department of English, University of Rochester, NY 14627, USA.

HORTON Felix Lee. *See:* **FLOREN Lee.**

HORTON Michael Scott, b. 11 May 1964, California, USA. President of a Theological Think Tank. *Education:* BA Humanities, History, Biola University; MAR Theo emphasis, Westminster Theological Seminary; Certificat, International Inst of Human Rights, Strasbourg, France; History Studies, University of Cambridge; PhD Candidate, Wycliffe Hall, Oxford. *Publications:* The Agony of Deceit, 1990; Made in America, 1991; Putting Amazing Back into Grace, 1991; Power Religion, 1992; Mission Accomplished, 1986. *Honours:* Book of the year for Contemporary Issues; Christianity Today; First Runner Up, Book of the Year, 1992. *Memberships:* Royal Institute of Philosophy; Oxford Union Society; Phi Alpha Theta. *Address:* 2034 E Lincoln 209, Anaheim, CA 92806, USA.

HORWOOD Harold Andrew, b. 2 Nov 1923, St John's Newfoundland, Canada. *Appointments:* Creative Writing Teacher, Memorial University, 1974; Writer in Residence: University of Western Ontario, 1976, University of Waterloo, 1980, 1982. *Publications:* Tomorrow will be Sunday, 1966; Th Foxes of Beachy Cove, 1967; Newfoundland, 1969; White Eskimo, 1972; Death on Ice, 1972; Voices Underground, 1972; Beyond the Road, 1976; Bartlett, 1977; Only the Gods Speak, 1979; Tales of the Labrador Indians, 1981; The Colonial Dream, 1981; A History of Canada, 1983; Pirates and Outlaws of Canada, 1984; Corner Brook, 1986; A History of Newfoundland Ranger Force, 1986; Bandits and Privateers, 1987; Dancing on the Shore, 1987; Joey: The Life and Political Times of Joey Smallwood, 1989. *Contributions to:* Numerous publications. *Honours:* Beta Sigma Phi first Novel, 1966; Best Scientific Book of the Year, 1967; Canada Council Senior Arts Awrad, 1975; Order of Canada, 1980. *Memberships:* Writers Union of Canada, Vice Chairman and Chairman. *Literary Agent:*

Bella Pomer Inc, 22 Shallmar Blvd, Toronto. *Address:* PO Box 489, Annapolis Royal, Nova Scotia, Canada BOS 1AO.

HOSIER Peter. *See:* **CLARK Douglas.**

HOSILLOS Lucila V, b. 29 June 1931, Tanza, Iloilo City, Philippines. *Education:* AB, English, Far Eastern University, Manila, 1958; AM Comparative Literature, 1962, PhD, 1964, Indiana University, USA. *Appointments:* Instructor, State University of NY at Buffalo, 1963-64; Asst Prof, Full Professor of Comparative Literature, University of Philippines, 1966-85; Visiting Professor, National University of Singapore, 1983-84; Cultural Consultant, freelance, 1985-. *Publications:* The Concentric Sphere and Other Essays in Comparative Literature, 1968; Philippine American Literary Relations, 1898-1941, 1969, 1976; Philippine Literature and Contemporary Events, 1970; Anthology of Third World Poetry, 1978; Originality as Vengeance in Philippine Literature, 1984; Perempuam (Woman), editor, 1987; Hiligaynon Literature: Texts and Contexts, 1992; Participation in International Congress: Plenary speaker at XIIIth Triennial International Congress, FILLM, Sydney, Australia, 1975; XIVth Congress, Association of Asian Institutions of Higher Learning, Hongkong, 1982; XVI FILLM Congress, Budapest, Hungary, 1984 (Federation International des Langues et Litteratures). *Contributions to:* Encyclopaedia Universalis; Cooperator: International Dictionary of Literary Terms; A Comparative History of Literature in European Languages; International Directory of Comparative Literature Studies. *Honours include:* First Prize, Hiligaynon Short Story Writing Contest, Liwayway Publications, 1969; First Prize, ASEAN Literary Contest, Manila, 1977; Grand Prize, Literary Criticism in English, Cultural Centre of the Philippines 10th Anniversary Literary Contest, 1979; Second Prize, UNESCO Contest on Least Developed Countries, 1981. *Memberships:* Féderation Internationale des Langues et Littératures Modernes; Association Internationale de Littérature Comparée; American Comparative Literature Association; ASEAN Writers Association; Founder, Chairman and President, Illonggo Language and Literature Foundation Inc. *Address:* 5 Peace Street, East Fairview 1121, Quezon City, Phillipines.

HOSKINS Robert, (Grace Corren, John Gregory, Susan Jennifer, Michael Kerr), b. 1933. America, Writer of Historical/Romance/Gothic, Science Fiction/ Fantasy. *Appointments:* Freelance writer since 1972. Worked in family business 1952-64; Attendant, Wassaic State School for the Retarded, New York City, 1964-66; House Parent, Brooklyn Home for Children, 1966-68; Sub-Agent, Scott Meredith Literary Agency, New York City, 1967-68; Senior Editor, Lancer Books, New York City, 1969-72. *Publications:* (ed) First Step Outward, 1969; (as Grace Corren) The Darkest Room, 1969; (ed) Infinity 1-5, 5 vols, 1970-73; (ed) The Stars Around Us, 1970; (ed) Swords Against Tomorrow, 1970; (ed) Tomorrow I, 1971; (ed) The Far-Out People, 1971; (as Grace Corren) A Place on Dark Island, 1971; (ed) Wondermakers 1-2, 2 vols, 1972-74; (ed) Strange Tomorrows, 1972; (as Grace Corren) Evil in the Family (science fiction) 1972; (as Susan Jennifer) The House of Counted Hatreds, 1973; (as Grace Corren) Mansions of Deadly Dreams, 1973; (ed) The Edge of Never, 1973; (ed) The Liberated Future, 1974; The Shattered People (science fiction) 1975; (as Susan Jennifer) Country of the Kind, 1975; (ed) Master of the Stars (science fiction) 1976; To Control the Stars (science fiction) 1977; Tomorrow's Son (science fiction) 1977; (as Grace Corren) Dark Threshold, 1977; (ed) The Future Now, 1977; Jack-in-the-Box Planet (science fiction) 1978; To Escape the Stars (science fiction), 1978; (as John Gregory) Legacy of the Stars (science fiction) 1979; (as Michael Kerr) The Gemini Run, 1979; (as Grace Corren) The Attic Child, 1979; (as Grace Corren) Survival Run (novelization of screenpplay) 1979; (ed) Against Tomorrow 1979; The Fury Bombs, 1983. *Address:* c/ o Harlequin, 225 Duncan Mill Road, Don Mills, Ontario, Canada M3B 3K9.

HOSTE Pol, b. 25 Mar 1947, Lokeren, Belgium. Writer. *Education:* Licentiate Germanic Philology, State University of Ghent, 1970. *Publications:* De Veranderingen, 1979; Vrouwelijk Enkelvoud, 1987; Een Schoon Bestaan, 1989; Brieven Aan Mozart, 1991; Ontroeringen van een Forens, 1993. *Address:* Kortedagsteeg 31, B-9000 Gent, Belgium.

HOSTRUP-JESSEN Paula Eugenie, b. 16 Jan 1930, London, England. Danish-English Translator. m. Carl Hostrup-Jessen, 24 Jan 1953, 2 sons, 1 daughter. *Education:* Royal Free Hospital School of Medicine, 1947-53, incomplete; University of Copenhaven, Philosophy, Modern Greek, 1969-90. *Appointments:* Chief Editor, Tordenskjold, literary magazine, 1988-90; Publisher's Reader, 1990-. *Publications:* Translations: Villy Sprensen: Tutelary Tales, 1988, The Downfall of the Gods, 1989, Harmless Tales, 1991; Steen Steensen Blicher: The Diary of a Parish Clerk, 1968, 1991; Hans Christian Andersen: Brothers Very Far Away and other Poems, 1991. *Contributions to:* Encounter, Stand Magazine, Scandinavian Review, Seattle Review, Translation, Cimarron Review, Sprint, World Literature Today. *Honours:* Christian Wilster Prize for Literary Translation, 1990. *Memberships:* Danish Writers Association, Chairwoman of Translators Group, 1989; American Literary Translator's Association. *Address:* Sortemosen 48, PO Box 122, DK-3450 Allerod, Denmark.

HOTCHNER A(aron) E(dward), b. 1920, USA. Author. *Appointments:* Articles Editor, Cosmopolitan magazine, 1948-50. *Publications:* The Dangerous American, 1958; For Whom the Bell Tolls, by Hemingway (adaptor), television play, 1958; The Killers, by Hemingway (adaptor), television play, 1959; Adventures of a Young Man, by Hemingway (adaptor), sceenplay, 1961; The White House, play, 1964; Papa Hemingway: A Personal Memoir, 1966; The Hemingway Hero, play, 1967; Treasure, 1970; Do You Take This Man, play, 1970; King of the Hill, 1972; Looking for Miracles, 1974; Doris Day: Her Own Story, 1976; Sophia: Living and Loving, 1979; Sweet Prince, play, 1980; The Man Who Lived at the Ritz, 1982; Choice People, 1984; Hemingway and His World, 1988; Welcome to The Club, Broadway Musical, 1989; Blown Away, 1990. *Address:* 14 Hillandale Road, Westport, CT 06880, USA.

HOUGH (Helen) Charlotte, b. 24 May 1924, Hampshire, England. Writer. m. Richard Hough, 17 July 1941, (div 1973), 4 daughters. *Publications:* The Bassington Murder, 1980; Red Biddy, 1966; Sir Frog, 1968; Educating Flora, 1968; Three Little Funny Ones, 1962; Jim Tiger, 1956; Morton's Pony, 1957; The Homemakers, 1959; The Story of Mr Pinks, 1958; The Hampshire Pig, 1958; The Animal Game, 1959; The Trackers, 1960; Algernon, 1962; Anna-Minnie, 1967; The Owl in the Barn, 1964; More Funny Ones, 1965; My Aunt's Alphabet, 1969; A Bad Child's Book of Moral Verse, 1970. *Memberships:* PEN Society of Authors; Crime Writers Association. *Literary Agent:* Curtis Brown. *Address:* 1A Ivor Street, London NW1 9PL, England.

HOUGH Michael, b. 5 Aug 1928. Landscape Architect. m. Bridget, 24 July 1956, 2 sons, 1 daughter. *Education:* DipArch, Edinburgh, 1955; MLA, Penn, 1958. *Publications:* City FOrm and Natural Process, 1984; Out of Place, 1990. Chapters in Green Cities, Land Conservation and Development, Examples of Land Use Planning projects and programmes; People and City Landscapes; The Urban Landscape; THe Hitten Frontier. *Contributions to:* Design Principles for Recreation on Urban Waterfronts; Recreation Research Review; Arborcultural journal. *Honours:* LA Bradford Williams Award for Journalistic Excellence, 1989; Arts Foundation of Greater Toronto Award, 1991. *Memberships:* American and Canadian Societies of Landscape Architects; Ontario Association of Landscape Architects; Royal Canadian Academy of Arts. *Address:* 29 Cornish Road, Toronto, Canada M4T 2E3.

HOUGH Richard Alexander, (Bruce Carter, Elizabeth Churchill, Pat Stong), b. 15 May 1922. Writer. m. (1) Helen Charlotte, 1943, div, 4 daughters, (2) Judy Taylor, 1980. *Appointments include:* Publisher 1947-70; Bodley Head until 1955; Director, Managing Director, Hamish Hamilton Childen's Books, 1955-70. *Publications:* The Fleet That Had to Die, 1958; Admirals in Collision, 1959; The Potemkin Mutiny, 1960; The Hunting of Force Z, 1963; Dreadnought, 1964; The Big Battleship, 1966; First Sea Lord: An Authorised Life of Admiral Lord Fisher, 1969; The Pursuit of Admiral von Spee, 1969; The Blind Horn's Hate, 1971; Captain Bligh and Mr Christian, 1972 (filmed as The Bounty, 1984); Louis and Victoria: the First Mountbattens, 1974; One Boy's War: per astra ad ardua, 1975; Editor, Advice to a Grand-daughter (Queen Victoria's Letters), 1975; The Great Admirals, 1977; The Murder of Captain James Cook, 1979; Man o' War, 1979; Nelson, 1980; Mountbatten: Hero of Our Time, 1980; Edwina: Countess Mountbatten of Burma, 1983; The Great War at Sea 1914-1918, 1983; Former Naval Person: Churchill and the Wars at Sea, 1985; The Ace of Clubs: a History of the Garrick, 1986; The Longest Battle: The War at Sea (1939-45), 1986; Born Royal: The Lives and Loves of the Young Windsors (1894-1937), 1988; (jointly with Denis Richards) The Battle of Britain: the Jubilee History, 1989; Winston & Clementine: the triumph of the Churchills, 1990; Bless our Ship: Mountbatten & the Kelly, 1981; Edward & Alecandra: their private & personal lives, 1982. (Novels) Angels One Five, 1978; The Fight of the Few, 1979; The Fight to the Finish, 1979; Buller's Guns, 1981; Razor Eyes, 1981; Buller's Dreadnought, 1982; Buller's Victory, 1984; Edward and Alexandra, 1992; numerous books on motoring, history and books for children under pseudonym Bruce Carter. *Address:* 31 Meadowbank, Primrose Hill, London NW3 IAY, England.

HOUGH Stanley Bennett, (Rex Gordon, Bennett Stanley), b. 25 Feb 1917, Preston, Lancashire, England, Author. m. Justa E C Wodschow, 1938. *Appointments:* Radio Operator, Marconi Company, 1936-38; Radio Officer, International Marine Radio, 1939-45; Professional Yachtsman, 1946-51. *Publications Include:* Frontier Incident, 1951; Moment of Decision, 1952; Mission in Guemo, 1953; The Seas South, 1953; The Primitives, 1954; The Bronze Perseus, 1959; The Tender Killer, 1962; Sea to Eden, 1954; Extinction Bomber, 1956; A Pound a Day Inclusive, 1957; Expedition Everyman, 1959; Beyond the Eleventh Hour, 1961; Where?, 1965; Dear Daughter Dead, 1965; Sweet Sister Seduced, 1968; Fear Fortune Father, 1974; No Man Friday, (as Rex Gordon), 1956; Government Contract, (as Bennett Stanley), 1956. *Honour:* Infinity Award for Science Fiction, 1957. *Memberships:* Chairman, Workers Education Association, South west District; Chairman, Secondary School Boards; President, Royal Cornwall Polytechnic Society, 1985-88. *Literary Agent:* A M Heath and Company Limited. *Address:* 21 St Michael's Road, Ponsanooth, Truro TR3 7ED, England.

HOUGHTON Eric, b. 4 Jan 1930, West Yorkshire, England, Teacher; Author. m. Cecile Wolffe, 4 June 1954, 1 son, 1 daughter. *Education:* Certificate in Education, Sheffield City College of Education, 1952. *Publications:* The White wall, 1961; Summer Silver, 1963; They Marched With Spartacus, 1963; A Giant Can Do Anything, 1975; The Mouse and the Magician, 1976; The Remarkable Feat of King Caboodle, 1978; Steps Out of Time, 1979; Gates of Glass, 1987; Walter's Wand, 1989; The Magic Cheese, 1991; The Backwards Watch, 1991; Vincent the Invisible, 1993. *Contributor to:* Review. *Honour:* Junior Book Award, Boys' Clubs of America, 1964. *Memberships:* Society of Authors, London; Children's Writers' Group. *Address:* The Crest, 42 Collier Road, Hastings, East Sussex TN34 3JR, England.

HOUGRON Jean (Marcel), b. 1 July 1923, Caen, France. Writer. m. (1) Noelle Desgouille, (div), (2) Victoria Sanchez, 2 sons, 3 daughters. *Education:* Faculty of Law, University of Paris. *Appointments:* Schoolmaster 1943-46; various positions 1946-49; Translator, American

Consulate, 1950; News Editor, Radio France Asie 1951; Bookseller, Nice, 1953-54. *Publications:* Tu Recolteras la Tempete, 1950; Rage Blanche, 1951; Soleil au Ventre, 1952; Mort en Fraude (film), 1953; La Nuit Indochinoise, 1953; Les Portes de l'aventure, 1954; Les Asiates, 1954; Je Reviendrai a Kandara (film), 1955; La Terre du Barbare, 1958; Par qui le Scandale, 1960; Le Signe du Chien, 1961; Histoire de Georges Guersant, 1964; Les Humilies, 1965; La Gueule Pleine de Dents, 1970; L'homme de Proie, 1974; L'anti-jeu, 1977; Le Naguen, 1979; La Chambre (novel), 1982; Coup de Soleil, 1984. *Honours include:* Prix Populiste, 1965; Grand Prix de la Science-Fiction, 1982; Chevalier des Arts et des Lettres. *Address:* 1 rue des Guillemites, 75004 Paris, France.

HOUSTON Douglas Norman, b. 18 Mar 1947, Cardiff, Wales. Writer; Lecturer; m. Karen Mary Pearce, 5 July 1986, 3 sons, 1 daughter. *Education:* BA English, 1969, PhD English, 1986, University of Hull. *Appointments:* Freelance reviewer, articles, poems etc in various journals, industrial copywriter; Visiting Lecturer, Trinity College, Dublin University College Dublin; Staff of English Department, University College of Wales, Aberystwyth. *Publications:* With the Offal Eaters, 1986; A Rumoured Cty, ed. Meic Stephens, 1982; The Bright Field, ed. Douglas Dunn, 1991; Casting a Spell, ed. Angela Huth, 1992. *Contributions to:* Poetry Review; London Magazine; Oxford Guide to Twentieth Century Literature in English. *Honours:* Welsh Arts Council Book Prize, 1987; Welsh Arts Council Bursary, 1990; Elected to Welsh Academy, 1987. *Address:* Brynheulog, Cumbrwyno, Aberystwyth, Dyfed, Wales.

HOUSTON James A(rchibald), b. 1921, Canada. Author; Artist. *Appointments:* Associate Director, 1962-72, Associate Designer, 1972-, Steuben Glass. *Publications:* Tikta-liktat, 1965; Eagle Mask, 1966; The White Archer, 1967; Eskimo Prints, 1967; Akavakm 1968; Wolf Run, 1971; The White Dawn, for adults, 1971; Ghost Paddle, 1972; Ojibwa Summer, 1972; Kiviok's Magic Journey, 1973; Frozen Fire, 1977; Ghost Fox, for adults, 1977; River Runners, 1979; Spirit Wrestler, for adults, 1980; Long Claws, 1981; Black Diamonds, 1982; Eagle Song, 1983; Ice Swords, 1985; The Falcon Bow, 1986; Whiteout 1988; Running West, for adults, 1989; Drifting Snow, 1992. *Honours:* Degree of Doctor of Literature, honoris causa, Carleton University, Ottawa, 1972; Book of the Year Medal, Canadian Library Associatiom, 1966, 1968, 1980; Canada Council's Children's Literature Prize, 1986; B.C. Book Prize, 1987; American Library Association Notable Book Award, 1967, 1968, 1971, 1977; Twice nominated from Canada, Hans Christian Andersen Award, IBBY, 1987, 1991; Max and Greta Ebel Memorial Award, 1989. *Memberships:* Board of Governors, Museum of Anthropology, Brown University; Board of Directors, Arctic Society of Canada, Inuit Tapirisat of Canada; Northern Arts Committee, Art Gallery of Ontario; Board of Directors, Alaska Indian Arts; Collections Committee, Mustic Seaport Museum; Honorary Vice-President, West Baffin Eskimo Co-Operative. *Address:* 24 Main Street, Stonington, CT 06378, USA.

HOUSTON R B. *See:* RAE Hugh Crawford.

HOVANNISIAN Richard G, b. 1932, USA. Professor of Armenian and Near Eastern History; Director, Near Eastern Center, UCLA; Holder, Armenian Educational Foundation Chair in Modern Armenian History since 1987. *Appointments:* Member, Editorial Board: Armenian Review; International Journal of Middle East Studies, Ararat; Haigazian Armenological Review, Beirut. *Publications:* Armenia on the Road to Independence, 1967, 4th Edition, 1984; The Republic of Armenia, vol I, 1971, 3rd Edition, 1984, vol II, 1982; The Armenian Holocaust, 1978, 2nd Edition, 1980; The Armenian Image in History and Literature, 1982; Ethics in Islam, 1985; The Armenian Genocide in Perspective, 1986; The Armenian Genocide: History, Politicis, Ethics, 1992. *Contributions to:* Read More About It; Armenian Review. *Honours:* Elected Armenian Academy of Sciences, 1990. *Memberships:* Society for Armenian

Studies, Chairman 1974-75, 1976-77, 1990-91, 1991-92; Middle East Studies Association; American Association for Advancement of Slavic Studies; Oral History Association; American Historical Association. *Address:* Department of History, University of California, Los Angeles, CA 90024, USA.

HOWARD Anthony Michell, b. 12 Feb 1934, London, England. Journalist. m. 26 May 1965. *Education:* BA, Jurisprudence, Christ Church, Oxford University, 1955; Called to Bar, Inner Temple, 1956. *Literary Appointments:* Editor, New Statesman 1972-78, Listener 1979-81; Deputy editor, Observer, 1981-88. *Publications:* The Making of the Prime Minister, with Richard West, 1965; The Crossman Diaries: Selections from the Diaries of a Cabinet Minister, editor, 1979; Rab: The Life of R. A. Butler, 1987; Crossman: The Pursuit of Power, 1990. *Contributions to:* Books: The Baldwin Age, 1960; The Age of Austerity, 1963. Journals: Sunday Times; Times Literary Supplement; New York Times Book Review; The Independent, London Review of Books, Spectator. *Literary Agent:* Peters, Fraser and Dunlop. *Address:* 17 Addison Avenue, London W11 4QS, England.

HOWARD Clark, b. 1934, USA. Author. *Publications:* The Arm, novel, 1967; Mystery novels: A Movement Toward Eden, 1969; The Doomsday Squad, 1970; The Killings, 1973; Last Contract, 1973; Summit Kill, 1975; Mark the Sparrow, 1975; The Hunters, 1976; The Last Great Death Stunt; Other: Six Against the Rock, 1977; The Wardens, 1979; Zebra: The True Account of the 179 Days of Terror in San Francisco, 1979, UK Edition The Zebra Killings, 1980; American Saturday, 1981; Brothers in Blood, 1983; Dirt Rich, 1986; Hard City, 1990. *Honours:* Edgar Allan Poe Award, 1980; Ellery Queen Award, 1985, 1986, 1988, 1990. *Literary Agent:* Ms Roslyn Targ. *Address:* The Roslyn Targ Agency, 105 W 13 St, Suite 15-E, New York, NY 10011, USA.

HOWARD Constance (Mildred), b. 1910, United Kingdom. Freelance Lecturer and Writer. *Appointments:* Part-time Lecturer, 1946-59, Full-time Senior Lecturer, 1959-73, Principal Lecturer, 1973-75, Goldsmiths School of Art, University of London; Member, Advisory Committee, London College of Fashion. *Publications:* Design for Embroidery from Traditional English Sources, 1956; Inspiration for Embroidery, 1966; Embroidery and Colour, 1976; Textile Crafts (editor), 1978; Constance Howard Book of Stitches, 1979; Twentieth Century Embroidery in Great Britain, 4 vols, 1981-84. *Contributions to:* articles and reviews of exhibitions to Embroidery magazine. *Honours:* MBE, 1975. *Memberships:* Council Member, Society of Designer Craftsmen; Art Workers Guild. *Address:* 43 Cambridge Road South, London W4 3DA, England.

HOWARD Deborah Janet, b. 26 Feb 1946, Westminster, London, England. University Lecturer. m. Malcolm S Longair, 26 Sept 1975, 1 son, 1 daughter. *Education:* BA Hons, Newnham College, Cambridge, 1968; Courtauld Institute of Art, University of London, 1968-72; MA, distinction, 1969, MA 1972, PhD, 1973. *Publications:* Jacopo Sansovino: Architecture and patronage in Renaissance Venice, 1975, 1987; The Architectural History of Venice, 1980, 1981, 1987. *Contributions to:* Numerous articles and book reviews in academic journals on the history of art and architecture and the TLS. *Honours:* Fellow, Society of Antiquaries, 1984; Fellow, Society of Antiquaries of Scotland, 1991. *Memberships:* Alice David Hitchock Medallion Committee; Royal Commission on the Ancient & Historical Monuments of Scotland; Royal Fine Art Commission for Scotland. *Address:* St John's College, Cambridge, CB2 1TP, England.

HOWARD Elizabeth Jane, b. 26 Mar. 1923, London, England. Author. m. 1 daughter. *Education:* Educated at home. *Literary Appointments:* Honorary Director, Cheltenham Literary Festival, 1962; Co-Director, Salisbury Festival, 1973. *Publications:* The Beautiful Visit, 1950; The Long View, 1956; The Sea Change,

1959; After Julius, 1965; Odd Girl Out, 1972; Something In Disguise, 1974; The Lovers' Companion (anthology); Getting It Right, 1982; Howard and Maschler on Food, 1987 (with Fay Maschler); Bettina (biography with Arthur Helps); The Light Years (first volume of The Cazalet Chronicle), 1990; Green Shades (gardening anthology), 1990; Collections of short stories; Mr Wong; We Are For The Dark (with R Aickman); Marking Time, 1991; 14 television plays; 3 film scripts. *Contributions to:* The Times; Sunday Times; Telegraph; Encounter; Vogue; Harpers; Queen; Others. *Honours:* John Llewellyn Rhys Memorial Prize, 1950; Yorkshire Post Novel of the Year, 1982. *Memberships:* Fellow of The royal Society of Literature; The Writers' Guild (Council Member 3 years); Authors Lending and Copyright Society (Council Member). *Literary Agent:* Jonathan Clowes, London, England. *Address:* c/o Jonathan Clowes, Ivan Bridge House, Bridge Approach, London NW1 8BD, England.

HOWARD Maureen, b. 1930, USA. University Educator. *Appointments:* Worked in advertising and publishing, 1953-54; Lecturer in English: New School for Social Research, New York City, 1967-68, 1970-71, 1974-; University of California, Santa Barbara, 1968-69; Amherst College, Amherst, Massachusetts; Brooklyn College, New York; Currently Member, English Department, Columbia University, New York City. *Publications:* Not a Word about Nightingales, novel, 1960; Bridgeport Bus, novel, 1965; Before My Time, novel, 1975; Facts of Life, autobiography, 1978; Grace Abounding, novel, 1982; Expensive Habits, novel, 1986. *Address:* c/o Summit Books, Simon and Schuster, 1230 Sixth Avenue, New York, NY 10020, USA.

HOWARD Philip Nicholas Charles, b. 2 Nov 1933, London, England, Writer; Literary Editor. m. Myrtle Janet Mary Houldsworth, 17 Oct 1959, 2 sons, 1 daughter. *Education:* MA, Major Scholar, Trinity College, Oxford, 1953-57. *Appointments:* Reporter, Feature Writer, Leader Writer, Parliamentary Correspondent, The Glasgow Herald, 1960-64; Reporter, Feature Writer, Columnist, Leader Writer, 1964-, Literary Editor, 1978-, The Times. *Publications:* The State of the Language, 1984; We Thundered Out, 200 Years of The Times, 1985; Winged Words, 1988; A Word in Time, 1990; Word-Watching, 1988; London's River, 1975; The Royal Palaces; The Black Watch; New Words for Old; Weasel Words; Words Fail Me; A Word in Your Ear; The Book of London. *Contributions to:* Diverse magazines and journals. *Honours:* Fellow, Royal Society of Literature, 1985; IPC Press Awards. *Memberships:* The Literary Society; The Society of Bookment; Council, The Classical Association; International PEN; Society of Authors; National Union of Journalists. *Address:* Flat 1, 47 Ladbroke Grove, London W11 3AR, England.

HOWARD Richard (Joseph) b. 13 Oct 1929, Cleveland, Ohio, Freelance literary and art critic and translator. Writer. *Education:* Educated at Shaker Heights High School, Ohio; BA 1951, MA 1952, Columbia University, New York; the Sorbonne, Paris, 1952-53. *Career:* Lexicographer, World Publishing Company, Cleveland, 1954-56 and in New York, 1956-58. Freelance literary and art critic and translator, 1958-; Poetry Editor, American Review, New York; Director, Braziller Poetry Series. *Publications:* Verse includes: Findings, 1971; Two-Part Inventions (includes radio plpay The Lesson of the Master) 1974; Fellow Feelings, 1976; Misgivings, 1979; Lining Up, 1984. Plays: The Automobile Graveyard, adaptation of a play by Fernando Arrabal (produced New York, 1961); Wildflowers (produced New York, 1976); Natures (produced New York, 1977); Two-Part Inventions (produced Chicago, 1979). Other publications. *Honours:* Guggenheim Fellowship, 1966; Harriet Monroe Memorial Prize, 1969 and Levinson Prize 1973 (Poetry, Chicago)l American Academy grant, 1970, and Award of Merit Medal, 1980; Pulitzer Prize, 1970; American Book Award for translation, 1983; Fellow, Morse College, Yale University, New Haven, Connecticut. Member, American Academy 1983.

HOWARD Roger, b. 19 June 1938, Warwick, England. Theatre Writer; Poet; Lecturer. *Education:* MA, Litt. Drama. *Appointments:* Writing Fellow, York University, 1976-78, East Anglia University 1979; Lecturer, Literature, University of Essex. *Publications:* New Short Plays, 1968; Slaughter Night and Other Plays, 1971; A Break in Berlin, 1979; Mao Tse Tung and the Chinese People, 1977; Contemporary Chinese Theatre, 1978; The Siege, 1981; Partisans, 1983; Senile Poems, 1988; The Tragedy of Mao, 1989. *Contributions to:* Transatlantic Review; Stand; Bananas; Times Literary Supplement; Double Space; New Society; Times Education Supplement; Minnesota Review; Theatre Quarterly; Plays and Players; Theatre Research International. *Address:* c/o Theatre Underground, Dept. of Literature, University of Essex, Wivenhoe Park, Colchester, Essex CO4 3SQ, England.

HOWARTH David Armine, b. 18 July 1912. Author. *Education:* Trinity College, Cambridge. *Appointments:* Talks Assistant, etc, BBC 1934-39; War Correspondent, 1939-40; RNVR 1940-45. *Publications:* The Shetland Bus, 1951; We Die Alone (also under title Escape Alone), 1955; The Sledge Patrol, 1957; Dawn of D-Day, 1959; The Shadow of the Dam, 1961; The Desert King, A Biography of Ibn Saud, 1964; The Golden Isthmus, 1966; A Near Run Thing: the Day of Waterloo, 1968; Trafalgar: The Nelson Touch, 1969; Sovereign of the Seas, 1974; The Greek Adventure, 1976; 1066, The Year of the Conquest, 1977; The Voyage of the Armada: The Spanish Story, 1981; Tahiti, 1983; Pursued by a Bear (autobiography), 1986; (with S. Howarth) The Story of P & O; (fiction) Group Flashing Two, 1952; One Night in Styria, 1953; (for children) Heroes of Nowadays, 1957; Great Escapes, 1969; Editor, My Land and My People (by HH The Dalai Lama), 1962. *Address:* Wildings Wood, Blackboys, Sussex, England.

HOWAT Gerald Malcolm David, (Gerald Henderson-Howat), b. 12 June 1928, Glasgow, Scotland. Writer; Former Lecturer & Schoolmaster. m. Dr Anne McGillivray Murdoch, 7 Aug 1951, 2 sons, 1 daughter. *Education:* MA, University of Edinburgh, 1950; DipEd, University of London; M.Litt., Exeter College, Oxford University; PhD, Pac. West, California. *Appointments:* RAF, 1950-52; Staff, Trinidad Leaseholds, 1952-55; Staff, Kelly College, Tavistock, 1955-60; Principal Lecturer, Culham College, Oxford University Department of Educational Studies 1960-74 (Principal Lecturer Emeritus 1974-), Radley College, Oxon, 1974-77, Lord Williams's Thame, 1977-86. *Publications:* Dictionary of World History, 1973; Stuart & Cromwellian Foreign Policy, 1974; Who Did What, 1975; From Chatham to Churchill, 1966; Story of Health, with Dr A Howat, 1967; Documents in European History, 1974; Learie Constantine, 1975; Village Cricket, 1980; Cricketer Militant, 1980; Culham College History, 1982; Walter Hammond, 1984; Plum Warner, 1987; Len Hutton, 1988; Cricket's Second Golden Age, 1989; Bud Finch Remembers, 1989. *Contributions to:* The Times; Journal of Cricket Society; Australian Cricket Journal; Wisden Cricket Monthly; The Cricketer; Glasgow Herald; Scotsman; British Journal of Educational Studies; Quarterly Review. *Honours:* Story Miller Prizeman, University of London, 1959; The Cricket Society Jubilee Literary Award, 1975. *Memberships:* Fellow, Royal Historical Society; Society of Authors; Marylebone Cricket Club; Moreton Cricket Club, Oxon, Secretary, 1961-; Chairman, Edinburgh University Club of Oxford. *Address:* Old School House, North Moreton, Oxon, England.

HOWATCH Susan, b. 14 July 1940, Leatherhead, Surrey, England. Writer. *Education:* LLB, King's College, University of London, 1958-61. *Publications:* The Dark Shore, 1965; The Waiting Sands, 1966; Call in the Night, 1967; The Shrouded Walls, 1968; April's Grave, 1969; The Devil on Lammas Night, 1970; Penmarric, 1971; Cashelmara, 1974; The Rich are Different, 1977; Sins of the Fathers, 1980; The Wheel of Fortune, 1984; Glittering Images, 1987; Glamorous Powers, 1988; Ultimate Prizes, 1989; Scandalous Risks, 1991; Mystical Paths, 1992. *Contributions to:* The Writer; The Church

Times; The Tablet. *Honour:* Winifred Mary Stanford Memorial Prize for Scandalous Risks, 1992. *Memberships:* PEN; Society of Authors; Authors League/Guild (USA); Royal Overseas League. *Literary Agents:* Brian Stone, Aitken & Stone, (UK); Claire Smith, Harold Ober Associates Inc, (USA). *Address:* c/o Aitken & Stone, 29 Fernshaw Road, London SW10 OT6, England.

HOWCROFT Wilbur Gordon, b. 28 Aug 1917, Kerang, Australia. Wheat & Sheep Farmer. m. Barbara Innes McLennan, 17 Aug 1942. *Publications:* The Bushman Who Laughed, 1982; The Bushman Who Laughed Again, 1983; The Wilbur Howcroft Omnibus, 1985; Bush Characters, 1986; This Side of the Rabbit Proof Fence, 1971; The Clancy That Overflowed, 1971; Bush Ballads & Bulldust, 1982; Hello Cocky, 1982; Sand in the Stew, 1974; Dungarees & Dust, 1978; Bush Ballads & Buffoonery, 1979; Nonsery Rhymes, 1978; The Farm that Blew Away, 1973; Random Ramblings, 1972; Outback Observations, 1970; Black with White Cockatoos, 1977; The Old Working Hat, 1975; The Eucalypt Trail, 1975; Facts, Fables & Foolery, 1973; Aussie Odes, 1988; Billabongs and Billy Tea, 1989; Mopokes and Mallee Roots, 1989. *Contributions to:* Frequent Radio and TV appearances; Professional journals, newspapers and magazines. *Membership:* Australian Society of Authors. *Literary Agent:* Caroline Lurie, Australian Literary Management. *Address:* Po Box 36, Culgoa, 3530 VIC, Australia.

HOWE Doris Kathleen, (Mary Munro, Kaye Stewart), b. United Kingdom. Novelist. *Publications:* This Girl Is Mine, 1978; 46 other novels including some as Mary Munro, and some as Newlyn Nash with Muriel Howe. *Address:* The Garden Flat, Middle Brig How, Skelwith Bridge, Ambleside, Cumbria, England.

HOWE Florence, b. 17 Mar 1929, New York, USA. Writer; Publisher; Educator. *Education:* AB, Hunter College, 1950; AM Smith College, 1951; DHL (hon), New England College, 1977; Honorary Degrees: Skidmore College, 1979; De Pauw University, 1987; State University of New York, College at Old Westbury, 1992. *Appointments include:* Assistant Professor of English, Goucher College, 1960-71; Professor of Humanities and American Studies, SUNY College at Westbury, 1971-87; Professor English City College, CUNY, 1985-; President, The Feminist Press, 1970-; Director, The Feminist Press at CUNY, 1985-. *Publications:* The Conspiracy of the Young, 1970; Seven Years Later: Women's Studies Programs in 1976, 1977; Myths of Coeducation: Selected Essays, 1964-84; Co-editor, No More Masks: An Anthology of Poems by Women, 1973; Editor, Women and the Power to Change, 1975; Co-editor, Women Working: An Anthology of Stories and Poems, 1979; Co-author, Everywoman's Guide to Colleges and Universities, 1982; Co-editor, With Wings: An Anthology of Literature by and about Disabled Women, 1987; Co-editor, Women and Higher Education in American History, 1988; Editor, Tradition and the Talents of Women, 1991; Editor, No More Masks! an Anthology of American Women Poets, Revised & Expanded Second Edition, 1993. *Honours:* Mina Shaughnessy Award Fund for Improvement of Post-Secondary Education, 1982-83; NEH Fellow, 1971-73; Ford Foundation Fellow, 1974-75; Fullbright Fellow, India, 1977; Mellon Fellow, Wellesley College, 1979; US Department of State Grantee, 1983. *Memberships:* Editorial Boards of: Women's Studies: An Interdisciplinary Journal; SIGNS: Women in Cultue and Society, 1974-80; Journal of Education; The Correspondence of Lydia Marie Child, 1977-81; Research in the Humanities. *Address:* 201 E 87th St Apt 11D, New York, NY 10128, USA.

HOWE James b. 2 Aug 1946, Oneida, New York, USA. Writer. m. Betsy Imershein, 5 Apr 1981, 1 daughter. *Education:* BFA, Boston University, 1968; MA, Hunter College, 1977. *Publications:* Bunnicula, 1979; Teddy Bear's Scrapbook, 1980; The Hospital Book, 1981; Howliday Inn, 1982; A Night Without Stars, 1983; The Celery Stalks at Midnight, 1983; Morgan's Zoo, 1984; The Day the Teacher Went Bananas, 1984; What Eric Knew, 1985; Stage Fright, 1986; When You Go to the Kindergarten, 1986; There's A Monster Under My Bed, 1986; Babes in Toyland, 1986; Eat Your Poison, Dear, 1987; Nighty-Nightmare, 1987; I Wish I Were a Butterfly, 1987; The Fright Before Christmas, 1988; Scared Silly, 1989; Hot Fudge, 1990; Dew Drop Dead, 1990; Pinky and Rex, 1990; Pinky and Rex Get Married, 1990; Pinky and Rex and the Spelling Bee, 1991; Pinky and Rex and the Mean Old Witch, 1991; Creepy-Crawly Birthday, 1991; Dances With Wolves: A Story for Children, 1991; Return to Howliday Inn, 1992; Pinky and Rex Go To Camp, 1992; Pinky and Rex and the New Baby, 1993; Rabbit-Cadabra! 1993; Bunnicula Fun Book, 1993. *Contributions to:* Writing for the Hidden Child in The Horn Book Magazine, 1985; School Library Journal; Writing Mysteries for Children - The Horn Book Magazine, 1990. *Honours:* Golden Sower Award, 1981; South Carolina Childrens Book Award, 1981; Dorothy Canfield Fisher Award, 1981; Alabama Young Readers Award, 1981; Iowa Childrens Choice Award, 1982; Sequoya Childrens Book Award, 1982; Young Readers Choice Award, 1982; Land of Enchantment Childrens Book Award, 1982; Nene Award, 1983; Sunshine State Young Readers Award, 1984; Boston Globe-Horn Book Honour Award, 1984; Tennessee Children's Choice Award, 1984; 1992 Flicker Tale Children's Book Award. *Memberships:* Authors Guild; Mystery Writers of America; Poets, Playwrights, Editors, Essayists and Novelists; Society of Childrens Book Writers; Writers Guild of America, East. *Literary Agent:* Amy Berkower, New York, USA. *Address:* Writers House, 21 West 26 Street, New York, NY 10010, USA.

HOWE Tina b. 21 Nov 1937, New York City, USA. Playwright; Professor. m. Norman Levy, 1961, 1 son, 1 daughter. *Education:* BA, Sarah Lawrence College, Bronxville, New York, 1959. *Career:* Adjunct Professor, New York University, 1983-; Visiting Professor, Hunter College, New York, 1990-. *Publications:* Productions: The Nest, (Provincetown, Massachusetts, 1969; New York, 1970); Museum (Los Angeles, 1976; New York, 1977), New York, Samuel French, 1979; The Art of Dining (Washington DC and New York, 1979-80) New York, Samuel French, 1980; Painting Churches (New York, 1983) New York, Samuel French, 1984; Coastal Disturbances (New York, 1986) New York, Samuel French, 1987; Approaching Zanzibar (New York, 1989) New York, Samuel French, 1990; One Shoe Off (New York, 1993), New York, Samuel French, 1993; Books: Coastal Disturbances: Four plays by Tina Howe (includes Museum, The Art of Dining, Painting Churches, Coastal Disturbances), Theatre Communications Group; 1989 Approaching Zanzibar, Theatre Communications Group, 1990. *Honours:* Rosamond Gilder Award, 1983; Rockefeller Grant, 1983; Obie Award, 1983; Outer Critics Circle award 1983, National Endowment for the Arts Grant, 1984; Honorary Degree, Bowdoin College, 1988; Guggenheim Fellow, 1990; Literature Award, American Acadamy of Arts and Letters, 1993; elected to Council of Dramatists Guild. *Literary Agent:* Flora Roberts Inc, 157 West 57th St, New York, NY 10019, USA.

HOWELL Paul Philip, b. 13 Feb 1917, London, England. Administrator, Diplomat, University of Cambridge. m. Bridgit Mary Radcliffe Luard, 10 Nov 1964, 2 sons, 2 daughters. *Education:* MA, PhD, Westminister School, Trinity College, Cambridge, 1935-38; MA, DPhil, Christ Church, Oxford, 1947-50. *Publications:* Nver Law, 1954; Editor: THe Equatorial Nile Project and its effects in the Sudan, 1954, Natural Resources and Development Potential in the Southern Provinces of theSudan, 1955, The Jonglei Canal: Impact and Opportunity, 1988. *Contributions to:* Journals in fields of social antropology and development studies. *Honours:* OBE, 1955; CMG, 1964. *Memberships:* Fellow: Royal Geographical Society, London; Royal Institute of International Affairs, London; Royal Anthropological Institute, London. *Address:* Burfield Hall, Wymondham, Norfolk NR18 9SJ, England.

HOWELL Virginia Tier. *See:* **ELLISON** Virginia Howell.

HOWES Barbara b. 1 May 1914, New York, USA. Poet; Anthologist. m. William Jay Smith, 1 Oct 1947, 2 sons. *Education:* Graduated from Bennington College, 1937. *Publications:* Books of Poetry: The Undersea Farmer, 1948; In the Cold Country, 1954; Light and Dark, 1959; Looking up at Leaves, 1966; The Blue Garden, 1972; A Private Signal: Poems New and Selected, 1977; Moving, 1983. Short stories: The Road Commissioner and Other Stories, 1983; Edited Anthologies: 23 Modern Stories, 1963; From the Green Antilles: writings of the Caribbean, 1966; The Sea-Green Horse, with Gregory Jay Smith, 1970; The Eye of the Heart: stories from Latin America, 1973, paperback 1974. *Contributions to:* Accent; Antaeus; The Atlantic; Berkshire Review; Partisan Review; Poetry; The New York Times; The Southern Review; The Sewanee Review; Stand; The Virginia Quarterly Review; Yale Review and others. *Honours:* Guggenheim Fellowship, 1955; Brandeis University Creative Arts Poetry Grant, 1958; Award in Literature from the National Institute of Arts and Letters, 1971; Golden Rose Award from the New England Poetry Club, 1973; Christopher Award for The Eye of the Heart, 1974; Bennington Award for Outstanding Contributions to Poetry, 1980. *Address:* Brook House, North Pownal, VT 05260, USA.

HOWITH Harry, b. 1934, Canada. Writer. *Appointments:* Ottawa Correspondent, Cooperative Press, Ottawa, 1957-59; Editor, Flight Comment, Royal Canadian Air Force, 1960-62; Research Assistant, Royal Commission on Publications, Ottawa, 1960-61; Editor, Publications Officer, Department of Northern Affairs and National Resources, Ottawa, 1962-64; Publications Officer, North York Board of Education, Toronto, 1964-65; Assistant to Academic Dean, 1970-71, English Master, 1972-73, Centennial College, Toronto. *Publications:* You Bet Your Love, play, 1957; Street Encounter, 1962; Burglar Tools, 1962; Two Longer Poems: The Seasons of Miss Nicky by Harry Howith and Louis Riel by William Hawkins, 1965; Total War, 1967; Fragments of the Dance, 1969; The Stately Homes of Westmount, 1973; Multiple Choices: New and Selected Poems 1961-76, 1976. *Address:* c/o 335 Crichton Street, Ottawa, Ontario, Canada.

HOWLAND Bette, b. 28 Jan 1937, Chicago, Illinois, USA, Writer. 2 sons. *Education:* AB, University of Chicago, 1955. *Appointments:* Visiting Professor, University of Chicago, 1993-; Committee on Social Thought, Literature. *Publications:* W-3, 1974; Blue in Chicago, 1978; Things to Come and Go, 1983; German Lessons, 1993. *Contributions to:* Various newspapers, journals and magazines. *Honours:* Rockefeller Foundation, 1969; Marsden Foundation, 1973; Guggenheim Foundation, 1978; MacArthur Foundation, 1984-89. *Address:* 102 Mulbarger Lane, Bellefonte, PA 16823, USA.

HOWLETT John Reginald, b. 4 Apr 1940, Leeds, England. Author; Scriptwriter. m. Ada Finocchiaro, 10 June 1967, 2 daughters. *Education:* BA, Jesus College, Oxford. *Publications:* James Dean, 1974; Christmas Spy, 1975; Tango November, 1976; Maximum Credible Accident, 1980; Orange, 1982; Murder of a Moderate Man, 1985; Frank Sinatra - Biography. *Literary Agent:* Elaine Green, Alan Brodie. *Address:* Orchard House, Stone-in-Oxney, Tenterden, Kent TN30 7JR, England.

HOY Linda, b. 27 Mar 1946, Sheffield, England. Author. m. Mike Hoy, 4 Apr 1964, 2 sons, 1 daughter. *Education:* Sheffield Polytechnic. *Appointments:* Shop Assistant; Barmaid; Civil Servant; English Teacher; Lecturer. *Publications:* Your Friend Rebecca; The Damned; Kiss; Nightmare Park; Ring Of Death; Emmeling Pankhurst; Poems for Peace; The Alternative Assembly Book; Haddock N Chips. *Memberships:* Society of Authors. *Literary Agent:* Gina Pollinger, 222 Old Brompton Road, London SW5 0B2, England.

HOYLAND Michael (David), b. 1 Apr 1925, Nagpur, CP, India. Retired Art Lecturer; Author. m. Marette Nicol Fraser, 21 July 1948, 2 sons, 2 daughters. *Appointments:* Schoolteacher, 1951-63; Lecturer, 1963-65, Senior Lecturer in Art, 1963-1980, Kesteven College of Education, Stoke Rochford, Lincolnshire. *Publications:* Introduction Three (co-author), 1967; Art for Children, 1970; Variations: An Integrated Approach to Art, 1975; A Love Affair with War, novel, 1981; The Bright Way In, poetry, 1984; 139 poems in journals and a collection; 3 short stories in Introduction 3; 3 other short stories. *Contributions to:* Reviewing for Ore; Jade. *Memberships:* Ex-Chairman, Stamford Writers Group; PEN; Welland Valley Art Society; East Anglian Potters Association. *Address:* Foxfoot House, South Luffenham, Nr Oakham, Rutland, Leicestershire LE15 8NP, England.

HOYLE Fred, b. 1915. Science Fiction/Fantasy, Astronomy, Physicis, Autobiography. *Appointments:* Honorary Fellow, St John's College, Cambridge, 1973- (Fellow 1939-72) and Emmanuel College, Cambridge, 1984-. Lecturer in Mathematics, 1945-58, Plumian Professor of Astronomy and Experimental Philosophy, 1958-72 and Director, Institute of Theoretical Astronomy, 1966-72, Cambridge University; Staff member, Mount Wilson and Palomar Observatories, California, 1956-62; Professor of Astronomy,Royal Institution, London, 1969-72; White Professor, Cornell University, Ithaca, New York, 1972-78. *Publications include:* (with Geoffrey Hoyle) Into Deepest Space, 1976; (with Geoffrey Hoyle) The Incandescent Ones, 1977; Ten Faces of the Universe, 1977; On Stonehenge, 1977; (with N C Wickramasinghe) Lifecloud, 1978; (with Geoffrey Hoyle) The Westminster Disaster, 1978; The Cosmogony of the Solar System, 1978; (with Chandra Wickramasinghe) Diseases from Space, 1979; (with Geoffrey Hoyle) Commonsense in Nuclear Energy, 1979; (with J V Narlikar) The Physics-Astronomy Frontier, 1980; Ice, 1981; (with C Wickramasinghe) Evolution from Space, 1981; (with C Wickramasinghe) Space Travellers: The Bringers of Life, 1981; Facts and Dogmas in Cosmology and Elsewhere (Rede Lecture) 1982; (with Geoffrey Hoyle) The Energy Pirate (for children) 1982; (with Geoffrey Hoyle) The Giants of Universal Park (for children) 1982; (with Geoffrey Hoyle) The Frozen Planet of Aruron (for children) 1982; (with Geoffrey Hoyle) The Planet of death (for children) 1982; The Intelligent Universe: A New View of Creation and Evolution, 1983; Comet Halley (novel) 1985; The Small World of Fred Hoyle (autobiography) 1986; (with N C Wickramasinghe) Life Force, 1987. *Honour:* KT, 1972. *Address:* St John's College, Cambridge, England.

HOYLE Geoffrey, b. 1942, United Kingdom. Author. *Appointments:* Worked in documentary films, 1963-67. *Publications:* Fifth Planet (with Fred Hoyle), 1963; Rockets in Ursa Major (with Fred Hoyle), 1969; Seven Steps to the Sun (with Fred Hoyle), 1970; Molecule Men (with Fred Hoyle), 1971; 2010, 1972; The Inferno (with Fred Hoyle), 1973; Disasters, 1975; Into Deepest Space (with Fred Hoyle), 1976; The Incandescent Ones (with Fred Hoyle), 1977; The Westminster Disasters (with Fred Hoyle), 1978; Commonsense in Nuclear Energy (with Fred Hoyle), 1979; The Energy Pirate (with Fred Hoyle), for children, 1982; The Giants of Universal Park (with Fred Hoyle), for children, 1982; The Frozen Planet of Azuron (with Fred Hoyle), for children, 1982; The Planet of Death (with Fred Hoyle), for children, 1982; Flight, 1984. *Address:* West Wissett, 8 Milner Road, Bournemouth, BH4 8AD, England.

HOYLE Peter, b. 25 Oct 1939, Accrington, Lancashire. Retired Librarian. m. Barbara Croop, 22 Oct 1983, 1 son, 1 daughter. *Education:* Ba English Literature, Liverpool University, 1959-62. *Publications:* The man in the Iron Mask, 1984; Brantwood, 1986. *Contributions to:* Stories in Stand and P N Review. *Honours:* Bursary NW Arts, 1986. *Memberships:* Former Associate of the Library Association. *Address:* 19 Hexham Avenue, Bolton, Lancs BL1 5PP, England.

HOYT Erich, b. 28 Sept 1950, Akron, Ohio, USA.

Writer. m. Sarah Elizabeth Wedden, 4 Mar 1989, 1 son. *Education:* Campion Jesuit High School, Prairie du Chien, Wisconsin, USA, 1964-67; Vannevar Bush Fellow in Science Journalism, Massachusetts Institute of Technology, Cambridge, Massachusetts, USA, 1985-86. *Appointments:* Contributing Editor, Equinox Magazine, Canada, 1982-; Field Correspondent, Defenders Magazine, USA, 1985-; Visiting Lecturer, Massachusetts Institute of Technology, 1986-87, and The Ohio State University, 1992; Consultant for science and botanical museums, 1987-. *Publications:* Orca: The Whale Called Killer, 1981, 2nd edition 1984, 3rd edition 1990; Seasons of the Whale, 1990; The Whale Watcher's Handbook, 1984, German edition 1987; Extinction A-Z, 1991; Meeting the Whales, 1991; Riding with the Dolphins, 1992; Conserving the Wild Relatives of Crops, 1988, French, Chinese, Portuguese and Spanish editions, 1992. *Contributions to:* Anthologies and textbooks; National Geographic; The New York Times; The Globe and Mail (Toronto); Discover; World and over 100 other journals. *Honours:* Francis H Kortright Award, 1st place, Magazines, 1983; Environment Canada Award for Best Magazine Article, 1986; BBC Wildlife Award for Nature Writing, 2nd place for Essay. 1988; James Thurber Writer-in-Residence, Thurber House, 1992. *Memberships:* The Writer's Guild; American Society of Journalists and Authors; International Science Writers Association; National Association of Science Writers; Outdoor Writers of Canada; Society for Marine Mammalogy. *Address:* 29 Dirleton Avenue, No.11, North Berwick EH39 4BE, Scotland.

HRUSKA Elias N, b. 7 July 1943, San Francisco, USA. Financial Planner; Writer; Translator. m. 29 Jan 1966, 1 son, 2 daughters. *Education:* AB, 1966; MA, 1968. *Appointment:* Translation Coordinator for Estuary Press, 1989. *Publications:* This Side & Other Things, 1974; Cantos y la Luna, 1975; For Neruda, For Chile, 1975. *Contributions to:* Various journals and magazines. *Honours:* Honorable Mention, Phelan Awards Competition for Poetry. *Membership:* Poets & Writers Inc. *Address:* 51 University Avenue, Suite G, Los Gatos, CA 95030, USA.

HSIA Hsiao. *See:* **LIU Wu Chi.**

HSU Kenneth Jinghwa, b. 28 June 1929, Nanking, China. m. Christine Eugster, 15 Sept 1966, 3 sons, 1 daughter. *Education:* BSc, National Nanking University, 1948; MA Ohio State University, 1950; PhD, UCLA, 1953. *Publications:* The Great Dying, 1986; The Mediterranean was a desert, 1984; Ein Schieff revolutioniert die Wissenschaft, 1982. *Honours:* Wollaston medal, Geological Society of London, 1984; Foreign Associate, US National Academy. *Memberships:* Pres, International Association of Sendimentologists, 1978-83. *Address:* Frohburgstrasse 96, 8006 Zurich, Switzerland.

HUBLER Richard G(ibson), b. 1912, American. *Appointments:* Public Relations Consultant, NYC and Los Angeles, 1938-60; Associate Book Reviewer, Los Angeles Times, CA, 1960-; Former Teacher, Ventura College, University of California at Santa Barbara, and Assistant to President, San Fernando Valley State College, Los Angeles (now California State University, San Francisco), 1964. *Publications:* Lou Gehrig, 1941; I Flew for China (with R Leonard), 1942; Flying Leathernecks (with J DeChant), 1944; I've Got Mine, 1945; The Quiet Kingdom, 1948; The Brass God, The Chase, 1952; In Darkest Childhood, 1954; The Pass, 1955; Man in the Sky, 1956; SAC: Strategic Air Command, 1958; St Louis Woman (with H Traubel), The Shattering of the Image, True Love True Love, 1959; Big Eight, 1960; Straight Up: History of the Helicopter, The Blue-and-Gold Man, The World's Shortest Stories (ed), 1961; Trial and Triumph (with L Morrison), Where's the Rest of Me (with Ronald Reagan), The Cole Porter Story, 1965; South of the Moon, Soldier and Sage, The Christianis, 1966; Wheeler, 3 volumes, 1967; In All His Glory, 1968; The Earthmaker Drinks Blood, 1975. *Address:* Box 793, Ojai, CA 93023, USA.

HUDDLE David, b. 1942, Ivanhoe, Virginia, USA. m. Lindsey M Huddle, 2 daughters. *Education:* BA Foreign Affairs, University of Virginia, 1968; MA English, Hollins College, 1969; MFA Writing, Columbia University, 1971. *Appointments include:* Faculty: Warren Wilson College MFA Programme for Writers, 1981-85, Goddard College, 1980, Bread Loaf School of English, 1979, 1975-; Professor of English, University of Vermont, 1982-. *Publications:* A Dream with no Stump Roots in it, 1975; Paper Boy, 1979; Only the Little Bone, 1986; Stopping by Home, 1988; The High Spirits, 1992; The Writing Habit: Essays on Writing, 1992; The Nature of Yearning, 1992; Intimates, 1993. *Contributions to:* Esquire, Harper's, The New York Times Book Review; Kentucky Poetry Review; Texas Quarterly; Poetry; Shenandoah; American Poetry Review. *Honours include:* Honorary Doctorate of Humanities, Shenandoah College and Conservatory, Virginia, 1989; Bread Loaf School of English Commencement Speaker, 1989; Rober Frost Professor of American Literature, 1991. *Address:* Department of English, University of Vermont, Burlington, VT 05405, USA.

HUDSON Christopher, b. 29 Sept 1946, England. Writer. m. Kirsty McLeod, 10 Mar 1978, 1 son. *Education:* Scholar, Jesus College, Cambridge. *Appointments:* Editor, Faber & Faber, 1968; Literary Editor, The Spectator, 1971, The Standard, 1981. *Publications:* Overlord, 1975; The Final Act, 1980; Insider Out, 1982; The Killing Fields, 1984; Colombo Heat, 1986; Playing in the Sand, 1989. *Agent:* Gill Coleridge. *Address:* 64 Westbourne Park Road, London W2, England.

HUDSON Helen. *See:* **LANE Helen.**

HUDSON Jan. *See:* **SMITH George H.**

HUDSON Jeffrey. *See:* **CRICHTON Michael.**

HUDSON Liam, b. 30 July 1933, London, England. Visiting Professor, Tavistock Clonic, London. m. Bernadine Jacot de Boinod, 2 July 1965, 3 sons, 1 daughter. *Education:* MA, Exeter College, Oxford, 1954-57; PhD, Psychological Laboratory, Cambridge University, 1957-61. *Publications:* Contrary Imaginations, 1966; Frames of Mind, 1968; The Ecology of Human Intelligence, (Editor), 1970; The Cult of the Fact, 1972; Human Beings, 1975; The Nympholepts, 1978; Bodies of Knowledge, 1982; Night Life, 1985; The Way Men Think, 1991. *Contributor to:* Times Literary Supplement. *Membership:* British Psychological Society. *Address:* Balas Copartnership, 34 North Park, Gerrards Cross, Buckinghamshire, England.

HUDSON Mark Marshall, b. 29 Mar 1957, Harrogate, Yorks, England. *Education:* Penarth Grammar School, 1968-72; Esher Grammar School, 1972-75; Chelsea School of Art, 1975-76; Winchester School of Art, 1976-79. *Publications:* Our Grandmothers' Drums, 1989. *Contributions to:* Daily Telegraph; Elle; World Beat; City Limits; Folk Roots. *Honours:* Thomas Cook Award, 1990; Somerset Maugham Award, 1990. *Memberships:* London Screenwriters Workshop, Chairman, 1983-85; Society of Authors. *Literary Agent:* Rogers, Coleridge & White. *Address:* c/o Rogers Coleridge & White, 20 Powis Mews, London W11 1JN, England.

HUDSON Miles Matthew Lee, b. 17 Aug 1925. Farmer. m. 17 May 1956, 3 sons, 1 daughter. *Education:* Sherbourne School, 1939-43; MA, Trinity College, Oxford, 1947-49. *Publications:* Triumph or Tragedy - Rhodesia to Zimbabwe. *Contributions to:* Journals concerned with foreign affairs. *Address:* The Priors Farm, Mattingley, Basingstoke, Hants, England.

HUELSMANN Carl Herman, b. 25 Nov 14, Amsterdam, Holland. Economist. m. (1) Erika Sprongel, 27 Dec 1939, dec 1982; 1 son, 3 daughters, (2) Irene

Haeck, 8 Oct 1984. *Education:* BA, School of Economics, 1938. *Publications:* Awakening of Consciousness, 1982; Bewusstwerdung, 1980. Many pamphlets in Dutch and German. *Literary Agent:* Hunter House Inc, Publishers, POB 1302 Claremont, CA 91711, USA; Servire, Cothen 3945 PG, Netherlands. *Address:* Lorentzweg 31, 1402 CB Bussum, Netherlands.

HUFANA Alejandrino G, b. 1926, Filipino. *Appointments:* Research Assistant in Social Science 1954-56, joined English Department 1956, Principal Researcher in Iloko Literature 1972-, Professor of English and Comparative Literature 1975-, University of Philippines; Co-Founding Editor, Signatures magazine, 1955, Comment magazine, 1956-67, Heritage magazine, 1967- 68 and University College (later General Education Journal), 1961-72; Editor, Panorama magazine, 1959-61; Managing Editor, University of the Philippines Press, 1965-66; Director of the Library 1970-, and Editor, Pamana magazine, 1971-, Cultural Centre of the Philippines, Manila. *Publications:* 13 Kalisud, 1955; Man in the Moon, 1956, 1972; Sickle Season: Poems of a First Decade 1948-58, 1959; Poro Point: An Anthology of Lives: Poems 1955-1960, 1961; Mena Pecson Crisologo and Iloko Drama, 1963; Curtain-Raisers: First Five Plays, 1964; Aspects of Philippine Literature (ed), 1967; A Philippine Cultural Miscellany (ed), parts I and II, 1970; The Wife of Lot and Other New Poems, The Unicorn, Salidomay, 1971; Notes on Poetry, 1973; Sieg Heil: An Epic on the Third Reich, I R Marcos: A Tonal Epic, 1975; Obligations: Poems on Cheers of Conscience, 1976; Philippine Writing: Poems, Stories and Essays (ed), 1977. *Address:* English Department, University of the Philippines, Diliman, Quezon City, Philippines.

HUFF Barbara A, b. 2 July 1929, Los Angeles, California, USA. Writer; Editor. *Education:* Marlborough School, Los Angeles; BA, University of California. *Publications:* Welcome Aboard - Travelling on an Ocean Liner, 1987; Greening the City Streets, 1990; Once Inside the Library, 1990. *Contributions to:* New York Times Travel Section; School Library Journal. *Memberships:* MENSA; Society of Children's Book Writers; Community Garden Association; Ocean Liner Museum; Steamship Historical Society. *Address:* One Christopher Street, New York, NY 10014, USA.

HUFF Robert, b. 3 Apr 1924, Evanston, Illinois, USA. Professor of English; Poet. 1 son, 2 daughters. *Education:* AB, English Literature, with distinction, 1949, AM Humanities, 1952, Wayne State University. *Literary Appointments:* Instructor of Composition: University of Oregon, Fresno State College, Oregon State University; Poet-in- Residence, University of Delaware, 1960-64; Associate Professor, Modern Poetry, Humanities etc. Western Washington State College, 1964-66; Writer-in-Residence, University of Arkansas, 1966-67; Professor, Modern Poetry, Humanities, Introductory Literature and The Writing of Poetry, Western Washington University, 1967-. *Publications:* Colonel Johnson's Ride, 1959; The Course, 1966; The Ventriloquist, 1977; Shore Guide to Flocking Names, 1985; Numerous poems recorded. Books in progress: Taking Her Sides on Immortality; Beginning in Winter. *Contributions to:* Numerous magazines, journals and newspapers, also anthologies. *Honours include:* Robert Huff Manuscript Collections at University of Kentucky, Wayne State University and Carnegie Library, Syracuse University; Student Fellowship, School of Letters, Indiana University, 1957; Writing Scholarship, Bread Loaf Writers Conference, 1961; Writing Fellowship, The MacDowell Colony, 1963; several other honours and awards. *Memberships include:* Northwest Poetry Circuit, Member, Selection Committee. *Address:* Department of English, Western Washington University, Bellingham, WA 98225, USA.

HUGGAN Jean Isabel, b. 21 Sept 1943, Canada. Writer; Teacher. m. Robert David Huggan, 31 Dec 1970, 1 daughter. *Education:* BA Hons English and Philosophy, University of Western Ontario, 1965. *Publications:* The Elizabeth Stories, 1984; You Never Know, 1993.

Honours: New Voices Award, Quality Paperback Book of the Month, 1987; Best Fiction Denver Quarterly Award, 1987. *Memberships:* PEN University, Canadian Centre; Writers' Union of Canada; Authors' Guild, USA.

HUGGETT Frank Edward, b. 1924, British. *Appointments:* Sub-Editor, Daily Telegraph, 1951-53; Editor, Look and Listen, 1956-57; Visiting Lecturer, Polytechnic of Central London, 1957-65 and Ministry of Defence, 1965-72. *Publications:* South of Lisbon, 1960; Farming, 1963, 3rd edition, 1975; The Newspapers, 1969, 1972; Modern Belgium, 1969; A Short History of Farming, 1970; Nineteenth Century Reformers, How It Happened, 1971; Nineteenth Century Statesman, Travel and Communications, A Day in the Life of a Victorian Farm Worker, The Modern Netherlands, 1972; The Battle for Reform 1815-32, A Day in the Life of a Victorian Factory Worker, Factory Life and Work, 1973; The Dutch Today, 2nd edition, 1974; History Not So Long Ago, 1974- 75; A Dictionary of British History 1815-1973, The Land Question and European Society, Life and Work at Sea, Slavery and the Slave Trade, 1975; Life Below Stairs, 1977; Victorian England as Seen by Punch, 1978; Goodnight Sweetheart, Carriages at Eight, 1979; Cartoonists at War, 1981; The Dutch Connection, 1982; Teachers, 1986.

HUGGETT Joyce, b. 16 Sept 1937, Exeter, England. Teacher. m. David John Huggett, 16 July 1960, 1 son, 1 daughter. *Appointments:* Teacher of the Deaf, Nutfield Priory School, Redhill, 1960-62; Peripatetic Teacher of the Deaf, Health Centre, Croydon 1963-65, Cambridge 1971-73; Director of Pastoral Care and Counselor, St Nicholas Church, Nottingham, 1973-; Regular Broadcaster on television and radio in England. *Publications:* Two Into One: Relating in Christian Marriage, 1981; Growing Into Love; We Believe in Marriage (Editor), 1982; Growing Into Freedom, 1984, (Living Free, 1986); Conflict: Friend or Foe? 1984, (Creative Conflict, 1984); Just Good Friends, 1985, (Dating, Sex and Friendship, 1985); The Joy of Listening to God, 1986; Approaching Easter; Marriage on the Mend; Approaching Christmas, 1987; Listening to Others; Life in a Sex-Mad Society, 1988; Writer of Scripture Notes; Open to God, 1989; The Smile of Love; Scripture notes for Scripture Union and Bible Reading Fellowship. *Contributions to:* Magazines and newspapers including, Decision; Christian Family; Today; Home and Family. *Address:* 18 Lenton Road, The Park, Nottingham NG7 1DU, England.

HUGHES Brenda. *See:* **COLLOMS Brenda.**

HUGHES Chip. *See:* **HUGHES Robert Saunders Jr.**

HUGHES Colin Anfield, b. 4 May 1930, Bahamas. Professor of Political Science. m. Gwen Glover, 6 Aug 1955, 1 son. *Education:* BA, 1949; MA, 1950, Columbia; PhD, London School of Economics, 1952. *Publications:* Readings in Australian Government, 1968; Images and Issues, 1969; Mr Prime Minister, 1976; The Government of Queensland, 1980; Race and Politics in the Bahamas, 1981; Handbook of Australian Government and Politics, 1975-84. *Address:* Department of Government, University of Queensland, St. Lucia 4072, Australia.

HUGHES David (John), b. 1930, British. *Appointments:* Assistant Editor, London Magazine, 1953-54; Editor, Town magazine, 1960-61; Film Writer in Sweden, 1961-68; lived in France, 1970-74; Editor, New Fiction Society, 1975-77, 1981-82; Film Critic, Sunday Times Newspaper, 1982-83. *Publications:* A Feeling in the Air (in US as Man Off Beat), 1957; J B Priestley: An Informal Study of His Work, 1958; Sealed with a Loving Kiss, 1959; The Horsehair Sofa, 1961; The Major, The Road to Stockholm and Lapland, 1964; The Cat's Tale (with Mai Zetterling), 1965; The Seven Ages of England, 1966; Flickorna, The Man Who Invented Tomorrow, 1968; The Rosewater Revolution:

Notes on a Change of Attitude, 1971; Memories of Dying, 1976; Evergreens (ed), 1977; A Genoese Fancy, 1979; The Imperial German Dinner Service, 1983; The Pork Butcher, 1984; But for Bunter, Winter's Tales 1 (ed), 1985; The Stories of Ernest Hemingway (ed), 1986. *Address:* C/o Anthony Sheil Associates, 43 Doughty Street, London WC1N 2LF, England.

HUGHES Elizabeth. *See:* **ZACHARY Hugh.**

HUGHES Glyn, b. 25 May 1935. Author. m. Jane Mackay, 5 Mar 1990. 1 son. *Education:* College of Art, Manchester, 1952-56; ATD (art teacher qualification), 1959. *Appointments:* Teaching, Lancashire and Yorkshire, 1956-72; Arts Council Fellow, Bishop Grosseteste College, Lincoln, 1979-81; Southern Arts Writer-in-Residence, Farnborough, Hampshire, 1982-84; Arts Council Writer-in-Residence, D H Lawrence Centenary Festival, Eastwood, Nottinghamshire, 1985. *Publications:* Novels: Where I Used To Play On The Green, 1982; The Hawthorn Goddess, 1984; The Rape Of The Rose, 1987; The Antique Collector, 1990; Roth, 1992; Autobiography: Fair Prospects, 1976; Millstone Grit, 1975, Revised Editions, 1985, 1987; Verse: Neighbours, 1970; Rest The Poor Struggler, 1972; Best of Neighbours (Selected Poems), 1979; Editor, Samuel Laycock, Selected Poems, 1981; Plays; Mary Hepton's Heaven, 1984; Oldham Coliseum; Various plays for BBC Schools Broadcasts on TV & Radio. *Honours:* Welsh Arts Council Poets Prize, 1970; Guardian Fiction Prize, 1982; David Higham Fiction Prize, 1982. *Literary Agents:* Shiel Land, 43 Doughty Street, London WC1N 2LF, England; Sanford Greenburger, New York, USA. *Address:* Mor's House, 1 Mill Bank Road, Mill Bank, Sowerby Bridge, W Yorks HX6 3DY, England.

HUGHES H Stuart, b. 7 May 1916, New York, New York, USA, Historian. m. Judith Markham, 26 Mar 1964, 2 sons, 1 daughter. *Education:* BA, Amherst College, 1937; MA, 1938, PhD, 1940, Harvard University. *Publications:* Consciousness and Society, 1958; History as Art and as Science, 1964; The Obstructed Path, 1968; The Sea Change, 1975; Prisoners of Hope, 1983; Sophisticated rebels, 1988; Gentleman Rebel, 1990; A Essay for Our Times, 1950; Oswald Spengler, 1952; The US and Italy, 1953; Contemporary Europe, 1961; An Approach to Peace, 1962. *Contributions to:* Commentary; The American Scholar; New York Review of Books; Times Literary Supplement; American Historical Review; Revista Storica Italiana. *Memberships:* American Academy of Arts and sciences; Accademia Nazionale dei Lincei, Rome; American Historical Association. *Address:* 8531 Avenida de las Ondas, La Jolla, CA 92037, USA.

HUGHES Jon Christopher, b. 30 Jan 1945, Elkhart, Indiana, USA. Professor of English. m. Susan Elaine Zavodny, 15 Jan 1968, 1 son, 1 daughter. *Education:* BS, Social Sciences, 1967; MA, Journalism, 1972. *Appointments:* Writing Programme Director, Department of English, University of Cincinnati; Journalism Programme Co-ordinator, 1975-; President, Radio Repertory Company, 1988-; Executive Producer, Dimension Radio Thearer, 1988-90. *Publications include:* The Tanyard Murder, 1982; Ye Giglampz, 1983; The Jolly Book, 1984; Period of the Gruesome, 1990; Dismal Man, 1990; numerous radio plays, screenplays. *Contributions to:* North American Union List of Victorian Serials; American humour magazines and comic papers; over 200 articles to journals, newspapers; Editor, Lafcadio Hearn Journal. *Honours:* Award of Distinction, American Association of Museums, 1984; OBIE, 1989 and 1990. *Memberships:* National Writers Union; American Association of University Professors; President, Lafcadio Hearn Society, USA. *Address:* 3440 Bishop, Cincinnati, OH 45220, USA.

HUGHES Matilda. *See:* **MacLEOD Charlotte.**

HUGHES Monica, b. 3 Nov 1925, Liverpool, England. Writer. m. Glen Hughes, 22 Apr 1957, 2 sons, 2 daughters. *Publications:* The Keeper of the Isis Light, 1980; Hunter in the Dark, 1982; Ring-Rise, Ring-Set, 1982; Crisis on Conshelf Ten, 1975; Invitation to the Game, 1990; The Crystal Drop, 1992. *Contributions to:* Short Stories in: Take your Knee off my Heart, 1990; Mother's Day, 1992; Owl Summer Fun; Articles: Creating Books for Children; Perception of Society through Children's Literature; Writing Science Fiction and Fantasy; My Search for Somewhere; What is a Child, After All?: Behind the Mask. *Honours:* Alberta Culture Juvenile Novel Award, 1981; Canada Council Prize for Children's Literature, 1981, 1982; R Ross Annett Award, 1982, 1983, 1986; Canadian Library Association Young Adult Book Award, 1983; Silver Feather Award, 1986; Boeken Leeuw, 1987. *Memberships:* PEN; IBBY. *Address:* 13816-110A Avenue, Edmonton, BA, Canada T5M 2M9.

HUGHES R S. *See:* **HUGHES Robert Saunders Jr.**

HUGHES Robert Saunders Jr, (Chip Hughes, R S Hughes), b. 19 Sept 1948. Professor; Writer. m. Charlene S Avallone, 25 May 1987, 1 son. *Education:* BA, California Western University, 1970; MA, California State University, 1976; PhD, Indiana University, 1981. *Publications:* Beyond the Red Pony, 1987; John Steinbeck: Study of the Short Fiction, 1989. *Contributions to:* Harvard Library Bulletin; Biography; Western American Literature; Steinbeck Quarterly. *Memberships:* Steinbeck Society International; Modern Language Association. *Address:* English Department, University of Hawaii, Honolulu, HI 96822, USA.

HUGHES Shirley, b. 1927, United Kingdom. Children's Fiction Writer and Illustrator. *Appointments:* Public Lending Right Registrars Advisory Committee, 1984-88; Library & Information Services Council, 1989-92. *Publications:* Lucy and Tom series, 6 vols, 1960-87; The Trouble with Jack, 1970; Sally's Secret, 1973; Helpers, 1975; It's Too Frightening for Me, 1977; Dogger, 1977; Moving Molly, 1978; Up and Up, 1979; Here Comes Charlie Moon, 1980; Alfie Gets in First, 1981; Alfie's Feet, 1982; Charlie Moon and the Big Bonanza Bust-Up, 1982; Alfie Gives a Hand, 1983; An Evening at Alfie's, 1984; The Nursery Collection, 6 vols, 1985-86; Another Helping of Chips, 1986; Tales of Trotter Street, 4 vols, 1988-90; The Big Alfie and Annie Rose Story Book, 1988; Out and About, 1989; The Big Alfie Out of Doors Story Book, 1992. *Honours:* Kate Greenaway Medal for Dogger, 1977; Eleanor Farjeon Award for Services to Children's Literature, 1984. *Membership:* Society of Authors, Committee of Management, 1983-86.

HUGHES Ted, b. 1930, British, Children's fiction, Plays/Screenplays, Poetry, Literature. Editor, Modern Poetry in Translation magazine, London, 1965-; Poet Laureate, 1984. *Publications include:* Sean, The Fool, The Devil and the Cats (play) 1971; Orghast (play) 1971; (ed) A Choice of Emily Dickinson's Verse, 1971; (ed) A Choice of Shakespeare's Verse (in US as Poems: With Fairest Flowers While Summer Lasts: Poems from Shakespeare) 1971; (ed) Selected Poems by Yehuda Amichai, 1971; (ed) Crossing the Water by Sylvia Plath (in US as Crossing the Water, Transitional Poems) 1971; Eat Crow (poetry) 1972; Selected Poems 1957-67, 1972; In the Little Girl's Angel Gaze (poetry) 1972; The Iron Man (play) 1972; The Story of Vasco (play) 1974; Season Songs, 1975; Cave Birds (poetry) 1975; Earth-Moon: Poems, 1976; Gaudete, 1977; Moon-Bells (for children) 1978; Sunstruck, 1977; Chiasmadon, 1977; Moortown Elegies, 1978; A Solstice, 1978; Orts, 1978; Adam and the Sacred Nine, 1979; Moortown, 1979; Remains of Elmet, 1979; Henry Williamson, 1979; (ed) Collected Poems, by Sylvia Plath, 1981; Under the North Star (verse for children) 1981; Selected Poems, 1957-1981 (in US as New Selected Poems) 1982; (ed with Frances McCullough) The Journals of Sylvia Plath, 1985; (ed with Seamus Heaney) The Rattle Bag: An Anthology, 1982; (ed verse; photographs by Peter Keen) 1983; What Is The Truth? (verse for children) 1984; (ed) Selected Poems, by Sylvia Plath 1985; Flowers and Insects (poetry) 1986; Wolfwatching, 1989, (poetry);

Moortown Diary, 1989; The Cat and the Cuckoo, 1991; Rain-Charm for the Dutchy, 1992. *Honour:* OBE, 1977; Signal Award, verse for children, 1978, 1981; Guardian Children's Fiction Award, 1985. *Address:* c/o Faber & Faber Ltd, 3 Queen Square, London WC1N 3AU, England.

HUGHES Thomas Alan, b. 1 Jan 1939, Toronto, Canada. Professor. m. Mary Elizabeth Welsman, 8 Aug 1990, 1 son, 5 daughters. *Education:* BA, 1960, MA, 1963, University of Toronto; PhD, University of Birmingham, 1972. *Publications:* Henry Irving, Shakespearean; Three Plays. *Contributions to:* Theatre Notebook; 19th Century Theatre Research; Theatre History in Canada; Modern Drama; Educational Theatre Journal; Shakespearean Criticism; Theatre Survey; BC Studies. *Address:* Department of Theatre, University of Victoria, PO Box 1700, Victoria, BC, Canada V8W 2YZ.

HUHNE Christopher Murray Paul, b. 2 July 1954, London, England. Journalist. m. Vasiliki Courmouzis, 19 May 1984, 1 son, 1 daughter. *Education:* BA Hons, Politics Philosophy Economics, Oxford University, 1975; Certificat en largue et civilisation francaise, University de la Sorbonne, Paris, 1972. *Publications:* The ECU Report, 1991; Real World Economics, 1990; Debt and Danger, 1985, 1987. *Contributions to:* New Statesman; Spectator; Political Quarterly; London Review of Books. *Honours:* Wincolt Award for financial journalism, 1990; Wincolt Award, 1981. *Memberships:* Royal Economics Society. *Literary Agent:* Michael Sissons, Peters Laser & Dunlop. *Address:* 8 Crescent Grove, London SW4 7AH, England.

HULL Eleanor, b. 1913, USA. Author. *Publications:* Tumbleweed Boy, 1949; The Third Wish, 1950; Papi, 1953; The Turquoise Horse, 1955; Suddenly the Sun, 1957; In the Time of the Condor, 1961; The Sling and the Swallow, 1963; Through the Secret Door, 1963; Everybody's Somebody, 1964; Noncho and the Dukes, 1964; The Church Not Made with Hands, 1965; A Trainful of Strangers, 1969; The Second Heart, 1973; Women Who Carried the Good News, 1975; Alice with Golden Hair, 1981; Baptist Life and Thought 1600-1980 (contributing editor), 1983; The Summer People, 1984. *Address:* c/o Macmillan, 866 Third Avenue, New York, NY 10022, USA.

HULME Keri, b. 9 Mar 1947, Christchurch, New Zealand. Writer; Fisher; Dreamer. *Appointments:* New Zealand State Literary Fund Advisory Committee, 1985; Literature Committee, Arts Council, 1986-89. *Publications:* The Bone People, 1984; Te-Kaihau - The Windeater, 1986; BAIT, 1993; The Silences Between, 1982; Lost Possessions, 1986; Homeplaces, 1989; Strands. *Contributions to:* Many and varied. *Honours:* NZ Writing Bursary, 1983; New Zealand Book of the year, 1984; Mobil Pegasus Prize for Maori Literature, 1984; Booker McConnell Award, 1985; The Special 1990 Scholarship in Letters. *Memberships:* Nga Puna Waihanga (Maori Artists' and Writers' Organization; New Zealand PEN. *Address:* Okarito Private Bag, Hokitika PO, Westland, New Zealand.

HULSE Michael William, b. 12 June 1955, Stoke-on-Trent, England. Freelance Translator; Critic; Poet. *Education:* MA, 1st Class, Honours, German, University of St Andrews, 1977. *Appointments:* English Editor, Benedikt Taschen Verlag, Cologne, West Germany, 1988. *Publications:* Monochrome Blood, 1980; Dole Queue, 1981; Knowing and Forgetting, 1981; Propaganda, 1985; Translations of German Literature for: Carcanet, Penguin, Farrar Straus & Giroux, Anvil Press, Macmillan. *Contributions to:* About 200 essays and reviews in literary publications in Britain, Canada, Australia, and West Germany. *Honours:* 1st Prize, National Poetry Competition, 1979; Eric Gregory Award, Society of Authors, 1980; 3rd Prize, Tate Gallery Poetry Competition, 1985; 2nd Prize, Times Literary Supplement/Cheltenham Literature Festival Poetry Competition, 1987. *Address:* c/o Secker & Warburg Ltd., 54 Poland Street, London W1V 3DF, England.

HUME (Alexander) Brit(ton), b. 22 June 1943, WA, USA. Reporter; Author. m. Clare Jacobs Stoner, 10 Feb 1965, 2 sons, 1 daughter. *Education:* BA, University of Virginia, 1965. *Appointments:* Reporter, Hartford Times, Hartford, CT, 1965-66; Reporter, United Press International, WA, 1967; Reporter, Evening Sun, Baltimore, MD, 1968; Freelance Reporter, 1969; Investigative Reporter for Jack Anderson's syndicated column, Washington Merry Go Round, 1970-72; Editor, More Magazine, 1973-75; Consultant to the ABC News Closeup documentary series 1973-79, General Correspondent 1976-77, Principal Correspondent to the US House of Representatives 1977-80, Chief Senate Correspondent, 1981-, Anchor of World News Tonight-The Weekend Report 1985-, Author (with T R Reid) of column The Computer Report distributed by the Washington Post Writers Group Syndicate, American Broadcasting Company Incorporated, WA; Host of Brit Hume: On Line, a weekly radio commentary on computers for ABC News. *Publications:* Death and the Mines: Rebellion and Murder in the United Mine Workers, 1971; Inside Story, 1974; Co-author and Narrator of Documentaries for ABC News Close-Up including Arson: Fire for Hire, 1978; The Killing Ground, Nobody's Children, Battleground Washington: The Politics of Pressure, 1979; St Alban's: An Illustrated History of St Alban's School, 1981. *Contributions to:* Articles Periodicals including New York Times Magazine; Harper's; Atlantic Monthly; New Republic. *Honour:* Fellow, Washington Journalism Center, 1969. *Membership:* Radio-Television Correspondents Association. *Address:* 5409 Blackistone Road, Bethesda, MD 20816, USA.

HUME George Haliburton (Basil Hume), b. 2 Mar 1923, Newcastle upon Tyne, England. *Education:* MA, St Benet's Hall, Oxford, 1947; STL, University of Fribourg, 1951; Honorary Degree, University of Surrey, 1992; honorary Doctorate of Law Degree, Newcastle Upon Tyne Polytechnic, 1992. *Appointments:* Entered Ordo Sancti Benedicti (Order of St Benedict, Benedictines, OSB), 1941, made the vows of a monk, 1945, ordained Roman Catholic Priest, 1950; Assistant Priest, Village Church, Teacher, Monastery's Secondary School for Boys 1950-63, Rugby Coach 1951-63, Head of Modern Languages Department 1952-63, Abbot 1963-76, Ampleforth Abbey, Ampleforth; Archbishop of Westminster, London, 1976-, Created Cardinal, 1976; Delegate to General Chapter of English Benedictine Congregation, 1957, Elected Magister Scholarum, 1957, 1961; Chairman of Benedictine Ecumenical Commission, 1972-76; President of Bishops' Conference of England and Wales, 1979-; President of Council of European Episcopal Conferences, 1978-87; Member of Vatican Secretariat for Christian Unity and Council of Synod on the Family; Member of Sacred Congregation for Religious and Secular Institutes, Pontifical Commission for the Revision of the Canon Law, and Joint Commission of the Holy See and Orthodox Church to promote theological discussion between the churches, 1980-; Vice-President of Council of Christians and Jews; President of Catholic Institute for International Relations and European Committee of Bishops' Conferences, 1979-87; Co-founder of Benedictine Monastery in St Louis, MO; Guest on television and radio programs. *Publications:* Searching for God, 1977; In Praise of Benedict, 1981; To Be a Pilgrim: A Spiritual Notebook, 1984; Towards A Civilisation of Love, 1988; Light in the Lord, 1991. *Contributions to:* British Periodicals. *Honours:* Honorary Degrees include DD from University of Newcastle upon Tyne and Cambridge University, 1979, University of London, 1980, Oxford University 1981, University of York 1982, University of Durham and Benedictine International Athenaeum of St Anselm, Rome, 1987, Hull, 1989, DHL, Manhattan College and Catholic University of America, 1980; Honorary Bencher of Inner Temple, 1976; Honarary Freeman of London and Newcastle upon Tyne, 1980. *Address:* Archbishop's House, Ambrosden Avenue, Westminster, London SW1P 1QJ, England.

HUME John Robert, b. 1939, British. *Appointments:* Lecturer 1964-82, Senior Lecturer in History, University of Strathclyde, Glasgow, 1982-; Chairman, Scottish Railway Preservation Society, 1966-75; Treasurer 1968-71, Editor 1971-79, Scottish Society for Industrial Archaeology; Member, Inland Waterways Amenity Advisory Council, 1974-; Director, Scottish Industrial Archaeology Survey, 1978-85; Seconded to Historic Scotland as Principal Inspector of Ancient Monuments, 1984-91; Principal Inspector of Historic Buildings, Historic Scotland, 1991-. *Publications:* Industrial History in Pictures: Scotland (with J Butt and L L Donnachie), 1968; The Industrial Archaeology of Glasgow, 1974; Glasgow As It Was (with Michael Moss), 3 volumes, 1975-76; A Plumber's Pastime (photographs) (with Michael Moss), 1975; The Industrial Archaeology of Scotland: The Lowlands and the Borders, 1976; The Workshop of the British Empire (with Michael Moss), The Industrial Archaeology of Scotland: The Highlands and the Islands, 1977; Beardmore: History of a Scottish Industrial Giant (with Michael Moss), 1979; the Making of Scotch Whisky (with Michael Moss), 1981; A Bed of Nails (with Michael Moss), 1983; Scottish Windmills (with G Douglas and M Oglethorpe), 1984; Scottish Brickmarks (with others), 1985; Shipbuilders to the World: A History of Harland Wolff, Belfast (with Michael Moss), 1986; Various Guidebooks to Historic Scotland Monuments in Cars. *Honour:* André Simon Prize for the Best Book on Drink, 1981. *Memberships:* Fellow, Society of Antiquaries; Fellow, Society of Antiquaries of Scotland. *Address:* Historic Scotland, 20 Brandon Stree, Edinburgh EH3 5KA, Scotland.

HUMPHREYS Emyr Owen, b. 15 Apr 1919. Author. m. Elinor Myfanwy, 1946, 3 sons, 1 daughter. *Education:* University College, Aberystwyth; University College, Bangor; Gregynog Arts Fellow, 1974-75. *Publications:* The Little Kingdom, 1946; The Voice of a Stranger, 1949; A Change of Heart, 1951; Hear and Forgive, 1952; A Man's Estate, 1955; The Italian Wife, 1957; Y Tri Llais, 1958; A Toy Epic, 1958; The Gift, 1963; Outside the House of Baal, 1965; Natives, 1968; Ancestor Worship, 1970; National Winner, 1971; Flesh and Blood, 1974; Landscapes, 1976; The Best of Friends, 1978; Penguin Modern Poets, No. 27, 1978; the Kingdom of Bran, 1979; The Anchor Tree, 1980; Pwyll a Riannon, 1980; Miscellany Two, 1981; The Taliesin Tradition, 1983; Jones : A Novel, 1984; Salt of the Earth, 1985; An Absolute Hero, 1986; Open Secrets, 1988; The Triple Net, 1988; Bonds of Attachment, 1990; Outside Time, 1991. *Honours:* Somerset Maugham Award, 1953; Hawthornden Prize, 1959; Society of Authors Travel Award, 1978; Welsh Arts Council Prize, 1983. *Literary Agent:* Richard Scott Simon. *Address:* Llinon, Penyberth, Llanfairpwll, Ynys Mon, Gwynedd LL61 5YT, Wales.

HUMPHREYS Josephine, b. 2 Feb 1945, Charleston, South Carolina, USA. Novelist. m. Thomas A Hutcheson, 30 Nov 1968, 2 sons. *Education:* AB Duke University, 1967; MA, Yale University, 1968. *Publications:* Dreams of Sleep, 1984; Rich in Love, 1987; The Fireman's Fair, 1991. *Contributions to:* Occasional Reviews; Travel Articles for the New York Times. *Honours:* PEN, Erners Hemingway Foundation, 1985; Guggenheim Foundation Fellowship, 1985; Lyndhurst Prize, 1986. *Literary Agent:* Harriet Wasserman. *Address:* c/o Harriet Wasserman, 137 E. 36 Street, NY, NY 10016, USA.

HUMPHRY Derek John, b. 29 Apr 1930, Bath, England. Journalist; Author; Broadcaster. *Appointments:* Messenger Boy, Yorkshire Post, London, 1945-46; Cub Reporter, Evening World, Bristol, 1946-51; Junior Reporter, Evening News, Manchester, 1951-55; Reporter, Daily Mail, 1955-61; Deputy Editor, The Luton News, 1961-63; Editor, Havering Recorder, 1963-67; Home Affairs Correspondent, The Sunday Times, London, 1967-78; Special Writer, Los Angeles Times, 1978-79; Roving Correspondent in North America, The Sunday Times, London, 1979-81. *Publications:* Because They're Black, 1971; Police Power and Black People, 1972; Passports and Politics, 1974; False Messiah, 1977; The Cricket Conspiracy, 1976; Jean's Way, 1978; Let Me Die Before I Wake, 1982; The Right to Die! Understanding Euthanasia, 1986. *Contributions to:* New Statesman; The Independent, London; USA Today; Joint Editor, The Euthanasia Review, New York. *Honours:* Martin Luther King Memorial Prize, 1972. *Memberships:* President-Elect, 1988-89, World Federation of Right-to-Die Societies. *Literary Agent:* Robert Ducasm 9 West 29th Street, New York, NY 10001, USA. *Address:* P O Box 11830, Eugene, OR 97440, USA.

HUNNICUTT Benjamin Kline, b. 16 Nov 1943, Raleigh, North Carolina, USA. University Professor. m. Francine Marderello, 8 June 1963, 2 sons, 1 daughter. *Education:* BA Philosophy/Religion, 1967, MA 1972, PhD, 1976, History, University of North Carolina, Chapel Hill. *Publications:* Work Without End, 1988; The New Deal: The Salvation of work and the End of the Shorter Hour Movement, 1988; Southern Leisure, 1989; the Jewish Sabbath Movement in the early 20th Century, 1979; Monsignor John A Ryan and the Shorter Hours of Labour: A Forgotten Vision of Genuine Progress, 1983. *Contributions to:* Labour History, 1984; The Wall Street Journal, 1990. *Honours:* Old Gold Fellowships, 1979, 1980, University of Iowa; Historian for the Society of Park and Recreation Educators, 1980-81. *Memberships:* Iow Parks and Recreation Association; National Recreation and Park Association; Society of Parks and Recreation Educators. *Address:* 1610 College Street, Iowa City, IA 52240, USA.

HUNT Bruce J, b. 23 June 1956, Historian. m. Elizabeth Hedrick. *Education:* BA History, BS Physics, University of Washington, 1979; PhD, History of Science, Johns Hopkins University, 1984. *Publications:* The Maxwellians, 1991. *Contributions to:* Isis; Historical Studies in the Physical Sciences; The British Journal for the History of Science. *Honours:* Schuman Prize, History of Science Society, 1980; Visiting Fellow, Clare Hall, Cambridge, 1989-90. *Memberships:* History of Science Society; British Society for the History of Science; Society for the History of Technology; Lone Star History of Science Group. *Address:* Dept of History, University of Texas, Austin, TX 78712, USA.

HUNT E(verette) Howard, (John Baxter, Gordon Davis, Robert Dietrich, David St John), b. 1918. America, Novels/Short stories, Mystery/Crime/Suspense. *Career:* Scriptwriter and editor, March of Time, newsreel series, 1942-43; War Correspondent, Life mag, 1943; screenwriter, 1947-48; Attache, American Embassy, Paris, 1948-49, Vienna, 1949-50 and Mexico City 1950-53; Political Officer, Far East Command, Tokyo, 1954-56; First Secretary, American Embassy, Montevideo, 1957-60; Consultant, Department of Defence, Washington DC, 1960-65; with Department of State, Washington 1965-70; Vice President and Creative Director, Robert R Mullen, public relations firm, 1970-72; Consultant to President Richard M Nixon, 1971-72 (served terms in federal prison for his role in Watergate scandal, 1973-74, 1975-77). *Publications include:* The Hargrave Deception, 1980; The Gaza Intercept, 1981; The Kremlin Conspiracy, 1985; Cozumel, 1985; mystery novels as Gordon Davis: I Came to Kill, 1953; House Dick, 1961, Washington Payoff (as E Howard Hunt) 1975; Counterfeit Kill, 1963; Ring Around Rosy, 1964; Where Murder Waits, 1965; mystery novels as Robert Dietrich: One for the Road, 1954; The Cheat, 1954; Be My Victim, 1956; Murder on the Rocks, 1957; The House on Q Street, 1959; End of a Stripper, 1959; Mistress of Murder, 1960; Murder on Her Mind, 1960; Angel Eyes, 1961; Steve Bentley's Calypso Caper, 1961; Curtains for a Lover, 1961; My Body, 1962; mystery novels as David St John: On Hazardous Duty, 1965; Return from Vorkuta, 1965; The Towers of Silence, 1966; Festival for Spies, 1966; The Venus Probe, 1966; One of Our Agents is Missing, 1967; The Mongol Mask, 1968; The Sorcerers, 1969; Diabolius, 1971; The Coven, 1972; other - Give Us This Day, 1973; Undercover Memoirs of an American Secret Agent, 1974.

HUNT Fay Ann, (Annie Hedley), b. 18 July 1935, Cornwall. Farmer; Teacher; Writer. div. 3 sons. *Education:* Teaching Certificate, Redland College of

Education, Bristol. *Publications:* Motherin Sunday, 1990; Creative Activities for the Mentally Handicapped, 1986; Listen Lets Make Music, 1980; Look at Home before you Look Away, 1983. *Contributions to:* TES; Lancet; Special Education; Cornish Scene, Observer, Correspondent, Western Morning News, Cornish Times. *Honours:* First Prize Winner, Ian S James Award, 1990. *Memberships:* West Country Writers Association. *Literary Agent:* Gill Coleridge, Coleridge, White and Taylor. *Address:* Clift Farmhouse, Anthony, Torpoint, Cornwall PL11 2PH, England.

HUNT Francesca. *See:* **HOLLAND Isabelle.**

HUNT Gill. *See:* **TUBB E C.**

HUNT Joyce, b. 31 Oct 1927, New York City, USA. Writer. m. Irwin Hunt, 25 June 1950, 2 sons. *Education:* BA, Brooklyn College; MA, Hunter College. *Publications:* Co-Author with Irwin Hunt, Watching Orangutans, 1983; Co-author with Millicent Selsam, series of science books for children: A First Look at: Leaves, 1972; Fish, 1972; Mammals, 1973; Birds 1973; Insects, 1974; Frogs and Toads, 1976; Animals Without Backbones, 1976; Flowers, 1977; Snakes, Lizards & Other Reptiles, 1977; Animals with Backbones, 1978; The World of Plants, 1978; Monkeys and Apes, 1979; Sharks, 1979; Whales, 1980; Cats, 1981; Dogs, 1981; Horses, 1981; Dinosaurs, 1982; Spiders, 1983; Seashells, 1983; Rocks, 1984; Bird Nests, 1984; Kangaroos, Koalas and Other Animals with Pouches, 1985; Poisonous Snakes, 1986; Caterpillars, 1987; Seals & Walruses, 1987; Keep Looking, co-author Millicent Selsam, 1989; A First Look At Animals With Horns, co-author Millicent Selsam, 1989. *Honours:* Outstanding Science Books for Children Award, 1977, 1979. *Address:* 131 Riverside Drive, New York, NY 10024, USA.

HUNT Michael Houston, b. 19 Dec 1942, Texas, USA. University Professor and Historian. m. Paula Schreiter, 2 daughters. *Education:* BS Georgetown University, 1965; MA 1967, PhD 1971, Yale University. *Publications:* Ideology and US Foreign Policy, 1987; The Making of a Special Relationship, 1983; Frontier Defense and the Open Door, 1973. *Contributions to:* Some 25 essays and articles contributed to scholarly journals and edited volumes. *Honours:* Phi Beta Kappa; NEH Fellowships, 1973, 1979; Bernath Awards, 1974, 1978, 1984; National Programme for Advanced Study and Research in China Award, 1989; Woodrow Wilson Centre Fellowship, 1990-91. *Memberships:* Society for Historians of American Foreign Relations, VP and President, 1989-90; American Historical Association; Association for Asian Studies; Organization of American Historians. *Address:* Department of History, University of North Carolina, Chapel Hill, NC 27599, USA.

HUNT Morton, b. 20 Feb 1920, Philadelphia, Pennsylvania, USA. Writer. m. (3) Bernice Weinick, 10 Sept 1951. *Education:* AB, Temple University, 1941. *Appointment:* Freelance Writer, 1949-. *Publications:* The Natural History of Love, 1959; Her Infinite Variety: The American Woman as Lover, Mate and Tival, 1962; The World of the Formerly Married, 1966; The Affair: A Portrait of Extramarital Love in Contemporary America, 1969; The Mugging, 1972; Sexual Behaviour in the 1970's, 1974; Prime Time: A Guide to the Pleasures and Opportunities of the New Middle Age, (co-author Bernice Hunt), 1975; The Divorce Experience, (co-author, Bernice Hunt), 1977; The Universe Within: A New Science Explores the Human Mind, 1982; Profiles of Social Research: The Scientific Study of Human Interaction, 1985; The Compassionate Beast: What Science Is Discovering About the Humane Side of Humankind, 1990; The Story pf Psychology, 1993. *Contributions to:* Over 400 articles in The New Yorker, The New York Times Magazine, Reeder's Digest and Others, 1949-. *Honours:* American Association for the Advancement of Science Westinghouse Award, 1952; Claude Bernard Award, 1971; American Society of Journalists and Authors, 1983. *Literary Agent:* Georges Borchardt Incorporated, 136 E 57, New York, NY, USA.

Address: 15 Kingstown Ave., East Hampton, NY 11937, USA.

HUNT Robert William Gainer, b. 28 July 1923, Colour Consultant. m. Eileen Mary Redhead, 26 July 1947, 2 sons, 2 daughters. *Education:* BSc, ARCS, 1943, PhD, 1954, DSc, 1968, London University; DIC, Imperial College, 1947. *Publications:* The Reproduction of Colour, 4th edition, 1987; Measuring Colour, 2nd edition, 1991. *Contributions to:* numerous scientific papers, journals including Colour Research and Application. *Honours:* Newton Medal, The Colour Group, 1974; Progress Medal, The Royal Photographic Society, 1984; Judd-AIC Gold Medal, International Colour Association, 1987; Gold Medal, Institute of Printing, 1989. *Memberships:* International Colour Association, President, 1981; The Royal Institution, Vice President, 1985-87. *Address:* Kewferry House, 10 Kewferry Road, Northwood, Middlesex HA6 2NY, England.

HUNT Sam, b. 1946, New Zealand. Poet. *Publications:* Between Islands, 1964; A Fat Flat Blues (When Morning Comes), 1969; Selected Poems 1965-1969, 1970; A Song about Her, 1970; Postcard of a Cabbage Tree, 1970; Bracken Country, 1971; Letter to Jerusalem, 1971; Bottle Creek Blues, 1971; Bottle Creek, 1972; Beware the Man, 1972; Birth on Bottle Creek, 1972; South into Winter, 1973; Roadsong Paekakariki, 1973; Time to Ride, 1976; Drunkard's Garden, 1978; Collected Poems 1963-80, 1980; Three Poems of Separation, 1981; Running Scared, 1982; Approaches to Paremata, 1985; Selected Poems, 1987. *Address:* PO Box 1, Mana, Wellington, New Zealand.

HUNT Timothy Arthur, (Tim Hunt), b. 22 Dec 1949, California, USA. College Teacher. m. Susan D Spurlock, 1 son, 1 daughter. *Education:* AB cum laude, 1970, MA 1974, PhD, 1975, Cornell University. *Appointments include:* Assistant, Associate Professor, English Department, Indiana- Purdue University, Fort Wayne, 1985-87; Academic Dean, Deep Springs College, California, 1987-90; Associate Professor of English, Coordinator for Humanities, Washington State University, Vancouver, 1990-. *Publications include:* The Collected Poetry of Robinson Jeffers: Volume I, 1920-28, 1988, Volume II, 1928-38, 1989, Volume III, 1938-62, 1991; Kerouac's Crooked Road: Development of a Fiction, 1981; Various articles and essays, papers and poems. *Contributions to:* South Coast Poetry Journal; The White Clouds Revue; High Plains Review; Montana Review 7; The Seattle Review; Quarterly West; Westigan Review; Epoch; Wind/Literary Journal. *Honours include:* NEH Grants, 1986, 1987, 1991, 1992; Outstanding Teacher, Cornell University, 1991; Certificate of Merit, Bookbuilder's West Book Show, 1989. *Memberships:* Judge, Programme of Fellowships to Writers, Oregon Institute of Literary Arts; Founding Member and Steering Committee, Robinson Jeffers Association, first president, 1993; Modern Language Association; American Literature Association; Society for Textual Scholarship. *Address:* 323 NW 74th Street, Vancouver, WA 98665, USA.

HUNTER Alan James Herbert, b. 25 June 1922, Hoveton St John, Norwich, England, Author. m. Adelaide Elizabeth Cecily Cubitt, 6 Mar 1944, 1 daughter. *Education:* RAF 1940-46. *Appointment:* Crime reviewer, Eastern Daily Press, 1955-71. *Publications:* Gently Go Man, 1961; Vivienne: Gently Where She Lay, 1972; The Honfleur Decision, 1980; Gabrielle's Way, 1981; The Unhung Man, 1984; Traitor's End, 1988; The Norwich Poems, 1945; Author of 38 crime novels including Gently Does It, 1955 and Gently In The Glens, 1993. *Contributions to:* Magazines and journals. *Memberships:* Society of Authors; Crime Writers' Association. *Literary Agent:* Gregory & Radice, London. *Address:* 3 St Laurence Avenue, Brundall, Norwich, NR13 5QH, England.

HUNTER Elizabeth. *See:* **DE GUISE Elizabeth (Mary Teresa).**

HUNTER Evan. See: **LOMBINO Salvatore A.**

HUNTER Kristin, b. 1931, USA. Author; University Educator. *Appointments:* Copywriter, Lavenson Bureau of Advertising, Philadelphia, Pennsylvania, 1952-59; Copywriter, Wermen & Schorr, Philadelphia, 1962-63; Senior Lecturer in English, University of Pennsylvania, Philadelphia, 1972-. *Publications:* God Bless the Child, 1964; The Double Edge, play, 1965; The Landlord, 1966; The Soul Brothers and Sister Lou, 1968; Boss Cat, 1971; The Pool Table War, 1972; Uncle Daniel and the Racoon, 1972; Guests in the Promised Land: Stories, 1973; The Survivors, 1975; The Lakestown Rebellion, 1978; Lou in the Limelight, 1981. *Literary Agent:* Jeremy Solomon. *Address:* First Books, 2040N, Milwaukee Avenue, Chicago, IL 60647, USA.

HUNTER Mollie, b. 30 June 1922, Longniddy. Writer. m. Thomas McIlwraith, 23 Dec 1940, 2 sons. *Publications:* 25 books including: The Smartest Man in Ireland; The Kelpie's Pearls; Thomas and the Warlock; The Walking Stones; The Haunted Mountain; The Wicked One; The Enchanted Whistle; A Furl of Fairy Wind; The Spanish Letters; The Lothian Run; A Pistol in Greenyards; The Ghosts of Glencoe; The Thirteenth Member; The Stronghold; A Sound of Chariots; The Dragonfly Years; The Third Eye; I'll Go My Own Way; The Mermaid Summer; nonfiction for adults: Talent is Not Enough. *Memberships:* Society of Authors; PEN. *Literary Agent:* A M Heath & Co., London. *Address:* The Sheiling, Milton by Drumnadrochit, Inverness-shire, IV3 6UA, Scotland.

HUNTER Muir Vane Skerrett, (Muir Hunter), b. 19 Aug 1913, Mitcham, Surrey, England. Queen's Counsel; Author. m. (1) 1 Daughter, (2) Gillian Victoria Joyce Petrie, 4 July 1986. *Education:* Christ Church College, Oxford, MA, MRI; Barrister, 1938, Queen's Counsel, 1965. *Publications:* Williams Muir Hunter On Bankruptcy; Muir Hunter On Personal Insolvency; Kerr On Receivers and Administrators; County Court Procedure and Precedents. *Contributions to:* Numerous. *Honours:* Lt Colonel; Queens Counsel. *Memberships:* Society of Authors; Poetry Society; International PEN; Grays Inn; Royal Institute of Great Britain. *Address:* Hunterston Donhead, St Andrews, Shaftesbury, Dorset SP7 8EB, England.

HUNTINGTON Samuel Phillips, b. 1927. America, Military/Defence, Politics/Government. *Appointments:* Eaton Professor of Science of Government, Harvard University, Cambridge, 1982- (joined faculty 1950; Dillon Professor of International Affairs, 1981-82); Director for International Affairs, Harvard University, 1978-89. Director, John M. Olin Institute for Strategic Studies, 1989-; Vice President 1984-85 and President, 1986-87, American Political Science Association; Assistant Director 1958-59, Associate Director 1959-62, Institute of War and Peace Studies, and Associate Professor of Government, 1959-62, Columbia University, New York City; Member of Council, American Political Science Association, 1969-71; Member, Presidential Task Force on International Development, 1969-70; Member, Commission on US/Latin American Relations, 1974-75; Member, Commission on Integrated Long Term Strategy, 1986-88; Co-ordinator of Security Planning, National Security Council, 1977-78; Co-editor, Foreign Policy journal, 1970-77. *Publications:* The Soldier and the State: The Theory and Politics of Civil-Military Relations, 1957; The Common Defence: Strategic Programs in National Politics, 1961; (ed)Changing Patterns of Military Politics, 1962; (co-author) Political Power USA/USSR 1964; Political Order in Changing Societies, 1968; (co-ed) Authoritarian Politics in Modern Society: The Dynamics of Established One-Party Sustems, 1970; (co-author) The Crisis of Democracy, 1975; (with J M Nelson) No Easy Choice: Political Participation in Developing Countries, 1976; American Politics: The Promise of Disharmony, 1981; (ed) The Strategic Imperative: New Policies for American Security, 1982; (co-author) Living with Nuclear Weapons, 1983; (co-ed) Global Dilemmas, 1985; (co-ed) Reorganizing America's Defence, 1985; (co-ed)

Understanding Political Development, 1987; The Third Wave: Democratization in The Late Twentieth Century, 1991. *Address:* 1737 Cambridge Street, Cambridge, MA 02138, USA.

HURD Douglas (Richard), Rt. Hon. b. 8 Mar 1930 (eldest son Baron Hurd d. 1966) Politician, Writer. m. (1) Tatiana Elizabeth Michelle, 1960, (diss 1982), 3 sons; (2) Judy 1982, 1 son, 1 daughter. *Education:* Eton (King's Scholar and Newcastle Scholar); Trinity College, Cambridge (Major Scholar), President, Cambridge Union, 1952. *Career:* H M Diplomatic Service 1952-66, served in Peking 1954-56, UK Mission to UN 1956-60, Private Secretaary to Permanent Under-Secretary of State, Foreign Office, 1960-63, Rome 1963-66; Joined Conservative Research Department 1966, Head of Foreign Affairs Section 1968, Private Secretary to Leader of Opposition 1968-70, Political Secretary to Prime Minister 1970-74; Member of Parliament (Conservative) for Mid-Oxon, 1974-83, for Witney 1983- Opposition Spokesman on European Affairs, 1976-79; Minister of State FCO 1979- 83; Minister of State Home Office 1983-84; Secretary of State for Northern Ireland 1984-85; Appointed Secretary of State for the Home Office, 1985; Currently Foreign Secretary; Visiting Fellow, Nuffield College, Oxford, 1978-86. *Publications:* The Arrow War, 1967; Truth Game, 1972; Vote to Kill, 1975; An End to Promises, 1979; (with Andrew Osmond) Send Him Victorious, 1968; The Smile on the Face of the Tiger, 1969, 1982; Scotch on the Rocks, 1971; War Without Frontiers, 1982; (with Stephen Lamport) Palace of Enchantments, 1985. *Honours:* CBE 1974; PC 1982. *Address:* House of Commons, London SW1, England.

HURD Edith Thacher, b. USA. Children's Author. *Publications:* Hurry, Hurry, 1960; Stop, Stop, 1961; Come and Have Fun, 1962; The SooSo Cat, 1963; Johnny Lion's Book, 1965, 2nd Edition, 1978; Who Will Be Mine, 1966; The Day the Sun Danced, 1966; What Whale Where, 1966; Little Dog Dreaming, 1967; The Blue Heron Tree, 1968; Johnny Lion's Bad Day, 1970; Catfish, 1970; The White Horse, 1970; Come with Me to Nursery School, 1970; The Mother Beaver, 1971; The Mother Deer, 1972; Wilson's World, UK Edition Wilkie's World, 1971; Johnny Lion's Rubber Boots, 1972; The Mother Whale, 1973; The Mother Owl, 1974; The Mother Kangaroo, 1976; Look for a Bird, 1977; The Mother Chimpanzee, 1978; Dinosaur My Darling, 1978; Under the Lemon Tree, 1980; The Black Dog Who Went into the Woods, 1989; I Dance in My Red Pyjamas, 1982; The Song of the Sea Otter, 1983. *Address:* 1635 Green Street, San Francisco, CA 94123, USA.

HURD Michael John, b. 19 Dec 1928, Gloucester, England, Composer; Author. *Education:* BA, 1953, MA, 1957, Pembroke College, Oxford. *Publications:* Immortal Hour, The Life and Period of Rutland Boughton, 1962; An Outline History of European Music, 1968; The Ordeal of Ivor Gurney, 1978; The Oxford Junior Companion to Music, 1979; Vincent Novello and Company, 1981; The Orchestra, 1981; Sailors' Songs and Shanties, 1965; Soldiers' Songs and Marches, 1966; The Composer, 1968; Elgar, 1969; Vaughan Williams, 1970; Mendelssohn, 1970; Rutland Boughton and the glastonbuty Festivals, 1993. *Contributor to:* The New Grove Dictionary of Music and Musicians, 1980; The New Oxford Companion to Music, 1983; The Oxford Illustrated Encyclopedia; The Oxford Children's Encyclopedia; The Athlone History of Music in Britain. *Address:* 4 Church Street, West Liss, Hampshire GU33 6JX, England.

HURGERFORD Pixie. See: **BRINSMEAD Hesba Fay.**

HUSSEY Leonard. See: **PEARCE Brian Leonard.**

HUTCHEON Linda Ann Marie, b. 24 Aug 1947, Toronto, Canada. m. Michael Alexander Hutcheon, 30 May 1970. *Education:* BA Modern Language and Literature, 1969, PhD Comparative Litearture, 1975,

University of Toronto; MA Romance Studies, Cornell University, 1971. *Appointments:* Assistant, Associate and full Professor of of English, McMaster , 1976-88; Professor of English and Comparative Literature, University of Toronto, 1988-. *Publications:* Books: Narcisisstic Narrative, 1980, 1984; Formalism and the Freudian Aesthetic, 1984; A Theory of Parody, 1985; A Poetics of Postmodernism, 1988; The Canadian Postmodern 1988; The Politics of Postmodernism, 1989; Splitting Images, 1991; Editor: Other Solitudes, 1990; Double-Talking, 1992; Likely Stories, 1992. *Contributions to:* Articles in Diacritics, Textual Practice, Cultural Critique, and other journals. *Honours:* Fellow, Royal Society of Canada; John P Robarts Professor of Canadian Studies, York University, 1988-89; Killam Research Fellow, 1986-88; Connaught Research Fellow, 1991-92; Guggenheim Fellow, 1992-93. *Memberships:* Modern Language Association of America, Executive Council, 1993-96; Editorial Board, 1990-92; Association of Canadian University Teachers of English, Executive, 1980-82; International Comparative Literature Association; Toronto Semiotic Circle, President, 1982; Canadian Comparative Literature Association, Secretary, 1983. *Address:* University of Toronto, Ontario, Canada M5S 1A1.

HUTCHINS Hazel Jean, b. 9 Aug 1952, Canada. Writer. m. James E Hutchins, 13 Jan 1973, 2 sons, 1 daughter. *Publications:* The Three and Many Wishes of Jason Reid, 1983; Anastasia, Morningstar, 1984; Leanna Builds a Genie Trap, 1986; Ben's Snow Song, 1987; Casey Webber and the Great, 1988; Norman's Snowball, 1989; Nicholas at the Library, 1990; Katie's Babbling Brother, 1991; A Cat of Artimus Pride, 1991; And You can Be the Cat, 1992. *Address:* c/o Annick Press, 15 Patricia Avenue, Willowdale, Ontario, Canada M2M 1H9.

HUTCHINS Maude (Phelps McVeigh), b. New York, USA. Author; Painter; Sculptress. m. Robert Maynard Hutchins, 1921, divorced, 3 daughters. *Publications:* Co-Author, Diagrammatics, 1932; Georgiana, 1948; A Diary of Love, 1950, reprinted, 1971; Love is a Pie, 1953; The Memoirs of Maisie, 1953; Victorine, 1959; The Elevator, 1962; Honey on the Moon, 1964; Blood on the Doves, 1965; The Unbelievers Downstairs, 1967. *Contributions to:* Poetry; New Yorker; Accent; Kenyon Review; Foreground; Mademoiselle; Quarterly Review of Literature; Quest; Harper's; Vogue; Ramparts. *Address:* c/o Andrew Emery Garson, 72 Ruane Street, Fairfield, CT 06430, USA.

HUTCHINS Pat, b. 18 June 1942, Yorkshire, England. Writer; Illustrator (childrens books). m. 20 Aug 1966. 2 sons. *Education:* Darlington School of Art, 1958-61; Leeds College of Art, 1961-63; National Diploma in Design. *Publications:* Rosie's Walk, 1968; Titch, 1971; Goodnight Owl, 1972; The Wind Blew, 1974; Happy Birthday Sam, 1979; The Very Worst Monster, 1985; Tom and Sam, 1968; The Surprise Party, 1969; Clocks and More Clocks, 1970; Changes, Changes, 1971; The Silver Christmas Tree, 1974; The House That Sailed Away, 1975; Follow That Bus, 1978; One Eyed Jake, 1978; The Best Train Set Ever, 1978; The Tale of Thomas Mead, 1980; The Mona Lisa Mystery, 1981; King Henry's Palace, 1983; One Hunter, 1982; You'll Soon Grow Into Them Titch, 1983; The Curse of the Egyptian Mummy, 1983; The Doorbell Rang, 1986; Where's The Baby?, 1988; Which Witch is Which?, 1989; Rats!, 1989; What Game Shall We Play?, 1990; Tidy Titch, 1991; Silly Billy, 1992; My Best Friend, 1992. *Honour:* Kate Greenaway Medal, 1975. *Address:* 75 Flask Walk, London NW3 1ET, England.

HUTCHINSON (William Patrick Henry) Pearse, b. 1927, Republic of Ireland. Poet; Translator. *Appointments:* Translator, International Labour Organisation, Geneva, Switzerland, 1951-53; Drama Critic, Radio Eireann, Ireland, 1957-61; Drama Critic, Telefis Eireann, 1968; Gregory Fellow in Poetry, University of Leeds, Leeds, England, 1971-73. *Publications:* Poems, by Josep Carner, translation, 1962; Tongue without Hands, 1963; Faoustin Bhacach (Imperfect Confession), 1968; Expansions, 1969; Friend Songs: Medieval Love-Songs from Galaico-Portuguese, translation, 1970; Watching the Morning Grow, 1973; Frost Is All Over, 1975; Selected Poems, 1982. *Address:* c/o Gallery Press, 19 Oakdown Road, Dublin 14, Republic of Ireland.

HUTCHINSON Ron, b. near Lisburn, County Antrim, Northern Ireland; brought up in Coventry, Warwickshire, England. *Education:* Educated in schools in Coventry. *Career:* Worked at various jobs including fish gutter, carpet salesman, scene shifter and bookseller all in Coventry; Clerk, Ministry of Defence and Ministry of Labour, Coventry; Social Worker and Claims Investigator, Department of Health and Social Security, Coventry, 5 years; Resident writer, Royal Shakespeare Company, London 1978-79. *Publications:* Plays include: The Dillen, adaptation of a work by Angela Hewins (produced Stratford-on-Avon, 1983); Rat in the Skull (produced, London 1984; New York, 1985), London Methuen, 1984; Mary, After the Queen, with Angela Hewins (produced Stratford-on-Avon, 1985); Curse of the Baskervilles, from a story by Arthur Conan Doyle (produced Plymouth, 1987); Novel: Connie (novelization of television series) London, Severn House, 1985; Radio plays include: Murphy Unchained, 1978; There Must Be a Door, 1979; Motorcade, 1980; Risky City, 1981; Television plays include: Deasy 1979; The Winkler 1979; Bull Week 1980; Bird of Prey (series) 1982 and 1984; Connie (series) 1985; The Marksman, from the novel by Hugh C Rae (Unnatural Causes, series) 1987. *Honours:* George Devine Award, 1978; John Whiting Award, 1984. *Literary Agent:* Judy Daish Associates, London. *Address:* c/o Judy Daish Associates, 83 Eastbourne Mews, London W2 6LQ, England.

HUTHMACHER J Joseph, b. 1929, American. *Appointments:* Instructor, Ohio State University, Columbus, 1956-57; Associate Professor, Georgetown University, WA, 1957-66; Professor, Rutgers University, New Brunswick, NJ, 1966-70; Richards Professor of History, University of Delaware, Newark, 1970-; General Co-Editor, The American Forum Series, Schenkman Publishing Company, 1972-. *Publications:* Massachusetts People and Politics 1919-1933, 1959; American History (overhead projection transparencies) (author and designer), Twentieth-Century America: An Interpretation with Readings (ed), 1966; America Past and Present (ed with B Labaree and V P de Santis), 2 volumes, A Nation of Newcomers: Ethnic Minority Groups in American History, 1967; Senator Robert F Wagner and the Rise of Urban Liberalism, 1968; From Colony to Global Power: A History of the United States (gen ed), 6 volumes, 1972-73; The Truman Years: The Reconstruction of Postwar America (ed), 1972; Trial by War and Depression: The United States 1917-1941, 1973. *Address:* c/o Athrneum, 115 Fifth Avenue, New York, NY 10003, USA.

HUTTON Ann, (Barbara Whitnell), b. 30 Mar 1929, Watford, Herts, England. Past Teacher. m. William West Hutton, 2 Sept 1950, 2 sons, 2 daughters. *Education:* St Mary's College, Cheltenham, 1946-48; Teaching Diploma, 1948. *Publications:* Ring of Bells, 1982; Song of the Rainburd, 1984; The Salt Rakers, 1986; Freedom Street, 1989; Loveday, 1990; Charmed Circle, 1992. *Contributions to:* Short stories and serials for many women's magazines, at home and abroad. *Honours:* Mary Elgin Award, 1984. *Memberships:* Society of Authors; PEN. *Literary Agent:* Serafina Clarke. *Address:* c/o Serafina Clarke, 98 Tunis Road, London W12 7EY, England.

HUTTON John Harwood, b. 21 Nov 1928, Manchester, England. Retired Teacher. m. Gladys May Lloyd, 31 July 1965. *Education:* BA Hons 1949, Teaching Diploma 1950, MA 1952, University College of North Wales, Bangor. *Publications:* 29, Herriott Street, 1979; Accidental Crimes, 1983. *Honour:* Gold Dagger Award of the Crime Writers' Association, 1983. *Memberships:* Crime Writers' Association; The Society of Authors. *Address:* Gwylfa, Old Holyhead Road, Berwyn, Llangollen, Wales.

HUTTON Ronald Edmund, b. 19 Dec 1953, Ootacamund, India. Historian. m. Lisa Radulovic, 5 Aug 1988. *Education:* BA Hons, Cantab, 1976; MA Cantab, 1980; DPhil, 1980. *Publications:* The Royalist War Effort, 1981; The Restoration 1985; Charles II 1989; The British Republic, 1990; The Pagen Religions of the Ancient British Isles, 1991. *Contributions to:* Essays in seven journals. *Honours:* FRHistS, 1981. *Memberships:* Royal Historiacl Society; Folklore Society. *Address:* 13 Woodland Road, Bristol, BS8 1TB, England.

HUXLEY Anthony Julian, b. 2 Dec 1920, Oxford, England. Writer; Editor; Photographer. *Education:* MA, Cambridge University. *Publications:* Standard Encyclopaedia of the World's Mountains, Oceans and Islands, Rivers and Lakes (Editor), 1962, 1968; Flowers of the Mediterranean (with O Polunin), 1965; Mountain Flowers, 1967, 1986; House Plants, Cacti and Succulents, 1972; Plant and Planet, 1974; The Financial Times Book of Garden Design, (Editor), 1975; Flowers of Greece and the Aegean (with W Taylor), 1977; An Illustrated History of Gardening, 1978; Success with House Plants (General Editor), 1979; Penguin Encyclopaedia of Gardening, 1981; Wild Orchids of Britain and Europe (with P & J Davies), 1983, 1988; The Macmillan World Guide to House Plants (Editor), 1983; Green Inheritance, 1985; The Painted Garden, 1988; Royal Horticultural Society's Dictionary of Gardening (Editor), 1988-. *Contributions to:* Country Life; The Garden. *Honour:* Award, Victoria Medal of Honour, Royal Horticultural Society. *Memberships:* Horticultural Club (London), President; Royal Horticultural Society (Council, various Committees). *Address:* 50 Villiers Avenue, Surbiton, Surrey, KT5 8BD, England.

HUXLEY Elspeth Josceline, b. 23 July 1907, London. Writer. m. Gervas Huxley, 12 Dec 1931, 1 son. *Education:* Dip Agriculture, Reading University, 1925-27; Special Course, Cornell University, New York, 1927-28. *Appointments:* Assistant Press Officer, Empire Marketing Board (now defunct) 1929-32; News Department, BBC, 1941-43. *Publications include:* The Flame Trees of Thika, 1959; The Mottled Lizard, 1961; Out in the Midday Sun, 1985; White Man's Country: Lord Delamere (biography) 1935; The African Poison Murders, (Crime) 1938, reprint 1989; Murder on Safari (Crime) 1937, reprint 1989; Nine Faces of Kenya, 1990; Peter Scott, Painter and Naturalist (biography), 1993. *Contributions to:* Many articles to the New York Times Magazine, Daily Telegraph, Encounter, Time and Tide. *Honour:* CBE, 1962. *Membership:* Society of Authors. *Literary Agent:* Heather Jeeves, 9 Dryden Place, Edinburgh, EH9 1RP, Scotland. *Address:* Green End, Oaksey, Malmesbury, Wilts SW16 9TL, England.

HUYLER Jean Wiley, b. 30 Mar 1935, Seattle, Washington, USA. Communications Management Consultant; Author-Writer; Editor; Photojournalist. divorced. 1 son, 1 daughter. *Education includes:* Business Administration, University of Washington, 1953-55; BA, Marylhurst College, 1978; MA, Pacific Lutheran University, 1979; DLitt, Fairfax University, 1989. *Literary Appointments:* Various newspaper and magazine editorships, 1963-75; Editor, books for Education System Managers, Washington School Directors Association, 1977-81; Designer and Editor, For The Record, A History of Tacoma Public Schools, Tacoma School District, 1985-. *Publications:* Demystifying the Media, 1980, 81; Crisis Communications, 1983; Campaign Savvy - School Support, 2nd edition, 1981; Communications is a People Process, 1981; How to Get Competent Communications Help, 1983; Sharing a Vision for Gifted Education with Business and Education Leaders, 1988; Lifespan Learning on Centerstage of the Future, 1988; Learning to Learn - New Techniques for Corporate Education, 1989. *Contributions to:* Press Woman; C:JET Communications: Journalism Education Today; Publishers Auxiliary; American Banker; The Lion; Kiwanis; Lottery Players Magazine; Travel Magazines. *Honours:* Over 150 awards for assorted writings including: Superior Performance, 1964, Torchbearer,

1984, Washington Press Association; Excellence in Educational Communications, National Association of State Education Department Information Officers, 1978; National Federation of Press Women; Woman (Communicator) of Achievement, 1988; and other awards. *Memberships include:* Past President and various other offices, National Federation of Press Women. *Literary Agent:* B J Simon. *Address:* 922 North Pearl A-27, Tacoma, WA 98406, USA.

HWANG David Henry, b. 11 Aug 1957, Los Angeles, California, USA. Playwright; Director. m. Ophelia Y M Chong, 1985. *Education:* AB, English, Stanford University, California, 1979; Yale University, School of Drama, New Haven, Connecticut, 1980-81. *Career:* Director: Plays: A Song for a Nisei Fisherman, 1980 and The Dream of Kitamura, 1982, both by Philip Kan Gotanda, San Francisco. *Publications include:* Family Devotions (produced New York 1981), Included in Broken Promises: Four Plays, 1983; Sound and Beauty (includes The House of Sleeping Beauties and The Sound of a Voice) (produced New York, 1983; The House of Sleeping Beauties in Broken Promises, produced London 1987) The House of Sleeping Beauties included in Broken Promises: Four Plays 1983; The Sound of a Voice published New York, Dramatists Play Service, 1984. Broken Promises: Four Plays, New York, Avon, 1983; Rich Relations (produced New York, 1986); As the Crow Flies (produced Los Angeles, 1986; Broken Promises (includes The Dance and the Railroad and The House of Sleeping Beauties) (produced London 1987). *Honours:* Drama-Logue Award, 1980, 1986; Obie Award 1981; Golden Eagle award, for television writing, 1983; Rockefeller fellowship, 1983; Guggenheim fellowship, 1984; National Endowment for the Arts fellowship, 1985. *Literary Agent:* Paul Yamamoto and William Craver, Writers and Artists Agency, New York. *Address:* c/o Paul Yamamoto and William Craver, Writers and Artists Agency, 70 West 36th Street, New York, NY 10018, USA.

HYDE Eleanor. *See:* **COWEN Frances.**

HYKISCH Anton, b. 23 Feb 1932, Ban Stiavnica, Slovakia. Economist Manager; Diplomat; Journalist. m. Eva Suchonova, 19 October, 1957, 1 daughter, 1 son. *Education:* Engineer of Economics, Economical University, Bratislava, 1956. *Appointments:* Managing Director, Mlade Leta Publishers, 1990-92; Ambassador of Slovakia to Canada. *Publications:* A Step in the Unknown, 1959; Nadja, 1964; The Square in the Town Mahring, 1965; The Time of Masters, 1977; Lets Love the Queen, 1984; Defending Mysteries, 1990; I've Met You, 1963; Canada is not a Fun, 1968; Atomic Summer, 1988; My Little Friend Chippy, 1989. *Contributions to:* Slovak and Czech literary Magazines and weeklies including: Kulturny Zivot, Mlada Tvorba, Slovenske Pohlady, Literarni Noviny, Nove SLovo, Literary Tyzdennik. *Honours:* Award for Fiction, 1988, Children's Book Award, 1989, Mlade Leta Publishing House, 1988. *Memberships:* Union of Slovak Writers, till 1971; Society of Slovak Writers, 1990, Past Chairman and Vice Chairman; PEN Slovak Centre, past Committee member, 1989; Chairman, Committee for Education and Culture, Slovak Parliament, 1990-92; Executive Committee, Pan-Europa Union, Slovak Centre, 1990-; Executive Council, Christian Social Union, 1992. *Literary Agent:* Lita Slovak Literary Agency, Bratislava, Partizanska, 17. *Address:* Lachova 18, 851 03 Bratislava, Slovakia.

HYLAND Paul, b. 15 Sept 1947, Poole, England. Author. m. Maggie Ware 8 Dec 1990. *Education:* BSc. *Honours:* Bristol University, 1968. *Publications:* Purbeck: The Ingrained Island, 1978; Wight: Biography of an Island, 1984; Poems of Z, 1982; The Stubborn Forest, 1984; The Black Heart: A Voyage into Central Africa, 1988; Getting into Poetry, 1992; poetry, drama & features for radio. *Contributions to:* Poems in many magazines. *Honours:* Alice Hunt Bartlett Award, 1985. *Memberships:* Poetry Society; Society of Authors; Orchard Theatre Company, Chairman. *Literary Agent:*

David Higham Associates Ltd. *Address:* 5 Gunswell Lane, South Molton, Devon EX36 4DH, England.

HYMAN Harold M(elvin), b. 1924. America, History. *Career:* William P Hobby Professor of History, Rice University, Houston, Texas, 1968- (Chairman of Department 1968-70). Member of Board of Editors, Reviews in American History, 1964-, Ulysses S Grant Association, 1968- and The American Journal of Legal History 1970-. Assistant Professor of History, Earlham College, Richmond, Indiana, 1952-55; Visiting Professor, 1955-56 and Professor of History 1957-63, University of California, Los Angeles; Associate Professor, Arizona State University, Tempe, 1956-57; Member, Board of Editors, Journal of American History, 1970-74. *Publications include:* (ed) Heard, Round the World: The Impact of the Civil War and Reconstruction, 1968; (ed with F B Hyman) The Circuit Court Opinions of Salmon Portland Chase, 1972; (ed) Sidney George Fisher: The Trial of the Constitution, 1972; (ed with H K Trefousse) The Political History of the United States During the Great Rebellion, 1860-1865, The Political History of the United States of America During the Period of Reconstruction, Apr 15 1865-July 15 1870, and the Handbook of Politics, 6 vols, 1972-73; A More Perfect Union: The Impact of the Civil War and Reconstruction on the Constitution, 1973; Crisis and Confidence 1860-1870, 1975; (with W Wiecek) Equal Justice under Law Constitutional Development, 1835-1875, 1982; American Singularity, 1987; Oleander Odyssey: The Kempners of Galveston, 1870-1980, 1990. *Address:* Department of History, Rice University, PO Box 1892, Houston, TX 77251, USA.

I

IBRAHIMOV Mirza Azhdar Oglu, b. 15 Oct 1911, Iran. Politician; Writer. m. Sarahanum Ibrahimli, 1938, 1 son, 3 daughters. *Education:* Institute of Oriental History, USSR; Academy of Sciences. *Publications:* Plays: Khaiat, 1935; Madrid, 1938; Mahabbeth, 1942; Kendchi Kyzy, 1962; Yakshy Adam, 1965; Kezaran ochzhaglar, 1967; Human Comedy of Don Juan, 1977; Novels: the Day Will Come, 1948; Beyuk Dayag, 1967; Parvane, 1971; Short Stories: Fyrtyna Gushu, 1966; On the Slopes of the Murovdag, 1967; Scholarly Works: Beyuk democrat, 1939; Hayat ve edebijath, 1947; Halgilik ve realizm jabhesinden, 1962; On the Laws of Beauty, 1964; Realism in Ashug Poetry, 1966; Sketches on Literature, 1971; Azerbaijani Prose : An Anthology, 1977. *Honours:* Red Banner of Labour; Order of Lenin (three times); Order of October Revolution 1971; Stalin Prize. *Address:* Writers' Union, 25 Khagany Baku, Azerbaijan, USSR.

ICHIKAWA Satomi, b. 15 Jan. 1949, Gifu, Japan. Author. *Appointments:* Author and illustrator of books for children, 1974-; Work exhibited at Gallery Printemps Ginza, 1984. *Publications:* A Child's Book of Seasons, 1975; Friends, Sophie and Nicky Go to Market, 1976; From Mornto Midnight, 1977; Keep Running, Allen!, Sophie and Nicky and the Four Seasons, Playtime, 1978; Under the Cherry Tree, Suzette and Nicholas and the Sunijudi Circus, 1979; Suzette et Nicolas au Zoo, Sun Through Small Leaves, 1980; Let's Play, Children Through Four Seasons, 1981; Suzette et Nicolas: L'Annee en fetes, 1982; Angels Descending From the Sky, The Wonderful Rainy Week: A Book of Indoor Games, Merry Christmas! Children at Christmastime Around the World, 1983; Children in Paris (two volumns), Suzette et Nicolas font le tour du monde, 1984; Here a Little Child I Stand: Poems of Prayer and Praise for Children, 1985; Nora's Castle, 1986; Happy Birthday! A Book of Birthday Celebrations, 1988. *Honour:* Special mention for Prix Critici in Erba, Bologna Children's Book Fair, 1978.

ICHIMURA Shinichi, b. 30 Mar 1925, Kyoto, Japan. Professor of Economics. m. Yukiko Kondo, 2 May 1956, 2 sons, 1 daughter. *Education:* BA, Economics, Kyoto University, 1949; PhD, MIT, USA, 1953; DEcon, Osaka University, 1961. *Publications:* The Str of Japanese Economy, 1957; The Development of Southeast Asia, 1980; Challenge of Asian Developing Countries, 1988; Econometric Models of Asian LINK, 1988; Japanese Management in Asia, 1990. *Honours:* Fellow (Econometrics Society), President (East Asian Economis Association), Dr of Economics. *Memberships:* East Asian Economic Association; Econometric Society; Association of Asian Politics and Economics. *Address:* 2-40 Minami- Kasugaoka, 4 Ibaraki, Osaka 576, Japan.

IDDINGS Kathleen, b. West Milton, Ohio, USA, Writer; Publisher, div, 1 son, 3 daughters. *Education:* BS Ed, Miami University, Oxford, Ohio, 1968; UCSD, Napa College, Mira Costa College, San Diego City College. *Appointments:* Editor/Publisher/Originator of San Diego Poets Press, 1981; La Jolla Poets Press, 1985; Poetry Consultant, GATE Programme (Gifted and Talented), San Diego City Schools; Poetry Editor, San Diego Writers' Monthly. *Publications:* The Way of Things, 1984; Invincible Summer, 1985; Promises to Keep, 1987; Selected and New Poems, 1980-1990, 1990. *Contributions to:* McGraw Hill college text, Literature, 1988, Over 250 in anthologies and quarterlies. *Honours:* National Endowment for the Arts/ COMBO Fellowship, 1986; 2 Carnegie and 2 PEN Writers Grants, 1988-1992; Djerassi Artists' Colony Residency, 1992. *Memberships:* Poetry Society of America; PEN; AWP; Academy of Am Poets, San Diego Independent Scholars. *Address:* PO Box 8638, La Jolla, CA 92038, USA.

IGGERS Georg Gerson, b. 7 Dec 1926, Hamburg, Germany, Historian. m. Wilma Abeles, 23 Dec 1948, 3 sons. *Education:* BA, University if Richmond, 1944; AM, 1945, PhD, 1951, University of Chicago; Graduate Student, New School for Social Research, 1945-46. *Publications:* German Conception of History, 1968; New Directions in European Historiography, 1975; Cult of Authority, Political Philosophy of the Saint Simonians, 1958; Social History of Politics, (Editor), 1985; leopold von Ranke, The Shaping of History, 1990; Aufklarung und Geschichte, (Co-editor), 1986; International Handbook of Historical Studies, (Co-editor) 1979; Leopold von Ranke, The Theory and Practice of History (co-editor), 1973; Leopold von Ranke and the Shaping of the Historical Discipline (co-editor), 1990; Marxist Historiography in Transition: Historical Writings in East Germany in the 1980's (editor), 1991; Geschichtswissenchaft 20, Jahrhunder, 1993. *Contributions to:* History and Theory; American Historical Review; Journal of Modern history; Geschichte und Gesellschaft; Historische Zeitschrift. *Honours:* Fellowships: Guggenheim Foundation; Rockefeller Foundation; National Endowment for the Humanities; Woodrow Wolson International Center of Scholars; Fulbright; Centre for Interdisciplinary Studies; Erasmus-Kittler Award, Technische Hochschule, Darmstadt. *Memberships:* International Commission on the History of Historiography, Vice President, 1980-; Conference Group on Central European History, Chair, 1990-91 American Historical Association. *Address:* Department of History, Park Hall, SUNY/Buffalo, Buffalo, NY 14260, USA.

IGGULDEN John Manners (Jack), b. 12 Feb 1917, Brighton, Victoria, Australia. Businessman, Writer. m. Helen Carrol Schapper, 2 daughters. *Publications:* Breakthrough, 1960; The Storms of Summer, 1960; The Clouded Sky, Macmillan, USA, 1965, Macdonald, UK. 1965; Dark Stranger, McGraw Hill, USA 1965, Macdonald, UK, 1966; Editor: Summer's Tales 3. Macmillan (Aust) 1966, Macmillan and St Martin's, USA; Manual of Standard Procedures, First edition 1964, Gliding Federation of Australia; Gliding Instructor's Handbook. First edition 1968, Gliding Federation of Australia; Non-fiction: The Promised Land Papers: Vol 1, The Revolution of the Good, 1986, Vol 2, How Things Are Wrong and How to Fix Them, 1988. *Honour:* Australian National Gliding Champion, 1959-60, represented Australia in Ninth World Gliding Championships in Argentina in 1963. *Memberships:* Director, Australian National Gliding School, 1960, 1961, 1962, 1963, 1964; Life-Governor, The Gliding Federation of Australia; Founding President, now Life-Governor, the Port Phillip Conservation Council (Victoria); Founding President, the North Coast Environment Council (NSW); Founding President, Bellingen and Plateau Conservation Society (NSW). *Literary Agents:* The Fox Chase Agency, Inc, The Public Ledger Building, Independence Squarer, Philadelphia, Pennsylvania. *Address:* Gleniffer Road, Promised Land, Bellingen, NSW 2454, Australia.

IHIMAERA Witi, b. 1944, New Zealand. Author. *Publications:* Pounamu, Pounamu (short stories), 1972; Tangi, 1973; Whanau, 1974; Maori, 1975; The New Net Goes Fishing, 1977; co-editor, Into the World of Light, 1980; The Matriarch, 1986; The Whale Rider, 1987; Dear Miss Mansfield, 1989. *Address:* c/o Ministry of Foreign Affairs, Private Bag, Wellington 1, New Zealand.

IMPEY Rosemary June, (Rose Impey), b. 7 June 1947, Northwich, Cheshire, England. 2 daughters. *Education:* Teacher's Certificate, 1970. *Publications include:* Who's A Clever Girl, Then?, 1985; The Baked Bean Queen, 1986; Desperate for a Dog, 1988; The Flat Man, 1988; The Girl's Gang, 1986; Letter to Father Christmas, 1988; Joe's Cafe, 1990; First Class, 1992; Trouble with the Tucker Twins, 1992; Revenge of the Rabbit, 1990; Instant Sisters, 1989; Orchard Book of Fairytales, 1992. *Honours:* 100 Most Borrowed Library Books Award; Shortlisted for the Smarties Children's Books Prize. *Literary Agent:* Caroline Sheldon. *Address:* 5 Carisbrooke Court, 55 Carisbrooke Road, Leicester LE2 3PF, England.

INCHBALD Peter Bingham, b. 1919, London,

England. 2 sons. *Education:* MA Oxon; Diploma Royal Academy School of Painting. *Publications:* Tondo for Short, 1981; The Sweet Short Grass, 1982; Short Break in Venice, 1983; Or the Bambino Dies, 1985. *Memberships:* Society of Authors; Crime Writers' Association; Cheltenham Writers Circle. *Literary Agent:* Curtis Brown.

INDICK Benjamin Philip, b. 11 Aug 1923, New Jersey, USA. Pharmacist; Writer. m. 23 Aug 1953, 1 son, daughter. *Education:* BS Biology, Rutgers University, New Brunswick, NJ, 1947; BS Pharmacy, Ohio State University, Columbus, Ohio, 1951; The New School, New York, 1960-61, no degree. *Publications include:* Plays: He, She and the End of the World, 1982; Incident at Cross Plains, 1976; The Children of King, 1989; Books: A Gentleman from Providence Pens a Letter, 1975; The Drama of Ray Bradbury, 1976; Ray Bradbury: Dramatist, 1989; Non Fiction: Exploring Fantasy Worlds, 1985; Discovering Modern Horror Fiction, I, 1985, II, 1988; Kingdom of Fear, 1986; Discovering H P Lovecraft, 1987; Reign of Fear, 1988; Penguin Encyclopaedia of Horror and the Supernatural, 1986. *Contributions to:* Eldritch Tales; Etchings and Odysseys; Twilight Zone Magazine; Lone Star Fictioneer; Castle Rock: The Stephen King Newsletter; The Scream Factory. *Honours:* First Prizes, Playwriting Contests, 1962, 1964, 1965. *Memberships:* The Dramatists Guild; Horror Writers of America; Rho Chi; Phi Lambda Epsilon. *Address:* 428 Sagamore Avenue, Teaneck, NJ 07666, USA.

ING Dean, b. 1931, American. Freelance Writer since 1977; Engineer. *Appointments:* Engineer, Aerojet-General, Sacramento, California, 1957-62 and Lockheed, San Jose, California, 1962, 1965-70; Assistant Professor of Speech, Missouri State University, Maryville, 1974-77. *Publications:* Soft Targets (novel), 1979; Anasazi (short stories), 1980; Systemic Shock (novel), 1981; High Tension (short stories) 1982; Pulling Through, (novel), 1983; (ed.) The Lagrangists, by Mack Reynolds, 1983; Single Combat (novel), 1983; (ed.) Home Sweet Home 2010 A.D., by Mack Reynolds, 1984; (ed.) Eternity, by Mack Reynolds, 1984; (ed.) The Other Time, by Mack Reynolds, 1984; Wild Country (novel), 1985; (ed.) Trojan Orbit, by Mack Reynolds, 1985.

INGALLS Jeremy, b. 2 Apr 1911. Poet; Retired University Professor; Translator. *Education:* BA, MA, LittD, Tufts University; University of Chicago. *Appointments:* Assistant Professor, English Literature, Western College, 1941-43; Professor, Head, English & American Literature, Director, Asian Studies, Rockford College, 1950s; Rockefeller Foundation Lecturer, American Poetry; Ford Foundation Fellowship, Asian Studies; Fulbright Professor, American Literature, Japan, 1957, 1958. *Publications:* A Book of Legends, 1941; The Metaphysical Sword, 1941; Tahl, 1945; The Galilean Way, 1953; The Woman from the Island, 1958; These Islands Also, 1959; Nakagawa's Tenno Yugao, 1975; The Malice of Empire, 1970; This Stubborn Quantum, 1983; Summer Liturgy, 1985; The Epic Tradition and Related Essays, 1989. *Contributions to:* Poetry Now; Michigan Quarterly Review; Christianity and Crisis; Religion in Life; The Classical Journal; Yearbook of General and Comparative Literature; Literature East and West; East-West Review; Poetry, New Republic; Saturday Review; Accent; American Mercury; American Prefaces; Atlantic Monthly; Beloit Poetry Journal; Chicago Review; Common Sense; Maryland Quarterly; Studia Mystica. *Honours:* Guggenheim Fellowship, Poetry, 1943; American Academy of Arts and Letters Grant, 1944; Shelley Memorial Award, 1950; Lola Ridge Memorial Awards, 1951, 1952; Honorary LHD, Rockford College, 1960; University of Arizona Poetry Centre Lectureship, 1964; Epic Poet Laureate, UPLI, 1965; Steinman Foundation. *Memberships:* Life Member, Poetry Society of America; several other professional organisations. *Address:* 6269 East Rosewood, Tucson, AZ 85711, USA.

INGHAM Daniel. See: **LAMBOT Isobel Mary.**

INGHAM Kenneth, b. 9 Aug 1921. Emeritus Professor of History. m. Elizabeth Mary Southall, 18 June 1949, 1 son, 1 daughter. *Education:* BA 1941, MA 1947, DPhil 1950, University of Oxford. *Publications:* Jan Christian Smuts, 1986; A History of East Africa, 1962; The Making of Modern Uganda, 1958, reprinted, 1983; Reformers in India, 1956, reprinted 1979; The Kingdom of Toro in Uganda, 1975; Politics in Modern Africa, 1990. *Contributions to:* Britannica Book of the Year. *Honour:* Military Cross, 1946; OBE, 1961. *Memberships:* Fellow, Royal Historical Society; Vice-President, The Royal African Society; Vice-President, British Institute in Eastern Africa. *Address:* The Woodlands, 94 West Town Lane, Bristol BS4 5DZ, England.

INGLE Stephen James, b. 6 Nov 1940, Ripon, Yorkshire, England. University Professor. m. Margaret Anne Farmer, 5 Aug 1964, 2 sons, 1 daughter. *Education:* BA Hons, 1962, DipEd, 1963, MA Econ, 1965, University of Sheffield; PhD, Victoria University Wgnton, New Zealand, 1967. *Publications:* Socialist thought in Imaginative Literature, 1979; Parliament and Health Policy, 1981; British Party System, 1989; George Orwell: A Political Life, 1993. *Contributions to:* Many in fields of politics, and literature. *Honours:* Commonwealth Scholar, 1964-67. *Memberships:* Political Studies Association, Secretary, 1987-88. *Address:* Department of Political Studies, University of Stirling, Scotland FK9 4LA.

INGLIS Brian, b. 31 July 1916, Dublin, Ireland. Journalist. m. Ruth Langdon, (div), 1 son, 1 daughter. *Education:* BA, Oxon; PhD, Dublin. *Publications:* The Story of Ireland, 1956; Revolution in Medicine, 1958; Fringe Medicine, 1964; Abdication, 1966; Poverty and the Industrial Revolution, 1971; Roger Casement, 1973; The Forbidden Game, 1975; Natural and Supernatural, 1977; Natural Medicine, 1978; The Alternative Health Guide (with Ruth West), 1983; Science and Parascience, 1984; The Paranormal : An Encyclopedia of Psychic Pheonomena, 1985; The Hidden Power, 1986; The Unkown Guest, 1987; The Power of Dreams, 1987; Trance, 1989; Downstart, (Autobiography), 1989. *Contributions to:* The Lancet; World Medicine; The Guardian; The Times; Spectator; Punch; Encounter; Vogue. *Membership:* Fellow, Royal Society of literature. *Literary Agent:* Curtis Brown. *Address:* Garden Flat, 23 Lambolle Road, London NW3 4HS, England.

INGRAMS Richard Reid, (Philip Reid), b. 11 Aug 1937, London, England. Journalist. m. 1962, 2 sons (1 dec), 1 daughter. *Education:* University College, Oxford. *Appointments:* Joined Private Eye 1962, Editor 1963-86, Chairman 1974-; TV Critic, The Spectator 1976-84. *Publications:* Private Eye on London (with Christopher Booker and William Rushton), 1962; Private Eye's Romantic England, 1963; Mrs Wilson's Diary (with John Wells), 1965; Mrs Wilson's Second Diary, 1966; The Tale of Driver Grope, 1968; The Bible for Motorists (with Barry Fantoni), 1970; The Life and Times of Private Eye, Editor, 1971; Harris in Wonderland (as Philip Reid with Andrew Osmond), 1973; Cobbett's Country Book, Editor, 1974; Beachcomber : the Works of J.B. Morton, Editor, 1974; The Best of Private Eye, 1974; God's Apology, 1977; Goldenballs, 1979; Romney Marsh (with Fay Godwin), 1980; Dear Bill : the Collected letters of Denis Thatcher (with John Wells), 1980; The Other Half, 1981; Piper's Places (with John Piper), 1983; Dr Johnson by Mrs Thrale, Editor, 1984; Down the Hatch (with John Wells), 1985; Just the One (with John Wells), 1986; John Stewart Collis : a Memoir, 1986; The Best of Dear Bill (with John Wells), 1986; John Stewart Collis, 1986; Mud in Your Eye (with J Wells), 1987; The Ridgeway, 1988; You Might As Well be Dead, 1988; England (anthology), 1989; Number 10 (with John Wells), 1989; On and On, 1990. *Address:* c/o Private Eye, 6 Carlisle Street, London, W1, England.

INMAN Robert (Anthony), b. 13 June 1931, San Francisco, California, USA. Writer; Editor. m. Joan Marshall, 18 June 1958, div, 2 sons. *Education:* BA, Great Distinction, Stanford University, 1952;

Universities of Graz and Vienna, Austria, 1952-54; Free University of Berlin, Germany, 1956-57; MA, University of Washington, USA, 1959. *Publications:* The Torturer's Horse, 1965; The Blood Endures, 1981. *Contributions to:* Fiction, articles, book reviews in periodicals; I'll Call You, story, selected for reprint in O Henry Prize Stories, 1971. *Honours:* Fulbright Scholarship, Graz, Austria, 1952-53; Fulbright Scholarship, Playwriting, Vienna, Austria, 1953-54. *Literary Agent:* Gunther Stuhlmann, Becket, MA. *Address:* 720 Gough Street 58, San Francisco, CA 94102, USA.

INNAURATO Albert, b. 2 June, 1947, Philadelphia, Pennsylvania, USA. Playwright; Director. *Education:* BA, Temple University, Philadelphia; BFA, California Institute of the Arts, Valencia, 1972; MFA, Yale University School of Drama, New Haven, Connecticut, USA, 1975. *Career:* Playwright-in-residence, Playwrights Horizons, New York, 1983; Adjunct Professor, Columbia University, New York and Princeton University, New Jersey, 1987; Director of plays, including The Transfiguration of Benno Blimpie, New York, 1983; Herself as Lust, New York, 1983; Coming of Age in Soho, Seattle 1984, New York, 1984 and 1985; Actor in play: I Don't Generally Like Poetry But Have You Read Trees?, New York, 1973. *Publications:* Plays include The Transfiguration of Benno Blimpie (produced New Haven, Connecticut, 1973, New York 1975, London 1978) New Haven, Connecticut, Yale/Theatre, 1976, London, TQ Publications, 1977; The Idiots Karamazov, with Christopher Durang, music by Jack Feldman, lyrics by Durang (also director: produced New Haven, Connecticut, 1974). New Haven, Connecticut, Yale/Theatre, 1974; augmented edition, New York Dramatists Play Service, 1981; Earth Worms (produced Waterford, Connecticut, 1974; New York 1977) Included in Bizarre Behavior, 1980; Gemini (produced New York, 1976). New York Dramatists Play Service, 1977; Ulysses in Traction (produced New York, 1977). New York Dramatists Play Service, 1978; Passione (also director: produced New York, 1980) New York, Dramatists Play Service, 1981. *Honours:* Guggenheim grant, 1975; Rockefeller Grant, 1977; Obie Award, 1977; National Endowment for the Arts Grant, 1986. *Literary Agent:* George Lane, William Morris Agency, New York. *Address:* 325 West 22nd Street, New York, NY 10011, USA.

INNES Brian, b. 4 May 1928, Croydon, Surrey, England. Writer and Publisher. m. (1) Felicity McNair Wilson, 5 Oct 1956; (2) Eunice Lynch, 2 Apr. 1971 (diss 1984) 3 sons. *Education:* Whitgift School, Croydon, 1938-46; BSc. (Special) Kings College, London, 1946-49. *Literary Appointments:* Assistant Editor, Chemical Age, 1953-55; Associate Editor, The British Printer, 1955-60; Art Director, Hamlyn Group, 1960-62; Director, Temperance Seven Ltd, 1961-; Director, Innes Promotions Ltd, and Animated Graphic and Publicity, 1964-65; Proprietor, Brian Innes Agency 1964-66; Proprietor, Immediate Books, 1966-70; Proprietor, FOT Library 1970-; Creative Director and Deputy Chairman, Orbis Publishing Ltd, 1970-86; Creative Director, British Magazine Publishing Corporation, 1986-88. *Publications:* Book of Pirates, 1966; Book of Revolutions, 1967; Book of Outlaws, 1968; Flight, 1970; Saga of The Railways, 1972; Horoscopes, 1976; The Tarot, 1977; Editor, Rococo To Romanticism, 1977; Book of Change, 1979; The Red Baron Lives!, 1981; The Red Red Baron, 1983; The Havana Cigar, 1983; Crooks and Conmen, 1993. *Contributions to:* Made numerous recordings, films and radio and TV broadcasts; many photographs published. *Honours:* Royal Variety Command Performance, 1961. *Memberships:* Fellow, Chartered Society of Designers; Fellow, Royal Society of Arts; Member, Institute of Printing. *Address:* Les Forges de Montgaillard, 11330 Mouthoumet, France.

INNES Hammond. *See:* **HAMMOND-INNES Ralph.**

INOUE Kenji, b. 15 Feb 1929, Tokyo, Japan. Professor of English. m. Midori Yoshiura, 10 May 1956, 1 son. *Education:* BA, University of Tokyo, 1951; Graduate School of University of Tokyo, 1953; Graduate Course, Oberlin College, USA, 1956-60. *Publications:* Amerika Dokushno Note, 1991; Amerika Bungakushi Nyumon, 1979; Salinger no Sekai, 1969; Amerika Bungakushi 1981; Works of Frank Norris, 1984; Translations: Faulkner: Wild Palms, 1968; Rabbit Redux, 1993; A Month of Sundays, 1988; Steinbeck: Cannery Row, 1989; The Slave, 1975; Winner TAke Nothing, 1982. *Contributions to:* Eigo Seinen; Kaoen; Dokushojin; Tosho Shinbun; Teinbeck Quarterly. *Honours:* Recognition Award, International John Steinbeck Society, 1991. *Memberships:* American Literature Society of Japan, President, 1986-90, Senior Consultant, 1991-; American Studies Association of Japan Nihon Bungeika Kyokai; International John Steinbeck Society. *Address:* 1-3-8 Sekimae, Musashino-shi, Tokyo 180, Japan.

INSINGEL Mark, b. 3 May 1935, Lier, Antwerp, Belgium. Author. 1 son. *Education:* MA, Koninklijk Vlaams Muziek-Conservatorium, 1959; French Litterature, Sorbonne, Paris, 1960-62. *Publications:* Reflections, 1970; A Course of Time, 1977; When a Lady..., 1982; That is to Say, 1986; MY Territory, 1987; Perpetuum Mobile, 1969; Modellen, 1970; Posters, 1984, (poetry). *Contributions to:* Major literary journals and magazines in Holland and Dutch-speaking Belgium. *Memberships:* Treasurer, PEN Centre, Belgium; Maatschappij voor Nederlandse Letterkunde te Leiden. *Address:* Rucaplein 205, B-2610 Antwerpen, Belgium.

IOANNIDES I D, b. 25 Nov 1931, Kavala, Greece. Professor of Educational Psychology (Retired). m. Rita Kalodemou, 30 Aug 1970, 1 daughter. *Education:* Diploma, Teachers College; Postgraduate degree, University of Athens, 1963; American University, Beirut, 1959; University of Thessaloniki, English, 1961; Master's degree, Temple University, Philadelphia, USA, 1965. *Appointments:* Teacher, Elementary School, 1952; Professor, Teachers' College, Thessalonika, 1965. *Publications include:* The Golden Bow, 1975; The White Horse, 1968; Secret Journeys, 1970; A Girl With Two Mothers, 1984; Educational Psychology, 1977; A Ship in the Shop Window, 1979; The Three Boys, 1980; Zaza: Elephant Dreams, 1986; A Story in a Blue Pencil,.1985; Without a Stem, 1984; Radiography, 1971; The Whip & the Umbrella, 1985; etc. *Contributions to:* Nea Estia; Nea Poria; Erevna; Skapti Ili; The Athenian; To Rhodi; etc. *Honours:* 2 awards, Womens Literary Association; Award, Greek Literary Association of Athens. *Memberships:* Greek Literary Association of Thessaliniki; Circle of Greek Children's Book Writers; Greek Educational Society. *Literary Agent:* Kedros, A S E, Kastaniotis. *Address:* 2 Arist. Stani Street, Kavala 65403, Greece.

IOANNOU Susan, b. 4 Oct 1944, Toronto, Canada. Writer; Editor. m. Lazaros Ioannou, 28 Aug 1967, 1 son, 1 daughter. *Education:* BA, 1966, MA, 1967, University of Toronto. *Appointments:* Managing Editor, Coiffure du Canada, 1979-80; Associate Editor, Cross-Canada Writers' Magazine, 1980-89; Poetry Editor, Arts Scarborough Newsletter, 1980-85; Poetry Instructor, Toronto Board of Education, 1982-; Poetry Instructor, University of Toronto, 1989-90. *Publications:* Spare Words, 1984; Motherpoems, 1985; The Crafted Poem, 1985; Familiar Faces, Private Griefs, 1986; Ten Ways To Tighten Your Prose, 1988; Writing Reader-Friendly Poems, 1989; Clarity Between Clouds, 1991. *Contributions to:* Numerous professional journals. *Honours:* Norma Epstein Foundation Award, University of Toronto, 1965; Honorary Member, Cross-Canada Writers' Workshop, 1980; Book Cellar Mother's Day Poem Award, 1982; Arts Scarborough City Poetry Contest (winner), 1987. *Memberships:* Canadian Poetry Association; Freelance Editors' Association of Canada; League of Canadian Poets. *Address:* PO Box 456, Station O, Toronto, Ontario M4A 2P1, Canada.

IPSEN David Carl, b. 15 Feb 1921, Schenectady, New York, USA, Freelance Writer. m. Heather Marian Zoccola, 28 Aug 1949, 2 sons. *Education:* BS, Engineering, University of Michigan, 1942; PhD, Mechanical Engineering, University of California, 1953.

Publications: Units, Dimensions and Dimensionless Numbers, 1960; The Riddle of the Stegosaurus, 1969; Units, Rattlesnakes and Scientists, 1970; What Does a Bee See? 1971; The Elusive Zebra, 1971; Eye of the Whirlwind: The Story of John Scopes, 1973; Isaac Newton: Reluctant Genius, 1985; Archimedes: Greatest Scientist of the Ancient World, 1988. *Membership:* The Authors Guild. *Address:* 655 Vistamont Avenue, Berkeley, CA 94708, USA.

IRBY Kenneth, b. 18 Nov 1936, Bowie, Texas, USA. Writer; Teacher. *Education:* BA, University of Kansas; MA, 1960, PhD, Studies, 1962-63, Harvard University; MLS, University of California, 1968. *Publications:* The Roadrunner Poem, 1964; Kansas-New Mexico, 1965; Movements/Sequences, 1965; The Flower of Having Passed Through Paradise in a Dream, 1968; Relation, 1970; T Max Douglas, 1971; Archipelago, 1976; Catalpa, 1977; Orexis, 1981; Riding the Dog, 1982; A Set, 1983; Call Steps, 1992. *Contributions to:* Anthologies and magazines including: Chicago Review; Paris Review; Poetry; Poetry Review; Parnassus; Conjunctions (contributing editor). *Address:* N-311 Regency Pl., Lawrence, KS 66049, USA.

IRELAND David, b. 1927, Australia. Author; Playwright; Freelance Writer. *Publications:* Image of Clay (play), 1962; The Chantic Bird, 1968; The Unknown Industrial Prisoner, 1971; The Flesheaters, 1972; Burn, 1975; The Glass Canoe, 1976; A Woman of the Future, 1979; City of Woman, 1981; Archimedes and the Seagle, 1984; Bloodfather, 1989.

IRELAND Kevin Mark, b. 18 July 1933, Auckland, New Zealand. Writer. m. Phoebe Caroline Dalwood. 2 sons. *Appointments:* Writer-in-Residence, Canterbury University, 1986; Sargeson Fellow 1987, Literary Fellow 1989, Auckland University. *Publications:* Poetry: Face to Face, 1964; Educating the Body, 1967; A Letter from Amsterdam, 1972; Orchids Hummingbirds and Other Poems, 1974; A Grammar of Dreams, 1975; Literary Cartoons, 1978; The Dangers of Art, 1980; Practice Night in the Drill Hall, 1984; The Year of the Comet, 1986; Selected Poems, 1987; Tiberius at the Beehive, 1990; Editor, The New Zealand Collection-A Celebration of the New Zealand Novel, 1989. *Honour:* New Zealand National Book Award for Poetry, 1979. *Membership:* President PEN, New Zealand. *Address:* 1 Anne St, Devonport, Auckland 9, New Zealand.

IRSFELD John Henry, b. 2 Dec 1937, Bemidji, Minnesota, USA. Vice President & Deputy to President, University of Nevada; Writer. m. (2) Janet Elizabeth Jones, 5 May 1984. 1 daughter, previous marriage. *Education:* BA 1959, MA 1966, PhD 1969, University of Texas. *Literary Appointments:* Senior editor, Las Vegan (city magazine) 1980-85, LV (magazine of Las Vegas) 1985-87; Editorial Board, University of Nevada Press, 1985-; Nevada Historical Society Quarterly, 1987-89. *Publications:* Little Kingdoms, 1976; Coming Through, 1975; Rats Alley, 1987. *Contributions to:* Kansas Quarterly; Nunc Dimittis; South Dakota Review; Halcyon; Los Angeles Reader; Library Journal; College English; The Sparrow; Western American Literature; Texas Observer; Robb Report; The Writer. *Honours:* Stories selected for mention in : Distinctive Short Stories, 1974, Martha Foley's Best American Short Stories, 1975. *Address:* University of Nevada, Las Vegas, Las Vegas, Nevada 889154, USA.

IRVING Clifford, (John Luckless), b. 1930, United States of America. Author; Screen Playwright. *Publications:* On a Darkling Plain, 1956; The Losers, 1957; The Valley, 1962; The 38th Floor, 1965; Spy (with H. Burkholz), 1969; The Battle of Jerusalem, 1970; Fake!, 1970; Global Village Idiot: Extracts from Nixon Tapes, 1973; Project Octavio, 1978; The Death Freak, 1979; The Hoax, 1981; Tom Mix and Pancho Villa, 1982; The Sleeping Spy, 1983; The Angel of Zin, 1984; Daddy's Girl, 1988; Trial, 1990; Final Argument, 1993. *Literary Agent:* Frank Cooper, 10100 Santa Monica Blvd, Los Angeles, CA 90067, USA. *Address:* c/o Frank Cooper.

IRVING John Winslow, b. 2 Mar 1942, New Hampshire, USA. Novelist. m. (1) Shyla Lery, 1964, div 1981, 2 sons; (2) Janet Turnbull, 1987, 1 son. *Education:* BA, University of New Hampshire; MFA, University of Iowa, 1967. *Publications:* A Prayer for Owen Meany, 1989; The Cider House Rules, 1985; The Hotel New Hampshire, 1981; The World According to Garp, 1978; The 158 Pound Marriage, 1974; The Water-Method Man, 1972; Setting Free the Bears, 1969. *Contributions to:* New York Times Book Review; The New Yorker; Rolling Stone; Esquire; Playboy. *Honours:* O'Henry Prize, Best Short Stories, 1981; Pushcard Prize, Best of the Small Presses, 1978; The American Book Award, 1979. *Memberships:* Executive Board, PEN American Centre. *Literary Agent:* Janet Turnbull, The Turnbull Agency. *Address:* c/o The Turnbull Agency, PO Box 757, Dorset, VT O5251, USA.

ISAACS Alan, (Alec Valentine), b. 14 Jan 1925, London, England. Writer, Lexicographer, Encyclopedist. m. Alison Coster, 1 son, 3 daughters. *Education:* St Paul's School 1938-42; Imperial College 1942-50; PhD, BSc, DIC, ACGI. *Publications include:* Introducing Science, Penguin, Basic Books, 1965; Survival of God in the Scientific Age, Penguin, 1967; Penguin Dictionary of Science (with Uvarov) 1964; Macmillan Encyclopedia (Editor) 1981; Collins English Dictionary (Science Editor) 1978; Longman Dictionary of Physics (with Gray) 1975; Brewster's Twentieth Century Phrase and Fable (editor), 1991. *Contributions to:* Nature; New Scientist. *Address:* 74 West Street, Harrow-on-the-Hill, HA1 3ER, England.

ISAACS Susan, b. 7 Dec 1943. Novelist; Screenwriter. m. 11 Aug 1968, 1 son, 1 daughter. *Education:* Queens College, Flushing, New York, 3 years. *Publications:* Compromising Positions, 1978; Close Relations, 1980; Almost Paradise, 1984; Shining Through, 1988; Magic Hour, 1991; Film scripts: Compromising Positions, 1985; Hello Again, 1987. *Contributions to:* Book reviews to: New York Times; Washington Post; Newsday; Detroit News; Essays to: New York Times Arts and Leisure; American Film. *Memberships:* National Book Critics Circle; PEN; Poets and Writers; Authors Guild; Mystery Writers of America; International Crime Writers Association. *Literary Agent:* Owen Laster, William Morris Agency. *Address:* c/o Harper Collins, 10 Eaast 53rd Street, New York, NY 10022, USA.

ISAACSON Judith Magyar, b. 3 July 1925, Kaposvar, Hungary. Writer; Retired Dean. m. Irving Isaacson, 24 Dec 1945, 2 sons, 1 daughter. *Education:* Matura, Gimnazium, Kaposvar, Hungary, 1943; BA, Bates College, 1965; MA Bowdoin College, 1967. *Publications:* Seed of Sarah, 1990, in German, 1991. *Contributions to:* The Yale Review. *Literary Agent:* Julian Bach, New York. *Address:* 13 Barkley Place, Auburn, ME 04210, USA.

ISHIGURO Kazuo, b. 1954. Japan, Novels/Short stories. Writer; Resettlement worker, West London Cyrenians Ltd, 1981-82. *Appointments:* Grouse-Beater for the Queen Mother, Balmoral, Scotland, 1973; Community worker, Glasgow, 1976; Residential Social Worker, London, 1979. *Publications:* Novels: A Pale View of Hills, 1982; An Artist of the Floating World, 1986; The Remains of the Day, 1989; Short stories include: The Summer After the War appeared in Granta, 1980; Family Supper appeared in Quarto and has also been published in Firebird and in The Penguin Collection of Modern Short Stories, edited by Malcolm Bradbury; Plays for Channel 4 TV: A Profile of Arthur J Mason, 1985 and The Gourmet, 1987. *Honours:* A Pale View of Hills was awarded the Winifred Holtby Prize by the Royal Society of Literature; An Artist of the Floating World was winner of the Whitbread Book of the Year Award and was shortlisted for the 1986 Booker Prize; The Remains of the Day, awarded Booker Prize, 1989; Honorary Doctor of Letters, University of Kent, 1990; Fellow, Royal Society of Literature, 1989; Fellow, Royal Society of Arts, 1990. *Address:* c/o Faber & Faber Ltd, 3 Queen Square, London WC1N 3AU, England.

IWASE Tsuneko, b. 26 Jan 1940, Tokyo, Japan. University Professor. *Education:* BA, 1966, MA, 1967, Western Michigan University. Certified General Travel Service Supervisor, 1986. *Publications:* English for the Hospitality Industry, 1987; How to Road Materials for the Travel Business, 1990; English for Tour Operators Tomorrow, 1989; An English Dictionary of Travel Business, 1990; Enjoyment of Classroom Reading, 1977. *Contributions to:* Journal of Transportation World, 1991. *Memberships:* International Steinbeck Society; Japan-American Literary Society; Japan-English Literary Society. *Address:* 14-9 Schome Suginami-ku, Tokyo 166, Japan.

J

J J. *See:* JUNOR John Donald Brown (Sir).

J K. *See:* MAYHAR Ardath (Frances).

JACK Donald. *See:* JACK Donald Lamont.

JACK Donald Lamont, (Donald Jack), b. 6 Dec 1924, Radcliffe, Manchester, England. Professional Writer. m. Nancy Tolhurst, 22 Nov 1952, (dec). 2 daughters. *Education:* Bury Grammar School, Lancs; Marr College, Troon, Ayrshire. *Publications:* Story of Canadian Medicine, 1981; Sinc, Betty and the Morning Man, 1977; The Bandy Papers, 1962, 1973, 1975, 1979, 1982, 1987, 1989. *Contributions to:* Weekend magazine; Books in Canada; MacLean's. *Honours:* Leacock Medal and Award for Humour, 1962, 1973, 1979; Author's Award, Periodical Distributors of Canada, 1983. *Literary Agent:* A L Hart, Philadelphia, USA. *Address:* Doubleday Canada, 105 Bond Street, Toronto, Canada M5B 1Y3.

JACK Ian (Robert James), b. 1923, British. *Appointments:* Lecturer, Fellow, Brasenose College, Oxford, 1950-61; Visiting Professor, University of Alexandria, 1960; de Carle Lecturer, University of Otago, New Zealand, 1964; Warton Lecturer, British Academy, 1967; Visiting Professor, University of Chicago 1968-69, University of California, Berkeley 1968-69, University of BC 1975, University of Virginia 1980-81, Tsuda College, Tokyo 1981; Fellow 1961-, Librarian 1965-75, Pembroke College; Lecturer in English 1961-73, Reader in English 1973-76, Professor of English Literature 1976-, Cambridge University. *Publications:* Augustan Satire, 1952; English Literature 1815-1832 (Oxford History of English Literature), 1963; Keats and the Mirror of Art, 1967; Browning's Major Poetry, 1973; The Brontës novels, Clarendon Ed (gen ed), E Brontë's Wuthering Heights (ed with H Marsden), 1976; Oxford English Texts Edition of Brownings Poetical Works (ed), Vol.1, 1983, reprinted, 1985, Vol.II, 1984, reprinted, 1992, Vol.III, 1988, Vol.IV, 1991, Vol.V, in preparation. *Address:* Highfield House, High Street, Fen Ditton, Cambridgeshire CB5 8ST, England.

JACKMAN Brian, b. 25 Apr 1935, Epsom, Surrey, UK. Journalist. m. 14 Feb 1964, 1 daughter. *Education:* Grammar school. *Appointment:* Staff, Sunday Times, 1970-. *Publications:* The Marsh Lions, 1982; The Countryside in Winter, 1986; We Learned to Ski, co-author, 1974; Dorset Coast Path, HMSO Guide, 1977; My Serengeti Years, editor, 1987. *Contributions to:* Country Living; Country Life; BBC Wildlife; Script consultant, Survival, Anglia TV. *Honours:* TTG Travel Writer of the Year, 1982; Wildscreen 1982 Award, Best Wildlife TV Commentary Script, Osprey. *Memberships:* Fellow, Royal Geographical Society; Past Council Member, Fauna & Flora Preservation Society. *Literary Agent:* Curtis Brown. *Address:* Way Cottage, Powerstock, Nr Bridport, Dorset DT6 3TF, England.

JACKMAN Stuart (Brooke), b. 1922, British. *Appointments:* Congregational Minister, Barnstaple, Devon 1948-52, Pretoria, South Africa 1952-55, Caterham, Surrey 1955-61, Auckland 1961-65, Upminster, Essex 1965-67, Oxted, Surrey 1969-; Editor, Council for World Mission, London, 1967-71, Oxted, Surrey, 1969-81, Melbourn, Cambs, 1981-87. *Publications:* Portrait in Two Colours, 1948; But They Won't Lie Down: Three Plays, The Numbererd Days, 1954; Angels Unawares, 1956; One Finger for God, 1957; My Friend, My Brother, 1958; The Waters of Dinyanti, 1959; The Lazy TV and Other Stories, The Daybreak Boys, 1961; This Desirable Property, The Davidson Affair, 1966; The Golden Orphans, 1968; Guns Covered with Flowers, 1973; Slingshot, 1975; The Burning Men, 1976; Operation Catcher, 1980; A Game of Soldiers, The Davidson File, 1981. *Address:* c/o Curtis Brown, 162-168 Regent Street, London W1R 5TB, England.

JACKOWSKA Nicki, b. 6 Aug 1942, Brighton, Sussex, England. Writer; Tutor. 1 daughter. *Education:* BA, Hons, Philosophy 1977, MA, Philosophy, 1978, University of Sussex. *Appointments:* Freelance writer; Short periods as writer-in-residence; Tutor to numerous workshops, weekend and residential courses throughout Britain; Founder and Tutor, The Brighton Writing School; Writer-in-Residence, Brighton Festival, 1987, 1988, 1989; Readings, forums, TV and Radio appearances. *Publications:* Fiction: Doctor Marbles and Marianne - A Romance, 1982; The Road to Orc, 1985; The Islanders, 1987; Poetry: The House that Manda Built, 1981; Earthwalks, 1982; Letters to Superman, 1984; Gates to the City, 1985; News from the Brighton Front, Sinclair-Stevson, 1993. *Contributions to:* Poetry and fiction: Ambit; Resurgence; Poetry Review; Outposts; Bananas; Poetry Wales; New Statesman; Tribune; Writing Women; Poetry Durham; Stand; The Rialto. *Honours:* Winner, Stroud Festival Poetry Competition, 1972; Continental Bursary SEARTS, 1978; C Day Lewis Fellowship 1982; Arts Council Writers Fellowship, 1984-85; Prizewinner Stand International Short Story Competition, 1986. *Membership:* The Poetry Society. *Literary Agent:* Judy Martin, 20 Powis Mews, London W11 1JN. *Address:* 98 Ewart Street, Brighton BN2 2VQ, East Sussex, England.

JACKS Oliver. *See:* GANDLEY Kenneth Royce.

JACKSON E F. *See:* TUBB E C.

JACKSON Everatt. *See:* MUGGESON Margaret Elizabeth.

JACKSON G Mark, b. 27 Aug 1952, Atlanta, Georgia, USA. *Education:* Spring Hill College, 1971-75; BA, University of Alabama, 1976; MA, University of Central Florida, 1988. *Appointments:* Writer, Jefferson Advertiser, Birmingham, 1978-79; Writer, Southside News and Sentinel Star, Orlando, 1979-81; Freelance Writer, 1981-. *Publications:* NINJA - Men of I ga, 1989. *Contributions to:* Martial Arts Movies; Action Films; Black Belt; Fighting Stars Ninja; American Karate and FLorida Automotive. *Honours:* Jesse Hill Ford's Creative Writing Workshop, 1978; Robert M Young's Film Directing Seminar, 1981. *Memberships:* Florida Freelance Writer Association. *Address:* 2043 SE Isabell Road, Port St Lucie, FL 34952, USA.

JACKSON Guida. *See:* JACKSON-LAUFER Guida Myrl Miller.

JACKSON Harold Hobson, b. 2 Oct 1932, London, England. Journalist.m. Christine Ann Harding, Oct 1977, 2 sons. *Education:* Brunce Court School, 1943-48; Wormwood Scrubbs, 1951. *Appointments:* Manchester Guardian, 1950-, including: Sub-Editor, 1952-66; Roving foreign correspondent, 1966-72; Features editor, 1972-78; Chief Washington correspondent, 1979-85; Chief systems editor, 1986-. *Publications:* The Two Irelands, 1970; Decade of Disillusion, co-author, 1972; The British Press: A Manifesto, co-author, 1978; Bedside Guardian 18, 1969. *Contributions to:* Numerous publications and broadcasting media in UK, USA, Ireland, Australia, New Zealand, Holland, Canada. *Honours:* News Reporter of the Year, British Press Awards, 1969; Commendation, reporting Northern Ireland, Granada Press Awards, 1970. *Address:* c/o The Guardian, 119 Farrington Road, London, EC1R 5ER, England.

JACKSON Kenneth T(erry), b. 1939, American. *Appointments:* Assistant Professor of History 1968-71, Director of Urban Studies 1970-77, Associate Professor 1971-76, Professor of History 1976-, Barzun Professor of History and the Social Sciences, 1990-, Columbia University, NYC; Executive Secretary, Society of American Historians Incorporated, 1970-1991; General Editor, Columbia History of Urban Life series, 1980-; Chairman, Bradley Commission on History in Schools, 1987-1990; Chairman, National Council for History

Education, 1990-1992. *Publications:* The Ku Klux Klan in the City 1915-1930, 1967; American Vistas, 2 volumes (ed with L Dinnerstein), 1971, 5th edition, 1987; Cities in American History (ed with S K Schultz), 1972; Atlas of American History, 1978; Crabgrass Frontier: The Suburbanization of the United States, 1985; Silent Cities: The Evolution of the American Cemetery, 1989. *Honours:* Bancroft Prize, 1986; Francis Parkman Prize, 1986. *Address:* Department of History, Columbia University, New York, NY 10027, USA.

JACKSON MacDonald Pairman, b. 13 Oct 1938, Auckland, New Zealand. University Professor. m. Nicole Philippa Lovett, 2 Sept 1964, 1 son, 2 daughters. *Education:* MA Hons, University of New Zealand, 60; BLitt, Oxford, 1964. *Appointments:* Lecturer in English, University of Auckland, 1964; Professor since 1989. *Publications:* Studies in Attribution: Middleton and Shakespeare, 1979; The Revenger's Tragedy: Attributed to Thomas Middleton, ed, 1983; The Oxford Book of New Zealing Writing Since 1945, ed, 1983; The Selected Plays of John Marston, ed, 1986; Shakespeare's A Lover's Complaint: Its Date and Authenticity, 1965. *Contributions to:* Chapters in the Cambridge Companion to Shakespeare Studies, 1968; The Oxford History of New Zealand Literature in English, 1991 and five other books; Academic and literary journals. *Honours:* Folger Shakespeare Library Fellowship, 1989. *Memberships:* International Shakespeare Association. *Address:* 21 Te Kowhai Pl, Remuera, Auckland 5, New Zealand.

JACKSON Neville. *See:* **GLASKIN Gerald Marcus.**

JACKSON Richard Paul, b. 17 Nov 1946, Lawrence, MA, USA. Poet; Critic; Editor; College Professor. m. Margaret McCarthy, 28 June 1970, 1 daughter. *Education:* BA English, Merrimack College, 1969; MA English, Breadloaf School of English, Middlesbury College, 1972; PhD English, Yale University, 1976. *Appointments:* English Professor, University Chattanouga, 1976; Director of McAcham Writer's Workshops, 1986; Staff, Vermont College MFA In Writing Programme, 1987; Staff, Bread Loaf Writers Conference, 1987. *Publications:* Poetry: Alive All Day, 1992; Worlds Apart, 1987; part of the Story, 1983; Dismantling Time in Contemporary Poetry, 1989; Acts of Mind, 1983; Four Slovene Poets, 1992; Selected Poems, 1992; The Poetry Miscellany, 1971; The Poetry Miscellany Chapbooks, 1989. *Contributions to:* Georgia Review; Prairie Schooner; Studies in romanticism; Boundary Z; Poetry; Poetry Northwest; Kenyon Review; Antioch Review; New England Review; Bread Loaf Quarterly. *Honours:* NEH Research Grant, 1980; NEA Creative Writing Grant, 1984; Agee Prize in Criticism, 1989; Pushcart Prizes in Poetry, 1987, 1992; Crazyhorse Magazine Poetry Prize, 1989; Cleveland State University Poetry Prize, 1991. *Memberships:* PEN; Associated Writing Programmes; MLA; SAMLA. *Address:* 3413 Alta Vista Dr, Chattanooga, TN 37411, USA.

JACKSON Robert Louis, b. 10 Nov 1923, New York, USA. Professor, Russian Literature. m. Elizabeth Mann Gillette, 18 July 1951, 2 daughters. *Education:* BA, Cornell University, 1944; MA 1949, Certificate, Russian Institute 1949, Columbia University; PhD, University of California, Berkeley, 1956. *Literary Appointments:* Instructor 1954, Assistant Professor 1958, Professor of Russian Literature 1967, Yale University. *Publications:* Dostoevsky's Underground Man in Russian Literature, 1958; Dostoevsky's Quest for Form: Study of his Philosophy of Art, 1966; The Art of Dostoevsky, 1981; Dialogues with Dostoevsky: The Overwhelming Questions, 1993. Editor: Chekhov: Collection, Critical Essays, 1967; Crime & Punishment, Collected Critical Essays, 1974; Dostoevsky: Collected Critical Essays, 1984; Reading Chekhov's Text, 1993. *Contributions to:* Yale Review; Yale French Studies; Comparative Literature; Slavic Review; Slavic & East European Journal; Scando-Slavica; Slavica Hierosolymitana; Russian Literature; Ricerche Slavistiche; Sewanee Review; Dostoevsky Studies; Voprosy Literatory. *Honours:* Fellow, American Council of Learned Societies, 1950, 1951; Yale Morse Fellowship, 1961-

62; Guggenheim Fellow, 1967-68; National Endowment for the Humanities Fellowship, 1974. *Memberships:* Phi Beta Kappa; President, North American Dostoevsky Society 1970-77, International Dostoevsky Society 1977-83, International Chekhov Society 1977-, Vyacheslav Ivanov Convivium 1981-; Director, Yale Conferences in Slavic Literatures and Culture, 1980- ; American Association for Advancement of Slavic Studies. *Address:* Box 3, Hall of Graduate Studies, Yale University, New Haven, CT 06520, USA.

JACKSON Stanley Webber, b. 17 Nov 1920, Montreal, Canada. Physician; Psychiatrist; Historian of Medicine; Psychoanalyst. *Education:* BCom, 1941, MD, CM, 1950, McGill University; Diploma, San Francisco Psychoanalytic Institute and Seattle Psychoanalytic Training Centre, 1962; MA Hons, Yale University, 1975. *Appointments:* Editorial Board, Journal of the History of Medicine and Allied Sciences, 1968-1972; Editorial Advisory Board: Classics of Psychiatry and Behavioural Sciences Library, 1987-, History of Psychiatry, 1990- ; Assistant Professor, Associate Professor, Professor, Psychiatry and History of Medicine, Yale University, 1966-1991; Professor Emeritus, 1991-; Editor, Journal of History of Medicine and Allied Sciences, 1992-. *Publications:* Melancholia and Depression: From Hippocratic times to Modern Times, 1986; Observations on Maniacal Disorders, editor and introduction, 1988; Numerous articles on the history of medicine and history of psychiatry. *Memberships:* Life Fellow, American Psychiatric Association; American Association for the History of Medicine; History of Science Society; American Historical Association; Life, American Psychoanalytic Association. *Address:* 72 Downs Road, Bethany, CT 06524, USA.

JACKSON William Godfrey Fothergill, b. 28 Aug 1917, Lancashire, England. Retired General, British Army; former Governor of Gibraltor, 1977-82. m. Joan Mary Buesden, 7 Sept 1946, 1 son, 1 daughter. *Education:* MA, Mechanical Science Tripos, King's College, Cambridge; Staff College, Camberley; Imperial Defence College. *Publications:* British Official History of The Mediterranean and Middle East Campaigs 1940-45, Vol VI, Pts I, II and III, 1986-88; Attack In The West, 1953; Seven Roads to Moscow, 1957; Battle For Italy, 1967; Battle For Rome, 1968; Alexander of Tunis, 1971; North African Campaigns, 1975; Overlord: Normandy 1944, 1978; Rock Of The Gibraltarians, 1986; Withdrawal From Empire, 1986; The Alternative Third World War, 1987; Britain's Defence Dilemmas, 1990; The Chiefs, 1992. *Honours:* GBE, 1975; KCB, 1971; OBE, 1958; MC, 1940; Bar to MC, 1944; Kings Medal, Royal Military Academy, Woolwich, 1937; Rusi Gold Medals, 1953 and 1964. *Address:* West Stowell, Marlborough, Wiltshire SN8 4JU, England.

JACKSON William Keith, b. 5 Sept 1928, Colchester, Essex, England. University Profesor. 3 sons. *Education:* Teachers Certificate, Borough Road Teachers Training College, London; BA, 1st Class Honours, University of Nottingham; PhD, University of Otago, New Zealand. *Publications:* NZ Politics in Action (with R M Chapman & A V Mitchell), 1962; New Zealand (with John Harré), 1969; The NZ Legislative Council, 1972; NZ Politics of Change, 1973; Beyond New Zealand (with J Henderson & R N Kennaway), 1980; The Dilemma of Parliament, 1987; Fight for Life: NZ, Britain & the EEC, 1971. *Contributions to:* Various popular and academic journals, also radio & tv current affairs commentaries within New Zealand and overseas. *Honours:* Mobil Award, Radio NZ, 1979 Best Spoken Current Affairs Programme; Henry Chapman Fellow, Institute of Commonwealth Studies, London, 1963; Canterbury Fellowship, 1986. *Memberships:* Editorial Advisory Boards: Journal of Commonwealth & Comparative Studies, 1972-90; Political Science, 1975-; Politics, 1981-; Electoral Studies, 1982-; NZ Journalism Review, 1988-. *Address:* 92 Hinau Street, Christchurch 4, New Zealand.

JACKSON-LAUFER Guida Myrl Miller, (Guida Jackson), b. Clarendon, Texas, USA. Author; University

Lecturer; Editor. m. (1) Prentice Lamar Jackson, 1954; (2) William Hervey Laufer, 1986. 3 sons, 1 daughter. *Education:* BA, Texas Tech University, 1954; MA, California State University, 1986; PhD, Greenwich University International Institute of Advanced Studies, 1989. *Appointments:* Managing Editor, Touchstone Literary Journal, 1976-; Lecturer in Writing, 1986-. *Publications:* Passing Through, 1979; The Lamentable Affair of the Vicar's Wife, 1981; Heart to Heart, 1988; Women Who Ruled, 1990; Virginia Diaspora, 1992; Encyclopaedia of Traditional Epic, 1993; Compiler, African Women Write, 1990; Co-author, The Three Ingredients, 1981; Contributor to New Growth, Contemporary Fiction by Texas Writers, 1988. *Contributions to:* University of North Texas Press New Texas 1991; University of North Texas Press New Texas 92; Texas Country; Thema; Town and Country; Conjunto; North American Mentor. *Honours:* Faulkner Award for Fiction; Huey Call Fiction Award, 1991; Porter Award, Associated Texas Writers, 1991; Chapter One Award, 1992. *Memberships:* Authors United of Houston; Welty Society, President; Associated Texas Writers. *Literary Agent:* Molly Friedrich; Aaron Priest Inc. *Address:* Touchstone, PO Box 8308, Spring, TX 77387, USA.

JACOB Anthony Dillingham, (Piers Anthony), b. 1934. Author. *Publications:* Chthon, 1967; Omnivore, 1968; Orn, 1971; Ox (novel trilogy), 1976; The Ring (with Robert E. Margroff), 1968; Macroscope, 1969; The E.S.P. Worm (with Robert E. Margroff), 1970; Prostho Plus, 1973; Race Against Time (juvenile), 1973; Rings of Ice, 1974; Triple Detente, 1974; Martial arts adventure series (with Roberto Fuentes)- Kiai!, 1974, Mistress of Death, 1974, Bamboo Bloodbath, 1974, Ninja's Revenge, 1975, Amazon Slaughter, 1976; Phthor, 1975; Steppe, 1976; But What of Earth? (with Robert Coulson), 1976; Hasan, 1977; Cluster, 1977; Chaining the Lady, 1978; Kirlian Quest, 1978; Thousandstar, 1980; Viscous Circle (novel quitology), 1982; Xanth series - A Spell for Chameleon, 1977, The Source of Magic, 1979; Castle Roogna, 1979 (1st 3 vols published as The Magic of Xanth, 1981), Centaur Aisle, 1982, Ogre, Ogre, 1982, Night Mare, 1983, Dragon on a Pedestal, 1983; Crewel Lye, 1985; Battle Circle, 1978 (novel trilogy); Var the Stick, 1973; Neq the Sword (with Frances Hall), 1975; The Pretender, 1979; God of Tarot, 1979; Vision of Tarot, 1980, Faith of Tarot, 1980 (novel in 3 vols); Mute, 1981; The Apprentice Adept, 1982 (novel trilog, Blue Adept, 1981, Juxtaposition, 1982; Incarnations os Immortality series, On a Pale Horse, 1983; Bearing an Hourglass, 1984, With a tangled Skein, 1985, Weilding a Red Sword, 1986, Bio of a Space Tyrant quintology - Refugee, 1983, Mecenary, 1984; Polition, 1985, Executive, 1985, Statesman, 1986; Anthology, 1985; Ghost, 1986; Shade of the Tree, 1986. *Address:* 7140 E. Entwood Court, Inverness, FL 32650, USA.

JACOB John, b. 27 Aug 1950, Chicago, IL, USA. 1 son, 1 daughter. *Education:* AB, University of Michigan, 1972; MA 1973, PhD 1989, University of Illinois at Urbana-Champaign. *Appointments:* Instructor in English, 1974-79, Instructor in English, 1984-, Northwestern University, Evanston, IL; Chief Writer, Illinois Legislative Investigating Commission, Chicago, 1979-82; Development director for Community Advancement Programs, Chicago, 1973-77; Lecturer, Roosevelt University, 1975-; Assistant Professor at North Central College, Naperville, IL, 1987-; Member of Board of Directors of Domestic and Violence Support Group, Sarah's Inn; Consultant to Illinois Arts Council. *Publications:* Scatter: Selected Poems, 1979; Hawk Spin, Summerbook, 1983; Wooden Indian, 1987; Long Ride Back, The Light Fandango, 1988. *Contributions to:* Margins; ALB Booklist, 1976-86. *Honours:* Carl Sandburg Award from Friends of Chicago Public Library, 1980; Grants from Illinois Arts Council, 1985 and 1987. *Memberships:* International PEN; Modern Languages Association of America; Associated Writing Programs; Authors Guild; Multi-Ethnic Literature Society of the United States. *Address:* 527 Lyman Street, Oak Park, IL 60304, USA.

JACOBS Arthur David, b. 1922, British. Musicologist; Critic. *Appointments:* Deputy Editor 1962-71, Member, Editorial Board, Opera, 1972-; Critic and Columnist, Hi Fi News and Record Review, 1964-89; Opera Record Reviewer, Sunday Times, London, 1964-89; Editor, British Music Yearbook, 1971-79; Professor, Royal Academy of Music, 1964-79; Professor and Head of the Department of Music, Huddersfield Polytechnic, 1979-84; Member of Advisory Board, New Grove Dictionary of Opera, 1988-; Visiting Scholar, Wolfson College, Oxford, 1991-92. *Publications:* Gilbert and Sullivan, 1951; A New Dictionary of Music, 1958; Choral Music (ed and contributor), 1963; Pan Book of Opera (in US as Great Operas in Synopsis) (with Stanley Sadie), 1966; reissued as The Opera Guide: A Short History of Western Music, 1972; Music Education Handbook (ed), 1976; Arthur Sullivan: A Victorian Musician, 1984; Penguin Dictionary of Musical Performers, 1990. *Contributions to:* The New Grove Dicitionary of Opera, 1992. *Address:* 7 Southdale Road, Oxford, OX2 7SE, England.

JACOBS Barbara, b. 6 Feb 1945, St Helens, England. Writer. m. Mark Jacobs, 26 Feb 1968, div, 1980, 1 son. *Education:* BA Hons English, 1966, PGCE, 1967, Leicester University. *Appointments:* Freelance Journalist, 1978-. *Publications:* Two Times Two, 1984; Stick, 1988; Just How Far, 1989; Not Really Working, 1990; Love's A Pain, 1990; Rigby Graham, 1982; The Fire-Proof Hero, 1986; Desperadoes, 1987; Listen to my Heartbeat, 1988; Goodbye my Love, 1989. *Contributions to:* My Guy; Just Seventeen; Girl; Jackie; Patches; Blue Jeans; Me; Catch; Mizz. *Address:* 29 Gotham Street, Leicester LE2 0NA, England.

JACOBS Leah. *See:* GELLIS Roberta Leah.

JACOBSON Dan, b. 7 Mar 1929, Johannesburg, South Africa. Writer. m. Margaret Pye, 3 sons, 1 daughter. *Education:* BA, University of the Witwatersrand, Johannesburg, South Africa. *Literary Appointments:* Fellow in Creative Writing, Stanford University, California, 1956; Professor, Syracuse University, New York, 1965-66; Fellow, State University of New York, Buffalo, New York, 1972; Fellow Royal Society of Literature, 1974; Lecturer 1975-80, Reader in English 1980-87, Professor of English, 1988-, University College, London, England; Fellow, Humanities Research Centre, Australian National University, 1981. *Publications:* The Trap, 1955; A Dance in the Sun, 1956; The Price of Diamonds, 1957; The Evidence of Love, 1960; The Beginners, 1965; The Rape of Tamar, 1970; The Wonder-Worker, 1973; The Confessions of Josef Baisz, 1979; The Story of the Stories, 1982; Time and Time Again, 1985; Her Story, 1987; Adult Pleasures, 1988; Hidden in the Heart, 1991; The God-Fearer, 1992. *Contributions to:* New Yorker; Commentary; Grand Street; London Magazine; London Review of Books; The Guardian. *Honours:* John Llewelyn Rhys Memorial Award, 1958; W Somerset Maugham Award, 1964; H H Wingate Award, 1979; J R Ackerley Award, 1986; Mary Elinore Smith Prize for Poetry, 1992. *Literary Agent:* A M Heath and Co Ltd, London. *Address:* c/o A M Heath and Co Ltd, 79 St Martins Lane, London WC2, England.

JACOBUS Lee A, b. 1935, American. *Appointments:* Faculty Member, Western Connecticut State College, 1960-68; Assistant Professor 1968-71, Associate Professor 1971-76, Professor of English 1976-, University of Connecticut. *Publications:* Improving College Reading, 1967, 4th edition, 1983; Aesthetics and the Arts, 1968; Issues and Response, 1968, revised edition, 1972; Developing College Reading, 1970, 1979; 17 from Everywhere: Short Stories from Around the World (ed), 1971; Poetry in Context, 1974; Humanities Through the Arts, 1974, 3rd edition, 1983; John Cleveland, 1975; Sudden Apprehension: Aspects of Knowledge in Paradise Lost, 1976; The Paragraph and Essay Book, 1977; The Sentence Book, 1980; Longman Anthology of American Drama (ed), 1982; Shakespeare and the Quest for Certainty, Signficances: A Rhetoric Reader of Ideas, 1983; Humanities: The Evolution of

Values, 1984. *Address:* c/o Harcourt Brace Jovanovich, 1250 Sixth Avenue, San Diego, CA 92101, USA.

JACOBUS Mary, b. 1944, British. *Appointments:* Lecturer, Department of English, Manchester University, 1970-71; Fellow and Tutor in English, Lady Margaret Hall, Lecturer in English, 1971-80, Oxford University; Associate Professor 1980-82, Professor 1982-, Department of English, Cornell University, Ithaca. *Publications:* Tradition and Experiment in Wordsworth's Lyrical Ballads (1798), 1976; Women Writing and Women about Women (ed), 1979; Reading Women, 1986. *Address:* Department of English, Cornell University, Ithaca, NY 14853, USA.

JADAV Kishore, b. 15 Apr 1938, Ambaliala, Gujarat, India. Government Service. m. Smt Kumsangkola Ao 4 Mar 1967, 2 sons, 3 daughters. *Education:* BCom, 1960; MCom, 1963. *Appointments:* General Secretary, 1976, Vice President, 1986, North Eastern Writers Academy. *Publications:* Pragaitihaski ane Shoksahba, 1969; Suryarohan 1972; Chhadmavesh 1982; Kishore Jadavni Vartao, 1984; Kishore Jadavni Shrestha Vartao, 1989 - all short stories; Nishachakra, 1979; Riktaraag, 1989 - novels; Navi Tunki Vartani Kalaminmasa, 1986, Critical essays; Aagantuk, 1990; Ed, Contempory Gujarati Short Stories, 1992. *Contributions to:* Kishore Jadav Sathe Vartalap, 1988; Mulakat: Kishore Jadavni, 1981; Sahityik Goshthi, 1988; Kishore Jadav Sathe Vartakala vishe Vartalap, 1982. *Honours:* Awards from Gujarat Government, 1972; Gujarati Sahitya Parishad, Award, 1988; Critics Sandham Award, 1988. *Memberships:* Gujarati Sahitya Parishad; Indian PEN; Lions Club. *Address:* POB 19 Nagaland, PO Kohima 797 001, India.

JAFFE (Dr) Betsy. *See:* **JAFFE Elizabeth Ross Latimer.**

JAFFE Elizabeth Ross Latimer, b. 22 Nov 1935, Washington DC, USA. Career Consultant. m. Morton I Jaffe, 16 June 1962. *Education:* BA Antioch College, 1958; MBA University of Connecticut, 1963; EdD, Columbia University, 1985. *Publications:* Altered Ambitions, 1991. *Contributions to:* National Business Employment Weekly; Training and Development; Management Review; Curtis Courier. *Honours:* Beta Gamma Sigma; Kappa Delta Pi; Am Society of Training and Development National Award, 1984; Chiar, Board, ASTD, 1980-83; Am Counseling Association; Academy of Management, Harvard Business School Club; International Alliance, Board. *Memberships:* Authors Guild. *Literary Agent:* Anne Edelstein. *Address:* 10 West 15 St 2017, New York City, NY 10011, USA.

JAFFE Rona, American. Freelance Writer and Television Personality. *Publications:* The Best of Everything, 1958; Away from Home, 1960; The Last of the Wizards, 1961; Mr Right is Dead, 1965; The Cherry in the Martini, 1966; The Fame Game, 1969; The Other Woman, 1972; Family Secrets, 1974; The Last Chance, 1976; Class Reunion, 1979; Mazes and Monsters, 1981; After the Reunion, 1985. *Address:* c/o Delacorte Press, 1 Dag Hammarskjold Plaza, New York, NY 10017, USA.

JAFFEE Annette Williams, b. 10 Jan 1945, Abilene, Texas, USA. Novelist. div. 1 son, 1 daughter. *Education:* BS Journalism, Boston University, 1966. *Publications:* Adult Education, 1981; Recent History, 1988, both novels. *Contributions to:* Ploughshares; Missouri Reviews; The Ontario Review. *Honours:* NJ Arts Council Grant, 1986; Dodge Fellow at Yaddo, 1991. *Memberships:* Authors Guild; PEN America. *Literary Agent:* Liz Darhansoff. *Address:* PO Box 26, River Road, Lumberville, PA 18933, USA.

JAGLOM Henry David, b. 26 Jan 1943, London, England. Film Writer; Director; Actor. m. Victoria Foyt Jaglom, 22 Oct 1991, 1 daughter. *Education:* University of Pennsylvania. *Publications:* Writer and Director of the

following films: A Safe Place, 1971; Tracks, 1976; Sitting Ducks, 1980; Can She Bake a Cherry Pie, 1983; Always But not forever, 1985; Someone to Love, 1987; New Year's Day, 1989; Eating, 1990; Venice/Venice, 1992. *Address:* International Rainbow Pictures, 9165 Sunset Blvd. The Penthouse, Los Angeles, CA 90069, USA.

JAIN Girilal, b. 21 Sept 1923, Pipli Khere, Haryana. Journalist. m. Sudarshan Jain, 1951, 1 son, 3 daughters. *Education:* Delhi University. *Appointments:* Entered Journalism, 1945, Sub- Editor, Times of India, Delhi, 1950, Reporter 1951, Chief Reporter, 1958, Foreign Correspondent, Pakistan, 1961, London 1962, Assistant Editor, Delhi, 1964, Resident Editor 1970, Editor, 1976, Editor in Chief, 1978-. *Publications:* What Mao Really Means, 1957; India Meets China in Nepal, 1959; Panchsila and After, 1960. *Address:* 22 Ashoka Apartment, Napean Sea Road, Bombay 6, India.

JAMES Alan, b. 1943, British. *Appointments:* Form Master, Junior School, Royal Grammar School, Newcastle upon Tyne, 1968-78; Deputy head, Runnymede First School, Ponteland, Northumberland, 1979-. *Publications:* Animals, Hospitals, 1969; The Post, Living Light Book One, 1970; Buses and Coaches, 1971; Tunnels, Sir Rowland Hill and the Post Office, Living Light Book Two, 1972; Money, Collecting Stamps, Submarines, Amphibians and Reptiles, 1973; Clocks and Watches, Zoos, 1974; Keeping Pets, Newspapers, Buildings, Living Light Book Five, 1975; Spiders and Scorpions, Newspapers and the Times in the Nineteenth Century, The Telephone Operator, The Vet, 1976; Stocks and Shares, 1977; Circuses, 1978; Let's Visit Finland, 1979; Let's Visit Austria, Let's Visit Denmark, 1984; Lapps: Reindeer Herders of Lapland, 1986; Homes in Hot Places, 1987; Homes in Cold Places, 1987; Castles and Mansions, 1988; Homes on Water, 1988. Gilbert and Sullivan: Their Lives and Times, 1990. *Address:* The Stable, Market Square, Holy Island, Northumberland TD15 2RU, England.

JAMES Andrew. *See:* **KIRKUP James.**

JAMES Anthony Stephen, b. 27 Oct 1956, South Wales. Freelance Writer. m. Penny Windsor, 24 May 1987. 1 daughter. *Education:* BA English, University College of Swansea, 1991. *Publications:* Author of novel, A House with Blunt Knives, The Literature For More Than One Year Group; Poetry published in: Acumen; Anglo Welsh Review; Collection of Poems: All That The City Has to Offer; Ambit; Borderlines; Celtic Dawn; Envoi; Foolscap; Hybrid; Krax; Nutshell; Orbis; Poetry Nottingham; Poetry Wales; Radical Wales; Social Care Education; Tears in the Fence; The White Rose Literary Magazine; Bradford Poetry Quarterly. Prose in: Agenda; Cambrensis; Celtic Dawn; Edinburgh Review; New Welsh Review; Passport; Social Care Education; Western Mail. *Honours:* Eileen Illtyd David Award, 1983. *Membership:* Welsh Union of Writers.*Address:* 7 Taplow Terrace, Pentrechwyth, Swansea SA1 7AD, Wales.

JAMES Clive Vivian Leopold, b. 7 Oct 1939. Writer; Broadcaster; Journalist. *Education:* Sydney University; Pembroke College, Cambridge. *Appointments Include:* Record Albums as Lyricist for Pete Atkin; TV Series Include: Cinema; Up Sunday; So It Goes; A Question of Sex; Saturday Night People; Clive James on Television; The Late Clive James; TV Documentaries include: Shakespeare in Perspective: Hamlet, 1981; The Return of the Flash of Lightning, 1982; Clive James live in Las Vegas, 1982; Clive James meets Roman Polanski, 1984; The Clive James Great American Beauty Pageant, 1984; Clive James in Dallas, 1985; Clive James on Safari, 1986; Feature Writer, The Observer, 1972- , TV Critic 1972-82. *Publications:* (non-fiction) The Metropolitan Critic, 1974; The Fate of Felicity Fark in the Land of the Media, 1975; Peregrine Prykke's Pilgrimage through the London Literary World, 1976; Britannia Bright's Bewilderment in the Wilderness of Westminster, 1976; Visions Before Midnight, 1977; At the Pillars of Hercules, 1979; First Reactions, 1980; The Crystal Bucket, 1981; Charles Charming's Challenges on the Pathway to the Throne, 1981; From the Land of Shadows, 1982; Glue to the Box, 1982; Flying Visits, 1984; Snakecharmers in Texas, 1988; Somewhere Becoming Rain, 1992; (fiction): Brilliant Creatures, 1983; (Verse): Fan Mail, 1977; Poem of the Year, 1983; Other Passports: Poems 1958-85, 1986; Autobiography, Unreliable Memoirs, 1980; Falling Towards England: Unreliable Memoirs II, 1985; May Week was in June; Unreliable Memoirs III, 1990.

JAMES Dana. *See:* **JACKSON Jane.**

JAMES John, b. 14 Mar 1939, Cardiff, Wales. *Education:* BA University of Bristol, 1960; MA, University of Keele, 1973. *Appointments:* Arts Council Creative Writing Fellow, University of Sussex, 1978-79. *Publications:* mmmm...ah yes, 1967; The Small Henderson Room, 1969; Letters from Sarah, 1973; Striking the Pavilion of Zero, 1975; A Theory of Poetry, 1977; Berlin Return, 1983; Dreaming Flesh, 1991. *Address:* 119 Ross Street, Cambridge CB1 3BS, England.

JAMES Noel David Glaves, b. 16 Sept 1911. Author; Retired Land Agent. m. Laura Cecilia Livingstone, 29 Dec 1949, (dec 23 Aug 1970), 3 sons (1 dec.). *Education:* Haileybury College, Hertford, 1925-28; Diploma in Estate Management, Royal Agricultural College, Cirencester, 1932. *Publications:* The Forester's Companion, 4th Edition, 1989; The Arboriculturist, 2nd Edition, 1990; Working Plans for Estates Woodlands, 1948; Notes on Estate Forestry, 1949; An Experiment in Forestry, 1951; Trees of Bicton, 1969; A Book of Trees, anthology, 1973; Before the Echoes Die Away, 1980; A History of English Forestry, 1981; A Forest Centenary, 1982; Gunners at Larkhill, 1983; Plain Soldiering, 1987; An Historical Dictionary of Forestry and Woodland Terms, 1991. *Honours:* Military Cross, 1945; Territorial Decoration, 1946; OBE, 1964; Gold Medal for Distinguished Services to Forestry, Royal Forestry Society; Bledisloe Gold Medal for Services to Agriculture and Forestry, Royal Agricultural College. *Memberships:* President, Chartered Land Agents Society, 1957-58; President, Royal Forestry Society of England, Wales and Northern Ireland, 1962-64. *Address:* Blakemore House, Kersbrook, Budleigh Salterton, Devon EX9 7AB, England.

JAMES P(hyllis) D(orothy), of Holland Park, Baroness, b. 3 Aug 1920, Oxford, England. Writer; Former Civil Servant. 2 daughters. *Publications:* Cover Her Face, 1962; A Mind to Murder, 1963; Unnatural Causes, 1967; Shroud for a Nightingale, 1971; An Unsuitable Job for a Woman, 1972; The Black Tower, 1975; Death of an Expert Witness, 1977; Innocent Blood, 1980; The Skull Beneath the Skin, 1982; A Taste for Death, 1986; Devices and Desires, 1989; The Children of Men, 1992. *Honours:* OBE, 1983; Fellow, Royal Society of Arts, 1986; Fellow, Royal Society of Literature, 1987; Associate Fellow, Downing College, Cambridge; JP; DBE, 1991. *Memberships:* Royal Society of Literature; PEN; Crime Writers' Association; Society of Authors; Detection Club. *Agent:* Elaine Greens Ltd.,London. *Address:* c/o Elaine Greens Ltd., 31 Newington Green, London N16 9PU, England.

JAMES R(obert) V(idal) Rhodes (Sir), b. 1933, British. *Appointments:* Assistant Clerk 1955-61, Senior Clerk 1961-64, House of Commons; Fellow, All Souls College, Oxford, 1964-68, 1979-81; Kratter Professor of European History, Stanford University, CA, 1968; Director, Institute for the Study of International Organisation, University of Sussex, Brighton, 1968-73; Principal Officer, Executive Office of the Secty, General of the UN, NYC, 1973-76; Conservative Member of Parliament (UK) for Cambridge, 1976-92; Parliamentry Private Secretary, Foreign and Commonwealth Office, 1979-81; Chairman, Parliament Trust, 1983-; Member of the Speakers's Panel of Chairman of the House of Commons, 1987-92. *Publications:* Lord Randolph Churchill, 1959; An Introduction to the House of Commons, 1961; Rosebery, 1963; Gallipoli, 1965; Chips: The Diary of Sir Henry Channon (ed), 1967; Memoirs of a Conservative: The Memoirs and Papers of J C C Davidson, 1968; The Czechoslovak Crisis (ed), 1968, 1969; Churchill: A Study in Failure 1900-1939, 1970; Britain's Role in the United Nations, 1970; Ambitions and Realities: British Politics 1964-1970, 1971; Complete Speeches of Sir Winston Churchill 1897-1963, 8 volumes, 1974; Victor Cazalet: A Portrait, 1976; The British Revolution 1880-1939, volume I, 1976, volume II, 1977; Albert, Prince Consort, 1983; Anthony Eden, 1986; Bob Boothby: A Portrait, 1991. *Address:* The Stone Horse, Great Gransden, Nr Sandy, Bedfordshire, SA19 3AF, England.

JAMES Robin (Irene), b. 24 Sept 1953, Seattle, WA, USA. Artist. m. Michael George Cosgrove, 1 July 1980. *Appointment:* Free-lance artist, 1971-. *Publications:* Tale of Three Tails, Wheedle on the Needle, Serendipity, Muffin Muncher, The Dream Tree, 1974; Little Mouse on the Prairie, Cap'n Smudge, The Gnome From Nome, In Search of the Saveopotomas, Morgan and Me, 1975; Bangalee, Creole, Kartusch, Jake O'Shawnasey, Hucklebug, 1976; Gabby, Leo the Lop, Leo the Lop: Tail Two, Leo the Lop: Tail Three, 1977; Snaffles, Flutterby, Catundra, Feather Fin, 1978; Grampa-Lop, 1979; Nitter Pitter, Raz-Ma-Taz, Trafalgar True, Trapper, 1980; Maui-Maui, Ming Ling, Tee-Tee, 1981; Morgan and Yew, Morgan Mine, 1982; Morgan Morning, Flutterby Fly, Kiyomi, 1983; Minikin, Dragolin, Shimmeree, Baby Pets, Baby Forest Animals, Babu Zoo Animals, Baby Farm Animals, 1984; Baby Puppies, Baby Kittens, Squeakers, Glitterby Baby, Jingle Bear, Crabby Gabby, 1985; Buttermilk, Fanny, Pish Posh, Mumkin, Baby Horses, Baby Unicorns, 1986; Misty Morgan, Buttermilk-Bear, Memily, Crickle-Crack, 1987; Persnickity, Sassafras, Sniffles, Rhubarb, 1988; Gigglesnitcher, Tippy Potter the Otter, Potty LaPush the Platypus, Perry P Plum the Possum, Andy McClark the Aardvark, 1989. *Memberships:* International Wildlife Federation; American Humane Association; Annimal Protection Institute; Humane Society of the United States; National Wildlife Federation; People for the Ethical Treatment of Animals; Delta Society. *Address:* Snohomish, WA, USA.

JAMES William M. *See:* **GILMAN George G.**

JANDL Ernst, b. 1 Aug 1925, Vienna, Austria. Writer. *Education:* Teacher's Diploma, 1949, PhD 1950, University of Vienna. *Publications include:* Laut und Luise (poems) 1966; Fünf Mann Menschen (radio play with F Mayröcker) 1968; Aus der Fremde (play) 1980; Der künstliche Baum (poems) 1970; Idyllen (poems) 1989; Gesammelte Werke 3 vol (poems, plays, prose) 1985. *Honours:* Hörspielpreis der Kriegsblinden, 1968; Georg- Trake-Prize, 1974; Prize of the City of Vienna, 1976; Mülheimer Dramatiker-Preis, 1980; Austrian State Prize, 1984; Georg-Büchner-Preis, 1984; Medal of Honour in Gold of the City of Vienna, 1986; Peter Huchel-Preis, 1990. *Memberships:* Academy of Arts, West Berlin; Academy of Arts of GDR; Deutsche Akademie für Sprache und Dichtung, Darmstadt; Academy of Fine Arts, Munich; Forum Stadtpark, Graz; Grazer Autorenversammlung, Vienna; Österreichischer Kunstsenat, Vice-President. *Literary Agent:* Luchterhand Literaturverlag, Hamburg, Kiepenheuer & Witsch Theaterverlag, Cologne. *Address:* P O Box 227, A-1041, Vienna, Austria.

JANES J Robert. *See:* **JANES Joseph Robert.**

JANES Joseph Robert, b. 23 May 1935, Toronto, Canada. Writer. m. Gracia Joyce Lind, 16 May 1958, 2 sons, 2 daughters. *Education:* BS.Sc, Mining Engineering, 1958, MEng Geology, 1967, University of Toronto. *Publications:* Children's books: Murder in the market, 1985; Spies for Dinner, 1984; Danger on the River, 1982; Theft of Gold, 1980; The Tree-Fort War, 1976. Adult Books: Carousel, 1992; Mayhem, 1992; The Alice Factor, 1991; The Hiding Place, 1984; The THird Story, 1983; The Watcher, 1982; The Toy Shop, 1981.

Non fiction: The Great Canadian Outback, 1978; Textbooks: Airphoto Interpretation and the Canadian Landscape, 1984 (co-authored with Dr J D Mollard); Geology and the New Global Tectonics, 1976; Earth Science, 1974; Rocks, Minerals and Fossils, 1973; Searching for Structure, 1977, (co-authored); Teachers' Guide Searching for Structure, 1977 (co-authored); Holt Geophoto Resource Kits, 1972. *Contributions to:* Toronto Star, Toronto Globe and Mail, The Canadian, The Winnipeg Free Press, The Canadian Children's Annual. *Honours:* Grants: The Canada Council, Ontario Arts Cuncil, J P Bickell Foundation; Thesis Award, Canadian Institute of Mining and Metallurgy; Works-in-progress Grant, Ontario Arts Council, 1991. *Memberships:* Association of Professional Engineers of Ontario; Writers' Union of Canada, Crime Writers of Canada. *Address:* c/o Acacia House, 51 Acacia Road, Toronto, Canada M4S 2K6.

JANES Percy Maxwell, b. 12 Mar 1922, St John's Newfoundland, Canada. Writer. *Education:* BA, University of Toronto. *Publications:* House of Hate, 1970; No Cage for Conquerors, 1980; Requiem for a Faith, 1984; Eastmall, 1985; Light Dark, 1982. *Memberships:* Newfoundland Writer's Guild. *Address:* Box 77, St Thomas, NF, Canada A1L 1C1.

JANET Lillian. *See:* **O'DANIEL Janet.**

JANICKI Jerzy, b. 10 Aug 1928, Czortkow, Poland. Writer. m. Krystyna Czechowicz-Janicka, 20 June 1964, 2 daughters. *Education:* MA, Department of Polish Philology, University of Wroclaw, 1948. *Publications include:* 6 novels, 5 selections of reportages, 4 selections of radio plays, 3 dramas, 18 film screenplays, over 40 TV screenplays. 3 TV serials: Polish Roads; The House; Action V. Radio novel, Matysiakowie, over 1600 episodes, running since 1956. *Contributions to:* Numerous journals & magazines. *Honours:* 2 State Awards, Minister of Culture. *Memberships:* Society of Polish Writers; Society of Polish Filmmakers; Society of Polish Journalists; Society of Stage Authors & Composers. *Address:* 02-928 Warsaw, Zelwerowicza 36, Poland.

JANIFER Laurence M. *See:* **HARRIS Laurence Mark.**

JANOSY Istvan Laszlo, b. 18 May 1919, Besztencebanya, Hungary. Poet; Writer. m. Katalin Nylkos, 18 Dec 1953, 1 son. *Education:* Arts Dept, University of Sciences, Budapest, 1937-44. *Publications:* Prometheus 1948; The Godess of Maize; The Depth of Well of Dreams is Fathomless, - all poems: Experience and Rememberances; Vanishing Faces; Translations include: Paradise Lost; Der Grune Heirich; Die Leute Von Seldvila; The Angloamerican Poetry of XX Century; Poems of John Berryman. *Honours:* Jozsef Attila Award, 1973; Dery Tibor Award, 1986. *Memberships:* Hungarian Pen Club; Association of Hungarian Writers; Ecumenical Society. *Address:* Mogyosodi ut 64B, H-1142 Budapest, Hungary.

JANOWITZ Phyllis, b. 3 Mar 1940, New York City, USA. Poet. (div), 1 son, 1 daughter. *Education:* BA, Queens College; MFA, University of Massachusetts, Amherts, 1970. *Literary Appointments:* Hodder Fellow in Poetry, Princeton University, 1979-80; Associate Professor in English and Poet in Residence, Cornell University, 1980-. *Publications:* Rites of Strangers, 1978; Visiting Rites, 1982; Temporary Dwellings, 1988. *Contributions include:* Poems in The New Yorker; Atlantic; The Nation; The New Republic; Paris Review; Ploughshares; Radcliffe Quarterly; Prairie Schooner; Esquire; Andover Review; Harvard Magazine Backbone; The Literary Review; The Mid-Atlantic Review; Anthology of Magazine Verse; Mississippi Review; Moving Out; Beyond Baroque; DeKalb Literary Review; Bellingham Review; Concerning Poetry. *Honours:* Fellow, Bunting Institute, 1973; National Endowment of the Arts Award, 1974-75; Stroud International Poetry

Festival Award, 1978; Alfred Hodder Fellow in Humanities, Princeton University, 1979-80; Emily Dickinson Award, Poetry Society of America, 1983. *Memberships:* PEN; Poetry Society of America; Association Writing Program; MacDowell Colony. *Address:* Cornell University, English Department, Ithacp, NY 14853, USA.

JANSEN Michael Elin, b. 16 Dec 1940, Bay City, Michigan, USA. Writer. m. Godfrey Henry Jansen, 31 Oct 1967, 1 daughter. *Education:* BA, Mount Holyoke College, Massachusetts; MA, American University of Beirut, Lebanon. *Publications:* The Battle of Beirut, (co-author), 1982; Dissonance in Zion, 1987; The Aphrodite Plot, 1983; The United States and the Palestinian People, 1970. *Contributions to:* The Irish Times; Middle East International; Gemini News Service. *Literary Agent:* Jacqueline Korn of David Higham, London, England. *Address:* 5 Metaxas Street, Ayios Dhometios, Nicosia 164, Cyprus.

JANSSENS Jessica Rolande Julienne, b. 8 July 1962, Deurne, Belgium. Editor; Literary Agent. *Education:* Degree in Theory of Music, 1976, Degree in Chamber Music, 1977, Academy of Music; Library Management Graduate, STLBW, 1980-83; Degree in Playing the Recorder (flute), Academy of Music, 1981; Degree in Public Library Management, STLBW, 1981. *Address:* Toneelfonds J Janssens BVBA, Kruikstraat 14, 2018 Antwerpen, Belgium.

JARMAN Mark Foster, b. 5 June 1952, Mt Sterling, Kentucky, USA. Poet; Teacher. m. Amy Kane Jarman, 28 Dec 1974, 2 daughters. *Education:* BA, University of California, Santa Cruz, MFA, University of Iowa. *Publications:* Far and Away, 1985; The Rote Walker, 1981; North Sea, 1978; Tonight is the Night of the Prom, a Chapbook of Verse, 1974; The Black Riviera, 1990; Iris, 1992. *Contributions to:* American Poetry Review; Hudson Review; New Yorker; Ohio Review; Partisan Review; Poetry; Prairie Schooner; The Reaper. *Honours:* Joseph Henry Jackson Award, 1974; Academy of American Poets Prize, 1975; NEA Grants, 1977, 1983; Guggenheim Fellowship (poetry), 1991-92; NEA Grant (poetry), 1992; The Poets' Prize, 1991, for The Black Riviera. *Memberships:* Associated Writing Programmes; The Poets' Prize Committee; MLA. *Address:* Dept. of English, Vanderbilt University, Nashville, TN 37235, USA.

JAROS Peter, b. 22 Jan 1940, Hybe, Slovakia. Writer. m. Maria Zuzana Kristova, 5 July 1980. 2 sons, 1 daughter. *Education:* Philosophical Faculty, Komensky University Bratislava, 1962. *Literary Appointments:* Editor, Kulturny Zivot, 1964-66; Editor, Literary Department, Slovak Radio, 1967-71; Slovak Film, 1972-91. *Publications:* Popoludnie na Terase (Afternoon of the Terrace), 1963; Zdesenie (Anxiety), 1965; Menuet, 1967; Krvaviny (Stories of Blood), 1970; Orechy (Nuts), 1972; Tisicrocna Vcela (1000 year old Bee), 1979; Neme Ucho, Hluche Oko (Dumb Ear, Deaf Eye), 1984; Lasky Hmat (A Clutch of Love), 1988. *Contributions to:* Kulturny Zivot; Slovenske Pohlady; Romboid; Nove Slovo; Mlada Tvorba; Inostrannaja Literatura (USSR); Literatura na Swiece (Poland). *Honours:* Ivan Krasko's Award for Popoludnie Na Terase, 1963; Award, Publishing House Smena, for Menuet, 1967; Award, Publishing House Slovenskyspisovatel for Krvaviny, 1968; Award of the Slovak Union of Writers, for Tisicrocna Vcela, 1979. *Membership:* Slovak Union of Writers. *Literary Agent:* LITA, Slovak Literacy Agency, Bratislava. *Address:* Klzava 11, 83101 Bratislava, Slovakia.

JARVIS Martin, b. 4 Aug 1941, Cheltenham, Gloucestershire, England. Actor; Writer. m. (2) Rosalind Ayres, 23 Nov 1974. 2 sons (from previous marriage). *Education:* Diploma (Hons), Royal Academy of Dramatic Art, 1962. *Appointments:* Numerous acting roles on stage, film and television productions; starred in Alan Aykbourn's Woman in Mind, Vaudeville Theatre, London, 1987; Co-star, feature film, "Buster", 1988;

Alan Aykbourn's Henceforward, Vaudeville Theatre, London, 1989; British Première of Yuri Trifanov's Exchange, 1989; Literary Consultant, Countdown, 1990; Co-produced, own adaptation of Frayn's Make and Break, Los Angeles, 1993; Co-produced, Directed, Tales From Shakespeare, Los Angeles, 1993; Co-produced, Best of Second World War Poetry, spoken word cassette, 1993; Co-starred as M de Renal in Scarlet and Black, BBC TV, 1993. *Major Publications:* Play: Bright Boy, 1977; Short stories: Name out of a Hat, 1967; Alphonse, 1972; Late Burst, 1976; adapted over 60 Just William stories of Richmal Crompton for BBC Radio and TV, 1972-76; adapted, Goodbye Mr Chips, by James Hilton for BBC Radio & Television, 1973; Founded Jarvis and Ayres Productions, 1986; Created Jarvis's Frayn for BBC Radio 4, 1986; Adapted, William at Easter, for BBC, 1987; William Stories: Personal Selection, (book), 1992. *Contributions to:* Scripted various TV and Radio Shows; "The Listener" and "Punch", 1988; Comic Relief and Children In Need, 1988-89; Solo reading on cassette tapes including: Just William, 1, 2 and 3; Plain Tales from the Hills, by Kipling and Classic Love Stories; regular contributor to fourth Column, BBC Radio 4. *Honours:* Vanbrugh Award, Silver Medal, Royal Academy of Dramatic Art, 1968; National Theatre Player, 1982-84; Emmy Award, 1991. *Membership:* Council member, National Youth Theatre; Board Member, Children's Film Unit. *Literary Agent:* Michael Whitehall Ltd. *Address:* 125 Gloucester Road, London SW1, England.

JARVIS Sharon, b. 1 Oct 1943, Brooklyn, New York, USA. Literary Agent; Editor; Writer. *Education:* BFA, Hunter College, 1964. *Appointments:* Copy Editor, Ace Books, 1969; Assistant Managing Editor, Popular Library, 1971; Editor, Ballantine Books, 1972; Editor, Doubleday & Co., 1975; Senior Editor, Playboy Books, 1978. *Publications:* The Alien Trace, with K. Buckley, 1984; Time Twister, 1984; Inside Outer Space, 1985; True Tales of the Unknown, 1985; True Tales of the Unknown: The Uninvited, 1989; True Tales of the Unknown: Beyond Reality, 1991; Dead Zones, Dark Zones, 1992. *Memberships:* Independent Literary Agents Association; Science Fiction Writers of America; Romance Writers Association; Westrn Writers Association; Mystery Writers of America; International Fortean Organization. *Address:* RR2 Box 16B, Laceyville, PA 18623, USA.

JASON Jerry. *See:* **SMITH George H.**

JASON Johnny. *See:* **GLUT Don F.**

JASON Katherine, b. 9 Feb 1953, NY, USA. Instructor. m. Peter Rondinone, 23 Apr 1984. *Education:* AB, Bard College, 1975; MFA, Columbia University, 1978; Doctural study at Graduate Center of the City University of New York, 1980-81. *Appointments:* Instructor in Writing and Literature, Hunter College of the City University of New York, NY, 1981-. *Publications:* Racers, What People!, 1984; Words in Commotion and Other Stories, 1986; Name and Tears: Forty Years of Italian Fiction, 1990. *Contributions to:* Poems and translations to periodicals, including Omni; New Yorker; City; The Phoenix; Folio; The Northern Review; Translation; Work represented in anthologies including, Italian Poetry Today, 1979; Armenian Poetry Through the Ages, 1980; The New Directions Anthology 45, 1982. *Honours:* Fulbright Fellow, 1978-79; Finalist for Renato Poggioli Award from PEN for translation, 1984; Finalist for the 'Discovery' The Nation Award for Unstringng, Grant from National Endowment for the Arts, 1985. *Address:* 348 West 11th Street, No 3B, New York, NY 10014, USA.

JASON Stuart. *See:* **FLOREN Lee.**

JASPER David, b. 1 Aug 1951, Stockton on Tees, England. University Teacher; Clergyman. m. Alison Elizabeth Collins, 29 Oct 1976, 3 daughters. *Education:* Dulwich College, 1959-69; BA, MA, 1976, Jesus College, Cambridge;, 1973-76; BA, MA, 1979, St Stephen's House, Oxford, 1973- 76; BD, Keble College Oxford, 1976-80; PhD, Hatfield College, Durham, 1979-83. *Appointments:* Director, Centre for the Study of Literature and Theology, Durham University, 1986-91, Glasgow University, 1991-; Editor, Literature and Theology Advisory Board *Publications:* Coleridge as Poet and Religious Thinker,1985; The New Testament and the Literary Imagination, 1987; The Study of Literature and Religion, 1989. General Editor of McMillan Series, Studies in Literature and Religion. *Contributions to:* Graphe; Literature and Translation. *Honours:* Dana Fellow, Emory University, Atlanta, 1991; Hon Fellow, Research Foundation, Durham University, 1991. *Memberships:* Sec, European Society for Literature and Religion; American Academy of Religion; Modern Language Association. *Address:* Netherwood, 124 Old Manse Road, Wishaw, Lanarkshire Scotland ML2 OEP.

JAY Antony Rupert, b. 20 Apr 1930, London, England. Writer; Producer. m. Rosemary Jill Watkins, 15 June 1957, 2 sons, 2 daughters. *Education:* Open Major Classical Scholarship 1948-52, BA, 1st Class Honours 1952, MA 1955, Magdalene College, Cambridge. *Publications:* Corporation Man, 1972; Yes Minister, Vol.1 1981, Vol.II, 1982, Vol.III, 1983; The Complete Yes, Minister, 1984; The Complete Yes, Prime Minister, 1989; Elizabeth R, 1992; Management & Machiavelli, 1967, 2nd Edition, 1987; To England With Love, with David Frost, 1967; Effective Presentation, 1970, 2nd Edition, 1993; Corporation Man, 1971. *Honours:* Knighthood, 1989; Honorary MA, Sheffield University, 1978; Honorary DBA, International Management College, 1988; CVO, 1992; FRSA, 1992; CIM, 1992. *Literary Agent:* Curtis Brown and Michael Imison Playwrights. *Address:* c/o Video Arts Ltd, Dumbarton House, 68 Oxford Street, London W1N 9LA, England.

JAY Charlotte. *See:* **JAY Geraldine Mary.**

JAY Geraldine Mary, (Geraldine Halls, Charlotte Jay), b. 1919, Australian. *Appointments:* Operates Oriental Antiques Business, Somerset, England 1958-71, Adelaide 1971-. *Publications:* (as Charlotte Jay) - The Knife is Feminine, 1951; Beat Not the Bones, The Fugitive Eye, 1953; The Yellow Turban, 1955; The Feast of the Dead (as G M Jay), 1956, (in US as Charlotte Jay, as the Brink of Silence, 1957); The Silk Project (as G Halls), 1956; (as C Jay) - The Man Who Walked Away (in US as The Stepfathers), 1958; Arms for Adonis, 1960; A Hank of Hair, 1964; (as Geraldine Halls) - The Cats of Benares, 1967; The Cobra Kite, 1971; The Voice of the Crab, 1974; The Last of the Men Shortage, 1976; The Felling of Thawle, 1979, in US as The Last Inheritor, 1980; Talking to Strangers, 1982. *Address:* 21 Commercial Road, Hyde Park, SA 5061, Australia.

JAY Peter, b. 7 Feb 1937, England. Editor; Writer; Broadcaster. m. (1) Margaret Ann Callaghan, 1961, 1 son, 2 daughters, (2) Emma Thornton, 1985, 2 sons. *Education:* Winchester College; Christ Church, Oxford; MA Oxon 1st Class Honours, 1960; Nuffield College, 1960. *Literary Appointments:* Economics Editor, The Times, 1967-77; Associate Editor, Times Business News, 1969-77; Director, The Economist Intelligence Unit, 1979-83; Consultant, Economist Group, 1979-81; Director, Landen Press Limited, 1982-; Editor, Banking World, 1986; Chief of Staff to Robert Maxwell, Publisher of Mirror Group Newspapers and Chairman of BPCC plc and Pergamon, 1986-; Editor, BBC, 1990-. *Publications:* The Budget, 1972; The Crisis for Western Political Economy and Other Essays, 1984; Apocalypse 2000, 1987. *Contributions to:* Numerous newspaper and magazine articles; Foreign Affairs - America and the World, 1979. *Honours:* Political Broadcaster of the Year, 1973; Harold Wincott Financial and Economic Journalist of the Year, 1973; Pye Award, Royal TV Society's Male Personalty of the Year, 1974; SFTA Shell International TV Award, 1974; FRGS, 1977; Honorary DH, Ohio State University, 1978; Honorary DLitt, Wake Forest University, 1979; Berkeley Citation, University of California, 1979. *Memberships:* Chairman, NACRO

Working Party on Children and Young Persons in Custody, 1976-77; Charities Aid Foundation (Trustee), 1981-86; Vice-President, National Council for Voluntary Organisations (Chairman 1981-86); Cinema and TV Benevolent Fund (Council 1982-83); Governor, Ditchley Foundation; Director, New National Theatre, Washington DC, 1979-81; President, The Union, Oxford, 1960; Chairman: United Way (UK) Limited, 1982-83; United Feasibility Steering Committee, 1982-83; United Funds Limited, 1983-85; United Funds Advisory Committee, 1983-84. *Address:* 39 Castlebar Road, London, W5 2DJ, England.

JEAL Tim, b. 27 Jan 1945, London, England. Author. m. Joyce Timewell, 11 Oct 1969. 3 daughters. *Education:* MA (English), Christ Church, Oxford. *Publications:* For Love or Money, 1967; Somehwere Beyond Reproach, 1968; Livingstone, 1973; Cushing's Crusade, 1974; Until The Colours Fade, 1976; A Marriage of Convenience, 1979; Carnfirth's Creation, 1983; Baden-Powell, 1989. *Honours:* Joint Winner, Llewelyn Rhys Memorial Prize, 1974; Writers' Guild's Laurel Award for Services to Writers. *Membership:* Writers' Guild of Great Britain, Chief Publishing Negotiator, 1980-90; Society of Authors. *Literary Agent:* Toby Eady Associates. *Address:* 29 Willow Road, London NW3 1TL, England.

JEFFERS E L. *See:* **JEFFERS Eugene Leroy.**

JEFFERS Eugene Leroy, b. 8 May 1926, Ohio, USA. Writer. m. Anne Elizabeth Eberhart, 28 Aug 1946. 3 sons, 4 daughters. *Education:* BA cum laude, Kent State University, 1951; Western Reserve University, Cleveland, 1953; US Air War College, Montgomery, 1969. *Appointments:* Reporter, The Plain Dealer, Cleveland, Ohio, 1948-54. *Contributions to:* Short stories and travel articles in Pulpsmith, Crosscurrents, Format; Art and the World; Virginia Country; World Travelling; Orbis. *Honours:* Individual Artist Award Fellowship in Fiction, Maryland State Arts Council, 1991. *Memberships:* The Writers Centre, Bethesda, Maryland. *Address:* 13412 Oriental Court, Rockville, MD 20853, USA.

JEFFERSON Alan, b. 1921. British. *Appointments:* Professor of Vocal Interpretation, Guildhall School of Music and Drama, London, 1967-74; Administrator, London Symphony Orchestra, 1967-68; Manager, BBC Concert Orchestra, 1968-73. *Publications:* The Operas of Richard Strauss in Great Britain, 1910-1963; The Lieder of Richard Strauss, 1971; Delius, 1972; The Life of Richard Strauss, 1973; Inside the Orchestra, 1973; Straus, (The Musicians), 1975; The Glory of Opera, 1976; The Complete Gilbert and Sullivan Opera Guide, 1984; Richard Straus: Der Rosenkavalier, 1986; Lotte Lehmann, 1988; Member, Royal Society of Musicians; Club Savile. *Address:* c/o Watson Little Ltd, 12 Egbert Street, London NW1 8LJ, England.

JEFFERSON Ian. *See:* **DAVIES Leslie Purnell.**

JEFFREY Francis, b. 1950, California, USA. Forecaster; Consultant; Software Developer. *Education:* BA Computational Neurophysiology, University of California, Berkeley, 1972. *Publications:* John Lilly, so far. . . , (a biography), 1990; Handbook of States of Consciousness, (co- author), 1986. *Memberships:* IEEE Computer Society; Founding member, Control Systems Group, American Society for Cybernetics; Co-Founder and Director, Great Whales Foundation, San Francisco; Co-Founding member, New Forum, Monterey. *Address:* PO Box 6847, Malibu, CA 90264, USA.

JEFFREY William. *See:* **WALLMANN Jeffrey M.**

JEFFS Julian, b. 5 Apr 1931, Sedgley, England. Barrister. m. Deborah Bevan, 21 May 1966, 3 sons. *Education:* MA, Downing College, Cambridge, 1950-53. *Appointment:* Chairman 1970-72, Vice President 1975-

91, President 1991-, Circle of Wine Writers. *Publications:* Sherry, 1971, 4th edition, 1992; Clerk & Lindsell on Torts (an editor) 13th edition 1969 to 16th edition 1989; The Wines of Europe, 1971; Little Dictionary of Drink, 1973; Encyclopedia of United Kingdom & European Patent Law, 1977. *Honours:* Glenfiddich Wine Writer Awards, 1974 and 1978. *Address:* Church Farm House, East Ilsley, Newbury, Berkshire, England.

JEFFS Rae. *See:* **SEBBEY Frances Rae.**

JELLICOE (Patricia) Ann, b. 15 July 1927. Playwright; Director. m. (1) C. E. Knight-Clark, 1950, divorced 1961, (2) Roger Mayne, 1962, 1 son, 1 daughter. *Publications:* The Sport of My Mad Mother, 1958; The Knack, 1961; Shelley, 1965; The Rising Generation, 1967; The Giveaway, 1969; Flora and the Bandits, 1976; The Bargain, 1979; (community plays): The Reckoning, 1978; The Tide, 1980; (with Fay Weldon and John Fowles) The Western Women, 1984; (Community Play for Holbaek, Denmark): En Tid Til At Tage I Favn, 1988; (plays for children): You'll Never Guess!, 1973; Clever Elsie, Smiling John, Silent Peter, 1974; A Good Thing or a Bad Thing, 1974; (Translations Include) Rosmersholm, 1960; the Lady from the Sea, 1961; The Seagull, 1963; Der Freischutz, 1964; (Books) Some Unconscious Influences in the Theatre, 1967; (with Roger Mayne) Shell Guide to Devon, 1975; (Community Plays): Har to Put Them On, 1988. *Honours:* OBE, 1984. *Address:* c/o Margaret Ramsay Ltd., 14a Goodwin's Court, St Martin's Lane, London WC2, England.

JEN Ssu. *See:* **KUO Nancy.**

JENCKS Charles Alexander, b. 21 June 1939, Baltimore, Maryland, USA. Writer; Architect; Professor. m. Margaret Keswick. 3 sons, 1 daughter. *Education:* BA, English 1961, BA & MA Architecture 1965, Harvard University, USA; PHP, London University, England, 1970. *Appointments:* Editor, Connections, Harvard, USA, 1963; Editorial Adviser, Architectural Design, London, England, 1979. *Publications:* The Language of Post- Modern Architecture, 1977, 6th edition 1986; Modern Movements in Architecture, 1973, 2nd edition, 1984; Architecture Today, 1982, 2nd edition 1988; What is Post-Modernism? 1986, 3rd edition 1990; Post-Modernism the New Clum? in Art & Architecture, 1987; Le Corvisier and The Tragic View of Architecture, 1974, 2nd edition 1987; Meaning in Architecture, edited 1969; Architecture 2000, 1971; Ad hocism, 1972; Daydream Houses of LA, 1978; Late-Modern Architecture, 1980. *Contributions to:* Architectural Forum; Architectural Review; Architectural Design; Times Literary Supplement; Encounter. *Honours:* Melbourne Oration, 1974; Boston Lectures, Royal Society of Arts, 1980. *Literary Agent:* Ed Victor. *Address:* Architectural Association, 36 Bedford Square, London WC1, England.

JENKIN Len (Leonard Jenkin), b. 2 Apr 1941, New York City, New York, USA. 1 daughter. *Education:* Columbia University, 1958-64, 1969- 71, BA, English, 1962, MA, 1964, PhD, 1972. *Appointments:* Lecturer in English, Brooklyn College, New York, 1965-66; Associate Professor of English, Manhattan Community College, 1967-79; Associate Professor, Tisch School of Arts, New York University, 1980-; Associate Artistic Director, River Arts Repertory Company, Woodstock, New York, 1983-. *Publications:* Plays: My Uncle Sam (also Director, produced New York, 1983) New York, Dramatists Play Service, 1984; A Country Doctor, adaptation of a story by Kafka (also Director: produced San Francisco, 1983, New York, 1986); Madrigal Opera, music by Phillip Glass (produced Los Angeles 1985); American Notes (also Director, produced, Los Angeles, 1986, New York, 1987); A Soldier's Tale, adaptation of a libretto by Ramuz, music by Stravinsky (produced New York, 1986). Screenplays: Merlin and Melinda 1977; Blame It on the Night, 1985. Various television plays; Novel: New Jerusalem, Los Angeles, Sun and Moon Press, 1986. *Honours:* Yaddo

Fellowship, 1975; National Endowment for the Arts Fellowship, 1979, 1982; Rockefeller fellowship, 1980; Christopher Award, 1981; American Film Festival Award, 1981; Creative Artists Public Service grant, 1981; Obie Award, 1981 (for writing and directing) 1984; MacDowell Fellowship, 1984; Guggenheim Fellowship, 1987. *Literary Agent:* Flora Roberts Inc, New York, *Address:* c/o Flora Roberts Inc, 157 West 57th Street, New York, NY 10019, USA.

JENKIN Leonard. *See:* **JENKIN Len.**

JENKINS Alan, b. 5 Sept 1914, Carshalton, Surrey, England. Journalism; Public Relations. m. Margaret Elizabeth Hoskin, 15 Dec 1956, 1 daughter. *Education:* BA (Hons) 1935, MA 1948, St Edmund Hall, Oxford. *Appointments:* Fiction Editor, Nash's Magazine, 1936-37; Assistant Editor, Argosy Magazine, 1938-39; Editor, Army Illustrated Magazine, 1941-46; Assistant Editor, World Review, Lilliput, Leader. *Publications:* The Twenties, 1974; The Thirties, 1976; The Forties, 1977; The Rich Rich, 1977; Stephen Potter, 1978; The Book of the Thames, 1983; The Young Mozart, 1961; Various company histories: Taylor Woodrow; Knight Frank & Rutley; The Stock Exchange Story. *Contributions to:* Most leading magazines and newspapers in USA and England. *Honours:* The Twenties, First, BCA Choice; The Thirties, BCA Choice; The Forties, BCA Choice. *Literary Agent:* David Higham Associates Ltd. *Address:* 7 Beech Close, Effingham, Surrey KT24 5PQ, England.

JENKINS Alan Roberts, b. 8 June 1926. Editorial Executive, The Times. m. (1) Kathleen Mary Baker, 1949, dec 1969, 4 sons, (2) Helen Mary Speed, 1971, 1 son. *Appointments:* Reporter, Reading Mercury and Berkshire chronicle, 1948; Sub-Editor, Daily Herald; Sub Editor, Night Editor 1962-69, Northern Editor 1969-71, Daily Mail; Assistant Editor, Evening Standard, 1971; Deputy Editor, Sunday People, 1971-72; Assistant Editor, Sunday Mirror, 1972-77; Editor, Glasgow Herald, 1978-80; Editorial Executive, The Times, 1981- . *Address:* 21 The Heights, 97 Frognal, Hampstead NW3, England.

JENKINS Dan, (Thomas B.), b. 2 Dec 1929, Fort Worth, TX, USA. Writer. m. (3) June Burrage, 2 sons, 1 daughter. *Education:* Texas Christian University. *Appointments:* Affiliated with Fort Worth Press, Fort Worth, 1948-60; Affiliated with Dallas Times Herald, Dallas, 1960-62; Affiliated with Sports Illustrated, New York, 1962-84; Affiliated with Playboy, Chicago, IL, 1985-; Writer. *Publications:* Sports Illustrated's The Best Eighteen Golf Holes in America, 1966; The Dogged Victims of Inexorable Fate, Saturday's America, 1970; Semi-Tough, 1972; Dead Solid Perfect, 1974; Limo (with Edwin Shrake), 1976; Baja Oklahoma, 1981; Life Its Ownself: The Semi-Tougher Adventures of Billy Clyde Puckett and Them, 1984; Football, 1986; Fast Copy, 1988. *Contributions to:* Author of film and television screenplays.

JENKINS Daniel Thomas, b.9 June 1914, Merthyr Tydfil, Wales. Minister and Professor of Theology. m. Agatha Helen Mary Cree, 15 Aug 1942, 2 sons, 3 daughters. *Education:* Edinburgh University, MA 1935, BD 1938; Yorkshire United College 1935-37; Mansfield College, Oxford, BA (Oxon) 1939. *Appointments:* Assistant Editor, Christian News-Letter, 1945-48; Commonwealth Fund Fellow, New York, 1948-49; Professor (part-time) University of Chicago, 1950-62; Reader and University Chaplain, University of Sussex, 1963-73; Professor, Princeton Theological Seminary, New Jersey, 1981-84; Also Minister of various United Reformed Churches. *Publications:* The Nature of Catholicity, 1942; The Gift of Ministry, 1947; The Strangeness of the Church, 1955; Beyond Religion, 1962; Equality and Excellence, 1961; The British, Their Identity and Their Religion,, 1975; The Christian Belief in God, 1964 and twelve others. *Contributions to:* Numerous journals in Britain and the USA; London Times and Times Literary Supplement. *Honours:* DD Knox College, Toronto, 1957; DD, Edinburgh University,

1964. *Membership:* Athenaeum, London. *Address:* 301 Willoughby House, Barbican, London EC2Y 8BL, England.

JENKINS Elizabeth, British Writer. *Education:* Newnham College, Cambridge. *Publications:* The Winters, 1931; Lady Caroline Lamb : A Biography, 1932; Portrait of an Actor, 1933; Harriet, 1934; The Phoenix Nest, 1936; Jane Austen - A Biography, 1938; Robert and Helen, 1944; Young Enthusiasts, 1946; Henry Fielding, English Novelist Series, 1947; Six Crlmlnal Women, 1949; The Tortoise and the Hare, 1954; Ten Fascinating Women, 1955; Elizabeth The Great, 1958; Elizabeth and Leicester, 1961; Brightness, 1963; Honey, 1968; Dr Gully, 1972; The Mystery of King Arthur, 1975; The Princes in the Tower, 1978; The Shadow and the Light, 1983. *Honour:* OBE, 1981; Femina Vie Heureuse Prize, 1934. *Address:* 8 Downshire Hill, Hampstead, London, NW3, England.

JENKINS John Geraint, b. 4 Jan 1929, Llangnrannog, Dyfed, Wales, Museum Curator. m. 8 Jan 1954, 3 sons. *Education:* BA, 1952, MA 1953, DSc Econ, 1980, University of Wales, Swansea and Aberystwyth. *Appointments:* Editor, Folk Life, 1963-78; President, Society for Folk Life Studies, 1983-86; Chairman, Society for the Interpretation of Britain's Heritage, 1975-81. *Publications:* The English Farm Wagon, 1963; Traditional Country Craftsmen, 1965; Nets and Coracles, 1974; The Welsh Woollen Industry, 1969; Life and Tradition in Rural Wales, 1973; The Coracle, 1985; Agricultural Transport in Wales, 1966; Exploring Museums, Wales, 1990; Interpreting the Heritage of Wales, 1990. *Contributions to:* Country Life; Folk Life; Agricultural History Review; Home and Country. *Honour:* Druid, Eorsedd of Bards, National Eisteddfod of Wales, 1969. *Address:* The Garden House, St Fagans, Cardiff CF5 6DS, Wales.

JENKINS Peter George James, b. 11 May 1934, Amersham, Buckinghamshire, England. Journalist. m. Polly Toynbee, 28 Dec 1970, 1 son, 3 daughters. *Education:* BA, Honours, Trinity Hall, Cambridge, 1957; University of Wisconsin, USA, 1957. *Appointments:* Financial times, 1958-60;; Reporter, 1960, Labour Correspondent, 1963-67, Political Columnist, 1967-72, Washington Correspondent, 1972-74, Policy Editor, Chief Political Commentator, 1974-85, The Guardian; Columnist, Sunday Times, 1985-87; Associate Editor, Political Commentator, The Independent, 1987-. *Publications:* The Battle of Downing Street, 1970; Mrs Thatcher's Revolution: The Ending of the Socialist Era, 1987; Play, Illuminations, 1980. *Contributions to:* Numerous professional journals. *Honours:* Visiting Fellow, Nuffield, Oxford, 1980-87. *Literary Agent:* A.D. Peters & Co., London. *Address:* The Independent, 40 City Road, London EC4, England.

JENKINS (John) Robin, b. 1912, British. *Appointments:* Teacher, Gjazi College, Khabul, 1957-59; British Institute, Barcelona, 1959-61, Gaya School, Sabah, 1963-68. *Publications:* Go Gaily Sings the Lark, 1951; Happy for the Child, 1953; The Thistle and the Grail, 1954; The Cone-Gatherers, 1955; Guests of War, 1956; The Missionaries, 1957; The Changeling, 1958; Love is a Fervent Fire, 1959; Some Kind of Grace, 1960; Dust on the Paw, 1961; The Tiger of Gold, 1962; A Love of Innocence, 1963; The Sardana Dancers, 1964; A Very Scotch Affair, 1968; The Holly Tree, 1969; The Expatriates, 1971; A Toast to the Lord, 1972; A Figure of Fun, 1974; A Would- Be-Saint, 1978; Fergus Lamont, 1979; The Awakening of George Darroch, 1985; Poverty Castle, 1991. *Address:* Fairhaven, Toward by Dunoon, Argyll, PA23 7UE, Scotland.

JENKINS Roy Harris, Rt. Hon., Lord Jenkins of Hillhead, b. 11 Nov 1920. Politician; Writer; Chancellor of Oxford University, 1987-; Former President, European Commission. m. Jennifer Morris, 2 sons, 1 daughter. *Education:* Balliol College, Oxford. *Appointments include:* MP, Labour, Central Southwark, London 1948-50, Stechford, Birmingham, 1950-77; Home Secretary,

1965-67, 1974-76; Chancellor of the Exchequer, 1967-70; Co-Founder, Social Democratic Party, 1981, Leader 1982-83; MP, SDP, Hillhead, Glasgow, 1982-87. *Publications:* Purpose and Policy, Editor, 1947; Mr Attlee : An Interim Biography, 1948; New Fabian Essays (contributor), 1952; Pursuit of Progress, 1953; Mr Balfour's Poodle, 1954; Sir Charles Dilke : A Victorian Tragedy, 1958; The Labour Case, 1959; Asquith, 1964; Essays and Speeches, 1967; Afternoon on the Potomac?, 1972; What Matters Now, 1973; Nine Men of Power, 1974; Partnership of Princple, 1985; Truman, 1986; Baldwin, 1987; Twentieth Century Portraits, 1988; European Diary, 1989. *Honours:* Life Peer, cr. 1987; Recipient, numerous honours and awards including: Hon. Fellow, Berkeley College, Yale, Balliol College, Oxford, Loughborough, University College, Cardiff; Honorary LL.D., Leeds 1971, Harvard 1972, Pennsylvania 1973, Dundee 1973, Oxford 1973; Bath 1978, Michigan 1978, Essex 1978, Wales 1978, Reading 1979, Bristol 1980; Numerous other honorary degrees; Charlemagne Prize, 1972; Robert Schuman Prize, 1972. *Address:* 2 Kensington Park Gardens, London, W11, England.

JENKINS Simon David, b. 10 June 1943, Birmingham, England. Times Columnist, Editor. m. Gayle Hunnicutt, 1978. *Education:* BA, St John's College, Oxford. *Appointments:* Staff, Country Life Magazine, 1965; News Editor, Times Educational Supplement, 1966-68; Leader Writer, Columnist, Features Editor, 1968-74, Editor, 1977-78, Evening Standard; Insight Editor, Sunday Times, 1974-76; Political Editor, The Economist, 1979-86; Director, Faber and Faber (Publishers) Ltd., 1981-90. *Publications:* A City at Risk, 1971; Landlords to London, 1974; Newspapers : The Power and the Money, 1979; The Companion Guide to Outer London, 1981; Images of Hampstead, 1982; The Battle for the Falklands, 1983; With Respect, Ambassador, 1985; Market for Glory, 1986. *Memberships:* Board, Old Vic Co., 1979-81; Part-time Member, British Rail Board, 1979-90; London Regional Transport Board, 1984-86; Museum of London, 1984-88; Vice Chairman, Thirties Society, 1979-90; Director, The Municipal Journal, 1980-90; Historic Buildings and Monuments Commission, 1985-90; South Bank Board, 1985-90. *Address:* 174 Regents Park Road, London, NW1, England.

JENKS Randolph, b. 17 Mar 1912, Morristown, New Jersey, USA. Cattle Rancher; Ornithologist; Naturalist. m. Julia Post Swan, 2 Sept 1936, 1 son, 3 daughters. *Education:* BS, Princeton University. *Publications:* Naming the Birds at a Glance (with Lou Blackly), 1962; Desert Quest (with Beverly Powell), 1990. *Contributions to:* Several articles to The Condor, Cooper Ornithological Society. *Honours:* Phi Beta Kappa, 1936; Associate, Society of Sigma Xi, 1935. *Memberships:* Explorers Club; American Ornithological Union; Cooper Ornithological Society; Princeton Club of Tucson; Audobon Society; Nature Conservancy; Arizona Historical Society; American Society for Range Management; Museum of Northern Arizona; Westerners. *Address:* 2146 East 4th Street, Tucson, AZ 85719, USA.

JENNIFER Susan. *See:* HOSKINS Robert.

JENNINGS Elizabeth (Joan). b. 18 July 1926, Boston, Lincolnshire, England. Writer. *Education:* Oxford High School, MA, English Language and Literature, St Anne's College, Oxford. *Appointments:* Assistant, Oxford City Library, 1950-58; Reader, Chatto and Windus Ltd, publishers, London 1958-60; Freelance writer 1961-; Guildersleeve Lecturer, Barnard College, New York, 1974. *Publications:* Verse includes: Relationships, 1972; Growing-Points: New Poems, 1975; Consequently I Rejoice, 1977; After the Ark (for children) 1978; Moments of Grace: New Poems, 1979; Selected Poems, 1979; Winter Wind, 1979; A Dream of Spring, 1980; Celebrations and Elegies, 1982. Author or edition of many other publications. *Honours:* Arts Council Award, 1953; Bursary 1965, 1968, 1981, Grant 1972; Somerset Maugham Award, 1956; Richard Hillary

Memorial Prize, 1966; WH Smith Award, 1987. *Literary Agent:* David Higham Associations Ltd, 5-8 Lower John Street, London W1R 4HA. *Address:* 11 Winchester Road, Oxford, OX2 6NA, England.

JENNINGS Marie Patricia b. 25 Dec 1930, Quetta, India. Author. m. Harry Brian Locke, 3 Jan 1976, 1 son. *Publications:* Women and Money, 1988; Money Guide, 1986; Getting the Message Across, 1988; A Guide to Good Corporate Citizenship, 1990; Money Go Round!, 1968; Moneyspinner Guides, 1987-88; Ten Steps To The Top, 1992. *Contributions to:* Finance Correspondent, Womans Journal; Good Housekeeping; Editor, Consumer Affairs; Money Wise: Accountancy. *Memberships:* Society of Authors; Institute of Directors; Institute of Public Relations; Fellow of the Royal Society of Arts. *Literary Agent:* Andrew Mann. *Address:* The Court House, Bisley, Stroud, Glos, GL6 7AA, England.

JENNINGS Paul (Francis), b. 20 June 1918. Writer. m. Celia Blom, 1952, 3 sons, 3 daughters. *Appointments:* Freelance work in Punch and Spectator began while still in Army (Lt. Royal Signals); Script-writer, Central Office of Information, 1946-47; Copy Writer, Colman Prentis Varley, 1947-49; Staff, The Observer, 1949-66. *Publications:* Oddly Enough, 1951; Even Oddlier, 1952; Oddly Bodlikins, 1953; Next to Oddliness, 1955; Model Oddlies, 1956; Gladly Oddly, 1957; Idly Oddly, 1959; I Said Oddly, Diddle I?, 1961; Oodles of Oddlies, 1963; The Jenguin Pennings, 1963; Oddly Ad Lib, 1965; I Was Joking of Course, 1968; The Living Village, 1968; Just a Few Lines, 1969; It's An Odd Thing, But . . . , 1971; Editor, The English Difference, 1974; Britain As She Is Visit, 1976; The Book of Nonsense, 1977; I Must Have Imagined It, 1977; Companion to Britain, 1980; Editor, A Feast of Days, 1982; Editor, My Favourite Railway Stories, 1982; Golden Oddlies, 1983; East Anglia, 1986; Novel: And Now for Something Exactly the Same,1977; for children: The Hopping Basket, 1965; The Great Jelly of London, 1967; The Train to Yesterday, 1974. *Memberships:* FRSL, FRSA. *Address:* 25 High Street, Orford, Woodbridge Suffolk, England.

JENNINGS Phillip C, b. 5 Mar 1946, Seattle, WA, USA. m. Deborah Louise McCarl, 6 Sept 1969, 1 son, 1 daughter. *Education:* BA, Macalester College, 1968. *Appointments:* Programmer and Analyst, State of Minnesota, St Paul, 1969-78; Programmer and Analyst, Control Data Corporation, Arden Hills, MN, 1978-79; Programmer and Analyst, United Information Services, Kansas City, MO, 1979-83; Writer, 1983-; Member of St John's Episcopal Church Choir. *Publications:* Tower to the Sky, 1988; The Bug-Life Chronicles, 1989. *Contributions to:* Stories in magazines, including Amazing Stories; Issac Asimov's Science Fiction; Argos Fantasy and Science Fiction; New Destinies; Tales of the Unanticipated; Far Frontiers; Work represented in anthologies including There Will Be War. *Memberships:* Science Fiction Writers of America; Planetary Society; National Organization for Women. *Address:* 32130 County Road 1, St Cloud, MN 56303, USA.

JENOFF Marvyne Shael, b. 10 Mar 1942, Winnipeg, Canada. Teacher. *Education:* BA University of Manitoba, 1964; Teacher Training. *Publications:* No Lingering Peace, 1972; Hollandsong, 1975; The Orphan and the Stranger, 1985, (all poetry); The Emperor's Body, (adult fables); Editor, New Poet's Handbook, 1984-85. *Contributions to:* Prism International; The Fiddlehead; The Antigonish Review; Matrix; The Canadian Forum. *Memberships:* League of Canadian Poets; The Writer's Union of Canada. *Address:* c/o The Writer's Union of Canada, 24 Ryerson Avenue, Toronto, Ontario, Canada M5T 2P3.

JENSEN De Lamar, b. 1925, American. *Appointments:* Instructor in History, New York University, NYC, 1954-57; Professor of History, Brigham Young University, Provo, UT, 1957-. *Publications:* Machiavelli: Cynic, Patriot or Political Scientist? (compiler and ed), 1960; Diplomacy and Dogmatism:

Bernardino de Mendoza and the French Catholic League, 1964; The Expansion of Europe: Motives, Methods and Meanings (compiler and ed), 1967; The World of Europe: The Sixteenth Century, Confrontation at Worms: Martin Luther and the Diet of Worms, 1973; Renaissance Europe, 1980, 2nd edition, 1991; Reformation Europe, 1981, 2nd edition, 1991. *Address:* 1079 Briar Avenue, Provo, UT 84604, USA.

JENSEN Laura Linnea, b. 16 Nov 1948, Tacoma, Washington, USA. Poet; Occasional Teacher. *Education:* BA, University of Washington, 1972; MFA, University of Iowa, 1974. *Literary Appointments:* Manuscript judge, NEA, 1977; Panel member, NEA, Washington DC, 1981; Prize judge, Poetry Society of America, 1982, 1985; Hopwood Awards, University of Michigan, 1986; Visiting Poet, Oklahoma State University, 1978. *Publications include:* Shelter, 1985; Memory, 1982; Bad Boats, 1977; Anxiety & Ashes, 1976. Also chapbooks & pamphlets: A Sky Empty of Orion, 1985 (award); Tapwater, 1978; The Story Makes Them Whole, 1979; After I Have Voted, 1972. *Contributions to:* American Poetry Review; Antaeus; Field; Iowa Review; Ironwood; New Yorker; Northwest Review; Poetry Northwest; Pushcart Prize No.3. *Honours:* Honours Award 1978, fellowship grant 1986-87; Washington State Arts Commission; Fellowship, National Endowment for the Arts, 1980-81; Grant, Ingram-Merrill Foundation, 1983; Theodore Roethke Award, poetry, Poetry Northwest, 1986; Guggenheim Fellowship, 1989-90. *Memberships:* Poets & Writers; Associated Writing Programmes; Academy of American Poets, 1970's. *Address:* 302 North Yakima C3, Tacoma, Washington 98403, USA.

JENSEN Ruby Jean, b. 1 Mar 1930. Author m. Vaughn Jensen, 1 daughter. *Publications:* Novels: House of Illusions, 1988; Chain Letter, 1987; Such a Good Baby, 1982; Pendulum 1989; Jump Rope 1988; Death Stone 1989; Annabelle 1987; The House that Samael Built, 1974; The Lake 1983; Seventh All Hallows' Eve, 1974; Dark Angel, 1978; Hear the Children Cry, 1981; Mama 1983; Home Sweet Home, 1985; Celia, 1991; Baby Dolly, 1991. *Literary Agent:* Marcia Amsterdam. *Address:* 41 West 82nd Street, New York, NY 10024, USA.

JERE. *See:* **VAN DYK Wilmer Gerald.**

JERINA Carol, b. 2 Sept 1947, Dallas, TX, USA. Writer. m. Drew Jerina, 20 Dec 1968, 4 sons. *Appointments:* Sales Clerk, Sanger-Harris (retail store), 1964-66; Tax and Data Processing Clerk, City of Dallas, 1966-68. *Publications:* Lady Raine, Gallagher's Lady, 1984; Fox Hunt, 1985; Brighter Than Gold, Embrace An Angel, 1987; Tropic Gold, The Tall Dark Alibi, Sweet Jeopardy, 1988. *Honours:* Reviewer's Choice Awards from Romantic Times for best Humourous Historical Romance, for Fox Hunt, 1985; Nomination for best post-Civil War romance, for Embrace An Angel, 1987. *Memberships:* Romance Writers of America; Greater Dallas Writers' Association. *Address:* 3109 Bluffview Drive, Garland, TX 75043, USA.

JERSILD Per Christian, b. 14 Mar 1935, Katrineholm, Sweden. Writer. m. Ulla J, 1960, 2 sons. *Education:* MD. *Publications:* The Animal Doctor, 1975, 1988; After the Flood, 1986; Childrens Island, 1987; The House of Babel, 1987; A Living Soul, 1988; also 29 books published in Sweden. *Honours:* Swedish Grand Novel Prize, 1981; Swedish Academy Award, 1982. *Memberships:* Swedish PEN, Board. *Address:* Rosensdalsv. 20, 5-19454 Uppl. Vasby, Sweden.

JESSUP Frances, b. 29 July 1936, England. Author. m. Clive Turner, 2 Jan 1960, 1 son, 3 daughters. *Education:* BA Hons Philosophy, King's College, London University, 1955-58. *Appointments:* Organiser of Theatre Writing in Halesmere, UNA, 1992. *Publications:* The Fifth Child's Conception, 1970, 1972. *Contributions to:* New Poetry, 1980; New Stories, 1981; Hard Lines, 1987; Words Etcetera 1973; Words Broadsheet, Pen Broadsheet, 1986; Weyfarers; Overspill; MTD Journal. *Honours:* First Prize for Fiction and Poetry, Moor Park College, 1972; UNA Trust Award (for Peace Play Festival), 1988; University of Surrey Arts Committee Literary Festival Award, 1991. *Memberships:* PEN; TWU. *Literary Agent:* Patricia Robertson. *Address:* Strone Grove Road, Hindhead, Surrey GU26 6QP, England.

JETHA Akbarali Hasambhoy, b. 6 Feb 1942, Bombay, India. Businessman. m. Suraiya, 18 Dec 1966, 2 sons, 1 daughter. *Education:* Junior Cambridge. *Publications:* Reflections I, II, and III, 1980, 1983 and 1989 respectively; Path to Enlightenment, 1985; Parables, 1987. *Memberships:* PEN All-India Centre; Beauty without Cruelty, President, India Branch; Rashtriya Ahinsa Pratishtan, Vice President; Indian Vegetarian Congress, Committee Member. *Address:* 65 Mount Unique, 9th Floor, Dr Gopalrao Deskmukh Road, Bombay 400 026, India.

JHABVALA Ruth Prawer, b. 7 May 1927, Cologne, Germany. Writer. m. 16 June 1951, 3 daughters. *Education:* BA 1948, MA 1951, DLitt,(Hon) London. *Publications:* The Householder, 1960; A New Dominion, 1971; Heat & Dust, 1975; Out of India, 1986; Three Continents, 1987; Poet and Dancer, 1993. *Honours:* Booker Prize, 1975; Neil Gunn International Fellowship, 1979; MacArthur Foundation Fellowship, 1984-89; Academy Award, 1987; Academy Award, 1993. *Memberships:* Fellow Royal Society of Literature; Authors Guild; Writers Guild of America. *Literary Agent:* Harriet Wasserman. *Address:* 400 East 52nd Street, New York, NY 10022, USA.

JIMENEZ Francisco, b. 29 June 1943, Mexico. University Professor and Administrator. m. Laura Facchini Jimenez, 17 Aug 1968, 3 sons, 3 daughters. *Education:* BA, Santa Clara 1u, 1966; MA 1969, PhD, 1972, Columbia University; Management Development Programme Certificate, Harvard University, 1989. *Appointments:* Editorial Board, The Bilingual Review, 1973-, West Coast Editor, 1974-; Board of Directors, Asociacion Literaria de Bellas Artes, 1978-; President, Chicano Literature Executive Committee of the Modern Language Association of AMerica. *Publications:* The Circuit; Cajas de Carton; Prosa chicana cubana puertorriquena; Los episodios nacionales de Victoriano Salado Alvarez; Identification and Analysis of Chicano Literature; Hispanics in the US: An Anthology of Creative Literature; Viva La Lengua; Poverty and Social Justice; Critical Perspectives. *Contributions to:* Cuadernos Americanos; Hispania; The Bilingual Review; La Luz; El Grito; Lector; Mensaje: Revista de Cultura y Arte; Arizona Quarterly; Journal of the Association of Mexican American Educators. *Honours:* Best Short Story, Arizona Quarterly Annual Award, 1973. *Memberships:* Board, Asociacion Literaria de Bellas Artes; Vice Chair, California Council for the Humanities; Chair, State commission for Teacher Credentialing; Accrediting Commission for Senior Colleges and Universities; Board, Far West Laboratory for Educational Research and Development; Board, Western Association of Schools and Colleges Accrediting Commission. *Address:* 624 Enos Court, Santa Clara, CA 95051, USA.

JOHANSSON-BACKE Karl Erik, b. 24 Nov 1914, Stockholm, Sweden. Teacher (Retired 1963); Author. m. Kerstin Gunhild Bergquist, (childrens author), 21 Nov 1943, 1 son, 3 daughters. *Education:* Degree, High School Teacher. *Publications:* A Pole in the River, (novel), 1950; Daybreak (novel), 1954; Lust and Flame (poetry), 1981; The Mountain of Temptation (novel), 1983; The Ghost Aviator (documentary), 1985; The Tree and the Bread, (novel), 1987; King of Mountains, (novel), 1993; Author, 30 books and 12 plays. *Honours:* Many litterary awards from 1961-93. *Memberships:* Swedish Authors Federation; Swedish Playwrights Federation. *Literary Agent:* Arbetarkultur, Stockholm; Bonniers, Stockholm; Proprius, Stockholm. *Address:* Kopmangstan 56, 83133, Ostersund, Sweden.

JOHN Katherine. *See:* **WATKINS Karen Christina.**

JOHN Nancy. *See:* **SAWYER John & SAWYER Nancy.**

JOHNS Kenneth. *See:* **BULMER Henry Kenneth.**

JOHNSON A E. *See:* **JOHNSON Annabel (Jones).**

JOHNSON A Findlay. *See:* **JOHNSON Alison Findlay.**

JOHNSON Alison Findlay, (A Findlay Johnson), b. 19 Nov 1947, Stafford, England. Author. m. Andrew J D Johnson, 1973, 1 daughter. *Education:* MA, Aberdeen University, 1968; BPhil, Oxford, 1970. *Publications:* A House by the Shore, 1986; Scarista Style, 1987; Children of Disobedience, 1989; Islands in the Sound, 1989; The Wicked Generation, 1992. *Contributions to:* West Highland Free Press; The Times. *Literary Agent:* Vivien Green. *Address:* c/o Vivien Green, 43 Goughty Street, London WC1N 2LF, England.

JOHNSON Annabel (Jones), (A E Johnson), b. 1921, American. *Publications:* As A Speckled Bird, 1956; The Big Rock Candy (with Edgar Johnson), 1957; The Black Symbol, 1959; Torrie, The Bearcat, 1960; The Rescued Heart, The Secret Gift (as A E Johnson), Pickpocket Run, 1961; Wilderness Bride, 1962; A Golden Touch, 1963; The Grizzly, 1964; A Peculiar Magic, 1965; The Burning Glass, 1966; Count Me Gone, 1968; A Blues I Can Whistle (as A E Johnson), 1969; The Last Knife, 1971; Finders Keepers, 1981; An Alien Music, 1982; The Danger Quotient, 1984; Prisoner of PSI, 1985; A Memory of Dragons, 1986; Gamebuster, 1990; I am Leaper, 1990. *Address:* 2925 S Teller, Denver, CO 80227, USA.

JOHNSON Barbara Ferry, b. 1923, American. *Appointments:* Association Editor, American Lumberman Magazine, Chicago, 1945-48; High School English Teacher, Myrtle Beach, 1960-62; Member of the English Department, Columbia College, 1964-. *Publications:* Lioners, 1975; Delta Blood, 1977; Tara's Song, 1978; Homeward Winds the River, 1979; The Heirs of Love, 1980; Echoes from the Hills, 1982. *Address:* c/o Warner Books, 660 Fifth Avenue, New York, NY 10103, USA.

JOHNSON Carlos Alberto, b. 26 June 1943, Lima, Peru. Writer. *Education:* BS Educ and Spanish, Brooklyn College, NY, 1972-74; MA Spanish, CYNY Graduate Centre, NY, 1974-76; Completed 60 credits toward PhD Spanish. *Appointments:* Correspondent and reporter for El Dominical of the Peruvian newspaper El Diario El Comercio, 1981-88. *Publications:* El Ojo-Cara del Professor, 1983; Adivina quien es?, 1976; El monologo del vendedor ambulante, 1984; Cuando me muera que me arrojen al Rimac en un cajon blanco, 1990. *Contributions to:* Centerpoint; Revista chicano-Riquena; Revista Casa de las Americas; Chasqi, Revista de Literatura Latinoamericana; Inti Rev de Lit Hispanica; Linden Lane Magazine; New Delhi Magazine; Sunday Sketch; El Dominical; El Guacamayo y la Serpiente; Rev de la Casa de la Cult; Ecuatoriana. *Honours:* Creative Writing Fellowship, National Endowment for the Arts, 1990. *Address:* 30-98 Crescent Street Apt 1C, Astoria, NY 11102, USA.

JOHNSON David, b. 26 Aug 1927, Meir, Staffs, England. *Education:* Repton; Sandhurst. *Publications:* Sabre General, 1959; Promenade in Champagne, 1960; Lanterns in Gascony, 1965; A Candle in Aragon, 1970; Regency Revolution, 1974; Napoleon's Cavalry and its Leaders, 1978; The French Cavalry 1792-1815, 1989. *Contributions to:* Military History, USA. *Address:* 16 Belgrave Gardens, London NW8 ORB, England.

JOHNSON Denis, b. 1949, American. *Publications:* The Man among the Seals, 1969; Inner Weather, 1976; The Incognito Lounge and Other Poems, 1982; Angels, 1983; Fiskadoro, 1985; The Stars at Noon, 1986.

Address: c/o Knopf Incorporated, 201 E 50th Street, New York, NY 10022, USA.

JOHNSON Diane Lain, b. 28 Apr, 1934, Illinois, USA. m. John Frederick Murray, 9 Nov 1969, 4 children. *Education:* AA, Stephens College, 1953; BA, University Utah, 1957; MA, PhD, UCLA, 1968. *Appointments:* Faculty, Dept of English, University California, Davis, 1968-87. *Publications:* Fair Game, 1965; Loving Hands at Home, 1968; Burning, 1970; The Shadow Knows, 1975; Lying Low, 1978; Lesser Lives, 1972; Terrorists and Novelists, 1982; Dashiell Hammett, 1983; Persian Nights, 1987; Health and Happiness, 1990; Natural Opium, 1993. *Contributions to:* New York Review of Books; New York Times Book Reviews; The New Yorker; Washington Post; Los Angeles Times. *Honours:* Nominee, National Book Awards, 1973, 1979; Recipient, Rosenthal Award American Academy of Arts and Letters, 1979; Mildred and Harold Strauss Living, American Academy and Institute of Arts and Letters, 1988. *Memberships:* PEN; Writers Guild of America. *Literary Agent:* Lynn Nesbit.

JOHNSON E(mil) Richard, b. 1938, American. Inmate at Stillwater, Minnesota State Prison, 1964-. *Publications:* Silver Street, 1968 (in UK as The Silver Street Killer, 1969); The Inside Man, Mongo's Back in Town, 1969; Cage Five Is Going To Break, The God Keepers, 1970; Case Lord - Maximum, The Judas, 1971; The Cardinalli Contract, 1975; Blind Man's Bluff, Fur: Food and Survival, 1987; The Hands of Eddy Loyd, 1988; Dead Flowers, 1990. *Address:* Box 55, Stillwater, MN 55082, USA.

JOHNSON George, b. 20 Jan 1952, Fayetteville, Arkansas, USA. Writer. *Education:* MA American University, 1979; BA University of New Mexicos, 1975. *Appointments:* Alicia Patterson Journalism Fellow, 1984. *Publications:* In the Palaces of Memory, 1991; Machinery of the Mind, 1986; Architects of Fear, 1984. *Contributions to:* New York Times Book Review; The Sciences; PM Magazine; New York Times Magazine. *Literary Agent:* Esther Newbery ICM. *Address:* c/o Esther Newbery ICM, 40 West 57th Street, NY 10019, USA.

JOHNSON (Hettie) Jean, b. 16 Jan 1937, Fort Collins, CO, USA. Teacher; Musician; Writer. m. LeRoy C Johnson, 22 Oct 1959, 2 sons. *Education:* BS, Mills College, 1959. *Appointments:* Second Chair Cellist, Portland Symphony, Portland, 1960-63; First Chair Cellist, Sacramento Symphony, Sacramento, CA, 1964-77; Cellist, New Mexico Symphony, Albuquerque, 1978-81; Free-lance writer and scientific editor, 1981-. *Publications:* Julia: Death Valley's Youngest Victim, 1981; Escape From Death Valley: As Told by William Lewis Manly and Other '49ers, 1987, (both with L C Johnson). *Contributions to:* Scientific Journals; Editor and Author of introduction, (with L C Johnson), of historical monograph Route of the Manly Party of 1849 to 1850 in Leaving Death Valley for the Coast, 1988. *Memberships:* American Association of University Women; Musicians Union (Albuquerque NM); Professional Editors' Network (Twin Cities, MN); Death Valley '49ers. *Address:* 2595 Cohansey Street, Roseville, MN 55113, USA.

JOHNSON Hubert Covington, b. 6 Jan 1930, Santa Rita, New Mexico, USA. Professor of History. m. Suzanne Marguerite Pasche, 20 Aug 1954, 3 sons. *Education:* BA San Diego State College, 1955; MA 1956, PhD, 1962, University of California, Berkeley. *Publications:* Frederick the Great and his Officials, 1975; The Midi in Revolution, 1986; Forthcoming: Breakthrough: The Evolution of Tactics on The Western Front, 1914-1918, 1994. *Contributions to:* Various reviews in journals. *Honours:* Fellowship, US Army Military History Institute, 1981. *Memberships:* American and Canadian Historical Associations; Society for Nautical Research. *Address:* Department of History, University of Saskatchewan, Saskatoon, Saskatchewan, Canada S7N OWO.

JOHNSON Hugh Eric Allan, b. 10 Mar 1939, London, England. Author; Editor. m. Judith Eve Grinling, 1965, 1 son, 2 daughters. *Education:* MA, King's College, Cambridge. *Appointments:* Feature Writer, Conde Nast Magazines, 1960-63; Editor, Wine and Food Magazine, 1963-65; Wine Correspondent, Sunday Times, 1965-67; Travel Editor 1967, Editor, Queen Magazine, 1968-70; Wine Editor, Cuisine Magazine, New York, 1983-84; Editorial Consultant, The Garden, 1975-. *Publications:* Wine, 1966; The World Atlas of Wine, 1971; The International Book of Trees, 1973; The California Wine Book (with Bob Thompson), 1975; Hugh Johnson's Pocket Wine Book, annually 1977-; The Principles of Gardening, 1979; Hugh Johnson's Wine Companion, 1983; How to Handle a Wine (video), 1984; Hugh Johnson's Cellar Book, 1986; The Atlas of German Wines, 1986; Understanding Wine (A Sainsbury Guide), 1986; Atlas of the Wines of France (with Hubrecht Duijker), 1987; A History of Wine, Channel 4 TV series, 1989; The Story of Wine, 1989; The Art and Science of Wine, 1992. *Honours:* Andre Simon Prize, 1967, 1984; Awards include: Glenfiddich Wine Award, 1990; Grand Prix de la Communication de la Vigne et du Vin, 1992 & 1993; Marques de Caceres Award, 1984; Masi Award, Verona, 1993. *Memberships:* President, Sunday Times Wine Club, 1973- ; Chairman, Winestar Productions Ltd., The Hugh Johnson Collection. *Address:* Saling Hall, Great Saling, Essex, CM7 5DT, England.

JOHNSON James Henry, b. 19 Nov 1930, University Professor. m. Jean McKane, 31 Mar 1956, 2 sons, 2 daughters. *Education:* BA, Belfast, Northern Ireland, 1953; MA, Wisconsin, USA, 1954; PhD, London, England, 1962. *Appointments:* Editor, Aspects of Geography Series, Macmillan, 1980-. *Publications:* Urban Geography: An Introductory Analysis, 1967; Trends in Geography, (Editor), 1969; Geographical Mobility of Labour in England and Wales, (Co-author), 1974; Surburban Growth, (Editor), 1974; Urbanisation, 1980; The Structure of Nineteenth Century Cities, (Co-editor), 1982; Labour Migration, (co-editor), 1990; Population Migration, (co-author), 1990. *Contributions to:* Geographical journals, 1956-90. *Honour:* President, Institute of British Geographers, 1989. *Memberships:* Institute of British Geographers, Vice President and President; Royal Geographical Society; Association of American Geographers. *Address:* The Coach-house, Wyreside Hall, Dolphinholme, Lancaster LA2 9DH, England.

JOHNSON James Ralph, b. 20 May 1922, Ft Payne, Alabama, USA, Writer; Artist. m. (1) 2 sons, 1 daughter, (2) Burdetta F Beebe, 11 Oct 1961. *Education:* BS, Economics, Howard College, Birmingham, Alabama; USN Intelligence School, Anacostia, Maryland, 1951; Armed Forces Staff College, Norfolk, Virginia, 1960. *Publications:* Mountain Bobcat, 1953; Lost on Hawk Mountain, 1954; The Last Passenger, 1956; Big Cypress Buck, 1957; Horsemen Blue and Gray, 1960; Anyone Can Live Off the Land, 1961; Best Photos of the Civil War, 1961; Wild Venture, 1961; Utah Lion, 1962; Anyone Can Camp in Comfort, 1964; American Wild Horses, 1964; Camels West, 1964; Anyone Can Backpack in Comfort, 1965; The Wolf Cub, 1966; Advanced Camping Techniques, 1967; Pepper, 1967; Ringtail, 1968; Blackie the Gorilla, 1968; Animal Paradise, 1969; Moses Band of Chimpanzees, 1969; Everglades Adventure, 1970; Southern Swamps of America, 1970; Zoos of Today, 1971; Photography for Young People, 1971; Animals and Their Food, 1972. *Contributions to:* Marine Corps Gazette; Leatherneck; Saga; Boys' Life; Field and Stream. *Honours:* Boys' Clubs of America Best Like of Year Selection, for Anyone Can Camp in Comfort, 1965. *Memberships:* Western Writers of America; Outdoor Writers of America; Santa Fe Society of Artists Incorporated. *Address:* Box 5295, Santa Fe, NM 87502, USA.

JOHNSON John H, b. 19 Jan 1918, Arkansas, USA. Publisher. m. Eunice Johnson, 1 son (dec), 1 daughter. *Education:* Chicago & Northwestern Universities. *Appointments:* Assistant Editor 1936, later Managing Editor, employees' publication, Supreme Life Insurance Co, America; Founder, Ebony, 1945, Jet 1951, Black Stars Black World, Ebony Jr.; Founder, President, Johnson Publishing Co. Inc.; Director, Chairman, Supreme Life Insurance Co; Director, Marina City Bank of Chicago. *Honours:* Hon. LL.D., several universities and colleges; Horatio Alger Award, 1966; named Publisher of the Year, Magazine Publishers' Association; 1st Black Businessman to be selected as one of 10 Outstanding Young Men of America, US Junior Chamber of Commerce. *Memberships include:* United Negro College Fund; Trustee, Institute of International Education; Tuskegee Insitute. *Address:* 3600 Wilshire Boulevard, Los Angeles, CA 90005, USA.

JOHNSON Kim, (Kim 'Howard' Johnson), b. 6 Aug 1955, USA. Writer; Performer. *Education:* BSc, Illinois State University, 1977; AA, Illinois Valley Community College, 1975. *Appointments:* Feature Writer: Prevue magazine, 1980-87, Starlog magazine, 1983-; Senior Writer, Comics Scene magazine, 1984-. *Publications:* The First 20 Years of Monty Python, 1989; And Now for Something Completely Trivial, 1991; Life after Python: The Solo Flights of the Flying Circus, 1993. *Contributions to:* Starlog, Comics Scene, Prevue, Fangoria, Video Action, V, Its Only a Movie; Life Before and AFter Monty Python: The Solo Flights of the Flying Circus. *Literary Agent:* Dominick Abel Literary Agency. *Address:* 3037 N Racine 2, Chicago, IL 60657, USA.

JOHNSON Kim 'Howard'. *See:* **JOHNSON Kim.**

JOHNSON LeRoy C, b. 13 Oct 1937, Little Falls, MN, USA. Forester; Writer. m. Jean Hornibrook, 22 Oct 1959, 2 sons. *Education:* BA 1962, MS 1965, Oregon State University. *Appointments:* Assistant Regional Geneticist in California, Department of Agriculture, WA, 1963-66; Director of Institute of Forest Genetics, Placerville, 1966-77; Research Forester, Berkeley, 1977-78; Regional Geneticist, Alberquerque, NM, 1978-81; Field Representative, St Paul, MN, 1981-. *Publications:* Julia: Death Valley's Youngest Victim, 1981; Escape From Death Valley: As Told by William Lewis Manly and Other '49ers, 1987, (both with Jean Johnson). *Contributions to:* Author of about 30 articles to scientific journals; Editor and Author of introduction, (with J. Johnson), of historical monograph Route of the Manly Party of 1849 to 1850 in Leaving Death Valley for the Coast, 1988. *Memberships:* Society of American Foresters; Western History Association; Professional Editors' Network (Twin Cities, MN); Death Valley '49ers. *Address:* 2595 Cohansey Street, Roseville, MN 55113, USA.

JOHNSON Louis Albert, b. 27 Sept 1924, Wellington, New Zealand. Teacher; Journalist. m. Cecilia Wilson, 14 Nov 1970, 1 son, 1 daughter. *Education:* Wellington Teachers' College. *Appointments:* Lecturer, Senior Lecturer, Mitchell College Advanced Education, (NSW), 1970-79; OIC Bureau Literature, (PNG), 1968-69; Writer in Residence, Victoria University, Wellington, 1980; Member, New Zealand Literary Fund Advisory Board, 1982-. *Publications:* True Confessions of the Last Cannibal, 1986; Coming & Going, 1982; Fires & Patterns, 1975; Land Like a Lizard, 1970; Bread and a Pension, 1964; New Worlds for Old, 1956; Founder, Editor, Numbers, 1953-60; Founder Editor, New Zealand Poetry Yearbook, 1951-64. *Contributions to:* Poetry Australia; The Bulletin; Quadrant; Poetry Chicago; Poetry London; London Magazine; Landfall. *Honours:* New Zealand Book Award, Poetry, 1975; Writers' Fellowship, Victoria University, 1980; OBE, 1987. *Memberships:* PEN, New Zealand Centre, Secretary, 1955-59, President 1986-87. *Address:* 4 Te Motu Road, Pukerua Bay, New Zealand.

JOHNSON Mel. *See:* **MALZBERG Barry Norman.**

JOHNSON Mike. *See:* **SHARKEY Jack.**

JOHNSON Nora, b. 31 Jan 1933, Hollywood, California, USA. Author. m. (1) Leonard Siwek, 1955; (2) John A Milici 1965. 2 sons, 2 daughters. *Education:* BA, Smith College, 1954. *Publications:* The World of Henry Orient, 1958; A Step beyond Innocence, 1961; Love Letter in the Dead Letter Office, 1966; Flashback, 1979; You Can Go Home Again, 1982; The Two of Us, 1984; Tender Offer, 1985; Uncharted Places, 1988; Perfect Together, 1991. *Contributions to:* New York Times Book Review, LA Times Magazine, LA Times Book Review, New Yorker, Seventeen, McCall's Sports Illustrated; Atlantic Monthly; Cosmopolitan. *Honours:* McCall's Short Story Prize, 1962; Nomination, Screen Writers Award, 1964; O Henry Award Story, 1982; NU Times Best Book, 1982, 1984. *Memberships:* Authors Guild; PEN. *Literary Agent:* Helan Brann, 94 Curtis Road, Bridewater, CT 06752, USA. *Address:* 1385 York Avenue 8G, New York City, NY 10021, USA.

JOHNSON Owen Verne, b. 22 Feb 1946, Madison, Wisconsin, USA. Historian; Professor. m. Marta Kucerova, 17 July 1969, 2 daughters. *Education:* BA, Washington State University, 1968; MA, 1970, Certificate, 1978, PhD, 1978, University of Michigan. *Appointments:* Sports Editor, General Assignment Reporter, Pullman Washington Herald, 1961-67; Reporter, Editor, Producer, WUOM, Ann Arbor, 1969-77; Administrative Assistant, Russian & East European Centre, University of Michigan, 1978-79; Assistant Professor, Journalism, Southern Illinois University, 1979-80; Assistant Professor, 1980-87, Associate Professor, 1987-, Journalism, Indiana University; Acting Director, Polish Studies Center, Indiana University, 1989-90; Director, Russian and East European Institute, Indiana U., 1991. *Publications:* Slovakia 1918-1938: Education and the Making of a Nation, 1985; Mobilizing and Mobilized: The Roles and Functions of the Mass Media in Eastern Europe, forthcoming. *Contributions to:* 20 articles or essays in Journalism Quarterly; Journalism History; Editor, Clio Among the Media, 1983-84, Czech Marks, 1982-84. *Honours:* Sigma Delta Chi Excellence in Journalism award, State of Washington, 1966; Stanley Pech Prize, Czechoslovak History Conference, 1989; Recipient, various other honours and awards. *Memberships:* AEJMC, many offices held; AHA; AAASS; OAH; IAMCR; Czechoslovak History Conference; Slovak Studies Association, President, 1988-90. *Address:* School of Journalism, Indiana University, Bloomington, IN 47405, USA.

JOHNSON Paul (Bede), b. 2 Nov 1928, Barton, England. Historian; Journalist; Broadcaster. m. Marigold Hunt, 1957, 3 sons, 1 daughter. *Education:* BA, Magdalen College, Oxford. *Appointments:* Assistant Executive Editor, Realites, Paris, 1952-55; Assistant Editor, New Statesman, 1955-60, Deputy Editor 1960-64, Editor 1965-70, Director, 1965-75; DeWitt Wallace Professor of Communications, American Enterprise Institute, Washington DC, 1980; Freelance Writer. *Publications:* The Offshore Islanders, 1972; Elizabeth I : A Study in Power and Intellect, 1974; Pope John XXIII, 1975; A History of Christianity, 1976; Enemies of Society, 1977; The National Trust Book of British Castles, 1978; The Civilization of Ancient Egypt, 1978; Civilizations of the Holy Land, 1979; British Cathedrals, 1980; Ireland : Land of Troubles, 1980; The Recovery of Freedom, 1980; Pope John Paul II and the Catholic Restoration, 1982; History of the Modern World : From 1917 to the 1980s, 1984; The Pick of Paul Johnson, 1985; A History of the Jews, 1986; The Oxford Book of Political Anecdotes, Editor, 1986; The Intellectuals, 1989; The Birth of the Modern World Society, 1815-30, 1991. *Honours:* Book of the Year Prize, Yorkshire Post, 1975; Francis Boyer Award for Services to Public Policy, 1979; Krag Award for Excellence, Literature, 1980. *Memberships:* Royal Commission on the Press, 1974-77; Cable Authority 1984-. *Address:* 29 Newton Road, London W2, England.

JOHNSON (John) Stephen, b. 1947, British. *Publications:* The Roman Forts of the Saxon Shore, 1976, 1979; Later Roman Britain, 1980; Late Roman Fortifications, 1983; Hadrian's Wall, 1989; Rome and its Empire, 1989. *Address:* 50 Holmdere Avenue, London SE24 9LF, England.

JOHNSON Stowers, British. *Appointments:* Principal, Dagenham Literary Institute, 1936-39; Headmaster, Aveley School, 1939-68; Editor, Anglo-Soviet Journal, 1966-68; Art Curator, National Liberal Club, London, 1974-79. *Publications:* Branches Green and Branches Black, 1944; London Saga, 1946; The Mundane Tree, 1947; Mountains and No Mules, Sonnets They Say, 1949; Before and After Puck, 1953; When Fountains Fall, 1961; Gay Bulgaria, 1964; Yugoslav Summer, 1967; Collector's Luck, 1968; Turkish Panorama, The Two Faces of Russia, 1969; Agents Extraordinary, 1975; Headmastering Man, 1986; Hearthstones in the Hills, 1987; Collector's World, 1989. *Address:* Corbiere, 45 Rayleigh Road, Hutton, Brentwood, Essex, England.

JOHNSON Terry, b. 20 Dec 1955. Playwright. *Education:* Queens School, Bushey, Hertfordshire, England; BA, Drama, University of Birmingham, 1976. *Career:* Actor in late 1970s and director. *Publications:* Plays: Amabel (produced London 1979); Days Here So Dark (produced Edinburgh and London 1981); Insignificance (produced London 1982, New York 1986) London, Methuen, 1982; Bellevue (produced on tour, 1982); The Idea (produced Bristol, 1983); Unsuitable for Adults (produced London, 1984; Costa Mesa, California, 1986), London, Faber, 1985; Cries from the Mammal House (produced Leicester aned London, 1984); Tuesday's Child with Kate Lock (televised 1985; produced London 1986) London, Methuen, 1987; Screenplays: Insignificance 1985; Killing Time, 1985; Way Upstream 1987. Television Plays: Time Trouble, 1985; Tuesday's Child with Kate Lock, 1985. *Honour:* Evening Standard Award, 1983. *Literary Agent:* Goodwin Associates, London. *Address:* c/o Phil Kelvin, Goodwin Associates, 12 Rabbit Row, London W8 4DX, England.

JOHNSON Warren A, b. 1937, American. *Appointments:* Civil Engineer, National Park Service, 1960-67; Assistant Professor 1969-71, Associate Professor 1971-75, Professor of Geography 1975-, Department Chairman 1976-79, San Diego State University, CA. *Publications:* Public Parks on Private Land in England and Wales, Economic Growth vs the Environment (co-ed), 1971; Muddling Toward Frugality, 1978; The Future is Not What It Used to Be, 1985. *Address:* Department of Geography, San Diego State University, San Diego, CA 92182, USA.

JOHNSON Wendell Stacy, b. 27 Dec 1927, Jackson County, Missouri, USA. Writer; University Professor. *Education:* BA, University of Missouri, 1948; MA, 1949, PhD, 1952, Ohio State University. *Publications:* The Voices of Matthew Arnold, 1961; An Introduction to Literary Criticism, 1962; Gerard Manley Hopkins, 1968; A Poetry Anthology, with M Danziger, 1968; Words Things & Celebrations, 1972; Sex and Marriage in Victorian Poetry, 1975; Living in Sin, 1979; Charles Dickens - New Perspectives, Editor, 1982; Browning Institute Annual, Editor, 1983; Sons and Fathers, 1985; W H Auden, 1989. *Contributions to:* various journals and magazines. *Honours:* Fulbright Fellowship, 1952; Howald Postdoctoral Fellowship, 1962; ACLS Grants, 1964, 1967; Guggenheim Fellowship, 1965; NEH Senior Research Fellowship, 1979; Huntington Library Grants, 1968, 1980. *Memberships:* MLA, Chairman Victorian Group; Golier Club; American Association of University Professors. *Literary Agent:* Charlotte Sheedy. *Address:* 65 Hampton Street, Southampton, NY 11968, USA.

JOHNSTON George Benson, b. 7 Oct 1913, Hamilton, Ontario, Canada. m. Jeanne McRae, 1944, 3 sons, 3 daughters. *Education:* BA 1936, MA 1945, University of Toronto; LLD, Queen's University, Kingston, Ontario, 1971; LitD, Carleton University, 1979. *Appointments:* Assistant Professor of English, Mount Allison 1t, Sackville, 1946-48; Staff, English

Department, Carleton University, Ottawa, 1950-79, now retired. *Publications:* Vers: The Crusing Auk, 1959; Home Free, 1966; Happy Enough, 1972; Between, 1976; Taking a Grip, 1979; Auk Redivivus: Selected Poems, 1981; Editor, Rocky Shores: An Anthology of Faroese Poetry, 1981; Translator: The Saga of Gisli, 1963; The Faroe Islanders' Saga, 1975; Te Greenlanders Saga; Wind over Romsdal: Selected Poems, 1981. *Address:* 2590 Cooks Line, RR 1, Athelstan, Quebec, Canada J0S 1A0.

JOHNSTON Jennifer, b. 12 Jan 1930. Author. m. (1) Ian Smyth, 1951, 2 sons, 2 daughters, (2) David Gilliland, 1976. *Education:* Trinity College, Dublin; FRSL, 1979. *Publications:* The Captains and the Kings, 1972; The Gates, 1973; How Many Miles to Babylon?, 1974; Shadows on Our Skin, 1978 (dramatised for TV, 1979); The Old Jest, 1979; Play: The Nightingale and not the Lark, 1980; The Christmas Tree, 1981; The Railway Station Man, 1984; Fools Sanctuary, 1987; Plays: Indian Summer, Belfast, 1983; The Porch, Dublin, 1986; The Invisible Man, Dublin, 1987; The Invisible Worm (novel), 1991; BBC Radio: O, Ananais, Azarais and Misael, 1990; Billy, 1990; Triptych, Dublin, 1989. *Honours:* Hon. DLitt., NUU, 1984; Hon D.Litt, TCD. *Membership:* AOSDANA. *Address:* Brook Hall, Culmore Road, Derry, Northern Ireland BT48 8JE.

JOHNSTON Jill, b. 1929 in England, American. *Appointments:* Columnist and Contributor, Village Voice, 1959-75; Contributor, Art News, 1959-65; Critic, Art in America, 1983-87. *Publications:* Marmalade Me, 1971; Lesbian Nation, 1973; Gullibles Travel, 1974; Mother Bound, 1983; Paper Daughter, 1985.

JOHNSTON Norma, (Elizabeth Bolton, Catherine E Chambers, Kate Chambers, Pamela Dryden, Lavina Harris, Adrian Robert, Nicole St John), American. Writer of novels, short stories, mystery, crime, suspense, historical, romance, Gothic, children's fiction, children's non-fiction, mythology, folklore. President, St John Institute of Arts and Letters. Has worked as a retailer, producer, director, actress, teacher and businesswoman. *Publications include:* Pride of Lions, 1979; A Nice Girl Like You, 1980; Myself and I, 1981; The Days of the Dragon's Seed, 1982; Timewarp Summer, 1982; Gabriel's Girl, 1983; The Carlisle Chronicles, 3 vol series, 1986; Shadow on Unicorn Farms, 1986; Watcher in the Mist, 1986; as Nicole St John: Wychwood, 1976; Guinever's Gift, 1977; as Pamela Dryden: Mask for my Heart, 1982; as Lavinia Harris: Dreams and Memories, 1982; The Great Rip-Off, 1984; A Touch of Madness, 1985; Soaps in the Afternoon, 1985; Cover-up, 1986; The Packaging of Hank and Celia, 1986; as Kate Chambers: Secrets on Beacon Hill, 1984; The Legacy of Lucian Van Zandt, 1984; The Threat of the Pirate Ship, 1984; as Catherine Chambers: Indian Days: Life in a Frontier Town, 1984; Log Cabin Home: Pioneers in the Wilderness, 1984; Texas Roundup: Life on the Range, 1984; Wagons West: Off to Oregon, 1984; as Elizabeth Bolton: The Secret of the Ghost Piano, 1985; The Secret of the Magic Potion, 1985; The Tree House Detective Club, 1985; as Adrian Robert: My Grandma, the Witch, 1985; The Secret of the Haunted Chimney, 1985; The Secret of the Old Barn, 1985.

JOHNSTON Ronald John, b. 30 Mar 1941, Swindon, England. University Professor. m. Rita Brennan, 16 Apr 1963, 1 son, 1 daughter. *Education:* BA 1962, MA 1964, University of Manchester, England; PhD, Monash University, Australia, 1967. *Publications:* Geography and Geographers, 1979, 1983, 1987, 1991; City and Society, 1984; A World in Crisis?, 1986, 1989; Dictionary of Human Geography, 1981, 1986; The New Zealanders, 1976; Bell-Ringing, 1986; On Human Geography; Environmental Problems; Geography of Elections; The Geography of English Politics; A Nation Dividing?; Geography and The State. *Contributions to:* Over 300. *Honours:* Murchison Award, 1984, Victoria Medal 1990, Royal Geographical Society. *Membership:* Institute of British Geographers, Secretary 1982-85,

President 1990. *Address:* Vice-Chancellor, University of Essex, Wivenhoe Park, Colchester, CU4 35Q, England.

JOHNSTON Ronald, b. 1926, British. *Appointments:* Associate, Chartered Insurance Institute; with Manufacturers Life Insurance of Canada, 1947-51; Salesman, General Manager, Director, Anglo-Dutch Cigar Company Limited, 1959-68. *Publications:* Disaster at Dungeness (in US as Collision Ahead), 1964; Red Sky in the Morning (in US as Danger at Bravo Key), 1965; The Stowaway, 1966; The Wrecking of Offshore Five, 1967; The Angry Ocean, 1968; The Black Camels (in US as The Black Camels of Qahran), 1969; Paradise Smith, 1972; The Eye of the Needle, 1975; Sea Story, 1980; Flying Dutchman, 1983. *Memberships:* Council Member, Scottish Arts Council, 1973-; Vice President, Scottish PEN, 1974-; Management Committee, Society of Authors, 1975-.

JOHNSTON William, b. 1925, Irish. *Appointments:* Ordained Catholic Priest, 1957; Professor of Theology, Sophia University, 1960-. *Publications:* The Mysticism of The Cloud of Unknowing, 1967, 1975; Silence by S Endo (trans), 1969; The Still Point: On Zen and Christian Mysticism, 1970; Christian Zen, 1971; The Cloud of Unknowing and the Book of Privy Counselling (ed), 1973; Silent Music: The Science of Meditation: The Inner Eye of Love: Mysticism and Religion, 1978; The Mirror Mind: Spirituality and Transformation, 1981; The Wounded Stag, The Bells of Nagasaki by T Nagai (trans), 1984; Being In Love: The Practice of Christian Prayer, 1988; Letters to Contemplatives, 1991; Lord, Teach us to Pray, 1992. *Address:* Sophia University, 7 Kioi-Cho, Chiyodaku, Tokyo 102, Japan.

JOHNSTONE Iain Gilmour, b. 8 Apr 1943, England. Film Critic. m. Maureen Hammond, 1957, 2 daughters. *Education:* LLB Honours; Distinction, Solicitor's finals. *Literary Appointments:* Film Critic, The Sunday Times. *Publications:* The Arnhem Report, 1977; The Man With No Name, 1980; Dustin Hoffman, 1984; Cannes: The Novel, 1990; Wimbledon 2000, 1992. *Address:* 16 Tournay Road, London SW6, England.

JOKOSTRA Peter, b. 5 May 1912. Literary Critic, Novelist, Poet. m. Annemarisa Hintz, 16 July 1965, 2 sons, 3 daughters. *Education:* Universities of Frankfurt, Munich, Berlin. *Literary Appointments:* Publishers Reader 1951; Press Officer 1958; Publicity Officer 1962. *Publications include:* Herzinfarkt, Roman, 1960; Die Gewendete Haut, Lyrik, 1967; Ala die Tuilerien brannten, History, 1971; Sudfrankreich fur Kenner, autobiography, 1979; Heimweh nach Masuren, autobiography, 1982; Damals in Mecklenburg, Roman, 1990. *Contributions to:* Die Welt, Rheinische Post, Akzente, Sinn und Form, Neue deursche Literatur; Voix des Poetes, Suddeutscher Rundfunk, Stuttgart; RIAS Berlin. *Honours:* Poetry Prize, Ministry of Culture, 1956, 1958; Andreas Gryphius Prize, 1965; Maj Art Prize Rheinland Pfalz, 1979; Ehrengast der Villa Massimo, Rom, 1990. *Memberships:* PEN - Zentrum der BRD; Verband deutscher Schriftsteller; Gesellschaft Amicus Poloniae. *Address:* In der Stehle 38, D-5460 Kasbach-Ohlenberg, Federal Republic of Germany.

JOLL James, b. 1918, British. *Appointments:* Fellow and Tutor in Modern History and Politics, New College, 1946-50; Fellow and Sub-Warden of St Antony's College, Lecturer in Modern History, Oxford University, 1951-67; Visiting Member, Institute for Advanced Study, Princeton, NJ, 1953, 1971; Stevenson Professor of International History 1967-81, Emeritus 1981-, London School of Economics. *Publications:* Britain and Europe from Pitt to Churchill (ed), 1950, 1961; The Second International 1889-1914, 1955, 1975; The Decline of the Third Republic (ed), 1959; Three Intellectuals in Politics, 1960; The Anarchists, 1964, 1979; Anarchism Today (ed with D Apter), 1971; Europe since 1870, 1973, 1983, 1990; Gramsci, 1977; The Origins of the First World War, 1984, 2nd edition 1992. *Membership:* Fellow of the British Academy. *Literary*

Agent: Peters, Fraser and Dunlop. *Address:* 24 Ashchurch Park Villas, London W12 9SP, England.

JOLLEY Elizabeth, b. 4 June 1923, Birmingham, England. Writer; Tutor. m. Leonard Jolley, 1 son, 2 daughters. *Education:* Nursing Training, 1940-46; Honorary Doctorate, Technology, Western Australian Institute of Technology, 1986. *Appointments:* Writer in Residence, Western Australian Institute of Technology, now Curtin University of Technology, Perth, 1980-; Citizen of the Year Arts Culture and Entertainment, 1987; Officer of the Order of Australia (AO) for Services to Australian Literature, 1988. *Publications:* Five Acre Virgin & Other Stories, 1976; The Travelling Entertainer, 1979; Woman in a Lampshade, 1983; (Novels) Palomino, 1980; The Newspaper of Claremont Street, 1981; Mr Scobie's Riddle, 1983; Miss Peabody's Inheritance, 1983; Foxbybaby, 1985; Milk and Honey, 1984; The Well, 1986; The Sugar Mother, 1988; My Father's Moon, 1989; Cabin Fever, 1990; Central Mischief, 1992. *Contributions to:* The New Yorker; New York Times; Los Angeles Times; Westerly Mennjin; Grand Street Magazine. *Honours:* Fellowship of Australian Writers Short Story Award, 1966, 1980, 1981; Awgie Award, Radio Drama, Two Men Running, 1982; The Age Book of the Year,1983; The Premier of NSW Award for Fiction, 1984; Barbara Ramsden Best Book of the Year Award, 1986; Miles Franklin Prize, The Well, 1987; Pater Award for Paper Children, 1988; Talking Book of the Year Award, My Father's Moon, 1988. *Memberships:* Fellowship of Australian Writers; Australian Society of Authors, President 1985, 1986; Foundation Member, Perth PEN International Club. *Literary Agent:* Australian Literary Management, Victoria, Australia. *Address:* 28 Agett Road, Claremont, WA 6010, Australia.

JONAS Ann, b. 15 July 1919, Joplin, Missouri, USA. Poet. m. 30 Mar 1944, 1 daughter. *Education:* Graduate, Goodman Theatre, Chicago, Illinois, USA. *Publications:* Anthologies: Dark Unsleeping Land, 1960; Deep Summer, 1963; The Diamond Anthology, 1971; Friendship Bridge/Anthology of World Poetry, 1979; Ipso Facto, 1975; The Kentucky Book, 1979; Kentucky Contemporary Poetry, 1964, 1967; Kentucky Harvest, 1968; Peopled Parables, 1975; Barbeque Planet Sampler, 1977; A Merton Concelebration, 1981; Dan River Anthology, 1985; Lawrence of Nottingham, 1985. *Contributions to:* Adena; Approaches; Bitterroot; Carolina Quarterly; Colorado Quarterly; Kentucky Poetry Review; The Poetry Review; The Southern Review; The Quest; Prism International (Canada). *Honours:* Yaddo Fellowship, 1968; Finalist, Poetry Society of America Annual Award, 1970; Cecil Hemley Memorial Award, Poetry Society of America, 1972; Henry Rago Memorial Award, New York Poetry Forum, 1972; Eleanor B North Award, International Poetry Society, England, one of 5 finalists, 1975; Edwin Markham Poetry Prize, Eugene V Debs Foundation, Co-winner, 1977; 1st Prize, Poetry, Caddo National Writer's Center, 1982. *Membership:* Poetry Society of America. *Address:* 2425 Ashwood Drive, Louisville, Kentucky 40205, USA.

JONAS Manfred, b. 9 Apr 1927, Mannheim, Germany, Historian. m. Nancy jane Greene, 19 July 1952, 2 sons, 2 daughters. *Education:* BS, City College of New York, 1949; AM, 1951, PhD, 1959, Harvard University. *Appointments:* Visiting Professor for North American History, Free University of Berlin, 1959-62; Assistant Professor to Professor of History, Union College, 1963-81; Washington Irving Professor in Modern Literary and Historical Studies, Union College, 1981-86; Dr Otto Salgo visiting Professor of American Studies, Eotvos Lorand University of Budapest, 1983-84; John Bigelow Professor of History, Union College, 1986-. *Publications:* Isolationism in America 1935-1941, 1966, 1990; Roosevelt and Churchill: Their Secret Wartime Correspondence, 1975, 1990; The United States and Germany: A Diplomatic History, 1984; American Foreign Relations in the 20th Century, 1967; New Opportunities in the New Nation, 1982; Die Unabhangigkeitserklarung der Vereingten Staaten, 1964. *Contributions to:* The Historian; Mid- America;

American Studies; Maryland Historical Magazine; Essex County Historical Collections; Jahrbuch fuer Amerikastudien. *Memberships:* Honorary Member, Mark Twain Society; Society for Historians of American Foreign Relations; American Historical Association; Organization of American Historians; American Association of University Professors, Chair, Government Relations Committee, New York Conference; Phi Beta Kappa, President, Alpha of New York, 1989-92. *Address:* Department of History, Union College, Schenectady, NY 12308, USA.

JONES Ann Maret, b. 3 Sept 1937, USA. Author. *Education:* MA, University of Michigan, 1961; PhD, University of Wisconsin, 1970. *Appointments include:* Writing Faculty, Mount Holyoke College, 1986-. *Publications:* Uncle Tom's Campus, 1973; Women Who Kill, 1980; Everyday Death: Case of Bernadette Powell, 1985. *Contributions to:* Nation; Ms; Vogue; American Heritage; New York Times; Newsday; Women's Rights Law Reporter. *Honour:* Author/Journalist of the Year, National Prisoners Rights Union, 1986. *Memberships:* PEN American Centre; Authors Guild; National Writers Union; National Book Critics Circle. *Literary Agent:* Frances Goldin. *Address:* 229 Sullivan Street, New York, NY 10012, USA.

JONES Aubrey, b. 20 Nov 1911, Merthyr Tydfil, Mid Glamorgan, Wales. Economist; Politician; Industrialist. Joan Godfrey-Isaacs, 7 Sept 1948, 2 sons. *Education:* BSc, Economics, 1st Class Honours, London School of Economics. *Publications:* The New Inflation: The Politics of Prices and Incomes, 1973; The Pendulum of Politics, 1946; Industrial Order, 1950; Oil: The Missed Opportunity, 1981; The Reform of Pay Determination, 1981; Britain's Economy: The Roots of Stagnation, 1985; Economics and Equality, (Editor), 1976; The End of the Keynesian Era, (Contributing Editor), 1977. *Contributions to:* The Technologist; Sunday Times; The Observer; The Guardian. *Honours:* Honorary fellow, LSE, 1959; Honorary DSc, Bath, 1968; Fellow Commoner, Churchill College, Cambridge, 1972-73, 1982-86; Hon Fellow, Science Policy Research Unit, University of Sussex, 1993. *Membership:* President, Oxford Energy Policy Club, 1976-86. *Address:* Arnen, 120 Limmer Lane, Felpham, Bognor Regis, West Sussex PO22 7LP, England.

JONES Brian, b. 1938, British. *Publications:* The Lady with a Little Dog, 1962; Poems, 1966; A Family Album, 1968; Interior, 1969; The Mantis Hand and Other Poems, 1970; For Mad Mary, 1974; The Spitfire on the Northern Line, 1975; The Island Normal, 1980; Children of Separation, 1985; Freeborn John, 1990. *Address:* c/o Caranet Press, 208 Corn Exchange Buildings, Manchester M4 3BQ, England.

JONES Christopher Dennis, b. 13 Dec 1949, New York, USA. Playwright. m. Gwendoline Shirley Rose, 18 Aug 1979, London, England. *Education:* BA English Literature, University of Pittsburgh. *Literary Appointments:* Resident Playwright, Carnaby Street Theatre, London, England, 1975-76; Resident Playwright, New Hope Theatre Company, London, 1977-78. *Publications:* Plays: Passing Strangers, 1975; Nasty Corners, 1977; New Signals, 1978; In Flight Reunion, 1979; Sterile Landscape, 1982; Ralph Bird's River Race, 1985; Dying Hairless With A Rash, 1985; Bitter Chalice, 1987; Begging The Ring, 1989; Burning Youth, 1989. *Contributions to:* Country Life; Arts Review. *Membership:* Writer's Guild of Great Britain. *Literary Agent:* Fraser and Dunlop. *Address:* c/o Richard Wakeley, Fraser and Dunlop, 91 Regent Street, London W1R 8RU, England.

JONES D(ennis) F(eltham), British. *Appointments:* Bricklayer; Market Gardener. *Publications:* Colossus, 1966; Implosion, 1967; Don't Pick the Flowers (in US as Denver is Missing), 1971; The Fall of Colossus, 1974; Earth Has Been Found (in UK as Xenos), 1979. *Address:* c/o Sedgwick and Jackson Limited, 1 Tavistock

Chambers, Bloomsbury Way, London WC1A 2SG, England.

JONES Diana Wynne, b. 16 Aug 1934, London, England, Writer, m. J A Burrow, 23 Dec 1956, 3 sons. *Education:* BA, Oxford University, 1956. *Appointments:* Panelist on Guardian Award, 1979-82; Panelist on Whitbread Award, Children's Book Section, 1988. *Publications:* Charmed Life, 1977; Archer's Goon, 1984; The Ogre Downstairs, 1974; Witch Week, 1974; Power of Three, 1976; Fire and Hemlock, 1985; Dogsbody, 1975; Eight Days of Luke, 1975; Cart and Cwidder, 1975; Wilkin's Tooth, 1973; Drowned Ammet, 1977; The Magicians of Caprona, 1979; The Spellgoats, 1980; Howl's Moving Castle; The Lives of Christopher Chant; A Tale of Time City; Wild Robert; Chairperson; The Homeward Bounders; The Four Grannies; Caste in the Air; Warlock at the Wheel; Who Got Rid of Angus Flint?; Black Maria; Yes Dear; A Sudden Wild Magic; The Crown of Dalemark; Hexwood. *Contributions to:* Reviews in The Guardian, The Daily Telegraph. *Honours:* Guardian Award for Children's Books, 1978; Honour Book, Boston Globe, Horn Book Award, 1984, 1986; Runner-up for Carnegie Award, 3 times. *Membership:* Society of Authors. *Literary Agent:* Laura Cecil. *Address:* 9 The Polygon, Bristol BS8 4PW, England.

JONES Glyn, b. 28 Feb 1905, Merthyr Tydfil, Wales, retired Schoolmaster. m. Phyllis Doreen Jones, Aug 1935. *Education:* St Paul's College, Cheltenham. *Appointments:* First Chairman, English Section, The Welsh Academy, 1968. *Publications:* Fiction: The Blue Bed, 1937; The Water Music, 1944; Selected Short Stories, 1971; Welsh Heirs, 1977; The Learning Lark, 1960; The valley the City the Village, 1956; The Island of Apples, 1965; Critism: The Dragon has Two Tongues, 1968; Profiles, (co-author John Rowlands), 1980. Poems: Poems, 1939; The Dream of Jake Hopkins, 1954; Selected Poems, 1975; Selected Poems, Fragments and Fictions, 1988 (Translations); The Saga of Llywarch the Old (with T J Morgan), 1955; When the Rosebush Brings Forth Apples, 1980; Honeydew on the Wormwood, 1984. *Contributions to:* Poetry Chicago; Wales; Welsh Review; Life and Letters Today; Adam; Rann; Dock Leaves; The Times; News Chronicle; Western Mail; London Welshman; Anglo-Welsh Review; Poetry Wales. *Honours:* DLitt, University of Wales, 1974; Fellow, The Welsh Academy, 1989. *Membership:* Welsh Academy, English Language Section. *Literary Agent:* Laurence Pollinger, Maddox Street, Mayfair, London, England. *Address:* 158 Manor Way, Whitchurch, Cardiff CF4 1RN, Wales.

JONES Hettie, b. 16 July 1934, Brooklyn, New York, USA. Writer. div. 2 daughters. *Education:* BA Mary Washington College of the University of Virginia, 1955; Graduate Study, Columbia University. *Appointments:* Associate Professor, Writing; Hunter College, 1984; Stte University of New York, 1989-91; The New School, 1991; University of Wyoming, 1993. *Publications:* How I Became Hettie Jones, 1991; Big Star Fallin' Mama, 1975; The Trees Stand Shining, 1971; Longhouse Winter, 1974; Coyote Tales, 1976; How to Eat your ABCs, 1978; I Hate to Talk About Your Mother, 1980. *Contributions to:* Stories and peoms in The Village Voice; Ikon, among others. *Honours:* Best Books for Young Adults Award, New York Public Llbrary, 1975; New York Times Recommended Reading List, Best Books of the year, 1991. *Memberships:* Phi Beta Kappa; PEN (Prison Writing Committee). *Literary Agent:* Berenice Hoffman. *Address:* c/o Berenice Hoffman Literary Agency, 215 West 75th Street, New York, NY 10022, USA.

JONES Joanna. *See:* **BURKE John Frederick**.

JONES John Philip, b. 3 July 1930, Caernarvon, Wales. University Professor. m. Wendy Maudlayne Hoblyn, 4 Oct 1958, 1 son, 1 daughter. *Education:* BA Hons, 1953, MA, 1957, Cambridge University. *Publications:* The Great Gray Spire, 1985; What's in a Name? Advertising and The Concept of Brands, 1986; Does It Pay to Advertise? Cases Illustrating Successful

Brand Advertising, 1989; How Much is Enough? Getting the Most From Your Advertising Dollar, 1992. *Contributions to:* International Journal of Advertising, Admap, Harvard Business Review; New York Times, among others. *Honours:* Distinguished Advertising Educator of the Year, American Advertising Federation, 1991. *Address:* 122 Edgehill Road, Syracuse, NY 13224, USA.

JONES Julia, b. 27 Mar 1923, Liverpool, England. Writer. m. Edmund Bennett, 10 Oct 1950, 1 son, 1 daughter. *Education:* Royal Academy of Dramatic Art, 1946-48. *Publications include:* The Navigators, 1986; Over 50 plays for theatre, television & radio, films; Numerous dramatisations. *Honour:* 'The Golden Prague'(1st prize, drama), Prague TV Festival, 1970. *Memberships:* Dramatists Club; Green Room Club; TV Committee, Writers Guild of Great Britain. *Literary Agent:* Jill Foster Ltd. *Address:* c/o Jill Foster Ltd, 35 Brompton Road, London SW3 1DE, England.

JONES Kenneth Westcott, b. 11 Nov 1921, London, England. Travel Writer & Author. *Literary Appointments:* Travel Editor, East Anglian Daily Times, 1951-93; Group Travel Correspondent, United Newspapers, 1960-83; Travel Contributor to The Bulletin, Scotland, 1953-60; Travel World & Business Travel, Focus Correspondent, 1962-83. *Publications:* New York, 1958; America Beyond the Bronx, 1961; Great Railway Journeys of the World, 1964; Exciting Railway Journeys of the World, 1967; To the Polar Sunrise, 1957; By Rail to the Ends of the Earth 1968; Business Air Travellers Guide, 1970; Romantic Railways, 1971; Steam in the Landscape, 1972; Railways for Pleasure, 1981; Scenic America, 1984; Where To Go in America, 1991; Rail Tales of The Unexpected, 1992. *Contributions to:* Go Magazine; Railway Magazine; Going Places; The Universe. *Honours:* Canton of Valais Award, 1964; Thomson Travel Award, Travel Writer of the Year, 1971 . *Memberships:* Croydon Writers Circle, 1954-61; British Guild of Travel Writers, Chairman 1975-76, Secretary 1959-62; Fellow, Royal Geographical Society. *Address:* Hillswick, Michael Road, London SE25 6RN, England.

JONES Le Roi, (Imanu Amiri Baraka), b. 7 Oct 1934, Newark, New Jersey, USA. Assistant Professor of African Studies; Writer. m. (1) Hettie Cohen, 1958 (div 1965), 2 daughters; (2) Sylvia Robinson, 1966, 2 step-daughters and one other daughter. *Education:* Educated at the Central Avenue School and Barringer High School, Newark; Howard University, Washington DC; Served in the US Air Force 1954-56. *Appointments:* Taught at the New School for Social Research, New York, 1961-64 and summers 1977-79; State University of New York, Buffalo, summer 1964; Columbia University, New York, 1964 and Spring 1980; Visiting Professor, San Francisco State College, 1966-67; Yale University, New Haven, Connecticut, 1977-78 and George Washington University, Washington DC, 1978-79. Assistant Professor of African Studies, State University of New York, Stony Brook, 1980-; Founder, Yugen magazine and Totem Press, New York, 1958; Editor, with Diana de Prima, Floating Bear magazine, New York, 1961-63; Founding Director, Black Arts Repeertory Theatre, Harlem, New York, 1964-66; Founding Director, Spirit House, Newark, 1966-; Involved in Newark politics; Member of the United Brothers, 1968 and Committee for United Newark, 1969-75; Chairman, Congress of Afrikan People, 1972-75. *Publications:* Verse includes: It's Nation Time, 1970; In Our Terribleness: Some Elements and Meaning in Black Style, with Fundi (Billy Abernathy) 1970; Spirit Reach, 1972; Afrikan Revolution, 1973; Hard Facts, 1976; Selected Poetry, 1979; AM/TRAK, 1979; Reggae or Not! 1982. Numerous plays, including The Motion of History (also director, produced New York, 1977) included in The Motion of History and Other Plays, 1978; What Was the Relationship of the Lone Ranger to the Means of Production? (produced New York, 1979); At the Dim'crackr Convention (produced New York, 1980); Boy and Tarzan Appear in a Clearing (produced New York, 1981); Weimar 2 (produced New York, 1981). Screenplays: Dutchman 1967; A Fable 1971. Novel: The

System of Dante's Hell, New York, Grove Press 1965; London, Macgibbon and Kee, 1966; Short stories and other publications. *Honours:* Whitney Fellowship, 1961; Obie Award for Drama, 1964; Guggenheim Fellowship, 1965; Dakar Festival Prize, 1966; Rockefeller Grant, 1981; DHL; Malcolm X University, Chicago, 1972. *Memberships:* Black Academy of Arts and Letters. *Address:* 808 South 10th Street, Newark, NJ 07108, USA.

JONES Madison Percy, b. 21 Mar 1925, Nashville, Tennessee, USA. Author; Retired Professor of English. m. Shailah McEvilley, 5 Feb 1951, 3 sons, 2 daughters. *Education:* Public and private schools in Nashville, Tennessee; BA, Vanderbilt University, 1949; MA, University of Florida, 1953. *Appointments:* Instructor in English, Miami University of Ohio, 1953- 54; Instructor in English, University of Tennessee, 1955-56; Professor and Writer-in-Residence, Auburn University, 1956-87. *Publications:* Novels: A Cry of Absence, 1971; A Buried Land, 1963; An Exile, 1967; Last Things, 1989; The Innocent, 1957; Passage Through Gehenna, 1978; Season of the Strangler, 1983; Forest of the Night, 1960; To The Winds, (novel), forthcoming. *Contributions to:* Short stories, essays and reviews in Sewanee Review, Southern Review, South Atlantic Quarterly, Studies in Short Fiction, New York . Times Book Review, Washington Post Book World. *Honours:* Sewanee Review Writing Fellowship, 1954-55; Rockefeller Foundation Fellowship, 1968; Book Award of Alabama Library Association, 1968; Guggenheim Foundation Fellowship, 1973-74. *Memberships:* Member, Fellowship of Southern Writers, 1988-; Member, Alabama Academy of Distinguished Authors. *Literary Agent:* Elizabeth McKee, McIntosh, McKee and Dodds, New York. *Address:* 800 Kuderna Acres, Auburn, AL 36830, USA.

JONES Malcolm Vince, b. 7 Jan 1940, Professor of Slavonic Studies. m. Jennifer Rosemary Durrant, 27 July 1963, 1 son, 1 daughter. *Education:* Cotham Grammar School, Bristol 1950-58; University of Nottingham, 1958-62; Postgraduate at University of Nottingham 1962-65. *Literary Appointment:* General Editor, Cambridge Studies in Russian Literature. *Publications:* Dostoyevsky, The Novel of Discord, Paul Elek, London, 1976; Barnes and Noble, New York, 1976; New Essays on Tolstoy, ed. Cambridge University Press, Cambridge, London, New York and Melbourne, 1978; New Essays on Dostoyevsky, ed. with Garth M Terry, Cambridge University Press, Cambridge, London, New York and Melbourne, 1983; Dostoyevsky after Bakhtin, Cambridge University Press, Cambridge, London, New York and Melbourne, 1990. *Contributions to:* Various academic journals in Slavonic Studies. *Memberships:* British Universities' Association of Slavists, 1966-68, President, 1986-88; President, Association of Teachers of Russian, 1985-86; Vice-President, International Dostoyevsky Society, 1983-86; President of Co-ordinating Council for Area Studies Association, 1991-93-; Vice-President, British Association for Soviet, Slavonic and East European Studies, 1988-91. *Address:* Department of Slavonic Studies, University of Nottingham, University Park, Nottingham NG7 2RD, England.

JONES Mervyn, b. 1922, British. *Appointments:* Assistant Editor 1955-60, Drama Critic 1958-66, Tribune; Assistant Editor, New Statesman, 1966-68, London. *Publications:* No Time to Be Young, 1952; The New Town, The Last Barricade, 1953; Helen Blake, 1955; Guilty Men (with Michael Foot), Suez and Cyprus, 1957; On the Last Day, 1958; Potbank, 1961; Big Two (in US as The Antagonists), 1962; Two Ears of Corn: Oxfam in Action (in US as In Famine's Shadow: A Private War on Hunger), A Set of Wives, 1965; John and Mary, 1966; A Survivor, 1968; Joseph, 1970; Mr Armitage Isn't Back Yet, 1971; Life on the Dole, 1972; Holding On (in US as Twilight of the Day), The Revolving Door, 1973; Lord Richard's Passion, Strangers, K S Karol: The Second Chinese Revolution (trans), 1974; The Pursuit of Happiness, 1975; The Oil Rush (with Fay Godwin), Scenes from Bourgeois Life, 1976; Nobody's Fault,

1977; Today the Struggle, 1978; The Beautiful Words, 1979; A Short Time to Live, 1980; Two Women and Their Men, 1982; Joanna's Luck, 1985; Coming Home, 1986; Chances, 1987; That Year In Paris, 1988; A Radical Life, 1991. *Address:* 10 Waterside Place, Princess Road, London NW1, England.

JONES Owen Marshall, b. 17 Aug 1941, Te Kuiti, New Zealand. Writer. m. Jacqueline Hill, Dec 1965, 2 daughters. *Education:* MA Hons, University of Canterbury, 1964; Diploma in Teaching, Christchurch Teachers' College, 1965. *Publications:* The Master of Big Jingles, 1982; The Day Hemingway Died, 1984; The Lynx Hunter, 1987; The Divided World, 1989; Tomorrow We Save the Orphans, 1991; Supper Waltz Wilson, 1979. *Contributions to:* Numerous magazines and journals. *Honours:* NZ Literary Fund Scholarship in Letters, 1988. *Literary Agent:* Glenys Bean. *Address:* 10 Morgans Road, Timaru, New Zealand.

JONES Peter (Austin), b. 1929, British. *Appointments:* Managing Director, Carcanet Press Limited, Manchester, 1970-. *Publications:* Rain, 1970; Seagarden for Julius, Tribute to Freud by Hilda Doolittle (ed), 1971; The Peace and The Hook, Imagist Poetry (ed), 1972; Shakespeare - The Sonnets: A Casebook, The Garden End: New and Selected Poems, 1977; An Introduction to Fifty American Poets: Critical Essays, 1979; British Poetry since 1970: A Critical Survey (ed), 1980. *Membership:* English Faculty, Christ's Hospital, Horsham, Sussex, 1954-69. *Address:* Carcanet Press, 208 Corn Exchange Building, Manchester M4 3BQ, England.

JONES Phyllis Marjory, b. 12 Mar 1923, Truro, Cornwall. Nursing Officer. m. Ivor Gordon Jones, 27 June 1959. *Education:* State Registered Nurse; OHNC, Occupational Health. *Publications:* They gave me a Lamp, 1992. Volumes of poetry: The Grass is not yet grown; Song of Gower. *Contributions to:* Nursing Times; Occupational health; Contry Quest; Anglo Welsh Review; New Welsh Review; Cornish Review; Cornish Scene; Athena. *Honours:* Runner Up, Theodora Doorae Award Novel of Literary Merit, 1972; Winner, Cornish Gorsedd, Poetry Rose Bowl, 1972. *Memberships:* Society of Women Writers and Journalists; Welsh Academy; West Country Writers; Chairman, Llanelli Writers Circle. *Address:* Pen-y-Bont, Heol Sylen, Pontyberem, Dyfed SA15 5NW, Wales.

JONES Rhydderch Thomas, b. 25 Dec 1935, North Wales. Television Producer. m. 3 Mar 1980. *Education:* Diploma, Education, Normal College, Bangor. *Appointments:* Teacher, English Literature & Dramatic Art, Croydon and Llanrwst; Joined BBC, Light Entertainment Dept., 1973-. *Publications:* Roedd Catarinao Gwmpas Ddoe, 1974; Mewn Tri Chyfrwng, 1979; Cofiant Ryan, 1979; Ryan, 1980 (English); TV Drama: Mr Lolipop M.A.; Man a Lle; Broc Môr; Gwenoliaid (Swallows); Lliwiau (Colours); Radio Plays: Edau Frau; Charlie's Aunt, Brandon Thomas: Trans Madam Siarli, 1962; Offshore Island, Margarita Laski: Trans A Oes Heddwch; Co-Writer, Sit-Com with G. Parry, Fo a Fe, Hafod Henri. *Honours:* Pye Award, Best Regional Drama, 1987; Royal TV Society Award for Outstanding Contribution to Creative Writing, 1987. *Membership:* Yr Academi Gymraeg. *Address:* 39 Heol Hir, Llanishen, Cardiff, Wales.

JONES Richard Andrew III, b. 8 Aug 1953, London, England. Poet. *Education:* BA, 1975, MA, 1976, University of Virginia. *Publications:* Country of Air, 1986; At Last We Enter Paradise, 1991; Rush, 1984. *Contributions to:* American Poetry REview; Poetry; Tri Quarterly. *Honours:* Illinois Arts Council Award, 1991; Literary Award, 1991; The Posner Prize, 1986. *Address:* Department of English, DePaul University, Chicago, IL 60614, USA.

JONES Robert Gerallt (Hamlet), b. 11 Sept 1934, Nefyn, Gwynedd, Wales. Writer; University

Administrator. m. Susal Lloyd Griffith, 15 Sept 1962, 2 sons, 1 daughter. *Education:* BA 1954, MA 1956, University College of North Wales. *Appointments:* Creative Writing Fellow, University of Wales, 1976-78; Senior Lecturer in Welsh Studies, University College, Aberystwyth, 1979-89; Editor of Taliesin, Welsh Academy Quarterly, 1988-. *Publications:* Triptych, 1977; Jamaican Landscape, 1969; Cerddi 1955-89, (poems), 1991; Cafflogion, 1979; Tair Drama, 1988; 30 volumes of poetry, novels and critism in Welsh language. *Honours:* Prose Medal, National Eisteddfed of Wales, 1977, 1979; Hugh McDiarmid Award, 1984; Welsh Arts Council Poetry Award, 1990. *Memberships:* Welsh Academy, Chairman, 1982-87; Welsh Arts Council, Chairman, Film Committee, 1987-; Welsh Fourth Channel Authority (S4C), 1990-. *Address:* Gregynog, University of Wales, Newtown, Powys SY16 3PW, Wales.

JONES Sally Roberts, b. 1935, United Kingdom. Author; Poet; Publisher. *Appointments:* Senior Assistant, Reference Library, London Borough of Havering, 1964-67; Reference Librarian, Borough of Port Talbot, Wales, 1967-70; Publisher, Alun Books, 1977-. *Publications:* Turning Away, 1969; Romford in the Nineteenth Century, 1969; About Welsh Literature (compiler), 1970; Elen and the Goblin, 1977; Strangers and Brothers, 1977; The Forgotten Country, 1977; Books of Welsh Interest: A Bibliography, 1977; Allen Raine, 1979; Margam Through the Ages (editor), 1979; Welcome to Town, 1980; Relative Values, 1985; The History of Port Talbot, 1991. *Memberships:* Founder Member, Welsh Academy; President, Afan Poetry Society.*Address:* 3 Crown Street, Port Talbot, Wales.

JONES-EVANS Eric (John Llewellyn), b. 2 Oct 1898, West Coker, Somerset, England. General Medical Practitioner (Retired); Former Actor, Theatre Historian. m. Agnes Maude Edwards, 27 Feb. 1922, 1 son (dec.) *Education:* Qualified in medicine, St Thomas' Hospital, London, 1921; LRCP; MRCS. *Literary Appointments:* Theatre historian, Hampshire Magazine, Southern Evening Echo, Kent Life, Bygone Kent. *Publications include:* Henry Irving & The Bells, memoir, edited by Dr David Mayer, 1980. Also: Character Sketches from Dickens; In the Footsteps of Barnaby Rudge, 1947; John Jasper's Secret, stage version (4 acts), Dickens' Edwin Drood; Suicide Isn't Murder, 1951; The Black Bag, 1957. Plays published: Death On the Line; Lucky Venture (3 acts); Death of a Lawyer, Scrooge the Miser, 1962; The Haunted Man, 1962; The Weaver of Raveloe, 1963; The Murder of Nancy, 1963; The Jackal, 1964; The Blue Cockade, 1951 (award winner); Mr Crummles Presents..., 1966; David Copperfield, 1970; Footlight Fever, autobiography; Death on the Line, radio play, 1971; The Dream Woman, 1973; The Music of Melodrama, Markheim, The Body-Snatchers, radio plays. *Honour:* 1st Prize, Festival of Britain playwriting competition, 1951. *Literary Agent (Plays):* Samuel French Ltd, Fitzroy Street, London W1P 6JR. *Address:* The Treshams, Fawley, Nr Southampton, Hampshire, England.

JONG Erica Mann, b. 26 Mar 1942, New York City, USA. Author; Poet. 1 daughter. *Education:* BA, Barnard College, 1963; MA, Columbia University, 1965. *Literary Appointments:* Faculty, English Department, City University of New York, 1964-65, 1969-70; Member, Literary Panel, New York State Council on Arts, 1972-74. *Publications include:* Fruits & Vegetables, poems, 1971; Half-Lives, poems, 1973; Fear of Flying, novel, 1973; Loveroot, poems, 1975; How to Save Your Own Life, novel, 1977; At the Edge of the Body, poems, 1979; Fanny: Being the True History of the Adventures of Fanny Hackabout-Jones, novel 1980; Witches, 1981; Ordinary Miracles, poems, 1983; Parachutes & Kisses, novel, 1984. *Honours:* Bess Hokin Prize, Poetry Magazine, 1971; Alice Faye di Castagnola Award, Poetry Society of America, 1972; Grant, National Endowment for Arts, 1973. *Memberships:* Director 1975, Authors Guild; Writers Guild of America; PEN; Phi Beta Kappa. *Literary Agent:* Ed Victor, Ltd. *Address:* 162 Wardour Street, London, IV 3AT, England.

JONG Eveline Dorothea de b. 23 Oct 1948, Bilthoven, The Netherlands. Author. m. Jan R Magnus, 25 Mar 1974, 1 son, 1 daughter. *Education:* BA, University of Amsterdam, 1973; MA, Communication Studies, Simon Fraser University, Burnaby, Canada, 1987. *Publications:* The Bilingual Experience, 1986; Isn't She Clever, 1988; Alternative Health Care for Children, 1989; Aren't they Wonderful, 1990; Grandma's Bag, 1992. *Address:* Minervalaan 108, 1077 PM Amsterdam, The Netherlands.

JORDAN June, (June Meyer), b. 1936, American. *Appointments:* Instructor, City College, City University of New York, 1967-69, Sarah Lawrence College, Bronxville, 1969-70, 1973-74; Columnist, The Black Poet Speaks of Poetry, American Poetry Review, 1974- ; Professor of English, 1981-; Director of The Poetry Center, 1986-; Director of Creative Writing Program, 1986-. *Publications:* Who Look at Me, 1969; Soulscript, Some Changes, His Own Where, The Voice of the Children (co-ed), 1971; Dry Victories, Fannie Lou Hamer, 1972; New Days, 1974; I Love You, New Life: New Room, 1975; Things I Do in the Dark: Selected Poetry, 1977; Passion: New Poems, 1980; Civil Wars, Kimako's Story, 1981; Living Room, 1985; On Call, 1986. *Address:* Department of English, State University of New York, Stony Brook, NY 11790, USA.

JORDAN Lee. *See:* **SCHOLEFIELD Alan.**

JORDAN Neil Patrick, b. 25 Feb 1950, Sligo, Republic of Ireland. Author; Director, 2 daughters. *Education:* BA, 1st Class Honours, History/English Literature, University College, Dublin, 1969-72. *Appointment:* Co-Founder, Irish Writers Co-operative, Dublin, 1974. *Publications:* Night in Tunisia, 1976; The Dream of a Beast, 1983; The Past, 1979; Films as a Director: Angel, 1982; Company of Wolves, 1984; Mona Lisa, 1986; Nigh Spirits, 1988; We're No Angels, 1989; The Crying Game, 1992. *Honours:* Guardian Fiction Prize for Night in Tunisia, 1979; Film Awards: Los Angeles Film Critics Award; New York Film Critics Award, 1986; London Critic Circle Award, 1986. *Literary Agent:* Jenne Casarotto, Casarotto Comp Limited, UK; Suzanne Gluck, ICM, USA. *Address:* c/o Jenne Casarotto Co Ltd, National House, 60-66 Wardour St, London, W1V 3HP, England.

JORGENSON Ivar. *See:* **SILVERBERG Robert.**

JOSEPH Jenny, b. 7 May 1932, Birmingham, England. Writer; Lecturer. m. C A Coles, 29 Apr 1961, 1 son, 2 daughters. *Education:* BA, Honours, English, St Hilda's College, Oxford University, 1950-53. *Publications:* The Unlooked-for Season, 1960; Warning, poem, 1961; Boots, 1966; Rose in the Afternoon, 1974; The Thinking Heart, 1978; Beyond Descartes, 1983; Persephone, 1986; The Inland Sea, 1989; Beached Boats, folio and book, with photographer Robert Mitchell, 1991; Selected Poems, 1992; Author of 6 books for children. *Contributions to:* Contributor of poems, articles and prose in various magazines and anthologies. *Honours:* Gregory Award, 1962; Cholmondely Award, 1974; Arts Council of Great Britain Award, 1975; James Tait Black Award for Fiction for Persephone, 1986. *Memberships:* National Poetry Society of Great Britain, Council, 1975-78. *Literary Agent:* John Johnson Limited, London. *Address:* 17 Windmill Road, Minchinhampton, Gloucestershire GL6 9DX, England.

JOSEPH Stephen M, b. 1938, American. *Appointments:* Teacher, NYC Board of Education, 1960-70, Lecturer, The Cooper Union and New York University, 1970-71; Lecturer, Wyoming State Arts Council, 1973-; Writer-in-Residence, New York State-New Jersey State Arts Council. *Publications:* The Me Nobody Knows (ed), 1969; The Shark Bites Back, Meditations (ed), 1970; Children in Fear, 1974; Mommy, Daddy, I'm Afraid, 1979. *Address:* 270 First Avenue, New York, NY 10009, USA.

JOSEPHY Alvin M Jr, b. 1915, American. *Appointments:* Director and Senior Editor, American Heritage Publishing Company Incorporated, NYC, 1960-79. *Publications:* The Long and Short and the Tall, 1946; The Patriot Chiefs, The American Heritage Book of Indians (ed), 1961; The American Heritage Book of Natural Wonders (ed), 1963; Chief Joseph's People and Their War, 1964; The American Heritage History of the Great West, The Nez Perce Indians and the Opening of the Northwest, 1965; RFK: His Life and Death, The Indian Heritage of America, 1968; The Artist was a Young Man, 1970; Red Power, The Horizon History of Africa (ed), 1971; American Heritage History of Business and Industry (ed), 1972; The Pictorial History of the American Indians by Oliver La Farge (reviser), The Law in America (ed), 1974; History of the US Congress, 1975; Black Hills, White Sky, 1978; On the Hill: A History of the American Congress, 1979; Now That the Buffalo's Gone, 1982; War on the Frontier, 1986; The Civil War in the American West, 1991; America in 1492, 1992. *Honour:* Doctor of Humanities, College of Idaho, 1987. *Memberships:* Society of American Historians; American Antiquarian Society; Western History Association. *Literary Agent:* Julian Bach, New York. *Address:* 4 Kinsman Lane, Greenwich, CT 06830, USA.

JOSHI Umashankar, b. 21 July 1911, Bamna, India. Teacher; Poet. m. Jyotsna, 25 May 1937, 2 daughters. *Education:* BA 1936, MA 1938, University of Bombay. *Appointments include:* Postgraduate Teacher, Literature, 1939-46; Professor, Director, School of Languages, Gujarat University, Ahmedabad, 1954-70. *Publications:* Poetry: Vishva Shanti, 1931; Gangotri, 1934; Nisheeth, 1939; Mahaprasthan, 1971; Dharavstra, 1981; Saptapadi, 1981. Also: Sapna Bhara, one-act play, 1936; Shravani Melo, short stories, 1937; Nireeksha 1960, Kavini Shraddha 1972, criticism; Samayrang, 1978. *Contributions to:* Poetry (Chicago); Indian Literature (New Delhi); etc. *Honours:* Ranajitram Gold Medal, 1939; Narmad Gold Medal, 1945; Joint Winner, Bharatiya Jnanpith Award, 1967; Sahitya Akademi Award, 1972; Soviet Land Nehru Award, 1979; Mahakavi Kumaran Asan Award, 1982; Honorary DLitt, 7 Universities. *Memberships:* Past President, Sahitya Akademi (National Academy of Letters), New Delhi; President 1985-, Past Vice President, All-India PEN. *Address:* 26 Sardar Patel Nagar, Ahmedabed 380 006, India.

JOSIPOVICI Gabriel David, b. 8 Oct 1940, Nice, France. Professor of English. *Education:* BA, Hons 1st Class, St Edmund Hall, Oxford, 1958-61. *Publications:* Novels: Migrations, 1977; The Air We Breathe, 1981; Contre-Jour, 1986; The Big Glen, 1990; In a Hotel Garden, 1991; The Inventory; Words; The Present; The Echo Chamber; Conversations in Another Room. Stories: Mobius the Stripper, 1974; In the Fertile Land. Essays: The World and the Book, 1971; The Lessons of Modernism; Writing and the Body; The Book of God: A Response to the Bible, 1988; Text and Voice, 1992. *Contributions to:* Encounter; New York Review of Books; London Review of Books; Times Literary Supplement. *Honours:* AG 1977 and Mr Vee 1989, radio plays, both BBC nominations for Italia Prize; Invited to give the 1981 Lord Northcliffe Lectures, University of London. *Literary Agent:* John Johnson. *Address:* 60 Prince Edwards Road, Lewes, Sussex, England.

JOSLIN Sesyle, (Josephine Gibson, G B Kirtland), b. 1929, America, Novels/Short stories. Children's fiction. Poetry. *Appointments:* Editorial Assistant, Holiday magazine, 1947-49; Assistant Fiction Editor, Westminster Press, 1950-52, and Book Editor, Country Gentleman magazine, 1950-52, all in Philadelphia; Production Assistant on Peter Brook's film, Lord of the Flies, Puerto Rico, 1963. *Publications:* What Do You Say Dear? 1058; Brave Baby Elephant, 1960; Baby Elephant's Trunk, 1961; What Do You Do Dear? 1961; There Is a Dragon in My Bed (French Primer) 1961; (with Al Hine, as G B Kirtland) One Day in Elizabethan England, 1962; Dear Dragon . . . and Other Useful Letter Forms for Young Ladies and Gentlemen Engaged in Everyday Correspondence, 1962; Senor Baby Elephant, The Pirate, 1962; Baby Elephant and the Secret Wishes, 1962; Baby Elephant Goes to China, 1963; (with Al Hine, as G B Kirtland) One Day in Aztec, Mexico, 1963; La Petite Famille (reader), 1964; Baby Elephant's Baby Book, 1964; Please Share That Peanut! 1965; Spaghetti for Breakfast (Italian primer), 1965; (with Al Hine, as Josephine Gibson), Is There a Mouse in the House? (verse), 1965; There Is a Bull on My Balcony (Spanish Primer), 1966; Pinkety, Pinkety, A Practical Guide to Wishing, 1966; La Fiesta (reader), 1967; The Night They Stole the Alphabet, 1968; Doctor George Owl, 1970; The Spy Lady and the Muffin Man, 1971; Last Summer's Smugglers, 1973; The Gentle Savages, 1979.

JOY David (Anthony Welton), b. 1942, British. *Appointments:* General Reporter, Yorkshire Post Newspapers, 1962-65; Editorial Assistant 1965-70, Books Editor 1970-88, Dalesman Publishing Company Limited, Editor 1988-. *Publications:* Settle-Carlisle Railway (with W R Mitchell), 1966; Main Line Over Shap, 1967; Cumbrian Coast Railways, 1968; Whitby-Pickering Railway, 1969; Railways in the North, Traction Engines in the North, 1970; George Hudson of York (with A J Peacock), 1971; Railways of the Lake Counties, 1973; Regional History of the Railways of Great Britain: South and West Yorkshire, Railways in Lancashire, Settle-Carlisle Centenary, 1975; Railways of Yorkshire: The West Riding, 1976; North Yorkshire Moors Railway (with P Williams), 1977; Steam on the North York Moors, 1978; Yorkshire Railways (with A Haigh), 1979; Steam on the Settle and Carlisle, 1981; Yorkshire Dales Railway, Settle: Carlisle in Colour, 1983; Regional History of the Railways of Great Britain: The Lake Counties, 1984; Portrait of the Settle: Carlisle, 1984; Yorkshire Dales in Colour, 1985; The Dalesman - A Celebration of 50 Years, 1989; Life in the Yorkshire Coalfield, 1989; Settle - Carlisle Celebration, 1990; Best Yorkshire Tales, 1991. *Address:* Hole Bottom, Hebden, Skipton, North Yorkshire, BD23 5D1, England.

JOY P K, b. 25 Sept 1940, Kerala, India. Business Manager and Consultant. m. Saramma (Dolly), 10 June, 1965, 2 sons. *Education:* PhD, Management Studies. *Publications:* Handbook of Construction Management, 1990; Total Project Management - The Indian Context, 1993; The Final Goal, 1986, reprinted, 1988; For a More Beautiful World, 1988; Forced Smiles, 1988; Convener of Indian Writers Club; Indian Editor for several foreign journals. *Contributions to:* Numerous Indian English newspapers and journals including The Hindu, Financial Express, The Indian management, Fortune India. *Honours:* DLitt from several universities and academies. *Memberships:* Director, International Liaison, World Poetry Society; British Institute of Management; American Management Association; Indian Society for Tech Education; Indian Council of Arbitration; Project Management Institute (USA); Institute of Industrial Engineers (USA). *Address:* C-23 Annanagar East, Madras 600 106, India.

JOYCE Graham William, b. 22 Oct 1954, Coventry, England. Writer. m. Suzanne Lucy Johnsen, 6 May 1989. *Education:* BED Hons, 1977; MA, 1980. *Publications:* Dreamside, 1991; Dark Sister, 1992. *Contributions to:* Numerous magazines, newspapers and journals. *Honours:* George Fraser Poetry Award, 1981; Oppenheim John Downs Award, 1991. *Memberships:* BSFA; BFS; Leicester Writer's Club. *Literary Agent:* David Grossman. *Address:* 66 Shanklin Drive, Stoneygate, Leicester LE2 3QA, England.

JOYNT Carey Bonthron, b. 7 Jan 1924, Hensall, Ontario, Canada. Professor. m. Anne Morgan, 21 Aug 1948, 1 son. *Education:* BA History and Economics, 1945, MA, 1948, University of Western Ontario; PhD, International Relations, Clarke University, 1951. *Publications:* Theory and Reality in World Politics, 1978; Ethics and International Affairs, 1982; Vietnam, 1967. *Contributions to:* Mind; The Journal of Philosophy; History and Theory; Canadian Journal of Economics and Political Science. *Honours:* Gold Medalist, 1945; Ford Foundation Fellow, 1957-58; John Simon Guggenheim

Foundation Fellow, 1963. *Memberships:* International Studies Association; International Institute for Strategic Studies. *Address:* 1415 Oakwood Drive, Bethlehem, PA 18017, USA.

JUDD Cyril. *See:* **MERRILL (Josephine) Judith Grossman.**

JUDD Denis, b. 28 Oct 1938, Byfield, Northants, England. Historian; Writer. m. Dorothy Woolf, 10 July 1964. 3 sons, 1 daughter. *Education:* BA Hons, Modern History, Oxford University, 1961; PGCEd 1962, PhD 1967, London University. *Publications:* Balfour & the British Empire, 1968; The Boer War, 1977; Radical Joe: Joseph Chamberlain, 1977; Prince Philip, 1981; Lord Reading, 1982; Alison Uttley, 1986; Sawaharlal Nehru, 1993; 2 novels/books and stories for children; Other history books and biographies. *Contributions to:* History Today; History; Journal of Imperial & Commonwealth History; Times Literary Supplement; Financial Times; New Statesman and Society. *Honours:* Fellow, Royal Historical Society, 1977; Awarded Professorship, 1990. *Literary Agent:* Bruce Hunter, David Highams, London. *Address:* 20 Mount Pleasant Road, London NW10 3EL, England.

JUDSON John, b. 1930, American. *Appointments:* Editor, Juniper Press, Northeast/Juniper Books, literary magazine and chapbook series, 1961-; Professor of English, University of Wisconsin, La Crosse, 1965-. *Publications:* Two from Where It Snows (co-author), 1963; Surreal Songs, 1968; Within Seasons, 1970; Voyages to the Inland Sea, 6 volumes, 1971-76; Finding Worlds in Winter; West of Burnam South of Troy, 1973; Ash Is the Candle's Wick, 1974; Roots from the Onion's Dark, A Purple Tale, 1978; North of Athens, Letters to Jirac II, 1980; Reasons Why I Am Not Perfect, 1982; The Carrabassett Sweet William Was My River, 1982. *Address:* 1310 Shorewood Drive, La Crosse, WI 54601, USA.

JUERGENSEN Hans, b. 17 Dec 1919, Myslowitz, Germany (now Mysiowice, Poland). m. Ilse Dina Loebenberg, 27 Oct 1945, 2 daughters. *Education:* BA, Upsala College, New Jersey, 1942; PhD, Johns Hopkins University, 1951. *Appointments include:* Associate Professor of English, Chairman, University of Quinnipiac College, Hamden, Connecticut, 1953-61; Assistant, Associate, Professor of Humanities, University of South Florida, 1961-; Acting Dean and Member of the Board, Silvermine College of Art, 1960-61; Coordinator, Poetry in Schools, Hillsborough County, Florida, 1972-76; Nominating Committee, Nobel Prize in Literature, 1975-; Professor Emeritus, University of South Florida, 1992. *Publications:* Poetry: I Need for Names, 1961; Existential Cannon and other Poems, 1965; Florida Montage, 1966; Sermons from the Ammunition Hatch of the Ship of Fools, 1968; From the Divide, 1970; Hebraic Modes, 1972; Journey toward the Roots, 1976; The Broken Jug, 1977; California Frescoes, 1980; General George H Thomas: A Summary in Perspective, 1980; The Record of a Green Planet, 1982; Books: Fire-Tested, 1983; Beachheads and Mountains, 1984; The Ambivalent Journey, 1986; Roma, 1987; Testimony, 1989. *Contributions to:* Editor: Ipso Facto, 1975; For Neruda, For Chile, 1975; The Anthology of American Magazine Verse, 1981; Children's Poetry Anthology, 1975; Gryphon, 1974-89; Co-Editor, Orange Street Poetry Journal, 1958-62, and, University of South Florida Language Quarterly, 1961-74. *Honours:* Florida Poet of the Year, 1965; Stephen Vincent Benet Awrd, 1970, 1974; Award for Services to American Literature, Hayden Library, Arizona State University, 1984. *Memberships:* Fellow, International Poetry Society; Pres, 1968-70, National Federation of State Poetry Societies; Poetry Societies of America and Florida; Fellow, Academy of Arts and Science. *Address:* Department of Humanities, University of South Florida, Tampa, FL 33620, USA.

JULIAN Jane. *See:* **WISEMAN David.**

JULIAN Norman Sebastian, b. 9 June 1939, Clarksburg, West Virginia, USA. Journalist. *Education:* Bachelor's in Journalism and English, West Virginia University, 1968. *Publications:* Cheat, 1984; Mountains and Valleys, 1976; Snake Hill, 1992. *Honours:* Best General Columnist in West Virginia, West Virginia Press Association, 1992; Second Prize, novels, West Virginia Writers Inc, 1983. *Address:* Rt 7 Box 222HH, Morgantown, WV 26505, USA.

JULL COSTA Margaret Elisabeth, b. 2 May 1949, England. Literary Translator. *Education:* BA First Class Hons, Hispanic Studies, Bristol University, 1977; MA Spanish and Portuguese, Stanford University, California, 1978; Post Graduate Diploma in English as a Second Language, Leeds University, 1982. *Publications:* Translations: All Souls by Javier Marías, 1992; Obabakoak by Bernardo Atxaga, 1992; The Book of Disquiet by Fernando Pessoa, 1991; The Witness by Juan Jose Saer, 1990; The Last Days of William Shakespeare, by Vlady Kociancich, 1990; The Resemblance by Alvaro Pombo, 1989; The Hero of the Big House by Alvaro Pombo, 1988. *Honours:* Joint Winner, Portuguese Translation Prize, 1992. *Membership:* Translators Association. *Address:* 316 Mayflower House, Manhattan Drive, Cambridge CB4 1JT, England.

JUNKINS Donald (Arthur), b. 1931, American. *Appointments:* Assistant Professor, Emerson College, Boston, 1961; Assistant Professor, California State College, Chico, 1963-66; Assistant Professor 1966-69, Associate Professor 1969-74, Director, Master of Fine Arts Program in English 1970-78, Professor of English 1974-, University of Massachusetts, Amherst. *Publications:* The Sunfish and the Partridge, 1965; The Graves of Scotland Parish, Walden 100 Years after Thoreau, 1968; And sandpipers She Said, 1970; The Contemporary World Poets (ed), 1976; The Uncle Harry Poems and Other Maine Reminiscences, 1977; Crossing by Ferry, 1978; The Agamenticus Poems, 1984; Playing for Keeps, 1991. *Contributions to:* Published poems in New Yorker; Atlantic; Sewanee Review; American Poetry Review; Published articles in Hemingway Review. *Honours:* NEA Fellowship Grants, 1974, 1979; John Masefield Award, 1973. *Memberships:* PEN; Hemingway Society. *Address:* Hawks Road, Deerfield, MA 01342, USA.

JUNOR John Donald Brown, Sir, (J.J.), b. 15 Jan 1919, Glasgow, Scotland. Journalist. m. Pamela Welsh, 1942, 1 son, 1 daughter. *Education:* MA, Glasgow University. *Appointments:* Political Columnist, Sunday Express, 1948-50; Assistant Editor, Daily Express, 1951-53; Deputy Editor, Evening Standard 1953-54; Editor, Sunday Express, 1954-86, Director 1956-, Chairman, 1968-; Director, Express Newspapers, 1960-86, Fleet Holdings PLC, 1982-. *Publications:* Proletariat of Westminster, 1949; Equal Shares, 1950; The Best of J.J., 1981; Listening For a Midnight Tram (memoirs), 1990. *Honours:* Hon. Dr. Law, New Brunswick, 1973; Kt, 1980. *Address:* c/o Bank of Scotland, 16 Piccadilly, London W1, England.

JURGENSEN Manfred, b. 26 Mar 1940, Flensburg, Germany. Professor. m. Uschi Fischer, 1986. *Education:* BA, 1964; Ma, 1966; PhD, 1968. *Appointments:* Editor, Outrider, Journal of Multicultural Literature; Co Editor, Seminar; Director, Phoenix Publications. *Publications:* Stations; places; Signs & Voices; A kind of Dying; A Winters Journey; South Africa Transit; State Security; The skin Trade; Waiting for Cancer; First Presence; Break Out; Experimental Man; A Difficult Love; Other inc. On Guenter Grass; Thomas Bernhard; Boell; Frisch; Intruders. *Contributions to:* Numerous. *Memberships:* Australian Fellowship of Writers; Australian Society of Authors; National Book Council of Australia; International PEN; Deutscher Schriftstellerverband; Humboldt Fellowship; AULLA. *Literary Agent:* Michael Meller, Munich. *Address:* c/o Department of German, University of Queensland, St Lucia, Brisbane 4072, Australia.

JURMAIN Suzanne, b. 1945, New York, USA. m. Richare B Jurmain, 1966, 1 son, 1 daughter. *Education:* BA Hons English, UCLA, 1966. *Appointments:* Assistant Editor, TV Guide, Los Angeles 1966; Editor, Legal Directories Publishing Company, 1967; Editor and Public Relations Coordinator, UCLA Museum of Cultural History, 1968-77. *Publications:* Once upon a Horse: A History of Horses and How they shaped our History, 1989; From Trunk to Tail: Elephants Legendary and Real, 1978. *Literary Agent:* c/o Dorothy Markinko, McIntosh & Otts, 310 Madison AVenue, New York 10017, USA. *Address:* c/o Dorothy Markinko, McIntosh & Otts, 310 Madison Avenue, New York, NY 10017, USA.

JUSTICAR. *See:* **POWELL-SMITH Vincent.**

JUSTICE Donald Rodney, b. 12 Aug 1925, Miami, Florida, USA. m. Jean Ross, 22 Aug 1947, 1 son. *Education:* BA, University of Miami, 1945; MA, University of North Carolina, 1947; PhD, University of Iowa, 1954. *Appointments:* University of Iowa, 1957-66, 1971-82; Syracuse University, 1966-70; University of California, Irvine, 1971; University of Florida, 1982-92. *Publications:* The Summer Anniversaries, 1960; Night Light, 1967; Departures, 1973; Selected Poems, 1979; The Sunset Maker, 1987; Platonic Scripts, Criticism, 1984; A Donald Justice Reader, 1992; The Collected Poems of Weldon Kees, Editor, 1960. *Contributions to:* numerous journals & magazines. *Honours:* Lamont Award, 1959; NEA Fellowships, 1967, 1973, 1980, 1989; Guggenheim Fellowship, 1976; Pulitzer Prize, Poetry, 1980; Academy of American Poets Fellow, 1988; NEA Fellowship, 1989; Co-Winner of Bollingen Prize, 1991. *Membership:* American Academy and Institute of Arts and Letters. *Address:* 338 Rocky Shore Drive, Iowa City, IA 52246, USA.

K

KAAVERI. *See:* **KANNAN Lakshmi.**

KAEL Pauline, b. 19 June 1919, Sonoma County, California, USA. Movie Critic. *Education:* University of California, Berkeley, 1936-40; Recipient of 8 Honorary Degrees. *Appointment:* Movie Critic, The New Yorker, 1968-1991. *Publications:* Books: I Lost it at the Movies, 1965; Kiss Kiss Bang Bang, 1968; Going Steady, 1970; Raising Kane in The Citizen Kane Book, 1971; Deeper into Movies, 1973; Reeling, 1976; When the Lights Go Down, 1980; 5001 Nights at the Movies, 1982; Taking It All In, 1984; State of the Art, 1985; Hooked, 1989; Move Love, 1991. *Contributions to:* Partisan Review; Vogue; The New Republic; McCall's; The Atlantic; Harpers. *Honours:* Guggenheim Fellow, 1964; George Polk Memorial Award for Criticism, 1970; The National Book Award (Arts & Letters), 1974 for Deeper into Movies; Front Page Awards, Newswomen's Club of New York: Best Magazine Column of 1974, Distinguished Journalism, 1983. *Address:* c/o The New Yorker, 25 West 43rd Street, New York, NY 10036, US.

KAFF Albert Ernest, b. 14 June 1920, Atchison, Kansas, USA. Journalist. m. Diana Lee-chuan Fong, 15 Oct 1960, 2 sons. *Education:* BA, Economics, University of Colorado, 1942; Radio Engineering, US Army Signals Corps, University of Kansas, 1943. *Appointments:* Reporter, Ponca City News (Oklahoma) 1946-48, Daily Oklahoman, Oklahoma City 1948-50; Editor, 45th Division News, Japan & Korea, 1950-52; Reporter/ Editor, United Press International, 1952-85; Business & International Editor, News Service, Cornell University, 1986-. Numerous articles published, newspapers in North & South America, Europe & Asia, while working as foreign correspondent in Asia, 1952-75, 1978-83. *Publications:* Crash: Ten Days in October . . . Will It Strike Again?. *Contributions to:* Catholic Digest; Holiday; Civil Air Transport Bulletin, Taiwan; Time; Sporting News; Editor & Publisher. *Memberships:* Past President, Foreign Correspondents Clubs, Republic of China (Taipei), Japan (Tokyo), Hong Kong; Vice President, Overseas Press Club of America, New York City. *Address:* News Service, Cornell University, 840 Hanshaw Road, Ithaca, NY 14850-1548, USA.

KAGAN Andrew Aaron, b. 22 Sept 1947, St Louis, Missouri, USA. Art Historian; Art Adviser; m. Jayne Wilner, 17 May 1987. *Education:* BA Washington University, 1969; MA 1971, PhD 1977, Harvard University. *Appointments:* Advisory Editor, Arts Magazine, 1975-89; Critic of Art, Music, Architecture, St Louis Globe Democrat, 1978-81. *Publications:* Paul Klee/Art and Music, 1983; Absolute Art, 1993; Marc Chagall, 1989; Troua, 1988; Rothko, 1987. *Contributions to:* McMillan Dictonary of Art; Arts Magazine and Burlington Magazine, among others. *Honours:* Harvard Prize Fellowship, 1970-77; Phi Beta Kappa, 1969; Kingsbury Fellowship, 1977-78; Goldman Prize, 1985. *Memberships:* Founder, Director, Wednesday Night Society. *Address:* 232 N Kingshighway No 1709, St Louis, MO 63108, USA.

KAHN James, b. 1947, American. *Appointments:* Resident, Los Angeles County Hospital, 1976-77, University of California at Los Angeles, 1978-79; Physician: Emergency Room Physician, Rancho Encino Hospital, Los Angeles, 1978-. *Publications:* Diagnosis Murder, Nerves in Petterns (with Jerome McGann), 1978; World Enough and Time, Time's Dark Laughter, Poltergeist, 1982; Return of the Jedi, 1983; Indiana Jones and the Temple of Doom, 1984; Goonies, 1985; Timefall, Poltergeist II, 1986. *Address:* c/o Jane Jordan Browne, 410 S Michigan Avenue, Suite 724, Chicago, IL 60605, USA.

KAHN Michele Anne, b. 1 Dec 1940, Nice, France. Writer. m. Pierre-Michel Kahn, 8 Jan 1961, 1 son. *Education:* Diploma in Social Sciences, University of Paris, 1976. *Publications include:* Contes du jardin d'Eden, 1983; Un Ordinateur pas Ordinaire, 1983; Juges et Rois, 1984; De l'autre cote du brouillard, 1985; Hotel Riviera, 1986; Rue du Roi-dore, 1989; La vague noire, 1990; Boucles d'Or et Bebe Ours (serie), 1990. *Contributions to:* Magazine Litteraire. *Honours:* Diplome Loisirs Jeunes, 1971; Diplome Loisirs Jeunes, 1983; Liste d'Honneur, Osterreichen und Jugenbuchpriesen, 1977. *Memberships:* International Pen Club; Secretaire Generale de la Societe des Gens de Lettres de France, 1982-86; Vice Presidente de la Societe des Gens de Lettres de France, 1986-91; Vice President de la Societe Civile des Auteurs Multimedia. *Literary Agent:* Claudia Vincent. *Address:* Residence Belloni, 192A Rue de Vaugirard, Paris 75015, France.

KAHN Peggy. *See:* **KATZ Bobbie.**

KAIKINI P R, b. 15 Feb 1912, Bombay, India. Editor; Translator. m. J Sita, 11 Oct 1952, 1 son. *Education:* MA English Literature, 1941; BT, 1942. *Appointments:* Editor, The Farmer, 1951-57. *Publications:* Flower Offerings, 1934; Songs of a Wanderer, 1936; This Civilization, 1937, 1955; Shanghai, 1939; Snake in the Moon, 1942; Look On Undaunted, 1944; Selected Poems, 1946; Poems of the Passionate East, 1948; Some of My Years, 1972. *Memberships:* Life, Authors Guild of India; The Indian PEN. *Address:* Banarasi Bhavan 10th Road, Khar, Bombay 400 052, India.

KAIM-CAUDLE Peter Robert, b. 14 Dec 1914, University Professor. m. Patricia Caudle, 24 May 1945, 2 sons, 2 daughters. *Education:* BSc, Economics, London School of Economics, 1935-39; Barrister at Law, Lincoln's Inn, 1953-56. *Publications:* Social Security in Ireland and Western Europe, 1964; Social Policy in the Irish Republic, 1967; Dental Services in Ireland, 1969; Comparative Social Policy and Social Security, 1973; Team Care in General Practice, 1976; Cost and Provision of Health Services in the Republic of China on Taiwan, 1979-81; Research, Development and Evaluation Commission, 1984; with J Keithley, Ageing and Society, 1993. *Contributions to:* Local Government Finance; Administration; New Christian; International Reiew of Administrative Sciences; Lloyds Bank Review; British Journal of Plastic Surgery; Irish Jurist; British Medical Journal; Journal of Social Policy; Community Care; Journal of the Chinese Public Health Association; Die Angstelltenversicherung; Journal of the Irish Medical Association. *Memberships:* Honorary Fellow, JUC for Social and Public Administration; Vice Chairman, Chairman, Vice President, Northern Region of the WEA; Chairman, Durham Citizens Advice Bureau; County Durham Social Services Committee; Royal Commonwealth Trust. *Address:* Beechwood, Princes Street, Durham DH1 4RP, England.

KAIN Philip Joseph, b. 21 May 1943, San Francisco, Calfornia, USA. Associate Professor of Philosophy. m. Helen Yuko Nakamura, 2 Apr 1967, 2 sons. *Education:* BA Philosophy, St Mary's College of California, 1966; PhD Philosophy, University of California, San Diego, 1974. *Publications:* Books: Marx and Ethics, 1988; Schiller Hegel and Marx, 1982; Marx Method, Epistemology and Humanism, 1986. *Contributions to:* Studies in Soviet Thought; Journal of the History of Philosophy; Hobbes's Science of Natural Justice; Annals of Scholarship; Clio; Idealistic Studies XiX; History of Philosophy Quarterly; Praxis International; Marx and Aristotle, among others. *Address:* Philosophy Department, Santa Clara University, Santa Clara, CA 95053, USA.

KALB Jonathan, b. 30 Oct 1959, New Jersey, USA. Theatre Critic; Professor of Theatre. m. Julie Heffernan, 18 June 1988, 1 son. *Education:* Ba English, Wesleyan University; MFA Dramaturgy and Dramatic Critcism, 1985, DFA Dramaturgy and Dramatic Criticism, 1987, Yale School of Drama. *Appointments:* Theatre Critic, The Village Voice, 1987-; Assistant Professor of Performance Studies, NYC, 1990-92; Assistant Professor of Theatre, Hunter College of CUNY, 1992-. *Publications:* Beckett in Performance, 1989. *Contributions to:* American Theatre; Michigan Quarterly

Review; Theatre Three; The Threepenny Review; Performing Arts Journal; Modern Drama; Theatre Journal; High Performance; Theatre reviews, book reviews and feature articles for the Village Voice and other newspapers. *Honours:* Fulbright Hays Grant, 1988-89; TCG Jerome Fellowship, 1989-90; George Jean Nathan Award for Dramatic Criticism, 1990-91. *Memberships:* MLA: Pen American Centre. *Address:* Hunter College of CUNY, Department of Theatre, 695 Park Avenue, NY 10021, USA.

KALECHOFSKY Roberta, b. 11 May 1931, New York, USA, Writer; Publisher. m. Robert Kalechofsky, 7 June 1953, 2 sons. *Education:* BA, Brooklyn College, 1952; MA, 1957, PhD, 1970, English, New York University. *Appointments:* Literary Editor, Branching Out, feminist Journal in Canada, 1973-74; Contributing Editor, Margins, 1974-77; Contributing Editor, On The Issues, feminist journal, 1987-. *Publications:* Bodmin 1349, 1988; Orestes in Progress, 1976; Stephen's Passion, 1975; Solomon's Wisdom, 1978; The 6th Day of Creation, 1986; La Hoya, 1976; Rejected Essays and Other Matters, 1980; Justice, My Brother, re-issued, 1993. *Contributions to:* Confrontation; Works; Ball State University Forum; Western Humanities Review; Rocky Mountain Review; Between the Species; So'western; Response; Reconstructionist. *Honours:* Literary Fellowship in Writing, National Endowment for the Arts, 1980; Literary Fellowship in Fiction, Massachusetts Council on the Arts, 1987. *Memberships:* The Authors' Guild; Committee of Small Press Magazine Editors and Publishers; National Writers Union; Association of Jewish Publishers. *Address:* 255 Humphrey Street, Marblehead, MA 01945, USA.

KALLEN Lucille Eve, b. Los Angeles, California, USA, Writer; Author. m. Herbert Engel, 22 Aug 1952, 1 son, 1 daughter. *Education:* Harbord Collegiate, Toronto, Canada; Toronto Conservatory of Music. *Publications:* Outside There, Somewhere, 1964; Introducing C B Greenfield, 1979; C B Greenfield: The Tanglewood Murder, 1980; C B Greenfield: No Lady in the House, 1982; C B Greenfield: The Piano Bird, 1984; C B Greenfield: A Little Madness, 1986; Television work includes Your Show of Shows, 1949-54; Maybe Tuesday, play, 1958. *Honour:* Introducing C B Greenfield nominated for American Book Award, 1980. *Memberships:* Mystery Writers of America; Authors Guild; Dramatists Guild; Writers Guild of America, East. *Literary Agent:* Arnold Goodman. *Address:* c/o Arnold Goodman, 500 West End Avenue, New York, NY 10024, USA.

KAMENKA Eugene, b. 4 Mar 1928, Cologne. Historian of Ideas, Social Philosopher. m. Alice Er-Soon Tay, 14 Nov 1964, 1 son, 1 daughter. *Education:* BA, Sydney, 1953; PhD, A.N.U., 1962. *Appointments:* Cable Sub-editor, The Jerusalem post, 1951; Journalist and Cable Sub-editor, Sydney Morning Herald, 1952- 55. *Publications include:* The Ethical Foundations of Marxism, 1972; The Philosophy of Ludwig Fenerbach, 1970; The Portable Karl Marx, (editor), 1983; Human Rights, (edited with A.E. -S.Tay), 1978. *Memberships:* Fellow, Academy of the Social Sciences in Australia; Fellow, Australian Academy of the Humanities, Honorary Secretary 1976-81. *Address:* The History of Ideas, Research School of Social Sciences, Australian National University, PO Box 4, Canberra, ACT 2600, Australia.

KAMINSKI Ireneusz Gwidon, b. 1 Mar 1925, Gniezno, Poland. Writer. m. Alicja Gardocka, 26 Aug 1960, 2 sons, 2 daughters. *Education:* MA, Liberal Arts, Mickiewicz University, Poznan, 1952. *Literary Appointments:* Journalist, teacher, librarian, 1950-70; War correspondent, Vietnam, 1968, 1972; 2nd editor-in-chief, Morze (Sea) monthly, 1971-85. *Publications:* 10 novels, 25 short stories, 1 reportage, 3 radio plays, numerous essays, etc. First published (poetry), 1950. Titles include: Wegierska opowiesc, 1954; Czerwony sokol, 1957; Msciciel przyplywa z Rugii, 1958; Czas slonca, 1960; Biale wrony, 1963; Anastazja, 1969; Paszcza smoka, 1970; Krystyna i rapier, 1971; Odro,

rzeko poganska, 1975; Swiety Ateusz, 1987; Kontredans, 1988; Retrospekcja, 1990; Diabelska ballada, 1992; Dziesiata planeta, 1994; Powracajaca fala, 1994. *Honours:* Literary Awards, City of Szczecin, 1958, 1975, 1985. *Memberships:* Executive, Polish Writers Union; Sea Yacht Club, Szczecin. *Address:* 70-791 Szczecin, ul. Kozia 16, Poland.

KAMINSKY Stuart, b. 1934, USA. Author; Professor. *Appointments:* Science Writer, University of Illinois, Champaign, 1962- 64; Editor, News Service, University of Michigan, Ann Arbor, 1965-66; Director of Public Relations, Assistant to Vice-President for Public Affairs, University of Chicago, 1969; Joined Faculty, 1972, currently Professor of Radio, Television and Film, Northwestern University, Evanston, Illinois. *Publications:* Don Siegel: Director, 1973; Clint Eastwood, 1974; American Film Genres: Approaches to a Critical Theory of Popular Film, 1974; Ingmar Bergman: Essays in Criticism (edited with Joseph Hill), 1975; John Huston: Maker of Magic, 1978; Bullet for a Star, novel, 1977; Murder on the Yellow Brick Road, novel, 1978; You Bet Your Life, novel, 1979; The Howard Hughes Affair, novel, 1979; Never Cross a Vampire, novel, 1980; Coop: The Life and Legend of Gary Cooper, 1980; Basic Filmaking (with Dana Hodgdon), 1981; Death of a Dissident, novel, 1981; High Midnight, novel, 1981; Catch a Falling Clown, novel, 1982; He Done Her Wrong, novel, 1983; When the Dark Man Calls, novel, 1983; Black Knight on Red Square, novel, 1983; American Television Genres (with Jeffrey Mahan), textbook, 1984; Down for the Count, novel, 1985; Red Chameleon, novel, 1985; Exercise in Terror, novel, 1985; Smart Moves, novel, 1987; A Fine Red Rain, novel, 1987. *Address:* School of Speech, Northwestern University, Evanston, IL 60201, USA.

KAMM Dorinda, b. 1952, USA; Novelist; Short Story Writer. *Publications:* Cliffs Head, 1971; Devil's Doorstep, 1972; The Marly Stones, 1976; Drearloch, 1977; Shadow Game, 1979; Kingsroads Legacy, 1981. *Address:* 82 New Hyde Park Road, Franklin Square, NY 11010, USA.

KANAME Hiroshi, b. 15 Dec 1940, Osaka Japan. Professor. m. Motoko Nakata, 29 Apr 1976, 1 son. *Education:* BA Kobe City University of Foreign Studies, 1964; MA, Osaka City University, 1969. *Appointments:* Lecturer, 1973, Associate Professor, 1976, Professor, 1991-, University of Osaka Prefecture. *Publications:* American Novels: Study and Appreciation, 1977; Alienation and American Novels, 1982; The Dream and Its Collapse in American Literature, 1988. *Memberships:* American Literature Society of Japan; The International John Steinbeck Society; John Steinbeck Society of Japan. *Address:* 1-10-14-741 Imafuku-Higashi, Joto-Ku, Osaka-shi, Japan 536.

KANAVA Zoe, b. 6 Jan 1933, Greece. Writer. m. John Kanavas, 2 sons. *Publications include:* Liontaria ston Hippodromo, 1977; Na Sas Po Mia Historia?, 1978; To Stichima, 1979; O Glaros Tou Aigiorgiou, 1980; Ta Genethlia Tis Chelonas, 1981; O Saligaros Vgainei Amaxada, 1982; me Tis Alyssides tis Eleftherias, 1982; Paschalia Me Autostop, 1983; Apo Kei Vgainei O helios, 1985; O Polemistis Tou Megalou Kastrou, 1987. *Contributions to:* Numerous magazines and journals; Radio & TV programmes. *Honours:* Literary Awards, Society of Christian Letters, Circle of Greek Children's Books, Youth Literature Honour of the University of Padova. *Memberships:* National Society of Greek Literature Authors; Awards Jury, Womens Literary Society Circle of Greek Children's Books. *Address:* Xenias 45, GR 15771 Athens, Greece.

KANDELL Alice S, b. 1938, USA. Children's Author. *Publications:* Sikkim: The Hidden Kingdom, 1971; Mountaintop Kingdom: Sikkim (with Charlotte Y Salisbury), 1971; Max the Music-Maker (with Miriam Stecher), 1980; Daddy and Ben Together (with Miriam Stecher), 1981; Friends (with Terry Berger), 1981; Ben's

ABC Day (with Terry Berger), 1982. *Address:* 11 East 68th Street, New York, NY 10021, USA.

KANE Aarno. *See:* **KAGAN Andrew Aaron.**

KANE Jim. *See:* **GERMANO Peter B.**

KANE Penny. *See:* **RUZICKA Penelope Susan.**

KANE Wilson. *See:* **BLOCH Robert.**

KANIGEL Robert, b. 28 May 1946, Brooklyn, New York, USA. Writer. m. Judith Schiff Pearl, 28 June 1981. 1 son. *Education:* BS Rensselaer Polytechnic Institute, Troy, New York, USA. *Appointments:* Instructor, Johns Hopkins University School of Continuing Studies, 1985-91; Visiting Professor of English, University of Baltimore and Senior Fellow, Institute of Publications Design, 1991-; Freelance Writer, 1970-. *Publications:* The Man who knew Infinity: A Life of the Genius Ramanujan, 1991; Apprentice to Genius: The Making of a Scientific Dynasty, 1986. *Contributions to:* New York Times Magazine; The Sciences; Health; Psychology Today; Science 85; Johns Hopkins Magazine; Washington Post. *Honours:* A D Emmart Award for Writing in the Humanities, 1979; Grady Stack Award for Interpreting Chemistry, 1989; American Society of Journalists and Authors outstanding article award, 1989; Los Angeles Times Book Prize finalist, 1991; National Book Critics Circle Award nominee, 1992. *Memberships:* American Society of Journalists and Authors; Authors Guild; National Association of Science Writers. *Literary Agent:* Vicky Bijur, 333 West End Avenue, NYC 10023, USA. *Address:* 2643 North Calvert Street, Baltimore, MD 21218, USA.

KANIN Garson, b. 24 Nov 1912, Rochester, NY, USA. Writer; Director. m. (1) Ruth Gordon, 4 Dec 1942, (dec), (2) Marian Seldes, 19 June 1990. *Education:* American Academy of Dramatic Arts. *Publications include:* Blow up a Storm, 1959; The Rat Race, 1960; Cast of Characters, 1969; Tracy and Hepburn: An Intimate Memoir, 1971; A Thousand Summers, 1973; Smash, 1980; Together Again, 1981; Cordelia, 1982. *Honours include:* Best Film of 1945, National Board Review, Academy Award; Citation NY Film Critics Circle; American Academy of Dramatic Arts Alumni Association Theatre Hall of Fame. *Memberships include:* Society of Stage Directors and Choreographers; Writers Guild; Dramatists Guild; Academy of Motion Pictures, Arts and Sciences; Authors Guild; ASCAP; Actors Fund; Actors Equity. *Address:* 200 W 57th St. Ste. 1204, New York, NY 10019, USA.

KANN Maria, b. 11 May, 1906, Poland. Writer. *Education:* MA, University of Warsaw, 1932. *Appointments:* Editor in Chief, Underground Magazine, Wzlot, 1943-44; Editor, Arts Department for Children and Teenagers, Odrodzenie, 1948-49; Founder and Editor-in-Chief, Underground Publishing House, Zaloga. *Publications include:* Gora Czterech Wiatrow, 1948; Dujawica, 1956; Niebo Niezanane, 1964; Na oczach swiata, 1943; A Case Concerning Honour, 1968; Nine Miseries and the One Luck, 1985. *Contributions to:* Magazines, journals and radio and television. *Honours:* Silver Cross of Merit, 1939; Medal of the Commission of National Education, 1981; International Award LBB, 1965; Award from the President of the City of Warsaw, 1987. *Memberships:* Society of Polish Authors; Warsaw Krakowskie Predmercie, 1987-89; Society of Authors Agency, Warsaw Hipoteczna 2. *Address:* Krasinskiego 35 50, Warsaw 01784, Poland.

KANN Mark E, b. 24 Feb 1947, Professor of Political Science. m. kathy Michael, 13 Feb 1969, 1 son. *Education:* BA 1968, MA 1972, PhD, 1975, University of Wisconsin, Madison, USA. *Publications:* On the Man in Question: Gender and Civic Virtue in America, 1991; Middle Class Radicals n Santa Monica, 1986; The American Left: Failures and Fortunes, 1983; Thinking About Politics: Two Political Sciences, 1980. *Contributions to:* Numerous newspapers, journals and magazines. *Honours:* Various research and teaching awards. *Memberships:* Vice President, Thomas Jefferson Centre. *Address:* The Graduate School, University of Southern California, Los Angeles, CA 90089, USA.

KANNAN Lakshmi, (Kaaveri), b. 13 Aug 1947, Mysore, India. Writer. m. L V Kannan, 2 sons. *Education:* BA Hons, MA, PhD, all in English. *Publications:* Rhythms, 1986; Parijata, 1992; Exiled Gods, 1985; Glow and the Grey, 1976; Laya Baddh, (Hindi), 1990 (translation); Wooden Cow, 1979 (translation); As Kaaveri: Osaigal, (Tamil), 1985; Athukku Poganum, (Tamil), 1986, 1989; Venmai Porthiyathu, (Tamil), 1992; . *Contributions to:* Critical articles on literary subjects, the sociology of literature and the Art of Translation and on Women Related Issues in Leading English and Tamil Journals at Home and Abroad. *Honours:* Scholar-in-Residence, American Studies Research Centre, Hyderabad, 1982, 1990; Honorary Fellow in Writing, University of Iowa, USA, 1987. *Memberships:* Founder and Executive Committee, The Poetry Society, India; Convenor, Tamil langauge Committee, KK Birla Foundation, Delhi; All-India PEN: Life, Anuvad Society for Translation, Delhi; Life, American Studies Research Centre Hyderabad. *Address:* A 2503 Netji Nagar, New Delhi 110023, India.

KANTARIS Sylvia, b. 9 Jan 1936. Poet. m. Emmanuel Kantaris, 11 Jan 1958. 1 son, 1 daughter. *Education:* BA Hons, 1957, CertEd, 1958, Bristol University; Diplôme d'Etudes de Civilisation Francaise, Sorbonne, Paris, 1955; MA 1967, PhD 1972, Queensland University, Australia, 1964-71. *Appointments:* Member of Literature Panel, South West Arts, 1983-87; Literary Consultant, SWA, 1990-. *Publications:* Time and Motion, 1975, 1986; The Tenth Muse, 1983, 1986; The Sea at the Door, 1985; The Air Mines of Mistila, 1988; Dirty Washing: New and Selected Poems, 1989; Stocking Up, 1981; News from the Front, 1983; Lad's Love, 1993. *Contributions to:* Essays in French Literature; Australian Journal of French Studies; New Poetry; Prospice; Stand; Poetry Review; Outposts Poetry Quarterly; The Observer; Times Literary Supplement; London Magazine; London Review of Books. *Honours:* Hon DLitt, University of Exeter, 1989; Major Arts Council Literature Award, 1991; Society of Authors Award, 1992. *Memberships:* Poetry Society of Grat Britain. *Address:* 14 Osborne Par, Helston, Cornwall TR13 8PB, England.

KANTO Peter. *See:* **ZACHARY Hugh.**

KANTOR Peter, b. 5 Nov 1949, Budapest, Hungary. Poet. *Education:* MA English and Russian Literature, 1973, MA Hungarian Literature, 1980, Budapest Elte University. *Appointments:* Literary Editor of Kortars (literary magazine), 1984-86. *Publications:* Naplo, 1987-89, 1991; Hogy no az eg, 1988; Gradicsok, 1985; Halmadar, 1981; Kavics, 1976; Sebbel Lobbal, 1982; Font lomb, lent avar, 1993; Selected Poems, 1993. *Contributions to:* Holmi, Kortars, Es, Agni; Raster 42, De Tweede Ronde, Storm. *Honours:* George Soros Fellowship, 1988-89; Wessely Laszlo Award, 1990; Dery Tibor Awad, 1991; Fulbright Fellowship, 1991-92; Fust Milan Award, 1992. *Memberships:* Hungarian Writers Union; International PEN Club. *Address:* Stollar Bela u 3/a, Budapest 1055, Hungary.

KAPICA Jack M, b. 11 Sept 1946, Riode, Brazil. Journalist. m. Eve J Drobot, 9 Apr 1983, 1 daughter. *Education:* BA, MA, McGill University. *Publication:* Shocked & Appalled. *Memberships:* PEN; Crime Writers of Canada. *Address:* 17 Simpson Avenue, Toronto, Ontario, Canada M4K 1A1.

KAPLAN Harold, b. 3 Jan 1916, Chicago, Illinois, USA. Professor Emeritus. m. Isabelle M Ollier, 29 July 1962, 1 son, 2 daughters. *Education:* BA, 1937, MA

1938, University of Chicago. *Appointments:* Instructor of English, Rutgers University, 1946-49; Professor of English, Bennington College, 1950-72; Professor of English, Northwestern University, 1972-86. *Publications:* Democratic Humanism and American Literature, 1972; The Passive Voice, 1966; Power and Order, 1981. *Contributor to:* Commentary; Nation; Partisan Review; Sewanee Review; Poetry Magazine; The New Leader; The Hudson Review. *Honours:* Rockefeller Foundation Humanities - Fellowship 1982; Fulbright Lecturer, 1967, 1981. *Memberships:* Chairman, American Culture Program, Northwestern University; Chairman, Department of English, Northwestern University. *Address:* Turnabout Lane, Bennington, UT 05201, USA.

KAPLAN Morton A, b. 9 May 1921, Pennsylvania, USA. Professor Political Science. m. Azie Mortimer Kaplan, 22 July 1967. *Education:* BS, Temple University, 1943; PhD, Columbia University, 1951. *Appointments:* Associate Editor, Journal of Conflict Resolution, 1961-72; Board of Editors, World Politics, 1956-71; Orbis, 1967-90; Member Advisory Board, Washington Times, 1982-; Editor, Publisher, World and I, 1985-. *Publications include:* System and Process in International Politics, 1965; Political Foundation of International Law, 1961; Justice, Human Nature and Political Obligation, 1976; Science, Language and the Human Condition, 1989; Law In A Democratic Society, 1939. *Memberships include:* American Political Science Association; International Political Science Association; International Institute for Strategic Studies; Hon. Member International Cultural Society of Korea. *Address:* The University of Chicago, Department of Political Science; 5828 South University Avenue, Chicago, IL 60637, USA.

KAPLAN William, b. 24 May 1957, Toronto, Canada. Lawyer. m. Susan Krever, 8 June 1985, 2 sons. *Education:* BA, MA, University of Toronto; LLB Osgoode Hall Law School; JSD Stanford University. *Publications:* Everything that Floats, 1987; State and Salvation: The Jehovah's Witnesses and the fight for Civil Rights, 1989; Labour Arbitration Yearbook, I, II, 1991, III, 1992; Belonging: The Meaning and Future of Canadian Citizenship, 1993. *Honour:* Osgoode Society Fellowship, 1989-1990. Memberships: American Society for Legal History; Association of Candian Law Teachers; Canadian Civil Liberties Association; Canadian Committee for the History of the Second World War; Canadian Historical Association; Law Society of Upper Canada; Lawyers Against Apartheid; Ontario Labour Management Arbitrator's Association; The Selden Society. *Address:* Faculty of Law, University of Ottawa, Canada K1N 6N5.

KAPUSCINSKI Ryszard, b. 4 Mar 1932, Pinsk, Poland. Journalist; Writer. m Alicja Mielczarek, 6 Oct 1952, 1 daughter. *Education:* MA Faculty of History, Warsaw University. *Appointments:* Sztandar Mlodych, daily, 1951; Polityka, weekly, 1957-61; Corr. Polish Press Agency (PAP) In Africa, Latin America, 1962-72; Kultura, weekly, 1974-81. *Publications:* The Emperor; The Soccer War; Another Day of Life; The Shah of Shahs; Bush Polish Style; Lapidarium; Notes; Imperium, 1993. *Contributions to:* Vanity Fair; Tempo; The Independent; The Guardian; Frankfurter Augemeine Zeitung. *Honours:* Gold Cross of Merit; Knight's Cross Order Polonia Restituta; Prize of International Journalists Org., 1976; State Prize. *Memberships:* PEN Club, Polish Centre Club; Board of Advisors, NPQ; Polish Association of Artistic Photographers; The Natural Council of Culture. *Literary Agent:* Ms Eva Koralnile, Liepman Ag, Meienburgweg 32, CH-8044, Zürich, Switzerland. *Address:* ul Prokuratorska 11m2, 02-074 Warsaw, Poland.

KARAVIA Lia Hadzopoulou, b. 27 June 1932, Athens, Greece. Writer; Philologue; Actress. m. Vassilis Caravias, 20 Sept 1953, 2 sons. *Education:* Diploma, English Literature, Pierce College, Athens, 1953; Diploma, French Literature, Institute of France, Athens, 1954; Diploma, Acting, Acting School, Athens, 1962; Classical Literature, University of Athens, 1972;

Doctorat Nouveau Regime, Comparative Literature, Paris, 1991. *Appointments:* Teacher, Acting, History of the Theatre, Public Schools, 1984-90. *Publications include:* Hypermnesia, 1979; Riki, 1980; The Silent Piano Keys, 1969; Trilingual Edition of The Lion-Riki-The Silent Piano Keys, 1984; The Censor, 1986; Our Neighbourhood, 1986; Oldsters and Youngsters, 1992; 10 collections of Poetry; 1 collection of Short Stories; 10 novels; 4 short plays; 5 long plays; scripts for Greek TV; radio plays for Greek Radio. *Contributions to:* Numerous journals, magazines; Romanian Poetry Anthology, 1987; French Poetry Anthologies; short story: Die Schwägerinnen in Frauen in Griechenland, dtv editions, Germany, 1991; essays in USA publications. *Honours including:* Menelaos Loudemis Prize, 1980; Michaela Averof's Prize, 1981; League of Philologues' Prize, 1986; Women's Literary Club Prizes, 1986 and 1988; National Prize "Best Play for the Young", 1989; National Playwrights' Prize for 'Generation Gaps', 1990; National Playwright' Prize for 'Bench in a Public Garden', 1991. *Memberships include:* World Academy of Arts and Culture; Founding member, Maison Internationale de Poeses, Liege; Society of Greek Writers; International Theatre Centre; Actors League of Greece; Society of Greek Translators; Union of Greek Playwrights; Society of Greek Women Scientists. *Address:* 51 Aghiou Polycarpou Str., Nea Smyrni 17124, Athens, Greece.

KARIN Sydney. *Education:* Be Mechanical Engineering, City College of New York, 1966; MSE 1967, PhD, 1973, Nuclear Engineering, University of Michigan. *Publications:* Co-author, book, The Supercomputer Era, 1987. Numerous technical papers and articles. *Honours:* Fellowship, Atomic Energy Commission; National Defence Education Act Fellowship; New York State Regents College Scholarship; 1989 Outstanding Alumnus, University of Michigan. *Memberships:* AAAS; Association for Computing Machinery; IEEE: American Nuclear Society. *Address:* San Diego Supercomputer Centre, PO Box 85608, San Diego, CA 92186, USA.

KARINTHY Ferenc, b. 2 June 1921, Budapest, Hungary. Writer. m. Agnes Boross, 1 son, 1 daughter. *Education:* Budapest University of Arts & Sciences. *Appointments:* Lecturer, History of Literature & Theatre, MIT, Columbia University, New York, University of California at Los Angeles and Chicago State University; Drama Adviser, National Theatre of Budapest, 1949-50, Madach Theatre, 1952-53, Hungarian TV 1965-70. *Publications:* Novels: Don Juan ejszakaja, 1943; Szellemidezes, 1946; Kentaur, 1947; Budapesti tavasz, 1953; Epepe, 1970; Ösbemutato, 1972; Alvilagi naplo, 1979; Budapesti Ösz, 1982; Uncle Joe, 1987; Short Stories: Irodalmi tortenetek, 1956; Ferencvarosi sziv, 1960; Kek-zold Florida, 1962; Hatorszag, 1965; Viz folott, viz alatt, 1966; Vegtelen szonyeg, 1974; Harmincharom, 1977; Marich Geza utolso kalandja, 1979; Mi van a Dunaban, 1980; Zenebona, 1986; Plays: Ezer ev, 1956; Bosendorfer, 1966; Goz, 1967; Dunakanyar, 1967; Het jatek, 1969; Gellerthegyi almok, 1972; Pesten esBudan, 1972; Korallzatony, 1976; Sketches: Hazai tudositasok, 1954; Teli furdo, 1964; Leanyfalu es videke, 1973; Studies: Olasz joveveny szavaink, 1947; Nyelveles, 1964; Dialogus, 1978; Ovilag es Ujvilag, 1985. *Honours:* Recipient various prizes including: Baumgarten Prize for Literature, 1947; Jozsef Attila Prize, 3 times; Kossuth Prize, 1955. *Memberships:* PEN; International Theatre Institute. *Address:* Menesi ut 71, 1118 Budapest, Hungary.

KARL Frederick Robert, b. 10 Apr 1927, Brooklyn, New York, USA. Professor; Writer. m. Dolores Mary Oristaglio, 8 June 1951, 3 daughters. *Education:* BA, 1948, Columbia College; MA 1949, Stanford University; PhD, 1957, Columbia University. *Appointments include:* Professor, City College of New York 1957-80, New York University 1981-. *Publications:* Joseph Conrad: The Three Lives, biography; American Fictions: 1940-1980; Modern & Modernism: Sovereignty of the Artist 1885-1925; The Quest, novel; The Adversary Literary. Editor, Volumes I & II (continuing), Collected Letters of Joseph

Conrad; William Faulkner: American Writer, 1989; Frank Kafka: Representative Man, 1991. Also: Reader's Guide to Joseph Conrad; An Age of Fiction; The Contemporary English Novel. *Contributions to:* Yale Review; Sewanee Review; Criticism; Nation; New Republic; 20th Century Literature; 19th Century Fiction; Midway; Mosaic; Comparative Literature; Journal of Modern Literature; Numerous essays in books, various subjects. *Honours:* Guggenheim Fellowship; Fulbright Award; Senior Research Grant, National Endowment for the Humanities; American Council of Learned Societies. *Memberships:* Director, Andiron Club; Modern Language Association; Board, Joseph Conrad Society. *Literary Agent:* Melanie Jackson. *Address:* 2 Settlers Landing Lane, East Hampton, NY 11937, USA.

KARLIN Wayne Stephen, b. 13 June 1945, Los Angeles, California, USA. Writer; Teacher. m. Ohnmar Thein, 27 Oct 1977, 1 son. *Education:* BA, American College, Jerusalem, 1972; MA Goddard College, 1976. *Appointments:* President; Co-Editor, First Casulty Press, 1972-73; Visiting Writer. William Joiner Centre for the Story of War and Social Consequences, University of Massachusetts, Boston, 1989-. *Publications:* Free Fire Zone, 1973, co-editor and contributor; Crossover, 1984; Lost Armies, 1988; The Extras, 1989; US, 1992. *Contributions to:* Prairie Schooner; Glimmer Train; Indiana Review; Swords and Ploughshares: An Anthology; Antietom Review; New Outlook; New Fiction from the South: The Best of 1993 (Anthology). *Honours:* Maryland State Arts Council Fellowship in Fiction, 1988 and Individual Artist Award, fiction, 1991; National Endowment for the Arts Fellowship, 1993. *Memberships:* Associated Writing Programmes. *Literary Agent:* Phyllis Webster, Harold Ober Associates, 925 Madison Avenue, New York 10017, USA. *Address:* Rurol Route 1, Box 268K, Luxington Park, MD20653, USA.

KARNOW Stanley, b. 4 Feb 1925, New York City, USA. Writer. m. Annette Kline, 21 Apr 1959, 2 sons, 1 daughter. *Education:* BA, Harvard University; Sorbonne, France; Ecole des Sciences Politiques; Nieman Fellow; Fellow, Kennedy School of Government & East Asia Research Centre, Harvard University. *Publications:* Southeast Asia, 1963, 1965; Mao and China : From Revolution to Revolution, 1972; Vietnam : A History, 1983; In Our Image: America's Empire in the Philippines, 1989. *Contributions to:* New York Times; GEO; Atlantic; Foreign Affairs; Foreign Policy; Esquire. *Honours:* Overseas Press Club, 1967, 1968, 1983; Dupont Polk and Emmy Awards, 1984. *Memberships:* Century Association; Authors Guild; Council on Foreign Relations; PEN. *Address:* 10850 Springknoll Drive, Potomac, MD 20854, USA.

KAROL Alexandra. *See:* **KENT Arthur.**

KARP David, (Adam Singer, Wallace Ware), b. 5 May 1922, New York City, USA. Writer. m. Lillian Klass, 25 Dec 1944, deceased 1987, 2 sons. *Education:* BSc., Social Sciences, City College of New York, 1948. *Appointment:* Guggenheim Fellow, Creative Writing, 1956-57. *Publications:* One, 1953; The Day of the Monkey, 1955; All Honorable Men, 1956; Leave Me Alone, 1957; Enter, Sleeping, 1960; non-fiction, with M.D. Lincoln, Vice President in charge of Revolution, 1960; The Last Believers, 1964; The Brotherhood of Velvet, 1952; Hardman, 1952; (Under Pseudonym) Platoon, 1953; The Charka Memorial, 1956. *Contributions include:* New York Times; National Saturday Review; Los Angeles Times. *Honours:* Guggenheim Fellow, 1956; Emmy Award, 1965; Look Magazine Award for Best TV Play, 1958; Edgar Award, 1959. *Memberships:* PEN; Writers Guild of America, President TV-Radio Branch, 1969-71, various other offices. *Address:* 300 East 56th Street, Apt 3C, New york, NY 10022, USA.

KARPF Anne, b. 8 June 1950, London, England. Journalist; Critic; Broadcaster; Sociologist. *Education:* BA, Honours, St Hilda's College, University of Oxford; MA, Oxon, 1976; MSc, with Distinction in Sociology of Health and Illness, part-time at Polytechnic of the South Bank, London, 1979-81. *Appointments:* Researcher with BBC TV, London, 1972-76; Freelance Journalist and Critic, Contributions Include - The Guardian, the Observer, the Sunday Times, 1976-; Weekly Radio Reviewer for the Observer, 1977-; Radio Critic for the Listener, 1980-83; Broadcasting Editor for The Times Health Supplement, 1981-82; Associate Editor for Radio Month, 1978-80; Critic for BBC Radio 4's Kaleidoscope Arts Programme, 1979-. *Publications:* Chapter on Women and Radio in Women & Media; Reported, presented and wrote TV items, including 2 editions of What the Papers Say, 1981, 1983; Member of Collective which wrote Women's Health & Food, 1983; Book on Health, Medicine and the Media. *Memberships:* National Union of Journalists; Women's Airwaves; The Politics of Health Group. *Address:* c/o The Peters Fraser and Dunlop Group, 503/4 The Chambers. Chelsea Harbour, London SW10 0XF, England.

KARSEN Sonja Petra, b. 11 Apr 1919, Berlin, Germany. (US Citizen, 1945-). Professor of Spanish Emerita. *Education:* BA, Carleton College, USA, 1939; MA, Bryn Mawr College, 1941; PhD, Columbia University, 1950. *Publications include:* Guillermo Valencia, Columbian Poet, 1873-1943, 1951; Educational Development in Costa Rica with UNESCO's Technicnal Assistance, 1951-54, 1954; Jaime Torres Bodet : A Poet in a Changing World, 1963; Selected Poems of Jaime Torres Bodet, 1964; Versos y prosas de Jaime Torres Bodet, 1966; Jaime Torres Bodet, 1971; Essays on Iberoamerican Literature and History , Peter Lang, 1988; Reviewer, World Literature Today, 1959-; Editor, Language Association Bulletin, 1980-82; Numerous papers on Foreign Languages, Literature and Culture, 1982-1987; Schenectady: New York State Association of Foreign Language Teachers, 1988. *Contributions to:* Texas Quarterly; Revista Interamericana de Bibliografia. *Honours:* Chevalier dans l'ordre des Palmes Académique, Paris, France, 1963; numerous grants and fellowships; Fulbright Lecturer, Freie Universität Berlin, 1968; National Distinguished Leadership Award, New York State Association of Foreign Languages Language Teachers, 1979; Alumni Achievement Award Carleton College, 1982; Member, Ateneo Doctor Jaime Torres Bodet, Mexico, 1984; Spanish Heritage Award, 1981; Honorary Member, Sigma Delta Pi, Phi Sigma Iota. *Memberships:* Mildenberger Medal Selection Committee, MLA; numerous committees. *Address:* PO Box 441, Saratoga Springs, NY 12866, USA.

KARVAS Peter, b. 25 Apr 1920, Banska Bystrica, CSFR. Writer; University Professor. m. Eva Ruhmann, 15 May 1969. 1 son. *Education:* PhD, 1946; University Professor, 1989. *Publications include:* Prose: Night in My Town, 1979; Humoresques, I, II, III, 1984, 1986, 1989; In the Nest, 1981; Fascicle S, 1988; Drama: The Seven Witnesses, 1969; Absolute Prohibition, 1970; Private party, 1972; Visit by Night, 1973; Back Entrance, 1976; The Twentieth Night, 1971; A Kingdom for a Murderer, 1988. *Contributions to:* Numerous studies and articles about the theory of literature, drama, theatre, film, television, radio. *Honours:* Czechoslovak State Prize, 1960; Czechoslovak Writers Union Prizes, 1960, 1963, 1967; Slovak Writers Association Prize, 1991. *Memberships include:* Committee of Slovak Writers Union; Central Committee Czechoslovak Writers Union; Member of Presidency of the Slovak Pen Centre; Club of Independent Writers; Slovak Writers Association. *Address:* Vlckova 7, 81106 Bratislava, Czechoslovakia.

KASDAGLIS Nikos, b. 10 Mar 1928. Retired Bank Manager. m. Irene Athanasiadou, 1 May 1957, 1 son, 1 daughter. *Education:* High School Graduate, 1946. *Publications:* The Cogs of the Millstone, 1955; Shaved Heads, 1959; Maria Wandering Over the Metropolis of the Waters, 1982; Highways of the Land and the Sea, 1988; Blessed are the Merciful, 1991; Squalls; I am the Lord Thy God, 1961; Thirst, 1970; Mythology, 1977; The Bowstring, 1985; The Swamp, 1988. *Contributions* *to:* Both Greek and Foreign press. *Honours:* Greek Novel National prize, 1955; Society of Writers, Greece. *Memberships:* Greek Section of Amenesty International. *Address:* End of Stockholm St, 85100 Rhodes, Greece.

KASSEM Lou. *See:* **KASSEM Louise Sutton Morreu.**

KASSEM Louise Sutton Morrell, b.10 Nov 1931, Tennessee, USA. Author. m. Shakeep Kassem, 17 June 1951, 4 daughters. *Education:* East Tennessee State University, 1949-51; Short courses: University of Virginia, 1982, Vassar College, 1985. *Publications:* Middle School Blues, 1986; Listen for Rachel, 1986; Dance of Death, 1984; Secret Wishes, 1989; A Summer for Secrets, 1989; A Haunting in Williamsburg, 1990; The Treasures of Witch Hat Mountain, 1992. *Honours:* ALA Notable Book in Social Studies, 1986. *Memberships:* Society of Childrens Book Writers; Writers in Virginia; Appalachian Writers. *Literary Agent:* Ruth Cohen. *Address:* 715 Burruss Dr NW, Blacksburg, VA 24060, USA.

KATKO ISTVAN b. 17 June 1923, Jaszjakohalma. Writer. m. (1) Zsuzsa Kalmar, 1949; (2) Anna-Maria Fridrich, 1979. 1 son, 1 daughter. *Education:* Literature Degree; Teacher's Diploma. *Appointments:* TV Editor of Hungarian Literatura Pensioner. *Publications:* Novels: Kokarda, 1993; Ahóhér, 1992; Haziorizet, 1981; Vadhajta's, 1973; Felszivu apostolok, 1958; Nap adja az arnyekot is, 1962; Ot ferfi komoly szandekkal. *Contributions to:* Elet es Irodalom, Nepszabasag, Vasarnapi Hirek. *Honours:* Andor Gabor Prize, 1970; SZOT Trade Union Prize, 1983. *Memberships:* Union of Hungarian Writers; PEN: Union of Film and Television Artists of Hungary. *Address:* Farkas Biro u. 8, Budapest 1011, Hungary.

KATO Shuichi, b. 19 Sept 1919, Tokyo, Japan. Writer; Professor. *Education:* Graduate, Faculty of Medicine 1943, MD 1950, Tokyo University. *Publications:* Form, Style, Tradition, Reflexions on Japanese Art and Society, 1969; Japan-China Phenomenon, 1973; Six Lives/Six Deaths. Portraits from Modern Japan (co-authors Robert Lifton & Michael Reich), 1979; A History of Japanese Literature, 3 volumes, 1979-1983; Chosakushu (Collected Works), 15 volumes, 1978-80. *Contributions to:* Asahi Shimbun; Many Japanese, French and American periodicals. *Honours:* Osaragi Jiro Prize for A History of Japanese Literature, 1980; Ordre des Arts et des Lettres, 1985. *Membership:* PEN Club, Japanese Branch. *Address:* Kaminage 1-8- 16, Setagaya-ku, Tokyo, 158-Japan.

KATTAN Naim, b. 26 Aug 1928. Writer. m. 21 July 1961, 1 son. *Education:* Law College, Baghdad, 1945-47; Sorbonne Paris, 1947-52. *Appointments:* Head of Writing and Publishing, Canada Council Ottawa, 1990-91; Associate Director, Canada Council, 1990-91; Writer in Residence, University of Quebec, Montreal, 1991- . *Publications:* Reality and Theatre, 1970; Farewell Babylon, 1974; La Memoire of La Promesse, 1980; Le Pere, 1988; Fari La, 1989. *Contributions to:* Critique; Quaizaire; Nouvelle Reme Francaise; Le Devoir; Canadian Literature. *Honours:* Prix Frances, Canada, 1971; Segal Awards, 1975; Order of Canada, 1987; Order of Arts and Letters of France, 1989; Order of Quebec, 1990. *Memberships:* Royal Society of Canada Academie de Lettres, Montreal; Union de Ecrivains du Quebec. *Address:* 3463 Rue Ste Famille 2114, Montreal, Canada H2X 2K7.

KATZ Bobbi, (Gail, Barbara George, Emily George, Peggy Kahn, Don E Plumme, Ali Reich), b. 2 May 1933. Writer; Editor. m. H D Katz, 1956, divorced 1979. 1 son, 1 daughter. *Education:* BA, with special honours, Fine Arts, Goucher College, Maryland, 1954. *Appointment:* Editor of Books for Young Readers, Random House, New York, 1982-. *Publications:* Collection of Own Poems: Upside Down and Inside Out; Poems for All Your Pockets, 1976; Poems for Small

Friends, 1988; Anthologies: Birthday Bear's Book of Birthday Poems, 1983; Bedtime Bear's Book of Bedtime Poems, 1984; A Popple in Your Pocket and Other Funny Poems, 1986; Ghosts and Goosebumps: Poems to Make You Shiver, 1991; Puddle Wonderful: Poems to Welcome Spring. Novels: The Manifesto and Me, Meg, 1978; and others. Non-fiction, The Creepy, Crawly Book, 1988; Over 80 books for children, over 100 poems. *Contributions to:* The Cousteau Almanac. *Membership:* Authors Guild. *Address:* 65 W 96 Street (21H), New York, NY 10025, USA.

KATZ Hilda, (Hulda Weber), b. 2 June 1909, USA. Fine Arts Artist; Author/Poet. *Education:* National Academy of Design; Full Art Scholarship, New School of Social Research, 1940-41. *Appointments:* Editor, Director, Tagore Institute of Creative Writing International, India, 1984-90. *Publications:* Poems in anthologies: Blue River Anthology; Treasures of Parnassus; Cavalcade of Poetry Anthology; Best Broadcast Poetry; 1st Anthology, International Poetry Society; The Golden Harvest Anthology; Album of International Poets, India; The Bloom Anthology, India; Perfume and Fragrance Anthology, India; Lightning and Rainbows, India. Special Poetry Collections: Yad Vashem Mem Mus. 9 poems, Holocaust, 1987; Pres. Chaim Herzog, Israel, 9 poems, Holocaust, 1987, also, 12 poems, American Genre-, 1989; Museum of Jewish Heritage, New York, 9 poems, Holocaust & American Genre, 1989; Jewish Theological Seminary of America, 15 poems, Holocaust/American Genre. 1989; Jewish National & University Library, Israel, Holocaust/American Genre. 18 poems, 1990; Simon Wiesenthal Center, USA, 21 poems, Holocaust/American, Genre. 1990. Archives, Hilda Katz/Hulda Weber, Smithsonian Institution Art Archives, 104 items, 1979; New York State Museum of Albany, USA, Art, 121 works, All original manuscripts, 1979; Archives: Permanent Collections: The Smithsonian Institution Archives of American Art: Smithsonian Archives of American Art has aquired both Art & Poetry, including Original Manuscripts & Honors since 1979-1992; New York State Museum/Archives of Albany, New York has aquired both Art & Poetry, 121 Paintings, Drawings, Prints & Original Manuscripts & Honors since 1979-1991. As an artist: All art, painting, drawing, prints, print blocks, have been acquired by 19 National & International Museums including the following, 1). Metropolitan Museum of Art, New York, 62 works, 1965, 1980; 2). New York, State Museum of Albany, New York, 121 works, 1979-90, containing acquisitions and all original manuscripts, stories and poetry; 3). New York Public Library, Main Branch, 67 works, 1971, 1978; 4). National Collection Fine Arts, D.C. 49 works, 1966, 1978; 5). National Gallery of Art, D.C. 3 works, 1966; 6). New Britain Museum of Art, CT. 43 works, 1978, 1979; 7). Israel Museum, Jerusalem, 30 works, 1980, others. *Contributions to:* Children's short stories in: Daily Forward; Scholastic Magazine; World Over Magazine; Young Judean Magazine; Southern Israelite Magazine; Cheer Magazine; Growing Up Magazine; Vacation Magazine; Humpty Dumpty Magazine; Short stories in: Forward Weekly. *Honours:* Membro Honoris Causa dell Accadenia Di Scienze. Letteri, Arti, nella Classe Accademica Nobel N.D. (Nobel Designate), Art, Hilda Katz, 1974; Classe Accademica Nobel, ND, Nobel Designate, Hulda Weber, 1975; Author, poet, Classe Nobel, ND, Nobel Designate, Hulda Weber, 1978; Consigliere Storia Letteratura Americana, Milan, Italy. Made Daughter of Mark Twain for contribution to Modern Art; Honourable Mention, Scourge of God, 1982, One Long-Burning Light, sonnet, 1985, One Star Within Yourself, ballade, 1985, Sacajawea, ballade, 1987, World Order of Narrative Poets; 2nd Award for John Brown and Abe Lincoln, ballade, New York Poetry Forum, 1983; Certificate of Merit for Sacajawea, National Federation of State Poetry Societies; Many other awards for poetry. *Memberships:* Founder Fellow, International Academy of Poets, International Biographical Association; Founder Fellow, ORBIS-HUB; International Poetry Shrine, USA; Fellow-for-Life, Metropolitan Museum of Art; Life Member, Executive and Professional Hall of Fame. *Address:* 915 West End Avenue 5D, New York, NY 10025, USA.

KAUFMAN Amy Rebecca, b. 8 Oct 1951, Long Beach, California, USA. Editor; Publisher. *Education:* BA, University of California, Berkeley. *Publications:* Founder, Editor, Publisher, Stories Magazine, 1982-. *Honours:* Selections from Stories have appeared in Best American Short Stories, 1984, and Prize Stories 1985 : The O Henry Awards. *Membership:* Magazine Publishers of America. *Address:* 14 Beacon Street, Boston, MA 02108, USA.

KAUFMAN Bel, b. Berlin, Germany. Writer; Lecturer; Educator. div. 1 son, 1 daughter. *Education:* BA magna cum laude, Hunter College, NYC; MA Columbia University; DLett, Nasson College. *Appointments:* Teacher of English, NYC High Schools; Creative Writing Workshops and seminars and various universities; Lecturer, 18th C English Literature, New School Social Research; Assistant and Adjunct Professor of English, CUNY; Keystone speaker at education conventions in USA. *Publications:* Up the Down Staircase, 1964, 57 editions, latest in 1991; Love, 1979; Translations of Russian poetry. *Contributions to:* Numerous short stories and articles in Saturday Review, McCalls Esquire; Today's Education; Ladies Home Joournal; The English Journal; NYT; Colliers; Todays Health; Fifty Plus; New Choices. *Honours include:* Scriptwriters Annual Award; National Human Resource Award; Paperback of the year Award; Anti Deformation League Award; United Jewish Appeal Plaque; Kentucky Colonel Award; Educaiton Association pf America Award. *Memberships:* Authors League; Dramatists Society; PEN American Center; English Graduate Union; Commission on Performing Arts; Advisory Council, Town Hall Foundation. *Literary Agent:* Maurice Greenbaum, 575 Madison Avenue, New York, USA. *Address:* 1020 Park Avenue, New York City, NY 10028, USA.

KAUFMANN Myron S, b. 27 Aug 1921, Boston, Massachusetts, USA. Novelist. m. Paula Goldberg, 6 Feb 1960, (div 1980). 1 son, 2 daughters. *Education:* AB, Harvard University, 1943. *Publications:* Remember Me To God, novel, 1957; The Love of Elspeth Baker, novel, 1982; Thy Daughter's Nakedness, novel, 1968. *Literary Agent:* Sterling Lord, New York City, USA. *Address:* 111 Pond Street, Sharon, MA 02067, USA.

KAUFMANN Thomas DaCosta, b. 7 May 1948, New York, USA. University Professor. m. Virginia Burns Roehrig, 1 June 1974, 1 daughter. *Education:* BA, MA, 1970, Yale University; MPhil, Warburg Institute, University of London, 1972; PhD, Harvard University, 1977. *Publications:* The School of Prague: Painting at the Court of Rudolf II, 1988; Drawings from the Holy Roman Empire, 1540-1650, 1982; Variations on the Imperial Theme, 1978; Central European Drawings, 1680-1800, 1989; Art and Architecture in Central Europe, 1550-1620, 1985; The Mastery of Nature, 1993. *Contributions to:* Art Journal; Journal of the Warburg and Courtauld Institutes and other scholarly journals. *Honours:* Finley Fellowship; American Council of Learned Societies Dissertation Prize; Alexander von Humboldt Senior Fellowship; Jan Mitchell Prize for the Best Book on Art History, 1988. *Memberships:* College Art Association of America; Renaissance Society of America. *Address:* Department of Art and Archaeology, McCormick Hall, Princeton University, Princeton, NJ 08544, USA.

KAUFMANN William J, b. 1942, USA. Astronomer; Writer. *Publications:* Relativity and Cosmology, 1973, 2nd Edition, 1977; Astronomy: The Structure of the Universe, 1977; The Cosmic Frontiers of General Relativity, 1977; Exploration of the Solar System, 1978; Stars and Nebulas, 1978; Planets and Moons, 1979; Galaxies and Quasars, 1979; Black Holes and Warped Spacetime, 1979; Particles and Fields (editor), 1980; Universe, 1985, 1988, 1991; Discovering the Universe, 1987, 1990. *Address:* 385 Paraiso Drive, Danville, CA 94526, USA.

KAVALER Lucy Estrin, b. 29 Aug 1930, New York City, New York, USA. Author. m. 9 Nov 1948, 1 son, 1 daughter. *Education:* BA magna cum laude, Oberlin College, Ohio; Fellowship in Advanced Science Writing, Columbia University Graduate School. *Literary Appointments:* Associate Editorial Director, PW Communications International, 1976-89; Vice-President, Editorial/Editorial Director, AJN Company, 1989-. *Publications:* Major Works: Private World of High Society, 1960; Mushrooms, Molds and Miracles, 1965; The Astors, 1966; Freezing Point, 1970; Noise the New Menace, 1975; A Matter of Degree, 1981; The Secret Lives of the edmonts, 1989; Others: Green Magic; Cold Against Disease; Life Battles Cold; The Wonders of Fungi; Artificial World Around Us; The Dangers of Noise; The Astors (for children); Wonders of Algae. *Contributions to:* Smithsonian; Natural History; McCalls; Readers Digest; Redbook; Female Patient; Woman's Day (and encyclopedia); Primary Cardiology. *Honours:* Listings in Best Books of the Year; American Library Association Best Book of the Year; American Association for the Advancement of Science Listing; Library Journal Best Books in Science and Technology. *Memberships:* Executive Board, American Center, and Chairman, Writers in Prison Committee, International Association of Poets, Playwrights, Editors, Essayists, and Authors; Exectutive Council, Workshop Moderator, American Society of Journalists and Authors; National Association of Science Writers; International Science Writers Association; Authors Guild; President 1986-87, Forum of Writers for Young People; New York Business Press Editors. *Literary Agent:* Harold Ober Associates, New York, USA. *Address:* c/o Claire Smith, Harold Ober Associates, 40 East 49th Street, New York, NY 10017, USA.

KAVALER Rebecca, b. 26 July 1930, Atlanta, Georgia, USA. Writer. m. Frederic Kavaler, 1955, 2 sons. *Education:* AB, University of Georgia. *Publications:* Tigers in the Woods, 1986; Doubting Castle, 1984; Further Adventures of Brunhild, 1978. *Honours:* Short Stories in Best of Nimrod, 1957-69; Best American Short Stores, 1972; AWP Award for Short fiction, 1978; NEA Fellowships, 1979, 1985. *Memberships:* PEN. *Literary Agent:* ICM AGency, Lisa Bankoff. *Address:* 425 Riverside Drive, New York, NY 10025, USA.

KAVANAGH Cynthia. *See:* **DANIELS Dorothy.**

KAVANAGH P J, b. 6 Jan 1931, Worthing, Sussex, England. Writer. m. (1) Sally Philipps, (2) Catherine Ward, 2 sons. *Education:* Merton College, Oxford. *Literary Appointment:* Columnist, The Spectator, 1983- . *Publications:* The Perfect Stranger (Memoir), 1966; Editor: Poems of Ivor Gurney, 1982; The Oxford Book of Short Poems (with James Michie), 1985; G.K. Chesterton (The Bodley Head Edition), 1985; A Book of Consolations, 1992; Poems: One and One, 1959; On the Way to the Depot, 1968; About Time, 1970; Edward Thomas in Heaven, 1974; Life Before Death, 1979; Selected Poems, 1982; 2nd Edition, 1987; Presences, 1987; Novels: A Song and Dance, 1968; A Happy man, 1972; People and Weather, 1978; Scarf Jack (The Irish Captain), 1978; Only By Mistake, 1986; Rebel for Good, 1980; People and Places (essays), 1988; Finding Connections (travel), 1990; Selected Poems of Ivor Gurney, 1990; Collected Poems, 1992. *Honours:* Richard Hillary Prize, 1966; Guardian Fiction Prize, 1968. *Membership:* Fellow, Royal Society of Literature. *Literary Agent:* The Peters Fraser and Dunlop Group Ltd. *Address:* Sparrowthorn, Elkstone, Gloucestershire, England.

KAWALEC Julian, b. 11 Oct 1916, Wrzawy, Poland. Writer. m. Irene Wierzbanowska, 2 June 1948, 1 daughter. *Education:* Graduate, Jagellonian University, Cracow. *Publications:* Paths Among Streets, 1957; Scars, 1960; Bound to the Land, 1962; Overthrown Elms, 1963; In the Sun, 1963; The Dancing Hawk, 1964; Black Light, 1965; Wedding March, 1966; Appeal, 1968; Searching for Home, 1968; Praise of Hands, 1969; To Cross the River, 1973; Gray Aureole, 1974; Great Feast, 1974; To Steal the Brother, 1982. *Contributions to:* Literary Life, Cracow; Literary Monthly, Warsaw. *Honours:* Prize Polish Editors, 1962; Prize of Minister of Culture and Art, 1967, 1985; Prize of State, 1975. *Memberships:* Polish Pen Club; Polish Writers Association; Society European Culture. *Address:* 39 Zaleskiego, 31-525 Krakow, Poland.

KAWIN Bruce Frederick, b. 6 Nov 1945, Los Angeles, California, USA. Professor of English and Film Studies; Poet; Critic; Screenwriter. *Education:* AB, cum laude, English and Comparative Literature, Columbia University, 1967; MFA, Creative Writing (poetry) and Filmmaking 1969, PhD Modern Literature and Film Aesthetics 1970, Cornell University. *Publications:* Telling It Again and Again: Repetition in Literature and Film; Mindscreen: Bergman, Godard and First-Person Film; The Mind of the Novel: Reflexive Fiction and the Ineffable; How Movies Work; Faulkner and Film; Faulkner's MGM Screenplays; Breakwater and Slides (poetry chapbooks); To Have and Have Not (edited); Gerald Mast, A Short History of the Movies, 5th edition, (edited); Several screenplays. *Contributions to:* Film Quarterly; Dreamworks; Paris Review; Rolling Stock. *Honour:* Mindscreen won University of Colorado Faculty Book Prize, 1978. *Memberships:* MLA; Executive Council, Society for Cinema Studies. *Literary Agent:* Rick Balkin, PO Box 222, Amherst, MA 01004, USA. *Address:* 915 15th Street, Boulder, CO 80302, USA.

KAWIŃSKI Wojciech, b. 22 May 1939, Poland. Poet. m. Helena Lorenz, 17 Apr 1964, 1 son, 1 daughter. *Education:* MA, 1964. *Appointments:* Pismo Literacko-Artystyczne, Sub-Director, 1985-1990. *Publications:* Odleglosci Posluszne, 1964; Narysowane We Wnetrzu, 1965; Ziarno Rzeki, 1967; Pole Widzenia, 1970; Spiew Bezimienny, 1978; Pod Okiem Slonca, 1980; Listy Do Ciebie, 1982; Milosc Nienawistna, 1985; Ciemna strona jasności, 1989; Wieczorne śniegi, 1989; Czysty zmierzch, 1990; Pamięć żywa, 1990; Zwierciadło sekund, 1991. *Contributions to:* Numerous journals & magazines including: Więz; Echo Krakowa. *Honours:* Prize, City of Cracow, 1985; Red Rose Prize for Poetry, Gdansk, 1985. *Membership:* Polish Writers Association. *Address:* ul. Stachiewicza 22a, 31-303 Kraków, Poland.

KAY Guy Gavriel, b. 7 Nov 1954, Weyburn, Canada. Author. m. Laura Beth Cohen, 15 July 1984, 1 son. *Education:* BA Philosophy, University of Manitoba, 1975; LLB, University, of Toronto 1978. *Appointments:* Principal Writer and Associate Producer, The Scales of Justice, CBC Radio Drama, 1981-90. *Publications:* A Song for Arbonne, 1992; Tigana, 1990; The Summer Tree, 1984; The Wandering Fire, 1986; The Darkest Road, 1986. *Contributions to:* Malahat Review; MacLean's. *Honours:* Aurora Prize, Best Work of Speculative Fiction, Canada, 1986, 1990; Award, Best Dramatic Treatment of a Legal issue, 1986. *Memberships:* Law Society of Upper Canada; Association of Canadian Radio and TV Artists. *Literary Agents:* (1) MGA, 10 St Mary Street, Toronto, Canada; (2) Curtis Brown, 162-168 Regent Street, London. *Address:* c/o Curtis Brown Agency, 162-168 Regent Street, London W1R 5TB, England.

KAY Mara, b. Europe. Retired. *Publications:* In Place of Katia, 1964; The Burning Candle, 1966; Masha, 1969; The Youngest Lady in Waiting, 1971; The Circling Star, 1973; The Storm Warning (hard cover), 1976; Restless Shadows, 1980; Lolo, 1981; One Small Clue, 1982. *Membership:* PEN, England. *Address:* 2 Lent Avenue, Hempstead, NY 11550, USA.

KAYE Geraldine, b. 14 Jan 1925, Watford, Herts, England. Writer. m. 1948, div. 1975. 1 son, 2 daughters. *Education:* BSc Economics, London School of Economics, 1946-49. *Publications:* Comfort Herself 1985; A Breath of Fresh Air, 1986; A Piece of Cake, 1991; Someone Else's Baby, 1990; Snowgirl, 1991; Stone Boy, 1991; Summer in Small Street, 1989. *Honours:* The Other Award, 1986. *Memberships:* PEN: West Country Writers; Society of Authors; Women Writers and Journalists. *Literary Agent:* A M Heath. *Address:* 39 High Kingsdown, Bristol BS2 8EW, England.

KAYE Marvin Nathan, b. 10 Mar 1938, Philadelphia, Pennsylvania, USA. Writer. m. Saralee Bransdorf, 4 Aug 1963, Wilkes-Barre, Pennsylvania. 1 daughter. *Education:* BA, MA, Pennsylvania State University; Graduate study, University of Denver, Colorado. *Literary Appointments:* Senior Editor, Harcourt Brace Jovanovich; Adjunct Associate Professor of Creative Writing, New York University. *Publications:* The Histrionic Holmes, 1971; A Lively Game of Death, 1972; A Toy is Born, The Stein and Day Handbook of Magic, 1973; The Grand Ole Opry Murders, The Handbook of Mental Magic, 1974; Bullets for Macbeth, Fiends and Creatures (Editor), 1975; Brother Theodore's Chamber of Horrors (Editor), 1975; Catalog of Magic, My Son the Druggist, The Laurel and Hardy Murders, 1977; The Masters of Solitude, with Parke Godwin, 1978; The Incredible Umbrella, My Brother the Druggist, 1979; Ghosts (Editor), 1981; The Amorous Umbrella, The Possession of Immanuel Wolf, 1981; Wintermind (with Parke Godwin), 1982; The Soap Opera Slaughters, 1982; A Cold Blue Light (with Parke Godwin), 1983; Masterpieces of Terror and the Supernatural (Editor), 1985; Ghosts of Night and Morning, Devils and Demons (Editor), 1987; Weird Tales, the Magazine That Never Dies (Editor), 1988; Witches and Warlocks (Editor), 1989; 13 Plays of Ghosts and the Supernatural (Editor), 1990. *Contributions to:* Amazing; Fantastic; Galileo; Family Digest. Columnist, Science Fiction Chronicle. *Honours include:* First runner-up, best novellas, British Fantasy Awards, 1978. *Memberships:* Several professional organizations. *Literary Agent:* Mel Berger, William Morris Inc. *Address:* c/o William Morris Inc, 1350 Avenue of the Americas, New York, NY 10019, USA.

KAYE Mary Margaret, (Mollie Hamilton), b. United Kingdom, 1911. Author. *Publications:* Six Bars at Seven, 1940; Death Walks in Kashmir, 1953, as Death in Kashmir, 1984; Death Walks in Berlin, 1955; Death Walks in Cyprus, 1956, as Death in Cyprus, 1984; Shadow of the Moon, Revised Edition, 1979; Later Than You Think, 1958, as Death in Kenya, 1983; House of Shade, 1959, as Death in Zanzibar, 1983; Night on the Island, 1960; Trade Wind, 1963, Revised Edition, 1981; The Far Pavilions, 1978; The Ordinary Princess, for children, 1980; The Golden Calm (editor), 1980; Thistledown, for children, 1981; Autobiography: Vol.1, The Sun in the Morning, 1990. *Address:* c/o St Martin's Press, 175 Fifth Avenue, New York, NY 10010, USA.

KAYODE. *See:* **SOYINKA Olykjayode Adedeji.**

KAZAN Elia, b. 7 Sept 1909. Writer/Director. m. (1) Molly Day Thacher, 12 Dec 1932 (dec) 2 sons, 2 daughters; (2) Barbara Loden, 5 June 1967 (dec) 1 son; (3) Frances Rudge, 28 June, 1982. *Education:* Williams College, 1930; Yale University, Postgraduate School of Drama, 1932; Honorary Degrees: Wesleyan University (DLitt) 1955; Yale University (MFA) 1959; Carnegie Institute of Technology (DLitt) 1962; Williams College (DLitt) 1964; Katholieka Universitait, Luuven, Belgium Doctor Honoris Causa, 1978. *Publications:* America, America, 1962; The Arrangement 1967; The Assassins, 1972; The Understudy, 1975; Acts of Love, 1978; The Anatolian 1982; Elia Kazan: A Life, 1988. *Contributions to:* The Writer and Motion Pictures in Sight and Sound, 1957; Theatre, New Stages, New Plays, New Actors, in New York Times Magazine, 1962; Mr Kazan Finds a Find, New York Herald Tribune, 1963; On What Makes a Director, Directors Guild of America, 1973; Inside a Turkish Prison, New York Times Magazine, 1979. *Literary Agent:* Irving Paul Lazar.

KEANE John B(rendan), b. 1928, Ireland. Author; Pub Owner. *Publications:* Sive, 1959; Sharon's Grave, 1960; The Highest House on the Mountain, 1961; Many Young Men of Twenty, 1961; The Street and Other Poems, verse, 1961; Hut 42, 1963; The Man from Clare, 1963; Strong Tea, 1963; The Year of the Hiker, 1964; Self-Portrait, 1964; The Field, 1965; The Rain at the End of the Summer, 1967; Letters of a Successful T D, 1967; Big Maggie, 1969; The Change in Mame Fadden, 1971; Moll, 1971; Letters of an Irish Parish Priest, 1972; Letters of an Irish Publican, 1973; Values,

1973; The Crazy Wall, 1973; The Gentle Art of Matchmaking, 1973; Letters of a Love-Hungry Farmer, 1974; Letters of a Matchmaker, 1975; Death Be Not Proud, stories, 1976; Letters of a Civic Guard, 1976; Is the Holy Ghost Really a Kerryman, 1976; The Good Thing, play, 1976; Letters of a Country Postman, 1977; Unlawful Sex and Other Testy Matters, 1978; The Buds of Ballybunion, 1979; Stories from a Kerry Fireside, 1980; The Chastitute, 1981; More Irish Short Stories, 1981; Letters of an Irish Minister of State, 1982; Man of the Triple Name, 1984; Owl Sandwiches, 1985; The Bodhran Makers, 1986; Love Bites, 1991; Duraneo, 1992; The Ram of God, 1992. *Honours:* Hon D Litt, Trinity College, Dublin, 1984; Hon Doc of Fine Arts, Marymount Manhattan College, 1984; Independent Irish Life Award, 1986; Sunday Tribune Award, 1986; Irish American Literary Award, 1988; Person of the Year Award, 1991. *Memberships:* Irish PEN, President 1973-74; Hon Life Membership, Royal Dublin Society, 1991. *Address:* 37 William Street, Listowel, Co Kerry, Republic of Ireland.

KEATING Bern, b. 1915, USA. Author. *Publications:* The Mosquiito Fleet, 1963; The Grand Banks, 1968; Alaska, 1969; Famous American Explorers; Northwest Passage, 1970; Mighty Mississippi, 1971; Florida, 1972; Gulf of Mexico, 1973; Famous American Cowboys, 1977; The Flamboyant Mr Colt and His Deadly Six-Shoter, 1978; Mississippi, 1984; Legend of the Delta Queen, 1986. *Address:* 141 Bayou Road, Greenville, MS 38701, USA.

KEATING Frank, b. 4 Oct 1937, Hereford, England. Journalist. m. Jane Anne Sinclair, 8 Aug 1987. *Appointments:* Editor, Outside Broadcasts, ITV, 1964-70; Columnist, The Guardian, 1975-; Punch, 1980-. *Publications:* Bowled Over, 1979; Up and Under, 1980; Another Bloody Day in Paradise, 1981; High, Wide & Handsome, 1985; Long Days, Late Nights, 1986; Gents & Players; Half-Time Whistle, 1992. *Contributions include:* Punch; New Statesman; Listener; Cricketer. *Honours:* Sportswriter of Year, 1978, 1980, 1989; Magazine Writer of Year, 1987; Sports Journalist of the Year, british Press Awards, 1988. *Address:* Church House, Marden, Hereford HR1 3EN, England.

KEATING Henry Reymond Fitzwalter, b. 31 Oct 1926, St. Leonards-on-Sea, Sussex, England. Author. m. 1953, 3 sons, 1 daughter. *Education:* BA, Trinity College, Dublin, Republic of Ireland. *Publications:* The Perfect Murder, 1964; Inspector Ghote Trusts the Heart, 1972; The Lucky Alphonse, 1982; Under A Monsoon Cloud, 1986; Dead on Time, 1989; The Iciest Sin, 1990; Crime Wave (ed), 1991; Cheating Dealth, 1992; The Man who (ed), 1992; The Rich Detective, 1993. *Contributions to:* Crime books reviews, The Times, 1967-83. *Honours:* Gold Dagger, Crime Writers Association, 1964, 1980. *Memberships:* Crime Writers Association (Chairman 1970-71); Society of Authors (Chairman 1982-84); The Detection Club (President 1986); Fellow, Royal Society of Literature, 1990. *Literary Agent:* The Peters Fraser and Dunlop Group Ltd. *Address:* 35 Northumberland Place, London, W2 5AS, England.

KEAY John, b. 1941, United Kingdom. Author. *Publications:* Into India, 1973; When Men and Mountains Meet, 1977; The Gilgit Game, 1979; India Discovered, 1981; Eccentric Travellers, 1982; Highland Drove, 1984; Explorers Extraordinary, 1985; The Royal Geographical Society's History of World Exploration, 1991; The Honourable Company, 1991. *Literary Agent:* David Higham and Assoc, 5-8 Lower John Street, London WI, England. *Address:* Succoth, Dalmally, Argyll, Scotland.

KEDYS Jonas Petras, b. 15 June 1914, Lithuania. Publisher; Editor. m. Justina Ankus, 15 Jan 1944, div 1977, 1 daughter. *Education:* Forestry Diploma, (Lith), 1938; Economics and Politics Degree, Erlangen, Germany, 1949. *Appointments:* Began Editing and publishing News Digest International, a quarterly magazine with the aim of educating the public on international politics; dictatorships of Communism, Facism, Military Tribal and Religious; Weaknesses of democracies and reviews of books and other publications. *Contributions:* Newspapers: Rebirth; Kaunas Echo; Free Lithuania (Chicago); The Worker (New York); Spring (English journal). *Memberships:* Founder member, Captive National Council in Australia, 1964; Delegate to State council, Ruling Body of the Liberal Party of Australia. *Address:* Box 533, Parramatta 2124, Australia.

KEE Robert, b. 5 Oct 1919, Calcutta, India. Journalist; Author; Broadcaster. m. (1) Janetta Woolley, 1948, (2) Cynthia Judah, 1960, 1 son (1 son dec), 2 daughters. *Education:* Magdalen College, Oxford. *Appointments:* Journalist, Picture Post 1948-51; Picture Editor, WHO 1952; Foreign Correspondent, Observer 1956-57, Sunday Times 1957-58; Literary Editor, Spectator, 1957; with BBC 1958-62, 1979-82, Independent Television 1962-79, 1984; now Freelnce Broadcaster, Presenter, 7 Days (Channel 4), TV series include: Ireland : a Television History (13 parts); The Writing on the Wall. *Publications:* A Crowd is Not Company, 1947; The Impossible Shore; The Impossible Shore; A Sign of the Times; Broadstrop in Season; Refugee World; The Green Flag, 1972; Ireland : A History, 1980; The World We Left Behind, 1939, 1984; 1945 : The World We Fought For, 1985; Trial and Error, 1986; Munich: The Eleventh Hour, 1988; The Picture Post Album, 1989. *Address:* c/o Lloyds Bank, 112 Kensington High Street, London W8, England.

KEEBLE Neil Howard, b. 7 Aug 1944, London, England. University Reader in English Literature. m. Jenny Bowers, 20 July 1968, 2 sons, 1 daughter. *Education:* BA Lampeter, 1966; DPhil, Oxford, 1974. *Publications:* Richard Baxter: Puritan Man of Letters, 1982; The Literary Culture of Nonconformity, 1987; Calendar of the Correspondence of Richard Baxter, 1991, co-author; Editor: John Bunyan: Conventicle and Parnassus, 1988; The Pilgrim's Progress, 1984; The Autobiography of Richard Baxter, 1974. *Contributions to:* numerous articles on cultural history, 1500-1700, in academic journals. *Honours:* Fellow of the Royal Historical Society, 1990. *Address:* Duncraggan House, Airthrey Road, Stirling FK9 5JS, Scotland.

KEEFE Susan E, b. 1 Dec 1947, Spokane, Washington, USA. Professor of Anthropology. m. Thomas K Keefe, 3 Sept 1971, 1 daughter. *Education:* BA 1969, Ma 1971, PhD 1974, Anthropology, University of California, Santa Barbara. *Publications:* Chicano Ethnicity, 1987; Appalachian Mental Health, editor, 1988; Negotiating Ethnicity, editor, 1989; Family and Mental Health in the Mexican American Community, co-editor, 1978. *Contributions to:* Human Organization; American Ethnologist; Hispanic Journal of Behavioural Sciences; American Journal of Community Psychology; Social Science and Medicine; Urban Anthropology; Ethnic Groups. *Honours:* Phi Kappa Phi. *Memberships:* Fellow, American Anthropological Association; Fellow, Society for Applied Anthropology; Southern Anthropological Society; Society for Medical Anthropology; Society for Urban Anthropology; Council on Anthropology and Education, Applachian Studies Association. *Address:* PO Box 949, Blowing Rock, NC 28605, USA.

KEEFFE Barrie (Colin). b. 31 Oct 1945, London, England. Playwright; Editor. m. (1) Dee Truman, 1969 (div 1979); (2) Verity Bargate, 1981 (dec 1981), two stepsons; 3. Julia Lindsay, 1983. *Appointments:* Actor at Theatre Royal Stratford East, London 1964 and National Youth Theatre, 3 years; Reporter, Stratford and Newham Express, London to 1969 and for news agency to 1975; Dramatist-in-residence, Shaw Theatre, London (Thames TV Playwright Scheme) 1977, and Royal Shakespeare Company, 1978. Since 1986, associate writer, Theatre Royal Stratford East; Since 1877 member of Council, National Youth Theatre; since 1978 member of the Board of Directors, Soho Poly Theatre, London. *Publications:* Plays include: A Mad World, My Masters (produced London 1977; San Francisco 1978, revised version produced London 1984) London, Eyre Methuen, 1977; Gimme Shelter, 1977; Frozen Assets (produced London and San Francisco, 1978 revised version produced London 1987), London, Eyre Methuen, 1978; Sus (produced London 1979, New York 1983) London. Eyre Methuen, 1979; Heaven Scent (braodcast 1979), published in Best Radio Plays of 1979, London, Eyre Methuen, 1980; Bastard Angel (produced London 1980) London, Eyre Methuen, 1980; Black Lear (produced Sheffield, 1980); She's So Modern (produced Hornchurch, Essex 1980); Chorus Girls, music by Ray Davies (produced London 1981); A Gentle Spirit, with Jules Croiset, adaptation of a story by Dostoevsky (also director: produced Amsterdam, 1981; London 1982); The Long Good Friday (screenplay) London, Methuen, 1984; Better Times (produced London 1985) London, Methuen, 1985; King of England, 1986; My Girl, 1989; Not Fade Away, 1990; Wild Justice, 1990; Gimme Shelter, 1990. Radio Plays: Good Old Uncle Jack, 1975; Pigeon Skyline, 1975; Self Portrait, 1977; Heaven Scent, 1979. Television plays include: Champions, 1978; Hanging Around, 1978; Waterloo Sunset, 1979; No Excuses series, 1983; King 1984. *Honours:* French Critics prize, 1978; Mystery Writers of America Edgar Allan Poe Award, for screenplay, 1982. *Literary Agent:* Harvey Unna and Stephen Durbridge Ltd, 24-32 Pottery Lane, London W11 4LZ or Gilbert Parker, William Morris Agency, 1350 Avenue of the Americas, New York, NY 10019, USA. *Address:* 110 Annandale Road, London SE10 0JZ, England.

KEEGAN Mary Constance, (Mary Heathcott, Mary Raymond), b. 1914, United Kingdom. Author. *Appointments:* Editorial positions: London Evening News, 1934-40; Straits Times and Singapore Free Press, 1940-42; MOI All-India Radio, 1944; Time and Tide, 1945; John Herling's Labor Letter, 1951-54. *Publications:* As Mary Keegan, Mary Heathcott or Mary Raymond: If Today Be Sweet, 1956; Island of the Heart, 1957; Love Be Wary, 1958; Her Part of the House, 1960; Hide My Heart, 1961; Thief of My Heart, 1962; Never Doubt Me, 1963; Shadow of a Star, 1963; Take- Over, 1965; Girl in a Mask, 1965; The Divided House, 1966; The Long Journey Home, 1967; I Have Three Sons, 1968; That Summer, 1970; Surety for a Stranger, 1971; The Pimpernel Project, 1972; The Silver Girl, 1973; Villa of Flowers, 1976; April Promise, 1980; Grandma Tyson's Legacy, 1982. *Address:* Cockenskell, Blawith, Ulverston, Cumbria, England.

KEEGAN William James, b. 3 July 1938, London, England. Journalist. m. Tessa Ashton, 7 Feb 1967, (div 1982), 2 sons, 2 daughters. *Education:* BA, honours, Cantab. *Appointments:* Economics Editor 1977-, Associate Editor 1983-, The Observer; Visiting Professor of Journalism, Sheffield University, 1989-90. *Publications:* Consulting Father Wintergreen, novel, 1974; A Real Killing, novel, 1976; Who Runs the Economy?, 1979; Mrs Thatcher's Economic Experiment, 1984; Britain Without Oil, 1985; Mr Lawson's Gamble, 1989. *Contributions to:* The Tablet; frequent Broadcaster. *Memberships:* Advisory Board, Department of Applied Economics, Cambridge, 1988- . *Address:* c/o Garrick Club, London WC2, England.

KEEN Geraldine. *See:* **NORMAN Geraldine.**

KEENE Donald, b. 1922, USA. Writer; Translator; Professor of Japanese. *Appointments:* Lecturer, Cambridge University, England, 1948-53; Currently: Shincho Professor of Japanese, Emeritus, Columbia University, New York City, USA; Former Guest Editor, Asahi Shimbun, Tokyo, Japan. *Publications:* The Battles of Coxinga, 1951; The Japanese Discovery of Europe, 1952, 2nd Edition, 1969; Japanese Literature: An Introduction for Western Readers, 1953; Anthology of Japanese Literature (editor), 1955; Modern Japanese Literature (editor), 1956; The Setting Sun, translation, 1956; Living Japan, 1957; Five Modern No Plays, translation, 1957; No Longer Human, translation, 1958; Sources of Japanese Tradition (editor), 1958; Major Plays of Chikamatsu, translation, 1961; The Old Woman, the Wife and the Archer, translation, 1961; After the

Banquet, translation, 1965; Bunraku, the Puppet Theatre of Japan, 1965; No: The Classical Theatre of Japan, 1966; Essays in Idleness, translation, 1967; Madame de Sade, translation, 1967; Friends, translation, 1969; Twenty Plays of the No Theatre (editor), 1970; Landscapes and Portraits, 1971; The Man Who Turned into a Stick, translation, 1972; Some Japanese Portraits, 1978; World Within Walls, 1978; Meeting with Japan, 1978; Travels in Japan, 1981; Dawn to the West, 1984; Travellers of a Hundred Ages, 1990; Seeds in the Heart, 1993; Three Plays of Kobo Abe, translation, 1993. *Memberships:* Japan Society, New York, Director 1979-82; Member American Academy of Arts and Letters; (foreign), Japan Academy, 1990. *Address:* 407 Kent Hall, Columbia University, New York, NY 10027, USA.

KEESING Nancy Florence, b. 7 Sept 1923, Sydney, Australia. Writer. m. Dr A M (Mark) Hertzberg, 2 Feb 1955. 1 son, 1 daughter. *Education:* Diploma of Social Studies, University of Sydney. *Literary Appointments:* Member Literature Board 1973-74, Chairman Literature Board 1974-77, Australia Council. *Publications include:* Poetry: Imminent Summer, 1951; Three Men and Syndey, 1955; Showground Sketchbook, 1968; Hails and Farewells, 1977. Garden Island People (Memoirs), 1975; Anthologies: Editor, with Douglas Stewart, Australian Bush Ballads, 1955 and Old Bush Songs, 1957; John Lang and The Forger's Wife, Biography, 1979; Lily on the Dustbin/Slang of Australian Women and Families, 1982, reprinted 1985; Riding the Elephant, 1988, reissued, 1989. *Contributions to:* Sydney Morning Herald; Australian; Bulletin; Overland; Southerly; Westerly. *Honour:* Member, Order of Australia (AM), 1979. *Memberships include:* Vice President, English Association (New South Wales); International PEN; Board Member, Overland magazine; Committee of Management, Australian Society of Authors; Royal Australian Historical Society; Australian Jewish Historical Society. *Literary Agent:* Curtis Brown Australia Ltd. *Address:* c/o Australian Society of Authors Ltd, P O Box 315, Redfern, NSW 2016, Australia.

KEIGER John Frederick Victor, b. 7 Dec 1952, Wembley, England. University Senior Lecturer. *Education:* Institut d'etudes Politiques d'Aix-en Provence, University of Aix Marseille III, FRance, 1971-74; PhD, University of Cambridge, 1975-78. *Publications:* France and the Origins of the First World War; Europe 1848-1914 (19 volumes in British Documents on Foreign Affairs, Reports and papers from the Foreign Office Confidential Print, 1988-92. *Contributions to:* Reviews for the Times Higher Education Supplement; History; International History Review. *Address:* Department of Modern Languages, Salford University, Manchester M5 4WT, England.

KEILLOR Garrison, b. 1942, Minnesota, USA. Writer. m. Ulla Skaerved, 4 children. *Education:* Graduated, University of Minnesota, 1966. *Appointments:* Worked on campus radio station, University of Minnesota; Presenter of live radio show, A Prairie Home Companion, 1974-87, by 1980 was being broadcast nationwide by satellite. Followed by The American Radio Company, 1989-. On both shows Garrison Keillor tells the story of the inhabitants of a mythical mid-Western town, Lake Wobegon. *Publications:* Lake Wobegon Days, novel derived from radio monologues, bestseller in United States, in UK, 1986, published in paperback 1987; Collection of short stories Happy To Be Here; Leaving Home, Short stories based on tales from Lake Wobegon published 1988, paperback 1989; We Are Still Married, collection of stories, essays and reflections, 1990; Radio Romance, 1992. *Honour:* Lake Wobegon Days, No 1 in Sunday Times Bestseller List, remained in list for over 20 weeks. *Address:* c/o Publishing Department, Faber and Faber, 3 Queens Square, London WC1N 3AU, England.

KEITH William John, b. 9 May 1934, London, England. University Teacher; Critic. m. Hiroko Teresa Sato, 26 Dec 1965. *Education:* BA Cantab, 1958; MA,

1959, PhD, 1961, Toronto. *Publications:* Richard Jefferies: A Critical Study, 1965; The Rural Tradition, 1974; The Poetry of Nature, 1980; Epic Fiction: The Art of Rudy Wiebe, 1981; Canadian Literature in English, 1985; Regions of the Imagination, 1988; A Sense of Style, 1989; An Independent Stance, 1991; Echoes in Silence, (poems), 1992; Literary Images of Ontarion, 1992. *Contributions to:* Frequent articles on Canadian literature to such journals as Canadian Literature, Essays on Canadian Writing. *Honours:* Fellow of the Royal Society of Canada, 1979-; Editor, University of Toronto, Quarterly, 1976-85. *Address:* University College, University of Toronto, Toronto, Canada M5S 1A1.

KELEN Stephen, b. 21 Mar 1912, Budapest, Hungary. m. Sylvia Margaret Steuart, 19 Jan 1951, 2 sons. *Appointments:* Managing Editor, Goodyear Tyre and Rubber Publications, Australia, 1960-77; Freelance Writer. *Publications:* I Remember Hiroshima, 1983; Uphill all the Way, 1974; Heed McGlarity, 1945; Jackals in the Jungle, 1941; Camp Happy, 1944; Goshu, 1965; I was There, 1940. *Contributions to:* various magazines, newspapers, and many radio documentaries, features and dramatised book reviews. *Honours:* 2nd Prize, Refugee Year Novel Contest; Order of Australia Medal, 1986. *Memberships:* Australian Society of Authors; International PEN, President Sydney Centre 1975-85, Life Member; Australian Journalists Association. *Address:* c/o Australian Society of Authors, P.O. Box 315, Redfern, NSW 2016, Australia.

KELLEHER Victor (Michael Kitchener), b. 19 July 1939, London, England. Lecturer; Writer. m. Alison Lyle, 2 Jan 1962, 1 son, 1 daughter. *Education:* BA, University of Natal, 1961; Diploma in Education, University of St Andrews, 1963; BA (with Honours), University of the Witwatersrand, 1969; MA 1970, D Litt et Phil 1973, University of South Africa. *Appointments:* Junior Lecturer in English, University of Witwatersrand, Johannesburg, 1969; Lecturer 1970-71; Senior Lecturer in English 1972-73, University of South Africa, Pretoria; Lecturer in English, Massey University, Palmerston North, New Zealand, 1973-76; Lecturer 1976-79, Senior Lecturer 1980-83, Associate Professor of English 1984-87, University of New England, Armidale, Australia. *Publications:* Voices From the River, Forbidden Paths of Thual, 1979; The Hunting of Shadroth, 1981; Master of the Grove, 1982; Africa and After, 1983; The Beast of Heaven, Papio, The Green Piper, 1984; Taronga, 1986; The Makers, 1987; Em's Story, 1988; Baily's Bones, 1988; The Red King, 1989; Wintering, 1990; Brother Night, 1990; Del-Del, 1991; To The Dark Tower, 1992; Micky Darlin, 1992. *Contributions to:* Articles and stories to magazines; Work represented in anthologies, including Introduction 6, 1977. *Honours:* Patricia Hackett Prize from Westerly magazine, 1978; Senior Writer's Fellowship from the Literature Board of the Australia Council, 1982; West Australian Young Readers' Book Award, 1982; West Australian Young Readers' Special Award, Australian Children's Book of the Year Award, 1983; Australian Science Fiction Achievement Award, 1984; Honour Award from the Children's Book Council of Australia, 1987; 3 Year Senior Writer's Fellowship, Literature Board of the Australia Council, 1989-91; Peace Prize for Australian Children's Literature, 1989; Honour Award, The Children's Book Council of Australia, 1991; Koala Award, 1991; Hoffman Award, 1992. *Membership:* Association of Australian Authors. *Literary Agent:* Curtis Brown, Australia. *Hobbies:* Running; Making Pottery; Working with Silver; Travel. *Address:* 1 Avenue Road, Glebe, NSW 2037, Australia.

KELLER Evelyn Fox, b. 20 Mar 1936, Professor of History and Philosophy of Science. 1 son, 1 daugher. *Education:* BA, Brandeis University, 1957; MA Radcliffe College, 1959; PhD, Harvard University, Department of Physics, 1963. *Publications:* A Feeling for the Organism: The Life and Work of Barbara McClintock, 1983; Reflections on Gender and Science, 1985, Secrets of Life, Secrets of Death: Essays on language, Gender and Science, 1992; ed, Women Science and Body, 1989;

Conflicts in Feminish, 1990; Keywords in Evolutionary Biology, 1992. *Contributions to:* Animals, Humans, Machines; Models of Scientific Practice; History of the Human Sciences; Journal of History of Biology; Social Studies of Science; Great Ideas Today; Perspective in Biology and Medicine; The Human Genome Initiative; The Annals of Scholarship. *Honours:* Distinguished Publication Award, Association for Women Psychology, 1986; Radcliffe Graduate Society Medal, 1985; AAUW's Educational Foundation 1990 Achievement Award; MacArthur, 1992; Honorary Doctorate, Mt Holyoke College, 1991; University of Amsterdam, 1993. *Memberships:* History of Science Society; Pres, West Coast History of Science Society. *Address:* Programme in Science Technology & Society, MIT, Cambridge, MA 02139, USA.

KELLER Janet Wynne Dixon, b. 12 Sept 1948, St Paul, Minnesota, USA. Anthropologist. m. Charles M Keller, 1 Aug 1980, 2 sons, 1 daughter. *Education:* BA Anthropology, UC Davis, 1970; PhD Anthropology, UC Berkeley, 1975; Postdoctoral appointment in linguistics, MIT, 1976. *Appointments:* Deputy Editor, American Enthnologist, 1983; Editor in Chief, American Anthropologist, 1989-93. *Publications:* Directions in Cognitive Anthropology, edotir, 1985; Book: Grammer and Dictionary of a Polynesian Outlier Language, 1983. *Contributions to:* Numerous to newspapers, and journals. *Memberships:* American Anthropological Association; American Ethnological Society. *Address:* Department of Anthropology, 109 Davenport Hall, 607 S Mathews Avenue, University of Illinois, Urbana, IL 61801, USA.

KELLER Mark, b. 21 Feb 1907, Austria. Editor; University Professor. m. 30 Dec 1930, 1 daughter. *Appointments:* Managing Editor, Editor, Quarterly Journal of Studies on Alcohol, Yale University, 1941-61; Editor, Journal of Studies on Alcohol, Rutgers University, 1962-77; Emeritus Professor, Documentation, Rutgers University, 1977-; Editor, Data (Johnson Institute), 1984-86. *Publications:* The Alcohol Language, with J R Seeley, 1958; CAAAL Manual, with V. Efron & E M Jellinek, 1965; A Dictionary of Words about Alcohol, with M McCormick and V Efron, 1982. *Contributions include:* British Journal of Addiction; Encyclopedia Britannica; Contemporary Psychology; Cancer Research; Medical Communications; Medical Tribune; Alkohologia, Budapest; Mercurio, Milan; Japanese Journal of Studies on Alcohol; Annals of the American Academy of Political and Social Science. *Honours:* Hammond Award for Distinguished Medical Journalism, American Medical Writers Association, 1976; Jellinek Memorial Award, 1977. *Memberships:* American Medical Writers Association; Council of Biology Editors; American Association for the Advancement of Science; American Professors for Peace in the Middle East; British Society for the Study of Addiction; American Public Health Association. *Address:* Centre of Alcohol Studies, Rutgers University, POB 969, Piscataway, NJ 08855, USA.

KELLEY Leo P(atrick), b. 1928, USA. Freelance Novelist and Short Story Writer. *Publications:* The Counterfeits, 1967; Odyssey to Earthdeath, 1968; The Accidental Earth, 1968; Time Rogue, 1970; The Coins of Murph, 1971; Brother John, novelisation of screenplay, 1971; Mindmix, 1972; Time: 110100, 1972, UK Edition The Man from Maybe, 1974; Themes in Science Fiction: A Journey into Wonder (editor), 1972; The Supernatural in Fiction (editor), 1973; Deadlocked, novel, 1973; Mythmaster, 1973; The Earth Tripper, 1973; Fantasy: The Literature of the Marvellous (editor), 1974; Science fiction novels for children: The Time Trap, 1977; Backward in Time, 1979; Death Sentence, 1979; Earth Two, 1979; Prison Satellite, 1979; Sunworld, 1979; Worlds Apart, 1979; Dead Moon, 1979; King of the Stars, 1979; On the Red World, 1979; Night of Fire and Blood, 1979; Where No Sun Shines, 1979; Vacation in Space, 1979; Star Gold, 1979; Good-bye to Earth, 1979; Western novels: Luke Sutton series, 9 vols, 1981-90; Cimarron series, 20 vols, 1983-86; Morgan, 1986; A Man Named Dundee, 1988; Thunder Gods' Gold,

1988. *Address:* 702 Lincoln Boulevard, Long Beach, NY 11561, USA.

KELLMAN Steven G, b 15 Nov 1947, Brooklyn, New York, USA. Critic; Professor. *Education:* BA, State University of New York, 1967; MA 1969, PhD, 1972, University of California, Berkeley. *Appointments:* Editor in Chief, Occident, 1969-70; Assistant Professor, Bemidji State University, Minnesota, 1972-73; Lecturer, Tel-Aviv University, 1973-75; Visiting Lecturer, University of California, Irvine, 1975-76; Fulbright Senior Lecturer, USSR, 1980; Assistant Professor, 1976-80, Visiting Associate Professor, University of California, Berkeley, 1982; Associate Professor, 1980-85, Professor, 1985-, University of Texas, San Antonio; Literary Scene Editor, USA Today; Partners of the Americas Lecturer in Peru, 1988. *Publications:* The Self-Begetting Novel, 1980; Editor, Approaches to Teaching Camus's The Plague, 1985; Loving Reading: Erotics of the Text, 1985; The Modern American Novel, 1991; The Plaque: Resistance and Ficiton, 1993. *Contributions to:* San Antonio Light; Village Voice; The Nation; Georgia Review; Moment; Newsweek; Modern Fiction Studies; Midstream; New York Times Book Review; The Washington Post Book World; The Gettysburg Review; Film Critic, The Texas Observer. *Honours:* Fulbright Senior Lectureship, American Literature USSR, 1980; Danforth Teaching Associate, 1981-86; ACLS Travel Grant, 1984, 1990, 1992, 1993; Finalist, NBCC Citation for Excellence in Reviewing 1984; H L Mencken Award, 1986. *Memberships:* PEN American Centre; National Book Critics Circle; MLA; Popular Culture Association. *Address:* 302 Fawn Drive, San Antonio, TX 78231, USA.

KELLMAN Tony, b. 24 Apr 1958, Barbados, West Indies. Journalist; Public Relations Practitioner. m. Pamela Emptage, 19 Dec 1981, 1 daughter. *Education:* Diploma, London School of Journalism, England; BA, English, History, University of The West Indies. *Appointments:* Participated, as Poet, Third International Book Fair of Radical and Third World Books, London, 1984. *Publication:* In depths of Burning Light, poetry, 1982. *Contributions to:* Articles, Art and Literary Reviews; Poems and Short Stories in, New Voices; Kyk-Over-Al; Bajan Magazine; Poems in North American Mentor Magazine; Wascana Review; Poetry Wales; Chelsea and Greenfield Review; Visions; Bim and Banja. *Honours:* 2 Awards, Creative Writing, Barbados National Independence Festival of Creative Arts, 1973; 2 Awards, Excellence, NIFCA, 1974; 2 Special Awards, Excellence, NIFCA, 1975; 2nd Award, North American Mentor Magazine's International Poetry Contest, 1984; Award of Merit, North American Mentor Magazine, 1985. *Memberships:* Fellow, World Academy of Literature; Barbados Museum and Historical Society. *Address:* First Avenue, Birds River, Deacons Road, St Michael, Barbados, West Indies.

KELLOGG Steven, b. 1941, USA. Children's Fiction Writer. *Publications:* The Wicked Kings of Bloon, 1970; Can I Keep Him, 1971; The Mystery Beast of Ostergeest, 1971; The Orchard Cat, 1972; Won't Somebody Play With Me, 1972; The Island of the Skog, 1973; The Mystery of the Missing Red Mitten, 1974; There Was an Old Woman, 1974; Much Bigger than Martin, 1976; Steven Kellogg's Yankee Doodle, 1976; The Mysterious Tadpole, 1977; The Mystery of the Magic Green Ball, 1978; Pinkerton Behave, 1979; The Mystery of the Flying Orange Pumpkin, 1980; A Rose for Pinkerton, 1981; The Mystery of the Stolen Blue Paint, 1982; Tallyho Pinkerton, 1982; Ralph's Secret Weapon, 1983; Paul Bunyan, 1984; Chicken Little, 1985; Best Friends, 1986; Pecos Bill, 1986; Aster Aardvark's Alphabet Adventure, 1987; Prehistoric Pinkerton, 1987; Johnny Appleseed, 1990; Mike Fink, 1992; The Christmas Witch, 1992. *Address:* Bennett's Bridge Road, Sandy Hook, CT 06482, USA.

KELLY A A. *See:* HAMPTON Angeline Agnes.

KELLY Charles M, b. 26 Feb 1932, Pittsburg, Kansas, USA. Management Consultant. m. 25 May 1989. *Education:* PhD, Purdue University, 1962. *Publications:* The Destructive Achiever: Power and Ethics in the American Corporation, 1988. *Contributions to:* Sloan Management Review; Business Horizons; Training and Development Journal; Productivity Review; Organizational Dynamics; Research Management. *Address:* 3050 Pointclear, Tega Cay, SC 29715, USA.

KELLY James Plunkett, b. 21 May 1920, Dublin, Ireland. Author. m. Valerie Koblitz, 4 Sept 1945, 3 sons, 1 daughter. *Education:* Synge Street Christian Brothers' School, Dublin Municipal College of Music, Dublin. *Appointments:* Assistant Head, Drama, Radio Eireann, 1955-61; Head, Features, Telefis Eireann, 1969-72. *Publications:* Strumpet City, 1969; Farewell Companions, 1977; The Gems She Wore, 1972; The Trusting and the Maimed, 1959; Collected Short Stories, 1977; The Risen People, 1958; The Boy on the Back Wall - and Other Essays, 1987; The Circus Animals, 1990. *Contributions to:* The Bell; Irish Writing; Bookman; Writing Today. *Honours:* Yorkshire Post Literary Award, 1969; Jacobs Television Script Awards, 1963, 1969. *Memberships:* Irish Academy of Letters, president 1974-76; Governor, Royal Irish Academy of Music, 1950-54; Council Member, Society of Irish Playwrights; Council Member, AOSDANNA. *Agent:* The Peters Fraser and Dunlop Group Ltd, London. *Address:* 29 Parnell Road, Bray, Co. Wicklow, Ireland.

KELLY M T (Terry). Author. m. 2 sons. *Education:* BA, English, Glendon College, 1970; B.Ed., University of Toronto, 1976. *Publications:* I Do Remember the Fall, 1979; County You Can't Walk In, 1979; The More Loving One, 1980; The Ruined Season, 1982; The Green Dolphin, 1982; County You Can't Walk In and Other Poems, 1984; A Dream Like Mine, 1987. *Contributions to:* Toronto Life; The Globe & Mail; Canadian Forum; Antigonish Review; many other professional journals and magazines. *Honours:* Finalist, Books of Canada Best First Novel of the Year Award, 1978; 7 Ontario Arts Council Grants for Creative Writing and Drama; Unbodied Souls, Nominated Best Short Story Fiction, National Magazine Awards, 1983; Winner, Toronto Arts Council Award for Poetry, 1986; Winner, Governor-Generals Award for literature, 1987, A Dream like Mine. *Memberships:* International PEN, Executive; The Champlain Society; Canadian Association in Solidarity with Native Peoples; Pollution Probe; Wilderness Canoe Association; Writers Union of Canada. *Address:* 60 Kendal Avenue, Toronto, Ontario M5R 1L9, Canada.

KELLY Patrick. *See:* ALLBURY Theo Edward Le Bouthillier.

KELLY Robert b. 24 Sept 1935, Brooklyn, New York, USA. Professor of English; Writer. *Education:* AB, City College of New York, 1955; Columbia UNiversity, New York, 1955-58. *Appointments:* Translator, Continental Translation Service, New York, 1956-58; Lecturer in English, Wagner College, New York, 1960-61; Instructor in German 1961-62, Instructor in English 1962-64, Assistant Professor 1964-69, Associate Professor, 1969-74, Professor of English 1974-, Director of Poetry 1981-, Avery Graduate School of the Arts, Bard College, Annandale-on-Hudson, New York; Assistant Professor of English, State University of New York, Buffalo, Summer 1964; Visiting Lecturer, Tufts University, Medford, Massachusetts, 1966-67; Poet-in- Residence, California Institute of Technology, Pasadena, 1971-72, University of Kansas, Lawrence, 1975 and Dickinson College, Carlisle, Pennsylvania, 1976; Editor, Chelsea Review, New York 1958-60; Founding Editor, with George Economou, Trobar magazine, 1960-64 and Trobar Books 1962-64, New York; Contributing Editor, Caterpillar, New York, 1969-73; Editor, Los I, 1977; Editor, Matter magazine and Matter publishing company, New York, later Annandale-on-Hudson, New York, 1963-; Contributing Editor, Alcheringa Ethnopoetics, New York 1977- and Sulfur, Pasadena, California 1981-. *Publications include:* Verse includes: Kill the Messenger Who Brings Nad News, 1979; Sentence, 1980; The Alchemist to Mercury, edited by Jed Pasula, 1981; Spiritual Exercises, 1981. Recording:

Finding the Measure, Black Sparros Press, 1968. Plays: The Well Wherein a Deer's Head Bleeds (produced New York, 1964) Published in A Play and Two Poems, with Diane Wakoski and Ron Loewinsohn, Los Angeles, Black Sparros Press, 1968; Eros and Psyche, music by Elie Yarden (produced New Platz, New York, 1971). Novels: The Scorpions, New York Doubleday 1967, London, Calder and Boyars, 1969; Cities, 1971; Short story: Wheres, 1978 and other publications. *Honours:* New York City Writers Conference Fellowship, 1967; Los Angeles Times Book Prize, 1980. *Address:* Department of English, Bard College, Annandale-on-Hudson, NY 12504, USA.

KELLY Russell John Cusack, b. 20 Sept 1949, Toronto, Canada. Writer; Editor. m. Joan McMahon, 1 May 1980, 1 son, 1 daughter. *Appointments:* Reporter, CBC Radio Halifax, 1972-75; Editor: CBC National Radio Newsroom, 1975-77; Editor in Charge, Edmonton CBC Radio News, 1977-80; Editor, British Columbia Bookworld, 1990-. *Publications:* Pattison, 1986; The Expo Story, 1987 (co-author). *Contributions to:* Toronto Globe and Mail; Vancouver Sun; New Internationalist Magazine; Edmonton Journal. *Memberships:* Writers Union of Canada; Canadian Society of Childrens Authors, Illustrators and Performers; Federation of British Columbia Writers. *Address:* 2218 West 13 Avenue, Vancouver, BC, Canada V6K 2S3.

KELLY Susan Croce, b. 6 Feb 1947, Berkeley, California, USA. Vice President, Corporate Affairs, Sandoz Agro Inc. m. Joel L Kirkpatrick, 16 March 1991. *Education:* BS, Psychology, Purdue University, 1969; MA AMerican History, St Louis University, 1973. *Publications:* Route 66, 1988; paperback, 1990. *Contributions to:* Numerous freelance articles to newspapers, small magazines. *Honours:* Missouri Press Women, 1975; Monsanto Communication Award, 1985; Chicago Women in Publishing Award, 1990; PR News Gold Key Award. *Memberships:* Chapter President, Public Relations Society of America; Chicago Communication Forum. *Address:* 1300 E Touhy, Des Plaines, IL 60018, USA.

KELLY Tim, b. 2 Oct 1937, Mass., USA. Playwright; Screenwriter. *Education:* BA, 1956; MA, 1957, Emerson College; American Broadcasting Co. Fellow, Yale University, 1965. *Publications include:* over 200 plays in print, including, Terror by Gaslight; Varney the Vampire; The Butler Did It; Fog on the Mountain. *Honours:* Numerous awards and grants, including, New England Theatre Conference Award; California Festival of Arts Drama Award; Aspen Playwrights Conference Award; Wayne State University Best Play Award. *Memberships:* Dramatists Guild; Authors League; Writers Guild of America. *Literary Agent:* William Talbot, Samuel French Inc., NY, NY. *Address:* 8730 Lookout Mountain Avenue, Hollywood, CA 90046, USA.

KELTON Elmer Stephen, (Alex Hawk, Lee McElroy), b. 29 Apr 1926. Novelist; Agricultural Journalist. m. Anna Lipp, 3 July 1947, 2 sons, 1 daughter. *Education:* BA, Journalism, University ofTexas. *Publications include:* The Time it Never Rained, 1973; The Good Old Boys, 1978; The Wolf and Buffalo, 1980; The Man Who Rode Midnight, 1987; The Day the Cowboys Quit, 1971; Stand Proud, 1984; Honor At Daybreak, 1991; Slaughter, 1992. *Contributions to:* Numerous articles for magazines and newspapers. *Honours:*4 Spur Awards, Western Writers of America; 4 Western Heritage Awards, National Cowboy Hall of Fame; Tinkle-McCombs Achievement Award, Texas Institute of Letters. *Memberships:* Western Writers of America, President 1963-64; Texas Institute of Letters, former Counselor; Sigma Delta Chi. *Literary Agent:* Sobel Weber & Associates, New York. *Address:* 2460 Oxford, San Angelo, TX 76904, USA.

KEMAL Yashar, b. 1923. Writer; Journalist. m. Thilda Serrero, 1952, 1 son. *Education:* Self Educated. *Publications:* (In English) Memed, My Hawk, 1961; The Wind from the Plain, 1963; Anatolian Tales, 1968; They Burn the Thistles, 1973; Iron Earth, Copper Sky, 1974; The Legend of Ararat, 1975; The Legend of the Thousand Bulls, 1976; The Undying Grass, 1977; The Lords of Akchasaz, Part I Murder in the Ironsmiths Market, 1979; The Saga of a Seagull, 1981; The Sea-Crossed Fisherman, 1985; The Birds Have Also Gone, 1987; To Crush The Serpent, 1991; novels, short stories, plays and essays in Turkish. *Honours:* Commander, Legion d'honneur, 1984; Prix Mondial Cino del Duca, 1982; Doctor Honoris Causa, Universite de Sciences Humaines, Strasburg, 1991. *Address:* PK 14, Basinkoy, Istanbul, Turkey.

KEMP Gene, b. 1926, United Kingdom. Children's Fiction Writer; Educator. *Appointments:* Teacher, St Sidwell's School, Exeter, 1962-74; Lecturer, Rolle College, 1963-79. *Publications:* Tamworth Pig series, 4 vols, 1972-78; The Turbulent Term of Tyke Tiler, 1977; Gowie Corby Plays Chicken, 1979; Ducks and Dragons (editor), 1980; Dog Days and Cat Naps, 1980; The Clock Tower Ghost, 1981; No Place Like, 1983; Charlie Lewis Plays for Time, 1984; The Well, 1984; Jason Bodger and the Priory Ghost, 1985; McMagus Is Waiting For You, 1986; Juniper, 1986; I Can't Stand Losing, 1987; Room With No Windows; Matty's Midnight Monster; Just Ferret; The Mink War. *Honours:* Children's Rights Award, 1977; Carnegie Medal, 1978; Hon MA, Exeter University, 1984; Runner-Up Whitbread, 1985. *Literary Agent:* Laurence Pollinger Ltd, England. *Address:* c/o Laurence Pollinger Ltd, 18 Maddox Street, London W1R 0EU, England.

KEMP Martin John, b. 5 Mar 1942, Windsor, Berkshire, England. University Professor. m. Jill Lightfoot, 27 Aug 1966, 1 son, 1 daughter. *Education:* MA, University of Cambridge, 1963; Academic diploma in the History of Art, University of London, 1965. *Publication:* Leonardo da Vinci, The Marvellous Works of Nature and Man, 1981; The Science of Art, 1990. *Contributions to:* Journals including: Art Journal-Art Bulletin; Burlington magazine; Bibliotheque de Humanisme et Renaissance; The Guardian; Journal of the Warburg and Courtauld Institutes; Medical History; Sunday Times; Viator. *Honour:* Mitchell Prize for the Best First Book on Art History, 1981; Armand Hammer Prize for excellence in Leonardo studies, 1992; British Academy Wolfson Research Professor, 1993-. *Literary Agent:* Caroline Dawnay, The Peters Fraser and Dunlop Group Ltd. *Address:* 45 Pittenweem Road, Anstruther, Fife, RY10 3OT, Scotland.

KEMP Patricia Penn, (Penn Kemp), 1 son, 1 daughter. *Education:* MEduc, University of Toronto, 1988; Honours in English Language and Literature, 1966. *Appointments:* Writer in Residence: Flesherton Library, 1988-89; Women and Words, University of Victoria, 1983; Niagara Eue Writers, New York State, 1984; Labrador, 1986. *Publications:* Binding Twine, 1984; Throo, 1990; Some Talk Magic, 1986; Eidolons, 1990; Bearing Down, 1972. *Contributions to:* Tessera; Prism. *Honours:* Arts Grants, Canada Council, 1979-80, 1981-82, 1991-92; Ontario Graduate Scholarship, 1987-88. *Memberships:* Writer's Union; Playwrithts' Union; League of Canadian Poets; CAPAC. *Address:* 136 Stephenson Ave, Toronto, Ontario, Canada M4C 1G4.

KEMP Penn. *See:* **PENN Patricia Penn.**

KEMPER Troxey, b. 29 Apr 1915, Oklahoma, USA. Editor; Novelist; Poet. m. Jeanne Doty, 31 July 1954, div 1964, 2 daughters. *Education:* BA University of New Mexico, Albuquerque, 1951. *Appointments:* Newspaper Reporter, 1951-69, Albuquerque Journal; Editor, Tucumcari Literary Review, 1988-. *Publications:* Comanche Warbonnet, 1991; Part Comanche, 1991; Mainly on the Plain, 1982; Whence and Whither, 1983; Folio and Signature, 1983. *Contributions to:* Poets and Writers Magazine; Small Press Review; Amarillo News Globe; Los Angeles Daily News; American Film Magazine. *Honours:* Honorable Mention, National Writers Club, 1990. *Memberships:* National Writers

Union; Sigma Delta Chi. *Address:* 3108 W Bellevue Avenue, Los Angeles, CA 90026, USA.

KENDALL Carol, b. 13 Sept 1917, Bucyrus, Ohio, USA, Writer, m. Paul Murray Kendall, 15 June 1939, 2 daughters. *Education:* AB, Ohio University, 1939. *Publications:* The Other Side of the Tunnel, 1956, 1957; The Gammage Cup, 1959 (as The Minnipins, 1960); The Big Splash, 1960; The Whisper of Glocken, 1965, 1967; Sweet and Sour Tales, retold by Carol Kendall and Yao Wen Li, 1978, 1979; The Firelings, 1981, 1982; Haunting Tales From Japan, 1985; The Wedding of the Rat Family, 1988; The Black Seven, 1946, 1950; The Baby Snatcher, 1952. *Contributions to:* Something About the Author Autobiography Series, Volume 7. *Honours:* Ohioana Award, 1960; Newbery Honour Book, 1960; American Library Association Notable Book, 1960; Parents Choice Award, 1982; Aslan Award, Mythopoeic Society, 1983. *Memberships:* PEN American Centre; Authors League of America; Authors Guild. *Address:* 928 Holiday Drive, Lawrence, KS 66049, USA.

KENEALLY Thomas Michael, b. 7 Oct 1935, Sydney, Australia. Author. m. Judith Mary Martin, 1965, 2 daughters. *Appointments:* Lecturer, Drama, University of New England, 1968-70; Visiting Professor, University California, Irvine, 1985; Berg Professor, New York University, 1988. *Publications:* Bring Larks and Heroes, 1967; Three Cheers for the Paraclete 1968; The Survivor, 1969; A Dutiful Daughter, 1970; The Chant of Jimmie Blacksmith, 1972; Blood Red, Sister Rose, 1974; Gossip from the Forest, 1975; Season in Purgatory, 1976; A Victim of the Aurora, 1977; Passenger, 1978; Confederates, 1979; Schindler's Ark, 1982; Outback, 1983; The Cut-Rate Kingdom, 1984; A Family Madness, 1985; The Play Maker, 1987; Towards Asmara, 1989; Flying Hero Class, 1991; The Place Where Souls are born, 1992; Now and in Time to be Woman of the Inner Sea, 1992. *Honours:* Booker Prize, 1983, Royal Society of Literature, 1983; Los Angeles Times Fiction Prize, 1983. *Memberships:* President, National Book Council of Australia, 1985-; Australia-China Council, Inaugural member, 1978-83; Chairman, Australian Society Authors, 1987-; Council, Australian Society Authors, 1985-; Literary Art Board Australia, 1985-88. *Address:* c/o Tessa Sayle Agency, 11 Jubilee Place, London SW3 3TE, England.

KENJO Takashi, b. 2 Feb 1940, Shizuoka, Japan. Professor; Technical Writer. m. 2 Apr 1968, 2 sons. *Education:* Tohoku University, 1964; Doctorate for Studies, Electric Machines, 1970,. *Publications:* Stepping Motors and Their microprocessor Controls; Electric Motors and Their Controls; Permanent Magnet and Brushless DC motors; Power Electronics for the Microprocessor Age; An Introduction to Ultrasonic Motors. *Contributions to:* Nikkei Sangyo Shimbun. *Address:* 3-4-17 Maehara-cho, Koganei-shi, Toyko, 184, Japan.

KENNAN George (Frost), b. 1904, America. History/ International relations Current affairs. Professor Emeritus, Institute of Advanced Study, Princeton. *Appointments:* Joined US Foreign Service, 1927; Vice Consul, Hamburg, 1927, Tallin USSR, 1928; Third Secretary, Riga Kovno and tallin, USSR 1929; Language Officer, Berlin, 1929; Third Secretary, Riga, 1931, Moscow, 1934; Consul, then Second Secretary, Vienna, 1935; Second Secretary, Moscow, 1935; with Department of State, Washington, 1937; Second Secretary 1938 and Consul, 1939, Prague, Second Secretary, 1939 and First Secretary, 1940, Berlin; Counsellor, Lisbon, 1942; Counsellor to US Delegation, European Advisory Committee, London 1944; Minister-Counsellor, Moscow, 1945; Deputy for Foreign Affairs, National War College, Washington, 1946; Director, Policy Planning Staff, Department of State, 1947-1950; on leave at Institute for Advanced Study, Princeton, 1950-51; Ambassador to the USSR 1952 until retirement from Foreign Services, 1963; numerous visiting professorships, 1954-60; Professor, Princeton Institute for Advanced Study, 1955; Ambassador to Yugoslavia, 1961-63; University Fellow in History and Slavic Civilizations, Harvard University, Cambridge, Massachusetts, 1966-70; Fellow, All Souls College, Oxford, 1969. President, National Institute of Arts and Letters 1865-68 and American Academy of Arts and Letters 1967-71. *Publications include:* Realities of American Foreign Policy, 1954; Soviet-American Relations 1917-1920, vol 1 Russia Leaves the War, 1956, vol 2 The Decision to Intervene, 1958; Russia, The Atom and the West (Reith Lectures) 1958; Soviet Foreign Policy, 1917-1945, 1960; Russia and the West under Lenin and Stalin, 1961; On Dealing with the Communist World, 1963; Memoirs 1925-50, 1967; Democracy and the Student Left, 1968; From Prague after Munich: Diplomatic Papers 1938-40, 1968; The Marquis de Custine and His Russia in 1839, 1971; Memoirs 1950-63, 1972; Cloud of Danger, 1978; The Decline of Bismarck's European Order: Franco-Russian Relations, 1875-1890, 1979; The Nuclear Delusion, 1982; The Fateful Alliance, 1984; Sketches From A Life, 1989; Around The Cragged Hill, 1992. *Honours include:* Numerous Honorific Academic Degrees including Oxford University, 1969; numerous literary prizes and distinctions; German, Order of Pour le Mérite for Arts and Sciences, 1979; The British Academy; The Presidential Medal of Freedom, 1990. *Address:* 146 Hodge Road, Princeton, NJ 08540, USA.

KENNEALLY Michael Anthony, b. 19 Sept 1945, Cork, Ireland. Professor. m. Rhona Richman, 25 June, 1978. 1 son. *Education:* BA Hons, University of British Columbia, Canada, 1968; MA McGill University, Montreal, 1971; PhD, University of Toronto, 1978. *Appointments:* Canadian Editor, Irish Literary Supplement, New York, 1981-; Co-Editor, Studies in English and Comparative Literature, 1986-; Editorial Board, The Canadian Journal of Irish Studies, 1990-. *Publications:* Portraying the Self: Sean O'Casey and the Art of Autobiography, 1988; Editor: Cultural Contexts and Literary Idioms in Comtemporary Irish Literature, 1988, Irish Literature and Culture, 1992; Editor, POetry in Contemporary Irish Literature, 1993. *Contributions to:* English Studies in Canada; Essays in several books of critical essays. *Memberships:* Canadian Association for Irish Studies, Pres, 1987-90; International Association for the Study of Anglo-Irish Literature, North American Vice-Chairman, 1991-. *Address:* Department of English, Marianopolis College, 3880 Cote des Neiges, Montreal, Quebec, Canada H3H 1W1.

KENNEDY Ludovic Henry Coverley, b. 3 Nov 1919, Edinburgh, Scotland. Writer; Broadcaster. m. Moira Shearer King, 1950, 1 son, 3 daughters. *Education:* Christ Church, Oxford. *Appointments include:* Editor, Feature, First Reading, BBC Third Programme, 1953-54; Lecturer, British Council, Sweden, Finland, Denmark, 1955, Belgium, Luxembourg, 1956; Introduced Profile, ATV 1955-56; Newscaster, ITV 1956-58; Introducer On Stage, Associated Rediffusion, 1957, This Week, 1958-59; Chairman BBC Features: Your Verdict, 1962; Your Witness 1967-70; Commentator, BBC Panorama, 1960-63; Election TV Broadcasts, 1966; Presenter, 24 Hours, BBC 1969-72, Ad lib, BBC L 1970-72, Midweek, BBC 1973-75, Newday BBC 1975-76; Interviewer, Tonight, BBC 1976-80; Presenter, Lord Mountbatten Remembers, 1980, Changes of Direction 1980, Did You See, 1980-, Great Railway Journeys of the World, 1980. *Publications:* Sub-Lieutenant, 1942; Nelson's Band of Brothers, 1951; One Man's Meat, 1953; Murder Story, 1956; Ten Rillington Place, 1961; The Trial of Stephen Ward, 1964; Very Lovely People, 1969; Pursuit : The Chase and Sinking of the Bismarck, 1974; A Presumption of Innocence: the Amazing Case of Patrick Meehan, 1975; The Portland Spy Case, 1978; Wicked Beyond Belief : The Luton Post Office Murder Case, 1980; A Book of Railway Journeys, 1980; A Book of Sea Journeys, 1981; A Book of Air Journeys, 1982; General Editor, The British at War, 1973-; Menace; The Life and Death of the Tirpitz, 1979; The Airman and the Carpenter: The Lindbergh Case and the Framing of Richard Hauptmann, 1985; On My Way to the Club (autobiography), 1989; Euthanasia, 1990; Truth To Tell (collected writings), 1991. *Honours:* Recipient, various honours and awards. *Literary Agent:* Rogers, Coleridge and White. *Address:* c/o 20 Powis Mews, London, W11 1JN, England.

KENNEDY Michael, b. 19 Feb 1926, Manchester, England. Journalist; Critic. m. Eslyn Durdle, 1947. *Appointments:* Staff Music Critic, The Daily Telegraph, 1950-; Chief Music Critic, Sunday Telegraph, 1989-; Northern Editor 1960-86, Associate Northern Editor, 1986-. *Publications:* The Halle Tradition, 1960; The Works of Ralph Vaughan Williams, 1964; Portrait of Elgar, 1968; History of Royal Manchester College of Music, 1971; Barbirolli, 1971; Portrait of Manchester, 1971; Mahler, 1974; Strauss, 1976; Britten, 1980; Concise Oxford Dictionary of Music, Editor, 1980; Oxford Dictionary of Music, 1985; Adrian Boult, 1987; Portrait of Walton, 1989. *Address:* 3 Moorwood Drive, Sale, Cheshire, England.

KENNEDY Moorhead, b. 5 Nov 1930, New York, USA. Educator; Retired US Foreign Service Officer. m. Louisa Livingston, 8 June 1955, 4 sons. *Education:* AB, Princeton University, 1952; JD, Harvard Law School, 1959; National War College, 1974-75. *Appointments:* Public lecturer and frequent guest on Network TV. *Publications:* The Ayatollah in the Cathedral, 1986; Co-author: (Think about) Terrorism, The New Warfare; Hostage Crisis; Death of a Dissident; Fire in the Forest; Nat-Tel 1995; Hinomaru; Metalfabriken. *Contributions to:* Criminal and Civil Investigation handbook, 1993; Collier's Encyclopaedia, all editions since 1962. *Honours:* LLD, Middlebury College, 1983; DPS, University od Pittsburgh, 1983; DPS, North Adams State College, 1991; Medal for Valor, Department of State, 1981; Gold Medal of National Institute of Social Sciences, 1991. *Memberships:* Church Club of NY; American Foreign Service Association; Board of Managers, International Programme Branch, YMCA of Greater New York; National Council. American for Middle East Understanding. *Address:* 55 Liberty Street Apt 7A, New York, NY 10005, USA.

KENNEDY Thomas Eugene, b. 9 Mar 1944, New York, USA. Writer; Editor; Translator; Teacher; Administrator. m. Monique M Brun, 28 Dec 1974, 1 son, 1 daughter. *Education:* BA, (summa cum laude), Fordham University, New York, USA; MFA, Vermont College, Norwich University, USA, 1985; PhD, Copenhagen University, 1988. *Literary Appointments:* Guest Editor, Nordic Section, Frank magazine, 1987; European Editor, Rohwedder, 1988-89; European Editor, Cimarron Review, 1989-; Contributing Editor, Pushcart Prize, 1990-; Advisory Editor, Short Story, 1990-. *Publications include:* Index of American Award Stories, 1970-90; Andre Dubus: A Study, 1988; Crossing Borders (novel) 1990; The American Short Story Today, 1990; Robert Coover: A Study, 1992; (ed) New Danish Fiction (forthcoming). *Contributions to:* Approx 200 stories, essays, poems, translations, interviews, reviews in: North American Review; Kenyon Review; Virginia Quarterly Review; American Book Review; American Fiction; Missouri Review; New Centers. *Honours:* T B Goodman Fund Grant 1969, 1970, 1971; Passages North, NEA Emerging Writer Award, 1987; Charles Angoff Award, The Literary Review, 1988; Pushcart Prize, 1990. *Memberships:* Executive Board, Danish Association for American Studies, 1988-92; Deputy Member, Executive Board, Nordic Association for American Studies, 1989-92; Danish Writers Union; Associated Writing Programs; Poets and Writers; Danish Chapter PEN. *Address:* Fragariavej 12, DK-2900 Hellerup, Denmark.

KENNEDY William Joseph, b. 16 Jan 1928, Albany, USA. Educator; Novelist. m. Ana Daisy Dana Segarra, 31 Jan 1957, 1 son, 2 daughters. *Education:* BA, Siena College, 1949; LHD, Hon, Russell Sage Collee, 1980; Dr Lit., Hon., 1984, D.Letters, Hon., Collee St Rose, 1985; Hon ArtsD, Hon LHD, Rensselaer Poly Inst, 1987; Hon Degree, Long Island University, 1989. *Appointments:* Assistant Sports Editor, Columnist, Glens Falls Post Star, 1949-50; Reporter, Albany Times-Union, 1952-56; Special Writer, 1963-70; Assistant Managing Editor, Columnist, PR, World Journal, San Juan, 1956; Reporter, Miami Herald, Florida, 1957; Correspondent, Time Life Publishers, in PR, 1957-59; Reporter, Knight Newspapers, 1957-59; Founding Managing Editor, San Juan Star, 1959-61; Lecturer, SUNY, 1974-82, Professor, English, 1983-. *Publications:* The Ink Truck, 1969; Legs, 1975; Billy Phelan's Greatest Game, 1978; Ironweed, 1983; Non-Fiction, O Albany!, with Francis Ford Coppola, 1983; The Cotton Club, 1983; Charlie Malarkey and the Belly Button Machine, 1986. *Contributions to:* various journals and newspapers. *Address:* Writers Institute, SUNY, 1400 Washington Ave., Albany, NY 12222, USA.

KENNEDY-MARTIN (Francis) Troy, b. 15 Feb 1932. Writer. m. Diana Aubrey, 1967, 1 son, 1 daughter. *Education:* BA, Honours, History, Trinity College, Dublin. *Publications:* TV Screenplays, BBC: Incident at Echo Six, 1959; Storyboard, and The Interrogator, 1961; Z Cars, 1962; Diary of a Young Man, 1964; Man Without Papers, 1965; Edge of Darkness, 1985; Thames TV: Reilly, Ace of Spies, 1983; Films: The Italian Job, 1969; Kelly's Heroes, 1970; (Books) Beat on a Damask Drum, 1961. *Honours:* BAFTA Scriptwriter's Award, 1962; Joint Screen Writers' Guild Award, 1962. *Address:* 6 Ladbroke Gardens, London W11 2PT, England.

KENNELLY Brendan, b. 17 Apr 1936, Ballylongford, Co Kerry, Ireland. Professor of Modern Literature. *Education:* BA (1st class Honours, English and French) 1961, MA 1963, PhD (Trinity College and Leeds University, Yorkshire England) 1966, Trinity College, Dublin. *Publications include:* Poetry: Good Souls to Survive, 1967; Dream of a Black Fox, 1968; Selected Poems, 1969, enlarged edition 1971; A Drinking Cup: Poems from the Irish, 1970; Bread, 1971; Love Cry, 1972; Salvation, the Stranger, 1972; The Voices, 1973; Shelley in Dublin, 1974, 2nd edition 1982; A Kind of Trust, 1975; New and Selected Poems, 1976, 1978; Islandman, 1977; The Visitor, 1978; A Small Light, 1979; The Boats Are Home, 1980; The House That Jack Didn't Build, 1982; Cromwell, 1983, reprinted 1984, 1986; Moloney Up and At It, 1984, reprinted 1987; Selected Poems, 1985; Mary, 1987; Love of Ireland, 1989. Novels: The Crooked Cross, 1963; The Florentines, 1967. Editor, The Penguin Book of Irish Verse, 1970, 1972, 1974, 1976, enlarged edition, 1981, 1988. *Contributions to:* International magazines. *Honours:* AE Memorial Prize for Poetry, 1967; Fellow, Trinity College, 1967; Critics' Special Harveys Award, 1988. *Address:* Department of English, Arts Building, Trinity College, Dublin 2, Republic of Ireland.

KENNET Lord (Wayland Young), b. 2 Aug 1923, London, England. Writer; Politician. m. Elizabeth Ann Adams, 1948, 1 son, 5 daughters. *Education:* Trinity College, Cambridge. Royal Navy, 1942-45. *Publications:* The Italian Left, 1949; The Deadweight, 1952; Now or Never, 1953; Old London Churches, with Elizabeth Young, 1956; The Montesi Scandal, 1957; Still Alive Tomorrow, 1958; Strategy for Survival, 1959; The Profumo Affair, 1963; Eros Denied, 1965; Preservation, 1972; The Futures of Europe, 1976; The Rebirth of Britain, 1982; London's Churches, with Elizabeth Young, 1987; Northern Lazio, 1990 with Elizabeth Young. *Address:* House of Lords, SW1A 0PW, England.

KENNEY Catherine, b. 3 Oct 1948, Memphis, Tennessee, USA. Writer; Professor. m. John Patrick Kenney, 1 June 1968, 1 son. *Education:* BA English, Siena College, 1968; MA and PhD English, 1970, 1974, Loyola University of Chicago. *Publications:* The Remarkable Case of Dorothy L Sayers, 1990; Thurber's Anatomy of Confusion, 1984. *Contributions to:* Dorothy L Sayers: A Centenary Celebration; Old Maids to Radical Women; 100 Great Detectives; Scholarly journals; Chicago Tribune; Christian Century; Chicago Sun Times; Arkansas Times. *Honours:* American Association of University Women Grant, 1983; Kilby Award from Wheaton College, 1984; Edgar Allan Poe Award Nominee, 1990. *Memberships:* Jane Austen Society of North America; Modern Language Association of America; Dorothy L Sayers Society; American Association of University Women; Sisters in Crime;

Mystery Writers of America. *Address:* 228 Stanley Avenue, Park Ridge, IL 60068, USA.

KENNEY Charles Colin, b. 8 July 1950, Boston, Massachussets, USA. Writer; Editor. m. Anne L Detmer, 27 Aug 1983, 1 son, 1 daughter. *Publications:* Dukakis: An American Odyssey, 1988; Riding the Runaway Horse - The Rise and Decline of Wang Laboratories, 1992. *Address:* 18 Cedarwood Road, Jamaica Plain, MA 02130, USA.

KENNY Adele,b. 28 Nov 1948. Poet; Teacher; Writing Consultant. *Education:* BA, English 1970; MS, Education, 1982. *Appointments:* Poetry/Writing Consultant 1980-; Artist in Residence, Middlesex County Arts Council, 1979-80; Poetry Editor, NJ Art Form, 1981-83; Grants Review Panelist, NJ State Council of the Arts, 1985; Henderson Award Judge, 1985; Japan Airlines Haiku Competition Judge, 1988; Associate Editor, Muse-Pie Press, 1988-. *Publications include:* Migrating Geese, 1987; Between Hail Marys, 1986; The Roses Open, 1984; Counseling Gifted, Creative and Talented Youth through the Arts, 1989; The Crystal Keepers Handbook, 1988; Illegal Entries, 1984; An Archaeology of Ruins, 1982; Starship Earth, 1990; Questi Momenti, 1990; Castles and Dragons, 1990. *Contributions to:* The Alchemist; Black Swan Review; Brussels Sprout; Home Planet News; Mirrors; Journal of NJ Poets, and others. *Honours:* Fellowships in Poetry, NJ State Council on the Arts, 1982, 1987; Merit Book Award, 1987, 1983; Writer Digest Award, 1981; Roselip Award, 1988; Haiku Quarterly Award, 1989. *Memberships:* The Poetry Society of America; The Haiku Society of America, President 1987, 1988, 1990. *Address:* 207 Coriell Avenue, Fanwood, NJ 07023, USA.

KENNY Sir Anthony (John Patrick), b. 1931, Liverpool, England. Philosopher; Fellow and Master, Balliol College, Oxford. *Publications:* Action, Emotion and Will, 1963; Blackfriars Edition of Aquinas' Summa Theologiae (editor and translator), 1964; Descartes, 1968; Aquinas, A Collection of Critical Essays (editor), 1969; The Five Ways, 1969; Descartes: Philosophical Letters, translation, 1969; The Nature of the Mind (with C Longuet-Higgins), 1972; Wittgenstein, 1973; Will, Freedom and Power, 1975; The Aristotelian Ethics, 1978; Aristotle's Theory of the Will, 1979; The God of the Philosophers, 1979; Aquinas, 1980; Thomas More, 1982; Wyclif, 1985; The Legacy of Wittgenstein, 1984; The Ivory Tower, 1985; Wyclif in His Times (editor), 1986; The Road to Hillsborough, 1986; God and Two Poets, 1988; The Metaphysics of Mind, 1989; Mountains: an anthology, 1991; Aristotle on the Perfect Life, 1992; What Is Faith? 1992; Aquinas on Mind, 1992. *Honour:* Knighted, 1992. *Memberships:* President, British Academy, 1989-; Member of British Library Board, 1991. *Address:* Rhodes House, Oxford OX1 3RG, England.

KENRICK Tony, b. 1935, Australia. Author. *Appointments:* Advertising Copywriter, Sydney, Toronto, San Francisco, New York and London, 1953-72. *Publications:* The Only Good Body's a Dead One, 1970; A Tough One to Lose, 1972; Two for the Price of One, 1974; Stealing Lillian, 1975, UK Paperback The Kidnap Kid, 1976; The Seven Day Soldiers, 1976; The Chicago Girl, 1976; Two Lucky People, 1978; The Nighttime Guy, 1979; The 81st Site, 1980; Blast, 1983; Faraday's Flowers, 1985; US Paperback Shanghai Surprise; China White, 1986; Neon Tough, 1988; Glitterbug, 1991. *Literary Agent:* Jean Naggar. *Address:* c/o 216 E 75th Street, New York, NY 10021, USA.

KENT Alexander. *See:* **REEMAN Douglas Edward.**

KENT Arthur (William Charles), (James Boswell, James Bradwell, M DuBois, Paul Granados, Alexander Karol, Alex Stamper, Brett Vane), b. 1925, United Kingdom; Author; Former Journalist. *Appointments:* Journalist: News Chronicle, London, 1943-46; Australian Daily Mirrors, 1947-53; Beaverbrook Newspapers, UK, 1957-69; BBC, London, 1970-71. *Publications:* Sunny (as Bret Vane), 1953; Gardenia (as Bret Vane), 1953; Broadway Contraband (as Paul Granados), 1954; El Tafile (as M Dubois), 1954; Legion Etrangere (as M Dubois), 1954; March and Die (as M Dubois), 1954; Revolt at Zaluig (as Alex Stamper), 1954; Inclining to Crime, 1957; Special Edition Murder, 1957; Kansas Fast Gun, 1958; Stairway to Murder, 1958; Wake Up Screaming, 1958; The Camp on Blood Island (with G Thomas), 1958; Last Action, 1959; Broken Doll, 1961; Action of the Tiger, 1961; The Weak and the Strong, 1962; The Counterfeiters, 1962; Long Horn, Long Grass, 1964; Black Sunday, 1965; Corpse to Cuba; Plant Poppies on My Grave, 1966; Red Red Red, 1966; Fall of Singapore (with I Simon), 1970; The Mean City (as James Bradwell), 1971; A Life in the Wind (with Z de Tyras), 1971; Sword of Vengeance (as Alexander Karol), 1973; Dark Lady (as Alexander Karol), 1974; The King's Witchfinder (as Alexander Karol), 1975; The Death Doctors; Maverick Squadron, 1975; The Nowhere War, 1975. *Address:* 26 Verulam Avenue, London E17, England.

KENT Helen. *See:* **POLLEY Judith Anne.**

KENT Philip. *See:* **BULMER Henry Kenneth.**

KENT Thomas Worrall, b. 3 Apr 1922, Stafford, England. Editor; Consultant. m. Phyllida A Cross, 1944, 3 sons. *Education:* MA, Corpus Christi College, Oxford; LLD, Dalhousie University, Canada, 1989. *Appointments:* Editorial Writer, Manchester Guardian, 1946-50; Assistant Editor, The Economist, 1950-54; Editor, Winnipeg Free Press, 1954-59; Vice President, Chemcell Ltd., Montreal, 1959-61; Special Consultant to Leader of Opposition, Ottawa, 1961-63; Co-ordinator, Programming, Policy Secretary to Prime Minister and Director of Special Planning Secretary Privy Council Office, 1963-65; Deputy Minister of Manpower and Immigration, 1966-68; Regional Economic Expanision, 1968-71; President, Chief Executive, Cape Breton Development Corporation, 1971-77, Sydney Steel Corporation, 1977-79; Chairman, Royal Commission on Newspapers, 1980-81; Dean, Administrative Studies, Dalhousie University, 1980-83; Professor, Public Administration, 1983-; Editor, Policy Options, 1980-88; Associate, School of Pilcy Studies, Queen's Unviersity, 1992-. *Publications:* Social Policy for Canada, 1962; Management for Development, 1985; A Public Purpose, 1988; Getting Ready for 1999: Ideas for Canada's Politics and Government, 1989. *Contributions to:* Numerous books of essays, journals and magazines. *Honours:* Officer of the Order of Canada, 1979. *Address:* RR 1, Box 29, Inverary, Ontario, K0H 1X0, Canada.

KENTON Maxwell. *See:* **SOUTHERN Terry.**

KENWARD Jean, b. 10 May 1920, Pangbourne, Berkshire, England. Writer. m. David Chesterman, 5 Sept 1945, 2 sons, 1 daughter. *Education:* Diploma, Speech & Drama, Central School. *Appointments include:* Lecturer, Complementary Studies, Harrow School of Art. *Publications:* A Flight of Words, 1971; The Forest, 1971; Old Mr Hotchpotch, 1974; Ragdolly Anna, 1979; Clutterby Hogg, 1980; Theme & Variations, 1981; 3 Cheers for Ragdolly Anna, 1985; Aesop's Fables, 1986; Ragdolly Anna's Circus, 1987; The Hotchpotch Horse, 1987; A Kettle Full of Magic, 1988; Ragdolly Anna's Treasure Hunt, 1989; Seasons, 1989. *Contributions to:* Country Life; Countryman; Script; Poetry Review; Middle Way; Child Education; Liberal Education; Over 60 Anthologies; Regular Broadcasts on BBC Schools. *Honours:* Premium Prize, Poetry Review, 3 times, 1940. *Address:* 15 Shire Lane, Chorleywood, Hertfordshire, England.

KENYON Bruce Guy, (Meredith Leigh, Daisy Vivian), b. 16 Aug 1929, Cadillac, Michigan, USA. Bookseller. m. Marian Long, 1950, (div 1954). *Publications:* As Daisy Vivian: Rose White, Rose Red, 1983; Fair Game, 1986; A Marriage of Inconvenience,

1986; The Counterfeit Lady, 1987. As Meredith Leigh: A Lady of Qualities, 1987; An Elegant Education, 1987. Also: The Forrester Inheritance, 1985; Wild Rose, 1986; Return to Cheyne Spa, 1988; A Certain Reputation, 1990. *Contributions to:* New Leaves; Harvest; Hidden Path; Manscape. *Memberships:* Authors Guild Inc; Authors League of America Inc. *Literary Agent:* Kearns and Orr. *Address:* c/o Kearns and Orr, 686 Lexington Avenue, New York, NY 10022, USA.

KENYON John (Philipps), b. 1927, United Kingdom. Professor of Modern History, St Andrews University. *Publications:* Robert Spencer, Earl of Sunderland, 1958; The Stuarts, 1958, 2nd Edition, 1970; The Stuart Constitution, 1966; The Popish Plot, 1972; Revolution Principles, 1977; Stuart England, 1978; The History Men, 1983. *Address:* 82 Hepburn Gardens, St Andrews, Fife KY16 9LN, Scotland.

KENYON Kate. *See:* **ADORJAN Carol.**

KENYON Michael, (Daniel Forbes), b. 26 June 1931, England. Author. 3 daughters. *Education:* MA History, Wadham College, Oxford, 1951-54. *Publications:* May You Die in Ireland, 1965; The 100,000 Welcomes, 1970; Mr Big, 1973; The Rapist, 1976; A Healthy Way to Die, 1986; Peckover Holds The Baby, 1988; Author of 35 articles in Gourmet Magazine, 1971-. *Memberships:* Detection Club. *Address:* 164 Halsey Street, Southampton, NY 11968, USA.

KEOGH Dermot Francis, b. 12 May 1945. Academic. m. Ann, 22 Aug 1973, 2 sons, 2 daughters. *Education:* BA 1970, MA 1974, University College, Dublin; PhD, 1980, European University Institute, Florence. *Appointments:* Lecturer, Department of Modern History, 1970-90, Jean Monnet Professor of European Integration, 1990-, University College, Cork. *Publications:* The Vatican, The Bishops and Irish Politics, 1919-1939, 1985; The Rise of the Irish Working Class 1890-1914, 1983; Ireland and Europe 1919-1989, 1989; Ireland, 1922-1993, (ed) Church and Politics in Latin America, 1990. *Contributions to:* Academic journals and national press. *Honour:* Fellow, Woodrow Wilson Centre for Scholars, Washington DC, 1988. *Address:* Department of Modern History, University College, Cork, Ireland.

KEOGH James, b. 29 Oct 1916, Nebraska, USA. Journalist; Government Official. *Appointments:* Joined Omaha Herald 1938, rising to Editor 1948-51; Contributor to Time, 1951, Editor 1956-68; Chief of Research, Presidential Election Campaign, 1968; Special Assistant to President Nixon, 1969-70; Director, US Information Agency, 1973-76; Executive Director, Business Roundtable, 1976-86. *Publications:* This is Nixon, 1956; President Nixon and the Press, 1972; Corporate Ethics: A Prime Business Asset, 1988; Centennial In Belle Haven, 1989. *Address:* Byram Drive, Belle Haven, Greenwich, CT 96830, USA.

KEPPEL Charlotte. *See:* **TORDAY Ursula.**

KERESZTURY Dezso, b. 6 Sept 1904. Literary Historian; Writer. m. Maria Seiber, 1934, Novàk Maria, 1986. *Education:* Budapest, Vienna and Berlin. *Appointments:* Lecturer, Librarian, Hungarian Institute, Berlin University, 1928-36; Lecturer, Hungarian Literature, Eötvös College, Budapest, 1935-45; Director of College 1945-48; Minister of Education 1945-47; Chief Librarian, Hungarian Academy, 1948-51; Head of Historical Collections, National Szechenyi Library until 1971. *Publications:* Arany Janos; Ungarn; A nemet irodalom kincseshaza; Balaton; helyunk a vilagban; A magyar irodalom kepeskonyve A magyar zenetortenet kepeskonyve; Magyar Opera es Balett Szcenika; A nemet elbeszeles mesterei; A nemet lira kincseshaza; Dunantuli hexameterek; Lassul a szel; emberi Nyelven; Festbeleuchtung auf dem Holzmarkt; S mi vagyok en; Uzenet; Orokseg; A Szepseg hasna; Egry breviarium; helyunk a Vilagban; A'rnyak Nyomában; Égö turelem;

Hatarok, frontok, Mindvegig; revised, adapted, 2 plays by Imre Madach. *Honours:* Banner Order of Hungarian Peoples Republic, 1974; Grillparzer Ring, Vienna, 1974; Herder Prize, 1976; State Prize, 1978; Ady Prize, 1978. *Address:* Semmelweis utca 4, 1052 Budapest V, Hungary.

KERFERD George Briscoe, b. 20 Jan 1915, Melbourne, Australia. Classical Scholar. m. Mariamna Clapiers de Collongues, 16 Dec 1944, 1 son, 1 daughter. *Education:* BA, University of Melbourne, 1936; BA University of Oxford, 1939; MA, 1943. *Publications:* The Sophistic Movement, 1981, 1984; Italian Translation, 1988. *Contributions to:* Numerous articles and reviews in classical and philosophical journals. *Honours:* Editor, journal, Phronesis, 1973-79. *Memberships:* Society for Promotion of Hellenic Studies, President, 1983-86, Member of Classical Association, President, 1990-91. *Address:* 31 Belfield Road, Manchester M20 OBJ, England.

KERMODE John Frank, Sir, b. 29 Nov 1919, Douglas, Isle of Man. Literary Critic. *Education:* BA, 1940; MA, 1947, Liverpool University; MA, Cambridge, 1974. *Publications include:* Romantic Image, 1957; The Sense of an Ending, 1967; The Classic, 1975; The Genesis of Secrecy, 1979; History and Value, 1988; An Appetite for Poetry, 1989; Uses of Error, 1991. *Contributions to:* The Guardian; NY Times; London Review of Books; New York Review of Books; New Republic, and others. *Honours:* Hon. Doctorates, Chicago University, 1975; Liverpool University, 1981; Amsterdam University, 1987; Newcastle University, 1993; Knighted, 1991. *Memberships:* FRSL; FBA; American Academy of Arts and Sciences. *Literary Agent:* The Peters Fraser and Dunlop Group Ltd. *Address:* 27 Luard Road, Cambridge CB2 2PJ, England.

KERN Gregory. *See:* **TUBB E C.**

KERNAGHAN Eileen Shirley, b. 6 Jan. 1939, Enderby, British Columbia, Canada. Writer. m. Patrick Walter Kernaghan, 22 Aug 1959, Enderby. 2 sons, 1 daughter. *Education:* Elementary Teaching Certificate, University of British Columbia. *Publications:* The Upper Left-Hand Corner: A Writer's Guide for the Northwest, co-author, 1975, revised, 1986; Journey to Aprilioth, 1980; Songs for the Drowned Lands, 1983; Sarsen Witch, 1988. *Contributions to:* Galaxy, USA; Room of One's Own, Canada; Womanspace, USA; The Window of Dreams, Canada; Northern Journey; Branching Out; Canadian Review; Origins; Nimbus; Tesseracts; Prism International, and others. *Honours:* Silver Porgy Award for original paperback (Journey to Aprilioth), West Coast Review for Books 1981; Canadian Science Fiction and Fantasy Award (for Songs from the Drowned Lands), 1985. *Memberships:* Writers Union of Canada; Federation of British Columbian Writers; Secretary, Treasurer, Newsletter editor, Burnaby Writers Society. *Literary Agent:* Jane Butler. *Address:* c/o Burnaby Arts Council, 6450 Gilpin Street, Burnaby, British Columbia, Canada V5G 2J3.

KERR Alex Arthur, (Andy Kerr), b. 11 Jan 1922, Sydney, Australia. Naval Officer; Attorney; Author. m. (1) Rusty Dreller, 1947, dec 1977, (2) Susan Jovovich, 1979, 1 son, 1 daughter. *Education:* BSc, US Naval Academy, 1944; JD, George Washington University Law School, 1954. *Publications:* A Journey Amongst the Good and the Great, 1987. *Contributions to:* Yachting magazines. *Address:* 98 Union Apt 1309, Seattle, WA 98101, USA.

KERR Andy. *See:* **KERR Alex Arthur.**

KERR Carole. *See:* **CARR Margaret.**

KERR Jean, b. July 1923, Scranton, USA. Writer. m. Walter Kerr, 1943, 5 sons, 1 daughter. *Education:* Catholic University of America. *Publications:* Jenny

Kissed Me (play), 1949; Touch and Go (play), 1950; King of Hearts (with Eleanor Brooke), 1954; Please Don't Eat the Daisies, 1957; The Snake Has All the Lines, 1960; Mary, Mary (play), 1962; Poor Richard (play), 1963; Penny Candy, 1970; Finishing Touches (play), 1973; How I Got to Be Perfect, 1978; Lunch Hour (play), 1980. *Honours:* Hon. LHD, Northwestern University, 1962; Campion Award, 1971; Laetare Medal, 1971. *Membership:* National Institute of Arts and Sciences. *Address:* 1 Beach Avenue, Larchmont, Manor, New York, NY 10538, USA.

KERR (Anne) Judith, b. 1923, Germany. Children's Fiction Writer. *Appointments:* Secretary, Red Cross, London, England, 1941-45; Teacher and Textile Designer, 1948-53; Script Editor, Script Writer, BBC-TV, London, 1953-58. *Publications:* The Tiger Who Came to Tea, 1968; Mog the Forgetful Cat, 1970; When Hitler Stole Pink Rabbit, 1971; When Willy Went to the Wedding, 1972; The Other Way Round, 1975; Mog's Christmas, 1976; A Small Person Far Away, 1978; Mog and the Baby, 1980; Mog in the Dark, 1983; Mog and Me, 1984; Mog's Family of Cats, 1985; Mog's Amazing Birthday Caper, 1986; Mog and Bunny, 1988; Mog and Barnaby, 1990; How Mrs Monkey Missed The Ark, 1992; The Adventures of Mog, 1993. *Address:* c/o Harper Collins Publishers, 77-85 Fulham Palace Road, London W6 8JB, England.

KERR M E. *See:* **MEAKER Marijane.**

KERR Michael. *See:* **HOSKINS Robert.**

KERSH Cyril, b. 24 Feb 1925. Author; Journalist. m. Suzanne Fajner, 1956. *Appointments:* Worked variously for newsagent, baker, woollen merchant and toy manufacturer, 1939-43; Reporter, then News and Features Editor, The People, 1943-54; Features Editor, Illustrated, 1954-59; Features Staff, London Evening Standard, 1959-60; Editor, Men Only, 1960-63; Daily Express (one day), 1963; Features Editor, then Senior Features Executive, 1963-76, Sunday Mirror; Editor, Reveille, 1976-79 (Fleet Street's First Photocomposition Editor); Assistant Editor, Features 1979-84, Managing Editor 1984-86, Sunday Mirror. *Publications:* The Aggravations of Minnie Ashe, 1970; The Diabolical Liberties of Uncle Max, 1973; The Soho Summer of Mr Green, 1974; The Shepherd's Bush Connection, 1975; Minnie Ashe at War, 1979; A Few Gross Words, 1990. *Address:* 14 Ossington Street, London W2 4LZ, England.

KERSHAW Peter. *See:* **LUCIE-SMITH John Edward McKenzie.**

KESSELMAN Wendy (Ann), b. America. *Appointments:* Teaching Fellow, Bryn Mawr College, Pennsylvania, 1987; Writer, composer and songwriter. *Publications:* Plays: Becca (for children) music and lyrics by Kesselman (produced New York, 1977); Maggie Magalita (produced Washington, DC 1980; New York, 1986); My Sister in This House, music by Kesselman (produced Louisville and London, 1987) New York, French, 1982; Merry-Go-Round (produced Louisville 1981; New York, 1983); I Love You, I Love You Not (one-act version produced Louisville, 1982; New York 1983; full-length version produced St Paul, 1986; New York, 1987); The Juniper Tree: A Tragic Household Tale, music and lyrics by Kesselman (produced Stockbridge, Massachusetts, 1982; New York, 1983) New York, French, 1985; Fiction for children includes: Time for Jody, 1975; Emma, 1980; There's a Train Going by My Window, New York, Doubleday, 1982, London, Hodder and Stoughton, 1983; Flick, 1983. *Honours:* Meet the Composer Grant, 1978, 1982; National Enodwment for the Arts Fellowship, 1979; Sharfman Award, 1980; Susan Smith Blackburn Prize, 1980; Playbiil Award, 1980; Guggenheim Fellowship, 1982; McKnight fellowship, 1985. *Literary Agent:* George Lane, William Morris Agency, 1350 Avenue of the Americas, New York, NY 10019, USA or Jane Annakin, William Morris

Agency Ltd, 31-32 Soho Square, London W1V 6AP, England. *Address:* P O Box 680, Wellfleet, MA 02667, USA.

KESSLER Jascha, b. 27 Nov 1929, New York, USA. Writer; Professor of English & Modern Literature. m. 17 July 1950, 2 sons, 1 daughter. *Appointments:* Professor of English and Modern Literature, University of California at Los Angeles, 1961-. *Publications:* American Poems: A Contemporary Collection, 1964; An Egyptian Bondage, 1967; Death Comes for the Behavioriest, 1983; Transmigrations: 18 stories, 1985; Classical Illusions: 28 Stories, 1985; Whatever Love Declares, 1969; After the Armies have Passed, 1970; In Memory of the Future, 1976; Bride of Acacias: The Poetry of Forough Farrokhzad, 1983; The Magician's Garden: 24 Stories by Geza Csath (with Charlotte Rogers), 1980; Opium, 1983; Under Gemini: The Selected Poetry of Miklos Radnoti, 1985; Medusa: The Selected Poetry of Nicolai Kantchev, 1986; The Face of Creation: 23 Contemporary Hungarian Poets, 1987; To Kolonos, 1988; Catullan Games, 1989. Writer of several plays and full length opera, The Cave. *Honours:* Recipient, various research grants and prizes, writing fellowships, 1952-; Major Hopwood Award for Poetry, University of Michigan, 1952; 2 Senior Fulbright Awards to Italy; Fellowship, National Endowment of the Arts, 1974; Rockefeller Fellow, 1979; Hungarian PEN Club Memorial Medal, 1979; George Soros Foundation Prize, 1989. *Memberships:* Poetry Society of America; ASCAP; American Literary Translators Association. *Address:* English Department, University of California at Los Angeles, 405 Hilgard Avenue, Los Angeles, CA 90024-1530, USA.

KESSLER Lauren Jeanne, b. 4 Apr 1950, New York City, USA. Author; Professor. m. Thomas Hager, 7 July 1984, 2 sons. *Education:* BS Northwestern University, 1971; MS University of Oregon, 1975; PhD, University of Washington, 1980. *Publications:* The Stubborn Twig: A Japanese Family in America, 1993; After All these years: Sixties Ideals in a Different World, 1990; Aging Well, 1990, 1987; The Dissident Press: Alternative Journ. in American History, 1984; When World Collede, 1984, 1988, 1992; The Search, 1991; Mastering the Message, 1989. *Contributions to:* Self, Working Mother, Modern Maturity, Us, Spring, Northwest magazine, Oregon magazine; Journalism Quarterly; Journalism History; American Journalism; Oregon Historical Quarterly. *Honours:* Council for Advancement of Secondary Education, Excellence in Periodical Writing, 1987; Sigma Delta Chi for Excellence in Journalism, 1987. *Memberships:* Association for Education in Journalism and Mass Communications; American Journalism Historians Association; Union for Democratic Communication. *Literary Agent:* Nat Sobel. *Address:* School of Communications, Allen Hall, University of Oregon, Eugene, OR 97405, USA.

KETTELKAMP Larry Dale, b. 1933, American. Writer of children's Fiction, Music, Psychology, Sciences, Supernatural/Occult topics. Freelance writer, editor, music teacher, composer, and lecturer, Institute of Graphic Design, Rider College, Lawrenceville, New Jersey, 1986-; Director, Bookarts Associates, Cranbury, New Jersey, 1982-. *Appointments:* Art Director, Garrard Publishing Co, Champaign, Illinois, 1959-60; Layout and Staff Artist, Highlights for Children magazine, Honesdale, Pennsylvania 1962-67; Director of Publications, Summy-Birchard Music, Princeton, New Jersey, 1981-82. *Publications:* Magic Made Easy, 1954, 1981; Spooky Magic, 1955; The Magic Sound, 1956, 1982; Shadows, 1957; Singing Strings, 1958; Kites 1959; Drums, Rattles and Bells, 1960; Gliders, 1961; Flutes, Whistles and Reeds, 1962; Puzzle Patterns, 1963; Spirals, 1964; Horns, 1964; Spinning Tops, 1966; Song, Speech and Ventriloquism, 1967; Dreams, 1968; Haunted Houses, 1969; Sixth Sense, 1970; Investigating UFIOs, 1971; Religions East and West, 1972; Astrology, Wisdom of the Stars, 1973; Tricks of Eye and Mind, 1976; Hypnosis, 1975; The Dreaming Mind, 1975; A Partnership of Mind and Body, Biofeedback, 1976; Investigating Psychics, 1977; The

Healing Arts, 1978; Lasers: The Miracle Light, 1979; Mischevious Ghosts: The Poltergeist and PK, 1980; Your Marvelous Mind, 1980; Electronic Musical Instruments: What They Do, How They Work, 1984; Starter Solos for Classical Guitar, 1984; Intermediate Etudes for Classical Guitar, 1984; The Human Brain, 1986; Modern Sports Science, 1986; Bill Cosby: Family Funny Man, 1987. *Address:* 2 Wynnewood Drive, Cranbury, NJ 08512, USA.

KEVILL-DAVIES Sally, b. 9 Jan 1945, London, England. Author. m. Rev. Christopher Kevill Davies, 16 May 1974, 2 sons, 1 daughter. *Education:* Queens Gate School, 1950-61. *Publications:* Yesterdays Children; The Price Guide to 18th Century English Pottery; The History of Jelly Moulds; Treasurers in Your Home (contributing editor); Christie's Wine Companion (contrib editor). *Contributions to:* The Times; Antique Collecting; Collectors Guide; Discovering Antiques; Barclaycard Magazine; Wine Press; Country. *Memberships:* Society of Authors; The English Ceromic Circle; Wedgwood Society. *Literary Agent:* Maggie Noach, 21 Redan Street, London W14 0AB. *Address:* The Old Bakery, Berden, Bishops Stortford, Herts CM23 1AE, England.

KEYES Daniel, b. 9 Aug 1927, New York, USA. Author. m. Aurea Georgina Vazquez, 14 Oct 1952, 2 daughters. *Education:* BA 1950; MA 1962. *Appointments:* Lecturer, Wayne State University, 1962-66; Professor, English, Ohio University, 1966-. *Publications:* Flowers for Algernon (Filmed as Charly), 1966; The Touch, 1968; The Fifth Sally, 1980; The Minds of Billy Milligan (non-fiction), 1981; Unveiling Claudia (non-fiction), 1986. *Honours:* Hugo Award, 1959; Nebula Award, 1966; Special Award, Mystery Writers of America, 1981; Baker Fund Award, Ohio University, 1986; Individual Artist Fellowship, Ohio Arts Council, 1986-87; Distinguished Alumnus Medal of Honour, Brooklyn College, City University of New York, 1988. *Memberships:* PEN; Associated Writing Programmes; Author's League of America; Dramatists Guild. *Literary Agent:* Ned Leavitt, William Morris Agency. *Address:* c/o William Morris Agency, 1350 Avenue of the Americas, New York, NY 10019, USA.

KEYISHIAN Marjorie Deiter, b. Brooklyn, New York, USA. English Instructor; Freelance Writer. *Education:* BA, MA, Columbia University. *Contributions to:* The New York Times; The Literary Review; New York Quarterly; Ararat; Phoebe; Fiction; Arts; Works; The English Record; The Massachusetts Review. *Memberships:* Northeast Modern Language Association; Shakespeare Association of America. *Address:* 110 Burnham Parkway, Morristown, NJ 07960, USA.

KGOSITSILE Kkeorapetse (William), b. 1938, South Africa. Poet; University Lecturer. *Appointments:* Currently: Lecturer in Literature, University of Nairobi, Kenya; African Editor-at-Large, Black Dialogue, San Francisco, California, USA. *Publications:* Spirits Unchanged, 1969; For Melba, 1970; My Name is Afrika, 1971; The Word is Here: Poetry from Modern Africa (editor), 1973; The Present Is a Dangerous Place to Live, 1974; A Capsule Course in Black Poetry Writing (with others), 1975; Places and Bloodstains: Notes for Ipelang, 1975. *Address:* Department of Literature, University of Nairobi, PO Box 30197, Nairobi, Kenya.

KHADDURI Majid, b. 27 Sept 1908, Mosul, Iraq. Educationist; Writer. m. Majdia Khadduri, 1942 (dec 1972), 1 son, 1 daughter. *Education:* American University, Beirut; University of Chicago, USA; BA; PhD; LHD, LLD. *Appointments Include:* Professor, Modern Middle-Eastern History, Higher Teachers College, Baghdad, 1948-49; Visiting Professor, Middle East Politics, Chicago & Harvard Universities, 1949-50; Professor, 1950-80, Professor Emeritus, 1980-, Johns Hopkins University; Director, Research & Education, Middle East Institute, 1950-80. *Publications:* The Liberation of Iraq from the Mandate (in Arabic), 1935; The Law of War and Peace in Islam, 1941; The Government of Iraq, 1944; The System of Government

in Iraq (in Arabic), 1946; Independent Iraq, 1951; War and Peace in the Law of Islam, 1955; Islamic Jurisprudence, 1961; Modern Libya, 1963; The Islamic Law of Nations, 1966; Republican Iraq, 1969; Political Trends in the Arab World, 1970; Arab Contemporaries, 1973; Socialist Iraq, 1978; Arab Personalities in Politics, 1981; The Islamic Conception of Justice, 1984; The Gulf War, 1988. *Memberships:* Secretary Treasurer, Baghdad PEN Club; American Society of International Law. *Address:* 4454 Tindall Street NW, Washington DC 20016, USA.

KHAN Masud Husain, b. 28 Jan 1919, Kaimganj, India. University Professor. m. 3 Feb 1948, 1 son, 4 daughter. *Education:* BA, University of Delhi, 1939; MA, 1941, PhD, 1945, Aligarh University; Doctorat d'Universite, Paris University; Professor Emeritus, Aligarh University, 1987. *Appointments:* Editor, Hamari Zaban (weekly), 1971; Editor, Qadim Urdu, 1971-78; Editor, Fikr-o-Nazar, 1971-73. *Publications:* Tarikh-e-Zaban-e-Urdu, 1948; Urdu Zaban Awr Adab, 1954; Do Neem, Poetry Collection, 1954; A Phonetic and Phonological Study of the 'Word' in Urdu, 1954; Dakhani Urdu Ki lughat, 1968; Sher-o-Zaban, (poetry & language), 1966; Edited, Old Texts: Qissa Mehrafroz-o-Dilbar, 1966, BiKat Kahani, 1966, Ashoor Nama, 1972; Ibrahim Nama, 1969. *Contributions include:* Urdu Adab, Fikro-Nazar; Qadim Urdu; Hamari Zaban. *Honours:* UP Urdu Academy Award, 1982; Sahilya Academy Award, 1984; Niaz Fatchpuri Award, 1985. *Memberships:* Taraqqi-e-Urdu, Anjuman; Taraqqi e Urdu Bureau, Ministry of Education, Vice Chairman; Vice-Chancellor, Jamia Urdu, Aligarh. *Address:* Javed Manzil, Jamia Urdu Road, Dodpur, Aligarh (UP) 202002, India.

KHATCHADOURIAN Haig, b. 22 July 1925, Old City, Jerusalem, Palestine. Professor of Philosophy. m. Arpine Yaghlian, 10 Sept 1950, Jerusalem. 2 sons, 1 daughter. *Education:* BA, MA, American University of Beirut, Lebanon; PhD, Duke University, USA. *Appointments:* American University of Beirut, Lebanon, 1948-49, 1951-67; Assistant Instructor - Full Professor of Philosophy; Professor of Philosophy, University of Southern California, 1968-69; Professor of Philosophy, University of Wisconsin-Milwaukee, 1969-. *Publications:* The Coherence Theory of Truth: A Critical Evaluation, 1961; (Poetry) Traffic with Time (with others), 1963; A Critical Study in Method, 1967; The Concept of Art, 1971; Shadows of Time (poetry), 1983; Music, Film & Art, 1985. *Contributions to:* Numerous professional & Literary journals. *Memberships include:* Various Philosophical Societies. *Honours include:* Phi Beta Kappa, 1956; J. Walker Tomb Essay Prize, Princeton University, 1958; 2nd prize, World Essay Contest, International Humanist & Ethical Union, Netherlands, 1959; 1st Prize, poetry contest, Ararat, New York, USA, 1962; Harvard University International Seminar, under the direction of Dr Henry Kissinger, 1962; Prize, essay contest, 1964, Ararat, USA; Outstanding Educators of America Award, 1973; Visiting Professor, University of Wisconsin-Milwaukee, 1967-68; Visiting Professor, University of Hawaii, 1977; Distinguished Visiting Professor, Unviersity of New Mexico, 1978-79; Liberal Arts Fellow, Philosophy & Law, Harvard Law School, 1982-83; University of Wisconsin-Milwaukee Foundation Research Award, 1983-94; Phi Kappa Phi, 1985; University of Wisconsin-Milwaukee Alumni Association's 1987 Award for Excellence in Teaching. *Address:* Department of Philosophy, University of Wisconsin, Milwaukee, WI 53201, USA.

KHATENA Joe, b. 25 Oct 1925, Singapore. University Professor. m. 17 Dec 1950, 2 sons, 2 daughters. *Education:* Normal Trained Certificate, Education, Singapore Teachers Training College, 1953; Certificate of Education, University of Malaya, 1957; BA (General) 1960; BA (Honours) English 1961; University of Malaya; MEd, Education, University of Singapore, 1965; PhD, Psychology , University of Georgia, 1969. *Literary Appointments:* Member of Editorial Boards of Gifted Child Quarterly 1975 and Journal of Mental Imagery

1982; Guest Editor of Gifted Child Quarterly 1975 and 1979. *Publications:* Thinking Creatively With Sounds and Words (co-author Torrance) 1973; Khatena-Torrance Creative Perception Inventory 1976; The Creatively Gifted Child, 1978; Educating The Ablest 2nd Edition (co-editors Gowan and Torrance) 1979; Teaching Gifted Children to Use Creative Imag. Imagery, 1979; Images of The Inward Eye: Poems 1981; Creative Imag. Imagery Actionbook, 1981; Creativity: Its Educational Implications 2nd Edition (co-editors Gowan and Torrance), 1981; Educational Psychology of The Gifted 1982; Imagery and Creative Imagination 1984; Khatena-Morse Multitalent Perception Inventory 1987. *Contributions to:* Over 100 contributions: Journal Articles; Journals: Perceptual and Motor Skills; Psychological Reports; Journal of Educational Psychology; Gifted Child Quarterly; Journal of Creative Behaviour; Sociology and Social Research; Art Psychotherapy; Educational Trends; Indian Journal of Psychology; Humanitas; Journal of Mental Imagery; APA Proceedings. *Honours:* University Scholarships, University of Malaya, 1956-61; Book Award, University of Malaya, 1957; Fellow of American Psychological Association, 1975; Marshall University Research Award, 1976; USOE Office of Gifted Certificate of Recognition 1976; Distinguished Scholar Award, 1982; Distinguished Service Award, 1983; (Both by National Association for Gifted Children) Life member of National Association for Gifted Children 1982; Distinguished Lecturer of Texas Womens' University 1985; Fulbright Senior Lecturer Award to India 1985. *Memberships:* National Association For Gifted Children, President 1977-79; American Psychological Association, Fellow 1975; Creative Education Foundation, Colleague 1983; American Education Research Association 1972; New York Academy of Sciences 1985; Kappa Delta Phi, 1968; Phi Kappa Phi 1984. *Address:* Department of Educational Psychology; Drawer EP, Mississippi State University, Mississippi State, MS 39762, USA.

KHAYAM Massoud, b. 5 May 1947, Tehran, Iran. Consultant Engineer. m. T Z Ganji, 7 Oct 1976, 2 sons, 1 daughter. *Education:* Diploma, 1966; MSc Engineering, 1975; BSc Engineering, 1971; Research Officer, 1976-79. *Appointments:* Lecturer, Tehran University of Science, 1990; Assistant Editor, Safar Quarterly 1991; Asst Editor in Chief, Donya Sokhan monthly magazine, 1990; Science Editor, Adine, monthly magazine, 1988; In charge of Homa University, 1986; Lecturer, Navy University, 1978. *Publications:* Human Zoo, novel, 1991; Shahnameh in Land Rover, (humour), 1990; Universal Construction of Knowledge, 1982; Earthly (collected essays), 1988; Black Hole, 1982; Omar Khayam and golden age of Mathematics, 1990; Mana and Nima, novel, in press; On War, collection of short stories; Narrow Stream; and a further five books mostly banned in Iran. *Contributions to:* Most of the Private journals in Iran. *Honours:* Best Lecturer Award. *Memberships:* Informatic Society. *Literary Agent:* Pary Ganji Tehran. *Address:* PO Box 15875, Tehran 3168, Iran.

KHERDIAN David, b. 1931, American, Writer - Poetry, Literature, Biography. Director, Two Rivers Press, 1978-. *Appointments:* Literary Consultant, Northwestern University, Evanston, Illinois, 1965; Publisher, Giligia Press, 1967-73; Poetry Judge, Institute of American Indian Arts, Santa Fe, New Mexico, 1968; Editor, Ararat magazine, 1970; Poet-in-the-Schools, State of New Hampshire, 1971. *Publications include:* (with G Hausman), Eight Poems, 1968; Six San Francisco Poets, 1969; On the Death of My Father and Other Poems, 1970; (ed with J Baloian), Down at the Santa Fe Depot: Twenty Fresno Poets, 1970; Homage to Adana, 1970; Looking Over Hills, 1972; (ed) Visions of America: By the Poets of Our Time, 1973; A David Kherdian Sampler, 1974; The Nonny Poems, 1974; (ed) Settling Smerica: The Ethnic Expression of Fourteen Contemporary Poets, 1974; Any Day of Your Life, 1975; (ed) Poems Here and Now, 1976; (ed) The Dog Writes on the Window with His Nose and Other Poems, 1977; (ed) Traveling America with Today's Poets, 1977; (ed) If Dragon Flies Made Honey, 1977; Country Cat, City Cat, 1978; I Remember Root River, 1978; (ed) I Sing

the Song of Myself, 1978; The Road from Home: The Story of an Armenian Girl, 1979; The Farm, 1979; (trans), The Pearl: Hymn of the Robe of Glory, 1979; It Started with Old Man Bean 1980; Finding Home, 1981; Beyond Two Rivers, 1981; Taking the Soundings on Third Avenue, 1981; The Farm: Book Two, 1981; (trans), Pigs Never See the Stars: Proverbs from the Armenian, 1982; The Song in the Walnut Grove, 1983; The Mystery of the Diamond in the Wood, 1983; Right Now, 1983; The Animal, 1984; Root River Run, 1984; Threads of Light, 1985.

KHOSLA Gurdial Singh, b. 15 Jan 1912, Lahore. Writer. m. Manorama, 16 Oct 1941, 1 son, 1 daughter. *Education:* BA Hons, 1931, MA, 1933, English, Punjab University, Lahore. *Appointments:* Lecturer in English, Khalsa College, Amritsar, 1934-35; General Manager, Western Railway, 1967-70; Adviser and Head, Department of Dramatic Arts, Pubjab University, 1970-72. *Publications:* Plays: The Daughter at the Doorstep; The Homeless and otehr one-act plays; Mar Milthn Wale; Before Doomsday; The Auction of a City; Literary and Other Essays, 1951. *Contributions to:* Punjabi Duniya, Punjabi Sahit, The Indian Express, Sun; Observer; The Statesman; Hundustan Times; Times of India. *Honours:* Eminent Theatreman, Delhi Natya Sangh and President of India at World Punjabi Conference; Drama Award, Punjabi Academy, Delhi, 1988 and Sahitya Academy Pubjab, 1989. *Memberships:* PEN: President, Pubjabi Theatre; Founder member and Treasurer, Authors Guild of India, 1974-81; Founder member and President, Conservation Society Delhi, 1983-86; Hon Secretary, General Indian Heritage Society. *Address:* D-103 Defence Colony, New Delhi 110- 024, India.

KHRUSHCHEV Sergei Nikitich, b. 2 July 1935, Moscow, Russia. Control Systems Engineer. m. Valentina N Golenko, 3 aug 1985, 3 sons. *Education:* Moscow Electrical Institute, 1952-58; PhD Eng, Moscow Technical University, 1967; Asst Prof, Moscow Technical University, 1968; Doctor's Degree Ukranian Academy of Science, 1988; Professor, Control Computer Inst, 1989. *Appointments:* Columnist, Asia Inc, business magazine for Pacific region, 1992-. *Publications:* Khrushchev on Khrushchev, 1990; Pensioner Sousnogo Znachenia, 1991; Khrushchev: Crises and Missiles, 1992. *Contributions to:* Magazines in USSR and Russia, including Ogonck. 150 different articles internationally. *Honours:* Lenin Prize of Engineering, 1959; Council of Ministers Prize, USSR, 1985; Hero of Socialist Labour, 1963. *Membership:* International Informatization Academy, Russian Computer Society. *Literary Agent:* Andrew Nurnberg, London. *Address:* 3 Laurelhurst Road, Cranston, RI 02930, USA.

KIBIROV Timur. See: ZAPOEV Timur.

KIDD Charles William, b. 23 May 1952, Danby, Yorkshire, England. Editor. *Education:* St Peter's School, York; Bede College, Durham. *Literary Appointments:* Assistant editor, Burke's Peerage 1972-77, Debrett's Peerage 1977-80; Editor, Debrett, 1980-90. *Publications:* Editor Debrett's Peerage, 1985; Debrett's Book of Royal Children, co-author, 1982; Debrett Goes To Hollywood, 1986. *Contributions to:* Times; Telegraph; Harper's & Queen. *Membership:* Society of Genealogists. *Address:* c/o Debrett's Peerage Ltd, 73-77 Britannia Road, London SW6 2JR, England.

KIDD Ian Gray, b. 6 Mar 1922, Chandernagore, India. University Professor Emeritus. m. Sheila Elizabeth Dow, 17 Dec 1949, 3 sons. *Education:* MA St Andrews Univ, 1947; BA, MA, Lit Hunamiores, Queen's College, Oxford, 1947-49. *Publications:* Posidonius I, The Fragments, 1972, 1989; Posidonius II, A-B, The Commentary, 1988. *Contributions to:* Literature and Western Civilisation Vol I, 1972; The Stoics, 1978; Problems in Stoicism, 1971; The Criterion of Truth, 1989; The Encyclopaedia of Philosophy, 1967; Articles and Reviews in learned journals including: Classical Quarterly; Classical Review; Journal of Hellenic Studies;

Philosophical Quarterly; Philosophical Books. *Honours:* Member, Institute for Advanced Study, Princeton, 1971-72, 1979-80; Honorary Fellow: St Leonard's College, St Andrews, and, Institute for Research in Classical Philosophy and Science, Princeton. *Address:* Ladebury, Lade Braes Lane, St Andrews, Fife KY16 9EP, Scotland.

KIDD Virginia, b. 2 June 1921, Germantown, Philadelphia, Pennsylvania, USA. Literary agent. m. (1) Jack Emden, 17 Apr 1943 (div 1947), (2) James Blish, 23 May 1947 (div 1964), 2 sons, 2 daughters. *Publications:* Saving Worlds (aka The Wounded Planet), 1973 (co-edited w Roger Elwood); The Best of Judith Merril (editor), 1976; Millennial Women, 1978; Edges (co-edited w Ursula K Le Guin), 1980; Interfaces (co-edited w Ursula K Le Guin) 1980. *Contributions to:* various journals and magazines including: The Mad River Review; Just Friends, Accent, Speculative Poetry Review; short stories: Galaxy, Venus, Quark. *Memberships:* Science Fiction & Fantasy Writers of America; Science Fiction Research Association; Science Fiction Poetry Association; Academy of American Poets; Authors Guild. *Address:* 538 E. Harford St, PO Box 278, Milford, PA 18337, USA.

KIDMAN Fiona Judith, b. 26 Mar 1940, Hawera, New Zealand. Writer. m. Ernest I R Kidman, 20 Aug 1960, 1 son, 1 daughter. *Publications:* A Breed of Women, 1979; Mandarin Summer, 1981; Paddy's Puzzle, 1983; The Book of Secrets, 1987; Unsuitable Friends, 1988; True Stars, 1990; Mrs Dixon and Friends, 1982; Going to the Chathams, 1985; Wakeful Nights, (poems), 1991. *Contributions to:* Numerous. *Honours:* Scholarship in Letters, 1981, 1985, 1991; QE II Arts Council Award for Achievement, 1988; OBE, 1988; New Zealand Book Award for Fiction, 1988. *Memberships:* Secretary, 1972-75, President, 1980-82, PEN International NZ Centre; Secretary Organiser, 1972-75, President, 1992-, New Zealand Book Council; New Zeland Writer's Guild; Media Women. *Literary Agent:* Ray Richards, Richards Literary Agency, PO Box 31-240 Milford, Auckland, New Zealand. *Address:* 28 Rakan Road, Hataitai, Wellington 3, New Zealand.

KIEFER Middleton. *See:* **KIEFER Warren & MIDDLETON Harry.**

KIEFER Warren (David), (Kiefer Middleton with Harry Middleton), b. 1930, USA. Author. *Appointments:* Director, Intercontinental Management Associates, Assistant Manager, International Public Relations, Chas Pfizer & Co Inc, 19544-57; Television Documentary Film Writer, 1958-74. *Publications:* Pax (with Harry Middleton with joint pseudonym Middleton Kiefer), 1958; Castle of the Living Dead, screenplay, 1964; The Outrider, screenplay, 1967; Juliette de Sade, screenplay, 1968; Michael Stroganoff, screenplay, 1969; The Last Rebel, screenplay, 1970; The Kidnappers, screenplay, 1971; By Force of Arms, screenplay, 1972; The Lingala Code, 1972; Farewell to the King (with Pierre Schoendoerffer), 1973; Pontius Pilate Papers, novel, 1976; The Snow Queen, novel, 1979. *Address:* Sarmiento 1881, Buenos Aires, Argentina.

KIELY Benedict, b. 1919, Dromore, Co Tyrone, Ireland. Writer. *Education:* Christian Brothers' School, Omagh and National University of Ireland; Visiting Professor & Writer in Residence at several US Universities. *Appointments:* Journalist in Dublin, 1940-65. *Publications include:* Novels: Land Without Stars, 1946; In a Harbour Green, 1949; Call for a Miracle, 1950; Honey Seems Bitter, 1952; The Cards of the Gambler: a Folktale, 1953; There was an Ancient House, 1955; The Captain with the Whiskers, 1960; Dogs Enjoy the Morning, 1968; Proxopera: a Novella, 1977; Nothing Happens in Carmincross, 1985; Drink To The Bird - A Memoir, 1991. Short story collections, Non-fiction and edited works; Selected Stories, 1993. *Honours:* American Irish Foundation Award, 1980; Irish Academy of Letters Award, 1980; Irish Independent Literary Award, 1985; D Litt (hc), National University of Ireland

and of Queen's University, Belfast. *Address:* 119 Morehampton Road, Donnybrook, Dublin 4, Eire.

KIENZLE William X, b. 11 Sept 1928, Detroit, Michigan, USA, Author. m. Javan Herman Andrews, Nov 1974. *Education:* BA, Sacred Heart Seminary College, 1950; St John's Seminary, 1950-54. *Publications:* The Rosary Murders, 1979; Death Wears a Red Hat, 1980; Mind Over Murder, 1981; Assault with Intent, 1982; Shadow of Death, 1983; Kill and Tell, 1984; Sudden Death, 1985; Deathbed, 1986; Deadline for a Critic, 1987; Marked for Murder, 1988; Eminence, 1989; Masquerade, 1990; Chameleon, 1991; Body Count, 1992; Dead Wrong, 1993. *Contributions To:* Editor, The Michigan Catholic, 1962-74; Editor, MPLS Magazine, 1974-76. *Honours:* Michigan Knights of Columbus Journalism Award for General Excellence, 1963; Honorable Mention, Catholic Press Association for Editorial Writing, 1974. *Memberships:* Authors Guild; Crime Writers Association; American crime Writers. *Address:* PO Box 645, Keego Harbor, MI 48320, USA.

KILBRACKEN John Godley, Lord, b. 17 Oct 1920, London, England- Nationality: Irish. Writer. m. (1) Penelope Reyne, 22 May 1943, (div), 2 sons (1 dec); (2) Susan Heazlewood, 15 May 1981, (div), 1 son. *Education:* Eton, 1934-39 (won Hervey English Verse Prize); Balliol, Oxford 1939-40 and 1945-47; BA and MA 1948. *Literary Appointments:* Reporter: Daily Mirror, 1947-49, Sunday Express, 1949-51; Editorial Director of WorldWatch, 1984-85. *Publications:* Even For An Hour (Poems), 1940; Tell Me The Next One, 1950; The Master Forger, 1951; Letters From Early New Zealand (Editor), 1951; Living Like A Lord, 1955; A Peer Behind The Curtain, 1959; Shamrocks and Unicorns, 1962; Van Meegeren, 1967; Bring Back My Stringbag, 1979; The Easy Way To Bird Recognition, 1982; The Easy Way To Wild Flower Recognition, 1984. *Contributions to:* Many UK and Foreign Newspapers and Magazines. *Honours:* Labour Peer, transferrd from Liberals in 1966 after inheriting the title in 1950; DSC, for Service as Naval Pilot in World War II, 1945; Times Ed Supp Senior Information Book Award, 1982 (for book The Easy Way To Bird Recognition). *Literary Agent:* Curtis Brown, England. *Address:* Killegar, Cavan, Ireland.

KILGORE James C, b. 2 May 1928. Professor. *Education;* BA, Wiley College, 1952; MA, English, University of Missouri, 1963; various other courses, workshops. *Publications:* The Big Buffalo, 1969; Midnight Blast, 1970; A Time of Black Devotion, 1971; Night Song, 1974; Let It Pass, 1976; A Black Bicentennial, 1976; Until I Met You, 1978; African Violet, 1982; I've Been in the Storm So Long, 1983; During Arabica Lunch, 1986. *Contributions to:* various journals and magazines. *Honours:* Recipient, honours and awards including: Ohio Poet of the Year, 1982; Ralph Besse Award for Teaching Excellence, 1983. *Memberships:* National Council of Teachers of English; MLA; Renaissance Society of America; Ohio Poets' Association; Phi Beta Sigma; many others. *Address:* 2531 Richmond Road, Beachwood, OH 44122, USA.

KILJUNEN Kimmo Roobert, b. 13 June 1951, Rauha, Finland. Development Researcher; Director. m. Marja Liisa Kiljunen, 17 Jan 1972, 2 sons, 2 daughters. *Education:* MA Helsinki University, 1973; MPhil, 1977, DPhil, 1985, Sussex University, England. *Publications:* Editor: Kampuchea, Decade of the Genocide, 1984; Namibia, the Last Colony, 1981; Region to Region Cooperation between Developed and Developing Countries, 1990; Author, Finland and the New International Division of Labour, 1992; Books published in Finland in Finish: Author: The underdeveloped world, 1976; Premises for Regional Policy in the 1980s, 1979; Three Worlds, 1989; You and the World Poor, 1991. *Memberships:* European Association of Development Research and Training Institutes, Executive Committee, 1987-. *Address:* Linnoittajanpolku 3 g 15, 01280 Vantaa, Finland.

KILLANIN The Lord (Michael Morris), b. 30 July 1914, London, England. Writer; Film Producer; Company Director. m. Mary Sheila Dunlop, MBE, 17 Dec 1945, 3 sons, 1 daughter. *Education:* Eton, 1928-31; Sorbonne, Paris, 1931-32; Magdalene College, Cambridge, 1932-35; BA, 1935; MA, 1939. *Literary Appointments:* Reporter: Daily Express, 1935; Daily Mail, 1936; Sunday Dispatch, 1938. *Publications:* Four Days, 1938; Sir Godfrey Knelier, 1947; Shell Guide To Ireland, with M.V. Duigan, 1956; The Olympic Games, with John Rodda, 1976, 1980, 1984; My Ireland - A Personal Impression 1987. Producer of Films including: The Rising of the Moon; The Playboy of the Western World; Gideon's Day. Wrote film commentary for Connemara and Its Pony. *Honours include:* MBE; Olympic Order (Gold) 1980; Honorary LLD, National University of Ireland, 1975, LLD(NUI); Honorary D.Litt(NUU), New University of Ulster, 1977; Chubb Fellowship, Yale, 1981; Chubb Scholar, 1981; Numerous foreign honours. *Memberships include:* President, Olympic Council of Ireland 1950-73, Honorary Life President, 1981-; MRIA, 1954; Elected Member, International Olympic Committee, 1952, Executive Board 1967, Vice-President 1968, President 1972-80, Honorary Life President 1980-; Member, French Academy of Sports, 1984; Honorary Life Member, Royal Dublin society, 1981; Fellow, Royal Society of Arts, Royal Society of Antiquaries of Ireland, 1984; Hon Life Member, National Union of Journalists and of the Association of Cinemaand Television Technicians, 1985; Hon Life Member, Chambers of Commerce of Ireland; Hon Member, Marketing Institute of Ireland; Honorary Consul General for the Principality of Monaco in Ireland 1961-844; Chairman, National Heritage Council, 1988-; Chairman Dublin Theatre Festival 1958-70, Patron 1971. *Literary Agent:* Scott Ferris Associates. *Address:* 9 Lower Mount Pleasant Avenue, Dublin 6, Ireland.

KILLDEER John. *See:* **MAYHAR Ardath (Frances).**

KILLOUGH (Karen) Lee, b. 1942, USA. Science Fiction Writer; Radiological Technologist. *Publications:* A Voice Out of Ramah, 1979; The Doppelganger Gambit, 1979; The Monitor, the Miners, and the Shree, 1980; Aventine, 1981; Deadly Silents, 1982; Liberty's World, 1985; Spider Play, 1986; Blood Hunt, 1987; The Leopard's Daughter, 1987; Bloodlinks, 1988; Dragon's Teeth, 1990. *Address:* Box 422, Manhattan, KS 66502, USA.

KILMARTIN Terence Kevin, b. 10 Jan 1922. Literary Editor. m. Joanna Pearce, 1952, 1 son, 1 daughter. *Appointments:* Private Tutor, France, 1938-39; Special Operations Executive, 1940-45; Assistant Editor, World Review, 1946-47; Freelance Journalist, Middle East, 1947-48; Assistant Editor, Observer Foreign News Service, 1949-50; Assistant Literary Editor, 1950-52, Literary Editor, 1952-86, The Observer. *Publications:* A Guide to Proust, 1983; translations of Henry de Montherlant: The Bachelors, 1960; The Dream, 1962; Chaos and Night, 1964; The Girls, 1968; The Boys, 1974; André Malraux: Anti-Memoirs, 1968; Lazarus, 1977; Charles de Gaulle: memoirs of Hope, 1971; Marcel Proust: Rev. trans. of Remembrance of Things Past, 1981. *Address:* 44 North Side, Clapham Common, London SW4, England.

KILROY Thomas, b. 23 Sept 1934, Ireland. Writer; University Teacher. m. Julia Lowell Carlson, 9 Dec 1981, 3 sons by first marriage. *Education:* BA, 1956, MA, 1959, University College, Dublin. *Publications:* Death and Resurrection of Mr Roche (Play), 1968 The Big Chapel, (novel), 1971; Talbots' Box, (play), 1977; The Seagull, (play adaptation), 1981; Double Cross (play), 1986; Ghosts, 1989; Madame McAdam's Travelling Theatre (play), 1990. *Contributions to:* Radio, TV Drama; numerous journals & magazines. *Honours:* Guardian Fiction Prize, 1971; Heinnmann Award for Literature, 1971; Irish Academy of Letters Prize, 1972; American-Irish Foundation award for Literature, 1974. *Memberships:* Fellow, Royal Society of Literature, 1971; Irish academy of Letters, 1973. *Address:* c/o Margaret

Ramsay Ltd., 14A Garden Court, St Martins Lane, London WC2 N4LC, England.

KILWORTH Garry, b. 5 July 1941, York, England. Writer. m. Annette Jill Bailey, 30 June 1962. 1 sons, 1 daughter. *Education:* HND, Business Studies, 1974; Honours Degree in English, 1985. *Publications:* Hunter's Moon, 1989; In the Hollow of the Deep-Sea Wave, 1989; Songbirds of Pain, 1984; Standing on Shamsan, 1992; Spiral Winds, 1987; The Drowners; Midnight's Sun; Abandonati; Cloudrock; Witchwater Country; In Solitary; The Electric Kids; The Rain Ghost; Frost Dancers. *Contributions to:* Omni Magazine; Isaac Asimov's Magazine; F&SF Magazine; Interzone; Sunday Times Review. *Honours:* Sunday Times, Gollancz Short Story Award Winner, 1974; Librarian Association's Carnegie Medal Commendation, 1991. *Memberships:* PEN. *Literary Agent:* Maggie Noach, 21 Redan Street, London, England. *Address:* Wychwater, The Chase, Ashingdon, Essex, England.

KIM Unsong William, b. 1 Sept 1924, North Korea. Retired Professor, Molecular Biology. m. Sue Kim, 18 Jan 1948, 4 sons. *Education:* BS, Biology, Seoul University, 1949; MS, 1956, PhD, 1958, Virology, University of Wisconsin, USA. *Publications:* 100 Classical Korean Poems (Sijo) Selected Translated, 1986; Classical Korean Poems, Translated in English, 1986; Search for Life, Poems by Kim Unsong, 1987; Poems by Mao Tsetung, Translated by Kim Unsong, 1988; General Biology, 1950; Introduction to Molecular Biology, 1975; Philosophy of Science, 1980; Lao Tza's Tao-Te Ching, lyrical trans in English and Korean, 1990; Poetry Kim Unsong, International Poets Book V, 1991. *Contributions to:* Over 30 scientific papers in various journals including: Science; Biochim, Biophys, Acta and other international journals. Poems in Poet; Korean-American Journal; American Anthology; New York Federal Anthology. *Honours:* Essay award, Governor General, 1937; 1st prize, Essay, Korea Times, 1975; 1st Prize, World Poetry International, 1987; Hon DLitt, World Academy of Arts and Culture, 1991; many other honours and awards. *Memberships:* Daly City Creative Writers Group; California Federation of Chapparal Poets; President, World Poetry International; Editor of the Poetry Journal, Poet 1990; Vice President, International Poets Academy. *Address:* PO Box No 1131, San Bruno, CA 94066, USA.

KIM Yong-ik, b. 15 May 1920, Korea. Writer. m. 11 Feb 1972, 3 daughters. *Education:* BA, Aoyama Jakuin College, Tokyo, 1942; BA Florida Southern College, 1951; MA, University of Kentucky, 1952. *Publications:* Moons of Korea, 1959; The Happy Days, 1960; The Diving Gourd, 1962; Blue in the Seed, 1964; The Wedding Shoes, 1984; Love in Winter, 1970; The Shoes from Yang San Valley, 1981. *Contributions to:* Harpers Bazaar; The New Yorker; Mademoiselle; Korea Journal; Hudson Review; The Yankee Magazine; Prism International. *Honours include:* First Oversea Korean Literature Prize, Korean Literary and Writers Association, 1990; Main Stream America Award for Excellence in Literature, Asian Pacific Council, 1991. *Memberships:* Korean American Literature Society. *Address:* 1030 Macon Avenue, Pittsburgh, PA 15218, USA.

KIMBALL Penn Townsend, b. 12 Oct 1915, New Britain, Connecticut, USA. Journalist; Professor Emeritus, Graduate School of Journalism, Columbia Unversity. m. (2) Julie M. Ellis, 27 July 1985 (1st wife dec.). 1 daughter. *Education:* BA, Princeton University School of Public & International Affairs, 1937; BA, MA, Balliol College, Oxford University, UK, 1939; PhD, Columbia University, 1988. *Appointments include:* Editor & writer for: US News, 1939; Newspaper PM, 1940; Time Magazine, 1946; New Republic, 1947; New York Times, 1951-54; Omnibus TV, CBS, 1954-55; Colliers, 1955-56; Columbia Journalism Review, 1960-87. Consulting editor, Harris Survey, 1963-74. *Publications include:* Bobby Kennedy & the New Politics, 1968; The Disconnected, 1972; The File, USA 1983, UK 1984; Keep Hope Alive, 1991. Chapter in, The

Professions in America, 1965. *Contributions to:* Journals as listed, also: Nation; Life Magazine; Saturday Review; Public Opinion Quarterly. *Honours:* Rhodes Scholar, 1937-39; War Service US Marine Corps, 1942-48; Guest Scholar, Woodrow Wilson International Center for Scholars, Washington DC, 1992-93. *Memberships:* American PEN; National Press Club, Washington DC; Authors Guild; American Society of Public Opinion Research. *Literary Agent:* Berenice Hoffman. *Address:* Box 240, Chilmark, Massachusetts 02535, USA.

KIMBALL Roger, b. 13 Aug 1953, Ohio, USA. Writer; Editor. m. Alexandra Mullen, 1993. *Education:* BA, Bennington College, 1975; MA, 1977, MPhil, 1978, Yale University. *Publications:* Tenured Radicals: How Politics has Corrupted our Higher Education, 1990. *Contributions to:* The New Criterion; The Wall Street Journal; The Times Literary Supplement; Commentary; The American Scholar; Architectural Record. *Literary Agent:* Writers Representatives, 25W 19th Street, NYC 10011, USA. *Address:* 850 7th Avenue, New York City, NY 10019, USA.

KIMBROUGH Robert (Alexander III), b. 1929, USA. Professor of English. *Appointments:* Instructor to Associate Professor, 1959-68, Professor of English, 1968; Chair, Integrated Liberal Studies Department, 1970-75, University of Wisconsin, Madison. *Publications:* Joseph Conrad, Heart of Darkness: An Authoritative Text, Backgrounds and Sources, Essays in Criticism (editor), 1963, 3rd Edition, 1987; Shakespeare's Troilus and Cressida and Its Setting, 1964; Henry James, The Turn of the Screw: An Authoritative Text, Backgrounds and Sources, Essays in Criticism (editor), 1966; Troilus and Cressida: A Scene-by-Scene Analysis with Critical Commentary, 1966; Sir Philip Sidney: Selected Prose and Poetry, 1969, 2nd Edition, 1982; Sir Philip Sidney, 1971; Christopher Marlowe, 1972; The Nigger of the Narcissus, by Joseph Conrad (editor), 1979; Youth, by Joseph Conrad (editor), 1984; Shakespear and the Art of Human Kindness: the essay toward androgyny, 1990. *Address:* 3206 Gregory Street, Madison, WI 53711, USA.

KIMENYE Barbara, b. United Kingdom. Social Worker; Author. *Publications:* Kalasanda, for adults, 1965; Kalasanda Revisited, for adults, 1966; The Smugglers, reader, 1966; Moses series, 9 vols, 1967-73; The Winged Adventure, 1969; Paulo's Strange Adventure, 1971; Barah and the Boy, 1973; Martha the Millipede, 1973; The Runaways, 1973; The Gemstone Affair, adult novel, 1978; The Scoop, adult novel, 1978. *Address:* c/o Nelson, Nelson House, Mayfield Road, Walton-on-Thames, Surrey KT12 5PL, England.

KIMES Beverly Rae, b. 17 Aug 1939, Aurora, Illinois, USA. Writer; Editor. m. James H. Cox, 6 July 1984. *Education:* BS, Journalism, University of Illinois; MA, Journalism, Pennsylvania State University. *Publications:* The Classic Tradition of the Lincoln Motor Car, 1968; Oldsmobile : The First Seventy-Five years, 1972 (co-author); The Cars that Henry Ford Built, 1978; Editor, Great Cars and Grand Marques, 1976; Editor, Packard : A History of the Motor Car and the Company, 1979; Editor, Automobile Quarterly's Handbook of Automotive Hobbies, 1981; My Two Lives : Race Car to Restauranteur, (co-author), 1983; Chevrolet : A History from 1911, (co-author), 1984; Standard Catalog of American Cars 1805-1942, 1985; The Star and the Laurel, 1986. *Contributions to:* American Heritage; Automobile Quarterly; The Classic Car; Automobiles Classiques; Wheels; Car and Driver; Road and Track. *Honours:* Cugnot Award, Society of Automotive Historians, 1978, 1979, 1984-86; McKean Trophy, Antique Automobile Club of America, 1984-86; Moto Award, National Automotive Journalism Association, 1984-86; many other honours and awards. *Membership:* Society of Automotive Historians, President, 1987-. *Address:* 215 East 80th Street, New York, NY 10021, USA.

KIMPEL Benjamin Franklin, b. 1905, USA. Emeritus Professor of Philosophy; Author. *Publications:* Principle of Contradiction in Idealistic Metaphysic, 1934; Religious Faith, Language and Knowledge, 1952; Faith and Moral Authority, 1953; Symbols of Religious Faith, 1954; Moral Principles in the Bible, 1956; Language and Religion, 1957; Principles of Moral Philosophy, 1960; Kant's Critical Philosophy, 1964; Hegel's Philosophy of History, 1964; Schopenhauer's Philosophy, 1964; Nietzsche's Beyond Good and Evil, 1965; A Philosophy of Zen Buddhism, 1966; Philosophies of Life of Ancient Greeks and Israelites: An Analysis of Their Parallels, 1980; Emily Dickinson as Philosopher, 1981; A Philosophy of the Religion of Ancient Israelites and Greeks, 1982; Stoic Moral Philosophies: Their Counsel for Today, 1985; Moral Philosophies in Shakespeare's Plays, 1987. *Address:* West Street, North Bennington, VT 05257, USA.

KINCAID Jamaica, b. 1949, St John's, Antigua, West Indies. Writer. *Appointments:* Contributor, currently Staff Writer, The New Yorker Magazine, New York City, 1974-. *Publications:* At the Bottom of the River, short stories, 1984; Annie John, novel, 1985; A Small Place, non-fiction, 1988; Lucy, novel, 1990. *Address:* c/o The New Yorker magazine, 25 West 43rd Street, New York, NY 10036, USA.

KINCAID Matt. See: **ADAMS Clifton.**

KING Betty Alice, b. 17 June 1919. Historical Novelist. m. D James King, 14 June 1941, 2 sons, 1 daughter. *Education:* Queenswood School, Hertfordshire; Open University. *Publications include:* The Lady Margaret, 1965; The Lord Jasper, 1967; The King's Mother, 1969; Margaret of Anjou, 1974; Emma Hamilton, 1976; Nell Gwyn, 1979; Claybourn, 1980; The French Countess, 1982; We Are Tomorrow's Past, 1984. *Contributions to:* Hertfordshire Countryside; Enfield Gazette. *Membership:* The Society of Authors. *Address:* Monkswood Cottage, Hadley Wood, Hertfordshire EN4 ONL, England.

KING Bruce (Alvin), b. 1933, USA. Professor of Literature. *Appointments:* Taught: Brooklyn College, 1960-61; University of Alberta, Calgary, 1961-62; University of Ibadan, 1962-65; University of Bristol, 1966-67; University of Lagos, 1967-70; University of Windsor, Ontario, 1970-73; Ahmadu Bello University, Zaria, Nigeria, 1973-76; Teacher, University of Paris, 1977-78; Rockefeller Foundation Humanities Fellow, 1977-78; University of Stirling, Scotland, 1979; University of Canterbury, New Zealand, 1979-83; Albert S Johnston Professor of Literature, University of North Alabama, Florence, 1983-; American Institute of Indian Studies Research Fellowship, 1984; Rockefeller Foundation Scholar in Residence, Bellagio Center, 1984. *Publications:* Dryden's Major Plays, 1966; Twentieth Century Interpretations of All for Love (editor), 1968; Dryden's Mind and Art (editor), 1969; Introduction to Nigerian Literature (editor), 1971; Literatures of the World in English (editor), 1974; A Celebration of Black and African Writing (co-editor), 1976; Marvell's Allegorical Poetry, 1977; West Indian Literature (editor), 1979; The New English Literatures, 1980; Ibsen's A Doll's House, 1980; G B Shaw's Arms and the Man, 1980; Fielding's Joseph Andrews, 1981; History of Seventeenth-Century English Literature, 1982; Modern Dramatists (series co-editor), 1982-.

KING Clive, b. 28 Apr 1924, Richmond, Surrey, England. Author. m. (1)Jane Tuke, 1948, 1 son, 1 daughter, (2)Penny Timmins, 1974, 1 daughter. *Education:* BA, Downing College, 1947. *Publications:* The Town that Went South, 1959; Stig of the Dump, 1963; The Twenty Two Letters, 1966; The Night the Water Came, 1973; Snakes and Snakes, 1975; Me and My Million, 1976; Ninny's Boat, 1980; The Sound of Propellers, 1986; The Seashore People, 1987; 7 other books. *Honours:* Boston Globe-Horn Book Award, Honour Book, 1980. *Memberships:* Chairman, Children's Writers Group, Society of Authors 1980-82.

Literary Agent: Murray Pollinger. *Address:* Pond Cottage, Low Road, Thurlton, Norwich NR14 6PZ, England.

KING Cynthia, b. 27 Aug 1925, USA. Writer. m. Jonathan King, 26 July 1944, 3 sons. *Education:* Bryn Mawr College, 1943-44; The University of Chicago, 1944-45; New York University Writer's Workshop, 1964-67. *Appointments:* Associate Editor, Hillman Periodicals, 1945-50; Managing Editor, Fawcett Publications, 1950-55. *Publications:* Beggars and Choosers, 1980; In the Morning of Time, 1970; Sailing Home, 1982; The Year of Mr Nobody, 1978. *Contributions to:* The New York Times Book Review; The Detroit News; Los Angeles Daily News; Short Stories; Good Housekeeping; Texas Stories and Poems; Encore. *Honours:* Artists Grant; Michigan Council for the Arts, 1986. *Memberships:* Author's Guild; Detroit Women Writer's, President, 1979-81, Treasurer, 1978; Poets and Writers; Fripp Island Audubon CLub, President, 1991-92, VP, 1989-91. *Literary Agent:* Philippa Brophy, Sterling Lord Literistic Inc. *Address:* 1112 Finney, College Station, TX 77845, USA.

KING David John, b. 31 Jan 1955, Melbourne, Australia. Freelance Writer/Photographer. *Education:* Diploma, Arts/Humanities, Gordon Institute of Technology, Geelong, 1975. *Appointments Include:* Freelance Scriptwriter, Editor, Story Consultant, ABC Education Department, Victoria & Queensland, 1980-84; Freelance Scriptwriter, Storyliner, ABC TV Drama Department, 1982-83; Freelance Scriptwriter, Australian Children's TV Foundation, 1983-84; Freelance Scriptwriter, Independent Producers, 1980-85; Freelance Travel and Features Journalist, Geelong Advertiser, 1980-92; Freelance Scriptwriter, ATV Channel 10, Melbourne, Victoria; Writer, Producer, ATV 10 Deafness Appeal Telethon, 1986; Editor, Dive Log Australia, National Scuba Diving Newspaper, 1988-89; Freelance Features Journalist, Melbourne Herald-Sun, 1991-92; Freelance Features Journalist, Townsville Bulletin Supplements Department; Casual Sports and Features Journalist Twin Cities Advertiser, 1992-93. *Publications:* Credits Include: Series of short, historical radio documentaries broadcast throughout South-East, West Asia, the Pacific and Europe by Radio Australia; Story World, What If..?, Listen and Read : TV drama/documentary, What Killed Cobb and Co? for Queensland ABC Education Department, Episodes 10, 18, 27, 28 of award winning young people's TV series Home for ABC TV Drama Department; Episodes 1- of science fiction tv series for young people, The Parallax Factor; Erotic Rock 'N' Roll Comedy video release feature film Coming of Age (with Brian Jones); Developed screenplay of original mystery thriller feature film Entangled, for David Hannay Production, Sydney; Developed Series of short original documentaries for Deafness Foundation Telethon, 1985, 1986. *Contributions to:* Geelong Advertiser; Bellaraine Echo; Australasian Post; Sportdiving; Heritage Australia; Scuba Diver; Pursuit; Inside Sport; Melbourne Herald-Sun; The Age; Sports & Classic Cars; Editions Review; Townsville Bulletin; Twin Cities Advertiser; Triathlon Magazine. *Honours:* Young Australian National Short Story Award, 1971; Winner, Walter Backholer National Award for Prose, 1986. *Memberships:* various professional organisations; Leader/Foundation Member of Wreckdive Expeditions, (Victoria). *Address:* c/o 9 Robertson Street, East Geelong, Victoria 3219, Australia.

KING Francis Henry, (Frank Cauldwell), b. 4 Mar 1923 Author; Drama Critic. *Education:* Balliol College, Oxford. *Appointments:* Drama Critic, Sunday Telegraph, 1978-88. *Publications:* Novels: To the Dark Tower, 1946; Never Again, 1947; An Air That Kills, 1948; The Dividing Stream, 1951; The Dark Glasses, 1954; The Widow, 1957; The Man on the Rock, 1957; The Custom House, 1961; The Last of the Pleasure Gardens, 1965; The Waves Behind the Boat, 1967; A Domestic Animal, 1970; Flights, 1973; A Game of Patience, 1974; The Needle, 1975; Danny Hill, 1977; The Action, 1978; Act of Darkness, 1983; Voices in an Empty Room, 1984;

Frozen Music, 1987; The Woman Who Was God, 1988; Punishment, 1989; Visiting Cards, 1990; The Ant Colony, 1991; (with Tom Wakefield and Patrick Gale), Secret Lives, 1991; Short Stories: So Hurt and Humiliated, 1959; The Japanese Umbrella, 1964; The Brighton Belle, 1968; Hard Feelings, 1976; Indirect Method, 1980; One is a Wanderer, 1985; (Poetry) Rod of Incantation, 1952; Biography: E M Forster and His World, 1978; Editor, My Sister and Myself: the Diaries of J R Ackerley, 1982; General: (Editor) Introducing Greece, 1956; Japan, 1970; Florence, 1982; Editor, Lafcadio hearne: Writings from Japan, 1984; Autobiography: Yesterday Came Suddenly, 1993. *Honours:* OBE, 1979; CBE, 1985; FRSL; Somerset Maugham Award, 1952. *Memberships:* International President, PEN, 1986-89; International Vice-President, PEN, 1989-; President, English Pen, 1978-86. *Literary Agent:* A M Heath & Co. *Address:* c/o 19 Gordon Place, London W8 4JE, England.

KING Larry L, b. 1 Jan 1929, Playwright; Author; Actor. m. Barbara S Blaine, 2 sons. 3 daughters. *Education:* Midland (Texas) High School, 1947; Texas Technical University 1949-50; Nieman Fellow, Harvard University 1969-70; Duke Fellow of Communications, Duke University, 1975-76; Visiting Ferris Professor of Journalism and Political Science, Princeton University, 1973-74. *Appointment:* Poet Laureat, Monahans (Texas) Sandhills Literary Society, 1977 (for life), *Publications:* The Best Little Whorehouse in Texas (play) 1978; The Night Hank Williams Died (play) 1988; Confessions of a White Racist (book), 1971; The Old Man and Lesser Mortals (book) 1974; None But a Blockhead (book) 1986; The One-Eyed Man (novel) 1966; ....And Other Dirty Stories, 1968; Of Outlaws, Whores, Conmen, Politicians and Other Artists, 1980; Warning: Writer at Work, 1985; Because of Lozo Brown, 1988; The Kingfish (play) 1979; Christmas: 1933, (play) 1986. *Contributions to:* Harper's; Atlantic Monthly; Life; New Republic; Texas Monthly; Texas Observer; New York; Playboy; Parade; Esquire; Saturday Evening Post; Nation Geographic, and many others. *Honours:* Texas Writers Roundup, 1968; Stanley Walker Journalism Award, 1971; Television Emmy 1981; Helen Hayes Award, 1988; Theatre Lobby Award, 1988; Nominated for National Book Award, 1971; Broadway Tony 1978-79. *Memberships:* Texas Institute of Letters; Mark Twain Society; PEN; Author's League; National Writers Union; Screenwriters Guild; Drama Guild; Washington Independent Writers; Actors Equity. *Literary Agent:* Barbara S Blaine, 700 13th Street, NW, (7th Floor), NW Washington, DC 20005, USA. *Address:* 3025 Woodland Drive, NW Washington, DC 20008, USA.

KING Margaret L, b. 16 Oct 1947, New York City, USA. Professor of History. m. Robert E Kessler, 12 Nov 1976. 2 sons. *Education:* BA, Sarah Lawrence College, 1967; MA 1968, PhD, 1972, Stanford University. *Publications:* Venetian Humanism in an Age of Patrician Dominance, 1986; Women of the Ranaissance, 1991; Her Immaculate Hand, 1983, co-author. *Contributions to:* Renaissance Quarterly; Journal of Mediaeval and Renaissance Studies; Studi Veneziani and others. *Honours:* Woodrow Wilson Fellow, 1967-68; Danforth Fellow, 1968-72; ALCS Fellow, 1971-78; NEH Fellow, 1986-87; Howard Marrard Prize of the ACHA, 1986. *Memberships:* American Historical Association; Editor, 1984-88, Executive Director, 1988-, Renaissance Society of America. *Address:* 324 Beverly Road, Douglaston, NY 11363, USA.

KING Michael, b. 15 Dec 1945, Wellington, New Zealand. Writer. m. 17 Oct 1987, 1 son, daughter. *Education:* BA, Victoria University, 1967; MA, 1968, DPhil, 1978, Wackato University. *Appointments:* Katherine Mansfield Fellow, 1976; Writing Fellow, Victoria University, 1983; National Library Fellow, 1990; Fellowship in Humanities, Wackato University, 1991-. *Publications:* Te Puea, 1977; Maori, 1983; Being Pakeha, 1985; Death of the Rainbow Warrior, 1986; Mariori, 1989. *Contributions to:* Columnist, and feature writer for variety of newspapers and magazines including New Zealand Listener, New Zealand Sunday

Times, Metro. *Honours:* Feltex Award, 1975; Cowan Prize, 1976; NZ Book Award, 1978; Wattie Book of the Year Prize, 1984, 1990; OBE, 1988; Literary Fund Achievement Award, 1989. *Memberships:* PEN, New Zealand President, 1979-80; New Zealand Aurhors Fund Advisory Committee, 1980-92; Frank Sargeson Trust, 1982-; Auckland Institute Museum Council, 1986-91; Chatham Islands Conservation Board, 1990-. *Address:* PO Box 109, Whangamata, New Zealand.

KING Paul. *See:* **DRACKETT Philip Arthur (Phil).**

KING Ronald, b. 1914, United Kingdom. Author. *Appointments:* Secretary, Royal Botanical Gardens, Kew, London, 1959-76. *Publications:* World of Kew, 1976; Botanical Illustration, 1978; Quest for Paradise, history of the world's gardens, 1979; Temple of Flora, 1981; Tresco: England's Island of Flowers, 1985; Royal Kew, 1985. *Address:* Kuranda, Northfield Place, Weybridge, Surrey KT13 ORF, England.

KING Stephen Edwin, (Richard Bachman), b. 21 Sept 1947, Portland, Maine, USA. Author. m. Tabitha J Spruce, 1971, 2 sons, 1 daughter. *Education:* University of Maine. *Appointments:* Teacher of English, Hampden Academy, Maine, 1971-73; Writer in Residence, University of Maine, Orono, 1978-79. *Publications include:* Carrie, 1974; Salem's Lot, 1975; The Shining, 1977; The Stand, 1978; The Dead Zone, 1979; Firestarter, 1980; Danse Macabre, 1981; Cujo, 1981; Christine, 1983; Pet Sematary, 1983; The Talisman (with Peter Straub), 1984; Cycle of the Werewolf, 1985; It, 1986; The Eyes of the Dragon, 1987; Misery, 1987; The Tommyknockers, 1987; The Dark Half, 1989; Four Past Midnight, 1990; Needful Things, 1991; Gerald's Game, 1992; The Dark Tower Stories: Volume 1: The Gunslinger, 1982; Volume 2: The Drawing of the Three, 1984; Short Story Collections: Night Shift, 1978; Different Seasons, 1982; Skeleton Crew, 1985; Gerald's Game, 1992; Dolores Claiborne, 1993. As Richard Bachman: Thinner, 1984; The Bachman Books: Rage, The Long Walk, Roadwork, The Running Man, 1985; Numerous other short stories. *Memberships:* Authors Guild of America; Screen Artists' Guild; Screen Writers of America; Writers Guild. *Address:* c/o Press Relations, Viking Press, 625 Madison Avenue, New York, NY 10022, USA.

KING Vincent. *See:* **VINSON Rex Thomas.**

KING-HELE Desmond George, b. 3 Nov 1927, Seaford, England. Author. *Education:* BA (Hons), 1948, MA, 1952, Trinity College, Cambridge. *Appointments:* Editor, Notes and Records of the Royal Society, 1989. *Publications include:* Shelley: His Thought and Work, 1960, 3rd edition 1984; Satellites and Scientific Research, 1962; Erasmus Darwin, 1963; Satellite Orbits in an Atmosphere, 1964 new edition 1987; Observing Earth Satellites, 1966, new edition 1983; The End of the Twentieth Century?., 1970; Poems and Trixies, 1972; Doctor of Revolution, 1977; The Letters of Erasmus Darwin, 1981; Animal Spirits, 1983; Erasmus Darwin and the Romantic Poets, 1986; A Tapestry of Orbits, 1992. *Contributions to:* Over 400 papers to various journals. *Honours:* Fellow of the Royal Society, 1966; Honorary Degrees: DSc., University of Aston, 1979, D. Univ, University of Surrey, 1986; several scientific awards. *Address:* 3 Tor Road, Farnham, Surrey GU9 7BX, England.

KING-SMITH Dick, b. 1922, United Kingdom. Freelance Writer; Former Farmer and Teacher. *Publications:* The Fox Busters, 1978; Daggie Dogfoot, 1980, US Edition Pigs Might Fly, 1982; The Mouse Butcher, 1981; Magnus Powermouse, 1982; The Queen's Nose, 1983; The Sheep-Pig, 1985; Harry's Mad, 1984; Lightning Fred, 1985; Saddlebottom, 1985; Noah's Brother, 1986; Dumpling, 1986; Yob, 1986; Pets for Keeps, 1986; E S P, 1986; H Prince, 1986; The Hodgehog, 1987; Tumbleweed, 1987; Friends and Brothers, 1987; Dodos Are Forever, 1987; Sophie's

Snail, 1988; Emily's Legs, 1988; The Trouble With Edward, 1988; George Speaks, 1988; Martin's Mice, 1988; The Jenius, 1988; The Water Horse, 1990; Ace, 1990; Paddy's Pot of Gold, 1990; Alphabeasts, 1992; The Hodgeheg, 1992; Martin's Mice, 1992. *Address:* Diamond's Cottage, Queen Charlton, near Keynsham, Avon BS18 2SJ, England.

KING-SMITH Ronald Gordon, b. 27 Mar 1922, Bitton, Gloucestershire, England. Children's Author. m. Myrle England, 6 Feb 1943, 1 son, 2 daughters. *Education:* Marlborough; BEd, Bristol University. *Publications:* The Fox Busters, 1978; Daggie Dogfoot, 1980; The Mouse Butcher, 1981; Magnus Powermouse, 1982; The Queen's Nose, 1983; The Sheep-Pig, 1984; Harry's Mad, 1984; Saddlebottom, 1985; Lightning Fred, 1985; Pets for Keeps, 1986; Noah's Brother, 1986; ESP, 1986; Yob, 1986; Dumpling, 1986; H.Prince, 1986; Tumbleweed, 1987; The Hodgeheg, 1987; Farmer Bungle Forgets, 1987; Friends and Brothers, 1987; Cuckoobush Farm, 1987; Country Watch, 1987; Town Watch, 1987. *Honour:* The Guardian Award for Children's Fiction, The Sheep-Pig, 1984. *Literary Agent:* Pamela Todd, A P Watt, London. *Address:* Diamond's Cottage, Queen Charlton, Keynsham, Avon, England.

KINGDON Robert McCune, b. 1927, USA. Professor of History, University of Wisconsin. *Publications:* Geneva and the Coming of the Wars of Religion in France, 1956; Registres de la Compagnie des Pasteurs de Geneve au temps de Calvin (edited with J-F Bergier), 2 vols, 1962, 1964; William Cecil: Execution of Justice in England, and William Allen: A True, Sincere and Modest Defence of English Catholics (editor), 1965; Geneva and the Consolidation of the French Protestant Movement, 1967; Calvin and Calvinism: Sources of Democracy (edited with R D Linder), 1970; Theodore de Beze: Du droit des magistrats (editor), 1971; Transition and Revolution: Problems and Issues of European Renaissance and Reformation History (editor and contributor), 1974; The Political Thought of Peter Martyr Vermigli, 1980; Church and Society in Reformation Europe, 1985; Myths about the St Bartholomew's Day Massacres, 1988; Jean de Coras, Question politique: s'il est licite anx subjects de capituler avec leur prince (editor), 1989; A Bibliography of the Works of Peter Vermigli (compiled with John Patrick Donnelly), 1990. *Address:* Institute for Research in the Humanities, Old Observatory, University of Wisconsin, Madison, WI 53706, USA.

KINGMAN Lee, b. 1919, USA. Freelance Writer and Editor. *Appointments:* Children's Book Editor, Houghton Mifflin Co, Boston, Massachusetts, 1944-46. *Publications:* Pierre Pidgeon, 1943; Ilenka, 1945; The Rocky Summer, 1948; The Best Christmas, 1949; Philippe's Hill, 1950; The Quarry Adventure, UK Edition Lauri's Surprising Summer, 1951; Kathy and the Mysterious Statue, 1953; Peter's Long Walk, 1953; Mikko's Fortune, 1955; The Magic Christmas Tree, 1956; The Village Band Mystery, 1956; Flivver, the Heroic Horse, 1958; The House of the Blue Horse, 1960; The Saturday Gang, 1961; Peter's Pony, 1963; Sheep Ahoy, 1963; Private Eyes, 1964; Newbery and Caldecott Medal Books: 1956-1965 (editor), 1965; The Year of the Raccoon, 1966; The Secret of the Silver Reindeer, 1968; Illustrators of Children's Books: 1957-1966 (edited with J Foster and R G Lontoft), 1968; The Peter Pan Bag, 1970; Georgina and the Dragon, 1971; The Meeting Post: A Story of Lapland, 1972; Escape from the Evil Prophecy, 1973; Newbery and Caldecott Medal Books: 1966-1975 (editor), 1975; Break a Leg, Betsy Maybe, 1976; The Illustrator's Notebook, 1978; Head over Wheels, 1978; Illustrators of Children's Books: 1967-1976 (edited with G Hogarth and H Quimby), 1978; The Refiner's Fire, 1981; The Luck of the Miss L, 1986; Newbery and Caldecott Medal Books: 1976-1985 (editor), 1986; Catch the Baby!, 1990. *Address:* PO Box 7126, Lanesville, Gloucester, MA 01930, USA.

KINGSTON Maxine Hong, b. 27 Oct 1940, Stockton, California, USA. Writer. m. 23 Nov 1962, 1 son. *Education:* AB, University of California, Berkeley, 1962,

Secondary Teaching Credential, UC, Berkeley, 1965. *Appointments:* Various teaching positions; currently at University of California, Berkeley, 1990. *Publications:* The Woman Warrior, 1976; China Men, 1980; Hawai'i One Summer, 1987; Tripmaster Monkey - His Fake Book, 1989. *Contributions to:* Numerous including: The Iowa Review; American Heritage; English Journal; The Michigan Quarterly; Mother Jones; New York Times; Los Angeles Times. *Honours:* The National Book Critics Circle Award, 1977; Madamoiselle Magazine Award, 1977; Anisfield-Wolf Race Relations Book Award, 1978; National Endowment for the Arts Writing Fellowship, 1980; Living Treasure of Hawaii, 1980; The National Book Award, 1981; Pulitzer Prize Runner-Up, 1981; The National Book Critics Circle nominee, 1981; Guggenheim Fellowship, 1981; Stockton Arts Commission Award, 1981; Asian/Pacific Women's Network Woman of the Year, 1981; Hawaii Award for Literature, 1982; The California Council for the Humanities Award, 1985; Honorary DEd, Eastern Michigan University, 1988; Governor's Award for the Arts, California, 1989; PEN USA West Award in Fiction, 1990; American Academy and Institute of Arts and Letters Award, 1990; DHL, honoris causa, Colby College, 1990; Bradeis University National Women's Committee Major Book Collection Award, 1990; Lila Wallace Reader's Digest Writers Award, 1992. *Memberships:* Authors Guild; PEN American Centre; PEN West; American Acadeym of Arts & Sciences. *Literary Agency:* Timothy Schaffner.

KINGTON Miles Beresford, b. 13 May 1941. Humorous Columnist. m. (1) Sarah Paine, 1964, divorced 1987, 1 son, 1 daughter, (2) Caroline Maynard, 1987, 1 son. *Education:* BA, Modern Languages, Trinity College, Oxford. *Appointments:* Freelance Writer, 1963- ; Part-time Gardener, 1964; Jazz Reviewer, The Times, 1965; joined staff of Punch, 1967, literary editor, 1973-80; Freelance Writer, 1980-; Regular Let's Parler Franglais Column in Punch and Daily Moreover Column in The Times, 1981-87; Member, Musical Group, Instant Sunshine; Jazz Player, 1970; Daily Columnist The Independent, 1987-. *Publications:* World of Alphonse Allais, 1977, reprinted as A Wolf in Frog's Clothing, 1983; 4 Franglais Books, 1979-82; Moreover, 1982; Miles and Miles, 1982; Nature Made Ridiculously Simple, 1983; Moreover, Too..., 1985; The Franglais Lieutenant's Woman, 1986; Welcome to Kington, 1985; Steaming Through Britain, 1990; Anthology of Jazz (ed), 1992. *Address:* Lower Hayze, Limpley Stoke, Bath BA3 6HR, England.

KINKLEY Jeffrey Carroll, b. 13 July 1948, Urbana, Illinois, USA. Professor of History. m. Chuchu Kang, 16 May 1981. *Education:* BA, University of Chicago, 1969; MA, 1971, PhD, 1977, Harvard University. *Publications:* The Odyssey of Shen Congwen, 1977; After Mao (editor), 1985; Hsio Ch'ien, Traveller Without a Map, (trans) 1990; Co-ed, Modern Chinese Writers, (co-editor) 1992; Chen Xuezhao, Surviving the Storm, (editor), 1990. *Memberships:* Asst Editor, China, of the Journal of Asian Studies; Editorial Board, Clear, Republican of China. *Address:* 8 Laurel Lane, Bernardsville, NJ 07924, USA.

KINNELL Galway, b. 1 Feb 1927, Providence, Rhode Island, USA. Writer. m. Ines Delgado de Torres, 1965, 1 son, 1 daughter. *Education:* Princeton University. *Publications:* Poetry: What a Kingdom it Was, 1960; Flower Herding on Mount Monadnock, 1963; Body Rags, 1966; The Book of Nightmares, 1971; The Avenue Bearing the Initial of Christ into the New World, 1974; Mortal Acts, Mortal Words, 1980; Selected Poems, 1982; The Past 1985; When One Has Lived A Long Time Alone, 1990; Novel: Black Light, 1966; Children's Story: How the Alligator Missed Breakfast, 1982; translation, The Poems of Francois Villon, 1965; On the Motion and Immobility of Douve, 1968; The Lackawanna Elegy, 1970; Interviews: Walking Down the Stairs, 1977. *Honours:* Award, National Institute of Arts and Letters 1962; Cecil Hemley Poetry Prize, 1969; Medal of Merit, 1975; Pulitzer Prize, 1983; American Book Award, 1983; MacArthur Fellowship, 1984. *Memberships:* PEN;

Poetry Society of America; New York Institute for the Humanities. *Address:* RFD, Sheffield, VT 05866, USA.

KINNEY Arthur F(rederick),b. 5 Sept 1933, New York, USA. Author; Editor; Teacher. *Education:* AB magna cum laude, Syracuse University, 1955; MS, Columbia University, 1956; PhD, University of Michigan, 1963. *Appointments:* Editor, English Literary Renaissance, 1971-; Editor, Twayne English Authors Series in the Renaissance, 1973-; President, Renaissance English Text Society, 1985-; Editor, Massachusetts Studies in Early Modern Culture. *Publications include:* Humanist Poetics, 1986; Continental Humanist Poetics, 1989; Renaissance Historicism, 1989; John Skelton, Priest as Poet, 1987; Elizabethan Backgrounds, 1990; Rogues, Vagabonds, and Sturdy Beggars, 1990. *Contributions to:* Renaissance Quarterly; Huntington Library Quarterly; Shakespeare Quarterly; Southern Review; Southern Quarterly, and others. *Honours:* Avery and Jules Hopwood Major Award in Criticism; Bread Loaf Scholar in Fiction and Criticism; Fulbright-Hays Scholar; NEH Senior Fellow, (twice); Huntington Library Senior Fellow, (3 times); Folger Shakespeare Library Senior Fellow, (twice). *Memberships:* Conference of Editors of Learned Journals, President 1971-73, 1980-82; Board/Consultant to many journals and publishers. *Literary Agent:* Elizabeth McKee. *Address:* 25 Hunter Hill Drive, Amherst, MA 01002, USA.

KINSEY-JONES Brian. *See:* **BALL Brian Neville.**

KINZIE Mary, b. 30 Sept 1944, Montgomery, Alabama, USA. Poet; Teacher. *Education:* MA, 1972, PhD, 1980, English, MA, Writing Seminars, 1970, Johns Hopkins University; BA, German, Northwestern University, 1967. *Appointments:* Executive Editor, Triquarterly Magazine, 1975-78; Instructor, 1975-78, Lecturer, English, 1978-85, Director, English Major in Writing, 1979-, Associate Professor, English, 1985-, Professor, 1990-, Northwestern University. *Publications:* The Threshold of the Year, (original verse), 1982; Masked Women and Summers of Vietnam, verse, 1990; Qutumn Eros, verse, 1992; Essays, Poems, articles and reviews in literary periodicals. *Honours:* Fulbright Scholarship, 1967-68; Illinois Arts Council Award for Poetry, 1977; Illinois Arts Council Award in Essay, 1978; DeWitt Wallace Fellow, The MacDowell Colony, 1979; Illinois Arts Council, Award in Poetry, 1981; Devins Award, University of Missouri Press, 1982; IAC Essay award, 1982; IAC Artist Grant, Summer, 1983; IAC Award in Poetry, 1984; Guggenheim Fellowship in Poetry, 1986. *Memberships:* PEN; Poetry Society of America; Society of Midland Authors. *Address:* English Dept., University Hall 102, Northwestern University, Evanston, IL 60201, USA.

KIPPENHAHN Rudolf, b. 24 May 1926, Barringen, Czechoslovakia. Astronomer. m. 19 Sept 1955, 3 daughters. *Education:* Studies in mathematics in Halle and Erlangen, 1945-51, Diploma, 1950, PhD, 1951. *Publications:* 100 Billion Suns, 1983; Light from the Depth of Time, 1987; Bound to the Sund, 1990; Stellar Structure and Evolution, 1990; Der Stern von dem wir leben, 1990; Abenteuer Weltall, 1991; Elementare Plasmaphysik, 1975. *Contributions to:* Artronomy and Astrophysics; Bild der Wissenschaft, among others. *Honours:* Carus Preis der Stadt Schweinfurt Lorenz Oken Medaille. *Memberships:* International Astron. Union, Vice President, 1991; Royal Astron. Society, Associate. *Address:* Rautenbreite 2, 3400 Gottingen, Germany.

KIRBY Louis, b. 30 Nov 1928, Liverpool, England. Journalist. m. (1) Marcia Teresa Lloyd, 1952, 2 sons, 3 daughters; (2) Heather Veronica Nicholson, 1976, 1 son, 1 daughter; (3) Heather Margaret McGlone, 1983, 1 daughter. *Appointments:* General Reporter, then Court Correspondent, 1953-60, Political Correspondent, 1960-62, Daily Mail; Chief Reporter, then Leader Writer and Political Editor, 1962-64, Assistant Editor 1964-67, Executive Editor, then Acting Editor, 1967-71, Daily

Sketch; Deputy Editor, Daily Mail, 1971-76; Editor, Evening News, 1976-80; Director, Associated Newspapers Group Ltd, and Vice-Chairman, Evening News, 1976-80; Editor, The New Standard, 1980-81, The Standard 1981-86; Editor, Evening Standard, 1980-86; Director, Mail Newspapers PLC, 1986-; Editorial Director, Associated Newspapers, 1986-88; Editorial Consultant, Daily Mail, 1988-. *Membership:* Member of Council, English Heritage and Commonwealth Press Union. *Address:* Northcliffe House, Derry Street, London W8 5EE, England.

KIRBY Rowan. *See:* **EDWARDS Rowan Judith.**

KIRK Geoffrey Stephen, b. 1921, United Kingdom. Classicist; Professor Emeritus. *Appointments:* Reader, 1958-64, Regius Professor of Greek, 1973-, currently Regius Emeritus Professor of Greek, Cambridge University; Professor of Classics: Yale University, New Haven, Connecticut, USA, 1965-71; University of Bristol, England, 1971-73. *Publications:* Heraclitus: The Cosmic Fragments (editor), 1952; The Presocratic Philosophers (with J E Raven), 1956; The Songs of Homer, 1962; The Language and Background of Homer (editor), 1964; Euripides: Bacchae (editor and translator), 1970; Myth, 1970; The Nature of Greek Myths, 1974; Homer and the Oral Tradition, 1977; The Iliad: A Commentary, vol I, 1985, vol II, 1990. *Address:* 12 Sion Hill, Bath, Avon, BA1 2UH, England.

KIRK Michael. *See:* **KNOX William.**

KIRK Russell, b. 19 Oct 1918, Plymouth, Michigan, USA, Writer; Editor, m. Annette Courtemanche, 19 Sept 1964, 4 daughters. *Education:* BA, Michigan State University, 1940; MA, Duke University, 1941; DLH, St Abndrews University, Scotland, 1952. *Appointments:* Editor, Modern Age, 1957-59; Editor, The University Bookman, 1960-; Director, Social Science Programme, Educational Research Council of America, 1979-84. *Publications:* The Conservative Mind, 1953; Eliot and His Age, 1971; The Roots of American Order, 1974; Edmund Burke, 1967; Old House of Fear, 1961; The Conservative Constitution, 1990; Randolph of Roanoke; St Andrews; Prospects for Conservatives; Enemies of the Permanent Things; The Intemperate Professor. *Contributions to:* Fortune; Yale Review; Modern Age; National Review; Chronicles; Sewanee review; Kenyon Review; Society; Contemporary Review; Fortnightly. *Honours:* Christopher Award, 1971; Weaver Prize of Ingersoll Awards, 1983; Constitutional Fellowship, National Endowment for the Humanities, 1985; Presidential Citizens Medal, 1989. *Literary Agent:* Kirby Macauley, 432 Park Avenue South, New York, NY 10016, USA. *Address:* PO Box 4, Mecosta, MI 49332, USA.

KIRK-GREENE Anthony (Hamilton Millard), b. United Kingdom. University Lecturer in Modern African History; Fellow, St Antony's College, Oxford. *Appointments:* Currently: Director, Foreign Service Programme, Oxford University, 1986-90. *Publications:* Adamawa Past and Present, 1958; The Cattle People of Nigeria (with Caroline Sassoon), 1959; The River Niger (with Caroline Sassoon), 1961; Barth's Travels in Nigeria, 1962; Principles of Native Administration in Nigeria, 1965; The Making of Northern Nigeria (editor), 1965; The Emirates of Northern Nigeria (with S J Hogben), 1966; Hausa Proverbs, 1966; A Modern Hausa Reader (with Y Aliyu), 1967; Lugard and the Amalgamation of Nigeria, 1968; Language and People of Bornu (editor), 1968; Crisis and Conflict in Nigeria, 1971; West African Narratives (with P Newman), 1972; Gazetteers of Northern Nigeria (editor), 1972; Teach Yourself Hausa (with C H Kraft), 1973; The Concept of the Good Man in Hausa, 1974; Nigeria Faces North (with Pauline Ryan), 1975; The Transfer of Power in Africa (editor), 1978; Stand by Your Radios: The Military in Tropical Africa, 1980; Biographical Dictionary of the British Colonial Governor, 1981; Nigeria since 1970 (with D Rimmer), 1981; The Sudan Political Service: A Profile, 1982; Margery Perham: West African Passage (editor), 1983; Pastoralists of the Western Savanna (with Mahdi Adamu), 1986; Margery Perham: Pacific Prelude (editor), 1988; The Sudan Political Service: A Preliminary Register of Second Careers (with Sir Gawain Bell), 1989; A Biographical Dictionary of the British Colonial Service, 1939-66, 1991. *Address:* St Antony's College, Oxford, England.

KIRKPARTICK Sidney Dale, b. 4 Oct 1955; Writer; Film Maker; m. 26 Nov 1983, 2 sons. *Education:* BA Hampshire College, Amherst, 1978; MFA, New York University, 1982. *Appointments:* Reader, Huntington Library, 1992. *Publications:* A Cast of Killers, 1986; Turning the Tide, 1991; Lords of Sipan, 1992. *Contributions to:* Los Angeles Times; American Film. *Honours:* Winner American Film Festival, 1982. *Memberships:* Board of Directors, PEN Centre West, 1991-92. *Literary Agent:* Tim Seldes, Russel and Volkening, 50W 29th Street, NY 10001, USA. *Address:* c/o Tim Seldes, Russell and Volkening, 50 W 29th St, New York, NY 10001, USA.

KIRKPATRICK Clayton, b. 8 Jan 1915, Waterman, Illinois, USA. Newspaper Editor. m. Thelma Marie De Mott, 1943, 3 sons, 2 daughters. *Education:* University of Illinois. *Appointments:* Reporter, City News Bureau, Chicago, 1938; Staff Member, 1938-, Day City Editor 1958-61, City Editor, 1961-63, Assistant Managing Editor, 1963-65, Managing Editor, 1965-67, Executive Editor 1967-69, Editor 1969-79, Chicago Tribune; Vice President, Chicago Tribune Co., 1967-77, Executive Vice President, 1977-79, President 1979-81, Chairman, 1981. *Honours:* Bronze Star Medal; Elijah Parish Lovejoy Award Colby College, 1978; William Allen White Award, University of Kansas, 1978; Fourth Estate Award, National Press Club, 1979. *Address:* 435 North Michigan Avenue, Chicago, IL 60611, USA.

KIRKUP James, (James Falconer, Andrew James, Ivy B Summerforest, Jun Terahata, Shig eru Tsuyuki), b. 23 Apr 1918, South Shields, England. Writer; Playwright; Broadcaster. *Education:* BA; FRSL; Durham University, Gregory Fellow, Poetry, Leeds University, 1950-52. *Publications include:* The Cosmic Shape, 1947; The Drowned Sailor, 1948; The Creation, 1950; The Submerged Village, 1951; A Correct Compassion, 1952; A Spring Journey, 1954; Upon This Rock, The Dark Child, The Triump of Harmony, 1955; The True Mystery of the Nativity, Ancestral Voices, The Radiance of the King, 1956; The Descent into the Cave, The Only Child (autobiography), 1957; The Peach Garden, Two Pigeons Flying High (TV plays), Sorrows, Passions and Alarms (autobiography), 1960; The Love of Others (novel), 1962; Tropic Temper (travel), 1963; Refusal to Conform, Last and First Poems, 1963; The Heavenly Mandate, 1964; Japan Industrial, Volumes I and II, 1964-65; Tokyo, 1966; Bangkok, 1967; Filipinescas, 1968; One Man's Russia, 1968; Streets of Asia, 1969; Hong Kong, 1969; Japan Behind the fan, 1970; Insect Summer (novel), 1971; Brand (Ibsen), 1972; Peer Gynt, 1973; Play Strindberg 1974; The Conformer, 1975; Don Carlos, 1975; Scenes from Sesshu, 1977; Enlightenment, 1979; Scences from Sutcliffe, 1981; Ecce Homo: My Pasolini, 1981; To the Unknown God, 1982; The Bush Toads, 1982; Folktales Japanesque, 1982; The Glory that Was Greece, 1984; Hearn in my Heart, 1984: Operas: An Actor's Revenge, 1979; Friends in Arms, Shunkinsho, 1980; No More Hiroshimas, 1982; The Damask Drum, 1984; The Sense of the Visit: New Poems, 1984; Trends and Traditions, 1985; Dictionary of Body Language, 1985; English with a Smile, 1986; Fellow Feelings (poems), 1986; Portraits and Souvenirs, 1987; The Mystery and Magic of Symbols, 1987; The Cry of the Owl : Native American Folktales and Legends, 1987; I, of All People: An Autobiography of Youth, 1988; The Best of Britain: Essays, 1989; First Firewoks, 1992; A Room in the Woods, 1991; Shooting Stars, 1992; Notes for an Autobiography, 1992; A Poet could not But be Gay, autobiography, 1992; Gaijin on the Ginza, novel, 1992; Queens have Died Young and Fair, novel, 1993; Me All Over: Memoirs of a Misfit, autobiography, 1993; Words for Contemplation; Mantras, poems, 1993; Look at it This Way, poems for children, 1993; others;

numerous poems, plays and essays and translations from French; German, Japanese, Italian and Norwegian. *Honours:* Recipient, numerous honours and awards including, Scott-Moncrieff Prize for Translation, 1992; JAL Foundation Grant, 1993. *Memberships:* Numerous professional organisations; President, The British Haiku Society. *Address:* c/o British Monomarks, Box 2780, London, WC1N 3XX, England.

KIRTLAND G B. *See:* **JOSLIN Sesyle.**

KISS Iren, b. 25 Sept 1947, Budapest, Hungary. Writer; University Professor. m. Laszlo Tabori, 10 June 1988. *Education:* PhD, History of Literature, Budapest University, 1992. *Publications:* Szelcsend, poems, 1977; Allokep, novel, 1978; Arkadiat Tatarozxak, poems, 1979; Maganrecept, (cycle), 1982; Kemopera, plays, 1988. *Contributions to:* Elet es Irodalom; Nagyuilag; Kortars; uj Iras; Eletunk; In Italy - Bollettario; Invarianti; per Approssimazione. *Honours:* Yeats Club Award, 1987; Golden Medal ofthe Brianza World Competition of Poetry, Italy, 1988. *Memberships:* Association of the Hungarian Writers; Hungarian PEN: The Berzenyi Daniel Literary Association. *Literary Agent:* (F)Anita Kenedi, *Hungarian Artis Jus. Address:* Somloi ut 60/B, Budapest 1118, Hungary.

KISS Karoly, b. 22 Aug 1930, Mako, Budapest, Hungary. Writer; Poet; Columnist. m. 27 Aug 1982, 2 sons. *Education:* BA Economics, Karoly Marx Economics University, 1969. *Appointments:* Staff, Daily Magyar Nemzet, 1973-87; Editor: Budapest (monthly), 1987-89, Hid, (quarterly), 1989-. *Publications:* Songs about Zrinyi, 1956; Songs about Hunyadi, 1956; Girl of Kosovo, 1957; Memory of Mohacs, 1976; Prey of Destruction, 1982. *Memberships:* Hungarian Writers Association; PEN Club. *Literary Agent:* Magyar Irodalmi Lexikon, Budapest. *Address:* Lajos u 116, Budapest 1036, Hungary.

KISSINGER Henry Alfred, b. 27 May 1923, Furth, Germany. Company Chairman. m. (1) Anne Fleischer, 1949, 1 son, 1 daughter, (2) Nancy Maginnes, 30 Mar 1974. *Education:* Graduated Summa Cum Laude, Harvard College, USA, 1950; MA, 1952, PhD, 1954, Harvard University. *Appointments:* 56th Secretary of State, 1973-77; Assistant to the President for national Security Affairs, 1969-75; Appointed by President Reagan to Chair the National Bipartisan Commission on Central America, 1983-85; Chairman, Kissinger Associates Incorporated; member, Commission on Integrated Longterm Strategy of the National Security Council and defence Department, 1986-88; Member iof Boards of Directors of several companies. *Publications:* A World restored: Castlereagh, Metternich and the Restoration of Peace 1812-1822; Nuclear Weapons and Foreign Policy; The Necessity for Choice: Prospects of American Foreign Policy; The Troubled Partnership: A Reappraisal of the Atlantic Alliance; Problems of National Strategy: A Book of Readings, Editor; American Foreign Policy, Three Essays; White House Years; For the record: Selected Statesments 1977-1980; Years of Upheaval, 1982; Observations: Selected Speeches and Essays 1982-1984, 1985. *Contributions To:* Numerous including: Los Angeles Times Syndication; National and international newspapers. *Honours:* Nobel Peace Prize, 1973; Presidential Medal of Freedom, 1977; Medal of Liberty, 1986. *Literary Agent:* International Creative Management. 40 W 57th Street, New York, NY 10019, USA. *Address:* 1800 K Street NW, Suite 400, Washington DC 20006, USA.

KITCHEN Bert. *See:* **KITCHEN Herbert Thomas.**

KITCHEN Herbert Thomas, (Bert Kitchen), b. 24 Apr 1940, Liverpool, England. Artist; Illustrator; Author. m. Muriel Chown, 2 Apr 1960, 2 daughters. *Education:* London Central School of Arts & Craft, 1958-61. *Publications:* Mythical Creatures; Tenrecs Twigs; Somewhere Today; Animal Alphabet; Animal Numbers; Gorilla, Chinchilla; Pig in a Barrow. *Memberships:* The

Society of Authors. *Literary Agent:* Gina Pollinger. *Address:* 222 Old Brompton Road, London SW5 0BZ, England.

KITCHEN Martin, b. 21 Dec 1936, Nottingham, England. University Professor. *Education:* BA Hons, 1963; PhD, 1966, School of Slavonic and East European Studies, University of London. *Publications include:* British Policy Towards the Soviet Union during the Second World War, 1986; Europe Between the Wars, 1988; The Political Economy of Germany 1815-1914, 1978; Fascism, 1976; The Silent Dictatorship, 1976; The German Officer Corps 1890-1914, 1968. *Contributions to:* International History Review; Central European History; Journal of the History of Ideas; Military Affairs; Slavonic Review, and others. *Honours:* Fellow, Royal Society of Canada; Royal Historical Society; Moncado Prize, American Military Academy, 1978. *Address:* Department of History, Simon Fraser University, Burnaby, BC, Canada.

KITCHENER Michael. *See:* **KELLEHER Victor.**

KITE L Patricia, b. 2 Feb 1940, New York, USA. Writer. 4 daughters. *Education:* BA, Rehabilitation Science, 1961; Biology Certificate, 1972; MS, Mass Communication and Journalism, 1982. *Appointments:* Staff, California State University, Journalism Department, 1983-84; Staff, Ohlone College, Journalism Department, 1984-87. *Publications include:* How To Be Successfully Interviewed by the Press, 1982; Interview Tips and Tricks, 1983; How to Self-Promote Your Book, 1983; Writing Fast Fun-Money Fillers, 1985; Controlling Lawn and Garden Insects, 1987; Syndicating Your Column, 1987. *Contributions to:* Over 1000 articles, short stories etc in numerous publications including: Highlights for Children, Bronx Botanical Garden Magazine, San Francisco Chronicle, San Jose Mercury, Writer's Digest. *Honours:* Stanford CWC Short Story Fiction Award, 1977; Romance Writers Award, 1984; Newspaper Columnist General Interest Award, 1984; Garden Writers of American Merit Award, 1988 and 1989. *Memberships:* Sigma Delta Chi; Society of Children's Book Writers; Writer's Connection; Vice President, National Society of Newspaper Columnists, 1986-88; Entomological Society of America; Pacific Coast Entomological Society; Garden Writers Association; Northern California Science Writers' Association. *Address:* PO Box 8318, Fremont, CA 94537, USA.

KITT Tamara. *See:* **DE REGNIRES Beatrice Schenk.**

KITTREDGE William Alfred, b. 14 Aug 1932, Portland, Oregon, USA. Professor. 1 son, 1 daughter. *Education:* BS Agriculture, Oregon State University, 1953; MFA, University of Iowa, 1969. *Appointments:* Professor of English, University of Montana, 1969-. *Publications:* The Van Gough Field, 1979; We are not in this Together, 1984; Owning It All, 1984; Hole in the Sky, 1992. *Contributions to:* Harpers; Atlantic; Esquire; Paris Review; TriQuarterly, among others. *Honours:* Governor's Award for Literature, Montana, 1987; Humanist of the Year, Montana, 1988. *Address:* English University of Montana, Missoula, MT 59801, USA.

KITZINGER Sheila Helena Elizabeth, b. 29 Mar 1929. Author; Social Anthropologist; Birth Educator. m. Uwe Kitzinger, 1952, 5 daughters. *Education:* St. Hughs College, Oxford; MLitt, University of Edinburgh, 1954. *Appointments:* Research Assistant, Dept of Anthropology, University of Edinburgh, 1952-53; Joost de Blank Award, research on problems facing West Indian mothers in Britain, 1971-73; Course Team Chairperson, Continuing Education Open University, 1981-83. *Publications include:* The Experience of Childbirth, 1987; The Experience of Breastfeeding, 1987; Pregnancy and Childbirth, 1989; Freedom and Choice in Childbirth, 1987; The Crying Baby, 1989; Womans Experience of Sex, 1983. *Contributions to:*

journals and magazines. *Membership:* Royal Society Medicine; President, Oxfordshire Royal College of Midwives; Patron Seattle School of Midwifery; Management Committee, Midwives' Information and Resource Service, 1985-87; Breastfeeding Your Baby, 1989; The Midwife Challenge, 1988; Homebirth, 1991; Ourselves as Mothers, 1988. *Literary Agent:* Mary Clemmy. *Address:* The Manor, Standlake, Nr Witney, Oxon OX8 7RH, England.

KLAITS Joseph Aaron, b. 23 Sept 1942, New York City, New York, USA. Historian. m. Barrie Gelbhaus, 5 Sept 1965, 2 sons. *Education:* BA, Columbia University, 1964; MA, 1966, PhD, 1970, University of Minnesota. *Appointments:* Professor, Department of History, Oakland University, Rochester, Michigan, 1970-; Visiting Professor, Catholic University of America, 1982-83. *Publications:* Animals and Man in Historical Perspective, 1974; Printed Propaganda under Louis XIV: Absolute Monarchy and Public Opinion, 1976; Servants of Satan: The Age of the Witch Hunts, 1985. *Contributions to:* Articles in: Journal of Modern History; Proceedings of the Western Society for French History; Church, State and Society under the Bourbon Kings of France. *Honours:* Fulbright Fellowship, 1967-68; Honourable Mention, Leo Gershoy Award, American Historical Association, 1976; National Endowment for the Humanities Fellowship, 1980-81; American Council of Learned Societies Fellowship, 1987; Folger Shakespeare Library Fellow, 1989. *Memberships:* Western Society for French History, Governing Council 1980-83; Society for French Historical Studies; American Historical Association; American Society for Eighteenth Century Studies. *Address:* Department of History, Oakland University, Rochester, MI 48309, USA.

KLAPPERT Peter, b. 14 Nov 1942, Rockville Center, New York, USA. Poet; Educator. *Education:* BA, Cornell University, 1964; MA 1967, MFA 1968, University of Iowa. *Literary Appointments:* Instructor, Rollins College, 1968-71; Briggs-Copeland Lecturer, Harvard University, 1971- 74; Visiting Lecturer, New College, Florida, 1972; Writer-in-Residence, 1976-77; Assistant Professor, 1977-88; College of William and Mary; Assistant Professor, 1977-81; Director of The Graduate Writing Program, 1979-80, 1985-88; Associate Professor, 1981-, George Mason University. *Publications:* Lugging Vegetables to Nantucket, 1971; Circular Stairs, Distress in the Mirrors, 1975; Non Sequitur O'Connor, 1977; The Idiot Princess of the Last Dynasty, 1984; 52 Pick-up; Scenes from The Conspiracy, A Documentary, 1984; Internal Foreigner (audio cassette), 1984. *Contributions to:* Antaeus; The Atlantic Monthly; Harper's; American Poetry Review; Agni Review; Ploughshares; Missouri Review; Paris Review; Parnassus: Poetry in Review. *Honours:* Yale Series of Younger Poets, 1971; NEA Fellowships in Creative Writing, 1973, 79; Lucille Medwick Award of Poetry, Society of America, 1977; Ingram Merrill Foundation Grant in Creative Writing, 1983; Resident Fellowships at Yaddo, The MacDowell Colony, The Virginia Center for the Creative Arts, The Millay Colony, La Fondation Karoly. *Memberships:* Academy of American Poets; Associated Writing Programs; PEN; Poetry Society of America; Washington Independent Writers; National Writers Union. *Literary Agent:* Sandra Hardy, Wald-Hardy Associates. *Address:* Graduate Writing Program, Department of English, George Mason University, Fairfax, VA 22030, USA.

KLASS Perri Elizabeth, b. 29 Apr 1958, Trinidad. Pediatrician; Writer. 1 son, 1 daughter. *Education:* AB, magna cum laude in Biology, Radcliffe College, Harvard University, 1979; MD, Harvard Medical School, 1986. *Publications:* Recombinations, novel, 1985; I Am Having An Adventure, short stories, 1986; A Not Entirely Benign Procedure, essays, 1987; Other Women's Children, novel, 1990. *Contributions to:* The New York Times Magazine; Massachusetts Medicine; Discover; Vogue; Glamour; Esquire; Boston Globe Magazine; Mademoiselle; Triquarterly; North American Review; and numerous others. *Memberships:* PEN; Media Spokesperson, American Academy of Pediatrics; American Medical Women's Association;

Massachusetts Medical Society; Tilling Society. *Literary Agent:* Maxine Groffsky. *Address:* Department of Pediatric Infectious Diseases, Maxwell Finland Building, Boston City Hospital, Boston, MA 02118, USA.

KLECZKOWSKA Krystyna Felicja, b. 24 June 1932, Stanislawow. Writer. m. Antoni Kleczkowski, 14 Oct 1953, 1 son. *Education:* BA, History of the Arts, Jagiellonian University, Krakow, 1953. *Publications:* Tomorrow I Will not Be a Mystery, 1959; The Four Walls of the World, 1964; A Visit to the Day Before Yesterday, 1968; The Little Partisan, 1969. *Contributions to:* Zycie Literackie; Wspolczesnesc; Zebra Odra; Ty i Ja; Zwierciadlo. *Honours:* Award, Contemporary Play Contest, 1963; Award, Polish Radio's Play Contest, 1982. *Memberships:* Association of Polish Writers; Club of Creative Intellectuals Kuznica, Krakow. *Literary Agent:* Wydawnictwo Literackie, Krakow. *Address:* Ul Grunwaldzka 21/2, 31 524 Krakow, Poland.

KLEIN Alexander, b. 1923, American (born Hungarian), *Appointments:* Consultant, Theatre for Ideas and Common Cause; Co- Founder, Arden House Annual Convocations on Foreign Policy, 1947-; Adjunct Professor of History, Political Science and Sociology, Fordham University, 1970-77; Director of Public Relations, CARE World Headquarters, 1972-82. *Publications:* Armies for Peace, 1950; Courage is the Key, 1953; The Empire City, Grand Deception, 1955; The Counterfeit Traitor, 1958; The Double Dealers, 1959; The Fabulous Rogues, 1960; The Magnificent Scoundrels, 1961; Rebels, Rogues, Rascals, 1962; That Pellett Woman!, 1965; Natural Enemies?: Youth and the Clash of Generations, 1969; Dissent, Power and Confrontation, 1972; Black Banana (co-author), 1974, filmed as Shalom, Baby!, 1975; The Savage, 1975. *Address:* 75 Bank Street, Apartment 3A, New York, NY 10014, USA.

KLEIN Theodore Eibon Donald, b. 15 July 1947, New York, USA. Writer; Editor. *Education:* AB, Brown University, 1969; MFA, Columbia University, 1972. *Appointments:* Editor in chief: Brown Daily Herald, 1968; Twilight Zone Magazine, 1981-85. *Publications:* The Ceremonies, (Novel), 1984; Dark Gods, (Story Collection), 1985. *Contributions to:* Sunday Features in New York Times: New York Daily News; Washington Post Book World; Film Column, Night Cry Magazine; Readers Digest. *Honours:* British Fantasy Society Award for Best Novel, 1985; World Fantasy award for Best Novella, 1986; Phi Beta Kappa, 1969. *Memberships:* Arthur Machen Society. Agent: Kirby McCauley, USA; Leslie Gardner, UK. *Address:* 210 West 89th Street, New York, NY 10024, USA.

KLEIN Zachary, b. 6 July 1948, New Jersey, USA. 2 sons. *Education:* Hillel Academy, Jewish Educational Centre, Mirrer Yeshia; University of Wisconsin. *Publications:* Still Among the Living, 1990; Two Way Toll, 1991. *Honours:* New York Time Notable Book of 1990; Drood Revied Editors Choice. *Literary Agent:* Herb Katz & Nancy Katz. *Address:* 5 Oakview Terrace, Boston, MA 02130, USA.

KLIAFA Maroula, b. 24 Mar 1937, Trikala, Greece. Author. m. Constantine Kliafas, 20 May 1961, 2 sons. *Education:* Diplome d'Etudes Superieures, French Institute, Athens, 1976; Diploma, Journalism, 1970. *Publications:* Storks Will Come Again, 1976; A Tree in our Yard, 1980; Tales of Thessaly, 1977; Let's Play Again, 1979; Thessaly 1881-1981: A Hundred Years' Life, 1983; People Are Bored With Reading Sad Stories, 1986. Also: The Ray of the Sun, 1974; Translations from French into Greek. *Contributions to:* Numerous magazines & journals. *Honours:* Award, Greek Children's Book Circle, 1974; Michaela Averof Awrd, Greek Authors Society, 1982; List of Honour, IX Premio Europeo di Litteratura Giovanile, Provinica di Trenton, 1983; Greek Academy Award, 1983. *Memberships:* Greek Children's Book Circle; Film Club of Trikala. *Address:* 10 Omirou Street, GR-42100 Trikala, Greece.

KLIMA Ivan, b. 14 Sept 1931, Prague, Czechoslovakia. Writer. m. Helena Mala-Klimova, 24 Sept 1958, 1 son, 1 daughter. *Education:* Master's degree, Czech Language and Esthetics, Philosophy Faculty, Charles University, Prague, 1956. *Appointments:* Editor, Ceskoslovensky spisorvatel, Publishing House, 1958-63; Editor, Literary Weeklies: Literarni noviny, 1963-67; Literarni Listy, 1968; Listy, 1968-69; Visiting Professor, Slavic Department, Ann Arbor, Michigan, USA, 1969-70; Freelance Author publishing abroad, 1970-89. *Publications:* Lod jmenem nadeje, (English: A Ship Named Hope, 1970) novel, 1968; Milostne leto, (English: A Summer Affair, 1987) novel, 1972; Ma vesela jitra, (English: My Merry Mornings, 1983) short stories, 1979; Moje prvni lasky, (English: My First Love, 1985) short stories, 1985; Laska a Smeti, (English: Love and Garbage, 1990) novel, 1987; Soudce z milosti, (English: Judge on Trial), novel, 1987; Plays: Zamek, (English: The Castle), 1964; The Master, 1967, English version, 1970; The Sweetshop Myriam, 1968, English version, 1969; President and the Angel, English version, 1975; Klara and Two Men, 1968, English version, 1969; Bridegroom for Marcela, 1968, English version, 1969; The Games, 1975, English version, 1985; Kafka and Felice, 1986; Moje Zlata Remesla, (English: My Golden Trades), 1992. *Contributions to:* Various magazines in various countries including: New York Review of Books; National; Granta; Index on Censorship. *Honours:* Hostovsky Award, New York, 1985. *Memberships:* Union of Czechoslovak Writers, Central Committee 1963-70; Executive President, Czech PEN Centre, 1990-; Council Member, Czech Writers, 1989-. *Literary Agents:* Adam Bromberg, Stockholm, Sweden; Theatre Agent: Projeklt Köln Brd.

KLINE Suzy Weaver, b. 27 Aug 1943, Berkeley, California, USA. Teacher; Childrens Author. m. Rufus Kline, 12 Oct 1968, 2 daughters. *Education:* BA, University of California, Berkeley; Standard Teachers Credential, California State University. *Publications:* Childrens Novels: Herbie Jones, 1985; What's the Matter with Herbie Jones?, 1986; Herbie Jones and the Class Gift, 1987; Herbie Jones and The Monster Ball, 1988; Orp; Orp and the Chop Suey Burgers; Horrible Harry series; Mary Marony and the Snake; Picture Books: Shhhh!, 1984; Don't Touch!, 1985; Ooops!, 1988. *Contributions to:* Instructor Magazine. *Honours:* Teacher of the Year, Torrington, 1986; Herbie Jones, Children's Choice for 1986, Winner of the West Virginia Children's Book Award, 1987-88, Omar Award of Indiana, 1987, Nominated for Sequoyah Children's Book Award, 1988; What's the Matter with Herbie Jones?, Children's Choice for 1987, IRA, Editors' Choice for 1986 Booklist, Nominated for Utah Children's Book Award; Nominated for Sunshine State Young Readers Book Award, 1988; Nominated for Georgia Childrens Book Award, 1988. *Memberships:* Society of Childrens Book Writers; Authors Guild; Connecticut Teachers Association; etc. *Address:* 124 Hoffman St., Torrington, CT 06790, USA.

KLINGER Mario D, b. 17 June 1946, 1 son, 2 daughters. *Publications:* Erotic Art in 30 volumes; American Quilts; Ambroius and Hans Holbein, catalogue raisonne; Intern. Guide of arts experts and catalgoue raisonnees; Alfred Kohler, biography/catalogue raisonne. *Address:* Hutergasse 4, D-8500 Nuernberg, Germany.

KLINKOWITZ Jerome, b. 24 Dec 1943, Milwaukee, Wisconsin, USA. Author. m. (1) Elaine Ptaszynaki, 29 Jan 1966, (2) Julie Huffman, 27 May 1978, 1 son, 1 daughter. *Education:* BA, 1966, MA, 1967, Marquette University; PhD, University of Wisconsin, 1970. *Appointments:* University Fellow, University of Wisconsin, 1968-69; Assistant Professor, English, Northern Illinois University, 1969-70; Associate Professor, English, 1972-75, Professor, 1975-, University Distinguished Scholar, 1985-, University of Northern Iowa. *Publications:* Literary Disruptions, 1975; The Life of Fiction, 1977; The American 1960s, 1980; The Practice of Fiction in America, 1980; Kurt Vonnegut, 1982; The Self Apparent Word, 1984; Literary

Subversions, 1985; The New American Novel of Manners, 1986; Rosenberg/Barthes/Hassan: The Postmodern Habit of Thought, 1988; Short Season and Other Stories, 1988; Their Finest Hours: Narratives of the RAF and Luftwaffe in World War II, 1989; Slaughterhouse-Five: Reinventing the Novel and the World, 1990; Listen: Gerry Mulligan/An Aural Narrative in Jazz, 1991; Donal Barthelme: An Exhibition, 1991; Writing Baseball, 1991; Structuring the Void, 1992. *Contributions to:* over 250 essays in Partisan Review, New Republic, Nation, American Literature; short stories in, North American Review, Chicago Tribune, The San Francisco Chronicle. *Honours:* NEA/PEN Syndicated Fiction Prizes, 1984, 1985. *Memberships:* MLA; PEN, American Centre. *Literary Agent:* Nat Sobel, 146 East 19th St, New York, NY 10003-2404, USA. *Address:* 1904 Clay Street, Cedar Falls, IA 50613, USA.

KNAAK Richard Allen, b. 28 May 1961, Chicago, Illinois, USA. Author. *Education:* Bachelor's Degree (LAS) Rhetoric, University of Illinois. *Publications:* The Legend of Huma, 1988; Firedrake, 1989; Ice Dragon, 1989; Kaz the Minotaur, 1990; Wolfhelm, 1990; Shadow Steed, 1990; The Shrowded Realm, 1991; Children of the Drake, 1991; Dragon Tome, 1992; The Crystal Dragon, 1993; King of The Grey, 1993. *Memberships:* Science Fiction and Fantasy Writers of America. *Literary Agent:* Peekner Literary Agency. *Address:* PO Box 8158, Bartlett, IL 60103, USA.

KNEBEL Fletcher,b. 1 Oct 1911, Ohio, USA.Writer. m. Constance Wood, 28 Apr 1985, 1 son. *Education:* BA, Miami University. *Publications include:* Seven Days in May, (with Charles Bailey), 1962; Dark Horse, 1972; Night of Camp David, 1965; Crossing in Berlin, 1981; No High Ground, (with Charles Bailey), 1960; Trespass, 1968. *Contributions to:* Look Magazine; Readers Digest; Honolulu Magazine. *Honours:* Doctor of Literature, Miami University, 1964; Drake UNiversity, 1967. *Memberships:* Gridiron Club, President 1964. *Address:* 1070 Oilipuu Place, Honolulu, HI 96825, USA.

KNECHT Robert Jean,b. 20 Sept 1926, London, England. Emeritus Professor of French History. m. (1) Sonia Hodge, 8 Aug 1956, (2) Maureen White, 28 Jul. 1986. *Education:* BA, 1948; MA, 1953, Kings College London; DLitt, Birmingham, 1984. *Publications:* The Voyage of Sir Nicholas Carewe, 1959; Francis I, 1982; French Renaissance Monarchy, 1984; The French Wars of Religion, 1989; Francis I and Absolute Monarchy, 1969; The Fronde, 1975; Richelieu, 1991. *Contributions to:* Times Literary Supplement; English Historical Review; History; Journal of Ecclesiastical History; Bulletin Monumental; and others. *Memberships:* Society of Renaissance Studies, Chairman 1989-; FR Historical Society; Societe de l'Histoire de France. *Address:* 79 Reddings Road, Moseley, Birmingham B13 8LP, England.

KNEF Hildegard, b. 28 Dec 1925, Ulm, Germany. Actress; Singer; Authoress. m. (2) David Cameron, 1 daughter, (3) Paul Rudolph Schell, 1977. *Education:* Art Studio, Ufa Babelsberg. *Publications:* Der Geschenkte Gaul, 1970; Ich brauche Tapetenwechsel, 1972; Das urteil, 1975; Heimwehblues, 1978; Nicht als Neugier, 1978; So nicht, 1982; Romy, 1983. *Honours:* Edison Prize, 1972; Bundesverdienstkreuz (1st Class), 1975; Award, Best Female Role, Karlsbad Film Festival, 1976; Bunesfilmpreis, 1977; Golden Tulip, Amsterdam, 1981; other film awards; Mark Twain Prize, for Das Urteil, 1980. *Address:* c/o Agentur Jovanovic, Perfallstr. 6, 8000 Munich 80, Federal Republic of Germany.

KNEVITT Charles Philip Paul, b. 10 Aug 1952, Dayton, Ohio, USA. (British). Journalist. m. Lucy Joan Isaacs, 4 June 1981, 1 daughter. *Education:* BA, Honours, School of Architecture, University of Manchester. *Appointments:* Freelance Journalist, 1974-; Editor, What's New in Building, 1978-80; Architecture Correspondent; Sunday Telegraph, 1980-84, The Times, 1984-; Architecture/Planning Consultant, Thames News, Thames TV, 1983- 86.

Publications: Community Architecture, 1987, with Nick Wates; Space on Earth, 1985; Perspectives, 1986, Editor; Monstrous Carbuncles, 1985, Editor; Connections, 1984; Manikata, 1980; Architecural Anecdotes, 1988, Co-editor. *Contributions to:* Guardian; Daily Telegraph; Architects' Journal; Architectural Review; Building; Building Design. *Honours:* Architectural Journalist of the Year, IBP, 1984; Special Commendation for Manikata, 1983 (Interarch); Commendation, Young Writer of the Year, IBP, 1978; Student Travel Award, Manchester Society of Architects, 1974. *Memberships:* Fellow, Royal Society of Arts, 1987; Architecture Club, 1985, Hon. Treasurer, 1986-; International Building Press, 1977, Executive Committee, 1977-80, Hon. Treasurer, 1978-80. *Address:* Crest House, 102-104 Church Road, Teddington, Middlesex, TW11 8PY, England.

KNIGHT Alanna, b. South Shields, Tyne & Wear, England. Novelist; Biographer. m. Alexander Harrow Knight, 2 sons. *Education:* Fellow, Royal Society of Antiquaries, Scotland. *Appointments include:* Founder, Chairman, Aberdeen Writers Workshop, 1967; Lecturer, Creative Writing, Workers Educational Association, and Andrews' University Summer School, 1971-75; Tutor, Arvon Foundation, 1982. *Publications include:* Legend of the Loch (award), 1969; This Outward Angel, 1971; October Witch, 1971; Castle Clodha, 1972; Lament for Lost Lovers, 1972; White Rose, 1974; A Stranger Came By, 1974; Passionate Kindness, 1974; A Drink for the Bridge, 1976; Black Duchess, 1980; Castle of Foxes, 1981; Colla's Children, 1982; Robert Louis Stevenson Treasury, 1985; The Clan, 1985; RLS in the South Seas, 1986; Estella, 1986. *Contributions include:* Scottish Field; Highlander; Aberdeen Leopard. Also radio documentaries, short stories, plays; short stories, features with world syndication. *Honour:* 1st novel Award, Romantic Novelists Association, 1969. *Memberships include:* Former Committees, Society of Authors, Scottish PEN; Crime Writers Association; Radiowriters Association; Romantic Novelists Association. Literary Agent: Giles Gordon, Anthony Shiel Associates, 43 Doughty Street, London WC1N 2LF. *Address:* 9 Dryden Place, Edinburgh EH9 1RP, Scotland.

KNIGHT Andrew Stephen Bower, b. 1 Nov 1939. Journalist; Newspaper Executive. m. (1) Victoria Catherine Brittain (div), 1966, 1 son, (2) Begum Sabiha Rumani Malik, 1975, 2 daughters. *Appointments:* Editor, The Economist, 1974-85; Chief Executive, Daily Telegraph, 1985-. *Memberships:* Director, Tandem Computers Inc., 1984-; Member, Advisory Board, Centre for Economic Policy Reseach, Stanford University, USA, 1981-; Council Royal Institute of International Affairs, 1976-; Council, Templeton College, Oxford, 1984-; Governor and member, Council of Man. Ditchley Foundation, 1982-; Atlantic Institute, 1985-; Steering Committee, Bilderberg Meetings, 1980; Council of Friends of Covent Garden, 1981; Trustee, Harlech Scholars Trust, 1985; Director of Hollinger Inc., 1987; Director of Reuters, 1988. *Address:* Daily Telegraph, Peterborough Court, South Quay, 181 Marsh Wall, London E14 9SR, England.

KNIGHT Arthur Winfield, b. 29 Dec 1937, San Francisco, USA. Writer. m. 25 Aug 1976. 1 daughter. *Education:* AA Santa Rosa Junior College, 1956-58; BA English, 1958-60; MA Creative Writing, 1960-62, San Francisco State University. *Appointments:* Professor of English, California University of Pennsylvania, 1966-93; Film Critic: Russian River News, Guerneville, 1991-92, Anderson Valley Advertiser, Boonville, CA, 1992-, Potpourri, Prarie Village, KS, 1993-. *Publications:* Basically Tender, 1991; Wanted!, 1988; King of the Beatniks, 1986; A Marriage of Poets, 1984; The Beat Vision, (co-editor), 1987; Cowboy Poems, 1993. *Contributions to:* New York Quarterly, Poet Lore, Oui, The Cape Rock college English, The Massachussetts Review, the Redneck Review of Literature, New Frontiers Vol II. *Honours:* 3rd Annual First Place Winner of the Joycean Lively Arts Guild Poetry Competition, 1982. *Memberships:* Friends of Jesse James Farm; Billy

the Kid Outlaw Gang. *Address:* PO Box 439, California, PA 15419, USA.

KNIGHT Bernard, (Bernard Picton), b. 1931, British. *Appointments:* Lecturer in Forensic Medicine, University of London, 1959-65; Medical Editor, Medicine, Science and the Law, 1960-63; Lecturer 1962-65, Senior Lecturer 1965-76, Reader 1976, Professor and Consultant in Forensic Pathology, University of Wales, College of Medicine; Senior Lecturer in Forensic Pathology, University of Newcastle, 1965-68. *Publications:* The Lately Deceased (as Bernard Picton), 1963; Thread of Evidence (as Bernard Picton), 1965; Mistress Murder (as Bernard Picton), 1966; Russian Roulette (as Bernard Picton), 1968; Policeman's Progress (as Bernard Picton), 1969; Tiger at Bay (as Bernard Picton), 1970; Murder, Suicide or Accident, 1971; Deg Y Dragwyddoldeb, 1972; Legal Aspects of Medical Practise, 1972, 3rd edition, 1982; In the Dead, Behold the Quick, Edfyn Brau, 1973; Discovering the Human Body, 1980; Forensic Radiology, 1981; Lawyer's Guide to Forensic Medicine, 1982; Sudden Death in Infancy, Coroner's Autopsy, 1983; Post-Modern Technicians Handbooks, 1984; Pocket Guide to Forensic Medicine, 1985; Simpson's Forensic Medicine, 10th edition, 1991; Forensic Pathology, 1991. *Address:* Wales Institute of Forensic Medicine, Royal Infirmary, Cardiff CF2 1SZ, Wales.

KNIGHT Cranston Sedrick, b. 10 Sept 1950, Chicago, Illinois, USA. m. Dolores Anderson, 5 Aug 1978, 2 sons, 1 daughter. *Education:* BA, History, Southern Illinois University, 1977; MA, East Asian and American History, Northeastern Illinois University, 1990. *Appointments:* Poetry Editor, Eclipses Magazine, University of Illinois, 1971; Editor, C'Est La Vie Magazine, Northwestern University, 1983- 86; Literary Consultant, Mystic Voyage, 1978-79; B.O.L.T, Southern Illinois University, 1979-80. *Publications include:* Tour of Duty, 1986; Freedsom Song, (poetry), 1988; Garden of the Beast, (poetry), 1989; Cadence Magazine, 1986; Samisdat Literary Anthology, 1987; Pearl Magazine Spring, (poem), 1989; Wide Open Magazine, (poem), 1989. *Contributions to:* The Otherwise Room Anthology; American Poetry Association; Walking Point; Black American Literature Forum; Deros Poetry Magazine; AIM Magazine. *Honours:* 1st Place, Trophy for Disabled Students, Southern Illinois University, 1974; 2nd Place Trophy, Kappa Alpha Psi, 1975; 1st Place Trophy, Kappa Psi Performing Arts Production, 1976; Literary Grant, Benjamin Henry Matchett Foundation, 1990. *Memberships:* Illinois Writers Inc.; International Black Writers Society; Westside Writers Guild; NAACP, Midwest Asian Association, Chicago Japanese Association; Phi Alpha Theta History Honor's Society. *Address:* 5935 N Magnolia Apt 1, Chicago, IL 60660, USA.

KNIGHT David. See: PRATHR Richard.

KNIGHT David Marcus, b. 30 Nov 1936, Exeter, England. University Professor. m. Sarah Prideaux, 21 July 1962, 2 sons, 4 daughters. *Education:* BA, Chemistry, 1960, Keble College; Diploma, History and Philosophy of Science, 1962; DPhil, 1964, Oxford University. *Appointments:* Editor, British Journal of History of Science 1982-88; General Editor, Blackwell Science Biographies, 1989-. *Publications:* The Age of Science, 1988; A Companion to the Physical Sciences, 1989; Humphry Davy, 1992; Ideas in Chemistry, 1992; Natural Science Books in English 1600-1900, 1989; Sources for the History of Science, 1984; Ordering the World, 1981; The Transcendental Part of Chemistry, 1978; Zoological Illustration, 1977. *Contributions to:* Isis; British Journal for the History of Science; Annals of Science; Ambix; Studies in Romanticism. *Literary Agent:* The Peters, Fraser and Dunlop Group Ltd. *Address:* Department of Philosophy, Durham University, 50 Old Elvet, Durham DH1 3HN, England.

KNIGHT Etheridge, b. 1931, American. *Appointments:* Poet- in-Residence, Lincoln University,

Jefferson City, MO, 1970-71; Poetry Editor, Motive, Nashville, TN, 1970-71; Co-Editor, Black Box, WA, 1971-72. *Publications:* Poems from Prison, The Idea of Ancestry, 2 Poems for Black Relocation Centers, Voce negre dal carcere (in US as Black Voices from Prison) (ed), 1968; For Black Poets Who Think of Suicide, A Poem for Brother Man, 1972; Belly Song and Other Poems, 1973; Born of a Woman: New and Selected Poems, 1980. *Address:* c/o Broadside Press, PO Box 04257, Detroit, MI 48204, USA.

KNIGHT Gareth. *See:* **WILBY Basil Leslie.**

KNIGHT William Edwards, b. 1 Feb 1922, Tarrytown, New York, USA. US Foreign Service Officer. m. Ruth L Lee, 14 Aug 1946, 2 sons. *Education:* BA, Yale College, 1942; Pilot Training, US Army Air Force, 1943-44; B-24 Co-Pilot, 1944-45; MA, Yale University, 1946; Industrial College of the Armed Forces, 1961-62; State Department Senior Seminar in Foreign Policy, 1971-72. *Appointments:* Foreign Service Officer, US Department of State, 1946-75. *Publications:* Mystery and suspense: The Tiger Game, 1986; The Bamboo Game, 1992-93; Screenplays in progress: Plague of Locusts; The Byte Fairy. *Contributions to:* Articles to journals of foreign policy and diplomatic affairs; President and Chief Executive Officer, The Araluen Press, 1992-. *Memberships:* Washington Independent Writers; Diplomatice and Consular Officers Retired; Army Navy Country Club of Washington; Army Navy Club of Manila, Treasurer 1970; Yale Club of Washington; Randolph Mountain Club, President 1985-87. *Literary Agent:* Lichtman, Singer and Ross, Washington, DC, USA. *Address:* 5000 Park Place, Bethesda, MD 20816, USA.

KNIGHT William Nicholas, b. 18 Apr 1939, Mount Vernon, New York, USA. Professor of English. m. 2 Sept 1961, 1 son, 3 daughters. *Education:* BA cum laude, Amherst College, 1961; MA, University of California, Berkeley, 1963; PhD, Indiana University, 1968; Postdoctoral, Institute of Advanced Legal Studies, University of London, 1969-70. *Appointments include:* Wesleyan University, 1966-75; Chairman, Humanities, University of Missouri, Rolla, 1975-. *Publications include:* Death of J.K., play, 1969; Shakespere's Hidden Life, 1974; Law in Spenser, in Spenser Encyclopaedia (Toronto), 1988. *Contributions to:* Numerous journals, USA, Europe, Japan, including: Christian Science Monitor; USA Today; Avalon to Camelot; Shakespeare Translation; Review of English Studies; Shakespeare Survey; Erasmus Review; Costerus Essays, American Legal Studies Association. Reviews, poems, short stories, various small magazines. *Honours include:* Scholar, Warburg Institute, University of London, 1969-70; Fellow, Wesleyan Centre for Humanities, 1971; Ford Foundation Fellow, 1972; Newberry Fellow, 1983; Numerous Teaching Awards, Research Grants. *Memberships include:* International Shakespeare Association; Shakespeare Association of America; Spenser Society; Modern Language Association; Missouri Philogical Association. *Literary Agents:* Arthur C. Pine Associates, NYC; Sterling Lord Associates, NYC. *Address:* 1313 Whitney Lane, Rolla, Missouri 65401, USA.

KNIGHTLEY Phillip George, b. 23 Jan 1929, Sydney, Australia. Author/Journalist. m. Yvonne Fernandes, 13 July 1964, 1 son, 2 daughters. *Publications:* The First Casualty, 1975; The Vestey Affair, 1980. The Second Oldest Profession, 1986; An Affair of State, 1988; Philby: KGB Masterspy, 1989. *Honours:* British Journalist of the Year, 1980 and 1988. *Memberships:* Society of Authors; NUJ. *Literary Agent:* Tessa Sayle Agency. *Address:* 4 Northumberland Place, London W2 5BS, England.

KNOLL Erwin, b. 17 July 1931, Vienna, Austria. Editor; Writer. m. Doris E. Ricksteen, 1 Mar 1954, 2 sons. *Education:* BA, New York University, 1953. *Appointments:* Staff, Editor & Publisher Magazine, 1948-53, 1955-56; Associate Editor, Better Schools

Magazine, 1956-57; Reporter, Assistant World Editor, Washington Post, 1957-62; Washington Editor, Los Angeles Times-Washington Post News Service, 1962-63; Washington Correspondent, Newhouse National News Service, 1963-68; Washington Editor, 1968-73; Editor, 1973-, The Progressive. *Publications:* Anything But the Truth, 1968; Scandal in the Pentagon, 1969; American Militarism, 1970; War Crimes and the American Conscience, 1970; No Comment, 1984. *Contributions to:* many periodicals. *Address:* c/o The Progressive, 409 East Main Street, Madison, WI 53703, USA.

KNOTT Bill. *See:* **KNOTT William Cecil.**

KNOTT Bill. *See:* **KNOTT William Kilborn.**

KNOTT Will C. *See:* **KNOTT William Cecil.**

KNOTT William Cecil, (Bill J Carol, Tabor Evans, Bill Knott, Will C Knott, Bryan Smith), b. 7 Aug 1927, Boston, MA, USA. Professor of English. *Education:* AA, 1949; BA, 1951, Boston University; MA, State University of New York, Oswego, 1966. *Publications include:* The Craft of Fiction, 1974; Circus Catch, 1963; Scatback, 1964; Long Pass, 1966; Lefty's Long Throw, 1967; High Fly to Center, 1972; Fullback Fury, 1974; Junk Pitcher, 1967; Night Pursuit, 1966; Taste of Vengeance, 1975; Lyncher's Moon, 1980; Longarm and the Railroaders, 1980; Longarm on the Yellowstone, 1980; Longarm and the Outlaws of Skull Canyon, 1990; Longarm and the Tattoed Lady, 1990; Mission Code: King's Pawn, 1981; The Trailsman Series (15 books 1984-86); The Golden Hawk Series, (9 books 1986-88); The Texan, 1987; numerous others. *Memberships:* Western Writer's of America, President 1980-81. *Address:* 216 Falls of Venice, South Venice, Florida 34292, USA.

KNOTT William Kilborn, (Bill Knott), b. 1940, American. *Publications:* The Naomi Poems, Book One: Corpse and Beans, 1968; Aurealism: A Study: A Poem, Are You Ready Mary Baker Eddy? (with J Tate), 1970; Auto-Necrophilia: The Bill Knott Poems, Book 2, Nights of Naomi, 1971; Love Poems to Myself, 1974; Rome in Rome, 1976; Selected and Collected Poems, Lucky Daryll (with James Tate), 1977; Becos, 1983. *Address:* c/o Random House, 201 East 50th Street, New York, NY 10022, USA.

KNOWLES Valerie Jean, b. 2 Aug 1934, Montreal, Quebec, Canada. Freelance Writer. m. David Clifford Knowles, 11 Mar 1961. *Education:* Smith College, Northampton, Massachusetts, USA, 1956; McGill University, Quebec, 1957; BJ, Carleton University, Ottawa, Ontario, 1964. *Publications:* Leaving With A Red Rose: A History of the Ottawa Civic Hospital School of Nursing, 1981; First Person: A Biography of Cairine Wilson, Canada's First Woman Senator, 1988; Strangers At Our Gates: Canadian Immigration and Immigraiton Policy, 1540-1990, 1992. *Contributions to:* Numerous Canadian publications including: Canadian Geographic; Vie des Arts; The Beaver; Foodservice and Hospitality; Horizon Canada. *Honours:* Ontario Arts Council Writers Reserve Grants, 1988, 1990. *Memberships:* Writers Union of Canada; Media Club of Ottawa, Hospitality Chairman 1977- 83. *Literary Agent:* Joanne Kellock. *Address:* 554 Piccadilly Avenue, Ottawa, Ontario, Canada K1Y 0J1.

KNOWLTON Derrick, b. 1921, British. *Appointment:* Local Gorvernment Administrative Assistant, 1948-69. *Publications:* The Naturalist in Central Southern England, 1973; The Naturalist in Scotland, 1974; Discovering Walks in the New Forest, 1976; The Naturalist in the Hebrides, 1977; Walks in Hampshire, Looking at Nature: A Beginner's Guide, 1978; Looking at Mammals: A Beginner's Guide, Tramp after God: The Story of Willie Mullan (co-author), 1979; Found by God: The Story of Vijay Menon, 1982. *Address:* The White House, Vicarage Lane, Curdridge, Southampton, Hampshire, England.

KNOX Bill. *See:* **KNOX William.**

KNOX Calvin. *See:* **SILVERBERG Robert.**

KNOX Ray, b. 23 Sept 1926, Wellington, New Zealand. Editor. m. Heather Douglas, 23 Feb 1955, 3 daughters. *Education:* Victoria University, Wellington. *Appointments include:* Feature Writer, 1956; Chief Reporter 1964, New Zealand Listener; Editor in Chief, New Zealand's Heritage, 1971; Editor in Chief, New Zealand Today, 1973; Editor in Chief, New Zealand's Nature Heritage, 1974. *Publications:* Editor, Collins Nature Heritage, series; A Thousand Mountains Shining, 1984. *Contributions to:* New Zealand Listener; Here and Now; New Zealand National Review; New Zealand Mirror; Radio Documentaries, talks and criticism to New Zealand Broadcasting Corporation; TV Documentaries on New Zealand novelists. *Membership:* PEN. *Address:* 1 Bayview Road, Paremata, New Zealand.

KNOX William, (Michael Kirk, Bill Knox, Robert MacLeod, Noah Webster), b. 20 Feb 1928, Glasgow, Scotland. Author; Journalist. m. Myra Ann MacKill, 31 Mar 1950, 1 son, 2 daughters. *Appointments:* Deputy News Editor, Evening News, 1957; Scottish Editor, Kemsley Newspapers, 1957-60; News Editor, Scottish Television, 1960-62; Freelance author and broadcaster 1962-; Presenter STV Crimedesk 1977-89; Editor, RNLI Scottish Lifeboat, 1984-. *Publications:* Over 60 novels of crime, sea and adventure; also radio and TV adaptations of own work. *Honours:* William Knox Collection established, Boston University, 1969; Police Review Award, 1986; Paul Harris Fellow, Rotary International, 1989. *Memberships include:* Association of Scottish Motoring Writers, past President, Hon. Member; Scottish Committee, Society of Authors; Crime Writers Association; Mystery Writers Association. *Literary Agent:* Random-Century Publishing, London. *Address:* 55 Newtonlea Avenue, Newton Mearns, Glasgow G77 5QF, Scotland.

KNOX-JOHNSTON Robin, b. 17 Mar 1939, Putney, London, England. Master Mariner; Author. m. 6 Jan 1962, 1 daughter. *Education:* Master's Certificate, 1965. *Publications:* A World of My Own, 1969; Sailing, 1974; Twilight of Sail, 1978; Last But Not Least, 1978; Seamanship, 1986; The BOC Challenge 1986-87, in 1987; The Cape of Good Hope, 1989; The History of Yachting, 1990; The Columbus Venture, 1991; Sea Ice Rock, (with Chris Bonington), 1992. *Contributions to:* Yachting World, UK; Yachting Monthly, UK; Cruising World, USA; The Guardian. *Honours:* Commander, Order of British Empire (CBE), 1969; Hon DSc, Maine Maritime Academy. *Memberships:* Younger Brother, Trinity House; Honourable Company of Master Mariners; F.R.G.S. (Fellow of the Royal Geographical Society). *Literary Agent:* John Farquarson Ltd. *Address:* 95 Nightingale House, Thomas More St, London E1 9VB, England.

KNOX-MAWER June Ellis, b. 10 May 1930, Wrexham, North Wales. Writer; Broadcaster. m. Ronald Knox-Mawer, 30 June 1951, 1 son, 1 daughter. *Education:* Grove Park Girls Grammar School, Wrexham, 1941-47. *Appointments:* Trained as Journalist, Chester Chronicle, 1948-50; Aden Correspondent, Daily Express, 1952-56; Presenter and Author, various literary and feature programmes, BBC Radio 4, 1970-. *Publications:* The Sultans Came to Tea, 1961; A Gift of Islands, 1965; A World of Islands, 1968; Marama, novel of 19th century Fiji, 1972; A South Sea Spell, 1975; Tales from Paradise, 1986; Marama of the Islands, 1986; Sandstorm (novel set in South Arabia), 1991. *Contributions to:* The Guardian; Various women's magazines. *Honours:* Sandstorm, Romantic Novel of the Year Award, 1992. *Memberships:* Council, Royal Commonwealth Society; Library Committee, Commonwealth Trust. *Literary Agent:* Bruce Hunter, David Higham Associates, England. *Address:* c/o David Higham Associates, 5-8 Lower John Street, Golden Square, London W1, England.

KNOX-MAWER Ronald, b. 3 Aug 1925, Wrexham, Wales. Retired Judge, HM Overseas Judiciory. m. 30 June 1952, 1 son, 1 daughter. *Education:* Emmanuel College, Cambridge, 1947-49; MA (Cantab); Barrister, Middle Temple. *Publications:* Palm Court, 1979; Tales from a Palm Court, 1986; Tales of a Man Called Father, 1989; A Case of Bananas and Other South Seas Trials, 1992; 4 volumes Commonwealth Law Reports; Law of Workmen's Compensation. *Contributions to:* Under pseudonym, latterly under own name: Punch; The Times; Argosy; Cornhill; Sunday Express; The Listener; Weekend Telegraph; The Independent; Saturday Review. *Address:* c/o Midland Bank, Ruabon, Clwyd, North Wales.

KNUDSON R(ozanne) R, b. 1932, American. *Publications:* Selected Objectives in the English Language Arts (with Arnold Lazarus), 1967; Sports Poems (ed with P K Ebert), 1971; Zanballer, 1972; Jesus Song, 1973; You Are the Rain, Fox Running, 1974; Zanbanger, 1977; Zanboomer, Weight Training for the Young Athlete (with F Columbo), Starbodies (with F Columbo), 1978; Rinehart Lifts, 1980; Just Another Love Story, Speed, Muscles, Punch, 1982; Zan Hagen's Marathon, 1984; Babe Didrikson, Frankenstein's 10 K, 1985; Martina Navratilova, Rinehart Shouts, 1986; Julie Brown, American Sports Poems (ed with May Swenson), 1987; The Wonderful Pen of May Swenson, 1993. *Address:* 73 Boulevard, Sea Cliff, New York, NY 11579, USA.

KNUTSON Roger Marvin, b. 3 Jan 1933, Montevideo, Minnesota, USA. College Professor. m. Sharon Louise Belding, 31 Aug 1957, 3 sons, 2 daughters. *Education:* BA, St Olaf College, Northfield, Minnesota; MS, 1961, PhD, 1965, Michigan State University. *Publications:* Flattened Fauna, 1987; Furtive Fauna, 1992. *Contributions to:* Plants in Heat, to Natural History, 1984; Plants that Make Heat while the Sun Shines, to Natural History, 1985. *Memberships:* American Association for the Advancement of Science; American Institute of Biological Sciences; Iowa Academy of Sciences. *Literary Agent:* Jeanne K Hanson. *Address:* Luther College, 700 College Drive, Decorah, IA 52101, USA.

KOBAK Annette Margot, b. 20 Nov 1943, London, England. Writer; Broadcaster. m. Reg Gadney, 16 July 1966, div, 1 son, 1 daughter. *Education:* Girton College, Cambridge, 1962-65. *Publications:* Isahelle: The Life of Isabelle Eberhardt; Vagabond. *Contributions to:* The New York Times Book Review; The Times Literary Supplement; Harpers & Queen. *Honours:* Society of Authors Travel Award. *Memberships:* Cheltenham Literary Festival; The Society of Authors; PEN. *Literary Agent:* Rachel Calder, Tessa Sayle Agency, 11 Jubilee Place, SW3. *Address:* 6 Park Place, Cheltenham, Glos GL50 2QR, England.

KOCH Christopher John, b. 16 July 1932. Author. m. Irene Vilnonis, 23 Apr 1960, 1 son. *Education:* BA Hons; DLItt, University of Tasmania. *Publications:* The Boys in the Island, 1958; Across the Sea Wall, 1965; The Year of Living Dangerously, 1978; The Doubleman, 1965; *Essays:* Crossing the Gap, 1987. *Honours:* National Book Council Award for Australian Literature, 1979; Miles Franklin Prize, 1985. *Literary Agent:* Curtis Brown Ltd., *Address:* P.O. Box 19, Paddington, NSW 2021, Australia.

KOCH Claude Francis, b. 28 Nov 1918, Philadephia, USA. Emeritus Professor. m. Mary P Kane, 7 Sept 1941, 5 sons, 1 daughter. *Education:* BS, La Salle University; MA, University of Florida. *Publications:* Island Interlude; Light in Silence; The Kite in the Sea; A Casual Company; Mother; Anne Askewe. *Contributions to:* Sewanee Review; Southern Review; Antioch Review; Kansas Quarterly; Four Quarters; Northwest Review; Ave Maria; Delta Review. *Honours:* Dodd, Mead Intercollegiate Literary fellowship; Sewanee Review Fellowship in Fiction; La Salle College Centenary Award; Rockerfeller Foundation Fellowship in Fiction; Lindback Award for

Distinguished Teaching. *Address:* 128 West Highland Avenue, Philadelphia, PA 19118, USA.

KOCH Joanne Barbara, b. 28 Mar 1941, Chicago, Illinois, USA. Author; Playwright. m. Lewis Z Koch, 30 May 1964, 1 son, 2 daughters. *Education:* BA Hons., Cornell University; MA (Woodrow Wilson Fellowship), Columbia University. *Appointments:* Guest Lecturer: Loyola University, DePaul University; Writer-in-Residence, Lake Forest College, Southern Illinois University. *Publications:* The Marriage Savers (with Lewis Koch), 1976; Contributor: Readings in Psychology Today, 1978; Children : Development through Adolescence, 1983; Marriage and the Family, 1983; Child Development : Topical Approach, 1985; Novels (as Joanna Z Adams), Makeovers, 1987; Rushes, 1988; Plays: Haymarket: Footnote to a Bombing; Teeth; Nesting Dolls; XX-XY; Grant 5742; Danceland (musical with Julie Shannon); Teleplays: Today I Am a Person; The Price of Daffodils. *Contributions to:* Psychology Today; Newsday; MaCalls; Washingtonian, etc; Syndicated Columnist, Newspaper Enterprise Association. *Honours include:* First Place Media Award, Family Service Association; Harris Media Award, American Psychoanalytic Association; Grants from Illinois Arts Council for Playwriting; 1st Place, International Playwriting Contest, Southern Illinois University & Piscator Foundation. *Memberships include:* Ph Beta Kappa; Phi Kappa Phi; Society of Midland Authors, President 1978-80; Chairperson, Drama Award, Society of Midland Authors, 1980-84; Dramatists Guild; Women in Theatre; Board of Directors, Women in Film. *Literary Agent:* Timoth Seldes, Russell & Volkening, New York City. *Address:* 343 Dodge Avenue, Evanston, IL 60202, USA.

KOCH Kenneth, b. 27 Feb 1925, Cincinnati, Ohio, 1925. Professor of English; Writer. m. Mary Janice Elwood, 1955, 1 daughter. *Education:* AB, Harvard University, Cambridge, Massachusetts, 1948; MA 1953, PhD 1959, Columbia University, New York; Served in the United States Army 1943-46. *Appointments:* Lecturer in English, Rutgers University, New Brunswick, New Jersey, 1953-54, 1955-56, 1957-58 and Brooklyn College 1957-59; Director of Poetry Workshop, New School for Social Research, New York, 1958-66, Lecturer 1959-61, Assistant Professor, 1962-66, Associate Professor, 1966-71, Professor of English 1971-, Columbia University. Associated with the magazine Locus Solus, 1960-62. *Publications:* Verse includes: The Art of Love, 1975; The Duplications, 1977; The Burning Mystery of Anna in 1951, 1979; From the Air, 1979; Days and Nights, 1982; Selected Poems, 1985; On The Edge, 1986; Seasons on Earth, 1987; Selected Poems, 1991; The First Step (forthcoming). Plays include: Rooster Redivivus (produced Garnerville, New York, 1975); The Art of Love, adaptation of his own poem (produced Chicago, 1976); The Red Robins, adaptation of his own novel (produced New York, 1978), New York, Performing Arts Journal Publications, 1970; The New Diana (produced New York, 1984); A Change of Hearts (produced New York, 1986); Popeye Amory The Polar Bears (produced New York, 1987); One Thousand Avant-Garde Plays, 1988. Screenplays: The Scotty Dog, 1967; The Apple, 1968. Novel: The Red Robins, New York, Random House, 1975; Hotel Lambusa (forthcoming). Short stories and other publications. *Honours:* Fulbright Fellowship, 1950, 1978; Guggenheim Fellowship, 1961; National Endowment for the Arts Grant, 1966; Ingram Merrill Foundation Fellowship, 1969; Harbison Award, for teaching, 1970; Frank O'Hara Prize (Poetry, Chicago) 1973; American Academy Award, 1976, 1985. *Literary Agent:* Maxine Groffsky, 2 Fifth Avenue, New York, NY 10011, USA. *Address:* 25 Claremont Avenue, Apt 2-B, New York, NY 10027, USA.

KOCH Klaus, b. 4 Oct 1926, Sulzbach, Thueringen, Germany. University Professor. m. Eva-Maria Koch, 28 Mar 1978. *Education:* Universities of Heidelberg, Mainz and Tuebingen, 1945-50; Dr theol, University of Heidelberg, 1953; Habilitation, University of Erlangen, 1956. *Appointments:* Assistant, University of Heidelberg, 1950; Pastor, Lutheran Church, Jena, 1954; Dozent, Old Testament, University of Erlangen, 1956; Dozent, University of Hamburg, 1957; Professor, Old Testament, Kirchliche Hochschule, Wuppertal, 1960; Professor, Old Testament, History of Ancient Near Eastern Religions, University of Hamburg, 1962-. *Publications:* Was ist Formgeschichte?, 1964, 5th Edition, 1989; English Edition: The Growth of Biblical Tradition, 1969; Ratlos vor der Apokalyptik, 1970; English Edition: The Rediscovery of Apocalyptic, 1972; Die Profeten I, Assyrische Zeit, 1978, 2nd Edition, 1987, English Edition: The Prophets I, 1982; Die Profeten II, Babylonisch-persische Zeit, 1980, 2nd Edition, 1988; English Edition: The Prophets II, 1984; Spuren des hebraischen Denkens, Gesammelte Aufsatze I, 1991. *Contributions to:* 70 scholarly journals. *Memberships:* Joachim-Jurgius Gesellschaft der Wissenschaften, Hamburg; Wissenschaftliche Gesellschaft fur Theologie. *Address:* Diekbarg 13 A, D 2000 Hamburg 65, Germany.

KOCHAN Miriam Louise, b. 5 Oct 1929, London, England. Freelance writer and translator. m. Lionel Kochan, 23 Dec 1951, 2 sons, 1 daughter. *Education:* BSc (Econ) Hons, London University, 1950. *Literary Appointments:* Sub-editor, Reuters Economic Services 1950-54; Assistant Sub-editor, Past and Present, a journal of historical research, 1977-81; General Editor, Berg Women's series 1985-88. *Publications:* Prisoners of England, 1980; Britain's Internees in the Second World War, 1983; The Last Days of Imperial Russia, 1976; Life in Russia under Catherine the Great, 1969; Numerous translations. *Contributions to:* Reviews to Jewish Quarterly. *Address:* 237 Woodstock Road, Oxford OX2 7AD, England.

KOEHN Ilse Charlotte, b. 6 Aug 1929, Berlin, Germany. Graphic Designer; Writer. *Education:* Illustration, Graphic Design, Fashion Graphics, Berlin Art Academy. *Publications:* Mischling, Second Degree, 1977; Tilla, 1981. *Honours:* Nominee, US National Book Awards, 1978; Boston Globe/ Horn Book Award, best non-fiction, 1978; Jane Addams Peace Association Honour Award, 1978; Lewis Carroll Shelf Award, 1978. *Memberships:* Authors Guild (USA); Graphic Artists Guild; Soroptimist International of the Americas. *Literary Agent:* Janet Loranger. *Address:* 322 Riverside Avenue, Riverside, Connecticut 06878, USA.

KOELB Clayton, b. 12 Nov 1942, New York City, New York, USA. Educator. m. Susan J Noakes, 1 Jan 1979, 1 son, 1 daughter. *Education:* BA, 1964, MA, 1966, PhD 1970, Harvard University. *Appointments:* Assistant Professor, Associate Professor, Professor of German and Comparative Literature, 1969-91, Chairman, Department of Germanic Languages, 1978-82, University of Chicago, Illinois; Visiting Professor, Purdue University, 1984-85; Visiting Professor, Princeton University, 1985-86; Visiting Eugene Falk Professor, 1990, Guy B Johnson Professor, 1991-, University of North Carolina, Chapel Hill. *Publications:* The Incredulous Reader, 1984; Thomas Mann's 'Goethe and Tolstoy' 1984; The Current in Criticism, 1987; Inventions of Reading, 1988; The Comparative Perspective on Literature, 1988; Kafka's Rhetoric, 1989; Nietzsche as Postmodernist, 1990. *Contributions to:* About 40 articles to literary- critical journals. *Honours:* Germanistic Society of America Fellow, 1964-65; Danforth Foundation Fellow, 1965-69; Woodrow Wilson Foundation Fellow, 1965; Susan Anthony Potter Prize, Harvard University, 1970. *Memberships:* Modern Language Association of America; International Association for Philosophy and Literature; Semiotics Society of America; Vice-President, President-Elect, Kafka Society of Anmerica. *Address:* University of North Carolina, 434 Dey Hall, Chapel Hill, NC 27599, USA.

KOEPPEL Mary Sue, b. 12 Dec 1939, Phlox, Wisconsin, USA. Educator; Writer. m. Robert B Gentry, 31 May 1980. *Education:* BA English, Alverno College, Milwaukee; MA English, Loyola University. *Appointments:* Editor, Kalliope, journal, 1988-; Editor, NewLit on the Block, 1990; Co-Editor, Tips for Teachers,

1985; Co-Editor, Instructional Network News, 1983-85. *Publications:* Writing, Resources for Conferencing and Collaboration, 1989. *Contributions to:* Clockwatch Review, Christian Science Monitor, Bittersweet, Poets for Liveable Planet, Single Parent, Florida Times Union. *Honours include:* Esmee Bradberry Comtemporary Poets Award, 1992; Poetry and Fiction Award, University of North Florida, 1989; Poetry Award, State Street Writers Festival, 1988, 1992; Florida Book Award, National League of American Pen Women, 1989. *Memberships:* National League of American Pen Women; Kalliope Writers' Collective; Friends of Library; Jacksonville Art Museum. *Address:* 3879 Oldfield Trail, Jacksonville, FL 32223, USA.

KOGAN Norman, b. 15 June 1919, Chicago, Illinois, USA. Professor Emeritus of Political Science. m. Meryl Reich, 18 May 1946, 2 sons. *Education:* BA, 1940, PhD, 1949, University of Chicago. *Appointments:* University of Connecticut 1949-88; University of Rome, 1973, 1979, 1987 (Visiting Fulbright Professorships). *Publications:* Italy and the Allies, 1956; The Government of Italy, 1962; The Politics of Italian Foreign Policy, 1963; A Political History of Postwar Italy, 1966; Storia Politica Dell' Italia Repubblicana, 1982; A Political History of Italy: The Postwar Years, 1983; 2nd Edition, revised and expanded of Storia Politica Dell' Italia Repubblicana, 1990. *Contributions to:* Yale Law Journal; Il Ponte; Western Political Quarterly; Journal of Politics; Comparative Politics; Indiana Law Journal. *Honours:* Honorable Mention, Beer Prize, 1957; Knight in the Order of Merit of the Italian Republic, 1971; Award for an Outstanding Academic Book of Modern History, 1984. *Memberships:* Conference Group on Italian Politics, President 1975-77; Society for Italian Historical Studies, Executive Secretary-Treasurer, 1967-75. *Address:* 7 Eastwood Road, Storrs, CT 06268, USA.

KOGAWA Joy, b. 6 June 1935, Vancouver, BC, Canada. Writer. 1 son, 1 daughter. *Appointment:* Writer-in-Residence, University of Ottawa, 1977. *Publications include:* Poetry: The Splintered Moon, 1967; A Choice of Dreams, 1974; Jericho Road, 1977; Woman in the Woods, 1985. Novels: Obasan, 1981; Naomi's Road, 1986. *Honours:* First Novel Award, Books in Canada; Book of the Year Award, Canadian Authors Association; Best Paperback Fiction Award, Periodical Distributors of Canada; The American Book Award, Before Columbus Foundation; Notable Book, American Library Association; Member of the Order of Canada. *Memberships:* Director, Canadian Civil Liberties Association; Patron, Canadian Tribute to Human Rights; Writers Union of Canada; PEN International. *Address:* c/o Writers Union of Canada, 24 Ryerson, Toronto, Ontario, Canada M5T 2P3.

KOGER Lisa Jan, b. 9 June 1953, Elyria, Ohio, USA. Writer. m. Jerry Lynn Koger, 28 Dec 1974, 2 sons. *Education:* BSW, West Virginia University, 1974; MS, Communications (Journalism), University of Tennessee, 1979; MFA, Creative Writing, Iowa Writers Workshop, University of Iowa, 1989. *Appointments:* Iowa Teaching and Writing Fellow, Writers Workshop, University of Iowa, 1988-89; Writing Instructor, Graduate Studies Center, Rock Island, Illinois, summer 1989; Visiting Lecturer, Creative Writing, Mississippi State University, 1990-91. *Publications:* Farlanburg Stories, 1990; Writing in the Smokehouse, essay, in The Confidence Woman, 1991. *Contributions to:* Book reviews to: The New York Times Book Review; Atlanta Journal-Constitution; Fiction to: Seventeen Magazine; Ploughshares; The American Voice; New Myths-MSS; The Chattahoochee Review; Highlights for Children; Others. *Honours:* Writing grant, Kentucky Foundation for Women, 1987; Teaching and Writing Fellowship, Iowa Writers Workshop, 1988; James Michener Award, 1989. *Memberships:* Authors Guild; Authors League of America; Kappa Tau Alpha; Phi Kappa Phi; Mortar Board. *Literary Agent:* Jane Gelfman, John Farquharson Ltd, USA.

KOLAKOWSKI Leszek, b. 23 Oct 1927, Radom, Poland. Academi. m. Tamera Dynenson, 19 Nov 1949,

1 daughter. *Education:* MA, Lodz University, 1950; Phd, Warsaw University, 1953. *Publications:* Individual and Infinity, 1959; Chrietieus sans eglise, 1969; Main Currents of Marxism, 1978; Religion, 1982; Metaphysical Horror, 1988. *Contributions to:* Many magazines, newspapers and journals in Britain, Poland, France, Germany and Italy. *Honours:* Friedenpreis des Deutschen Bouchhandels, 1977; Erasmus Prize, 1982; Prix Europea d'essai; Jefferson Award, 1985; McArthur Fellowship, 1985. *Memberships include:* Polish Writers Association; PEN club; British Academy; International Institute of Philosophy; American Academy of Arts and Sciences; Philosophical Societies in Oxford and in Poland. *Address:* 77 Hamilton Road, Oxford OX2 7QA, England.

KOLKO Joyce, b. 19 Aug 1933, Cleveland, Ohio, USA. Writer. m. Gabriel Kolko, 11 June 1955. *Publications:* The Limits of Power (with Gabriel Kolko), 1972; America and the Crisis of World Capitalism, 1974; Restructuring the World Economy, 1988. *Address:* 330 Spadina Rd, Apt 305, Toronto, Ontario, Canada M5R 2V9.

KOLLER James, b. 30 May 1936, Oak Park, Illinois, USA. Writer; Artist. div, 2 sons, 4 daughters. *Education:* BA, North Central College, Naperville, Illinois, 1958. *Publications:* Poetry: Two Hands, 1965; Brainard and Washington Street Poems, 1965; The Dogs and Other Dark Woods, 1966; Some Cows, 1966; I Went To See My True Love, 1967; California Poems, 1971; Bureau Creek, 1975; Poems for the Blue Sky, 1976; Messages-Botschaften, 1977; Andiamo, 1978; O Didn't He Ramble-O ware er nicht umhergezogen, 1981; Back River, 1981; One Day at a Time, 1981; Great Things Are Happening-Grossartoge Dige passieren, 1984; Give The Dog A Bone, 1986; Graffiti Lyriques (with Franco Beltrametti), graphics and texts, 1987; Openings, 1987; Fortune, 1987; This Is What He Said, graphics and texts, 1991; Prose: Messages, 1972; Working Notes 1960-82, 1985; Gebt dem alten Hund'nen Knochen (Essays, Gedichte and Prosa 1959-85), 1986; The Natural Order, essay and graphics, 1990; Fiction: If You Don't Like Me You Can Leave Me Alone, English Edition, 1974, US Edition, 1976; Shannon Who Was Lost Before, 1975. *Address:* PO Box 629, Brunswick, ME 04011, USA.

KOLLER Marvin Robert, b. 24 Feb 1919, Cleveland, Ohio, USA. Professor of Sociology. m. Pauline Esther Steinfeld, 27 Jan 1945, 1 son. *Education:* BS, Education, Kent State University, 1940; MA, Sociology, 1947, PhD, Sociology, 1950, Ohio State University. *Publications:* Sociology of Childhood, 1964, 2nd Edition, 1978; Modern Sociology, 1965, 3rd Edition, 1974; Social Gerontology, 1968; Families, 1974; Foundations of Sociology, 1975; Humor and Society, 1988; 5-4-3-2-1-0, A Docudrama on the May 4, 1970 Shootings at Kent State University, presented at Ripon College, Wisconsin, 1981. *Contributions to:* Residential Propinquity of White Mates at Marriage in Relation to Age and Occupations of Males, Columbus, Ohio, to American Sociological Review, 1938, 1946; Some Changes in Courtship Behavior in Three Generations of Ohio Women, to American Sociological Review, 1951. *Honours:* Fellowship in Social Gerontology, 1959; National Science Foundation Grant in Anthropology, 1962; National Endowment for the Humanities in Tragi-Comedy, 1980. *Memberships:* American Sociology Association; National Council on Family Relations; American Gerontological Society; American Association of University Professors. *Address:* Sociology Department, Kent State University, Kent, OH 44242, USA.

KOLM Ronald Akerson, b. 21 May 1947, Pittsburgh, Pennsylvania, USA; Writer, Editor, Publisher. m. Donna Sterling, 5 Sept 1984, 2 sons. *Education:* BA, Albright college, 1970. *Publications:* Plastic Factory, 1989; Welcome to the Barbecue, 1990; Suburban Ambush, 1991; Rank Cologne, 1991. *Contributions to:* Cover Magazine; Appearances Magazine; New Observations; Semiotext(e); Red Tape. *Address:* 30-73 47th Street, Long Island City, NY 11103, USA.

KOMAR Kathleen Lenore, b. 11 Oct 1949, Joliet, Illinois, USA. Professor of German and Comparative Literature. m. 16 June 1988. *Education:* BA with honours, English, University of Chicago; Universities of Bonn and Freiburg, 1971-72; MA. Comparative Literature, 1975, PhD, Comparative Literature, 1977, Princeton University. *Appointments:* Assistant Professor, 1977-84, Associate Professor, 1984-90, Full Professor, 1990-, Department of Germanic Languages and Programme in Comparative Literature, Chair, Programme in Comparative Literature, 1986-89, Director, Humanities Cluster Programme, 1991-1992, University of California, Los Angeles; Associate Dean of the graduate Division, UCLA, 1992-. *Publications:* Pattern and Chaos: Multilinear Novels by Dos Passos, Faulkner, Döblin, and Koeppen, 1983; Transcending Angels: Rainer Marie Rilke's 'Duino Elegies', 1987; Re-Visions of the Women of the Trojan War: Contemporary Women Authors' Rewriting of the Figures of Helen, Kassandra, Klytemnestra, and Penelope, forthcoming. *Contributions to:* The Germanic Review; The German Quarterly; Twentieth Century Literature; Comparative Literature Studies; Comparative Literature; Modern Austrian Literature; Euphorion: Zeitschrift fur Literaturgeschichte; Modern Fiction Studies; Germanisch- Romanische Monatsschrift; Others. *Honours include:* Goethe Prize, University of Chicago, 1970; Phi Beta Kappa, 1971; DAAD Fellow, 1971-72; Kent Fellow, Danforth Foundation, 1974-77; Distinguished Teaching Award, University of California, Los Angeles, 1988-89; Several grants. *Memberships:* Modern Language Association, Chair of 20th Century Comparative Studies Board; American Comparative Literature Association, Advisory Committee; International Comparative Literature Association; German Studies Association; Philological Association of the Pacific Coast; American Association of Teachers of German; Society for Values in Higher Education. *Address:* Program in Comparative Literature, Royce Hall 334, UCLA, Los Angeles, CA 90024, USA.

KONDOLEON Harry, b. 1955, American. *Appointment:* Taught Playwriting, New School for Social Research, NYC, 1983-84. *Publications:* Slacks and Tops, Christmas on Mars, 1983; The Vampires, Self Torture and Strenuous Exercise (in The Best Short Plays 1984), 1984; Linda Her and The Fairy Garden, The Cote d'Azur Triangle, Anteroom, 1985; The Brides (in Wordplays 2), The Death of Understanding, 1986; Andrea Rescued, The Whore of Tjampuan, 1987. *Address:* C/o George Lane, William Morris Agency, 1350 Avenue of the Americas, New York, NY 10019, USA.

KONER Pauline, b. 26 June 1912, New York City, New York, USA. Choreographer; Writer; Lecturer; Teacher. m. 23 May 1939. *Education:* Columbia University, 1928; Professional training with Michel Fokine, Michio Ito and Angel Cansino. *Publications:* Solitary Song - An Autobiography, 1989; Elements of Perforance, 1993; Essays: The Truth about The Moor's Pavane, 1966; Intrinsic Dance, 1966; Pauline Koner Speaking, 1966. *Contributions to:* Dance Magazine; Ballet Review; Dance Chronicle. *Honours:* Dance Magazine Award, 1963; Honorary Doctorate of Fine Arts, Rhode Island College, 1985; Special Citation, De La Torre Bueno Award, 1989. *Membership:* American Dance Guild. *Address:* 263 West End Ave, 9F, New York, NY 10023, USA.

KONIGSBERG Allen Stewart, (Woody Allen), b. 1 Dec 1935, Brooklyn, New York, USA. Actor; Writer; Producer; Director. m. (1) Harlene Rosen, (div), (2) Louise Lasser, 1966, (div 1969). *Education:* City College of New York. *Appointments:* Actor in numerous films, stage & TV productions. *Publications:* Plays: Play It Again Sam; The Floating Light Bulb, 1981. Films: What's New Pussycat?, 1965; Casino Royale, 1967; What's Up, Tiger Lily?, 1967; Take the Money and Run, 1969; Bananas, 1971; Everything You Always Wanted To Know About Sex, 1972; Play It Again Sam, 1972; Sleeper, 1973; Love and Death, 1976; The Front, 1976; Annie Hall, 1977; Interiors, 1978; Manhattan, 1979; Stardust Memories, 1980; A Midsummer Night's Sex Comedy,

1982; Zelig, 1983; Broadway Danny Rose, 1984; The Purple Rose of Cairo, 1985; Hannah and Her Sisters, 1985; Husbands and Wives, 1992; Shadows and Fog, 1992. Books: Getting Even, 1971; Without Feathers, 1975; Side Effects, 1980. Written for TV Performer: Herb Shriner; Sid Caesar; Art Carney; Jack Parr and Carol Channing. Writer for the Tonight Show and Gary Moore Show. *Honours:* Academy Award, Best Director and Best Writer for Annie Hall. *Address:* 930 Fifth Avenue, New York, NY 10021, USA.

KONING Hans, b. 12 July 1924, Amsterdam, Netherlands. Writer. m. Kathleen Scanlon, 1 son, 3 daughters. *Education:* Universities of Amsterdam, Zurich & Paris-Sorbonne. *Publications:* The Affair, 1958; A Walk with Love and Death, 1960; The Revolutionary, 1967; Death of a Schoolboy, 1974; A New Yorker in Egypt, 1976; The Kleber Flight, 1981; America Made Me, 1983; DeWitt's War, 1983; Acts of Faith, 1986; Nineteen Sixty-Eight, A Report, 1987. *Contributions to:* New Yorker; Nation; Atlantic Monthly; others. *Honours:* NEA Award, 1978; Connecticut Arts Award, 1980. *Literary Agent:* Lantz Office, New York. *Address:* c/o The Lantz Office, 888 Seventh Avenue, New York, NY 10106, USA.

KONOPINSKI Lech Kazimierz, b. 16 Mar 1931, Poznan, Poland. Writer; Journalist; Doctor of Economics. m. Hanna Zapytowska, 26 July 1956, 1 son, 1 daughter. *Education:* Master's degree, Higher School of Economics, 1955; Doctorate, University of Lodz, 1973. *Appointments include:* Columnist, Szpilki (Needles) 1954-, Kaktus (Cactus) 1957-60, Karuzela 1958-, satirical weekly journals. *Publications:* 17 books, 3 plays, over 300 songs. Titles include: The Amor Alphabet, 1977, 1989; Funny Resentments, 1981; Prince Lech & the Three Friends, 1984; Jocular Leaflets, 1980; Paradise Apples, 1971; Eyes of a Peacock's Tail, 1975; Devil's Dodges, 1968; Actions & Reactions, 1960; Jokes from Warta River, 1983. Children's books include: Fabulous Stories, 1970; What Creeps & Frisks in the Woods & Fields, 1979; From Flower to Flower, 1983; From Pole to Pole, 1986; What Flies and Walks in Our Farm, 1988; What Jumps and Runs Among Trees and Flowers, 1989; The Mysterious Signs, 1989. *Contributions to:* Szpilki; Karuzela; Plomyczek; Swierszczyk; Mis; Gazeta Poznanska; Express Poznanski. *Honours include:* Golden Book, 1971; Golden Ring, 1973, 1980; Awards of Honour, Poznan; Golden Order of Merit; Chivalry Order of Merit; Prize in Reward for Universalize of Culture. *Memberships include:* Various offices, Polish Writers Association, Polish Authors & Composers Association; Association of Authors; Polish Philatelists Association; Officer, Association International des Journalistes Philateliques. *Literary Agent:* Wydawnictwo Poznanskie, Poznan, ul. Fredry 8. *Address:* ul. Michalowska 18 m.3, PL-60-645 Poznan, Poland.

KONVITZ Jeffrey, b. 1944, American. *Appointments:* Admitted to the Bar of New York, 1969; Attorney and Agent, Creative Management Associations, 1969-70; in Private Law Practise, 1970-72; General Counsel, Jerry Lewis Theater Chain, 1971-72; Film Executive, Metro-Goldwyn- Meyer, Culver City, 1972-73; Screenwriter and film producer, 1973-; Entertainment Attorney, Finley Kumble Wagner, Beverly Hills, 1983- . *Publications:* Silent Night, Bloody Night (co-author), 1971; The Sentinel, 1974, screenplay, 1975; The Guardian, Gorp, 1979; Monster: A Tale of Lock Ness, 1982. *Address:* 12660 Mulholland Drive, Beverly Hills, CA 90211, USA.

KOONTS J(ones) Calvin, b. 19 Sept 1924. Educator. m. 1 son, 1 daughter. *Education:* AB 1945, Litt D, 1979, Catawba College, North Carolina; MA 1949, PhD 1958, George Peabody College, Nashville; postdoctoral study: Harvard University, 1960, Smithsonian/Oxford Seminar, Oxford University, England. *Publications:* I'm Living in a Dream, song, 1947; You Know, Love, song, 1989; Since Promontory, 1967; Under the Umbrella, book of poetry, 1971; Editor, Green Leaves in January, 1972; A Slice of the Sun, 1976; Poems represented in National Poetry Anthology, 1957, 1959, 1960, 1962; Editor, Inklings, 1983; A Stone's Throw, book of poetry, 1986. *Honours:* Fulbright Grantee, 1964; Winner, William Gilmore Simms Poetry Prize, South Carolina, 1973; Unicorn Poetry Prize, 1974; Lyric Poetry Prize, 1975; Elizabeth B Coker Poetry Award, 1977. *Memberships include:* NEA; Academy of American Poets; AACTE; ATE; Phi Delta Kappa. *Address:* Box 163, Erskine College, Due West, SC 29639, USA.

KOONTZ Dean R, (David Axton, Brian Coffey, K R Dwyer), b. 9 July 1945, Everett, PA, USA. Novelist; Screenwriter. m. Gerda Ann Cerra, 15 Oct 1966. *Education:* BS, Shippensburg University, 1966. *Publications include:* The Bad Place, 1990; Midnight, 1989; Lightning, 1988; Watchers, 1987; Twilight Eyes, 1987; Strangers, 1986; Darkness Comes, (in USA as Darkfall), 1984; Phantoms, 1983; Whispers, 1980; plus over 40 others; numerous contributions to journals and magazines. *Honours:* Doctor of Letters, Shippensburg University, PA, 1989; Daedalus Award for Twilight Eyes, 1988. *Literary Agent:* Claire M Smith, Harold Ober Associates Inc. *Address:* PO Box 5686, Orange, CA 92613, USA.

KOONZ Claudia, American. Author; Educator. *Appointments:* Professor of History at College of the Holy Cross in Worcester, Massachusetts; Associate Professor, History Department, Duke University, Durham, North Carolina. *Publications:* Co-edited, Becoming Visible, revised edition, 1987; Women in European History, 1977; Mothers in the Fatherland: Women, Politics & The Family in Nazi Germany, translated into Dutch, French, Japanese, 1987, revised German edition, Mütter in Vaterland, 1991; Forthcoming: The Biopolitics of Race and Gender in Nazi Germany. *Contributions to:* Periodicals: New York Times Book Review, 1988; SIGNS; Women's Review of Books; American Journal of Sociology; Journal of Oral History; Feministische Studien; Gesichichte und Gesellschaft. *Honours:* Nomination for National Book Award for Mothers in the Fatherland: Women, the Family and Nazi Politics, 1987; Winship Prize; Berkshire Conference Prize; Feminist Fortnightly Prize; US Library Association Prize; National Association Jesuit Colleges Prize. *Memberships:* American History Association (Research Division); Berkshire Conference (Executive Committee); German Studies Association; PEN International. *Literary Agent:* Charlotte Sheedy Inc, 41 King Street, New York, NY 10014, USA. *Address:* Department of History, Duke University, Durham, NC 27705, USA.

KOOSER Theodore John (Ted), b. 25 Apr 1939, Ames Iowa, USA. Insurance Executive. m. 14 Sept 1977, 1 son. *Education:* BA Iowa State University, 1962; MA, University of Nebraska, 1968. *Publications:* Sure Signs, 1980 (poems); One World at a Time, 1985 (poems). *Contributions to:* Poems published in many literary magazines including The Nation, Poetry, The New Yorker. *Honours:* 1976 and 1984 National Endowment Fellowships; 1980 Midlands Poetry Prize for Best Book of Poetry published in that year. *Membership:* PEN. *Address:* Rt 1 Box 10, Garland, NE 68360, USA.

KOPIT Arthur (Lee), b. 1937, American. *Publications:* Oh Dad, Poor Dad, Mama's Hung You in the Closet and I'm Feelin' So Sad: A Pseudoclassical Tragiface in a Bastard French Tradition, 1960; The Day the Whores Came Out to Play Tennis and Other Plays (in UK as Chamber Music and Other Plays), 1965; Indians, An Incident in the Park, 1968; Wings, Secrets of the Rich, 1978; Good Help Is Hard to Find, 1982; Nine, 1983; Ghosts, End of the World (with a Symposium to Follow), 1984. *Address:* c/o Audrey Wood, International Creative Management, 40 West 57th Street, New York, NY 10019, USA.

KORANDA J Timothy, b. 26 July 1950, Fort Wayne, Indiana, USA. Speechwriter. *Education:* SB, MIT; AB, Colgate; SM, MIT; MBA, New York University. *Appointments:* Writer, N.W. Ayer & Son, 1973-75; Financial Writer/Broker, Bache, 1975-76; Financial Writer, Doremus, 1976-78; Corporate Speechwriter, Citibank, 1978-84; Executive Speechwriter, AT & T, 1984-85; Director, Editorial Services, RCA/NBC, 1985-86; Partner, Korda, Koranda & Huynh, 1986-. *Publications:* Successful Telemarketing; The Tao : China's Religion; Ghostwriter, several books. *Contributions to:* New York Times; New Yorker; Business Week; Esquire; Saturday Review; etc. *Honours:* Saturday Review, World Award; Esquire Award. *Memberships:* Phi Beta Kappa; Copy Club; NATL Committee on US China Relations; China Institute; International Centre of New York. *Literary Agent:* Helen Pratt. *Address:* 135-10 Grand Central Parkway, Kew Gardens, NY 11435, USA.

KORBAR Marcia M, b. 20 Nov 1955, Gowanda, New York, USA. Mental Health Therapist. *Education:* Jamestown Community College, 1978. *Publications:* Poetry, various anthologies. *Contributions to:* World Poetry Anthology; American Collegiate Poets; Young American Poets. *Honours:* Special Award, American Collegiate Poets; Golden Poet Awards, 1985, 1986; Award of Merit, Honourable Mention, 1985. *Address:* 106 Chestnut Street, Gowanda, NY 14070, USA.

KORDA Michael Vincent, b. 8 Oct 1933, London, England. Writer. m. (1) Carolyn Keese, 1 son, (2) Margaret Mogford. *Education:* BA, Magdalen College, Oxford University, 1958. *Appointments Include:* Publishing Entrpreneur; Editor-in-Chief, Simon and Schuster Publishing House; Bestselling Author. *Publications:* Male Chauvinism! Hot It Works, 1973; Power! How to Get it, How to Use it, 1975; Success!, 1977; Charmed Lives: A Family Romance, 1979; Worldly Goods, 1982; Queenie, 1985; The Fortune. *Honours:* Pulitzer Prize, the National Book Award, National Book Critics Circle Award for editing Richard Rhodes The Making of the Atomic Bomb; The Fortune on the New York Times Bestsellers List 1989 10 weeks; The Fortune main selection of the Literary Guild.

KORFIS Tasos. *See:* **ROMBOTIS Anastassios.**

KORG Jacob, b. 1922, American. *Appointments:* Assistant and Associate Professor 1955-65, Professor of English 1965-, University of Washington, Seattle; Former Staff Member, English Department, Bard College, Annandale-on-Hudson, University of Maryland, College Park and City College of New York; Visiting Professor, 1960, National Taiwan University, 1959-61, University of Washington; Professor, 1965-91, Professor Emeritus, 1991-. *Publications:* Westward to Oregon (ed with S F Anderson), Thought in Prose (ed with R S Beal), 1958, 3rd edition, 1966; An Introduction to Poetry, 1959; London in Dickens' Day (ed), 1960; The Complete Reader (ed with R S Beal), 1961; George Gissing's Commonplace Book (ed), 1962; George Gissing: A Critical Biography, 1963; Dylan Thomas, 1965, updated edition, 1991; The Force of Few Words (author and ed), 1966; Twentieth Century Interpretations of Bleak House (ed), 1968; The Poetry of Robert Browning (ed), 1971; Thyrza, by George Gissing (ed), 1974; The Unclassed, by George Gissing (ed), 1976; George Gissing on Fiction (ed with C Korg), 1978; Language in Modern Literature, 1979; Browning and Italy, 1983. *Memberships:* Modern Language Association; International Association of University Professors of English. *Address:* 6530 51st Avenue NE, Seattle, WA 98115, USA.

KORMAN Gordon Richard, b. 23 Oct 1963, Montreal, Quebec, Canada. Author of Juvenile & Young Adult Fiction. *Education:* Bachelor of Fine Arts, New York University, 1985. *Appointments:* Short-term reading consultant to schools, libraries, teachers' groups, reading groups in Canada and the USA. *Publications include:* This Can't Be Happening at MacDonald Hall, 1977; Go Jump In The Pool, 1979; Beware The Fish, 1980; Who is Bug's Potter?, 1980; I Want to go Home, 1981; Our Man Weston, 1982; The War with Mr Wizzle, 1982; Bugs Potter LIVE at Nickaninny, 1983; No Coins Please, 1984; Don't Care

High, 1985; Son of Interflux, 1986; A Semester in the Life of a Garbage Bag, 1987; The Zuechini Warriors, 1988; Radio 5th Grade, 1989; Losing Joe's Place, 1990; Macdonald Hall Goes Hollywood, 1991; The Twinkle Squad, 1992; The D-Poems of Jeremy Bloom (with Bernice Korman), 1992; In Progress: The Toilet Paper Tigers & The Three Z's. *Contributions to:* The Toronto Star; Quill & Quire; and numerous scholastic magazines. *Honours:* Canadian Authors Association Air Canada Award, 1981; Ontario Youth Medal, 1985; International Reading Association Children's Choice Award (I Want to Go Home), 1986; American Library Association Best Book List (Son of Interflux), 1987; Markham Civic Award for the Arts, 1987; IRA Children's Choice Award (Our Man Weston), 1987; ALA Best Book List (A Semester in the Life of a Garbage Bag), 1988; Manitoba Young Readers' Choice Award for The Zuccini Warriors, 1992. *Memberships:* Canadian Society of Children's Authors, Illustrators and Performers; Writers' Union of Canada; Canadian Authors' Association; American Society of Children's Book Writers; ACTRA. *Literary Agent:* Marilyn Marlow, Curtis Brown Ltd.*Address:* 20 Dersingham Crescent, Thornhill, Ontario, Canada, L3T 4EZ.

KORMONDY Edward J(ohn), b. 1926, American. *Appointments:* Assistant Professor, Associate Professor and Professor of Biology, 1957-68, Oberlin College, OH; Director, Commission on Undergraduate Education in the Biological Sciences and Director Office of Biological Education, American Institute of Biological Sciences, WA, 1968- 71; Member of the Faculty 1971-79, Interim Acting Dean, 1972-73, Vice-President and Provost 1973-78, Evergreen State College, Olympia, WA; Senior Professional Associate, National Science Foundation, 1979; Provost and Professor of Biology, University of Southern Maine, Portland, 1979-82; Vice-President, Academic Affairs and Professor of Biology, California State University, Los Angeles, 1982-86; Senior Vice President and Chancellor and Professor of Biology, University of Hawaii, Hilo and University of Hawaii-West Oahu, 1986-93. *Publications:* Introduction to Genetics, 1964; Readings in Ecology (ed), 1965; Readings in General Biology (ed), 2 volumes, 1966; Concepts of Ecology, 1969, 1976, 1983; Population and Food (ed with Robert Leisner), Pollution (ed with R Leisner), Ecology (ed with R Leisner), 1971; General Biology: The Natural History and Integrity of Organisms (with T Sherman et al), 1977; Handbook of Contemporary Developments in World Ecology (with F McCormick), 1981; Environmental Science: The Way the World Works (with B Nebel), 1981, 1987; Biology (with B Essenfeld), 1984, 1988; International Handbook of Pollution Control, 1989. *Address:* 1388 Lucile Avenue, Los Angeles, CA 90026, USA.

KORNFELD Robert Jonathan, b. 3 Mar 1919, Newtonville, Massachusetts, USA. Author/Playwright. m. Celia Seiferth, 23 Aug 1945, 1 son 1 daughter. *Education:* AB, Harvard University, 1941. Also attended Columbia, Tulane, New York University, The New School, Circle-in-the-Square School of Theatre; Playwrights Horizons theatre school and laboratory. *Literary Appointments:* Founder 1965 and Chair, Riverdale Contemporary Theatre; Director, 1979-81, Broadway Drama Guild. *Publications:* Landmarks of the Bronx, 1990; Libretto, A Dream Within a Dream, 1987; Great Southern Mansions, 1977; Two plays written in 1979 in summer stock at Hangar Theatre, Ithaca, New York; Acting Out at Samuel Beckett Theatre, New York City, Fall 1989, and at Southern Repertory Theatre, Spring 1990; Music for Saint Nicholas, performed in Alice Tully Hall, Lincolln Center, 1992. *Contributions to:* Many travel articles in New York Times; Poems in French in Cahiers d'Art et D'Amitie, in English in Botteghe Oscure, Rome. *Honours:* Many early National Drama Awards; Best new play, San Francisco Playwrights Center, 1988; BRIO Award for playwrighting, by Bronx Council on the Arts, 1989. *Memberships:* Dramatists Guild; Authors League; Co-Chair, Literary Committee and Chair, Literary Scholarship Committee, The National Arts Club; Vice President, Bronx Society of Science and Letters; Vice President, Historic Districts Council; Victorian Society; Elected to PEN, member of Freedom to Write Committee.

Address: 5286 Sycamore Avenue, Riverdale, NY 10471, USA.

KORNHAUSER Julian, b. 20 Sept 1946, Gliwice, Poland. Writer. m. Alicja Wojna, 1971, 1 son, 1 daughter. *Education:* Slavic Philology, Jagiellonian University, 1965-70; PhD, 1975; Habilitation, 1982. *Appointments:* Institute of Slavic Philology, University of Cracow, 1970- ; Member, Editorial Staff, Pismo, 1981-83. *Publications:* And the Lazy Will Have Their Feast, 1972; In Factories We Pretend to Be Sad Revolutionaries, 1973; The Unportrayed World (with Adam Zagajewski), 1974 A Few Moments, 1975; The Potato Eaters, 1978; Exceptional Conditions, 1978; Basic Difficulties, 1979; The Procurer of Ideas, 1980; Hurrraaa!, 1981; 148 poems (selection), 1982; Internal Light, 1984; For us, with us, 1985; Another Order, 1985; Poems of 80-ies, 1991; six books on Serbian and Croatian Literatures, 1978, 1980, 1981, 1983, 1991, 1993. *Contributions to:* Kultura; Tworczosc; Pismo; Student; Naglos; Arka; Zeszyty Literackie. *Honours:* Koscielski Foundation, 1975; Andrzej Bursa Award, 1981; DAAD FEllowship in West Berlin, 1986; European Literary Award, Yugoslavia, 1989. *Membership:* SPP, Poland. *Address:* Boleslawa Chrobrego 29-3, Cracow, Poland.

KORZENIK Diana, b. 15 Mar 1941, New York City, New York, USA. College Educator. *Education:* Oberlin College; BA, Vassar College; Master's programme, Columbia University; EdD, Graduate School of Education, Harvard University. *Appointments:* Professor, Massachusetts College of Art, Boston, Massachusetts. *Publications:* Art and Cognition, 1977; Drawn to Art, 1986; Art Making: Its Uses in Education, 1992; Chapter in Framing the Past. *Contributions to:* Studies in Art Education; Art Education Magazine; Boston Magazine; Manchester Magazine. *Honours:* Publication Grant for Drawn to Art, J P Getty Trust, 1985; Boston Globe Literary Award, 1986; L L Winship Award, 1986; June McFee Award, Women's Caucus, National Art Education Association, 1986. *Memberships:* National Writers Union; National Art Education Association; American Association of Historians of Art. *Address:* Massachusetts College of Art, 621 Huntington Avenue, Boston, MA 02115, USA.

KOSSOFF David, b. 24 Nov 1919 (Russian parentage). Actor; Designer; Illustrator. *Publications:* Bible Stories retold by David Kossoff, 1968; The Book of Witnesses, 1971; The Three Donkeys, 1972; The Voices of Masada, 1973; You Have a Minute Lord? 1975; The Little Book of Sylvanus, 1975; A Small Town is a World, 1979; Sweet Nutcracker, 1985; Own Bible Storytelling programmes (writer & teller) on radio & TV; Appeared, many plays & films & on radio & TV; since 1972, one-man performances: As According to Kossoff, A Funny Kind of Evening, The Kossoff Storytellings (to children). *Honours:* British Academy Award, 1956; Elected Member, Society Industrial Artists, 1958; FRSA, 1969; Hon D.Litt, 1990. *Membership:* Society of Authors. *Address:* 45 Roe Green Close, Hatfield, Hertfordshire, England.

KOSTELANETZ Richard, b. 14 May 1940, New York City, New York, USA. Writer; Artist. div. *Education:* AB with honours, American Civilisation, Brown University, 1962; Fulbright Scholar, King's College, University of London, 1964-65; MA, American History, Columbia University, 1966; Music, Theatre, Morley College, London and New School, New York. *Appointments:* Co-Founder, President, Assembling Press, 1970-82; Senior Staff, Indiana University Writers Conference, July 1976; Literary Director, The Future Press, Cultural Council Foundation, 1976-; Co-Editor, Publisher, Precisely: A Critical Magazine, 1977-; Visiting Professor, American Studies, English, University of Texas, Austin, spring 1977; Sole Proprietor, RK Editions, 1978-; Coordinator-Interviewer, American Writing Today, Voice of American Forum Series, 1979-81. *Publications:* The End of Intelligent Writing: Literary Politics in America, 1974, 2nd Edition, 1977; Numbers: Poems and Stories (author, designer), booklet, 1976; The Old Poetries and the New, 1980; The Old Fictions and the New, 1987; Conversing with Cage, 1989; Wordworks: Poems Selected and New, 1993; On Innovative Performance(s), 1994; The Dictionary of the Avant-Gardes, 1993; Many others; Editor: Merce Cunningham, 1992; Writings about John Cage, 1993; John Cage: Writer, 1993. *Contributions to:* Essays, reviews, poetry, fiction, prose to numerous US and UK newspapers, magazines, anthologies, others. *Honours:* Phi Beta Kappa; Numbers: Poems and Stories, 1 of Best Books of 1976, American Institute of Graphic Art; Pulitzer Fellow in Critical Writing, 1965; Guggenheim Fellow, 1967; Visual Arts Senior Fellow, National Endowment for the Arts, 1985; Other fellowships and grants. *Memberships:* American PEN; Audio Independents; International Association of Art Critics; National Writers Union; Foundation for Independent Video and Film; National Artworkers; Society for Origination of Horspiel in America; American Society of Composers, Authors and Publishers. *Address:* PO Box 444, Prince St, New York, NY 10012, USA.

KOSUSAM. *See:* **SAMPUTAANAE Kosu.**

KOT Jozef, b. 1 Sept 1936, Bratislava, Slovakia. Writer. m. Dagmar Kirüdova, 13 Feb 1965. 1 son, 1 daughter. *Education:* University of Comenius, Bratislava, 1958. *Literary Appointments:* Editor, Mlada tvorba, 1956-59; Editor, Slovenske pohlady, 1961-66; Editor, Revue avetovej literatury, 1966-67; Editor-in-Chief, Publishing House, Tatran, 1968-71. *Publications:* The Last Ones, 1963; The Ascension of the Centre-Forward, 1965; Welcoming of the Spring, 1968; The Fever, 1973; The Birthday, 1978; The Skittle-ground, 1983; The Foot-race without End, 1986; Film adaptation of The Fever, 1975. Translations from English into Slovak: William Shakespeare, James Joyce, Carl Sandburg, EL Masters, Eugene O'Neill, William Faulkner, E Hemingway, H Miller, J Updike. *Contributions to:* Numerous literary magazines and journals. *Honours:* Honour, for the Eminent Work, 1975; The Slovak National Prize, 1976; Honourable title, Meritorious Writer, 1980; Honour, for the Merits, 1987; Literary Awards of the publishing houses. *Membership:* Society of Slovak Writers. *Literary Agent:* Slovak Literary Agency, Bratislava. *Address:* Hrdlčkova 1, 831 01 Bratislava, SLovakia.

KOTOW Piotr, b. 25 Aug 1919, Pokrowka, USSR. Teacher. m. Anna Kremzo, 14 Mar 1953, 2 daughters. *Education:* Masters degree, Russian Philology Department, Warsaw University, 1963. *Publications:* Poetry: Z Tamtego Brzegu, 1980; Slady, 1986; Stara Pieśń, 1988; Widziakczem Kotlas, 1989; Za Kregiem Polarnym, 1990; Wecnyj Ogoń, 1973; Sledy, 1986; Weczernij Zwol, 1989. *Contributions to:* Numerous poems, scholarly articles and book reviews in professional magazines in Russian and Polish. *Memberships:* Polish Writers Association; Stage Authors and Composers Association. *Address:* Ul Siennicka 11m 37, 80-703 Gdansk-Przeròlka, Poland.

KOTSIRAS Georgis, b. 9 June 1921, Athens, Greece. Lawyer; Poet; Writer; Essayist; Translator. m. Despina Mikhailidi, 22 Aug 1954, 1 daughter. *Education:* Political Sciences and Law, University of Athens, 1939-45. *Appointments:* Self-employed Lawyer and Notary Public. *Publications:* The Home, fiction, 1947; Herostratus, tragedy, 1970; Poetry: I Hora ton Lotofagon, 1948; Frouri tis Siopis, 1949; Poliorkia tou Hronou, 1955; Sinomilia me ton sisifo, 1958; Aftognosia, 1959; Anatomia Englimatos, 1964; Mythologia ton Pragmaton, 1968; Metallages, 1974; To 'Alfa' tou Kentaurou, 1975; Aftopsia Englimatos, 1978; Ta poiimata, 1980-87; I Lampas kai to Teras Engomio, 1983; Translations: Don Camilo (Giovanni Guareschi), 1954; The Stranger (Albert Camus), 1955, later editions; The Home of Bernarda Alba (F G Lorca), 1957, 2nd Edition, 1959; The Sacred Comedy (Dante Alighieri), rhymed translation, Hell, Purgatory, Havens, 3 cols, 1987. *Contributions to:* Kathemerini; Vradeni; Ethnos; Acropolis; Nea Estia; Eflhini; Others. *Honours:* 2 State Awards for Poetry, 1958, 1975; Award of the Twelve for Poetry, 1964; 2 Awards for Poetry, Academy of Athens, 1980, 1989; Award, Greek Association of Translators of Literature, 1988. *Memberships:*

Association of Greek Writers; PEN Club of Greece, former Vice-President, former President; Bar Association of Greece. *Address:* 22 Adrianou, GR 145 61 Kifissia, Greece.

KOTT Jan, b. 27 Oct 1914, Warsaw, Poland. University Professor. m. Lidia Steihaus, 17 June 1939, 1 son, 1 daughter. *Education:* LLM, University of Warsaw, 1936; PhD, Lodz University, Poland, 1947. *Appointments:* Professor of Polish Literature, University of Warsaw, 1952-59; Professor of Drama and Slavic Literature, 1969-73; Professor of Comparative Literature and English, 1985. *Publications:* Shakespeare our Contemporary, 1961; The Eating of the Gods, 1973; The Theatre of Essence, 1984; The Bottom Translation, 1987; La Vie en Sursis, 1991; Four Decades of Polish Essays, 1990; The Memory of the Body, 1992; Pisma Wybrane, 1991; Przyczynek do bigrafii, 1990; The Gender of Rosalind, 1992; Leben auf Raten, 1993; Still Alive, 1994 *Contributions to:* NY Review; NYT: Formations; New Theatre Quarterly, England; Lettre Internationale; Zeszyty Literackie, Paris-Warsaw; Theatre Yale. *Honours:* Herder Award, Vienna, 1964; Alfred Jurzykowski Award, NY, 1976; Goerge G Nathan Award, 1985; Guggenheim Fellow, 1972-73; Getty Scholar, 1985; Officier Ordre des Arts et des Lettres, 1991; Robert Levis Medal, 1993. *Memberships:* Polish PEN Club; Centre for Medieval and Renaissance Studies, UCLA. *Address:* 29 Quaker Path, Stony Brook, NY 11790, USA.

KOTZ Nathan K (Nick), b. 16 Sept 1932, San Antonio, Texas, USA. Journalist; Author; Educator. m. Mary Lynn Booth, 7 Aug 1960, 1 son. *Education:* BA magna cum laude, International Relations, Dartmouth College, 1955; London School of Economics, England, 1955-56. *Appointments:* Reporter, Des Moines Register, 1958-64; Washington Correspondent, Des Moines Register and Minneapolis Tribune, 1964-70; National Correspondent, The Washington Post, 1970-73; Author, Freelance Journalist, 1973-; Adjunct Professor, The American University, School of Communication, 1978-87; Senior Journalist in Residence, Duke University, 1983. *Publications:* Let Them Eat Promises: The Politics of Hunger in America, 1970; The Unions (co-author), 1972; A Passion for Equality: George Wiley and the Movement (co-author), 1977; Wild Blue Yonder: Money, Politics and the B-1 Bomber, 1988. *Contributions to:* Atlantic Monthly; Columbia Journalism Review; Harper's; Look; The Nation; The New Republic; New York Times Magazine; The Progressive; Technology Review; Washington Monthly; Washington Post Outlook; The Washingtonian. *Honours:* Phi Beta Kappa; Reynolds Scholarship for Graduate Study, 1955; A P Writing Awards, 1961, 1962, 1963, 1964; The Chautauqua Society, 1963; Sigma Delta Chi Award for Washington Correspondents, 1966; Raymond Clapper Memorial Award, 1966, 1969, 2nd place, 1973; Pulitzer Prize for National Reporting, 1968; Robert F Kennedy Memorial Award, 1969; Olive Branch Award, 1989. *Memberships:* PEN/Faulkner, Board of Directors; Black Student Fund, Board of Directors 1980-86; Fund for Investigative Journalism, 1980-88, Chairman 1982-86; Washington Press Club; White House Correspondents Association; National Press Club; Cosmos Club; Authors Guild. *Literary Agent:* Arnold Goodman, Goodman Associates, 500 West End Avenue, New York, NY 10024, USA. *Address:* Galemont Farm, Broad Run, VA 22014, USA.

KOTZIAS Alexandros, b. 27 Jan 1926, Athens, Greece. Writer; Journalist; Translator. m. Eleni Apostolou, 25 Feb 1954, 1 son, 1 daughter. *Education:* Law School, University of Athens. *Appointments:* Literary Editor and Book Reviewer: Mesimvrini, newspaper, 1961-67; Book Reviewer, Vma, nespaper, 1971-72; Co-editor, Synechid, magazine, 1973; Literaty Editor and Book Reviewer, Kathmerini, newspaper, 1976-82. *Publications:* Novels: Siege, 1953; The Attempt, 1964; The Usurpation of Authority, 1979; Imaginary Adventure, 1955; Jaguar, 1987. *Contributions to:* Ikoner, Tachydzomos, Nex Pozia, Synechia, Tzam, Haztis, Anti, Gzammata ke Technes. *Honours:* Proze Prise of The 12, 1965; Ford Foundation

Grant, 1970; State Proze Prize, 1986. *Memberships:* Founding member, Soicety of Greek Writers, 1981; VP, 1982-84, Board member, 1984-; Journalists Union of the Athens Daily Newspapers. *Address:* 162 Papadiamontopoulou Street, 15773 Athens, Greece.

KOTZWINKLE William, b. 1938, American. Freelance Writer. *Publications:* The Fireman, 1969; The Ship That Came Down the Gutter, Elephant Boy: A Story of the Stone Age, The Day the Gang Got Rich, 1970; The Oldest Man and Other Timeless Stories, Return of Crazy Horses, 1971; Hermes 3000, 1972; The Supreme, Superb, Exalted and Delightful, One and Only Magic Building, 1973; The Fan Man, Night-Book, Up the Alley with Jack and Joe, 1974; Swimmer in the Secret Sea, 1975; Doctor Rat,The Leopard's Tooth, 1976; Fata Morgana, 1977; Herr Nightingale and the Satin Woman, The Ant Who Took Away Time, 1978; Dream of Dark Harbor, The Nap Master, Jack in the Box, 1980; Christmas at Fountaine's, E T: The Extra-Terrestrial, The Extra Terrestrial Storybook, 1982; Superman III, Great World Circus, Trouble in Bugland: A Collection of Inspector Mantis Mysteries, 1983; Queen of Swords, 1984; E T: The Book of the Green Planet, Seduction in Berlin, The Book of the Green Plant, 1985; Hearts of Wood, The World Is Big and I'm So Small, 1986. *Address:* c/o Putnam's, 200 Madison Avenue, New York, NY 10016, USA.

KOUHI Elizabeth, b. 11 Nov 1917, Lappe, Ontario, Canada. Writer. m. George A Kouhi, 1 July 1951, 1 son, 3 daughters. *Education:* BA, McGill University, 1949; Teaching Certificate, Ontario College of Education, 1964. *Appointments:* Schoolteacher in Raith, Ontario, Canada, 1950-52; Home-maker and mother 1952-63; Teacher, Lakehead Board of Education, Thunder Bay, Ontario, 1963-82; Writer 1982-. *Publications:* Jamie of Thunder Bay (juvenile novel) 1977; North Country Spring (juvenile poetry) 1980; The Story of Philip (juvenile) 1982; Sarah Jane of Silver Islet (juvenile novel) 1983; Round Trip Home (adult poetry) 1983. *Contributor to:* Poetry for anthologies for children; Editor of newsletter of Lakehead Association for the Mentally Retarded. *Memberships:* League of Canadian Poets; Writers Union of Canada; Canadian Society of Children's Authors, Illustrators and Performers; Lakehead Association for the Mentally Retarded (member of board of directors).

KOURKOV Andrei, b. 23 Apr 1961, Leningrad. Writer. m. Elizabeth Sharp, 25 June 1988. *Education:* BA, Kiev Institute; Moscow Culture Institute. *Appointments:* Editor, Dnipro; Senior Lecturer, Film Script Writing; Theatre Institute, Kiev. *Publications:* Napadenie; DeKlassirovannie; Dont Take Me to Kengaraks; The Cosmopolitans Favorite Song; Bickfords World; Goshas Stories; The School for Flying Cats; Flying South; Eleven Odd Stories. *Honours:* Ukrainian Literary Fund Prize; Renaissance Short Story Competition 2nd Prize. *Memberships:* PEN; Cinematographer's Union of the Ukraine. *Address:* Drive Mayakovskovo 46 k17, 253232 Kiev, Ukraine.

KOURTOVIK Dimosthenis, b. 15 July 1948, Athens, Greece. Author; Literary Critic; Translator; Anthropologist. m. Vibeke Espholm, 10 Aug 1988. *Education:* Doctor, University of Wroclaw. *Appointments:* Literary Critic, O Scholiastis; Eleftherotypia; Ta Nea. *Publications:* Three Thousand Kilometres; the Last Earthquake; The Greek Autumn of Eva Anita Bengtsson; The Dust of the milky Way; Doct Thesis on The Evolution of Human Sexuality; Greek Intellectuals and the Greek Movie; Domestic Exile. *Contributions to:* Numerous. *Honour:* Greek Publishers Award. *Memberships:* European Anthropological Association. *Address:* 23 Amynandrou Street, 117 41 Athens, Greece.

KOURVETARIS George A, b. 21 Nov 1933, Greece. Professor of Sociology; Author; Editor. m. Toula Savas, 22 Aug 1966, div. 1987, 2 sons, 1 daughter. *Education:* Teacher's Diploma, Tripolis, Greece, 1955; BS, Loyola University, Chicago, USA, 1963; MA with honours, Roosevelt University, Chicago, 1965; PhD, Northwestern University, Evanston, Illinois, 1969. *Publications:* First and Second Generation Greeks in Chicago; An Inquiry Into Their Stratification and Mobility Patterns, 1971; Co-author: Social Origins and Political Orientations of Officer Corps in a World Persepctive, 1973; Society and Politics: An Overview and Reappraisal of Political Sociology, 1980; A Profile of Modern Greece: In Search of Identity, 1987; Co-editor: World Perspectives in the Sociology of the Military, 1977; Political Sociology; Readings in Research and Theory, 1980; A book of poetry in Greek and in part in English, 1992; Articles in books. *Contributions to:* Over 60 articles to: American Sociological Review; The American Sociologist; Greek Review of Social Research; International Journal of Contemporary Sociology; Journal of Political and Military Sociology; Journal of Social, Political and Economic Studies; Journal of the Hellenic Diaspora; East European Quarterly; Others; Book reviews to: Social Science; Contemporary Sociology: A Journal of Reviews; Journal of Political and Military Sociology; International Migration Review; Others. *Honours include:* Doctoral Research Fellowship, Council of Intersocial Studies, Northwestern University, 1968-69; Heritage Award, Greek American Community Services, Chicago, 1987; Recognition Award, Hellenic Council on Education, Chicago, 1991; Faculty Career Enhancement Grant, Graduate School, College of Liberal Arts and Sciences, and Sociology Department, 1992. *Memberships:* Delta Tau Kappa, International Social Science Honor Society; American Sociological Association; Modern Greek Studies Association. *Address:* 109 Andresen Ct, DeKalb, IL 60115, USA.

KOVEL Ralph, Author; Company President. m. 1 son, 1 daughter. *Publications:* Dictionary of Marks, Pottery and Porcelain, 1953; A Directory of American Silver, Pewter and Silver Plate, 1958; American Country Furniture 1780-1875, 1963; Kovels' Know Your Antiques, 1967, 3rd edition 1981; Kovels' Antiques & Collectibles Price List, annually 1968-; Kovels; Bottles Price List, Biennially 1971-; Kovels' Collector's Guide for Collector Plates, Figurines, Paperweights and Other Limited Edition Items, 1974, 1978; Kovels; Collector's Guide to American Art Pottery, 1974; Kovels' Organizer for Collectors, 1978, 1983; Kovels' Illustrated Price Guide to Royal Doulton, 1980, 1984; Kovels Illustrated Price Guide to Depression Glass and American Dinnerware, 1980, 1983; Kovels' Know Your Collectibles, 1981; Kovels; Book of Antique Labels, 1982; Kovels; Collectors Source Book, 1983; Kovels; New Dictionary of Marks, Pottery and Porcelain 1850-Present, 1985; Kovels' Advertising Collectibles Price List, 1986; Kovels Guide to Selling Your Antiques & Collectibles, 1987; Kovels American Silver Marks, 1650 to the Present, 1989; Kovels Collectibles 1990 Calender, 1989. *Contributions to:* Monthly Column, House Beautiful, 1979-; Newspaper Column, Kovels Antiques & Collecting; Editor, Publisher, Kovels on Antiques & Collectibles, Newsletter, 1974-. *Honours:* Recipient, numerous honours and awards. *Address:* 9090 Bank Street, Valley View, OH 44125, USA.

KOWALCZYK David Theodore, (Slade Adamsson), b. 22 Nov 1952, New York, USA. Teacher. *Education:* BA, 1974, MA English Creative Writing, 1988, State University of New York. *Appointments:* English Instructor: Arizona State University, 1983-84, Genesee Community College, 1987-. *Contributions to:* Albany Review; Maryland Review; Oxalis; Artifacts; Crazy Quitt; Pure Light; City; Bogg; Pinchpenny; Rectangle. *Honours:* First Prize, Poetry Competition, City Magazine, 1984; First Prize, Fiction, Chavtavgua Council on Arts Awards, NY, 1990. *Memberships:* Former VP, Grand Canyon Literary Guild, 1981; Phi Beta Kappa. *Address:* 9318 Creek Road, Batavia, New York, NY 14020, USA.

KOWALSKI Kazimierz Maria, b. 18 Aug 1926, Chelmno, Poland. Writer. m. Stanislawa Nowak, 12 June 1948. 1 son, 1 daughter. *Education:* University of Wroclaw. *Appointment:* Polish Radio, Opole, 1954-1992. *Publications:* Fighter Will never Give Up, 1964,

1969; Strip Tease Without Fun, 1977; Both Our Hearts, 1777, 1978; Crazy With Love, 1984; Escape to the Green Meadows, 1985; The One Whom I love, 1989; Long Odysses Return (collection of the radio performances), 1989; Neither too early, nor too late, 1992; 27 books. Radio plays include: Not Far from a Dead Forest; Ophelia, Hamlet's Lover; Daddy in Some Other Clothes; Call controlled; La mort on the Marat's bath. Dramas: To Dearest Catherine. Screenplay: It Was a Beautiful Funeral, People Cried. Numerous translations. Contributions to: Kwartalnik Opolski; Tak i nie; Osnowa; Zycie Literackie; Opole. Honours: Voivodship Literary Awards, 1959, 1984, 1991; Jan Langowski Award, 1981; Main Award, President of Polish Radio and TV, 1982. Memberships: Society of Polish Writers; National Council of Culture. Literary Agent: Authors Agency Ltd, Warsaw. Address: ul Strzelcow Bytomskich 5 m.6, 45-084 Opole, Poland.

KOWALSKI Marian, b. 8 Sept 1936, Szymonki, near Rawicz, Poland. Editor. m. Jadwiga Abrahamow, 13 Jan 1961, 1 daughter. Education: MA, Literature, Department of Polish Philology, Wroclaw University. Publications: Novels, short stories, screen plays, theatrical plays: Chtopiec z ortem, 1971; Ktoś obey, 1974; Sydonia, 1984. Titles include: Koty, 1958; Jesienna, 1964; Odnajdywanie siebie, 1965; Blinda, 1973; Wszedzie i Nigdzie, 1973; Junga, 1977; Wszedzie i Donikad, 1980; Moj przyjaciel Delfin, 1981; Skarb Morza Sargassowego, 1983. Also: Galapagos, 1982; W Oczekiwaniu, 1984; Przed Kurtyna, 1984; Karczowiska, 1985; Dom na Klifie, 1986; Moj najwiekszy nieprzyiaciel, 1987; Cecylia i Eryk, 1990; Wiatraki na biekicie, 1990. Contributions to: Odra; Nowe Sygnaly; Teatr; Scena, Student; Kurier Szczecinski; Glos Szczecinski; Morze i Ziemia. Honours: Award, J. Czechowicz competition, 1970; 1st Prize for play, 1971; Grand Prix for film screenplay, Joseph Conrad Prize for novel, 1971. Memberships: Polish Writers Union; Polish Marine Writers Association. Address: ul. Szafera 130 m. 12, 71-245 Szczecin, Poland.

KOZAK Henryk Jozef, b. 15 July 1945, Krasna, Poland. Writer, Poetry & Prose. m. Maria Tomasiewicz, 1 July 1967, 2 sons. Education: MA, History, University of Maria Curie-Sklodowskiej, 1969. Publications: First poems published, Lublin local press, 1968. Titles include: W krajobrazie lagodnych slow, poem, 1973; Podroze do zrodel, poem, 1978; Chwila, poem, 1979; W cieniu ciszy, poem, 1982; Coraz cichsze lata, poem, 1985; Kupic smierc, novel, 1985; Kiedy konczy sie milosc, detective novel, 1987; Nie dokończona powieść o miłości, detective novel, 1990. Participant, numerous literary events, 1968-. Contributions include: Numerous journals & magazines including: Kamena; Tygodnik Kulturalny; Poezja; Akcent; Kierunki. Honours: Josef Czechowicz Literary Awards, selections of poems (1st prize), 1980, 1987. Membership: Society of Polish Writers. Address: 20-854 Lublin, ul. Paryska 7 m. 6, Poland.

KOZOL Jonathan, b. 5 Sept 1936, Boston, USA. Author. Education: Harvard College, and Magdalen College, Oxford, England. Appointments: Teacher Boston area, 1964-72; Lecturer, numerous Univerisities, 1973-85. Publications: Death At An Early Age, 1967; Free Schools, 1972; The Night is Dark, 1975; Children of the Revolution, 1978; On Being a Teacher, 1979; Prisoners of Silence, 1980; Illiterate America, 1985; Rachel and Her Children, 1988; Savage Inequalities, 1991. Honours: Rhodes Scholar, 1954; National Book Award, 1968; Guggenheim Fellow, 1972, 1984, 1985; Field Foundation Fellow, 1973, 1974; Rockefeller Fellow, 1978; Senior Fellow, 1983; Robert F Kennedy Memorial Book Award, 1989. Address: PO Box 145, Byfield, MA 01922, USA.

KRAFT Joseph, American. Appointments: Staff Writer, New York Times, 1951-57; Washington Correspondent, Harpers Magazine, NY, 1961-66; Syndicated Columnist, Los Angeles Times Syndicate. Publications: The Struggle for Algeria, 1961; The Grand Design, 1962; Profiles in Power, 1966; The Chinese Difference, 1973; The Mexican Debt Rescue, 1985. Address: 2101 Connecticut Avenue, NW Washington, DC 20008, USA.

KRAMER Aaron, b. 13 Dec 1921, Brooklyn, New York, USA. Professor of English; Poet. m. Katherine Kolodny, 10 Mar 1942, 2 daughters. Education: BA, 1941, MA 1951, Brooklyn College; PhD, New York University, 1966. Publications: The Glass Mountain, 1946; The Poetry and Prose of Heinrich Heine, 1948; Roll The Forbidden Drums! 1954; The Tune of the Calliope, 1958; Rumshinsky's Hat, 1964; Rilke, Visions of Christ, 1967; The Prophetic Tradition in American Poetry, 1968; Melville's Poetry, 1972; On Freedom's Side, 1972; On the Way to Palermo, 1973; Carousel Parkway, 1980; The Burning Bush : Poems and Other Writings 1940-1980, 1983; A Century of Yiddish Poetry, 1988; Indigo, 1991. Contributions to: Numerous magazines and journals including: West Hills Review Co-Editor, 1978-85; American Annals of the Deaf; Massachusetts Review; Midstream; Modern Poetry Review; New York Times; Village Voice; Kenyon, Missouri and New England Reviews; Writers Forum; Journal of Poetry Therapy. Honours: Numerous honours and awards including: ASCAP Awards 1971-74, 1976-79, 1981-92; All Nations Poetry Contests, 1975-79; Fellowship Memorial Foundation for Jewish Culture, 1978-79; Eugene O'Neill Theatre Centre Award, 1983; Abraham Jenofsky Yiddish Culture Award, 1983; Zhitlowsky Foundation Award, 1989; National Endowment for the Humanities Award, 1993 . Memberships: PEN; International Academy of Poets; NE MLA; Association for Poetry Therapy, Executive Board, 1969-84; ASCAP. Literary Agent: John K Payne Literary Agency, Inc. Address: English Dept., Dowling College, Oakdale, NY 11769, USA.

KRAMER Dale, b. 1936, American. Appointments: Instructor 1962-63, Assistant Professor of English 1963-65, Ohio University, Athens; Assistant Professor 1965-67, Associate Professor 1967-71, Professor of English 1971-, Associate Dean, College of Liberal Arts and Sciences, 1992-, University of Illinois, Urbana; Associate Vice Provost, 1990, University of Oregon, Eugene; Editor, Journal of English and German Philology. Publications: Charles Maturin, 1973; Thomas Hardy: The Forms of Tragedy, 1975; Critical Approaches to the Fiction of Thomas Hardy (ed), 1979; The Woodlanders, by Thomas Hardy (ed), 1981, 1985; The Mayor of Casterbridge, by Thomas Hardy (ed), 1987; Critical Essays on Thomas Hardy (ed), 1990; Thomas Hardy: Tess of the d'Urbervilles, 1991. Address: Department of English, University of Illinois, Urbana, IL 61801, USA.

KRAMER Jane, b. 7 Aug 1938, Providence, Rhode Island, USA. Writer. m. Vincent Crapanzano, 30 Apr 1967, 1 son. Education: BA, Vassar College; MA, Columbia University. Appointments: Morningsider, 1962; Village Voice, 1963; New Yorker, 1964-. Publications: Off Washington Square, 1963; Allen Ginsberg in America, 1969; Honor to the Bride, 1970; The Last Cowboy, 1978; Unsettling Europe, 1981. Contributions to: New Yorker; New York Review of Books; many others. Honours: Front page Award, 1977; mademoiselle Woman of the Year Award, 1968; Emmy Award, 1966; American Book Award for Non Fiction, 1980. Memberships: PEN; Writers Guild; Authors Guild; National Book Critics Circle; Authors League. Literary Agent: Georges Borchardt. Address:The New Yorker, 25 West 43 Street, New York, NY 10036, USA.

KRAMER Larry, b. 25 June 1935, Bridgeport, CT, USA. Screenwriter; Playwright; Novelist. Education: BA, Yale University, 1957. Appointments: Associated with training programs, NY for William Morris Agency 1958 and Columbia Pictures 1958-59; Assistant Story Editor, Columbia Pictures, 1960-61; Production Executive, London, England, 1961-65; Assistant to the President of United Artists, 1965; Associate Producer of motion picture, Here We Go Round the Mulberry Bush, 1967; Producer of motion picture Women in Love, 1969; Co-founder of Gay Men's Health Crisis in NY, 1981; Founder of ACT UP (AIDS Coalition to Unleash Power), 1988. *Publications:* Women in Love, 1969; Faggots, 1978; The Normal Heart, 1985; Just Say No, 1988; Reports from the Holocaust: The Making of an AIDS Activist, Sissies' Scrapbook, The Furniture of Home, 1989. *Contributions to:* Political writings to periodicals, including New York Times; Village Voice. *Honours:* Academy Award nomination for Best screenplay from the Academy of Motion Picture Arts and Sciences, British Film Academy for Best Screenplay, 1970, for Women in Love; Dramatists Guild Matron Award, City Lights Award, Sarah Siddons Award, (all for best play of the year), Olivier Award for best play, 1986, for Normal Heart; Arts and Communication Award from the Human Rights Campaign Fund, 1987. *Address:* NY, USA.

KRAMER Leonie Judith, (Professor Dame) b. 1 Oct 1924, Melbourne, Australia. Professor. m. Dr Harold Kramer, 2 Apr 1952 (dec), 2 daughters. *Education:* BA, University of Melbourne, 1945; DPhil, University of Oxford, UK, 1953. *Appointments include:* Professor, Australian Literature, University of Sydney, 1968-1989; Visiting Professor, Chair of Australian Studies, Harvard University, USA, 1981-82; Chair, Australian Brodcasting Commission, 1982-83; Member, Universities Council, 1974-86; Director, Quadrant Magazine Company; Chairman, Board of Directors, National Institute of Dramatic Art (NIDA), 1987-1992; Deputy Chairman, Senior Fellow, Institute of Public Affairs (IPA), 1988-; Professor, Australian Literature, University of Sydney, 1968-89; Deputy Chancellor, University of Sydney, 1989-1991, Chancellor, 1991-. *Publications include:* Author of: Henry Handel Richardson & Some of her Sources, 1954; Companion to Australia Felix, 1962; Myself When Laura: Fact & Fiction in Henry Handel Richardson's School Career, 1966; Henry Handel Richardson, 1967; Language & Literature: A Synthesis, with R.D. Eagleson, 1976; Guide to Language & Literature, with R.D. Eagleson, 1977; A.D. Hope, 1979. Editor/co-editor: Coast to Coast, 1963-64, 1965; Hal Porter, Selected Stories, 1971; Oxford History of Australian Literature, 1981; Oxford Anthology of Australian Literature, 1985; My Country: Australian Poetry & Short Storis, 200 Years, 2 volumes, 1985; James McAuley: Poetry, Essays and Personal Commentary, 1988; David Campbell: Collected Poems, 1989. *Contributions to:* Numerous journals. *Honours:* Dame of British Empire (DBE), 1982. AC, 1993; Inaugural Britannica Award, 1986; Honorary doctorates, Tasmania, Melbourne, Australian National University, Queensland & NSW. *Memberships include:* Fellow, Australian Academy of Humanities, College of Education; Vice President, Australian Council for Educational Standards. *Address:* 12 Vaucluse Road, Vaucluse, NSW 2030, Australia.

KRAMER Lotte Karoline, b. 22 Oct 1923, Mainz, Germany. Poet; Painter. m. Frederic Kramer, 20 Feb 1943, 1 son. *Education:* Mainz, 1930-38; Evening classes, Richmond, England, 1958-68. *Publications:* Scrolls, 1979; Ice Break, 1980; Family Arrivals, 1981; A Lifelong House, 1983; The Shoemaker's Wife, 1987; Poetry in anthologies including: PEN New Poetry; Writers of East Anglia; Chaos of the Night; Poetry of Chess; Shades of Green; Contemporary Women Poets; In the Gold of the Flesh. *Contributions to:* Agenda; Ambit; Ariel; Chapman; The Christian Science Monitor; The New York Times; The Spectator; The New Statesman; Encounter; The Jewish Chronicle; The Jewish Quarterly; Stand; Literary Review; The Observer; The PEN; Outposts; The Month; The Rialto; Passport; Others. *Honours:* 2nd Prize, York Poetry Competition, 1972. *Memberships:* PEN; Ver Poets; Writers in Schools; Poetry Society, Peterborough Museum Society; Decorative and Fine Arts Society. *Address:* 4 Apsley Way, Longthorpe, Peterborough PE3 9NE, England.

KRAMER-BADONI Rudolf, b. 22 Dec 1913, Rudesheim, Germany. Freelance Writer. *Education:* PhD. *Publications:* 8 novels including: Jacobs Jahr, 1943, 1978; Bewegliche Ziele (French translation, Les realites mouvantes), 1962; Gleichung mit einer Unbekannten, 1977. Political works including:

Anarchismus, 1970; Die niedliche revolution, 1973. Religious works including: Revolution in der Kirche-Lefebvre und Rom, 1980. Also: Galileo Galilei, biography, 1983; Zwischen allen Stuhlen, autobiography, 1985. *Contributions to:* Die Welt, Bonn. *Honour:* Konrad Adenauer Literature Prize, 1979. *Memberships include:* Past German secretary, PEN Club, Switzerland. *Address:* Brunnenstrasse 6, D-6200 Wiesbaden, Federal Republic of Germany.

KRANTZ Hazel Newman, b. 29 Jan 1920, Brooklyn, New York, USA, Writer; Teacher. m. Michael Krantz, 7 June 1942, 2 sons, 1 daughter. *Education:* BS, Journalism, New York University; MS, Elementary Education, Hofstra University. *Appointments:* Classroom Teacher, Nassau County, New York; Copy Editor, DB, The Sound Engineering Magazine; Editor, True Frontier Magazine. *Publications:* 100 Pounds of Popcorn; Freestyle for Michael; The Secret Raft; Tippy; A Pad of Your Own; Pink and White Striped Summer; None But The Brave; Daughter of my People: The Story of Henrietta Szold; For Love of Jeremy; Ellen Baker: Space Doctor; Look to the Hills, in progress. *Contributions to:* Numerous magazines and journals. *Membership:* Society of Children's Book Writers. *Address:* 1306 Stoney Hill Drive, Ft Collins, CO 80525, USA.

KRANTZ Judith, American. *Appointments:* Contributor, Good Housekeeping 1948-54, McCalls 1954-59 and Ladies Home Journal 1959-71; Contributing Editor, Cosmopolitan, 1971-79. *Publications:* Scruples, 1978; Princess Daisy, 1980; Mistral's Daughter, 1982; I'll Take Manhattan, 1986; Till We Meet Again, 1989; Dazzle, 1990; Scruples Two, 1992. *Membership:* PEN. *Literary Agent:* Morton Janklow. *Address:* c/o Morton Janklow - Lyn Nesbitt Associates, 598 Madison Avenue, New York, NY 10022, USA.

KRAPF Norbert, b. 14 Nov 1943, Jasper, Indiana, USA. Professor of English. m. 13 June 1970, 1 son, 1 daughter. *Education:* BA, English, magna cum laude, St Joseph's College, Indiana, 1965; MA, English, 1966, PhD, English and American Literature, 1971, University of Notre Dame. *Literary Appointment:* Professor of English, Long Island University, joined 1970, appointed full Professor 1984. *Publications include:* Lines Drawn from Dürer, 1981; A Dream of Plum Blossoms, 1985; ed: Under Open Sky: Poets on William Cullen Bryant, 1986; Trans and ed: Beneath the Cherry Sapling: Legends from Franconia, 1988; Arriving on Paumanok, 1979; Circus Songs, 1983; Trans and ed: Shdows on the Sundial: Selected Early Poems of Rainer Maria Rilke, 1990; Somewhere in Southern Indiana: Poems of Midwestern Origins, 1993; Blue-Eyed Grass: Poems of Germany, in progress. *Contributions to:* American Scholar; Poetry; New Letters; Kansas Quarterly; Confrontation. *Honours:* Senior Fulbright Professor of American Literature, University Freiburg, 1980-81 and University Erlangen/Nuremberg, 1988-89; Trustees Award for Scholarly Achievement, Long Island University, 1984. *Memberships:* Modern Language Association; Poetry Society of America; Academy of American Poets; Society for German-American Studies; Walt Whitman Birthplace Society; Indiana German Heritage Society. *Address:* English Department, Long Island University, Brookville, NY 11548, USA.

KRASILOVSKY Phyllis, b. 1926, American. *Publications:* The Man Who Didn't Wash His Dishes, 1950; The Very Little Girl, 1953; The Cow Who Fell in the Canal, 1957; Scaredy Cat, 1959; Benny's Flag, 1960; The Very Little Boy, 1961; Susan Sometimes, 1962; The Girl Who Was a Cowboy, 1965; The Very Tall Little Girl, 1969; The Shy Little Girl, 1970; The Popular Girls Club, 1972; LC Is the Greatest, 1975; The Man Who Tried to Save Time, 1979; The Man Who Entered a Contest, 1980; The First Tulips in Holland, The Man Who Cooked for Himself, 1982; The Happy Times Story Book, 1987. *Address:* 1177 Hardscrabble Road, Chappaqua, NY 10514, USA.

KRASNER William, b. 8 June 1917, St Louis, Missouri, USA. Writer, semi-retired. m. Juanita Frances Frazier, 12 Oct 1956. 4 sons. *Education:* Washington University, ST Louis, 1935-36; Army Air Force Meteorology Schools, 1942-46; BS, Psychology, Columbia University, 1948. *Appointments:* Writer-producer, CBS St Louis, Radio-TV, 1957-59; Development Staff Writer, Washington University, 1962; Articles Editor, Trans-Action magazine, 1963-69; Senior Assistant Editor, Psychiatric Reporter, 1969; Staff Writer- Editor, University of Pennsylvania, 1970-74; Staff Writer, Temple University, 1977; Writer (contract), NIMH, 1977-78; Freelance, 1946-. *Publications:* Novels: Walk the Dark Streets, 1949, 1950, 1986; The Gambler, 1950, 1951, 1987; North of Welfare, 1954; The Stag Party, 1957, 1958; Francis Parkman, Dakota Legend, 1983; Death of a Minor Poet, 1984; Resort to Murder, 1985; Drug Trip Abroad (non-fiction, collaboration), 1972; Look For The Dancer (German), 1993. *Contributions to:* Yank; The World; American Meteorological Bulletin; Harper's; Saturday Evening Post; St Louis Post-Dispatch; New Society; Philadelphia Inquirer. *Honours:* National Institute of Arts & Letters Grant, 1955; Newsweek's Best 10 Mysteries List, 1949; Grant from Pennsylvania Council on the Arts, 1980; Speaker for Pennsylvania Council on the Humanities; Krasner Collection Repository in Special Collections, Boston University.*Membership:* Author's Guild. *Literary Agent:* Scott Meredith Literary Agency, 845 Third Avenue, New York City, NY 10022, USA. *Address:* 538 Berwyn Avenue, Berwyn, PA 19312, USA.

KRAUS Robert, (Eugene H Hippopotamus), b. 1925, America, Writer of children's fiction; Cartoonist and illustrator. Founding President, Windmill Books 1966- and Springfellow Books, 1972-. *Publications include:* Don't Talk to strange Bears, 1969; The rabbit Brothers, 1969; Vip's Mistake Book, 1970; How Spider Saved Christmas, 1970; Whose Mouse Are You? 1970; Bunya the Witch, 1971; Shaggy Fur Face, 1971; The Tail Who Wagged the Dog, 1971; Ludwig, The Dog Who Snored Symphonies, 1971; Pip Squeak Mouse in Shining Armor, 1971; Lillian, Morgan and Teddy, 1971; Leo the Late Bloomer, 1971; The Tree That Stayed Up until Next Christmas, 1972; Good Night, Little A B C, 1972; Good Night, Little One, 1972; Good Night, Richard Rabbit, 1972; Milton, the Early Riser, 1972; Big Brother, 1973; How Spider Saved Halloween, 1973; Poor Mister Splinterfitzi, 1973; Herman the Helper, 1974; The Night-Lite Story Book, 1974; Rebecca Hatpin, 1974; Owliver, 1974; Pinchpenny Mouse, 1974; I'm a Monkey, 1975; Three Friends, 1975; The Gondolier of Venice, 1976; Kittens for Nothing, 1976; Boris Bad Enough, 1976; The Good Mousekeeper, 1977; The Detective of London, 1977; Noel the Coward, 1977; Springfellow, 1978; Another Mouse to Feed, 1979; Meet the Blunt, 1980; Box of Brownies, 1980; The King's Trousers, 1981; See the Christmas Lights, 1981; Tubby Books, 6 vols, 1981-82; Leo the Late Bloomer Takes a Bath, 1981; Herman the Helper Cleans Up, 1981; Squeaky Books, 2 vols, 1982; Tony the Tow truck, 1985; Freddy the Fire Engine, 1985; How Spider Saved Valentine's Day, 1986; Mrs Elmo of Elephant House, 1986; Where Are You Going Little Mouse? 1986; Come Out and Play, Little Mouse, 1987. *Address:* c/o Greenwillow Books, 105 Madison Avenue, New York, NY 10016, USA.

KRAUSS Bruno. *See:* **BULMER Henry Kenneth.**

KRAUSS Clifford, b. 30 July 1953, New York, USA. Journalist. *Education:* BA Vassar College, 1975; MA History, University of Chicago, 1976; MS Jurnalism, Columbia University, 1977. *Publications:* Inside Central America: Its People, Politics and History, 1991. *Contributions to:* The Nation; Foreign Affairs; The Wilson Quarterly; Times Literary Supplement. *Literary Agent:* Gloria Loomis. *Address:* 1305 Corcoran Street NW, Washington DC 20009, USA.

KRAUSS Ruth (Ida), b. 25 July 1911, Baltimore, Maryland, USA. Writer. m. David Johnson Leisk, 1940, (dec 1975). *Education:* Educated at Public Elementary Schools; at Peabody Institute of Music, Baltimore; New

School for Social Research, New York; Maryland Institute of Art, Baltimore; Graduate, Parsons School of Art, New York. *Publications:* Poem-Plays include: This Breast Gothic, 1973; If I Were Freedom (produced Annandale-on- Hudson, New York, 1976); Re-examination of Freedom (produced Boston 1976); Under 13, 1976; When I Walk I Change the Earth, 1978; Small Black Lambs Wandering in the Red Poppies (produced New York, 1982); Ambiguity 2nd (produced 1985). Productions include: A Beautiful Day; There's a Little Ambiguity Over There Among the Bluebells; Re-examination of Freedom; Newsletter; The Cantilever Rainbow; In a Bull's Eye; Pineapple Play; Quartet, A Show, A Play - It's a Girl! Onward Duet (or Yellow Umbrella); Drunk Boat, If Only, This Breast, many with music by Al Carmines, Bill Dixon and Don Heckman, produced in New York, New Haven, Boston and other places, since 1964. Fiction and verse for children. *Address:* c/o Scholastic Books, 730 Broadway, New York, NY 10003, USA.

KRAUT Richard Henry, b. 27 Oct 1944, Brooklyn, New York, USA. Professor of Philosophy. m. Susan Nancy Hyman, 11 Sept 1966, 1 son, 2 daughters. *Education:* BA, University of Michigan, 1965; PhD, Princeton University, 1969. *Appointments:* Currently Professor of Philosophy, University of Illinois, Chicago. *Publications:* Socrates and the State, 1984; Aristotle on the Human Good, 1989; Cambridge Companion to Plato (editor), 1992. *Address:* Philosophy Department, University of Illinois, MC 267, Box 4348, Chicago, IL 60680, USA.

KRAUZER Steven M, (J W Baron, Terry Nelson Bonner, Cole Harding, Adam Lassiter, Richard Marks, Owen Roundtree), b. 9 June 1948, Jersey City, USA. Writer. m. Dorri T Karasek, 2 Nov 1992. 2 daughters. *Education:* BA Yale University, 1970; MA, English Literature, University of New Hampshire, 1974. *Publications include:* The Cord Series, 1982-86; Blaze, 1983; The Diggers, 1983; The Dennison's War Series, 1984-86; The Executioner Series, 1982-83; Frame Work, 1989; Brainstorm, 1991; Rojak's Rule, 1992; Anthologies: Great Action Stories, 1977; The Great American Detective, 1978; Stories into Film, 1979; Triquarterly 48: Western Stories, 1980. *Contributions to:* American West; Montana: The Magazine of Western History; Outside. *Memberships:* Writers Guild of America West Inc; Authors Guild; Authors League; Mystery Writers of America. *Literary Agent:* Ginger Barber, Virginia Barber Literary Agency Inc, 101 5th Avenue, NY 10003, USA. *Address:* c/o Virginia Barber Literary Agency, 101 5th Avenue, New York, NY 10003, USA.

KREISEL Henry, b. 5 June 1922, Vienna, Austria, Professor Emeritus of English and Comparative Literature. m. Esther Lazerson, 22 June 1947, 1 son. *Education:* BA, 1947, MA, 1947, University of Toronto, Canada; PhD, University of London, 1954. *Appointments:* Lecturer to Professor of English, University of Alberta, 1947-60; University Professor, 1975-87. *Publications:* The Rich Man, 1948; The Betrayal, 1964; The Almost Meeting, 1981; Another Country: Writings By and About Henry Kreisel, 1985; The Rich Man, play, 1987. *Contributions to:* Canadian Literature; Canadian Forum; prism; Literary Review, Chicago; University of Toronto Quarterly; Queen's Quarterly. *Honours:* President's Medal, University of Western Ontario, 1960; I I Segal Foundation Award for Fiction, 1983; Sir Frederick Haultain Prize, 1986; Officer of the Order of Canada, 1987. *Memberships:* Association of Canadian University Teachers of English, President, 1962-63; Canadian Writers' Union. *Address:* Department of Comparative Literature, University of Alberta, Edmonton, Alberta, Canada T6G 2E1.

KREMP Herbert, b. 12 Aug 1928, Munich, Germany. Journalist. m. Brigitte Steffal, 1956, 2 daughters. *Education:* Munich University. *Appointments:* Reporter, Frankfurter Neue Presse, 1965-7; Political Editor, 1957-59, Bonn Correspondent 1961-63, Editor in Chief, 1963-68, Rheinische Post; Director, Political dept., Der Tag,

Berlin, 1959-61; Editor in Chief, 1969-77, Editor in Chief, 1981-85, Publisher, 1985-87, Die Welt; Chief Correspondent, Peking, 1977-81, Chief Correspondent, Brüssal, 1987-, Die Welt, Springer Group Newspapers. *Publications:* Am Ufer der Rubikon : Eine Politische Anthropologie 1972; Die Bambusbrucke : Ein Asiatisches Tagebuch, 1982. *Honour:* Konrad Adenauer Prize, 1984; Theodor-Wolff Prize, 1980. *Address:* St Hubertusdreef 24. 1900 Overÿse, Belgium.

KRESS Nancy, b. 20 Jan 1948, Buffalo, NY, USA. Teacher. m. (1) Michael Kress, (div) 2 sons, (2) Mark P Donnelly, 19 Aug 1988. *Education:* BS, State University of NY College at Plattsburgh, 1969; MS (Education) 1978, MA (English) 1979, State University of NY College at Brockport. *Appointments:* Elementary School Teacher, Penn Yan, 1970-73; Adjunct instructor, State University of NY College at Brockport, 1980-; Senior Copywriter, Stanton and Hucko, Rochester, 1984-. *Publications:* The Prince of Morning Bells, 1981; The Golden Grove, 1984; The White Pipes, 1985; Trinity and Other Stories, 1985; An Alien Light, 1988; Brain Rose, 1990. *Contributions to:* Periodicals, including Isaac Astimov's Science Fiction; Omni; Fantasy and Science Fiction; Twilight Zone; Work represented in anthologies, including The Best Science Fiction of the Year 12; Universe 12; Full Spectrum, 1982. *Honours:* Nebula Award from Science Fiction Writers of America, 1985, for Out of All Them Bright Stars. *Memberships:* Science Fiction Writers of America (director of speakers bureau). *Address:* 50 Sweden Hill Road, Brockport, NY 14420, USA.

KRETZMER Herbert, b. 5 Oct 1925, South Africa. Journalist; Lyric Writer. m. Elisabeth Margaret Wilson, 1961, (div 1973), 1 son, 1 daughter. *Appointments:* Entered Journalism, 1946; Reporter, Entertainment Columnist, Sunday Express, Johannesburg, 1951-54; Feature Writer, Columnist, Daily Sketch, London, 1954-59; Columnist, Sunday Dispatch, London, 1959-61; Theatre Critic, Daily Express, 1962-78; TV Critic, Daily Mail, 1979-87. *Publications:* Our Man Crichton, 1965; (jointly) Every Home Should Have One, 1970; Lyricist, Ivor Novello Award Song, Goodness Gracious Me, 1960; Lyricist, contributed to weekly songs to That Was the Week..; Not So Much A Programme...BBC3, That's Life. *Honours:* ASCAP Award, 1969; Gold Record for She, 1974; 'Tony' Award for lyrics of RSC's, Les Miserables, 1987; Grammy Award, 1988; TV Critic of the Year, Philips Industries Award, 1980; commended British Press Awards, 1981. *Address:* c/o London Management, 235/241 Regent Street, London W1A 2JT, England.

KRIEGER Murray, b. 27 Nov 1923, Newark, New Jersey, USA. Professor; Literary Critic. m. Joan Alice Stone, 15 June 1947, 1 son, 1 daughter. *Education:* MA, University of Chicago, 1948; PhD, Ohio State University, 1952. *Appointments:* Assistant, Associate Professor, English, Universiy of Minnesota, 1952-58; Professor, English, University of Illinois, 1958-63; Carpenter Professor, Literary Criticism, University of Iowa, 1963-66; Professor, English, Univerity of California, Irvine, 1966-, Los Angeles, 1973-82; University Professor, University of California, 1974-, Director, University of California, Humanities Research Institute, 1987-89. *Publications:* New Apologists for Poetry, 1956; The Tragic Vision, 1960; A Window to Criticism : Shakespeare's Sonnets and Modern Poetics, 1964; The Play and Place of Criticism, 1967; The Classic Vision, 1971; Theory of Criticism, 1976; Poetic Presence & Illusion, 1979; Arts on the Level : The Fall of the Elite Object, 1981; Words About Words About Words : Theory Criticism and the Literary Text, 1988; A Reopening of Closure: Organicism Against Itself, 1989; Ekphrasis: The Illusion of the Natural Sign, 1992; The Ideological Imperative: Repression and Resistance in Recent American Theory, 1993. *Contributions to:* Many literary and scholarly journals. *Honours:* Guggenheim Fellowships 1956-57, 1961-62; Fellowship, American Council of Learned Societies, 1966-67; Humanities Fellowship, Rockefeller Foundation, 1978; Elected Fellow, American Academy of Arts and Sciences, 1983;

Research Prize, A.V. Humboldt Foundation, Federal Republic of Germany, 1985-86; Residency at Rockefeller Study and Conference Center, Bellagio, Italy, 1990. *Memberships:* various professional organisations including: Modern Language Association of America; English Institute, Chairman 1982-83; International Association of University Professors of English; Academy of Literary Studies. *Address:* Dept. of English & Comparative Literature, University of California, Irvine, CA 92717, USA.

KRIEGLER Lyn. *See:* **KRIEGLER-ELLIOTT Carolyn Patricia.**

KRIEGLER-ELLIOTT Carolyn Patricia, b. 14 Apr 1949, Niagara Falls, New York, USA. Children's Book Author and Illustrator. m. Tom Elliott, 8 Apr 1983. *Education:* BFA with honours, Illustration, Virginia Commonwealth University; Early Childhood Education, St Petersburg Junior College, Tarpon Springs, Florida, 1987. *Appointments:* Children's Book Agent, Richards Literary Agency, 1990; Guest, Aim Children's Book Week, National Library Service, Whangarei, New Zealand, 1992. *Publications:* The Magpies Said, 1980; Legend of the Kiwi, 1981; A Bundle of Birds, 1985; Come Back, Ginger (with Dorothy Butler), 1986; Rosie Moonshine (with Anthony Holcroft), 1989; A Lollipop, Please, 1989; Good Night, Little Brother, 1989; Pins and Needles, 1989; Rain, 1990; Chen Li and the River Spirit (with Anthony Holcroft), 1990; Lulu, 1990; Lucky for Some, 1990; Cat Concert, 1990; A Present for Anna, 1990; Higgledy Piggledy Hobbledy Hoy, 1991; Woodsmoke, 1991; The Cave, 1991; Googer in Space, 1991; Night Cat, 1991; By Jingo!, 1992; What Peculiar People, 1992; Good Night, Alice, 1992; Island in the Lagoon (with Anthony Holcroft), 1992; A Dog for Keeps (with Pauline Cartwright), 1992. *Contributions to:* Mobil Oil New Zealand Wildlife Heritage Series; Time Magazine; Reader's Digst; New Zealand Listener, 1978-79. *Honours:* Art Award, Junior Women's League, Hopewell, Virginia, 1967; Outstanding Departmental Senior Award, Virginia Commonwealth University, 1971; Guest Promotion Art Director (Award), Mademoiselle Magazine, 1971; Legend of the Kiwi presented to HRH Prince Charles and HRH Princess Diana, RNZAF, 1983. *Memberships:* New Zealand Book Council; New Zealand Children's Book Foundation; PEN (Writers Guild of New Zealand); Writers in Schools, New Zealand Book Council; Sathya Sai Organization of New Zealand; Education in Human Values Wing, Values, Education and Service Trust, New Zealand. *Literary Agent:* Ray Richards, Richards Literary Agency, Auckland, New Zealand. *Address:* c/o Richards Literary Agency, PO Box 31240, Milford, Auckland 9, New Zealand.

KRISHNA CHAR H R, (Kanteerava (Soopsar)), b. 1 Jan 1929, Shinoga. Teacher; Press Woman. m. 15 Oct 1970, 1 son, 1 daughter. *Education:* BA, 1980. *Publications:* Samasdye; Kanda Sapdge; Nane Bharama. *Contributions to:* Several. *Honours:* Audhuneeka Sarwagma. *Memberships:* Mysore Jilla Barahagarara Balaga Mysore; Graduates Cooperative Bank; Sarwa Bhoma Theatre Mysore. *Literary Agent:* Associated Editor, Chamundeshwari A Kannada Weekly B'Lore.

KRISHNAN-KUTTY G, b. 16 Apr 1931, Kerala State, India. Economist; Writer. *Education:* MA Economics; PhD Economics. *Publications:* Anguish, novel, 1965; Perroux's Theory of Dominant Economy, 1964; Colonialism in India: Roots of Underdevelopment; Peasantry in India, 1987. *Contributions to:* Several articles in English, French and Malayalam. *Honours:* Fellowship, French Government, 1955; University Grant Commission Award; Senior Fellowship, Indian Council of Social Science Research, 1982, 1990; International Fellowship, Indo-French Cultural Exchange, 1987. *Memberships:* Indian Economic Association; Authors Guild of India; Association Tiers-Mondes; Indian Institute of Public Administration. *Address:* Vallauris VII/15 Prasant Nagar, Ulloor, Trivandrum 695011, India.

KRISHNASWAMY IYENGAR H S, (Echeske (HSK), Samadarshi, Vicharapriya), b. 26 Aug 1920, Haleyur, Karnataka, India. Professor; Editor; m. 2 July 1945, 1 son, 1 daughter. *Education:* LCom Diploma, 1943; BCom Degree, University of Mysore, 1948; MA Economics, Banaras Hindu University, 1951. *Publications include:* Bayakeya Bele (novel), 1954; Vyavaharika Kannada, 1960; Sri Ramanuja, (biography), 1963; Surahonne, (essays) 1980; Etharada Vyktigalu, (profiles), 1966. *Contributions to:* Sudha, (weekly); Prajavani, (daily). *Honours:* Nama Abhivridhi Yoganegalu, State Government, 1961; Karnetaka Sahitya Academy Award, 1981. *Memberships:* Indian PEN Society; Editor, Banking Parapancha, quarterly. *Address:* 41 6th Main Road , Saraswathipuram, Mysore 570009, India.

KROETSCH Robert, b. 26 June 1927, Canada, Writer; Professor. *Education:* BA, University of Alberta, 1948; MA, Middlebury College, Vermont, USA, 1956; PhD, University of Iowa, 1961. *Appointments:* Assistant Professor, 1961, Professor, 1967, State University of New York at Binghampton; Professor, University of Manitoba, 1978. *Publications:* The Studhorse Man, 1969; Badlands, 1975; What the crow Said, 1978; Alibi, 1983; Completed Field Notes, poetry, 1989; The Lovely Treachery of Words, essays, 1989; But We Are Exiles; The Words of My Roaring; Gone Indian; Alberta, travel. *Honours:* The Governor General's Award, Canada, 1969; Fellow, The Royal Society of Canada, 1986. *Membership:* Writers' Union of Canada. *Literary Agent:* MGA Agency, 10 St Mary Street, Suite 510, Toronto, M4Y 1P9, Canada. *Address:* Department of English, University of Monitoba, Winnipeg, Canada R3T 2N2.

KROPP Lloyd, American. *Appointments:* Teacher, University of North Carolina, Greenboro, 1970-75; Teacher, Southern Illinois University, Edwardsville, 1975-. *Publications:* The Drift, 1969; Who is Mary Stark?, 1974; One Hundred Times to China, 1979; Greencastle, 1987. *Address:* 32 South Meadow Lane, Edwardsville, IL 62025, USA.

KRUGER Lorenz, b. 3 Oct 1932. Professor. m. Christa Krug, 1967, 1 son, 2 daughters. *Education:* Physics Diploma, 1957; Graduation Dr rer nat, 1959; Habilitation for Philosophy, 1972. *Publications:* Rationalismus und universale logik bei Leibniz, 1969; Der Begriff des Empirismus, 1973; The Probabilistic Revolution, 1987; The Empire of Chance, How Probability changed Science and Everyday Life, 1989. *Honours:* Visiting Professor Berkeley, 1972; Fellow, Princeton University, 1973-74; Research Fellow, University of Pittsburgh, 1978-79. *Memberships:* Akademie der Wissenschaften zu Gottingen; Allg Ges. f. Philosophie in Deutschland; Philosophical American Association; Philosophy of Science Association; Academia Europaea. *Address:* Philosophisches Seminar, Georg-Agust-Universitat, D-3400 Gottingen, Humboldtalle 19, Germany.

KRUKOWSKI Lucian Wladyslaw, b. 22 Nov 1929, New York City, New York, USA. Professor of Philosphy. m. Marilyn Denmark, 17 Jan 1955, 1 daughter. *Education:* BA, Brooklyn College, 1952; BFA, Yale University, 1955; MS, Pratt Institute, 1958; PhD, Washington University, 1977. *Publications:* Art and Concept, 1987; Aesthetic Legacies, 1992; Anthologies: The Arts, Society, and Literature, 1984; The Reasons of Art, 1985; Cultural Literacy and Arts Education, 1990; Ethics and Architecture, 1990; The Future of Art, 1990. *Contributions to:* Over 25 articles to professional philosophical journals. *Memberships:* American Society for Aesthetics; American Philosophical Association. *Address:* 24 Washington Terrace, St Louis, MO 63112, USA.

KRUPAT Arnold, b. 22 Oct 1941, New York City, New York, USA. Professor. 1 son, 1 daughter. *Education:* BA, New York University, 1962; MA, 1965, PhD, 1967, Columbia University. *Publications:* For Those Who Come After, 1985; I Tell You Now (edited with Brian Swann), 1987; Recovering the Word (edited with Brian Swann), 1987; The Voice in the Margin,1989; Ethnocriticism: Ethnography, History, Literature, 1992; New Voices: Essays on Native American Literatures (editor), 1933; Native American Autobiography (editor), 1993. *Contributions to:* Dozens to critical journals. *Address:* Sarah Lawrence College, Bronxville, NY 10708, USA.

KRZYZAGORSKI Klemens, b. 1 Oct 1930, Zduny. Journalist. m. *Education:* Academy of Political Sciences, Warsaw. *Appointments:* Head, Artistic Programmes, Section of TV Wroclaw, 1965-67; Editor in Chief, Odra, Wroclaw, 1967-72, Kontrasty, Bialystok, 1974-79; Editor in Chief, Prasa Polska, 1981-85; Editor in Chief, Kultura, 1985-86, Literatura, 1986-89. *Publications:* Collected Journalism Klopoty z cialem, 1969; Co-author, Co-editor, 10 volumes of prose, essays in literary and socio-cultural journals, theatre scenarios: Albertus Return, 1966, Long Live the King, 1966. *Honours:* Prizes, City of Wroclaw, 1956, City of Walbrzych, 1964, City of Bialystok, 1975; Julian Brun Prize (1st class), 1956; Boleslaw Prus Prize, (2nd Class), 1981; Journalists' Prize of Toj, 1987 (International Organization of Journalists); Kt's and Officers Cross, Polonia Restituta Order. *Memberships:* National Council of Culture; Press Council; Polish Writers Association; President, Association of Journalists of Polish People's Republic, 1982-87; many other professional organisations. *Address:* ul Dobra 29 m 10, 00-344 Warsaw, Poland.

KUBE-MCDOWELL Michael Paul, b. 29 Aug 1954, Philadelphia, Pennsylvania, USA. Freelance Writer/ Novelist. m. Karla Jane Kube, 12 Dec 1975, (div 7 Oct 1987), 1 son. *Education:* BA, Honours, Michigan State University, 1976; MS, Education, Indiana University, 1981. *Appointments:* Writing Instructor, Miles Laboratories, 1978-80, Goshen College, 1984-85; Correspondent, Elkhart Truth, 1982-84; Jurist, Nebula Award, 1989; Instructor, Clarion Workshop, 1990. *Publications:* Emprise, 1985; After the Flames, 1985; Enigma, 1986; Empery, 1987; Thieves of Light (As Michael Hudson), 1987; Odyssey (Isaac Asimov's Robot City), 1987; Alternities, 1988; The Quiet Pools, 1990. Teleplays for Tales from the Darkside: Lifebomb, Effect and Cause, The Bitterest Pill, 1985-86. *Contributions to:* Numerous fiction and non-fiction in various magazines. *Honours:* National Merit Scholar, 1972; Courier-Post Journalism Award, 1972; Hoosier State Press Association Honourable Mention, 1983; Presidential Scholar Distinguished Teacher, 1985; Philip K. Dick Award Finalist, 1986. *Memberships:* Science Fiction Writers of America; Writers Guild of America; National Space Society; Planetary Society; many other professional journals. *Literary Agent:* Scott Meredith Literary Agency. *Address:* PO Box 706, Okemos, MI 48805-0706, USA.

KUBLY Herbert Oswald, b. New Glarus, Wisconsin, USA. Novelist; Author; Retired Educator. (div), 1 son. *Education:* BA, University of Wisconsin. *Literary Appointments:* Professor Emeritus of English, University of Wisconsin - Parkside, Kenosha; Fellow, Wisconsin Academy of Science, Arts & Letters, 1989. *Publications:* American in Italy, 1955; Easter in Sicily, 1956; Varieties of Love, Short Stories, 1958; Italy, 1961; The Whistling Zone, novel, 1963; Switzerland, 1964; At Large, essays, 1964; Gods and Heroes, 1969; The Duchess of Glover, novel, 1975; The Native's Return, 1981; The Parkside Stories, 1985; Amazing Grace, 1990. Plays: Men to the Sea, National Theater, New York; The Cocoon, Playhouse Theater, London; The Virus, University of Wisconsin Parkside Theater; Perpetual Care, University of Wisconsin Parkside Theater. *Contributions to:* Esquire; Atlantic; Saturday Review and other magazines; Editor, Time Magazine and Writer for Life and Holiday magazines; Gourmet and Travel Writer for Sunday Magazine of Milwaukee Journal, 1969-84. *Honours:* Rockefeller Grants, 1947, 1948; Fulbright Research Grant, Italy, 1950; National Book Award, 1956; First Award, Wisconsin Council for Writers, 1970, 1976; Citations for Distinguished Service in Letters by Wisconsin State Legislature and Wisconsin Academy of Science, Arts and Letters, 1982. *Memberships:* Authors League of America; Dramatists Guild of America (National Secretary, 1947-49); Council of

Wisconsin Writers; Wisconsin Academy of Science, Arts and Letters; Poetry Society of America. *Literary Agent:* Harold Ober Associates, New York City. *Address:* W4970 Kubly Road, New Glarus, WI 53574, USA.

KUBRICK Stanley, b. 26 July 1928, New York, USA. Film Writer; Producer; Director. m. Suzanne Harlan, 1958, 3 daughters. *Education:* City College of New York. *Appointments:* Staff Photographer, Look, 1946-50; produced, directed and photographed documentaries for RKO, 1951; has produced written and directed feature films, 1952-. *Publications:* Fear and Desire, 1953; Killer's Kiss, 1955; The Killing, 1965; Paths of Glory, co-writer, 1948; Dr Strangelove, 1963; 2001: A Space Odyssey, co-author, 1968; A Clockwork Orange, 1971; Barry Lyndon, 1975; The Shining, 1978; Full Metal Jacket, 1987. *Honours:* New York Critics' Best Film Award, Dr Strangelove, 1964; Oscar, 1968; Best Director Award, 1971. *Address:* c/o Loeb & Loeb, 10100 Santa Monica Boulevard Suite 2200, Los Angeles CA 90067, USA.

KUHN Thomas S, b. 1922, American. *Appointments:* With the radio research laboratory, AM-British Laboratory, ORSD, 1943-45; Member of Faculty, 1948-57, Harvard University, Cambridge, MA, University of California, Berkeley, 1957-64; Professor 1964-68, M Taylor Pyne Professor of the History of Science 1968-79, Princeton University, NJ; President, History of Science Society, 1968-70; Member, Institute for Advanced Study, Princeton, 1972-79; Professor, Philosophy and History of Science, Massachusetts Institute of Technology, Cambridge, 1979-. *Publications:* The Copernican Revolution: Planetary Astronomy in the Development of Western Thought, 1957, 1959; The Structure of Scientific Revolutions, 1962, 1970; Sources for History of Quantum Physics: An Inventory and Report (with John L Heilbron, Paul L Forman ad Lim Allen), 1966; The Essential Tension: Selected Studies in Scientific Tradition and Change, 1977; Black-Body Theory and the Quantum Discontinuity 1894-1912, 1978.

KULICKI Krzysztof Bogdan, b. 7 Feb 1938, Warsaw, Poland. Chemist. m. Danuta Kulicka, 10 July 1973. *Education:* BS, Chemistry, 1961; Doctor of Technical Sciences, 1966. *Publications:* Bad Streets, 1978; Escapers from the Street of Dreams, 1979; Square of Harmony, 1982; Kif 1989; Straight Ahead, 1972; After Storm, 1979; These Few People, 1974; Welcome the Second Year, 1975. *Contributions to:* Life of Warsaw since 1978; Polityka, since 1975. *Honours:* Prize of the Publishing House of MON (Ministry of National Defence), 1974; Competition of the Ministry of Culture, 1975. *Memberships:* The Union of Polish Writers, since 1976; Vice-President of Polish Section of AIEP. *Literary Agent:* Publishing House of Bellona, Grzybowska 77, Warsaw, Poland. *Address:* Sanocka 11a/26, 02-110 Warszawa, Poland.

KULTERMANN Udo, b. 1927, American (b. German), *Appointments:* Director, Museum Schloss Morsbroich, Leverkusen, West Germany, 1959-84; Professor of Architecture 1967-86, Ruth and Norman Moore Professor of Architecture 1986-, Washington University, St Louis; Member, National Faculty of Humanities, Arts and Sciences, Atlanta, Georgia, 1986-; Member, Architecture Committee, Venice Biennale, 1979-82. *Publications:* Architecture of Today Hans und Wassili Luckhardt: Bauten und Entwuerfe, 1958; Dynamische Architektur, 1959; New Japanese Architecture, 1960; Der Schluessel zur Architektur von heute; Junge deutsche Bildhauer; New Architecture in Africa, 1963; New Architecture in the World, 1965; History of Art History, 1966; Architektur der Gegenwart: Kunst der Welt; The New Sculpture, 1967; Gabriel Grupello, 1968; The New Painting; New Directions in African Architecture, 1969; Modern Architecture in Color (with Werner Hofmann); Kenzo Tange: Architecture and Urban Design; Art and Life, 1970; New Realism, 1972; Ernest Trova, 1977; Die Architektur im 20 Jahrhundert, 1978; I Contemporanei (volume XIV of Storia della Scultura del Mondo), 1979; Architecture of the

Seventies; Architekten der Dritten Welt, 1980; Zeitgenoessische Architektur in Osteuropa, 1985; Kleine Geschichte der Kunsttheorie, 1987; Visible Cities - Invisible Cities, 1988; Kunst und Wirklichkeit von FiedlerbBis Derrida Zehn Annaeherungen, 1991. *Address:* School of Architecture, Washington University, St Louis, MO 63130, USA.

KUMAR Satish, b. 27 May 1933, Moga, India. University Professor. m. Manjari, 7 May 1963, 2 daughters. *Education:* MA, Political Science, Delhi University; PhD, Indian School of International Studies, Delhi University, 1962. *Appointments:* Assistant Professor, South Asian Studies, Indian School of International Studies, 1961-67, Senior Research Officer (Pakistan), Ministry of External Affairs, 1967-72; Associate Professor, 1972-83, Professor, Diplomacy, School of International Studies, Jawaharlal Nehru University, 1983-. *Publications:* Rana Polity in Napal, 1967; The New Pakistan, 1978; CIA and the Third World: A Study in Crypto Diplomacy, 1981; Bangladesh Documents, two volumes, 1971, 1972; Documents on India's Foreign Policy, 3 volumes, 1975, 1976, 1977; Yearbook on India's Foreign Policy, 1982-83, 1983-84, 1984-85, 1985-86, 1987-88, 1989, 1990-91. *Contributions to:* About 40 research articles in Indian and foreign journals. *Honours:* Senior Fulbright Fellowship, School of Advanced International Studies, John Hopkins University, Washington, USA, 1978; Ford Foundation Fellowship, University of California, Berkeley, 1978. *Memberships:* Authors Guild of India; Institue of Defence Sudies and Analysis; Indian Council of World Affairs; India International Centre. *Literary Agent:* Third World Book Review, London. *Address:* 66 Dakshinapuram, New Campus, Jawaharlal Nehru University, New Delhi 110067, India.

KUMAR Shiv K(umar), b. 16 Aug 1921, Lahore, Punjab. Writer. m. Madhu Kumar, 1967, 2 sons, 2 daughters. *Education:* BA 1941, MA 1943, Forman Christian College, Panjab University, Lahore; PhD, Fitzwilliam College, Cambridge, 1956. *Appointments:* Lecturere, DAV College, Lahore, 1945-47, and Hansraj College, Delhi 1948-49; Programme Executive, All India Radio, Delhi, 1949; Broadcaster, BBC, 1951-53; Senior Lecturer and Chairman of the Department of English, Government College, Chandigarh 1953-56; Reading in English, Panjab University, Hoshiarpur, 1956-59; Professor and Chairman of the Department of English, Osmania University, Hyderabad, 1959-76; Professor and Chairman of the Department of English and Dean of the School of Humanities, 1976-79 and Acting Chancellor, 1979-80, University of Hyderabad; Visiting Professor, Elmira College, New York, 1965-57, Marshall University, Huntington, West Virginia, 1968, and University of Northern Iowa, Cedar Falls, 1969; Cultural Award Visitor, Australia, Summer 1971; Visiting Professor, Drake University, Des Moines, Iowa, 1971-72, Hofstra University, Hempstead, New York, 1972, University of Kent, Canterbury, 1977-78, Oklahoma University, Norman, 1980-82 and Franklin and Marshall College, Lancester, Pennsylvania, 1982-84; President, All India English Teachers Conference, 1975; Member, Advisory Board (English), Sahitya Akademy, 1978-83. *Publications include:* Verse: Articulate Silences, 1970; Cobwebs in the Sun, 1974; Subterfuges, 1976; Woodpeckers, 1979. Play: The Last Wedding Anniversary (produced Hyderabad 1974) New Delhi, Macmillan, 1975; Novels: The Bone's Prayer, 1979; Nude Before God, 1983. *Honours:* Smith-Mundt Fellowship, 1962; Fellow, Royal Society of Literature, 1978. *Address:* 2-F/Kakatiya Nagar, P O Jamia Osmania, Hyderabad 500 007, India.

KUMIN Maxine Winokur, b. 6 June 1925, Philadelphia, Pennsylvania, USA. Writer. m. Victor M. Kumin, 29 June 1946, 1 son, 2 daughters. *Education:* AB, 1946, AM, 1948, Radcliffe College. *Appointments include:* Brandeis University, 1975; Hurst Professor, Literature, Washington University, 1977; Woodrow Wilson Visiting Fellow, 1979; Consultant in Poetry, Library of Congress, 1981-82; Poet-in-Residence, Bucknell University, 1983; Master Artist, Atlantic Centre for the Arts, Florida, 1984. *Publications include:* Poetry: Halfway, 1961; The Privilege, 1965; The Nightmare Factory, 1970; Up Country, 1972; The Retrieval System, 1978; Our Ground Time Here Will Be Brief, 1982; Closing the Ring, 1984; The Long Approach, 1985; Nurture, 1988. Novels: Through Dooms of Love, 1965; The Passions of Uxport, 1968; The Abduction, 1971; The Designated Heir, 1974; In Deep: Country Essays, 1987; short stories, essays, children's books. *Contributions to:* Numerous magazines & journals. *Honours include:* Various honorary degrees; Eunice Tietjens Memorial Prize, Poetry Magazine, 1972; Pulitzer Prize, Poetry, 1973; 1st Prize, Borestone Mountain, 1976; Recognition Award, Radcliffe College Alumnae, 1978; Award, American Academy & Institute, Arts & Letters, 1980; Academy of American Poets Fellowship, 1985; Levinson Award, Poetry Magazine, 1986; Poet Laureate, State of New Hampshire, 1989; Fellowships, Scholarships. *Memberships:* Poetry Society of America; PEN; Writers Union. *Literary Agent:* Emilie Jacobson, Curtis Brown Ltd. *Address:* c/o Curtis Brown Ltd., 10 Astor Place, New York, NY 10003, USA.

KUNCA John, b. 7 Nov 1919, Lithuania. Surgeon. m. Agnes Plavskis, 6 Sept 1957, 3 daughters. *Education:* MD, 1945; Surgeon, Registered in Argentina and Australia. *Appointments:* Columnist: Vision, international; Free Lithuania, Chicago, USA; World Lithuanian, USA; Teviskes Aidai, Australia; Tiesa Lithuania. *Publications:* The Man and the Atomic Era, 1985; Lithuania's Future, 1992; Encyclopaedia contributor: The Australian People, 1991; Religion and the Ethnic Identity, 1991. *Contributions to:* Vision; Free Lithuania; World Lithuanian. *Memberships:* Lithuanian Journalists Society; Australian Medical Association. *Address:* 112 High St, Doncaster, Victoria 3108, Australia.

KUNDERA Milan, b. 1 Apr 1929, Brno, Czechoslovakia. Writer. m. Vera Hrabankova, 1967. *Education:* Film Faculty, Academy of Music and Dramatic Arts, Prague. *Appointments:* Assistant, Assistant Professor, Film Faculty, Academy of Music and Dramatic Arts, Prague, 1958-69; Professor, University of Rennes, 1975-80; Professor, Ecole des hautes etudes en sciences sociales, Paris, 1980-. *Publications:* Drama: Jacques et son maitre 1971-81; Short Stories: Laughable Loves, 1970; Novels: The Joke, 1967; Life is Elsewhere, 1973; La Valse aux adieux, 1976; Livre du rire et de l'oubli, 1979. Essays: L'art Du Rohan, 1986; The Unbearable Lightness of Being, 1984. *Honours:* Union of Czechoslovak Writers' Prize, 1968; Czechoslovak Writers' Publishing House Prize, 1969; Prix Medicis, 1973; Premio Letterario Mondello, 1978; Commonwealth Award, 1981; Prix Europa-Litterature, 1982; Los Angeles Times Prize, 1984; Jerusalem Prize, 1985; Prix de le Critique de l'Academie Française, 1987; Prix Nelly Sachs, 1987; Ostereichischere staatspreis für europeische litterateur, 1987. *Memberships:* Editorial Board, Literarni noviny, 1963-67, 1968; Editorial Board, Listy 1968-69. *Address:* Ecole des hautes etudes en sciences sociales, 54 boulevard Raspail, Paris 75006, France.

KUNITZ Stanley (Jasspon), b. 1905. America, Poet, Writer of Literary Essays. *Appointments:* Editor, Wilson Library Bulletin, New York City, 1928-43; Member of Faculty, Bennington College, Vermont, 1946-49; Professor of English, State University of New York, Potsdam, 1949-50; Lecturer, New School for Social Research, New York City, 1950-57; Visiting Professor, University of Washington, Seattle, 1955-56, Queens College, Flushing, New York, 1956-57, and Brandeis University, Waltham, Massachusetts, 1958-59; Director, YM-YWHA Poetry Workshop, New York City, 1958-62; Danforth Visiting Lecturer, US 1961-63; Lecturer, 1963-67 and Adjunct Professor of Writing 1967-85, Columbia University, New York City; Editor, Yale Series of Younger Poets, Yale University Press, New Haven, Connecticut, 1969-77; Visiting Professor, Yale University, New Haven, Connecticut, 1970 and Rutgers University, Camden, New Jersey, 1974; Consultant in Poetry, Library of Congress, Washington

DC, 1974-75; Visiting Professor and Senior Fellow in Humanities, Princeton University, New Jersey, 1978; Visiting Professor, Vassar College, Poughkeepsie, New York, 1981; Montgomery Fellow, Dartmouth College, Hanover, New Hampshire, 1991. *Publications include:* On Intellectual Things (verse), 1930; Passport to the War: A Selection of Poems, 1944; (ed with H Haycraft) British Authors Before 1800: A Biographical Dictionary, 1952; Selected Poems 1928-1958, 1958; (ed)Poems by John Keats, 1964; (ed with V Colby) European Authors 1000-1900: A Biographical Dictionary of European Literature, 1967; The Testing-Tree Poems, 1971; (ed and trans with M Hayward) Poems of Akhmatova, 1973; The Terrible Threshold: Selected Poems 1940-1970, 1974; (trans)Story Under Full Sail by A Voznesensky, 1974; A Kind of Order, A Kind of Folly (essays) 1975; (ed and co-trans) Orchard Lamps by Ivan Drach, 1978; The Poems of Stanley Kunitz, 1928- 1978, 1979; The Wellfleet Whale and Companion Poems, 1983; Next-to-Last Things (poems and essays) 1985; (ed)The Essential Blake, 1987. *Address:* 37 West 12th Street, New York, NY 10011, USA.

KUNSTLER William M, b. 1919, American. *Appointments:* Partner, Kunstler and Kunstler, lawyers, 1949-; Associate Professor of Law, New York Law School, 1950-, and Pace College, 1951-; Lecturer, New School for Social Research, 1966-. *Publications:* Our Pleasant Vices, 1941; The Law of Accidents, 1954; First Degree, 1960; Beyond a Reasonable Doubt, 1961; The Case for Courage, 1962; ...And Justice for All, 1963; The Minister and the Choir Singer, 1964; Deep in My Heart, 1966; The Hall-Mills Murder Case, 1980; Trials and Tribulations, 1985. *Address:* 13 Gay Street, New York, NY 10014, USA.

KUNZE Reiner Alexander, b. 16 Aug 1933, Oelsnitz, Germany. Writer. *Education:* Studies of philosophy & journalism, literary history, art history, music history, University of Leipzig, 1951-55; MA. *Publications:* Poetry, Prose, translations, films; Sensible Wege, 1969; Der Loewe Leopold, 1970; Zimmerlautstaerke, 1972; Brief mit blauem Siegel, 1973; Die wunderbaren Jahre, 1976; Film Script, Die wunderbaren Jahre, 1979; Auf eigene Hoffnung, 1981; Eine stadtbekannte Geschichte, 1982; In Deutschland zuhaus, 1984; Gespraech mit der Amsel, 1984; Eines jeden einziges Leben, 1986; Zurueckgeworfen auf sich selbst, 1989; Das weisse Gedicht, 1989; Deckname Lyrik, 1990; Wohin der Schlaf rich schlafen legt, 1991; Mensch ohne Macht, 1991; Am Sonnenhang, 1993; Begehrte, unbegneme Freiheit, 1993; Deckname Lyrik, 1990; Wohin der Schlaf legt, 1991; mensch ohne Macht, 1991; Am Connenhang, 1993; Beghrte, Unbegueme Freiheit, 1993. *Honours:* Translation Prize, Czech Writers Association, 1968; German Young People's Book Prize, 1970; Moelle Literary Prize, Sweden, 1973; Literary Prize, Bavarian academy of Fine Arts, 1973; Georg Trakl Prize, Austria, 1977; Andreas Gryphius Prize, 1977; Georg Buechner Prize, 1977; Bavarian Film Prize, 1979; Geschwister Scholl Prize, 1981; Eichendorff Prize, 1984; Bundesverdienstkreuz 1 Klasse, 1984; Bayerischer Verdienstorden, 1988; Kulturpreis Ostbayern, 1989; Herbert und Elsbeth Weichmann - Preis und Hanns Martn Schleyer - Preis, 1990; Kulturpreis Deutscher Freimaurer, 1993; Großes Verdienst - Kreuz der Bundesrepublik Deutschland. *Memberships:* Bavarian academy of Fine Arts; Academy of Arts, Berlin, 1975-1992; German Academy for Language & Literature, Darmstadt; PEN. *Address:* Am Sonnenhang 19, D 94 130, Obernzell 1-Erlau, Federal Republic of Germany.

KUO Gloria Liang-Hui, b. 10 July 1926, Kaifeng, Henan, China. Author. m. 1949, 2 sons. *Education:* BA, National Szechuan University, Chengtu, 1948. *Appointment:* Journalist, Hsin Ming Evening News, Shanghai, 1948-49. *Publications:* 34 novels, 20 novelettes, 2 non-fiction books. Some in English translations. Titles include: Debt of Emotion, 1959; The Lock of a Heart, 1962; Far Far Way to Go, 1962; Stranger in Calcutta, 1973; Taipei Women, 1980; Appreciating Chinese Art (non-fiction), 1985; Untold Tales of Chinese Art, 1987. *Contributions to:* Major newspapers: China

Times, United Daily News, Taiwan; World Journal, New York; Sing Tao Daily News, Sing Tao Evening News, Sing Tao Express, Hong Kong; Morning Post, Sabah Times, Malaysia. Major magazines: Artist, Taiwan; Art of China Monthly, Hong Kong & Taiwan. *Memberships:* Chinese Literature Association, Taiwan; Executive director 1978-, Chinese Antique Collectors Association. *Literary Agent:* International Art Promotions Centre, 906 Eastern Centre, 1065 King's Road, Quarry Bay, Hong Kong. *Address:* 11F, 126-23 Chung Hsiao East Road, Sec.4, Taipei, Taiwan, Republic of China.

KUO Nancy, (Nany Kuo, Nanse, Ssujen) b. 8 Apr 1921, Shanghai, China. Writer; Artist; Designer; Director; Dancer. m. Guy Davis, 1 Oct 1949, 1 daughter. *Education:* Diplomas, Xin Hua Art Academy, Shanghai, 1936. *Appointments:* Editor, Suixi Weekly, 1937; Member, Editorial Board, Jun Zhi You, 1946; Art Critic, Arts Review, London, England, 1967-70; Honorary President, Voice of Qing Yuan, 1989. *Publications:* Chinese Paper-Cut Pictures, 1964, paperback, 1965; Chinese Painting, 1967-70; The Mount Trust Collection of Chinese Art, 1970; The Harari Collection, 1970; The Fantastic Landscape of Kweilin, 1973; Chinese Acrobats, Past and Present in China, 1973; Chinese Exhibition in London, 1974; Chinese Way, 1975-76; I Tai-P'ing, I Protagonisti della Rivoluzione, 1975; The Magic of Chinese Gardens, 1980; Japanese Ceramics Today Exhibition, 1983; Chinese Cinema Past and Present, 1984; The Sky is Singing and Other Poems, 1984; Rolling and Folding, 1985; The Amazing Chinese Puppet Theatre, 1987; Art reviews on Courbet, Leonardo and other exhibitions. *Contributions to:* In English: Arts and Sciences in China, 1963; Arts Review, Canvas and Amateur Artist, 1967-70; Leisure Painter, Eastern Horizon (Hong Kong), Dancing Times, 1973; BBC Springboard, 1975-76; In-House, 1980; Artrage, 1982-87; In Chinese: Chen Kuang Daily, 1945; Hsin Min Daily, Da Gong Daily, 1946; Hua Shang Daily, Hong Kong, 1947; People's Daily, 1954-56; Wild Angle, Hong Kong, 1970; The Seventies, Hong Kong, 1978-79; Hong Kong New Digest, 1978; Chinese World, Beijing, 1986; Xing Dao Daily, London, 1987; Qing Yuan's Voice, 1988; Feixi Ashikan Poetry Collection, 1989; Yang Ching Daily, Guang Zhou, 1991; In English and Pushtu: Bakhtar News Bulletin and Afghanistan News, 1958-62. *Memberships:* Director, Founder. Chinese Arts Institute; Advisor, British Association of Writers in Chinese; PEN International; Fellow, World Association of Writers; International Association of Art Critics; British Actors Equity Association; International Association of Art. *Address:* 35 Artillery Road, Ramsgate, Kent CT11 8PT, England.

KUO Nany. *See:* KUO Nancy.

KUPFERBERG Herbert, b. 1918, American. *Appointments:* With New York Herald Tribune, 1942-66; Senior Editor, Parade Magazine, 1967-. *Publications:* Those Fabulous Philadelphians, 1969; The Mendelssohns, 1971; Felix Mendelssohn, 1972; A Rainbow of Sound, 1973; Opera, 1975; Tanglewood, 1976; Basically Bach, The Book of Classical Music Lists, 1985; Amadeus: A Mozart Mosaic, 1986. *Address:* 113-14 72 Road, Forest Hills, NY 11375, USA.

KUREISHI Hanif, b. 5 Dec 1954, London, England. *Education:* BA, Philosophy, King's College, University of London. *Appointment:* Writer-in-residence, Royal Court Theatre, London, 1981 and 1985-86. *Publications:* Plays: Soaking the Heat (produced London), 1976; The Mother Country (produced London), 1980; The King and Me (produced London), 1980; Included in Outskirts, The King and Me, Tomorrow-Today!, 1983; Outskirts (produced London), 1981; Included in Outskirts, The King and Me, Tomorrow-Today! 1983; Tomorrow-Today! (produced London), 1981; Included in Outskirts, The King and Me, Tomorrow-Today! 1983; Cinders, from a play by Janusz Glowacki (produced London), 1981; Borderline (produced London, 1981;) Artists and Admirers, with David Leveaux, from a play by Alexander Ostrovsky (produced London), 1981; Birds of Passage, 1983; Outskirts, The King and Me, Tomorrow - Today!

London, and New York, 1983; Mother Courage, adaptation of a play by Brecht (produced London), 1984; The Buddha of Suburbia. My Beautiful Laundrette (screenplay, includes essay The Rainbow Sign, London, 1986; Sammy and Rosie Get Laid (screenplay) London, 1988; Radio Plays: You Can't Go Home, 1980; The Trial, from a novel by Kafka, 1982. *Honours:* George Devine Award, 1981; Evening Standard Award for Screenplay, 1985. *Literary Agent:* Sheila Lemon. *Address:* c/o Sheila Lemon, Lemon and Durbridge Ltd, 24 Pottery Lane, London W11 4LZ, England.

KURLAND Michael (Joseph), (Jennifer Plum), b. 1938, American. *Appointments:* News Editor, KPFK-Radio, Los Angeles, 1966; Teacher of English, Happy Valley School, Ojai, CA, 1967; Editor, Crawdaddy, 1969; Editor, Pennyfarthing Press, San Francisco, 1976-; also former play director, road manager for a band, advertising copywriter and freelance ghostwriter and writer of SF short stories. *Publications:* Ten Years to Doomsday (with Chester Anderson), 1964; Mission: Third Force, 1967; Mission: Tank War, 1968; Mission: Police Action, 1969; A Plague of Spies, The Unicorn Girl, 1969; Transmission Error, 1970; The Secret of Benjamin Square (as J Plum), 1972; The Whenabouts of Burr, Plurisbus, 1975; Tomorrow Knight, 1976; The Princes of Earth, The Redward Edward Papers, by Avram Davidson (ed), 1978; The Best of Avram Davidson (ed), The Infernal Device, 1979; The Last President (with S W Barton), Psi Hunt, 1980; Death by Gaslight, 1982.

KURTZ Katherine Irene, b. 18 Oct 1944, Florida, USA. Author. m. Scott Roderick MacMillan, 9 Apr 1983, 1 son. *Education:* BS, University of Miami, 1966; MA, University of California, Los Angeles, 1971. *Publications:* Deryni Rising, 1970; Deryni Checkmate, 1972; High Deryni, 1973; Camber of Culdi, 1976; Saint Camber, 1978; Camber the Heretic, 1981; The Bishop's Heir, 1984; The King's Justice, 1985; The Quest for Saint Camber, 1986; Lammas Night, 1983; The Legacy of Lehr, 1986; The Deryni Archives, 1986; The Harrowing of Gwynedd, 1989; Deryni Magic: A Grimoire, 1990; King Javan's Year, 1992; with Deborah Turner Harris: The Adept, 1991; Lodge of The Lynx, 1992; The Templar Treasure, 1993; various short stories. *Honours:* The Edmund Hamilton Memorial Award, 1977; The Balrog Award, 1982. *Memberships:* Authors Guild; Science Fiction Writers of America. *Literary Agent:* Russell Galen, Scott Meredith Literary Agency. *Address:* Holybrooke Hall, Kilmacanogue, Bray, Co. Wicklow, Ireland.

KURUP O N V, b. 27 May 1931, India. University Teacher; Professor Emeritus. m. Sarojini, 5 June 1958, 1 son, 1 daughter. *Education:* BA, Economics 7 History; MA, Malayalam Literature & Kerala History. *Appointments:* Sahitya Akademi, Delhi; Professor Emeritus, Calicut University. *Publications:* Porutunna Soundariam, 1950; Dahikkunna Pana Patram, 1956; Mayilppeeli, 1964; Oru Tulli Velicham, 1966; Agni Salabhangal, 1971;Aksharam, 1974; Karutha Pakshiyude Pattu, 1977; Uppu, 1980; Bhoomikkoru Charamageetam, 1984; Sarngaka pakshikal, 1987. *Contributions to:* various journals and magazines. *Honours:* Kerala State Sahitya Akademi Award for Poetry, 1971; National Sahitya Akademi Award, 1975; Soviet Land Nehru Award, 1982; Vayalar Literary Award, 1981. *Memberships:* Executive Board: State Sahitya Akademi, 1972-84, National Sahitya Akademi, New Delhi, 1982-87; Kerala Sahitya Parishad. *Address:* Indeevaram, Cotton Hill, Trivandrum 695014, India.

KURZMAN Dan, b. 1929, American. m. Florence Knopf. *Appointments:* Correspondent, International News Service, 1948, Feature Writer, Marshall Plan Information Office, 1948-49, Paris; Correspondent, National Broadcasting Company, Middle East, 1950-53; Bureau Chief, McGraw Hill World News Service, Tokyo, 1954-59; Correspondent, Washington Post, 1962-69; Contributor, Washington Star, 1975-, Independent News Alliance, 1979-1984, San Francisco Chronicle, 1991-92. *Publications:* Kishi and Japan: The Search of the Sun, 1960; Subversion of the Innocents, 1963;

Santo Domingo: Revolt of the Damned, 1965; Genesis, 1968; The First Arab-Israeli War, 1970; The Race for Rome, 1975; The Bravest Battle: The Twenty Eight Days of the Warsaw Ghetto Uprising, 1976; Miracle of November: Madrid's Epic Stand 1936, 1980; Ben-Gurion: Prophet of Fire, 1983; Day of the Bomb: Countdown to Hiroshima, 1985; A Killing Wind: Inside Union Carbide and The Bhopal Catastrophe, 1987; Fatal Voyage: The Sinking of the USS Indianapolis, 1990. *Honours:* Overseas Press Club Award, Best Book on Foreign Affairs, Subversion of the Innocents, 1963; George Polk Memorial Award, Washington Post, 1965; Front Page Award, Washington Post, 1965; Cornelius Ryan Award, Overseas Press Club, Best Book of Foreign Affairs, Miracle of November: Madrid's Epic Seige 1936, 1980; National Jewish Book Award, Ben-Gurion: Prophet of Fire, 1984. *Memberships:* Overseas Press Club of America; National Press Club; Tokyo Foreign Correspondents Club; PEN Club. *Literary Agent:* Julian Bach Literary Agency, New York, USA. *Address:* c/o H Knopf, 187 Boulevard, Apartment 9-H, Passaic, NJ 07055, USA.

KUSCHE Lothar, b. 2 May 1929, Berlin, Germany. Author. *Publications:* Satirical novels and essays including: Das bombastische Windei, 1958; Nanu wer schiesst denn da?, 1960; Ueberall ist Zwergenland, 1960; Quer durch England in anderthalb Stunden, 1961; Kaese und Loecher, 1963; Kein Wodka fur den Staatsanwalt, 1967; Wie man einen Haushalt aushaelt, 1969; Patientenfibel 1971; Kusches Drucksachen, 1974; Kellner Willi serviert, 1978; Knoten im Taschentuch, 1980; Donald Duck siehe unter Greta Garbo, 1981; Leute im Hinterkopf, 1983; Der Mann auf dem Kleiderschrank, 1985; Nasen die man nicht vergisst, 1986. *Contributions to:* Die Weltbuehne; Eulenspiegel, Berlin. *Honours:* Heinrich Heine Prize, 1960; Heinrich Greif Prize, 1973; National Prize, DDR, 1984. *Memberships:* International PEN; Writers Association of Democratic German Republic; Association of Journalists of Democratic German Republic. *Address:* Woelckpromenade 5, DDR 1120 Berlin, Democratic German Republic.

KUSHNER Aleksandr Semyonovich, b. 14 Sept 1936, Leningrad, Russia. Poet. m. Elena Vsevolodovna Nevzgliadova, 21 July 1984, 1 son. *Education:* Graduate, Pedagogical Institute, 1959. *Appointments:* Editor in Chief, Publishing House, Biblioteka Poeta. *Publications:* First Impression, 1962; Omens, 1969; Letter, 1974; Voice, 1978; The Tavrichesky GArden, 1984; The Hedgerow, 1988; A Night Melody, 1991; Apollo in the Snow - essays on Russian poetry and personal memoirs, 1991. *Contributions to:* Novii Mir; Znamya; Zvezda; Unost; Voprosi Literaturi. *Memberships:* Union of Writers; PEN Club. *Address:* Kaluzhsky Pereulok 9, apt 48, St Petersburg 193015, Russia.

KUSHNER Donn Jean, b. 29 Mar 1927, Lake Charles, USA. Scientist; Author. m. Eva Milada Ruth Dubska, 15 Sept 1949, 3 sons. *Education:* SB Chemistry, Harvard, 1948; MSc, 1950, PhD, 1952, Biochemistry, McGill. *Publications:* The Witnesses and other Stories, 1980; The Violin- Maker's Gift, 1980; Uncle Jacob's Ghost Story, 1984; A Book Dragon, 1987; The House of the good Spirits, 1990; The Dinosaur Duster, 1992. *Contributions to:* Scientific articles in professional journals. *Honours:* Canadian Library Association Book of the Year Award, 1981; Imperial Order of Daughters of the Empire, Canada Chapter Award, 1988. *Memberships:* Writer's Union of Canada; Canadian Society of Children's Authors, Illustrators and Performers; Poets Essayists and Novelists; American Society for Microbiology; Canadian Society of Microbiologists, President, 1980-81. *Address:* 63 Albany Avenue, Toronto, Ontario, Canada M5R 3C2.

KUSHNER James Alan, b. 14 Apr 1945, Philadelphia, Pennsylvania, USA. Law Professor; Author. m. Jacqueline Fregeau, 15 May 1970, 2 sons, 1 daughter. *Education:* BBA, University of Miami, 1967; JD, University of Maryland, 1968. *Appointments:* Assistant Editor, Maryland Law Review, 1967-68.

Publications: Apartheid in America, 1980; Housing and Community Development, 1981, 2nd Edition, 1989; Fair Housing, 1983; Government Discrimination, 1988; Subdivision Law and Growth Management, 1991. *Honours:* Appointed Irwin R Buchalter Professor of Law, Southwestern University School of Law, Los Angeles, 1989; Hulen Visiting Professor of Law, University of Missouri, Kansas City, 1985-86. *Memberships:* American Civil Liberties Union of Southern California, Board Member 1983-85; Fair Housing Congress of Southern California, Board Member, President, Chairman of Board 1983-86. *Address:* 675 South Westmoreland Avenue, Los Angeles, CA 90005, USA.

KUSKIN Karla Seidman, (Nicholas Charles), b. 1932, American, Writer and illustrator of children's fiction and verse. *Publications:* Roar and More (verse) 1956, new edition-1990; James and the Rain (verse) 1957; In the Middle of the Trees (verse) 1958; The Animals and the Ark (verse) 1958; Just Like Everyone Else (fiction) 1959; Which Horse is William? (fiction) 1959, new edition 1992; Square as a House (verse) 1960; The Bear Who Saw the Spring (verse) 1961; All Sizes of Noises (verse) 1962; (as Nicholas Charles), How Do You Get from Here to There? (verse) 1962; Alexander Soames: His Poems, 1962; ABCDEFGHIJKLMNOPQRSTUVWXYZ (verse) 1963; The Rose on My Cake (verse) 1964; Sand and Snow (verse) 1965; (as Nicholas Charles), Jane Ann June Spoon and Her Very Adventurous Trip to the Moon (verse) 1966; The Walk the Mouse Girls Took (fiction) 1967; Watson, The Smartest Dog in the USA, (fiction) 1968; In the Flaky Frosty Morning (verse)1969; Any Me I Want to Be: Poems (verse) 1972; What Did You Bring Me? (fiction) 1973; What Do You Mean by Design? (screenplay) 1973; An Electric Talking Picture (screenplay) 1973; Near the Window Tree: Poems and Notes, 1975; A Boy Had a Mother Who Brought Him a Hat (verse) 1976; A Space Story, 1978; Herbert Hated Being Small (verse) 1979; Dogs and Dragons, Trees and Dreams (poetry collection), 1980; (contributing Author), The State of the Language, 1980; Night Again (verse) 1981; The Philharmonic Gets Dressed (fiction) 1982; Something Sleeping in the Hall (verse) 1985; The Dallas Titans Get Ready for Bed, 1986; Jerusalem, Shining Still, 1987; Soap Soup, 1992. *Contributions to:* New York Mag; House and Garden; Horizon Magazine; Wilson Lib Bulletin; New York Times Book Section; Contributing Editor, Saturday Review, 1973. *Honours:* Best Children's Books, AIGA, 1956 and 1958; Poetry Award, National Council Teachers of English, 1979; New York Academy of Sciences, 1979; Notable Books, ALA, Best Picture Books, 1982; Nominee, American Book Award, 1983 and 1992. *Address:* 96 Joralemon Street, Brooklyn, NY 11201, USA.

KUSTOW Michael (David), b. 1939, British. *Appointments:* Director, Institute of Contemporary Arts, 1967-71; Associate Director, National Theatre of Great Britain, 1973-81; Lecturer in Dramatic Arts, Harvard University, Cambridge, MA, 1980-82; Commissioning Editor, Channel 4 TV, 1981-. *Publications:* Productions: The Book of Us (ed), Jose Triana: Night of the Assassins (trans), 1968; Tank, Roger Planchon and People's Theatre, 1975; Stravinsky: The Soldier's Story, 1980; Charles Wood's Has Washington Legs, Harold Pinter's Family Voices, 1981; The Manhabbaraten, 1989; The War That Never Ends, 1991. *Address:* c/o Tom Corrie, The Peters Fraser and Dunlop Group Ltd, The Chambers, Chelsea Harbour, Lots Road, London, SW10 OXF, England.

KUYK Dirk Adriaan Jr, b. 27 Apr 1934, Roanoke, Virginia, USA. Professor of English and American Literature. m. Betty Louise McNulty, 27 May 1954, 1 son. *Education:* AB, University of Virginia, 1955; PhD, Brandeis University, 1970. *Appointments:* Trinity College, Hartford, Connecticut, 1970-. *Publications:* Threads Cable-strong, 1983; Sutpen's Design, 1990. *Address:* Department of English, Trinity College, Hartford, CT 06106, USA.

KWAN William Chao-Yu, b. 7 Aug 1916,

Shanhaikuan, China. Writer; Adman; Artist. m. Emily Wei-tan Wang, 24 Feb 1940, 1 son, 2 daughters, (one adopted). *Education:* Diplomas in Advertising and English, ICS, Scranton, Pennsylvania; Creative and Article Writing, Palmer School of Authorship, Hollywood, CA, USA. *Appointments:* Associate Editor, The Advertiser magazine, China; Ad Copywriter, Layout Man, China Press, Shanghai; Editor, HAECO Newsletter, Hong Kong; Editorial Advisor, HAECO Welfare Society magazine, Hong Kong; Contributing Editor, Border Crossings Magazine, USA; Seminar, Chinese University of Hong Kong for Asia/Pacific Editors & Correspondents of Lutheran Press Services. *Publications:* English Precis & English Composition Eton Publications, Hong Kong, 1978-79. *Contributions to:* Hong Kong Tiger Standard; China Mail; The Asia Magazine; NAEC Newsletter; Kong Gei News; Fate Magazine; Beyond; Successful Beekeeping; Elite; American Poetry Anthology; 5-Star Music Masters of Boston; Small Town; Our Town; Alms House Press Yellow Ribbons Poetry Anthology; Rockland Journal News; Silver Kris - Singapore Airline In-Flight Magazine, Singapore. *Honours:* Fellow, World Literary Academy, England; Certificate of Merit, Poster Designing, Latham Foundation, USA. *Memberships:* Past Associate member, Society of Authors, London; Past Member, Hong Kong Journalist Association; Professional Member, National Writers Club, USA; Charter Member, East-West Literary Foundation, San Francisco, USA; Past Chapter Member, National Writers Club, Hudson Valley Chapter, USA. *Address:* 12 Carol Lane, Tappan, NY 10983, USA.

KYGER Joanne, b. 1934, United States of America. Poet. *Publications:* The Tapestry and the Web, 1965; The Fool in April: A Poem. 1966; Places to Go, 1970; Joanne, 1970; Desecheo Notebook, 1971; Trip Out and Fall Back, 1974; All This Ever Day, 1975; The Wonderful Focus of You, 1980; Mexico Blonde, 1981; Japan and India Journal, 1981; Going On: Selected Poems 1958-1980, 1983. *Address:* c/o Dutton, 2 Park Avenue, New York, NY 10016, USA.

KYLE Duncan, (James Meldrum), Author. *Publications:* A Cage of Ice, 1970; Flight into Fear, 1972; A Raft of Swords, 1974; The Semonov Impulse (as James Meldrum), 1975; Terror's Cradle, 1975; In Deep, 1976; Black Camelot, 1978; Green River High, 1979; Stalking Point, 1981; The King's Commissar, 1983; The Dancing Men, 1985. *Address:* c/o William Collins Limited, 8 Grafton Street, London, W1X 3LA, England.

L

L'ENGLE Madeleine, b. 29 Nov 1918, New York City, USA. Author. m. Hugh Franklin, 26 Jan 1946, 1 son, 2 daughters. *Education:* AB, Smith College, 1941. *Appointments:* Writer-in-Residence, Cathedral St John the Divine, New York City, 1965-. *Publications:* A Wrinkle in Time; A Wind in the Door; A Swiftly Tilting Planet; Circle of Quiet; A Severed Wasp; A Ring of Endless Light; (for Younger Readers) Many Waters; A House Like A Lotus; The Sphinx at Dawn; Prayers for Sunday; Prayers for Everyday; Dragons in the Waters; Dance in the Desert; The Young Unicorns; The Arm of the Starfish; The Moon By Night; A Wrinkle in Time; The Anti-Muffins; Meet the Austins; Camilla; And Both Were Young. *Honours:* Recipient, Newberry Medal, 1963; Sequoyah Award, 1965; Runner up Award, Hans Christian Anderson International Award, 1965; Lewis Carroll Shelf Award, 1965; Austrian State Literary Award, 1969; Bishop's Cross, 1970; University of Southern Mississippi Medal, 1978; Regina Medal, 1984. *Memberships:* Authors Guild; Authors League; Writers Guild. *Literary Agent:* Robert Lescher. *Address:* 924 West End Ave, Apt. 95, New York, NY 10025, USA.

L'ESTRANGE Anna. *See:* **ELLERBECK Rosemary.**

LA FRENAIS Ian, b. 7 Jan 1937. Writer; Screenwriter; Producer. m. Doris Vartan, 1984, 1 stepson. *Publications include:* Writer or Co-Writer (with Dick Clement) TV: The Likely Lads, 1965-68; The Adventures of Lucky Jim, 1968; Whatever Happened to the Likely Lads, 1971-73; Seven of One, 1973; Thick as Thieves, 1974; Comedy Playhouse, 1975; Porridge, 1974-77; Going Straing, 1978; Further Adventure of Lucky Jim, 1983; Auf Wiedershen Pet, 1983-84; Mog, 1985; Lovejoy, 1986; Freddy and Max, 1989; Spender, 1990; Old Boy Network, 1992; Full Stretch, 1992; The Rainbow, 1993. US TV: On The Rocks, 1976-77; Billy, 1979; Sunset Limousine, 1983. Films: Writer or Co-Writer (with Dick Clement) The Jokers, 1967; The Touchables, 1968; Otley, 1968; Hannibal Brooks, 1969; The Virgin Soldiers, 1969; Villian, 1971; The Likely Lads, 1974; Porridge, 1979; To Russia with Elton, co-produced and co-directed 1979; Prisoner of Zenda, 1981; Bullshot, produced, 1983; Water, 1984; Vice Versa, co-written, co-produced, 1988; The Commitments, 1991. Stage: writer, Billy 1974; Co-Producer, Anyone for Denis?, 1982; Partner (with Dick Clement and Allan McKeown), Witzend Productions. *Honours:* Awards from BAFTA, Broadcasting Guild, Evening News, Pye, Screen Writers' Guild, Society of TV Critics, London Film Critics, Evening Standard Film Awards, and Writers Guild of America. *Address:* 2557 Hutton Drive, Beverly Hills, CA 90211, USA.

LA TOURETTE Jacqueline, b. 1926, USA. Novelist. *Publications:* The Joseph Stone, 1971; A Matter of Sixpence, 1972; The Madonna Creek Witch, 1973; The Previous Lady, 1974; The Pompeii Scroll, 1975; Shadows in Umbria, 1979; The Wild Harp, 1981; Patarran, 1983; The House on Octavia Street, 1984; The Incense Tree, 1986. *Address:* c/o Raines and Raines, 71 Park Avenue, New York, NY 10016, USA.

LACEY Nicola Mary, b. 3 Feb 1958. University Teacher. *Education:* LLB Hons, University College, London, 1979; BCL, University College, Oxford, 1981; MA Oxon, 1984. *Publications:* State Punishment, 1988; Reconstructing Criminal Law (with C Wells and D Meure), 1990. *Contributions to:* Many articles to law journals and edited collections on legal theory, criminal justice, anti-discrimination law, feminist theory. *Address:* New College, Oxford OX1 3BN, England.

LACEY Robert, b. 1944, Author. *Appointments:* Assistant Editor, Sunday Times Magazine, London, 1969-73; Editor, Look! pages, Sunday Times, 1973-74. *Publications:* The French Revolution 2 vols (author, editor), 1968; The Rise of Napoleon (author, editor), 1969; The Peninsular War (author, editor), 1969; 1812: The Retreat from Moscow (author, editor), 1969; Robert, Earl of Essex: An Elizabethan Icarus, 1971; The Life and Times of Henry VIII, 1972; The Queens of the North Atlantic, 1973; Sir Walter Raleigh, 1973; Sir Francis Drake and the Golden Hinde (author, editor), 1975; Heritage of Britain (editor, contributor), 1975; Majesty: Elizabeth II and the House of Windsor, 1977; The Kingdom: Arabia and the House of Saud, 1981; Princess, 1982; Aristocrats, 1983; Ford: The Men and the Machine, 1986; God Bless Her: Her Majesty Queen Elizabeth the Queen Mother, 1987; Little Man: Meyer Lansky and the Gangster Life, 1991. *Address:* 12783-E West Forest Hill Boulevard, Suite 105, West Palm Beach, FL 33414, USA.

LACKEY Mercedes, b. South Bend, Indiana, USA. Writer. m. 14 Dec 1990. *Education:* BSci Biology, Purdue University, 1972. *Appointments:* Artist's model, 1975-81; Computer Programmer, Associates Data Processing, 1979-82; Surveyor, Layout Designer, Analyst, CAIRS (survey and data processing firm), 1981-82, South Bend, IN; Computer Programmer, American Airlines, Tulsa, OK, 1982-. *Publications:* Arrows of the Queen, Arrow's Flight, 1987; Arrow's Fall, Oathbound, 1988; Oathbreakers, Reap the Whirlwind, Magic's Pawn, Burning Water, 1989; Magic's Promise, 1990; The Magic-Winds Books: Winds of Change, 1992; Winds of Fury, 1993; The Bard's Tale Series: Fortress of Frost and Fire, 1993; Prison of Souls, 1993; Forthcoming Firebird Arts and Music Inc: Oathbound; Oathbreakers; Freedom, Flight and Fantasy. Written lyrics for and recorded nearly 50 songs for Off-Centaur. *Honour:* Arrows of the Queen, Best Books, American Library Association, 1987. *Membership:* Science Fiction and Fantasy Writers of America. *Literary Agent:* Scott Meridith, New York, USA. *Hobby:* Scuba diving. *Address:* PO Box 8309, Tulsa, OK 74101-8309, USA.

LADERO QUESADA Miguel-Angel, b. 14 Jan 1943, Valladolid, Spain. Professor of Mediaeval History. m. Isabel Galan Parra, 22 June 1968, 2 sons, 1 daughter. *Education:* Doctorate in History, University of Valladolid, 1967. *Appointments:* Professor of Mediaeval History, La Laguna University, Canary Islands, 1970; Professor of Mediaeval History, University of Seville, 1974; Professor of Mediaeval History, 1978-, Director, Mediaeval History Department, 1980-93, University Vice-Rector, 1986-87, Complutensian University, Madrid. *Publications:* Castilla y la conquista del reino de Granada, 1967, 2nd Edition, 1987; Granada. Historia de un pais islamico, 1969, 3rd Edition, 1988; La Hacienda Real de Castilla en el siglo XV, 1973; Historia de Sevilla. La ciudad Medieval, 1976, 3rd Edition, 1988; Historia Universal. Edad Media, 1987, 2nd Edition, 1992; Los mudejares de Castilla y otros estudios, 1988; Los Reyes Catolicos, La Corona y la unidad de España, 1988; Andalusia en torno a 1492, 1992; Fiscalidad y Poder Real en Castilla (1252-1369), Madrid, 1993. *Contributions to:* Hispania; Anuario de Estudios Medievales; En la España Medieval, Madrid; Historia, Instituciones, Documentos, Sevilla; Annales ESC, Paris; Sefarad, Madrid; Cuadernos de Historia de España, Buenos Aires. *Honours:* Menendez Pelayo Prize for History, 1974; Officier, Ordre des Palmes Academiques, 1987. *Memberships:* Full Member, Royal Historical Academy of Spain; International Commission of Urban History; International Commission of Representative and Parliamentary Institutions; Society for Spanish and Portuguese Historical Studies, USA. *Address:* Departamento de Historia Medieval, Facultad de Geografia e Historia, Universidad Complutense, 28040 Madrid, Spain.

LADIA Eleni, b. 13 Aug 1945, Athens, Greece. Writer. *Education:* Graduated, Archaeology, University of Athens, 1970. *Publications:* Figures on a Krater, short stories, 1973; The Fragmentary Relationship, novel, 1974, 3rd Edition, 1983; Articles on the poetry of Kavafis, 1974, 1975; The Black Hermes, short stories, 1977; The Copper Sleep, short stories, 1980; The Schizophrenic God, short stories, 1983; Poets and Ancient Greece, essay, 1983; X, the Lion-Faced, novel, 1986; Horography, short stories, 1990; Frederic and John, narrative, 1991. *Contributions to:* Short stories, essays and archaeological articles to various journals and magazines, Athens and abroad. *Honours:* 2nd State Prize for Copper Sleep, 1981; Prize, Academy of Athens-Uranis Foundation, for Horography, 1991. *Memberships:* National Greek Literary Society; PEN Club. *Address:* 44 Kavatha St, 157 73 Athens, Greece.

LAFFERTY R(aphael) A(loysius), b. 1914, USA. Freelance Writer; Former Buyer. *Publications:* Past Master, 1968; The Reefs of Earth, 1968; Space Chantey, 1968; Fourth Mansions, 1969; Nine Hundred Grandmothers, short stories, 1970; The Devil Is Dead, 1971; Arrive at Easterwine, 1971; The Fall of Rome, historical novel, 1971; The Flame Is Green, historical novel, 1971; Okla Hannali, historical novel, 1972; Strange Doings, short stories, 1972; Does Anyone Else Have Something Further to Add, short stories, 1974; Funnyfingers, and Cabrito, short stories, 1976; Horns on Their Heads, short stories, 1976; Not to Mention Camels, 1976; Apocaplypses, 1977; Archipelago, 1979; Aurelia, 1982; The Annals of Klepsis, 1983; Golden Gate and Other Stories, 1983; Four Stories, 1983; Heart of Stone Dear and Other Stories, 1983; Snake in His Bosom and Other Stories,1983; Through Elegant Eyes, stories, 1983; Ringing Changes, stories, 1984; The Man Who Made Models and Other Stories, 1984; Half a Sky, 1984; Slippery and Other Stories, 1985. *Address:* 1715 South Trenton Avenue, Tulsa, OK 74120, USA.

LAFFIN John, b. 21 Sept 1922, Sydney, Australia. Author; Journalist; Lecturer. m. Hazelle Stonham, 6 Oct 1943, 1 son, 2 daughters. *Education:* MA; D.Litt. *Appointments:* Battlefield Archaeologist; Advisor/Consultant, War and Military History. *Publications:* 114 books including: Dagger of Islam, 1979; Damn the Dardanelles!, 1980, 2nd edition 1985; Brassey's Battles, 1986; The Arab Mind, 1974; The Hunger to Come, 1966; Digger - Story of Australian Soldier, 1958, and 1990; Fight for the Falklands, 1982; War Annual 1, 1986; War Annual 2, 1987; On the Western Front, 1985; Man the Nazis Couldn't Catch, 1984; Battlefield Archaeology, 1987; Know the Middle East, 1985; Devils Goad, 1970; Western Front, 1916-17: The Price of Honour, 1988; Western Front, 1917-18: The Cost of Victory, 1988 (both Time/Life books); Holy War - Islam Fights, Collins; War Annual 3, 1987; War Annual 4, 1988; War Annual 5, 1990; War Annual 6, 1992; British Butchers and Bunglers of World War I, 1989; The Western Front Illustrated, 1991; Dictionary of Africa Since 1960, 1991; Guidebook to Australian Battlefields of France and Flanders 1916-18, 1992. *Contributions to:* Magazines and Journals: Special Correspondent for the Daily Mail, London, on Islam, Arab World and Middle East. *Memberships:* Society of Authors, UK; Society of Authors, Australia; FRGS; FRHists; Royal Commonwealth Society. *Address:* Oxford House, Church St, Knighton, Powys LD7 1AG, Wales.

LAHTINEN Anni, b. 2 Feb 1914, Kuhmalahti, Finland. Writer. *Publications:* Ystavani Elviira, Mustalaistytto, 1973; Hiiret, 1974; Kakstoista Meren Rannalla, 1976; Jattilaisen Tasku, 1980; Voi Elaman J Kevat, 1981; Sinappia, Olkaa Hyva, 1982; Tuku Tuku Lampaitani, 1983; Tunturikurmitsa Kutsuu, 1984; Kyynelia Joulupuurossa, 1985; Tukikohdan Mirja, 1987; Kyllä, herra tohtori, 1988; Vetehisen kutsu, 1989. *Contributions to:* Various publications and broadcasting productions: Rivien Välistä and Heitä luetaan, 1992. *Honours:* Country Award for Literature, 1980; Finnish State Prize for Literature, 1981; City Prize, 1981; Publishing Company's Prize, 1983. *Memberships:* Finnish Writers' Society; Finnish Provincial Writers' Society; Finnish Dramatists' Society; Local Literary Society. *Address:* Yrjönkatu 3-5 A 7, 33100 Tampere, Finland.

LAIRD Elizabeth Mary Risk, b. 21 Oct 1943, New Zealand. Writer. m. David Buchanan McDowall, 19 Apr 1975, 2 sons. *Education:* BA, Bristol University; MLitt, Edinburgh University. *Publications:* The Miracle Child, 1985; The Road to Bethlehem, 1987; Red Sky in the Morning, 1988; Crackers, 1989; Arcadia, 1990; Kiss the Dust, 1991; Toucan Tecs, 1992. *Honours:* Children's

Book Award, The Burnley Express. *Membership:* Society of Authors. *Literary Agent:* Gill Coleridge, (Rogers, Coleridge & White). *Address:* 31 Cambrian Road, Richmond, Surrey TW10 6JQ, England.

LAIT Robert, b. 1921, United Kingdom. Lecturer in Criminology and Social Science. *Publications:* The Second Yoke, 1960; The Africans, 1961; Massacre, 1963; The Fireworks, 1965; Mrs Hardwick's Private War, 1966; A Chance to Kill, 1968; Pit, 1970; Switched Out, 1970; Once Too Often, 1980. *Address:* Department of Social Administration, University of Wales, Swansea, Wales.

LAIZER S J. *See:* **LAIZER Sheri J.**

LAIZER Sheri. *See:* **LAZIER Sheri J.**

LAIZER Sheri J, (Shirin Agri, Sheri Laizer, S J Laizer), b. 10 Oct 1955, New Zealand. Writer; Broadcast Journalist; Photographer. m. (1) Richard John Creser, 16 Jan 1979, (2) Mehmet Teymur, 15 Jan 1988, (3) Dursun Sen, 18 June 1990. *Education:* BA, English, French, 1977; MA Hons, English, 1978. *Appointments:* Assignments: Arcomundi Films, 1990; Planet Television, 1991; BBC Foreign News Reports, 1991; Insight News Television, 1991-92. *Publications:* Maelstrom, poems and photographs, 1981; Into Kurdistan - Frontiers under Fire, 1991; Love-Letters to a Brigand, photographs and poems, 1992. *Contributions to:* Kurdish Times, New York, USA; Kurdistan Report, UK; The Non-Violent Activist, USA; The New Zealand Listener; New Departures. *Memberships:* PEN English Centre, UK; Chartered Institute of Journalists, UK. *Address:* 30A Weston Park, Crouch End, London N8 9TJ, England.

LAKATOS Menyhert, b. 11 Apr 1926, Budapest, Hungary. Writer. div, 2 daughters. *Education:* Matriculation Diploma; Technical University. *Appointments:* Chief Editor. *Publications:* Smoked Faces, novel, 1975; Angarka-Buslodorfi, tales, 1977; Seven bearded wolves, tales, 1978; Paramisches' descendants, novel, 1980; The secret of the old pot, tales, 1981; Those who wanted to live, novel, 1982; Csandra's Caravan, short stories, 1984; Various plays and scripts including: Curse and Love; Nationality is Unwanted; Those who wanted to live. *Contributions to:* Hundreds of articles to newspapers. *Honours:* Milan Fust Literary Prize, 1977; Order of Magnitude with Gold Wreath, Hungarian Republic, 1991. *Memberships:* Society of Hungarian Writers; Literary Foundation of the Hungarian Republic; Club of Gipsy Intelligentsia; Vice-President, Auswitz Foundation. *Address:* Fust Milan u 22, 1039 Budapest, Hungary.

LAKE David John, b. 26 Mar 1929, Bangalore, India. University Professor. m. Marguerite Ivy Ferris, 30 Dec 1964, 1 daughter, 3 stepchildren. *Education:* BA, MA, DipEd, Trinity College, Cambridge, 1949-53; Diploma of Linguistics, University of Wales (Bangor), 1964-65; PhD, University of Queensland, Australia, 1974. *Publications:* The Canon of Thomas Middleton's Plays, 1975; The Gods of Xuma, 1978; The Man who Loved Morlocks, 1981; The Changelings of Chaan, 1985; Hornpipes and Funerals, poems, 1973; Walkers on the Sky, 1976; The Right Hand of Dextra, 1977; The Wildings of Westron, 1977; The Fourth Hemisphere, Warlords of Xuma, The Ring of Truth, West of the Moon. *Contributions to:* Extrapolation; Science Fiction Studies; Foundation; Notes and Queries; The Explicator; The Ring Bearer. *Honours:* Ditmar Awards for best Australian Science Fiction Novel, 1977 (for Walkers on the Sky) and 1982 (for The Man Who Loved Morlocks). *Memberships:* Science Fiction Research Association; Mythopoeic Society of Australia. *Literary Agent:* Pamela Buckmaster. *Address:* 7 8th Avenue, St Lucia, Queensland 4067, Australia.

LAKEHURST Diana. *See:* **AYRES Philip James.**

LAKER Rosalind. *See:* **OVSTEDAL Barbara Kathleen.**

LAL P, b. 1929, India. Poet; Writer; Translator; Professor of English. *Appointments:* Professor of English, 1952-67, Honorary Professor, 1967-, St Xavier's College, Calcutta; Editor, Orient Review and Literary Digest, 1954-58; Visiting Professor, Hofstra University, Hempstead, New York, USA, 1962-63; Professor of English, University of Calcutta, India, 1967-; Robert L Morton Visiting Professor, Ohio University, Athens, USA, 1973- 74; Founder, Secretary, Writers Workshop, Publishers, and Editor, Writers Workshop Miscellany, Calcutta. *Publications:* The Art of the Essay, 1951; The Merchant of Venice, by William Shakespeare (editor), 1952; Modern Indo-Anglian Poetry (edited with K R Rao), 1959; The Parrot's Death and Other Poems, 1960; Love's the First: Poems, 1962; Change, They Said: New Poems, 1066; Draupadi and Jayadratha and Other Poems, 1967; An Annotated Mahabharata Bibliography, 1967; T S Eliot: Homage from India: A Commemoration Volume of 55 Essays and Elegies (editor), 1967; The First Workship Story Anthology (editor), 1967; The Concept of an Indian Literature: Six Essays, 1968; Creations and Transcreations: Three Poems, Selected from the Subhasita-Ratna- Kosa, and the First 92 Slokas from the Mahabharata, 1968; Yakshi from Didarganj: Poems, 1969; Modern Indian Poetry in English: The Writers Workshop Literary Reader (editor), 1973; The Man of Dharma and the Rasa of Silence, 1974; Nepal: Where the Gods Are Young, 1976; Calcutta, 1977; Collected Poems, 1977; The Alien Insiders: Indian Writing in English, 1979; Personalities: Meetings with Writers, 1979. *Address:* 162/92 Lake Gardens, Calcutta 45, India.

LAM Truong Buu, b. 1933, Vietnam. Associate Professor of History. *Publications:* Patterns of Vietnamese Response to Foreign Intervention, 1967; New Lamps for Old, 1983; Resistance, Rebellion, Revolution in Vietnamese History, 1984. *Address:* History Department, University of Hawaii, 2530 Dole Street, Honolulu, HI 96822, USA.

LAMANTIA Philip, b. 1927, USA. Poet. *Appointments:* Assistant Editor, View Magazine, New York City, 1944. *Publications:* Erotic Poems, 1946; Narcotica: I Demand Extinction of Laws Prohibiting Narcotic Drugs, 1959; Ekstasis, 1959; Destroyed Works, 1962; Touch of the Marvelous, 1966; Selected Poems, 1943-1966, 1967; Penguin Modern Poets 13 (with Charles Bukowski and Harold Norse), 1969; The Blood of the Air, 1970; Becoming Visible, 1981; Meadowlark West, 1986. *Address:* c/o City Lights Books, 261 Columbus Avenue, San Francisco, CA 94133, USA.

LAMB Andrew Martin, b. 23 Sept 1942. Investment Manager. m. Wendy Ann Davies, 1 Apr 1970, 1 son, 2 daughters. *Education:* Corpus Christi College, Oxford, 1960-63; MA (Hons), Oxford. *Publications:* Jerome Kern in Edwardian London, 1985; Ganzl's Book of the Musical Theatre (with Kurt Ganzl), 1988; Editor: The Moulin Rouge, 1990; Light Music from Austria, 1992; Substantial contributions to: The New Grove Dictionary of Music and Musicians; The New Grove Dictionary of American Music; The New Grove Dictionary of Opera; Others. *Contributions to:* Gramophone; The Musical Times; Classic CD; American Music; Music and Letters; Wisden Cricket Monthly; The Cricketer; The Listener; Others. *Memberships:* Fellow, Society of Actuaries; Associate Member, Institute of Investment Management & Research; Lancashire County Cricket Club. *Address:* 12 Fullers Wood, Croydon CR0 8HZ, England.

LAMB Charlotte. *See:* **HOLLAND Sheila.**

LAMB Elizabeth Searle, (K L Mitchell), b. 22 Jan 1917, Topeka, Kansas, USA. Writer/Editor. m. F Bruce Lamb, 11 Dec 1941, Port of Spain, Trinidad. 1 daughter. *Education:* BA 1939, BMus 1940, University of Kansas. *Literary Appointment:* Editor, Frogpond, Haiku Quarterly, 1984-91, Co-editor, Haiku Southwest, 1993-. *Publications:* Pelican Tree and Other Panama Adventures, co-author, 1953; Today and Every Day, 1970; Inside Me, Outside Me, 1974; In this Blaze of Sun, 1975; Picasso's Bust of Sylvette, 1977; 39 Blossoms, 1982; Casting Into a Cloud: Southwest Haiku, 1985; Lines for My Mother, Dying, 1988. *Contributions to:* Americas; Etude; Family Circle; Christian Science Monitor; East West Journal; Studia Mystica; Lookout; The Mennonite; Daily Word; Purpose; Ideals; Augsburg Christmas Annual; The World of English (China); Ko (Japan); Literatura na Swiecie (Poland); Opole (Poland); Plainwraps (New Zealand); Neblina (Colombia); Ant Farm. Juvenile journals: Jack and Jill; The Children's Friend; Highlights for Children; Wee Wisdom. Poetry journals: Frogpond; Cicada; Haiku; Tweed; Outch; Poets On; Blue Unicorn; Modern Haiku; Bonsai. *Honours:* Ruth Mason Rice Awards, 1966, 1967, 1972, 1975 and 1977; Graham Peace Award, 1965 and 1969; Ruben Dario Memorial Award (2nd Place, from OAS) 1972; National League of American Pen Women Awards, 1964, 1968, 1976 and 1978; Henderson Awards, 1978, 1981 and 1991; Dellbrook Poetry Award, 1979; Yuki Teikei, 1981; Mainichi Daily News (Tokyo) Award, 1984 (Haiku), 1989; Poetry Soc of Japan, 1987; World Haiku Contest (Japan), 1989. *Memberships:* Past President and Vice-President, Haiku Society of America; Past Vice-President, New York Women Poets; National League of American Pen Women; Poetry Society of America. *Literary Agent:* Bertha Klausner, New York. *Address:* 970 Acequia Madre, Sante Fe, NM 87501, USA.

LAMB Geoffrey Frederick, (Balaam), b. London, England. Author. *Education:* BA (Hons), Teacher's Diploma, MA (English) 1939, King's College, London. *Publications:* English for General Certificate, 1954; Chalk in My Hair (under pseudonym Balaam), 1953; Victorian Magic, 1976; Magic, Witchcraft, & The Occult, 1977; Pocket Companion Quotation Guide, 1983; Harrap Book of Humorous Quotations, 1990; Franklin - Happy Voyager, 1956; The Happiest Days, 1959; Modern Adventures at Sea, 1970; One Hundred Good Stories, 1969-70; Animal Quotations, 1985; Shakespeare Quotations, 1992. *Memberships:* Society of Authors (Honorary Secretary Children's Writers Group 1962-67); Magic Circle. *Address:* Penfold, Legion Lane, Kings Worthy, Winchester, England.

LAMB Hubert Horace, b. 22 Sept 1913, Bedford, England. Meteorologist, Climatologist and University Professor. m. Moira Milligan, 7 Feb 1948, 1 son, 2 daughters. *Education:* Oundle School, 1927-32; Trinity College, Cambridge University, 1932-35, BA 1935, MA 1947, ScD 1983. *Publications:* Climate, Present, Past and Future, Vol 1 1972, Vol 2 1977; Climate, History and the Modern World, 1982; Weather, Climate and Human Affairs, 1988; Historic Storms of the North Sea, British Isles and NW Europe, 1991; Volcanic Dust in the Atmosphere and Assessment of its Meteorological Significance, 1970; The Changing Climate, 1966; The English Climate, 1964; Entry on Climate in Encyclopaedia Britannica 1975 edition; Chapter on Climatic Fluctuations in World Survey of Climatology, Vol 2, 1969. *Contributions to:* Leading meteorological and geographical magazines and journals in England, Scotland, also Nature, Geografiska Annaler (Sweden), Geologische Rundschau & Meteorologische Rundschau (Germany), Ymer (Sweden), Forskning och Framsteg (Sweden); Pure and Applied Geophysics (Switzerland); Atmospheric Physics & Geojournal (Germany); Chinook (Canada); Bulletin of the American Meteorological Society. *Honours:* Groves Prizes 1960 and 1971, UK Meteorological Office; Darton Prize, Royal Meteorological Society, 1963; Murchison Award, Royal Geographical Society, 1974; Emeritus Professor, University of East Anglia, 1978; Vega Medal, Royal Swedish Geographical Society, 1984; Symons Memorial Medal, Royal Meteorological Society, 1987; Hon LLD, Dundee University, 1981; Hon DSc, University of East Anglia, 1981. *Memberships:* Life Fellow, Royal Meteorological Society, Former Vice President; Fellow, Royal Geographical Society; Corresponding Member, Danish Natural History Society; Corresponding Member, Royal Academy of Arts and Sciences, Barcelona.

Address: Climatic Research Unit, University of East Anglia, Norwich NR4 7TJ, England.

LAMB Larry, (Sir) b. 15 July 1929, Fitzwilliam, Yorkshire, England. Editor. m. Joan Mary Denise Grogan, 2 sons, 1 daughter. *Appointments:* Journalist, Brighouse Echo, Shields Gazette, Newcastle Journal, London Evening Standard; Sub editor, Daily Mirror; Editor, (Manchester) Daily Mail, 1968-69; The Sun, 1969-72, 1975-81; Director 1970-81, Editorial Director, 1971-81, News International Ltd; Deputy Chairman, News Group, 1979-81; Director, The News Corporation (Australia) Ltd, 1980-81; Deputy Chairman, Editor in Chief, Western Mail Ltd, Perth, Australia, 1981-82; Editor in Chief, The Australian, May 1982-83; Editor, Daily Express, 1983-86; Chairman, Larry Lamb Associates, 1986-. *Publications:* Sunrise, 1989. *Address:* Bracken Cottage, Bratton Fleming, N Devon, EX31 4TG, England.

LAMB Patricia Frazer, b. 15 Jan 1931, California, USA. Writer. Divorced, 2 sons. *Education:* BA, Boston University, 1966; MA, Brandeis University, 1968; PhD, Cornell University, 1977. *Appointments:* Assistant Professor of English, University of Kentucky 1974-76; Professor of English 1978-90, currently Emeritus Professor of English, Westminster College, Pennsylvania. *Publications include:* Touchstones: Letters Between Two Women 1953-64, 1983; Erotic Universe Sexuality and Fantastic Literature, 1986, 2 essays in no 2; Write This Way: A Classical Rhetoric Handbook, 1980. *Contributions to:* Essays in College English Association Forum, Westminster Magazine, Women's Review of Books, Bulletin of the PCTE. *Honours:* Bunting Fellowship, Radcliffe College, 1984-85; Distinguished Visiting Scholar, Sacramento State University, California, 1983; Jane Bakerman Award, best published essay, Popular Culture Association, 1986. *Literary Agent:* Martha Casselman, San Francisco, California, USA. *Address:* 1718 N Decatur, no 5, Las Vegas, NV 89108, USA.

LAMBERT Derek (William), (Richard Falkirk), b. 1929, United Kingdom. Novelist. *Appointments:* Journalist for Devon, Norfolk, Yorkshire and National newspapers, 1950-68. *Publications:* Novels: For Infamous Conduct, 1970; Grand Slam, 1971; The Great Land, 1977; The Lottery, 1983. Mystery novels: Angels in the Snow, 1969; The Kites of War, 1970; The Red House, 1972; The Yermakov Transfer, 1974; Touch the Lion's Paw, 1975, US Paperback Edition, Rough Cut, 1980; The Saint Peter's Plot, 1978; The Memory Man, 1979; I, Said the Spy, 1980; Trance, 1981; The Red Dove, 1982; The Judas Code, 1983; The Golden Express, 1984; The Man Who Was Saturday, 1985; Chase, 1987; Triad, 1988. Mystery novels as Richard Falkirk: The Chill Factor, 1971; The Twisted Wire, 1971; Blackstone, 1972; Beau Blackstone, 1973; Blackstone's Fancy, 1973; Blackstone and the Scourge of Europe, 1974; Blackstone Underground, 1976; Blackstone on Broadway, 1977. Other: The Sheltered Days: Growing Up in the War, 1965; Don't Quote Me - But, 1979; And I Quote, 1980; Unquote, 1981; Just Like the Blitz: A Reporter's Notebook, 1987; The Night and the City, 1989; The Gate of the Sun, 1990. *Literary Agent:* Robert I Ducas. *Address:* 350 Hudson Street, New York, NY 10014, USA.

LAMBERT Gavin, b. 1924, USA. Author. *Appointments:* Editor, Sight and Sound, London, 1950-55. *Publications:* The Slide Area, 1959; Sons and Lovers (co-author), screenplay, 1960; The Roman Spring of Mrs Stone, screenplay, 1961; Inside Daisy Clover, novel and screenplay, 1963, 1965; Norman's Letter, 1966; A Case for the Angels, 1968; The Goodby People, 1971; On Cukor, 1972; GWTW: The Making of Gone with the Wind, 1973; The Dangerous Edge, 1976; In the Night All Cats are Grey, 1976; I Never Promised You a Rose Garden, screenplay, 1977; Running Time, 1982. *Address:* c/o Macmillan, 866 Third Avenue, New York, NY 10022, USA.

LAMBOT Isobel Mary, (Daniel Ingham, Mary Turner), b. 21 July 1926, Birmingham, England. Novelist. m. Maurice Edouard Lambot 19 Dec 1959 (dec). *Education:* BA, Liverpool University; Teaching Certificate, Birmingham University. *Appointments:* Tutor in Creative Writing, Lichfield Evening Institute, 1973-80. *Publications:* 20 detective stories, latest: The Flower of Violence (detective novel), 1992; How to Write Crime Novels, 1992; 4 historical novels, latest, Runaway Lady, 1980. *Contributions to:* Women's journals. *Memberships:* Crime Writers' Association; Society of Authors; Writers' Guild of Great Britain. *Literary Agent:* Mary Irvine. *Address:* 45 Bridge Street, Kington, Herefordshire HR5 3DW, England.

LAMONT Marianne. *See:* RUNDLE Anne.

LAMONT-BROWN Raymond, b. 20 Sept 1939, Horsforth, England. Author; Broadcaster. m. (2) Dr Elizabeth Moira McGregor, 6 Sept 1985. *Education:* MA; AMIET; FSA (Scot). *Appointment:* Managing Editor, Writers Monthly, 1984-86. *Publications:* Discovering Fife, 1988; The Life & Times of Berwick-Upon-Tweed, 1988; The Life & Times of St Andrews, 1989; Royal Murder Mysteries, 1990; Scottish Epitaphs, 1990; Scottish Superstitions, 1990. *Contributions to:* Magazines and newspapers. *Memberships:* Society of Authors, Secretary in Scotland 1982-89; Rotary International, Past President, St Andrews Branch, 1984-85. *Address:* 3 Crawford House, 132 North Street, St Andrews, Fife KY16 9AF, Scotland.

LAMPITT Dinah, b. 6 Mar 1937. Author. m. L F Lampitt, 28 Nov 1959 dec, 1 son, 1 daughter. *Education:* Regent Street Polytechnic, London, 1950s. *Appointments:* Worked on Fleet Street for The Times, The Evening News and various magazines, 1950s. *Publications:* Sutton Place Trilogy: Sutton Place, 1983, The Silver Swan, 1984, Fortune's Soldier, 1985; To Sleep No More, 1987; Pour the Dark Wine, 1989; The King's Women, 1992; As Shadows Haunting, 1993; Serials: The Moonlit Door; The Gemini Syndrome; The Staircase; The Anklets; The Wardrobe. *Contributions to:* Numerous short stories to women's magazines. *Membership:* The Society of Authors; Romantic Novelists' Association. *Literary Agent:* Rupert Crew Ltd, London, England. *Address:* c/o Rupert Crew Ltd, 1A King's Mews, London WC1N 2JA, England.

LAMPLUGH Lois Violet, b. 9 June 1921, Barnstaple, Devon, England. Author. m. Lawrence Carlile Davis, 24 Sept 1955, 1 son, 1 daughter. *Education:* BA Honours, Open University, 1980. *Appointments include:* Editorial staff, Jonathan Cape publishers, 1946-56. *Publications include:* The Pigeongram Puzzle, 1955; Nine Bright Shiners, 1955; Vagabonds' Castle, 1957; Rockets in the Dunes, 1958; Sixpenny Runner, 1960; Midsummer Mountains, 1961; Rifle House Friends, 1965; Linhay on Hunter's Hill, 1966; Fur Princess & Fir Prince, 1969; Mandog, 1972; Sean's Leap, 1979; Winter Donkey, 1980; Falcon's Tor, 1984; Barnstaple: Town on the Taw, 1983; History of Ilfracombe, 1984; Minehead & Dunster, 1987; A Shadowed Man: Henry Williamson, 1990; Take Off From Chivenor, 1990; Sandrabbit, 1991; Lundy: Island Without Equal, 1993. *Contributions to:* Western Morning News. *Memberships:* Society of Authors; West Country Writers Association. *Address:* Springside, Bydown, Swimbridge, Devon EX32 0QB, England.

LAMPPA William R, b. 1928, USA. Poet; Social Worker. *Publications:* The Crucial Point and Other Poems, 1971; In Familiar Fields with Old Friends, 1972; The Ancient Chariot and Other Poems, 1973. *Address:* PO Box 81, Embarrass, MN 55732, USA.

LAN David Mark, b. 1 June 1952, Cape Town, South Africa. Writer; Social Anthropologist. *Education:* BA, University of Cape Town, 1972; BSc 1976, PhD 1983, London School of Economics, UK. *Publications include:* Book: Guns & Rain: Guerrillas & Spirit Mediums in Zimbabwe, 1985. Plays: Painting a Wall, 1979; Bird

Child, 1974; Homage to Been Soup, 1975; Paradise, 1975; The Winter Dancers, 1977; Not in Norwich, 1977; Red Earth, 1977; Sergeant Ola & His Followers, 1979; Flight, 1986; A Mouthful of Birds, with Caryl Churchill, 1986; Desire, 1990. Television plays: The Sunday Judge, 1985; Crossing the Sky, 1988; Welcome Home Comrades, 1989; Dark City, 1990. *Contributions include:* Guardian; London Review of Books; Journal of Southern African Studies; New Society; New Statesman. *Honours:* John Whiting Award, 1977; George Orwell Memorial Award, 1983. *Literary Agent:* Judy Daish Associates, 83 Eastbourne Mews, London W2, England.

LANCASTER David. *See:* **HEALD Timothy Villiers.**

LANCASTER Sheila. *See:* **HOLLAND Sheila.**

LANCASTER-BROWN Peter, b. 13 Apr 1927, Cue, Western Australia. Author. m. Johanne Nyrerod, 15 Aug 1953, 1 son. *Education:* Astronomy; Surveying; Mining Engineering; Civil Engineering. *Appointments include:* Full-time author, 1970-. *Publications include:* Halley's Comet & the Principia, 1986; Halley & his Comet, 1985; Megaliths & Masterminds, 1979; Megaliths, Myths & Men, 1976; Fjord of Silent Men, 1983; Astronomy in Colour, 1972; Comets, Meteorites & Men, 1973; Planet Earth in Colour, 1976; What Star is That?, 1971; Australia's Coast of Coral & Pearl, 1972; Call of the Outback, 1970; Twelve Came Back, 1957; Astronomy, 1984; etc. *Contributions to:* Blackwood's; Nature; New Scientist; Sky & Telescope. *Membership:* Society of Authors. *Address:* 10A St Peter's Road, Aldeburgh, Suffolk IP15 BG, UK.

LANCE Betty Rita Gomez, b. 28 Aug 1923, Costa Rica. Professor of Romance Languages and Literatures; Writer. 2 sons. *Education:* Teaching Diploma, Universidad Nacional, Costa Rica, 1941; BS, Central Missouri State University, 1944; MA, University of Missouri, 1947; PhD, Washington University, 1959. *Publications:* La Actitud Picaresca en la Novela Espanola del Siglo XX 1969; Poetry: Vivencias, 1981, Bebiendo Luna, 1983, Vendimia del Tiempo, 1984, Alas en el Alba, 1987; Hoy Hacen Corro las Ardillas, (short story), 1985. *Contributions to:* Americas; Letras Femeninas: Caprice. *Memberships:* Poets and Writers of America; Asociacion de Escritores de Costa Rica; Asociacion Prometeo de Poesia, Madrid; Asociacion Iberoamericana de Poesia, Madrid; American Association of University Professors; American Association of University Women; American Association of Teachers of Spanish and Portuguest. *Address:* 1562 Spruce Dr, Kalamazoo, MI 49008, USA.

LAND Thomas. *See:* **ORSZAG-LAND Thomas.**

LANDERT Walter, b. 3 Jan 1929, Zurich, Switzerland. Merchant. *Education:* Higher School of Commerce, Neuchatel; merchant Apprentice w. diploma; Diploma, Swiss Mercantile School, London; Student Trainee, Westminster Bank, London. *Publications:* Manager auf Zeit (novel), 1968; Selbstbefragung (poems), 1969; Entwurf Schweiz (literary essay), 1970; Koitzsch (novel), 1971; Traum einer besseren Welt (short stories & poems), 1980; UnKraut im helvetischen Kulturgartchen (literary essay), 1981; meine Frau baut einen Bahnhof (short stories), 1982; S huus us Pilatusholz (monodrama), 1st performance, 1985; Klemms Memorabilien - Ein Vorspiel (novel), 1989; Umwerfende Zeiten - Ein Prozess (novel), 1990; Treffpunkt: Fondue Bourguignonne (novel), 1993. *Contributions to:* various newspapers. *Honours:* Artemis Jubilee Prize, 1969; Poetry Prize, Literary Union, Saabrucken, 1977. *Memberships:* Swiss Authors; Olten Group. *Address:* Lendikonerstrasse 54, CH 8484 Weisslingen/ZH Switzerland.

LANDESMAN Jay, b. 15 July 1919, St Louis, Missouri, USA. Publisher; Author; Playwright; Producer. m. Frances Deitsch, 15 July 1950, 2 sons. *Education:* University of Missouri, 1938-40; Rice Institute, Houston, 1940-42. *Publications:* Editor: Neurotica, The Complete, 1981; Rebel Without Applause, 1987 (memoir); The Nervous Set novel, 1954, Broadway Musical, 1959; A Walk on the Wild Side (musical) 1960; Molly Darling (musical) 1963; Small Day Tomorrow (major film in production 1990); Bad Nipple (novel) 1970; The Babies (play) 1969; Nobody Knows the Trouble I've Been (play). *Memberships:* Dramatists Guild; AFTRA; Groucho Club, London. *Address:* 8 Duncan Terrace, London N1 8BZ, England.

LANDIS J D. *See:* **LANDIS James David.**

LANDIS James David, (J D Landis), b. 30 June 1942, Springfield, MA, USA. Writer. m. (1) Patricia Lawrence Straus, 15 Aug 1964, (div), 1 daughter, (2) Denise Evelyn Tillar, 20 July 1983, 2 sons. *Education:* BA (magna cum laude), Yale College, 1964. *Appointments:* Assistant Editor, Abelard Schuman, 1966-67; Editor, Senior Editor, William Morrow & Co, 1967-1980; Editorial Director, Senior Vice-President, Publisher, Quill trade paperbacks, 1980-85; Senior Vice-President, William Morrow & Co, 1985-91; Publisher, Editor-in-Chief, Beech Tree Books, 1985-1987; Publisher, Editor-in-Chief, William Morrow & Co, 1988-91. *Publications:* The Sisters Impossible, 1979; Love's Detective, 1984, Daddy's Girl, 1984; Joey and the Girls, 1987; The Band Never Dances, 1989; Looks Aren't Everything, 1990. *Contributions to:* American Review; The Bennington Review. *Honours:* Roger Klein Award for Editing, 1973; Advocate Humanitarian Award, 1977. *Memberships:* Phi Beta Kappa; PEN. *Literary Agent:* Kathy Robbins, The Robbins Office. *Address:* 350 Central Park West, New York, NY 10025, USA.

LANDON H(oward) C(handler) Robbins, b. 1926, USA. Professor of Music. *Publications:* The Symphonies of Joseph Haydn, 1955; The Mozart Companion (co-editor), 1956, 2nd Edition, 1970; The Collected Correspondence and London Notebooks of Joseph Haydn, 1959; Complete Symphonies, by Haydn (editor), 1965-68; Complete String Quartets, by Haydn (co-editor), 1968-83; Beethoven, 1970; Complete Piano Trios, by Haydn (editor), 1970-78; Haydn: Chronicles and Works, biography, 5 vols, 1976-80; Mozart and the Masons, 1982; Handel and his World, 1984; 1791: Mozart's Last Year, 1987; Mozart: The Golden Years, 1989; The Mozart Compendium (ed), 1990; Mozart and Vienna, 1991; Five Centuries of Music in Venice, 1991; Une Journée Particuliere De Mozart, 1993. *Address:* Château de Foncoussières, 81800 Rabastens (Tarn), France.

LANE David Stuart, b. 1933, United Kingdom. Professor of Sociology. *Publications:* The Roots of Russian Communism, 1960; Politics and Society in the USSR, 1970; The End of Inequality, Social Stratification Under State Socialism, 1971; Social Groups in Polish Society (with G Kolankiewicz), 1973; The Socialist Industrial State, 1976; The Soviet Industrial Worker (with F O'Dell), 1978; Leninism: A Sociological Interpretation, 1981; The End of Social Inequality, 1982; State and Society in the USSR, 1985; Soviet Economy and Society, 1985; Current Approaches to Down's Syndrome (edited with B Stratford), 1985; Labour and Employment in the USSR (editor), 1986; Soviet Labour and the Ethic of Communism, 1987; Soviet Society Under Penestroika, 1990, 2nd Edition 1992; Russia in Flux, (ed), 1992. *Address:* Emmanuel College, Cambridge CB2 3AP, England.

LANE Gary (Martin), b. 1943, United States of America. Writer (Literature). *Publications:* A Concordance to the Poems of Theodore Roethke, 1971; A Concordance to the Poems of Hart Crane, 1972; As Concordance to the Poems of Marianne Moore, 1972; A Concordance to Personae: The Poems of Ezra Pound, 1972; A Word Index to Joyce's Dubliners, 1972; A Concordance to the Poems of Sylvia Plath, 1974; I Am: A Study of Cummings' Poems, 1976; A Concordance to the Poems of Dylan Thomas, 1976; Sylvia Plath: A Bibliography (with Maria Stevens), 1978; Sylvia Plath,

1979. *Address:* Department of English, University of Miami, Coral Gables, FL 33124, USA.

LANE Helen, (Helen Hudson), b. 31 Jan 1920, New York City, New York, USA. Writer. m. Robert Lane, 15 Nov 1944, 2 sons. *Education:* BA, Bryn Mawr College, 1941; MA, 1943, PhD, 1950, Columbia University. *Publications:* Tell The Time To None, 1966; Meyer Meyer, 1967; The Listener, 1968; Farnsbee South, 1971; Criminal Trespass, 1986; A Temporary Residence, 1987. *Contributions to:* Short stories to: Antioch Review; Sewannee Review; Virginia Quarterly; Northwest Review; Mademoiselle; Quarterly Review of Literature; Red Book; Ellery Queen; Mid-Stream; Best American Short Stories; O Henry Prize Stories; Others. *Honours:* Virginia Quarterly Prize Story, 1963. *Memberships:* Authors Guild; Authors League; American PEN. *Literary Agent:* Candida Doncedio. *Address:* 558 Chapel Street, New Haven, CT 06511, USA.

LANE M Travis (Millicent Elizabeth Travis), b. 23 Sept 1934, USA. Writer. m. Lauriat Lane, 26 Aug 1957, 1 son, 1 daughter. *Education:* MA, PhD, Cornell University. *Appointments:* Assistantships, Cornell University, University of New Brunswick; Honorary Research Associate, University of New Brunswick. *Publications:* Five Poets: Cornell, 1960; An Inch Or So Of Garden, 1969; Poems 1968-72, 1973; Homecomings, 1977; Divinations and Shorter Poems, 1973-78, 1980; Reckonings, Poems 1979-85, 1988; Solid Things: Poems New and Selected, 1989; Temporary Shelter, 1993. *Contributions to:* Canadian Literature; Dalhousie Review; Ariel; Essays on Canadian Writing; University of Toronto Quarterly; Fiddlehead Magazine; Essays on Canadian Writing *Honour:* Pat Lowther Prize, League of Canadian Poets, 1980. *Address:* 807 Windsor Street, Fredericton, New Brunswick, Canada E3B 4G7.

LANE Patrick, b. 26 Mar 1939, Nelson, Canada. Writer; Poet. 4 sons, 1 daughter. *Appointments:* Editor, Very Stone House, Publishers, Vancouver, 1966-72; Writer-in- Residence: University of Manitoba, Winnipeg, 1978-79; University of Ottawa, 1980; University of Alberta, Edmonton, 1981-82; Saskatoon Public Library, 1982-83; Concordia University, 1985; The Globe Theatre Co, Regina, Saskatchewan, 1985-. *Publications:* Letters from the Savage Mind, 1966; For Rita - In Asylum, 1969; Calgary City Jail, 1969; Separations, 1969; Sunflower Seeds, 1969; On the Street, 1970; Mountain Oysters, 1971; Hiway 401 Rhapsody, 1972; The Sun Has Begun to Eat the Mountain, 1972; Passing into Storm, 1973; Beware the Months of Fire, 1974; Certs, 1974; Unborn Things: South American Poems, 1975; For Riel in That Gawdam Prison, 1975; Albino Pheasants, 1977; If, 1977; Poems, New and Selected, 1978; No Longer Two People (with Lorna Uher), 1979; The Measure, 1980; Old Mother, 1982; Woman in the Dust, 1983; A Linen Crow, A Caftan Magpie, 1985; Selected Poems, 1987. *Contributions to:* Most major Canadian Magazines, American & English journals. *Honour:* Governor-General's Award for Poetry, 1979. *Membership:* League of Canadian Poets; Writers Union of Canada. *Address:* c/o League of Canadian Poets, 24 Ryerson Avenue, Toronto, Ontario, Canada M5T 2P3.

LANE Roumelia, b. 31 Dec 1927, Bradford, West Yorkshire, England. Writer. m. Gavin Green, 1 Oct 1949, 1 son, 1 daughter. *Appointment:* Writer, Bournemouth Echo, mid 1950's. *Publications:* Cafe Mimosa, 1971; Stormy Encounter, 1974; Dream Island, 1981; Night of the Beguine, 1986; Second Spring, 1980; Sea of Zanj, 1969; Hideaway Heart; A Summer to Love; House of the Winds; Summer of Conflict; Desert Haven; The Fires of Heaven; Lupin Valley; Hidden Rapture; The Brightest Star, 30 Books: TV and Film Scripts: Phantom of the Oscar; Icebound; Tender Saboteur; Chantico; Turn of the Tide. *Contributions to:* various journals and magazines including Bournemouth Echo. *Honours:* Featured Writer, Writers of Distinction, Harlequin USA and Canada, 1970's; Featured Writer, Coast to Coast Press Promotion for Coca Cola (Books) USA; Featured Writer, Coast to Coast Promotion of Books, Avon

Cosmetics, USA, 1970's. *Memberships:* Society of Authors of Great Britain; Writers Guild of Great Britain; Affiliate Member, Writers Guild of America (East and West); ALCS. *Address:* Casa Mimosa, Santa Eugenia, Majorca, Beleares, Spain.

LANG David Marshall, b. 1924, United Kingdom. Professor Emeritus of Caucasian Studies. *Publications:* Studies in the Numismatic History of Georgia in Transcaucasia, 1955; Lives and Legends of the Georgian Saints (compiler and translator), 1956; The Wisdom of Balahvar, translation, 1957; The First Russian Radical: Alexander Radishchev, 1959: A Modern History of Georgia, 1962; Catalogue of the Georgian Books in the British Museum (compiler), 1962; The Georgians, 1966; The Balavariani, translation, 1966; Penguin Companion to Literature. vol 4 (co-editor), 1969; Armenia, Cradle of Civilization, 1970; The Peoples of the Hills: Ancient Ararat and Caucasus (with C Burney), 1971; Guide to Eastern Literatures (editor and compiler), 1971; The Bulgarians, 1976; The Armenians: A People in Exile, 1981. *Address:* School of Oriental and African Studies, University of London, London WC1, England.

LANG Grace. *See:* FLOREN Lee.

LANG Jean. *See:* LANG-CROWE Jean E.

LANG King. *See:* TUBB E C.

LANG-CROWE Jean E, (Jean Lang), b. Dongara, Western Australia. Teacher; Writer; Illustrator. m. Courthope Farquhar Crowe, 7 Mar 1940, 1 son, 2 daughters. *Education:* Linton Institute of Art, 1931-33; Perth Technical College, 1931-33; Secondary Teachers Certificate, 1934; Certificate of Art Studies, 1970. *Appointments:* Archivist Tom Collins House. *Publications:* Bobby and Anne in Beeloo; Living Tradition; At The Toss of a Coin; Pillows on the Thorn; Pathway to Magic; My Animal Book; Albany Pitcher Plant; Open Door. *Contributions to:* Several. *Honours:* W A Newspapers Jubilee Award; Tom Collins Award; Canning Nat; SWW Bronze; Walter Stone Nat; Ric Throssell Award; WA Citizen of the Year; Aquinas Academy Nat Award. *Memberships:* Australian Society of Authors; Association for Study of Australian Literature; Fellowship of Australian Writers; Society of Women Writers. *Address:* 6/99 McCabe Street, Mosman Park, Western Australia 6012, Australia.

LANGDALE Cecily, b. 27 July 1939, USA. Art Dealer; Art Historian. m. Roy Davis, 24 July 1972. *Education:* Swarthmore College, 1961. *Publications:* Gwen John: Paintings and Drawings from the Collection of John Quinn and Others (with Betsy G Fryberger), 1982; Monotypes by Maurice Prendergast in the Terra Museum of Art, 1984; Gwen John: An Interior Life (with David Fraser Jenkins), 1985, 1986; Gwen John: with a Catalogue Raisonne of the Paintings and a Selection of the Drawings, 1987, paperback, 1989; Maurice Brazil Prendergast, Charles Prendergast: A Catalogue Raisonne (contributor), 1990. *Contributions to:* The Connoisseur, 1979; Antiques, 1987; Drawing, 1990, 1992; Dictionary of National Biography: Supplementary Volume: From the beginnings to 1985. *Membership:* Cosmopolitan Club, New York. *Address:* 231 East 60 Street, New York, NY 10022, USA.

LANGDON Philip Alan, b. 6 Jan 1947, Greenville, Pennsylvania, USA. Journalist; Author. m. Maryann Dunkle, 12 June 1971. *Education:* BA, Allegheny College, 1969; Certificate in American Studies, 1973, MA, History, 1977, Utah State University. *Appointments:* Reporter, The Patriot, Harrisburg, Pennsylvania, 1969-71; Reporter, Columnist, Architecture Critic, The Buffalo Evening News, Buffalo, New York, 1973-82; Journalist-in-residence, University of Michigan, 1979-80; Writer, Home column, Design column, The Atlantic Monthly, 1987-90. *Publications:* Orange Roofs, Golden Arches, 1986; American Houses, 1987; Urban Excellence, 1990; This Old House Kitchens (with Steve Thomas), 1992; This Old House Bathrooms (with Steve Thomas), 1993. *Contributions to:* Many articles to The Atlantic Monthly, 1984-, including 2 cover articles: The American House, 1984, A Good Place to Live, 1988; Planning; Landscape Architecture; Others. *Honours:* Professional Journalism Fellowship, National Endowment for the Humanities, 1979; Architectural Fellowship, New York State Council on the Arts, 1982; Golden Hammer Award, National Association of Home Builders, 1984; National Endowment for the Arts USA Fellowship, 1990. *Membership:* New Haven Preservation Trust. *Address:* 178 East Rock Road, New Haven, CT 06511, USA.

LANGE John. *See:* **CRICHTON Michael.**

LANGFORD Gary,b. 21 Aug 1947, Christchurch. Writer; Senior Lecturer. 1 daughter. *Education:* BA, 1969; MA, (Hons) History, 1971; MA, (Hons) English, 1973, University of Canterbury; Diploma of Teaching Drama, Christchurch Sec Teachers College, 1973. *Appointments:* Senior Lecturer, Creative Writing, University of Western Sydney, 1986; Writer in Residence, University of Canterbury (part), 1989. *Publications:* 19 Books, including 7 novels such as Death of the Early Morning Hero, 1975; Players in the Ballgame, 1979; Vanaties, 1984; Pillbox, 1986; Newlands, 1990 and 7 books of poetry such as Four Ships, 1982; The Pest Exterminator's Shakespeare, 1984; Bushido, 1987; Love at the Traffic Lights, 1990; Poetry and Anthologies; 150-200 performances of scripts and plays on stage, television and radio. *Honours:* Young Writers Fellowship, Australia Council, 1976; Alan Marshall Award, 1983. *Address:* c/o Curtis Brown (Aust) Ptg Ltd, Box 19, Paddington, NSW 2021, Australia.

LANGHOLM Neil. *See:* **BULMER Henry Kenneth.**

LANGLEY Gill. *See:* **LANGLEY Gillian Rose.**

LANGLEY Gillian Rose, (Gill Langley), b. 10 Aug 1952, London, England. Scientific Consultant and Writer. m. Christopher Kenneth Langley, 11 Aug 1979. BA (Hons) Cantab, Zoology, Class 2:I, 1974; MA Cantab, 1975; PhD, Neurochemistry, Cantab, 1978. *Appointments:* Member, Editorial Board, Humane Education Journal, 1979-81; Editor, Alternative News, 1981-. *Publications:* Biogenic Amines in the Nervous System of the Cockroach Periplaneta americana, 1979; Redundancy for the Laboratory Guinea-Pig, 1984; Blinded by Science, 1987; Vegan Nutrition: A Survey of Research, 1988; Animal Experimentation: The Consensus Changes, 1989; Faith, Hope and Charity: An Enquiry into Charity-Funded Research, 1990. *Contributions to:* New Scientist; The Guardian; The Independent; Outrage; Liberator; Alternative News; Natural Choice; Me Magazine. *Memberships:* Fellow, Royal Society of Medicine; Member, Institute of Biology. *Address:* 46 Kings Road, Hitchin, Herts SG5 1RD, England.

LANGTON Jane, b. 30 Dec 1922, Boston, Massachusetts, USA. Writer. m. William Langton, 10 June 1943. 3 sons. *Education:* BS 1944, MA 1945, University of Michigan; MA 1948, Radcliffe College. *Publications:* Adult Suspense Novels: The Transcendental Murder, 1964; The Memorial Hall Murder, 1978; Emily Dickinson Is Dead, 1984; Murder At the Gardner, 1988; Dark Nantucket Noon, 1975; Natural Enemy, 1982; Good and Dead, 1986; The Dante Game, 1991; God in Concord, 1992. For Children: Diamond in the Window, 1962; Paper Chains, 1977; The Fledgling, 1980; The Fragile Flag, 1984. Her Majesty, Grace Jones, 1961; The Swing in The Summerhouse, 1967; The Astonishing Stereoscope, 1971; The Boyhood of Grace Jones, 1972. *Honours:* Newbery Honor Book, 1981 for The Fledgling; Nero Wolfe Award, for Emily Dickinson is Dead. *Literary Agent:* Meg Ruley Inc for adult books: McIntosh & Otis

for children's books. *Address:* Baker Farm Road, Lincoln, MA 01773, USA.

LANIER Sterling E(dmund), b. 1927, USA. Writer; Sculptor. *Appointments:* Research Historian, Winterthur Museum, Switzerland, 1958-60; Editor: John C Winston Co, 1961; Chilton Books, 1961-62, 1965-67; Macrae-Smith Co, 1963-64; Full-time Writer and Sculptor, 1967-. *Publications:* The War for the Lot, juvenile, 1969; The Peculiar Exploits of Brigadier Ffellowes, short stories, 1972; Hiero's Journey, 1973; The Unforsaken Hiero, 1983; Menace under Marwood, 1983; The Curious Quest of Brig Ffellowes, 1986. *Literary Agent:* Curtis Brown Ltd, USA. *Address:* c/o Curtis Brown Ltd, 575 Madison Avenue, New York, NY 10022, USA.

LANOUETTE William, b. 14 Sept 1940, New Haven, Connecticut, USA. Writer; Editor. m. Joanne M Sheldon, 12 Apr 1969, St Paul, Minnesota. 2 daughters. *Education:* BA, Fordham College, New York City, New York, 1963; MSc 1966, PhD 1973, London School of Economics. *Literary Appointments:* Researcher, Reporter, Newsweek, 1961-64; Staff Writer, The National Observer, 1969-70, 1972-77; Staff Correspondent, 1977-82, Contributing Editor, 1982-83, National Journal, Washington; Communications Director, 1983-85, Senior Associate 1985, World Resources Institute, Washington; Fellow, John F. Kennedy School of Government, Harvard University, 1988-89. Author of a biography of Leo Szilard, Genius in the Shadow, 1993. *Contributions to:* Arms Control Today; The Atlantic Monthly; The Bulletin of the Atomic Scientists; Commonweal; The Economist; Environment; The Far Eastern Economic Review; New York; Parliamentary Affairs; The Wilson Quarterly. *Honour:* Forum Award for significant print media contributions to public understanding of atomic energy, 1974. *Literary Agent:* F Joseph Spieler. *Address:* 326 Fifth Street South East, Washington, DC 20003, USA.

LANSIDE Luke. *See:* **CRAGGS Robert S.**

LANTRY Mike. *See:* **TUBB E C.**

LAPINSKI Susan, b. 27 May 1948, Baltimore, Maryland, USA. Magazine Writer; Author. m. 31 Dec 1973, 2 daughters. *Education:* BA, College of Notre Dame, Maryland, 1970; MA, Communications, University of North Carolina, Chapel Hill, 1977. *Appointments:* Editor in Chief, Lady's Circle, 1979-80; Senior Editor, Family Weekly, 1980; Columnist, American Baby, 1985-. *Publications:* In a Family Way, 1982. *Contributions to:* numerous journals and magazines including: Family Circle; Glamour; Ladies Home Journal; McCall's; Redbook, others. *Honours:* Honourable Mention, Atlantic Monthly Poetry Competition, 1970; Runner up, Front Page Award, 1987. *Memberships:* American Society of Journalists and Authors; Newswomen's Club; Writers' Network. *Literary Agent:* Aaron Priest Literary Agency. *Address:* 152 Remsen Street Brooklyn Heights, NY 11201, USA.

LAPPÉ Frances Moore, b. 10 Feb 1944, Pendleton, Oregon, USA. Educator. m. Paul Martin Du Bois, 19 Aug 1991, 1 son, 1 daughter. *Education:* BA, Earlham College, Indiana. *Publications:* Diet for a Small Planet, 1971; Food First: Beyond the Myth of Scarcity, 1977; World Hunger, Ten Myths, (co-author), 1979; Aid as Obstacle, 1980; World Hunger: Twelve Myths, 1986; Betraying the National Interest, (co-author), 1987; Mozambique and Tanzania: Asking the Big Questions and Casting New Molds: First Steps Toward Worker Control in a Mozambique Factory, (co-author), 1980; What To Do After You Turn Off the TV : Fresh Ideas for Enjoying Family Time, 1985; Rediscovering America's Values, 1989; Taking Population Seriously, 1989. *Contributions to:* New York Times; Harper's; Readers Digest; Journal of Nutrition Education; War on Hunger. *Honours:* Honorary LLD, Star King School of Religious Leadership, St Mary's College, MacAlester College, Lewis and Clark College, Hamline University,

Kenyon College and Earlham College; JFK University, Unviersity of Michigan, Niagara College; Right Livelihood Award, Sweden's Alternative Nobel Prize, 1987. *Address:* Center for Living Democracy, Black Fox Road, Brattleboro, Vermont 05301, USA.

LAPPING Brian (Michael), b. 1937, United Kingdom. Television Producer; Journalist; Editor. *Appointments:* Reporter, Daily Mirror, London, 1959-61; Reporter and Deputy Commonwealth Correspondent, The Guardian, London, 1961-67; Editor, Venture, Fabian Society monthly journal, 1965-69; Feature Writer, Financial Times, London, 1967-68; Deputy Editor, New Society, London, 1968-70; Television Producer, Granada Television Ltd, 1970-88; Executive Producer, World in Action, 1976-78, The State of the Nation, 1978-80, End of Empire, 1980-85; Chief Executive of Brian Lapping Associates, 1988-; Executive Producer, Countdown to War, 1989; Hypotheticals (three programmes annually for BBC 2); Question Time (weekly for BBC 1); The Second Russian Revolution (for BBC 2), 1991; The Washington Version (for BBC 2), 1992. *Publications:* More Power to the People (co-editor), 1968; The Labour Government 1964-70, 1970; The State of the Nation: Parliament (editor), 1973; The State of the Nation: The Bounds of Freedom, 1980; End of Empire, 1985; Apartheid: A History, 1986. *Address:* 61 Eton Avenue, London NW3, England.

LAQUEUR Walter, b. 26 May 1921, Breslau, Germany. History Educator. m. Barbara Koch, 29 May 1941. 2 daughters. *Appointments:* Journalist, Freelance Author, 1944-55; Editor of Survey, 1955-65; Co-editor, Journal of Contemporary History, 1966-. *Publications:* Communism and Nationalism in the Middle East, 1956; Young Germany, 1961; Russia and Germany, 1965; The Road to War, 1968; Europe Since Hitler, 1970; Out of the Ruins of Europe, 1971; Zionism, a History, 1972; Confrontation: The Middle East and World Politics, 1974; Weimar: a Cultural History 1918-33, 1974; Guerrilla, 1976; Terrorism, 1977; The Missing Years, 1980; A Reader's Guide to Contemporary History (edited jointly), 1972; Fascism: a reader's guide (editor), 1978; The Terrible Secret, 1980; Farewell to Europe, 1981; Germany Today: a personal report, 1985; World of Secrets: the uses and limits of intelligence, 1986; The Long Road to Freedom: Russia and Glasnost, 1989; Thursday's Child Has Far To Go, 1993. *Honours:* Recipient 1st Distinguished Writer's Award, Center Strategic and International Studies, 1969; Inter Nations Award, 1985. *Address:* Center for Strategic and International Studies, 1800 K Street NW, Washington, DC 20006, USA.

LARDNER Ring W Jr, b. 19 Aug 1915, Chicago, Illinois, USA. Writer. m. Frances Chaney, 28 Sept 1946. *Education:* Phillips Academy, Andover, Massachusetts; Princeton University, 2 years. *Publications:* The Ecstasy of Owen Muir, UK Edition, 1954, USA Edition, 1955; The Lardners: My Family Remembered, 1976; All for Love, 1985. *Honours:* Best Original Screenplay for Woman of the Year (with Michael Kanin), Academy of Motion Pictures, 1942; Best Screenplay Based on Material from Another Medium for M A S H, Academy of Motion Picture Arts and Sciences, 1970; Best Comedy Award for M A S H, Writers Guild of America, 1970; Laurel Award for Lifetime Achievement in Screenwriting, Writers Guild of America, West, 1989. *Memberships:* Vice-President, Screen Writers Guild, 1945; Writers Guild of America, East; PEN. *Literary Agent:* Jim Preminger Agency, USA. *Address:* c/o Jim Preminger Agency, 1650 Westwood Boulevard, Los Angeles, CA 90024, USA.

LARKIN Rochelle, b. 1935, USA. Author. *Appointments:* Editor, Countrywide Publications, New York City, 1963; Editor, Kanrom Inc, New York City, 1964-70; Editor, Pinnacle Books, New York City, 1970; Editor-in-Chief, Lancer Books, New York City, 1973-74; Editor-in-Chief, Female Bodybuilding Magazine, 1986-89; Editor-in-Chief, Bodybuilding Lifestyles Magazine, 1990-91; Editor, Waldman Publishing, 1992-. *Publications:* Soul Music, 1970; Supermarket

Superman, 1970; Teen Scene (with Milburn Smith), 1971; The Godmother, 1971; Honour Thy Godmother, 1972; For Godmother and Country, 1972; 365 Ways to Say I Want to Be Your Friend (with M Smith), 1973; Black Magic, 1974; The Beatles: Yesterday, Today, Tomorrow, 1974; The Greek Goddess, 1975; Call Me Anytime, 1975; International Joke Book, 1975; The Raging Flood, 1976; Hail Columbia, 1976; The First One, 1976; Valency Girl (with Robin Moore), 1976; Pusher, 1976; Sexual Superstars, 1976; Harvest of Desire, 1976; Kitty, 1977; Mafia Wife (with Robin Moore), 1977; Mistress of Desire, 1978; Instant Beauty (with Pablo Manzoni), 1978; Tri (with Robin Moore), 1978; Torches of Desire, 1979; Glitterball, 1980; Beverly Johnson's Guide to a Life of Health and Beauty (with Julie Davis), 1981; Only Perfect, 1981; Golden Days, Silver Nights, 1982; Amber series (as Darrell Fairfield), 6 vols, 1982; The Crystal Heart, 1983; Angels Never Sleep, 1984. *Address:* 351 East 84th Street, New York, NY 10028, USA.

LARSEN Eric Everett, b. 29 Nov 1941, USA. College Educator; Writer. m. Anne Schnare, 5 June 1965, 2 daughters. *Education:* BA, Carleton College, 1963; MA, 1964, PhD, 1971, University of Iowa. *Appointments:* Professor of English, John Jay College of Criminal Justice, City University of New York, 1971-. *Publications:* Novels: An American Memory, 1988; I Am Zoe Handke, 1992. *Contributions to:* Harper's; The New Republic; The Nation; Los Angeles Times Book Review; The North American Review; The New England Review; Others. *Honours:* The Heartland Prize for An American Memory, Chicago Tribune, 1988. *Literary Agent:* Brandt and Brandt, Literary Agents Inc, New York, USA. *Address:* c/o Brandt and Brandt, Literary Agents Inc, 1501 Broadway, New York, NY 10036, USA.

LASHMAR Paul Christopher, b. 18 Dec 1954, Essex, England. Journalist. *Education:* Diploma, Communication Design, North-East London Polytechnic, 1975-1978. *Appointments:* Investigative Researcher, The Observer, 1978-89; Researcher, World in Action, Granada TV, 1989-. *Publication:* Scotland Yard's Cocaine Connection, 1990. *Contributions to:* The Observer; The Guardian; Folk Roots. *Honour:* Reporter of the Year, UK Press Awards, (with David Leigh), 1985. *Membership:* National Union of Journalists. *Address:* 3 Upper James Street, London W1, England.

LASKA Vera, b. 21 July 1928, Kosice, Czechoslovakia. Professor; Lecturer; Columnist; Author. m. Andrew J Laska, 5 Nov 1949, 2 sons. *Education:* MA, History, 1946, MA, Philosophy, 1946, Charles University, Prague; PhD, History, University of Chicago, 1959. *Appointment:* Professor of History, Regis College, Weston, Massachusetts, USA, 1966-. *Publications:* Remember the Ladies, Outstanding Women of the American Revolution, 1976; Franklin and Women, 1978; Czechs in America, 1633-1977, 1978; Benjamin Franklin the Diplomat, 1982; Nazism, Resistance and Holocaust: A Bibliography, 1985; Women in the Resistance and in the Holocaust, 1983, 1988. *Contributions to:* Over 200 articles and book reviews in newspapers and professional journals. *Honours:* Outstanding Educator of America, 1972; Kidger Award in History, 1984; George Washington Medal from Freedom Foundation, 1984. *Memberships:* PEN Club of New England; Czech Society of Arts and Sciences in America; American Historical Association; New England Historical Association, Vice-President; Massachusetts Bicentennial Commission; Chairman, Weston Historical Society; National Association of Foreign Student Affairs. *Address:* 50 Woodchester Drive, Weston, MA 02193, USA.

LASKER David Raymond, b. 21 Apr 1950, New York City, New York, USA. Writer; Musician, Double-bassist. *Education:* BA, 1972, MMus, 1974, Yale University; studies, Juilliard School of Music, New York, 2 years. *Appointments:* Editor, Contract Magazine, Toronto, Canada, 1989. *Publications:* The Boy Who Loved Music, 1979. *Contributions to:* Interior Design; Progressive Architecture; Architectural Digest; Los Angeles Times;

ID; House & Home; Canadian Interiors; Ontario Living; City & Country Home; Toronto Life; Maclean's. *Honours:* Notable book, for Boy Who Loved Music, American Library Association, 1980. *Memberships:* Fees Committee, Periodical Writers Association of Canada. *Address:* Contract Magazine, Victor Publishing Company Ltd, 7777 Keele Street, Unit 8, Concord, Ontario L4K 1Y7, Canada.

LASKOWSKI Jacek Andrzej, b. 4 June 1946, Edinburgh, Scotland. Author; Translator. m. Anne Grant Howieson, 8 July 1978. 2 daughters. *Education:* MagPhil, Jagiellonian University, Krakow, Poland, 1973. *Appointments:* Literary Manager, Haymarket Theatre, Leicester, 1984-87. *Publications:* Plays Produced: Dreams to DAmnation, BBC Radio 3, 1977; Pawn Takes Pawn, BBC Radio 4, 1978; The Secret Agent, BBC Radio 4, 1980; Nostromo, BBC Radio 4, 1985. *Memberships:* Theatre Writers Union, General Secretary, 1981-82; Society of Authors, V-Chairman, Broadcasting Committee, 1982-83. *Literary Agent:* Penny Tackaberry. *Address:* c/o Penny Tackaberry, Tessa Sayle Agency, 11 Jubilee Place, London SW3 3TE, England.

LASKY Jesse Louis Jr, (David Love, Francis Smeed), b. 1910, USA. Writer. *Appointments:* Scriptwriter, BBC and ITV Television, London; Former Vice President, Screen Branch, Writers Guild of America; Writers Guild of Great Britain; Company of Military Historians. *Publications:* Songs from the Heart of a Boy, 1926; Listening to Silence, 1928; Curtain of Life, 1934; Singing in Thunder, 1935; No Angels in Heaven, 1938; Spindrift, 1948; Naked in a Cactus Garden, 1960; Cry the Lonely Flesh: Whatever Happened to Hollywood, 1973; Men of Mystery (with Pat Silver), US version Dark Dimensions, 1978; Love Scene (with Pat Silver), 1978; The Offer (with Pat Silver), 1981. *Contributions to:* Cosmopolitan; Writers Guild of America Book on TV and Screen Writing; Writers Guild of Great Britain publication Lookout; Spanish Home; Sunday Times Book Review; Poetry Reviews: Los Angeles Times; La Prensa, Argentina. *Honours:* Poetry Awards; Short Story Award for 1 of 10 best published in Cosmopolitan, Christopher Award; American University Woman's Award for most original play for verse play Ghost Town (with Pat Silver). *Memberships:* Writers Guild of America, Vice-President, Screen Writers Branch, 1955; Writers Guild of Great Britain. *Literary Agent:* Andrew Mann, London; Lantz Office, New York. *Address:* c/o Andrew Mann Ltd., 1 Old Compton Street, London W1, England.

LASKY Victor, b. 1918, USA. Writer. *Appointments:* Columnist, Say It Straight, North American Newspaper Alliance, New York City, 1962-80. *Publications:* Seeds of Treason (with R de Toledano), 1950; American Legion Reader (editor), 1953; J F K: The Man and the Myth, 1963; The Ugly Russian, 1965; Robert F Kennedy: The Myth and the Man, 1968; Say, Didn't You Used to be George Murphy (with George Murphy), 1970; Arthur J Goldberg: The Old and the New, 1970; It Didn't Start with Watergate, 1977; Jimmy Carter: The Man and the Myth, 1979; Never Complain, Never Explain: The Story of Henry Ford II, 1981. *Address:* 3133 Connecticut Avenue NW, Washington, DC 20008, USA.

LASSITER Adam. *See:* **KRAUZER Steven M.**

LATHAM Mavis. *See:* **THORPE-CLARK Mavis.**

LATOW Roberta, b. 27 Sept 1931, Springfield, Massachusetts, USA. Author. *Education:* Whitney School of Interior Design, New York City. *Appointments:* International Interior Designer, USA, the Middle East, Europe, Africa, United Kingdom, 1952-81; Art Dealer, owning galleries in Springfield, Massachusetts and New York City, 1954-62. *Publications:* Three Rivers, 1981; Tidal Wave, 1983; Soft Warm Rain, 1985; This Stream of Dreams, 1986. *Honours:* The Romantic Erotica Award, USA, 1984. *Membership:* Authors Guild. *Address:* Wiltshire, England.

LAUGHTON Bruce Kyle Blake, b. 6 June 1928, Northampton, England. Professor of Art History. m. (1) Mary Shields, 1953, 1 son, 1 daughter, (2) Doris Brebner, 1973. *Education:* MA, Oxford University, 1953; Camberwell School of Art; Slade School of Fine Art, London; PhD, London University, 1968. *Publications:* Philip Wilson Steer (1860-1942), 1971; The Euston Road School, 1986; The Drawings of Daumier and Millet, 1991. *Contributions to:* Articles and reviews to: Apollo Magazine; Burlington Magazine; Master Drawings; Racar (Canadian Art Review). *Membership:* Fellow, Royal Society of Arts. *Address:* Department of Art, Queen's University, Kingston, Ontario, Canada K7L 3N6.

LAUMER Keith, b. 1925, American, Writer of Mystery, Crime, Suspense, Science fiction, Fantasy, Recreation, Leisure, Hobbies. *Appointments:* Freelance writer since 1964. Staff Member, University of Illinois, Urbana, 1952; Foreign Service Vice-Consul and Third Secretary, Rangoon, 1956-59. *Publications include:* Greylorn (short stories, in UK as The Other Sky) 1968; It's a Mad, Mad, Mad Galaxy (short stories) 1968; The Afrit Affair (suspense, novelization of TV series) 1968; The Drowned Queen (suispense, novelization of TV series) 1968; The Gold Bomb (suspense, novelization of TV series) 1969; The World Shuffler, 1970; The House in November, 1970; Time Trap, 1970; (ed)Five Fates, 1970; Retief's Ransom, 1971; The Star Treasure, 1971; Deadfall, 1971, as Fat Chance, 1975; Dinosaur Beach, 1971; Retief of the CDT (short stories) 1971; Once There Was a Giant (short stories) 1971; The Infinite Cage, 1972; Night of Delusions, 1972; The Shape Changer, 1972; The Big Show (short stories) 1972; Timetracks (short stories) 1972; The Glory Game, 1973; The Undefeated (short stories) 1974; Retief, Emissary to the Stars (short stories) 1975; Bolo: The Annals of the Dinochrome Brigade, 1976; The Best of Keith Laumer (short stories) 1976; The Ultimax Man, 1978; Retief Unbound (short story omnibus) 1979; Retief at Large (short stories) 1979; The Star Colony, 1981; The Breaking Earth (short stories) 1981; Worlds of the Imperium (short stories) 1982; The Other Sky, 1982; Retief to the Rescue (short stories) 1983; The Galaxy Builder (short stories) 1984; The Return of Retief, 1985; Rogue Bolo, 1985; End as a Hero, 1985. *Address:* Box 972, Brooksville, FL 33512, USA.

LAURENT Jacques, b. 5 Jan 1919, Paris, France. Author; Journalist. (div). *Education:* Faculte des Lettres, Paris. *Appointments:* Literary Review, La Parisienne, 1953; President, Director-General, Arts, 1954-59; has written screenplay for several films. *Publications:* Under Pseudonym Cecil Saint-Laurent: Caroline Cherie; Le fils de Caroline Cherie; Lucrece Borgia; prenom Clotilde; Ici Clotilde; Les passagers pour Alger; Les agites d'Alger; Hortense 1914-18; A Simon l'honneur; L'histoire imprevue des dessous feminins; La Communarde; La Bourgeoise, 1974; la Mutante, 1978; Clarisse 1980; as Jacques Laurent: Les corps tranquilles, Paul et Jean-Paul; Le petit canard; mauriac sous de Gaulle, 1964; Les Bêtises, 1971; Dix perles de culture, 1972; Histoire Egoiste, 1976; Roman du roman, 1977; Le Nu vetu et devetu, 1979; Les sous-ensembles flous, 1981; Les dimanches de Mademoiselle Beaunon, 1982; Stendhal comme Stendhal, 1984; Le dormeur debout, 1985. *Honours:* Prix Goncourt, 1971; Grand Prix de Litterature, Academy Francaise 1981; Prix Litteraire Prince Pierre de Monaco, 1983; Election to Academie of Française. *Address:* Ed Grasset, 61, rue des Saints-Pères, 75006 Paris, France.

LAURENTS Arthur, b. 14 July 1917, New York, USA. Playwright. *Education:* Cornell University. *Appointments:* Radio Scriptwriter, 1939-40. *Publications:* Novels: The Way We Were, 1972; The Turning Point, 1977; Screenplays: The Snake Pit, 1948; Rope, 1948; Caught, 1948; Anna Lucasta 1949; Anastasia, 1956; Bonjour Tristesse, 1958; The Way We Were, 1972; The Turning Point, 1977; Plays: Home of the Brave, 1946; The Bird Cage, 1950; The Time of the Cuckoo, 1952; A Clearing in the Woods, 1956; Invitation to a March, 1960; The Enclave, 1973; Scream,

1978; Musical Plays: West Side Story, 1957; Gypsy, 1959; Anyone Can Whistle, 1964; Do I Hear a Waltz?, 1964; Hallelulah Baby, 1967; Screenwriter, Co-producer, film, The Turning Point, 1977; writer, director, several Broadway plays including I can get it for You Wholesale, 1961; Anyone Can Whistle, 1964; La Cage aux Folles, 1983; Broadway Musical, Author and Director, Nick and Nora, 1991. *Honours:* Recipient, various awards including: American Academy of Arts and Letters, 1946; Sidney Howard Award, 1946; Writers Guild of America Award, 1977; Tony Award, 1967, 1984; Drama Desk Award, 1974. *Memberships:* Screenwriters Guild; Academy of Motion Picture Arts and Sciences; Council, Dramatists Guild; SSD&C; PEN; Theatre Hall of Fame. *Literary Agent:* Shirley Bernstein, 1414 Avenue of the Americas, New York, NY 10019, USA. *Address:* Quogue, New York, NY 11959, USA.

LAURIE Rona, b. 16 Sept 1916, Derby, England. Actress; Writer; Drama Lecturer; Professor of Speech and Drama, Guildhall School of Music and Drama. m. Edward Lewis Neilson, 1961. *Education:* Derby High School; Penrhos College; University of Birmingham; Royal Academy of Dramatic Art. BA (Hons), FGSM. LRAM, LGSM, FRSA. *Literary Appointments:* Dramatic Critic, Teachers' World; Dramatic Critic, On Stage (Australia). *Publications:* Festivals and Adjudication, 1975; A Hundred Speeches from the Theatre, 1966; Adventures in Group Speaking, 1967; Speaking Together I & II, 1966; Scenes and Ideas, 1967; Children's Plays from Beatrix Potter, 1980; Mrs Tiggywinkle and Friends, 1986; Auditioning, 1985. *Contributions to:* Speaking Shakespeare Today (Speech and Drama); Speaking the Sonnet (Speech and Drama). *Memberships:* Guild of Drama Adjudicators, Chairman; Society of Teachers of Speech and Drama, Chairman; Chairman, Drama Advisory Committee Guildhall School; Adjudicator, Gold Medal, The Poetry Society; Adjudicator, British Federation of Music Festivals. *Address:* 21 New Quebec Street, London W1H 7DE, England.

LAURO Shirley (Shapiro) Mezvinsky, b. 18 Nov 1933, Des Moines, IA, USA. m. (1) Norton Mezvinsky, (div) 1 daughter, (2) Louis Paul Lauro, 18 Aug 1973. *Education:* BS (cum laude), Northwestern University, 1955; MS, University of Wisconsin-Madison, 1957. *Appointments:* Instructor in drama and literature, University of Wisconsin-Madison, 1959; Professional film, television and stage actress, NY, Boston, MA, Detroit, MI, Chicago, IL, Wisconsin, 1959-; Writer, 1961-; Instructor in speech and theatre, City College of the City University of NY, 1967-71; Instructor in speech, theatre and playwriting, Yeshiva University, 1971-76; Literary Consultant 1975-80, Production Critic 1975-, Member's Council 1975-, Resident Playwright 1976-, Ensemble Studio Theatre; Instructor in Speech, Manhattan Community College, 1978; Instructor in English and Creative Writing, Marymount Manhattan College, 1978-79; Resident Playwright, Alley Theatre, Houston, 1987; Adj Professor Playwriting, Tisch School of The Arts, New York University, 1989-; Actress and Free-lance Editor; Afiliated with American Place Theatre Women's Project. *Publications:* The Edge, 1965; The Contest, 1975; Open Admissions, Nothing Immediate, I Don't Know Where You're Coming From at All!, The Coal Diamond, Margaret and Kit, 1979; In the Garden of Eden, 1982; Sunday Go to Meetin' 1986; Pearls on the Moon, 1987; AA Piece of My Heart, 1992. *Contributions to:* Short stories, periodicals, including Jewish Horizon and New Idea; The Christian Science Monitor. *Honours:* Recipient of numerous honours and awards for professional services including The John Simon Guggenheim. *Memberships:* Writers Guild of America; PEN; League of Professional Theatre Women (vice-president); Authors League; Authors Guild; Dramatists Guild. *Address:* 275 Central Park West, New York, NY 10024, USA.

LAVERS Norman b. 21 Apr 1935, United States. Teacher. m. Cheryl Dicks, 20 July 1967, 1 son. *Education:* BA 1960, MA 1963, San Francisco State University; PhD, University of Iowa, 1969. *Publications:*

Mark Harris (criticism) 1978; Selected Short Stories, 1979; Jerzy Kosinski (criticism) 1982; The Northwest Passage (novel) 1984; Pop Culture Into Art: The Novels of Manuel Puig (criticism) 1988. *Contributions:* Contributing Editor, Bird Watcher's Digest. *Honours:* National Endowment for the Arts Fellowship in Creative Writing, 1982, 1991; O Henry Award 1987; Editor's Choice Award, 1986; Hohenberg Award, 1986; Pushcart Award, 1992; William Peden Prize, 1992. *Literary Agent:* Sobel Weber Associates Incorporated, 146E 19th Street, New York, NY 100003, USA. *Address:* Rt 5 Box 203, Jonesboro, AR 72401, USA.

LAVIN Mary, b. 12 June 1912, E. Walpole, Massachusetts, USA. Writer. m. (1) William Walsh, 1942, (dec 1954), (2) Michael MacDonald Scott, 1969, 3 daughters. *Education:* University College, Dublin. *Publications:* Tales from Bective Bridge 1942; The Long Ago, 1944; The House in Clewe Street 1945; The Becker Wives, 1946; At Sallygap, 1947; Mary O'Grady, 1950; A Single Lady, 1956; The Patriot Son, 1956; A Likely Story, 1957; Selected Stories, 1959; The Great Wave, 1961; The Stories of Mary Lavin, Volume I, 1964, Volume II, 1973, Volume III, 1985; The Middle of the Fields, 1967; Happiness, 1969; Collected Stories, 1971; The Second Best Children in the World (illustrated by Edward Ardizzone), 1972; A Memory, 1972; The Shrine, 1977; A Family Likeness, 1985. *Honours:* James Tait Black Memorial Prize, 1943; Guggenheim Fellowship, 1959-60; Katherine Mansfield Prize, 1961; Ella Lyman Cabot Award, 1972; Eire Society Gold Medal, 1974; Gregory Medal, Supreme Literary Award of the Irish Nation, 1975; American Irish Foundation Literary Award, 1979; Allied Irish Banks Literary Award 1981; Honorary D.Litt., Univerity College Dublin. *Memberships include:* President, Irish PEN, 1964-65, 1985-86; President, Irish Academy of Letters 1972-73; Board of Governors, School of Irish Studies, Dublin, 1974-. *Address:* The Abbey Farm, Bective, Co. Meath, Ireland.

LAVRENTIEV Alexander Nikolaevich, b. 12 May 1954, Moscow, Russia. Designer; Art Historian. m. Presnetsova irina Sergeevna, 6 Nov 1974, 1 daughter. *Education:* Grad, Faculty of Industrial Art, Moscow Indsitute of Industrial and Applied Arts, 1976; PhD, Art History, 1983. *Appointments:* Freelance Critic, Soviet Photo, 1977; Freelance Author, Sovetsky Khudosznik, 1982. *Publications:* Varvara Stepanova: A Constructivist Life, 1988; Rodchenko Photography, 1982; Rodchenko Stepanova Family Workshop, 1989; Rodtschenko Stepanova, Die Zukunft ist unser einziges Ziel; Exhibition Catalogue, 1991. *Contributions to:* Soviet Photo; Tehnicheskaya Estetica; DAPA, Journal of Agitational and Propaganda Art; Art and Design; Interpressgraphic. *Membership:* Union of Journalists; Union of Designers; Union of Photo-Artists. *Address:* Miasnitskaya 21 apt 18, Moscow 101000, Russia.

LAWLER Patrick, b. 12 Sept 1948, Syracuse, New York, USA. Professor. m. Janet Dimento, 7 Sept 1974, 1 daughter. *Education:* MA Creative Writing, Syracuse University, 1981; BA English, LeMoyne College, 1976. *Appointments:* Writing Project Coordinator, SUNY Environmental Science and Forestry, 1990-; Creative Writing Teacher, Onondago Community College, Syracuse, 1978-. *Publications:* A Drowning Man is Never Tall Enough, 1990. *Contributions to:* American Poetry Review; Central park; The Iowa Review; The Literary Review; New York Times Book Review; Ohio Journal; Poetry Wales; Southern Humanities Review. *Honours:* NY State Foundation for the Arts, 1989; National Enndowment for the Arts, 1990. *Memberships:* Poets and Writes; Community Writers Project, Board, 1989. *Address:* 103 Saltwell Drive, Liverpool, NY 13090, USA.

LAWRENCE Berta, b. United Kingdom. Author. *Publications:* A Somerset Journal, 1951; Quantock Country, 1952; The Bond of Green Withy, 1954; The Nightingale in the Branches, 1955; Coleridge and Wordsworth in Somerset, 1970; Somerset Legends, 1973; Discovering the Quantocks, 1974; Exmoor

Villages, 1984. *Address:* 17 Wembdon Hill, Bridgwater, Somerset, TA6 7PX, England.

LAWRENCE Clifford Hugh, b. 28 Dec 1921, London, England. Professor of Mediaeval History. m. Helen Maud Curran, 11 July 1953, 1 son, 5 daughters. *Education:* Lincoln College, Oxford, 1946-51; BA Hons, Class I, History, 1948; MA, 1953; DPhil (Oxon), 1955. *Publications:* St Edmund of Abingdon: A Study of Hagiography and History, 1960; The English Church and the Papacy, 1965; Medieval Monasticism. Forms of Religious Life in Western Europe in the Middle Ages, 1984, 2nd Edition, 1989; The University in State and Church, 1984. *Contributions to:* Articles and reviews to: English Historical Review; History; Journal of Ecclesiastical History; The Month; The Tablet; Times Literary Supplement; Times Higher Education Supplement; The Spectator; Other. *Memberships:* Fellow, Royal Historical Society; Society of Antiquaries; Reform Club. *Address:* 11 Durham Road, London SW20 0QH, England.

LAWRENCE Jerome, b. 1915, USA. Playwright; Lyricist; Biographer. *Appointments:* Partner, 1942-, President, 1955, Lawrence and Lee Inc, New York City and Los Angeles; Professor of Playwriting: University of Southern California, New York University, Baylor University and Ohio State University; Member, Board of Directors: American Conservatory Theatre, National Repertory Theatre, American Playwrights' Theatre. *Publications:* Look, Ma, I'm Dancin' (co-author), musical, 1948; Inherit the Wind (with Robert E Lee), 1955; Auntie Mame (with Lee), 1957; The Gang's All Here (with Lee), 1960; Only In America (with Lee), 1960; Checkmate (with Lee), 1961; Mame (co-author), musical, 1967; Dear World, musical, 1969; Sparks Fly Upward (co-author), 1969; The Night Thoreau Spent in Jail (with Lee), 1970; Live Spelled Backwards, 1970; The Incomparable Max (with Lee), 1972; The Crocodile Smile (with Lee), 1972; Actor: The Life and Times of Paul Muni, 1974; Jabberwock (with Lee), 1974; First Monday in October (with Lee), 1975; Whisper in the Mind (with Lee and Norman Cousins), 1987. *Memberships:* Board of Directors, Dramatists Guild; Board of Directors, Authors League. *Address:* 21056 Las Flores Mesa Drive, Malibu, CA 90265, USA.

LAWRENCE Karen, b. 18 Mar 1949, NY, USA. Professor. m. Peter F. Lawrence, 27 June 1971, 2 sons. *Education:* BA, Yale University, 1971; MA, Tufts University, 1973; PhD, Columbia University, 1978. *Appointments:* Assistant Professor 1978-82, Associate Professor of English 1982-, Chairperson of Department 1984-89, University of Utah, Salt Lake City; Member of Board of Trustees of James Joyce Foundation; Member of Executive Committee of Association of Departments of English; Professor, 1989-. *Publications:* The Odyssey of Style in Ulysses, 1981; The McGraw-Hill Guide to English Literature (with Betsy Siefter and Lois Ratner), 1985; Decolonizing Tradition: New Views of Twentieth-Century 'British' Literary Canons (ed), 1991. *Contributions to:* The Cambridge Companion to Joyce Studies; Literature Journals, including English Literary History, Nineteenth-Century Literature, and Western Humanities Review. *Honour:* Guggenheim Foundation Fellowship, 1989-90. *Memberships:* Modern Language Association of America; President, International James Joyce Foundation; Society for the Study of Narrative; Utah Women's Forum. *Address:* Department of English, University of Utah, Salt Lake City, UT 84112, USA.

LAWRENCE Karen Ann, b. 5 Feb 1951, Windsor, Ontario, Canada. Writer. m. Robert Gabhart, 18 Dec 1982, 1 son. *Education:* BA (Hons), University of Windsor, 1973; MA, University of Alberta, 1977. *Publications:* The Life of Helen Alone, 1986; Springs of Living Water, 1990; The Life of Helen Alone, Screenplay 1987; Nekuia: The Inanna Poems, 1980. *Honours:* W H Smith/Books in Canada First Novel Award, 1987; Best First Novel Award, PEN, Los Angeles Center, 1987. *Memberships:* Authors Guild; Writers' Union of Canada; ACTRA, (Canada). *Literary Agent:*

Esther Newberg, ICM Inc, 40 W 57th Street, NY 10019, New York, USA. *Address:* 2153 Pine Street, San Diego, CA 92103-1522, USA.

LAWRENCE Louise, b. 5 June 1943, Surrey, England. Novelist. m. Graham Mace, 28 Aug 1987, 1 son, 2 daughters. *Education:* Leatherhead Poplar Road Primary School, 1948-56; Lydney Grammar School, Gloucestershire, 1956-61. *Publications:* Andra, 1971; Power of Stars, 1972; Wyndcliffe, 1974; Sing and Scatter Daisies, 1977; Star Lord, 1978; Cat Call, 1980; Earth Witch, 1981; Calling B for Butterfly, 1982; Dram Road, 1983; Children of the Dust, 1985; Moonwind, 1986; Warriors of Taan, 1986; Extinction is Forever, 1990. *Address:* 22 Churxh Road, Cinderford, Gloucestershire GL14 2EA, England.

LAWRENCE P. *See:* **TUBB E C.**

LAWRENCE Steven C. *See:* **MURPHY Lawrence Agustus.**

LAWSON Chet. *See:* **TUBB E C.**

LAWSON James, b. 1938, USA. Author; Company Vice-President. *Appointments:* Copywriter, McCann-Marschalk Advertising, 1961-62; Reporter, Aspen Times, Colorado, 1962; Copywriter, J Walker Thompson Advertising, New York City, 1963-64; Copywriter, Al Paul Lefton Advertising, Philadelphia, Pennsylvania, 1964-66; Vice-President, Copy Supervisor, Doyle Dane Bernbach Advertising, New York City, 1966-78; Senior Vice-President, Director of Creative Services, Doremus and Co, New York City, 1978-80; Senior Vice President, Creative Director, DDB Needham Worldwide, New York City, 1982-. *Publications:* XXX, 1963; Disconnections, 1972; The American Book of the Dead, 1974; Crimes of the Unconcious, 1975; The Girl Watcher, 1976; The Copley Chronicles, 1980; The Fanatic, 1981; Forgeries of the Heart, 1981; The Madman's Kiss, 1987; Frederick Law Olmsted (teleplay), 1990. *Address:* 756 Greenwich Street, New York, NY 10014, USA.

LAYTON Andrea. *See:* **BANCROFT Iris.**

LAYTON Irving (Peter), b. 1912. Canadain, Poet; Professor of English Literature, York University, Toronto, 1968-78. *Appointments:* Associate Editor, First Statement, later Northern Review, Montreal, 1941- 43; former Associate Editor, Contact magazine, Toronto and Black Mountain Review, North Carolina; Lecturer, Jewish Public Library, Montreal, 1943-58; High School Teacher in Montreal, 1945-60; Part-time Lecturer, 1949-68 and Poet-in-Residence, 1965-69, Sir George Williams University, Montreal; Writer-in-Residence, University of Guelph, Ontario, 1969-70; Writer-in-Residence, University of Toronto, 1981; Adjunct Professor of Writer-in-Residence, Concordia University, 1988-89. *Publications include:* Collected Poems, 1965; (ed) Anvil: A Selection of Workshop Poems, 1966; Periods of the Moon: Poems, 1967; The Shattered Plinths, 1968; The Whole Bloody Bird (obs, aphs and pomes) 1969; Selected Poems, 1969; (ed) Poems to Colour: A Selection of Workshop Poems, 1970; Collected Poems, 1971; Nail Polish, 1971; Engagements: The Prose of Irving Layton, 1972; Lovers and Lesser Men, 1973; (ed) Anvil Blood: A Selection of Workshop Poems, 1973; The Pole-Valuter, 1974; Seventy- Five Greek Poems, 1974; Selected Poems, 2 vols, 1975; For My Borther Jesus, 1976; The Uncollected Poems, 1936-59, 1976; The Poems of Irving Layton, 1977; The Covenant, 1977; Taking Sides: The Collected Social and Political Writings, 1977; The Tightrope Dancer, 1978; Droppings from Heaven, 1979; The Love Poems of Irving Layton, 1979; There Were No Signs, 1979; An Unlikely Affair: The Correspondence of Irving Layton and Dorothy Rath, 1979; For My Neighbors in Hell, 1980; Europe and Other Bad News, 1981; A Wild Peculiar Joy, 1982; The Gucci Bag 1983; With Reverence and Delight: The Love Poems, 1984; A Spider Danced a Cozy Jig, 1984; Fortunate Exile, 1987; The Complete Correspondence

1953-1978 (with Robert Creeley), 1990. *Address:* 6879 Monkland Avenue, Montreal, Quebec, Canada H4B 1J5.

LAZARUS Arnold Leslie, b. 20 Feb 1914, Revere, Massachusetts, USA. Writer. m. Keo Felker, 24 July 1938, 2 sons, 2 daughters. *Education:* BA, English and Classics, University of Michigan, 1935; BS, Middlesex Medical School, 1937; MA, 1939; PhD, 1957, UCLA. *Appointments:* English and Drama Teacher, Santa Monica, CA, 1945-53; Literature Teacher, Technical Direcotr, Theatre, Santa Monica City College, 1953-58. *Publications:* Harbrace Adventures in Literature, (with R. Lowell and E. Hardwick), 1970; Modern English, (with others), 1970; The Indiana Experience, 1977; Best of George Ade, 1985; Some Light, (new and selected verse), 1988; A George Jean Nathan Reader, 1990; Entertainments and Valedictions, 1970; A Suit of Four, 1973; Beyond Graustark (with Vicotr H. Jones), 1981; Glossary of Literature and Compopsition, (with H. Wendell Smith), Urbana: Note, 1983. *Contributions to:* over 200 poems and reviews in various periodicals. *Honours:* Ford Foundation Fellow, 1954; Purdue University, Best Teacher Award, 1974; Kemper McComb Award, 1976; US. Office of Education Grant, 1963; Chief Midwest Judge, Book of the Month Club Writing Fellowships, 1967-70. *Memberships:* Phi Beta Kappa; Academy of American Poets; Poetry Society of America; American Society for Theatre Research; Comparative Literature Association; Screenwriters Association of Santa Barabara; Modern Language Association of America; National Council of Teachers of English; College English Association. *Literary Agent:* Andrea Brown, 319 East 52nd Street, New York, NY 10022, USA. *Address:* 709 Chopin Drive, Sunnyvale, CA 94087, USA.

LE CARRE John. *See:* **CORNWELL David John Moore.**

LE GUIN Ursula K(roeber), b. 1929, USA. Fiction Writer; Poet; Essayist. *Publications:* Rocannon's World, 1966; Planet of Exile, 1966; City of Illusion, 1967; A Wizard of Earthsea, 1968; The Left Hand of Darkness, 1969; The Tombs of Atuan, 1971; The Lathe of Heaven, 1971; The Farthest Shore, 1972; The Dispossessed, 1974; The Wind's Twelve Quarters, short stories, 1975; Wild Angels, poetry, 1975; A Very Long Way from Anywhere Else, 1976; The Word for World Is Forest, 1976; Orsinian Tales (short stories), 1976; Nebula Award Stories 11 (editor), 1977; The Language of the Night, essays, 1978; Leese Webster, 1979; Malafrena, 1979; The Beginning Place, UK Edition Threshold, 1980; Interfaces (edited with Virginia Kidd), 1980; Edges (edited with Virginia Kidd), 1981; Hard Words and Other Poems, (poetry), 1981; The Compass Rose, short stories, 1982; The Eye of the Heron, 1983; In the Red Zone, poetry, 1983; The Visionary, 1984; Always Coming Home, 1985; Buffalo Gals and Other Animal Presences, (short stories) 1987; Solomon Leviathan's 931st Trip Around the World, 1988; A Visit From Dr Katz, 1988; Wild Oats and Fireweed, (poetry), 1988; Catwings, 1988; Catwings Return, 1989; Fire and Stone, 1989; Dancing at the Edge of the World, (essays), 1989; Tehanu: The last Book to Earthsea, 1990; Searoad, 1991; A Ride on the Red Mare's Back, 1992; Fish Soup, 1992. *Honour:* Boston Globe-Hornbook Award, 1968; Hugo Award, 1969, 1972, 1973, 1975, 1988; Nebula Award, 1969, 1975, 1991; Newbery Honor Medal, 1972; National Book Award, 1972; Gandalf Award, 1979; Janet Heidinger Kafka Award, 1986; Prix Lectures-Jeunesse 1987; International Fantasy Award 1988; Pushcart Prize Story 1991; Harold D Vursell Award, American Academy & Institute of Letters, 1991; Writers of Distinction Award, National Council for Research on Women, 1992. *Literary Agent:* (All Rights), Virginia Kidd, *Address:* c/ o Virginia Kidd, Box 278, Milford, PA 18337, USA.

LE ROI David de Roche, (John Roche), b. 1915, United Kingdom. Freelance Journalist, Writer and Editor. *Appointments:* Associate Editor, New Universal Encyclopedia, 1945-49; Executive Editor, Household Encyclopedia, 1950-51; Assistant Editor, Waverley Technical Publications, 1962; Executive Editor, World of Wonder, 1953-54; Science and Technical Editor, Book of Knowledge, 1955-56; Science Editor, Children's Encyclopedia, 1957-59; Science Editor, Chief Feature Writer, 1960-64, currently Advisory Science Editor, IPC Publications, London; Editor, Marts Press, 1977. *Publications:* Book of Jets, 1949; Aeronautics, 1950; Things to Make and Do, 1951; Sea, Land and Air Weapons, 1952; Hamsters and Guinea Pigs, 1955; The Aquarium, 1955; Pigeons, 1957; Town Dogs, 1957; Book of Inventions, 1957; Tortoises and Lizards, 1958; Cage Birds, 1958; Book of Flight, 1958; Modern Wonders, 1958; Jets and Rockets, 1959; Nuclear Power, 1959; Radio, Radar and Television, 1959; Modern Agriculture, 1960; Man-Made Materials, 1960; Modern Medicine, 1960; Look at Roads, 1961; How We Get Our Oil, 1962; Aluminium, 1963; Cats, 1963; Science Today and Tomorrow, 1964; Treasure Book of Animals, 1966; Second Treasure Book of Animals, 1967; How it Works, 1967; Book of Wonders of Nature, 1967; Third Treasure Book of Animals, 1968; Second Book of Wonders of Nature, 1968; 1001 Questions and Answers, 1968; Fourth Treasure Book of Animals, 1969; New Ideas for this Modern Age, 1969; Third Book of Wonders of Nature, 1969; The Channel Tunnel, 1969; Book of Firsts, 1973; In the Days of the Dinosaurs, 1974; Rabbits, 1974; Prehistoric Life, 1975; Stars and Planets, 1975; Mice and Gerbils, 1976; Ponies and Donkeys, 1976; Goats, 1977. *Address:* 12 Kirklees Road, Thornton Heath, Surrey CR4 6HP, England.

LE ROY Claude, b. 13 Mar 1937, Orne, France. Headmaster. *Literary Appointment:* Director of magazine NOREAL founded in 1972. *Publications:* Anthologies of Norman Poets, 1971, 1972, 1980; Picking, Drinking and Eating, 1981; The Memory of the Streets, 1982; In the Shady Corner of the Mirror, 1985; Poems from a 50 Years Old Man, 1987; Fingers of Light for Gloomy Ways, 1989; The Templar's Cry, 1969, (all in French except Fingers of Light for Gloomy Ways, which was written in English); Gens De Chez Nous (People From Here), 1991. *Contributions to:* International Poetry (USA); World Poetry 1989 (COREA), several magazines in Italy and France. *Membership:* Societe des Gens de Lettres, Paris. *Address:* College Jean Moulin, Rue de Broceliande, 14000 Caen, France.

LEA Tom, b. 1907, USA. Writer; Artist; Illustrator. *Appointments:* Freelance Artist and Illustrator, 1936- ; Artist, Correspondent, Life magazine, 1941-45; Freelance Writer, 1947-. *Publications:* John W Norton, American Painter 1876-1934 (with Thomas E Tallmadge), 1935; George Catlin Westward Bound a Hundred Years Ago, 1939; Randado, 1941; A Grizzly from the Coral Sea, short stories, 1944; Peleliu Landing, 1945; A Calendar of Twelve Travelers Through the Pass of the North, 1946; Bullfight Manual for Spectators, 1949; The Brave Bulls, novel, 1949; The Wonderful Country, novel, 1952; Western Beef Cattle: A Series of Eleven Paintings, 1950; Tom Lea: A Portfolio of Six Paintings, 1953; The Stained Glass Designs in McKee Chapel, Church of Saint Clement, El Paso, Texas, 1953; The King Ranch, 1957; The Primal Yoke, novel, 1960; Maud Durlin Sullivan 1872- 1944: Pioneer Southwestern Librarian: A Tribute, 1962; The Hands of Cantu, novel, 1964; A Picture Gallery, 1968; In the Crucible of the Sun, 1974. *Address:* 2401 Savannah Street, El Paso, TX 79930, USA.

LEACH Penelope, b. 19 Nov 1937, London, England. Psychologist. m. Gerald Leach, 23 Mar 1963, 1 son, 1 daughter. *Education:* BA, Cantab, 1959; Graduate Diploma in Social Sciences, LSE, 1961; PhD, Psychology, London 1964. *Publications include:* Baby and Child (American: Your Baby and Child) 1977, 1989; The Parents' A-Z (American: Your Growing Child) 1985; Babyhood, Revised edition 1983; The First Six Months: Coming to Terms with your Baby, 1986; The Babypack (American: The Babykit) 1990. Videos: England: Becoming a Family; Baby to Toddler; Toddler to Child, Virgin Video, 1988; USA: Your Baby, Sidney Place Communications, 1990; Your Baby and Child With Penelope Leach. *Contributions to:* Numerous journals and magazines; Year-long series in Parenting Magazine,

1990-91; Year-long series in Redbook Magazine, 1992-93. *Honours:* Fellow, British Psychological Society, 1989; CableAce Award, Best Informational Television Presentation, 1993. *Membership:* Society of Authors. *Address:* 3 Tanza Road, London NW3 2UA, England.

LEALE B C, b. 1 Sept 1930, Ashford, Middlesex, England. Bookseller; Poet. *Publications:* Under a Glass Sky, 1975; Preludes, 1977; Leviathan and other poems, 1984; The Colours of Ancient Dreams, 1984. *Contributions to:* Magazines and journals including: Ambit; Encounter; The Fiction Magazine; Kayak; The Listener; The Literary Review; London Review of Books; Montana Gothic; The Observer; Pacific Quarterly; Poetry Review; A Review of English Literature; Second Aeon; The Spectator; Stand; The Times Literary Supplement; Tribune. Anthologies: Best of the Poetry Year 6; A Group Anthology; New Poems 1963 and 1977-78; New Poetry 1, 2, 4, 6, 7 and 9; New Writing and Writers 16 and 18; PEN New Poetry 1; The Poetry Book Society Anthology 1986/87; Voices in the Gallery; Double Vision. *Address:* Flat E10, Peabody Estate, Wild Street, London WC2B 4AH, England.

LEAN Geoffrey, b. 21 Apr 1947, London, England. Journalist; Author. m. Judith Eveline Wolfe, 24 June 1972, 1 son, 1 daughter. *Education:* BA, Oxford University. *Appointments:* Graduate Trainee, 1969; Feature Writer 1973, Environment Correspondent, 1973, Yorkshire Post; Reporter, 1977, Environment Correspondent, 1979-, The Observer; Environment Consultant, Country Life, 1987-89; Presented 'Go For Green', magazine environment programme, BSB, 1990; Director, Central Observer, 1990-. *Publications:* Rich World, Poor World, 1978; Chernobyl, The End of the Nuclear Dream, co-author, 1986; Atlas of the Environment, general editor, 1990-92. *Contributions To:* Numerous contributions to International and Specialist Journals; Consultancies to Food and Agriculture Organisation, 1981; United Nations Environment Programme, 1982-; World Bank, 1992; Edited, State of the Environment Report, UNEP, 1983, 1984, 1986, 1988, 1989; Environment: A Dialogue Among Nations, UNEP, 1985; Radiation, Doses, Effects, Risks, UNEP, 1985, revised 1992; Action on Ozone, UNEPP, 1989, 1990. *Honours:* Runner Up, Young Journalist of the Year, British National Press Awards, 1972; Yorkshire Council for Social Service Press Award, 1972; Glaxo Travelling Fellowship, 1973; World Environment Festival Rose Award, 1986; UN Global 500, 1987; Special Awareness Award, British Environment and Media Awards, 1991; Clear Award, 1989; Design Award of Excellence, 1986; Runner-Up, RSPB Press Award, 1988. *Literary Agent:* Caradoc King, A P Watt and Son. *Address:* The Observer, Chelsea Bridge House, Queenstown Road, London SW8 4NN, England.

LEAPMAN Michael Henry, b. 24 Apr 1938, London, England. Writer; Journalist. m. Olga Mason, 15 July 1965, 1 son. *Appointments:* Journalist, The Times, 1969-81. *Publications:* One Man and His Plot, 1976; Yankee Doodles, 1982; Companion Guide to New York, 1983; Barefaced Cheek, 1983; Treachery, 1984; The Last Days of the Beeb, 1986; Kinnock, 1987; The Book of London (Editor), 1989; London's River, 1991; Treacherous Estate, 1992. *Contributions to:* numerous magazines & journals. *Honours:* Campaigning Journalist of the Year, British Press Award, 1968; Thomas Cook Travel Book Award, Best Guide Book of 1983. *Memberships:* Society of Authors; National Union of Journalists. *Literary Agent:* Felicity Bryan. *Address:* 13 Aldebert Terrace, London SW8 1BH, England.

LEAR Cyril James, b. 9 Sept 1911. Editorial Manager. m. Marie Chatterton, 5 sons, 1 daughter. *Appointments:* Western Morning News, 1928-32; Torquay Times, 1932-34; Daily Mail, 1934-38; Daily Telegraph, 1938-39; Features Editor, Assistant Editor, Deputy Editor, News of the World, 1946-70; Editorial Manager, News Group Newspapers, 1974-76. *Address:* c/o News International Ltd., 30 Bouverie Street, London EC4, England.

LEAR Martha Weinman, b. 1932, USA. Writer. *Appointments:* Assistant Editor, Collier's magazine, New York City, 1951-55; Associate Editor, Women's Home Companion, New York City, 1955-56; Writer, NBC, New York City, 1956-57; Editor, The New York Times Sunday Magazine, 1957-61. *Publications:* The Child Worshipers, 1964; Heartsounds, 1980. *Address:* c/o Simon and Schuster, 1239 Avenue of the Americas, New York, NY 10020, USA.

LEAR Peter. *See:* **LOVESEY Peter.**

LEASOR (Thomas) James, b. 20 Dec 1923, Erith, Kent, England. Author; Member of Lloyds. m. Joan Margaret Bevan (LLB, Barrister-At-Law), 1 Dec 1951, 3 sons. *Education:* City of London School; Oriel College, Oxford, BA Honours, 1948, MA Honours 1952. *Literary Appointments:* Feature Writer, Foreign Correspondent, Daily Express, London, 1948-55; Editorial Advisor, Publishing Company, Newnes and Pearson, Later IPC, 1955-69; Director, Publishing Company, Elm Tree Books, 1970-73. *Publications:* novels and works of non-fiction; several have been filmed and many published in up to 19 foreign editions; Most recent pub's inc, Boarding Party, 1977; Who Killed Sir Harry Oakes, 1983; The Maine from Mandalay, 1988; The Unknown Warrior, 1980. *Memberships:* FRSA (Fellow of Royal Society of Arts); O.St.J. (Order of St. John). *Address:* Swallowcliffe Manor, Salisbury. Wiltshire, SP3 5PB, England.

LEAVER Ruth. *See:* **TOMALIN Ruth.**

LEBIODA Dariusz Thomas, b. 23 Apr 1958, Bydgoszcz, Poland. University Teacher. m. Danuta Mary Futyma, 25 June 1983, 1 son. *Education:* MA, Higher Pedagogical School, 1984. *Appointments:* Teacher 1983-84, Grammar School Teacher, 1984-85, University Teacher, Higher Pedagogical School, 1985-; Editor, quarterly magazine Metorfora, 1989-. *Publications:* Poems: Suicides from Under the Charles' Wain, 1980; Mary, 1982; The Newest Testament, 1983; A Moment Before the End of the World, 1988; The Ground of Dying European Roller, 1988; Cry My Generation (Selected Poems 1980-1990), 1990; Stories: Pilots of the Ultra-Violet Distances, 1987, 1990; The Wounded of the Childhood in preparation; Novels: Trilogy (in preparation). *Contributor to:* The Art; Miesiecznik Literacki, Literature Life; Culture, Poetry and numerous other magazines. *Honours:* Andrzej Bursa Prize for Poetry, 1984; Red Rose prize, 1984; Klemens Janicki Prize, 1988; Stanislav Wyspianski Artistic Prize for Literature, 1989. *Memberships:* Adam Mickiewicz Literary Society; Henryk Sienkiewicz Literary Society; Polish Writers Union. *Address:* Osiedlowa 18 m 16, 85-792 Bydgoszcz, Poland.

LEBOW Jeanne, b. 29 Jan 1951, Richmond, Virginia, USA. Writer; Teacher. m. (1) Howard Lebow, (2) Steve Shepard, 5 July 1985. *Education:* AB, College of William and Mary, 1973; MA, Hollins College, 1982; PhD, University of Southern Mississippi, 1989. *Appointments:* Instructor, Memphis State University, 1982-84; Graduate Teaching Assistant, University of Southern Mississippi, 1984-87; Fulbright Professor, University of Ouagadougou, West Africa, 1987-88; Assistant Professor, Northeast Missouri State University, 1988-92; Currently Adjunct Professor, University of Southern Mississippi, Gulf Coast. *Publications:* The Outlaw James Copeland and the Champion-Belted Empress, 1991. *Contributions to:* Poems to; New Virginia Review; South Florida Poetry Review; Nimrod; Chariton Review; Poems and essays to various anthologies. *Honours:* National Award, Georgia State Poetry Society, 1983; Fulbright Grant to West Africa, 1987-88; Runner- up, Norma Farber First Book Award, 1991. *Memberships:* Associated Writing Programs; Modern Language Association; Session Chair for Regional Groups. *Literary Agent:* Mark Rosoff of Scott Meredith. *Address:* PO Box 290, Gautier, MS 39553, USA.

LEBRUN Claude Odile, b. 13 Aug 1929, France. Professor. m. Francois Lebrun, 7 Apr 1956, 2 sons. *Education:* Lic de Lettres Modernes, 1953; Lic Libre d'Anglais, 1953; Diplome detudes Superieures de Letteres, 1954; Capes de Lettres Modernes, 1956. *Publications:* Invitation a Jean Sulivan, 1981; 1000 mots pour seussir (an lycie), 1987. *Contributions to:* Little Brown Bear. *Address:* Alle Cassandie, 41899 Couture sur Loir, France.

LEDOUX Paul Martin, b. 4 Nov 1949, Halifax, Nova Scotia, Canada. Dramatist. m. Ferne Downey. *Education:* BA, Dalhousie University, Halifax; Postgraduate work, NSCAD, Halifax. *Publications include:* Love is Strange, 1985; Children of the Night, 1986; Fire, 1987. Also numerous teleplays & radio dramas. *Honours:* Best play, Quebec Drama Festival, 1975; Outstanding Drama, Chalmer Award, 1989; Dora Manor Moore Award, Best Canadian Drama, Toronto, 1990. *Memberships:* Chairman 1985-87, Playwrights Union of Canada; ACTRA; Dramatists Guild; CAPAC; Dramatists Cooperative of Nova Scotia. *Literary Agent:* Katherine Martin. *Address:* 41 Cowan Avenue, Toronto, Ontario, Canada M6K 2N1.

LEE Dennis Beynon, b. 31 Aug 1939, Toronto, Canada. Writer. m. (1) 1 son, 2 daughters, (2) Susan Perly, 1985. *Education:* BA, 1962, MA 1965, University of Toronto. *Appointments:* Editor, House of Anansi Press, 1967-72; Consulting Editor, Macmillan of Canada, 1972-78; Poetry Editor, McClelland and Stewart, 1981-84. *Publications:* Children's Poetry: Wiggle to the Laundromat, 1970; Alligator Pie, 1974; Nicholas Knock, 1974; Garbage Delight, 1977; Jelly Belly, 1983; Lizzy's Lion, 1984; The Ice Cream Store, 1991. Children's Tale: The Ordinary Bath, 1979. Adult Poetry: Kingdom of Absence, 1967; Civil Elegies, 1972; The Gods, 1979; The Difficulty of Living on Other Planets, 1988; Riffs, 1993. Adults Non-Fiction: Savage Fields, 1977. *Contributions to:* Magazines and journals. *Honour:* Governor General's Award for Poetry, 1972. *Memberships:* Writers' Union of Canada; PEN, Canada. *Address:* c/o MGA, 10 St Mary Street No 510, Toronto, Canada M4Y 1P9.

LEE Don L, b. 1942, USA. Writer; Poet; Editor; Publisher. *Appointments:* Editor, Publisher, Third World Press, Chicago, Illinois, 1967-; Writer-in-Residence, Cornell University, Ithaca, New York, 1968-69; Poet-in-Residence, Northeastern Illinois State College, Chicago, 1969-70; Lecturer, University of Illinois, Chicago, 1969-71; Writer-in-Residence, Howard University, Washington, District of Columbia, 1971-75; Writer-in- Residence, Morgan State College, Baltimore, Maryland, 1972-73; Editor, Black Books Bulletin, Chicago, 1972-. *Publications:* Think Black, 1967; Black Pride, 1968; Back Again, Home, 1968; One Sided Shoot-Out, 1968; For Black People (and Negroes Too), 1968; Don't Cry, Scream, 1969; We Walk the Way of the New World, 1970; Dynamite Voices: Black Poets of the 1960s, 1971; To Gwen with Love (edited with P L Brown and F Ward), 1971; Directionscore: Selected and New Poems, 1971; Book of Life, poetry, 1973; From Plan to Planet: Life Studies; The Need for Afrikan Minds and Institutions, 1973; Enemies: The Clash of Races, 1978. *Address:* Third World Press, 7524 S Cottage Grove, Chicago, IL 60619, USA.

LEE Elsie, (Elsie Cromwell, Norman Daniels, Jane Gordon, Lee Sheridan), b. 1912, American, Writer of Historical, Romance, Gothic, Cookery, Gardening publications. *Appointments:* Librarian, Waterhouse and Co, New York City, 1937-42; Office Manager, Reeves Laboratories, New York City, 1942-45; Librarian, Gulf Oil Co, New York City, 1947-51; Executive Secretary, Andrews Clark and Buckley, New York City, 1951-53; Currently full-time writer. *Publications:* Novels: The Spy at the Vila Miranda, 1967, in Uk as The Unhappy Parting, 1973; Doctor's Office, 1968; (as Elsie Cromwell), The Governess, 1969, in UK as Guardian of Love, 1972; Satan's Coast, 1969, in UK as Mystery Castle, 1973; Fulfilment, 1969; Barrow Sinister, 1969, in UK as Romantic Assignment, 1974; (as Elsie Cromwell), Ivorstone Manor, 1970; Silence Is Golden, 1971; Wingarden, 1971; The Diplomatic Lover, 1971; Star of Danger, 1971; The Passions of Medora Graeme, 1972; A Prior Betrothal, 1973; The Wicked Guardian, 1973; Second Season, 1973; An Eligible Connection, 1974; Roommates, 1976; The Habob's Widow, 1976; Mistress of Mount Fair, 1977; other: (as Lee Sheridan, with Michael Sheridan), How to Get the Most Out of Your Tape Recording, 1958; (as Lee Sheridan, with Michael Sheridan), More Fun with Your Tape Recorders and Stereo, 1958; The Exciting World of Rocks and Gems, 1959; Easy Gourmet Cooking, 1962; (as Lee Sheridan; with Michael Sheridan), The Bachelor's Cookbook, 1962; At Home with Planets: A Guide to Successful Indoor Gardening, 1966; Second Easy Gourmet Cookbook, 1968; Book of Simple Gourmet Cookery, 1971; Party Cookbook, 1974. *Address:* c/o Bill Berger Associates, 444 E 58th Street, New York, NY 10022, USA.

LEE Hamilton, b. 10 Oct 1921, Chowhsien, Shandong, China. Professor Emeritus (Education). m. Jean C. Chang, 24 Aug 1945, 1 son, 3 daughters. *Education:* BS, National Peking Teachers University, 1948; MA, University of Minnesota, Minneapolis, USA, 1958; EdD, Wayne State University, Detroit, Michigan, 1964. *Appointments:* English Teacher, Taiwan High Schools, Taiwan, China, 1948-56; Research Associate, Wayne State University, Detroit, Michigan, USA, 1958-64; Visiting Professor of Chinese Literature, Seton Hall University, summer 1964; Assistant Professor, Moorhead State University, 1964-1965; Associate Professor, University of Wisconsin, 1965-66; Professor, East Stroudsburg University, 1966-84; Visiting Scholar, Harvard University, summer 1965 and 1966; Visiting Fellow, Princeton University, 1976-78; Professor Emeritus, East Stroudsburg University, East Stroudsberg, Pennsylvania, 1984-. *Publications:* Readings In Instructional Technology, 1970; Reflection, chap book, 1988; Chap book, Revelation, 1989; Golden Voices, anthology, 1989; Works in numerous anthologies, 1974-. *Contributions to:* Education Tomorrow, 1974-76; World Future Society; Byline; Poetry Norwest; Today Poetry; Various small literary magazines, 1974-. *Honours:* Numerous honourable mentions and awards in poetry contests, 1974-. *Memberships:* Poetry Society of America; Pennsylvania Poetry Society; Phi Delta Kappa; Former Member, numerous societies including: World Future Society; American Association of University Professors; AACI. *Address:* 961 Long Woods Drive, Stroudsburg, PA 18360, USA.

LEE John, b. 1931, USA. Writer; Former Professor. *Appointments:* Photographer: Fort Worth Star-Telegram, Fort Worth, Texas, 1952-57; Denver Post, Denver, Colorado, 1958-60; Professor of Journalism: American University, Washington, District of Columbia, 1965-67; University of Arizona, Tucson, 1967-71; New York University, 1971-74; California State University, Long Beach, 1975-76; Memphis State University, 1984-. *Publications:* Caught in the Act, 1968; Diplomatic Persuaders, 1968; Assignation in Algeria, 1971; The Ninth Man, 1976; The Thirteenth Hour, 1978; Lago, 1980; Stalag Texas, 1990. *Literary Agent:* Don Congdon Associates Inc. *Address:* c/o Don Congdon Associates Inc, 156 Fifth Avenue, Suite 625, New York, NY 10010, USA.

LEE Joyce Isabel, b. 19 June 1913, Murtoa, Australia. Pharmacist; Lecturer. m. Norman Edward, 18 Dec 1937, 2 sons. *Education:* Methodist Ladies' College; Registered Pharmacist, Victorian College of Pharmacy, Melbourne. *Literary Appointments:* Lecturer/Tutor (Poetry Writing) Victoria College of Advanced Education, Toorak Campus, 1981-. *Publications:* Sisters Poets 1, 1979, reprinted 1979, 1980; Abruptly from the Flatlands, 1984 reprinted 1984; Plain Dreaming, 1991. *Contributions to:* Meanjin; Poetry Australia; The Age; The Bulletin; Luna; Compass; Contempa; New Europe; Premier Poets and various anthologies; New Oxford Book of Australian Verse, 1986; The Penguin Book of

Australian Women Poets, 1986. *Honours:* Literature Board Grants 1977 and 1982; Maryborough Golden Wattle Festival, 1st Prize for Poetry; Grenfull Henry Lawson Prize for Verse, 1978; Poetry Prize, Communicating Arts Centre, 1981; McWarana Prize for Poetry, 1982. *Memberships:* International PEN Melbourne; Fellowship of Australian Writers; Poets Union; Treasurer, Past-President, Parish Press Co-op Ltd; Australian Society of Authors, 1989; The Association for the Study of Australian Literature, ASAL, 1989. *Address:* 13/205 Burke Road, Glen IRIS, Victoria 3146, Australia.

LEE Kuei-shien, b. 19 June 1937, Taipei, Taiwan. Patent Agent; Chemical Engineer; Corporation President. m. Huei-uei Wang, 1965. 1 son, 1 daughter. *Education:* Chemical Engineering, Taipei Institute of Technology, 1958; German Literature, European Language Center of Educational Ministry, 1964; PhD, Chemical Engineering (Honoris Causa), Marquis Giuseppe Scicluna International University Foundation, 1985. *Literary Appointments:* Director, Li Poetry Society; Publisher, Inventors Journal; Examiner, Wu yong-fu Critique Prize. *Publications:* Essays include: Journey to Europe, 1971; Profile of the Souls, 1972; Essays on German Literature, 1973; On International Patent Practices, 1975; Critical Essays on Chinese Translation of English Poetry, 1976; Critical essays: On Taiwanese Poems, 1987. Poetry includes: Pagoda and Other Poems, 1963; The Loquat, 1964; Poems on Nankang, 1966; Naked Roses, 1976; Collected poems, 1985; Formation of Crystal, 1986; Transfusion, 1986; Eternal Territory, 1990. Anthologies include: Anthology of German Poems, 1970; Anthology of Black Orpheus, 1974; Year Book of Taiwanese Poems, 1987; Selected Poems of Li Poetry Society, 1992; Translations include: The Trial by Franz Kafka, 1969; Cat and Mouse by Gunter Grass, 1970; Rainer Maria Rilke by H E Holthusen, 1969; Duineser Elegien by R M Rilke, 1969; Die Sonnete an Orpheus by R M Rilke, 1969; Das Buch der Bilder, by R M Rilke, 1977; Selected Poems by Giosue Carducci, 1981; Selected Poems by Giogos Seferis, 1981; Selected Poems by Salvatore Quasimodo, 1981; Prussian Night by Alexander Solzhenitsyn, 1983. *Contributions to:* Numerous magazines and journals including: Taiwan Literature; Li Poetry; Capital Morning Posts; Liberty Times. *Honours include:* Outstanding Poet Award, 1967; Wu Tzu-lieu New Poetry Award, 1975; Chung Hsing Literary Medal for Poetry, 1978; Diploma di Merito, Universita delle Arti, Italy, 1982; The Poetic Critique Award of Li Poetry Society, 1984; Albert Einstein International Academy Foundation Bronze Medal for Peace, 1986; Critique Prize of Wu Yong-fu, 1986; Albert Einstein International Academy Foundation Alfred Nobel Medal for Peace, 1991. *Memberships include:* Founder Fellow, International Academy of Poets; Rilke-Gesellschaft; Vice President, Taiwan PEN, 1987. *Address:* Room 705, Asia Enterprise Center, No 142 Minchuan East Road, Sec 3, Taipei, Taiwan.

LEE Lance, b. 25 Aug 1942, New York, USA. Writer; Poet; Playwright. m. Jeanne Barbara Hutchings, 30 Aug 1962, 2 daughters. *Education:* Boston University; BA, Brandeis Univesity, 1964; MFA, Yale School of Drama, 1967. *Appointments include:* Lecturer, Bridgeport University, 1967-68; Instructor, Southern Connecticut State College, 1968; Assistant Professor, Senior Lecturer, 1968-71; University of Southern California, Lecturer, University of California, Los Angeles, 1971-73; Lecturer, Screenwriting, California State University, 1981-. *Publications:* Plays: Fox Hounds and Huntress, 1973; Time's Up, 1979; Productions: Time's Up; Gambits; Fox Hound and Huntress; Rasputin; Textbook: The Understructure of Writing for Film and Television, 1988; Wrestling with the Angel (poetry), 1990. *Contributions to:* Numerous journals & magazines including: Glass Onion; The Journal; Poem; Lake Superior Review; Midwest Poetry Review; Cottonwood Review; Embers; Cross Currents; Los Angeles Times; California Writers Issue; Poetry Northwest; Poetry LA; Negative Capability. *Honours:* Fellowships: Arts of the Theatre Foundation, 1967; University of Southern California Research and Publication Grants, 1970-71; Rockefeller Foundation, 1971; NEA, 1976; Theatre

Development Fund, 1976; Squaw Valley Community of Writers, 1982; Port Townsend (Centum), 1985; Theron Bamberger Award, Brandeis University. *Memberships:* Dramatists Guild; Authors League; American Acadmey of Poets; Poetry Society of America. *Literary Agent:* Samuel French, New York. *Address:* 1127 Galloway Street, Pacific Palisades, CA 90272, USA.

LEE Laurie, b. 1914, United Kingdom. Author; Poet. *Appointments:* Scriptwriter, Crown Film Unit, 1942-44; Publications Editor, Ministry of Information, 1944-46; Member, Green Park Film Unit, 1946-47; Caption Writer-in-Chief, Festival of Britain, 1950-51. *Publications:* The Dead Village, by Avigdor Dagan, translation, 1943; The Sun My Monument, 1944; Land at War, 1945; The Voyage of Magellan: A Dramatic Chronicle for Radio, 1946; The Bloom of Candles, 1947; Peasants' Priest: a Play, 1947; We Make a Film in Cyprus (with R Keene), 1947; New Poems 1954 (edited with C Hassall and Rex Warner), 1954; My Many-Coated Man, 1955; A Rose for Winter: Travels in Andalusia, 1956; Cider with Rosie, US Edition The Edge of Day, 1959; Poems, 1960; The Firstborn, essay on childhood, 1964; As I Walked Out One Midsummer Morning, autobiography, 1969; Pergamon Poets 10 (with Charles Causley), 1970; I Can't Stay Long, 1975; Innocence in the Mirror, 1978; Two Women, 1983; Selected Poems, 1983; A Moment of War, 1991. *Address:* c/o Andre Deutsch Ltd, 105 Great Russell Street, London WC1B 3LU, England.

LEE Robert E(dwin), b. 1918, USA. Dramatist; University Lecturer. *Appointments:* Director, Radio Station WHK-WCLE, Cleveland, Ohio, 1937- 38; Director, Young & Rubicam, New York City and Hollywood, California, 1938- 42; Partner, Lawrence & Lee, 1942-; Vice-President, Lawrence & Lee Inc, New York City and Los Angeles, California, 1955-; Professor of Playwriting, College of Theatre Arts, Pasadena Playhouse, California, 1962-63; Adjunct Professor, University of California, Los Angeles, 1966-; Co-Founder, American Playwrights Theatre. *Publications:* Television: The Revolutionary Industry, 1944; Shangri-La (with J Lawrence and James Hilton), 1956; With Jerome Lawrence: Inherit the Wind, 1955; Auntie Mame, 1956, Musical Version Mame, 1966; The Gang's All Here, 1959; Only in America, 1959; A Call on Kuprin, 1961; Sparks Fly Upward, 1967; The Incomparable Max, 1969; The Night Thoreau Spent in Jail, 1970; Jabberwock, 1972; The Crocodile Smile, 1972; First Monday in October, 1975; Sounding Brass, 1975; Whisper in the Mind (with Norman Cousins), 1990. *Honour:* Elected to Hall of Fame of American Theatre, 1990. *Address:* 15725 Royal Oak Road, Encino, CA 91436, USA.

LEE Tanith, b. 1947. United Kingdom. Freelance Writer (Science Fiction, Radio Plays, Children's Fiction). *Publications:* The Betrothed, short stories, 1968; The Dragon Hoard, juvenile, 1971; Princess Hynchatti and Some Other Surprises, juvenile, 1972; Animal Castle, juvenile, 1972; Companions on the Road, juvenile, 1975, US Edition Companions on the Road, and the Winter Players, 1977; The Birthgrave, 1975; Don't Bite the Sun, 1976; The Storm Lord, 1976; The Winter Players, juvenile, 1976; East of Midnight, juvenile, 1977; Drinking Sapphire Wine, 1977, 1977, UK Edition same title but including Don't Bite the Sun, 1979; Volkhavaar, 1977; Vazkor, Son of Vazkor, 1978, UK Edition Shadowfire, 1979; Quest for the White Witch, 1978; Night's Master, 1978; The Castle of Dark, juvenile, 1978; Shon the Taken, juvenile, 1979; Death's Master, 1979; Electric Forest, 1979; Sabella; or, The Blood Stone, 1980; Kill the Dead, 1980; Day by Night, 1980; Delusion's Master, 1981; The Silver Metal Lover, 1982; Cyrion, short stories, 1982; Prince on a White Horse, juvenile, 1982; Sung in Shadow, 1983; Anackire, 1983; Red as Blood; or, Tales from the Sisters Grimmer, 1983; The Dragon Hoard, 1984; The Beautiful Biting Machine, short stories, 1984; Tamastara, or, The Indian Nights, short stories, 1984; Days of Grass, 1985; The Gorgon and Other Beastly Tales, 1985; Dreams of Dark and

Light, 1986. *Address:* c/o Macmillan London Ltd, 4 Little Essex Street, London WC2R 3LF, England.

LEE Warner. *See:* **BATTIN B W.**

LEE Wayne C, (Lee Sheldon), b. 1917, USA. Author. *Publications:* Prairie Vengeance, 1954; Broken Wheel Ranch, 1956; Slugging Backstop, 1957; His Brother's Guns, 1958; Killer's Range, 1958; Bat Masterson, 1960; Gun Brand, 1961; Blood on the Prairie, 1962; Thunder in the Backfield, 1962; Stranger in Stirrup, 1962; The Gun Tamer, 1963; Devil Wire, 1963; The Hostile Land, 1964; Gun in His Hand, 1964; Warpath West, 1965; Fast Gun, 1965; Brand of a Man, 1966; Mystery of Scorpion Creek, 1966; Trail of the Skulls, 1966; Showdown at Julesburg Station, 1967; Return to Gunpoint, 1967; Only the Brave, 1967; Doomed Planet (as Lee Sheldon), 1967; Sudden Guns, 1968; Trouble at Flying H, 1969; Stage to Lonesome Butte, 1969; Showdown at Sunrise, 1971; The Buffalo Hunters, 1972; Suicide Trail, 1972; Wind Over Rimfire, 1973; Son of a Gunman, 1973; Scotty Philip, the Man Who Saved the Buffalo, 1975; Law of the Prairie, 1975; Die Hard, 1975; Law of the Lawless, 1977; Skirmish at Fort Phil Kearney, 1977; Gun Country, 1978; Petticoat Wagon Train, 1978; The Violent Man, 1978; Ghost of a Gunfighter, 1980; McQuaid's Gun, 1980; Trails of the Smoky Hill, non-fiction, 1980; Shadow of the Gun, 1981; Guns at Genesis, 1981; Putnam's Ranch War, 1982; Barbed Wire War, 1983; The Violent Trail, 1984; White Butte Guns, 1984; War at Nugget Creek, 1985; Massacre Creek, 1985; The Waiting Gun, 1986; Hawks of Autumn, 1986; Wild Towns of Nebraska, 1988; Arikaree War Cry, 1992. *Memberships:* Western Writers of America, President 1970-71; Nebraska Writers Guild, President 1974-76. *Address:* PO Box 906, Imperial, Nebraska 69033, USA.

LEE SIX Abigail Etta, b. 30 June 1960. University Lecturer. m. Jean-Louis Six, 1 Apr 1989, 1 son. *Education:* Sidney Sussex College, Cambridge University, 1979-88; BA, 1983; MA, 1086; PhD, 1988. *Publications:* Juan Goytisolo: The Case for Chaos, 1989; Juan Goytisolo: Campos de Nijar, in press. *Contributions to:* Reviews to: Times Literary Supplement; BHS; MLR; Articles to: BHS; MLS; Renaissance and Modern Studies. *Honours:* Elected to Research Fellowship, Cambridge University, 1986. *Membership:* Association of Hispanists of Great Britain and Ireland. *Address:* Department of Hispanic Studies, Queen Mary and Westfield College, Mile End Rd, London E1 4NS, England.

LEECH Geoffrey Neil, b. 16 Jan 1936, Gloucester, England. University Professor. m. Frances Anne Berman, 29 July 1961, Watford. 1 son, 1 daughter. *Education:* BA, English Language and Literature, 1959, MA 1963, PhD 1968, University College, London. *Publications:* English in Advertising, 1966; A Linguistic Guide to English Poetry, 1969; Towards a Semantic Description of English, 1969; Meaning and the English Verb, 1971, 2nd edition, 1987; A Grammar of Contemporary English, with R Quirk, S Greenbaum and J Svartvik, 1972; Semantics, 1974, 2nd edition, 1981; A Communicative Grammar of English, with J Svartvik, 1975; Explorations in Semantics and Pragmatics, 1980; Style in Fiction, with Michael H Short, 1981; English Grammar for Today, with R Hoogenraad and M Deuchar, 1982; Principles of Pragmatics, 1983; A Comprehensive Grammar of the English Language, with R Quirk, S Greenbaum and J Svartvik, 1985; The Computational Analysis of English (ed with R Gatside and G Sampson), 1987; An A-Z of English Grammar and Usage, 1989; Introducing English Grammar, 1992. *Contributions to:* A Review of English Literature; Lingua; New Society; Linguistics; Dutch Quarterly Review of Anglo-American Letters; TLS; Prose Studies; The Rising Generation; Transactions of the Philological Society. *Honours:* FilDr, University of Lund, 1987; FBA, 1987. *Membership:* Academia Europaea. *Literary Agent:* The Peters, Fraser & Dunlop Group Ltd, 503/4 The Chambers, Chelsea Harbour, London SW10 0XF, England.

LEEDOM-ACKERMAN Joanne, b. 7 Feb 1947, Dallas, Texas, USA. Novelist. m. Peter Ackerman, 3 June 1972, 2 sons. *Education:* BA, Principia College, 1968; MA, Johns Hopkins University, 1969; MA, Brown University, 1974. *Publications:* Marble Angels, 1985; The Dark Path to the River, 1988; Articles or poems in: What You Can Do: Practical Suggestions for Action on Some Major Problems in the Seventies, 1971; Bicentennial Collection of Texas Short Stories, 1974; Fiction and Poetry by Texas Women, 1975; Beyond Literacy, 1991. *Contributions to:* Articles to: The Christian Science Monitor; The Los Angeles Times; The Houston Post. *Memberships:* President, PEN Center, USA West; Board of Trustees, International PEN Foundation; Executive Board, Poets and Writers; English PEN; American PEN; Authors Guild. *Honours:* Honourable Mention, National Council for Advancement of Education Writing, 1970, 1971; Sevellon Brown Memorial Award, 1971; Finalist, Newspaper Woman of the Year, New England Press Association, 1971; Finalist, Best Newspaper Series, New England Press Association, 1971. *Literary Agent:* Michael Congdon, Don Congdon Associates, New York City, New York, USA. *Address:* 48 Phillimore Gardens, London W8 7QG, England.

LEES-MILNE James, b. 1908, United Kingdom. Author. *Appointments:* Private Secretary to Baron Lloyd, 1931-35; Staff Member, Reuters, 1935-36; Staff Member, National Trust, 1936-66. *Publications:* The National Trust (editor), 1945; The Age of Adam, 1947; National Trust Guide: Buildings, 1948; Tudor Renaissance, 1951; The Age of Inigo Jones, 1953; Roman Mornings, 1956; Baroque in Italy, 1959; Baroque in Spain and Portugal, 1960; Earls of Creation, 1962; Worcestershire: A Shell Guide, 1964; St Peter's, 1967; English Country Houses: Baroque, 1970; Another Self, 1970; Heretics in Love, novel, 1973; Ancestral Voices, 1975; William Beckford, 1976; Prophesying Peace, 1977; Round the Clock, novel, 1978; Harold Nicolson, 2 vols, 1980-81; The Country House, anthology, 1982; The Last Stuarts, 1983; Enigmatic Edwardian, 1986; Some Cotswold Country Houses, 1987; Venetian Evenings, 1988; The Fool of Love, 1990; Bachelor Duke, 1991; People and Places, 1992. *Honours:* FRSL; FSA. *Address:* Essex House, Badminton, Avon GL9 1DD, England.

LEESON Robert (Arthur), b. 31 Mar 1928, Barnton, Cheshire, England. Writer and Journalist. m. Gunvor Hagen, 25 May 1954, 1 son, 1 daughter. *Education:* Sir John Deane's Grammar School, Northwich, Cheshire, 1939-44; External Degree in English (Hons), London University, 1972. *Literary Appointment:* Literary Editor, Morning Star, London 1960-80. *Publications:* Third Class Genie (Childrens) 1975; Silver's Revenge (Childrens) 1978; It's My Life (Teen Fiction), 1980; Slambash Wangs of a Compo Gormer (Fantasy), 1987; Travelling Brothers (Six centuries history of travelling Craftsmen), 1979; Reading and Righting (Past, Present and Future of Fiction for the Young), 1985; Candy For King (Teen fiction), 1983; Grange Hill Rules OK (School), 1980; Coming Home (Teen Fiction), 1991; Zarnia Experiment 1-6 (Science Fiction), 1993. *Contributions to:* Occasional contributions to: The Guardian, Times Education Supplement, Book for Your Children, Books for Keeps, School Librarian, Children's Literature in Education. *Honour:* Eleanor Farjeon Award for services to Children and Literature, 1985. *Memberships:* Writers' Guild of Great Britain (Chairman 1985-86); International Board on Books for Young People (British Section) Treasurer 1972-. *Address:* 18, McKenzie Road, Broxbourne, Hertfordshire, EN10 7JH, England.

LEFEBURE Molly, b. United Kingdom. Author. *Publications:* Evidence for the Crown, 1955; Murder with a Difference, 1958; The Lake District, 1963; Scratch and Co, 1968; The Hunting of Wilberforce Pike, 1970; Cumberland Heritage, 1971; The Loona Balloona, 1974; Samuel Taylor Coleridge: A Bondage of Opium, 1974; Cumbrian Discovery, 1977; The Bondage of Love: A Life of Mrs Samuel Taylor Coleridge, 1986; The Illustrated Lake Poets, 1987; Blitz: A Novel of Love and War, 1988;

The Coleridge Connection (Essays, ed with Richard Gravil), 1990; Thunder In the Sky (novel), 1991. *Address:* c/o Watson Little Ltd, 12 Egbert Street, London, NW1 8LJ, England.

LEFF Leonard J, b. 23 Jan 1942, Houston, Texas, USA. Professor of English. m. Linda Ringer, 26 Jan 1969, 1 son. *Education:* BBA, University of Texas, Austin, 1963; MA, University of Houston, 1965; PhD, Northern Illinois University, 1971. *Appointments:* Instructor, English: McNeese State University, 1965-68; University of Illinois, Urbana-Champaign, 1971-72; Northern Illinois University, 1972-73; Assistant Professor, Associate Professor, Head of English, Bellevue College, 1973-79; Assistant Professor, 1979-82, Associate Professor, 1983-91, Interim Head of English, 1989-90, Professor, 1991-, Oklahoma State University, Stillwater. *Publications:* Film Plots, vol I, 1983, vol II, 1988; Hitchcock and Selznick: The Rich and Strange Collaboration of Alfred Hitchcock and David O Selznick in Hollywood, 1987, paperback, 1988, UK Edition, 1988, UK paperback, 1990, French translation, 1990, Spanish translation, 1992; The Dame in the Kimono: Hollywood, Censorship, and the Production Code from the 1920s to the 1960s (with Jerold Simmons), 1990. *Contributions to:* Cinema Journal; Historical Journal of Film, Radio and Television; Western Humanities Review; The Georgia Review; Film Quarterly; PMLA; Critique; Restoration and 18th Century Theatre Research; Film Heritage; The Southern Quarterly; Journal of Popular Film and Television; Quarterly Review of Film Studies; Theatre Journal; Manuscripts; New Orleans Review; Journal of Film and Video; Literature and Film Quarterly. *Honours:* New York Times Book Review, Notable Books of the Year, 1987, 1990; British Film Institute Book Award, 1988; Oklahoma Book Award for Nonfiction, 1989; Finalist: Outstanding Teacher Award, AMOCO, 1983, Burlington Northern Faculty Achievement Award, 1989. *Memberships:* Modern Language Association; Society for Cinema Studies; University Film and Video Association. *Literary Agent:* Sobel Associates, New York City, New York, USA. *Address:* 3002 Loma Verde Ln, Stillwater, OK 74074, USA.

LEFFLAND Ella Julia, b. 25 Nov 1931, Martinez, California. Writer. *Education:* BA, Fine Arts, San Jose State College, 1953. *Publications:* Mrs Munck, 1970; Love out of Season, 1974; Last Courtesies, 1979; Rumors of Peace, 1980; The Knight, Death of the Devil, 1990. *Contributions to:* New Yorker; Harper's; Atlantic Monthly; Mademoiselle; New York Magazine; New York Times. *Honours:* Gold Medal for Fiction, 1974, 1979, Silver Medal, 1991, Commonwealth Club of California; O Henry First Prize, 1977; Bay Area Book Reviewers Award for Fiction, 1990. *Literary Agent:* Lois Wallace. *Address:* Wallace Literary Agency, 177 East 70th Street, New York, NY 10021, USA.

LEGAT Michael Ronald, b. 24 Mar 1923, London, England. Writer. m. Rosetta Clark, 20 Aug 1949, 2 sons. *Appointments:* Editorial Director, Transworld Publishers Limited, 1956-73; Editorial Director, Cassell Limited, 1973-78. *Publications:* Dear Author..., 1972, revised 1989; Mario's Vineyard, 1980; The Silver Fountain, 1982; An Author's Guide to Publishing, 1983, revised 1991; Putting on a Play, 1984; The Shapiro Diamond, 1984; The Silk Maker, 1985; Writing for Pleasure and Profit, 1986; The Cast-Iron Man, 1987, revised 1993; The Illustrated Dictionary of Western Literature, 1987; We Beheld His Glory, 1988; The Nuts and Bolts of Writing, 1989; How to Write Historical Novels, 1990; Plotting the Novel, 1992; Understanding Publishers' Contracts, 1992. Non-Fiction: A Writer's Guide, 1993. *Contributions to:* The Author; Writers' Monthly. *Memberships:* President, The Weald of Sussex Writers; Vice-President, Uckfield Writers' Circle; Chairman, Writers' Holiday, Caerleon; Society of Authors; Hon Sec, Society of Sussex Authors. *Literary Agent:* Campbell Thomson and McLaughlin Limited. *Address:* Brevic, Lewes Road, Horsted Keynes, Haywards Heath, West Sussex RH17 7DP, England.

LEGERE Werner, b. 28 May 1912, Hohenstein-Ernstthal, Germany. Author. m. Ruth Corsa, 20 Oct. 1942, 2 sons. *Publications;* Ich war in Timbuktu, 1955; Unter Korsaren verschollen, 1955; Die Verschwoerung vom Rio Cayado, 1956; Schwester Florence, 1956; Der Ruf von Castiglione, 1960; Stern aus Jakob, 1963; Die Stiere von Assur, 1969; Der gefuerchtete Gaismair, 1976; In allen meinen Taten, 1982. *Honours:* 1st Prize Group, Adventure Books for Children and Young People, Board of literature of the GDR, 1953; Art Prize, County Karl-Marx-Stadt, 1961; Artur Becker Medal, Silver, Free German Youth Organization, 1962; Johannes R. Becher Medal, Silver, Kulturbund Association of the GDR, 1982; Culture Prize, County Karl-Marx-Stadt, 1982. *Address:* Lutherstrasse 20, Hohenstein-Ernstthal, D-09337, Germany.

LEGGATT Alexander Maxwell, b. 18 Aug 1940, Trafalgar Twp. Ontario, Canada. University Teacher. m. Margaret Anna Leggatt, 4 daughters. *Education:* BA, University of Toronto, 1962; MA 1963, PhD 1965, University of Birmingham. *Literary Appointments:* Associate Editor, Modern Drama, 1972-75; Editorial Board, English Studies in Canada, 1984-91. *Publications include:* Shakespeare's Comedy of Love, 1974; Shakespeare's Political Drama, 1988; Citizen Comedy in the Age of Shakespeare, 1973; Ben Jonson: his Vision and his Art, 1981; English Drama: Shakespeare to the Restoration 1988; Harvester/Twayne New Critical Introductions to Shakespeare: King Lear, 1988; Shakespeare in Performance: King Lear, 1991; Jacobean Public Theatre, 1992. *Contributions to:* Contributions to many scholarly journals including: Shakespeare Quarterly; Shakespeare Studies; Shakespeare Survey; Essays in Criticism; Studies in English Literature; Modern Language Review. *Honour:* Guggenheim Fellowship 1985-86. *Memberships:* Shakespeare Association of America, Trustee 1986-89; International Shakespeare Association, Executive Committee 1987-; International Association of University Professors of English; Association of Canadian University Teachers of English. *Address:* University College, University of Toronto, Toronto, Canada M5S 1A1.

LEGUM Colin, b. 3 Jan 1919, Kestell, South Africa. Journalist. m. 27 July 1960, 1 son, 3 daughters. *Education:* Secondary School, Kestell, South Africa. *Appointments include:* Political Correspondent, Sunday Express, Johannesburg, 1936; Editor, The Forward, Johannesburg, 1939; Editor, Illustrated Bulletin, Johannesburg, 1942; Associate Editor, The Observer, London 1949; Editor, Africa Contemporary Record; Co-Editor, Middle East Contemporary Survey, 1976; Editor, Third World Reports, 1982-. *Publications include:* Pan-Africanism; Congo Disaster; Must We Lose Africa; Attitude to Africa (with others); South Africa - Crisi for the West (co-author); The Battlefronts of Southern Africa, 1987. *Contributions to:* Journal of Contemporary African Affairs; New York Times; Washington Post; Christian Science Monitor; Jerusalem Post; London Review of Books. *Memberships:* Royal Institute of African Affairs; International Institute of Strategic Studies; African Publications Trust (Chairman); Africa Education Trust; Africa Studies Association of US; Diplomatic and Commonwealth Writers. *Address:* Wild Acre, Plaw Hatch, Nr Sharpthorne, West Sussex RH19 4JL, England.

LEHMAN Yvonne, b. 1936, USA. Author. *Publications:* Red Like Mine, 1970; Dead Men Don't Cry, 1973; Fashions of the Heart, 1981; In Shady Groves, 1983; Smoky Mountain Sunrise, 1984; Taken By Storm, 1984; More Than A Summer's Love, 1985. *Contributions to:* Several magazines and journals annually. *Membership:* Founder and Director, Blue Ridge Writers Conference, 1975-. *Address:* PO Box 188, Black Mountain, NC 28711, USA.

LEHMANN Geoffrey, b. 1940, Australia. Tax Lawyer. m. 1981, 3 sons, 2 daughters. *Education:* BA, LLM, University of Sydney. *Appointment:* Partner, Price Waterhouse. *Publications:* Spring Day in Autumn 1974;

Ilex Tree with Les A Murray, 1967; A Voyage of Lions 1970; Conversation with a Rider 1972; Selected Poems, 1975; Ross' Poems, 1978; Nero's Poems, 1981; Children's Games, 1990; Spring Forest, 1992; editor, co-editor of anthologies. *Honour:* Grace Levin Prize, 1967, 1981. *Memberships:* Literature Board of Australia Council, 1982-85. *Literary Agent:* Curtis Brown, Australia. *Address:* Curtis Brown (Australia) Pty Ltd, 27 Union Street, Paddington, NSW 2021, Australia.

LEIGH Meredith. *See:* **BRUCE Guy Kenyon.**

LEIGH Mike, b. 20 Feb 1943, Salford, Lancashire, England. Dramatist; Film and Theatre Director. m. Alison Steadman 1973, 2 sons. *Education:* Royal Academy of Dramatic Art; Camberwell School of Arts and Crafts; Central School of Art and Design; London Film School. *Publications:* Plays: The Box Play, 1965; My Parents Have Gone to Carlisle, The Last Crusade of the Five Little Nuns, 1966; Nenaa, 1967; Individual Fruit Pies, Down Here and Up There, Big Basil, 1968; Epilogue, Glum Victoria and the Lad with Specs, 1969; Bleak Moments, 1970; A Rancid Pong, 1971; Wholesome Glory, The Jaws of Death, Dick Whittington and His Cat, 1973; Babies Grow Old, The Silent Majority, 1974; Abigail's Party, 1977 (also TV play); Ecstasy, 1979; Goose-Pimples, 1981; TV Films: A Mug's Game, Hard Labour, 1973; The Permissive Society, The Birth of the 2001 F.A. Cup, Final Goalie, Old Chums, Probation, A Light Snack, Afternoon, 1975; Nuts in May, Knock for Knock, 1976; The Kiss of Death, 1977; Who's Who, 1978; Grown Ups, 1980; Home Sweet Home, 1981; Meantime, 1983; Four Days in July 1984; Feature Films: Bleak Moments, 1971; The Short & Curlies, 1987; High Hopes, 1988; Life Is Sweet, 1990; Radio Play: Too Much of a Good Thing, 1979. *Honours:* Golden Leopard, Locarno Film Festival, Golden Hugo, Chicago Film Festival, for Bleak Moments, 1972; George Devine Award, 1973; London "Evening Standard" and "Drama" London Critics' Choice best Comedy Awards, 1981. *Address:* The Peters Fraser and Dunlop Group Ltd, 503/4 The Chambers, Chelsea Harbour, London SW10 0XF, England.

LEIGH Richard Harris b. 16 Aug 1943, New Jersey, USA. Writer. *Education:* BA Programme, Tufts University, 1961-65; MA Programme University of Chicago, 1965-67; PhD Programme, State University of New York at Stony Brook, 1967-70. *Appointments:* Special Collections Librarian, Simon Fraser University, Vancouver, 1970-72. *Publications:* The Holy Blood and the Holy Grail (with Michael Baigent and Henry Lincoln) 1982; The Messianic Legacy (with Michael Baigent and Henry Lincoln) 1986; The Temple and the Lodge (with Michael Baigent) 1989; The Dead Sea Scrolls Deception (with Michael Baigent), 1991; Various short pieces particularly Madonna in Random Review, 1982. *Contributions to:* Various journals and anthologies of short stories, some introductions to books by other people, particularly essay on contemporary fiction as preface to Song of a Man Who Came Through by Douglas Lockhart, 1978. *Honour:* Madonna selected among best short stories of 1982 published in Random Review (hardback and paperback). *Memberships:* Co-Founder of Pushkin Prize Programme in Ireland (together with Seamus Heaney, Bernard McCabe, the Earl of Mount Charles and the Duchess of Abercorn). *Literary Agent:* Barbara Levy. *Address:* 21 Kelly Street, London, NW1 8PG, England.

LEIGH FERMOR Patrick (Michael), b. United Kingdom. Author. *Publications:* The Traveller's Tree, 1950; Julie de Carneilhan and Chance Acquaintances, by Colette, translation, 1951; A Time to Keep Silence, 1953; The Violins of Saint-Jacques, 1953; Mani, 1958; Roumeli, 1966; A Time of Gifts, 1977; Between the Woods and the Water, 1986. *Honours:* DSO, OBE. *Address:* c/o John Murray Ltd, 50 Albemarle Street, London W1, England.

LEISY James Franklin, (Frank Lynn), b. 1927, USA. Writer; Publisher; Company Director. *Appointments:*

Editor, Prentice-Hall, 1949-54; Editor, Allyn and Bacon, 1954-56; Founder, Chairman of Board, Chief Executive Officer, Wadsworth, 1956-85; Co-Owner, Stephen Greene Press, 1978-85; Deputy Chairman, International Thomson Organisation, 1979-85; Chairman, International Thomson Books, 1980-85; Founder, Chairman of Board, Science Books International, 1981-83; Founder, Chairman of Board, Linguistics International, 1983-85; Co- Founder, Franklin Beedle and Associates, 1985-; Director, Advisor, Mayfield Publishing Co, 1985-. *Publications:* Abingdon Song Kit (editor), 1957; Let's All Sing (editor), 1959; Songs for Swinging Housemothers (edited as Frank Lynn), 1961, 1963; Songs for Singing (edited as Frank Lynn), 1961; Songs for Pickin' and Singin' (editor), 1962; The Beer Bust Songbook (edited as Frank Lynn), 1963; Hootenanny Tonight, 1964; Folk Song Fest: Songs and Ideas for Performance Artistry, 1964; The Folk Song Abecedary, 1966; Alpha Kappa Psi Sings (editor), 1967; The Good Times Songbook, 1974; Scrooge: The Christmas Musical, 1978; Alice: A Musical Play, 1980; Cuckoo Clock in a Music Box, 1980; Pinocchio: A Musical Play, 1981; Tiny Tim's Christmas Carol, 1981; The Pied Piper, 1982; The Nutcracker and Princess Pirlipat (as Julia Ericson), 1982; A Visit from St Nicholas, 1983; Pandora, 1983; Talkin' 'bout America, 1986; Mouse Country, 1987; The Dingalong Circus Holiday, 1987. *Address:* 183 Patricia Drive, Atherton, CA 94025, USA.

LEITCH Maurice, b. United Kingdom. Radio Producer; Novelist; Dramatist. *Appointments:* Features Producer, BBC, Belfast, Northern Ireland, 1962-70; Radio Drama Producer, BBC, London, 1970-. *Publications:* The Liberty Lad, 1965; Poor Lazarus, 1969; Stamping Ground, 1975; Silver's City, 1981. *Address:* c/o Drama Department, Radio 4, BBC, Broadcasting House, Portland Place, London W1, England.

LEITH Linda Jane, b. 13 Dec 1949, Belfast, Northern Ireland. Writer; Critic; Editor. m. Andras Gollner, 19 July 1974, 3 sons. *Education:* BA, 1st class honours, McGill University, Montreal, Canada, 1970; PhD, English Literature, London University, England, 1976. *Appointments:* Associate Editor, Montreal Review, Canada, 1978-79; Publisher, Co-Editor, Matrix magazine, 1988-; Fiction Editor, Vehicule Press, Montreal, 1989-. *Publications:* Telling Differences: New English Fiction from Quebec, 1989; Introducing Hugh MacLennan's Two Solitudes, 1990; Birds of Passage (novel), 1993. *Membership:* Vice-President, Quebec Society for the Promotion of English Language Literature. *Address:* English Department, John Abbott College, POB 2000, Ste-Anne de Bellevue, Quebec, Canada H9X 3L9.

LELAND Christopher Towne, b. 17 Oct 1951. Writer; Professor. *Education:* BA English, Pomona College, Claremont, CA, 1973; MA, Spanish, 1980, PhD, Comparative Literature, University of California, San Diego, 1982. *Appointments:* Professor of English, Wayne State University, 1990-. *Publications:* The Book of Marvels, 1990; Mrs Randall, 1987; Mean Time, 1982; The Last Happy Men: The Generation of 1922; Fiction and the Argentine Reality, 1986. *Contributions to:* Principal Translator, Open Door by Luise Valengnela, 1988. *Honours:* Finalist, PEN Hemingway Award, 1982; Fellow, Massachusetts Artists Foundation, 1985. *Memberships:* Poets and Writers; MLA. *Literary Agent:* M. Marmur. *Address:* c/o Department of English, Wayne State University, Detroit, MI 48202, USA.

LELAND Jeremy Francis David, b. 1932. Novelist; Short Story Writer. *Publications:* A River Decrees, 1969, 1972; The Jonah, 1970; The Tower, 1972; Lirri, 1973; The Last Sandcastle, 1983; Bluff, 1987, 1988; Breaking Up, 1987; Tenant's Rights, 1987. *Address:* 7 Swansea Road, Norwich, NR2 3HU, England.

LELCHUK Alan, b. 15 Sept 1938, New York City, New York, USA. Writer. m. Barbara Kreiger, 7 Oct 1979, 2 sons. *Education:* BA, Brooklyn College, 1960; MA,

1963, PhD, English Literature, 1965, Stanford University. *Appointments:* Brandeis University, 1966-81; Associate Editor, Modern Occasions, 1980-82; Amherst College, 1982-84; Dartmouth College, 1985-; Fulbright Writer-in-Residence, Haifa University, Israel, 1986-87; Visiting Writer, City College of New York, autumn 1991. *Publications:* American Mischief, 1973; Miriam at Thirty-Four, 1974; Shrinking: The Beginning of My Own Ending, 1978; 8 Great Hebrew Short Novels (co-editor), in English translation, 1983; Miriam in Her Forties, 1985; On Home Ground, for young adults, 1987; Brooklyn Boy, 1989. *Contributions to:* New York Times Book Review; Sewanee Review; The Atlantic; The New Republic; Dissent; New York Review of Books. *Honours:* Guggenheim Fellowship, 1976-77; Mishkenot Sha'Ananim Resident Fellow, 1976-77; Fulbright Award, 1986-87; Manuscript Collection, Mugar Memorial Library, Boston University. *Memberships:* PEN; Authors Guild. *Literary Agent:* Georges Borcharat Inc, 136 E 57th St, New York, NY 10022, USA. *Address:* RFD 2, Canaan, NH 03741, USA.

LELYVELD Joseph (Salem), b. 5 Apr 1937, Ohio, USA. Writer; Editor; Correspondent. *Appointments:* Staff Member, New York Times, 1962; Correspondent in the Congo and South Africa, 1965-66, in London, England, 1966, in India and Pakistan, 1966-69, in Hong Kong, 1973-75, in South Africa, 1980-83; Staff Writer for New York Times Magazine, 1984-85; London Bureau Chief, 1985-86; Foreign Editor, 1987. *Publications:* Move Your Shadow: South Africa Black and White, 1985. *Honours:* Fulbright Fellowship to Burma, 1960; Page One Award, 1970; George Polk Memorial Award, 1972 and 1984; John Simon Guggenheim Fellowship, 1984; Pulitzer Prize and Los Angeles Times Book Award, 1986.

LEM Stanislaw, b. 12 Sept 1921, Lvov, USSR. Author. m. Barbara Lesnik, 11 Aug 1953, 1 son. *Education:* Studied Medicine in Lvov, 1939-41, and Krakow, Poland, 1944-45. *Literary Appointments:* Lecturer, University of Krakow, part-time, 1973-. *Publications:* 40 books translated into 35 languages including: Eden, 1959; The Star Diaries, 1957, many later editions; Solaris, 1961; Memoirs Found in a Bathtub, 1961; The Invincible, 1964; The Cyberiad, 1965; His Master's Voice, 1968; Tales of Pirx the Pilot, More Tales of Pirx the Pilot, 1968; A Perfect Vacuum, 1971; The Futurological Congress, 1971; The Chain of Chance, 1976; Fiasco, 1986. *Contributions to:* The New Yorker; Encounter; Penthouse; Omni; many others. *Honours include:* Awards of Polish Ministry of Culture, 1965 and 1973; Polish State Prize for Literature, 1976; Austrian State Award for European Literature, 1985; Prize of the Alfred Jurzykowski Foundation for Literature, 1987; Honorary PhD, University of Wroclaw. *Membership:* International Association of Poets, Playwrights, Editors, Essayists and Authors. *Literary Agent:* Franz Rottensteiner, Vienna, Austria. *Address:* c/o Franz Rottensteiner, Marchettigasse 9/17, A-1060 Vienna, Austria.

LEMAIRE Michael, (Desert Roving Reporter), b. 6 Aug 1936, Bordeaux, France. Writer. *Education:* BSCE, major Civil Engineering, 1957; Minors Literature and Journalism, 1958. *Appointments:* Proprietor, Lemaire Enterprises, Desert Hot Springs, California, USA; Covering and publishing for many jazz festivals, worldwide. *Publications:* Love me or at least let me love you, 1988; A Romantic Interlude, 1990 Poems published by Hallmark Publishing Corporation, 1990-91; Vindicated Episode at Salton Sea, novel, 1993; Tracks Through Time and Space, (Fantasy Novel), 1993. *Contributions to:* San Diego Union; San Bernardino Bee; St Louis Post Dispatch; Kansas City Star; Washington Globe; London Times; Fresno Dixieland Society Jazz News Journal; St Louis Jazz on the River Publications; 1 Paris newspaper; 2 German newspapers (Frankfurt and Hamburg). *Honours:* Honorary Membershp, International Writers and Artists Association; Rollex watch presented for coverages. *Memberships:* Writers Guild; National Writers Club; Jazz Journalists Association. *Literary Agent:* Suzanne Berwick Inc. *Address:* 6030 Shady Creek Road, Agoura, CA 92549, USA.

LEMANN Nancy Elise, b. 4 Feb 1956, New Orleans, USA. Writer. m. Mark Paul Clein, 5 Oct 1991. *Education:* BA, Brown University, 1978; Mfa, Columbia University, 1984. *Publications:* Lives of the Saints; The Ritz of the Bayou; Sportsmans Paradise. *Contributions to:* Chicago Tribune; Los Angeles Times; New Republic; New York Review of Books; New York Times; People; Washington Post. *Memberships:* PEN; Authors Guild. *Address:* 254 West 73rd Street, no.5 New York, NY 10023, USA.

LEMMON David Hector, b. 4 Apr 1931, London, England. Writer. m. (Jean) Valerie Fletcher, 16 Aug 1958, 2 sons. *Education:* Teachers Certificate, College of St Mark and John, 1953, BA Hons, English, 1968, London University; Associate, College of Preceptors, 1967; Final Certificate, English Speaking Board, 1967. *Appointments:* English and Games Master, Bound's Green Secondary Modern School, 1953-57; English Tutor, Ankara College, Turkey, 1957-60; Professional Director, Ankara American Little Theatre, 1958-59; Head of English: Kingsbury High School, Warwickshire, England, 1960-63; Torells Girls School, Thurrock, 1963-68; Nicholas Comprehensive School, Basildon, 1973-83; Examiner, A Level Theatre Studies, 1980-; Editor, TCCB's Official Tour Guide, Compiler, Test Match and Texaco Trophy programmes, 1984-89. *Publications:* Books on cricket (more than any other writer in game's history) including: Pelham Cricket Year, yearly 1979-81; Benson and Hedges Cricket Year, yearly 1982-; Summer of Success, Great One Day Cricket Matches, Tich Freeman, 1982; Wisden Book of Cricket Quotations I, 1982, II, 1990; Johnny Won't Hit Today, The Book of One-Day Internationals, 1983; The Great Wicket-Keepers, A Walk to the Wicket (with Ted Dexter), Cricket Heroes (editor), 1984; Ken McEwan, Percy Chapman, Cricket Reflections (with Ken Kelly), Cricket Mercenaries, 1985; The Great All-Rounder, 1987; The Official History of Essex CCC (with Mike Marshall), 1987, of Middlesex CCC, 1988, of Worcestershire CCC, 1989, of Surrey CCC, 1989; One-Day Cricket, The Crisis of Captaincy, 1988; Know Your Sport-Cricket (with Chris Cowdray) 1989; British Theatre Yearbook, 1989, 1990; Len Hutton, a Pictorial Biography, 1990; Cricket's Champion Counties, The Cricketing Greigs, 1991; Guinness Book of Test Cricket Captains, Benson and Hedges British Theatre Yearbook, 1992. *Contributions to:* Cricket World; The Guardian; Various. *Membership:* Cricket Writers Club. *Literary Agent:* Malcolm Hamer, Headline Enterprises. *Address:* 26 Leigh Road, Leigh-on-Sea, Essex SS9 1LD, England.

LEMON Lee Thomas, b. 9 Jan 1931, Kansas City, Kansas, USA. Professor. m. Maria Mullinaux, 5 May 1973, Lincoln, Nebraska. 3 sons, 3 daughters. *Education:* BS, St Louis University, 1951; MA, Southern Illinois University, 1952; PhD, University of Illinois, 1961. *Publications:* Russian Formalist Critics, 1965; Glossary of Literary Terms, 1971; Partial Critics, 1965; Portraits of the Artist in Contemporary Fiction, 1985. *Contributions to:* Various articles on Modern Fiction, Literary Theory, Previews. *Memberships:* Associate Editor, Prairie Schooner. *Address:* 224 Andrews, WNL, Lincoln, NE 68588, USA.

LENGYEL Balazs, b. 21 Aug 1918, Budapest, Hungary. Writer. m. (1) Agnes Nemes Nagy, 1944; (2) Veronika Kerek. *Education:* Doctor of Law. *Publications:* Collections of essays: Green and Gold, 1988; Returning, 1990; Editor, Ujhold (New Moon), Literary year-book. *Honours:* Literary Award, Hungarian Writer's Union. *Memberships:* Presidium, Hungarian Writer's Union; Founding Member, Hungarian Academy of Arts, 1992. *Address:* 4 Apat utca, Budapest, 1033 Hungary.

LENT Blair, (Ernest Small), b. 1930, USA. Children's Fiction Writer. *Appointments:* Freelance Writer and Illustrator, 1963-. *Publications:* Pistachio, 1963; The Wave (with M Hodges), 1964; Baba Yaga (as Ernest Small), 1966; John Tabor's Ride, 1966; From King Boggen's Hall to Nothing-at-All, 1967; Why the Sun and the Moon Live in the Sky (with E Dayrell), 1968, as animated film, 1970; The Little Match Girl, by Hans Christian Andersen, 1968; Tikki Tikki Tembo (with A

Mosel), 1968; The Angry Moon (with W Sleator), 1970; The Funny Little Woman (with A Mosel), 1972; Tales Told in India (with V Haviland), 1973; The Telephone (with K Chukovsky), 1977; I Stood Upon a Mountain (with A Fisher), 1979; Bayberry Bluff, 1987. *Address:* 10 Dana Street, Cambridge, MA 02138, USA.

LEONARD Constance, b. 1923, USA. Author. *Publications:* The Great Pumpkin Mystery, 1971; The Other Maritha, 1972; Steps to Nowhere, 1974; Hostage in Illyria, 1976; Shadow of a Ghost, 1978; The Marina Mystery, 1981; Stowaway, 1983; Aground, 1984; Strange Waters, 1985. *Address:* Box 126, Francestown, NH 03043, USA.

LEONARD Dick (Richard L), b. 12 Dec 1930, Ealing, Middlesex, England. Journalist; Former Member of Parliament. m. Irene Heidelberger, 29 Mar 1963, 1 son, 1 daughter. *Education:* MA, Essex University, 1969. *Literary Appointments:* Assistant Editor, The Economist, 1974-85; various other editorial posts in magazines and broadcasting. *Publications:* Elections in Britain, 1968, 1991; The Backbencher and Parliament, (co-author), 1972; Paying for Party Politics, 1975; The Socialist Agenda (co-author), 1981; World Atlas of Elections (co-author), 1986; The Economist Guide to the EC, 1988, 1992. *Contributions to:* Guardian; Observer; Sunday Times; New Society; Encounter; Leading newspapers, USA, Canada, Australia, New Zealand, Japan, India. *Memberships:* Fabian Society (Former Chairman); Reform Club. *Address:* 22 rue du Gruyer, 1170 Brussels, Belgium.

LEONARD Elmore, b. 11 Oct 1925, New Orleans, Louisiana, USA. Novelist. m. Joan Shepard, 15 Sept 1979, 3 sons, 2 daughters. *Education:* BA, University of Detroit, 1950. *Publications Include:* 21 novels including: Hombre, 1961; City Primeval, 1980; Split Images, 1981; Cat Chaser, 1982; Stick, 1983; Labrava, 1983; Glitz, 1985; Bandits, 1986; Touch, 1987; Freaky Deaky, 1988; Killshot, 1989; Get Shorty, 1990; Maximum Bob, 1991; Rum Punch, 1992. *Honours:* Edgar Allen Poe Award, Mystery Writers of America, 1984; Michigan Foundation for the Arts Award for Literature, 1985. *Memberships:* Writers Guild of America Inc. West; PEN; Authors Guild; Western Writers of America; Mystery Writers of America. *Address:* c/o H N Swanson Literary Agent, 8523 Sunset, Los Angeles, CA 90069, USA.

LEONARD Hugh, (John Keyes Byrne), b. 9 Nov 1926, Dublin, Ireland. Playwright. m. Paule Jacquet, 1955, 1 daughter. *Publications:* Stage Plays Include: the Big Birhday, 1957; A Leap in the Dark, 1957; Madigan's Lock, 1958; A Walk on the Water, 1960; The Passion of Peter Ginty, 1961; Stephen D, 1962; The Poker Session, 1963; Dublin 1, 1963; The Saints Go Cycling In, 1965; Mick and Mick, 1966; The Quick and the Dead, 1967; The Au Pair Man, 1968; The Barracks, 1969; The Patrick Pearse Motel, 1971; Da, 1973; Thieves, 1973; Summer, 1974; Times of Wolves and Tigers 1974; Irishmen, 1975; Time Was, 1976; A Life, 1977; Moving Days, 1981; The Mask of Moriarty, 1984; Writing for TV includes: Silent Song 1967; Nicholas Nickleby, 1977; London Belongs to Me, 1977; The Last Campaign, 1978; The Ring and the Rose, 1978; Strumpet City, 1979; The Little World of Don Camillo, 1980; Kill, 1982; Good Behaviour, 1982; O'Neill, 1983; Beyond the Pale, 1984; The Irish RM, 1985; A Life, 1986; Troubles, 1987; Films: Herself Surprised, 1977; Da, 1984; Widows' Peak, 1984; Troubles, 1984; Autobiography: Home Before Night, 1979; Out After Dark, 1988. *Honours:* Hon. DHL (RI), Writers Guild Award, 1966; Tony Award; Critics Circle Award; Drama Desk Award; Outer Critics Award, 1978; Doctor of Literature, Trinity College, Dublin, 1988. *Address:* 6 Rossaun Pilot View, Dalkey, Co. Dublin, Ireland.

LEONARD Tom, b. 22 Aug 1944, Glasgow, Scotland. Writer. m. Sonya Maria O'Brien, 24 Dec 1971. 2 sons. *Education:* MA, Glasgow University, 1976. *Appointment:* Writer-in-Residence, Renfrew District Libraries, 1986-88 and 1988-89. *Publications:* Intimate Voices (writing 1965-83), 1984; Radical Renfrew (editor), 1990; Situations Theoretical & Contemporary, 1986; Nora's Place, 1990. *Contributions to:* Edinburgh Review. *Honour:* Joint Winner, Saltire Scottish Book of the Year Award, 1984. *Address:* 56 Eldon Street, Glasgow G3 6NJ, Scotland.

LEONG Gor Yun. *See:* **ELLISON Virginia Howell.**

LEONI Edgar (Hugh), b. 6 May 1925, New York City, New York, USA. Book Dealer. *Education:* BA, Harvard University, 1947; MA, Columbia University, 1952. *Appointments:* Translator, Japanese, Russian, US Army, 1943-46, 1950-51; Liability Insurance Claims Examiner, 1951-64; Editor-in-Chief, Pageant Book Co Inc, New York City, 1964-66; Associate Editor, Oxford Book Co Inc, New York City, 1967-72; Semi-retired Book Dealer in out-of-print books, 1972-. *Publications:* Nostradamus: Life and Literature, 1961, reprinted as Nostradamus and His Prophecies, 1982. *Address:* PO Box 266, Clearwater, FL 34617, USA.

LEONOV Leonid Maximovich, b. 31 May 1899, Moscow, Russia. Novelist; Playwright. m. Tatiana Mikhailovna Sabashnikova, 25 July 1923, 2 daughters. *Education:* Moscow 3rd Public School, 1910-1918. *Appointments:* Editor, bulletin of 15th Inzenskaia Division, 1920; Secretary, Editorial Division, Kpa Krashnyi voin, newspaper of Moscow Military District, 1921-22. *Publications:* The Petushikino Breakthrough, 1922; The End of Insignificant Man, 1922; Barsuki, 1924; Vor, 1927; A Provincial Story, 1927; Untilovsk, 1926; Untilovsk, was staged in 1927 in Moscow Art Theatre by K Stanislavski; Sot, 1929; The Humbling of Badadoshkin, 1929; Saranchuki, 1930; Skutarevski, 1932; Doroga na okean, 1935; Evgenia Ivanovna, 1938; The Wolf, 1938; The Orchards of Polovchansk, 1939; The Snowstorm, 1939; An Ordinary Man, 1941; The Invasion, 1942; Staged in Moscow Mali Theatre in 1943; Lyonushka, 1943; The Taking of Velikoshumsk, 1944; The Golden Coach, 1946; Russkii Ies, 1953; Mr McKinley's Escape, 1961; Other stories, dramatisations of 4 novels, essays. *Memberships:* USSR Union of Writers, Chairman of Board 1929-32, Secretary of Board; USSR Academy of Sciences; Serbian Academy of Sciences and Arts. *Address:* Gerzena 37, flat 10, 121069 Moscow, Russia.

LEPAN Douglas Valentine, b. 25 May 1914, Toronto, Canada. Separated, 2 sons. *Education:* BA, University of Toronto, 1935; BA 1937, MA 1948, Oxford University. *Appointments include:* Counsellor and later Minister Counsellor at the Canadian Embassy in Washington 1951-55; Secretary and Director of Research of the Royal Commission on Canada's Economic Prospects, 1955-58; Assistant Under Secretary of State for External Affairs, 1958-59; Professor of English Literature, Queens University, Kingston, 1959-64; Principal of University College, University of Toronto, 1964-70, Principal Emeritus, 1983-; University Professor, University of Toronto 1970-79, University Professor Emeritus, 1979-; Senior Fellow of Massey College, 1970-85; Senior Fellow Emeritus 1985-. *Publications:* The Wounded Prince and other poems, 1948; The Net and the Sword, 1953; Final Report on the Royal Commission on Canada's Economic Prospects, Ottawa 1957 chapters 1-7; The Deserter, 1964; Bright Glass of Memory, 1979; Something Still to Find, new poems, 1982; Weathering It complete poems 1948-87, 1987; Far Voyages poems, 1990. *Honours:* Guggenheim Fellowship 1948-49; Governor-General's Award for Poetry 1953; Governor-General's Award for Fiction, 1964; Lorne Pierce Medal, Royal Society of Canada 1976. *Address:* c/o Massey College, 4 Devonshire Place, Toronto, Ontario, Canada M5S 2E1.

LEPOSKY George C, b. 25 Mar 1943, Chicago, Illinois, USA. Writer: Educator; Public Relations Consultant. m. Rosalie E. Leposky, 2 Sept 1973, 1 son, 1 daughter. *Education:* BA, Political Science, 1963, MA, Political Science, 1964, Washington University, St

Louis, Missouri; Fellow in Advanced Science Writing Programme, Graduate School of Journalism, Columbia University, New York, 1967-68. *Appointments:* Reporter, City News Bureau, Chicago, Illinois, 1964-65; Reporter, Science Writer, Chicago's American, Chicago Today, 1965-69; Editor, Ampersand Communications, 1982-; Adjunct Professor, Department of English: Florida International University, 1984-, University of Miami, Florida, 1986-; Managing Editor, Vacation Industry Review, 1985-91; Editor, 1992-. *Publications:* An Employer's Guide to Preferred Provider Organizations, 1984; Fodor's 89 Florida (with Rosalie Leposky), 1988; Fodor's 89 Greater Miami, Fort Lauderdale, Palm Beach (with Rosalie Leposky), 1988; Fodor's 90 Florida (with Rosalie Leposky), 1988; Fodor's 90 Greater Miami, Fort Lauderdale, Palm Beach (with Rosalie Leposky), 1988; Chapter on career opportunities in the vacation ownership industry, Travel and Hospitality Directory, 1989; Chapter on public relations, The Law and Business of Resort Development, 1990. *Contributions to:* Born of the Sun, Florida Bicentennial Commemorative Journal Inc, 1975; Traveling the South, syndicated travel column (with Rosalie Leposky), newspapers, SE USA, 1989-; Numerous newspapers, magazines and trade journals. *Honours:* Phi Beta Kappa, 1963; Science Writer's Award, American Dental Association, 1974; National Media Award, American Psychological Foundation; MacEachern Award, Academy of Hospital Public Relations, 1978; President's Award, South Florida Chapter, International Association of Business Communications, 1988. *Memberships:* Florida Freelance Writers Association; International Association of Business Communicators (South Florida Chapter), Treasurer 1984-85, Chairman, Professional Development Workshop Committee 1988, Newsletter Editor 1986-87; President, Oneco Community Association, 1972-75. *Address:* 2311 South Bayshore Drive, Miami, FL 33133, USA.

LEPOSKY Rosalie E, b. 24 Sept 1942, St Louis, Missouri, USA. m. George C Leposky, 2 Sept 1973, 1 son, 1 daughter. *Education:* BS, 1965, Washington University, St Louis, Missouri; MA, 1971, St Louis University, St Louis, Missouri. *Publications:* With George Leposky: Fodor's 89 Florida, 1988; Fodor's Greater Miami, Fort Lauderdale, Palm Beach, 1988; Fodor's 90 Florida, 1988; Fodor's Greater 90 Miami, Fort Lauderdale, Palm Beach, 1988. *Contributions to:* Many trade and consumer publications in areas of health (nursing), hospitality, travel, business; Syndicated travel column (with George Leposky), newspapers, SE USA; Syndicated home-improvement column, Home & House, newspapers in Florida and California; Syndicated cooking column, Food for Thought, newspapers in Florida and Mississippi. *Address:* 2311 South Bayshore Drive, Miami, FL 33133, USA.

LEPOWITZ Helena Waddy, b. 13 June 1945, Winchester, England. Associate Professor. div, 1 son. *Education:* BA, 1966, MA, 1970, Cambridge University; PhD, University of California, San Diego, 1984. *Appointments:* Teaching, Modern European History, Department of History, State University of New York, Geneseo. *Publications:* Images of Faith: Expressionism, Catholic Folk Art, and the Industrial Revolution, 1991. *Contributions to:* Articles to: Past and Present, 1983; Notebooks in Cultural Analysis, 1984; German History, 1989; Journal of Social History, 1990; Historical Reflections, 1992. *Memberships:* American Historical Association; German Studies Association. *Address:* 415 W Lake Road, Geneseo, NY 14454, USA.

LEPSCHY Anna Lavra, b. 30 Nov 1933, Turin, Italy. University Professor. m. 20 Dec 1962. *Education:* BLitt, MA, Somerville college, Oxford, 1952-57. *Publications:* Viaggio in Terrasanta, 1480, 1966; The Italian Language Today, 1977, 1991, (co-author); Tintoretto Observed, 1983; Narrativa e Teatro fra due Secoli, 1984. *Contributions to:* Italian Studies, Romance Studies, Studi Francesi, Studi sul Boccaccio, Studi Novecenteschi, Yearbook of the Pirandello Society, Modern Language Notes, Lettere Italiane. *Memberships:* President, Pirandello Society, 1988-92; Chair, Society

for Italian Studies, 1988-; Association for the Study of Modern Italy; Associazione Internazionale di Lingua e Letterat ura Italiana. *Address:* Department of Italian, University College, Gower Street, London WC1E 6BT, England.

LERMAN Rhoda, b. 18 Jan 1936, New York, USA. Writer. m. Robert Lerman, 15 Sept, 1957, 1 son, 2 daughter. *Education:* BA, University of Miami, 1957. *Appointments:* Visiting Professor of Creative Writing: SUNY, Buffalo, 1988, 1990, University of Colorado, 1982, 1984; NEA Distinguished Professor of Creative Writing, Hartwick College, 1985; Chair of English Literature, SUNY, Buffalo, 1990. *Publications:* Call me Ishtar, 1973, 1977; Girl That he Marries, 1976; Eleanor, A Novel, 1979; Book of the Night, 1984; God's Ear, 1989. *Literary Agent:* Owen Laster. *Address:* William Morris Literary Agency, 1350 Avenue of the Americas, New York, NY 10019, USA.

LERNER Robert Earl, b. 8 Feb 1940, New York, USA. Historian. m. Erdmut Krumnack, 25 Oct 1963, 2 daughters. *Education:* BA, University of Chicago, 1960; MA, 1962, PhD, 1964, Princeton University. *Publications:* The Age of Adversity, 1968; The Heresy of the Free Spirit in the Later Middle Ages, 1972; One Thousand Years, co-author, 1974; The Powers of Prophecy, 1983; Western Civilizations, co-author, 12th edition, 1993. *Contributions to:* numerous articles and reviews in professional journals. *Honours:* Fulbright Fellow, 1967; National Endowment for the Humanities Fellow, 1972; American Council of Learned Societies Fellow, 1979; Guggenheim Foundation Fellow, 1983; American Academy in Rome Fellow, 1983; Institute for Advanced Study, 1988. *Address:* Dept. of History, Northwestern University, Evanston, IL 60208, USA.

LESCHAK Peter M, b. 11 May 1951, Chisholm, MN, USA. Writer. m. Pamela Cope, May 1974. *Education:* BA, Ambassador College, 1974. *Appointments:* Lumberjack, Roseburg, OR, 1973; Printer, Baton Rouge, LA, 1974; Water Plant Operator, Chisolm, 1975-79; Operator of Waste Water Plant, City of Hibbing, 1979-84; Writer, 1984-; Fire Chief of French, MN; Depot Outreach Artist, 1990-91. *Publications:* Letters From Side Lake, 1987; The Bear Guardian, 1990. *Contributions to:* Author of regular column in TWA Ambassador, 1985-86; Magazines; Editor of Twin Cities, 1984-86; Minnesota Monthly, 1984-. *Honour:* Minnesota Book Award, 1991. *Memberships:* Authors Guild; Minnesota Fire Chiefs Association. *Address:* Box 51, Side Lake, MN 55781, USA.

LESLIE Desmond, b. 29 June 1921, London, England. Author; Composer of Electrophonic Music. *Education:* Trinity College, Dublin. *Publications:* (Novels)Careless Lives, 1944; Angels Weep, 1945; Hold Back the Night, 1950; The Amazming Mr Lutterworth, 1955; The Jesus File, 1975; How Britain Won the Space Race, with Patrick Moore, 1973; (Non-Fiction)Flying Saucers Have Landed, with Geroge Adamski, 1953; 18 English Editions, 21 for Translations. *Contributions to:* Life; Picture Post; Sunday Telegraph; Vogue; Life. *Address:* Castle Leslie, Glaslough, Co Monaghan, Republic of Ireland.

LESLIE O H. *See:* **SELSAR Henry.**

LESOURD Leonard Earle, b. 20 May 1919, Columbus, Ohio, USA. Editor; Publisher; Author. m. (1) Evelen Chester, 21 May 1948, div. 1958, (2) Catherine Marshall, 14 Nov 1959, dec. 1983, (3) Sandra Simpson, 22 June 1985, 3 sons, 1 daughter. *Education:* AB, Ohio Wesleyan University, 1941. *Appointments:* Associate Editor, Executive Editor, Editor, Guideposts Magazine, 1946-74; Executive Editor, Deputy Publisher, Chosen Books, 1974-92; Founder, Board Chairman, Breakthrough, Intercessory Prayer Ministry, 1980-. *Publications:* Skybent, 1944; Personal Prayer Diary (with Catherine Marshall), 1978; Touching the Heart of God (editor), 1989; Strong Men, Weak Men, 1990.

Contributions to: Over 100 articles to Guideposts Magazine; Articles to: Christian Herald; Charisma; Decision; Christian Life; Logos Journal; Others. *Memberships:* Rotary Club; Dutch Treat Club. *Address:* Bar Harbour, 86 MacFarlane Dr, Delray Beach, FL 33483, USA.

LESSER David Coleman, b. 6 June 1928, England. Curative Hypnotherapist. m. 10 July 1960, div, 4 daughters. *Education:* Various Certifictes and Diplomas, 1966-77; Teaching Diploma, 1978; Certificate in Curative Hypnotherapy, 1981; Diploma, 1985. *Publications:* Hypnotherapy Explained; The Book of Hypnosis. *Contributions to:* Aesthetics International; Healthy Living; Les Nouvelles Aesthetiques; New Health; Hypnotherapy Journal. *Memberships:* Association of Qualified Curative Hypnotherapists; Curative Hypnotherapy Examination Committee. *Address:* 8 Balaclava Road, Kings Heath, Birmingham, B14 7SG, England.

LESSING Charlotte, Journalist. m. 3 daughters. *Education:* University of London Diploma in English Literature. *Literary Appointments:* Editorial Assistant, Lilliput Magazine, 1945-50; Deputy Editor 1964-73, Editor 1973-87, Good Housekeeping; Editor in Chief also Country Living, 1985-86. *Contributions to:* Freelance features and short stories to a variety of magazines including Wine Writer for The Lady magazine. *Honours:* Editor of the Year, PPA Award, 1983. *Address:* 2 Roseneath Road, London SW11 6AH, England.

LESSING Doris May, b. 22 Oct 1919, Persia. Writer. m. (1) Frank Charles Wisdom, 1939 (div 1943), 1 son, 1 daughter, (2) Gottfried Anton Nicholas Lessing, 1945 (div 1949), 1 son. *Publications include:* The Golden Notebook, 1962; The Children of Violence; Canopus in Argos: Archives, 1979; African Stories, 1964; The Grass Is Singing; Briefing for a Descent into Hell, 1971; The Good Terrorist, 1985; Prisons We Choose To Live Inside, 1986; The Wind Blows Away Our Words - And Other Documents Relating to the Afghan Resistance, 1987; The Fifth Child, 1988; Doris Lessing Reader, 1990; London Observed (short stories), 1992; African Laughter: Four Visits to Zimbabwe, 1992. *Honours include:* Somerset Maugham Award, 1954; Prix Medici, 1976; Austrian State Prize for European Literature, 1981; Shakespeare Prize, 1982; W H Smith Literary Award, 1986; Grinzane Cavour Prize, Italy, 1989; Honorary Doctor of Literature, Princeton, 1989; Distinguished Fellow in Literature, University of East Anglia, 1991. *Memberships Include:* Associate member, American Association for Arts & Letters; National Institute of Arts & Letters, USA; Institute for Cultural Research; Honorary Fellow, Modern Languages Association. *Literary Agent:* Jonathan Clowes Ltd. *Address:* c/o Jonathan Clowes Ltd, Iron Bridge House, Bridge Approach, London NW1 8BD, England.

LESTER Andrew D, b. 8 Aug 1939, Coral Gables, Florida, USA. Professor of Pastoral Care and Pastoral Counselling. m. Judith L Laesser, 8 Sept 1960, 1 son, 1 daughter. *Education:* BA, Mississippi College, Clinton, 1961; BD, 1964, PhD, 1968, Southern Baptist Theological Seminary, Louisville, Kentucky; Clinical Pastoral Education, Central State, Louisville General, Jewish and Children's Hospitals, Louisville, 1964-68; Clinical Training in Pastoral Counselling Service, Clarksville, Indiana; 1964-69; Diplomate, Association of Pastoral Counselors, 1979. *Appointments:* General Editor, Resources for Living series, 1989-90, Editor, series on Pastoral Counselling, 1992-, Westminster-John Knox Press. *Publications:* Pastoral Care in Crucial Human Situations (editor with Wayne Oates), 1969; Sex Is More Than A Word, 1973; It Hurts So Bad, Lord! The Christian Encounters Crisis, 1976; Understanding Aging Parents (with Judith L Lester), 1980; Coping With Your Anger: A Christian Guide, 1983; Pastoral Care with Children in Crisis, 1985; Spiritual Dimensions of Pastoral Care: Witness to the Ministry of Wayne E Oates (editor with Gerald L Borchert), 1985; When Children Suffer: A Sourcebook for Ministry with Children in Crisis, 1987; In preparation: Pastoral Care of the Angry Person;

The Centrality of Hope in Pastoral Care and Counselling. *Contributions to:* The Baptist Student, 1967; Church Administration, 1967; Home Missions, 1970; Review and Expositor, 1971, 1986. *Memberships:* Association of Clinical Pastoral Education, Membership Committee 3 terms; American Association of Pstoral Counselors, Membership Committee 3 terms, Ethics Committee 2 terms; Fellow, College of Chaplains, American Protestant Hospital Association; American Association of Marriage and Family Therapists, Legislation Committee 2 years; Society for Pastoral Theology; International Society of Theta Phi. *Address:* Brite Divinity School, Texas Christian University, PO Box 32923, Fort Worth, TX 76129, USA.

LESTER Julius, b. 1939, USA. Professor of Judaic Studies; Writer; Musician; Singer. *Appointments:* Contributing Editor, SING OUT, New York, 1964-69; Contributing Editor, Broadside of New York, 1964-70; Director, New Port Folk Festival, Rhode Island, 1966-68. *Publications:* The 12-String Guitar as Played by Leadbelly: An Instructional Manual (with Pete Seeger), 1965; To Praise Our Bridges: An Autobiography by Fanny Lou Hamer (edited with Mary Varela), 1967; Our Folk Tales: High John, The Conqueror, and Other Afro-American Tales (edited with Mary Varela), 1967; The Mud of Vietnam: Photographs and Poems, verse, 1967; Revolutionary Notes, 1969; Ain't No Ambulances for No Nigguhs Tonight, by Stanley Couch (editor), 1969; Look Out Whitey, Black Power's Gon' Get Your Mama, 1968; To Be a Slave, 1968; Black Folktales, 1969; Search for the New Land: History as Subjective Experience, 1969; The Seventh Son: The Thought and Writings of W E B Du Bois (editor), 2 vols, 1971; The Knee-High Man and Other Tales, 1972; Long Journey Home: Stories from Black History, 1972; Two Love Stories, 1972; Who I Am, 1974; All Is Well, autobiography, 1976; This Strange New Feeling, short stories, 1982; Do Lord Remember Me, 1984; The Tales of Uncle Remus: The Adventures of Brer Rabbit, 1987; More Tales of Uncle Remus: Further Adventures of Brer Rabbit, His Friends, Enemies and Others, 1988; How Many Spots Does A Leopard Have? and Other Tales, 1989; Further Tales of Uncle Remus: The Misadventure of Brer Rabbit, Brer Fox, Brer Wolf, the Dooding and Other Creatures, 1990; Falling Pieces of the Broken Sky, 1990. *Address:* 600 Station Road, Amherst, MA 01002, USA.

LETTE Kathy, b. 11 Nov 1958, Sydney, Australia. Writer. m. Geoffrey Robertson, 1 May 1990. 1 son, 1 daughter. *Publications:* Plays: Wet Dreams, 1985; Perfect Mismatch, 1985; Grommitts, 1986; Play, radio, I'm So Happy For You, I Really Am, 1991; Books: Puberty Blues, 1979; Hit and Ms, 1984; Girls' Night Out, 1988; The Llama Parlour, 1991; Foetal Attraction, 1993. *Contributions to:* Satirical columnist for the Sydney Morning Herald; The Bulletin; Cleo magazine; Irregular contributor to the Guardian. *Honours:* Australian Literature Board Grant, 1982. *Memberships:* Judge and Organiser, The Hooker Prize, a yearly feminist spoof of The Booker Prize. *Literary Agent:* Mic Cheetan, Sheil Land and Associates. *Address:* c/o Sheil Land, 43 Doughty Street, London WC1N 2LF, England.

LEVANT Victor Avrom, b. 26 Nov 1947, Winnipeg, Manitoba, Canada. Professor; Film Consultant; Practising Gestalt Therapist. *Education:* BA Honours, Economics, Political Science, 1968, MA, Political Science, 1975, PhD, Political Philosophy and International Relations, 1981, McGill University; Institut des Sciences Politiques, Sorbonne, Paris, 1968-69. *Appointments:* Film Consultant: The World Challenge, TV series, 1984; Studio B, Office National du Film, 1984-86; Maximage Productions, 1987; Communications for The Making of an Etching: P Buckley Moss, 1988. *Publications:* How to Make a Killing; Canadian Military Involvement in the Indo-China War, 1972; How to Buy a Country: Monograph on Global Pentagon Contracts (co-editor), 1973; Capital and Labor: Partners?, 1976; Capital et Travail, 1977; Quiet Complicity; Canada and the Vietnam War, 1987; The Neighborhood Gourmet, 1989; Le Gourmet du Quartier, 1989, 1990; Secrete Alliance: Le Canada dans las guerre du Vietnam, 1990.

Contributions to: This Magazine; Le Devoir; La Presse; The Canadian Encyclopedia; Interventions Economiques. *Honours:* National Wolfson Scholarship, 1965-66; Guy Drummond Fellowship, 1968-69, 1969-70; McConnell Fellowship, 1970-71, 1971-72, 1972-73; Canada Council Fellowship, 1976-77. *Address:* 4341 Old Orchard Ave, Montreal, Quebec, Canada H4A 3B5.

LEVENDOSKY Charles (Leonard), b. 4 July 1936. Journalist; Poet. *Education:* BS, Physics, 1958, BA, Mathematics, 1960, University of Oklahoma; MA, Secondary Education, New York University, 1963. *Appointments:* HS Teacher, US Virgin Islands, 1963-65; Tutor, Kyoto University, Japan, 1965-66; HS Tutor, New York, USA, 1966-67; Instructor of English, New York University, 1967-71; Visiting Poet (Poetry in the Schools) New York State, Georgia, New Jersey, 1971-72; Poet-in-Resident, Wyoming Council on the Arts, 1972-82; Editor for annual arts edition for the Casper Star-Tribune; Columnist for the Casper Star-Tribune, Wyoming, USA; Poet Laureate of Wyoming, 1988. *Publications:* Perimeters, 1970; Small Town America, 1974; Words and Fonts, 1975; Aspects of the Vertical, 1978; Distances, 1980; Wyoming Fragments, 1981; Nocturnes, 1982; Hands and Other Poems, 1986. *Contributions include:* Numerous magazines and journals including: El Corno Emplumado; New York Quarterly; Thoreau Journal Quarterly; American Poetry Review; Poetry Now; Writers Forum; Northwest Review; Sun Dog; Sulphur River; Negative Capability; Posts on; Blue Light Review; Dacotah Territory. *Honours:* National Endowment for the Arts Fellowship as Librettist; Small Town America, silver medal at Internationale Buchkunst-Austellung in Leipzig for book design, 1977; Wyoming Governor's Award for the Arts, 1983; Wyoming Writers' Arizola Magnenat Award, 1984; Wyoming Press Association Pacemaker Award, 1985; Wyoming Education Association's Friend of Education Award, 1987; Hugh M Hefner First Amendment Award for Print Journalism, 1987; John Phillip Immroth Memorial Award for Intellectual Freedom, 1987; H L Mencken Award, 1988; Manufacturers Hanover Art/World Cultural Award for editing the Star-Tribune's annual Arts Edition, 1988. *Memberships include:* PEN; Wyoming Writers; Poetry Progs of Wyoming (Founder and Director, 1973-78); Poets & Writers Inc. *Address:* PO Box 3033, Casper, WY 82602, USA.

LEVENS David George, b. 3 Apr 1939, London, England. Sales Manager. m. (1) Maureen Rose, 1961, 2 sons, 1 daughter; (2) Pamela Joy, 25 Aug 1973, 2 sons. *Education:* City and Guilds Certificates: Final Radio Servicing, 1955, Telecoms Intermediate, 1955. *Appointment:* BAAB Senior Marathon Coach, 1985. *Publications:* Jacob the Jumping Spider, Ratel and Guide, The Animal Marathon, Ragwort and Cinnabar, Farmer and the Fox, Sally and the Scamp and the Vandals, all in 1983; How to Love a Worm, 1989. *Contributions to:* Writers' Monthly; Poetry read on Radio Nottingham; Two children's series commissioned for East Midlands BT's Storyline. *Memberships:* Ilkeston Salvation Army, Young People's Sergeant Major; Chairman, Derby Writers' Guild, 1989-92; Founder and Deputy Chairman and Club Captain, Heannor Running Club; Founder and Chairman, NCH Relay League. *Address:* 16 Queen Street, Langley Mill, Nottingham NG18 4EJ, England.

LEVENSON Christopher, b. 1934, United Kingdom. Educator; Poet; Translator. *Appointments:* Taught: International Quaker School, Eerde, Netherlands, 1957-58; University of Münster, Federal Republic of Germany, 1958-61; Rodway Technical High School, Mangotsfield, Gloucestershire, 1962-64; Member, English Department, Carleton University, Ottawa, Canada, 1968-; Editor, Arc, 1978-88. *Publications:* Poetry from Cambridge (editor), 1958; New Poets 1959 (with I Crichton Smith and K Gershon), 1959; Van Gogh, by Abraham M W J Hammacher, translation, 1961; The Golden Casket: Chinese Novellas of Two Millennia, translation, 1965; The Leavetaking and Vanishing Point, by Peter Weiss, translation, 1966; Cairns, 1969; Stills,

1972; Into the Open, 1977; The Journey Back, 1978; No-Man's Land, 1980; Seeking Hearts Solace (translations), 1981; Light of the World (translations), 1982; Arriving at Night, 1986; The Return, 1986; Half Truths, 1991. *Address:* Department of English, Carleton University, Ottawa, Ontario, Canada K1S 5B6.

LEVER Tresham Christopher Arthur Lindsay, b. 9 Jan 1932, London, England. Naturalist. m. Linda Weightman McDowell Goulden, 6 Nov 1975. *Education:* Eton College, 1945-49; Trinity College, Cambridge, BA, 1954, MA, 1957. *Publications:* Goldsmiths and Silversmiths of England, 1975; The Naturalized Animals of the British Isles, 1977; Naturalized Mammals of the World, 1985; Naturalized Birds of the World, 1987; The Mandarin Duck, 1990; They Dined on Eland: The Story of the Acclimatisation Societies, 1992. Contributor to several books on natural history. *Contributions to:* The Connoisseur, Apollo, Country Life, The Field, Illustrated London News, New Scientist, Oryx, Ibis, The Listener, Times Literary Supplement, Species, London Naturalist, Journal of Natural History. *Honours:* Honorary Life Member, Bronte Society, 1988. *Memberships:* Fellow, Linnean Society of London. *Address:* Newell House, Winkfield, Berkshire SL4 4SE, England.

LEVERICH Kathleen Cameron, b. 2 Feb 1948, Connecticut, USA. Writer. m. Walter H Lorraine, 23 Jan 1988. *Appointments:* Editor, CRICKET Magazine, 1974-75; Children's Books Editor, Addison-Wesley Publishing Co, 1975-78. *Publications:* CRICKET's Backyard Expeditions, 1978; The Hungry Fox, 1979, paperback, 1991; Best Enemies, 1989; Best Enemies Again, 1991; Hilary and the Troublemakers, 1992. *Address:* Somerville, Massachusetts, USA.

LEVERTOV Denise, b. 24 Oct 1923, Ilford, Essex, England. Professor; Writer. m. Mitchell Goodman, 1947, 1 son. Emigrated to US in 1948, naturalized in 1955. *Education:* Private education. *Appointments:* Teacher, YM-YMCA Poetry Center, New York, 1964; City College of New York, 1965 and Vassar, Poughkeepsie, New York, 1966-67; Visiting Lecturer: Drew University, Madison, New Jersey, 1965, University of California at Berkeley, 1969, Visiting Professor: Massachusetts Institute of Technology, Cambridge, 1969-70; University of Cincinnati, Ohio, Spring 1973; Professor, Tufts University, Medford, Massachusetts, 1973-79; Fannie Hurst Professor (Poet in Residence), Brandeis University, Waltham, Massachusetts, 1981-83; Professor, Stanford University, Stanford, California, 1981-; Poetry editor, The Nation, New York, 1961-62 and Mother Jones, San Francisco 1976-78. *Publications include:* Verse: Life in the Forest, 1978; Collected Earlier Poems 1940-60, 1979; Candles in Babylon, 1982; Poems 1960-67, 1983; Oblique Prayers 1984; Selected Poems, 1986; Poems 1968-72, 1987; Breathing the water, 1987; A Door in the Hive, 1989; Evening Train (new Poems), 1992; New and Selected Essays, 1992. Recordings, essays and edited works. *Honours:* Honorary Scholar, Radcliffe Institute for Independent Study, Cambridge, Massachusetts, 1964-66; Longview Award, 1961; Guggenheim Fellowship, 1962; National Institute of Arts and Letters grant, 1966; Seven Honorary Doctorates; Receipient, NEA Senior Fellowship, 1991. *Memberships:* American Academy and Institute of Arts and Letters, 1980; Elmer Bobst Award, 1983; Corresponding Member, Academie Mallarme. *Address:* New Directions, 80 Eighth Avenue, New York, NY 10011, USA.

LEVEY Michael (Vincent) (Sir), b. 1927, United Kingdom. Writer; Director, National Gallery. *Appointments:* Slade Professor of Fine Art, Cambridge University, 1963-64; Assistant Keeper, 1951-66, Deputy Keeper, 1966- 68, Keeper, 1968-73; Director, 1973-86, National Gallery, London. *Publications:* Painting in XVIIIth Century Venice, 1959, 2nd Edition, 1980; From Giotto to Cezanne, 1962; Durer, 1964; Later Italian Pictures in the Collection of HM The Queen, 1964; Rococo to Revolution, 1966; Early Renaissance, 1967; The Life and Death of Mozart, 1971; Painting at Court, 1971; Art and Architecture of the 18th Century in France (with W W Kalnein), 1972; High Renaissance, 1974; The World of Ottoman Art, 1976; The Case of Walter Pater, 1978; Sir Thomas Lawrence, exhibition catalogue, 1979; The Painter Depicted, 1982; Tempting Fate, 1982; An Affair on the Appian Way, 1984; Tiepolo, 1986; Men at Work, 1988; The Soul of the Eye (anthology), 1990; Painting and Sculpture in France 1700-1789, 1992. *Honours:* Hawthornden Prize for Early Renaissance, 1968. *Address:* 36 Little Lane, Louth, Lincolnshire LN11 9DU, England.

LEVI Peter, (Chad Tigar), b. 1931, United Kingdom. Professor of Poetry; Author. *Appointments:* Fellow, St Catherine's College, Oxford, 1977-; Professor of Poetry, Oxford University, 1984-. *Publications:* Earthly Paradise, 1958; The Gravel Ponds: Poems, 1960; Beaumont: 1861- 1961, 1961; Orpheus Head, 1962; Water, Rock and Sand, 1962; Selected Poems of Yevtushenko (translated with R Milber-Gulland), 1962; The Shearwaters, 1965; Fresh Water, Sea Water: Poems, 1965; Pancakes for the Queen of Babylon: Ten Poems for Nikos Gatsos, 1968; Ruined Abbeys, 1968; Life is a Platform, 1971; Death is a Pulpit, 1971; Guide to Greece, by Pausanias, translation, 2 vols, 1971; The Light Garden of the Angel King: Journeys in Afghanistan, 1972; Penguin Modern Poets 22 (with Adrian Mitchell and John Fuller), 1973; The English Bible from Wycliff to William Barnes (editor), 1974; Pope (editor), 1974; John Clare and Thomas Hardy, 1975; Collected Poems, 1976; The Psalms, translation, 1977; The Noise Made by Poems, 1977; Five Ages, 1978; The Head in the Soup, novel, 1979; The Hill of Kronos, 1980; Atlas of the Greek World, 1980; Private Ground, 1981; The Flutes of Autumn, 1983; The Echoing Green: Three Elegies, 1983; Grave Witness, novel, 1984; Shakespeare's Birthday, 1985; A History of Greek Literature, 1985; The Frontiers of Paradise: A Study of Monks and Monasteries, 1987; Goodbye to the Art of Poetry, 1989; Shadow and Bone, 1989; Shade Those Laurels (with Cyril Connolly), 1990; The Art of Poetry, Lectures, 1991; Life of Lord Tennyson, 1993. *Memberships:* Society of Jesus, 1948-77. *Address:* Prospect Cottage, Frampton on Severn, Glostershire, England.

LEVIN (Henry) Bernard, b. 19 Aug 1928. Journalist; Author. *Education:* BSc., Economics, London School of Economics, University of London. *Appointments:* Writer, regular and occasional, many newspapers and magazines, UK and abroad including: The Times, London; Sunday Times; Observer; Manchester Guardian; Truth; Spectator; Daily Express; Daily Mail; Newsweek; International Herald Tribune; Writer, Broadcaster Radio and TV, 1952-. *Publications:* The Pendulum Years, 1971; Taking Sides, 1979; Conducted Tour, 1981; Speaking Up, 1982; Enthusiasms, 1983; The Way We Live Now, 1984; Hannibal's Footsteps, 1985; In These Times, 1986, To The End of The Rhine, 1987; All Things Considered, 1988; A Walk Up Fifth Avenue, 1989; Now Read On, 1990; If You Want My Opinion, 1992. *Honours:* Numerous awards for journalism; Honorary Fellow, London School of Economics, 1977; CBE, 1990. *Membership:* Member, Order of Polonia Restituta (by Polish Government in Exile). *Address:* c/o Curtis Brown Ltd., 162-168 Regent Street, London W1R 5TB, England.

LEVIN Michael Graubart, b. 8 Aug 1958, New York City, New York, USA. Novelist. *Education:* BA, Amherst College, 1980; JD, Columbia University Law School, 1985. *Appointments:* Writers Programme, University of California, Los Angeles, 1990-. *Publications:* Journey to Tradition, 1986; The Socratic Method, 1987; Settling the Score, 1989; Alive and Kicking, 1993. *Contributions to:* New York Times; Jerusalem Post. *Honours:* John Woodruff Simpson Fellowship, 1982, 1983. *Memberships:* Treasurer, Authors Guild Foundation, Inc., PEN, Authors Guild and Writers Guild of America, East, Inc. *Literary Agents:* Kristine Dahl, International Creative Management, New York City, New York, USA. *Address:* Box 181, Boston, MA 02101, USA.

LEVIN Torres, (Tereska Torres), b. 3 Sept 1920, Paris,

France. Writer. m. Meyer Levin, 25 Mar 1948, 3 sons, 1 daughter. *Education:* French Baccalaureat. *Publications:* Women's barracks, 1951; Not Yet, 1952; The Dangerous Games, 1953; The Golden Cage, 1954; By Colettes, 1955; The Converts, 1971; Les Annees Anglaises, 1980; Le Pays des Chuchotements, 1983; Les Poupees de Cendre, 1978; Les maisons hantees de Meyer Levin, 1990. *Address:* 65 Boulevard Arago, Studio 13, Paris 75013, France.

LEVINE Norman, b. 22 Oct. 1923, Canada. m. (1) Margaret Emily Payne, 2 Jan. 1952, (dec 1978), 3 daughters. (2) Anne Sarginson, 10 Aug 1983. *Education:* BA 1948, MA 1949, McGill University, Montreal; Trinity College, Cambridge, England 1945; King's College, London, 1949-50. *Publications:* Canada Made Me (travel), 1958; Short stories: One Way Ticket, 1961; Thin Ice, 1979-1980; Champagne Barn, 1984-1985; I Don't Want to Know Anyone Too Well (stories), 1971; From A Seaside Town (novel), 1970; Something Happened Here, (stories), 1991-92. *Contributions to:* Atlantic Monthly; Sunday Times; New Statesman; Spectator; Vogue; Harper's Bazaar; Encounter; Times Literary Supplement; Saturday Night. *Literary Agent:* Dr Ruth Liepman, Zurich, Switzerland. *Address:* c/o Liepman AG, Maienburgweg 23, CH-8044, Zurich.

LEVINE Stuart, b. 25 May 1932, New York, USA. College Professor; Editor. m. Susan Fleming Matthews, 6 June 1963, 2 sons, 1 daughter. *Education:* AB, Harvard University, 1954; MA 1956, PhD 1958, Brown University. *Appointments:* Founding Editor, American Studies, 1959-89; Exchange Professor, University of the West Indies, 1988. *Publications:* Materials for Technical Writing, 1963; The American Indian Today (with N O Lurie), 2nd edition 1970; Charles Caffin: The Story of American Painting, Editor, 1972; Edgar Poe: Seer and Craftsman, 1972; The Short Fiction of Edgar Allan Poe (with Susan Levine), 1976, 1989; Editor, with Susan Levine, Eureka and the Major Criticism, in The Collected Writing of Edgar Allan Poe (ongoing). *Contributions to:* American Quarterly; American Studies; Comparative Literature; Canadian Review of American Studies. *Honours:* Phi Beta Kappa, 1954; Anisfield-Wolf Award in Race Relations, 1968; Citation, National Conference of Christians & Jews, 1969; Exxon Intra-University Professorship, 1982-83; Gabriel Prize Jury, 1983-85; Chairman of Jury, 1985; 5 Fulbright Awards. *Memberships:* American Studies Association; Chairman, Prize Committees; Chairman, Major Speakers Committee, 1967, National Convention Executive Board, Mid America American Studies Association, 1960-. *Address:* 1846 Barker, Lawrence, KS 66044, USA.

LEVINSON Deirdre, b. 1931, United Kingdom. Novelist; Short Story Writer. *Publications:* Five Years, 1966; Modus Vivendi, 1984. *Address:* 220 W 93rd Street, New York, NY 10025, USA.

LEVINSON Harry, b. 16 Jan 1922, Port Jervis, New York, USA. Clinical Psychologist; Management Consultant. m. Roberta Freiman, 11 Jan 1946, (div June 1972), 2 sons, 2 daughters. *Education:* BSEd, 1943, MSEd, 1947, Psychology, Emporia (Kansas) State University; PhD, Clinical Psychology, University of Kansas, 1952. *Appointments:* Editorial Advisory Board, Consultation, 1981-83; Editorial Review Board, Academy of Management Executive, 1986-89; Editorial Board, Family Business Review, 1987-; Panel of Editorial Advisors, Human Relations, 1990-. *Publications include:* Men, Management, and Mental Health, 1962; Organizational Diagnosis, 1972; The Great Jackass Fallacy, 1973; Executive Stress, 1975; Psychological Man, 1976; Emotional Health in the World of Work, 1980; Executive, 1981; Ready, Fire, Aim: Avoiding Management by Impulse, 1986; Designing and Managing Your Career (editor), 1989; Career Mastery, 1992. *Contributions to:* Numerous professional journals and magazines. *Honours include:* Distinguished Alumnus Award, 1967, Distinguished Lecturer in Business, 1979, Emporia (Kansas) State University, 1967; McKinsey Foundation Awards, Best Management

Book, 1968, Best Article, 1969, 1981; Academy of Management Award, Best Management Book, 1968; Book Award, James A Hamilton Hospital Administrators, 1970; James A Hamilton Book Award, American College of Healthcare Executives, 1986; Distinguished Professional Contributions to Knowledge, American Psychological Association, 1992. *Memberships:* Authors Guild; Academy of Management; Fellow, American Psychological Association; Massachusetts and New England Psychological Associations; Past President, Kansas Psychological Association; American Association for the Advancement of Science; New York Academy of Sciences; Associate, Topeka Psychoanalytic Society; Affiliate, American Medical Association; Affiliate Scholar, Boston Psychoanalytic Society and Institute. *Address:* The Levinson Institute, 404 Wyman Street, Ste 400, Waltham, MA 02154, USA.

LEVINSON Riki, Friedberg, b. Brooklyn, New York, USA. Author; Associate Publisher; Art Director. m. Morton Levinson, 7 Mar 1944, 1 daughter. *Education:* BA, Cooper Union School of Art & Sciences. *Publications:* Watch the Stars Come Out, 1985; I Go with My Family to Grandma's, 1986; DinnieAbbieSister-r-r!, 1987; Touch! Touch! 1987; Our Home is the Sea, 1988. *Honours:* Watch the Stars Come Out, American Library Association Notable Book, 1985; Redbooks Top Ten Picture Books, 1985, I Go with My Family to Grandma's, Virginia Library Association's Jefferson Cup Honour Book, 1987; Georgia Book Award for DinnieAbbieSister-r-r-r!, 1987. *Memberships:* Authors Guild; American Institute of Graphic Arts.

LEVIS Larry, b. 1946, USA. University Educator; Poet. *Appointments:* Instructor, California State University, Fresno, 1970; Lecturer, Calfornia State University, Los Angeles, 1970-72; Visiting Lecturer, University of Iowa, Iowa City, 1972; Assistant Professor, University of Missouri, Columbia, 1974-80; Associate Professor of English, University of Utah, Salt Lake City, 1980-. *Publications:* Wrecking Crew, 1972; The Rain's Witness, 1975; The Afterlife, 1977; The Dollmaker's Ghost, 1981; Winter Stars, 1985. *Address:* Department of English, University of Utah, Salt Lake City, UT 84112, USA.

LEVY Alan, b. 1932, USA. Journalist; Author; Editor. *Appointments:* Reporter, Courier-Journal, Louisville, Kentucky, 1953-60; Investigator, Carnegie Commission on Educational Television, 1966-67; Foreign Correspondent, 1967-, including Life magazine and Good Housekeeping magazine in Prague, Czechoslovakia, 1967-71; New York Sunday Times and International Herald Tribune in Vienna, Austria, 1971-91; Dramaturg, Vienna's English Theatre Ltd, 1977-82; Foundeing Editor-in-Chief, The Prague Post, weekly English language newspaper, Prague, Czechoslovakia, 1991-. *Publications:* Draftee Confidential Guide (with B Krisher and J Cox), 1957, Revised Edition (with R Flaste), 1966; Operation Elvis, 1960; The Elizabeth Taylor Story, 1961; Wanted: Nazi Criminals at Large, 1962; Interpret Your Dreams, 1962, 2nd Edition, 1975; Kind-Hearted Tiger (with G Stuart), 1964; The Culture Vultures, 1968; God Bless You Real Good: My Crusade with Billy Graham, 1969; Rowboat to Prague, 1972; Good Men Still Live, 1974; The Bluebird of Happiness, 1976; Forever, Sophia, 1979, 2nd Edition, 1986; So Many Heroes, 1980; The World of Ruth Draper, play, 1982; Ezra Pound: The Voice of Silence, 1983; W H Auden: In the Autumn of the Age of Anxiety, 1983; Treasures of the Vatican Collections, 1983; Vladimir Nabokov: The Velvet Butterfly, 1984; Ezra Pound: A Jewish View, 1988. *Contributions to:* International Herald Tribune, Paris; ARTnews, New York City; New York Sunday Times; Reader's Digest; Travel & Leisure. *Honours:* New Republic Magazine's Younger Writer Award, Washington DC, 1957; Sigma Delta Chi, Regional Award for Best Enterprise Reporting in Coverage of Cuban Revolution, 1959; Bernard De Voro Fellowship in Prof Bread Loaf Writers Conference, Middlebury College, Vermont, USA, 1963; Best Article of 1978, Pacific Area Travel Assn, San Francisco, 1978; Golden Johann Strauss Medal of City of Vienna for Services to Culture and Tourism, 1981; (with Rene Staar), Ernst Krenck Prize of City of Vienna for Best Work of New Music, 'Just and Accident', 1983. *Memberships:* Authors Guild; Dramatists Guild; American PEN; Overseas Press Club of America; American Society of Journalists and Authors; Foreign Press Association of Vienna; Foreign Correspondents Association of Prague; Czech Union of Journalists. *Literary Agent:* Seratina Clarke, England. *Address:* c/o Seratina Clarke, Literary Agent, 96 Tunis Road, London W12 7EY, England.

LEVY Faye, b. 23 May 1951, Washington, District of Columbia, USA. Syndicated Columnist; Cooking Teacher. m. Yakir Levy, 28 Sept 1970. *Education:* BA, Sociology, Anthropology, Tel Aviv University, Israel, 1973; Grand Diplome, Ecole de Cuisine la Varenne, Paris, 1979. *Appointments:* Cokkery Editor, La Varenne, Paris, France, 1977-81; Columnist, Bon Appetit Magazine, 1982-88; Columnist, At Magazine, Israel, 1988-; Syndicated Columnist, Los Angeles Times, USA, 1990-; Columnist, Jerusalem Post, 1990-. *Publications:* La Cuisine du Poisson, 1984; French Cooking without Meat, in Hebrew, 1984; French Desserts, in Hebrew, 1985; Faye Levy's Chocolate Sensations, 1986; Fresh from France: Vegetable Creations, 1987; Fresh from France: Dinner Inspirations, 1989; Sensational Pasta, 1989; Fresh from France: Dessert Sensations, 1990; Faye Levy's International Jewish Cookbook, 1991; Faye Levy's International Chicken Cookbook, 1992. *Contributions to:* Gourmet; Bon Appetit; Chocolatier; Cooks Magazine. *Honours:* Best Dessert and Baking Book of the Year, 1986, Best General and Basic Cookbook of the Year, 1986, 2nd Prize, Vegetable and Fruit Books, 1987, International Association of Culinary Professionals. *Memberships:* International Association of Culinary Professionals; Newspaper Food Editors and Writers Association. *Literary Agent:* Maureen Lasher. *Address:* 835 4th St, Santa Monica, CA 90403, USA.

LEVY Jonathan Frederick, b. 20 Feb 1935, New York City, USA. Teacher; Writer. m. Geraldine Carro (deceased), 24 Nov 1968, 1 daughter. *Education:* MA; PhD. *Appointments:* Playwright in Residence, Manhattan Theatre Club, New York, 1973-78; National Endowment for the Arts (Chairman, Theatre for Youth Panel, 1979-81, Policy Panel, 1980-81; Literary Advisor, Manhattan Theatre Club, 1982-. *Publications:* Turandot, 1967; The Play of Innocence and Change, 1967; The Marvellous Adventures of Tyl, 1971; Boswel's Journal, 1972; Marco Polo, 1977; Charlie the Chicken, 1982. *Contributions to:* New York Times; Village Voice. *Honours:* Charlotte Chorpennig Award, Best Short Plays of 1983. *Memberships:* the Dramatists Guild; ASCAP; Playwrights for Children's Theatre, President 1971-75. *Literary Agent:* Susan Schulman. *Address:* 1165 Fifth Avenue, New York, NY 10029, USA.

LEWANDOWSKI Jan, b. 23 Feb 1933, Warsaw, Poland. Journalist; Writer. m. Iwona. *Education:* Warsaw University, 1951-54. *Publications:* Without the Song, 1965; The Stars of Small Orfelon, 1975; Do You Believe in UFO, M-mum?, 1981; Everybody is Waiting for the Sentence, 1979; The Grenadier's Tomb, 1986. *Contributions include:* Kierunki; Prawo i zycie; Slowo Powszechne; Tygodniowy Magazyn Tim. *Honours:* Wlodziemierz Pietrzak Award, 1986; Awards, Union of Polish Journalists, 1974, 1976, 1978, 1980. *Memberships:* Union of Polish Writers; Union of Polish Journalists. *Address:* ul. Prozna 12 m 17, 00-107 Warsaw, Poland.

LEWIN Leonard C, b. 2 Oct 1916, New York, USA. Writer. 1 son, 1 daughter. *Education:* BA, Harvard University. *Publications:* A Treasury of American Political Humor; Report from Iron Mountain; Triage. *Contributions to:* Numerous Professional Journals, Magazines, Newspapers. *Memberships:* Various Professional Organizations. *Literary Agent:* L. Wallace. *Address:* 6 Long Hill Farm, Guilford, CT 06437, USA.

LEWIN Michael Zinn, b. 21 July 1942, Cambridge, Massachusetts, USA. Writer. m. Marianne Ruth Grewe,

11 Aug 1965, 1 son, 1 daughter. *Education:* AB, Harvard University, 1964; Churchill College, Cambridge, England. *Appointments:* High School Teacher, 1966-69; Freelance Writer, 1969-. *Publications:* How to Beat College Tests; Ask the Right Question; The Way we Die Now; The Enemies Within; Night Cover; The Silent Salesman; Missing Woman; Outside In; Hard Line; Out of Season, (Out of Time in UK); Late Payments; And Baby Will Fall (Child Proof in UK); Called By A Panther, 1991; various radio plays, stage plays and short stories. *Honours:* Edgar Nominations for Ask the Right Question, 1972 and The Reluctant Detective, 1985; Maltese Falcon Society Best Novel for Hard Line, 1987; Raymond Chandler, Society of Germany Best Novel, 1992, Called By A Panther. *Memberships:* Crime Writers Association; Mystery Writers of America; Private Eye Writers Association; Authors Guild. *Literary Agent:* Wallace Literary Agency (NY), A M Heath (London). *Address:* 5 Welshmill Road, Frome, Somerset BA11 2LA, England.

LEWIS Anthony, b. 27 Mar 1927, New York City, USA. Newspaper Columnist; Legal Lecturer. m. (1) Linda Rannells, 8 July 1951, divorced, 1982, 1 son, 2 daughters, (2) Margaret Hilary Marshall, 23 Sept. 1984. *Education:* BA, Harvard University, 1948; Hon.D.Litt., Adelphi University, 1964, Rutgers University, 1973, Williams College, 1978, Clark University, 1982; Hon. LLD, Syracuse University, 1979, Colby College, 1983, Northeastern University, 1987. *Appointments:* Desk Editor, New York Times, 1948-52; Supreme Court Reporter, 1957-64; Chief, London Correspondent, 1964-72; Columnist, 1969-; Reporter, Washington Daily News, 1952-55; Lecturer, Law, Law School, Harvard University, 1975-90; James Madison Visiting Professor, Columbia University, 1983-. *Publications:* Gideon's Trumpet, 1964; Portrait of a Decade, 1964; Make No Law: The Sullivan Case and the First Amendment, 1991. *Honours:* Winner, Pulitzer Prize for National Correspondence, 1955, 1964. *Address:* New York Times, 2 Faneuil Hall Marketplace, Boston, MA 02109, USA.

LEWIS Charles. *See:* **DIXON Roger.**

LEWIS Ernest Michael Roy, (Roy Lewis), b. 6 Nov 1913, England. Author and Journalist. m. Christine May Tew, 1938, 2 daughters. *Education:* MA, University College Oxford: London School of Economics and University College London. *Appointments:* Editor and Washington Correspondent, The Economist, 1956-60; Editor, New Commonwealth, 1957-58; Leaader Writer and Commonwealth Correspondent, The Times, 1961-81. *Publications:* The English Middle Classes, 1949; Professional People, 1952; The British Business Man, 1961; The Evolution Man, 1960; Enoch Powell, 1979; Sierra Leone, 1954; The British in Africa, 1971; the Extraordinary Reign of King Ludd, 1990; A Force for the Future, 1976; A Walk with Mr Gladstone, 1991. *Contributions to:* Various newspapers, magazines and journals. *Address:* 2 Park House Gardens, Twickenham TW1 2DE, England.

LEWIS F R. *See:* **LEWIS Frances R.**

LEWIS Frances R (F R Lewis), b. 30 Apr 1939, USA. Writer. m. Howard D Lewis, 16 Apr 1961, 2 sons, 1 daughter. *Education:* BA, University of Albany, 1960. *Appointments:* Fiction Writing Instructor, 1989; Literary Manager, Public Radio Book Show, 1988. *Publications:* Short stories include: Cash on Delivery, 1991; How the World Grew Up, The Present, Husbands, 1992; Wanting, School Days, School Days, What You Eat, 1993; In Anthologies: Secrets, 1986, Next to the Last Straw, 1987, Gribiness, 1992, Vital Signs, 1993. One-act Play: Fourth Floor Follies: A literary Revue, 1989. *Contributions to:* Cream City Review; Salmon; San Jose Studies; Alasqa Quarterly Review; Kalliope; The William and Mary Review; The American Voice; Buffalo Spree; Blue Moon; Chariton Review; Albuquerque Journal; Alabama Literary Reveiew. *Honours:* Fellow, The MacDavell Colony fir the Arts; Fellow, The Millay Colony for the Arts; PEN NEA Syndicated Fiction Project

Awards, 1988, 1986; Finalist, Capricorn First Book Contest, The Writer's Voice, 1992. *Memberships:* Hudson Valley Writers Guild, (President, Secretary); Poets and Writers Inc., Associated Writing Programs; International Women's Writing Guild. *Address:* PO Box 12093, Albany, NY 12212, USA.

LEWIS Linda Joy, b. 20 June 1946, New York City, New York, USA. Writer. m. 31 Mar 1965, 1 son, 1 daughter. *Education:* BA, City College of New York, 1972; MEd, Florida Atlantic University, 1976. *Publications:* We Hate Everything But Boys, 1985; Is There Life After Boys, 1987; We Love Only Older Boys, 1988; 2 Young 2 Go 4 Boys, 1988; My Heart Belongs to That Boy, 1989; All for the Love of That Boy, 1989; Want to Trade 2 Brothers for a Cat, 1989; Dedicated to That Boy I Love, 1990; Loving Two is Hard to Do, 1990; Tomboy Terror in Bunk, 1991. *Membership:* Authors Guild. *Address:* 4469 Poinciana St, Lauderdale by the Sea, FL 33308, USA.

LEWIS Margaret Beatrice, b. 8 Sept 1942, Northern Ireland. Writer; Teacher. m. Peter Elvet Lewis, 15 May 1965, 1 son, 2 daughters. *Education:* BA, University of Alberta, Canada, 1962; MA, University of Leeds, England, 1964; PhD, University of Newcastle-upon-Tyne, 1984. *Appointments:* Committee Member, Literary and Philosophical Society, Newcastle-upon-Tyne, 1986-89; Board Member, Northern Arts, 1991-. *Publications:* Paul Scott, in British Novelists since 1960, 1983; Ngaio Marsh: A Life, 1991; Ngaio Marsh, in Twentieth Century Crime and Mystery Writers, 1991; Roderick Alleyn, in 100 Great Detectives, 1991; Natural Powers, short story; Death in Hard Covers (short Story), 1992. *Contributions to:* Ngaio March, Artist in Crime, to Pacific Way, 1989. *Honours:* Nominated for Talking Book of the Year, New Zealand, 1992. *Membership:* Crime Writers Association; Society of Authors. *Literary agent:* Brian Stone, Aitken and Stone, London, England. *Address:* 4 Mitchell Avenue, Jesmond, Newcastle-upon-Tyne NE2 3LA, England.

LEWIS Maynah, b. 1919, United Kingdom. Writer; Former Professional Musician and Teacher. *Publications:* No Place for Love, 1963; Give Me This Day, 1964; See the Bright Morning, 1965; Make Way for Tomorrow, 1966; The Long, Hot Days, 1966; The Future Is Forever, 1967; Till Then, My Love, 1968; Of No Fixed Abode, 1968; Symphony for Two Players, 1969; A Corner of Eden, 1970; A Pride of Innocence, 1971; Too Late for Tears, 1972; The Town That Nearly Died, 1973; The Miracle of Lac Blanche, 1973; The Unforgiven, 1974; The Other Side of Paradise, 1975; Yesterday Came Suddenly, 1975; A Woman of Property, 1976; These My Children, 1977; Love Has Two Faces, 1981; Barren Harvest, 1981; Hour of the Siesta, 1982; Whisper Who Dares, 1983. *Address:* c/o Robert Hale Ltd, 45-47 Clerkenwell Green, London EC1R 0HT, England.

LEWIS Mervyn. *See:* **FREWER Glyn Mervyn Louis.**

LEWIS Robert William, b. 15 Dec 1930, Elrama, Pennsylvania, USA. Professor; Editor. *Education:* BA, English, University of Pittsburgh, 1952; MA, English, Columbia University, New York, 1958; PhD, English, University of Illinois, Urbana, 1963. *Literary Appointments:* University of Nebraska, Lincoln, 1955-58; University of Illinois, Urbana, 1958-63; University of Texas, Austin, 1963-69; University of Catania, Italy, 1967-68; University of North Dakota, 1969-; American University in Cairo, Egypt, 1975; Ain Shams University, Cairo, Egypt, 1975-76; Editor, North Dakota Quarterly, 1982-. *Publications:* Hemingway on Love, 1965; Contributions to 'Seven Contemporary Authors' 1966, Editor, Thomas B Whitbread; Literature in Critical Perspectives, 1968, Editor Walter K Gordon; Hemingway's African Stories, 1969, Editor John M Howell; Hemingway: In Our Time, 1974, Editors Jackson J Benson and Richard Astro; The Short Stories of Ernest Hemingway, 1975, Editor Jackson J Benson; Ernest Hemingway: The Writer in Context, 1984, Editor James

Nagel; Hemingway in Italy & Other Essays, 1990; A Farewell to Arms: The War of the Words, 1992. *Contributions to:* The Humanist; North Country. *Honours include:* Outstanding Educator of America, 1975 and several other honours. *Memberships:* Modern Language Association; Executive Committee, Conference on College Composition and Communication, 1970-73; Executive Committee, 1980-83, President, 1987-92, The Hemingway Society; Editorial Board, The Hemingway Review, 1980-; Iota Tau Alpha; Chair, Board of Directors, The Ernest Hemingway Foundation, 1987-92. *Address:* Department of English, University of North Dakota, PO Box 7209, Grand Forks, ND 58202, USA.

LEWIS Roy. *See:* **LEWIS Ernest Michael Roy.**

LEWIS Thomas P(arker), b. 1936, USA. Children's Fiction Writer; Company President. *Appointments:* Coordinator, Institutional and Corporate Marketing Departments, Harper and Row, Publishers, Inc, New York City, 1964-82; President, Pro/Am Music Resources, White Plains, New York, 1982-. *Publications:* Hills of Fire, 1971; The Dragon Kite, 1974; Clipper Ship, 1978; A Call for Mr Sniff, 1981; Mr Sniff's Motel Mystery, 1983; The Blue Rocket Fun Show, 1986. *Address:* 63 Prospect Street, White Plains, NY 10606, USA.

LEWIS-SMITH Anne Elizabeth, b. 14 Apr 1925, London, England. Writer; Poet. m. Peter Lewis-Smith, 17 May 1944, 1 son, 2 daughters. *Appointments:* Editor, 1st WRNS Magazine, Aerostat International Balloon and Airship, 1973-78; Editor, WWNT Bulletin, BAFM Newsletter, 1967-83; Assistant Editor, 1967-83, Editor, 1983-91, Envoi; Editor, British Association of Friends of Museums Yearbook, 1985-91; Publisher, Envoi Poets Publications, 1986-. *Publications:* Poetry: Seventh Bridge, 1963; The Beginning, 1964; Flesh and Flowers, 1967, 3 editions; Dandelion Flavour, 1971; Dinas Head, 1980; Places and Passions, 1986; In the Dawn, 1987. *Contributions to:* Poetry to over 40 magazines; Numerous articles to newspapers and magazines; Own Woman's page, 6 years; Features to Cambridgeshire Life and Northamptonshire Life. *Honours include:* Tissadier Diploma, services to International Aviation; Debbie Warley Award, services to International Aviation; Dorothy Tutin Award, services to poetry. *Membership:* Fellow, PEN. *Address:* Pen Ffordd, Newport, Pembrokeshire, Dyfed SA42 0QT, Wales.

LEWISOHN Leonard. *See:* **LEWISOHN Leonard C.**

LEWISOHN Leonard C, b. 28 Aug 1953, New York, USA. Translator. m. Jane Ferril, 1973. *Education:* BA, International Relations, Pahlavi University, 1973-78; PhD, Persian Literature, University of London, 1983-88. *Publications:* Translations: Masters of the Path (A History of the Masters of the Nimatullahi Sufi Order), 1980; The Truths of Love: Sufi Poetry, 1982; Sufi Women, 1983; Jesus in the Eyes of the Sufis, 1983; Books: The Legacy of Medieval Persian Sukism, editor, 1992; Divan-i Muhammad Shirin Maghribi, 1993; Persian Sufism from its Origins to Rumi, editor, 1993; Forthcoming, The Nimatullahi Sufi Order in India and Iran. *Contributions to:* Shabistari's Garden of Mysteries, 1989; Iranian Studies; Iran Numeh; Annemarie Schimmel Festschrift, 1993. *Memberships:* Society of Authors; Middle Eastern Studies Association of North America; British Institute of Persian Studies. *Address:* 41 Chepstow Place, London W2 4TS, England.

LEXAU Joan M, (Joan L Nodset), American. Writer of Children's fiction. *Appointments:* Editorial Secretary, Catholic Digest, St Paul, 1953-55; Advertising Production Manager, Glass Packer magazine, New York City, 1955-56; Reporter, Catholic News, New York City, 1956-57; Correspondent, Religious News Service, New York City, 1957; Children's Books Production Liaison, Harper and Row, Publishers, New York City, 1957-61. *Publications:* Olaf Reads, 1961; Cathy is Company, 1961; Millicent's Ghost, 1962; The Trouble with Terry,

1962; Olaf is Late, 1963; That's Good, That's Bad, 1963; Jose's Christmas Secret, 1963, revised edition as The Christmas Secret, 1973; (as Joan L Nodset) Who Took the Farmer's Hat? 1963; (as Joan L Nodset) Go Away, Dog, 1963; Banjie, 1964; Maria, 1964; (as Joan L Nodset) Where Do You Go When You Run Away? 1964; (ed)Convent Life: Catholic Religious Orders for Women in North America, 1964; I Should Have Stayed in Bed! 1965; More Beautiful Than Flowers, 1966; The Homework Caper, 1966; A Kite over Tenth Avenue, 1967; Finders Keepers, Losers Weepers, 1967; Every Day a Dragon, 1967; Three Wishes for Abner, 1967; Striped Ice Cream! 1968; The Rooftop Mystery, 1968; A House So Big, 1968; Archimedes Takes a Bath, 1969; Crocodile and Hen, 1969; It All Began with a Drip, Drip, Drip...., 1970; Benjie on His Own, 1970; Me Day, 1971; A T for Tommy, 1971; That's Just Fine, and Who-o-o Did It? 1971; Emily and the Klunky Baby and the Next-Door Dog, 1972; (as Joan L Nodset) Come Here Cat, 1973; The Tail of the Mouse, 1974; I'll Tell on You, 1976; Beckie and the Bookworm, 1979; I Hate Red Rover, 1979; The Spider Makes a Web, 1979; Jack and the Beanstalk, 1980; The Poison Ivy Case, 1984; The Dog Food Caper, 1985; Don't Be My Valentine, 1985. *Address:* P O Box 270, Otisville, NY 10963, USA.

LEY Alice Chetwynd, b. 12 Oct 1913, Halifax, Yorkshire, England. Novelist. m. Kenneth James Ley, 3 Feb 1945. 2 sons. *Education:* Diploma in Sociology, London University. *Literary Appointments:* Tutor, Creative Writing, Harrow College of Further Education, 1962-84; Lecturer, Sociology & Social History, Harrow College of Further Education, 1968-71. *Publications:* 19 novels published in UK, USA, Germany, Holland, Scandinavia, Iceland, and Australia including: The Georgian Rake, 1960 (dramatised and broadcast on BBC Saturday Night Theatre, Radio, 1962 and 1966). *Contributions to:* Numerous journals. *Honour:* Gilchrist Award for Diploma in Sociology, 1962. *Memberships:* Romantic Novelists Association, Chairman 1970, Honorary Life Member, 1987; Society of Women Writers & Journalists; Jane Austen Society. *Literary Agent:* Curtis Brown Ltd, London. *Address:* 42 Cannonbury Avenue, Pinner, Middlesex HA5 1TS, England.

LEYTON Sophie. *See:* **WALSH Sheila.**

LEZENSKI Cezary Jerzy, b. 6 Jan 1930, Poznan, Poland. Journalist; Novelist. m. Antonina Czebatul, 1958, 1 son, 1 daughter. *Education:* Journalism, 1951, MA, Polish Philology, 1952, Jagiellonian University, Cracow. *Appointments:* Editor-in-Chief, Kurier Polski, 1969-81; Editor- in-Chief, Epoka Literacke, 1981-90; Editor-in-Chief, Poland Today, edited monthly in 7 languages in 104 countries 1991-. *Publications:* 21 books including: Powrot, novel, 1963; Zolnierskie Drogi, story, 1971; Pozostaly Tylko Slady Podkow, essay, 1978, 1984; Kwatera 139, biography, 1989; Kawaleria Polska XX Wieku, essay, 1991; 6 novels for young people. *Contributions to:* Noweksiaski literary and science magazine, 1978-89. *Honours:* Commander, Polonia Restituta, 1978; Order of Smile for young people's novels, 1979. *Memberships:* Society of Polish Writers; Vice-Chairman, Mazurek Dabrowski Society; Chancellor of Chapter of the Order of Smile (Internationa); Board, Authors Agency, Poland; Polish Section, UNICEF. *Literary Agent:* Authors Agency, ul Danilowiczowska, Warsaw, Poland. *Address:* ul Frascati 8/10A, 00-483 Warsaw, Poland.

LI Tien-yi, b. 14 Mar 1915, Juyzng, Honan, China. Professor. m. 14 Sept 1963, 1 son, 1 daughter. *Education:* BA, Nankai University, 1937; MA 1946, PhD 1950, Yale University. *Appointments:* Editor and Executive Secretary, Tsing Hua Journal of Chinese Studies, 1955-88; Director and Editor-in-Chief, Far Eastern Publications, Yale University, 1960-69. *Publications:* A Study of Thomas Hardy, 1937; Woodrow Wilson's China Policy, 1913-1917, 1952; P'ai-an Ching-ch'i, editor, 2 vols, 1967; Chinese Fiction, a Bibliography pf Books and Articles in Chinese and English, 1968; Chinese Historical Literature, 1970; Erh-k'o P'ai-an Ching-ch'i, editor, 2 vols 1980; Editor, Life and Letters.

Contributions to: Tsing Hua Journal of Chinese Studies; Journal of Asian Studies; American Historical Review. *Honours:* Phi Tau Phi Honorary Society; Award from National Science Council, Taiwan; Award from Tunghai University, Taiwan. *Memberships:* American Oriental Society; Association for Asian Studies; American Historical Society; Board Member, American Chinese Language Teachers Association; Board Member and President, American Association for Chinese Studies; Director, Institute of Chinese Literature, The Chinese University of Hong Kong. *Address:* Department of East Asian Languages and Literatures, The Ohio State University, Columbus, OH 43210, USA.

LI Xueqin, b. 28 Mar 1933, Beijing, China. Professor. m. Xu Weiying, 20 Aug 1956, 2 sons. *Education:* Department of Philogophy, Tsinghua University, Beijing, 1952. *Publications:* On Geography of the Yin Dynasty, 1959; The Wonder of Chinese Bronzes, 1980; Eastern Zhou and Qin Civilizations, 1985; Essays on Comparative Archaeology, 1991; Origins of I- Ching, 1992; Selected works of Li Xueqin, 1989; Studies of Recently Discovered Bronzes, 1990. *Memberships:* Chiarman, Association of the History of Pre-Qin Dynasties; Honorary Member, The American Oriental Society. *Address:* Institute of History, Chinese Academy of Social Sciences, 6 Ritan Lu, Beijing 100020, China.

LIBBY Ronald Theodore, b. 20 Nov 1941, Los Angeles, California, USA. University Professor. m. Kathleen Christina Jacobson, 6 June 1982, 2 daughters. *Education:* BA, Political Science, Washington State University, 1965; MA, Political Science, 1966, PhD, Political Science, 1975, University of Washington. *Appointments:* Book Reviewer, numerous professional journals and magazines including Comparative Politics, ORBIS, Journal of Modern African Studies, American Political Science Association, Social Science Quarterly. *Publications:* Toward an Africanized US Policy for Southern Africa, 1980; The Politics of Economic Power in Southern Africa, 1987; Hawke's Law: The Politics of Mining and Aboriginal Land Rights in Australia, 2nd Edition, 1992; Protecting Markets: US Policy and the World Grain Trade, 1992. *Contributions to:* Listen to the Bishops, to Foreign Policy, 1983; Transnational Class Alliances in Zambia, to Comparative Politics, 1983; The United States and Jamaica: Playing the American Card, to Latin American Perspectives, 1990; 11 more peer- reviewed articles to journals. *Honours:* Grant, University of Michigan, 1969; Carnegie Endowment Grant, 1971; Book nominated by American Political Science Association for Woodrow Wilson Foundation Award for Best Book of the Year, 1988; Choice Award for Outstanding Academic Book, 1991; Protecting Markets: US Policy and the World Grain Trade nominated for the Gladys M Kammerer Award, American Political Science Association, Best Publication in the field of US National Policy. *Memberships:* New Zealand Political Science Association, Treasurer-Elect 1989; American Political Science Association; Australian Political Studies Association. *Literary Agent:* Oscar Collier, Collier Associates, 2000 Flat Run Rd, Seaman, OH 45679, USA. *Address:* Department of Political Science, Southwest State University, Marshall, MN 56258, USA.

LIBERMAN Serge Israel, b. 14 Nov 1942, Fergana, Russia. Medical Practitioner; Writer; Editor; Reviewer; Bibliographer. m. Eva Matzner, 19 Jan 1969, 1 son, 2 daughters. *Education:* MBBS, Melbourne University, Australia, 1967. *Appointments:* Editor, Melbourne Chronicle, 1977-84, re-appointed 1991; Associate Editor, Outrider, 1984-86; Literary Editor, Menorah, 1986; Literary Editor, Australian Jewish News, Melbourne, 1987-; Literary Editor, Australian Jewish Times, Sydney, 1987-; Member, Editorial Committee, Australian Jewish Historical Society Journal, 1988-. *Publications:* On Firmer Shores, 1981; A Universe of Clowns, 1983; The Life That I Have Led, 1986; A Bibliography of Australian Judaica, 1987, updated and revised 1991; The Battered and the Redeemed, 1990; Anthologies: Shalom; Jewish Writing Down Under; Transgressions; Joseph's Coat; The Greatest Game;

Pomegranates; Ethnic Australia; Displacements 2; Neighbours. Editorial Committee of GESHER: Journal of One Council for Christians and Jews. *Contributions to:* Biala; Nepean Review; Australian Jewish News; Melbourne Chronicle; Overland; Outrider; Inprint; Menorah; Story-Teller; Brave New Word; Jewish Quarterly, London. *Honours:* Alan Marshall Award, 1979, 1980, 1983; New South Wales Premier's Literary Award, 1984. *Memberships:* Fellowship of Australian Writers; Australian Society of Authors; PEN International, Melbourne Centre, Vice-President 1986-87; Honorary Treasurer, Australian Jewish Historical Society, Victorian Branch. *Address:* 2/64 Hotham Street, Balaclava, Victoria 3183, Australia.

LICHTENBERG Jacqueline, b. 1942, American, Writer. *Publications:* House of Zeor, 1974, 3rd Ed. 1981; (with S Marshak and J Winston), Star Trek Lives! 1975; Unto Zeor, Forever, 1978, 1980; (with J Lorrah), First Channel, 1980, 1981; Channel's Destiny, 1982, Ren Sime, 1984; City of a Million Legends, 1985; Dushau, 1985; Farfetch, 1985; Outreach, 1986; (with Jean Lorrah), Zelerod's Doom, 1986: Those of My Blood, 1988.

LIDDELL (John) Robert, b. 1908, British, Writer of Novels/Short stories, Literature, Travel, Translations. *Appointments:* Senior Assistant, Department of Western Manuscripts, Bodleian Library, Oxford, 1933-38; Lecturer, University of Helsingfors, Finland, 1939, and Farouk I University, Alexandria, 1941-46; Lecturer 1946-51 and Assistant Professor, 1951-52, Fuad I University, Cairo; Head of English Department, Athens University, 1963-68. *Publications:* The Almond Tree, 1938; Kind Relations (in US as Take This Child) 1939; The Gantillons, 1940; Watering Place (stories) 1945; A Treatise on the Novel, 1947; The Last Enchantments, 1948; Unreal City, 1952; Some Principles of Fiction, 1953; Aegean Greece, 1954; The Novels of Ivy Compton-Burnett, 1955; Byzantium and Istanbul, 1956; The Morea, 1958; The Rivers of Babylon, 1959; (trans) Demetrios Sicilianos: Old and New Athens, 1960; The Novels of Jane Austen, 1963; Mainland Greece, 1965; An Object for a Walk, 1966; The Deep End, 1968; Stepsons, 1969; Abbé Tigrane: Ferdinand Fabre (trans), 1988; Cavafy: A Critical Biography, 1974; The Novels of George Eliot, 1977; Elizabeth and Ivy (memoir) 1986; The Aunts (novel), 1987; Twin Spirits (Emily and Anne Brontë), 1990. *Honour:* Hon DLitt, 1987. *Address:* c/o Barclays Bank, High Street, Oxford, England.

LIDDLE Peter (Hammond), b. 1934. British, Writer on History. Keeper of the Liddle Collection, University of Leeds. *Appointments:* History Teacher, Havelock School, Sunderland, 1957; Head, History Department, Gateacre Comprehensive School, Liverpool, 1958-67; Lecturer, Notre Dame College of Education, 1967; Lecturer 1967-70, Senior Lecturer in History, 1970-, Sunderland Polytechnic; Tutor, British Council, Lesotho and Chairman, Sunderland Industrial Archaeological Society, 1969; Fellow of the Royal Historical Society, 1982; Vice-President, British Audio-Visual Trust; Keeper of the Liddle Collection, University of Leeds, 1988. *Publications:* Men of Gallipoli, 1976; World War One: Personal Experience Material for Use in Schools, 1977; Testimony of War 1914-18, 1979; The Sailor's War 1914-18, 1985; Gallipoli: Pens, Pencils and Cameras at War, 1985; 1916: Aspects of Conflict, 1985; (ed and contributor) Home Fires and Foreign Fields, 1985; The Airman's War 1914-18, 1987; The Soldier's War 1914-18, 1988; Voices of War, 1988; The Battle of the Somme, 1992. *Address:* Dipity House, 282 Pudsey Road, Leeds, LS13 4HK, England.

LIDE Mary Ruth, (Harry Lomer), b. Cornwall, England. Writer. 3 sons, 1 daughter. *Education:* MA, History, Oxford University. *Publications:* The Bait (as Mary Lomer), 1961; Ann of Cambray, 1985; Gifts of the Queen, 1985; Hawks of Sedgemont, 1987; Diary of Isobelle, 1988; Tregaran, 1989; Command of the King, 1990; Robert of Normandy (as Mary Lomer), 1991; The Legacy, 1991; The Homecoming, 1992. *Contributions to:* Short stories; Poetry; Book reviews. *Honours:* Avery

Hopwood Award for Poetry, 1955; Best Historical Novel for Ann of Cambray, USA, 1984. *Membership:* Writers Guild, USA. *Literary Agent:* Goodman Associates, USA. *Address:* c/o Goodman Associates, 500 West End Avenue, New York, NY 10024, USA.

LIDSTONE John Barrie Joseph, b. 21 July 1929, Salisbury, England. Marketing Consultant; Author. m. Primrose Vivien Russell, 30 Mar 1957, 1 daughter. *Education:* Presentation College Reading, University of Manchester, RAF Education Officers' Course. *Career:* National service RAF 1947-48; English Master Repton 1949-52; Shell-Mex and BP and Assoc cos 1952-62, dep md Vicon Agricultural Machinery Ltd 1962-63, Director and General Manager, Marketing Selections Ltd 1969-72; Marketing Improvements Group Plc: joined 1965, Director 1968-, Director and General Manager 1972-74, dep md 1974-88, dep Chairman 1988-89; Non-executive Director 1989-; Non-executive Director: Kalamazoo Plc, 1986-91, North Hampshire Trust Co Ltd 1986-, St Nicholas' School Fleet Educational Trust Ltd 1982-90; UK Management Consultancies Association 1978-88 (Chairman 1986-87). *Publications:* Training Salesmen on the Job, 1975, 2nd edition, 1986; Recruiting and Selecting Successful Salesmen, 1976, re-issued as 'How to Recruit and Select Successful Salesmen' 1983; Negotiating Profitable Sales, 1977, Made into two part film by Video Arts, 1979; Motivating Your Sales Force, 1978; Making Effective Presentation, 1985; The Sales Presentation, co-author, 1985; Profitable Selling, 1986; Marketing Planning for the Pharmaceutical Industry, 1987; Manual of Sales Negotiation, 1991; Manual of Marketing, (for University of Surrey,) 1991; Beyond the Pay Packet, 1991; Face the Press, 1992. *Contributions to:* The Times; Financial Times; Observer; Daily Telegraph; Director; Management To-Day; Marketing Week; Chief Executive: International Management. *Honours:* Two books filmed by Rank and Video Arts; Award for Creative Excellence for film of book 'Training Salesmen on the Job' USA, 1981; Freeman, City of London, 1978; Voted Top Speaker on Marketing in Europe, 1974. *Membership:* British Academy of Film and Television Arts; National Executive Committee Chartered Institute of Marketing 1985-90; FIMC; FIM; FIOD; FCIM (MCIM 1980). *Address:* 17 Ulster Terrace, Regents Park, London NW1 4PJ, England.

LIEBER Robert James, b. 29 Sept 1941, Chicago, Illinois, USA. Professor of Government. m. Nancy Lee Isaksen, 20 June 1964, 2 sons. *Education:* BA, High Honours, University of Wisconsin, 1963; PhD, Harvard University, 1968. *Publications:* British Politics and European Unity, 1970; Theory and World Politics, 1972; Oil and the Middle East War: Europe in the Energy Crisis, 1976; Eagle Entangled: US Foreign Policy in a Changing World (co-editor, co-author) 1979; The Oil Decade, 1983, 1986; Eagle Defiant, co-editor, co-author, 1983; Eagle Resurgent, co-editor, co- author, 1987; No Common Power, 1988 and 1991; Eagle in a New World, co-editor, co-author, 1992. *Contributions to:* International Affairs; American Political Science Review; International Security; Foreign Policy; Politique Etrangere; Washington Quarterly; Washington Post; New York Times; Harpers. *Honours:* Graduate Prize Fellowship, Harvard University, 1964; Guggenheim Fellow, 1972; Council on Foreign Relations International Affairs Fellow, 1972; Rockefeller Foundation International Relations Fellowship, 1978; Woodrow Wilson International Centre for Scholars Fellow, 1980. *Memberships:* Phi Beta Kappa; International Institute for Strategic Studies; Council on Foreign Relations. *Address:* Department of Government, Georgetown University, Washington, DC 20057, USA.

LIEBERMAN Herbert Henry, b. 22 Sept 1933, New Rochelle, New York, USA. Novelist; Playwright; Editor. m. Judith Barsky, 9 June 1963, 1 daughter. *Education:* AB, City College of New York, 1955; AM, Columbia University, 1957. *Publications:* The Adventures of Dolphin Green, 1967; Crawlspace, 1971; The Eighth Square, 1973; Brilliant Kids, 1975; City of the Dead, 1976; The Climate of Hell, 1978; Nightcall from a Distant Time Zone, 1982; Night Bloom, 1984; The Green Train, 1986; Shadow Dancers, 1989; Sandman Sleep, 1993. *Honours:* Charles Sergel, 1st Prize for Playwriting, University of Chicago, 1963; John Simon Guggenheim Fellow, Playwrighting, 1964; Grand Prix de Litterature Policiere, Paris, France, 1978. *Memberships:* Mystery Writers of America Inc; International Association of Crime Writers. *Literary Agent:* Georges Borchardt, New York, USA. *Address:* c/o Georges Borchardt, 136 East 57th St, New York, NY 10022, USA.

LIEBERMAN Robert Howard, b. 4 Feb 1941, New York City, USA. m. Gunilla Anna Rosen, 9 Sept 1911, 2 sons. *Education:* Cornell University, 1958-59; BS, Electrical Engineering, Polytechnic Institute of Brooklyn, 1962; MS, Electronic Engineering/Biophysics, Cornell University, 1965. *Publications:* Baby, 1981; Paradise Rezoned, 1974; Goobersville Breakdown, 1979; Perfect People, 1986; Faces in a Famine, documentary film, 1984. *Contributions to:* numerous articles and stories in US and Swedish Magazines. *Honours:* G.K. Hall Distinguished Fiction Series, 1980; CINE Golden Eagel for Faces in a Famine, 1984 *Membership:* American Film Institute. *Literary Agent:* Maureen Walters, Curtis Brown Ltd. *Address:* 400 Nelson Road, Ithaca, NY 14850, USA.

LIEBERTHAL Kenneth Guy, b. 9 Sept 1943, Asheville, North Carolina, USA. Professor of Political Science. m. Jane Lindsay, 15 June 1968, 2 sons. *Education:* BA with distinction, Dartmouth College, 1965; MA, 1968, Certificate, East Asian Institute, 1968, PhD, Political Science, 1972, Columbia University. *Appointments include:* Instructor, 1972, Assistant Professor, 1972-75, Associate Professor, 1976-82, Professor, 1982-83, Political Science Department, Swarthmore College; Postdoctoral Scholar, Center for Chinese Studies, 1974, Visiting Professor, 1983, Professor, 1983-, University of Michigan, Ann Arbor; Editorial Boards: China Economic Review; China Quarterly. *Publications include:* Policy Making in China: Leaders, Structures, and Processes (with Michel Oksenberg), 1988; Paths to Sino-American Cooperation in the Automotive Sector (with Michael Flynn and others), 1989; Research Guide to Central Party and Government Meetings in China, 1949-1986 (with Bruce Dixon), 1989; Co-editor, contributor: Perspectives on Modern China: Four Anniversaries, 1991; Bureaucracy, Politics and Policy Making in Post-Mao China, 1991. *Contributions to:* Quarterly publication for Atlantic Council; Book reviews to: American Political Science Review; China Economic Review; China Quarterly. *Honours:* Rufus Choate Scholar, 1964-65; National Defense Foreign Language Fellow, Herbert H Lehman Graduate Fellow, 1967-69; Reynolds Scholarship, 1969-70; NDEA-Related Fulbright Hays Fellow, 1970; Foreign Area Fellow, 1971, 1972; National Endowment for the Humanities Fellow, 1979; AMOCO Award, Distinguished University Teaching, 1986; LS&A Excellence in Education Award, 1991; Many grants. *Memberships:* Council on Foreign Relations; American Political Science Association; Association of Asian Studies; Board of Directors, National Committee on US-China Relations; Joint Committe on Chinese Studies, ACLS and SSRC. *Address:* Center for Chinese Studies, 104 Lane Hall, 204 S State St, University of Michigan, Ann Arbor, MI 48109, USA.

LIEBMAN Herbert, b. 29 Mar 1935, Brooklyn, NY, USA. Associate Professor of English. m. Heather Denwood, 12 Aug 1976, 2 sons. *Education:* BA 1957; MA 1964; MPhil, 1992. *Publications:* Plays produced: Off Off Broadway; Alex and Joanna, 1985; Positions, 1984; The Breakers, 1982; Survivors, 1978. *Contributions to:* Short stories: Paris Transcontinental; Confrontation; Chelsea; Pen Syndicated Fiction; Outerbridge. *Honours:* McDowell Fellow, 1979; NEA Fellow, 1979; Wurlitzer Foundation, 1986, 1988, 1990; VCCA Fellow, 1990; Creative Incentive Award, CUNY, 1987. *Memberships:* The Dramatists Guild. *Literary Agent:* Letti Lee, Ann Elmo Agency Inc. *Address:* c/o English Department, College of Staten Island, 715 Ocean Terrace, New York 10301, USA.

LIEBMANN Irina, b. 23 July 1943, Moscow, USSR. Writer; Scripter; Reporter. 2 daughters. *Education:* MA, Sinology and Arts, Leipzig University. *Publications:* Berliner Mietshaus (Berlin Apartment House), 1983; Neun Berichte uber Ronald, der seine Grossmutter begraben wollte (Nine Reports on Ronald, Who Wanted to Bury His Grannie), radio play reprinted in Dialog, 1981; henschelverlag : Sie Mussen jetzt gehen, Frau Muhsam (You'd Better Go Now, Frau Muhsam), radio play reprinted in Dialog; Hast du die Nacht genutzt? Story, reprinted in Neue Rundschau, Nr 4, 1987, and in Neue Deutsche Lite Ratur, Nr 2, 1988; Playwrights: Berliner Kindl, Schwerin 1988. *Contributions to:* Wochenpost; Temperamente, Berlin 1975-80. *Honours:* 2nd Prize, Radio Drama Competition, 1979; Radiodrama Award for the GDR (Preis der Horer), 1980; 1st Prize, radio drama Competition, 1981; Award for the Benefit of Young writers, 1984; Ernst-Willner Prize of the Editors, Klagenfurt, 1987. *Memberships:* Schriftstellerverband der DDR. *Literary Agent:* Mitteldeutscher Verlag Halle/Saale. *Address;* Wolfshagener Str., DDR 1100 Berlin, Democratic Republic of Germany.

LIFTON Betty Jean, American; Writer of Children's fiction; Plays/Autobiography/Memoirs/Personal. *Education:* PhD, (UMM Inst), 1992. *Publications:* Joji and the Dragon, 1957; Mogo the Mynah, 1958; Joji and the Fog, 1959; Kap the Kappa, 1960, play 1974; The Dwarf Pine Tree, 1963; Joji and the Amanojaku, 1965; The Cock and the Ghost Cat, 1965; The Rice-Cake Rabbit, 1966; The Many Lives of Chio and Goro, 1966; Taka-Chan and I: A Dog's Journey to Japan, 1967; Kap and the Wicked Monkey, 1968; The Secret Seller, 1968; The One-Legged Ghost, 1968; A Dog's Guide to Tokyo, 1969; Return to Hiroshima, 1970; The Silver Crane, 1971; The Mud Snail Son, 1971; Good Night, Orange Monster, 1972; (with Thomas C Fox) Children of Vietnam, 1972; (ed) Contemporary Children's Theater, 1974; Twice Born: Memoirs of an Adopted Daughter, 1975; Jaguar, My Twin, 1976; Lost and Found: The Adoption Experience, 1979; I'm Still Me, 1981; A Place Called Hiroshima, 1985; The King of Children, A Biography of Janusz Korczak, 1988; Tell Me A Real Adoption Story, 1991; Forthcoming: The Adoptee's Journey. *Address:* 300 Central Park W, New York, NY 10024, USA.

LILIENTHAL Alfred M, b. 25 Dec 1913, New York City, USA. Author; Historian; Attorney. *Education:* BA, Cornell University, 1934; LLD Columbia University School of Law, 1938; JD, 1969. *Appointments:* Editor, Middle East Perspective, 1968-85. *Publications:* What Price Israel? 1953; There Goes the Middle East, 1958; The Other Side of the Coin, 1965; The Zionist Connection I, 1978; The Zionist Connection II, 1982, Czech trans 1989, Japanese trans 1991. *Contributions to:* Numerous journals including: Readers Digest; Mercury. *Honour:* National Press Club Book Honours, 1982. *Memberships:* University Club; Cornell Club; National Press Club; Capitol Hill Club. *Address:* 800 25 NW, Washington DC 210378, USA.

LILLINGTON Kenneth (James). b. 1916. British, Writer of Novels/Short stories, Children's fiction, Plays/Screenplays, Literature. Lecturer in English Literature, Brooklands Technical College, Weybridge, Surrey, now retired. *Publications:* The Devil's Grandson, 1954; Soapy and the Pharoah's Curse, 1957; Conjuror's Alibi, 1960; The Secret Arrow, 1960; Blue Murder, 1960; A Man Called Hughes, 1962; My Proud Beauty, 1963; First (and Second) Book odf Classroom Plays, 1967-68; Fourth (and Seventh) Windmill Book of One-Act Plays, 1967-72; Cantaloup Crescent, 1970; Olaf and the Ogre, 1972; (ed)Nine Lives, 1977; For Better for Worse, 1979; Young Man of Morning, 1979; What Beckoning Ghost, 1983; Selkie, 1985; Full Moon, 1986. *Address:* 90 Wodeland Avenue, Guildford, Surrey GU2 5LD, England.

LIM Shirley Geok-Lin, b. 27 Dec 1944, Malacca, Malaysia. Author. m. Dr Charles Bazerman, 27 Nov 1972, 1 son. *Education:* BA, Ist Class Honours 1967, MA, English & American Literature 1971, PhD 1973, Brandeis University, USA. *Appointments include:* Writer-in-residence, National University of Singapore, 1985. *Publications:* Crossing the Peninsula, 1980; Another Country, 1982; No Man's Grove, 1985; Modern Secrets, 1988. *Contributions include:* Ariel; Asia; Asia Week; Commentary; Contact II; Journal of Ethnic Studies; Kunapipi; Meanjin; Pacific Quarterly Moana; Chelsea; Solidarity; Tengarra; Waves. *Honours:* Commonwealth Poetry Prize, 1980; 2nd Prize, Asia Week Short Story Competition, 1982; Summer Seminar Fellowship, National Endowment for the Humanities, 1978, 1987; Mellon Fellowships, 1983, 1987; Fulbright Award, Wien Aard, ISIAS Fellowship. *Memberships include:* Offices, Modern Languge Association. *Address:* Stuart Lane, Katonah, NY 10536, USA.

LIMA Robert, b. 7 Nov 1935, Havana, Cuba. University Professor; Writer. m. Sally Murphy, 27 June 1964. 2 sons, 2 daughters. *Education:* BA, English & Philosophy 1957, MA, Theatre & Drama 1961, Villanova University; PhD, Romance Literatures, New York University, 1968. *Appointments:* Professor of Spanish and Comparative Literature, 1965-; Poet-in-Residence, Pontificia Universidad Catolica del Peru, 1976-77; Writer-in-Residence, USIA, 1986. *Publications:* Criticism: The Theatre of Garcia Lorca, 1963; Ramon del Valle-Inclan, 1972; An Annotated Bibliography of Valle-Inclan, 1972; Dos Ensayos sobre Teatro Espanol de Los 20, 1984; The Lamp of Marvels by Valle-Inclan (editor and translator), 1986; Valle-Inclan: The Theatre of His Life, 1988; Reader's Encyclopedia of American Literature (Editor of Revised edition), 1962; Barrenechea's Borges The Labyrinth Maker (Editor & Translator), 1965; Poetry: Fathoms, 1981; The Olde Ground, 1985; Mayaland Poetry, 1992; Savage Acts: Four Plays by Valle-Inclán, 1993. *Contributions to:* Articles in USA and Hispania including: Revista de Estudios Hispánicos; Romantic Review; Saturday Review; Americas; Chicago Review; Washington Post; The Lima Times; The Philadelphia Inquirer; Modern Drama; The Chicago Tribune; The Philadelphia Bulletin; The Christian Science Monitor; Over 300 poems published in journals, newspapers, books and anthologies in USA and abroad. *Honours:* Cintas Fellow in Poetry, 1971- 72; Senior Fulbright Fellow, 1976-77; Honorary Fellow: Phi Sigma Iota, 1979; Phi Kappa Phi, 1984; Fellow, Institute for the Arts and Humanistic Studies, 1986; Initiated Elder, Menda Nkwe Tribe (Bamenda, Cameroon), 1986. *Memberships:* Poetry Society of America; Poets and Writers; International PEN-American Center; Academia Norteamericana de la Lengua Espanola. *Address:* Pennsylvania State University, N346 Burrowes Building, University Park, PA 16802, USA.

LIMBURG Peter R, b. 1929. American, Writer on Marine Science/Oceanography, Natural history. *Appointments:* Special Editor, Harper Encyclopaedia of Science, 1960-61; Senior Technology Editor, The New Book of Knowledge, 1961-66; Editor, School Department, Harcourt, Brace and World, publishers, 1966-69; Co-ordinating Editor, Collier's Encyclopaedia, 19969-70, all New York City. President, Forum Writers for Young People, 1975-76, 1980-81. *Publications:* The First Book of Engines, 1969; The Story of Corn, 1971; What's in the Names of Fruit, 1972; What's in the Names of Antique Weapons, 1973; (with James B Sweeney) Vessels for Underwater Exploration: A Pictorial History, 1973; Watch Out, It's Poison Ivy! 1973; What's in the Names of Flowers, 1974; (with James B Sweeney), 102 Questions and Answers about the Sea, 1975; What's in the Name of Birds, 1975; Chickens, Chickens, Chickens, 1975; What's in the Names of Stars and Constellations, 1976; Poisonous Plants, 1976; What's in the Names of Wild Animals, 1977; Oceanographic Institutions, 1979; The Story of Your Heart, 1979; Farming the Waters, 1980; Stories Behind Words, 1986. *Memberships:* American Society of Journalists and Authors (Chairman, Membership Committee, 1991-92); National Association of Science Writers. *Address:* RR 4, Banksville Road, Bedford, NY 10506, USA.

LIMES Victor. *See:* **HATAR** Victor Gyozo George John.

LIMONOV Eduard, b. 1952, Dzerzhinsk, Gorky District. Poet; Writer. m. Yelena Limonova, 1971. *Appointments:* in Kharkov 1965-67, moved to Moscow, 1967, where acquired reputation of "unofficial" poet; forced to leave USSR, 1974, settled in New York 1975. *Publications:* verse and prose in Kontinent, Ekho, Kovcheg, Apollon, 1977 (in translations in England, USA, Austria, Switzerland); It's Me-Eddie (novel), 1979; and Russian (Russkoye), Verse, 1979. *Address:* c/o Index Publishers, New York, USA.

LINCOLN Alan Jay, b. 1 Aug 1945, Boston, Massachusetts, USA. Professor. m. Carol Zall, 3 Mar 1967, 2 daughters. *Education:* BS, Psychology, 1967; MS, Social Psychology, 1969; MA, Sociology, 1971; PhD, Sociology, 1973; Postdoctoral study in Family Violence, 1981. *Appointments:* Professor, University of Massachusetts-Lowell, 1984-; Editor, Library and Archival Security, Haworth Press, 1989-92. *Publications:* Crime in the Library, 1984; Crime and the Family, 1985; Library Crime and Security: An International Perspective, 1986. *Contributions to:* Articles on crime and violence, and series of articles on library security, to journals. *Honours:* Fulbright Professor, The Netherlands, 1974. *Address:* Department of Criminal Justice, University of Massachusetts-Lowell, Lowell, MA 01854, USA.

LINCOLN Bruce Kenneth, b. 5 Mar 1948, Philadelphia, USA. University Professor. m. Louise Gibson Hassett, 17 Apr 1971, 2 daughters. *Education:* BA (High Honours), Haverford College, 1970; PhD (Distinction), University of Chicago, 1976. *Publications:* Priests, Warriors and Cattle: A Study in the Ecology of Religions, 1981; Emerging from the Chrysalis: Studies in Rituals of Women's Initiation, 1981; Religion, Rebellion, Revolution, Editor, 1985; Myth Cosmos and Society, 1986; Discourse and the Construction of Society, 1989; Death, War and Sacrifice, 1991. *Contributions to:* Articles in Comparative Studies in Society and History; History of Religions; Journal of Indo-European Studies & other scholarly journals. *Honours:* American Council of Learned Societies Award for Best New Book in History of Religions for Priests, Warriors and Cattle, 1981; John Simon Guggenheim Memorial Fellowship, 1983-84. *Address:* Dept. Cultural Studies and Comparative Literature, 350 Folwell Hall, University of Minnesota, Minneapolis, MN 55455, USA.

LINCOLN Geoffrey. *See:* **MORTIMER John Clifford.**

LIND Levi Robert, b. 1906. American, Literature, Translations. University Distinguished Professor of Classics, University of Kansas, Lawrence, 1940-. *Publications:* Medieval Latin Studies: Their Nature and Possibilities, 1941; The Vita Sancti Malchi of Reginald of Canterbury, 1942; (trans) The Epitome of Andreas Vesalius, 1949; (trans) Lyric Poetry of the Italian Renaissance, 1954; (trans) Ten Greek Plays in Contemporary Translations, 1957; (trans) Latin Poetry in Verse Translation, 1957; (ed and trans) Ecclesiale by Alexander of Villa Dei, 1958; (trans) Berengario da Carpi, A Short Introduction to Anatomy, 1959; (trans) Vergil's Aeneid, 1963; (trans) Aldrovandi on Cickens: The Ornithology of Ulisse Aldrovandi (1600), 1963; Epitaph for Poets and Other Poems, 1966; (ed)Problemata Varia Anatomica: The University of Bologna MS 1165, 1968; Twentieth Century Italian Poetry: A Bilingual Anthology, 1974; (trans) Johann Wolfgang von Goethe, Roman Elegies and Venetian Epigrams, 1974; (trans) Studies in Pre-Vesalian Anatomy, 1974; (trans) Ovid, Tristia, 1975; (trans) Andre Chenier, Elegies Camille, 1978; (trans) Gabriele Zerbi, Gerontocomia: On the Care of the Aged, and Maximianus, Elegies on Old Age and Love, 1988; An Epitaph Years After (poems), 1990; Berengario da Caspi, On Fracture of the Skull or Cranium, (trans from Latin); Transactions of the American Philosophical Society Vol

80, Part 4, 1990; (Ed) The Letters of Giovanni Garzoni, Bolognese Humanist and Physician (1419-1505), 1992. *Contributions to:* Articles in Classical and Modern Literature, 1980-. *Address:* 1714 Indiana Street, Lawrence, KS 66044, USA.

LIND William Sturgiss, b. 9 July 1947, Lakewood, Ohio, USA. Writer. *Education:* AB, Dartmouth College, 1969; MA, Princeton University, 1971. *Appointments:* Currently Associate Publisher, The New Electric Railway Journal. *Publications:* Maneuver Warfare Handbook, 1985; America Can Win: The Case for Military Reform (with Gary Hart), 1986; Cultural Conservatism: Toward a New National Agenda (with William H Marshner), 1987; Cultural Conservatism: Theory and Practice (editor with William H Marshner), 1991. *Contributions to:* Many articles to military journals including: Marine Corps Gazette; US Naval Institute Proceedings; Military Review; Parameters; General publications including: Washington Post; Harper's. *Address:* Free Congress Foundation, 717 2nd St NE, Washington, DC 20002, USA.

LINDEY Christine, b. 26 Aug 1947. Art Historian. *Education:* BA Hons, History of European Art, Courtauld Institute, University of London. *Publications:* Superrealist Painting and Sculpture, 1980; 20th Century Painting: Bonnard to Rothko, 1981; Art in the Cold War, 1990. *Address:* c/o West Herts College, The Art School, Ridge Street, Watford, Herts WD2 5BY, England.

LINDGREN Charlotte Holt, b. 5 Jan 1924, Ipswich, Massachusetts, USA, Professor Emeritus. m. Donald J Winslow, 11 Aug 1978. *Education:* AB, 1945, AM, 1947, PhD, 1961, Boston University. *Appointment:* Professor of Writing, Literature and Publishing, Emerson College, 1960-89. *Publications:* William Barnes: The Dorset Engravings, (Co-author Laurence Keen), 1986; The Love Poems and Letters of William Barnes and Julia Miles, 1986. *Contributions to:* Thomas Hardy Journal; Dorset Year Book; Fiction, Literature and the Arts Review; Notes and Queries for Somerset and Dorset; History Today; Antigonish Review; Tennessee Folklore Bulletin; American Reference Books Annual. *Honours:* Phi Beta Kappa, 1976; Mansel-Pleydell Award, Dorset, England, 1986. *Memberships:* Thomas Hardy Society; William Barnes Society; Herman Melville Society; Dorset Natural History and Archaeological Society. *Address:* 23 Maple Street, Auburndale, MA 02166, USA.

LINDGREN Gustav Torgny, b. 16 June 1938, Raggsjo, Sweden. m. Stina Andersson, 19 June 1959, 1 son, 2 daughters. *Education:* DPhil. *Publications:* Batseba, 1984; Ormens vag pa halleberget, 1983; Merabs skonhet, 1983; Legender, 1986; Ljuset, 1987; Skrammer dig minuten, 1981; Ovriga tragor, 1973; Karleksguden Fro, 1988; Brannvinsfursten, 1979; Till Sanningens lov, 1991. *Honours:* Prix Fomina, 1986; Guralid Prize, 1990. *Memberships:* Swedish Academy; PEN. *Address:* Trollenas, S-598 36 Vimmerby, Sweden.

LINDMAN-STRAFFORD Kerstin Margareta, b. 30 May 1939, Abo, Finland. Writer; Critic. 2 children. *Education:* BA, Hum.Kand, 1961; MA, 1962. *Appointments:* Critic, Hufvudstadsbladet, Helsinki, 1964-; Cultural Presenter, OBS Kulturkvarten, Swedish Radio, 1975-. *Publications:* Sandhogen and Other Essays, 1974; Tancred Borenius, 1976; Landet med manga ansikten, 1979; English Writers in Literaturhandboken, 1984; Faeder och Dottrar, 1986. *Contributions to:* Numerous journals and magazines. *Honour:* Finland's Swedish Literary Society Prize, 1976. *Memberships:* PEN; Finlands Svenska Litteraturforening. *Address:* 16 Church Path, Merton Park, London SW19 3HJ, England.

LINDSAY Hilarie Elizabeth, b. 18 Apr 1922, Sydney, Australia. Writer; Museum Curator; Company Director. m. Philip Singleton Lindsay, 19 Feb 1944, 1 son 2 daughters. *Education:* Graduate William's Business College, 1938; BA (Deakin), 1985; Mm AVE (NSW),

1992. *Appointments:* President, Terrey Hills Library, 1957- 63, now patron. *Publications:* You're On Your Own - Teenage Survival Kit, 1977; One for the Road, Short Stories, 1978; Murder at the Belle Vue, 1983; Echoes of Henry Lawson, 1981; The Gravy Train, 1981; One Woman's World, 1980; The Naked Gourmet, 1979. *Contributions to:* The Sydney Morning Herald Literary Supplement; Freemantle Arts Review; Westerly; Mattoid; SCARP; The Bulletin; First Hearing ABC; The Author; The Australian Women's Weekly; Dolly; Woman's Day; New Idea; SCOPP; Rotary Down Under; TV Times. *Honours:* MBE for Services to Literature, 1974; Queen's Silver Jubilee Medal, 1977; Hilarie Lindsay Award, The Society of Women Writers NSW, 1981; Bi-Centennial Medal, The Society of Women Writers NSW, 1988. *Memberships include:* Society of Women Writers of Australia, Treasurer 1969-70, President 1971-73, 1975-77; Federal President of Council of Society of Women Writers of Australia 1978-80; Federal President, Fellowship of Australian Writers, 1982-84, 1992-; Governing Council, National Book Council, 1982-84; President NSW State Council Fellowship of Australian Writers. *Address:* 19-25 Beeson Street, Leichhardt, NSW 2020, Australia.

LINDSEY Alton Anthony, b. 7 May 1907, Pittsburgh, Pennsylvania, USA. Ecologist; Writer; Explorer. m. Elizabeth Smith, 2 June 1939, 1 son, 1 daughter. *Education:* BS, Allegheny College, 1929; PhD, Cornell University, 1937. *Appointments:* Editor, Indiana Academy, 1963-65; Editor, Indiana Sesquicentennial Volume, 1965-67; Ford Foundation Grantee, researching and writing a book, 1967-69. *Publications:* Natural Features of Indiana, 1966; Natural Areas in Indiana and Their Preservation, 1969; Naturalists, Explorers, and Pioneers, 1980; North American Wildlife, 1982; Naturalist on Watch, memoirs, 1983; The Bicentennial of John James Audubon, 1985. *Contributions to:* 72 technical articles to journals; 10 popular articles to quality magazines including: Presidential Farewell to Passenger Pigeons, to Natural History. *Honours:* Phi Beta Kappa, 1929; Special Congressional Medal, 1935; Sigma Xi, 1936; Participant, Ice Party, Byrd Antarctic Expedition II, 1933-35; Lindsey Islands, off Antarctica, (named for), 1960; Private papers in US National Archives, District of Columbia, 1960; Indiana Sesquicentennial Medal, 1966; Eminent Ecologist, Ecological Society of America, 1976; Honorary ScD, Allegheny College, 1988. *Memberships:* Ecological Society of America, Managing Editor; Indiana Academy, President; Antarctican Society; Fellow, American Association for the Advancement of Science; Life Trustee, Indiana Nature Conservancy. *Address:* 191 Drury Lane, West Lafayette, IN 47906, USA.

LINETT Deena, b. 30 Aug 1938, Boston, Massachusetts, USA. College Professor. 2 sons, 1 daughter. *Education includes:* EdD, Rutgers University, 1982. *Publications:* On Common Ground, novel, 1983; The Translator's Wife, novel, 1986; Visit, 1990. *Contributions to:* Harvard Magazine; Sun Dog; South Coast Poetry Journal; Kalliope; Calliope; Taos Review; Phoebe; Mississippi Valley Review. *Honours:* Fellowships to Yaddo, 1981, 1985; Prizes for both novels; Visit chosen for PEN-Syndicated Fiction Project, 1990. *Memberships:* PEN; Modern Language Association; National Council of Teachers of English; Co-Director (with Martin White Ed.D.), New Jersey (USA), Writing Project ;Listed Writer, Poets and Writers. *Address:* English Department, Montclair State College, Upper Montclair, NJ 07042, USA.

LINGARD Joan Amelia, b. 8 Apr 1932, Edinburgh, Scotland. Author. 3 daughters. *Education:* Bloomfield Collegiate School, Belfast, 1943-48; General Teaching Diploma, Moray House Training College, Edinburgh. *Appointments:* Council Member, Member, Literary Committee, Scottish Arts Council, 1981-85; Edinburgh Book Festival Board, 1982-84; Chairman, Meet the Author Committee, Edinburgh. *Publications:* Childrens Books: The Twelfth Day of July, 1970; Frying As Usual, 1971; Kevin & Sadie, Quintet, 1972-76; Across the

Barricades, 1972; Into Exile, 1973; Maggie, Quartet, 1974-77; The Clearance, 1974; A Proper Place, 1975; The Resettling, 1975; Hostages to Fortune, 1976; The Pilgrimage, 1976; The Reunion, 1977; The Gooseberry, 1978; The File on Fraulein Berg, 1980; Strangers in the House, 1981; The Winter Visitor, 1983; The Freedom Machine, 1986; The Guilty Party, 1987; Rags and Riches, 1988; Tug of War, 1989; Glad Rags, 1990; Between Two Worlds, 1991; Hands Off Our School! 1992; Night Fires, 1993; Novels: Liam's Daughter, 1963; The Prevailing Wind, 1964; The Tide Comes In, 1966; The Headmaster, 1967; A Sort of Freedom, 1968; The Lord on Our Side, 1970; The Second Flowering of Emily Mountjoy, 1979; Greenyards, 1981; Sisters By Rite, 1984; Reasonable Doubts, 1986; The Women's House, 1989; After Colette, 1993. *Honours:* Scottish Arts Council Bursary, 1967-68; Preis Der Leseratten ZDF, W. Germany, 1986; Buxtehuder Bulle, W. Germany, 1987. *Memberships:* Society of Authors in Scotland, Chairman, 1982-86; Scottish PEN. *Literary Agent:* David Higham Associates Ltd. *Address:* c/o David Higham Associates Ltd., 5-8 Lower John St., Golden Square, London W1R 4HA, England.

LINGEMAN Richard, b. 2 Jan 1931, USA. Editor; Writer. m. Anthea Judy Lingeman, 3 Apr 1965, 1 daughter. *Education:* BA, Haverford College, Haverford, PA. *Appointments:* Executive Editor, The Nation, 1978-; NY Times Book Review, 1969-78. *Publications:* Drugs from A to Z: A Dictionary, 1969; Don't You Know There's a War On?, 1970; Small Town America, 1980; Theodore Dreiser: At The Gates of the City 1871-1907, 1986; Theodore Dreiser: An American Journey 1908- 1945, 1990; Theodore Dreiser: An American Journey, (paperback), 1993. *Memberships:* National Book Critics Circle; PEN American Center, Authors Guild. *Address:* The Nation, 72 Fifth Avenue, New York, NY 10011, USA.

LINK Arthur S(tanley), b. 1920, American. History, Biography. George Henry Davis Professor of American History, Princeton University Emeritus. *Appointments:* Instructor in History, 1945-48, Assistant Professor, 1948-49, Member, Institute for Advanced Study 1949; Professor 1960-65; Edwards Professor of American History, 1965-76; Associate Professor of History, 1949-54 and Professor 1954-60, Northwestern University, Evanston, Illinois. *Publications:* Wilson: The Road To The White House, 1947; Wilson: The New Freedom, 1956; Wilson: The Struggle For Normality, 1960; (with D S Muzzey) Our American Republic, 1963; (with D S Muzzey) Our Country's History, 1964; Wilson: Confusions and Crises, 1915-1916, 1964; Woodrow Wilson, Pequena Biografia, 1964; Historia Moderna dos Estados Unidos, 3 vols, 1965; Wilson: Campaigns for Progressivism and Peace, 1916-1917, 1965; (ed)The Papers of Woodrow Wilson, 1966-1993; (ed) The First Presbyterian Church of Princeton: Two Centuries of History, 1967; (ed with R W Patrick), Writing Southern History: Essays in Historiography in Honor of Fletcher M Green, 1967; The Growth of American Democracy: An Interpretive History, 1968; Woodrow Wilson: A Profile, 1968; The Impact of World War I, 1969; (with W M Leary), The Progressive Era and the Great War, 1896-1920, 1969; (ed with W M Leary), The Diplomacy of World Power: The United States 1889-1920, 1970; The Higher Realism of Woodrow Wilson and Other Essays, 1971; (with S Coben), The Democratic Heritage: A History of the United States, 1971; Woodrow Wilson: Revolution, War and Peace, 1979; (co-author), The American People, 1981, 1987; (ed) Woodrow Wilson and a Revolutionary World, 1982; Trans and ed, The Deliberations of Four by Paul Mantoux, 2 vols, 1992. *Address:* 5322 Bermuda Village, Advance, NC 27006, USA.

LINKLETTER Art(hur Gordon), b. 1912. American. Writer on Human relations, Social commentary/ phenomena, Autobiography, Memoirs, Personal, Humour, Satire. Television entertainer. Head, Linkletter Enterprises. *Publications:* People Are Funny, 1947; Kids Say the Darndest Things, 1957; (with A Gordon) Secret World of Kids, 1959; (with D Jennings) Confessions of a Happy Man, 1960; Kids Still Say the Darndest Things,

1961; Kids Sure Rite Funny, 1962; Oops! 1967; Wish I'd Said That, 1968; Linkletter Down Under, 1968; Drugs at My Doorstep, 1973; How to be a Super Salesman, 1973; Women Are My Favorite People, 1973; Yes, You Can! 1979; I Didn't Do It Alone, 1980; Hobo on the Way to Heaven, 1981; Public Speaking for Private People, 1981; Old Age is Not for Sissies, 1988. *Address:* 8484 Wilshire Bl. Ste 205, Beverley Hills, CA 90211, USA.

LINSCOTT Gillian, b. 27 Sept 1944, Windsor, England. Journalist; Writer. m. Tony Geraghty, 18 June 1988. *Education:* Somerville College, Oxford, 1963-66; Honours degree, English Language and Literature, Oxford University, 1966. *Publications:* A Healthy Body, 1984; Murder Makes Tracks, 1985; Knightfall, 1986; A Whiff of Sulphur, 1987; Unknown Hand, 1988; Murder, I Presume, 1990; Sister beneath the Sheet, 1991. *Memberships:* Society of Authors; Crime Writers Association; Mystery Writers of America. *Literary Agent:* Anthony Goff, David Higham Associates, London, England. *Address:* c/o David Higham Associates, 5-8 Lower John St, Golden Square, London W1R 4HA, England.

LIPKA J R. *See:* **KARVAS Peter.**

LIPMAN David, b. 13 Feb 1931, Springfield, Missouri, USA. Journalist. m. 10 Dec 1961, 1 son, 1 daughter. *Education:* BA, Journalism, University of Missouri, 1953. *Appointments:* Sports Editor, Jefferson City Post Tribune, 1958; Reporter, Springfield Daily News, 1953-54, Springfield Leader and Press, 1956-57; Reporter, Copy Editor, Kansas City Star, 1957-60; Sports Reporter, St Louis Post Dispatch, 1960-66; Assistant Sports Editor, 1966-68, News Editor, 1968-71, Assistant Managing Editor, 1971-78, Managing Editor, 1979-92, Director of Strategic Planning and Development, Pulitzer Publishing Co. 1992-; Vice President, Director, 1981-88, Pulitzer Productions Inc. *Publications:* Maybe I'll Pitch Forever, 1962, re-issued 1993; Mr Baseball, The Story of Branch Rickey, 1966; Ken Boyer, 1967; Joe Namath, 1968; Co-author, The Speed King, The Story of Bob Hayes, 1971; Bob Gibson Pitching Ace, 1975; Jim Hart, Underrated Quarterback, 1977. *Honours:* Distinguished Service Medal, University of Missouri Alumni-Faculty, 1988; Missouri Honor Medal, Distinguished Service to Journalism, 1989; St Louis Jeremiah Award, 1991. *Memberships:* American Press Insitute; American Society of Newspaper Editors; Chairman, Board of Advisors of University of Missouri School of Journalism; President, Missouri Society of Newspaper Editors, 1993; President, Missouri Editors and Publishers Association; Missouri Press Association; Board Member, Mis America Press Institute; Chairman, Press Club of Metropolitan St Louis, 1990; Football Writers Association of America. *Address:* 900 North Tucker Blvd., St Louis, MO 63101, USA.

LIPMAN Elinor, b. 16 Oct 1950, Massachusetts, USA. Fiction Writer. m. Robert M Austin, 29 July 1975, 1 son. *Education:* AB, Simmons College, Boston, 1972. *Appointments:* Managing Editor, The Massachusetts Teacher, monthly magazine, and MTA Today, monthly tabloid, 1975- 81; Correspondent, Patriot Ledge, West Edition, 1973-74; Staff Writer, Promotion Department, WGBH-TV, Boston, 1973. *Publications:* Into love and out Again, stories, 1987; Then she found me, 1990, The Way Men Act, 1992, both novels. *Contributions to:* Short stories in: Yankee; Playgirl; Ascent; Ladies Home Journal; Cosmopolitan; Self; New England Living; Redstart; Wigwag. *Honours:* Distinguished story citations in Best American Short Stories, 1984, 1985; Massachusetts Artists Foundation, Finalist in Playwriting, 1983. *Memberships:* The Authors' Guild; PEN. *Literary Agent:* Elizabeth Grossman. *Address:* 67 Winterberry Lane, Northampton, MA 01060, USA.

LIPSEY David Lawrence, b. 21 Apr. 1948. Editor. m. Margaret Robson, 1982, 1 daughter. *Education:* 1st Class Honours, PPE, Magdalen College, Oxford. *Appointments:* Research Assistant, General and Municipal Workers' Union, 1970-72; Political Adviser to Anthony Crosland, MP, 1972-77 (Dept. of the Environment, 1974-76; FCO 1976-77); Prime Minister's Staff, 10 Downing Street, 1977-79; Journalist, 1979-80, Editor, 1986- , New Society; Political Staff, 1980-83, Economics Editor, 1982-86, Sunday Times. *Publications:* Labour and Land, 1972; Editor, with Dick Leonard, The Socialist Agenda : Crosland's Legacy, 1981; Making Government Work, 1982. *Memberships:* Secretary, Streatham Labour Party, 1970-72; Chairman, Fabian Society, 1981-82; Fabin Executive, 1986-; Executive Committee, Charter for Jobs, 1984-86. *Address:* 44 Drakefield Road, London SW17 8RP, England.

LIPSON Charles, b. 1 Feb 1948, Clarksdale, Mississippi, USA. Associate Professor of Political Science. m. Susan Bloom, 13 July 1980, 2 sons. *Education:* BA magna cum laude, Political Science, Economics, Yale University, 1970; AM, Political Science, 1974, PhD, Political Science, 1976, Harvard University. *Appointments:* Assistant Professor, 1977-84, Associate Professor, 1984-, Principal Investigator, Chicago-Pew Project to Integrate the Study of Economics and National Security, 1987-91, Director, Programme on International Politics, Economics and Security, 1987-, Director of Graduate Studies, Department of Political Science, 1989-, University of Chicago, Illinois; Visiting Scholar, Center for International Affairs, Harvard University, 1979-80; Visiting Fellow, Centre for International Studies, London School of Economics, England, 1988-89. *Publications:* Standing Guard: Protecting Foreign Capital in the Nineteenth and Twentieth Centuries, 1985. *Contributions to:* International Cooperation in Economic and Security Affairs, to World Politics, 1984; Bankers' Dilemmas: Private Cooperation in Rescheduling Sovereign Debts, to World Politics, 1985; Why are Some International Agreements Informal?, to International Organization, 1991; Others. *Honours:* Chase Prize, Research in International Relations, Harvard, 1977; Board of Editors, 1984-90, Executive Committee of the Board, 1987-90, International Organization; University of Chicago Faculty Achievement Award, Outstanding Graduate Instruction, Burlington Foundation, 1986; British- American Conference for the Successor Generation, 1987-. *Memberships:* Secretary, American Political Science Association; American Society for International Law; British-American Conference for the Successor Generation; Chicago Council on Foreign Relations; International Institute for Strategic Studies, London; International Studies Association; Royal Institute for International Affairs, London. *Address:* 5828 So University Avenue, Chicago, IL 60637, USA.

LIPTZIN Sol, b. 1901, American, Writer on Cultural/ Ethnic topics, Literature, Biography. *Appointments:* Professor, City University, New York City, 1923-63 and American College, Jerusalem, 1968-74. *Publications:* Shelley in Germany, 1924; The Weavers in German Literature, 1926; Lyric Pioneers of Modern Germany, 1928; (ed)Heine, 1928; (ed)From Vovalis to Nietzsche, 1929; Arthur Schnitzler, 1932; Historical Survey of German Literature, 1936; Richard Beer-Hofmann, 1936; Germany's Stepchildren, 1945; (trans. and ed)Peretz, 1946; Eliakum Zunser, 1950; English Legend of Henrich Heine, 1954; Generation of Decision, 1958; Flowering of Yiddish Literature, 1963; The Jew in American Literature, 1966; Maturing of Yiddish Literature, 1970; History of Yiddish Literature, 1972; (co-author) Einfuhrung in die jiddische Literatur, 1978; Biblical Themes in World Literature, 1985. *Address:* 21 Washington Street, Jerusalem, Israel.

LISSENS René Felix, b. 27 Mar 1912, Louvain, Belgium. Emeritus Professor. m. Berthe van den Begin, 29 June 1938, 1 son, 1 daughter. *Education:* PhD, University of Louvain, 1933; Postgraduate studies, University of Hamburg, Rostock, Berlin and Paris. *Appointments:* Founder, Director, Centre for Studies of Guido Gezelle, Antwerp, 1966-81; Co-Editor, Vormen, 1937-40; Founder, Editor in Chief, De Periscoop, 1950-59; Co-Editor, Dietsche Warande Len Belfort, 1960-,

Gezelliana, 1970-. *Publications:* Het Impressionisme in de Vlaamsche letterkunde, 1934; Brieven van A Rodenbach, 1942; Rien que l'homme, 1944; De Vlaamse letterkunde van 1780 tot heden, 1967, 4th edition; Gezellebriefwisseling 1, 1970; Letter en geest, 1982. *Contributions to:* various English, Dutch, American, French, Italian Encyclopedias and reference books. *Honours:* Commander, Order of Leopold II, 1962; Commander, Order of Leopold, 1966; Grand Officer, Order of the Crown, 1974; Grand Officer, Order of Leopold, 1981; Beernaert Prize, Royal Flemish Academy, 1952-53; Prize, Flemish Provinces, 1955. *Memberships:* Ex-President, Royal Flemish Academy of Language & Letters; South Netherlands Society of Language, Literature & History; Dutch Society of Literature; Commission for National Biographical Dictionary; Consultant, Commission of Archives and Museum of Flemish Cultural Life; Guido Gezelle Society; Accademia Internationale de Leonardo da Vinci; Society of Flemish Men of Letters; Flemish Pen Club; Past President, Scriptores Christiani. *Address:* Gebladertelaan 2A, 1180 Brussels, Belgium.

LISTER Raymond George, b. 1919, British, Writer on Arts, Crafts. *Appointments:* Managing Director and Editor, Golden Head Press, Cambridge, 1952-72; Senior Research Fellow, 1975-85, Fellow 1985-86, now Emeritus, Wolfson College, Cambridge, Litt D (Cantab). *Publications:* The British Miniature, 1951; Silhouettes, 1953; Thomas Gosse, 1953; The Muscovite Peacock: A Study of the Art of Leon Bakst, 1954; Decorated Porcelains of Simon Lissim, 1955; Decorative Wrouoght Ironwork in Great Britain, 1957; The Loyal Blacksmith, 1957; Decorative Cast Ironwork in Great Britain, 1960; The Craftsman Engineer, 1960; Edward Calvert, 1962; Great Craftsmen, 1962; The Miniature Defined, 1963; Beulah to Byzantium, 1965; How to Identify Old Maps and Globes, 1965; Victorian Narrative Paintings, 1966; The Craftsman in Metal, 1966; Great Works of Craftsmanship, 1967; William Blake, 1968; Samuel Palmer and His Etchings, 1969; Hammer and Hand: An Essay on the Ironwork of Cambridge, 1969; British Romantic Art, 1973; Samuel Palmer, 1974; (ed)The Letters of Samuel Palmer, 2 vols, 1974; International Methods: A Study of William Blake's Art Techniques, 1975; Apollo's Bird, 1975; For Love of Leda, 1977; Great Images of British Printmaking, 1978; Samuel Palmer: A Vision Recaptured, 1978; Samuel Palmer in Palmer Country, 1980; George Richmond, 1981; Bergomask, 1982; There Was a Star Danced, 1983; Prints and Printmaking, 1984; Samuel Palmer and The Ancients, 1984; The Paintings of Samuel Palmer, 1985; The Paintings of William Blake, 1986; Catalogue Raisonné of the Works of Samuel Palmer, 1988; British Romantic Painting, 1989; A M St Léon's Stenochoreography (translation), 1992. *Address:* 9 Sylvester Road, Cambridge CB3 9AF, England.

LISTER Richard Percival, b. 23 Nov 1914, Nottingham, England. Author; Painter. m. Ione Mary Wynniatt-Husey, 24 June 1985. *Education:* BSc., Manchester University. *Publications:* Novels: The Way Backwards, 1950; The Oyster and the Torpedo, 1951; Rebeca Redfern, 1953; The Rhyme and the Reason, 1963; The Questing Beast, 1965; One Short Summer, 1974; Poems: The Idle Demon, 1958; The Albatross, 1986; Travel: A Journey in Lapland, 1965; Turkey Observed, 1967; Biography: The Secret History of Genghis Khan, 1969; Marco Polo's Travels, 1976; The Travels of Herodotus, 1979. *Contributions to:* Punch; New Yorker; Atlantic Monthly; others. *Honour:* FRSL, 1970. *Membership:* International Pen. *Address:* Flat H, 81 Ledbury Road, London W11 2AG, England.

LITOWINSKY Olga Jean, b. 9 Feb 1936, Newark, New Jersey, USA. Writer; Editor. *Education:* BS Hons History, Columbia University, 1965. *Publications:* The High Voyage, 1977, 1991; Writing and Publishing Books for Children in the 1990s, 1992; The New York Kids Book, 1978. *Contributions to:* Atlas; Publishers Weekly; The Writer; Writer's Digest; SCBW Bulletin. *Honours:* The Christopher Award, 1979. *Memberships:* Society of CHildren's Book Writers and Illustrations. *Literary*

Agent: Curtis Brown Ltd, New York. *Address:* c/o Simon and Schuster, 15 Columbus Circle, NY 10023, USA.

LITT Iris, b. 18 Mar 1928, New York City, New York, USA. Freelance Writer; Poet. m. Gilbert Burries, 11 July 1948, 2 sons. *Education:* BA with honours in English, Ohio State University, 1948; Exchange student, Universidad de Las Americas, Mexico City, 1947. *Appointments:* New York Market Editor, Columnist, The Writer, 1949-54; Copywriter, The Gumbinner Agency, 1954-59; Copywriter, Ellington & Co, 1960- 62; Copywriter, Norman, Craig & Kummel, 1960-62; Copywriter, Benton & Bowles, 1962-64; Copywriter, Clinton E Frank Advertising, 1964-70; Copywriter, ACR Advertising, 1971-1984. *Contributions to:* Poetry: Poetry Now; Earth's Daughters; Woodstock Poetry Review; DeKalb Literary Arts Journal; Central Park; Blue Unicorn; Poet Lore; West End; Stone Country; Lactuca; Icarus; Cape Rock Journal; Pearl; Bitterroot; Bardic Echoes; The Green Fuse; Scholastic; Compact; Poetry Chap-Book; Atlantic Monthly (special college edition); Poetry and articles in many other journals and magazines. *Honours:* Award for College Poetry, Atlantic Monthly, 1948; 2nd Prize for Poetry, League of American Pen Women, Boston, 1974; Numerous others. *Membership:* Poetry Society of America. *Address:* 252 West 11th Street, New York, NY 10014, USA.

LITTELL Robert, b. 1935, American, Writer of Mystery/Crime/Suspense. Formerly an editor on Newsweek magazine, based in Eastern Europe and the Soviet Union. *Publications:* (with Richard Z Chesnoff and Edward Klein) If Israel Lost the War (non-fiction) 1969; The Czech Black Book, 1969; The Defection of A J Lewinter, 1973; Sweet Reason, 1974; The October Circle, 1976; Mother Russia, 1978; The Debriefing, 1979; The Amateur, 1981; The Sisters, 1985. *Address:* c/o Simon and Schuster, 1230 Sixth Avenue, New York, NY 10020, USA.

LITTEN Julian William Sebastian, b. 6 Nov 1937, Wolverhampton, England. Museum Curator. *Education:* South West Essex Technical College and School of Art, Walthamstow; University of Wales, College of Cardiff, currently working on PhD. *Publications:* The English way of Death, 1991; St Mary's Woodford, Essex, 1978. *Contributions to:* Society of Genealogists; Post-Medieval Arahceology' Essex Archaeological Society; Somerset Archaeological Society; Various county magazines. *Memberships:* Commissioner, Cathedrals Fabric Commission for England; Chairman, Portsmouth Cathedral Fabric Advisory Committee; Committe, Victorian Siocety; President, Friends of Kensal Green Cemetery; Westminster Abbey Architectural Advisory Panel; Royal Archaeological Institute. *Literary Agent:* John Pawsey, Worthing. *Address:* The Vicarage, St Barnabas Road, Walthamstow, London E17 8JZ, England.

LITTLE Bryan Desmond Greenway, b. 22 Feb 1913, Deal, Kent, England. Author; Lecturer. m. Margaret Maud Day, 3 July 1965, deceased 1988. *Education:* MA, 1st Class, Classical tripos, Jesus College, Cambridge, 1932-36. *Publications:* The Building of Bath, 1947; The Life and Work of James Gibbs, 1955; The Monmouth Episode, 1956; Sir Christopher Wren, 1975; Portrait of Somerset (4 editions), 1969-; Portrait of Exeter, 1983; Numerous other books on Topography, Local History and Architecture including Cambridge. *Contributions to:* Country Life; West Country Magazine; Numerous county and regional magazines. *Membership:* West Country Writers' Association (Chairman 1980-81). *Address:* c/o Lloyd's Bank, 58 Queen's Road, Bristol 8, England.

LITTLE Charles Eugene, b. 1 Mar 1931, Los Angeles, California, USA. Writer. m. Ila Dawson. *Education:* BA with distinction in Creative Writing, Wesleyan University, Connecticut, 1955. *Appointments:* Editorial Director, Open Space Action Magazine, 1968-69; Editor-in-Chief, American Land Forum, 1980-86; Books Editor, Wilderness Magazine, 1987-; Consulting Editor, Johns Hopkins University Press, 1989-. *Publications:*

Challenge of the Land, 1969; Space for Survival (with J G Mitchell), 1971; A Town is Saved... (with photos by M Mort), 1973; The American Cropland Crisis (with W Fletcher), 1980; Green Fields Forever, 1987; Louis Bromfield at Malabar (editor), 1988; Greenways for America, 1990; Hope for the Land, 1992. *Contributions to:* Number of magazines and journals including: American Forests; Amicus Journal; Country Journal; Garden; Garden Design; Harrowsmith; Journal of Soil and Water Conservation; Smithsonian; Air and Space; Utney Reader; Wilderness; others. *Membership:* Washington Environmental Writers Association. *Literary Agent:* Max Gartenberg, New York City, New York, USA. *Address:* 3929 Washington Street, Kensington, MD 20895, USA.

LITTLE Geraldine Clinton, b. 20 Sept 1925, Portstewart, Ireland. Adjunct College Professor of English; Writer. m. Robert Knox Little, 26 Sept 1953, 3 sons. *Education:* BA, English, Goddard College, Plainfield, 1971; Master's in English, Trenton State College, 1976. *Publications:* Heloise & Abelard: A Verse Play, 1989; A Well-Tuned Harp, 1988; Hakugai: Poem from a Concentration Camp, 1983; Star-Mapped, 1989; Beyond the Boxwood Comb, 1988; Seasons in Space, 1983; Contrasts in Keening: Ireland, The Spinalonga Poems; forthcoming: Women: In the Mask and Beyond; More Light Larger Vision; Out of Darkness. *Contributions to:* Shenandoah; The Literary Review; Massachusetts Review; Confrontation; Seneca Review. *Honours:* 5 from The Poetry Society of America; AWP Anniversary Award, 1986; Pablo Neruda Award, Nimrod, 1989; 3 grants from New Jersey Council on the Arts. *Memberships:* Poetry Society of America, former Vice President; Haiku Society of America, President; PEN. *Address:* 519 Jacksonville Road, Mt Holly, NJ 08060, USA.

LITTLE Jean, b. 2 Jan 1932, Taiwan. Children's Writer. *Education:* BA, Victoria College, University of Toronto, Canada, 1955. *Publications:* Mine For Keeps, 1962; Home From Far, 1965; Spring Begins In March, 1966; When The Pie Was Opened, 1968; Take Wing, 1968; One To Grow On, 1969; Look Through My Window, 1970; Kate, 1971; From Anna, 1972; Stand In The Wind, 1975; Listen For The Singing, 1977; Mama's Going to Buy You A Mockingbird, 1984; Lost And Found, 1985; Different Dragons, 1986; Hey, World, Here I Am! 1986; Little By Little, 1987. *Honours:* Little, Brown Canadian Children's Book Award, 1961; Vicky Metcalf Award, 1974; Canada Council Children's Book Award, 1977; Canadian Library Association Children's Book of the Year Award, 1984; Ruth Schwartz Award, 1984; Boston Globe Horn Book Honor Book, 1988; Short-listed for the 1988 Governor General's Children's Literature Award, 1989. *Memberships:* Writers' Union of Canada; CANSCAIP (Canadian Society for Children's Authors, Illustrators & Performers); Canadian Authors' Association; PEN; IBBY. *Address:* 198 Glasgow North, Guelph, Ontario, Canada N1H 4X2.

LITTLEDALE Freya Lota, b. New York City, USA. Writer. 1 son. *Appointments:* Adjunct Professor, English Dept, Writing for Children and Adolescents, Fairfield University, 1984, 1986-92. *Publications:* The Magic Fish, 1967; King Fox and Other Old Tales, 1971; The Boy Who Cried Wolf, 1975; The Elves and the Shoemaker, 1975; Seven at One Blow, 1976 (revised under the title, The Brave Little Tailor, 1990); The Snow Child, 1978; Pinocchio, adaptation, 1979; I Was Thinking (poems), 1979; The Magic Plum Tree, 1981; The Wizard of Oz, adaptation, 1982; Frankenstein, adaptation, 1983; Sleeping Beauty, 1984; The Little Mermaid, adaptation, 1986; The Farmer in the Soup, 1987; The Twelve Dancing Princesses, 1988; Peter and the North Wind, 1988; King Midas and the Golden Touch, 1989; Rip Van Winkle, adaption, 1991; Editor, various books including: A Treasure Chest of Poetry, 1964; Andersen's Fairy Tales, 1966; Thirteen Ghostly Tales, 1966; Ghosts and Spirits of Many Lands, 1970; Strange Tales from Many Lands, 1975; etc; Plays include: Stop That Pancake, 1975; The King and Queen Who Wouldn't Speak, 1975; The Giant's Garden, 1975; The Big Race,

1976. *Contributions to:* various journals and magazines. *Honours:* One of the Childen's Books of the Year, Child Study Association of America, Ghosts and Spirits of Many Lands, 1970; Children's Book Council/IRA Liaison Committee, 70 Favourite Paperbacks, 1986; International Reading Association Children's Choice Selection, The Magic Fish, 1987; IRA Children's Choice Selection, The Farmer in the Soup, 1988. *Memberships:* PEN; Authors Guild; Society of Children's Book Writers. *Literary Agent:* Curtis Brown. *Address:* c/o Curtis Brown Ltd, Ten Astor Place, New York, NY 10003, USA.

LITVINOFF Emanuel, b. 1915. British, Writer of Novels/Short stories, Plays/Screenplays, Poetry. Director, Contemporary Jewish Library, London, 1958-88; Founder, Jews in Eastern Europe, journal, London. *Publications:* Conscripts: A Symphonic Declaration, 1941; The Untried Soldier, 1942; A Crown for Cain, 1948; The Lost Europeans, 1959; The Man Next Door, 1968; Journey Through a Small Planet, 1972; Notes for a Survivor, 1973; A Death Out of Season, 1974; (ed)Soviet Anti-Semitism: The Paris Trial, 1974; Blood on the Snow, 1975; The Face of Terror, 1978; (ed) The Penguin Book of Jewish Short Stories, 1979; Falls the Shadow, 1983. *Address:* c/o David Higham Associates, 5-8 Lower John Street, London W1R 4HA, England.

LIU Shaotang, b. 29 Feb. 1936, Beijing, China. Writer. m. Zeng Caimei, 1 May 1955, 1 son, 2 daughters. *Education;* Beijing University, 1954-55. *Appointments:* Managing Director, Beijing Writers' Association, 1980; Director, Chinese Writers' Association, 1985; President, Beijing Learned Society of Writing, 1986; Vice President, Chinese Learned Society of Popular Literature, 1987. *Publications:* The Sound of Oars on the Grand Canal, 1955; Catkin Willow Flats, 1980; The Flower Street, 1980; The Budding Lotus, 1981; The Suburbs of Beijing, 1984; Bean Shed, Melon Hut, Drizzle, 1985; This Year, 1986; Story-telling by Jing Liuting, 1987; Flowers Within Reach, 1987; Rural Weddings, 1988; Happiness and Sorrow beside the River, 1990; Vigin Pond, 1991; A Solitary Village, 1993. 11 novels, 28 novelettes, 60 short stories, 4 collections of prose, 9 collections of poems. *Contributions to:* many influential literary magazines in China. *Honours:* Winner, China Novelettes, 1980; Winner, China Stories, 1980; Elected, Advanced Worker of Beijing, 1982; Award by the Beijing Government, for success in literary creation, 1985. *Memberships:* PEN, China Centre; Chinese Writers' Association. *Address:* Beijing Writers' Association, Beijing, China.

LIU Wu-chi, (Hsiao Hsia), b. 1907. Chinese-American, Writer on History, Literature, Philosophy, Biography. Emeritus Professor. *Appointments:* Visiting Professor of Chinese Language and Literature, 1951-53 and Senior Editor and Associate Director of Research, Human Relations Area Files, 1955-60, Yale University, New Haven, Connecticut; Professor of Chinese and Director of Chinese Language and Area Center, University of Pittsburgh, Pennsylvania, 1960-61; Professor 1961-76, Chairman 1962-67, Emeritus Professor 1976-, Department of East Asian Languages and Culture, Indiana University, Bloomington; Chairman of Board, Tsing Hua Journal of Chinese Studies, 1978-87; President, International Association for Nan-shê, Studies, 1989-. *Publications:* (Co-ed) Readings in Contemporary Chinese Literature, 5 vols, 1953-58, revised edition, 3 vols 1964-68; A Short History of Confucian Philosophy, 1955; Confucius: His Life and Time, 1955; (ed as Hsiao Hsia) China: Its People, Its Society, Its Culture, 1960; An Introduction to Chinese Literature, 1966; Su Man-shu, 1972; (co-ed and trans) Sunflower Splendor: Three Thousand Years of Chinese Poetry, 1975; (co-ed) K'uei Yeh Chi, 1976. *Membership:* Hon President, China Association of Nan-shê and Liu Ya-tzu Studies. *Address:* 2140, Santa Cruz Avenue, Menlo Park, CA 94025, USA.

LIVAS Harriet (Haris) Parker, b. 1 Apr 1936, USA. Journalist; Author; Professor. m. John Livas, 18 June 1962, dec. 1976, 3 sons, 3 daughters. *Education:* BS, Syracuse University, 1958; MLitt, University of

Pittsburgh, 1960; PhD, Pacific Western University, 1990. *Appointments:* English Department, University of Maryland Overseas Faculty, 1966-78; Foreign Correspondent, 1978-82; Director of Feature Service, Athens News Agency, Greece, 1982-88; Director, Hellenic Features International, Ministry of the National Economy, Greece, 1988-90; Creative Writing, Adult Education Programme, UK, 1991. *Publications:* Contemporary Greek Artists, 1992. *Contributions to:* All articles for international distribution: Athens News Agency, 1982-88; Hellenic Features International, 1988-90. *Honours:* University Award for Creative Writing, Ohio Wesleyan University, 1954. *Memberships:* International PEN; Travel Writers of the Mediterranean; National Federation of Press Women, USA; Foreign Press Association of Greece; UNESCO, Group B; Board Member, Hellenic Animal Welfare; Hellenic-American Union; Greek-Irish Society; Multi-National Women's Liberation Movement; Beverley Operatic Society; Beverley Garland Dancers. *Address:* 19 Thurlow Ave, Beverley HU17 7QJ, England.

LIVELY Penelope Margaret, b. 17 Mar 1933, Cairo, Egypt. Writer. m. 27 June 1957, 1 son, 1 daughter. *Education:* Honours Degree, Modern History, Oxford University, England. *Publications:* (Fiction) The Road to Lichfield, 1977; Nothing Missing But The Samovar, and other Stories, 1978; Treasures of Time, 1979; Judgement Day, 1980; Next to Nature, Art, 1982; Perfect Happiness, 1983; Corruption and Other Stories, 1984; According to Mark, 1984; Pack of Cards : Stories, 1978-86; Moon Tiger, 1986, 1987; Passing On, 1989; City of the Mind, 1991; Cleopatra's Sister, 1993; (Non-Fiction) The Presence of the Past : An Introduction to Landscape History, 1976; (Children's Books) Astercote, 1970; The Whispering Knights, 1971; The Driftway, 1972; Going Back, 1973; The Ghost of Thomas Kempe, 1974; A Stitch in Time, 1976; The Voyage of QV66, 1978; The Revenge of Samuel Stokes, 1981; The Stained Glass Window, 1976; Boy Without a Name, 1975; Fanny's Sister, 1976; Fanny and the Monsters, 1978; Fanny and the Battle of Potter's Piece, 1980; Uninvited Ghosts and Other Stories, 1984; Dragon Trouble, Debbie and the Little Devil 1984; A House Inside Out, 1987; Passing On, 1989; City of the Mind, 1991. *Contributions include:* numerous journals and magazines including: Quarto; Good Housekeeping; Vogue; Options; Over 21. *Honours include:* OBE, 1989; Treasures of Time, Arts Council National Book Award; Nothing Missing But the Samovar Southern Arts Literature Prize; Shortlisted for the Booker Prize: The Road to Lichfield, and According to Mark; Carnegie Medal, The Ghost of Thomas Kempe; A Stitch in Time, Whitbread Award; Moon Tiger, Booker Prize. *Address:* c/o Murray Pollinger, 222 Old Brompton Road, London SW5 0B2, England.

LIVERSAGE Toni, b. 31 Jan 1935, Hellerup, Denmark. Writer. m. 19 May 1962, 1 son, 1 daughter. *Education:* Magister artium in Slavonic Languages, Copenhagen University, 1965. *Publications:* 10 books including: Women and History, 1972; Mary and the Revolution, 1974; Father and Daughters, 1977; From Gandhi to Greenham Common, 1987; The Great Goddess, 1990. *Contributions to:* Numerous articles about women's history, grass roots movements and other topics to magazines and journals. *Honours:* The Thit Jensen Award for Women's Literature, 1989. *Membership:* Danish Writers Union (International Committee Secretary). *Address:* Morlenesvej 26, 2840 Holte, Denmark.

LIVERSIDGE (Henry) Douglas, b. 12 Mar 1913, Swinton, Yorkshire, England. Journalist/Author. m. Cosmina Pistola, 25 Sept 1954, Holburn, London. 1 daughter. *Publications include:* White Horizon, 1951; The Last Continent, 1958; The Third Front, 1960; The Whale Killers, 1963; Saint Francis of Assisi, 1968; Peter the Great, 1968; Lenin, 1969; Joseph Stalin, 1969; Saint Ignatius of Loyola, 1970; The White World, 1972; Queen Elizabeth II, 1974; Prince Charles, 1975; Prince Phillip, 1976; Queen Elizabeth the Queen Mother, 1977; The Mountbattens, 1978. *Contributions to:* Numerous

journals and newspapers. *Address:* 56 Love Lane, Pinner, Middlesex, HA5 3EX, England.

LIVINGS Henry, b. 1929. British, Writer of Short stories, Plays/Screenplays, History. *Publications:* Eh? 1965; The Little Mrs. Foster Show, 1967; Good Grief! 1968; Honour and Offer, 1969; The Ffinest Ffamily in the Land, 1970; Pongo Plays 1-6, 1971; This Jockey Drives Late Nights, 1972, 1976; (adaptor) Cinderella, 1976; Six More Pongo Plays, 1974; Jonah, 1975; That the Medals and the Baton Be Put in View: The Story of a Village Band, 1875-1975, 1975. Pennine Tales, 1983; Flying Eggs and Things: More Pennine Tales, 1986. *Address:* 49 Grains Road, Delph, Oldham OL3 5DS, England.

LIVINGSTON Myra Cohn, b. 17 Aug 1926, Omaha, Nebraska, USA. Writer. m. Richard Roland Livingston, 14 Apr 1952, (dec 1990), 2 sons, 1 daughter. *Education:* BA, Sarah Lawrence College, 1948. *Appointments:* Poet-in-Residence, Beverly Hills Unified School District, 1966-84; Senior Instructor, University of California, Los Angeles, 1972-. Whispers and Other Poems, 1958; The Malibu and Other Poems, 1972; No Way of Knowing: Dallas Poems, 1980; The Child as Poet: Myth of Reality, 1984; Climb into the Bell Tower, essays on poetry, 1990; 60 other books. *Contributions to:* The Horn Book; Top of the News; Childhood Education; Psychology Today; School Library Journal; The Reading Teacher; The Advocate; The New Advocate; Cricket Magazine; Many others. *Honours include:* Texas Institute of Letters, 1961, 1980; Southern California Council on Literature, 1968, 1971, 1989; Excellence in Poetry Award, National Council of Teachers of English, 1980; Juvenile Award, Commonwealth Club of California, 1984. *Memberships include:* PEN International; Texas Institute of Letters; Society of Children's Bookwriters; USBBY and IBBY. *Literary Agent:* Dorothy Markinko, McIntosh and Otis, 310 Madison Avenue, New York, NY 10017, USA. *Address:* 9308 Readcrest Drive, Beverly Hills, CA 90210, USA.

LIVINGSTON Paisley Nathan, b. 25 Dec 1951, Mississippi, USA. Professor. m. Anne M Hjort. *Education:* BA, Stanford University Department of Philosophy, 1974; Département d'Etudes et do Recherches Cinematographiques, University of Paris III, 1974-75; PhD, Comparative Literature, Johns Hopkins University, 1980. *Appointments include:* Lecturer, Department of English Language and Literature, University of Michigan, 1980-81; Assistant Professor, 1981-85, Associate Professor, 1985, Professor, 1991-, Department of English, McGill University. *Publications:* Books: Models of Desire: Rene Girard and the Psychology of Mimesis, 1992; Literature and Rationality: Ideas of Agency in Theory and Fiction, 1991; Literary Knowledge: Humanistic Inquiry and the PHilosophy of Science, 1988; Editor, Disorder and Order: Proceedings of the Stanford International Symposium, 1984. Several translations. *Contributions to:* Articles included in Stanford French Review, Spiel, Realism and Representation, A Companion to Epistemology; Poetics; Modern Language Studies; Discours social. *Honours:* Outstanding Academic Book,1988; Social Sciences and Humanities Research Council Fellowship, 1986-87; FCAR TEam Research Grant, 1991-94; SSHRC Research Grant, 1982-85. *Memberships include:* Humanities advisory Committee for le Conseil des universites, Government of Quebec; Evaluation Committee for Faculty Research Grants in Humanities, Quebec Government, 1984-86; Executive COmmittee, Modern Language Association, 1989-94, President, Division Committee, 1992-93. *Address:* 4657 Hutchinson, Montreal, Quebec, Canada H2V 4A2.

LIYONG Taban lo, Ugandan, b. 1938. Writer of Novels/short stories, poetry, Cultural/Ethnic topics. Member of the Institute of Development Studies Cultural Division, 1968-, and Lecturer in English, University of Nairobi. *Publications:* The Last Word: Cultural Synthesism, 1969; Fixions and Other Stories, 1969; Eating Chiefs: Lwo Culture from Lolwe to Malkal, 1970; Meditations in Limbo (novel) 1970; Franz Fannon's

Uneven Ribs: With Poems More and More, 1971; The Uniformed Man (short stories) 1971; Another Nigger Dead: Poems, 1972; Popular Culture of East Africa: Oral Literature, 1972; Thirteen Offensives Against Our Enemies, 1973; Ballads of Underdevelopment, 1974; (ed)Sir Apolo Kagwa Discovers England, 1974; Meditations, 1977; To Still a Passion, 1977; Meditations, 1978. *Address:* Department of English, University of Nairobi, P O Box 30197, Nairobi, Kenya.

LLARENA Elsa de, b. 11 Mar 1921, Mexico. Teacher. Divorced, 1 son. *Education:* Diploma, Literature, Mexican Writers Centre, 1957; Diploma, Spanish-American Literature, Hispanic Culture, 1962; etc. *Appointments:* El Sol De Mexico Cultural Supplement, 1977; El Universal Cultural Supplement, 1978; Novedades Cultural Supplement, 1980. *Publications:* El Rehilete; Prosas, 1960; Sevres, 1965; Short Stories, 1974; Durero, 1978; Ayotzin, Childrens Stories, 1980; etc. *Contributions to:* many articles in journals and magazines; Art Column, Brecha; Co- Editor, Imaginaria Magazine; Co-Editor, Trilingual Magazine Folios. *Honours:* 1st Prize, Children's Book, 1980; Diploma, First Cervantine Festival, 1976; 2 Diplomas for childrens Stories, AL INPI, 1975. *Memberships:* PEN; Asociacion Mexicana de Escritores; World Association of Women Writers and Journalists, Co-ordinator of Publications. *Address:* Patricio Sanz 21, Mexico 03100 DF, Mexico.

LLEWELLYN Sam, b. 2 Aug 1948, Isles of Scilly. Author. m. Karen Wallace, 15 Feb 1975, 2 sons. *Education:* St Catherine's College, Oxford; BA (Hons), Oxford University. *Appointments:* Editor, Picador, 1973-76; Senior Editor, McClelland and Stewart, 1976-79; President, Publisher, Arch Books, 1982-; Captain, SY Loon, 1988-. *Publications:* Hell Bay, 1980; The Worst Journey in the Midlands, 1983; Dead Reckoning, 1987; Blood Orange, 1988; Death Roll, 1989; Pig in the Middle, 1989; Deadeye, 1990; Blood Knot, 1991; Riptide, 1992; Clawhammer, 1993. *Contributions to:* Occasionally to: Country Living; The Telegraph. *Memberships:* Society of Authors; Former Member, Crime Writers Association; The Academy. *Literary Agent:* Andrew Hewson, John Johnson, London, England. *Address:* c/o John Johnson, Clerkenwell House, Clerkenwell Green, London EC1, England.

LLOSA Mario Vargas, b. 1936, Arequipa, Peru. Novelist; Football Commentator. *Education:* Law & Literature, Peru. *Publications:* The Bosses; The Time of the Herd; The Green House; Conversation in the Cathedral; Pantaleon and the Visitors; Aunt Julia and the Scriptwriter; The War at the End of the World; The Real Life Alejandra Mayta; Who Killed Palomino Molero?; The Perpetual Orgy. *Contributions to:* Numerous. *Honours:* Ritz Paris Hemingway Award; Ingersoll TS Eliot Prize. *Membership:* PEN. *Address:* Lima, Peru.

LLOYD David Tecwyn, b. 22 Oct 1914, Llawrbetws, Corwen, North Wales. University Tutor (Retd) . m. (1) Frances M. Stubbs, (2) Gwyneth Elizabeth Owen, 1984. *Education:* BA (Wales), 1937; MA (Liverpool), 1961; Honorary DLitt (Wales), 1989. *Appointments:* Deputy Editor, Y Cymro, 1956-61; University Tutor in Welsh Literature, 1961-82; Editor, Taliesin, 1965-87; Adjudicator, National Eisteddfod of Wales, various times, 1945-. *Publications:* Trwy Diroedd y Dwyrain (translation of H I Bell), 1946; Erthyglau Beirniadol (literary studies), 1946; Safle'r Gerbydres (literary studies), 1970; Lady Gwladys a Phobl Eraill (essays), 1971; Bore Da Lloyd (essays), 1980; Llen Cyni a Rhyfel (literary studies), 1987; John Saunders Lewis (biography), 1988; Cymysgadw, 1986; Drych o Genedl, 1987; Cofio Rhai Pethe, 1988; Editor: Tannau'r Cawn, 1965; Saunders Lewis, 1975. *Contributions to:* Some 700 About 25 Welsh journals and papers; Reviews, essays, some major articles and studies in Literature and History. *Honours:* National Eisteddfod Prize for Biography, 1943; Elected Fellow, Welsh Academy of Letters, 1961; Honorary Fellow of University College, Bangor, N Wales, 1990; Literature Award, Arts Council in Wales, 1970, 1971, 1989; Elected F S A, 1991.

Memberships: Academi Gymreig; The Honourable Society of Cymmrodorion; Society for the Promotion of Hellenic Studies; Vice-Chairman, The Edeirnion Literary Society; Merioneths Historical Society. *Address:* Maes-yr-Onnen, Maerdy, Corwen, Clwyd LL21 9NY, Wales.

LLOYD Geoffrey Ernest Richard, b. 25 Jan 1933. Professor. m. Janet Elizabeth Lloyd, 1956, 3 sons. *Education:* Charterhouse 1946-51; King's College, Cambridge, 1951-54, BA 1954, MA 1958, PhD 1958. *Appointments:* Fellow, King's College, Cambridge 1957; Honorary Fellow, 1990. Cambridge University: Assistant Lecturer in Classics 1965-67, Lecturer in Classics, 1967-74, Reader in Ancient Philosophy and Science, 1974-83, Senior Tutor, King's College, Cambridge 1969-73; Bonsall Professor, Stanford University, 1981; Fellow, Japan Society for the Promotion of Science, 1981; Fellow, The British Academy, 1983-; Sather Professor, University of California at Berkeley, 1984; Visiting Professor, Peking University and Academy of Sciences, Beijing, 1987; A D Professor at Large, Cornell, 1990; Professor of Ancient Philosophy and Science, Cambridge University, 1983-, Master, Darwin College, Cambridge 1989-. *Publications include:* Books include: Polarity and Analogy, 1966; Early Greek Science: Thales to Aristotle, 1970, translations: Spanish 1973, French 1974, Italian 1978; Greek Science After Aristotle, 1973, translations: Italian 1978, French 1990; Magic, Reason and Experience, 1979, translations: Italian 1978, French 1990; Science, Folklore and Ideology, 1983, translations: Italian 1987, Spanish forthcoming; Science and Morality in Greco-Roman Antiquity (Inaugural lecture) 1985; The Revolutions of Wisdom, 1987; Demystifying Mentalities, 1990; Methods and Problems in Greek Science, 1991, translation Italian, 1993; Editor: Hippocratic Writings (introduction by GERL) 1978; Co-editor with G E L Owen, Aristotle On Mind and the Senses (Proceedings of the Seventh Symposium Aristotelicum) Cambridge Classical Studies, 1978. *Contributions to:* Numerous articles and books. *Honour:* Sarton Medal, 1987. *Address:* 2 Prospect Row, Cambridge CB1 1DU, England.

LLOYD John Nicol Fortune, b. 15 Apr 1946. Editor. m. (1) Judith Ferguson, 1974, (div 1979), (2) Marcia Levy, 1983. *Education:* MA, Honours, Edinburgh University. *Appointments:* Editor, Time Out, 1972- 73; Reporter, London Programme, 1974-76; Producer, Weekend World, 1976-77; Industrial Reporter, Labour Correspondent, Industrial and Labour Editor, Financial Times, 1977-86; Editor, New Statesman, 1986-87; Financial Times, 1987-. *Publications:* (with Ian Benson) The Politics of Industrial Change, 1982; (with Martin Adeney) The Miners' Strike: Loss Without Limit, 1986. *Contributed to:* Counterblasts, 1989. *Honours:* Journalist of the Year, Granada Awards, 1984; Specialist Writer of the Year, IPC Awards, 1985. *Address:* Flat 8, 14 Kutuzovsky Prospekt, Moscow, Russia.

LLOYD Kathleen Annie, (Kathleen Conlon), b. 4 Jan 1943, Southport, England. Writer. m. Frank Lloyd, 3 Aug 1962, div, 1 son. *Education:* BA (Hons), King's College, Durham University. *Publications:* Apollo's Summer Look, 1968; Tomorrow's Fortune, 1971; My Father's House, 1972; A Twisted Skein, 1975; A Move in the Game, 1979; A Forgotten Season, 1980; Consequences, 1981; The Best of Friends, 1984; Face Values, 1985; Distant Relations, 1989; Unfinished Business, 1990. *Contributions to:* Atlantic Review; Cosmopolitan; Woman's Journal; Woman; Woman's Own. *Memberships:* Society of Authors; British Psychological Society. *Literary Agent:* Gill Coleridge, Rogers, Coleridge and White. *Address:* 26A Brighton Rd, Birkdale, Southport PR8 4DD, England.

LLOYD Levannah. See: PETERS Maureen.

LLOYD Nicholas Markley, b. 9 June 1942. Editor. m. (1) Patricia Sholliker, 1968, (div 1978), 2 sons, 1 daughter, (2) Eve Pollard, 1979, 1 son. *Education:* MA, St Edmund Hall, Oxford; Harvard University, USA.

Appointments: Reporter, Daily Mail, 1964; Education Correspondent, 1966, Deputy News Editor, 1968, Sunday Times; News Editor, 1970, Assistant Editor, 1976, The Sun; Assistant Editor, News of the World, 1972; Deputy Editor, Sunday Mirror, 1980; Editor, Sunday People, 1982-83; Editor, News of the World, 1984-85; Editor, Daily Express, 1986-. *Address:* Daily Express, Ludgate House, 245 Blackfriars Road, London SE1 9UX, England.

LLOYD Trevor Owen, b. 30 July 1934, London, England. University Teacher. *Education:* BA, Merton College, Oxford, 1956; MA, D Phil, Nuffield College, Oxford, 1959. *Appointments:* Lecturer 1959, Professor 1973, Department of History, University of Toronto. *Publications:* Canada in World Affairs 1957-59, 1968; The General Election of 1880, 1968; Suffragettes International, 1971; The Growth of Parliamentary Democracy in Britain, 1973; The British Empire 1558-1983, 1984; Empire to Welfare State: English History 1906-1992, 1993. *Contributions:* Various journals. *Honours:* Guggenheim Fellowship, 1978-79. *Memberships:* William Morris Society; Victorian Studies Association of Ontario. *Address:* Department of History, University of Toronto, Toronto M5S 1A1, Canada.

LLOYD-JONES (Peter) Hugh (Jefferd) (Sir), b. 21 Sept 1922, St Peter Port, Jersey, Channel Islands. Classical Scholar. m. (1) Frances Hedley, 1953, (div 1981), 2 sons, 1 daughter, (2) Mary R. Lefkowitz, 1982. *Education:* Westminster School; Christ Church, Oxford; MA (Oxon), 1947. *Publications:* The Justice of Zeus, 1971, 2nd Edition, 1983; Blood for the Ghosts, 1982; Supplementum Hellenisticum (with P J Parsons), 1983; Sophoclis Fabulae (with N G Wilson), 1990; Sophoclea (with N G Wilson), 1990; Academic Papers (2 vols), 1990; Greek in a Cold Climate, 1991. *Contributions to:* Numerous. *Honours:* Honorary DHL, Chicago, 1970; Honorary PhD, Tel Aviv, 1984; Knight Bachelor, 1989. *Memberships:* Fellow, British Academy; Corresponding Fellow, Academy of Athens; American Academy of Arts and Sciences; American Philasophical Society; Rheinisch-Westfälische Akademie; Bagerische Akademie der Wissenschaften; Accademia di Lettere, Archeologia e Belle Arti, Naples. *Address:* 15 West Riding, Wellesley, MA 02181, USA.

LLYWELYN Morgan, b. 3 Dec 1937, New York City, USA. Novelist. m. Charles Winter, 1 Jan 1957, 1 son. *Publications:* The Wind from Hasings, 1978; Lion of Ireland, 1980; The Horse Goddess, 1982; Bard:Odyssey of the Irish, 1984; Grania, 1986; Red Branch (also title On Ravens Wing, in UK, 1990), 1988; Isles of the Blest, 1988; Xerxes, A Biography, 1986. *Contributions to:* A number of short stories, many anthologies, various journals and magazines. *Honours:* Irish/American Cultural Achievement Award, 1981; Best Novel, Anerican Association of Penwomen, 1982; Spanish Poetry in Prose Award, 1985; Woman of the Year, Irish/American Heritage Committee, 1986; Resolution Honourable Literary Contribution, 1986. *Memberships:* Authors Guild; Science Fiction Writers of America; MENSA. *Literary Agent:* Edward J. Acton, New York, USA. *Address:* Oaklanos, Newcastle, Co. Wicklow, Ireland.

LOADES David Michael, b. 19 Jan 1934. Academic. m. Judith Anne Atkins, 18 Apr 1987. *Education:* Perse School for Boys, Cambridge, 1945-53; Emmanuel College, Cambridge, 1955-61, BA 1958, MA, PhD 1961, Litt D 1981. *Appointments:* Lecturer in Political Science, University of St Andrews, 1961-63; Lecturer in History, University of Durham, 1963-70; Senior Lecturer, 1970-77, Reader 1977-80, Professor of History, University College of North Wales, Bangor, 1980-. *Publications include:* The Tudor Conspiracies, 1965; The Reign of Mary Tudor, 1979; The Tudor Court, 1986; Mary Tudor, a life, 1989; The Tudor Mary, 1992; The Papers of George Wyatt (ed) 1968; The End of Strife (ed) 1984; Faith and Identity (ed) 1987. *Contributions to:* Journal of Ecclestical History and others. *Memberships:* Fellow of the Royal Historical Society; Fellow, Society of Antiquaries of London. *Address:* Department of History,

University College of North Wales, Bangor, Gwynedd LL57 2DG, Wales.

LOBEL Anita, b. 1934, American (born Polish), Writer of children's fiction. *Publications:* Sven's Bridge, 1965; The Troll Music, 1966; Potatoes, Potatoes, 1967; The Seamstress of Salzburg, 1970; Under a Mushroom, 1970; A Birthday for the Princess, 1973; King Rooster, Queen Hen, 1975; The Pancake, 1978; The Straw Maid, 1983. *Address:* c/o Harper & Row, Inc, 10E 53rd Street, New York, NY 10022, USA.

LOCHHEAD Douglas Grant, b. 25 Mar 1922, Guelph, Ontario, Canada, Writer. m. Jean St Clair Beckwith, 17 Sept 1949, 2 daughters. *Education:* BA, McGill University, 1943; MA, University of Toronto, 1947; BLS, McGill University, 1951. *Appointments:* Writer-in-Residence, Mount Allison University, 1987-90. *Publications:* High Marsh Road, 1980, Dykelands, 1989; The Full Furnace, 1976; Upper Cape Poems, 1989; Tiger in the Skull, selected poems, 1986; Millwood Road Poems, 1970; The Heart is Fire, 1959; It Is All Around, 1960; Poet Talking, 1964; A & B & C &, poems, 1969; Prayers in a Field, 1974. *Contributions to:* Canadian literary journals. *Honours:* Golden Dog Award, 1974; Fellow, Royal Society of Canada, 1976; DLitt, St Mary's University, 1987; LLD, Dalhousie University, 1987. *Memberships:* League of Canadian Poets, Vice Chairman, 1968-72; President, Bibliographical Society of Canada. *Address:* PO Box 1108, Sackville, New Brunswick, Canada E0A 3C0.

LOCHHEAD Liz, b. 1947, British, Writer of Plays, Screenplays, Poetry. Art Teacher, Bishopsbriggs High School, Glasgow. *Publications:* Memo for Spring (poetry) 1972; Now and Then (screenplpay) 1972; The Grimm Sisters, (poetry) 1981; Blood and Ice (play) 1982; Dreaming Frankenstein, and Collected Poems, 1984; Silver Service (play) 1984; True Confessions and New Cliches, 1985. *Address:* c/o Salamander Press, 18 Anley Road, London W14 0BY, England.

LOCKE Elsie Violet, b. 17 Aug 1912, New Zealand. Writer. m. John Gibson Locke, 7 Nov 1941, 2 sons, 2 daughters. *Education:* BA, Auckland University, 1933; Hon DLitt, University of Canterbury, Christchurch, 1987. *Publications:* The Runway Settlers, 1965; Two Peoples One Land, 1988; the Kauri and the Willow, 1984; Student at the Gates, 1981; Peace People, 1992; The End of the Harbour, 1968; Journey under Warning, 1984; A Canoe in the Mist, 1984; The Boy with the Snowgrass Hair, 1976. *Contributions to:* New Zealand School Journal among others. *Honours:* Katherine Mansfield Award for Non-Fiction, essay, 1959; Children's Literature Association of New Zealand award for distinguished services to children's literature, 1992. *Memberships:* Childrens Literature Association; Children's Book Foundation; NZ PEN. *Address:* 392 Oxford Tce, Christchurch 1, New Zealand.

LOCKE Hubert Gaylord, b. 30 Apr 1934, Detroit, Michigan, USA. University Professor. 2 daughters. *Education:* BA, Latin and Greek, Wayne University, 1955; BD, New Testament Studies, University of Chicago, 1959; MA. Comparative Literature, University of Michigan, 1961. *Literary Appointments:* Associate Editor, Journal of Holocaust: Genocide Studies, 1989; Editorial Board, Studies in the Shoah, 1990. *Publications:* Detroit Riot of 1967, 1969; Care and Feeding of White Liberals, 1970; German Church Struggle and the Holocaust (with F Littell) 1974; Church Confronts the Nazis, 1984; Exile in the Fatherland, 1986. *Honours:* Doctor of Divinity (hc), Payne Theological Seminary, 1967; Doctor of Humane Letters (hc), University of Akron, 1970; Doctor of Divinity (hc), Chicago Theological Seminary, 1971; Doctor of Humane Letters, University of Nabraska, 1992. *Memberships:* National Academy of Public Administration; Society for Values in Higher Education. *Address:* 7717 57th Avenue NE, Seattle, WA 98115, USA.

LOCKE Ralph P, b. 9 Mar 1949, Boston, Massachusetts. USA. Teacher; Musicologist; Author. *Education:* BA, cum laude Music, Harvard University, 1970; MA, 1974, and PhD 1980 in History & Theory of Music, University of Chicago. *Literary Appointments:* Music Critic, Boston After Dark and the Boston Phoenix, 1967-70; Associate and Acting Editor, Journal of Musicological Research; Senior Editor, Eastman Studies in Music. *Publications:* Music, Musicians, and the Saint-Simonians, 1986. Chapters in: Mendelssohn and Schumann, 1984; Music in Paris in the 1830s, 1987; Les Saint-Simoniens et l'Orient, 1989; Music and Society: The Early Romantic Era, 1991. Articles in: New Grove Dictionary of Music, 1980; New Harvard Dictionary of Music, 1986; Royal Opera (Covent Garden) Programme Book, 1991-. *Contributions to:* 19th-Century Music, Cambridge; Opera Journal; Journal of the American Musicological Society; Opera Quarterly; Revue de musicologie; Fontes artis musicae; Fenway Court. *Honours:* Music Library Association, Best Article, 1980; Galler Dissertation Prize, 1981; Grants from American Council of Learned Societies, National Endowment for the Humanities, Andrew Mellon Foundation. *Memberships:* Program Committee, American Musicological Society; Board Member, Institute for Gounod Studies. *Address:* Dept of Musicology, 26 Gibbs Street, Rochester, NY 14604-2599, USA.

LOCKE Robert Howard, (Bess Clayton), b. 30 Dec 1944, Vallejo, California, USA. Librarian; Playwright; Author. *Education:* BA, Speech Arts, California State University, Chico, 1965; MA, Drama, San Francisco State University, 1967; MS, Library Science, Simmons College, Boston, 1973. *Publications:* Written under the pen name: Clayton Bess: Story for a Black Night, 1982; The Truth about the Moon, 1984; Big Man and the Burn-Out, 1985; Tracks, 1986; The Mayday Rampage, 1993; Plays: The Dolly; Play; Rose Jewel and Harmony; On Daddy's Birthday; Murder and Edna Redrum; Premiere. *Honours:* Best First Novel for Story for a Black Night, Commonwealth Club of California, 1982; Tracks, A Best Book for Young Adults, American Library Association. *Address:* 900 53rd Street, Sacramento, CA 95819, USA.

LOCKERBIE D(onald) Bruce, b. 1935, American. Writer of Plays/Screenplays, Education, Literature, Theology/Religion. Scholar-in- Residence, Stony Brook School, New York, 1957-91; Visiting Consultant at American Schools in Asia and Africa, 1974; Visiting Lecturer/Consultant to American universities. *Publications:* Billy Sunday, 1965; Patriarchs and Prophets, 1969; Hawthorne, 1970; Melville, 1970; Twain, 1970; Major American Authors, 1970; (with L Westdahl) Success in Writing, 1970; Purposeful Writing, 1972; The Way They Should Go, 1972; The Liberating Word, 1974; The Cosmic Center: The Apostles' Creed, 1977; A Man under Orders: Lt Gen William K Harrison, 1979; Who Educates Your Child? 1980; The Timeless Moment, 1980; Asking Questions, 1980; Fatherlove, 1981; In Peril on the Sea, 1984; The Christian, The Arts and Truth, 1985; Thinking and Acting Like a Christian, 1989; Take Heart (with L Lockerbie), 1990; College: Getting In and Staying In (with D Fonseca), 1990. *Address:* PO Box 26, Stony Brook, NY 11790, USA.

LOCKLIN Gerald Ivan, b. 1941, American, Writer of novels/short stories, poetry. Professor of English, California State University - Long Beach, 1965-. *Appointments:* Instructor, California State University, Los Angeles, 1964-65. *Publications:* (with Ronald Koertge and Charles Stetler) Tarzan and Shane Meet the Toad (poetry); Poop and Other Poems, 1972; Son of Poop, 1973; Locked In (short stories) 1973; Toad's Europe, 1973; The Toad Poems, 1974; The Chase: A Novel, 1976; The Criminal Mentality (poems) 1976; The Four-Day Work Week and Other Stories, 1977; Toad's Sabbatical (poetry) 1978; Frisco Epic (poetry) 1978; Pronouncing Borges (poetry) 1978; The Cure: A Novel for Spreadreaders, 1979; A Weekend in Canada (short stories) 1979; Two Summer Sequences (poetry and

prose) 1979; Two Weeks on Mr. Stanford's Farm (poetry) 1980; The Last Toad (poetry) 1980; Two for the Seesaw and One for the Road (poetry) 1980; Scenes from a Second Adolescence and Other Poems, 1981; By Land, Sea and Air (poetry) 1982; Why Turn a Perfectly Good Toad into a Prince? (poems and story) 1984; The Case of the Missing Blue Volkswagen (novella) 1985; Gringo and Other Poems, 1985; (with Ray Zepeda) We Love LA: The Olympic Boxing Poems, 1985; The Clubford Midget Shoots Pool (poems) 1986; The English Mini-Tour (poems) 1987; A Constituency of Dunces, 1988; Return to Ronnie Scott's, 1988; Toad Comes To Cleveland, 1988; On The Rack, 1988; Maybe The Confused Me With Ezra Pound, 1989; Lost and Found (poems), 1989; Toad On The Half-Shell, 1989; The Gold Rush, 1989; The Rochester Trip, 1990; The Conference, 1990. *Address:* English Department, California State University-Long Beach, Long Beach, CA 90840, USA.

LOCKRIDGE Ernest Hugh, b. 28 Nov 1938, USA. Novelist. m. Laurel Richardson, 12 Dec 1981, 2 sons, 3 daughter. *Education:* BA Indiana 1t, 1960; MA Yale University, 1961; PhD, 1964. *Appointments:* Professor, Yale, 1963-71; Ohio State, 1971-; Visiting Writer, Eastern Kentucky University, 1977. *Publications:* Novels: Prince Elmo's Fire, 1974; Flying Elbows, 1975; Hartspring Blows His Mind, 1968; Criticism: 20th Century Studies of the Great Gatsby, 1968. *Contributions to:* Sewanee Review; Yale Review; The Ohio Journal; Journal of Literary Technique. *Honours:* Book of the month club selection, 1974; Distinguished Teaching Award, the Ohio State University, 1985. *Memberships:* Phi Beta Kappa. *Address:* 143 W South St, Worthington, OH 43085, USA.

LOCKRIDGE Laurence S, b. 1 July 1942, Bloomington, Indiana, USA. Writer; Professor of English. *Education:* AB with highest distinction, Indiana University, 1964; MA, 1968, PhD, 1969, Harvard University. *Appointments:* Assistant Professor, English, Rutgers College, New Brunswick, New Jersey, 1969-76; Visiting Lecturer, Northwestern University, 1977-78; Associate Professor, English, 1978-89, Professor, English, 1989-, New York University. *Publications:* Coleridge the Moralist, 1977; The Ethics of Romanticism, 1989; Nineteenth-Century Lives (editor), 1989. *Honours:* Woodrow Wilson Fellowship, 1964-65; Danforth Fellowship, 1964-69, Summer Stipend, National Endowment for the Humanities, 1978; Guggenheim Fellowship, 1984-85. *Memberships:* PEN American Center; Modern Language Association. *Literary Agent:* Lescher and Lescher Ltd. *Address:* 2 Washington Square Village, Apt 10M, New York, NY 10012, USA.

LOCKYER Roger Walter, (Philip Francis), b. 1927, British, Writer of History, Biography. *Appointments:* Senior Lecturer in History, Royal Holloway College, University of London, 1964-. *Publications:* (ed) The Trial of Charles I, 1959; (with J Thorn and D Smith), A History of England, 1961; (ed) Cavendish's Life of Cardinal Wolsey, 1962; (ed as Philip Francis), A Selection from the Diary of John Evelyn, 1963; Tudor and Stuart Britain, 1471-1714, 1964; The Monarchy, 1965; (ed) A Selection from Clarendon's History of the Great Rebellion, 1967; Henry VII, 1968; (ed) Bacon's History of the Reign of King Henry VII, 1971; Hapsburg and Bourbon Europe 1420-1720, 1974; Buckingham, 1981.

LODGE David John, b. 28 Jan 1935. Honorary Professor of Modern English Literature. m. Mary Frances Jacob, 1959, 2 sons, 1 daughter. *Education:* BA, Honours, MA (London); PhD, Birmingham; National Service, RAC, 1955-57. *Appointments:* British Council, London, 1959-60; Assistant Lecturer, 1960-62, Lecturer, 1963-71, Senior Lecturer, 1971-73, Reader, English, 1973-76, University of Birmingham; Harkness Commonwealth Fellow, 1964-65; Visiting Associate Professor, University of California, Berkeley, 1969; Henfield Writing Fellow, University of East Anglia, 1977. *Publications:* (Novels) The Picturegoers, 1960; Ginger, You're Barmy, 1962; The British Museum is Falling Down, 1965; Out of the Shelter, 1970, revised edition

1985; Changing Places, 1975; How Far Can You Go?, 1980; Small World, 1984; Nice Work, 1988; Paradise News, 1991; (Criticism) Language of Fiction, 1966; The Novelist at the Crossroads, 1971; The Modes of Modern Writing, 1977; Working with Structuralism, 1981; Write On, 1986; After Bakhtin (essays), 1990; The Art of Fiction, 1992. *Honours:* Yorkshire Post Fiction Prize, 1975; Hawthornden Prize, 1976; Whitbread Book of the Year Award, 1980; Sunday Express, Book of the Year Award, 1988. *Address:* Department of English, University of Birmingham B15 2TT, England.

LOESER Katinka Elizabeth, b. 2 July 1913, Ottumwa, Iowa, USA. Writer. m. 16 Oct 1943, 2 sons, 2 daughters 1 dec. *Education:* BA, University of Chicago. *Publications:* Tomorrow Will Be Monday, 1964; The Archers At Home, 1968; A Thousand Pardons, 1983. *Contributions to:* New Yorker Magazine; Many short stories. *Membership:* Authors Guild. *Literary Agent:* Ms G Loomis, Watkins-Loomis Agency. *Address:* 170 Cross Highway, Westport, CT 06880, USA.

LOEWE Michael Arthur Nathan, b. 2 Nov 1922, Oxford, England. University Lecturer (retired). *Education:* Magdalen College, Oxford, 1941; BA Hons, 1951, PhD, 1962, University of London; MA, Cambridge, 1963. *Publications:* Records of Han Administration, 1967; Everyday Life in Early Imperial China, 1968, 2nd Edition, 1988; Crisis and Conflict in Han China, 1974; Ways to Paradise: the Chinese Quest for Immortality, 1979; Chinese Ideas of Life and Death, 1982; The Cambridge History of China, Vol 1, 1986; The Pride that was China, 1990. *Contributions to:* T'oung Pao; Bulletin of Museum of Far Eastern Antiquities; Asia Major; Bulletin of School of Oriental and African Studies. *Membership:* Fellow, Society of Antiquaries, 1972. *Address:* Willow House, Grantchester, Cambridge CB3 9NF, England.

LOEWINSOHN Ron(ald William), b. 1937, American, Poet. *Appointments:* Taught poetry workshops at San Francisco State College, 1960-61; Teaching Fellow, Harvard University 1968-70; Member of the English Department, University of California at Berkeley, 1970-. *Publications:* Watermelons, 1959; The World of the Lie, 1963; Against the Silences to Come, 1965; l'Autre, 1967; Lying Together, Turning the Head and Shifting the Weight, The Produce District and Other Places, Moving A Spring Poem, 1967; Three Backyard Dramas with Mamas, 1967; The Sea Around Us, 1968; The Step, 1968; These Worlds Have Always Moved in Harmony, 1968; Meat Air: Poems, 1957-1969, 1970; The Leaves, 1973; (ed)Embodiment of Knowledge, by William Carlos Williams, 1974; Eight Fairy Tales, 1975; Goat Dances, 1976; Magnetic Field(s) (novel) 1983. *Address:* Department of English, University of California, Berkeley, CA 94720, USA.

LOGAN Jake. *See:* **RIFKIN Shepard.**

LOGAN Matt. *See:* **WHITEHEAD David Henry.**

LOGIE Roderick. *See:* **ROBERTS Andrew.**

LOGUE Christopher, (Count Palmiro Vicarion), b. 1926, British, Plays/Screenplays, Poetry, Documentaries/Reportage, Translations. Contributor to Private Eye, London. *Publications:* Wand and Quadrant, 1953; Devil, Maggot, and Son, 1955; (trans) The Man Who Told His Love: Twenty Poems Based on Pablo Neruda's Los Cantoos d'Amores, 1958; The Trial of Cob and Leach: A News Play, 1959; Songs, 1959; Trials by Logue (Antigonne and Cob and Leach) 1960; Songs from The Lily-White Boys, 1960; Patrocleia, 1962; True Stories, 1966; Pax, 1967; The Girls, 1969; New Numbers, 1969; Twelve Cards, 1972; Savage Messiah (screenplay) 1972; True Stories from Private Eye, 1973; Puss-in-Boots Pop-up, 1976; Ratsmagic, 1976; The Crocodile, 1976; Abecedary, 1977; (ed) The Children's Book of Comic Verse, 1978; The Magic Circus (juvenile), 1979; Bumper Book of True Stories, 1980; Ode to Dodo: Poems, 1953-1978, 1981; War Music: An Account of Books 16-19 of the Iliad, 1981; Kings: An Account of Books 1-2 of the Iliad, 1992; (ed) London in Verse, 1982; (ed) Sweet and Sour: An Anthology of Comic Verse, 1983; (ed) The Oxford Books of Pseuds, 1983; (ed) The Children's Book of Children's Rhymes, 1987. *Address:* 41 Camberwell Grove, London SE5 8JA, England.

LOGUE John, b. 7 July 1933, Bay Minette, AL, USA. Writer. m. Helen Roberts, 15 Aug 1959, 3 sons. *Education:* BA, Auburn University, 1955. *Appointments:* Police Reporter, Montgomery Adviser, 1955; Reporter, United Press, 1957; Sportswriter, Atlanta Journal, 1957-67; Feature Writer, Southern Press Corporation, Birmingham, 1967-68; Managing Editor 1968- 73, Creative Editor 1988-, Southern Living Magazine; Editor in chief of Oxmoor House, 1973-. *Publications:* Follow the Leader, 1979; Replay: Murder, 1983; Flawless Execution, 1986; Boats Against the Current, 1987. *Honours:* Edgar Allen Poe Award nomination for Best First Novel from Mystery Writers of America, 1979. *Memberships:* PEN; Mystery Writers of America. *Address:* 2737 11th Avenue South, Birmingham, AL 35205, USA.

LOMAX Marion, b. 20 Oct 1953, Newcastle-upon-Tyne, England. Poet; Lecturer. m. Michael Lomax, 29 Aug 1974. *Education:* BA (Hons), University of Kent, 1979; DPhil, University of York, 1983. *Appointments:* Creative Writing Fellow, University of Reading, 1987-88; Lecturer, Senior Lecturer in English, St Mary's College, Strawberry Hill, Middlesex, 1987-; Writer-in-Residence, Cheltenham Festival of Literature, Oct 1990. *Publications:* Stage Images and Traditions: Shakespeare to Ford, 1987; The Peepshow Girl, poems, 1989; Editor: Time Present and Past: Poets at the University of Kent 1965-1985, 1985; Four Plays of John Ford, in press. *Contributions to:* Over 60 poems to anthologies, magazines and journals including: Times Literary Supplement; London Magazine; Poetry Review; Writing Women; Reviews to: Times Literary Supplement; Poetry Wales; Modern Language Review. *Honours:* E C Gregory Award, Society of Authors, 1981; 1st Prize, Cheltenham Festival Poetry Competition, 1981; 3rd Place, Southern Arts Literature Award, 1992. *Membership:* Poetry Society. *Address:* c/o Bloodaxe Books, England.

LOMBINO Salvatore A, (Curt Cannon, Hunt Collins, Ezra Hannon, Evan Hunter, Richard Marsten, Ed McBain), b. 15 Oct 1916, New York, USA. Writer, Editor, Cooper Union and Hunter College. m. (1) Anita Melnick, 1949, 3 sons, (2) Mary Vann Finley, 1973, 1 step daughter. *Publications:* The Blackboard Jungle, 1954; Second Ending, 1956; Strangers When We Meet, 1958 (screenplay 1959); A Matter of Conviction, 1959; Mother and Daughters, 1961; The Birds (screenplay), 1962; Happy New Year Herbie, 1963; Buddwing, 1964; The Easter Man (play), 1964; The Paper Dragon, 1966; A Horse's Head, 1967; Last Summer, 1968; Sons, 1969; The Conjurer (play), 1969; Nobody Knew They Were There, 1971; Every Little Crook and Nanny, 1972; The Easter Man, 1972; Come Winter, 1973; Streets of Gold, 1974; The Chisholms, 1976; Me and Mr Stenner, 1976; Love, Dad, 1981; 87th Precinct Mysteries, Far From The Sea, 1983; Lizzie, 1984; (under pseudonym Ed McBain): Cop Hater, 1956; The Mugger, 1956; The Pusher, 1956; The Con Man, 1957; Killer's Choice, 1957; Killer's Payoff, 1958; Lady Killer, 1958; Killer's Wedge, 1959; 'Til Death, 1959; King's Ransom, 1959; Give the Boys a Great Big Hand, 1960; The Heckler, 1960; See Them Die, 1960; Lady, Lady, I Did It, 1961; Like Love, 1962; The Empty Hours (three novelettes), 1962; Ten Plus One, 1963; Ax, 1964; He Who Hesitates, 1965; Doll, 1965; The Sentries, 1965; Eighty Million Eyes, 1966; Fuzz, 1968 (screenplay 1972); Shotgun, 1969; Jigsaw, 1970; Hail, Hail, The Gang's All Here, 1971; Sadie When She Died, 1972; Let's Hear It for the Deaf Man, 1972; Hail To The Chief, 1973; Bread, 1974; Where There's Smoke, 1975; Blood Relatives, 1975; So Long As You Both Shall Live, 1976; Long Time No See, 1977; Goldilocks, 1977; Calypso, 1979; Ghosts, 1980; Rumpelstiltskin, 1981; Heat, 1981; Ice, 1983; Beauty and the Beast, 1983; Jack and The Beanstalk, 1984; Lightening, 1984; Snow White and Rose Red, 1985; Eight Black Horses, 1985;

Cinderella, 1986; Another Part of the City, 1986; Poison, 1987; Puss in Boots, 1987; Tricks, 1987; McBain's Ladies, 1988; The House That Jack Built, 1988; Lullaby, 1989; McBain's Ladies, Too, 1989; Downtown, 1989; Vespers, 1990; Three Blind Mice, 1990. *Address:* c/o John Farquharson Ltd, 250 West 57th Street, New York, NY 10019, USA.

LOMER Mary. *See:* **LIDE Mary Ruth.**

LOMPERIS Timothy John, b. 6 Mar 1947, Guntur, A P, India. University Professor. m. Ana Maria turner, 15 May 1976, 1 son, 1 daughter. *Education:* AB magna cum laude, Augustana College, Rock Island, Illinois, USA, 1969; MA, Johns Hopkins School of Advanced International Studies, Washington, District of Columbia, 1975; MA, Political Science, 1978, PhD, Political Science, 1981, Duke University, Durham; Olin Postdoctoral Fellow, Harvard University, 1985-86. *Appointments:* Assistant Professor, Political Science, Louisiana State University, Baton Rouge, 1980- 83; Assistant Professor, Political Science, Duke University, Durham, North Carolina, 1983-; Fellow, Woodrow Wilson Center, Smithsonian Institution, 1988- 89. *Publications:* The War Everyone Lost - And Won, 1984; The Hindu Influence on Greek Philosophy, 1984; Reading the Wind, 1987; From People's War to People's Rule: Insurgency, Intervention, and the Lessons of Vietnam. *Contributions to:* Vietnam: The Lesson of Legitimacy, to Conflict Quarterly, 1986; Giap's Dream, Westmoreland's Nightmare, to Parameters, 1988. *Honours:* Bronze Star, 1973; Vietnamese Army Staff Medal, First Class, 1973; Helen Dwight Reid Award for Best Dissertation in International Relations, American Political Science Association, 1981; Finalist, Furniss Award for Best First Book in National Security, 1984. *Membership:* American Political Science Association. *Address:* Department of Political Science, Duke University, Durham, NC 27706, USA.

LONDON Herbert I, b. 1939, American, Writer on Education and Sociology. Professor of Social Studies, 1967-92, and Dean of the Gallatin Division, New York University, New York City (formerly Director of University Without Walls Programme). Presently, the John M Olin Professor of Humanities at New York University; Consultant, Hudson Institute, 1969-; Candidate for Governor of New York State, 1990. *Publications:* (ed and contrib) Education in the Twenty-First Century, 1969; Non-White Immigration and the White Australia Policy, 1970; Fitting In: Crosswise at Generation Gap, 1974; (ed and contrib) Social Science Theory, Structure and Application, 1975; The Overheated Decade, 1976; The Seventies: Counterfeit Decade, 1979; Myths That Rule America, 1981; Closing the Circle: A Cultural History of the Rock Revolution, 1984; Why Are They Lying to Our Children? 1984; Military Doctrine and the American Character, 1984; Armageddon In The Classroom, 1986; A Strategy For Victory Without War, 1989; The Broken Apple: Notes On New York In The 1980's, 1989. *Address:* 2, Washington Square Village, New York, NY 10012, USA.

LONG A(nthony) A(rthur), b. 1937. British, Writer on Classics, Philosophy. Professor of Classics, University of California, Berkeley, 1983-. *Appointments:* Lecturer and Reader in Greek and Latin, University College, London 1966-73; Professor of Greek, University of Liverpool, 1973-83; Joint Editor, Classical Quarterly, 1975-81. *Publications:* Language and Thought in Sophocles, 1968; (ed)Problems in Stoicism, 1971; Hellenistic Philosophy, 1974, 1986; (co-ed) Theophrastus of Erseus, 1985; (with D N Sedley) The Hellenistic Philosophers, 1987; (co ed) The Question of Eclecticism, 1988. *Address:* Department of Classics, University of California, Berkeley, CA 94720, USA.

LONG Cynthia, b. 9 Oct 1956, Toronto, Ontario, Canada. Writer. m. Michael Waldin, 29 July 1984, 1 son. *Education:* BA (with honours), Trent University, 1978. *Publications:* Wishbones, 1985; Monroe.

Honours: Grants from Canada Council and Ontario Arts Council.

LONG Gerald, b. 22 Aug 1923, York, England. Journalist. m. Anne Hamilton Walker, 1951, 2 sons, 3 daughters. *Education:* BA, Emmanuel College, Cambridge. *Appointments:* Reuters 1948-81, Correspondent in France, Germany and Turkey, 1950-60, Assistant General Manager, 1960-63, Chief Executive, 1963-81, General Manager, 1963-73, Managing Director, 1973-81; Chairman, Visnews Ltd., 1968-79; Managing Director, Times Newspapers Ltd., 1981-82; Deputy Chairman, News International, 1982-84; Chairman, Executive Committee, International Institute of Communication Ltd, 1973-78. *Honours:* Commander, Royal Order of the Phoenix, Greece, 1964; Grand Officier, Order of Merit, Italy, 1973; Commander, Order of the Lion of Finland, 1979; Chevalier, Legion d'Honneur, France, 1979; Commander's Cross, Order of Merit of the Federal Republic of Germany, 1983. *Address:* 15 rue d'Aumale, 75009 Paris, France.

LONG Robert Emmet, b. 7 June 1934, New York, USA. Literary Critic; Freelance Writer. *Education:* BA,1956, PhD, 1968, Columbia University; MA, Syracuse University, 1964. *Appointments:* Instructor, English Department, State University of New York, 1962-64; Assistant Professor, City University of New York, 1968-71. *Publications:* The Achieving of the Great Gatsby : F. Scott Fitgerald, 1920-25, 1979; The Great Succession : Henry James and the Legacy of Hawthorne, 1979; Henry James : The Early Novels, 1983; John O'Hara, 1983; Nathanael West, 1985; Barbara Pym, 1986; James Thurber, 1988; James Fenimore Cooper, 1990; The Films of Merchant Ivory, 1991. Editor, 18 Reference Books including: American Education, 1985; Drugs and American Society, 1985; Vietnam Ten Years After, 1986; Mexico, 1986; The Farm Crisis, 1987; The Problem of Waste Disposal, 1988; AIDS, 1989; The Welfare Debate, 1989; Energy and Conservation, 1989; Japan and the USA, 1990; Censorship, 1990. *Contributions to:* several hundred articles in magazines, journals and newspapers. *Address:* 254 South Third Street, Fulton, NY 13069, USA.

LONGFORD Francis Aungier Pakenham 7th Earl of (cr. 1975), (cr. Baron 1945), b. 5 Dec 1905. Politician; Writer. m. Elizabeth Harman, 1931, 4 sons, 4 daughters (1 dec). *Education:* MA, New College, Oxford. *Appointments include:* Tutor, University Tutorial Courses Stoke-on-Trent, 1929-31; with Conservative Party Economic Research Dept. 1930-32; Lecturer, Politics, Christ Church, Oxford, 1932; Student in Politics, Christ Church, 1934-46, 1952-64. *Publications:* Peace by Ordeal (The Anglo-Irish Treaty of 1921); Born to Believe, 1953; The Causes of Crime, 1958; Five Lives, 1963; Humility, 1969; De Valera (with T P O'Neill), 1970; The Grain of Wheat, 1974; The Life of Jesus Christ, 1974; Abraham Lincoln, 1974; Kennedy, 1976; Francis of Assisi: A Life for All Seasons, 1978; Nixon, 1980; Ulster, 1981; Pope John Paul II (biography), 1982; Diary of a Year, 1982; Eleven at No. 10: A Personal View of Prime Ministers 1931-84, 1984; One Man's Faith, 1984; The Search for Peace, 1985; The Bishops: A Study of Leaders in the Church Today, 1986; Saints, 1987; A History of the House of Lords, 1989; Suffering and Hope, 1990; Punishment and the Punished, 1991; Prisoner or Patient, 1992. *Honours:* Recipient, numerous honours and awards. *Memberships:* Lord Privy Seal and Leader of House of Lords, 1964-65, 1966-68; Secretary of State for Colonies, 1965-66; Chairman, National Youth Employment Council, 1968-71. *Address:* Bernhurst, Hurst Green, East Sussex, TN19 7QN, England.

LONGMATE Norman Richard, b. 15 Dec 1925, Newbury, Berkshire, England. Freelance Writer. *Education:* BA, Modern History, 1950, MA 1952, Worcester College, Oxford. *Appointments:* Leader Writer, Evening Standard, 1952; Feature Writer, Daily Mirror, 1953-56; Administrative Officer, Electricity Council, 1957-63; Schools Radio Producer, 1963-65, Senior, subsequently Chief Assistant, BBC Secretariat,

1965-83, BBC; Freelance Writer, 1983-. *Publications:* Editor, A Socialist Anthology, 1953; Oxford Triumphant, 1955; various detective stories, 1957-61; 3 career books for boys, 1961-64; King Cholera, 1966; The Waterdrinkers, 1968; Alive and Well, 1970; How We Lived Then, 1971; If Britain had Fallen, 1972; The Workhouse, 1974; The Real Dad's Army, 1974; The GI's, 1975; Milestones in Working Class History, 1975; Air Raid, 1976; When We Won the War, 1977; The Hungry Mills, 1978; The Doodlebugs, 1981; The Bombers, 1982; The Breadstealers, 1984; Hitler's Rockets, 1985; Defending the Island, From Cæser to the Armada, 1989. *Memberships:* Vice-Chairman, North Surrey Area, Oxford Society; Society of Authors; Fortress Study Group; United Kingdom Fortification Club; Historical Association; Ramblers Association; Society of Sussex Downsmen; Prayer Book Society; Fellow, Royal Historical Society. *Address:* c/o Century Hutchison, 62-65 Chandos Place, London WC2 4NW, England.

LONGRIGG Roger Erskine, (Laura Black, Ivor Drummond, Rosalind Erskine), b. 1 May 1929. Author. m. Jane Chichester, 1957, 3 daughters. *Education:* BA, Honours, Modern History, Magdalen College, Oxford. *Publications:* A High Pitched Buzz, 1956; Switchboard, 1957; Wrong Number, 1959; Daughters of Mulberry, 1961; The Paper Boats, 1963; The Artless Gambler, 1964; Love among the Bottles, 1967; The Sun on the Water, 1969; The Desperate Criminals, 1971; The History of Horse Racing, 1972; The Jevington System, 1973; Their Pleasing Sport, 1975; The Turf, 1975; The History of Foxhunting, 1975; The Babe in the Wood, 1976; The English Squire and His Sport, 1977; Bad Bet, 1982. *Address:* Orchard House, Crookham, Hants, England.

LONGWORTH Philip, b. 1933, British/Canadian. Writer on History; Professor of History, McGill University, Montreal, 1984-. *Publications:* (trans) A Hero of Our Time, by Lermontov, 1962; The Art of Victory, 1965; The Unending Vigil, 1967, 1985; The Cossacks, 1969; The Three Empresses, 1971; The Rise and Fall of Venice, 1974; Alexis, Tsar of All the Russias, 1984; The Making of Eastern Europe, 1992. *Contributions to:* The Times Literary Supplement. *Address:* c/o A M Heath and Co, 79 St Martin's Lane, London WC2N 4AA, England.

LONGYEAR Barry (Brookes), b. 1942. American, Science fiction. Freelance writer 1977-. *Appointments:* Publisher, Sol III Publications, Philadelphia, 1968-72, and Farmington, Maine 1972-77. *Publications:* City of Baraboo, 1980; Manifest Destiny (stories) 1980; Circus World (stories) 1980; Elephant Song, 1981; The Tomorrow Testament, 1983; It Came from Schenectady, 1984; Sea of Glass, 1986; Enemy Mine. *Address:* PO Box 100, Vienna Road Rt 41, New Shanon, ME 04955, USA.

LOOMIE Albert Joseph, b. 1922, American, History. Professor of History, Fordham University, 1968- (member of faculty 1958-) Member of the Jesuit Order 1939-. *Publications:* (with C M Lewis), The Spanish Jesuit Mission in Virginia 1570-72, 1953; Toleration and Diplomacy: The Religious Issue in Anglo-Spanish Relations 1603-1605, 1963; The Spanish Elizabethans: The English Exiles at the Court of Philip II, 1964; Guy Fawkes in Spain, 1971; Spain and the Jacobean Catholics, vol I, 1973, vol II, 1978; Ceremonies of Charles I: The Notebooks of John Finet 1628-41, 1987. *Address:* Department of History, Fordham University, New York, NY 10458, USA.

LOPACH James Joseph, b. 23 June 1942, Great Falls, Montana, USA. Professor; Academic Administrator. m. 31 July 1965, div. Dec 1991, 1 son, 1 daughter. *Education:* AB, Carroll College, 1964; MA, 1967, MAT, 1968, PhD, University of Notre Dame; Terminal degree, Government and International Studies, 1973. *Publications:* Co-author: A State Mandates Local Government Review, 1979; We the People of Montana (also editor), 1983; Planning Small Town America, 1990; Tribal Government Today, 1990. *Contributions to:* National Civic Review; State and Local Government Review; Social Education; Montana Law Review. *Address:* Political Science Department, University of Montana, Missoula, MT 59812, USA.

LOPATE Phillip, b. 16 Nov 1943, Writer. m. Cheryl Cipriani, 31 Dec 1990. *Education:* BA, Columbia College, 1964; PhD, Union Institute, 1979. *Appointments:* Associate Professor: English, University of Houston, 1980-88, Creative Writing, Columbia University, 1988-91; Professor of English, Bennington College, 1992-. *Publications:* Bachelorhood, 1981; The Rug Merchant, 1987; Being with Children, 1975; Against Joie de Vivre, 1989; The Daily Round, 1976; Confessions of Summer, 1979; The Eyes Don't Always Want to Stay Open, 1972. *Contributions to:* Paris Review; Esquire; Vogue; New York Times; Film Comment; Journal of Contemporary Fiction; Harper's; Tikkun; Ploughshares. *Honours:* Christopher Medal, 1975; National Endowment for the Arts Grant, 1978, 1985; Guggenheim Foundation Fellowship, 1988; NY State Foundation for the Arts Grant, 1991. *Memberships:* PEN American Centre; Judge, Pulitzer Prize in poetry, 1984; Judge, National Book Award in Fiction, 1990; NY Film Festival Selection Committee, 1987-91; Municipal Art Society. *Literary Agent:* Wendy Weil Agency. *Address:* 260 West 10th Street, NY 10014, USA.

LOPES Henri, b. 12 Sept 1937, Leopoldville, Belgian Congo. Writer (Novelist). m. Nirva Pasbeau, 13 May 1961, 1 son, 3 daughters. *Education:* Licence es lettres, 1962, Diplome d'Etudes Superieures, History, 1963, University of Paris (Sorbonne). *Publications:* Tribaliques, 1971, English translation as Tribaliks, 1989; La Nouvelle Romance, 1976; Sans Tam- Tam, 1977; The Laughing Cry, 1988; Le Chercheur d'Afriques, 1990; Sur l'Autre Rive, 1992. *Honours:* Grand Prix de la Litterature d'Afrique Noire, 1972; Prix Jules Verne, 1990; Doctor Honoris Causa, University Paris-Val de Marne, France. *Address:* UNESCO, 1 rue Miollis, 75015 Paris, France.

LOPEZ Barry Holstun, b. 6 Jan 1945, USA. m. Sandra Jean Landers, 10 June 1967. *Education:* BA cum laude, University of Notre Dame, 1966; MA, 68; LDH Honorary, Whittier College, 1988. *Publications:* Arctic Dreams, 1986; Crossing Open Ground, 1988; Of Wolves and Men, 1978; Crow and Weasel, 1990; Winter Count, 1981; Desert Notes, 1976; Giving Birth to Thunder, 1978; River Notes, 1978; The Rediscovery of North America, 1991. *Contributions to:* Harper's; New York Times; North American Review; National Geographic. *Honours:* John Burroughs Medal, 1979; Christopher Medal, 1979, 1987; National Book Award, 1987; Award in Literature, American Academy, 1986; Guggenheim Fellowship, 1987; Lannan Foundation Award, 1990. *Memberships:* PEN American Center. *Literary Agent:* Peter Matson, Sterling Lord Literistic, *Address:* Peter Mason, Sterling Lord Literistic, 1 Madison Avenue, NY 10010, USA.

LORD Bette Bao, b. 3 Nov 1938, Shanghai, China. Writer. m. 4 May 1963, 1 son, 1 daughter. *Education:* BA, Tufts University, USA, 1959; MA, Fletcher School of Law & Diplomacy, 1960. *Publications:* Eighth Moon, 1964; Spring Moon, 1981; In the Year of the Boar & Jackie Robinson, 1984; Legacies, A Chinese Mosaic, 1990. *Contributions to:* Numerous magazines & journals including, Los Angeles Times; Newsweek; New York Times; USA Today. *Honours include:* Nomination, American Book Award (1st novel), 1981; Honorary Doctor of Letters, Tufts University, 1982; Award, American Library Association, 1984; Honorary Doctor of Humanities, Notre Dame University, 1985; Honorary Doctorates: Skidmore College; Marymount College; Bryant College; Dominican College; American Women for International Understanding Award; Barnard College Medal of Distinction; The International Women's Hall of Fame. *Memberships:* Council on Foreign Relations; Authors Guild; PEN Organisation of Chinese Americans. *Literary Agent:* Irving Lazar. *Address:* 740 Park AVenue, New York, NY 10021, USA.

LORD Graham John, b. 16 Feb 1943, Mutare, Zimbabwe. Journalist. m. Jane Carruthers, 12 Sept 1962, 2 daughters. *Education:* BA Honours, Cambridge University, 1965. *Literary Appointments:* Literary Editor, Sunday Express, London, 1969-; Originator of Sunday Express Book of the Year Award, 1987, Judge, 1987, 1988, 1989. *Publications:* Novels: Marshmallow Pie, 1970; A Roof Under Your Feet, 1973; The Spider and the Fly, 1974; God and All His Angels, 1976; The Nostradamus Horoscope, 1981; Time Out of Mind, 1986. *Literary Agent:* A M Heath, London. *Address:* Sunday Express, 245 Blackfriars Road, London SE1, England.

LORD Robert Needham, b. 18 July 1945, New Zealand, Playwright. *Education:* BA, Victoria University of Wellington; Diploma of Teaching, Wellington Teachers' College. *Appointment:* Burns Fellow, Otago University, 1987. *Publications:* Heroes and Butterflies, 1973; Well Hung, 1974; Bert and Maisy, 1987; The Travelling Squirrel, 1987; The Affair, 1987; Country Cops, 1988; China Wars, 1988; Glorious Ruins, 1990. *Honours:* Katherine Mansfield Young Writers Award, 1969; CAPS Grant, New York State, 1984; Burns Fellowship, 1987. *Memberships:* PEN; Dramatists Guild. *Literary Agent:* Gilbert Parker, William Morris Agency, New York, USA. *Address:* Apartment 145, 250 West 85, New York, NY 10024, USA.

LORD Walter, b. 8 Oct 1917, Baltimore, Maryland, USA. Author. *Education:* BA, Princeton University, 1939; LLB, Yale University, 1946. *Publications include:* The Fremantle Diary, 1954; A Night to Remember, 1955, illustrated edition 1976; Day of Infamy, 1957; The Good Years, 1960; A Time to Stand, 1961; Peary to the Pole, 1963; The Past That Would Not Die, 1965; Incredible Victory, 1967; Dawn's Early Light, 1972; Lonely Vigil, 1977; Miracle of Dunkirk, 1982; The Night Lives On, 1986. *Contributions include:* Various magazines & journals including: American Heritage; Life; Look, Readers Digest. *Honours:* Summerfield Roberts Award, 1961; Colonial Dames Award, American history, 1972; Andrew White Medal, Maryland history, 1984. *Memberships:* American Society of Authors, Composers & Publishers; Council, Authors Guild; Authors League; Trustee, New York Historical Society; Century Association. *Literary Agent:* Sterling Lord, New York City. *Address:* 116 East 68th Street, New York, NY 10021, USA.

LORENZ Sarah E. *See:* **WINSTON Sarah.**

LORRIMER Claire. *See:* **CLARK Patricia Denise.**

LOSCHIAVO Linda Ann, b. 24 Oct 1947, New York City, USA. Freelance Writer; Non Fiction Author. m. Sergei Brozski PE (divorced), 3 Sept 1977. *Education:* BA 1971, MA 1976, Hunter College, New York City; PhD Candidate, New York University. *Appointments:* E P Dutton Book Company, 1968; MacFadden Bartell Publishers, 1969; Universal Publishing Co., 1970; Reese Publishing Co., 1971; American Journal of Nursing Publishers, 1975. *Publications:* Contributor to various international magazines. *Honours:* Marquis Award, 1964; Writer's Digest Writing Competition (won 1978, 1980, 1987); Mensa Journalist Awards, 1979. *Memberships:* Sigma Tau Delta; American Society of Journalists and Authors; American Mensa Ltd (Editor 1978-79, Board Member 1979-80). *Address:* 24 Fifth Avenue, New York, NY 10011-8817, USA.

LOTT Bret, b. 8 Oct 1958, Los Angeles, CA, USA. Professor. m. Melanie Kai Swank, 28 June 1980, 2 sons. *Education:* BA, California State University, Long Beach, 1981; MFA, University of Massachusetts, Amherst, 1984. *Appointments:* Cook's Trainer, Big Yellow House Incoparated, Santa Barbara, 1977-79; Salesman, RC Cola, 1979-80; Reporter, Daily Commercial News, 1980-81, Los Angeles; Instructor in Remedial English, Ohio State University, Columbus, 1984-86; Assistant Professor of English, College of Charleston, 1986-. *Publications:* The Man Who Owned Vermont, 1987; A

Stanger's House, 1988; A Dream of Old Leaves, 1989. *Contributions to:* Short stories represented in anthology, Twenty Under Thirty, 1986; Fiction to periodicals, including Missouri Review; Michigan Quarterly Review; Iown Review; Yale Review; Yankee; Seattle Review; Redbook; Confrontation; Literary Reviews to periodicals, including New York Review of Books; Los Angeles Times; Michigan Quarterly Review. *Memberships:* Associated Writing Programs; Poets and Writers. *Honours:* Syndicated fiction Project Award from PEN/National Endowment for the Arts; Ohio Arts Council Fellowship in Literature, 1986; South Carolina Arts Commission Fellowship in literature, 1987-88; South Carolina Syndicated Fiction Project Award, 1987. *Address:* Department of English, College of Charleston, Charleston, SC 29424, USA.

LOUDEN J Keith, b. 4 Mar 1905, Duquesne, Pennsylvania, USA. Business Executive. m. 4 June 1932, 1 daughter. *Education:* BBA, Ohio State University, 1928. *Publications:* Wage Incentives (with J W Deegan), 1959; Job Evaluation (with Thomas Newton), 1967; The Corporate Director (with J M Juran), 1967; Making It Happen - The Unit President Concept, 1971; The Effective Director in Action, 1975; Managing at the Top, 1977; Think Like a President, 1981; The Director, 1982. *Honours:* Worcester Reed Warner Medal, Contribution to Engineering Literature, American Society of Mechanical Engineers; Gilbreth Medal, Contribution to Management Literature, Society of Advancement Management. *Memberships:* Fellow, International Academy of Management; American Society of Mechanical Engineers, Chairman of Management, Director; American Management Association, Director, Executive Committee, Manufacturing, Planning and Fellow; Honorary Life President, Society of Advancement Management. *Address:* 257 Brook Farm Rd, Lancaster, PA 17601, USA.

LOUW Raymond, b. 13 Oct 1926, Cape Town, South Africa. Publisher/Editor, Southern Africa Report. m. Jean Ramsay Byres, 1950, 2 sons, 1 daughter. *Appointments:* Journalist, Rand Daily Mail, 1946-50, Worthing Herald, 1951-52, North Western Evening Mail, 1953-54, Westminster Press Provincial Newspapers (London) 1955-56; Night News Editor, Rand Daily Mail, 1958-59, News Editor, 1960-65, Editor 1966-77; Chairman, S.A. Morning Newspaper Group, 1975-77; General Manager, SA Associated Newspapers, 1977-82; Executive Board, International Press Institute, London, 1979-87. *Honour:* Pringle Medal for services to Journalism, 1976. *Memberships:* Anti-Censorship Action Group; Chairman, Media Defence Trust. *Address:* Southern Africa Report, PO Box 261579, Excom, Johannesburg, 2023, South Africa.

LOVE David. *See:* **LASKY Jesse Louis.**

LOVE William F, b. 20 Dec 1932, Oklahoma City, Oklahoma, USA. Writer. m. Joyce Mary Athman, 30 May 1970, 2 daughters. *Education:* BA, St John's University, Minnesota, 1955; MBA, University of Chicago, 1972. *Publications:* The Chartreuse Clue, 1990; The Fundamental of Murder, 1991; Bloody Ten, 1992. *Contributions to:* The Enduring Legacy of Rex Stout, article, to Mostly Murder, 1991. *Honours:* Nominations (1 of top 5) for Macavity and Agatha Awards, for The Chartreuse Clue, 1991-. *Memberships:* Mystery Writers of America, Chairman of Committee to select winner of 1992 Edgar Award in category on Biographical-Critical Works; International Association of Crime Writers; Private Eye Writers of America; Authors Guild; Society of Midland Authors; PEN Midwest; Hinsdale Area United Way, Chairman 1991-83; Love Christian Clearing House, Theatre of Western Springs. *Literary Agent:* Arthur Pine Associates, 250 W 57th St, New York, NY 10019, USA. *Address:* 940 Cleveland, Hinsdale, IL 60521, USA.

LOVELACE Earl, b. 1935, Trinidadian. Writer of novels and short stories. Agricultural Assistant,

Jamaican Civil Service. *Publications:* While Gods Arer Falling, 1965; The Schoolmaster, 1968; The Dragon Can't Dance, 1979; The Wine of Astonishment, 1982; Jestina's Calypso and Other Plays, 1984. *Address:* c/o Andre Deutsch, 105, Great Russel Street, London WC1B 3LJ, England.

LOVELL (Sir) (Alfred Charles) Bernard, b. 1913, British, Astronomy. Professor of Radio Astronomy and Director of Nuffield Radio Astronomy Laboratories at Jodrell Bank, University of Manchester, 1951-81. President, Royal Astronomical Society, 1969-71. *Publications:* Science and Civilization, 1939; World Power Resources and Social Development, 1945; (with J A Clegg), Radio Astronomy, 1952; Meteor Astronomy, 1954; (with R Hanbury Brown), The Exploration of Space by Radio, 1957; The Individual and the Universe, 1959; The Exploration of Outer Space, 1962; (with M Joyce Lovell), Discovering the Universe, 1963; Our Present Knowledge of the Universe, 1967; The Story of Jodrell Bank, 1968; Out of the Zenith: Jodrell Bank, 1957-70, 1973; The Origins and International Economics of Space Exploration, 1973; Man's Relation to the Universe, 1975; P M S Blackett: A Biographical Memoir, 1976; In the Center of Immensities, 1978; Emerging Cosmology, 1981; The Jodrell Bank Telescopes, 1985; (with F G Smith), Pathways to the Universe, 1988; Voice of the Universe, 1987; Astronomer by Chance, 1990; Echoes of War, 1991. *Honours include:* OBE, 1940; Kt, 1961. *Address:* Jodrell Bank, Macclesfield, Cheshire, England.

LOVELOCK Yann Rufus, b. 11 Feb 1939, Birmingham, England. Writer; Translator; Co-ordinator of Angulimala, Buddhist Prison Chaplaincy Organisation. m. Ann Riddell, 28 Sept 1961. *Education:* BA, English Literature, St Edmund Hall, Oxford, 1963. *Literary Appointments:* Resident Writer in a number of schools also at Long Lartin Prison (1984) and other appointments for West Midlands Art Link. *Publications:* The Vegetable Book, 1972; The Line Forward, 1984; The Colour of the Weather, editor and translator, 1980; A Vanishing Emptiness, editor and part translator, 1989; A Townscape of Flanders, Versions of Grace (translation of Anton van Wilderode), 1990; Blue Cubes for a Catarrh and Songs of Impotence, poem, 1990. Some 25 other books of poems, experimental prose, anthologies and translations since 1960. *Contributions to:* Regular features in Dutch Crossing (London University); Poems in PN Review, Poetry Review, Ambit, Stand and others. *Honour:* Silver Medal, Haute Academie d'Art et de litterature de France, 1986. *Memberships:* Freundkreis Poesie Europe, Assistant Director. *Address:* 80 Doris Road, Birmingham, West Midlands B11 4NF, England.

LOVESEY Peter, (Peter Lear), b. 10 Sept 1936, Whitton, Middlesex, England. Writer. m. Jacqueline Ruth May 1959, 1 son, 1 daughter. *Education:* BA, Honours, English, University of Reading, 1958. *Publications:* The Kings of Distance, non-fiction sports, 1968; Wobble to Death, crime fiction, 1970; The Detective Wore Silk Drawers, 1971; Abracadaver, 1972; Mad Hatters Holiday, 1973; Invitation to a Dynamite Party, 1974; A Case of Spirits, 1975; Swing, Swing Together, 1976; Goldengirl, as Peter Lear, 1977; Waxwork, 1978; Official Centenary History of the Amateur Athletic Association, 1979; Spider Girl, as Peter Lear, 1980; The False Inspector Dew, 1982; Keystone, 1983; Butchers, short stories, 1985; The Secret of Spandau, as Peter Lear, 1986; Rough Cider, 1986; Bertie and the Tinman, 1987; On The Edge, 1989; Bertie and the Seven Bodies, 1990; The Last Detective, 1991; Diamond Solitaire, 1992. *Honours:* Macmillan/Panther 1st Crime Novel Award, 1970; Crime Writers Association Silver Dagger, 1978, Gold Dagger, 1982; Grand Prix de Littérature Policière, 1985; Prix du Roman D'Aventures, 1987; Anthony Award, 1992. *Memberships:* Crime Writers Association; Detection Club; Society of Authors. *Literary Agent:* Vanessa Holt Associates Ltd. *Address:* 59 Crescent Road, Leigh-on-Sea, Essex SS9 2PF, England.

LOVETT Albert Winston, b. 16 Dec 1944, Abingdon,

England. Academic. *Education:* BA, 1965, PhD, 1969, Cambridge. *Publications:* Philip II and Mateo Vazquez, 1977; Modern Europe 1453-1610, 1979; Early Habsburg Spain 1516-1598, 1986. *Contributions to:* Historical Journal (Cambridge); European History Quarterly; English Historical Review; Others. *Memberships:* Fellow, Royal Historical Society. *Address:* 26 Coney Hill Rd, West Wickham, Kent BR4 9BX, England.

LOW Dorothy Mackie. *See:* LOW Lois.

LOW Lois, (Zoë Cass, Dorothy Mackie Low, Lois Paxton), b. 1916, British, Writer of Mystery/Crime/Suspense. Historical/Romance/Gothic fiction. *Publications:* Isle for a Stranger, 1962; Dear Liar, 1963; A Ripple on the Water, 1964; The Intruder, 1965; A House in the Country, 1968; (as Lois Paxton), The Man Who Died Twice, 1969; To Burgundy and Back, 1970; (as Lois Paxton), The Quiet Sound of Fear, 1971; (as Lois Paxton), Who Goes There? 1972; (as Zoë Cass), Island of the Seven Hills, 1974; (as Zoë Cass), The Silver Leopard, 1976; (as Zoë Cass), A Twist in the Silk, 1980; (as Lois Paxton), The Man in the Shadows, 1983. *Memberships:* Crime Writers Association; Society of Authors; Romantic Novelists Association, Chairman 1969-71. *Literary Agent:* A M Heath & Company Ltd, 79 St Martin's Lane, London WC2N 4AA, London. *Address:* 6 Belmont Mews, Abbey Hill, Kenilworth, Warwickshire CV8 1LU, England.

LOW Rachael, British. *Appointments:* Film, Researcher engaged in a history of British cinema: with British Film Institute, London, 1945-48, and Gulbenkian Research Fellow, Lucy Cavendish College, Cambridge, 1968-71; Fellow Commoner of Lucy Cavendish College, 1983. *Publications:* History of the British Film, 1896-1906, 1948; (with Roger Manvell) 1906- 1914, 1949, 1914-1918, 1950, 1918-1929, 1971, 1929-39, 2 vols, 1979, 3rd vol, 1985. *Address:* c/o Allen & Unwin Ltd, 40 Museum Street, London WC1, England.

LOWBURY Edward Joseph Lister, b. 6 Dec 1913, London, England. Writer (Poet); Retired from medicine. m. Alison Young, 12 June 1954, 3 daughters. *Education:* Oxford University; London Hospital Medical College; BM BCh, 1939; MA, 1940; DM, 1957; FRCPath, 1963. *Publications:* Time for Sale, 1961; Daylight Astronomy, 1968; Thomas Campion: Poet, Composer, Physician, 1970; Green Magic, 1973; The Night Watchman, 1974; Selected Poems, 1978; Selected & New Poems, 1990; Drug Resistance in Anti-microbial Therapy, 1973; Control of Hospital Infection (with others), 1974, 1981, 1991. *Contributions to:* Over 200 medical and scientific papers in professional journals. Poems in: Times Literary Supplement; New Statesman; Encounter; London magazine. *Honours:* FRSL, 1974; OBE, 1979; FRCP, 1977; FRCS, 1978; Member of Literature Panel, West Midlands Arts, 1970's; President, Smethwick Arts Club, 1970's; Keats Memorial Lecturer, 1973; Honorary DSc, Aston University, 1977; Honorary Visiting Professor of Medical Microbiology, Aston University 1979; Honorary LLD, Birmingham University, 1980. *Memberships:* Society of Authors; Fellow, Royal Society of Literature. *Address:* 79 Vernon Road, Birmingham B16 9SQ, England.

LOWDEN Desmond Scott, b. 27 Sept 1937, Winchester, Hants. England. Writer. m. 14 July 1962, 1 son, 1 daughter. *Education:* Pilgrims' School, Winchester; Marlborough College. *Publications:* Bandersnatch, 1969; The Boondocks, 1972; Bellman and True, 1975; Boudapesti 3, 1979; Sunspot, 1981; Cry Havoc, 1984; The Shadow Run, 1989; Chain, 1990. *Honour:* Crime Writers' Association Silver Dagger Award, 1989, for Shadow Run. *Membership:* Crime Writers' Association. *Literary Agent:* Deborah Rogers. *Address:* c/o Deborah Rogers, Rogers, Coleridge and White Ltd, 20 Powys Mews, London W11 1JN, England.

LOWE John Evelyn, b. 23 Apr 1928, London,

England. Writer. m. (1) Susan Sanderson, 1956, 2 sons, 1 daughter, (2) Yuki Nomura, 1989, 1 daughter. *Education:* English Literature, New College, Oxford, 1950-52. *Appointments:* Associate Editor, Collins Crime Club, 1953-54; Editor, Faber Furniture Series, 1954-56; Deputy Story Editor, Pinewood Studios, 1956- 57; Literary Editor, Kansai Time Out Magazine, 1985-89. *Publications:* Thomas Chippendale, 1955; Cream Coloured Earthenware, 1958; Japanese Crafts, 1983; Into Japan, 1985; Into China, 1986; Corsica - A Traveller's Guide, 1988; A Surrealist Life - Edward James, 1991; A Short Guide to the Kyoto Museum of Archaeology, 1991; Major contribution to the Encyclopaedica Britannica and the Oxford Junior Encyclopaedia. *Contributions to:* The American Scholar; Country Life; Listener; Connoisseur; Apollo; Others. *Honours:* Honorary Fellow, Royal College of Art. *Memberships:* Fellow, Society of Antiquaries; Fellow, Royal Society of Arts. *Address:* Paillole-Basse, 47360 Prayssas, France.

LOWE Richard Grady, b. 5 July 1942, Eunice, Louisiana, USA. Historian. m. Cheron Fontenot, 22 July 1962, dec 3 May 1989, 3 sons. *Education:* BA, History, University of Southwestern Louisiana, 1964; AM, History, Harvard University, 1965; PhD, History, University of Virginia, 1968. *Appointments:* Visiting Lecturer, Virginia Polytechnic Institute, summer 1967; Professor, History, University of North Texas, Denton, 1968-; Visiting Assistant Professor, University of Virginia, summer 1970. *Publications:* Wealth and Power in Antebellum Texas (co-author), 1977; Planters and Plain Folk (co-author), 1987; Republicans and Reconstruction in Virginia, 1856-70, 1991. *Contributions to:* William and Mary Quarterly, 1968; Journal of American History, 1976; Journal of Southern History, 1976; Civil War History, 1988; Others. *Memberships:* Southern Historical Association; Texas State Historical Association; Society of Civil War Historians. *Address:* Department of History, University of North Texas, Denton, TX 76203, USA.

LOWE Robson, b. 7 Jan 1905, London, England. Editor; Author; Auctioneer. m. Winifred Marie Devine, 7 Mar 1928, 2 daughters. *Education:* Fulham Central School. *Publications:* Regent Catalogue of Empire Postage Stamps, 1933; The Encyclopaedia of Empire Postage Stamps (1 vol) 1935; Handstruck Postage Stamps of the Empire, 1937; The Birth of the Adhesive Postage Stamp, 1939; Masterpieces of Engraving on Postage Stamps, 1943; The Encyclopaedia of Empire Postage Stamps (7 vols) 1950-90; Sperati & His Work, 1956; The British Postage Stamp 1968; Many monographs; Leeward Islands, 1990; The House of Stamps, Imitations, 1993. *Contributions to:* Edited the Philatelist 1935-74, 1982-; Contributed many articles to philatelic and postal history journals at home and abroad. *Honours:* Lichtenstein Award (US) 1970; RPS of Canada, Gold Medal, 1973; Crawford Medal (GB) 1974; Milan Special Award 1977; India Special Award, 1980; Carl Lindberg Medal (Germany) 1980; New Zealand Award of Honour, 1982; First Signatory of the US Roll of Distinguished Philatelists, 1988; Elected to Roll of Distinguished Philatelists in South Africa, 1990; Hon Fellow of the Royal Philatelic Society. *Memberships:* Co-founder, Postal History Society, 1935; Chairman of Expert Committee, British Philatelic Association 1941-61; President 1979-81, founded Society of Postal Historians, 1950; Collectors Club, New York. *Address:* c/o The East India Club, 16 St James's Square, London SW1, England.

LOWE Stephen, b. 1 Dec 1947, Nottingham, Engalnd. Playwright. m. (1) Tina Barclay; (2) Tany Myers, 1 son, 1 daughter. *Education:* BA Hons, English and Drama, 1969, Postgraduate Research, 1969-70. *Appointments:* Senior Tutor in Writing for Performance, Dartington College of Arts Prerformance, 1978-82; Resident Playwright, Riverside Studios, London, 1982-84; Senior Tutor, Birmingham University, 1987-88; Nottingham Trent University Advisory Board to Theatre Design Degree, 1987-. *Publications:* Stage Plays: Touched, 1981; Ragged Trousered Philanthropists, 1991; Moving

Pictures and othe Plays, 1985; Divine Gossip/Tibetan Inroads, 1988; Body and Soul in Peace Plays, Vol I, 1985, Vol 2, 1990; Cards, 1983. *Contributions to:* Englisch Amerikanische Studien, 1986; Debut on 2: A Guide to TV Writing, 1990; The Breath of Inspiration. *Honours:* George Devine Award for Playwriting, 1977. *Memberships:* Theatre Writers Union; Writers Guild; PEN. *Literary Agent:* S Stroud, Judy Daish Associates. *Address:* S Stroud, Judy Daish Associates, 83 Eastbourn Mews, London W2 6LQ, England.

LOWE-WATSON Dawn, b. 12 June 1929, London, England. Writer. m. David Lowe-Watson, 22 Oct 1951, sep, 3 sons. *Education:* Modern Arts Diploma, Queen's College, 1946. *Appointments:* Editorial Assistant, Weldons Publications, 1947; Editor, Markets and People, British Export Trade Research Organisation, 1950; Editorial Director, Perry Press Productions, 1951-54. *Publications:* The Good Morrow, 1980; Sound of Water, 1982; Black Piano, 1986; 12 radio plays, BBC Radio 4. *Contributions to:* As Dawn Valery, fiction to magazines; Features to many newspapers including Sunday Times. *Honours:* Authors Club 1st Novel Award for The Good Morrow, 1980; Elgin Prize for Sound of Water, 1983. *Memberships:* PEN; Society of Authors; Authors Club, Committee Member. *Literary Agent:* Rogers, Coleridge and White, England.

LOWELL Susan Deborah, b. 27 Oct 1950, Chihuahua, Mexico. Writer. m. William Ross Humphreys, 21 Mar 1975, 2 daughters. *Education:* BA, 1972, MA, 1974, Stanford University, USA; MA, PhD, Princeton University, 1979. *Appointments:* University of Arizona, USA, 1974-76; University of Texas, Dallas, 1979-80; University of Arizona, 1989. *Publication:* Ganado Red: A Novella and Stories, 1988. *Honour:* Milkweed Editions National Fiction Prize, 1988. *Membership:* Southern Arizona Society of Authors. *Address:* c/o Milkweed Editions, PO Box 3226, Minneapolis, MN 55403, USA.

LOWEN Alexander, b. 1910. American, Writer on Human relations, Psychiatry, Psychology, Sex. Psychiatrist in private practice since 1953; Associate Director, New England Heart Center; Executive Director, Institute for Bioenergetic Analysis, New York City. *Publications:* Physical Dynamics of Character Structure, 1958; Love and Orgasm, 1965; The Betrayal of the Body, 1967; Depression and the Body, 1973; Pleasure, 1975; Bioenergetics, 1975; (with Leslie Lowen) The Way to Vibrant Health, 1977; Fears of Life, 1980; Narcissism, 1983; Love, Sex and Your Heart, 1989; The Spirituality of the Body, 1990. *Literary Agent:* Raines and Raines, 71 Park Avenue, New York, NY 10016, USA. *Address:* Puddin Hill Road, New Canaan, Connecticut, USA.

LOWING Anne. *See:* **GEACH Christine.**

LOWNDES Robert A(ugustine) W(ard), b. 1916, American, Writer of Science fiction/Fantasy, Children's fiction, Literature. Production Associate, Radio Electronics magazine, 1978-; Editor, Airmont Classics, also freelance writer of science fiction short stories under various pseudonyms. *Appointments:* Worked for the Civilian Conservation Corps, 1934, 1936- 37, 1939; Assistant on a squab farm; salesman; porter, Greenwich Hospital Association, Connecticut, 1937-38; Literary Agent, Fantastory Sales Service, 1940-42; Editor, Future Fiction, 1940-42, and Science Fiction Quarterly, 1940- 42, 1951-58; Editor, Director, Columbia magazines, 1942-60; Editor, Future Science Fiction, 1950-60, Dynamic Science Fiction 1952-54 and Science Fiction Stories, 1953-60; Editor, Avalon science-fiction series, Thomas Bouregy, 1955- 67; Editor, Famous Science Fiction, 1960-69, Magazine of Horror, 1962-71, Startling Mystery Stories, 1966-71, Weird Terror Tales, 1969-70, and Bizarre Fantasy Fiction, 1970-71; Associate Editor 1971-77 and Managing Editor, 1977- 78, Sexology and Luz magazines; Production Chief 1978-81 and Editor in English 1982-84, Luz magazine. *Publications:* Mystery of the Third Mine (juvenile) 1953; (with James Blish)

The Duplicated Man, 1959; The Puzzle Planet, 1961; Believer's World, 1961; Three Faces of Science Fiction, 1973; (ed)The Best of James Blish, 1979. *Address:* 717 Willow Avenue, Hoboken, NJ 07030, USA.

LOWNIE Andrew James Hamilton, b. 11 Nov 1961, Kenya. Literary Agent. *Education:* Magdalene College, Cambridge, 1981-84; BA (Cantab); MA (Cantab); MSc, Edinburgh University, 1989. *Appointments:* Trustee, Iain Macleaod Award, 1984; Hodder and Stoughton Publishers, 1984-85; Joined, 1985, Director, 1986-88, John Farquharson Literary Agents; Andrew Lownie Associates, 1988-; Denniston and Lownie, 1991-; Parliamentary Candidate, Monklands West, 1992. *Publications:* North American Spies, 1992; Edinburgh Literary Guide, 1992. *Contributions to:* Regularly to: Times; Spectator; Telegraph; Scotland on Sunday. *Honours:* English Speaking Union Scholarship to Asheville School, North Carolina, USA, 1979-80; Fellow, Royal Geographical Association; Fellow Royal Society of Arts; Fellow, Royal Historical Society. *Address:* 122 Bedford Court Mansions, Bedford Square, London WC1B 3AH, England.

LOWRY Robert James, b. 28 Mar 1919, Cincinnati, Ohio, USA. Writer. 3 sons. *Publications include:* Casualty, 1946; Find Me in Fire, 1948; The Wolf That Fed Us, 1949; The Big Cage, 1949; The Violent Wedding, 1953; Happy New Year, Kamerades!, 1954; What's Left of April, 1956; New York Call Girl, 1959; The Prince of Pride Starring, 1959; Party of Dreamers, 1962. *Address:* Hotel Fort Washington, 421 Main Street, Cincinnati, Ohio, USA.

LUARD Nicholas (James McVean), b. 1937, British, Writer of Mystery/Crime/Suspense, Environmental science/Ecology. Worked for NATO and in theatre and publishing. *Publications:* Mystery novels: The Warm and Golden War, 1967; The Robespierre Serial, 1975; Travelling Horseman, 1975; The Orion Line, 1976; in US as Double Assignment, 1977; (as James McVean) Bloodspoor, 1977; The Dirty Area (in US as The Shadow Spy) 1979; (as James McVean) Seabird Nine, 1981; (as James McVean) Titan, 1984; Other: (with Dominick Elwes) Refer to Drawer, 1964; The Last Wilderness: A Journey Across the Great Kalahari Desert, 1981; The Wildlife Parks of Africa, 1985. *Address:* 227 South Lambeth Road, London SW8, England.

LUBINGER Eva, b. 3 Feb 1930, Steyr, Austria. Writer. m. Dr Walter Myss, 7 Oct 1952, 2 sons. *Appointment:* Wort und Welt, Innsbruck, Austria. *Publications:* Paradies mit Kleinen Fehlein, 1976; Gespenster in Sir Edward's Haus, 1978; Pflucke den Wind, (lyric), 1982; Verlieb Dich nicht in Mark Aurell, 1985; Zeig mir Lamorna, 1985; Fleig mit Nach Samarkand, 1987. *Contributions to:* Prasent, weekly newspaper. *Honours:* Literature Prize for Lyrics, Innsbruck, 1963; Literature Prize for Drama, Innsbruck, 1969. *Membership:* PEN, Austria. *Literary Agent:* Wort und Welt, Innsbruck. *Address:* Lindenbuhelweg 16, 6020 Innsbruck, Austria.

LUCAS Celia, b. 23 Oct 1938, Bristol, England. Writer. m. Ian Skidmore, 20 Oct 1971. *Education:* BA, Hons, Modern History, St Hilda's College, Oxford, 1961. *Publications:* Steel Town Cats, 1987; The Adventures of Marmaduke Purr Cat, 1990; Prisoners of Santo Tomas, 1975, paperback 1988; Anglesey Rambles (with husband) 1989 (under Skidmore); Glyndwr Country (with husband) 1988 (under Skidmore). *Contributions to:* Numerous journals and magazines. *Honour:* TIR NA N-OG Award for junior fiction with Welsh background, 1988. *Membership:* Welsh Academy (elected 1989). *Address:* Aberbraint, Llanfairpwll, Isle of Anglesey, Gwynedd LL61 6BP, Wales.

LUCAS John Randolph, b. 18 June 1926, London, England. Don. m. Helen Morar Portal, 17 June 1961, 2 sons, 2 daughters. *Education:* Scholar, Winchester, 1942-47; Scholar, Balliol, Oxford, 1947-51; 1st Class Mathematics Mods, 1948; 1st Class Lit Hum. 1951; BA, 1951; Harmsworth Senior Scholar, Merton College, Oxford, 1951-53; MA, 1954. *Publications:* Principles of Politics, 1966, 2nd Edition, 1985; The Concept of Probability, 1970; The Freedom of the Will, 1970; A Treatise on Time and Space, 1973; Democracy and Participation, 1973; Essays on Freedom and Grace, 1976; On Justice, 1980, 1989; Space, Time and Causality, 1985; The Future, 1989; Spacetime and Electromagnetism, 1990; Responsibility, 1993. *Honours:* John Locke, 1952; FBA, 1988. *Address:* Merton College, Oxford OX1 4JD, England.

LUCAS Stephen E, b. 5 Oct 1946, White Plains, New York, USA. Professor. m. Patricia Vore, 14 June 1969, 2 sons. *Education:* BA, University of California, Santa Barbara, 1968; MA, 1970, PhD, 1973, Pennsylvania State University. *Publications:* Portents of Rebellion: Rhetoric and Revolution in Philadelphia, 1765-1776, 1976; The Art of Public Speaking, 1983, 1986, 1989, 1992; Justifying America: The Declaration of Independence as a Rhetorical Document, 1989. *Contributions to:* The Schism in Rhetorical Scholarship, to Quarterly Journal of Speech, 1981; The Renaissance of American Public Address, to Quarterly Journal of Speech, 1988; The Stylistic Artistry of the Declaration of Independence, to Prologue, 1990. *Honours:* Golden Anniversary Book Award, Speech Communication Association, 1976. *Memberships:* Speech Communication Association; International Society for the History of Rhetoric; Society for Eighteenth-Century Studies; Organization of American Historians. *Address:* Department of Communications Arts, University of Wisconsin, Madison, WI 57306, USA.

LUCIA Ellis Joel, b. 6 June 1922, Watsonville, California, USA. Author; Freelance Writer. m. Elsie Eleanor Kemmling, 6 Nov 1965, North Plains Oregon. *Education:* BA, History, Literature, Political Science, 1944, Honorary Doctor of Letters, 1965, Pacific University. *Publications:* The Saga of Ben Holladay, 1959; Klondike Kate, 1962; Tough Men, Tough Country, 1963; The Big Blow, 1963; Don't Call It Or-E-Gawn, 1964; Head Rig, 1965; Wild Water, 1964; Sea Wall, 1966; This Land Around Us, 1969; Mr Football: Amos Alonzo Stagg, 1970; Editor, The Gunfighters, 1971; (with Mike Hanley) Owyhee Trails, 1974; The Big Woods, 1975; Cornerstone, 1975; Magic Valley, 1976; Editor, Oregon's Golden Years, 1976; Seattle's Sisters of Providence, 1978; Tillamook Burn Country, 1983. *Contributions to:* Over 1,000 magazine, newspaper, journal and anthologie articles including, New York Times; The nation; King Features. *Honours:* Best Western, The Wrangler, Western Heritage, 1974; Trophy, Citation, Founder-Public Relations Director, All Northwest Barber Shop Ballad Contest and Gay 90's Festival, 1948; Consultant, national Award-Winning TV documentary for Public Television, Greening of the Tillamook, 1983-84. *Memberships:* Authors Guild of America; Western Writers of America; Oregon Freelance Club, President, twice, 1950's. *Address:* P O Box 17507, Portland, OR 97217, USA.

LUCIE-SMITH John Edward McKenzie, (Peter Kershaw), b. 27 Feb 1933, Kingston, Jamaica, West Indies. Writer. *Education:* King's School, Canterbury; MA, Hons, Modern History, Merton College, Oxford. *Appointments:* Settled in England in 1946; Education Officer, Royal Air Force, 1954-56; Advertising copywriter 1956-66; Freelance author, journalist and broadcaster 1966-; Consultant, curator or co-curator of a number of exhibitions of in Britain and the USA and author of exhibition catalogues. *Publications include:* Moments in Art since 1945 (entitled Late Modern in the US) 1969; A Concise History of French Painting, 1971; Symbolist Art, 1972; Eroticism in Western Art, 1972; Fantin-Latour, 1977; A Concise History of Furniture, 1979; A Cultural Calender of the Twentieth Century, 1979; Art in the Seventies, 1980; The Story of Craft, 1981; A History of Industrial Design, 1983; A Thames and Hudson Dictionary of Art Terms, 1984; Art of the 1930s, 1985; American Art Now, 1985; Lives of the Twentieth Century Artists, 1986; Sculpture Since 1945, 1987; Art of the Eighties, 1990; Art Deco Painting,

1990; Art and Civilization, 1992; The Faber Book of Art Anecdotes, 1992; Wendy Taylor, 1992; Alexander, 1992. Other publications include four collections of his own verse, two standard anthologies (the Penguin Book of Elizabethan Verse and British Poetry Since 1945), a biography of Joan of Arc, a history of piracy and an autobiography; Fletcher Benton, 1990; Jean Rustin, 1991; Harry Holland, 1992. *Membership:* Fellow, Royal Literary Society. *Address:* c/o Rogers, Coleridge and White, 20 Powis Mews, London W11 1JN, England.

LUCKLESS John. *See:* **IRVING Clifford.**

LUCZAK Alojzy Andrzej, . 12 June 1930, Poznan, Poland. Writer; Journalist. m. Wanda, 22 Dec 1954, 2 sons, 1 daughter. *Education:* Academy of Economyics, Poznan, 1956. *Publications:* Hungry, 1974; Against the Wind With Music, 1988; You Will Still be a Eagle for Me, 1976; Pro Sinfonika - the Life-art Among People, 1978; Music Itinerarium, 1979; Pro Sinfonica's Leading Ideas, 1980; Cinema Film: Go and Come Back with Poland, 1987. *Contributions to:* various journals and magazine. *Honours:* Prize, Polish Government (twice); Prize, Journal Polityka; Prize Children, Smile Order; Polish Literary Society; Polish Journalists Society; President, Great Polish Cultural Society; President, Pro Sinfonica. *Address:* ulica Nowowiejskiego 12 m. 5, 61-731 Poznan, Poland.

LUDLUM Robert, (Jonathan Ryder, Michael Shepherd), b. 25 May 1927, New York, United States of America. Author; Writer. m. Mary Ryducha, 31 Mar 1951, 2 sons, 1 daughter. *Education:* BA, Wesleyan University, 1951. *Appointments include:* Early Career devoted to the Theatre and Television as an Actor and Producer; Became Full-Time Writer, 1975. *Publications:* The Scarlatti Inheritance, 1971; Trevayne (as Jonathan Ryder), 1973; The Cry of the Halidon (as Jonathan Ryde), 1974; The Road to Gandolfo (as Michael Shepherd), 1975; The Gemini Contenders, 1976; The Chancellor Manuscript, 1977; The Icarus Agenda, 1988. *Honours:* The Scarlatti Inheritance became bestseller and Book of the Month; The Icarus Agenda, New York Times Bestseller List, 1988.

LUEBKE Frederick Carl, b. 1927, American, Writer on History. *Appointments:* Charles Mach Distinguished Professor of History, University of Nebraska, Lincoln, since 1987 (Professor, 1972-87, associate Professor, 1968-72); Director, Center for Great Plains Studies, 1983-88; Associate Editor, Great Plains Quarterly, 1985- (Editor 1981-84). *Publications:* Immigrants and Politics, 1969; (ed)Ethnic Voters and the Election of Lincoln, 1971; Bonds of Loyalty: German Americans and World War I, 1974; (ed)The Great Plains: Environment and Culture, 1979; (ed)Ethnicity on the Great Plains, 1980; (ed)Vision and Refuge: Essays on the Literature of the Great Plains, 1981; (co-ed) Mapping the North American Plains, 1987; Germans in Brazil: A Comparative History of Cultural Conflict During World War I, 1987; Germans in the New World: Essays in the History of Immigration, 1990; (ed) A Harmony of the Arts: The Nebraska State Capitol, 1990. *Address:* 3117 Woodsdale Boulevard, Lincoln, NE 68502, USA.

LUELLEN Valentina. *See:* **POLLEY Judith Anne.**

LUHRMANN Tanya Marie, b. 24 Feb 1959, Ohio, USA. Associate Professor of Anthropology. *Education:* BA summa cum laude, Harvard University, 1981; MPhil, Social Anthropology, 1982, PhD, Social Anthropology, 1986, University of Cambridge. *Appointments:* Research Fellow, Christ's College, Cambridge, England, 1985-89; Dept of Anthropolgy, University of California at San Diego, USA, 1989-. *Publication:* Persuasions of the Witch's Craft, 1989. *Contributions to:* Popoc Vuh and Lacan, to Ethos, 1984; The Magic of Secrecy, to Ethos, 1989; Witchcraft, Morality and Magic in Contemporary England, to International, Journal of Moral Social Studies; Others. *Honours:* Bowdoin Prize, 1981; National Science Foundation Graduate Fellow,1982-85;

Emanuel Miller Prize, 1983; Partingdon Prize, 1985; Stirling Prize, 1986; Fulbright Award, 1990. *Memberships:* American Anthropology Association; Society for Psychological Anthropology, Nominations Committee; Royal Anthropological Institute. *Literary Agent:* Jill Kneerim, Palmer and Dodge Agency. *Address:* UCSD-0101, La Jolla, CA 92093, USA.

LUKAS Richard Conrad, b. 1937. American. Writer on History. *Appointments:* Research Consultant, US Air Force Historical Archives, 1957-58; Assistant Professor 1963-66, Associate Professor 1966-69, Professor 1969-, University Professor of History, 1983-, Tennessee Technological University, Cookeville. *Publications:* Eagles East: The Army Air Forces and the Soviet Union, 1941-45, 1970; (ed)From Metternich to the Beatles, 1973; The Strange Allies: The United States and Poland, 1941-45, 1978; Bitter Legacy: Polish-American Relations in the Wake of World War II, 1982; Forgotten Holocaust: The Poles under German Occupation, 1986. *Address:* Department of History, Tennessee Technological University, Cookeville, TN 38501, USA.

LUKE Peter, b. 12 Aug 1919, England. Writer; Dramatist. m. June Tobin, 23 Nov 1963, 3 sons (1 dec), 4 daughters. *Education:* Eton 1932-37; Byam Shaw School of Art, 1938; Atelier Andre Lhote, Paris, 1938-39. *Appointments:* Sub-Editor, Reuters, 1946-47; Story Editor, ABC-TV, 1958-62, Editor, The Bookman, 1962-63, Editor, Tempo, 1963-64, ABC-TV; Drama Producer, BBC-TV, 1963-67; Director, Dublin Gate Theatre Co, 1977-80. *Publications:* The Play of Hadrian the Seventh, 1968; Sisyphus and Reilly, 1972; Telling Tales, short stories, 1981; The Other Side of the Hill, 1984; The Mad Pomegranate and the Praying Mantis, 1985; Yerma, translation, 1987; West End productions: Hadrian VII, 1968; Bloomsbury, 1974; Yerma (NT), 1987; Married Love, 1988; Editor: Enter Certain Players, Edwards-MacLiammoir, 1978; Paquito and the Wolf, for children, 1981. *Contributions to:* Envoy, Dublin; Cornhill; Pick of Today's Short Stories; Winter's Tales; Era, Ireland; New Irish Writing; Irish Times; Daily Telegraph; Independent on Sunday. *Honours:* MC 1944; Prix Italia, 1967; Nomination for Antoinette Perry Award, 1968-69; Nomination for Sony Award, 1990. *Memberships:* Writers Guild of Great Britain; Society of Authors; International PEN. *Literary Agent:* Lemon, Unna and Durbridge Ltd, England. *Address:* c/o Lemon, Unna and Durbridge Ltd, 24 Pottery Lane, Holland Park, London W11 4LZ, England.

LUKE Thomas. *See:* **MASTERTON Graham.**

LUKER Nicholas John Lydgate, b. 26 Jan 1945, Leeds, England. University Senior Lecturer in Russian. 1 son. *Education:* Hertford College, Oxford, 1964-68; MA, French, Russian, Oxford; Lecteur d'Anglais, University of Grenoble, France, 1967; Postgraduate Scholar, Department of Slavonic Studies, 1968-70, PhD, 1971, University of Nottingham. *Publications:* Alexander Kuprin, 1978; Alexander Grin: The Seeker of Adventure, 1978; Alexander Grin: The Forgotten Visionary, 1980; An Anthology of Russian-Neorealism, 1982; Fifty Years On: Gorky and his Time, 1987; Alexander Grin: Selected Short Stories, 1987; From Furmanov to Sholokhov, 1988; In Defence of a Reputation, 1990; The Russian Short Story, 1900-1917, 1991. *Contributions to:* Numerous articles in various journals in field of Russian literature. *Honours:* Visiting Lecturer in Russian, Victoria University of Wellington, New Zealand, 1976; Visiting Fellow, Department of Russian, University of Otago, Dunedin, New Zealand, 1991. *Memberships:* British Association of Slavists; Executive Committee, RLUSC for UK Universities. *Address:* Department of Slavonic Studies, University of Nottingham, Nottingham NG7 2RD, England.

LULUA Abdul-Wahid, b. 16 July 1931, Mowsil, Iraq. Professor of English Literature. m. Mariam Abdul-Bagi, 22 July 1962, 1 son, 1 daughter. *Education:* Licence-es-Lettres, English, Ecole Normale Superieure,

University of Baghdad, 1952; EdM, English, Harvard University, USA, 1957; PhD, English, Western Reserve University, Cleveland, Ohio, 1962. *Appointments:* Lecturer, Assistant Professor, English Literature, Head, Department of European Languages, College of Education (formerly Ecole Normale Superieure), Baghdad, 1962-67; Assistant Professor, English Literature, University of Kuwait, 1967-70; Associate Professor, English Literature, Faculty of Arts, 1970-71, 1972-77; Visiting Scholar, Cambridge University, England, 1971-72; Freelance Translator, 1977; Associate Professor, English Literature, 1983, Professor, English Literature, 1983-89, Chairman, Department of English Language and Literature, 1983-84, Yarmouk University, Jordan; Professor, English Literature, United Arab Emirates University, 1989-. *Publications:* Critical studies: In Search of Meaning, 1973, 2nd Edition, 1983; T S Eliot, The Waste Land. The Poet and the Poem, 1980, 2nd edition, 1986; Blowing into Ashes, 1982, 2nd Edition, 1989; Aspect of the Moon, 1990; Arabic Poetry and the Rise of European Love Lyrics; English-Arabic translations: The Waters of Babylon and Sergeant Musgrave's Dance (John Arden), 1976; Timon of Athens (Shakespeare), 1977, 2nd Edition, 1984; Left-Handed Liberty and The Hero Rises Up (John Arden), 1978; William Blake (D G Gillham), 1982; The Critical Idion, 44 vols, 1969-82; Trends and Movements in Modern Arabic Poetry (Salma K Jayyusi); Cymbeline, Pericles (Shakespeare); Psychoanlytic Criticism (Elizabeth Wright); Arabic-English translations: Culture and Arts in Iraq, 1978; Revolution and Development in Iraq, 1980; Iraq: The Eternal Fire, 1981; The Long Days, novel, 1982; Battlefront Stories from Iraq, 1983; Modern Iraqi Poetry, 1987. *Contributions to:* Major Arabic magazines, Iraq and Middle East. *Memberships:* Modern Humanities Research Association, Cambridge; Association Internationale de Litterature Comparative. *Literary Agent:* Riad El-Rayyes Books, 56 Knightsbridge, London SW1X 7NJ, England.

LUMLEY Joanna, b. Kashmir, India. Actress. *Publications:* Stare Back and Smile: Memoirs, 1990. *Contributions to:* Columns in the Times.

LUND Gerald Niels, b. 12 Sept 1939, Fountain Green, Utah, USA. Educator. m. Lynn Stanard, 5 June 1963, 3 sons, 4 daughters. *Education:* BA, Sociology, 1965, MS Sociology, 1969, Brigham Young University; Further graduate studies in New Testament at Pepperdine University, Los Angeles. *Publications:* The Alliance, 1983; Freedom Factor, 1987; One in Thine Hand, 1981; The Coming of the Lord, 1971; This Is Your World, 1973; Leverage Point, 1986; Pillar of Light (vol 1 in 5-part series called The Work and The Glory) Oct 1990; Like A Fire is Burning, vol 2, 1991; Truth Will Prevail, vol 3, 1992. *Contributions to:* Numerous articles in magazines and monographs on Biblical and religious themes. *Honour:* Outstanding Teacher, Continuing Education, Brigham Youong University, 1985; Awarded Best Novel by Association of Mormon Letters, 1991. *Address:* 1157 E 1500 S, Bountiful, UT 84010, USA.

LUNN Janet Louise, b. 28 Dec 1928, Dallas, Texas, USA. Writer. m. Richard Lunn, 2 Mar 1950, 4 sons, 1 daughter. *Education:* Three years at Queen's University, Kingston, Ontario. *Publications:* The County, 1967; Double Spell, 1968; Larger Than Life, 1979; The Twelve Dancing Princesses, 1979; The Root Cellar, 1981; Shadow in Hawthorn Bay, 1986; Amos's Sweater, 1988; Duck Cakes for Sale, 1989; One Hundred Shining Candles, 1990; The Story of Canada for Children, 1992; (Ed) Collection of Ghost Stories for Children, 1993. *Contributions to:* Magazine articles, book reviews, radio talk and interviews. *Honours include:* IODE Children's Book Award, 1979, Children's Book of the Year, 1982, both from Canadian Library Association; Ruth Schwartz Children's Book of the Year runner up, Canadian Boosellers Association, 1981; Honour List, University Board of Books for Young People, 1984; Hon Doctorate of Laws, Queens University, 1992. *Memberships:* Canadian Children's Book Centre: VP, 1990; Board, IBBY Canada, 1989; Board, Canadian Children's Book Centre,

1989; Writer's Union of Canada, Chair, 1984-85; First Vice, 1983-84, Second Vice Chair, 1979-80; Canadian Society of Children's Authors, Illustrators and Performers; PEN International. *Literary Agent:* Lee Davis-Creole, Lucinda-Davey Agency. *Address:* RR No.2 Hillier, Ontario, Canada KOK 2JO.

LUO Bin Ji (Zhang Pujun), b. 17 Feb 1917, Jilin, China. Author/Novelist; Historian; Philologist. m. Zou Min Cai, 6 Oct 1949, 1 son, 1 daughter. *Education:* Completed Junior Middle School, 1933; Auditor, Peking University, 1934; Self-study, Peking Library, 1934-35. *Appointments:* Writer, 1936-; Propagandist, Shanghai, 1936; Minister, Chengxian County Propaganda Department, 1938; Chief Editor, magazines: Zhan Qi and Wen Xue Bao, 1939, 1941, North-East Culture, 1945. *Publications:* One Week and One Day, 1937; One Day of Shanghai, 1938; On the Border Line, 1939; Busy Summer, 1939; FEI YOU-WU, 1941; CHILDHOOD, 1944; An Unbending Man, 1944; Spring over Bei-Wang-Yuan and Other Stories, 1947; Blue River Tu-Men, 1947; May Lilac, play, 1947; Mother Wang, 1953; Old Wei Jun and Fang-rang, 1958; A Trading Post in the Mountains, 1963; Selected Short Stories, 1980; New Textual Research of Inscriptions on Bronze Objects, 1987; On Dragon, historical scientific paper (Japanese), 1987; Recollections of General Li Yan Lu, 1978; A Window for Looking at the Age, essays, 1988; The Rear Area, short stories, 1990; Short Stories, 1990; The Ancient Society of China, 1990. *Contributions to:* Feng Huo; Literature; Lü Zhou; Ren Ming Ri Bao; Ren Ming Wen Xue; Writer; Centre Daily News, USA. *Honours:* October Literature Prixe for A Brief Biography of Xiao Hong, 1984; Named Greqat Master of Short Story, The Muse of the Novel, The Father of Jin Wen. *Memberships:* Chinese Writers Association, Council Member 1979-, Vice-Chair, Beijing Branch, 1963-88; Standing Council Committee Member, Chinese Literature and Art Association, 1979-; Standing Council Committee Member, Academy of Pacific History; Vice-Chair: Lao She Foundation, 1989-; Association of Literature and Art, Shandong. *Literary Agent:* Zhang Xiao-xin. *Address:* The Beijing Branch of the Association of Chinese Writers, Liubukou, Beijing, China.

LUPOFF Richard Allen, b. 21 Feb 1935. Author. m. Patricia Enid Loring, 27 Aug 1958, 2 sons, 1 daughter. *Education:* BA, University of Miami, Florida, USA, 1956. *Appointments:* Editor, Canaveral Press, 1963-70; Contributing Editor, Crawdaddy Magazine, 1968-71; Contributing Editor,Science Fiction Eye, 1988-90; Editor, Canyon Press, 1986-. *Publications:* Edgar Rice Burroughs: Master of Adventure, 1965; All in Colour for a Dime, 1971; Sword of the Demon, 1977; Space War Blues, 1978; Sun's End, 1984; Circumpolar!, 1984; Lovecrafts Book, 1985; The Forever City, 1987; The Comic Book Killer, 1988 and many others. *Contributions to:* Ramparts; Los Angeles Times; Washinton Post; San Francisco Chronicle; New York Times; Magazine of Fantasy and Science Fiction, and many others. *Honour:* Hugo Award, 1963. *Literary Agent:* Henry Morrison, PO Box 235, Bedford Hills, NY 10507, USA. *Address:* 3208 Claremont Avenue, Berkeley, CA 94705, USA.

LURIE Alison. *Appointments:* Currently, Frederic J Whiton Professor of American Literature, Cornell University; Editor, The Oxford Book of Modern Fairy Tales; Co-Editor, The Garland Library of Children's Classics. *Publications:* Love and Friendship, 1962; The Nowhere City, 1965; Imaginary Friends, 1967; Real Peple, 1969; The War Between the Tates, 1974; V R Lang: Poems and Plays, 1975; Only Children, 1979; Clever Gretchen and other Forgotten Folktales, 1980; The Heavenly Zoo, 1980; The Language of CLothes, 1981; Fabulous Beasts, 1981; Foreign Affairs, 1984. The Truth about Lorin Jones, 1988; Don't Tell the Grownups: Subversive Children's Literature, 1990. *Contributions to:* Art and Antiques, Children's Literature, Harper's, House and Garden; Lear's, Ms, The New York Times Book Review, New York Woman, The Observer, Psychology Today, The Times Literary Supplement, Vanity Fair, Vogue. *Honours:* American Academy of Arts and Letters Award in Fiction, 1984; Radcliffe College

Alumnae Award, 1987; Pulitzer Prize in Fiction, 1985; Prix Femina Etranger, 1989. *Address:* English Department, Cornell University, Ithaca, NY 14853, USA.

LURIE Morris, b. 30 Oct 1938, Melbourne, Australia. Writer. *Education:* Architecture studies, Royal Melbourne Institute of Technology, 1957-60, no degree. *Appointments:* Writer in Residence, Latrobe University, 1984; Holmesglen Tafe, 1992. *Publications:* Rappaport, 1966; Flying Home, 1978; The Twenty Seventh Annual African Hippopotamus Race, 1969; Whole Life, 1987; Outrageous Behaviour, 1984. *Contributions to:* Virginia Quarterly Review; The Times; Punch; Telegraph Magazine; The Age, National Times, Nation Review; Stories broadcast on BBC, and plays on ABC. *Honours:* Bicentennal Banjo Aard, 1988; State of Victoria Short Story Award, 1973; State of Victoria Short Story Award, 1973; National Book Council Selection, 1980. *Address:* 2/3 Finchley Court, Hawthorn, Victoria 3122, Australia.

LUSTBADER Eric, b. 1946, American, Writer of novels, science fiction. *Publications:* The Sunset Warrior, 1976; Shallows at Night, 1977; Dai-San, 1978; Beneath an Opal Moon, 1978; The Ninja, 1980; Sirens, 1982; Black Heat, 1983; The Miko, 1984; Jian, 1985; Shan, 1986; French Kiss, 1989. *Address:* c/o Henry Morrison, Inc, Box 235, Bedford Hills, NY 10507, USA.

LUSTGARTEN Celia Sophie, b. 24 Oct 1941, New York City, New York, USA. Freelance Consultant; Writer. *Publications:* Short story in book, Shock Treatment, 1988. *Contributions to:* US publications: Shameless Hussy Review, 1978; Cow in the Road, 1986; Egad!, 1986-87; Z Miscellaneous, 1987; Bad Haircut, 1987; Ransom, 1988; For Poets Only, 1988; Famous Last Words, 1988; Perceptions, 1989, 1990, 1992; Stellanova, 1989; The Cacanadada Review, 1990; Grasslands Review, University of North Texas, 1990; The Key Move, 1992; Canadian publications: Room of One's Own, 1981; New Canadian Review, 1989; Chanticleer, 1989; Herspectives, 1990, 1991; New Zealand publications: Rhythm-and-Rhyme, 1985, 1986; UK publications: Spokes, 1985, 1986; T.O.P.S. 10 Poetry Magazine, 1985, 1986, 1987. *Honours:* First Prize, Short Story, Alternate Realities Society and Imaginative Fiction Society, Victoria, British Columbia, Canada, 1986. *Address:* 317 Third Avenue, San Francisco, CA 94118, USA.

LUSTIG Arnost, b. 21 Dec 1926, Prague, Czechoslovakia. Came to US in 1970. Writer; Screenwriter; Educator. m. Vera Wieislitz, 24 July 1949, 1 son, 1 daughter. *Education:* MA, College of Political and Social Science, Prague, 1951, Ing 1954; Doctor of Hebrew Letters (hon), Spertus College, Judaica, 1986. *Appointments:* Arab-Israeli Correspondent, Radio Prague, 1948-49; Correspondent, Czechoslovak Radio, 1950-68; Screenwriter, Barrandov Film Studies, Prague, 1960-68; Writer, Kibutz Hachotrim, Israel, 1968-69; Screenwriter, Jadran Film Studio, Zagreb, 1969-70; Member, International Writers Program, University of Iowa, Iowa City, 1970-71, Visiting Lecturer, English 1971-72; Visiting Professor, English, Drake University, Des Moines, 1972-73; Professor, Literature and Film, American University, Washington, 1973-; Head, Czechoslovak film delegation, San Sebastian Film Festival, 1968; Member, Jury, Karlovy Vary International Film Festival, 1968; Jury member, International Neustad Prize, 1981; Lecturer in field. *Publications:* Night and Hope, 1958; Diamonds of the Night, 1958; Street of Lost Brothers, 1959; Dita Saxova, 1962; My Acquaintance Vili Feld, 1962; A Prayer for Katarina Horovitzova, 1964; Nobody Will Be Humiliated, 1964; Bitter Smell of Almonds, 1968; Darling, 1969; The Unloved (From the Diary of a Seventeen Year Old), 1986; Indecent Dreams, 1988. *Films/Screenplays:* Transport from Paradise, 1963; Diamonds of the Night, 1964; Dita Saxova, 1968; A Bit to Eat, 1960; The Blue Day, 1960; A Prayer for Katerina Horovitzova, 1965; Terezin, (with Ernest Pendrell for ABC) 1965; Stolen Childhood, 1966 (text for symphonic poem) Night and Hope, 1961; (text for cantata) The Beadl from Prague, 1984; Precious Legacy, 1984; (commentary to documentary) The

Triumph of Memory, 1989; Correspondent to literary magazines, 1950-58; Editor, Mlady svet magazine, 1958-60. *Honours:* 1st prize Mlada fronta Publishing House, 1962; 1st prize, Monte Carlo Film Festival, 1966; 1st prize, Czechoslovak Radio Corp, 1966, 67; Klement Gottwald State prize, 1967; San Sebastian Film Festival, 2nd prize, 1968; B'nai B'rith prize 1974; National Book Award, Nomination, 1974; National Jewish Book Award, 1980; National Jewish Book Award, 1986; Emmy Award, 1986. *Memberships:* Authors Guild; Authors League; Czech PEN; Film Club (Prague). *Address:* 4000 Tunlaw Road NW, Apt 825, Washington, DC 20007, USA.

LUTTWAK Edward (Nicolae), b. 1942. American, Writer on History, International relations/Current affairs, Politics/Government. *Appointments:* Associate, Center of Strategic and International Studies, Washington DC, 1978-87; Visiting Professor, Johns Hopkins University, Baltimore, 1974-78; Holder of Chair in Strategy, Center for Strategic and International Studies, Washington, DC; Director of Geo-Economics, Centre for Strategic and International Studies, 1991. *Publications:* Coup D'Etat, 1968; Dictionary of Modern War, 1971; The Strategic Balance 1972, 1972; The US-USSR Strategic Balance, 1974; The Political Uses of Sea Power, 1974; (co-author) The Israeli Army, 1975; The Grand Strategy of the Roman Empire, 1977; Strategy and Politics, 1980; The Grand Strategy of the Soviet Union, 1983; The Pentagon and the Art of War, 1985; Strategy and History: Collected Essays, 1985; (co-author) Yearbook of International Politics 1983-84, 1984, 1984-85, 1985; Strategy: The Logic of War and Peace, 1987. *Address:* CSIS, 1800 K Street NW, Washington, DC 20006, USA.

LUTYENS Mary, (Esther Wyndham), b. 1908, British, Writer of Historical/Romance/Gothic publications, Biography. *Publications:* Forthcoming Marriages, 1933; Perchance to Dream, 1935; Rose and Thorn, 1936; Spider's Silk, 1938; Family Colouring, 1940; A Path of Gold, 1941; Together and Alone, 1942; So Near to Heaven, 1943; Julie and the Narrow Valley, 1944; And Now There Is You, 1953; Weekend at Hurtmore, 1954; The Lucian Legend, 1955; Meeting in Venice, 1956; To Be Young, 1959; (ed) Lady Lytton's Court Diary, 1961; Effie in Venice, 1965; Millais and the Ruskins, 1967; (ed) Freedom from the Known, by Krishnamurti, 1969; (ed) The Only Revolution by Krishnamurti, 1970; (ed) The Urgency of Change, by Krishnamurti, 1971; The Ruskins and the Grays, 1972; Cleo, 1973; Krishnamurti: The Years of Awakening, 1975; The Lyttons of India, 1979; Edwin Lutyens, 1980; Krishnamurti: The Years of Fulfilment, 1982; Krishnamurti: The Open Door, 1988; The Life and Death of Krishnamurti, 1989; Repv, 1991. *Honours:* FRSL. *Literary Agent:* Jane Turnbull, 13 Wendall Road, London W12 9RS. *Address:* 8 Elizabeth Close, Randolph Avenue, London W9 1BN, England.

LUTZ, John Thomas, b. 11 Sept 1939, Dallas, Texas, USA. Writer. m. Barbara Jean Bradley, 15 Mar 1958, 1 son, 2 daughters. *Education:* Meramac Community College. *Publications:* The Truth of the Matter, 1971; Buyer Beware, 1976; Bonegrinder, 1977; Lazarus Man, 1979, 1980; Jericho Man, 1980, 1981; The Shadow Man, 1981, 1982; Exiled, with Steven Greene, 1982; The Eye with Bill Pronzini, 1984; Nightlines, 1985; The Right to Sing the Blues, 1986; Tropical Heat, 1986; Ride the Lightning, 1987; Scorcher, 1987; Kiss, 1988; Shadowtown, 1988; Time Exposure, 1989; Flame, 1990; Diamond Eyes, 1990; SWF Seeks Same, 1990; Bloodfire, 1991; Hot, 1992; Dancing with the Dead, 1992; Spark, 1993. *Contributions to:* Ellery Queens Mystery Magazine; Hitchcocks Mystery Magazine; Mike Shayne Mystery Magazine; Executioner; Charlie Chan Mystery Magazine; Cavalier; Espionage; Works featured in numerous foreign publications, textbooks and anthologies; several adaptations for radio mystery dramas. *Honours:* Scroll, Mystery Writrs of America, 1981; Shamus Award, 1982; Shamus Nominee, 1983; Private Eye Writers of America; Peer Award Nominee, 1985; MWA Edgar Award, 1986; Shamus Award, 1988.

Memberships: Board of Directors, Private Eye Writers of America; Midwest Chapter, Mystery Writers of America. *Literary Agent:* Dominick Abel, New York. *Address:* 880 Providence Avenue, Webster Groves, MO 63119, USA.

LYALL Gavin Tudor, b. 9 May 1932, Birmingham, England. Author; Journalist. m. Katherine Whitehorn, 4 Jan 1958, 2 sons. *Education:* MA, Pembroke College, Cambridge, 1956; MA 1986. *Literary Appointments:* Staff, Picture Post, 1956-57; Worked on BBC TV's Tonight programme 1958-1959; Staff, Sunday Times, 1959-63. *Publications:* The Wrong Side of the Sky, 1961; The Most Dangerous Game, 1964; Midnight Plus One, 1965; Shooting Script, 1966; Freedom's Battle Vol II, 1968; Venus With Pistol, 1969; Blame the Dead, 1972; Judas Country, 1975; Operation Warboard, 1976; The Secret Servant, 1980; The Conduct of Major Maxim, 1982; The Crocus List, 1985; Uncle Target, 1989; Spy's Honour, 1993. *Contributions to:* The Observer; Sunday Telegraph; Punch; London Illustrated News. *Honours:* Silver Dagger, Crime Writers' Association, 1964, 1965. *Memberships:* Crime Writers' Association, (Chairman 1966-67); Detection Club; Society of Authors. *Literary Agent:* The Peters Fraser and Dunlop Group Ltd. *Address:* 14 Provost Road, London NW3 4ST, England.

LYKIARD Alexis, b. 1940, British, Writer of novels/short stories, poetry; translator. Creative Writing Tutor, Arvon Foundation, 1974-. Writer-in-Residence, Sutton Central Library (C Day Lewis Fellowship), 1976-77; Loughborough Art College (Arts Council of GB) 1982-83; Tavistock (Devon Libraries) 1983-85; HMP Channings Wood, 1988-89; HMP Haslar, 1992. *Publications:* Lobsters, 1961; Journey of the Alchemist, 1963; The Summer Ghosts, 1964; (ed)Wholly Communion, 1965; Zones, 1966; Paros Poems, 1967; A Sleeping Partner, 1967; Robe of Skin, 1969; Strange Alphabet, 1970; (trans) Lautréamont's Maldoror, 1970; (ed)Best Horror Stories of J Sheridan Le Fanu, 1970; Eight Lovesongs, 1972; The Stump, 1973; Greek Images, 1973; Lifelines, 1973; Instrument of Pleasure, 1974; (trans) The Piano Ship, 1974; (ed) The Horror Horn, by E F Benson, 1974; Last Throes, 1976; Milesian Fables, 1976; A Morden Tower Reading, 1976; (trans) Laure, by Emmanuelle Arsan, 1977; The Drive North, 1977; (ed)New Stories 2, 1977; (trans) Nea. by Emmanuelle Arsan, 1978; (trans) Lautréamont Poésies, etc, 1978; (ed)A Man with a Maid, 1982; Scrubbers, 1983; (ed)The Memoirs of Dolly Morton by Hugues Rebell, 1984; Cat Kin, 1985; Out of Exile, 1986; (trans) Secrets of Emmanuelle, by E Arsan, 1980; Vanna, by E Arsan, 1981; Oh Wicked Country! 1982; Nostradamus Countdown to Apocalypse by J-C de Fontbrune, 1983; Joy by Joy Laurey, 1983; Indiscreet Memoirs, by Alain Dorval, 1984; Nostradamus 2, by J-C de Fontbrune, 1984; Florian by Antoine S, 1986; Violette, by Marquise de Mannoury d'Ectot, 1986; The Exploits of a Young Don Juan, by Apollinaire/Irene by Aragon, 1986; (ed) Beat Dreams and Plymouth Sounds, 1987; (ed) Out of the Wood, 1989; (trans) Days and Nights, by Alfred Jarry, 1989; Safe Levels, 1990; (trans) Emmanuelle Exposed, by E Arsan, 1991; Living Jazz, 1991; Surrealist Games by André Breton, 1991; Beautiful Is Enough, 1992. *Address:* c/o A M Heath and Co Ltd, 79 St Martin's Lane, London WC2N 4AA, England.

LYLE-SMITH Alan. *See:* **CAILLOU Alan.**

LYNCH Audry Louise, b. 18 July 1933, Cambridge, Massachusetts, USA. Guidance Counsellor; Community College English Instructor. m. Gregory Lynch, 8 Sept 1956, 1 son, 2 daughters. *Education:* BA, Harvard University, 1955; EdM, Boston University, 1968; EdD, University of San Francisco, 1983. *Publications:* With Steinbeck in the Sea of Cortez, 1991; Father Joe Young: A Priest and His People, 1993. *Contributions to:* Yankee Magazine; West Magazine; Parade Magazine; The Writer; The International Herald Tribune. *Memberships:* California Writers Club; The Writers Connection. *Address:* 20774 Meadow Oak Road, Saratoga, CA 95070, USA.

LYNCH Frances. *See:* **COMPTON David Guy.**

LYNCH John, b. 1927. British, Writer on History. Emeritus Professor. *Appointments:* Lecturer in History, University of Liverpool, 1954-61, Lecturer, Reader and Professor of Latin American History, University College, London, 1961-74, Professor of Latin American History and Director of Institute of Latin American Studies, University of London, 1974-87. *Publications:* Spanish Colonial Administration, 1782-1810: The Intendant System in the Viceroyalty of the Rio de la Plata, 1958; Spain Under the Habsburgs, 2 vols, 1964-69, 2nd rev ed 1981; (ed with R A Humphreys) The Origins of the Latin American Revolutions 1808-1826, 1965; The Spanish American Revolutions 1808-1826, 1973, 2nd rev ed 1986; Argentine Dictator: Juan Manuel de Rosas 1829-1852, 1981; (with others) The Cambridge History of Latin America, vol 3 1985, vol 4 1986; Bourbon Spain 1700-1808, 1989; Caudillos In Spanish America 1800-1850, 1992. *Honours:* Order of Andres Bello, Venezuala, 1979; Encomienda Isabel La Catolica, Spain 1988; Doctor, Honoris Causa, University of Seville, 1990. *Membership:* FRHistS. *Address:* 8 Templars Crescent, London N3 3QS, England.

LYNDS Dennis, (William Arden, Nick Carter, Michael Collins, John Crowe, Carl Dekker, Maxwell Grant, Mark Sadler), b. 15 Jan 1924, St Louis, Missouri, USA. Writer. m. (1) Doris Flood, 1949 (div 1956), (2) Sheila McErlean, 1961 (div 1985), 2 daughters, (3) Gayle Hallenbeck Stone, 1986. *Appointments include:* Assistant Editor, Chemical Week, New York, 1951-52; Editorial Director, American Institute of Management, NY, 1952-54; Editor, Managing Editor, Chemical Engineering Progress, 1955-61; Editor (part-time), Chemical Equipment, Laboratory Equipment, NY, 1962-66; Instructor, Adult Education, Santa Barbara City College, California, 1966-68; Self-Employed Writer, 1961-. *Publications include:* Combat Soldier, 1962; Uptown Downtown, 1963; Why Girls Ride Sidesaddle, short stories, 1980; The Slasher, 1980, 1981; Freak, 1983; Deadly Innocents, 1986; Minnesota Strip, 1987; Red Rosa, 1988; Castrato, 1989; Chasing Eights, 1990. *Contributions to:* Numerous short stories, various journals & anthologies. *Honours:* Edgar Allan Poe Award 1968, Special Award 1969, Mystery Writers of America; Special Commendation, entire body of work, Arbeitsgemeinschaft Kriminalliteratur, 1981; Shamus nominee, Private Eye Writers of America, 1984; Guest of honour, 8th Festival du Roman et du Film Policiers, Reims, France, 1986; Life Time Achievement Award, Private Eye Writers of America, 1988. *Memberships include:* Past President, Private Eye Writers of America. *Literary Agent:* Bleecker Street Associates, 88 Bleecker Street, Suite 6P, New York, NY 10012, USA. *Address:* 12 St Anne Drive, Santa Barbara, California 93109, USA.

LYNN Frank. *See:* **LEISY James Franklin.**

LYNN Jonathan, b. 1943, British. Theatre and film director, actor, writer of novels/short stories, plays/screenplays. *Appointments:* Artistic Director, Cambridge Theatre Company, 1976-81; Company Director of National Theatre, 1987. *Publications:* (with George Layton) Doctor in Charge, Doctor at Sea, Doctor on the Go (television series) 1971-74; (with George Layton) My Name is Harry Worth (television series), 1973; Pig of the Month (play) 1974; (with Barry Levinson) The Internecine Project (screenplay) 1974; (with George Layton) My Brother's Keeper (2 television series) 1975, 1976; A Proper Man (novel) 1976; (with Antony Jay) Yes Minister (television series) 1980-83; Yes Prime Minister, 1986, 1987; (hardback) The Complete Yes Minister, 1984; Yes Prime Minister, vols I and II, 1986, 1987; Clue (screenplay and direction), 1985; Nuns on the Run (screenplay and direction), 1990; My Cousin Vinny (director), 1992; The Distinguished Gentleman (director), 1992; Greed (director), 1993; Mayday (novel), 1993. *Address:* C/o Peters, Fraser and Dunlop Ltd, The Chambers, Chelsea Harbour, Lots Road, London SW10.

LYNN Mary. *See:* **JACOBS Barbara.**

LYNNE James Broom, (James Quartermain), b. 1920. British, Writer of novels/short stories, plays/screenplays. Freelance graphic designer, specialising in book design. *Appointments:* Art Director, William Larkins Studio, London 1962-66; Art Editor, Macdonald & Co, London, 1966-69; Art School Lecturer, London, 1970-72 and Suffolk College of Higher and Further Education, 1972-78. *Publications:* The Trigon, 1962; Ketch, 1963; Tobey's Wednesday (in US as The Wednesday Visitors), 1967; The Marchioness, 1968; Drag Hunt, 1969; (as James Quartermain), The Diamond Hook, 1970; (as James Quartermain), The Man Who Walked on Diamonds, 1972; (as James Quartermain), Rock of Diamonds, 1972; The Commuters (in US as Collision), 1973; The Colonel's War, 1975; Verdict, 1977; Jet Race, 1978; Rogue Diamonds, 1980. *Address:* Gissings, East Bergholt, Colchester, Essex, England.

LYNTON Ann. *See:* **RAYNER Claire.**

LYON Bryce Dale, b. 22 Apr 1920, Bellevue, OH, USA. Professor. m. Mary Elizabeth Lewis, 3 June 1944, 1 son, 1 daughter. *Education:* AB, Baldwin-Wallace College, 1942; PhD, Cornell University, 1949. *Appointments:* Assistant Professor of History, University of Colorado, Boulder, 1949-51; Assistant Professor of History, Harvard University, Cambridge, MA, 1951-56; Associate Professor of History, University of Illinois at Urbana-Champaign, 1956-59; Professor of History, University of California, Berkeley, 1959-65; Barnaby and Mary Critchfield Keeney Professor of History 1965-, Chairman of Department 1968-, Brown University, Providence. *Publications:* Medieval Institutions: Selected Essays, 1954; From Fief to Indenture: The Transition From Feudal to Non-Feudal Contract in Western Europe, 1957; A Constitutional and Legal History of Medieval England, 1960, 2nd edition 1980; A History of the World (with others), 1960; Medieval History (with Stephenson), 4th edition, 1962; The High Middle Ages 1000-1300, 1964; Medieval Finance: A Comparison of Financial Institutions in Northwestern Europe (with A E Verhulst), 1967; Frankish Institutions Under Charlemagne (with M Lyon), 1968; A History of the Western World, 1969, 2nd edition, 1974; The Origins of the Middle Ages: Pirenne's Challenge to Gibbon, 1972; Henri Pirenne: A Biographical and Intellectual Study, 1974; The Journal de Guerre of Henri Pirenne (with M Lyon), 1976; Studies of West European and Medieval Institutions, 1978; Magna Carta, the Common Law and Parliament in Medieval England, 1980; The Wardrobe Book of William de Norwell: 12 July 1338 to 27 May 1340 (with H S Lucas and M Lyon), 1983. *Contributions to:* History Journals. *Memberships:* American Academy of Arts and Sciences (Fellow); Medieval Academy of America (Fellow); American Historical Association; Economic History Association; Conference on British Studies; Royal Historical Society (Fellow); Belgian Royal Academy (Fellow). *Honours:* Fellow of Belgian American Education Foundation, 1951-52; American Council of Learned Societies, 1962-63; National Endowment for the Humanities, 1973-74; Guggenheim fellow, 1954-55, 1972-73. *Address:* Department of History, Brown University, Brown Station, Providence, RI 02912, USA.

LYONS Arthur, b. 1946. American, Writer of mystery/crime/suspense. Owner of gift shop and restaurant, Palm Springs, California, 1967-. *Publications:* The Second Coming: Satanism in American (non-fiction) 1970, in UK as Satan Wants You: The CUlt of Devil Worship, 1971; The Dead Are Discreet, 1974; All God's Children, 1975; The Killing Floor, 1976; Dead Ringers, 1977; Castles Burning, 1980; Hard Trade, 1982; At the Hands of Another, 1983; Three with a Bullet, 1985.

LYONS Christine, b. 11 Dec 1943, Detroit, Michigan. Journalist. m. John T Lyons, 3 Apr 1965, div, 1985, 2 sons, 1 daughter. *Education:* BA English, St Mary's College, Notre Dame, Indiana, 1965. *Publications:* How do we tell the Children, 1985, co-author. *Contributions to:* USA Today; New York Daily News; Country Living; Longevity; Bride's. *Honours:* Columbia Du Pont Citation for Public Service; Radio-TV News Director's Association National Investigative Reporting Award for Radio; Billboard Magazine Award for Best Radio Documentary; Ohio and San Francisco State Awards; Aviation Space Writers Awards; New York State AB Broadcasters Awards. *Memberships:* American Society of Journalists and Authors; Foreign Press Association and UN Singers. *Literary Agent:* Nancy Love. *Address:* 515 E14th Street Apt 9B, New York, NY 10009, USA.

LYONS Dorothy Marawee, b. 1907. American, Writer of children's fiction. *Publications:* Silver Birch, 1939; Midnight Moon, 1941; Golden Sovereign, 1946; Red Embers, 1948; Harlequin Hullabaloo, 1949; Copper Khan, 1950; Dark Sunshine, 1951; Blue Smoke, 1953; Java Jive, 1955; Bright Wampum, 1958; Smoke Rings, 1960; Pedigree Unknown, 1973; The Devil Made the Small Town, 1984. *Address:* 900 Calle de los Amigos, C 102, Santa Barbara, CA 93105, USA.

LYONS Elena. *See:* **FAIRBURN Eleanor M.**

LYONS Garry Fairfax, b. 5 July 1956, Kingston-upon-Thames, England. Writer. m. Ruth Caroline Willis, 6 Apr 1985, 1 son, 1 daughter. *Education:* BA, English Literature, University of York, 1978; MA, Drama & Theatre Arts, University of Leeds, 1982. *Literary Appointments:* Playwright in Residence, Manor Road Theatre Company, 1983; Fellow in Theatre, University of Bradford, 1984-88. *Major Productions:* Echoes from the Valley, 1983; Mohicans, 1984; St Vitus' Boogie, 1985; Urban Jungle, 1985; The Green Violinist, 1986; Irish Night, 1987; Divided Kingdoms, 1989; The People Museum, 1989; Dream Kitchen, 1992; Frankie and Tommy, 1992. *Membership:* Theatre Writer's Union. *Literary Agent:* Alan Brodie Representation. *Address:* c/o Alan Brodie Representation, 91 Regent Street, London W1R 7TB, England.

LYONS Gene, b. 20 Sept 1943, Elizabeth, NJ, USA. Writer. m. Diane Haynie, 10 June 1967, 2 sons. *Education:* BA, Rutgers University, 1965; MA 1966, PhD 1969, University of Virginia. *Appointments:* Assistant Professor of English, University of Massachusetts at Amherst, 1969-72; Associate Professor of English, University of Arkansas, Little Rock, 1972-75; Visiting Professor of English, University of Texas at Austin, 1975-76; Free-lance magazine writer, 1976-80; Associate Editor, Texas Monthly, Austin, 1980; General Editor, Newsweek, NY, 1981-86; Free-lance writer and television commentator, 1986-. *Publications:* The Higher Illiteracy, 1988; Willow's Web, 1993. *Contributions to:* Author of monthly column in Arkansas Times and weekly news; KATV-TV; Articles and reviews to magazines and newspapers, including Harper's; Newsweek; Nation; Esquire; Inside Sports; Inquiry. *Honours:* National Magazine Award from Graduate School of Journalism at Columbia University, Clarion Award from Women in Communications, 1980, for article Why Techers Can't Teach. *Memberships:* International PEN; American Civil Liberties Union. *Address:* 204 Crystal Court, Little Rock, AR 72205, USA.

LYONS Thomas Tolman, b. 1934, American, Writer on Civil liberties/Human rights, History, Race relations. *Appointments:* History Teacher, Mount Hermon School, 1958-63; History Teacher, Phillips Academy, Andover, Massachusetts, 1963-. *Publications:* (ed)Presidential Power in the Era of the New Deal, 1964; (ed) Realism and Idealism in Wilson's Peace Program, 1965; (ed)Reconstruction and the Race Problem, 1968; Black Leadership in American History, 1970; The Supreme Court in Contemporary American Life, 1975; The Expansion of the Federal Union, 1978; After Hiroshima, 1979, 1985; The President: Teacher, Preacher, Salesman, 1984. *Address:* 38 Phillips Street, Andover, MA 01818, USA.

M

MABBETT Ian William, b. 27 Apr 1939. University Academic. m. Jacqueline Diana June Towns, 11 Dec 1971, 2 daughters. *Education:* Cranbrook School, 1950-57; Jesus College, Oxford, 1957-63, BA (Oxon) 1960, MA (Oxon) 1964, D Phil (Oxon) 1963. *Publications:* A Short History of India, 1968, 2nd edition 1983; Modern China, The Mirage of Modernity, 1985; Kings and Emperors of Asia, 1985; (ed) Patterns of Kingship and Authority in Traditional Asia, 1985. *Contributions to:* Hemisphere, Canberra; Asian Pacific Quarterly, Seoul; The Cambridge History of Southeast Asia, Cambridge. *Memberships:* Federation of Australian Writers; Australian Society of Authors. *Address:* c/o Department of History, Monash University, Clayton, Victoria 3168, Australia.

MABEY Richard Thomas, b. 20 Feb 1941, Berkhamsted, England. Writer; Broadcaster. *Education:* Hon. BA, 1966, MA, 1971, St Catherine's College, Oxford. *Appointment:* Senior Editor, Penguin Books, 1966-73. *Publications:* The Pop Process, 1969; Food for Free, 1972; Unofficial Countryside, 1973; Street Flowers, 1976; Plants with a Purpose, 1977; The Common Ground, 1980; The Flowering of Britain, 1980; In a Green Shade, 1983; Oak and Company, 1983; Frampton Flora, 1985; Gilbert White, 1986; The Flowering of Kew, 1988; Home Country, 1990. *Contributions to:* Times; Listener; Telegraph; Sunday Times; Observer; The Countryman; Nature; Modern Painters; The Independent. *Honours:* Times Educational Supplement Information Book Award, 1977; New York Academy of Science Childrens Book Award, 1984; Whitbread Biography Award, 1986. *Memberships:* Guild of Food Writers; Botanical Society of British Isles, Council 1981-83; London Wildlife Trust, President, 1982-92. *Literary Agent:* Richard Simon, London. *Address:* 10 Cedar Road, Berkhamsted, Herts HP4 2LA, England.

MABIE Margot Cauldwell Jones, b. 9 Nov 1944, Utica, New York, USA. Writer; Freelance Editor. m. James T Mabie, 26 June 1971, 2 daughters. *Education:* BA, Mills College, Oakland, California, 1966. *Publications:* Vietnam There and Here, 1985; The Constitution: Reflection of a Changing Nation, 1987; Bioethics and the New Medical Technology, forthcoming. *Contributions to:* America's Cup: New Look for the Tradition of Race, to Oceans, 1988. *Literary Agent:* Robin Rue. *Address:* 13 Oval Avenue, Riverside, CT 06878, USA.

MAC AVOY Roberta Ann, b. 1949, American. *Publications:* Tea with the Black Dragon, Damiano, 1983; Damiano's Lute, Raphael, 1984; The Book of Kells (co-author), 1985; Twisting the Rope, 1986; The Grey Horse, 1987; The Third Eagle, 1989; Lens of the World, 1990. *Address:* Underhill at Nelson Farm, 1669 Nelson Road, Scotts Valley, CA 95066, USA.

MACCREIGH James. *See:* POHL Frederick.

MACAULEY Robie Mayhew, b. 3 May 1919. Editor; Writer. m. 19 July 1978, 1 son. *Education:* AB, Kenyon College, Gambier, Ohio, 1941; MA, University of Iowa, 1950; Postgraduate study, University of London, England, 1965-66. *Appointments:* Editor, The Kenyon Review, 1958-66; Executive Editor, Houghton Mifflin Co, 1977-88. *Publications:* The Disguises of Love, novel, 1952; The End of Pity, stories, 1957; A Secret History of Time to Come, novel, 1978; Technique in Fiction, non-fiction, 1988; The Seven Basic Quarrels of Marriage, non-fiction, 1990. *Contributions to:* Esquire; Cosmopolitan; The Paris Review; Encounter; The Virginia Quarterly Review; New York Times Review of Books; Others. *Honours:* Rockefeller Foundation Grant, 1958-59; Guggenheim Foundation Grant, 1965-66; Honorary DLitt, Kenyon College, 1986. *Membership:* American PEN Center. *Literary Agent:* Kimberley Witherspoon, Witherspoon and Chernoff, New York, USA. *Address:* c/o Witherspoon and Chernoff, 136 W 57th St, New York, NY 10019, USA.

MACCAIG Norman Alexander, b. 14 Nov 1914, Edinburgh, Scotland. Teacher; Lecturer. m. Isabel Munro, 6 Apr 1940. 1 son, 1 daughter. *Education:* MA, Hons, Classics, University of Edinburgh, 1928-32. *Appointment:* Writer-in-Residence, Edinburgh University, 1967-69. *Publications:* Collected Poems, 1985; Riding Lights, 1955; A Round of Applause, 1962; Tree of Strings, 1977; The Equal Skies, 1980; Voiceover, 1983; Measures, 1965; A Common Grace, 1960; Surroundings, 1966; A Man in My Position, 1969; The White Bird, 1973; The World's Room, 1974; A World of Difference, 1983; The Sinai Sort, 1957; Rings on a Tree, 1968; Collected Poems, 1985; Voice Over, 1988. *Contributions to:* The Listener; Sunday Observer; Spectator; New Statesman; Lines Review; Chapman; Agenda; Poetry Chicago. *Honours:* 8 Scottish Arts Council Awards, 1954-86; Society of Authors Awards, 1964 and 1967; Heinemann Award, 1967; Cholmondeley Award, 1975; OBE, 1979; DUniv (Stirling); ARSA, 1981; DLitt; FRSE, 1983; FRSL, 1965; Saltire Award, 1985; Queen's Gold Medal. *Membership:* Scottish Arts Club. *Address:* 11 Leamington Terrace, Edinburgh, Scotland.

MACCARTHY Fiona, b. 23 Jan 1940, London, England. Writer; Critic. m. David Mellor, 1966, 1 son, 1 daughter. *Education:* Oxford University, 1958-61; MA, English Language and Literature, Oxford. *Appointments:* Reviewer, The Times, 1981-91; Reviewer, The Observer, 1991-. *Publications:* The Simple Life: C R Ashbee in the Cotswolds, 1981; The Omega Workshops: Decorative Arts of Bloomsbury, 1984; Eric Gill, 1989. *Contributions to:* The Times; The Observer; The Guardian; Times Literary Supplement; New York Times Review of Books. *Honours:* Royal Society of Arts Bicentenary Medal, 1987; Honorary Fellowship, Royal College of Arts, 1989. *Memberships:* PEN Club. *Literary Agent:* Peters, Fraser, Dunlop. *Address:* The Round Building, Hathersage, Sheffield S30 1BA, England.

MACCOBY Michael, b. 5 Mar 1933, Mt Vernon, New York, USA. Consultant. m. Sandylee Weille, 19 Dec 1959, 1 son, 3 daughters. *Education:* BA 1954, PhD 1960, Harvard University; New College, Oxford, 1954-55; University of Chicago, 1955-56; Diploma, Mexican Institute of Psychoanalysis, 1964. *Publications:* The Gamesman, 1977; The Leader, 1981; Why Work, 1988; Social Character in a Mexican Village (with E Fromm) 1970; Sweden at the Edge, 1991; Social Change and Character in Mexico and the United States, 1970. *Memberships:* PEN; Signet Society; Cosmos; American Psychological Association; American Anthropological Association; National Academy of Public Administration. *Address:* 4825 Linnean Avenue NW, Washington, DC 20008, USA.

MACCRACKEN Mary, b. 1926, American. *Appointments:* Teacher of emotionally disturbed children, 1965-70; Supplemental teacher, 1970-73; Resource Room Teacher, 1973-79; In private practise as a specialist in learning disabilities, Englewood, NJ, 1973-. *Publications:* A Circle of Children, 1973; Lovey: A Very Special Child, 1976; City Kid, 1980; Turnabout Children, 1986. *Address:* 325 Morrow Road, Englewood, NJ 07631, USA.

MACDONALD Alastair A, b. 24 Oct 1920, Aberlour, Scotland. Poet; University Professor Emeritus. *Education:* MA (Hons), Aberdeen University, 1948; BLitt, Christ Church, Oxford, 1953; PhD, Manchester University, 1956. *Appointments:* Senior Studentship in Arts (English), Manchester, 1953- 55; Professor of English, Memorial University, Newfoundland, Canada, 1955-87; Professor Emeritus, 1992. *Publications:* Academic: Prose and verse in Fearful Joy. Papers from the Thomas Gray Bicentenary Conference, Ottawa 1971, 1974; A Festschrift for Edgar Ronald Seary (co-editor, contributor), 1975; Introduction and Notes to reproduction in facsimile of Thomas Gray. An Elegy...The Eton Manuscript and First Edition 1751, 1976;

Numerous essays, articles, book reviews; Books of Poetry: Between Something and Something, 1970; Shape Enduring Mind, 1974; A Different Lens, 1981; Towards the Mystery, 1985; A Figure on the Move, 1991; Selected and New Poems, in preparation; Collected Longer Poems, in preparation; Poetry in many anthologies, etc; Flavian's Fortune, novel, 1985. *Contributions to:* Aberdeen University Review; Dalhousie Review; Bulletin of Humanities Association of Canada; Review of English Studies; Queen's Quarterly, Canada; Studies in Scottish Literature; The University Review, USA. *Honours:* Prizes and mentions for poetry: Honourable Mention, Stroud Festival, 1967; Canadian Author and Bookman Prize for Best Poem in Vol 47, 1972; Prize for Best Poem in New Voices in American Poetry 1973, Vantage Press, New York, 1973; 1st Prize for Poetry, 1976, Honourable Mention, 1978, 2nd Prize, 1982, Newfoundland Government Arts and Letters Competition; Readings of own poetry: Many public readings, the most recent, by invitation, for Habourfront Reading Series, Toronto, Canada, 1992. *Membership:* Writers' Alliance of Newfoundland and Labrador. *Address:* c/o Department of English, Arts and Administration Building, Memorial University, St John's, Newfoundland, Canada A1C 5S7.

MACDONALD Alexa Eleanor Fiona, (Fiona MacDonald), b. 25 Apr 1945, India. Writer. *Publications:* The Duke Who Had Too Many Giraffes; Little Bird I Have Heard. *Contributions to:* International Construction; Construction News; Underground Engineering. *Memberships:* PEN. *Address:* 41 Denne Place, London, SW3 2NH, England.

MACDONALD Amy. *See:* **MACDONALD Margaret A.**

MACDONALD Elizabeth Anne, b. 15 May 1954, Great Yarmouth, Norfolk. Translator; Writer. m. Alastair Livingstone MacDonald, 4 June 1983, 1 daughter. *Education:* BA Hons, Cambridge, 1973-76; MA Hons, 1979; PhD Spanish, 1983; Institute of Linguists Diploma in Translation. *Publications:* Translation: Venus Unveiled, 1989; Japanese Paper. *Contributions to:* Medium Aevum; The Linguist. *Honours:* Newnham College Progress Prize, 1976, Scholarship, 1976-77, Research Studentship, 1977-79. *Memberships:* Winchester Writer's Circle; Society of Authors; Institute of Linguists. *Address:* 4 Burnett Close, Weeke, Winchester, Hampshire SO22 5JQ, England.

MACDONALD Fiona. *See:* **MACDONALD Alexa Eleanor Fiona.**

MACDONALD Jake M, b. 6 Apr 1949, Winnipeg, Manitoba, Canada. Writer. m. Carolyn MacKinnon, 18 June 1983, 1 daughter. *Education:* BA, University of Manitoba, 1971. *Appointments:* Writer, Fishing guide in nothern Onterio, summers 1969-. Freelance writer. *Publications:* Novels: Indian River, 1981; Stonehouse; Radio Plays: Becoming, CBC Winnipeg, 1982; The Man From the Boy, CBC Winnipeg, 1983; Men Who Say No, CBC Winnipeg, 1984; The Highway Is for Gamblers, CBC Winnipeg, 1985; The Longest Night of the Year, CBC 1986; Tax Dodge Lodge, Real Special Productions, 1986; Short Stories: The Bridge Out of Town (collection) 1986. *Contributions to:* Short stories in various anthologies; Articles contributed to periodicals. *Memberships:* Writers Union of Canada; Manitoba Writers Guild; Ducks Unlimited. *Literary Agent:* Sarah Parker and Associates, Toronto.

MACDONALD Malcolm. *See:* **ROSS-MACDONALD Malcolm.**

MACDONALD Margaret A, (Amy MacDonald), b. 14 June 1951, Boston, Massachusetts, USA. Journalist. m. Thomas A Urquhart, 26 June 1976, 2 sons, 1 step-daughter. *Education:* Univeristy of Pennsylvania, PA, 1969-73; BA, Centre de Formation et Perfectionement des Journalistes, 1982-83. *Appointments:* Stonecoast

Writers conference; Harvard University, Teacher. *Publications:* Little Beaver and the Echo; Rachel Fister's Blister; Let's Try, Let's Make A Noise, Let's Play, Let's Do It; A Very Young Housewife. *Contributions to:* Parents Magazine; Earthwatch Magazine; The Times; New Scientist; Guardian. *Honours:* Silver Stylus Award. *Memberships:* Society of Childrens Book Writers. *Address:* 10 Winslow Road, Falmouth, ME 04105, USA.

MACDONALD Nancy Gardiner Bodman, b. 24 May 1910. m. Dwight MacDonald, 1934, div, 2 sons. *Education:* Vassar College, BA, 1932. *Appointments:* Institute of Persian Art & Archeology, 1932-33; Common Sensa Magazine, 1932-35; Partison Review, Business Manager, 1936-42; Political Magazine, 1943-47; Politics Packages Abroad, Director, 1945-50; International Rescue Committee, 1951-52; Spanish Refugee Aid, 1953-84. *Publications:* Are Hospitals Made for People? Homage to the Spanish Exiles. *Honours:* Dama de la Order de la Liberacion de Espana; American Committee for Iberian Freedom; Spanish Civil War Historical Society; El Lazo de Dama de la Orden de Isabel La Catolica. *Address:* Spanish Refugee Aid, 386 Park Avenue South, New York, NY 10016, USA.

MACDONOGH Giles Malachy Maximilian, b. 6 Apr 1955, London, England. Author; Journalist. *Education:* Balliol College, Oxford, 1975- 78; BA (Hons), Modern History, Oxford University, 1978; Ecole des Hautes Etudes Pratiques, France, 1980-83; MA (Oxon), 1992. *Appointments:* Freelance Journalist, 1983-; Editor, Made in France, 1984; Columnist, Financial Times, 1989-; Contributor to various magazines and annual publications. *Publications:* A Palate in Revolution, Grimod de La Reynière and the Almanach des Gourmands, 1987; A Good German: Adam von Trott zu Solz, 1990; The Wine and Food of Austria, 1992; Brillat Savarin: the Judge and his Stomach, 1992; Syrah Grenache, Mourvèdre, 1992; *Contributions in:* Webster's Wine Guide, 1990-; Sainsbury's Pocket Wine Guide, 1992-; The Companion to Wine, 1992; Berghs Jahrbuuch der Gastronomie, 1992-; Le Guide BCBG, 1984. *Contributions to:* Financial Times (regularly); WINE; Decanter; Wine and Spirit; Food and Entertaining; Homes and Gardens; Opera Now. *Honours:* Shortlisted, Andre Simon Award, 1987; Glenfiddich Special Award, 1988. *Memberships include:* International PEN; Guild of Food Writers; Octagon of Wine Writers; The Academy. *Literary Agent:* Peter Robinson, Curtis Brown, London, England. *Address:* c/o Curtis Brown, 162 Regent Street, London W1, England.

MACDOUGALL Ruth Doan, b. 19 Mar 1939, Laconia, New Hampshire, USA. Writer. m. Donald K MacDougall, 9 Oct 1957. *Education:* Bennington College, 1957-59; BEd, Keene State College, 1961. *Publications:* The Lilting House, 1965; One Minus One, 1971; The Cost of Living, 1971; The Cheerleader, 1973; Wife and Mother, 1976; Aunt Pleasantine, 1978; The Flowers of the Forest, 1981; A Lovely Time Was Had By All, 1982; Snowy, 1993. *Contributions to:* Book Reviewer: The New York Times Book Review; Newsday; Others. *Honours:* Winner, PEN Syndicated Fiction Project, 1983, 1984, 1985. *Membership:* National Writers Union. *Literary Agent:* Emilie Jaconson, Curtis Brown Ltd. *Address:* RRI, Box 286, Center Sandwich, NH 03227, USA.

MACDOWELL Douglas Maurice, b. 1931, British. *Appointments:* Assistant Lecturer, Lecturer, Senior Lecturer, Reader in Greek and Latin, University of Manchester, 1958-71; Professor of Greek, University of Glasgow, 1971-. *Publications:* Andokides: On the Mysteries (ed), 1962; Athenian Homicide Law, 1963; Aristophanes: Wasps (ed), 1971; The Law in Classical Athens, 1978; Spartan Law, 1986; Demosthenes: Against Meidias (ed), 1990. *Honours:* Fellow, Royal Society of Edinburgh (FRSE). *Address:* University of Glasgow, Glasgow G12 8QQ, Scotland.

MACDOWELL John. *See:* **PARKS T(imothy) Harold.**

MACEACHERN Diane, b. 29 May 1952, Detroit, Michigan, USA. President, Vanguard Communications; Author. *Education:* BA, Literature, Science, Arts, 1974, MS, School of Natural Resources, 1977, University of Michigan. *Publications:* Save Our Planet: 750 Everyday Ways You Can Help Clean Up The Earth, 1990, translated into Chinese, Japanese, Italian. *Contributions to:* Frequently to: Family Circle; Good Housekeeping; Also articles to: Ladies Home Journal; Self; Lady's Circle; Bottom Line; National Wildlife; Syndicated column in Washington Post Writer's Group. *Honours:* William J Branstrom Freshman Prize, 1970; Honorary Alumni Award, 1990. *Literary Agent:* Ms Gail Ross. *Address:* 102 Tulip Avenue, Takoma Park, MD 20912, USA.

MACER-STORY Eugenia, b. 20 Jan 1945, Minneapolis, Minnesota, USA. Writer. m. Leon A Story, 1970, (div 1975), 1 son. *Education:* BS, Speech, Northwestern University, 1965; MFA, Playwriting, Columbia University, New York City, 1968. *Appointments:* Fond du Lac Commonwealth Reporter, 1970; Polyarts, Boston, 1970-72; Joy of Movement, Boston, 1972-75; Magik Mirror, Salem, 1975-76; Magick Mirror Communications, Woodstock and New York City, 1977-. *Publications include:* Books: Congratulations: The UFO Reality, 1978; Angels of Time: Astrological Magic, 1981; Du Fu Man Chu Meets The Lonesome Cowboy: Sorcery and the UFO Experience, 1991, 2nd edition, 1992. Articles: 'Espionage: Has Mind Control Supplanted the Cloak and Dagger', Pursuit, 1982; 'The Skyo UFO Sighting', Metascience, 1980. Plays: The Little Old Hermit of the Northwest Woods, 1972; Aphrodite-The Witch Play, 1979; Red Riding Hood's Revenge, 1980; The Observation Chamber, 1981; The UFO Show, 1981; The Sky Moth Project at Location 30, 1982; Six Way Time Play, 1983; Eternal Flowers of Ghost Mountain, 1985; Robin Hood's Nightgown, 1985; Cancelled & Interrupted Performances, 1986; All Souls Banquet, 1986; Poems With Percussion and Songs, 1986; Archaological Politics, 1986; Strange Inquiries, 1988; Divine Appliance, 1989; I Was Madelaine, 1989; The 13th Wife, 1989; The Zig Zag Wall, 1990; The Only Qualified Huntress, 1990; Wars With Pigeons, 1992; Battles With Dragons: Certain Tales of Political Yoga, 1993. *Contributions to:* Tri-Quarterly; Shadows; Woodstock Times; Omni; Frontiers of Science. *Honour:* Shubert Fellowship, 1968. *Memberships:* Dramatists Guild; US Psychotronics Association. *Address:* Magick Mirror Communications; Box 741 - JAF Building, New York, NY 10116, USA.

MACEWAN J(ohn) W(alter) Grant, b. 1902, Canadian. *Appointments:* Dean, Faculty of Agriculture and Home Economics, University of Manitoba, Winnipeg, 1946-51; Liberal Member for Calgary, Legislative Assembly of Alberta, 1955-59; Leader of the Liberal Party in Alberta, 1958-60; Mayor of Calgary, Alta, 1963-65; Lieutenant Governor of Alberta, 1965-74. *Publications:* Canadian Animal Husbandry (co-author), 1936; General Agriculture (co-author), 1939; Breeds of Farm Livestock in Canada, 1941; Feeding of Farm Animals, 1945; Sodbusters, 1948; Agriculture on Parade, Between the Red and the Rockies, Eye Opener Bob, 1957; Fifty Mighter Men, Calgary Cavalcade, 1958; Blazing the Old Cattle Trails, 1965; Hoofprints and Hitchingposts, 1967; Tatanga Mani, 1968; Poking into Politics, West to the Sea, Harvest of Bread, 1969; Portraits from the Plains, Power for Prairie Plows, 1971; Sitting Bull, 1973; Battle for the Bay, And Mighty Women Too, 1975; Memory Meadows, 1976; Cornerstone Colony, 1977; Rhyming Horseman of the Qu'Appelle, Pat Burns Cattle King, 1979; History of Western Canadian Agriculture, 1980; Metis Makers of History, 1981; Highlights of Shorthorn History, 1982. *Address:* 132 Hallbrook Drive, Calgary, Alta, Canada.

MACGIBBON Jean, b. 1913, British. *Appointment:* Editorial Director, MacGibbon and Kee, Publishers, London, 1948-54. *Publications:* When the Weather's Changing, 1945; Peter's Private Army, 1960; Red Sail White Sail, Women of Islam by Assia Djebar (trans), 1961; The Red Sledge, Girls of Paris by Nicole de Buron

(trans), Pam Plays Doubles, 1962; The View-Finder, 1963; A Special Providence, 1964; Sandy in Hollow Tree House, 1967; Liz, 1969; The Tall Ship, 1973; Hal, 1974; Jobs for the Girls, 1975; After the Raft Race, 1976; Three's Company, 1978; I Meant to Marry Him, 1985. *Address:* 8 Quay Street, Manningtree, Essex CO11 1AU, England.

MACGOWAN Christopher John, b. 6 Aug 1948, London, England. Educator. m. Catherine Levesque, 10 July 1988. *Education:* BA, Cambridge University (Kings College), 1976; MA, 1979, PhD, 1983, Princeton University, USA. *Appointments:* Research Assistant, The Writings of Henry D Thoreau, Princeton, 1981-83; Assistant Professor, 1984-90, Associate Professor, 1990-, College of William and Mary, Williamsburg, Virginia; Co- Editor, Editor, various works of William Carlos Williams, 1984-92. *Publications:* William Carlos Williams' Early Poetry: The Visual Arts Background, 1984; The Collected Poems of William Carlos Williams, Vol I, 1909-1939 (co-editor), 1986, Vol II, 1939-62 (editor), 1988; William Carlos Williams' Paterson (editor), 1992. *Contributions to:* Several articles to William Carlos Williams Review; John Witherspoon to Dictionary of Literary Biography, 1984; Editing William Carlos Williams: Paterson, 1991; Short articles on Harriet Monroe, Alfred Kreymborg and William Carlos Williams to Encyclopedia of American Writers. *Honours:* James Prize, King's College, Cambridge, England, 1976, 1977; Teaching Assistantship, Pennsylvania State University, 1976-77; Graduate Fellowship, Princeton University, 1977-81; Summer Grant, College of William and Mary, 1985, 1987, 1989; Summer Stipend, 1986, Fellowship, 1990-91, National Endowment for the Humanities. *Memberships:* Modern Language Association; William Carlos Williams Society, President 1989-91. *Address:* Department of English, College of William and Mary, Williamsburg, VA 23187, USA.

MACGREGOR David Roy, b. 26 Aug 1925, London, England. Author. m. Patricia Margaret Aline Purcell-Gilpin, 26 Oct 1962, London. *Education:* BA 1948, MA 1950, Trinity College, Cambridge University; Hammersmith School of Building, 1954-55; Associate, Royal Institute of British Architects, 1957. *Publications:* The Tea Clippers, 1952, revised edition 1983; The China Bird, 1961; Fast Sailing Ships 1775-1875, 1973; Clipper Ships, 1977; Merchant Sailing Ships, 1775-1815, 1980; Merchant Sailing Ships, 1815-1850, 1984; Merchant Sailing Ships, 1858-1875, 1984. *Contributions to:* Mariner's Mirror; Journal of Nautical Archaeology. *Honours:* Gold Medal from Daily Express for Best Book of the Sea in 1973 for Fast Sailing Ships. *Memberships:* Fellow, Royal Historical Society, 1957; FSA, 1975; Council Member, Society of Nautical Research, 1959-63, 1965-69, 1974-77, 1980-85, Hon Vice-President, 1985; Ship's Committee, Maritime Trust, 1974. *Address:* 99 Lonsdale Road, London SW13 9DA, England.

MACGREGOR-HASTIE Roy Alasdhair Niall, b. 28 Mar 1929. Author; University Professor. m. Maria Grazia, 25 Dec 1977, 1 son. *Education:* New College, Royal Military Academy, Sandhurst, 1947-48; BA, University of Manchester; MFA, University of Iowa, USA; MEd, PhD, University of Hull. *Appointments:* Editor, The New Nation, 1955-56; Joint Editor, Miorita, 1977-; Editor, Prospice, 1967-77; Contributing Editor, numerous magazines and journals; Foreign Editor, Time and Tide, 1960-65; Japan Correspondent, 1989-. *Publications:* Books include: The Man from Nowhere, 1960; The Red Barbarians, 1961; Pope John XXIII, 1962; The Day of The Lion - a history of Eascism, 1964; Pope Paul VI, 1966; The Throne of Peter, 1967; Never to Be Taken Alive, 1985; Nell Gwyn, 1987; History of Western Civilisation, 1989; Getting it Right, 1990. Travel: The Compleat Migrant, 1962; Don't Send Me to Omsk, 1964; Signor Roy, 1967; Africa, 1968. Art history: Picasso, 1988. Poetry and Criticism: A Case for Poetry, 1960; Interim Statement, 1962; Eleven Elegies 1969; Frames, 1972; The Great Transition, 1975; Poems of Our Lord and Lady, 1976; Poeme, 1980. UNESCO collection of rep works: Eminescu, The Last Romantic, 1972;

Anthology of Contemporary Romanian Poetry (1969, 2 edn 1977, 3 edn 1982); Anthology of Bulgarian Poetry, 1978; Eminescu Centennial Commem Volume, 1989. Politics: The Mechanics of Power, 1966. Novel in translation, The Gypsy Tribe, 1974. *Contributions to:* Punch; Time and Tide; Twentieth Century; Spectator; New Statesman; Commonwealth Journal; Times Literary; Daily Yoniuri; The Scotsman. *Honours:* Victoria Poetry Prize, 1986; UNESCO Author, 1989. *Memberships:* PEN; Society of Authors; British Association for Romanian Studies, Secretary 1966-77, President 1977-; International Association of Translators, President 1978-80; Asian History Association; Scottish Record Society. *Literary Agent:* Kurt Singer, Anahein, California, CA 72801, USA. *Address:* c/o Osaka Gakuin University, Kishibe, Suita, Osaka 564, Japan.

MACHUNG Anne, b. 30 Jan 1947, Long Beach, California, USA. Sociologist. m. Ron Rothbart, 27 Sept 1986. *Education:* BA summa cum laude, Seattle University, 1968; MA, 1972, PhD, 1983, University of Wisconsin. *Publications:* The Second Shift (with Arlie Hochschild), 1989. *Contributions to:* Talking career, thinking job: Gender differences to work and family expectations of Berkeley seniors, to Feminist Studies, 1989. *Honours:* Distinguished Achievement for Bay Area Women Writers, National Women's Political Caucus, 1991. *Memberships:* American Sociological Association; National Women's Studies Association. *Address:* Institute for Study of Social Change, University of California-Berkeley, Berkeley, CA 94720, USA.

MACINTYRE Stuart Forbes, b. 21 Apr 1947, Australia. Historian. m. (1) Margaret Geddes, 1971, (2) Martha Bruton, 1976, 2 daughters. *Education:* BA, University of Melbourne, 1968; MA, Monash University, 1971; PhD, Cambridge University, 1975. *Appointments:* Ernest Scott Professor, University of Melbourne, 1990- . *Publications:* A Proletarian Science; Little Moscows; Militant; Winners and Losers; Oxford History of Australia; A Colonial Liberalism. *Honours:* Blackwood Prize; Premiers Literary Award. *Memberships:* Academy of the Social Sciences in Australia; Council of the National Library of Australia. *Address:* History Department, University of Melbourne, Parkville, Victoria, Australia 3052.

MACKAY Claire Lorraine, b. 21 Dec 1930, Toronto, Ontario, Canada. Writer. m. Jackson F. Mackay, 12 Sept 1952, 3 sons. *Education:* BA, Political Science, University of Toronto, 1952; Social work studies, University of British Columbia, 1968-69; Certificate, rehabilitation counselling, University of Manitoba, 1971. *Appointments include:* Writer-in-residence, Metropolitan Toronto Library, 1987. *Publications:* Mini-Bike Hero, 1974, 1978, 1984; Mini-Bike Racer, 1976, 1979, 1984; Mini-Bike Rescue, 1982; Exit Barney McGee, 1979; One Proud Summer, 1981; Minerva Program, 1984; Pay Cheques & Picket Lines, 1987. *Contributions include:* Articles, columns, short stories, verse, book reviews, in various newspapers & magazines. *Honours include:* Award, best children's book, Ruth Schwartz Foundation, 1982; Vicky Metcalf Award, Body of Work for Children, 1983; Vicky Metcalf Award, Best Children's Short Story, 1988; City of Toronto Award of Merit, 1991. *Memberships:* Various offices, Canadian Society of Children's Authors, Illustrators & Performers; Writers Union of Canada; Canadian Authors Association; Children's Book Centre; Writers Development Trust; etc. *Literary Agent:* MGA Agency, 10 St Mary Street, Ste 510, Toronto, Ontario, M4Y 1P9, Canada. *Address:* 6 Frank Crescent, Toronto, Ontario, Canada M6G 3K5.

MACKAY Eric Beattie, b. 31 Dec 1922. Editor. m. Moya Margaret Mayes Connolly, 1954, (dec 1981), 3 sons, 1 daughter. *Education:* MA, Aberdeen University. *Appointments:* Aberdeen Bon-Accord, 1948; Elgin Courant, 1949; The Scotsman, 1950; Daily Telegraph, 1952; London Editor, 1957, Deputy Editor, 1961, Editor, 1972-85, The Scotsman. *Address:* 5 Strathearn Place, Edinburgh, EH9 2AL, Scotland.

MACKAY James Alexander, (Ian Angus, William Finlay, Bruce Garden, Peter Whittington), b. 21 Nov 1936, Inverness, Scotland. Author and Journalist. m. (1) Mary Patricia Jackson, 24 Sept 1960, (diss 1972), 1 son, 1 daughter, (2) Renate Finaly-Freundlich, 11 Dec 1992. *Education:* MA (Hons) History, Glasgow University, 1958. *Literary Appointments:* Philatelic columnist, The New Daily, 1962-67; Collecting Wisely in Financial Times, 1967-85; Editor-in-Chief, IPC Stamp Encyclopaedia, 1968-72; Antiques Advisory Editor, Ward Lock, 1972-79; Editor, The Burns Chronicle 1977- , The Burnsian, 1986-89; Editor, The Postal History Annual, 1978-90; Editor, Seaby Coin and Medal Bulletin, 1990-92; Consultant Editor, Antiques Today, 1992-. *Publications:* The Tapling Collection, 1964; Glass Paperweights, 1973, 1977, 1988; The Dictionary of Stamps in Colour, 1973; The Guinness Book of Stamps Facts and Feats, 1982, 1988; The Dictionary of Western Sculptors in Bronze, 1977; Complete Works of Robert Burns, 1986, 1990; 140 titles from 1961 to date on philately, numismatics, applied and decorative arts, biography and Scottish literature. *Contributions to:* Regular columnist in: Stamps; Stamp Magazine; Gibbons Stamp Monthly; British Philatelic Bulletin; Stamp and Coin Mart; Coin News; Coin Monthly; Seaby Coin and Medal Bulletin; Coin Digest (Singapore); Studies in Scottish Literature (USA); Occasional contributor to many others worldwide. *Honours:* Silver Medal Amphile (Amsterdam) 1965; Vermeil Medal, Spellman Foundation (USA 1982, 1987, 1990); Thomas Field Award for services to Irish Philatelic Literature, 1983. *Membership:* The Burns Federation (Executive Council 1977-). *Address:* 5/75 Lancefield Quay, Glasgow G3 8HA, Scotland.

MACKAY Simon. *See:* **NICOLE Christopher Robin.**

MACKELWORTH R(onald) W(alter), b. 1930, British. *Appointments:* Insurance, 1950; Life Insurance Marketing Manager, 1985- ; Freelance writer. *Publications:* Firemantle, 1968, (in US as the Diabols, 1969); Tiltangle, 1970; Starflight 3000, 1972; The Year of the Painted World, 1975; Shakehoue, 1979. *Address:* 32 Mark Way, Godalming, Surrey, England.

MACKENZIE Andrew Carr, b. 30 May 1911, Oamaru, New Zealand. Journalist and Author. m. Kaarina Sisko Sihvonen, 1 Mar 1952, 1 son, 2 daughters. *Education:* Wellington College, Wellington, New Zealand, 1924-26; Victoria University College, New Zealand, 1930-32. *Literary Appointment:* London News Editor, Sheffield Morning Telegraph, 1963-76. *Publications:* The Unexplained, 1966; Frontiers of the Unknown, 1968; Apparitions and Ghosts, 1971; A Gallery of Ghosts (Ed) 1972; Riddle of the Future, 1974; Dracula Country, 1977; Hauntings and Apparitions, 1982; Romanian Journey, 1983; A Concise History of Romania (Ed) 1985; Archaeology in Romania, 1986; The Seen and the Unseen, 1987; A Journey into the Past of Transylvania, 1990. *Contributions to:* The Journal of the Society of Psychical Research. *Memberships:* Vice President 1989, Council Member 1970-91, Society for Psychical Research. *Literary Agent:* A M Heath, 79 St Martin's Lane, London WC2N 4AA. *Address:* 18 Castlebar Park, London W5 1BX, England.

MACKENZIE David, b. 10 June 1927, Rochester, New York, USA. Professor of History. m. Patricia Williams, 8 Aug 1953, 3 sons. *Education:* AB, University of Rochester, 1951; MA, & Certificate of Russian Institute, 1953; PhD, 1962, Columbia University. *Appointments:* US Merchant Marine Academy, 1953-58; Princeton University, 1959-61; Wells College, 1961-68; University of North Carolina, Greensboro, 1969-. *Publications:* The Serbs and Russian Pan-Slavism, 1875-1878, 1967; The Lion of Tashkent: The Career of General M G Cherniaev, 1974; A History of Russia and the Soviet Union, 1977, 1982, 1987, 1993; Ilija Garasanin: The Balken Bismarck, 1985; A History of the Soviet Union, 1986, 1991; Ilija Garasanin Drzavirik i Diplomata, 1987; Apis: The Congenial Conspirator, 1989; Imperial Dreams/Harsh Realities: Tsarist Russian Foreign Policy, 1815-1917, 1993. *Contributions to:* The

Journal of Modern History; Slavic Review; Canadian Slavic Studies; Russian Review; International History Review; East European Quarterly; Serbian Studies. *Honours:* Phi Beta Kappa, 1950; Ellison Prize, 1951; Elected to the Serbian Academy of Sciences, 1988; Fellowships from Ford Foundation, ACLS, Inter-University Committee on Travel Grants, IREX, American Philosophical Society. *Address:* 1000 Fairmont St, Greensboro, NC 27401, USA.

MACKENZIE Donald, b. 11 Aug 1918, Canada. Writer. *Education:* England, Switzerland, Canada. *Publications include:* 32 novels published Macmillan, Houghton Mifflin Company, Doubleday. *Contributions to:* Colliers; Saturday Evening Post; Newsweek; Esquire. *Membership:* Writers Guild. *Literary Agent:* Russell & Volkening Inc. *Address:* c/o Russell & Volkening Inc, 50 West 24th Street, New York City, NY 10001, USA.

MACKENZIE Kelvin Calder, b. 22 Oct 1946. Editor. m. Jacqueline Mary Holland, 1969, 2 sons, 1 daughter. *Appointments:* Assistant Night Editor, 1976, Night Editor, 1980, Editor, 1981-, The Sun; Managing Editor, New York Post, 1978; Night Editor, Daily Express, 1981. *Address:* The Sun, 1 Virginia Street, London E1 9XP, England.

MACKENZIE Lee. *See:* BOWDEN Jean.

MACKENZIE Norman Hugh, b. 8 Mar 1915, Salisbury, Rhodesia. Educator; Writer. m. Rita Mavis Hofmann, 14 Aug 1948, 1 son, 1 daughter. *Education:* BA, 1934, MA, 1935, Diploma in Education, 1936, Rhodes University, South Africa; PhD, University of London, England, 1940. *Appointments include:* Professor of English, 1966-80, Emeritus Professor, 1980-, Queen's University, Kingston, Ontario, Canada. *Publications:* South African Travel Literature in the 17th Century, 1955; The Outlook for English in Central Africa, 1960; Hopkins, 1968; A Reader's Guide to G M Hopkins, 1981; Editor: The Poems of Gerard Manley Hopkins (with W H Gardner), 1967, Revised Edition, 1970; Poems by Hopkins, 1974; The Early Poetic Manuscripts and Notebooks of Gerard Manley Hopkins in Facsimile, 1989; The Poetical Works of Gerard Manley Hopkins, 1990; The Later Poetic Manuscripts of Gerard Manley Hopkins in Facsimile, 1991; Various book chapters. *Contributions to:* International Review of Education; Bulletin of the Institute for Historical Research; Times Literary Supplement; Modern Language Quarterly; Queen's Quarterly; Others. *Honours:* British Council Scholar, 1954; Killam Senior Fellow, 1979-81; Martin D'Arcy Lecturer, Oxford University, 1988-89; Honorary DLitt, St Joseph's University, Philadelphia, 1989. *Memberships:* Fellow, Royal Society of Canada; Past President, English Association of Rhodesia; Former Vice-Chairman, Southern Rhodesia Drama Association; Past President, Hopkins Society; Life Member, Yeats Society; Life Member, Modern Language Association; Board of Scholars, International Hopkins Association; International Association for the Study of Anglo-Irish Literature. *Address:* 416 Windward Place, Kingston, Ontario, Canada K7M 4E4.

MACKENZIE Suzanne, b. 22 Mar 1950, Vancouver, Canada. University Professor. m. Alan Eric Nash, 29 May 1984. *Education:* BA Hons Simon Fraser University, BC, 1976; MA, University of Toronto, 1978; DPhil Geography, Sussex University, England. *Publications:* Visible Histories: Gender and Environment in a Post-War British City, 1989; Remaking Human Geography, 1989, co-editor; Gender Sensitive Theory and the Housing Needs of Mother led familes, 1987, co-author. *Contributions to:* Cahiers de Geographie des Quebec, 1987, among others. *Memberships:* Canadian Association of Geographers; National Executive, 1988-90; Co-Founder, CAG Women and Geography Studies Group; International Geographic Union, Executive Genere and Geography Working Group, 1989-. *Address:* Department of Geography, Carleton University, Ottawa, Ontario, Canada K1S 5B6.

MACKERRAS Colin Patrick, b. 26 Aug 1939, Sydney, Australia, Academic. m. Alyce Barbara Brazier, 29 June 1963, 2 sons, 3 daughters. *Education:* BA, Melbourne, 1961; BA Hons, Australia National University, 1962; M.Litt, Cambridge, 1964; PhD, Australia National University, 1970. *Publications:* Western Images of China, 1989; The Rise of the Peking Opera 1770-1870, 1972; China: The Impact of Revolution, A Survey of Twentieth Century China, 1976; China Observed, 1967; The Chinese Theatre in Modern Times, 1975; Modern China, A Chronology from 1842 to the Present, 1982. *Honour:* Shared a Gold Citation of the Media Peace Prize awarded by the United Nations Assocation of Australia, 1981. *Membership:* Australian Writers' Guild. *Address:* Division of Asian and International Studies, Griffith University, Nathan, Qld 4111, Australia.

MACKESY Piers Gerald, b. 1924, British. *Appointments:* Harkness Fellow, Harvard University, 1953-54; Fellow, Pembroke College, Oxford, 1954-87, Emeritus, 1988-; Visiting Fellow, Institute for Advanced Study, Princeton, NJ, 1961-62; Visiting Professor, California Institute of Technology, 1966. *Publications:* The War in the Mediterranean 1803-1810, 1957; The War for America 1775-1783, 1964; Statesmen at War: The Strategy of Overthrow 1798- 1799, 1974; The Coward of Minden: The Affair of Lord George Sackville, 1979; War without Victory: The Downfall of Pitt 1799-1802, 1984. *Memberships:* Council of National Army Museum, 1983-92; Council of the Society for Army Historical Research, 1985-. *Address:* Leochel Cushnie House, Alford, Aberdeenshire AB33 8LJ.

MACKINLAY Leila Antoinette Sterling, (Brenda Grey), b. 5 Sept 1910, London, England. Novelist. *Education:* Diploma, English Literature, London University, 1950. *Literary Appointments:* Dancing Times, 1930's; Amateur Stage, 1946-; Writing and English Literature, London County Council and Greater London Council to 1965; Teacher of Ordinary Level English Literature. *Publications:* Little Mountebank, 1930; No Room for Loneliness, 1965; numerous other books published, 3 before the age of 21 years. *Contributions to:* Romantic Novelists Association News, Editor. *Honours:* Presidents Prize, Romantic Novelists Association, 1965; Adjudicator, Waterford Festival of Light Opera, 3 years. *Memberships:* Life Member, Society of Authors and NBL; Romantic Novelists Association; Society of Literature. *Address:* 4P Portman Mansions, Chiltern Street, London W1M 1LF, England.

MACKINNON Marianne H J, b. 4 June 1925, Berlin, Germany. Retired, 1986. 3 sons. *Education:* Translator Diploma, Hannover, 1946; Cambridge University Language Exam (English), 1949; State Registered Nurse, 1953; English Language and Literature, Strathclyde University, Scotland, 1983-85. *Appointments:* Author, Scottish Arts Council Register for Speakers in Schools and Public Schemes. *Publications:* Autobiographies: The Naked Years, 1987, paperback, 1989; The Alien Years, sequel, 1991; The Deluge, 1993. *Honours:* Constable Trophy, Scotland, 1982; Poetry and short story prizes, 1982-87; Research and Travel Award, 1989, Writer's Bursary, 1990, Scottish Arts Council. *Memberships:* PEN International; Society of Authors. *Literary Agent:* A D Peters, London, England. *Address:* 54 Rosehill, Torrance, Glasgow G64 4HF, Scotland.

MACKSEY K(enneth) J(ohn), b. 1923, British. *Appointments:* Officer, Royal Tank Regiment, British Army, 1941, until retirement with rank of Major, 1968; Deputy Editor, History of the Second World War, History of the First World War, Purnell, London, 1968-70. *Publications:* The Shadow of Vimy Ridge, To the Green Fields Beyond, 1965; Armoured Crusader: General Sir Percy Hobart, 1967; Africa Korps, Panzer Division, 1968; Crucible of Power: The Fight for Tunisia, 1969; Tank Force, Tank: A History of AFVs, 1970; Tank Warfare, Beda Fomm, 1971; The Guinness History of Land (Sea Air) Warfare, 3 volumes, 1973-76; Battle (in US as Anatomy of a Battle), 1974; The Partisans of Europe in the Second World War, The Guinness Guide to

Feminine Achievements, Guderian Panzer General, 1975; The Guinness Book of 1952 (1953 1954), 3 volumes, 1977-79; Kesselring, 1978; Rommel's Campaigns and Battles, 1979; The Tanks, volume III of the History of the Royal Tank Regiment, 1979; Invasion: The German Invasion of England, July 1940, 1980; The Tank Pioneers, 1981; History of the Royal Armoured Corps 1914-1975, 1983; Commando Strike, First Clash, 1985; Technology in War, 1986; Godwin's Saga, Military Errors of World War 2, 1987; Tank Versus Tank, 1988; For Want of a Nail, 1989; Penguin Encyclopedia of Modern Warfare, 1991. *Address:* Whatley Mill, Beaminster, Dorset DT8 3EN, England.

MACKWORTH Cecily, b. Llantillio Pertholey, Gwent, Wales. Writer. m. Marquis de Chabannes la Palice, 1956, 1 daughter (by 1st husband). *Publications:* I Came Out of France, 1942; Francois Villon, A Study, 1947; A Mirror for French Poetry, 1942; The Mouth of the Sword, 1949; The Destiny of Isobella Eberhardt, 1952; Springs Green Shadow (novel), 1953; Guillaume Apollinaire and the Cubist Life, 1961; English Interludes, 1974; Ends of the World, Memoirs, 1987; Lucy's Nose (novel), 1992. *Contributions to:* Horizon; Life and letters Today; Poetry Quarterly; Cornhill; Twentieth Century; Cultures for all Peoples (UNESCO); Critique; Les Lettres Nouvelles and several others. *Honour:* Darmstadt Award, 1965. *Memberships:* PEN (French); Association Internationale des Critiques Litteraires; Society of Authors, GB. *Address:* 6 Rue des Countures-St-Gervais, Paris 75003, France.

MACLAINE Allan H(ugh), b. 1924, American. *Appointments:* Instructor, Brown University, Providence, RI, 1947-50; Instructor, University of Massachusetts, Amherst, 1951-54; Assistant Professor 1954-56, Associate Professor 1956-62, Texas Christian University, Fort Worth; Professor of English 1962-, Dean of Division of University Extension 1967-71, University of Rhode Island, Kingston. *Publications:* The Student's Comprehensive Guide to the Canterbury Tales, 1964; Robert Fergusson, 1965; Allan Ramsay, 1985. *Membership:* President, College English Association, 1965-66. *Address:* Department of English, University of Rhode Island, Kingston, RI 02881, USA.

MACLEAN Art. *See:* **SHIRREFFS Gordon Donald.**

MACLEAN Arthur. *See:* **TUBB E C.**

MACLEAN Fitzroy, Sir, b. 1911, British. *Appointments:* Former Conservative MP: Under Secretary of State for War, 1954-57. *Publications:* Eastern Approaches, 1949; Disputed Barricade, 1957; A Person from England, 1958; Back to Bokhara, 1959; Jugoslavia, 1969; A Concise History of Scotland, 1970; To the Back of Beyond, 1974; To Caucasus, 1976; Take Nine Spies, 1978; Holy Russia, 1979; Tito, 1980; The Isles of the Sea, 1985; Bonnie Prince Charlie, 1988; Portrait of the Soviet Union, 1988; All The Russias - The End of an Empire, 1992. *Address:* Strachur House, Strachur, Argyll, PA27 8BX, Scotland.

MACLEAN Katherine, b. 1925, American. *Appointments:* Research Laboratory Assistant 1943-45; Electrocardiograph Technician 1951- 56; Lecturer, University of Connecticut and University of Maine, 1961-74. *Publications:* Cosmic Checkmate (with C de Vet), 1962; The Diploids, 1966, 1974; The Man in the Birdcage, 1971; Missing Man, Garbage In Garbage Out, The Kid in the Computer, 1974; Dark Wing (with Carl West), 1979; The Trouble with You Earth People, 1980. *Address:* PO Box 1563, Biddeford, ME 04005, USA.

MACLEOD Alison, b. 1920, British. *Publications:* Dear Augustine, 1958; The Heretics (in US as The Heretic), 1965; The Hireling (in UK as The Trusted Servant), 1968; City of Light (in UK as No Need of the Sun), 1969; The Muscovite, 1971; The Jesuit (in US as Prisoner of the Queen), 1972; The Portingale, 1976.

Address: 63 Muswell Hill Place, London N10 3RP, England.

MACLEOD Charlotte, (Alisa Craig, Matilda Hughes), b. 1922, American. *Appointment:* Former Vice-President, NH Miller advertising agency, Boston (member of staff 1952-). *Publications:* As Charlotte MacLeod: Mystery of the White Knight, 1964; Next Door to Danger, 1965; The Fat Lady's Ghost, 1968; Mouse's Vineyard (juvenile), 1968; Ask me No Questions, 1971; Brass Pounder (juvenile), 1971; Astrology for Sceptics (non-fiction), 1972; King Devil, 1978; Rest You Merry, 1978; The Family Vault, 1979; The Luck Runs Out, 1979; The Withdrawing Room, 1980; We Dare Not Go a-Hunting, 1980; The Palace Guard, 1981; Wrack and Rune, 1982; Cirak's Daughter (juvenile), 1982; The Bilbao Looking Glass, 1983; Something the Cat Dragged In, 1983; Maid of Honour (juvenile), 1984; The Convival Codfish, 1984; The Curse of the Giant Hogweed, 1985; The Plain Old Man, 1985; Grab Bag, 1987; The Corpse in Oozak's Pond, 1987; The Recycled Citizen, 1988; The Silver Ghost, 1988; Vane Pursuit, 1989; The Gladstone Bag, 1990. As Matilda Hughes: The Food of Love, 1965; Headlines for Caroline, 1967. As Alisa Craig: A Pint of Murder, 1980; The Grub-and-Stakers Move a Mountain, 1981; Murder Goes Mumming, 1981; The Terrible Tide, 1983; The Grub and Stakers Quilt a Bee, 1985; The Grub-and-Stakers Pinch a Poke, 1988; Trouble in the Brasses, 1989; The Grub-and-Stakers Spin a Yarn, 1990. *Address:* c/o Jed Mattes, 175 W 73rd Street, New York, NY 10023, USA.

MACLEOD Ellen Jane, (Ella Anderson), b. 17 May 1918, Glasgow, Scotland. Author. m. 15 Dec 1953. *Education:* Educated in Scotland and the United States. *Publications:* Orchids for a Rose, 1963; Stranger in the Glen, 1968; The Broken Melody, 1969; The Kelpie Ledge, 1972; Isle of Shadows, 1974; 14 Youth Books. *Contributions to:* Radio 2 Plays, One Stormy Night, 1964; Something Fishy, 1966, Serials and Short Stories to various magazines. *Memberships:* Society of Authors; Radio Writers Association. *Address:* 12 Montgomery Place, Buchlyvie, Stirlingshire, FK8 3NF, Scotland.

MACLEOD Robert. *See:* **KNOX William.**

MACMANUS Yvonne, b. 18 Mar 1931, Los Angeles, California, USA. Editor; Writer; Videoscripter. *Education:* Sundry courses at UCLA & USC, New York University and University of London, England. *Publications:* The Presence, 1982, 1987; You Can Write a Romance, 1983; Hugo, (2 act play), 1990. Over 30 books published mostly pseudonymously; Corporate videoscripting. *Contributions to:* Training and Development Journal; Business Digest and Greater New Haven; Litchfield County Times. *Honours:* Honary Daughter of Mark Twain, 1977. *Memberships:* American Society of Training and Development. *Address:* c/o Write On, Ste 1304, 4040 Mountain Creek Road, Chattanooga TN 34715, USA.

MACNAB Roy Martin, b. 17 Sept 1923, Durban, South Africa. Retired Diplomat. m. Rachel Heron-Maxwell, 6 Dec 1947, 1 son, 1 daughter. *Education:* Hilton College, Natal, South Africa; MA, Jesus College, Oxford, England, 1955; DLitt et Phil, University of South Africa, 1981. *Publications:* The Man of Grass and other Poems, 1960; The French Colonel, 1975; Gold Their Touchstone, 1987; For Honour Alone, 1988; Co-editor Oxford Poetry, 1947; Poets in South Africa, 1958; Journey Into Yesterday, 1962. *Contributions to:* Times Literary Supplement; Spectator; Poetry Review; History To-day. *Honour:* Silver Medal, Royal Society of Arts, 1958. *Address:* c/o Travellers Club, London SW1, England.

MACNEACAIL Aonghas, b. 7 June 1942, Uig, Isle of Skye, Scotland. Writer. m. Gerda Stevenson, 21 June 1980, 1 son. *Literary Appointments:* Writing Fellowships - The Gaelic College, Isle of Skye, 1977-79; An Comunn Gaidhealachm Oban, 1979-81; Ross-Cromarty District

Council, 1988-90. *Publications:* Poetry Quintet, 1976; Imaginary Wounds, 1980; Sireadh Bradain Sicir/Seeking Wise Salmon, 1983; An Cathadh Mor/The Great Snowbattle, 1984; An Seachnadh/The Avoiding, 1986; Rock and Water, 1990. *Contributions to:* Gairm (Gaelic) Cencrastus; Words; Acuarius; Cracked Locking Glass; Chapman Lines Review; Scottish Review; Edinburgh Review; Scotsman; West Highland Free Press; Akros Poetry, Australia; Pembroke Magazine, USA; International Poetry Review, USA; Tijdschrift Voor Poezie, Belgium; Honest Ulsterman, Ireland. *Honours:* Grampian TV Gaelic Poetry Award; Diamond Jubilee Award, Scottish Association for the Speaking of Verse, 1985; An Comunn Gaidhealach Literary Award, 1985. *Memberships:* Council Member, Poetry Society London, 1974-77; Council Member, Scottish Poetry Library Association, 1984-. *Address:* 1 Roseneath Terrace, Marchmont, Edinburgh EH9 1JS, Scotland.

MACNEIL Duncan. *See:* **MCCUTCHAN Philip Donald.**

MACPHERSON (Jean) Jay, b. 1931, Canadian. *Appointments:* Joined faculty 1957, Professor of English 1974-, Victoria College, University of Toronto, Ontario. *Publications:* The Boatman, 1957; Four Ages of Man, 1962; Welcoming Disaster: Poems 1970-1974, 1974; Poems Twice Told, 1981; The Spirit of Solitude: Conventions and Continuities in Late Romance, 1982. *Address:* Victoria College, Toronto, Ontario, Canada M5S 1K7.

MACSHANE Frank (Sutherland), b. 1927, American. *Appointments:* Assistant Professor of English, University of California, Berkeley, 1959- 64; Associate Professor, Williams College, Williamstown, MA, 1964-67; Professor, Writing Division 1967-, Dean 1971-72, School of the Arts, Columbia University, NYC. *Publications:* The Visits of the Queen of Sheba by Miguel Serrano (trans), The Mysteries by Miguel Serrano (trans), 1960; Many Golden Ages, 1962; Impressions of Latin America (ed), The Serpent of Paradise by Miguel Serrano (trans), 1963; Critical Writings of Ford Madox Ford (ed), 1964; The American in Europe (ed), The Life and Work of Ford Madox Ford, 1965; C G Jung and Hermann Hesse: A Record of Two Friendships by Miguel Serrano (trans), 1966; The Ultimate Flower by Miguel Serrano (trans), 1969; El/Ella by Miguel Serrano (trans), Ford Madox Ford: The Critical Heritage (ed), 1972; Borges on Writing (ed with D Halpern and N T di Giovanni), 1973; The Life of Raymond Chandler, The Notebooks of Raymond Chandler, 1976; The Life of John O'Hara, Selected Letters of Rayond Chandler, 1981; The Collected Stories of John O'Hara (ed), Into Eternity: The Life of James Jones American Writer, 1985. *Memberships:* Director, Columbia Trans Center, NYC; Authors Guild. *Address:* c/o Aaron M Priest Literary Agency, 122 E 42nd Street, Suite 3902, New York, NY 10168, USA.

MACSWEENEY Barry, b. 1948, British. Writer. *Appointments:* Director Blacksuede Boot Press; Editor Harvest and the Blacksuede Boot, Barnet, Herts. Former Freelance Journalist. *Publications:* Poems, 1965-68: The Boy from the Green Cabaret Tells of His Mother, 1969; The Last Bud, 1969; (with P. Bland) Joint Effort, 1970; Flames on the Beach at Viareggio: Poems, 1970; Our Mutual Scarlet Boulevard, 1970; Elegy for January: An Essay Commemorating the Bi-Centenary of Chatterton's Death, 1970; The Official Biography of Jim Morrison, Rock Idol (poetry), 1971; Brother Wolf, 1972; 5 Odes, 1972; Dance Steps, 1972; Fog Eye, 1973; 6 Odes, 1973; Pelt Feather Log, 1975; Odes, 1979; Blackbird: Elegy for William Gordon Calvert, Being Book Two of Black Torch, 1980; Ranter, 1986.

MACVEAN Jean, b. Bradford, England. Writer. m. James Bernard Wright, 11 Oct 1952, 1 son, 1 daughter. *Education:* Sorbonne, Paris. *Publications:* The Intermediaries, novel; The Adjacent Kingdom (introduction, editing of Thomas Blackburn poems), 1980; Eros Reflected, poems, 1981; The Dolorous Death

of King Arthur, 1992; The Price of an Eye, radio feature; Flight of the Swan, radio play; The Image of Freedom, play; Ideas of Love, poems. *Contributions to:* Another Look at Edith Sitwell, to Agenda and Contemporary Literary Criticism, USA; Thomas Blackburn, George MacKay Brown, to Temenos; The Poetry and Prose of Moelwyn Merchant, to Agenda; Poems to: Encounter; Yale Literary Magazine; Meridien; Agenda; The Tablet; Pen Anthology; Mandeville Press; Big Little Poems; Poetry London (Apple). *Membership:* Fellow, International PEN Society. *Address:* 21 Peel Street, London W8 7PA, England.

MACVEY John Wishart, b. 1923, British. *Appointments:* Research Chemist 1956-61, Company Technical Information Officer 1971-80, Nobel's Explosives Limited, Division of ICI; Plant Manager, 1961-62; Assistant Technical Information Officer, 1962-71. *Publications:* Speaking of Space (with C P Snow, B Lovell and P Moore), 1962; Alone in the Universe?, 1963; Journey to Alpha Centauri, 1965; How We Will Reach the Stars, 1969; Whispers from Space, 1973; Interstellar Travel, Past, Present and Future, 1977; Space Weapons/Space War, 1979; Where Will We Go When the Sun Dies?, 1980; Colonizing Other Worlds, 1984; Time Travel, 1987. *Address:* Mellendean, 15 Adair Avenue, Saltcoats, Ayrshire KA21 5QS, Scotland.

MADDEN Tara Roth, b.16 Nov 1942, Pittsburgh, Pennsylvania, USA. Writer. m. Edward E Madden, 24 May 1980. *Education:* BA, Kent State University, 1970; MBO, Walsh College, 1975; also attended Miami College, Oxford, Ohio, Glassboro State College and University of Seattle. *Appointments:* Communications specialist for public schools in Cuyahoga Falls, Ohio, 1970; Communications Specialist, American Red Cross, Northern Ohio Blood Services, Cleveland, 1978-79; Communications Specialist, Ohio Edison Electric Co, Akron, 1979; Manager of Publicity and Public Relations, Laser Images Inc, Van Nuys, California, 1980; Promotion Manager and Assistant Production Director, Marketing Association Services, Los Angeles, California, 1980; Editor of Marketing Communications, Pertec Computer Corporation, Los Angeles, 1980-81; Manager of Marketing Communications Services, Microdata Computer Corporation, Newport Beach, California, 1981-83; Direcctor of Development for Laguna Art Museum; Lecturer at colleges, corporations and management seminars. *Publications:* Women vs Women: The Uncivil War, AMACOM, 1987; Screenplay based on Women vs Women in progress.

MADDISON Angela Mary, (Angela Banner), b. 1923, European. *Publications:* Ant and Bee, 1950; More Ant and Bee, 1955; One, Two, Three with Ant and Bee, 1958; Around The World with Ant and Bee, 1960; More and More Ant and Bee, 1961; Ant and Bee and the Rainbow, 1962; Ant and Bee and King Dog, 1963; Happy Birthday with Ant and Bee, 1964; Ant and Bee and the ABC, 1966; Ant and Bee Time, 1969; Ant and Bee and the Secret, 1970; Ant and Bee and the Doctor, 1971; Ant and Bee Big Buy Bag, 1971; And and Bee Go Shopping, 1972; Which Two Will Meet?, 1972; Kind Dog on Monday, 1972; Kind Dog Up and Down The Hill, 1972; Dear Father Christmas, 1984. *Address:* The Ant and Bee Partnership, c/o Grindleys Bank Ltd, 13 St James Square, London SW1Y 4LF, England.

MADDISON Tyler. *See:* **SMITH Moe Sherrard.**

MADDOCK R(eginald) B(ertram), b. 1912, British. *Appointments:* Headmaster, Evelyn Street School, 1949-57, Richard Fairclough Secondary School, 1957-73, Warrington. *Publications:* Corrigan and the White Cobra (Tomb of Opi, Yellow Peril, Black Riders, Golden Pagoda, Dream-Makers, Blue Crater, Green Tiger, Red Lions and Little People) 10 volumes, 1956-63; Rocky and the Lions, 1957; The Time Maze, 1960; The Last Horizon, 1961; The Willow Wand, The Tall Man from the Sea, Rocky and the Elephant, 1962; One More River, 1963; The Widgeon Gang, The Great Bow, 1964; The Pit, 1966; The Dragon in the Garden, 1968; Sell-Out (in US as Danny Rowley), 1969; Northmen's Fury, 1970; Thin Ice, The Big Ditch, 1971; Home and Away, 1980. *Address:* 116 Dudlow Green Road, Appleton, Warrington WA4 5EH, England.

MADDOX Carl. *See:* **TUBB E C.**

MADELEY John, b. 14 July 1934, Salford, England. Writer; Broadcaster. m. Alison, 10 Mar 1962, 1 son, 1 daughter. *Education:* BA Hons Econ, 1972. *Publications:* When Aid is no Help, 1991; Trade and the Poor, 1992; Diego Garcia: Contrast to the Falklands, 1982; Human Rights Begin with Breakfast, 1981. *Contributions to:* Financial Times; The Observer; The Guardian; The Independent; International Agricultural Development (editor and publisher); Broadcasting: BBC and Deutsche Welle. *Memberships:* Society of International Development; Development Journalists Group (Secretary). *Address:* 19 Woodford Close, Caversham, Reading, Berks RG4 7HN, England.

MADGETT Naomi Long, b. 5 July 1923, Norfolk, Virginia, USA. Poet; Publisher; Professor. m. Leonard P Andrews Snr. *Education:* BA, Virginia State College, 1945; MEd, English, Wayne State University; PhD, International Institute for Advanced Studies, 1980. *Appointments:* Staff Writer, The Michigan Chronicle; Service Representative, Michigan Bell Telphone Co; Teacher of English, Northwestern High School, Detroit, Michigan; Research Associate, Oakland University; Lecturer in English, University of Michigan, Ann Arbor; Associate Professor, Professor of English, now Emeritus Professor, Eastern Michigan University; Editor, Lotus Press, 1974-. *Publications include:* Songs to a Phantom Nightingale, 1941; One and the Many, 1956; Star By Star, 1965, 1970; Pink Ladies in the Afternoon, 1972; Exits and Entrances, 1978; A Student's Guide to Creative Writing, 1980; Phantom Nightingale: Juvenilia, 1981. *Contributions to:* Numerous anthologies and journals including: Beyond the Blues, 1962; Afro-Amerikaanse Poezie, 1964; Ik Ben De Nieuwe Negar, 1965; Kaleidoscope, 1967; Ten, 1968; Black Voices, 1968; Black Poetry, 1969; Michigan Signatures, 1969; Black America, Yesterday and Today, 1969; The Harlem Renaissance and Beyond, 1969; Poems to Enjoy, 1970; Soulscript, 1970; Britain America, 1970; The Black Poets, 1971; New Black Voices, 1972; Modern and Contemporary Afro-American Poetry, 1972; Afro-American Writing, 1972; The Poetry of Black America, 1973; Within You, Without You, 1973; Love Has Many Faces, 1973; American Negro Poetry (revised edition), 1974; The Touch of a Poet, 1975; One Little Room, an Everywhere, 1975; The Freelance; Poet; English Journal; Ebony; Phylon; Negro Digest; Michigan Challenge; Freedomways; Poetry Digest; American Pen; Journal of Black Poetry; Negro History Bulletin; Detroit News; Michigan Chronicle; Obasidian; Callaloo; Metropolitan Detroit; Michigan Quarterly Review; Woman Poet; The Midwest; The Zora Neale Hurston Forum. *Honours:* Poetry Award, National Writers' Club, 1955; Robert Hayden Runagate Award, 1985; Wayne State University Arts Achievement Award; Creative Artist Award (Michigan Council for the Arts), 1987. (Literature), 1985. *Membership:* Detroit Women Writers. *Address:* 16886 Inverness Ave, Detroit, MI 48221, USA.

MADIA Chunilal Kalidas, b. 12 Aug 1922. Writer. *Education;* H.L. College of Commerce, Ahmedabad. *Appointments:* Editorial Staff, prabhat and Navsaurashtra, 1942-44; Editor, Varta 1943; Editorial Staff, janmabhoomi Group of Newspaper, Bombay, 1945-50; Language Editor, US Information Service, Bombay, 1950-62; Editor, Ruchi; Literay Editor, Sandesh. *Publications:* (in Gujarati) Novels: Vyajano Varas; Velavelani Chhanyadi; liludi Dharati; Kumkum Ane Ashaka; Short Stories: Ghooghavatan Pur; padmaja Champo Ane Kel; Tej Ane Timir; Roop-Aroop; Antastrota; Plays: Rangada; Vishavimochan; Raktatilak; Shoonyashesh; Poems: Sonnet (collected Sonnets); Criticism: Granthagarima; Shahamrig; Suvarnamrig; in Malayalam: Gujarati Kathakal. *Honours:* Narmad Gold Medal, 1951; Ranajitram Gold Medal, 1957; numerous other prizes. *Membership:* PEN. *Address:* B-213

Chandralok, Manav Mandir Road, Malabar Hill, Bombay, India.

MADSEN Richard Paul, b. 2 Apr 1941, California, USA. Sociologist. m. Judith Rosselli, 12 Jan 1974, 1 daughter. *Education:* BA, Maryknoll College, 1963; MTh, Maryknoll Seminary, 1968; MA, Esat Asian Studies, 1972, PhD, Sociology, 1977, Harvard University. *Publications:* Morality and Power in a Chinese Village, 1984; Chen Village (with Anita Chen and Jonathan Unger), 1984; Habits of the Heart (with Bellah, Sullivan, Swidler, Tipton), 1985; The Good Society (with Robert Bellah, Sullivan, Swidler, Tipton), 1991. *Honours:* C Wright Mills Award, for Morality and Power in a Chinese Village, 1985; For Habits of the Heart: Los Angeles Times Book Award, 1985; Jury nomination for Pulitzer Prize, 1986. *Memberships:* Association of Asian Studies, Governing Council for China and Inner Asia 1989-91; American Sociological Association. *Address:* Department of Sociology, University of California at San Diego, La Jolla, CA 92093, USA.

MAESTRO Giulio, b. 1942, American. *Appointments:* Assistant to Art Director, Design Organization Incorporated, 1965-66; Assistant Art Director, Warren A Kass Graphics Incorporated, 1966-69; Freelance Writer, Designer and Illustrator, 1969-. *Publications:* The Tortoise's Tug of War, 1971; The Remarkable Plant in Apartment 4, 1973; One More and One Less, 1974; Leopard Is Sick, 1978; Leopald and the Noisy Monkeys, 1980; A Raft of Riddles, 1982; Riddle Romp, Just Enough Rosie, 1983; What's a Frank Frank?, 1984; What's Mite Might?, 1986.

MAGEE Bryan, b. 12 Apr 1930, London, England. Writer. m. Ingrid Söderlund, 1954, (dec 1986), 1 daughter. *Education:* MA, Oxford, 1956; Yale University, 1955-56. *Appointments:* Theatre Critic, The Listener, 1966-67; Regular Columnist, The Times, 1974-76. *Publications include:* Go West Young Man, 1958; To Live in Danger, 1960; The New Radicalism, 1962; The Democratic Revolution, 1964; Towards 2000, 1965; One in Twenty, 1966; The Television Interviewer, 1966; Aspects of Wagner, 1968; Modern British Philosophy, 1971; Popper, 1973; Facing Death, 1977; Men of Ideas, 1978; The Philosophy of Schopenhauer, 1983; The Great Philosophers, 1987. *Contributions to:* numerous journals. *Honour:* Silver Medal, Royal Television Society, 1978. *Memberships:* President, Critics Circle; Society of Authors. *Literary Agent:* Peters, Fraser & Dunlop Group Limited. *Address:* 12 Falkland House, Marloes Road, London W8 5LF, England.

MAGEE Wes, b. 20 July 1939, Greenock, Scotland. Former Headteacher; Broadcaster; Full Time Author. m. Janet Elizabeth Parkhouse, 10 Aug. 1967, 1 son, 1 daughter. *Education:* Teaching Certificate, 1967; Advanced Certificate in Education, 1972. *Publications:* Poetry: Urban Gorilla, 1972; No Man's Land, 1978; A Dark Age, 1982; Flesh of Money, 1990; Other: Oliver the Daring Birdman, 1978; The Real Spirit of Christmas, 1979; All the Day Through, 1982; Dragon' Smoke, 1985; A Shooting Star, 1985; Story Starters 1986; A Calendar of Poems, 1986; Don't Do That, 1987; A Christmas Stocking, 1987; Morning Break, 1989; The Witch's Brew, 1989; A Big Poetry Book, 1989; Read A Poem, Write A Poem, 1989; Madtail Miniwhale, 1989; Legend of The Ragged Boy, 1992; Scribblers of Scumbagg School, 1993. *Contributions to:* Journals and publications including poetry & reviews. *Honours:* New Poets Award, 1972; Poetry Book Society Recommendation, 1978; Cole Scholar (Florida, USA), 1985. *Membership:* Poetry Society of Great Britain. *Address:* Santone House, Low Street, Sancton, York, YO4 3QZ, England.

MAGISTER X. *See:* **HERMANUS Dirk Baars.**

MAGNUSSON Magnus, b. 12 Oct. 1929. Writer; Broadcaster. m. Mamie Baird, 1954, 1 son, 3 daughters (1 son dec). *Education:* MA, Jesus College, Oxford.

Publications: Introducing Archaeology, 1972; Viking Expansion Westwards, 1973; The Clacken and the Slate, 1974; Hammer of the North, 1976, 2nd edition, Viking Hammer of the North, 1980; BC, The Archaeology of the Bible Lands, 1977; Landlord or Tenant? a View of Irish History, 1978; Iceland, 1979; Vikings!, 1980; Magnus on the Move, 1980; Treasures of Scotland, 1981; Lindisfarne: The Cradle Island, 1984; Iceland Saga, 1987; translations (all with Hermann Palsson): Njal's Saga, 1960; The Vinland Sagas, 1965; King Harald's Saga, 1966; Laxdaela Saga, 1969; (all by Halldor Laxness): The Atom Station, 1961; Paradise Reclaimed, 1962; The Fish Can Sing, 1966; World Light, 1969; Christianity under Glacier, 1973; (by Samivel) Golden Iceland, 1967; Contributor: The Glorious Privilege, 1967; The Future of the Highlands, 1968; Strange Stories, Amazing Facts, 1975; Pass the Port, 1976; Book of Bricks, 1978; Chronicle, 1978; Discovery of Lost Worlds, 1979; Pass the Port Again, 1981; Second Book of Bricks, 1981; Introduced: Ancient China, 1974; The National Trust for Scotland Guide, 1976; Karluk, 1976; More lives Than One?, 1976; Atlas of World Geography, 1977; Face to Face with the Turin Shroud, 1978; Modern Bible Atlas, 1979; Living Legends, 1980; The Hammer and the Cross, 1980; Household Ghosts, 1981; Great Books for Today, 1981; The Voyage of Odin's Raven, 1982; Robert Burns: Bawdy Verse & Folksongs, 1982; Mastermind 4, 1982; Northern Voices, 1984; The Village, 1985; Secrets of the Bible Seas, 1985. Edited: Echoes in Stone, 1983; Readers Digest Book of Facts, 1985; Chambers Biographical Dictionary, 1990; The Nature of Scotland, 1991. *Honours:* Knight of the Order of the Falcon, Iceland, 1975; Knight Commander, 1986; Silver Jubilee Medal, 1977; Iceland Media Award, 1985; Hon KBE, 1989; Hon Fellow, Jesus College, Oxford, 1990; Honorary Degrees, and many other honours and awards. *Memberships:* Fellow, Society of Antiquaries of London, 1991; Fellow, Royal Scottish Gergraphical Society, 1991. *Literary Agent:* Deborah Rogers, Rogers, Coleridge & White, 20 Powis Mews, London W11 1JN, England. *Address:* Blairskaith House, Balmore-Torrance, Glasgow, G64 4AX, Scotland.

MAGNUSSON Sigurdur A, b. 31 Mar 1928, Reykjavik, Iceland. Writer. Twice married, twice divorced, 2 sons, 3 daughters. *Education:* BA, New School for Social Research, New York, 1955. *Appointments:* Literary & Drama Critic, Morgunbladid, 1956-67; Editor in chief, Samvinnan, 1967-74; Member, International Writing Programme, University of Iowa, 1976, 1977; Member, West Berlin International Artists' Programme, 1979- 80; Member, 11 Man 1986 Jury, Neustadt International Prize for Literature, Oklahoma; Member of Jury, Nordic Council's Prize for Literature, 1990-. *Publications:* Poems: Scribbled in Sand, 1958; The Sea & the Rock, 1961; This is Your Life, 1974; In the Light of Next Day, 1978; Tropics - Selected Poems 1952-82, 1988. Essays: the Emperor's New Clothes, 1959; Sown to the Wind, 1967; In the Limelight, 1982. Novels: Night Visitors, 1961; Under a Dead Star, 1979; The Meshes of Tomorrow 1981; Jacob Wrestling, 1983; The Tree of Knowledge, 1985; From the Snare of the Fowler, 1986. Short Stories: Trivialities, 1965. Play: Visiting, 1962. Biography: Bishop Sigurbjörn - Life and Work, 1988. Travel Books on Greece, 1992 and India, 1953, 1962 (In Greek) Death of Balder and Other Poems, 1960; (In English) Northern Sphinx - Iceland and the Icelanders from the Settlement to the Present 1977, 2nd edition 1984; Iceland Country and People, 1978, 1987; The Iceland Horse, 1978; The Postwar Poetry of Iceland, 1982; Icelandic Writing Today, 1982; Iceland Crucible - A Modern Artisic Renaissance, 1985; The Icelanders, 1989. *Contributions to:* Numerous professional journals. *Honours:* Golden Cross of Phoenix, Greece, 1955; Cultural Council's Prize for Best Play, 1961; Cultural Prize for Best Novel, 1980. *Memberships:* Society of Icelandic Drama Critics, Chairman, 1963-71; Writers Union of Iceland, Chairman, 1971-78; Greek-Icelandic Cultural Society, Chairman 1985-88; Amnesty International, Chairman 1988-89. *Address:* Barónsstig 49, Haaleitisbraut 22, 108 Reykjavik, Iceland.

MAGORIAN James b. 24 Apr 1942, Palisade, Nebraska, USA. Writer; Poet; Author of children's stories. *Education:* BS, University of Nebraska, 1965; MS, Illinois State University, 1969; Graduate studies: Oxford University, 1972, Harvard University 1973. *Publications:* Author of 56 books including: The Garden of Epicus (poetry) 1971; Distances (poetry) 1972; School Daze (children's book) 1978; Safe Passage (popetry) 1977; The Edge of the Forest (poetry) 1980; Keeper of Fire (children's book) 1984; Ground-Hog Day (children's book) 1987; The Bad Eggs (children's book) 1989; The Invention of the Afternoon Nap (children's book) 1989. *Contributions to:* Western Poetry Quarterly; Poetry View; Nebraska Review; San Francisco Poetry Journal; Kansas Quarterly; The Louisville Review; Illinois Quarterly. *Address:* 1225 North 46th Street, Lincoln, NE 68503, USA.

MAGORIAN Michelle Jane, b. 6 Nov 1947, Southsea, Portsmouth, Hampshire, England. Writer; Actress. m. Peter Keith Venner, 18 Aug 1987, 1 son. *Education:* Diploma, Speech & Drama, Rose Bruford College of Speech and Drama, Kent, 1969; Ecole Internationale de Mime Marcel Marceau, Paris, 1969-70. *Publications:* Novels: Goodnight Mister Tom, 1981, US Edition, 1982, also book and lyrics as musical; Back Home, 1984, 1985; A Little Love Song, 1991; Poetry: Waiting for My Shorts To Dry, 1989; Orange Paw Marks, 1991; In Deep Water, short story collection, 1992; Picture books; Short stories. *Contributions to:* Puffin Post. *Honours:* For Goodnight Mister Tom: Guardian Award for Children's Fiction, UK, 1981; Commended for Carnegie Medal, UK, 1981; Children's Award, International Reading Association, USA, 1982; Notable Children's Books of 1982, Best Book for Young Adults, 1982, YA Reviewers Choice, 1982, American Library Association; Western Australia Young Readers Book Award, 1983; Teachers Choice, NCTE, 1983; For Back Home: Best Books for Young Adults, American Library Association, 1984; Western Australia Young Readers Book Award, 1987; Goodnight Mister Tom (musical) winner, Buxon Opera Hosue Quest for New Musicals. *Memberships:* Society of Authors, Children's Writers and Illustrators Committee; PEN; British Actors Equity. *Literary Agent:* Patricia White, Rogers, Coleridge and White. *Address:* 803 Harrow Road, Wembley, Middlesex HAO 2LP, England.

MAGUIRE Michael, b. 1945, British. *Publications:* Shot Silk, Slaughter Horse, 1975; Scratchproof, 1976; Mylor, The Most Powerful Horse in the World, 1977; Mylor: The Kidnap, 1978; Superkids, 1979; Hot Metal, 1982. *Address:* c/o Crescent, W H Allen, 44 Hill Street, London W1X 8LB, England.

MAHANAIM Anna. *See:* **MORIZOT YOUNG Carol Ann.**

MAHESHWARI Shriram,b. 27 Nov 1931, Kanpur. Teaching. m. Bimla, 30 May 1955, 3 sons, 2 daughters. *Education:* BA, 1951; MA Economics, 1953; MA Political Science, 1955, Agra University; MGA, Wharton School, University of Pensylvania, 1964; PhD, University of Delhi, 1965. *Appointments:* Professor of Political Science and Public Administration at Indian Institute of Public Administration 1973-; Guest faculty at Jawaharla Nehru University, New Delhi, 1979-83. *Publications:* Rural Development in India: A Public Policy Approach, 1986; The Higher Civil Service in Japan, 1987; The Higher Civil Service in France, 1990. *Contributions to:* Various journals. *Honours:* Sardar Patel Prize for best work in Hindi, instituted by the Government of India, 1988. *Memberships:* President of Indian Public Administration Association, 1988-89; Indian Political Science Association. *Address:* 156 Golf Links, New Delhi 110003, India.

MAHFOUZ Naguib, b. 11 Dec 1911, Gamalia, Cairo, Egypt. Writer. m. 27 Sept 1954, 2 daughters. *Education:* BA, Philosophy, Cairo University, 1934. *Appointments:* Office Director, Egyptian Arts Association, 1955-66; Head, The Egyptian Cinema Organisation, 1966-68;

Consultant to Egyptian Minister of Culture, 1968-71. *Publications:* In English: Midaq Alley, 1966; Miramar, 1978; The Thief and the Dogs, 1984; Wedding Song, 1984; The Beginning and The End, 1985; Autumn Quail, 1985; The Beggar, 1986; The Search, 1987; Respected Sir, 1987; The Time and The Place and Other Stories, 1991; The Cairo Trilogy: Vol I Palace Walk, 1990, Vol II Palace of Desire, 1991, Vol III Sugar Street, 1992. *Contributions to:* Numerous Egyptian magazines. *Honours:* National Merit Award, Egypt, 1968; Nobel Prize for Literature, 1988. *Memberships:* International Member, American Academy and Institute of Arts and Letters; Story Club, Cairo; Authors Union, Cairo; Authors Society, Cairo. *Literary Agent:* The American University in Cairo Press. *Address:* The American University in Cairo, 113 Kasr El Aini Street, Cairo, Egypt.

MAHON Derek, b. 1941, British. *Appointments:* English Teacher, Belfast High School, Newtownabbey, Co Antrim, 1967-68; Lecturer in English, The Language Centre of Ireland, Dublin, 1968-70; Poet-in-Residence, Emerson College, Boston, 1976-77, New University of Ulster, Coleraine, 1977- 79; Poetry Editor, New Statesman, London; Dream Critic; The Listener, London. *Publications:* Twelve Poems, 1965; Night-Crossing, 1968; Ecclesiastes, Beyond Howth Head, 1970; Modern Irish Poetry (ed), Lives, The Man Who Built His City in Snow, 1972; The Snow Party, 1975; Light Music, 1977; The Sea in Winter, Poems 1962-1978, 1979; Courtyards in Delft, 1981; The Chimeras by Nerval (trans), The Hunt by Night, 1982; A Kensington Notebook, 1984; Antarctica, 1985. *Address:* c/o Deborah Rogers Limited, 49 Blenheim Crescent, London W11 2EF, England.

MAHONEY Rosemary, b. 28 Jan 1961, Boston, Massachusetts, USA. Writer. *Education:* BA, Harvard College, 1983; MA, Johns Hopkins University, 1985. *Publications:* The Early Arrival of Dreams; A Year in China; Whoredom In Kimmage; Irish Women Coming of Age, 1993. *Honours:* C E Horman Prize for Fiction, Harvard College, 1982; Henfield-Transatlantic Review Award for Fiction, 1985. *Literary Agent:* Wylie, Aitken and Stone, 250 West 57th St, New York, NY 10107, USA. *Address:* Houghton Mifflin Company, 215 Park Avenue South, New York, NY 10003, USA.

MAHY Margaret, b. 1936 New Zealander, Full-time writer of children's fiction, poetry and history. *Appointments:* Former Librarian, School Library Service, Christchurch; Writer-in-Residence, Canterbury University, 1984 and College of Advanced Education in Western Australia, 1985. *Publications:* The Dragon of an Ordinary Family, 1969; A Lion in the Meadow, 1969; Mrs. Discombobulous, 1969; Pillycock's Shop, 1969; The Procession, 1969; The Little Witch, 1970; Sailor Jack and the 20 Orphans, 1970; The Princess and the Clown, 1970; The Boy with Two Shadows, 1971; Seventeen Kings and Forty Two Elephants (verse) 1972; The First (Second, Third) Margaret Mahy Story Book: Stories and Poems, 3 vols, 1972-75; The Man Whose Mother Was a Pirate, 1972; The Railway Engine and the Hairy Brigands, 1973; Rooms for Rent (in Uk as Rooms to Let) 1974; The Witch in the Cherry Tree, 1974; Clancy' Cabin, 1974; The Rare Spotted Birthday Party, 1974; Stepmother, 1974; New Zealand: Yesterday and Today, 1975; The Bus under the Leaves, 1975; The Ultra-Violet Catastrophe! or, The Unexpected Walk with Great-Uncle Magnus Pringle, 1975; The Great Millionaire Kidnap, 1975; Leaf Magic, 1975; The Boy Who Was Followed Home, 1975; The Wind Between the Stars, 1976; David's Witch Doctor, 1976; The Pirate Uncle, 1977; Nonstop Nonsense, 1977; The Great Piratical Rumbustification, 1979; Fearsome Robots and Frightened Uncles, 1980; Raging Robots and Unruly Uncles, 1981; The Chewing- Gum Rescue, 1982; The Haunting, 1983; The Changeover, 1983; The Pirate's Mixed-up Voyage, 1983; The Birthday Burglar and a Very Wicked Headmistress, 1984; The Catalogue of the Universe, 1985; Jam 1985; Aliens in the Family, 1986; The Tricksters, 1986; The Downhill Crocodile Whizz and Other Stories, 1986; Memory, 1987; The Horrible Story and Others, 1987. *Honours:* Carnegie Medal and Esther

Glen Medal for The Haunting. *Address:* RD No 1, Lyttelton, New Zealand.

MAI Gottfried Erhard Willy, b. 11 May 1940, Finsterwalde, Federal Republic of Germany. Theologian. m. Gunhild Flemming, 1 Sept 1962, 2 sons, 2 daughers. *Education:* Navigation Certificate, Nautical School, Bremen; Study of Theology and History, Universities of Bonn, Gottingen, Hamburg and Copenhagen; Dr Theol; Dr Phil. *Appointments:* Freelance Writer. *Publications include:* The Protestant Church and the German Emigration to North America (1815-1914), 1972; Die niederdeutsche Reformbegwegung, 1979; The German Federal Armed Forces 1815-1864, 1977/1982; Geschichte der stadt Finsterwalde, 1979; Der Uberfall des Tigers, 1982; Chronicle of the 4th Minesweeper Squadron Wilhelmshaven, 1985; Buddha, 1985; Napoleon -Temptation of Power, 1986; Zwischen Polor und Wonderkreis, 1987; Lenin - The Perverted Moral, 1987. *Contributions include:* Hospitium ecclesiae (Society for History), Bremen; Annual Books of Hermannsburg Mission Society; Annual Books of Gustav-Adolf-Werk Kassel; Readers Digest of world Mission, erlangen; Annual Book of Lower Saxonian Church History, Blomberg; German Soldier Annual Book, Bonn. *Honour:* International Book Prize for History of AWMM, 1983. *Address:* Harlinger Weg 2, D 2948 Grafschaft, Germany.

MAIBAUM Matthew, b. 14 Aug 1946, Chicago, Illinois, USA. Consulting Social Scientist; Writer. *Education:* AB, Honours, University of California, Berkeley, 1969; MPA, University of California, Los Angeles; PhD, California School Professional Psyhology, 1975; PhD, Political Sciences, Claremont Graduate School, 1980. *Publications include:* Sly Times, (play), 1985; Wiggling in the Rain, (play), 1987; The Lilac Bush 1990; monographs, articles and funded studies in ethnic studies, politics, intergroup relations. *Contributions to:* Various journals, books. *Honours:* California State Psychological Association Best Paper, 1975; Society for the Psychological Study of Social Issues, Grant Aid Award, 1972; other awards. *Memberships:* Authors Guild; Dramatists Guild; Pi Gamma Mu; Sigma Xi; UC Berkeley; Society of Authors (UK). *Address:* 15237 Sunset Blvd '24, Pacific Palisades, California 90272, USA.

MAIER Paul Luther, b. 1930, American. *Appointments:* Professor of Ancient History, Campus Chaplain to Lutheran students, Western Michigan University, Kalamazoo, 1958-. *Publications:* A Man Spoke, A World Listened: The Story of Walter A Maier, 1963; Pontius Pilate, 1968; First Christmas, 1971; First Easter, 1973; First Christians, 1976; The Best of Walter A Maier (ed), 1980; The Flames of Rome, 1981; Josephus - The Jewish War (associate ed), 1982; Josephus: The Essential Writings, 1988; In The Fullness of Time, 1991; A Skeleton in God's Closet, 1994. *Honours:* Alumni Award for Teaching Excellence, Western Michigan University, 1974; Distinguished Faculty Scholar Award, WMU, 1981; Professor of the Year Citation, Council for Advancement and Support of Education, 1984; The Academy Citation, Michigan Academy of Science Arts, and Letters, 1985; The Gold Medallion Book Award, Evangelical Christian Publishers Association (for: Josephus, The Essential Writings), 1989. *Membership:* Advisory Board, Christian Herald Family Bookshelf 1967-; Resource Scholar, Christianity Today Institute; Board for Higher Education, the Lutheran Church - Missouri Synod. *Address:* Department of History, Western Michigan University, Kalamazoo, MI 49008, USA.

MAILER Norman Kingsley, b. 31 Jan 1923, Long Beach, USA. Writer. m. (1) Beatrice Silverman, 1944, (div 1951), 1 daughter, (2) Adele Morales, 1954, (div 1962), 2 daughters, (3) Lady Jeanne Campbell, 1962, (div 1963), 1 daughter, (4) Beverly Rentz Bentley, 1963, (div 1980), 2 sons, 1 daughter, (5) Carol Stevens, (div), 1 daughter, (6) Norris Church, 1980, 1 son. *Education:* BS, Harvard University. *Publications:* The Naked and The Dead, 1948; Barbary Shore, 1951; The Deer Park, 1955 (dramatised 1967); Advertisements for Myself, 1959; Deaths for the Ladies (poems), 1962; The Presidential Papers, 1963; An American Dream, 1964; Cannibals and Christians, 1966; Why are We in Vietnam? (novel), 1967; The Armies of the Night 1968; Miami and the Siege of Chicago, 1968; Moonshot, 1969; A Fire on the Moon, 1970; The Prisoner of Sex, 1971; Existential Errands, 1972; St George and the Godfather, 1972; Marilyn, 1973; The Faith of Graffiti, 1974; The Fight, 1975; Some Honourable Men, 1976; Genius and Lust - A Journey Through the Writings of Henry Miller, 1976; A Transit to Narcissus, 1978; The Executioner's Song, 1979; Of Women and Their Elegance, 1980; The Essential Mailer, (Selections), 1982; Pieces and Pontifications, 1982; Ancient Evenings (novel), 1983; Tough Guys Don't Dance (novel), 1983; Haulot's Ghost, 1991. *Contributions to:* numerous journals and magazines. *Honours:* National Book Award for Arts and Letters, 1969; Pulitzer Prize for Non-fiction, 1969; 14th Annual Award for Outstanding Service to the Arts, McDowell Colony, 1973. *Memberships:* President, PEN, US Chapter, 1984-86; American Academy of Arts and Letters. *Literary Agent:* Scott Meredith Literary Agency, 845 Third Avenue, New York, NY 10022, USA. *Address:* c/o Rembar, 19 W 44th Street, New York, NY 10036, USA.

MAIMANE Arthur John, b. 5 Oct 1932, South Africa. Journalist. m. twice, 5 daughters. *Education:* Johannesburg, South Africa. *Appointments:* Drum Magazine, 1952-56; Golden City Post, 1956-58; Drum (West Africa), 1958-60 (Accra); Ghana Radio Times, 1960-61; Fleet Street, Radio & TV. *Publications:* Victims, novel; Short Stories including: Hungry Flames, 1955; Radio Plays including: The Opportunity, 1964, Where The Sun Shines, 1964; Stage Plays including, The Dung Heap Flower, 1970, The Prosecution, 1971. *Honours:* Pringle Award for Creative Writing, English Academy of South Africa, 1978; Commonwealth Radio Play, The Opportunity, 1964. *Membership:* Society of Authors. *Literary Agent:* Shelley Power, Surbitan, Surrey, England. *Address:* 15 Homefield Road, London W4 2LN, England.

MAINE David. *See:* **BARBET Pierre Claude Avice.**

MAIR Alexander Craig, b. 3 May 1948. School Teacher. m. Anne Olizar, 1 Aug 1970, 2 sons, 1 daughter. *Education:* BA, Stirling University, 1968-71. *Publications:* A Time in Turkey, 1973; A Star for Seamen, 1978; Britain at War 1914-19, 1982; The Lighthouse Boy, 1981; Mercat Cross and Tolbooth, 1988; David Angus, 1989; Stirling, The Royal Burgh, 1990; The Incorporation of Glasgow Maltmen: A History, 1990. *Memberships:* Fellow of Scottish Society of Antiquaries; Educational Institute of Scotland; Various Local History Groups. *Address:* 21 Keir Street, Bridge of Allan, Stirling, Scotland.

MAIRS Nancy Pedrick, b. 23 July 1943, Writer. m. George Anthony Mairs, 18 May 1963, 1 son, 1 daughter. *Education:* AB cum laude, Wheaton College, Massachusetts, 1964; MFA, 1975, PhD, 1984, University of Arizona. *Publications:* Instead It Is Winter, 1977; In All the Rooms of the Yellow House, 1984; Plaintext, 1986; Remembering the Bone House, 1989; Carnal Acts, 1990; Ordinary Time, 1993. *Contributions to:* The American Voice; MSS; TriQuarterly. *Honours:* Western States Book Award, 1984; Fellowship, National Endowment for the Arts, 1991. *Memberships:* The Authors Guild; Poets and Writers; National Women's Studies Association. *Literary Agent:* Barbara S Kouts. *Address:* 1527 East Mabel Street, Tucson, AZ 85719, USA.

MAJA-PEARCE Adewale, b. 3 June 1953, London, England. Researcher; Consultant; Writer. *Education:* BA, University of Wales, University College of Swansea, 1975; MA, School of Oriental and African Studies, 1986. *Appointments:* Researcher, Index on Censorship, London, 1986-; Consultant, Heinemann International, Oxford, 1986-. *Publications:* (ed) Christopher Okigbo: Collected Poems, Heinemann, 1986; In My Father's Country: A Nigerian Journey (nonfiction) Heinemann, 1987; Loyalties (stories) Longman, 1987; How Many Miles to Babylon? (nonfiction) Heinemann, 1990; (ed) The Heinemann Book of African Poetry in English, 1990; Who's Afraid of Wole Soyinka? Essays on Censorship, 1991; A Mask Dancing: Nigerian Novelists of the Eighties, 1992. *Contributions to:* Various periodicals. *Memberships:* PEN; Society of Authors. *Literary Agent:* David Grossman, Literary Agency, London. *Address:* 33 St George's Road, Hastings, E Sussex, TN34 3NH, England.

MAJEWSKI Janusz, b. 5 Aug 1931, Lvov, Poland. Film Director; Scriptwriter. m. Zofia Nasierowska, 1960, 1 son, 1 daughter. *Education:* Cracow Polytechnic; State School of Drama and Film, Lodz, 1960. *Appointments:* Feature Film Set Designer, 1955-60; Short Film Director, 1961-67, Feature Film Director, 1967-; Professor, Higher State School of Film, TV and Drama, Lodz. *Publications:* Shorts: Rondeau, 1959; Fleischer's Album, 1963; Duel, 1964; Avatar, 1965; Feature Films: The Lodger, 1966; Lokis, 1970; Jealousy and Medicine, 1973; Hotel Pacific, 1975; The Gorgonowa Case, 1977; Lesson of the Dead Language, 1979; The Epitaph for Barbara Radziwillowna, 1983; Daydream, 1985; Deserters, 1986; The Black Gorge, 1989. TV plays; TV Series Bona the Queen, 1982; TV Series Napoleon and Europe (Moscow episode), French production, 1989. *Honours:* Numerous awards and citations at National & International Festivals; several Polish Awards including: Gold Cross of Merit, 1975; Kt's Cross, order of Polonia Restituta, 1981. *Memberships:* Polish Film-makers Association, Secretary, General Board, 1970-74, President 1983-; ZAIKS. *Address:* ul. Forteczna 1a, 01-540 Warsaw, Poland.

MAJOR Kevin (Gerald), b. 12 Sept 1949, Stephenville, Newfoundland, Canada. Writer. m. Anne Crawford, 3 July 1982, 2 sons. *Education:* BSc, Memorial University, Newfoundland, 1972. *Publications:* Hold Fast, 1978; Far From Shore, 1980; Thirty-Six Exposures, 1984; Dear Bruce Springsteen, 1987; Blood Red Ochre, 1989. *Honours:* Award, Children's Literature, Canada Council, 1979; Book of Year, Canadian Association of Children's Literature, 1979; Ruth Schwartz Award, 1979; Hans Christian Andersen Honour List, 1980; Canadian Young Adult Book Award, 1981. *Membership:* Writers Union of Canada. *Literary Agency* MGA Agency. *Address:* Box 85, Eastport, Newfoundland, Canada A0G 1Z0.

MAKAREWICZ Roman, b. 13 Aug 1905, Cracow, Poland. Writer; Retired Senior Auditor. m. Irene Unverman, 19 Mar 1945, 2 sons. *Education:* Academy of Commerce, Poland, 1925; Diploma, Konsularakademie, Vienna, Austria, 1929; Postgraduate course, Hautes Etudes Internationales, Paris, France, 1929-30. *Career includes:* Several poems in Gazeta Poranna and Gazeta Lwowska, Lwow, 1923-26; 1st public appearance, An Evening With The Authors, Municipal Casino, Lwow, 1923; Wrote, directed, "Hold on till Spring" show, Artillery Officers School, Wlodzimierz, 1930; Press Attache, Polish Consulate, Breslau and Correspondent, Polish Telegraph Agency, 1932-34; Co- Editor, Dzennik Zwiazkowy, Polish daily, Chicago, Illinois, USA, 1946-48. *Publications:* Poems: Wiosna i Zima, 1972; Rapsody Kalifornijskie, 1983; Fraszki Frasujace, 1988; Postcards from Hawaii and Old Stories; Unpublished, registered drama: Gay Nineties on Broadway, Part I, 1990, Part II, 1991. *Contributions to:* Dziennik Polski daily and Tydzien Polski weekly, London, 1970-80; New Horizon, New York, 1981-86. *Honours:* Participant, 9-hour docu-drama Struggles for Poland, WNET, 1986; Silver Poet Award, 1986, Golden Poet Award, 1987, World of Poetry, San Francisco; Certificate of Merit, Poetry in Paradise Association, Hawaii, 1987; Award of Merit, Iliad Press and National Authors Registry, 1991. *Memberships:* Past President, Los Angeles Municipal Accountants and Auditors Association; Commander, Polish Veterans in Exile, Southern California, 1966- 67. *Address:* PO Box 575, Kilauen, Kauai, HI 96754, USA.

MAKARSKI Henryk, b. 17 Aug 1946, Biala, Podlaska, Poland. Writer. m. Maria Anna Koziolkiewicz, 24 July 1971, 1 son, 1 daughter. *Education:* MA, Polish Philology, Maria Curie-Sklodowska University of Lublin, 1969. *Appointments:* Co-Editor of Youth Literary Columns, 1965-1980. *Publications:* Drowning in the Hardened Soil, 1972; Desire, 1978; The Endless Staircase, 1980; The Easiest, The Hardest, 1984; 5 volumes of poetry; critical literary essays, short criminal sensational forms. *Honours:* Boleslaw Prus Literary; Award for Prose, 1984; Main Jozef Czechowicz Award for Poetry, 1985; Over 25 Awards and Honours for prose, poetry and reportage. *Membership:* Polish Writers Association, Lublin Regional Board. *Address:* 20-850 Lublin, ul Radzynska 18 m 23, Poland.

MAKOWIECKI Andrzej, b. 5 Aug 1938, Warsaw, Poland. Writer; Reporter; Jazzman; Traveller. m. 6 Jan 1973, 1 son. *Education:* State School of Music, Lodz, 1962; MA, Polish Philology, Lodz University, 1968. *Literary Appointments:* Editor, reporter, Odgiosy literary weekly, 1965-87; Correspondent, Polityka weekly, 1970-72; Reporter, Zwierciadlo, weekly, 1973-75. *Publications include:* Novels: Every Day Nearer to Heaven, 1972 (film, 1983); The Catcher's Return, 1977, 1985; The Night of Saxophones, 1984; There Are No Trains to Barcelona, 1987; The Quarter of the Sleeping Beauty, 1979; Napoleon's Rapier, 1986. Also short stories. *Contributions to:* Polityka; Odglosy; Kultura; Tygodnik Kulturalny; Zycie Warszawy; Zwierciadlo. *Honours:* 1st place, short story competition (sports subjects), Chief Committee for Physical Culture & Tourism, 1969; Various other literary awards & prizes. *Memberships:* Union of Polish Writers (ZLP); Association of Polish Journalists (ZDP); Association of Polish Authors (ZAIKS). *Literary Agent:* Dr Jacek Zaorski, Publishing House of Lodz, Lodz, ul. Piotrkowska 171. *Address:* 90-440 Lodz, ul. Piotrkowska 147 m. 1, Poland.

MALAND David, b. 1929, British. Barrister. *Appointments:* Senior History Master, Stamford School, Lincolnshire, 1956-66; Headmaster, Cardiff High School, Glamorgan, 1966-69; Headmaster, Denstone College, Uttoxeter, 1969-78; High Master, Manchester Grammar School, 1978-86. *Publications:* Europe in the Seventeenth Century, 1966; La Guerre de Trente Ans by G Pages (co-trans), 1970; Culture and Society in Seventeenth Century France, 1971; Europe in the Sixteenth Century, 1973; Europe at War 1600-1650, 1980. *Address:* Windrush, Underhill Lane, Westmeston, Nr Hassocks, East Sussex BN6 8XG, England.

MALCOLM John. See: **ROSS-MACDONALD Malcolm.**

MALGONKAR Manohar (Dattatray), b. 1913, Indian. *Appointments:* Professional Big-game Hunter, 1935-37; Cantonment Executive Officer, Government of India, 1937-42; Owner, Jagalbet Mining Syndicate, 1953-59; Self employed Farmer in Jagalbet, 1959-. *Publications:* Kanhoji Angray, Maratha Admiral: An Account of His Life and His Battles with the English, 1959; Distant Drum, 1960; Combat of Shadows, 1962; Puars of Dewas Senior, The Princes, 1963; A Bend in the Ganges, 1964; Spy in Amber, The Chhatrapatis of Kolhapur, 1971; The Devil's Wind: Nana Saheb's Story, 1972; Bombay Beware, 1974; A Toast in Warm Wine, 1975; Rumble Tumble, 1976; Dead and living Cities, Line of Mars, 1977; Shalimar (with K Shah), The Men Who Killed Gandhi, 1978; Cue from the Inner Voice, The Garland Keepers, 1980; Inside Goa, Bandicoot Run, 1982; Princess, 1985.

MALING Arthur (Gordon), b. 1923, American. *Appointments:* Reporter, The Journal, San Diego, CA, 1945-46; Executive, Maling Brothers Incorporated, Retail Shoe Chain, Chicago, 1946-72. *Publications:* Decoy, 1969; Go-Between, 1970, (in UK as Lambert's Son, 1972); Loophole, 1971; The Snowman, 1973; Dingdong, 1974; Bent Man, 1975; Ripoff, 1976; Schroeder's Game, When Last Seen (ed), 1977; Lucky

Devil, Mystery Writers' Choice (ed), 1978; The Rheingold Route, The Koberg Link, 1979; From Thunder Bay, 1981; A Taste of Treason, 1983; Lover and Thief, 1988. *Address:* 111 East Chestnut Street, Chicago, IL 60611, USA.

MALINS Penelope, (Penelope Hobhouse), b. 20 Nov 1929, Northern Ireland. Writer; Designer. m. John Malins, 1 Nov 1985, 2 sons, 1 daughter. *Education:* Cambridge Hons, Economics, 1951. *Publications:* The Country Gardener; Colour in Your Garden; Garden style; Flower Gardens; Guide to the garden of Europe; The Smaller Garden; Painted Gardens; Private Gardens of England; Borders; Flower Gardens; Plants in Garden History; Garden Style. *Contributions to:* The Garden; Horticulture; Vogue; Antiques; Plants & Gardens. *Literary Agent:* Felicity Bryan. *Address:* Tintinhull House, Yeovil, Somerset, BA22 8PZ, England.

MALKIN Lawrence, b. 30 July 1930, Richmond Hill, New York, USA. Writer. m. Edith Stark, 1960, 2 daughters. *Education:* AB, University of Chicago, 1949; AB (honours) Columbia University, 1951. *Appointments:* Correspondent, Associated Press, United Nations Bureau, London, England, 1954-69; Time: National Economics Correspondent in Washington, DC, European Cultural Correspondent in London, Bureauchief in New Delhi, India, European Correspondent in Paris, France and correspondent in Boston, Massachusetts, 1969-88. *Publication:* The National Debt, Holt, 1987. *Contributions to:* Magazines and newspapers, including Horizon, Commentary, Times Literary Supplement and Atlantic Monthly. *Honour:* E W Fairchild Award for Foreign Financial Reporting from Overseas Press Club of America, 1967. *Memberships:* Phi Beta Kappa; St Botolph's Club (Boston); Reform Club (London). *Literary Agent:* Wallace and Shiel, New York. *Address:* c/o Wallace and Shiel, 170 East 77th Street, New York, NY 10021, USA.

MALLINSON Jeremy John Crosby, b. 16 Mar 1937, Ilkley, Yorkshire, England. Zoological Director, Jersey Wildlife Preservation Trust. m. Odette Louise Guiton, 26 Oct 1963, 1 son, 1 daughter. *Education:* Mowden Hall School, Northumberland; The King's School, Canterbury. *Publications:* Okavango Adventure, 1973 UK; 1974 USA; Earning Your Living With Animals, 1975 UK; Modern Classic Animal Stories (Editor) 1977 UK, in USA as Such Agreeable Friends 1978; The Shadow of Extinction, 1978 UK; The Facts About a Zoo, 1980 UK; Travels in Search of Endangered Species, 1989. *Contributions to:* 135 articles in over 30 different journals/magazines. *Honour:* C Biol, F I Biol 1990 (Chartered Biologist, Fellow of the Institute of Biology). *Memberships:* Chairman of the Editorial Board of International Zoo Yearbook; International Union of Zoo Directors; Honorary Director of Wildlife Preservation Trust International (Philadelphia, USA) and Wildlife Preservation Trust Canada (Toronto, Ontario); UK Trustee of The Dian Fossey Gorilla Fund; Member of Species Survival Commission of IUCN. *Literary Agent:* Curtis Brown Ltd, London. *Address:* Jersey Wildlife Preservation Trust, Les Augres Manor, Trinity, Jersey, Channel Islands.

MALLOY Michael Terrence, b. 26 Feb 1936, Chicago, USA. Journalist. m. Ruth Lor, 5 June 1965, 1 son, 1 daughter. *Appointments:* City News Bureau, 1956-58; Stars & Stripes, 1959-60; United Press International, 1960-67; National Observer, 1967-77; Asian Wall Street Journal, 1977-84; Dow Jones Canada, 1984-. *Publications:* Racing Today; The Art of Retirement. *Address:* c/o Dow Jones canada Inc, Suite 706, 155 University Avenue, Toronto, Ontario, Canada M5H 3B7.

MALONE Joseph Lawrence, b. 2 July 1937, New York City, USA. Professor. m. 31 Jan 1964, 2 sons. *Education:* AB, University of California, 1963; PhD, 1967. *Appointments:* Consultant, Contributing Editor, Member Advisory Boar, The Academic American Encyclopedia, 1977-; Member Editorial Board, Itellas, 1990-. *Publications:* The Science of Linguistics in the

Art of Translation; Tiberian Hebrew Phonology. *Contributions to:* Chicago Review; Yellow Silk; New York Times; Hellas; New Press; Reflect; Feasta; Webster Review; Paintbrush. *Honours:* Prize Story in the PEN Syndicated Fiction Project. *Memberships:* Linguistics Society of America; American Oriental society; North American Conference on Afro Asiatic Linguistics. *Address:* 169 Prospect Street, Leonia, NJ 07605, USA.

MALOUF David, b. 1934, Australian. *Appointment:* Lecturer, University of Sydney, 1968-77. *Publications:* Four Poets (with others), 1962; Bicycle and Other Poems, 1970, (in US as The Year of the Foxes and Other Poems, 1979); We Took Their Orders and Are Dead: An Anti-War Anthology (ed with others), 1971; Neighbours in a Thicket, 1974; Gesture of a Hand (ed), Johnno, 1975; Poems 1975-76, 1976; An Imaginary Life, 1978; First Things Last, 1981; Child's Play, Fly Away Peter (in US as The Bread of Time to Come), 1982; Harland's Half Acre, 1984; Antipodes, 12 Edmondstone, 1985; Voss, 1986; Blood Relations, 1987; The Great World, 1990; Remembering Babylon, 1993; Baa Baa Black Sheep, 1993. *Address:* 53 Myrtle Street, Chippendale, NSW 2008, Australia.

MALPASS Eric Lawson, b. 14 Nov 1910, Derby, England. m. 3 Oct 1936, 1 son. *Education:* King Henty VIII School, Coventry, England. *Publications:* Morning's At Seven; At the Height of th Moon; Shakespeare Trilogy: Sweet Will, The Cleopatra Boy, A House of Women; 12 other novels. *Contributions to:* Argosy; BBC. *Honours:* Palma d'Oro Italian Award; Goldene Leinwand, Germany; Observer SHort Stores Competition Award. *Memberships:* President, Nottingham Writer's Club; President, Derby Writers' Club. *Address:* 3 Cedar Court, Rareridge Lane, Bishops Waltham, Hants SO3 1DX, England.

MALZBERG Barry Norman, (Mike Barry, Claudine Dumas, Mel Johnson, Lee W Mason, Francine de Natale, K M O'Donnell, Gerrold Watkins), b. 1939, American. Mystery/Crime/Suspense; Historical/ Romance/Gothic; Science fiction/Fantasy; Freelance writer; author of many novels under various pseudonyms for Midwood, Oracle, Soft Cover Library and Traveler's Companion Series; Investigator, New York City Department of Welfare, and Reimbursement Agent, New York State Department of Mental Hygiene; Editor, Scott Meredith Literary Agency, New York City; Editor, Amazing and Fantastic magazines, 1968; Managing Editor, Escapade, 1968. *Publications include:* Science fiction: Chorale, 1978; (ed with Bill Pronzini), Shared Tomorrows: Collaboration in SF, 1979; The Who Who Loved the Midnight Lady (stories), 1980; (ed with Martin Greenberg), Neglected Vision, 1980; (ed with Martin Greenberg), The Science Fiction of Mark Clifton, 1980; The Cross of Fire, 1982; (ed with Martin Greenberg), The Science Fiction of Kris Neville, 1984; The Remaking of Sigmund Freud, 1985; (ed with others), Uncollected Stars, 1986; Suspense and romance: (as Mike Barry), Miami Marauder, 1974; (as Mike Barry), Peruvian Nightmare, 1974; (as Mike Barry), Detroit Massacre, 1975; (as Mike Barry), Harlem Showdown, 19795; (as Mike Barry), The Killing Run, 1975; (as Mike Barry), Philadelphia Blow-up, 1975; (as Mike Barry), Phoenix Inferno, 1975; (with Bill Pronzini), The Running of Beasts, 1976; (as Lee W Mason), Lady of a Thousand Sorrows, 1977; (with Bill Pronzini), Acts of Mercy, 1977; (with Bill Pronzini), Night Screams, 1979; (with Bill Pronzini), Prose Bowl, 1980; (ed with Bill Pronzini and Martin H Greenberg), The Arbor House Treasury of Horror and the Supernatural, 1981. *Address:* Box 61, Teaneck, NJ 07666, USA.

MAMLEYEV Yuri, b. 11 Dec 1931, Moscow, Russia. Professor; Writer. m. Farida Mamleyev, 14 Apr 1973. *Education:* Forestry Institute, Moscow, 1955. *Publications:* The Sky Above Hell, 1980; Chatouny, 1986; La Dernier Comedie, 1988; Der Morder aus dem Nichts, 1992; Iznanka Gogena, 1982; Zivaja Smert, 1986; Shatuny, 1987; Ytopi Moyu goloru, 1990; Golos iz Nichto, 1990; Vechnyi dom, 1991. *Contributions to:* Russian Literary Triquarterly; Apollon; Neue Russische

Literatur; Russica New York; Kontinent. *Memberships:* French PEN Centre. *Address:* 142 rue Legendre, 75017 Paris, France.

MANCHEL Frank, b. 1935, American. *Appointments:* Professor of English, College of Arts and Science, University of Vermont, Burlington; Film Reviewer and Critic-at-Large. *Publications:* Movies and How They are Made, When Pictures Begin to Move, The Lamancha Project, 1968; La Mancha Plus One, When Movies Began to Speak, 1969; Terrors of the Screen, La Mancha Plus Two, 1970; Cameras West, 1971; Yesterday's Clown: The Rise of Film Comedy, Film Study: A Resource Guide, 1973; An Album of Great Science Fiction Films, 1976; Women on the Hollywood Screen, 1977; The Talking Clowns, Gangsters on the Screen, 1978; The Box-Office Clowns, 1979; An Album of Great Sports Movies, 1980; An Album of Great Science Fiction Movies, 1982; An Album of Modern Horror Films, 1983; Film Study: An Analytical Bibliography 4 vols, 1990. *Address:* Department of English, Old Mill, College of Arts and Science, University of Vermont, Burlington, VT 05405, USA.

MANCHESTER William, b. 1 Apr 1922, Attleboro, Masschusetts, USA. Writer. m. 27 Mar 1948, 1 son, 2 daughters. *Education:* AB, LHD, University of Massachusetts; AM, University of Missouri, 1947; Graduate study, University of New Haven. *Appointments include:* Faculty, Wesleyan University, Connecticut, 1968-; Official historian, Kennedy assassination, 1963-67. *Publications include:* Disturber of the Peace, 1951; City of Anger, 1953; Shadow of the Monsoon, 1956; Beard the Lion, 1958; Rockefeller Family Portrait, 1959; The Long Gainer, 1962; Portrait of a President, 1962; Death of a President, 1967; Arms of Krupp, 1968; Glory & the Dream 1932-72, 1974; Controversy & Other Essays in Journalism, 1976; American Caesar, 1978; Goodbye Darkmen, 1980; Last Lion: Winston Spencer Churchill 1874-1932, Volume 1, Visions of Glory, 1983; One Brief Shining Moment: Remembering Kennedy, 1983; Last Lion: Winston Spencer Churchill 1932-1940, Volume 2, Alone, 1988; The Caged Lion, 1989; This is Our Time, 1989; A World Lit Only By Fire, 1992. *Honours include:* Hammarskjold International Prize, literature, 1966-67; Best Book, Foreign Affairs, Overseas Press Club, 1969; Literary Lion, New York Public Library, 1983; Frederick S. Troy Award, 1980; Abraham Lincoln Literary Award, 1985; Distinguished Public Service Award, Conncticut Bar Association, 1985; Various fellowships, honorary degrees. *Memberships include:* PEN; Authors Guild; Society of American Historians. *Address:* Olin Library, Wesleyan University, Middletown, Connecticut 06457, USA.

MANDEL Eli(as Wolf), b. 1922, Canadian. *Appointments:* Associate Professor 1957-63, Professor of English 1964-65, University of Alberta, Edmonton; Associate Professor 1965-66, Professor of English and Humanities 1967-1987 (retired), York University. *Publications:* Trio (with G Turnbull and P Webb), 1954; Fuseli Poems, 1960; Poetry 62 (ed with Jean-Guy Pilon), 1961; Black and Secret Man, 1964; Criticism: The Silent Speaking Words, 1966; An Idiot Joy, 1967; Irving Layton, 1969; Five Modern Canadian Poets (ed), 1970; English Poems of the Twentieth Century (ed with D Maxwell), Contexts of Canadian Criticism (ed), 1971; Poets of Contemporary Canada 1960-70 (ed), Eight More Canadian Poets (ed), 1972; Crusoe: Poems Selected and New, Stony Plain, 1973; Out of Place, Another Time, The Poems of Irving Layton (ed), 1977; Dreaming Backwards: Selected Poems, Life Sentence: Poems and Journals 1976-80, The Poetry of Irving Layton, 1981; The Family Romance, 1986; A Passion For Identity (ed with D Taras), 1986. *Address:* Department of English, York University, Downsview, Ontario, Canada M3J 1P3.

MANDEL Ernest, b. 1923, Belgian. *Appointment:* Professor, Free University of Brussels, Flemish Section, 1970-90. *Publications:* Marxist Economic Theory, 1962; Formation of the Economic Thought of Karl Marx, 1967; Contradictions of Imperialism: Europe vs America?, Workers Control Workers Councils Workers Self-

Management (ed), 1971; Late Capitalism, 1972; The Decline of the Dollar, 1973; From Stalinism to Eurocommunism, The Second Slump, 1978; Trotsky, Revolutionary Marxism Today, 1979; The Long Waves of Capitalist Development, 1980; Delighted Murder, 1984; The Meaning of the Second World War, 1986; Beyond Perostroika, 1989; Power and Money: The Marxist Theory of Bureaucracy, 1992. *Address:* 127 Rue Jos, Impens 1030, Brussels, Belgium.

MANDEL Oscar, b. 24 Aug 1926. Writer; Professor. *Education:* BA, NYC, 1947; MA, Columbia, 1948; PhD, Ohio State University, 1951. *Publications:* A Definition of Tragedy; The Theatre of Don Juan; Chi Po and The Sorcerer; The Gobble-Up Stories; Seven Comedies by Marivavy; Five Comedies of Medieval France; Others inc, The Land of Upside Down; Ariadne and French Classical Tragedy; Sigismund, Prince of Poland. *Memberships:* MLA; CAA. *Address:* Humanities and Social Sciences, Cal. Institute of Technology, Pasadena, CA 91125, USA.

MANEA Norman, b. 19 July 1936, Suceava, Romania. Writer. m. Josette Cella Manea, 28 June 1969. *Education:* Institute of Construction, Bucharest, Romania, 1959. *Publications:* Octobrie, Ora Opt; De Trenchcoat; Fenster zur Arbeiterklasse; On Clowns: The Dictator and the Artist; Plicul Negru; Others inc. Pe Contur; Primele Porti. *Contributions to:* Romania Literara; Contrapunct; 22; Akzente; Neue Rundschau; Lettre; Les Temps Modernes; Lettre International; Linea d'Ombra; The New Republic; Partizan Review; Comparative Criticism. *Honours:* S Guggenheim, MacArthur Award; DAAD Berliner Künstlerprogramm; Association of Bucharest Writers; Writers Union of Romania. *Memberships:* Romanian Writers Union; American PEN. *Literary Agent:* A. Wylie, 250 West 57th Str, Suite 2114, New York, NY 10107, USA. *Address:* Bard College, Annandale-on-Hudson, NY 12504, USA.

MANER Martin Wallace, b. 16 June 1946, Sturgis, Michigan, USA. Educator. m. Elizabeth Marie Noel Geer, 22 Apr 1982, 2 daughters. *Education:* BA, Occidental College, 1968; MA, University of Virginia, 1972; PhD, 1975. *Appointments:* Teaching assistant, University of Virginia, 1974-75; Lecturer, 1975-76; Assistant Professor, Wright State University, 1976-81; Associate Professor, 1981-89; Director of Graduate Studies, 1986-88; Professor, 1989-. *Publications:* The Philosophical Biographer. *Contributions to:* Genre; PBSA; Studies in English Literature 1500-1900; American Imago; English Studies; Philological Quarterly; Biography; Age of Johnson; English Literature in Transition; South Atlantic Review; Modern Philology. *Honours:* NCTE Award for Writing; Danforth career Teaching Fellowship. *Memberships:* Modern Language Association; American Society for 18th Century Studies; Johnson Society. *Address:* Department of English Language & Literature, Wright State University, Dayton, OH 45435, USA.

MANES Christopher S, b. 24 May 1957, Chicago, Illinois, USA. Author. 1 daughter. *Education:* BA, UCLA, 1979; MA, University of Wisconsin, 1981; JD, University of Calif, 1992. *Publications:* Green Rage; Technology & Mountain Thinking; Radical Environmentalism. *Contributions to:* Environmental Ethics; Orion Nature Quarterly; Penthouse; American Country; Wild Earth Journal; Lear's; Amicus Journal; Encylopeadia of the Environment. *Memberships:* Phi Beta Kappa. *Literary Agent:* Patricia Van der Leun. *Address:* 34542 Paseo Real, Cathedral City, CA 92234, USA.

MANFRED Frederick Feikema, (Feike Feikema), b. 6 Jan 1912, Doon, Iowa, USA. Writer. (div), 1 son, 2 daughters. *Education:* BA, Calvin College; Honorary Litt.D., Augustana College; Honorary DHL, Morningside College and Buena Vista College. *Appointments:* Writer in residence, Macalaster College, St Paul, 1949-51; University of South Dakota, 1968-82; Chair, Regional Heritage, Augustana College, Sioux Falls, Dakota, 1984. *Publications:* Author, 25 books including: This is the Year, 1947; Lord Grizzly, 1954; Conquering Horse, 1959; Wanderlust Trilogy, 1962; King of Spades, 1966; Milk of Wolves, 1976; the Manly-Hearted Woman, 1976; Green Earth, 1977; Sons of Adam, 1980; Winter Count II, 1978; Prime Fathers, 1988; Selected Letters of Frederick Manfred, 1988. *Contributions to:* New Republic; Esquire; Minnesota History; American Scholar; The New Republic. *Honours:* Grant in Aid, American Academy of Arts and Letters, 1945; Honorary Life Membership, Western Literature Association, 1967; Iowa's Most Distinguished Contribution to Literature, 1980. *Memberships:* Authors League; Society of Midland Writers; The Players. *Address:* Roundwind, RR3, Luverne, MN 56156, USA.

MANGUEL Alberto (Adrian), b. 13 Mar 1948, Buenos Aires, Argentina. div, 1 son, 2 daughters. *Education:* Colegio Nacional de Buenos Airs, 1961-67; Universidad de Buenos Aires, 1967-68; London University, 1976. *Appointments include:* Theatre Critic, CBLT Morning, 1984-86; Head of the Contemporary Reading Group, McGill Club, 1986-89; Contributing Editor, Saturday Night, Toronto, 1988; Contributing Editor, Grand Street, NY, 1991. *Publications:* The Oxford Book of Canadian Ghost stories; Black Water; Dark Arrows; The Dictionary of Imaginary Places; News from a Foreign Country Came (novel); Other Fires; The Gates of Paradise. *Contributions to:* Saturday Night; The Washington Post; New York Times; The Village Voice; The Ottawa Citizen; Destinations; Impulse; Exile; Rubicon; The Whig Standard. *Honours:* Juan Angel Fraboschi Gold Medal; Ricardo Monner Sans Gold Medal. *Address:* 45 Geneva Avenue, Toronto, Ontario, Canada M5A 2J9.

MANHEIM Werner, b. 17 Feb 1915, Poland. Pianist-Musicologist; Professor of Modern Foreign Languages. m. Eliane Housiaux, 18 Aug 1951, Chicago, USA. *Education:* BEd, University of Berlin, Germany; BMus, MMus, Cincinnati Conservatory of Music; Doctor of Fine Arts, Chicago Musical College. *Publications:* Monograph Martin Buber, 1974; Sonette von der Verganglichkeit, 1975; Klange der Nacht, 1977; Im Abendrot versunken, 1983; A Spark of Music, 1983; Wenn das Morgenrot aufbluht, 1985; Monograph: Albert Conradi, 1985; Schatten uber Blutentau, 1987; Noch flieben die Tranen, 1987; An Die Musik, 1988; Landschaft in Moll, 1988; In Nebel Gehüllt, 1989; Im Atem Der Nacht, 1990; Geheimnisvoll Das Licht, 1991; Herbstmusik, 1991; Many translations and contributions in anthologies. *Contributions to:* Encounter; Poet; Poesie und Prosa; Lyrikmappe; Ocarina; Nachrichten aus den Staaten; UNIO; World Poetry, Gauke Jahrbuch; Anthology on World Brotherhood and Peace. *Honours:* Medal studiosis humanitatis, Poetenmunze zum Halben Bogen; Certificate of Merit, Adolf-Bartels-Gedachtais Ehrung; Distinguished Service: United Poets Laureate, International, 1987; Golden Poet Awards, 1989, 1990. *Memberships:* International Circle of Authors; Plesse International; Board of German Senryu Center Regensburg Autorenkreis; International Contributing Editor, Ocarina; International Poets Academy, 1987; German Haiku Society; World Poetry Society; American Association of Teachers of German. *Address:* 2906 Hazelwood Avenue, Fort Wayne, IN 46805, USA.

MANHIRE Bill, b. 1946, New Zealander. *Appointments:* Editor, Amphedesma Press, Dunedin, 1971-75; Reader in English, Victoria University, Wellington. *Publications:* New Zealand Universities Arts Festival Yearbook 1969 (ed), 1969; Malady, 1970; The Elaboration, 1972; How to Take Off Your Clothes at the Picnic, 1977; New Zealand Listener Short Stories (ed), 1977, volume II, 1978; Dawn/Water, 1979; Zoetropes, 1981; Good Looks, 1982; Locating the Beloved and Other Stories, 1983; Zoetropes: Poems 1972-82, Some Other Country: New Zealand's Best Short Stories (ed with M McLeod), 1984; Maurice Gee, 1986. *Address:* Department of English, Victoria University of Wellington, Private Bag, Wellington, New Zealand.

MANKOWITZ Wolf, b. 7 Nov 1924, Bethnal Green, London, England. Writer; Theatrical Producer. m. Ann

Margaret Seligmann, 1944, 4 sons. *Education:* MA, Downing College, Cambridge. *Appointments:* Extensive work in journalism, Radio, TV, films and as a Theatrical Producer; Expert in English Ceramics; Hon. Consul to Republic of Panama in Dublin, 1971; Professor of Film and Dance, University of Mexico, 1982-89. *Publications:* Novels: Make Me an Offer, 1952; A Kid for Two Farthings, 1953; Laugh till You Cry, 1955; My Old Man's A Dustman, 1956; Cockatrice, 1963; The Biggest Pig in Barbados, 1965; Penguin Wolf Mankowitz, 1967; Raspberry Reich, 1978; Abracadabra!, 1980; The Devil in Texas, 1984; Gioconda, 1987; The Magic Cabinet of Professor Smucker, 1988; Exquisite Cadaver, 1989; A Night With Casanova, 1991. Short Stories: The Mendelman Fire, 1957; The Blue Arabian Nights, 1972; The Day of the Women and the Night of the Men, 1975; Plays: The Bespoke Overcoat and other Plays, 1955; Expresso Bongo, 1961; The Samson Riddle, 1972; Histories: The Portland Vase, 1953; Wedgwood, 1953; An Encyclopedia of English Pottery and Porcelain, 1957; Dickens of London (TV Script also), 1976; Biography: The Extraordinary Mr Poe, 1978, Mazeppa, 1981. *Honours:* Venice Film Festival Award, British Film Academy Award, Hollywood Oscar, 1955; British Film Academy Award, 1961; Critic's Prize, Cork International Film Festival, 1972; Grand Prix, Cannes, 1973. *Address:* Bridge House, Ahakista, Co. Cork, Ireland.

MANN Anthony Phillip, b. 7 Aug 1942, North Allerton, Yorkshire, England. Writer; Theatre Director. *Education:* BA Hons, English and Drama, Manchester University, England, 1966; MA Design and Directing, Humboldt State University, California, USa, 1969. *Publications:* Eye of the Queen, 1982; Master of Paxwax, 1986; Fall of the Families, 1987; Pioneers, 1988; Wulfsyarn - A Mosaic, 1990. *Memberships:* PEN New Zealand; SFWA; British Society of Dowsers. *Literary Agent:* Glenys Bean, Auckland, New Zealand. *Address:* 22 Bruce Avenue, Booklyn, Wellington, New Zealand.

MANN Christopher Michael Zithulele, b. 6 Apr 1948, Port Elizabeth, South Africa. Director; Writer. m. Julia Georgina Skeen, 10 Dec 1980. 1 son, 1 daughter. *Education:* BA, Witwatersrand University, Johannesburg, 1969; MA, Oxford University, England, 1973; MA, London University 1974. *Publications:* First Poems, 1977; A New Book of South African Verse, edited with Guy Butler, 1979; New Shades, 1982; Kites, 1990; Mann Alive, a video & book presentation of aural poems, 1991. *Contributions to:* Numerous magazines and journals. *Honours:* Rhodes Scholar; Newdigate Prize for Poetry, Oxford; Olive Schreiner Prize for Poetry, South African Academy of English; Hon D.Litt University of Duban-Westville. *Address:* Box 444, Bothas Hill, Natal, South Africa 3660.

MANN Francis Anthony, b. 10 June 1914, Bolton, England. Foreign Correspondent; Journalist; Author. m. Traute Eichwede, 8 Oct 1937, 2 daughters. *Education:* BA (Hons.) Oxford. *Appointments:* London Staff, Daily Telegraph, 1937; Thereafter Vienna, Berlin; chief Berlin Correspondent at outbreak of WWII, 1939; Copenhagen; interned on German invasion of Denmark, 1940; Correspondent, Germany, 1945-; Nuremberg Tribunal; Berlin, Dusseldorf, Bonn; Chief Correspondent for Mediterranean and Middle East, Rome, 1952; Chief European Correspondent, Sunday Telegraph, 1961; Chief Paris Correspondent, Daily Telegraph, 1965-73; Special Correspondent, numerous European and African Countries and USA; Retired from Daily Telegraph, 1973. *Publications:* Where God Laughed: The Sudan Today, 1954; Well Informed Circles, 1961; Zelezny: Portrait Sculpture 1917-70, 1970; Tiara (novel), 1973; Comeback : Germany, 1945-52, 1980. *Contributions to:* Daily Telegraph; Sunday Telegraph; Sunday Telegraph Magazine; Politiken; publications in USA, Canada, Italy, Germany; Articles mainly on Foreign affairs. *Honours:* Humboldt Medallist of German Academy, Munich; Rustichello da Pisa Prize for International Journalism, Italy. *Memberships:* Ex President, Anglo American Press Association, Paris. *Agent:* Clark Conway Gordon, London. *Address:* 58018 Porto Ercole, Prov. Grosseto, Italy.

MANN Jessica, British. *Publications:* A Charitable End, 1971; Mrs Knox's Profession, 1972; The Only Security, 1973; The Sticking Place, 1974; Captive Audience, 1975; The Eighth Deadly Sin, 1976; The Sting of Death, 1978; Funeral Sites, Deadlier Than the Male, 1981; No Man's Island, 1983; Grave Goods, 1984; A Kind of Healthy Grave, 1986; Death Beyond the Nile, 1988; Faith, Hope and Homicide, 1991; Telling Only Lies, 1992. *Contributions to:* Daily Telegraph; Sunday Telegraph; various magazines and journals. *Memberships:* Dectection Club; Society of Authors; PEN; Crime Writers Association. *Literary Agent:* Gregory & Radice, Riverside Studios, Crisp Road, London W6, England. *Address:* Lambessow, St Clement, Cornwall, England.

MANN Peter H(enry), b. 1926, British. *Appointments:* Research Worker, University of Liverpool, 1950-52; Research Fellow, University of Nottingham, 1952-54; Lecturer 1954-64, Senior Lecturer 1964-72, Reader in Sociology 1972-83, University of Sheffield; Director, Centre for Library and Information Management 1983-87, Director, Library and Information Statistics Unit 1987-90, Loughborough University. *Publications:* An Approach to Urban Sociology, 1965; Methods of Sociological Enquiry, 1968; Books and Reading (with J L Burgoyne), 1969; Books: Buyers and Borrowers, 1971; Students and Books, 1974; From Author to Reader: A Social Study of Books, 1982; A Readers' Guide to Fiction Authors, 1985. *Address:* 158 Station Road, Cropston, Leicestershire LE7 7HF, England.

MANNERS Alexandra. See: RUNDLE Anne.

MANNERS David, b. 23 Feb 1912, Zanesville, Ohio, USA. Public Relations Counsel. m. Ruth Ann Bauer, 22 Feb 1945, 4 sons. *Education:* BA, University of Cincinnati, 1933. *Appointments:* Editor, Popular Publications Inc., New York City, Standard Magazines, New York City; Editorial director, Universal Publishing Co., New York City; Editor, Hearst Magazines, New York City; Chairman, David X Manners, Co. Inc. *Publications:* Complete Book of Home Workshops, 1969; Memory of a Scream, 1946; Dead to the World, 1947; Handyman's Handbook, 1958; The Great Tool Emporium, 1980; Isn't It A Crime, 1947; original story, film, Humphrey Bogart in Conflict; 8 other non-fiction books. *Contributions to:* numerous journals and magazines including: Ellery Queen's Mystery Magazine; Alfred Hitchcock's Mystery Magazine; House Beautiful; Readers Digest. *Honours:* Silver Platter Award, Water Quality Association, 1979; Superior Achievement in Press Relations, 1982. *Memberships:* Authors Guild; Water Quality Research Council; Canadian Water Quality Association, Press Director. *Address:* 237 East Rocks Road, Norwalk, CT 06851, USA.

MANNING Marsha. See: GRIMSTEAD Hettie.

MANNING Paul, b. 22 Nov 1912, Pasadena, California, USA. Author. m. Louise Margaret Windels, 22 Mar 1947, 4 sons. *Education:* Alumnus Occidental College, Los Angeles, California. *Appointments:* Editor, Time-Life, New York City, 1937-38; Editor, Everyweek, 1939; Chief European Correspondent in London, Newspaper Enterprise Association and Scripps Howard Newspaper Group, 1939-42; Joined Edward R Murrow as CBS News Commentator from London, England, 1942. *Publications:* Martin Bormann, Nazi in Exile, 1986; The Silent War, KGB Against the West, 1987; Mr England, Biography of Winston Churchill, 1941; Years of War, 1988; Hirohito: The War Years, 1986, 1989; Was the only journalist to witness and broadcast both German surrender ceremonies at Reims, France and Japanese Surrender aboard the USS Missouri, Tokyo Bay. *Contributions to:* The New York Times; Reader's Digest; Saturday Evening Post; Contributor of articles in numerous journals including 8th Air Force News. *Honours:* Nominated 3 times for Pulitzer Prize, 1943, 1971, 1986; Special Citations, Secretary of War Robert Patterson and Secretary of Navy James Forrestal:

Nominated for Congressional Medal for War Coverage, 1947; Medal of Honour, American Biographical Institute, 1987. *Memberships:* The Eighth Air Force Historical Society; Fellow, International Biographical Association. *Address:* P.O. Box 3129, Jersey City, NJ 07302, USA.

MANNING Robert Joseph, b. 25 Dec 1919, Binghamton, New York, USA. Journalist. m. Margaret Marinda Raymond, 1944, 3 sons. *Appointments:* State Department and White House Correspondent, United Press, 1944-46; Chief UN Correspondent, United Press, 1946-49; Writer, Time Magazine, 1949-55, Senior Editor, 1955-58, Chief of London Bureau, Time, Life, Fortune, Sports Illustrated Magazines, 1958-61; Sunday Editor, New York Herald Tribune, 1961-62; Assistant Secretary of State for Public Affairs, US Dept. of State, 1962-64; Executive Editor, Atlantic Monthly, 1964-66; Editor in Chief, 1966-80; Vice President, Atlantic Monthly Co., 1966-80; Editor in Chief, Boston Publishing Co., 1981-. *Honours:* Nieman Fellow, Harvard Univesity, 1945-46; Fellow, Kennedy Institute of Politics, Harvard University, 1980. *Address:* 191 Commonwealth Avenue, Boston, MA 02116, USA.

MANNING Rosemary, (Mary Voyle), b. 1911, British. *Publications:* Green Smoke, 1957; Dragon in Danger, 1959; Look Stranger (in US as The Shape of Innocence), 1960; Dragon's Quest, 1961; The Chinese Garden, 1962; Man on a Tower, 1965; Heraldry, Boney Was a Warrior, 1966; A Grain of Sand: Selections from Blake (ed), 1967; The Rocking Horse, 1970; Railways and Railwaymen, 1977; A Dragon in the Harbour, 1980; Down by the Riverside, 1983; A Time and a Time, 1986. *Address:* 20 Lyndhurst Gardens, London NW3 5NR, England.

MANNING Stanley (Arthur), b. 1921, British. *Appointments:* Biology and Mathematics teacher in various English independent schools, 1948-70; with local Government services, Cambridge, 1970-77. *Publications:* The Right Way to Understand the Countryside, 1948; Broadland Naturalist: The Life of Arthur H. Patterson, 1948; Trees and Forests, 1964; Bakers and Bread, 1964; A Ladybird Book of Butterflies, Moths and Other Insects, 1965; Systematic Guide to Flowering Plants of the World, 1965; The Insect World, 1971; The Woodland World, 1972; The Naturalist in South-East England, 1974; Nature in East Anglia, 1976; Portrait of Essex, 1977; Portrait of Cambridgeshire, 1978; Nature in the West Country, 1979; Portrait of Broadland, 1980.

MANO D Keith, b. 12 Feb 1942, New York, USA. Novelist; Screenwriter. m. Laurie Kennedy, 18 July 1980, 2 sons. *Education:* BA, Columbia University; Kellett Fellow, Clare College, Cambridge, England; Woodrow Wilson Fellow, Columbia. *Appointments:* Cont. Editor: National Review, 1975-, Playboy, 1980-; Book Editor, Esquire, 1979-80. *Publications:* Bishop's Progress, 1968; Horn, 1969; War is Heaven!, 1970; The Death & Life of Harry Goth, 1971; The Proselytizer, 1972; Take Five, 1982; The Bridge, 1973; Resistance, play, 1984; Topless, novel, 1991. *Contributions to:* Regular Columnist for National Review Magazine; Playboy; Esquire; New York Times; People Magazine. *Honours:* MLA Award, Best Religious Novel, 1968; Playboy Award, Non-fiction, 1975; Literary Lion, New York Public Library, 1987. *Address:* c/o National Review Magazine, 150 E 35th St., New York, NY 10016, USA.

MANOFF Robert Karl, b. 23 Apr 1944, New York New York, USA. m. Katherine De Saulles Ellis, 3 Nov 1979, 1 son, 1 daughter, 2 stepchildren. *Education:* BA, Haverford College, 1968; MCP, Massachusetts Institute of Technology, 1973. *Career:* Senior Editor, More magazine, New York, 1977-78; Editor, Columbia Journalism Review, New York City, 1978-80; Managing Editor, Soho News, New York City, 1980-82; Managing Editor, Harper's, New York City, 1983-84; Director, Center for War, Peace and News Media, New York City, 1984-; Member, International board, Alderdinck

Foundation, The Hague, Netherlands, 1986-; Member, Board of Directors, Earthview Foundation. *Publications:* (ed with Michael Schudson) Reading the News (essays) 1987. *Contributions to:* Author of Media, a column for Progressive, 1985-87; Articles to periodicals, including Bulletin of the Atomic Scientists, Harper's International Herald Tribune, Nation, Journal of Communication, New York Times and Quill. *Honours:* Japanese Newspaper Publishers Association, 1983; Olive Branch Award for outstanding coverage of the Nuclear Arms Issue from Editor's Organizing Committee, 1984, for article The Silencer; Lowell Mellet Award (special citation) for Improving Journalism Throuogh Critical Evaluation from Pennsylvania State University School of Communications, 1987, for work of New York University's Center for War, Peace and the News Media; Joel R Seldin Award, contribution to Understanding the Psychology of International Conflict, 1988. *Memberships:* International Communications Association; American Association for the Advancement of Slavic Studies; Association for Education in Journalism and Mass Communication. *Literary Agent:* Diane Cleaver, Inc/Sanford J Greenburger Associates, New York. *Address:* Diane Cleaver, Inc/Sanford J Greenburger Associates, 55 Fifth Avenue, New York, NY 10003, USA.

MANOR Jason. See: **HALL Oakley Maxwell.**

MANSEL Philip Robert Rhys, b. 19 Oct 1951, Writer. *Education:* Eton College, 1964-69; Balliol Oxford, MA, 1974; University College, London, PhD, 1978. *Publications:* Louis XVII; The Eagle in Splendor; Sultans in Splendor; The Court of Fame; Le Charmer Re l'Europe; Charles Joseph de Lyne. *Contributions to:* History Today; Past & Present; Architectural Digest; Harpers and Queen; Spectator; International Heald Tribune. *Memberships:* PEN; Society d' Histoire de la Ristuaraton Association. *Literary Agent:* Murray Pollinger. *Address:* 13 Prince of Wales Terrace, London W8 5PG, England.

MANSER Martin Hugh, b. 11 Jan 1952. Reference Book Editor. m. Yusandra Tun, 1979, 1 son, 1 daughter. *Education:* BA, Honours, University of York, 1974; M.Phil., C.N.A.A., 1977. *Publications:* Concise Book of Bible Quotations, 1982; A Dictionary of Contemporary Idioms, 1983; A Dictionary of Everyday Idioms, 1983; Listening to God, 1984; Pocket Thesaurus of English Words, 1984; Children's Dictionary, 1984; Macmillan Student's Dictionary, 1985; Penguin Wordmaster Dictionary, 1987; Guiness Book of Words, 1988; Dictionary of Eponyms, 1988; Visual Dictionary, 1988; Bloomsbury Good Word Guide, 1988; Printing and Publishing Terms, 1988; Marketing Terms, 1988; Bible Promiser: Outlines for Christian Living, 1989; Oxford Learner's Pocket Dictionary, 2nd Edition, 1991; Guiness Book of Words, 1st Edition, 1991; Guiness Book of Words, 2nd Edition, 1991; Get to the Roots: A Dictionary of Word & Phrase Origins, 1992; The Lion Book of Bible Quotations, 1992; Oxford Learner's Pocket Dictionary with Illustrations, 1992; In Progress: Good Word Guide, 3rd Edition. *Address:* 102 Northern Road, Aylesbury, Bucks HP19 3QY, England.

MANTEL Hilary, b. 6 July 1952, Derbyshire, England. Author. m. Gerald McEwen, 23 Sept 1972. *Education:* London School Econs and Sheffield Univ; Bach, Jurisprudence, 1973. *Publications:* Every Day Is Mother's Day, 1985; Vacant Possession, 1986; Eight Months on Ghazzah Street, 1988; Fludd, 1989; A Place of Greater Safety, UK Edition, 1992, US Edition, 1993. *Contributions to:* Film column, Spectator, 1987-91; Book reviews to range of papers. *Honours:* Shiva Naipaul Prize, 1987; Winifred Holtby Prize, 1990; Cheltenham Festival Literary Prize, 1990; Southern Arts Literature Prize, 1991. *Memberships:* FRSL. *Literary Agent:* A M Heath, London, England. *Address:* c/o A M Heath and Co, 79 St Martin's Lane, London WC2, England.

MANWARING Randle (Gilbert), b. 3 May 1912, London, England. Poet; Author; Retired Company Director. m. Betty Violet Rout, 9 Aug 1941, 3 sons, 1

daughter. *Education:* Private Schools; MA, Keele, 1982; FSS: FPMI. *Publications:* Satires and Salvation, Poetry 1960; The Heart of This People, 1954; Christian Guide to Daily Work, 1963; Under the Magnolia Tree, Poetry, 1965; In a Time of Unbelief, Poetry, 1977; The Swifts of Maggiore, Poetry, 1981; The Run of The Downs, 1984; Collected Poems, Poetry, 1986; From Controversy to Coexistence, 1985; The Singing Church, 1990; Some Late Lark Siging, 1992. *Contributions to:* Anglo-Welsh Review; British Weekly; Poetry Review; Outposts; Envoi; This England; Country Life; The Field; SE Arts Review; John O'London's Weekly; Church of England Newspaper; The Lady; Pick; The Cricketer; Sussex Life; Limbo; Scrip; English; Oxford Magazine. *Memberships:* Downland Poets (Chairman 1981-83); Kent and Sussex Poetry Society; President of Society of Pension Consultants, 1968-70; Fellow of the Statistical Society. *Address:* Marbles Barn, Newick, East Sussex, BN8 4LG, England.

MAPES Mary A. *See:* **ELLISON Virginia Howell.**

MAPLE Eric William, b. 1915, British. *Appointments:* Consultant, Man, Myth and Magic, 1967-70; Freelance Writer, Broadcaster, and Lecturer on the occult and folklore. *Publications:* The Dark World of Witches, 1962; The Realm of Ghosts, 1964; The Domain of Devils, 1966; Magic, Medicine and Quackery, 1968; Superstition and the Superstitious, 1971; The Magic of Perfume, Witchcraft - The Story of Man's Quest for Psychic Power, 1973; The Ancient Art of Occult Healing, Incantations and Words of Power, 1974; Deadly Magic, 1976; Supernatural England, 1977; Ghosts: Monsters, 1978; The Secret Lore of Plants and Flowers, 1980; Old Wives' Tales, 1981. *Contributions to:* The Flower Arranger Magazine; Atlantis Magazine. *Address:* 52 Buckingham Road, Wanstead, London E11, England.

MAPLE Gordon Extra, b. 6 Aug 1932, Jersey, Channel Islands, England. Writer. m. Mabel Atkinson-Frayn, 29 Jan 1953, 1 son, 1 daughter. *Publications:* Plays: Limeade, 1963; Dog, 1967; Here's A Funny Thing, 1964; Elephant, 1968; Tortoise, 1974; Singo, 1975; Napoleon has Feet, 1977; Pink Circle, 1984; Chateau Schloss, 1985; Popeye, Theatr Hafren, 1985; Keeping in Front, memoirs, 1986; Sour Grapes (award), with Miles Whittier, 1986; Yet Another Falklands Film, 1987. *Honours:* Evening Standard Awards, 1964, 1973; Oscar nomination, 1964; SWEAT Award, 1986. *Memberships:* BPM, Oxford Yec; Fellow, Royal Society of Letters. *Literary Agent:* (Scripts), Fraser & Dunlop Ltd. *Address:* The Manor, Milton, near Banbury, Oxfordshire, England.

MAPLES Evelyn Lucille Palmer, b. 7 Feb 1919, Ponce de Leon, MO, USA. Editor/Author. m. William Eugene Maples, 23 Dec 1938, 2 sons, 1 daughter. *Education:* Southwest Missouri State University, 1936-38. *Appointments:* Proofreader/Contributing Author 1953, Copy Editor/Editor 1963-1981, Herald House. *Publications:* The Many Selves of Ann-Elizabeth, 1973; Norman Learns About the Sacraments, 1961; That Ye Love (poetry), 1971, 1973; Endnotes (poetry), 1989; Contributor to various journals. *Honour:* The Many Selves of Ann-Elizabeth, winner, Midwestern Books Competition, 1973. *Memberships:* Reorganised Church of Jesus Christ of Latter Day Saints, minister; American Association of Retired Persons; Scroll Club; Missouri Writers Guild. *Address:* Route 1, Box 137, Niangua, MO 65713, USA.

MARAS Karl. *See:* **BULMER Henry Kenneth.**

MARCEAU Felicien, b. 16 Sept 1913, Cortenberg, Belgium. Author; Playwright. *Education:* Law Faculty, Louvain University. *Publications:* Plays: L'Oeuf, 1956; La Bonne Soupe, 1958; La Preuve par Quatre, 1964; Madame Princesse, 1965; Le Babour, 1968; L'Homme en Question, 1973; A Nous de Jouer, 1979; Novels: Bergere Legere, 1953; Les Elans du Coeur, 1955; Creezy, 1969; Le Corps de mon Ennemi, 1975; Appelez-mois Mademoiselle, 1984; La Carriole du Pere Juniet,

1985; Les Passions partagees, 1987; Un Oiseau Dans Le Ciel, 1989; La Terrasse de L'ucrezia 1993; Memoirs: Les Anneés Courtes, 1968; Une insolente Liberte ou Les Aventures de Casanova, 1983. *Honours:* Prix Pellman du Theatre, 1954; Prix Interallie, 1955; Prix Goncourt, 1969; Grand Prix Prince Pierre de Monaco, 1974; Grand Prix du Theatre, 1975. *Membership:* Academie Francaise, 1975. *Address:* c/o Eds. Gallimard, 5 Rue Sebastien-Bottin, Paris 75007, France.

MARCH Jessica. *See:* **AFRICANO Lillian.**

MARCHANT Catherine. *See:* **COOKSON Catherine.**

MARCHBANKS Samuel. *See:* **DAVIES Robertson.**

MARCHI Jason J, b. 24 July 1960, New Britain, Connecticut, USA. Editor for Text Book Publisher. *Education:* BS, Geology, English, Northeastern University, Boston, Massachusetts, 1983. *Publications:* Treasures from the Shell Heap, 1990. *Contributions to:* Amazing Stories; Weird Tales Magazine; Pandora; Byline Magazine. *Honours:* Special Honourable Mention, 5th Place for poem Waiting For Father, Honourable Mention for Summerhood Child, Byline Any Theme Poetry Contest, 1989. *Memberships:* Science Fiction and Fantasy Writers of America; Horror Writers of America; Society of Children's Book Writers and Illustrators. *Address:* 29 Horseshoe Rd, Guilford, CT 06437, USA.

MARCUS Frank Ulrich, b. 30 June 1928, Breslau, Germany. Playwright; TV Critic. m. Jacqueline, 1951, 1 son, 2 daughters. *Appointments:* Theatre Critic, Sunday Telegraph, 1968-78. *Publications:* The Formation Dancers, 1964; The Killing of Sister George, 1965; The Window, 1968; Mrs Mouse Are You Within?, 1969; Notes on a Love Affair, 1972; Blank Pages, 1973; Beauty and the Beast, 1977; Blind Date, 1977. *Contributions include:* Behind the Scenes, 1972; Those Germans, 1973; On Theatre, 1974; London Magazine; Plays and Players; Dramatists' Quarterly; New York Times. *Address:* 8 Kirlegate, Meare, Glastonbury, Somerset BA6 9TA, England.

MARCUS Joanne. *See:* **ANDREWS Lucilla.**

MARCUS Steven, b. 13 Dec 1928. University Professor; Literary Critic. m. Dr Gertrud Lenzer, 20 Jan 1966. 1 son. *Education:* AB 1948, PhD 1961, Columbia University. *Publications:* Dickens: From Pickwick To Dombey, 1965; The Other Victorians, 1966; Engels, Manchester and The Working Class, 1974; Representations: Essays on Literature & Society, 1976; Doing Good (with David Rothman, et al), 1978; Freud and The Culture of Psychoanalysis, 1984. Editor: The Life & Work of Sigmund Freud (with Lionel Trilling), 1960; The World of Modern Fiction (2 volumes), 1968; The Continental Op, 1974. *Contributions to:* Partisan Review; Commentary; New York Review of Books; New Statesman; Times Literary Supplement; New York Times Book Review. *Honours:* Fulbright Fellowship, 1982-84; Guggenheim Fellowship, 1967-68; ACIS Award, 1961; Center for Advanced Study in The Behavioral Sciences, 1972-73; National Humanities Center, 1980-82; Honorary Visiting Professor, University of Leicester, England, 1968; DHL, Clark University, 1985. *Memberships:* American Academy of Arts & Sciences; Academy of Literary Studies; PEN. *Literary Agent:* Berenice Hoffman, New York City, USA. *Address:* Department of English & Comparative Literature, Columbia University, New York, NY 10027, USA.

MAREK Richard (William), b. 14 June 1933, New York, New York, USA. Company President, Writer. m. Margot Lynn Ravage, 17 June 1954, (dec 29 Sept 1987), 1 son, 1 daughter. *Education:* BA, Haverford College, 1955; MA, Columbia University, 1956. *Appointments:* Editor, McCalls, New York, 1958-64; Senior Editor,

Macmillan Publilshing Co, New York City, 1964-69; Associate Director, World Publishing, New York City, 1969-72; Editor-in-Chief, Dial Press, New York City, 1972-76; Publisher, Richard Marek Books, New York City, 1977-81; Publisher, St Martin's Press/Marek, New York City, 1981-85; President, E P Dutton, New York City, 1985-. *Publication:* Works of Genius, 1987. *Contributions to:* Various periodicals. *Membership:* Phi Beta Kappa. *Address:* 12 West 96th Street, New York, NY 10025, USA.

MARGENAU Henry, b. 1901, American. *Appointments:* Eugene Higgins Professor of Physics and Natural Philosophy Emeritus, Yale University, New Haven, 1969-; Executive Director, Center for Integrative Education, New Rochelle, NY, 1969-; Editor, Foundation of Physics, 1969-; Consultant to Argonne National Laboratory, Bureau of Standards, Avco Rand Corporation, Social Science Research Council, National Research Council, General Electric Company, Radiation Weapons Committee of the Lockhead Corporation. *Publications:* Foundations of Physics, 1936; Mathematics and Physics and Chemistry, volume I, 1943, volume II, 1964; Physics: Principles and Application, 1949, 1953; The Nature of Physical Reality, The Nature of Concepts, 1950; Open Vistas, 1961; Ethics and Science, 1964; The Scientist, 1965; Theory of Intermolecular Forces, 1969; Integrative Principles of Modern Thought, 1972; Physics and Philosophy: Selected Essays, 1978; Einstein's Space and Van Gogh's Sky, 1983; The Miracle of Existence, 1984. *Memberships:* Trustee, Connecticut College President, Philosophy of Science Association, 1954-64; Committee Atomic Age, World Council of Churches, 1955-57. *Address:* 173 Westwood Road, New Haven, CT 06515, USA.

MARGULIES James Howard, (Margulies), b. 8 Oct 1951, Brooklyn, New York, USA. Editorial Cartoonist. m. Marha Ann Golub, 21 May 1978, 1 son, 1 daughter. *Education:* BA, Carnegie-Mellon University, Pittsburgh. *Appointments:* Editorial Cartoonist, Journal Newspapers, 1980-84; Houston Post, 1984-90; The Record Hackensack, 1990-; Syndicated by King Features, North America Syndicate, 1991-. *Publications:* My Husband Is Not A Wimp. *Contributions to:* Cartoonist PRD Files; Target The Political Cartoon Quarterly. *Memberships:* Association of American Editorial Cartoonists. *Literary Agent:* Michael Doran, Southern Literary Agency. *Address:* The Record 150 River Street, Halkensack, NJ 07601, USA.

MARK Jan(et Marjorie), b. 1943, British. *Appointment:* Arts Council Writer Fellow, Oxford Polytechnic, 1982-84. *Publications:* Thunder and Lightning, 1976; Under the Autumn Garden, 1977; The Ennead, 1978; Divide and Rule, 1979; The Short Voyage of the Albert Ross, Nothing to be Afraid Of, 1980; Hairs in the Palm of the Hand, 1981; Aquarius, The Dead Letter Box, The Long Distance Poet, 1982; Handles, Feet, 1983; Childermas, 1984; At the Sign of the Dog and Rocket, Trouble Half-Way, 1985; Frankie's Hat, Out of the Oven, 1986; Zeno Was Here, 1987; Man in Motion, 1989, (Children's Fiction).

MARKANDAYA Kamala. *See:* **TAYLOR Kamala.**

MARKERT Joy, b. 8 May 1942, Tuttlingen, Germany. Author. *Publications:* Asyl, 1985; Malta, 1986. Also: Film scripts: Harlis, 1973; Der Letzte Schrei, 1975; Belcanto, 1977; Das Andere Lacheln, with R. Van Ackeren, 1978; Ich Fuhle Was, Was du Nicht Fuhlst, 1982. Theatre: Asyl, 1984; Erich's Tag, 1985. 30 radio plays, 1976-. *Contributions to:* German & Austrian radio stations; Various Literary Publications. *Honours:* German Film Prize, 1972; German Film Awards, 1977, 1980; Berlin Literary Awards, 1982, 1984. *Memberships:* German Authors Association; Berlin Film Makers. *Address:* Bredowstrasse 33, D-1000 Berlin, Federal Republic of Germany.

MARKFIELD Wallace (Arthur), b. 1926, American. *Appointment:* Film Critic, New Leader, NYC, 1954-55. *Publications:* To an Early Grave, 1964; Teitlebaum's Window, 1970; You Could Live if They Let You, 1974; Multiple Orgasms, 1977. *Address:* c/o Alfred A Knopf Incorporated, 201 East 50th Street, New York, NY 10022, USA.

MARKHAM Marion Margaret, b. 12 June 1929, Chicago, Illinois, USA. Writer. m. Robert Bailey Markham, 30 Dec 1955, 2 daughters. *Education:* BS, Northwestern Univ. *Appointments:* Contributing Editor, The Magazine Silver, 9 years. *Publications:* Escape From Velos, 1981; The Halloween Candy Mystery, 1982; The Christmas Present Mystery, 1984; The Thanksgiving Day Parade Mystery, 1986; The Birthday Party Mystery, 1989; The April Fools Day Mystery, 1991; The Valentines Day Mystery, 1992; Strangler's Hands, for radio; Works in anthologies: The Handy Man; Hurricane Five. *Contributions to:* Short fiction to: 'Teen; Alfred Hitchcock's Mysgtery Magazine; London Mystery Magazine; Mike Shayne Mystery Magazine; Buffalo Spree; Women's magazines, USA, UK, Australia; Over 200 articles to: Ford Times; Weight Watchers; Chicago Tribune; Others. *Memberships:* Board Member, Society of Midland Authors; Regional Vice-President, Mystery Writers of America; Authors Guild of America; Society of Children's Book Writers. *Literary Agent:* Alice Orr. *Address:* 2415 Newport Rd, Northbrook, IL 60062, USA.

MARKHAM Robert. *See:* **AMIS Kingsley.**

MARKO Katherine Dolores, b. 26 Nov 1913, Allentown, Pennsylvania, USA. Writer. m. Alex Marko, 20 Oct 1945, Allentown. 2 sons, 1 daughter. *Publications:* Juvenile books: The Sod Turners, 1970; God, When Will I Ever Belong? 1979; Whales, Giants of the Sea, 1980; How The Wind Blows, 1981; God, Why Did Dad Lose His Job? 1982; Away To Fundy Bay, 1985; Animals in Orbit, 1991; Hang Out The Flag, 1992. *Contributions to:* Children's Encyclopedia Britannica; Jack and Jill; Highlights for Children; Children's Playmate; Straight; Alive; The Friend; On The Line; Childlife; Christian Science Monitor; Young Catholic Messenger; Wow. *Honours:* Prizes for short stories, 1967; Child Study Association List, 1970; Honorable Mention for Manuscript at conference, 1973. *Memberships:* Children's Reading Round Table, Chicago; Society of Children's Book Writers, Los Angeles; Off Campus Writer's Workshop, Winnetka. *Address:* 471 Franklin Boulevard, Elgin, IL 60120, USA.

MARKS Paula Mitchell, b. 29 Mar 1951, El Dorado, Arkansas, USA. Professor; Writer. m. Alan Ned Marks, 2 Apr 1971, 1 daughter. *Education:* BA, St Edward's University, Austin, Texas, 1978; MA, 1980, PhD, American Civilisation, 1987, University of Texas, Austin. *Publications:* And Die in the West, 1989; Turn Your Eyes Toward Texas, 1989. *Contributions to:* American History Illustrated; Civil War Times; True West; Old West. *Honours:* T R Fehrenbach Texas History Award, 1990; Finalist, Non- Fiction Book Award, Western Writers of America, 1990; Certificate of Commendation, American Association for State and Local History, 1990; Kate Broocks Bates Texas History Research Award, 1991. *Memberships:* Authors Guild; Western Writers of America; Western History Association; Texas State Historical Association. *Literary Agent:* Robert Gottlieb. *Address:* St Edward's University, 3001 S Congress, Austin, TX 78704, USA.

MARKS Richard. *See:* **KRAUZER Steven M.**

MARKS Stanley, b. London, England. Writer. *Education:* Coursework (part) for Diploma of Journalism, Melbourne University, Australia. *Appointments:* Worked Australia and overseas (UK, USA, Canada) for various Australian newspapers including Melbourne Herald and Sydney Daily Telegraph; British Commonwealth Press Union Exchange, Montreal Star and Toronto Telegram, Canada; New York Correspondent for Australian journals; Publicity Supervisor, Australian Broadcasting Commission; Public Relations Manager, Australian Tourist Commission. *Publications:* God Gave You One Face, UK, 1964, Paperback, 1966; Fifty Years of Achievement (scouting in Victoria); Animal Olympics, 1972; St Kilda Sketchbook, 1980; Welcome to Australia, 1981; Malvern Sketchbook, 1982; Out and About in Melbourne, 1988; Children Everywhere series, 1970s-80s; Ketut Boy of Bali, republished in Danish, Hebrew and Braille; Graham Is An Aboriginal Boy, Rarua Lives In Papua New Guinea; Is She Fair Dinkum; Montague Mouse Who Sailed With Captain Cook And Discovered Australia (recorded). *Contributions to:* Features to newspapers and journals worldwide; Most Australian magazines and newspapers; MS Daily Cartoon Strip; M Australian and New Zealand papers. *Memberships:* Australian Society of Authors; Fellowship of Australian Writers; Australian Travel Writers Society. *Address:* 348 Bambra Road, South Caulfield, Melbourne, Victoria 3162, Australia.

MARLATT Daphne Shirley, b. 11 July 1942, Melbourne, Australia. Writer; Teacher. m. Gordon Alan Marlatt, 24 Aug 1963, (div 1970). 1 son. *Education:* BA, English & Creative Writing, University of British Columbia, 1964; MA, Comparative Literature, Indiana University, 1968. *Appointments:* Writer-in-Residence, University of Manitoba, Autumn, 1982; Writer-in-Residence, McMaster University & Hamilton Poetry Center, Jan. 1985; Writer-in-Residence, University of Alberta, 1985-86; Writer-in- Residence, Mount Royal College in Calgary, May 1987; Poetry Instructor, Creative Writing Department, University of British Columbia, 1989-90; Writer-in-residence, University of Western Ontario, 1993. *Publications:* Steveston, poetry, 1974; What Matters: Writing 1968-70, 1980; How Hug a Stone, 1983; Touch to my Tongue, 1984; Ana Historic, novel, 1988; Frames of a Story, 1968; Vancouver Poems, 1972; Our Lives, 1975; Zocalo, 1977; Net Work: Selected Writing, 1980; Double Negative (with Betsy Warland), 1988; Ghost Works, 1993. *Contributions to:* Origin III; Imago; The Capilano Review; How(ever) I; Ellipse; Line; Co-editor, Tessera. *Honours:* MacMillan Award; Brissenden Award; Canada Council Grants. *Memberships:* West Coast Women and Words Society (Board Member 1982-83, 1986-87); PEN; Writers' Union of Canada (second Vice-Chair 1987-88); Federation of BC Writers; The Writer's Union of Canada. *Address:* c/o 24 Byerson Avenue, Toronto, Ontario M5T 2P3.

MARLIN Brigid, b. 16 Jan 1936, Washington, District of Columbia, USA. Artist; Writer. div, 2 sons. *Education:* National College of Art, Dublin; Centre d'Art Sacre, Paris; Studio Andre L'Hote, Paris; Beaux-Arts Academie, Montreal; Art Students League, New York; Atelier of Ernest Fuchs, Vienna. *Publications:* Author: From East to West, 1989; Paintings in the Mische Technique, 1990; Illustrator: King Oberon's Forest (Hilda von Stockern); Celebration of Love (Mary O'Hara); Bright Sun, Dark Sun (Nickolas Fisk); The Leap from the Chess-Board (Charles Sprague). *Contributions to:* Several contributions to The Artists magazine; Article to: The Horn Book; The Lady; The Architect's Review. *Honours:* Special Children's Book Award, USA, 1958; 1st Prize, American Art Appreciation award, 1987; 1st Prize, Visions of the Future, New English Library. *Memberships:* PEN Club; Authors Club; Free Painters Society; President, Inscape Group; Co-Chairman, WIAC. *Address:* 15 Pixies Hill Cres, Hemel Hempstead, Herts HP1 2BU, England.

MARLOW Joyce, b. 1929, British. *Appointment:* Professional Actress, 1950-65. *Publications:* The Man with the Glove, 1964; A Time to Die, 1966; Billy Goes to War, 1967; The House on the Cliffs, 1968; The Peterloo Massacre, 1969; The Tolpuddle Martyrs, 1971; Captain Boycott and the Irish, The Life and Times of George I, 1973; The Uncrowned Queen of Ireland, 1975; Mr and Mrs Gladstone, Kings and Queens of Britain, 1977; Kessie, 1985, Sarah, 1987. *Address:* 109 St Albans Road, Sandridge, St Albans AL4 9LH, England.

MARLOWE Derek, b. 1938, British. *Publications:* Scarecrow, 1961; A Dandy in Aspic, 1966; The Memoirs of Venus Lackey, 1968; A Single Summer with LB: The Summer of 1816, 1969 (in US as S Single Summer with Lord B, 1970); Echoes of Celadine, 1970, as The Disappearance, 1977; Do You Remember England?, 1972; Somebody's Sister, 1974; Nightshade, 1975; The Rich Boy from Chicago, 1980; Nancy Astor, 1982.

MARLOWE Hugh. *See:* **PATTERSON Harry.**

MARLOWE Piers. *See:* **GRIBBLE Leonard (Reginald).**

MARLOWE Stephen, b. 7 Aug 1928, New York City, USA. Novelist. m. (1) Leigh Lang, 1950, (2) Ann Humbert, 1964, 2 daughters. *Education:* AB, College of William and Mary in Virginia, 1949. *Appointments:* Writer in Residence, College of William and Mary, 1974-75, 1980-81. *Publications:* The Death and Life of Miguel de Cervantes, 1991; The Memoirs of Christopher Columbus, 1987; Translation, 1976; Colossus, 1972; The Shining, 1962; Nineteen Fifty-Six, 1981; The Valkyrie Encounter, 1978; The Summit, 1970; Come Over Red Rover, 1968; Many works in genres of suspense and sci-fi. *Honours:* Prix Gutenberg du Livre, 1988. *Literary Agent:* Campbell Thompson and McLaughlin Ltd, London, England. *Address:* c/o Campbell Thomson & McLaughlin Ltd, 1 Kings Mews, London WC1N 2JA, England.

MARMARIADES Yannis, (Petros Haris), b. 26 Aug 1902, Athens, Greece. Writer. m. Fetula Haris, 14 Feb 1943. *Education:* Diploma, University of Athens Law School. *Publications:* The last night of the earth; Days of wrath; 10 volumes of short stories; 9 volumes of critical essays. *Contributions to:* Elefteria daily newspaper; Nea Hestid literary review. *Honours:* Recipient, several decorations of high degree. *Memberships:* Athens Academy; Society of Men of Letters; Union of Journalists. *Address:* Nikis 16, Athens 10557, Greece.

MAROWITZ Charles, b. 26 Jan 1934, New York City, USA. Writer. m. Jane Elizabeth Allsop, 14 Dec 1982. *Appointments include:* West Coast correspondent, London Times, 1980; Senior editor, Matzoh Ball Gazette; Theatre critic, LA Herald Examiner, 1989. *Publications:* The Method as Means, 1961; The Morowitz Hamlet, 1966; The Shrew, 1972; Artaud at Rodez, 1975; Confessions of a Counterfeit Critic, 1976; Marowitz Shakespeare, 1980; Act of Being, 1980; Sex Wars, 1983; Sherlock's Last Case, 1984; Prospero's Staff, 1986; Potboilers, play collection, 1986; Recycling Shakespeare, 1990; Burnt Bridges, 1991; Directing The Action, 1992. *Contributions to:* New York Times; Guardian, UK; Sun Times; Plays & Players; Encore; New Statesman, UK; Spectator, UK; Village Voice; LA Times; LA Herald Examiner; American Theatre Magazine. *Honours:* Order of Purple Sash, Denmark, 1965; Whitbread Award, drama, 1967; 1st prize, Louis B. Mayer Award, 1984. *Memberships:* Dramatists Guild; Writers Guild. *Literary Agent:* Gary Salt, c/o Paul Kohner Agency, California. *Address:* 3058 Sequit Drive, Malibu, California 90265, USA.

MARQUEZ Gabriel Garcia, b. 6 Mar 1928, Aracataca, Colombia. Writer. m. Mercedes Barcha, 1958, 2 sons. *Education:* Studied, University of Bogota, 1946-51. *Appointments:* Journalist in Colombia and abroad, including several years in Paris; originally writer of short stories for magazines and newspapers. Well-known social activist. Recently forced to flee his native Colombia for alleged involvement with Colombian guerrillas. Maintains homes in Paris and Mexico City. *Publications:* One Hundred Years of Solitude, published in US 1970; The Autumn of the Patriarch, 1976; Chronicle of a Death Foretold, 1982; (with P. Mendoza) Fragrance of Guava, 1983; Love in the Time of Cholera, 1988, (Fiction); Claudestine in Chile, 1989, (Non-Fiction); The General in His Labyrinth, 1991. *Honours:*

1982 Nobel Prize for Literature; Love in the Time of Cholera remained on both the New York Times and Publishers Weekly bestseller lists for more than six months and was awarded the Los Angeles Times Book Prize for fiction. *Address:* Agencia Literaria Carmen Balcelos, Diagonal 580, Barcelona, Spain.

MARQUIS Edward Frank, (Max Marquis), b. Ilford, Essex, England. Author. m. (1) 1 son, (2) Yvonne Cavenne, 1953. *Appointments:* News Writer and Reader, RDF French Radio, 1952; Sub Editor and Columnist: Continental Daily Mail, 1952, Evening News, London, 1955; Chief British Correspondent, L'Equipe, Paris, 1970. *Publications:* Sir Alf Ramsey: Anatomy of a Football Manager, 1970; The Traitor Machine, 1980; Bodyguard to Charles, 1989; Vegeance, 1990; Deadly Doctors, 1992; The Caretakers 1975; A Matter of Life, 1976; The Shadowed Heart, 1978. *Literary Agent:* Rupert Crew Ltd. *Address:* c/o Rupert Crew Ltd, 1A Kings Mews, London WC1N 2JA, England.

MARQUIS Max. *See:* **MARQUIS Edward Frank.**

MARR William W, b. 3 Sept 1936, China. Engineer. m. Jane J Liu, 22 Sept 1962, 2 sons. *Education:* MS, Marquette University, 1963; PhD, University of Wisconsin, 1969. *Appointments:* Editing Advisor, Li Poetry Magazine, 1985, New Mainland Poetry Magazine, 1992; Editor, Chinese Poets, 1993. *Publications:* In the Windy City, 1975; Selected Poems, 1983; White Horse, 1984; Selected Poems of Fei Ma, 1985; The Galloping Hoofs, 1986; Road, 1987; Selected Short Poems, 1991; Fly! Spirit, 1992. *Contributions to:* Li Poetry Magazine; Literary Taiwan; First Line; New Mainland; Unitas Literary Magazine; Hong Kong Literature Monthly; Renmin Wenxue; Chinese Poets. *Honours:* Wu Cho Liu Poetry Award, 1982; Li Poetry Translation Award, 1982; Li Poetry Award, 1984. *Memberships:* Li Poetry Society; First Line Poetry Society; Chinese Artists' Association of North America; Illinois State Poetry Society; The American Society of Mechanical Engineers. *Address:* 737 Ridgeview Street, Downers Grove, IL 60516, USA.

MARRECO Anne. *See:* **ACLAND Alice.**

MARSDEN Peter Richard Valentine, b. 29 Apr 1940, Twickenham. Archaeologist. m. Frances Elizabeth Mager, 7 Apr 1979, 2 sons, 1 daughter. *Education:* Frien Barnet Grammar School 1952-54; Kilburn Polytechnic 1956-59; Currently studying for Higher Degree, Oxford University. *Publications:* The Wreck of the Amsterdam, 1974 (British, Dutch and USA editions) revised 1985; Roman London, 1980; The Marsden Family of Paythorne and Nelson (privately published) 1981; The Roman Forum Site in London, 1987; Londinium, 1971; The Historic Shipwrecks of South-East England, 1987. *Contributions to:* Geographical Magazine; The Independent; The Times Literary Supplement; Illustrated London News; The Telegraph Colour Magazine; various academic journals. *Memberships:* Fellow, Society of Antiquaries of London; Institute of Field Archaeologists. *Address:* 21 Meadow Lane, Lindfield, West Sussex RH16 2RJ, England.

MARSDEN Philip John, b. 11 May 1961, Bristol, England. Writer. *Publication:* A Far Country: Travels in Ethiopia, 1990. *Address:* Church Farm, Burrington, Bristol BS18 7AD, England.

MARSH J E. *See:* **MARSHALL Evelyn.**

MARSH Jean. *See:* **MARSHALL Evelyn.**

MARSHALL Evelyn, (Lesley Bourne, J E Marsh, Jean Marsh), b. 2 Dec 1897, Pershore, England. Journalist; Author; Broadcaster. m. 26 June, 1917, Lt Gerald Eric Marshall, 1 son, 1 daughter. *Education:* Halesowen Grammar School; Oxford Junior and Senior Student Teacher Course (during WWI). *Literary*

Appointments: Contract as serial and ghost writer to Amalgamted Press Ltd of Farrington Street, London; Broadcaster and script writer, BBC Midland Region, during WWII. *Publications include:* The Shore House Mystery, 1931; Murder Next Door, 1933; Death Stalks the Bride, 1943; On Trail of the Albatross 1950; Valley of Silent Sound; Sand Against the Wind; Identity Unwanted 1951; Death Visits the Circus, 1953; Pattern is Murder, 1954; Death Among the Stars 1954; Death at Peak Hour, 1957; numerous Romances to the present day. *Contributions to:* Numerous magazines and journals, including Woman's Story, Woman's Weekly. *Memberships:* Society of Authors; Broadcasting Group. *Literary Agent:* Miss Shirley Russell, Rupert Crew Ltd, Gray's Inn Road, London. *Address:* Bewdley, Worcestershire, England.

MARSHALL Jack, b. 1937, American. *Publications:* The Darkest Continent, 1967; Bearings, 1970; Floats, 1972; Bits of Thirst, 1974; Bits of Thirst and Other Poems and Translations, 1976; Arriving on the Playing Fields of Paradise, 1983; Arabian Nights, 1986. *Address:* 1056 Treat Avenue, San Francisco, CA 94110, USA.

MARSHALL James Vance. *See:* **PAYNE Donald Gordon.**

MARSHALL Joanne. *See:* **RUNDLE Anne.**

MARSHALL Owen. *See:* **JONES Owen Marshall.**

MARSHALL Paule, b. 1929, American. *Appointment:* Staff Writer, Our World Magazine, 1953-56. *Publications:* Brown Girl, Brownstones, 1959; Soul Clap Hands and Sing, 1961; The Chosen Place, The Timeless People, 1969; Reena and Other Stories, Praisesong for the Widow, 1983. *Address:* 407 Central Park West, New York, NY 10025, USA.

MARSHALL Rosalind Kay, b. Dysart, Scotland. Historian. *Education:* MA, Dip Ed, PhD, FRSL, FSA Scot, Edinburgh University, Scotland. *Literary Appointments:* Associate Editor of The Review of Scottish Culture, 1983-. *Publications:* The Days of Duchess Anne, 1973; Mary of Guise, 1977; Virgins and Viragos: A History of Women in Scotland, 1983; Queen of Scots, 1986; Bonnie Prince Charlie, 1988; Henrietta Maria, 1990; Elizabeth I, 1992. *Contributions to:* Various publications on social history. *Honours:* Hume Brown Senior Prize for PhD Thesis, also Jeremiah Dalziel Prize, 1970; Scottish Arts council New Writing Award, 1973; Fellow of the Royal Society of Literature, 1974. *Memberships:* Many historical societies. *Address:* Scottish National Portrait Gallery, Edinburgh, Scotland.

MARSHALL Ruth, b. 13 Dec 1961, Singapore. Reporter. *Education:* MSc, Economics, Distinction, London School of Economics. *Appointment:* Paris Correspondent, Newsweek, 1985-. *Contributions to:* Newsweek and other magazines and newspapers. *Honour:* Polk Award, foreign reporting, 1987. *Membership:* Anglo Press Association, Paris. *Address:* Newsweek, 162 rue du Faubourg St Honore, 75008 Paris, France.

MARSHALL Tom, b. 9 Apr 1938, Niagara Falls, Ontario, Canada. Professor of English. *Education:* BA, history, 1961; MA, English, 1965, Queens University, Kingston, Ontario, Canada. *Appointments:* Professor of English, Queen's University, Kingston; Editor of Quarry, 1965-66, 1968-70; Poetry Editor, Canadian Forum, 1973-78. *Publications:* The Beast With Three Backs (poems), 1965; The Silences of Fire (poems), 1969; A M Klein (criticism), 1970; The Psychic Mariner: A Reading of the Poems of D H Lawrence (criticism), 1970; Magic Water (poems), 1971; Fourteen Stories High (fiction), 1971; The Earth-Book (poems), 1974; The White City (poems), 1976; Rosemary Goal (fiction), 1978; Harsh and Lovely Land: the major Canadian poets and the making of a Canadian tradition (criticism), 1979;

The Elements: Poems 1960-1975, 1980; Playing With Fire (poems), 1984; Dance of the Particles (poems), 1984; Glass Houses (fiction), 1985; Adele at the End of the Day (fiction), 1987; Voices on the Brink (fiction), 1989; Changelings, (fiction), 1991; Ghost Safari (poems), 1991; Goddess Disclosing (Fiction), 1992; Multiple Exposures, Promised Lands (criticism), 1992. *Contributions to:* Various journals. *Memberships:* Writer's Union of Canada, League of Canadian Poets, PEN. *Address:* Department of English, Queen's University, Kingston, Ontario, Canada K7L 3N6.

MARSTEN Richard. *See:* **LOMBINO Salvatore A.**

MARTELLARO Joseph A., b. 20 July 1924, Rockford, IL, USA. Professor of Economics. m. Loretta W. Kowalski, 25 Aug 1945, 3 sons. *Education:* AB, 1956; MA, 1958, PhD, 1962, University of Notre Dame, US Army Command and General Staff School; Commissioned in US Army, Direct Appointment to 1st Lieutenant, 1959, total service eight and a half years, highest rank: Major, Awarded Honorary Retirement as Major; Associate Dean, Full Dean Northern Illinois University Graduate School, 1969-73; Corporation President & Board Chairman, 11 years. *Publications:* Economic Development in Southern Italy, 1956-60; Perspectives for Teachers of Latin American Culture, (co-author), 1970; Essays in Honour of Tullio Bagiotti, 1985; Economic Reform in China, Hungary and the USSR, 1989. *Contributions:* Over 50 articles in professional journals; Newspaper editorialist; Poetry. *Honours:* Research Scholar, International Centre of Asian Research, Hong Kong; Excellence in Teaching Award, Northern Illinois University, 1978, 1993; 4 Fulbright Grants; Nominated for Fulbright to Yugoslavia, 1992; Special Chair, Professor of Economics, National Taiwan University, 1988. *Memberships:* International Editorial Board, Journal of Economics and International Relations; Comparative Economics Association; European Association of Comparative Economics; Midwest Economics Society; Knights of Columbus (3rd and 4th Degree); American Legion; General Clair Chennault Post; ROC; Disabled American Veterans; Charter Member of Battle of Normandy Foundation appointed on Council for Planning 50th Anniversary of Battle of Normandy. *Address:* 1702 Margaret Lane, DeKalb, IL 60115, USA.

MARTER Joan M, b. 13 Aug 1946, Philadelphia, Pennsylvania, USA, Professor of Art History. *Education:* AB magna cum laude, Temple University, 1968; MA, 1970, PhD, 1974, University of Delaware. *Publications:* Vanguard American Sculpture, 1913-1939, 1979; José de Rivera, 1980; Design in America: The Cranbrook Vision, 1983; Alexander Calder, 1991. *Contributions to:* Archives of American Art Journal; Art Journal; Arts Magazine; American Art Journal; Sculpture Magazine; Tema Celeste; Women's Studies Quarterly. *Honours:* Charles F Montgomery Prize, Decorative Arts Society, Society of Architectural Historians, 1984; George Wittenborn Award, Art Libraries Society of North America, 1985. *Memberships:* International Association of Art Critics; College Art Association of America; Women's Caucus for Art. *Address:* Department of Art History, Voorhees Hall, Rutgers University, New Brunswick, NJ 08903, USA.

MARTI Rene, b. 7 Nov 1926, Frauenfeld, Switzerland. Freelance Author and Journalist. m. Elisabeth Wahrenberger, 13 Oct 1955, 1 son, 2 daughter. *Education:* Commercial School, Lausanne; Cambridge Proficiency class, Polytechnic School, London; Eidgenossisches Fahigkeitszeugnis fur kaufmanniscen Abschluss (commercial qualification); Diploma, French and English; Further study, Neuchatel and Zurich; Literature Science, Philosophy, Konstanz University, 9 terms. *Publications:* Das unausloschliche Licht, 1954, French translation as La lumiere qui ne s'eteint point, 1975; Die funf Unbekannten, lyric poetry, stories (main author), 1970; Stories: Der unsichtbare Kreis, 1975; Stationen, 1986; Poetry: Dom des Herzens, 1967; Weg an Weg, 1979; Besuche dich in der Natur (with Lili Keller), 1983; Gedichte zum Verschenken (with Lili Keller), 1984; Die verbrannten Schreie (9 of them set to music and recorded), 1989; Gib allem ein bisschen Zeit, haikus, 1993. *Contributions to:* Over 90 anthologies; Poems translated to English, French, Persian, Polish; Regular books reviews, English and French grammars, radio, several poems set to music; Numerous newspapers and periodicals. *Honours:* AWMM Lyric Poetry Prize, Luxembourg, 1985; Publication grants: Rosicrucians, Baden-Baden, 1984; Thurgau Canton, 1986; Cultura- Stiftung, Weinfelden, 1986. *Memberships:* Board, Swiss-German PEN Centre; PEN Centre of German-Speaking Writers Abroad, London; Internationaler Bodensee Club, Board Member, Arbitration Committee; Schweiz-Schriftsteller-Verband; Freier Deutscher Autorenverband; Berner Schriftsteller Verein; Zurcher Schriftstellerverband, Board Member; Founder Member, Interessengemeinschaft deutschsprachiger Autoren, Board Vice-Chairman, Committee Member; Regensburger Schriftstellergruppe international; TURM-Bund, Innsbruck. *Address:* Haus am Herterberg, Haldenstr 5, CH-8500 Frauenfeld, Switzerland.

MARTIN Alexander George, b. 8 Nov 1953, Baltimore, USA. Writer. m. 28 July 1979, 2 sons. *Education:* Winchester College, 1967-71; MA English, Cambridge University, 1972-75; Diploma in Theatre, University College Cardiff, 1975-76. *Publications:* Boris the Tomato, 1984; Snow on the Stinker, 1988; The General Interruptor, 1989; Modern Poetry, 1990; Modern Short Stories, 1991. *Honours:* Betty Trask Award, 1988. *Memberships:* Society of Authors. *Literary Agent:* David Higham Associates, London. *Address:* c/o D Higham Associates, 5-8 Lower John Street, London W1R 4HA, England.

MARTIN David Alfred, b. 30 June 1929, London, England. Professor. m. 30 June 1962, 3 sons, 1 daughter. *Education:* Westminster College, Oxford, 1950-52, Teachers Diploma; London External Degree (BSc) 1959, PhD (London) 1964. *Publications:* Pacifism, 1966; A General Theory of Secularization, 1978; Dilemmas of Contemporary Religion, 1979; (Ed)Cries for Cranmer and King James (PN Review 13) 1979; The Breaking of the Image, 1980; Divinity in a Grain of Bread, 1989; Tongues of Fire, 1990. *Contributor to:* Regular contributor to The Times Supplements. *Address:* Cripplegate Cottage, 174 St John's Road, Woking, Surrey, England.

MARTIN David, b. 1915, British. Writer; Author. *Publications:* Battlefields and Girls, 1942; Tiger Bay, 1946; The Shoes Men Walk In, 1946; The Shepherd and the Hunter, 1946; The Stones of Bombay, 1949; Poems, 1938/58, 1958; Spiegel the Cat, 1961; The Young Wife, 1962; The Hero of Too (in U.S. as The Hero of the Town), 1965; The King Between, (in U.S. as The Littlest Neutral), 1966; The Gift, 1966; The Idealist, 1968; Where a Man Belongs, 1969; On the Road to Sydney, 1970; Hughie, 1971; Frank and Francesca, 1972; Gary, 1972; The Chinese Boy, 1974; The Cabby's Daughter, 1975; Mister P and His Remarkable Flight, 1975; The Devilish Mystery of the Flying Man, 1977; The Man in the Red Turban, 1978; The Mermaid Attack, 1979; Peppino Says Goodbye, 1980; I Rhyme My Time, 1980; Armed Neutrality for Australia, 1984.

MARTIN F(rancis) X(avier), b. 1922, Irish. *Appointments:* Assistant Lecturer 1959-62, Professor of Medieval History 1962-, University College, National University of Ireland, Dublin; Chairman, Council of Trustees, National Library of Ireland, 1977-. *Publications:* The Problem of Giles of Viterbo 1469-1532, 1960; Medieval Studies presented to Aubrey Gwynn (ed with J A Watt and J B Morrall), 1961; Friar Nugent: A Study of Francis Lavalin Nugent 1569-1635, 1962; The Irish Volunteers 1913-1915 (ed), 1963; The Howth Gun-running 1914: Recollections and Documents (ed), 1964; 1916 and University College, Dublin (ed), 1966; The Course of Irish History (ed with T W Moody), 1967, 1984; Leaders and Men of the Easter Rising, Dublin 1916 (ed), The 1916 Rising - Myth Fact and Mystery, 1967; The Scholar Revolutionary: Eoin MacNeil 1867-1945 and the making of the New Ireland (ed with F J Byrne), 1973; A New History of Ireland (ed with T W Moody and F J Byrne), volume III, 1974, volume VIII, 1982, volume IX 1984, volume IV, 1986, volume II, 1987, volume V, 1989; No Hero in the House: The Coming of the Normans to Ireland, 1977; The Conquest of Ireland by Giraldus Cambrensis (ed with A B Scott), 1978; Lambert Simnel: The Crowning of a King at Dublin, 24th May 1487, 1988. *Address:* Department of Medieval History, University College, Dublin 4, Ireland.

MARTIN Janette Gould, b. 25 Mar 1957, Jamestown, New York, USA. Freelance Writer; College Instructor. m. Rick Allen Martin, 12 Aug 1978, 1 son. *Education:* BA, 1980, MA, 1982, State University of New York, Fredonia; PhD Candidate, State University of New York, Buffalo. *Appointment:* Judge, JCC Literary Festival. *Publications:* Visual Puns, printed in Newspaper on weekly basis. *Contributions to:* The Old House Journal; Art Times; Seek; The Volunteer Fireman; The Abbey; New Poetry; The Haven; Aevum; Encore; People in Action; American Painting. *Honours:* Kentucky State Poetry Society Poetry Award, 1980; Essay Award, The Humanist, 1981,1983; National Federation of State Poetry Societies, Poetry, 1982. *Memberships:* International Save the Pun Foundation; Authors Guild; Society for Children's Book Writers; Northern New York Women Writers Alliance; International Women's Writing Guild; others. *Address:* RD No 3, Box 173, Forest Avenue Ext., Jamestown, NY 14701, USA.

MARTIN Laurence Woodward, b. 30 July 1928, United Kingdom. Professor. m. Betty Parnall, 19 Aug 1951, 1 son, 1 daughter. *Education:* Christ's College, Cambridge 1945-48, BA, History 1948, MA 1952; Yale University 1950-55, MA, International Politics, 1951, PhD, with distinction 1955. *Publications:* The Anglo-American Tradition in Foreign Affairs (with Arnold Wolfers) 1956; Peace Without Victory, 1958; The Sea in Modern Strategy, 1966; Arms and Strategy, 1973; Retreat From Empire (joint author) 1973; Strategic Thought in the Nuclear Age (Editor/Contributor) 1979; The Two- Edged Sword: Armed Force in the Modern World, 1982; Before the Day After, 1985; The Changing Face of Nuclear Warfare, 1987. *Honours:* Fellow, King's College, London, 1983-; Honorary Professor, University of Wales, 1985-. *Memberships:* International Institute of Strategic Studies; European Strategy Group. *Address:* The Royal Institute of International Affairs, 10 St James's Square, London SW1Y 4LE, England.

MARTIN Lori Anne, b. 15 Sept 1958, New York City, USA. Author; Advertising Copywriter. m. Flavian Cresci, 25 May 1986. *Education:* BA, English Literature, New York University, 1980. *Publications:* The Darkling Hills, 1986; Sequel schedule for publication, 1988; German Edition, The Darkling Hills, 1988. *Membership:* Author's Guild. *Literary Agent:* Henry Morrison. *Address:* c/o Henry Morrison, PO Box 235, Bedford Hills, NY 10507, USA.

MARTIN (Roy) Peter, (James Melville), b. 5 Jan 1931, London, England. Author. 2 sons. *Education:* BA, Philosophy, 1953, MA, 1956, Birkbeck College, London University; Tubingen University, Germany, 1958-59. *Appointments:* Crime Fiction Reviewer, Hampstead and Highgate Express, 1983-; Occasional Reviewer, Times Literary Supplement. *Publications:* The Superintendent Otani mysteries, 13 in all; The Imperial Way, 1986; A Tarnished Phoenix, 1990. *Honours:* MBE, 1970. *Memberships:* FRSA; Crime Writers Association; Mystery Writers of America; The Detection Club. *Literary Agent:* Curtis Brown, London, England. *Address:* c/o Curtis Brown, 162-168 Regent Street, London W1R 5TB, England.

MARTIN Philip (John Talbot), b. 28 Mar 1931, Melbourne, Australia. Poet; Teacher; Translator; Critic; Radio Broadcaster. *Education:* BA, University of Melbourne. *Appointments include:* English tutor, University of Melbourne, 1960-62; Lecturer, Australian National University, 1963; Lecturer, Senior Lecturer, English, Monash University, 1964-; Visiting Lecturer/Professor, University of Amsterdam 1967, Venice 1976, Carleton College, Northfield, Minnesota, USA 1983. *Publications:* Voice Unaccompanied, poems, 1970; Shakespeare's Sonnets: Self, Love & Art, criticism, 1972; A Bone Flute, poems, 1974; Translation, Lars Gustafsson: Selected Poems, 1982; A Flag for the Wind, poems, 1982; New & Selected Poems, 1988. Also co-editor, Directory of Australian Poets, 1980. *Contributions to:* Australian journals: Age; Australian; Helix; Meanjin; Overland; Scripsi. USA: Carleton Miscellany; Hiram Poetry Journal; Poetry Chicago. UK: Ambit; Stand; Times Literary Supplement. European: Lyrikvannen; New Hungarian Quarterly. Also represented in many anthologies, from Australian Poetry 1957, to Anthology of Australian Religious Poetry, & New Oxford Book of Australian Verse, 1986. Poems & Features Broadcast, Australian Brodcasting Corporation; Poems on BBC, US Public Radio. *Memberships include:* Amnesty; PEN; Past chairperson, Poets Union of Australia; Fellowship of Australian Writers; Association for Study of Australian Literature; American Association of Australian Literary Studies. *Address:* 25/9 Nicholson Street, Balmain 2041, Australia.

MARTIN Ralph Guy, b. 4 Mar 1920, Chicago, USA. Writer. m. Marjorie Jean Pastel, 17 June 1944, 1 son, 2 daughters. *Education:* BJ, University of Missouri, 1941. *Appointments:* Reporter, Managing Editor, Box elder News Journal, Brigham, Utah, 1940-41; Associate Editor, New Republic Magazine, 1945-48; Associate Editor, Newsweek Magazine, 1953-55; Executive Editor, House Beautiful magazine, 1955-57; Publisher, President, Bandwagon Inc. *Publications:* Boy from Nebraska, 1946; The Best is None Too Good, 1948; Ballots and Bandwagons: Five Key Conventions since 1900, 1964; Skin deep, 1964; The Bosses, 1964; President from Missouri, 1964; Wizard of Wall Street, 1965; World War II, Pearl Harbor to V-J Day, 1966; The GI War, 1967; A Man for All People, 1968; Jennie: The Life of Lady Randolph Churchill, The Romantic Years, 1969, Volume II, The Dramatic Years, 1971; Lincoln Centre for the Performing Arts, 1971; The Woman He Loved: The Story of the Duke and Duchess of Windsor, 1974; Cissy, The Extraordinary Life of Eleanor Medill Patterson, 1979; A Hero for Our Times, An Intimate Study of the Kennedy Years, 1983; Charles and Diana, 1985; Golda: Golda Meir, The Romantic Years, 1988; Henry & Clare: An Intimate Portrait of the Luces, 1990. Co-author: Eleanor Roosevelt: Her Life in Pictures, 1958; The Human Side of FDR, 1960; Front Runner, Dark Horse, 1960; Money Money Money, 1960; Man of Destiny: Charles DeGaulle, 1961; Man of the Century: Winston Churchill, 1961; The Three Lives of Helen Keller, 1962; World War II: From D-Day to VE-day, 1962. *Contributions to:* Numerous journals and magazines. *Memberships:* Author's League; Authors Guild; Century Association. *Literary Agent:* Sterling Lord. *Address:* 135 Harbor Road, Westport, CT 06880, USA.

MARTIN Reginald, b. 15 May 1956, Memphis, Tennessee, USA. Editor; Director of professional writing programs, Writer. *Education:* Feature Editor and Reporter, News, Boston, Massachusetts, 1974-77; Instructor in English, Memphis State University, 1979-80; Research Fellow, Tulsa Center for the Study of Women's Literature, 1980-81; Instructor in English, Tulsa Junior College, Tulsa, 1982; Assistant Instructor in English, University of Tulsa, 1982-83; Assistant Professor, 1983-87, Associate Professor of Composition, 1988-, Memphis State University; Visiting Lecturer, Mary Washington College, 1984; Lecturer in Literary Criticism, University of Wisconsin - Eau Claire, 1988. Editor, Continental Heritage Press 1981; Director of professional Writing Programs 1987-. *Publications:* Ntozake Shange's First Novel: In the Beginning Was the Word, 1984; Ishmael Reed and the New Black Aesthetic Critics, 1988; An Annotated Bibliography of New Black Aesthetic Criticism (in press). *Contributions to:* Stories, poems, articles and reviews to various anthologies and periodicals. *Honours:* Mark Allen Everell Poetry Contest winner 1981; Friends of the Library Contest winner in fiction, 1982 and in poetry 1983; Award in Service for Education from Alpha Kappa, 1984; Award for Best Novel from Deep South writers Competition, 1987; Award for best critical article from South Atlantic Modern Language Association, 1987; Award for Best Critica/Article, College English Association, 1988. *Memberships:* Numerous professional associations. *Address:* PO Box 111306, Memphis, TN 38111, USA.

MARTIN Rhona. *See:* **MARTIN Rhona Madeline.**

MARTIN Rhona Madeline, (Rhona Martin), b. 3 Jun 1922, London, England. Writer; Artist. m. (1) Peter Wilfrid Alcock, 9 May 1941, (div), (2) Thomas Edward Neighbour, (div), 2 daughters. *Appointments:* Fulltime Writer, 1979-; Former Fashion Artist, Freelance Theatrical Designer, Cinema Manager and Accounts Secretary & Office Manager; Served on Panel of S E Arts (Regional Arts Council), 1978-84; Part-Time Tutor, Creative Writing for University of Sussex, 1986-91. *Publications:* Gallows Wedding, 1978; Mango Walk, 1981; The Unicorn Summer, 1984; Goodbye Sally, 1987; Writing Historical Fiction, 1988. *Contributions to:* London Evening News; S E Arts Review; Cosmopolitan; Prima. *Honour:* Georgette Heyer Historical Novel Award, 1979. *Memberships:* Romantic Novelists Association; Society of Authors; Society of Women Writers and Journalists; PEN; Friends of the Avron Foundation; Society of Limners. *Literary Agent:* Campbell, Thomson & McLaughlin, London. *Address:* 25 Henwood Crescent, Pembury, Kent TN2 4LJ, England.

MARTIN Robert Allen, b. 25 June 1930, Toledo, Ohio, USA. Teacher; Writer; Editor. m. 2 sons, 2 daughters. *Education:* BA, University of Toledo, 1958; MA 1959, PhD 1965, University of Michigan. *Publications:* Editor: The Theater Essays of Arthur Miller, 1978; Arthur Miller: New Perspectives, 1981; The Writer's Craft, 1982; Editor (with others) Rewriting the Good Fight: Critical Essays on the Literature of the Spanish Civil War, East Lansing MI: Michigan State University Press, 1989. *Contributions to:* Michigan Quarterly Review; Theatre Journal; Studies in American Fiction; Mid America; Modern Drama; American Notes and Queries; CEA Critic; The Hemingway Review; Studies in the Literary Imagination; Journal of Popular Culture; Michigan Academician; Philosophy and Literature; The Centennial Review; Notes on Contemporary Literature; Arizona Quarterly; College Literature. *Honours:* Several Academic, Thomas Clarkson Trueblood Fellowship, 1958; Fellowships 1958-81; Woodrow Wilson Fellowship, 1964; Editorial Consultant for several presses and journals, 1975-. *Memberships:* Phi Kappa Phi; Modern Language Association; Michigan College English Association; Society for the Study of Midwestern Literature; American Literature section, Modern Language Association; The Hemingway Society; F Scott Fitzgerald Society; Eugene O'Neill Society. *Literary Agent:* International Creative Management, New York. *Address:* Department of English, Michigan State University, East Lansing, MI 48824, USA.

MARTIN Robert Bernard, (Robert Bernard), b. 11 Sept 1918, La Harpe, Illinois, USA. Writer. *Education:* AB, University of Iowa, 1943; AM, Harvard University, 1947; BLitt, Oxford University, England, 1950. *Appointments:* Professor of English, Princeton University, 1950-1975; Emeritus Professor, 1975; Citizens Professor of English, University of Hawaii, 1980-81, 1984-88, Emeritus Citizens Professor, 1988. *Publications:* The Dust of Combat: A Life of Charles Kingsley, 1959; Enter Rumour: Four Early Victorian Scandals, 1962; The Accents of Persuasion: Charlotte Bronte's Novels, 1966; The Triumph of Wit: Victorian Comic Theory, 1974; Tennyson: The Unquiet Heart, 1980; With Friends Possessed: A Life of Edward Fitzgerald, 1985; Gerard Manley Hopkins: A Very Private Life, 1991; 3 other critical books and 4 novels. *Contributions to:* Numerous magazines and journals.

Honours: Fellow, ACLS, 1966-7; Fellow, Guggenheim Foundation, 1971-72, 1983-84; Senior Fellow, NEH, 1976-77; Fellow, Rockefeller Research Center, 1979; Duff Cooper Award, Biography, 1981; James Tait Black Award, Biography, 1981; Royal Society's Heinemann Award, 1981; Christian Gauss Award, 1981; DLitt, Oxford, 1987; Fellow, National Humanities Center, 1988-89. *Memberships:* Fellow, Royal Society of Literature; Honorary Vice President, Tennyson Society. *Literary Agent:* Curtis Brown. *Address:* 8 Walton Street, Oxford OX1 2HG, England.

MARTIN Ruth. *See:* **RAYNER Claire.**

MARTIN Stoddard H (Chip), b. 15 Dec 1948, Bryn Mawr, Pennsylvania, USA. Writer; Editor; Lecturer. m. Edin Harper Beard, 28 Sept 1974, separated. *Education:* BA, History, Stanford University, 1970; MA, English, California State University, 1974; PhD, University College, London, England, 1978. *Appointments:* Guest Lecturer, California State University, 1984; Guest Lecturer, University of Gottingen, West Germany, 1987; Lecturer, Harvard University, 1987-. *Publications include:* Wagner to the Wasteland: A Study of the Relationship of Wagner to English Literature, 1982; California Writers: Jack London, John Steinbeck, The Tough Guys, 1983; Art, Messianism and Crime: A Study of Antinomianism in Modern Literature and Lives, 1986; Orthodox Heresy: The Rise of Magic in Religion and its Relation to Literature, 1988; (Fiction) as Chip Martin, The Jew Hater, 1979, A Revolution of the Sun, 1982-86. *Contributions to:* Reviews; Times Literary Supplement; Numerous articles in professional and arts journals; Co-Founder and Editor, Starhaven Books, La Jolla, 1979-; Co-Founder, Starhaven Productions, Brawley, 1983-. *Literary Agent:* Jane Conway-Gordon, London W11 2SE. *Address:* c/o 21 Humbolt Road, London W6, England; 601 Franklin St., Cambridge, MA 02139.

MARTIN Victoria Carolyn, b. 22 May 1945, Windsor, Berkshire, England. Writer. m. Tom Storey, 28 July 1969, 4 daughters. *Education:* Challow Court School, 1950-53; Silchester House School, Bucks. 1953-61; Winkfield Place, Berks. 1961-62; Byam Shaw School of Art, 1963-66. *Publications:* September Song, 1970; Windmill Years, 1975; Seeds of the Sun, 1980; Opposite House, 1984; Tigers of the Night, 1985; Obey the Moon, 1987. *Contributions to:* Woman; Woman's Own; Woman's Journal; Good Housekeeping; 19; Woman's Realm; Woman's Weekly; Redbook; Honey, 1967-87. *Literary Agent:* Vanessa Holt. *Address:* Newells Farm House, Lower Beeding, Horsham, Sussex RH13 6CN, England.

MARTIN-JENKINS Christopher Dennis Alexander, b. 20 Jan 1945. Editor. m. Judith Oswald Hayman, 1971, 2 sons, 1 daughter. *Education:* BA, Modern History, MA, Fitzwilliam College, Cambridge. *Appointments:* Deputy Editor, 1967-70, Editor, 1981-87, Editorial Director, 1988-, The Cricketer; Sports Broadcaster, 1970-72; Cricket Corespondent, 1973-80, 1984-, BBC; Cricket Correspondent, Daily Telegraph, 1991-. *Publications:* Testing Time, 1974; Assault on the Ashes, 1975; MCC in India, 1977; The Jubilee Tests and the Packer Revolution, 1977; In Defence of the Ashes, 1979; Cricket Contest, 1980; The Complete Who's Who of Test Cricketers, 1980; The Wisden Book of County Cricket, 1981; Bedside Cricket, 1981; Sketches of a Season, 1981; Twenty Years On : Cricket's Years of Change, 1984; Cricket : A Way of Life, 1984; Editor: Cricketer Book of Cricket Eccentrics, 1985, Seasons Past, 1986; Joint Editor, Quick Singles, 1986; Grand Slam, 1987; Cricket Characters, 1987; Sketches of a Season, 1989; Ball by Ball, 1990. *Address:* Daily Telegraph, Canada Square, Canary Wharf, London E14 9DET, England.

MARTINET Gilles, b. 8 Aug 1916, Paris, France. Journalist; Politician; Diplomat. m. Iole Buozzi, 1938, 2 daughters. *Appointments:* Editor in Chief, Agence France Presse, 1944-49, Observateur, 1950-61; Director, Observateur, 1960-64; Board of Directors,

Nouvel Observateur, 1964-87, Matin 1973-81; Member European Parliament, 1979-81; Ambassador in Italy, 1981-85; Ambassadeur de France (dignity), 1984. *Publications:* Le marxisme de notre temps, 1961; La conquete des pouvoirs, 1968; Les cinq communismes, 1971; Le systeme Pompidou, 1973; L'avenir depuis vingt ans, 1975; Les septs syndicalismes, 1977; Cassandre et les tueurs, 1986; Les It'alicus, 1990. *Address:* 12 rue Las Cases, 75007 Paris, France.

MARTINGAY Claude, b. 30 Dec 1920, Geneve, Switzerland. Bookseller and Publisher. m. Jacqueline Tuscher, 1 July 1948, 1 son, 1 daughter. *Publications:* Le Conte du Huitieme Jour, 1986; Kleman pacha et le Jeu de Mar-Lah-Klem, 1964; D'un instant a l'autre 1976; Pour la Sainte Liturgie, 1982; Pour Saint Maurice et ses compagnons martyrs, 1989. *Address:* 40 rue du Nord, CH 1248 Hermance, Switzerland.

MARTINI Teri, b. 1930, American. *Appointments:* Former Teacher; Tenafly, NJ Board of Education. *Publications:* The Fisherman's Ring, True Book of Indians, 1954; Treasure of the Mohawk, True Book of Cowboys, 1956; Sandals on the Golden Highway, 1959; What a Frog Can Do, 1962; Mystery of the Hard Luck House, 1965; The Lucky Ghost Shirt, 1971; Patrick Henry, Patroit, 1972; Mystery of the Woman in the Mirror, 1973; John Marshall, 1974; Mystery Writers of Tunbridge Wells, 1975; The Dreamer Lost in Terror, 1976; To Love ad Beyond, 1977; Dreams to Give, 1979; The Arrundel Touch, 1980; Love's Lost Melody, 1986.

MARTINUS Eivor Ruth, b. 30 Apr 1943, Goteborg, Sweden. Writer; Translator. m. Derek Martinus, 27 Apr 1963, 2 daughters. *Education:* Double Degree, English and Swedish Literature, Universities of Lund and Goteborg, 1981. *Publications:* Five original novels in Swedish; Strindberg Translations: Thunder in the Air, 1989; Chamber plays, 1991, The Great Highway, 1990, three one act plays. Other Translations: My Life as a Dog; The Mysterious Barricades; A Matter of the Soul; Barabbas. *Contributions to:* Swedish Book Review; Swedish Books; Scandinavica. *Memberships:* Society of Authors; Swedish Writers Union; Swedish Playwrights Union; Swedish English Translators Association; SVEA-BRITT. *Literary Agent:* Tony Peake, Peake Associates, 18 Gratton Crescent, NW1 8SL, London, England. *Address:* 16 Grantham Road, London W4 2RS, England.

MARTONE Michael, b. 22 Aug 1955, Fort Wayne, Indiana, USA. Writer. m. Theresa Pappas, 3 Apr 1984. *Education:* AB, English, Indiana University, 1977; MA, The Writing Seminars, Johns Hopkins University, 1979. *Publications:* Alive and Dead in Indiana, 1984; Safety Patrol, 1988; A Place of Sense: Essays in Search of the Midwest (Editor), 1988; Fort Wayne is Seventh on Hitler's List, stories, 1990; Townships, (editor), 1990. *Contributions to:* Stories in: Antaeus; Ascent; Benzene; Shenandoah; Iowa Review; Harpers; Northwest Review; Indiana Review; Denver Quarterly; Windless Orchard; Gargoyle; Mississippi Review. *Honours:* National Endowment for the Arts Literary Fellowship, 1984; Pen Syndicated Fiction Awards, 1983, 1984, 1986; National Endowment for the Arts, 1988; Ingram-Merrill Foundation Award, 1988; Pushcart Prize, 1989. *Memberships:* National Writers Union; PEN; Associated Writing Programs. *Literary Agent:* Sallie Gouverneur. *Address:* 348 Fellows Avenue, Syracuse, NY 13210, USA.

MARTY. *See:* **CAMPBELL Martin Crafts.**

MARTY Martin E, b. 5 Feb 1928, West Point, Nebraska. Professor; Editor. m. (1) Elsa, (dec), (2) Harriet Julia, 23 Aug 1982, 4 sons, 1 daughter. *Education:* M Div, Concordia, St Louis, 1952; STM, Lutheran School of Theology, Chicago, 1954; PhD, University of Chicago, 1956. *Appointments:* Fairfax M Cone Distinguished Service Professor, University of Chicago, 1963; Senior Editor, the Christian Century, Chicago, 1986. *Publications:* Modern American Religion Vol 1, The Irony

of it All; Religion and Republic, 1986; Righteous Empire 1972; Modern American Religion, Vol 2, The Noise of Conflict: 1919-1941; (co-edited with R Scott Appleby), Fundamentalisms Observed, Fundamentalisms and Society, Fundamentalisms and the State, 1993. *Contributions to:* Various magazines/journals. *Honours:* Recipient of numerous honours and awards for professional services; 45 Honorary Degrees; National Book Award, for Righteous Empire, 1972. *Address:* University of Chicago Divinity School, 1025 E 58th Street, Chicago, Il 60637, USA.

MARTZ Louis (Lohr), b. 1913, American. *Appointments:* Instructor 1938-44, Assistant Professor 1944-48, Associate Professor 1948-54, Professor of English 1954-57, Chairman of Department 1956-62, Douglas Tracy Smith Professor of English and American Literature 1957-71, Director of Humanities 1959-62, Sterling Professor of English 1971-, Yale University, New Haven; Editorial Chairman, Yale Edition of the Works of Thomas More. *Publications:* The Later Career of Tobias Smollett, 1942; Pilgrim's Progress, by John Bunyan (ed), 1949; The Poetry of Meditation: A Study in English Religious Literature of the Seventeenth Century, 1954, 1962; The Meditative Poem (compiler), 1963; The Paradise Within: Studies in Vaughan, Traherne, and Milton, 1964; The Poem of the Mind: Essays on Poetry English and American, Milton: A Collection of Critical Essays (ed), 1966; Thomas More's Prayer Book (ed with Richard Sylvester), The Wit of Love: Donne Carew Crashaw Marvell, 1969; Seventeenth Century Verse (compiler), volume I, 1969; Hero and Leander, by Christopher Marlowe (ed), 1972; Thomas More's Dialogue of Comfort (ed with Frank Manley), 1976; The Author in His Work: Essays on a Problem in Criticism (ed with Aubrey Williams), 1978; Poet of Exile: A Study of Milton's Poetry, 1980; H D: Collected Poems 1912-1944 (ed), 1983; George Herbert and Henry Vaughan (ed), 1986; H D: Selected Poems, 1988; Thomas More: The Search for the Inner Man, 1990; From Renaissance to Baroque: Essays on Literature and Art, 1991. *Memberships:* American Academy of Arts and Sciences; British Academy of Arts and Sciences. *Address:* 994 Yale Station, New Haven, CT 06520, USA.

MARUTA Leszek, b. 8 Nov 1930, Torun, Poland. Writer; Journalist. (div), 1 son, 1 daughter. *Education:* Jagellonian University, 1949-52. *Appointments:* Staff, Gazeta Krakowska, Editor, 1969-71; Staff, Estrada Krakowska, Art Director, Scenarist, 1962-69; Director, WOK, Culture Centre of Tarnow, 1975-77. *Publications:* Almanach Mlodych, 1958; Martwa Natura Z Wasami, 1960; Haml-op Mopm C Ycamu, 1973; Austriackie Gadanie, 1975; Hejnal Z Wiezy Wariackiej, 1986; Gulasz Z Serc, 1989; W Pustyni, W Puszczy I W Polsce, 1992; Krakowski Zart - Centa Wart, 1993; Adaptations for Radio, TV and Theatre. *Contributions to:* Numerous journals and magazines including: Zycie Literackie; Tak I Nie; Szpilki; Karuzela. *Honours:* Karuzela Literary Award, 1958; Medal of Millenium, 1966; Award of The District Council of Cracow, 1972; Polish Radio Award, 1973; Award of The Governor of District Tarnow, 1976; Golden Cross of Merit, 1988; Golden Badge of The City of Cracow, 1988. *Memberships:* Polish Writers Union; Polish Journalistic Association, Secretary, Cracow Branch; Society of Authors; Society for Humour of the Peoples; German Society for Military Music. *Address:* Ul. Krupnicza 22/12, 31-123 Cracow, Poland.

MARVIN Blanche, b. 17 Jan 1926, New York, New York, USA. Actress; Writer; Critic of London Theatre Reviews; Director; Agent; Producer. m. Mark Marvin 31 Oct 1950, 1 son, 1 daughter. *Education:* BA, Antioch College. *Appointments:* Secretary, PMA; Secretary, Royal Academy of Dancing; Editor and Artistic Director, Merri-Mimes. *Publications:* Sleeping Beauty, 1961, 1990; Scarface and Blue Water, 1971, 1990; Firebird, 1990; The Infanta, 1990; Pied Piper, 1990; and 11 other plays; four plays 4 children, volume 1; 11 plays for children volume 2. *Contributions to:* Articles in: Dance Magazine; Theatre, New York City. *Honours:* Cue Magazine, Hall of Fame; Community Services, New York City; Children's Theatre Association Award; Emmy

Award, TV film, Gertrude Stein & A Companion. *Memberships:* Writers Guild; Theatre Writers Union; PMA, Secretary; Equity; Screen Actors Guild; BAFTA; Royal Academy of Art. *Literary Agent:* Blanche Marvin. *Address:* 21a St Johns Wood High Street, London NW8 7NG, England.

MARWICK Arthur, b. 1936, British. *Appointments:* Assistant Lecturer, University of Aberdeen, 1959-60; Lecturer, University of Edinburgh, 1960-69; Professor of History 1969-, Dean of Arts 1978-84, The Open University. *Publications:* The Explosion of British Society 1914-1962, 1963, 1971; Clifford Allen: The Open Conspirator, 1964; The Deluge: British Society and the First World War, 1965, 1991; Britain in the Century of Total: War, Peace and Social Change 1900-1967, 1968; The Nature of History, 1970, 1981, 1989; War and Social Change in the Twentieth Century, 1974; The Home Front: The British and the Second World War, 1976; Women at War 1914-1918, 1977; Class: Image and Reality in Britain France and the USA since 1930, 1980, 1990; Thames and Hudson Illustrated Dictionary of British History (ed), 1980; British Society since 1945, 1982, 1990; Britain in Our Century: Images and Controversies, 1984; Class in the Twentieth Century (ed), 1986; Beauty in History: Society, Politics and Personal Appearance, c. 1500 to the present, 1988; Total War and Social Change (ed), 1988; The Arts Literature and Society (ed), 1990; Culture in Britain since 1945, 1991. *Address:* Flat 5, 67 Fitzjohn's Avenue, Hampstead, London NW3 6PE, England.

MARX Arthur, b. 1921, American. Film Writer; TV Writer and Director; Playwright. *Publications:* The Ordeal of Willie Brown, 1951; Life with Groucho, 1954; Not as a Crocodile, 1958; Son of Groucho, 1972; Everybody Loves Somebody Sometime - Especially Himself, 1974; Goldwyn, 1976; Red Skelton, 1979; The Nine Lives of Mickey Rooney, 1986; My Life With Groucho, 1988. Plays: The Impossible Years, 1965; Minnie's Boys, 1970; My Daughter's Rated X, 1975; Sugar and Spice, 1974; Groucho: A Life in Revue, 1986; The Ghost and Mrs Muir, 1987. *Contributions to:* Los Angeles Magazine. *Honour:* Groucho: A Life in Revue - Nominated for Laurence Olivier Award, Best Comedy Production, 1987. *Memberships:* Dramatists Guild; Writers Guild of America. *Address:* c/o Scott Meredith, 845 Third Avenue, NY 10022, USA.

MARX Robert (Frank), b. 1936. American, Archaeology/Antiquities, History, Travel/Exploration/Adventure. Director of Operations, Phoenician Explorations, 1979-; Member, Council of Nautical Archaeology, London and Council of Underwater Archaeology. *Appointments:* Oceanographic Consultant, International Minerals and Chemicals, 1959-60; Adventure Editor, Saturday Evening Post magazine, 1960-63; Underwater Archaeologist, Jamaica Government, 1965-58; Underwater Archaeological Consultant, Real Eight Co, Melbourne, Florida, 1968-71; Director, Salvage for Seafinders Corporation, Bahamas, 1971-74; has taught underwater archaeology and maritime history at Scripps Institution of Oceanography, La Jolla, California, and the University of California at San Diego, 1974-75; Consultant, Planet Ocean: International Oceanographic Foundation, 1974; President, Sea World Enterprises Inc, 1974-76; Contributing Editor, Aquarius magazine, 1972-76; Expedition Leader, LOST, Inc, 1978. *Publications include:* The Battle of Lepanto 1571, 1966; They Dared the Deep: A History of Diving, 1967; History of the Sunken City of Port Royal, 1967; Always Another Adventure, 1967; Treasure Fleets of the Spanish Main, 1968; Shipwrecks in Florida Waters, 1969; Shipwrecks in Mexican Waters, 1971; Shipwrecks of the Western Hemisphere, 1971; Sea Fever: Famous Underwater Explorers, 1972; Port Royal Rediscovered, 1973; The Lure of Sunken Treasure, 1973; The Underwater Dig, 1975; Still More Adventures, 1976; Capture of the Spanish Plate Fleet 1628, 1976; Spanish Treasures in Florida Waters, 1978; Burried Treasures of the United States, 1978; Into the Deep: A History of Man's Underwater Explorations, 1978; Diving for Adventure,

1979; Quest for Treasure: Discovery of the Galleon Maravillas, 1982. *Address:* 205 Orlando Boulevard, Indialantic, FL 32903, USA.

MASA Hikaru. *See:* **MASATSUGU Mitsuyuki.**

MASATSUGU Mitsuyuki, b. 25 Jan 1924, Taiwan. Writer. m. Kiyoko Takeda, 3 Nov 1951, 1 son, 1 daughter. *Education:* BS, Osaka University of Foreign Studies, Japan, 1945; Course, Industrial Management, Tokyo, 1952. *Publications:* How To Run A Successful Business, 1969; The Turning Point of Japanese Enterprises Overseas, 1972; The Modern Samurai Society, 1982; Zigzags To The Meiji Restoration - The Divine Puppet Dazzled The Blue- eyed Imperialists, 1994. *Contributions to:* Occasionally to Japanese papers and magazines. *Address:* 3-35-16 Tomioka-nishi, Kanazawa-ku, Yokohama 236, Japan.

MASCHLER Thomas Michael, (Mark Caine), b. 16 Aug 1933. Publisher. m. (1) Fay Coventry, 1970, 1 son, 2 daughters. (2) Regina Kulinicz, 1987. *Appointments:* Production Assistant, Andre Deutsch, 1955-56; Editor, MacGibbon and Kee, 1956-58; Fiction Editor, Penguin Books, 1958-60; Editorial Director, Jonathan Cape 1960-70, Chairman 1970-; Director, Random House, 1987-. *Publications:* Editor, Declarations, 1957; New English Dramatists Series 1959-63; Publisher, Jonathan Cape Children's Books, since 1991. *Address:* 20 Vauxhall Bridge Road, London, SW1V 2SA, England.

MASEFIELD Geoffrey (Bussell), b. 1911, British. *Appointments:* Agricultural Officer, Uganda, 1935-48; Lecturer in Tropical Agriculture 1948-76, Fellow, Wolfson College, Oxford University; Editor, Tropical Agricultural Journal, 1953-65. *Publications:* I Am Not Armed, 1938; This Springing Wilderness (with S Wood), 1942; The Uganda Farmer, 1948; Handbook of Tropical Agriculture, 1949; Short History of Agriculture in the British Colonies, 1950; Famine: Its Prevention and Relief, 1963; Food and Nutrition Procedures in times of Disaster, 1967; The Oxford Book of Food Plants (with S G Harrison, M Wallis and B E Nicholson), 1969; Farming Systems of the World (with A N Duckham), 1970; History of the Colonial Agricultural Service, 1972. *Address:* Steepway, Adey's Lane, Wotton-under-Edge, Gloucestershire GL12 7PS, England.

MASINI Eleonora Barbieri, b. 19 Nov 1928, Guatemala. Sociologist. m. Francesco Maria Masini, 31 Jan 1953, 3 sons. *Education:* BA, 1948, Law Degree, 1952; Comparative Law Specialisation, 1953, Sociology Specialisation, 1969, Rome, Italy. *Publications:* Visions of Desirable Societies, 1983; Women - Households and Change (with Susan Stratigeo), 1991; Why Futures Studies?, 1992. *Contributions to:* Various articles to: Futures; Technological Forecasting and Social Change; Futurist. *Memberships:* Executive Council Chair, Past Secretary-General, Past President, World Futures Studies Federation; President for Europe, World Academy of Art and Science. *Address:* Via A Bertolini 23, 00197 Rome, Italy.

MASLOW Jonathan Evan, b. 4 Aug 1948, Long Branch, New Jersey, USA. Writer. *Education:* BA, high honors, American Literature, Marlboro College, Vermont; Masters of Science, Columbia University Graduate School of Journalism. *Publications:* Bird of Life, Bird of Death: A Political Ornithology of Central America, 1986; The Owl Papers, 1983; A Tramp in the Darien, film for BBC-WGBH-TV, 1990. *Contributions to:* Over 200 magazine articles in Atlantic Monthly; Saturday Review; GEO. *Honours:* George Varsell Award, American Academy of Arts & Letters, 1988; Guggenheim Fellow, 1989-90. *Memberships:* Authors Guild; National Writers Union. *Literary Agent:* The Robbins Office, New York City, USA. *Address:* Cutter's Way, Rd 3, Woodbine, NJ 08270, USA.

MASON Douglas Rankine, (R M Douglas, Douglas Rankine, John Rankine), b. 26 Sept 1918, Hawarden,

England. Headmaster (Retired). m. 26 May 1945, 2 sons, 2 daughters. *Education:* BA, Manchester University, 1947; Teachers Diploma, 1948. *Publications include:* Landfall is a State of Mind, 1968; From Carthage Then I Came, 1968; The Janus Syndrome, 1969; The Phaeton Condition, 1973; Pitman's Progress, 1976; The Typhon Intervention, 1981. Also: The Darkling Plain, as R.M. Douglas, 1979; The Star of Hescock, as John Rankine, 1980; Total, 40 titles published. *Contributions to:* Short stories in: Vision of Tomorrow; Impulse; New Writing in SF. *Literary Agent:* Carnell Literary Agency, Danescroft, Goose Lane, Little Hallingbury, Bishop's Stortford, Herts CM22 7RG. *Address:* 101 Millans Court, Ambleside, Cumbria, LA22 9BW, England.

MASON Ellsworth (Goodwin), b. 25 Aug 1917, Waterbury, Connecticut, USA. Library Consultant; Writer. m. (1) Rose Ellen Maloy, 13 May 1951 (div Oct 1961) 2 daughters; (2) Joan Lou Shinew, 16 Aug 1964, 1 son. *Education:* BA 1938, MA 1942, PhD 1948, Yale University. *Appointments:* Instructor in English, Williams College, Williamstown, Massachusetts, 1948-50; Instructor in English 1951-52, Librarian 1951-52, Marlboro College, Marlboro, Vermont; Serials Librarian, University of Wyoming, Laramie, 1952-54; Lecturer in English 1954-63, Reference Librarian 1954-58, Librarian 1958-63, Colorado College, Colorado Springs; Director of Library Services and Professor 1963-72, Hofstra University, Hempstead, New York; Director of Libraries and Professor, 1972-76, Head of Special Collections Department 1976-82, Consultant to the Library 1982-, University of Colorado, Boulder; Director of Theses and Member of Dissertation Committees at Colorado College, Hofstra University and University of Colorado, 1965-79; Adjunct Professor at the Graduate School of Library Science at the University of Illinois, 1968; Member of the Chancellor's Council, University of Texas; Consultant to numerous school and university libraries. *Publications:* Editor and author of introduction, with Stanislaus Joyce, The Early Joyce: The Book Reviews, 1902-1903, 1955 reprinted 1978; Editor with Richard Ellmann, The Critical Writings of James Joyce, 1959; Author of Historical Background and Chapter Commentaries, A Portrait of the Artist as a Young Man: A Critical Commentary, 1966; James Joyce's Ulysses and Vico's Cycle, 1973; Mason on Library Buildings, 1980. Translator from the Italian of a memoir on James Joyce by his brother. *Contributions to:* Articles to many periodicals. *Honours include:* Design Award from the New York State Association of Architects/American Institute of Architects, 1974, for consulting on the Sarah Lawrence College Library, Progressive Architecture Award, 1975, for consulting on the Ohio State University Library addition; Harry Bailly Speaker's Award, 1975; designated Honorary Librarian by the University of Lethbridge, 1977. *Memberships:* Many professional associations. *Address:* 756 6th Street, Boulder, CO 80302, USA.

MASON Francis K(enneth), b. 1928, British. *Appointments:* Editor, Flying Review International, 1963-64; Managing Director, Profile Publications Limited, 1964-67; Managing Editor, Guinness Superlatives Limited, Enfield, Middlesex, 1968-71; Managing Director, Alban Book Services Limited, Watton, Norfolk; Archivist and Researcher. *Publications:* Hawker Aircraft since 1920, 1961, 1972; Hawker Hurricane, 1962; Gloster Gladiator, North American Sabre (ed), 1963; The Hawker Hunter, 1965; The Hawker Sea Hawk, The Westland Lysander, 1966; The Hawker Siddley Kestrel, The Hawker Hunter Two-Seater, The Hawker Tempest, 1967; British Fighters of the Second World War, 1968; Air Facts and Feats, Battle Over Britain, 1969; British Gallantry Awards (ed), 1970; Know Britain, 1972; Know Aviation, 1973; Ribbons and Medals (ed), 1974; A Dictionary of Military Biography, 1975; Harrier, Famous Pilots and Their Planes, 1981; Lockheed Hercules, Phantom, 1984; War in the Air, 1985; Tornado, Luftwaffe Aircraft (with M Turner), 1986. *Address:* Beechwood, Watton, Norfolk, England.

MASON Haydn Trevor, b. 1929, British. *Appointments:* Instructor in French, Princeton University, NJ, 1954-57; Lecturer, University of Newcastle, 1960-63; Lecturer 1964-65, Reader 1965-67, University of Reading; Professor of European Literature, University of East Anglia, Norwich, 1967-79; Editor, Studies on Voltaire and the Eighteenth Century, 1977-; Professor of French Literature, University de Paris III, 1979-81; Professor of French, University of Bristol, 1981-; Scholar in Residence, University of Maryland, 1986; Chairman, Association of University Professors of French, 1981-82; President, Society for French Studies, 1982-84, British Society for Eighteenth Century Studies, 1984-86; Chairman, Board of Directors, Voltaire Foundation, University of Oxford, 1989-; President, International Society for Eighteenth-Century Studies, 1991-. *Publications:* Pierre Bayle and Voltaire, 1963; Marivaux: Les Fausses Confidences (ed), 1964; Leibniz-Arnauld Correspondence (trans and ed), 1967; Voltaire: Zadig and Other Stories (ed), 1971; Voltaire, 1974; Voltaire: A Life, 1981; French Writers and Their Society 1715-1800, 1982; Cyrano de Bergerac: L'Autre Monde, (ed), 1984; Candide: Optimisim Demolished, 1992. *Honours:* Officier dans L'Ordre des Palmes Academiques, 1985; Medaille D'Argent de la Ville de Paris, 1989. *Address:* Department of French, University of Bristol, Bristol BS8 1TE, England.

MASON Herbert (Molloy), b. 1927, American. *Publications:* The Lafayette Escadrille, 1964; High Flew the Falcons, Famous Firsts in Exploration, 1965; The Texas Rangers, 1966; Bold Men, Far Horizons, The Commandos, 1967; The New Tigers, 1968; Duel for the Sky, 1969; The Great Pursuit, 1970; Death From the Sea, 1972; The Rise of the Luftwaffe, 1973; Missions of Texas, The Fantastic World of Ants, 1974; Secrets of the Supernatural, 1975; The United States Air Force, 1976; To Kill the Devil, 1979; The Luftwaffe, 1981; Hitler Must Die, 1985. *Address:* c/o John Hawkins and Association, 71 West 23rd Street, NY 10010, USA.

MASON Lee W. *See:* **MALZBERG Barry Norman.**

MASON Ronald Charles, b. 30 July 1912, Thames Ditton, England. Retired Staff Tutor, London University Extra Mural Department. m. Margaret Violet Coles, 8 Sept 1936, 2 sons, 1 daughter. *Education:* BA, London University, 1947; Barrister at Law, Lincolns Inn, Called to the Bar 1935. *Publications include:* The Spirit Above the Dust (study of Herman Melville) 1951; Batsman's Paradise (cricket book) 1955; Jack Hobbs, 1960; Walter Hammond, 1962; Sing all a Green Willow (essays on cricket) 1967; Plum Warner's Last Season, 1970; Warwick Armstrong's Australians, 1971; Ashes in the Month, 1982. Novels: Timbermills, 1938; The Gold Garland, 1939; Cold Pastoral 1946; The House of the Living, 1947; Songs: Songs from a Summer School, 1974 (with music by Geoffrey Bush); More Songs from a Summer School, 1980. *Contributions to:* Horizon; Penguin New Writing; Tribune; The Cricketer; Modern Reading; Notes and Queries. *Memberships:* MCC; Surrey County Cricket Club. *Literary Agent:* David Higham Associates Ltd. *Address:* 22 Rosehill Farm Meadow, Park Road, Banstead, Surrey, England.

MASON Stanley, b. 16 Apr 1917, Blairmore, Alberta, Canada. Editor; Translator. m. Cloris Ielmini, 29 July 1944, 1 daughter. *Education:* MA, English Literature, Oriel College, Oxford. *Appointments:* Literary Editor, Graphis Magazine, 1963-83; Editor, Elements, Dow Chemical Europe House Organ, 1969-75. *Publications:* Modern English Structures (with Ronald Ridout), 4 volumes, 1968-72; A Necklace of Words, poetry, 1975; A Reef of Hours, poetry, 1983; Send Out the Dove, play, 1986; The Alps, verse translation of Albrecht von Haller's poem, 1987; The Everlasting Snow, poetry, 1993. *Contributions to:* UK: Adelphi; Poetry Review; Envoi; Orbis; Doors, Pennine Platform; others; Canada: Canadian Forum; Dalhousie Review. *Honours include:* 2 poems in Best Poems of 1964, Borestone Mountain Poetry Awards, 1965; 4 diplomas, Scottish National Open Poetry Competitions, including, 1984, 1985, 1986; Living Playwrights Award, Send Out The Dove, 1986; Writers Merit Award of the New York Art Directors Club, 1988. *Address:* Im Zelgli 5, 8307 Effretikon, Switzerland.

MASSINGHAM Harold (William), b. 1932, British. *Appointments:* Tutor, Extra-Mural Department, University of Manchester, since 1971. School Teacher, Manchester Education Committee, 1955-70. *Publications:* Black Bull Guarding Apples, 1965; Creation, 1968; The Magician: A Poem Sequence, 1969; Storm, 1970; Snow-Dream, 1971; The Pennine Way, 1971; Frost-Gods, 1971; Doomsday, 1972; Mate in Two (on chess), 1976.

MAST Gerald, b. 1940, American. *Appointments:* Instructor of English, New York University, 1964-65, Oberlin College, OH, 1965-67, Assistant Professor 1967-73, Associate Professor of Humanities 1974-78, Richmond College, City University of New York; Professor, Department of English, the College, the Committee on General Studies in the Humanities, the Committee on Art and Design, University of Chicago, 1978-. *Publications:* A Short History of the Movies, 1971, 4th edition, 1986; The Comic Mind: Comedy and the Movies, 1973, 1979; Film Theory and Criticism: Introductory Readings (ed with Marshall Cohen), 1973, 3rd edition, 1985; Filmguide to Rules of the Game, 1974; The Movies in Our Midst: Readings in the Cultural History of Film America (ed), Howard Hawks Storyteller, 1982; Can't Help Singin': The American Musical on Stage and Screen, 1987. *Address:* c/o University of Chicago, 5811 S Ellis Avenue, Chicago, IL 60637, USA.

MASTERS Hilary Thomas, b. 2 Mar 1928, Kansas City, USA. Novelist and Short Sotry Writer; Professor of English, Carnegue Mellon University. div. 1 son, 2 daughters. *Education:* AB from Brown University, 1952. *Appointments:* Freedom to Write Committee, PEN, 1984. *Publications:* Last Stands: Notes from Memory, 1982; The Harlem Valley Trio: Strickland, 1990; Cooper, 1987; Clemmons, 1985; Hammertown Tales, 1986; Success, 1992; Palace of Strangers, 1971; An American Marriage, 1969; The Common Pasture, 1967. *Contributions to:* Sports Illustrated; North American Review; Sewanne Review; The Georgia Review; New England Review; Kenyon Review. *Honours:* In 25 years, I've managed to escape any honors or awards. *Memberships:* PEN: New York Centre; The Authors Guild. *Literary Agent:* Kit Ward. *Address:* c/o Kit Ward, Box 515, North Scituate, MA 02060, USA.

MASTERTON Graham, (Thomas Luke), b. 16 Jan 1946, Edinburgh, Scotland. Author. m. Wiescka Walach, 11 Nov 1975, Guildford, Surrey, England. 3 sons. *Publications:* The Manitou, 1975; Charnel House, 1976; Rich, 1977; Railroad, 1980; Solitaire, 1983; Maiden Voyage, 1984; Tengu, 1984; Lady of Fortune, 1985; Corroboree, 1985; Family Portrait, 1986; Night Warriors, 1987; Headlines, 1987; Silver, 1987; Death Trance, 1987. *Contributions to:* The Writer, article on technique, 1985; article on horror writing, 1987; Twilight Zone, 1988. *Honours:* Special Award, Mystery Writers of America, 1977; Silver Medal, West Coast Review of Books, 1984. *Membership:* Authors Guild. *Literary Agent:* Wiescka Masterton. *Address:* c/o Sphere Books, 27 Wrights Lane, London W8 5TZ, England.

MASTROLIA Lilyan Spitzer, b. 28 Mar 1934, Brooklyn, New York, USA. Teacher; Writer. m. Edmund J. Mastrolia, 28 Aug 1956, 2 sons. *Education:* BS, Chemistry, Brooklyn College, 1955; Postgraduate, University of Southern California, 1955-56; MEd., California State University, Los Angeles, 1957; Postgraduate, California State University, Sacramento, 1959-60, 1980-81. *Appointments:* Artist in Residence, Cameron Ranch School, 1967-68; President, California Writers Club, 1981-82; President, National League of American Penwomen, Sacramento Branch, 1985; Vice President, California Writers Club, Sacramento, 1987-88. *Publications:* Teachers Guide to Physical Science, 1979; Observations from the Back Room, poetry, 1977. *Contributions to:* The Science Teacher; Cardiology News; MDX; Sacramento Bee; Canoe; Sacramento Union; New Yorker; Writers Digest; Science and Children. *Honours:* Grant, NSF, 1960, 1983, 1984; Consultant to SMUD, 1985-86; Consultant to Science Museum, 1985-86; Facilitator, Reaching Out Drug Abuse, 1985-86. *Memberships:* National Writers Club; California Writers Club; American Association of Medical Writers; National Science Teachers Association; American Medical Writers Association; International Food, Wine and Travel Writers Association. *Address:* 4706 Cameron Ranch Drive, Sacramento, CA 95841, USA.

MASTROSIMONE William, b. 1947, American. *Publications:* The Woolgather, 1981; Extremities, Shivaree, 1984; A Tantalizing, 1985; Nanawatai, 1986, Cat's-Paw, 1987. *Address:* c/o George Lane, William Morris Agency, 1350 Avenue of the Americas, New York, NY 10019, USA.

MATCHETT William H(enry), b. 1923, American. *Appointments:* Teaching Fellow, Harvard University, Cambridge, MA, 1953-54; Instructor 1954-56, Assistant Professor 1956-60, Associate Professor 1960-66, Professor of English 1966-82, Professor Emeritus, 1983-, University of Washington, Seattle; Modern Language Quarterly, 1963-82. *Publications:* Water Ouzel and Other Poems, 1955; Poetry: From Statement to Meaning (with J Beaty), The Phoenix and the Turtle: Shakespeare's Poem and Chester's Loues Martyr, 1965; The Life and Death of King John, by William Shakespeare (ed), 1966; Fireweed and Other Poems, 1980. *Honours:* Furioso Poetry Award, 1952; Washington State Governor's Award, 1982. *Membership:* Editorial Board, Poetry Northwest, Seattle, 1961-. *Address:* 1017 Minor Avenue, 702, Seattle, WA 98104, USA.

MATHESON Don(ald S), b. 17 Feb 1948, Charlotte, North Carolina, USA. Writer and Estate Manager. m. Vickie Diaz, 12 Dec 1981. *Education:* BA Vanderbilt University, 1972; Graduate study at Purdue University, 1972. *Appointments:* Kendall Co, began as salesman in hospital products division in Atlanta, Georgia, 1973, District Manager in Dallas, Texas, beginning in 1978 and Kansas City, Missouri, beginning in 1979, Regional Manager in Boston, Massachusetts, beginning in 1980, Strategic Planning Manager, beginning in 1982, leaving company as national accounts manager, 1983; Writer and Estate Manager 1983-. *Publications:* Stray Cat, 1987; Ninth Life, 1989. *Contributions to:* Local newspapers. *Memberships:* International Association of Crime Writers; Ashawagh Hall Writers Workshop. *Literary Agent:* Liz Darhansoff, New York. *Address:* Liz Darhansoff, 1220 Park Avenue, New York, NY 10128, USA.

MATHESON Richard (Burton), b. 1926, American. Freelance writer, especially of screenplays and TV plays. *Publications:* Someone Is Bleeding, 1953; Fury on Sunday, I Am Legend, Born of Man and Woman, 1954; Third from the Sun, 1955; The Shrinking Man, 1956; The Shores of Space, 1957; A Stir of Echoes, 1958; Ride the Nightmare, 1959; The Beardless Warriors, 1960; Shock!, 1961; Shock III, 1964; Shock III!, 1966; Shock Waves, 1970; Hell House, 1971; Bid Time Return, 1975; What Dreams May Come, 1978; Shock 4, 1980; Earthbound, 1989; Collected Stories, 1989. *Address:* PO Box 81, Woodland Hills, CA 91365, USA.

MATHIAS Roland Glyn, b. 4 Sept 1915, Talybont-on-Usk, Breconshire, Wales. Schoolmaster. m. Mary (Molly) Hawes, 4 Apr 1944, Chipping Norton, Oxfordshire, England. 1 son, 2 daughters. *Education:* BA, Modern History, 1936, BLitt (by thesis) 1939, MA, 1944, Jesus College, University of Oxford, England; Doctor of Humane Letters (honoris causa), Georgetown University, Washington, USA, 1985. *Literary Appointments:* Editor, The Anglo-Welsh Review, 1961-76; Member, Welsh Arts Council, 1970-79; Chairman, Literature Committee, Welsh Arts Council, 1976-79; Visiting Professor, University of Alabama at Birmingham, 1971; Extra-Mural Lecturer, University College, Cardiff, 1970-77. *Major Publications:* Poems: Break in Harvest, 1946; The Roses of Tretower, 1952; The Flooded Valley, 1960; Absalom in the Tree, 1971; Snipe's Castle, 1979; Burning Brambles, selected poems, 1983. The Eleven Men of Eppynt, short stories, 1956; Whitsun Riot, Historical Research, 1963; Vernon Watkins, literary criticism, 1974; John Cowper Powys as Poet, literary criticism, 1979; A Ride Through the Wood, critical essays, 1985; Anglo-Welsh Literature - An Illustrated History, 1987. *Contributions to:* Very many periodicals and literary journals. *Honours:* Welsh Arts Council Prizes for Poetry, 1972, 1980; Honorary Doctorate, Georgetown University (USA) for services to literature of Wales. *Memberships:* The Welsh Academy of Writers, Chairman 1975-78; The Powys Society; The David Jones Society. *Address:* Deffrobani, 5 Maescelyn, Brecon, Powys, LD3 7NL, Wales.

MATHIS-EDDY Darlene, b. 19 Mar 1937, Indiana, USA. Poet; Professor; Editor. m. Spencer Livingston Eddy, Jr. 23 May 1964, deceased 1971. *Education:* BA, Goshen College, 1959; MA, 1961, PhD, 1967, Rutgers University. *Appointments:* Poetry Editor, Forum, 1985-1989; Poet-in-Residence, Ball State University, 1989-1993. *Publications:* The Worlds of King Lear, 1968; Leaf Threads Wind Rhymes, 1985; Weathering, 1991; May Sarton: Woman and Poet, 1983; Contributor, Florilegia, 1987. *Contributions to:* American Literature; English Language Notes; The Old Northwest. *Honours:* Woodrow Wilson National Fellow, 1959-62; Rutgers University Graduate Honours Fellowship and Dissertation Award, 1964-65, 1966; numerous research, creative arts awards; Notable Woodrow Wilson Fellow, 1991. *Memberships:* Associated Writing Programme; Academy of American Poets; Modern Language Association; American Association of University Profesors; National Council of Teachers of English. *Address:* Dept. of English, RB 248, Ball State University, Muncie, IN 47306, USA.

MATRAY James Irving, b. 6 Dec 1948, Evergreen Park, Illinois, USA. University Professor. m. Mary Karin Heine, 14 Aug 1971, 1 son, 1 daughter. *Education:* BA, Lake Forest College, 1970; MA, 1973, PhD, 1977, University of Virginia. *Appointments:* Glenville State College, 1976-77; California State College, Bakersfield, 1978-79; University of Texas, Arlington, 1979-80; New Mexico State University, Las Cruces, 1980-; University of Southern California, 1988-89. *Publications:* Truman's Plan for Victory, 1979; The Reluctant Crusade: American Foreign Policy in Korea, 1941- 1950, 1985; Spoils of War, 1989; Historical Dictionary of the Korean War, 1991; Korea and the Cold War: Division, Destruction, and Disarmament, 1993. *Honours:* Stuart L Bernath Article Award, 1980; Best Book Award, Phi Alpha Theta, 1986; Best Reference Book Award, Library Journal, 1992. *Memberships:* American Historical Association, Pacific Coast Branch, Board of Editors; Society for Historians of American Foreign Relations; Organization of American Historians. *Address:* Box 3H, Department of History, New Mexico State University, Las Cruces, NM 88003, USA.

MATSAS Nestoras, b. Athens, Greece. Author; Director. *Publications include:* Childrens Books, Withour Love; The Girl With The Stars; Peektock the Astronomer; Novels. Sealed Heavens; The Messiah; The Little Soldier. *Contributions to:* Nea Estia. *Honours include:* The Award of Academy of Athens; National Greek Award for Fictional Biography; French Award for literature and Art. *Memberships:* Ethnographic Cinema, Greece. *Address:* Oubliamis Street, 16121 Athens, Greece.

MATSON Clive, b. 13 Mar 1941, Los Angeles, California, USA. Poet; Playwright; Teacher. *Education:* Undergraduate work, University of Chicago, 1958-59; MFA, Poetry, School of the Arts, Columbia University. *Publications:* Mainline to the Heart, 1966; Space Age, 1969; Heroin, 1972; On the Inside, 1982; Equal in Desire, 1983; Hourglass, 1987; Breath of Inspiration, essay, 1987. *Contributions to:* Anthologies of poetry: 31 New American Poets, 1969; Loves, Etc, 1973; Take It to the Hoop, 1980; Hang Together, 1987; 8 others; Over 100 poetry journals including: Exquisite Corpse; Hanging Loose; Nine Items or Less; Yellow Silk; Jeopardy; Hawaii Review; Factor, Mexico City; Berkeley Poetry Review; Blue Unicorn; The Centennial Review;

Dalmo'ma; Silver; Intrepid; The Floating Bear. *Honours:* Columbia University Graduate Writing Fellowship, 1987-88. *Memberships:* Poets and Writers; Dramatists Guild; Theatre Bay Area; Bay Area Mineralogists. *Literary Agent:* Peter Beren, Berkeley, California, USA. *Address:* 472 44th Street, Oakland, CA 94609, USA.

MATSUMURA Takao, b. 7 Jan 1942, Yokohama, Japan. Professor of Economics. m. Rumiko Fukuoka, 20 May 1967, 1 son, 1 daughter. *Education:* BA, Economics, 1964, MA, Economics, 1966, Keio University; PhD, Social History, University of Warwick, England, 1976. *Appointments:* Associate Professor, 1972-81, Professor, 1982-, Department of Economics, Keio University; Visiting Fellow, Social History, Warwick University, 1987-88. *Publications:* The Labour Aristocracy Revisited: The Victorian Flint Glass Makers, 1850-1880, 1983. *Contributions to:* Journal of Historical Studies (in Japanese); Mita Economic Journal (in Japanese); Bulletin of the Society for the Study of Labour History. *Honours:* 7th Prize for Excellent Labour Publications, Japan Institute of Labour, 1984. *Memberships:* Japan Socio-Economic Society, Editorial Board; Japan Social Policy Society; Society for the Study of Labour History, International Board. *Address:* 7 chome 28-2, Okusawa, Setagaya-ku, Tokyo, Japan.

MATTHEW Christopher Charles Forrest, b. 8 May 1939, London, England. Writer; Broadcaster. m. Wendy Mary Mallinson, 19 Oct 1979, 2 sons, 1 daughter. *Education:* BA (Hons), Oxford; MA (Hons), St Peter's College, Oxford. *Literary Appointment:* Editor, Times Travel Guide, 1972-73. *Publications:* A Different World: Stories of Great Hotels, 1976; Diary of a Somebody, 1978; Loosely Engaged, 1980; The Long Haired Boy, 1980; The Crisp Report, 1981; Three Men in a Boat (annotated with Benny Green), 1982; The Junket Man, 1983; How to Survive Middle Age, 1983; Family Matters, 1987; The Simon Crisp Diaries, 1988; A Perfect Hero, 1991; Radio Play: A Portrait of Richard Hillary; TV Scripts: The Good Guys, LWT, 1993; Radio: Writer & Presenter: Fourth Column R4, 1990-93; Something to Declare, 1971-82; Points of Departure, 1980-82; Invaders, 1982-83; The Travelling Snow (R4), 1984-85; Plain Tales from the Rhododendrons (R4), 1991; Cold Print (R4), 1992. *Contributions to:* Punch; Vogue; Daily Telegraph; Sunday Telegraph; High Life; World of Interiors; London Evening Standard; The Observer. *Membership:* Society of Authors. *Address:* c/o Michael Whitehall Ltd, 125 Gloucester Road, London SW7 4TE, England.

MATTHEWS Patricia Anne, (P A Brisco, Patty Brisco, Laura Wylie), b. 1 July 1927, San Fernando, California, USA. Author. m. (1) Marvin Owen Brisco, 1946 (div 1961), 2 sons, (2) Clayton Hartly Matthews, 1971. *Education:* Pasadena Junior College; California State University, Los Angles; Freelance Writer. *Appointments:* Secretary and Administrator, California State University, 1959-77. *Publications:* As Patricia Matthews: Love's Avenging Heart, 1977; Love's Wildest Promise, 1977; Love, Forever More, 1977; Love's Daring Dream, 1978; Love's Pagan Heart, 1978; Love's Magic Moment, 1979; Love's Golden Destiny, 1979; Love's Many Faces (poetry), 1979; Love's Raging Tide, 1980; Love's Sweet Agony, 1980; Love's Bold Journey, 1980; Tides of Love, 1981; Embers of Dawn, 1982; Flames of Glory, 1983; Dancer of Dreams, 1984; Gambler in Love, 1985; Tame The Restless Heart, 1986; Destruction at Dawn (juvenile), 1986; Twister (juvenile), 1986; Enchanted, 1987; Thursday and the Lady, 1987; The Night Visitor (occult), 1987; Mirrors (suspense), 1988; The Dreaming Tree, 1989; Sapphire, 1989; Oasis, 1989; The Death of Love (mystery), 1990; The Unquiet, 1991. As Patricia Matthews with Clayton Matthews (suspense): Midnight Whispers, 1981; Empire, 1982; Midnight Lavender, 1985. As Laura Wylie (occult): The Night Visitor, 1979, 1987. As Patty Brisco (juveniles): Merry's Treasure, 1969; The Carnival Mystery, 1976; The Campus Mystery, 1977; Raging Rapids, 1978; Too Much In Love, 1979; The Other People (science fiction), 1970; Gothics: Horror at Gull House, 1972; The Crystal Window, 1973; The House of Candles, 1973; Mist of

Evil, 1976. *Contributions to:* Short stories in: Escapade; Motive; Alfred Hitchcock's Mystery Magazine; Ellery Queen Mystery Magazine; Mike Shane Mystery Magazine; Azimov's Miniature Mysteries; Azimov's Microcosmic Tales; Magazine of Fantasy & Science Fiction. Poetry in: The Oregonion; The American Bard; Ladies Home Journal; Statement Magazine; Cosmopolitan; Ellery Queen's Mystery Magazine. Anthologies in: Escapade Annual; Alfred Hitchcocks Anthology; Miniature Mysteries; Microcosmic Tales. Articles in: Los Angeles Time; Valley People. Others: Your First Romance; My First Romance; Love's Leading Ladies; Writing The Romance; Writer's Digest; Candlelight, Romance and You. *Honours:* Porgie Award, West Coast Review of Books - Silver Medal, 'The Night Visitor', 1979; Silver Medal, 'Empire', 1983; Bronze Medal, 'Flames of Glory', 1983; Romantic Times, Team Writing Award with Clayton Matthews, 1983; Romantic Times, Reviewers Choice Awards, Best Historical Gothis, 'Enchanted', 1986-87; Affaire de Couer Silver Pen Reader's Award, 'Mirrors', 1989. *Memberships:* RWA; MWA; Charter Member, Novelists Inc. *Literary Agent:* Mr Jay Garon. *Address:* c/o Mr Jay Garon, 415 Central Park West, New York, NY 10025, USA.

MATTHEWS Peter John, b. 6 Jan 1945, Fareham, Hampshire, England. Freelance Author; Athletics Commentator, ITV. m. Diana Randall, 1975, 2 sons. *Appointments:* Editorial Director, Guinness Publishing 1981-84, 1989-; Sports Editor, Guinness Book of Records, 1982-91; Editor, Guiness Book of Records, 1991-. *Publications:* Guinness Book of Athletics Facts and Feats, 1982; International Athletics Annual, yearly from 1985; Track and Field Athletes - The Records (Guinness), 1986; Guinness Encyclopaedia of Sports Records and Results, 1987; Cricket Firsts (with Robert Brooke), 1988. *Contributor to:* Athletics publications. *Address:* 10 Madgeways Close, Great Amwell, Ware, Hertfordshire SG12 9RU, England.

MATTHEWS Robert Andrew James, b. 23 Sept 1959, Carshalton, Surrey, England. Journalist. m. Fiona J Bacon, 29 Sept 1989. *Education:* BA, Honours, Physics, Corpus Christi College, Oxford, 1981. *Appointments:* Associate Editor, Technology Week, 1981-82; Technology Editor, Building, 1982-86, Design, 1986- 87; Technology Correspondent, The Times, 1987-89; Science Correspondent, The Sunday Correspondent, 1989-. *Publications:* Consultant Editor, Physics Today, 1984. *Contributions to:* Sunday Times; The Times; Economist; Science Now; New Scientist; Popular Astronomy. *Honours:* Periodical Publishers Association Campaigning Features of the Year Award, 1984. *Memberships:* Fellow, Royal Astronomical Society; Associate Member, Institute of Physics; Association of British Science Writers; Oxford & Cambridge University Club. *Address:* 10 Park House, 55 Highbury Park, London N5 1TH, England.

MATTHEWS William, b. 11 Nov 1942, Cincinnati, Ohio, USA. Writer; Teacher. m. (1) Marie Harris, 4 May 1963, div. 1973, (2) Arlene Modica, 1984, (3) Patricia Smith, 1989, 2 sons. *Education:* BA, Yale University, 1965; MA, University of North Carolina, Chapel Hill, 1966. *Appointments:* Co-Editor, Co-Founder, Lillabulero Press, Lillabulero Magazine, 1966-74; Member, Editorial Board for Poetry, 1969-73, New Poets Editorial Board, 1988- 90, Wesleyan University Press; Poetry Editor, Iowa Review, 1976-77; Teaching positions include: Bread Loaf Writers Conference, 1981-89, 1991; Brooklyn College, 1983-85; Columbia University, 1983-85, 1988, 1990-92; Prof, English, City College. NY, 1985-; University of Michigan, 1987; Guest Poetry Editor, Indiana Review, 1987. *Publications:* Poetry books: Ruining The New Road, 1970; Sleek for the Long Flight, 1972; Sticks and Stones, 1975; Rising and Falling, 1979; Flood, 1982; A Happy Childhood, 1984, UK Edition, 1985; Foreseeable Futures, 1987; A World Rich in Anniversaries (translations with Mary Feeney from Jean Follain's prose poems), 1979; Curiosities, essays, 1989; Selected Poems and Translations 1969-1991, 1992. *Contributions to:* The Atlantic Monthly; The New Yorker; Ohio Review; Poetry; Others. *Honours:*

Fellowships: National Endowment for the Arts, 1974, 1983; John Simon Guggenheim Memorial Foundation, 1980-81; Ingram Merrill Foundation, 1984; Governors Award for Literature, State of Washington, 1983; Oscar Blumenthal Award, 1983, Eunice Tietjens Memorial Prize, 1989, Poetry magazine; Residencies: Rockefeller Foundation Study and Conference Center, Bellagio, Italy, 1988; Harthornden Castle International Writers Retreat, Scotland, 1990. *Memberships:* Past Member, Past Chairman, Literature Panel, National Endowment for the Arts; Associated Writing Programs, Past Member, Board of Directors, Past President; PEN; Authors Guild; Poetry Society of America, Past President. *Address:* 523 W 121st St, New York, NY 10027, USA.

MATTHIAS John (Edward), b. 1941, American. *Appointments:* Assistant Professor of English 1967-73, Associate Professor 1973-81, Professor of English 1981, University of Notre Dame. *Publications:* Bucyrus, Other Poems, 1970; Contemporary British Poetry (ed), Twenty-Three Modern British Poets, 1971; Herman's Poems, 1974; Turns, 1975; Crossing, Introducing David Jones, Contemporary Swedish Poetry (ed and trans with Goran Printz-Pahlson), Five American Poets, 1979; Bathory and Lermontov, 1980; Rainmaker, by Jan Ostergren (trans with Goran Printz-Pahlson), 1983; Northern Summer: New and Selected Poems 1963-83, 1984; The Battle of Kosovo (translated with Vladeta Vuckovic), 1987; David Jones: Man and Poet, 1989; Tva Dikter, 1989; A Gathering of Ways, 1991; Reading Old Friends, 1992. *Address:* Department of English, University of Notre Dame, Notre Dame, IN 46556, USA.

MATTHIESSEN Peter, b. 22 May 1927, New York, United States of America. Writer. m. (1) Patricia Southgate, 8 Feb 1951 (divorced), 1 son, 1 daughter; (2) Deborah Love, 16 May 1963 (deceased), 1 son, 1 daughter; (3) Maria Eckhart, 28 Nov 1980. *Education:* Sorbonne, University of Paris, 1948-49; BA, Yale University, 1950. *Appointments Include:* Writer, 1950-; Co-founder, 1951, Editor, 1951-, Paris Review, New York City (originally Paris, France). *Publications:* Race Rock, 1954; Partisans, 1955; Wildlife in America, 1959; Raditzer, 1961; The Cloud Forest: A Chronicle of the South American Wilderness, 1961; Under the Mountain Wall: A Chronicle of Two Seasons in the Stone Age, 1962; At Play in the Fields of the Lord, 1965; Oomingmak: The Expedition to the Musk Ox Island in the Bering Sea, 1967; The Shorebirds of North America, 1967, (The Wind Birds, 1973); Sal Si Puedes: Cesar Chavez and the New American Revolution, 1970; Blue Meridian: The Search for the Great White Shark, 1971; Everglades: With Selections from the Writings of Peter Matthiessen, 1971; The Tree Where Man Was Born/ The African Experience, 1972; Seal Pool (juvenile) (in United Kingdom as The Great Auk Escape, 1974), 1972. Far Tortuga, 1975; The Snow Leopard, 1978; Sand Rivers, 1981; In the Spirit of Crazy Horse, 1983; Indian Country, 1984; Men's Lives:The Surfmen and Baymen of the South Fork, 1986; Nine-Headed Dragon River: Zen Journals 1969- 82, 1986; (Midnight Turning Gray, 1984), On the River Styx, 1989; Killing Mister Watson, 1990; African Silences, 1991; Shadows of Africa, 1992; BAIKAL: Sacred Sea of Siberia, 1992. *Memberships:* American Academy and Institute of Arts and Lecturers, Trustee of New York Zoological Society, 1965-78. *Honours:* Various Awards and Honours including Atlantic Prize, 1950, for best first story; National Book Award for contemporary thought, 1979 (for the Snow Leopard); American Book Award, 1980 for paperback edition of The Snow Leopard; John Burroughs Medal and African Wildlife Leadership Foundation Award, 1982 (for Sand Rivers); Gold Medal for Distinction in Natural History from the Philadelphia Academy of Natural Sciences, 1985. *Address:* PO Box 392, Bridge Lane, Sagaponack, NY 11962, USA.

MATTINGLEY Christobel Rosemary, b. 26 Oct 1931, Adelaide. South Australia. Writer. m. Cecil David Mattingley, 17 Dec 1953, 2 sons, 1 daughter. *Education:* BA, 1st Class Hons. in German, 1951; Registration Certificate and Associate of the Library Association of Australia, 1971. *Publications include:* Windmill at

Magpie Creek, 1971; The Great Ballagundi Damper Bake, 1975; Rummage, 1981; The Angel with the Mouth Organ, 1984; The Miracle Tree, 1985; Survival in Our Own Land: Aboriginal Experiences in South Australia since 1836, 1988; The Butcher, the Beagle and The Dog Catcher, 1990; Tucker's Mob, 1992. *Contributions to:* Australian Library Journal; New Zealand Libraries; Landfall (NZ); Reading Time; Classroom. *Honours:* 1972 Highly Commended, Children's Book Council of Australia Awards; 1975, 1983 Australia Council Literature Board Fellowships; 1982 Inaugural Children's Book Council of Australia Medal for Outstanding Book for Junior Readers; 1983 National Parks and Wildlife Services NSW Writers Award; 1985 Australian Christian Children's Book of the Year Award; 1987 Notable Book Award USA; 1990 Advance Australia Award for Services to Literature. *Membership:* Australian Society of Authors. *Literary Agent:* A P Watt, 20 John Street, London WC1N 2DR. *Address:* 18 Allendale Grove, Stonyfell, SA 5066, Australia.

MATURA Mustapha, b. 1939, Trinidadian. *Publications:* As Times Goes By, and Black Pieces, 1972; Play Mas, 1976; Nice, Rum an Coca Cola and Welcome Home Jacko, 1980; Play Mas, Independence and Meetings, 1982. *Address:* c/o Judy Daish Associates, 83 Eastbourne Mews, London W2 6LQ, England.

MATURA Thaddee, b. 24 Oct 1922, Poland. Monk. *Education:* Master in Theology; Master in Biblical Studies. *Publications:* Celibat et Communaute, 1967; La vie religieuse au tournant, 1971; Naissance d'un charisme, 1973; Le projet evangelique de Francois d'Assise, 1977; Le radicalisme evangelique, 1980; Ecrits de Francois d'Aroise, 1981; Ecrits de Claire d'Assise, 1985; Suivre Jesus, 1983; Une absence ardente, 1988; Dieu le Pere tres saint, 1990. *Contributions to:* About 150 items to various publications. *Address:* 84240 Grambois, France.

MATUTE AUSEJO Ana Maria, b. 26 July 1925, Barcelona, Spain. Writer. m 1952, divorced 1963, 1 son. *Appointment include:* Editor, Damas Negras, French Nus College; collaborator, Destino; Visiting Lecturer, Indiana University, 1965-66, Oklahoma Univerity, 1969-; Writer in Residence, Univerity of Virginia, 1978-79. *Publications:* Los Abel, 1947; Fiesta Al Noroeste, 1952; Pequeno Teatro, 1954; Los ninos tontos, 1956; Los Hijos Muertos, 1959; primera Memoria, 1959; Tres y un sueno, 1961; historias de la Artamila, 1961; El Rio, 1963; El Tiempo, 1963; Los Soldados lloran de noche, 1964; El Arrepentido y otras Narraciones, 1967; Algunos Muchachos, 1968; La Trampa, 1969; la Torre Vigia, 1971; Olvidado Rey Gudu, 1974; Children's Books: El Pais de la Pizarra, 1956; Paulina, 1961; El Sal Tamonte Verde, 1961; Caballito Loco, 1961; El Aprendiz, 1961; Carnavalito, 1961; El Polizon del "Ulises" 1965. *Honours:* Cafe Gijon Prize, 1952; Planeta Prize, 1954; National Literary Prize & Critics Prize, 1959; Nadal Prize, 1959; Fastenrath Prize(1969; Lazarillo Prize, 1965. *Address:* Provenza, 84-At. 3a, Barcelona 29, Spain.

MAUMELA Titus Ntsieni, b. 25 Dec 1924, Sibasa, Venda, Southern Africa. Teacher. m. Rose Maumela, 27 June 1949, 2 sons, 1 daughter. *Education:* BA, University of South Africa, 1961. *Publications:* Novels: Elelwani, 1954; Mafangambiti, 1956 (English, 1986); Vhavenda Vho-Matshivha, 1958; Vhuhosi Vhu tou Bebelwa, 1962; Zwa Mulovha Zwi a Fhela, 1963; Maela wa Vho-Mathavha, 1967; Musandiwa na Khotsi Vho-Liwalaga, 1968; Kanakana (youth), 1975; Ndi Vho-Muthukhuthukhu, 1977; Vho-Rammbebo, 1981; Tshiphiri Tsho Bvela Khagala, 1986; Talukanyani (youth), forthcoming. Dramas: Tshililo, 1957; A Hu Bebiwi Mbilu, 1975; Vhuhosi A Vhu Thetshelwi, 1975; Edzani, 1985; Tomolambilu, 1989. Short stories: Matakadzambilu, 1965; Zwiitavhathu, 1965; Maungedzo, 1972; Mihani Ya Shango, 1972; Mithetshelo, 1981; Mmbwa Ya La Inwe a i Noni, 1983; Nganea pfufhi dza u takadza, 1989. Essay: Maanea A Pfadzaho, 1992. Folktales: Dzingaho na Dzithai dza Tshivenda, 1968; Salungano! Salungano!, 1978. Language Manuals: Thikho ya Luvenda ya Fomo I, 1970;

Thikho ya Luvenda ya Fomo II, na III, 1970; Luvenda Iwa Murole wa 5, 1975; Luvenda Iwa Fomo I, 1975; Luvenda Iwa Murole wa Fomo II, 1976; Luvenda Iwa Murole wa 8, 1978; Tshivenda tsho tambaho tsha, Murole wa 5 (with Prof T W Muloiwa and B H Maumela), 1986; Gondo la Tshivenda, Murole wa 5, 1987; Gondo la Tshivenda, Murole wa 6 (with M R Madiba), 1990; Gondo la Tshivenda, Murole wa 7 (with M R Madiba), 1990; Gondo la Tshivenda, Murole wa 8 (with M R Madiba and F K Maselesele), 1992; Gondo la Tshivenda, Murole wa 9 (with M R Madiba), 1992; Gondo la Tshivenda, Murole wa 10 (with M R Madiba), 1992. *Contributions to:* Muvenda. *Honours:* Bantu Education novel writing competition, 1966; Die Suid Afrikaanse Akademie vir Vetenskan en Kuns, 1967; SABC Venda short story competition, 1971; Diploma, Venda Language Board, Dept of Education, 1989; Silver Medal, De Jager-Haum Publishing House, 1992. *Address:* PO Box 2, Vhufuli, Venda, Southern Africa.

MAVOR Elizabeth (Osborne), b. 1927, British. *Publications:* Summer in the Greenhouse, 1959; The Temple of Flora, 1961; The Virgin Mistress: A Biography of the Duchess of Kingston (in US as The Virgin Mistress: A Study in Survival: The Life of the Duchess of Kingston), 1964; The Redoubt, 1967; The Ladies of Llangollen: A Study in Romantic Friendship, 1971; A Green Equinox, 1973; Life with the Ladies of Llangollen, 1984; The Grand Tour of William Beckford, 1986; The White Solitaire, 1988; The American Journals of Fanny Kemble, 1990. *Address:* 11 Gorwell, Watlington, Oxon, England.

MAXWELL D E S, b. 1925, Irish. *Appointments:* Lecturer, University of Ghana, 1956-61; Assistant Director of Examinations, Civil Service Commission, England, 1961-63; Professor of English, Head of Department, University of Ibadan, Nigeria, 1963-67; Professor of English, York University, Toronto 1967-. *Publications:* The Poetry of TS Eliot, 1952; American Fiction: The Intellectual Background, 1963; Cozzens, 1964; Herman Melville, 1968; WB Yeats Centenary Essays (ed with S B Bushrui), 1965; Poets of the Thirties, 1969; Brian Friel, 1973; Modern Irish Drama, 1984. *Address:* Department of English, York University, Downsview, Ontario, Canada M3J 1P3.

MAXWELL Glyn Meurig, b. 7 Nov 1962, Welwyn Garden City, England. Writer. *Education:* Worcester College, Oxford, 1982-85; BA Hons 1st Class, English, 1985; MA, Creative Writing, Boston University, USA, 1987-1988. *Publications:* Tale of the Mayor's Son, poems, 1990; Out of the Rain, poems, 1992; Gnyss the Magnificent, verse-plays, 1993. *Contributions to:* Reviews to: Independent; Times Literary Supplement; Vogue; Poetry Review; Verse; Poems to: Times Literary Supplement; LRB; Sunday Times; Spectator; Independent; Atlantic Monthly; Partisan Review; Verse; The New Yorker. *Honours:* Poetry Book Society Choice, summer 1990; Shortlisted, John Llewellyn Rhys Memorial Prize, 1991; Poetry Book Society Recommendation, summer 1992;7000 Eric Gregory Award, 1992; Somerset Mauham Trabel Prize. *Memberships:* PEN; Poetry Society. *Address:* c/o Bloodaxe Books, PO Box 1SN, Newcastle-upon-Tyne NE99 1SN, England.

MAXWELL Gordon Stirling, b. 21 Mar 1938, Edinburgh, Scotland. Archaeologist. m. Kathleen Mary King, 29 July 1961, 2 daughters. *Education:* MA (hons) St Andrews, 1959. *Appointments:* Curatorial Officer, Royal Commission Ancient & Historical Monuments, Scotland, 1964-. *Publications:* Rome's Northwest Frontier: the Antonine Wall, 1983; The Romans in Scotland, 1989; A Battle Lost: Romans and Caledonians at Mons Graupius, 1990; Editor: The Impact of Aerial Reconnaissance on Archaeology, 1983. *Contributor to:* Britannia; Proceedings, Society, Antiquaries, Scotland; Glasgow Archaeological Journal. *Memberships:* Fellow, Royal Society of Arts; Fellow, Society of Antiquaries of London; Fellow, Society of Antiquaries of Scotland. *Address:* Micklegarth, 72a High Street, Aberdour, Fife KY3 0SW, Scotland.

MAXWELL Patricia Anne, (Jennifer Blake, Maxine Patrick, Patricia Ponder, Elizabeth Trehearne), b. 9 Mar 1942, Louisiana, USA. Author. m. Jerry R Maxwell, 1 Aug 1957, 2 sons, 2 daughters. *Appointments:* Writer in Residence, University of Northeastern Louisiana. *Publications:* Love's Wild Desire, 1977; Tender Betrayal, 1979; The Storm and the Splender, 1979; Golden Fancy, 1980; Embrace and Conquer, 1981; Royal Seduction, 1983; Surrender in Moonlight, 1984; Midnight Waltz, 1985; Fierce Eden, 1985; Royal Passion, 1986; Prisoner of Desire, 1986; Louisiana Dawn, 1987; Southern Rapture, 1987; Perfume of Paradise, 1988; Love and smoke, 1989; Spanish Serenade, 1990. *Honour:* Historical Romance Author of the Year 1985. *Address:* Route 1, Box 133, Quitman, LA 71268, USA.

MAXWELL Vicky. *See:* **WORBOYS Annette Isobel.**

MAXWELL William. *See:* **ALLEN Ted.**

MAY Derwent James, b. 29 Apr 1930, Eastbourne, Sussex, England. Author; Journalist. m. Yolanta Izabella Sypniewska, 1 son, 1 daughter. *Education:* Lincoln College, Oxford, 1949-52; MA (Oxon). *Appointments:* Theatre and Film Critic, Continental Daily Mail, Paris, France, 1952-53; Lecturer in English, University of Indonesia, 1955-58; Senior Lecturer in English, Universities of Lodz and Warsaw, Poland, 1959-63; Chief Leader Writer, Times Literary Supplement, 1963-65; Literary Editor, The Listener, 1965-86; Literary and Arts Editor, Sunday Telegraph, 1986-90; Literary and Arts Editor, The European, 1990-91; European Arts Editor, The Times, 1992-. *Publications:* Novels: The Professionals, 1964; Dear Parson, 1969; The Laughter in Djakarta, 1973; A Revenger's Comedy, 1979. Non-fiction: Proust, 1983; The Times Nature Diary, 1983; Hannah Arendt, 1986. *Contributions to:* Encounter; Hudson Review. *Honours:* Member, Booker Prize Jury, 1978; Hawthornden Prize Committee, 1987-. *Membership:* Beefsteak Club. *Address:* 201 Albany Street, London NW1, England.

MAY Gita, b. 16 Sept 1929, Brussels, Belgium. Professor of French, Columbia University, New York, USA. m. Irving May, 21 Dec 1947. *Education:* BA, Hunter College, New York, 1953; MA 1954, PhD 1957, Columbia University, New York. *Literary Appointments:* Professor of French, Columbia Unviersity; Chair of Department, 1983-92, Columbia Unviersity, New York, USA; Chair, American Society for Eighteenth-Century Studies, Gottschalk Prize Committee, 1979; Member, Executive Committee of the Division on European Literary Relations of the Modern Language Association of America, 1981-85; Elected to the Academy of Literary Studies, 1986. *Publications:* Stendhal and the Age of Napoleon, 1977; Madame Roland and the Age of Revolution, 1970; Diderot et Baudelaire, critiques d'art, 1957; De Jean-Jacques Rousseau a Madame Roland; Essai sur la sensibilite preromantique et revolutionnaire, 1964; Diderot Studies III, co-editor with O Fellows, 1961; Critical edition of Diderot's Essais sur la peinture, vol XIV for the edition of complete works, 1984, paperback edition 1984. *Contributions to:* Publications of the Modern Language Association of America; French Review; Romanic Review; Stendhal Club. Also contributions to numerous volumes, eg. sections on Diderot and on George Sand in European Writers, ed, G Stade. Editorial boards of several journals. *Honours:* Hunter College Award for Outstanding Achievement, 1963; Guggenheim Fellowship 1964; Decorated Chevalier dans l'Ordre des Palmes Academiques, 1968, promoted to rank of Officier, 1981; Senior Fellow, National Endowment for the Humanities, 1971; Columbia University's Van Amringe Distinguished Book Award for Madame Roland and the Age of Revolution, 1971. *Memberships:* Executive Council of the Modern Language Assoication of America, 1980-83; President of the American Society of Eighteenth-Century Studies, 1985-86; on Editorial Board of Romanic Review, French Review, 1975-86, Eighteenth-Century Studies, 1975-76. *Address:* Departmenrt of French, Columbia University, 516 Philosophy Hall, New York, NY 10027, USA.

MAY Julian, b. 10 July 1931, Chicago, USA. Writer. m. Thaddeus E Dikty, 1953. 2 sons, 1 daughter. *Publications:* The Many-Colored Land, 1981; The Golden Torc, 1982; The Nonborn King, 1983; The Adversary, 1984; Intervention, 1987; Black Trillium, co-author with Marion Zimmer Bradley and Andre Norton, 1990; Jack the Bodiless, 1991; 254 other books published and 8 under pseudonyms, mostly juvenile non-fiction. *Literary Agent:* Scott Meredith Inc, New York City. *Address:* Box 851, Mercer Island, WA 98040, USA.

MAY Naomi Young, b. 27 Mar 1934, Glasgow, Scotland. Novelist; Journalist; Painter. m. Nigel May, 3 Oct 1964, 2 sons, 1 daughter. *Education:* Slade School of Fine Art, London, 1953-56; Diploma, Fine Art, University of London. *Publications:* At Home, 1969, radio adaptation, 1987; The Adventurer, 1970; Troubles, 1976. *Contributions to:* Short stories to anthologies: New Writing and Writers; Rapunzel laas dein Haar herunter, in German translation; Also to magazines: Nova; London Review of Books; Encounter; PN Review; Articles mostly on positive aspects of life in Northern Ireland to: The Daily Telegraph; The Times; The Independent; The Observer; New Statesman and Society. *Honours:* History of Art Prize, Slade School of Fine Art. *Memberships:* PEN. *Address:* 6 Lion Gate Gdns, Richmond, Surrey TW9 2DF, England.

MAY Robin (Robert) Stephen May, b. 26 Dec 1929, Deal, Kent, England. Writer. 2 sons, 1 daughter. *Education:* Bradfield College, 1943-48; Central School of Speech and Drama, 1950-53. *Publications:* Operamania, 1966; Theatremania, 1967; Wit of the Theatre, 1969; Wolfe's Army, 1974; Who Was Shakespeare? 1974; The Gold Rushes, 1977; History of the American West, 1984; History of the Theatre, 1986; A Guide to the Opera, 1987. *Contributions to:* Miscellaneous magazines for young people. *Membership:* Society of Authors. *Literary Agent:* Rupert Crew Ltd, Kings Mews, London WC1, England. *Address:* 23 Malcolm Road, London SW19 4AS, England.

MAY Stephen James, (Julian Poole), b. 10 Sept 1946, Toronto, Canada. College Professor and Advisor; Educator; Novelist; Essayist; Historian; Critic. m. Caroline C May, 13 Oct 1972. *Education:* BA 1975, MA 1977, California State University, Los Angeles, USA; DLitt, International University, Bombay, India, 1992. *Publications:* Pilgrimage, 1987; Fire from the Skies, 1990; Footloose on the Santa Fe Trail, 1992; A Land Observed, 1993; Zane Grey: The Making of a Legend, 1993. *Contributions to:* Southwest Art; Artists of the Rockies; National Geographic. *Membership:* Colorado Authors League. *Literary Agent:* Carl Brandt, New York City, USA. *Address:* 610 Country Drive, Monument, CO 80132, USA.

MAYBURY Anne. *See:* **BUXTON Anne.**

MAYER, b. 27 Feb 1902, Paris, France. Music Critic; Writer. m. Therese Raynal, 19 Feb 1929. *Education:* Licence, Law; Licence, English; Diploma, Ecole des Sciences Politiques. *Publications:* La Vie Anglaise, 1960; L'Humour Anglais, 1962. *Contributions to:* Numerous, mainly to: The Times (films); Opera; La Vie Francais. *Address:* 84560 Menerbes, France.

MAYER Anne, b. 29 Oct 1953, Dayton, Ohio, USA. Freelance Writer. m. David Gross Mayer, 15 Aug 1976, 2 daughters. *Education:* Ohio University; Trinity College, Oxford University, England; BA(hons) English, 1976. *Literary Appointments:* Assistant Editor, Morgan Guaranty News, 1977-78; Full-Time Freelancer for Seventeen, Lady's Circle, and Today's Secretary, 1978-79; Associate Editor, Lady's Circle, 1979-81; Assistant Features Editor, Harper's Bazaar, 1981-82. *Publications:* The Bride (co-author), 1984; Poems in From The Hudson To The World (anthology), 1978. *Contributions to:* The New York Times; Die Weltwoche; McCall's; Harper's Bazaar; Parents; Mademoiselle; Bride's; Working Mother; Seventeen; Parenting; American Baby;

Childbirth Educator; Family Weekly; Health. *Honours:* Member of College Board, Mademoiselle, 1974-76; Honourable Mention, Mademoiselle's Guest Editor Competition, 1975; 2nd place, Writer's Digest National Article Writing Contest, 1975. *Membership:* American Society of Journalists and Authors Inc. *Literary Agent:* The Jeff Herman Agency Inc. *Address:* 344 Riviera Drive, San Rafael, CA 94901, USA.

MAYER Robert, b. 24 Feb 1939, Bronx, New York, USA. Writer. m. La Donna Cocilovo, 24 Feb 1989, 1 stepdaughter. *Education:* BA, City College of New York, 1959; MS Journalism, Columbia University, 1960. *Appointments:* Reporter and Columnist, Newsday, 1961-71; Santa Fe Reporter, managing Editor, 1988-90. *Publications:* Superfolks, 1977; The Execution, 1979; Midge and Decker, 1982; The Dreams of Ada, 1987; I, JFK, 1989; Sweek Salt, 1984; The Grace of Shortstops, 1984; The Search, 1986. *Contributions to:* Vanity Fair; New York Magazine; Travel and Leisure; Rocky Mountain Magazine; New Mexico Magazine; Santa Fe Reporter; Newsday. *Honours:* National Headliner Award, 1968; Mike Berger Award, 1969, 1971; Nominee, Edgar Allen Poe Award, 1988. *Literary Agent:* Philip Spitzer, New York. *Address:* 135 Cedar Street, Santa Fe, NM 87501, USA.

MAYER-KOENIG Wolfgang, b. 28 Mar 1946, Vienna, Austria. Author; University Professor; Industrial Director. *Education:* Extraordianry University Professor; Founder, Director, Austria University Cultural Centre; Dr.h.c.f.litt. *Appointments:* Editor, International Literature Magazine, LOG. *Publications:* Sichtbare Pavillons, 1968; Stichmarken, 1969; Vorlaeufige Versagung, 1985; Colloqui nella stanza, 1986; Chagrin non dechifre, 1986; In den armen unseres Waerters, 1979; Texte und Bilder, 1972; Karl Kraus als Kritiker, 1975; Robert Musils Moeglichkeitsstil, 1977; Sprache-Politik-Aggression, 1975; Schreibverantwortung, 1986; Ahatalom bonyolult angyala, 1988; A Complicated Angel, 1989; Colloquios Nelcuarto, 1990. *Contributions to:* Various journals including: Neue Wege-Wien; Lieratur und Kritik-Wien; Meanjin Quarterly, Melbourne. *Honours:* Theodor Koerner Prize for Literature, 1974; Wiener Kunstfonds Prize for Literature, 1975; Premio Prometeo aurero per la Literatura delle Provinzie di Lazio; Cross of Honour for Science and Arts of Republic of Austria; Ordre des Arts et des Lettres de la Republique Française; Many other honours and awards. *Memberships:* Academy of Science and Art, Tiberina and Cosentina; President, International Mozart Company. *Address:* Hernalser Guertel 41, A 1170 Vienna, Austria.

MAYHAR Ardath (Frances), (J K, John Killdeer), b. 20 Feb 1930, Timpson, Texas, USA. Writer; Teacher. m. Joe E Mayhar, 7 June 1958, Nacogdoches, Texas. 2 sons. *Publications:* How The Gods Wove in Kyrannon, 1979; Seekers of Shar-Nuhn, 1980; Soul-Singer of Tyrnos, 1981; Warlock's Gift, 1982; Golden Dream: A Fuzzy Odyssey, 1982; Runes of the Lyre, 1982; Khi to Freedom, 1983; Lords of the Triple Moons, 1983; Exile on Vlahil, 1984; The Absolutely Perfect Horse, 1983; The World Ends in Hickory Hollow, 1985; The Saga of Grittel Sundotha, 1985; Medicine Walk, 1985; Carrots and Miggle, 1986; Makra Choria, 1987; Bloody Texas Trail, 1988; A Place of Silver Silence; BattleTech: The Sword and the Dagger, 1987; Trail of the Seahawks, 1987; The Wall, Space & Time, 1987; Monkey Station (with Ron Fortier), 1989; People of the Mesa, 1992; Island in the Swamp, 1993; Towers of the Earth, in progress; as John Killdeer: Wild Country, 1992; Blood Kin, 1993; as J.K: The Untamed, 1992; Wilderness Rendezvous, 1992. *Contributions to:* stories: The Twilight Zone Magazine; Isaac Asimov's Science Fiction Magazine; Espionage Magazine; Mike Shayne's Mystery Magazine, and many small and literary magazines; Narrative poetry to: Fantasy Book; Pulpsmith; Tempest. *Honour:* Balrog Award, Best Poet, 1985. *Memberships:* Science Fiction Writers of America; Western Writers of America. *Literary Agent:* Donald Maass. *Address:* PO Box 180, Chireno, TX 75937, USA.

MAYNARD Christopher, b. 1949, Canadian. *Appointments:* Editor, Macdonald Educational, 1972-74, Intercontinental Book Productions, Maidenhead, Berkshire, 1976-77; Director, The Strip Limited, Maynard and How Publishing, London. *Publications:* Planet Eart, Prehistoric World, 1974; Great Men of Science (with Edward Holmes), 1975; The Amazing World of Dinosaurs, The Real Cowboy (with others), 1976; The Amazing World of Money, 1977; Smimitar Paperbacks (ed), 1977-78; Economy Guide to Europe (with others), New York (with Gail Rebuck), Indians and Palefaces (with Marianne Gray), The Razzmataz Gang, 1978; Father Christmas and His Friends, 1979; The First Great Kids Catalogue, 1987. *Address:* 78 Carlton Mansions, Randolph Avenue, London W9, England.

MAYNARD Fredelle Bruser, b. 9 July 1922, Foam Lake, Canada. Writer; Lecturer; TV Host. Divorced, 2 daughters. *Education:* BA, Honours, University of Manitoba, 1942; MA, University of Toronto, 1943; PhD, Phi Beta Kappa, Harvard University, USA, 1947. *Appointments:* Radcliffe Institute Scholar, 1967-69; Writer in Residence, University of Illinois, USA, 1974. *Publications:* Raisins and Almonds, 1972; Guiding Your Child to a More Creative Life, 1973; The Child Care Crisis, 1985; The Tree of Life, 1988. *Contributions to:* Numerous journals in USA, Canada, England, Australia & South Africa. *Honours:* Governor General's Medal, Canadian Federation of University Women's Fellowship; Flavelle Fellowship (Harvard); University of Missouri Award for Excellence in Women's Journalism; Canada Council Senior Arts Award. *Memberships:* Periodical Writers Association of Canada; Distinguished Affiliate, Ontario Association of Marriage and Family Therapy; Honorary Member, International Association for Promotion of Humanistic Studies in Gynaecology. *Address:* 25 Metcalfe St, Toronto, Ontario, Canada M4X 1R5.

MAYNARD Richard, b. 30 Sept 1936, London, England. Construction Manager. m. Margaret, 6 July 1973, 2 sons. *Publications:* The Coconut Book, 1985; The Quiet Place, (also known as The Return, in USA), 1987; Trail of the Warrigal, 1988; The Gundabara Legacy, 1989. *Address:* 86 Donaldson Street, Corinda, Queensland, Australia.

MAYNE Richard (John), b. 2 Apr 1926, London, England. Writer; Editor; Broadcaster. m. Jocelyn Mudie Ferguson, 2 daughters. *Education:* MA, PhD, Trinity College, Cambridge, 1947-53. *Appointments:* Rome Correspondent, New Statesman, 1953-54; Paris Correspondent, 1963-73, Co-Editor, 1985-90, Encounter. *Publications:* The Community of Europe, 1962; The Institutions of the European Community, 1968; The Recovery of Europe, 1970; The Europeans, 1972; Europe Tomorrow, (ed), 1972; The New Atlantic Challenge, (ed), 1975; The Memoirs of Jean Monnet, (translation), 1978; Postwar: The Dawn of Today's Europe, 1983; Western Europe: A Handbook, (ed), 1987; Federal Union: The Pioneers (with John Pinder), 1990; Europe: A History of its Peoples (translation), 1990; History of Europe (translation), 1993. *Contributions to:* Numerous in UK, USA, France and Germany. *Honour:* Scott-Moncrieff Prize for Translation from French, 1978. *Memberships:* Society of Authors; Royal Institute of International Affairs; Council member, Federal Trust for Education & Research; Franco-British Council; UK Council of European Movement. *Address:* Albany Cottage, 24 Park Village East, Regent's Park, London NW1 7PZ, England.

MAYNE Seymour, b. 18 May 1944, Montreal, Canada. Poet; Editor; Translator. *Education:* BA, McGill University, 1965; MA, 1966; PhD, University of british Columbia. *Appointments:* Managing Editor, Vary Stone House, 1966-69; Editor, Ingluvin Publications, 1970-73; Editor, Mosaic Press, 1974-83. *Publications:* Mouth; Name; Diaporas; The Impossible Promised Land; Vanguard of Dreams; Children of Abel; Simple Ceremony; Essential Words; Killing Times, 1992; Locust of Silence, 1993. *Honours:* Chester Macnaghten First Prize; J I Segal Prize; York Poetry Workshop Award;

American Literary Translators Association, Poetry Translation Award, 1990. *Memberships:* PEN; AM Klein Research & Publication Committee. *Address:* Department of English, University of Ottawa, Ottawa, Ontario, Canada K1N 6N5.

MAYNE William, b. 16 Mar 1928. Writer. *Appointments:* Lecturer, Creative Writing, Deakin University, Geelong, Australia, 1976, 1977. *Publications:* Published about 66 stories for children and young people, 1953-. *Honours:* Library Association's Carnegie Medal for Best Children's Book of the Year, (1956) 1957. *Memberships:* Fellow, Creative Writing, Rolle College, Exmouth, 1979-80. *Address:* c/o David Higham Associates, 5-8 Lower John Street, Golden Square, London W1R 4HA, England.

MAYO James. *See:* **COULTER Stephen.**

MAYRÖCKER Friederike, b. 20 Dec 1924, Vienna, Austria. Writer; Poetess. *Publications include:* More than 50 books of poetry, childrens' books, novels, prose, radio plays, most recent being: Reise durch die Nacht, 1984; Das Herzzerreiszende der Dinge, 1985; Winterglück, 1986; Magische Blätter I, II, III, 1983 and 1987; Stilleben, Dasbesessene Alter. *Contributions include:* Numerous articles in literary journals and magazines since 1946. *Honours:* Hörspielpreis der Kriegsblinden, 1968; Osterreichischer Würdigungspreis, 1975; Preis der Stadt Wien, 1976; Georg Trakl-Preis, 1977; Roswitha-von-Gandersheim-Preis, 1982; Anton-Wildgans-Preis, 1982; Grosser Osterreichischer Staatspreis, 1982; Literaturpreis des Südwestfunk, 1985; Hauptpreis fur Literatur der Deutschen Industrie, 1989; Friedrich-Hölderlih Preis, 1993. *Memberships:* Osterreichischer Kunstsenat Wien; Kurie für Wissenschaft und Kunst; Akademie der Künste Berlin-West; Internationales Künstlergremium; Grazer Autorenversammlung; Deutsche Akademie für Sprache und Dichtung Darmstadt; Forum Stadtpark; Graz. *Address:* Zentagasse 16/40, A-1050 Vienna, Austria.

MAYSON Marina. *See:* **ROGERS Rosemary.**

MAZER Norma Fox, b. 15 May 1931, New York City, USA. Writer. m. Harry Mazer, 12 Feb 1950, 1 son, 3 daughters. *Publications:* After the Rain, 1987; Dear Bill, Remember Me?, 1976; A Figure of Speech, 1973; Silver 1988; Taking Terri Mueller, 1981; I Trissy, 1971; Saturday the Twelfth of October, 1975; The Solid Gold Kid, 1977; Up in Setho's Room, 1979; Mrs Fish, Ape, and Me the Dump Queen, 1980; Summer Girls, Love Boys, and other Stories, 1982; When We First Met, 1982; Someone to Love, 1983; Supergirl, the Novel, 1984; Downtown, 1984; Three Sisters, 1986; A My Name is Ami, 1986; B, My Name is Bunny, 1987; Heartbeat, 1989; Waltzing on Water, poetry, 1989; Babyface, 1990; C, My Name is Cal, 1990; Bright Days, Stupid Nights, 1991; D, My Name is Danita, 1992; E, My Name is Emily, 1992; Out of Control, 1993. *Contributions to:* English Journal; Alan Review; The Writer; Signal; Writing; Redbook; Playgirl; Voice; Ingenue. *Honours include:* National Book Award Nominee, 1974; Califronia Young Reader's Medal, Edgar Allen Poe Award, 1983; Newbery Honor Book; School Library Journal Best Book of the Year, ALA Notable Book, ALA Best Books for Young Adults, Association of Booksellers for Children Choices; Canadian Children's Book Council CHoice; Horn Book Fanfare Book, all 1988; ALA Best Books for Young Adults, 1989; Iowa Teen Choice Award, 1989; CBC IRA Children's Choice, 1990; American Bookseller Pick of the Lists, IRA Teachers' Choice, 1991. *Memberships:* PEN; Authors Guild. *Literary Agent:* Elaine Marksson Literary Agency, 44 Greenwich Avenue, NYC 10011, USA. *Address:* Brown Gulf Road, Jamesville, NY 13078, USA.

MAZLISH Bruce, b. 15 Sept 1923, New York City, USA. Historian; WrldEb. *Education:* BA, Columbia College, 1944; MA 1946, PhD 1955, Columbia University. *Publications include:* The Western Intellectual Tradition: From Leonardo to Hegel, with J Bronowski, 1960; In Search of Nixon: A psychohistorical study, 1972; Kissinger: The European Mind in American Policy, 1972; The Revolutionary Ascetic, 1976; The Meaning of Karl Marx, 1984; A New Science: The Breakdown of Connection and the Birth of Society, 1989. *Contributions to:* Various journals and magazines. *Honours:* Fellow, American Academy of Arts and Sciences, 1967; Clement Staff Essay Award, 1968; The Toynbee Prize, 1986-87. *Address:* 11 Lowell Street, Cambridge, MA 02138, URA.

MAZUMDAR Maxim William, b. 27 Jan 1953, Bombay, India. Actor; Playwright. m. 16 Aug 1984. *Education:* BA, Loyola College, 1972; Dip.Ed., McGill University, 1973; MA, City University of New York, USA, 1986. *Appointments:* Head, Theatre Programme, Acadia University, 1985; Performance Studies, Memramcook School of Performing Arts, 1987. *Publications:* Oscar Remembered, 1978; Dance for Gods, 1980; Invitation to the Dance, 1981; Journeys, 1987; Tennessee and Me, 1983; Rimbaud, 1979; Conversations with Diaghilev, Nijinsky, 1980; Unholy Trinity, 1986. *Contributions to:* various journals and magazines. *Honours:* ACTRA Award Nominee, 1976; Anik Award, CBC TV Script, The Fun of Being with Oscar, 1977; Canada Council Project Award Winner, 1987. *Memberships:* Dramatists Guild, 1981; Playwrights Union of Canada, 1987; Canadian Actors Equity, Advisory Board, Atlantic Region; Artistic Director, Stephenville Festival. *Address:* c/o The Stephenville Festival, Box 282 Stephenville, Newfoundland, Canada A2N 2Z4.

MAZUR Bridget, b. 9 Jan 1958, Buffalo, New York, USA. Writer. m. Christopher Mazur, 1 Aug 1981, 1 son, 1 daughter. *Education:* BS Medical Technology, State University New York, 1980; MPH, University of California, 1981; MFA in Writing, Vermont College, 1990. *Appointments:* Instructor, Fiction and Non-Ficton Writing, Lebanon College, 1990-. *Publications:* The Art of Baking, the Politics of Love, 1991; Atlas's Revenge, 1992; Our Lady of the Keyboard, 1989; A Woman's Place is Intuition, 1990; The Eye of the Needle, 1991; The Problems and Pitfalls of Writing About Sex, 1989. *Contributions to:* Associate Editor, AIDS and Society: An International Research and Policy Bulletin. *Honours:* Fellowship, Vermont Council on the Arts, 1992. *Memberships:* Poets and Writers. *Address:* PO Box 656, Norwich, VT 05055, USA.

MAZZARO, Jerome Louis, b. 25 Nov 1934, Detroit, Michigan, USA. College Professor; Freelance Writer. *Education:* AB, Wayne State University, 1954; MA, University of Iowa, 1956; PhD, Wayne State University, 1963. *Literary Appointments:* Editor: Fresco 1959-60, Modern Poetry Studies 1970-78, Poetry Review 1965-66; Contributing editor: Salmagundi 1967-, American Poetry Review 1972-, Italian-Americana 1974-88. *Publications include:* Poetic Themes of Robert Lowell, 1965; Changing the Windows: Poems, 1966; Transformations in the Renaissance English Lyric, 1970; William Carlos Williams: Later Poems, 1973; Figure of Dante, 1981; Caves of Love, 1985; Rubbings, 1985. Also: Juvenal's Satires, 1965; Postmodern American Poetry, 1980. *Contributions to:* Numerous journals including: Accent; Bennington Review; Choice (Chicago); Epoch; Georgia Review; Hudson Review; Literary Review; Humanist; Nation; New Republic; New Letters; Salmagundi; Shenandoah; Sewanee Review. *Honours:* John Simon Guggenheim Memorial Fellowship, 1964-65; Hadley Fellowship, 1979-80. *Memberships:* Past member, governing councils: Dante Society of America, Poetry Society of America. *Address:* 147 Capen Boulevard, Buffalo, New York 14226, USA.

MBURUMBA Kerina, b. 6 June 1932, Tsumeb, Namibia. Professor amd Member Parliament. m. Jane M Miller, Los Angeles, California, 1957, 2 sons, 2 daughters. *Education:* BA, Lincoln University, Oxford, Pennsylvania, USA, 1957; Legal courses, American Extension School of Law, Chicago Correspondence

School, 1953-57; Graduate courses, Graduate Faculty, New School for Social Research, 1957-59; PhD, H C Political Science, Padjajaran University, Badung, Indonesia, 1962. *Appointments include:* Diplomatic Attache of Republic of Liberia to United Nations, Legal Researcher for Republic of Liberia and Ethiopia, International Court of Justice, 1960-63; Adjunct Assistant Professor, School of Education, 1968-70, Associate Professor, Afro-Americnan Studies, 1970-71, Associate Professor, Africana Studies Dept, 1972-75, Brooklyn College, City University of New York; Visiting Professor, Livingston College, Rutgers University, 1970-71; In Namibia: Director of Communications, Namibia Foundation, 1976-78; Member of the Constituent Assembly and currently Member of the National Assembly of Namibia, 1990; Consultant and Lecturer. *Publications include:* Leadership and Responsibility, 1962, Vol 2 No 2; Co-editor with H Newman, Malcolm X: The Apostle of Defiance, An African View in Malcolm X. The Man and His Times, John H Clarke (Ed) 1969; The Political History of Namibia 1884-1972, 1979; Namibia the Making of a Nation. *Contributions to:* Ghanian Times; The New African; Africa South; Egytian Review. *Address:* PO Box 24861, Windhoek, Namibia, South West Africa.

MCADAM Douglas John, b. 31 Aug 1951, Pasadena, California, USA. Professor of Sociology. m. Tracy Lynn Stevens, 20 Feb 1988. *Education:* BA, Occidental College, Los Angeles, California, 1973; MA, 1977, PhD, 1979, SUNY at Stony Brook. *Publications:* Freedom Summer, 1988; Political Process and the Development of Black Insurgency 1930-1970, 1982; Politics of Privacy, 1980. *Contributions to:* Numerous articles in American Journal of Sociology, American Sociological Review. *Honour:* Finalist for 1989 Sorokin Award (given annually for best book in Sociology). *Membership:* American Sociological Association. *Address:* Department of Sociology, University of Arizona, Tucson, AZ 85721, USA.

MCALINDON Thomas Edward, b. 14 Sept 1932, Belfast, Northern Ireland. University Teacher. m. Margot King, 11 July 1962, 3 sons. *Education:* BA 1953, MA 1955, PhD 1961. Cambridge University. *Appointments:* Assistant Lecturer, University College, Cork, 1960-61; Lecturer 1961-70, Senior Lecturer 1970-86, Reader 1986-, Professor 1992-, University of Hull; Visiting Professor, University of Ottawa, 1978-79. *Publications:* Shakespeare and Decorum, 1973; English Renaissance Tragedy, 1986; Shakespeare's Tragic Cosmos, 1991. *Contributions to:* Review of English Studies; Modern Language Review; Publications of the Modern Language Association of America, Modern Philology, Mosaic. *Honours:* Mellon Research Fellow, Huntington Library, San Marino, California, 1989. *Memberships:* Modern Language Association of America; Marlowe Society of America; Shakespeare Association of America. *Address:* Department of English, The University of Hull, Hull, HU6 7RX, England.

MCALLISTER Bruce (Hugh), b. 1946, American. *Appointments:* Visiting Instructor 1971-74, Assistant Professor 1974-79, Associate Professor 1979-83, Director of the Writing Program 1979-, Professor of English 1983-, University of Redlands, CA; Consultant, VSP Associate, Sacramento, 1982-. *Publications:* Humanity Prime, 1971; SF Directions (ed), 1972; Their Immortal Hearts (ed), 1980; The Faces Outside, 1985. *Address:* 935 Aaron Drive, Redlands, CA 92374, USA.

MCALLISTER Casey. *See:* BATTIN B W.

MCAULEY James J, b. 1936, Irish. *Appointments:* Journalist, Literary Critic, Lecturer, Dublin, 1954-66; Teaching Assistant, English Department, University of Arkansas, Fayetteville, 1966-68; Assistant Professor, Director of Creative Writing, 1968-70, Lycoming College, Williamsport, PA; Assistant Professor 1970-73, Associate Professor 1973-78, Director, Creative Writing Program, 1970-, Professor of English, 1978-, Eastern Washington University, Cheney. *Publications:*

Observations, 1960; A New Address, 1965; The Revolution, 1966; Draft Balance Sheet, 1970; After the Blizzard, The Exile's Recurring Nightmare, 1975; An Irish Bull and Praise, 1981; The Exile's Book of Hours, 1982. *Address:* Department of English, Eastern Washington University, Cheney, WA 99004, USA.

MCBAIN Ed. *See:* LOMBINO Salvatore A.

MCBAIN Laurie (Lee), b. 1949, American. *Publications:* Devil's Desire, 1975; Moonstruck Madness, 1977; Tears of Gold, 1979; Chance the Winds of Fortune, 1980; Dark Before the Rising Sun, 1982; Wild Bells to the Wild Sky, 1983; When the Splendor Falls, 1985. *Address:* c/o Harold Ober Associates, 425 Madison Avenue, New York, NY 10017, USA.

MCCABE Helen, b. 3 Mar 1942, Worcester, England. Novelist; Scriptwriter; Poet. div. 1 son, 2 daughters. *Education:* BA Hons English, University of London, 1974; MA, University of Keele, 1984. *Appointments:* Assistant Teacher of English, 1975-84, Lecturer, University of Birmingham, 1975-84. *Publications:* Several novels. *Contributions to:* Financial Times; BBC Radio; Country Quest; MENSA. *Memberships:* Writers Guild of Great Britain; Romantic Novelists Association; MENSA. *Address:* 81 Corbett Avenue, Droitwich, Worcs WR9 8BH, England.

MCCAFFREY Anne (Inez), b. 1926, American. *Appointments:* Copywriter, Liberty Music Shops, 1948-50; Copywriter and Executive Secretary, Helen Rubinstein Incorporated, 1950-54. *Publications:* Restoree, 1967; Dragon-flight, 1968; Decision at Doona, Alchemy and Academe (ed), 1969; Ship Who Sang, 1970; Dragonquest, The Mark of Merlin, Ring of Fear, 1971; To Ride Pegasus, Cooking Out of This World (ed), 1973; Kilternan Legacy, 1975; Dragonsong, 1976; Dragonsinger, Get Off the Unicorn, 1977; The White Dragon, Dinosaur Planet, 1978; Dragondrums, 1979; The Worlds of Anne McCaffrey, 1981; Crystal Singer, 1982; The Coelura, Moreta Dragonlady of Pern, 1983; Dinosaur Planet Survivors, Stitch in Snow, 1984; Killashandra, 1985; Nerilka's Story, The Year of the Lucy, 1986; The Carradyne Touch, 1987; Dragons Dawn, 1988; Renegades of Pern, 1989; Sassinak (with Elizabeth Moon), 1990; The Death of Sleep (with Jody-Lynn Nye), 1990; The Rowan, 1990; Pegasus in Flight, 1990; All the Weyrs of Pern, 1992; Crystal Like, 1992. *Address:* Dragonhold, Kilaquade, Greystones, Co Wicklow, Ireland.

MCCALL Mabel Bunny, b. 6 Feb 1923, Bronx, New York, USA. Retired. m. T Ross, 31 Oct 1947, dec. 1973. *Publications:* Poetry includes: Africa...Sings; The Rape of the Lady Called Harlem; She Walked to the Tune of a Different Drummer; Did I Pass You God?; Carnival Time; A Full Moon in the West Indies; Ode to a Rose of Darker Hue; Sweet Memories of Dixie Land; The Night My Spirit Took Flight; The Chosen One; My Trip to the Holy Land; In These Gardens of Granite, 1989; The Road Not Taken, 1990; Poems for All Seasons, collection of poems, 1991; Poetry in various anthologies including: Ode to a Cockroach, 1985; My Heart Speaks to Thee, 1985; The Heart of a Poet, 1985; The Art of Poetry, 1985; Dreams and Wishes, 1986; Sands of Time, 1986; Others. *Contributions to:* Unification News; News World; Voice in the Wilderness; Many other journals and magazines. *Honours:* Numerous honours and awards including: Golden Poet Award, Wrld of Poetry, 1985, 1986, 1887, 1988, 1989, 1990, 1991; Award of Merit Certificate, World of Poetry, 1990; 4th Place, Mug Poetry Contest, 1991; Guest Poet, Annual International Festival of Literary and Creative Arts, New York City, 1991. *Memberships:* World of Poetry; American Poetry Association; International Society of Poets. *Address:* 41-12 10th Street 4F, Long Island City, NY 11101, USA.

MCCARRY Charles, b. 1930, American. *Appointments:* Editor, Lisbon Evening Journal, OH, 1952-55; Reporter and Columnist, Vindicator,

Youngstown, Ohio, 1955-56; Assistant to the Secretary of Labor 1956-58, Central Intelligence Agency 1958-60, 1960-67; Freelance Journalist and Writer, 1967-83; Editor-at-Large, National Geographic, WA, 1983-90. *Publications:* Citizen Nader, 1972; The Miernik Dossier, 1973; The Tears of Autumn, 1975; The Secret Lovers, 1977; Double Eagle, 1979; The Better Angels, 1979; The Great Southwest, 1981; The Last Supper, 1983; The Bride of the Wilderness, 1988; Second Sight, 1991. *Address:* c/o William Morris Agency, 1350 Avenue of the Americas, New York, NY 10019, USA.

MCCARTHY Gary W, b. 23 Jan 1943, California, USA. Western & Historical Novelist. m. Virginia Kurzwell, 14 June 1969, 1 son, 3 daughters. *Education:* BS, Agriculture, California State University; MS, Economics, University of Nevada. *Appointments:* Labor Economist, State of Nevada, Carson City, 1970-77; Economist, Copley International Corporation, La Jolla, CA, 1977-79; Full-time Writer, 1979-. *Publications:* The Derby Man, 1976; Showdown at Snakegrass Junction, 1978; The First Sheriff, 1979; Mustang Fever, The Pony Express War, Winds of Gold, 1980; Silver Shot, Explosion at Donner Pass, The Legend of the Lone Ranger, 1981; North Chase, Rebel of Bodie, 1982; The Rail Warriors, Silver Winds, 1983; Wind River, 1984; Powder River, The Last Buffalo Hunt, 1985; Mando, 1986; The Mustangers, Transcontinental, 1987; Sodbuster, 1988. *Literary Agent:* Joseph Elder Agency. *Address:* 323 Matilija Street, No 204, Ojai, CA 93023, USA.

MCCARTHY Rosemary P, b. 21 Oct 1928, Newark, New Jersey, USA. Public Health Nurse; Retiree, NYC Health Dept; Family Historian, Genealogist, Archivist; Artist; Lecturer. *Education:* BSN, St John's University, 1963; MEd, Columbia University Teachers College, 1973; Catholic University of American, Institute of Adult Education, 1980-81; Long Island University, Southampton Campus, Summer 1986. *Publications include:* The Family Tree of the Connors-Walsh Family of Kiltimagh, County Mayo, Eire, & USA, with Branches in Great Britain & throughout the world, 1979; Grandma, 1986; Editor, International Family Tree newsletter 1979-; International Family Directory 1983-. *Contributions to:* O'Lochlainn's Journal of Irish Families; The Irish Genealogical Foundation. *Memberships:* Various nursing and public health organizations, civic & historical societies. *Address:* 814A Jefferson Street, Alexandria, VA 22314-4255, USA.

MCCARTHY Shaun, (Theo Callas, Desmond Cory), b. 1928, British. *Appointments:* Freelance Journalist and Translator in Europe, 1951-54; Language Teacher in Spain and Sweden, 1954-60; Lecturer, University of Wales Institute of Science and Technology, Cardiff, 1960-77; Lecturer, University of Qatar, 1977-80; Associate Professor of English, University College, Bahrain, 1980-. *Publications:* Secret Ministry (in US as The Nazi Assassins, 1970), Begin Murderer!, 1951; This Traitor Death (in US as The Gestapo File, 1971), This is Jezebel, 1952; Dead Man Falling (in US as The Hitler Diamonds, 1979), Lady Lost, 1953; Intrigue, 1954 (in US as Trieste, 1968); The Shaken Leaf, Height of Day (in US as Dead Men Alive, 1969), City of Kites (as Theo Callas), The Phoenix Sings, 1955; High Requiem, Johnny Goes North (in US as The Swastika Hunt, 1969), 1956; Pilgrim at the Gate, 1957; Johnny Goes East, 1958 (also as Mountainhead, 1966); Johnny Goes West, Johnny Goes South (also as Overload, 1964), Pilgrim on the Island, Ann and Peter in Southern Spain (as Theo Callas), 1959; Jones on the Belgrade Express, The Head, 1960; Stranglehold, 1961; Undertow, 1962; Hammerhead, 1963 (in US as Shockwave, 1964); The Name of the Game, 1964; Deadfall, 1965; Feramontov, 1966; Timelock, 1967; The Night Hawk, 1969; Sunburst, Take My Drum to England (in US as Even If You Run, 1972), 1971; A Bit of a Shunt Up the River, 1974; The Circle Complex, 1975; Bennett, Lucky Ham (as Shaun McCarthy), 1977. *Address:* c/o George Greenfield, John Farquharson Limited, 162-168 Regent Street, London W1R 5TB, England.

MCCARTHY William E(dward) J(ohn), b. 1925, British. *Appointments:* Research Fellow of Nuffield College 1959-63, Staff Lecturer and Tutor in Industrial Relations 1964-65, Fellow, Nuffield College and Centre for Management Studies 1968-, Oxford University; Director of Research, Royal Commission on Trade Unions and Employers' Association, London, 1965-68; Senior Economic Adviser, Department of Employment, 1968-70; Special Adviser, European Economic Commission, 1974-75. *Publications:* The Future of the Unions, 1962; The Closed Shop in Britain, 1964; The Role of Shop Stewards in British Industrial Relations: A Survey of Existing Information and Research, 1966; Disputes Procedures in Britain (with Arthur Ivor Marsh), Employers' Associations: The Result of Two Studies (with V G Munns), 1967; The Role of Government in Industrial Relations, Shop Stewards and Workshop Relations: The Results of a Study, 1968; Industrial Relations in Britain: A Guide for Management and Unions (ed), 1969; The Reform of Collective Bargaining: A Series of Case Studies, 1971; Trade Unions, 1972, 1985; Coming to Terms with Trade Unions (with A J Collier), 1972; Management by Agreement (with N D Ellis), 1973; Wage Inflation and Wage Leadership (with J F O'Brien and V C Dowd), 1975; Making Whitley Work, 1977; Change in Trade Unions (co-author), 1981; Strikes in Post War Britain (with J W Durcun), 1985; Freedom at Work, 1985; The Future of Industrial Democracy, 1988. *Address:* 4 William Orchard Close, Old Headington, Oxford, England.

MCCAULEY Martin, b. 1934, British. *Appointments:* Senior Lecturer in Soviet and East European Studies 1968-91; Senior Lecturer in Politics, 1991-; Member of Council 1976, School of Slavonic and East European Studies, University of London. *Publications:* The Russian Revolution and the Soviet State 1917-1921 (ed and trans), 1975, 1980; Khrushchev and the Development of Soviet Agriculture: The Virgin Land Programme 1953-64, 1976; Communist Power in Europe 1944-1949 (ed and co-author), 1977, 1980; Marxism - Leninism in the German Democratic Republic: The Socialist Unity Party (SED), The Stalin File, 1979; The Soviet Union Since 1917, 1981; The Soviet Union, 1917-1991, 2nd edition 1993; Stalin and Stalinism, The Origins of the Cold War, The Soviet Union since Brezhnev (ed and contrib), 1983; The German Democratic Republic since 1945, Octobrists to Bolsheviks: Imperial Russia 1905-1917, 1984; Leadership and Succession in the Soviet Union, Eastern Europe and China (ed and contrib), 1985; The Origins of the Modern Russian State 1855-81 (with Peter Waldron), The Soviet Union under Gorbachev (ed), 1987; Gorbachev and Perestroika (ed), 1990; Khrushchev, 1991; Directory of Russian MPs (ed), 1993. *Membership:* Politics and Society Group; Economic and Social Research Council; East-West Initiative Group, 1991-93. *Address:* School of Slavonic and East European Studies, Senate House, Malet Street, London WC1E 7HU, England.

MCCAULEY Sue. *See:* **HAMMOND Susan Montgomery.**

MCCGWIRE Michael Kane, b. 9 Dec 1924, Madras, India. m. Helen Jean Scott, 22 Nov 1952, 2 sons, 3 daughters. *Education:* RNC Dartmouth, 1938-42; University of Wales, BSc, 1967-70. *Appointments:* Office, Royal Navy (Commander), 1942-67; Professor, Dalhousie University, 1971-79; Senior Fellow, The Brookings Institution, Washington, DC, 1979-90; Visiting Professor, Global Security Programme, Camrbidge University, 1990-1993. *Publications:* Author: Perestroika & Soviet National Security; Military Objectives & Soviet Policy; Editor: Soviet Naval Influence; Soviet Naval Policy; Soviet Naval Developments. *Contributions to:* Numerous. *Honours:* Order of the British Empire. *Address:* Hayes, Durlston, Swanage, Dorset, BH19 2JF, England.

MCCLANE Kenneth A Jr, b. 19 Feb 1951, New York, USA. W.E.B. Du Bois, Professor of English. m. Rochelle Evette Woods, 22 Oct 1983. *Education:* AB, 1973, MA 1974, MFA, 1976, Cornell University. *Appointments:*

Visiting Professor, Colby College, 1975-76; Luce Visiting Professor, Williams College, 1983; Associate Professor, English, Cornell University, 1983-, Full Professor of English, Cornell University, 1989-; Martin Luther King Visiting Professor, Wayne State University, 1987. *Publications:* Walls: Essays, 1985-1990; Take Five, collected Poems, 1971-86; A Tree Beyond Telling, 1983; At Winter's End, 1982; To Hear the River, 1981; Moons and Low Times, 1978; Out Beyond the Bay, 1975; These Halves Are Whole, 1983; Running Before the Wind, 1972. *Contributions to:* Antioch Review; Northwest Review; Community Review; Black Scholar. *Honours:* George Harmon Coxe Award, 1973; Corson Morrison Poetry Prize, 1973; Phi Beta Kappa, 1973; Lamont Poetry Prize Nominee, 1978. *Memberships:* Poets and Writers; Associated Writing Programme. *Address:* Dept. of English, Rockefeller Hall, Cornell University, Ithaca, NY 14853, USA.

MCCLINTOCK David, b. 4 July 1913, Newcastle upon Tyne, England. Writer. m. Elizabeth Anne Dawson, 6 July 1940, 2 sons, 2 daughters. *Education:* BA, 1934, MA, 1940, Trinity College, Cambridge. *Publications include:* Pocket Guide to Wild Flowers, with R.S.R. Fitter, 1956; Supplement to Pocket Guide to Wild Flowers, 1957; Natural History of the Garden of Buckingham Palace, jointly, 1964; Companion to Flowers, 1966; Guide to the Naming of Plants, 1969, 2nd edition 1980; Wild Flowers of Guernsey, 1975, Supplement, 1987; Wild Flowers of the Channel Islands, with J. Bichard, 1975; Joshua Gosselin of Guernsey, 1976; The Heather Garden by H van de Laar, 1978, edited and rewritten; Guernsey's Earliest Flora, 1982. *Contributions:* over 900 to 80 publications, in British Isles and abroad; 25 contributions to other books. *Memberships include:* Fellow, Linnean Society, Vice President, 1971-74, Editorial Secretary, 1974-78, Council, 1970-78; Botanical Society of the British Isles, President 1971-73; Heather Society, President, 1990-. *Address:* Bracken Hill, Platt, Sevenoaks, Kent TN15 8JH, England.

MCCLURE Gillian Mary, b. 29 Oct 1948, Bradford, England. Author; Illustrator. m. 26 Sept 1971, 3 sons. *Education:* Horsham High School for Girls; BA, Combined Honours in French, English and History of Art, Bristol University; Teaching Diploma, Moray House. *Publications:* What's the Time Rory Wolf? 1982; Prickly Pig, 1976; Cat Flap, 1990; What Happened to the Picnic? 1987; Fly Home McDoo, 1979; The Emperor's Singing Bird, 1974; Collaboration with Father Paul Coltman:- Tog the Ribber, 1985; Witch Watch, 1989; Tinker Jim, 1992. *Honours:* Tog Ribber, Highly Commended: Smarties Award, 1985, and Highly Commended: Kate Greenaway Award, 1985; Shortlisted for the Smarties Award for Tinker Jim, 1992. *Membership:* CWIG Society of Authors, Committee Member 1989-; PLR Advisory Committee, 1992. *Literary Agent:* Curtis Brown. *Address:* The Mill House, Mill Lane, Whittlesford, Cambs. CB2 4NE, England.

MCCLURE James, b. 1939, British. *Appointments:* Photographer and Teacher, Natal, 1958-63; Journalist, Natal, Edingburgh, Oxford, 1963-69; Deputy Editor, Oxford Times Group, 1971-74; Managing Director, Sabensa Gakula Limited, Oxford, 1975-. *Publications:* The Steam Pig, 1971; The Caterpillar Cop, 1972; Four and Twenty Virgins, 1973; The Gooseberry Fool, 1974; Snake, 1975; Rogue Eagle, Killers, 1976; The Sunday Hangman, 1977; The Blood of an Englishman, Spike Island: Portrait of a British Police Division, 1980; The Artful Egg, 1984; Copworld, 1985. *Address:* 14 York Road, Headington, Oxford OX3 8NW, England.

MCCOLGAN John Joseph, b. 5 May 1946, Boston, MA, USA. Records and Information Management Consultant; President, MC Records Management Enterprises. m. Donna Blythe, 26 Nov 1989, 1 Son. *Education:* Diploma in Archival Studies, National University of Ireland, 1979; PhD, National University of Ireland, 1976; Bachelor of Science, Boston College, 1968. *Publication:* British Policy and the Irish Administration 1920-22. *Contributions to:* Irish Historical Studies, Administration; Irish Archives

Bulletin. *Memberships:* Association of Records Managers & Administrators. *Address:* 69 Houston Avenue, Milton, MA 01286, USA.

MCCOLLEY Diane Laurene Kelsey, b. 9 Feb 1934, Riverside, California, USA. University Professor. m. Robert M McColley, 30 Aug 1958, 1 son, 5 daughters. *Education:* AB, University of California; PhD, University of Illinois. *Publications:* Miltons Eve; A Gust for Paradise; Others inc. Cambridge Companion to Milton; Medieval and Renaissance Texts and Studies. *Contributions to:* Milton Studies; Various Journals. *Memberships:* Milton Society of America; Modern Language Association; Renaissance Society of America. *Address:* Dept of English, Rutgers, The State University of New Jersey, Camden, NJ 08102, USA.

MCCOLLINS. *See:* **PASZKOWSKI Kazimierz.**

MCCONICA James Kelsey, b. 1930, Canadian. *Appointments:* Instructor 1956-57, Assistant Professor of History 1957-62, University of Saskatchewan, Saskatoon; Associate Professor 1967-70, Professor 1976-, Pontifical Institute of Medieval Studies, Toronto; Visiting Fellow 1969-71, 1977, Research Fellow 1978-, All Souls College, Oxford; Associate Director, Center for Medieval Studies, 1973-76; President, University of St Michael's College, Toronto, 1984-; Research Fellow, All Souls College, Oxford, 1990-. *Publications:* English Humanists and Reformation Politics, 1965; The Correspondence of Erasmus 1515-1517 (ed), volumes III and IV of Collected Works of Erasmus, 1976, 1977; Thomas More: A Short Biography, 1977; The History of the University of Oxford: The Collegiate University, volume 3, 1986; Erasmus, 1991. *Honours:* Fellow, Royal Society of Canada, 1987; Foreign Member, Royal Belgian Academy. *Memberships:* American Society for Reformation Research; Renaissance Society of America; Royal Historical Society. *Address:* All Souls College, Oxford OX1 4AL, England.

MCCONKEY James Rodney, b. 2 Sept 1921, Educator; Writer. m. Gladys Jean Voorhees, 6 May 1944, 3 sons. *Education:* BA, Cleveland College, 1943; MA, Western Reserve University, 1946; PhD, University of Iowa, 1953. *Appointments:* Director, Morehead Writers' Workshop, 1951-56; Director, Antioch Seminar in Writing and Publishing, 1957-59; Editorial Staff, Currently Advisory Editor, Epoch Magazine, 1956-. *Publications:* Court of Memory, 1983; The Tree House Confessions, 1979; To a Distant Island, 1984; Crossroads, 1968; The Novels of E M Forster, 1957; Kayo: The Authentic and Annotated Autobiographical Novel from Outer Space, 1987; Night Stand, 1965; A Journey to Sahalin, 1971; Editor: Chekov and Our Age, 1985; The Structure of Prose, 1963; Kentucky Writing, 1954; Kentucky Writing II, 1956; Stories from My Life with the Other Animals, 1993. *Contributions to:* The New Yorker; Hudson Review; Shenandoah; American Poetry Review; Yale Review; Sewanee Review; The New York Times Book Review; Washington Post Book World. *Honours:* Saxton Literary Fellowship, 1962; National Endowment for the Arts Essay Award, 1968; Guggenheim Fellowship, 1969; Award in Literature, American Academy and Institute of Arts and Letters, 1979. *Literary Agent:* Jane Gelfman, John Farquharson Limited. *Address:* 402 Aiken Road, Trumansburg, NY 14886, USA.

MCCONNELL Will. *See:* **SNODGRASS W D.**

MCCORD Anne, b. 1942, British. *Appointments:* Teacher, 1964-71; Higher Scientific Officer, British Museum of Natural History, London, 1971-78; Assistant Registrar, University of Reading, 1978-. *Publications:* All About Early Man, 1974; Dinosaurs, Prehistoric Mammals, Early Man, 1977; Children's Encyclopaedia of Prehistoric Life, 1980. *Address:* School of Education, The University, London Road, Reading RG1 5AQ, England.

MCCORMICK John Owen, b. 20 Sept 1918, Thief River Falls, Minnesota, USA. Professor, Comparative Literature. m. Mairi MacInnes, 4 Feb 1954, 3 sons, 1 daughter. *Education:* BA 1941, MA 1947, University of Minnesota; PhD, Harvard University, 1951. *Appointments:* Senior Tutor and Teaching Assistant, Harvard University, Cambridge, MS, 1946-51; Lecturer, Salzburg Seminar in American Studies, Austria, 1951-52; Professor of American Studies, Free University of Berlin, 1952-53, 1954-59; Professor of Comparative Literature, 1959-, now Emeritus, Rutgers University, New Brunswick, NJ. *Publications:* Catastrophe and Imagination, 1957; Versions of Censorship (with Mairi MacInnes), 1962; The Complete Aficionado, 1967; The Middle Distance: A Comparative History of American Imaginative Literature, 1919-1932, 1971; Fiction as Knowledge: The Modern Post-Romantic Novel, 1975; George Santayana: A Biography, 1987. *Contributions to:* numerous magazines & journals. *Honours:* Guggenheim Fellow, 1964-65, 1980-81; Longview Award for Non-Fiction, 1960; Senior Fellow, NEH, 1983-84; American Academy and Institute of Arts and Letters Prize, 1988. *Agent:* ICM (International Creative Management), New York. *Address:* Hovingham Lodge, Hovingham, York, YO6 4NA, England.

MCCORQUODALE Barbara Hamilton, (Dame Barbara Cartland). Writer; Lecturer; Public Speaker. *Publications:* Author of more than 521 books including: The Explosion of Love, 1980; A Heart is Stolen, 1980; The Power and the Prince, 1980; Free From Fear, 1980; A Song Of Love, 1980; Love For Sale, 1980; Little White Doves of Love, 1980; The Perfection of Love, 1980; Lost Laughter, 1980; Punished With Love, 1980; Lucifer and the Angel, 1980; Ola and the Sea Wolf, 1980; The Prude and the Prodigal, 1980; The Goddess and the Gaiety Girl, 1980; Signpost to Love, 1980; Money, Magic and Marriage, 1980; Love in the Moon, 1980; Pride and the Poor Princess, 1980; The Waltz of Hearts, 1980; From Hell to Heaven, 1981; The Kiss Of Life, 1981; Afraid, 1981; Dreams Do Come True, 1981; In the Arms of Love, 1981; For All Eternity, 1981; Pure and Untouched, 1981, 1981; Coutn the Stars, 1981; Kneel for Mercy, 1982; Call of the Highlands, 1982; A Miracle in Music, 1982; From Hate to Love, 1983; Lights, Laughter and a Lady, 1983; Diona and a Dalmatian, 1983; Moonlight on the Sphinx, 1984; Bride to a Brigand, 1984; Love Comes West, 1984; A Witch's Spell, 1984; White Lilac, 1984; Miracle for a Madonna, 1984; Royal Punishment, 1985; The Devilish Deception, 1985; Secrets of the Heart, 1985; A Caretaker of Love, 1985; The Devil Defeated, 1985; Love in the Ruins, 1989; The Duke's Dilemma, 1989; Beyond The Stars, 1990; Love Runs in, 1991; A Secret Passage to Love, 1992; A Train to Love, 1992; The Man of Her Dreams, 1993; Captured by Love, 1993; Love or Money, 1993; Danger to the Duke, 1993; The King without a Heart, 1993; A Battle of Love, 1993; Lovers in London, 1993. *Honours include:* DBE, 1991; Gold Medal, City of Paris for Achievement, 1988; Achiever of the Year Award, National Home Furnishing Association, 1981; Bishop Wright Air Industry Award, 1984. *Address:* Camfield Place, Hatfield, Herts, England.

MCCRAW Thomas K, b. 1940, American. *Appointments:* Newcomen Research Fellow, Harvard University, Cambridge, MA, 1973-74; Associate Professor, University of Texas at Austin, 1974-78; Visiting Associate Professor 1976-78, Professor of Business Administration 1978-, Straus Professor of Business History, 1989-, Harvard Business School, Boston. *Publications:* Morgan vs Lilienthal: The Feud Within the TVA, 1970; TVA and the Power Fight 1933-1939, 1971; Regulation in Perspective: Historical Essays (ed and contrib), 1981; Prophets of Regulation, 1984; America vs Japan (ed), 1986. *Honour:* Recipient of Pulitzer Prize for History, 1985. *Address:* Harvard Business School, Soldiers Field, Boston, MA 02163, USA.

MCCREADY Jack. *See:* **POWELL Talmage.**

MCCRUMB Sharyn Elaine Arwood. b. 26 Feb 1948, Wilmington, North Caroline, USA. m. David McCrumb, 9 Jan 1982, 1 son, 2 daughters. *Education:* BA, University of North Carolina, 1970; MA, Virginia Tech, 1987. *Publications:* The Hangmans Beautiful Daughter; If Ever I Return Pretty Peggy O; Bimbos of the Death Sun; Missing Susan; Highland Laddie Gone; Sick of Shadows; Lovely in Her Bones; Paying the Piper; The Windsor Knot; Zombies of the Gene Pool; MacPhersons Lament. *Contributions to:* Ellery Queen; Crescent Review; Appalachian Heritage; Yorker; Mystery Scene. *Honours:* New York Times Notable Book; Sherwood Anderson Short Story Contest; Best Appalachian Novel Award; Edgar Award; Macavity Award; Agatha Award. *Memberships:* Mystery Writers of America; Sisters in Crime; Appalachian Writers Association; Whimsey Foundation. *Literary Agent:* Dominick Abel. *Address:* Rowan Mountain Inc, PO Box 10111, Blacksburg, VA 24062, USA.

MCCULLAGH Sheila Kathleen, b. 3 Dec 1920, England. Writer.*Education:* Bedford Froebel College, 1939-42; MA, University of Leeds, 1949. *Publications:* Pirate Books, 1957-64; One, Two, Three and Away, 1964-92; Tim Books, 1974-83; Buccaneers, 1980-84; Hummingbirds, 1976-92; Puddle Lane, 1985-88; Dragon Books, a Series, 1963-70; Whizzbang Adventures, 1980; Into New Worlds, 1974; Where Wild Geese Fly, 1981; Tales & Adventures, 1961; Penguins; Sea Animals; The Big Cats; Caterpillars & Butterflies; How Birds Live; Garden Birds; The Sea Shore, 1992. *Honour:* MBE, 1987. *Membership:* Society of Authors. *Literary Agent:* A.P. Watt. *Address:* 27 Royal Crescent, Bath, Avon BA1 2CT, England.

MCCULLOUGH Kenneth Douglas, b. 18 July 1943, Staten Island, New York, USA. Writer; Teacher. 1 son. *Education:* BA, University of Delaware, 1966; MFA, University of Iowa, 1968. *Publications:* New and Selected Poems, 1993; Sycamore Oriole, 1991; Travelling Light, 1987; Elegy for Old Anna, 1983; Creosote, 1976; Migrations, 1973; The Easy Wreckage, 1971. *Contributions to:* New Letters; Confluence; Nimrod; Studia Mystica; The Devils Millhoppers; Crab Creek Review; Longhouse. *Honours:* Academy of American Poets Award, 1969; National Endowment for the Arts Fellowship, 1974; Capricorn Book Award of the Writer's Vice, 1985; Pablo Neruda Award, 1989. *Memberships:* Science Fiction Writers of America; Associated Writing Programmes; National Association of College Acaemic Advisers; Rocky Mountain Language Association. *Address:* 4869 Rapid Creek Rd NE, Iowa City, IA 52240, USA.

MCCUNN Ruthanne Lum, b. 21 Feb 1946, San Francisco, California, USA. Writer. m. Donald H. McCunn, 15 June 1965. *Education:* BA, English Literature, 1968. *Publications:* Chinese American Portraits, 1988; Sole Survivor, 1985; Pie-Biter, 1983; Thousand Pieces of Gold, 1981; Illustrated History of the Chinese in America, 1979; Bibliography of Chinese & Chinese American Resource Materials; Directory of Language Resources. *Contributions to:* Yihai, literary magazine, People's Republic of China. *Honour:* Before Columbus Foundation American Book Award, 1983. *Memberships:* Chinese Historical Society of America; Asian Women United; American Civil Liberties Union; Chinese For Affirmative Action; Amnesty International. *Address:* 1007 Castro Street, San Francisco, CA 94114, USA.

MCCUTCHAN Philip Donald, (Robert Conington Galway, Duncan MacNeil, T I G Wigg), b. 13 Oct 1920, Cambridge, England. Author. m. Elizabeth May Ryan, 30 June 1951, 1 son, 1 daughter. *Publications include:* More than 100 novels, 1957-, including series featuring Commander Shaw; Detective Chief Superintendent Simon Shard; Lieutenant St Vincent Halfhyde RN; Donald Cameron RNVR; Commodore John Mason Kemp, RNR; As Duncan MacNeil, series featuring Captain James Ogilvie, of the 114th Highlanders, fighting Indian NW Frontier, 1890's; non-fiction: Tall Ships: The Golden Age of Sail, 1976; Great Yachts, 1979. *Honour:* Knight of Mark Twain, USA, 1978;

Chairman, Crime Writers Association, 1965-66. *Address:* Myrtle Cottage, 107 Portland Road, Worthing, West Sussex BN11 1QA, England.

MCCUTCHEON Elsie Mary Jackson, b. 6 Apr 1937, Glasgow, Scotland. Author. m. James McCutcheon, dec, 14 July 1962, 1 daughter. *Education:* BA, Glasgow University, 1960; Jordanhil College of Education, 1961. *Appointments:* English Teacher, Glasgow, 1961-63; Publicity Officer, norfolk Archaeological Rescue Group, 1976078; Editor, Newsletter of Friends of the Suffolk Record Office, 1984-91. *Publications:* Summer of the Zeppelin; The Rat War; Smokescreen; Storm Bird; Twisted Truth. *Contributions to:* She; Good Housekeeping; Ideal Home; Scotlands Magazine; Scottish Field; Suffolk Fair; Eastern Daily Press. *Honours:* Runner up, Guardian Award for Childrens Fiction. *Memberships:* Bury St Edmunds Library Users Group; Writers Guild of Great britain; Suffolk Local History Council; Suffolk Institute of Archaeology. *Literary Agent:* Vanessa Hamilton. *Address:* Wendover, Sharpers Lane, Horringer, Bury St Edmunds, Suffolk IP29 5PS, England.

MCCUTCHEON Hugh, (Hugh Davie-Martin, Griselda Wilding), b. 1909, British. *Appointment:* Town Clerk of Renfrew, Scotland, 1945-74. *Publications:* Alamein to Tunis, 1946; The Angel of Light (in US as Murder at the Angel), 1951; None Shall Sleep Tonight, Prey for the Nightingale, 1954; Cover Her Face, 1955; The Long Night Through, 1956; Comes the Blind Fury, 1957; To Dusty Death, 1960; Yet She Must Die, 1961; The Deadly One, 1962; Suddenly in Vienna, 1963; Treasure of the Sun, 1964; The Black Attendant, 1966; Killers Moon (in US as The Moon Was Full), 1967; The Scorpion's Nest, 1968; A Hot Wind from Hell, 1969; Brand for the Burning, Something Wicked, 1970; Red Sky at Night, 1972; Instrument of Vengeance, 1975; The Girl in My Grave (as Hugh Davie-Martin), 1976; The Pearl of Oyster Island (as Hugh Davie-Martin), 1977; Night Watch, 1978; Spaniard's Leap (as Hugh Davie-Martin), 1979; The Cargo of Death, 1980; Death's Bright Angel (as Hugh Davie-Martin), 1982; Promise of Delight (as Griselda Wilding), 1988; Beloved Wolf (As Griselda Wilding), 1991. *Address:* 19 Bentinck Drive, Troon, Ayrshire, Scotland.

MCDONALD Forrest, b. 7 Jan 1927, Orange, Texas, USA. Historian. m. Ellen Shapiro, 1 Aug 1963, 3 sons, 2 daughters. *Education:* BA, 1949, MA 1949, PhD, 1955, University of Texas, Austin. *Publications:* Novus Ordo Seclorum, 1985; We the People: The Economic Origins of the Constitution, 1958; Alexander Hamilton: A Biography, 1979; Insull, 1962; E Pluribus Unum, 1965; The Presidency of George Washington, 1974; Requiem: Variations on 18th Century Themes, 1988; The Presidency of Thomas Jefferson, 1976; The Phaeton Ride, 1974. *Contributions to:* Many publications. *Honours:* Guggenheim fellow, 1962-63; Fraunas Tavern Book Award, 1980; American Revolution Round Table Book Award, 1986; 16th Jefferson Lecturer in the Humanities 1987 (NEH); Ingersoll Prize, Richard Weaver Award in the Humanities, 1990. *Memberships:* Philadelphia Society, President 1988- 90; American Antiquarian Society. *Address:* P O Box 155, Coker, AL 35452, USA.

MCDONALD Gregory, b. 1937, American. Full-time writer. *Appointment:* Arts and Humanities Editor, Critic-at-Large, Boston Globe, 1966-73. *Publications:* Running Scared, 1964; Fletch series, 9 volumes, 1974-86; Flynn series, 3 volumes, 1977-85; Love among the Mashed Potatoes, 1978; Who Took Toby Rinaldi?, 1980; The Education of Gregory McDonald, Safekeeping, 1985; The Last Laugh (ed), 1986; A World Too Wide, 1987.

MCDONALD Robert Francis, b. 25 Oct 1943, Vancouver, BC, Canada. Writer; Broadcaster. m. Catherine Donna Napier, 28 Aug 1965. *Education:* BA, 1964. *Publications:* Pillar & Tinderbox; The Problem of Cyprus; Greece in the 1990s; Greek Privatisation. *Contributions to:* The World Today; Economist

Intelligence Unit Country Report Greece and Cyprus. *Memberships:* Commonwealth Journalists Association, London Management Committee. *Address:* 10 Chelwood Gardens, Richmond, Surrey TW9 4JQ, England.

MCDONALD Roger, b. 1941, Australian. Author; Poet. *Appointment:* Poetry Editor, University of Queensland Press, 1969-76. *Publications:* Citizens of Mist, 1968; The First Paperback Poets Anthology, 1974; Airship, 1975; 1915: A Novel, 1979; Slipstream (novel), 1982. *Address:* c/o University of Queensland Press, P.O. Box 42, St. Lucia, Qld, 4067, Australia.

MCDONALD Walter R(obert), b. 18 July 1934, Lubbock, Texas, USA. Professor of English. m. Carol Ham, 28 Aug 1959, 2 sons, 1 daughter. *Education:* BA 1956, MA 1957, Texas Technological College; PhD, University of Iowa, 1966. *Appointments include:* Faculties, US Air Force Academy, University of Colorado, Texas Tech University; Currently Paul W Horn Professor of English and Poet in Residence, Texas Tech University. *Publications:* Poetry, Caliban in Blue, 1976; One Thing Leads to Another, 1978; Anything, Anything, 1980; Working Against Time, 1981; Burning the Fence, 1981; Witching on Hardscrabble, 1985; Flying Dutchman, 1987; After the Noise of Saigon, 1988; Rafting the Brazos, 1988; fiction: A Band of Brothers: Stories of Vietnam, 1989; Night Landings, 1989; The Digs in Escondido Canyon, 1991. *Contributions to:* Numerous journals & magazines including: Poetry; American Poetry Review; The Atlantic; The New York Review of Books; The Paris Review; The Nation; The Sewanee Review. *Honours:* Poetry Award, The Texas Institute of Letters, 1976, 1985, 1987; George Elliston Poetry Prize, 1987; The Juniper Prize, 1988; National Cowboy Hall of Fame's Western Heritage Award for Poetry, 1990, 1992. *Memberships:* Past President, Texas Association of Creative Writing Teachers; PEN; Poetry Society of America; Associated Writing Programmes; Councilor, The Texas Institute of Letters; Past President, Conference of College Teachers of English of Texas. *Address:* Department of English, Texas Tech University, Lubbock, TX 79409, USA.

MCDONELL Marcella Anne, b. 4 Nov 1945, Author. 1 son, 1 daughter. *Education:* Marymount College, 1970; University of California. *Publications:* Barney the Magical Snail; The cambridge Collection, Blue Bells & Other Dreams; Moonlight End. *Honours:* Santa Monica Journalism Award; Suwannee Press Poetry Award. *Memberships:* Poetry Society; American Poetry Association; Sierra Club. *Address:* 320 Mesa Road, Santa Monica, CA 90402, USA.

MCDOUGALL Bonnie Suzanne, b. 12 Mar 1941, Sydney, Australia. Professor. m. H Anders Hansson, 1980, 1 son. *Education:* BA, University of Sydney, 1965; MA, 1967; phD, 1970. *Publications:* Introduction of Western Literary Theories into China; Mao Zedongs Talks at the Yanan Conference; Popular Chinese Literature and Performing Arts; The Yellow Earth: A Film By Chen Kaige; The August Sleepwalker; Old Snow; Brocade Valley. *Contributions to:* Journal of the Oriental Society of Australia; Modern Chinese Literature; Renditions; Contemporary China; Stand; Grand Street; New Directions. *Memberships:* PEN; Edgar Wallace Society; British Association of Chinese Studies; Universities China Committee in London; Amnesty International. *Literary Agent:* David Higham. *Address:* Dept of East Asian Studies, University of Edinburgh, 8 Buccleuch Place, Edinburgh EH8 9LW, Scotland.

MCDOUGALL Walter A(llan), b. 3 Dec 1946, Washington, DC, USA. Professor of History; Writer. m. Elizabeth Swoope, 8 Aug 1970, divorced 1979. *Education:* BA, cum laude, Amherst College, 1968; MA 1971, PhD 1974, University of Chicago. *Appointments:* Assistant Professor 1975-83, Associate Professor 1983-87, Professor of History 1987-, University of California, Berkeley; Vestryman at St Peter's Episcopal Church. *Publications:* France's Rhineland Diplomacy

1914-1924: The Last Bid for a Balance of Power in Europe (adaptation of PhD thesis) 1978; Editor with Paul Seabury, The Grenada Papers, forward by Sidney Hook, Institute of Contemporary Studies, 1984; Contributor: T Stephen Cheston, Charles M Chafer and Sallie Birket Chafer, eds. Social Sciences and Space Exploration: New Directions for University Instruction, 1984; ...the Heavens and the Earth: A Political History of the Space Age, 1985. *Contributions to:* Numerous articles and reviews to periodicals. *Honours include:* Finalist for American Book Award nonfiction, Association of American Publishers, 1985; Winner of Pulitzer Prize, History, Columbia University Graduate School of Journalism, 1986, both for ...the Heavens and the Earth; Visiting scholar at Hoover Institution, 1986; Selected by Insight, America's Ten Best College Professors, 1987; Dexter Prize, for best book, Society for the History of Technology, 1987. *Memberships:* American Church Union; Pumpkin Papers Irregulars; Delta Kappa Epsilon. *Address:* Department of History, University of California, Berkeley, CA 94720, USA.

MCDOWALL David Buchanan, b. 14 Apr 1945, London, England. Writer. m. 19 Apr 1975, 2 sons. *Education:* St Johns College Oxford, MA. *Publications:* Palestine & Israel: The Uprising and Beyond; The Kurds: A Nation Denied; An Illustrated History of Britain; Britain in Close Up; Other inc. The Spanish Armada; The Kurds; Europe and the Arabs: Discord or Symbiosis?; Lebanon: A Conflict of Minorities. *Honours:* The Other Award. *Address:* 31 Cambrian Road, Richmond, Surrey TW0 6JQ, England.

MCDOWELL Edwin S, b. 13 May 1935, Somers Point, New Jersey, USA. Journalist. m. Sathie Akimoto, 7 July, 1973, 1 son, 2 daughters. *Education:* BS, Temple University, 1959. *Publications:* Novels: The Lost World, 1988; To Keep Our Honor Clean, 1980; Three Cheers and a Tiger, 1966. *Membership:* Authors Guild. *Address:* c/o New York Times, 229 W 43rd Street, New York, NY 10036, USA.

MCDOWELL Michael, b. 1950, United States of America. Author. *Publications:* The Amulet, 1979; Cold Moon over Babylon, 1980; Vermilion (with Dennis Schuetz, as Nathan Aldyne), 1980; Gilded Needles, 1980; The Elementals, 1981; Blood Rubies (with Dennis Schuetz, as Axel Young), 1981; Katie, 1982; Cobalt, 1982; Wicked Stepmother, 1983; Blackwater, 6 vols, 1983; Slate, 1984; Toplin, 1985; Jack and Susan, 3 vols, 1985-87. *Address:* c/o The Otte Company, 6 Goden Street, Belmont, MA 02178, USA.

MCELDOWNEY Richard Dennis, b. 1926, New Zealand. Writer. *Appointments:* Editor, 1966-72, Managing Editor, 1972-86, Auckland University Press. *Publications:* The World Regained, 1957; Donald Anderson: A Memoir, 1966; Tikera by Sygurd Wisniowski, 1972; Arguing with My Grandmother, 1973; Frank Sargeson in His Time, 1976; Full of the Warm South, 1983; Presbyterians in Aotearoa, 1990; Shakinf the Bee Tree, 1992. *Address:* 54a Challenger Street, St. Heliers, Auckland, New Zealand.

MCELFRESH (Elizabeth) Adeline, (John Cleveland, Jane Scott, Elizabeth Wesley), b. 1918. American. Writer of mystery/crime/suspense, historical/romance/Gothic, children's fiction. *Appointments:* Proofreader 1936-42, Feature Editor 1943-46, Staff Writer 1973-75, City Editor 1975-78, Managing Editor, 1978-82, Feature Writer 1982-83, Sun-Commercial newspaper, Vincennes; Reporter, Daily News, Troy, Ohio, 1942-43; Director of Public Relations, Good Samaritan Hospital, Vincennes, Indiana, 1966-70. *Publications include:* Team-Up for Ann, 1959; (as Elizabeth Wesley), Jane Ryan, Dietician, 1959; (as Jane Scott), Nurse Nancy, 1959; Wings for Nurse Bennett, 1960; Ann Kenyon, Surgeon, 1960; (as Elizabeth Wesley), Doctor Dee, 1960; (as Jane Scott), A Nurse for Rebel's Run, 1960; Summer Change (juvenile), 1960; Dr Jane's Choice, 1961; To Each Her Dream, 1961; Night Call, 1961; Hospital Hill, 1961; Romantic

Assignment, 1961; Jeff Benton MD, 1962; Jill Nolan, Surgical Nurse, 1962; Jill Nolan, RN, 1962; (as Elizabeth Wesley), Dr Dee's Choice, 1962; Challenge for Dr Jane, 1963; Jill Nolan's Choice, 1963; (as Elizabeth Wesley), Dr Dorothy's Choice, 1963; The Magic Scalpel of Dr Farrer, 1965; Nurse Nolan's Private Duty, 1966; Dr Jane Interne, 1966; Nurse for Mercy's Mission, 1969; Assignment in the Islands, 1970; Nurse in Yucatan, 1970; Skye Manor, 1971; Flight Nurse, 1971; Ellen Randolph, 1971; Doctor for Blue Hollow, 1971; Patient in 711, 1972; Danger at Aldurrai, 1972; Evil Island, 1974; Kanesbroke, 1975; Dangerous Assignment, 1975; Lone Shadow, 1976; To Last a Lifetime, 1977. *Address:* R R 3, Vincennes, IN 47591, USA.

MCELROY Colleen J, b. 30 Oct 1935, St Louis, Missouri, USA. Teacher; Writr. (div), 1 son, 1 daughter. *Education:* BS, 1958, MS, 1963, Kansas State University; PhD, University of Washington, 1973. *Appointments:* Professor, Creative Writing Programme, University of Washington, 1973-; Editor, Dark Waters, 1973-78. *Publications:* Poetry: Queen of the Ebony Isles, 1984; Lie and Say You Love Me, 1981; Winters Without Snow, 1979; Music From Home: Selected Poems, 1976. Short Fiction: Jesus and Fat Tuesday, 1987; Follow The Drinking Gourd: A Play About Harriet Tubman, 1987; The Halls of Montezuma, The New Voice, WGBH-TV, 1979; Speech and Language of the Preschool Child, (text), 1972. Fiction: Driving Under the Cardboard Pines, 1990. *Contributions to:* 200 poems and short stories in various journals including: Obsidian; Essence; Nimrod; Massachusetts Review; Calyx; Epoch; Southern Poetry Review; Georgia Review; Callaloo; Missouri Review. *Honours:* Bridgman Scholarship, Breadloaf Writers Conference, 1974; Pushcart Prize, Poetry, 1975; NEA Creative Writing, 1978; Callaloo First Place Fiction, 1981; Cincinnati Poetry Review, 1st Place, 1983; Before Columbus American Book Award, 1985; Fulbright Fellowship, 1987; Washington State Governor's Award, 1988. *Memberships:* Writers Guild of America East; Dramatist Guild; Authors Guild. *Literary Agent:* Julie Fallowfield, MacIntosh & Otis, New York. *Address:* Creative Writing Program GN-30, Dept. of English, University of Washington, Seattle, WA 98195, USA.

MCELROY Joseph (Prince), b. 1930, United States of America. Author. *Publications:* A Smuggler's Bible, 1966; Hind's Kidnap, 1969; Ancient History, 1971; Lookout Cartridge, 1974; Plus, 1977; Ship Rock, 1980; Women and Men, 1987. *Address:* c/o Georges Borchadt, 136 E. 57th Street, New York, NY 10022, USA.

MCELROY Lee. See: KELTON Elmer Stephen.

MCEVEDY Colin (Peter), b. 1930. Writer. *Publications:* The Penguin Atlas of Medieval History, 1961; The Penguin Atlas of Ancient History, 1967; The Atlas of World History, 3 vols (with Sarah McEvedy), 1970-73; The Penguin Atlas of Modern History, 1972; Atlas of World Population History (with Richard Jones), 1980; The Penguin Atlas of African History, 1980; The Penguin Atlas of Recent History (Europe since 1815), 1982; The Century World History Factfinder, 1984; Penguin Atlas of North American History, 1988. *Address:* 7 Caithness Road, London, W14, England.

MCEVOY Marjorie, (Gillian Bond, Marjorie Harte), b. York City, England. Novelist. m. William Noel McEvoy, Cramlington, Northumberland. 1 son, 1 daughter. *Publications:* Doctors in Conflict, 1962; The Grenfell Legacy, 1967; Dusky Cactus, 1969; Echoes from the Past, 1978; Calabrian Summer, 1980; Sleeping Tiger, 1982; Star of Randevi, 1984; Temple Bells, 1985; Camelot Country, 1986; The Black Pearl, 1988. *Contributions to:* The Caravan; Modern Caravan; various newspapers and magazines. *Membership:* RNA. *Address:* 54 Miriam Avenue, Chesterfield, Derbyshire, England.

MCEWAN Ian Russell, b. 21 June 1948. Author.

m. Penny Allen, 1982, 2 sons, 2 daughters. *Education:* BAQ, Honours, English Literature, University of Sussex; MA, University of East Anglia. *Publications:* Films: The Ploughman's Lunch, 1983; Last Day of Summer, 1984; (Books) First Love, Last Rites, 1975; In Between the Sheets, 1978; The Cement Garden, 1978; The Imitation Game, 1981; The Comfort of Strangers, 1981; Or Shall We Die? (oratorio), 1982; The Innocent, 1989; Black Dogs, 1992. *Address:* c/o Jonathan Cape, 32 Bedford Square, London WC1B 3EL, England.

MCFADDEN David, b. 1940, Canada. Author. *Publications:* The Poem Poem, 1967; The Saladmaker, 1968; Letters from the Earth to the Earth, 1968; The Great Canadian Sonnet (novel), 1970; Intense Pleasure, 1972; The Ova Years, 1972; Poems Worth Knowing, 1973; A Knight in Dried Plums, 1975; The Poet's Progress, 1977; On the Road Again, 1978; I Don't Know, 1978; A New Romance, 1978; The Individual Human Being, 1978; A Trip around Lake Huron (novel), 1980; My Body Was Eaten by Dogs: Selected Poems, 1981; A Trip Around Lake Erie (novel), 1981; Three Stories and Ten Poems, 1982; Country of the Open Heart, 1982; Animal Spirits: Stories to Live By, 1983; A Pair of Baby Lambs, 1983; The Art of Darkness, 1984.

MCFADDEN Roy, b. 14 Nov 1921, Belfast, Northern Ireland. *Publications:* The Garryowen, 1971; Verifications, 1977; A Watching Brief, 1979; The Selected Roy McFadden, 1983; Letters to the Hinterland, 1986; After Seymour's Funeral, 1990. *Address:* c/o Blackstaff Press, Dundonald, Belfast, Northern Ireland.

MCFARLAND John Bernard, b. 16 Jan 1943, Cambridge, Massachusetts, USA. Economist; Writer. *Education:* BS, Massachusetts Institute of Technology, 1964; MA, Johns Hopkins University, 1974. *Publications:* The Exploding Frog and Other Fables from Aesop, 1981. *Contributions to:* Short stories to: Ararat, Caliban, Cricket, Fiction 84, Image, On the Edge, Letters Magazine, Seniority, Wiggansnatch. *Honours:* Best Illustrated book, Parents Choice Magazine, 1981. *Memberships:* Society of Children's Book Writers; Poets and Writers; American Economic Association. *Address:* 2320 10th Avenue East, Apt 5, Seattle, Washington 98102, USA.

MCFARLAND Violet Sweet, b. 26 Feb 1908, Seattle, Washington, USA. Author. m. Glen W McFarland, 1958, div, 1965. *Education:* BA, Washington State University, 1928; MA, Columbia University, 1933. *Appointments:* Social Editor, Japan Times, Toyko, Japan, 1930-31; Social Editor, Hong Kong Telegraph, 1940; Currator, Oriental Art & Literature. *Publications:* As Violet Sweet Haven: Hong kong for Weekend; Many Ports of call; Gentlemen of Japan. *Contributions to:* Professional Journals. *Honours:* Numerous International Literary Awards. *Memberships:* International Institute of Arts & Letters; National Press Club; California Board of Realtors; Delta Zeta. *Address:* PO Box 872, Lake Elsinore, CA 92330, USA.

MCFARLANE James Walter, b. 1920. Writer. *Publications:* Translator, Knut Hamsun Pan, 1955; Ibsen and the Temper of Norwegian Literature, 1960; The Oxford Ibsen, 8 vols, 1960-77; Discussions of Ibsen, 1962; Thorkild Hansen: Arabia Felix, 1964; North West to Hudson Bay, 1970; Henrik Ibsen: A Critical Anthology, 1970; Modernism: European Literature 1890- 1930, 1976; Knut Hamsun: Wayfarers, 1980; Slaves of Love and Other Norwegian Short Stories, 1982; Sigbjósn Obstfelder: A Priest's Diary, 1987; Ibsen and Meaning, 1988; Knut Hamson, Letters 1879-1898, 1989. *Address:* The Croft, Stody, Melton Constable, Norfolk, NR24 2EE, England.

MCGAHERN John, b. 12 Nov 1934. Author. m. Madeline Green, 1973. *Appointments:* Research Fellow, University of Reading, 1968-71; O'Connor Professor, Colgate University, 1969, 1972, 1977, 1979, 1983; Visiting Fellow Trinity College, 1988. *Publications:* The

Barracks, 1963; The Dark, 1965; Nightlines, 1970; The Leavetaking, 1975; Getting Through, 1978; The Pornographer, 1979; High Ground, 1985; The Rockingham Shoot, BBC 2, 19871 Amongst Women, 1990. *Honours:* A E. Memorial Award, 1962; McCauley Fellowship, 1964; British Arts Council Award, 1967; Society of Authors Award, 1975; American Irish Foundation Literary Award, 1985; Galway Festival 10th Anniversary Award, 1987. *Memberships:* Aosdana Irish Academy of Letters; British Northern Arts Fellow, 1974-76. *Address:* c/o Faber & Faber, 3 Queen Square, London WC1N 3AU, England.

MCGARRITY Mark, (Bartholomew Gill), b. 1943, United States of America. Author; Freelance Writer. *Publications:* Novels as Mark McGarrity: Little Augie's Lament, 1973; Lucky Shuffles, 1973; A Passing Advantage, 1980; Neon Caesar, 1989; White Rush/ Green Fire, 1991. Mystery Novels as Bartholomew Gill: McGarr and the Politician's Wife, 1977; McGarr and the Sienese Conspiracy, 1977; McGarr on the Cliffs of Moher, 1978; McGarr at the Dublin Horse Show, 1980; McGarr and the P.M. of Belgrave Square, 1983; McGarr and the Method of Descartes, 1984; McGarr and the Legacy of a Woman Scorned, 1986; The Death of a Joyce Scholar, 1989; The Death of Love, 1992. *Contributions to:* New Jersey Monthly; New Jersey Herald. *Honours:* Fellow, New Jersey Council of the Arts, 1981-82; 1st Place, New Jersey Press Association, Critical Writing. *Memberships:* PEN. *Literary Agent:* Anita Diamant Agency, New York. *Address:* 159 North Shore Road, Andover, NJ 07821, USA.

MCGARRY Jean, b. 18 June 1952, Providence, Rhode Island, USA. Writer; Teacher. *Education:* BA, Harvard University, 1970; MA, Johns Hopkins University, 1983. *Appointment:* Teacher, The John Hopkins University. *Publications:* Airs of Providence, 1985; The Very Rich Hours, 1987; The Courage of Girls, 1992. *Contributions to:* Various US journals including: Antioch Review; Southern Review; Southwest Review; Sulfur; New Orleans Review. *Honour:* Short fiction Prize, Southern Review/Louisiana State University, 1985. *Membership:* Associated Writing Programmes. *Address:* 100 West University Parkway, Baltimore, Maryland 21210, USA.

MCGILL Ian. *See:* **ALLEGRO John Marco.**

MCGINNISS Joe, b. 1942, United States of America. Writer. *Appointment:* Newspaper Reporter, 1964-68. *Publications:* The Selling of the President, 1968; The Dream Team, 1972; Heroes, 1976; Going to Extremes, 1980; Fatal Vision, 1983; Blind Faith, 1989. *Address:* c/o Morton L. Janklow, 598 Madison Avenue, New York, NY 10022, USA.

MCGIVERN Maureen Daly. *See:* **DALY Maureen.**

MCGOUGH Roger, b. 9 Nov 1937, Liverpool, England. Poet. m. 20 Dec 1986, 3 sons, 1 daughter. *Education:* St Mary's College, Crosby; BA and Graduate Certificate of Education, Hull University. *Literary Appointments:* Fellow of Poetry, The University of Loughborough, 1973-75; Writer-in- Residence at West Australian College of Advanced Education, Perth, 1986. *Publications include:* The Mersey Sound (with Brian Patten and Adrian Henri), 1967; Strictly Private (editor) 1982; An Imaginary Menagerie, 1989; Blazing Fruit (selected poems 1967-87), 1990; Summer with Monika, reissued 1990; Pillow Talk, 1990; Melting in the Foreground, Poems; The Lighthouse that Ran Away, 1991; You at the Back (selected poems 1967-87, volume 2), 1991; My Dad's Fire Eater, 1992; Defying Gravity, 1992; The Elements, 1993. *Honours:* Signal Award for Best Book of Children's Poetry, 1984; BAFTA Award for writing and performing in a children's film, Banff TV Festival: First Prize (Popular Science) Royal Television Society Award: Best Adult Education Programme, 1985. *Memberships:* Member, Executive Council, The Poetry Society, 1989-; Chairman, The Chelsea Arts Club, 1984-

86. *Literary Agent:* The Peters, Fraser and Dunlop, Group Ltd, London. *Address:* c/o The Peters, Fraser and Dunlop Group Ltd, 5th Floor, The Chambers, Chelsea Harbour, Lots Road, London SW10 0XF, England.

MCGOVERN Ann, b. 25 May 1930, New York, USA. Author. m. Martin L. Scheiner, 6 June 1970, 3 sons, 1 daughter. *Education:* BA, University of New Mexico. *Appointment:* Publisher, The Privileged Traveler, 1986-1990. *Publications:* Published, over 50 books including: The Secret Soldier, 1975; Sharks, 1976; Shark Lady, The Adventures of Eugenie Clark, 1978; Elephant Baby, 1982; Night Dive, 1984; Stone Soup, 1968; Swimming With Sea Lions and Other Adventures in the Galapagos Islands, 1992; Too Much Noise, 1967; If You Lived in Colonial Times, 1964. *Contributions to:* Signature; Saturday Review. *Honours:* Author of the Year, Scholastic Publishing Inc., 1978; Outstanding Science Book, National Science Teacher Association, 1976, 1979, 1984, 1993. *Memberships:* Explorers' Club; PEN; Authors Guild; Society of Childrens Book Writers; Society of Journalists and Authors. *Literary Agent:* Kirchoff Wohlberg Inc, New York. *Address:* 30 E 62nd Street, New York, NY 10021, USA.

MCGOWAN John Patrick, b. 12 July 1953, New York, USA. Professor. m. Jane Danielewicz, 24 July 1982, 1 son, 1 daughter. *Education:* AB, Georgetown University, 1974; PhD, State University of NY, 1978. *Appointments:* University of Michigan, 1979-83; University of Rochester, 1984-92; University of North Carolina, 1992-. *Publications:* Postmodernism and its Critics; Representation and Revelation: Victorian Realism from Carlyle to Yeats. *Honours:* National Endowment for Humanities Fellowship. *Memberships:* Modern Language Association. *Address:* Dept of English, Greenlaw Hall, University of North Carolina, Chapel Hill, NC 27599, USA.

MCGOWAN Robert Oliver, b. 17 Nov 1944, Luton, England. Journalist. m. Pauline Frances Langley, 19 June 1970, 1 son, 1 daughter. *Appointments:* Staff, London Evening Standard, 1968-75; Staff, London Daily Express, 1975-. *Publications:* Don't Cry for Me Sergeant-Major, 1983; Try Not to Laugh Sergeant, 1984. *Contributions To:* Coverage of Yom Kippur War, Uganda War, Beirut, Russian Invasion of Afghanistan, Turkish Invasion of Cyprus, Falklands War for London Evening Standard, and London Daily Express, 1973-82. *Honours:* British Press Awards Reporter of the Year, 1980; South Atlantic Medal, 1982. *Address:* The Beacon, Beacon Lane, Staplecross, Robertsbridge, East Sussex, TN32 5QP, England.

MCGRATH John (Peter), b. 1935. Playwright; Director. *Appointments:* Over 40 plays performed; Director for Film and TV; Screenplays for TV and films. *Publications:* Events While Guarding the Bofors Gun, 1966; Adaptor: Bakke's Night of Fame, 1968; Random Happenings in the Hebrides: or, The Social Democrat and the Stormy Sea, 1970; Rules of the Game (translation with M.Teitelbaum), 1970; The Fish in the Sea, 1973; The Cheviot, the Stag, and the Black, Black Oil, 1973; The Game's a Bogey, 1974; Little Red Hen, 1975; Yobbo Nowt, 1975; Joe's Drum, 1979; Swings and Roundabouts, 1981; Blood Red Roses, 1981; A Good Night Out: Popular Theatre: Audience, Class and Form (non-fiction), 1981; The Bone Won't Break (non-fiction), 1990. *Address:* c/o Freeway Films, 67 George Street, Edinburgh EH.

MCGRATH Morgan. *See:* **RAE Hugh Crawford.**

MCGRAW Eloise Jarvis, b. 9 Dec 1915. Writer. m. William Corbin McGraw, 29 Jan 1940. 1 son, 1 daughter. *Education:* BA, Principia College, Elsah, Illinois. *Publications:* Moccasin Trail, 1952; Mara, Daughter Of The Nile, 1953; The Golden Goblet, 1961; A Really Weird Summer, 1977; The Money Room, 1981; The Seventeenth Swap, 1986; Sawdust In His Shoes, 1950; Crown Fire, 1951; Pharaoh, 1958; Techniques

of Fiction Writing, 1959; Merry Go Round In Oz, 1963; Greensleeves, 1968; Master Cornhill, 1973; Joel and The Great Merlini, 1979; Forbidden Fountain of Oz, 1980; Hideaway, 1983; The Trouble with Jacob, 1988; Steady Stephanie (Play), 1962; The Striped Ships, 1991; Tangled Webb, 1993. *Contributions to:* The Writer Magazine; Cricket Magazine. *Honours:* Honor Book, NY Herald Tribune Children's Spring Book Festival; Deutschen Jugendbuch Sonderpreis, 1956; Newbery Medal Honor Book, 1952; Lewis Carroll Shelf Award, 1952; Golden Goblet, Newbery Honor Book, 1962; Mystery Writers of America Edgar Award, 1977; Evelyn Sibley Lampman Award, 1983; L Frank Baum Award, 1983; Oregon Book Award, 1992. *Memberships:* Authors' League of America; Authors' Guild. *Literary Agent:* Emilie Jacobson, Curtis Brown Ltd, New York, USA. *Address:* 1970 Indian Trail, Lake Oswego, OR 97034, USA.

MCGREEVY Susan Brown, b. 28 Jan 1934, Chicago, Illinois, USA. Lecturer; Writer. m. Thomas J McGreevy, 16 June 1973, 3 children. *Education:* Attended Mount Holyoke College 1951-53; BA, hons, Roosevelt University, 1969; MA, Northwestern University 1971. *Appointments:* Staff Consultant, Heart of America Indian Center, Kansas City, Missouri, 1973-75; Curator of North American ethnology, Kansas City Museum of History and Science, Kansas City, 1975-77; Director 1978-82, Research Associate 1983-, Member of Board of Trustees 1987, Wheelwright Museum of the American Indian, Santa Fe, New Mexico; Adjunct Professor, Ottowa University, Kansas City campus, 1976-77; Guest lecturer at colleges and museums 1978-; Member of faculty, Northwestern University, Gallina, New Mexico, 1980-; Member of various Boards of Directors. *Publications:* (ed)Woven Holy People: Navajo Sandpainting Textiles, 1983; (with Andrew Hunter Whiteford), Translating Tradition: Basketry Arts of the San Juan Paiutes (catalogue) 1985; (with Katherine Spencer Halpern), Guide to Microfilm Edition of the Washington NMatthews Papers, 1985. *Contributions to:* Various art journals. *Honours:* Grants from National Historic Publications and Records Commission, 1980; National Endowment of the Humanities, 1981 and National Endowment for the Arts, 1985. *Memberships include:* American Anthropological Association; American Association of Museums; American Ethnological Society. *Address:* Route 7, Box 129-E, Santa Fe, NM 87505, USA.

MCGREGOR Iona, b. 7 Feb 1929, Aldershot, England. Writer. *Education:* BA Hons, University of Bristol, 1950. *Publications:* Historical fiction for children: An Edinburgh Reel, 1968, 4th edition, 1986; The Popinjay, 1969, 2nd Edition, 1979; The Burning Hill, 1970; The Tree of Liberty, 1972; The Snake and the Olive, 1974, 2nd Edition, 1978; Death Wore A Diadem, feminist crime novel, 1989; Non-fiction: Edinburgh and Eastern Lowlands, 1979; Wallace and Bruce, 1986; Importance of Being Earnest, Penguin Passnote, 1987; Huckleberry Finn, Penguin Passnote, 1988; Various radio scripts. *Honour:* Writer's Bursary, Scottish Arts Council, 1989. *Membership:* Scottish PEN. *Address:* 9 Saxe Coburg Street, Edinburgh EH3 5BN, Scotland.

MCGRORY Edward, b. 6 Nov 1921, Stevenston, Ayrshire, Scotland. Retired Sales Consultant. m. Mary McDonald, 20 Nov 1948, 1 son, 1 daughter. *Education:* BA, Open University, 1985. *Publications:* Selected Poems, 1984; Plain and Coloured, 1985; Pied Beauty, 1986; Orchids and Daisies, 1987; Light Reflections - Mirror Images (foreword by Iris Murdoch), 1988; Chosen Poems by Celebrities: Eddie McGrory's Poems, 1988; Masks and Faces (introduction by Duncan Glen), 1989; Illuminations, 1990; Letters From Flora (From My Correspondence with Dame Flora Robson DBE), 1991; Candles and Lasers (poetry) Lyrics For Musicla Settings, 1992; My Brother Cain, novel, in progress. *Memberships:* Various literary societies. *Address:* 41 Sythrum Crescent, Glenrothes, Fife KY7 5DG, Scotland.

MCGUCKIAN Medbh, b. 1950, Ireland. Poet. *Publications:* Single Ladies: Sixteen Poems, 1980;

Portrait of Joanna, 1980; Trio Poetry (with Damian Gorman and Douglas Marshall), 1981; The Flower Master, 1982; Venus and the Rain, 1984; On Ballycastle Beach, 1988; Marconis Cottage, 1991. *Address:* c/o Peter Fallon, Gallery Press, Loughcrew, Oldcastle, Co Neath, Ireland.

MCGURN James Edward, b. 21 Oct 1953, Newcastle upon Tyne, England. Writer; Publisher. m. Elizabeth Sally McGurn, 17 Feb 1980, 5 sons. *Education:* BA Hons, University of Leeds. *Appointments:* Founder and Editor of New Cyclist Magazine, 1988-. *Publications:* On Your Bicycle: A Social History of Cycling, 1987; Tolles Theater, 1984; Vous Êtes en Scène, 1986; Comparing Languages: English and its European Relatives, 1987; Cross-country Cycling, 1993; Encyclopaedia: An Alternative Guide to Specialised Bicycles, 1993. *Memberships:* Veteran Cycle Club. *Address:* 4 New Street, York YO1 2RA. England.

MCILVANNEY William, b. 1936. Author; Poet. *Publications:* Remedy Is None (novel), 1966; A Gift from Nessus (novel), 1968; The Longships in Harbour (poetry), 1970; Landscapes and Figures (poetry), 1973; Docherty (novel), 1975; Laidlaw (mystery novel), 1977; The Papers of Tony Veitch (mystery novel), 1983; Weddings and After (poetry), 1984; The Big Man (novel), 1985; Glasgow 1956-1986, 1986; Walking Wounded (short stories), 1989. *Address:* c/o Vivienne Schuster, John Farquharson Limited, 162-168 Regent Street, London, W1R 5TB, England.

MCINERNY Jay, b. 1955, United States of America. Author. *Appointments:* Editor, Time-Life Publishers, Japan; Reader, Random House Publishers, New York City; Fact-checker, New Yorker Magazine, 1980. *Publication:* Bright Lights, Big City, 1984; Ransom, 1985. *Address:* c/o ICM, 40 W. 57th Street, New York, NY 10019, USA.

MCINERNY Ralph,b. 24 Feb 1929. Professor. m. 2 sons, 4 daughters. *Education:* BA, St Paul Seminary, St Paul, MN, 1951; MS, University of Minnesota, Minneapolis, MN, 1953; PhL, Philosophy, 1953, PhD, summa cum laude, 1954, Universite Laval Quebec, Canada. *Publications:* Novels: The Priest, 1973; The Gate of Heaven, 1975; Connolly's Life, 1983; The Noonday Devil, 1985; Frigor Mortis, 1989; Four on the Floor, 1989; The Search Committee, 1990; Sisterhood, 1991; Chambre Froide, 1991; Le Demon de Midi, 1992; Desert Sinner, 1992; Basket Case, 1992; Body and Soil, 1993; Philosophical Books: Art and Prudence, 1988; First Glance at Thomas Aquinas, 1989;p Beothius and Aquinas, 1990; Aquinas on Human Action, 1992. *Honours:* Fellow, Pontifical Roman Academy of St Thomas Aquinas, 1987; Honorary Doctor of Letters, St Benedict College, 1978; Honorary Doctor of Letters, University of Steubenville, 1984; Sigma Nat'l Scholastic Honor Society, 1990; Thomas Aquinas Medal, University of Dallas, 1990; St Thomas Aquinas Medallion, Thomas Aquinas College, 1991; Thomas Aquinas Medal, American Catholic Philosophical Association, 1993; Board of Governors, Thomas Aquinas College, 1993. *Memberships:* Authors Guild; Mystery Writers of America; Homeland Foundation Executive Director, 1990-1992; The New Scholasticism, Editor, 1975-89; Metaphysical Society of America, President, 1992-93; Fellowship of Catholic Scholars, President, 1991-93. *Address:* 2158 Portage Avenue, South Bend, IN 46616, USA.

MCINTIRE Carl Thomas, b. 4 Oct 1939, Philadelphia, Pennsylvania, USA. Professor. m. Rebekah Smick, 7 June 1980, 2 sons, 2 daughters. *Education:* BA, Shelton College, 1961; MA, University of Pennsylvania, 1962; MDiv, Faith Theol Seminary, 1966; PhD, University of Pennsylvania, 1976. *Publications:* England Against the Papacy; God, History and Historians; History and Historical Understanding; Toynbee: Reappraisals; Herbert Butterfield: Writings on Christianity and History; Butterfield as Historian; The Legacy of Herman Dooyeweerd; Canadian Protestant and Catholic

Missions. *Contributions to:* Many Articles and Reviews. *Honours:* 12 Fellowships & Research Grants. *Memberships:* American Historical Association; American Society of Church History; Canadian Church Historical Society. *Address:* Trinity College, University of Toronto, Toronto, Ontario, Canada M5S 1H8.

MCINTOSH Christopher (Angus), b. 1943. Writer (History). *Appointments:* Former Assistant Editor, Country Life Magazine, London; Illustrated London News. *Publications:* The Astrologers and Their Creed, 1969; Astrology, 1970; Eliphas Levi and the French Occult Revival, 1972; The Rosy Cross Unveiled, 1980; The Swan King, 1982; The Devil's Bookshelf,1985. *Address:* 2 Abbey Road, Oxford, OX2 0AE, England.

MCKEAN John Maule Laurie, b. 7 Nov 1943, Glasgow, Scotland. Critic; Teacher; Designer. m. Polly Eupalinos, 1 son, 1 daughter. *Education:* B.Arch, Honours, University of Strathclyde, 1968; MA, Theory of Architecture, University of Essex, 1971. *Appointments:* Editor, The Architects' Journal, 1971-75; UK Correspondent, Architecture, 1975-80; Architecture Correspondent, City Limits, London, 1984. *Publications:* Essex University: A Case Study, 1971; The First Era of Modern Architecture of the Western World, 1980; Building Materials & Architectural Quality, 1982; Style Structure & Design, 1982; Masterpieces of Architectural Drawing, 1982; The Word Crystal, 1984; Learning from Segal, 1987; Suburban Prototype, 1986; Two Essays in Glasgow: Form Structure & Image of the City, 1987; The Royal Festival Hall, 1990. *Contributions to:* spazio E Societa (CH); Building Design; Architects Journal; A A Files. *Honour:* Elected to CICA, 1990. *Memberships:* Royal Society of Arts; International Building Press, UK Branch, Committee Member, 1974-76; Chartered Society of Designers; Royal Incorporation of Architects, Scotland; Design History Society; Construction History Society. *Address:* 34 Dukes Avenue, Muswell Hill, London N10, England.

MCKENZIE Mary Ellen (Kindt), b. 24 June 1928, Kenosha, Wisconsin, USA. Music Teacher; Writer. m. Arthur V. McKenzie, 4 Nov 1950, 2 sons, 1 daughter. *Education:* Chicago Musical College, 1946-49. *Publications:* Taash & the Jesters, 1968; Drujienna's Harp, 1971; Kashka, 1987. *Honour:* Notable Book Award, American Library Association, 1968. *Membership:* Society of Children's Book Writers. *Literary Agent:* Kendra Bersamin. *Address:* 27920 Moody Road, Los Altos, California 94022, USA.

MCKEON Zahava Karl, b. 11 Mar 1927, Chicago, Illinois, USA. Emeritus Associate Professor of English. m. (1) 1 son, 1 daughter, (2) 11 Mar 1979. *Education:* AB, 1952; AM, 1963; PhD, 1974. *Publications:* Novels and Arguments: Inventing Rhetorical Criticism, 1982; Freedom and History and Other Essays: An Introduction to the Thought of Richard McKeon (editor), 1990; The Collected Essays of Richard McKeon, Vol I, Essays on Classical Antiquity (editor and introduction), forthcoming. *Contributions to:* American Literature; The Armchair Detective; Was Philosophinnen Denken (Zurich); Reviews in: Theological Studies. *Honours:* University Scholarship, University of Chicago, 1967; Danforth Fellow, 1968-71. *Memberships:* National Council of Teachers of English; American Association of University Professors. *Address:* 2336 SW Osage, Apt 505, Portland, OR 97205, USA.

MCKINLEY Hugh, b. 18 Feb 1924, Oxford, England. m. Deborah Waterfield, 15 Sept 1979. *Appointments:* Literary Editor, Athens Daily Post, 1966-77; European Editor, Poet, India, 1967-1991; Editorial Panel, Bitterroot, USA, 1980-1989. *Publications:* Poetry: Starmusic, 1976; Transformation of Faust, 1977; Poet in Transit, 1979; Exulting for the Light, 1983; Skylarking, 1993. *Contributions to:* Publications worldwide including: London Magazine; Orbis; Weyfarers; Pennine Platform; Candelabrum; Poetry Wales; Poet's Voice, UK; Hibernia; Kilkenny Magazine; Dublin Magazine, Ireland;

Malahat Review, Canada; Bitterroot, The Smith Poetry International, USA; Laurel Leaves, Philippines; Poet India; Skylark, India. *Honours:* LittLD, International Academy of Leadership & President Marcos Medal, Philippines, 1967; Hon. D.Litt., Free University of Asia, Karachi, India, 1973; Directorate, Academia Pax Mundi, Israel, 1978. *Memberships:* Suffolk Poetry Society; Life Member, Baha'i World Faith. *Address:* Roseholme, Curlew Green, Kelsale, Suffolk, England.

MCKINNEY Jack. *See:* **DALEY Brian Charles.**

MCKINNON Ronald Ian, b. 10 July 1935, Edmonton, Alberta, Canada. Economist. m. Margaret McQueen Learmonth, 2 sons, 1 daughter. *Education:* Royal Roads, Victoria, BC, 1952-54; University of Alberia, BA, 1954-56; University of Minnesota, PhD, 1956-60. *Appointments include:* Royal Canadian Air Force, 1952-56; Lecturer, Syracuse University, 1960-61; Associate Professor, Stanford University, 1966-69; William D Eberle Professor, 1984-. *Publications:* Money and Capital in Economic Development; Money and finance in Economic Growth and Development; Money in International Exchange; An International Standard for Monetary stabilization; The Order of Economic Liberalization. *Contributions to include:* International Finance; Quarterly Journal of Economics; The Journal of Political Economy. *Honours:* Gold Medal of Economics; Doctoral Dissertation Grant; Gave Frank D Graham Memorial Lecturer; Kenan Enterprise Award. *Memberships:* Various inc. AEA; Royal Economic Society. *Address:* Dept of Economics, Stanford University, Stanford, CA 94305, USA.

MCKNIGHT Reginald, b. 26 Feb 1956, Germany. Writer; Professor. m. Michele Davis, 25 Aug 1985, 1 daughter. *Education:* AA, Liberal Arts & Sci; BA; MA. *Publications:* Moustaphas Eclipse; I Get on the Bus; The kind of Light That Shines on Texas. *Contributions to:* Prairie Schooner; Players; Kenyon Review; Massachusetts Review; New York Times Book Review. *Honours:* Bernice M Slote Award; drue Heinz Prize; Pen American Special Citation; Henry Award; Kenyon Rev Award for Literary Excellence. *Memberships:* PEN America; African Literary association. *Literary Agent:* Flannery, White & Store. *Address:* Dept of English, BH228D, Carnegie Mellon, Pittsburgh, PA 15213, USA.

MCKUEN Rod, b. 29 Apr 1933, Oakland, California, USA. Poet; Composer; Author; Performer; Columnist; Classical Composer. *Appointments:* Appeared in numerous films, TV, concerts, nightclubs and with symphony orchestras; Composer, modern classical music; scores for films and TV; President, Stanyan Records, Discus Records, Tamarack Books, Stanyan Books, Rod McKuen Enterprises. *Publications include* Poetry: And Autumn Came, 1954; Stanyan Street and Other Sorrows, 1966; Listen to the Warm, 1967; Lonesome Cities, 1968; Twelve Years of Christmas, 1968; In Someone's Shadow, 1969; A Man Alone, 1969; With Love, 1970; Caught in the Quiet, 1970; new Ballads, 1970; Fields of Wonder, 1971; The Carols of Christmas, 1971; And to Each Season, 1972; Pastorale, 1972; Grand Tour, 1972; Come to Me in Silence, 1973; America an Affirmation, 1974; Seasons in the Sun, 1974; Moment to Moment, 1974; Beyond the Boardwalk, 1975; The Rod McKuen Omnibus, 1975; Alone, 1975; Celebrations of the Heart, 1975; Finding My father; One Man's Search for Identity (prose), 1976; The Sea Around Me, 1977; hand in Hand, 1977; Coming Close to the Earth, 1978; We Touch the Sky, 1979; Love's Been Good to Me, 1979; Looking for a Friend, 1980; An Outstretched Hand (prose), 1980; The Power Bright and Shining, 1980; Too Many Midnights, 1981; Rod McKuen's Book of Days, 1981; The Beautiful Strangers, 1981; The Works of Rod McKuen : Volume 1, Poetry, 1950-82, 1982; Watch for the Wind..., 1982; Rod McKuen - 1984 Book of Days, 1983; The Sound of Solitude, 1983; Suspension Bridge, 1984; Another Beautiful Day, 1984, volume 2, 1985; Valentines, 1986; Major Classical Works: Symphony No One; Concerto for Guitar and Orchestra; Concerto for Four Harpsichords; Concerto for Cello and Orchestra; Film

and TV Scores include: Joanna, 1968; Travels with Charley, 1968; The Prime of Miss Jean Brodie, 1969; Me, Natalie, 1969; The Loner, 1969; A Boy Named Charlie Brown, 1970; Intervals, 1987; and others. *Honours include:* 41 Gold and Platinum Records internationally; Nominated Pulitzer Prize, Classical Music for The City, 1973; Grand Prix Du Disc, Paris, 1966, 1974, 1975, 1982; Golden Globe Award, 1969; Grammy for best spoken word album, Lonesome Cities, 1969; Entertainer of the Year, 1975; Man of the Year Award, University of Detroit, 1978; Freedoms Foundation Patriot Medal, 1981; Salvation Army Man of the Year, 1982; Academy Award Nominations. *Memberships:* Member, numerous professional and civic organisations. *Address:* PO Box G, Beverly Hills, CA 92013, USA.

MCLANATHAN Richard, b. 12 Mar 1916, Methuen, USA. Author; Art Historian. m. Jane Fuller, 3 Jan 1942. *Education:* AB, 1938, PhD, 1951, Harvard University. *Appointments:* Visiting Professor, number of US and European Universities; Museum Curator, Director, Trustee, etc. *Publications:* Images of the Universe: Leonardo da Vinci, The Artist as Scientist, 1966; The Pageant of Medieval Art and Life, 1966; The American Tradition in the Arts, 1968; A Guide to Civilisation: The Kenneh Clark Films on he Cultural Life of Western Man, 1970; The Brandywine Heritage, 1971; Art in America, A Brief History, 1973; East Building, A Profile, National Gallery of Art, 1978; The Art of Marguerite Stix, 1977; World Art in American Museums, 1983; Gilbert Stuart, 1986; Leonardo de Vinci, 1990, (French, German and Japenese eds, 1991); Michelangelo, 1993. *Contributions to:* Numerous journals and magazines. *Honours include:* Society of Fellows, Harvard University, 1943; Prix de Rome, Art History, 1948; Distinguishd Service Award, USIA, 1959; Rockefeller Senior Fellow, Metropolitan Museum of Art, 1975; US National Commission for UNESCO, 1976-79. *Memberships:* American Association of Museums, Executive Director, 1976-79; Founding Member, New York State Council on the Arts, 1960. *Literary Agent:* Lucy Kroll Agency. *Address:* The Stone School House, Phippsburg, ME 04562, USA.

MCLAREN Colin Andrew, b. 14 Dec 1940, Middlesex, England. Manuscript Librarian. m. Jan Foale, 25 Mar 1964, 1 son, 1 daughter. *Education:* BA, MPhil, DipArch Admin. University of London. *Publications:* Rattus Rex, 1978; Crows in a Winter Landscape, 1979; Mother of the Free, 1980; A Twister over the Thames, 1981; The Warriors Under the Stone, 1983. *Contributions to:* Writes, broadcasts and adapts regularly for BBC Radio 3 and 4. *Honour:* Winner, Society of Authors' Award, best adaptation, Munchansen, 1986. *Memberships:* Society of Authors; Crime Writers' Association. *Literary Agent:* A P Watt Ltd. *Address:* c/o The Library, University of Aberdeen, Aberdeen, Scotland.

MCLAREN John David, b. 7 Nov 1932, Melbourne, Australia. Professor; Academic. *Education:* BA (Hons), BEd, PhD, Melbourne University; MA, Monash, University. *Appointments:* Associate Editor, Overland, 1968-; Editor, Australian Book Review, 1978-86. *Publications:* Our Troubled Schools, Melbourne, 1968; A Nation Apart, Melbourne, 1983 (editor); Australian Literature, an historical introduction, Melbourne, 1989; Xavier Herbert's Capricornia and Poor Fellow My Country, Melbourne 1981; Towards a New Australia, Melbourne (editor); 1972; The New Pacific Literatures: culture and environment in the European Pacific, 1993. *Address:* Humanities Department, FIT, PO Box 64, Footscray, Victoria 3011, Australia.

MCLAUGHLIN Dean, b. 22 July 1931, Ann Arbor, Michigan, USA. Writer. *Education:* AB, University of Michigan, 1953. *Publications:* Hawk Among The Sparrows, 1976; Dome World, 1962; The Furs From Earth, 1963; The Man Who Wanted Stars, 1965. *Contributions to:* Analog; Isaac Asimov's; Magazine of Fantasy & Science Fiction. *Membership:* Science Fiction Writers of America. *Literary Agent:* Owlswick Literary

Agency and Ed Cornell. *Address:* 1214 W Washington Street, Ann Arbor, MI 48103, USA.

MCLEAN Allan Campbell, b. 1922. Author. *Publications:* The Hill of the Red Fox, 1955; The Islander (in United States of America as The Gates of Eden), 1962; The Glasshouse, 1969; The Year of the Stranger, 1971; The Highlands and Islands of Scotland, 1976; Ribbon of the Fire, 1985; A Sound of Trumpets, 1985. *Address:* Anerley Cottage, 16 Kingsmills Road, Inverness, IV2 3JS, Scotland.

MCLEAN Antonia Maxwell, 1 Aug 1919, Retired. m. Rvari McLean, 24 Jan 1945, 2 sons, 1 daughter. *Education:* MA, Downs School Seaford, Sussex; Somerville College, Oxford. *Publications:* Humanism and the Rise of Science in Tudor England; Benjamin Fawcett, Victorian Colour Printer. *Contributions to:* Sunday Mail Supplement. *Address:* Carsaig, Pennyghael, Isle of Mull PA70 6HD, Scotland.

MCLEAN Iain Sinclair, b. 13 Sept 1946, Edinburgh, Professor. m. Jo, 8 Sept 1984, 1 son, 1 daughter. *Education:* University of Oxford, BA, 1967; B Phil, 1969; D Phil, 1972. *Publications:* Public Choice; Keir Hardie; Elections; The Legend of Red Clydeside; Democracy and New Technology; Dealing in Votes. *Contributions to:* Scholarly Journals. *Address:* Department of Politics & International Studies, University of Warwick, Coventry, CV4 7AL, England.

MCLEES Ainslie Irene Armstrong, b. 17 Feb 1947, Philadelphia, Pennsylvania, USA. Writer; Professor. m. John Hill McLees Jr. *Education:* BA, Ursinus College, 1968; MA, Mawr College, 1969; PhD, University of VA, 1980. *Appointments:* Mary Washington College, 1969-70; University of Virginia, Instructor, 1973-77; Northern Virginia Community College, 1979-85; Virginia Meuseum of Fine Arts, 1985-; Randolph Macon College, Associate Professor, 1985-. *Publications:* Baudelarie's Argot Plastique: Poetic Caricature and Modernism, 1989; Argot Plastique. *Contributions to:* Mosaic; Symposium; Explorations in the 19th Century; The Other Arts. *Honours:* Nominated Cane Award; MLA Award; Gauss Award; VA Bookstore Associate Award. *Memberships:* South Atlantic Modern Language Association; womens Studies Caucus; Foreign Language Association of Va; American Association of Teachers of French. *Address:* 1628 Park Avenue, Richmond, VA 23220, USA.

MCLEISH Kenneth, b. 10 Oct 1940, Glasgow, Scotland. Author; Translator. m. Valerie Elizabeth Heath, 30 May 1967, 2 sons. *Education:* BA, B.Mus., MA, Worcester College, Oxford, 1963. *Publications:* The Theatre of Aristophanes, 1980; Penguin Companion to 20th Century Arts, 1985; Listener's Guide to Classical Music, 1986; Shakespeare's People, 1986; The Good Reading Guide, 1988; over 50 childrens books including: The Oxford First Companion to Music, 1979; Children of the Gods (Myths & Legends of Ancient Greece), 1984; Myths and Folktales of Britain and Ireland 1986; Stories from the Bible, 1988; Translator: Ibsen, Feydeau, Labiche, Sophocles, Aristophanes. *Contributions to:* Reviewer, General Books, Sunday Times. *Literary Agent:* A P Watt & Co. *Address:* c/o A P Watt Ltd, 20 John Street, London WC1N 2DL, England.

MCLELLAN David Thorburn, b. 10 Feb 1940, Hertford, England. University Teacher. m. Annie Brassart, 1 July 1967. 2 daughters. *Education:* MA 1962, DPhil 1968, St John's College, Oxford. *Publications:* Simone Weil: Utopian Pessimist, 1989; Karl Marx: His Life and Thought, 1974; Marxism and Religion, 1987; Ideology, 1986; Marxism After Marx, 1980; Engels, 1977; The Young Hegelians and Karl Marx, 1969. *Literary Agent:* The Peters, Fraser & Dunlop Group Ltd. *Address:* Eliot College, University of Kent, Canterbury CT2 7NS, England.

MCLERRAN Alice, b. 24 June 1933, West Point,

New York, USA. Writer. m. Larry Dean McLerran, 8 May 1976, 2 sons, 1 daughter. *Education:* BA Anthropology, 1965, PhD, 1969, University of California at Berkeley; MS Behavioural Sciences, 1973, MPH, 1974, Harvard School of Public Health. *Publications:* The Mountain that Loved a Bird, 1985; Secrets, 1990; Roxaboxen, 1991; I Want to go Home, 1992; Dreamsong, 1992; Hugs, 1993; Kisses, 1993. *Honours:* Southwest Book Award, 1991. *Memberships:* The Authors Guild; Society of Children's Book Writers and Illustrators. *Address:* 2524 Colfax Avenue South, Minneapolis, MN 55405, USA.

MCMANUS James, b. 22 Mar 1951, New York City. USA. Poet; Novelist. m. Jennifer Arra, 9 July 1992, 1 son, 1 daughter. *Appointments:* Professor, The School of the Art Institute, Chicago, 1981. *Publications:* Great America; Girl with Electric Guitar; Ghost Waves; Chin Music; Curtains; Out of the Blue; Antonio Salazar is Dead. *Contributions to:* Paris Review; Atlantic Monthly; Parnassus; New York Times; American Poetry Review; Honest Ulsterman; Tri Quarterly. *Memberships:* PEN; AWP. *Literary Agent:* Kathy Robbins. *Address:* SAIC, 37 S Wabash, Chicago, IL 60603, USA.

MCMASTER Juliet Sylvia, b. 2 Aug 1937, Kenya. University Professor. m. Rowland McMaster, 10 May 1968, 1 son, 1 daughter. *Education:* BA 1959, MA 1962, St Anne's College, Oxford; MA, 1963, PhD, 1965, University of Alberta. *Appointments:* Assistant Professor, 1965-70, Associate Professor, 1970-76, Professor, 1976-86, University Professor, 1986-, English, University of Alberta. *Publications:* Thackeray: The Major Novels, 1971; Jane Austen's Achievement (editor), 1976; Trollope's Palliser Novels, 1978; Jane Austen on Love, 1978; The Novel from Sterne to James (with R D McMaster), 1981; Dickens the Designer, 1987. *Contributions to:* Nineteenth-Century Fiction; Victorian Studies; Modern Language Quarterly English Studies in Canada. *Honours:* Canada Council Post-Doctoral Fellowship, 1969-70; Guggenheim Fellow, 1976-77; McCalla Professorship, University of Alberta, 1982-83; University of Alberta Research Prize, 1986; Killam Research Fellowship, 1987-88. *Memberships:* Jane Austen Society of North America, Board Member, 1979-, Editor 1987-88; Dickens Society, Trustee, 1989-. *Address:* Dept. of English, University of Alberta, Edmonton, Alberta Canada T6G 2E5.

MCMILLAN James, (Coriolanus), b. 30 Oct 1925. Journalist. m. Doreen Smith, 7 Apr 1953, 3 sons, 1 daughter. *Education:* MA (Economics), Glasgow University, Scotland. *Publications:* American Take-Over, 1967; Anatomy of Scotland, 1969; British Genius (with Peter Grosvenor), 1972; The Way Were 1900-1950 (trilogy), 1977-80; Five Men at Nuremberg, 1984; The Dunlop Story, 1989; The Glass Lie, 1964; The Honours Game, 1970; Roots of Corruption, 1971; From Finchley to The World-Margaret Thatcher, 1990. *Literary Agent:* Curtis Brown, London. *Address:* Thurleston, Fairmile Park Road, Cobham, Surrey KT11 2PL, England.

MCMILLEN Neil Raymond, b. 1939, American. *Appointments:* Assistant Professor of History, Ball State University, Muncie, IN, 1967- 69; Assistant Professor 1969-70, Associate Professor 1970-78, Professor of History 1978-, University of Southern Mississippi, Hattiesburg. *Publications:* The Citizens' Council: Organized Resistance to the Second Reconstruction, 1971; Thomas Jefferson: Philosopher of Freedom, 1973; A Synopsis of American History (with C Sellers and H May), 1984, 7th ed, 1992; Dark Journey: Black Mississippians in the Age of Jim Crow, 1989. *Honour:* Bancroft Prize, 1990. *Address:* Department of History, University of Southern Mississippi, Hattiesburg, MS 39401, USA.

MCMILLIN Harvey Scott, b. 29 June 1934, Pittsburgh, Pennsylvania, USA. Scholar. m. 11 May 1957, 3 sons. *Education:* Princeton University, BA, 1956; George Washington University, MA, 1960; Stanford University, PhD, 1965. *Appointments:* Professor, Cornell University, NY, 1964-. *Publications:*

Elizabethan Theatre and Book of Sir Thomas More; Shakespeare in Performance; Norton Critical Edition of Restoration and Eighteenth Century Comedy. *Contributions to:* Shakespeare Quarterly; Review of English Studies; Studies in English Literature; Renaissance Drama; Medieval & Renaissance Drama; English Literary Renaissance. *Honours:* Fellowship, National Endowment for Humanities; Distinguished Teaching Award. *Memberships:* Shakespeare Association of America; Theatre History Seminar of Shakespeare Association of America; Modern Language Association; American Society for Theatre Research. *Address:* English Department, Cornell University, Ithaca, NY 14853, USA.

MCMULLEN Mary, b. 1920, American. *Publications:* Stranglehold, 1951, in UK as Death of Miss X, 1952; The Doom Campaign, 1974; A Country Kind of Death, The Pimlico Plot, 1975; Funny, Jonas, You Don't Look Dead, 1976; A Dangerous Funeral, Death By Request, 1977; Prudence Be Damed, The Man with Fifty Complaints, 1978; Welcome to the Grave, But Nellie Was So Nice, 1979; My Cousin Death, Something of the Night, 1980; The Other Shoe, 1981; Better Off Dead, Until Death Do Us Part, 1982; A Grave Without Flowers, 1983; The Gift Horse, 1985; The Bad-News Man, 1986. *Address:* C/o Doubleday and Company Incorporated, 245 Park Avenue, New York, NY 10017, USA.

MCMURTRY Larry (Jeff), b. 1936, American. *Publications:* Horseman Pass By (in UK as Hud), 1961; Leaving Cheyenne, 1963; The Last Picture Show, 1966; screenplay with Peter Bogdanovitch, 1971; In a Narrow Grave, 1968; Moving On, 1970; All My Friends Are Going to be Strangers, 1972; It's Always We Rambled, 1974; Terms of Endearment, 1975; Somebody's Darling, 1978; Cadillac Jack, 1982; The Desert Rose, 1983; Lonesome Dove, 1985; Texasville, 1987; Anything For Billy, 1989. *Address:* C/o Simon and Schuster, 1230 Sixth Avenue, New York, NY 10020, USA.

MCNALLY Terrence, b. 1939, American. *Appointments:* Stage Manager, Actors Studio, NYC, 1961; Tutor, 1961-62; Film Critic, The Seventh Art, 1963-65; Assistant Editor, Columbia College Today, 1965-66. *Publications:* Apple Pie, Sweet Eros Next and Other Plays, 1969; Three Plays: Cuba Si!, Bringing It All Back Home, Last Gasps, 1970; Where Has Tommy Flowers Gone?, 1972; Bad Habits: Ravenswood and Dunelawn, 1974; The Ritz and Other Plays, 1976; The Rink, 1985. *Address:* 218 West 10th Street, New York, NY 10014, USA.

MCNAMARA Dennis Louis, b. 11 Mar 1945, USA. Professor. *Education:* BA Philosophy, St Louis University, 1969; MA Sociology, Fordham University, 1976; MDiv, 1976, STM, 1977, Jesuit School of Theology, Berkeley, 1976; PhD, Sociology, Harvard University, 1983. *Publications:* Colonial Origins of Korean Enterprise, 1990; Articles: The Keisho and the Korean Business Elite, 1989; Entrepreneurship in Colonial Korea, 1988; Reincorporation and the American State, 1992; A Corporatist Anomaly, 1992. *Honours:* Fulbright Fellowships, 1981, 1987, 1992; National Science Foundation Fellowship, 1991. *Memberships:* International Sociological Association; American Sociological Association; Association for Asian Studies. *Address:* Sociology Department, Georgetown University, 37th and O St NW, Washington DC 20057, USA.

MCNAMARA Eugene Joseph, b. 18 Mar 1930, Oak Park, Illinois, USA. Professor; Editor; Poet; Writer. m. Margaret Lindstrom, 19 July 1952, Chicago, Illinois, USA. 4 sons, 1 daughter. *Education:* BA, MA, DePaul University; PhD, Northwestern University, 1964. *Literary Appointments:* Editor, Mainline, 1967-72; Editor, University of Windsor Review, 1965-; Editor, Sesame Press, 1973-80. Professor of English, University of Windsor. *Major Publications:* Poems: For the Mean Time, 1965; Outerings, 1970; Dillinger Poems, 1970; Love Scenes, 1971; Passages, 1972; Screens, 1977;

Forcing the Field, 1980; Call it a Day, 1984. Short Stories: Salt, 1977; Search for Sarah Grace, 1978; Spectral Evidence, 1985; The Moving Light, 1986. *Contributions to:* Queens Quarterly; Saturday Night; Chicago; Quarry; Denver Quarterly, and others (several hundred poems). *Address:* 166 Randolph Place, Windsor, Ontario, N9B 2T3, Canada.

MCNEIL Elisabeth. *See:* TAYLOR Elisabeth Dewar.

MCNEIL Florence Ann, b. 8 May 1940, Vancouver, British Columbia, Canada. Writer. m. David McNeal, 3 Jan 1973. *Education:* BA 1960, MA 1965, University of British Columbia, Vancouver. *Publications:* Fiction: Miss P and Me, 1982; All Kings of Magic, 1984; Catriona's Island, 1989. Poetry: Emily, 1975; A Balancing Act, 1979; Ghost Towns, 1975; Poems: Selected and New, 1990; Barkerville, 1984; The Overlanders, 1982; Rim of the Park, 1972; Walhachin, 1972. Play: Barkerville, produced in 1987. *Contributions to:* Many magazines, journals and anthologies. *Honours:* Thea Koetner Award for Creative Writing, 1963; The MacMillan Prize for Poetry, 1963; National Magazine Award for Poetry, 1980; The BC Book Awards, Sheila Egoff Prize for Children's Literature, 1989; Our Choice, Toronto Childrens Book Centre, 1985; Many Canada Council Grants. *Memberships:* League of Canadian Poets (Chair, Education Committee); Canadian Writers' Union; Canadian Society For Children's Authors, Illustrators and Performers; British Columbia Writers Federation. *Address:* 20 Georgia Wynd, Delta, British Columbia, Canada V4M 1A5.

MCNEIL John, b. 16 Dec 1939, Oxford, England. Writer. m. Mary Sweron, 2 Apr 1962, 1 son. *Education:* Imperial College, London, BSc, 1958-61. *Publications:* The Consultant; Spy Game; Little Brother; The Hoolet; Crossfire. *Memberships:* Writers Guild of Great Britain. *Literary Agent:* Carol Smith. *Address:* Greenpark, Charlotte Street, Helensburgh G84 7ST, Scotland.

MCNEISH James, b. 1931, New Zealander. *Appointment:* Writer-in-Residence, Berlin Kunstler-program, 1983. *Publications:* Tavern in the Town, 1957; Fire Under the Ashes, 1965; Mackenzie, 1970; The Mackenzie Affair, 1972; Larks in a Paradise (co-author), 1974; The Glass Zoo, 1976; As for the Godwits, 1977; Art of the Pacific (with Brian Brake), 1980; Belonging: Conversations in Israel, 1980; Joy, 1982; Walking on My Feet, 1983; the Man from Nowhere: A Berlin Diary, 1985; Lovelock, 1986; Penelope's Island, 1990. *Address:* c/o Vivienne Schuster, John Farquharson Limited, 162/168 Regent Street, London W1R 5TB, England.

MCNULTY Faith, b. 1918, American. *Appointment:* Staff Writer, The New Yorker magazine, 1953-. *Publications:* Arty the Smarty, Wholly Cats (with E Keiffer), When a Boy Wakes Up in the Morning, 1962; When a Boy Goes to Bed at Night, 1963; The Whooping Crane, 1966; Must They Die?, 1971; Prairie Dog Summer, 1972; The Great Whales, Woodchuck, 1974; Whales, 1975; Mouse and Tim, 1978; How to Dig a Hole to the Other Side of the World, 1979; The Burning Bed, The Wildlife Stories of Faith McNulty, 1980; Hurricane, 1983; The Lady and the Spider, 1986. *Address:* c/o The New Yorker, 25 West 43rd Street, New York, NY 10036, USA.

MCPHEE John, b. Princeton, New Jersey, USA. *Education:* Princeton High School; Deerfield Academy; Princeton University; Cambridge University. *Appointments:* Staff Writer, The New Yorker; Teacher of Writing Course, Princeton University. *Publications:* A Sense of Where You Are; The Headmaster; The Pine Barrens; A Roomful of Hovings; Oranges; Levels of the Game; The Crofter and the Laird; The Deltoid Pumpkin Seed; Pieces of the Frame; The Survival of the Bark Canoe; Encounters with the Archdruid; The Curve of Binding Energy; The John McPhee Reader; Coming into the Country, 1977; Giving Good Weight (collection of essays), 1979; Books on geology and geologists: Basin and Range, 1981, In Suspect Terrain, 1982, Rising from the Plains, 1986, La Place de la Concorde Suisse, 1984; Table of Contents, 1986; Heirs of General Practice, 1986; The Control of Nature, 1989; Looking for a Ship, 1990. *Honours:* Nominated for National Books Awards in the category of science: Encounters with the Archdruid, 1973, The Curve of Binding Energy, 1974; Award from American Academy and Institute of Arts and Letters, 1977. *Address:* c/o Ruth Weiner, Farrar, Straus and Giroux, 19 Union Square West, New York, NY 10003, USA.

MCPHERSON James Allen, b. 16 Sept 1943, Savannah, Georgia, USA. Writer; Teacher. 1 daughter. *Education:* BA, Morris Brown College, Atlanta, Georgia, 1965; LLB, Harvard Law School, 1968; MFA, University of Iowa, 1971. *Appointments include:* University of California, Santa Cruz, 1969-70; Morgan State University, Baltimore, Maryland, 1974-75; University of Virginia, Charlottesville, 1976-81; University of Iowa, 1981-. *Publications include:* Hue & Cry, 1969; Railroad, 1976; Elbow Room, 1977; A World Unsuspected, 1987. *Contributions to:* Contributing editor, Atlantic Monthly; Atlantic; Esquire; New York Times, Magazine, Book Review; Reader's Digest; Chicago Tribune; Playboy; Ploughshares; Iowa Review. *Honours:* Atlantic First Award, 1968; Atlantic Grant, 1969; Award, Literature, National Academy of Arts & Letters, 1970; Guggenheim Fellowship, 1973; Pulitzer Prize, 1978; McArthur Award, 1981. *Membership:* Authors League. *Literary Agent:* Carl Brandt. *Address:* c/o Carl Brandt, 1501 Broadway, New York, NY 10036, USA.

MCPHERSON James Munro, b. 11 Oct 1936, Valley City, North Dakota, USA. m. Patricia Rasche, 28 Dec 1957, 1 daughter. *Education:* BA, Gustavus Aldophus College, 1958; PhD, The Johns Hopkins University, 1963. *Appointments:* Instructor in History, 1962-65, Assistant Professor of History, 1965-66, Associate Professor, 1966-72, Professor of History, 1972-82, Edwards Professor of American History, 1982-91, George Henry Davis Professor of American History, 1991-; Princeton University; Commonwealth Fund Lecturer, University College, London, England, 1982. *Publications:* Battle Cry of Freedom: The Civil War Era, 1988; The Struggle for Equality, 1964; The Negro's Civil War, 1965; The Abolitionist Legacy, 1975; Ordeal by Fire: The Civil War and Reconstruction, 1982; Abraham Lincoln and the Second American Revolution, 1991. *Contributions to:* Atlantic Monthly; New York Review of Books; New Republic; American Historical Review; Journal of American history; Southern Historical Review; New England Quarterly. *Honours:* Anisfield-Wolf Award, 1965; Pulitzer Prize in History, 1989; Michael Award of New Jersey Literary Hall of Fame, 1989; DHL Gustavus Adolphus College, 1990. *Memberships:* American Historical Association; Organization of American Historians; Society of American Historians; Southern Historical Association; American Philosophical Society. *Address:* 15 Randall Road, Princeton, NJ 08540, USA.

MCPHERSON Sandra, b. 2 Aug 1943, San Jose, California, USA. Writer; Teacher. m. Henry Carlile, 24 July 1966, (div), 1 daughter. *Education:* BA, English, San Jose State, 1965; University of Washington, 1965-1966. *Publications:* Elegies for the Hot Season, 1970, 1982; Radiation, 1973; The Year of Our Birth, 1978; Sensing, 1980; Patron Happiness, 1983; Pheasant Flower, 1985; Responsibility for Blue, 1985; Floralia, 1985; Streamers, 1988; The God of Indeterminacy, 1993. *Contributions to:* (Poetry) American Poetry Review; Field; Grand Street; The Yale Review; New Republic; The New Yorker; many others. *Honours:* Ingram Merrill Foundation Grant, 1972, 1984; NEA Grant, 1974, 1980, 1985; Guggenheim Foundaiton Fellowship, 1976; National Book Award Nominee, 1979; Oregon Arts Commission Fellowship,1984; American Acdemy and Institute of Arts and Letters Award in Literature, 1987. *Address:* c/o English Dept., University of California, Davis, CA 95616, USA.

MCQUOWN Norman Anthony, b. 30 Jan 1914, Peoria, Illinois, USA. Teacher. m. 7 Nov 1942, 2 daughters. *Education:* AB 1935, AM 1936, University of Illinois; PhD, Yale University. *Appointments:* University of Illinois 1935-36; Escuela Nacional de Antropologia (Mexico) 1939-42; Hunter College of the City of New York, 1945-46; University of Chicago, 1946-. *Publications include:* Language, Culture and Education, Stanford, 1982; El Microanalisis de Entrevistas, Mexico, 1983; Spoken Turkish, New York, 1946; Konusulan Ingilizce, Washington DC, 1954; El Tzeltal Hablado, Chicago, 1957; Handbook of Middle American Indians 5: Linguistics, Texas, 1967. *Contributions to:* International Journal of American Linguistics; American Anthropologist; Revista Mexicana de Antropologia; Estudios de Cultura Maya. *Honours:* Diploma, Sociedad Mexicana de Antropologia, 1981; Certificate of Merit, Ministry of Education, Guatemala, 1983; Alexander von Humboldt-Stiftungspreis, 1988. *Memberships:* Linguistic Society of America; American Anthropological Association; Programa Interamericano de Linguistica y Ensenanza de Idiomas (President 1967-77). *Address:* 1126 East 59th Street, Chicago, IL 60637, USA.

MCRAE Hamish Malcolm Donald, b. 20 Oct 1943, Barnstaple, Devon, England. Journalist. m. Frances Anne Cairncross, 10 Sept 1971. 2 daughters. *Education:* Fettes College, Edinburgh 1957-62; Trinity College, Dublin, 1962-66, Honours Degree Economics & Political Science. *Literary Appointments:* Editor, Euromoney, 1972; Financial Editor, The Guardian, 1975; Editor, Business and City, The Independent, 1989. *Publications:* Capital City - London as a Financial Centre (with Frances Cairncross), 1973, 5th Edition 1991; The Second Great Crash (with Frances Cairncross), 1975; Japan's role in the emerging global securities market, 1985. *Contributions to:* Numerous magazines and journals. *Honours:* Financial Journalist of the Year, Wincott Foundation, 1979; Special Merit Award, Amex Bank Review Essays, 1987. *Address:* 6 Canonbury Lane, London N1 2AP, England.

MCSHANE Mark, (Marc Lovell), b. 28 Nov 1929, Sydney, Australia. Writer. m. Rosemary Armstrong, 15 Oct 1963, 2 sons, 1 daughter. *Publications:* Over 40 novels. *Literary Agent:* Collier Associates, 875 Fifth Avenue, New York, USA. *Address:* Can Tumi, La Cabaneta, Majorca, Spain.

MCSHARRY Deirdre, b. 4 Apr 1932, London, England. Journalist. *Education:* Trinity College, Dublin. *Appointments:* Women's Editor, Daily Express, 1962-66; Fashion Editor, The Sun, 1966-72; Editor, Cosmopolitan, 1973-85; Editor in Chief, Country Living, 1986-89. *Honour:* Magazine Editor of the Year, 1981 and 1987, for Country Living. *Address:* Bath, Avon, England.

MCVEAN James. See: LUNARD Nicholas.

MCWHIRTER George, b. 26 Sept 1939, Belfast, County Antrim, Northern Ireland. Writer; Translator; University Professor. m. Angela Mairead Cold, 26 Dec 1963, Belfast. 1 son, 1 daughter. *Education:* BA Honours, Diploma in Education, Queen's University, Belfast; MA, University of British Columbia, Canada. *Literary Appointments:* Co-editor in chief 1977, Advisory Editor, 1978-89, 'Prism' international magazine; Head, Department of Creative Writing, University of British Columbia, Canada, 1982-. *Publications:* Catalan Poems, 1971; Bodyworks, 1974; Queen of the Sea, 1976; Twenty-five, 1978; God's Eye, 1981; Coming To Grips With Lucy, 1982; The Island Man, 1980; Fire Beofre Dark, 1983; Paula Lake, 1984; Selected poems of Jose Emilio Pacheco (translation), 1987; Cage, 1987; The Listener, 1991; A Bad Day To Be Winning, 1992; A Staircase For All Souls, 1993. *Contributions to:* Poetry Australia; The Irish Universities Review; The Malahat Review; The London Magazine; Saturday Night; The Meanjin Quarterly; Helix; The Honest Ulsterman; Quarry; The Canadian Forum; Prism International; The

Beloit Poetry Journal; Epoch; Poetry Review anada; CBC's Anthology; Books in Canada; Interface; Canadian Literature; The Fiddlehead; Event; Ariel. *Honours:* Macmillan Prize for Poetry, 1969; Commonwealth Poetry Prize, shared with Chinua Achebe, 1972; F R Scott Prize for Translation, League of Canadian Poets & F R Scott Foundation, 1988; Ethel Wilson Fiction Prize, B C Book Awards, 1988. *Memberships:* League of Canadian Poets; Writer's Union of Canada. *Address:* 4637 West 13th Avenue, Vancouver BC, Canada, V6R 2V6.

MCWHIRTER Norris Dewar, b. 12 Aug 1925, London, England. Author; Editor; Broadcaster. m. (1) Carole Eckert, 28 Dec 1957 (dec 1987), 1 son, 1 daughter, (2) Tena Mary Pocock, 26 Mar 1991. *Education:* BA, 1947, MA, 1948, Trinity College, Oxford. *Appointments:* Athletics Correspondent, Observer, 1951-67, Star 1951-60; Editor, Athletics World, 1952-56; Founder Editor, Guinness Book of Records, 1955. *Publications:* Get To Your Marks, 1951; Guinness Book of Records, 1955-86 (30 languages); Dunlop Book of Facts, 1964-73; Guinness Book of Answers 1976-; Ross, Story of a Shared Life, 1976; Guinness Book of Essential Facts, 1979. *Contributions to:* Encyclopaedia Brittanica; Whitakers Almanack. *Honour:* CBE, 1980. *Memberships:* Royal Institution. *Address:* c/o Guinness Publishing Co, 33 London Road, Enfield, Middlesex, EN2 6DJ, England.

MCWILLIAM Candia Frances Juliet, b. 1 July 1955, Edinburgh, Scotland. Writer. m. (1) Earl of Portsmouth, 10 Feb 1981, (2) F E Dinshaw, 27 Sept 1986, 2 sons, 1 daughter. *Education:* Sherborne School for Girls, 1968-73; Girton College, Cambridge, BA, 1973-76. *Publications:* A Case of Knives; A Little Stranger. *Honours:* Betty Traske Prize; Scottish Arts Council Prize. *Memberships:* Society of Authors; PEN. *Literary Agent:* Janklow & Nesbit. *Address:* c/o Bloomsbury Publishing, 2 Soho Square, London W1V 5DE, England.

MEAD Matthew, b. 1924, British. *Appointment:* Editor, Satis magazine, Edinburgh, 1960-62. *Publications:* A Poem in Nine Parts, 1960; Identities, 1964; Kleinigkeiten, 1966; Identities and Other Poems, 1967; The Administration of Things, Penguin Modern Poets 16 (with Harry Guest ad J Beeching), 1970; In the Eyes of the People, 1973; Minusland, 1977; The Midday Muse, 1979; A Roman in Cologne, 1985. *Address:* c/o Anvil Press, 69 King George Street, London SE10 8PX, England.

MEAD (Edward) Shepherd, b. 1914, American. *Appointments:* With Benton and Bowles Incorporated, 1936-56; Consultant to S H Benson, 1958-62; Director, Nouvelles Editions, S A, Lausanne, Switzerland, 1969- . *Publications:* The Magnificant MacInnes, 1949; Tessie, the Hound of Channel One, 1951; How to Succeed in Business Without Really Trying, 1952, musical version 1961; The Big Ball of Wax, 1954; How to Get Rich in TV Without Really Trying, 1956; How to Succeed with Women Without Really Trying, 1957; The Admen, 1958; Readers Digest Book Club, 1959; The Four Window Girl, 1959; 'Dudley, There Is No Tomorrow!' 'Then How About This Afternoon?', 1963; How to Live Like a Lord Without Really Trying, 1964; The Carefully Considered Rape of the World, 1966; How to Succeed at Business Spying by Trying, 1968; ER: or, The Brassbound Beauty, the Bearded Bicyclist, and the Gold-Colored Teen-Age Grandfather, 1969; How to Stay Medium-Young Practically Forever Without Really Trying, 1971; Free the Male Man! The Manifesto of the Men's Literature Movement, 1972; How to Get to the Future Before It Gets to You, 1974; How to Succeed in Tennis Without Really Trying, 1977; Tennessee Williams: An Intimate Biography (with Dakin Williams), 1983. *Honour:* Pulitzer Prize. *Address:* 53 Rivermead Court, Ranelagh Gardens, London SW6 3RY, England.

MEADES Jonathan Turner, b. 21 Jan 1947, Salisbury, Wiltshire, England. Journalist; Writer; Broadcaster. m. (1) Sally Browne. (2) Frances Bentley.

3 daughters. *Education:* Kings College, Taunton, 1960-64; Royal Acaedmy of Dramatic Art, 1967-69. *Publications:* Filthy English; Peter Knows What Dick Likes; Pompey. *Contributions to:* The Times; Sunday Times; The Observer; The Independent. *Memberships:* Water Rats; Pro Celeb Golfers. *Literary Agent:* Peters, Fraser & Dunlop. *Address:* c/o Jonathan Cape, Vauxhall Bridge Road, London SW1, England.

MEAKER Marijane, (M E Kerr, Vin Packer), b. 1932, USA. Children's Fiction Writer. *Publications:* Dinky Hocker Shoots Smack, 1972; If I Love You, Am I Trapped Forever, 1973; The Son of Someone Famous, 1974; Is That You, Miss Blue, 1975; Love Is A Missing Person, 1975; I'll Love You When You're More Like Me, 1977; Gentlehands, 1978; Little, Little, 1980; What I Really Think of You, 1982; Me Me Me Me Me, 1983. *Address:* 12 Deep Six Drive, East Hampton, NY 11937, USA.

MEASHAM Donald Charles, b. 19 Jan 1932. Retired Teacher, Higher Education. m. Joan Doreen Barry, 15 Dec 1954. 1 son, 1 daughter. *Education:* BA (Hons), Birmingham University, 1953; MPhil, Nottingham University, 1971. *Appointments:* Member (Deputy Chairman) Literature Panel, East Midlands Arts, 1980-84; Founding Editor 1983, Business Manager and Continuing Co-Editor 1988-, Staple Magazine. *Publications:* Leaving, 1965; Fourteen, 1965; English Now & Then, 1965; Larger Than Life, 1967; Quattordicenni, 1967; The Personal Element, 1967; Lawrence & The Real England, 1985; Ruskin: The Last Chapter, 1989. *Contributions to:* Tribune; TLS; Teacher; Renaissance and Modern Studies; Other People's Clerihews, edited G Ewart. *Address:* Tor Cottage, 81 Cavendish Road, Matlock, Derbyshire DE4 3HD, England.

MEDNICK Murray, b. 1939, American. *Appointment:* Playwright-in-Residence and Artistic Director, Theatre Genesis, NYC, 1970-73; Founder and Artistic Director, the Padua Hills Playwrights' Workshop/Festival, Los Angeles, CA, 1978-. *Publications:* The Hawk: An Improvisational Play (with Tony Barsha), 1968; The Hunter, 1969; The Deer Kill, 1971; Taxes, 1983; The Coyote Cycle, 1984. *Address:* 2242 Lake Shore Avenue, Los Angeles, CA 90039, USA.

MEDOFF Mark, b. 18 Mar 1940. Playwright. m. Stephanie Thorne, 3 daughters. *Education:* BA, University of Miami; MA, Stanford University; DHL, Gallaudet College. *Appointments:* Dramatist in Residence, New Mexico State University, Las Cruces, New Mexico; Literature and Theatre Panel, National Endowment for the Arts. *Publications:* Plays: When You Comin' Back, Red Ryder, 1973-74; The Wager; Children of a Lesser God, 1979; The Majestic Kid, 1981, Revised Edition, 1989; The Hands Of Its Enemy, 1984; The Heart Outright, 1986; Big Mary, 1989; Stumps, 1989; The Hero Trilogy (When You Comin' Back, Red Ryder, The Heart Outright, The Majestic Kid), 1989; Stephanie Hero, 1990; Kringle's Window, 1991; Others; Film scripts: Good Guys Wear Blakc, 1977; When You Comin' Back, Red Ryder, 1978; Off Beat, 1985; Apology, 1986; Children of a Lesser God, 1987; Clara's Heart, 1988; City of Joy, 1992. *Contributions to:* The Washington Post; Los Angeles Times; Journal of Teachers of English; Dramatics Magazine; Reader's Digest; New York Times Magazine; Albuquerque Journal Impact; Esquire. *Honours include:* For When You Comin Back, Red Ryder: OBIE Award, Drama Desk Award, New York Outer Critics Award, Best Plays, 1973-74; Westhafer Award for Excellence in Creative Activity, New Mexico State University, 1974; Guggenheim Fellowship in Playwriting, 1974-75; Best Plays for The Wager, 1974-75; Outstanding Play Script for Firekeeper, Texas Review of Books, 1978; Governor's Award for Excellence in the Arts, State of New Mexico, 1980; For Children of a Lesser God: Antoinette Perry Award for Best Play, Drama Desk Award, New York Outer Critics Circle Award, 1979-80, Best Plays, 1980-81, Los Angeles Drama-Logue Critics Award, Best Play, Society of West End Theatre, 1981; Distinguished Alumnus, University of Miami, 1987; John Conley Scholar, American

Academy of Otolaryngology-Head and Neck Surgery, 1987; California Media Access Award for film script of Children of a Lesser God. *Memberships:* Writers Guild of America; Actors Equity Association; Screen Actors Guild. *Literary Agent:* Gilbert Parker, William Morris Agency. *Address:* Box 3585, Las Cruces, NM 88003, USA.

MEDVEDEV Roy (Alexandrovich), b. 1925, Russian. *Appointments:* School Teacher, Sverdlovsk region, 1952-54; School Director, Leningrad region; Deputy Editor-in-Chief, Prosveshchenic Publishing House, 1957-60; Head of Department of Vocational Education, Research Institute of Education, Moscow, 1961-71; Deputy of the Supreme Soviet of the USSR 1989-. *Publications:* Let History Judge, Questions of Madness (with Zhores A Medvedev), 1971; On Socialist Democracy, 1975; Khrushchev: The Years in Power (with Zhores A Medvedev), Political Essays, 1976; Problems in the Literary Biography of Mikhail Sholokov, 1977; Samizdat Register (ed), 2 volumes, 1977-80; The October Revolution, On Stalin and Stalinism, 1979; On Soviet Dissent, Nikolai Bukharin: The Last Years, 1980; Leninism and Western Socialism, 1981; All Stalin's Men, 1983; China and the Superpowers, 1986; Let History Judge, 1989. *Address:* Abonement Post Box 258, Moscow A-475, 125475, USSR.

MEDVEDEV Zhores (Alexandrovich), British, b. Russian, 1925. *Appointments:* Senior Research Fellow, MRC National Institute for Medical Research Division of Genetics, London, since 1973; Associate Ed, Experimental Gerontology; Senior Research Scientists K Timiriasev Academy of Agricultural Sciences, Moscow, 1951-62; Head of Laboratory of Molecular Radiobiology, Research Institute of Medical Radiology, Obninsk, Kaluga Region, USSR, 1963-69; Senior Research Scientist, Laboratory of Proteins, Research Institute of Biochemistry and Physiology of Farm Animals, Borovsk, Kaluga region, USSR, 1970-72. *Publications:* Protein Biosynthesis, 1966; The Rise and Fall of T D Lysenko, 1969; Molecular-Genetic Mechanisms of Development, 1970; (with Roy A Medvedev), Questions of Madness, 1971; Medvedev Papers, 1971; Ten Years After Ivan Denisovich; (with Roy A Medvedev) Khrushchev: The Years in Power, 1976; Soviet Science, 1978; Nuclear Disaster in the Urals, 1979; Andropov, 1983; Gorbachev, 1986; Soviet Agriculture, 1987.

MEDVEI Victor Cornelius, (C Monk), b. 6 June 1905, Budapest, Hungary. Consultant Physician. m. Sheila Mary Wiggins, (dec 1989), 9 May 1946, 1 son, 2 daughters. *Education:* Prince Eszterhazy Symnasium, Vienna, 1916-24; MD, University of Vienna, 1930; MRCS LRCP, St Bartholomews Hospital, London, 1941; MRCP, 1943; FRCP, 1965. *Publications include:* The Mental and Physical Effects of Pain, 1949; The Royal Hospital of St Bartholomews 1923-1973, (joint editor), 1974; A History of Endocrinology, 1982, reprinted 1984, 2nd edition 1993. *Contributions to:* About 80 papers for Medical Scientific Journals, 1931-92. *Honours:* CBE, 1965; Chevalier de l'ordre National du Merite, 1981; Buckston Browne Prize, Harveian Society of London, 1948; Golden MD, Diploma of the University of Vienna, 1991. *Memberships:* London PEN, 1946; Harveian Society, President 1970; Osler Club of London, President 1983; Section of History of Medicine (Royal Society of Medicine), President 1986-87; The Garrick Club, 1972-. *Address:* 38 Westmoreland Terrace, London SW1V 3HL, England.

MEEK Jay, b. 23 Aug 1937, Grand Rapids, Michigan, USA. Professor; Writer. m. Martha George, 29 Aug 1966, 1 daughter. *Education:* BA, University of Michigan; MA, Syracuse University. *Appointments:* Guest Member, Writing Faculty, Sarah Lawrence College, Bronxville, 1980- 82; Associate Professor, MIT, 1982-83; Writer in Residence, Memphis State University, 1984; Professor, University of North Dakota, current. *Publications:* The Week the Dirigible Came, 1976; Drawing on the Walls, 1980; Earthly Purposes, 1984; Stations, 1989; After the Storm: Poems on the

Persian Gulf War, 1992; Windows, (book of poems), 1993. *Contributions to:* Poetry; Paris Review; Yale Review; Virginia Quarterly Review; numerous others. *Honours:* Award, NEA, 1972-73; Award, John Simon Guggenheim Memorial Foundation, 1985; Co-editor in poetry, Pushcart Prize, XIII, 1988; Bush Artist Fellowship, 1989. *Memberships:* Poetry Editor, North Dakota Quarterly, 1985-. *Address:* University of North Dakota, University Station, 7209, Grand Forks, ND 58202, USA.

MEGGED Aharon, b. 10 Aug 1920, Wloclawek, Poland. Writer. m. Eda Zoritte, 11 May 1944, 2 sons. *Appointments:* Editor, MASSA, 1953-55; Literary Editor, Lamerchav Daily, 1955-68; Cultural Attaché, Israel Embassy, London, 1968-71; Columnist Davar Daily, 1971-85. *Publications:* Fortunes of a Fool,1960; Living on the Dead, 1965; The Short Life, 1971; Asahel, 1978; The Flying Camel and the Golden Hump, 1982; Foiglmann, 1987; The Turbulent Zone, (essays), 1985; The Writing Desk, (literary essays), 1988; The Selvino Children, (documentary), 1984; Anat's Day of Illumination, 1992. Plays: Hedva and I, 1955; Hannah Senesh, 1963; Genesis, 1965; The High Season, 1968. *Contributions to:* Atlantic Monthly; Encounter; Midstream; the Listener; Moment; Present-Tense; Partisan Review. *Honours:* Ussishkin Prize, 1955, 1966; Brenner Prize, 1957; Shlonsky Prize, 1963; Prime Minister Award, 1973; Bialik Prize, 1973; Fichman Prize, 1979; Kenneth B. Smilen Literature Award, 1983; Gatmon Prize, 1987; Polak Prize, 1989; Newman Prize, 1991. *Memberships:* Hebrew Writers Association; Israel PEN Club, President 1980-87; Israel Journalists Association. *Literary Agent:* In USA, Gloria Stern 1230 Park Avenue, New York 10128; In Europe, Liepman AG, Maienburgury 23, Zurich. *Address:* 26 Rupin Street, Tel Aviv 63457, Israel.

MEGGS Brown (Moore), b. 1930, USA. Author; Record Company President. *Appointments:* Various positions including Executive Vice- President, Chief Operating Officer, and Member of Board of Directors, Capitol Records, Hollywood, California, 1958-76; Executive Vice-President, Nanbrook Corporation, Pasadena, California, 1976-84; President, Angel Records, Los Angeles, California, 1984-. *Publications:* Saturday Games, 1974; The Matter of Paradise, 1975; Aria, 1978; The War Train, 1981. *Address:* 1450 El Mirado Drive, Pasadena, CA 91103, USA.

MEGHANEE Taru, (Kajaia), b. 4 Feb 1953, Calcutta, India. Journalist. m. 29 Dec 1975, 1 son. *Education:* BA Political Science and Philosophy, 1973; MA, Literature and Journalism. *Publications:* Pavitra Bhoomi, 1991; Alice Ajayabnagarima, 1990 (trans); Leelachham Graphics (in press). *Contributions to:* Short stories and essays in: Dharmyug; Narbharat Times; Afternoon Despatch; Navneet Samarpan; Femina; Janmabhoomi; Pravasi. *Memberships:* Life, PEN International; Life, Gujarati Sahitya Parishad, (literary organisation); Gujarati PatrakarSangh; Bombay Union of Journalists. *Address:* Magazine Editor, Janmabhoomi Pravasi, Janmbhoomi Marg, Bombay 400001, India.

MEHTA Ved, (Parkash), b. 21 Mar 1934, Lahore, India. Writer. m. Linn Fenimore Cooper Cary, 1983, 2 daughters. *Education:* Arkansas School for the Blind; BA, Pomona College, 1956; BA, Hons, Modern History, Oxford University, England, 1959, MA, 1962; MA, Harvard University, 1961. *Appointments:* Staff Writer, The New Yorker, 1961-; Visiting Scholar, Case Western Reserve, 1974; Writer and Commentator on Television Documentary Film Chachaji, My Poor Relation, PBS, 1978, BBC, 1980; Beatty Lecturer, McGill University, 1979; Visiting Professor of Literature, Bard College, 1985, 1986; Noble Foundation Visiting Professor of Art and Cultural History, Sarah Lawrence College, 1988; Visiting Fellow of Literature, Balliol College, Oxford, 1988-89; Visiting Professor of English, New York University, 1989-90; Yale University: Rosenkranz Chair in Writing, 1990-93; Lecturer in History, 1990, 1991, 1992; Lecturer in English, 1991-93; Associate Fellow, 1988-, Residential Fellow, 1990-93, Berkeley College;

Arnold Bernhard Visiting Professor of English and History, Williams College; Randloph Distinguihed Professor, Vassar College. *Publications:* Face to Face, 1957; Walking the Indian Streets, 1960, revised edition, 1971; Fly and the Fly-Bottle, 1963, 2nd edition 1983, introduction by Jasper Griffin; The New Theologian, 1966; Delinquent Chacha, 1967; Portrait of India, 1970, 2nd edition, 1993; John is Easy to Please, 1971; Mahatma Gandhi and his Apostles, 1977, reissued 1993; The New India, 1978; Photographs of Chachaji, 1980; A Family Affair: India Under Three Prime Ministers, 1982; Three Stories of the Raj, 1986; Rajiv Ganghi's Legacys, in progress. Continents of Exile (autobiographical series): Daddyji, 1972; Mamaji 1979; Vedi 1982; The Ledge Between the Streams, 1984; Sound-Shadows of the New World, 1986; The Stolen Light, 1989; Up At Oxford, 1993. *Honours:* Phi Beta Kappa, 1955; Hazen Fellow, 1956-59; Harvard Prize Fellow, 1959-60; Guggenheim Fellow, 1971-72, 1977-78; Ford Foundation Travel and Study Grantee, 1971-76; Public Policy Grantee, 1979-82; Member Council on Foreign Relations, 1979-; Member Usage Panel, American Heritage Dictionary, 1982; MacArthur Prize Fellow, 1982-87; Fellow, New York Institute for the Humanities, 1988-92; Association of Indians in America Award, 1978; Distinguished Service Award, Asian/ Pacific American Library Association, 1986; New York City Mayor's Liberty Medal, 1986; Centenary Barrows Award, Pomona College, 1987; Honorary D Litt, Pomona, 1972, Bard 1982; Williams, 1986; Honorary D Univ, Stirling (Scotland) 1988. *Literary Agent:* Anthony Sheil, Georges Borchardt. *Address:* c/o The New Yorker, 20 West 43rd Street, New York, NY 10036, USA.

MEIDINGER Ingeborg Lucie, b. 16 Mar 1923, Berlin. Writer. *Education:* Studies of History & German Literature; DPhil. *Publications include:* 50 works of novels, poetry, stories, radio plays, essays & critiques including: Welterlebnis in deutscher Gegenwartsdichtung, 1956; Der Mond von Gestern (novel), 1963; Ordentliche Leute (stories), 1976; Zukunfts-chronik (poetry), 1978 and others. *Contributions to:* ORF, Vienna; Die Presse, Vienna; Zeitwende; Die Welt; Nurnberger Zeitung and others. *Honours include:* Hans Sachs Drama Prize, 1976; Max Dauthendey Plaque, 1979; International Molle Literary Prize, Sweden, 1979 and others. *Memberships:* PEN; European Authors Association Die Kogge (Chairman 1967-1988). *Address:* Schobertweg 1 a, D 8520 Erlangen, Germany.

MEIER Carl Alfred, b. 19 Apr 1905, Switzerland. Psychiatrist. m. Johanna Fritzsche, 1936, 1 son, 1 daughter. *Education:* MD, University of Zurich, 1929; ETH, 1948; Prof, 1952. *Appointments:* Editor, Zentralblatt fur Psychotherapie, 1938-45; Co Editor, Analytische Psychologie, 1974-. *Publications:* Ancient Incubation and Modern Psychotherapy; The Unconscious and Its Empirical Manifestations; The Meaning and Significance of Dreams; Consciousness; Personality; Body & Soul; Wolfgang Pauli und C G Jung. *Contributions to:* Too Numerous. *Memberships:* Swiss Society of Psychiatry; Naturforschende Gesellschaft Zurich; International Association of Jungian Psychology. *Address:* Steinwiesstrasse 37, 8032 Zurich, Switzerland.

MEIGS Mary Roberts, b. 27 Apr 1917, Philadelphia, Pennsylvania, USA. Writer; Painter. *Education:* Bryn Mawr College, BA, 1939. *Appointments:* Bryn Mawr College, Instructor, 1940-43. *Publications:* Lily Briscoe: A Self Portrait; The Medusa Head; The Box Closet; Tn, The Company of Strangers. *Contributions to:* The Womens Review of Books; Canadian Women Studies; Exile; Room Of Ones Own; Brick; Broadside. *Literary Agent:* The Colbert Agency Inc. *Address:* 427 Grosvenor Avenue, Westmount, Quebec, Canada H3Y 2S5.

MEINKE Peter, b. 29 Dec 1932, Brooklyn, New York, USA. Writer; Teacher. m. Jeanne Clark, 14 Dec 1957, 2 sons, 2 daughters. *Education:* AB, Hamilton College, 1955; MA, University of Michigan, 1961; PhD, University of Minnesota, 1965. *Appointments:* Director,

Writing Workshop, Eckerd College, St Petersburg, Florida, 1966-1993 (retired); Fulbright Senior Lecturer, University of Warsaw, Poland, 1978-79; Jenny Moore Writer-in- Residence, Washington DC, 1981-82; James Thurber Writer-in-Residence, Columbus, Ohio, 1987; McGee Writer-in-Residence, Davidson College, North Carolina, 1989; Writer-in-Residence, University of Hawaii. *Publications:* The Piano Tuner, 1986; Night Watch on the Chesapeake, 1987; Trying to Surprise God, 1981; The Night Train and the Golden Bird, 1977; Far from Home, 1988; Underneath the Lantern, 1987; The Rat Poems, 1978; Liquid Paper: New & selected Poems, 1981. *Contributions to:* Poems and stories in The Atlantic, The New Yorker, Poetry, Yankee, Grand Street, The Virginian Quarterly. *Honours:* NEA Creative Writing Fellowships, 1974, 1989; Gustav Davidson Award. PSA, 1976; Lucille Medwick Award, PSA 1984; Emily Dickinson Award, PSA, 1992; Emily Clark Balch Award for Short Fiction, 1982; Flannery O'Connor Award for Short Fiction, 1986; Robert A Staub, Outstanding Teacher Award, Eckead College, 1990. *Memberships:* PSA; PEN. *Address:* 147 Wildwood Lane SE, St Petersburg, FL 33705, USA.

MEISLER Stanley, b. 14 May 1931, New York, USA. Journalist. m. Elizabeth Fox, 21 Jan 1984, 5 sons, 1 daughter. *Education:* BA, City College of New York, 1952; Graduate Studies, University of California, Berkeley,1952-53, 1961-62. *Appointments:* Foreign Correspondent, Los Angeles Times, 1967-. *Contributions To:* Atlantic; Foreign Affairs; Smithsonian Magazine; Nation; Washington Journalism Review; Columbia Journalism Review; Progressive. *Memberships:*Association de La Presse Anglo-Americaine de Paris. *Agent:* Emilie Jacobson, New York, USA. *Address:* c/o Los Angeles Times, 73 Champs-Elysees, 75008, Paris, France.

MEJIA GONZALEZ Eduardo, b. 13 Oct 1948. Editor. m. Lourdes Eguiluz, 9 Aug 1973, 1 son, 1 daughter. *Appointments:* Journalist, Novedades, 1973-85; Contenido, 1990-: Editor, Universidad Veracruzana, 1980- 84; Fondo de Cultura Economica, 1985-90; Dragon, 1990-. *Publications:* Leave Me Space; For Example, You; A Wave Smash on the Rock; Matrimonial Promise. *Contributions to:* Revista de la Universidad de Mexico; La Palabra y el Hombre; Sabado; Siemprol; Nexos. *Address:* Thiers 213-5, 11590 Mexico, DF Mexico.

MELCHIOR Ib (Jorgen), b. 1917, Copenhagen, Denmark. Naturalized citizen of United States of America, 1944. Author; Playwright; Freelance Writer. *Appointments Include:* Actor, Stage Manager, Company Director, English Players, 1937-39; Stage Manager, Radio City Music Hall, Center Theatre, New York City, 1941-42; Television Writer, Actor, Director, New York City, 1947-50; Associate Producer, G-L Enterprises, 1952- 53; Writer and/or Director, 12 feature films, 1959-76, Hollywood. *Publications:* Rosmersholm, by Henrik Ibsen, 1946; Hedda Grabler, by Henrik Ibsen, 1947; Order of Battle (novel), 1972; Sleeper Agent (novel), 1975; The Haigerloch Project (novel), 1977; The Watchdogs of Abaddon (novel), 1979; The Marcus Device (novel), 1980; Hour of Vengeance (stage play), 1982; The Tombstone Cipher (novel), 1983; Eva (novel), 1984; V-3 (novel), 1985; Code Name: Grand Guignol (novel), 1987; Steps & Stairways (non-fiction with Cleo Baldon), 1989; Quest (non-fiction), 1990. *Address:* 8228 Marmont Lane, Los Angeles, CA 90069, USA.

MELDRUM James. See: **KYLE Duncan.**

MELEAGROU Evie, b. 28 May 1930, Nicosia, Cyrpus. Author. m. Dr John Meleagros, MD, 26 Nov 1952, 1 son, 2 daughters. *Education:* Pancyprian Gymnasium, Nicosia; High School Diploma, Ecole Saint Joseph, Nicosia; Diplome de la Literature Francaise, Athenaeum Institute, Athens; Philosophical Studies, University of London; BA Classics. *Literary Appointments:* Producer Literary Programmes, CBC, 1952-55; Editor, Cyprus Chronicles, 1960-72; Secretary, Cyprus Chronicles

Cultural Centre, 1960-74; Cyprus Representative, World Writers Conference, 1965. *Publications:* Solomons Family, 1957; Anonymous City, 1963; Eastern Mediterranean, 1969; Conservations with Che, 1970; Penultimate Era, 1981; Persona is the unknown Cypriot Woman (literary essays and poetry), 1993; The Virgin Plunge in the Ocean Depths (short stories and novelles), 1993; Cyprus Chronaca (historical essay), 1974-1992; Translations. *Honours:* Severian Literary Prize, 1945; 1st Pancyprian Prize Short Story Competition, 1952; Pancyprian Novella Competition, 1957; Cyprus National Novel Award, 1970, 82; Panhellenic National Novel Award, 1982. *Memberships:* Cyprus Chronicles Cultural Centre, General Secretary; Cyprus Cultural Association of Women, General Secretry; The First Cypriot Writers Association, Secretary, 1961-70; Association of Greek Writers, Athens; Cyprus State Literary Awards Committee, 1969-79. *Agent:* Dodoni Publishing House, 3 Asklipios Street, Athens 10679, Greece. *Address:* 22 Messolongi Street, Micosia, Cyprus.

MELFI Leonard, b. 1935, United States of America. Playwright. *Publications:* Encounters: 6 One-Act Plays, 1967; Stars and Stripes, 1968; Jack and Jill, 1969; Fantasies at the Frick, 1980; Porno Stars at Home, 1980; Later Encounters: 7 One-Act Plays, 1980; Tales of a New York Playwright, 1985. *Address:* c/o Helen Harvey, 410 W. 24th Street, New York, NY 10011, USA.

MELLEN Joan, b. 1941, United States of America. Writer. *Publications:* A Film Guide to the Battle of Algiers, 1973; Marilyn Monroe, 1973; Women and Their Sexuality in the New Film, 1973; Voices from the Japanese Cinema, 1975; The Waves at Genji's Door: Japan Through Its Cinema, 1976; Big Bad Wolves: Masculinity in the American Film, 1978; The World of Luis Bunuel, 1978; Natural Tendencies, 1981; Priviledge: The Enigma of Sacha Bruce, 1983; Bob Knight: His Own Man, 1988. *Address:* PO Box 359, 25 Elm Ridge Road, Pennington, NJ 08534, USA.

MELLERS Wilfrid Howard, b. 26 Apr 1914. University Teacher. 3 daughters. *Education:* Leamington College, 1933; BA, 1936; MA, 1938, Cambridge University; DMus, Birmingham University. *Appointments:* University Teacher, 1945-1981. *Publications:* Man and his Music, 1957, revised edition, 1987; Francois Couperin and the French Classical Tradition, 1950, revised, 1987; Bach and the Dance of God, 1980; Beethoven and the Voice of God, 1984; Music in a New Found Land 1987; Vaughan Williams and the Vision of Albion, 1989; The Music of Percy Grainger, 1992. *Contributions to:* Various journals and encyclopaedias. *Honours:* OBE, 1982; D Phil (city University), 1980; Honorary member of the Sonneck Society (for services to American music). *Address:* Oliver Sheldon House, 17 Aldwark, York YO1 2BX, England.

MELLOW James R, b. 28 Feb. 1926, Gloucester, Massachusetts, USA. Writer; Biographer; Art Critic. *Education:* BS, Northwestern University, 1950. *Appointments:* Staff, 1955-61, Editor in Chief, 1961-65, Arts Magazine; Art Critic, Art International, 1965-69; Art Critic, The New Leader, 1969-72; Art Critic, New York Times, 1969-74. *Publications:* Charmed Circle: Gertrude Stein & Co, 1974; Nathaniel Hawthorne in His Times, 1980; Invented Lives: F Scott and Zelda Fitzgerald, 1984; Editor: The Best in Arts, 1962, New York - The Art World, 1964; Hemingway: A Life Without Consequences, 1993. *Contributions include:* New York Times; Washington Post; Chicago Tribune; Chicago Sun Times; Saturday Review; Gourmet; Horizon. *Honours:* Nominated, National Book Award, 1974; National Book Award, 1983. *Memberships:* National Book Critics Circle; Authors Guild. *Agent:* Georges Borchardt Inc, New York. *Address:* PO Box 297, Clinton, CT 06413, USA.

MELLY (Alan) George (Heywood), b. 1926. Writer; Jazz Singer. *Appointments:* Jazz Singer, Mick Mulligan's Band, 1949-61; Writer, Flook Strip Cartoon, 1956-71; Pop Music Critic, 1965-67, TV Critic, 1967-71, Film Critic, 1971-73, Observer Newspaper, London; Compere, George, Granada TV Show, 1974. *Publications:* 1 Flook, 1962; Owning Up, 1965; Revolt into Style, 1970; Flook by Trog, 1970; Rum, Bum and Concertina, 1977; Media Mob (with B. Fantoni), 1980; Great Lovers, 1981; Tribe of One, 1981; Mellymobile, 1982; Swans Reflecting Elephants, 1982; Scouse Mouse, 1984; It's All Writ Out For You, The Life and Works of Scottie Wilson, 1986; Paris and the Surealists, with Michael Woods, 1991. *Address:* 33 St. Lawrence Terrace, London, W10 5SR, England.

MELNIKOFF Pamela Rita, b. London, England. Journalist; Author. m. Edward Harris, 29 Mar 1970. *Education:* North London Collegiate School. *Appointments:* Reporter, Feature Writer, The Jewish Chronicle, 1960-70; Film Critic, The Jewish Chronicle, 1970-. *Publications:* The Star and the Sword; Plots and Players; Prisoner in Time; Others inc, The Ransomed Menorah. *Contributions to:* The Jewish Quarterly; Poetry Review. *Honours:* Golden Pen Award; Poetry Societys Greenwood Prize. *Memberships:* PEN; Society of Authors; Guild of Jewish Journalists; Critics Circle. *Address:* 25 Furnival Street, London, EC4A 1JT, England.

MELTON David, b. 1934, United States of America. Children's Writer, Poet. *Publications:* Todd (autobiographical), 1968; I'll Show You the Morning Sun (poem), 1971; Judy: A Remembrance (biography/poetry), 1971; When Children need Help, 1972; This Man, Jesus (children's book), 1972; Burn the Schools, Save the Children, 1975; Children of Dreams, Children of Hope (with Raymundo Veras), 1975; A Boy Called Hopeless (children's novel), 1976; Happy Birthday, America! (anthology), 1976; How to help Your Preschooler Learn More, Faster and Better, 1976; And God Created....(poems), 1976; Theodore, 1978; The Survival Kit for Parents and Teenagers, 1979; The One and Only Autobiography of Ralph Miller, 1979; Harry S. Truman, 1980; Promises to Keep, 1984; Written and Illustrated by.....1985. *Address:* 7422 Rosewood Circle, Prairie Village, KS 66208, USA.

MELVILLE Anne. See: POTTER Margaret.

MELVILLE Arabella, b. 23 Aug 1948, Cheshire, England. Writer. *Education:* BSc, University of Birmingham, 1970; PhD, 1974. *Publications:* Cured to Death: The Effect of Prescription Drugs; Fat Yourself Thin; Fat Free Forever; The Good Sex Diet; Natural Hormone Health; Immunity Plus; Alternatives to Drugs; The Long Life Heart. *Contributions to:* Vogue; Cosmopolitan; Womens Own; Womens Journal; The Observer; The Guardian; Manchester Evening News. *Memberships:* Womens Environmental Network. *Literary Agent:* David Grossman, c/o David Grossman, 110/114 Clerkenwell Road, London EC1M 55A, England.

MELVILLE James. See: MARTIN (Roy) Peter.

MELVILLE Jennie. See: BUTLER Gwendolyn (Williams).

MELWOOD (Eileen) Mary. Children's Fiction Writer; Playwright. *Publications:* Plays: It Isn't Enough (radio), 1957; The Tingalary Bird, 1964; Five Minutes to Morning, 1965; Masquerade, 1970; The Small Blue Hoping Stone, 1976; Fiction: Nettlewood, 1974; The Watcher Bee, 1982; Reflections in Black Glass, 1987. *Address:* 5 Hove Lodge Mansions, Hove Street, Hove, Sussex, BN3 2TS, England.

MENASHE Samuel, b. 16 Sept 1925, New York, USA. *Education:* BA, Queens College; Doctorat d'Universite, University of Paris, France. *Publications:* The Many Named Beloved, 1961; No Jerusalem But This, 1971; Fringe of Fire, 1973; To Open, 1974; Collected Poems, 1986. *Contributions to:* Poems in the

Times Literary Supplement; Temonos; Poetry Nation Review; Poetry Durham; Proteus. *Honour:* Longview Foundation Award, 1957. *Membership:* PEN. *Address:* 75 Thompson Street, New York NY 10012, USA.

MENDEL David, b. 4 Mar 1922, London, England. Translator and Medical Writer. m. Margaret Graty, 13 Jan 1960, 2 daughters. *Education:* Physician, St Thomas' Hospital, MBBS, University of London, 1948; FRCP, London, 1968. *Publications:* A Practice of Cardiac Catheterisation, 1966; Proper Doctoring, 1984. *Contributions to:* Articles in the Observer, The Times, The Independent, Sunday Telegraph and journals. *Memberships:* Society of Authors; Translators Association. *Address:* Gilhams Cottage, Eastling near Faversham, Kent ME13 OBP, England.

MENDELSOHN Martin, b. 6 Nov 1935, London. Solicitor. m. 20 Sept 1959, 2 sons. *Education:* Solicitor, with hons. *Appointments:* Editor, Journal of International Franchising and Distribution Law; Visiting Professor of Franchising, City University Business School, London. *Publications:* The Guide to Franchising, (5th edition), 1992; How to Evaluate a Franchise (5th edition), 1989; How to Franchise Internationally, 1989; How to Franchise your Business, (co-author) (3rd edition), 1989; The Ethics of Franchising, 1987; Franchisor Manual, 1987; Franchising and Business Development, 1992; Franchising in Europe (editor and contributor); International Franchising - An Overview (editor and contributor); UK and EC Sections of 'Survey of Foreign Laws and Regulations Affecting International Franchising' and of 'The Canadian Franchise Guide'. *Contributions to:* Business and legal magazines and journals worldwide. *Memberships:* Law Society; International Bar Association; American Bar Association; Fellow, Royal Society of Arts; Fellow, Chartered Insitute of Arbitrators. *Address:* 9 Sandown Court, Marsh Lane, Stanmore, Middlesex HA7 4HZ, England.

MENDES Bob. *See:* **MENDES David.**

MENDES David, (Bob Mendes), b. 15 May 1928, Antwerp, Belgium. Accountant. *Education:* Graduate in Accountancy, 1953. *Publications:* Day of Shame, 1988; The Chunnel Syndrome, 1989; The Fourth Sura, 1990; The Fraud Hunters, 1991; Vengeance, 1992; Riots, 1993. *Contributions to:* VIT Magazine; Sodipa. *Memberships:* Flemish Writers Guild; PEN Club. *Literary Agent:* Dan Wright, Ann Wright Literary Agency, 136 East 56 Street, NY 10022, USA. *Address:* Wezelsebann 191, B 2900 Schoten, Belgium.

MENDYK Stan James Anthony, b. 31 July 1953, Oshawa, Ontario, Canada. Professor. *Education:* BA, 1976; MA, 1977; BEd, 1983; PhD, 1983. *Publications:* Speculum Britanniae. *Contributions to:* Variety of International Scholarly Journals. *Honours:* American Society for 18th Century studies Fellowship. *Address:* 216 Chadburn Street, Oshawa, Ontario, Canada L1H 5V6.

MENENDEZ Albert J, b. 1942, United States of America. Writer. *Publications:* The Bitter Harvest: Church and State in Northern Ireland, 1974; Church-State Relations: An Annotated Bibliography, 1975; The Sherlock Holmes Quiz Book, 1975; The American Political Quiz Book, 1976; Religion at the Polls, 1977; Classics of Religious Liberty, 1978; John F. Kennedy: Catholic and Humanist, 1974; The Dream Lives On, 1982; Christmas in the White House, 1983; Religious Conflict in America, 1985; School Prayer and Other Religious Issues in American Education, 1985; The Subject is Murder, 1985; The Road to Rome, 1986; Religion and the US Presidency, 1986; The Catholic Novel, 1987. *Address:* 8120 Fenton Street, Silver Spring, MS 20910, USA.

MENZIES Grant Michael, b. 2 June 1964, Mariposa, California, USA. *Education:* Private Study of Literature

& Music; Under Guidance of Playwright William Luce & Mrs Oswald H Milmore. *Publications:* Poems in The Divine Orlando; Lucifers Child; Augustaeum, Newsletter of The Augustan Society, (editor). *Contributions to:* Omnibus, Quarterly of the Augustan Society of Torrance; Journal of Ancient & Mediaeval Studies; The Octavian Society of Torrance; The Genealogist, ed by Dr Neal Thompson. *Memberships:* Mariposa County Library Board. *Address:* PO Box 370, Depoe Bay, OR 97341, USA.

MERCHANT William Moelwyn, (Rev. Prof.) b. 5 June 1913. Writer; Sculptor. m. Maria Eluned Hughes, 1938, 1 son, 1 daughter. *Education:* Exhibitioner, University College, Cardiff, BA, 1st Class English Honours, 1933; 2nd Class 1st div. History, 1934; MA, 1950; DLitt, 1960. *Publications:* Wordsworth's Guide to the Lakes, 1952, USA, 1953; Reynard Library Wordsworth, 1955, USA, 1955; Shakespeare and the Artist, 1959; Creed and Drama, 1965; Editor, Merchant of Venice, 1967; Editor, Marlowe's Edward the Second, 1967; Comedy, 1972; Tree of Life (libretto, music by Alun Hoddinott), 1972; Breaking the Code (poems), 1975; Editor, essays and Studies, 1977; No Dark Glass, (Poems), 1979; R. S. Thomas, a critical evaluation, 1979; Confrontation of Angels (poems), 1986; Jeshua (novel), 1986; Five from the Heights (novel), 1989; A Bundle of Papyrus (novel), 1989; Fragments of a Life (Autobiography), 1990; Inherit the Land (short stories), 1992; Triple Heritage (novel), 1992. *Contributions include:* The Times Literary Supplement; Warburg Journal; Shakespeare Survey; Shakespeare Quarterly; Shakespeare Jahrbuch; Encyclopedia Britannica. *Honours:* FRSL, 1976; Founder, Llanddewi Brefi Arts Festival, 1975; Honorary Fellow, University College of Wales, 1975; Hon. HLD, Wittenberg University, Ohio, 1973; Welsh Arts Council Literary Award, 1991. *Address:* 32A Willes Road, Leamington Spa, Warwickshire, England.

MEREDITH Christopher, b. 15 Dec 1954, Tredegar, Wales. Writer; School teacher. m. V Smythe, 1 June 1981. 2 sons. *Education:* BA (Joint Honours), Philosophy and English, University College Wales, Aberystwyth, 1976. *Publications:* Poems: This, 1984; Snaring Heaven, 1990. Novel: Shifts, 1988. *Contributions to:* Literary magazines in Wales, England and USA. *Honours:* Eric Gregory Award, 1984; Welsh Arts Council Young Writer's Prize, 1985; Welsh Arts Council Fiction Prize, 1989. *Membership:* Yr Academi Gymreig (English language Section). *Address:* c/o Seren Books, Andmar House, Tondu Road, Bridgend, Mid Glamorgan, Wales.

MEREDITH Donald Clynton, b. 12 Apr 1938, Inglewood, California, USA. Writer. m. Jo Ann, 15 Oct 1962. *Education:* AA, Orange Coast College, 1959; Long Beach State College, 1959-60; San Francisco State College, 1961-62. *Publications:* Morning Line, 1980; Home Movies, 1982. *Contributions to:* Image magazine; Teh Greensboro Review; The Texas Review; The Short Story Review; Kingfisher; Folio; Slipstream; Poets and Writers Magazine; Modern Maturity Magazine. *Honours:* National Endowment for the Arts Grant in Fiction, 1982, 1988; Pushcart Prize Anthology VIII, 1983-84; Best Story Award, Folio, The American University, Washington DC, 1990. *Memberships:* Poets and Writers; National Writers Union. *Address:* 16700 Fitzpatrick Lane, Occidental, CA 95465, USA.

MEREDITH Leigh. *See:* **KENYON Bruce Guy.**

MERLIN Christina. *See:* **KEEGAN Mary.**

MERRILL Christopher L, b. 24 Feb 1957, Northampton, Massachusetts, USA. Writer. m. 4 June 1983. *Education:* BA, Middlebury College, 1975- 79; MA, University of Washington, 1979-82. *Appointments:* Ingram Merrill Fellow, 1991. *Publications:* Workbook; Fevers & Tides; The Forgotten Language; From The Faraway Nearby; The Grass of Another Country; Outcroppings. *Contributions to:* The Paris Review;

Poetry East; Poetry Wales; Poetry Northwest; Mississippi Review; Prairie Schooner; New Virginia Review; Sierra Magazine; Northern Lights; Seneca Review. *Honours:* Sherman Brown Neff Fellow; Columbia: A Magazine of Poetry & Prose Editors Award; Ingram Merrill Award; Prairie Schooner's Readers Choice; John Ciardi fellow; *Memberships:* PEN; Poets & Writers; AWP. *Literary Agent:* Elizabeth Grassman, Sterling Lird Literistic, One Madison Avenue, New York, NY 10010, USA. *Address:* 2214 SE 57th Avenue. Portland, OR 97215, USA.

MERRILL (Josephine) Judith Grossman, (Cyril Judd), b. 1923, Canada. Writer. *Appointments Include:* Freelance Writer and Lecturer, 1949-; Research Assistant, Ghostwriter, 1943-47; Editor, Bantam Books, New York City, 1947-49; Director, Milford Science Fiction Writers Conference, 1956-61; Writing Teacher, Adult Education Programme, Port Jervis, New York, 1963-64; Book Editor, Fantasy and Science Fiction, 1965-69; Radio Documentaries for Canadian Broadcasting Corporation, 1971-75; Video Documentaries and commentaries for TV Ontario, 1978-81; Writer-in-Residence: Centennial College (Toronto), 1983, Toronto Public Libraries, 1987, Brampton Public Libraries, 1989. *Publications:* Shadow on the Hearth, 1950; Shot in the dark, 1950; Beyond the Human Ken, 1952; As Cyril Judd: Gunner Cade, 1952, Outpost Mars, 1952, as Sin in Space, 1956; Beyond the Barriers of Space and Time, 1954; Human?, 1954; Galaxy of Ghouls, 1955, as Off the Beaten Orbit, 1959; S-F: The Year's Greatest Science Fiction and Fantasy 1-6, continued as The Year's Best S-F, 7th-11th Annual, 12 vols, 1956-68, as SF '57-'59, 3 vols, 1957-59 (in United Kingdom as Annual SF and the Best of Sci-Fi, 5 vols, 1965-70; The Tomorrow People, 1960; Out of Bounds (short stories), 1960; SF: The Best of the Best, 1967; Daughters of Earth (short stories), 1968; England Swings SF, 1968 (in United Kingdom abridged edition as The Space-Time Journal), 1972; Survival Ship and Other Stories, 1973; The Best of Judith Merril (short stories), 1976; Tesseracts: Canadian S-F, 1985; Daughters of Earth and Other Stories, 1985. *Address:* 40 St George Street, Toronto, Ontario, Canada M5S 2E4.

MERRITT E B. *See:* **WADDINGTON Miriam.**

MERTZ Barbara Louise Gross (Barbara Michaels, Elizabeth Peters), b. 29 Sept 1927, Canton, Illinois, USA. Writer. (div), 1 son, 1 daughter. *Education:* PhD, University of Chicago, 1952. *Publications:* As Barbara Mertz: Temples, Tombs & Hieroglyphs: The Story of Egyptology, 1964, 1978, 1990; Red Land, Black Land: The World of the Ancient Egyptians, 1966, 1978, 1990; Two Thousand Years in Rome (with Richard Mertz), 1968. As Barbara Michaels: The Master of Blacktower, 1966; Sons of the Wolf, 1967; Ammie, Come Home, 1968; Prince of Darkness, 1969; The Dark on the Other Side, 1970; Greygallows, 1972; The Crying Child, 1973; Witch, 1973; House of Many Shadows, 1974; The Sea King's Daughter, 1975; Patriot's Dream, 1976; Wings of the Falcon, 1977; Wait For What Will Come, 1978; The Walker in Shadows, 1979; The Wizard's Daughter, 1980; Someone in the House, 1981; Black Rainbow, 1982; Here I Stay, 1983; The Grey Beginning, 1984; Be Buried in the Rain, 1985; Shattered Silk, 1986; Search for Shadows, 1987; Smoke and Mirrors, 1988; Into the Darkness, 1990. As Elizabeth Peters: The Jackal's Head, 1968; The Camelot Caper, 1969; The Dead Sea Cipher, 1970; The Night of the Four Hundred Rabbits, 1971 (UK Shadows in the Moonlight, 1975); The Seventh Sinner, 1972; Borrower of the Night, 1973; The Murders of Richard III, 1974; Crocodile on the Sandbank, 1975; Legend in Green Velvet, 1976 (UK Ghost in Green Velvet, 1977); Devil-May-Care, 1977; Street of the Five Moons, 1978; Summer of the Dragon, 1979; The Love Talker, 1980; The Curse of the Pharaohs, 1981; The Copenhagen Connection, 1982; Silhouette in Scarlet, 1983; Die for Love, 1984; The Mummy Case, 1985; Lion in the Valley, 1986; Trojan Gold, 1987; Deeds of the Disturber, 1988; Naked Once More, 1989; The Last Camel Died at Noon, 1991. *Contributor to:* The Writer; Washington Post; Baltimore Sun; Encyclopaedia

Britannica; Americana, World Book. *Memberships:* Authors Guild; Mystery Writers of America. *Literary Agent:* Dominick Abel. *Address:* c/o Dominick Abel, 498 West End Avenue, New York, NY 10024, USA.

MESERVE Walter Joseph Jr, b. 1923, United States of America. Playwright; Writer. *Publications:* The Complete Plays of W.D. Howells, 1960; Outline History of American Drama, 1965; Discussions of Modern American Drama, 1966; Co-editor, American Satiric Comedies, 1969; Robert E Sherwood, 1970; Co-editor, Modern Drama from Communist China, 1970; The Rise of Silas Lapham, by W.D. Howells, 1971; Studies in Death of a Salesman, 1972; Co-editor, Modern Literature from China, 1974; An Emerging Entertainment: The Drama of the American People to 1828, 1977; co-author, The Revels History of Drama in English VIII: American Drama, 1977; American Drama to 1900: A Guide to Information Sources, 1980; Cry Woolf (play with Mollie Ann Meserve), 1982; Heralds of Promise: The Drama of the American People During the Age of Jackson 1829-1849, 1986; Who's Where in the American Theatre (with Mollie Ann Meserve), 1990. *Address:* PhD Program in Theatre, Graduate School, CUNY, 33 West 42nd Street, NY 10036, USA.

MESSENT Peter Browning, b. 24 Oct 1946, Wimbledon, England. University Lecturer. m. Brenda 10 July 1972, div. 1 son, 1 daughter. *Education:* BA Hons, American Studies, Manchester University, 1969; MA, 1972; PhD, Nottingham, 1991. *Appointments:* Temporary Lecturer in American Literature, Manchester University, 1972-73; Lecturer in American Studies, Nottingham University, 1973-. *Publications:* Ernest Hemingway, 1992; New Readings of the American Novel, 1990; Henry James: Selected Tales, 1992 (editor); Twentieth Century Views: Literature of the Occult, 1981, (editor). *Contributions to:* Books and journals and magazines including Journal of American Studies. *Memberships:* Hemingway Society; British Association for American Studies. *Address:* Department of American and Canadian Studies, University of Nottingham, Nottingham NG7 2RD, England.

MESSER Thomas M, b. 1920, United States of America. Writer (Art). *Appointments:* Teaching Assignments: Harvard University, 1960; Barnard College, 1965-71; Weslyan University, 1966; Vienna Hochschule Feur Angewandte Kunst, 1984; Frankfurt Goethe University, 1991-92. *Publications:* The Emergent Decade: Latin American Painters and Painting in the 1960's; Edvard Munch, 1973; Pablo Picasso, 1974; Sixty Works: The Peggy Guggenheim Collection, 1982; Acquisition Priorities, 1983; Munch, 1986. *Memberships include:* Honorary Chairman, International Committee, Museums and Collections of Modern Art, International Council of Museums; Past, Museum Advisory Panel, National Endowment for the Arts; Past, Commission on US-Latin American Relations; Chairman: Board of Trustees, National Gallery, Prague; Vice President, Kandinsky Society, Paris; Trustee: Institute of International Education, NY; Americas Senior Advisor: Americas Society, NY; La Caixa Foundation, Barcelona; Art Advisory Boards: Palazzo Grazzi, Venice; Hans Hinterreiter Foundation, Zurich. *Address:* 1105 Park Avenue, New York, NY 10028, USA.

MESSERLI Douglas John, b. 30 May 1947, Waterloo, Iowa, USA. Publisher; Poet; Fiction Writer. *Education:* BA, University of Wisconsin; MA, 1974, PhD, 1979, University of Maryland. *Appointments:* Assistant Professor, Literature, Temple University, 1979-85; Director, Contemporary Arts Educational Project Inc, 1982-; Publisher, Sun & Moon Press, 1976-. *Publications:* Djuna Barnes: A Bibliography, 1976; Dinner on the Lawn, 1982; Some Distance, 1982; River to Rivet: A Poetic Manifesto, 1984; Language, Poetries, Editor, 1987; Maxims from My Mother's Milk/Hymns to Him: A Dialogue, 1988; Contemporary American Fiction, Editor, 1983; Silence All Round Marked: An Historical Play in Hysteria Writ, 1992; Along Without: A Film for Poetry, 1992. *Contributions to:* Roof;

Mississippi Review; Paris Review, Boundry 2; Art Quarterly; Los Angeles Times. *Membership:* Modern Language Association. *Address:* c/o Sun & Moon Press, PO Box 481170, Los Angeles, CA 90048, USA.

MESTAS Jean-Paul, b. 15 Nov 1925, Paris, France. Engineer; Poet; Critic; Essayist; Lecturer; Translator; Consultant. m. Christiane Schoubrenner, 23 Dec 1977, 2 sons, 1 daughter. *Education:* Graduated, Institute of Political Studies, Paris, 1947; LLB, 1947; BA, 1947. *Publications:* Soleils noirs, 1965; Part de Vivre, 1968; Résurgences, 1969; Romance limousine, 1970; Château de Paille, 1971; Plaise aux souvenirs, 1972; L'Aventure des choses, 1973; Le retour d'Ulysse, 1974; Traduire la Mémoire, 1975; Pays Nuptial, 1977; Mémoire d'Exil, 1978; Cette idée qui ne vivra pas, 1979; En ce royaume d'ombre et d'eau, 1982; Entre deux temps, 1983; En Ecoutant vieillir les lampes, 1983; Ismène, 1984; Entre les colonnes du vent, 1984; Dans la longue automne du coeur, 1985; L'ancre et le cyclone, 1987; La terre est pleine de haillons, 1988; Entre les violons du silence, 1988; Chant pour Chris, 1989; La Lumière arriva des mains, 1990; Roses de Sable, 1990. Works in anthologies; Monographs, essays, including: Rencontre avec Manes Sperber, 1979; En prenant ainsi conscience du Monde...Ilarie Voronca, 1979; Sur les portes et aux fronts des hommes: Alberto E Mazzocchi, 1981; Comme une vie Qui marche: Mara Guimaraes, 1981; Present de Voronca, 1982; Dans sa harpe d'oiseaux lilas: Henry Rougier, 1984; Privire Asupra Poeziei Romane de Azi: Revista de Istoriei si teorie literara 1, 1985, 2, 1986; Seigneur, que ne m'as-tu fait pierre: Ion Caraion, 1986; Dans ce pays comme au début du monde: Audrey Bernard et Jeanne Maillet, 1986; Nichita Stanescu ou les épines de la gloire, 1988. *Contributions to:* Numerous magazines and journals in some 50 countries. *Honours:* Excellence in Poetry, Int Poet, NY, 1982; Premio della Cultura Carlo Alianello, Palermo, 1991. *Memberships:* Associate, Emeritus Academician: International Academy of Madras; Academy of Human Sciences, Brazil; Accademia Internazionale, Naples; Life Member, International Writers and Artists, New York. *Address:* 65 Avenue du Parc d Proce, 44 100 Nantes, France.

MESTERHÁZI Marton, b. 7 July 1941, Budapest, Hungary. Radio Drama Scipt Editor. m. Ágnes Pécsvari, 7 July 1962, 1 son, 1 daughter. *Education:* MA, Hungarian English and French, Budapest, 1964; PhD, English Literature, 1987. *Publications:* The World of Sean O'Casey, 1983; Translations: The Selected Essays of Arnold J Toynbee, 1971; Ian McEwan: The Comfort of Strangers, 1984; Brian Friel: The Communication Cord, 1990. *Contributions to:* Nagyvilag, (literary monthly). *Honours:* Outstanding Programmes Prizes, Hungarian Radio. *Memberships:* Hungarian Irish Cultural Society; Chamber of Hungarian Radio Programme Makers. *Literary Agent:* Artisjus, Hungarian Copyright Office. *Address:* Hungarian Radio, Drama H-1800, Budapest, Hungary.

METCALF John Wesley, b. 12 Nov 1938, Carlisle, England. Writer. m. Myrna Teitelbaum, 3 sons, 2 daughters. *Education:* BA, English, Bristol University, 1960. *Literary Appointments:* Writer-in-Residence: University of New Brunswick, 1972-73, Loyola of Montreal, 1976, University of Ottawa, 1977, Concordia University (Montreal) 1980-81, University of Bologna, 1985. *Publications:* The Lady Who Sold Furniture, 1970; The Teeth of My Father, 1975; Girl in Gingham, 1978; Kicking Against the Pricks, 1982 Adult Entertainment 1986. Some 25 texts and anthologies edited. *Contributor to:* Many publications in Canada and the USA. *Honours:* Canada Council Arts Awards 1968, 69, 71, 74, 76, 78, 80, 83, 85. *Literary Agent:* Susan Schulman, 454 West 44th Street, New York, USA. *Address:* 128 Lewis Street, Ottawa, Ontario, Canada K2P 0S7.

METCALF Paul, b. 7 Nov 1917, East Milton, Massachusetts, USA. Writer. m. Nancy Harman Blackford, 30 May 1942, 2 daughters. *Education:* Taft School, Watertown, 1936. *Appointments:* University of Kansas, Writer in Residence; University of Indiana

Writers Conference, Lecturer, Teacher; University of California, San Diego, Visiting Professor; The Centrum Foundation, Writer in Residence; State University of NY, Writer in Residence. *Publications:* Genoa; Apalache; Waters of Potowmack; Where Do You Put The Hourse?; Headlands. *Contributions to:* Innumerable. *Honours:* The Morton Dauwen Zabel Award, American Academy and Institute of Arts and Letters. *Address:* RFD 1, Box 60, Chester, MA 01011, USA.

METZ Jerred, b. 5 May 1943, Lakewood, New Jersey, USA. Writer; Social Service Administrator. m. Sarah Barker, 14 May 1978, 1 son, 1 daughter. *Education:* BA, 1965, MA, 1967, University of Rhode Island; PhD, University of Minnesota, 1972. *Appointment:* Poetry Editor, Webster Review, 1973-. *Publications:* Halley's Comet, 1910: Fire in the Sky, 1985; Drinking the Dipper Dry: Nine Plain-Spoken Lives, 1980; Angels in the House, 1979; Three Legs Up, Cold as Stone; Six Legs Down, Blood and Bone, 1977; The Temperate Voluptary, 1976; Speak Like Rain, 1975. *Contributions to:* Numerous poems and short stories in magazines and journals. *Literary Agent:* Mary Yost. *Address:* 6200 Jackson Street, Pittsburgh, PA 15206, USA.

METZGER Deena, b. 17 Sept 1936, Brooklyn, New York, USA. Writer (Novelist, Poet, Playwright, Essayist); Teacher; Lecturer; Healer; Counselor. m. (1) H Reed Metzger, 26 Oct 1957, (2) Michael Ortiz Hill, 20 Dec 1987, 2 sons. *Education:* BA cum laude, Literature and Philosophy, Brooklyn College; MA, English and American Literature, University of California, Los Angeles; PhD, Creative Writing & Education, International College, Los Angeles. *Appointments:* Faculty Member, California Institute of the Arts, 1970-75; Professor, English, Los Angeles Valley College, 1966-69, 1973-74, 1975-79; Founded & Directed, Writing Program of the Feminist Studio Workship and the Woman's Buildong, 1973-77; Teaching writing privately, 1976-. *Publications:* Dark Milk, 1978; The Book of Hags, 1978; The Axis Mundi Poems, 1981; Dreams Against the State (play, performed 1981, 1986); The Woman Who Slept with Men to Take the War out of Them and Tree, 1981 1983; What Dinah Thought, 1989; Looking For The Faces Of God, 1989; A Sabbath Among the Ruins, 1992; Writing For Your Life: A Guide and Companion to the Inner World, 1992. *Contributions to:* World Futures; ReVision; Anima; American Journal of Psychiatry; New Letters; Yoga Journal; Utne Reader; Jacaranda Review; Zero; Bachy; Semiotica; Numerous anthologies. *Honours:* California Federation of Teachers, First Academic Freedom Aware, 1975; National Endowment for the Arts, Creative Writing Fellowship, 1978; First Annual Woman's Building Vesta Award, 1982. *Memberships:* International PEN US Center West; PEN American Club; Author's Guild; National Writer's Union. *Literary Agent:* Beth Vesell. *Address:* PO Box 186, Topanga, CA 90290, USA.

MEURANT Georges, b. 18 Mar 1948, Brussels. Painter. m. Kellens Anne, 18 Nov 1985, 1 son. *Publications:* Shoowa Design; Traumzeichen; Analogies. *Contributions to:* Arts d'Afrique Noire; Tanzanie Méconnue. *Literary Agent:* Hansjorg Mayer, London, Stuttgart. *Address:* 50 Rue Souveraine, 1050 Brussels, Belgium.

MEWSHAW Michael, b. 1943, United States of America. Author. *Publications:* Man in Motion, 1970; Walking Slow, 1972; The Toll, 1974; Earthly Bread, 1976; Intro 9, 1978; Land Without Shadow, 1979; Life for Death, 1980; Short Circuit, 1983; Year of the Gun, 1984; Blackballed, 1986. *Address:* c/o Owen Laster, William Morris Agency, 1350 Sixth Avenue, New York, NY 10019, USA.

MEYER Ben F, b. 5 Nov. 1927, Chicago, USA. Professor, Religious Studies. m. Denise Oppliger, 27 Mar 1969. *Education:* BA, Santa Clara, 1952; MA, Gonzaga, 1953; PhL, Mount St Michael's, 1952; SSL, Istituto Biblico, 1961; STD, Gregorian University, Rome, 1965. *Publications:* The Man for Others, 1970; The

Church in Three Tenses, 1971; Spanish Translation, El Hombre Para Los Demas, 1973; The Aims of Jesus, 1979; The Early Christians, 1986; TV Script, Christianity, 1974; Critical Realism and the New Testament, 1989; Lonergan's Hermeneutics, editor, 1989; Christus Faber: The Master Builder and the House of God, 1992; One Loaf, One Cup (editor), 1992. *Contributions to:* Editorial Consultant: Method, Los Angeles, Ex Auditu, Princeton; articles in various journals. *Memberships:* Canadian Society of Biblical Studies, President, 1988-89; Studiorum Novi Testamenti Societas. *Address:* Dept. of Religious Studies, McMaster University, Hamilton, Ontario L8S 4K1, Canada.

MEYER E Y, b. 11 Oct 1946, Liestal, Switzerland. Novelist; Essayist; Dramatist. m. Florica Malureanu. *Publications:* Ein Reisender in Sachen Umsturz, 1972; In Trubschachen, 1973; Eine entfernte Aehnlichkeit, 1975; Die Ruckfahrt, 1977; Die Halfte der Erfahrung, 1980; Playdoyer, 1982; Sundaymorning, 1984. *Contributions to:* Numerous periodicals. *Honours:* Literature Prize of the Province of Basel, 1976; Gerhart Hauptmann-Prize, 1983; Prize of the Swiss Schiller-Foundation, 1984; Welti-Prize for The Drama, 1985. *Memberships:* Swiss Writers Association; Swiss-German PEN Centre. *Address:* Brunnen-Gut, CH 3027 Berne, Switzerland.

MEYER June. *See:* JORDAN June.

MEYER Lawrence, b. 1941, United States of America. Author; Journalist. *Publications:* A Capitol Crime, 1977; False Front, 1979; Israel Now: Portrait of a Troubled Land, 1982. *Address:* 3311 Ross Place, N.W., Washington, DC 20008, USA.

MEYER Michael, b. 11 June 1921, London, England. Freelance Writer. 1 daughter. *Education:* MA, Christ Church, Oxford. *Publications:* (Editor with Sidney Keyes, and Contributor) Eight Oxford Poets, 1941; Editor, Collected Poems of Sidney Keyes, 1945, Editor, The Minos of Crete, by Sidney Keyes, 1948; The End of the Corridor (novel), 1951; The Ortolan (play), 1967; Henrik Ibsen: The Making of a Dramatist, 1967; Henrik Ibsen: The Farewell to Poetry, 1971; Henrik Ibsen: The Top of a Cold Mountain, 1971; Lunatic and Lover (play), 1981; Editor, Summer Days, 1981; Ibsen on File, 1985; Strindberg, a Biography, 1985; File on Strindberg, 1986; Not Prince Hamlet (memoirs), (USA Words Through a Windowpane), 1989; The Odd Women, (play), 1993; Numerous translations including all the major plays of Ibsen (1960-86) and of Strindberg, (1964-91). *Honour:* Gold Medal of the Swedish Academy, 1964; Whitbread Biography Prize, 1971; FRSL, 1971; Knight Commander of the Order of the Polar Star (Swedish), 1977. *Literary Agent:* David Higham Associates Ltd. *Address:* 4 Montagu Square, London W1H 1RA, England.

MEYER Michael Jon, b. 7 Oct 1943, Moline, Illinois, USA. Professor of English. m. Loralee Ann Klotz, 10 June 1967, dec, 2 sons, 1 daughter. *Education:* BA Concordia Teachers College, 1965; MA, 1969, PhD, 1985, Loyola University, Chicago. *Appointments:* Assistant editor, Steinbeck Quarterly; Guest Editor, CLLA Quarterly. *Publications:* The Short Novels of John Steinbeck, 1990; The Steinbeck Question, 1992; Teaching Approaches to Steinbeck, 1994; Steinbeck Monograph on the Short Novels, 1991. *Contributions to:* Steinbeck Qtr; Steinbeck Newsletter; The Cresset; Children's Literary Quarterly. *Honours:* National Endowment Humanities Summer Seminar, 1989, 1992. *Memberships:* MLA, MMLA, Chair and Secretary, Children's Lit, Christianity and Literature; International John Steinbeck Soc; NCTE. CHLA. *Address:* 1416-5 Cypress, Mt Prospect, Il 60056, USA.

MEYER Nicholas, b. 1945, United States of America. Author. *Publications:* Target Practice, 1974; The Seven PerCent Solution, 1974; The West End Horror, 1976; Black Orchid (with Barry J Kaplan), 1978; Confessions of a Homing Pigeon, 1981. *Address:* c/o Bloom and

Dekom, 9255 Sunset Boulevard, Los Angeles, CA 90069, USA.

MEYEROWITZ Patricia, b. 29 Mar 1933. London, England. Artist. m. 27 Oct 1957. *Education:* Studied techniques of jewelry making at Central School of Arts and Crafts, London 1959-60. *Appointments:* Practised jewelry making 1960-; Sculpture construction in metal 1962- and in wood 1967-; Writer 1965-. *Publications:* Jewelry and Sculpture Through Unit Construction, 1967, republished as Making Jewelry and Sculpture Through Unit Construction (paperback) 1978; And a Little Child, 1982; Introduction to How to Write (Gertrude Stein) 1975; Editor of Gertrude Stein: Writing and Lectures 1909-45. 1967, 1971, 1984, 1986 1989. Numerous exhibitions of sculpture and jewelry. *Honour:* Aug 1989 - Grant from City of Easton, Pennsylvania with matching funds from Pennsylvania Council on the Arts to construct a monumental sculpture for the City of Easton, work completed June 1990. *Address:* PO Box 8, Easton, PA 18044, USA.

MEYERS Jeffrey, b. 1939, United States of America. Writer (Biography & Literature). *Publications include:* Fiction and the Colonial Experience, 1973; The Wounded Spirit: A Study of Seven Pillars of Wisdom, 1973; T E Lawrence: A Bibliography, 1974; A Reader's Guide to George Orwell, 1975; George Orwell: The Critical Heritage, 1975; Painting and the Novel, 1975; A Fever at the Core, 1976; George Orwell: An Annotated Bibliography of Criticism, 1977; Married to Genius, 1977; Homosexuality and Literature, 1890-1930, 1977; Katherine Mansfield: A Biography, 1978; The Enemy: A Biography of Wyndham Lewis, 1980; Wyndham Lewis: A Revaluation. 1980; D H Lawrence and the Experience of Italy, 1982; Hemingway: The Critical Heritage, 1982; Disease and the Novel 1860-1960, 1984; Hemingway: A Biography, 1985; D H Lawrence and Tradition, 1985; The Craft of Literary Biography, 1985; The Legacy of D H Lawrence, 1987; Manic Power: Robert Lowell and His Circle, 1987; Robert Lowell: Interviews and Memoirs, 1988; The Biographer's Art, 1989; T E Lawrence: Soldier, Writer, Legend, 1989; The Spirit of Biography, 1989; Graham Greene: A Revaluation, 1989; D H Lawrence: A Biography, 1990; Joseph Conrad: A Biography, 1991; Edgar Allan Poe: his Life and Legacy, 1992; Scott Fitzgerald: A Biography, 1994. *Address:* 84 Stratford Road, Kensington, California 94707, USA.

MEYLAKH Michael, b. 20 Dec 1944, Tashkent. Translator; Journalist; Literary Critic; Poet. m. Rita Ilukhin, 24 Dec 1989. *Education:* University of Leningrad, 1967; Institute of Linguistics, Academy of Science, 1967-70. *Appointments:* La Pensée Russe, Correspondent, 1988-. *Publications:* V Nabokov, (translations); The Language of the Troubadours; Daniel Harms Collected Works; Alexander Vvedensky Complete Works; Anna Akhmatova Poems. *Contributions to:* La Pensée Russe; Financial Times; Apollo; Times Literary Supplement; Continent. *Honours:* Political Prisoner in Russia, 1983-87. *Memberships:* PEN; Association Internationale d'Etudes Occiaties. *Address:* Bolshoy 21-V Komarovo, Petersburg, 189643, Russia.

MEYNELL Hugo Anthony, b. 23 Mar 1936, England. m. 24 Feb 1969, 1 Adopted son, 3 daughters. *Education:* Eton College, 1949-54; Cambridge University, BA, 1959; PhD, 1963. *Appointments:* Lecturer, University of Leeds, 1961-81; Visiting Professor, Emory University, 1978; Professor, Religious Studies, University of Calgary, 1981. *Publications:* Introduction to the Philosophy of Bernard Lonergan; The Intelligible Univerce; Freud; The Art of Handels Operas; The Nature of Aesthetic Value; Others inc, God and the World. *Contributions to:* The New Scholastic; Heythrop Journal, Sex and Catholicism; New Blackfriars. *Memberships:* Canadian Society for Religious Studies; Canadian Philosophical Association. *Address:* Department of Religious Studies, University of Calgary, Calgary, Alberta, Canada T2N 1N4.

MEZEY Katalin, b. 30 May 1943, Budapest, Hungary.

General Secretary of Hungarian Writers Trade Union. m. Janos Olah 1 Mar 1971, 2 sons, 1 daughter. *Education:* Zurich University, Philology, German Literature, 1964; Philology, Hungarian Literature and Adult Education, Eotvos University in Budapest. *Appointments:* Journalist and translator, 1970-; Secretary, 1987, General Secretary, 1992, Trade Union of Hungarian Writers, 1987-; Founder and Editor of publishers, Szephalom Konyvmuhely, 1989-. *Publications:* Books: Waiting for the Bus, 1970; Materials Study, 1977; Green Jungle, 1978; Csutka-Jutka's Teles, 1981; Live Film, 1984; Again and again, 1985; Holes in the Classbook, 1987; Letters to the Native country, 1989; Paul Whowas in Nopossible-Land, 1987; Continental Winter, 1991. *Contributions to:* Texas Review; Poetry East; Artful Dodge; Iowa Review; Remetei Keziratok. *Honours:* Fust Milan Literary Prize, 1985; Ibby Prize, Hungarian Book of the year, 1989. *Memberships:* Hungarian Writers Association; Hungarian Pen Club; Trade Union of Hungarian Writers; Demokratic League of Free Trade Unions in Hungary, National Secretary, Bucher Frauen, Germany. *Literary Agent:* Artijus, Budapest, V Vorosmarty ter 1. *Address:* Pesthidegkut 2 pf 5, Budapest 1286, Hungary.

MIALL Robert. *See:* **BURKE John Frederick.**

MIANOWSKA Aleksandra Jadwiga, b. 16 July 1912, Rusocice. Voluntary Nurse; Literary Chief; Lecturer; Actress; Stage Director; Author. m. Walery Bigay Mianowski, 27 June 1936 (dec). *Education:* School of Political Sciences, 1936; Polish & Classical Philology, 1937; Doctor of Law, 1947; Diploma of Stage Director; Doctor of Philosophy, 1968. *Appointments:* Appointments with Voluntary Audience in Cracow and towns of Southern Poland, 1956-81. *Publications:* 1944 as the Underground Print: Polish Society in the novels of Eliza Orzesz Kova; 1945 Adaptation of too Volumes, Robinson Cruzoe; Stories for a Little Brother; Sutkowski of Stephan Zerömeki on the Polisg Stages, 1972; The Rose of Stephan Zerömeki on the Polish Stages, 1975; Theatre. *Contributions to:* Odra; Przekroj; The Litterary Life; Newspaper of Polish Underground; Polish Daily. *Memberships:* Society of Authors. *Address:* Karmelicka 9/3, 31-133 Krakow, Poland.

MICHAEL John. *See:* **CRICHTON Michael.**

MICHAELIS Bo Tao, b. 19 July 1948, Copenhagen, Denmark. Teacher; Critic; Author. m. Annette Gertrud Begtorp, 9 Oct 1976, 1 son, 1 daughter. *Education:* Studied Sorbonne, Paris, 1969-70; University of Copenhagen. *Appointments:* Critic, Berlingske Tidende, 1984-89; Reader, Gyldendal, 1985-; Chairman, palle Rosenkrantz, 1989-; Film Critic, Teacher, Danish Filmschool, 1989-. *Publications:* Portrait of the Private Eye as a petit Bourgeois; An Analysis of the Philip Marlowe Novels by Raymond Chandler; Lyst og Labyrint. *Contributions to:* Levende Billeder; Kosmorama; Dansk Noter; Essays on inc, Jorgen Gustava Brandt; Paul Auster; John Le Carre. *Memberships:* The Danish Writers Union; The Academy of Danish Crime Literate; Union of Grammar School Teachers. *Address:* Standboulevarden 7, 4th 2100 Copenhagen O, Denmark.

MICHAELS Barbara. *See:* **MERTZ Barbara Louise G.**

MICHAELS Dale. *See:* **RIFKIN Shepard.**

MICHAELS Kirstin. *See:* **WILLIAMS Jeanne.**

MICHAELS Steve. *See:* **AVALLONE Michael.**

MICHENER James Albert, b. 3 Feb 1907, New York, USA. Writer. m. (1) Patti Koon, 1935, (div), (2) Vange Nord, 1948, divorced, (3) Mari Yoriko Sabusawa, 1955. *Education:* Swarthmore College; Colorado State College of Education; Ohio State University; Universities of

Pennsylvania, Virginia, Harvard and St Andrews (Scotland). *Appointments:* Teacher, 1929-36; Professor, Colorado State College of Education, 1936-41; Associate Editor, Macmillan Co, 1941-46; US Naval Reserve 1944-46. *Publications:* Unit in the Social Studies, 1940; Tales of the South Pacific, 1947; The Fires of Spring, 1949; Return to Paradise 1951; The Voice of Asia, 1951; The Bridges at Toko-ri, 1953; Sayonara 1954; Floating World 1955; The Bridge at Andau, 1957; Rascals in Paradise (with A Grove Day), 1957; Selected Writings, 1957; The Hokusai Sketchbook, 1958; Japanese Prints, 1959; Hawaii, 1959; Report of the County Chairman, 1961; Caravans, 1963; The Source 1965; Iberia, 1968; Presidential Lottery, 1969; The Quality of Life, 1970; Kent State, 1971; The Drifters 1971; The Fires of Spring, 1972; A Michener Miscellany, 1973; Centennial, 1974; Sports in America, 1976; Chesapeake, 1978; The Covenant, 1980; Space, 1982; Poland, 1983; Texas, 1985; Legacy, 1987; Alaska, 1988; Journey, 1988; Caribbean, 1989; Six Days in Havana 6with John Kings), 1989; The Novel, 1990; The Eagle and the Raven, 1990; The World Is My Home, 1992; Writer's Handbook, 1992; Mexico, 1992; My Lost Mexico, 1992. *Honours:* Pulitzer Prize, 1947; Einstein Award 1967; Medal of Freedom, 1977; Gold Medal Spanish Institute 1980. *Memberships:* Chairman, President Kennedy's Food for Peace Programme, 1961; Board Member, International Broadcasting, 1984-91; Member Advisory Council, NASA, 1980-83. *Address:* Texas Center for Writers, University of Texas Austin, TX 78713, USA.

MICHIE James, b. 1927, British. *Appointments:* Director, The Bodley Head, Publishers, London; Formerly, Lecturer at London University. *Publications:* Oxford Poetry 1949 (ed with Kingsley Amis), 1949; Possible Laughter, 1959; The Odes of Horace (trans), 1964; The Poems of Catullus: A Bilingual Edition (trans), 1969; The Epigrams of Martial (trans), 1973; The Bodley Head Book of Longer Short Stories (in US as The Book of Longer Short Stories) (ed), 1974; Selected Fables, by La Fontaine (trans), 1979; The Helen of Euripides (trans with Colin Leach), 1981; New and Selected Poems, 1983. *Address:* c/o The Bodley Head, 32 Bedford Square, London WC1B 3EL, England.

MICHIE Jonathan, b. 25 Mar 1957, London, England. Economist. m. Carolyn Downs, 5 Nov 1988, 1 son. *Education:* Balliol College, Oxford University, 1976-79; Queen Mary College, London University, 1979-80; Balliol College, Oxford University, 1980-85. *Publications:* The Economic Legacy; Wages in the Business Cycle; Beyond the Casino Economy; The Economics of Restructuring and Intervention; Inflation, Employment, Wage Barganing and the Law. *Memberships:* Cambridge Journal of Economics. *Address:* Robinson College, Cambridge, CB3 9AN, England.

MIDDLETON Christopher, b. 10 June 1926, Truro, Cornwall, England. University Teacher. *Education:* BA 1951, DPhil 1954, University of Oxford, England. *Publications:* Poems: Torse 3, 1962; Nonsequences, 1965; Our Flowers & Nice Bones, 1969; The Lonely Suppers of W V Balloon, 1975; Carminalenia, 1980; Serpentine, 1985; Two Horse Wagon Going By, 1986; Selected Writings, 1989; The Balcony Tree, 1992; The Pursuit of the Kingfisher, Essays, 1983. *Honours:* Sir Geoffrey Faber Memorial Prize, 1963; Guggenheim Poetry Fellowship, 1974-75; Schlegel- Tieck Translation Prize, 1985. *Address:* Germanic Languages, E.P.S 3.154, University of Texas, Austin, Texas 78712, USA.

MIDDLETON Osman Edward, b. 25 Mar 1925, Christchurch, New Zealand. Writer; Author. m. 1949 (div), 1 son, 1 daughter. *Education:* Auckland University College, 1946, 1948; University of Paris, France, 1955-56. *Appointments include:* Robert Burns Fellow, University of Otago, 1970-71; Visiting lecturer, University of Canterbury 1971, also Universities of Zurich, Frankfurt, Giessen, Kiel, Erlangen, Regensburg, Turin, Bologna, Pisa, Venice, Rome, 1983; Writer in residence, Michael Karolyi Memorial Foundation,

Vence, France, 1983. *Publications:* The Stone & Other Stories, 1959; A Walk on the Beach, 1964; The Loners, 1972; Selected Stories, 1976; Confessions of an Ocelot, 1979. Also: 10 Stories, 1953; From the River to the Tide, juvenile, 1962. *Contributions to:* Anthologies worldwide; Numerous magazines & journals. *Honours:* Achievement award 1959, Scholarship in Letters 1965, NZ Literary Fund; Hubert Church Prose Award, 1964; NZ Government Bursary winner, study in France, 1955-56; Joint winner, NZ Prose Fiction Award, 1976; Joint winner, John Cowie Reid Award, 1989. *Memberships:* PEN, 1959-80; Committee, NZ Association of the Blind & Partially Blind, 1970. *Address:* 20 Clifford Street, Dalmore, Dunedin, New Zealand.

MIDDLETON Roger, b. 19 May 1955, England. *Education:* BA, first class honours, Victoria University of Manchester, 1976; PhD, Cambridge University, 1981. *Appointments:* Lecturer in Economic History, University of Durham, Durham, England, 1979-87; Senior Lecturer in Economic History, University of Bristol, Bristol, England, 1987-. *Publication:* Towards the Managed Economy, 1985. *Contributions to:* Economic, history and computing journals. *Honours:* T S Ashton Prize from Economic History Society, 1980, for best paper of the year by a young scholar in the society's journal, Economic History Review. *Memberships:* Royal Economic Society; Economic History Society; Conference of Socialist Economists; Association of History and Computing; Institute of Fiscal Studies; Software Review; Economic History Review. *Address:* Department of Economic and Social History, University of Bristol, Bristol BS1 1TB, England.

MIDDLETON Stanley, b. 1 Aug 1919, Writer. m. Margaret Shirley Charnley (nee Welch), 21 Dec 1951, 2 daughters. *Education:* BA London, 1940; MEd, 1952, MA, (Hons) 1975, Nottingham. *Publications:* Holiday, 1974; Harris's Requiem, 1960; Entry into Jerusalem, 1983; Valley of Decision, 1990; Changes and Chances, 1990; Teo Beothers, 1978; In a Strange Land, 1979; Blind Understanding, 1982; Recovery, 1988; Vacant Places, 1990; A Place to Stand, 1992. *Contributions to:* Critical Quarterly; Fiction Magazine; Cambridge Review. *Honours:* Booker Prize, 1974. *Memberships:* Fellow of PEN. *Literary Agent:* Hutchinson. *Address:* 42 Caledon Road, Sherwood, Nottingham, England.

MIDWOOD Barton A, b. 10 Mar 1938, Brooklyn, New York, USA. Writer. m. Laura Melim, 10 Oct 1988, 3 sons, 2 daughters. *Education:* BA, University of miami, 1959. *Appointments:* Fiction Reviewer, Esquire Magazine, 1970-72. *Publications:* Bodkin; Phantoms; The Nativity; Bennetts Angel. *Contributions to:* Esquire; Atlantic; Paris Review; Dutton Review; Transatlanic Review; Columbia Magazine. *Honours:* Robert Frost Prize; NEA; Aga Khan Prize; Guggenheim. *Memberships:* PEN. *Address:* 64 Meadow Street, Garden City, NY, 11530, USA.

MIESEL Sandra Louise, b. 25 Nov 1941, New Orleans, Los Angeles, USA. Freelance Writer. m. John Louis Miesel, 20 June 1964, 1 son, 2 daughters. *Education:* BS, College of St Frances, 1962; MS, University of Illinois, 1965; AM, 1966; Indiana University, 1990. *Publications:* Shaman; Dreamrider; Against Times Arrow; A Seperate Star; Heads to the Storm. *Contributions to:* Amazing; American Book Review; Destines; Mystics Quarterly. *Honours:* John W Campbell Award. *Memberships:* Lambden Iota Tan Honor Society; Science Fiction Fantasy Writers Of America; Delta Epsilon Sigma College Honor Society; Phi Alpha Theta History Honor Society. *Address:* 8744 N Pennsylvania Street, Indianafalls, IN 46240, USA.

MIHAJLOV Mihajlo, b. 26 Sept 1934, Pancevo, Yugoslavia. Scholar; Author; Journalist. *Education:* BA, Comparative Literature, 1953; Graduate Study, 1960-61; Zagreb University. *Publications:* Moscow Summer; Russian Themes; Underground Notes; Unscientific Thoughts; The Yugoslav Paradox; Tyranny & Freedom. *Contributions to:* New Leader; Chronicles; Encounter;

Survey; Kontinent; Kasper Hauser; RCDA Magazine; Forum Magazine; Tribuna Magazine. *Honours:* Ford Foundation Award; Free German Authors Oranization. *Memberships:* International PEN American Branch. *Address:* Radio Free Europe/ Radio Liberty Inc, 1201 Connecticut Avenue, NW Washington, DC 20036, USA.

MIJUSKOVIC Ben Lazare, b. 20 June 1937, Budapest; Hungary. College Teacher; Psychotherapist. m. Ruth Rykse Mijuskovic, 26 Nov 1965, 2 Daughters. *Education:* University of California, 1972; San Diego State University, 1987; University of Cal, San Diego, 1991. *Appointments:* Newberry Library Fellow, 1975; PostDoctoral Fellow, Yale University, 1975-76. *Publications:* Loneliness; Contingen Immateriacism; Achilles of Rationalist Argumonts. *Contributions to:* Psychiatry; Philosophical Quarterly; Psychoanlythic Review. *Address:* 428 Carnation Avenue, Corona Del Mar, CA 92625, USA.

MIKHAIL Edward H, b. 1928, Canadian. *Appointments:* Lecturer, Assistant Professor, University of Cairo, 1949-66; Associate Professor of English 1966-72, Professor of English Literature 1972-, University of Lethbridge, Alta. *Publications:* The Social and Cultural Setting of the 1890's, 1969; John Galsworthy the Dramatist, 1971; Comedy and Tradegy: A Bibliography of Criticism, Sean O'Casey: A Bibliography of Criticism, A Bibliography of Modern Irish Drama 1899-1970, 1972; Dissertations on Anglo-Irish Drama, 1973; The Sting and the Twinkle: Conversations with Sean O'Casey (co-ed), 1974; J M Synge: A Bibliography of Criticism, 1975; Contemporary British Drama 1950-1976: An Annotated Critical Bibliography, 1976; W B Yeats: Interviews and Recollections, J M Synge: Interviews and Recollections, English Drama 1900-1950, Lady Gregory: Interviews and Recollections, 1977; Oscar Wilde: An Annotated Bibliography of Criticism, 1978; A Research Guide to Modern Irish Dramatists, Oscar Wilde: Interviews and Recollections, The Art of Brendan Behan, 1979; Brendan Behan: An Annotated Bibliography of Criticism, 1980; An Annotated Bibliography of Modern Anglo-Irish Drama, 1981; Lady Gregory: An Annotated Bibliography of Criticism, Brendan Buhan: Interviews and Recollections, 1982; Sean O'Casey and His Critics, 1985; The Abbey Theatre, 1987. *Address:* 6 Coachwood Point West, Lethbridge, Altberta, Canada T1J 4B3.

MIKHALKOV Sergey Vladimirovich, b. 13 Mar 1913, Moscow, Russia. Poet; Playwright; Childrens Writer. *Education:* Literary Institute, Moscow. *Publications:* Uncle Steve, 1936; Collected Works, 2 volumes; Film Script: Frontline Friends, 1941; Plays: After Mark Twain, 1938; Red Neckerchief; Selected Works, 1947; I Want to Go Home, 1949; Lobsters, 1952; Zaika-Zasnaika, 1955; Basni Mikhalkova, 1957; Sombrero, 1958; A Monument to Oneself 1958; Campers, 1959; Collected Works, 4 volumes, 1964; Green Grasshopper, 1964; We Are Together, My Friend and I, 1967; In the Museum of Lenin, 1968; Fables, 1970; Disobedience Day, 1971; The Funny Bone (articles), 1971; Collected Works, 3 volumes 1970-71; Selected Works, 1973; Bibliographical Index, 1975. *Honours:* 4 Orders of Lenin; Hero of Socialist Labour, 1973; Red Banner; Red Banner of Labour; Red Star; Lenin Prize, 1970; 4 State Prizes; Merited Worker of Arts of RSFSR. *Memberships:* Academy of pedagogical Sciences; Commission for Youth Affairs. *Address:* USSR Union of Writers ulitsa Vorovskogo 52, Moscow, USSR.

MIKKOLA Marja-Leena (Pirinen), b. 18 Mar 1939, Salo, Finland. Writer. *Education:* Candidate of Philosophy, Helsinki University, 1963. *Publications:* Naisia, 1962; Raskas Puuvilla, 1971; Laakarin Rouva, 1972; Anni Manninen, 1977; Maailman Virrassa, 1981; Jalkeen Kello Kymmenen, 1984. *Contributions to:* Parnasso; Kultuurivihkot. *Honours:* Eino Leino Award, 1968; State Prize for Literature, 1971, 1972, 1977, 1984. *Membership:* Finnish Writers Union. *Literary Agent:* Otava, Helsinki. *Address:* Kalervonk 12.C. 16, 00610 Helsinki, Finland.

MIKLOWITZ Gloria D, b. 18 May 1927, New York State, USA. Writer. m. Julius Miklowitz, 28 Aug 1948, 2 sons. *Education:* Hunter College of New York, 1944-45; BA, University of Michigan, Ann Arbor, 1948; Graduate study (no degree) New York University, 1948. *Appointment:* Instructor, Pasadena City College, 1970-80. *Publications include:* Did You Hear What Happened to Andrea?; Close to the Edge; The Day the Senior Class Got Married; The War Between the Classes; Anything to Win; The Emerson High Vigilantes; Suddenly Super Rich; Standing Tall, Looking Good. *Contributor to:* Numerous journals, magazines, newspapers. *Honours:* 3 novels made into TV Specials for children (Did You Hear What Happened to Andrea?, The Day the Senior Class Got Married, The War Between the Classes); Western Australia Young Book Award, 1984. *Memberships:* PEN Center West, Treasurer; Society of Children's Book Writers; SC Council of Literature for Children and Young People. *Literary Agent:* Curtis Brown, New York. *Address:* 5255 Vista Miguel Drive, La Canada, CA 91011, USA.

MILBURN Robert Leslie Pollington, b. 28 July 1907. Clerk in Holy Orders. m. Margery Kathleen Mary Harvie, 15 Apr 1944, 1 son, dec, 1 daughter. *Education:* Oundle, 1921-26; Sidney Sussex College, Cambridge; Worcester College, Oxford, 1934-57; Dean of Worcester, 1957-68; Master of the Temple, 1968-80. *Publications:* Early Christian Interpretation of History; early Christian Art & Architecture; Saints and their Emblems in English Churches. *Contributions to:* Many Articles. *Memberships:* Society of Antiquaries. *Address:* 5 St Barnabas, Newland Malvern, Worcs WR13 5AX, England.

MILENSKI Paul, b. 15 Nov 1942, Adams, Massachusetts, USA. Author. m. Beverly Jean Milenski, 17 Nov 1979, 1 son, 1 daughter. *Education:* Middlebury College, VT; North Adams State, BA, 1966; University Iowa, MFA, 1968; University Mass, EdD, 1973. *Appointments:* Fiction Writer. *Publications:* Sexual Rhythms; Tickits: The Movie. *Contributions to:* Hundreds of Short Stories in: Quarterly West; Paper Radio; Phoebe; Calypso; Potato Eyes; Great River Review; Pinchpenny; Asylum; Facet; Ransom; Wind; Pale Fire Review. *Honours:* Four Time Winner Pen Syndicated Fiction Prize; Finalist, AWP Competition; Bobst Award; Capricorn Award. *Memberships:* Poets & Writers; Associated Writing Programs; Berkshire Writers Room. *Address:* 26A Highview Drive, Pittsfield, MA 01201, USA.

MILES Betty, b. 1928, American. *Publications:* A House for Everyone, 1958; The Cooking Book, What Is the World?, 1959; Having a Friend, A Day of Summer, 1960; Mr Turtle's Mystery, 1961; A Day of Winter, 1962; The Feast on Sullivan Street, 1963; The Bank Street Readers (assoc ed), 1965; A Day of Autumn, 1967; Joe Finds a Way, 1969; A Day of Spring, 1970; Just Think!, 1971; Save the Earth!, The Real Me, 1974; Just the Beginning, 1975; All It Takes Is Practise, 1976; Looking On, 1977; The Trouble with Thirteen, 1979; Maudie and Me and the Dirty Book, 1980; The Secret Life of the Underwear Champ, 1981; I Would If I Could, 1982; Sink or Swim, 1986; Save the Earth An Action Handbook for Kids, 1991. *Address:* 94 Sparkill Avenue, Tappan, NY 10983, USA.

MILES John. *See:* BICKHAM Jack Miles.

MILIONIS Christoforos, b. 4 Nov 1932, Greece. Writer. m. Tatixma Tsxliki, 28 Dec 1969, 1 daughter. *Education:* Diploma, Classical Greek Literature. *Appointments:* Conferences, University of Kolu; University of Milamo, Italy; Union Santove Santarosx, Tovino; University of Tvieste; University of Kolm; Congress, University of Trieste. *Publications:* Kalamxs ke Achevontos; Silvestvos Novel; Dytiki Sinikix; Acrokevaunia; The Shirt of Ceytauracs; The Short Stories of Trial. *Contributions to:* Endochora; Dokimxsix; I Lexi; To Dentro; Anti Grammxta Ke Technes; Ta Nea. *Honours:* 1st State Award of Short Stories.

Memberships: Society of Greek Writers; Union of Greek Philologist. *Address:* ssa 001 Agathiou Street, Athens, 11472, Greece.

MILKOMANE George Alexis Milkomanovich, (George Bankoff, George Borodin, George Braddin, Peter Conway, Alec Redwood, George Sava), b. 15 Oct 1903. Author; Consulting Surgeon. m. Jannette Hollingdale, 1939, 2 sons, 2 daughters. *Publications:* (Autobiography, Medical) The Healing Knife, 1937; Beauty from the Surgeon's Knife, 1938; A Surgeon's Destiny, 1939; Donkey's Serenade, 1940; Twice the Clock Round, 1941; A Ring at the Door, 1941; Surgeon's Symphony, 1944; The Come by Appointment, 1946; The Knife Heals Again, 1948; The Way of a Surgeon, 1949; Strange Cases, 1950; A Doctor's Odyssey, 1951; Patients' Progress, 1952; A Surgeon Remembers, 1953; Surgeon Under Capricorn, 1954; The Lure of Surgery, 1955; A Surgeon at Large, 1957; Surgery and Crime, 1957; All this and Surgery Too, 1958; Surgery Holds the Door, 1960; A Surgeon in Rome, 1961; A Surgeon in California, 1962; Appointments in Rome, 1963; A Surgeon in New Zealand, 1964; A Surgeon in Cyprus, 1965; A Surgeon in Australia, 1966; Sex, Surgery, People, 1967; he Gates of Heaven are Narrow, 1968; Bitter Sweet Surgery, 1969; One Russian's Story, 1970; A Stranger in Harley Street 1970; A Surgeon and his Knife, 1978; Living with your Psoriasis (essays), 1978; (Politica and Historical Books): Rasputin Speaks, 1941; Valley of Forgotten People, 1942; The Chetniks, 1943; School for War, 1943; They Stayed in London, 1943; Russia Triumphant, 1944; A Tale of Ten cities, 1944; War Without Guns, 1944; Caught by Revolution, 1952; (Novels): Land Fit for Heroies, 1945; Link of Two hearts, 1945; Gissy, 1946; Call it Life, 1946; Boy in Samarkand, 1950; Flight from the Palace, 1953; Pursuit in the Desert, 1955; The Emperor Story, 1959; Punishment Deferred, 1966; Man Without Label, 1967; Alias Dr Holtzman, 1968; City of Cain, 1969; The Imperfect Surgeon, 1969; Nothing Sacred, 1970; Of Guilt Possessed, 1970; A Skeleton for My Mate, 1971; The Beloved Nemesis, 1971; On the Wings of Angels, 1972; The Sins of Andrea, 1972; Tell Your Grief Softly, 1972; Cocaine for Breakfast, 1973; Return from the Valley, 1973; Sheilah of Buckleigh Manor, 1974; Every sweet Hath Its Sour, 1974; The Way of the Healing Knife, 1976; mary Mary Quite Contrary, 1977; Crusader's Clinic, 1977; pretty Polly, 1977; No Man is Perfect, 1978; A Stranger in his Skull, 1979; Secret Surgeon, 1979; Crimson Eclipse, 1980; Innocence on Trial, 1981; The Price of Prejudice, 1982; The Killer Microbes, 1982; Betrayal in Style, 1983; Double Identity, 1984; A Smile Through Tears, 1985; Bill of Indictment, 1986; Rose By Any Other Name, 1987; The Roses Bloom Again, 1988; numerous novels as George Borodin. *Address:* c/o A P Watt Ltd, 20 John Street, London WC1N 2DR, England.

MILLAR Margaret (Ellis) b. 5 Feb 1915, Kitchener, Ontario, Canada. Writer. m. Kenneth Millar (Ross Macdonald) 1938 (dec 1983), 1 daughter (dec). *Education:* Kitchener-Waterloo Collegiate 1929-33; University of Toronto, 1933-36. *Appointments:* Screenwriter, Warner Brothers, Hollywood, 1945-46; Freelance writer. *Publications include:* Crime Publications include: The Listening Walls, 1959; A Stranger in My Grave, 1960; How Like an Angel, 1962; The Fiend, 1964; Beyond This Point Are Monsters, 1971; Ask For Me Tomorrow, 1977; The Murder of Miranda, 1980; Mermaid, 1982; Banshee, 1983; Spider Webs, 1986, 1987. Novels: Experiment in Springtime, 1947; It's All in the Family, 1948; The Cannibal Heart, 1949, 1950; Wives and Lovers, 1954; Autobiography: The Birds and Beasts Were There, 1968; various short stories. *Honours:* Mystery Writers of America Edgar Allan Poe Award, 1956; Grand Master Award, 1982; Los Angeles Times Woman of the Year Award, 1965. *Membership:* President, Mystery Writers of America, 1957-58. *Literary Agent:* Harold Ober Associates. *Address:* Harold Ober Associates, 425 Madison Avenue, New York, NY 10017, USA.

MILLAR Ronald (Graeme) (Sir), b. 1919, British.

Appointment: Deputy Chairman, Theatre Royal, Haymarket, London, 1977-. *Publications:* Plays: Frieda, 1947; Waiting for Gillian, 1955; The Bride and the Bachelor, 1958; A Ticklish Business, 1959; The More the Merrier, The Bride Comes Back, 1960; The Affair, 1962; The Affair, The New Men, The Masters: Three Plays Based on the Novels and with a Preface by C P Snow, 1964; Robert and Elizabeth, Number 10, 1967; They Don't Grow on Trees, 1969; Abelard and Heloise, 1970; The Case in Question, 1975; A Coat of Varnish, 1982; A View from the Wings (autobiography), 1993. *Honour:* Kt, 1980. *Address:* 7 Sheffield Terrace, London W8 7NG, England.

MILLER Arthur, b. 17 Oct 1915, New York, USA. Playwright. m. (1) Mary Grace Slattery, 1940, (div 1956), 1 son, 1 daughter, (2) Marilyn Monroe, 1956, (div 1961), (3) Ingeborg Morath, 1962, 1 daughter. *Education:* University of Michigan. *Publications:* The Man Who Had All the Luck, 1943; Situation Normal, 1944; Focus, 1945; All My Sons, 1947; Death of a Salesman, 1949; The Crucible, 1953; A View from the Bridge, 1955; A Memory of Two Mondays, 1955; Collected Plays, 1958; The Misfits (screenplay), 1959; After the Fall, 1964; Incident at Vichy, 1964; I Don't Need You Any More (short stories), 1967; The Price (play), 1968; In Russia (with Inge Morath), 1969; Chinese Encounters (with Inge Morath), 1972; The Creation of the World and Other Business (play), 1972; Up From Paradise, (musical) 1974; The American Clock, 1980; Playing for Time (play), 1981; Elegy for a Lady (play), 1983; Some Kind of Love Story (play), 1983; Salesman in Beijing (journal), 1984; The Archbishop's Ceiling, 1986; Danger, Memory! (two one-acts), 1987; Timebends (autobiog), 1987. *Honours:* Theatre Guild National Award, 1938; New York Drama Critics Circle Award, 1947, 1949; Pulitzer Prize for Drama, 1949; Antoinette Perry Award, 1953; American Academy of Arts and Letters Gold Medal for Drama, 1959; Anglo-American Award, 1966; Creative Arts Award Brandeis University, 1970; Kennedy Centre Award, 1984; Hon. D.Litt., University of East Anglia, 1984. *Membership:* President, International PEN, 1965-69. *Address:* c/o ICM, 40 W. 57th Street, New York, NY 10019, USA.

MILLER Christian, b. 3 Dec 1920. Writer. m. John Miller, 2 Jan 1953, 2 daughters. *Publications:* A Childhood in Scotland, 1981; Daisy, Daisy (travel), 1981; Champagne Sandwich (novel), 1968 *Contributions to:* Numerous magazines and journals. *Honour:* Scottish Arts Council Literary Award, 1982. *Membership:* Society of Authors. *Literary Agent:* Anthony Sheil. *Address:* Old Stables, Newtown, Newbury, Berkshire RG15 9AP, England.

MILLER Danny, b. 15 Nov 1947, Montreal, Canada. Professor. *Education:* B Comm, Sir George Williams, 1968; MBA, University of Toronto, 1970; PhD, McGill University, 1976. *Publications:* The Icarns Paradox; Unstable at the Top; The Neurotic Organization; Organizations: A Quantum View. *Contributions to:* Academy of Management Journal; Administrative Science Quarterly; Management Science; Academy of Management Review; Org Studies; Psychology Today; Harpers. *Address:* 4642 Melrose Avenue, Montreal, Quebec, Canada H4A 2S9.

MILLER David Lindsay, b. 2 Oct 1950, Melbourne, Australia. Librarian. *Education:* BA, Middlesex Polytechnic, 1981; PhD, Royal Holloway College, University of London, 1986. *Publications:* Pictures of Mercy; Darkness Enfolding; W H Hudson and the Elusive Paradise; In the Midst; Primavera. *Contributions to:* Artscribe; London Magazine; Agenda; Origin; Art Press; Acts; Text; Longhouse; American Literary Review; La Carta de Oliver. *Address:* 66 Oakfield Road, London N4 4LB, England.

MILLER Donald George,b. 30 Oct 1909, PA, USA. Clergyman; Professor. m. Eleanor Chambers, 21 July 1937, 2 sons, 1 daughter. *Education:* AB, Greenville College, 1930; STB, 1933; STM, 1934, Biblical Seminary in New York; MA, 1934; PhD, 1935, New York University; LLD, Waynesburg College, 1963; LittD, Washington and Jefferson College, 1965. *Appointments:* Co-editor, Interpretation, 1947-62; Associate Editor, Layman's Bible Commentary, 1957-65; Editorial Board, Ex Auditu, 1985-. *Publications include:* Nature and Mission of the church, 1957; Fire in thy Mouth, 1954; The Way to Biblical Preaching, 1957; The Gospel according to Luke, 1959; The Scent of Eternity: A Biography of Harris E. Kirk, 1990; On This Rock: A Commentary on I Peter, 1993. *Contributions to:* Over 35 journals. *Membership:* Society of Biblical Literature. *Address:* 401 Russell Avenue, Apt. 405, Gaithersburg, MD 20877, USA

MILLER Douglas Taylor, b. 27 May 1937. Professor of History; Author. m. Susanne Elin Nielsen, 22 May 1982. 1 son, 1 daughter. *Education:* BA, Colby College, 1958; MA, Columbia University, 1959; PhD, Michigan State University, 1965. *Publications:* Jacksonian Aristocracy: Class and Democracy in New York, 1830-1860, 1967; The Birth of Modern America, 1820-1850, 1970; Then Was the Future: The North in the Age of Jackson, 1973; The Fifties, 1977; Visions of America: Second World War to the Present, 1988; Frederick Douglass and the Fight For Freedom, 1988; Henry David Thoreau: A Man for All Seasons, 1991; Editor, The Nature of Jacksonian America, 1972. *Contributions to:* American Quarterly; Educational Theory; New York History; Journal of Popular Culture; Americana; Tijdschrift Voor De Studie Van Nord-America. *Literary Agent:* Virginia Barber, New York, USA. *Address:* Department of History, Michigan State University, East Lansing, Michigan 48824, USA.

MILLER Eugene Ernest, b. 18 Apr 1930, Akron, Ohio, USA. Professor. m. Margaret E Kelly, 28 Dec 1962, 2 daughters. *Education:* University of Notre Dame, BA, 1950-55; Ohio University, MA, 1961-62; University of Illinois, PhD, 1962-67; Howard University, 1971-72. *Appointments:* Albion College, 1967-. *Publications:* Voice of a Native Son; Some Black Thoughts on Don L Lees's Think Black; Voodoo Parallels in Native Son; Richard Wright and Gertrude Stein; Folkloric Aspects of Richard Wrights, The Man Who Killed a Shadow. *Memberships:* MLA; American Culture Association; National Association of Scholars. *Address:* English Department, Albion College, Albion, MI 49224, USA.

MILLER Frederick Walter Gascoyne, b. 1904, New Zealander. *Appointments:* Former Journalist, Otago Daily Times, Dunedin: The Press, Christchurch: Southland Daily News: and Southland Times: (journalist from 1922). *Publications:* Gold in the River, 1946; Golden Days of Lake County, 1949, 5th edition 1973; Beyond the Blue Mountains, 1954, 1978; West to the Fiords, 1954, 1976; Waikaia: The Golden Century, 1966; Ink on My Fingers, 1967; The Story of the Kingston Flyer, 1976; King of Counties: A History of the Southland County: Hokonui: The School and the People, 1982; Murihiku - The Tail, an epic poem dealing lightly with the history of Southland for the 1990 commemoration. *Honour:* OBE. *Memberships:* Life Member, NZ Journalists Union; Invercargill Lions Club. *Address:* 191 Princes Street, Invercargill, New Zealand.

MILLER Hugh, b. 1937, British. *Appointments:* Editorial Assistant, Scottish ITV, Glasgow, 1958-60; Technical and Photographic Assistant to a Forensic Pathologist, University of Glasgow, 1960-62; Manager 1963-64, Co-Owner 1965-70, Unique Studios, London; Editor, Bulletin 1967-69, General 1968-71. *Publications:* A Pocketful of Miracles, 1969; Secrets of Gambling, 1970; Professional Presentations, 1971; The Open City, Levels, Drop Out, Short Circuit, Koran's Legacy, 1973; Kingpin, Double Deal, Feedback, 1974; Ambulance, 1975; The Dissector, A Soft Breeze from Hell, 1976; The Saviour, 1977; The Rejuvenators, Terminal 3, 1978; Olympic Bronze, Head of State, 1979; District Nurse, 1984; Honour a Physician, 1985; EastEnders, Teen EastEnders, 1986; Snow on the Wind, 1987; Silent Witnesses, 1988; The Paradise Club, 1989;

An Echo of Justice, 1990; Home Grown, 1990. *Address:* 40 St John's Court, Warwick, England.

MILLER Jake C, b. 28 Dec 1929, Hobe Sound, Florida, USA. College Professor. m. Nellie Carrol, 22 Dec 1956, 3 sons. *Education:* BS, Bethune Cookman College, 1951; MA, University of Illinois, 1957; PhD, University of North Carolina, 1967. *Publications:* Black Presence in American Foreign Affairs; Plight of Haitian Refugees. *Contributions to:* Journal of Black Studies; Africa Today; Middle East Journal; TransAfrica Forum. *Honours:* Faculty Excellence in Research Award; National Professorof the Year Finalist; Dstinguished Alumni Award. *Memberships:* American Political Science Association; National Conference of Black Political Scientists. *Address:* 1103 Lakewood Park Drive, Daytona Beach, Fl 32117, USA.

MILLER Jim Wayne, b. 21 Oct 1936, Leicester, North Carolina, USA. Professor; Writer. m. Mary Ellen Yates, 17 Aug 1958, 2 sons, 1 daughter. *Education:* AB, English, Berea College, 1958; PhD, German and American Literature, Vanderbilt University, 1965. *Appointments:* Invited Reader, 50th Anniversary Meeting, South Atlantic Modern Language Association, Atlanta, 1978; Invited Reader, Folger Shakespeare Library, Washington, 1981; Writer-in-Residence, The Centre College of Kentucky, 1984; East Tennessee State University, 1985. *Publications:* Poems: The Mountains Have Come Closer, 1980; Dialogue With a Dead Man, 1974, 1978, 1990; Brier, His Book, 1988; Vein of Words, 1984; Nostalgia for 70, 1986. Novels: Newfound, 1989; I Have a Place, editor, 1981; The Figure of Fulfillment, translations from poetry of Emil Lerperger, 1975; His First Best Country (chapbook, fiction), 1987; The Examined Life: Family, Community, Work in American Literature, 1989. *Contributions to:* The Writer; Appalchian Journal; Appalachian Heritage; Modern Philology. *Honours:* Alice Lloyd Memorial Award, 1967; Western Kentucky Award, 1976; Thomas Wolfe Literary Award, 1980; Zoe Kinkaid Brockman Memorial Award for Poetry. *Memberships:* Kentucky Poetry Society; Appalachian Studies Conference. *Address:* IWFAC 258, Western Kentucky University, Bowling Green, KY 42101, USA.

MILLER Jonathan (Wolfe), b. 1934, British. *Appointments:* Co-author and appeared in Beyond the Fringe, London and NYC, 1961-64; Editor of Monitor (BBC TV documentary series), 1965; Research Fellow in the History of Medicine, University College, 1970-73; Associate Director, National Theatre, 1973-75; Produced The Body in Question (BBC series), 1978; Executive Producer, BBC Shakespeare Series, 1979-80; Research Fellow in Neuropsychology, University of Sussex, Brighton. *Publications:* McLuhan, 1971; Freud: The Man, His World, His Influence (ed), 1972; The Body in Question, 1978; Darwin for Beginners, 1982; Subsequent Performances, 1986; Editor, The Don Giovanni Book: Myths of Seduction and Betrayal, 1990. *Honour:* CBE, 1983. *Address:* c/o IMG Artists (Europe), Media House, 3 Burlington Lane, London W4 2TH, England.

MILLER Karl (Fergus Connor), b. 1931, British. *Appointments:* Assistant Principal, HM Treasury, 1956-57; Producer, BBC Television, 1957-58; Literary Editor, The Spectator, 1958-61 and the New Statesman, 1961-67; Editor, The Listener, 1967-73; Lord Northcliffe Professor of Modern English Literature, University College, London, 1974-92; Editor, London Review of Books, 1979-89, co-editor, 1989-92. *Publications:* Poetry from Cambridge 1952-54 (ed), 1955; Writing in England Today: The Last Fifteen Years (ed), 1968; Memoirs of a Modern Scotland (ed), A Listener Anthology August 1967-June 1970 (ed), 1970; A Second Listener Anthology (ed), 1973; Cockburn's Millennium, 1975; Robert Burns (ed), 1981; Doubles: Studies in Literary History, 1985; Authors, 1989; Rebecca's Vest, 1993. *Honour:* James Tait Black Award for Cockburn's Millennium. *Membership:* Fellow, Royal Society of Literature. *Address:* 26 Limerston Street, London SW10, England.

MILLER Kerby A, b. 30 Dec 1944, Phoenix, Arizonia, USA. Professor. m. Patricia Mulholland, June 1979, 2 sons, 1 daughter. *Education:* BA, Pomona College, California, 1966; MA, University of California, CA, 1967; PhD, 1976. *Appointments:* Assistant Professor, University of Missouri, 1978-84; Associate Professor, 1984-89; Professor, 1989-. *Publications:* Emigrants and Exiles. *Contributions to:* Irish Historical studies; Journal of American Ethnic History. *Honours:* Merle Curti Award; Theodore Saloutos Award; Finalist, Pulitzer Prize. *Memberships:* American Historical Association; Organization of American Historians; Irish Historical Society; Imigration History Society; Irish Social & Economic History Society. *Address:* History Department, 101 Read Hall, University of Missouri, Columbia, MO 65211, USA.

MILLER Lily Poritz, b. 7 June 1938, Cape Town, South Africa. Editor; Writer. m. Stephen Harris Miller, 6 Aug 1966. *Education:* The Fay School, Boston, Massachusetts; The American Academy of Dramatic Arts, New York; The New School for Social Research, New York. *Appointments:* Editor with Collier-Macmillan and McGraw-Hill, New York; Teacher of Creative Writing, City University of New York; Senior Editor, McClelland and Stewart Ltd, Book Publishers, Toronto, Canada; Lily Poritz Miller Editorial Services. *Publications:* The Proud One, play produced in Toronto, 1974, published by Playwrights Canada; My Star of Hope, play produced off-Broadway, 1962; Stories published in American Scene: New Voices, 1963. *Honour:* The Proud One (play) received Samuel French Award, 1974. *Memberships:* PEN International; Dramatists Guild of Author's League of America; Playwrights Union of Canada. *Address:* 17 Lascelles Boulevard, Suite 1105, Toronto, Ontario, Canada M4V 2B6.

MILLER Linda Patterson, b. 27 Jan 1946, Detroit, Michigan, USA. Professor. m. Randall M Miller, 3 Aug 1968, 1 son. *Education:* Hope College, BA, 1968; Ohio State University, MA, 1971; University of Delaware, PhD, 1979. *Appointments:* Penn State University, Professor, 1980-. *Publications:* Letters from the Lost Generation; Friends. *Contributions to:* Studies in American Fiction; Mosaic; Renascence; Hemingway Review; Journal of Modern Literature; American Transcendental Quarterly; North Dakota Quarterly; Journal of the Early Republic. *Honours:* Lilly Foundation Post Doctoral Fellow; Danforth Foundation Associate. *Memberships:* Hemingway Society; F Scott Fitzgerald Society; Modern Language Association. *Address:* 244 Sagamore Road, Havertown, PA 19083, USA.

MILLER Marc William, b. 29 Aug 1947, Annapolis, Maryland, USA. Writer. m. Darlene File, 24 Sept 1981, 1 son, 1 daughter. *Education:* BA, Sociology, University of Illinois, 1969. *Appointments:* Staff, Grenadier Magazine, 1977-79, Journal of the Travellers' Aid Society, 1979-85; Staff, Challenge Magazine, 1986-92; Contributing Editor, Fire & Movement Magazine, 1977-84. *Publications:* Traveller, 1977; Imperium, 1977; 2300 AD, 1986; MegaTraveller, 1988; MegaTraveller II, Quest for the Ancients, 1991; Spellbound, 1992; 8 science fiction simulation games; 8 historical simulation games; 4 role-playing games, 3 computer games. Triplanetary, 1973; Chaco, 1974; Coral Sea, 1974; Their Finest Hour, 1976; The Russo-Japanese War, 1976; Battle for Midway, 1976; Mayday, 1978; Belter, 1979; Asteroid, 1980; Twilight's Peak, 1980; Verdun, 1980; 1942!, 1981; Safari Ship, 1984. Translations: various editions in German, French, Spanish, Portuguese, Swedish, Italian and Japanese. *Contributions to:* Journal of Travellers' Aid Society; Moves; the Travellers' Digest; Fire & Movement; other professional journals. *Honours:* Charles Roberts Award, 1978, 1979, 1980, 1981; H.G. Wells Award, 1979, 1980; Game Designers Guild Select Award, 1978, 1980, 1981; Games 100, 1981, 1982, 1983, 1984, 1991; Elected to Adventure Gaming Hall of Fame, 1982. *Memberships:* Science Fiction Writers of America; Game Designers' Guild, President, 1979-81; Academy of Adventure Gaming Arts & Sciences; United States Army Air Defense Artillery, 1969-89,

Captain, 1975-89; The Children's Foundation, Board of Directors; City of Bloomington Human Relations Commission; Rotary; Scabbard & Blade. *Address:* PO Box 193, Normal, IL 61761, USA.

MILLER Margaret. *See:* **DALE Margaret Jessy.**

MILLER (Hanson) Orlo, b. 1 Apr 1911, London, Ontario, Canada. Anglican Priest, retired. m. Maridon Gordon-Wylie, 29 Dec 1934, 1 son. *Literary Appointments:* Night Telegraph Editor, Science Editor, London (Canada) Free Press, 1940-45; Lecturer, School of Journalism, University of Western Ontario, 1954-61. *Publications include:* 17 books, 10 stage plays, 2000 credits in radio & television for networks & independent broadcasting stations in Canada, UK, USA. Book titles include: Raiders of the Mohawk, 1954; The Donnellys Must Die, 1962; Death to the Donnellys, 1975; The Day-Spring, 1976; 20 Mortal Murders, 1978; This Was London, 1988. *Contributions to:* Canadian Science Digest; New Liberty; Papers & records, Ontario Historical Society; Families, magazine of Ontario Genealogical Society. *Honours:* Fellow, Institute of American Genealogy, 1939; 9 Awards, Institute for Education by Radio & Television, Ohio State University, 1946-68. *Memberships include:* Numerous local, national & international societies, science, history, archaeology, genealogy. Honorary President, London & Middlesex Historical Society. *Address:* 183 Gammage Street, London, Ontario, Canada N5Y 2B4.

MILLER Thomas Eugene, b. 4 Jan 1929, Bryan, Texas, USA. Attorney; Editor; Writer. *Education:* BA Texas A & M University, 1950; MA, 1956; JD, 1966, University of Texas at Austin. *Appointments:* Editor, Bancroft Whitney, San Francisco, 1966-92. *Publications:* Nonfiction book published under pseudonym, 1984. *Contributions to:* American Law Reports Annotated; Texas Jurisprudence; Federal Procedural Forms; American Jurisprudence Pleading and Practice Forms; American Jurisprudence Legal Forms; Texas Pleading and Practice Forms; Williston on Contracts. *Honours:* Phi Eta Sigma, 1947; Phi Kappa Phi, 1950; Psi Chi, 1952; Medal of Honour, 1988; Grand Ambassador of Achievement, 1987; Man of the Year, 1990. *Memberships:* World Literary Academy; National Writers Club; Press Club of San Francisco (Vice Chair, Admissions Committee); United Writers Association of India; National Association of Legal Writers and Editors; Texas and American Bar Associations. *Address:* 101N Haswell Drive, Bryan TX 77803 USA.

MILLER Vassar (Morrison), b. 1924, American. *Appointment:* Instructor in Creative Writing, St John's School, Houston, 1975-76. *Publications:* Adam's Footprint, 1956; Wage War on Silence: A Book of Poems, 1960; My Bones Being Water: Poems, 1963; Onions and Roses, 1968; If I Could Sleep Deeply Enough, 1974; Small Change, Approaching Nada, 1977; Selected and New Poems, 1982; Struggling to Swim on Concrete, 1984; Despite This Flesh (ed), 1985. *Address:* 1615 Vassar Street, Houston, TX 77006, USA.

MILLER Walter M(ichael), b. 1922, American. *Appointments:* Engineer; Freelance Writer, mainly of SF Short Stories and Novellas. *Publications:* A Canticle for Leibowitz, 1960; Conditionally Human, 1962; The View from the Stars, 1964; The Best of Walter M Miller Jr, 1980; The Darfstellar and Other Stories, 1982; The Science Fiction Stories of Walter M Miller Jr, 1984; Beyond Armegeddon (co-ed), 1985.

MILLETT John, Australian. *Appointments:* Lawyer; Editor, South Head Press and Poetry Australia, 1972-. *Publications:* Calendar Adam, 1971; The Silences, 1973; Love Tree of the Coomera, 1975; West of the Cunderand, 1977; Last Bride at Longsleep (with Grace Perry), 1981; Tail Arse Charlie, 1982; Come Down Cunderang, 1985; Blue Dynamite, 1986; Nine Lives of Big Meg O' Shannessy, 1989. *Address:* Market Place, Berrima, New South Wales 2577, Australia.

MILLETT Kate (Katherine Murray Millett), b. 1934, American. Leader in the Feminist movement. *Publications:* Sexual Politics, 1970; Flying, 1974; The Prostitution Papers, 1976; Sita, 1977; The Basement, 1980; Going to Iran, 1982; The Loony Bin Trip, 1990. *Address:* c/o Georges Borchardt Incorporated, 136 East 57th Street, New York, NY 10022, USA.

MILLHISER Marlys, b. 27 May 1938, Charles City, Iowa, USA Author. m. David Millhiser, 25 June 1960, 1 son, 1 daughter. *Education:* BA, History, University of Iowa, 1960; MA, History, University of Colorado, 1963. *Publications:* Novels: Michael's Wife, 1972, 1973; Nella Waits, 1974, 1975; Willing Hostage, 1976, 1977; The Mirror, 1978, 1979; Nightmare Country, 1981, 1982; The Threshold 1984, 1985; Murder at Moot Point, 1992; Death of the Office Witch, 1993. *Contributions to:* Column for Mystery Scene Magazine. *Honours:* Top Hand Award for adult novel, Colorado Authors League, 1975 for Nella Waits and again in 1985 for The Threshold. *Memberships:* The Authors Guild; Mystery Writers of America; Sisters in Crime; Western Writers of America; Colorado Author's League, current Board Member. *Literary Agent:* Deborah Schneider, John Farqueharson Ltd, 250 West 57th Street, NY 10107, USA. *Address:* 1743 Orchard Avenue, Boulder, CO 80304, USA.

MILLIEX Tatiana Gritsi, b. 20 Oct 1920, Athens, Greece. Writer. m. Roger Millex, 1 June 1939, 1 son, 1 daughter. *Education:* Diploma, French Institute in Athens, 1938. *Publications:* Imeroloyio, 1951, 3 editions; Allazoume?, 1958, French translation, 1985, 3 editions; Kai Idou Ippos Chloros, 1963, 6 editions; Anadromes, 1983, 2 editions; Apo Tin Alli Oxhtitou Chronou, 1988, French translation, Paris, 1992, 3 editions; H Tripoli Tou Pontou, 1977, 4 editions; Se Proto Prosopo, 1958, 5 editions; Onirika, 1991. *Contributions to:* Variety of Greek and Cypriot magazines and Journals. *Honours:* State Prize for short story, 1951, 1985, Novel, 1964 and 1974; Prize of Athens Academy, 1973. *Memberships:* Greek Writers Society. *Literary Agent:* Castaniotis, Zoodochou Piyis 3, 16078, Athens, Greece. *Address:* 20 Odos Metsovou, BP 26180 Exarchin, Athens, Greece.

MILLIGAN Spike. *See:* **MILLIGAN Terence Alan.**

MILLIGAN Terence Alan, (Spike Milligan), b. 1918, Irish, Writer of Plays/Screenplays, Poetry, Humour/Satire. Radio and TV personality: The Goon Show, BBC Radio; Show Called Fred, ITV; World of Beachcomber, Q5-Q10, BBC-2 Television; Curry and Chips, BBC; Oh in Colour, BBC; A Milligan for All Seasons, BBC. *Publications:* (with J Antrobus) The Bed Sitting Room (play); Oblommov (play); Son of Oblomov (play); Silly Verse for Kids, 1959; A Dustbin of Milligan, 1961; Puckoon, 1963; The Little Pot Boiler, 1963; A Book of Bits, 1965; The Bedside Milligan, 1968; Milliganimals, 1968; The Bald Twit Lion, 1970; Milligan's Ark, 1971; Adolf Hitler: My Part in His Downfall, 1971; The Goon Show Scripts, 1972; Small Dreams of a Scorpion, 1972; Rommel? Gunner Who? 1973; Badjelly the Witch, 1973; More Goon Show Scripts, 1974; Spike Milligan's Transports of Delight, 1974; Dip the Puppy, 1974; The Great McGonagal Scrapbook, 1975; (with Jack Hobbs) The Milligan Book of Records, Games, Cartoons and Commercials, 1975; Monty: His Part in My Vistory, 1976; Mussolini: His Part in My Downfall, 1978; A Book of Goblins, 1978; Open Heart University (verse) 1979; Indefinite Articles and Slunthorpe, 1981; The 101 Best and Only Limericks of Spike Milligan, 1982; The Goon Cartoons, 1982; Sir Nobonk and the Terrible Dragon, 1982; The Melting Pot, 1983; More Goon Cartoons, 1983; There's a Lot About, 1983; Further Transports of Delight, 1985; Floored Masterpieces and Worse Verse, 1985; Where Have All the Bullets Gone, 1985; Goodbye Soldier, 1986; The Mirror Running, 1987; Startling Verse For All The Family, 1987; The Looney, 1987; William McGonall Meets George Gershwin, 1988; It Ends With Magic..., 1990; Peacework, 1991; Condensed Animals, 1991; Dear Robert, Dear Spike, 1991; Depression And How To Survive It, (with Anthony

Clare), 1993; Hidden Words, 1993. *Honours:*TV Writer of the Year Award, 1956; Writing and Appearing: Awarded Golden Rose and Special Comedy Award, Montreux, 1972; CBE, 1992. *Address:* Spike Milligan Productions, 9 Orme Court, London W2, England.

MILLINGTON Barry John, b. 1st Nov 1951, Essex, England. Music Journalist. *Education:* BA, cambridge University, 1974. *Publications:* Wagner; Selected Letters of Richard Wagner; Wagner Compendium; Wagner in Performance; Reviews Editor BBC Music Magazine; Wagners Ring of the Nibelung: a Companion. *Contributions to:* Times; Opera. *Membership:* Critics Circle. *Address:* 55 Cobbold Road, London, NW10 9SU, England.

MILLS Barbara Kleban, b. 20 Jan, Manchester, England. m. Eugene Kleban, 10 Feb 1951, (div 1979). *Appointments:* Editorial Assistant, Business Week, 1953-56; Letters Correspondent, 1956-60; Business Reporter, 1961-70, Time; Features Editor, Playboy, 1970-77; Correspondent, People Weekly, 1977-. *Address:* 1200 N. Lake Shore Drive, Chicago, IL 60610, USA.

MILLS Claudia, b. 21 Aug 1954, New York City, USA. Writer. m. Richard W Wahl, 19 Oct 1985, 2 sons. *Education:* BA, Philosophy, Wellesley College, 1976; MA, Philosophy, Princeton University, 1979; PhD, Philosophy, Princeton University, 1991. *Publications:* Luisa's American Dream, 1981; At the Back of the Woods, 1982; The Secret Carousel, 1983; All the Living, 1983; Boardwalk with Hotel, 1985; The One and Only Cynthia Jane Thornton, 1986; Melanie Magpie, 1987; Cally's Enterprise, 1988; After Fifth Grade, the World!, 1989; Dynamite Dinah, 1990; Hannah on Her Way, 1991; Dinah for President, 1992; A Visit to Amy-Claire, 1992; Dinah in Love, 1993. *Memberships:* Authors Guild; Washington Children's Book Guild, President 1986-87; Society of Children's Book Writers. *Address:* 2575 Briarwood Drive, Boulder, Co 80303, USA.

MILLS Ralph Joseph Jr, b. 16 Dec 1931. University Professor of English. m. 25 Nov 1959, 1 son, 2 daughters. *Education:* BA, English, Lake Forest College, 1954; MA, English, 1956, PhD, English, 1963, Northwestern University. *Appointments:* Teaching: Northwestern University, 1957-59; University of Chicago, 1959-65; University of Illinois at Chicago, 1965-. *Publications:* Criticism: Theodore Roethke, 1963; Contemporary American Poetry, 1965; Edith Sitwell, 1966; Kathleen Raine, 1967; Poetry: Living with Distance, 1979; March Light, 1983; Each Branch: Poems 1976-85, 1986; A While, 1989; A Window in Air, 1993; Edited: Selected Letters of Theodore Roethke, 1968. *Contributions to:* Accent; Boundary 2; New York Times Book Review; Poetry; New Letters; Kayak; Tar River Poetry; The Nation; New England Review; Mississippi Valley Review. *Honours:* English Speaking Union Fellowship, 1956-57; Poetry Prize, Society of Midland Authors, 1979; Carl Sandburg Prize for Poetry, 1983-84. *Address:* 1451 North Astor Street, Chicago, IL 60610, USA.

MILNE Christopher Robin, b. 21 Aug 1920, London, England. Author. m. Lesley Elizabeth De Selincourt, 25 July 1948, 1 daughter. *Education:* BA, Honours, Trinity College, Cambridge. *Appointments:* Bookseller, 1951-76; Writer, 1976-. *Publications:* The Enchanted Places, 1974; The Path through the Trees, 1979; The Hollow on the Hill, 1982; The Windfall, 1985; The Open Garden, 1988. *Membership:* Fellow, Royal Society of Arts. *Address:* Embridge Forge, Dartmouth, Devon, England.

MILNE W(illiam) Gordon, b. 1921, American. *Appointments:* Joined faculty 1951, Professor of English 1964-, Chairman, Department of English 1964-75, Chairman of American Studies 1976-, Lake Forest College, IL. *Publications:* George William Curtis and the Genteel Tradition, 1956; The American Political Novel, 1966; The Sense of Society: A History of the American

Novel of Manners, 1977; Stephen Crane at Brede: An Anglo-American Literary Circle of the 1890's, 1980; Ports of Call: A Study of the American Nautical Novel, 1986. *Address:* Box 273, Rye Beach, NH 03871, USA.

MILOSZ Czeslaw, b. 30 June 1911, Lithuania, naturalised US Citizen, 1970. Poet; Author; Professor. *Education:* University of Wilno, Mjuris, 1934. *Publications:* Poemat o czasie zastyglym, 1933; Trzy zimy, 1936; Ocalenie, 1945; Zniewolony umysl, 1953; Zdobycie wladzy, 1953; Dolina Issy, 1955; Traktat poetycki, 1957; Rodzinna Europa, 1958; Postwar Polish Poetry, 1965; Widzenia nad Zatoka San Francisco, 1969; The History of Polish Literature, 1970; Prywatne obowiazki, 1972; Selected Poems, 1973; Ziemia Ulro, 1977; Emperor of the Earth, 1977; Bells in winter, 1978; Hymn o perle, 1982; Visions from san Francisco Bay, 1983; The Witness of Poetry, 1983; Separate Notebooks, 1984; The Land of Ulro, 1985; Nieobjeta Ziema, 1986; Unattainable Earth, 1987; Kroniki, 1987; Collected Poems, 1988; Provinces, 1991. *Honours:* Prix Littératire Europèen, 1953; Neustadt International Prize for Literature, 1978; Nobel Prize in Literature, 1980; National Medal of Arts, 1989. *Memberships:* American Academy and Institute of Arts and Letters. *Address:* Dept. of Slavic Languages and Literatures, 5416 Dwinelle Hall, University of California, Berkeley, CA 94720, USA.

MILSTED David, b. 5 Jan 1954, Sussex, England. Writer. m. (2) Janet Holt, 1 Dec 1984, 4 sons. *Education:* University of Newcastle Upon Tyne, 1976. *Publications:* Chronicles of Craigfieth; Market Forces; Telling Stories. *Contributions to:* The Guardian. *Membership:* Society of Authors. *Address:* Keston, Newbury, Gillingham, Dorset SP8 4HZ.

MILWARD Alan Steele, b. 19 Jan 1935, Stoke-on-Trent, England. University Teacher. *Education:* BA 1956, PhD 1960, London University. *Publications include:* War, Economy and Society 1939-1945, 1979; The Reconstruction of Western Europe, 1945-1951, 1984; The Economic and Social Effects of the Two World Wars on Britain, 1971, 1984; The German Economy at War, 1965; The New Order and the French Economy, 1970; The Fascist Economy in Norway, 1972; The European Rescue of the Nation-State, 1992. *Contributions to:* History and Economics journals, Times Literary Supplement, London Review of Books. *Honours:* Honorary MA, Manchester University, 1976; FBA 1987. *Memberships:* Economic History Society; Economic History Association; German History Society; University Association for Contemporary European Studies (former President); British Academy. *Address:* Department of Economic History, London School of Economics, Houghton Street, London WC2A 2AE, England.

MINARIK Else H(olmelund), b. 1920, American (born Danish). *Publications:* Little Bear, 1957; No Fighting, No Biting!, 1958; Father Bear Comes Home, 1959; Cat and Dog, Little Bear's Friend, 1960; Little Bear's Visit, 1961; Little Giant Girl and the Elf Boy, 1963; The Winds That Come from Far Away and Other Poems, 1964; A Kiss for Little Bear, My Grandpa Is a Pirate, by Jan Loof (trans), 1968; What If!, 1987; It's Spring!, 1989; Percy and The Five Houses, 1989; The Little Girl and The Dragon, 1991; Am I Beautiful?, 1992. *Memberships:* PEN Club; Authors Guild. *Address:* c/o Green Willow Books, 1350 Avenue of the Americas, New York, NY 10016, USA.

MINARIK John Paul, b. 6 Nov 1947, McKeesport, Pennsylvania, USA. Engineer; Poet. *Education:* BS, Mechnical Engineering, Carnegie Mellon University, 1970; BA, magna cum laude, English & Psychology, University of Pittsburgh, 1978. *Appointments include:* Editor, Academy of Prison Arts, 1973-. *Publications:* A Book, 1974, 1977; Patterns in the Dusk, 1977; Past the Unknown, Remembered Gate, 1980; Editor, Kicking Their Heels with Freedom, 1980; Advisory Editor, Light from Another Country: Poetry from American Prisons, 1984. *Contributions include:* Bulletin, Poetry Society of

America; New Orleans Review; Prison Writing Review; Journal of Popular Culture; Small Pond; Interstate; Backspace; Gravide; Joint Conference; Nitty Gritty. *Honour:* Honorable mention, International PEN, 1976-77. *Address:* PO Box 99901, Pittsburgh, Pennsylvania 15233, USA.

MINEAR Richard H, b. 31 Dec 1938, Illinois, USA. Historian. m. Edith Christian, 1962. 2 sons. *Education:* BA, Yale University, 1960; MA 1962, PhD 1968, Harvard University. *Appointments:* Assistant Professor of History, Ohio State University, 1967-70; Associate Professor of History, University of Massachusetts at Amherst, 1970-; Professor of History, University of Massachusetts at Amherst, 1975-. *Publications:* Hiroshima: Three Witnesses (editor & translator), 1990; Requiem for Battleship Yamato (editor & translator), 1985; Through Japanese Eyes, 1974 and later editions; Victors' Justice, 1971; Japanese Tradition and Western Law, 1970. *Contributions to:* Numerous magazines and journals. *Membership:* Association for Asian Studies. *Address:* History Department, University of Massachusetts, Amherst, MA 01003, USA.

MINER Earl Roy, b. 21 Feb 1927, Wisconsin, USA. Professor of English and Comparative Literature. m. Virginia Lane, 15 July 1950, 1 son, 1 daughter. *Education:* BA, 1949; MA, 1955; PhD, University of Minnisota. *Publications include:* The Japanese Tradition in British and American Literature, 1958; Japanese Court Poetry (with R.H. Brower), 1961; Dryden's Poetry, 1967; Comparative Poetics, 1992. *Contributions to:* Professional journals. *Honours:* Fulbright Lectureships, 1960-61, 1966-67, 1985; American Council of Learned Societies, Fellow, 1963; Guggenheim Fellow, 1977-78; Yamagato Banto Prize, 1988; Kizumi Yakomu Prize, 1991; Howard T. Behrman Prize, 1993. *Memberships:* American Society for 18th Century Studies, former President; Milton Society of America, former President; International Comparative Literature Association, President 1988-91; Association for Asian Studies; Renaissance Society of America. *Address:* 22 McCosh, Princeton University, Princeton, NJ 08544, USA.

MINGAY Gordon Edmund, b. 20 June 1923, Long Eaton, Derbyshire, England. Emeritus Professor. m. Mavis Tippen, 20 Jan 1945. *Education:* BA, 1st class, 1952, PhD 1958, University of Nottingham. *Appointment:* Editor, the Agricultural History Review, 1972-84. *Publications:* English Landed Society in the Eighteenth Century, 1963; the Agricultural Revolution 1750-1880 (with J D Chambers), 1966; Britain and America: a study of economic change 1850-1939 (with P S Bagwell), 1970; The Gentry, 1976; Rural Life in Victorian England, 1976; The Victorian Countryside, 1981; Enclosure and the Small Farmer in the Age of the Industrial Revolution, 1968; Arthur Young and his Times, 1975; The Transformation of Britain 1830-1939, 1985; The Agrarian History of England and Wales, Volume VI (edited), 1989. *Contributions to:* The Economic History Review; The Agriculture History Review; Agricultural History. *Honour:* FRHS, 1968. *Memberships* Head, British Agricultural History Society, Editor 1972-84, President 1987-89; Economic History Society. *Address:* Mill Field House, Selling Court, Selling, Faversham, Kent ME13 9RJ, England.

MINHINNICK Robert, b. 1952, British. *Appointments:* Has worked as a Clerk; Postman; Salvage Worker; Teacher; Co-ordinator of Friends of the Earth, Wales. *Publications:* A Thread in the Maze, 1978; Native Ground, 1979; Life Sentences, 1983; The Dinosaur Park, 1985; The Looters, 1989. *Address:* 11 Park Avenue, Porthcawl, Mid- Glamorgan, Wales.

MINO Carlos Felix, b. 2 Feb 1932, Peru. Journalist and Writer. m. Laura, 3 daughters. *Education:* Journalist, 1966. *Publications:* Books of Short Stories: Escoba al Reves, 1960; Relatos Esobianos, 1974. As well as essays and articles. *Contributions:* El Comercio, Lima; Veriedades, La Cronica; Lima. *Memberships:* The National Writer's Club; Instituto Literario y Cultural

Hispanico; The Translators' Guild. *Literary Agent:* Daniel P King. *Address:* 22276 Caminito Mescalero, Laguna Hills, CA 92653, USA.

MINOGUE Valerie Pearson, b. 26 Apr 1931, Llanelli, South Wales. Research Professor. m. Kenneth Robert Minogue, 16 June 1954, 1 son, 1 daughter. *Education:* BA, Girton College, Cambridge, 1952; M Litt, 1956. *Appointments:* Assistant Lecturer, University College Cardiff, 1952-53; Contributor, Cambridge Italian Dictionary, 1956-61; Lecturer, Queen Mary College, London, 1962-81; Professor, University College Swansea, 1981- 88; Research Professor, 1988-. *Publications:* Nathalie Sarraute: The War of the Words; Proust: Du Coté de chez Swann; Zola: L'Assommoir; Romance Studies. *Contributions to:* Quadrant; The Literary Review; Modern Language Review; French Studies; Romance Studies; Forum for Modern Language Studies. *Memberships:* Association of University Professors of French; Modern Humanities Research Association; Society for French Studies; Romance Studies Institute. *Address:* 92 Eaton Crescent, Swansea, West Glamorgan SA1 4QP, Wales.

MINOT Susan Anderson, b. 7 Dec 1956, Botson, Massachusetts, USA. Writer. m. Davis McHenry, 30 Apr 1988. *Education:* BA (Writing), Brown University, 1978; MFA (Fiction Writing), Columbia University, 1983. *Publications:* Monkeys, 1986; Lust & Other Stories, 1989. *Contributions to:* The New Yorker; Grand Street; The Paris Review; Mademoiselle; Harper's; GQ; New England Monthly; Conde Nast's Traveler. *Honour:* Prix Femina Etranger, 1987. *Literary Agent:* Georges Borchardt. *Address:* c/o Georges Borchardt, 136 E 57th, New York City, NY 10021, USA.

MINTER David Lee, b. 1935, American. *Appointments:* Universitatslektor, University of Hamburg, 1965-66; Lecturer, Yale University, New Havem CT, 1966-67; Assistant Professor 1967-69, Associate Professor 1969-74, Professor of English 1974-80, Rice University, Houston; Professor of English, Dean of Emory College and Vice-President for Arts and Sciences, Emory University, Atlanta, 1981-90; Professor of English, Rice University, Houston, 1991-. *Publications:* The Interpreted Design as a Structural Principle in American Prose, Twentieth Century Interpretations of Light in August (ed), 1969; William Faulkner: His Life and Work, 1980; The Harper American Literature (co-ed), 1986; The Norton Critical Edition of The Sound and the Fury (ed), The Columbia Literary History of the United States (co-ed), 1987; Forthcoming: Heirs of Changing Promise: A Cultural History of the American Novel, 1840-1940, 1994. *Address:* Department of English, Rice University, PO Box 1892, Houston, TX 77251, USA.

MINTZ Samuel I(saiah), b. 1923, United States of America. Writer. *Publications:* The Hunting of Leviathan: Thomas Hobbes in the Seventeenth Century, 1962; From Smollett to James, 1981. *Address:* Department of English, City College of New York, New York, NY 10031, USA.

MIRABELLI Eugene, Jr., b. 1931, United States of America. Author. *Publications:* The Burning Air, 1959; The Way In, 1968; No Resting Place, 1972; The World at Noon, 1993. *Address:* 29 Bennett Terrace, Delmar, NY 12054, USA.

MIRENBURG Barry L, b. 1952, United States of America. *Appointments:* Book Publisher, Barlenmir House Publishers, New York City, 1970-; President, Barlenmir House of Graphics, 1970-; Barlenmir House of Music, Barlenmir House Foundation on the Arts, 1972-; Barlenmir House Theatres Inc., 1974-; Advisory Board, East Coast Writers. *Publications:* Barlenmir House Anthology (poetry and short stories); The Joy of Living. *Address:* 413 City Island Avenue, New York, NY 10064, USA.

MIRVISH Robert F, b. 17 July 1921, Washington DC, USA. Author. m. 1 June 1963, 2 sons. *Education: (*University of Toronto, 1947. *Publications:* A House of Her Own, 1953; The Eternal Voyagers, 1953; Texana, 1954; The Long Watch, 1954; Red Sky at Midnight, 1955; Woman in a Room, 1959; Two Women, Two Worlds, 1960; Dust on the Sea, 1960; Point of Impact, 1961; Cleared Narvik 2000, 1962; The Last Capitalist, 1963; Business is People, 1963; There You Are, But Where Are You?, 1964; Holy Loch, 1964; Radio Scripts; magazine short stories. *Membership;* Author's Guild of America. *Address:* 110 Bloor Street West No 605, Toronto, Ontario, Canada M5S 2W7.

MIRZA Mohd Z Ahan Azurdah, b. 17 Mar 1945, India. Teacher. m. Haleema Begum, 3 Oct 1963, 2 sons, 1 daughter. *Education:* MA, Urdu, 1970; B.Ed., 1971; PhD, 1977. *Publications:* Mirza Salamet Ali Debeer, 1981, 1985; Ghubar Kalwan, 1984; Essay, 1983; Thorns & Thistles, 1986; Sheereen Ke Khatoot, 1974; Ghubari Khayal, 1973; Fibori Hing Tibrir, 1980, 1981; Ratan Nath Sarshar, 1987; Kante, 1975. *Contributions to:* Indian Literature; Enquiry; many other professional journals. *Honours:* WP, 1981, 1985, AP, 1981, WB, 1981, urdu Academy; National Academy of Letters 1984. *Memberships Include:* General Secretary, Brazni Iqbal Kind.; Vice President, Kaharrin Cultural League; ChairMan, Haghmin Council of Historical and Cultural Research. *Address:* Hasanabad Rainawari, Srinagar, Kashmir, India 190003.

MISHAN E J b. 1917. Writer. *Publications:* The Cost of Economic Growth, 1967; Twenty-one Economic Fallacies, 1969; Cost Benefit Analysis, 1971; Making the World Safe for Pornography, 1973; The Economic Growth Debate, 1977; An Introduction to Normative Economics, 1980; Economic Efficiency and Social Welfare, 1980; Pornography, Psychedelics and Technology, 1981; Introduction to Political Economy, 1982; Economic Myths and the Mythology of Economics, 1986.

MISHLER William Thomas Earle, b. 14 Oct 1947, USA. Political Science Professor. m. Catherine Tenner, 5 Aug 1972. *Education:* BA, Stetson University, 1969; MA, Duke University, 1971; PhD, 1973. *Appointments:* Duke University, 1972-78; University of Strathelyde, 1976-77; State University of NY, 1978-86; University of South Carolina, 1986-. *Publications:* Influence in Parliement; Political Participation in Canada; Representative Democracy in the Canadian Provinces; Resurgence of Conservatism in Angloa American Democracies; Controvesies in Political Economy. *Honours:* Phi Beta Kappa; Woodrow Wilson Fellow; James B Duke Fellow. *Memberships:* American Political Science Association; Southern Political Science Association. *Address:* Department of Government, University of South Carolina, Columbia SC 29208, USA.

MISS Read. *See:* **SAINT Dora.**

MITCHAM Hank. *See:* **NEWTON Dwight Bennett.**

MITCHELL Adrian, b. 24 Oct 1932, London, England. Writer. *Education:* Christ Church, Oxford. *Appointments:* Granada Fellow, University of Lancaster, 1968-69; Fellow, Centre for the Humanities, Wesleyan University, 1972; Resident Writer, Sherman Theatre, Cardiff, 1974-75; Visiting Writer, Billericay Comprehensive School, 1978-80; Judith Wilson Fellow, Cambridge University, 1980-81; Resident Writer, Unicorn Theatre for Children, 1982-83. *Publications:* Tyger, 1971; Man Friday, 7:84, 1973; For Beauty Douglas; On the Beach at Cambridge, 1984; Nothingmas Day, 1984; The Pied Piper, 1986; Adaptations, various works including: Peer Gynt, 1980; Novels; Strawberry Drums, 1989; TV plays. *Contributions include:* Oxford Mail; London Magazine; Times Literary Supplement; Observer; New Yorker; Peace News Tribune; New Statesman; Sunday Times; Daily Mail; Evening Standard; Sanity. *Memberships;* Theatre Writers Union. *Agent:* The Peter Fraser &

Dunlop Group Ltd. *Address:* c/o The Peter Fraser and Dunlop Group Ltd, 5th Floor, The Chambers, Chelsea Harbour, Lots Road, London SW10 0XF, England.

MITCHELL David John, b. 24 Jan 1924, London, England. Freelance Writer. m. 1955, 1 son. *Education:* Bradfield College, Berkshire; Trinity College, Oxford, 1944-47; MA (Hons), Modern History. *Appointments:* Staff Writer, Picture Post, 1947-52. *Publications:* Women on the Warpath, 1966, as Monstrous Regiment, USA; The Fighting Pankhursts, 1967; 1919 Red Mirage, 1970, translated as L'Annata Rossa dell'Europa, Italy, 1972; Pirates, 1976; Queen Christabel, 1977; The Jesuits: A History, 1980; The Spanish Civil War, 1982; Travellers in Spain, 1990, translated as Viajeros por Espana. *Contributions to:* Articles and reviews to: Times; Times Literary Supplement; New Statesman; New Society; Guardian; Daily Telegraph; London Magazine; History Today. *Honours:* US Literary Guild Alternate Choice for Pirates, 1976; UK Historical Guild Selection for Pirates, 1976. *Memberships:* Society of Authors. *Address:* 20 Mountacre Close, Sydenham Hill, London SE26 6SX, England.

MITCHELL (Sibyl) Elyne Keith, b. 30 Dec 1913, Melbourne, Australia. Author; Grazier. m. Thomas Walter Mitchell, 4 Nov 1935, deceased. 2 sons (1 dec), 1 daughter. *Publications:* Australia's Alps, 1942; Silver Brumby Series (for children), 1958-1977; Light Horse, the Story of Australia's Mounted Troops, 1978; Discoverers of the Snowy Mountains, 1985; A Vision of the Snowy Mountains, 1988; Towong Hill, Fifty years on an Upper Murray Cattle Station, 1989; Speak to the Earth, 1945; Chauvel Country, 1983; Light Horse to Damascus, 1971; The Snowy Mountains, 1980; Kingfisher Feather (children), 1962; Winged Skis (children), 1964; Colt from Snowy River series, 1979-81; Flow River, Blow Wind, 1953; Soil & Civilization, 1946. *Contributions to:* Quadrant; Poetry Australia; The Canberra Times; The Age; The Australian. *Honours:* Children's Book Week Award: Silver Brumby, Highly Commended, Winged Skis and Silver Brumby's Daughter, Commended; Order of Australia Medal, 1990. *Membership:* Australian Society of Authors. *Literary Agent:* Curtis Brown Ltd. *Address:* Towong Hill, Corryong, Victoria 3707, Australia.

MITCHELL Geoffrey Duncan, British. *Appointments:* Senior Research Worker, University of Liverpool, 1950-52; Lecturer in Sociology, University of Birmingham, 1952-54; Lecturer and Senior Lecturer 1954-67, Professor 1967-86, Emeritus Professor of Sociology and Research Fellow, Institute of Population Studies, University of Exeter. *Publications:* Neighbourhood and Community (with T Lupton, M W Hodges and C S Smith), 1954; Sociology: The Study of Social Systems, 1959, 1972; A Dictionary of Sociology (ed and contributor), A Hundred Years of Sociology, 1968; A New Dictionary of Sociology (ed and contributor), 1979; The Artificial Family (with R Snowden), 1981; Artificial Reproduction (with R and E Snowden), 1983. *Contributions to:* New Scientist; Journal of Medical Ethics; Sociological Review. *Honours:* MBE, 1946; OBE, 1984. *Address:* 26 West Avenue, Exeter, Devon, England.

MITCHELL Ian. *See:* **MITCHELL John MacKinnon.**

MITCHELL Jerome, b. 7 Oct 1935, Chattanooga, Tennessee, USA. University Lecturer. *Education:* BA, Emory University, 1957; MA, 1959, PhD, 1965, Duke University. *Appointments:* Assistant Professor, University of Illinois, 1965-67; Associate Professor, 1967-72, Professor, 1972-, University of Georgia; Fulbright Guest Professor, University of Bonn, 1972-73; Visiting Exchange Professor, University of Erlangen, summer semester, 1975; Richard Merton Guest Professor, University of Regensburg, 1978-79. *Publications:* Thomas Hoccleve: A Study in Early 15th Century English Poetic, 1968; The Walter Scott Operas, 1977; Scott, Chaucer, and Medieval Romance, 1987; Hoccleve's Works: The Minor Poems, revised with A I Doyle, 1970; Chaucer, The Love Poet, Editor with

William Provost, 1973. *Contributions to:* various scholarly journals. *Memberships:* South Atlantic Modern Language Association, Associate Editor, South Atlantic Bulletin, 1970-76; Gesellschaft für Englische Romantik; Edinburgh Sir Walter Scott Club. *Address:* English Dept, University of Georgia, Athens, GA 30602, USA.

MITCHELL John MacKinnon, (Ian Mitchell), b. 4 Apr 1935, Ayr, Scotland. Freelance Translator. m. Mary E A Neilson, 9 Aug 1961, 2 sons. *Education:* MA Hons, French and German, Glasgow University, 1958; Secondary Teacher's Diploma, Jordanhill College of Education, Glasgow, 1959; MEd (TEFL), Manchester University, 1980. *Publications:* Translations: Erich Loest: The Monument, 1987; Schottland-ein Reisebuch, 1988 (Co-editor and contributor); Veza Canetti: Yellow Street, 1990; Herbert Rosendorfer: The Night of the Amazons, 1992; Thomas Strittmatter: Raven, 1993; Hanns Werner Schwarze: The GDR Today, 1973. *Contributions to:* GDR Monitor, 1984 and 1987; East Central Europe; VDI Nachrichten Magazin; Esquire (German). *Memberships:* Society of Authors; Translator's Association. *Address:* 76 South Mains Road, Milngavie, Glasgow G62 6DG, Scotland.

MITCHELL (Charles) Julian, b. 1935, United Kingdom. Author. *Appointments:* Midshipman, Royal Naval Volunteer Reserve, 1953-55. *Publications:* Imaginary Toys, 1961; A Disturbing Influence, 1962; As Far as You Can Go, 1963; The White Father, 1964; A Heritage and Its History (adapter), 1965; A Circle of Friends, 1966; The Undiscovered Country, 1968; Jennie Lady Randolph Churchill: A Portrait with Letters (with Peregrine Churchill), 1974; A Family and a Fortune (adpater), 1974; Half-Life, play, 1977; The Enemy Within, play, 1980; Another Country, play, 1982, film, 1984; Francis, play, 1983; After Aida, play, 1985. *Contributions to:* Welsh History Review, The Monmouthshire Anti Quary. *Literary Agent:* The Peters, Fraser & Dunlop Group Ltd. *Address:* The Peeters Fraser and Dunlop Group Ltd, The Chambers, Chelsea Harbour, Lots Road, London SW10 0XF, England.

MITCHELL Juliet, b. 1940, New Zealand. Full-time Psycho-Analyst; Freelance Writer; Broadcaster and Lecturer. *Appointments:* Lecturer in English, University of Leeds, England, 1962-63; Lecturer in English, University of Reading, 1965-70; Luce Lecturer, Yale University, 1984-85. *Publications include:* Women: The Longest Revolution, 1966; Woman's Estate, 1972; Psycho-Analysis and Feminism, 1974; Rights and Wrongs of Women (co-editor), 1977; Feminine Sexuality (co-editor), 1982; Women: The Longest Revolution, 1983; What Is Feminism (co-editor), 1986; The Selected Writings of Melanie Klein, 1986. *Literary Agent:* Deborah Rogers. *Address:* c/o Deborah Rogers, 20 Powis Mews, London W11 IJN, England.

MITCHELL K L. *See:* **LAMB Elizabeth Searle.**

MITCHELL Margaretta Meyer Kuhlthau, b. 27 May 1935, Brooklyn, New York, USA. Photographer. m. 23 May 1959, 3 daughters. *Education:* BA, Smith College, 1957; MA University of Callifornia, 1985. *Appointments:* Teacher: Academy of Art, San Francisco, 1990-93; University of California Ext. Program, 1976-78; City College 1980; Civic Arts, Walnut Creek 1980-84; Carleton College, Visiting Professor 1988, RISD 1983, CCAC 1984, University of California, Berkeley, 1986, Academy of Art, 1990. *Publications include:* Recollections: Ten Women of Photography, 1979; To a Cabin 1973; Gift of Place, 1969; Introduction to After Ninety by Imogen Cunningham, 1977; Dance For Life, 1985; Flowers, 1991. *Contributions to:* Ramparts; Vermont Life; Camera Arts. *Honour:* Phi Beta Kappa, Alpha Award, 1957. *Memberships:* American Society of Media Photographers, President 1990-92; Institute for Historical Study. *Address:* 280 Hillcrest Road, Berkeley CA 94705, USA.

MITCHELL Michael Robin, b. 10 Apr 1941, Rochdale, Lancashire. University Lecturer. m. Jane Speakman, 3 Jan 1970. 3 sons. *Education:* MA, 1960-64, BLitt, 1966-68, Lincoln College, Oxford. *Publications:* Translator: Gyorgy Sebestyen: The Works of Solitude, 1991; Gustav Meyrink: The Angel of the West WIndow, 1991; Meyrink: The Green Face, 1992; Herbert Rosendorfer: The Architect of Ruins, 1992; The Dedalus Book of Austrian Fantasy (Editor and translator), 1992. Peter Hacks: Theatre for a Socialist Society, 1991, (author); Harrap's German Grammar, 1989, (co-author). *Address:* 4 Mount Hope, Bridge of Allan, Stirling, Scotland.

MITCHELL Roger, b. 8 Feb 1935, Boston, Massachusetts, USA. Poet; Teacher. 2 daughters. *Education:* AB, Harvard College, 1957; MA, University of Colorado, 1961; PhD, Manchester University, England, 1963. *Appointments:* Editor, The Minnesota Review, 1973-81; Director, Indiana University Writers' Conference, 1975-85; Director, Creative Writing Program, Indiana University, 1978-. *Publications:* Letters From Siberia & Other Poems, 1971; Poems: Moving, 1976; A Clear Space On A Cold Day, 1986; Adirondack, 1988. Non-fiction: Clear Pond, 1991. *Contributions to:* Poetry; Poetry Northwest; Triquarterly; Ploughshares; New Republic; Times Literary Supplement; Poetry East; Massachusetts Review. *Honours:* Abby M Copps Award, 1971; Midland Poetry Award, 1972; Borestone Mountain Award, 1973; PEN Award, 1977; Arvon Foundation Award, 1985, 1987; NEA Creative Writing Fellowship, 1986; Chester H Jones Award, 1987. *Membership:* Associated Writing Programs. *Address:* 1010 E First Street, Bloomington, IN 47401, USA.

MITCHELL W(illiam) O(rmond), b. 1914, Canada. Author. *Publications:* Who Has Seen The Wind, 1947; The Alien, 1954; Jake and The Kid, 1961; The Kite, 1962; The Black Bonspiel of Wullie MacCrimmon, 1965, play, 1966; The Vanishing Point, 1973; Back to Beulah, play, 1976; How I Spent My Summer Holidays, 1981; The Dramatic W O Mitchell, plays, 1982; Since Daisy Creek, 1984. *Address:* 3031 Roxboro Glen Road, Calgary, Alberta, Canada.

MITCHELL William John Thomas, b. 24 Mar 1942, Anaheim, California, USA. College Professor; Editor. m. Janice Misurell, 11 Aug 1968. 1 son, 1 daughter. *Education:* BA, Michigan State University, 1963; MA, PhD 1968, Johns Hopkins University. *Appointment:* Editor, Critical Inquiry, 1979-. *Publications:* Iconology, 1986; Blake's Composite Art, 1977; The Language of Images, 1980; The Politics of Interpretation, 1983; Picture Theory, 1994; Landscape amd Power, 1993; Art and The Public Sphere, 1993. *Contributions to:* Times Literary Supplement; London Review of Books; Raritan Review; Salmagundi; After Image; New Literary History; Representations. *Honours:* American Philosophical Society Essay Prize, 1968; National Endowment for the Humanities Fellowship, 1978, 1986; Guggenheim Fellow, 1983. *Memberships:* Modern Language Association; PEN; Academy of Literary Studies. *Address:* English Dept, University of Chicago, 1050 E 59th Street, Chicago, IL 60637, USA.

MITCHELL-HAYES Minnie Marie, b. 30 Nov 1948, Chicago, USA. Formerly Journalist; Copy Writer; PR Writer, Political Campaign Worker. m. James E Hayes, 12 July 1969. 2 sons. *Education:* BAS, University of Illinois; MFA, Vermont College, 1991; Residency Fellow at Ragdale, Lake Forest, Illinois. *Literary Appointment:* Co-Editor, Story Quarterly No 20, 1985. *Contributions to:* 2 Plus 2, 1987; North American Review, 1986; Ball State University's Forum; The Connecticut Writer, 1987; Other Voices (forthcoming); Novel in progress; Global Tapestry, 1987; Prospice, 1987; Green Feather, 1987; Hawaii Review, 1987; High Plains Quarterly Review, 1988; Listed one of 25 Dist Stories of 1988, Best of the Rest 3, 1989; Gallery Magazine, 1991; Whetstone Magazine, 1991. *Honours:* 2nd Prize, Redbook Magazine, 1986; Honourable Mentions: Writers Digest, 1986, 1987, 1990; National Writers Club, 1986; Manuscripts International, 1987; Science

Writers of the Future Contest, 1987; Best of the Rest 3, one of 25 Distinguishing Stories of 1989. *Memberships:* Poets & Writers; The Writers, Vice-President 1989-92; PEN, Midwest Associate; Off Campus Writers Workshop. *Literary Agent:* Philip G Spitzer. *Address:* 431 Sheridan Road, Kenilworth, Ill 60043, USA.

MITCHISON Naomi, b. 1 Nov 1897, Edinburgh, Scotland. Novelist; Farmer. m. Gilbert Richard Mitchison, 1916, 3 sons, 2 daughters. *Publications:* The Conquered, 1923; When the Bough Breaks, 1924; Cloud Cuckoo Land, 1925; Black Sparta, 1928; Anna Comnena, 1928; Nix-Nought-Nothing, 1928; Barbarian Stories, 1929; The Corn King and the Spring Queen, 1931; The Delicate Fire, 1932; We Have Been Warned, 1935; The Fourth Pig, 1936; Socrates (with R.H.S. Crossman), 1937; Moral Basis of Politics, 1938; The Kingdom of Heaven, 1939; As it Was in the Beginning (with L.E. Gielgud), 1939; The Blood of the Martyrs, 1939; Among You Taking Notes, 1945; Re-Educating Scotland, 1945; The Bull Calves, 1947; Men and Herring (with D. Macintosh), 1949; The Big House 1950; Lobsters on the Agenda, 1952; Travel Light, 1952; Swan's Road, 1954; Graeme and the Dragon, 1954; Land the Ravens Found, 1955; Chapel Perilous, 1955; Little Boxes, 1956; Behold Your King, The Far Harbour, 1957; Other People's Worlds, Five Men and a Swan, 1958; Judy and Lakshmi, 1959; Rib of the Green Umbrella, 1960; The Young Alexander, 1960; Karensgaard 1961; memoirs of a Spacewoman, 1962; The Fairy Who Couldn't Tell a lie, 1963; When We Became Men, 1964; Return to the Fairy Hill, 1966; Friends and Enemies, 1966; African Heroes, 1968; The Famiy at Ditlabeng, 1969; The Africans: A History, 1970; Sun and Moon, 1970; Cleopatra's People, 1972; A Danish Teapot, 1973; A Life for Africa, 1973; Sunrise Tomorrow, 1973; Small Talk (autobiography), 1973; All Change Here 1975; Solution Three, 1975; Snake!, 1976; The Two Magicians, 1979; The Knife and other poems, 1979; You May Well Ask : A Memoir 1920-40, 1979; Images of Africa, 1980; The Vegetable War, 1980; Mucking Around, 1981; What Do You Think Yourself?, 1982; Not By Bread Alone, 1983; Among You Taking Notes, 1985; Early in Orcadia, 1987; A Girl Must live, 1990; Sea-Green Ribbons, 1991; The Oathtakers, 1991. *Honours:* CBE, 1985; Member, Bakgatla Tribe S.E. Botswana; Hon. D.Litt., Strathclyde 1983, Stirling, Dundee. *Address:* Carradale House, Carradale, Campbeltown, Scotland.

MITCHISON Rosalind Mary, b. 11 Apr 1914, Manchester, England. m. 21 June 1947, 1 son, 3 daughters. *Education:* Oxford University, 1938- 42; MA 1945. *Publications:* A History of Scotland, 2nd edition, 1982; Life in Scotland, 1978; Lordship to Patronage: Scotland 1603-1749, 1989; Sexuality and Social Control: Scotland 1660-1780, (Co-author Leah Leneman), 1989. *Contributions to:* London Review of Books. *Memberships:* Fellow, Royal Historical Society; The Scottish History Society, President, 1981-84. *Address:* Great Yew, Ormiston, East Lothian EH35 5NJ, Scotland.

MITEHAM Hank. *See:* NEWTON Dwight Bennett.

MITFORD Jessica, b. 11 Sept 1917. Writer. m. (1) Esmond Marcus David Romilly, (dec 1941), 1 daughter, (2) Robert Edward Treuhaft, 1 son. *Publications:* Hons and Rebels (autobiography), 1960; The American Way of Death, 1963; The Trial of Dr Spock, 1970; The American Prison Business, 1973; A Fine Old Conflict, 1977; The Making of a Muckraker (essays), 1979; Faces of Philip: A Memoir of Philip Toynbee, 1984; Grace Had an English Heart, The Story of Grace Darling, Heroine and Victorian Superstar, 1988; The American Way of Birth, 1992. *Memberships:* Authors Guild, USA; National Writers Union, USA. *Literary Agent:* Renee Wayne Golden, 8983 Norma Place, West Hollywood, CA 90069, USA. *Address:* 6611 Regent Street, Oakland, CA 94618, USA.

MITSON Eileen Nora, b. 22 Sept 1930, Langley, Essex, England, Housewife; Author. m. Arthur Samuel Mitson, 22 Sept 1951, 2 daughters, (1 dec). *Education:* Cambridge Technical College and School of Art, 1946-47. *Publications:* Beyond the Shadows, 1968; The Inside Room, 1973; Reaching for God, 1978; Creativity, (Co-author), 1985; Amazon Adventure, 1969; A Kind of Freedom, 1976; Author of 2 other adult and 2 children's novels. *Contributions to:* Regular Columnist for Christian Woman Magazine (now Woman Alive), 1982-. *Address:* 39 Oaklands, Hamilton Road, Reading, Berkshire RG1 5RN, England.

MIURA Chizuko, (Ayako Sono), b. 17 Sept 1931, Toyko, Japan. Author. m. Shumon Miura, 19 Oct 1953, 1 son. *Education:* University of Sacred Heart, Bachelor of Arts, 1954. *Appointments:* Mansfield American Pacific Lecture given, Library of Congress, Washington. *Publications:* The Heavenly Blue; Watcher from the Shore; Monuments Withour Inscription; A photograph; The Babies for Whom Time Stopped; The House of Lies; The Tadami River; The Desert, This Gold's Land; The Birth of a Lake; In This World of Grief; The Blessing of the City. *Contributions to:* Shinchosha Magazine; PHP Research Institute Magazine; Shogakukan Magazine. *Honours:* La Croce Pro Ecclesia et Pintifice, The Vatican; Father Damien Award; Civil Engineering Society Writers Award; Shikanai Nobutaka Seiron Prize. *Memberships:* United States Japan Foundation; Bulletin of the pontifical Council for Culture; Canada Japan Forum; Japan Association of Authors; Japan Medical Association; Economic Council of Quality Of Life; Matsushita Institute of Government and Management; Sasakawa Peace Foundation. *Literary Agent:* Ms Machiko Moriyasu, Kodansha Internationa inc. *Address:* 3-5-13, Denechofu, Ohta-Ku, Toyko, Japan.

MO Timothy, b. 1950, Hong Kong. Novelist. *Publications:* The Monkey King, 1978; Sour Sweet, 1982; An Insular Possession, 1986; The Redundancy of Courage, 1991. *Literary Agent:* A P Watt Ltd. *Address:* c/o A P Watt, 20 St John Street, London WC1N 2DL, England.

MOAT John, b. 1936, United Kingdom. Author; Poet. *Publications:* 6d per Annum, 1966; Heorot, novel, 1968; A Standard of Verse, 1969; Thunder of Grass, 1970; The Tugen and the Toot, novel, 1973; The Ballad of the Leat, 1974; Bartonwood, juvenile, 1978; Fiesta and the Fox Reviews His Prophecy, 1979; The Way to Write (with John Fairfax), 1981; Skeleton Key, 1982; Mai's Wedding, novel, 1983; Welcombe Overtures, 1987; The Missing Moon, 1988; Firewater and the Miraculous Mandarin, 1990. *Address:* Crenham Mill, Hartland, N. Devon, EX39 6HN, England.

MODIANO Patrick Jean, b. 30 July 1945. Novelist. m. Dominique Zehrfuss, 1970, 2 daughters. *Publications:* La place de l'etoile, 1968; La ronde de nuit, 1969; Les boulevards de ceinture, 1972; Lacombe Lucien (screenplay), 1973; La polka (play), 1974; Villa triste (novel), 1975; Interrogatoire d'Emmanuel Berl, 1976; Livret de famille (novel), 1977; Rue des boutiques obscures, 1978; Une Jeunesse, 1981; Memory Lane, 1981; De si Braves Garcons (novel), 1982; Poupee blonde, 1983; Quartier perdu, 1985; Dimanches d'Aout, 1986; Une aventure de Choura, 1986; Remise de Peine, 1987; l'enfance, 1989; Voyage de Noies, 1990; Fleurs de Ruine, 1991; Un Cirque Passe, 1992. *Honours:* Prix Roger Nimier, 1968; Prix Goncourt, 1978; Chevalier des Arts et des Lettres. *Address:* c/o Editions Gallimard, 5 rue Sebastien Bottin, 75007 Paris, France.

MOFFAT Gwen, b. 3 July 1924, Brighton, Sussex, England. Author. m. Gordon Moffat, 1948. 1 daughter. *Publications:* Space Below My Feet, 1961; The Corpse Road, 1974; The Buckskin Girl, 1982; The Storm Seekers, 1989; The Stone Hawk, 1989; Rage, 1990; Lady with a Cool Eye, 1973; Deviant Death, 1973; Miss Pink at the Edge of the World, 1975; Over the Sea to Death, 1976; A Short Time to Live, 1976; Persons Unknown, 1978; Die like a Dog, 1982; Last Chance

Country, 1983; Grizzly Trail, 1984; Hard Option, 1975; Two Star Red, 1964; On My Home Ground, 1968; Survival Count, 1972; Hard Road West, 1981; Snare, 1987; The Raptor Zone, 1990; Pit Bull, 1991; Veronica's Sisters, 1992; The Outside Edge, 1993. *Contributions to:* Guardian; Sunday Times; Sunday Telegraph; Sunday Express; Glasgow Herald; Scotsman; Argosy; Good Housekeeping; Homes and Gardens; She; The Lady. *Memberships:* The Society of Authors; The Crime Writers Association; Mystery Writers of America. *Literary Agent:* Gregory and Radice, London. *Address:* c/o Gregory and Radice, Riverside Studios, Crisp Road, Hammersmith, London W6 9RL, England.

MOFFEIT Tony A, b. Claremore, Oklahoma, USA. Poet; Librarian. *Education:* MLS., University of Oklahoma; BS, Psychology, Oklahoma State University, 1964. *Appointments:* Director, Pueblo Poetry Project, 1980-; Poet in Residence, University of Southern Colorado, 1987-88. *Publications:* Pueblo Blues, 1986; Dancing with the Ghosts of the Dead, 1986; Black Cat Bone, 1986; The Spider Who Walked Underground, 1985; Hank Williams Blues, 1985; Coyote Blues, 1985; Shooting Chant, 1984; Outlaw Blues, 1983; La Nortenita, 1983; Luminous Animal, 1989; Boogie Alley, 1989. *Contributions to:* Numerous journals and magazines. *Honours:* Jack Kerouac Award for Pueblo Blues, 1986; President's Research Fellowship, University of Southern Colorado, 1987-88, 1989-90. *Membership:* American Library Association. *Address:* 1501 E. 7th., Pueblo, Colorado 81001, USA.

MOFFETT Judith, b. 1942, USA. Author; Poet; University Educator. *Appointments:* Assistant Professor, Behrend College, Pennsylvania State University, Erie, 1971-75; Visiting Lecturer, Programme in Creative Writing, University of Iowa, Iowa City, 1977-78; Visiting Lecturer, 1978-79, Assistant Professor of English, 1979-, University of Pennsylvania, Philadelphia. *Publications:* Keeping Time, verse, 1976; Gentleman, Single, Refined, and Selected Poems 1937-59, by Hjalmar Gullberg, translation, 1979; Whinny Moor Crossing, verse, 1984; James Merrill: An Introduction to the Poetry, criticism, 1984; Pennterra, science fiction, 1987; The Ragged World, science fiction, 1991; Two That Came True, science fiction, 1991. *Address:* 39 Rabbit Run, Wallingford, PA 19086, USA.

MOHAMED N P, b. 1 July 1929, Calicut, India. Author. m. 27 Nov 1954, 4 sons, 3 daughters. *Education:* Intermediate, Madras University. *Appointments:* Assistant Editor, Kerala Kaumudi, 1987. *Publications:* Thopplyum Thattavum, 1952; Maram, 1959; Hiranya Kashipu, 1976; Abudabi-Dubai, 1978; Ennapadam, 1981; Avar Nalupaer, 1987. *Contributions to:* Various literary journals, periodicals. *Honours:* Madras Government Award, Short Stories, 1959; Kerala Sahitya Academy Award, 1969, 1981. *Memberships:* Kerala Sahitya Academy, Executive Committee; Central Academy of Letters, Advisory Member in Malaysian. *Address:* Suthalam, Calicut-Pin 6730007, Kerala, India.

MOHL Ruth, b. 1891, USA. University Educator (retired). *Appointments:* Associate Professor of English Language and Literature, Brooklyn College, City University of New York, 1942-62. *Publications:* The Three Estates in Medieval and Renaissance Literature, 1933; Studies in Spenser, Milton, and the Theory of Monarchy, 1949; John Milton's Commonplace Book (translator and editor), 1953; John Milton and His Commonplace Book, 1969; Edmund Spenser: His Life and Works, 1987.

MOHLER James Aylward, b. 22 July 1923, Ohio, USA. Professor; Writer; Clergyman. *Education:* LittB, Xavier University, 1946; PhL, 1949; STL, 1956, Jesuit School of Theology of Loyola University; MSIR, Loyola University, 1959; PhD, University of Ottawa, 1964; STD, University of St. Paul, 1966. *Publications* include: Speaking of God, (co-author), 1967; Man Needs God, 1967; Dimension of Faith, 1969; The School of Jesus, 1973; Dimension of Love, 1975; Dimensions of Prayer,

1981; Love, Marriage and the Family, 1982; Paradise, Gardens of the Gods, 1985; Late Have I Loved You, 1991. *Contributions to:* a few articles and book reviews in journals and magazines. *Literary Agent:* Bill Holub. *Address:* Rodman Hall, John Carroll University, Cleveland, Ohio 44118, USA.

MOHR Steffen b. 24 July 1942, Leipzig, Germany. Author. 3 sons 4 daughters. *Education:* Diplomas of Theatre, University of Leipzig and Institute of Literature, Leipzig. *Publications:* At the Beginning of this Travel, 1975; Andy, Set the Fashion, 1975; A Day Full of Music, 1976; Interrogation Withour Order, 1979; Remarkable Causes of Captain Merks, 1980; Flowers from the Heaven-meadow, 1982; Today I'll Kill 10 past 12, 1980; Moritz and the Golden Princess, 1986; Don't Look too Closely, 1989 co-author with Professor Bosetzky of West Berlin, (the first book written by an author of the GDR with an author of the FDR); The Corpse in the Baobab, 1992; Films: Women With and Without (TV film) 1985; Five Minutes to Six (TV film) 1989-90; Radio-drama: Wriggling, 1990; Youth and the dog of the Lord, 1992. *Memberships:* SYNDIKAT, Union of Crime Writers of Federal Republic of Germany; AIEP; Free Society of Literatur (founder and 2nd chairman). *Address:* Liechtensteinstr 35, Leipzig, Germany.

MOHRT Michel, b. 28 Apr 1914, Morlaix, France. Writer; Editor. m. Francoise Jarrier, 1955, 1 son. *Education:* Law School, Rennes. *Appointments:* Lawyer, Marseilles Bar until 1942; Professor, Yale University, 1947-52; Editor, Head of English Translations, Les Editions Gallimard, 1952-. *Publications:* Novels: Le repit; Mon royaume pour un cheval, 1949; Les nomades; Le serviteur fidele; La prison maritime, 1961; La campagne d'Italie, 1965; L'ours des Adirondacks, 1969; Deux Americaines a Paris, 1974; Les moyens du bord, 1975; La guerre civile, 1986; Le Télésieje, 1989. Essays: Motherlant, homme libre, 1943; Le nouveau roman americain, 1956; L'air du large, 1969; Vers l'Ouest, 1988; Benjamin on Lettes sur l'Incorestauce, 1989. Plays: Une jeu d'enfer, 1970 (narration); La maison du pere, 1979; Vers l'Ouest, 1988; Benjammiz on Lettes sur l'Inconstance, 1989; Le Télésieze, 1989; Un Soiz, à Loudres, 1991; Ou Liquðe et ou s'en Va, 1992. *Honours:* Chevalier Legion d'honneur, Croix de guerre; Grand Prix du roman de l'Academie francaise for La Prison Maritime, 1962; Grand Prix de la Criique Litteraire, 1970; Grand prix de Litterature de l'Academie francaise, 1983. *Memberships:* Académic Française, 1985; Garrick club. *Address:* c/o Editions Gallimard, 5 rue Sebastien-Bottin, Paris 75007, France.

MOJTABAI Ann Grace, b. 8 June 1937, New York City, USA. Author; Educator. m. Fathollah Mojtabai, 27 Apr 1960, div 1966, 1 son, 1 daughter. *Education:* BA Philosophy, Antioch College, 1958; MA Philosophy, Columbia University, 1968; MS in LS, Columbia University, 1970. *Appointments:* Lecturer in English, Harvard University, 1978-83; Writer in Residence, University of Tulsa, 1983-. *Publications:* Mundome, 1974; The 400 Eels of Sigmund Freud, 1976; A Stopping Place, 1979; Autumn, 1982; Blessed Assurance, 1986; Ordinary Time, 1989. *Contributions to:* The New York Times Book Review; The New Republic; Philosophy Today; The Philosophical Journal. *Honours:* Radcliffe Institute Fellow, 1976-78; Guggenheim Fellow, 1981-82; Richard and Hinda Rosenthal Award, American Academy and Institute of Arts and Letters, 1983; Academy Award in Literature, The American Academy of Arts and Letters, 1993. *Memberships:* The Mark Twain Society; PEN; Texas Institute of Letters; Phi Beta Kappa. *Literary Agent:* Georges Borchardt. *Address:* 2102 S Hughes, Amarillo, TX 79109, USA.

MOLDON Peter Leonard, b. 31 Mar 1937, London, England. Writer; Freelance Designer. *Education:* Hampton Grammar School, 1948-55; Regent Street Polytechnic, 1958-59. *Publications:* Your Book of Ballet (illustrated & designed by author), 1974, revised edition 1980; Nureyev (designed by author), 1976; The Joy of Knowledge Encyclopaedia, (ballet articles), 1976. *Contributions to:* The Dancing Times. *Honours:* Your

Book of Ballet, selected as one of the Children's Books of the Year, National Book League, 1974, shown at Frankfurt Book Fair by British Council, 1974. *Address:* 11 Oxlip Road, Witham, Essex, CM8 2XY, England.

MOLE John Douglas, b. 12 Oct 1941, Taunton, Somerset, England. Teacher; Writer. m. Mary Norman, 22 Aug 1968. 2 sons. *Education:* MA, Magdalene College, Cambridge, 1961-64. *Publications include:* In & Out Of The Apple, 1984; Homing, 1987; Boo To A Goose (for children), 1987; The Mad Parrot's Countdown, 1990; The Conjuror's Rabbir, 1992; Depending on The Light, 1993; Passing Judgements: Poetry In The Eighties, (critical essays), 1989. *Contributions to:* Encounter; TLS; TES; Spectator. *Honours:* Eric Gregory Award Winner, 1970; Signal Award, for the year's outstanding contribution to children's poetry, 1988. *Memberships:* Council Member, National Poetry Society; Society of Authors. *Address:* 11 Hill Street, St Albans, Hertfordshire AL3 4QS, England.

MOLLENKOTT Virginia Ramey, b. 1932, USA. Professor of English. *Appointments:* Faculty Member, Shelton College, 1955-63; Faculty Member, Nyack College, 1963-67; Assistant Editor, Seventeenth-Century News, 1964-73; Professor of English, William Paterson College of New Jersey, 1967-. *Publications:* Adamant and Stone Chips: A Christian Humanist Approach to Knowledge, 1967; In Search of Balance, 1969; Adam Among the Televion Trees: An Anthology of Verse by Contemporary Christian Poets (editor), 1971; Women, Men, and the Bible, 1977, 1988; Is the Homosexual My Neighbour (with Letha Scanzoni), 1978; Speech, Silence, Action, 1980; Views from the Intersection (with Catherine Barry), 1983; The Divine Feminine, 1983; Godding: Human Responsibility and the Bible, 1987; Women of Faith in Dialogue (editor), 1987; Sensuous Spirituality: Out From Fundamentalsim, 1992. *Memberships:* Modern Language Association; Milton Society of America. *Address:* 11 Yearling Trail, Hewitt, NJ 07421, USA.

MOLLOY Michael (Joseph), b. 1917, Ireland. Playwright; Author. *Publications:* The King of Friday's Men, 1954; The Paddy Pedlar, 1954; The Will and the Way, 1957; Old Road, 1961; The Wood of the Whispering, 1961; Daughter from Over the Water, 1963; The Bitter Pill, 1965; The Visiting House, 1967; The Making of Folkplays, 1977; Petticoat Loose, 1982. *Address:* Milltown, Tuam, Co Galway, Republic of Ireland.

MOLLOY Michael John, b. 22 Dec 1940. Editor. m. Sandra June Foley, 1964, 3 daughters. *Appointments:* Sunday Pictorial, 1956; Daily Sketch, 1960; Daily Mirror, 1962-85; Editor, Daily Mirror, 1969, Assistant Editor, Daily Mirror, 1970, Deputy Editor, 1975, Editor, Daily Mirror, 1975-85; Director, Mirror Group Newspapers, 1976- ; Editor in Chief, Mirror Group, 1985-; Editor, Sunday Mirror, 1986-. *Publications:* The Black Dwarf, 1985; The Kid from Riga, 1986; The Harlot of Jericho, 1988; The Century. *Address:* 62 Culmington Road, London W13, England.

MOMADAY Navarre Scott, b. 27 Feb 1934, Lawton, Oklahoma, USA. Writer; Painter; Professor. m. Regina Heitzer, 21 July 1978, 4 daughters. *Education:* BA, University of New Mexico, 1958; MA, 1960, PhD, 1963, Stanford University. *Appointments:* Visiting Professor, Columbia University, Princeton, 1979; Writer in Residence, Southeastern University, 1985; Aspen Writers Conference, 1986. *Publications:* House Made of Dawn, 1968; The Way to Rainy Mountain, 1969; The Names, 1976; The Gourd Dancer, 1976. *Honours:* Pulitzer Prize, Fiction, 1969; Premio Mondello, Italy 1979; Honorary Degrees, various Universities. *Memberships:* PEN. *Literary Agent:* Julian Bach Agency, New York. *Address:* c/o Julian Bach Literary Agency, New York, NY, USA.

MOMI Balbir Singh, b. 20 Nov 1935, Amargarh, PB, India. Teacher; Education Officer; Writer; Translator. m. Baldev Kaur, 28 Oct 1954, 4 daughters. *Education:* Honours in Punjabi, 1953, MA in Punjabi, 1970, Honours in Persian, 1974, Doctor of Philosophy, 1977, Panjab University, Chandigarh (Candidate); OT, Education Department, PB Government, 1957. *Appointments:* School Teacher, various PB Government High Schools and Higher Secondary Schools, 1954-71; Research and Evaluation Officer, Editor of Pankhrian, 1971-73, Subject Officer, 1976-79, Public Relations Officer, Subject Expert, 1979-82, PB School Education Board, Chandigarh; Lecturer, Research Assistant, GND University, Amritsar, 1974-76; Literary Editor, Perdesi Punjab, Toronto, Canada, 1982-; worked with literary magazines in Toronto, including: Dooron Ner-eon, Perdesi Punjab Canasia Sanjh-Svera Weekly. *Publications:* Short story collections: Masale Wala Ghora, 1959; Je Main Mar Jawan, 1965; Sheeshe Da Samunder, 1968; Sar Da Boojha, 1973; Novels: Jeeja Jee, 1964; Peela Gulab, 1975; Ek Phul Mera Vi, 1986; Dramas: Laudha Vela and Noukrian Hi Nukrian, 1960-64; Translations into Punjabi: Tobha Tek Singh; Nangian Awazan; Sat Gawache Lok; Jai Kantan Ki Kahanian; From Urdu and Hindi short stories and novels, 1975, 1977, 1978-79; Science, Education and National Development (English to Punjabi). *Contributions to:* Short stories, pen portraits, research articles and book reviews to various Punjabi magazines including: Amar Kahanian; Panj Darya; Preet Lari; Kavita; Lok Sahit; Pritam, Punjabi Sahit; Khoj Darpan; Jan Sahit; Punjabi Duniya; Arsee; Ajit; Punjabi Tribune; Sardal; Navat Sahit; Indo Canadian Times; Punjabi Tribune; The Sikh Press, Canasia. *Honours:* Promotion of Culture Award, Government of Punjab, 1968; Literary Awards: Kala Kendar Amritsar, 1975; Guru Nanak Dev University, Amritsar, 1989; Sahit Sameekhia Board, Jalandhar, 1989; CIPSA Award, Toronto, Canada, 1990; Baltimore, Punjabi Society Award, 1993. *Memberships:* General Secretary, Panch Kala Ferozohur, 1950-70; Punjabi Sahit Sabha Chandigarh, 1971-82; President, International Perdesi Punjab Sahit Sabha, Toronto, 1982-90. *Address:* Balbir Singh Momi, 17 Donaldson Drive, Brampton, Ontario, Canada, L6Y 3H1.

MOMMSEN Katharina Zimmer, b. 18 Sept 1925, Berlin, Germany. Professor of Literature. m. Momme H. Mommsen, 23 Dec 1948. *Education:* Abitur, Berlin, 1943; Dr.Phil., Tubingen, 1956; Dr.Phil.Habil., Berlin, 1962. *Appointments:* Researcher, German Academy ofSciences, Berlin, 1949-61; Docent, Professor, Free University of Brlin, 1962-70; Professor, German Literature, Carleton University, Ottowa, 1970-74, Stanford University, USA, 1974-. *Publications:* Goethe und 1001 Nacht, 1960; Goethe und Diez, 1961; Goethe und der Islam, 1964; Natur und Fabelreich in Faust II, 1968; Schillers Anthologie, 1973; Kleists Kampf mit Goethe, 1974; Gesellschaftskritik bei Fontane und Thomas Mann, 1974; Herders Journal Meiner Reise, 1976; Hofmannsthal und Fontane, 1978; Who is Goethe?, 1983; Goethe - Warum?, 1984; Goethes Marchen, 1984; Goethe und die arabische Welt, 1988. *Contributions to:* numerous journals and magazines. *Honours:* Guggenheim, 1976; Alexander von Humboldt Forschungspreis, 1980; Bundesverdienstkreuz I Klasse, 1985; Endowed Chair as Albert Guerard Professor of Literature, Stanford University. *Memberships:* various professional organisations. *Address:* Stanford University, Dept. of German Studies, Stanford, CA 94305, USA.

MONACO James Frederick, b. 15 Nov 1942, New York, USA. Writer; Publisher. m. Susan R. Schenker, 24 Oct 1976, 2 sons, 1 daughter. *Education:* AB, Muhlenberg College, 1963; MA, Columbia University, 1964. *Publications:* How to Read A Film, 1977, 1981; American Film Now, 1979, 1984; Connoisseurs Guide to the Movies, 1985; The New Wave, 1976; Media Culture, 1977; Celebrity, 1977; The International Encylopeadia of Film, 1991; The Movie Guide, 1992; Cinemania: Interactive Movie Guide, 1992. *Contributions to:* Numerous professional journals including: New York Times; Village Voice; American Film; Christian Science Monitor; many other publications. *Memberships:* Authors Guild, Writers Guild. *Literary Agent:* Virginia Barber. *Address:* UNET Inc, 31 E 12 St, New York, NY 10003, USA.

MONAGAN John Stephen, b. 23 Dec 1911, Waterbury, Connecticut, USA. Attorney at Law. m. Rosemary Brady, 23 May 1949, 2 sons, 3 daughters. *Education:* Dartmouth College, AB, 1933; Harvard Law School, JD, 1937. *Publications:* Horace Priest of the Poor; The Grand Panjandrun Mellow Years of Justice Holmes. *Contributions to:* NY Times Magazine; NY Times Book Review; Washington Post Book World; Washington Times; NY State Bar Journal; Am Bar Association Journal; Boston Globe Magazine; US Supreme Court Historical Society, Journal; Hartford Courant. *Memberships:* Cosmos Club; Am Conn and DC Bar Associations; Association Former Members of Congress, 1959-1973. *Address:* 3043 West Lane Keys, NW, Washington, DC 20007, USA.

MONCURE Jane Belk, b. 16 Dec 1926, Orlando, Florida. Teacher; Author; Consultant. m. James Ashby Moncure, 14 June 1952, 1 son. *Education:* BS Degree, Viginia Commonwealth University, 1952; Masters Degree, Columbia University, 1954. *Appointments:* Instructor, Early Childhood Ed, University of Richmond, Virginia, 1972-73; Burlington Day School, Burlington, North Carolina, 1974-78. *Publications:* First Steps To Reading-Sound Box Books/The Child's World, (24 books), 1970's; Magic Castle Books/The Child's World, (27), 1980's. *Honours:* Outstanding Service to Young Children, 1979; C S Lewis Gold Medal Award, Best Childrens Book of the Year, 1984. *Address:* Cove Cottage, Seven Lakes Box 3336, West End, NC 27376, USA.

MONES James J, b. 25 Nov 1952, Brooklyn, USA. Journalism. m. 13 Aug 1977, 1 son. *Education:* BS, New York University, 1974. *Literary Appointments:* Staff, Port Chester Daily Item, 1974-78; Lifestyles Editor, Westchester Rockland Newspapers, 1978-80; Copy Editor, Newsday, 1978-80; Entertainment Editor, 1980-86, Assistant News Editor, 1986-87, New York Post; Makeup Editor, New York Times, 1987-. *Honours:* Associated Press Award for Feature Writing in 1978, The Two-Clown Circus. *Address:* 74 Hudson Road, Bellerose Village, New York 11001, USA

MONET Jacques, b. 1930, Canada. Historian. *Appointments:* University of Toronto, 1982-92; President, University of Sudbury, 1992-. *Publications:* The Last Cannon Shot: A Study of French-Canadian Nationalism, 1969; The Canadian Crown, 1979; Jules Leger: A Selection of His Writings on Canada, 1982. *Address:* University of Sudbury, Sudbury, Ontario P3E 2C6, Canada.

MONETTE Madeleine, b. 3 Oct 1951, Montreal, Canada. Author. m. William R. Leggio, 27 Dec 1979. *Education:* MA, Literature, University of Quebec. *Publications:* Le Double suspect, 1980; Petites Violences, 1982; Fuites et Poursuites, 1982; Plages, 1986; L'Aventure, la Mesaventure, 1987; Amandes et melon, 1991; Nouvelles de Montréal, 1992. *Contributions to:* Quebec français; Possibles; Arcade; Le Devoir; Trois; Moebius; Ecrits du Canada-Français; Nuit Blanche; Le Sabord (Canada); Sud; Europe (France); Beacon and Romance Language Annual (USA). *Honours:* Robert-Cliche Award, Quebec City International Book Fair, 1980; Grants, Canadian Council of Arts, 1981, 1984, 1991, 1993. *Membership:* Quebec Writers Union. *Address:* 2 Charlton Street, 11K, New York, NY 10014, USA.

MONEY David Charles, b. 5 Oct 1918, Oxford, England, Schoolmaster. m. Madge Matthews, 30 Nov 1945, 1 son. *Education:* Honours Degree, Chemistry, 1946, Honours Degree, Geography, 1947, St John's College, Oxford University. *Publications:* Human Geography, 1954; Climate, Soils and Vegetation, 1965; The Earth's Surface, 1970; Patterns of Settlement,

1972; Environmental Systems, series, 1978-82; Foundations of Geography, 1987; Climate and Environmental Systems, 1988; China-The Land and the People, 1984, revised 1989; China Today, 1987; Australia Today, 1988. *Honours:* Honorary Member, for Services to Education, The Geographical Association. *Memberships:* Fellow, The Royal Geographical Society; The Farmers' Club. *Address:* 52 Park Avenue, Bedford MK40 2NE, England.

MONEY Keith, b. 1935, Auckland, New Zealand. Author; Artist; Photographer. *Publications include:* Salute the Horse, 1960; The Horseman in Our Midst, 1963; The Equestrian World, 1963; The Art of The Royal Ballet, 1964, 1967; The Art of Margot Fonteyn, 1965, 1975; The Royal Ballet Today, 1968; Fonteyn: The Making of a Legend, 1973; John Curry, 1978; Anna Pavlova: Her Life & Art, 1982; The Bedside Book of Old-fashioned Roses, 1985; Some Other Sea: The Life of Rupert Brooke, 1988-89; Forteyn and Nureyev: the Great Years, 1993; Margot, assoluta, 1993-94. Collaborations: Pat Smythe, Peter Beales. *Contributions to:* Numerous journals & magazines. Also screenplays, anthologies. *Address:* Carbrooke Hall Farm, Thetford, Norfolk, England.

MONK C. *See:* **MEDVEI Victor.**

MONK Raymond, b. 21 Oct 1925, Derby, England. Writer. *Publications:* Elgar Studies; Edward Elgar: Music & Literature; Edward Elgar: An Iconograhy. *Contributions to:* Elgar Society Journal. *Membership:* Royal OVerseas Club. *Address:* 19 Severn Street, Leicester LE2 0NN, England.

MONOD Jean, b. 19 Oct 1941, Paris, France. Writer; Ethrologist; Film Maker. m. (1) Marie Laure Chaude, 1962, (2) Kagumi Onodera, 1989, 3 sons, 2 daughters. *Education:* University Paris, 1974. *Appointments:* Lecturer, 1970; Editor in Chief, Aiou, 1987; Editorial Board, Ethnies, 1989; Editorial Board, Dock(k)s, 1991. *Publications:* Les Barjots; Un Riche Cannibale; Wora, La Deesse Cachee; Lumiere d Ailleurs; Raid; Le Foetus Astral; Others inc. L'eau Du Premier Soir. *Contributions to:* Le Monde; Canal; Liberation; Les Temps Modernes; Journal de la Societe des Americanistes; L'Autre Journal. *Honours:* Prix Georges Sadoul; Prix Louis Marin de L'Academie des Sciences; d'Outre-Mer. *Address:* L'Espinassounel, 48330 Saint Etienne Vallé Française, France.

MONSARRAT Ann Whitelaw, b. 8 Apr 1937, Walsall, England, Writer. m. Nicholas Monsarrat, 22 Dec 1961. *Publications:* An Uneasy Victorian: Thackeray the man, 1980; And the Bride Wore...The Story of the White Wedding, 1973. *Contributions to:* Journalist, West Kent Mercury, 1954-58; Daily Mail, London, 1958-61; Assistant Editor, Stationery Trade Review, 1961. *Literary Agent:* Campbell Thomson and McLaughlin, London, England. *Address:* San Lawrenz, Gozo, Malta.

MONTAG Tom, b. 1947, USA. Poet; Editor; Publisher. *Appointments:* Formerly Researcher, Center for Venture Management; Editor, Publisher, Monday Morning Press, Milwaukee, 1971-; Editor, Publisher, Margins Books, 1974-. *Publications:* Wooden Nickel, 1972; Twelve Poems, 1972; Measures, 1972; To Leave This Place, 1972; Making Hay, 1973; The Urban Ecosystem: A Holistic Approach (edited with F Stearns), 1974; Making Hay and Other Poems, 1975; Ninety Notes Toward Partial Images and Lover Prints, 1976; Concerns: Essays and Reviews, 1977; Letters Home, 1978. *Address:* c/o Sparrow Press, 193 Waldron Street, West Lafayette, IN 47906, USA.

MONTAGU Robert, b. 25 Nov 1949. Writer; Businessman. m. Marzia Brigante Colonna, 23 May 1970, 2 sons, 2 daughters. *Education:* Eton College, 1962-66; Diploma in Communications Studies, Polytechnic of Central London, 1973. *Publication:* Coming to Terms, 1988. *Honour:* Shortlisted for Faber

Prize, 1988. *Literary Agent:* Jane Conway- Gordon, 1 Old Compton Street, London W1, England. *Address:* The Old Manor, Evershot, Dorset, England.

MONTAGU OF BEAULIEU Edward John Barrington Douglas-Scott-Montagu, (Lord), b. 1926, United Kingdom. Author; Founder/Trustee, National Motor Museum, Beaulieu. *Appointments:* Founder, Publisher, Veteran and Vintage Magazine, 1956-79. *Publications:* The Motoring Montagus, 1959; Lost Causes of Motoring, 1960; Jaguar: A Biography, 1961, 1962, 1967, 1981, 1982, 1986, 1990; The Gordon Bennett Races, 1963; Rolls of Rolls Royce, 1966; The Gilt and the Gingerbread, 1967; Lost Causes of Motoring in Europe, vol I, 1969, vol II, 1971; More Equal Than Others, 1970; History of the Steam Car (with A Bird), 1971; The Horseless Carriage, 1975; Early Days on the Road, 1976; Behind the Wheel, 1977; Royalty on the Road, 1980; Home, James, 1982; The British Motorist, 1987; English Heritage, 1987. *Address:* Palace House, Beaulieu, Brockenhurst, Hants SO42 7ZN, England.

MONTAGUE John (Patrick), b. 1929, Ireland. Author; Educator. *Appointments:* Worked for State Tourist Board, Dublin, 1956-61; Currently Lecturer in Poetry, University College, Cork. *Publications:* Forms of Exile, 1958; The Old People, 1960; Poisoned Lands and Other Poems, 1961; The Dolmen Miscellany of Irish Writing (editor), 1962; Death of a Chieftain and Other Stories, 1964; All Legendary Obstacles, 1966; Patriotic Suite, 1966; A Tribute to Austin Clarke on His Seventieth Birthday, 9 May 1966 (edited with Liam Miller), 1966; Home Again, 1967; A Chosen Light, 1967; The Rough Field, 1972; Hymn to the New Omagh Road, 1968; The Bread God: A Lecture, with Illustrations in Verse, 1968; A New Siege, 1969; The Planter and the Gael (with J Hewitt), 1970; Tides, 1970; Small Secrets, 1972; The Rough Field, play, 1972; A Fair House, translation from Irish, 1973; The Cave of Night, 1974; O'Riada's Farewell, 1974; The Faber Book of Irish Verse (editor), 1974; A Slow Dance, 1975; The Great Cloak, 1978; Selected Poems, 1982; The Dead Kingdom, 1984; Mount Eagle, 1989. *Address:* Department of English, University College, Cork, Republic of Ireland.

MONTE Bryan Robert, b. 3 Nov 1957, Cleveland, Ohio, USA. Writer; Editor. *Education:* BA, English Literature, University of California, Berkeley, 1983; MA, Graduate Writing Programme, Brown University, 1986. *Appointments:* California Poet in the Schools, 1983-84; University Fellow, Brown University, 1984-86; Writing Specialist, Massachusetts Public Schools, 1986-87; Assistant Bibliographer, John Carter Brown Library, 1986. *Publications:* No Apologies, Editor, 1983- ; The Mirror of the Medusa, poetry, 1987; Neurotika, poetry, 1988. *Contributions to:* James White Review; Bay Windows; Advocate. *Honours:* Youth and Creative Arts Award Winner, The Saints Herald, 1976-78; Joan Lee Yang Memorial Poetry Prize Winner, University of California, 1982; many other honours and awards. *Literary Agent:* Jayne Walker. *Address:* 1835 Ednamary Way, No E, Mountain View, CA 94040, USA.

MONTELEONE Thomas Francis, b. 14 Apr 1946, Baltimore, Maryland, USA. Writer. div, 2 sons. *Education:* BS, Psychology 1964, MA, English Literature 1973, University of Maryland. *Publications:* The Time-Swept City, 1977; The Secret Sea, 1979; Night Things, 1980; Dark Stars and Other Illuminations, 1981; Guardian, 1981; Night Train, 1984; Lyrica, 1987; The Magnificent Gallery, 1987; Crooked House, 1988; Fantasma, 1989; Borderlands, 1990; Borderlands 2, 1991; Borderlands 3, 1992; The Blood of the Lamb, 1992; Borderlands 4, 1993. *Contributions to:* National & International Science Fiction, Dark Fantasy, and Suspense magazines, anthologies. *Honours:* Finalist: John W. Campbel Award 1973; Nebula Award, best short story, 1976, 1977. Winner: Gabriel Award, best television drama, 1984; Bronze Award, International Film & TV Festival, New York (best drama), 1984. *Memberships:* Secretary, 1976-79, Science Fiction Writers of America; Vice-President, 1987-88, Horror Writers of America. *Literary Agent:* Howard Morhaim, 175 Fifth Avenue, New York, NY 10010, USA. *Address:* PO Box 5788, Baltimore, MD 21208, USA.

MONTGOMERY David, b. 6 Nov 1948, Bangor, Northern Ireland. Journalist. m. Heidi Kingstone, 6 May 1989. *Education:* BA, Politics & History, Queens's University, Belfast, 1967-1970. *Appointments:* Sub-editor, Daily and Sunday Mirror, Manchester, 1973-1976; Back Bench Executive, Daily and Sunday Mirror, London, 1976-1980; Chief Sub-Editor, The Sun, 1980-1982; Assistant Editor, Sunday People, 1982-1984; Assistant Editor, News of the World, 1984-1985; Editor, News of the World, 1985-1987; Director, Sky Television plc, 1986-1990; Editor, Today, Managing Director, News (UK), Publisher, Today, 1987-1991; Director, London Live Television Ltd, 1991; Director, Caledonian Newspaper Publishing Ltd, owner of George Outram, 1992; Chief Executive, Mirror Group Newspapers, 1992. *Honours:* Newspaper of the Year, (Granada TV), 1988; Newspaper Design Award, Best Colour & Outstanding Contribution to Newspaper Design, 1988; Media Week Consumer Press, 1989; The British Environment & Media Awards, 1989. *Address:* 13 Warrington Crescent, London W9, England.

MONTGOMERY David Bruce, b. 30 Apr 1938, Professor; Management Consultant. m. Toby Marie Franks, 11 June 1960, 2 sons, 1 daughter. *Education:* BS, Electrical Engineering, 1960, MBA, Graduate School of Business, 1962; MS, Mathematical Statistics, 1964, PhD, Management Science, 1966, Stanford University. *Publications:* Stochastic Models of Buying Behaviour, (Co-authors W F Massy and D G Morrison), 1970; Management Science in Marketing, (Co-author G L Urban), 1969; Cases in Computer and Model Assisted Marketing, I, Planning (Co-authors G S Day, E J Eskin and C B Weinberg), 1973, II, Data Analysis, (Co-author E J Eskin), 1975; Author of 4 other books. *Contributions to:* Over 70 professional articles in: Strategic Management Journal; Management Science; Journal of Marketing; Journal of Marketing Research; Decision Science; Journal of Finance; Applied Statistics; Journal of Advertising Research; Sloan Management Review; Journal of Business Research; Communications of the ACM. *Memberships:* American Marketing Association, Institute of Management Science; Associate Editor, Journal of Marketing and Journal of Marketing Research; Departmental editor for Marketing Management Science. *Address:* Graduate School of Business, Stanford, CA 94305, USA.

MONTGOMERY Derek. See: SIMMONS J S A.

MONTGOMERY Marion, b. 16 Apr 1925. Teacher; Writer. m. Dorothy Carlisle, 20 Jan 1952, 1 son, 4 daughters. *Education:* AB, 1950; MA, 1953, University of Georgia; Creative Writing Workshop, University of Iowa, 1956-58. *Appointments:* Associate Editor, Modern Age; Managing Editor, Western Review, 1957-58; Assistant Director, University of Georgia Press, 1950-52. *Publications:* Dry Lightening, (Poems), 1960; The Wandering Desire, 1962; Fugitive, 1974; The Propehtic Poet and the Popular Spirit, 3 vols., 1981, 1983, 1984; Possum and other Receits for the Recovery of Southern Being, 1987; The Reflective Journey toward Order, 1974; Darrell, 1964; Liberal Arts and Community, 1990; Virtue and Modern Shadows of Turning, 1990; The Men I Have Chosen for Fathers: Literary and Philosophical Passages, 1990. *Contributions to:* Over 200 essays, 300 poems, 30 stories in periodicals. *Honours:* Best American Short Stories, 1971; Eugene Saxton Memorial Award, 1960; Earhart Foundation Fellowship, 1973-74. *Membership:* Philadelphia Society. *Address:* Box 115, Crawford, GA 30630, USA.

MONTI Nicolas, b. 8 Jan 1956, Milan, Italy. Architect; Writer. *Education:* Liceo Gonzaga, Milan, 1974; Paris VI University, 1976; Polytechnic School of Architecture, Milan, 1984. *Publications:* Mediterranean Houses; Cunha Moraes, Viagens en Angola; Italian Modern: A Design Heritage; Africa Then; Emilio Sommariva; Luca Comerio, Fotografo e Cineasta. *Contributions to:* AI;

Area; Camera Mainichi; Corto Maltese; Domina; Domus; Geodes; IlGiornale dell'Ingegnere; Lagola; La Mia Casa; Modo; PM; Personal Time; Progresso Fotografico; Zoom. *Honour:* Study Tour of Japan Essay Contest. *Memberships:* Ordine Degli Architetti; Collegio Degli Ingegneri. *Literary Agent:* Melanie Jackson Agency, 250 West 57 Street, New York. *Address:* Via Borghetto 5, 20122, Milano, Italy.

MOODY Peter Richard Jr, b. 13 Oct 1943, San Francisco, USA. Teacher. m. Margaret Shahan, 18 June 1966, 4 sons, 2 daughters. *Education:* Vanderbilt University, AB, 1965; Yale University, PhD, 1971. *Publications:* Opportion, Dissient in Contemporary China; Chinese Politics After Mao; Political Opposition in Post Conlrian Society; Political Change on Taiwan. *Contributions to:* World Politics; China Quarterly; Asian Survey. *Address:* Department of Government, University of Notre Dame, Notre Dame, IN 46556, USA.

MOONEY Bel, b. 8 Oct 1946, Liverpool, England. Writer; Broadcaster. m. Jonathan Dimbleby, 23 Feb 1968, 1 son, 1 daughter. *Education:* BA, Honours, 1st Class, University College, London, 1968. *Publications:* The Year of the Child, 1979; Liza's Yellow Boat, 1980; The Windsurf Boy, 1983; Differences of Opinion, 1984; I Don't Want To!, 1985; The Anderson Question, 1985; Father Kissmass and Mother Claws, 1985; The Stove Haunting, 1986; The Fourth of July, 1988; From This Day Forward, 1989; A Flower of Jet, 1990; But You Promised!, 1990; Why Not?, 1990; I Know!, 1991; Perspectives for Living Conversations on Bereavement and Love, 1992; Lost Footsteps, 1993. *Contributions include:* All major British Newspapers and Magazines (Freelance), 1970-87; Columnist, Daily Mirror, 1979-80, Sunday Times, 1982-83; Book Reviews; Interviews. *Literary Agent:* David Higham Associates. *Address:* c/o David Higham Associates, 5-8 Lower John Street, London W1R 3PE, England.

MOONEY Ted (Edward Comstock), b. 19 Oct 1951, Dallas, Texas, USA. Writer; Editor. *Education:* BA, Bennington College, USA, 1973. *Appointments:* Managing Editor, Fiction Magazine, 1975-77; Senior Editor, Art in America Magazine, 1977-. *Publications:* Traffic and Laughter; Easy Travel to Other Planets. *Contributions to:* Los Angeles Times; Granta; Esquire; Art in America. *Honours:* Guggenheim Fellowship; Ingram Merrill Foundation; Sue Kaufman Prize; Creative Public Service Award; Nominated for Amerscam Book Award. *Memberships:* PEN. *Literary Agent:* Harviet Wasserman Literary Agency, NYC, USA. *Address:* 127 West 96th Street, Apt 11B, New York, NY 10025, USA.

MOONMAN Eric, b. 29 Apr 1929, Liverpool, England. Professor, City University (Health Management); Director of Research. m. Jane, 10 Sept 1962, 2 sons, 1 daughter. *Appointments:* Professor, City University (Health Management), 1990-; Director of Research; Consultant, International Red Cross (Africa), 1992-. *Education:* MSc, Management Science, Manchester University, 1966; Dip Social Sciences, Liverpool University, 1955. *Publications:* The Manager and the Organization, 1961; The Violent Society, 1987; The Relevant Partnership, 1971; The Alternative Government, 1984; Communications in an Expanding Organization, 1970. *Contributions to:* Times; New York Times; Observer. *Honour:* OBE. *Memberships:* Fellow, British Institute of Management; fellow, Royal Society of Arts. *Address:* 1 Beacon Hill, London N7 9LY, England.

MOORCOCK Michael (John), b. 1939. British, Writer of Novels/Short stories, Science fiction/Fantasy. Editor, Tarzan Adventures, 1956-58, Sexton Blake Library, 1959-61 and New Worlds, London, 1964-79. *Publications include:* The Stealer of Souls and other Stories, 1961, (as Desmond Read with James Cawthorn); Caribbean Crisis, 1962; The Fireclown, 1965, as The Winds of Limbo, 1969; The Sundered World, 1965, as The Blood Red Game, 1970; Stormbringer, 1965; (ed.) The Best of New Worlds, 1965; (as Edward P Bradbury) Michael Kane series: Warriors

of Mars, 1965 as The City of the Beast, 1970; (with Philip James) The Distant Suns, 1975; The Quest for Tanelorn, 1975; The Adventures of Una Persson and Catherine Cornelius in the Twentieth Century, 1976; The End of All Songs, 1976; Moorcock's Book of Martyrs, 1976; The Lives and Times of Jerry Cornelius, 1976; Legends from the End of Time, 1976; The Sailor on the Seas of Fate, 1976; (ed) England Invaded, 1977; The Transformation of Miss Mavis Ming, 1977, as Messiah at the End of Time, 1978; The Weird of the White Wolf, 1977; The Bane of the Black Sword, 1977; Sojan (for children), 1977; Condition of Muzak, 1977; Glorianna, 1978; Dying for Tomorrow, 1978; The Golden Barge, 1979; My Experiences in the Third World War, 1980; The Russian Intelligence, 1980; The Great Rock 'n' Roll Swindle, 1980; Byzantium Endures, 1981; The Entropy Tanga, 1981; The Warhound and the World's Pain, 1981; The Brothel in Rosenstrasse, 1982; The Dancers at the End of Time (omnibus) 1983; The Retreat from Liberty, 1983; (ed) New Worlds: An Anthology, 1983; The Laughter of Carthage, 1984; The Opium General and Other Stories, 1984; The Chronicles of Castle Brass, 1985; Letters from Hollywood, 1986; The City in the Autumn Stars, 1986; The Dragon in the Sword, 1986; Death is No Obstacle, 1992. *Address:* c/o Anthony Sheil Associates, 43, Doughty Street, London WC1N 2LFF, England.

MOORE Barbara, b. 1934, USA. Writer. *Appointments:* Reporter: Fort Worth Star-Telegram, Fort Worth, Texas, 1955-57; Denver Post, Denver, Colorado, 1958-60; San Antonio Light, San Antonio, Texas, 1963-65. *Publications:* Hard on the Road, 1974; The Fever Called Living, 1976; Something on the Wind, 1978; The Doberman Wore Black, 1983; The Wolf Whispered Death, 1986. *Literary Agent:* Harold Matson Co Inc, USA. *Address:* c/o Harold Matson Co Inc, 276 Fifth Avenue, New York, NY 10001, USA.

MOORE Brian, b. 25 Aug 1921, Belfast, Ireland. Author. m. Jean Denney, Oct 1967. 1 son. *Publications:* The Lonely Passion of Judith Hearne, 1955; The Feast of Lupercal, 1957; The Luck of Ginger Coffey, 1960; An Answer from Limbo, 1962; The Emperor of Ice-Cream, 1965; I am Mary Dunne, 1968; Fergus, 1970; The Revolution Script, 1971; Catholics, 1972; The Great Victorian Collection, 1975; The Doctor's Wife, 1976; The Mangan Inheritance, 1979; The Temptation of Eileen Hughes, 1981; Cold Heaven, 1983; Black Robe, 1985; The Color of Blood, 1987; Lies of Silence, 1990; No Other Life, 1993. *Honours:* Que. Literary Prize, 1958; US National Arts and Letters Award, 1961; Fiction Award, Governor Genral of Canada, 1961; 75 WH Smith Award, 1973; Heinemann Award, Royal Society of Literature, 1986; Sunday Express Book of the Year Award, 1987; Guggenheim Fellow, 1959; Canadian Council Senior Fellow, 1962, 1976; Scottish Arts Council International Fellow, 1983. *Address:* 33958 Pacific Coast Highway, Malibu, CA 90265, USA.

MOORE Carman, b. 1936, USA. Writer; Music Critic. *Appointments:* Formerly Member of Faculty: New York University, New York City; Yale University, New Haven, Connecticut; Brooklyn College, New York City; Queens College, New York City; Currently Music Critic: New York Times; The Village Voice, New York City. *Publications:* Somebody's Angel Child: The Story of Bessie Smith, 1970; Growth of Black Sound in America, 1981. *Address:* 148 Columbus Avenue, New York, NY 10023, USA.

MOORE Charles Hilary, b. 31 Oct 1956. Editor. m. Caroline Mary Baxer, 1981. *Education:* BA, Trinity College, Cambridge. *Appointments:* Joined Editorial Staff, Daily Telegraph, 1979, leader Writer, 1981-83; Assistant Editor, Political Columnist, 1983-84, Editor, 1984-90, The Spectator; Weekly column in Daily Express, 1987-; Weekly Column, Daily Express, 1987-90; Fortnightly Columnist, The Spectator, 1990-; Deputy Editor, The Daily Telegraph, 1990-92; Editor, The Sunday Telegraph, 1992-. *Publications:* Editor with (C. Hawtree) 1936, 1986; (with A.N. Wilson and G. Stamp) The Church in Crisis, 1986; (ed with Simon Heffer) A

Tory Seer, 1989. *Membership:* Beefsteak Club. *Address:* 16 Thornhill Square, London N1 1BQ, England.

MOORE Christopher Hugh, b. 9 June 1950, England. Historian; Writer. m. Louise Brophy, 7 May 1977. *Education:* BA, Honours, University of British Columbia, 1971; MA, University of Ottawa, 1977. *Publications:* Louisbourg Portraits, 1982; The Loyalists, 1984; Co- author, The Illustrated History of Canada, 1987; and many Radio Documentaries, School Texts, Educational Software Programmes, Historical Guidebooks on Canadian History. *Contributions to:* Numerous scholarly journals and magazines. *Honours:* Governor General's Literary Award, 1982; Secretary of State's Prize for Excellence in Canadian Studies, 1985; Canadian Historical Association Award of Merit, 1984. *Memberships:* Writers' Union of Canada; Canadian Historical Association; Ontario Historical Society; Heritage Canada Foundation. *Address:* 620 Runnymede Road, Toronto, Ontario, M6S 3A2, Canada.

MOORE Elizabeth. See: ATKINS Meg Elizabeth.

MOORE John Evelyn, (Captain), b. 1 Nov 1921, Sant'llario, Italy. Editor; Author; Retired Naval Officer. m. (1) Joan Pardoe, 1945, 1 son, 2 daughters, (2) Barbara Kerry. *Appointments Include:* Editor, jane's Fighting Ships, 1972-; Editor, Jane's Naval Review, 1982-1987. *Publications:* Jane's Major Warships, 1973; The Soviet Navy Today, 1975; Submarine Devlopment, 1976; Soviet War Machine (jointly), 1976; Encyclopaedia of World's Warships, 1978 (jointly); World War 3, 1978 (jointly); Seapower and Politics, 1979; Warships of the Royal Navy, 1979; Warships of the Soviet Navy, 1981; Submarine Warfare: Today and Tomorrow (jointly), 1986. *Address:* Elmhurst, Rickney, Hailsham, Sussex BN27 1SF, England.

MOORE Maureen Audrey, b. 13 Aug 1943, Canada. Writer. m. 1966, 1 son. *Education:* BA, 1971; MA, 1973. *Publication:* The Illumination of Alice Mallory. *Memberships:* The Society of Authors. *Address:* PO Box 71528, Hillcrest Post Office, White Rock, BC, Canada V4B 5JS.

MOORE Nicholas, b. 1918, United Kingdom. Author; Poet. *Appointments:* Editor, Seven, 1938-40; Editor, New Poetry, 1944-45. *Publications:* A Wish in Season: Poems, 1941; The Island and the Cattle, 1941; A Book for Priscilla: Poems, 1941; The Fortune Anthology (edited with J Bayliss and D Newton), 1942; Buzzing Around with a Bee and Other Poems, 1942; The Cabaret, The Dancer, The Gentleman: Poems, 1942; Henry Miller, 1943; The Glass Tower: Poems 1936-43, 1944; Three Poems (with F Marnau and W Gardiner), 1944; Thirty-Five Anonymous Odes, 1944; The War of the Little Jersey Cows; Poems by Guy Kelly, 1945; The P L Book of Modern American Short Stories (editor), 1945; Atlantic Anthology (edited with D Newton), 1945; Recollections of the Gala: Selected Poems, 1943-1948, 1950; The Tall Bearded Iris, horticulture, 1956; Identity: Poems, 1969; Resolution and Identity, 1970; Spleen, 31 Versions of Baudelaire's poem, 1973. *Address:* 89 Oakdene Road, St Mary Cray, Kent BR5 2AL, England.

MOORE Patrick Alfred Caldwell, b. 4 Mar 1923, Pinner, Middlesex, England. Astronomer; Author. *Appointments:* BBC TV Series, The Sky at Night 1957- ; Radio Broadcasts; Editor, Year Book of Astronomy, 1962-; Director, Armagh Planetarium, 1965-68; Composer, Perseus and Andromeda (opera), 1975, Theseus 1982; Editor, Astronomy Now, monthly periodical. *Publications:* Numerous, including Guide to the Moon, 1976; Atlas of the Universe, 1980; History of Astronomy, 1983; Guinness Book of Astronomy (revised edition), 1983; The Story of the Earth (with Peter Cattermole), 1985; Halley's Comet (with Heather Couper), 1985; Patrick Moore's Armchair Astronomy, 1985; Stargazing, 1985; Exploring the Night Sky with Binoculars, 1986; The A-Z of Astronomy, 1986; Astronomy for the Under Tens, 1987; Stargazing, 1988;

Men of the Stars, 1988; The Planet Neptune, 1989; Mission to the Planets, 1990; A Passion for Astronomy, 1991; The Earth for Under Tens, 1992; Fireside Astronomy, 1992. *Honours:* Goodacre Medal, British Astronomical Association, 1968; Jackson Gwilt Gold Medal, Royal Astronomical Society, 1977; Klumpke Medal, Astronical Society of the Pacific, 1979; Hon. D.Sc., Lancaster, 1974; OBE, 1968; CBE, 1988; Minor Planet No 2602 named 'Moore' in his honour. *Memberships:* Past President, British Astronomical Association. *Address:* Farthings, 39 West Street, Selsey, West Sussex, England.

MOORE Peter Dale, b. 20 June 1942, Nantyglo, Wales. University Lecturer. m. Eunice P Jervis, 18 Dec 1966, 2 daughters. *Education:* University of Wales, BSc, 1963; PhD, 1966. *Publications:* Peatlands; Biography; Pollen Analysis; Atlas of Living World; Encyclopedia of Animal Ecology; Mitchell Beazeley Guide to Wild Glowers; European mires; Methods in Plant Ecology. *Contributions to:* New Scientist; Nature; Plants Today; Journal of Ecology. *Memberships:* British Ecological Society; Cambridge Philosophic Society; Botanical Society of British Isles. *Address:* Department of Life Sciences, Kings College, Campden Hill Road, London W8 7AH, England.

MOORE Ruth Nulton, b. 19 June 1923, Easton, Pennsylvania, USA. Writer. m. Carl Leland Moore, 15 June 1946, 2 sons. *Education:* BA, Bucknell University; MA, Columbia University. *Publications:* Frisky the Playful Pony, 1966; Hiding the Bell, 1968; Peace Treaty, 1977; Ghost Bird Mystery, 1977; Mystery of the Lost Treasure, 1978; Tomas and the Talking Birds, 1979; Wilderness Journey, 1979; Mystery at Indian Rocks, 1981; The Sorrel Horse, 1982; Danger in the Pines, 1983; In Search of Liberty, 1983; Mystery of the Missing Stallions, 1984; Mystery of the Secret Code, 1985. *Contributions to:* Jack and Jill; Children's Activities. *Honours:* C.S. Lewis Honor Book Medal, 1983; Religion in Media Silver Angel Award, 1984. *Membership:* Children's Authors and Illustrators of Philadelphia. *Literary Agent:* McIntosh and Otis. *Address:* 3033 Center Street, Bethlehem, PA 18017, USA.

MOORE Wilbert E(llis), b. 1914, USA. Emeritus Professor of Sociology and Law, University of Denver. *Publications:* Economic Demography of Eastern and Southern Europe, 1945; Twentieth Century Sociology (edited with G Gurvitch), 1945; Industrial Relations and the Social Order, 1946, 2nd Edition 1951; Industrialization and Labor, 1951; Economy and Society, 1955; Economic Growth: Brazil, India, Japan (edited with S Kuznets and J J Spengler), 1955; Labor Commitment and Social Change in Developing Areas (edited with A S Feldman), 1960; Conduct of the Corporation, 1962; Social Change, 1962, 2nd Edition, 1974; Man, Time and Society, 1963; Industrialization and Society (edited with B F Hoselitz), 1963; The Impact of Industry, 1965; Readings on Social Change (edited with R M Cook), 1967; Order and Change, 1967; Indicators of Social Change, 1968; Trusteeship and the Management of Foundations (with D R Young), 1969; Professions: Roles and Rules, 1970; American Negro Slavery and Abolition, 1971; Technology and Social Change (editor), 1972; World Modernization: The Limits of Convergence, 1981. *Address:* 7207 South Vine Street, Littleton, CO 80122, USA.

MOOREHEAD Caroline, b. 1944, United Kingdom. Writer; Journalist. *Appointments:* Reporter, Time magazine, Rome, Italy, 1968-69; Feature Writer, Telegraph Magazine, London, England, 1969-70; Features Editor, Times Educational Supplement, 1970-73; Feature Writer, The Times newspaper, London, 1973-1988; Human Rights Columnist Independent, 1988-. *Publications:* Myths and Legends of Britain (editor and translator), 1968; Fortune's Hostages, 1980; Sidney Bernstein: A Biography, 1983; Freya Stark: A Biography, 1985; Troublesome People, 1988; Betrayal Children in Today's World, 1989; Bertrand Runei: A Life, 1992. *Address:* 36 Fitzroy Road, London NW1, England.

MOORHOUSE Frank, b. 21 Dec 1938, Nowra, Australia. Writer. *Education:* University of Queensland, WEA. *Appointments:* President, Australian Society of Authors, 1979-82; Chairman, Copyright Council of Australia, 1985. *Publications:* Futility and Other Animals, 1969; The Americans, Baby, 1972; The Electrical Experience, 1974; Conference-Ville, 1976; Tales of Mystery and Romance, 1977; Everlasting Secret Family and Other Secrets 1980; Days of Wine and Rage, 1980; Room Service, 1986; Forty-Seventeen, 1988. *Contributions to:* Bulletin. *Honours:* Henry Lawson Short Story Prize, 1970; National Award for Fiction, 1975; Winner, Awgie Award, Best Script, Conference-Ville; Australian Literary, Gold Medal for Literature, 1989. *Memberships:* Australian RAC (Sydney); Crouchos Club (London); Member, Order of Australia. *Literary Agent:* Rosemary Creswell. *Address:* c/o Rosemary Cresswell, Private Bag 5, PO Balmain, NSW 2041, Australia.

MOORHOUSE Geoffrey, b. 29 Nov 1931, Bolton, Lancashire, England. Author. m. Marilyan Isobel Edwards, 2 sons, 1 daughter, previous marriage. *Publications:* The Other England, 1963; Against All Reason, 1969; Calcutta, 1971; The Missionaries, 1973; The Fearful Void, 1974; The Diplomats, 1977; The Boat & the Town, 1979; The Best Loved Game, 1979; Lord's., 1983; India Britannica, 1983; To the Frontier, 1984; Apples in the Snow, 1990; Hell's Foundation: a town, it's myth and Gallipolis, 1992. *Contributions to:* The Guardian; The Times; Observer; London magazine; Books & Bookmen. *Honours:* Fellow, Royal Geographical Society, 1972; Fellow, Royal Society of Literature, 1982; Cricket Society Literary Award, 1979; Thomas Cook Literary Award, 1984. *Literary Agent:* A P Watt Ltd, London. *Address:* Park House, Gayle, Near Hawes, N Yorks DL8 3RT, England.

MORAES Dominic, b. 19 July 1938. Writer; Poet. *Education:* Jesus College, Oxford. *Appointments:* Consultant, UN Fund for Population Activities, 1973-, (on loan to India); Managing Editor, the Asia Magazine, Hong Kong, 1972-. *Publications Include:* A Beginning, 1957; Gone Away, 1960; My Son's Faher (autobiography), 1968; The Tempest Within, 1972-73; The People Time Forgot, 1972; A Matter of People, 1974; Voices for Life (essays), 1975; Mrs Gandhi, 1980; Bombay, 1980; books of poems and travel books on India. *Honour:* Hawthornden Prize for A Beginning, 1957. *Address:* c/o 521 Fifth Avenue, New York, NY 10017, USA.

MORAN John Charles, b. 4 Oct 1942, Nashville, Tennessee, USA. Editor; Foundation Director; Researcher; Librarian. *Education:* BA, 1967, MLS, 1968, George Peabody College, Nashville, Tennessee. *Appointments:* Director, F Marion Crawford Memorial Society, Nashville, Tennessee, 1975-; Editor, The Romantist, 1977-; Editor, The Worthies Library, 1980-. *Publications:* An F Marion Crawford Companion, 1981; Seeking Refuge in Torre San Nicola, 1980; In Memoriam: Gabriel Garcia Moreno 1875-1975, 1975; Editor, Francesca Da Rimini, (1902), 1980; Bibliography of Marketing of Fruits and Vegetables in Honduras, 1975-85, 1985; Editor, The Satanist, (1912) Forthcoming; Last Days and Death of Dr. & Gen., William Walker, Forthcoming; Editor, Anne Crawford von Rabe's, A Shadow on a Wave 1891, 1991. *Contributions to:* Numerous professional journals and magazines. *Honours:* Special Guest, Il Magnifico Crawford - Conference on Francis Marion Crawford, Sant' Agnello Di Sorrento, 1988. *Membership:* Director, F. Marion Crawford Memorial Society, 1975-. *Address:* F. Marion Crawford Memorial Society, Saracinesca House, 3610 Meadowbrook Ave., Nashville, TN 37205, USA.

MORAY WILLIAMS Ursula, b. 19 Apr 1911, Petersfield, Hampshire, England. Writer, Children's Books. m. Conrad Southey John, 28 Sept 1935, 4 sons. *Education:* Winchester Art College. *Publications:* Approximately 70 titles, 1931-, including: Jean-Pierre; Adventures of the Little Wooden Horse; Gobbolino the Witch's Cat; Further adventures of Gobbolino & the Little Wooden Horse; Nine Lives of Island Mackenzie; The

Noble Hawks; Bogwoppit; Jeffy the Burglar's Cat; Good Little Christmas Tree; Cruise of the Happy-Go-Gay; Bellabelinda & the No-Good Angel; The Moonball. *Contributions to:* Cricket USA; Puffin Post; The EGG; Storyteller 1, 2, Christmas numbers; Various Australian magazines. *Membership:* West of England Writers Guild. *Literary Agent:* Curtis Brown. *Address:* Court Farm House, Beckford, near Tewkesbury, Gloucestershire, England.

MOREHOUSE Thomas Alvin, b. 26 May 1937, Minneapolis, Minnesota, USA. University Professor. m. (1) Karen Bornfleth, 1959, (2) Dolores Sauberlich, 1978, 1 son, 2 daughters. *Education:* Harvard College, AB, 1960; University of Minnesota, MAPA, 1961; PhD, 1968. *Appointments:* Editor, Editorial Advisory Board, The Northern Review, 1987-; MS Reviewer, American Review of Public Administration, 1988-; University of Alaska Press, 1989-. *Publications:* Issues in Alaska Development; Dynamics of Alaska Native Self Government; Alaska's Urban and Rural Governments; Alaska Resource Development; Alaska State Government and Politics; Native Claims and Political Development. *Contributions to:* Polar Record; Arctic. *Memberships:* American Association for the Advancement of Science; American Society for Public Administration. *Address:* 3900 Amber Bay, Anchorage, AL 99515, USA.

MORENCY Pierre, b. 8 may 1942, Quebec, Canada. Writer. *Education:* BA, College de Levis, 1963; Licence es Lettres, Universite Laval, Quebec, Canada, 1966. *Appointments:* Freelance Writer at Radio Canada, 1967-91. *Publications:* Lumiere des Oiseaux, 1992; L'Oeil Americain, 1989; The Eye is an Eagle, 1992; A Season for Birds, selected poems, 1990; Quand nous serons, 1988; Effets Personnels, 1986; Les Passeuses, 1976; Glimmer on the Mountain, 1992. *Honours:* Prix Alain-Grandbois, 1987; Prix Quebec-Paris, 1988; Prix Ludger-Duvernay, 1991; Prix France-Quebec, 1992. *Memberships:* Union Des Ecrivains Quebecois; PEN Club; Ordre Des Arts et Des Lettres de France, (Chevalier). *Address:* 1211 Avenue Preston, Sillery, Quebec, Canada.

MORENO Armando, b. 19 Dec 1932, Porto, Portugal. University Professor and Medical Doctor. m. Maria Guinot Moreno, 3 Oct 1987. *Education:* Licentiate in Medicine, 1960; Doctor of Medicine, 1972; Aggregation in Medicine, 1984; Licentiate in Literature, 1986. *Literary Appointments:* 1st Congresso Luso-Brasileiro de Literatura, Porto, 1984; Oratio Sapientia, Universidade Tecnica de Lisboa, Lisbon; 1st Congresso Internacional de Lingua Portuguesa, Lisbon, 1989; Ciclo de Conferencias O Corpo Morfologico, Porto, 1990. *Publications include:* Historias Quase Clinicas (short stories) 3 vols, 1982, 1984, 1988; A Chamada (short stories) 1982; As Carreiras (Romance) 1982; O Bojador (Romance) 1982; Biologia do Conto (literary study about short story) 1987; Cais do Sodre (short stories) 1988; Also, Medical books (6 vols), poetry. plays. *Contributions to:* Magazines, including Noticias Medicas, Geofarma, Espaco Medico, Intercidades, and journals, such as O Diario, Jornal de Letras, Letras e Letras. *Honours:* Theatre Play Award, Fialho de Almeida, 1982; Literary Award, Abel Salazar, 1986; Great Award to Romance, Cidade da Amadora, 1990. *Memberships include:* Associacao Portuguesa de Escritores; Sociedade Portuguesa de Escritores Medicos; Sociedade de Ciencias Medicas de Lisboa; Sociedade Portuguesa de Anatomia. *Address:* Rua Almirante Matos Moreira 7, 2775 Carcavelos, Portugal.

MORGAN Alison Mary, b. 2 May 1930. Childrens Writer. m. 23 Apr 1960, 2 sons. *Education:* BA, Somerville College, Oxford, 1952; Postgraduate Certificate of Education, London University, 1952-53. *Publications:* Fish, 1971; Pete, 1972; Ruth Crane, 1973; At Willie Tuckers Place, 1975; River Song, 1976; Leaving Home, 1979; Paul's Kite, 1981; the Eyes of the Blind, 1986; The Raft, 1976; Brighteye, 1984; Christabel, 1984; Staples for Amos, 1987; A Walk with Smudge the Wild Morgans, 1988; Smudge and the Danger Lion,

1989; Macrae, 1989; The Biggest Birthday Card in the World, 1989; Caroline's Coat, 1991. *Contributions to:* Various journals. *Honours:* Welsh academy Award for Pete, 1973; Shortlisted Carnegie for Chistabel, 1985; Guardian Childrens Book of the Year, Leaving Home, 1981. *Literary Agent:* A.P. Watt. *Address:* Talcoed, Llanafan, Builth Wells, Powys, Wales.

MORGAN Austen Jude, b. 4 July 1949, Derry, Northern Ireland. *Education:* University of Bristol, BSc, 1968-72; Queens University, Belfast, PhD, 1972-75. *Publications:* Harold Wilson; J Kamsay MacDonald; James Connolly: A Political Biography; Labour and Partition: The Belfast Working Class, 1908-23; Ireland: Divied Nation Divided Class. *Memberships:* Writers Guild of Great Britain. *Literary Agent:* A M Heath, 79 St Martins Lane, London WC2W 4AA. *Address:* 76 Inderwick Road, London N8 9JY, England.

MORGAN Claire. *See:* **HIGHSMITH (Mary) Patricia.**

MORGAN Dan, b. 1925, United Kingdom. Writer; Managing Director. *Appointments:* Formerly Lecturer on Contemporary Novel, Extra-Mural Department, University of Nottingham; Currently Managing Director, Dan Morgan Ltd (retail menswear). *Publications:* Guitar, 1965; The New Minds, 1967; The Several Minds, 1969; Mind Trap, 1970; Inside, 1971; Thunder of Stars (with J Kippax), 1974; Seed of Stars (with J Kippax), 1974; The Neutral Stars (with J Kippax), 1975; The Country of the Mind, 1975; The Concrete Horizon, 1976; Spanish Guitar, 1982; Beginning Windsurfing, 1982; You Can Play the Guitar (with Nick Penny), 1983. *Address:* 1 Chapel Lane, Spalding, Lincs PE11 1BP, England.

MORGAN Edwin (George), b. 1920, United Kingdom. Writer; Poet; Emeritus Professor. *Appointments:* Assistant Lecturer, 1947-50, Lecturer, 1950-65, Senior Lecturer, 1965-71, Reader, 1971-75, Titular Professor of English, 1975-80, University of Glasgow; Visiting Professor, University of Strathclyde, 1987-90; University College of Wales, Aberystwyth, 1990-. *Publications:* The Vision of Cathkin Braes, 1952; Beowulf, translation, 1952; The Cape of Good Hope, 1955; Poems from Eugenio Montale, translation, 1959; Sovpoems: Brecht, Neruda, Pasternak, Tsvetayeva, Mayakovsky, Martynov, Yevtushenko, translation, 1961; Collins Albatross Book of Longer Poems: English and American Poetry from the Fourteenth Century to the Present Day (editor), 1963; Starryveldt, 1965; Scotch Mist, 1965; Sealwear, 1966; Scottish Poetry One to Six (edited with G Bruce and M Lindsay), 1966-72; Emergent Poems, 1967; The Second Life, 1968; Gnomes, 1968; Proverbfolder, 1969; Penguin Modern Poets 15 (with Alan Bold and Edward Brathwaite), 1969; The Horseman's Word: A Sequence of Concrete Poems, 1970; Twelve Songs, 1970; New English Dramatists 14 (editor), 1970; Sandor Weores and Ferenc Juhasz: Selected Poems (translated with David Wevill), 1970; The Dolphin's Song, 1971; Glasgow Sonnets, 1972; Instamatic Poems, 1972; Wi the Haill Voice: Poems by Mayakovsky, translation, 1972; The Whittrick: A Poem in Eight Dialogues, 1973; From Glasgow to Saturn, 1973; Essays, 1974; Fifty Renascence Love-Poems, translation, 1975; Rites of Passage: Selected Translations, 1976; East European Poets, 1976; Hugh MacDiarmid, 1976; The New Divan, 1977; Colour Poems, 1978; Platen: Selected Poems, translation, 1978; Star Gate: Science Fiction Poems, 1979; Scottish Satirical Verse (editor), 1980; Poems of Thirty Years, 1982; Grafts/Takes, 1983; 4 Glasgow Subway Poems, 1983; Sonnets from Scotland, 1984; Selected Poems, 1985; From the Video Box, 1986; Newspoems, 1987; Themes on a Variation, 1988; Tales from Limerick Zoo, 1988; Collected Poems, 1990; Nothing Not Giving Messages (interviews), 1990; Crossing the Border: Essays on Scottish Literature, 1990; Hold Hands Among the Atoms, 1991; Evening Will Come They Will Sew the Blue Sail, 1991; Rostand's Cyrano de Bergerac (translation), 1992. *Address:* 19 Whittingehame Court, Glasgow G12 0BG, Scotland.

MORGAN Elaine (Neville), b. 1920, United Kingdom. Author. *Publications:* The Descent of Woman, 1972, 2nd Edition, 1985; Falling Apart, 1976; The Aquatic Ape: A Theory of Human Evolution, 1982; The Scars of Evolution, 1990. *Literary Agent:* Lemon Unna & Durbridge. *Address:* 24 Aberffrwd Road, Mountain Ash, Glamorgan, Wales.

MORGAN Mary. *See:* **WRIGHT Mary Morgan.**

MORGAN Michaela, b. 7 Apr 1951, Manchester, England. Writer; Teacher. m. Colin Holden, 1 son. *Education:* BA, University of Warwick, 1970-73; PGCE, University of Leicester, 1975. *Appointments:* Writer in Residence, H M Prison, Ashwell, Leicester, 1992. *Publications:* The Monster is Coming; The Edward Stories; Dinostory; The Helpful Betty Stories; Harraps Junior and Longmans Project. *Contributions to:* Poetry Anthologies for Children. *Honours:* Included, Childrens Book of the year; Childrens Choice of International Reading Association. *Memberships:* Society of Authors; NAWE. *Literary Agent:* Rosemary Sandberg, Bowerdean Street, SW6. *Address:* 9 Main Street, Bisbrooke, Oakham, Rutland, Leics, LE15 9EP, England.

MORGAN Patricia, b. 1944, United Kingdom. Writer. *Appointments:* Teacher, 1967-71; Research Fellow, London School of Economics, 1979-82. *Publications:* Child Care: Sense and Fable, 1975; Delinquent Fantasies, 1978; Criminal Welfare on Trial (co-author). *Address:* c/o Maurice Temple Smith Ltd, Gower House, Croft Road, Aldershot GU11 3HR, England.

MORGAN Robert, b. 17 Apr 1922, South Wales, Former Schoolmaster; Artist; Writer. m. Dec 1953, 2 daughters. *Education:* ONC, School of Mines, Treforest, South wales, 1947-50; Teaching Diploma, College of Education, Bognor Regis, 1951-53; Advanced Diploma in Special Education, Southampton University, 1968-70. *Publications:* The Night's Prison, 1967; Poems and Extracts, 1968; On the Banks of the Cynon, 1974; The Storm, 1974; My Lamp Still Burns (autobiography), 1981; The Miners and Other Stories, 1986; Memoir, 1988; Landmarks, 1989; Poems and Drawings, 1984; Broadcast Plays: Rainbow Valley, 1967; The Master Miners, 1972; Voices in the Dark (verse-play), 1976. *Contributions to:* Short stories and articles in magazines and journals at home and abroad. *Membership:* Full Member, The Welsh Academy. *Address:* 72 Anmore Road, Denmead, Hampshire PO7 6NT, England.

MORGAN Ted, b. 1932, USA. Writer. *Appointments:* Member of Staff, Associated Press, New York City, 1958-59; Member of Staff, New York Herald Tribune, New York City, Paris and Rome, 1959-64. *Publications:* On Becoming American, 1979; Maugham, 1980; Rowing Toward Eden, 1981; Churchill: Young Man in a Hurry 1874-1915, 1982; F D R: A Biography, 1985; An Uncertain Hour, 1989.

MORGAN-GRENVILLE Gerard, b. 1931, United Kingdom. Chairman of Companies; Writer. *Publications:* Barging into France, 1972; Barging into Southern France, 1973; Holiday Cruising in France, 1973; Cruising the Sahara, 1974; Barging into Burgundy, 1975; Nuclear Power: What It Means to You, 1980.

MORGAN-WITTS Maxwell, b. 27 Sept 1931, Detroit, USA. Author; Film and Video Producer/Director. m. Pauline A L Lawson, 4 Jan 1958, 1 son, 1 daughter. *Education:* Mount Royal College, Calgary, Canada; Honours, University of Toronto, Academy of Radio & TV Arts. *Publications:* The Day the World Ended, 1969, as film, When Time Ran Out, 1977; Earthquake, 1971; The Strange Fate of the Morro Castle, 1973; Voyage of the Damned, 1974, as film, 1976; The Day Guernica Died, 1975; Enola Gay (Ruin From the Air, in UK), 1977, film, 1978; The Day the Bubble Burst, 1979, as film, 1981; Trauma, 1981; Pontiff, 1983; The Year of Armageddon, 1984. *Contributions to:* The Listener; Times; Daily Mail; Reader's Digest. *Honours:* Edgar Allan

Poe Award, 1974; Knight of Mark Twain, 1978. *Memberships:* Authors Guild; Society of Authors; Hurlingham Club; Club des hauts de Vaugrenier. *Literary Agent:* Andrew Lownie. *Address:* c/o Andrew Lownie, 15/17 Meddon Street, London W1R 7LF, England.

MORHANGE Michele. *See:* **DE WAELE Michele.**

MORIARTY Frederick L., b. 1913, USA. Professor of Biblical Studies. *Appointments:* Professor of Biblical Studies, Weston School of Theology, Cambridge, Massachusetts, 1950-70; Professor of Theology, Boston College, Massachusetts, 1960-78; Professor of Biblical Studies: Gregorian University, Rome, Italy, 1963-77; Loyola University, Chicago, Illinois, USA, 1979-81; Gonzaga University, Spokane, Washington, 1981-. *Publications:* Introducing the Old Testament, 1960; Foreword to the Old Testament Books, 2nd Edition, 1964. *Address:* Boston College, Chestnut Hill, MA 02167, USA.

MORICE Anne. *See:* **SHAW Felicity.**

MORIER Henri, b. 23 May 1910, Geneva, Switzerland. *Education:* Licence es lettres, distinction, Modern Romance Languages, University of Geneva, 1933; Doctorat es lettres, 1944. *Appointments:* High School Teacher of Literature, 1945-1947; Extraordinary Professor, History of the French Language, University of Geneva, 1952; Ordinary Professor, and dissertation, 1956; Director, Centre of Poetics and Experimental Phonetics, 1962; Emeritus Professor, 1980. *Publications:* Dictionnaire de Poetique et de Rhetorique, 1961, (4 editions); Le Rythme du Veis-libre Symboliste, 1943-44, (3 volumes); La Psychologie des Styles, 1985; La Technique de l'Examen, 1941; Poemes nocturnes, 1944; Aubades, 1947; Le Rythme du Vers libre symboliste, 1944 (re-edition, 1975); La Psychologie des Styles, 1959; Dictionaire de Poétique et de Rhetorique, 1st edition, 1961, 4th edition, 1989. *Honours:* Lacharanne Prize for Poetry, 1934; Hentsch Prize for Literature, 1934; First Prize, Competition for Sonnets, Journal de Geneve, 1940; Bordin Prize for Literature, 1946, Prize for the French Language, Academie Francaise, 1959, Saintour Prize, 1962, Academie Francaise; First Prize for Short Story, Institute National Genevois, 1957; Vangelas Prize, 1979. *Memberships:* Conseil International de la Langue Francaise; Honorary Committee Association pour la sauvegarde de la langue francaise, 1991; l'Institut National Genevois. *Address:* Les Caryatides, 7 Rue du Bief, 74100 Ambilly, France.

MORIZOT-YOUNG Carol Ann, (Anna Mahanaim), b. 21 Sept 1944, Shreveport, USA. Poet; Writer; Teacher. m. Bruce L. Young, 7 Sept 1982, 2 sons by previous marriage. *Education:* BA, 1966; BS, 1971, Northeast Louisiana University. *Appointments:* Harold House Publishers, 1977-79; Poet in the Schools, Arkansas Arts Council, 1979-80. *Publications:* Just This Side of Madness, 1978; Survivors and Other Poems, 1977. *Contributions to:* Numerous magazines and journals. *Honours:* Mary B. Patton Award, 1963; Poet Laureate Award Arkansas Democrat, 1986, 1987; many other honours and awards. *Memberships:* Poets & Writers Inc, National Education Association; Arkansas Education Association. *Literary Agent:* Bertha Klausner, New York.

MORLAND Dick. *See:* **HILL Reginald (Charles).**

MORLEY David, b. 1923, United Kingdom. Emeritus Professor of Tropical Child Health. *Appointments:* Member, Editorial Board, Medicine Digest, Postgraduate Doctor, and Journal of Environmental Paediatrics and Tropical Child Health. *Publications:* Paediatric Priorities in the Developing World, 1973; See How They Grow (with Margaret Woodland), 1979; Practising Health for All (with J R Rohde and G Williams); My Name Is Today (with Hermione Lovel), 1986; Releasing Stone, 1989. *Address:* Institute of Child Health, 30 Guilford Street, London WC1N 1EH, England.

MORLEY Don, b. 28 Jan 1937, Derbyshire, England. Photographer; Journalist. m. Josephine Mary Munro, 17 Sept 1961, 2 sons. *Education:* National Certificates Electrical Engineering & Photography. *Appointments:* Former Picture Editor, The Guardian; Former Chief Photographer, Sports World Magazine, British Olympic Association; Chief Photographer, Moto Course. *Publications:* Action Photography, 1975; Motorcycling, 1977; Everyone's Book of Motorcycling, 1981; The Story of the Motorcycle, 1983; Motorbikes, 1983; Classic British Trials Bikes, 1984; Classic British Moto Cross Machines, 1985; The Classic British Two Stroke Trials Bikes, 1987; The Spanish Trials Bikes, 1987; Trials: A Riders Guide, 1990; BSA (History in Colour), 1990; Triumph (History in Colour), 1990; Norton (History in Colour), 1990; BMW, (History in Colour), 1993. *Contributions to:* Magazines & journals worldwide. *Honours:* 17 times national and international photography award winner. *Memberships:* Founder, 5 years Chairman, Hon. Life Member, Professional Sports Photographers Association. *Address:* 132 Carlton Road, Reigate, Surrey RH2 OJF, England.

MORLEY John(athan) David, b. 21 Jan 1948, Singapore. *Education:* BA, First Class Honours, Merton College, Oxford, 1969; Diploma from Language Research Institute, Waseda University, 1975. *Appointments:* Japan Broadcasting Corporation, free-lance interpreter, translator, researcher and general co-ordinator in Western Europe, 1976-. *Publications:* Pictures From the Water Trade: Adventures of a Westerner in Japan (autobiographical novel) 1985; In the Labyrinth, 1986; The Case of Thomas N (novel) 1987. *Contributions to:* Newspapers and magazines in the United states, Australia, West Germany and Denmark, including New York Times and Vanity Fair. *Honours:* Pictures From the Water Trade won an award for best first work from Yorkshire post and was nominated by Time magazine as one of the five best nonfiction books of the year, both 1985. *Literary Agent:* A P Watt, London. *Address:* c/o A P Watt, 20 John Street, London WC1N 2DR, England.

MORLEY Patricia Marlow, b. 25 May 1929, Toronto, Canada. Writer; Educator. m. Lawrence W. Morley, (div), 3 sons, 1 daughter. *Education:* BA Hon, English Language and Literature, University of Toronto, 1951; MA, English, Carleton University, 1967; PhD, English Literature, University of Ottowa, 1970. *Appointments:* Asst Professor 1972-75; Assoc Professor 1975-80; Professor of English and Canadian Studies 1980-89; Fellow, Simone de Beauvoir Institute, Concordia University, 1979-89; Lifetime Honorary Fellow, Simone de Beauvoir Institute, 1989-. *Publications include:* Kurelek, 1986; Margaret Laurence, 1981; Morley Callaghan, 1978. *Contributions to:* Reviews, Articles to professional journals. *Honours:* Award for non-fiction, 1987; Ottawa-Carleton Literary Award, 1988. *Memberships:* The Writers Union of Canada; Canadian Association of University Teachers; Association of Commonwealth Language and Literature Studies (exec. 1976-78). *Address:* Box 137, Manotick, Ontario KOA 2NO, Canada.

MORLEY Sheridan Robert, b. 5 Dec 1941, Ascot, Berkshire, England. Journalist; Biographer; Broadcaster. m. Margaret Gudejko, 18 July 1965 (div 1990), 1 son, 2 daughters. *Education:* MA, Honours, Merton College, Oxford, 1964. *Appointments:* Arts Editor, Punch, 1974-88; Drama Critic, International Herald Tribune, 1975-; Drama Critic, Spectator, 1992-; Film Critic, Sunday Express, 1992-. *Publications:* A Talent to Amuse (1st Biography of Noel Coward), 1969; The Other Side of the Moon (1st Biog of David Niven), 1979; Odd Man Out (1st Biog of James Mason), 1984; Gladys Cooper; Gertrude Lawrence; Oscar Wilde; Tales From The Hollywood Raj; Elizabeth Taylor; Marlene Dietrich; Katharine Hepburn; Review Copies; Our Theatres In The 80's; Spread A Little Happiness, 1986; Shooting Stars; Our Theatres in the Eighties, 1990; Methuen Book of Theatrical Shot Stories, 1992. *Contributions to:* The Times; Punch; Herald Tribune; Spectator; Sunday Times; Playbill (US); Variety (US); The Australian. *Honour:* BP

Arts Journalist of the Year, 1990. *Memberships:* Critics Circle; Garrick Club. *Literary Agent:* Curtis Brown, 162 Regent St, London, England. *Address:* 19 Carlyle Court, Chelsea Harbour, London SW10 0XD, England.

MORNELL Pierre, b. 22 Jan 1935, Chicago, Illinois, USA. Psychiatrist. m. Linda Carol Whitney, 16 Oct 1966, 1 son, 2 daughters. *Education:* UCLA, BA, 1952-56; UCSF, MD, 1959-63; Langley Porter Institute. *Publications:* Passive Men, Wild Women; Thank God It's Monday; The Lovebook. *Memberships:* American Psychiatric Association. *Literary Agent:* Don Congdon. *Address:* 1 Park Avenue, Mill Valley, CA 94941, USA.

MORNER (Carl) Magnus (Birgersson), b. 31 Mar 1924, Mellosa, Sweden. University Professor. m. Aare Ruth Puhk, 2 Dec 1947, 2 sons, 1 daughter. *Education:* University Studies, Stockholm, PhD, 1946-54. *Publications:* The Political And Economic Activities of the Jesuits in the Plata Region; Race Mixture in the History of Latin America; La Corona Espanola y los Foraneos en los Puehlos de indios de America; Historia Social Latinoamericana; The Andean Past and others. *Contributions to:* Numerous. *Honours:* Loubat Prize; Doctor H Causa (2); President, 48th International Congress of Americanists. *Memberships:* Regia Societatis Scientiarum et Litterarum Gothoburgensis; Association of European Latin Americanist Historians; International Congress of Americanists. *Address:* Äppelstigen 5, S-647 00 Mariefred, Sweden.

MOROWITZ Harold J, b. USA. Robinson Professor of Biology and Natural Philosophy, George Mason University. *Publications:* Proceedings of the First National Biophysics Conference (edited with H Quastler), 1959; Theoretical and Mathematical Biology (edited with T Waterman), 1961; Life and the Physical Sciences, 1963; Energy Flow in Biology, 1968; Entropy for Biologists, 1970; Life on the Planet Earth (with L Morowitz), 1975; Ego Niches, 1977; Foundations of Bioenergetics, 1978; The Wine of Life, 1979; Mayonnaise and the Origin of Life, 1982; Cosmic Joy and Local Pain, 1987. *Address:* 56 Ox Bow Lane, Woodbridge, CT 06525, USA.

MORPURGO Jack Eric, b. 26 Apr 1918, London, England, Author; Literary Agent; University Professor. m. Catherine Noel Kippe Cammaerts, 16 July 1947, 3 sons, 1 daughter. *Education:* Christ's Hospital; University of New Brunswick, Canada; BA, College of William and Mary, USA, 1938; Durham University, England, 1939; Institute of historical Research, 1946. *Appointments:* Editor, Penguin Books, 1945-69; Editor, Penguin Parade, 1949-50; General Editor, Penguin History of England and Penguin History of the World, 1949-69; Assistant Director, Nuffield Foundation, 1951-54; Director General, National Book League, 1954-69; Professor of American and Canadian Studies, University of Geneva, Switzerland, 1968-70; Professor of American Literature, University of Leeds, 1969-83. *Publications:* American Excursion, 1949; History of the United States, (Co-author), 2 volumes, 1955, 1959, 1971, 1976; Barnes Wallis: A Biography, 1972; Allen lane: King Penguin, 1979; The Road to Athens, 1963; Their Majesties; Royall Colledge, 1976; Leigh Hunt: Autobiography, (Editor), 1949; Editions of Lamb, Trelawny, Keats, Cobbett, Fenimore Cooper, Lewis Carroll, Marlowe and others; Master of None: An Autobiography, 1990; Christ's Hospital, (Co-author G A T Allan), 1986; Christ's Hospital: An Introductory History, 1990; Charles Lamb and Elia, 1993. *Contributions to:* Times Literary Supplement; Daily Telegrph; Yorkshire Post; Quadrant, Australia; Mayfair, Canada. *Honours:* 4 Honorary Doctorates from USA Institutions; Yorkshire Post Special Literary Award, 1980. *Memberships:* Army and Navy Club, Pilgrims. *Literary Agent:* Sexton Agency and Press Limited. *Address:* 12 Laurence Mews, Askew Road, London W12 9AT, England.

MORRESSY John, b. 8 Dec 1930, USA. Writer; Educator. m. Barbara Ann Turner, 11 Aug 1956. *Education:* MA, English, New York University, 1961. *Appointments:* Writer in Residence, Worcester Consortium for Higher Education, 1977; Visiting Lecturer, Creative Writing, & Lloyd C. Elliott Professor, English, University of Maine, Orono, 1977-78; Writer in Residence, Professor, English, Franklin Pierce College, Rindge, 1978-; Writer in Residence, Lynchburg College, 1987. *Publications:* The Addison Tradition, 1968; Starbrat, 1972; A Long Communion, 1974; Frostworld and Dreamfire, 1977; Ironbrand, 1980; A Voice for Princess, 1986; The Blackboard Cavalier, 1966; Nail Down the Stars, 1973; Under a Calculating Star, 1975; Graymantle, 1981; Kingsbane, 1982; The Mansions of Space, 1983; Other Stories, 1984; The Time of the Annihilator, 1985; The Questing of Kedrigern, 1987; Kedrigern in Wanderland, 1988. *Contributions to:* Esquire; Playboy; many other professional journals & magazines. *Honours:* Balrog Award, Best Short Story Fantasy Fiction, 1984; Pandora Award for Science Fiction, 1984. *Memberships:* Authors Guild; Science Fiction Writers of America. *Literary Agent:* William Morris Agency Inc, New York, USA. *Address:* East Sullivan, NH 03445, USA.

MORRIS Christopher Hugh, b. 28 Mar 1938, Luton, England. Journalist; Author. m. 31 Mar 1962, 1 daughter. *Education:* Diploma, Luton College; National Council for Training of Journalists, 1958. *Appointments:* Reporter, Film & Music Critic, Home Counties Newspapers, Luton, 1953-58; Reporter, Daily Sketch, London, 1958-62; Freelance Foreign Correspondent, Madrid Spain, 1962-72, BBC TV/Radio, ITN, NBC, Canadian and Australian Broadcasting, Daily Mail and Daily Express; Reporter, Special Correspondent, BBC TV and Radio News, 1972-. *Publications:* The Day They Lost the H Bomb, 1966; The Big Catch, 1966; Don't They Know It's Christmas - Bob Geldof in Africa, documentary film, BBC TV, 1985. *Contributions to:* various journals. *Honours:* Golden Nymph Monte Carlo, 1983; Silver Award, New York International Film and TV Festival, 1982. *Address:* BBC TV News, Wood Lane, London W12 7RJ, England.

MORRIS Colin, b. Liverpool, Englnd. Writer; Producer; Director; Actor; Interviewer, BBC TV & ITV. *Publications:* Stage Play Productions: Desert Rats, 1945; Italian Love Story, 1945; Reluctant Heroes, 1950; Television Plays: the Unloved, 1954; Who Me, 1959; Jacks and Knaves, 1960; Women in Crisis, 1963; The Newcomers, 1965; King of the River, 1967; Walk with Destiny, 1974; Television Serials: Reluctant Bandit, 1966; The Dragon's Opponent, 1973; Television Series: The Carnforth Practice, 1974; Heart to Heart; Turning Point; My Way; Women of Today; My Life; My Marriage; My Family, 1986; numerous dramatized documentaries, 1954-74. *Contributions to:* Evening Standard; Sunday Mirror. *Honours:* Atlantic Award in Literature, 1946; 4 Best Scripts Awards, 1955, 1956, 1958, 1961. *Address:* 75 Hilway, London N6, England.

MORRIS Desmond John, b. 24 Jan 1928, Purton, Wiltshire, England. Zoologist. m. Ramona Baulch, 30 Jul 1952, 1 son. *Education:* Dauntsey's School, Wiltshire; BSc, Birmingham University, 1951; D Phil, Oxford University, 1954. *Publications include:* The Biology of Art, 1962; The Naked Ape, 1967; The Human Zoo, 1969; ManWatching, 1977; Catwatching, 1986; Dogwatching, 1986; The Animal Contract, 1990; Animal-Watching, 1990; Babywatching, 1991. *Contributions to:* Many journals, magazines. *Membership:* Scientific Fellow, Zoological Society of London. *Address:* c/o Jonathan Cape, Random Century House, 20 Vauxhall Bridge Road, London SW1V 2SA, England.

MORRIS (Clifford) Eric, b. 1940, United Kingdom. Political/Defence Analyst and Consultant; Former Lecturer, Royal Military Academy. *Publications:* Berlin and the Cold War, 1973; Tanks: An Illustrated History, 1975; Weapons and Warfare of the Twentieth Century, 1976; The Russian Navy: Myth and Reality, 1977; War in Peace: An Illustrated History of Conflict since 1945, 1981; Corregidor, 1982; Salerno, 1983; Churchill's

Private Armies, 1986; Terrorism - Threat & Response (with Alan Hoe), 1988; Guerrillas in Uniform, 1989. *Address:* 23 Marine Drive, Barry, South Glamorgan CF6 8QP, Wales.

MORRIS Harry, b. 1924, USA. Professor of English; Poet. *Appointments:* Assistant Professor, 1961-63, Associate Professor, 1963-67, Professor of English, 1967-, Florida State University, Tallahassee. *Publications:* Poetry: A Critical and Historical Introduction (with I Ribner), 1962; Richard Barnfield: Colin's Child, 1963; The Sorrowful City, 1966; Birth and Copulation and Death, 1969, 1969; The Snake Hunter, 1970; Last Things in Shakespeare, 1985. *Address:* Department of English, Florida State University, Tallahassee, FL 32306, USA.

MORRIS James. *See:* **MORRIS Jan.**

MORRIS James Cliftonne, b. Talladega, Alabama, USA. Junior High School and College English Teacher. m. Gladys P Morris. *Education:* BS, Columbia University, 1949; Teachers College, MA, 1950. *Publications:* Cleopotra and Other Poems; From a Tin mouth God to His Brass Eared Subjects; Love Poems for a Black Indian Grandma; Good Evenin, Midnight Blues This Mornin; Call Them Heros; Dusty Shells from the Peanut Gallery. *Contributions to:* Phylon Review; Beyond the Blues; New Voices in the Wind; Apple Blossom. *Honours:* Silver & Gold Awards; World of Poetry Award. *Memberships:* NY Poetry Forum; NY Shelley Society; Am Poetry Society; Poets and Writers; Queens Council of the Arts; Am academy of Poets; Int Clover Poetry Association; association of teachers of England. *Address:* 174-31 126 Avenue, Springfield Gardens, New York City, NY 11434, USA.

MORRIS Jan, (James Morris), b. 2 Oct 1926. Writer. *Appointments:* Editorial Staff: The Times, 1951-56, The Guardian 1957-62. *Publications:* (as James Morris) Coast to Coast, 1956; Sultan in Oman, 1957; The Market of Seleukia, 1957; Coronation Everest, 1958; South African Winter, 1958; The Hashemite Kings, 1959; Venice, 1960; The Upstairs Donkey (for children), 1962; The Road to Huddersfield, 1963; Cities, 1963; The Presence of Spain, 1964; Oxford, 1968; Pax Britannica, 1968; The Great Port, 1970; Places, 1972; Heaven's Command, 1973; Farewell The Trumpets, 1978; (as Jan Morris) Conundrum, 1974; Travels, 1976; The Oxford Book of Oxford, 1978; Spain, 1979; Destinations; The Venetian Empire; My Favourite Stories of Wales, 1980; The Small Oxford Book of Wales; Wales the First Place; A Venetian Bestiary; Spectacle of Empire, 1982; Stones of Empire, 1983; Journeys, 1984; The Matter of Wales, 1984; Among the Cities, 1985; Last Letters from Hav, 1985; Stones of Empire: The Buildings of the Raj, 1986; Manhattan '45, 1987; Hong Kong, 1988; Pleasures of a Tangled Life (Autobiography), 1989; Ireland, Your Only Place, 1990; City to City, 1990; Sydney, 1992. *Honours:* Commonwealth Fellowship, USA, 1954; George Polk Memorial Award for Journalism, USA, 1961; Heinemann Award for Literature; Hon Fellow, University College of Wales, Aberystwyth; Hon D.Litt, University of Wales. *Membership:* Yr Academi Gymreig. *Address:* Trefan Morys, Llanystumdwy, Cricieth, Gwynedd, LL52 OLP, Wales.

MORRIS Janet Ellen, b. 25 May 1946, Boston, Massachusetts, USA. Writer. m. 31 Oct 1970. *Publications include:* Silistra Quartet 1976- 78; 1983-84; Dream Dance Trilogy 1980-83; Heroes in Hell, series 1984-88 (10 volumes); Beyong Sanctuary 1985-86 (3 volumes); Warlord! 1986; I, the Sun, 1984; with Chris Morris: The 40-Minute War, 1983; Medusa 1984; The Little Helliad, 1986; Outpassage, 1987; City at the Edge of Time, 1988; Tempus Vabound, 1989; with David Drake: Target 1989; Kill Ratio 1987. *Contributions to:* 50 short stories in various publications including The Yacht; Argos; New Destinies. *Honours:* Hellva Award for Best Novel for 40 Minute Wars, 1985. *Memberships:* Science Fiction Writers of America; Mystery Writers of America; BMI (Broadcast Music Inc); New York Academy

of Science; National Intelligence Studyn Center; Association of Old Crows. *Literary Agent:* Perry Knowlton, Curtis Brown Ltd. *Address:* c/o Curtis Brown Ltd, 10 Astor Place, New York, NY 10003, USA.

MORRIS John. *See:* **HEARNE John.**

MORRIS Katharine, b. 22 May 1910, England. *Publications:* New Harrowing; The Vixens Cub; Country Dance; The Long Meadow; The House by the Water. *Memberships:* International PEN; English Speaking Union. *Address:* Little Dower House, Bleasby, Nottingham, NG14 7EX, England.

MORRIS Mary, b. 14 May 1947, Chicago, Illinois, USA. Writer. m. Larry O'Connor, 20 Aug 1989, 1 daughter. *Education:* BA, Tufts College, 1969; MA, Columbia University, 1973; M Phil, 1977. *Appointments:* Princeton University, 1980-87, 1991-; New York University, 1988-. *Publications:* A Mother's Love, Nothing to Declare: Memoirs of A Women Traveling Alone; The Waiting Room; Vanishing Animals & Other Stories; The Bus of Dreams; Wall to Wall; Crossroads. *Contributions to:* The Paris Review; The New York Times; Triquarterly; New Women; Vogue; McCalls; Ontario Review; Agni Review. *Honours:* National Endowment for the Arts; Rome Prize; Guggenheim; Creative Public Service Award; Friends of American Writers Award; Princeton University Fellowship. *Memberships:* American PEN; Authors Guild; Friends of the American academy, Rome. *Literary Agent:* Amanda Urban, ICM. *Address:* c/o Amanda Urban, ICM 40 W, 57th Street, New York, NY 10019, USA.

MORRIS Robert K, b. 1933, USA. Professor of English. *Appointments:* Professor of English, City College, City University of New York, 1974-87, retired. *Publications:* The Novels of Anthony Powell, 1968; Continuance and Change, 1972; The Consolations of Ambiguity, 1972; The Achievement of William Styron (edited with Irving Malin), 1974, 2nd Edition, 1981; Paradoxes of Order, 1975; Old Lines, New Forces, 1977; Fables, 1985. *Address:* Rt 1, Box 263, South Road, Denmark, ME 04022, USA.

MORRIS Sara. *See:* **BURKE John Frederick.**

MORRIS Stephen, b. 1935, United Kingdom. Educator; Poet. *Appointments:* Assistant Lecturer, 1967-69, Lecturer, 1969-72, Senior Lecturer, 1972-85, Faculty of Art, The Polytechnic, Wolverhampton; Full Time Writer, Journalist & TV Script Writer. *Publications:* Alien Poets, 1965; Wanted for Writing Poetry (with Peter Finch), 1968; Penny Farthing Madness, 1969; Born Under Leo, 1972; The Revolutionary, 1972; The Kingfisher Catcher, 1974; Death of a Clown, 1976; Widening Circles, 1977; The Moment of Truth, 1978; Too Long at the Circus, 1980; The Umbrellas of Mr Parapluie, 1985; Rolling Dice, 1986. *Address:* Rue Las Cours, Aspiran 34800, France.

MORRIS Terry, b. 19 Feb 1914, New York City, USA. Freelance Writer. m. Eugene J. Morris, 29 Mar 1934, 1 son. *Education:* BA, 1933, MA, 1937, Hunter College. *Appointments:* Reporter, Feature Writer, Battle Creek, Michigan Enquirer, 1943-44; Lecturer, Writers' Workshops, New York University, Queens College, New School for Social Research. *Publications:* No Hiding Place, 1945; Dr America: The Story of Tom Dooley, 1963; Shalom, Golda, 1973; A New You: How Plastic Surgery Can Change Your Life, 1977; Just Sixteen, 1983; On Your Toes, 1984; Editor, Contributor, Prose by Professionals, 1963; Contributor, Writing the Magazine Article, 1970. *Contributions to:* professional journals including; Good Housekeeping; Redbook; Readers' Digest. *Honours:* American Heart Association Blakeslee Award, 1964; President, American Society of Journalists & Authors, 1974-75. *Memberships:* American Society of Journalists & Authors, various offices; Women's City Club. *Address:* 200 Central Park South, New York, NY 10019, USA.

MORRIS Willie, b. 1934, USA. Author. *Appointments:* Editor-in-Chief, The Texas Observer, 1960-62; Executive Editor, 1965-67, Editor-in-Chief, 1967-71, Harper's Magazine, New York City. *Publications:* North Toward Home, 1967; Yazoo: Integration in a Deep Southern Town, 1971; Good Old Boy, 1972; The Last of the Southern Girls, 1973; James Jones, 1978; Terrains of the Heart, 1981; The Courting of Marcus Dupree, 1983; Always Stand in Against the Curve, 1984.

MORRISON Anthony James, (Tony Morrison), b. 5 July 1936, United Kingdom. TV Producer; Writer. *Appointments:* South American Pictures (Partner) Nonesuch Expeditions Ltd, Director. *Publications:* Steps to a Fortune (co-author), 1967; Animal Migration, 1973; Land Above the Clouds, 1974; The Andes, 1976; Pathways to the Gods, 1978; Lizzie: A Victorian Lady's Amazon Adventure (co-editor), 1985; The Mystery of the Nasca Lines, Nonesuch Expeditions 1987; Margaret Mee, In Search of Flowers of the Amazon Forests (Editor) Nonesuch Expeditions 1988. *Address:* 48 Station Road, Woodbridge, Suffolk, IP12 4AT, England.

MORRISON Bill, b. 22 Jan 1940, Ballymoney, Northern Ireland. Playwright; Theatre Director. (Div), 1 son, 1 daughter. *Education:* LLB (Hons), Queen's University, Belfast, 1958-62. *Appointments:* Resident Playwright, Victoria Theatre, Stoke-on-Trent, England, 1969-71; Resident Playwright, Everyman Theatre, Liverpool, 1976-79; Associate Director, 1981-83, Artistic Director, 1983-85, Liverpool Playhouse. *Publications:* Stage plays: Flying Blind, 1979; Scrap, 1982; Be Bop A Lula, 1988. Radio and stage plays: Sam Slade Is Missing, 1971; The Love of Lady Margaret, 1972; Ellen Cassidy, 1975; The Emperor of Ice Cream, 1977; Blues in a Flat, 1989; The Little Sister, 1990. Radio plays: The Great Gun-Running episode, 1973; Simpson and Son, 1977; Maguire, 1978; The Spring of Memory, 1981; Affair, 1991; Three Steps To Heaven, 1992. TV plays: Shergar, 1986; A Safe House, 1990; Force of Duty, 1992. *Honours:* Best Programme, Pye Radio Awards, for The Spring of Memory, 1981. *Memberships:* Director, Lagan Pictures Ltd; Chairman, Merseyside Young People's Theatre. *Literary Agent:* Alan Brodie, Representation. *Address:* c/o Alan Brodie, Representation, 91 Regent Street, London W1R 7TB, England.

MORRISON Dorothy Jean Allison, b. 17 Feb 1933, Glasgow, Scotland. Author; Lecturer. m. James F T Morrison, 12 Apr 1955, 1 son, 1 daughter. *Education:* MA, Honours, Glasgow University. *Appointments:* Principal Teacher of History, Montrose Academy, 1968-73; Lecturer in History, Dundee College of Education, 1973-83; Advisor to the Series, Scottish History, & History at Hand, for Scottish TV. *Publications:* (Textbooks for Schools and Colleges): The Great War, 1916-18, 1981; The Romans in Britain, 1978, 2nd edition, 1980; Ancient Greeks, with John Morrison, 1984; Story of Scotland, with J. Halliday, I, 1979, 1980, II, 1982; People of Scotland, I, 1983, II, 1985; History Around You, 1983; Handbook on Money Management, 1985; Historical Sources for Schools, I Agriculture, 1982; Social Studies Topics: Old Age, 1972; Young People, 1973; Health and Hospitals, 1973; The Civilian War, with M. Cuthbert, 1975; Billy Leaves Home, 1979; Travelling in China, 1977; Modern China, 1987. *Contributions to:* Numerous including: Scottish Association of Teachers of History; Northern Review; Times Literary Supplement; Education in the North; History Teaching Review; Produced Teachers' Handbooks for each series of Scottish History programmes for schools. *Memberships:* Fellow, Society of Antiquaries of Scotland; Society for Asian Studies, Committee, 1979-82. *Address:* Craigview House, Usan, Montrose, Tayside, Scotland DD10 9SD.

MORRISON Joan, b. 20 Dec 1922, Hinsdale, Illinois, USA. Writer. m. Robert Thornton Morrison, 19 June 1943, 2 sons, 1 daughter. *Education:* BA, University of Chicago, 1944. *Publications:* American Mosaic; From Camelot to Kent State. *Contributions to:* Numerous inc.

New York Times; McCalls; Mademoiselle. *Honours:* Ambassador Award; New York Times Notable Book of the Year. *Memberships:* Authors Guild; National Society of Arts & Letters; Oral History Association; American Studies Association. *Literary Agent:* John Ware, 392 Central Park West, New York, NY 10025. *Address:* Morristown, NJ 07960, USA.

MORRISON Kristin Diane, b. 1934, USA. Professor of English. *Appointments:* Assistant Professor of English, New York University, New York City, 1967-69; Assistant Professor of English, 1969-71, Associate Professor, 1971-84, Professor of English, 1984-, Boston College, Chestnut Hill, Massachusetts; Academic Dean, Professor of English, Newton College, Massachusetts, 1972-74. *Publications:* Crowell's Handbook of Contemporary Drama (with M Anderson, J Guicharnaud and J D Zipes), 1971; Handbook of Contemporary Drama, 1972; In Black and White, 1972; Canters and Chronicles: The Use of Narrative in the Plays of Samuel Beckett and Harold Pinter, 1983; William Trevor, 1993. *Address:* Department of English, Boston College, Chestnut Hill, MA 02167, USA.

MORRISON Tony. *See:* **MORRISON Anthony James.**

MORRISON Wilbur Howard, b. 21 June 1915, Plattsburgh, New York, USA. Freelance Writer. *Education:* Plattsburgh State Normal School, 1922-30; Plattsburgh High School, 1930-34. *Publications:* Hellbirds, The Story of the B-29s in Combat, 1960; The Incredible 305th: The Can Do Bombers of WWII, 1962; Wings Over the Seven Seas: US Naval Aviation's Fight for Survival, 1974; Point of No Return: The Story of the Twentieth Air Force, 1979; Fortress Without a Roof: The Allied Bombing of the Third Reich, 1982; Above and Beyond 1941-45, 1983; Baja Adventure Guide, 1990; The Elephant and the Tiger: The Full Story of the Vietnam War, 1990; Donald W Douglas: A Heart With Wings, 1991. *Membership:* Dramatists Guild. *Address:* 2036 E Alvarado Street, Fallbrook, CA 92028, USA.

MORRISS Frank, b. 28 Mar 1923, Pasadena, California, USA. Writer; Teacher. m. Mary Rita Moynihan, 11 Feb 1950, 1 son, 3 daughters. *Education:* BS, Regis College, Denver, Colorado, 1943; LLD, Georgetown University School of Law, Washington DC, 1948; Doctor of Letters, Register College of Journalism, Denver, Colorado, 1953. *Appointments:* News Editor, Denver Catholic Register, 1960; Associate Editor, Vermont Catholic Tribune, 1961; News Editor, National Register, 1963; Founding Editor, Twin Circle, 1967; Contributing Editor, Wanderer, St Paul, Minnesota, 1968-. *Publications:* The Divine Epic, 1973; The Catholic as Citizen, 1976; Abortion (co-author) 1979; Saints for the Small, (children's book) 1965; Alfred of Wessex, (children's book) 1959; Submarine Pioneer (children's book) 1961;; The Conservative Imperative, 1970; The Adventures of Broken Hand (children's book) 1957; Boy of Philadelphia (children's book) 1955; The Forgotten Revelation; A Christmas Celebration, 1985, Editor and Contributor; A Neglected Glory, 1976; A Little Life of Our Lord, 1993. *Contributions to:* The Wanderer, columns, fiction, poetry; The World of Poetry, anthology of prizewinners. *Honours:* George Washington Award for newspaper writing on two occasions; Honorable Mention, World of Poetry. *Membership:* The Fellowship of Catholic Scholars (USA). *Address:* 3505 Owens Street, Wheat Ridge, CO 80033, USA.

MORROW Ann Patricia, (Morrow), b. Dublin, Ireland. m. (2) G W K Fenn Smith, 19 May 1984, 2 stepsons, 1 stepdaughter. *Education:* University College of Dublin. *Appointments:* Fleet Street, Daily Express, IPC Magazines, Daily Telegraph. *Publications:* The Queen; The Queen Mother; Highness; Picnic in a Foreign Land; Princess. *Contributions to:* Times; Daily Telegraph. *Memberships:* PEN. *Literary Agent:* Michael Shaw, Curtis Brown. *Address:* c/o Curtis Brown & John

Farquharson, 162-168 Regent Street, London W1R 5TB, England.

MORSBERGER Robert Eustis, b. 10 Sept 1929, Baltimore, Maryland, USA. Professor; Writer. m. Katharine Miller, 17 June 1955, 1 daughter. *Education:* BA, Johns Hopkins University, 1950; MA, 1954, PhD English, 1956, The University of Iowa. *Appointments:* Assistant Professor of English: Miami University, 1956-59, Utah State University, 1959-61; Assistant, Associate Professor of American Thought and Language, Michigan State University, 1961-68; Professor of English: Eastern Kentucky University, 1968- 69, California State Polytechnic University, 1969-; Chairman of the Department, 1974-78. *Publication:* James Thurber, 1964; Lew Wallace: Militant Romantic, 1980; Commonsense Grammar and Style, 1965, 1972; American Screenwriters, co-editor, 1984, 1986; John Steinbeck's Viva Zapata!, editor, 1975; How to Improve Your Verbal Skills, 1963; Swordplay and the Elizabethan and Jacobean Stage, 1974. *Contributions to:* American Literature; American Quarterly; American History Illustrated; Civil War Times Illustrated; Natural History Magazine; New England Quarterly; Steinbeck Quarterly; Alfred Hitchcock Mystery Magazine. *Honours:* Winner of Burkhardt Award for Distinguished Steinbeck Criticism, 1991. *Memberships:* PEN Western American Literature Association; International John Steinbeck Society; Head of Editorial Board, Steinbeck Quarterly. *Literary Agent:* Mike Hamilburg. *Address:* 1530 Berea Court, Claremont, CA 91711, USA.

MORSY Magali, b. 18 Oct 1933, Prague, Checkoslavakia. University Professor. 1 son. *Education:* BA, Kings College, 1956. *Appointments:* University Mohammed, 1960-70; University de la Sorbonne Nouvelle, 1970-. *Publications:* Les Femmes Du Prophete; History of North Africa 1800-1900; Lexique de Monde Arabe Moderne; La Relation de Thomas Pellow; Les Africains. *Contributions to:* Liberation; Jeune Afrique; Maghrea Mashrek. *Honours:* Palmes Academiques; Officier; Order of Science and Arts. *Memberships:* Academie du Vaucause; Societe des Amis D'Ismayl Urbain. *Address:* University de la Sorbonne, Nouvelle, 17 Rue de la Sorbonne, 75005, Paris, France.

MORT Graham Robert, b. 11 Aug 1955, Middleton, England. Poet. m. Maggie Mort, 12 Feb 1979, 3 sons. *Education:* BA, Liverpool University, 1977; St Martins College, Lancaster, 1980. *Appointments:* Creative Writing Course Leader for Open College of the Arts, 1989-. *Publications:* A Country on Fire; Into The Ashes; A Halifax Cider Jar; Sky Burial; Snow From the North; Starting To Write; The Experience of Poetry, Storylines. *Contributions to:* Numerous Literary Magazines and Journals. *Honours:* Major Eric Gregoy Award; Chelterton Poetry Competition 1st Prize; Duncan Launie Prize. *Memberships:* Society of Authors; Northern Association of Writers in Education. *Address:* The Beeches, Riverside, Clapham, Lancaster LA2 8DT, England.

MORTIMER John Clifford, (Geoffrey Lincoln), b. 21 Apr 1923. Barrister; Playwright; Author. m. (1), Penelope Ruth Fletcher, 1 son, 1 daughter, (2) Penelope Gallop, 2 daughters. *Education:* Brasenose College, Oxford. *Appointments:* Called to the Bar, 1948; QC, 1966; Master of the Bench, Inner Temple, 1975. *Publications include:* Novels: Charade, 1947; Rumming Park, 1948; Answer Yes or No, 1950; Like Men Betrayed, 1953; Three Winters, 1956; Will Shakespeare, 1977; Rumpole of the Bailey, 1978; The Trials of Rumpole, 1979; Rumpole's Return, 1981; Clinging to the Wreckage (autobiography), 1982; In Character, 1983; Rumpole and the Golden Thread, 1983; Rumpole's Last Case, 1986; Paradise Postponed, 1986; Character Parts (interviews), 1986; Summers Lease 1988; Titmuss Regained, 1989. Full length plays: The Wrong Side of the Park, 1960; Two Stars for Comfort, 1962; Come as You Are, 1970; The Judge, 1967; The Bells of Hell. Film scripts: John and Mary, 1970; Edwin, 1984. TV Series: Rumpole of the Bailey (4 series); Brideshead

Revisited, 1981; Unity Mitford, 1981; The Ebony Tower, 1984; Paradies Postponed, 1986; Summer Lease, 1989. Plays: The Dock Brief and Other Plays, 1959; Collaborators, 1973; Rumpole à la Carte, 1990; Dunster, 1992; Rumpole on Trial, 1992; Villians, 1992. *Contributions to:* Various periodicals. *Honours include:* Italia Prize for Short Play, 1958; British Academy Writers Award, 1979; BAFTA Writer of the Year Award, 1980; Book of the Year Award, Yorkshire Post, 1982; Susquehanna University, 1985; CBE, 1986; Hon LLD, Exeter, 1986; St. Andrews, 1987; Hon. DLitt, Nottingham, 1989. *Memberships:* Royal Society of Literature, Chairman. *Address:* c/o The Peter Fraser and Dunlop Group Ltd, 5th Floor, The Chambers, Chelsea Harbour, Lofs Road, London SW10, England.

MORTIMER Penelope (Ruth), (Penelope Dimont, Ann Temple), b. 1918, United Kingdom. Author. *Appointments:* Film Critic, The Observer, London, 1967-70. *Publications:* Johanna (as Penelope Dimont), 1947; A Villa in Summer, 1954; The Bright Prison, 1956; With Love and Lizards (with John Mortimer), travel, 1957; Daddy's Gone A-Hunting, US Edition Cave of Ice, 1958; Saturday Lunch with the Brownings, 1960; The Pumpkin Eater, 1962; My Friend Says It's Bullet-Proof, 1967; The Home, 1971; Long Distance, 1974; About Time: An Aspect of Autobiography, 1979; The Handyman, 1983; Queen Elizabeth: A Life of the Queen Mother, 1986; Screenplay: Portrait of a Marriage, 1990. *Honours:* Whitbread Prize, 1979. *Literary Agent:* Anthony Sheil, 43 Doughty Street, London WC1N 2LF, England. *Address:* 19 St Gabriel's Road, London NW2 4DS, England.

MORTON Henry Albert, b. 20 July 1925, Gladstone, Manitoba, Canada. Writer; Associate Professor of History (retired). *Education:* BA, BEd, University of Manitoba; MA, University of Cambridge, UK; PhD, University of Otago, New Zealand. *Publications:* And Now New Zealand, 1969; The Wind Commands (award), 1975; Which Way New Zealand, 1975; Why Not Together?, 1978; The Whale's Wake, 1982; The Farthest Corner, 1988. *Honour:* Sir James Wattie Award, book of the year, 1976 *Memberships:* Blenheim Club; PEN, New Zealand. *Address:* 23 Mountain View Road, Blenheim, Marlborough, New Zealand.

MORTON Henry W, b. 1929, USA. Professor of Political Science. *Publications:* Soviet Sport: Mirror of Soviet Society, 1963; Soviet Policy-Making (with others), 1967; The Soviet Union and Eastern Europe, 1971; Soviet Policy and Society in the 1970's (with others), 1974; The Contemporary Soviet City (co-author), 1984. *Address:* 12 Francis Terrace, Glen Cove, NY 11542, USA.

MOSBY Aline, b. 27 July 1922, Misosula, Montana, USA. Journalist. *Education:* BA, University of Montana School of Journalism, 1943; Postgraduate studies at Columbia University, New York City, 1965. *Appointments:* Journalist, Time Magazine, 1943; Journalist, Foreign Correspondent, United Press International, 1943-85; Freelance Writer, based in Paris, 1985; Lecturer, Keedick Agency; Guest Instructor, University of Montana. *Publications:* The View from Number 13 People's Street, 1963. *Contributions to:* Periodicals including the New York Times, France Magazine, Art News, Hors Ligne of Switzerland, International Herald Tribune. *Honours:* Montana State Hall of Fame, 1967; Cabanes International Prize for Wire Service Reporting, Bernard Cabanes Foundation, 1980; Honorary Doctorate Degree, University of Montana, 1985. *Memberships:* Anglo- American Press Association of Paris, Board of Directors, 1982-. *Address:* 1 Rue Maitre Albert, Paris 75005, France.

MOSES Elbert Raymond Jr, b. 31 Mar 1908, New Concord, Ohio, USA. Professor Emeritus. m. (1) Mary M. Sterrett, 21 Sept 1933, (dec 1984), 1 son, (2) Caroline M. Chambers, 19 June 1985. *Education:* AB, University of Pittsburgh; MSc, PhD, University of Michigan. *Publications:* A Guide to Effective Speaking, 1956, 1957;

Phonetics : History & Interpretation, 1964; Three Attributes of God, 1983; Adventure in Reasoning, 1988; Beating the Odds, 1992. *Contributions to:* American Speech & Hearing Magazine; Journal of American Speech; Speech Monographs; Veterans Voices. *Honours include:* Paul Harris Fellow, Rotary, 1971; Certificate, humanitarian services, Nicaraguan Government, 1974; Phi Delta Kappa Service Key, 1978; Certificate, Services to Education, 1981; Life Patron, American Biographical Institute, 1985; Grand Ambassador of Achievement, HE, American Biographical Institute, 1985; Life Fellow, World Literary Academy, 1987. *Address:* 2001 Rocky Dells Drive, Prescott, AZ 86303-5685, USA.

MOSKOWITZ Faye Stollman, b. 31 July 1930, Detroit, Michigan, USA. English Professor; Writer. m. Jack Moskowitz, 29 Aug 1948, 2 sons, 2 daughters. *Education:* George Washington University, BA, 1970; MA, 1979; PhD (abd), 1974. *Publications:* A Leak in the Heart; Whoever Finds this: I Love You; And The Bridge Is Love. *Contributions to:* The New York Times; Washington Post; Chronicle of Higher Education; Womans Day; Feminist Studies; Calyx; Christian Science Monitor; Wigwag Magazine. *Honours:* Michael Karolyi Foundation; Breadloaf Scholar; EdPress Merit Award; Pen Syndicated Fiction award; Literary Friends of DC Library. *Memberships:* Jenny McKean Moore Fund for Writers. *Literary Agent:* Russell & Volkenning. *Address:* 3306 Highland Place, NW Washington, DC 20008, USA.

MOSLEY Jonathan Philip, b. 8 June 1947, Grimsby, England. University Professor. m. Shu Ching Huang, 11 Aug 1988. *Education:* Leeds University, BA, 1968; University of East Anglia, MA, 1970; PhD, 1976. *Publications:* Ingmar Bergman: The Cinema as Mistress; Bruges-La-Morte; Tea Masters, Tea Houses. *Contributions to:* Numerous articles & Reviews. *Memberships:* British, American & International Comparative Literature Associations; International Council of Francophone Studies; Society for Cinema Studies. *Address:* Pennsylvania State University, Worthington Scranton Campus, 120 Ridge View Drive, Dunmore, PA 18512, USA.

MOSLEY Leonard, b. 1931, United Kingdom. Author; Former Critic. *Appointments:* Formerly Drama and Film Critic, Daily Express, London. *Publications:* Backs to the Wall; On Borrowed Time; Hirohito; Curzon; Gideon Goes to War; The Last Days of the British Raj; Faces from the Fire; Power Play, 1973; Reich Marshal: A Biography of Herman Goering, 1974; Charles Lindbergh, 1976; The Battle of Britain, 1977; Dulles, 1978; The Druid, 1982; Zanuck: The Rise and Fall of Hollywood's Last Tycoon, 1984; The Real Walt Disney, 1986. *Address:* c/o Weidenfeld and Nicolson Ltd, 91 Clapham High Street, London SW4, England.

MOSLEY Nicholas (Lord Ravensdale), b. 1923, United Kingdom. Author. *Publications:* Spaces of the Dark, 1951; The Rainbearers, 1955; Corruption, 1957; African Switchback, 1958; The Life of Raymond Raynes, 1961; Meeting Place, 1962; Accident, 1965; Experience and Religion: A Lay Essay in Theology, 1965; Assassins, 1966; Impossible Object, 1968; Natalie, Natalia, 1971; The Assassination of Trotsky, 1972, screenplay, 1973; Impossible Object, screenplay, 1975; Julian Grenfell: His Life and the Times of His Death 1888- 1915, 1976; Catastrophe Practice, 1979; Image Bird, 1980; Serpent, 1981; Rules of the Game: Sir Oswald and Lady Cynthia Mosley 1969-1933, 1982; Beyond the Pale: Sir Oswald Mosley and Family 1933-1980, 1983; Judith, 1986; Hopeful Monsters, 1990. *Honour:* Whitbread Prize, 1990. *Address:* 2 Gloucester Crescent, London NW1 7DS, England.

MOSS Norman Bernard, b. 30 Sept 1928, London. m. Hilary Sesta, 21 July 1963, 2 sons. *Education:* High Schools in New York City, Hamilton College, New York, 1946-47. *Appointments:* Staff Journalist with Newspapers, New Agencies and Radio Networks. *Publications:* Men Who Played God - The Story of the Hydrogen Bomb, 1968; A British/American Dictionary, 1972, revised editions, 1978, 1982, 1990; The Pleasures of Deception, 1976; The Politics of Uranium, 1982; Klaus Fuchs: The Man Who Stole the Atom Bomb, 1987; The Politics of Global Warming, 1992. *Contributions to:* Various journals. *Honours:* Magazine Writer of the Year, Awarded by Periodical Publishers' Association, 1982. *Memberships:* International Institute of Strategic Studies. *Address:* 21 Rylett Crescent, London W12 9RP, England.

MOSS (Victor) Peter (Cannings), b. United Kingdom. Author; Former Lecturer, Lewes Technical College. *Publications:* Our Own Homes Through the Ages, 1956; Meals Through the Ages, 1958; Sports and Pastimes Through the Ages, 1962; Tombstone Treasure, 1965; Hermit's Hoard, 1965; History Alive, 5 vols, 1967-71; Today's English, 2 vols, 1968; Town Life Through the Ages, 1973; The Media, 1974; Crime and Punishment, 1974; Medicine and Morality, 1974; Statistics Alive, 1975; People and Politics, 1976; Prejudice and Discrimination, 1976; Ghosts over Britain, 1977; Work and Leisure, 1978; Family and Friends, 1978; History Scene, I, II and III, 1978-80; Modern World History 1900-1977, 1978; Encounters with the Past, 1979; Commerce in Action (with Joan Moss), 1981; The Private Past, 1983; Religion and the Supernatural (with S Lamont), 1985; History Scene IV, 1985; France - Enchantment of the World Series, 1986; Oxford History Project for Chinese Schools in Hong Kong (6 books), 1986-89; History Scene: Into the Modern World, 1987; Society in Action (with Joan Moss), 1988; Word Patterns, Books 1-5 (with Joan Moss), 1988-89; Kisértetek Britannia Felet (with Judit Toth), 1990; Találkozott Már Kísértetekkel? (with Judit Toth), 1991. *Membership:* Society of Authors (Committee Member, Educational Group). *Literary Agent:* Mark Paterson, Wivenhoe, Colchester, England. *Address:* Brook Cottage, Ripe, Lewes, Sussex BN8 6AR, England.

MOSS Rose, b. 2 Jan 1937, South Africa. Writer; Managment Consultant. div, 1 son. *Education:* BA, University of Natal, 1960; BA, Boston University, 1983. *Publications:* Shouting at the Crocodile; Exile; The Terrorist; The Family Reunion; Darwin's Beetle. *Contributions to:* Los Angeles Times; New York Times; Harvard Business Review; Agni Christian Science Monitor; Cross Currents. *Honours:* Arts Festival Prize; Quill Prize; New Fiction Society Choice; PEN Syndicated Fiction Award; MacDowell Fellow; Yaddo. *Memberships:* PEN American Center; Authors Guild; Writers Union. *Literary Agent:* Christina Ward. *Address:* c/o Christina Ward, PO Box 515, N Scituate, MA 02060, USA.

MOSTYN-OWEN Gaia. *See:* **SERVADIO Gaia Cecilia.**

MOTION Andrew Peter, b. 26 Oct 1952, London, England. Writer. m. Jan Dalley, 9 June 1985, 2 sons, 1 daughter. *Education:* Radley College, Oxfordshire, 1965-70; BA (1st Class Honours), M Litt, University College, Oxford, 1970-76. *Literary Appointments:* Editor, Poetry Review, 1980-82; Editorial Director, Chatto and Windus, 1982-89. *Publications:* Dangerous Play, Selected Poems, 1979-84; Natural Causes (Poems) 1987; The Lamberts (Biography) 1986; The Pale Companion (Novel) 1989; Love in a Life (Poems) 1991; Famous for the Creatures (Novel) 1991. *Contributions to:* LRB; TLS; Observer, all regular. *Honours:* ARVON/Observer Prize; John Llewelyn Rhys Prize; Dylan Thomas Prize; Somerset Maugham Award. *Membership:* Fellow, Royal Society of Literature. *Literary Agent:* Pat Kavanagh, The Peters, Frazer and Dunlop, Group Ltd. *Address:* c/o Faber and Faber, 3 Queen Square, London WC1 3AU, England.

MOTT Michael, (Charles Alston), b. 8 Dec 1930, London, England. Writer. m. (1) Margaret Ann Watt, 6 May 1961 (dec 1990), 2 daughters, (2) Emma Lou Powers, 16 Nov 1992. *Education:* Diploma, Central School of Arts & Crafts, London; Intermediate Law

Degree, Law Society, London; BA, History of Art, Courtauld & Warburg Institutes, London; Honorary Doctor of Letters, St Mary's College, Notre Dame, 1983. *Literary Appointments:* Editor, Air Freight, 1954-59; Assistant Editor, Adam International Review, 1956-66; Editor, Books on Fine Arts, Thames and Hudson, 1961-64; Assistant Editor, The Geographical Magazine, 1964-66; Poetry Editor, The Kenyon Review, 1966-70; 25 years teaching experience including positions as Visiting Professor and Writer-in-Resident at Kenyon College, 1966-70; SUNY, Buffalo, 1968; Concordia University, Montreal, Canada, 1970 and 1974; Emory University, 1970-77; The College of William and Mary, 1978-79, 1985-86; Professor of English, Bowling Green State University, 1980-1992; Retired Professor Emeritus, 1992. *Publications include:* Novels: The Notebooks of Susan Berry, 1962; Master Entrick, 1964; Helmet and Wasps, 1964; The Blind Cross, 1968. Poetry: Absence of Unicorns, Presence of Lions, 1977; Counting the Grasses, 1980; Corday, 1986; Piero do Cosimo: The world of Infinite Possibility, 1990; Taino, 1992. Biography: The Seven Mountains of Thomas Merton, 1984. *Contributions to:* Encounter; Poetry Chicago; The Sunday Times (London); The Kenyon Review; Southern Review; Sewanee Review; Iowa Review; Pearl (Denmark) Reviews in, The Sunday Times, Balitmore Sun, Poetry and many others. *Honours:* Governor's Award in Fine Arts, State of Georgia, 1974; Guggenheim Fellowship, 1979-80; Runner-up Pulitzer Prize in Biography, 1984; The Christopher Award, 1984; Ohiona Book Award, 1985; Olscamp Research Award, 1985; Nancy Dasher Book Award, 1985. *Memberships:* Arts Club; Fellow, Royal Geographical Society, 1953-; Associated Writing Programs; Author's Guild; Amnesty International; British Lichen Society. *Literary Agent:* The Peter Frazer and Dunlop Group Ltd, London. *Address:* 122 The Colony, Williamsburg, VA 23185, USA.

MOULD Daphne Desire Charlotte Pochin, b. 15 Nov 1920, Salisbury, England. Author *Education:* BSc 1st Class Honours, Geology, 1943; PhD, Geology, 1946, University of Edinburgh. *Publications include:* Captain Roberts of the Sirius, 1988; The Aran Islands, 1972; Ireland from the Air, 1972; Irish Monastiries, 1976; The Celtic Saints, 1956; The Irish Saints (critical biographies) 1963. *Contributions to:* Numerous and various. Also Broadcaster on Radio Telefis Eireann. *Membership:* Aircraft Owners and Pilots Association. *Address:* Aherla House, Aherla, Co Cork, Irish Republic.

MOULES Joan Margaret, b. 4 Feb 1931, Hastings, Sussex, England. Writer. m. Leon Moules, 16 Sept 1956, 2 daughters. *Publications:* Our Gracie, biography, 1983; Gracie, memoir, 1980; Precious Inheritance, 1979; A Golden Flame, 1980; Passionate Enchantment, 1980; Richer than Diamonds, 1982; Strand of Gold, 1978; From this Day Forward, 1987; Paid in Full, 1986; In Progress: Softly, Softly, (The Story of Ruby Murray). *Contributions to:* Lady, Woman's Realm, Womans Own, She, My Weekly, Retail Newsagent, National Newsagent, British Digest Illustrated. *Memberships:* Society of Authors; Society of Women Writers and Journalists; West Country Writers; Warminister Writers Circle, Chairman; British Music Hall Society. *Address:* Linford 14 Upton Lovell, Warminster, Wilts BA12 OJW, England.

MOUNT William Robert Ferdinand, b. 2 July 1939, London. Novelist, Journalist & Editor. m. Julia Lucas, 20 July 1968, 2 sons, 1 daughter. *Literary Appointment:* Editor, Times Literary Supplement, 1991-. *Education:* BA, Christ Church, Oxford, 1961. *Appointments:* Political Correspondent, Spectator, 1977-82; Head of Prime Minister's Policy Unit, 1982-84; Literary Editor, Spectator, 1984-85; Columnist, Daily Telegraph, 1985-. *Publications:* Very Like a Whale, 1967; The Theatre of Politics, 1972; The Man Who Rode Ampersand, 1975; The Clique, 1978; The Subversive Family, 1982; The Selkirk Strip, 1987; Of Love and Asthma, 1991; The British Constitution Now, 1992. *Contributions to:* Spectator, Encounter, National Interest, Politique Internationale. *Honour:* Hawthornden Prize for Of Love and Asthma, 1991. *Address:* 17 Ripplevale Grove, London N1, England.

MOUNTBETTEN Richard. *See:* **WALLMANN Jeffrey M.**

MOUNTFIELD David. *See:* **GRANT Neil David Mountfield**.

MOUNTJOY Roberta Jean. *See:* **SOHL Gerald A.**

MOUNTZOURES Harry Louis, b. 9 July 1934, Fishers Island, NY, USA. Writer. m. Mary Ann Cawley, 8 Oct 1964, 1 son. *Education:* BA, Wesleyan University, 1956. *Publications:* The Empire of Things; The Bridge. *Contributions to:* The New Yorker; The Atlantic; Redbook McCalls. *Honours:* Atlantic First Prize. *Memberships:* Pen International. *Address:* 29 Old Black Point Road, Niantic, CT 06357, USA.

MOUZELIS Nicos, b. 22 Jan 1939, Athens, Greece. Professor. m. 1966, 1 daughter. *Education:* University of Geneva, 1957-62; London School of Economics, PhD, 1966. *Appointments:* Assistant Lecturer, University of Leicester, 1965-66; Lecturer, 1966-69; Lecturer, London School of Economics, 1970; Senior Lecturer, 1977; Reader, 1987; Professor, 1990-. *Publications:* Modern Greece; Organisation and Bureaucracy; Politics in the Semi Periphery; Post Marxist Alternatives; Back to Sociological Theory. *Contributions to:* Sociology; Encyclopaedia Britannica; British Journal of Sociology; Comparative Studies in Society and History; The Journal of Peasant Studies; New Left Review; Les Tempa Modernes. *Address:* 35 Holly Croft Avenue, London NW3 7QJ, England.

MOWAT Farley McGill, b. 12 May 1921, Belleville, Ontario, Canada. Author. m. (1) Frances Thornhill, 1947, (2) Claire Wheeler, 1963, 2 sons. *Education:* BA, University of Toronto, 1949. *Publications:* Over 11 million copies, over 120 editions, 33 foreign languages. Titles include: People of the Deer, 1952, 1975; The Regiment, 1955, 1973; Lost in the Barrens, 1956; The Dog Who Wouldn't Be, 1957; The Grey Seas Under, 1958; Coppermine Journey, 1958; The Desperate People, 1959, 1975; Ordeal by Ice, 1960, 1973; Owls in the Family, 1961; The Serpent's Coil, 1961; The Black Joke, 1962; Never Cry Wolf, 1963, 1973; Westviking, 1965; The Curse of the Viking Grave, 1966; Canada North, 1967; The Polar Passion, 1967, 1973; This Rock Within the Sea (with John de Visser), 1968; The Boat Who Wouldn't Float, 1969, 1974; Sibir (The Siberians - USA), 1970, 1973; A Whale for the Killing, 1972; Tundra, 1973; Wake of the Great Sealers (with David Blackwood), 1973; The Snow Walker, 1975; Canada North Now (The Great Betrayal - USA), 1976; And No Birds Sang, 1979; The World of Farley Mowat (ed Peter Davison), 1980; Sea of Slaughter, 1984; My Discovey of America, 1985; Virunga, 1987; The New Founde Land, 1989; Rescue the Earth, 1990; My Fathers Son. 1992; Born Naked, 1993. *Contributions to:* Numerous magazines & journals. *Honours include:* President's Medal, University of Western Ontario, 1952; Governor General's Medal (Canada), 1957; Book of the Year Medal, Canadian Library Association, 1958; Canadian Centennial Medal, 1967; Leacock Medal for Humour (Canada), 1970; Queen Elizabeth II Jubilee Medal, 1978; Officer, Order of Canada, 1981; Author's Award, Advancement of Canadian letters, 1985; Author of the Year, 1988; Book of the Year, Periodical Marketers of Canada, Foundation for the Advancement of Canadian Letters, 1988; Torgi Talking Book of the Year Award, 1989; Gemini Award, Best Documentary Script, 1989; Award of Excellence, Atlantic Film Festival, 1990; Canadian Achievers Award, 1990; Conservation Film of the Year, 1990; Finalist, American Cable Entertainment Awards, 1990; Take Back the Nation Award, Council of Canadians, 1991. Numerous awards, Canada, USA, France; 6 honorary doctorates, Canada, 1970-86. *Address:* c/o Writers Union of Canada, 24 Ryerson Avenue, Toronto, Ontario, Canada M4T 2P3.

MOYES Gertrude Patricia, b. 19 Jan 1923, Bray, Ireland. Author. m. (1) John Moyes, 29 Mar 1952. (2) John Haszard, 13 Oct 1962. *Publications:* Henry Tibbett Mysteries 1959-89: Dead Men Don't Ski; The Sunken Sailor; Death On The Agenda; Murder A La Mode; Johnny Underground; Murder Fantastical; Death & The Dutch Uncle; Many Deadly Returns; Season of Snows & Sins; The Curious Affair Of The Third Dog; Black Widower; The Coconut Killings; Who Is Simon Warwick?; Angel Death; A 6-Letter Word for Death; Night Ferry to Death; Black Girl, White Girl, 1989; Twice in a Blue Moon, 1993; How To Talk To Your Cat; Helter Skelter; Time Remembered, translation, 1958. *Contributions to:* Ellery Queen Mystery magazine. *Honour:* Edgar Special Scroll, Mystery Writers of America for Many Deadly Returns, circa 1963. *Memberships:* Crime Writers Association; Mystery Writers of America; Detection Club; Authors Guild. *Literary Agent:* Curtis Brown Ltd, London and The Karpfinger Agency New York. *Address:* PO Box 1, Virgin Gorda, British Virgin Islands.

MOYNAHAN Molly, b. 15 May 1957, Princeton, New Jersey, USA. Writer; Teacher. *Education:* BA, Rutgers University, 1979; MFA, Brooklyn College, 1990. *Appointments:* Professor, Rutgers University. *Publications:* Parting Is All We Know of Heaven; Living In Arcadia. *Contributions to:* Mademoiselle Magazine. *Honours:* Djerassi Foundation; Helena Wurlitzir Award. *Memberships:* Authors Guild; MLA. *Address:* 3439 Lawrenceville Road, Princeton, NJ 08540, USA.

MOYNIHAN Daniel Patrick, b. 1927, USA. United States Senator; Author. *Publications:* Beyond the Melting Pot (with Nathan Glazer), 1963; Defenses of Freedom: The Public Papers of Arthur J Goldberg (editor), 1966; Equal Educational Opportunity (co-author), 1969; Maximum Feasible Misunderstanding: Community Action in the War on Poverty, 1969; On Understanding Poverty: Perspectives from the Social Sciences (editor), 1969; Toward a National Urban Poverty (editor), 1970; The Politics of a Guaranteed Income, 1973; Coping, 1973; Ethnicity: Theory and Experience (edited with Nathan Glazer), 1975; A Dangerous Place (with S A Weaver), 1978; Counting Our Blessings: Reflections on the Future of America, 1980; Loyalties, 1984; Family and Nation, 1986; Came the Revolution: Argument in Reagan Era, 1988; On the Law of Nations, 1990. *Address:* United States Senate, Washington, DC 20510, USA.

MOYNIHAN John Dominic, b. 31 July 1932, London, England. Journalist; Author. 1 son, 2 daughters. *Education:* Felsted School; Chelsea School of Art. *Literary Appointments:* Bromley Mercury, 1953-54; Evening Standard, 1954-63; Daily Express, 1963-64; The Sun, 1964-65; The Sunday Telegraph, 1965-89, (Assistant Literary Editor, Sports Correspondent); Freelance, Sunday Telegraph, 1992-; The Independent on Sunday (Sportswriter), 1990. *Publications:* The Soccer Syndrome, 1966, 1987; Not All a Ball (autobiography), 1970; Park Football, 1970; Football Fever, 1974; Soccer, 1974; The Chelsea Story, 1982; The West Ham Story, 1984; Soccer Focus, 1989; Black and White, 1993. *Contributions to:* Sunday Telegraph Magazine; New Statesman; Spectator; Harpers and Queen; The Observer; The Melbourne Age; Sunday Supplement, Australia; The Radio Times; Now Magazine, Evening Standard; Daily Express; The Sunday Times; Country Life; Catholic Herald; Badminton, Tennis World; The European; World Soccer. *Memberships:* The Society of Authors; Sports Writers Association; Football Writers Association; Lawn Tennis Writers Association; Chelsea Arts Club; Scribes. *Literary Agent:* Scott Ferris Associates, London. *Address:* 102 Ifield Road, London SW10, England.

MPHAHLELE Ezekiel (Es'kia Mphahlele), b. 1919, South Africa. Author; Professor of African Literature. *Appointments:* Teacher of English and Afrikaans, Orlando High School, Johannesburg, 1942-52; Fiction Editor, Drum magazine, Johannesburg, 1955-57; Lecturer in English Literature, University of Ibadan, Nigeria, 1957-61; Director of African Programmes, International Association for Cultural Freedom, Paris, France, 1961-63; Director, Chem-chemi Creative Centre, Nairobi, Kenya, 1963-65; Lecturer: University College, Nairobi, 1965-66; University of Denver, Colorado, USA, 1966-74; University of Pennsylvania, Philadelphia, 1974-77; Professor of African Literature, University of the Witwatersrand, Johannesburg, 1979-. *Publications:* Man Must Live and Other Stories, 1947; Down Second Avenue, autobiography, 1959; The Living Dead and Other Stories, 1961; The African Image, essays, 1962, 2nd Edition, 1974; Modern African Stories (edited with E Komey), 1964; African Writing Today (editor), 1967; In Corner B and Other Stories, 1967; The Wanderers, novel, 1971; Voices in the Whirlwind and Other Essays, 1972; Chirundu, novel, 1979; The Unbroken Song, 1981; Bury Me at the Marketplace, 1984; Father Come Home, 1984; Afrika My Music: An Autobiography 1957-1983, 1986. *Address:* African Studies Institute, University of the Witwatersrand, Johannesburg 2001, South Africa.

MRABET Mohammed, b. 1939, Tangier, Morocco. Storyteller. *Publications:* The Lemon, 1969; Love with a Few Hairs, 1968; The Boy who set the Fire, 1974; Harmless Poison, Blameless Sins, 1976; Look and Move on, 1976; The Chest, 1976; Marriage with Papers, 1986; Translations into ten languages. *Contributions to:* D4, (Switzerland). *Literary Agent:* Roberto de Hollanda. *Address:* c/o Roberto de Hollanda, Bonn, Germany.

MUAMBA Muepu, b. 23 Nov 1946, Tshilundu, Zaire. Journalist; Writer. *Education:* Institute St Ferdinand, Jernappes, Belgium. *Appointments:* Literary Director, Editions Les Presses Africaines, Kinshasa, Zaire; Literary Critic, Salongo and Elima. *Publications include:* Ventre Creux Short Stories; Supplique; Anthologie d'une jeune Litterature, slected by Oliver Dubuis; Afrika in eigener Sache, essays on Africa with jochen klicker and Klaus Paysan, 1980; Poems in various anthologies; Devoir d'ingérence, Nouvelles et poémes, Kjivouvon-Verlag Editions Bantoues. Heidleberg - Brazzaville, 1988; Ma Terre d' O, Poems (sous presses). *Contributions to:* Salongo; Elima; Culture et Authenticite (Kinshasa, Zaire); Beto (Dusseldorf, Germany). *Honours:* 1st Prize, Short Story, La Chambree, Literary Competition of L'Association Cultures et d'Expressions Minorities, Paris 1986. *Memberships include:* National Council of Culture; Union of Writers of Zaire, Office for Foreign Relations; National Association of Publishers of Zaire, Union Internationales des Journalises et de la Presse de Langue Francaise. *Literary Agent:* Dr Jochon Klicker, Berlin and Barcelona. *Address:* c/o Dr M Kohlert Nemeth, Schaumainkai 99, 6000 Frankfurt am Main 70, Germany.

MUCHA Jiri, b. 12 Mar 1915, Prague, Czechoslovakia, Author, m. Geraldine Thomson, 1 son. *Education:* Faculty of Medicine, Faculty of Letters, Charles University, Prague, 1934-39. *Appointments:* Co- editor, New Writing and Daylight, London, 1944. *Publications:* Problems of Lieutenant Knap, 1945; The Scorched Crop, 1947; Living and Party Living, 1967; Alphouse Mucha, His Life and Art, 1963; The Probable Face, 1965; Marieta by Nigth, 1968; Fire Braves Frire; The War Continues; Lloyd's Head; Strange Loves. *Contributions to:* New Writing; The Nation; Lidore Noviny; Kmen. *Honours:* M F Award for Black and White, New York 1967; C S Award for Living and Party Living, 1968; Honorary Degree, Dundee University, 1969. *Memberships:* Czechoslovak PEN Club, President; The Garrick Club. *Address:* Hradcanske Nam 6, 118 00 Prague 1, Czechoslovakia.

MUEHL Lois Baker, b. 29 Apr 1920, Oak Park IL. Teacher; Writer. m. Siegmar Muehl, 15 Apr 1944, 2 sons, 2 daughters. *Education:* BA, English, Oberlin College, 1941; MA, English-Education, University of Iowa, 1967. *Appointments:* Director, Developmental Reading Lab, University of Iowa, 1965-85; ESL Teacher, Kyungnam University, Masan, Korea, 1985; ESL Teacher, Postgraduate Program, Hohai University, Nanjing PRC, 1987-88. *Publication:* My Name is ---

Holiday House, 1959; Worst Room in the School --- Holiday House, 1961. *Contributions to:* Various magazines. *Honours:* Phi Bete Kappo, Oberlin, 1941; Old Gold Creative Fellowship, 1970; Developmental Leave to prepare Communications Exhibit, 1980. *Memberships:* University Women's Club, Chair of Writers' Group, 1989-90. *Address:* 430 Crestview Avenue, Iowa City, IA 52245, USA.

MUELLER Robert Emmett, b. 1925, USA. Novelist; Short Story Writer; Poet; Essayist. *Publications:* Inventivity, 1963, 2nd Edition, 1967; Inventor's Notebook, 1964; Eyes in Space, 1965; The Science of Art, 1967; Abracadabra, fiction, 1970; Rainbows Always Recede, fiction, 1975; Cyberthetics, 1982; Flutestruck, 1983; Shadows on the Nile, 1988; Terror Love, 1990; The Making of A Modern Dilattante, 1992. *Contribution to:* Schema: The Evolution of A Minimal Visual Art Form, Leonardo, vol 24, no 3, 1991. *Literary Agent:* Robert Ducas, 350 Hudson St, New York, NY 10014, USA.*Address:* Britton House, Roosevelt, NJ 08555, USA.

MUGGESON Margaret Elizabeth, (Margaret Dickinson, Everatt Jackson), b. 30 Apr 1942, Gainsborough, Lincolnshire, England. Partner in Retail Store. m. Dennis Muggeson, 19 Sept 1964, 2 daughters. *Education:* Lincoln College of Technology, 1960-61. *Publications:* Pride of The Courtneys, 1968; Brackenbeck, 1969; Portrait of Jonathan, 1970; Abbeyford Trilogy, 1981; Lifeboat!, 1983; Beloved Enemy, 1984; (as Margaret Dickinson), The Road to Hell, 1975 (as Everatt Jackson). *Address:* 17 Seacroft Drive, Skegness, Lincolnshire, PE25 3AP, England.

MUHRINGER Doris Agathe Annemarie, b. 18 Sept 1920, Graz, Austria. Writer. *Major Publications:* Gedichte 1, 1957; Das Marchen von den Sandmannlein (kinderbilderbuch), 1961; Gedichte II, 1969; Staub offnet das Auge (Gedichte III), 1976; mein Tag, mein Jahr, (with H. Valencak), 1983; Vogel, die ohne Schlaf sind, (Gediche IV), 1984; Tanzen unter d. Netz (Kurzprosa), 1985; Das hatten die Ratten vom Schatten (Ein Lachbuch), 1989, 2nd edition, 1992. *Contributions to:* numerous literary magazines in 9 countries. *Honours:* Georg Trakl Prize, 1954; Award of Achievement, Vienna, 1961; Lyrics Prize of Steiermark, 1973; Austrian State Scholarship, 1976; Award of Achievement, Board of Austrian Literar-Mechana, 1984; Großer Literaturpreis des Landes Steiermark, 1985. *Memberships:* PEN; Association of Austrian Writers; Poium; Kogge. *Address:* Goldeggasse 1, A-1040 Vienna, Austria.

MUINZER Genevieve, Writer. m. Nicholas A Segal, 11 Sept 1982, 1 son. *Education:* Princeton University, BA; University Warwick, LLB. *Appointments:* Founder, The Lady Gregory Short Story Competition; Founder, The Muinzer Bursary. *Publications:* New to the UK A Guide to your Life and Rights; Report on Post secondary Education in New Jersey. *Contributions to:* The Wall Street Jounral; The Guardian; Country Life; Whats On; Emirates in Flights; BBC Radio 4; Women Magazine. *Memberships:* PEN International. *Address:* 30 Hurlingham Road, London SW6 3RF, England.

MUIR Dexter. *See:* **DRIBBLE Leonard (Reginald).**

MUIR Frank, b. 1920, United Kingdom. Freelance Writer and Broadcaster. *Appointments:* Assistant Head, BBC Light Entertainment Group, London, 1964-67; Head of Entertainment, London Weekend Television, 1967-69; Member of Panel, My Word, and Call My Bluff, BBC Television. *Publications:* Call My Bluff (with Patrick Campbell), 1972; You Can't Have Your Kayak and Heat It (with Denis Norden), 1973; Upon My Word (with D Norden), 1974; Christmas Customs and Traditions, 1975; The Frank Muir Book, US Edition An Irreverent and Thoroughly Incomplete Social History of Almost Everything, 1976; What-a-Mess series, 17 vols, 1977-90; Frank Muir Goes Into... (with Simon Brett), 4 vols, 1978-81; Take My Word for It (with D Norden), 1978; The Glums (with D Norden), 1979; Frank Muir on Children (with S Brett), 1980; Oh, My Word (with D Norden), 1980; The Big Dipper (with P Muir), 1981; The Oxford Book of Humorous Prose, 1990; What-a-Mess and the Hairy Monster, 1990; Frank Muir Retells: Three Little Pigs, Jack and the Beanstalk, Goldilocks and the Three Bears, 1991. *Honour:* CBE, 1980. *Address:* Anners, Thorpe, Egham, Surrey TW20 8UE, England.

MUIR Kenneth (Arthur), (Mark Finney), b. 1907, United Kingdom. Emeritus Professor. *Appointments:* King Alfred Professor of English Literature, 1951-74, Emeritus Professor, 1974-, University of Liverpool; Editor, Shakespeare Survey, 1965-79. *Publications:* Collected Poems of Sir Thomas Wyatt (editor), 1949; Elizabethan Lyrics, 1953; John Milton, 1955; The Pelican Book of English Prose, 1 (editor), 1956; Shakespeare's Sources, 1957; The Life and Death of Jack Straw (edited with F Wilson), 1957; John Keats (editor), 1958; Shakespeare and the Tragic Pattern, 1959; Five Plays of Jean Racine, translation, 1960; Shakespeare as a Collaborator, 1960; Unpublished Poems of Sir Thomas Wyatt (editor), 1961; Last Periods, 1961; Life and Letters of Sir Thomas Wyatt, 1963; Introduction to Elizabethan Literature, 1967; New Companion to Shakespeare Studies with S Schoenbaum), 1971; Shakespeare's Tragic Sequence, 1972; Shakespeare the Professional, 1973; Three Plays of Thomas Middleton (editor), 1975; The Singularity of Shakespeare, 1977; The Sources of Shakespeare's Plays, 1977; Shakespeare's Comic Sequence, 1979; Four Comedies of Calderon, translation, 1980; Troilus and Cressida, by Shakespeare (editor), 1982; Interpretations of Shakespeare (editor), 1985; Shakespeare, Contrasts and Controversies, 1985; King Lear, 1986; Antony and Cleopatra, 1987; The Schism in England (with Ann L Mackenzie), translation, 1990; Calderon's Jealousy the Worst Monster (trans with Ana L Mackenzie), 1993. *Honours:* Hon Doctorate, Rouen, 1967, Dijon, 1976; Fellow, British Academy, 1970; Chairman, International Shakespeare Association, 1974-86, Vice President, 1986; Fellow, Royal Society of Literature, 1978; President, English Association, 1987; Three collections of essays in his honour, 1974, 1980 and 1987. *Address:* 6 Chetwynd Road, Oxton, Birkenhead, Merseyside L43 2JJ, England.

MUIR Richard, b. 18 June 1943, Yorkshire, England. Author; Photographer. *Education:* 1st class honours, Geography, 1967; PhD 1970, Aberdeen University, Scotland. *Appointment:* Editor, National Trust Regional Histories and Countryside Commission National Park Series. *Publications:* Modern Political Geography, 1975; Geography, Politics and Behaviour, with R Paddison; The English Village; Shell Guide to Reading the Landscape; Lost Villages of Britain; History from the Air; National Trust Guide to Prehistoric and Roman Britain, with Humphrey Welfare; Visions of the Past, with C Taylor; East Anglian Landscapes, with J Ravensdale; Shell Countryside Book, with E Duffey; Reading the Celtic Landscape; National Trust Guide to Dark Age and Medieval Britain; Landscape and Nature Photography; National Trust Book of Rivers, with N Muir; Hedgerows: Their History and Wildlife, with N Muir, 1987; Old Yorkshire, 1987; The Countryside Encyclopaedia, 1988; Fields (with Nina Muir), 1989; Portraits of the Past, 1989; Barleybrigde (fiction), 1989; The Dales of Yorkshire, 1991; The Villages of England, 1992; The Coastlines of Britain, 1993. *Contributions to:* Geographical Magazine; Sunday Times Magazine; Observer Magazine; various academic articles. *Honours:* Yorkshire Arts Literary Prize, 1982-83. *Address:* Waterfall Close, Station Road, Birstwith, Harrogate, Yorkshire, England.

MUKHERJEE Bharati, b. 1940. Associate Professor; Author. *Appointments:* Associate Professor, McGill University, Montreal, Canada, 1966-. *Publications:* Tiger's Daughter, 1972; Wife, 1975; Kautilya's Concept of Diplomacy, 1976; Days and Nights in Calcutta (with Clark Blaise), 1977; The Middleman, 1989. *Address:* Department of English, McGill University, Montreal, Quebec, Canada.

MULDOON Paul, b. 1951, Ireland. Radio Producer; Poet. *Appointments:* Radio Producer, BBC, Northern Ireland; Lecturer, Princeton University. *Publications:* Knowing My Place, 1971; New Weather, 1973; Spirit of Dawn, 1975; Mules, 1977; Names and Addresses, 1978; Why Brownlee Left, 1980; Immram, 1980; Quoof, 1983; The Wishbone, 1984; Meeting the British, 1987; Madoc: A Mystery, 1990. *Address:* Faber and Faber, 3 Queen Square, London WC1N 3AU, England.

MULLAN Eugene, b. 10 Oct 1958, Kettering, Northants, England. Teacher. m. Wendy Anne Maxted, 28 Mar 1986. *Education:* Warwick University, BA, 1981. *Contributions to:* Panurge; Stand; Iron. *Honours:* Betty Trask Prize. *Address:* 23 Welney Place, Birley Carr, Sheffield, S6 1JX, England.

MULLARD Chris(topher), b. 1944, United Kingdom. Writer; Former Community Relations Officer. *Publications:* Black Britain, 1973; Racism in Society and Schools, 1980; Race, Power, and Resistance, 1985. *Address:* c/o George Allen and Unwin, Ruskin House, 40 Museum Street, London WC1A 1LU, England.

MULLER Marcia b. 28 Sept 1944, Detroit, Michigan, USA. Crime Writer. *Education:* BA, English Literature, 1966, MA, Journalism, 1971, University of Michigan. *Publications:* Novels include: The Legend of the Slain Soldiers, 1985; There's Nothing to be Afraid Of, 1985; The Cavalier in White, 1986; Beyond the Grave, with Bill Pronzini, 1986; The Lighthouse, with Bill Pronzini, 1987; Eye of the Storm, 1988; There Hangs the Knife, 1988; There's Something in a Sunday, 1989; Dark Star, 1989; The Shape of Dread, 1989. Anthologies and criticism include: The Deadly Arts (with Bill Pronzini), 1985; Kill or Cure (with Bill Pronzini), 1985; Chapter and Hearse (with Bill Pronzini), 1985; The Wickedest Show on Earth (with Bill Pronzini), 1985; 1001 Midnights: The Aficianado's Guide to Myster and Detective Fiction (with Bill Pronzini), 1986; Lady on the Case (with Bill Pronzini and Martin H Greenberg), 1988. *Contributions to:* Short stories, articles and essays in various anthologies, A Matter of Crime, Alfred Hitchcock's Mystery Magazine, Boy's Life and The Writer. *Honour:* Mystery Writers of America Scroll Award for Critical/Biographical Work. *Literary Agent:* Molly Friedrich, Aaron M Priest Literary Agency, New York. *Address:* P O Box 1349, Sonoma, CA 95476, USA.

MULLIN Chris John, b. 12 Dec 1947, Chelmsford, England. Member of Parliament. m. Nguyen Thi Ngoc, 14 Apr 1987, 1 daughter. *Publications:* Error of Judgement: The Truth About The Birmingham Bombings; A very British Coup; The Last Man Out of Saigon; The Year of the Fire Monkey. *Honours:* Befta Award; US Emmy, Best drama. *Literary Agent:* Pat Kavanaget, Peters, Fraser & Dunlop. *Address:* The House of Commons, London SW1, England.

MULLINS Edwin, b. 14 Sept 1933, London, England. Writer. 1 son, 2 daughters. *Education:* MA, Oxford University. *Publications:* Alfred Wallis, 1967; Braque, 1968; The Pilgrimage to Santiago, 1974; Angels on the Point of a Pin, 1979; Great Paintings, 1981; Sirens, 1983; The Arts of Britain, 1983; The Painted Witch, 1985; A Love Affair with Nature, 1985; The Golden Bird, 1987; The Lands of the Sea, 1988; The Royal Collection, 1992; and others under a pseudonym, 1992, 1993. *Literary Agent:* Curtis Brown, London.

MULVIHILL Maureen Esther, b. 2 Oct 1944, Detroit, Michigan, USA. Writer, Scholar, Teacher. m. Daniel Harris, 18 June 1983. *Education:* B Phil, Monteith College, Wayne State University, 1966; MA, 1968; PhD, University of Wisconsin-Madison, (English Lit), 1983; Post-Doctoral, Yale University, 1983; Columbuia University Rare Book School, 1986. *Appointments:* Writer, State of Wisconsin, Office of the Governor & Office of the Mayor, 1975-82; Corporate Communications Director, Gruntal & Co, Inc, Wall St, New York, 1983-85; Communications Consultant, NY,

1985-; Visiting Scholar, Lecturer: New York University, Princeton University, Brooklyn Museum, Utah State University, McMaster University, (Canada), Georgian Court College, (NJ), Metropolitan State College, (Denver, CO). *Publications:* book, Poems by Ephelia, 1992; essays in Restoration, 1987, Scriblerian, 1989, Curtain Calls, 1991, Studies in 18th Century Culture, 1992; biographical profiles in Dictionary of Britain & American Women Writers, 1986; Encylopeadia of Continental Women Writers, 1991; British Women Writers, 1991; Medieval Women Writers, 1993-94; British Publishers To 1830, 1993-94; Work-in-Progress: Stewardess of Culture: Stuart Women Writers & Paronesses, 1660-1714: A Multimedia Source Book. *Honours:* Frances Hutner Award, Princeton Research Forum, Princeton, NJ; Under Graduate and Graduate Scholarships; Fellow, National Endowment for the Humanities, 1990; Reader, Clifford Award Committee, American Society for 18th Century Studies, 1990. *Memberships:* Princeton Research Forum; Modern Language Association; American Society for 18th Century Studies; Society for Textural Scholarship; Grolier Club; Friends of the Yale Art Gallery; Close Friend, Book Arts Press, Columbia University, Rare Book School. *Address:* 45 Plaza Street, West Park Slope, Brooklyn, NY 11217, USA.

MUMFORD Ruth, (Ruth Dallas), b. 1919, New Zealand. Writer of children's fiction and poetry. *Publications:* Country Road and Other Poems, 1953; The Turning Wheel, 1961; Day Book: Poems of a Year, 1966; Shadow Show, 1968; The Children in the Bush, 1969; Ragamuffin Scarecrow, 1969; A Dog Called Wig, 1970; The Wild Boy in the Bush, 1971; The Big Flood in the Bush, 1972; The House on the Cliffs, 1975; Walking on the Snow, 1976; Songs for a Guitar, 1976; Shining Rivers, 1979; Steps of the Sun, 1979; Holiday Time in the Bush, 1983; Collected Poems, 1987; Curved Horizon (autobiography), 1991. *Address:* 448 Leith Street, Dunedin, New Zealand.

MUNDIS Hester (Jane), b. 1938, USA. Author; Former Editor. *Appointments:* Assistant Copy Director, Fawcett Publications, New York City, 1961-63; Associate Editor, Macfadden-Bartell Corporation, New York City, 1963-64; Copy Chief, Associate Editor, Dell Books and Delacorte Press, New York City, 1964-67; Executive Editor, Popular Library, New York City, 1967-70; Senior Editor, Avon Books, New York City, 1970-71. *Publications:* Jessica's Wife, 1975; No He's Not a Monkey, He's an Ape and He's My Son, 1976; Separate Ways, 1978; Working Girl, 1981; Powerman, 1984; 101 Ways to Avoid Reincarnation: OR Getting it Right the First Time, 1989. *Address:* Moonshaw Road, West Shokan, NY 12494, USA.

MUNDSTOCK Karl b. 26 Mar 1915, Berlin, Germany. Writer m. 10 July 1943, 1 son, 1 daughter. *Education:* Schoolfarm isle of Scharfenberg, 1928-32; Classical School, 1939-40, studied Machine Engineering. *Publications include:* Helle Nadrte (novel) 1952; Alicund die Bande van Lanseplatz (children's book) 1955; Gespenster Edes Tod und Auferstehung (children's book), 1956; Tod an der Grenze (shortstories) 1961; Meine 1000 Jahre Jugend (autobiography) 1980; Zeit der Zauberin, 1985. *Honours:* Medal for Anti-Facism, 1958; Order of Merit (Silver) 1974; FDGB Prize for Literature, 1982; Goethe Prize of Berlin, 1984; GDR National Prize (second class) 1985. *Memberships:* German Writers Union; PEN. *Literary Agent:* Mitteldentscher Verlag Halle, Verlag Neues Leben, Berlin. *Address:* Wolfshagener Str 75, 0 - 1100 Berlin, Germany.

MUNIZ-HUBERMAN Angelina, b. 29 Dec 1936, Hyeres, France. Writer; University Professor. m. Alberto Huberman, 9 June 1959, 1 son, 1 daughter. *Education:* MA, Spanish Literature, 1955-58, Degree, 1967, Postdoctoral studies, 1975-76, National Autonomous University of Mexico; PhD studies, University of Pennsylvania, City University of New York, 1967-69. *Publications:* El mundo de la mujer (co-author), essay, 1967; Morada interior, novel, 1972; Cancionero folklorico de Mexico (co-author), 1975; Tierra adentro,

1977; Vilano al viento, poetry, 1982; La guerra del Unicornio, novel, 1983; Huerto cerrado, huerto sellado, short stories, 1985; De magias y prodigios, short stories, 1987; Dulcinea encantada, novel; El ojo de la creacion, poetry; A Garden Enclosed, short stories. *Contributions to:* 1960-87-: Cuadernos del Viento; El rehilete; Diorama de la cultura; Dialogos; Vuelta; Sabado; Mississippi Review; Mundus Artium; Pacific Moana Quarterly; Leviathan. *Honours:* Magda Donato National Literary Prize, 1972; National System of Research, 1984; Xavier Villaurrutia International Literary Prize, 1985. *Memberships:* Asociacion de Escritores de Mexico; PEN Club, Mexico; Asociacion de escritores judios de habla espanola y portuguesa; Asociacion de Poetas; International Comparative Literature Association; Association of Literary Translators of America. *Address:* Cadiz 108-703, Insurgentes-Mixcoac, 03920 Mexico, D F Mexico.

MUNRO Alice, b. 1931, Canada. Author. *Publications:* Lives of Girls and Women, novel, 1971; Dance of the Happy Shades, short stories, 1968; Something I've Been Meaning to Tell You, short stories, 1974; Who Do You Think You Are, US Edition The Beggar Maid, 1979; The Moons of Jupiter, 1982; Progress of Love, 1986. *Address:* 1648 Rockland, Victoria, British Columbia, Canada.

MUNRO David Mackenzie, b. 28 May 1950. Freelance Geographical Reference Editor. m. Wendy Jane Nimmo, 22 Nov 1985. *Education:* BSc (Edinburgh), 1973; PhD (Edinburgh), 1983. *Appointment:* Editor, Chambers World Gazetteer, 1984-. *Publications:* Chambers World Gazetteer (editor), 1988; Ecology and Environment in Belize (editor), 1989; A World Record of Major Conflict Areas (with Alan J Day), 1990; Contributor to Longman's Encyclopedia, Hutchinson's Encyclopedia, Oxford Encyclopaedic English Dictionary; The Hutchinson Paperbook Guide to the World (assoc ed), 1990. *Contributions to:* Geographical Magazine. *Honour:* Research Fellow, University of Edinburgh, 1984. *Memberships:* Chairman, Michael Bruce Trust; Fellow, Society of Antiquaries of Scotland; Member of Council, Royal Scottish Geographical Society; Scottish Arts Club; Chairman, Kinross-shire Civic Trust. *Address:* Department of Geography, University of Edinburgh, Drummond Street, Edinburgh EH8 9XP, Scotland.

MUNRO John Murchison, b, 29 Aug 1932, Wallasey, Cheshire, England. University Administrator. m. Hertha Ingrid Bertha Lipp, 12 Aug 1956, 2 sons, 2 daughters. *Education:* BA, English Literature, University of Durham, 1955; PhD, English Literature, Washington University, St Louis, USA, 1960. *Literary Appointments:* Part-time Instructor of English, Washington University, St Louis, Missouri, USA, 1959-60; Instructor, University of North Carolina, 1960-63; Assistant Professor, University of Toronto, Canada, 1963-65, Professor, American University of Beirut, Lebanon, 1965-87; Director, Outreach Services and Professor of Mass Communications, American University in Cairo, Egypt, 1987-. *Publications:* English Poetry in Transition, 1968; Arthur Symons, 1969; The Decadent Poets of the 1890's, 1970; Selected Poems of Theo Marzials, 1974; James Elroy Flecker, 1976; A Mutual Concern: The Story of the American University of Beirut, 1977; Cyprus: between Venus and Mars (with Z Khuri), 1984; Selected Letters of Arthur Symons (with Karl Beckson), 1988; Theatre of the Absurd: Lebanon, 1982-88, 1989; Senior Editor, Middle East Times. *Contributions to:* Various scholarly articles in literary journals; Journalism on Middle Eastern subjects. *Honour:* Fulbright Research Award, University of California, Los Angeles, summer 1987. *Address:* American University in Cairo, 113 Kasr el Aini Street, Cairo, Egypt.

MUNRO Mary. *See:* **HOWE Doris Kathleen.**

MUNRO Ronald Eadie. *See:* **GLEN Duncan Munro.**

MUNSCH Robert, b. 11 June 1945, Pittsburgh, PA, USA. Author. m. Ann Metta, 20 Jan 1973, 1 son, 2 daughters. *Education:* BA History, Fordham University, 1969; MA Anthropology, Boston University, 1971; MEd, Child Studies, Tufts University, 1973. *Publications:* Mud Puddle, The Dark, 1979; The Paper Bad Princes, 1980; Jonathan Cleaned Up, 1981; The Boy in the Drawer, Mortimer, Fire Station, Murmel Murmel Murmel, 1982; David's Father, 1983; Millicent and the Wind, 1984; Thomas' Snowsuit, 1985; 50 Below Zero, Love You Forever, 1986; I Have to Go, Moira's Birthday, 1987; A Promise is a Promise, Angela's Airplane, 1988; Pigs, Giant, 1989; Something Good, Good Familes Don't, Show and Tell, 1991; Get me Another One, Purple Green and Yellow, 1992. *Honours:* Author of the Year, Canadian Booksellers Association, 1991. *Memberships:* Writer's Union of Canada; Canadian Association of Children's Authors, Illustrators and Performers; Canadian Authors Association. *Address:* c/o Writer's Union of Canada, 24 Ryerson Avenue, Toronto, Canada M5T 2P3.

MURATA Kiyoaki, b. 19 Nov 1922, Ono, Hyogo. Educator; Author. m. (1) Minako Iesaka, 1960, (div 1981), 2 sons, 1 daughter. (2) Kayoko Matsukura, 1987. *Education:* MA; University of Chicago, USA. *Appointments:* Editorial Writer, The Japan Times, 1957-66; Managing Editor, 1971-76, Executive Editor, 1976-77, Managing Director 1976-1983, Editor in Chief, 1977-83; Director, Japan Graphic Inc., 1977-1982; Professor, International Communication, Yachiyo International University, 1988. *Publications:* Japan's New Buddhism - An Objective Account of Soka Gakkai, 1969; Japan - The State of the Nation, 1979; Kokuren Nikki-Suppon Wan no Kaiso (UN Diary - Recollections of Turtle Bay), 1985; An Enemy Among Friends, 1991. *Honours:* Hon. LL.D., Carleton College; Vaughn Prize, Japan Newspaper Editors and Publishers Association. *Address:* 19-12 Hiroo 2 chome, Shibuya-ku, Tokyo 150, Japan.

MURDOCH Iris (Jean), Dame, b. 15 July 1919, Dublin, Ireland. Writer; Philosopher. m. John O. Bayley. *Education:* Froebel Educational Institute, London; Badminton School, Bristol; Somerville College, Oxford. *Publications:* Sartre : Romantic Rationalist, 1953; Under the Net, 1954; The Flight from the Enchanter, 1955; The Sandcastle, 1957; The Bell, 1958; A Severed Head, 1961 (play 1963); An Unofficial Rose, 1962; The Unicorn, 1963; The Italian Girl, 1964 (play 1967); The Red and the Green, 1965; The Time of the Angels, 1966; The Nice And the Good, 1968; Bruno's Dream, 1969; A Fairly Honourable Defeat, 1970; The Sovereignty of Good, 1970; The Servants and the Snow (play), 1970; An Accidental Man, 1971; The Three Arrows (play), 1972; The Black Prince, 1973; The Sacred and Profane Love Machine, 1974; A Word Child, 1975; Henry and Cato, 1976; The Sea, the Sea, 1978; The Fire and the Sun, 1978; Nuns and Soldiers, 1980; Art and Eros (play), 1980; The Philosopher's Pupil, 1983; The Good Apprentice, 1985; Acastos (Platonic Dialogues), 1986; The Book of the Brotherhood, 1987; The Message to the Planet, 1989; Metaphysics as a Guide to Morals, 1992. *Honours Include:* Hon.D. Litt., Universities of Sheffield, Belfast, Norwich, Caen, London; Fellow, St Anne's College, Oxford, 1948-63, Hon. Fellow, 1963; James Tait Black Prize for Fiction, 1974; Whitbread Literary Award for Fiction, 1974; Booker Prize for Fiction, 1978; Gifford Lecture, University of Edinburgh, 1982; DBE, 1987. *Memberships:* Various professional organisations.

MURDOCH (Keith) Rupert, b. 11 Mar 1931, Melbourne, Australia. Newspaper Publisher. m. Anna Maria Torv, 1967, 2 sons, 2 daughters. *Education:* Worcester College, Oxford. *Appointments:* Inherited Adelaide News, 1952; has since built up Cruden Investments, a Murdoch family company which owns 43 per cent of News Corporation; has acquired newspapers, magazines and other interests in Australia, UK, USA and Hong Kong including: Australia-newspapers: The Australian, Telegraph Mirror (Sydney), Sunday Sun (Brisbane), The News and Sunday Mail (Adelaide), The Sunday Times (Perth); USA-The Boston Herald, Mirror Newspapers Ltd., Nationwide News Pty.

Ltd., Southdown Press Ltd., Cumberland Newspapers Ltd.; UK-Newspapers: Sun, News of the World (national, acquired 1969), Berrows Org. (regional newspapers), acquired Times Newspapers Ltd., 1981; Television includes: Channel 10 (Sydney); Channel 10 (Melbourne), News Group Productions (USA); BSkyB PLC (UK), 1984-. *Honours:* Commander of the White Rose (First Class), 1985; AC. *Address:* c/o News America Publishing, 1211 Avenue of the Americas, New York, NY 10036, USA.

MURDOCK Eugene Converse, b. 30 Apr 1921, Lakewood, Ohio, USA. Retired Professor of History. m. Margaret McColl, 7 Oct 1950. 1 son, 1 daughter. *Education:* BA, Wooster College, 1943; MA 1948, PhD 1951, Columbia University. *Appointments:* Editorial Board, Ohio History, 1964-74; Pro Football Digest, 1967-69; Journal of Sport History, 1974-78. *Publications:* Ohio's Bounty System in the Civil War, 1963; Patriotism Limited, 1967; One Million Men: the Civil War Draft in the North, 1971; Ban Johnson: Czar of Baseball, 1982; Mighty Casey: All-American, 1984; The Civil War in the North: A Selective Annotated Bibliography, 1987; The Buckeye Empire: An Illustrated History of Ohio Enterprise, 1988; Bernard P McDonough: The Man and His Work, 1989; Co-author, Fenton Glass, 1978, 1980, 1989. *Contributions to:* Historical and sport journals including: Encyclopedia of Southern History; Insider's Baseball; Biographical Dictionary of American Sport; Baseball, Football. *Address:* 415 Columbia Avenue, Williamstown, WV 26187, USA.

MURPHEY Rhoads, b. 13 Aug 1919, Philadelphia, Pennsylvania, USA. Professor, History & Asian Studies. m. Eleanor Albertson, 12 Jan 1952, 2 sons, 2 daughters. *Education:* AB 1941, AM 1942, History, Harvard University; AM China 1948, PhD Eastern History & Geography 1950, ibid. *Publications include:* Shanghai: Key to Modern China, 1953; Introduction to Geography, 1961, 4th edition 1978; Scope of Geography, 1969, 4th edition 1987; Mozartian Historian, 1976; Outsiders (award), 1977; Fading of the Maoist Vision; The Chinese, 1986. Also: A New China Policy, 1965; Approaches to Modern Chinese History, 1967; Treaty Ports, 1975; The Human Adventure, 1990; A History of Asis, 1992; Civilizations of the World, 1993. *Contributions to:* Various professional journals. *Honour:* Best Book of Year, 1978. *Memberships include:* Board of Directors 1959-, President 1986-, Editor, Monographs, Association for Asian Studies. *Address:* Department of History, University of Michigan, Ann Arbor, Michigan 48109, USA.

MURPHY C L. *See:* **MURPHY Lawrence Agustus.**

MURPHY Clive Hunter. b. 28 Nov 1935, Liverpool, England. Writer. *Education:* BA, LL.B, Trinity College, Dublin, 1958; Incorporated Law Society of Ireland, 1958. *Publications:* Freedom for Mr Mildew and Nigel Someone; Oral History: The Good Deeds of a Good Woman; Born to Sing; Four Acres and a Donkey; Love, Dears!; A Funny Old Quist; Oiky; At The Dog in Dulwich; a Stranger in Gloucester. *Contributions to:* PEN; Over 21; Cara; Books & Bookmen. *Honours:* Adam International Review 1st Novel award. *Memberships:* PEN; Society of Authors; Authors' Club; The Academy Club; Associate Royal Society of Literature. *Address:* 132 Brick Lane, London E1 6RU, England.

MURPHY Dervla, b. 28 Nov 1931, Ireland. Author. 1 daughter. *Publications:* Full Tilt, 1965; Tibetan Foothold, 1966; The Waiting Land, 1967; In Ethiopia with a Mule, 1968; On Shoestring to Coorg, 1976; Where the Indus is Young, 1977; A Place Apart, 1978; Wheels Within Wheels, 1979; Race to the Finish?, 1981; Eight Feet in the Andes, 1983; Muddling Through in Madagascar, 1985; Ireland, 1985; Tales from Two Cities, 1987; Cameroon with Egbert, 1989; Translvania and Beyond, 1992. *Contributions to:* various journals and magazines. *Honours:* American Irish Foundation Literary award, 1975; Ewart-Biggs Memorial Prize, 1978; Irish American Cultural Institute Literary Award, 1985. *Memberships:* Fellow, Royal Geographical

Society; Royal Society for Asian Affairs. *Address:* The Old Market, Lismore, County Waterford, Ireland.

MURPHY Gavin Martin Hedd, b. 10 Jan 1934. Teacher. *Education:* Downside School, 1947-52; Clare College, MA, 1952-55; University of Fribourg, 1959-61. *Publications:* Blanco White; St Gregorys College, Seville; Ovid, Metamorphoses Book XI. *Contributions to:* History Today; Recusant History. *Memberships:* Conference Secretary, Catholic Record Society of England & Wales. *Address:* 58 Stratford Street, Oxford, OX4 1SW, England.

MURPHY Jill, b. London. Writer and Illustrator. *Education:* Chelsea Art School; Croydon Art School. *Publications:* The Worst Witch, 1974; Peace At Last; Five Minutes' Peace, 1986; All in One Piece, 1987; Worlds Apart, 1988; Five Minutes' Peace (miniature) 1989; A Piece of Cake, 1989. *Honours:* Commended in Kate Greenaway Award for Peace At Last; Parents Magazine Best Books for Babies Award for Five Minutes' Peace, also shortlisted for the Children's Book Award. *Address:* c/o Walker Books Ltd, 87 Vauxhall Walk, London SE11 5HJ. England.

MURPHY Joseph Edward, b. 13 Mar 1930, Minneapolis, Minnesota, USA. Writer. m. Diana E Kuske, 4 July 1958, 2 sons. *Education:* Princeton University, BA, 1952; University of Minnesota. *Publications:* South of the Pole by Ski; The Randoam Character in Interest Rates; Stock market Prohability; With Interest; Adventure Beyound the Clouds. *Contributions to:* Princeton Alumni Journals; American Alpine Journals; Journal of Quantitative; Financial Analysis. *Memberships:* Authors Guild; American Alpine Club; Explorers Club; Chartered Financial Analyits. *Literary Agent:* Vicki Lansky, Minneapolis, MN, USA. *Address:* 2116 W Lake Isles, Minneapolis, MN 55405, USA.

MURPHY Lawrence Agustus, (Steven C Lawrence, C L Murphy), b. 1924, USA. Educator; Author. *Appointments:* English Teacher, Department Chairman, South Junior High School, Brockton, Massachusetts, 1951-85; President, Treasurer, Steven C Lawrence Productions, Brockton; Instructor in Creative Writing, Stonehill College, North Easton, Massachusetts, 1967. *Publications:* The Naked Range, 1956; Saddle Justice, 1957; Brand of a Texan, 1958; The Iron Marshal, 1960; Night of the Gunmen, 1960; Gun Fury, 1961; With Blood in Their Eyes, 1961; Slattery, and Bullet Welcome for Slattery, 1961, Slattery published separately as The Lynchers, 1975; Walk a Narrow Trail, and A Noose for Slattery, 1962; Longhorns North, and Slattery's Gun Says No, 1962; A Texan Comes Riding, 1966; Buffalo Grass (jointly with Charlotte Murphy as C L Murphy), 1966; That Man from Texas, 1972; Edge of the Land, 1974; Six-Gun Junction, 1974; North to Montana, 1975; Slattery Stands Alone, 1976; A Northern Sage: The Account of the North Atlantic-Murmansk, Russia, Convoys, 1976; Trial for Tenihan, 1976; Day of the Comancheros, 1977; Gun Blast, 1977; Slattery Stands Alone, 1979; Through Which We Serve, 1985; The Green Concord Stagecoach, 1988. *Address:* 30 Mercedes Road, Brockton, MA 02401, USA.

MURPHY Norman Thomas Philip, b. 20 May 1933, Croydon, Surrey, England. Soldier. m. Charlotte Archibald, 7 Jan 1961, 1 son, 1 daughter. *Education:* MA, Oxford, 1957. *Publications:* In Search of Blandings; One Man's London; A True and Faithful Account of the Wodehouse Society Pilgrimage; NATO Logistics Handbook. *Contributions to:* Blackwood's Punch & Country Life. *Membership:* Savage Club. *Address:* Gill Cottage, Gosforth, Cumbria CA20 1AJ, England.

MURPHY Peter John, (P J Murphy), b. 25 May 1946, Birmingham, England. English Professor. m. Jennifer Edith Stott, 3 Dec 1977, 2 daughters. *Education:* BA, 1968, MA, 1970, University of BC; HDip, Anglo Irish, Trinigh College, Dublin, 1971; PhD, University of

Reading, England, 1979. *Publications:* Reconstructing Beckett, 1990; Critique of Beckett Criticism, 1993; Under Contract: Critical Beckett. *Contributions to:* Journal of Beckett Studies; Prison Journal, (editor, 1982-90); Textual Studies in Canada; English Studies in Canada. *Honours:* Canada Council Exploration Grant, 1987; Standard Grant, Social Sciences Humanities Research Council of Canada, 1992. *Memberships:* PMLA; ACCUTE: Beckett Society. *Address:* Box 613 Yarrow, BC, Canada VOX 7AO.

MURPHY Richard, b. 6 Aug 1927, Co Mayo, Ireland. *Education:* Baymount School, Dublin, 1935-37; Canterbury Cathedral Choir School 1937-40; The Kings' School, Canterbury, 1941-42; Wellington College, 1943-44; BA, Hons, Magdalen College, Oxford, 1948, MA 1968; Sorbonne 1954-55. *Literary Appointments:* Visiting Lecturer, Reading University, England, 1968; Compton Lecturer in Poetry, Hull University, England, 1969; Visiting O'Connor Professor of Literature, Colgate University, 1971; Visiting Professor, Bard College, 1972; Visiting Professor, Princeton University, 1974; Visiting Professor, Iowa University, 1976; Visiting Professor, Syracuse University, 1977; Distinguished Visiting Poet, Catholic University, Washington DC, 1983; Distinguished Writer-in-Residence, Pacific Lutheran University, Tacoma, Washington, 1985; Distinguished Poet in Residence, Wichita State University, 1987; Visiting Poet, Institute of Fundamental Studies, Kandy, Sri Lanka, 1988-90. *Publications include:* Volumes of Poetry: Sailing to an Island, 1963; The Battle of Aughrim, 1968; High Island, 1974; The Price of Stone, 1985; New Selected Poems, 1989; The Mirror Wall, 1989. *Contributions to:* Times Literary Supplement; Irish Literary Supplement, New York; New York Review of Books; Grand Street; Sewanee Review; Massachusetts Review; Yale Review; The Reporter; New Statesman; Listener; Irish Times; Poetry Australia. *Honours:* Poetry Book Society Choice for Sailing to an Island, 1963; Poetry Book Society Recommendation for The Battle of Aughrim, 1968, and The Price of Stone, 1985; Poetry Book Society Translation Award in Britain for The Mirror Wall, 1989; American Irish Foundation Literary Award, 1983. *Memberships:* Aosdána, Ireland; Fellow, Royal Society of Literature. *Literary Agent:* John Johnson Ltd, 45 Clerkenwell Green, London EC1R OHT. *Address:* Knockbrack, Glenalua Road, Killiney, County Dublin, Ireland.

MURPHY Sylvia, b. 6 Feb 1937, Jaffa, Palestine. Writer; Retired Teacher. m. David Greenland, 21 Feb 1986. *Education:* CertEd, Saint Luke's College, Exeter, 1969; BA Hons (1st class) Open University, 1974; MPhilosophy, Exeter University, 1984. *Publications:* Novels: The Complete Knowledge of Sally Fry, 1983; The Life & Times of Barly Beach, 1987. *Contributions to:* Jennings; Woman's Own; Classic Boat; Practical Boat Owner; Yachting Monthly; South-West Yacht & Boat; Journal of Moral Education. *Honours:* Joint 1st Prize, Cosmopolitan Magazine Novel Competition, 1981; First Prize, Western Morning News Playwriting Competition, 1986. *Memberships:* Society of Authors; Educational Writers Association. *Literary Agent:* David Higham Associates, London. *Address:* Exmouth Business Bureau, 15 South Street, Exmouth, Devon, England.

MURPHY Thomas (Tom), b. 23 Feb 1935, Tuam, County Galway, Republic of Ireland. Playwright. m. Mary Hamilton Hippisley, 14 Nov 1966, Palma, Majorca. 2 sons, 1 daughter. *Education:* Vocational Engineering Teachers Diploma, 1957. *Literary Appointments:* Writer in association, Druid Theatre Company, Galway, 1983-; Writer in association, Abbey Theatre Dublin (Irish National Theatre), 1986-1989. *Publications include:* Stage Plays: On The Outside, 1959; A Whistle in the Dark, 1961; Famine, 1966; The Orphans, 1968; Epitaph Under Ether, 1968; The Fooleen: A Crucial Week in the Life of a Grower's Assistant, 1969; The Morning After Optimism, 1971; The White House, 1973; On The Inside, 1974; The Vicar of Wakefield, adaptation, 1974; The Sanctuary Lamp, 1975; The J Arthur Maginni, Story, 1976; The Blue Macushla, 1980; The Informer, adaptation, 1981; She Stoops to Conquer, adaptation,

transplantation, 1982; The Gigli Concert, 1983; Conversations on a Homecoming, 1985; Bailegangaire, 1985; Bailegangaire II (A Thief of a Christmas), 1985; Too Late for Logic, 1989; The Patriot Game, 1991; Television plays for BBC, Thames and RTE. *Honours:* Irish Academy of Letters Award for Distinction in Literature, 1973; Harvey's and Independent Newspaper Awards for Play of the Year, 1983-84; Harvey's Play of the Year, 1985-86; Sunday Tribune Theatre Award, 1986. *Memberships:* Irish Academy of Letters; Acadana; Writer's Guild of Great Britain; Society of Irish Playwrights; Board of Directors, Irish National Theatre, The Abbey Theatre, 1972-83; International Committee on English in the Liturgy, 1972-75; Founder Member, Moli Productions, 1974. *Literary Agent:* Alexandra Cann, 337 Fulham Road, London SW10 9TW, England. *Address:* 4 Garville Road, Dublin 6, Republic of Ireland.

MURPHY Walter Francis, b. 21 Nov 1929, Charleston, South Carolina, USA. McCormick Professor of Jurisprudence, Princeton University. m. Mary Therese Dolan, 28 June 1952, 2 daughters. *Education:* AB magna cum laude, University of Notre Dame, 1950; AM, George Washington University, 1954; PhD, University of Chicago, 1957. *Publications include:* Upon this Rock, fiction, 1987; The Vicar of Christ, fiction, 1979; Elements of Judicial Strategy, 1964; American Democracy, several editions 1963-83; Courts, Judges & Politics, editions 1961- 86; The Roman Enigma, fiction, 1981; Congress & the Court, 1962; Comparative Constitutional Law, 1977; American Constitutional Interpretation, 1986; Wiretapping on Trial, 1965. *Contributions to:* Numerous legal, academic & professional journals. *Honours:* Chicago Foundation for Literature, 1980; Guggenheim Fellowship, 1973; Fulbright Award, 1980. *Memberships:* Fellow, American Academy of Arts & Sciences; Various offices, American Political Science Association, Law & Society Association. *Literary Agent:* Robert Lantz, Lantz Office, 888 7th Avenue, NYC. *Address:* Department of Politics, Princeton University, Princeton, New Jersey 08544, USA.

MURRAY Albert, b. 12 May 1916, Nokomis, Alabama, USA. Writer. b. 31 May 1941, 1 daughter. *Education:* BS, Tuskegee University, 1939; MA, New York University, 1948. *Publications:* The Omni-Americans, 1970; South to a Very Old Place, 1971; The Hero and the Blues, 1973; Train Whistle Guitar, 1974; Stomping the Blues, 1976; Good Morning Blues, 1985; The Spyglass Tree, (novel7, 1991. *Honours:* Lillian Smith Award for Fiction for Train Whistle Guitar, 1974; Deems Taylor Award for Music Criticism for Stomping the Blues, American Society of Composers, Authors and Publishers, 1977; Honorary DLitt, Colgate, 1975; The Lincoln Center Alumni Emerito Award, 1991. *Memberships:* American PEN; Authors Guild. *Literary Agents:* Wylie, Aitken and Stone. *Address:* 45 West 132nd Street, New York, NY 10037, USA.

MURRAY Beatrice. *See:* **POSNER Richard.**

MURRAY Frances. *See:* **BOOTH Rosemary.**

MURRAY Les(lie) A(llan), b. 1938, Australia. Poet. *Appointments:* Scientific and Technical Translator, Australian National University, Canberra, 1963-67; Co-Editor, Poetry Australia, 1973-80; Literary Editor, Quadrant, 1990-; Poetry Reader, Angus & Robertson Publishers, 1976-91. *Publications:* The Ilex Tree (with Geoffrey Lehmann), 1965; The Weatherboard Cathedral, 1969; Poems Against Economics, 1972; Lunch and Counter Lunch, 1974; Selected Poems: The Vernacular Republic, 1976, 2nd Edition, 1982; Ethnic Radio, 1978; The Peasant Mandarin, prose, 1978; The Boys Who Stole the Funeral, 1980; The Vernacular Republic: Poems 1961-1981, 1982; Equanimities, 1982; The People's Otherworld, 1983; Persistence in Folly, 1984; The Australian Year (with Peter Solness), 1986; The Daylight Moon, 1986; Dog Fox Field, 1991; Collected Poems, Aust 1991, USA & UK 1992; Blocks and Tackles (prose), 1991; The Paperbark Tree: Selected Prose, UK 1992; Editor, New Oxford Book of Australian Verse,

1986; Collins Dove Anthology of Australia, Religious Verse, 1986. *Address:* c/o Curtis Brown Australia, 21 Unionist Paddington, NSW 2021, Australia.

MURRAY Robin, b. 14 Sept 1940, Westmoreland, England. University Lecturer. m. 21 Dec 1965, 2 daughters. *Education:* Ballion College, Oxford, BA; College of Europe, Bruges; London school of Economics, MSC. *Publications:* vietnam; Multinational Companies & Nation States; Multinational Beyound the Market; London Industrial Strategy; Breaking with Bureaucracy; Local Space. *Address:* 88 Albion Drive, London E8 4LY, England.

MURRAY Virginia R, b. 8 Nov 1914, Virginia, USA. Secondary English Teacher, Retired. m. Herbert H. Murray, 27 Feb 1943, 1 son, 1 daughter. *Education:* BA, Randolph-Macon Woman's College (Phi Beta Kappa), 1936; Graduate work: English, University of Virginia, 1938-40, Physics and Law, George Washington University, 1946. *Appointments:* Newspaper Advisor and Editor, Literary Magazine, Randolph School, Huntsville, 1965- 72. *Publications include:* Poems, published in various journals and anthologies; Poetry programmes. *Honours include:* Edwin Morkham Poetry Society Awards, 1959, 1960; Several awards in Alabama State Poetry Society and the Alabama Conclave Annual Contests, 1983-90; Poet/Author Contest Award, 1983. *Memberships:* Alabama State Poetry Society; Alabama Writers Conclave; Huntsville Branch National League of American Pen Women; Past President, Alabama State Association NLAPW; Alpha Delta Kappa; Poets and Writers; Academy of American Poets. *Address:* 8905 Strong Avenue SE, Huntsville, AL 35802, USA.

MURRAY William Hutchison, b. 18 Mar 1913. Author. m. Anne Burnet Clark, 1 Dec 1960. *Education:* Glasgow Academy; Prison camps of Central Europe, 1942-45. *Publications include:* Mountaineering in Scotland, 1947; Undiscovered Scotland, 1951; Scottish Himalayan Expedition, 1951; The Story of Everest, 1953; Five Frontiers, 1959; The Spurs of Troodos, 1960; Maelstrom, 1962; Highland Landscape, 1962; Dark Rose the Phoenix, 1965; The Hebrides, 1966; Companion Guide to West Highlands, 1968; The Real Mackay, 1969; The Western Islands of Scotland, 1973; The Scottish Highlands, 1976; The Curling Companion, 1981; Rob Roy MacGregor, 1982; Scotland's Mountains, 1987. *Contributions to:* Innumerable publications. *Honours:* Mungo Park Medal of the Royal Scottish Geographical Society, 1950; Literary Award of USA Educational Board, 1954; OBE 1966; Honorary Doctorates, Stirling University, Strathclyde University. *Memberships:* Scottish Mountaineering Club, Honorary President; Alpine Club, Vice President 1971; British Mountaineering Council, Hon Member; Ramblers Association, Vice-President. *Address:* Lochwood, Loch Goil, Argyll PA24 8AE, Scotland.

MURTI Kotikalapudi Venkata Suryanarayana, b. 31 May 1928, Parlakemidi, India. Retired Professor of English; Teacher; Research Guide; Researcher; Creative Writer; Journalist; Linguist. *Education:* MA English Language and Literature, 1963, PhD English, 1972, Andhra University (India); Certificate Linguistics, Central Institute of English and Foreign Languages, Hyderbad, 1969. *Publications:* The Allegory of Eternity, 1975; The Triple Light, 1975: Sparks of the Absolute, 1976; Spectrum, 1976; Symphony of Discords, 1977; Anaku, 1982; Waves of Illumination, 1978; Iham lo Param, 1979; Lilahela, 1981; The Sword and the Sickle: A Study of Mulk Raj Anand's Novels, 1981; Kohimoon in the Crown: Critical Studies in Indian English Literature, 1987; Old myth and New Myth: Letters from MRA to KVS, 1991. *Contributions to:* number of journals the world over including POET (Indian Edition), World Literature Today (Review Comm). *Honours include:* Hon DLitt, University Asia, 1976, World University, 1977. *Memberships:* International Academy of Poets; World University Round Table, Tucson, USA. *Address:* 43-21-9A Venkatrazu Nagar, Visakhapatnam 530 016, (AP) India.

MUSAPHIA Joseph, b. 1935, New Zealand. Dramatist; Freelance Radio and Television Writer. *Appointments:* Commercial Artist: Stuart Wearn, Christchurch, 1954-55; Wood and Braddock, Wellington, 1955; John Haddon, London, England, 1956-57; Agencies in Wellington, 1958-60; Cartoonist, The New Zealand Listener, Wellington, 1958-60; Columnist, The Dominion, and The Sunday Times, Wellington, 1974-; Writers Fellow, Victoria University of Wellington, 1979. *Publications:* The Guerrilla, 1976; Mothers and Fathers, 1978; Shotgun Wedding, 1981. *Address:* 75 Monro Street, Wellington 3, New Zealand.

MUSGRAVE Susan, b. 1951, Canada. Writer; Poet. *Appointments:* Writer-in-Residence, University of Waterloo, Ontario, 1983-85. *Publications:* Songs of the Sea-Witch, 1970; Skuld, 1971; Mindscapes, 1971; Birthstone, 1972; Entrance of the Celebrant, 1972; Equinox, 1973; Kung, 1973; Grave-Dirt and Selected Strawberries, 1973; Gullband, 1974; Against, 1974; Two Poems, 1975; The Impstone, 1976; Kistkatinaw Songs (with Sean Virgo), 1977; Selected Strawberries and Other Poems, 1977; Becky Swan's Book, 1978; A Man to Marry, A Man to Bury, 1978; Conversation During the Omelette Aux Fine Herbes, 1979; The Charcoal Burner, novel, 1980; Hag Head, for children, 1980; Taboo Man, 1981; Tarts and Muggers: Poems New and Selected, 1982; The Plane Put Down in Sacramento, 1982; I Do Not Know if Things That Happen Can be Said to Come to Pass or Only Happen, 1982; Cocktails at the Mausoleum, 1985; The Dancing Chicken, novel, 1987. *Address:* Box 2421, Sidney, British Columbia, Canada V8L 3Y3, Canada.

MUSGROVE Frank, b. 1922, United Kingdom. Professor Emeritus of Education, University of Manchester. *Publications:* The Migratory Elite, 1963; Youth and the Social Order, 1964; The Family, Education and Society, 1966; Society and the Teacher's Role (with P H Taylor), 1969; Patterns of Power and Authority in English Education, 1971; Ecstasy and Holiness, 1974; Margins of the Mind, 1977; School and the Social Order, 1979; Education and Anthropology, 1982; The North of England: A History from Roman Times to the Present, 1990. *Address:* DIB SCAR, The Cedar Grove, Beverley, East Yorkshire, HU17 7EP, England.

MUSSER Joe, b. 1936, USA. Writer; Company President. *Appointments:* Director, Creative Services, 1966-73, President, 1963-, Four Most Productions Inc, Wheaton, Illinois. *Publications:* The Centurian, radio play, 1963; Dawn at Checkpoint Alpha, radio play, 1966; Behold, a Pale Horse, 1970; Doctor in a Strange Land (co-author), 1968; Road to Spain, screenplay, 1971; The Rapture, screenplay, 1972; Joni (with Joni Eareckson), 1976; Josh, 1981; The Coming World Earthquake, 1982; A Skeptic's Quest, 1984. *Address:* c/o Tyndale House, 336 Gundersen Drive, Wheaton, IL 60187, USA.

MUSSEY Virginia T H. *See:* ELLISON Virginia Howell.

MUSTO Barry, (Robert Simon), b. 1930, United Kingdom. Novelist; Short Story Writer. *Appointments:* Public Relations Consultant. *Publications:* The Lawrence Barclay File, 1969; Storm Centre, 1970; The Sunless Land (as Robert Simon); The Fatal Flaw, 1974; Code Name, Bastille; No Way Out; The Weighted Scales; The Lebanese Partner, 1984. *Memberships:* Crime Writers Association. *Address:* Thistles, Little Addington, Kettering, Northants, England.

MYDDLETON Robert. *See:* HEBBLETHWAITE Peter.

MYERS Harriet Kathryn. *See:* WHITTINGTON Harry.

MYERS Jack Elliott, b. 29 Nov. 1941, Lynn, Massachusetts, USA. Professor of English. m. Willa

Naomi Robins, 15 Aug 1980, Atlanta. 3 sons, 1 daughter. *Education:* BA, University of Massachusetts, 1970; MFA, University of Iowa, 1972. *Literary Appointments:* Poetry Editor of Cimarron Review, 1989. *Publications:* Black Sun Abraxas, 1970; Will it Burn, 1974; The Family War, 1977; I'm Amazed That You're Still Singing, 1981; A Trout in the Milk, 1982; New American Poets of the '80's, 1984; The Longman Dictionary & Handbook of Poetry, 1985; As Long As You're Happy, 1986; New American Poets of the 90's, 1991; A Profile of 20th Century American Poetry, 1992; Blindsided, 1993. *Contributions include:* Esquire; American Poetry Review; Antaeus; Poetry; A Magazine of Verse; Iowa Review; Minnesota Review; Virginia Quarterly Review; Georgia, Missouri and Southern Poetry Reviews; Ploughshares; South-west Review; Fiction International; The Nation. *Honours:* Texas Institute of Letters Poetry Award, 1978; Elliston Book Award, 1978; National Endowment for the Arts Fellowship, 1982 and 1986. *Memberships:* PEN; Associated Writing Programs; Texas Institute of Letters; Texas Association of Creative Writing Teachers. *Address:* Dept of English, Southern Methodist University, Dallas, TX 75275, USA.

N

NABOKOV Dmitri, b. 10 May 1934, Berlin, Germany. Operatic Bass; Writer; Translator. *Education:* AB cum laude, Harvard University; Longy School of Music, 1955-57. *Publications:* Translator: Numerous works of Vladimir Nabokov, 1957-; Other translations; Editor and-or Commentator: The Man from the USSR and Other Plays (Vladimir Nabokov), 1984; The Enchanter, 1986; Selected Letters 1940-1977, 1989. *Contributions:* Articles and essays to various collections and periodicals. *Honours:* Participant; award-winning recording Madrigals by Gesualdo, 1963; Served with AUS, 1957-59; Winner, International Opera Contests, Reggio Emilia, 1960, Parma, 1966; Chevalier du Tastevin. *Memberships:* Offshore Powerboat Racing Association; American Powerboat Racing Association; American Alpine Club; Ferrari Club in Switzerland. *Literary Agent:* Smith and Slolnik, New York, USA. *Address:* Chemin de la Caudraz, CH-1820 Montreux, Switzerland.

NADICH Judah, b. 13 May 1912, Baltimore, MD, USA. Rabbi. m. 26 Jan 1947, Martha Hadassah Ribaloe, 3 daughters. *Education:* AB, College of the City of New York, 1928-1932; MA, Columbia University, 1935-1936; Jewish Theological Seminary of America, 1932-1936; Rabbi, Doctor of Hebrew Literature, 1953, Doctor of Divinity, (Honoris Causa), 1966. *Publications:* Eisenhower and the Jews, 1953; Translator of The Flowering of Modern Hebrew Literature by Menachem Ribalow, 1957; Editor, Al Halakhah Ve-Aggadah, by Louis Ginzberg, 1960; Jewish Legends of the Second Commonwealth, 1983; Yom Kippur, a brochure for Armed Forces of USA; Articles on Eisenhower and Jews in the Military in Encyclopeadia Judaica and Jewish-American History and Culture, an Encyclopeadia. *Contributions to:* Articles published in The Reconstructionist; Hadoar; Jewish Book Annual; Essays in Jewish Booklore; Congress Weekly; Conservative Judaism; Shma; The Jewish Frontier; Journal of Jewish Social Studies. *Memberships:* President, The Jewish Book Council of America, 1970-72; The Rabbinical Assembly, Prsident, 1972-74. *Address:* Park Avenue Synagogue, 50E 87th Street, New York, NY 10028, USA.

NADOLNY Sten, b. 29 July 1942, Zehdenick/Havel, Germany. Author. *Education:* Abitur, 1961; Dr phil, Modern History, 1977. *Publications:* Netzkarte, 1981; Die Entdeckung der Langsamkeit, 1983; Selim oder die Gabe der Rede, 1990; Das Erzählen und die guten Absidhten, 1990. *Honours:* Ingeborg Bachmann Prize, 1980; Hans Fallada Prize, 1985; Vallombrosa Prize, Florence, 1986. *Memberships:* PEN; Bayerishe Akademie der Schönen Künste. *Literary Agent:* R Piper & Co Verlag, Germany. *Address:* c/o R Piper & Co Verlag, Georgenstrasse 4, D 8000 Munich 40, Germany.

NAEF Adrian, b. 10 Jan 1948, Zurich, Switzerland. Educator; Writer; Journalist; Musician; Songwriter. 1 son. *Education:* Phil I, Economics, Universities of St Gallen and Zurich, 1969-75; Diploma, Language History, University of Zurich, 1978. *Appointments:* Teacher, several school; Currently Teacher, Hospital for Children, Zurich. *Publications:* Lagebericht, 1976; Gott ist krank, sein Sohn hort Punk; Die beste aller Zeiten; Religion ohne Gott und Teufel. *Contributions to:* Merkur; Tages-Anzeiger Magazin; Weltwoche; Einspruch; Several others. *Honours:* Anerkennungs-Preis, Darmstadt Akademie, 1976. *Address:* Hohenweg 11, CH-8032 Zurich, Switzerland.

NAGARAJA RAO C K (Rajanna, Haritas, Haida), b. 12 June 1915, Chellakere, India. Author; Journalist. m. Rajamani Nagarajo Rao, 18 May 1934. Author and journalist. 2 sons, 6 daughters. *Education:* Intermediate Engineering Exam, Mysore University, 1933; Hindi Preaveshika Exam, 1937. *Publications:* Wild Jasmine, 1937; Mushrooms, 1942; Place and Aate of Mahakavi Lakshmeeshana, 1969; Pattamahadevi Shantaladevi, 1978; Sankole Basava, 1979; Sangama, 1944; Savilladavaru, 1982; Shoodramuni, 1943; Sampanna Samaja, 1979; Kuranganayani, 1983; Veeranganga

Vishnuvardhana, 1992; Ekalavya, 1988. *Contributions to:* Illustrated Indian Weekly; Mirror; Quarterly Journal of Mythic Society; PEN; Vani; Prabhata; Prakasha; Janapragati?; Subodha; Vakchitra; Prajamata; Prajavani. *Honours:* Kernataka State Sahitya Akademi Award for Research and Criticism, 1969-70, Best Creative Literature of the Year, 1978; Moorthidevi Sahiyta Puraskar of Bharatiya Jnanpith, 1983. *Memberships:* Kannada Sahitya Parishat; Karnataka Lekhakar Sangha; PEN All India Centre; Mythic Society; Author's Guild of India. *Address:* 7/61/2 Mandaara, 1 Main Road, Padmanabhanagar, Bangalore 560 070, India.

NAGATSUKA Ryuji, b. 20 Apr 1924, City of Nagoya, Japan. Professor. m. 20 July 1949. *Education:* Graduated, Section of French Literature, University of Tokyo, 1948. *Appointments:* Professor, Nihon University, 1968-. *Publications:* Napoleon tel qu'il etait, 1969; J'etais un kamikaze, 1972; George Sand, sa vie et ses oeuvres, 1977; Napoleon, 2 vols, 1986; Talleyrand, 1990. *Contributions to:* The Yomiuri Shimbun. *Honours:* Prix Pierre Mille, 1972; Prix Senghor, 1973. *Membership:* Association International des Critiques Litteraires, Paris. *Address:* 7-6-37 Oizumigakuen-Cho, Nerima-Ku, Tokyo, Japan.

NAGEL Paul C, b. 1926, American, Writer on History & Biography. Distinguished Lee Scholar, R E Lee Memorial Foundation, 1986-. *Appointments:* Professor of History 1964-69, Dean, College of Arts and Sciences, 1965-69, University of Kentucky, Lexington; Professor of History 1969-78, and Vice-President for Academic Affairs, 1970-74, University of Missouri, Columbia; Professor of History and Head of Department, University of Georgia, Athens, 1978-81; Director, Virginia Historical Society, 1981-85; Contributing Editor, American Heritage Magazine, 1983-; Visiting Scholar, Duke University, 1991-92; Visiting Scholar, University of Minnesota, 1992-93. *Publications:* One Nation Indivisible: The Union in American Thought 1776-1861, 1964; This Sacred Trust: American Nationality 1798-1898, 1971; Missouri: A History, 1977; Descent from Glory: Four Generations of the John Adams Family, 1983; (co-author) Extraordinary Lives: The Art and Craft of American Biography, 1986; The Adams Women, 1987; The Lees of Virginia, Seven Generations of An American Family, 1990; George Caleb Bingham, co-author, 1990; Massachusetts and the New Nation, 1992. *Honour:* Virginia Cultural Laureate, 1988-. *Memberships:* Fellow, Pilgrim Society; Fellow, Society of American Historians; President, Southern Historical Assocation. *Address:* 12800 Marion Lane West, Apt 502, Minnetonka, MN 55305, USA.

NAGY Paul, b. 23 Aug 1934, Hungary. Writer. div. *Education:* Bachelor's degree, Hungary, 1953; Diploma, French Language and Literature, Sorbonne, Paris, 1962. *Appointments:* Les faineants de Hampstead; Co-Founder, Atelier Hongrois, 1962; Co-Founder, D'Art, video-review, 1987. *Creative works:* Books: Lea faineants de Hampstead, 1969; Sadisfaction S, 1977; Journal in-time, 1984; Projections-performances, 1978-; Visual multimedia works, 1980-. *Contributions to:* Change; Change International; Rampike; Lotta poetica; Others. *Membership:* Union des Ecrivains Francais. *Address:* 141 Ave Jean Jaures, 92120 Montrouge, France.

NAHAL Chaman, b. 1927, Indian, Writer of novels/short stories, literature, philosophy. Member of Department of English, Delhi University, 1963-. *Appointments:* Columnist, Taking About Books, The Indian Express newspaper, 1966-73; Associate Professor of English, Long Island University, New York, 1968-70. *Publications:* The Weird Dance (short stories) 1965; A Conversation with J Kristnamurti, 1965; D H Lawrence: An Eastern View, 1970; (ed)Drugs and the Other Self, 1971; The Narrative Pattern in Ernest Hemingway's Fiction, 1971; My True Faces (novel) 1973; Azadi (novel) 1975; Into Another Dawn (novel) 1977; The English Queens (novel) 1979; The Crown and the Loincloth (novel) 1982; The New Literatures in English, 1985; The Bhagavad-Gita: A New Rendering, 1987;

Sunrise in Fiji (novel) 1988; The Salt of Life (novel) 1990. *Address:* 2/1 Kalkaji Extension, New Delhi 110019, India.

NAIMAN Anatoly G, b. 23 Apr 1936, Leningrad, Russia. Poet; Writer. m. Galina Narinskaia, 1969. 1 son, 1 daughter. *Education:* Degree in Organic Chemistry, Leningrad Technoogical Institute, 1958; Postgraduate Diploma in Screenwriting, Moscow, 1964. *Appointments:* Visiting Professor in Russian and Poetry, Bryn Mawr College, USA, 1991; Visiting Fellow, All Souls College, Oxford, UK, 1991-92. *Publications:* Remembering Anna Akhmatova, 1989; The Poems of Anatoly Naiman, 1989; The Statue of A Commander and other Stories, 1992; Translations into Russian include: Songs of Troubadours, 1979; Flemanca, 1983, 1984; Floire et Blanceflor, 1985; Le Roman de Renard, 1986; Le Roman de Sept Sages, 1989; The Poems of Giacomo Leopardi, 1967, 1989. *Contributions to:* The New Worlds; October; The Star; Literaturnaia Gazeta; Russkaia Mysl; L'Espresso; TLS. *Honours:* Lativian Union of Writers Translators Prize. *Memberships:* Leningrad Four (group of poets), 1960-66; Writers Committee, Leningrad, 1965-70, Moscow, 1970-; PEN Club, France, 1989-. *Literary Agent:* Andrew Nurnberg Assoicates, London. *Address:* Dmitrovskoye Schosse 29 fl 56, Moscow, Russia.

NAIPAUL Vidiadhar Surajprasad, b. 17 Aug 1932, Trinidad. Writer. m. Patricia Hale, 1955. *Education:* BA, Honours, English, University College, Oxford, 1954. *Publications:* The Mystic Masseur, 1957; The Suffrage of Elvira, 1958; Miguel Street, 1959; A House for Mr Biswas, 1961; The Middle Passage, 1962; Mr Stone and the Knights Companion, 1963; An Area of Darkness, 1965; The Mimic Men, 1967; A Flag on the Island, 1967; The Loss of Eldorado, 1969; In a Free State, 1971; India : A Wounded Civilisation, 1977; A Bend in the River, 1979; The Return of Eva Peron, 1980; Among the Believers, 1981; Finding the Centre, 1984; The Enigma of Arrival, 1987; A Turn in the South, 1989. *Contributions to:* Various journals and magazines. *Honours:* Recipient, numerous honours and awards including: Rhys Memorial Prize, 1958; W.H. Smith Literary Award, 1968; Booker Prize, 1971; Bennet Award, 1980; Jerusalem Prize, 1983; Ingersoll Prize, 1986; D.Litt., Cambridge University, 1983. *Memberships:* Fellow, Royal Society of Literature; Society of Authors. *Literary Agent:* Gillon Aitken. *Address:* c/o Aitken & Stone, 29 Fernshaw Road, London SW10 0TG, England.

NAKAYAMA Kiyoshi, b. 30 Mar 1935. Professor of English. 1 son, 1 daughter. *Education:* BA French, Tenri University, Nara 1955; MA English Literature, Kansai University, Osaka, 1959-62. *Publications:* Steinbeck in Japan: A bibliography, 1992; John Steinbeck: Asian Perspectives, 1992; John Steinbeck's Writings: The California Years, 1989; Uncollected Stories of John Steinbeck, 1986; Selected Essays of John Steinbeck, 1981; Tanoshii Mokuyobi, 1984. *Contributions to:* Kansai University English Literature Society Bulletin; San Jose Studies; Essays on Collecting John Steinbeck's Books; Steinbeck Quarterly; Monterey Life. *Honours:* The Richard W and Dorothy Burkhardt Award, 1992. *Memberships:* John Steinbeck Society of Japan, Executive Director; International John Steinbeck Society, Executive Board; The Japan American Literature Society. *Address:* 594 Takabatake Honyakushi-cho, Nara-shi, Nara 630, Japan.

NAKAYAMA Shigeru, b. 22 June 1928, Japan, Professor. m. Motoko Watanabe, 8 July 1962, 1 son, 1 daughter. *Education:* BA, Tokyo University, 1951; PhD, Harvard University, 1959. *Publications:* Academic and Scientific Traditions, 1984; History of Japanese Astronomy, 1969; Chinese Science, 1973; Science and Society in Modern Japan, 1974; Characteristics of Scientific Development in Japan, 1977. *Memberships:* International Council for Science Policy Studies; Academie Internationale d'Histoire des Sciences. *Address:* 3-7-11 Chuo, Nakano, Tokyo, Japan.

NANDA Bal Ram, b. 11 Oct 1917, Rawalpindi, India (now in Pakistan). Historian; Writer. m. Janak Khosla, 24 May 1946, 2 sons. *Education:* MA History, 1st class, University of Punjab, Lahore, 1939. *Appointment:* Director, Nehru Memorial Museum & Library, New Delhi, 1965-79. *Publications:* Mahatma Gandhi, A Biography, 1958; The Nehrus, Motilal and Jawaharlal, 1962; Gokhale, The Indian Moderates and the British Raj, 1977; Gandhi and His Critics, 1986; Gandhi, Pan-Islamism, Imperialism and Nationalism in India, 1989; In Gandhi's Footsteps: Life and Times of Jamnalal Bajaj, 1990; Gandhi, A Pictorial Biography, 1972; Jawaharlal Nehru, A Pictorial Biography, 1980; Edited: Indian Foreign Policy: The Nehru Years, 1975; Socialism in India, 1972; Science and Technology in India, 1977; Essays in Modern Indian History, 1980. *Contributions to:* Numerous newspapers, magazines and journals. *Honours:* Rockefeller Fellowship, 1964; National Fellowship, Indian Council of Social Science Research, New Delhi, 1979; Dadabhai Naoroji Memorial Prize, 1981; Padma Bhushan, 1988. *Memberships:* Indian Historical Records Commission; Institute for Defence Studies and Analyses, New Delhi. *Address:* S-174 Panchshila Park, New Delhi 110017, India.

NANDY Pritish, b. 1947, Indian, Poet, Translator. Editor, Dialogue Calcutta, later Dialogue India, 1968- . *Publications:* Of Gods and Olives: 21 Poems, 1967; I Hand You in Turn My Nebbuk Wreath: Early Poems, 1968; On Either Side of Arrogance, 1968; (ed) Getting Rid of Blue Plastic: Poems Old and New, by Margaret Randall, 1968; (ed) Some Modern Cuban Poems, 1968; Rites for a Plebeian Statue: An Experiment in Verse Drama, 1969; From the Outer Bank of the Brahmaputra, 1969; (ed) Selected Poems of Subhas Mukhopadhyay, 1969; (ed)Selected Poems of Parvez Shadedi, 1969; (ed) Selected Poems of G Sankara Kurup, 1969; (ed)Selected Poems of Agyeya, 1969; (trans) Ravana's Lament: A Selection from the Abhiseka Swarga of the Meghnad-Badh Kavya of Michael Madhusudhan Data, 1969; Masks to Be Interpreted as Messages, 1970; (ed and trans) The Complete Poems of Samar Sen, 1970; (ed)Selected Poems of Amrita Pritam, 1970; Collected Poems, 1973; (ed)Indian Poetry in English Today, 1973; (ed)Modern Indian Poetry, 1974; (ed)Bengali Poetry Today, 1974; Riding the Midnight River: Selected Poems, 1975; Lone Song Street, 1975; Stranger Called I, 1976; In Secret Anarchy, 1976; Nowhere Man, 1978; Anywhere Is Another Place, 1979; Tonight This Savage Rite: The Love Poetry of Kamala Das and Pritish Nandy, 1979; The Rainbow Last Night, 1981; Some Friends, 1983. *Address:* 5 Pearl Road, Calcutta 17, India.

NANSE. See: KUO Nancy.

NAPIER Bill. See: NAPIER William McDonald.

NAPIER Mary. See: WRIGHT Patricia.

NAPIER William McDonald, (Bill Napier), b. 29 June 1940, Perth, Scotland. Astronomer. m. Nancy Miller Baillie, 7 July 1965, 1 son, 1 daughter. *Education:* BSc, 1963; PhD, 1966. *Publications:* The Cosmic Serpent, 1982; The Cosmic Winter, 1990; The Origin of Comets, 1990. *Contributions to:* Occasionally to: New Scientist; Astronomy Today. *Honours:* Joint recipient, Arthur Beer Memorial Prize, 1986-87. *Membership:* Fellow, Royal Astronomical Society. *Address:* Royal Observatory, Blackford Hill, Edinburgh EH9 3HJ, Scotland.

NARANG Gopi Chand, b. 1 Jan 1931, Dukki, Baluchistan, India. Professor, urdu Language & Literature, Delhi University. m. Manorama, 9 Dec 1973, 2 sons. *Education:* MA, First Class First, Urdu 1954, Phd 1958, Diploma in Linguistics, First Division 1961, University of Delhi; Post-doctoral Courses in Acoustic Phonetics and Transformational Grammar, Indiana University, 1964; Hons. Persian, First Class First, 1958, Hons. Urdu, First Class First, 1948, Punjab University. *Publications include:* Karkhandari Dialect of Delhi Urdu, 1961; Puranon Ki Kahaniyan, 1976; Anthology of

Modern Urdu Poetry, 1981; Safar Ashna, 1982; Usloobiyat-e-Mir, 1985; Saniha-e-Karbala bataur Sheri Istiara, 1987; Amir Khusrau ka Hindaui Kalaam, 1988; Adabi Tanqeed aur Usloobiyat, 1989; Under Language & Literature: Critical Perspectives, 1991. *Honours:* President of Pakistan Gold Medal for distinguished research work on Iqbal, 1977; Ghalib Award, 1985; Hindi Urdu Sahitya Award from President of India, 1985; Mohd. Husain Azad Aalmi Urdu Award, 1987; Amir Khusrau Award, 1987; Canadian Association for Language & Literature Award, 1987; President of India's State honours and decoration, Padma Shri, 1992. *Memberships:* Fellow, Royal Asiatic Society; Linguistic Society of India; Association for Asian Studies; All India PEN; Linguistic Society of America. *Address:* D-252 Sarvodaya Enclave, New Delhi, India 110017.

NARDON Anita Lucia, b. 2 Apr 1931, Belgium. Multi Lingual Secretary; Art Critic. m. div, 3 sons. *Appointments:* Staff, Peau de Serpent, 1962-78; Le Drappeau Rouge, 1980-1991; IDEART, 1989; Montrer, 1991. *Publications:* Poetry. La Terre au Gout de Sel; Le Manteau d'Arlequin; Frontieres; La Chanson d'Isis; Novel. L'Objet et la Chute; Tale. Contes Pour Yannick. *Contributions to:* Panarte; La Critque; Le Drapeau Rouge; Medaille d'argent Arthur Rimbaud; Prix Ville de Toulon, France; Prix Silarus Francia; Medaille de Bronze Poesiades de Paris. *Memberships:* PEN; Association of French Speaking Belgian Writers; Association International des Critiques d'Art. *Address:* Rue Jourdan 57, 1060 Brussels, Belgium.

NARULA Surinder Singh, b. 8 Nov 1917, Amritsar, India. Teacher. m. Pritama, 10 Apr 1950, 3 daughters. *Education:* MA, English, 1942. *Appointments:* Former Principal & Head, Post Graduate Dept. of English and American Literatures, Government College, Ludhiana. *Publications:* 13 novels, 6 collections of short stories, 8 books of literary criticism, 3 collections of poetry and 12 books on socio cultural subjects including: Peo Puttar, 1946; Sil Alune, 1963; History of Panjabi Literature, 1958; Gatha, epic poem, 1985; Gali Gwand, 1971; Nili Bar; Rang Mahal. *Contributions to:* numerous professional journals. *Honours:* Rattingon Gold Medalist, 1938; J. S. Hailey Prizeman, 1938; Panjab Government Shiromani Sahityakar; Panjab Arts council award; Sahitya Shri Award, Bhartiya Bhasha Sangam; Rotary International Award; Panjabi Sahitya Akademi Silver Jubilee Robe of Honour; Vishav Panjabi Sammelan Gold Medal; many other honours and awards. *Memberships:* various professional organisations. *Address:* 684 Gurdevnagar, Civil Lines, Ludhiana 141001, India.

NASH Gary B, b. 1933, American, Writer on History. Professor of History, University of California at Los Angeles, 1966-. *Appointments:* Assistant Professor of History, Princeton University, New Jersey, 1964-66; Associate Director, National Center for History in the Schools, 1988-. *Publications:* Quakers and Politics: Pennsylvania 1618-1726, 1968; Class and Society in Early America, 1970; (ed with Richard Weiss), The Great Fear: Race in the Mind of America, 1970; Red, White and Black: The Peoples of Easrly America, 1974, 1982-91; The Urban Crucible: Social Change, Political Consciousness and the Origins of the American Revolution, 1979; (ed with David Sweet), Struggle and Survival in Colonial American, 1980; (co-ed) The Private Side of American History, 2 vols, 1983-87; (with J R Jeffrey), The American People, 2 vols, 1985-89; Retracing the Past, 2 vols, 1985-89; Race, Class and Politics, 1986; Forging Freedom: The Formation of Philadelphia's Black Community, 1720-1840, 1988; Race and Revolution, 1991. *Address:* 16174 Alcima Avenue, Pacific Palisades, CA 90272, USA.

NASH Gerald David, b. 16 July 1928, Berlin, Germany. University Professor. m. 19 Aug 1967, 1 daughter. *Education:* BA, New York University, 1950; MA, Columbia University, 1952; PhD, University of California, Berkeley, 1957. *Appointments:* Stanford University, 1957- 58, 1959-60; Northern Illinois University, 1959-60; Harvard University, 1960- 61; University of New Mexico, 1961-. *Publications:* State Government & Economic Development, 1964; US Oil Policy, 1968; The Great Transition, 1971; The American West in 20th Century, 1973; The Great Depression & World War II, 1979; American West Transformed, World War Ii, 1985; Editor, Issues in American Economic History, 1964; F.D. Roosevelt, 1967; Urban West, 1979; Half Century of Social Security, 1988; Perspectives on 20th Century West, 1988; World War II and the West: Re-shaping the Economy, 1990; Creating the West: Historical Interprettions 1890- 1990, 1991; A P Giannninni and the Bank of America, 1992. *Contributions to:* 40 articles in professional journals. *Honours:* Phi Beta Kappa, 1950; Newberry Fellow, 1955; Huntington Library Fellow, 1979; NEH Fellow, 1981. *Memberships:* Phi Alpha theta, historian, 1974-84, Editor, The Historian; Organisation of American Historians; Western History Association. *Address:* Dept. of History, University of New Mexico, Albuquerque, NM 87131, USA.

NASH Padder. *See:* **SEWART Alan**.

NASSAUER Rudolf, b. 1924, British, Writer of novels/short stories, poetry. *Publications:* Poems 1947; The Holigan, 1959; The Cuckoo, 1962; The Examination, 1973; The Unveiling, 1975; The Agents of Love, 1976; Midlife Feasts, 1977; Reparations, 1981; Kramer's Goats, 1986. *Address:* 51, St James' Gardens, London W11, England.

NATALE Francine de. *See:* **MALZBERG Barry Norman**.

NATHAN David, b. 9 Dec 1926, Manchester, England, Journalist. m. Norma Ellis, 31 Mar 1957, 2 sons. *Appointments:* Copy boy, Copy taker, News Chronicle, Manchester, 1942-44, 1947; Reporter, St Helens Reporter, 1947- 49; Reporter, Feature Writer, Theatre Critic, London Editor, Nottingham Guardian, 1949-52; Daily Mail, 1952-54; Associated Press, 1954-55; Reporter, Feature Writer, Theatre Critic, Daily Herald/Sun, 1955-69; Theatre Critic, Jewish Chronicle, 1970-; Deputy Editor, 1978-1991. *Publications:* Hancock, (Co-author Freddie Hancock), 1969; A Good Human Story, television play, 1978; The Laughtermakers, 1971; The Freeloader, 1970; Co-contributor (with Dennis Potter) to That Was The Week That Was, Not So Much a Programme, BBC3; Glenda Jackson, a critical profile, 1984; John Hurt, An Actor's Progress, 1986; The Story So Far, 1986; The Belman of London, 1982; The Bohemians, 1983 radio plays; Shaw and Politics, (Contributor), 1991. *Contributions to:* The Times Saturday Review; Daily and Sunday Telegraph, Independent; Harpers and Queens; TV Times; Observer Colour Magazine. *Honours:* Highly Commended, Writer's Award, Royal Television Society, 1978. *Memberships:* President, Critics Circle, 1986-88, trustee. *Literary Agent:* Harvey Unna and Stephen Durbridge Limited. *Address:* 16 Augustus Close, Brentford Dock, Brentford, Middlesex, England.

NATHAN Edward Leonard, b. 8 Nov 1924, Los Angeles, California, USA Teacher; Poet. m. Carol G. Nash, 27 June 1949, 1 son, 2 daughters. Publications: Western Reaches, 1958; Glad and Sorry Seasons, 1963; The Day the Perfect Speakers Left, 1969; Returning Your Call, 1975; Dear Blood, 1980; Holdings Patterns, 1982; Carrying On : New & Selected Poems, 1985; Translations Include: First Person, Second Person by Agyeya, 1971; The Transport of Love, 1976; Grace and Mercy in Her Wild Hair, 1982; Songs of Something Else, 1982; Happy as a Dog's Tail, 1986; On the Skin, (translation with C Milosz of poetry of Aleksander Wat) 1989. *Contributions to:* Salmagundi; New Yorker; New Republic; Kenyon Review. *Honours:* Guggenheim Fellowship, 1976-77; Nominee, National Book Award, 1975; National Institute of Arts and Letters Award for Creative Literature, 1971; American Institute of Indian Studies Fellowship, 1965-66; Creative Arts Fellowship, UCB, 1973-74, 1963-64. *Address:* 40 Beverly Road, Kensington, CA 94707, USA.

NATHAN Robert S, b. 13 Aug 1948. *Education:* BA cum laude, Amherst College, 1970. *Appointments:* Producer, NBC Television Series, Law and Order. Writer and Co-writer; Writer, television film, In the Deep Woods, 1992. *Publications:* The White Tiger, 1988; Rising Higher, 1981; Amusement Park, 1977; In the Deep Woods, 1989; The Legend, 1986; The Religion, 1982. *Contributions to:* All Things Considered; The New Republic; New York; Harper's; The New York Times Book Review. *Honours:* Notable Book of the Year, New York Times; Book of the Month Club Selection. *Address:* c/o Adam Berkowitz, William Morris Agency, New York, USA.

NATHANSON Carol, b. 24 Apr 1922, Pittsburgh, Pennsylvania, USA. Author; Lecturer. *Education:* BA, Carnegie Mellon University, Pittsburgh, 1943. *Publications:* The Constellations, 1988, 1991. *Memberships:* New York Academy of Sciences; National Academy of Television Arts and Sciences. *Address:* 2200 Walton Avenue, Apt 6E, Bronx, NY 10453, USA.

NATSUKI Shizuko, b. 21 Dec 1938, Tokyo, Japan. m. 1963. *Education:* Graduate, Keio University. *Publications:* 30 novels, 220 novelettes and short stories, and 25 books, including: The Angel Vanishes, 1970; Disappearance, 1973; The Tragedy of W, 1984; The Third Lady, 1984; mystery novel, A Different Sort of Death, rewritten into a screenplay called, Only I Know. *Contributions to:* Ellery Queen's Mystery Magazine, and other magazines and periodicals. *Honours:* Literary Award, Fukuoka City, 1972; 26 Mystery Writers of Japan Award, 1973; Delegate, 3rd International Congress of Mystery Writers, Stockholm, 1981; Prix du Roman d'Adventures, France, 1984. *Address:* Woodbell Co Ltd, 2-12-3 Komaba 2-chome, Meguro-ku, Tokyo 153, Japan.

NATUSCH Sheila Ellen, b. 14 Feb 1926, New Zealand. Writer; Illustrator. m. Gilbert G. Natusch, 28 Nov 1950. *Education:* MA, Otago University, 1948. *Publications:* Animals of New Zealand, 1967; Brother Wohlers, 1969, 2nd edition, 1992; New Zealand Mosses, 1970; Wild Fare for Wilderness Foragers, 1970; Native Plants, Revised Edition, 1976; Hell and High Water, 1977, 2nd edition, 1992; The Cruise of the Acheron, 1978; On the Edge of the Bush, 1978; Wellington, 1981; A Bunch of Wild Orchids, 3rd Edition, 1983; A Pocketful of Pebbles, 1983; Southward Ho, 1985; William Swainson of Fern Grove, 1987; Roy Trail of Stewart Island, 1991; An Island Called Home, 1992. *Contributions to:* Occasional articles in: Marine News; New Zealand Gardener; NZ Fisherman. *Honours:* Hubert Church Award for Brother Wohlers, PEN, New Zealand, 1969. *Address:* 46 Owhiro Bay Parade, Wellington 2, New Zealand.

NAU Henry Richard, b. 10 Dec 1941, USA. Associate Dean; Professor of Political Science and International Affairs. m. Marion M Nau, 1 daughter. *Education:* BS, Economics, Politics, Science, Massachusetts Institute of Technology, 1963; MA with distinction, International Relations, 1967, PhD, International Relations, 1972, School of Advanced International Relations, Johns Hopkins University. *Publications:* National Politics and International Technology: Nuclear Reactor Development in Western Europe, 1974; Technology Transfer and US Foreign Policy, 1976; Domestic Trade Policies and the Uruguay Round (editor, contributor), 1989; The Myth of America's Decline: Leading the World Economy into the 1990s, 1990; 18 book chapters; Monographs. *Contributions to:* Perspective; Orbis; International Organization; Columbia Journal of World Business; Journal of International Affairs; Policy Studies Journal; The Washington Quarterly; World Affairs; Geopolitics of Energy; Economic Impact; Foreign Policy; Western Political Quarterly; The National Interest; International Economy; Dokumentation; National Review; CEO International Strategies. *Honours:* Dean's List, Massachusetts Institute of Technology; Proctor and Gamble Fellowship, Massachusetts Institute of Technology, 1958-63; NDEA Title IV Fellownshsip, 1965-68; Ford Foundation Foreign Area Fellowship Grant,

1968-70; Phi Beta Kappa, 1973; National Science Foundation Grant, 1974-75; International Affairs Fellowship, Council on Foreign Relations, 1975-76; Superior Honor Award, Department of State, 1977; Fellowship, Woodrow Wilson International Center for Scholars, 1987; Fellowship, Smith-Richardson Foundation, 1987. *Memberships:* North-South Roundtable on Trade, Society for International Development, Islamabad; Board of Editors and Executive Committee, International Organization, 1977-81. *Address:* 7409 River Falls Drive, Potomac, MD 20854, USA.

NAUMOFF Lawrence Jay, b. 23 July 1946, Charlotte, North Carolina, USA. Author. (div), 1 son. *Education:* BA, University of North Carolina, Chapel Hill, 1969. *Publications:* Novels: The Night of the Weeping Women, 1988; Rootie Kazootie, 1990; Taller Women, 1992. *Contributions to:* Various Literary Magazine, Short Stories. Honours: Thomas Wolfe Memorial Award, 1969; National Endowment for the Arts Grant, 1970, $30,000; Whiting Foundation Writers Award. *Membership:* PEN. *Literary Agent:* Barbara Lowenstein (USA); Adam Stein (UK). *Address:* PO Box 901, Carrboro, NC 27510, USA.

NAVON Robert, b. 18 May 1954, New York City, New York, USA. Editor; Philosopher. *Education:* BA, Lehman College, City University of New York, 1975; MS, State University of New York, Geneseo, 1978; MA studies, New School, 1982-86; PhD candidate, University of New Mexico, 1991-. *Publications:* Patterns of the Universe, 1977; Autumn Songs: Poems, 1983; The Pythagorean Writings, 1986; Healing of Man and Woman, 1989; Harmony of the Spheres, 1991; Cosmic Patterns, Volume I, 1993; Great Works of Philosophy, 7 vols (editor). *Honours:* New York State Regents Scholar, 1971; Phi Beta Kappa, 1975; Intern, Platform Association, 1980. *Memberships:* Society of Ancient Greek Philosophy; American Philosophical Association. *Address:* PO Box 81702, Albuquerque, NM 87198, USA.

NAVRATIL Jan, b. 13 May 1935, Slovakia. Writer. m. Libusa Nigrovicova, 5 Sept 1959, 1 son, 1 daughter. *Education:* Pedagogic Faculty at University, 1959. *Publications:* Lampas maleho plavcika, 1980, 1983, 1989; Gulata Kocka, 1985, 1987; Kto vidi na dno, 1981; Len srdce prvej velkosti, 1970, 1984; Pramienok, 1983, 1989; Plachetnica Nonsens, 1967; Diskoteka L, 1983; Z hliny a rosy, 1981; Riekanky, 1988; Belasy majak, 1985; Kral s gitarou, 1988; Ciarky na dlani, 1989; Tri cervene klobuciky, 1973; Rozpravka o duhovej lodi, 1984. *Honours:* Janusz Korczak Award, 1981; Frano Kral Award, 1980; Union of Slovak Writers Award, 1981, 1985; Mlade leta Award, 1966, 1970, 1990; Maxim Gorki diploma, 1987; HCh Andersen Diploma, 1982. *Memberships:* ssa 00Union of Slovak Writers; Friends of Children's Book Club. *Literary Agent:* Agence Litteraire Slovaque, Partizánska ul c 21, 815 30 Bratislava, Slovakia. *Address:* Obezna Street 13, 926 01 Sered, Slovakia, Slovaki.

NAYAK Harogadde Manappa, b. 5 Feb 1931, Hosamane, India. Teacher. m. Yashodharamma, 11 May 1955, 1 son, 1 daughter. *Education:* BA, Honours, University of Mysore, 1955; MA, Calcutta University, 1959; PhD, Indiana, USA, 1964. *Appointments:* Editor, Prabuddha Karnataka, 1967-84; Adviser, Grantha Loka, 1976-. *Publications:* Namma Maneya Deepa, 1956; Ravindranath Tagiore, 1960; Kannada - Literary and Colloquial, 1967; Sulangi, 1975; Sangati, 1987; Janapada Swarupa, 1971; more than 60 books. *Contributions to:* Indian PEN; Kannada Prabha; Prajamata; Prajavani; Inchara; Prabuddha Karnataka; Sudha; Taranga. *Honours:* Calcutta University Gold Medal, 1959; Mysore University Golden Jubilee Award, 1978; Karnataka State Award, 1982; Karnataka Sahitya Akademy award, 1985; Presided over 57th All India Kannada Literary Conference, 1985. *Memberships:* Indian National Academy of Letters, Executive Committee; National Book Trust, India, Trustee; Indian PEN; Kannada Sahitya Parisht; Karnataka Janapada

Parisht, President. *Address:* Godhuli, Jayalakshmi Puram, Mysore 570-021, Karnataka, India.

NAYLOR Gloria, b. 1950, American, Novelist. *Appointments:* Missionary for the Jehovah's Witnesses, New York, North Carolina and Florida, 1968-75; Telephone operator, New York City hotels, 1975-81; Writer-in-Residence, Commington Community of the Arts, Massachusetts, 1983; Visiting Professor, George Washington University, Washington DC, 1983-84; Visiting Writer, New York University, 1986; Columnist, New York Times, 1986. *Publications:* The Women of Brewster Place: A Novel in Seven Stories, 1982; Linden Hills, 1985. *Address:* c/o Ticknor and Field, 52 Vanderbilt Avenue, New York, NY 10017, USA.

NEAL Ernest Gordon, b. 20 May 1911, Boxmoor, Hertfordshire, England, Retired School Teacher; Biologist, m. Helen Elizabeth Thomson, 30 Apr 1937, 3 sons. *Education:* BSc, MSc, PhD, London University and Extension, 1931-35. *Publications:* Exploring Nature with a Camera, 1946; The Badger, 1948; Woodland Ecology, 1953; Topsy and Turvy My Two Otters, 1961; Uganda Quest, 1971; Biology for Today, (Co-author K R C Neal), 1974; Badgers, 1977; Badgers in Closeup, 1984; Naural History of Badgers, 1986; On Safari in East Africa, A Background Guide, 1991. *Contribution to:* Country Life; The Field; Illustrated London News; Times; Wildlife Magazine; Sunday Times; Countryman; Countryside Magazine; Mammal Review. *Honours:* Stamford Raffles Award, Zoological Society of London, 1965; MBE, 1976; Fellow, Institute of Biology, 1965. *Memberships:* Society of Authors; Mammal Society, Chairman, President; British Ecological Society; Somerset Trust for Nature Conservation, Chairman, Vice President. *Address:* 42 Park Avenue, Bedford MK40 2NF, England.

NEAL Harry Edward, b. 1906, American, History, Politics/Government, Social sciences (general), Writing/Journalism. Freelance writer since 1957. *Appointments:* Member, US Secret Service 1926-57, retired as Assistant Chief. *Publications:* Writing and Selling Fact and Fiction, 1949; The Story of the Kite, 1954; Nature's Guardians: Your Career in Conservation, 1956; Pathfinders: USA, 1957; The Telescope, 1958; Skyblazers1958; Six Against Crime, 1959; Diisease Detectives, 1959; (co- author) The United States Secret Service, 1960; Communication: From Stone Age to Space Age, 1960; Engineers Unlimited, 1960; Treasures by the Million, 1961; Money Masters, 1961; The Hallelujah Army, 1961; Diary of Democracy, 1962, 1970; Your Career in Electronics, 1963; From Spinning Wheel to Spacecraft, 1964; Nonfiction: From Idea to Published Book, 1964; Your Career to Foreign Service, 1965; The Mystery of Time, 1966; Money, 1967; The Pennsylvania Colony, 1967; The Protectors, 1968; The Virginia Colony, 1969; Oil, 1970; Of Maps and Men, 1970; The People's Giant, 1970; The Story of the Sceret Service, 1971; The Story of Offshore Oil, 1977; The Secret Service in Action, 1980; Before Columbus: Who Discovered America? 1981. *Address:* 210 Spring Street, Culpeper, VA 22701, USA.

NEEDLE Jan, b. 1943, British, Writer of children's and adults, Literature. *Publications:* Albeson and the Germans, 1977; My Mate Shofiq, 1978; A Fine Boy for Killing, 1979; The Size Spies, 1979; Rottenteeth, 1980; The Bee Rustlers, 1980; A Sense of Shame, 1980; Wild Wood, 1981; Losers Weepers, 1981; Another Fine Mess, 1981; (with Peter Thomson) Brecht, 1981; Piggy in the Middle, 1982; Going Out, 1983; A Game of Soldiers (TV serial) 1983, and book 1985; A Pitiful Place, 1984; Great Days at Grange Hill, 1984; Tucker's Luck, 1984; Behind the Bike Sheds, 1985; Tucker in Control, 1985; Behind the Bike Sheds (TV series) 1985; Wagstaffe, The Wind-Up Boy, 1987; Soft Soap (TV play) 1987, as TV series, 1988; Truckers (TV series), 1987; Uncle in the Attic, 1987; Skeleton at School, 1987; In the Doghouse, 1988; The Sleeping Party, 1988; Mad Scramble, 1989; As Seen on TV, 1989; The Thief (TV series), 1989; The Thief (novel), 1990. *Address:* (For Drama), c/o Rochelle Stevens and Co, 2 Terretts Place,

Upper Street, London, N1 1QZ, England; (For Novels), David Higham Associates, 5-8, Lower John Street, London, W1R 4HA, England.

NEELY Richard, American. Fulltime Writer of Mystery, Crime, Suspense. Formerly an advertising executive. *Publications:* Death to My Beloved, 1969; The Plastic Nightmare, 1969; While Love Lay Sleeping, 1969; The Walter Syndrome, 1970; The Damned Innocents, 1971, in US paperback as Dirty Hands, 1976; The Japanese Mistress, 1972; The Sexton Women, 1972; The Smith Conspiracy, 1972; The Ridgway Women, 1975; A Madness of the Heart, 1976; Lies, 1978; No Certain Life, 1978; The Obligation, 1979; An Accident Woman, 1981; Shadows from the Past, 1983. *Address:* c/o Delacorte Press, 1 Dag Hammarskjold Plaza, New York, NY 10017, USA.

NEHAMAS Alexander, b. 22 Mar 1946, Athens, Greece. University Professor. m. Susan Glimcher, 22 June 1983, 1 son. *Education:* BA, Swarthmore College, USA, 1967; PhD, Princeton Universitry, 1971. *Publications:* Nietsche: Life As Literature, 1985; Plato's Symposium, 1989. *Contributions to:* Many articles to journals, including Cauafy's World of Art, and Sartre's Freud Scenario, to Grand Street. *Honours:* Fellow, National Endowment for the Humanities, USA, 1977-78; Guggenheim Fellow, 1984-85; Phi Beta Kappa, Romanwell Professor, 1991; Sather Professor of Classical Literature University of Califonia, Berkeley, 1993. *Memberships:* American Philosophical Association, Executive Committee 1989-92; American Society for Aesthetics; Modern Language Association; Modern Greek Studies Association. *Address:* Department of Philosophy, Princeton University, Princeton, NJ 08544, USA.

NEILAN Sarah, b. Newcastle-upon-Tyne. m. 4 children. *Education:* MA (Oxon). *Publications:* The Braganza Pursuit; An Air of Glory; Paradise; The Old Enchantment. *Contribution to:* Observer; Guardian; Evening Standard; Bookseller; Times Ed Supplement; Reader's Digest; Woman Magazine. *Honour:* Mary Elgin Award. *Membership:* PEN. *Literary Agent:* The Peters, Fraser and Dunlop Group Ltd. *Address:* c/o The Peters, Fraser and Dunlop Group Ltd, 503/4 The Chambers, Chelsea Harbour, London SW10 0XF, England.

NEILSON Andrew, b. 15 Nov 1946, Ordsall, Nottinghamshire, England. Writer. m. Sally, 19 July 1980, 1 son, 1 daughter. *Education:* BA, Honours, Liverpool University, 1968. *Publications:* Braking Point, 1983; Dead Straight, 1984; The Monza Protest, 1985. *Literary Agent:* Julian Friedmann, Blake Friedmann Agency. *Address:* Las Nayas, Partida Lluca, Javea (Alicante), Spain.

NELSON Marguerite. *See:* FLOREN Lee.

NELSON Mildred (Pearson), b. 28 Mar 1915, Arkansas, USA. Writer. m. Arthur Lee Nelson, 7 July 1935, 1 son, 1 daughter. *Education:* BA, English Literature, University of Arkansas, 1936. *Publicatins:* Taste of Power, 1964; The Dark Stone, 1972; The Island, 1973. *Contributions to:* Fiction and poetry to many journals and magazines including: Crosscurrents; McCall's; Georgia Review; Christian Science Monitor; Colorado Quarterly; Light Year Anthology '86. *Honours:* PEN Syndicated Fiction Award, 1984; World Order of Narrative Poets Award, 1985; Poetry Arts Project Award, 1989. *Memberships:* Authors League of America; Authors League of America; PEN; Poets and Writers. *Literary Agent:* Jay Garon, New York, USA. *Address:* 1508 Circa del Lago B-307, Lake San Marcos, CA 92069, USA.

NELSON Richard, b. 1950, American, Writer of Plays/Screenplays. *Appointments:* Literary Manager, BAM Theatre Co, Brooklyn, 1979-81; Associate Director, Goodman Theatre, Chicago, 1980-83; Dramaturg, Guthrie Theatre, Minneapolis, 1981-82. *Publications:*

The Vienna Notes (in Word Plays I) 1980; II Campiello (adaptation) 1981; An American Comedy and Other Plays, 1984; Between East and West (in New Plays USA 3) 1986; Principia Scriptoriae, 1986; (ed)Strictly Dishonorable and Other Lost American Plays, 1986; Rip Van Winkle, 1986; Jungle Coup (in Plays from Playwrights Horizons) 1987; Accidental Death of an Anarchist (adaptations) 1987. *Address:* 32 South Street, Rhinebeck, NY 12572, USA.

NELSON-HUMPHRIES Tessa, b. Yorkshire, England. Professor of English Literature; Lecturer; Writer. m. (1) Kenneth Nelson Brown, 1 June 1957, London (dec 1962), (2) Cecil H. Unthank, 26 Sept 1963, New Mexico, USA (dec 1979). *Education:* BA, MA, University of North Carolina, USA; PhD, University of Liverpool, UK, 1973. *Contributions to:* Michigan Quarterly Review; Southern Folklore Quarterly; Dalesman; Let's Live; Cats Magazine; Bulletin, Society of Children's Book Writers; Child Life; Vegetarian Times; Bulletin, Society of Women Writers & Journalists; The Lookout; Joycean Literary Arts Guild magazine; Alive; British Vegetarian; Blue Unicorn; Candles & Lamps; Outposts. Poetry in: Z, 1987; Miscellaneous, 1988. *Honours:* Short story prize, Society of Women Writers, UK, 1975; Julia Cairns Trophy, poetry (UK), 1978; Mellon Award, writing & travel in China, 1981; James Still Fellowship in Humanities, University of Kentucky, for biography of L.E. Landon, 1983. Also Danforth, Fulbright, AAUW Awards; Article Prize 1985, Fiction Prize 1987, SWWJ; Poetry Prizes, (Julia Cairns Competition), 1988, 1989; Mellon Awards, a travel study, Spain, 1988, 1989. *Memberships:* Society of Childrens Book Writers, USA: Society of Women Writers & Journalists. *Address:* York Cottage, Route 4, Box 944, Williamsburg, Kentucky 40769, USA.

NEMEROV Howard, b. 29 Feb 1920, New York City, USA. English Teacher. m. Margaret Russell, 26 Jan 1944, 3 sons. *Education:* AB, Harvard College, 1941. *Appointments include:* Faculties, Hamilton College 1946-48, Bennington 1948-66, Brandeis University 1966-69, Washington University, Missouri 1969- (Edward Mallinckrodt Distinguished University Professor, English, 1976-); Consultant in Poetry, Library of Congress, 1963-64; Poet Laureate of the United States, 1988-. *Publications include:* Collected Poems of HN, 1977; Journal of the Fictive Life, 1965; The Homecoming Game, novel, 1958; Sentences, poems, 1980; Inside the Onion, poems, 1984; New & Selected Essays, 1985; Total, 26 books, poetry, fiction, criticism, memoirs; Most recent: The Oak in the Acorn: On Remembrance of Things Past & On Teaching Proust, Who Will Never Learn, 1987; War Stories: Poems About Long Ago & Now, 1987; Trying Conclusions, 1991. *Contributions to:* Numerous magazines & journals. *Honours include:* National Book Award, Pulitzer Prize, 1978; Bollingen Prize, poetry, 1980; Aiken/Taylor Award, poetry, 1987; National Medal of Arts, poetry, 1987. *Memberships:* American Academy of Arts & Letters; American Academy of Arts & Sciences; Chancellor, Academy of American Poets. *Address:* Department of English, Washington University, St Louis, Missouri 63130, USA.

NEMSER Cindy, b. 26 Mar 1937, Writer. m. Charles Nemser, 16 Dec 1956, 1 daughter. *Education:* BA Education, 1958, MA English and American Literature, 1964, Brooklyn College; MA Art History, NYU Institute of Fine Arts, 1966. *Publications:* Art Talk: Conversations with 12 women artists, 1975; Eve's Delight, 1982; Ben Cunningham: A Life with Color, 1989. *Contributions to:* Ms; The Village Voice; Art Forum; Art in America; Arts Magazine; The Feminist Art Journal; Opera Monthly; Newsday; Art Education; New York Law Journal. *Honours:* Arts Critic's Fellowship, NEA, 1975; Commencement Speaker Minneapolis College of Art and Design, 1977. *Memberships:* PEN, 1990; Advisory Board of Women's Caucus for Art: College Art Association, 1975- 78, Poets and Writers Authors Guild, Dramatists Guild; Drama Desk, 1992; American Theatre Critics Association, 1992-93; The New York Press Club, Inc, 1992-93; American Society of Journalists and Authors, Inc, 1992-93. *Literary Agent:* Helmus Meyer. *Address:* 41 Montgomery Place, Brooklyn, NY 11215, USA.

NEUBAUER Alexander, b. 17 Jan 1959, New York City, New York, USA. Writer. m. April Stevens, 1 Oct 1988. *Education:* BA, Haverford College, 1981. *Publications:* Nature's Thumbprint: The New Genetics of Personality, 1990. *Membership:* Authors Guild. *Literary Agent:* Mel Berger, William-Morris Inc. *Address:* 308 West 103rd Street, New York, NY 10025, USA.

NEUBERGER Julia Babette Sarah, b. 27 Feb 1950, London, England. Rabbi; Author; Broadcaster. m. Anthony John Neuberger, 17 Sept 1973, 1 son, 1 daughter. *Education:* Newnham College, Cambridge, 1969-73; BA, Assyriology, Hebrew, Cambridge; MA, 1975; Rabbinic Ordination, Leo Baeck College, 1977. *Publications:* Judaism, for children, 1986; Caring for Dying People of Different Faiths, 1987; Days of Decision, 4 vols (editor), 1987; Whatever's Happening to Women?, 1991; A Necessary End (editor with John White), 1991; Ethics and Healthcare: Research Ethics Committees in the UK, 1992; The Things that Matter (ed), an anthology of Women's Spiritual Poetry, 1993. *Contributions to:* Jewish Chronicle; Journal of STD and AIDS; Vogue; Cosmopolitan; Others; Reviews to: Sunday Times; Telegraph; Sunday Express; Mail on Sunday; Evening Standard. *Membership:* Fellow, Royal Society of Arts. *Literary Agent:* Carol Smith. *Address:* 36 Orlando Road, London SW4 0LF, England.

NEUFELD Peter Lorenz, b. 1931. Canadian. Writer on Animals/Pets, History. *Appointments:* Developer of new Domestic Animal Breeds; School Trustee and former Executive Table Officer of Manitoba Association of School trustees; School teacher in Manitoba, 1952-67. *Publications:* Aurora, 1968; The Invincible White Shepherd, 1970. *Address:* PO Box 81, Minnedosa, Manitoba, Canada R0J 1E0.

NEUGEBOREN Jay, b. 30 May 1938, New York, USA. Writer. 2 sons, 1 daughter. *Education:* BA, Columbia University, 1959; MA, Indiana University, 1963. *Appointments:* Visiting Writer, Stanford University, 1966-67; Writer in Residence, University of Massachusetts, 1971-. *Publications:* The Stolen Jew, 1981; Before My Life Began, 1985; Big Man, 1966; Sams Legacy, 1974; POLI, 1989; Corkys Brother, 1969. *Contributions to:* The Atlantic; The American Scholar; Tri Quarterly; Sport, and others. *Honours:* Transatlantic Revew Novella Award, 1967; National Endowment for Arts Fellow, 1974, 1989; Guggenheim Fellow, 1978; Present Tense Award, Best Novel, 1981; Wallant Memorial Prize, Best Novel, 1985; PEN Syndicated Fiction Prize, 1982-1988. *Memberships:* Authors Guild; PEN. *Literary Agent:* Elaine Markson, New York City, USA. *Address:* 35 Harrison Avenue, Northampton, MA 01060, USA.

NEUMEYER Peter F, b. 4 Aug 1929. Professor; Writer. m. Helen Wight Snell, 27 Dec 1953, 3 sons. *Education:* BA 1951, MA 1955, PhD 1963, University of California, Berkeley. *Appointments:* Assistant Professor, Harvard University, 1963-69; Associate Professor, SUNY (Stony Brook), 1969-75; Professor, Chairman, Department of English, West Virginia University, 1975-78; Professor, San Diego State University, 1978-. *Publications:* Kafkas, The Castle, 1969; Donald and the ...., 1969; The Faithful Fish, 1971; Homage to John Clare, 1980; Image and Makes (co-ed) 1984; The Phantom of the Opera (adapted) 1988; Donald Has a Difficulty, 1970; Why We Have Day and Night, 1970; Elements of Fiction (co-ed) 1974. *Contribution to:* The Creation of Charlotte's Web from Drafts to Book, Horn Book, Oct and Dec 1982; Franz Kafka, Sugar Baron, Modern Fiction Studies, Spring 1971. *Address:* 7968 Windsor Drive, La Mesa, CA 92041, USA.

NEUSTADT Richard E, b. 1919. American. Writer

on Politics/Government. *Appointments:* Associate Dean of Kennedy School of Government, 1965-75, Director Institute of Politics, 1966-71, Lucius Littauer Professor 1975-86, Douglas Dillon Professor of Government, 1987-89, Emeritus, 1989-, Harvard University, Cambridge, Massachusetts; Economist, Office of Price Administration, Washington DC, 1942; US Navy, 1942-1946, Staff Member, Bureau of the Budget 1946- 50; Member, White House Staff 1950-53; Professor of Government, Columbia University, New York City, 1954-65; Special Consultant, Sub-Committee on National Policy Machinery, US Senate, Washington, DC, 1959-61; Member, Advisory Boardr, Commission on Money and Credit, 1960-61; Special Consultant to President Kennedy, 1961-63; Bureau of the Budget, 1961-70; Department of State, 1963 and to President Johnson, 1964-66; Council on Foreign Relations, 1963; Associate Member, Nuffield College, Oxford, 1964-1967, 1990-93. *Publications:* Presidential Power, 1960, 1990; Alliance Politics, 1970; (with H V Finiberg), The Swine Flu Affair, 1978; The Epidemic That Never Was, 1982; (with E R May), Thinking in Time, 1986. *Memberships:* International Institute of Strategic Studies, 1968. *Address:* 1010 Memorial Drive, Cambridge, MA 02138, USA.

NEUSTATTER Angela Lindesay, b. 24 Sept 1943, Buckinghamshire, England. Journalist; Author. 2 sons. *Education:* Regent Street Polytechnic; Diploma in Journalism. *Publications:* Twiggy - Health & Beauty, 1985; Mixed Feelings, 1986; Getting the Right Job; Working for Yourself. *Contributions to:* Guardian; The Times; Observer; Sunday Telegraph; Daily Telegraph. *Honours:* Mixed Feelings Selected for Feminist Top Twenty List, 1986. *Literary Agent:* Vivienne Schuster, John Farquarson. *Address:* 32 Highbury Place, London N5, England.

NEVILLE Alison (Edward Candy), b. 1925, British. *Appointments:* Reviewer, The Times and The Sunday Times, London, 1967-76; Physician: worked in hospitals in Norwich, Sheffield, Northwood and Liverpool. *Publications:* Which Doctor, 1953; Bones of Contention, 1954; The Graver Trive, 1958; A Lady's Hand, 1959; A Season of Discord, 1964; Strokes of Havoc, 1966; Parent's Day, 1967; Doctor Amadeus, 1969; Words for Murder, Perhaps, 1971; Scene Changing, 1977; Voices for Children, 1980. *Address:* 2 Mile End Road, Newmarket Road, Norwich NR4 7QY, England.

NEVILLE Robert Cummings, b. 1 May 1939, St. Louis, MO. Philosophy and religion educator. m. Elizabeth Egan, 3 daughters. *Education:* BA, 1960; MA, 1962; PhD, 1963, Yale University; Ordained Elder, United Methodist Church, 1966. *Publications:* God the Creator, 1968; The Cosmology of Freedom, 1974; (ed with Gaylin and Meister); Operating on the Mind (ed), 1975; Soldier, Sage, Saint, 1978; Creativity and God, 1980; Reconstruction of Thinking, 1981; The Tao and the Diamon, 1982; The Puritan Smile, 1987; (Ed), New Essays in Metaphysics), 1987; The Recovery of the Measure, 1989; Behind the Masks of God, 1991; The Highroad around Modernism, 1992; Eternity and Time's Flow, 1993. *Contributions to:* Articles to professional journals. *Memberships:* American Academy of Religion, Board of Directors 1982-; Chairman, Research and Scholarship Committee, 1984-89; Program Committee, 1990-92; Long-range Planning Cmmittee, 1985-92; Vice- President, President Elect, President, 1990-92; Executive Committee, 1990-92; Missouri East Annual Conference, United Methodist Church; American Theological Society (Exec. Comm. 1980-83); American Philosophical Association; (Exec. Comm. 1983-85); Metaphysical Society of America, President, 1988. *Address:* Boston University School of Theology, 745 Commonwealth Avenue, Boston, MA 02215, USA.

NEVINS Francis M(ichael) Jr. b. 1943, American. Writer of Mystery/Crime/Suspense, Literature. *Appointments:* Assistant Professor, 1971-75, Associate Professor 1975-78, Professor, 1978-, St Louis University School of Law; Admitted to the New Jersey Bar 1967; Assistant to the Editor- in-Chief, Clark Boardrman Co, law publishers, New York City, 1967; served in the US Army 1968-69; Staff Attorney, Middlesex County Legal Services Corp, New Brunswick, New Jersey, 1970-71. *Publications:* Novels: Publish and Perish; Corrupt and Ensnare, 1978; The 120-Hour Clock, 1987; The Ninety Million Dollar Mouse, 1987. Non-fiction: Detectionary (with four co-authors), 1971; Royal Bloodline: Ellery Queen, Author and Detective, 1974; Missouri Probate: Intestacy, Wills and Basic Administration, 1983; The Films of Hopalong Cassidy, 1988; Cornell Woolrich: First You Dream, Then You die, 1988. Fiction Edited or Co-Edited: Nightwebs, 1971; The Good Old Stuff, 1983; Exeunt Murderers, 1983; Buffet For Unwelcome Guests, 1983; More Good Old Stuff, 1985; Carnival of Crime, 1985; Hitchcock In Prime Time, 1985; The Best of Ellery Queen, 1985; Leopold's Way, 1985; The Adventures of Henry Turnbuckle, 1987; Better Mousetraps, 1988; Mr President-Private Eye, 1988; Death on Television, 1989; Little Boxes of Bewilderment, 1989; The Night My Friend, 1991; Non-fiction Edited or Co-Edited: The Mystery Writer's Art, 1970; Multiplying Villainies, 1973. *Honours:* Edgar Award from Mystery Writers of America for Royal Bloodline: Ellery Queen, Author and Detective, 1975; Edgar Award from Mytery Writers of America for Cornell Woolrich: First You Dream, Then You Die, 1988. *Literary Agent:* Curtis Brown Ltd, New York, USA. *Address:* 7045 Cornell, University City, MO 63130, USA.

NEVZGLIADOVA Elena Vsevolodovna, (Elena Ushakova), b. 2 June 1939, Leningrad, Russia. Poet; Literary Critic. m. Aleksandr Semyonovich Kushner. 1 son. *Education:* Graduate, 1962, PhD, 1974, Philological Faculty, Leningrad University. *Publications:* Nochnoe Solntse, (A Night Sun), 1991. *Contributions to:* Neva; Znamya; Syntaxis; Raduga; Zvezda; Novii Mir; Almanakh Petropol. *Memberships:* Writers' Union. *Address:* Kaluzhskii per 9 apt 48, St Petersburg 193015, Russia.

NEW Anthony Sherwood Brooks, b. 14 Aug 1924, London, England. Architect. m. Elizabeth Pegge, 11 Apr 1970, 1 son, 1 daughter. *Education:* Highgate School, 1937-41; Northern Polytechnic School of Architecture, 1941-43, 1947-51. *Publications:* Observer's Book of Postage Stamps, 1967; Observer's Book of Cathedrals, 1972; A Guide to the Cathedrals of Britain, 1980; A Guide to the Abbeys of England and Wales, 1985; New Observer's Book of Stamp Collecting, 1986; A Guide to the Abbeys of Scotland, 1988. *Memberships:* Fellow, Society of Antiquaries; Fellow, Royal Institute of British Architects; Institution of Structural Engineers. *Address:* 26 Somerset Road, New Barnet, Herts EN5 1RN, England.

NEWALL Venetia June, b. 1935, British. Writer on Mythology/Folklore. *Appointments:* Honorary Research Fellow in Folklore, Department of English, University of London, 1971-; General Editor, The Folklore if the British Isles series, Batsford Ltd, London 1972-78. *Publications:* A Egg at Easter: A Folklore Study, 1971; The Folklore of Birds and Beasts, 1971; (ed and author with C Blacker et al), The Witch Figure, 1973; (with Russell Ash et al), Folklore Myths and Legends of Britain, 1973; Encyclopaedia of Witchcraft and Magic, 1974; (ed) Folklore Studies in the Twentieth Century, 1980. *Address:* University Women's Club, 2 Audley Square, South Audley Street, London W1Y 6DB, England.

NEWBY (Percy), Howard, b. 25 June 1918, Crowborough, Sussex, England. Author. m. 12 July 1946, 2 daughters. *Education:* St Paul's College, Cheltenham. *Publications:* A Journey to the Interior, 1945; The Picnic at Sakkara, 1955; Something to Answer For, 1968; Kith, 1977; Feelings have Changed, 1981; Leaning in the Wind, 1986; Coming in with the Tide, 1991; 12 other novels; 3 historical studies; 2 works of literary criticism; 2 children's books. *Honours:* Atlantic Award, 1946; Somerset Maugham Prize, 1948; Yorkshire Post Fiction Award, 1968; Booker Prize, 1969; CBE 1972. *Membership:* Society of Authors. *Literary Agent:* David Higham Associates. *Address:* Garsington House, Garsington, Oxford OX44 9AB, England.

NEWCOMER James William, b. 14 Mar 1912, Gibsonburg, Ohio, USA. College Professor; Vice Chancellor Emeritus. m. 17 Aug 1946, 1 son, 2 daughters. *Education:* PhB, Kenyon College; MA, University of Michigan; PhD, University of Iowa. *Publications:* Criticism: Maria Edgeworth the Novelist, 1967; Maria Edgeworth, 1973; Lady Morgan the Novelist, 1990. Poetry: The Merton Barn Poems, 1979; The Resonance of Grace, 1984. The Grand Duchy of Luxembourg (History), 1984; The Nationhood of Luxembourg (essays), 1990. *Contributions to:* College English; Nineteenth Century Fiction; Criticism; Books at Iowa; Arlington Quarterly; Descant; Sands. *Honours:* Phi Beta Kappa; Officer in Order of Merit and Honorary Member, L'Institut Grand-Ducal, Grand Duchy of Luxembourg. *Address:* 1100 Elizabeth Boulevard, Fort Worth, Texas 76110, USA.

NEWELL Crosby. *See:* **BONSALL Crosby Newell.**

NEWLANDS Willy, (William Newlands of Lauriston), b. 5 Nov 1934, Perth, Scotland. Travel Writer. m. (1) 1 son, 2 daughters. (2) Dorothy Walker, 1985. *Appointments:* Travel Correspondent, Daily Mail, 1980-. *Contributions to:* Articles on Wildlife and travel for: The Field; Shooting Times; Country Life. *Honours:* Churchill Fellow, 1968; Travel Writer of the Year, 1983-84 and 1987-88. *Memberships:* Caledonian Club; British Association of Travel Editors, Founder. *Address:* Lauriston Castle, St. Cyrus, Kincardineshire, Scotland.

NEWLOVE John (Herbert), b. 1938, Canadian. Poet. Formerly Senior Editor, McClelland and Stewart Ltd, Publishers, Toronto. *Publications:* Grave Sirs: Poems, 1962; Elephants, Mothers and Others, 1963; Moving in Alone, 1965; Notebook Pages, 1966; Four Poems, 1967; What They Say, 1967; Black Night Window, 1968; The Cave, 1970; Lies, 1972; (ed) Canadian Poetry: The Modern Era, 1977; The Fat Man: Selected Poems 1962-1972, 1977; (with John Metcalf) Dreams Surround Us, 1977; The Green Plain, 1981; (ed) The Collected Poems of F R Scott, 1981.

NEWMAN Andrea, b. 7 Feb 1938, Dover, England. Writer, (div). *Education:* BA, Honours, English, 1960, MA, 1972, London University. *Publications:* A Share of the World, 1964; Mirage, 1965; The Cage, 1966; Three Into Two Won't Go, 1967; Alexa, 1968; A Bouquet of Barbed Wire, 1969; Another Bouquet, 1977; An Evil Streak, 1977; Mackenzie, 1980; A Sense of Guilt, 1988; Triangles, 1990; A Gift of Poison, 1991. *Contributions to:* Woman; Woman's Own; Woman's Realm; Marie-Claire; GQ; Living; T.V. Scripts for Bouquet of Barbed Wire; Another Bouquet; Mackenzie; A Sense of Guilt. *Memberships:* PEN; Writers' Guild. *Literary Agent:* A P Watt. *Address:* A.P. Watt, 20 John St, London WC1N 2DR, England.

NEWMAN Aubrey N, b. 1927, British. Writer on History, Biography. Professor in History, University of Leicester. *Appointments:* Research Fellow, Bedford College, University of London, 1954-55; President, Jewish Historical Society of England, 1977-79. *Publications:* The Parliamentary Diary of Sir Edward Knatchbull 1722-1730, 1963; The Stanhopes of Chevening: A Family Biography, 1969; (compiler with Helen Miller) A Bibliography of English History, 1485-1760; The United Synagogue 1870-1970, 1977; The Jewish East End 1840-1939, 1981; The Board of Deputin, 1760-1985, a brief survey, 1987; The World Turned Inside Out, new views on George II, 1988. *Address:* Department of History, University of Leicester, Leicester, England.

NEWMAN Edwin Harold, b. 25 Jan 1919, New York, USA. Journalist. m. Rigel Grell, 1 daughter. *Education:* University of Wisconsin; Louisiana State University. *Appointments:* Washington Bureau, International News Service, 1941, United Press, 1941-42, 1945-46; US Navy, 1942-45; CBS News, Washington, DC, 1947-49; Freelance, London 1949-52; NBC News, London Bureau, 1952-57, Rome Bureau 1957-58, Paris Bureau 1958-61; Correspondent, Commentator, NBC News, New York 1961-84; Columnist, King Features Syndicate, 1984-; Freelance Journalist, Lecturer. *Publications:* Strictly Speaking, 1974; A Civil Tongue, 1976; Sunday Punch, 1979. *Contributions to:* Punch; Esquire; Atlantic; Harper's; New York Times; Saturday Review; Chicago Tribune; TV Guide; Sports Illustrated. *Honours:* Peabody, Overseas Press Club, Emmy, University of Missouri School of Journalism Awards and many others. *Address:* c/o Richard Fulton Inc., 101 W. 57th Street, New York, NY 10019, USA.

NEWMAN G F, b. 22 May 1945, England. Writer. *Publications:* Sir, You Bastard, 1970; You Nice Bastard, 1972; You Flash Bastard, 1974; The Govnor, 1977; The Nation's Health, 1982; Law and Order, 1977, 1983; The List, 1984; The Men With Guns, 1985; Set a Thief, 1986; The Testing Ground, 1987; Operation Bad Apple, play; An Honourable Trade, play. *Literary Agent:* Elaine Steel. *Address:* Wessington Court, Woolhope, Hereford HR1 4QN, England.

NEWMAN John Kevin, b. 17 Aug 1928, Bradford, Yorkshire, England. Classics Educator. m. Frances M Stickney, 8 Sept 1970, 1 son, 2 daughters. *Education:* BA, Lit Humaniores, 1950, BA, Russian, 1952; MA, 1953, Oxford University; PhD, Bristol University, 1967. *Appointments:* Classics Master, St Francis Xavier College, Liverpool, 1952-54; Classics Master, Downside School, Somerset, 1955-69; Faculty, 1969-, Professor, Classics, 1980-, University of Illinois, Urbana, USA; Editor, Illinois Classical Studies, 1982-87. *Publications:* Augustus and the New Poetry, 1967; The Concept of Vates in Augustan Poetry, 1967; Latin Compositions, 1976; Golden Violence, 1976; Dislocated: An American Carvival, 1977; Pindar's Art, 1984; The Classical Epic Tradition, 1986; Roman Catullus, 1990; Lelio Guidiccioni, Latin Poems, 1992. *Honours:* Silver Medals, Vatican, Rome, 1960, 1962, 1965. *Membership:* Senior Common Room, Corpus Christi College, Oxford, 1985-86. *Address:* 703 W Delaware Ave, Urbana, IL 61801, USA.

NEWMAN Leslea, b. 5 Nov 1955, Brooklyn, New York, USA. Writer; Teacher of Women's Writing Workshops. *Education:* BS, Education, University of Vermont, 1977; Certificate in Poetics, Naropa Institute, 1980. *Appointment:* Massachusetts Artists Fellowship in Poetry, 1989. *Publications:* A Letter to Harvey Milk, 1988; Good Enough to Eat, 1986; Love Me Like You Mean It, 1987; Heather Has Two Mommies, 1989; Bubbe Meisehs by Shayneh Maidelehs, 1989; Secrets, 1990. *Contributions to:* Sojourner, Heresies, Dark Horse, Sinister Wisdom, Telephone, Common Lives, Lilith, New Age Magazine. *Honour:* 2nd Place Finalist, Raymond Carver Short Story Competition, 1987. *Memberships:* Authors Guild and Authors League of America; Poets and Writers, Inc. *Address:* P.O.Box. 815, Northampton, MA 01061, USA.

NEWMAN Margaret. *See:* **POTTER Margaret.**

NEWMAN Peter Charles, b. 10 May 1929, Vienna. Author, journalist. *Education:* MA, Economics, University of Toronto and McGill. *Appointments:* Assistant Editor, The Financial Post, 1951-55; Ottawa Editor, Maclean's Magazine, 1955-64; Ottawa Editor, Toronto Daily Star, 1964-69; Editor-in-Chief, Toronto Daily Star, 1969-71; Editor-in-Chief, Maclean's Magazine, 1971-82; Director, Maclean Hunter Limited, 1972-83; Weekly interview show, Global Television Network, 1981-87; Senior Contributing Editor, Macleans. *Publications:* Flame of Power, 1959; The Distemper of our Times, 1968; The Canadian Establishment, 1975; The Establishment Man, 1982; Company of Adventurers, 1985; Caesers of the Wilderness, 1987; Empire of the Bay, 1989. *Honours:* Companion Order of Canada, National Newspaper Award, Feature Writing, 1966; President's Medal, University of Western Ontario, 1974; Quill Award as Journalist of Year, 1977; Knight-Commander in the

Order of St. Lazarus, 1983; National Business Writing Achievement Award, 1986; The Bob Edwards Award, 1989. *Address:* 2594 Panorama Drive, Deep Cove, North Vancouver, British Columbia, Canada V7G 1V5.

NEWMAN Shirley S, b. 13 Feb 1924, New York City, New York, USA. Teacher; Writer. m. Louis Newman, 3 Sept 1945, 2 sons, 1 daughter. *Education:* BA, 1944; Bachelor of Hebrew Literature, 1944; MA, 1949. *Publications:* Child's Introduction to torah, 1972; Child's Introduction to Early Prophets, 1975; Introduction to Kings, Later Prophets and Writings, 1981. *Address:* 680 Beacon Street, Newton Center, MA 02159, USA.

NEWTON D(wight) B(ennett) (Dwight Bennett, Clement Hardin, Ford Logan, Hank Miteham, Dan Temple), b. 1916. American. Writer of Westerns/Adventure. *Appointments:* Freelance writer since 1946; Story consultant and staff writer for TV series Wagon Train, 1957, Death Valley Days, 1958 and Tales of Wells Fargo. *Publications:* Shotgun Guard, 1950, in Uk as Stagecoach Guard, 1951; Six-Gun Gamble, 1951; Guns along the Wickiup, 1953; Rainbow Rider, 1954, in US paperback as Triple Trouble, 1978; Syndicate Gun, 1972; Massacre Valley, 1973; Range Tramp, 1973; Trail of the Bear, 1975; The Land Grabbers, 1975; Bounty on Bannister, 1975; Broken Spur, 1977; as Dwight Bennett - Stormy Range, 1951, in UK (as D B Newton) Range Feud, 1953; Lost Wolf River, 1954; Border Graze, 1952; Top Hand, 1955; The Avenger, 1956; Cherokee Outlet, 1961; The Oregon Rifles, 1962; Rebel Trail, 1963; Crooked River Canyon, 1966; Legend in the Dust, 1970; The Big Land, 1972; The Guns of Ellsworth, 1973; Hangman's Knot, 1975; The Cheyenne Encounter, 1976; West of Railhead, 1977; The Texans, 1979; Disaster Creek, 1981; as Clement Hardin - Hellbent for a Hangrope, 1954; Cross Me in Gunsmoke, 1957; The Lurking Gun, 1961; The Badge Shooters, 1962; Outcast at Ute Bend, 1965; The Ruthless Breed, 1966; The Paxman Feud, 1967; The Oxbow Deed, 1967; Ambush Reckoning, 1968; Sheriff of Sentinel, 1969; Colt Wages, 1970; Stage Line to Rincon, 1971; as Dan Temple - Outlaw River, 1955; The Man from Idaho, 1956; Bullet Lease, 1957; The Love Goddess, 1962; Gun and Star, 1964; as Hank Mitchum - Station I: Dodge City, 1982; Station 2: Laredo, 1982; Station 3: Tombstone, 1983; Station 6: Santa Fe, 1983; Station 11; Deadwood, 1984; Station 13: Carson City, 1984; Station 20: Leadville, 1985; Station 26: Tulsa, 1986. *Memberships:* Founding Member 1953, Secretary/Treasurer 1953-58, 1967-71, Western Writers of America. *Literary Agent:* Golden West Literary Agency, Oregon, USA. *Address:* 11 N W Kansas Avenue, Bend, OR 97701, USA.

NEWTON David Edward, b. 18 June 1933, Grand Rapids, Michigan, USA. University Educator; Science Writer. *Education:* AS, Grand Rapids Junior College, 1953; BS with high distinction, Chemistry, 1955, MA, Education, 1961, University of Michigan; DEd, Science Education, Harvard University, 1971; Various short courses, Cornell University, Oregon State University, Atlanta University, Hampshire College. *Publications:* Many books including: Chemistry Problems, 1962, 3rd Edition, 1984; Understanding Venereal Disease, 1973, 2nd Edition, 1978; Math in Everyday Life, 1975, 2nd Edition, 1991; Scott Foresman Biology (with Irwin Slesnick, A LaVon Blazar, Alan McCormack, Fred Rasmussen), 1980, 2nd Edition, 1985; Science and Social Issues, 1983, 3rd Edition, 1992; Biology Updated, 1984, 2nd Edition, 1987; Chemistry Updated, 1985, 2nd Edition, 1989; An Introduction to Molecular Biology, 1986; Science Ethics, 1987; Particle Accelerators, 1989; Taking a Stand Against Environmental Pollution, 1990; Land Use, 1991; James Watson and Francis Crick: A Search for DNA and Beyond, 1992; Contributions to books; Numerous teaching aids. *Contributions to:* The Bulletin of the National Association of Secondary School Principals; School Science and Mathematics; The High School Journal; Journal of Homosexuality; Appraisal; Several others. *Honours:* Sloane Scholarship, University of Michigan, 1958; Star '60 Award, National Science Teachers Association; William Payne Scholar, Horace Rackham Graduate School, University of Michigan,

1961-62; Shell Merit Fellow, 1964; Outstanding Young Science Educator of the Year, AETS, 1968. *Memberships:* Phi Beta Kappa; Phi Kappa Phi; Phi Lambda Upsilon; Delta Pi Alpha; National Science Teachers Association; Association for the Education of Teachers in Science; American Association for the Advancement of Science; National Association of Science Writers, Reviewer; Reviewer, Children's Science Book Review Committee. *Address:* Instructional Horizons Inc, 297 Addison Street, San Francisco, CA 94131, USA.

NEWTON Suzanne, b. 1936, American. Writer of children's fiction. Consultant in creative writing in North Carolina public schools, 1972-; Freelance writer. Writer-in-Residence, Meredith College, Raleigh, North Carolina. *Publications:* Purro and the Prattleberries, 1971; C/O Arnold's Corners, 1974; What Are You Up To, William Thomas, 1977; Reubella and the Old Focus Home, 1978; MV Sexton Speaking, 1981; I Will Call It Georgie's Blues, 1983; An End to Perfect, 1984; A Place Between, 1986; Where Are You When I Need You? 1991. *Address:* 841-A Barringer Drive, Raleigh, NC 27606, USA.

NEYREY Jerome H, b. 5 Jan 1940, New Orleans, Louisiana, USA. Professor. *Education:* BA, 1963; MA, 1964; MDiv, 1970; MTh, 1972; PhD, 1977; STL, 1987. *Appointments:* Weston School of Theology, 1977-92; University of Notre Dame, Notre Dame, Indiana, 1992-. *Publications:* The Passion According to Luke, 1983; Christ Is Community, 1983; An Ideology of Revolt, 1988; Calling Jesus Names, 1988; The Resurrection Stories, 1988; Paul, In Other Words, 1990; The Social World of Luke - Acts, 1991. *Contributions to:* Articles regularly to: Catholic Biblical Quarterly; Journal of Biblical Literature; Biblica; Novum Testamentum; New Testament Studies. *Honours:* Bannan Fellowship, Santa Clara University, 1984-85; Young Scholars Grant, 1984; ATS Grant, 1989; Visiting Professor, Pontifical Biblical Institute, Rome, 1989; Lilly Foundation, 1989; Plowshares, 1990. *Memberships:* Catholic Biblical Association; Society of Biblical Literature, New England Region President 1990; Executive Secretary, Context Group. *Address:* Department of Theology, University of Notre Dame, Notre Dame, IN 46556, USA.

NGUGI J(ames) T, (Wa Thiongio Ngugi), b. 1938, Kenya. Literary and Political Journalist; Author. *Appointments:* Former Editor, Penpoint magazine, Kampala. *Publications:* As J T Ngugi or Ngugi Wa Thiong'o: The Black Hermit, play, 1962; This Time Tomorrow, play, 1964; Weep Not, Child, 1964; The River Between, 1965; A Grain of Wheat, 1967; Homecoming: Essays on African and Caribbean Literature, Culture and Politics, 1972; Secret Lives, 1974; Petals of Blood, 1977; The Trial of Dedan Kimathi (with M G Mugo), 1977; Writers in Politics, 1980; Devil on the Cross, 1981; Detained: A Writer's Prison Diary, 1981; Education for a National Culture, 1981; I Will Marry When I Want, play, 1982; Barrel of a Pen: Resistance to Repression in Neo-Colonial Kenya, 1983. *Contributions to:* Sunday Nation, Nairobi. *Address:* c/o William Heinemann Ltd, 10 Upper Grosvenor Street, London W1X 9PA, England.

NGUGI Wa Thiongio. *See:* **NGUGI J(ames) T.**

NGUYEN Ngoc Huy, b. 2 Nov 1924, Cholon, Vietnam, immigrated to the USA 1975. Research Associate; Writer. m. Thu Thi Duong, 1952 (dec 1974), 1 son, 1 daughter. *Education:* Graduate of Institute of Political Studies, 1958, Licence en Droit 1959, DES en Science Politique, 1960, Doctorat en Science Politique, 1963, University Paris. *Appointments include:* Member of central executive committee of Vietnam's Dai Viet Nationalist Party 1945-64; Founder and General Secretary of Vietnam's Neo Dai Viet Party, 1964-75; Research Associate, Harvard Law School, Harvard University, Cambridge, Massachusetts, 1976-. *Publications:* Hon Viet (Vietnamese Soul) poems 1950, 2nd edition (Paris) 1984, 3rd edition (San Jose, California) 1985; Dan toc sinh ton (The Doctrine of the

Nation's Survival) 2 vols Dai Viet Party, 1964; De tai nguoi uu tu trong chanh tri Trung Quoc co thoi (Elite Notions in Traditional Chinese Political Thought) 1969; Lich su cac hoc thuyet chanh tri (A History of Political Theories) 2 vols, 1970-71; (Translator from Chinese into Vietnamese) Han Fei, Han Phi Tu (Master Han Fei) 2 vols, Lua Thieng, 1974; (with Stephen B Young) Understanding Vietnam, 1982; A New Strategy to Defend the Free World Against Communist Expansion, 1985; Pour une strategie de defense du monde libre contre l'expansion communiste (A New Strategy to Defend the Free World Against Communist Expansion) 1985; Cac an so chanh tri trong tieu thuyet vo hiep Kim Dung (The Hidden Political Thoughts in Jin Yung's Martial-Arts Fiction Novels) 1986; (with Ta Van Tai and Tran Van Liem) The Le Code: Law in Traditional Vietnam: A Comparative Sino-Vietnamese Legal Study With Historical-Juridicial Analysis and Annotations, 1987; (with Stephen B Young) Virtue and Law: Human Rights in Traditional China and Vietnam, 1988. *Contributions to:* Poems in periodicals. *Address:* 72-74, Shirley Ave, Revere, MA 02151, USA.

NI CHUILLEANAIN Eilean b. 28 Nov 1942. Lecturer. m. Macdara Woods, 27 June 1978, 1 son. *Education:* BA 1962, MA 1964, University College, Cork; B Litt, Lady Margaret Hall, Oxford, 1969. *Appointments:* Lecturer in Mediaeval and Renaissance English, Trinity College, Dublin, 1966-; Professor of American History & Institutions, Oxford University, 1969-78. *Publications:* Acts and Monuments, 1972; Site of Ambush, 1975; Cork, 1977; The Second Voyage, 1977, 1986; The Rose-Geranium, 1981; Irish Women: Image and Achievement (editor) 1985; The Magdalene Sermon, 1989. *Contributions to:* An Editor of Cyphers Literary Magazine; Articles in Journal of Ecclesiastical History; Poems in many magazines. *Honours:* Irish Times Poetry Prize, 1966; Patrick Kavanagh Prize 1972. *Address:* 2 Quarry Hollow, Headington, Oxford OX3 8JR, England.

NICHOL B(arrie) P(hillip), b. 1944, Canadian. Novels/Short Stories, Poetry. *Appointments:* Co-Editor, Gronk Magazine, Toronto. *Publications include:* Cycles Etc., 1965; Scraptures 2-4, 10-11, 5 vols., 1965-67; (with D. Aylward) Strange Grey Town, 1960; Tonto or, 1966; Calendar, 1966; A Little Pome for Yur Fingertips. 1966; Fodder, Fodder, 1966; Portrait of David, 1966; A Vision of the U of T Stacks, 1966; Langwedge, 1966; Alaphbit, 1966; Stan's Ikon, 1966, The Birth of O, 1966, followed by later titles including: The Teaching of Arress Kinken, 1982; Three Drafts, 1982; Ruins of C, 1983; Song for Saint Ein, 1983; New H Blues, 1983; Haiku (for David A), 1983; Hologram 4, 1983; Wall, 1983; Possibilities of the Poem, 1984; To the End of the Block, (for children), 1984; Theory 1-4, 1984; Zygal, 1985; The Martyrology Book 6, 1987.

NICHOLAS David, b. 25 Jan 1930, Tregaron, England. Editor; TV Executive. m. Juliet Nicholas, 1952, 1 son, 1 daughter. *Education:* University College of Wales. *Appointments:* National Service, 1951-53; Journalist, Yorkshire Post, Daily Telegraph, Observer; Joined ITV, 1960, Deputy Editor, Independent Television News, 1963, Editor and Chief Executive, 1977-; Chief Executive, 1977-91; Chairman, Independent Television News, 1989-91; Director, Channel Four Television, 1992-. *Honours:* Producers' Guild Award, 1967; CBE, 1982; Cyril Bennett Award, 1985; Kt, 1989; Hon LLD, Wales, 1990; Judge's Award, 1991. *Address:* ITN, ITN House, 48 Wells Street, London, W1P 4DE, England.

NICHOLAS Herbert George, b. 8 June 1911. Retired. *Education:* BA, New College Oxford, 1934; Yale University, USA, 1935-37. *Publications:* The United Nations as a Political Institution, 1959; Britain and the United States, 1963; The British General Election of 1950, 1951; The USA and Britain, 1975; Washington Despatches, (editor), 1981; The American Union, 1948; To the Hustings, 1956; The Nature of American Politics, 1980. *Contributions to:* The Listener; The Economist, and various learned journals. *Honour:* Hon. D.C.L., University of Pittsburgh, 1968. *Memberships:* British Academy, Fellow, Vice President 1975-76; Royal

Historical Society, Fellow. *Address:* 3 William Orchard Close, Old Headington, Oxford OX3 9DR, England.

NICHOLLS Christine Stephanie, b. 23 Jan 1943, Bury, Lancashire, England. Editor. m. Anthony James Nicholls, 12 Mar 1966, 1 son, 2 daughters. *Education:* BA, 1964, MA, 1968, Lady Margaret Hall, Oxford; DPhil St Antony's College, Oxford, 1968. *Appointments:* Henry Charles Chapman Research Fellow, Institute of Commonwealth Studies, London University, 1968-69; Freelance Writer, BBC, 1970-74; Research Assistant, 1975-76; Joint Editor, 1977-89, Editor, 1989-, Dictionary of National Biography Supplements. *Publications:* The Swahili Coast, 1971-; Cataract (with P Awdry), 1985; Power, 1990; Dictionary of National Biography, 1961-70 (joint editor), 1981, 1971-80 (joint editor), 1986, 1981-85 (joint editor), 1990, Missing Persons (editor), 1990. *Address:* 27 Davenant Road, Oxford OX2 8BU, England.

NICHOLS Janet Louise, b. 3 Oct 1952, Sacramento, California, USA. Writer; Pianist. m. Timothy Lynch, 30 June 1984, 1 son, 1 daughter. *Education:* BA, Music, California State University, Sacramento, 1974; MMus, Piano, Arizona State University, 1976. *Publications:* American Music Makers, 1990; Women Music Makers, 1992. *Contributions to:* Fiction to: The New Yorker; Seventeen. *Membership:* Adjudicator, National Guild of Piano Teachers. *Literary Agent:* Diana Fince, Ellen Levine Agency. *Address:* 123 S Cottonwood Ct, Visalia, CA 93291, USA.

NICHOLS John, b. 1940, USA. Freelance Writer and Photographer. *Publications:* The Sterile Cuckoo, 1965; The Wizard of Loneliness, 1966; The Milagro Beanfield War, 1974; The Magic Journey, 1978; A Ghost in the Music, 1979; If Mountains Die, 1979; The Nirvana Blues, 1981; The Last Beautiful Days of Autumn, 1982; On The Mesa, 1986; American Blood, 1987; A Fragile Beauty, 1987; The Sky's The Limit, 1990. *Address:* Box 1165, Taos, NM 87571, USA.

NICHOLS Peter Richard, b. 31 July 1927. Playwright. m. Thelma Reed, 1960, 1 son, 2 daughters (1 daughter deceased). *Appointments:* Actor, 1950-55; Teacher, Primary and Secondary Schools, 1958-60; Arts Council Drama Panel, 1973-75; Playwright in Residence, Guthrie Theatre, Minneapolis, 1976. *Publications:* TV Plays: Walk on the Grass, 1959; Promenade, 1960; Ben Spray, 1961; The Reception, 1961; The Big Boys, 1961; Continuity Man, 1963; Ben Again, 1963; The Heart of the Country, 1963; The Hooded Terror, 1963; The Brick Umbrella, 1968; When the Wind Blows, 1964 (later adapted for radio); Daddy Kiss It Better, 1968; The Gorge, 1968; Hearts and Flowers, 1971; The Common, 1973; See Me, (in 5 parts), 1984; (Films): Catch Us If You Can, 1965; Georgy Girl, 1967; Joe Egg, 1971; The National Health, 1973; Privates on Parade, 1983; Changing Places, 1984. (Stage Plays): A Day in the Death of Joe Egg, 1967; The National Health, 1969; Forget-me-not Lane, 1971; Chez Nous, 1973; The Freeway, 1974; Privates on Parade, 1977; Born in the Gardens, 1979 (televised 1986); Passion Play, 1980; A Piece of My Mind, 1986; (Musical) Poppy, 1982; Feeling You're Behind, autobiography, 1984; About Turner, (stage play), 1989; Private View, (film of Passion Play), 1989; Ravishing!, 1991; Blue Murder, 1992. *Honours:* Standard Best Play Award (Joe Egg), 1967 & National Health, 1969; Tony Award, 1985; Evening Standard Best Comedy, Society of West End Theatres Best Comedy, Ivor Novello Best Musical Awards, 1977; SWET Best Musical (Poppy), 1982; Standard Best Play Award, Passion Play, 1981; FRSL, 1983. *Literary Agent:* c/o Rochelle Stevens, 2 Terrett's Place, London N1 8PS, England. *Address:* 22 Belsize Park Gardens, London NW3 4LH, England.

NICHOLS (Joanne) Ruth, b. 4 Mar 1948, Toronto, Canada. Novelist; Theologian. m. W N Houston, 21 Sept 1974. *Education:* BA Hons, University of British Columbia, 1967; MA Religious Studies, 1972, PhD, Theology, 1977, McMaster University. *Publications:* A

Walk Out of the World, 1969; The Marrow of the World, 1972; Song of the Pearl, 1976; The Left- Handed Spirit, 1978; What Dangers Deep: A Story of Philip Sidney, 1992; Ceremony of Innocence, 1969; The Burning of the Rose, 1989. *Honours:* Award, Shankar's International Literary Contest for Children, 1965, 1963; Gold Medal, Canadian Association of Children's Librarians, 1972; Woodrow Wilson Fellow, 1968; Fellow of The Canada Council, 1971-72; Research Fellow of The Canada Council, 1978. *Address:* 276 Laird Drive, Toronto, Ontario, Canada MY6 3XY.

NICHOLSON Christina. *See:* **NICOLE Christopher Robin.**

NICHOLSON Geoff. *See:* **NICHOLSON Geoffrey Joseph.**

NICHOLSON Geoffrey Joseph, b. 4 Mar 1953, Sheffield, England. Writer. m. Tessa Robinson, 31 Jan 1984, div. 1989. *Education:* Gonville and Caius College, Cambridge, 1972-75; MA, English, Cambridge; MA, Drama, University of Essex, Colchester, 1978. *Publications:* Street Sleeper, 1987; The Knot Garden, 1989; What We Did On Our Holidays, 1990; Hunters and Gatherers, 1991; Big Noises, 1991; The Food Chain, 1992; The Errol Flynn Novel, 1993. *Contributions to:* Regularly, Ambit magazine. *Honours:* Shortlisted, Yorkshire Post 1st Work Award, 1987. *Literary Agent:* A P Watt, London, England. *Address:* 23 Sutherland Avenue, London W9 2HE, England.

NICHOLSON Margaret Beda, (Margaret Yorke), b. 1924. Author. *Appointments:* Assistant Librarian, St. Hilda's College, Oxford, 1959-60; Library Assistant, Christ Church, Oxford, 1963-65; Chairman Crime Writers Association, 1979-80. *Publications:* Summer Flight, 1957; Pray Love Remember, 1958; Christopher, 1959; Deceiving Mirror, 1960; The China Doll, 1961; Once a Stranger, 1962; The Birthday, 1963; Full Circle, 1965; No Fury, 1967; The Apricot Bed, 1968; The Limbo ladies, 1969; Dead in the Morning, 1970; Silent Witness, 1972; Grave matters, 1973; No Medals for the Major, 1974; Mortal Remains, 1974; The Small Hours of the Morning, 1975; Cast for Death, 1976; The Cost of Silence, 1977; The Point of Murder, 1978; Death on Account, 1979; The Scent of Fear, 1980; The Hand of Death, 1981; Devil's Work, 1982; Find Me a Villain, 1983; The Smooth Face of Evil, 1984; Intimate Kill, 1985; Safely to the Grave, 1986; Evidence to Destroy, 1987; Speak for the Dead, 1988; Crime in Question, 1989; Admit to Murder, 1990; A Small Deceit, 1991; Criminal Damage, 1992; Dangerous To Know, 1993. *Address:* c/o Curtis Brown, 162-168 Regent Street, London, W1R 5TB, England.

NICHOLSON Robin. *See:* **NICOLE Christopher Robin.**

NICK Dagmar, b. 30 May 1926, Breslau, German. Writer. *Education:* Studies of Psychology and Graphology, Munich, 1947-50. *Publications:* Poetry: Martyrer, 1947; Das Buch Holofernes, 1955; In den Ellipsen des Mondes, 1959; Zeugnis und Zeichen, 1969; Fluchtlinien, 1978; Gezahte Tage, 1986; Im Stillstand der Stunden, 1991; Prose: Einladung nach Israel, 1963; Rhodos, 1967; Israel gestern und haute, 1968; Sizilien, 1976; Gotterinseln der Agais, 1981; Medea, ein Monolog, 1988; Lilith, eine Metamorphose, 1992. *Contributions to:* Zeit; Frankfurter Allgemeine Zeitung; Akzente; Merian; Westermanns Monatshefte; Horen; Chicago Review; International Poetry Review; Chariton Review. *Honours:* Liliencron Prize, Hamburg, 1948; Eichendorff-Prize, 1966; Honorary Award, Gryphius Prize, 1970; Roswitha Medal, 1977; Kulturpreis 'Schlesien' des Landes Niedersachsen, 1986; Gryphius Prize, 1993. *Memberships:* PEN Club; Association of German Writers. *Address:* Kuglmullerstrasse 22, D 80638 Munich, Germany.

NICOL Abioseh (Davidson Sylvester Hector Willoughby Nicol), b. 1924, Sierra Leone. Author; Honorary Fellow, Christ's College, Cambridge; Former Diplomat. *Publications:* Alienation: An Essay, 1960; Africa: A Subjective View, 1964; The Truly Married Woman and Other Stories, 1965; Two African Tales, 1965; Africanus Horton: The Dawn of Nationalism in Modern Africa, US Edition Black Nationalism in Africa, 1867, 1969; New and Modern Roles for Commonwealth and Empire, 1976; The United Nations and Decision Making, 1978; Nigeria and the Future of Africa, 1980; Paths to Peace, 1981; The United Nations Security Council, 1981; Creative Women, 1982. *Memberships:* President, World Federation of United Nations Associations, 1983-87. *Address:* Christ's College, Cambridge CB2 3BU, England.

NICOL Dominik, b. 25 Sept 1930, North Oltenia, Rumania. Writer; Photographer. *Education:* Baccalaureat Diploma, Rm Valcea Lyceum, 1949; Diploma in Technology and Chemistry of Antibiotics, Technical School of Antibiotics, Bucharest, 1954. *Publications:* Self encounter, 1979; Vacuum (colocviu de abis), 1979; Ten oneiric sketches, 1980; Rendez-Vous sau Intalnire cu mine insumi, 1987; Vacuum-Void (bilingual edition), play, 1988. *Contributions to:* Micro-Magazin, New York; Tricolorul magazine, Ontario; Stindardul magazine, Munich; Saptamana Muncheneza magazine, Munich; Meridiane magazine, New York; Lupta magazine, Providence, Rhode Island. *Address:* PO Box 411, Times Square Sta, New York, NY 10108, USA.

NICOL Donald MacGillivray, b. 1923, United Kingdom. Historian; Koraes Professor of Modern Greek and Byzantine History, Language and Literature, King's College, University of London, retired, 1988. *Publications:* The Despotate of Epiros, 1957; Meteora: The Rock Monasteries of Thessaly, 1963, 2nd Edition, 1975; The Byzantine Family of Kantakouzenos 1100-1460, 1968; The Last Centuries of Byzantium 1261-1453, 1972; Byzantium: Its Ecclesiastical History and Relations with the Western World, 1972; Church and Society in the Last Centuries of Byzantium, 1979; The End of the Byzantine Empire, 1979; The Despotate of Epiros 1267-1479: A Contribution to the History of Greece in the Middle Ages, 1984; Studies in Late Byzantine History and Prosopography, 1986; Byzantium and Venice, 1988; Joannes Gennadios - The Man, 1990; A Biographical Dictionary of the Byzantine Empire, 1991; The Immortal Emperor, 1992. *Address:* 16 Courtyards, Little Shelford, Cambridge CB2 5ER.

NICOLAEFF Ariadne, b. 27 Nov 1915, Odessa. Writer/Translator. *Education:* English High School for Girls, Istanbul; Bedford College, London University. *Publilcations:* As translator of Aleksei Arbazov: The Promise, 1967; Old-World, 1977; Selected Plays of Aleksei Arbazov, 1982; Chance Vistor, 1986; Radio (BBC) and stage plays; play reviews and articles. *Membership:* Society of Authors. *Address:* 27, Great Livermere, Bury St Edmunds, Suffolk IP31 1JT, England.

NICOLAYSEN (F.) Bruce, b. 1934, USA. Writer. *Appointments:* Copy Chief, Carson/Roberts Advertising, Los Angeles, California, 1966-70; Creative Director, Ogilvy and Mather, Los Angeles, 1970-74. *Publications:* Perilous Passage, UK Edition The Passage, novel, 1977, as The Passage, screenplay, 1978; The Brinks Job (co-author), screenplay, 1979; From Distant Shores, novel, 1980; On Maiden Lane, novel, 1981; Beekman Place, novel, 1982; The Pirate of Gramercy Park, novel, 1983; Gracie Square, novel, 1984. *Address:* Apple Hill Road, Bennington, VT 05201, USA.

NICOLE Christopher. *See:* **NICOLE Christopher Robin.**

NICOLE Christopher Robin (Daniel Adams, Leslie Arlen, Robin Cade, Peter Grange, Nicholas Grant, Caroline Gray, Mark Logan, Simon Mackay, Christina Nicholson, Robin Nicholson, Christopher Nicole, Alan Savage, Alison York, Andrew York), b. 7 Dec 1930,

Georgetown, Guyana. Novelist. m. Diana Bachmann, 8 May 1982, 4 sons, 3 daughters. *Education;* Harrison College, Barbados; Queen's College, Guyana; Fellow, Canadian Bankers Association. *Publications:* As Christopher Nicole: Ratoon, 1962; Caribee Series, 1974-78; Byron, 1979; The Haggard Series, 1980-82; The China Series, 1984-86; The Japan Series, 1984-86; Black Majesty, 2 volumes, 1984-85; The Old Glory series, 1986-88; Ship with No Name, 1987; The High Country, 1988; The Regiment, 1988; The Pearl of the Orient, 1988; As Andrew York: The Eliminator Series (9 Spy Thrillers), 1966-75; The Operation Series, 1969-71; Where the Cavern Ends, 1971; The Tallant Series, 1977-78; Dark Passage, 1976; The Combination, 1984; As Peter Grange: King Creole, 1966; The Devil's Emissary, 1968; As Robin Cade: The Fear Dealers, 1974; As Mark Logan: The Tricolour Series, 1976-78; As Christina Nicholson: The Power and the Passion, 1977; The Savage Sands, 1978; The Queen of Paris, 1983; As Alison York: The Fire and the Rape, 1979; The Scented Sword, 1980; As Robin Nicolson: The Friday Spy, 1981; As Leslie Arlen: The Borodin Series, 1980-85; As Daniel Adams: The Brazilian Series, 1982-83; As Simon Mackay: The Anderson Series, 1984-85; As Caroline Gray: First Class, 1984; Hotel de Luxe, 1985; White Rani, 1986; Victoria's Walk, 1986; The Third Life, 1988; Shadow of Dealth, 1989; Blue Water, Black Depths, 1990; The Daughter, 1992; Golden Girl, 1992; Spares, 1993; Spawn of the Devil, 1993; As Christopher Nicole: The Happy Valley, 1989; The Triumph, 1989; The Command, 1989; Dragon'd Blood, 1989; Dark Sun, 1990; Sword of Fortune, 1990; Sword of Empire, 1990; Days of Wine & Roses, 1991; The Titans, 1992; Resumption, 1992; The Last Battle, 1993; Bloody Sunrse, in progress; Bloody Sunset, in progress; As Alan Savage: Ottoman, 1990; Mughal, 1991; The Eight Banners, 1992; Queen of Night, 1993; The Last Bannerman, 1993; Queen of Lions, in progess; As Nicholas Grant: Khan, 1993. Total of 114 Books - 107 novels, 4 juveniles, 1 history, 1 sporting history and 1 technical Also several books written jointly with wife, Diana Bachmann. *Contributions to:* Numerous journals and magazines. *Memberships:* Society of Authors; Literary Guild of America; Mark Twain Society. *Literary Agent:* David Higham Associates Ltd, 5-8 Lower John Street, Golden Square, London W1R 4HA, England. *Address:* Curtis Brown & John Farquharson Ltd., 162-168 Regent St., London W1R 5TB, England.

NICOLSON Nigel, b. 19 Jan 1917. Author; Director. m. Philippa Janet, 1953, (div 1970), 1 son, 2 daughters. *Education:* Balliol College, Oxford. *Publications include:* The Grenadier Guards, 1939-45, 1949 (official history); People and Parliament, 1958; Lord of the Isles, 1960; Great Houses of Britain, 1965, revised edition 1978; Editor, Harold Nicholson: Diaries and Letters, 3 volumes, 1966-68; Great Houses, 1968; Alex (FM Alexander of Tunis), 1973; Portrait of a Marriage, 1973; Editor, Letters of Virginia Woolf, 1975-80 (6 volumes); The Himalayas, 1975; Mary Curzon, 1977; Napoleon: 1812, 1985; The World of Jane Austin, 1991; Vita and Herald: The Letters of Vita Sackville-West and Harold Nicolson, 1910-1962, 1992. *Honours:* Whitbread Award; MBE, 1945; FSA; FRSL. *Address:* Sissinghurst Castle, Kent, England.

NIEDZIELSKI Henryk Zygmunt, b. 30 Mar 1931, France. Educator. m. 26 July 1977, 3 sons, 1 daughter. *Education:* BA, 1959, MA, 1963, PhD, 1964, Romance Philology, University of Connecticut, USA. *Appointments:* Editor in chief, Language & Literature in Hawaii, 1967-72; Correspondent, France Amerique, 1969-72; Editorial Board, Conradiana, 1971-76; Editorial Board, Science et Francophonie, 1985-1991. *Publications:* Le Roman de Helcanus, 1966; the Silent Language of France, 1975; Studies on the Seven Sages of Rome, 1978; Jean Misrahi Memorial Volume, 1977; 6 language teaching books; The Silent Language of Poland, 1989; Polish Body Language, (film). *Contributions to:* La Democratie au foyer La Tribune des l'enfance, 1970; articles in various professional journals; Journal of American Literary Translators Association. *Honours:* Distinguished Fellow University of Auckland, New Zealand, Foundation 1989; Silver Cross of Merit of the Polish Peoples Republic, 1989.

Memberships: Medieval Academy of America; International Arthurian Society; American Association of Teachers of French, President, Hawaii, 1981-83; Hawaii Association of Translators, Founding President, 1982; International Association of Teachers of English As A Foriegn Language. *Address:* 2425 W. Orange Avenue, Anaheim, CA 92804, USA.

NIELSEN Helen Berniece, (Kris Giles), b. 1918, USA. Author. *Publications:* The Kind Man, 1951; Gold Coast Nocturne, 1951, UK Edition, Murder by Proxy, 1952, US Paperback, Dead on the Level, 1954; Obit Delayed, 1952; Detour, 1953, US Paperback, Detour to Death, 1955; The Woman on the Roof, 1954; Stranger in the Dark, 1955; The Crime Is Murder, 1956; Borrow the Night, 1957, US Paperback, Seven Days Before Dying, 1958; The Fifth Caller, 1959; False Witness, 1959; Sing Me a Murder, 1960; Woman Missing and Other Stories, 1961; Verdict Suspended, 1964; After Midnight, 1966; A Killer in the Street, 1967; Darkest Hour, 1969; Shot on Location, 1971; The Severed Key, 1973; The Brink of Murder, 1976; Line of Fire, 1987.

NIEMANN Linda Grant, b. 22 Sept 1946, Pasadena, California, USA. Railroad Brakeman. *Education:* BA, University of California, Santa Cruz, 1968; PhD, University of California, Berkeley, 1975. *Publications:* Boomer: Railroad Memoirs, 1990. *Honours:* Non-Fiction Award, Bay Area Book Reviewers Association, 1991. *Memberships:* PEN West; National Writers Union. *Address:* PO Box 7409, Santa Cruz, CA 95061, USA.

NIEMINEN Kai Tapani, b. 11 May 1950, Helsinki, Finland. Poet; Translator. m. 1991. 1 daughter. *Publications:* Joki vie ajatukseni, 1971; Syntymästä, 1973; Kiireettä, 1977; Tie jota oli kuljettava, 1979; Vain mies, 1981; Elämän vouteessa, 1982; Oudommin kuin unessa, 1983; En minä tiedä, 1985; Milloin missäkin hahmossa, 1987; Keinuva maa, 1989; Fuuga/Fugue (English translation by Herbert Lomas), 1992; Translations from Japanese include: Joutilaan mietteitä, 1978; Kapea tie pohjoiseen, 1981; Harhojen maja, 1984; Kokoro, 1985; Rakasta sinä vain, 1986; Genjin tarina vol. 4, 1990; Makiokan sisarukset, 1981; Kwaidan, 1981. *Contributions to:* numerous translations of Japanese poetry, essays on Japanese literature & culture. *Honours:* National Literary Awards for translations, Ministry of Education, 1978, 1982, 1991; National Literary Award for Poems, 1986, 1990. *Memberships:* Finnish Authors' Society; Finnish PEN (president since 1981); Eino Leinon Seura Society. *Literary Agent:* Tammi Publishers. *Address:* Baggböle 99 A, 07740 Gammelby, Finland.

NIGG Joseph Eugene, b. 27 Oct 1938, Davenport, Iowa, USA. Editor; Writer. m. (1) Gayle Madsen, 20 Aug 1960, divorced 1979, 2 sons, (2) Esther Muzzillo, 27 Oct 1989. *Education:* BA, Kent State University, 1960; MFA, Writers Workshop, University of Iowa, 1963; PhD, University of Denver, 1975. *Appointments:* Assistant Editor, Essays in Literature, 1974-75; Associate Editor, Liniger's Real Estate, 1979-81; Co-Editor, Pendragon, 1981- 85; Fiction Editor, Wayland Press, 1985-1992. *Publications:* The Book of Gryphons, 1982; A Guide to the Imaginary Birds of the World, 1984; Winegold, 1985; The Strength of Lions and the Flight of Eagles, 1982; The Great Balloon Festival, 1989. *Contributions to:* various journals and magazines. *Honours:* Non-fiction Book of the Year, 1983, 1985, Colorado Authors League; Mary Chase Author of the Year, Rocky Mountain Writers Guild, 1984; Non-fiction Book of the Year, 1989, Colorado Authors League. *Memberships:* Colorado Authors League, Publicity Chairman, Membership Chairman; Rocky Mountain Writers Guild, Board of Directors. Address: 1114 Clayton St., Denver, CO 80206, USA.

NIHAL SINGH Surendra, b. 30 Apr 1929, Rawalpindi (now in Pakistan). Journalist. m. Geertje Zuiderweg, 1957. *Education:* BA, Delhi Univerity. *Appointments:* Sub-Editor, The Times of India, Delhi, 1951-53; Staff Reporter, Parliamentary Correspondent, The Statesman,

Calcutta, 1954-61, Special Corespondent for SE Asia and Far East, Singapore, 1962-67, Pakistan 1967, for USSR and Eastern Europe, Moscow, 1968-69, Political Correspondent, Delhi, 1969-71, Special Correspondent, London, 1971-74, Resident Editor, Delhi, 1974-75, Editor, Calcutta, 1975-80; Editor in Chief, Indian Express, 1981-82. *Publications:* Malaysia - A Commentary, 1971; From the Jhelum to the Volga, 1972; Indira's India, 1978; The Gang and 900 Million, 1979; My India, 1981. *Honours:* International Editor of the Year Award, Atlas World Press Service, New York, 1978. *Address:* Indian Express, Bahadur Shah Zafar Marg, New Delhi 2, India.

NIKLAUS Robert, b. 18 July 1910, London, England. Professor of French, m. (1) Thelma Elinor Florence, 25 July 1936, (dec 1970), 2 sons, 1 daughter, (2) Kathleen Anne, 27 Jan 1973. *Education:* University College, London, 1928-34; L es L, University of Lille, France, 1930; BA, 1st Class Honours, 1931, PhD, 1934, London; Dr University of Rennes, honoris causa, 1963; DLit, Exon, honoris Causa, 1981. *Publications:* Jean Moreas, poete lyrique, 1936; A Literary History of France, The 18th century, 1970; Beaumarchais, Le Barbier de Seville, 1968; Beamarchais, le Mariage de Figaro, 1983; critical Editions of: J J Rosseau, Les Reveries du promeneur solitaire, 1942; Diderot: eds of pensee philosophhiques, 1950; Lettre sur les aveugles, 1951, Co-author Thelma Niklaus, Marivaux Arlequin poli par l'amour, 1959; Sedaine, La Gageure imprevue, 1970; Diderot, Oeuvres completes, Volume 2, 1975, volume 4, 1979; general Editor, Textes Francais Classiques et Modernes. *Contributions to:* The Year's Work in Modern Language Studies VII-XIII; The John Rylands Library, 1941; Diderot Studies, 4, 1963, 6, 1964; Studies on Voltaire and the 18th Century, XXVI, 1963, 99, 1972; Contemporary review; Modern Languages Review, French Studies. *Honour:* Hon Dr, University of Rennes, 1963; Hon D.Litt, Exon, 1981; Officier de l'Ordre National du Merite, 1972. *Memberships Include:* Association Of University Teachers, President, 1954-55, Executive Committee, 1948-62; International Association of University Professors and Lecturers, President, 1958-62, Vice President, 1957-58, 1964-66; 18th Century Studies, 1970-72; Treasurer, International Society for 18th Century Studies, 1969-79. *Address:* 17 Elm Grove Road, Topsham, Exeter, Devon EX3 0EQ, England.

NILE Dorothea. *See:* **AVALLONE Michael.**

NIMS John Frederick, b. 20 Nov 1913, Chicago. Professor; Editor of Poetry. m. Bonnie Larkin, 1 son, 2 daughters. *Education:* AB 1937, MA 1939, University of Notre Dame; PhD, University of Chicago, 1945. *Appointments:* Professor, numerous Universities including: University of Notre Dame, University of Florence, University of Madrid, University of Illinois, Harvard University, Williams College; Editor, Poetry Chicago, 1978- 84. *Publications:* The Iron Pastoral, 1947; A Fountain in Kentucky, 1950; The Poems of St John of the Cross, translation, 1958, 3rd edition, 1979; Knowledge of the Evening, 1960; Of Flesh and Bone, 1967; Sappho to Valery: Poems in Translation, 1971, 3rd edition, 1990; Western Wind: An Introduction to Poetry, 1974, 3rd edition, 1992; The Harper Anthology of Poetry, 1980; The Kiss: A Jambalaya, poems, 1982; Selected Poems, 1982; A Local Habitation: Essays on Poetry, 1985; The Six-Cornered Snowflake, 1990; Zany in Denim, 1990. *Contributions to:* Numerous magazines, journals and reviews including: Poetry; Hudson Review; Atlantic; Harpers; Times Literary Supplement; Saturday Review. *Honours include:* National Institute of Arts and Letters Award, 1967; Creative Arts Poetry Award, Brandeis University, 1972; Fellowship, Academy of American Poets, 1982; Guggenheim Fellowship, 1986-87; Aiken-Taylor Award, 1991; Melville Cane Award, 1992; Hardison Poetry Prize, 1993. *Address:* 3920 Lake Shore Drive, Chicago, IL 60613, USA.

NIOSI Jorge Eduardo, b. 8 Dec 1945, Buenos Aires, Argentina. University Professor. m. Graciela Ducatenzeiler, 25 Nov 1971, 2 daughters. *Education:* Licence, Sociology, National University of Buenos Aires, 1967; Advanced degree, Economics, IEDES, Paris, 1970; Doctorate, Sociology, Ecole Pratique, Paris, 1973. *Publications:* Technology and National Competitiveness, 1991; Les entrepreneurs dans la politique argentine, 1976; The Economy of Canada, 1978; Canadian Capitalism, 1981; Firmes multinationales et autonomie nationale, 1983; Canadian Multinationals, 1985; La montee de l'ingenierie canadienne, 1990. *Contributions to:* Nearly 30 magazines and journals including: Recherches sociographiques; Sociologie et societe; Tiers Monde; World Development; Technovation; Revue francaise d'economie. *Honours:* John Porter Award, Canadian Sociology and Anthropology Association, 1983; Fellow, Statistics Canada, 1989-92. *Memberships:* International Sociological Association; Canadian Sociology and Anthropology Association. *Address:* CREDIT, UQAM, PO Box 8888, Station A, Montreal, Quebec, Canada H3C 3P8.

NISBET Jim, b. 20 Jan 1947. Writer. *Publications:* Poems for a Lady, 1978; Gnachos for Bishop Berkeley, 1980; The Gourmet, novel, 1980; Morpho (with Alastair Johnston), 1982; The Visitor, 1984; Lethal Injection, novel, 1987; Death Puppet, novel, 1989; Laminating the Conic Frustum, 1991; Small Apt, 1992. *Contributions to:* Poetry to numerous little magazines. *Literary Agent:* William Morris Agency, New York, USA. *Address:* c/o Mr Matthew Bialer, William Morris Agency, 1350 Avenue of the Americas, New York, NY 10019, USA.

NISH Ian Hill, b. 3 June 1926, Edinburgh, Scotland. Professor; Retired. m. Rona Margaret Speirs, 29 Dec 1965, 2 daughters. *Education:* University of Edinburgh, 1943-51; University of London, 1951-56. *Appointments:* University of Sydney, 1957-62; London School of Economics and Political Science, 1962-1991. *Publications:* Origins of Russo-Japanese war, 1986; Anglo-Japanese Alliance, 1966; Alliance in Decline, 1972; The Story of Japan, 1968; Japanese Foreign Policy, 1978; Contemporary European Writing on Japan, 1988; Anglo-Japanese Alienation 1919-52, 1982; Japan's Struggle with Internationalism, 1931-33, 1993. *Honour:* CBE, 1990; Order of the Rising Sun, 1991. *Memberships:* European Association of Japanese Studies, President, 1985-88; British Association of Japanese Studies, President, 1986. *Address:* Oakdene, 33 Charlwood Drive, Oxshott, Surrey KT22 0HB, England.

NITCHIE George Wilson, b. 19 May 1921, Chicago, Illinois, USA. retired Professor of English. m. Laura Margaret Woodard, 19 Jan 1947, 3 daughters. *Education:* BA, Middlebury, 1943; MA 1947, PhD, 1958, Columbia University. *Appointments:* Instructor of English, 1947, Assistant Professor, 1950, Associate Professor, 1959, Professor, 1966, Chairman, English Department, 1972-79, Professor Emeritus, 1986-, Simmons College. *Publications:* Human Values in the Poetry of Robert Frost, 1960; Marianne Moore: An Introduction to the Poetry, 1969; Various critical essays on Robert Frost, Robert Lowell, Randall Jarrell, Howard Nemerov, T S Eliot, John Donne and John Milton. *Contributions to:* Poems in various publications. *Memberships:* American Association of University Professors. *Address:* 50 Pleasantview Avenue, Weymouth, MA 02188, USA.

NIVEN Alastair Neil Robertson, b. 25 Feb 1944, Edinburgh, Scotland. Director of Literature, Arts Council of Great Britain. m. Helen Margaret Trow, 22 Aug 1970, 1 son, 1 daughter. *Education:* BA, 1966, MA, 1968, University of Cambridge; MA, University of Ghana, 1968; PhD, University of Leeds, 1972. *Appointments:* Lecturer, English: University of Ghana, 1968-69; University of Leeds, England, 1969-70; Lecturer, English Studies, University of Stirling, Scotland, 1970-78; Visiting Professor, Aarhus University, Denmark, 1975-76; Honorary Lecturer, University of London, 1979-84; Chapman Fellow, Institute of Commonwealth Studies, 1984-85; Visiting Fellow, Australian Studies Centre, London, 1985; Director of Literature, Arts Council of Great Britain, 1987-; Editor, Journal of Commonwealth

Literature, 1979-92. *Publications:* D H Lawrence: the Novels, 1978; The Yoke of Pity: The Fictional Writings of Mulk Raj Anand, 1978; The Commonwealth of Universities (with Hugh W Springer), 1987; Truth into Fiction or Raja Rao's The Serpent and the Rope, 1988; Edited: The Commonwealth Writer Overseas, 1976; Under Another Sky, 1987; Study guides on William Golding, R K Narayan, Elechi Amadi. *Contributions to:* Articles or book chapters to: The Times; Ariel; The Literary Criterion; Commonwealth Essais et Etudes. *Honours:* Commonwealth Scholar, 1966-68. *Memberships:* Chairman, Greater London Arts Association Literature Advisory Panel, 1980-84; Secretary, Association for Commonwealth Literature and Language Studies, 1986-89; Chairman, Executive Committee, UK Council for Overseas Student Affairs, 1987-92; Commonwealth Trust. *Address:* Eden House, 28 Weathercock Lane, Woburn Sands, Buckinghamshire MK17 8NT, England.

NIVEN Larry, (Laurence Van Cott), b. 30 Apr 1938, Los Angeles, California, USA. m. Marilyn Joyce Wisowaty, 6 Sept 1969. *Education:* California Institute of Technology, 1956-58, BA, Mathematics, Washburn University, Kansas, 1962. *Publications:* Neutron Star, 1966; Ringworld, 1970; Inconstant Moon, 1971; The Hole Man, 1974; The Borderland of Sol, 1975; Protector, 1974; N-Space; Playgrounds, 1991; Achilles' Choice, (co-author); Footfall, with Jerry Pournelle, 1985; The gripping Hand, with Jerry Pournelle, 1993; Dream Park, with Steven Barnes, 1981; The California Voodoo Game. Articles, speeches, TV scripts, contributions to books, magazines and comics. *Honours:* Honorary Doctor of Letters, Washburn University, 1984; Science Fiction Achievement Awards, 1966, 1970, 1971, 1974, 1975; Nebula Best Novel, 1970; Australian Best International Science Fiction, 1972, 1974; Inkpot Award, San Diego Comic Convention, 1979. *Literary Agent:* Eleanor Wood, Spectrum Literary Agency, 111 8th Avenue 1501, New York 10011, USA. *Address:* 3961 Vanalden Ave, Tarzana, CA 91356, USA.

NIVEN (Cecil) Rex (Sir), b. 1898, United Kingdom. Author; Former Member of Nigerian Administrative Service; Former Speaker, Northern House of Assembly, Nigeria. *Publications:* Short History of Nigeria, 1937: 13 editions, Nigeria's Story, 1939; Nigeria - Outline of a Colony, 1946; How Nigeria is Governed, 1950; West Africa, 1958; Short History of the Yoruba Peoples, 1958; You and Your Government, 1958; My Life (with Sardauna of Sokolo), 1962; Nine Great Africans, 1964; Nigeria (Nations of the Modern World), 1967; War of Nigerian Unity, 1970; A Nigerian Kaleidoscope, 1982. *Honour:* Kt, 1960. *Address:* 12 Archery Square, Walmer, Kent, CT4 7HP, England.

NIXON Richard (Milhous), b. 1913, USA. Former Lawyer; Former US Senator; Former President of the United States; Author. *Publications:* Six Crises, 1962; Memoirs, 1978; The Real War, 1980; Leaders, 1982; Real Peace: A Strategy for the West, 1983; No More Vietnams, 1985; Victory Without War, 1988; In The Arena; A Memoir of Victory, Defeat and Renewal, 1990; Seize the Moment: America's Challenge in a one Superpower World, 1992. *Address:* 577 Chestnut Ridge Road, Woodcliff Lake, NJ 07675, USA.

NIZALOWSKI Edward Michael, b. 4 Nov 1947, Jersey City, New Jersey, USA. Library Media Specialist. *Education:* BA, English; SUC, Potsdam, New York, 1970; MLS, Syracuse University, 1988. *Publications:* Section on Ethnic Groups and Immigrant Groups for Bicentennial History Book, Tioga County, New York. *Contributor to:* Several articles in Afro-Americans in New York Life and History. *Honour:* Award of Merit from Regional Conference of Historical Agencies in 1985 for research into Afro-American History in Tioga County, New York. *Address:* 441 Brown Road, Berkshire, NY 13736, USA.

NKOSI Lewis, b. 1936, South Africa. Novelist; Playwright; Essayist. *Appointments:* Staff Member:

Ilange Lase Natal (Zulu newspaper), Durban, South Africa, 1955-56; Drum magazine and Golden City Post, Johannesburg, 1956-60; South African Information Bulletin magazine, Paris, France, 1962-68; Radio Producer, BBC Transcription Centre, London, England, 1962-64; Literary Editor, New African magazine, London, 1965-68. *Publications:* The Rhythm of Violence, 1964; Home and Exile, essays, 1965; The Transplanted Heart: Essays on South Africa, 1975; Tasks and Masks: Themes and Styles of African Literature, 1981; Mating Birds, novel, 1986. *Address:* Flat 4, Burgess Park Mansions, Fortune Green Road, London NW6, England.

NOAKES Vivien, b. 16 Feb 1937, England. Writer. m. Michael Noakes, 9 July 1960, 2 sons, 1 daughter. *Education:* BA, First Class Honours, English, Senior Scholar, Somerville College, Oxford University. *Publications:* Edward Lear: The Life of a Wanderer, 1968, revised 1979, revised 1985; Edward Lear 1812-1888, The Catalogue of the Royal Academy Exhibition, 1985; The Selected Letters of Edward Lear, 1988; The Painter Edward Lear, 1991. *Contributions to:* The Times; The Times Literary Supplement; Daily Telegraph; New Scientist; Punch; Harvard Magazine; Tennyson Research Bulletin. *Literary Agent:* Watson, Little Limited. *Address:* 12 Egbert Street, London N81 8LJ, England.

NOBLE Miss Jayne. *See:* **DOWNES Mary Raby (Jayne).**

NOBLE John Appelbe, b. 1914, Australian. Travel, Exploration and Adventure. *Appointments:* Ship's Captain, Unioon Steamship Co., New Zealand, 1951-58; Ship's Pilot, Port Phillip Sea Pilots, Williamstown, Victoria, 1959-79. Editor, Journal of the Co. of Master Mariners of Australia, Harbour Press, Sydney, 1966-71; Melbourne Branch Master., Co. of Master Mariners of Australia, 1974-75. *Publications:* Australian Lighthouse, 1967; Hazards of the Sea, 1970; Port Phillip: Pilots and Defence, 1973, 1978; Port Phillip Panorama, 1975; The Golden Age of Sail, 1985.

NODSET Joan L. *See:* **LEXAU Joan M.**

NOEL Gerard Eyre Wriothesley, (Hon.) b. 20 Nov 1926. Author; Publisher; Journalist. m. Adele Julie Patricia Were, 1958, 2 sons, 1 daughter. *Education:* MA, Modern History, Exeter College, Oxford; Called to bar, Inner Temple, 1952. *Appointments:* Director, Herder Book Co., 1959-66; Search Press Ltd., 1972-; Literary Editor, Catholic Times, 1958-61; Editor, 1970-76, Editorial Director 1976-81, Catholic Herald. *Publications:* Paul VI, 1963; Harold Wilson, 1964; Goldwater, 1964; The New Britain, 1966; The Path from Rome, 1968; Princess Alice : Queen Victoria's Forgotten Daughter, 1974. *Contributions to:* The Prime Ministers, 1974; The Great Lock-Out of 1926, 1976; The Anatomy of the Roman Catholic Church, 1980; Ena: Spain's English Queen, 1984; Cardinal Basil Hume, 1984; Translations: The Way to Unity after the Council, 1967; The Holy See and the War in Europe, 1968. *Address:* 105 Cadogan Gardens, London SW3, England.

NOEL-HUME Ivor, b. 1927, United Kingdom. Author; Archaeological Researcher. *Appointments:* Archaeological Director, Colonial Williamsburg Foundation, Williamsburg, Virginia, USA, 1957-; Research Associate, Smithsonian Institution, 1959-; Vice-President, Society for Post-Medieval Archaeology, UK, 1967-76; Council Member, Institute of Early American History and Culture, 1974-76; Board Member, Jamestown Yorktown Foundation, 1987-. *Publications:* Archaeology in Britain, 1953; Tortoises, Terrapins and Turtles (co-author), 1954; Treasure in the Thames, 1956; Great Moments in Archaeology, 1957; Here Lies Virginia, 1963; 1775: Another Part of the Field, 1966; Historical Archaeology, 1969; Artifacts of Colonial America, 1970; All the Best Rubbish, 1974; Early English Delftware from London and Virginia, 1976;

Martin's Hundred, 1982. *Address:* PO Box 1711, Williamsburg, VA 23187, USA.

NOF Shimon Y, b. 22 Mar 1946, Haifa, Israel. Professor of Industrial Engineering. m. Nava C Vardinon, 1972. 2 daughters. *Education:* BSc, 1969, MSc, 1972, Industrial Engineering and Management, Technion, Haifa, Israel; PhD, Industrial and Operations Engineering, University of Michigan, Ann-Arbor, USA, 1976. *Appointments:* Deputy Editor, Computer and Knowlede Engineering, 1984-; Special issue Editor, Material Flow, 1984-85; Consulting Editor, Encyclopaedia of Robotics, 1984-88; Editorial Board: Handbook of IE, 1989-92, International Journal of Production Planning and Control, 1991-; Advisory Board, International Journal of Informatics. *Publications:* Handbook of Industrial Robotics, 1985; International Encyclopaedia of Robotics and Automation, 1988; Robotics and Material Flow, 1986; Co-editor: Concise Encyclopaedia of Robotics and Automation, 1990, Advanced Information Technology for Industrial Material Flow Systems, 1989. *Contributions to:* Journals and Proceedings articles on computer applications in manufacturing and industrial robotics. *Honours:* Fulbright Grant, 1972; The Silent Hoist Doctoral Award, 1975; American Association of Publishers Awards of Excellence, 1975, 1988; Fellow, Institute of I.E, 1991. *Memberships:* Institute of Industrial Engineers; Association of Computing Machinery; Institute of Management Science; Japan Industrial Management Association; Society of Manufacturing Engineers; International Federation of Production Research. *Address:* 1287 Grissom Hall, Purdue University, W Lafayette IN 47907, USA.

NOGEE Joseph L. b. 16 June 1929, Schenectady, NY. Teacher; Writer. m. Jo Nahor, 17 Dec 1960, 1 son, 1 daughter. *Education:* BSFS, Georgetown School Foreign Service, 1950; MA, University of Chicago, 1952; PhD, Yale University, 1958. *Publications:* Soviet Policy Toward International Control Atomic Energy, 1962; The Politics of Disarmament (co-author), 1963. *Contributions to:* Various journals. *Memberships:* American Political Science Association, Council Member, 1968-70; Southwest Political Science Association, President, 1973-74; American Association Advancement Slavic Studies; International Studies Association. *Address:* 8735 Link Terrace, Houston, TX 77025, USA.

NOLAN David Joseph, b. 27 June 1946, Boston, Massachusetts, USA. Author; Lecturer. 1 son, 1 daughter. *Education:* University of Virginia, Charlottesville, 1963-65; Columbia University, New York City, 1964. *Appointments:* Editor, New South Student magazine, Nashville, Tennessee, 1966-69; Historic Sites Specialist, Historic St Augustine Preservation Board, 1978-80. *Publications:* Fifty Feet In Paradise: The Booming of Florida, 1984; The Book Lover's Guide to Florida, 1992. *Contributions to:* Frequently to magazines and newspapers. *Honours:* Annual Authors Award, Council for Florida Libraries, 1985. *Memberships:* Trustee, Marjorie Kinnan Rawlings Society; Editorial Board, Journal of Florida Literature; Friends of St Augustine Architecture. *Address:* 30 Park Terrace Drive, St Augustine, FL 32084, USA.

NOLAN Patrick, b. 1 Feb 1933, Bronx, New York, USA. Teacher. 3 sons. *Education:* MA, University of Detroit, 1969; PhD, English Literature, Bryn Mawr College. *Appointments include:* Instructor, University of Detroit; Professor, Villanova University. *Publications include:* Films: Hourglass Moment, 1969; Jericho Mile, 1978; Plays: Chameleons, 1981; Midnight Rainbows, 1991. *Contributions:* Origin of Fear in the Emperor Jones, in O'Neill Newsletter, 1980; Jungian View of Desire Under the Elms, ibid, 1981. *Honours:* Emmy Award, Academy of TV Arts & Sciences, 1979; Citation, Teaching Excellence, Philadelphia Magazine, 1980. *Membership:* Writers Guild of America, West. *Literary Agent:* Richard Barber, 544 E. 82nd Street, New York, NY 10028, USA. *Address:* English Department,

Villanova University, Villanova, Pennsylvania 19085, USA.

NOLAN William F(rancis) (Frank Anmar, Mike Cahill, F E Edwards, Michael Phillips), b. 1928, American. Writer of novels/short stories, mystery/crime/suspense, science fiction/fantasy, poetry, film, literature, sports, biography. *Publications:* Over 600 appearances in 255 publications Worldwide, 200 anthology appearances and 40 scripts for films and television; (ed)Ray Bradbury Review, 1952; (ed with C Beaumont) Omnibus of Speed, 1958; (with J Fitch) Adventure on Wheels, 1959; Barney Oldfield, 1961; Phil Hill: Yankee Champion, 1962; Impact 20 (stories), 1963; (ed with C Beaumont) When Engines Roar, 1964; Men of Thunder, 1964; John Huston: King Rebel, 1965; (ed)Man Against Tomorrow, 1965; (ed)The Pseudo-People, 1965; Sinners and Supermen, 1965; (ghost ed) Il Meglio della Fantascienza, 1967; (with G C Johnson) Logan's Run, 1967; (ed)3 to the Highest Power, 1968; Death Is for Losers, 1968; The White Cad Cross-Up, 1969; (ed)A Wilderness of Stars, 1969; Dashiell Hammett: A Casebook, 1969; (ed)A Sea of Space, 1970; (ed)The Future Is Now, 1970; (ed)The Human Equation, 1971; (ghost ed)The Edge of Forever, 1971; Space for Hire, 1971; Steve McQueen: Star on Wheels, 1972; Carnival of Speed, 1973; Alien Horizons (stories) 1974; Hemingway: Last Days of the Lion, 1974; The Ray Bradbury Companion, 1975; Wonderworlds (stories) 1977; Logan's World, 1977; Logan's Search, 1980; (ed with M Greenberg) Science Fiction Origins, 1980; (ed)Max Brand's Best Western Stories, 3 vols, 1981-87; Hammett: A Life at the Edge, 1983; McQueen, 1984; Things Beyond Midnight (stories) 1984; Look Out for Space, 1985; The Black Mask Boys, 1985; The Work of Charles Beaumont (bibliography) 1986; Dark Encounters (poems), 1986; (ed)Max Brand: Western Giant, 1986; Logan: A Trilogy, 1986, (with Boden Clarke) The Work of William F. Nolan, (bibliography), 1988; (as Terence Duncan) Rio Renegades, 1989; (ed. with M Greenberg) Urban Honnons, 1990; How to Write Horror Fiction, 1990; Blood Sky, 1991; Helltracks, 1991; (ed with M Greenberg) The Bradbury Chronicles, 1991; 3 Fon Space, 1992; Helle On Wheels, 1992; Saturday's Shadow, 1992; Six in Darkness (stories), 1993; (ed) Max Brand's Best Detective Stories, 1993; Night Shapes (stories), 1993. *Address:* Loni Perkins Associates Literary Agency, 301 W 53rd St, New York, NY 10019, USA.

NONHEBEL Clare, b. 7 Nov 1953, London, England. m. Robin Nonhebel, 30 Aug 1975. *Education:* BA, Honours, French Studies, University of Warwick. *Appointments:* Freelance Feature Writer, 1980-84. *Publications:* Cold Showers, 1985; The Partisan, 1986; story in Winter's Tales anthology, 1987; Incentives, 1988; Child's Play, 1991. *Contributions to:* Annabel, various other womens magazines; Mind Your Own Business, & other business journals; occasional items for Newspapers. *Honour:* Betty Trask Award, (Joint Winner), 1984. *Literary Agent:* Curtis Brown. *Address:* c/o 162-168 Regent Street, London W1R 5TB, England.

NOON Ed. *See:* **AVALLONE Michael.**

NOONAN Lowell Gerald b. 11 Feb 1922, San Francisco, California, USA. Professor Emeritus, Political Science. m. Mary-Joan Westfall, 2 Sept 1949, 2 daughters. *Education:* AB, San Francisco State University, Social Science, 1944; MA, Stanford University, Political Science, 1946; PhD, University of California, Berkeley, Political Science, 1951. *Appointments:* Instructor, Political Science, Pennsylvania State University, 1948-49; Instructor, Assistant and Associate Professor, University of Southern California, 1949-60; Professor, California State University, Northridge, 1960-. *Publications:* France: The Politics of Continuity in Change, 1970; Co-author: European Politics and Government, 1962; Contributor: Western European Party Systems, 1980. *Contributions to:* Journal of Politics, Decline of the Liberal Party in British Politics, 1954; articles in World Affairs Interpreter and other publications. *Honours:*

Fellow of the Fund for the Advancement of Education 1952-53; Faculty Fulbright Research Professor, L'Institut d'Études Politiques, Paris, 1957-58; Fulbright Lecturer, University of Innsbruck, Austria, 1966-67; Creative Fellow, California State Universities, 1970-71. *Memberships:* American Political Science Association. *Address:* 20444 Acre Street, Canoga Park, CA 91306, USA.

NOONE Edwina. *See:* **AVALLONE Michael.**

NORDBRANDT Henrik, b. 21 Mar 1945, Copenhagen, Denmark. Writer. *Education:* Turkish & Arabic Studies. *Publications:* Digte, 1966; Miniaturer, 1967; Syvsoverne, 1969; Omgivelser, 1972; Opbrud og ankomstr, 1974; Ode til blaeksprutten, 1976; Guds hus, 1977; Selected Poems, 1978; Armenia, 1982; Violinbyggernes by, 1985; Glas, 1986; Istid, 1987. *Contributions to:* various journals and magazines. *Honours:* 12 Literary Awards including big prize of Danish Academy, Danish Critic's Prize for Best Book of the Year & Life Grant of Honour, Danish State. *Address:* Gyldendal, Klareboderne 3, Copenhagen 1001 K, Denmark.

NORDLAND Rodney Lee, b. 17 July 1949, USA. Journalist. *Education:* BA, Pennsylvania State University. *Appointments:* Foreign Correspondent, Asia, Philadelphia Inquirer, 1972-83; Bureau Chief, Newsweek Magazine, 1984-85; Correspondent-at-Large, Newsweek Magazine, 1986-. *Publications:* Names and Numbers: A Journalist's Guide, 1978; The Watergate File, 1974. *Contributions to:* numerous newspapers and magazines in USA, France, Germany. *Honours:* Pulitzer prize, Local Reporting, 1978; Thomas L Stokes Award, 1978; Edward J Meeman Award, 1978; Pulitzer Prize, 1st Finalist, Foreign Reporting, 1982; George Polk Special Award, Foreign Correspondent, 1982. *Memberships:* Board of Governors, Pen & Pencil Club; Society of Professional Journalists; Investigative Reporters & Editors; Overseas Press Club. *Literary Agent:* Betty Martin, New York. *Address:* 496 La Guardia Pl, No. 450, New York, NY 10012, USA.

NORGAARD Erik Lykke, b. 26 July 1929, Soro, Denmark. Author; Journalist. m. Ruth Berner Hansen, 2 Oct 1960, 4 sons, 1 daughter. *Education:* As Journalist. *Appointments:* Former Head, Culture Division, Danmarks Radio. *Publications:* About 50 books, some also appearing in UK, USA, Germany, Sweden, Norway, Finland, Japan. *Contributions to:* Numerous to magazines and journals. *Honours:* Cavling Prize; PH-Prize. *Memberships:* Dansk Forfatterforening, Former Member of Board; Dansk Journalistforbund. *Address:* Mollegarden, Spodbjergvej 243, DK-5900 Rudkobing, Denmark.

NORLING Bernard, b. 23 Feb 1924, Hunters, Washington, USA. Retired University Professor. m. Mary Pupo, 30 Jan 1948. *Education:* BA, Gonzaga University, 1940-42, 1946-48; Military, Bard College, 1943-44; Military, Hamilton College, 1944; Military, Washington and Lee College, 1945; MA 1949, PhD, 1955, Notre dame University. *Appointments:*Instructor, 1952-55, Assistant Professor, 1955-61, Associate Professor, 1961-71, Professor, 1971-86, History Department, University of Notre Dame. *Publications:* Towards a Better Understanding of History, 1960; Timeless Problems in History, 1970; Understanding History Through the American Experience, 1976; Return to Freedom, 1983; Behind Japanese Lines, 1986; The Nazi Impact On A German Village, 1993 . *Contributions to:* Numerous articles magazines and journals. *Honour:* Best Teacher of Freshman, University of Notre Dame, 1968. *Memberships:* Indiana Association of Historians; Michiana Historians, President, 1972. *Address:* 504 E Pokagon, South Bend, IN 46617, USA.

NORMAN Barry Leslie, b. 21 Aug 1933, London, England. Writer; Broadcaster. m. Diana Narracott, 1957, 2 daughters. *Appointments:* Entertainments Editor, Daily Mail, London, 1969-71; Weekly Columnist, The Guardian, 1971-80; Writer & Presenter, BBC 1 Film, 1973-81, 1983-88, The Hollywood Greats, 1977-79, 1984, The British Greats 1980, Omnibus, 1982, Film Greats 1985; Talking Pictures, 1988; Radio 4 Today 1974-76, Going Places 1977-81, Breakaway 1979-80. *Publications:* Novels: The Matter of Mandrake, 1967; The Hounds of Sparta, 1968; End Product, 1975; A Series of Defeats, 1977; To Nick a Good Body, 1978; Have a Nice Day, 1981; Sticky Wicket 1984; Non-fiction: Tales of the Redundance Kid, 1975; The Hollywood Greats, 1979; The Movie Greats, 1981; Talking Pictures, 1987; 100 Best Films of the Century, 1992; Thriller: The Birddog Tape, 1992. *Honours:* BAFTA Richard Dimbleby Award, 1981. *Address:* c/o Curtis Brown, 162-168 Regent Street, London, W1R 5TA, England.

NORMAN Geraldine, (Geraldine Keen, Florence Place), b. 13 May 1940, Wales, UK. Journalist. m. Frank Norman, July 1971. *Education:* MA Honours, Mathematics, St Anne's College, Oxford University; University of California, USA. *Publications:* 19th Century Painters & Paintings: A Dictionary, 1977; The Fake's Progress, co-author, 1977; The Tom Keating Catalogue, editor, 1977. The Sale of Works of Art (as Geraldine Keen), 1971; Mrs Harper's Neice (as Florence Place), 1982; Biedermeier Painting, 1987. *Contributions to:* The Independent, regular reports. *Honour:* News Reporter of the Year, 1977. *Literary Agent:* Gillon Aitken. *Address:* 5 Seaford Court, 220 Great Portland Street, London W1, UK.

NORMAN Hilary, b. London, England. *Education:* Attended Queen's College, London. *Appointments:* Director, Henry Norman (textile manufacturing and retail firm) London, England, 1971-79; Production Assistant, 1980-82, Capital Radio, London; Production Assistant 1982-85, British Broadcasting Corporation; Writer 1985-. *Publications:* In Love and Friendship (novel) Hodder and Stoughton 1986, Delacorte 1987; Chateau Ella (novel) Hodder & Stoughton, 1988, Delacorte, 1988; Shattered Stars (novel) Hodder & Stoughtn, 1991, Delacorte, 1991; Fascination (novel) Hodder & Stoughton, 1992, Nal/Dutton, 1992. *Contributions to:* Stories to Woman's Own. *Literary Agents:* John Hawkins Associates, 71 West 23rd Street, New York, NY 10010, USA; A. M. Heath & Company, London. *Address:* c/o A.M Heath Co Ltd., 79 St Martins Lane, London, WC2N 4AA, England.

NORMAN John, b. 20 July 1912, Syracuse, New York, USA. Professor Emeritus. m. Mary Lynott, 28 Dec 1948, Pittsburgh, Pennsylvania, 4 daughters. *Education:* BA 1935, MA 1938, Syracuse University; PhD, Clark University, 1942. *Publications include:* Edward Gibbon Wakefield: A Political Reappraisal, 1963; Labor and Politics in Lybia and Arab Africa, 1965; Poem in anthology, Our World's Most Treasured Poems, 1991. *Contributions to:* Funk and Wagnall's Encyclopedia Yearbook; Encyclopedia Americana: Industrial and Labor Relations Review; Far Eastern Historical Review. *Honours:* Prizes for Poetry by World Poetry, 1991. *Address:* 94 Cooper Road, John's Pond, Ridgefield, CT 06877, USA.

NORMAN Marsha, b. 1947, USA. Novelist; Dramatist. *Appointments:* Teacher, Brown School, Louisville, and Book Reviewer, Louisville Times, mid-1970s; Resident Writer, Actors Theatre, Louisville, 1977-80. *Publications:* Plays: Getting Out, 1977; Third and Oak: The Laundromat, The Pool Hall, 2 vols, 1980-85; 'Night, Mother, 1983; The Holdup, 1987; Novel: The Fortune Teller, 1987; Traveler in the Dark, 1988, Four Plays; Sarah and Abraham; Musical Book & Lyrics - The Secret Garden. 1991. *Literary Agent:* The Tantleff Agency, Jack Tantleff, 375 Greenwich, Suite 700, New York, NY 10019, USA. *Address:* c/o Samuel Liff, William Morris Agency, 1350 Avenue of the Americas, New York, NY 10019, USA.

NORSE Harold George, b. 6 July 1916, New York City, USA. Author. *Education:* BA, Brooklyn College,

1938; MA, New York University, 1951. *Appointments:* Instructor in English, Cooper Union College, New York, 1949-52, Lion School of English, Rome, 1956-57, United States Information Service School, Naples, 1958-59; Instructor in Creative Writing, San Jose State University, California, 1973-75; Currently freelance writer. *Publications:* Beat Hotel (novel) 1975 (Germany), 1983 (USA), 1985 (Italy, Switzerland); Karma Circuit (poetry) 1967 (London), 1974 (USA); Carnivorous Saint (poetry) 1977; Hotel Nirvana (poetry) 1974; Love Poems (poetry) 1986; Memoirs of a Bastard Angel (autobiography) 1989, 1990 (UK), 1991 (France); Mysteries of Magritte (poetry) 1984; The Roman Sonnets of Giuseppe Gioacchino Belli (translations) 1960, 1974. *Contributions to:* Antaeus; City Lights Review; Kayak; Kenyon Review; Poetry Flash; The Advocate; Exquisite Corpse; Semiotexte; Commentary; Harpers & Queen; Transatlantic Review; Christopher Street; Isis (Oxford); Paris Review; Saturday Review; Sewanee Review. *Honours:* National Endowment for the Arts, Poetry Fellowship, 1974; R H de Young Museum Grant, 1974. *Membership:* PEN. *Literary Agent:* Writers House. *Address:* Box 263, 537 Jones Street, San Francisco, CA 94102, USA.

NORTH Andrew. *See:* **NORTON Alice Mary.**

NORTH Carol Sue, b. 6 May 1954, Keokuk, Iowa, USA. Physician; Author. m. 23 Sept 1989. *Education:* BS, General Science, University of Iowa, Iowa City, 1976; MD, 1983, Internship, Residency in Psychiatry, 1983-87, Postdoctoral Fellow, Psychiatric Epidemiology, 1987-90, Washington University School of Medicine, St Louis. *Appointments:* Editorial Board, Journal of Traumatic Stress, 1990-. *Publications:* Welcome, Silence, 1987, 1989; 1st Author: Multiple Personalities, Multiple Disorders: Psychiatric Classification and Media Influence, 1993. *Contributions to:* Archives of General Psychiatry; American Journal of Psychiatry; Annals of Internal Medicine; Hospital and Community Psychiatry; Journal of Traumatic Stress; Comprehensive Therapy; Journal of Family Practice; Journal of Chemical Physics; Others. *Honours:* Omicron Delta Kappa, 1976; Richard S Brookings Medical School Award, 1983; Sandoz Award, Psychiatry, 1983; National Institute of Mental Health Postdoctoral Fellowship, 1987-90. *Memberships:* American Psychiatric Association; American Psychopathological Association; Eastern Missouri Psychiatric Society, Executive Council; National Alliance for the Mentally Ill; Life History Research Society. *Address:* Washington University School of Medicine, Department of Psychiatry, 4940 Children's Place, St Louis, MO 63110, USA.

NORTH Elizabeth (Stewart), b. 1932, United Kingdom. Author; Teacher of Creative Writing. *Appointments:* Writer-in-Residence, Bretton Hall College of Higher Education, 1984-85. *Publications:* Make Thee an Ark, radio play, 1969; Wife Swopping, radio play, 1969; The Least and Vilest Things, novel, 1971; Pelican Rising, novel, 1975; Enough Blue Sky, novel, 1977; Everything in the Garden, novel, 1978; Florence Avenue, novel, 1979; Dames, novel, 1981; Ancient Enemies, novel, 1982; The Real Tess, radio feature, 1984; Jude the Obscure, adaptation for radio, 1985. *Address:* 8 Huby Park, Huby, Leeds, England.

NORTH Sara. *See:* **BONHAM Barbara.**

NORTON Alice Mary (Andrew North, André Norton), b. 1912. USA. Writer of science fiction/fantasy, children's fiction. Former Librarian, Children's Department, Cleveland Public Library. *Publications include:* Spell of Witch World (short stories) 1972; Breed to Come, 1972; Crystal Gryphon, 1972; Garan the Eternal (short stories) 1973; (ed) Gates to Tomorrow, 1973; Forerunner Foray, 1973; Here Abide Monsters, 1973; Lavender-Green Magic, 1974; Jargoon Pard, 1974; (co-author) Many Worlds of Andre Norton, 1974; Iron Cage, 1974; (ed) Small Shadows Creep, 1974; (co-author) Day of the Ness, 1975; Outside, 1975; White Jade Fox, 1975; Merlin's Mirrow, 1975; No Light

Without Stars, 1975; Knave of Dreams, 1975; Perilous Dreams, 1976; (with Dorothy Madlee) Star Ka'at, 1976; Wraiths of Time, 1976; Red Hart Magic, 1976; Velvet Shadows, 1977; Opan-Eyed Fan, 1977; Trey of Swords (short stories) 1977; Quag Keep, 1978; (with Dorothy Madlee) Star Ka'at World, 1978; Yurth Burden, 1978; (with Dorothy Madlee) Star Ka'ats and the Plant People, 1979; Zarathor's Bane, 1979; (with Phyllis Miller) Seven Spells to Sunday, 1979; Snow Shadow, 1979; Iton Butterflies, 1980; Voorloper 1980; Lore of Witchworld, (short stories) 1980; Gryphon in Glory, 1981; Forerunner, 1981; Horn Crown, 1981; Ten Mile Treasure, 1981; (with Dorothy Madlee) Star Ka'ats and Winged Warriors, 1981; Moon Called, 1982; (with Enid Cushing) Caroline, 1982; Wheel of Stars, 1983; Ware Hawk, 1983; Stand and Deliver, 1984; (with Phyllis Miller) House of Shadows, 1984; (with A C Crispin) Gryphon's Eyrie, 1984; Werewrath, 1984; Wings in Nektor, 1986; Gate of Cat, 1987; Serpents' Tooth, 1988; sa Collectionsa; Moon Mirror, 1988; Grand Master's Choice, 1989; Wizard's World, 1989; Dare to go hunting, 1990; (with Bradley & May) Black Trillium, 1990; Sekyll Legacy (with Bloch), 1990; Storms of Victory (with Griffin), 1991; Eirenbane (with Hackey), 1991; Anthologies ed: Magic in Itker I, 1986; Magic in Itker II, 1987; Tales of Witch World I, 1987; Tales of Witch World II, 1988; Four from Witch World, 1989; Cat Fantastic, 1989; Tales of Witch World III, 1990; Cat Fantastic, 1991. *Literary Agent:* Scott Meredith (Russell Galen). *Address:* Address: 1600 Spruce Avenue, Winter Park, FL 32789, USA.

NORTON André. *See:* **NORTON Alice Mary.**

NORTON Augustus Richard, b. 2 Sept 1946, New York, USA. Professor; Army Officer (Colonel). m. Deanna J Lampros, 27 Dec 1969, 1 son. *Education:* BA, magna cum laude 1974, MA, Political Science 1974, University of Miami; PhD, Political Science, University of Chicago, 1984. *Publications:* Amal and the Shia: Struggle For the Soul of Lebanon, 1987; International Terrorism, 1980; Studies in Nuclear Terrorism, 1979; NATO, 1985; Touring Nam: The Vietnam War Reader, 1985; The International Relations of the Palestine Liberation Organization, 1989; UN Peacekeepers: Soldiers With a Difference, 1990; Political Tides in the Arab World, 1992. *Contributions to:* Numerous magazines including Survival & Foreign Policy; Current History; New Outlook; New Leader; Middle East Journal. *Address:* Dept of Social Science, USMA, West Point, NY 10996, USA.

NORTON Natascha. *See:* **SCOTT-STOKES Natascha.**

NORWICH John Julius, b. 15 Sept 1929. Writer; Broadcaster. m. (1) Ann Clifford, 5 Aug 1952, 1 son, 1 daughter, (2) Mollie Philipps, 14 June 1989. *Education:* University of Strasbourg, 1947; New College, Oxford, 1949-52. *Publications:* A History of Venice, 1977, 1981; The Normans in the South, 1967; The Kingdom in the Sun, 1970; Byzantium: The Early Centuries, 1988; The Architecture of Southern England, 1985; Mount Athos, 1966; Sahara, 1968; Glyndebourne, 1985; Christmas Crackers 1970-79, 1980; More Christmas Crackers 1980-89, 1990; A Taste for Travel, 1985; Vencie: A Traveller's Companion, 1990; (ed) The Oxford Illustrated Encyclopeadis of the Arts, 1990; Byzantium, the Apogee, 1991. *Contributions to:* Numerous magazines and journals. *Honours:* C.V.O. Commendatore, Ordine al Merito della Republica Italiana. *Memberships:* FRSL; FRGS; Garrick Club; Beefsteak. *Literary Agent:* Felicity Bryan, 2A North Parade, Oxford. *Address:* 24 Blomfield Road, London W9 1AD, England.

NORWOOD Victor George Charles, b. 1920. British. Writer of: mystery/crime/suspense, westerns/adventure, science fiction/fantasy, children's fiction, plays/screenplays, poetry, travel/explporation/adventure. *Appointments:* Managing Director, Westcliff Literary Agency, 1947-77; Founder and Chairman, North Lincs Writers' Circle, 1960. *Publications:* Most recent publications include: (as Victor G C Norwood)

The Saphire Seekers (non-fiction) 1979; Venom, 1980; A Lifetime of Cheating Death (non-fiction) 1980; Miracles of Cardiac Surgery (non-fiction) 1980; Across Australia by Volkswagen (non-fiction) 1980; as Victor G C Norwood in the United States: The Know-How of Prospecting, 1976; A Guide to General Prospecting, 1977; Walkabout, 1977; Tressidy's Last Case (fiction) 1977; Where the River Ends, 1978; Holocaust, 1978; The Beast of Bulgalloth, 1978; as Victor G C Norwood in Canada: Legends of the Forests, 1978; The Carib Hordes, 1978; Diamonds Are Forever (fiction), 1979; Also numerous publications under pseudonyms in the 1950's, 60's and 70's. *Address:* 194 W Common Lane, Westcliff, Scunthorpe DN17 1PD, England.

NORWOOD Warren, b. 1945, USA. Science Fiction Writer. *Appointments:* Assistant Manager, University Bookstore, University of Texas, Arlington, 1973-76; Manager, Century Bookstore, Ft Worth, Texas, 1976-77; Publisher's Representative in Fort Worth, 1978-83; Taught Creative Writing, Tarrant County Junior College, 1983. *Publications:* The Windhover Tapes, comprising An Image of Voices, 1982, Flexing the Warp, 1983; Fize of the Gabriel Ratchets, 1983, and A Planet of Flowers, 1984; The Seren Cenacles (with Ralph Mylius), 1983; Double Spiral War, comprising Midway Between, 1984, Polar Fleet, 1985, and Final Command, 1986.

NOSKOWICZ-BIERON Helena, b. 5 July 1931, Sobolow, Poland. Journalist. m. Wladystaw Bieron, 27 Dec 1956, 2 sons. *Education:* BA, Journalism, Jangiellonian University, Cracow, 1964; MA Journalism, University of Warsaw, 1964. *Appointments:* Reporter for the Polish Radio in Cracow, 1953-63; Columnist for Echo Krakowa, daily, 1964-81; Editor, Underground Press, 1981-89; Columnist, Gazeta Krakowska and Dziennik Polski, 1989-. *Publications:* Ciagle czekaja z obiadem, 1978; Kto Ukradl Zloty Fon, 1991. *Contributions to:* Zycie Literackie weekly; St Uzba Zdrowia monthly; Polityka, weekly; Architektura i Biznes; Solidarnosc matopolska. *Honours:* Book of the Year about Cracow, 1978; Association of Polish Journalists prizes and awards. *Memberships:* Association of Polish Journalists, Secretary, Cracow Chapter, 1981-82. *Address:* ul Batorego 19/16, 31-135 Krakow, Poland.

NOSSITER Bernard Daniel, b. 10 Apr 1926. Journalist. m. Jacqueline Robinson, 1950, 4 sons. *Education:* BA, Dartmouth College; MA, Harvard University. *Appointments:* National Economics Correspondent, 1955-62, European Economics Correspondent, 1964-67, South Asia Correspondent, 1967-68, National Bureau Reporter, 1968-71, London Correspondent, Washington Post; UN Bureau Chief, New York Times, 1979-83. *Publications:* The Mythmakers, 1964; Soft State, 1970; Britain : A Future that Works, 1978; The Global Struggle for More, 1987. *Contributions to:* American Economics Review; Harvard Business Review; Annals American Academy Political Science. *Memberships:* Nieman Fellow, Harvard, 1962-63; Reform Club, Council on Foreign Relations. *Address:* 6 Montagu Place, London W1H 1RF, England.

NOTLEY Alice, b. 8 Nov 1945, Bisbee, Arizona, USA. Poet. m. Douglas Oliver, 10 Feb 1988, 2 sons (Ted Berrigan). *Education:* BA Barnard College, 1967; MFA, The Writer's Workshop, University of Iowa, 1970. *Publications:* Alice Ordered Me To Be Made, 1976; When I Was Alive, 1980; How Spring Comes, 1981; Waltzing Matilda, 1981; Margaret and Dusty, 1985; At Night the States, 1988; Beginning with a Stain; Homer's Art, 1991; The Scarlet Cabinet (with Douglas Oliver), 1992. *Contributions to:* Co-Editor of Scarlet & frequent contributor. *Honours:* NEA Award, 1979; The Poetry Center Book Award, 1982; GE Foundation Award, 1984; NYFA Fellowship, 1991. *Address:* 61 rue Lepic, 75018, France.

NOVAK Maximillian Erwin, b. 26 Mar 1930, New York City, USA. University Professor. m. Estelle Gershgoren, 21 Aug 1966, 2 sons, 1 daughter. *Education:* PhD, University of California, 1958; DPhil,

St John's University, Oxford, 1961. *Appointments:* Assistant Professor, University of Michigan, 1958-62; Assistant Professor-Professor, University of California, Los Angeles, 1962-. *Publications:* Economics and the Fiction of Daniel Defoe, 1962; Defoe and the Nature of Man, 1963; Congreve, 1970; Realism Myth and History in the Fiction of Daniel Defoe, 1983; Eighteenth Century English Literature, 1983; Editor, The Wild Man Within, 1970; English Literature in the Age of Disguise, 1977; California Dryden Volumes X and XIII, 1971, 1984. *Contributor To:* Essays in Criticism; PMLA; JEGP; MP; PQ; SEL; Kenyon Review; SP; Studies in the Literary Imagination; MLR; TSLL. *Honours:* Fulbright Fellowship, 1955-77; Guggenheim Fellowship, 1965-66, 1985-86; NEH, 1981-82; University of California President's Fellowship, 1991-1992; Beinecke Library Fellowship, 1991; Mellon Fellowship at Huntingdon Library, 1992. *Memberships:* MLA; American Society for Eighteenth Century Studies. *Address:* Dept. of English, University of California, Los Angeles, CA 90024, USA.

NOVAK Michael, b. 1933, Johnstown, Pennsylvania, USA. Professor. m. Karen Laub, 1 son, 2 daughters. *Education:* AB, Stonehill College 1956; BT, Gregorian University, Rome, 1958; Theological studies at Catholic University; MA, History and Philosophy of Religion, Harvard University, 1966. *Appointments:* Teaching Fellow, Harvard University; Assistant Professor of Humanities, Stanford University, 1965-68; Teacher, College at SUNY Old Westbury, 1968-73; Launched new humanities programme at Rockefeller Foundation, 1973-74; University Professor and Ledden-Watson Distinguished Professor of Religion, Syracuse University 1976-78; Resident Scholar, American Enterprise Institute, 1978-, currently holds George Frederick Jewett Chair in Religion and Public Policy and is Director of Social and Political Studies at the Institute in Washington DC; W Harold and Martha Welch chair as Professor of American Studies at the University of Notre Dame for autumn semesters of 1987 and 1988; Headed US Delegation to the Experts' Meeting on Human Contacts at the Conference on Security and Co-operation in Europe (continuation of the Helsinki Accord negotiations) March 1986. *Publications include:* Confession of a Catholic, 1983; Freedom with Justice: Catholic Social Thought and Liberal Institutions, 1984; Will It Liberate? Questions About Liberation Theology, 1986; Taking Glasnost Seriously, 1988; Free Persons and the Common Good, 1989; together with the Lay Commission on Catholic Social Teaching and the US Economy, Toward the Future: Catholic Social Thought and the US Economy, 1984; Wrote text of New Consensus on Family and Welfare, 1987; Works of fiction include: The Tiber was Silver, 1961 and Naked I Leave, 1970; Free Persons and the Common Good, 1989. *Contributions to:* Author and editor of numerous monographs and over 200 articles; Articles and essays in popular journals; Twice weekly column entitled Illusions and Realities, syndicated nationally from 1970-80, 1984-; Column, Tomorrow and Tomorrow appeared monthly in National Review, 1979-86; Column, The Larger Context in Forbes Magazine, 1989-. Member, editorial board of several publications; co-founder of This World and Crisis, Columnist for Forbes Magazine, 1989. *Honours include:* Freedom Award, Coalition for a Democratic Majority, 1979; George Washington Honor Medal, Freedoms Foundation, 1984; Award of Excellence, Religion in Media, 8th Annual Angel Awards, 1985; Column, Illusions and Realities, was Pulitzer finalist in 1979; First US Member, Argentine National Academy of Sciences, Norals and Politics, 1985; Ellis Island Medal of Honor, 1986; The Anthony Fisher Award for Spirit of Democratic Capitalism, 1992; 12 honorary degrees. *Memberships include:* Presidential Task Force on Project Economic Justics, 1985; Appointed Board of International Broadcasting, 1984; Founder, Ethnic Millions Political Action Committee (EMPAC) in 1974. *Address:* American Enterprise Institute, 1150 17th Street NW, Washington, DC 20036, USA.

NOVE Alec, b. 1915, United Kingdom. Emeritus Professor of Economics, University of Glasgow. *Publications:* The Soviet Economy, 1961; Was Stalin

Really Necessary, 1964; The Soviet Middle East (with J A Newth), 1967; An Economic History of the USSR, 1969, 3rd edition, 1993; Socialist Economics (edited with D M Nuti), 1972; Efficiency Criteria for Nationalised Industries, 1973; Stalinism and After, 1975; The Soviet Economic System, 1977; Political Economy and Soviet Socialism, 1979; The Economics of Feasible Socialism, 1983; Socialism, Economics and Development, 1986. Studies in Economics and Russia, 1990; Glasnost in Action, 1990; The Stalin Phenomenon (editor), 1993. *Address:* Hamilton Drive, Glasgow G12 8DP, Scotland.

NOYES Stanley Tinning, b. 7 Apr 1924, San Francisco, California, USA. Teacher; Writer. m. Nancy Black, 12 Mar 1949, 2 sons, 1 daughter. *Education:* BA, English, 1950, MA, English, 1951, University of California, Berkeley. *Appointments:* Literary Arts Coordinator, New Mexico Arts Division, 1972-86. *Publications:* No Flowers for a Clown, novel, 1961; Shadowbox, novel, 1970; Faces and Spirits, poems, 1974; Beyond the Mountains Beyond the Mountains, poems, 1979; The Commander of Dead Leaves, poems, 1984; Los Comanches: The Horse People, 1751-1845, history, 1993. *Contributions to:* San Francisco Review; New Mexico Quarterly; Sumac; The Cold Mountain Review; San Marcos Review; Puerto del Sol; The Greenfield Review; High Plains Literary Review; Floating Island; Others. *Honours:* MacDowell Fellow, 1967. *Membership:* PEN American Center. *Literary Agent:* Marie Theresa Caen, 2901 Scott St, San Francisco, CA 94123, USA. *Address:* 634 East Garcia, Sante Fe, NM 87501, USA.

NUDELSTEJER Sergio, b. 24 Feb 1924, Warsaw, Poland. Writer; Journalist. m. Tosia Malamud. *Education:* National University of Mexico. *Publications:* Theodor Herzl, Prophet of our Times, 1961; The Rebellion of Silence, 1971; Albert Einstein: A Man in his Time, 1980; Franz Kafka: Concience of an Era, 1983; Borges: Getting Near to his Literary Work, 1987; Rosario Castellanos: The Voice, the Word, the Memory, Anthology, 1984; Elais Canetti: The Language of Passion, 1990; Spies of God-Authors of end of Century, 1992 ans Stefan Zweig: The Concience of Man, 1992. *Contributions to:* Writer, daily newspaper Excelsior; Writer, Revista de Revistas, Plural and Coloquio published in Argentina Magazines; Editor: Tribuna Israelita. *Honours:* Award to Intelectual Merit by the World Jewish Congress in 1990, Recipient of various honors and awards including Honorary Fellowship, Mexican Institute of Science and Humanities. *Memberships:* Mexican Institute of Culture; Mexican Writer's Association; Mexican Society of Geography and History; Mexican Institute of Science and Humanities, Mexican Academy of Human Rights. *Address:* Heraclito 331 Apt. 601, Polanco, Mexico 11560, Mexico DF.

NUGENT Henry Neill, b. 22 Mar 1947, Newcastle-on-Tyne, England. Lecturer. m. Maureen Nugent, 12 Sept 1969, 2 daughters. *Education:* BA, Politics, Social Administration, University of Newcastle, 1969; MA, Government, University of Kent, 1970; London School of Economics, 1970-71. *Publications:* The British Right (with R King); Respectable Rebels (with R King); The Left in France (with D Lowe); The Government and Politics of the European Communities. *Contributions to:* Numerous articles on aspects of British and European politics to academic journals. *Memberships:* Political Studies Association; University Association for Contemporary European Studies; European Community Studies Association, USA. *Address:* Department of Social Sciences, Manchester Metropolitan University, Undercroft Building, Manchester M15 6BR, England.

NUNIS Doyce B(lackman) Jr, b. 1924. American. Professor of History; Writer. *Appointments:* Associate Professor, 1965-68, Professor of History, 1968-, Emeritus, 1989, University of Southern California, Los Angeles; Editor, Southern Californian Quarterly, 1962-; President, Board of Trustees, Mission Santa Barbara Archive, 1971-; Historian, El Pueblo de Los Angeles State Historic Park, 1971-80. *Publications include:* Andrew Sublette, Rocky Mountain Prince, 1960; (ed)The

Golden Frontier, 1962; (ed)Josiah Belden, 1841 California Overland Pioneer, 1962; (ed)Letters of a Young Miner, 1964; (ed)California Diary of Farm Dean Atherton, 1964; (ed)Journey of James A Bull, 1967; (trans with L Jay Oliva) A California Medical Journey, by Pierre Garnier, MD, 1967; Trials of Issac Graham, 1968; Past Is Prologue: Centennial Profile of Pacific Mutual Life Insurance Co, 1968; (ed)Hudson's Bay Company's First Fur Brigade to Sacramento Valley: Alexander McLeod's 1829 Hunt, 1968; (ed)Sketches of a Journey on the Two Oceans, by Abbe Henri-J-A Alric, 1971; (ed)San Francisco Vigilance Committee of 1856: Three Views, 1971; (ed)The Drawing of Ignacio Tirsch, SJ, 1972; (ed) Los Angeles and Its Environs in the Twentieth Century: A Bibliography of a Metropolis, 1973; A History of American Political Thought, 2 vols, 1975; The Mexican War in Baja, California, 1977; (ed)A Frontier Doctor, by Henry F Hoyt, 1979; (ed)Los Angeles from the Days of the Pueblo, 1981; (ed)The Letters of Jacob Baegart, 1749-1761: Jesuit Missionary in Baja. California, 1982; (ed)The 1769 Transit of Venus: The First Planned Scientific Expedition in Baja California, 1982; Men, Medicine and Water: The Building of the Los Angeles Aqueduct 1908-1913, 1982; (ed)Frontier Fighter by George W Coe, 1984; (ed)Southern California Historical Anthology, 1984; (ed)The Life of Tom Horn, 1987; (co-ed.) A Guide to the History of California, 1988. *Memberships:* Sheriff, Los Angeles Corral of Westerners, 1973; President, Zamorano Club, 1975-76; Atheneaum, London. *Address:* Department of History, University of Southern California, Los Angeles, CA 90089, USA.

NUNN Frederick McKinley, b. 1937, United States of America. Writer (History, Politics/Government). *Appointments include:* Editorial Advisory Board, Military Affairs, 1973-78; Board of Editors, Latin America Research Review, 1984-85. *Publications:* Chilean Politics, 1920-31; The Honorable Mission of the Armed Forces, 1970; The Military in Chilean History: Essays on Civil-Military Relations 1810-1973, 1976; Yesterdays Soldiers: European Military Professionalism in South America 1890-1940, 1983; The Time of The Generals: Latin American Profesional Militarism in World Perspective, 1992. *Address:* Department of History, Portland State University, P.O. Box 751, Portland, OR 97207, USA.

NUNN John, b. 1955. Writer. *Publications:* The Pirc for the Tournament Player, 1980; Tactical Chess Endings, 1981; Sicilian Defence Najdorf Variation (with M. Stean), 1982; The Benoni for the Tournament Player, 1982; Beating the Sicilian, 1984; Solving in Style, 1985. *Address:* 228 Dover House Road, London, SW15 5AH, England.

NURENBERG Philip Robert, b. 21 July 1949, Newton, Massachusetts, USA. Author; Researcher; Photographer; Documentary Movie Maker; Manuscript Editor; Consultant. *Education:* BS, Management, Boston University School of Management, Bachelor of Science Degree, 1972; Diploma, Legal Investigation, Universal Schools, Washington, DC, 1973. *Appointments:* Founder, Editor-in-Chief, Happy Rock Press, 1980; Affiliated with Maine Writers and Publishers Alliance. *Creative works include:* Bern Porter Interviewed, 1983, recorded, 1980; Over 400 Interview Copyrights and Permissions with friends and acquaintances of Anais Nin and Henry Miller; Copyrights to thousands of photos of The Friends and Aquaintances of Henry Miller and Anais Nin and other celebrities. *Contributions to:* Information and correspondence to editors of Stroker Magazine (on Henry Miller), New York City, and Anais: An International Journal, Los Angeles. *Honours:* Authorised Biographer, the late Eddie Schwartz, President and Founder of the authorised-by-Miller Henry Miller Literary Society; Authorised Biographer of the late Emil White and the authorised by Henry Miller Memorial Library, Big Sur, California. *Memberships:* Henry Miller Literary Society; Boston University Alumni Organization; Maine Writers and Publishers Alliance; Buckminster Fuller Institute; Registered Democrat

Voter. *Literary Agent:* Los Angeles, USA. *Address:* PO Box 24453, Los Angeles, CA 90024, USA.

NUTTALL Jeffrey b. 8 July 1933, Clitheroe, Lancashire, England. Artist. (div), 5 sons, 1 daughter. *Education:* Intermediate Examination in Arts and Crafts, Hereford School of Art, 1951; NDD in Painting (Special Level), Bath Academy of Art, Corsham, 1953; ATD, Institute of Education, London University, 1954. *Appointments:* Sergeant Instructor, Royal Army Education Corps, 1954-56; Art Master, Green Lane Secondary Modern School, Leominster, 1956-59; Art Master, Alder Secondary Modern School, East Finchley, London, 1959-63; Art Master, Ravenscroft Secondary Modern School, Barnet, Herts, 1963-67; English Master, Greenacre Secondary Modern School, Great Yarmouth, 1967-68; Lecturer, Foundation Course, Bradford College of Art, 1968-70; Senior Lecturer, Fine Art Department, Leeds Polytechnic, 1970-81; Head of Department, Fine Art Department, Liverpool Polytechnic, 1981-84; Took early retirement in 1984; Number of part-time teaching appointments. *Publications include:* Verse: Objects, 1973; Sun Barbs, 1974; Grape Notes/Apple Music, 1979; Scenes and Dubs, 1987; Mad with Music, 1987. Fiction: The Gold Hole, 1968; Snipe's Spinster, 1973; Anatomy of my Father's Corpse, 1976; What Happened to Jackson, 1977; Muscle, 1980; The Patriarchs, 1975. Non-Fiction: King Twist, A Portrait of Frank Randle, 1978; Performance Art Vol I: Memoirs, 1979; Performance Art, Vol II: Scripts, 1979; The Pleasures of Necessity, 1989; The Bald Soprano, 1989. Graphics: Come Back Sweet Prince, 1965; Oscar Christ and the Ommaculate Conception, 1970; The Fox's Lair, 1972. *Contributions to:* Knuckleduster Funnies (comic book - four issues, co-edited Robert Bank) 1986; Poetry criticism for The Guardian, 1979-82; Criticism and comment in numerous journals. Occasional broadcasts for London Weekend Television, Granada Television, Yorkshire Television, BBC Radio. Paintings exhibited in numerous exhibitions. *Address:* 71 White Hart Lane, Barnes, London SW13 OPP, England.

NUWER Henry Joseph (Hank), b. 19 Aug 1946, Buffalo, New York, USA. Author. m. (1) Alice Cerniglia, 28 Dec 1968, (div 1980), (2) Jenine Howard, 9 Apr 1982, 2 sons. *Education:* BS, State University College of New York, Buffalo, 1968; MA, New Mexico Highlands University, 1970; PhD equivalency, Ball State University, 1988. *Appointments:* Assistant Professor of English, Clemson University, 1982-83; Associate Professor of Journalism, Ball State University, 1985-89; Senior Writer, Rodale Press Book Division, Emmaus, Pennsylvania, 1990-1991; Historian, Cedar Crest College, 1991-1993. *Publications:* Non-fiction: Strategies of the Great Football Coaches, 1988; Strategies of the Great Baseball Managers, 1988; Rendezvousing with Contemporary Writers, 1988; Recruiting in Sports, 1989; Steroids, 1990; Sports Scandals, 1993; Broken Pledges: The Deadly Rite of Hazing, 1990; Come Out, Come Out Wherever you are (with Carole Shaw), 1982; Fiction: The Bounty Hunter series (with William Boyles), 4 vols, 1980-82; Blood Kin, novel (with James Noble), in progress; Nonfiction Biography of Jesse Owens in progress; History of Cedar Crest College in progress; How to Write Like an Expert, in progress. *Contributions to:* Over 700 articles in: Inside Sports; Saturday Evening Post; Human Behavior; Sport; Outside; The Nation; Gentlemen's Quarterly. *Honours:* College Media Advisers Magazine Adviser of the Year, 1988. *Memberships:* Society of Professional Journalists; Investigative Reporters and Editors; Phi Kappa Phi. *Address:* PO Box 776, Fogelsville, PA 18051, USA.

NYE Joseph S(amuel) Jr, b. 1937, New Jersey, USA. University Professor. m. Molly Harding, 3 sons. *Education:* BA summa cum laude, Princeton University, 1958; Degree in Philosophy, Politics, Economics, Oxford University, England; PhD, Political Science, Harvard University, 1964. *Appointments:* Instructor, 1964-66, Associate Professor, 1966-69, Associate Professor, 1969-71, Professor of International Security, 1971-, Director, Center for Science and International Affairs, 1985-90, Director Center for Internatioal Affairs, 1990-, Harvard University, Cambridge, Massachusetts; Deputy to Under-Secretary of State for Security Assistance, Science and Technology, 1977-79; Editorial Board, Foreign Policy and International Security magazines. *Publications:* Pan-Africanism and East African Integration, 1965; International Regionalism (editor), 1968; Peace in Parts: Integration and Conflict in Regional Organization, 1971; Conflict Management by International Organizations, 1972; Transnational Relations and World Politics (author, edited with R O Keohane), 1972; Power and Independence, 1977; Energy and Security (edited with David Deese), 1980; Living with Nuclear Weapons, 1983; The Making of America's Soviet Policy, 1984; Global Dilemmas (edited with Samuel P Huntington), 1985; Hawks, Doves, and Owls (co-author), 1985; Nuclear Ethics, 1986; Fateful Visions (co-editor), 1988; Bound to Lead: The Changing Nature of American Power, 1990; Understanding International Conflicts, 1993. *Contributions to:* Professional and scholarly journals; New York Times; Washington Post; Los Angeles Times; Boston Globe; Christian Science Monitor; Atlantic Monthly; New Republic. *Honours:* Rhodes Scholar, Oxford; Distinguished Honor Award, Department of State, 1979. *Memberships:* Fellow, American Academy of Arts and Sciences; Senior Fellow, Aspen Institute; International Institute for Strategic Studies; Advisory Committee, Institute for International Economics; Director, United Nation Association. *Address:* Center for International Affairs, Harvard University 1737 Cambridge Street, Cambridge, MA 02138, USA.

NYE Nelson (Clem Colt, Drake C Denver), b. 28 Sept 1907, Chicago, USA. Writer. m. (1) 1 daughter, (2) Ruth Hilton, 1937. *Education:* Studied art and engineering. *Publications:* Pistols for Hire, 1941; Not Grass Alone, 1961; Maverick Marshal, 1958; Riders by Night, 1950; Horse Thieves, 1987; Mule man, 1988; Wild Horse Shorty, 1944; The Parson of Gunbarrel Basin, 1955; Wide Loop, 1952; Gunfight at the OK Corral; Trail of Lost Skulls, 1967. *Contributions to:* Ford Times; The Speed Horse; Quarter Horse Journal; Western Horseman; Thoroughbred Record;' Blood Horse. *Honours:* Spur Award for Best Western Critic, 1954; Spur Award for Best Western Novel, 1959; Editorial Award, Quarter Racing Owners of America, 1972. *Memberships:* Western Writers of America Incorporated, Co-Founder, twice President, twice Judge, Director; Judge, Best Western category, 1989. *Address:* 2290 W Ironwood Ridge Drive, Tucson, AZ 85745, USA.

NYE Robert, b. 1939. Poet; Novelist; Literary Critic. *Appointments:* Poetry Editor, The Scotsman, 1967-; Poetry Critic, The Times, London, 1971-. *Publications:* Juvenilia 1, (poems), 1961; Juvenilia 2, (poems) 1963; Taliesin (juvenile), 1966; March Has Horse's Ears (juvenile), 1966; Doubtfire (novel), 1967; Beowulf, 1968; Tales I Told My Mother, 1969; Sawney Bean (with Bill Watson), 1969; Sisters, 1969; Darker Ends (poems), 1969; Wishing Gold, 1970; Fugue (screenplay), 1971; Poor Pumpkin, 1971; Cricket, 1972; A Choice of Sir Walter Ralegh's Verse, 1972; The Mathematical Princess and Other Stories, 1972; A Choice of Swinburne's Verse, 1973; The Faber Book of Sonnets, 1976; Falstaff (novel), 1976; Penthesilia, 1976; The English Sermon 1750-1850, 1976; Divisions on a Ground (poems), 1976; Out of the World and Back Again (juvenile), 1977; Merlin (novel), 1978; The Bird of the Golden Land (juvenile), 1980; Faust (novel), 1980; Harry Pay the Pirate (juvenile), 1981; The Voyage of the Destiny (novel), 1982; The Facts of Life and Other Fictions, 1983; Three Tales (for children), 1983; editor, PEN New Poetry, 1, 1986; editor, William Barnes, selected poems, 1988; The Memoirs of Lord Byron (novel) 1989; A Collection of Poems 1955-1988, 1989; The Life and Death of My Lord Gilles de Rais (novel), 1990; Editor (with Elizabeth Friedmann and Alan J Clark), First Awakenings: The Early Poems of Laura Riding, 1992; Mrs Shakespeare (novel) 1993. *Address:* c/o Sheil Land Associates, 43 Doughty Street, London, WC1N 2LF, England.

NYE Russel (Blane), b. 1913, United States of America. Writer (History, Biography). *Publications:* George Bancroft, Brahmin Rebel, 1944; Civil Liberty and Slavery, 1948; Midwestern Progressive Politics, 1951; The History of the United States (with J. E. Morpurgo), 1955, 1970; A Baker's Dozen, 1956; Cultural Life of the New Nation, 1960; The Almost Chosen People, 1966; The Unembarrassed Muse, 1970. *Membership:* President, Popular Culture Association, 1969-72. *Address:* 301 Oxford Road, East Lansing, MI 48823, USA.

NYE Simon Beresford, b. 29 July 1958, Burgess Hill, Sussex, England. Writer. *Education:* BA, French, German, Bedford College, London University, 1980; Diploma, Technical Translation, Polytechnic of Central London, 1985. *Publications:* Men Behaving Badly, 1989, 1992, as situation comedy, Thames TV, 1992; Wideboy, 1991, comedy-drama series, Carlton TV, 1993; Translator: The Vienna Opera, 1985; Braque, 1986; Matisse: Graphic Works, 1987. *Literary Agent:* Rod Hall, A P Watt Ltd, London, England. *Address:* 84b Delancey St, London NW1 7SA, England.

O

O'BALLANCE Edgar, b. 1918. Freelance Writer; Journalist. *Publications:* The Arab-Israeli War, 1956; The Sinai Campaign, 1956, 1959; The Story of the French Foreign Legion, 1961; The Red Army of China, 1962; The Indo-China War 1945-1954, 1964; The Red Army of Russia, 1964; The Greek Civil War 1944-1949, 1966; Malaya: The Communist Insurgent War 1948-1960, 1966; The Algerian Insurrection 1954-1962, 1967; Korea 1950-1953, 1969; War in the Yemen 1962-1967, 1971; The Third Arab-Israeli War 1967, 1972; The Kurdish Revolt 1961-1970, 1973; Arab Guerilla Power, 1974; The Electronic War in the Middle East 1968-1970, 1974; The Wars in Vietnam 1954-1972, 1975; The Secret War in the Sudan 1955-1972, 1977; No Victor, No Vanquished, 1978, The Language of Violence, 1979; Terror in Ireland, 1979; The Bloodstained Cedars of Lebanon, 1980; The Tracks of the Bear, 1982; The Gulf War, 1988; The Cyanide War, 1989; Terrorism in the 1980s, 1989; Wars in Afghanistan: 1839-1990, 1991; The Second Gulf War; The Civil War in Yugoslavia. *Address:* Wakebridge Cottage, Wakebridge, Matlock, Derbyshire, England.

O'BRIEN Conor Cruise, (Donat O'Donnell), b. 1917, Ireland. Writer (History, Politics/Government). *Appointments include:* Consultant Editor, The Observer Newspaper, London, 1981-; Pro-Chancellor, Dublin University, 1973-. *Publications:* Maria Cross, 1952; Parnell and His Party, 1957; The Shaping of Modern Ireland, 1959; To Katanga and Back, 1962; Conflicting Concepts for the U.N., 1964; Writers and Politics, 1965; The United nations: Sacred Drama, 1967; Murderous Angels (play), 1968; Power and Consciousness, 1969; Albert Camus, 1969; Edmund Burke: Reflections on the Revolution in France, 1969; Conor Cruise O'Brien Introduces Ireland, 1969; The Suspecting Glance (with M.Cruise O'Brien), 1970; A Concise History of Ireland, 1971; States of Ireland, 1972; King Herod Advises (play), 1973; Neighbours, 1980; The Siege: The Saga of Israel and Zionism, 1986; The Great Melody, a thematic biography of Edmund Burke, 1992. *Memberships:* Irish Delegation to the UN New York City, 1956-60; Labour Member of the Dail Eirann (Irish Parliament) for Dublin North East, 1969-77; Minister of Posts and Telegraphs, 1973-77; Passion and Cunning and Godland, 1988; Reflections on Religion and Nationalism, 1988. *Address:* Whitewater, Howth Summit, Dublin, Ireland.

O'BRIEN Edna, b. 15 Dec 1936, Co Clare, Ireland. Author. m. 1954, (div 1964), 2 sons. *Education:* Pharmaceutical College of Ireland. *Publications:* The Country Girls, 1960 (film 1983); The Lonely Girl, 1962; Girls in Their Married Bliss, 1963; August is a Wicked Month, 1964; Casualties of Peace, 1966; The Love Object, 1968; A Pagan Place, 1970 (play 1971); Night, 1972; A Scandalous Woman (short stories), 1974; Mother Ireland, 1976; Johnny I Hardly Knew You (novel), 1977; Arabian Days, 1977; Mrs Reinhardt and Other Stories, 1978; The Wicked Lady (screenplay), Virginia (play), 1981; The Dazzle (children's book); Returning: A Collection of New Tales, 1982; A Christmas Treat, 1982; Home Sweet Home (play), 1984; Stories of Joan of Arc (film), 1984; A Fanatic Heart (Selected Stories), 1985; Flesh and Blood (play), 1987; Madame Bovary (play), 1987; Vanishing Ireland, 1987; Tales for the Telling (children's book), 1987; The High Road, 1989, (Fiction); Lantern Slides (short stories), 1990; Time and Tide, 1992. *Honours:* Yorkshire Post Novel Award, 1971; Kingsley Amis Award. *Address:* c/o Douglas Rae Management, 28 Charing Cross Road, London WC2 0DB, England.

O'CASEY Brenda. *See:* **HAYCRAFT Anna Margaret.**

O'CONNELL Richard (James), b. 25 Oct 1928, New York City, USA. Poet; Educator. m. Beryl Evelyn Reeves, 14 Nov 1978, 1 son, 2 daughters. *Education:* BS, Temple University, 1956; MA, Johns Hopkins University, 1957. *Publications:* Brazilian Happenings, 1966; Terrane, 1967; Epigrams from Martial, 1976; Hudson's Fourth Voyage, 1978; Irish Monastic Poems, 1984; Temple Poems, 1985; Hanging Tough, 1986; Battle Poems, 1987; Slected Epigrams, 1990; New Epigrams from Martial, 1991; The Caliban Poems, 1992; RetorWorlds, 1993; Simulations, 1993. *Contributions to:* New Yorker; Paris Review; Atlantic Monthly; National Review; Quarterly Review of Literature; Littack; Acumen; Texas Quarterly, etc. *Honours:* Fulbright Lecturer, University of Brazil, 1960; Fulbright Lecturer, University of Navarre, Pamplona, Spain, 1962-63; Contemporary Poetry Prize, 1972; Yaddo Foundation Writing Residency, 1974, 1975. *Memberships:* American PEN Club; Modern Language Association. *Address:* 1150 Hillsboro Mile, Hillsboro Beach, Florida 33062, USA.

O'CONNOR Alan, b. 6 Aug 1955, Dublin, Ireland. Teacher; Writer. *Education:* BA Mod, 1st Class, Sociology, Trinity College, Dublin, 1977; PhD, Sociology, York University, Toronto, Canada, 1987. *Appointments:* Associate Professor, Culture Studies Programme, Trent University, Peterborough, Ontario, Canada. *Publications:* Raymond Williams: Writing Culture Politics, 1989; Raymond Williams on Television (editor), 1989. *Contributions to:* Miners Radios in Bolivia: A Culture of Resistance, to Journal of Communication, 1990; The Emergence of Culture Studies in Latin America, to Critical Studies in Mass Communications, 1991. *Memberships:* International Communication Association; Union for Democratic Communication; International Association for Mass Communication Research. *Address:* Cultural Studies Programme, Trent University, Peterborough, Ontario, Canada K9J 7B8.

O'CONNOR Anthony Michael, b. 1939. Writer (Geography). *Publications:* Railways and Development in Uganda, 1965; An Economic Geography of East Africa, 1966, 1971; The Geography of Tropical African Development, 1971, 1978; Urbanization in Tropical Africa, 1981; The African City, 1983; Poverty in Africa, 1991. *Address:* 42 Crossways, Sutton, Surrey, SM2 5LB, England.

O'CONNOR Patrick, b. 8 Sept 1949, London, England. Writer; Editor. *Appointments:* Deputy Editor, Harpers and Queen, 1981-86; Contributing Editor, F M R, 1986; Editor-in-Chief, Publications, Metropolitan Opera Guild, 1987-89; Consulting Editor, The New Grove Dictionary of Opera, 1989-91. *Publications:* Josephine Baker (with B Hammond), 1988; Toulouse-Lautrec: The Nightlife of Paris, 1991; The Amazing Blonde Woman, 1991. *Contributions to:* The Times Literary Supplement; Literary Review; Daily Telegraph; Gramophone; Opera; House and Garden; Music and Letters; The Independent. *Memberships:* National Union of Journalists; PEN. *Literary Agent:* Deborah Rodgers, London, England. *Address:* c/o Rodgers, Coleridge and White, 20 Powis Mews, London W11 1JN, England.

O'CONNOR Stephen, b. 21 May 1952, New York City, New York, USA. Writer; Teacher. m. Helen Benedict, 10 May 1980, 1 son, 1 daughter. *Education:* BA, English Literature, Columbia University, 1974; MA, English, University of California, Berkeley, 1978. *Publications:* Rescue, 1989. *Contributions to:* Partisan Review; The Quarterly; Fiction International; The Massachusetts Review; Hubbub; Journal of Temporary Culture. *Honours:* Cornell Woolrich Fellowship, Columbia University, 1974; Residency, Yaddo, 1983; Residencies, Cummington Community of the Arts, 1988, 1989, 1990. *Memberships:* Authors Guild; Poets and Writers. *Literary agent:* Witherspoon and Chernoff Associates, New York, USA. *Address:* c/o Witherspoon and Chernoff Associates, 130 West 57th St 14C, New York, NY 10009, USA.

O'DANIEL Janet, (Lillian Janet), b. United States of America. Author. *Publications:* Touchstone (novel with L. Ressler), 1947; City Beyond Devil's Gate (with L. Ressler), 1950; O Genesee, 1958; The Cliff Hangers, 1961; Garrett's Crossing (children), 1969; A Part for Addie (children), 1974; As Evelyn Claire: Storm Remembered, 1984; No More Heartache, 1986;

Prescription for Love, 1987; As Amanda Clark: Flower of the Sea, 1985. *Address:* 211 Birchwood Avenue, Upper Nyack, NY 10960, USA.

O'DEA Agnes Cecilia, b. 24 Apr 1911, St John's, Newfoundland, Canada. Librarian. *Education:* BA, 1931, Diploma, Library Science, 1932, BLS, 1940, University of Toronto. *Appointments:* Assistant Librarian, Gosling Memorial Library, St John's, 1934-39; Circulation Librarian, Toronto Public Library, 1940-49; Assistant Librarian, Ontario Research Foundation, 1949-52; Assistant Librarian, 1952-55, Librarian, Department of History, 1955-60, Cataloguer, 1961-64, Head, Centre for Newfoundland Studies, 1964-76, Memorial University of Newfoundland. *Publications:* A Bibliography of Newfoundland (compiler), 1986. *Honours:* Certificate of Merit, 1976, Regional Certificate of Merit, 1988, Canadian Historical Society, 1976; Heritage Award, Newfoundland Historical Society, 1977; Merit Award, Arlandie Provinces Library Association, 1980; Tremaine Medal, Bibliographical Society of Canada, 1987; Honorary LLD, Memorial University of Newfoundland, 1987; Distinguished Graduate Medal, Faculty of Library and Information Science, University of Toronto, 1989. *Memberships:* Newfoundland Library Association; Atlantic Provinces Library Association; Canadian Federation of University Women; Beathie Chapter, IODE; Newfondland Historical Society. *Address:* 69 Le Marchant Rd, St John's, Newfoundland, Canada A1C 2G9.

O'DONNELL K M. *See:* **MALZBERG Barry Norman.**

O'DONNELL Kevin Jr, b. 1950, United States of America. Author. *Appointments:* Assistant Lecturer in English, Hong Kong Baptist College, 1972-73; American English Language Institute, Taipei, 1973-74; Managing Editor, 1979-81, Publisher, 1983-83, Empire, New Haven, Conneticut. *Publications:* Bander Snatch, 1979; Mayflies, 1979; Caverns, 1981; Reefs, 1981; War of Omission, 1982; Lava, 1982; ORA:CLE, 1984; The Electronic Money Book (non-fiction with the Haven Group), 1984; Cliffs, 1986.

O'DONNELL Lillian, b. 15 Mar 1920, Trieste, Italy. Writer. m. James Leonard O'Donnell, 13 Feb 1954. *Education:* American Academy of Dramatic Arts. *Publications:* Norah Mulcahaney Series; The Phone Calls, 1972; Dial 577 - R.A.P.E.; A Good Night To Kill, No Business Being a Cop (also TV Movie - Prime Target); A Wreath for the Bride; Lady Killer, Casual Affairs; The Other Side of the Door; The Baby Merchants; Contibuted several stories to magazines. *Literary Agent:* Roberta Kent, STE Representation.

O'DONNELL Michael, b. 20 Oct 1928. Author; Broadcaster. m. Catherine Dorrington Ward, 1953, 1 son, 2 daughters. *Education:* MB.BChir., St Thomas's Hospital Medical School, London. *Appointments:* Editor, Cambridge Writing, 1948; Scriptwriter, BBC Radio 1949-52; General Medical Practitioner, 1954-64; Editor, World Medicine, 1966-82; Scientific Adviser: O Lucky Man, 1972; Inside Medicine, 1974; Don't Ask Me, 1977; Don't Just Sit There, 1979-80; Where There's Life, 1981-83. *Publications:* (TV Plays): Suggestion of Sabotage, 1963; Dangerous Reunion, 1964; Resolution, 1964; (TV Documentaries): You'll Never Believe It, 1962; Cross Your Heart and Hope to Live, 1975; The Presidential Race, 1976; From Europe to the Coast, 1976; Chasing the Dagon, 1979; Second Opinion, 1980; Judgement on Las Vegas, 1981; Is Your Brain Really Necessary, 1982; Plague of Hearts, 1983; Medical Express, 1984; Can You Avoid Cancer, 1984; O'Donnell Investigates...booze, 1985; O'Donnell Investigates..food, 1985; O'Donnell Investigates...the food business, 1986; Health, Wealth and Happiness, 1989; What is this thing Called Health, 1990; Radio: Serious Professional Misconduct, 1992. *Contributor to:* Stop the Week (BBC), 1976-; Chairman, My Word (BBC), 1983; (Books) Cambridge Anthology, 1952; The Europe We Want, 1971; My Medical School, 1978; The Devil's Prison, 1982; Doctor! Doctor! an Insider's Guide to the

Games Doctors Play, 1986; The Long Walk Home, 1988; Dr. Michael O'Donnell's Executive Health Guide, 1988. *Contributions to:* Punch; New Scientist; Vogue; The Times; Sunday Times; Daily Telegraph; Daily Mail; The Listener. *Literary Agent:* A P Watt. *Address:* Handon Cottage, Markwick Lane, Loxhill, Godalming, Surrey GU8 4BD, England.

O'DONNELL Patricia Eileen, b. 14 July 1952, Waterloo, Iowa, USA. College Teacher; Writer. m. 22 July 1989, 1 son, 2 daughters. *Education:* BA, University of Northern Iowa, 1978; MA, University of Northern Iowa, 1981; MFA, University of Massachusetts, Amherst, 1986. *Appointments:* Assistant Professor, Southern Connecticut State University, 1986-87; Assistant Professor, Associate Professor, English, University of Maine, Farmington, 1987-. *Contributions to:* New Yorker; North American Review; Agni Review; Short Story; Epiphany; The Eloquent Edge; 4-Minute Fiction; Others. *Memberships:* Poets and Writers; Maine Writers and Publishers Association. *Address:* PO Box 438, Wilton, ME 04294, USA.

O'DONNELL Peter, b. 1920. Author. *Appointments:* Writer of Strip Cartoons: Garth, 1953-66, Tug Transom, 1954-66, Romeo Brown, 1956-62, Modesty Blaise, 1963-. *Publications:* Modesty Blaise, 1965; Sabre-Tooth, 1966; I, Lucifer, 1967; A Taste for Death, 1969; The Impossible Virgin, 1971; Pieces of Modesty (short stories), 1972; The Silver Mistress, 1973; Murder Most Logical (play), 1974; Last Day in Limbo, 1976; Dragon's Claw, 1978; The Xanadu Talisman, 1981; The Night of Morningstar, 1982; Dead Man's Handle, 1985; (as Madeleine Brent): Tregaron's Daughter, 1971; Moonraker's Bride, 1973; Kirkby's Changeling, 1975; Merlin's Keep, 1977; The Capricorn Stone, 1979; The Long Masquerade, 1981; A Heritage of Shadows, 1983; Stormswift, 1984; Golden Urchin, 1986. *Address:* 49 Sussex Square, Brighton, BN2 1GE, England.

O'DONOVAN Joan Mary, b. 31 Dec 1914, Mansfield, England. *Appointment:* General Adviser for Education, Oxfordshire, retired 1977. *Publications:* Dangerous Worlds, 1958; The Visited, 1959; Shadows on the Wall, 1960; The Middle Tree, 1961; The Niceties of Life, 1964; She, Alas, 1965; Little Brown Jesus, 1970; Argument with an East Wind, 1986. *Contributions to:* Times Educational Supplement; The Guardian; Punch; Vogue; Harpers and Queen. *Memberships:* Society of Authors; International PEN. *Literary Agent:* Rivers Scott (Scott-Ferris Associates) *Address:* 98 (B) Banbury Road, Oxford OX2 6JT, England.

O'FAOLAIN Julia, b. 6 June 1932, London, England. Writer. m. Lauro Rene Martines, 14 Dec 1957, 1 son. *Education:* BA, 1952, MA, 1953, University College, Dublin; Scholarship, Italian Government for Study at Rome University, 1952-53; Travelling Studentship, National University of Ireland, 1953-55. *Publications:* No Country for Young Men, 1980; Women in the Wall, 1975; The Obedient Wife, 1982; The Irish Signorina, 1984; Daughters of Passion, 1982; Man in the Cellar, 1974; We Might See Sights! and Other Stories, 1968; Godded and Codded, 1970; Editor, Not in God's Image: Women in History from the Greeks to the Victorians, with Lauro Martines, 1973; Novel, The Judas Cloth, 1992. *Contributions to:* numerous magazines & newspapers. *Membership:* Society of Authors. *Literary Agent:* Deborah Rogers Ltd. *Address:* c/o Rogers, Coleridge & White Ltd., Literary Agency, 20 Powis Mews, London W11 1JN, England.

O'FARRELL Patrick James, b. 17 Sept 1933, Greymouth, New Zealand. University Professor of History. m. Deirdre Genevieve MacShane, 29 Dec 1956. 3 sons, 2 daughters. *Education:* MA, New Zealand, 1956; PhD, Australia National University, 1961. *Publications:* Vanished Kingdoms Irish in Australia and New Zealand, 1990; The Irish in Australia, 1986; Letters From Irish Australia, 1984; The Catholic Church and Community. An Australian History, 1985; England and Ireland Since 1800, 1975; Ireland's English Question,

1971; The Catholic Church in Australia, A Short History, 1968; Documents in Australian Catholic History, 2 Volumes, 1969; Harry Holland, Militant Socialist, 1969. *Contributions to:* Historical, literary and religious journals. *Honour:* NSW Premiers Literary Award, 1987. *Memberships:* Australian Society of Authors; Fellow, Australian Academy of the Humanities. *Address:* School of History, University of New South Wales, P O Box 1, Kensington, NSW 2033, Australia.

O'FLAHERTY Patrick Augustine, b. 6 Oct 1939, Long Beach, Newfoundland, Canada. Professor; Writer. 3 sons. *Education:* BA (Hons); MA; PhD. *Publications:* The Rock Observed, 1979; Part of the Main: An Illustrated History of Newfoundland and Labrador (with Peter Neary), 1983; Summer of the Greater Yellowlegs, 1987; Priest of God, 1989; A Small Place in the Sun; By Great Waters (with Peter Neary). *Contributions to:* Weekend Magazine; Saturday Night; Canadian Forum; Queen's Quarterly; Globe and Mail; Ottawa Citizen; Others. *Membership:* The Writers Union of Canada. *Address:* Box 2676, St John's, Newfoundland, Canada A1C 6K1.

O'GORMAN Edward Charles. *See:* **O'GORMAN Ned.**

O'GORMAN Ned, (Edward Charles O'Gorman), b. 1929, United States of America. Children's Fiction Writer, Poet. *Appointments include:* Editor, Jubilee Magazine, New York City, 1962-65; Headmaster, The Children's Storefront School, 1966-. *Publications:* The Night of the Hammer: Poems, 1959; Adam Before His Mirror, 1961; The Buzzard and the Peacock, 1964; The Harvesters' Vase, 1969; Prophetic Voices: Essays and Words in Revolution, 1969; The Storefront: A Community of Children on Madison Avenue and 129th Street, 1970; The Blue Butterfly, 1971; The Wilderness and the Laurel Tree: A Guide to Parents and Teachers on the Observation of Children, 1972; The Flag the Hawk Flies, 1972; The Children Are Dying, 1978; Perfected Crystal, Terrible Steel: An Unconventional Source Book of Spiritual Readings in Prose and Poetry, 1981; How to Put Out a Fire, 1984. *Honours:* 2 Guggenheim Fellowships, 1954 & 1962; Lamont Poetry Award, 1960. *Address:* 2 Lincoln Square, New York, NY 10023, USA.

O'GRADY Desmond James Bernard, b. 27 Aug 1935, Limerick City, Ireland. Poet. 1 son, 2 daughters, 2 step-sons. *Education:* MA, 1964; PhD, 1982, Harvard University, USA. *Publications include:* Chords and Orchestrations, 1956; Reilly, 1961; Separazioni, 1965; The Dying Gaul, 1968; Separations, 1973; Sing Me Creation, 1977; Alexandrian Notebook, 1989; The Seven Arab Odes, 1990; Ten Modern Arab Poets, 1991. *Contributions to:* Batteghe Oscure; The Transatlantic Review; The Atlantic Monthly; Poetry Ireland; Translation, and others. *Memberships:* The Irish Aosdana; Irish Academy of Letters; Amnesty International. *Address:* Kinsele, Co. Cork, Ireland.

O'GRADY Rohan. *See:* **SKINNER June O'Grady.**

O'GRADY Tom, b. 26 Aug 1943. Teacher; Poet; Vintner. *Education:* BA, University of Baltimore, 1966; MA, Johns Hopkins University, 1967; Advanced Studies of English and American Literature, University of Delaware, 1972-74. *Appointments:* Lecturer in English, Johns Hopkins University, 1966-67; Catonsville College, 1969-71; University of Delaware, 1972-74; Hampden-Sydney College 1974-76; Adjunct Professor, English, Poet-in-Residence, Hampden-Sydney College, 1976-. *Publications:* Unicorn Evils (pamphlet), 1973; Establishing a Vinyard, (sonnet sequence), 1977; Photographs, 1980; The Farmville Elegies, 1981; Co-Founder, Editor, The Hampden-Sydney Poetry Review; Translation of, Jaroslav Siefert (1984 Nobel Laureate in Literature); The Casting of Bells; Mozart in Prague; Eight Days; In The Room of The Just Born (a collection of poems), 1989. *Contributions to:* Newsletters; Dryad; Enoch; Scene; Pyx; Nimrod; New Laurel Review.

Honours include: Leache Prize for Poetry; Chrysler Museum, Arts Poetry Residency, 1976-77; Impact Book Award, 1980; Virginia Prize for Poetry, 1989. *Memberships:* Co-Ordinator, Council of Literary Magazine, COSMEP South. *Address:* PO Box 126, Hampden-Sydney, VA 23943, USA.

O'HEHIR Diana, b. 23 May 1922, USA. Writer; Professor of English. (div), 2 sons. *Education:* MA, Aesthetics of Literature 1957, PhD, Humanities 1970, Johns Hopkins University, Baltimore. *Publications:* I Wish This War Were Over (a novel), 1984. Poetry: Summoned, 1976; The Power to Change Geography, 1979; Home Free, 1988; The Bride Who Ran Away (a novel), 1988. *Honours:* Devins Award for Poetry, 1974; Helen Bullis Poetry Award, 1977; Di Castagnola Award in Poetry, 1981; Runner-up, Pulitzer Prize in Fiction, 1984; Guggenheim Award in Fiction, 1984; NEH Award in Fiction, 1984. *Memberships:* Poetry Society of America; Modern Language Association; Authors Guild; Poets and Writers. *Literary Agent:* Ellen Levine. *Address:* English Department, Mills College, Oakland, CA 94613, USA.

O'HIGGINS Paul, b. 5 Oct 1927. Emeritus University Professor of Law; Vice-Master, Christ's College, Cambridge. m. Rachel Elizabeth Bush, 1952, 1 son, 3 daughters. *Education:* MA, 1960, LLD, 1987, Trinity College Dublin; MA, 1961, PhD, 1961, LLD, 1988, Cambridge University; Barrister of the Kings Inn, Dublin, 1957, of Lincoln's Inn, 1959. *Appointments:* Editorial Committee, Industrial Law Journal, 1972-; Advisory Editorial Committee, Managerial Law, 1975-; Joint General Editor, Mansell Series of Studies in Labour and Social Law, 1978-; Ed. Adv. Board, Northern Ireland Legal Quarterly, 1972-; Trustee, Varsity Publications, 1975-. *Publications:* Censorship in Britain, 1972; Workers' Rights, 1976; Biobliographyh of Irish Trials, 1986; Bibliography of the Literature on British and Irish Social Security Law, 1986; Bioliography of Periodical Literature on Irish Law, 1966, 1975, 1983. *Contributions to:* British Yearbook of International Law; Criminal Law Review; Industrial Law Journal. *Honours:* Gilbert Murray Prize, 1968; Joseph L Andrews Bibliographical Award of American Association of Law Libraries, 1987. *Memberships:* Defence of Literature and Arts Society and Committee, 1979-82; Royal Irish Academy; Governor, British Institute of Human Rights; Irish Society for Labour Law, Chairman, 1985-87; Executive Committee International Society for Labour Law & Social Security, 1965-; Bureau European Institute of Social Security, 1972-; Vice-President Institute of Employment Rights, 1989-. *Address:* Christ's College, Cambridge CB2 3BU, England.

O'LEARY Liam, b. 25 Sept 1910, Youghal, County Cork, Eire. Film Historian. *Education:* University College, Dublin. *Appointments:* Editorial Staff, Ireland Today, 1936-37. *Publications:* Invitation to the Film, 1945; The Silent Cinema, 1965; Rex Ingram, Master of the Silent Cinema, 1980; International Dictionary of Films and Filmmakers, 1985; Cinema Ireland: A History, in progress. *Contributions to:* Ireland Today, Film Critic; Irish Times; Films and Filming; Kosmorama; The Leader; Irish Press; Envoy; The Bell; film scripts, 1948; gaelic translations of Shakespeare Masterlinck, 1946. *Honours:* Medal for services in film section, Brussells International Film Fair, 1958; Medal for contribution to Irish Film Industry, National Film Studios of Ireland. *Address:* The Garden Flat, 2 Otranto Place, Sandycove, Co. Dublin, Ireland.

O'MORRISON Kevin, b. St Louis, Missouri. Playwright; Novelist; Lyricist; Director; Actor. m. Linda Soma, 30 Apr 1966. *Education:* Private tutoring to BA equivalent in European Philosophy. *Appointments include:* Playwright in Residence, University of Minnesota, 1966, Trinity University, San Antonio, Texas, 1974, Dallas Theatre Center, 1974, University of Montana, 1977. Artist in Residence, KCRCHE, 1975; Actor, The Watergate Coverup Trial, TV Documentary Film, 1975; Concealed Enemies, TV Documentary Film, 1986; Funny Farm, Theatrical Film, 1987; Lonesome

Dove, TV Mini-Series, 1988; Law & Order, TV Drama Series, 1990, 1991; Sleepless In Seattle, Theatrical Film, 1992. Adjunct Professor, Theatre, University of missouri, Kansas City, 1976; Director, The Morgan Yeard, Missouri Repertory Theatre, 1976. *Publications include:* TV Plays: The House of Paper, 1959; And Not a Word More, 1960; A Sign for Autumn, 1962; Radio play: Ladyhouse Blues, (adaptation of Stage Play, in English, German, Norweigian), 1981; Stage Plays: The Long War, 1967; The Morgan Yard, 1971; The Realist, 1974; A Report to the Stockholders, 1975; Ladyhouse Blues, 1976; Requiem, Dark Ages, 1979-80; The old Missouri Jazz, musical (book & lyrics), 1985; The Mutilators, 1988; Songs In A Strange Land, 1989, 50 monologues for Men & Women, 1989, The Nightgatherers, (on hold); Screenplays: The Cosmic Connection (rewrite of Next Time, Dynamite & Honey), 1992; Ladyhouse Blues, 1992 (adaption of stage plays). Novels: The Deadfile, 1992; The Medea Principle (in progress). Lyrics for Songs: The Dark Wind of missouri; I Need Someone, 1992. *Honours:* Creative Artists Public Service Playwright Fellowship, 1975; NEA Playwright Fellowship, 1981. *Memberships:* Dramatists' Guild of America, West; Authors League of America; PEN; ASCAP; Screen Actors Guild; American Federation of Radio & TV Artists; Actors Equity Association; Amnesty International. *Address:* 10120 240th Place SW, Edmonds, Washington 98020, USA.

O'NEIL Anil Ranjan. *See:* **BISWAS Anil Ranjan.**

O'NEILL Michael Stephen Charles, b. 2 Sept 1953, Aldershot, England. University Lecturer. m. Rosemary Ann McKendrick, 1977, 1 son, 1 daughter. *Education:* Exeter College, Oxford, 1972-75; BA Hons Class I, English, 1975; MA (Oxon), 1981; DPhil, Oxford University, 1981. *Appointments:* Co-Founder, Editor, Poetry Durham, 1982-. *Publications:* The Human Mind's Imaginings: Conflict and Achievement in Shelley's Poetry, 1989; Percy Bysshe Shelley: A Literary Life, 1989; The Stripped Bed, poems, 1990; Auden, MacNeice, Spender: The Thirties Poetry (with Gareth Reeves), 1992. *Honours:* Eric Gregory Award, 1983; Cholmondeley Award, 1990. *Address:* School of English, University of Durham, Durham DH1 3JT, England.

O'NEILL Patrick Geoffrey, b. 1924. Writer. *Publications:* A Guide to No, 1953; Early No Drama, 1958; An Introduction to Written Japanese, 1963; Respect Language in Modern Japanese, 1966; Japanese Kana Workbook, 1967; A Programmed Introduction to Literary Style Japanese, 1968; Japanese Names, 1972; Essential Kanji: 2000 Japanese Characters, 1973; Tradition and Modern Japan (ed), 1982; A Reader of Handwritten Japanese, 1984; Japan on Stage (tr), 1990. *Address:* School of Oriental and African Studies, University of London, Thornaugh Street, London, WC1E 7HP, England.

O'NEILL Paul, b. 26 Oct 1928, St John's Newfoundland, Canada. Author. *Education:* National Academy of Theatre Arts, NY, USA. *Publications:* Spindrift & Morning Light, 1968; The Oldest City, 1975; Seaport Legacy, 1976; Legends of a Lost Tribe, 1976; A Sound of Seagulls, 1984; Upon this Rock, 1984. Also: The City in Your Pocket, 1974; The Seat Imperial, 1983; Breakers, 1982; Radio and stage plays; TV and film scripts. *Contributions to:* Numerous magazines and journals, poetry publications, newspapers, and reviews. *Honours include:* Regional History Prize, Canadian Historical Association; Literary Heritage Award, Newfoundland Hstorical Society; Robert Weaver Award, National Radio Producers Association of Canada, 1986; Honorary Doctor of Laws, Memorial University of Newfoundland, 1988; Order of Canada, 1990; Newfoundland and Labrador Arts Hall of Honour, 1991; Canaada Commemorative Medal, 1992. *Memberships:* Former VP, Canadian Authors Association; Former President, Newfoundland Writers Guild; Executive, Atlantic Region Representative, Writers Union of Canada; Canadian Radio Producers Association; Chairman, Newfoundland and Labrador Arts Cuncil,

1988-89. *Address:* 115 Rennies Mill Road, St John's, Newfoundland, Canada A1B 2P2.

O'ROURKE Andrew Patrick, b. 26 Oct 1933, Plainfield, New Jersey, USA. County Executive, Westchester County, New York. Separated, 1988, 1 son, 2 daughters. *Education:* BA, Fordham College, 1954; JD, Fordham Law School, 1962; LLM, New York University Graduate Law School, 1965. *Publications:* Red Banner Mutiny, 1986; Hawkwood, 1989. *Contributions to:* Bar journals and digests; The Proceedings of the Naval Institute; Journal of Ancient and Medieval Studies. *Honours:* Honorary DHL, Mercy College, 1984; Honorary LLD, Manhattanville College, 1986; Honorary JD, Pace University, 1988. *Literary Agent:* Jane Dystel, Acton and Dystel Inc, 928 Broadway, New York City, NY 10010, USA. *Address:* 148 Martine Avenue, White Plains, NY 10601, USA.

O'TOOLE James, b. 15 Apr 1945, San Francisco, California, USA. Professor of Management; Writer. m. Marilyn Louise Burrill, 17 June 1967, 2 children. *Education:* BA, magna cum laude, University of Southern California, 1966; D Phil Oxford University, 1970. *Appointments:* Correspondent, Time-Life News Service, Los Angeles, California and Nairobi, Kenya, 1967-68; Management Consultant, McKinsey and Co, San Francisco, California, 1969-70; Special Assistant to Secretary 1970-73; Chairman of Secretary's Committee on Work in America, 1971-72, US Department of Health, Education and Welfare, Washington DC; Assistant Professor 1973-77, Associate Professor 1977-79, Professor of Management, 1980-, University Associate's Chair of Management, 1982-, Director of Twenty Year Forecast Project for Center for Futures Research, 1973-81, Co-ordinator of general field investigations for President's Commission on Campus Unrest, 1970, University of Southern California, Los Angeles; Director of Aspen Institute Project on Education, Work and the Quality of Life, 1973-74; Executive Director of Town Hall of California Study of Los Angeles Public Pension Plans, 1978-79; Host of Why in the World, a television series broadcast by Public Broadcasting System, 1981, 1983; Speaker for US Information Agency in Italy, and West Germany, 1976; Executive Director, The Leadership Institute, 1991-. *Publications:* Watts and Woodstock, Identity and Culture in the United States and South Africa, 1973; Work in America: Report of a Special Task Force to the Secretary of Health, Education and Welfare, 1973; (ed)Work and the Quality of Life, 1974; Energy and Social Change, 1976; Work, Learning and the American Future, 1977; (with others) Tenure, 1979; Making America Work, 1981; (ed) Working: Changes and Choices, 1981; Vanguard Management: Redesigning the Corporate Future, 1985; The Executive's Compass: Business And The Good Society, 1993. *Contributions to:* Various journals. *Honours include:* George and Cynthia Mitchell Prize 1979 for a paper on sustained growth; Vanguard Management was named one of the ten best business and economics books of 1985 by Business Week. *Memberships:* American Association for higher Education, Board of Directors 1977-79; Phi Beta Kappa. *Address:* 19912 Pacific Coast Highway, Malibu, CA 90265, USA.

OAKES James, b. 1953, USA. Professor of History. *Publications:* The Ruling Race: A History of American Slaveholders, 1982; Slavery and Freedom: An Interpretation of the Old South, 1990. *Address:* Department of History, Northwestern University, Evanston, IL 60208, USA.

OAKES John Bertram, b. 23 Apr 1913, Elkins Park, USA. Journalist. m. Margery C. Hartman, 1945, 1 son, 3 daughters. *Education:* Princeton University; Queen's College, Oxford; AM; LL.D. *Appointments:* Reporter, Trenton Times, 1936-37; Political Reporter, Washington Post, 1937-41; served US Army, 1941-46; Editor, Review of the Week, Sunday New York Times, 1946-49; Editorial Board 1949-61, Editorial Page Editor 1961-76, Senior Editor 1977-78, Contributing Columnist, 1977-90. *Publications:* The Edge of Freedom, 1961.

Contributions to: Essays Today, 1955; Foundations of Freedom, 1958; Tomorrow's American, 1977; On the Vineyard, 1980. *Honours:* Carnegie Foundation Travel Award, 1959; Columbia Catherwood Award, 1961; George Polk Memorial Award, 1966; Silurian Society Award, 1969; Garden Club of America Award, 1969; Woodrow Wilson Award, Princeton University, 1970; John Muir Award, Sierra Club, 1974; Audubon Medal, National Audubon Society, 1976; Hon. MBE; Croix de Guerre, etc. *Address:* 1120 Fifth Avenue, New York, NY 10128, USA.

OAKES Philip, b. 1928, United Kingdom. Author. *Appointments:* Scriptwriter for Granada TV and BBC, London, 1958-62; Film Critic: The Sunday Telegraph, London, 1963-65; Assistant Editor, Magazine, 1965-67; Arts Columnist, 1969-80, Sunday Times, London. *Publications:* Unlucky Jonah: Twenty Poems, 1954; The Punch and Judy Man (with Tony Hancock), screenplay, 1962; Exactly What We Want, novel, 1962; In the Affirmative, 1968; The God Botherers, US Edition Miracles: Genuine Cases Contact Box 340, novel, 1969; Married/Singular, 1973; Experiment at Proto, novel, 1973; Tony Hancock: A Biography, 1975; The Entertainers (editor), 1975; A Cast of Thousands, novel, 1976; The Film Addict's Archive, 1977; From Middle England, memoirs, 1980; Dwellers All in Time and Space, memoirs, 1982; Selected Poems, 1982; At the Jazz Band Ball: A Memory of the 1950's, 1983. *Literary Agent:* Elaine Greene Ltd, England. *Address:* c/o Elaine Greene Ltd, 37 Goldhawk Road, London W12 8QQ, England.

OAKLEY Ann, b. 1944, United Kingdom. Sociologist; Director, Research Unit. *Publications:* Sex, Gender and Society, 1972; Housewife, 1974; The Sociology of Housework, 1974; The Rights and Wrongs of Women (edited with J Mitchell), 1976; Becoming a Mother, 1979; Women Confined, 1980; Subject Women, 1981; Miscarriage (with A McPherson and H Roberts), 1984; Taking It Like a Woman, 1984; The Captured Womb, 1984; What Is Feminism (edited with J Mitchell), 1986; Telling The Truth About Jerusalem, 1986; The Men's Room, 1989; Matilda's Mistake, 1990; The Secret Lives of Eleanor Jenhuison, 1992; Social Support and Netherland, 1992. *Literary Agent:* Tessa Sayle Agency, 11 Jubilee Place, London SW3, England. *Address:* c/o Curtis Brown Ltd, 162-168 Regent Street, London W1R 5TB, England.

OAKLEY Graham, b. 1929, United Kingdom. Children's Fiction Writer. *Appointments:* Scenic Artist, theatres and Royal Opera House, 2 years. Designer, BBC TV, 1962-77. *Publications:* The Church Mouse, 1972; The Church Cat Abroad, 1973; The Church Mice series, 1974-; Magical Changes, 1979; Hetty and Harriet, 1981; Henry's Quest, 1986. *Address:* c/o Macmillan Children's Books, 4 Little Essex Street, London WC2R 3LF, England.

OANDASAN William Cortes, b. 17 Jan 1947, Santa Rosa, California, USA. Poet; Educator. m. 28 Oct 1973, 2 daughters. *Education:* BA, 1974; MA, 1981; MFA, 1984; Instructor Credential, 1989. *Appointments:* Editor, A Publications, 1976-; Senior Editor, American Indian Culture and Research Journal, University of California, Los Angeles, 1981-86; Instructor, English Department, University of Orleans, Louisiana State University, 1988-90. *Publications:* Moving Inland, 1983; Round Valley Songs, 1984; Summer Night, 1989; The Way to Rainy Mountain: Internal and External Structures, in Approaches to Teaching World Literature, 1988; Poetry in Harper's Anthology of 20th Century Native American Poetry, 1988. *Contributions to:* Colorado Review; Southern California Anthology; California Courier; American Indian Culture and Research Journal. *Honours:* Publishing Grant, National Endowment for the Arts, 1977; American Book Award, 1985; Summer Scholar Award for Writers, 1989; Research Council Grant, 1989. *Memberships:* Associated Writers Program; Executive Director, A Writers Circle; Modern Language Association; Society for the Study of Multi-Ethnic Literatures; Association for the Study of American Indian Literatures; National Association on Ethnic Studies; Philological Society of the Pacific Coast. *Literary Agent:* Florence Feiler. *Address:* 3832 West Avenue 43, No 13, Los Angeles, CA 90041, USA.

OATES Stephen B(aery), b. 1936, United States of America. Writer (History). *Publications:* Confederate Cavalry West of the River, 1961; Rip Ford's Texas, 1963; The Republic of Texas, 1968; Visions of Glory: Texans on the Southwestern Frontier, 1970; To Purge This Land with Blood: A Biography of John Brown, 1970; Portrait of America: From the Cliff Dwellers to the End of Reconstruction, 1973; Portrait of America: From Reconstruction to the Present, 1973; The Fires of Jubilee: Nat Turner's Fierce Rebellion, 1975; With Malice Toward None: The Life of Abraham Lincoln, 1977; Our Fiery Trial: Abraham Lincoln, John Brown and the Civil War Era, 1979; Let the Trumpet Sound: The Life of Martin Luther King, Jr, 1982; Abraham Lincoln: The Man Behind the Myths, 1984; Biography as High Adventure, 1986; William Faulkner, The Man and the Artist, 1987. *Contributions to:* New York Times; American Heritage; The New Republic; The Nation; Timeline. *Honours:* Christopher Award, 1977, 1982; Robert F Kennedy Memorial Book Award, 1983; Nevins-Freeman Award for Life-time Achievement, 1993. *Memberships:* Member, Author's Guild, USA; Elected Member of the Society of American Historians; The American Antiquarian Society; Gerard McCauley Agency. *Address:* 10 Bride Path, Amherst, MA 01002, USA.

OBARSKI Marek, b. 2 July 1947, Poznan, Poland. Novelist; Poet; Critic. m. Aleksandra Zaworska, 27 Mar 1982, 2 sons, 1 daughter. *Appointments:* Director, The Flowering Grass Theatre, 1974-79; Director - Literary Department, Nurt (literary magazine), 1985-; Critic, Art for Child (magazine), 1989-. *Publications:* The Sunken Pipes, 1969; The Countries of Wolves, 1971; The Lighting of Flight, 1978; The Body of Cloud, 1983; The Dancing Stoat, 1985; The Flower of Embryo, 1987; The Straw Giant, 1987; The Forest Altar, 1989; The Face of Demon, forthcoming. *Contributions to:* Various journals. *Honours:* Medal of Young Art, 1984; Stanislaw Pietak Award, 1985. *Memberships:* The Ecologic Association of Creators; Union of Polish Letters, 1979-83; Union Des Gens De Lettres Polonais. *Address:* O W1. Lokietka 13 F m 58, 61-616 Poznan, Poland.

OBERDORF Charles (Donnell), b. 25 Feb 1941, Sunbury, Pennsylvania, USA. Freelance journalist. m. Mechtild Hoppenrath, 25 Oct 1977, 1 daughter. *Education:* BFA, Carnegie Institute of Technology (now Carnegie-Mellon University), 1963. *Appointments:* Story Editor, WCAU-TV, Philadelphia, Pennsylvania, 1963-66; Writer/Interviewer, Canadian Broadcasting Corporation, Toronto, 1966-69; Editor, Weekend Magazine, Toronto, 1977-78; Editor in magazine division, Maclean Hunter, Toronto, 1983-1992; Producer and consultant on multi-media presentations to the National Film Board of Canada and private production houses; Freelance journalist in all media 1968-. *Publications:* (Associate editor) Between Friends/Entre Amis, 1976; (With Mechtild Hoppenrath and others) Fodor's Toronto, 1984; (With Hoppenrath) First-Class Canada, 1987. *Contributions to:* Contributor of articles and reviews, some under pseudonym Esmond Donnelly, to various periodicals. *Honours:* Canadian National Magazine Award, 1979, 1980, 1984, 1992; La Pluma de Plata from the Mexican Government, 1977 and 1984 for magazine articles about Mexico; Howell Thomas Award, 1988. *Memberships:* Society of American Travel Writers; Association of Canadian Television and Radio Artists; Canadian Society of Magazine Editors. *Address:* 93 Duplex Avenue, Toronto, Canada, M5P 2A6.

OBSTFELD Raymond, (Pike Bishop, Jason Frost, Don Pendleton, Carl Stevens), b. 22 Jan 1952, Williamsport, Pennsylvania, USA. Writer; Teacher. *Education:* BA, Johnston College, University of Redlands, 1972; MA, University of California, Davis, 1976. *Appointments:* Lecturer, Assistant Professor, 1976-, English, Orange Coast College. *Publications:*

(Novels) The Whipping Boy, 1988; Brainchild, 1987; Redtooth, 1987; Masked Dog, 1986; The Remington Factor, 1985; Dead Bolt, 1982; Dead Heat, 1981; Dead-End Option, 1980; The Golden Fleece, 1979; (As Jason Frost): Invasion USA, 1985; Warlord No.5: Terminal Island, 1985; Warlord No.4: Prisonland, 1985; Warlord No.3: Badlands, 1984; Warlord No.2: Cutthroat, 1984; Warlord, 1983; (As Don Pendleton): The Fire Eaters, 1986; Savannah Swingsaw, 1985; Flesh Wounds, 1983; Bloodsport, 1982; (As Pike Bishop): Judgement at Poisoned Well, 1983; Diamondback, 1983; (As Carl Stevens): Ride of the Razorback, 1984; The Centaur Conspiracy, 1983; Poetry Book, The Cat With Half a Face, 1978; poetry in various anthologies; Plays; Screenplays. *Contributions to:* numerous journals and magazines. *Honour:* Nominee, Edgar Allen Poe Award for Dead Heat, 1981. *Memberships:* Mystery Writers of America. *Address:* 190 Greenmoor, Irvine, CA 92714, USA.

ODA Beth Brown, b. 7 Mar 1953, Cleveland, Ohio, USA. Writer. m. 2 sons, 1 daughter. *Education:* AB, Bryn Mawr College; MFA, Goddard College; EdD. Temple University; PhD, University of Pennsylvania. *Appointments include:* Professor of English, Nassau State College, New York City, 1982. *Publications:* Poetry: Lightyears: 1973-1976, 1982; Blue Cyclone, 1982; Kaze, 1985; Satin Tunnels, 1988; Boca Raton, 1986; Riccardo, 1986. Also: Book of Hours, translation of Rainer Maria Rilke; Modern German Poetry, translation; Sun Stone, translation of Octavio Paz. *Contributions to:* Pennsylvania Review; Philadelphia Inquirer; Callaloo; Journal of Black Studies. *Honours:* CBS Writing fellowships, 1981-82; Publication Fellowship, Pennsylvania Council on the Arts; Goddard College Scholarship, 1977; Bread Loaf Writers Conference Scholarship, 1977. *Memberships:* Poetry Society of America; Academy of American Poets; Poets & Writers. *Literary Agent:* Riccardo Muti, conductor, Philadelphia Orchestra. *Address:* 4238 Chestnut Street No.4, Philadelphia, PA 19104, USA.

ODAGA Asenath (Bole), b. 1938 Kenyan, Writer of Novels/Short stories, Children's fiction, Plays/Screenplays, Mythology/Folklore. Freelance writer 1982-. *Appointments:* Tutor, Church Missionary Society Teacher Training College, Ngiya, 1957-58; Teacher, Butere Girls School, 1959-60; Headmistress, Nyakach Girls School 1961-63; Assistant Secretary, Kenya Dairy Board, Nairobi, 1965-67; Secretary, Kenya Library Services, Nairobi, 1968; Advertising Assistant, East African Standard newspaper and Kerr Downey and Selby Safaris, both Nairobi, 1969-70; Assistant Director, Curriculum Development Programme, Christian Churches Educational Association, Nairobi, 1974-75; Research fellow, Institute of African Studies, University of Nairobi, 1976-81. *Publications include:* Kip Goes to the City (children's fiction) 1977; Poko Nyar Mugumba (Poko Mugumba's Daughter, children's folktale) 1978; (ed with David Kirui and David Crippen) God, Myself and Others (pastoral handbook) 1976; Thu Tinda: Stories from Kenya (folktales) 1980; The Two Friends (folktales) 1981; Miaha (in Luo: The Bride, play) 1981; Simbi Nyaima (The Sunken Village, play) 1982; Oral Literature: A School Certificate Course (school text book non-fiction) 1982; Ange ok Tel (Regret Never Comes First; children's fiction), 1982; Kenyan Folk Tales, 1982; Sigendini gi Timbe Luo Moko (Stories and Some Customs of the Luo) 1982; A Reed on the Roof, Block Ten, With Other Stories, fiction, 1982; Mouth and Pen: Literature for Children and Young People in Kenya, Research on Childrens Lit in Kenya 1983; My Home (reader) 1983; The Shade Changes (fiction) 1984; Yesterday's Today: The Story of Oral Literature, 1984; The Storm (fiction) 1986; Nyamgondho the Son of Ombare and Other Luo Stories, 1986; Between the Years (fiction) 1987; A Bridge in Time (fiction), 1987; Munde and his Friends (children's fiction), 1987; Munde goes to the Market, (children's fiction), 1987; The Rag Ball, (children fiction), 1987; The Silver Cup (children fiction), 1988; The Storm (adolescent's fiction), 1988; Rianan, (children's fiction), 1990; A Night on A Tree (Fiction) 1991; Luo Sayings, 1992. *Address:* P O Box 1743, Kisumu, Kenya, Africa.

ODELL Peter Randon, b. 1930. Writer (Earth Sciences, Economics, Geography). *Publications:* An Economic Geography of Oil, 1963; Oil: The New Commanding Height, 1966; Natural Gas in Western Europe: A Case Study in the Economic Geography of Energy Resources, 1969; Oil and World Power: A Geographical Interpretation, 1970, 8th Edition, 1986; Economics and Societies in Latin America: A Geographical Interpretation (with D A Preston), 1973, 1978; Energy Needs and Resources, 1974, 1978; The North Sea Oil Province (with K E Rosing), 1975; The West European Energy Economy: The case for Self-Sufficiency, 1976; Optimal Developments of North Sea Oilfields (with K E Rosing), 1976; The Pressures of Oil: A Strategy for Economic Revival, (with L Valenilla) 1978; British Offshore Oil Policy: A Radical Alternative, 1980; The Future of Oil (with K E Rosing), 1980, 1983; Energie: Geen Probleem? (with J A van Reyn), 1981; The International Oil Industry: An Inter-disciplinary Perspective, (with J Rees)1986; Global and Regional Energy Supplies: Recent Fiction and Fallacies Revisited, 1991. *Honours:* Prize for Outstanding Contributions to Energy Economics and its Literature. *Address:* 7 Constitution Hill, Ipswich, IP1 3RG, England.

ODELL Robin Ian, b. 19 Dec 1935, Totton, Hampshire, Editor. m. Joan Bartholomew, 19 Sept 1959. *Publications:* Jack the Ripper in Fact and Fiction, 1965; Exhumation of a Murder, 1975; The Murderers' Who's Who, (Co-author J H H Gaute), 1979; Lady Killers, (Co-author J H H Gaute), 1980; Murder Whatdunit, (Co-author J H H Gaute), 1982; Murder Whereabouts, (Co-author H.H Gaute, 1986; Dad Help Me Please, (Co-author Christopher Berry-Dee), 1990; A Question of Evidence, (co-author, Christopher Berry-Dee), 1992; Lady Killer, (co-author, Christopher Berry-Dee), 1992; The Long Drop, (co-author, Christopher Berry-Dee), 1993. *Contributions to:* Crimes and Punishment; The Criminologist. *Honours:* FCC Watts Memorial Prize, 1957; International Humanist and Ethical Union, 1960; Mystery Writers of America Edgar Award, 1980. *Memberships:* Paternosters; Our Society (Crimes Club). *Literary Agent:* Curtis Brown. *Address:* 11 Red House Drive, Sonning Common, Reading RG4 9NT, England.

ODENWALD Sylvia Lavergne (Burr), b. 24 June 1928, USA. Writer; Publisher. m. Robert Owen Odenwald, 21 May 1954, 1 son, 3 daughters. *Education:* BA, Speech, Blue Mountain College, Mississippi, 1950; MA, English, Austin Peay State University, Clarksville, Tennessee, 1970; PhD, English (ABD), Baylor University, Waco, Texas. *Appointments:* High School Teacher, English, Writing, 1967-71; Editorial Assistant, Journal of Church and State, 1972-74; College Assistant Professor, English, Writing, 1974-77; President, Professional Communications, 1978-81; Manager, Instructional Design and Writing, Texas Instruments, 1981-84; President, The Odewnwald Connection and Odenwald Press, 1984-. *Publications:* Desktop Presentations (with Margaret Cole), 1990; Global Training: How To Design A Program for the Multinational Corporation, 1993. *Contributions to:* Training Makes Dollars and Sense, to Training and Development, 1988; Million Dollar Award, to Training and Development, 1989; Rewards Have Value, to Personnel Journal, 1990. *Honours:* Outstanding Member of the Year, ASTD Dallas Chapter, 1985; National Torch Award, 1988, International Leadership Award, 1990, ASTD. *Memberships:* Book Publishers of Texas; ASTD, National Secretary and Board of Directors 1986-88; International ASTD Executive Committee; Advisory Council, North Texas Space Business Roundtable. *Literary Agent:* The Odenwald Connection. *Address:* 3010 LBJ Freeway, Suite 1296, Dallas, TX 75234, USA.

ODGERS Sally Patricia Farrell, (Sally Darroll), b. 26 Nov 1957, Tasmania, Australia. Freelance Writer. m. Darrel Allan Odgers, 26 May 1979, 1 son, 1 daughter. *Education:* School's Board Education, 1963-72. *Publications:* Dreadful David, 1984; The Follow Dog, 1990; Tasmania: A Guide, 1989; Kayak!, 1992; Amy Amaryllis, 1992. Others include: Three Loony Months; Just like Emily; The Magician's Box; Pardon my Garden,

1992; Rosina and the Show; Rosina and Kate; The Bunyip Wakes; Storytrack: A Practical Guide to Writing for Children in Australia and New Zealand; Welcome to the Weirdie Club; The Follow Dog; Drummond; The Window Book; Summer Magic; Polly's Party; What a Day!; The Cat and the King; That's Enough; The Witch; Henry's Ears; Maria and the Pocket; Amy Claire and the Legs My Aunt Agatha; Stick in the Mud; Hey Mum; Kelly and the Mess; There were Cats; Elizabeth; How to Handle a Vivid Imagination; Blue Moon Animal Day; The Suitcase; The Haunting of Ace; Down River; Time Off; Winter-Spring Garden; Ex-Spelled; The Ghost Collector; The Powerful Pickle Problem. *Contributions to:* Organic Growing; Australian Women's Weekly; Australian Author; Lucky Magazine; Rippa Reading; Lu Rees Archive Journal. *Memberships:* Australian Society of Authors; Society of Women Writers; Hon Secretary, Book Worm Club. *Literary Agent:* Katya Public Relations Agents. *Address:* PO Box 87, Latrobe, Tasmania 7307, Australia.

OFFEN Yehuda, b. 4 Apr 1922, Altona, Germany. Writer. m. Tova Arbisser, 28 Mar 1946, 1 daughter. *Education:* BA, London University, UK, 1975; MA, Comparative Literature, Hebrew University, Jerusalem, Israel, 1978. *Publications:* Poems: L'Lo L'An, 1961; Har Vakhol, 1963; Lo Agadat Khoref, 1969; Nofim P'nima, 1979; N'Vilat Vered, 1983; Shirim Bir'hov Ayaif, 1984; P'Gishot Me'ever Lazman, 1986; Massekhet Av, 1986; Who Once Begot a Star, 1990; Silly Soil, 1992. B'Magal Sagur, short stories, 1979; Stoning on the Cross Road, short stories, 1988. *Contributions to:* Most magazines, literary journals & publications in Israel, also various publications in USA, Poland, Germany, Italy, India. Some songs recorded. *Honours:* ACUM Prize, Literature, 1961, 1979, 1984; Talpir Prize, Literature, 1979; Efrat Prize for Poetry, 1989. *Memberships:* Hebrew Writers Association, Israel; International Academy of Poets, USA; PEN Centre, Israel; ACUM (Societe des Auteurs, Compositeurs et Editeurs en Israel); National Federation of Israeli Journalists; International Federation of Journalists, Brussels. *Address:* 8 Gazit Street,Tel-Aviv 69417, Israel.

OFFUTT Andrew J(efferson V), b. United States of America. Author. *Publications:* Author of over 100 works including: Evil is Live Spelled Backwards, 1970; The Great 24 Hour Thing, 1971; The Castle Keeps, 1972; Messenger of Zhuvastou, 1973; Ardor on Aros, 1973; The Galactiv Rejects (juvenile), 1973; Operation: Super Ms, 1974; Sword of the Gael, 1975; The Genetic Bomb (with D Bruce Berry), 1975; Chieftain of Andor, 1976 (in United Kingdom as Clansman of Andor, 1978); The Undying Wizard, 1976; Demon in the Mirror (with Richard K Lyon), 1977; Sign of the Moonbow, 1977; The Mists of Doom, 1977; My Lord Barbarian, 1977; Swords Against Darkness 1-5, 5 vols, 1977-79; Conan and the Sorcerer, 1978; The Sword of Skelos, 1979; The Iron Lords, 1979; Shadows Out of Hell, 1979; King Dragon, 1980; When Death Birds Fly (with Keith Taylor), 1980; The Tower of Death (with Keith Taylor), 1980; The Eyes of Sarsis (with Richard K Lyon), 1980; Conan the Mercenary, 1980; Web of the Spider (with Richard K Lyon), 1981; The Tower of Death (with Keith Taylor), 1982; The Lady of the Snowmist, 1983. *Address:* Funny Farm, Haldeman, KY 40329, USA.

OGAWA Masaru, b. 1915, Los Angeles, USA. Journalist. m. Ayame Fukuhara, 1942, 1 son, 2 daughters. *Education:* University of California, Los Angeles; Tokyo Imperial, and Columbia Universities. *Appointments:* Domei News Agency, 1941-46; Kyodo News Service, 1946-48; The Japan Times, 1948-, Chief, Political Section 1949, assistant Managing Editor, 1950, chief Editor, 1952, Managing Editor, 1958-64, Director, 1959-, Executive Editor 1964-68, Senior Editor 1968-71, Chief Editorial writer 1969- 71, Editor 1971-77, Adviser 1977-, weekly columnist; Chairman, Asia-Pacific Magazine, Manila, 1981-. *Honours:* Hon.D.Litt., Lewis and Clark College, Portland, Oregon; Phi Beta Kappa, 1937 UCLA; Vaughn-Uyeda (Journalism) Prize, 1967. *Memberships:* Life Member, Foreign Correspondents Club of Japan, 1973-; Executive

Director, America Japan Society, 1981-; Tokyo Club, 1986-. *Address:* 2, 14-banchi, 5 chome, Mejiro, Toshima-ku, Tokyo, Japan.

OGBURN Charlton, b. 15 Mar 1911, Atlanta, USA. Writer. m. (1) Mary C. Aldis, 6 June 1945, (div 1951), 1 son, (2) Vera Weidman, 24 Feb 1951, 2 daughters. *Education:* SB, cum laude, Harvard, 1932; Graduate, National War College, 1952. *Publications:* The White Falcon, 1955; The Bridge, 1957; Big Caesar, 1958; The Marauders, 1959; US Army, 1960; The Gold of the River Sea, 1965; The Winter Beach, 1966; The Forging of our Continet, 1968; The Continent in Our Hands, 1971; Winespring Mountain, 1973; The Southern Appalachians : A Wilderness Quest, 1975; The Adventure of Birds, 1976, Railroads: The Great American Adventure (National Geographical Society), 1977; The Mysterious William Shakespeare : the Myth and the Reality, 1984. *Contributions to:* magazines & journals. *Address:* 403 Hancock St, Beaufort, SC 29902, USA.

OGILVIE Elizabeth (May), b. 1917, United States of America. Author. *Publications:* High Tide at Noon, 1944; Storm Tide, 1945; Honeymood (novelization of screenplay), 1947; The Ebbing Tide, 1947; Rowan Head, 1949; My World Is an Island (reminiscences), 1950; The Dawning of the Day, 1954; Whislte for a Wind: Maine 1820 (juvenile), 1956; The Fabulous Year (juvenile), 1958; The Witch Door, 1959; How Wide the Heart (juvenile), 1959; The Young Islanders (juvenile), 1960; Becky's Island (juvenile), 1961; Call Home the Heart, 1962; Turn Around Twice (juvenile), 1962, as Mystery on Hopkins Island, 1966; Ceiling of Amber (juvenile), 1964; Masquerade at Sea House (juvenile), 1965; There May Be Heaven, 1966; The Seasons Hereafter, 1966; The Pigeon pair (juvenile), 1967; Waters on a Starry Night, 1968; Come Aboard and Bring Your Dory (juvenile), 1969 (in United Kingdom as Nobody Knows about Tomorrow, 1971); Bellwood, 1969; The Face of Innocence, 1970; A Theme for Reason, 1970; Weep and Know Why, 1972; Strawberries in the Sea, 1973; Image of a Lover, 1974; Where the Lost Aprils Are, 1975; The Dreaming Swimmer, 1976; An Answer in the Tide, 1978; A Dancer in Yellow, 1979; The Devil in Tartan, 1980; The Silent Ones, 1981; Too Young to Know (juvenile), 1983; The Road to Nowhere, 1983; Jennie About To Be, 1984.

OGLETREE Thomas Warren, b. 1933, United States of America. Writer (Philosophy, Theology/Religion. *Publications:* Christian Faith and History: A Critical Comparison of Ernst Troelsch and Karl Barth, 1965; The Death of God Controversy, 1966; Openings for Marxist-Christian Dialogue, 1968; From Hope to Liberation: Toward a New Marxist-Christian Dialogue (with H Apthekerand S Bliss), 1974; Lifeboat Ethics: The Moral Dilemmas of World Hunger (with George Lucas Jr), 1976; The Use of the Bible in Christian Ethics, 1983; Hospitality to the Stranger: Dimensions of Moral Understanding, 1985. *Address:* Office of the Dean, Drew University, Theological School, Madison, NJ 07940, USA.

OHL Paul, b. 1 Oct 1940, Strasbourg, Alsace. Public Administrator. 2 sons, 1 daughter. *Education:* Royal Military College, Canada; Diploma, Royal Canadian Officers School; Social Sciences, University of Montreal; Diploma, Public Administration School, University of Quebec. *Appointment:* Permenent Assessor, Canadian Arts Council, 1980- . *Publications:* Katana, 1987; La Guerre Olympique, 1977; Le Dieu Sauvage, 1980; les Gladiateurs De L'Amerique, 1977; Les Arts Martiaux, 1975; La Machine a Tuer, 1981; Knockout Inc, 1979. *Contributions to:* Numerous journals and magazines in Quebec. *Honours:* Selections as Book of the Month; Latest Publication, Katana submitted to 3 Literary Awards. *Memberships:* L'Union Des Ecrivains Quebecois; International Olympic Academy; Canadian Olympic Academy, Studies Committee. *Address:* 932 Avenue Manrese, Quebec, Canada G1S 2X1.

OJALA Ossi Arne Atos, b. 22 Mar 1933, Savonlinna, Finland. Amateur Theatre Director; Teacher; Copywriter. *Education:* BA, University of Helsinki. *Publications include:* Novels: Saarella Tapahtuu (The Island), 1963; Valkoinen Vaara (White Danger), 1966; Kahvila Sinuhe (Sinuhe Cafe), 1967; Toisenlainen Rakkaustarina (Different Love Story), 1981; Ja Aika Pysahtyi (Time Stopped), 1985; Ennen Hiljaisuutta Mina Huudan (Before Stillness I Will Cry Out), 1985; Suolintu (The Crane), 1966. Also over 30 broadcast plays, including Haapaveden Kannel, 1986. *Contributions to:* Theater; Ita-Hame; Kaleva; Kainuun Sanomat; Opistolehti. *Honours:* Otava Prize, 1964; 1st Prize, novel competition, 1966; Best Finnish novel for young people, 1967. *Memberships:* Suomen Kirjailijaliitto; Suomen Noytelmakirjailijaliitto; Salpausselan Kirjailijat; Pirkkalaiskirjailijat. *Literary Agents:* WSOY, Helsinki; Kustannusoy Pohjoinen, Oulu. *Address:* Keskustie 39, 19600 Hartola, Finland.

OKAZAKI Tadao, b. 7 Apr 1943. Physician; Poet. *Education:* MD, Prefectual Medical School, Fukushima, Japan; Department of Medicine, School of Medicine, State University of New York USA; Writers Digest School, Cinicinnatti, Ohio. *Appointment:* Editor, New Cicada, Japan, 1984-. *Publications:* Haiku. Essays on Haiku-Ballard Theory. *Contributions to:* Cicada; Modern Haiku; Frogpond; New Cicada. *Honours:* Cicada Prize, 1976; Special Mention Award, 1979, Modern Haiku. *Memberships:* Hiaku Society of America; Haiku Canada; Canadian Poetry Association. *Address:* 13 Shimizu, Fushiguro, Fukushima 960-05, Japan.

OKON Zbigniew Waldemar, b. 21 July 1945, Chelm, Poland. Teacher. m. Halina Pioro Maciejewska, 6 Oct 1969, 2 sons, 1 daughter. *Education:* Maria Curie-Sklodowska University, Lublin. *Publications:* Outlooks and Reflections, 1968; The Soldiers of the Chalk Hills, 1970; Impatience of the Tree, 1979; Intimidation By Twilight, 1986; Calling Up the Darkness, 1987. *Contributions to:* Poetry in various journals and magazines. *Honours:* 1st Prize Winner, Poetry Competitions, 1964, 1966, 1968, 1974; The Czechowicz Literary prize, 1987. *Memberships:* Stowarzyszenie Ziemi Chelmskiej; Chairman, Pryzmaty, 1983; Union of Polish Literary Men. *Address:* Ul Kolejowa 86/19, 22-100 Chelm, Poland.

OKPAKU Joseph (Ohiomogben), b. 1943, Nigeria. Playwright. *Appointments:* President, Publisher, The Third Press, Joseph Okpaku Publishing Company Inc, New York City, 1969-; Executives Board, African Studies Association, 1971-. *Publications:* Born Astride the Grave (play), 1966; The Virtues of Adultery (radio play), 1967; Verdict!: The Exclusive Picture Story of the Trial of the Chicago 8, 1970; New African Literature and the Arts vol I and II, 1970, vol III, 1973; Nigeria-Biafra: Dilemma of Nationhood, 1971; Superfight No 11, 1974.

OKRENT Daniel, b. 2 Apr 1948, Detroit, Michigan, USA. Editor; Writer. m. Rebecca Lazear, 28 Aug 1977, 1 son, 1 daughter. *Education:* BA, University of Michigan, 1969. *Appointments:* Editor, Alfred A Knopf Inc., 1969-73; Editorial Director, Grossman Publishers, 1973-76; Editor in Chief, Harcourt Bruce Journovich, 1976-77; President, Texas Monthly Press, 1979-83; Editor, President, New England Monthly Inc., 1983-89. *Publications:* Nine Innings, 1985; The Ultimate Baseball book, 1979. *Contributions to:* Esquire; New York Times Book Review; New York Times Magazine; Sports Illustrated. *Honours:* Winner, National Magazine Award for General Excellence, 1986, 1987; Baseball Anecdotes, 1989; The Way We Were, 1989. *Membership:* Member Executive Committe, American Society of Magazine Editors. *Literary Agent:* Elizabeth Darhansoff. *Address:* Box 417, Worthington, MA 01098, USA.

OLDKNOW Antony, b. 15 Aug 1939, Peterborough, England. Poet, literary translator, professor. *Education:* BA, Leeds, 1961; postgraduate Diploma, phoenetics, Edinburgh, 1962; Phd, University of North Dakota, USA,

1983. *Appointments:* Editor, publisher, Scopcraeft Press Inc, 1966-; Editor, The Mainstreeter, 1971-78; Poet-in-the-schools, North Dakota, 1971-72; Traveling writer, The Great Plains Book Bus, 1979-81; Writer-in-residence, Wisconsin Arts Board, 1980-83; Poetry Staff, Cottonwood, 1984- 87; Associate Professor Literature, Eastern New Mexico University, 1987-. *Publications:* Lost Allegory, 1967; Tomcats and Tigertails, 1968; The Road of the Lord, 1969; Consolation for Beggars, 1978; Anthem for Rusty Saw and Blue Sky, 1975; Anthem for Rusty Saw and Blue Sky, 1975; Consolation for Beggars, 1978; Miniature Clouds, 1982; Ten Small Songs, 1985. *Contributions to:* Numerous journals, magazines, reviews. *Honours:* University of North Dakota Poetry Prize, 1973; North Dakota State Arts Board Literary Grant, 1974; Wisconsin State Arts Board Literary Grants, 1978, 1980. *Address:* Department of Languages and Literature, Eastern New Mexico University, Portales, NM 88130, USA.

OLDSEY Bernard, b. 18 Feb 1923, Wilkes-Barre, Pennsylvania, USA. Professor; Editor; Writer. m. Ann Marie Re, 21 Sept 1946, New York City. 1 son, 1 daughter. *Education:* BA 1948, MA 1949, PhD 1955, Pennsylvania State University. *Appointments:* Instructor to Associate Professor, English, Pennsylvania State University, 1951-69; Senior Fulbright Professor, American Literature, Universidad de Zaragoza, Spain, 1964-65; Professor, English, West Chester University, 1969-; Editor, College Literature, 1974-; University Professor, University of Innsbruck, Austria, 1985. *Publications:* From Fact to Judgement, 1957; The Art of William Golding, 1967; The Spanish Season, novel, 1970; Hemingway's Hidden Craft, 1979; Ernest Hemingway: Papers of a Writer, 1981; British Novelists, 1930- 1960, 1983; Critical Essays on George Orwell, 1985. *Contributions to:* Nation; American Literature; Modern Fiction Studies; Studies in American Fiction; College English etc. *Honours:* Senior Fulbright Appointment, Universidad de Zaragoza, 1964-65; Distinguished and Academic Service Award, Pennsylvania State Colleges and Universities Award, 1978. *Memberships:* Modern Language Association; Council of Editors of Learned Journals; Hemingway Society; Literary Fellowship of Philadephia. *Address:* 1003 Woodview Lane, West Chester, PA 19380, USA.

OLINTO Antonio, b. 10 May 1919, Uba, Brazil. Professor; Writer. m. Zora Seljan, 10 Dec 1955. *Education:* Philosophy, 1935-37; Theology, 1938-41. *Appointments:* Literature Professor, University of Rio Janeiro, Brazil; Visiting Professor, University of Columbia, New York, USA. *Publications:* The Water House, 1969; Brazilians in Africa, 1964; The Truth of Fiction, 1966; Copacabana, 1975; The Day of Wrath, 1959; the King of Ketu, 1980; Theories and Other Poems; The Movies in the Village; The Invention of Truth. *Contributions to:* Literary Critic, O Globo, 25 years; articles in various journals, magazines and newspapers. *Honours:* Saci/Jabuti Prize, Best Book of Criticism, 1959; Estacio de Sa Prize, Best Book of Poems, 1957. *Memberships:* PEN, Brazil; International PEN; Uba's Academy of Letters. *Address:* 34 Landward Court, Harrowby Street, London W1, England.

OLIVER (Symmes) Chad(wick), b. 1928, United States of America. Author. *Publications:* Shadows in the Sun, 1954; Mists of Dawn (juvenile fiction), 1952; Another Kind (short stories), 1955; The Winds of Time, 1957; Unearthly Neighbors, 1960; Ecology and Cultural Continuity as Contributing Factors in the Social Organization of the Plains Indians, 1962; The Wolf Is My brother (western novel), 1967; The Shores of Another Sea, 1971; The Edge of Forever edited by William F. Nolan (short stories), 1971; Giants in the Dust, 1976; Cultural Anthropology: The Discovery of Humanity, 1980; Broken Eagle, Winner Western Heritage Award for Best Novel of 1989. *Address:* 301 Eanes Road, Austin, TX 78746. USA.

OLIVER Douglas Dunlop, b. 14 Sept 1937, Southampton, England. Poet; Novelist; Prosodist. m. (1) Janet Hughes, July 1962, (2) Alice Notley, Feb 1988,

2 stepsons, 2 daughters. *Education:* BA, Literature, 1975, MA, Applied Linguistics, 1982, University of Essex. *Appointments:* Journalist, newspapers in England, Agence France-Presse, Paris, 1959-72; University Lecturer, Literature, English, various, 1975-; Editorial Board, Franco-British Studies; Co-Editor, Scarlet magazine. *Publications:* Oppo Hectic, 1969; The Harmless Building, 1973; In the Cave of Suicession, 1974; The Diagram Poems, 1979; The Infant and the Pearl, 1985; Kind, 1987; Poetry and Narrative in Performance, 1989; Three Variations on the Theme of Harm, 1990; Penniless Politics, 1991; The Scarlet Cabinet (with Alice Notley), 1992. *Contributions to:* Anthologies including: A Various Art, 1987; The New British Poetry 1968-1988, 1988; Numerous poems, articles, fiction to magazines and journals. *Honours:* Eastern Arts Grant, 1977; South-East Arts Grant for publication of Kind, 1987; Fund for Poetry Grants, 1990, 1991. *Address:* c/o British Institute in Paris, 11 Rue de Constantine, 75007 Paris, France.

OLIVER John Laurence, b. 14 Sept 1910, Journalist, m. Renee Mary Webb, 9 Nov 1946, 2 sons. *Appointment:* Staff, Popular Flying, 1932-33; Editor, The Sphere,1960-64; The Tater, 1961-65. *Publications:* Saint John's Wood Church, (Co-author Rev Peter Bradshaw), 1955; Malcolm Morley at the Everyman, 1977. *Contributions to:* Punch; The Bystander; Britannia and Eve; The Times; Evening Standard. *Memberships:* The Society for Theatre Research; Garrick Club; MCC. *Address:* 10 Wellington Place, London NW8 9JA, England.

OLIVER Mark. *See:* **TYLER-WHITTLE Michael Sidney.**

OLIVER Paul H. b. 25 May 1927, Nottingham, England. Author; Lecturer in Architecture and Popular Music. m. Valerie Grace Coxon, 19 Aug 1950. *Education:* Drawing Exam Distinction, 1945; Painting Exam, National Diploma in Design, 1947; Art Teachers' Diploma, 1948, Diploma in Humanities, History of Art, Distinction, 1955, University of London. *Literary Appointments:* Editor, Architectural Association Journal, 1961-63; Reviewer for Arts Review, 1965-70; Member, Cambridge University Press Popular Music Editorial Board, 1980-. *Publications:* Bessie Smith, 1959; Blues Fell This Morning, 1960; Conversation with the Blues, 1965; Screening the Blues, 1968; The Story of the Blues, 1969; Shelter and Society (ed), 1970; Savannah Syncopators: African Retentions in the Blues, 1970; Shelter in Africa, 1971; Shelter, Sign and Symbol, 1975; Dunroamin' The Suburban Semi and its Enemies (with Ian Davis and Ian Bentley), 1981; Songsters and Saints: Vocal Traditions on Race Records, 1984; Blues Off The Record: Thirty Years of Blues Commentary, 1984; Dwellings: The House Across the World, 1987; Blues FellThis Morning (1960); revised edition, 1990; Black Music in Britain (ed) 1990; Blackwell's Guide to Blues Records (ed), 1989; Architecture - An Invitation (with Richard Hayward), 1990. *Contributions to:* Articles and reviews published in: RIBA Journal; Architects Journal; Architectural Association Journal and Quarterly; Arts Review; Architectural Review; Third World Planning Review; Habitat International: Building Design; Building; Architectural Design; Hi-Fi News and Record Review; Journal of Musicology; Popular Music Yearbook; Black Music Research; Musical Traditions; Jazz Review; Blues Unlimited; MELUS. *Honours:* Prix d'Etrangers, Paris for Le Monde du Blues, French translation of Blues Fell This Morning, 1962; Prix du Disque, Paris, for The Story of the Blues, 1979; Honorary Fellow, AmCAS Univesity of Exter, 1986; Honorary Fellow, Oxford Polytechnic, 1988; Sony Radio Award Best Special Music Programme, 1988. *Memberships:* Fellow, Royal Anthropological Institute; Architectural Association; International Association for the Study of Popular Music; Standing Committee, and Honorary Fellow, Centre for American and Commonwealth Arts & Studies, University of Exeter, Society of Architectural Historians (USA), Vernacular Architecture Forum, (USA). *Address:* Wootton-by-Woodstock, Oxon, England.

OLIVER Reginald Rene St John, b. 7 July 1952, London, England. Actor; Dramatist. *Education:* BA Hons, University College, Oxford, 1975. *Literary Appointments:* Literary Consultant to Drama Panel, Arts Council of Great Britain, 1983-86; Director of Publications, Seeds Ltd, 1986-. *Publications:* Zuleika, 1975; Interruption to the Dance, 1977; You Might As Well Live, 1978; The Shewstone, 1981; Passing Over, 1982; Absolution, 1984; Back Payments, 1985; Rochester (A Dramatic Biography), 1986; A Portrait of Two Artists, 1986; Imaginary Lines, 1987. *Contributions to:* Numerous magazines and journals. *Honours:* Time Out Award Best Fringe Play; International Theatre Award, 1985. *Memberships:* Honorary President, Dramatist's Club; British Actors Equity; Theatre Writers Union. *Literary Agent:* Margaret Ramsay (Ltd). *Address:* The Bothy, Wormington Grange, Broadway, Worcs, England.

OLIVER Richard, b. 9 Aug 1945, Etterbeek, Belgium. Playwright; Film Producer. m. Monique Licht, 16 Sept 1967, 1 son. *Education:* Institut des Arts et Diffusion. *Publications:* Amin Dada ler Empereur de Belgique, 1980; Adaptation of Gulliver for children's television; Films include: Leurs Trucs en Plumes; Le Charme de l'Ambiguite; Strip School; Black Paris; Marivn Gaye Transit Ostende; La Chanson Rebelle; Le Buteur Fantastique; Musical Comedy: King Singer; Big Dady Dad; L'Irresistible Ascension de John Travol'rat; Theatre: Un Amour de Vitrine, 1987. *Contributions to:* Le Soir Illustre; Pourquoi Pas?; Moustique. *Honours:* Prix RTBF? La Louviere, 1969; Prix Ondas, Spain 1974; Prix Label of Quality CNC, 1977, 1981 and 1983; Prix du Jury de Festival Automoto, Paris, 1980; Prix Belgian Authors Write SABAM, 1982, 1984; Prix BNP, Rennes, 1984. *Membership:* Administrateur de la commission Audio-visuelle SABAM. *Address:* 24 avenue de Messidor, 1180 Brussels, Belgium.

OLIVER Roland Anthony, b. 1923. Writer (Area Studies, History). *Publications:* The Missionary Factor in East Africa, 1952; Sir Harry Johnston and the Scramble for Africa, 1957; The Dawn of African History, 1958; A History of East Africa (with G Mathew), 1961; A Short History of Africa (with J D Fage), 1961; The Middle Age of African History, 1966; Africa Since 1800 (with A Atmore), 1967; Papers in African Prehistory (with J D Fage), 1970; Africa in the Iron Age (with B M Fagan), 1975; Cambridge History of Africa, 8 vols, 1975-86; The African Middle Ages 1400-1800 (with A Atmore), 1980; The African Experience, 1991. *Address:* Frilsham Woodhouse, Newbury, Berkshire, RG16 9XB, England.

OLLARD Richard, b. 1923. Writer (History, Biography). *Appointments include:* Editor, William Collins and Sons, London, 1960-83. *Publications:* Historical Essays 1600-1750 (ed with H E Bell), 1963; The Escape of Charles II, 1967; Man of War: Sir Robert Holmes and the Restoration Navy, 1969; Pepys, 1974; This War Without an Enemy: A History of the English Civil Wars, 1976; The Image of the King: Charles I and Charles II, 1979; An English Education: A Perspective of Eton, 1982; For Veronica Wedgwood These: Studies in 17th Century History (ed with Pamela Tudor Craig), 1986; Clarendon and His Friends, 1987; Fisher & Cunningham: a study in the personalities of the Churchill era, 1991, Pepys new illus Edn, 1991. *Honours:* FRSL, 1970; FSA, 1984. *Address:* c/o Curtis Brown Limited, 162-168 Regent Street, London, W1, England.

OLMSTEAD Andrea Louise, b. 5 Sept 1948, Dayton, Ohio, USA. Musicologist. m. Larry Thomas Bell, 2 Jan 1982. *Education:* BM, Hartt College of Music, 1972; MA, New York University, 1974. *Appointments:* Faculty: The Julliard School, 1972-80; The Boston Conservatory, 1980-. *Publications:* Books: Roger Sessions and His Music, 1985; Conversations with Roger Sessions, 1987; The New Grove 20th-Century American Masters, 1987; The Correspondence of Roger Sessions, 1992. *Contributions to:* Journal of the Arnold Schoenberg Institute; American Music; Musical Quarterly; Tempo;

Musical America; Perspectives of New Music. *Honours:* Outstanding Academic Book, Choice, 1986. *Membership:* Sonneck Society. *Address:* 73 Hemenway St, apt 502, Boston, MA 02115, USA.

OLNEY Ross R(obert), b. 1929. American, Writer of Children's non-fiction, Recreation/Leisure/Hobbies, Sports-Physical education/Keeping fit, Biography. *Appointments:* Writing Instructor UCLA, USC, UCSB, and Several Community Colleges. *Publications include:* (with P Olney) Quick and Easy Magic Fun, 1974; Light Motorcycle Repair, 1975; Motorcycling, 1975; Photographing Action Sports, 1976; Simple Appliance Repair, 1976; Superstars of Auto-Racing, 1976; Gymnastics, 1976; Hang Gliding, 1976; How to Understand Soccer, 1976; Auto Racing's Young Lions, 1977; (with Chan Bush) Better Skateboarding for Boys and Girls, 1977; (with Mary Ann Duganne) How to Make Your Car Run Better, 1977; This Game Called Hockey, 1978; The Young Runner, 1978; A J Foyt, 1978; Illustrated Auto Racing Dictionary for Young People, 1978; Janet Guthrie, 1978; Modern Auto-Racing Superstars, 1978; Modern Racing Cars, 1978; (with Chan Bush) Roller Skating, 1979; Tricky Discs, 1979; How to Understand Auto Racing, 1979; (with Pat Olney) Magic, 1979; Out to Launch: Model Rockets, 1979; Modern Motorcycle Superstars, 1980; Auto Racing: Micro Style, 1980; (with Chan Bush) Better Kite Flying for Boys and Girls, 1980; The Amazing Yo-Yo, 1980; Model Airplanes, R/C Style, 1980; The Young Bicyclist, 1980; Listen to Your Car, 1981; Farm Giants, 1982; Modern Speed Record Superstars, 1982; Windsurfing, 1982; Winners, 1982; Construction Giants, 1983; (with Pat Olney) How to have More of It, 1983; (with Pat Olney) How Long? 1984; The Farm Combine, 1984; Super-Champions of Auto Racing, 1984; Ocean-Going Giants, 1985; Car of the Future, 1986; The Shell Auto Car Guide, 1986; (with Ross D Olney) The Amazing Transistor, 1986. *Contributions to:* Reader's Digest, all editions, Westways and others. *Memberships:* Board of Directors, Greater Los Angeles Press Club; Immediate Past President, American Auto Racing Writers and Broadcasters. *Literary Agent:* Gloria R Mosesson. *Address:* GRM Associates, 290 West End Ave, New York, NY 10023, USA.

OLSEN Lance, b. 14 Oct 1956, USA. Writer; Critic; Teacher. m. Andrea Hirsch, 3 Jan 1981. *Education:* BA Hons, University of Wisconsin, 1978; MFA, University of Iowa, 1980; MA, 1982, PhD, 1985, University of Virginia. *Publications:* Live from Earth, 1991; William Gibson, 1992; Circus of the Mind in Motion, 1990; Ellipse of Uncertainty, 1987; Lolita, due 1995; Short stories, poems, essays, reviews in journals and magazines. *Contributions to:* Hudson Review; Fiction International; Iowa Review; VLS; Mississippi Review; Mondo 2000; Alaska Quarterly; New Stories from the South; Shenandoah; College English. *Honours:* Distinguished Young Alumni Award, University of Iowa, 1991; Idaho State Board of Education Grant in Creative Writing, 1991-92. *Memberships:* National Book Critics Circle; Associated Writing Programs; Modern Languages Association. *Literary Agent:* Anita Diamant. *Address:* Rt 1 Box 214, Bear Creek Cutoff, Deary, ID 83823, USA.

OLSEN Otto H, b. 1925, United States of America. Writer (History, Humanities, Race Relations, Social Sciences). *Publications:* Carpetbagger's Crusade: The Life of Albion W Tourgee, 1965; The Thin Disguise: Turning Point in Negro History - Plessy vs Ferguson, 1967; The Negro Question: From Slavery to Caste 1863-1910, 1971; The Reconstruction and Redemption of the South, 1979. *Address:* 565 Garden Road, DeKalb, IL 60115, USA.

OLSEN Theodore Victor, (Joshua Stark, Christopher Storm, Cass Willoughby), b. 25 Apr 1932, Rhinelander, Wisconsin, USA. Freelance Writer. m. Beverly Butler, 25 Sept 1976, Sun Prairie. *Education:* BSc English, University of Wisconsin, 1955. *Publications:* 49 books including: Haven of the Hunted, 1956; The Rhinelander Story, 1957; The Man from

Nowhere, 1959; McGivern, 1960; High Lawless, 1960; Gunswift, 1960; Ramrod Rider, 1960; Brand of the Star, 1961; Brothers of the Sword, 1962; Savage Sierra, 1962; The Young Duke, 1963; Break the Young Land, 1964; The Sex Rebels, 1964; A Man Called Brazos, 1964; Canyon of the Gun, 1965; Campus Motel, 1965; The Stalking Moon, 1965; The Hard Men, 1966; Autumn Passion, 1966; Bitter Grass, 1967; The Lockhart Breed, 1967; Blizzard Pass, 1968; Arrow in the Sun, 1969; Keno, 1970; A Man Named Yuma, 1971; Eye of the Wolf, 1971; There Was a Season, 1972; Summer of the Drums, 1972; Starbuck's Brand, 1973; Mission to the West, 1973; Run to the Mountain, 1974; Track the Man Down, 1975; Day of the Buzzard, 1976; Westward They Rode, 1976; Bonner's Stallion, 1977; Rattlesnake, 1979; Roots of the North, 1979; Allegories for one Man's Moods, 1979; Our First Hundred Years, 1981; Blood of the Breed, 1982; Birth of a City, 1983; Red is the River, 1983; Lazlo's Strike, 1983; Lonesome Gun, 1985; Blood Rage, 1987; A Killer is Waiting, 1988; Under The Gun, 1989; The Burning Sky, 1991; The Golden Chance, 1992. *Contributions to:* 20 short stories in Ranch Romances, 1956-57. *Honour:* Award of Merit, State Historical Society of Wisconsin, 1983; WWA Spur Award for Best Western Paperback Novel, 1992. *Membership:* Western Writers of America. *Literary Agent:* Jon Tuska, Golden West Literary Agency, 2327 S E Salmon St, Portland, OR 97214. *Address:* PO Box 856, Rhinelander, WI 54501, USA.

OLSON David John, b. 18 May 1941, Brantford, North Dakota, USA. Professor, Chairman, Political Science. m. Sandra Jean Crabb, 11 June 1966, 1 daughter. *Education:* BA, Concordia College, 1963; MA, 1966, PhD, 1971, University of Wisconsin. *Publications:* Black Politics, 1971; Theft of the City, 1974; To Keep the Republic, 1975; Commission Politics, 1976; Governing the United States, 1977. *Contributions to:* Journal of Politics; Transactions; American Political Science Review. *Honours:* Rockefeller Fellow, 1964; Vilas Fellow, 1966; Brookings Predoctoral Fellow, 1968; Frederick Bachman Lieber Distinguished Teaching Award, 1973; Harry Bridges Endowed Chair in Labor Studies, 1992. *Memberships:* Western Political Science Association, Vice President 1984, President, 1985; American Political Science Association; Midwest Political Science Association; Southern Political Science Association. *Address:* 6512 E Green Lake Way North, Seattle, WA 98103, USA.

OLSON Robert William, b. 14 Dec 1940, North Dakota, USA. Professor. m. Judith Levore Peterson, 31 Jan 1970. 2 daughters. *Education:* BSc, 1962; MA, 1967; PhD, 1973. *Publications:* The Emergence of Kurdish Nationalism: 1880-1925, 1989; The Bath and Syria: 1947-1982, 1982; The Siege of Mosul and Ottoman Persian Relations, 1718-1743. *Contributions to:* Articles to magazines and journals. *Memberships:* Middle East Studies Association; Turkish Studies Association; Kundish Studies Association. *Address:* 616 Springridge Drive, Lexington, KY 40503, USA.

OLSON Toby, b. 17 Aug 1937, Berwyn, Illinois, USA. Poet; Novelist. m. Miriam Meltzer, 27 Nov 1966. *Education:* BA, Occidental College, California, 1965; MA, Long Island University, 1968. *Appointments include:* Associate Director, Aspen Writers Workshop, Colorado, 1965-69; Faculty, New School for Social Research, New York City, 1968-73; Assistant Professor, Long Island University, 1968-74; Professor of English, Temple University, 1975-. *Publications:* Life of Jesus, 1976; Seaview, 1982; We Are the Fire, 1984; Woman Who Escaped From Shame, 1986; Utah, 1987; Dorit in Lesbos, 1990; At Sea, 1993; Unfinished Building, 1993. *Contributions to:* Numerous magazines including: Arts in Society; New Directions in Prose & Poetry; American Book Review; Inside Outer Space; American Experience; Radical Reader; Nation; Ohio Review; Minnesota Review; New York Quarterly; New York Times; Choice; Sun; Caterpillar; American Poetry Review; Boundary 2; Conjunctions; Sun & Moon. *Honours include:* CAPS Award, poetry, 1974; PEN/Faulkner Award, Most Distinguished Work of American

Fiction, 1983; Fellowships, Fiction, Pennsylvania Council for the Arts 1983, National Endowment for the Arts 1985, Guggenheim 1985; Rockefeller Foundation Fellowship, Italy, 1987. *Memberships:* PEN; Poets & Writers; CCLM. *Literary Agent:* Ellen Levine. *Address:* 329 South Juniper Street, Philadelphia, Pennsylvania 19107, USA.

OLSON Walter Karl, b. 20 Aug 1954, Detroit, Michigan, USA. Writer; Editor. *Education:* BA, Yale University, 1975. *Publications:* New Directions in Liability Law (editor), 1988; The Litigation Explosion, 1991. *Address:* Manhattan Institute, 52 Vanderbilt Ave, New York, NY 10017, USA.

OLUDHE-MACGOYE Marjorie Phyllis, b. 21 Oct 1928, Southampton, England. Bookseller. m. D G W Oludhe-Macgoye, 4 June 1960, dec. 1990, 3 sons, 1 daughter. *Education:* BA, English, 1948, MA, 1953, London University. *Publications:* Growing Up at Lina School, juvenile, 1971, 2nd Edition, 1988; Murder in Majengo, novel, 1972; Song of Nyarloka and Other Poems, 1977; Coming to Birth, novel, 1986; The Story of Kenya, history, 1986; The Present Moment, novel, 1987; Street Life, novella, 1988; Victoria and Murder in Majengo, 1993. *Contributions to:* London Magazine; Literary Review; Ghala; Zuka; Alfajiri; Most anthologies of East African poetry; Heinemann Book of African Poetry in English. *Honours:* BBC Arts in Africa Poetry Award (3), 1982; Sinclair Prize for Fiction, 1986. *Address:* PO Box 70344, Nairobi, Kenya.

OMAN Julia Trevelyan, b. 11 July 1930, Kensington, England. Designer. m. Sir Roy Strong, 10 Sept 1971. *Education:* Royal College of Art, London. *Appointments include:* Designer, BBC Television, 1955-67; Art Director, The Charge of the Light Brigade, 1967; Art Director, Laughter in the Dart, 1968; Designer, 40 Years on, 1968; Production Designer, Julius Ceasar, 1969; The Merchant of Venice, 1970; Eugene Onegin, 1971; The Straw Dogs, 1971; Othello, 1971; Samual Pepys, 1971; Getting On, 1971; Othello, 1972; The Consul, 1985; Mr & Mrs Nobody, 1986; A Man for All Seasons, 1987; The Best of Friends, 1988. *Publications:* Street Children; Elizabeth R; Mary Queen of Scots; The English Year. *Contributions to:* Architectural Review; Vogue. *Honours:* Designer of the Year Award; Award for Cable Excellence. *Memberships include:* DES; RCA; FCSD. *Literary Agent:* Felicity Bryan. *Address:* Oman Productions Limited, The Laskett, Much Birch, Hereford, HR2 8HZ, England.

OMANG Joanne B, b. 7 January 1943, Seattle, Washington, USA. Journalist; Writer. m. David Bright Burnham, 23 Oct 1985. *Education:* BA, Newcomb College, 1964; Tulane University; London School of Economics. *Appointments:* Reporter, 1973-91, Foreign Correspondent, Latin America, 1975-78, Diplomatic Correspondent, Central America, 1982-87, Assistant National Editor, 1989-91, The Washington Post. *Publications:* Incident at Akabal, 1992. *Honours:* Phi Beta Kappa; Class Speaker; Co-recipient, Latin American Studies Association Reporting Award, 1982; United Nations Environment Programme Reporting Award, 1982. *Memberships:* Washington Independent Writers; National Writers Union. *Literary Agent:* Kathy Robbins, The Robbins Agency, New York, USA. *Address:* c/o Kathy Robbins, The Robbins Agency, 2 Dag Hammarskjold Plaza, New York, NY 10017, USA.

OMOLEYE Mike, b. 26 Jan 1940, Oye Ekiti, Ondo State, Nigeria. Journalist; Publisher. m. M. A Omoleye, 1970, 4 sons, 3 daughters. *Education:* Diploma, Journalism. *Appointments:* Freelance Journalist, 1960-63; Reporter, Morning and Sunday Post, 1964-69; Special Roving Features Writer, Daily and Sunday Sketch, 1969-71; News Editor, 1972-73, Assistant Editor, 1974-76, Daily and Sunday Sketch; Managing Director, Omoleye Publishing Company Limited, 1976-. *Publications:* You Can Control Your Destiny, 1974; Fascinating Folktales, 1976; Great Tales of the Yorubas, 1977; Mystery World Under the Sea, 1979; Awo As

I Know Him, 1982; The Book of Life, 1982; Self Spiritual Healing, 1982; Issues at Stake, 1983; Make the Psalms Perform Wonders for You, 1987. *Contributions to:* numerous articles in Nigerian newspapers: Former Columnist, Sunday Post, Daily Sketch, Sunday Sketch, Sunday Tribune; Publisher, Sunday Glory, 1986-. *Address:* GPO Box 1265, ibadan, Oyo State, Nigeria.

OMURA Jimmie Matsumoto, b. 27 Nov 1912, Winslow, Washington, USA. Journalist; Editor/Publisher. m. Haruko Motoishi, 8 Mar 1951, 2 sons. *Education:* Graduated, Broadway High School, Seattle, Washington, 1932; Home courses, Landscape Construction. *Appointments:* Editor, Junior High newspaper, 1928-29; Journalism Delegate to State of Washington Student Leaders Conference, 1931; Editor, New Japanese American News, Los Angeles, California, 1933-34; Editor, New World Daily News, San Francisco, California, 1934-35; Editor, New World Sun, San Francisco, 1935-36; Publisher, Current Life Magazine, San Francisco, 1940-42; Selected among All-Timme Nisei essayist, 1941 Special Edition, Japanese American News, San Francisco, California; Editor and Public Relations, The Rocky Shimpo, Denver, Colorado, 1944, 1947. *Publications:* The Passing Show Column, Japanese American News, 1939-40; Nisei America: Know the Facts, Rocky Nippon, 1943; The Passing Parude, The Colarado Times, 1942; Plain Speaking, The Hokube Mainichi, 1984-88; Editorials, Current Life Magazine, 1940-42; Testimony Against Eviction, Tolan Congressional Committee, San Francisco Hearings, 1942; Wartime Editorials Advocating Restoration of Civil Liberties as Prelude to Military Service, Rocky Shimpo, 1944; Debunking JACL Fallacies, The Rafu Shimpo, 1989; Japanese American Journalism in World War II, Frontieers of Asian American Studies, 1989. *Contributions to:* The Formation of Nisei Perspectives, UCLA's Amerasia Journal, 1983 a requested commentary and two book reviews, 1984 (requested) and volunteered Japan- Californian Daily; Great Northern Daily; Colorado Times; Rocky Nippon; Hokubei Mainichi; Asian Week; Hawaii Herald; New York Nichibei; Rikka Magazine, Canada. *Honours:* Tolan Testimony included in Americans Betrayed, Morton Grodzin, 1949, as Introductory Feature in Japanese section, To Serve the Devil, Paul Jacobs and Saul Landau, 1971, Chapter apborism in Years of Infamy, Michi Weglyn, 1976; Over 400 editorials used for UCLA classroom studies, 1945; Historical book Dedication and Tolan Statement Epigraph in Keeper of Concentration Camps, Richard Drinnon, 1986; Symbol of Wartime Resistance, Smithsonian Institution Bi-Centennial Exhibit, For A More Perfect Union: Japanese Americans and the US Constitution, 1987; 1st and only recipient, Lifetime Achievement Award, Asian American Journalists Association, 1989. *Memberships:* Vice-President, Associated Landscape Contractors of America; President, Landscape Contractors of Colorado, 2 terms; Nursery Advisory Committee, Colorado Department of Agriculture, 7 terms; Life Member, World Parliament of Chivalry, Sidney, Australia, 1990; Maison Internationale des Intellectuels, the Academie M.I.D.I. Paris, France, 1992; Liberty Lobby, Charter Member, US Committee for Battle of Normandy Museum; National Trust for Historic Preservation; Wilson Center Associate; American Museum of Natural History; Public Citizen; People For the American Way; HALT; The Statue of Liberty/Ellis Island Centennial Foundation. *Address:* 1455 South Irving Street, Denver, CO 80219, USA.

ONDAATJE Michael, b. 1943, Canada. Playwright; Poet; Novelist; Film Maker. *Publications:* The Dainty Monsters, 1967; The Collected Works of Billy the Kid, 1970, play 1973; Leonard Cohen, 1970; The Broken Ark, 1971; Rat Jelly, 1973; Elimination Dance, 1978; Coming Through Slaughter (novel), 1979; Rat Jelly and Other Poems, 1979; The Long Poem Anthology, 1979; Running in the Family, 1983; Secular Love (poems), 1985; In The Skin of a Lion, (novel), 1986; The Collected Works of Billy the Kid, 1989; The Cinnamon Peeler, 1989, (Poetry); The English Patient, 1992. *Honour:* Joint Winner, Barry Unsworth, Booker Prize, 1992. *Address:* Department of English, Glendon College, York

University, 2275 Bayview Avenue, Toronto, Ontario, Canada.

ONEAL Elizabeth, b. 1934, United States of America. Children's Fiction and Non Fiction Writer. *Publications:* War Work, 1970; The Improbable Adventures of Marvelous O'Hara Soapstone, 1971; The Language of Goldfish, 1980; A Formal Feeling, 1982; In Summer Light, 1985; Grandma Moses, Painter of Rural American, 1986. *Address:* 501 Onondaga Street, Ann Arbor, MI 48104, USA.

ONG Walter Jackson, b. 30 Nov 1912, Kansas City, Missouri, USA. Priest, Society of Jesus; University Professor. *Education:* BA, Rockhurst College, 1933; PhL 1940, MA 1941, STL 1948, St Louis University; PhD, Harvard University, 1955; Various honorary doctorates: University of Glasgow, University of Missouri, Southern Illinois University, University of Notre Dame, Catholic University of America; Carnegie-Mellon University; etc. *Appointments:* Instructor in English and French, Regis College, Denver; Instructor in English 1953-54, Assistant Professor 1954-57, Associate Professor 1957-59, Professor 1959-, Professor of Humanities in Psychiatry, 1970-, University Professor of Humanities 1981-, Emeritus Professor 1984-, St Louis University; Visiting Professor, Yale University, Cornell University, Indiana University, New York University etc; Lincoln Lecturer 1974, Zaire, Cameroun, Nigeria, Senegal; Wolfson College Lecturer, Oxford University, 1985; Lecturer, Finland, Austria, 1968; Israel, Egypt, 1969; USIA Lecturer, Sweden, Tunisia, Morocco, 1975; Korea and Japan, 1980. *Publications include:* Orality and Literacy, 1982; Ramus, Method and the Decay of Dialogue, 1958; The Presence of the Word, 1967; Interfaces of the Word, 1977; Fighting for Life: Contest, Sexuality and Consciousness, 1981; Rhetoric, Romance and Technology, 1971; Hopkins, the Self, and God, 1986; Faith and Contexts, 2 vols, 1992. *Contributions to:* Over 300 articles across the USA, Europe and other continents. *Honours:* Guggenheim Fellow 1949-50, 1951-52; Fellow, Center for Advanced Studies, Wesleyan University, Middletown, Connecticut, 1961-62; Fellow, Center for Advanced Study in Behavioural Sciences, Stanford, California, 1973-74; William Riley Parker Award, Modern Language Association of America, 1975. *Memberships:* Modern Language Association of America, President 1978; Milton Society of America, President 1967; Fellow, American Academy of Arts and Sciences; Chevalier dans l'Order des Palmes Academiques, France; Academy of Literary Studies, USA. *Address:* St Louis University, St Louis, MO 63103, USA.

ONYEAMA Charles Dillibe Ejiofor, b. 6 Jan 1951, Enugu, Nigeria. Publisher; Author; Journalist. m. Ethel Ekwueme, 15 Dec 1984, 4 sons. *Education:* Premier School of Journalism, Fleet Street, London, England. *Appointments:* Member, Anambra Book Fair Planning Committee, 1987-90; Member, Board of Directors, Star Printing & Publishing Company Limited, 1992-; Managing Director, Delta Publications (Nigeria) Limited. *Publications:* Nigger at Eton, 1972; John Bull's Nigger, 1974; Sex Is A Nigger's Game, 1975; The Book of Black Man's Humour, 1975; I'm The Greatest, 1975; Juju, 1976; Secret Society, 1977; Revenge of the Medicine Man, 1978; The Return, 1978; Night Demon, 1979; Female Target, 1980; The Rules of the Game, 1980; The Story of an African God, 1982; Modern Messiah, 1983; Godfathers of Voodoo, 1985; African Legend, 1985; Correct English, 1986; Notes of a So- Called Afro-Saxon, 1988. *Contributions to:* Books and Bookmen; The Spectator; The Times; Daily Express; Sunday Express; Drum; West Africa; Roots; The Guardian; Evening News. *Memberships:* President, Delta Book Club. *Literary agent:* Elspeth Cochrane Agency, London, England. *Address:* 8B Byron Onyeama Close, New Haven, Enugu, Enugu State, Nigeria.

OPIE Iona, b. 1923. Writer. *Publications:* All with Peter Opie: The Oxford Dictionary of Nursery Rhymes, 1951; The Oxford Nursery Rhyme Book, 1955; The Lore and Language of Schoolchildren, 1959; Puffin Book of Nursery Rhymes, 1963; A Family Book of Nursery Rhymes, 1964; Children's Games in Street and Playground, 1969; The Oxford Book of Children's Verse, 1973; Three Centuries of Nursery Rhymes and Poetry for Children, 1973; The Classic Fairy Tales, 1974; A Nursery Companion, 1980; The Oxford Book of Narrative Verse, 1983; The Singing Game, 1985; A Dictionary of Superstitions, (with Moira Tatem), 1989; Babies: an unsentimental anthology, 1990; I Saw Esau (2nd ed with Peter Opie); The People in the Playground, 1993. *Honours:* Hon, MA, Oxon, 1962; Hon, MA, OU, 1987; Hon D.Litt, Southampton, 1987; Hon D.Litt, Nottingham, 1991. *Address:* Westerfield House, West Liss, Hants, GU33 6JQ, England.

OPPENHEIMER Joel (Lester), b. 1930 United States of America. Playwright; Poet. *Publications:* The Dancer, 1952; The Dutiful Son, 1957; The Great American Desert (play), 1961; The Love Bit and Other Poems, 1962; Miss Right (play), 1962; Like a Hill (play), 1963; A Treatise, 1966; Sirventes on a Sad Occurrence, 1967; In Time: Poems 1962-1968, 1969; On Occasion, 1973; The Wrong Season (on baseball), 1973; The Woman Poems, 1975; Pan's Eyes (short fiction), 1975; Names, Dates and Places, 1978; Just Friends/Friends and Lovers, 1978; At Fifty, 1982; Marilyn Lives!, 1981; Poetry: The Ecology of the Soul, 1983; New Spaces, 1985. *Address:* P.O. Box 281, Henniker, NH 03242, USA.

ORDWAY Frederick I, III. b. 1927. American, Writer on Air/Space topics. *Appointments:* Special Assistant to the Director, Saturn Systems Office, Army Ballistic Missile Agency, 1957-60; Chief, Space Systems Information Branch, Marshall Space Flight Center, NASA, 1960-65; Scientific and Technical Consultant, MGM cinerama film 2001, 1965-66; Senior Research Associate, Research Institute, 1967-69, and Professor of Science and Technology, Applications and Evaluation, School of Graduate Studies and Research, 1967-73, University of Alabama, Huntsville; Consultant, Office of Science and Technology Policy, 1974-75; Special Assistant to the Administrator, Energy Research and Development Administration, 1975-77, and policy and internationl affairs positions, US Department of Energy, 1977-. *Publications:* (co-author) Space Flight, 1958; (ed)Advances in Space Science and Technology, vols I-XI and 2 supplements, 1959-67; (co-author) International Missile and Spacecraft Guide, 1960; (co-author) Annotated Bibliography of Space Science and Technology, 1962; (co-author) Basic Astronautics: An Introduction to Space Sciences, Engineering and Medicine, 1962; (co-author) Careers in Astronautics and Rocketry, 1962; (co-author) From Peenemünde to Outer Space, 1962; (co-ed) astronautical Engineering and Science, 1963; (co- author) Applied Astronautics: An Introduction to Space Flight, 1963; (co- author) Conquering the Sun's Empire, 1963; Life in Other Solar Systems, 1965; (co-author) Intelligence in the Universe, 1966; (co-author) History of Rocketry and Space Travel, 1966, 1969, 3rd ed 1975; (co-author) Histoire Mondiale de l'Astronautique, 1968; (co-author) Dividends from Space, 1971; (co-author) Antares Space Filmstrips, 1972; (co-author) Pictorial Guide to the Earth. 1974; (co-author) The Rocket's Glare, 1976; (co-author) New Worlds: Discoveries from Our Solar System, 1979; (co-author) The Rocket Team, 1979; (co-author) Space Travel: A History, 1985; editor History of Rocketry and Astronautics, 1989; editor and contributor, Blueprint for Space, 1992, Book, 1 hour Video, Laser disc and Slide/ Cassette set, co-author, Wernham von Braun; Aufbruck in den Weltraum-Die Biographic, 1992; Forthcoming, Wernham von Braun Crusader for Space, two volumes; plus several hundred papers. *Contributions include:* encyclopedias, chapters to books. *Address:* 2401 N Taylor Street, Arlington, VA 22207, USA.

ORFALEA Gregory Michael, b. 9 Aug 1949, Los Angeles, California, USA. Writer; Editor. m. Eileen Rogers, 4 Aug 1984, 3 sons. *Education:* AB with honours, English, Georgetown University; MFA, Creative Writing, University of Alaska. *Appointments:* Reporter, Northern Virginia Sun, 1971-72; Professor,

Santa Barbara City College, Santa Barbara, California, 1974-76; Editor, Political Focus, 1979-81; Editor, Small Business Administration, 1985-91; Editor, Resolution Trust Corporation, 1991-. *Publications:* Before the Flames, 1988; The Capital of Solitude, 1988; Grape Leaves, 1988; Imagining America: Stories of the Promised Land, 1991. *Contributions to:* Triquarterly; Epoch; The Christian Science Monitor; The Washington Post. *Honours:* California Arts Council Award, 1976; American Middle East Peace Research Award, 1983; District of Columbia Commission on the Arts and Humanities, 1991. *Membership:* American PEN. *Literary Agent:* Thomas Wallace, The Wallace Group, New York City, New York, USA. *Address:* 6001 34th Pl NW, Washington, DC 20015, USA.

ORGEL Doris, (Doris Adelberg), b. 15 Feb 1929, Vienna, Austria. Writer. m. Shelley Orgel, 25 June 1949, 2 sons, 1 daughter. *Education:* BA, Barnard College, 1950. *Publications:* Sarah's Room, 1963; The Devil in Vienna, 1978; My War with Mrs Galloway, 1985; Whiskers Once and Always, 1986; Midnight Soup and a Witch's Hat, 1987; Starring Becky Suslow, 1989; Nobodies And Somebodies, 1991; Next Time I Will, 1993; The Mouse Who Wanted To Marry, 1993; Some 30 others - retellings, translations, light verse and original stories for children; Novels for young adults: Risking Love, 1985; Crack in the Heart, 1989. *Contributions to:* Several stories to Cricket magazine. *Honours:* Lewis Carroll Shelf Award, 1960; Best Books, New York Times, 1963, 1978; Notable Book, American Library Association, 1976, 1978; Horn Book Honour List, 1978; Golden Kite Honour Book, Society of Children's Book Writers, 1978; 36th Annual Award, Child Study Association, 1978; Book of the Year, Association of Jewish Libraries, 1978. *Memberships:* PEN; Authors Guild; Society of Children's Book Writers. *Literary Agent:* Writers House, USA. *Address:* c/o Writers House, 21 West 26th Street, New York, NY 10010, USA.

ORIOL Jacques, (Jacques F G Vandievoet), b. 1 Oct 1923, Brussels, Belgium. Geography Teacher (retired); Poet; Essayist; Critic. 1 son. *Education:* Agregation, secondary school teaching, 1951. *Publications:* Travel writing, poetry, essays; Titles include: Les Belges au Kenya pour l'éclipse du siècle, series of 5 newspaper articles, 1973, book edited, 1991; Quarantaine, 1983; Dédicaces, 1984; Midi, déjà Minuit, 1985; Nous ferons se lever une clarté très haute, 1985; L'Un, Le Multiple et le Tout, 1985; Voyage, 1986; Co-author with Années Quatre-Vingts group: L'an prochain a Valparaiso, 1986; Etat critique, 1987; Bruxelles à venir, 1987; Icare selon les écrivains grecs et latins (in Phréatique, Paris), 1988; Icare ou l'éternelle jeunesse (id), 1988; Poète aujourd'hui, comment dire?, 1989; Douze chants pour renouer les liens d'amour en floréal, 1989; Demi-deuil, 1990; Contre la réforme de l'orthographe (collective work), 1990; Un un not comme en cent (ana), 1992; Dilecta, 1993. *Contributions to:* Reviews to various literary journals. *Honours:* 1st Prize, Classical Poetry, Rosati Society, Arras, 1985; Cup, Nord Pas-de-Calais Regional Council, 1985; Francois Villon Prize, National Association of French Writers, 1986; Silver Medal, High School of French Contemporary Culture, 1987; 1st Prize, Classical Poetry, Ecole de la Loire, Blois, 1989. *Memberships include:* Belgian Section, PEN Club; Association of Belgian Authors; Executive, Union of Walloon Writers and Artists; Sociedad de Escritores de Chile; Leader, Années Quatre-Vingts group; Association pour la au suavegarde et l'expansion de la langue française; Collaborator in Belgium of the parisian review, Vericuetos. *Address:* 210 avenue Moliere, boite 10, B-1060 Brussels, Belgium.

ORLEDGE Robert Francis Nicholas, b. 5 Jan 1948, Bath, Avon, England. Professor of Music. *Education:* Associate, Royal College of Organists, 1964; Clare College, Cambridge; BA Hons, Music, 1968, MA, 1972, PhD, 1973, Cambridge University. *Publications:* Gabriel Faure, 1979, Revised Edition, 1983; Debussy and the Theatre, 1982; Charles Koechlin (1867- 1950): His Life and Works, 1989; Satie the Composer, 1990.

Contributions to: Articles and reviews to: Music and Letters; Musical Quarterly; Musical Times; Music Review; Current Musicology; Journal of the Royal Musical Association. *Memberships:* Royal Musical Association; Centre de Documentation Claude Debussy; Association des Amis de Charles Koechlin; Fondation Erik Satie. *Address:* Windermere House, Windermere Terrace, Liverpool L8 3SB, England.

ORLOVA Alexandra, b. 22 Feb 1911, Russia. Musicologist. m. (1) Georgi Orlov, 1935, dec. 1940, 2 sons, (2) Mikhail Glukh, 23 Apr 1963, dec. 1973. *Education:* Leningrad Institute of Art History, 1928-30; Extra- mural studies, Leningrad University, 1930-33. *Career:* Freelance Writer, 1950-. *Publications:* Glinka: Literary Legacy, vol I, 1952, vol II, 1953; Glinka in the memory of contemporaries, 1955; Rimsky-Korsakov. Chronicle of his life and works (in Russian), 4 vols, 1969-71; Glinka in Petersburg, 1971; Musorgsky in Petersburg, 1974; Mikhail Glukh. Essay on his life and works, 1977; Musorgsky: Days and Works. Biography in documents, 1983; Glinka's Life in Music. Biography in documents, 1988; Tchaikovsky: A self- portrait, 1990; Musorgsky Remembered, 1991. *Contributions to:* Numerous contributions to collection, newspapers and magazines, USSR, USA, France, Germany. *Membership:* Former Member, Union of Societ Composers. *Address:* 97 Van Wagenen Ave, Apt 1D, Jersey City, NJ 07300, USA.

ORLOWSKI Wladyslaw, b. 27 June 1922, Warsaw, Poland. Writer. m. Halina Radzikowska, 4 Nov. 1954, 2 sons. *Education:* MA, University of Lodz, 1947; PhD, Institute of Art, Polish Academy of Sciences, Warsaw, 1970. *Publications:* Other's Love, Other's Suffering, 1976; The Splinters, 1987; Call from the Empty Space, 1982; The Sunrise of the Passed Day, 1988; From the Book to the Screen, 1961; The Justice in Kyoto, play, 1961. *Contributions to:* 400 articles to numerous journals and magazines. *Honours:* Literary Prize: Minister of Defence, 1965, City of Lodz, 1987. *Memberships:* Society of Polish Writers, President, Lodz Branch, 1984-. *Address:* ul. Brzezna 18 m 5, 90-303 Lodz, Poland.

ORMEROD Roger, Author. *Publications:* Time to Kill, 1974; The Silence of the Night, 1974; Full Fury, 1975; A Spoonful of Luger, 1975; Sealed with a Loving Kill, 1976; The Colour of Fear, 1976; A Glimpse of Death, 1976; Too Late for the Funeral, 1977; The Murder Come to Mind, 1977; A Dip into Murder, 1978; The Weight of Evidence, 1978; The Bright Face of Danger, 1979; The Amnesia Trap, 1979; Cart Before the Hearse, 1979; More Dead than Alive, 1980; Double Take, 1980; One Breathless Hour, 1981; Face Value, 1983; Seeing Red, 1984; The Hanging Doll Murder, 1984; Dead Ringer, 1985; Still Life with Pistol, 1986; A Death to Remember, 1986; An Alibi Too Soon, 1987; The Second Jeopardy, 1978; An Open Window, 1988; By Death Possessed, 1988; Guilt on the Lily, 1989; Death of an Innocent, 1989; No Sign Of Life, 1990; Hung In The Blance, 1990; Farewell Gesture, 1990. *Address:* c/o Constable, 10 Orange Street, London, WC2H 7EG, England.

ORMSBY Frank, b. 30 Oct 1947, Enniskillen, County Fermanagh, Northern Ireland, Schoolmaster. *Education:* BA, English, 1970, MA, 1971, Queen's University, Belfast. *Appointment:* Editor, The Honest Ulsterman, 1969-89. *Publications:* A Store of Candles, 1977, 1986; A Northern Spring, 1986; Poets from the North of Ireland, editor, 1979, new edition, 1990; Northern Windows: An Anthology of Ulster Autobiography, Editor, 1987; The Long Embrace: Twentieth Century Irish Love Poems, editor, 1987; Thine in Storm and Calm: An Amanda McKittrick Ros Reader, Editor, 1988. *Address:* 36 Strathmore Park North, Belfast BT15 5HR, Northern Ireland.

ORSZAG-LAND Thomas, b. 12 Jan 1938, Budapest, Hungary. Writer. *Publications:* Berlin Proposal, 1990; Free Women, 1991; Translations: Bluebeard's Castle, 1988; Splendid Stags, 1992; 33 Poems by Radnoti,

1992. *Contributions to:* Nature; Contemporary Review; Spectator; New York Times; Observer; Guardian; Financial Times; Times Higher Education Supplement; Others. *Memberships:* Fellow, International PEN; Foreign Press Association; Royal Institute of International Affairs; Society of Authors. *Address:* PO Box 1213, London N6 5HZ, England.

ORTEGA Julio, b. 29 Sept 1942, Peru. Writer; Professor. m. Claudia J. Elliott, 21 Mar 1986. *Education:* Doctoral of Literature, Catholic University, Lima, Peru. *Appointments:* Professor, University of Texas, Austin, 1978-86, Brandeis University, 1987-; Correspondent, Diario 16, Madrid, Republica, Lima, Unomasuno, Mexico. *Publications:* Poetics of Change, 1984; Adios Ayachucho, 1986; Latin America in its Literature, 1980; La Contemplacion y la fiesta, 1969; Figuracion de la persona, 1971; The Land in the Day, 1978; Rituales, 1976; Ceremonias, 1974; Acto subersivo, 1984; Mediodia, 1970; Relato de la Utopia, 1973; Teoria poetica de Vallejo, 1986; La Lima del 900. 1986; Antologia de la poesia hispanoamericana, 1987. *Contributions to:* London Magazine; TriQuarterly; L'Arc; Sulfur; New Orleans Review; Syntaxis; Vuelta; Mundo Nuevo. *Honours:* Guggenheim Fellowship, 1974; Director, NEH, 1981, 1987; Premio Cope for Short Story, Lima, 1981; National Prize, Theatre, Peru, 1968, 1971. *Memberships:* President, Peruvian Association of Culture; Archives de la Litterature Latinoamericaine, Paris; Latin American Studies Association. *Literary Agent:* Carmen Balcells, Barcelona. *Address:* Romance and Comp Lit, Brandeis University, Waltham, MA 02254, USA.

ORTIZ Simon J, b. 1941 United States of America. Author; Poet. *Appointments include:* Editor, Quetzal Chinle, Arizona, 1970-73; Consultant Editor, Pueblo of Acoma Press, 1982-. *Publications:* Naked in the Wind, 1970; Going for the Rain, 1976; A Good Journey, 1977; The People Shall Continue, 1977; Howbah Indians (short stories), 1978; Song, Poetry, Language, 1978; Fightback, 1980; From Sand Creek, 1981; A Poem Is a Journey, 1981; Blue and Red (for children), 1982; The Importance of Childhood, 1982; Fightin': New and Collected Stories, 1983. *Address:* 308 Sesame S.W., Albuquerque, NM 87105, USA.

OSBORN Carolyn Culbert, b. 7 Nov 1934, Nashville, Tennessee, USA. Fiction Writer. m. Joe A Osborn, 11 June 1955, 1 son, 1 daughter. *Education:* BJ, 1955, MA, 1959, University of Texas. *Publications:* The Fields of Memory, 1984; A Horse of Another Color, 1977; Warriors and Maidens, 1991. *Contributions to:* Granta; The Paris Review; The Georgia Review; Antioch Review; Texas Quarterly; New Letters; Shenandoah. *Honours:* Best Book-Length Fiction, Texas Book Review, 1977; Best Short Story, Texas Institute of Letters, 1978; PEN Syndicated Fiction Award, 1985; The O Henry Award, 1990. *Memberships:* Texas Institute of Letters. *Address:* 3612 Windsor Road, Austin, TX 78703, USA.

OSBORNE Charles, b. 24 Nov 1927, Brisbane, Queensland, Australia. Author; Critic; Musicologist; Chief Drama Critic of The Daily Telegraph, Opera Critic of The Jewish Chronicle. *Publications include:* The Complete Operas of Verdi, 1969; Ned Kelly, 1970; The Concert Song Companion, 1974; Russell Drysdale, 1976; William Dobell, 1976; Sidney Nolan, 1976; The Opera House, Album, 1976; Wagner and His World, 1977; The Complete Operas of Mozart, 1977; The Opera House Album, 1979; W.H. Auden; The Life of a Poet, 1979; The Complete Operas of Puccini, 1981; The Life and Crimes of Agatha Christie, 1982; The World Theatre of Wagner, 1982; The Dictionary of Opera, 1983; Letter to W.H. Auden and Other Poems, 1984; Schubert and his Vienna, 1985; Giving It Away (memoirs), 1986; Verdi: A Life in the Theatre, 1987; The Complete Operas of Strauss, 1988; The Complete Operas of Wagner, 1990; Edited and translated numerous volumnes. *Contributions to:* Radio and TV; London Magazine; Times Literary Supplement; New Statesman; Spectator; Sunday Times; Observer; Harvard Advocate. *Memberships:* Director, Poetry International; Secretary,

Poetry Book Society. *Literary Agent:* Aitken and Stone Ltd. *Address:* 125 St George's Road, London, SE1 6HY, England.

OSBORNE David. *See:* **SILVERBERG Robert.**

OSBORNE John (James), b. 1929. Writer; Playwright. *Appointments:* Co-Director, Woodfall Films, 1958-; Director, Oscar Lowenstein Plays Limited, London, 1960-; Council, English Stage Company, 1960-. *Publications:* Look Back in Anger, 1956; The Entertainer, 1958, sreenplay, 1960; Epitaph for George Dillon (with A Creighton), 1957; The World of Paul Slickey, 1959; A Subject for Scandal and Concern, 1961; Luther, 1961; Plays for England: The Blood of the Bambers, Under Plain Cover, 1963; Tom Jones (screenplay), 1964; Innadmissible Evidence, 1965; (adaptor) A Bond Honoured, 1966; A Patriot for Me, 1966; Time Present and The Hotel in Amsterdam, 1968; The Right Prospective: A Play for Television, 1969; Very Like a Whale, 1970; West of Suez, 1971; (adaptor) Hedda Gabler, 1972; The Gifts of Friendship, 1972; A Sense of Detachment, 1972; A Place Calling Itself Rome, 1973; Four Plays, 1973; (adaptor) The Picture of Dorian Gray, 1973; The End of Me Old Cigar, 1975; Watch It Come Down, 1975; You're Not Watching Me, Mummy, and Try a Little Tenderness, 1978; A Better Class of Person (autobiography), 1981; Too Young to Fight, Too Old to Forget, 1985; A Better Class of Person and God Rot Tunbridge Wells, 1985; The Father (adapt & trans), 1989; Déjàvu (play), 1991; Almost a Gentleman (autobiography), 1991. *Contributions to:* Various Newspapers and Journals. *Address:* The Hurst, Clunton, Craven Arms, Shropshire, England.

OSBORNE Maggie (Margaret Ellen), b. 10 June 1941, Hollywood, California, USA. Author; Novelist. m. George M Osborne II, 27 Apr 1972. 1 son. *Publications:* Partners (with Carolyn Bransford), 1989. As Margaret St George: Castles and Fairy Tales, 1986; Dear Santa, 1989; Winter Magic, 1986; The Heart Club, 1987; Where There's Smoke, 1987; Heart's Desire, 1988; Jigsaw, 1990; American Pie, 1990; Lady Reluctant, 1991; Chase The Heart, 1987; Alexa, 1980; Salem's Daughter, 1981; Portrait in Passion, 1981; Yankee Princess, 1982; Rage to Love, 1983; Flight of Fancy, 1984, As Maggie Osborne. *Honours:* Rocky Mountain Writers Guild, Writer of the Year 1981, Resident Writer, 1982-84; Romance Writers of America, Denver Chapter, Writer of the Year, 1984. *Memberships:* Romance Writers of America, National President, 1984-86 and Board of Directors 1987-88; Novelists Inc, Founding Member, National Secretary. *Literary Agent:* Meg Ruley, Jane Rotrosen Agency, 318 E 51st St, New York City, NY 10022. *Address:* Box E, Dillon, CO 80435, USA.

OSBORNE Mary Pope, b. 20 May 1949, Fort Sill, Oklahoma, USA. Writer. m. Will Osborne, 16 May 1976. *Education:* BA, University of North Carolina. *Publications:* Run, Run, As Fast As You Can, 1982; Love Always, Blue, 1983; Best Wishes, Joe Brady, 1984; Mo to the Rescue, 1985; Last One Home, 1986; Beauty & the Beast, 1987; Christopher Columbus, Admiral of the Ocean Sea, 1987; Pandora's Box, 1987; Jason and the Argonauts, 1988, The Deadly Power of Medusa, 1988, (co-authored with Will Osborne); Favorite Greek Myths, 1989; A Vist to Sleep's House, 1989; Mo and His Friends, 1989. *Literary Agent:* Gail Hochman, Brandt & Brandt. *Address:* Knopf Books for Young Readers, 225 Park Lane South, New York, NY 10003, USA.

OSBOURNE Ivor Livingstone, b. 6 Nov 1951, Jamaica. Author; Publisher. Partner: Charline Mertens, 2 daughters. *Publications:* Novels: The Mango Season, 1979, 1987; Prodigal 1987; The Mercenary 1976; The Rasta Cookbook, Optima 1990, The Exotic Cookbook of Optima, 1990. *Contributions to:* Various journals and magazines. *Literary Agent:* Peter Bryant Writers, 3 Kidderpire Gardens, Hampstead, London. *Address:* 27c Chippenham Road, Maida Vale, London W9 2AH, England.

OSERS Ewald, b. 13 May 1917, Prague, Czechoslovakia. Translator; Author. m. Mary Harman, 3 Aug 1942, 1 son, 1 daughter. *Education:* Prague University; BA Hons, University of London. *Appointments:* Chairman, Translators Association, 1971, 1980-81; Chairman, Translators Guild, 1975-79; Vice-Chairman, Institute of Linguists, 1975-80; Vice-President, International Federation of Translators, 1977-81, 1984-87; Editorial Director, Babel, 1979-87; Member, International Book Committee, 1981-87. *Publications:* Poetry: Wish You Were Here, 1976; 1 volume of own poetry translated into Czech, 1986; Translator, over 110 books including: 31 volumes of poetry; English translation of Jaroslav Seifert, Czech Nobel Prize winner. *Contributions to:* Over 30 magazines, UK, USA, Canada, Australia, India, Germany, Poland, Yugoslavia, Bulgaria. *Honours:* Schlegel-Tieck Prize, 1971; C B Nathhorst Prize, 1977; Gold Medal, Czechoslovak Society of International Relations, 1986; European Poetry Translation Prize, 1987; Bulgarian Cyril and Methodius Order 1st Class, 1987; Austrian Translation Prize, 1989; Dr hc, Olomouc University, Czechoslovakia, 1990; Officer's Cross, German Order of Merit; 11 other honours and awards. *Memberships:* Fellow, Royal Society of Literature; Poetry Society; Society of Authors; Institute of Translation and Interpreting; Translators Association; Honorary Member, German Translators Union. *Address:* 33 Reades Lane, Sonning Common, Reading, Berks RG4 9LL, England.

OSTRIKER Alicia, b. 11 Nov 1937, New York City, USA. m. 1 Dec 1958, 1 son, 2 daughters. *Education:* BA, Brandeis Universty, 1959; PhD, Univerity of Wisconsin, 1964. *Appointment:* Faculty, English Department, Rutgers University, 1965-. *Publications:* Poetry: The Mother/Child Papers, 1980; A Woman Under the Surface, 1982; The Imaginary Lover, 1986; Green Age, 1989. Criticism: Vision & Verse in William Blake; Writing Like a Woman; Stealing the Language: Emergence of Women's Poetry in America. *Contributions to:* New York Times Book Review; Nation; Partisan Review; Hudson Review; Poetry; American Poetry Review; Iowa Review; New Yorker. *Honours:* Poetry Fellowship, National Endowment for the Arts, 1977; Guggenheim Fellowship, 1984-85; William Carlos Williams Award, Poetry Society of America, 1986. *Memberships:* PEN; Poetry Society of America; Modern Language Association. *Address:* 33 Philip Drive, Princeton, New Jersey 08540, USA.

OSTROM Hans Ansgar, b. 29 Jan 1954, USA. Writer; Teacher. m. Jacqueline Bacon, 18 July 1983, 1 son. *Education:* BA, 1975, PhD, English, 1982, University of California, Davis. *Appointments:* Contributing Reviewer, Choice, 1987-; Columnist, Morning News Tribune, Tacoma, Washington, 1990-. *Publications:* The Living Language, 1984; Lives and Moments, 1991; Three To Get Ready, 1991; The Coast Starlight, 1992; Water's Night (with Wendy Bishop), 1992; Colors of a Different Horse, 1993; Langston Hughes: The Short Fiction, 1993. *Contributions to:* Reviews, poems, stories to: Ploughshares; San Francisco Chronicle; Poetry Northwest; Webster Review; San Francisco Review of Books. *Honours:* Harvest Prize in Poetry, 1978; Redbook Prize in Fiction, 1985. *Memberships:* National Book Critics Circle; Modern Language Association; Mystery Writers of America. *Address:* English Department, University of Puget Sound, Tacoma, WA 98416, USA.

OTTEN Charlotte F, b. 1 Mar 1926, Chicago, Illinois, USA. Professor of English. m. Robert T Otten, 21 Dec 1948, 2 sons. *Education:* AB, 1949; MA, 1969; PhD, 1971. *Publications:* Environ: D with Eternity, 1985; A Lycanthropy Reader, 1986; The Voice of the Narrator in Children's Literature, 1989; English Women's Voices, 1991. *Contributions to:* Shakespeare Quarterly; Milton Studies; N&Q; English Literary Renaissance; Huntington Library Quarterly; English Language Notes; Spenser Encyclopedia; English Studies; Chaucer Review; Signal; Concerning Poetry. *Honours:* ACLS Fellowship, 1973; Grand Valley Research Grant, 1976; Calvin Foundation Scholarship, 1987; Newberry Library Fellowship, 1985-

86. *Memberships:* Modern Language Association; Milton Society; Shakespeare Association of America. *Address:* English Department, Calvin College, Grand Rapids, MI 49546, USA.

OTTO Major, b. 4 Apr 1924, Budapest, Hungary. Author; Journalist. *Education:* Faculity of Arts, University of Pazmany Peter, Budapest, 1948. *Appointments:* President of Literary Society. *Contributions to:* Several magazines and journals. *Honours:* Literary Prizes, 1952, 1956, 1986. *Memberships:* Hungarian PEN Club. *Address:* Szalag utra 7, 1011 Budapest, Hungary.

OTTO-RIEKE Gerd, b. 3 Mar 1950, Schlagsdorf. Journalist. *Education:* Diplom-Volkswirt, Hamburg University, 1977. *Appointments:* Chairman, Junge Presse Schleswig-Holstein, 1968-73; Vice Chairman, Deutsche Jugendpresse, 1969-73; Staff, Interpress and F. Reinecke Verlag, Hamburg, 1977-81; Editor in Chief, Deutscher Verkehrsverlag, Hamburg, 1981-85; Editor in Chief, Jaeger Verlag, Darmstadt, 1985-87; Editor in Chief, Check-in, Verlag Industriemagazin, Munich, 1988-. *Publications:* Der Formalitaeten-Wegweiser, 1982; Der Grosse Hobby und Erlebnis-Urlaubsfuehrer, 1986; Landgangfuehrer fuer Schiffsbesatzungen, 1986. *Contributions to:* various articles in professional journals. *Memberships:* Hamburger Journalisten-Verband; Luftfahrt Presse Club. *Address:* Wrangelstrasse 28, D 2000 Hamburg 20, Germany.

OTTONE Piero, b. 3 Aug 1924, Genoa. Journalist. m. Hanne (Winslow) Ottone, 1958, 1 son, 1 daughter. *Education:* University of Turin. *Appointments:* Reporter, Corriere Ligure, 1945; Reporter, gazzetta del Popolo, 1945-58, London Correspondent 1948-50, Bonn Correspondent 1950-53; London and Moscow Correspondent, Corriere della Sera, 1953-61, Special Correspondent in Italy 1962, Editor in Chief, 1972-77; Editor, Secolo XIX, 1968; Managing Director, La Repubblica, 1977; General Manager, Mondadori Nov. 1977-. *Publications:* Gli industriali si confessano, 1965; Fanfani, 1966; La nuova Russia, 1967; De Gasperi, 1968; Potere economico, 1968; Intervista sul gionalismo Italiano, 1978; Come finira 1979. *Address:* c/o Arnoldo Mondadori, Via Marconi 27, 20090 Segrate, Milan, Italy.

OUSMANE Sembene, b. 1 Jan 1923, Ziguinchor, Casamance Region. Writer; Film-maker. *Appointments:* Plumber; Bricklayer; Apprentice Mechanic; studied film production in USSR under Marc Donski; Founder, Editor, 1st Wolof Language Monthly, Kaddu. *Publications:* Novels: Le docker noir, 1956; O pays mon beau peuple, 1957; les bouts de bois de Dieu, 1960; Voltaique, 1962; L'harmattan, 1964; Vehi-Ciosane suivi du mandat, 1966; Xala, 1974;Fat ndiay Diop, 1976; Dernier de l'empire, 1979. *Honours:* 1st Prize, Novelists, World Festival of Negro Arts, Dakar, 1966; Numerous international awards. *Address:* PO Box 8087, Yoff, Dakar, Senegal.

OUTHWAITE Richard William, b. 9 Dec 1949, Bradford, England. University Teacher. *Education:* BA (Oxon), 1971; MA (Sussex), 1972; DPhil (Sussex), 1980. *Publications:* Understanding Social Life, 1975; Concept Formation in Social Science, 1983; New Philosophies of Social Science, 1987. *Memberships:* International Sociological Association; British Sociological Association; Association of University Teachers. *Address:* School of European Studies, University of Sussex, Brighton BN1 9QN, England.

OVERTON Jenny Margaret Mary, b. 1942, Cranleigh, Surrey, England. Book Editor. *Education:* MA, Cantab, 1966. *Publications:* Creed Country, 1969; The Thirteen Days of Christmas, 1972; The Nightwatch Winter, 1973; The Ship from Simnel Street, 1986. *Address:* c/o Wyndene, Crest Hill, Peaslake, Guildford, Surrey GU5 9PE, England.

OVERY Paul (Vivian), b. 1940. Writer. *Appointments:*

Art Critic, The Listener, London, 1966-68; Art Critic, The Financial Times, London, 1968-70; Chief Art Critic, The Times, London, 1973-78; Literary Editor, New Society, London, 1970-71. *Publications:* Edouard Manet, 1967; De Stijl, 1969; Kandinsky: The Language of the Eye, 1969; Paul Neagu: A Generative Context, 1981; The Rietveld Schroder House, (co-author), 1988; De Stijl, 1991. *Contributions to:* Lions and Unicorns: The Britishness of Postwar British Sculpture; Art in America, 1991; Carpentering the Classic; A Very Perculiar Practice; The Furniture of Gerrit Rietveld, Journal of Design History, 1991. *Memberships:* Society of Authors; National Union of Journalists. *Literary Agent:* John Johnson. *Address:* 92 South Hill Park, London,NW3 25N.

OVESEN Ellis, b. 18 July 1923, Writer; Artist; Composer. m. 27 Aug 1949, 2 sons. *Education:* MA, cum laude, University of Wisconsin, 1948; California Teachers Credential, San Jose State University. 1962; Extra classes in poetry writing. *Appointments:* Teacher of English, University of Wisconsin, 1946-48; Writer, Advertising Department, Du Pont Mag, Delaware, 1948-49; Publicity Chairman, AAUW, Eastern Seaboard, 1949-53; Teacher of English, San Jose State U, 1962-63; Teaching Poetry, 1963-90. *Publications:* Gloried Grass, 1970; Haloed Paths, 1973; To Those Who Love, 1974; The Last Hour; Lives Touch, 1975; A Time For Singing, 1977; A Book of Praises, 1977; The Green Madonna, 1984; The Keeper of The Word, 1985; The Wing Brush, 1986; The Year of the Snake, 1989; The Flowers of God, 1985, 1990; Beloved I, 1980, II 1990; The Year of the Horse, 1990; A Time for Singing; Another Man's Mocassins; Memories of South Dakota. *Contributions to:* Poet India; Los Altos Town Crier; Paisley Moon; Fresh Hot Bread; Samvedana; The Plowman. *Honours:* National Honour Society, 1941; Los Altos Hills Poet, 1976-90; Honorary Doctorate, World Academy of Arts and Culture, 1986; Dame of Merit, Knights of Malta, 1988; World Poet, 1989; Golden Poet Award, 1988, 1989, 1991; Reearch Fellow, 1992. *Memberships include:* National Writers Club; California Writers Club; Poetry Society of America; California State Poetry Society, President; Peninsula Poets, Founder and President; NLAPW; Womens Museum of Art, Charter Member, Washington DC; San Francisco Poetry Society' South Dakota Music Composers. *Address:* Box 482, Los Altos, CA 94023, USA.

OVSTEDAL Barbara Kathleen, b. England. Writer. m. Inge Ovstedal, 1945, 1 son, 1 daughter. *Education:* West Sussex College of Art. *Publications:* The Warwyck Trilogy, 1979-80; This Shining Land,1985; The Silver Touch, 1987; To Dance With Kings, 1988; The Golden Tulip, 1991; The Venetian Mask, 1992; The Sugar Pavilion, 1993. *Contributions to:* Good Housekeeping; Country Life; Woman; Woman's Own; Woman's Weekly; Others. *Memberships:* Society of Authors; Romantic Novelists Association. *Literary Agent:* Laurence Pollinger Ltd, 18 Maddox Street, London W1R 0EU, England.

OWEN Alun (Davies), b. 24 Nov 1925. Writer. m. Mary O'Keeffe, 1942, 2 sons. *Publications include:* Everyday Except Christmas, 1957; I'm All Right Jack, 1959; The Servant, 1963; (Television) Glas y Dorlan, BBC Wales; Author, Stage Productions: The Rough and Ready Lot, 1959; Progress to the Park, 1959; Progress to the Park, 1959; The Rose Affair, 1966; A Little Winter Love, 1963; Maggie May, 1964; The Game, 1965; The Goose, 1967; Shelter, 1971; There'll Be Some Changes Made, 1969; Norma, 1969; We Who Are About To, 1969; The Male of the Species, 1974; (Screen)The Criminal, 1960; A Hard Day's Night, 1964; Caribbean Idyll, 1970; (Radio) Two Sons, 1957; It Looks Like Rain, 1959; Earwig, series, 1984; (Television) No Trams to Lime Street, 1959; After the Funeral, 1960; Lena, Oh My Lena, 1960; The Ruffians, 1960; The Ways of Love, 1961; Dare to be a Daniel, 1962; The Hard Knock, You Can't Wind'em All, 1962; The Strain, Let's Imagine Series, The Stag, A Local Boy, 1963; The Other Fella, The Making of Jericho, 1966; The Wake, 1967; The Web, 1972; Ronnie Barker Show (3 scripts); Buttons,

Flight, 1973; Lucky Norma, 1974; Left, 1975; Forget Me Not, 6 plays, 1976; The Look, 1978; The Runner, 1980; Sealink, 1980; Cafe Society, 1982; Colleagues, 1982; Tiger, 1984; Lovers of the Lake, 1984; Widowers, 1985. *Membership:* Chelsea Arts Club. *Literary Agent:* Blake Friedmann, London. *Address:* c/o Julian Friedmann, Blake Friedman Literary Agency, 37-41 Gower Street, London WC1E 6HH, England.

OWEN Douglas David Roy, b. 17 Nov 1922, Norton, Suffolk, England. University Professor (retired). m. Berit Mariann Person, 31 July 1954, 2 sons. *Education:* University College, Nottingham, 1942-43; St Catharine's College, Cambridge; BA, 1948, MA, 1953, PhD, 1955, Cambridge; Sorbonne and College de France, Paris, 1950-51. *Appointments:* Founder, General Editor, Forum for Modern Language Studies, 1965-. *Publications:* The Evolution of the Grail Legend, 1968; The Vision of Hell, 1970; The Song of Roland, translation, 1972, new expanded edition, 1990; The Legend of Roland: a Pageant of the Middle Ages, 1973; Noble Lovers, 1975; Chretien de Troyes: Arthurian Romances, translation, 1987; Guillaume le Clerc: The Romance of Fergus, translation, 1989; A Chat Round The Old Course (by D D R O), 1990; Eleanor of Aguitaine; Queen and Legnd, 1993; Edition with R C Johnston: Fabliaux, 1957; Two Old French Gauvain Romances, 1972. *Contributions to:* Over 30 Festschrift papers; Articles to British and foreign journals; Many reviews including about The Times Literary Supplement; 3 broadcast talks. *Memberships:* International Arthurian Society; Société Rencesvals; International Courtly Literature Society. *Address:* 7 West Acres, St Andrews, Fife KY16 9UD, Scotland.

OWEN Eileen, b. 27 Feb 1949, Concord, New Hampshire, USA. Editor; Writer. m. John D Owen, 19 June 1971, Chichester, New Hampshire. *Education:* BA, Spanish, University of New Hampshire, 1971; BA, English, 1979, MA, Creative Writing, 1981, University of Washington. *Publication:* Facing the Weather Side, 1985. *Contributions to:* Poetry Northwest; Dark Horse; Tar River Review of Poetry; Passages North; Sojourner; Welter; The Seattle Review; Mississippi Mud; Hollow Springs Review; Signpost; Back Door Travel; Arts and Artists; and other publications. *Honours:* Artist-in-Residence, Ucross Foundation, Wyoming, 1984 and 1988; Poems selected King County Arts Commission, 1983; Poems selected in competition Seattle Arts Commission, 1983 and 1987; Honorable Mention, Washington Poets Association, 1981. *Address:* 18508 90th Avenue W, Edmonds, WA 98020, USA.

OWEN Morman G, b. 23 Jan 1944, Los Angeles, California, USA. University Teacher. m. 4 Oct 1969, 1 son, 1 daughter. *Education:* BA summa cum laude, Occidental College, 1964; BA 1st class honours, University of London, 1967; MA, 1971, PhD, 1976, University of Michigan. *Publications:* Prosperity without Progress, 1984; Co-author and editor: Compadre Colonialism, 1971; The Philippine Economy and the United States, 1983; Death and Disease in Southeast Asia, 1987. *Contributions to:* Articles to: Pacific Historical Review; Journal of Southeast Asian Studies; Journal of the Siam Society; Philippine Studies; Asian Studies; Other journals; Annales de Demographie Historique. *Memberships:* Association for Asian Studies; Asian Studies Association of Australia; Royal Asiatic Society, Malaysian and Hong Kong Branches. *Address:* Department of History, University of Hong Kong, Pokfulam Road, Hong Kong.

OWEN Warwick (Jack Burgoyne), b. 1916, New Zealand. Writer. *Appointments:* Asst Lecturer/ Lecturer/Senior Lecturer in English, University College of North Wales, 1946-65; Professor/Emeritus Professor of English, McMaster University, 1965-. *Publications:* Wordsworth's Preface to Lyrical Ballads, 1957; Wordsworth and Coleridge Lyrical Ballads 1798, 1967, 1969; Wordsworth as Critic, 1969, 1971; Prose Works of William Wordsworth, 3 vols (with J W Smyser), 1974; Wordsworth's Literary Criticism, 1974; William Wordsworth: The Fourteen-Book Prelude, 1985.

Honours: Canada Council Research Fellow and Fellow, Inst for Advanced Studies in Humanities, Edinburgh University, 1973-74; Fellow, Royal Soc of Canada, 1975; Guggenheim Fellow, 1980-81; Hon D Litt, 1988. *Memberships:* Modern Lang Assoc of America; Assoc of Canadian College and University Teachers of English; Modern Humanities Research Assoc; International Assoc of University Professors of English. *Address:* Department of English, McMaster University, Hamilton, Ontario, Canada L8S AL9.

OXLEY William, b. 1939. Poet; Philosopher; Translator; Actor; Traveler; Freelance Writer. *Publications:* The Dark Structures, 1967; New Workings, 1969; Passages from Time: Poems from a Life, 1971; The Icon Poems, 1972; Sixteen Days in Autumn (travel), 1972; Opera Vetera, 1973; Mirrors of the Sea, 1973; Eve Free, 1974; Mundane Shell, 1975; Superficies, 1976; The Exile, 1979; The Notebook of Hepaestus and Other Poems, 1981; Poems of a Black Orpheus, 1981; The Synopthegms of a Prophet, 1981; The Idea and Its Imminence, 1982; Of Human Consciousness, 1982; The Cauldron of Inspiration, 1983; A Map of Time, 1984; The Triviad and Other Satires, 1984; The Inner Tapestry, 1985; Vitalism and Celebration,1987; The Mansands Trilogy, 1988; Mad Tom on Tower Hill, 1988; The Patient Reconstruction of Paradise, 1991; Forest Sequence, 1991; In The Drift of Words, 1992; Cardboard Troy, 1993; The Playboy, 1992. *Address:* 6 The Mount, Furzeham, Brixham, South Devon, TQ5 8QY, England.

OZ Amos, b. 4 May 1939, Jerusalem, Israel. Author. m. Nily Zuckerman, 5 Apr 1960, 1 son, 2 daughters. *Education:* BA cum laude, Hebrew Literature and Philosophy, Hebrew University, Jerusalem, 1965. *Appointments:* Teacher, Literature and Philosophy, Hulda High School and Givat Brenner Regional High School, 1963-86; Visiting Fellow, St Cross College, Oxford, England, 1969-70; Writer in Residence, Hebrew University, Jerusalem, 1975, 1990; Visiting Professor, University of California, Berkeley, USA, 1980; Writer in Residence, Professor of Literature, The Colorado College, Colorado Springs, 1984-85; Writer in Residence, Visiting Professor of Literature, Boston University, Massachusetts, 1987; Full Professor of Hebrew Literature, Ben Gurion University, Beer Sheva, Israel, 1987-; The Slopes of Lebanon. *Publications:* 13 books (novels, short stories and essays), 1965-90, including My Michael, 1982; Black Box, 1988. *Contributions to:* 280 articles and essays on literary, political and ideological topics in Israeli and world papers and magazines. *Honours:* Holon Prize, 1965; Brenner Prize, 1976; Zeev Award for Children's Books, 1978; Bernstein Prize, 1983; Bialik Prize, 1986; Officer, Order of Arts and Letters, France, 1984; Writer of the Year, Lotos Club, New York, 1985; Prix Femina Etranger for Best Foreign Novel of the Year, France, 1988; Wingate Prize, London, for Black Box, 1988; Honorary Doctorates: Hebrew Union College, Cincinnati and Jerusalem; Western New England College, Springfield, Massachusetts. *Address:* c/o Deborah Owen Ltd, 78 Narrow Street, London E14, England.

OZICK Cynthia b. 17 Apr 1928, New York City, USA. Author. m. Bernard Hallote, 7 Sept 1952, 1 daughter. *Education:* BA, cum laude, English, New York University, 1949; MA, Ohio State University, 1950; LHD (Hon) Yeshiva University, 1984; Hebrew Union College, 1984; Williams College, 1986, Hunter College 1987; Jewish Theological Seminary America, 1988; Adelphi University 1988; SUNY 1989; Brandeis University 1990. *Publications:* Trust 1966; The Pagan Rabbi and Other Stories, 1971; Bloodshed and Three Novellas, 1976; Levitation: Five Fictions, 1982; Art and Ardor: Essays, 1983; The Cannibal Galaxy, 1983; The Messiah of Stockholm, 1987; Metaphor and Memory: Essays, 1989; The Shawl, 1989. *Contributions to:* Poetry, criticism, reviews, translations, essays and fiction in numerous periodicals and anthologies. *Honours:* Phi Beta Kappa orator, Harvard University, 1985; Mildred and Harold Strauss Living Award, American Academy of Arts and Letters, 1983; Rea Award for short story, 1986; Guggenheim Fellow, 1982. *Memberships:* PEN; Authors League; American Academy of Arts and Sciences; American Academy and Institute of Arts and Letters; Phi Beta Kappa. *Address:* c/o Raines & Raines, 71 Park Avenue, New York, NY 10016, USA.

P

PAANANEN Eloise Engle, b. April 12, 1923. Writer. m. (1) P R Engle, 1 son, 1 daughter, (2) Lauri A Paananen, 26 Oct 1973. *Education:* Bachelor Degree, Foreign Affairs, George Washington University, Washington D.C. *Publications:* 29 books on military history, culture, travel, nutrition and foods and hundreds of articles and stories for magazines and newspapers; The Winter War - The 1939-40 the Russo-Finnish Conflict, reissued in America as The Soviet Attack on Finland; Man in Flight, 1979; America's Maritime Heritage; The Military, 1993. *Memberships:* Society of Woman Geographers, American Society of Journalists and Authors. *Honours:* Outstanding Books for Children; CINDY Award for film, More than Shelter; Best Book Awards for The Winter War, American's Maritime Heritage, Man in Flight. *Address:* 6348 Crosswoods Drive, Falls Church, VA 22044, USA.

PACI F G, b. 5 Aug 1948, Pesaro, Italy. Teacher; Writer. m. Christine Dunn, 11 June 1979, 1 son. *Education:* BA; BEd; MA. *Publications:* The Italians, 1978; Black Madonna, 1982; The Father, 1984; Black Blood, 1991; Under the Bridge, 1992; Sex and Character, 1993. *Address:* c/o Oberon Press, 400-350 Sparks St, Ottawa, Ontario, Canada K1R 7S8.

PACKARD Vance, b. 22 May 1914, Granville Summit, USA. Author; Teacher. m. Virginia Mathews, 1938, 2 sons, 1 daughter. *Education:* AB; MS; Pennsylvania State University; Columbia University. *Appointments:* Reporter, Boston Record, 1937-38; Writer, Editor, Associated Press Feature Service, 1938-42; Editor, Staff Writer, American Magazine, 1942-56; Staff Writer, Collier's Magazine, 1956. *Publications:* The Hidden Persuaders, 1957; The Status Seekers, 1959; The Waste Makers, 1960; The Pyramid Climbers, 1962; The Naked Society, 1964; The Sexual Wilderness, 1968; A National of Strangers, 1972; The People Shapers, 1977; Our Endangered Children, 1983; The Ultra Rich, 1989. *Honours:* Distinguished Alumni Awards, Pennyslvania State University, Columbia University. *Memberships:* Board, National Book Committee; Authors' Guild; President, Society of Magazine Writers, 1961; American Academy of Political and Social Sciences; American Sociology Association. *Address:* 87 Mill Road, New Canaan, CT 06840, USA.

PACKER Vin. *See:* **MEAKER Marijane.**

PACNER Karel, b. 29 Mar 1936, Janovice n-Uhl, Czechoslovakia. Science Journalist. m. 1971-1973 . *Education:* Dipl Ing (Master's degree), Economics, Economics University, Prague, 1959. *Appointments:* Mlada fronta (now Mlada fronta Dnes) daily newspaper, 1959-. *Publications:* In Czech: On both sides of Space, 1968; ...and the giant leap for mankind (Apollo 11), 1971, 1972; We are searching extra-terrestrial civilisation, 1976; Columbuses of Space, 1976; Soyuz is calling Apollo, 1976; The constructor-in-chief, 1977; Nine space days, 1978; Message of space worlds, 1978; The trip on Mars, 1979; Towns in space, 1986; The humanized of Galaxy, 1987; Discovered secrets of UFO, 1991. *Contributions to:* Several Czech magazines especially Letectvi a kosmonautika. *Honours:* Literary awards for several books from publishing houses. *Memberships:* Community of Writers in Czech Republic; Czechoslovak Society of Arts and Sciences in USA, Czechoslovak Branch. *Address:* K Vidouli 216, 15500 Prague 5, Czech Republic.

PADEL Ruth, b. 8 May 1946, London, England. Writer. m. Myles Burnyent, 15 Aug 1984, 1 daughter. *Education:* Greats, Lady Margaret Hall, Oxford; BA, 1969; MA, 1975; PhD, 1976. *Publications:* Alibi, poems, 1985; Summer Snow, poems, 1990; In and Out of the Mind: Greek Images of the Tragic Self, 1992; Collections on: Women in Antiquity; The Anthropology of the Self; Essays on George Steiner. *Contributions to:* Essays to: Encounter; Bete Noire; Gender and History; Articles on ancient and modern Greek poetry to: Classical Quarterly;

Proceedings of Cambridge Philological Society; Poems and reviews to: Times Literary Supplement, 1975-93; Poems to: The Times, The Sunday Times, London Review of Books, Acumen, Oxford magazine, Critical Quarterly, The Observer; New Statesman; Poetry Nation Review; Kenyon Review; Poetry; Poetry Review; Cambridge Review; Bete Noire; Various anthologies including Virago Book of Women's Love Poetry. *Honours:* Royal Literary Fund Grant, 1991; Wingate Fellowship, 1992; Prize-Winning Poems: National Poetry competition, 1985, 1992-. *Memberships:* Royal Zoological Society; Hellenic Society; PEN. *Address:* 5a Thurlow Road, London NW3 5PJ, England.

PADFIELD Peter Lawrence Notton, b. 3 Apr 1932, Calcutta, India. Author. m. Dorothy Jean Yarwood, 23 Apr 1960, Dodleston, Chester. 1 son, 2 daughters. *Publications:* The Titanic and the Californian, 1965; An Agony of Collisions, 1966; Aim Straight: A Biography of Admiral Sir Percy Scott, 1966; Broke and the Shannon: A Biography of Admiral Sir Philip Broke, 1968; The Battleship Era, 1972; Guns at Sea: A History of Naval Gunnery, 1973; The Great Naval Race: Anglo-German Naval Rivalry 1900-1914, 1974; Nelson's War, 1978; Tide of Empires: Decisive Naval Campaigns in the Rise of the West, Volume I 1481-1654, Volume II 1654-1763, 1979 and 1982; Rule Britannia: The Victorian and Edwardian Navy, 1981; Beneath The Houseflag of the P & O, 1982; Dönitz, The Last Führer, 1984; Armada, 1988; Himmler, Reichsführer - SS, 1990; Hess: Flight for the Führer, 1991, revised, updated ed. 1993; Novels: The Lion's Claw, 1978; The Unquiet Gods, 1980; Gold Chains of Empire, 1982; Salt and Steel, 1986. *Address:* Westmoreland Cottage, Woodbridge, Suffolk, England.

PADHY Pravat Kumar, b. 27 Dec 1954, India. Geologist. m. Namita Padhy, 6 Mar 1983, 2 daughters. *Education:* MSc, Applied Geology, 1979; MTech, Mineral Exploration, 1980; PhD, Applied Geology. *Career include:* Wrote 4-line poem at age 13; Currently Senior Geologist, ONGC, Baroda, Gujarat. *Publications:* Silence of the Seas, 1992; Anthologised in: RJES Intercontinental Poetry, 1979; Modern Trends in Indo-Anglian Poetry, 1982; Prevalent Aspects of Indian-English Poetry, 1983-84; Premier Poets, 1986; Anti-War, Vol II, 1988; East-West Voices, 1988; Contemporary Indian English Poetry, 1988; Snows to the Seas, 1989; Contemporary Indian English Love Poetry, 1990; World Poetry, 1991; World Poetry, 1992. *Contributions to:* Hesperus Review; Writer's Life Line; Skylark; Poetry; Poesie; Poetry Time; Commonwealth Quarterly; Canopy; Creative Forum; Poet Crit; Kavita India; Literary Horizon; By Word; Creative Art and Poetry; Others. *Honours:* Certificate of Honour for poem I Wish Every Day, Writer's Life Line, Canada, 1986. *Address:* 166 HIG Complex, Chandrasekharpur, Sailashri Vihar, Bhubaneshwar, Orissa, India.

PADMANABHAN Neela, b. 26 Apr 1938, Thiruvanantha Puram. Deputy Chief Engineer. m. U Krishnammal, 3 July 1963, 1 son, 3 daughters. *Education:* SSLC, 1953; Kekala University, Intermediate, 1956; BSC, 1959, Bsc (Engg), 1963; FIE, Institute of Engineers, Calcutta, 1991. *Publications:* Thalaimurakal; Pallikondapuram; Uravukal; Therodum Veedhi; Paavam Seyyathavargal; Samuka Chintaanai; Moondravathu Naal. *Contributions to:* Ezhutthu; Ilakkiavattam Nadai; Caravan; Mirror; Indian Literature; Indian Writing today; Kumudam. *Honours:* Rajah Sir Annamalai Chettiar Award; Tamil Annai Prize; Tamil Development Council of Tamil Nadu Government. *Memberships:* Authors Guild of India; PEN; Poetry Society of India; Centre of Indian Writers. *Address:* 39 1870 Kuriyathi Road, Manacaudpo, Thiruvanantha Purah 695009, India.

PADOVANO Anthony Thomas, b. USA. Professor. *Education:* BA magna cum laude, Seton Hall University, South Orange, New Jersey, 1956; STB magna cum laude, 1958, STL magna cum laude, 1960, STD magna cum laude, 1962, Pontifical Gregorian University, Rome; PhL magna cum laude, St Thomas Pontifical International University, Rome, 1962; MA, American

Literature, New York University, 1971; PhD, Fordham University, New York, 1980. *Appointments:* Professor of Systematic Theology, Darlington School of Theology, Mahwah, New Jersey, 1962-74; Professor of American Literature, Ramapo College of New Jersey, Mahwah, 1971-. *Publications:* The Cross of Christ, the Measure of the World, 1962; The Estranged God, 1966, Paperback, 1967, Spanish Edition, 1968; Who is Christ, 1967, Chinese Edition, 1969, Spanish Edition, 1972; Belief in Human Life, 1969; American Culture and the Quest for Christ, 1970, Paperback, 1971; Dawn Without Darkness, 1971, German Edition, 1984; Free to be Faithful, 1972; Eden and Easter, 1974; A Case for Worship, 1975; Presence and Structure, 1975; America: Its People, Its Promise, 1975; Trilogy, 1982; The Human Journey: Thomas Merton, Symbol of a Century, 1982, Paperback, 1984; Contemplation and Compassion, 1984; Winter Rain, play, 1985; His Name is John, play, 1986; Christmas to Calvary, 1987; Love and Destiny, 1987; Summer Lightening, play, 1988; Conscience and Conflict, 1989; The Church Today: Belonging and Believing, 1990; Reform and Renewal, 1990; A Celebration of Life, 1990; Scripture in the Streets, 1992. *Contributions to:* Ave Maria; The Catholic World; Preaching; National Catholic Reporter; St Anthony Messenger; New Catholic World; The Beacon; Creation. *Honours:* Catholic Book Club Selection, 1966, 1970; National Catholic Press Association Award, 1970; Angel Award, 1985; 2 New Jersey Writers Conference Awards, 1985; Silver Angel Award, 1986; Fred and Florence Thomases Award; Merit Award, Ramapo College. *Memberships:* President, Corpus; Vice-President, International Federation of Married Catholic Priests; Catholic Theological Society of America; Theta Alpha Kappa; Board of Directors, National Multiple Sclerosis Society; Priests for Equality; Advisory Board, Federation of Christian Ministries; Theological Consultor, Global Education Association; WEORC; National Federation of Priests Councils; Catholics Speak Out; Founding Member, International Thomas Merton Society. *Address:* 9 Millstone Drive, Morris Plains, NJ 07950, USA.

PAGE Bruce, b. 1 Dec 1936, London, England. Journalist; Publisher. m. (1) Anne Gillison, 1964, (div 1969), (2) Anne L Darnborough, 1969, 1 son, 1 daughter. *Education:* Melbourne University. *Appointments:* Trained as Journalist, Melbourne Herald, 1956-60; Evening Standard, London, 1960-62; Daily Herald, London, 1962-64; various executive posts, Sunday Times, 1964-76; Associate Editor, Daily Express, 1977; Editor, New Statesman, 1978-82; Managing Director, Executive Producers Ltd., 1983-. *Publications:* Co-Author: Philby, the Spy who Betrayed a Generation; An American Melodrama; Do You Sincerely Want to be Rich?; Destination Disaster; Ulster (Contributor): The Yom Kippur War; The British Press. *Honours:* Various awards for journalism. *Address:* 35 Duncan Terrace, London N1 8AL, England.

PAGE Diana (Preuthun), b. 17 Aug 1946, Detroit, Michigan, USA. m. Horacio Villalobos, 21 Feb 1973, (diss 12 Apr 1980). *Education:* BA, University of Michigan, 1968; MA, Johns Hopkins School of Advanced International Studies, 1982. *Appointments:* Volunteer worker in Bahia, Brazil, US Peace Corps, 1968-70; Correspondent from Rio de Janeiro, Brazil, 1970-72 and Buenos Aires, Argentina 1972-79, United Press International, Washington DC; Correspondent, El Dia/Noticias Argentinos, Washington DC, 1980-83; Correspondent, St Petersburg Times, St Petersburg, Florida, 1984-85; Director of Public Affairs, International Institute for Environment and Development, Washington DC, 1986-. *Publication:* (with Jose Napoleon Duarte) Duarte: My Story, 1986. *Literary Agent:* Elizabeth Grossman, Literistic Ltd, New York. *Address:* c/o Elizabeth Grossman, Literistic Ltd, 1 Madison Avenue, New York, NT 10010, USA.

PAGE Eleanor. *See:* **COERR Eleanor Beatrice.**

PAGE Emma. *See:* **TIRBUTT Honoria.**

PAGE Geoff, b. 7 July 1940, Grafton, New South Wales, Australia. Teacher; Writer. m. Carolyn Mau, 4 Jan 1972, 1 son. *Education:* BA Hons; DipEd. *Appointments:* Writer-in-Residence: Australian Defence Force Academy, Curtin University, Wollongong University and Edith Cowan University. *Publications:* The Question, in Two Poets, 1971; Smalltown Memorial, 1975; Collecting the Weather, 1978; Cassandra Paddocks, 1980; Clairvoyant in Autumn, 1983; Shadows from Wire: Poems and Photographs of Australian in the Great War (editor), 1983; Benton's Conviction, novel, 1985; Century of Clouds: Selected Poems of Guillaume Apollinaire (translator with Wendy Coutts), 1985; Collected Lives, 1986; Smiling in English, Smoking in French, 1987; Footwork, 1988; Winter Vision, novel, 1989; Invisible Histories, stories and poems, 1990; Selected Poems, 1991; Gravel Corners, 1992; On the Move (editor), 1992. *Honours:* Literature Board Grants, Australia Council, 1974, 1983, 1987, 1989, 1992. *Memberships:* Australian Society of Authors; Australian Teachers Union. *Address:* 8 Morehead St, Curtin, ACT 2605, Australia.

PAGE Katherine Hall, b. 9 July 1947, New Jersey, USA. Writer. m. Alan Hein, 5 Dec 1975, 1 son. *Education:* AB, Wellesley College, 1969; EdM, Tufts University, 1974; EdD, Harvard University, 1985. *Publications:* Faith Fairchild mystery series: The Body in the Belfry, 1990, 1991; The Body in the Bouillon, 1991, 1992; The Body in the Kelp, 1991, 1992; The Body in the Vestibule, 1992, 1993. *Honours:* Agatha for Best First Domestic Mystery, Malice Domestic, 1991. *Memberships:* Mystery Readers International; Mystery Writers of America; The Authors Guild; Sisters in Crime; The American Crime Writers League; Society of Children's Bookwriters and Illustrators. *Literary Agent:* Faith Hamlin, Greenburger Associates Inc, New York, NY, USA. *Address:* c/o St Martin's Press, 175 Fifth Avenue, New York, NY 10010, USA.

PAGE Louise, b. 1955. Writer; Playwright. *Appointment:* Resident Writer, Royal Court Theatre, London, 1982-83. *Publications:* Tissue (in Plays by Women 1), 1982; Salonika, 1983; Real Estate, 1985; Golden Girls, 1985; Beauty and the Beast, 1986. *Address:* c/o Phil Kelvin, Goodwin Associates, 12 Rabbit Row, London, W8 4DX, England.

PAGE Norman, b. 8 May 1930, University Teacher; Author. m. Jean Hampton, 29 Mar 1958, 3 sons, 1 daughter. *Education:* BA 1951, MA 1955 Emmanuel College, Cambridge; PhD University of Leeds, 1968. *Publications include:* The Language of Jane Austen, 1972; Speech in the English Novel, 1973, 2nd edition 1988; Thomas Hardy, 1977; A E Housman: A Critical Biography, 1983; A Kipling Companion, 1984; E M Forster, 1988; Tennyson: An Illustrated Life, 1992. *Contributions to:* London Review of Books; Modern Language Review; Notes and Queries; Etudes Anglaises; Bulletin of the New York Public Library. *Honours:* Guggenheim Foundation Fellowship, 1979; Fellow, Royal Society of Canada, 1982; University of Alberta Research Prize, 1983; *Memberships:* Thomas Hardy Society, Vice President, Editor of Thomas Hardy Journal; Newstead Abbey Byron Society; Tennyson Society, Chairman, Publications Board. *Address:* 23 Braunston Road, Oakham, Rutland LE15 6LD, England.

PAGE Patricia Kathleen, b. 23 Nov 1916, Dorset, England. Writer; Painter. m. Arthur Irwin, 16 Dec 1950, 1 stepson, 2 stepdaughters. *Publications:* Novel: The Sun and the Moon, 1944; Poetry: As Ten as Twenty, 1946; The Metal and the Flower, 1954; Cry Ararat!-Poems New and Selected, 1967; The Sun and the Moon and Other Fictions, 1973; Poems Selected and New, 1974; Editor, To Say the Least, 1979; Evening Dance of the Grey Flies (poems and a short story), 1981; The Travelling Musicians, text, 1984; The Glass Air, poetry, essays and drawings, 1985; Brazilian Journal, prose, 1988; I-Sphinx, A Poem for Two Voices; A Flask of Sea Water, fairy story, 1989; The Glass Air, Poems Selected and New, 1991; The Travelling Musicians, children's book, 1991. *Contributions to:* Numerous magazines and anthologies in Canada, USA and UK. *Honours:* Officer of the Order of Canada, 1977; Winner, Oscar Blumenthal Award, 1944; Governor- General's Award for Poetry, 1954; National Magazines Award (Gold), 1986; Canadian Authors' Association Literary Award for Poetry, 1986; Short listed for Governor-General's Award for Non-Fiction, 1988; BC Book Awards Hubert Evans Prize, 1988; Banff Centre School of Fine Arts National Award, 1989. *Memberships:* The League of Canadian Poets; The Writers' Union. *Literary Agent:* Denise Bukowski. *Address:* 3260 Exeter Road, Victoria, BC, Canada V8R 6H6.

PAGE Robin, b. 1943. Writer. *Publications:* Down with the Poor, 1971; The Benefits Racket, 1972; Down Among the Dossers, 1973; The Decline of an English Village, 1974; The Hunter and the Hunted, 1977; Weather Forecasting: The Country Way, 1977; Cures and Remedies: The Country Way,1978; Weeds: The Country Way, 1979; Animal Cures: The Country Way, 1979; The Journal of a Country Parish, 1980; Journeys into Britain, 1982; The Country Way of Love, 1983; The Wildlife of the Royal Estates, 1984; Count One to Ten, 1986; The Fox's Tale, 1986; The Duchy of Cornwall, 1987; The Fox and the Orchid, 1987. *Address:* Bird's Farm, Barton, Cambridgeshire, England.

PAGE Vicki. *See:* **AVEY Ruby Doreen.**

PAGTER Carl Richard, b. 13 Feb 1934, Baltimore, Maryland, USA. Attorney. m. (1) 1 son, (2) Judith Cox, 3 May 1978. *Education:* AA, Diablo Valley College, Concord, California, 1953; BA, San Jose State University, 1956; JD, Boalt Hall School of Law, University of California, Berkeley, 1964. *Publications:* Books with Alan Dundes: Work Hard and You Shall Be Rewarded, 1978; When You're Up to Your Ass in Alligators, 1987; Never Try to Teach a Pig to Sing, 1991; Persian Gulf Warlore (with Alan Dundes), Western Folklore, 1991. *Contributions to:* Various minor articles to magazines and journals. *Memberships:* American Folklore Society; California Folklore Society; American Bar Association; California Bar Association; District of Columbia Bar Association. *Address:* 17 Julianne Court, Walnut Creek, CA 94595, USA.

PAINE Lauran Bosworth, b. 25 Feb 1916, Duluth, Minnesota, USA. Author. m. Mona Margarette Lewellyn, 26 June 1982, 1 son, 4 daughters. *Education:* Pacific Military Academy, 1930-32; St Alban's Episcopal School, 1932-34. *Publications:* numerous psuedonyms: Over 600 westerns include: Geronimo, 1950; Decade of Deceit, 1955, as Dakota Death-Trap, 1986; Outpost, 1963; The Border Guns, 1965, as Arizona Drifter, 1966; Avenger's Trail, 1967; Rainey Valley, 1971; The Blue Hills, 1975; Mule-Train, 1978; The Loner, 1978; Deuce, 1979; The Trail Drive, 1983; The Sand Painting, 1987; The Bushwhacker, 1989; The Sheridan Stage, 1989; The Bandoleros, 1990; Alamo Jefferson, 1990; The Left-Hand Gun, 1991; Strangers in Buckhorn, 1991; The Undertaker (The Legend of El Cajonero), 1991; The Squaw Men, 1992; Devil's Canyon, 1992; Over 75 mysteries include: Case of the Hollow Men, 1958; Murder Now Pay Later, 1969; The Killer's Conscience, 1971; The Ivory Penguin, 1974; The Underground Men, 1975; Over 100 romances include: Beyond This Valley, 1964; Love and a Rusty Moon, 1968; A Fortune for Love, 1971; The Sunday Lover, 1973; A Scarlet Dawn, 1978; A Gentle Spring, 1980; April d'Auriac, 1990; Science fiction: This Time Tomorrow, 1963; The Undine, 1972; 8 more; Adventure: Blue Sea and Yellow Sun, 1967; The Night of the Crisis, 1968; Non-fiction includes: Northwest Conquest (Conquest of the Great Northwest), 1959; The General Custer Story, 1960; Tom Horn: Man of the West, UK Edition, 1962, US Edition, 1963; Viet-Nam, 1965; Bolivar the Liberator, 1970; The Hierarchy of Hell, 1972; Gentleman Johnny: The Life of General John Burgoyne, 1973; Saladin: A Man for All Ages, 1974; Witches in Fact and Fantasy, 1972; The CIA at Work, 1977; The Technology of Espionage, 1978; D-Day, 1981; America and the Americans, 1984; The Abwehr (German Military Intelligence in World War Two), 1984. *Literary Agent:* Jon Tuska, 2327 Salmon Street, Portland, OR 97214, USA. *Address:* 9413 North Hiway 3, Fort Jones, CA 96032, USA.

PAINE Theodor. *See:* **PETAJA Emil.**

PAJOR Johnjoseph, b. 5 Feb 1948, South Bend, Indiana, USA. Poet. m. Cass Pajor, 18 Nov 1989, 3 sons, 1 daughter. *Education:* Graduate Welder and Medical Assistant, Vocational College; College credits, University. *Career includes:* Readings and poetry concerts, radio drama, Italy, USA, Canada, over 30 years. *Publications:* Dies Faustus, Revised Edition, 1976; In Transit, 1978; A collection of 3, 1979; Auditions, 1979; Traveler, 1979; Works: On Tour; African violets, 1989; Challenger, 1990; Sacred fire, 1990; Chiaroscuro, 1991; Wilderness - land of the raining moon, 1991; THE tErpslchOrd I & II, registered 1992 & 93, unpublished; Numerous other works, 1965-92. *Contributions to:* Numerous small contributions to various publications, over last 30 years. *Honours:* Literary Honorarium, National Poetry Awards, USA, 1978. *Literary Agent:* Elaine Bertoldi, 900 Norway, Norway, MI 49870, USA. *Address:* PO Box 31742, Seattle, WA 98103, USA.

PALIN Michael Edward, b. 5 May 1943. Freelance Writer and Actor. m. Helen M. Gibbins, 1966, 2 sons, 1 daughter. *Education:* BA, Brasenose College, Oxford. *Appointments:* Actor, Writer: Monty Python's Flying Circus, BBC TV, 1969-74; Ripping Yarns, BBC TV 1976-80; Writer, East of Ipswich, BBC TV, 1986; Films: Actor and Joint Author: And Now for Something Completely Different, 1970; Monty Python and the Holy Grail, 1974; Monty Python's Life of Brian, 1978; Time Bandits, 1980; Monty Python's The Meaning of Life, 1982; Actor, Writer, Co-Producer, The Missionary, 1982; Around the World in 80 Days, BBC, 1989. Actor: Jabberwocky, 1976; A Private Function, 1984; Brazil, 1985; A Fish Called Wanda, 1988; Contributor, Great Railway Journeys of the World, BBC TV, 1980; Actor, Co-Writer, American Friends (film), 1991; Actor, GBH (TV Channel 4), 1991. *Publications:* Monty Python's Big Red Book, 1970; Monty Python's Brand New Book, 1973; Dr Fegg's Encyclopaedia of All World Knowledge, 1984; Limericks, 1985; For Children: Small Harry and the Toothache Pills, 1981; The Mirrorstone, 1986; The Cyril Stories, 1986; Around The World In 80 Days, 1989; Pole To Pole, 1992. *Honours:* Writers Guild, Best Screenplay Award for American Friends, 1991. *Address:* 68a, Delancey Street, London, NW1 7RY, England.

PALMER Alan Warwick, b. 28 Sept 1926, Ilford, Essex. Retired Schoolmaster. m. Veronica Mary Cordell, 1 Sept 1951. *Education:* Bancroft's School, Woodford Green, Essex. MA 1950, M Litt 1954, Oriel College, Oxford. *Publications:* Alexander I, Tsar of War and Peace, 1974; The East End, 1989; Bernadotte: Napoleon's Marshal, Sweden's King, 1990; The Chancelleries of Europe, 1982; Crowned Cousins: The Anglo-German Royal Connection, 1986; Penguin Dictionary of Twentieth Century History, 4th edition, 1990; The Decline and Fall of the Ottoman Empire, 1992. *Contributions to:* History Today; The Times etc. *Memberships:* Fellow of the Royal Society of Literature, 1979; International PEN, 1989. *Literary Agent:* Campbell, Thomson and McLaughlin Ltd. *Address:* 4 Farm End, Woodstock, Oxford OX20 1XN, England.

PALMER Frank Robert, b. 1922. Writer. *Publications:* Morphology of the Tigre Noun, 1962; Linguistic Study of the English Verb, 1965; Selected Papers of J.R. Firth 1951-1958, 1968; Prosodic Analysis, 1970; Grammar, 1971, 1984; The English Verb, 1974, 1987; Semantics, 1976, 1981; Modality and the English Modals, 1979, 1990; Mood and Modality, 1986. *Contributions to:* Over 50 learned journals. *Memberships:* Member of Linguistic Society of America; Vice-President of Philological Society; Academia Europaea; Fellow of the British Academy. *Address:* Whitethorns, Roundabout Lane, Winnersh, Wokingham, Berks, RG11 5AD, England.

PALMER John, b. 13 May 1943, Sydney, Nova Scotia, Canada. Playwright; Director. *Education:* BA, English, Carleton University, Ottawa, Canada, 1965. *Appointments:* Dramaturge, Associate, Factory Theatre Lab, Toronto, Canada, 1970-73; Co-Founder, Co-Artistic Director, Literary Manager, Toronto Free Theatre, 1972-76; Resident Playwright, Canadian Rep Theatre, Toronto, 1983-87; Course Director, Final Year Playwrighting, York University, Toronto, 1991-93. *Publications:* 2 Plays: The End, and A Day at the Beach, 1991; Before the Guns, Memories for my Brother, Part I, Dangerous Traditions: Four Passe-Muraille Plays, 1992; Henrik Ibsen On the Necessity of Producing Norwegian Drama, 1992-93; Selected Plays. *Contributions to:* Theatre Byline, Woodstock Sentinel Review, 1968; The Man Behind the News, short story, to Canadian Forum, 1973; Henrik Ibsen to: Canadian Theatre Review and This Magazine, 1977. *Honours:* Various Canada Council and Ontario Arts Council grants. *Memberships:* Co-Founder, Playwrights Union of Canada; Canadian Actors Equity Association. *Literary Agents:* Ronda Cooper, Characters Talent, 150 CArleton St, Toronto, Ontario, Canada M5A 2K1; Joyce Ketay, 334 w 89th St, New York NY 10024, USA. *Address:* 32 Monteith St, Toronto, Ontario, Canada M4Y 1K7.

PALMER Peter John, b. 20 Sept 1932, Melbourne, Australia. Teacher. m. Elizabeth Fischer, 22 Dec 1955, 1 son, 1 daughter. *Education:* BA, 1953, BEd 1966, University of Melbourne. *Publications:* The Past and Us, 1957; The Twentieth Century, 1964; Editor, Contributor and Illustrator: Confrontation 1971, Interaction 1974, Expansion 1975, Survival, 1976, Three Worlds 1978; Earth and Man, 1980, Man on the Land, 1981, Man and Machines 1983, Challenge 1985; Geography 10 (Author and Illustrator), 1992. *Contributions to:* Executive Editor: Macmillan Australian Atlas, 1983, 3rd edition 1990. 4th edition 1993. *Address:* 34 Ardgower Court, Lower Templestowe, Victoria 3107, Australia.

PALMER Tony, b. 29 Aug 1941, London, England. Film Director; Author. *Publications:* Born Under A Bad sign; Trials of Oz; Electric Revolution; Biography of Liberace; All You Need Is Love; Charles II; Julian Bream, A Life On The Road; Mienuhin, A Family Portrait. *Contributions to:* Observer; Sunday Times; New York Times; Spectator; Punch; Daily Mail; Life Magazine. *Honours:* Italia Prize (twice); Gold Medal, New York Film & TV Festival (6 times); Fellini Prize; Critics Prize Sao Paolo; Special Jury Prize, San Francisco. *Membership:* Garrick Club. *Address:* Nanjizal, St Levan, Cornwall, England.

PALOMINO Angel, b. 2 Aug 1929, Toledo, Spain. Novelist; Journalist; Television Writer. *Education:* Studies of Linguistics, Science and Chemistry, Central University, Madrid; Technician in Management. *Publications:* Numerous works of poetry, short stories, essays and novels include: El Cesar de Papel, 1957; Zamora y Gomora, 1968; Torremolinos Gran Hotel, 1971; Memorias de un Intelectual Antifranquista, 1972; Un Jaguar y una Rubia, 1972; Madrid Costa Fleming, 1973; Todo Incluido, 1975; Divorcio Para una Virgen Rota, 1977; La Luna se Llama Perez, 1978; Plan Marshall para 50 Munutos, 1978; Las Otras Violaciones, 1979. *Contributions to:* Estafeta Literaria; ABC; Semana. *Honours:* Numerous Literary prizes including: Miguel de Cervantes National Literary Prize, 1971; Finalist, Planeta Prize, 1977; International Prize, Press Club, 1968, others. *Memberships:* Royal Academy of Fine Arts and Historical Sciences; National Academy of Gastronomy; Spanish Association of Book Writers; UInternational Federation of Tourism Writers; International Association of Literary Critics. *Literary Agent:* Editorial Planeta, Barcelona. *Address:* Conde de Penalver 17, 28006 Madrid, Spain.

PÁLSSON Einar, b. 10 Nov 1925, Reykjavik, Iceland. Headmaster. m. Birgitte Laxdal, 24 Dec 1948, 2 sons, 1 daughter. *Education:* Cand phil, University of Iceland, 1946; Certificate of Merit, Royal Academy of Dramatic Art, London, 1948; BA, Danish and English Literature, University of Iceland, 1957. *Appointments:* Chairman, Reykjavik City Theatre (Leikfélag Reykjaviku), 1950-53; Play Producer, Reykjavik City Theatre, National Theatre and Icelandic State Radio, 1952-63. *Publications:* Spekin og Sparifotin, essays, 1963; The Roots of Icelandic Culture, 10 vols: 1. The Background of Njals Saga, 1969; 2. Religion and the Settlement of Iceland, 1970; 3. Time and Ekpyrosis, 1972; 4. Stone Cross, 1976; 5. The Ominous Beat, 1978; 6. The Celtic Heritage, 1981; 7. The Dome of Heaven, 1985; 8. The Theme. Paganism and Hrafnkels Saga, 1988; 9. Egils Saga and the Two Wolves, 1990; 10. The Ancient Althing at Thingvellir, 1991; Icelandic in Easy Stages, textbook, I, 1975, II, 1977. *Contributions to:* Numerous to Icel Morgunbladid; Lesbók; Special prints: monographs and lectures. *Honours:* Prize for 1-act play Trillan, Icelandic Cultural Council, 1962. *Memberships:* Rithøfundasamband Islands; The Nordic Society, Director 1966-69; The Reykjavik City Theatre. *Address:* Sólvallagata 28, 101 Reykjavik, Iceland.

PAMA Cornelis, b. 5 Nov 1916, Rotterdam, the Netherlands. Editor; Author. m. Heather Myfanwy Woltman, 1 Mar 1977. 1 son, 2 daughters. *Education:* Dutch Publishing Diploma. *Appointments:* Manager, Bailliere, Tindall & Cox Ltd, London, 1948-55; General Manager, W & G Foyle, Cape Town, 1955-67; Director, A A Balkema Publishers, Cape Town, 1967-72; Editor, Tafelberg Publishers, Cape Town, 1972-80; Editor-in-Chief, Nederlandse Post, Cape Town, 1980-; Honorary Editor: Familia, 1965-; Arma, 1955-. *Publications include:* Handboek der Heraldiek, 5th edition 1987; Lions & Virgins, 1964; Genealogies of Old South African Families, 3 volumes, 2nd edition 1966; The South African Library 1818-1968, 1968; The Heraldry of South African Families, 1970; Vintage Cape Town, 1973; Bowler's Cape Town, 1975; Regency Cape Town, 1978; 21 other books on genealogy and heraldry. *Contributions to:* Historical, genealogical and heraldic journals. *Honours include:* Extraordinary Gold Medal, SA Academy of Arts & Sciences, 1966; J Bracken Lee Award, Salt Lake City; Gold Medal Pro Merito Genealogicae, Deutsche Zentralstelle fur Familiengeschichte, Germany, 1976; Distinguished Fellow, American College of Heraldry and New Zealand Heraldry Society. *Memberships:* PEN South African Centre; South African Academy of Arts & Sciences; Afrikaanse Skrywerskring. *Address:* P O Box 4839, Cape Town 8000, South Africa.

PAMPEL Martha Maria, b. 4 Apr 1913, Muhlheim, Ruhr, Germany. Author. m. Adolf Pampel, 1 June 1936, 1 daughter. *Education:* Business Training; Correspondence Course, English; Organist's Examination; International Famous Writers School. *Publications:* Die Tur steht offen, 1965, 1976; Heilige mitkleinen Fehlern, 1977; Land der dunklen Walder, 1977; Wer in der Liebe bleibt, 1978; Ein Streiter vor dem Herrn, 1979; Das Freuen lernen, 1979, recorded on tape 1983; 7 small volumes, series, Die Feierabendstende. Various little books: Die Kleinen Freuden des Alltags, 1986; Calendars, children's devotions book. *Honours:* Diploma of Merit, Universityie delle Arti, Italy, 1982; Albert Einstein Academy Bronze Medal, peace proposition, Universal Intelligence Data Bank of America, 1986; Honorary Doctorate, International University Foundation, USA, 1986. *Address:* Lortzingstrasse 9, Bad Sachsa, 3423, Federal Republic of Germany.

PANICHAS George Andrew, b. 21 May 1930, Springfield, Massachusetts, USA. Educator; Literary Critic; Scholar. *Education:* BA, American International College, 1951; MA, Trinity College, Hartford, Connecticut, 1952; PhD, Nottingham University, UK, 1962. *Appointments include:* Instructor, Assistant/Associate Professor, Professor of English, University of Maryland, 1962-. Editor, Modern Age, quarterly review; Advisory editor, Continuity, history journal. *Publications include:* Adventure in Consciousness: The Meaning of D H Lawrence's Religious Quest, 1964; Epicurus, 1967; The Reverent Discipline: Essays in Literary Criticism & Culture, 1974; The Burden of Vision: Dostoevsky's Spiritual Art, 1977, 1985; The Courage of Judgement:

Essays in Literary Criticism, Culture & Society, 1983. Co-author, Renaissance & Modern Essays (presented to Vivian de Sola Pinto, 70th birthday), 1966. Editor, numerous books including: Politics of 20th Century Novelists; Modern Age: The First 25 Years. *Contributions to:* Articles, translations, reviews, essays, to books, anthologies, journals, USA & Europe. *Honours include:* Fellow, Royal Society of Arts, UK, 1971-; Grant, Earhart Foundation, 1982. *Memberships include:* Awards committee, Richard M Weaver Fellowship, 1983-; Jury panel, Ingersoll Prizes, 1986-; Academic Board, National Humanities Institute, 1985-; etc. *Address:* Department of English, University of Maryland, College Park, MD 20742, USA.

PANIKER Ayyappa, b. 12 Sept 1930, Kavalam, India. Professor. m. Sreeparvathy, 6 Dec 1961, 2 daughters. *Education:* BA, Honours, Travancore, 1951; MA, Kerala, 1959; CTE, Hyderabad, 1966; AM & PhD, Indiana, USA, 1971. *Appointments:* Founder Editor, Kerala Kavita, 1965; General Editor, Kerala Writers in English; Editor, World Classics Retold in Malayalam Editor, Indian Journal of English Studies; Director, Workshop in Literary Translation, 1987. *Publications:* Ayyappa Panikerude Kritikal 1, 1974, 1981; Ayyappa Panikerude Lekhanangal, 1982; Ezhukavitalum Patanangalam, 1984; Ayyappa Panikerude Kritikal, 1984; Cuban Poems, translation, 1984; Granth Sahib, translation, 1986; Mayakovskis Poems, 1987; Dialogues, 1988; Editor, Vallathol: A Centenary Perspective; Ayyappa Panikerude Kritikal 1981-89, 1989; Pattu Kavitakal, Patanangalum, 1989; Thakazhi Sivasankara Pillai, 1989; Gotrayanam, 1989; Indian Literature in English, A Perspective of Malayalain Literature, 1990; Spotlight on Comparative Indian Literature, 1992. *Contributor to:* Indian Journal of English Studies; Literary Criterion. *Honours:* Kerala Sahitya Akademi Award for Poetry, 1975; Kalyani Krishna Menon Prize, 1976; SPCS Award, 1978; Kerala Sahitya Akademi Award for Criticism, 1982; Central Sahitya Akademi Award for Poetry, 1984; Bharatiya Bhasha Parishad Bhilwara Award, 1988; Mahakaru Kuttamath Award, 1989; Mahakais Ulloov Award, 1991; Asan Prize, 1992. *Memberships:* Indian Association for English Studies, Life Member; American Studies Research Centre; Dravidian Language Association; Indian Sub Commission for Unesco. *Address:* 111 Gandhinagar, Trivandrum 695014, India.

PANIKER Salvador, b. 1 Mar 1927, Barcelona, Spain. Publisher; Writer. *Education:* Lic. Philos; Dr Indl. Engrng. *Publications:* Conversaciones en Cataluna, 1966; Los Signos y las Cosas, 1968; Conversaciones en Madrid, 1969; La Difficultad der Ser Espanol, 1979; Approximacion al Origen, 1982; Primer Testamento, 1985; Ensayos retroprogresivos, 1987; Segunda Memoria, 1988; Lectura De Los Griegos, 1992. *Contributions to:* La Vanguardia; El Pais; Convivum; Revista de Occidente; Ciencia y Pensamiento. *Honour:* International Press Prize, 1969. *Address:* Numancia 117-121, Barcelona 08029, Spain.

PANSHIN Alexei, b. 14 Aug 1940, Lansing, Michigan, USA. Writer. m. Cory Seidman, 4 June 1969, 2 sons. *Education:* BA, Michigan State University, 1965; MA, University of Chicago, 1966. *Publications:* Heinlein in Dimension, 1968; Rite of Passage, 1968; Star Well, 1968; The Thurb Revolution, 1968; Masque World, 1969; SF in Dimension, 1976, revised edition 1980 (with Cory Panshin); Farewell to Yesterday's Tormorrow, 1975; Earth Magic, with Cory Panshin, 1978; Transmutations : A Book of Personal Alchemy, 1982; The World Beyond the Hill, with Cory Panshin, forthcoming. *Contributions to:* various journals and magazines. *Honours:* Hugo Award, 1967; Nebula Award, 1968. *Address:* RD1, Box 168, Riegelsville, PA 18077, USA.

PANTEA Aurel, b. 1 Mar 1952, Transylvania, Romania. Teacher. m. Katia, 17 Apr 1975, 2 sons, 1 daughter. *Education:* BA, Romanian Literature. *Publications:* House with Rheters, 1980; The Afternoon Person, 1984; Days with Bouvard and Pecuchet. *Contributions to:* Echinex; Tribuna; Vatra; Amfiteatru.

Honour: Award, Albatros Editor. *Address:* Strada Zidariler 2, 2500 Alba Iulia, Romania.

PAPADIMITRAKOPOULOS Elias, b. 23 Aug 1930, Pyrgos, Ilias, Greece. Physician. m. Niobe Kataki, 30 Dec 1957. *Education:* Thessaloniki's University Medical School, 1949-55; Military Medical School, 1949-55. *Appointments:* Co Editor, Skapti Ili, 1965-66; O Chartis, 1983-87; Yiati, 1985-. *Publications:* Toothpaste with Chlorophyll; Maritime Hot Baths; The General Archivist. *Contributions to:* Tram; To Dendro; Anti; Yiati; I Lexi; O Chartis; To Tetarto. *Memberships:* Society of Greek Writers. *Address:* 23 Lazaradon Street, 11363 Athens, Greece.

PAPAGEORGIOU Kostas G, b. 4 July 1945, Athens, Greece. Author; Producer, Greek Radio. *Education:* Law Diploma, 1968; Literature, Philology, University of Athens, 1969-72. *Appointments:* Editor, Grammata ke Technes, 1982-; Member, Commission for Literary Awards, Ministry of Culture, 1982-84; Member, Commission for Authors' Pensions, 1991-. *Publications:* Piimata, 1966; Sillogi, 1970; Epi pigin kathise, 1972; Ichnographia, poetry, 1975; To Giotopato, prose, 1977; To Ikogeniako dendro, poetry, 1978; To skotomeno ema, 1982; Kato ston ipno, poetry, 1986; I genia tou 70, 1989; Rammeno Stoma, poetry, 1990. *Contributions to:* Anti; Diavazo; Lexi; Dendro; Tram; Tomes; Chronico. *Membership:* Eteria sigrafeon (Greek Authors Union). *Literary Agent:* Kedros Publishing House, Athens, Greece. *Address:* Kerasountos 8, 11528 Athens, Greece.

PAPAKOU-LAGOU Avgi, b. 1923, Greece. Schoolteacher; Writer. m. 23 De. 1948, 2 sons. *Education:* Diploma of Schoolteacher, 1946. *Appointment:* Agricultural News, 1978-82. *Publications:* (In Greek) The Fairy Child and Other Fairy Tales, 3rd edition; A Summer Different from the Ohers; The Festival Stories; The Little Maestro; Father's Secret, 1980; A Sunbeam Tells a Tale; In the Chestnut Grove; The Wonderful Sunbeams; Like a Fairy Tale I, II, III, IV; The Animals Warning, 1983; The Little Boatbuilder; Toto and His Kite, 1981; The Superior Truth; Once Upon a Time in a Marvellous City; Biographies : Modern Persons and Literary Works (in co-operation); Joyful Return, 1988; Editor: Andronikos a' KomnInos (Historical), 1988; What and Where : The Heroic Mouse; Don't Cry My Little Girl; The Golden Pomegranate, 1974; The Golden Apple, 1976; The Brave Ringworm, 1984; Christmas - New Year, Happy Holidays, 1986; Happy Return, 1987. *Contributions to:* Agricultural News; Act of Roumeli; Studies; Student; Farm Youth; Hunting News; Attican; Intellectual Problems; Essays. *Honours:* 1st Prize, Literary Company, 1978; 1st Prize, Circle of Children's Books, 1979; Award, Circle of Children's Books, 1979. *Memberships:* Circle of Children's Book Writers, 1975; Society of Greek Writers; Greek Committee, 1983, UNICEF, 1981-. *Address:* Vasiliadou 9, GR 11141 Athens, Greece.

PAPALEO Joseph, b. 13 Jan 1926. Professor of Literature and Writing; Fiction Writer. m. 4 sons. *Education:* BA, Sarah Lawrence College, 1949; Diploma di Profitto, University of Florence, Italy, 1951; MA, Columbia University, 1952. *Appointments:* Teacher, Fieldston Prep School, 1952-60; Professor, Literature, Writing, Sarah Lawrence, 1960-68, 1969-92; Guest Professor, Laboratorio de Cibernetica, Naples, Italy, 1968-69. *Publications:* All the Comforts, novel, 1968, paperback, 1969; Out of Place, novel, 1971; Picasso at Ninety One, 1988; The Bronx Book of the Dea, short stories; My Life Story (Sicilian Zen Version), short stories; Collection of 37 short stories; Original new stories in 3 anthologies: Delphinium Blossoms, From The Margin, Imagining America, 1991, 1992. *Contributions to:* Short stories and poems to: Harper's; New Yorker; Penthouse; Commentary (many); Patterson Literary Review; Rolling Coulter; Attenzione; Accent Review (Oberlin University); Remington Review; The Dial; Swank; Grove Press Review; Sarah Lawrence Journal; Many others. *Honours:* Guggenheim Fellowship, 1974; Ramapo College Poetry Prize, 1986.

Memberships: Authors Guild; Italian American Writers Association; American Association of University Professors. *Address:* 60 Puritan Avenue, Yonkers, NY 10710, USA.

PAPAS William, b. 1927, South Africa. Author. *Appointments:* Formerly Cartoonist, The Guardian, The Sunday Times Newspapers, Punch Magazine; Book Illustrator, Painter and Print Maker. *Publications:* The Press, 1964; The Story of Mr. Nero, 1965; The Church, 1965; Parliament, 1966; Freddy the Fell-Engine, 1966; The Law, 1967; Tasso, 1967; No Mules, 1967; Taresh, the Tea Planter, 1968; A Letter from India, 1968; A Letter from Israel, 1968; Theodore, or, The Mouse Who Wanted to Fly, 1969; Elias the Fisherman, 1970; The Monk and the Goat, 1971; The Long- Haired Donkey, 1972; The Most Beautiful Child, 1973; The Zoo, 1974; People of Old Jerusalem, 1980. *Address:* c/o Oxford University Press, Children's Books, Walton Street, Oxford, OX2 6DP, England.

PAPASTRATU Danae, b. 20 Mar 1935, Patras, Greece. Author; Journalist. *Education:* Diploma, Law, Athens University, 1959; Universite de Paris-Sorbonne, 1969; Greek-American Institute, 1965. *Appointments:* Protevoussa Journal: News of Municipalitis; Collector Magazine; Nautical Greece. *Publications:* Travels with the Polar Book, 1978; We Will See in Philippi, 1981; Without Periphrasis, Poetry Collection, 1981; A Vol d'oiseau, 1979; An Essay about the Poetry, 1983; A Study About the Women in General; Editor, Director, Perigramma, 1985-; Runnings Through Time and Space; Diadromes sto Horo and Hrono, travel book, 1989. *Contributions to:* Various professional journals including: Thessaliki Estia; Davlos; Cameiros; Nautiki Ellas; Perigramma; Vue Touristique (de Bruxelles); Meteora; Touristiki Zoi; Nautical Greece; Research Soc and Economist; Tourist Life. *Honours:* 1st Prize, Association Hellénique des Journalistes-Ecrivains du Tourisme, 1979; Cup Vermeil, Académie Internationale de Lutéce, Paris, 1980; Grand Prix des Jeunesses Culturelly de Wallonie, Belgium, 1980, 1983, 1989; Giovanni Gronchi, 1st Prize, 1990; Ass Journ-Writers of Tourism Greek, 1991. *Memberships:* Council, Special Secretary, 1985-87, EDSTE; Panhellenic Union of Authors; Federation of International Journalists; Society of Greek Authors; Syndicat des Journalistes et Ecrivains; Assoc des Journalistes - Ecrivains du Tourisme; Syndicat des Journalistes de France (Paris); Académie de Felgueiras (Portugal); UPLI, USA. *Literary Agent:* Koridis, editor, Mariomihali str.49, Athens 10680, Greece. *Address:* Bouboulinas la, Hilioupolis 16345, Athens, Greece.

PAPAZOGLOU Orania, b.13 July 1951, Bethel, Connecticut, USA. Writer. m. William L DeAndrea, 1 Jan 1984, 2 sons. *Education:* AB, Vassar College, 1973; AM, University of Connecticut 1975; Doctoral study at Michigan State University 1975-80. *Career:* Assistant to the Editor, 1980-81, Executive Editor 1981-83, Greek Accent (magazine); Full-time writer 1983-. *Publications:* Sweet, Savage Death (novel) 1984; Wicked Loving Murder, (novel) 1985; Death's Savage Passion (novel) 1986; Sanctity (novel) 1986; Rich, Radiant Slaughter, 1988. *Contributions to:* Columnist for Mystery Scene; Contributor to magazines, including Working Woman, Mother and Intro. *Literary Agent:* Meredith Bernstein, New York. *Address:* c/o Meredith Bernstein, 470 West End Avenue, New York, NY 10024, USA.

PAPIER Tadeusz Zenon, b. 9 July 1914, Writer, m. Helena Grochowska, 15 July 1944, 2 daughters. *Education:* University of Warsaw, 1936-39; University of Lodz, 1946-50. *Appointments:* Editor, Orka na ugorze, 1938; Teacher, 1939-44; Editor, Wies, 1945-49; Editor, Lodz Teatralna, 1949; Editor, Wytwornia Filmow Fabularnych, 1950-55; Editor, Osnowa, 1966-67; Editor in Chief, Socio-political Department, Wydawnictwo, Lodz, 1968-74. *Publications:* Powtorna smierc Boryny, 1965; Narodziny Gerty, 1968; Ciche jeziora, 1976; Cienie na piaskowej gorze, 1976; Wiktoria i general, 1980; Moje Lipce, 1986; Rodzina Szafrancow, 1988; Magdalena w nocy, 1971; Anita, 1979; Szum jodly w

miescie, 1984; Author of short stories and reports. *Contributions to:* numerous journals and magazines. *Honours:* Literary Award, Lodz Region, 1965; Literary Award, Lodz, 1983. *Memberships:* Country Department, Polish Writers' Society; Society of Authors. *Address:* Al Kosciuszki 98 m 14, 90-442 Lodz, Poland.

PAPINEAU David Calder, b. 30 Sept 1947, Como, Italy. Philosopher. m. Rose Wild, 6 July 1986, 1 daughter. *Education:* BSc (Hons), University of Natal, 1967; BA (Hons), Cambridge University, 1970; PhD, Cambridge. *Publications:* For Science in the Social Sciences, 1978; Theory and Meaning, 1979; Reality and Representation, 1987; Philosophical Naturalism, 1993. *Address:* Department of Philosophy, King's College, London WC2R 2LS, England.

PARGETER Edith, (Ellis Peters), b. 1913. British. Mystery/Crime/Suspense, Historical, Translations. *Publications include:* The Hounds of Sunset, 1976; Afterglow and Nightfall, 1977; The Marriage of Meggotta, 1979. (As Ellis Peters: Never Pick Up Hitch Hikers! 1976; A Morbid Taste for Bones, 1977; Rainbow's End, 1978; One Corpse Too Many, 1979; Monk's-Hood, 1980; Saint Peter's Fair, 1981; The Laper of Saint Giles, 1981; The Virgin in the Ice, 1982; The Sanctuary Sparrow, 1983; The Devil's Novice, 1983; Dead Man's Ransom, 1984; The Pilgrim of Hate, 1984; An Excellent Mystery, 1985; The Raven in the Foregate, 1986; The Rose Rent, 1986; The Hermit of Eyton Forest, 1987; The Confession of Brother Haluin, 1988; The Heretic's Apprentice, 1989; The Potters Field, 1989; The Summer of the Danes, 1991; The Holy Thief, 1992. Translations include: Legends of Old Bohemia, by Alois Jirasek, 1963; May, by Karlel Hynek Macha, 1965; The End of the Old Times, by Vladislav Vancura, 1965; A Close Watch on the Trains, by Bohumil Hrabal, 1968; Report on My Husband, by Josef Slaska, 1969; A Ship Named Hope, by Ivan Klima, 1970; Mozart in Prague, by Jaroslav Seifert, 1970. *Honour:* Crime Writers Association, Cartier Diamond Dagger Award, 1993. *Memberships:* The Welsh Academy, 1990; Society of Authors; Crime Writers Association; Mystery Writers of America. *Literary Agent:* Deborah Owen Ltd, 78 Narrow Street, London E14 8DP, England. *Address:* Troya, 3 Lee Dingle, Madeley, Telford, Shropshire TF7 5TW, England.

PARIS Bernard Jay, b. 19 Aug 1931, Baltimore, Maryland, USA. Univerity Professor. m. Shirley Helen Freedman, 1 Apr 1949, 1 son, 1 daughter. *Education:* AB, 1952, PhD, 1959, Johns Hopkins University. *Appointments:* Instructor, Lehigh University, 1956-60; Assistant Professor, 1960-64, Associate Professor, 1964-67, Professor, 1967-81, Michigan State University; Professor, English, University of Florida, 1981-; Director, Institute for Psychological Study of the Arts, 1985-1992; Director, International Karen Horney Society, 1991-. *Publications:* Experiments in Life, George Eliot's Quest for Values, 1965; A Psychological Approach to Fiction : Studies in Thackeray, Stendhal, George Eliot, Dostoevsky and Conrad, 1974; Character and Conflict in Jane Austen's Novels, 1978; Editor, Third Force Psychology and the Study of Literature, 1986; Shakespeare's Personality (co-ed), 1989; Bargains with Fate: Psychological Crises and Conflicts in Shakespeare and His Plays, 1991; Character as a Subversive Fura in Shakespeare: The History and The Roman Plays, 1991. *Contributions to:* Numerous essays in scholarly and literary journals. *Honours:* Phi Beta Kappa, 1952; Fellow, NEH, 1969; Fellow, John Simon Guggenheim Foundation, 1974. *Memberships:* Modern Language Association of America; Honorary Member, Association for the Advancement of Psychoanalysis; Scientific Associak, American Academy of Psychoanalysis. *Address:* Department of English, University of Florida, Gainesville, FL 32611, USA.

PARIS Erna, b. 6 May 1938, Toronto, Canada. Author; Journalist. m. Thomas More Robinson, 26 Apr 1981, 1 son, 1 daughter. *Education:* BA Honours, University of Toronto; Diplome Superieur, University of Paris, Sorbonne, France, 1961. *Appointments:* Member of the

Board of the Canadian Reprography Collective (CRC), 1987-. *Publications:* Unhealed Wounds: France & the Klaus Barbie Affair, 1985; Jews: An Acount of their Experience in Canada, 1980; Stepfamilies: Making Them Work, 1984; The Garden and the Gun: A Journey Inside Israel, 1988. Co-author, Her Own Woman: Profiles of Canadian Women, 1975. Book reviews, radio documentries, columns. *Contributions to:* Various magazines. *Honours:* Feature writing awards 1969, 1974, Radio documentary awards 1973, 1974, Media Club of Canada; Gold Medal, National Magazine Awards, 1983. *Memberships:* Past executive officer, Writers Union of Canada; Founding member, past president, Periodical Writers Association of Canada; Past executive officer, International PEN (Canada). *Literary Agent:* Lucinda Vardey, 297 Seaton Street, Toronto, Ontario, Canada M5A 2T6. *Address:* 126 Felstead Avenue, Toronto, Ontario, Canada M4J 1G4.

PARISH James (Robert), b. 1944. Writer on the film media. *Appointments:* Executive, MCRB, N, Hollywood, 1977-78 and 1981-; President, Entertainment Copyright Research Co Inc, New York City, 1965-68; Reviewer-Interviewer, Variety, New York City, 1968-69. *Publications include:* (with M R Pitts) The Great Spy Pictures, 1974; (with S Whitney) The George Raft File, 1974; (with S Whitney) Vincent Price Unmasked, 1974; (with M R Pitts) Film Directors Guide: United States, 1974; The RKO Gals, 1974; Hollywood's Great Love Teams, 1974; The Great Movie Heroes, 1974; Good Dames, 1974; (with D E Stanke) The Glamour Girls, 1975; (with D E Stanke) The Debonairs, 1975; (with L DeCarl) Hollywood Players: The 40's, 1975; (with J Ano) Liza!: Liza Minnelli Story, 1975; (with M R Pitts) The Great Gangster Pictures, 1975; (co-author) Film Directors Guide: Western Europe, 1975; The Elvis Presley Scrapbook, 1975; Great Western Stars, 1976; The 30's, 1976; The Tough Guys, 1976; (with M R Pitts) The Great Science Fiction Pictures, 1976; (with M R Pitts) The Great Western Pictures, 1976; (with Don E Stanke) The Swashbucklers, 1976; Film Actors Guide: Western Europe, 1977; (with Don E Stanke) The All-Americans, 1977; (with Don E Stanke) The Leading Ladies, 1977; Hollywood Character Actors, 1978; (with others) The Hollywood Beauties, 1978; (with M R Pitts) Hollywood on Hollywood, 1978; (with W T Leonard) The Funsters, 1979; (with D Stanke) The Forties Gals, 1979; (as Frances Maugham) Hollywood Happiness, 1979; (with G Mank) The Hollywood Regulars, 1980; (with G Mank) The Best of MGM, 1980. *Address:* 14406 Benefit Street, Sherman Oaks, CA 91403, USA.

PARISI Joseph Anthony, b. 18 Nov 1944, Duluth, Minnesota, USA. Editor; Writer; Consultant. *Education:* BA Honours, College of St Thomas, 1966; MA, University of Chicago, 1967; PhD, Honours, ibid, 1973. *Appointments include:* Associate Editor 1976-83, Acting Editor 1983-85, Editor 1985-, Poetry magazine. *Publications include:* Editor, The Poetry Anthology 1912-77, 1978; Marianne Moore: The Art of a Modernist, 1989. *Contributions to:* Articles, Reviews to: Yale Review; Georgia Review; Shenandoah; Modern Philology; TriQuarterly; Booklist; Poetry; Mandarin Oriental; Chicago Tribune Book World; Chicago Sun-Times Book Week; Sewanee Review; etc. *Honours:* Fellowship, University of Chicago, 1966-69; Alvin M. Bentley Scholarship; Delta Epsilon Sigma. *Memberships:* Society of Midland Authors; Modern Language Association. *Address:* c/o Poetry, 60 West Walton Street, Chicago, Illinois 60610, USA.

PARK Bert E, b. 5 June 1947, St Louis, Missouri, USA. Neurological Surgeon. 1 daughter. *Education:* AB, History, Duke University, 1969; MD, University of Missouri Medical School, 1973; Vanderbilt University Hospitals, 1973-79; American Board of Neurological Surgery, 1981. *Appointments:* Editorial Advisory Board to The Papers of Woodrow Wilson (Arthur S Link, Editor), Princeton University, 1988-92. *Publications:* The Impact of Illness on World Leaders, 1986; Catastrophic Illness, and the Family: A Physician's Perspective, 1991; Contributing author, The Papers of Woodrow Wilson, 1988, 1989, 1990. *Contributions to:* Journal of

Neurosurgery; Surgical Neurology; Leaders, Politics and the Life Sciences; Amrican Historical Review. *Membership:* Congress of Neurological Surgeons. *Literary Agent:* Bert Holtje, James Peter Associates. *Address:* 1965 S Fremont, Suite 3700, Springfield, MO 65804, USA.

PARK (Rosina) Ruth (Lucia), b. Australia. Author; Playwright. *Publications:* The Uninvited Guest (play), 1948; The Harp in the South, 1948; Poor Man's Orange (in United States of America as 12 and a Half Plymouth Street), 1949; The Witch's Thorn, 1951; A Power of Roses, 1953; Pink Flannel, 1955; The Drums Go Bang (autobiographical with D'Arcy Niland), 1956; One-a-Pecker, Two-a-Pecker (in United States of America as The Frost and the Fire), 1961; The Good Looking Women, 1961; The Ship's Cat, 1961 (in United States of America as Serpent's Delight, 1962); Uncle Matts's Mountain, 1962; The Road to Christmas, 1962; The Road Under the Sea, 1962; The Hole in the Hill (in USA as The Secret of the Maori Cave), 1964; The Muddle-Headed Wombat series, 11 vols, 1962-76; Shaky Island, 1962; Airlift for Grandee, 1964; Ring for the Sorcerer, 1967; The Sixpenny Island (in United States of America as Ten-Cent Island), 1968; Nuki and the Sea Serpent, 1969; The Companion Guide to Sydney, 1973; Callie's Castle, 1974; The Gigantic Balloon, 1975; Swords and Crowns and Rings, 1977; Come Danger, Come Darkness, 1978; Playing Beatie Bow, 1980; When the Wind Changed, 1980; The Big Brass Key, 1983; The Sydney We Love, 1983; Missus, 1985; My Sister Sif, 1986; The Tasmania We Love, 1987; Callie's Family; James, 1991; A Fence Around the Cuckoo, 1992; Fishing in the Styx, 1993. *Address:* c/o Curtis Brown Pty Limited, PO Box 19, Paddington, NSW 2021, Australia.

PARKER Edna Mae, b. 17 Mar 1910, near Leith, North Dakota, USA. Private Secretary; Former Postmaster; Teacher (in home). m. Laurence Yale Parker, 19 Aug 1938, 1 son, 2 daughters. *Education:* Diploma, Freeport High School, 1932; Graduate CTF, Newspaper Institute of America, 1985. *Publications:* Every Memory Precious, 1984; My Unforgettable ABCs, 1986; My Backyard Jungle, 1987; Twenty Years in the Post Office, 1988; Tempus Fugit, 300-year Calendar Book, 1989; Whatever Happened to Common Sense, 1990. *Contributions to:* Illinois magazine Museum, 1986; Monroe Evening Times, Northwest Illinois Farmer, Freeport Journal Standard, 1983-90. *Honours:* American Poetry Association Award; Editors Choice, National Library of Poetry. *Memberships:* Life Member, Cedarville Area Historical Society; Presidents Club, College of the Americas; National Association of Retired Federal Employees; International Association of Chiefs of Police; Illinois Sheriffs Association. *Literary Agent:* Jim Field, Monroe Graphics, Wisconsin, USA. *Address:* 125 West Cherry Street, Cedarville, IL 61013, USA.

PARKER Franklin, b. 2 June 1921, New York, USA. Writer; Educationalist. m. Betty June Parker, 1950. *Education:* BA, Berea College, 1949; MS, University of Illinois, 1950; EdD, Peabody College of Vanderbilt University, 1956. *Publications include:* African Development and Education in Southern Rhodesia, 1960, reprinted, 1974; Government Policy and International Education, 1965; Church and State in Education, 1966; Strategies for Curriculum Change: Cases from 13 Nations, 1968; International Education: Understandings and Misunderstandings, 1969; George Peabody, A Biography, 1971; American Dissertations on Foreign Education: Abstracts of Doctoral Dissertations (20 vols), 1971-90; What We Can Learn From the Schools of China?, 1977; Education in Puerto Rico and of Puerto Ricans in the USA, Vol. 1, 1978; Vol 2, 1984; British Schools and Ours, 1979; Women's Education (2 vols), 1979, 1981; US Higher Education: Guide to Information Sources, 1980; Education in the People's Republic of China, Past and Present: Annotated Bibliography, 1986; Education in England and Wales: An Annotated Bibliography, 1991 . *Contributions to:* Over 500 articles and book reviews in magazines and journals. *Honours include:* Distinguished Alumnus Award, Peabody College of Vanderbilt University, 1970;

Claude Worthington Benedum Professor of Education, Emeritus, West Virginia University, 1968-86; Distinguished Alumnus Award, Berea College, Berea, KY, 1989. *Address:* School of Education and Psychology, Western Carolina University, Cullowhee, NC 28723, USA.

PARKER Gordon, b. 1940. Author; Playwright. *Appointment:* Book Reviewer, BBC Radio and ITV. *Publications:* The Darkness of the Morning, 1975; Lightning in May, 1976; The Pool, 1978; Action of the Tiger, 1981; radio plays: The Seance, 1978; God Protect the Lonely Widow, 1982. *Address:* 14 Thornhill Close, Seaton Delaval, Northumberland, England.

PARKER Jean. *See:* **SHARAT Chandra G S.**

PARKER Keith John, b. 30 Dec 1940. Editor. m. Marilyn Ann Edwards, 1962, 1 son. *Appointments:* Various Editorial Appointments; Editor, Shropshire Star, 1972-77; Editor, Express and Star, Wolverhampton, 1977-. *Memberships:* President of the Guild of British Newspaper Editors, 1987-88; Guild of British Newspaper Editors; Association of British Editors. *Address:* 94 Wrottesley Road, Tettenhall, Wolverhampton, West Midlands, WV6 8SJ, England.

PARKER Kristy Kay, b. 3 May 1957, Decatur, Illinois, USA. Professional Freelance Writer; Homemaker. m. Thomas, 19 Aug 1978, 1 son, 2 daughters. *Education:* BA, Elementary Education (Language Arts), University of Illinois, 1979. *Publications:* My Dad the Magnificent, 1987. *Honours:* 1st Place, beginners category, for essay Lookout Superman and Honourable Mention, religious category, for essay The One Who Suffered First, Mississippi Valley Writers Conference, 1985; Honourable Mention foressay Tender Moments, National League of American Pen Women Literary Contest, 1986. *Memberships:* National League of American Pen Women. *Address:* 4897 Chimney Springs Drive, Greensboro, NC 27407, USA.

PARKER Maynard Michael, b. 28 July 1940, Los Angeles, California, USA. Journalist. m. (1) Judith K Seaborg, 1965, (div), 1 daughter, (2) Susan Fraker, 1985, 1 son. *Education:* MS, Stanford University; Columbia Graduate School of Journalism. *Appointments:* Public Affairs Reporter, Life Magazine, New York, 1963-64; US Army, 1964-66; Correspondent, Life Magazine, Hong Kong, 1966-67; Saigon Bureau Chief, 1969-70, Hong Kong Bureau Chief, 1970-73, Newsweek; Managing Editor, Newsweek International, 1973-75; Senior Editor, National Affairs, 1975-77, Assistant Managing Editor, 1977-80, Executive Editor, 1980-82, Editor, 1982-, Newsweek. *Publications:* Articles in various journals. *Address:* Newsweek, 444 Madison Avenue, New York, NY 10022, USA.

PARKER Robert B(rown), b. 1932, United States of America. Author. *Appointments include:* Technical Writer, Group leader, Raytheon Company, 1957-59; Copywriter, Editor, Prudential Insurance Company, Boston, 1959-62; Partner, Parker Farman Company, Advertising Agency, Boston, 1960-62. *Publications:* Fiction: The Godwulf Manuscript, 1973; God save the Child, 1974; Mortal Stakes, 1975; Promised Land, 1976; The Judas Goat, 1978; Wilderness, 1979; Looking for Rachel Wallace, 1980; Early Autumn, 1981; A Savage Place, 1981; Surrogate, 1982; Ceremony, 1982; The Widening Gyre, 1983; Love and Glory, 1983; Valediction, 1984; A Catskill Eagle, 1985; Taming a Sea Horse, 1986; Pale Kings and Princes, 1987; Crimson Joy, 1988; Playmates, 1989; Poodle Springs (completion of unfinished novel by R Chandler), 1989; Stardust, 1990; Perchance to Dream, 1991; Pastime, 1991; Double Deuce, 1992. Other: The Personal Response to Literature, 1971; Order and Diversity, 1973; Sports Illustrated Training with Weights, 1974; Three Weeks in Spring (with Joan H Parker), 1978; Playmates, (USA). *Address:* Helen Brann Agency, 94 Curtis Road, Bridgewater, CT 06752, USA.

PARKES Roger Graham, b. 15 Oct. 1933, Chingford, Essex, England. Novelist; Scriptwriter. m. Tessa Isabella McLean, 5 Feb 1964, London. 1 son, 1 daughter. *Education:* National Diploma of Agriculture; Member, Royal Agricultural College. *Literary Appointments:* Editor, Farming Express, 1963. *Publications:* Death Mask, 1970; Line of Fire, 1971; The Guardians, 1973; The Dark Number, 1973; The Fourth Monkey, 1978; Alice Ray Mortons Cookham, 1981; Them and Us, 1985; Riot, 1986; Y-E-S, 1986; An Abuse of Justice, 1988; Troublemakers, 1990; Gamelord, 1991; The Wages of Sin, 1992. *Contributions to:* Daily Express; Sunday Express; Farming Express and Scottish Daily Express, staff writer, 1959-63; Staff script editor, drama, British Broadcasting Corporation Television, London, 1964-70. *Honours:* Grand Prix de Literature, Paris, France, for The Dark Number, 1974; Runner Up, Prix Jeunese, with television play, Secrets, Munich, Germany. *Membership:* Writers Guild of Great Britain. *Literary Agent:* Watson Little Ltd, London. *Address:* Cartlands Cottage, Kings Lane, Cookham Dean, Berkshire SL6 9AY, England.

PARKIN Molly, b. 1932. Author. *Appointments:* Former Fashion Editor, Nova Magazine, Harper's Bazaar Magazine, The Sunday Times Newspaper, London. *Publications:* Love All, 1974; Uptight, 1975; Full Up, 1976; Write Up, 1977; Switchback, 1978; Good Golly, Ms Molly, 1978; Fast and Loose, 1979; Molly Parkin's Purple Passages, 1979; Up and Coming, 1980; Bite of the Apple, 1981; Love Bites, 1982; Breast Stroke, 1983; Cock-a-Hoop, 1985. *Address:* c/o St. Martin's Press, 175 Fifth Avenue, New York, NY 10010, USA.

PARKINSON Michael, b. 28 Mar 1935, Yorkshire, England. TV Presenter; Writer. m. Mary Heneghan, 3 sons. *Appointments:* Began career as Journalist with local paper, then worked on the Guardian, Daily Express, Sunday Times, Punch, The Listener; joined Granada TV as interviewer/reporter, 1965; Executive Producer and Presenter, London Weekend TV, 1968; Presenter, Cinema, 1969-70, Tea Break, Where in the World, 1971; hosted own chat show "Parkinson" (BBC), 1972-82, "Parkinson One to One" Yorkshire TV, 1987-; Presenter, Give Us a Clue 1984-, All Star Secrets, 1985, Desert Island Discs, 1986-88; Parky, 1989; LBC Radio, 1990; Help Squad, 1991; Daily Telegraph, 1991-. *Publications:* Football Daft, 1968; Cricket Mad, 1969; Sporting Fever, 1974; George Best: An Intimate Biography, 1975; A-Z of Soccer (joint author), 1975; Bats in the Pavilion, 1977; The Woofits, 1980; Parkinson's Lore, 1981; The Best of Parkinson, 1982. *Address:* c/o Michael Parkinson Enterprises Ltd, IMG, 23 Eyot Gardens, London W6 9TR, England.

PARKS Michael, b. 17 Nov 1943, Detroit, Michigan. USA. Journalist. m. Linda K Durocher, 26 Dec 1964, 2 sons, 1 daughter. *Education:* AB, University of Windsor, 1964. *Appointments:* Reporter. Detroit News, Detroit, Michigan, 1962-65; Correspondent, Time-Life News Service, New York, 1965-66; Assistant City Editor, Suffolk Sun, Deer Park, New York, 1966-68; Political Reporter 1968-70, Southeast Asia Correspondent 1970-72, Moscow Correspondent 1972-75, Mideast Correspondent 1975-78, Peking Correspondent 1978-80, Sun (Baltimore) Baltimore, Maryland; Peking Correspondent 1980-84, Southern Africa Correspondent 1984-88, Moscow Correspondent 1988-, Los Angeles Times, Los Angeles, California. *Honours:* Pulitzer Prize, 1987 for international reporting. *Memberships:* Hong Kong Foreign Correspondents Club. *Address:* Los Angeles Times, Times Mirror Square, Box 387, Los Angeles, CA 90012, USA.

PARKS T(imothy) Harold, (John MacDowell), b. 19 Dec 1954. Manchester, England. British educator, translator and author. *Publications:* Tongues of Flame, 1985; Loving Roger, 1986; Home Thoughts, 1987; Family Planning, 1989; Cara Massimina (as John MacDowell), 1990; Goodness, 1991; Italian Neighbours, 1992; Shear, 1993; Short Stories: Keeping Distance, 1988; The Room, 1992; Translations: La Cosa, (short stories), 1985; L'uomo che guarda (novel), 1989; Viaggo a Roma, (novel), 1989; Notturo indiano, (novel), 1988; Il filo dell'orizzonto, (novel), 1989; La donna di Porto Pim, I volatili del Beato Angelico, (short story collections), 1991; C'un punto della terra, 1991; I beati anni del castigo, (novel), 1991; Le nozzo di Cadmo e Armonia, 1993; La strada di San Giovanni, (stories), 1993 . Contributions to: Numerous articles, reviews and talks for BBC Radio 3. Honours: Somerset Maugham, 1986; Betty Trash 1st Prize, 1986; Llewellyn Rhys, 1986; Winner, Joh Florio Prize for Best Translation from Italian. Membership: Author's Society. Literary agent: Curtis Brown. Address: Via delle Primule 6, Montorio, 37033 Verona, Italy.

PARLAKIAN Nishan, b. 11 July 1925, New York City, New York, USA. Professor of Drama; Playwright. m. Florence B Mechtel, 1 son, 1 daughter. Education: BA, Syracuse University, 1948; MA, 1950, MA, 1952, PhD, 1967, Columbia University. Appointments: Editorial Board, Aravat, 1970-; Editorial Board, MELUS, 1977-80; Editor, Pirandello Society Newsletter; Editor, Armenian Church Magazine; Associate Editor, Pirandello Society Annual. Publications: Original plays: The Last Mohigian, 1959; Plagiarized, 1962; What Does Greta Garbo Mean to You?, 1973; Grandma, Pray for Me, 1988; Translated plays: For the Sake of Honor, 1976; Evil Spirit, 1980; The Bride, 1987; Be Nice, I'm Dead, 1990. Contributions to: Armenian Literature Between East and West, to Review of National Literature, 1984. Honours: Prizewinner, Stanley Awards, 1961; International Arts Award for Playwriting, Columbus: Countdown, 1992. Memberships: Modern Language Association; Vice-President, Pirandello Society of America. Literary Agent: Ann Elmo. Address: 415 W 115th St, New York City, NY 10025, USA.

PARMET Herbert Samuel, b. 28 Sept 1929, New York City, USA. Historian; Author. m. 12 Sept 1948. 1 daughter. Education: BA, State University of New York at Oswego; MA, Queens College, The City University of New York. Publications: Richard Nixon and His America, 1990; JFK: The Presidency of John F Kennedy, 1983; Jack: The Struggles of John F Kennedy, 1980; Eisenhower and the American Crusades, 1972; The Democrats: The Years After FDR, 1976; Never Again: A President Runs for a Third Term, 1968; Aaron Burr: Portrait of an Ambitious Man, 1967. Contributions to: American Historical Review; Journal of American History; Journal of Southern History. Memberships: The Authors Guild; The Authors League. Literary Agent: Timothy Seldes, Russell & Volkening. Address: Marsten Lane, Hillsdale, NY 12529, USA.

PARODI Anton Gaetano, b. 19 May 1923, Castanzaro Lido (Calabria), Italy. Journalist; Playwright. m. Piera Somino, 1952, 2 children. Education: Universita degli Studi, Turin and Genoa. Appointments: Journalist, 1945-; Professional Journalist, 1947-; Correspondent, Unita, Budapest, 1964-. Publications: Plays Include: Il gatto; Il nostro scandalo quotidiano; L'ex-maggiore Hermann Grotz; Adolfo o della nagia; Filippo l'Impostore; Una corda per il figlio di Abele; Quel pomeriggio di domenica; Dialoghi intorno ad un'uovo; Una storia della notte; Pioggia d'estate; Cielo di pietra; I giorni dell'Arca; Quello che dicono. Honours: Premio nazionale di teatro dei giovani, 1947; numerous other prizes. Address: Via Benvenuto Cellini 34/7, Genoa, Italy.

PARQUE Richard, b. 8 Oct 1935, Los Angeles, California, USA. Writer; Teacher. m. Vo Thi Lan, 1 May 1975, 3 sons. Education: BA, 1958, MA, 1961, California State University, Los Angeles; California State Teaching Credential, 1961; Postgraduate studies, University of Redlands. Publications: Sweet Vietnam, 1984; Hellbound, 1986; Firefight, 1987; Flight of the Phantom, 1988; A Distant Thunder, 1989. Contributions to: Numerous articles to magazines, many poems to poetry journals; commentary for newspapers. Honours: Bay Area Poets Award, 1989; Vietnam novels have been placed in the Colorado State University Vietnam War Collection. Memberships: Authors Guild; Academy of American Poets. Address: PO Box 327, Verdugo City, CA 91046, USA.

PARRINDER John Patrick, b. 11 Oct 1944, Wadebridge. Literary Critic. 2 daughters. Education: Leighton Park School, 1957-61; MA, PhD, Christ's College, Cambridge, 1962-65; Darwin College, Cambridge, 1965-57. Appointments: Fellow, King's College, Cambridge, 1957-74; Lecturer in English 1974-80, Reader 1980-86, Professor 1986-, University of Reading. Publications: H. G. Wells, 1970; Science Fiction: Its Criticism and Teaching, 1980; James Joyce, 1984; The Failure of Theory, 1987; Authors and Authority, 1977, 2nd enlarged edition 1991; Ed. H.G. Wells: The Critical Heritage, 1972; Ed. Science Fiction: A Critical Guide, 1979. Contributions to: London Review of Books and many academic journals. Honours: World S.F. President's Award, 1987. Memberships: Vice-President, H G Wells Society; Science Fiction Foundation. Address: Department of English, University of Reading, PO Box 218, Reading, Berks. RG6 2AA, England.

PARSON Mary Jean, Writer; Teacher; Consultant. Education: BA, cum laude, Birmingham-Southern College; MFA, Yale University, School of Drama. Appointments: Producer and manager of touring theatre companies, regional theatre and off-Broadway; Director of production exhibits for the Better Living Centre at the 1964-65 New York World's Fair; Supervisor of Entertainment Unit Managers, Manager of ABC News Programme Controllers, Associate Director of Planning, Associate Director of Employee Relations, Director of Planning, Development and Administration, Leisure Attractions, Director of Planning, Corporate Relations, American Broadcasting Companies, Inc; Vice President of Planning and Administration, Blair TV/Radio Representation, New York; Visiting Associate Professor, Yale University for 5 years; Lecturer on Entainment Management, Fordham University Graduate School of Business; Currently, teaches graduate management courses at Birmingham Southern College and conducts business planning seminars at University of Alabama, Birmingham and around the country. Publications: Back to Basics: Planning, 1985; An Executive's Coaching Handbook, 1986; The Single Solution, 1987; Managing the One Person Business, 1988; Financially Managing the One Person Business, 1991; How to be a Partner, 1992. Several music-dramas produced in Washington, Birmingham and North Carolina. Contributions to: Sylvia Porter's Personal Finance; Savvy; New Woman; Source; Birmingham; Working Woman. Honours: Phi Beta Kaapa; Distinguished Alumna, Birmingham Southern College, 1986. Memberships include: Partnership Birmingham; Network Birmingham; Women's Network; Birmingham Area Chamber of Commerce; Alabama Yale Club; Lambs Club of New York; Dramatists' Guild; American Society of Journalists and Authors. Address: 2812, Rhodes Circle, Birmingham, AL 35205, USA.

PARTNOY Alicia, b. 7 Feb 1955, Bahia Blanca, Argentina. Literature Professor; Translator; Human Rights Lecturer. m. Antonio Leiva, 2 daughters. Education: Certificate of Translation, English/Spanish, American University, USA, 1986; MA, Latin American Literature, The Catholic University, USA, 1991. Appointments: Lecturer on Latine American Literature, The Maryland Institute - College of Arts, Baltimore, USA, -1992; Acquisitions Editor, Latin American Series, Cleis Press, San Francisco, USA, 1989-. Publications: The Little School: Tales of Disappearance and Survival in Argentina, 1986 (USA), 1987 (UK); Ed. You Can't Drown the Fire: Latin American Women Writing in Exile, 1988 (USA), 1989 (UK); Revenge of the Apple - Venganza de la Manzana, 1992. Honours: Writer's Choice, Pushcart Foundation, juror Tobias Wolff, Sept. 1986; Writer's Choice, Pushcart Foundation, juror Bobbie Ann Mason, Oct 1986. Membership: Board of Directors, Amnesty International, USA, 1992. Address: PO Box 21425, Washington, DC 20009, USA.

PARTRIDGE Derek, b. 24 Oct 1945, London, England. Professor of Computer Science. m. 27 Aug 1971, 2 daughters. Education: BSc, Chemistry, University College, London, 1968; PhD, Computer Science, Imperial College, London, 1972. Appointment:

Editor, Computational Science, book series, Ablex Publishing Corporation, Norwood, NJ, USA. *Publications:* Artificial Intelligence: Applications in the Future of Software Engineering, 1965; A New Guide to AI, 1991; Engineering AI Software, 1992. *Contributions to:* More than 100 articles to professional magazines and journals. *Memberships:* American Association for Artificial Intelligence; Society for Artificial Intelligence and Simulation of Behaviour. *Address:* Department of Computer Science, University of Exeter, Exeter, EX4 4PT, England.

PARTRIDGE Frances Catherine, b. 15 Mar 1900, London, England. Writer. m. Ralph Partridge, 2 Mar 1933, 1 son. *Education:* Bedales School, 1915-17; BA, Hons., English/Moral Sciences, Newnham College, Cambridge, 1921. *Appointments:* Worked at Antiquarian Bookshop, 1922-28; Edited The Greville Memoires with Husband, Ralph Partridge, 1928-38; Translator of 20 books from French and Spanish. *Publications:* A Pacifist's War, 1978; Memories, 1981; Julia, 1983; Everything to Lose, 1985; Friends in Focus, 1987; The Pasque Flower, 1990; Hanging On, 1990; Many book reviews, obituaries. *Memberships:* FLS; International PEN. *Address:* 16 West Halkin Street, London SW1X 8JL, England.

PASCALIS Stratis, b. 4 Mar 1958, Athens, Greece. Poet; Translator. m. Sophie Phocas, 28 Feb 1982, 2 daughters. *Education:* Graduated, Political Sciences, University of Athens, 1983. *Publications:* Poetry: Anactoria, 1977; Excavation, 1984; Hermaphrodite's Night, 1989; Sour Cherry Trees in the Darkness, 1991; Translations: 49 Scholia on the poems of Odysseys Elytis (Jeffrey Carson), 1983; Phaedra (Racine), 1990; The Horla and other stories of madness and terror (Guy de Maupassant), 1992. *Contributions to:* Poems, translations, essays, articles to Greek magazines: Efthini; Lexi; To Dendro; Spira; Chartis; To Vima, newspaper. *Honours:* Maria P Ralli Prize for 1st book of a young poet, 1977. *Membership:* Society of Greek Writers. *Address:* Diamandidou 36, Palio Psychiko, Athens 15452, Greece.

PASCHEN Elise Maria, b. 4 Jan 1959, Chicago, Illinois, USA. Arts Administrator. *Education:* BA with honours, Harvard University, 1982; M Phil, 1984, D Phil, 1988, Oxford University, England. *Appointments:* Executive Director, Poetry Society of America. *Publications:* Houses: Coasts, 1985. *Contributions to:* Poems to: Poetry Magazine; Poetry Review, England; Oxford Magazine; Poetry Ireland Review; Oxford Poetry; The Harvard Advocate. *Honours:* Lloyd McKim Garrison Medal for poetry, Harvard, 1982; Joan Grey Untermyer Poetry Prize, Harvard/Radcliffe, 1982; Richard Selig Prize for poetry, Magdalen College, Oxford, 1984. *Memberships:* Harvard Club; National Arts Club; Former Member: Signet Literary Society, Harvard; John Florio Society, Magdalen College; Oxford University Poetry Society. *Address:* Poetry Society of America, 15 Gramercy Park, New York, NY 10003, USA.

PASCU Stefan, b. 14 Oct 1914, Apahida, Romania. Professor. m. Victoria Lascu, 14 Nov 1945, 1 daughter. *Education:* BA magna cum laude, 1938; MA magna cum laude, History, 1942; Graduate magna cum laude, School of Palaeography, Diplomatics and Archivistics, Vatican, 1942. *Literary Appointments:* Assistant Lecturer in History, 1943-44, Lecturer in History, 1944-48, Assistant Professor, 1948-62, Professor, 1962-, Dean, Faculty of History and Philosophy, 1962-68, Rector, 1968-76, Chief, Department of History, 1976-, University of Cluj-Napoca, Romania; Department Chief, 1948-68, Assistant Director and Director, 1968-75, Institute of History, Cluj-Napoca. *Publications include:* Istoria Transilvaniei (The History of Transylvania), 1944; Mestesugurile din Transilvania pina la sfirsitul secolului al XV1-lea (Handicrafts in Transylvania Up to the End of the 16th Century), 1954; Marea Adunare Nationala de la Alba Iulia (The Great National Assembly in Alba Iulia), 1968; Volevodatul Transilvaniei (The Voivodate of Translyvania) volumes 1-111, 1972-86; A Formacao de estado nacional unitario romeno, 1979; A History

of Transylcania, 1982; Faurirea statului national unitar roman (The Formation of the National Unitary State) volumes 1-11, 1983. *Contributions to:* Over 700 articles; Editor-in-Chief, Yearbook of the Institute of History and Archaeology of Cluj-Napoca (27 volumes), and Memorials of the Department of Historical Sciences of the Romanian Academy (10 volumes); Several editorial boards. *Honours include:* Prize of the Ministry of Education, 1943, 1966; Prize of the Romanian Academy, 1945, 1956; Honoured Professor, 1969; Honoured Man of Science, 1972; Honorary Fellow, Portuguese Academy of History, 1978; Honorary President, International Commission of Historical Demography, 1985-. *Memberships:* Fellow, 1974, President, Department of History, 1974-, President, Cluj-Napoca Section 1980-, Romanian Academy; Fellow, 1976, Academy of Social and Political Science of Romania; President, 1977-, Society of Historical Sciences in Romania. *Address:* Institutul de istoriesi archeologie, Strada Napooca nr 11, 3400 Cluj-Napoca, Romania.

PASK Raymond Frank, b. 27 May 1944, Melbourne. Teacher, Writer. *Education:* BA, 1964; Diploma of Education, 1965, Monash. *Publications:* People and Place, 1969; Australia and New Zealand, 1980; China, 1982; Using the Earth, 1981; People in Australia, 1986; The Changing Earth, 1985; Jacaranda Junior Geography, Book 1, 1989, Book 2, 1990; The Heinmann Atlas, 1993; Handbook of Geography, 1993. *Contributor to:* The Geographical Magazine, UK. *Address:* 41 Yarra Street, Abbotsford, Australia 3067.

PASKANDI Geza, b. 18 May 1933, Szatmarhegy-Viile Satumare, Romania. Writer. m. Anna-Maria Sebok, 24 Apr 1970, 1 daughter. *Education:* Szatmarnemeti-Satumare, Kolozsvar-cluj, 1944-53; Bolyai-Kolozsvar-Cluj, 1953-57. *Appointments:* Journalist, Szatmarnemati, Bucuresti, Kolozsvar, 1949-54; Redactor: Ed. Kriterion-Kolozsvar, 1970-73; Rev. Kortars - Budapest, Hungary. *Publications:* Poetry, 1972, 1979, 1989; Drama, 1970, 1975, 1987; Novels, 1988, 1989; Essays 1984; Tales, Radio Play, Screenplay, 1970-90. His works have appeared in 8 other languages; 40 of his dramas have been performed in Hungary and 7 in other countries. *Contributions to:* Magazines: Kortars, Helikon, Tiszataj, Nagyvilag, Eletunk, Hitel, Kelet-Nyugat, Irodalmi Szemle; Journals: Magyar Nemzet, Magyarorszag. *Honours:* Award of Romanian Writers Association, 1970; Jozsef Attila Award, Hungary, 1977; Award for Hungarian Art, 1991; Kossuth Award, Hungary, 1993. *Memberships:* Pen Club; Hungarian Writers' Association; Moricz Zsigmond Literary Society; Hungarian Academy of Arts. *Address:* Nagyszalonta u 50, 1112 Budapest XI, Hungary.

PASTERNAK Bogdan, b. 30 July 1932, Poland. Journalist. (div), 1 son, 2 daughters. *Education:* Magister, University of Lodz, 1965. *Appointments:* Contributing Editor, Przemianv; Editor in Chief, Gossip, 1981-; Head, House of Creative People, Kielce, 1984-. *Publications:* Poetry: Wicker Words, 1965; The Cage, 1973; Returns, 1975; The Simplest Dimension, 1980; The Secret Message, 1985; Novel, Black Angel, in print. *Contributions to:* Tygodnik Kulturalny (Cultural Weekly); Zycie Literackie (Literary Life); Radar; Okolice (Surroundings). *Honours:* Transformations Award, 1981; President of Kielce Award, Outstanding Achievements in Literature, 1983. *Membership:* Polish Writers' Association. *Address:* Checinska St 11/95, 25-020 Kielce, Poland.

PASTOS Spero, b. 18 Feb 1940, Chicago, Illinois, USA. *Education:* BS, Northwestern University, 1962; MA, University of California, Los Angeles, 1973. *Career:* Professional actor and singer 1959-70; Special Education Teacher, Los Angeles Board of Education, Los Angeles, California, 1970-. *Publications:* Pin-Up: The Tragedy of Betty Grable, 1986. *Literary Agent:* Ray Powers, New York. *Address:* c/o Ray Powers, 417 East 72nd Street, New York, NY 10036, USA.

PASZKOT Jan. *See:* **PASZKOWSKI Kazimierz Jan.**

PASZKOWSKI Kazimierz Jan, (Rideamus, Jan Paszkot, McCollins, Vapuru), b. 19 Sept 1895, Lvov, Poland. Writer; Publicist; Publisher. m. 1925-1969, 2 daughters. *Education:* Military College, Vienna, 1915; High School of Political Science, Warsaw, 1925; Privat Akademie dur Buchwesen und Litteraturewissenschaft, Meyers Institut, Leipzig, 1926-28. *Appointments:* Charter Member, Polish Writers Association, 1918; Director, Ignis publishing company, Warsaw, 1924; Served to Colonel, Polish Army. *Publications:* Grzech utajony, novel, 1923; Milosc na Wschodzie, story, 1923; Madrosci Wschodu, poems, 1923; Przygody Wicka i Wacka, comics, 1924; RAF kontra Luftweaffe, story, 1947; Swiat basni i legend, story, 1947; Translations: Mysli (R Tagore); Odrodzenie (R Tagore). *Contributions to:* Verses to the press. *Membership:* Polish Writers Association. *Address:* ul Kasprzaka 40 m 24, Lodz, Poland.

PATERAKIS Yolanda, b. 27 Oct 1934, Greece. Author. m. Andreas Paterakis, 14 Sept 1963, 1 son, 1 daughter. *Education:* Greek Literary Certificate, 1954; University of Cambridge, 1958. *Appointments:* Member, Circle of the Greek Children's Book, 1976-; General Secretary, National Society of Greek Authors, 1979-. *Publications:* Grandma's Lace Cap, 1976; My Brother My Little Man, 1977; Moonmen Come to Earth, 1977; Three Stories and a Truth, 1978; A Trick that Becomes True, 1978; The Lady of the Aegean Sea, 1978; The Ship Comes from Psaza, 1978; The Lionhearted, 6 volumes, 1979; The Secret of the Blessed Island, 1979; A Pearl Swims on the Sea, 1979; An Adventure in the Big Forest, 1981; Glory and Sacrifice, 1981; Under the Sun of Cephalonia, 1982; A Child that Conquers the Victory, 1984. *Contributor to:* numerous magazines and journals. *Honours:* State Award, 1977; National Academy Award, 1980; Awards & Distinctions, Literary Woman's Association. *Address:* 17 Kritonos Str, 116 34 Athens, Greece.

PATERSON Alistair (Ian Hughes), b. 1929. Full-time poet and writer; Formerly Lt Cdr, RNZN; Dean of general studies NZ Police; Education Officer with NZ Dept of Education. *Publications:* Caves in the Hills (selected poems), 1965; Birds Flying, 1973; Cities and Strangers, 1976; The Toledo Room: a poem for voices, 1978; 15 Contemporary New Zealand Poets (editor), 1980; Qu'appelle, 1982; The New Poetry, 1982; Incantations for Warriors, 1982; Oedipus Rex, 1986; Short Stories from New Zealand (editor), 1988; Climate and mate (Journals of NZ literature), (editor), 1972-82. *Honours:* Fulbright Fellow, 1977; The Auckland University's John Cowie Reid Award for Longer Poems, 1982. *Memberships:* Chairman, Auckland Branch PEN (Int), 1982-86; Member, NZ PEN (Int), National Council, 1982-87. *Address:* PO Box 9612, Newmarket, Auckland, New Zealand.

PATERSON Neil, b. 31 Dec 1915, Greenock, Scotland. Author. m. 6 July 1939, 1 son, 2 daughters. *Education:* MA, Edinburgh University, 1936. *Appointments:* Variously Member, Chairman of Production, Director and Consultant, Films of Scotland 1954-79; Director, Grampian Television 1960-86; Chairman, Literature Committee, Scottish Arts Council, 1967-76; Member, Arts Council Great Britain, 1973-76; Governor, British Film Institute, 1958-60; Governor, National Film School, 1970-80; Governor, Pitlochry Theatre, 1966-76. *Publications:* The China Run; Behold Thy Daughter; And Delilah; Man on the Tightrope; The Kidnappers; Stories & Screenplays. *Honours:* Atlantic Award in Literature, 1946; American Film Academy Award (Oscar), 1959. *Address:* St Ronans, Crieff, Perthshire, Scotland.

PATERSON Ronald (William Keith), b. 1933, United Kingdom. Senior Lecturer in Philosophy, University of Hull. *Publications:* The Nihilistic Egoist: Max Stirner, 1971; Values, Education, and the Adult, 1979. *Address:* Department of Philosophy, University of Hull, Hull, England.

PATHAK Jayant Himatlal, b. 20 Oct 1920, India. Retired Professor. m. 7 Feb 1945, 1 son, 1 daughter. *Education:* BA, 1943; MA 1945; PhD 1960. *Appointments:* Professor, Gujarati, 1953-80; Director, C.G. Vidyabhavan Institute of Learning & Research, 1963-75; Sectional president, Gujarati Sahitya Parishad Ahmedabad, 1974. *Publications:* Vananchal, 1967; Modern Trends in Gujarati Poetry, 1963; Anunaya (poems), 1978; Mrugaya (poems), 1983; Bhavayitree, 1974; Kimapidravyam, 1987; Taru Raga, 1987; Shuli Upar Sej, 1988. *Contributions to:* Sanskriti; Kavita; Kavyalok; Akhand Anand. *Honours:* Kumar Medal, 1957; Narmad Gold Medal, 1976; Ranjitram Gold Medal, 1976; Akademie Award, 1978; Dhanji Kanji Gold Medal, 1987. *Memberships:* Vice President, Narmad Sahitya Sabha; Board Member, Studies, South Gujarat University; Board Member, Publications, South Gujarat University; President, Gujarati Sahitya Parishad, Ahmedabad, 1989-91. *Address:* 23 Kadambpalli, Nanpura, Surat 395001, Gujarat State, India.

PATILIS Yannis, b. 21 Feb 1947, Athens, Greece. Teacher of Literature. m. Elsa Liacopoulou, 2 sons. *Education:* Degree, Law School, University of Athens, 1971; Degree, Department of Byzantine and Neo-Hellenic Studies, School of Philosophy, University of Athens, 1977. *Publications:* Poetry: The Little Guy and the Beast, 1970; But Now Be Careful!..., 1973; In Favour of Fruition, 1977; Tokens, 1980; Non-Smoker in the Land of Smokers, poems 1970-80 (above volumes collected, 1982); Warm Midday, 1984; The Scribe's Mirror, 1989; 1983-85 - co-founder and co-editor of poetry and music journal, Nesus (Island) and of the critical journal Kritike Kai Keimena (Critique and Texts); 1986- editor and publisher of Planodion, a journal of literature and the politics of culture. Many poems translated into various languages, notably English, French, German, Italian, Russian, Hungarian and Serbo-Croatian. *Membership:* Society of Greek Writers. *Address:* 23 G Mistriotou str., 112 55 Athens, Greece.

PATON WALSH Jill, b. 1937, United Kingdom. Children's Fiction Writer. *Publications:* Hengest's Tale, 1966; The Dolphin Crossing, 1967; Fireweed, 1969; Wordhoard (with Kevin Crossley-Holland), 1969; Goldengrove, 1972; Farewell Great King, for adults, 1972; Toolmaker, 1973; The Dawnstone, 1973; The Emperor's Winding Sheet, 1974; The Huffler, 1975; The Island Sunrise: Prehistoric Culture in the British Isles, 1975; Unleaving, 1976; Children of the Fox: Crossing to Salamis, 1977; The Walls of Athens, 1978; Persian Gold, 1978; A Chance Child, 1978; The Green Book, 1981; Babylon, 1982; A Parcell of Patterns, 1983; Lost and Found, 1984; Gaffer Samson's Luck, 1985; Lapsing, 1985. *Address:* 72 Water Lane, Histon, Cambridge CB4 4LR, England.

PATRICK John. *See:* **AVALLONE Michael.**

PATRICK John, b. 17 May 1905, Louisville, USA. Dramatist. *Education:* Harvard and Columbia Universities. *Appointments:* Radio Writer, 1932-35; Film Writer, Hollywood, 1936-37; Free-lance Dramatist, London and New York, 1940-. *Publications:* Plays; The Willow and I, 1942; The Hasty Heart, 1945; The Story of Mary Surratt, 1947; The Curious Savage, 1950; Lo and Behold, 1951; The Teahouse of the August Moon, 1953; Good as Gold, 1957; Everybody Loves Opal, 1962; It's Been Wonderful, 1965; Everybody's Girl, 1966; Scandal Point, 1967; Love is a Time of Day, 1969; Macbeth Did It, 1971; The Dancing Mice, 1971; Lovely Ladies, Kind Gentlemen (Musical), 1971; The Small Miracle (TV), 1972; Anybody Out There?, 1972; The Enigma, 1974; Opal's Husband, 1975; Divorce Anyone?, 1976; Suicide, Anyone?, 1976; Love Nest for Three, Sex on the Sixth Floor, 1977; Girls of the Garden Club; A Barrel Full of Pennies, 1960; Opal is a Diamond, 1972; The Savage Dilemma, 1972; Noah's Animals, 1973; Opal's Baby, 1974; People!, 1976; Opals Million Dollar Duck, 1979; The Magenta Moth, 1983; The Reluctant Rogue, 1984; Cheating Cheaters, 1985; The Gay Deceiver, 1988; Sense and Nonsense (verse), 1989; The Doctor Will See You Now, 1991. Films: Enchantment,

1948; The President's Lady, 1952; Three Coins in the Fountain, 1954; Mister Roberts, 1954; A Many Splendoured Thing, 1955; High Society, 1956; Les Girls, 1957; Some Came Running, 1958; The World of Suzie Wong, 1960; Gigot, 1961; Main Attraction, 1963; Shoes of the Fisherman, 1968. *Honours:* Pulitzer Prize, 1954; Drama Critics Circle Award Tony Award and Donelson Award, 1954; Screen Writers' Guild Award, 1957; Foreign Correspondent Award, 1957; Hon. DFA, 1972; Doctor Humane Letter, Camrus College; William Inge Award for Lifetime Achievement in the Theater, 1986. *Address:* Fortuna Mill Estate, Box 2386, St Thomas, US Virgin Islands 00801, USA.

PATRICK Maxine. *See:* **MAXWELL Patricia Anne.**

PATRICK Robert (Robert Patrick O'Connor), b. 1937, USA. Dramatist. *Appointments:* Feature Editor, Astrology Magazine, 1971-72. *Publications:* Robert Patrick's Cheap Theatricks, 1972; Play-by-Play: A Spectacle of Ourselves, 1972; Kennedy's Children, 1973; My Cup Runneth Over, 1978; Mutual Benefit Life, 1978; One Man, One Woman: Six One Act Plays, 1978; Mercy Drop and Other Plays, 1980.

PATRICK Susan. *See:* **CLARK Patricia Denise.**

PATRIDES C(onstantinos) A(postolos), b. 1930, USA. Professor of English. *Appointments:* Lecturer to Associate Professor, University of California, Berkeley, 1957-64; Lecturer to Professor, University of York, 1964-78; G B Harrison Professor of English, University of Michigan, Ann Arbor, 1978-. *Publications:* Milton's Lycidas: The Tradition and the Poem (editor), 1961; Milton and the Christian Tradition, 1966; Milton's Epic Poetry (editor), 1967; Approaches to Paradise Lost (editor), 1968; The Cambridge Platonists (editor), 1969; Sir Walter Raleigh's The History of the World (editor), 1971; The Poetry of John Milton (general editor), 1972; The Grand Design of God: The Literary Form of the Christian View of History, 1972; John Milton: Selected Prose (editor), 1974; The English Poems of George Herbert (editor), 1974; Aspects of Time (editor), 1976; Sir Thomas Browne: The Major Works (editor), 1977; Approaches to Marvell (editor), 1978; The Age of Milton (co-editor), 1980; Approaches to Sir Thomas Browne (editor), 1982; Premises and Motifs in Renaissance Thought and Literature, 1982; George Herbert: The Critical Heritage (editor), 1983; The Apocalypse in English Renaissance Thought and Literature (co-editor), 1984; The Complete English Poems of John Donne (editor), 1985. *Address:* Department of English, University of Michigan, Ann Arbor, MI 48109, USA.

PATTEN Brian, b. 7 Feb 1946, Liverpool, England, Poet. *Publications:* Little Johnny's Confession, 1967; Notes to the Hurrying Man, 1969; The Irrelevent Song, 1975; Mr Moon's Last Case, 1975; Vanishing Trick, 1976; Gossip, 1979; Love Poems, 1980; Gargling with Jelly, 1985; Storm Damage, 1989; Grave Thawing Frozen Frogs, 1990; Grinning Jack, 1990; The Puffin Book of 20th century Children's Verse, (Editor), 1991. *Contributor to:* TLS; Sunday Times; Independent; Guardian; Sunday telegraph. *Literary Agent:* Rogers Coleridge and White.

PATTERSON Bradley H Jr, b. 5 Dec 1921, Wellesley, Massachusetts, USA. Public Administrator. m. Shirley Jane DoBos, 26 Dec 1943, 3 sons, 1 daughter. *Education:* BA, 1942, MA, 1943, University of Chicago; Diploma, National War College, US Department of Defense, 1966. *Appointments:* Department of State, 1945-54; Assistant Cabinet Secretary, White House, 1954-61; Executive Secretary, Peace Corps, 1961-62; Executive Assistant, White House Staff, 1969-76; Senior Staff Member, The Brookings Institution, 1977-88. *Publications:* The Ring of Power: The White House Staff and Its Expanding Role in Government, 1988. *Contributions to:* Monograph: The President's Cabinet: Issues and Questions, 1976; Organizing the Reagan White House, to The Washingtonian, 1980. *Honours:*

Named 1 of the 10 Outstanding Young Men in the Federal Service, Arthur S Fleming Award, 1960. *Membership:* American Society for Public Administration, President 1984-85. *Address:* 6705 Pemberton Street, Bethesda, MD 20817, USA.

PATTERSON Harry, (Martin Fallon, James Graham, Jack Higgins, Hugh Marlowe, Henry Patterson), b. 27 July 1929. Novelist. m. (1) Amy Margaret Hewitt, 1958, (div 1984), 1 son, 3 daughters, (2) Denise Lesley Anne Palmer, 1985. *Education:* BSc., Honours, London School of Economics (external student); FRSA. *Appointments:* NCO, The Blues, 1947-50, 1950-58. *Publications include:* As Jack Higgins: Prayer for the Dying, 1973 (filmed 1985); The Eagle has Landed, 1975 (filmed 1976); Storm Warning, 1976; Day of Judgement, 1978; Solo, 1980; Luciano's Luck, 1981; Touch the Devil, 1982; Exocet, 1983; Confessional, 1985 (filmed 1985); Night of the Fox, 1986 (filmed 1990); Season in Hell, 1989; Coldharbour, 1990; The Eagle Has Flown, 1991. As Harry Patterson: The Valhalla Exchange, 1978; To Catch a King, 1979 (filmed 1983); Dillinger, 1983. Many others including: The Violent Enemy, filmed 1969; and The Wrath of God, filmed 1972, under pseudonyms; some books translated into 42 languages. *Address:* c/o Ed Victor, 162 Wardour Street, London W1V 3AT, England.

PATTERSON Henry. *See:* **PATTERSON Harry.**

PATTERSON Michael Wyndham, (formerly RICHARDS), b. 7 Sept 1939, London. University Lecturer. m. (1) Ellinor von Einsiedel, (2) Diana (Dixi) Patterson, 3 sons, 5 daughters. *Education:* BA, Mediaeval and Modern Languages, Oxford, 1962; D Phil, Oxford, 1968. *Publications:* The Revolution in German Theatre 1900-1933, 1981; Peter Stein, 1981; German Theatre Today, 1976; Georg Büchner: Collected Works, ed, 1987; The First German Theatre, 1990. *Contributions to:* Various journals. *Address:* Department of English, Media and Theatre Studies, University of Ulster, Coleraine, Northern Ireland.

PATTERSON Peter, (Peter Terson), b. 1932, British. Associated with the Victoria Theatre, Stoke on Trent and the National Youth Theatre, London. *Publications:* The Apprentices, 1968; The Adventures of Gervase Beckett; or, The Man Who Changed Places, 1969; Zigger Zagger, and Mooney and His Caravans, 1970; Rattling the Railings, 1979; Prisoners of the War, 1983. *Address:* C/o Harvey Unna and Stephen Durbridge, 24 Pottery Lane, London W11 4LZ, England.

PATTISON Robert, b. 28 Oct, 1945, Orange, New Jersey, USA. Teacher. *Education:* AB, Yale University; MA, University of Sussex, 1968; PhD, Columbia University, 1974; Languages: Greek, Latin, French. *Appointments:* Adjunct Lecturer, Richmond College, CUNY, 1974; Adjunct Instructor, Queensborough Community College, CUNY, 1974-75; Instructor, English, St. Vincent's College, St. John's University, New York, 1975-77; Professor of English, Southampton College, Long Island University, Southampton, New York, 1978-. *Publications:* The Child Figure in English Literature, 1978; Tennyson and Tradition, 1980; On Literacy, 1982; The Triumph of Vulgarity, 1987; The Great Dissent: John Henry Newman and the Liberal Heresy, 1991. *Contributions to:* The Nation; ADE Bulletin; University of Toronto Quarterly; Mosaic; The New York Times; Dickens Studies Newsletter; and various edited volumes. *Honours:* Long Island University Trustees Award for Scholarship, 1979 and 1985; Rockefeller Foundation Fellowship, 1980-81; Guggenheim Fellowship, 1986-87. *Address:* P O Box 2106, Southampton, NY 11969, USA.

PAUL Barbara Jeanne, b. 5 June 1931, Maysville, Kentucky, USA. Writer. (div), 1 son. *Education:* AB, Bowling Green State University, 1953; MA, University of Redlands, 1957; PhD, University of Pittsburgh, 1969. *Appointments:* Mellon Fellow, University of Pittsburgh,

1967-69. *Publications:* An Exercise for Madmen, 1978; The Fourth Wall, 1979; Pillars of Salt, 1979; Bibblings, 1979; First Gravedigger, 1980; Under the Canopy, 1980; Your Eyelids Are Growing Heavy, 1981; Liars and Tyrants and People Who Turn Blue, 1982; A Cadenza for Caruso, 1984; The Renewable Virgin, 1984; Prima Donna at Large, 1985; Kill Fee, 1985; But He Was Already Dead When I Got There, 1986; A Chorus of Detectives, 1987; The Three-Minute Universe, 1988; He Huffed and He Puffed, 1989; Good King Sauerkraut, 1989; In-Laws and Out Laws, 1990; You Have The Right To Remain Silent. *Contributions to:* various magazines & journals. *Memberships:* Treasurer, American Crime Writers League; Science Fiction and Fantasy Writers of America; Sisters in Crime; Mystery Writers of America; Novelists Inc. *Literary Agent:* Joshua Bilmes, Scott Meredith Agency. *Address:* c/o Scott Meredith Literary Agency, 845 Third Avenue, New York, NY 10022, USA.

PAUL Bette. *See:* **CHILDS Bette.**

PAUL Jeremy, b. 29 July 1939, Bexhill, Sussex, England. Writer. m. Patricia Garwood, 26 Nov 1960, 4 daughters. *Education:* King's School, Canterbury; St Edmund Hall, Oxford. *Appointments:* Has written numerous TV plays, series and adaptations, 1960-, including: Upstairs Downstairs, 1971-75; Country Matters, 1972; The Duchess of Duke Street, 1976; Danger, UXB, 1977; A Walk in the Forest, 1980; The Flipside of Dominick Hide, 1980, with Alan Gibson; Sorrell and Son, 1983; Adventures and Return of Sherlock Holmes, 1984, 1985, 1987, 1989; By the Sword Divided, 1983-85; Theatre Includes: David Going Out, 1971; Manoeuvres, 1971; Visitors, 1980, with Carey Harrison; The Secret of Sherlock Holmes, 1988; The Watcher, 1989; Scraps, Musical with Leslie Stewart, Keith Strachan; The Lady or the Tiger, musical with Michael Richmond, Nola York, 1976; Countess Dracula, film, 1970. *Memberships:* MCC; Writers Guild of Great Britain; Director, Parachute Production. *Address:* 8 Park Road, East Twickenham, Middlesex, TW1 2PX, England.

PAUL John. *See:* **WEBB Charles.**

PAULIN Tom, b. 1949, United Kingdom. Author. *Publications:* Thomas Hardy: The Poetry of Perception, 1975; Theoretical Locations, 1975; A State of Justice, 1977; Personal Column, 1978; The Strange Museum, 1980; The Book of Juniper, 1981; Liberty Tree, 1983; Ireland and the English Crisis, 1985; The Riot Act, play, 1985; The Faber Book of Political Verse (editor), 1986; Hard Lines 3 (co-editor), 1987. *Address:* Faber and Faber Ltd, 3 Queen Street, London WC1N 3AU, England.

PAULSON Ronald (Howard), b. 1930, USA. Professor of English. *Appointments:* Instructor, 1958-59, Assistant Professor, 1959-62, Associate Professor, 1962-63, University of Illinois; Professor of English, Rice University, Houston, Texas, 1963-67; Professor of English, Johns Hopkins University, Baltimore, Maryland, 1967-75, 1984-; Professor of English, Yale University, New Haven, Connecticut, 1975-84. *Publications:* Theme and Structure in Swift's Tale of a Tub; Fielding: The Critical Heritage (edited with T Lockward); Fielding: 20th Century Views (editor); Hogarth's Graphic Works; The Fictions of Satire; Satire and the Novel; Hogarth: His Life, Art and Times; Rowlandson: A New Interpretation; Emblem and Expression in English Art of the 18th Century; Satire: Modern Essays in Criticism (editor); The Age of Hogarth; Popular and Satire Art in the Age of Hogarth and Fielding; Literary Landscape: Turner and Constable; Representations of Revolution; Book and Painting; Shakespeare, Milton, and the Bible, 1982; Breaking and Remaking, 1989; Hogarth's Graphic Works (rev ed), 1989; Figure and Abstraction in Contemporary Painting, 1990; Hogarth, I: The Modern Moral Subject, 1991; Hogarth, II: High Artaud Law, 1992; Hogarth, III: Antaud Politics, 1993. *Address:* Johns Hopkins University, Baltimore, MD 21218, USA.

PAUWELS Rony, (Claude Van De Berge), b. 30 Apr 1945, Assenede, Belgium. Docent of Declamation. m. Drongen Pauwells, 30 Jan 1973. *Education:* Koninklijk Conservatorium, Gent. *Appointments:* Docent, Declamation, Academy of Arts, Ecklo; Universities of Brussels, Gent, Louvain-La-Neuve; University of Bonn, Germany, 1989. *Publications:* De koude wind du over het zand waeut, 1977; Het bewegen van her hoge gras op de top van de hevvel, 1981; Hiiumaa, 1987; Attu, 1988; Aztlan, 1990; Poetry: De zang van de maskers, 1988; De Mens in de ster, 1991; Het Silhouet, 1993. *Contributions to:* Journals: De Standaard: Literary magazines: Diogenes; Letters; Randschrift; DW and B; Bzulletin; Poeziekrant. *Honours:* 1st Prize, Declamation, Koninklijk Conservatorium, 1966; Scriptores Christianie, 1973; Dirk Martens Prize for Prose, 1975; E Bayie Prize, 1976; A De Pesseroy Poetry prize, 1982; Inter-Provincial Prize, Flanders, 1983. *Membership:* VVF (Flemish Writers). *Address:* Oude Molenstraat 2, 9960 Assenede, Belgium.

PAVEY Don, (Jack Adair), b. 1922, United Kingdom. Former Senior Lecturer (Art and Design), Kingston Polytechnic. *Appointments:* Editor, Athene, Journal of Society for Education Through Art, 1972-80. *Publications:* Methuen Handbook of Colour and Colour Dictionary (editor), 1963, 1967, 1978; Art-Based Games, 1979; Genius, 1980; Colour, 1981; The Artist's Colourmen's Story, 1985. *Contributions to:* Journal of the Royal College of Art; Athene;; Inscape; Colour Group Journal; Journal of Academic Gaming and Simulation in Education and Training; Times Educational Supplement. *Honours:* Freedom of the City of London, 1987 (Guild of Painter Stainers). *Memberships:* Council Member, Society for Education Through Art, 1972-83; Founder, Chairman, Junior Arts and Science Centres, 1970-80; Life Fellow, Royal Society of Arts; Design Research Society; Colour Group (Great Britain); Founder, Trustee of the National Art Education Archives at Bertton Hall, Wakefield, 1985-86. *Address:* 30 Wayside, London SW14 7LN, England.

PAXTON Lois. *See:* **LOW Lois.**

PAYNE Donald Gordon (Ian Cameron, Donald Gordon, James Vance Marshall), b. 3 Jan 1924, London, England. Author. m. Barbara Back, 20 Aug 1947, 4 sons, 1 daughter. *Education:* MA, History, Oxford. *Publications Include:* Walkabout, 1959; A River Ran Out of Eden, 1963; The Island at the Top of the World, 1970; To the Farthest Ends of the Earth, History of the Royal Geographical Society, 1980; Mountains of the Gods, 1984; Lost Paradise: The Exploration of the Pacific, 1987; many other books. *Contributions to:* Reader's Digest; National Geographic. *Literary Agent:* John Johnson. *Address:* Pippacre, Westcott Heath, Dorking RH4 3J2, Surrey, England.

PAYNE Laurence, b. 1919, United Kingdom. Author; Actor. *Appointments:* Numerous stage, film, television and radio roles; Drama Teacher: Royal College of Music, London; St Catherines's School, Guildford, Surrey. *Publications:* The Nose on My Face, 1962, US Paperback Edition The First Body, 1964; Too Small For His Shoes, 1962; Deep and Crisp and Even, 1964; Birds in the Belfry, 1966; Spy for Sale, 1969; Even My Foot's Asleep, 1971; Take the Money and Run, 1982; Malice in Camera, 1983; Vienna Blood, 1984; Dead for a Ducat, 1985; Late Knight, US Edition Knight Fall, 1987. *Address:* c/o Hodder and Stoughton, 47 Bedford Square, London WC1B 3DP, England.

PAYNE Peggy, b. 8 Jan 1949, Wilmington, North Carolina, USA. Writer. m. Dr Bob Dick, 8 Dec 1983. *Education:* AB, English, Duke University. *Publications:* Revelation, 1988; co-author, The Healing Power of Doing Good, 1992. *Contributions to:* Cosmopolitan; Ms; Family Circle; Travel & Leisure; New York Times; Washington Post; McCall's. *Honours:* Annual Fiction Award, given by Crucible, 1978; NEH Fellowship, 1979. *Memberships:* Society of American Travel Writers;

American Society of Journalists and Authors. *Address:* 512 St Mary's Street, Raleigh, NC 27605, USA.

PAZ Octavio, b. 31 Mar 1914, Mexico City. Poet; Philospher; Essayist; Critic; Director; Revista Vuelta. m. Marie José Tramini, 1 daughter. *Education:* National University of Mexico; Guggenheim Fellowship, USA, 1944. *Appointments:* Secretary, Mexican Embassy, Paris, 1946; New Delhi, 1952; Chargé d'Affaires ad interim, Japan, 1952; Posted Minister Secretariat for External Affairs, Mexico, 1953-58; Extraordinary and Plenintentiary Minister to Mexican Embassy, Paris, 1959-62; Ambassador to India, 1962-68; Simon Bolivar Professor of Latin American Studies, Cambridge, 1970; Visiting Porfessor of Spanish American Literature, University of Texas, Austin and Pittsburgh University, 1969-70; Charles Eliot Norton Professor of Poetry, Harvard University, 1971-72; Editor, Plural Mexico City, 1971-75. *Publications include:* Poetry: Hombre, 1937; Libertad bajo Palabra, 1949; Aguila o Sol?, 1951 (trans: Eagle or Sun?, 1970); Semillas para un Himno, 1956; Piedra de Sol, 1957 (trans: Sun Stone, 1960); La Estación Violenta, 1958; Discos Visuales, 1968; Ladera Este, 19969; La Centena, 1969; Topoemas, 1971; Renga, 1971; New Poetry of Mexico (Anthol), 1972; Pasado en Claro, 1975; Vuelta, 1976; Poemas 1935-1975, 1979; Arbol adentro, 1987; in English: Early Poems (1935-57), 1963; Configurations, 1971; A Draft of Shadows and Other Poems, 1979; Airborn/Hijos del Aire, 1981; Selected Poems, 1984; Collected Poems (1957-87), 1987; Prose: El Laberinto de la soledad, 1950; El Arco y la Lira, 1956; Las Peras del Olmo, 1957; Postdata, 1970; El Mono Gramático, 1971. *Honours:* Prizes include: Internat Poetry Grand Prix, 1963; National Prize for Literature, Mexico, 1977; Golden Eagle, Nicé, 1978; Ollin Yoliztli, Mexico, 1980; Cervantes, Spain, 1982; Neustadt International Prize for Literature, USA, 1982; T S Eliot Prize, Ingersoll Foundation, USA, 1987; Nobel Prize for Literature, 1990. *Address:* c/o Revista Vuelta, Presidente Canonza 210, Coyascán, Mexico 4000 DF, Mexico.

PEACOCK Daniel Joseph, b. 3 Oct 1919, Amityville, Long Island, New York, USA. Educator; Librarian. m. Shirley M Green, 12 Sept 1946, 1 son. 2 daughters. *Education:* BA, Earlham College, Richmond, Indiana, 1948; Graduate studies, University of Pennsylvania; MSinLS, Drexel University, 1959. *Publication:* Lee Boo of Belau, A Prince in London, 1987; Editor of numerous bibliographies and educational publications. *Contributions to:* Numerous articles to Pacific Islands periodicals. *Membership:* Charter Member, Mark Twain Association of America. *Address:* 500 University Avenue 935, Honolulu, HI 96826, USA.

PEAKE Lilian, b. United Kingdom. Writer. *Appointments:* Reporter, High Wycombe; Fashion Writer, London; Writer for Daily Herald, and Woman magazine, London. *Publications:* Man of Granite, 1971; This Moment in Time, 1971; The Library Tree, 1972; Man Out of Reach, 1972; The Real Thing, 1972; A Girl Alone, 1972; Mist Across the Moors, 1972; No Friend of Mine, 1972; Gone Before Morning, 1973; Man in Charge, 1973; Familiar Stranger, 1973; Till the End of Time, 1973; The Dream on the Hill, 1974; A Sense of Belonging, 1974; Master of the House, 1974; The Impossible Marriage, 1975; Moonrise over the Mountains, 1975; Heart in the Sunlight, 1975; The Tender Night, 1975; The Sun of Summer, 1975; A Bitter Loving, 1976; The Distant Dream, 1976; The Little Imposter, 1976; Somewhere to Lay My Head, 1977; Passionate Involvement, 1977; No Second Parting, 1977; This Man Her Enemy, 1977; Day of Possession, 1978; Rebel in Love, 1978; Run for Your Love, 1978; Dangerous Deception, 1979; Enemy from the Past, 1979; Stranger on the Beach, 1979; Promise at Midnight, 1980; A Ring for a Fortune, 1980; A Secret Affair, 1980; Strangers into Lovers, 1981; Gregg Barratt's Woman, 1981; Across a Crowded Room, 1981; Stay Till Morning, 1982.

PEARCE Ann Philippa, b. Great Shelford, Cambridgeshire, England. Freelance Writer of Childrens Books. m. Martin James Graham Christie, 9 May 1963, 1 daughter. *Education:* MA, Cambridge University. *Appointments:* Script Writer, Producer, School Broadcasting, Radio, 1945-58; Children's Editor, Andre Deutsch Limited, 1960-67. *Publications:* Minnow on the Say, 1954; Tom's Midnight Garden, 1958; Mrs Cockle's Cat, 1961; A Dog So Small, 1962; (with Sir Brian Fairfax-Lucy) The Children of the House, 1968, re-issued as The Children of Charlecote, 1989; The Squirrel Wife, 1971; What the Neighbours Did and other Stories, 1972; The Shadow Cage and other Stories of the Supernatural, 1977; The Battle of Bubble and Squeak, 1978; The Elm Street Lot, 1979; The Way to Sattin Shore, 1983; Lion at School and Other Stories, 1985; Who's Afraid? and Other Strange Stories, 1986; Emily's Own Elephant, 1987; The Toothball, 1987; Freddy, 1988; Old Belle's Summer Holiday, 1989; Here Comes Ted, 1992. *Contributions to:* Times Literary Supplement; The Guardian, Children's Book Reviewer, 1960-75. *Honours:* Carnegie Medal, for Tom's Midnight Garden, 1959; New York Herald Tribune Spring Festival Prize, for A Dog So Small; Whitbread Prize for Battle of Bubble and Squeak, 1979. *Membership:* Society of Authors. *Address:* c/o Viking-Kestrel Books, 27 Wright's Lane, London W8 5TZ, England.

PEARCE Brian Leonard, (Joseph Redman), b. 8 May 1915, Weymouth, Dorset, England. Translator. m. (1) Lilla Fox, 1940, 1 son, 2 daughters, (2) Fanny Greenspan, 1954, (3) Margaret Mills, 1966. *Education:* University College, London, 1934-37; BA Honours (Upper IInd), History, London, 1937. *Appointments:* Honorary Visiting Fellow: Aberdeen University; Glasgow University; School of Slavonic and East European Studies, University of London, 1992. *Publications:* How Haig Saved Lenin, 1987; Translations: The New Economics (E Preobrazhensky), 1965; Islam and Capitalism (M Rodinson), 1974; The Communist Movement, Part 1 (F Claudin), 1975; How the Revolution Armed (L D Trotsky), 1979-81; The Thinking Reed (Boris Kagarlitsky), 1988; Bread and Circuses (Paul Veyne), 1990; Others. *Contributions to:* Sbornik and its successor Revolutionary Russia. *Honours:* Scott-Moncrieff Prize, 1975, 1979, 1990. *Membership:* Translators Association. *Address:* 42 Victoria Road, New Barnet, Herts EN4 9PF, England.

PEARCE Brian Louis, b. 4 June 1933, West London, England. Poet; Author; Lecturer; Former Librarian. m. Margaret Wood, 2 Aug 1969, 1 daughter. *Education:* University College, London; MA; FLA; FRSA. *Appointments:* Examiner in English Literature, Library Association, 1964-70; Member, Writers in Schools Scheme, Greater London Arts, 1984-; Tutor in Creative Writing, Richmond upon Thames College. *Publications:* Victoria Hammersmith, novel, 1988; London Clay, stories, 1991; The Bust of Minerva, 1992; Poetry: Selected Poems 1951-73, 1978; The Vision of Piers Librarian, 1981; Office Hours, 1983; Browne Study, 1984; Dutch Comfort, poetry, prose, translations, 1985; Gwen John Talking, poetry, 1985; Jack o'Lent, 1991; Leaving the Corner: Selected poems, 1973-1985, 1992; Old Ascot: diaries (edited), 1964; Palgrave: Selected poems (edited), 1985; Thomas Twining of Twickenham, 1988; Plays: The Eagle and the Swan, 1966; Shrine Rites, 1990. *Contributions to:* New Poems, PEN, 1976, 1977; New Poetry, Arts Council anthologies, 1977, 1980, 1983; Voices of Today, The Least Thing, anthology, 1989; Emotional Geology: The Writings of Brian Louis Pearce, 1993; Many journals. *Honours:* 5th-6th, Place, 1-Act Verse Play Competition, Poetry Society, 1964; 1st Prize, Christian Poetry Competition, 1989. *Memberships:* PEN; Browning Society; Chairman, Richmond Poetry Group, 1974-84. *Address:* 72 Heathfield South, Twickenham, Middlesex TW2 7SS, England.

PEARCE Floyd Earl, b. 5 Feb 1935, Lewis, Iowa, USA. Printer; Publisher. *Education:* BA, State University of Iowa, 1960. *Appointments:* Literature Advisory Board, Iowa Arts council, 1984-87; Advisory Board, Thurber Country, Columbus, Ohio, 1987-90. *Publications:* As Publisher: Heinrich Himmler: Platoons & Files, 1982;

Joy, 1983; tidings, 1974; The Fountain and Other Fables, 1984; Reading Ourselves to sleep, 1986; Stoneboat, 1987; Lying, Stealing & Cheating, 1984; The Sacrifice Consenting, 1981; The King of the Golden River, 1986. *Honours:* Literary Advisory Board, Iowa Arts Council, 1984-87; Honour Books, Chicago Book Clinic, 1984, 1985; Advisory Board, Thurber Country 1987-90; Bay Area Critics Award, 1987. *Memberships:* Great Books Club; President, Hot Type Fraternity; Councilman, City of Cumberland, 1986-90. *Address:* Post Office Box 205, Cumberland, IA 50843, USA.

PEARCE Mary Emily, b. 7 Dec 1932, London, England. Writer. *Publications:* Apple Tree Lean Down, 1973; Jack Mercybright, 1974; The Sorrowing Wind, 1975; Cast a Long Shadow, 1977; The Land Endures, 1978; Seedtime and Harvest, 1980; Polsinney Harbour, 1983; The Two Farms, 1985; The Old House at Railes, 1993. *Memberships:* Society of Authors; National Book League. *Address:* Owls End, Shuthonger, Tewkesbury, Gloucestershire, England.

PEARSALL Derek Albert, b. 28 Aug 1931, Birmingham, England. Professor of English. m. Rosemary Elvidge, 30 Aug 1952, 2 sons, 3 daughters. *Education:* BA, 1951, MA, 1952, University of Birmingham. *Appointments:* Assistant Lecturer, Lecturer, King's College, University of London, 1959-65; Lecturer, Senior Lecturer, Reader, 1965-76, Professor, 1976-87, University of York; Visiting Professor, 1985-, Gurney Professor of English, 1987-, Harvard University, Cambridge, Massachusetts, USA. *Publications:* John Lydgate, 1970; Landscapes and Seasons of the Medieval World (with Elizabeth Salter), 1973; Old English and Middle English Poetry, 1977; Langland's Piers Plowman: An Edition of the C-Text, 1978; The Canterbury Tales: A Critical Study, 1985; The Life of Geoffrey Chaucer: A Critical Biography, 1992. *Memberships:* Council Member, Early English Text Society; Fellow, Medieval Academy of America, 1988-90; New Chaucer Society, President 1988-90; Fellow, American Academy of Arts and Sciences. *Address:* Harvard University, Department of English, Warren House, Cambridge, MA 02138, USA.

PEARSALL Ronald, b. 1927, United Kingdom. Author. *Publications:* Worm in the Bud, 1969; The Table-Rappers, 1972; Victorian Sheet Music Covers, 1972; Victorian Popular Music, 1973; Collecting Mechanical Antiques, 1973; Edwardian Life and Leisure, 1973; Collecting and Restoring Scientific Instruments, 1974; Inside the Antique Trade (with G Webb), 1974; Night's Black Angels, 1975; Collapse of Stout Party, 1975; Edwardian Popular Music, 1975; Popular Music of the 1920's, 1976; The Belvedere, 1976; The Alchemists, 1976; Public Purity, Private Shame, 1976; Conan Doyle, 1977; Tides of War, 1978; The Iron Sleep, 1979; Tell Me Pretty Maiden, 1981; Practical Painting, 1984. *Address:* Garden Cottage, 22 East Street, Ashburton, Devon TQ13 7AZ, England.

PEARSON Diane (Margaret), b. 1931, United Kingdom. Writer; Senior Editor. *Appointments:* With Production Department, Jonathan Cape Ltd, London, 1948-52; With Advertising Department, Purnells Publishing, London, 1962-63; Senior Editor, Transworld Publishers Ltd, London, 1963-. *Publications:* Bride of Tancred, 1967; The Marigold Field, 1969; Sarah Whitman, 1971; Csardas, 1975; The Summer of the Barshinskeys, 1984. *Address:* c/o Macmillan Ltd, 4 Little Essex Street, London WC2, England.

PEARSON John, b. 1934, USA. Novelist. *Appointments:* Served as Methodist Minister, Windsor and Napa, California; Extension Programme Coordinator, Department of Arts and Humanities, University of California, Berkeley, 1966-74. *Publications:* To Be Nobody Else, 1968; Kiss the Joy as It Flies, 1970; The Sun's Birthday, 1973; Begin Sweet World, 1976; Magic Doors, 1977; Love Is Most Mad and Moonly, 1978; The Calligraphy of Nature, 1984.

Address: 1343 Sacramento Street, Berkeley, CA 94702, USA.

PEARSON Ridley, b. 13 Mar 1953, Glen Cove, New York, USA. Author. m. Colleen Daly, 10 Aug 1984. *Education:* Kansas University, 1972; Brown University, 1974. *Publications:* Never Look Back, 1985; Blood of the Albatross, 1986; The Seizing of Yankee Green Mall, 1987; Undercurrents, 1988; Probable Cause, 1990; Hard Fall, 1992; The Angel Maker, 1993. *Honours:* Raymond Chandler Fulbright Fellow, 1990-91. *Memberships:* Writers Guild of America; Mystery Writers of America; The Authors Guild Inc; International Crime Writers Association. *Literary Agent:* Al Zuckerman. *Address:* PO Box 670, Hailey, ID 83333, USA.

PEARSON William Harrison (Bill), b. 18 Jan 1922, Greymouth, New Zealand. Writer and Retired University Teacher. *Education:* Greymouth Technical High School, 1934-38; MA, Canterbury University College, Christchurch, 1948; PhD, King's College, University of London, England, 1952. *Publications:* Coal Flat, 1963, 5th edition, 1985; Henry Lawson Among Maoris, 1968; Fretful Sleepers and Other Essays, 1974; Rifled Sanctuaries, 1984; Six Stories, 1991. *Honours:* Joint Recipient, Landfall Readers Award, 1960; New Zealand Book Award for non-fiction, 1975. *Address:* 49 Lawrence Street, Herne Bay, Auckland, New Zealand.

PECK Richard, b. 5 Apr 1934, Decatur, Illinois, USA. Writer. *Education:* BA, DePauw University, 1956; MA, Southern Illinois Uiversity, 1959. *Publications:* The Ghost Belonged to Me, 1975; Are You in the House Alone?, 1976; Amanda/Miranda, 1980; This Family of Women, 1983; Remembering the Good Times, 1985; Prinbers Ashley, 1987; Don't Look and It Won't Hurt, 1972; Secrets of the Shopping Mall, 1979; New York Time, 1981; Close Enough To Touch, 1981; Blossom Culp and the Sleep of Death, 1986; Princess Ashley, 1987; Those Summer Girls I Never Met, 1988; Unfinished Portrait of Jessica, 1991. *Contributor to:* New York Times; School Library Jurnal. *Honours:* Edgar A. Poe Award, American Society of Mystery Writers, 1977; Citations for 3 Young Adult Novels, American Library Associations Best of the Best Listing; American Library Association Margaret Edwards Young Adult Author Award, 1990. *Memberships:* Authors Guild; Authors League. *Literary Agent:* Sheldon Fogelman, New York. *Address:* 155 E. 72nd St., New York, NY 10021, USA.

PECK Robert Newton, b. USA. Author. *Publications:* A Day No Pigs Would Die, 1972; Millie's Boy, 1973; Path of Hunters: Animal Struggle in a Meadow, 1973; Soup, 1974; Soup for Me, 1975; Wild Cat, 1975; Bee Tree and Other Stuff, verse, 1975; Fawn, 1975; I Am the King of Kazoo, 1976; Rabbits and Redcoats, 1976; Hamilton, 1976; Hang for Treason, 1976; King of Kazoo (music and lyrics), play, 1976; Last Sunday, 1977; Trig, 1977; Patooie, 1977; The King's Iron, 1977; Soup for President, 1978; Eagle Fur, 1978; Trig Sees Red, 1978; Basket Case, 1979; Hub, 1979; Mr Little, 1979; Clunie, 1979; Soup's Drum, 1980; Secrets of Successful Fiction, 1980; Trig Goes Ape, 1980; Soup of Wheels, 1981; Justice Lion, 1981; Trig or Treat, 1982; Banjo, 1982; Soup in the Saddle, 1983; Soup's Goat, 1984; Spanish Hoof, 1985; Soup on Ice, 1985; Jo Silver, 1985; Soup on Fire, 1987; My Vermont, 1987; Hallapoosa, 1988; Arly, 1989; Soup's Hoop, 1990; Higbee's Halloween, 1990; Little Soup's Hayride, 1991; Little Soup's Birthday, 1991; Arly II, 1991; Soup in Love; Fort Dog July. *Honour:* Mark Twain Award, Missouri, 1981. *Address:* 500 Sweetwater Club Circle, Longwood, FL 32779, USA.

PECKHAM Morse, b. 1914, USA. Distinguished Professor Emeritus of English and Comparative Literature. *Appointments:* Instructor, 1946-47, Assistant Professor, 1948-49, Rutgers University, New Brunswick, New Jersey; Assistant Professor, 1949-52, Associate Professor, 1952-61, Director, Institute for Humanistic Education for Business Executives, 1953-54; Director, University Press, 1953-55, Professor,

1961-67, University of Pennsylvania, Philadelphia; Distinguished Professor of English and Comparative Literature, 1967-80, Distinguished Professor Emeritus, 1980-, University of South Carolina, Columbia. *Publications:* On the Origin of Species: A Variorum Text, by Charles Darwin (editor), 1959; Humanistic Education for Business Executives: An Essay in General Education, 1960; Word, Meaning, Poem: An Anthology of Poetry (edited with Seymour Chapman), 1961; Beyond the Tragic Vision: The Quest for Identity in the Nineteenth Century, 1962; Man's Rage for Chaos: Biology, Behaviour and the Arts, 1965; Romanticism: The Culture of the Nineteenth Century (editor), 1965; Paracelsus, by Robert Browning (editor), 1969; Art and Pornography: An Experiment in Explanation, 1969; The Triumph of Romanticism: Collected Essays, 1970; Victorian Revolutionaries; Speculation on Some Heroes of a Culture Crisis, 1970; Pippa Passes, by Robert Browning (editor), 1971; Luria, by Robert Browning (editor), 1973; Romanticism and Behavior: Collected Essays II, 1976; Sordello, by Robert Browning (editor), 1977; Explanation and Power: The Control of Human Behavior, 1979; Romanticism and Ideology, 1985; The Birth of Romanticism, 1986. *Address:* 6478 Bridgewood Road, Columbia, SC 29206, USA.

PEEBLES Anne. *See:* **GALLAWAY Priscilla.**

PEET Bill, b. 1915, USA. Children's Fiction Writer. *Appointments:* Formerly Artist and Screenwriter for Walt Disney Productions. *Publications:* Hubert's Hair-Raising Adventure, 1959; Huge Harold, 1961; Smokey, 1962; The Pinkish Purplish Bluish Egg, 1963; Ella, 1964; Randy's Dandy Lions, 1964; Kermit the Hermit, 1965; Chester the Worldly Pig, 1965; Capyboppy, 1966; Farewell to Shady Glade, 1966; Jennifer and Josephine, 1967; Buford the Little Big-Horn, 1967; Fly Homer Fly, 1969; The Whingdingdilly, 1970; The Wump World, 1970; How Droofus the Dragon Lost His Head, 1971; The Caboose Who Got Loose, 1971; Countdown to Christmas, 1972; The Ant and the Elephant, 1972; The Spooky Tail of Preewit Peacock, 1973; Merle the High Flying Squirrel, 1974; The Gnats of Knotty Pine, 1975; Big Bad Bruce, 1976; Eli, 1978; Cowardly Clyde, 1979; Encore for Eleanor, 1981; The Luckiest One of All, 1982; No Such Things, 1983; Pamela Camel, 1984; The Kweeks of Kookatumdee, 1985; Zella Zack and Zodiak, 1986; Jethro and Joel Were a Troll, 1987; Bill Peet - An Autobiography, 1989; Cock-A-Doodle Dudley, 1990. *Address:* c/o Houghton Mifflin Ci, 1 Beacon Street, Boston, MA 02107, USA.

PEIRCE Neal R, b. 1932, USA. Writer; Editor. *Appointments:* Political Editor, Congressional Quarterly, 1960-69; Fellow, Woodrow Wilson Center for Scholars, 1971-74; Co-Founder, Contributing Editor, The National Journal, Washington, District of Columbia, 1969-; Syndicated Columnist, Washington Post Writers Group. *Publications:* The People's President, 1968, 2nd Edition, 1981; The Megastates of America, 1972; The Pacific States of America, 1972; The Mountain States of America, 1972; The Great Plains States of America, 1973; The Deep South States of America, 1974; The Border South States, 1975; The New England States, 1976; The Mid-Atlantic States of America, 1977; The Great Lakes States of America, 1980; The Book of America, 1983; Corrective Capitalism, 1987; Enterprising Communities, 1989; Citistates, 1993. *Address:* 610 G Street SW, Washington, DC 20024, USA.

PELLI Moshe, b. 1936, Israel; Came to USA 1957, US citizen. Professor. m. 2 children. *Education:* BS, Journalism/Liberal Studies, New York University, 1960; PhD, Modern Hebrew Literature/Jewish Intellectual History/Bible, The Dropsie College for Hebrew and Cognate Learning, Philadelphia, Pennsylvania, 1967; Visiting Scholar, Oxford Centre for Postgraduate Hebrew Studies, 1984, 1991; Visiting Scholar, Institute of Jewish Studies, The Hebrew University, Jerusalem, 1991. *Appointments:* Assistant Professor, University of Texas, Department of Oriental Language and Literature, Austin, Texas, 1967-71; Senior Lecturer, Ben-Gurion University, Department of Hebrew Literature, Beer Sheva, Israel, 1971-74; Associate Professor of Modern Hebrew Language and Literature, Cornell University, Department of Near Eastern Studies, Ithaca, New York, 1974-78; Associate Professor, Yeshiva University, Erna Michael College, New York, 1978-84; Associate Professor, Department of Foreign Languages, 1985-88; Director, Judaic Studies Programme, 1985-, Interdisciplinary Programme in Judaic Studies placed in the Office of the Dean of Arts and Sciences, 1988-, Professor, 1989-, University of Central Florida. Various visiting appointments in USA, Israel and Australia. Other appointments include: Founding Editor, Lamishpaha, Hebrew Illustrated Monthly, New York, 1964-66; Abstractor, Religious and Theological Abstracts, 1968-71; Editor, Lamishpaha, 1983-85; Editor, Niv, Hebrew Literary Quarterly, New York, 1957-1966. *Publications:* Books: Moses Mendelssohn: Bonds of Tradition, (Hebrew) 1972; The Age of Haskalah: Studies in Hebrew Literature of the Enlightenment in Germany (1770-1820), 1979; Getting By in Hebrew, 1984; Struggle for Change: Studies in the Hebrew Enlightenment in Germany at the End of the 18th Century, 1988; Numerous journal research articles, review articles, 2 novels, 1961, 1965; 8 children's books, 1963-80; 15 short stories. *Honours include:* Short Story Prize, Haboker, Tel Aviv, 1955; Fellow, Dropsie College, 1962; Scroll plaque for sustained research activities, University of Central Florida, 1988; Appointed to Executive Council, National Association of Professors of Hebrew, 1988; Inducted into The Quill, University of Central Florida Authors Club, 1989; 1991, Abraham Friedman Prize for Hebrew Culture in America by Hebrew Language & Culture Association of America for Life Time Contribution to Hebrew Culture, in teaching, research & editing Hebrew periodicals, 1992; Many grant awards. *Memberships include:* Association for Jewish Studies; American Academy of Religion; American Society of 18th Century Studies; National Association of Professors of Hebrew; World Union of Jewish Studies; American Academy for Jewish Research. *Address:* 1140 Washington Avenue, Winter Park, FL 32789, USA.

PELLY David Fraser, b. 19 June 1948, Toronto, Canada. Writer. m. Laurie McGinnis Pelly. *Education:* BSc, Royal Military College of Canada. *Publications:* Expedition, 1981; Qikaaluktut - Images of Inuit Life, 1986; Inuit of the North, 1987; The Kazan, 1991. *Contributions to:* Numerous articles to Canadian Geographic and at least 30 other publications in Canada, US and UK. *Memberships:* Fellow, Royal Canadian Geographical Society; Periodical Writers Association of Canada. *Address:* 193-55 McCaul Street, Toronto, Canada M5T 2W7.

PELUFFO Luisa, b. 20 Aug 1941, Buenos Aires, Argentina. Writer. m. Pablo Masllorens, 24 Apr 1971, 2 sons. *Education:* Degree, Drawing Teacher, National Fine Arts School, 1959; Stage Direction, National Drama School, 1975. *Literary Appointments:* Staff: Panorama Magazine, Buenos Aires, 1969-70; Channel 7 TV, Buenos Aires, 1970-71; La Nacion newspaper, 1971-76. *Publications include:* Materia Viva, poems, 1976; Conspiraciones, short stories, 1982; Materia de Revelaciones, poems, 1983; Todo eso oyes (novel), 1989; La otra orilla (poems), 1990; La Doble Vida (novel), 1993, (Editorial Atlántida, Buenos Aires, Argentina). *Contributions to:* Various anthologies of short stories; Newspapers La Nacion, La Opinion, La Prensa, Rio Negro. *Honours:* 2nd Prize short stories 1978, 'Honour Band' 1983, Argentine Writers Society; 1st prize, Victoria Ocampo Award, Buenos Aires Bank Province Foundation, 1981; Special mention, National Poetry Award, National Secretary of Culture, 1983; National Arts Found 30th Anniversary Poetry Regional Award, 1988; Emecé Editors Literary Award, 1988-89. *Memberships:* Argentine Writers Society; San Carlos de Bariloche Writers Society; Hispanic Cultural & Literary Institute, California, USA; PEN Club, Mexico. *Address:* Palacios 465, (8400) Bariloche, Provincia de Rio Negro, Argentina.

PEMBERTON Margaret, b. 10 Apr 1943, Bradford, England. Writer. m. 1 son, 4 daughters. *Appointments:* Chairman, Romantic Novelists' Association, 1989. *Publications include:* Harlot, 1981; Lion of Languedoc, 1981; The Flower Garden, 1982; Silver Shadows, Golden Dreams, 1985; Never Leave Me, 1986; Multitude of Sins, 1988; White Christmas In Saigon, 1990. Also numerous other novels including: Forever, Pioneer Girl; African Enchantment; Guilty Secret; Vengeance in the Sun. *Memberships:* Crime Writers Association; Romantic Novelists Association; PEN; Society of Authors. *Literary Agent:* Carol Smith. *Address:* 13 Manor Lane, London SE13 5QW, England.

PENA MUNOZ Margarita, b. 21 Aug 1937, Mexico. Writer; Scholar. m. B. Lima, 6 Nov 1971, 1 son. *Education:* BD, Hispanic Literature, 1963, MD, Hispanic Literature, 1965, University of Mexico; PhD, El Colegio de Mexico, 1968. *Appointments:* Researcher, Literary Researching Centre, 1969-75, Professor, 1975-87, University of Mexico. *Publications:* Flores de varia poesia, 1980, 1987; America's Discovery and Conquest, An Anthology of Chronicles, 1982; To Pass Over in Silence, 1983; Mofarandel, 1986; Living Again, 1980. *Contributions to:* various journals and magazines. *Memberships:* International Hispanists Association; PEN; International Institute of Latin-American Literature; Latin-American Linguistics Association, University of Mexico. *Address:* Cerrada del Convento 45, Casa 2, Tlalpan, Mexico DF 14420.

PENDLETON Don. *See:* **OBSTFELD Raymond.**

PENDLETON Don(ald Eugene), (Dan Britain, Stephen Gregory). b. 1927, American, Writer of novels, short stories, mystery, crime, suspense, sex. *Appointments:* Telegrapher, Southern Pacific Railroad, San Francisco, 1948-55; Air Traffic Control Specialist, Federal Aviation Administration, Western Region, 1957-61; Engineering Supervisor, Martin Co, Denver, 1961-64; Engineering Administrator, General Electric, 1964-66 and Lockheed Corporation, Marietta, Georgia, 1966-67; Senior Editor and Columnist, Orion magazine, 1967-70. *Publications include:* mystery novels include: Colorado Kill-Zone, 1976; Acapulco Rampage, 1976; Dixie Convoy, 1976; Savage Fire, 1977; Command Strike, 1977; Cleveland Pipeline, 1977; Arizona Ambush, 1977; Tennessee Smash, 1978; Monday's Mob, 1978; Terrible Tuesday, 1979; Wednesday's Wrath, 1979; Thermal Thursday, 1979; Friday's Feast, 1979; Stan's Sabbath, 1980; Sicilian Slaughter, 1981; Bloodsport, 1982; Double Crossfire, 1982; The Iranian Hit, 1982; The Libyan Connection, 1982; The New War, 1982; Paramilitary Plot, 1982; Renegade Agent, 1982; Return to Vienna, 1982; Terrorist Summit, 1982; The Violent Streets, 1982. Other publications as Stephan Gregory: Society and the Sexual Life, 1968; Sex and the Supernatural, 1968; ESP and the Sex Mystique, 1968; Dialogues of Human Sexuality, 1968; Secret Sex Desires, 1968; The Sexuality Gap, 1968; The Olympians (novel) 1969; Cataclysm (novel) 1969; Hypnosis and the Free Female, 1969; The Truth about Sex, 1969; The Guns of terra 10 (novel) 1970, 1989; Population Doomsday (novel) 1970. As Dan Britain: The Godmakers (novel) 1970; The Executioner's War Book, 1977. *Address:* c/o Scott Meredith Literary Agency, 845 Third Avenue, New York, NY 10022, USA.

PENICK John Edgar, b. 2 Jan 1944, Langley, Virginia, USA. Professor. m. Nell Inman, 24 July 1966, 1 son, 1 daughter. *Education:* BS, Zoology and Chemistry, 1966, MA, Junior College Teaching of Biology, 1969, University of Miami; PhD, Science Education, Biology, Florida State University, 1973. *Appointments:* Teaching Experience: Teacher of Biology and Botany, Miami-Dade Junior College, summer 1968; Head of Science Department, Miami Jackson High School, 1967-70; Instructor of Science Methods and Plant Physiology, Florida State University, 1970-73; Assistant Professor and Director of Teacher Education, Loyola University, Chicago, 1973-75; Professor and Co-ordinator, University of Iowa, 1975-. Various international lecture engagements and teaching appointments. *Publications include:* Numerous journal articles and contributions to textbooks including: Developing creativity through science instruction in What Research Says to the Science Teacher, Volume IV R E Yager (Ed) 1982;with R E Yager, The Search for Excellence in Science Education in Phi Delta Kappan 64(9) May 1983; with R E Yager and R Bonnstetter, Teachers Make Exemplary Programs in Educational Leadership 44(2) Oct 1986; with R E Yager, Science Education, Chapter 33 of Houston R E (Ed), Handbook of Research on Teacher Eduxcation, Mar 1990. Numerous monographs, reviews and learned papers. *Honours include:* Gustav Ohaus Award (NSTA) for Innovations in College Science Teaching (with V N Lunetta), 1986; Distinguished Educator Award, Florida State University, 1987; Outstanding Science Educator in the United States, AETS 1987; Burlington Northern Award for Outstanding Career Achievements, 1992. *Memberships:* Numerous professional organizations. *Address:* 733 S Summit, Iowa City, IA 52240, USA

PENN John. *See:* **TROTMAN Jack.**

PENNANT-REA Rupert Lascelles, b. 23 Jan 1948, Zimbabwe. Journalist. m. Helen Jay, 2 sons, 1 daughter, 2 step-daughters. *Education:* BA, Economics, Trinity College, Dublin, 1970; MA, Economics, University of Manchester, 1972. *Appointments:* Economics Correspondent, 1977, Economics Editor, 1981, Editor, 1986-93, The Economist; Deputy Govcernor, Bank of England, 1993-. *Publications:* Gold Foil, 1979; Who Runs the Economy?, (jointly), 1979; The Pocket Economist (jointly), 1982; The Economist Economics (jointly), 1986. *Honours:* Winner, Wincott Prize for Financial Journalism, 1984. *Memberships:* Reform Club; MCC; Harare. *Literary Agent:* Curtis Brown. *Address:* Bank of England, Treadneedle Street, London EC1, England.

PENSLAR Derek Jonathan, b. 12 Aug 1958, Los Angeles, California, USA. Associate Professor of History. m. 12 June 1983, 1 son, 1 daughter. *Education:* BA, Stanford University, 1978; MA, 1980, PhD, 1987, University of California, Berkeley. *Appointments:* Currently Associate Professor, History, Indiana University, Bloomington. *Publications:* Zionism and Technocracy, 1991. *Contributions to:* Journal of Contemporary History, 1990; Cathedra, 1990, 1991; Leo Baeck Institute Yearbook, 1993. *Memberships:* American Historical Association; Association for Jewish Studies; Leo Baeck Institute. *Address:* Department of History, Indiana University, Bloomington, IN 47405, USA.

PEPPE Rodney Darrell, b. 24 June 1934, Eastbourne, East Sussex, England. Author; Artist. m. Tatjana Tekkel, 16 July 1960, 2 sons. *Education:* St Bede's School, Eastbourne, 1941-48; St Edward's School, Oxford, 1948-51; Eastbourne School of Art, 1951-53 and 1955-57; LCC Central School of Art (London) 1957-59, NDD Illustration (Special Subject) Central School Diploma. *Publications include:* The Alphabet Book, 1968; The House That Jack Built, 1970; Odd One Out, 1974; Henry (series) 1975-84; The Mice Who Lived in a Shoe, 1981; Huxley Pig (series) 1989. *Contributions to:* Books for Your Children, Autumn 1978: Making First Books by Rodney Peppe. *Membership:* Society of Authors. *Address:* Barnwood House, Whiteway, Stroud, Gloucestershire GL6 7ER, England.

PERCY Herbert Roland, b. 6 Aug 1920. Marine Engineer. m. Mary Davina James, 28 Mar 1942, 2 sons, 1 daughter. *Education:* Royal Navy Artificers Training Establishment, 1936-40; Royal Canadian Navy Prep School, Esquimalt, British Columbia, 1954-56; Royal Navy Engineering College, Manadon, 1956. *Appointments:* Editor, Canadian Author and Bookman, 1963-65. *Publications:* The Timeless Island, 1960; Joseph Howe, 1976; Flotsam, 1978; Thomas Chandler Haliburton, 1980; Painted Ladies, 1983; A Model Lover, 1986; Tranter's Tree, 1987; An Innocent Bystander, 1989, UK Edition, 1991; The Mother Tongue, 1992.

Contributions to: Short Story International, USA; Canadian Fiction Magazine; Prism International; Queen's Quarterly; Vanity Fair, UK; Wascana Review; Others. *Honours:* Allan Sangster Memorial Award, 1974; Nova Scotia Novel Award, 1975; Nove Scotia Cultural Life Award, 1992. *Memberships:* Writers Union of Canada, Membership Chair; Writers Federation of Nova Scotia, Founding Chair; International PEN; Canadian Authors Association. *Literary Agent:* Bella Pomer Agency, Toronto, Canada. *Address:* c/o TWUC, 24 Ryerson Ave, Toronto, Ontario, Canada M5T 2P3.

PERERA Victor Haim, b. 12 Apr 1934, Guatemala. Writer. m. Padma Hejmadi, 8 Aug 1960 (div 1974). *Education:* BA, Brooklyn College, 1956; MA, University of Michigan, 1958. *Appointments:* Editorial Staff, The New Yorker, 1963-66; Reporter, The New York Times Magazine, 1971-75; Contributing Editor, Present Tense, 1974-89; Editorial Board, Tikkun, 1990-. *Publications:* The Conversion, 1970; The Loch-Ness Monster Watchers, 1974; The Last Lords of Palenque (with Robert D Bruce), 1982; Rites: A Guatemalan Boyhood, 1986; Testimony: Death of A Guatemalan Village, by Victor Montejo (trans from Spanish), 1987; Unfinished Conquest: The Guatemalan Tragedy, 1993. *Contributions to:* New Yorker; Atlantic Monthly; The Nation; The New York Review of Books; Harper's; Paris Review; Antioch Review; Partisan Review. *Honours:* Avery Hopwood Major Award in the Essay, 1962; National Endowment of the Arts Writing Award, 1980; PEN Fiction, (Short Story) Award, 1984; Present Tense/ Joel Cavior Award in Biography, 1987; Lila Wallace, Reader's Digest Writing Award, 1992-94. *Memberships:* PEN American Centre. *Literary Agent:* Gloria Loomis, Watkins-Loomis Agency. *Address:* c/o Watkins-Loomis Agency, 150 East 35th Street, New York, NY 10016, USA.

PERI ROSSI Chistina, b. 12 Nov 1941, Montevideo, Uruguay, Writer. *Education:* Professor of Comparative Literature, 1963. *Appointments:* Professor of Literature, Montevideo, 1963-72; Professor of Comparative Literature and Latin American Literature, Universidad Autonoma de Barcelona, Spain, 1983. *Publications:* La nave de los locos, novel; Solitano de amor, novel; Babel barbara, poetry; El museo de los esfuerzos inutiles, short stories; La rebelion de los ninos, short stories; Europa despues de la Uwia, poetry; Una pasion prohibida, short stories; La tarde del dinosaurio, short stories. *Contributions to:* Marcha, Uruguay; In Spain: Quimera; El Viejo Topo; El Pais; La Vanguardia; Efe. *Honours:* ARCA Prize, narrative, Uruguay, 1968; 1st Prize, MARCHA, novel, Uruguay, 1969; In Spain: Inventarios Provisionales de Poesia, poetry, 1974; Civdad de Palma, poetry, 1975; Benito Perez Galdos Prize, narrative, 1979; Civtat de Barcelona Award, poetry, 1991; Award for Babel barbara in English, Quarterly Review of Literature Poetry Series, Princeton, USA, 1992. *Membership:* Asociacion Colegial de Escritores de Espana. *Literary Agent:* International Editors, Barcelona, Spain. *Address:* Travessera de les Corts No 171 4o 1a, 08028 Barcelona, Spain.

PERIN Roberto, b. 3 Apr 1948, Montreal, Canada. Professor of History. m. Yvonne Kaspers, 9 May 1970, 3 sons. *Education:* BA, Hons, Universite de Montreal, 1968; MA, Carleton University, 1970; PhD, University of Ottawa, 1975. *Appointments:* Lecturer, Centre of Canadian Studies, University of Edinburgh, 1975-77; Assistant Professor of History, York University, Canada, 1977-81; Director, Canadian Academic Centre in Italy, Rome, 1983-85; Associate Professor of History, York University, Canada, 1981-. *Publications:* Rome in Canada: The Vatican and Canadian Affairs in the Late Victorian Age, 1990; Arrangiarsi: The Italian Immigration Experience in Canada, 1989. *Contributions to:* Canadian Historical Review; International Journal of Canadian Studies; Il Veltro (Rome); Dictionary of Canadian Biography; British Bulletin of Canadian Studies. *Honour:* John W Dafoe Foundation Book Prize, 1990. *Memberships:* Institut d'Histoire de L'Amerique Francaise; Canadian Historical Association; Association of Canadian Studies; Canadian Catholic Historical

Association. *Address:* 440 Gladstone Avenue, Toronto, Canada M6H 3H9.

PERKINS Dwight Heald, b. 20 Oct 1934, Chicago, Illinois, USA. Professor of Economics. m. Julie Rate, 5 June 1957, 2 sons, 1 daughter. *Education:* BA, Cornell University, 1956; AM, 1961, PhD, 1964, Harvard University. *Publications:* Agricultural Development in China, 1368- 1968, 1969; China: Asia's Next Economic Giant, 1986; Market Control and Planning in Communist China, 1966; Economics of Development (co-author) 2nd edition, 1987; Economic and Social Modernization of Korea (co-author) 1980; Rural Development in China (with S Yusuf) 1984 and four other edited or co-authored books. *Contributions to:* Over 50 articles. *Memberships:* American Economic Association; Association for Asian Studies; Association of Comparative Economic Systems (Past President). *Address:* Harvard Institute for International Development, One, Eliot Street, Cambridge, MA 02138, USA.

PERKINS George Burton, b. 16 Aug 1930, USA. University Professor. m. Barbara Miller, 9 May 1964, 3 daughters. *Education:* AB, Tufts College, 1953; MA, Duke University, 1954; PhD, Cornell University, 1960. *Appointments:* Teaching Assistant, Cornell University, 1957-60; Assistant Professor, Baldwin Wallace College, 1960-63; Assistant Professor, Farleigh Dickinson University, 1963-66; Lecturer, American Literature, Edinburgh University, 1966-67; Professor, Eastern Michigan University, 1967-; General Editor, Journal of Narrative Technique, 1970-92. *Publications:* Writing Clear Prose, 1964; The Theory of the American Novel, 1970; Realistic American Short Fiction, 1972; American Poetic Theory, 1972; The American Tradition in Literature (with Bradley, Beatty, Long), 4th 5th, 6th, 7th editions, 1974, 1981, 1985, 1990; The Practical Imagination, (with Frye, Baker), 1981; The Harper Handbook to Literature (with Frye, Baker), 1985; Contemporary American Literature, (with B Perkins), 1987; Benet's Reader's Encyclopeadia of American Literature (with B Perkins), 1991; Kaleidoscope (with B Perkins), 1993. *Contributions to:* Essays and reviews in Nineteenth-Century Fiction; Journal of American Folklore; The Dickensian; New England Quarterly; others. *Honours:* Duke University Fellow, 1953-54; Cornell University Fellow, 1954-55; Phi Kappa Phi, 1956; Distinguished Faculty Award, Eastern Michigan University, 1978; Fellow, Institute for Advanced Studies in the Humanities, Edinburgh University, 1981; Senior Fulbright Scholar, University of Newcastle, Australia, 1989. *Memberships:* various professional organisations. *Address:* 1316 King George Bulevard, Ann Arbor, MI 48108, USA.

PERKINS Michael b. 11 Nov 1942, Lansing, Michigan, USA. Writer; Arts Programme Director. m. Renie (Shoemaker) McCune, 20 June 1960, 1 son 2 daughters. *Education:* Ohio University, Athens, 1963; New School for Social Research, 1962; City College New York, 1966. *Appointments:* Editor, Tompkins Square Press, 1966-68; Editor, Croton Press Ltd, 1969-72; Editor, Vister Arts Magazine, 1978-79. *Publications:* Evil Companions, 1968 and 1992; Down Here 1969; The Secret Record, 1977 and 1992; The Persistence of Desiro, 1977. *Contributions to:* Mother Jones; The Nation; Village Voice; Choice; Eleven. *Honour:* Panelist, New York Foundation for the Arts. *Memberships:* Authors Guild; National Book Critics Circle. *Literary Agent:* John Brockman. *Address:* 750 Ohayo Mt Road, Glenford, NY 12433, USA.

PERRETT Bryan b. 9 July, 1934, Liverpool, England. Author and Military Historian. m. Anne Catherine Trench, 13 Aug, 1966. *Education:* Liverpool College. *Appointment:* Defence Correspondent to Liverpool Echo during Falklands War and Gulf War. *Publications include:* A History of Blitzkrieg, 1983; The Czar's British Squadron (with A Lord) 1981; Knights of the Black Cross - Hitler's Panzerwaffe and its Leaders, 1986; Desert Warfare, 1988; Encyclopeadia of the Second World War (with Ian Hogg) 1989; Canopy of War, 1990; Liverpool: A City at War, 1990; Last Stand - Famous Bettles Against

The Odds, 1991; The Battle Book - Crucial Conflicts in History from 1469BC to the Present, 1992; At All Costs - Stories of Impossible Victories, 1993. *Contributions to:* War Monthly; Military History; World War Investigator; War in Peace (partwork); The Elite (partwork). *Memberships:* Rotary Club of Ormskirk; Royal United Services Institute. *Literary Agent:* Watson Little Ltd, London; McIntosh and Otis, New York. *Address:* 7, Maple Avenue, Burscough, Nr Ormskirk, Lancashire L40 5SL, England.

PERRIAM Wendy Angela, b. 23 Feb 1940, London, England. Author. m. (1) 22 Aug 1964, 1 daughter, (2) John Alan Perriam, 29 July 1974. *Education:* St Anne's College, Oxford, 1958-61; BA (Hons), History, 1961, MA, 1972, Oxford; London School of Economics, 1963-64. *Publications:* Absinthe for Elevenses, 1980; Cuckoo, 1981; After Purple, 1982; Born of Woman, 1983; The Stillness The Dancing, 1985; Sin City, 1987; Devils, for a Change, 1989; Fifty-Minute Hour, 1990; Bird Inside, 1992; Michael, Michael, 1993. *Contributions to:* Stories and articles to magazines and newspapers including: She; Cosmopolitan; Penthouse; Esquire; Sunday Times; Evening Standard; Poems and short stories to Arts Council Anthology and South East Arts anthologies: Seven Deadly Sins, 1985; The Literary Companion to Sex, 1992; Best Short Stories, 1992. *Memberships:* PEN; The Society of Authors; British Actors Equity Association. *Literary Agent:* Curtis Brown, London, England. *Address:* c/o Curtis Brown and John Farquharson, 162-168 Regent Street, London W1R 5TB, England.

PERRIE Walter, b. 5 June 1949, Scotland. Poet; Critic. *Education:* MA, Honours, Mental Philosophy, University of Edinburgh, 1975; MPhil, University of Stirling, 1989. *Appointments:* Scotland/Canada Exchange Fellow, 1984-85; Co-Editor, Margin, 1986-. *Publications:* Lamentation for the Children, 1977; By Moon and Sun, 1980; Out of Conflict, 1982; Concerning the Dragon, 1985; Metaphysics & Poetry, with Hugh MacDiarmid, 1974; Poem on a Winter Night, 1976; Roads that Move: A Journey through Eastern Europe, 1991. *Contributions to:* Chapman; Lines Review; New Edinburgh Review; numerous others. *Honours:* Gregory Award for Poetry, 1978; Scottish Arts Council Book Award, 1978; 2 Scottish Arts Council Writer's Bursaries, 1976, 1983; Merrill-Ingram Foundation Award, New York, 1986; Writing Fellow, University of Stirling, 1991. *Memberships:* PEN, Scotland; Society of Authors. *Address:* The Square Inch, Lower Granco St, Dunning, Perthshire PH2 0SQ, Scotland.

PERRY George Cox, b. 7 Jan 1935, London, England. Writer. m. 1 July 1976, 1 son. *Education:* BA, 1957, MA, 1961, Trinity College, Cambridge. *Publications:* The Films of Alfred Hitchcock, 1965; A Competitive Cinema, co-author, 1966; Penguin book of Comics, 1967, 1971; The Great British Picture Show, 1974, 1985; Rule Britannia-The Victorian World, 1974; Hitchcock, 1975; Movies from the Mansion, 1976; Forever Ealing, 1981; Diana-A Celebration, 1982; Life of Python, 1984; Rupert: A Bear's Life, 1985; Bluebell, 1986; The Complete Phantom of the Opera, 1987. *Contributions to:* The Times; Sunday Times; Radio Times; Los Angeles Times; Illustrated London News, Film Critic, 1982-. *Literary Agent:* Deborah Rogers Ltd., London, England. *Address:* 7 Roehampton Lane, London SW15 5LS, England.

PERRY Marion Judith Helz, b. 2 June 1943, Takoma Park, Maryland, USA. Poet. m. Franklyn A. H. Perry, 17 July 1971, 1 daughter, 1 son. *Education:* BA, English & Philosophy, 1964; MA, 20th Century Literature; MFA, Poetry, 1966; MA Reading Specialist, 1979, PhD English Instruction, 1986. *Appointments:* West Liberty State College, 1966-68; Albright College, 1968-70; SUNY, 1970-79; Associate Faculty, Empire State College, 1979-82; Assistant Professor, Erie Community College, 1980-. *Publications:* Icarus, 1980; The Mirror's Image, 1981; Establishing Intimacy, 1982; Dishes, 1989; The Training of Professional Writers, 1986. *Contributions to:* Intrepid; Buckle; Earth's Daughters; A Different Drummer; Poetry Section, Buffalo Evening News;

Golden Fleece; The Coffee House; Black Mountain II Review; The Hiram Poetry Review; Footwork; Esprit. *Honours:* College Arts Poetry Contest, 1967; All Nations Poetry Contest, 1980, 1981; Serendipity, The Poem Finds its Place Contest, 1980. *Memberships:* Poets & Writers; Poetry Society of America; Academy of American Poets; Ph. Delta Kappa, MLA, International Reading Association. *Address:* Erie Community College, 4140 Southwestern Boulevard, Orchard Park, NY 14127, USA.

PERRY Ritchie, (John Allen), b. 1942, United Kingdom. Teacher; Author. *Publications:* The Fall Guy, 1972; Nowhere Man, US Edition A Hard Man to Kill, 1973; Ticket to Ride, 1973; Holiday with a Vengeance, 1974; Your Money and Your Wife, 1975; One Good Death Deserves Another, 1976; Dead End, 1977; Brazil: The Land and Its People, 1977; Copacabana Stud (as John Allen), 1977; Dutch Courage, 1978; Bishop's Pawn, 1979; Up Tight (as John Allen), 1979; Grand Slam, 1980; Fool's Mate, 1981; George H Ghastly, for children, 1982; Foul Up, 1982; George H Ghastly to the Rescue, for children, 1982; MacAllister, 1984; George H Ghastly and the Little Horror, for children, 1985; Kolwezi, 1985; Fenella Fang, for children, 1986; Presumed Dead, 1987; Fenella Fang and the Great Escape, for children, 1987. *Address:* 4 The Close, Limbury, Luton, Beds, England.

PERUTZ Kathrin, b. 1939, USA. Author; Executive. *Appointments:* Executive Director, Contact Program Inc. *Publications:* The Garden, 1962; A House on the Sound, 1964; The Ghosts, 1966; Mother is a Country: A Popular Fantasy, 1968; Beyond the Looking Glass: America's Beauty Culture, UK Edition Beyond the Looking Glass: Life in the Beauty Culture, 1970; Marriage Is Hell: The Marriage Fallacy, 1972; Reigning Passions, 1978; Writing for Love and Money, 1991. Also as Johanna Kingsley: Scents, 1985; Faces, 1987. *Memberships:* PEN; Authors Guild. *Literary Agent:* Elaine Markson. *Address:* 16 Avalon Road, Great Neck, NY 10021, USA.

PESEK Boris Peter, b. 1926, USA. Professor of Economics. *Publications:* A Study of Contemporary Czechoslovakia (co-author), 1955; Gross National Product of Czechoslovakia, 1965; Money, Wealth, and Economic Theory (co-author), 1967; The Foundations of Money and Banking (co- author), 1968. *Address:* Department of Economics, University of Wisconsin, Milwaukee, WI 53201, USA.

PESETSKY Bette, b. 16 Nov 1932, Milwaukee, Wisconsin, USA. Writer. m. Irwin Pesetsky, 25 Feb 1956, 1 son. *Education:* BA, Washington University, 1954; MFA, University of Iowa, 1959. *Publications:* Stories Up to A Point, 1982; Author from a Savage People, 1983; Midnight Sweets, 1988; Digs, 1988; Confessions of a Bad Girl, 1989; Late Night Muse, 1991. *Contributions to:* The New Yorker; Vanity Fair; Ms; Vogue; Paris Review; Ontario Review; Stand. *Honours:* Creative Writing Fellowship, National Endowment for the Arts, 1979-80; Creative Writing Public Service Award, New York Council for the Arts, 1980-81. *Membership:* PEN. *Literary Agent:* Goodman Associates, USA. *Address:* Hilltop Park, Dobbs Ferry, NY 10522, USA.

PESSEN Edward, b. 31 Dec 1920, New York, USA. Historian; Author. m. Adele Barlin, 25 Nov 1940, Brooklyn, New York. 2 sons, 3 daughters. *Education:* BA 1947, MA 1948, PhD 1954, Columbia University, New York, USA. *Literary Appointments:* City College of New York, 1948- 54; Fisk University, Nashville, Tennessee, 1954-56; Staten Island Community College, 1956-70; Baruch College and Graduate School & University Centre, City University of New York, 1970-. *Major Publications:* Most Uncommon Jacksonians, 1967; Jacksonian America: Society, Personality & Politics, 1969, revised edition, 1978; Riches, Class & Power before the Civil War, 1973; Three Centuries of Social Mobility in America, 1974; The Log Cabin Myth: Social Backgrounds of the Presidents, 1984; Richer, Class and Power, (new ed.) 1989. *Contributions to:*

Journal of American History; American Historical Review. *Honours:* National Book Award Finalist, 1974; Guggenheim Foundation Fellowship, 1977; Rockefeller Foundation Fellow, 1978; Fulbright Lecturer, Moscow State University, USSR, 1985. *Memberships:* President, Society of Historians of the Early American Republic, 1985-86; American Historical Association; American Antiquarian Society; Organisation of American Historians; Southern Historical Association. *Address:* City University of New York, 17 Lexington Avenue, New York, NY 10010, USA.

PETAJA Emil (Theodore Pine), b. 1915, USA. Writer; Publisher. *Appointments:* Full-time Writer, 1963-; Owner, SISU Publications, San Francisco, California, 1972-; Chairman, Bokonalia Memorial Foundation. *Publications:* Alpha Yes, Terra No, 1965; The Caves of Mars, 1965; Saga of Lost Earths, 1965; The Star Mill, 1965; Tramontane, 1966; The Stolen Sun, 1967; Lord of the Green Planet, 1967; The Prism, 1968; Doom of the Green Planet, 1968; The Time Twister, 1968; And Flights of Angels, non-fiction, 1968; The Path Beyond the Stars, 1969; The Nets of Space, 1969; Seed of the Dreamers, 1970; Stardrift and Other Fantastic Flotsam, short stories, 1971; As Dream and Shadow, poetry, 1972; The Hannes Bok Memorial Showcase of Fantasy (editor), 1974; Photoplay Edition (edition), 1975; Lost Earths, omnibus, 1979. *Address:* PO Box 14126, San Francisco, CA 94114, USA.

PETECKI Bohdan Antoni, b. 5 July 1931, Krakow, Poland. Writer. m. Janina Rogowska, 19 July 1966, 1 daughter. *Education:* MA, Oriental Studies, Jagiellonian University, cracow. *Appointments:* Journalist, Polish Radio Station Katowice, 1958-68; Sub-Editor, TV Broadcasting Station, Katowice, 1968-72; 1st Sub Editor, Polish Radio Broadcasting Station, 1972-75; Sub Editor, Weekly Magazine, Panorama, 1978-. *Publications:* 1001 Swiatow, 1983; X-A Uwolnij gwiazdy, 1977, 1981; Strefy zerowe, 1972; Tylko cisza, 1974; Bal na pieciu ksiezycach, 1981; Pierwszy Ziemianin, 1983; Youth Novels: Sola z nieba polnocnego, 1977; Wiatr od Slonca, 1980; Krolowa kosmosu, 1979; Science Fiction Novels: Operocja wieczuosc, 1975; Rubin przerywa milczeniel, 1976. *Contributions to:* various journals and magazines. *Honours:* Diploma of Honour, National Publishers Iskry, Warsaw, 1977; Novel of the Year, Magazine Fantastyka, 1984. *Memberships:* Polish Writers' Association, Vice President, Katowice, 1985-. *Address:* ul. Baltycka 51A, 40-778 Katowice, Poland.

PETERFREUND Stuart Samuel, b. 30 June 1945, Brooklyn, New York, USA. English Professor. m. 12 Sept 1981. *Education:* AB, Cornell University, 1966; MFA, University of California, Irvine, 1968; PhD, University of Washington, 1974. *Appointments include:* University of Arkansas, 1975-78; Assistant Professor, 1978-82; Associate Professor 1982-91, Full Professor, 1991-, Chair, 1991-, Northeastern University. *Publications:* The Hanged Knife & Other Poems, 1970; Harder Than Rain, poems, 1977; Interstatements, poems, 1986; Literature and Sciences: Theory and Practice, 1990. *Contributions to:* Poetry in various journals including: Cimarron; Cincinnati Poetry Review; Epoch; Poetry Northwest; Shenandoah; and others. Articles, English Romantic Literature, various scholarly journals. *Honours:* Poetry prize, Writers Digest, 1970; Poet-in-residence, Southern Literary Festival, 1977; Fellowship, Southern Federation of State Arts, 1977; Curbstone Literary Prize, 1981. *Memberships:* Poets & Writers Inc; New England Poetry Club; Publications Editor, Society for Literature & Science, Interdisciplinary 19th Century Studies; Divisional Delegate, Literature & Science, Modern Language Association. *Address:* Department of English - 406 HO, Northeastern University, 360 Huntington Avenue, Boston, Massachusetts 02115, USA.

PETERKIEWICZ Jerzy, b. 29 Sept 1916, Poland. Novelist; Poet. *Education:* University of Warsaw; MA, University of St Andrews, Scotland, 1944; PhD, King's College, London, England, 1947. *Publications:* Prowincja, 1936; Wiersze i poematy, 1938; Pogrzeb

Europy, 1946; The Knotted Cord, 1953; Loot and Loyalty, 1955; Polish Prose and Verse, 1956; Antologia liryki angielskiej, 1958; Future to Let, 1958; Isolation, 1959; (with Burns Singer) Five Centuries of Polish Poetry, 1960 (enlarged edition 1970); The Quick and the Dead, 1961; That Angel Burning at my Left Side, 1963; Poematy Londynskie, 1965; Inner Circle, 1966; Green Flows the Bile, 1969; The Other Side of Silence (The Poet at the Limits of Language), 1970; The Third Adam, 1975; (Editor and translator) Easter Vigil and other Poems, by Karol Wojtyla (Pope John Paul II), 1979; Kula magiczna (Poems 1934-52), 1980; (editor and translator) Collected Poems, by Karol Wojtyla (Pope John Paul II), 1982; Poezje wybrane (Selected Poems), 1986; Literatura polska w perspektywie europejskiej (Polish Literature in its European context; essays translated from English), 1986; Essays, poems; Radio plays, BBC 3. *Contributions to:* Numerous periodicals. *Address:* 7 Lyndhurst Terrace, London NW3 5QA, England.

PETERNEL Joan, b. 9 Dec 1936, Chicago, Illinois, USA. Writer. *Education:* BA, St. Mary-of-the-Woods, Indiana, 1976; MA, Indiana State University, Indiana, 1977; PhD, English, Indiana University, Bloomington, 1981. *Appointments:* Instructor in Writing, Indiana University, 1981-83; Instructor in Writing, American University, 1984; Lecturer in Literature, Georgetown University, 1991-. *Publications:* Dissertation, Ann Arbor, UMI, The Hero and the Bride: Four Modern Quest Novels, 1982; Songs: The Thousandth Love Song, music by Ailene Goodman, 1990, The Winter of My Loneliness, music by Jeff Ichihashi, 1990; Essay: The Double in Light in August: Narcissus or Janus? Notes on Mississippi Writers 15.1 1983, 19-37. *Contributions to:* Reviews, poems, articles, fiction to America, Writer's Digest, Amelia, Illinois Writers Review, Nassau Review, The Washington Review, South Coast Poetry Journal. *Honours:* Terre Haute Literary Club Award, 1977; Ellis Literary Award, Bloomington, 1981; Roberts Memorial Prize, The Lyric, 1991. *Memberships:* Poetry Society of America; Academy of American Poetry; Modern Language Association; Writers Centre, Bethesda, Maryland. *Address:* 4615 North Park Avenue 704, Chevy Chase, MD 20815, USA.

PETERS Catherine Lisette, b. 30 Sept 1930, London, England. Lecturer; Writer. m. (1) John Glyn Barton,, 14 Jan 1952, 3 sons, (2) Anthony Storr, 8 Oct 1970. *Education:* BA (1st Class Hons) 1980, MA 1984, Oxford University. *Appointments:* Editor, Jonathan Cape, 1966-74; Lecturer in English, Somerville College, Oxford, 1981-92. *Publications:* Thackeray's Universe, 1987; The King of Inventors: A Life of Wilkie Collins, 1991. *Contributions to:* Dickens Studies Annual; Victorian Periodicals Review; Editions of Armadale and Hide and Seek by Wilkie Collins (World's Classics), Vanity Fair by W M Thackeray and The Moonstone by Wilkie Collins (Everyman Books). *Memberships:* Wilkie Collins Society; Society of Authors; Fellow, Royal Society of Literature. *Address:* 45 Chalfont Road, Oxford OX2 6TJ, England.

PETERS Dr. *See:* PRVULOVICH Zika Rad.

PETERS Elizabeth. *See:* MERTZ Barbara Louise G.

PETERS Ellis. *See:* PARGETER Edith Mary.

PETERS Lawrence. *See:* DAVIES Leslie Purnall.

PETERS Lance, b. 8 May 1934, Auckland, New Zealand. Author; Screenwriter. m. Laura Chiang, 25 Feb 1981, 2 sons, 2 daughters. *Appointments:* Feature Writer, TV Times London Correspondent, 1974-76; London Representative, Seymour Theatre Centre, 1973-75. *Publications:* Carry on Emmannuelle, 1978; The Dirty Half Mile, 1981; Cut-Throat Alley, 1982; Enemy Territory, 1988; God's Executioner, 1988; Extensive TV writing - comedy, documentary and drama; Five feature film screenplays; Stage Play, Assault with a Deadly Weapon. *Contributions to:* numerous popular magazines. *Memberships:* Honorary Life Member,

Australian Writers Guild, President 1970-72; Australian Society of Authors; Writers Guild of Great Britain; BAFTA. *Literary Agent:* William Morris Agency, New York, London, Los Angeles, Sydney. *Address:* 14/70-78 Cook Road, Centennial Park, Sydney 2021, Australia.

PETERS Margot McCullough, b. 13 May 1933, USA. Writer; Professor. 1 son, 1 daughter. *Education:* BA, 1961, MA, 1965, PhD, 1969, University of Wisconsin-Madison. *Appointments:* Kathe Tappe Vernon Professor of Biography, Dartmouth College, 1978; Professor Emerita, University of Wisconsin; Reviewer, New York Times Book Review. *Publications:* Charlotte Bronte: Style in the Novel, 1973; Unquiet Soul: A Biography of Charlotte Bronte, 1975; Bernard Shaw and the Actresses, 1980; Mrs Pat: The Life of Mrs Patrick Campbell, 1984; The House of Barrymore, 1990; As Lonely As God, in The Genius of Shaw; Editor, Bernard Shaw's Mrs Warren's Profession Facsimile edition. *Contributions to:* Biography: Language and Style; The Annual of Bernard Shaw Studies; The Southwest Review; The British Studies Monitor; Harvard Magazine; Bronte Society Transactions. *Honours:* Best Prose Award, Friends of American Writers, 1975; Banta Award, 1980, 1984; George Freedley Memorial Award for Best Drama Book, 1980, 1984; English Speaking Union Ambassador Award, 1990; American Council of Learned Societies Fellow; Guggenheim Fellow; Wisconsin Institute for the Humanities Fellow; Rockefeller Fellow. *Memberships:* Bernard Shaw Society; Bronte Society; Tennessee Williams Society; Authors Guild. *Literary Agent:* Lynn Nesbit, Janklow and Nesbit. *Address:* 511 College Street, Lake Mills, WI 53551, USA.

PETERS Maureen, (Veronica Black, Catherine Darby, Belinda Grey, Levannah Lloyd, Judith Rothman, Sharon Whitby). b. 1935, British, Writer of mystery/crime/suspense, historical/romance/Gothic, biography. *Publications include:* (as Sharon Whitby), No Song at Morningside, 1981; (as Belinda Grey), Daughter of Isis, 1981; (as Belinda Grey), Glen of Frost, 1981; (as Levannah Lloyd), A Maid Called Wanton, 1981; (as Levannah Lloyd) Mail Order Bride, 1981; (as Levannah Lloyd), Cauldron of Desire, 1981; (as Levennah Lloyd), Dark Surrender, 1981; (as Veronica Black), The Dragon and the Rose, 1982; Red Queen, White Queen, 1982; Imperial Harlot, 1983; My Lady Troubadour, 1983; Alianor, 1983; Lackland's Bride, 1983; (as Veronica Black), Bond Wife, 1983; (as Sharon Whitby), Children of the Rainbow, 1983; (as Catherine Darby), A Circle of Rowan, 1983; A Song for Marguerite, 1984; My Philippa, 1984; (as Veronica Black), Hoodman Blind, 1984; (as Catherine Darby), The Rowan Maid, 1984; (as Catherine Darby), Song of the Rowan, 1984; (as Catherine Darby), Sangreal, 1984; Fair Maid of Kent, 1985; Isabella, The She Wolf, 1985; The Vinegar Seed, 1985; (as Catherine Darby), Sabre, 1985; (as Catherine Darby), Sabre's Child, 1985; (as Catherine Darby), House of Sabre, 1986; (as Catherine Darby), Heart of Flame, 1986; The Vinegar Blossom, 1986; (as Catherine Darby), A Breed of Sabres, 1987; (as Catherine Darby), Morning of a Sabre, 1987; The Luck Bride, 1987; The Vinegar Tree, 1987. *Address:* c/o Hale, 45-47 Clerkenwell Green, London EC1R 0HT, England.

PETERS Natasha, Author. *Publications:* Savage Surrender, 1977; Dangerous Obsession, 1978; The Masquers, 1979; The Enticers, 1981; The Immortals: A Novel of Shanghai, 1983; Darkness into Light, 1984; Wild Nights, 1986. *Address:* c/o Ballantine Books, 201 E 50th Street, New York, NY 10022, USA.

PETERS Richard Stanley, b. 31 Oct 1919, Missouri, India, Emeritus Professor. m. Margaret Lee Duncan, 16 July 1943, 1 son, 2 daughters. *Education:* Queens College, Oxford; Birkbeck College, London; BA, Oxon; BA, London PhD, London 1949. *Appointments:* Part-time Lecturer, Birkbeck College, University of London, 1946-49, full-time, 1949-58; Reader in Philosophy, 1958-62; Visiting Professor, Harvard University, USA, 1961; Visiting Fellow, Australian National University, 1969; Part-time Lectureships, Bedford College and LSE,

1966; professor, Philosophy of Education, Institute of Education, London, 1962; Emeritus Professor, 1982. *Publications:* Hobbes, 1956; Social Principals Democratic State, (Co-author), 1958; Ehics and Education, 1945; Logic of Education, (Co-author), 1970; Authority, responsibility and Education, 1960; Psychology and Ethical development, 1974; Reason and Compassion, 1973; Essays on Educators, 1981; Moral Education and Moral Development, 1981; Editor, International Library of the Philosophy of Education. *Contributions to:* Mind; Aristotelian Society Journal; Philsophy of Education; Analysis; British Journal Educational Psychology; British Journal Educational Studies; British Journal Philosophy of Science. *Honour:* American National Academy of Education, 1966. *Membership:* President, Philosophy of Education of Great Britain. *Address:* Flat 3, 16 Shepherd's Hill, Highgate, London N6 5AQ, England.

PETERS Robert Louis, b. 20 Oct 1924, Wisconsin, USA. Poet; Critic; Actor; Professor of Literature. 3 sons, 1 daughter. *Education:* BA, 1948; MA, 1949; PhD, MacDowell and Yallo Colonies. *Publications:* The Crowns of Apollo: Swinburne's Principles of Literature and Art, 1965; Songs for a Son, 1967, (poems); The Gift to be Simple, 1975, poems; The Great American Poetry Bake-Off: First, Second, Third & Fourth Series, 1979, 1985, 1987 & 1990; What Dillinger Meant To Me, 1984; Hawker, 1984; The Peters Black and Blue Guide to Current Literary Periodicals, 1983, 1985, 1987; Kane, 1985; Shaker Light, 1987; Hawker, 1989; Goodnight Paul, 1992; Snapshots For A Serial Killer, 1992; Poems: Selected & New, 1992; Zapped: two Novellas, 1993; Lone Poems For Robert Mitchum, 1993. *Contributor to:* American Book Review; Poetry Now; Contact 11; Pearl; Western Humanities Review; numerous others. *Honours:* Guggenheim Fellow, 1966-67; NEA Fellowship, 1974; Alice Faye de Castagnola Prize, 1984; Larry P. Fine Award for Criticism, 1985; Jack Kerouac Award for Poetry. *Memberships:* PEN: Authors Guild. *Address:* Dept. of English, University of California, Irvine, CA 92717, USA.

PETERSEN P(eter) J(ames), b. 23 Oct 1941, Santa Rosa, California, USA. Writer; Teacher. m. Marian Braun, 6 July 1964, 2 daughters. *Education:* AB, Stanford University; MA San Francisco State University; PhD, University of New Mexico. *Appointments:* English Instructor, Shasta College. *Publications:* Would You Settle for Improbable, 1981; Nobody Else Can Walk It for You, 1982; The Boll Weevil Express, 1983; Here's to the Sophomores, 1984; Corky & the Brothers Cool, 1985; Going for the Big One, 1986; Good-bye to Good O' Charlie, 1987; The Freshman Detective Blues, 1987; I Hate Camping, 1991; Liars, 1992. *Honour:* Fellow, NEH, 1976-77. *Membership:* Society of Children's Book Writers. *Literary Agent:* Ellen Levine Inc. *Address:* 1243 Pueblo Court, Redding, CA 96001, USA.

PETERSON Chester Jr, b. 24 Mar 1937, Salina, Kansas, USA. Writer; Photographer; Software developer. m. (1) 3 sons, 1 daughter, (2) Mary Lindshield, 5 Oct 1988. *Education:* BS, 1959, BS, 1960, MS, 1960, Kansas State University. *Appointments:* Assistant Editor, then Associate Editor, Successful Farming, 1960-64; Freelance Writer-Photographer, 1964-73, 1987-; Publisher, Editor, Simmental Shield, 1973-87; Publisher, Kansas Business News, 1980-88; Contributing Editor, Private Pilot, 1991-; Contributing Editor, Kansas Farmer, 1991-. *Publications:* Chet Peterson's Aviation Spreadsheet Templates, 1991. *Contributions to:* Articles to 130 magazines; Photographs to 158 magazines. *Honours:* NAMA regional and national awards; Certificate of Merit, New York City Art Directors Club; BIF Ambassador Award. *Memberships:* Sigma Delta Chi; National Writers Club; American Agricultural Editors Association. *Address:* PO Box 71, Lindsborg, KS 67456, USA.

PETERSON Donald Macandrew, b. 23 June 1956. Lecturer in Cognitive Science. *Education:* MA, Philosophy and Psychology, Edinburgh University, 1978; PhD, Philosophy, University College London, 1985, MSc,

DIC, in Foundations of Advanced Information Technology, Imperial College London,1986. *Publication:* Wittgenstein's Early Philosophy - Three Sides of the Mirror, 1990. *Contributions to:* a number of professional journals and magazines. *Membership:* Society of Artificial Intelligence and the Simulation of Behaviour. *Address:* Department of Computer Science, University of Birmingham, Birmingham B15 2TT, England.

PETERSON Richard F, b. 14 Apr 1939, Pittsburgh, Pennsylvania, USA. Professor of English. m. 17 July 1965, 1 son, 2 daughters. *Education:* BS, Edinburgh University, 1965; MA, 1967, PhD, 1969, Kent University. *Appointment:* Department of Englilsh, Southern Illinois University, 1969-. *Publications:* Mary Lavin, 1978; William Butler Yeats, 1982; James Joyce Revisited, 1992. *Contributions to:* Essays in various journals, annuals and collections devoted to modern and Anglo-Irish literature. *Honours:* College Outstanding Teaching Award, 1977, 1978; University Outstanding Teaching Award, 1978. *Memberships:* Modern Language Association; American Conference for Irish Studies; James Joyce Society. *Address:* Department of English, Southern Illinois University, Carbondale, IL 62901, USA.

PETERSON Richard Scot, b. 14 July 1938, Ayr, Scotland. Professor of English. m. Lin Kelsey, 28 Aug 1965, 1 son. *Education:* BA, Princeton University, 1960; MA, 1963, PhD, 1968, University of California, Berkeley. *Appointments:* Instructor in English, 1966-69, Assistant Professor of English, 1969-72, Princeton University; Lecturer in English, University of Virginia, 1972-75; Assistant Professor of English, Yale University, 1976-80; Associate Professor of English, 1980-86, Professor of English 1986-, University of Connecticut. *Publications:* Imitation and Praise in the Poems of Ben Jonson, 1981; ed. Essays in Literature and the Visual Arts, 1986. *Contributions to:* Spenser Redivivus in Princeton University Library Chronicle, 1986; Icon and Mystery in Jonson's Masque of Beautie in John Donne Journal, 1986; In from the Cold: an Englishman at Rome, 1595, in American Notes and Queries, 1992; New Light Spenser Studies, 1994. *Honours:* Fulbright Scholar, Oxford, St Catherine's, 1960-61; Fellow, Institute of Advanced Studies, Edinburgh, 1975; NEH, Newberry Fellow, 1976; APS Fellow, 1976; Newberry - British Academy Fellow, 1984; ACLS Fellow, 1984-85; Bibliography Society of America Fellow, 1986; Editorial Board, John Donne Journal. 1981-. *Memberships:* Modern Language Association; Renaissance Society of America. *Address:* 1693 Main Street, Glastonbury, CT 06033, USA.

PETERSON Robert, b. 2 June 1924, Denver, Colorado, USA, 1 daughter. *Education:* BA, University of California, Berkeley, 1947; MA, San Francisco State College, 1956. *Appointment:* Writer-in-Residence, Reed College, Portland, Oregon, 1969-71. *Publications:* Home for the Night, 1962; The Binnacle, 1967; Wondering Where You Are, 1969; Lone Rider, 1976; Under Sealed Orders, 1976; Leaving Taos, 1981; The Only Piano Player in La Paz, 1985; Waiting for Garbo: 44 Ghazals, 1987. *Honours:* Grant in Poetry, National Endowment for the Arts, 1967; Amy Lowell Travelling Fellowship, 1972-73; National Poetry Series, Leaving Taos, 1981. *Memberships:* Authors Guild; PEN. *Address:* PO Box 417, Fairfax, CA 94978, USA.

PETERZEN (Anna Karin) Elisabet, b. 15 Apr 1938, Stockholm, Sweden, Author, 1 daughter. *Education:* London School of Foreign Trade, 1960; Stockholm University, 1980-83. *Appointment:* Women's Committee, Swedish Union of Authors, 1985-88. *Publications:* Marmor och Ebenholts, 1964; Njutning, 1967; Trygghet, 1968; Aktenskaps Brott, 1969; Den konstgjorda mannen, 1973; En mans liv (Mustafa Said), 1974; Roman, 1976; Ljusnatten, 1981; Lura Livet, 1981; Sista Sticket, 1983; Mamsell Caroline, 1986; Djursager, 1987; Nubiens Hjarta, 1989. *Honours:* 1st Prize, Best 3rd World Novel, Mustafa Said, 1976; 1st Prize, Best Book Club Novel, Mamsell Caroline, 1986. *Membership:* Swedish Union of Authors, 1970-. *Address:* Osmo, Sweden.

PETESCH Natalie L M, b. Detroit, Michigan, USA. Author; University Professor. m. Donald Anthony Petesch, 30 Aug 1959, 1 son, 1 daughter. *Education:* BS, magna cum laude, Boston University, 1955; MA, Brandeis University, 1955; PhD, University of Texas, 1962. *Appointments:* University of Texas, Austin, 1959-60; San Francisco State University, 1961; Distinguished Visiting Professor, University of Idaho, 1982. *Publications:* After the First Death There is No Other, 1974; The Odyssey of Katinou Kalokovich, 1974, 1979; Seasons Such as These: 2 novels The Long Hot Summers of Yasha K, and The Leprosarium, 1979; Soul Clap its Hands and Sing, 1981; Duncan's Colony, 1982; Wild with All Regret, 1986; Flowering Mimosa, 1987; Justina of Andalusia (short stories), 1990; The Laughter of Hastings Street: An Autobiographical Memoir, (Autobiography), 1990. *Contributions to:* Anthologies & journals including: Different Drummers: A College Anthology, 1973; Fiction Omnibus; California Quarterly; North of the Border: An Anthology of 100 years of the Mexican-American Experience, 1990; Finding Courage, (Women's anthology), 1989; Word of Mouth, (Women's anthology), 1990; autobiographical essay in The Confidence Woman, 1991. *Honours:* Iowa School of Letters Award for Short Fiction, 1974; Kansas Quarterly Fiction Award, 1976; New Letters Summer Prize Book Award, 1978; Louisville Review First Prize for Fiction, 1978; Fellowship, Literature, Pennsylvania Council on the Arts, 1980; Twice nominated for Governor's Award for Excellence in Arts; Winner, 1985, Swallow's Tale Short Fiction for Wild with All Regret; Contemporary Authors Autobiography series, (an international series) 1990; Winner, 1989, Harvey Curtis Webster Award for Best Story, autobiographical essay in The Confidence Woman, 1991; Pittsburgh Cultural Trust Award for Outstanding Established Artist, 1991. *Address:* 6320 Crombie Street, Pittsburgh, PA 15217, USA.

PETOCZ Andras, b. 27 Aug 1959, Budapest, Hungary. Writer Poet. 2 daughters. *Education:* Graduated, Faculty of Arts, Lorand Eotvos University, Budapest, 1986. *Appointments:* Chief Editor, literary periodical Jelenlet (Presence) 1981-83; An editor of literary periodical Magyar Muhely (Hungarian Workshop) 1989-91; Editor and publisher of Medium-Art, an underground literary periodical during the communist regime, 1983-89; Leader of the Medium-Art Studio, a centre of experimental art. *Publications:* Letter Pyramid (Betupiranis) 1984, poems; Attempts at an Autobiography (Oneletrajzi kiserletek), 1984; Non-figurative, 1989 poems and visual poems; Invisible presence (Lathatatlan jelenlet) 1990, poems; Europe, Metaphorically (Europa metaforaja) 1991, poems; Scale with no Meaning, (A jelentes nelkuli hangsor) poems, 1988; Dignity of Existence-in-Gesture (A jelben-letezes meltosaga) essay, 1990; Wake up, Gergely Csutoras! (Csutoras Gergely ebresztese) poems for children, 1991; The Typed Fear (Az irogepelt felelem) poems. 1992; Writer and director of two video films: Dialogue (Parbeszed) 1989 and Approaches to a Thing-Found (Kozelitesek egy talalt targyhoz) 1991; Author of a record of acoustic poetry, Approaching and Departing (Kozeledesek es tavolodasok) 1990. *Contributions to:* DOC/K/S. France; Rampike, Canada; Magyar Muhely, Budapest; Holmi, Budapest; New Hungarian Quarterly, Budapest. *Honours:* Lajos Kassak, 1987; Robert Graves Prize for best Hungarian poem of the year, 1990; Prize for best book by Szepirodalmi Publishers, 1989. *Memberships:* Hungarian Writers Association; Art Association of the Hungarian Republic; Hungarian Workshop Committee; Member of Advisory Board of Writers' Committee in Tokaj; Young Artists Club, Budapest. *Address:* Studio of Medium-Art, Donáti u 6, H-1015 Budapest, Huungary.

PETRIE Rhona. *See:* **BUCHANAN Eileen Marie.**

PETRINGENARU Adrian, b. 19 Oct 1933, Bucharest, Romania. Film Director; Author. m. Liliana Lazar, 1970, 1 daughter. *Education:* PhD, University of Paris, 1981. *Appointments:* Art Critic, Romanian Weekly Magazine, Contemporanul, 1963-70. *Publications:* Image and symbol in the Work of Brancusi, 1983;

(Films)The Prodigal Father, 1974; Pyre and Flame, 1979; The Woman from the Great Bear, 1982; The Hidden Castle, 1987; (Documentary Films) Steps to Brancusi, 1966; 6000 Years, 1967; (Animated Films) Brezaia, 1968; In John's Forrest, 1970; Byzance After Byzance, 1972; Long Way, 1976; The Principle of the Field, 1979; Art Expertise, 1980; Competition, 1981; The Final, 1982; Perpetual Reborn, 1986. *Contributions to:* various journals, magazines & newspapers. *Honours:* Golden Prize, Film Festival Santarem, 1975, 1980; Silver Prize, Film Festival, Mamaia, 1970; Honour Diplomas, Film Festivals: London, 1970, Salonica, 1977, Leipzig, 1979, 1984, Lucca, 1984, 1986; National Romanian Prizes for Films, 1977, 1981. *Memberships:* ASIFA; CIDALC; Romanian Film-makers Institution. *Address:* Str. Ciucea 5, Bloc L. 19, Apt. 33, Bucharest, CP 7210, Romania.

PETROSKI Catherine b. 7 Sept 1939, St Louis, Missouri, USA. Writer. m. Henry Petroski, 15 July 1966, 1 son, 1 daughter. *Education:* BA MacMurray College, 1961; MA University of Illinois, 1962. *Appointments:* National Endowment for the Arts Writing Fellowship, 1978-79; Alan Collins Fellow, Bread Loaf, 1982; National Endowment for the Arts Writing Fellow, 1983-84. *Publications:* Gravity and Other Stories, 1981; Beautiful My Mane in the Wind, 1983; The Summer That Lasted Forever, 1984. *Contributions to:* Short fiction in Virginia Quarterly Review, Mississippi Review, Southern Humanities Review, North American Review, Prairie Schooner and others; reviews of fiction and non-fiction to Chicago Tribune and others. *Honours:* Berlin Prize, 1960; Texas Institute of Letters Prize, 1976; PEN Syndicated Fiction Prizes, 1983, 1984, 1985, 1988; O Henry Award, 1989; AAUW North Carolina Literary and Historical Association Book Prize; 1984 Honorary D Lit conferred by MacMurray College. *Memberships:* The Author's Guild; The Author's League of America; National Book Critics Circle. *Literary Agent:* Georges Borchardt, 136 East 57th Street, New York, NY 10022, USA. *Address:* 2528 Wrightwood Avenue, Durham, NC 27705, USA.

PETROVITS Loty, b. 12 Aug 1937, Athens, Greece. Author. m. Andreas Andrutsopulos, 23 July 1966, 1 son, 1 daughter. *Education:* University of Michigan; Istituto Italiano di Cultura in Atene, 1960. *Appointments:* Editorial Correspondent, Phaedrus, 1980-88; Associate Editor, Bookbird, 1982-; Co-Editor, Diadromes, 1986-. *Publications:* O Mikros Adelfos, 1976 (translated into Japanese, published in Tokyo, 1988); Tris Fores Ki Enan Kero, 1977; Gia Tin Alli Patrida, 1978; Sto Tsimentenio Dasos, 1981; Zetete Mikros, 1982; Spiti Gia Pente, 1987, translated into Japanese, 1990; Istories pou kanenas den xerei, 1984; Istories me tous dodeca mines, 4 vols. 1988; Lathos Kyrie Noyger! 1989. Twelve more books for children and 2 for adults. Translations from English into Greek include: Blowfish Live in the Sea, by Paula Fox, 1979; The Camelthorn Papers, by Ann Thwaite, 1987. *Contributions to:* Phaedrus; Bookbird; Diadromes; Efthini; Diavazo; Kypriaki Martyria; Helidonia; Gia Hara. *Honours:* Women's Literary Club Prizes, 1975, 1979, 1981, 1987; Circle of the Greek Children's Book Prize, 1977; Kifissia YWCA Honour List for Short Stories, 1979; Ourani Prize, Academy of Athens, 1984; Hestia Tranouli Prize, 1988; Greek Society of Christian Letters Prize, 1992; University of Padova Honour List, 1989; IBBY Honour List, 1992. *Memberships:* Circle of the Greek Children's Book, Secretary General, 1984-1990; Greek Authors National Society; Association for the Dissemination of Good Books. *Address:* 129 Aristotelous Street, GR 112 51, Athens, Greece.

PETRY Alice Hall, b. 8 July 1951, Hartford, Connecticut, USA. College Professor; Scholar. *Education:* BS, Highest Hons., University of Connecticut, 1973; MA, Connecticut College, 1976; PhD, Brown University, 1979. *Appointment:* Currently, Professor of English, Rhode Island School of Design, Providence, Rhode Island. *Publications:* A Genius in his Way: The Art of Cable's Old Creole Days 1988; Fitzgerald's Craft of Short Fiction: The Collected Stories 1920-35, 1989; Understanding Anne Tyler, 1990; Critical Essays on Anne Tyler, 1992. *Contributions to:* American Literature; The Southern Quarterly; Studies in American Fiction; Studies in Short Fiction; The Southern Literary Journal. *Honours:* Senior Postdoctoral Fellow, American Council of Learned Societies, 1987-88; Fulbright Scholar in Brazil, 1985; United States Information Agency lecturer in Japan, 1991. *Memberships:* Executive Council, Society for the Study of Southern Literature (SSSL); Advisory Board, F Scott Fitzgerald Society; Modern Language Association; Northeast Modern Language Association; National Women's Studies Association; American Studies Association. *Address:* Department of English, Liberal Arts Division, Rhode Island School of Design, Providence, RI 02903, USA.

PETTIFER Julian, b. 21 July 1935. Freelance Writer; Broadcaster. *Education:* St John's College, Cambridge. *Appointments:* TV Reporter, Writer and Presenter: Southern TV, 1958-62, Tonight BBC, 1962-64, 24 Hours, BBC, 1964-69, Panorama, BBC 1969-75; Presenter, Cuba - 25 Years of Revolution (Series), ITV, 1984; Host, Busman's Holiday, ITV 1985-86; numerous TV documentaries, including: Vietnam War without End, 1970; The World About Us, 1976; The Spirit of 76, 1976; Diamonds in the Sky, 1979; Nature Watch, 5 series, 1981-90; Automania, 1984; The Living Isles, 1986; TV documentaries, Africawatch, 1989, Missionaries, 1990. *Publications:* (jointly) Diamonds in the Sky : a social history of air travel, 1979; (jointly) Nature Watch, 1981; (jointly) Automania, 1984; (jointly) The Nature Watchers, 1985; (jointly) Missionaries, 1990. *Honours:* Reporter of the Year Award, Guild of Television Directors and Producers, 1968. *Address:* c/o Curtis Brown, 163-168 Regent Street, London W1R 5TA, England.

PEYREFITTE (Pierre), Roger, b. 17 Aug 1907, Castres (Tarn). Author. *Education:* Ecole des Sciences Politiques, Paris; BA. *Publications:* Les amities particulieres, 1944-45; Mademoiselle de Murville, 1946; Le prince des neiges, 1947; L'oracle, 1948; les amours singulieres, 1949; la mort d'une mere, 1950; Les ambassades, 1951; Du Vesuve a l'Etna, 1952; Les cles de St. Pierre, 1955; Jeunes proies, 1956; Chevaliers de Malte, 1957; L'exile de Capri, 1959; Le spectateur nocturne, 1960; Les fils de la lumiere, 1961; La nature du prince, 1963; Les Juifs, 1965; Notre amour, 1967; Les Americains, 1968; Des Francais, 1970; La Coloquinte 1971; Manouche, 1972; La muse garconniere, 1973 Tableaux de chasse ou la vie extraordinaire de Fernand Legros, 1976; propos secrets, 1977; La jeunesse d'Alexandre, 1977; L'enfant de coeur, 1978; Roy, 1979; Les conquetes d'Alexandre, 1979; Propos Secrets, Ii, 1980; Alexandre le Grand, 1981; L'Illustre ecrivain, 1982; La soutane rouge, 1983; Henry de Montherlent-Roger Peyrefitte correspondence, 1983; Voltaire, sa Jeunesse et son Temps, 1985; L'Innominato, nouveaux propos secrets, 1989; Reflexion sur De Gaulle, 1992. *Honours:* Prix Theophraste Renaudot. *Address:* 9 avenue du Marechal Maunoury, 75016 Paris, France.

PEYTON K M. *See:* PEYTON Kathleen Wendy.

PEYTON Kathleen Wendy, (Kathleen Herald, K M Peyton), b. 2 Aug 1929. Writer. m. Michael Peyton, 1950, 2 daughters. *Education:* ATD, Manchester School of Art. *Publications:* (As Kathleen Herald): Sabre, the Horse from the Sea, 1947, USA 1963; The Mandrake, 1949; Crab the Roan, 1953; (as K.M. Peyton): North to Adventure, 1959, USA, 1965; Stormcock Meets Trouble, 1961; The Hard Way Home, 1962; Windfall, (USA as Sea Fever, 1963), 1963; Brownsea Silver, 1964; The Maplin Bird, 1964 (USA 1965); The Plan for Birdsmarsh, 1965 (USA 1966); Thunder in the Sky, 1966 (USA 1967); Flambards Triology, 1969-71; The Beethoven Medal, 1971 (USA 1972); The Pattern of Roses, 1972 (USA 1973); Pennington's Heir, 1973 (USA 1974); The Team, 1975; The Right-Hand Man, 1977; Prove Yourself a Hero, 1977 (USA, 1978); A Midsummer Night's Death, 1978 (USA 1979); Marion's Angels, 1979 (USA 1979); Flambards Divided, 1981; Dear Fred, 1981; Going Home, 1983 (USA 1983); The Last Ditch, 1984 (USA as Free Rein, 1983); Froggett's Revenge, 1985; The Sound of Distant Cheering, 1986; Downhill All The

Way, 1988; Darkling, 1989; Skylark, 1989; No Roses Round The Door, 1990; Poor Badger, 1991, USA, 1991; Late to Smile, 1992; The Boy Who Wasn't There, 1992, USA, 1992. *Honours:* New York Herald Tribune Award, 1965; Carnegie Medal, 1969; Guardian award, 1970. *Address:* Rookery Cottage, North Fambridge Chelmsford, Essex CM3 6LP, England.

PFANNER Anne Louise, (Louise Pfanner), b. 6 Mar 1955, Sydney, New South Wales, Australia. Illustrator; Writer. m. (1) Glenn Woodley, 24 Dec 1976, (2) Tim Maddox, 12 Jan 1987, 4 sons. *Education:* Diploma, Graphic Design, 1977; BA, Visual Communication, 1986. *Publications:* Louise Builds a Boat, 1986; Louise Builds a House, 1987; Illustrator: Your Book of Magic Secrets (R Deutch), 1991. *Contributions to:* Illustrations to various magazines and regularly to Sydney's Child; Exhibits Illustrations regularly; Contributed Illustrations for Favourite Stories from Playschool, 1991; Written and Illustrated Story, El Nido for Playschool; . *Membership:* Society of Book Illustrators, Sydney. *Literary Agent:* Barbara Mobbs. *Address:* 4 Catalpa Av, Avalon, New South Wales 2107, Australia.

PFANNER Louise. See: **PFANNER Anne Louise.**

PFEFFER Susan Beth, b. 1948, USA. Children's Fiction Writer. *Publications:* Just Morgan, 1970; Better Than All Right, 1972; Rainbows and Fireworks, 1973; The Beauty Queen, 1974; Whatever Words You Want to Hear, 1974; Marly the Kid, 1975; Kid Power, 1977; Starring Peter and Leigh, 1979; Awful Eveline, 1979; Just Between Us, 1980; About David, 1980; What Do You Do When Your Mouth Won't Open, 1981; A Matter of Principle, 1982; Courage, Dana, 1983; Fantasy Summer, 1984; Paperdolls, 1984; On the Move, 1985; Starting with Melodie, 1985; Make Me a Star series, 6 vols, 1986; The Friendship, 1986; Getting Even, 1986; Hard Times High, 1986. *Address:* 14 S Railroad Avenue, Middletown, NJ 10940, USA.

PHELAN Mary Kay, b. 1914, USA. Children's Author. *Publications:* The White House, 1962; The Circus, 1963; Mother's Day, 1965; Mr Lincoln Speaks at Gettysburg, 1966; The Fourth of July, 1966; Election Day, 1967; Four Days in Philadelphia, 1967; Midnight Alarm: The Story of Paul Revere's Ride, 1968; Probing the Unknown: The Story of Dr Florence Sabin, 1969; The Great Chicago Fire, 1971; Martha Berry, 1971; Mr Lincoln's Inaugural Journey, 1972; The Story of the Boston Tea Party, 1973; The Burning of Washington 1914, 1975; The Story of the Boston Massacre, 1976; Waterway West: The Story of the Erie Canal, 1977; The Story of the Louisiana Purchase, 1979; The Story of the United States Constitution, 1987.

PHELPS Barry, b. 26 Jan 1941, England. 1 son, 1 daughter. *Publications:* The Inflation Fighters Handbook, 1974; Power and the Party - A History of the Carlton Club, 1982; Endeavour: The Venetian Tramway System 1857-1902, 1988; P G Wodehouse: Man and Myth, 1992; Wooster of Yaxley and Wodehouse of Kimberley - Parallel Peerages, privately printed, 1992. *Contributions to:* Antiquarian Book Monthly Review; Daily Mail; Euromoney; The Times, Daily Telegraph. *Membership:* Society of Authors. *Address:* 25 Kenway Road, London SW5 0RP, England.

PHELPS Gilbert Henry, b. 23 Jan 1915, Writer. m. (1) 1 son, 1 daughter, (2) Kay Batchelor, 23 Oct 1972, 3 stepsons. *Education:* BA, 1st Class Honours, Fitzwilliam, Cambridge, 1934-39; Research and Teaching, St John's College, Cambridge, 1937-39; MA, 1941. *Appointments:* Lecturer and Tutor, Cambridge University Board of Extra-Mural Studies, 1937-39; Senior Producer, BBC Third Programme, 1950-55; Editor, Latin-American Series, 1972-77; Broadcaster & BBC Script Writer; Introductions for Folio Society. *Publications include:* Novels: The Dry Stone, 1953; The Heart in the Desert, 1954; A Man in His Prime, 1955; The Centenarians, 1958; The Love Before the First,

1960; The Winter People, 1963; Tenants of the House, 1971; The Old Believer, 1973; The Low Roads, 1975; Non-fiction: The Russian Novel in English Fiction, 1956; The Last Horizon: Travels in Brazil, 1964; A Survey of English Literature, 1965; The Byronic Byron, 1971; The Tradegy of Paraguay, 1975; Squire Waterton, 1976; An Introduction to Fifty British Novels 1600-1900, 1979; From Myth to Modernism: A Short Guide to the World Novel, 1988; Post-War Literature and Drama, 1988. *Contributions to:* The Pelican Guide to English Literature, 1987; The Cambridge Journal; Slavonic Review; World Review; New Statesman; Times Literary Supplement. *Memberships:* Fellow, Royal Society of Literature; Society of Authors, Panel of Judges for various literary Awards; Southern Arts, Chairman, Literature Panel, 1976-79; PEN; Fellow, Royal Commonwealth Society. *Address:* The Cottage, School Road, Finstock, Oxford OX7 3DJ, England.

PHILIPP Elliot Elias, (Anthony Havil, Victor Tempest) b. 20 July 1915, London, England. Surgeon. m. 22 Mar 1939, dec 4 July 1988, 1 son, 1 daughter. *Education:* St. Paul's School, 1928-33; BA, MA, St. John's College. Cambridge, 1933-36; MRCS, LRCP, 1939, MBBCh, 1947, MRCOG 1947, FRCS 1951, FRCOG 1962, Middlesex Hospital, London. *Appointments:* Medical Correspondent, RCS Chronicle 1947-52, Sunday Times 1952-54, *Publications:* The Technique of Sex (Anthony Havil) 1939; Obstetrics and Gynaecology for Students, 1962 and 1970; Scientific Foundation of Obstetrics and Gynaecology, co-editor, 1970, 1977, 1986, 1991; Caesareans, 1988; A History of Obstetrics and Gynaecology, 1993; Several books and booklets for nurses, midwives and the lay public on Gynaecology; Several books translated from French. *Contributions to:* British Medical Journal; Journals of Obstetrics and Gynaecology, English, American and French (over 300 papers). *Honour:* Chevalier de la Legion d'Honneur, 1971. *Memberships:* Society of Authors; PEN; Orator and President, Hunterian Society; President Elect, Medical Society of London. *Address:* 78 Nottingham Terrace, York Gate, London NW1 4QE, England.

PHILIPS Steve. See: **WHITTINGTON Harry.**

PHILIPS Thomas. See: **DAVIES Leslie Purnell.**

PHILLIPS Edward O, b. 26 Nov 1931, Montreal, Canada. Teacher; Writer. *Education:* BA, McGill University, 1953; LIL, University of Montreal, 1956; AMT, Harvard University, 1957; MA, Boston University, 1962. *Publications:* Sunday's Child, 1981; Where There's A Will, 1984; Buried on Sunday, 1986; Hope Springs Eternal, 1988; Sunday Best, 1990; The Landlady's Niece, 1992. *Contributions to:* Short stories to various Canadian journals. *Honours:* Arthur Ellis Award, 1986. *Memberships:* Canadian Writers Union; Union des ecrivains quebecois; PEN. *Literary Agent:* Lucinda Vardey Agency, Toronto, Canada. *Address:* 425 Wood Ave, Westmount, Quebec, Canada H3Y 3J3.

PHILLIPS Jayne Anne, b. 1952, USA. Writer. *Appointments:* Has taught: Humboldt State University, Arcata, California; Boston University, Massachusetts; Williams College, Williamstown, Massachusetts. *Publications:* Sweethearts, short stories, 1976; Counting, short stories, 1978; Black Tickets, short stories, 1979; How Mickey Made It, short stories, 1981; Fast Lanes, short stories, 1984; Machine Dreams, novel, 1984. *Literary Agent:* Lynn Nesbit, ICM, USA. *Address:* c/o Lynn Nesbit, ICM, 40 West 57th Street, New York, NY 10019, USA.

PHILLIPS Louis Christopher, b. 1939, USA. Writer; Poet; Educator. *Appointments:* Associate Professor, Director of Creative Writing, Central State University, Wilberforce, Ohio, 1966-. *Publications:* Dream Winners, novel, 1967; Love Ode: Plastic Surgical Pill Surreal, 1968; Sistine Cartoons, 1969; Bloodlines, 1971; Cheap Zoom Shots, 1974; Disco Candy and Other Stories,

1979; Twelve Muscle Tones, 1980; Bulkington, 1982. *Address:* 1812 Pueblo Drive, Xenia, OH 45385, USA.

PHILLIPS Michael. *See:* **NOLAN William Francis.**

PHILLIPS Michael Joseph, b. 2 Mar 1937, Indianapolis, Indiana, USA. Poet; Educator. *Education:* Purdue University, 1955-56; University of Edinburgh, 1957-58, 1959-60; Alliance Francaise, 1958; BA cum laude, Wabash College, 1959; Graduate study, New York University, 1960-61, Oxford University, 1969, 1971, Harvard University, 1970; MA, 1964, PhD, 1971, Indiana University; Postdoctoral study, Free University of Indianapolis, 1972-75, Butler University, 1973-75, Indiana University-Purdue University, Indianapolis, 1975, Cambridge and Oxford Universities, 1978. *Appointments:* Bookstore Manager, Bloomington, Indiana, 1961-63; College Traveller, Bobbs-Merrile Co Inc, Publisher, Indianapolis, 1964-65; Instructor, English, Free University of Indianapolis, 1973, 1977-79; Lecturer, English, University of Wisconsin, Milwaukee, 1973-78; Visiting Fellow, Harvard University. *Publications:* 9 Concrete Poems, 1967; Girls, Girls, Girls, 1967; 4 Poster Poems, 1968; 4 Poems for a Chocolate Princess, 1968; 7 Poems for Audrey Hepburn, 1968; Libretto for 23 Poems, 1968; Kinetics and Concretes, 1971; The Concrete Book, 1971; 8 Page Poems, 1971; Love, Love, Love, 1973; Concrete Sonnets, 1973; Concrete Haiku, 1975; Visual Sequences, 1975; Haiku II,1975, Visual Poems, 1975; A Girl, 1977; More Women, 1978; Movie Star Poems, 1978; 22 Concrete Poems Written While at Harvard, 1978; Abstract Poems, 1978; Underworld Love Poems, 1979; Erotic Concrete Sonnets for Samantha, 1979; Beginning of Samantha, 1979; Erotic Haiku for Samantha, 1979; 3 Visual Waka, 1979; Edwin Muir, criticism, 1979; Selected Love Poems, 1980; 4 Major Visual Poets (editor), 1980; 35 Boogie Woogie Haiku, 1980 Bebop Beuts, 1982; Indy Dolls, 1982; Superbeuts, 1983; Poems in anthologies. *Contributions to:* Over 1500 800 poems to magazines, newspapers, journals. *Memberships:* International Comparative Literature Association; Modern Language Association of America; American Comparative Literature Association; Society for the Study of Midwestern Literature; Midwest Modern Language Association; Phi Beta Kappa; Mensa.

PHILLIPS Samantha. *See:* **GELLES COLE Sandi.**

PHILLIPSON Charles Michael, (Michael Phillipson), b. 16 June 1940, Gatley, Cheshire, England. Freelance Painter; Writer. m. Julia Hauxwell, 1 Sept 1971, 1 son, 2 daughters. *Education:* BA, 1961, MA, 1964, Nottingham University. *Publications:* Making Fuller Use of Survey Data, 1968; Sociological Aspects of Crime and Delinquency, 1971; co-author, New Directions in Sociological Theory, 1972; Understanding Crime and Delinquency, 1974, co-author, Problems of Reflexivity and Dialectics in Sociological Inquiry, 1975; Painting, Language and Modernity, 1985; In Modernity's Wake, 1989. *Contributions to:* Reviews across Sociology journals; Articles and reviews for Artscribe International between 1986-88. *Address:* Derlwyn Glandwr, Hebron, Whitland, Dyfed SA34 0YD, Wales.

PHILLIPSON Michael. *See:* **PHILLIPSON Charles Michael.**

PHILP Peter, b. 10 Nov 1920, Cardiff, Wales. Writer. m. 25 Sept 1940, 2 sons. *Education:* Penarth Grammar School. *Publications:* Beyond Tomorrow, 1947; The Castle of Deception, 1952; Love and Lunacy, 1955; Antiques Today, 1960; Antique Furniture for the Smaller Home, 1962; Furniture of the World, 1974. *Contributions to:* The Times; Antique Dealer and Collectors Guide; Antique Collecting; Antique Furniture Expert, with Gillian Walking, 1991. *Honours:* Arts Council Award, 1951; C H Foyle Award, 1951. *Membership:* Society of Authors. *Address:* 77 Kimberley Road, Cardiff CF2 5DP, Wales.

PHIPPS Christine, b. 5 Dec 1945, Bristol, England. University Lecturer; Counsellor. Divorced. *Education:* Colston's Girls' School, Bristol, 1957-65; BA, Hons. 1st Class, Hull University, 1968; M Litt, St. Hugh's College, Oxford University, 1968; Advanced Diploma in Linguistics, Lancaster University, 1986; Advanced Diploma in Counselling, Wigan College of Technology, 1989. *Publications:* Buckingham: Public and Private Man (George Villiers 1628-1687), 1985. *Contributions to:* Notes and Queries Journal (Oxford University). *Address:* 21 Hurstway, Fulwood, Preston, Lancashire PR2 4TT, England.

PHIPSON Joan. *See:* **FITZHARDINGE Joan Margaret.**

PHOENIX Dawn. *See:* **JACOBS Barbara.**

PICANO Felice, b. 22 Feb 1944, New York City, New York, USA. Author. *Education:* BA cum laude, Queens College, City of New York University, 1960. *Publications:* Smart As the Devil, 1975; Eyes, 1976; Deformity Lover and Other Poems, 1977; The Lure, 1979; Late in the Season, 1980; An Asian Minor, 1981; Slashed to Ribbons in Defense of Love and Other Stories, 1982; House of Cards, 1984; Ambidextrous, 1985; Men Who Loved Me, 1989; To the Seventh Power, 1989; The New Joy of Gay Sex, 1992. *Contributions to:* Numerous magazines and journals. *Honours:* Finalist, Ernest Hemingway Award; PEN Syndicated Short Fiction Award; Chapbook Award, Poetry Society of America. *Memberships:* PEN Club; Writers Guild of America; Authors Guild; Publishing Triangle. *Address:* 95 Horatio Street 423, New York City, NY 10014, USA.

PICARD Barbara Leonie, b. 4 Dec 1917, Richmond, Surrey, England. Author. *Publications:* Ransom for a Knight, 1956; Lost John, 1962; One is One, 1965; The Young Pretenders, 1966; Twice Seven Tales, 1968; Three Ancient Kings, 1972; Tales of Ancient Persia, 1972; The Iliad and Odyssey of Homer, 1986; French Legends, Tales and Fairy Stories, 1992. *Address:* Oxford University Press, Walton Street, Oxford, England.

PICARD Robert George, b. 15 July 1951, Pasadena, California, USA. Professor; Author. m. Elizabeth Carpelan, 15 Sept 1979, 2 daughters and 1 son. *Education:* BA, Loma Linda University, 1974; MA, California State University-Fullerton, 1980; PhD, University of Missouri, 1983. *Appointments:* Editor, Journal of Media Economics, 1988-; Associate Editor, Political Communication and Persuasion, 1989-. *Publications:* Media Economics: Concepts and Issues, 1989; Press Concentration and Monopoly, 1988; The Ravens of Odin: The Press in the Nordic Nations, 1988; The Press and the Decline of Democracy, 1985; In The Camera's Eye: News Coverage of Terrorist Events, 1991; Media Portrayals of Terrorism: Functions and Meaning of News Coverage, 1993. *Contributions to:* Over 200 articles in magazines and journals. *Honours:* Herrick Fellowship, 1981; C.F. Denman Freedom of Information Award, 1981; Frank Luther Mott Historical Research Award, 1982; Phi Kappa Phi Award, outstanding research in social sciences and humanities, 1986; International Scholarship Award, Association for Advancement of Policy, Research and Development in Third World. *Memberships:* American Association of University Professors, Chapter President 1985-86, 1988-90; Association for Education in Journalism and Mass Communication; Mass Communication Division, President 1988-89; Chair, Professional Freedom and Responsibility Committee, 1993-94. *Address:* 2806 Gertrude Street, Riverside, CA 92506, USA.

PICK Frederick Michael, b. 21 June 1949, Leicestershire, England. Antique Dealer; Designer/ Decorator; Author; Lecturer. *Education:* MA, History & Law, Gonville & Caius College, Cambridge. *Publications:* The English Room, 1985; The National Trust Pocket Guide to Furniture, 1985; The English Country Room, 1988; Biography of the late Sir Norman Hartnell KCVO in progress. *Contributions to:* Antique Collector; Apollo; Art and Auction (USA); Antique & New Art; Connoisseur; Harpers and Queen; Journal of the Thirties Society; The Times; Vogue (Germany). *Honour:* 1969 Exhibitioner in History, Gonville and Caius, Cambridge. *Memberships:* Society of Authors; Founder Committee Member, The Twentieth Century Society; The Royal Society for Asian Affairs; The British Antique Dealer Association; Committee & Council Member The Landsdowne Club. *Address:* 114 Mount Street, London W1Y 5RA, England.

PICKARD Tom, b. 7 Jan 1946, Newcastle-on-Tyne, England. Writer/Director (Freelance). m. Joanna Voit, 22 July 1978, 2 sons, 1 daughter. *Publications:* Guttersnipe - City Lights, novella, 1971; Hero Dust, poetry, 1979; Jarrow March, oral history, 1982; Custom and Exile, poetry, 1985; We Make Ships, oral history, 1989; Tell Them in Gdansk, TV documentary (director), 1989; Word of Mouth, international poetry series (director and series editor). *Honours:* Arts Council Writer-in-Residence at Warwick University, 1979-80. *Memberships:* General Council, ACTT. *Literary Agent:* Judy Daish Associates, England. *Address:* c/o Judy Daish Associates, 83 Eastbourne Mews, London W2 6LQ, England.

PICKERING Edward Davies, Sir b. 4 May 1912. Journalist. *Appointments:* Chief Sub Editor, Daily Mail, 1939; RA 1940-44; Staff, Supreme HQ Allied Expeditionary Force, 1944-45; Managing Editor, Daily Mail, 1947-49, Daily Express 1951-57; Editor, Daily Express, 1957-62; Director, Beaverbrook Newspapers, 1956-63; Managing Director, Beaverbrook Publications, 1962-63; Editorial Director & Director, The Daily Mirror Newspapers Ltd., 1964-68; Editorial Director, International Publishing Corporation, Chairman IPC, Newspaper Division, Chair, Daily Mirror Newspapers Ltd., 1968-70; Chairman, IPC Magazines Ltd., 1970-74; Chairman, Mirror Group Newspapers Ltd., 1974-77; Director, Reed Publishing Holdings, 1977-81, Times Newspapers Holdings, 1981-, William Collins, 1981-. *Honours;* Hon.D.Litt., City University, London, 1986. *Memberships:* Vice President, Periodical Publishers Association, 1971-. *Address:* Chatley House, Norton St Philip, Somerset, England.

PICKERING Robert Easton, b. 1934, United Kingdom. Author. *Publications:* Himself Again, US Edition The Uncommitted Man, 1966; In Transit, 1968; The Word Game, 1982. *Address:* 07150 Lagorce, France.

PICOULT Jodi Lynn, b. 19 May 1966, New York, USA. m. Timothy van Leer, 18 Nov 1989, 1 son. *Education:* AB, Princeton University, 1987; MEd, Harvard University, 1990. *Publication:* Songs of the Humpback Whale, 1992. *Address:* 14 Muddy Pond Road, Sterling, MA 01564, USA.

PICTON Bernard. *See:* **KNIGHT Bernard.**

PIECHOCKI Stanislaw Ryszard, b. 8 Feb 1955, Olsztyn, Poland. Lawyer. m. Elzbieta, 29 Oct 1979, 1 daughter. *Education:* MSc, Department of Law, University of Torun, 1978. *Publications:* Na krancu drogi (On the End of Way), story, 1975; Przedostatni przystanek (The Last But One Stop), novel, 1980; Tekturowe czolgi (The Cardboard Tanks), novel, 1983; Przyladek burz (Cape of Storm), novel, 1989; Czysciec Zwany Kortau (Puratory called Kortau), report, 1993; Przysposobienie dziecka (Adoption of Child), science material, 1983. *Contributions to:* Local magazines & journals, Olsztyn; Historical publications relating to the former Eastern Prussia. *Honours:* Ignacy Krasicki Memorial Medal, best first novel, 1980; Award, Minister of Culture & Art, 1984. *Memberships:* Polish Writers Association; President, Revisory Commission, Olsztyn; Polish Lawyers Association; Society of the Friends of Warmia and Masuriás Literature - member of the authorities. *Address:* ul. Iwaszkiewicza 16 m. 28, 10-089 Olsztyn, Poland.

PIEL Gerard, b. 1 Mar 1915, New York, USA. Editor; Publisher. m. (1) Mary Tapp Bird, 1938, (div 1955), 2 sons (1 deceased), (2) Eleanor Virden Jackson, 1955, 1 daughter. *Education:* AB, Harvard College. *Appointments:* Editorial Associate, Science Editor, Life, 1938-45; Assistant to President, Henry J. Kaiser Co., and Associated Enterprises, 1945-46; Organiser, President, Scientific American Inc., Publisher, Scientific American, 1947-84, Chairman of the Board, 1984-87; Chairman Emeritus, 1987-. *Publications:* Science in the Cause of Man, 1962; The Acceleration of History, 1972; Only One World, 1992. *Honours:* George Polk Award, 1961; Kalinga Prize, 1962; Bradford Washburn Award, 1966; Arches of Science Award, 1969; Rosenberger Medal, University of Chicago, 1973; A.I. Djavakhishvili Medal, University of Tbilisi; Publisher of the Year, Magazine Publishers Association, 1980. *Memberships include:* Trustee, American Museum of Natural History; Phillips Academy; New York Botanical Garden; Henry J. Kaiser Family Foundation; Mayo Foundation; Fellow, American Philosopical Society, American Academy of Arts and Sciences. *Address:* 415 Madison Avenue, New York City, NY 10017, USA.

PIELMEIER John, b. 1949, USA. Dramatist; Actor. *Publications:* Agnes of God, 1983; Haunted Lives (A Witch's Brew, A Ghost Story, A Gothic Tale), 1984. *Literary Agent:* Artists Agency, USA. *Address:* c/o Artists Agency, 230 West 55th Street, New York, NY 10019, USA.

PIERACCINI Giovanni, b. 25 Nov 1918, Viareggio, Italy. Journalist; Politician. m. Vera Verdiani. *Education:* University of Pisa. *Appointments:* Organizer, Young Socialist Federation; Editorial Staff, La Nazione del Popolo, 1944-46; Joint Editor, Nuovo Corriere, 1946-48; Editor, Avanti, 1959-63. *Memberships:* President, Commercial Industry, Commerce and Tourism; Minister for Scientific and Technological Affairs; President, Socialist Group in Senate; President, Assitalia Insurance Co., SEC; ISLE, SIAC (from 1979; Minister Public Affairs (1963/64); Minister, Budget Affairs (1964/68); Minister Merchant Navy (1973/74); Member of Parliament in six legislatures (Deputy and Senator); Management of the Italian Socialist Party; Board of Directors of STET and UNIORIAS; Board of Management of ANIA.

PIERARD Richard V., b. 1934, USA. Professor of History. *Appointments:* Member, Indiana Governor's Advisory Commission on Libraries and Information Services, 1980-81. *Publications:* Protest and Politics: Christianity and Contemporary Affairs (edited with R G Clouse and R D Linder), 1968; The Unequal Yoke: Evangelical Christianity and Political Conservatism, 1970; The Cross and the Flag (edited with R G Clouse and R D Linder), 1972; Politics: A Case for Christian Action (with R D Linder), 1973; Twilight of the Saints (with R D Linder), 1978; Streams of Civilization, vol II (with R G Clouse), 1980; Bibliography on the Religious Right in America, 1986; Civil Religion and the Presidency (with R D Linder), 1988; Two Kingdoms: The Church and Culture Through the AGes (with R G Clouse and E M Yamanchi), 1993. *Address:* Department of History, Indiana State University, Terre Haute, IN 47809, USA.

PIERCE Meredith Ann, b. 5 July 1958, Seattle, Washington, USA. Novelist. *Education:* AA Liberal Arts 1976, BA English 1978, MA English 1980, University of Florida. *Publications:* The Darkangel, 1982; A Gathering of Gargoyles, 1984; The Woman Who Loved Reindeer, 1985; Birth of the Firebringer, 1985; Where the Wild Geese Go, 1988; Rampion (novella) in Four From the Witch World, 1989, Andre Norton, (ed.); The Pearl of the Soul of the World, (vol. III of the Darkangel Trilogy), 1990. *Contributions to:* Scholastic Magazine; Mythlore XXXI; The Horn Book; The Alan Review; The New Advocate. *Honours:* National First Prize, Scholastic Creative Writing Awards Contest, Scholastic Magazine, 1973; Graduate Teaching Assistant Award, University of Florida, English Department, 1979-80; The Darkangel: International Reading Association's Children's Book Award, Listed on American Language

Association's Best Books for Young Adults Roster; ALA Best of the Best Books List, Chosen for New York Times Notable Children's Book List; Appeared on Parents' Choice Award Book roster, 1982; Jane Tinkham Broughton Fellow in Writing for Children, Bread Loaf Writers' Conference, 1984; A Gathering of Gargoyles: ALA Best Books for Young Adults semifinalist, 1985; The Woman Who Loved Reindeer: Parents' Choice Book Award for Literature, 1985, ALA Best Book for Young Adults, 1985, New York Public Library's Books for the Teen Age participant, 1986; The Darkangel: California Young Reader Medal, 1986; Where the Wild Geese Go: Florida Department of State's Division of Cultural Affairs Individual Artist Fellowship Special Award for Children's Literature, 1987. *Memberships:* Phi Beta Kappa; Secretary-Treasurer Children's Literature Association's annual convention, 1982; The Author's Guild Inc; Science Fiction Writers of America. *Address:* 703 NW 19th Street, Gainesville, FL 32603, USA.

PIERCE Patricia Jobe, b. 18 May 1943, Seattle, Washington, USA, Writer; Historian; Art Dealer; Literary Agent for the Estate of poet Kahlil Gibran, 1978-; drug and narcotic abuse Counsellor to teenagers, m. Dr Norman B Pierce, 26 June 1965-89, 1 son, 1 daughter. *Education:* BFA, Boston University, 1965; Extension courses, University of Connecticut, 1965-66; Harvard University, 1989-90; Black belt, karate, 1968-. *Appointments:* Speaker Boston Book Festival, 1980; Chairman/Writer, National Rules Committee, Karate Illustrated, 1985-86; Historian Lecturer, Nantucket Art Association '88, University of Massachusetts, Boston, 1987; Hyde Park Historical Society, 1978, 1983, 1988. *Publications:* The Ten American Painters, 1976; Edmund C Tarbell and The Boston School of Painting, 1980; Richard Earl Thompson, American Painter, 1981; The Watercoloured World of J.W.S. Cox, 1982; John Joseph Enneling, American Impressionist, 1972; Introduction, Jane Peterson, American painter, 1982; Edward Henry Potthast, More Than One Man, 1988; Heads, film, 1989; The Test, film, 1988; An Impressionist Painter, Film, 1991; Victim Under Siege, novel and film, 1989; Secrets, 3 act stage play, 1989; Terrorists, film, 1989; Forthcoming: The Ultimate Elvis, the history of Rock 'n' Roll; Catalogue Raisçonnes on J W S Cox, W S Barrett, Edmund C Tarbell, J J Enneking. *Contributions to:* International Fine Arts collector, 1990-; Antique Monthly; Antique Journal; Art and Antique Weekly; karate Illustrated; Southwest Art; Tarbill; Animals. *Honours:* Golden Poet Award, World of Poetry, California, 1987, 1988, 1989; Citation, El Paso Museum of Art, Texas, 1974; Presidential Medal, Patriotism, Presidential Task Force, Washington DC, 1989. *Memberships:* National Writers Club; National Writers Union; International Society of Poets, London; International Platform Society; American Biographical Institute, Research Board of Advisers; Karate Illustrated, Chairman, Rules Committee; Appraisers Association of America; Archives of American Art, Advisory Board; Karate referee Association of New England; Presidential Task Force, Washington DC, 1989-90; League of American Women Vioters; National Federation of Wildlife; Hingham Historical Society, Donor; Brockton Museum, Donor; Appraisers Association of American; National Writer's Club; National Writer's Union. *Address:* 721 Main Street, Hingham, MA 02043, USA.

PIETRUSZA David, b. 22 Nov 1949, Amsterdam, New York, USA. m. Patricia Basford, 7 July 1990. *Education:* BA, 1971, MA, 1972, State University of New York at Albany. *Appointment:* Columnist, Old Tyme Baseball News, 1991-; Associate Editor, Total Baseball, 3rd edition, 1993. *Publications:* Baseball's Canadian-American League, 1990; Major Leagues, 1991; Lights On!, 1993. *Contributions to:* Books: Total Baseball (2nd & 3rd editions) 1991, 1993; The Empire State of Baseball, 1988; Journals and magazines: USA Today Baseball Weekly; Baseball America; The National Pastime; Baseball Research Journal; Elysian Fields Quarterly; Catholic Digest; National Review. *Memberships:* Society of American Baseball Research; North American Society for Sports History. *Address:* 49 Heritage Parkway, Scotia, NY 12302, USA.

PIETRZYK Leslie Jeanne, b. 24 June 1961, Boston, Massachusetts, USA. Writer; Editor. m. Robert Rauth Jr, 23 Aug 1986. *Education:* BA, English, Creative Writing, Northwestern University, 1983; MFA, Creative Writing, The American University, 1985. *Contributions to:* Epoch; The Iowa Review; The Gettysburg Review; North Dakota Quarterly; South Carolina Review; The Nebraska Review. *Honours:* 2nd Place, Virginia Prize for Fiction, 1990. *Membership:* Poets and Writers. *Literary agent:* Charlotte Sheedy. *Address:* 3201 Elmwood Drive, Alexandria, VA 22303, USA.

PIKE Charles R. *See:* **BULMER Henry Kenneth.**

PIKE Charles R. *See:* **GILMAN George G.**

PILCHER Rosamunde (Jane Fraser), b. 1924. British, Romance. Plays/Screenplays. m. Graham Pilcher, 4 children. During World War II worked for Foreign Office in Bedfordshire; Served with Women's Royal Naval Service in Portsmouth and Trincomalee, Sri Lanka, with the East Indies fleet. *Publications:* As Rosamunde Pilcher - A Secret to Tell, 1955; April 1957; On My Own, 1965; Sleeping Tiger, 1967; Another View, 1969; The End of the Summer, 1971; Snow in April, 1972; The Empty House, 1973; The Day of the Storm, 1975; Under Gemini, 1977; Wild Mountain Thyme, 1978; The Carousel, 1981; Voices in Summer, 1984; The Blue Bedroom and Other Stories, 1985; The Shell Seekers, 1988; September, 1989; Flowers In The Rain, 1991; plays with C C Gairdner: The Piper of Orde; The Dashing White Sergeant, 1955; The Tulip Major, 1959. *Contributions to:* Woman and Home; Good Housekeeping. *Address:* Over Pilmore, Invergowrie, by Dundee, Scotland.

PILGRIM Anne. *See:* **ALLAN Mabel Ester.**

PILGRIM Constance Maud Eva, b. 3 Dec 1911, London, England. Writer. m. (1) Paul Smither, 29 Dec 1934 (dec, 2 Sept 1943), 1 son, 1 daughter. (2) Richard Pilgrim, 10 Sept 1957 (dec, 5 June 1979). *Education:* Textile design, Eastbourne School of Art; English literature course, Oxford. *Publications:* Dear Jane, biographical research, Jane Austen, 1971, re-print, 1991; This is Illyria, Lady, life/rambles & friends of Jane Austen, 1991. Also: You Precious Winners All, study of The Winter's Tale completed & left in MSS by Rev.Richard Pilgrim (1979), seen through press by C.Pilgrim, published 1983. *Contributions to:* Persuasions, 1988 (the journal of JASNA, the Jane Austen Society of North America); Various journals & magazines. *Memberships:* The Society of Authors; West Country Writers Association; The Jane Austen Society, Bath & Bristol. *Address:* 24 Withington Court, Abingdon, Oxfordshire OX14 3QB, England.

PILGRIM Derral. *See:* **ZACHARY Hugh.**

PILKINGTON Roger Windle, b. 17 Jan 1915, St Helens, England. Author. m. (1) Miriam Jaboor, 27 July 1937; (2) Ingrid Geijer, 11 Oct 1972. *Education:* Rugby School, 1928-33; Magdalene College, Cambridge, 1933- 37; MA (Cantab); PhD. *Publications:* 20 volumes in Small Boat series, 1959-89, including: Small Boat down the Years, 1988; Small Boat in the Midi, 1989; Children's books including The Ormering Tide, 1974; Scientific philosophy and Christianity, notably: World Without End, 1960; Heavens Alive, 1962; Books on Inland Waterways; I Sailed on the Mayflower, 1990; One Foot in France, 1992. *Contributions to:* Sunday Telegraph; Guardian. *Honours:* Chevalier, Compagnons du Minervois. *Memberships:* Master, Glass Sellers Company, 1968. *Address:* Les Cactus, Montouliers 34 310, France.

PILLING Christopher (Robert), b. 20 Apr 1936, Birmingham, England. Writer; Teacher. m. Sylvia Hill, 6 Aug 1960. 1 son, 2 daughters. *Education:* BA, Hons, University of Leeds, 1954-57; Diplome d'Etudes

Francaises, Institut d'Etudes Francaises, La Rochelle, 1955; Certificate of Education, Loughborough College, 1958-59. *Appointment:* Assistant d'Anglais, Ecole Normale d'Instituteurs, Moulins, Allier, France, 1957-58; Teacher of French & PE Wirral Grammer School, Cheshire, 1959-61; Teacher of French & PE, King Edwards School for Boys, Camp Hill, Brimingham, 1961-62; Teacher of French, Housemaster, Ackworth School, Yorkshire, 1962-73; Head of Modern Languages Housemaster Knottingley High School, West Yorkshire, 1973-78; Head of French, teacher of German & latin, Keswick School, Cumbria, 1980-88; Reviewer, Times Literary Supplement, 1973-74. *Publications:* Snakes & Girls, 1970; In All The Spaces On All The Lines, 1971; Broadsheets from University of Leeds School of English Press; Sceptre Press; Cellar Press; Starwheel Press. Other books containing poems: Oxford Book of Christmas Poems; Speak to the Hills; Voices of Cumbria; New Christian Poetry; A Mandeville 15; Poetry and Audience 21; Between Comets. *Contributions to:* Observer; Times Literary Supplement; London Magazine; Critical Quarterly; Encounter; New Statesman; Ambit; Arts Council New Poetry; PEN Anthologies; Peterloo Anthologies; Oxford Book of Verse in English Translation. *Honours:* New Poets Award, 1970; Arts Council Grant, 1971; Arts Council Translators Grant, 1977; Kate Collingwood Award, 1983; Northern Arts Award, 1985. *Membership:* Cumbrian Poets. *Address:* 25 High Hill, Keswick, Cumbria CA12 5NY, England.

PILON Jean-Guy, b. 12 Nov 1930, St Polycarpe, Quebec, Canada. Writer; Radio Producer & Broadcaster *Education:* Law graduate, University of Montreal, 1954. *Appointments include:* Founder 1959, director 1959-79, review, Liberte; Head, Cultural Broadcast Service, 1970-85; Producer, Radio Canada. *Publications include:* Poetry: La Fiancee du Matin, 1953; Les Cloitres de l'Ete, 1955; L'Homme et le Jour, 1957; La Mouette et le Large, 1960; Recours au Pays, 1961; Pour Saluer une Ville, 1963; Comme eau retenue, 1969, revised 1985; Saisons pour la Continuelle, 1969; Silences pour une Souveraine, 1972. Articles: tourism, literature, writers, poets. *Contributions to:* La Presse, Le Devoir, 1960-80; Frequent service, various national juries including Prix David, international juries including Prix Gilson, Prix Canada-Belgique. *Honours include:* Quebec Poetry Prize, Prix David, 1956; Louise Labe Prize, 1969; France-Canada Prize, 1969; Van Lerberghe Prize, Paris, 1969; Governor-General of Canada's Prize, 1970; Athanase David Prize, 1984; Officer, Order of Canada, 1987. *Memberships:* President, International Quebec Writers Union; Royal Society of Canada; President de l'Academie des lettes du Quebec, depuis, 1982; Officier de l'Ordre des Atrts et des lettres (France), 1993. *Address:* 5724 Cote Saint-Antoine, Montreal, Quebec, Canada H4A 1R9.

PINCHER (Henry) Chapman, b. 29 Mar 1914, Ambala, India. Freelance Writer; Novelist; Business Consultant. m. Constance Wolsenholme, 1965, 1 son, 1 daughter (by previous marriage). *Education:* BSc., Honours, Botany, Zoology, 1935. *Appointments:* Staff, Liverpool Institute, 1936-40; Royal Armoured Corps, 1940; Defence Science and Medical Editor, Daily Express, 1946-73; Assistant Editor, Daily Express, Chief Defence Correspondent, Beaverbrook Newspapers, 1972-79. *Publications:* Breeding of Farm Animals, 1946; A Study of Fishes, 1947; Into the Atomic Age, 1947; Spotlight on Animals, 1950; Evolution, 1959; (with Bernard Wicksteed) It's Fun Finding Out, 1950; Sleep, and How to Get More of It, 1954; Sex in Our Time, 1973; Inside Story, 1978; Their Trade is Treachery, 1981; Too Secret Too Long, 1984; The Secret Offensive, 1985; Traitors - the Labyrinths of Treason, 1987; A Web of Deception, 1987; The Truth about Dirty Tricks, 1991; One Dog & Her Nan, 1991; Pastoral Synphony, 1993; A Box of Chocolates, 1993; (Novels): Not with a Bang, 1965; The Giantkiller, 1967; The Penthouse Conspiritors, 1970; The Skeleton at the Villa Wolkonsky, 1975; The Eye of the Tornado, 1976; The Four Horses, 1978; Dirty Tricks, 1980; The Private World of St John Terrapin, 1982; Contamination, 1989. *Honours:* Hon.D.Litt., Newcastle upon Tyne, 1979; Granada

Award, Journalist of the Year, 1964; Reporter of the Decade, 1966. *Address:* The Church House, 16 Church Street, Kintbury, Near Hungerford, Berkshire RG15 0TR, England.

PINGET Robert, b. 19 July 1919, Geneva, Switzerland. Writer. *Education:* University of Geneva. *Appointments:* Former Barrister, later Painter; Teacher, French in England; literary career, 1951-. *Publications:* Fantoine et Agapa, 1951; Mahu et la materiau, 1952; Le renard et la boussole, 1955; Graal Flibuste, 1956; Baga, 1958; Le fiston, 1959; Lettre morte (play), 1959; La manivelle (play), 1960; Clope au dossier, 1961; Architruc (play), 1961; L'hypothese (play), 1961; L'inquisitoire, 1962; Quelqu'un, 1965; Autour de Mortin (dialogue), 1965; Le libera, 1968; La passacaille, 1969; Fable, 1971 Identite, Abel et Bela (play), 1971; Paralchimie, 1973; Cette voix, 1975; L'Apocryphe, 1980; Monsieur Songe, 1982; Le harnais, 1984. *Honours:* Prix des Critiques, 1963; prix Femina, 1965. *Address:* c/o Editions de Minuit, 7 rue Bernard-Palissy, 75006, Paris, France.

PINNER David John, b. 6 Oct 1940. Writer. m. Catherine, 23 Oct 1965, 1 son, 1 daughter. *Education:* Royal Academy of Dramatic Art, 1959-60. *Publications:* Stage Plays: Dickon, 1965; Fanghorn, 1966; The Drums of Snow, 1969; The Potsdam Quartet, 1973; An Evening with the GLC, 1974; The Last Englishman, 1975; Lucifer's Fair, 1979; Screwball, 1985; The Teddy Bears' Picnic, 1988; TV Plays: Juliet and Romeo, 1975; 2 Crown Courts, 1978; The Potsdam Quartet, 1980; The Sea Horse; Novels: Ritual, 1967, 1968; With My Body, 1968; Corgi, 1969; There'll Always be an England, 1984. *Address:* Barnes, London, England.

PINNEY Lucy Catherine, b. 25 July 1952, London, England. Author; Journalist. m. Charles Pinney, 14 June 1975, 1 son, 1 daughter. *Education:* BA Honours, English, Education, York University, 1973. *Publications:* The Pink Stallion, 1988; Tender Moth, in progress; Short story in The Best of the Fiction Magazine anthology, 1986. *Contributions to:* The Sunday Times; The Observer; The Daily Mail; The Telegraph; Company; Cosmopolitan; Country Living; Country Homes and Interiors; Contributing editor, She magazine. *Honours:* Runner-up, Betty Trask Prize, 1987. *Membership:* West Country Authors Association. *Literary Agent:* Lisa Eveleigh, A P Watt Ltd. *Address:* Egremont Farm, Payhembury, Honiton, Devon EX14 0JA, England.

PINNINGTON Geoffrey Charles, b. 21 Mar 1919. Editor. m. Beryl, 1941, 2 daughters. *Education:* University of London. *Appointments:* On staff of (successively): Middlesex Independent; Kensington Post (Editor); Deputy News Editor, 1955, Northern Editor, 1957, Deputy Editor, 1958, Daily Herald; Night Editor, 1961, Assistant Editor, 1964, Deputy Editor, 1968, The Daily Mirror; Director, Mirror Group Newspapers, 1976-82; Editor, Sunday People, 1972-82. *Memberships:* Press Council, Joint Vice Chairman, 1983-86. *Address:* 23 Lauderdale Drive, Richmond, Surrey TW10 7BS, England.

PINSDORF Marion Katheryn, b. 22 Jun 1932, Teaneck, New Jersey, USA. Corporate Officer; Journalist; Professor. div. *Education:* BA, cum laude, Drew University, Madison, New Jersey, 1954; MA 1967, PhD 1976, Brazilian Economic History, Graduate School of Arts and Sciences, New York University. *Appointments:* Business include: Vice President, Corporate Communications, Textron Inc, 1977-1980, Ina Corporation, 1980-82; Director, Financial Communications, Smithkline Beckman Corporation, 1982-83; Member, Board of Directors, AMFAC Inc, 1982-88; Vice-President, 1971-77, Senior Consultants Programme and Senior Consultant, Hill and Knowlton, Inc, 1988-90. Academic appointments include: Adjunct Assistant Professor of Brazilian Studies, Brown University, Providence, Rhode Island, 1979-; Visiting Associate Professor, Business Faculties 1987-88, Associate Professor, Center for Communications and

Media Management, Graduate School of Business, 1988-, Fordham University. *Publications:* Books: Communicating When Your Company is Under Seige: Surviving Public Crises, 1987, 2nd ed. underway; German-Speaking Entrepreneurs: Builders of Business in Brazil South, 1990; Executive Ego: The Expensively Kept Secret, 1993. Numerous articles, reviews and academic presentations. *Contributions to:* Public Relations Journal; Drew Magazine; PR Quarterly; Executive Challenge; Business Journalism Review; Executive Communications; Risk Management and a number of others. *Memberships include:* Board of Directors, The Americas Society, 1990-; The Arthur Page Society; The Northeast Brazilianists; Authors Guild, 1992-. *Address:* 114 Leonia Avenue, Leonia, NJ 07605, USA.

PINTER Harold, b. 10 Oct 1930. Actor; Playwright. m. Lady Antonia Fraser. *Publications:* Plays: The Room, 1957; The Birthday Party, 1957; The Dumb Waiter, 1957; The Hothouse, 1958; A Slight Ache, 1958; A Night Out, 1959; The Caretaker, 1959; Night School, 1960; The Dwarfs, 1960; The Collection, 1961; The Lover, 1962; Tea Party, 1964; The Homecoming, 1964; The Basement, 1966; Landscape, 1967; Silence, 1968; Old Times, 1970; Monologue, 1972; No Man's Land, 1974; Betrayal, 1978; Family Voices, 1980; A Kind of Alaska, 1982; Victoria Station, 1982; One for the Road, 1984; Mountain Language, 1988; The New World Order, 1991; Party Time, 1991; Screenplays: The Caretaker, 1962; The Servant, 1962; The Pumpkin Eater, 1963; The Quiller Memorandum, 1965; Accident, 1966; The Birthday Party, 1967; The Go-Between, 1969; The Homecoming, 1969; Langrishe Go Down, 1970; A La Recherche du Temps Perdu, 1972; The Last Tycoon, 1974; The French Lieutenant's Woman, 1980; Betrayal, 1981; Turtle Diary, 1984; The Handmaid's Tale, 1987; Reunuion, 1988; The Heat of the Day, 1988; The Comfort of Strangers, 1989; The Trial, 1989; The Remains of The Day, 1991. *Honours include:* Recipient, various honorary degrees from Reading, 1970, Birmingham, 1971, Glasgow, 1974, East Anglia, 1974, Stirling, 1979, Brown (US), 1982, Hull, 1986 Universities; Awards Include: Evening Standard Drama Award, 1960; Screenwriters Guild Best British Screenplay, 1963; The Italia Prize, 1963; New York Film Critics Award, Best Screen Writing of the Year, The Servant, 1964; British Film Academy Award, The Pumpkin Eater, 1964; Whitbread Award, 1967; Writers Guild Prize, Best Screenplay Award, 1971; Donatello Prize, Italy, 1982; Ennio Flaiano Award, 1982; Elmer H. Bobst Award, New York University, and many others. *Memberships:* Fellow, Royal Society of Literature; Honorary Member, American Academy and Institute of Arts & Letters. *Address:* c/o Judy Daish Associates Ltd., 83 Eastbourne Mews, London W2 6LQ, England.

PIONTEK Heinz, b. 15 Nov 1925, Kreuzburg, Silesia. Writer. m. Gisela Dallmann, 1951. *Education:* Theologisch-Philosophische Hochschule, Dillengen. *Publications:* Poems: Die Furt, 1952; Die Rauchfahne, 1953; John Keats : Poems, 1960; Mit einer Kranichfeder, 1962; Klartext, 1966; Fruh im September, 1982; Helldunkel, 1987; Stories: Vor Augen, 1955; Kastanien aus dem Feuer, 1963; Wintertage-Sommernachte, 1977; Novels: Die mittleren Jahre, 1967; Dichterleben, 1976; Juttas Neffe, 1979; Windrichtungen (journey reports), 1963; Liebeserklarungen (essays), 1969; Leid und Zeit und Ewigkeit, Anthology, 1981; Das Buch vom Schreiben, Anthology, 1987. *Honours:* Tukan Preis, 1971; Literatur preis des Kulturkreises im BDI, 1974; Georg-Buchner Presi, 1976; Werner-Egk Preis, 1981; Obserschlesischer Kulturpreis, 1984; Bundesverdienstkreux, 1st class, 1985. *Address:* Dulfer Strasse 97, 8000 Munchen 50, Germany.

PIRIE David Tarbat, b. 4 Dec 1946, Dundee, Scotland. Writer. m. Judith Harris, 21 June 1983, 1 son, 1 daughter. *Education:* University of York; University of London. *Appointment:* Tutor, Film Critic/Editor, Time Out Magazine, 1980-84. *Publications:* Rainy Day Women, 1989, (film); Wild Things, 1988, (film);

Inhertage of Korror, 1974; Anatomy of the Movies, 1981; Mystery Story, 1980; Never Come Back, (BBC adaptation), 1989; Ashenden (BBC serial), 1990; Natural Lies (TV serial), 1991. *Contributions to:* Various journals. *Membership:* Screenwriters Studio, Dartington Hall, 1990. *Address:* c/o Lemon Unna and Durbridge, 24 Pottery Lane, London W11, England.

PIROT Alison T Lohans, b. 13 July, 1949, Reedley, California, USA. Writer. 2 sons. *Education:* BA Music, California State University, Los Angeles, 1971; Diploma in Elementary Education, University of Victoria, 1976. *Publications:* Can You Promise Me Spring?, 1986; Who Cares About Karen? 1983. *Contributions to:* Anthologies: Prairie Jungle; Canadian Children's Annual, No 11; Stories: Crackers; Read; Ahoy; Health Explorer; Canadian Author & Bookman; Wee Wisdom; Vision; Regina Women's Guide; Articles & Poems: First Teacher. *Honours:* Student Creative Writing Contest, Fiction Winner, 1985. *Memberships:* The Writers' Union of Canada; Canadian Society of Children's Authors, Illustrators & Performers, Prairie Representative, 1985-; Society of Children's Book Writers; Saskatchewan Writers' Guild, Treasurer, 1985-86. *Address:* 2629 Garnet Street, Regina, Saskatchewan, S4T 3A8, Canada.

PISERCHIA Doris (Elaine), b. 1928, USA. Author. *Publications:* Mister Justice, 1973; Star Rider, 1974; A Billion Days of Earth, 1976; Earthchild, 1977; Spaceling, 1978; The Spinner, 1980. *Address:* c/o DAW Books, New American Library, PO Box 120, Bergenfield, NJ 07621, USA.

PISKOR Stanislaw, b. 13 Aug 1944, Poland. Writer; Art Historian. m. 29 Sept 1969, 1 son, 1 daughter. *Education:* Degree in History of Art, Adam Mickiewicz University, Poznań, 1969; Doctor, Philology, Silesian University, Katowice, 1985. *Publications:* Confessions, 1975; Dispute Over Poetry, 1977; The Moveable Country, 1980; The Polish Identity, 1988; On The Bridge of Europe, 1992; (Plays): The Glass Pane, 1976; The Overflow, 1979; The Slaughter House, 1980. *Contributions to:* Editor in Chief, a literary-artistic magazine, Studio, 1981-93; articles in Nowy Wyraz; Tworczosc; Pismo; Odra; Poezja; Poglady. *Honours:* Private Artistic Award - Julian Przyboś, Medal for vanguard creation and promotion; Award of W Rzymowski, Warzawa, 1988; Award of Literary Foundation, Warszawa, 1988; Literary Award of Solidarity, Katowice, 1993. *Memberships:* Association of Polish Writers, 1980; Association of Art Historians in Poland. *Literary Agent:* ZAIKS, Warsaw, ul. Hipoteczna 2. *Address:* Ul. Jaworznicka 38, 32-520 Jaworzno, Poland.

PISTORIUS Vladimir, b. 10 Jan 1951, Ostrava, Czechoslovakia. Editor. m. Jitka Pistoriusova, 17 Apr 1976, 1 son. *Education:* Graduated, Faculty of Mathematics and Physics, Charles University, Prague, 1974, majoring in Cosmology. *Appointments:* Directed KE-78, one of Czech samizdat book editions, 1978-89; Editor-in-Chief, Mlada fronta Publishers, 1990-. *Publications:* A prece, KE.78, Praha, 1978; Jak se chyta slunce, Albatros, Praha, 1981; Filkovi na kalhoty, KE 78, Praha, 1984; Starnouci literatura, SPN, Praha, 1991. *Contributions to:* Kriticky sbornik; Literarni noviny; Lidove noviny. *Membership:* Czech Writers' Society. *Address:* Skalecka 17, 170 00 Praha 7, Czechoslovakia.

PITCHER George, b. 1925, USA. Emeritus Professor of Philosophy. *Publications:* Truth (editor), 1964; The Philosophy of Wittgenstein, 1964; Wittgenstein: A Collection of Critical Essays (editor), 1966; Ryle (edited with O P Wood), 1970; A Theory of Perception, 1971; Berkeley, 1977; A Life of Grace, 1987. *Address:* 18 College Road West, Princeton, NJ 08540, USA.

PITCHER Harvey John, b. 26 Aug 1936, London, England. Writer. *Education:* BA, 1st Class Honours, Russian, Oxford University. *Publications:* Understanding the Russians, 1964; The Chekhov Play : A New Interpretation, 1973, 1985; When Miss Emmie was in Russia, 1977, 1984; Chekhov's Leading Lady, 1979; Chekhov : The Early Stories, 1883-1888, with Patrick Miles, 1982; The Smiths of Moscow, 1984; Lily: An Anglo-Russian Romance, 1987. *Contributions to:* The Times Literary Supplement. *Address:* 37 Bernard Road, Cromer, Norfolk NR27 9AW, England.

PITCHFORD Kenneth S(amuel), b. 1931, United States of America. Poet; Freelance Editor. *Appointments Include:* Associate Editor, The New International Yearbook, New York City, 1960-66. *Publications:*The Blizzard Ape: Poems, 1958; A Suite of Angels and other Poems, 1967; Color Photos of the Atrocities: Poems, 1973; The Sonnets to Orpheus by Rilke, 1981. *Address:* c/o Purchase Press, PO Box 5, Harrison, NY 10528, USA.

PITT Barrie William Edward, b. 7 July 1918, Galway, Ireland. Historian. m. (1) Phyllis Kate Edwards, 1943, 1 son (dec.), (2) Sonia Deirdre Hoskins, 1953, diss. 1971, (3) Frances Mary Moore, 1983. *Appointments:* Historical Consultant to BBC Series, The Great War, 1963; Editor, Purnell's History of the Second World War, 1964; Editor-in-Chief, Ballantine's Illustrated History of World War 2, US Book Series, 1967; Editor, Purnell's History of the First World War, 1969; Editor-in-Chief, Ballantine's Illustrated History of the Violent Century, 1971; Editor, British History Illustrated, 1974-78. *Publications:* The Edge of Battle, 1958; Zeebrugge, St George's Day 1918, 1958; Coronel and Falkland, 1960; 1918 The Last Act, 1962; The Battle of the Atlantic, 1977; The Crucible of War: Western Desert 1941, 1980; Churchill and the Generals, 1981; The Crucible of War: Year of Alamein 1942, 1982; Special Boat Squadron, 1983. *Contributions to:* Encyclopaedia Britannica; The Sunday Times. *Address:* 10 Wellington Road, Taunton, Somerset, TA1 4EG, England.

PITT David Charles, b. 15 Aug 1938. Social Anthropologist; Ecologist; Sociologist. m. Carol Haigh, 13 Feb 1959, 3 sons, 4 daughters. *Education:* BA, University of New Zealand, 1959-61; B.Litt, M.Litt, D Phil, Balliol College, Oxford University, England, 1962-66. *Appointments:* Professor, School of Social Sciences, University of Waikato, New Zealand, 1968-71; Professor, Sociology, University of Auckland, New Zealand, 1972-80; Consultant, United Nations and World Health Organisation, Geneva, 1980-. *Publications:* Tradition and Economic Progress - OUP, 1970; Social Dynamics of Development - Pergamon, 1976. *Honours:* Vernadsky Medal, USSR Academy of Sciences, 1989. *Memberships:* Fellow, Royal Anthropological Institute; Commission Chairman, International Union of Anthropological and Ethnological Sciences. *Address:* 1265 La Cure, Switzerland.

PITT David George, b. 12 Dec 1921, Musgravetown, Newfoundland, Canada. Author; University Professor (retired). m. Marion Woolfrey, 5 June 1946, 1 son, 1 daughter. *Education:* BA (Hons. English, Mt Allison University, 1946; MA, 1948, PhD, 1960, University of Toronto. *Appointment:* Professor of English Literature, Memorial University of Newfoundland, 1949-83. *Publications:* Elements of Literacy, 1964; Windows of Agates, 1966; Critical Views on Canadian Writers: E J Pratt, 1969; Toward the First Spike: the Evolution of a Poet, 1982; Goodly Heritage, 1984; E J Pratt: The Truant Years, 1984; E J Pratt: The Master Years, 1987; Tales from the Outer Fringe, 1990. *Honours:* Medal for Biography, University of British Columbia, 1984; Artist of the Year, Newfoundland Arts Council, 1988; Honorary LLD, Mt Allison University, 1989. *Memberships:* Association of Canadian University Teachers of English; Humanities Association of Canada. *Address:* 7 Chestnut Place, St John's, Newfoundland, Canada A1B 2T1.

PITT-KETHLEY Fiona, b. 21 Nov 1954, Edgware, Middlesex. Writer and Poet. *Education:* BA, Hons, Fine Art, Chelsea School of Art, 1976. *Publications:* Sky Ray Lolly, 1986, Re-issue 1990; Private Parts, 1987, re-

issue, 1991; Journeys to the Underworld 1988, paperback, 1989; The Perfect Man, 1989; London, privately printed 1984; Rome, 1985; The Tower of Glass, 1985; Gesta, 1986; The Misfortunes of Nigel, 1991; The Literary Companion to Sex, 1992, paperback, 1993; Dogs, 1993; The Maiden's Progress, 1992; Too Hot to Handle, 1992. *Contributor to:* Numerous magazines and newspapers, including The Independent and The Guardian. *Memberships:* Society of Sussex Authors; Chelsea Arts Club; Film Artistes Association. *Literary Agent:* Giles Gordon, Sheil Land Associates, 43 Doughty Street, London. *Address:* 7 Ebenezer Road, Hastings, East Sussex TN34 3BS, England.

PITTOCK Murray George Hornby, b. 5 Jan 1962, Nantwich, England. Academic. m. Anne Grace Thornton Martin, 15 Apr 1989, 1 daughter. *Education:* MA, 1st Class, English Language and Literature, Glasgow University, 1983; Snell Exhibitioner, Balliol College, Oxford, 1983-86; DPhil, Oxford, 1986; British Academy Postdoctoral Research Fellow, University of Aberdeen, 1988-89. *Appointments:* Daily Express schools work, 1982-83; Lecturer, Pembroke College, Oxford, 1986-87; Editorial Assistant, Waverley Novels Project, 1987-88; Junior Research Fellow, Linacre College, Oxford, 1988-; Lecturer, University of Edinburgh, 1989-. *Publications:* Lionel Johnson: Selected Letters (editor), 1988; The Invention of Scotland, 1991; Clio's Clavers, 1992; Spectrum of Decadence, 1993. *Contributions to:* Over 50 articles to journals including: Victorian Poetry; Scottish Literary Journal; Irish University Review; Nineteenth-Century Fiction; British Journal for Eighteenth-Century Studies; Press, radio and TV appearances, UK, USA. *Honours:* Winner, 1 of 10 1st Prizes, National Childrens's Writing Contest, 1973; Sir James Robertson Prize for Literature, 1976; Buchanan Prize, 1979; Bradley Medal, 1983; English-Speaking Union Scholar, 1984; BP Humanities Research Prize, Royal Society of Edinburgh, 1992. *Memberships:* Council, Association for Scottish Literary Studies; Fellow, Royal Historical Society. *Address:* Department of English Literature, David Hume Tower, George Square, Edinburgh EH8 9JX, Scotland.

PIVOT Bernard, b. 5 May 1935, Lyons, France. Journalist. m. Monique Dupuis, 1959, 2 daughters. *Education:* Centre de formation des Journalistes. *Appointments:* Staff, Figaro Litteraire, then Literary Editor, Figaro 1958-74; Chronique pour sourire, on Europe 1, 1970-73; Columnist, Le Point, 1974-77; producer, presenter, Ouvrez les guillemets, 1973-74; Apostrophes, Channel 2, 1975-; Editor, Lire, 1975-. *Publications:* L'Amour en vogue (novel), 1959; La vie oh la la!, 1966; Les critiques litteraires, 1968; Beaujolaises, 1978; Le Football en vert, 1980. *Honours:* Grand Prix de la Critique l'Academie Francaise, 1983. *Address:* 7 Avenue Niel, 75017 Paris, France.

PLACE Florence. *See:* **NORMAN Geraldine.**

PLAGEMANN Bentz, b. 1913, United States of America. Author. *Appointments:* Bookstores, Cleveland, Chicago, Detroit, New York, 1932-42; Instructor, Journalism, New York University, 1946-47. *Publications:* William Walter, 1941; All for the Best, 1946; Into the Labyrinth, 1948 (in United States of America paperback as Downfall, 1952, 2nd United States paperback edited as The Sin Underneath, 1956; My Place to Stand (autobiography), 1949; This is Gogle, or, The Education of a Father (in United Kingdom as My Son Goggle), 1955; The Steel Cocoon, 1958; Half the Fun, 1961; Father to the Man, 1964; The Best is Yet To be, 1966; The Heart of Silence, 1967; A World of Difference, 1969; This Happy Place: Living the Good Life in America (reminiscences), 1970; How To Write a Story (juvenile), 1971; The Boxwood Maze (gothic novel), 1972; Wolfe's Cloister (gothic novel), 1974. *Address:* c/o Harold Matson Company, 276 Fifth Avenue, New York, NY 10001, USA.

PLAIN Belva, b. 1918, United States of America. Author. *Publications:* Evergreen, 1978; Random Winds,

1980; Eden Burning, 1982; Crescent City, 1984; The Golden Cup, 1986; Blessings, 1989.

PLANO Jack Charles, b. 1921, United States of America. Writer. *Appointments include:* Editor, New Issues Press, Western Michigan University, Kalamazoo. *Publications:* The United Nations and the India- Pakistan Dispute, 1966; The American Political Dictionary (with M. Greenberg), 1962, 9th Edition, 1993; Forging World Order (with R.E. Riggs), 1967, 1971; The International Relations Dictionary (with R. Olton), 1969, 4th edition, 1988; Dictionary of Political Analysis (with R.E. Riggs), 1973, revised edition with R.E.Riggs and H.S. Robin, 1982; Political Science Dictionary (with M. Greenberg, R. Olton and R.E. Riggs), 1973; International Approaches to the Problems of Marine Pollution; The latin American Political Dictionary (with Ernest E.Rossi), 1980, 2nd edition, 1993; The Public Administration Dictionary (with R. Chandler), 1982, 1988; The United nations (with R.E.Riggs), 1987, 2nd edition, 1993. *Address:* Department of Political Science, Western Michigan University, Kalamazoo, MI 49008, USA.

PLANT Richard, (Stefan Brockhoff) b. 22 Aug 1910. *Education:* PhD, University of Basel, Switzerland, 1936. *Publications:* Die Kiste mit dem Grossen S, 1935; Taschenbuch des Films, 1938; The Dragon in the Forest, 1950-51; Lizzie Borden (opera text) 1966; The Pink Triangle, 1986, 1991; Detective novels under Stefan Brockhoff 1936-38, reissued 1950. *Contributions to:* The New Yorker; The Saturday Review; The New York Times. *Honours:* Best Non-fiction Book for The Pink Triangle, 1991; Best Non Fiction Book, Lambda Report. *Membership:* American PEN. *Address:* 23 Perry Street, apt. 4, New York, NY 10014, USA.

PLANTE David (Robert), b. 1940, United States of America. Author. *Publications:* Argo, or The Voyage of a Balloon, by A. Embiricos (translation with N. Stangos), 1967; The Ghost of Henry James, 1970; Slides, 1971; Relatives, 1972; The Darkness of the Body, 1974; Figures in Bright Air, 1976; The Family, 1978; The Country, 1980; The Woods, 1982; Difficult Women, 1983; The Foreigner, 1984; The Catholic, 1985; The Native, 1987. *Address:* c/o Deborah Rogers Agency, 44 Blenheim Crescent, London, W11 2EF, England.

PLANTEY Alain, b. 19 July 1924, Mulhouse, France. Author; Councellor of State; Diplomat; Chairman of the International Court of Arbitration of the International Chamber of Commerce; Member of the French Academie des Sciences Morales et Politiques. m. Christiane Wioland, 4 daughters. *Education:* University of Bordeaux; LLD, University of Paris, 1949; Diploma, National School of Public Administration, Paris, 1949. *Publications include:* Traite Pratique de la Fonction Publique, 1955, 3rd edition 1971; Prospective de L'Etat Paris, 1974; La Fonction Publique Internationale Paris, 1977; La Negociation Internationale, 1980; De La Politique Entre Les Etats, 1987; International Civil Service, 1981; La Funcion Publica Internacional y Europea, 1982. *Contributions to:* various journals and magazines including: Le Monde. *Honours:* Award, Academy of Moral and Political Sciences, 1979; Award Academy Française, 1982; Commander, Legion d'Honneur, Palmes Academiques. *Memberships:* Various professional organisations. *Address:* 6 Av. Sully Prudhomme, Paris 75007, France. I.C.C., 38 Cours Albert Ier, 75008 Paris, France.

PLATE Andrea Margolis, (Darvi) b. 29 July 1952, Writer; Journalist; Lecturer; Media and Editorial Consultant. m. Thomas Plate, 22 Sept 1979, 1 daughter. *Education:* MA, English, University of California, Berkeley, 1974; MA, School of Journalism, University of South Carolina, 1978. *Appointments:* Adjunct Lecturer, Fordham University, New York City, 1988-90; Senior Lecturer, University of Southern California, 1990-92. *Publications:* Secret Police, 1980; Pretty Babies, 1983. *Contributions to:* Chicago Tribune; New York Times; New York Newsday; TV Guide; Harper's

Bazaar. *Address:* 812 16th Street 2, Santa Monica, CA 90403, USA.

PLATER Alan Frederick, b. 15 Apr. 1935. Freelance Writer. m. (1) Shirley Johnson, 1958, (div 1985), 2 sons, 1 daughter, (2) Shirley Rubinstein, 1986, 3 stepsons. *Publications:* Theatre: A Smashing Day (also televised); Close the Coalhouse Door; And a Little Love Besides; Swallows on the Water; Trinity Tales; The Fosdyke Saga; Fosdyke Two; On Your Way, Riley!; Skyhooks: A Foot on the Earth; Prez; Rent Party, 1989; Sweet Sorrow, 1990; Going Home, 1990; I Thought I Heard A Rustling, 1991. Films: The Virgin and the Gypsy; It Shouldn't Happen to a Vet; Priest of Love; Television Plays: So Long Charlie; See the Pretty Lights; To See How Far It Is (trilogy); Land of Green Ginger; Willow Cabins; The Party of the First Part; The Blacktoft Diaries; Thank You, Mrs Clinkscales; A Day In Summer, 1989; Misterioso, 1991. Biographies: The Crystal Spirit; Pride of our Alley; Edward Lear - at the Edge of the Sand; Coming Through. Television Series and Serials: Z Cars; Softly Softly; Shoulder to Shoulder; Trinity Tales; The Good Companions; The Consultant; The Beiderbecke Connection, 1989; Fortunes of War, 1987; A Very British Coup, 1988; Maigret, 1992. Radio: The Journal of Vasilije Bogdanovic. Books: The Beiderbecke Affair, 1985; The Beiderbecke Tapes, 1986; Misterioso, 1987; The Beiderbecke Connection, 1992. Plays and shorter pieces in various anthologies. *Contributions to:* Punch; The Guardian; The Listener. *Honours:* Writer's Guild Radio Award, 1972; Sony Radio Award, 1983; Honorary Fellow, Humberside College of Higher Education, 1983; Hon. D.Litt., Hull, 1985; RTS Writer's Award, 1984-85; Broadcasting Press Guild, Best Drama Series, 1987 and 1988; BAFTA, Best Drama Series, 1988; BAFTA, The Writer's Award, 1988; Royal Television Society, Best Drama Series, A Very British Coup, 1988; A Very British Coup also won: The International Emmy (USA), The Golden Fleece of Georgia (USSR), Best Series and Grand Prix of the Banff Television Festival (Canada). *Memberships:* President, Writer's Guild of Great Britain, 1991; FRSL, 1985; FRSA, 1991. *Literary Agent:* Alexandra Cann. *Address:* c/o 68e Redcliffe Gardens, London SW10 9HE, England.

PLATH James, b. 29 Oct 1950, Chicago, Illinois, USA. Editor- publisher; Assistant Professor of English. m. Carol Lynn Jacobson, 15 Nov 1973, (div 1980), 2 sons, 2 daughters. *Education:* BA, English, California State University, Chico, 1980; MA, English, 1982, PhD, English, 1988, University of Wisconsin-Milwaukee. *Appointments:* Founding editor-publisher, Clockwatch Review: A Journal of the Arts, 1983; Director, Hemingway Days Writer's Workshop and Conference, Key West, Florida, 1988; Literature Panel, Indiana Arts Council, 1990; Literature Panel, Illinois Arts Council, 1992; Illinois College Press Association, 2nd Vice President, 1991. *Publications:* Clockwatch Review, 1983-; Men of Our Time: Contemporary Male Poetry, 1992; Gathering Place of the Waters: 30 Milwaukee Poets, 1983. *Contributions to:* Men of Our Time: Contemporary Male Poetry, 1992; Gathering Place of the Waters: 30 Milwaukee Poets, 1983; Criticism, fiction and poetry in: Modern Short Stories; Studies in Short Fiction; Kansas Quarterly; Black Warrior Review; The Cream City Review; Amelia; The Writer; The Writer's Handbook; criticism forthcoming in an antholgy of Hemingway criticism, Hemingway Repossessed, 1993, and others. *Honours:* Graduate of the Last Decade, University of Wisconsin-Milwaukee Alumni Association, 1992; Editor's Award for Non-Fiction, The Cream City Review, 1991; CCLM Editor's Award, 1990; Tinsley Helton Dissertation Fellowship, University of Wisconsin-Milwaukee, 1987. *Memberships:* Academy of American Poets; Associated Writing Programmes; Council of Literary Magazines and Presses (formerly CCLM); Hemingway Society; College Media Advisors; Vice President, Illinois College Press Association, 1993. *Address:* Department of English, Illinois Wesleyan University, Bloomington, IL 61702, USA.

PLATT Charles, b. 1944. Author; Poet; Freelance Writer. *Appointments:* Formerly Worked for Clive

Bingley Publishers, London; Designer, Production Assistant, New Worlds Magazine, London. *Publications* The Garbage World, 1967; The City Dwellers, 1970; Highway Sandwiches (poetry), 1970; The Gas (poetry), 1970; Planet of the Voles, 1971; New Worlds 6 (edited with Michael Moorcock), 1973 (in United States of America as New Worlds 5, 1974); New Worlds 7 (edited with Hilary Bailey), 1974 (in United States of America as New Worlds 6, 1975); Sweet Evil, 1977; Dream Makers: The Uncommon People Who Write Science Fiction, 1980. *Address:* c/o Gollancz, 14 Henrietta Street, London, WC2E 8QJ, England.

PLAYER Corrie Lynne, (Oborn), b. 14 Oct 1942, Ogden, Utah, USA. Journalist; Technical Writer; Teacher. m. Gary Farnsworth Player, 5 sons, 3 daughters. *Education:* AA, English, Speech, Weber College; BA, English, Creative Writing, 1964, MA, Education, 1965, Stanford University. *Publications:* Anchorage Altogether, non-fiction, 1972, Revised Edition, 1977. *Contributions to:* Baby Talk, 1986; Parents Magazine, 1986; McCall's, 1987; American Baby, 1988; Woman's Day, 1988; Ladies Home Journal, 1989; Family Circle, 1992; I'd Rather Raise an Elephant, column, Daily Spectrum, 1990-. *Honours:* Non-Fiction Book, Oklahoma Writers Federation, 1986, 1988; Article, League of Utah Writers, 1991; Inspirational Article, National Writers Club, 1991. *Memberships:* Founder, 1st President, San Luis Obispo Nightwriters, 1988-89; Founder, 1st President, Cedar City Nightwriters; Oklahoma Writers Federation; League of Utah Writers; National Writers Club; National Foster Parents Association; Former Member, American Society of University Professors. *Address:* 429 West 400th South, Cedar City, UT 84720, USA.

PLEIJEL Agneta, b. 26 Feb 1940, Stockholm, Sweden. Author. m. Maciej Zaremba, 27 Nov 1982, 1 daughter. *Education:* MA, 1970. *Appointments:* Norstedts Publishing Co, Stockholm. *Publications:* Kollontay, play, 1979; Angels, Dwarfs, poetry volume, 1981; The Hill on the Black Side of the Moon, film, 1983; Eyes of a Dream, poetry volume, 1984; He Who Observeth the Wind, novel, 1987; Dog Star, novel, 1989. *Contributions to:* Several, mostly in Sweden/ Scandinavia. *Memberships:* President, Swedish PEN Club. *Address:* Tantogatan 45, 117 42 Stockholm, Sweden.

PLOWDEN Alison, b. 18 Dec 1931, Simla, India. Writer. *Publications:* Elizabethan Quartet: The Young Elizabeth, 1971; Danger to Elizabeth, 1973; Marriage with My Kingdom, 1977; Elizabeth Regina, 1980; The House of Tudor, 1976; Elizabethan England, 1982; The Young Victoria; Jane Grey and the House of Suffolk; 2 Queens in One Isle; Caroline and Charlotte; Lords of the Land; The Elizabethan Secret Service, in preparation; Dramatised documentaries for BBC Radio and TV; Radio plays. *Honours:* Writers Guild of Great Britain Award; Best British Educational TV Script for Mistress of Hardwick, BBC I, 1972. *Literary Agent:* John Johnson, England. *Address:* c/o John Johnson, Authors Agents, Clerkenwell House, 45-47 Clerkenwell Green, London EC1R OHT, England.

PLUCKROSE Henry Arthur (Richard Cobbett). British, b. 1931. Writer of children's fiction, Education. Head, Teacher, Prior Weston School, London 1968-, Editor, Let's Go series. *Appointments:* Teacher of elementary school-aged children in Inner London, 1954-68. *Publications:* Let's Make Pictures, 1965; Creative Arts and Crafts: A Handbook for Teachers in Primary Schools, 1966; Introducing Crayon Techniques, 1967; Lets WorkLarge: A Handbook of Art Techniques for Teachers in Primary Schools, 1967; Introducing Acrylic Painting, 1968; (compiler) The Art and Craft Book, 1969; (ed with Frank Peacock) A Dickens Anthology, 1970; Creative Themes, 1970; (ed)A Book of Crafts, 1971; Art and Craft Today, 1971; (ed)Let's Use the Locality, 1971; (ed)Let's Paint, 1971; (ed)Let's Print, 1971; (ed)Let's Make a Picture, 1971; (ed)Let's Make a Puppet, 1971; Art 1972; Churches, 1975; Castles, 1975; Open School, Open Society, 1975; Houses, 1976; Monastries, 1976;

Seen in Britain, 1978; (with Peter Wilby) The Condition of English Schooling, 1979; Saxon and Norman England, 1979; Mediaeval England, 1979; Children in Their Primary Schools, 1980; (with Peter Wilby) Education, 2000, 1980; Victorian Britain, 1981; 20th Century Britain, 1981; Tudor Britain, 1981; Stuart Britain, 1981; Ancient Greeks, 1981; Arctic Lands, 1982; Hearing, 1985; Smelling, 1985; Tasting, 1985; Touching, 1985; Seeing, 1985; Growing, 1986; Shape, 1986; Floating and Sinking, 1986; Moving 1987; Counting 1987. *Address:* 3 Butts Lane, Danbury, Essex, England.

PLUHAR Zdenek, b. 16 May 1913, Brno, Czechoslovakia. Writer; Author. m. Marie Janir, 6 Dec 1979. 1 daughter. *Education:* Diploma Jugenieur, 1937. *Publications:* V sest vecer v Astorii 1982; Opustis-li mne, 1957; At hodi kamenem, 1962; Minutu ticha za me lasky, 1969 Konecna stanice, 1971; Jeden stribrny, 1974; Opona bes poblesku, 1985; Krize rostou k Pacifiku, 1974; Mraky tahnou nad Savojskem, 1949; Bronzova spirala, 1953; Modre udoli, 1954 and numerous other novels. *Contributions to:* Literalrm mesicmk; Kmen and numerous others. *Honour:* National Artist, State Prize. *Membership:* Srak cescosloveurlch spisorarelu. *Address:* Narvdru 37, Praha 1, Czechoslovakia.

PLUM Jennifer. See: KURLAND Michael.

PLUMB John Harold (Sir), b. 20 Aug 1911, Leicester, England. Historian; Professor of Modern English History at University of Cambridge. *Education:* University College, Leicester; Christ's College, Cambridge; BA, PhD, LittD. *Literary Appointments:* Editor, History of Human Society, 1959-; European advisory editor, Horizon, 1959-; Historical advisor, Penguin Books. *Publications include:* England in the Eighteenth Century, 1950 and 1953; Sir Robert Walpole volume I, 1956, volume II 1960, both reprinted 1972; The First Four Georges, 1956; The Renaissance, 1961; Crisis in the Humanities, 1964; The Growth of Political Stability in England 1675-1725, 1967; Death of the Past, 1969; In the Light of History, 1972; The Commercialisation of Leisure, 1974; Royal Heritage the book of the BBC television series, advisor and co-author with Huw Wheldon, 1977; New Light on the Tyrant, George III, 1978; The Making of an Historian, 1988; The American Scene, 1988. *Honours include:* Knight; Several honorary degrees. *Memberships include:* Fellow, British Academy; Fellow, Royal Historical Society; Fellow, Society of Antiquaries; Fellow, Royal Society of Literature; Honorary foreign member, American Academy of Arts and Sciences. *Address:* Christ's College, Cambridge, England.

PLUMLY Stanley, b. 1939, United States of America. Poet. *Appointments Include:* Poetry Editor, Ohio Review, Athens, 1970-75; Poetry Editor, Iowa Review, Iowa City, 1976-78. *Publications:* In the Outer Dark, 1970; Giraffe, 1973; How the Plains Indians Got Horses, 1975; Out-of-the-Body Travel, 1977; Summer Celestial, 1983. *Address:* Department of English, University of Houston, Houston, TX 77004, USA.

PLUMME Don E. See: KATZ Babbie.

POAGUE Leland Allen, b. 15 Dec 1948, San Francisco, USA. English Professor. m. Susan Aileen Jenson, 24 Aug 1969, 2 daughters. *Education:* BA, English, San Jose State College, 1970; PhD, English, University of Oregon, 1973. *Appointments:* Instructor 1973-74, Assistant Professor 1974-78, SUNY Geneseo; visiting Assistant Professor, University of Rochester, 1977; Assistant Professor 1978-81; Associate Professor 1981-86; Professor 1986-, Iowa State University. *Publications:* A Hitchcock Reader, (edited with Marshall Deutelbaum), 1986; Howard Hawks, 1982; Billy Wilder and Leo McCarey, 1980; The Cinema of Ernst Lubitsch: The Hollywood Films, 1978; The Cinema of Frank Capra: An Approach to Fim Comedy, 1975; The Possibility of Film Criticism (with William Cadbury), 1989; All I Can See is the Flags, 1988; Cavell and the Fantasy of

Criticism, 1987. *Contributions to:* Various journals. *Address:* English Department, Iowa State University, Ames, Iowa 50011, USA.

POCOCK Tom (Guy Allcot), b. 18 Aug 1925, London, England. Author; Journalist. m. Penelope Casson, 26 Apr 1969, 2 daughters. *Publications:* Nelson and His World, 1968; Chelsea Reach, 1970; Fighting General, 1973; Remember Nelson, 1977; The Young Nelson in the Americas, 1980; 1945: The Dawn Came Up Like Thunder, 1983; East and West of Suez, 1986; Horatio Nelson, 1987; Alan Moorehead, 1990; The Essential Venice, 1990. *Contributions to:* numerous newspapers and magazines. *Literary Agent:* Andrew Lownie. *Address:* 22 Lawrence Street, London SW3 5NF, England.

PODOPULU Soula, b. 16 Aug 1935, Greece. Schoolmistress. m. 26 Dec 1963, 2 sons. *Education:* Pedagogic Academy Arsakiou Psihiku of Athens, 1955. *Publications:* Small Stories, 1977; Difficult Years, 1979; The Forty Sifters, 1983; With the Sea-gulls, 1986; Myrtle or Mirsini, 1985; Konstadi's and the Pigeon, 1987; Uneasy Days, 1981; The Consent of Silence, 1986. *Contributions to:* Numerous journals and magazines including: Instructivestep; Kycladiko Light; New Thoughts; New Fireside; Open School; Free Spirit; The Modern Woman; Fire Grand. *Honours:* Literary Award, Pedagogic Academia, 1955; Prize, Lyceum of Greek Women, 1982; Prize, Delphian Amphictionion, 1982; Award, Feminine Company, 1982; Award, Delphian Amphictionion, 1984; Award, Union Literary Men of the Prefecture Karolicha, 1985; Prize, Hellenic Organisation of Tourism, 1986. *Memberships:* Company of Greek Authors; Circle of Hellenic Childrens Book Authors; Union of Greek Scientist Women. *Address:* Ragavi 98, Athens 114-75, Greece.

POGREBIN Letty Cottin, b. 9 June 1939, New York City, USA. Author. m. Betrand B Pogrebin, 1963, 1 son, 2 daughters. *Education:* BA, cum laude, Brandeis University, 1959. *Publications:* Free To Be..A Family, Editor, 1987; Among Friends, 1986; Family Politics, 1983; Growing Up Free, 1980; Getting Yours, 1975; How to Make it in a Man's World, 1970; Stories for Free Children Editor, 1982; Editor, Ms Magazine, 1971-; Contributor to numerous Anthologies, 1974-. *Contributions to:* Colmnist, Ms. 1988-, Newsday 1986-; New York Times, 1983; Ladies Home Journal, 1971-81; Moment Magazine; TV Guide; McGill Journal of Education; Boardroom Reports. *Honours:* Recipient, numerous honours and awards including, Poynter Fellow, Yale University, National Honorary Life Member, Pioneer Women, 1984; Matrix Award, 1981; Emmy Award, 1974; Clarion Award, Women in Communication, etc. *Memberships:* Founding Member, National Women's Political Caucus; Women's Forum; National Commission for Women's Equality of the American Jewish Congress; UJA Federation Task Force on Women; New York Network; Board of Directors: Action for Children's Television; Authors Guild; Child Care Action Campaign; Women's Action Alliance; Jewish Fund for Justice; International Centre for Peace in the Middle East; Board of Trustees: Public Education Association. *Address:* c/o Ms Magazine, 1 Times Square, New York, NY 10036, USA.

POHL Frederik, (James MacCreigh), b. 1919, American, Writer of novels/short stories, science fiction/fantasy. Member of the Council, Author's Guild, 1976-. *Appointments:* Book Editor and Associate Circulation Manager, Popular Science Publishing Co, New York City, 1946-49; Literary Agent, New York City, 1949-53; Editor, Galaxy Publishing Co, New York City, 1960-69; Executive Editor, Ace Books, New York City, 1971-72; Science Fiction Editor, Bantam Books, New York City, 1973-79. *Publications include:* The Space Merchants, 1953; Gladiator-at-Law, 1954; Search the Sky, 1956; Wolfbane, 1957 (all novels in collaboration with C M Kornbane); Slave Ship, 1957; Drunkard's Walk, 1960 (solo novels); Other Short Novels, 1962; (with C M Kornbluth) The Wonder Effect, 1962; A Plague of Pythons, 1963, revised edition as Demon in the Skull,

1984; The Abominable Earthman, 1963; (ed)The Seventh Galaxy Reader, 1964; (with Jack Williamson) The Reefs of Space, 1964; (with Jack Williamson)Starchild, 1965; (ed)Star Fourteen, 1966; (ed)The If Reader of Science Fiction, 1966; The Frederik Pohl Omnibus, 1966; Digits and Dastards, 1968; The Age of Pussyfoot, 1969; (with Jack Williamson) Rogue Star, 1969; Day Million (short stories) 1970; (ed) Nightmare Age, 1970; Practical Politics 1972, 1971; (ed with C Pohl) Science Fiction: The Great Years, 1974; Man Plus, 1977; Gateway, 1978; Jem, 1979; Beyond the Blue Event Horizon, 1980; The Cool War, 1981; Syzygy, 1982; Starburst, 1982; (with Jack Williamson) Wall Around a Star, 1983; Midas World, 1983; Hecchee Rendezvous, 1984; The Years of the City, 1984; Black Star Rising, 1985; The Coming of the Quantum Cats, 1986; The Annals of the Heechee, 1987; Chernobyl, 1987; Narabedla, 1988; The Day the Martians Came, 1988; Homegoing, 1989; The World at the End of Times, 1990; The Gateway Trip, 1990; Outnumbering the Dead, 1990; Mining the Oort, 1991; with Jack Williamson, The Singers of Time, 1991; Stopping at Slowyear, 1992. *Memberships:* President, Science Fiction Writers of America, 1974-76; President, World SF, 1980-82. *Address:* c/o World, 855 S Harvard Drive, Palatine, IL 60067, USA.

POIRIER Louis (Julien Grace), b. 27 July 1910, St Florent le Vieil, Maine-et-Loire, France. *Education:* Diplome, Ecole des Sciences, Politiques, 1933; Agregation d'histoire, Ecole Normale Superieure, 1934. *Appointments:* Professor of History at numerous public schools in French cities; Assistant to faculty, Caen University, Normandy, France 1935-47; Professor of History, Lycee Claude Bernard, Paris, 1947-70; Guest Professor of Literature, University of Wisconsin, Madison, USA 1970; Writer 1939-. *2Publications include:* Au Château d'Angel 1939; Un Beau Teribeux, 1945; Liberti Grande, 1946; Andre Buton, 1948; Le Roi Pecfeur, 1948; Le Revage des Syrtes, 1951; Un Balcon un Ferêt; Ouferences, 1961; Lettrines, I, 1967; La Presqu'ile (contains La Presqu'ile, La Route and Le Roi Cophetua, 1970; Lettrines 2, 1974; Les Eaux etroites, 1976; En lisant, en ecrivant, 1981; La Forme d'une ville, 1985; Autour des F Collins, 1988; Cavrets du guard chemin, 1992. *Honours:* Prix Goncourt, 1951 for Le Rivage des Syrtes (refused by author). *Address:* 61 rue de Grenelle, 75007 Paris, France.

POIRIER Richard, b. 9 Sept 1925, Gloucester, Massachusetts, USA. Literary Critic. *Education:* University of Paris, France, 1946; BA, Amherst College, USA, 1949; MA, Yale University, 1950; Fulbright Scholar, Cambridge University, England, 1952; PhD, Harvard University, 1960. *Appointments:* Williams College, 1950-52; Harvard University, 1955-62; Rutgers University, 1962-; Editor, Partisan Review, 1963-71; Vice President, Founder, Library of America, 1980-; Editor, Raritan Quartelry, 1980-. *Publications:* Comic Sense of Henry James, 1960; A World Elsewhere, 1966; The Performing Self, 1971; Norman Mailer, 1976; Robert Frost: The Work of Knowing, 1977; The Renewal of Literature, 1987; Poetry and Pragmatism, 1992; In Defense of Reading, co-editor, 1962. *Contributions to:* Daelalus; New Republic; Partisan Review; New York Review; London Review of Books; various others. *Honours:* Phi Beta Kappa, 1949; Fulbright Fellow, 1952; Bolingen Fellow, 1963; Guggenheim Fellow, 1967; NEH Fellow, 1972; HHD Amherst College, 1978; Award, American Academy of Arts & Letters, 1980; Literary Lions of NY, 1992. *Memberships:* Poets, Playwrights, Editors, Essayists and Novelists; American Academy of Arts and Sciences; Century Club. *Address:* 104 West 70th Street 9B, New York, NY 10023, USA.

POLAND Dorothy Elizabeth Hayward (Alison Farely, Jane Hammond), b. 1937. Author. *Publications:* As Alison Farely: The Shadows of Evil, 1963; Plunder Island, 1964; High Treason, 1966; Throne of Wrath, 1967; Crown of Splendour, 1968; The Lion and the Wolf, 1969; Last Roar of the Lion, 1969; Leopard from Anjou, 1970; King Wolf, 1974; Kingdom under Tyranny, 1974; Last Howl of the Wolf, 1975; The Cardinal's Nieces,

1976; The Tempetuous Countess, 1976; Archduchess Arrogance, 1980; Scheming Spanish Wueen, 1981; Spain for Mariana, 1982. As Jane Hammond: The Hell Raisers of Wycombe, 1970; Fire and the Sword, 1971; The Golden Courtesan, 1975; Shadow of the Headsman, 1975; The Doomtower, 1975; Witch of the White House, 1976; Gunpowder Treason, 1976; The Red Queen, 1976; The Queen's Assassin, 1977; The Silver Madonna, 1977; Conspirators' Moonlight, 1977; Woman of Vengeance, 1977; The Admiral's Lady, 1978; The Secret of Petherick, 1982; The Massingham Topaz, 1983; Beware the King's Enchantress, 1983; Moon in Aries, 1984; Eagle's Talon, 1984; Death in the New Forest, 1984. Address: Horizons, 95 Dock View Road, Barry Glamorgan, Wales.

POLE Jack Richon, b. 14 Mar 1922, Historian. m. Marilyn Mitchell, 31 May 1952 (diss 1988) 1 son, 2 daughters. Education: BA Oxon 1949, MA 1979; PhD Princeton, 1953; MA, Cantab 1963. Publications: Political Representation in England and the Origins of the American Republic, 1966, 1971; Foundations of American Independence, 1972; The Pursuit of Equality in American History, 1978; Paths to the American Past, 1979; The Gift of Government, 1983; Colonial British America ed. 1983; The American Constitution, for and against, (ed.) 1987; The Blacksell Encyclopeadia of the American Revolution, (co-ed.) 1991; The Pursuit of Equality in American History, revised 2nd edition, 1993. Contributions to: Numerous articles in British and American historical journals, also in The Spectator, The New York Times, TLS, London Review of Books. Honours: New Jersey Scholar, Princeton, 1953; Charles Randall Award, Southern Historical Association, USA, 1959. Memberships: FBA; FR Hist S; MCC. Address: 20 Divinity Road, Oxford OX4 1LJ, England.

POLENBERG Richard, b. 1937, United States of America. Writer (History). Publications: Reorganizing Roosevelt's Government 1936-1939, 1966; America at War: The Home Front 1941-1945, 1968; War and Society: The United States 1941-1945, 1972; Radicalism and Reform in the New Deal, 1972; The American Century: A History of the United States since the 1890's (with Walter LaFeber and Nancy Woloch), 1975, 4th edition. 1991; One Nation Divisible: Class, Race, and Ethnicity in the United States since 1938, 1980; Fighting Faiths: The Abrams Case, The Supreme Court, and Free Speech, 1987. Address: Department of History, McGraw Hall, Cornell University, Ithaca, NY 14853, USA.

POLIAKOFF Stephen, b. 1953, United Kingdom. Dramatist. Publications: Lay-By (co-author), 1972; Hitting Town and City Sugar, 1976; Strawberry Fields, 1977; Shout Across the River, 1979; American Days, 1979; The Summer Party, 1980; Favourite Nights and Caught on a Train, 1982; Banners, and Soft Targets, 1984; Breaking the Silence, 1984; Coming In to Land, 1987; Plays One, 1989. Literary Agent: Margaret Ramsay Ltd, England. Address: c/o 33 Devonia Road, London N1 8JQ, England.

POLING-KEMPES Lesley Ann, b. 9 Mar 1954, Batavia, New York, USA. Writer. m. James Kempes, 31 May 1976, 1 son, 1 daughter. Education: Bachelor of University Studies cum laude, University of New Mexico, 1976. Publications: Harvey Girls: Women Who Opened the West, 1989. Contributions to: Short fiction to: Puerto del Sol; Writers' Forum 16; Best of the West 3; Higher Elevations; Articles to New Mexico Magazine. Honours: Zia Award for Excellence, New Mexico Press Women, 1991. Literary Agent: Sydelle Kramer-Frances Goldin Agency. Address: PO Box 36, Abiquiu, NM 87510, USA.

POLLAND Madeleine Angela (Frances Adrian), b. 1918, United Kingdom. Novelist; Short Story Writer; Children's Fiction Writer. Appointments: Assistant Librarian, Letchworth Public Library, Hertfordshire, 1939-42, 1945-46. Publications: Children of the Red King, 1960; The Town Across the Water, 1961; Born

the Proud, 1961; Fingal's Quest, 1961; The White Twilight, 1962; Chuiraquimba and the Black Robes, 1962; City of the Golden House, 1963; The Queen's Blessing, 1963; Flame over Tara, 1964; Thicker Than Water, 1964; Mission to Cathay, 1965; Queen Without Crown, 1965; Deirdre, 1967; The Little Spot of Bother, US Edition Minutes of a Murder, 1967; To Tell My People, 1968; Stranger in the Hills, 1968; Random Army, US Edition Shattered Summer, 1969; To Kill a King, 1970; Alhambra, 1970; A Family Affair, 1971; Package to Spain, 1971; Daughter to Poseidon, US Edition Daughter of the Sea, 1972; Prince of the Double Axe, 1976; Double Shadow (as Frances Adrian), 1977; Sabrina, 1979; All Their Kingdoms, 1981; The Heart Speaks Many Ways, 1982; No Price Too High, 1984; As It Was in the Beginning, 1987; Rich Man's Flowers, 1990; The Pomegranate House, 1992. Address: Edificio Hercules 634, Avenida Gamonal, Arroyo de la Miel, Malaga, Spain.

POLLARD Jane (Dana James), b. 22 Nov 1944, Goole, Yorkshire, England. Author. m. (3) Michael Pollard, 2 June 1992, 2 sons, 1 daughter. Publications: Historical romances: Harlyn Tremayne, 1984; The Consul's Daughter, 1986. Contemporary romance: Desert Flower, 1986; Doctor in the Andes, 1984; Doctor in New Guinea, 1986; Rough Waters, 1986; The Marati Legacy, 1986; The Eagle and the Sun, 1986; Heart of Glass, 1987; Tarik's Mountain, 1988; Snowfire, 1988; Pool of Dreaming, 1988; Dark Mood Rising, 1989; Love's Ransom, 1989; A Tempting Shore, 1992; Bay of Rainbows, 1993. Contributions to: Falmouth Packet; West Briton; Western Morning News; Woman's Way; Radio Cornwall; BFBS Gibraltar, GIB TV. Memberships: Executive, Royal Cornwall Polytechnic Society; Romantic Novelists Association; Society of Authors. Address: 32 Cogos Park, Comfort Road, Mylor, Falmouth, Cornwall TR11 5SE, England.

POLLARD John (Richard Thornhill), b. 1914, United Kingdom. Retired Senior Lecturer in Classics. Publications: Journey to the Styx, 1955; Adventure Begins in Kenya, 1957; Africa for Adventure, 1961; African Zoo Man, 1963; Wolves and Werewolves, 1964, 2nd ed 1991; Helen of Troy, 1965; Seers, Shrines and Sirens, 1965; The Long Safari, 1967; Virgil: The Aeneid Appeciation (with C Day Lewis), 1969; Birds in Greek Life and Myth, 1977; Divination and Oracles: Greece, Civilization of the Ancient Mediterranean, 1986. Address: The Yard, Red Wharf Bay, Anglesey LL75 8RX, Wales.

POLLARD John Stanley (Stan Pollard), b. 23 Nov 1922, Salford, Manchester, England. Retired Headmaster; Freelance Travel Writer. m. (2) June Elizabeth Ashley, 2 sons, 3 daughters. Education: BA (part 1); DipEd., Liverpool University. Appointments: Part-time Overseas Correspondent, NOMAD, 1962-69; Travel editor, MMM, 1982-. Contributions: Variety of journals, in field of camping, caravanning, caring, travel and geography. Memberships: Institute of Journalists; National Association of Head Teachers Caravan Writers Guild; Probus, past President; University of the Third Age Chairman. Address: 24 Town Farm Court, Braunton, Devon EX33 1QJ, England.

POLLEY Judith Anne, (Valentina Luellen, Judith Stewart, Helen Kent), b. 15 Sept 1938, London, England. Author. m. Roy Edward Polley, 28 Mar 1959, 1 son. Education: High School, Belgravia and Maida Vale, London. Publications: About 50 romance novels including: The Countess, 1967; Marie Elena, 1968; Journey into Love, 1968; Master of Karatangi, 1968; Slightly Scarlet, 1969; Children of the Devil, 1970; The Flowering Desert, 1970; A Man for Melanie, 1970; Madelon, 1970; The King's Cavalier, 1971; Dangerous Deception, 1972; Castle of the Mist, 1972; The King's Shadow, 1975; Francesca, 1977; Keeper of the Flame, 1977; The Laird's French Bride, 1978; The Captive Heart, 1978; Place of Happiness, 1978; To Touch the Stars, 1980; Beloved Enemy, 1980; Don't Run from Love, 1981; Moonshadow, 1981; Prince of Deception, 1981; Beloved Adversary, 1981; Shadow of the Eagle, 1982;

Silver Salamander, 1982; The Wind of Change, 1982; The Measure of Love, 1983; The Peaceful Homecoming, 1983; The Valley of tears, 1984; Moonflower, 1984; Elusive Flame of Love, 1984; Mistress of Tanglewood, 1984; Black Ravenswood, 1985; The Lord of Darkness, 1985; Devil of Talland, 1985; Passionate Pirate, 1986; Where the Heart Leads, 1986; Love the Avenger, 1986; The Devil's Touch, 1987; My Lady Melisande, 1987; Dark Star, 1988; Love and Pride (Book I), 1988; The Web of Love (Book II), 1989; Winter Embers, Summer Fire, 1991; To Please A Lady, 1992; One Love, 1993; Hostage of Love, in progress; Many foreign editions and translations. *Contributions to:* Woman's Weekly Library; Woman's Realm; Woman's Weekly Fiction Series; The Museum of Peace and Solidarity, Samarkand, Uzbekistan. *Membership:* Founding Member, English Romantic Novelists Association. *Address:* Calcada, 8150 Sao Braz de Alportel, Algarve, Portugal.

POLLOCK John Charles (Rev), b. 1923, London, England. Clergyman; Writer. *Education:* MA, Trinity College, Cambridge; Ridley Hall, Cambridge. *Publications include:* A Cambridge Movement, 1953; Earth's Remotest End, 1960; Hudson Taylor and Maria, 1962; Moody Without Sankey, 1963; The Keswick Story, 1964; The Christians from Siberia, 1964; Billy Graham, 1966, revised edition 1969; The Apostle, 1969; A Foreign Devil in China, USA, 1971, UK, 1972; George Whitefield and The Great Awakening, USA 1972, Uk, 1973; Wilberforce, UK 1977, USA, 1978; Billy Graham Evangelist To the World, 1979; The Siberian Seven, UK 1979, USA, 1980; Amazing Grace : John Newton's Story, 1981; The Master: A Life of Jesus, UK, 1984, USA, 1985; Billy Graham : Highlights of the Story, 1984, in USA 1985 as To All the Nations : The Cambridge Seven, revised centenary edition 1985; Shaftesbury : the Poor Man's Earl, UK 1985; A Fistful of Heroes: Great Reformers and Evangelists, 1988; John Wesley, 1989; On Fire for God: Great Missionary Pioneers, 1990; Fear No Foe: A Brother's Story, 1992. *Contributions to:* Churchman; Church of England Newspaper; Christianity Today; Sunday Telegraph. *Membership:* English Speaking Union. *Address:* Rose Ash House, South Molton, Devon EX36 4RB, England.

POLLOCK Sharon, Canadian. *Appointments:* Member of the Drama Department, University of Alberta, Edmonton, 1976-77; Head of Playwright's Colony, Banff Centre of Fine Arts, 1977-80; Playwright-in- Residence, Alberta Theatre Projects, 1977-79; Artist-in-Residence, National Arts Centre, Ottawa, 1981, 1982; Member 1978-80, Chairman 1979-80, Advisory Arts Panel, Canada Council; Member of the Advisory Committee, National Theatre School, 1979-80. *Publications:* A Compulsory Option: Walsh, 1973; The Komagata Maru Incident, 1978; Blood Resolutions and Other Plays, 1981. *Address:* 319 Manora Drive, North East Calgary, Altberta Canada T2A 4R2.

POLONSKY Anthony, b. 1940, British. *Appointments:* Lecturer in East European History, University of Glasgow, 1968-70; Lecturer in International History, London School of Economics, 1970-, London University, 1981-; Secretary, Association of Contemporary Historians, London, 1975-. *Publications:* Politics in Independent Poland, 1972; The Little Dictator, 1975; The Great Powers and the Polish Question, 1976; The Beginnings of Communist Rule in Poland (with B Druckier), 1978; The History of Poland since 1863 (co-author), 1981. *Address:* 27 Dartmouth Park Road, London NW5, England.

POLUKHINA Valentina, b. 18 June 1936, Urlup, Russia. Reader. div. *Education:* BA, Tula State University, USSR, 1959; MA, Moscow State University, 1972; PhD, Keele University, Newcastle, Staffs., England, 1985. *Appointments:* Teacher of Russian, Kajakent, DASR, 1959- 61; Lecturer in Russian, Moscow Friendship University, 1962-68, 1972-73; Language Assistant, 1973-76, Lecturer in Russian Studies, 1976-, Keele University. *Publications:* Joseph Brodsky: A Poet for Our Time, 1989; ed: Brodsky's Poetics and Aesthetics, 1990; Brodsky Through the Eyes

of his Contemporaries, 1992. *Contributions to:* Russian Literature; Wiener Slavistischer Almanach; Essays in Poetics. *Honours:* British Academy's Research Awards, 1979, 1987, 1990. *Memberships:* British Association of Slavonic and East European Studies; British Neo-Formalist Circle; 20th Century Russian Literature Study Group. *Address:* Department of Modern Languages, Russian, Keele University, Newcastle, Staffs. ST5 5AX, England.

POLUNIN Nicholas, b. Hammonds Farm, Checkendon, Oxford, England. m. Helen Eugenie Polunin, 3 Jan 1948, 2 sons, 1 daughter. *Education:* Open Scholar, Christ Church, 1928-32, BA, 1st Class Honours, Botany, Oxford University; subsequently MA, D.Phil., DSc., Oxon; MS, Yale University (Henry Fellow), 1933-34; Research Associate, 1936-37, Foreign Research Associate, 1937-, Fellow 1950-54, Harvard University. *Appointments:* various positions, Oxford University, 1934-46; Visiting Professor, then Macdonald Professor of Botany, McGill University, Montreal, 1946-55; Professor of Plant Ecology & Taxonomy, Head, Botany, Founding Director of Botanical Garden, Director of University Herbarium, University of Baghdad, Iraq, 1956-59; Professor of Botany, University of Ife, Ibadan, Nigeria, 1962-66; Founding Dean, Faculty of Science, Planned Campus for Ile-Ife; Guest Professor, University of Geneva, 1959-61, 1975-76; Founder, Editor, Biological Conservation, 1967-74, Environmental Conservation 1974-; President, Foundation for Environmental Conservation, 1975-, and of World Council for the Biosphere, 1984-; Originator of Biosphere Day (21 Sept, first in 1991). *Publications:* More than 600 Research and other Scientific papers, editorials, reviews, and books including: 3 Volumes on Botany of the Canadian Eastern Arctic, 1940-48; Circumpolar Arctic Flora, 1959; Arctic Unfolding, 1949; Introduction to Plant Geography and Some Related Sciences, 1960; Eléments de Géographie Botanique, 1967; Editor, The Environmental Future, 1972; Growth Without Ecodisasters?, 1980; Ecosystem Theory and Application, 1986; (with Sir John John Burnett) Maintenance of The Biosphere, 1989, (similarly) Surviving With The Biosphere, 1993. Editor about 30 volumes (including new editions) of Plant Science Monographs and World Crops Books, 1954-72; Convener and General editor, Environmental Monographs & Symposia, 1979-; Chairman of Board, Cambridge Studies in Environmental Policy, 1984-. *Honours:* Recipient, various honours and awards including International Sasakawa Environment Prize, 1987. *Address:* Environmental Conservation, 7 Chemin Taverney, 1218 Grand Saconnex, Geneva, Switzerland.

POLYAKOV Vasiliy Ivanovich, b. 10 Dec 1913, Kursk, USSR. Retired 1985. Agricultural Journalist; Politician. *Education:* Agricultural Technical School, Voronezh; Institute of Journalism, Leningrad. *Appointments:* Agronomist, 1933-38; CPSU, 1939-; head of Department Executive Secretary Editorial Board, Sotsialisticheskoe Zemldelie, 1938-41; Pravda, 1946-60, later Editor, Agricultura Dept., and Member, Editorial Board; Editor, Rural life, 1960-62; Head Agriculture, Central Committee of CPSU, 1962; Chairman, USSR Bureau of Agriculture, 1962-64; Secretary, Central Committee, CPSU, 1962-64; Deputy Chief Editor, Ekonomicheskaya Gazeta, 1964-; Deputy to USSR Supreme Soviet until 1970. *Honours:* Orders of Lenin, Red Banner of Labour, Patriotic War 1st and 2nd Classes, Red Star.

POMERANCE Bernard, b. 1940, American. *Appointment:* Founder, Foco Novo Theatre Group, London. *Publications:* The Elephant Man, 1979; Quantrill in Lawrence, 1981. *Address:* c/o Faber and Faber Limited, 3 Queen Square, London WC1N 3AU, England.

PONDER Particia. *See:* MAXWELL Patricia Anne.

POOLE Julian. *See:* MAY Stephan James.

POPE Deborah, Professor; Poet. m. 2 sons. *Education:* BA summa cum laude, Denison University; MA, PhD, University of Wisconsin. *Publications:* A Separate Vision: Isolation in Contemporary Women's Poetry, critical study, 1984; Ties That Bind: Essays on Mothering and Patriarchy; Fanatic Heart, poetry, 1992. *Contributions to:* Poetry; Southern Review; Prairie Schooner; Poetry Northwest; Southern Poetry Review; Poetry Miscellany; Seattle Review; Numerous others. *Membership:* Phi Beta Kappa. *Address:* Department of English, Duke University, Durham, NC 27708, USA.

POPE Dudley Bernard Egerton, b. 29 Dec 1925, Kent. Author. m. Kathleen Patricia Hall, 17 Mar 1954, 1 daughter. *Education:* Ashford Grammar School. *Publications:* The Ramage series, (18 volumes), the York series, (5 volumes), The Battle of the River Plate, 1956; 73 North, 1958; England Expects, 1959; At 12 Mr Byng Was Shot, 1962; The Black Ship, 1963; Ficiton: Ramage Series include: Ramage's Trial, 1984; Ramage's Challenge, 1985; Ramage and the Dido, 1989. *Honours:* Book Society Choice (1) Ramage; Book Society Alternative Choice (2) Ramage and the Drumbeat, Ramage and the Freebooters; Book Club Associates' Choice (1) Buccaneer; World Book Club Choice (1) Decoy. *Address:* c/o Campbell Thomson and McLaughlin, 31 Newington Green, London N16 9PU, England.

POPE Lester Neal, b. 17 May 1946, Georgia, USA. Writer; Teacher; Publisher. m. Nancy Jo Martin, 1967, 2 sons, 1 daughter. *Education:* ABJ, 1968; MA, 1972. *Appointments:* Managing Editor, Louisville Defender, 1969; News Editor, Gwinnett Daily News, 1972; City Editor, Columbia Missourian, 1976; Instructor, Communications, Bemidji State University, 1974; Assistant Professor, Journalism, University of Missouri, 1976; President, Lokman Publishing, 1986. *Publications:* Selling's Magic Words, 1986; Trickle, Trickle, Fountain Flow, 1981; The Mingled Seed, 1981; The Timechange Imperative, 1982; Mindtrapped!, 1982; Christmas Lost: A Fable, 1983; Hold Your Nose for America and Other Stories, 1982; About Blocks, 1985; various short stories, literary criticism. *Contributions to:* Missouri Life; Personal Selling Power; Bounty; many others. *Honours:* Best Editorial, 1967, Best Feature, 1968, University of Georgia William Randolph Hearts Award; Best Spot News, University of Georgia William Randloph Hearst Award, 1968. *Memberships:* Science Fiction Writers of America; Mystery Writers of America; Society of Children's Book Writers. *Literary Agent:* Jay Garon-Brooke Associates. *Address:* 5902 S. Spring Ct., Columbia, MO, USA.

POPE Pamela Mary Alison, b. 26 Apr 1931, Lowestoft, Suffolk, England. Novelist. m. Ronald Pope, 3 Apr 1954, 2 daughters. *Education: Newland High School, Hull. Publications:* The Magnolia Seige, 1982; The Candleberry Tree, 1982; Eden's Law, 1983; The Wind in the East, 1989; The Rich Pass By, 1990; Neither Angels Nor Demons, 1992. *Contributions to:* Good Housekeeping; Woman; Woman's Realm; Vanity Fair; True; Loving; Hampshire Magazine; Hampshire Life; London Evening News. *Memberships:* Romantic Novelists Association; Society of Authors; Society of Women Writers and Journalists. *Address:* 1 Rhiners Close, Sway, Lymington, Hants SO41 6BZ, England.

POPE Ray, b. 1924, British. *Appointment:* Geography Teacher, Chippenham High School for Girls, 1966-. *Publications:* Strosa Light, 1965; Nut Case, 1966; Salvage from Strosa, 1967; The Drum, Desperate Breakaway, 1969; One's Pool, 1969; The Model-Railway Men series, 3 volumes, 1970-78; Is It Always Like This?, 1970; Telford series, 5 volumes, 1970-79; Hayseed and Company, 1972. *Address:* The Vatican, 49 High Street, Marshfield, Chippenham, Wiltshire, England.

POPE-HENNESSY John Wyndham (Sir), b. 13 Dec 1913, London, England. Art Historian. *Education:* Balliol College, Oxford. *Publications:* Giovanni di Paolo, 1937; Sassetta, 1939; Sienese Quattrocento Painting, 1947; A Sienese Codex of the Divine Comedy, 1947; The Drawings of Domenichino at Windsor Castle, 1948; A Lecture on Nicholas Hilliard, 1949; Paolo Uccello, 1950, Revised Edition, 1969; Fra Angelico, 1952, Revised Edition, 1974; Italian Gothic Sculpture, 1955, 3rd Revised Edition, 1985; Italian Renaissance Sculpture, 1959, 3rd Revised Edition, 1985; Italian High Renaissance and Baroque Sculpture, 3rd Revised Edition, 1985; Catalogue of Italian Sculpture in the Victoria and Albert Museum, 1964; Renaissance Bronzes in The Kress Collection, 1965; The Portrait in the Renaissance, 1967; Essays on Italian Sculpture, 1968; The Frick Collection, Sculpture, 1970; Raphael, 1970; Westminster Abbey (co-author), 1972; Luca della Robbia, 1980; The Study and Criticism of Italian Sculpture, 1981; Benvenuto Cellini, 1985; The Robert Lehman Collection, I: Italian Paintings, 1987; Learning To Look (autobiography), 1991; The Piero Delle Francesca Trail, 1991; Donatello Sculptor, 1992; Paradiso, 1993. *Honours:* CBE, 1959; Created Knight, 1971; Grand Officer, Republic of Italy, 1988; Hon Citizen, City of Siena, 1982; Hon Fellow, Balliol College; Hon Fellow, Pierpoint Library, New York; LLD (hon), University of Aberdeen, 1972; Serena Medal, British Academy of Italian Studies, 1961; Medal, New York University, 1965; Torch of Learning Award, Hebrew University, Jerusalem, 1977; Mitchell Prize, 1981; Mangia d'Oro, 1982; Award, Art Dealers Association of America, 1984; Premio del Presidente del Consiglio, 1992. *Memberships:* Fellow, British Academy; Fellow, Society of Antiquaries; Fellow, Royal Society of Literature; American Academy of Arts and Sciences; American Philosophical Society; Accademia Senese degli Intronati; Bayerische Akademie der Wissenschaften; Honorary Academician, Accademia del Designo; Accademia Clementina, Bologna; Ateneo Veneto. *Address:* 28 via dé Bardi, 50125 Florence, Italy.

POPESCU Christine (Christine Pullein-Thompson), b. 30 Oct 1930, London, England. Author. m. Julian Popescu, 6 Oct 1954, 2 sons, 2 daughters. *Literary Appointment:* Speaker, Eastern Arts, 1984. *Publications:* 95 books for children including Phantom Horse series, 1956; Pony Patrol series 1970's; Black Pony Inn series; Father Unknown, 1980; A Home for Jessie series, 1986; Stay at Home Ben, Careless Ben, 1987, 88; The Road Through The Hills, 1988; Across the Frontier, 1990; The Long Search, 1991; I Want That Pony, 1993; Collection: Horse and Pony Stories. *Contributions to:* Riding magazines. *Memberships:* PEN; Society of Authors; Eastern Arts; The Book Trust; Chairman, Mellis Parish Council. *Literary Agent:* Jennifer Luithlen Agency. *Address:* The Old Parsonage, Mellis, Eye, Suffolk, IP23 8EE, England.

POPHAM Hugh b. 1920. British. Writer; Author. *Publications:* Against the Lightning, 1944; The Journey and the Dream, 1945; To the Unborn-Greetings, 1946; Beyond the Eagle's Rage, 1951; Sea Flight, 1954; Cape of Storms, 1957; Monsters and Marlinspikes (in U.S. as The Fabulous Voyage of the Pegasus), 1958; The Sea Beggars, 1961; The Shores of Violence, 1963; The House at Cane Garden, 1965; The Somerset Light Infantry, 1968; Gentlemen Peasants, 1968; Into Wind, 1969; The Dorset Regiment, 1970; A Thirst for the Sea, 1979; F.A.N.Y: The Story of the Women's Transport Service, 1985.

PORAD Francine Joy, b. 3 Sept 1929, Seattle, Washington, USA. Poet; Painter. m. Bernard L Porad, 12 June 1949, 3 sons, 3 daughters. *Education:* BFA, University of Washington, 1976. *Appointments:* Editor: Brussels Sprout, Haiku Journal, 1988-. *Publications:* Pen and Inklings, 1986; Connections, 1986; After Autumn Rain, 1987; Blues on the Run, 1988; Free of Clouds, 1989; Without Haste, 1990; Round Renga Round, 1990; A Mural of Leaves, 1991; Hundreds of Wishes, 1991. *Contributions to:* Leading Haiku journals in the USA, Canada, Japan, England and Romania (total of 49 poetry publications). *Honours:* Cicada Chapbook Award, 1990; San Francisco International Haiku, Honorable Mention, 1991; International Tanka Awards (3) 1991; Juror, International Haiku, Senryu & Tanka Competition, 1992. *Memberships:* President, Haiku

Society of America; Association of International Renku; Treasurer, National League of American Pen Women. *Address:* 6944-SE 33rd, Mercer Island, WA 98040, USA.

PORKERT Manfred Bruno, b. 16 Aug 1933, Decin, Czechoslovakia. University Professor of Chinese Studies and Chinese Medicine. div, 1 daughter. *Education:* PhD, Universite de Paris (Sorbonne) 1957; Dr. phil habil, Chinese Medicine, Munich University, 1969. *Appointments:* Editor, translator, Kindlers Literatur-Lexikon, 1959-62; Executive Editor-in-Chief: International Normative Dictionary of Chinese Medicine, China Academy, Peking, 1989-. *Publications:* The Theoretical Foundations of Chinese Medicine, 1974; Essentials of Chinese Diagnostics, 1976, 1983; Klinische chinesische Pharmakologie, 1978; Klassische chinesische Rezeptur, 1984; (with C H Hempen) Systematische Akupunktur, 1985; Booklength literary translation of Chinese "Pingyozhuan: Der Aufstand der Zauberer, 1987; Some 400 professional articles, 200 translations. *Memberships:* International Chinese Medicine Society (SMS), Founding President 1978-85, Honorary President 1985-. *Address:* Institut fur Ostasienkunde der Universitat Munchen, Kaulbachstrasse 51a, 8000 Munchen 22, Germany.

PORTAL Ellis. *See:* **POWE Bruce.**

PORTER Bernard (John), b. 1941, British. *Appointments:* Fellow, Corpus Christi College, Cambridge, 1966-68; Lecturer 1968-78, Senior Lecturer in History 1978-, University of Hull; Reader in History, 1986-92; Professor of Modern History, University of Newcastle, 1992-. *Publications:* Critics of Empire: British Radical Attitudes to Colonialism in Africa 1896-1914, 1968; The Refugee Question in Mid-Victorian Politics, 1979; Britain, Europe and the World 1850-1982; Delusions of Grandeur, 1983, 1987; The Lion's Share: A Short History of British Imperialism 1850-1982, 1984; The Origins of the Vigilant State: The London Metropolitan Police Special Branch Before the First World War, 1987; Plots and Parania: A History of Political Espionage in Britain 1790-1988, 1989. *Address:* Department of History, The University, Newcastle on Tyne NE1 7RU, England.

PORTER Bernard Harden (Bern Porter), b. 14 Feb 1911, Porter Settlement, Maine, USA. Writer. *Education:* BS, Colby College, 1932; ScM, Brown University, 1933; DSc (Hon), Institute of Advanced Thinking, 1969. *Publications:* Author, 86 books including: Dieresis, 1976; The Wastemaker, 1980; I've Left, 1982; The Book of Do's, 1984; Here Comes Everybody's Don't Book, 1984; Sweet End, 1984; Last Acts, 1985; Dear Me, 1985; Gee-Whizzels, 1986; H L Mencken: A Bibliography, 1987; First Publications of F Scott Fitgerald, 1987; Sounds That Arouse, 1992. *Contributions to:* various magazines, 1932-1989. *Honours:* Carnegie Authors Award, 1976; PEN Award, 1976; NEA, 1981. *Memberships:* Fellow, Society of Programed Instruction, 1970-; Member, Maine Writers & Publishers Alliance, 1980-. *Address:* 22 Salmond Way, Belfast, ME 04915, USA.

PORTER Brian (Ernest), b. 1928, British. *Appointments:* Lecturer in Political Science, University of Khartoum, 1963-65; Lecturer 1965-71, Senior Lecturer in International Politics 1971-85, University College, Aberystwyth; Acting Vice-Counsel, Muscat, 1967; Honorary Lecturer in International Relations, University of Kent, Canterbury, 1984-. *Publications:* Britain and the Rise of Communist China, 1967; The Aberystwyth Papers: International Politics 1919-1969 (ed), 1972; The Reason of States (joint author), 1978; The Community of States (joint author), 1982; Home Fires and Foreign Fields: British Social and Military Experience in the First World War (joint author), 1985; The Condition of States (jt author), 1991; (co-edited) Martin Wright's International Theory, 1991. *Address:* Rutherford College, University of Kent, Canterbury, Kent, England.

PORTER Burton F, b. 22 June 1936. University Professor; Author. m. 31 Dec 1981, 1 son, 1 daughter, 1 stepdaughter. *Education:* BA cum laude, University of Maryland, 1959; PhD, St Andrews and Oxford Universities, UK, 1962. *Appointments:* Associate Professor, Russell Sage College, 1971-87; Full Professor and Department Head, Drexel University, 1987-. *Publications:* Deity and Morality, 1968; Philosophy: A Literary and Conceptual Approach, 1974, 2nd Edition, 1980; Personal Philosophy, 1976; The Good Life, 1980; Reasons for Living, 1988; Religious Belief: A Philosophic View, 1992. *Contributions to:* Excerpt from The Moebius Strip, in Boulevard, 1990. *Memberships:* American Philosophical Association; Modern Language Association; Association of Departments of English. *Address:* 151 Erdenheim Road, Philadelphia, PA 19118, USA.

PORTER Catherine Marjorie, b. 27 June 1947, Oxford, England. Writer; Translator. 1 son, 1 daughter. *Education:* BA Hons, Russian, Czech, School of Slavonic Studies, University of London, 1970. *Publications:* Fathers and Daughters, 1976; Alexandra Kollontai: A Biography, 1980; Blood and Laughter: Images of the 1905 Revolution, 1983; Moscow in World War 2, 1987; Women in Revolutionary Russia, 1987; Larissa Reisner: A Biography, 1988; Translations: Sofia Tolstoya's Diary, 1985; Love of Worker Bees, 1977; A Great Love, 1981; Ship of Widows, 1985; Arise and Walk, 1990; The Best of Ogonyok, 1990; Little Vera, 1990. *Contributions to:* Articles and book reviews to: Independent; Guardian; New Statesman and Society; Independent on Sunday. *Honours:* People's Publishing Prize for translation of Ship of Widows, 1986; Shortlisted, Independent Foreign Fiction Award for Wagibin's Arise and Walk, 1990; numerous drama translations. *Membership:* Society of Authors. *Literary Agent:* Ann McDermid, Curtis Brown.

PORTER Cathy. *See:* **PORTER Catherine Marjorie.**

PORTER Joseph Ashby b. 21 July 1942, Madisonville, Kentucky, USA. University Professor. *Education:* Harvard University 1960-64; Pembroke College, Oxford, 1964-65; University of California, Berkeley, 1965-70. *Publications:* Books: Eelgrass, 1977; The Drama of Speech Acts, 1979; The Kentucky Stories, 1983; Shakespeare's Mercutio 1988; Lithuania, 1990. *Honour:* National Endowment for the Arts Grants 1979, 1985. *Membership:* Associated Writing Programs. *Address:* Department of English, Duke University, Durham, NC 27708, USA.

PORTER Joshua Roy, b. 1921, British. *Appointments:* Fellow, Chaplain and Tutor, Oriel College, Oxford and University Lecturer in Theology, Oxford University, 1949-62; Canon and Prebendary of Wightring, Chichester Cathedral and Theological Lecturer, 1965-; Dean, Faculty of the Arts 1968-71, Department Head and Professor of Theology 1972-86, University of Exeter. *Publications:* Eight Oxford Poets (with J Heath-Stubbs and S Keyes), 1941; Poetry from Oxford in War-Time (with W Bell), World in the Heart, 1944; Promise and Fulfilment (with F F Bruce), Moses and Monarchy, 1963; The Extended Family in the Old Testament, 1967; A Source Book of the Bible for Teachers (with R C Walton), Proclamation and Presence (ed with J I Durham), 1970; The Non-Juring Bishops, 1973; The Journey to the Other World (with H R E Davidson), 1975; The Book of Leviticus, 1976; Animals in Folklore (ed with W D M Russell), The Monarchy, The Crown and the Church, 1978; Tradition and Interpretation (with G W Anderson), 1979; A Basic Introduction to the Old Testament (with R C Walton), Folklore Studies in the Twentieth Century (co-ed), 1980; Divination and Oracles (with M Loewe and C Blacker), The Folklore of Ghosts (with H R E Davidson),1981; Israel's Prophetic Tradition (co-author), 1982; Tracts for Our Times (co-author), 1983; The Hero in Traditional Folklore (with C Blacker), 1984; Arabia and the Gulf: From Traditional Society to Modern States (with I Netton), 1986; (contributor to:) The Seer in Celtic & Other Traditions, 1989; Schöpfung und Befreiung, 1989; Synodical Government in the Church of England, 1990;

Christianity & Conservatism, 1990; Oil of Gladness, 1993; Boundaries & Thresholds (H R E Davidson), 1993. *Membership:* Wiccamical Canon & Prebendary of Exceit, Chichester Cathedral, 1988-. *Address:* 36 Theberton Street, Barnsbury, London N1 0QX, England.

PORTER Peter Neville Frederick, b. 16 Feb 1929, Brisbane, Australia. Freelance Writer; Poet. m. Jannice Henry, 1961, (dec 1974), 2 daughters. *Appointments:* Journalist, Brisbane before coming to England, 1951; Clerk, Bookseller and Advertising Writer, before becoming full-time Poet, Journalist, Reviewer and Broadcaster, 1968-. *Publications:* Once Bitten, Twice Bitten, 1961; Penguin Modern Poets No 2, 1962; Poems, Ancient and Modern, 1967; A Porter Folio, 1969; The Last of England, 1970; Preaching to the Converted, 1972; Translator, After Martial, 1972; (with Arthur Boyd) Jonah, 1973, The Lady and the Unicorn, 1975; Living in a Calm Country, 1975; Joint Editor, New Poetry 1, 1975; The Cost of Seriousness, 1978; English Subtitles, 1981; Collected Poems, 1983; Fast Forward, 1984; (with Arthur Boyd) Narcissus, 1985; Possible Worlds, 1989; The Chain of Babel, 1992. *Honour:* Duff Cooper Prize, 1983. *Address:* 42 Cleveland Square, London W2, England.

PORTERFIELD Nolan, b. 26 Feb 1936, Milliken, Colorado, USA. Writer; Teacher. m. (1) Peggy Pearce, 1956, 1 daughter; (2) Erika Brady, 1981. *Education:* BA, 1962, MA, 1964, Texas Tech University; PhD, University of Iowa, 1970. *Publications:* Trail to Marked Tree, 1968; A Way of Knowing, 1971; Jimmie Rodgers: The Life and Times of America's Blue Yodeler, 1979. *Contributions to:* Book: Country: The Music and The Musicians, 1988; Many short stories and articles in national publications, such as Harpers, North American Review, Sewanee Review, Chicago; Contributions to anthologies. *Honours:* Jesse H Jones Award for Best Novel, Texas Institute of Letters, 1971; ASCAP/Deems Taylor Award, 1979; Grammy Nominee (Best LIner Notes) 1988. *Memberships:* Association for Recorded Sound Collections; American Folklore Association; Authors Guild. *Address:* Greenwood Farm, 564 Boyce-Fairview Road, Alvaton, KY 42122, USA.

PORTIS Charles McColl, b. 28 Dec 1933, El Dorado, Arkansas, USA. Writer. *Education:* BA, University of Arkansas, 1958. *Publications:* Novels: Norwood, 1966; True Grit, 1968; The Dog of the South, 1979; Masters of Atlantis, 1985; Gringos, 1991. *Literary Agent:* Janklow and Nesbit Associates, 598 Madison Avenue, New York, NY 10022, USA. *Address:* 7417 Kingwood, Little Rock, AR 72207, USA.

PORTWAY Christopher, b. 30 Oct 1923, Halstead, Essex, England. Travel Journalist; Author; Novelist; Travel Editor. m. Jaroslava Anna Krupickova, 4 Apr 1957, 1 son, 1 daughter. *Publications:* Journey to Dana, 1955; The Pregnant Unicorn, 1969; All Exits Barred, 1971; Corner Seat, 1972; Lost Vengeance, 1973; Double Circuit, 1974; The Tirana Assignment, 1974; The Anarchy Pedlars, 1976; The Great Railway Adventure, 1983; Journey Along the Spine of the Andes, 1984; The Great Travelling Adventure, 1985; Czechmate, 1987; Indian Odyssey, 1993; A Kenyan Adventure, 1993. *Contributions to:* Times; Daily Telegraph; Times Educational Supplement; Guardian; Country Life; The Lady; Railway Magazine; In-Flight Magazines; Various holiday and Travel Magazines. *Honours:* TD; FRCS; Winston Churchill Fellow, 1993. *Address:* 22 Tower Road, Brighton BN2 2GF, England.

POSNER Richard (Jonathan Craig, Iris Foster, Beatrice Murray, Paul Todd, Dick Wine), b. 1944, American. *Appointments:* English Teacher, Sachem High School, Ronkonkoma, NY; Instructor of Composition, Queenborough Community College, Bayside. *Publications:* The Dark Sonata (as B Murray), 1971; The Moorwood Legacy (as I Foster), The New York Crime Book (as J Craig), Deadly Sea Deadly Sand (as I Foster), 1972; Nightshade (as I Foster), The Sabbath Quest (as I Foster), The Crimson Moon (as I Foster),

Allegro with Passion (as D Wine), The Mafia Man, The Seven-Ups, 1973; The Trigger Man, Welcome Sinner, 1974; Blood All Over (as P Todd), The Image and the Flesh, Lucas Tanner: A Question of Guilt, Lucas Tanner: A Matter of Love, Lucas Tanner: For Her to Decide, 1975; The Lovers, 1978; Impassioned, 1980; Infidelities, 1982; Tycoon, 1983; Jade Moon, The Goldshield (with Marie Castoire), 1984; Bright Desire, 1985.

POSTER Carol, b. 5 Aug 1956, New York City, New York, USA. Writer. m. David Chris Allen, July 1986. *Education:* BA cum laude, Hollins College, 1977; MFA, Eastern Washington University, 1992; Doctoral Fellow, University of Missouri, 1992-. *Appointments:* Contributing Editor, The Sports Guide, 1987-; Teaching Assistant, Eastern Washington University, 1991-92. *Publications:* Unnatural Fauna, non-fiction, 1992; Poetry: Blackbird, 1979; Deceiving the Worms, 1984; Selected Poems of Jacques Prevert, translations, 1987; Surrounded by Dangerous Things, 1993; Anthologised in: Elvis in Oz, 1992; Brand-X Anthology of Poetry; Intro 9; New Poetry 6; Others. *Contributions to:* Ski Magazine; Snow Country; Backpacker; Utah Holiday; The Formalist; Ploughshares; Philosophy and Rhetoric; Rhetoric Society Quarterly. *Honours:* Pullet Surprise, Poultry Magazine, 1984; 2nd Place, Poem Sequence, Utah Original Writing Competition, 1986; Elected, Phi Kappa Phi, 1991; G Ellsworth Huggins Doctoral Fellowship, 1992-. *Memberships:* Modern Language Association; Rocky Mountain Modern Language Association; Rhetoric Society of America; International Society for History of Rhetoric; American Culture Association. *Address:* English Department, 107 Tate Hall, University of Missouri, Columbia, MO 65211, USA.

POSTER Mark, b. 1941, American. *Appointments:* Professor of History, University of California at Irvine, 1978-; Member, Editorial Board, The 18th Century: A Journal of Interpretation. *Publications:* The Utopian Thought of Restif de la Bretonne, Harmonian Man: Selected Writings of Charles Fourier (ed), 1971; Existential Marxism in Postwar France, 1976; Critical Theory of the Family, 1978; Sartre's Marxism, 1979; Foucault, Marxism and History, 1984; Baudrillard: Selected Writings, (ed. and Intro., Mark Poster), 1988; Critical Theory and Poststructuralism, 1989; The Mode of Information, 1990; Postsuburban California: The Social Transformation of Orange County Since 1945, (ed. Rob Kling, Spencer Olin and Mark Poster), 1991. *Address:* History Department, University of California at Irvine, Irvine, CA 92717, USA.

POSTMA Johannes, b. 14 Jan 1935. University Professor. *Education:* BA, Graceland College, 1962; MA, University of Kansas, 1964; PhD, Michigan State University, 1970. *Appointments:* Instructor, Western Michigan University, 1964-68; Assistant Professor to full Professor, Mankato State University, 1969-; Visiting Professor, Leiden Rijksuniversiteit, 1986-87. *Publication:* The Dutch in the Atlantic Slave Trade, 1600-1815, 1990. *Memberships:* American Historical Association; Social Science History Association; Royal Institute of Linguistics and Anthropology. *Address:* 50 Woodview Drive, Mankato, MN 56001, USA.

POTTER Beverley Ann, b. 3 Mar 1944, Summit, New Jersey, USA. Psychologist; Publisher; Business Executive. *Education:* BA, 1966, MS, 1968, San Francisco State University; PhD, Stanford University, 1974. *Publications:* Chlorella: The Amazing Alchemist; Turning Around: Keys to Motivation and Productivity, 1980, 81, 85, 89; Beating Job Burnout: How to Transform Work Pressure into Productivity, 1980, 81, 85; The Way of the Ronin: Riding the Waves of Change at Work, 1985, 86, 89; Preventing Job Burnout: A Work Book, 1987; Drug Testing at Work: A Guide for Employers and Employees, 90; The Paathfinder's Craft: Tools for Personal Leadership, 1993; Brain Boosters: Foods & Drugs That Make You Smarter, 1993. *Contributions to:* Numerous contributions to journals and magazines. *Memberships:* North California Book Publicists Association; North California Booksellers Association; Bay Area Organisation Development

Network - formerly National Speakers Association. *Address:* PO Box 1035, Berkeley, CA 94701, USA.

POTTER Clarkson Nott, b. 17 May, 1928, New Jersey, USA. Editor; Writer. m. (1) Ruth Delafield, 1949, (2) Pamela Howard, 1974, (3) Helga Maass, 1981-. 3 sons, 2 daughters. *Education:* Graduated, St Andrew's School, Middletown, Delaware, 1946; BA, Union College, Schenectady, New York, 1950. *Appointments:* Editor, 1952-55, Senior Editor 1955-58, Advertising Manager, 1958-59, Doubleday & Co.; Managing Editor, The Dial Press 1959-60; President and Editor-in-Chief, 1960-64, Editor-in-Chief, 1964-77, Clarkson N Potter, Inc, Publisher; President, The Brandywine Press, 1979-82; President, The Kestrel Press, 1991-; Adjunct Professor, Department of English, Brown University, Providence, Rhode Island, 1982-. *Publications:* Who Does What and Why in Book Publishing, 1990; Writing for Publication, 1990, 1991. *Honour:* The Carey-Thomas Awards, Special Citation for Creative Publishing, 1970. *Membership:* The Century Association, New York. *Address:* 5 Westwood Road, Jamestown, RI 02835, USA.

POTTER Dennis (Christopher George), b. 17 May 1935. Playwright; Author; Journalist. m. Margaret Morgan, 1959, 1 son, 2 daughters. *Education:* BA, Honours in PPE, Oxon, 1959. *Appointments:* BBC TV, Current Affairs, 1959-61; Daily Herald, Feature Writer, then TV Critic, 1961-64; Contested (Labour) East Herts, 1964; Leader Writer, The Sun, 1964; TV Critic, Sunday Times, 1976-78. *Publications:* First TV Play, 1965; (Television Plays) Vote Vote Vote for Nigel Barton, 1968; Stand Up Nigel Barton; Where the Buffalo Road; A Beast with Two Backs; Son of Man; Traitor; Paper Roses; Casanova; Follow the Yellow Brick Road; Only Make Believe; Joe's Ark; Schmoedipus; Late Call, (adapted from novel by Angus Wilson), 1975; Brimstone and Treacle, 1976; Double Dare, 1976; Where Adam Stood, 1976; Pennies from Heaven (sextet), 1978; Blue Remembered Hills, 1979; Blade on the Feather, Rain on the Roof, Cream in My Coffee, 1980; Tender is the Night (sextet from Scott Fitzgerald), 1985; The Singing Detective (sextet), 1986; Blackeyes, 1990; (Screenplays) Pennies from Heaven, 1981; Brimstone and Treacle, 1982; Gorky Park, 1983; Dreamchild, 1985; (Stage Play) Sufficient Carbohydrate, 1983; The Glittering Coffin; Waiting for the Boat (3 plays), 1984; Lipstick On Your Collar, (televised 1993); Novels include: Hide and Seek, 1973; Ticket to Ride, 1986. *Honours:* BAFTA Award, 1978, 1980; Prix Italia, 1982. *Address:* Morecambe Lodge, Duxmere, Ross-on-Wye, Herefordshire, HR9 5BB, England.

POTTER Jeremy, b. 25 Apr 1922, London, England. Writer; Publisher. m. 11 Feb 1950, 1 son, 1 daughter. *Education:* MA, Queen's College, Oxford. *Publications:* Good King Richard?, 1983; Pretenders, 1986; Independent Television in Britain, vol.3: Politics and Control, 1968-80, (1989) and vol.4: Companies and Programmes, 1968-80, (1990). Novels: Hazard Chase, 1964; Death in Office, 1965; Foul Play, 1967; The Dance of Death, 1968; A Trail of Blood, 1970; Going West, 1972; Disgrace and Favour, 1975; Death in the Forest, 1977; The Primrose Hill Murder, 1992. *Address:* The Old Pottery, Larkins Lane, Headington, Oxford, OX3 9DW, England.

POTTER Margaret (Anne Betteridge, Anne Melville, Margaret Newman), b. 21 June 1926, Harrow, Middlesex, England. Author. m. Jeremy Potter, 11 Feb 1950, 1 son, 1 daughter. *Education:* Major Scholar, Modern History, St Hugh's College, Oxford; MA (Oxon); Book Production course, London School of Printing. *Appointments:* Editor, children's missionary magazine, 5 years. *Publications:* Murder To Music (as Margaret Newman); The Touch-and-Go Year; The Blow-and-Grow Year; Sandy's Safari; The Story of the Stolen Necklace; Tony's Special Place; The Boys Who Disappeared; Trouble on Sunday; The Motorway Mob; Tilly and the Princess; Unto The Fourth Generation; Lochandar; As Anne Betteridge: The Foreign Girl; The Young Widow; Spring in Morocco; The Long Dance of Love; The

Younger Sister; Return to Delphi; Single to New York; The Truth Game; A Portuguese Affair; A Little Bit of Luck; Shooting Star; Love in a Rainy Country; The Girl Outside; Journey from a Foreign Land; The Sacrifice; A Time of Their Lives, short stories; The Temp; A Place for Everyone, short stories; The Tiger and the Goat; As Anne Melville: The Lorimer Line; The Lorimer Legacy; Lorimers at War; Lorimers in Love; The Last of the Lorimers; Lorimer Loyalties; The House of Hardie; Grace Hardie; The Hardie Inheritance; The Dangerfield Diaries; Sirocco; The Stranger on the Beach; The Tantivy Trust; A Clean Break; Snapshots, short stories. *Contributions to:* Fiction reviews; Travel articles; Short stories in magazines. *Memberships:* Adviser, Citizens Advice Bureau, 8 years; Grant Allocation Committee, King Edward VII Fund, 5 years. *Address:* c/o Peters Fraser and Dunlop, 5th Floor, The Chambers, Chelsea Harbour, Lots Road, London SW10 0XF, England.

POTTS Richard, b. 1938, British. *Appointment:* Head Teacher, Great Ouseburn Primary School, York. *Publications:* An Owl for His Birthday, 1966; The Haunted Mine, 1968; A Boy and His Bike, 1976; Tod's Owl, 1980; Battleground, 1987; Molly With Ginger, 1993. *Address:* 142 Main Street, Fulford, York YO1 4PS, England.

POTTS Willard C, b. 26 Dec 1929. Professof of Englilsh. m. Patricia C Cotter, 2 Oct 1954, 1 son, 1 daughter. *Education:* BA, 1952, MA, 1956, PhD, 1969, University of Washington. *Appointments:* Department of Englilsh, Oregon State University, 1959-, currently Professor of English. *Publication:* Portraits of the Artist in Exile, 1979. *Contributions to:* James Joyce Quarterly; James Joyce Annual. *Memberships:* American Conference for Irish Studies; International James Joyce Foundation. *Address:* 115 NW 32, Corvallis, OR 97330, USA.

POULIN Gabrielle, b. 21 June 1929, St Prosper, Quebec, Canada. Writer. *Education:* MA University Montreal; Lic Letters; Dip Higher Studies; DLitt, University Sherbroke. *Appointments:* Writer in residence, Ottawa Public Library, 1988. *Publications:* Les Miroirs d'un poete: image et reflets de Paul Eluard, 1969; Cogne la caboche, 1979; L'Age de l'interrogation, 1937-52, 1980; Romans du pays, 1968-79, 1980; Un cri trop grand, 1980; Les Mensonges d'Isabelle, novel, 1983; All the Way Home, originally published as Cogne la caboche, translated by Jane Pentland, 1984. *Contributions to:* Voix et images; Lettres quebecoises; Relations. *Honours:* Prize, Swiss Embassy, 1967; Grant, Arts Council of Canada on 11 occasions, 1968-83, 1985. Press Lit. prize, 1979; Champlain Lit Prize, 1979. *Memberships:* Union Quebecois Writers; Société des écrivains canadieux de l'Ontaouais. *Literary Agent:* Rene Dionne, Lettres Francaises, University of Ottawa. *Address:* 1997 Avenue Quincy, Ottawa, Ontario, Canada K1J 6B4.

POUPLIER Erik, b. 16 June 1926, Svendborg, Denmark. Writer. m. Annalise Hansen, 28 Sept 1947, 1 daughter. *Education:* Trained as Journalist. *Publications:* In Danish: Lend Me Your Wife, 1957; My Castle in Lardeche, 1968; the Gentle Revolt, 1970; The Discreet Servant of the Death, 1972; The Adhesive Pursuer, 1973; Murder, Mafia and Pastis'er, 1974; My Castle in Provence, 1979; The Old Man in Provence, 1980; The Clumsy Kidnappers, 1981; The World of Annesisse, 1982; The Galic Cock, 1984; My Own Provence, 1984; The Cuisine of Provence, 1985; Panic in Provence, 1986; All year Round in Provence, 1987; Machiavelli, 1987; The Anaconda-coup in Provence, 1988; Long Live the grandparents, 1988; Barbaroux and the Flood, 1989; Always around the next corner (memoirs), 1990; Pearls of Provence, 1991; Barbaroux and the nuns, 1992; Merry-go-round, 1993. *Contributions to:* Jyllands Posten, Denmark. *Memberships:* Danish Authors Society; Danish Press Association. *Address:* Les Charmettes, Chemin de Plateau, 83550 Vidauban, France.

POURNELLE Jerry Eugene (Wade Curtis), b. 1933, USA. Freelance Writer, Lecturer and Consultant. *Publications:* Red Heroin (as Wade Curtis), novel, 1969; The Strategy of Technology: Winning the Decisive War (with Stefan Possony), 1970; Red Dragon (as Wade Curtis), novel, 1971; A Spaceship for the King, 1973; Escape from the Planet of the Apes, novelization of screenplay, 1973; The Mote in God's Eye (with Larry Niven), 1974; 20/20 Vision (editor), 1974; Birth of Fire, 1976; Inferno (with Larry Niven), 1976; West of Honor, 1976; High Justice, short stories, 1977; The Mercenary, 1977; Lucifer's Hammer (with Larry Niven), 1977; Exiles to Glory, 1978; Black Holes (editor), 1979; A Step Further Out, non-fiction, 1980; Janissaries, 1980; Oath of Fealty (with Larry Niven), 1981; Clan and Crown (with Roland Green), 1982; There Will Be War (co-editor), 1983; Mutual Assured Survival (with Dean Ing), 1984; Men of War (co-editor), 1984; Blood and Iron (co-editor), 1984; Day of the Tyrant (co-editor), 1985; Footfall (with Larry Niven), 1985; Warriors (co-editor), 1986; Imperial Stars: The Stars at War, Republic and empire (co-editor), 2 vols, 1986-87; Guns of Darkness (co-editor), 1987; Storms of Victory (with Roland Green), novel, 1987; Legacy of Heorot (with Larry Niven), novel, 1987; Prince of Mercenaries, 1989; The Gripping Hand (with Larry Niven), 1993. *Contributions to:* Non-fiction articles to Galaxy magazine, 1974-78; Consulting Editor and Columnist, Byte Magazine. *Memberships:* Fellow, Operations Research Society of America; Fellow, American Association for the Advancement of Science; President, Science Fiction Writers of America, 1974. *Address:* 12190 1/2 Ventura Blvd, Box 372, Studio City, CA 91604, CA, USA.

POWE B W (Bruce William), b. 23 Mar 1955, Ottawa, Ontario, Canada. Author; Teacher. m. Robin Leslie Mackenzie, 7 Sept 1991, 1 son, 1 daughter. *Education:* BA, Special Honours, York University, Toronto; MA, University of Toronto. *Publications:* A Climate Charged, 1984; The Solitary Outlaw, 1987; Noise of Time, text for Glenn Gould Profile, 1989; A Tremendous Canada of Light, 1993; Outage: A Journey into the Electric City, 1994. *Contributions to:* The Globe and Mail; The Toronto Star; The Antigonish Review; The Bennington Review; Exile; Modern Drama. *Honours:* York University Book Award, 1977; Special MA Scholarship to University of Toronto, 1979; Explorations Grant, Canada Council, 1980; Maclean-Hunter Fellowship, 1989. *Literary Agent:* Dean Cooke, Livingston Cooke-Curtis Brown, Canada. *Address:* 253 Bedford Park Avenue, Toronto, Ontario, Canada M5M 1J6.

POWE Bruce Allen (Ellis Portal), b. 1925, Canadian. *Appointments:* Special Assistant, Minister of Mines and Technical Surveys, 1951-57; Editorial Assistant, Imperial Oil Limited, 1957-60; Executive Director, Ontario Liberal Association, 1960-63; Vice-President, Public Relations, Baker Advertising Limited, 1964-66; Vice-President of Public Affairs, Canadian Life and Health Insurance Association, Toronto, 1966-90. *Publications:* Expresso '67, 1966; Killing Ground: The Canadian Civil War (as E Portal), 1968, under own name, 1972; The Last Days of the American Empire, 1974; The Aberhart Summer, 1983; The Ice Eaters, 1987. *Address:* 158 Ridley Boulevard, Toronto, Ontario M5M 3M1, Canada.

POWELL Anthony (Dymoke), b. 21 Dec 1905, British. Writer. m. Lady Violet Pakenham, 1934, 2 sons. *Education:* Balliol College, Oxford. *Appointments:* With Duckworth, publishers, 1926-35; Literary Editor, Punch, 1953-59; Trustee, National Portrait Gallery, 1962-76, London. *Publications:* Afternoon Men, 1931; Venusburg, 1932; From a View to a Death (in US as Mr Zouch: Superman: From a View to a Death), 1933; Agents and Patients, 1936; What's Become of Waring, 1939; Novels of High Society from the Victorian Age (ed), 1947; John Aubrey and His Friends, 1948, 1963; Brief Lives and Other Selected Writings of John Aubrey (ed), 1949; A Question of Upbringing, 1951; A Buyer's Market, 1952; The Acceptance World, 1955; At Lady Molly's, 1957; Casanova's Chinese Restaurant, 1960; The Kindly Ones, 1962; The Valley of Bones, 1964; The

Soldier's Art, 1966; The Military Philosophers, 1968; The Garden God and The Rest I'll Whistle: The Text of Two Plays, Books Do Furnish a Room, 1971; Temporary Kings, 1973; Hearing Secret Harmonies, 1975; Infants of the Spring, 1976; Messengers of Day, 1978; Faces in My Time, 1980; The Strangers All Are Gone, 1982; O, How the Wheel Becomes It!, 1983; To Keep the Ball Rolling, (abridged Memoirs), 1983; The Fisher King, 1986; Miscellaneous Verdicts, (Criticism), 1990; Under Review (criticism), 1992. *Honours:* CBE, 1956; CH, 1988; Orders of White Lion (Czechoslovakia) Leopold II (Belgium), Oaken Crown and Croix de Guerre (Luxembourg); James Tait Black Prize; Hon. D.Litt., Sussex, Leicester, Kent, Oxford, Bristol; Hon. Fellow, Balliol College, Oxford, 1974; W.H.Smith Award, 1974; The Hudson Review Bennett Award, 1984; Ingersoll Foundation; Hon D Litt, Wales, 1992. *Address:* The Chantry, Nr Frome, Somerset BA11 3LJ, England.

POWELL Barry Bruce, b. 30 Apr 1942, Sacramento, California, USA. Professor of Classics. m. Patricia Cox, 27 Sept 1967, 1 son, 1 daughter. *Education:* BA, Classics, 1963, PhD, Classics, 1970, University of California, Berkeley; MA, Classics, Harvard University, 1965. *Appointments:* Northern Arizona University, 1969-73; University of Wisconsin, Madison, 1973-; University of California, Berkeley, 1984. *Publications:* Composition by Theme in the Odyssey, 1977; The Origin of the Puzzling Supplementals, 1987; The Dipylon O'nochoe Inscription and the Spread of Literacy in 8th Century Athens, 1988; Why Was the Greek Alphabet Invented: The Epigraphic Evidence, 1989; Homer and the Origin of the Greek Alphabet, 1991; Classical Myth, 1993. *Honours:* General Motors National Scholarship, 1959-63; Phi Beta Kappa, 1962; Woodrow Wilson Fellowship, 1964- 65. *Memberships:* American Philological Association; President, Phi Beta Kappa; Archaeological Institute of America; Classical Association of Midwest and South. *Address:* 1210 Sweetbriar Road, Madison, WI 53705, USA.

POWELL (Elizabeth), Dilys, TV Film Critic; Film Critic. m. (1) Humfry Payne, 1926, (dec 1936), (2) Leonard Russell, 1943, (dec 1974). *Education:* Somerville College, Oxford. *Appointments:* Editorial Staff, Sunday Times, 1928-31, 1936-41; Film Critic, 1939-76, TV Film Critic, 1976-, The Sunday Times; Film Critic, Punch, 1979-1992. *Publications:* Descent from Parnassus, 1934; Remember Greece, 1941; The Traveller's Journey is Done, 1943; Coco, 1952; An Affair of the Heart, 1957; The Villa Ariadne, 1973; The Golden Screen, (Collected Reviews), 1989; The Dilys Powell Film Reader, (Collected reviews), 1991. *Honour:* CBE, 1974; Hon Fellow, Somerville College, 1992. *Memberships:* Board of Governors, British Film Institute, 1948-52, Fellow, 1986; Independent Television Authority, 1954-57; Cinematograph Films Council, 1965-69; President, Classical Association, 1966-67; Honorary Member, ACTT. *Address:* 14 Albion Street, Hyde Park, London W2 2AS, England.

POWELL (John) Enoch, b. 1912, British. Poetry, Classics, History, Politics/Government. Translations. *Appointments:* Ulster Unionist Member of Parliament (U.K.) for South Down, N. Ireland., 1974-87, (Conservative M.P. for Wolverhampton South-West, 1950-74). *Publications:* The Rendel Harris Papyri, 1936; First Poems, 1937; A Lexicon to Herodotus, 1938; The History of Herodotus, 1939; Casting Off and Other Poems, 1939; Herodotus, Book VIII, 1939; Llyfr Blegywryd, 1942; Thucydidis, Historia, 1942; (trans.) Herodotus, 1949; (with others) One Nation, 1950; Dancer's End and the Wedding Gift, 1951; The Social Services: Needs and Means, 1952; (with others) Change Is Our Ally, 1954; (with A. Maude) Biography of a Nation, 1955; Saving in a Free Society, 1960; Great Parliamentary Occasions, 1960; A Nation Mot Afraid, 1965; A New Look at Medicine and Politics, 1966; (with K. Wallis) The House of Lords in the Middle Ages, 1968; Freedom and Reality, 1969; Income Tax at 4/3 in the Pound, 1970; The Common Market: The Case Against, 1971; Still to Decide, 1972; No Easy Answers, 1973; Wrestling with the Angel, 1977; Joseph Chamberlain,

1977; A Nation or No Nation, 1978; Collected Poems, 1990; Enoch Powell on 1992 (ed E Ritchie), 1992. *Address:* 33 South Eton Place, London SW1, England.

POWELL Geoffrey Stewart, (Tom Angus), b. 25 Dec 1914, Scarborouogh, Yorkshire, England. Soldier; Writer. m. Felicity Wadsworth, 15 July 1944, 1 son, 1 daughter. *Education:* Scarborough College 1923-31; Army Staff College, 1945-46; United States Command and General Staff College, 1950-51; Joint Services Staff College, 1953-54; BA, Open University, 1981. *Publications:* The Green Howards, 1968; The Kandyan Wars, 1973; Men at Arnhem, 1978; Suez: The Double War (with Roy Fullick) 1979; The Book of Campden, 1982; The Devil's Birthday: The Bridges to Arnhem, 1984; Plumer: The Soldiers' General, 1990; The Green Howards: 300 Years of Service, 1992. *Contributions to:* Numerous contributions to journals and magazines. *Honours:* Fellow, Royal Historical Society, 1989. *Address:* c/o Army and Navy Club, Pall Mall, London SW1, England.

POWELL Joseph E, b. 22 Jan. 1952, Ellensburg, Washington, USA. Teacher. *Education:* BA, English Literature, University of Washington, 1975; MA, English Literature, 1978; BA, Education, Central Washington University, 1982; MFA, Creative Writing, University of Arizona, 1981. *Publications:* Counting the Change, 1986; Winter Insomnia, 1993. *Contributor include:* Science Monitor; Alaska Quarterly Review; Seattle Review; Southern Poetry Review; Hawaii Review. *Honours:* Book Award, Quarterly Review of Literature's International Poetry Contest, 1986. *Memberships:* President, Ellensburg Arts Commission; Alpine Lakes Protection Society. *Address:* Route 4, Box 241, Ellensburg, Washington 98926, USA.

POWELL Neil, b. 11 Feb 1948, London, England. Writer; Editor. *Education:* BA, 2:1 English & American Literature 1966-69, MPhil, English Literature 1969-71, University of Warwick. *Publications:* At The Edge, (poems), 1977; Carpenters of Light (criticism), 1979; A Season of Calm Weather (poems), 1982; Selected Poems of Fulke Greville (edited), 1990; True Colours: New & Selected Poems, 1991; Unreal City (novel), 1992; The Stones on Thorpeness Beach (poems), forthcoming. *Contributions to:* Critical Quarterly; Encounter; Gay Times; The Guardian; the Listener; London Magazine; New Statesman; PN Review; Poetry Review; Times Literary Supplement. *Honours:* Society of Authors Gregory Award, 1969; Authors' Foundation Award, 1992. *Memberships:* Greenpeace; Poetry Society; Society of Authors. *Literary Agent:* A.P. Watt. *Address:* c/o Carcanet Press Limited, 208-212 Corn Exchange Buildings, Manchester M4 3BQ, England.

POWELL Padgett, b. 25 Apr 1952, Gainesville, Florida, USA. Professor of Creative Writing. m. Sidney Wade, 22 May 1984, 2 daughters. *Education:* BA, College of Charleston, 1975; MA, University of Houston, 1982. *Appointments:* Freight handler, household mover and orthodontic technician in southern United States, including Jacksonville, Florida; Florence, South Carolina and Charleston, South Carolina, 1968-75; Day labourer, Houston, Texas, 1975; Roofer in Texas 1975-82, Writer 1983-; Professor of Creative Writing, University of Florida, Gainesville, 1984-. *Publications:* Edisto (novel) 1984; A Woman Named Drown (novel) 1987; Contributor, Alex Harris (ed) A World Unsuspected: Portraits of Southern Childhood, 1987; Typical (stories), 1991. *Contributions to:* Stories to periodicals, including Esquire, The New Yorker and Grand Street. *Honours:* Edisto named one of the year's five best books, 1984 by Time; American Book Award nominee for first fiction, 1984 and Whiting Foundation Writers' Award 1986, both for Edisto; American Academy and Institute of Arts and Letters Rome Fellowship in Literature 1987. *Memberships:* P.E.N.; Authors Guild; Writers Guild of America, East. *Literary Agent:* Cynthia Cannell, Janklow & Nesbit, 598 Madison Avenue, New York, NY 10022, USA. *Address:* Department of English, University of Florida, Gainesville, Fl 32611, USA.

POWELL Talmage (Jack McCready, Ellery Queen, Anne Talmage), b. 1920, USA. Author. *Publications:* Novels: The Girl from the Big Pine, 1961; The Cage, 1969; Mission: Impossible - The Priceless Particle, 1969; The Thing in B-3, 1969; Mission: Impossible - The Money Explosion, 1979; Dark over Arcadia (as Anne Talmage), 1971; Mystery novels: The Killer Is Mine, 1959; The Smasher, 1959; The Girl's Number Doesn't Answer, 1960; Man-Killer, 1960; The Girl Who Killed Things, 1960; What a Madman Behind Me, 1962; Start Screaming Murder, 1962; The Raper (as Jack McCready), 1962; Murder with a Past (as Ellery Queen), 1963; Beware the Young Stranger (as Ellery Queen), 1965; Corpus Delectable, 1965; Where is Bianca (as Ellery Queen), 1966; Who Spies, Who Kills (as Ellery Queen), 1966. Other: Cellar Team, juvenile, 1972. *Contributions to:* Anthologies: Numerous including: Bad Girls, 1958; The Saint Mystery Library, 1959; Best Detective Stories of The Year, 1961; The Fireside Treasury of Modern Humor, 1963; Mink Is For a Minx, 1964; Alfred Hitchcock's Witches' Brew, 1965; Treasury of Great Western Stories, 1966; Alfred Hitchcock's Games Killers Play, 1967; Alfred Hitchcock's Coffin Corner, 1968; Alfred Hitchcock's Death Mate, 1973 and many more. More recent works include: Alfred Hitchcock's A Choice of Evils, 1983; Alfred Hitchcock's Grave Suspicions, 1984; Alfred Hitchcock's Crime Watch, 1984; Alfred Hitchcock's A Brief Darkness, 1987; 14 Vicious Valentines, 1988; Dixie Ghosts, 1988; More Wild Westerns, 1989; A Treasury of American Mysteries, 1989; Curses! 1989; Lighthouse Horrors, 1990; Back From the Dead, 1990; Loaded for Bear, 1990. A volume of short stories, written for Hitchcock, 25 Twisted Tales of Revenge and Intrigue, 1989; 25 TV/ Motion pictures, stories and/or screenplays; Translations in 11 languages. *Address:* 33 Caledonia Road, Kenilworth, Asheville, NC 28803, USA.

POWELL Violet, b. 1912, British. *Publications:* Five Out of Six, 1960; A Substantial Ghost, 1967; The Irish Cousins, 1970; A Compton-Burnett Compendium, 1973; Within the Family Circle, 1976; Margaret, Countess of Jersey, 1978; Flora Annie Steel, Novelist of India, 1981; The Constant Novelist, 1983; The Album of Anthony Powell's Dance to the Music of Time (ed), 1987; The Life of A Provincial Lady: A Study of E M Delafield and Her Works, 1988; A Jane Austen Compendium, 1993. *Address:* The Chantry, Nr Frome, Somerset, BA11 3LJ, England.

POWELL-SMITH Vincent (Francis Elphinstone, Justiciar, Santa Maria), b. 28 Apr 1939, Westerham, Kent, England, Advocatem, m. (1) 2 daughters, (2) Martha Marilyn Du Barry, 4 Apr 1989. *Education:* University of Birmingham; International Faculty of Comparative Law, Luxembourg; Inns of Court School of Law, London; Gray's Inn; LLB, Honours; LLM; DLitt; Dip Com; DSL. *Appointments:* Professor of Construction Law, Universiti Teknologi Malaysia, 1990-; Joint Editor, Construction Law Reports, 1984-; Consultant Editor, Emden's Building Contracts and Practice, 1980; Series Editor, Architectural Press Library of Building Control. *Publications:* The Building Regulations Explained, 8th edition, 1990; Building Contract Claims, 2nd edition, 1988; Horse and Stable Management, 1984; The JCT Standard Building Contract, 2nd edition, 1989; Building Contract Casebook, 2nd edition, 1990; Building Contract Dictionary, 2nd edition, 1990; Horse Business Management, 1989; Engineering Contract Dictionary, 1989; Law of Boundaries and Fences; You and the Law, 1986; Author of over 60 books. *Contributions to:* Legal Correspondent, Contract Journal, 1974-; Legal Correspondent, Surveyor, 1980-; Architect's Journal; Law Society's Gazette; Financial Times; Daily Telegraph; The Field; New Law Journal. *Honours:* Liveryman, Worshipful Company of Paviors; Freeman of the City of London; Knight of Honour, Royal Yugoslavian Order of St John; Kt Cdr, Order of Polonia Restituta. *Memberships:* Fellow, Chartered Institute of Arbitrtators; Fellow, British Academy of Experts. *Address:* Apartado 127, 8126 Quarteira Codex, Portugal.

POWER Edward, b. 16 June 1951, Mooncoin, Co.

Kilkenny, Ireland. Writer; Historian. *Education:* Mooncoin BNS; Mooncoin Vocational and Technical School. *Appointments:* Worked for photographic firm in London; Literature Officer, Waterford Arts Centre, 1986-87; Publisher and Editor, Riverine literary magazine; Press correspondent, Kilkenny People newspaper; Local historian. *Publications:* Poetry and short stories included in: The Second Blackstaff Book of Short Stories, 1991, The Kilkenny Anthology, 1991, The Cloverdale Anthology of Irish Poets, 1992. *Contributions to:* New Irish Writing (Irish Press & Sunday Tribune); Poetry Ireland Review; Cyphers; Cloverdale Anthology; Kilkenny Magazine; Passages 4; The Salmon; Criterion. *Honours:* Winner, Waterford Literary Competition for Short Fiction, 1981; Shortlisted for Hennessy Literary Award, 1987; Story, entitled Faith Healer, won first place in a competition organised by Kilkenny County Council in conjunction with The Book Centre and Radio Kilkenny, 1991; Shortlisted for US based Cloverdale Library Prize for Irish Poetry, 1992. *Memberships:* Poetry Ireland Society, Dublin. *Address:* Chapel Street, Mooncoin, Co. Kilkenny, Ireland.

POWERS J(ames) F(arl), b. 1917, USA. Academic; Author. *Appointments:* Faculty Member: Marquette University, Milwaukee, 1949- 51; University of Michigan, Ann Arbor, 1956-57; Smith College, Northampton, Massachusetts, 1965-66; St John's University, Collegeville, Minnesota, 1976-. *Publications:* Prince of Darkness and Other Stories, 1947; The Presence of Grace, short stories, 1956; Morte d'Urban, novel, 1962; Look How the Fish Live, 1975; *Address:* c/o Alfred Knopf Inc, 201 East 50th Street, New York, NY 10022, USA.

POWERS M L. *See:* TUBB E C.

POWERS Robert M, b. 9 Nov 1942, Levington, Kentucky, USA. Author. m. 1 Sept 1961, 1 daughter. *Education:* BA, University of Arizona, 1969; University of Edinburgh, Scotland, 1968; MA, University of Western New Meixco. *Appointments:* Aerospace Editor, Revisa Aerea, 1980-; Contributing Editor, Final Frontier, 1987. *Publications:* Planetary Encounters, 1978, 1980; Shuttle, 1979; The Coattails of God, 1981; Mars, 1986; Other Worlds Than Ours, 1983; Moonboot, a Novel, (in progress); Viking Mission to Mars, with others, 1975. *Contributions to:* Over 200 magazine articles, 1970-.*Honours:* Best Book on Science, Library Journal, for Shuttle, 1980; Best Space Book, Av. Space Writers International, 1979, 1980, 1982. *Memberships:* Authors League and Guild; Fellow, Royal Astronomical Society, UK; Aviation Space Writers Association International; Royal Astronomical Society of Canada; Société Astronomique de France. *Agent:* Maggie Nouch, London, England. *Address:* Valencia Mountain Observatory, HCR-1, Box 470, Tucson, AZ 85736, USA.

POWNALL David, b. 1938, United Kingdom. Author. *Appointments:* Resident Writer: Century Theatre touring group, 1970-72; Duke's Theatre, Lancaster, 1972-75; Paines Plough Theatre, Coventry, 1975-80. *Publications:* Verse: An Eagle Each (with J Hill), 1972; Another Country, 1978; Fiction: The Raining Tree War, 1974; African Horse, 1975; My Organic Uncle and Other Stories, 1976; God Perkins, 1977; Light on a Honeycomb, 1978; Beloved Latitudes, 1981; Plays: The Dream of Chief Crazy Horse, 1975; Music to Murder By, 1978; Motocar, and Richard III, Part Two, 1979; An Audience Called Edouard, 1979; Beef (in Best Radio Plays of 1981), 1982; Master Class, 1983; Ploughboy Monday (in Best Radio Plays of 1985), 1986; Other: Between Ribble and Lune: Scenes from the North-West, 1980; The Bunch from Bananas, for children, 1980. *Address:* 136 Cranley Gardens, London N10 3AH, England.

POYER Joe, b. 30 Nov 1939, Battle Creek, Michigan, USA. Author. m. Bonnie Prichard, Oct 1987. *Education:* BA, Communications, Michigan State University, 1961. *Appointments include:* Field Editor, International Combat Arms, Journal of Defence Technology;

Freelance Specialist, high technology military affairs & weaponry; Novalist; Owner and Publisher, North Cape Publications. *Publications:* North Cape, 1968; Balkan Assignment, 1971; Chinese Agenda, 1972; Shooting of the Green, 1973; Devoted Friends, 1982; Time of War, 2 volumes, 1983, 1985. Also: The Contract; Vengeance 10; Tunnel War; Day of Reckoning. *Contributions to:* Journals as listed, also International Defence Images. *Literary Agent:* Diane Clever, 55 5th Avenue, New York City. *Address:* 380 Tustin Avenue, Orange, California 92666, USA.

PRABHASHANKAR T G, (Premi), b. 7 May 1942, Tumkur, India. Reader in Hindi. m. Anu Prabha, 16 Mar 1969, 1 son, 1 daughter. *Education:* MA, Hindi, Mysore University, Mysore, 1965; PhD, Karnatak University, Dharwar, 1977. *Appointments:* Editor, Basava Marg, half-yearly Hindi magazine, Basava Samiti publishers, Bangalore. *Publications:* Kavyabala, poetry in Hindi, 1975; Kannada Aur Hindi Sahitya Ka Tulanatmak Adyayan, 1977; Adhunik Hindi Kavita Par Gandhivad Ka Prabhav, PhD thesis, 1981; Basava Darshan, essay, translation, 1983; Shresta Jeevania, biographies, 1984; Talash, poetry in Hindi, 1988; Kanasugala Kannadi, poetry in Kannada. *Contributions to:* Hindi poems and articles to leading Hindi magazines: Kadambini; Aaj Kal; Samakaleen Bharalia Sahitya; Bhasha. *Honours:* Karnatak State Monetary Award for translation of Basava Darshan, 1983; Souhardh Samman cash award, Uttar Pradesh Government, 1990. *Memberships:* Vice-President, Poets International, Bangalore; Convenor, Authors Guild of India, Bangalore Chapter. *Address:* Prabhu Priya 391, VI Main III Block, III Stage, Basaveswar Nagar, Bangalore 560079, India.

PRABHJOT Kaur b. 6 July 1927, Langarlal, India. Poet; Politician. m. Brigadier Narenderpal Singh, 1948, 2 daughters. *Education;* Punjab University. *Publications:* 35 books including: Poems: Supne Sadhran, 1949; Do Rang, 1951; Pankheru, 1956; lala (in Persian), 1958; Bankapasi, 1958; Pabbi, 1962; Khali, 1967; Waddarshi Sheesha, 1972; Madhiantar, 1974; Chandra Yug, 1978; Dreams Die Young, 1979; Him Hans, 1982; Samrup, 1982; ishq Shara Ki Nata, 1983; Short Stories: Kinke 1952; Aman de Na, 1956; Zindgi de Kujh Pal, 1982. *Honours:* Most Distinguished Order of Poetry, World Poetry Society, 1974; Woman of the year, UPLI, Philippines, 1975; Sewa Sifti Award, 1980; NIF Cultural award, 1982; Josh Kenya Award, 1982; Delhi State Award, 1983; Poet Laureat, Punjab Government. *Memberships:* Legislative Council, Punjab, 1966-; Sahitya Akademi. *Address:* D-203 Defence Colony, New Delhi 110024, India.

PRALL Stuart Edward, b. 2 June 1929, Saginaw, Michigan, USA. Professor of History; Author. m. Naomi Shafer, 20 Jan 1958, 1 son, 1 daughter. *Education:* BA, Michigan State University, 1951; MA, University of Rhode Island, 1953; University of Manchester, England, 1953-54; PhD, Columbia University, 1960. *Appointments:* Queens College, City University of New York, 1955-58, 1960-; Newark State College, New Jersey, 1958-60; Executive Officer, Ph.D Program in History, Graduate School, CUNY, 1988-. *Publications:* The Agitation for Law Reform during the Puritan Revolution, 1640-1660, 1966; The Puritan Revolution: A Documentary History, 1968, 1969, 1973; The Bloodless Revolution: England, 1688, 1972, 1974, 1985; A History of England, 1984, 1991; Church and State in Tudor and Stuart England, 1993. *Contributions to:* The Development of Equity in Tudor England, to American Journal of Legal History. *Honours:* Fulbright Scholar, University of Manchester, 1953-54; Fellow, Royal Historical Society, 1978. *Memberships:* American Historical Association; North American Conference on British Studies. *Address:* 1479 Court Place, Hewlett, NY 11557, USA.

PRANDOTA Miroslaw, b. 4 Nov 1938, Czersk. Journalist. m. Ewa Umiecka, 30 Mar 1987, 2 sons. *Education:* Polish Philology, 1963; Psychology, 1970, both Catholic Universities of Lublin. *Appointments:* Psychiatric Hospital, Gniezno, 1970; The Cultural

Weekly, Warsaw. *Publications:* The Last Fight of Gladiators, 1982; Dance of Life, 1983; The Catch Those Days, 1977; The Four Minors and One Major, 1979; Queers, 1985; Waiting for the Wind, 1985; Hazardsmen and Magicians, 1986; The Image of the Public Man, 1986; On the Black, 1987. *Contributions to:* Renaissance. *Honours:* Literary Award, President of the Union of Polish Writers, 1977; Ministry of Culture Prize, 1987. *Membership:* Union of Polish Writers. *Address:* Karolkowa 66/74 m. 46, 01-193, Warsaw, Poland.

PRANTERA Amanda, b. 23 Apr 1942, England. Author. *Publications:* Strange Loop, 1984; The Cabalist 1985; Conversations with Lord Byron on Perversion, 163 Years After His Lordship's Death, 1987; The Side of the Moon, 1991; Proto-Zoe, 1992. *Literary Agent:* Jane Conway-Gordon, London. *Address:* Jane Conway-Gordon, 1 Old Compton Street, London W1V 5PH, England.

PRASAD Madhusudan, b. 30 Oct 1950, Allahabad, India. Reader in English, University of Allahabad, India. m. Kiran Srivastava, 29 May 1971, 4 daughters. *Education:* BA, 1967, MA, English, 1969, D Phil, 1974, University of Allahabad. *Appointments:* Associate Editor, Orbit, 1983-, Gaya, Bihar, India; Literary Editor, Fantasy, 1992-, Allahabad, India. *Publications:* D H Lawrence: A Study of His Novels, 1980; Anita Desai: The Novelist, 1981; In the Dark/Stories, 1982; ed. Indian-English Novelists: An Anthology of Critical Essays, 1982; ed. Contemporary Indian-English Stories, 1983, 1984, 1988; ed. Perspectives of Kamala Markandaya, 1984; ed. The Poetry of Jayanta Mahapatra: A Critical Study, 1986; ed. Living Indian- English Poets: An Anthology of Critical Essays, 1989. *Contributions to:* Numerous research papers published in journals, magazines and books, which include: World Literature Today (USA); Journal of South Asian Literature (USA); World Literature Written in English (Canada); Indian Literature; Thought; The Literary Half-Yearly (Mysore). *Address:* 134/112 Kothaparcha, off G T Road, Allahabad-211 003, India.

PRATCHETT Terry, b. 1948, England. Author. m. 1 daughter. *Appointments:* Worked as Journalist, now full-time writer. *Publications:* The Colour of Magic, 1983; Wyrd Sisters, 1989; Truckers, 1990; Small Gods, 1991; Reaper Man, 1991; Lords and Ladies, 1992; Witches Abroad, 1992; The Light Fantastic; Equal Rites; Mort; Sorcery; Strata; The Dark Side of the Sun. *Address:* c/o Corgi.

PRATHER Richard (David Knight, Douglas Ring), b. 1921, USA. Author. *Publications:* Case of the Vanishing Beauty, 1950; Bodies in Bedlam, 1951; Everybody Has a Gun, 1951; Find This Woman, 1951; Way of a Wanton, 1952; Darling It's Death, 1952; Lie Down, Killer, 1952; Dagger of Flesh, 1952; Pattern for Murder (as David Knight), 1952; The Peddler (as Douglas Ring), 1952; Too Many Crooks, 1953; Always Leave 'em Dying, 1954; Pattern for Panic, 1954; Strip for Murder, 1955; The Wailing Frail, 1956; Dragnet: Case No 561 (as David Knight), 1956; Have Gat, Will Travel, collection, 1957; Three's a Shroud, collection, 1957; Slab Happy, 1958; Take a Murder, Darling, 1958; Over Her Dear Body, 1959; Double in Trouble (with Stephen Marlowe), 1959; Dance with the Dead, 1960; The Comfortable Coffin (editor), anthology, 1960; Shell Scott's Seven Slaughters, collection, 1961; Dig That Crazy Grave, 1961; Kill the Clown, 1962; The Cockeyed Corpse, 1964; Dead Heat, 1964; The Trojan Hearse, 1964; Kill Him Twice, 1965; Dead Man's Walk, 1965; The Meandering Corpse, 1965; The Kubla Khan Caper, 1966; Gat Heat, 1967; The Cheim Manuscript, 1969; The Shell Scott Sampler, 1969; Kill Me Tomorrow, 1969; Shell Scott's Murder Mix, 1970; Dead-Bang, 1971; The Sweet Ride, 1972; The Sure Thing. *Memberships:* Former Director, Mystery Writers of America.

PRATLEY Gerald Arthur, b. 3 Sept 1923, London, England. Director, Ontario Film Institute. *Education:* Queen's University, Kingston, Ontario. *Literary*

Appointments: Seneca College; University of Toronto; York University. *Publications:* Cinema of John Frankenheimer, 1969; Cinema of Otto Preminger, 1971; Cinema of David Lean, 1974; Cinema of John Huston, 1977; Torn Sprockets: The Uncertain Projection of the Canadian Film, 1985. *Contributions to:* International Film Guide; International TV and Video Guide; Variety, Tribute, Films and Filming; Films in Review, etc. *Honour:* Order of Merit, Poland, 1980; Member, Order of Canada, 1984. *Memberships:* University Film Association; St George's Society; Arts and Letters Club, Toronto. *Address:* Ontario Film Institute, 770 Don Mills Road, Don Mills, Ontario, Canada M3C 1T3.

PRATNEY Winkie (William Alfred),b. 3 Aug 1944, Auckland, New Zealand. Writer; Communicator. m. Facona, 3 Mar 1968, 1 son. *Publications:* Youth Aflame, 1967, 2nd Edition, 1982; Doorways to Discipleship, 1963, 2nd Edition, 1980; Handbook for Followers of Jesus, 1978; Devil Take the Youngest, 1986; Revival-Principles to Change the World, 1984; The Thomas Factor, 1990. *Contributions to:* Accent on Action; BU22, Impact; Forerunner; Grapevine; Challenge; Last Days Magazine; Decision. *Honours:* Nominated Internationl Platform Association 156th year, 1988; Winner Decision Magazine Essay Contest, 1970. *Memberships:* Founder Member of Communication Foundation, Director Youth for Christ, Auckland, New Zealand, 1965. *Address:* PO Box 876, Lindale, TX 75771, USA.

PRATT John Clark (John Winton), b. 19 Aug 1932, St Albans, USA. Writer; Educator. m. (2) Doreen Goodman, 28 June 1968, 1 son, 5 daughters. *Education:* BA, University of California, 1954; MA, Columbia University, New York, 1960; PhD, Princeton University, 1965. *Appointments:* Instructor, English, 1960-66; Assistant Professor, 1965-69, Associate Professor, 1969-73, Professor, 1973-75, USAF Academy; Professor, Colorado State University, 1975-. *Publications:* The Meaning of Modern Poetry, 1962; John Steinbeck, 1970; One Flew Over the Cuckoo's Nest (Editor), 1973; Middlemarch Notebooks, 1978; Vietnam Voices, 1984; The Laotian Fragments, 1985; Co-Author, Reading The Winds, The Literature of the Vietnam War, 1986; Writing from Scratch: The Essay, 1987. *Contributions to:* Vietnam War Literature; Vietnam Perhasie. *Honours:* Fulbright Lecturer, University of Lisbon, Portugal, 1974-75; Fulbright Lecturer, Leningrad State University, USSR, 1980. *Education:* Dept. of English, Colorado State University, Ft. Collins, CO 80523, USA.

PRAWER Siegbert Salomon, b. 15 Feb 1925, Cologne, Federal Republic of Germany. Author and Artist; Educator. *iterary Appointments:* Honorary Fellow and Dean of Degrees, Queen's College, Oxford; Professor of German, emeritus, Oxford University; Lecturer, Birmingham University, 1948-63; Professor of German, Westfield College, London University, 1964-69; Co-Editor: Oxford German Studies, 1971-75; Anglica Germanica, 1973-79. *Publications:* German Lyric Poetry, 1952; Mörike und seine Leser, 1960; Heine's Buch der Lieder: A Critical Study, 1960; Heine, The Tragic Satirist, 1962; (ed) The Penguin Book of Lieder, 1964; The Uncanny in Literature (lecture), 1965; (co-ed), Essays in German Language, Culture and Society, 1969; (ed) The Romantic Period in Germany, 1970; Heine's Shakespeare (lecture), 1970; (ed) Seventeen Modern German Poets, 1971; Comparative Literary Studies, 1973; Karl Marx and World Literature, 1976; Caligari's Children: The Film as Tale of Terror, 1980; Heine's Jewish Comedy, 1983; Frankenstein's Island: England and the English in the Writings of Heinrich Heine, 1986; Israel at Vanity Fair, Jews and Judisum of the Writings of W M Thackeray, 1992. *Honours:* Fellow, British Academy; Corresponding Fellow, German Academy pf Language and Literature; Hon. Fellow, (Hon. Director, 1965-68), London University Institute of Germanic Studies; Hon. Member of Modern Language Association of America; President, Hon Fellow, British Comparative Literature Association, 1984-86; Holder of the Goethe Medal in Gold; Honorary Doctorates from the Universities of Birmingham,

(England) and Cologne, (Germany). *Address:* Queen's College, Oxford, England.

PREBBLE John (Edward Curtis), b. 1915, United Kingdom. Author. *Publications:* Where the Sea Breaks, 1944; The Edge of Darkness, US Edition The Edge of the Night, 1948; Age Without Pity, 1950; The Mather Story, 1954; The Brute Streets, 1954; The High Girders, US Edition Disaster at Dundee, 1956; My Great-Aunt Appearing Day, 1958, reissued with additions as Spanish Stirrup, 1973; Mongaso (with John A Jordan), US Edition Elephants and Ivory, 1959; Spanish Stirrup, 1959; The Buffalo Soldiers, 1959; Culloden, 1961; The Highland Clearances, 1963; Glencoe, 1966; The Darien Disaster, 1968; The Lion in the North, 1971; Mutiny, 1975; John Prebble's Scotland, 1984; The King's Jaunt: George IV in Edinburgh, 1988; Landscapes and Memories, 1993. *Membership:* FRSL. *Address:* Hill View, The Glade, Kingswood, Surrey KT20 6LL, England.

PRELUTSKY Jack, b. 1940, USA. Full-time Writer. *Publications:* The Bad Bear, translation, 1967; A Gopher in the Gardens and Other Animal Poems, 1967; No End of Nonsense, translation, 1968; Lazy Blackbird and Other Verses, 1969; Three Saxon Nobles and Other Verses, 1969; The Terrible Tiger, verse, 1969; Toucans Two and Other Poems, 1971; Circus, verse, 1974; The Pack Rats' Day and Other Poems, 1974; Nightmares: Poems to Trouble Your Sleep, 1976; It's Halloween (Christmas, Thanksgiving, Valentine's Day), verse, 4 vols, 1977-83; The Snopp on the Sidewalk and Other Poems, 1977; The Mean Old Mean Hyena, verse, 1978; The Queen of Eene, verse, 1978; The Headless Horseman Rides Tonight: More Poems to Trouble Your Sleep, 1980; Rainy Day Saturday, verse, 1980; Rolling Harvey Down the Hill, verse, 1980; The Sheriff of Rottenshot, verse, 1982; Kermit's Garden of Verses, 1982; The Baby Uggs Are Hatching, verse, 1982; The Random House Book of Poetry for Children, 1983; It's Snowing, It's Snowing, 1984; What I Did Last Summer, 1984; New Kid on the Block, 1984; My Parents Think I'm Sleeping, 1985; Ride a Pink Pelican, 1986. *Address:* c/o Greenwillow Books, 105 Madison Avenue, New York, NY 10016, USA.

PREMI. *See:* **PRABHASHANKAR T G.**

PRESCOTT J(ohn) R(obert) V(ictor), b. 1931, Australia. Professor of Geography, University of Melbourne. *Publications:* The Geography of Frontiers and Boundaries, 1965, Revised Edition as Frontiers and Boundaries, 1978; The Geography of State Policies, 1968; The Evolution of Nigeria's International and Regional Boundaries 1861-1971, 1971; Political Geography, 1972; The Political Geography of the Oceans, 1975; The Map of Mainland Asia by Treaty, 1975; Our Fragmented World: An Introduction to Political Geography (with W G East), 1975; The Frontiers of Asia and Southeast Asia (with H J Collier and D F Prescott), 1976; The Last of Lands: Antarctica (with J Lovering), 1979; Australia's Continental Shelf (with others), 1979; Maritime Jurisdiction in Southeast Asia, 1981; Australia's Maritime Boundaries, 1985; The Maritime Political Boundaries of the World, 1985; Political Frontiers and Boundaries, 1987; Aboriginal Frontiers and Boundaries in Australia, with S Davis, 1992. *Address:* Department of Geography, University of Melbourne, Parkville, Victoria 3052, Australia.

PRESS John Bryant, b. 11 Jan 1920, Norwich, England. Retired Officer of the British Council. m. Janet Crompton, 20 Dec 1947, 1 son, 1 daughter. *Education:* Corpus Christi College, Cambridge, England. *Publications include:* The Fire and the Fountain, 1955; The Chequer'd Shade, 1958; A Map of Modern English Verse, 1969; The Lengthening Shadows, 1971; John Betjeman, 1974; Poets of World War II, 1984; A Girl wih Beehive Hair, 1986. *Contributions to:* Encounter; Southern Review; Art International. *Honours:* Royal Society of Literature Heinemann Award, 1959; 1st Prize Cheltenham Poetry Festival, 1959. *Memberships:* Fellow of Royal Society of Literature, 1959; Member

of Council, 1960-88. *Address:* 5 South Parade, Frome, Somerset BA11 1EJ, England.

PRESS Lloyd Douglas Jr, (Skip Press), b. 26 July 1950, Commerce, Texas, USA. Writer. m. Debra Ann Hartsog, 30 July 1989, 1 son, 1 daughter. *Education:* Honours Programme, East Texas State University, Commerce. *Publications:* A Woman's Guide to Firearms, 1986; Cliffhanger, 1992; The Devil's Forest Fire, 1993; Knuclehood, 1993; A Rave of Snakes, 1993; The Omportance of Mark Twain, 1993. *Contributions to:* Boys' Life; Disney Adventures; Reader's Digest; Writer's Digest; Many others. *Honours:* Silver Medal, New York International Film Festival, 1987. *Memberships:* Dramatists Guild; Poets and Writers; Independent Writers of Southern California, Vice-President 1990-91; Poets, Essayists and Novelists. *Address:* 2132 Palos Verdes Drive West 6, Palos Verdes Estates, CA 90274, USA.

PRESS Simone Naomi Juda, b. 12 Apr 1943, Cambridge, Massachusetts, USA. Playwright; Poet. m. 14 June 1969, 2 daughters. *Education:* BA 1965, Bennington College; MA 1967, Columbia University. *Literary Appointments:* Lecturer, 1968, Long Island University; Instructor, 1969-72, City University of New York; Associate Professor of English, 1973-, Siena Heights College; Visiting Lecturer in the Arts in Psychiatry, 1980, University of Michigan; Lecturer, Creative Writing, University of Michigan, 1988. *Publications:* Poetry: Thaw, 1969; Lifting Water, 1974; Play: Willing, 1983. *Contributions to:* Boston/Phoenix After Dark; The New York Times; Quadrille; Ann Arbor Review; Anon; The Village Voice; Greenhouse; Astraea. *Honours:* Artist Apprenticeship Grant, 1982, 1983; Creative Artist Award, 1983, Michigan Council for the Arts. *Memberships:* Creative Writing Chair, Midwest Modern Language Association; Associate Member, The Dramatists Guild; American Association of University Professors; American Theatre Association; American Association of Teachers of English and Language Arts. *Address:* 2215 Chaucer Court, Ann Arbor, Michigan 48103, USA.

PRESS Skip. *See:* **PRESS Lloyd Douglas Jr.**

PRESTON Ivy Alice Kinross, b. 11 Nov 1913. Writer. m. Percival Edward James Preston, 14 Oct 1937, 2 sons, 2 daughters. *Publications:* The Silver Stream, autobiography, 1958; Hospital on the Hill, 1967; Voyage of Destiny, 1974; The House above the Bay, 1976; Fair Accuser, 1985; Stranger from the Sea, 1987; 40 romance novels, reprinted in 9 languages and 130 editions. *Contributions to:* Short stories, articles, radio talks, to most New Zealand publications including The Listener. *Honours:* Award in Recognition of Achievement, Holme Station Arts Festival, 1990. *Memberships:* President, Secretary, South Canterbury Writers Guild; New Zealand Women Writers Society; Life Member, South Island Writers Association; Romance Writers of America; Romantic Novelists Association, London. *Literary Agent:* Robert Hale Ltd, London, England. *Address:* 95 Church Street, Timaru, South Canterbury, New Zealand.

PRESTON Peter John, b. 23 May 1938. Editor. m. Jean Mary Burrell, 1962, 2 sons, 2 daughters. *Education:* MA, English Literature, St John's College, Oxford. *Appointments:* Editorial Trainee, Liverpool Daily Post, 1960-63; Political Reporter, 1963-64; Education Correspondent, 1965-66; Diary Editor, 1966-68; Features Editor, 1968-72; Production Editor, 1972-75, The Guardian; British Executive Chairman and European Vice-Chairman, IPI, 1988-. *Honour:* Hon.D.Litt., Loughborough, 1982. *Address:* The Guardian, 119 Farringdon Road, London EC1R 3ER, England.

PRESTON Richard McCann, b. 15 Aug 1954. m. 11 May 1985. *Education:* BA, summa cum laude, Pomona College, 1977; PhD, English and American Literature, 1983. *Appointments:* Lecturer in English,

Princeton University, 1983; Regular contributor to The New Yorker Magazine, 1986-. *Publications:* First Light, 1987; American Steel, 1991. *Contributions to:* The New Yorker; The New York Times; Los Angeles Times; National Geographic Traveler; Mercury; Blair & Ketchum's Country Journal. *Honours:* American Institute of Physics Science Writing Award, 1988; M.I.T. McDermott Award, 1993; A.A.A.S., Westinghouse Award, 1993. *Membership:* The Authors' Guild. *Address:* c/o Sallie Gouverneur, 10 Bleecker Street No. 4A, New York, NY 10012, USA.

PREUSS Paul F, b. 7 Mar 1942, Albany, Georgia, USA. Writer. m. (1) Marsha May Pettit, 1963, (2) Karen Reiser, 1973; 1 daughter. *Education:* BA, cum laude, Yale University, 1966. *Publications:* The Gates of Heaven, 1980; Re-entry, 1981; Broken Symmetries, 1983; Human Error, 1985; Starfire, 1988; Volumes of the Venus Prime Series, with Arthur C Clarke, 1987-991; Short stories in The Planets, 1985, The Microverse, 1989; The Ultimate Dinosaur, 1992. *Contributions to:* Science writer, principally for Science 80 - Science 85 and Discover; Numerous book reviews, currently for The Washington Post. *Memberships:* National Book Critics' Circle; Bay Area Book Reviewers' Association; Science Fiction Writers of America. *Address:* PO Box 590773, San Francisco, CA 94159, USA.

PREVOTS Naima Wallenrod, b. 27 May 1935, Brooklyn, New York, USA. Professor, The American University, Washington DC. m. Martin Wallen, 26 Aug 1979, 1 son, 1 daughter. *Education:* BA, Brooklyn College, 1955; MS, University of Wisconsin, 1960; Attended Juilliard School, 1957-58; PhD, University of Southern California. *Publications:* A Vision for Music, 1984; Sound Waves, 1985; Dancing in the Sun - Hollywood Choreographer, 1987; American Pageantry: A Movement for Art and Democracy, 1990. *Contributions to:* Dance Magazine; Dance Research Journal; Dance Chronicle; California Historical Society. *Honours:* Phi Beta Kappa; Fulbright Fellowship; National Endowment for the Humanities Fellowship; University-wide Award for Research and Professional Contribution. *Memberships:* ssa 00Board member, Dance History Scholars; Board member, Fulbright Association. *Address:* 5219 Mass Avenue, Bethesda, MA 20816, USA.

PRICE (Alan) Anthony, b. 16 Aug 1928. Author; Journalist; Editor. m. (Yvonne) Ann Stone, 1953, 2 sons, 1 daughter. *Education:* Exhibitioner, MA, Merton College, Oxford. *Appointments:* Editor, The Oxford Times, 1972-88. *Publications:* The Labyrinth Makers, 1970; The Alamut Ambush, 1971; Colonel Butler's Wolf, 1972; October Men, 1973; Other Paths to Glory, 1974; Our Man in Camelot, 1975; War Game, 1976; The '44 Vintage, 1978; Tomorrow's Ghost, 1979; The Hour of the Donkey, 1980; Soldier No More, 1981; The Old Vengeful, 1982; Gunner Kelly, 1983; Sion Crossing, 1984; Here Be Monsters, 1985; For The Good of the State, 1986; A New Kind of War, 1987; A Prospect of Vengeance, 1988; The Memory Trap, 1989; The Eyes of The Fleet, 1990. *Honours:* CWA Silver Dagger, 1970; CWA Gold Dagger, 1974; Swedish Academy of Detection Prize, 1978. *Literary Agent:* A P Watt. *Address:* Wayside Cottage, Horton-cum-Studley, Oxford, OX9 1AW, England.

PRICE Glanville, b. 16 June 1928, Rhaeadr, Wales. University Professor. m. Christine Winifred Thurston, 18 Aug 1954, 3 sons, 1 daughter. *Education:* University of Wales, Bangor, 1946-50, University of Paris, 1950-53: BA (Wales) 1949, MA (Wales) 1952, Docteur de l'Université de Paris, 1956. *Appointments:* Professor of French, University of Stirling, 1967- 72; Professor of French, University of Wales, Aberystwyth, 1972-92, research Professor, 1992-; Joint Editor, The Year's Work in Modern Language Studies, 1972-92. *Publications:* The Present Position of Minority Languages in Western Europe, 1969; The French Language, Present and Past, 1971; ed. William, Count of Orange: Four Old French Epics, 1975; (with Kathryn F Bach) Romance Linguistics and the Romance Languages, 1977; The Languages of

Britain, 1984; Ireland and the Celtic Connection, 1987; An Introduction to French Pronunciation, 1991; A Comprehensive French Grammar, 1992. *Contributions to:* Romance Philology; Romania; Studia Neophilologia; Revue de Linguistique Romane; Zeitschrift fur Romanische Philologie; Archivum Linguisticum. *Memberships:* Modern Humanities Research Association (Chairman 1979-90); Philological Society; Society for French Studies. *Address:* Department of European Languages, University of Wales, Aberystwyth, Dyfed, Wales SY23 3DY.

PRICE Jennifer. *See:* **HOOVER Helen.**

PRICE (Edward) Reynolds, b. 1933, USA. Professor of English; Writer. *Appointments:* Editor, The Archive, Durham, North Carolina, 1954-55; Faculty Member, 1958-, James B Duke Professor of English, 1977-, Duke University, Durham; Advisory Editor, Shenandoah, Lexington, Virginia, 1964-. *Publications:* A Long and Happy Life, 1962; The Names and Faces of Heroes, short stories, 1963; A Generous Man, 1966; Love and Work, 1968; Late Warning: Four Poems, 1968; Permanent Errors, short stories, 1970; Things Themselves, essays, 1972; Presence and Absence: Version from the Bible, 1973; The Surface of Earth, 1975; Early Dark, play, 1977; A Palpable God, 1978; The Source of Light, 1981; Vital Provisions, 1982; Mustian, 1983; Private Contentment, 1984; Clear Pictures: First Lover First Guides. *Address:* 4813 Duke Station, Durham, NC 27706, USA.

PRICE Roger (David), b. 1944, United Kingdom. Historian; Professor of European History, University of East Anglia. *Publications:* The French Second Republic: A Social History, 1972; The Economic Modernization of France, 1975; Revolution and Reaction: 1948 and the Second French Republic (editor and contributor), 1975; 1848 in France, 1975; An Economic History of Modern France, 1981; The Modernization of Rural France: Communications Networks and Agricultural Market Structures in 19th Century France, 1983; A Social History of 19th-Century France, 1987; The Revolutions of 1848, 1989; A Concise History of France, 1993. *Honours:* DLitt, University of East Anglia, 1985. *Membership:* Fellow, Royal Historical Society, 1983. *Address:* School of Modern Languages and European History, University of East Anglia, Norwich NR4 7TL, England.

PRICE Stanley, b. 12 Aug 1931, London, England. Writer. m. Judy Fenton, 5 July 1957, 1 son. *Education:* MA, University of Cambridge, England. *Publications:* Novels: Crusading for Kronk, 1960; A World of Difference, 1961; Just for the Record, 1962; The Biggest Picture, 1964; Stage Plays: Horizontal Hold, 1967; The Starving Rich, 1972; The Two of Me, 1975; Moving, 1980; Why Me?, 1985; Screenplays: Arabesque, 1968; Gold, 1974; Shout at the Devil, 1975; Television plays: All Things Being Equal, 1970; Exit Laughing, 1971; Minder, 1980; The Kindness of Mrs Radcliffe, 1981; Moving, 1985; Star Quality, series, 1986; The Bretts, 1990, Close Relations, 1986-87. *Contributions to:* The Observer; Sunday Telegraph; New York Times; Los Angeles Times; Punch; Plays and Players; New Statesman; The Independent; Town. *Memberships:* Writers Guild; Dramatists Club. *Literary Agent:* Douglas Rae, England. *Address:* Douglas Rae, 28 Charing Cross Road, London WC2, England.

PRICE Susan, b. 1955, United Kingdom. Children's Fiction Writer. *Publications:* Devil's Piper, 1973; Twopence a Tub, 1975; Sticks and Stones, 1976; Home from Home, 1977; Christopher Uptake, 1981; The Carpenter, stories, 1981; In a Nutshell, 1983; From Where I Stand, 1984; Ghosts at Large, 1984; Odin's Monster, 1986; The Ghost Drum, 1987; The Bone Dog, 1989; Forbidden Doors, 1990. *Honours:* The Other Award, 1975; The Carnegie Medal, 1987. *Membership:* The Society of Authors. *Literary Agent:* A M Heath & Co Ltd, 79 St Martins Lane, London. *Address:* c/o Faber and Faber Ltd, 3 Queen Square, London WC1N 3AU, England.

PRICE Victor, b. 10 Apr 1930, Newcastle, Co Down, Northern Ireland. m. Colette Rodot, 20 Oct 1956, 2 sons. *Education:* BA Hons, Modern Languages (French and German), Queen's University, Belfast, 1947-51. *Appointments:* With the BBC, 1956-90, ending as Head of German Language Service. *Publications:* Novels: The Death of Achilles, 1963; The Other Kingdom 1964; Caliban's Wooing, 1966; The Plays of Georg Buchner, 1971; Two Parts Water (poems), 1980. *Contributions to:* Financial Times; The Statesman; BBC World Service; Deutschland Funk, Channel Four. *Address:* 23 Hereford Square, London SW7 4TS, England.

PRIEST Christopher (McKenzie), b. 1943, United Kingdom. Freelance Writer. *Publications:* Indoctrinaire, 1970; Fugue for a Darkening Island, US Edition Darkening Island, 1972; Inverted World, 1974; Your Book of Film-Making, 1974; Real-Time World, 1974; The Space Machine, 1976; A Dream of Wessex, US Edition The Perfect Lover, 1977; Anticipations (editor), 1978; An Infinite Summer, 1979; Stars of Albion (co-editor), 1979; The Affirmation, 1981; The Glamour, 1984; The Quiet Woman, 1990. *Literary Agent:* Maggie Noach. *Address:* c/o Bloomsbury Publishing Ltd, 2 Soho Square, London, W1V 5DE, England.

PRIESTLAND Gerald Francis, b. 26 Feb 1927, Berkhamstead, England. Author; Broadcaster. m. Helen Sylvia Rhodes, 14 May 1949, 2 sons, 2 daughters. *Education:* Scholar, Charterhouse School 1940-45, New College, Oxford 1945-48; BA Honours (Oxon), PPE, 1948. *Literary Appointments:* BBC correspondent: Foreign affairs 1954-69, Religious affairs 1976-82. *Publications:* Priestland's Progress, 1981; The Case Against God, 1984; Something Understood, autobiography, 1986; The Future of Violence, 1974; The Dilemmas of Journalism, 1979; Frying Tonight, 1970; America the Changing Nation, 1968; Yours Faithfully, 2 volumes, 1979, 1981; Gerald Priestland at Large, 1983; Priestley Right & Wrong, 1983; West of Hayle River, 1980. *Contributions include:* Numerous articles on religious, ethical & social issues in UK newspapers & magazines, including: Listener; Times; Sunday Telegraph; Observer; International Christian Digest. *Honours:* Honorary Fellow, Manchester Polytechnic, 1978; Honorary Master, Open University, 1985; Sandford St Martin Prize, religious broadcasting, 1981. *Membership:* West Country Writers. *Literary Agent:* MBA, 45 Fitzroy Street, London W1P 5HR. *Address:* 4 Temple Fortune Lane, London NW11 7UD, England.

PRIESTLEY Brian, b. 10 July 1946, Manchester. Writer; Musician. *Education:* BA (Hon), French; Diploma of Education, Leeds University. *Publications:* Mingus, A Critical Biography, 1982; Charlie Parker, 1984; John Coltrane, 1987; Jazz - The Essential Companion (with Ian Carr and Digby Fairweather), 1987; Jazz on Record, A History, 1988; Jazz Piano (Volumns 1-6), 1983-90. *Contributions to:* Reviews and articles. *Address:* Flat 3, 43 Ponder Street, London N7 8UD, England.

PRIETO Mariana Beeching, b. 1912, USA. Children's Writer; Teacher. *Appointments:* Teacher of Creative Writing, Dade County Schools Adult Division, Miami, Florida, 1956-; Teacher of Creative Writing, University of Miami, 1960-62. *Publications:* Spanish and How, 1944; Pattern for Beauty, 1945; His Cuban wife, novel, 1954; The Wise Rooster, 1962; El Gallo and Itzo, 1964; A Kite for Carlos, 1965; Tomato Boy, 1966; Johnny Lost, 1969; When the Monkeys Wore Sombreros, 1969; Play It in Spanish (editor), 1973; The Birdman of Papantla, 1973; Fun Jewelry, 1973; Hickless Cocktails and Harmless Highballs, 1980. *Contributions to:* Travel articles to International Travel News, 1982. *Address:* 2499 SW 34th Avenue, Miami, FL 33145, USA.

PRINCE Alison, b. 26 Mar 1931, Kent, England. Writer. m. Goronwy Siriol Parry, dec 26 Dec 1957, 2 sons, 1 daughter. *Education:* Beckenham Grammar School; Slade School Diploma, London University; Art Teacher's Diploma, Goldsmiths College. *Appointment:* Fellow in Creative Writing, Jordanhill College, Glasgow, 1988-90. *Publications:* The Doubting Kind (young adults), 1974; How's Business (children's book) 1985; The Ghost Within (supernatural stories) 1987; The Blue Moon Day, (childrens) 1989; The Necessary Goat (essays on creativity) 1992. Other publications: A Haunting Refrain; Haunted Children; A Job for Merv; Goodbye Summer; Nick's October; The Sinister Airfield; The Type One Robot. *Contributions to:* New Statesman; The Scotsman; The Herald; Scottish Child; various educational journals. *Honour:* Runner-up for Smarties Prize, 1986. *Memberships:* Scottish PEN; Society of Authors. *Address:* Burnfoot, Whiting Bay, Isle of Arran, Scotland KA27 8QL.

PRINCE Charming. *See:* **THOMAS Rosanne Daryl.**

PRINCE F(rank) T(empleton), b. 1912, United Kingdom. Former Professor of English; Author; Poet. *Appointments:* Professor of English, University of Southampton, 1957-74; Professor of English, University of the West Indies, Jamaica, 1975-78; Fannie Hurst Professor, Brandeis University, Waltham, Massachusetts, USA, 1978-80. *Publications:* Poems, 1938; Soldiers Bathing and Other Poems, 1954; The Italian Element in Milton's Verse, 1954; The Stolen Heart, 1957; Samson Agonistes, by Milton (editor), 1957; The Poems, by Shakespeare (editor), 1960; Sir Thomas Wyatt, by Sergio Baldi, translation, 1961; Paradise Lost, books I and II, by Milton (editor), 1962; The Doors of Stone: Poems 1938-62, 1963; William Shakespeare: The Poems, 1963; Comus and Other Poems, by Milton (editor), 1968; Memoirs in Oxford, 1970; Penguin Modern Poets 20 (with John Heath-Stubbs and Stephen Spender), 1971; Drypoints of the Hasidim, 1975; Afterword on Rupert Brooke, 1977; Collected Poems, 1979; The Yuan Chen Variations, 1981; Later On, 1983; Walks in Rome, 1987; Collected Poems, 1993. *Address:* 32 Brookvale Road, Southampton, Hants SO2 1QR, England.

PRINCE Jennifer. *See:* **HOOVER Helen Mary.**

PRINGLE-JONES Jennifer Suzanne, b. 26 May 1946, Tasmania, Australia. Journalist. m. 21 July 1967, 1 son, 2 daughters. *Education:* Dux of School, St Michael's Collegiate School, 1962. *Appointments:* Staff, Mercury newspaper, 1962-67; Journalist, ABC Radio/TV 1967-71, TAS/TV 1978-86, Commonwealth Scientific & Industrial Research Organisation 1986-. *Publications:* Discovering Tasmania, 1981. Explore Tasmania, First edition, 1983; Tasmania is a Garden, 1985; Explore Tasmania, Second Edition, 1989; Tasmania The Beautiful Island, 1989. *Contributions to:* Fodor's Travel Guides; Herald & Weekly Times publications; Ansett Transport Industries publications; Tasmanian Chamber of Mines publications; Vogue Australia; The Design Series; Australian Country Style; Contrasts Australia Logies 1981 and 1983; numerous scripting awards; National Tourism Award 1984; TV News Reporters' Award. *Honours:* Numerous scripting awards; National Tourism Award; TV News Reporters Award. *Membership:* Australian Journalists Association; Australian Day Council; Queen Elizabeth II Silver Jublilee Trust for Young Australians; Advisory Board, St John's Hospital. *Address:* 29 Amanda Crescent, Sandy Bay, Tasmania 7005, Australia.

PRIOR Allan, b. 1922, United Kingdom. Author. *Publications:* A Flame in the Air, 1951; The Joy Ride, 1952; The One-Eyed Monster, 1958; One Away, 1961; The Interrogators, 1965; The Operators, 1966; The Loving Cup, 1968; The Contract, 1970; Paradiso, 1972; Affair, 1976; Never Been Kissed in the Same Place Twice, 1978; Theatre, 1981; A Cast of Stars, 1983; The Big March, 1983; Her Majesty's Hit Man, 1986; Fuhrer - the Novel, 1991. *Address:* Summerhill, Waverley Road, St Albans, Herts, England.

PRITCHARD R(obert) John, b. 30 Nov 1945, Los Angeles, USA. Freelance Writer and Broadcaster. m. (1) Sonia Magbanna Zaide, 15 Aug 1969, div 1984, 1 son, 1 daughter, (2) Lady Antonia Lodge, 20 Dec 1989. *Education:* AB, University of California, 1967; MA, 1968, PhD,1980, London School of Economics, England. *Appointments:* Managing Editor, Millennium: Journal of International Studies, 1974-78; Research Assistant in History, 1973-81; Consultant, Tokyo War Trial Project, The London School of Economics, 1981-87; Director/ Secretary, Integrated Dictionary Systems Ltd, 1988-90; Lecturer in History, University of Kent, 1990-93; Fellow in War Studies, Kings College, London, 1990-93; Simon Senior Research Fellow in History, University of Manchester, 1993. *Publications include:* Reichstag Fire: Ashes of Democracy, 1972; Tokyo War Crimes Trial Complete Transcripts, Proceedings of International Military Tribunal for Far East (with S M Zaide) 22 volumes, 1981; Tokyo War Crimes Trial, Index and Guide (with S M Zaide), 5 volumes, 1981-87; co-author: General History of the Philippines, volume 1, American Half-Century, 1898-1946, 1984; Far Eastern Influences on British Strategy Towards the Great Powers 1937-39, 1987; Overview of Historical Importance of the Tokyo War Trial, 1987; co-author: Total War: Causes & Courses of 2nd World War, 1989; co-author: The Japanese Army's Secret of Secrets, 1989; Japan and the 2nd World War (with Lady Toshiko Marks) 1989; ed. The British War Crimes Trials in the Far East, 1946-48, (21 volumes) 1993; co-author, From Pearl Harbour to Hiroshima, 1993; The Misconduct of War and the Rule of Law, forthcoming. *Contributions to:* Numerous professional journals; The Tokyo War Crime Trial: An International Symposium, 1984-1986; The Cambridge Encylopeadia of Japan, 1993. *Honours include:* California State Graduate Fellowship, 1967; Book Collection Prizes, Zeitlin & ver Brugge, 1969, 1970; Numerous research grants include: Social Science Research Council, Japan Foundation, International Centre for Study of Economics & Related Disciplines, 27 Foundation, British Academy, MacArthur Foundation; Nuffield Foundation. *Memberships:* American Historical Association; Association of Contemporary Historians; British Association for Japanese Studies; British Institute of Management. *Address:* 11 Charlotte Square, Margate, Kent CT9 1LR, England.

PRITCHARD William H, b. 12 Nov 1932, Binghamton, New York. Professor. m. 24 Aug 1957, 3 sons. *Education:* BA, Amherst College, 1953; Ma; PhD, Harvard University, 1960. *Appointments:* Teaching, Amherst College, 1958-. *Publication:* Randall Jarrell, A Literary Life, 1990; Frost, A Literary Life Reconsidered, 1984; Lives of the Modern Poets, 1980; Seeing Through Everything, English Writers 1918-1940, 1977; Wyndham Lewis, 1968. *Honours:* Fellowships from Guggenheim; National Endowment for the Humanities; American Council of Learned Societies. *Membership:* Harvard Club of New York City; Modern Language Association. *Address:* 62 Orchard Street, Amherst, MA 01002, USA.

PRITCHETT Victor Sawdon, (Sir), b. 16 Dec 1900, Ipswich, Suffolk, England. Author; Critic. m. Dorothy Rudge Roberts, 1936, 1 son, 1 daughter. *Appointments:* Lectured in 4 Universities in USA; Resident Writer, Smith College, 1967, 1970-72; Clark Lectures Cambridge 1969. *Publications:* Marching Spain; Clare Drummer; The Spanish Virgin; Shirley Sanz; Nothing Like Leather; Dead Man Leading; You Make Your Own Life; In My Good Books; It May Never Happen; Why Do I Write? (with Elizabeth Bowen & Graham Greene); The Living Novel; Mr Beluncle; Books in General; The Spanish Temper; Collected Short Stories; When My Girl Comes Home; London Perceived; The Key to My Heart; Foreign Faces; New York Proclaimed; The Living Novel and Later Appreciations; Dublin; A Cab at the Door (autobiography), 1968; Blind Love (short stories); George Meredith and English Comedy, 1970; Midnight Oil, (autobiography volume II), 1971; Balzac, 1973; The Camberwell Beauty (stories), 1974; Turgenev, 1977; The Gentle Barbarian, 1977; Selected Stories, 1978; The Myth Makers (essays), 1979; On the Edge of the Cliff (stories), 1979; The Tale Bearers 1980; Oxford Book of Short Stories, Editor, 1981; Collected Stories, 1982; The Turn of the Years, 1982; more Collected Stories, 1983; A Man of Letters; Chekhoo, 1988; (stories), A Careless Widow, 1989; At Home & Abroad, 1990; Lasting Impression, 1990; The Complete Essays, 1991. *Honours:* Hon D.Lit., Leeds, 1972, Columbia University, New York, Sussex University, 1978, Harvard, 1985; PEN Biography Award for Balzac, 1974; Knighted, 1975; CBE, 1968; CLIT (Royal Society of Literature), 1988. *Memberships:* President, Society of Authors, 1977-. *Address:* 12 Regent's Park Terrace, London, NW1, England.

PRIVATEER Paul, b. 15 Aug 1946, Buffalo, New York, USA. University Professor, Writer, Consultant. div 1 son, 1 daughter. *Education:* BA, MA, California State University, Tunlock, California; PhD, University of California, Davis, 1980. *Appointments:* Lecturer, San Jose State University, 1980-84; Professor, University of Southern Mississippi, 1984-86; Professor, Georgia Institute of Technology, 1986-89; Lecturer, Arizona State University, 1990-; Consultant in Information Technology, Marcopa Community College District. *Publications:* Romantic Voices: Ideology and Identity in British Literature, 1991; Literature and Science, 1992. *Honours:* British Council Prize for the Humanities, nomination 1992; Fulbright Fellow, 1976-77, Switzerland. *Address:* English Department, Arizona State University, Tempe, AZ 85258, USA.

PROCASSION Michael (Michael Cristofer), b. 1946, USA. Playwright. *Publications:* The Shadow Box, 1977; Black Angel, 1984; The Lady and The Clarinet, 1985; Ice; Breaking Up; The Bonfire of the Vanities. *Honours:* Pultizer Prize and Antoinette Perry 'Tony' Award for The Shadow Box. *Literary Agent:* Dramatists Play Service, USA. *Address:* c/o Dramatists Play Service, 440 Park Avenue South, New York, NY 10016, USA.

PROCHNOW Herbert Victor, b. Wilton, Wisconsin, USA. Various positions with The First National Bank of Chicago between 1933 and 1969. President, 1961-69; Secretary to Federal Advisory Council of the Federal Reserve System. m. Laura Virginia Stinson (dec 1977), 1 son. *Education:* BA; MA, University of Wisconsin; PhD, Northwestern University. *Appointments:* Financial Columnist, Chicago Tribune, 1968-70. *Publications include:* Practical Bank Credit, 1939; The Public Speaker's Treasure Chest, 1986; The Changing World of Banking, 1974; The Toastmaster's Treasure Chest, 1988; Inspirational Thoughts on the Ten Commandments, 1970; American Financial Institutions, 1970; The Federal Reserve System, 1960; The Eurodollar, 1970; Dilemmas Facing the Nation, 1979; Bank Credit, 1981; Editor and co-author of over 80 books. *Honours:* Order of Vesa, Sweden; Commanders Cross of the Order of Merit, Federal Republic of Germany; Business Statesmanship Award, Harvard Business School Association; Ayres Leadership Award, Reutgers University; Silver Plaque Highest Award, National Conference of Christians and Jews; Hon. LLD, University of Wisconsin and Northwestern University; Hon. Lett D, Millikin University; Hon. LLD, Ripon College, Lake Forest University; DHL, Thiel College. *Memberships include:* Beta Gamma Sigma. *Address:* 1st National Bank Plaza, Chicago, IL 60670, USA.

PROFESSER X. *See:* **BOORSTIN Daniel Joseph.**

PROSSER Harold Lee, b. 31 Dec 1944, Springfield, Missouri, USA. Author; Composer. div 1988, 2 daughters. *Education:* AA, Santa Monica College, 1968; BS, 1974, MSED, 1982, Southwest Missouri State University. *Publications:* Dandelion Seeds: 18 Stories, 1974; Goodbye Lon Chaney, Jr., Goodbye, 1977; Desert Woman Visions: 100 Poems, 1987; Jack Bimbo's Touring Circus Poems, 1988; Charles Beaumont (biography) 1994; Contributed several essays to book, Reader's Guide to 20th Century Science Fiction (ed. M.P. Fletcher) 1989; Over 900 publications since 1963;

Numerous musical compositions for publication. *Contributions to:* Antaeus; Doppleganger; Imagine; Dialogue; Moon; Night Music; Singing Guns Journal; Social Education; Fantasy; Several Essays to book, New Encyclopeadia of Science Fiction (editor James Gunn). *Honours:* Manuscripts permanently housed and stored at the following universities under title: The H L Prosser Collection: 1. Golden Library, Eastern New Mexico University at Portales, New Mexico; 2. Archival Heritage Centre, University of Wyoming at Laramie, Wyoming; 3. Donnelly Library, New Mexico Highlands University at Las Vegas, New Mexico. *Memberships:* Composer member of ASCAP; Vedanta Society. *Address:* 1313 South Jefferson Avenue, Springfield, MO 65807, USA.

PRUITT William O, b. 1 Sept 1922, Easton. University Professor. m. Erna Nauert, 5 Feb 1951, 1 son, 1 daughter. *Education:* BSc, University of Maryland, 1947; MA, University of Michigan, 1948; PhD, University of Michigan, 1952. *Publication:* Wild Harmony; Boreal Ecology; Author of 65 Scientific Papers; Author of 40 Popular Articles. *Honours:* Fellow, Arctic Institute of North America; Fellow, The Explorers Club; Seton Medal, Manitoba Naturalists Society; Northern Science Award and Centenary Medal, Government of Canada; Stefansson Award, University of Manitoba; DSc (Hon) University of Alaska, 1993. *Memberships:* American Society of Mammalogists, Arctic Institute, Sigma Xi. *Address:* Department of Zoology, The University of Manitoba, Winnipeg, Manitoba, Canada R3T 2N2.

PRUTKOV Kozma. *See:* **SNODGRASS W D.**

PRVULOVICH Žika Rad, (Dr Peters), b. 4 Dec 1920, Vlahovo, Serbia, Yugoslavia. Retired University Senior Lecturer. m. Janet Mary Atkins, 11 Aug 1959, 1 son, 1 daughter. *Education:* BA (Mod), Trinity College, Dublin, 1951; BA (Oxon), 1952; DPhil (Oxon), 1956; MA (Oxon), 1957. *Publications:* Njegoseva Teorija Saznauja i Sistem, 1981; Prince-Bishop Njegosh's Religious Philosophy, 1984; Serbia between the Swastika and the Red Star, 1986; Tajna Bogai Tajna Sveta, Pt 1 of a Trilogy, 1991; The Ray of the Microcosm, translation of Prince-Bishop Njegosh's poem Luča Mikrokozma (bilingual edition with critical commentary and Introduction in English), 1992. *Contributions to:* Many contributions to various literary, political, religious and philosophical journals and magazines. *Honours:* The Wray Prize in Philosophy, Dublin University, 1951. *Memberships:* Honorary Librarian, Dublin University Philosophical Society; PEN, English Section; Honorary Member, Serbian Writers Club; Society of Serbian Writers and Artists, England; Philosophy of Education Society of Great Britain; Oriel Society; University of Birmingham Common Room. *Address:* 26 Wheeler's Lane, King's Heath, Birmingham B13 0SA, England.

PRYBYLA Jan, b. 21 Oct 1927, Poland. Professor of Economics. m. Jacqueline Meyer, 1958, 1 son, 1 daughter. *Education:* BComm, 1949; MES, 1950, PhD, 1953, National University of Ireland; Diploma in Higher European Studies, University of Strasbourg, France, 1952. *Appointments:* Currently Professor of Economics, Pennsylvania State University, University Park, USA. *Publications:* The Political Economy of Communist China, 1970; The Chinese Economy: Problems and Policies, 1978, 1981; Issues in Socialist Economic Modernization, 1980; Market and Plan Under Socialism: The Bird in the Cage, 1987; Reforms in China and Other Socialist Economies, 1990; China and the Crisis of Marxism-Leninism (co-author), 1990; Editor, Comparative Economic Systems, 1969. *Contributions to:* Current History; Asian Survey; Problems of Communism; Slavic Review; Comparative Economic Studies; Review of World Economy; Social Research; The Annals; Pacific Affairs. *Memberships:* President, Conference on European Problems; Board of Directors, American Association for Chinese Studies; Association for Comparative Economic Studies. *Address:* 523 Kern Building, University Park, PA 16802, USA.

PRYCE-JONES David, b. 29 July 1959, Vienna,

Austria. Author. 1 son, 2 daughters. *Education:* BA, MA, Magdalen College, Oxford, 1956-59. *Appointments:* Literary Editor: Time & Tide, 1961; Spectator, 1964. *Publications:* Owls & Satyrs, 1961; The Sands of Summer, 1963; Next Generation, 1964; Quondam, 1965; The Stranger's View, 1967; The Hungarian Revolution, 1969; Running Away, 1969; The Face of Defeat, 1971; The England Commune, 1973; Unity Mitford, 1976; Shirley's Guild, 1981; Paris in the Third Reich, 1983; Cyril Connolly, 1984; The Afternoon Sun, 1986; The Closed Circle, 1989; Inheritance, 1992. *Contributions to:* numerous journals and magazines. *Honour:* Wingate Prize, 1986. *Membership:* Royal Society of Literature. *Literary Agent:* The Peters Fraser and Dunlop Group Ltd. *Address:* Lower Pentwyn, Gwenddwr, Powys, Wales.

PRYER Vanessa. *See:* **YARBRO Chelsea Quinn.**

PRYNNE J.H., b. 24 June 1936, England. *Publications include:* Kitchen Poems, 1968; Day light Songs, 1968; The White Stones, 1969; Brass, 1971; Into The Day, 1972; Wound Response, 1974; High Pink on Chrome, 1975; News of Warring Clans, 1977; Down Where Changes, 1979; Poems, 1982; The Oval Window, 1983; Bands around the Throat, 1987; Word Order, 1989; Not-You, 1993. *Address:* Gonville & Caius College, Cambridge CB2 1TA, England.

PRYOR Adel. *See:* **WASSERFALL Adel.**

PRYOR Bonnie Helen, b. 22 Dec 1942, Los Angeles, California, USA. Author. m. Robert E Pryor, 2 sons, 4 daughters. *Publications:* Grandpa Bear, 1985; Rats, Spiders and Love, 1986; Amanda and April, 1986; Grandpa Bear's Christmas, 1986; Mr Z and the Time Clock, 1986; Vinegar Pancakes and Vanishing Cream, 1987; House on Maple Street, 1987; Mr. Munday and Rustlers, 1988; Seth of Lion People, 1989; Plumtree War, 1989; Porcupine Mouse, 1989; Perfect Percy, 1989; Mr Munday and Space Creatures, 1989; Merry Christmas Amanda and April, 1990; 24 Hour Lipstick Mystery, 1990; Greenbrook Farm, 1991; Jumping Jenny, 1992; Beaver Boys, 1992; Lottie's Dream, 1992; Poison Ivy and Eyebrow Wigs, 1993. *Contributions to:* Women's Circle, 1983; Woman's World, 1984; Writers, 1989. *Honours:* Irma Simonton Black Award from Bank Street College, 1989 for Procupine Mouse; Children's Choise, 1986 for Mr Z and the Time Clock; Outstanding Book List, National Society of Science Teachers, and National Society of Social Studies, 1987, for House on Maple Street; National Society of Science Teachers award for Seth of Lion People, 1990. *Membership:* Society of Children's Book Writers. *Address:* 19600 Baker Road, Gambier, OH 43022, USA.

PRZYBYSZ Janusz Anastazy, b. 31 May 1926, Poznan, Poland. Journalist; Writer. m. Danuta Maria Magolewska, 10 Sept 1951, 1 daughter. *Education:* Poznan University, 1950. *Publications:* The Note-book of one Untermensch, 1972; The Dog Which in Sopot Get Out, 1980; A Short Fragment of a Family Story, 1981; Eintopfkommando, 1986; The Long Lesson of Gymnastics, 1990; Stories: Family Secrets, 1972; Thirteenth on Friday, 1975; In the Almonds and Icings Smell, 1978; Short Satirical Works: The Adventures of Gentlemen, 1962; My Good Unknown, 1966; Our Beloved Little World, 1968; Dreadful Lovely is this World, 1973. *Contributions to:* Kaktus, 1957-61; Tydzien, 1973-81; Wprost, 1982; Karuzela, 1966-; Gazeta Poznanska, 1966-. *Honours:* Reymont Literary Prize, 1987; City of Poznan Prize for Cultural Activity and Arts, 1988. *Memberships:* Polish Writers Association, Vice-Chairman Poznan Association, 1978-81; Association of Authors and Composers; Polish Journalists Association. *Address:* ul. Galileusza 6A, m 6, 60-161 Poznan, Poland.

PRZYMANOWSKI Janusz, b. 20 Jan 1922, Warsaw, Poland. Author; Journalist. m. Aleksandra Nowinska, 2 June 1984. 1 daughter. *Education:* MA, History,

University of Warsaw, 1964. *Publications:* Four from the Tank Corps and the Dog (novel, TV film 21 x 1 hour, translated into 18 languages), 1963; 101 Nights on the Front; Studzianki, 1964; Novels: Summoned; Dogged; Tired; Wire Entanglement, (film 1.5 hour); All and Nobody, (film 1.5 hour); Turnout; Who Speak Yes? (TV film, 7 x 15 mins.); Nest of Bricks; Tricks of Jonatan Kost; Who I am?; Memory; Over 200 songs. *Honours:* Literary Prize, Ministry of National Defense, 1959, 1961, 1966, 1967, 1987; Literary Prize, Prime Minister, 1977; Literary Prize, Minister of Culture and Art, 1967. *Membership:* Union of Polish Authors. *Address:* ul. Deuga, 30/34 m. 40 00-238 Warzawa, Poland.

PRZYPKOWSKI Andrzej Jozef, b. 9 July 1930, Poland. writer. m. Halina Sienska, 17 Mar 1980, 1 daughter. *Education:* University of Warsaw, 1952. *Publications:* Gdzies we Francji, 1966; Gdy wrocisz do Montpellier, 1969; Na ma jutra w Saint-Nazaire, 1971; Taniec Marihuany, 1977; Palm City, 1978; Victoria, 1980; 18 novels, 1 travel book including latest novel Miraz, 1987. *Contributions to:* Nike; Argumenty. *Honour:* Order of Polonia Restituta, 1980. *Memberships:* Union of Polish Writers; National Council of Culture. *Literary Agent:* Authors Agency Limited, Warsaw. *Address:* Graniczna 62, 05-540 Zalesie Gorne, Poland.

PUGH Dan. *See:* **PUGH Daniel Lovelock.**

PUGH Daniel Lovelock, (Dan Pugh), b. 11 Mar 1924, England. Engineers' Buyer (retired); Poet. m. Doris Irene Wheatcroft, 22 Sept 1951, 1 son, 4 daughters. *Education:* Evening and correspondence courses in Trades Unionism and Local Government, 1944-46; Old Testament, New Testament, Art of Teaching, Preaching, Child Psychology, 1951-55; Work Study, 1974. *Contributions to:* Poetry and creative articles to various publications, mainly UK, also South Africa, New Zealand, USA. *Honours:* Poem in Top 5 %, Rhyme Revival Competition, 1981, published in 1982 Anthology; Haiku in Top 100 (of 5200), BHA-JA: Contest, 1991; Sonnet commendeed, Age Concern Competition, 1991; Winner, Hrafnhon Magazine International Literary Competition, 1991; Mirrors, Tanka Award Poet, (USA), 1992. *Memberships:* Christian Writers Forum; Fellowship of Christian Writers. *Literary Agent:* Gerald England, New Hope International (overseas placements). *Address:* 8 Wyvern Terrace, Melton Mowbray, Leicestershire LE13 1AD, England.

PUGLISI Angela Aurora, b. 28 Jan 1949, Messina, Italy. University Lecturer. *Education:* BA cum Laude, Dunbarton College, USA, 1972; MFA, Painting, 1974, MA, Art History, MA, Language and Literatures, 1977, PhD, Comparative Literature, 1983, Catholic University of America; Georgetown University DC, 1986-. *Publications:* Towards Excellence in Education through the Liberal arts, 1984; Homage, 1985; Nature's Canvas, 1985; Sonnet, 1985; Primavera, 1986; Sand Dunes, 1986; Sun's Journey, 1986; Jet d'Eau, 1986; Ocean Waves, 1986; Prelude, 1987; Ethics in Journalism, 1989; Woodland Revisited, 1988. *Contributions to:* Catholic Academy of Sciences, 1989-90. *Honours include:* Certificate in Recognition of Outstanding Service to Education and Education Reform. *Memberships:* Academician, Catholic Academy of Sciences, Co-Chairperson, Admission Committee; Founding Member, Italian Cultural Center Casa Italiana; Corcoran College of Art Association; Charter Member, N Museum of Women in the Arts; Board of Directors, SEE. *Address:* 1500 Licoln Circle 101-McLean, VA 22102, USA.

PULSFORD Petronella, b. 4 Feb 1946, Leeds, Yorkshire, England. Actress; Writer; Director. *Education:* BA, Hons, English, St Hilda's College, Oxford. *Publication:* Lee's Ghost, novel, 1990. *Honour:* Constable Trophy for Fiction, 1989. *Memberships:* Society of Authors; Equity. *Address:* 8 Thomas Street West, Savile Park, Halifax, West Yorks. HX1 3HF, England.

PUNNOOSE Kunnuparambil P, b. 26 Mar 1942, Kottayam, India. Editor. m. Santhamma, 9 Jan 1967, 1 son, 2 daughters. *Education:* College graduate, 1962. *Appointments:* Managing Editor, Concept Publishing Co., 1974-75; Managing Edutor, Asian Literary Market Review, 1975-; Director, Darsan Books (P) Ltd, 1983-; General Convener, Kottayam International Book Fair, 1984-. *Publications:* Directory of American University Presses, 1979; American Book Trade in India, 1981; Bookdealers in India and the Orient, 1992. *Contributions to:* More than 100 articles on the art and craft of writing and the business of book and magazine publishing. *Honour:* Kottayam International Book Fair Award, 1989. *Memberships:* Authors Guild of India; Kerala Book Society. *Address:* Kunnuparambil Buildings, Kurichy, Kottayam 686549, India.

PURDUE Arthur William, b. 29 Jan 1941. University Lecturer. m. 29 Aug 1979, 1 daughter. *Education:* King's School, Tynemouth, 1951-59; BA, Hons, History, King's College, London, 1962; Diploma of Education, King's College, Durham University, 1963; Master of Letters, University of Newcastle- upon-Tyne, 1974. *Publications:* The Civilization of the Crowd (with J M Golby) 1984; The Makingn of the Modern Christmas (with J M Golby) 1986; The Monarchy and the British People (with J M Golby) 1988. *Contributions to:* Salisbury Review; Times Higher Education Supplement; New Society; Country Life; Northern History; International Review of Social History. *Memberships:* Trollope Society; Fellow, Royal Historical Society. *Address:* The Old Rectory, Allendale, Hexham, Northumberland NE47 9DA, England.

PURDY Carol Ann, b. 5 Jan 1943, Long Beach, California, USA. Writer; Social Worker. m. John Purdy, 8 June 1963, 1 son, 2 daughters. *Education:* BA, California State University, Long Beach, 1964; MSW, California State University, Sacramento, 1990. *Publications:* Iva Dunnit And The Big Wind, 1985; Least of All, 1987; The Kid Power Program, Groups for High Risk Children, 1989; Mrs Merriwether's Musical Cat, 1994. *Memberships:* Society of Children's Book Writers; National Association of Social Workers. *Literary Agent:* Faith Hamlin, Sanford J Greenburger Literary Agency. *Address:* 25310 68th Ave, Los Molinos, CA 96055, USA.

PURDY James, b. 23 July, Ohio, USA, Writer. *Publications:* Malcolm, 1959 The Nephew, 1960; 63 Dream Place, 1957; The House of the Solitary Maggot, 1974; In a Shallow Grave, 1976; Narrow Rooms, 1978; Eustace Chisholm and the Works, 1967; On Glory's Course, 1983; In the Hollow of His Hand, 1986; The Candles of Your Eyes, 1987; Garments The Living Wear, (novel) 1989; (play), Souvenirs, 1989; Collected Poems, 1989; Ruthanna Elder, (full-length play), 1990. *Contributions to:* Esquire; Antioch Review. *Honours:* Guggenheim, 1958, 1962; Ford Fellowship, 1960. *Literary Agent:* William Morris Incorporated. *Address:* 236 Henry Street, Brooklyn, NY 11201, USA.

PURSER Philip John, b. 28 Aug 1925, Letchworth, England. Journalist; Author. m. Ann Elizabeth Goodman, 18 May 1957, 1 son, 2 daughters. *Education:* MA, St Andrews University, 1950. *Appointments:* Staff, Daily Mail, 1951-57; Television critic, Sunday Telegraph, 1961-87. *Publications:* Four Days to the Fireworks, 1964; The Twentymen, 1967; Night of Glass, 1968; The Last Great Tram Race, 1974; Where Is He Now?, 1978; A Small Explosion, 1979; Peregrination 22, 1962; The Holy Father's Navy, 1971; The One & Only Phyllis Dixey, 1978; Halliwell's Television Companion, with Leslie Halliwell, 1982, 1986; Shooting the Hero, 1990; Poet ed: The Final Quest of Edward James, 1991; Done Viewing, 1992. *Contributions to:* Numerous magazines & journals. *Memberships:* Writers Guild of Great Britain; British Academy of Film & Television Arts; The Academy Club. *Literary Agent:* David Highams Associates. *Address:* 10 The Green, Blakesley, Towcester, Northamptonshire, England.

PURVES Libby (Elizabeth Mary), b. 2 Feb 1950, London, England. Journalist/Broadcaster. m. Paul

Heiney, 2 Feb 1980, 1 son, 1 daughter. *Education:* BA 1st class honours, Oxford, 1971. *Appointments:* Presenter/Writer, BBC, 1975-; Editor, Tatler, 1983. *Publications:* Adventures under Sail (editor), 1962; Britain At Play, 1982; The Sailing Weekend Book, 1984; How Not To Be A Perfect Mother, 1987; Where Did You Leave The Admiral, 1987; The English and Their Horses, 1988; One Summer's Grace, 1989; How Not To Raise a Perfect Child, 1991. *Contributions to:* Regularly to The Times and Sunday Express; Many magazines, Britain and Australia. *Honours:* Best Book of the Sea, 1984. *Literary Agent:* A P Watt, 20 John Street, London WC 1, England. *Address:* Vale Farm, Middleton, Saxmundham, Suffolk IP17 3LT, England.

PUSKAS Jozef, b. 9 Feb 1951, Michalovce, Czechoslovakia. Journalist. m. Melania Balintova, 8 Nov 1975, 1 son, 1 daughter. *Education:* High School of Arts (Film and Television), Bratislava, 1974. *Publications:* Hra na zivot a na smrt, 1972; Utesene sklamania, 1977; Priznanie, 1979; Stvrty rozmer, 1980; Zahrada v piatom obdobi roka, 1984; Sny, deti, milenky, 1985; Smrt v jeseni, 1992; Vreckovy labyrint, 1992. *Address:* Mlynarovicova 10, 851 04 Bratislava, Slovakia.

PYNCHON Thomas, b. 8 May 1937, Glen Cove, Long Island, New York, United States of America. Writer. *Education:* BA, Cornell University, 1958. *Appointments include:* Boeing Aircraft, Seattle, Washington. *Publications:* V (novel), 1963; The Crying of Lot 49 (novel), 1966; Gravity's Rainbow (novel), 1973; Been Down So Long It Looks Like Up to Me, 1983; Slow Leaner, 1984; Several Short Stories including: Mortality and Mercy in Vienna, 1976; Lowlands, 1978. *Contributions to:* Short Stories and Essays to periodicals including New York Times Magazine, New York Times Book Review, Cornell Writer, Holiday, Cornell Alumni News, Saturday Evening Post, Kenyon Review. *Honours:* William Faulkner Novel Award for V, 1963; Rosenthal Foundation Award from National Institute of Arts and Letters for The Crying of Lot 49, 1967; National Book Award for Gravity's Rainbow, 1974.

Q

QAZI Moin b.4 Apr 1956, Nagpur, India. Bank Executive and Author. m. Nahid Qazi, 30 Dec 1984, 2 sons. *Education:* LLB 1983, MA 1989. *Publication:* A Wakeful Heart (collection of poems) 1990 published by Writers' Workshop, Calcutta; The Real Face, 1991; The Elegant Costumes of the Deccan, The Mission of Muhammad. *Contributions to:* About 500 articles and 150 poems to Indian and foreign publications including The Times of India, The Statesman, Indian Express, The Economic Times, Financial Express, The Hindustan Times, Business Standard, The Hindu, Mainstream, Third World Features (Malaysia), SIDA Rapport (Sweden), Depth News, (Philippines), Poetry International, Asiaweek (Hongkong); First Time Symphony; New Hope International and Irish Poetry Review, UK; Prophetic Voices, USA, Resurgence, Australia. *Honours:* University World Politics Essay Gold Medal, 1977; Certificates of Poetic Accomplishment from Amherst Poetry Society, Baltimore and Poetry Center, California; Awarded Doctorate in Literature (D.Litt) at World Center. *Memberships:* Fellow International Poets Academy Manas (India), Fellow and Member, Advisory Council, International Biographical Association, Cambridge and American Biographical Inst, North Carolina, USA. *Address:* Samiullah Khan Marg, Sadar, Nagpur 440001, India.

QUARRY Nick. *See:* **ALBERT Marvin H.**

QUARTERMAIN James. *See:* **LYNNE James** Broom.

QUEEN Ellery. *See:* **POWELL Talmage.**

QUEST Erica. *See:* **SAWYER John & SAWYER** Nancy.

QUICK Barbara, b. 28 May 1954, Los Angeles, California, USA. Writer. m. John Quick, 1 Aug 1988. *Education:* BA, Hons, Literature, University of California, Santa Cruz. *Publication:* Northern Edge (novel) 1990. *Contributions to:* New York Times Book Review. *Honours:* Northern Edge was selected as one of 26 books for B Dalton's Discover: Great New Writers series, 1990; 2nd place, Ina Coolbrith Poetry Prize, 1977. *Address:* P O Box 2416, Berkeley, CA 94702, USA.

QUIJADA Rodrigo, b. 23 Nov 1942, Punta Arenas, Chile. Lawyer. m. Broughton Maria Isabel, 6 May 1979, 1 daughter. *Education:* Lawyer, Chile University, 1971; Criminology Researcher, 1970; Sexologist and Marriage Counsellor, 1970. *Appointments:* Public Relations Manager, Orbe Publishers, 1966-69; Executive Editor, Hera Magazine, 1967-69; Creative Director, Multivision Audiovisual, 1976-; Literature Coordinator, Fonatur, Mexico Latinoamerican Section Editor, Le Monde Diplomatique, Mexico. *Publications:* Graduacion, 1970; Tiempo de Aranas, 1967; Bajo un Silencio, 1963; Techo Circular, 1973; Manual de Educacion Sexual, 1972; Elementos de Derecho Penal, 1975; Short stories, essays. *Contributions to:* numerous journals and magazines. *Honours:* Zig-Zag Publishers Prize, 1966; Municipal Prize, 1967. *Memberships:* PEN; Chilean Association of Writers; Mexican Association of Writers; Chilean Association of Sexology; Cultural Multivision Institute. *Address:* Matias Romero 227, Mexico 12, CP 03100, Mexico.

QUILLER Andrew. *See:* **BULMER Henry Kenneth.**

QUINAN John Francis, (Jack Quinan) b. 28 Nov, 1939, Somerville, Massachusetts, USA. Professor of Architectural History. m. Colleen Mullaney, 25 July, 1990, 1 son. *Education:* BA, Dartmouth College, 1962; MA, 1970, PhD, 1973, Brown University. *Publication:* Frank Lloyd Wright's Larkin Building: Myth and Fact, 1987. *Contributions to:* Casabella; Antiques; Winterthur Portfolio; Journal of the Society of Architectural Historians; Arts and Crafts Quarterly; Vermont History. *Membership:* Society of Architectural Historians, Secretary 1989-93. *Address:* Department of Art History, 611 Clemens Hall, SUNY at Buffalo, Amherst, NY 14260, USA.

QUINCE Peter. *See:* **THOMPSON John William** McWear.

QUINN Martin. *See:* **SMITH Martin Cruz.**

QUINN Simon. *See:* **SMITH Martin Cruz.**

QUINNEY Richard, b. 16 May, 1934. University Professor. *Education:* BS, Carroll College, 1956; MA, Northwestern University, 1957; PhD, University of Wisconsin, 1962. *Appointments:* Instructor, Department of Sociology and Anthropology, St Lawrence University, 1960-62; Assistant Professor, Department of Sociology, University of Kentucky, 1962-65; Associate Professor, 1965-70, Professor 1970-73, Department of Sociology, New York University; Research and writing leaves, Department of Sociology, University of North Carolina at Chapel Hill, Sabbatical from New York University 1971-74; Visiting Professor 1975-78, Adjunct Professor 1980-83, Department of Sociology, Brown University; Distinguished Visiting Professor 1978-79, Adjunct Professor 1980-83, Department of Sociology, Boston College; Professor, Department of Sociology, Northern Illinois University, 1983-. *Publications:* Many books including: Criminology: Analysis and Critique of Crime in America, 1975, 1979; Class, State and Crime: On the Theory and Practice of Criminal Justice, 1977, 1980; ed. Capitalist Society: Readings for a Critical Sociology, 1979; Providence: The Reconstrtuction of Social and Moral Order, 1980; Marxism and Law, co-editor Piers Beirne, 1982; Social Existence: Metaphysics, Marxism and the Social Sciences, 1982; Criminology as Peacemaking, co-editor Harold E Pepinsky, 1991; Journey to a Far Place: Autobiographical Reflections, 1991. *Contributions to:* Numerous articles contributed to professional journals including: Social Problems; Southwestern Social Science Quarterly; Journal of Criminal Law, Criminology and Police Science; Journal of Research in Crime and Delinquency; Sociometry; American Behavioral Scientist; British Journal of Criminology. *Honours:* Edwin Sutherland Award, for contributions to criminological theory, American Society of Criminology, 1984; Delegate, Crime Prevention and Criminal Justice Delegation to the People's Republic of China, sponsored by the Eisenhower Foundation and Northern Illinois University, 1985; Fulbright Award, lectureship at University College, Galway, Ireland, 1986; President's Award, Western Society of Criminology, 1992. *Address:* Department of Sociology, Northern Illinois University, Dekalb, IL 60115, USA.

QUINOT Raymond G.A., b. 12 Feb 1920, Brussels, Belgium. Director; Writer. m. Suzanne Cambron, 3 Sept 1952. *Appointments:* General Secretary, International PEN Club, French Speaking Centre Belgium; Administrator: Association of Belgian Writers, Royal Association of Walloon Writers, Foundation Charles Plisnier, International Biennal of Poetry of Liege. *Publications:* 48 books (essays and poetry) including: The Adventures of Jaune and Jaunette; Charles de Ligne, Walloon and European Prince; Thoughts of a Gentleman; My Cities; The Nice October; Solo for a Reader; Langston Hughes or the Black Star; Present. *Contributions to:* numerous, magazines, journals and anthologies throughout the World. *Honours:* Jury Member, Prize of the Ministery of the French Community in Belgium; Max Rose, Interfrance, Davaine (Academie Française, Paris) Ville de Bruxelles, Rime d'Or; Bouvier-Parvillez, Royal Academy, Brussels. *Address:* Le Bel-Air, 76 Avenue du Onze Novembre (bte 7), 1040, Brussels, Belgium.

QUINTAVALLE Uberto Paolo, b. 1 Nov 1926, Milan, Italy. Writer. m. Josephine Hawke, 1970, 5 sons. *Education:* D Litt, University of Milan, 1949; Playwriting,

Yale Drama School, 1950. *Publications:* La festa, 1953; Segnati a dito, 1956; Capitale mancata, 1959; Tutti compromessi, 1961; Rito romano, rito ambrosiano, 1964; Carolinda, 1974; Il Dio riciclato, 1989; La Diecimila canzoni di Putai, 1992. *Contributions to:* Il corriere della sera; Il gionale. *Memberships:* PEN Club, Secretary General of the Italian Division. *Address:* Via Mangili 2, 20121 Milan, Italy.

QUIRK Randolph, b. 12 July 1920, Isle of Man, England. Academic; President, The British Academy. *Education:* BA, 1947, MA 1949, PhD 1951, DLitt, 1961, University College, London; Yale University, USA. *Publications:* The Use of English, 1968; Elicitation Experiments in English, 1970; Grammar of Contemporary English, 1972; University Grammar of English, 1974; The Linguist & the English Language, 1974; Style & Communication in the English Language, 1982; Comprehensive Grammar of the English Language, 1985; Words at Work, 1987; A Students Grammer of the English Language, 1990; English in Use, 1990; An Introduction to Standard English, 1993. *Honours:* CBE, 1976; KT, 1985; Honorary Doctorates: Paris & 20 other Universities. *Address:* University College London, Gowen Street, London WC1E 6BT, England.

QUIROGA Elena, Writer. *Publications:* Viento del Norte, 1951; La Sangre, 1952; Algo Pasa en la Calle, 1954; La Enferma, 1954; La Careta, 1955; Placida, La Joven, 1956; la Ultima Corrida, 1958; Tristura, 1960; Escribo tu Nombre, 1965. *Honours:* Nadal Prize, 1950; Critics Prize, 1960; Escribo tu Nombre chosen to represent Spain in Romulo Gallegos Literary Competition, 1965. *Address:* Real Academia de la Historia, Leon 21, Madrid 14, Spain.

QURESHI Bashir, b. 25 Sept 1935, Doctor; Writer. *Education:* FRCGP; DCH; AFOM(RCP); FRSH; MICGP; FRIPHH. *Appointments:* Editor, Faculty News, Royal College of GPs, 1981-86; Editor, London Medicine, 1986-88; Editor, Writer, Journal of the GP Writer Association, 1992; Editor, Faculty Newsletter, Faculty of Community Health, 1988-92. *Publications:* Transcultural Medicine - Dealing with Patients from Different Cultures, 1989; Chapters in: Rehabilitation of the Elderly, 1989; Health Care for Asians, 1990; Screening and Surveillance in General Practice, 1992; RCGP Members Reference Books, 1983. 1985; The Medical Annual, 1984, 1986. *Contributions to:* British Medical Journal; Sunday Times; Journal of the Royal Society of Medicine; Pulse, GP and Doctor; Journal of the Royal Society of Health. *Memberships:* Society of Authors; PEN; Council Member: Royal College of GPs, Royal Society of Health, Society of Public Health; Chairman, South Middlesex Division, British Medical Association; Editorial Representative, G P Section, Royal Society of Medicine. *Address:* 32 Legrace Avenue, Hounslow West, Middlesex TW4 7RS, England.

R

RABE Berniece, b. 11 Jan 1928. Author. m. 30 July 1946, 3 sons, 1 daughter. *Education:* BSEd, National College; Graduate work in Psychology and Administration, Northern Illinois and Roosevelt Universities; Master's degree, Columbia College, Chicago. *Appointments include:* Writing Instructor, Columbia College, Chicago, 2 years; Consultant, Missouri Council of the Arts. *Publications:* Rass, 1973; Naomi, 1975; The Girl Who Had No Name, 1977; The Orphans, 1978; Who's Afraid, 1980; Margaret's Moves, 1987; A Smooth Move, 1987; Rehearsal for the Bigtime, 1988; Where's Chimpy, 1988; Joey Caruba, 1988; Tall Enough To Own The World; Picture books: The Balancing Girl, 1982; Can They See Me; Two Peas in a Pod; 2 film scripts. *Contributions to:* Short stories and articles. *Honours include:* 3rd Place, Mark Twain Award, 1973; Honor Book, 1975; Golden Kite Award, 1977, National Society of Children's Book Writers Award, 1975; Midland Author's Award, 1978; Notable Book of the Year, American Library Association, 1982; Book of the Year, Child Study Association, 1982; National Children's Choice Award, 1987. *Memberships include:* Board of Directors, Society of Midland Authors; Board of Directors, Off Campus Writers; Board of Directors, Fox Valley Writers. *Address:* 860 Willow Lane, Sleepy Hollow, IL 60118, USA.

RACHLIN Nahid, b. 6 June 1944, Abadan, Iran. Writer; Instructor. m. Howard Rachlin, 1 daughter. *Education:* BA, Psychology, Lindenwood College, St Charles, Missouri, USA; 24 credits in Creative Writing, Columbia University. *Appointments:* New York University, School of Continuing Education, 1978-90; Marymount Manhattan College 1986-87; Hofstra University, 1988-90; Yale University, 1989-90; Hunter College, 1990; Barnard College, 1991-. *Publications:* Foreigner, W W Norton 1978, John Murray 1978; Married to a Stranger, 1983; Veils, 1992. *Contributions to:* Redbook; Shenandoah; Crosscurrents; Fiction; Prism International; Ararat; Confrontation; Minnesota Review; Four Quarters; Columbia Magazine; New Laurel Review; Blueline; New Letters; Mississippi Mud; City Lights Journal; Pleiades; North Atlantic Review; Chanteh. *Honours:* Doubleday-Columbia Fellowship; Stegner Fellowship, Stanford; National Endowment for the Arts grant; Bennet Certificate Award; PEN Syndicated Fiction Project. *Membership:* PEN. *Address:* Apt. PHC, 501E, 87th Street, New York, NY 10128, USA.

RADER Dotson Carlyle, b. 25 July 1942, Evanston, Illinois, USA. Writer. *Education:* Columbia University. *Appointments:* Editor, Defiance, radical review, Warner Books, 1969-71; Contributing Editor, Evergreen Review, 1969-73; Contributing Editor, Esquire, 1973-77; Vice-Chairman, National Committee for the Literary Arts, Lincoln Center, 1980-86; Contributing Editor, Parade Magazine, 1984-; Member, Special Board, New Politics. *Publications:* I Aint Marchin' Anymore, 1969; Gov't Inspected Meat and Other Summer Things, 1971; Blood Dues, 1973; The Dream's On Me, 1976; Miracle, 1978; Beau Monde, 1981; Tennessee: Cry of the Heart: An Intimate Memoir of Tennessee Williams, 1985. *Contributions to:* London Review; Paris Review; Vanity Fair; New Republic; Partisan Review; Rolling Stone; New York Magazine; Village Voice; Harper's Bazaar; New York Times. *Honours:* Honorary Ambassador, State of West virginia, 1982; National Journalism Award, Odyssey Institute, 1982; Special Olympics Award, National Journalism, Joseph P Kennedy Foundation, 1985. *Memberships:* PEN; Overseas Press Club; The Dramatists Guild; Actors Studio, Playwright-Directors Unit; Westhampton Writers Festival. *Literary Agent:* Anne Sibald, Janklow- Nesbit, New York, USA. *Address:* c/o Janklow-Nesbit, 598 Madison Avenue, New York, NY 10022, USA.

RADFORD Richard Francis, b. 15 Feb 1939, Boston. Executive Director, Home For Now, Inc. m. 20 Aug 1966, 1 son, 1 daughter. *Education:* BA, Hons, Boston State College 1979; Ordained Permanent Deacon, St John's Seminary, 1988; MEd, EdD, 1992, University of Massachusetts, Amherst. *Publications:* Having Been There, 1979; Dream of Spring, 1982; One White Rose, 1982; Tournament of Love, 1982; Trooper, 1985; Golfers' Book of Trivia, 1987; Drug Agent USA, 1991. *Contributions to:* Theory and Pedagogy; Creativity and Madness; 20th Century's Greatest Poems; Pegasus; Not the Boston Globe. *Honours:* National Council in Alcoholism, 1980; Nomination, Pushcart Prize; Tenet's Award (Shriners) 1992. *Address:* 8 Juniper Street 29, Brookline, MA 02146, USA.

RADLEY Shelia. *See:* **ROBINSON Shelia Mary.**

RADTKE Gunter, b. 23 Apr 1925, Berlin, Germany. Author. *Education:* Trainee Journalist. *Publications:* Davon Kommst du Nicht Los, 1971; Die Dunne Haut Der Luftballons, 1975; Der Krug Auf Dem Weg Zum Wasser, 1977; Gluck aus Mangel an Beweisen, 1978; Suchen Wer Wir Sind, 1980; Gedanken zum Selbermachen, 1987; Wolkenlandschaften, 1988. *Contributions to:* Numerous literary magazines, newspaper and broadcasting stations. *Honours:* German Short Story Prize, 1971; George Mackensen Prize, 1973; The First Roman Literature Prize, 1975; Literature Prize, Markische Culture Conference, 1979. *Memberships:* Die Kogge; Association of German Writers; NGL Hamburg and Berlin; PEN. *Literary Agent:* Deutsche Verlags-Anstalt. *Address:* Postfach 86, Keitúm/Sylt, Germany.

RAE Hugh Craufurd (James Albany, Robert Crawford, R B Houston, Morgan McGrath, Stuart Stern, Jessica Sterling), b. 22 Nov 1935, Glasgow, Scotland. Novelist. m. Elizabeth Dunn, 3 Sept 1960, Glasgow, 1 daughter. *Appointments:* Scottish Arts Council 1975-80. *Publications include:* Skinner, 1965; Night Pillow, 1966; A Few Small Bones, 1968; The Saturday Epic, 1970; Harkfast, 1976; Sullivan, 1978; Haunting at Waverley Falls, 1980; Privileged Strangers 1982; As Jessica Stirling: The Spoiled Earth, 1974; The Hiring Fair, 1976; The Dark Pasture, 1978; The Deep Well at Noon, 1980; The Blue Evening Gone, 1982; The Gates of Midnight, 1983; Treasures on Earth, 1985; Creature Comforts, 1986; Hearts of Gold, 1987; As James Albany: Warrior Caste, Mailed Fist, Deacons's Dagger, 1982; Close Combat, Matching Fire, 1983; Last Bastion, Borneo Story, 1984. *Membership:* Scottish Association of Writers. *Address:* Drumore Farm Cottage, Balfron Station, Stirlingshire, Scotland.

RAE John Malcolm, b. 20 Mar 1931, London, England. Director, The Portman Group. *Education:* MA, Sidney Sussex College, Cambridge University, 1955; PhD, King's College, London University. *Publications:* The Custard Boys, 1960; Conscience and Politics, 1970; The Golden Crucifix, 1974; The Treasure of Westminster Abbey, 1975; Christmas is Coming, 1976; Return to the Winter Palace, 1979; The Third Twin: A Ghost Story, 1980; The Public School Revolution, 1981; Letters from School, 1987; Too Little, Too Late?, 1989; Delusions of Grandeur, 1993. *Contributions to:* Encounter; Times Literary Supplement; Times Educational Supplement; The Times; Sunday Telegraph. *Honour:* Recipient, United Nations Award for Film Script, Reach for Glory, 1962. *Literary Agent:* The Peters Fraser Dunlop Group Ltd. *Address:* 101 Millbank Court, 24 John Islip St., London SW1P 4LG, England.

RAELIN Jospeh A, b. 10 Apr 1948, Cambridge, Massachusetts, USA. Professor of Management. m. Abby P Dolin, 4 Aug 1974, 2 sons. *Education:* Diplome, University of Paris, Sorbonne, 1969; BA, 1970, EdM, 1971, Tufts University; PhD, State University of New York at Buffalo, 1977. *Appointments:* The Wallace E Carroll School of Management, Boston College, Chestnut Hill, Massachusetts, 1976-, currently Professor of Management. *Publications:* Building A Career: The Effect of Initial Job Experiences and Related Attitudes on Later Employment, 1980; The Salaried Professional: How to Make the Most of Your Career, 1984; The Clash of Cultures: Managers Managing Professionals, 1986, paperback 1991. *Contributions to:*

Some 50 articles in professional journals, proceedings and magazines. *Memberships:* Academy of Management (US), Chair of Careers Division, 1991. *Address:* The Wallace E Carroll School of Management, Boston College, Chestnut Hill, MA 02167, USA.

RAES Hugo L, b. 26 May 1929, Antwerp, Belgium. Author. m. Marie- Therese Vandebotermet, 1965, 1 son, 1 daughter. *Education:* Germanic Languages. *Publications:* Novels: De vadsige koningen; Een faun met kille horentjes; De lotgevallen; Reizigers in de anti-tijd; De verwoesting van Hyperion; Het smaran; De strik; Many short stories. *Honours:* L van der Hoogt Prize, 1969; Literaire Staatsprijs, 1976. *Membership:* International PEN Club. *Address:* Nachtegaallaan 55, B 2660 Antwerp, Belgium.

RAFFEL Burton Nathan, b. 27 Apr 1928, New York City, USA. Writer; Translator; Editor; Teacher; Lawyer. m. Elizabeth Clare Wilson, 16 Apr 1974, 3 sons, 3 daughters. *Education:* BA, Brooklyn College, 1948; MA, Ohio State University, 1949; JD, Yale University, 1958. *Appointments include:* Editor, Foundation News, 1960-63; Denver Quarterly, 1976-77. *Publications include:* Beowulf, translation, 1963; How To Read A Poem, 1984; Signet Book of American Stories, anthology, 1985; After Such Ignorance, novel, 1986; Four Humours, poems, 1979; The Voice of the Night: Complete Poetry and Prose of Chairil Anwar, translation, 1993; Chretien de Troyes, Yvain, translation, 1987; Rabelais, Gargantua and Portaguel, translation, 1990; Cervantes, Don Quijote, translation, 1994; Various other books of criticism, history. *Contributions to:* Hudson Review; Saturday Review of Literature; Asian Wall Street Journal; Arion; Tri-Quarterly; Atlantic Monthly; Literary Review; Times Literary Supplement; Yale Review; Books Abroad; Science Digest; Thought; London Magazine; East-West Review. *Honour:* Frances Steloff Prize, fiction, 1978. *Address:* Raffel, 203 Mannering Avenue S, Lafayette, LA 70508, USA.

RAGEN Naomi, b. 10 July 1949, Brooklyn, New York, USA. Writer. m. Alex Ragen, 23 Nov 1969, 2 sons, 2 daughters. *Education:* BA, cum laude, English specialising in writing, Brooklyn College, 1971; MA, English, Hebrew University of Jerusalem, 1977. *Appointments:* Editor, Israel Environment Bulletin, Ministry of the Interior; Freelance Journalist, Jerusalem Post, Hadassah Magazine, Wisconsin Jewish Chronicle, Denver Jewish News. *Publications:* Jephte's Daughter, 1988; Sotah, 1992. *Membership:* Authors Guild. *Address:* POB 23004, Ramot, Jerusalem, Israel.

RAGON Michel, b. 24 June 1924, Marseille, France. Author. m. Francoise Antoine, 28 Dec 1968. *Education:* Docteur es-Lettres. *Publications:* Droles de Metiers (novel), 1953; L'Accent de ma mere (novel), 1980; Les Mouchoirs rouges de Cholet (novel), 1982; Histoire mondiale de l'architecture et de l'urbanisme modernes, 3 vols, 19781-78; Histoire de la litterature proletarienne, 1974; 25 ans d'art vivant, 1986; 12 other novels; 15 monographs about painters and architects; Numerous works conveyning modern art and architecture. *Honours:* Member of the Royal Academy of Denmark; Member of the Academy of Brittany; Laureate, Academie Francaise; Grande Medaille d'Argent and Grande Medaille de Vermeil, Academie d'Architecture. *Memberships:* Societe des Gens de Lettres; International Association of Art Critics. *Address:* 4 rue du Faubourg Poissonniere, 75010 Paris, France.

RAHAM Richard Gary, b. 12 Nov 1946, Ann Arbor, Michigan, USA. Graphic Artist; Illustrator; Writer. m. Sharon S Waufle, 8 Apr 1971, 2 daughters. *Education:* BA. Biology, 1968, MA, Biology, 1969, University of Michigan; Postgraduate work, Colorado State University. *Publications:* Dinosaurs in the Garden, 1988; Sillysaurs: The Dinosaurs That Could Have Been, 1990; 3 filmstrips on lichens, 1980. *Contributions to:* Articles and short fiction to: Earth Magazine; Highlights for Children; The Friend; The American Biology Teacher; From the Canyons; Backyard Bugwatching; Stimuli for

Writers; Aboriginal Science Fiction; Scientists and Science Teachers; On the Wing; Guild of Natural Science Illustrators Newsletter; Fusion; Backyard Biology monthly column in Northern Newsline, 1988-91. *Honours:* Honourable Mention, Writers Digest Magazine Writing Competition, Article Category, 1986; Science Article of the Year Award, Highlights for Children, 1987; Poster-cover design accepted for Society of Illustrators 30th Annual Exhibition and inclusion in Illustrators 30; Honourable Mention, National Writers Club Annual Short Fiction Contest, National Writers Club, 1991; Quarter-Finalist, L Ron Hubbard Writers of the Future Contest, 1991. *Memberships:* National Writers Club; Society of Children's Book Writers; Guild of Natural Science Illustrators; Art Director, Rivers-Srtudies in the Science, Environmental Policy and Law of Instream Flow. *Address:* 3714 Grant Ave, Wellington, CO 80549, USA.

RAI Indra Bahadur, b. 3 Feb 1927, Darjeeling, India. Author; Farmer. m. Maya Devi, 7 Aug 1950, 1 son, 2 daughters. *Education:* MA, Literature. *Publications:* These Days A Show, 1964; Glimpses of Realities, 1961; Belief and Stories, 1972; Notes and Jottings, 1966; Examining the Bases of Nepali Novels, 1974; With Reference to Peoms by Ishvar Vallachka Kavita, 1976; Half a Century of Indian Nepali Drama, 1984; Literature : A Caste of Attempted Kidnapping, 1983; Studying Bhanubhakta's Works, Editor, 1969. *Contributions to:* Numerous professional journals. *Honours:* Sahitya Akademi Award, 1977. *Memberships:* Executive Member, Sahitya Akademi Delhi, 1978-87; President, Nepali Sahitya Parishad, Darjeeling. *Literary Agent:* Maya Devi Rai. *Address:* Seclusion House, 15/1 Toong Soong Road, Darjeeling, India 734101.

RAIJADA Rajendrasinh, b. 1 July 1943, Sondarda, India. Headmast, High School, Keshod. m. Gulabkumari Raijada, 21 Feb 1969, 2 sons, 1 daughter. *Education:* BEd, Gujarati, 1973, MA, Gujarati, 1975, Saurashtra University, Rajkot; PhD, Mysticism in Modern Gujarati Poetry, Sardar Patel University, Vallabhvidyanagar, 1979. *Appointments:* Central Committee Member, Gujarati Sahitya Parishad, Amdavad, 1975-77; Language Expert, Gujarat State Text Book Board, Gandhinagar, 1975-82; Resource Person, National Education Policy, 1986; Adviser, Gujarat Sahitya Academy, Gandhinagar, 1991. *Publications:* Radha Madhav, translation from Hindi), 1970; Farva avyo chhun, poetry, 1976; Gulmahor ni niche, short stories, 1977; Rahasyavad, essays, 1980; Hun, Kali chhokari ane Suraj, poetry, 1982; Darsdhan ane Itihas, collection of articles, 1983; Sant Parampara Vimarsh, criticism, 1989. *Contributions to:* Numerous papers, articles on religion, yoga, philosophy, tantra, literature, archaelogy, history, culture, criticism, others, to prominent Gujarati, Hindi and English magazines and journals. *Honours:* 2nd Prize, Painting, Gujarat State Youth Festival, 1964; 1st Prize in Short Story, Patnik, 1976; 1st Prize in Short Story, Kumar, 1980; National Award for Best Teacher, 1990. *Memberships include:* Life Member, Puratatva Mandal, Porbandar; Life Member, Gujarati Sahitya Parishad, Amdavad; Akhil Gujarat Kalapi Sahitya Parishad, Junagadh District, 1989; Central Committee, District Acharya Sangh, Junagadh, 1975; Central Committee; Saurashtra Itihas Parishad, Junagadh, 1976-77; Chairman, Nature Club, Keshod, 1982; Secretary, Ramkrishna Education Trust, Keshod, 1982-87; Trustee, Saraswati Education Trust, Sondarda, 1982; Coral Nature Foundation, Jamnagar, 1991; President, All India Student Union, Keshod, 1986. *Address:* Sondarda, Via Kevadra 362227, Gujarat, India.

RAILSBACK Brian Evan, b. 24 Sept 1959, Glendale, California, USA. Assistant Professor of English. m. Sandra Lea Railsback, 6 Aug 1983, 2 sons, 1 daughter. *Education:* AA, 1981; BA, Journalism, 1982; MA, English, 1985; PhD, English, 1990. *Appointments:* John Cady Fellow, Ohio University, 1989; Assistant Professor, English, Western Carolina University, North Carolina, 1990-. *Contributions to:* Scholarly articles to: San Jose Studies; Steinbeck Quarterly; Short story to Tamaqua; Reviews to various magazines and journals.

Memberships: American Writing Programs; Modern Language Association; International Steinbeck Society. *Address:* PO Box 1001, Cullowhee, NC 28723, USA.

RAINBOW. *See:* **YANO Shigeharu.**

RAINE Craig Anthony, b. 3 Dec 1944, Shildon. Writer. m. Ann Pasternak Slater, 27 Apr 1972, 3 sons, 1 daughter. *Education:* Honours degree in English Language and Literature, Oxford, 1966; B Phil, English Studies, Oxford, 1968. *Literary Appointments:* Reviews Editor at the New Review, 1977-79; Editor of Quarto 1979-80; Poetry Editor, New Statesman, 1981; Poetry Editor, Faber 1981-91. *Publications include:* A Martian Sends a Postcard Home, 1979; The Onion Memory, 1978; Rich, 1984; The Electrification of the Soviet Union, 1987; '1953', 1990; Haydn and the Valve Trumpet, 1990. *Contributions to:* Observer; Sunday Times; Independent on Sunday; New Statesman; Listener; Encounter; London Review of Books; TLS; Literary Review; Grand Street; New Yorker. *Honours:* Southern Arts Literature Award, 1980; Cholmondeley Award, 1983; Fellow, New College, Oxford, 1991-. *Memberships:* PEN; Royal Society of Literature. *Address:* New College, Oxford, England.

RAINE Kathleen Jessie, b. 1908. Poet, Scholar. m. Charles Madge, divorced, 1 son, 1 daughter. *Education; Girton College, Cambridge. Publications:* Stone and Flower, 1943; Living in Time, 1946; The Pythoness, 1949; The Year One, 1952; Collected Poems, 1956; The Hollow Hill (poems), 1965; Defending Ancient Springs (criticism), 1967; Blake and Tradition (Andrew Mellon Lectures, Washington), 1962; William Blake, 1970; The Lost Country (verse), 1971; On a Deserted Shore (verse), 1973; Yeats, the Tarot and The Golden Dawn (criticism), 1973; Faces of Day and Night, 1973; Farewell Happy Fields, autobiography, 1973; Death in Life and Life in Death (on Yeats), 1974; The Land Unkown, autobiography, 1975; The Oval Portrait, (verse), 1977; The Lion's Mouth, autobiography, 1977; David Jones and the Actually Loved and Known, (criticism), 1978; From Blake to a Vision (criticism), 1979; Collected Poems, 1981; The Human Face of God, 1982; The Inner Journey of the Poet and other Papers (criticism), 1982; L'Imagination Creatice de William Blake: French translation of verse : Isis errant, 1978; Sur un rivage desert, 1978; Le Premier Jour, 1980; Spanish translation: En una desierta orilla, 1980; Co-Editor, Temenos, 1981-; Yeats the Initiate, 1986; La bueul du Lion, 1987; The Preserve (verse), 1988; Selected poems, 1988; Le Royaume Invisible, 1991. *Honours:* Hon. Doctorates from Universities of Leicester, 1974, Durham, 1979, Caen (France), 1987; Prix de Heilleur Liore Etranger, 1978; W.H. Smith & Son Award, 1972. *Address:* 47 Paultons Square, London SW3, England.

RAJA P, b. 7 Oct 1952, Pondicherry, India. Lecturer in English. m. Periyanayaki, 6 May 1976, 2 sons, 1 daughter. *Education:* BA, English, 1973; MA, English Language and Literature, 1975; PhD, Indian Writing in English, 1992. *Appointments:* Regular contributor to about 15 journals in India; Literary Editor to Pondicherry Today (fortnightly). *Publications:* From Zero to Infinity (poems) 1987; Folktales of Pondicherry, 1987; A Concise History of Pondicherry, 1987; Tales of Mulla Nasruddin, 1989; The Blood and Other Stories, 1991; Translations from Tamil: The Stupid Guru and his Foolish Disciples, 1981, The Sun and the Stars, 1982. *Contributions to:* Contributed poems, stories, one-act plays, interviews, essays, skits and reviews to more than 120 newspapers and magazines both in India and abroad. *Honours:* Literary Award, Pondicherry University, 1987; Michael Madhusudan Academy (Calcutta) Award, 1991. *Memberships:* Youth Literary Club, Pondicherry; Poetry Society, New Delhi. *Address:* 74 Poincare Street, Olandai-Keerapalayam, Pondicherry 605004, India.

RAJIC Negovan, b. 24 June 1923, Belgrade, Yugoslavia. Writer. m. Mirjana Knezevic, 28 Mar 1970, 1 son, 1 daughter. *Education:* Attended University of Belgrade 1945-46; Diplome d'etudes techniques superieures, 1962, Diploma in Electrical Engineering, 1968, Conservatoire des Arts et Metiers, Paris. *Appointments:* Fought with Resistance during World War II, escaped Yugoslavia 1946, arrived Paris, 1947, resumed studies in Engineering; Research Engineer, Physics Laboratory, Ecole Polytechnique de Paris, 1956-63; Researcher in Electronics, France 1963-69; Came to Canada, 1969 becoming Professor of Mathematics, Cegep Trois Rivieres to 1987. *Publications:* Les Hommes-Taupes, 1978, English translation The Mole Men, 1980; Propos d'un vieux radoteur, 1982, English translation The Master of Srappado, 1984; Sept roses pour une boulangere, 1987, English translation, Seven Roses for a Baker, 1988; Service penitentiaire, 1988, English translation The Shady Business, 1989; Numerous articles and short stories. *Honours:* Prix Esso du Cercle du Livre de France, 1978; Prix Air Canada best short story, 1980; Prix Slobodan Yovanovitch Association des ecrivains et artistes serbes enexil, 1984; Prix litteraire de Trois-Rivieres, 1988. *Memberships:* PEN International; Association of Writers of Quebec; Honorary member, Association of Serbian Writers, Belgrade. *Address:* 300 Dunant, Trois- Rivieres, Quebec, Canada G8Y 2W9.

RAMA RAO Vadapalli Vijaya Bhaskara, b. 1 Jan 1938, Srikakulam District, A P, India. Educator. m. Ramani Rama Rao, 15 Apr 1959, 1 son, 3 daughters. *Education:* BA, Economics, 1957; BA, English, 1958; MA, English, 1961; Diploma in Teaching English, 1966; Diploma in French, 1979; PhD, 1980. *Publications:* In English: Poosapati Ananda Gajapati Raju, biography, 1985; Tapaswi, novel, 1989; Graham Greene's Comic Vision, criticism, 1990; Into That Heaven of Freedom, novel, 1991; Warm Days Will Never Cease, forthcoming; Translation, Trapped, novel, from English to Telugu, 1991; 6 novels in Telugu: Sparasarekhalu, 1977; Neetikireetalu, 1977; Maguvalu - Manasulu, 1980; Gaalipadagalu - Deepakalikalu, 1981; Tapaswi, 1985; Avagaahana, forthcoming. *Contributions to:* 15 literary reviews in English and about 125 short fiction in Telugu to magazines and journals; About 400 English and about 20 Telugu feature and newspaper articles. *Honours:* Prize for novel in Telugu, popular weekly's contest, 1975; Merit Award,, British Council Short Story Contest, South India, 1988; A P State Award for College and University Teachers, 1989-90. *Memberships:* Indian Society of Authors, New Delhi; Life Member, Indian PEN, Bombay. *Address:* 19-5- 13 Kanukurti st, Vizianagaram 531 202, India.

RAMA RAU Santha, (Rama Rau Wattles), b. 24 Jan 1923, Madras, India. Freelance Writer. m. (1) Faubion Bowers, 24 Oct 1951, divorced 1966, 1 son, (2) Gurdon W. Wattles, 1970. *Education:* BA, Honours, Wellesley College, USA, 1945. *Publications:* Home to India, 1945; East of Home, 1950; This India, 1953; Remember the House, 1955; View to the South-East, 1957; My Russian Journey, 1959; A Passage to India, 1962 (Dramatisation of E.M. Forster's Novel); Gifts of Passage, 1962; The Cooking of India, 1970; The Adventuress, 1970; A Princess Remembers, 1976; An Inheritance, 1977. *Contributions to:* numerous journals and magazines. *Honours:* Honorary Degrees: Bates College, 1960, Roosevelt University, 1962, Brandeis University, 1962, Russell Sage College, 1965; Awards: Asia Society, 1962; Secondary Education Board, 1963; Mlle Mag. Merit Award, 1965; Association of Indians in America, 1977. *Literary Agent* William Morris Agency. *Address:* c/o William Morris Agency, 1350 6th Avenue, New York, NY 10019, USA.

RAMAMURTI Krishnamurthy Sitaraman, (Madhuram Ramamurti), b. 4 Nov 1930, Madras, India. Professor of English; Dean. m. Rajesnari Ramamurti, 4 July 1958, 2 daughters. *Education:* BSc, Physics, 1950, MA, English Language and Literature, 1954, University of Madras; MA, English Literature, Muslim University, Aligarh, 1963; Diploma, Teaching of English, Central Institute of English, Hyderabad; PhD, Madurai University, 1975. *Appointments:* Lecturer, English, St Aloysius College, Mangalore, 1954- 65; Professor, Head, Department of English, Sri Palaniasndowar Arts

College, Palmi, 1965-76; Lecturer, 1976-78, Reader, 1978-84, Professor, 1984-91, Dean, College Development Council, 1991-, Bharathidasan University, Tiruchirapalli. *Publications:* Vazhithunai, novel, 1980; Rise of the Indian Novel in English, 1986; Editor: The Spanish Tragedy (Thomas Kyd), 1978; Perspectives on Modern English Prose, 1985; Variety in Short Stories, 1988. *Contributions to:* About a dozen short novels and short stories in Tamil to leading journals; About a dozen feature articles to leading newspapers including: The Hindu; Indian Express; About 70 research papers to standard literary journals; About 20 book reviews and review articles. *Honours:* Prize for novel, 1980. *Memberships:* Indian Association of English Teachers; Comparative Literature Association of India; Executive Committee, Indian Association of Canadian Studies. *Address:* Bharatidasan University, Tiruchirapalli 620024, India.

RAMAMURTI Madhuram. *See:* **RAMAMURTI Krisnamurthy Sitaraman.**

RAMDIN Ronald Andrew, b. 20 June 1942, Marabella, Trinidad. Historian; Writer; Lecturer. m. Irma de Freitas, 20 Dec 1969, 1 son. *Education:* Diploma in Speech and Drama, New Era Academy of Drama and Music, 1963; Diploma in Industrial Relations and Trade Union Studies, University of Middlesex, 1977; BSc, Econ, London School of Economics and Political Science, 1982. *Publications:* From Chattel Slave to Wage Earner, 1982; Introductory Text: The Black Triangle, 1984; The Making of the Black Working Class in Britain, 1987; Paul Robeson: The Man and His Mission, 1987; World in View: West Indies, 1990; Arising From Bondage: A History of East Indians in the Caribbean 1838-1991, forthcoming. *Contributions to:* Anglo-British Review; City Limits; Dragon's Teeth; Race Today; Caribbean Times; West Indian Digest; History Workshop Journal. *Honours:* Scarlet Ibis (Gold Medal) Award, Trinidad and Tobago High Commission (London) 1990; Hansib (Caribbean Times) Community Award (Britain) 1990. *Address:* The British Library, Humanities and Social Science Section, Great Russell Street, London WC1B 3DG, England.

RAMI Sonia, b. 14 May 1953, Cairo, Egypt. Writer. *Education:* PhD, Harvard University, 1984. *Publication:* Antiquity Street (novel, love story) 1992. *Contributions to:* New York Times; New York Review of Books. *Address:* c/o Elaine Markson, Literary Agent, 44 Greenwich Avenue, New York City, NY 10011, USA.

RAMIREZ-DE-ARELLANO Diana, b. 3 June 1919, New York City, USA. Professor Emeritus; Poet; Writer. *Education:* BA, University of Puerto Rico, 1941; MA TC, University of Columbia, 1946; Licentiate Degree and Title, University of Madrid, 1959; Doctorate Degree and Title, 1952 and 1961. *Appointments:* Poetry Chair, City College, City University of New York, 1970-; President and Director of Publications, Ateneo de New York. *Publications include:* Los Ramirez de Arellano de Lope De Vega, literary editor, 1954; Caminos de la Creacion Poetica en Pedro Salinas, literary criticism, 1957; Angeles de Coniza (poetry) 1958; Privilegio (poetry), 1959; Poesia Contemporanea en Langua Espanola 1961; Tree at Vespers (bilingual) (poetry), ed 1987; Un Vuelo Casi Humano (poetry); Albatros Sobre el Alma (poetry); Poesia Diacunista de Taller, CUNY; Memorias del Ateneo Pr de NY 1961-67; Adelfazar (Elegia) 1990. *Contributions to:* Numerous journals in Puerto Rico and Spain. *Honours:* First Prize in Literature, Institute of Literature, Puerto Rico, 1958; Prize for Literary Criticism, Institute of Literature, Puerto Rico, 1961; Order of Merit, Republic of Ecuador, 1971; International Prize for Poetry, Ministry of Education and Arts, Bolivia, 1964; Professor Emeritus, City University of New York, 1984. *Memberships include:* American Association of Spanish and Portuguese (Professor Emeritus); President, Josefina Romo Arregon Memorial Foundation; PEN Club International, Puerto Rican Chapter; Royal Academy of Doctors of Madrid, USA Representative. *Address:* 23 Harbor Circle, Centerport, NY 11721, USA.

RAMKE Bin, b. 19 Feb 1947, Pt. Neches, Texas, USA. Teacher; Editor; Poet. m. 31 May 1967, 1 son. *Education:* BA, Louisiana State University, 1970; MA, University of New Orleans, 1971; PhD, Ohio University, 1975. *Appointments:* Professor, English, Columbus College, Georgia, 1976-85; Professor, English, University of Denver, 1985-; Editor, Contemporary Poetry Series, University of Georgia Press, 1984-; Poetry Editor, The Denver Quarterly, 1985-. *Publications:* The Language Student, 1987; The Difference Between Night and Day, 1978; White Monkeys, 1981; The Erotic Light of Gardens, 1989. *Contributions to:* Poetry, New Yorker, Paris Review, Poetry; Essays and Reviews in Georgia Law Review, Denver Quarterly. *Honours:* Yale Younger Poets Award, 1977; Texas Institute of Arts and Letters Award (Poetry), 1978. *Memberships:* PEN, American Centre; Associated Writing Programmes. *Address:* Department of English, University of Denver, Denver, CO 80208, USA.

RAMNEFALK (Sylvia) Marie Louise, b. 21 Mar 1941, Stockholm, Sweden. *Education:* FK, 1964, FL, 1968, FD, 1974, Stockholm University. *Appointments:* Script Supervisor, TV-theatre, 1967-68; University Teacher, Stockholm University, 1960s; Umea University, 1970s; School for Librarians, Boras, 1970s, 1980s; Karlstad University, 1986-87; Literary critic, several papers and magazines. *Publications:* Nagon har jag sett, poems, 1979; Author of 6 other poetry books including: Adam i Paradiset, 1984; Tre larodiktare, Studier i Harry Martinsons, Gunnar Ekelofs och Karl Vennbergs lyrik, 1974; Opera librettos: Love Love Love, 1973; Nagon har jag sett, 1987. *Contributions to:* numerous newspapers and magazines including: Aftonbladet; Var Losen. *Honours:* Recipient of several Scholarships. *Memberships:* Statens Kulturrad, 1981-89; Forfattarforlaget, Executive Board, 1977-82, President, 1982-84; Sveriges Forfattarforbund, Executive Board, 1979-83; Forfattarnas Fotokopieringsfond, President, 1985-87; Swedish PEN. *Address:* Vastra Valhallavagen 25 A, S-182 63 Djursholm, Sweden.

RAMSAY Jay. *See:* **RAMSAY-BROWN John Andrew.**

RAMSAY-BROWN John Andrew, (Jay Ramsay), b. 20 Apr 1958, Guildford, Surrey, England. Poet; Writer; Translator; Administrator; Editor; Teacher. *Education:* Charterhouse School; BA, Hons, English Language and Literature, Pembroke College, Oxford, 1980; Foundation Year diploma in Psychosynthesis, London Institute, 1987. *Appointments:* Co-founder and administrator of Angels of Fire 1983-88: 4 major festivals in London of poetry and related media (music, dance, video), appearing on ITV South of Watford and BBC2 Open Space, two documentaries, 1985; Project Director of Chrysalis - The Poet In You (founded 1990), including its two-part course by post for students in Britain and abroad, editing, one-to-one sessions, retreats, and the workshop The Sacred Space of the Word. *Publications:* Psychic Poetry - a manifesto, 1985; co-editor, Angels of Fire, an anthology of radical poetry in the 80's, 1986; The White Poem, with photographs by Carole Bruce, 1988; ed. Transformation - the poetry of spiritual consciousness, 1988; The Great Return bks 1-5, published in 2 vols, 1988; Raw Spiritual - Selected Poems, 1986, Trwyn Meditations, 1987, Transmissions, 1989, Strange Days, 1990, Journey to Eden (with Jenny Davis) 1991, For Now (with Geoffrey Godbert) 1991, The Rain, The Rain, 1992, St. Patrick's Breastplate. 1992; Tao Te Ching, a new translation, 1993. *Contributions to:* Poetry Review; Literary Review; City Limits; Acumen; Resurgence; Jungle (Paris); Apart (West Germany); Island (Athens); Forum - the journal of Psychosynthesis. *Memberships:* Poetry Society; Psychosynthesis Education and Trust (London). *Address:* c/o The Diamond Press, 5 Berners Mansions, 34-6 Berners Street, London W1P 3DA, England.

RANA J. *See:* **BHATIA Jamunadevi.**

RAND Peter, b. 23 Feb 1942, San Francisco,

California, USA. Writer. m. Bliss Inui, 19 Dec 1976, 1 son. *Education:* MA, Johns Hopkins University, 1975. *Appointments:* Fiction Editor, Antaeus, 1970- 72; Editor, Washington Monthly, 1973-74; Teaching Fellow, Johns Hopkins University, 1975; Lecturer-in-English, Columbia University, New York City, 1976-91. *Publications:* Firestorm, 1969; The Time of the Emergency, 1977; The Private Rich, 1984; Gold from Heaven, 1988. *Contributions to:* New York Times; Washington Post; Penthouse; Washington Monthly; Antaeus; Others. *Honours:* CAPS, 1977. *Memberships:* PEN; Authors Guild; Poets and Writers; East Asian Institute, Columbia University; Research Associate, Fairbank Center, Harvard University. *Literary Agent:* Wendy Weil. *Address:* 24 Winslow Rd, Belmont, MA 02178, USA.

RANDALL Clay. *See:* **ADAMS Clifton.**

RANDALL Michael Bennett, b. 12 Aug 1919. *Appointments:* Assistant Editor, Sunday Chronicle, 1952-53; Editor, Sunday Graphic, 1953; Assistant Editor, Daily Mirror, 1953-56; Assistant Editor, News Chronicle, 1956-57; Assistant Editor, Daily Mail, 1957-61, Deputy Editor 1961-63, Editor 1963-66; Managing Editor, News, Sunday Times, 1967-72, Senior Managing Editor, 1972-78. *Publication:* The Funny Side of the Street, 1988. *Honours:* Hannen Swaffer Award, Journalist of 1965-66. *Address:* 39 St Anne's Crescent, Lewes, East Sussex, BN7 1SB, England.

RANDALL Robert. *See:* **SILVERBERG Robert.**

RANDALL Rona b. Birkenhead, Cheshire, England. Free-lance Journalist; Short Story Writer; Novelist; Non-Fiction Writer. m. 1 son. *Literary Appointments:* Editorial Dept, UK Magazine, Woman's Journal, 4 years. *Publications:* 56 published novels including: Dragonmede, 1974; The Watchman's Stone, 1976; The Eagle at the Gate, 1978; The Mating Dance, 1979; The Ladies of Hanover Square, 1981; Curtain Call, 1982; The Drayton Trilogy: The Drayton Legacy, 1985; The Potter's Niece, 1987; The Rival Potters, 1990. Non-fiction: Jordan & the Holy Land, 1968; The Model Wife, 19th Century Style, 1989; Writing Popular Fiction, 1992. *Honours include:* Joint winner, RNA Major Ward, 1969, ; US Literary Guild Alternate Selection, 1974; US Doubleday Book Club Exclusive Selection, 1974; US Literary Guild Exclusive Selection for Young Adult Division, 1976. *Memberships:* Fellow, International PEN; Vice-Chair, Women's Press Club of London; Committee, Society of Sussex Authors; Member, Society of Women Writers & Journalists; Associate Member, South East Arts Association; Founder/Chair Tunbridge Wells Writers Weekends; Founder and Director: Fiction Forum Consultancy Service for Authors. *Literary Agent:* Curtis Brown Ltd. *Address:* Conifers, Pembury Road, Tunbridge Wells, Kent, TN2 4ND England.

RANGELY E R. *See:* **ZACHARY Hugh.**

RANGLEY Olivia. *See:* **ZACHARY Hugh.**

RANKINE Douglas. *See:* **MASON Douglas Rankine.**

RANKINE John. *See:* **MASON Douglas Rankine.**

RANSLEY Peter, b. 10 Dec 1931, Leeds, England. Writer. m. Cynthia Harris, 14 Dec 1974, 1 son, 1 daughter. *Plays include:* Numerous TV plays including, Plays for Today, Minor complications, Kate the Good Neighbour; Series, Bread or Blood, BBC, 1982, The Price (Channel 4), 1985; Books: The Price, based on the series; The Hawk, 1988; Theatre: Runaway, Royal Court, 1974; Ellen & Disabled, Hampstead Theatre Club, 1972. *Honours:* Gold Medal, Kate, 1st Commonwealth TV Film Festival, 1980; Award, Royal Television Society's Writer's, Minor Complications, 1981. *Agent:* Norman North, The Peters Fraser Dunlop Group Ltd. *Address:*

The Chambers, Chelsea Harbour, Lots Road, London SW10, England.

RANSOM Bill, b. 6 June 1945, USA. Writer. 1 daughter. *Education:* BA, University of Washington. *Appointments:* NDEA Title IV Fellow, American Minority Literature, University of Nevada, Reno, 1971-72; Poetry in the Schools, Master Poet, NEA, 1974-77. *Publications:* Novels: The Jesus Incident, 1979; The Lazarus Effect, 1983; The Ascension Factor, 1988; Jaguar, 1990; Viravax, 1993; Poetry: Finding True North, 1974; The Single Man Looks at Winter, 1983; Last Call, 1984; Waving Arms at the Blind, 1975; Last Rites, 1979. *Contributions to:* Numerous journals and magazines. *Honour:* NEA Discovery Award, 1977. *Memberships:* Poetry Society of America; Poets Essayists & Novelists; International Association of Machinists and Aerospace Workers; Science Fiction, Fantasy Writers of America; Poet's Writers, Inc. *Literary Agent:* Ralph Vicinanza, New York. *Address:* PO Box 284, Grayland, WA 98547, USA.

RAPHAEL Adam Eliot Geoffrey, b. 22 Apr 1938, London, England. Journalist. m. Caroline Rayner Ellis, 15 May 1970, 1 son, 1 daughter. *Education:* BA, Honours, History, Oxford Univesity. *Appointments:* London 1965-68, Foreign Correspondent in Washington, USA, 1969-73, The Guardian; Political Correspondent, 1976-82, Political Editor, 1982-87, The Observer; Presenter, BBC Newsnight, 1987-88; Assistant Editor, The Observer, 1988-. *Publications:* My Learned Friend, (non fiction), 1989. *Honours:* Journalist of the Year, Granada Awards, 1973; Journalist of the Year, IPC Awards 1973. *Address* 50 Addison Avenue, London, W11 4QP, England.

RAPHAEL Frederic Michael, b. 14 Aug 1931, Chicago, USA. Writer. m. 17 Jan 1955, 2 sons, 1 daughter. *Education:* St John's College, Cambridge, England. *Publications:* Obbligato, 1956; The Earlsdon Way, 1958; The Limits of Love, 1960; The Trouble With England, The Graduate Wife, 1962; Lindmann, 1963; Darling, 1965; Orchestra and Beginers, 1967; Two For The Road (film script with preface), 1968; Like Men Betrayed, 1970; Who Were You With Last Night?, 1971; April, June and November, 1972; Richard's Things, 1973; California Time, 1975; The Glittering Prizes, 1976; Somerset Maugham (biography), 1977; Sleeps Six (short stories), 1979; Cracks In The Ice: views and reviews, 1979; Oxbridge Blues (short stories), 1980; Byron (biography), 1982; Heaven and Earth, 1985; Think of England (short stories), 1986; After The War, 1988; The Hidden I, 1990; A Double Life, 1993; Of Gods And Men (Greek mythology revisited), 1992; Forthcoming, The Empty Jew (short stories); Translations (with Kenneth McLeish) The poems of Catullus, 1978; The Plays of Aeschylus (with introduction, two volumes), 1991. *Contributions to:* Sunday Times (London); Times Literary Supplement; The Spectator. *Honours:* Lippincott Prize, 1961; Writers' Guild, 1965, 1966; USA Academy Award, 1966; British Academy Award, 1966; Royal TV Society Award, 1976; ACE (US Cable TV) Award, 1985, 1991. *Membership:* Fellow, Royal Society of Literature. *Literary Agent:* Deborah Rogers, Rogers, Coleridge and White, 20 Powis MMews, London W11 1JJN, England.

RASKIN Abraham Henry, b. 26 Apr 1911, Edmonton, Alberta, Canada. m. 27 Sept 1933, 1 son, 1 daughter. *Education:* BA, City College of New York, 1931; Woodrow Wilson Visiting Fellow, 1981-. *Appointments:* Staff, New York Times, 1934-77; Adjunct Profesor, Columbia 1976, Stanford, 1984; Associate Director, National News Council, 1978-84. *Publication:* David Dubinsky: My Life With Labor, 1977. *Contributions to:* New Yorker; Fortune; Forbes; Atlantic; Annals, American Academy of Political Science; numerous others. *Honours:* Distinguished Service Medal, US Army, 1945; Sidney Hillman Memorial Award, 1950; George Polk Award, 1953, 1963; Heywood Broun Memorial Citation, 1964; Columbia Journalism Award, 1967; Silurians Award, 1970. *Memberships:* New York Newspaper Guild, Vice Chairman, 1955-61; Phi Beta Kappa, President, Gamma Chapter, New York, 1983.

Address: 136 East 64th Street, New York, NY 10021, USA.

RASKY Harry, b. 9 May 1928, Canada. Writer; Director; Producer; Commentator. m. Ruth Arlene Werkhoven, 21 Mar 1965, 1 son, 1 daughter. *Education:* BA, 1949, LLD, 1982, University of Toronto. *Publications:* Nobody Swings on Sunday, 1980; Tennessee Williams - A portrait in Laughter and Lamentation; Teresa Stratas; 40 feature-length documentaries including: Tennessee Williams' South, 1972; Homage to Chagall - The Colours of Love, 1975; The War against the Indians, 1992. *Contributions to:* The Nation; Saturday Night; Financial Post; Directors Guild of America News. *Honours:* Canadian Radio Award, 1951; Nominations, Writers Guild of America Award, 1972, 1978, 1980; 10 Awards, Writers Guild of Canada. *Memberships:* Writers Guild of Canada; Writers Guild of America; Writers Union of Canada; Directors Guild of America; Academy of Motion Pictures Arts and Sciences, Hollywood; Academy of TV Arts and Sciences, New York; Academy of Canadian Cinema, Toronto. *Literary Agent:* Lucinda Vardey Agency. *Address:* CBC, Box 500, Terminal A, Toronto, Ontario, Canada.

RASS Rebecca Rivka, b. 9 Dec 1936, Israel. Writer; Journalist; College Professor. 1 daughter. *Education:* Tel-Aviv University, 1958- 60; BA, Empire State College, New York, 1977; MFA, Brooklyn College, New York, 1979. *Appointments:* New York Cultural Correspondent, Yediodth Ahronoth, Tel-Aviv, Israel, 1965-; New York Art Critic, Zero Magazine, Amsterdam, 1978-80. *Publications:* From A to Z, prose-poetry, 1969, 1984; From Moscow to Jerusalem, 1976; The Fairy Tales of My Mind, novel, 1978, Spanish Edition, 1986; The Mountain, 1982, Hebrew Edition, 1988; Word War I and Word War II, 1984. *Contributions to:* Algemeen Handelsbladt, Amsterdam; Aftenposten, Norway; Rotterdam Courant; Vrij Nederland; San Francisco Chronicle. *Honours:* Grants, PEN American Center, 1976, 1977; CAPS Award for Fiction, 1981; Yaddo Grant, 1982. *Memberships:* New York Press Club; PEN; Poets and Writers. *Address:* 54 West 16th St, New York, NY 10011, USA.

RATHER Dan, b. Oct 1931. Broadcaster; Journalist. m. Jean Goebel, 1 son, 1 daughter. *Education:* University of Houston; South Texas Schoolo of Law. *Appointments:* Writer, Sports Commentator with KSAM-TV; Teacher, Journalism, Houston Chronicle; with CBS; with radio station KTRH, Houston, 4 years; News and Current Affairs Director, CBS Houston TV affiliate KHOU-TV late 1950s; joined CBS News, 1962; Chief, London Bureau, 1965-66; worked in Viet-Nam, White House, 1966; Anchorman CBS Reports, 1974- 75; Co-anchorman, 60 minutes CBS TV 1975-81; Anchorman, Dan Rather Reporting CBS Radio Network, 1977- ; Co-Editor, Show Who's Who, CBS TV, 1977; Anchorman, Managing Editor, CBS Evening News with Dan Rather, 1981-. *Publications:* The Palace Guard, 1974 (with Gary Gates); The Camera Never Blinks, (with Mickey Herskowitz), 1977. *Address:* CBS News, 524 West 57th Street, New York, NY 10019, USA.

RATNER Rochelle, b. 2 Dec 1948, Atlantic City, USA. Poet; Novelist; Critic. *Appointments:* Poetry Columnist, Soho Weekly News, 1976-82; Executive Editor, American Book Review, 1978-; Small Press Columnist, Library Journal, 1985. *Publications:* A Birthday of Waters, 1971; False Trees, 1973; Pirate's Song, 1976; The Tightrope Walker, 1977; Quarry, 1978; Combing the Waves, 1979; Sea Air in a Grave Ground Hog Turns Toward, 1980; Hide & Seek, 1980. Practicing to Be a Woman: New & Selected Poems, 1982; Trying to Understand What It Means to Be a Feminist, 1984; Bobby's Girl, 1986. *Contributions to:* New York Times; Hanging Loose; Shenandoah; Antaeus; Salmagundi. *Memberships:* PEN; National Book Critics Circle; Poetry Society of America. *Address:* 314 E. 78 St., New York, NY 10021, USA.

RAUBENHEIMER George H (George Harding), b. 26 June 1923, Pretoria, South Africa. Ceramics Manufacturer; Writer. m. Shirley Hall, 26 Apr 1958, 2 sons, 2 daughters. *Education:* Matriculation, 1940. *Publications:* North of Bushman's Rock, 1965; Dragon's Gap, 1967; The Gun Merchants, 1969; The Skytrap, 1972; Crossfire, 1980; Screenplay: Mr Kingstreets War, (co-writer), 1970; TV Scripts: Taskforce, 1981; Tilly, 1985; currently working on TV Scripts for SATV. *Memberships:* South African Military History Association; South African Air Force Association. *Address:* 19 Lystanwold Road, Saxonwold 2196, Johannesburg, Republic of South Africa.

RAVEN Simon (Arthur Noël), b. 28 Dec 1927, London, England. Author. m. Susan Mandeville Kilner, 1951, divorced, 1 son. *Education:* Charterhouse, King's College, Cambridge, 1948-52, Honours Degree in Classics. *Publications:* Alms for Oblivion, 10 volumes, 1964-76; Shadows on the Grass, memoirs, 1982; The First Born of Egypt, 7 vols, 1984-1992; In The Image of God; Bird of Ill Omen, 1989; Is There Anybody There? Said The Traveller, memories of a private nuisance, 1991. TV: The Pallisers, in 26 Episodes; Edward & Mrs Simpson, 7 episodes; In the Image of God. *Contributions to:* The Observer; The Listener; The Spectator. *Membership:* PEN; Royal Society of Literature. *Literary Agent:* Curtis Brown. *Address:* c/o Curtis Brown, 162 Regent Street, London W1R 5IB, England.

RAVVIN Norman, b. 26 Aug 1963, Calgary, Alberta, Canada. Novelist; University Instructor. *Education:* BA (Hons), 1986, MA, English, 1988, University of British Columbia; PhD in progress, University of Toronto, 1989- . *Publications:* Café des Westens, novel, 1991. *Contributions to:* Stories: My Father and the Sky, to West Coast Review, 1986; Family Architecture, to Western Living; Articles: Strange Presences on the Family Tree: The Unacknowledged Literary Father in Philip Roth's 'The Prague Orgy' to English Studies in Canada, 1991; An Irruption of the Archaic: Poe and the Grotesque, to Mosaic, 1992. *Honours:* Alberta Culture and Multiculturalism New Fiction Award, 1990; PhD Fellowship, Social Sciences and Humanities Research Council of Canada. *Memberships:* Writers Guild of Alberta; Association of Canadian College and University Teachers of English; Modern Language Society of America. *Address:* c/o Red Deer College Press, 56 Ave and 32nd St, Box 5005, Red Deer, Alberta, Canada T4N 5H5.

RAWORTH Thomas Moore, b. 19 July 1938, London, England. Writer. m. Valarie Murphy. 4 sons, 1 daughter. *Education:* MA, University of Essex, 1967-70. *Literary Appointments:* Poet-in-Residence, Literature Department, University of Essex, England, 1969-70; Poet-in-Residence, Northeastern Illinois University, Chicago, USA, 1973-74; Poet-in-Residence, King's College, Cambridge, England, 1977-78; London and Cambridge Correspondent, Rolling Stock, Boulder, USA; Editor, designer & publisher, Infolio, 1986. *Publications:* The Relation Ship, 1967, (USA 1969); The Big Green Day, 1968; A Serial Biography, 1969, (USA 1977); Lion Lion, 1970; Moving, 1971; Act, 1973; Ace, 1974, (USA 1977); Common Sense, 1976; Logbook, 1977; Nicht Wahr, Rosie?, 1979; Writing, 1982; Tottering State (Selected Poems 1963-83) USA 1984, UK 1988; Lazy Left Hand, 1986; Visible Shivers, 1987; Eternal Sections, 1991. *Contributions to:* Numerous magazines and journals in UK, USA, France, Italy, Spain, Romania, Hungary, Germany. *Honours:* Alice Hunt Bartlett Prize, 1969; Cholmondeley Award, 1971. *Membership:* PEN. *Address:* 3 St Philip's Road, Cambridge CB1 3AQ, England.

RAWSON Claude Julien, b. 8 Feb 1935, Shanghai, China. George M Bodman Professor of English, Yale University. m. Judith Ann Hammond, 14 July 1959, 3 sons, 2 daughters. *Education:* Magdalen College, Oxford, England, 1952-57; BA, 1955; MA, BLitt, 1959. *Appointments:* Editor, Modern Language Review, and Yearbook of English Studies, 1974-88; General Editor, Unwin Critical Library, 1975-; Executive Editor,

Cambridge History of Literary Criticism, 1983-; General Editor, Blackwell Critical Biographies, 1986-; Chairman and General Editor, Yale Editions of the Private Papers of James Boswell, 1990-. *Publications:* Henry Fielding, 1968; Focus Swift, 1971; Henry Fielding and the Augustan Ideal under Stress, 1972; Gulliver and the Gentle Reader, 1973; Fielding: A Critical Anthology, 1973; The Character of Swift's Satire, 1983; English Satire and the Satiric Tradition, 1984; Order from Confusion Sprung: Studies in 18th Century Literature, 1985; Thomas Parnell's Collected Poems (edited with F P Lock), 1989; Satire and Sentiment 1660-1800, 1993. *Contributions to:* Times Literary Supplement; London Review of Books; New York Times Book Review; Raritan; Review of English Studies; Modern Language Review; Essays in Criticism; Others. *Honours:* Special Certificate of Merit, Conference of Editors of Learned Journals, 1988; Andrew Mellow Fellow, Clark Library, 1980; Andrew Mellon Fellow, Huntington Library, 1990; Guggenheim Fellow, 1991-92; Clifford Lecturer, American Society for 18th Century Studies, 1992. *Memberships:* British Society for 18th Century Studies, President 1974, 1975, Vice-President 1972, 1973; American Society for 18th Century Studies; Modern Humanities Research Association, Committee 1974-88, Honorary Life Member 1988-; Modern Language Association of America. *Literary Agent:* The Peters, Fraser and Dunlop Group Ltd. *Address:* 50 Malthouse Lane, Kenilworth, Warwickshire CV8 1AD, England.

RAY David Eugene, b. 20 May 1932, Oklahoma, USA. Writer; Professor of English. m. Suzanne Judy Morriah, 21 Feb 1970, 1 son, 3 daughters. *Education:* BA, 1952; MA, 1957, University of Chicago. *Appointments:* Instructor in English, Wright Junior College, 1957-58; Northern Illinois University, 1958-60; also Associate Editor, Epoch, Cornell University, 1960-64; Assistant Professor, Reed College, 1964-66; Lecturer in Writers Workshop, University of Iowa, 1969-70; Visiting Associate Profesor, Bowling Green State University, 1970-71; Professor of English, University of Missouri, 1971-; Editor, New Letters, 1971-85; Visiting Professor, Syracuse University, 1978-79; University of Rajasthan, India, 1981-82; Exchange Professor, University of Otago, New Zealand, 1987; Visiting Fellow, University of Western Australia, 1991. *Publications include:* X-Rays, 1965; Dragging the Main, 1968; Gathering Firewood, 1974; The Touched Life, 1982; Sam's Book, 1987; The Maharani's New Wall, 1989; Not Far From The River, 1990. *Contributions to:* numerous journals and newspapers, including New York Times; The Paris Review; Harpers; Ontario Review; Poetry; The London Magazine; The Saturday Review, and many others. *Honours include:* New Republic Magazine, Young Writers Award, 1958; Kansas City Star Poetry Award, 1974; Associated Writing Programs Poetry Contest, Winner, 1982, 1983; National Endowment for the Arts Fellowship, 1983; PEN, Syndicated Fiction Award, 1983, 1984, 1986; Amelia Magazine, Poem Prize, 1987; Maurice English Award for Poetry, 1988. *Memberships:* PEN, Poetry Society of America; Authors Guild; National Writers Union; Phi Kappa Phi Honorary Society; Friends Association for Higher Education. *Address:* 5517 Crestwood Drive, Kansas City, MO 64110, USA.

RAY Robert Henry, b. 29 Apr I940, San Saba, Texas, USA. Professor of English. m. Lynette Elizabeth Dittmar, 1 Sept 1962, 2 daughters. *Education:* BA, 1963, PhD, 1967, University of Texas at Austin. *Appointments:* Assistant Professor of English, 1967-75, Associate Professor of English 1975-85, Professor of English, 1985-, Baylor University. *Publications:* The Herbert Allusion Book, 1986; Approaches to Teaching Shakespeare's King Lear, 1986; A John Donne Companion, 1990. *Contributions to:* Recent Studies in Herbert in English Literary Renaissance, 1988; Herbert's Words in Donne's Mouth, Modern Philology, 1987, and many others. *Honour:* Phi Beta Kappa, 1962. *Memberships:* Modern Language Association of America; South Central Modern Language Association; John Donne Society. *Address:* Department of English, P O Box 97406, Baylor University, Waco, TX 76798, USA.

RAY Robert J, b. 15 May 1935, Amarillo, Texas, USA. m. (1) Ann Allen, (div), (2) Margot M Waale, July 1983. *Education:* BA, 1957, MA 1959, PhD 1962, University of Texas, Austin. *Appointments:* Instructor 1963- 65, Assistant Professor 1965-68, Associate Professor 1968-75, Professor 1976, Beloit College, Beloit, Wisconsin; Certified Tennis Instructor, San Diego, California, 1976-81; Freelance writer 1981-; Partner of Owning the Store, 1983-88; Writing Teacher, Valley College, 1984-88 and at University of California, Irvine, 1985-88; Adjunct Professor at Chapman College, 1988-. *Publications:* (with Ann Ray) The Art of Reading: A Handbook on Writing, 1968; The Heart of the Game, (novel) 1975; Cage of Mirrors (novel) 1980; (with L A Eckert and J D Ryan) Small Business: An Entrepreneur's Plan, 1985; Bloody Murdock (novel) 1987; Murdock for Hire, (novel) 1987; The Hitman Cometh (novel) 1988; Dial M for Murdock (novel) 1988; Murdock in Xanadu, (novel) 1989. *Membership:* Mystery Writers of America, Fictionaries. *Literary Agent:* Ben Kamsler, H N Swanson, Inc, Los Angeles. *Address:* c/o Ben Kamsler, H N Swanson, Inc, 8523 Sunset Boulevard, Los Angeles, CA 90069, USA.

RAYMOND Derek. *See:* **COOK Robert William Arthur.**

RAYMOND Diana Joan, b. 25 Apr 1916, London, England. Novelist. m. Ernest Raymond, 20 Aug 1940, 1 son. *Publications:* Incident on a Summer Day, 1974; Emma Pride, 1981; House of the Dolphin, 1985; The Dark Journey, 1978; The Dancers All Are Gone, 1983; Horseman Pass By, 1977; 22 novels including: Strangers' Gallery, 1958; Guest of Honour, 1960; The Climb, 1962; The Small Rain, 1954; The Best of the Day, 1972; Lily's Daughter, 1988. *Honours:* Book Society Choice, The Small Rain, 1954. *Membership:* Society of Authors. *Literary Agent:* A.P. Watt Ltd. *Address:* 22 The Pryors, East Heath Road, London NW3 1BS, England.

RAYMOND Mary. *See:* **KEGAN Mary.**

RAYMOND Patrick Ernest, b. 25 Sept 1924, Cuckfield, Sussex, England. Royal Air Force, Retired. m. Lola Pilpel, 27 May 1950, 1 son. *Education:* Art School, Cape Town, South Africa. *Appointments:* RAF, rising to Group Captain, 1942-77. *Publications:* A City of Scarlet & Gold, 1963; The Lordly Ones, 1965; The Sea Garden, 1970; The Last Soldier, 1974; A Matter of Assassination, 1977; The White War, 1978; The Grand Admiral, 1980; Daniel and Esther, 1989. *Literary Agent:* A.P. Watt Ltd. *Address:* 24 Chilton Road, Chesham, Buckinghamshire HP5 2AU, England.

RAYNER Claire Berenice, (Sheila Brandon, Ann Lynton, Ruth Martin), b. 22 Jan 1931, London, England. Writer; Broadcaster. m. Desmond Rayner, 23 June 1957, 2 sons, 1 daughter. *Education:* State Registered Nurse (Gold Medal), Royal Northern Hospital, London, 1954; Midwifery, Guy's Hospital. *Appointments include:* 'Agony Aunt' for Petticoat, The Sun, Sunday Mirror; Today; Medical Correspondent for Womans Own; Woman; various other journals. Regular radio series, TV appearances: consumer affairs, family advice, personal problems, Kitchen Garden (with Keith Fordyce). *Publications:* Over 80 books: broad range of medical subjects, fiction. Medical titles include: Mothers & Midwives, 1962; Your Baby, 1965; Essentials of Out-Patient Nursing, 1967; 101 Key Facts of Practical Baby Care, 1967; Home Nursing & Family Health, 1967; Parents Guide to Sex Education, 1968; Childcare made Simple, 1973; Safe Sex, 1987; The Don't Spoil Your Body Book, 1989; 7 romantic novels (as Sheila Brandon); 12 volume saga, medical/theatrical fiction, The Performers, 1973-86; Various other novels including, Clinical Judgements, 1989; Postscripts, 1991. *Contributions to:* Papers & magazines as above; professional journals including The Lancet, Medical World, Nursing Times, Nursing Mirror. *Honour:* Freeman, City of London, 1981; Award, Medical Journalists Association, 1987; Hon Fellow, University of N London, 1988; Best Specialist Consumer Columnist

Award, 1988. *Memberships include:* Fellow, Royal Society of Medicine; Fellow, Royal Society of Arts; Society of Authors. *Literary Agents:* Desmond Rayner, Holly Wood House, Roxborough Avenue, Harrow-on-the-Hill, Middlesex HA1 3BU, UK; Aaron M. Priest Literary Agency Inc, 708 Third Avenue, 23rd Floor, New York, NY 10017, USA.

RAYNER Mary Yoma, b. 30 Dec 1933, Mandalay, Burma. Author. m. (1) Eric Rayner, 6 Aug 1960, 2 sons, 1 daughter, (2) Adrian Hawksley, 9 Mar 1985. *Education:* Honours Degree, English, University of St Andrews, Scotland. *Publications:* The Witch-Finder, 1975; Mr & Mrs Pig's Evening Out, 1976; Garth Pig & the Icecream Lady, 1977; The Rain Cloud, 1980; Mrs Pig's Bulk Buy, 1981; Crocodarling, 1985; Mrs Pig Gets Cross, 1986; Reilly, 1987; Oh Paul!, 1988; Rug, 1989; Marathon and Steve (USA), 1989. *Membership:* Society of Authors. *Literary Agent:* Laura Cecil. *Address:* c/o Victor Gollancz Ltd, 15 Henrietta Street, London WC2.

RAZ Joseph, b. 21 Mar 1939, Israel. Lecturer. *Education:* Magister Juris, Hebrew University, Jerusalem, 1963; D Phil, Oxford University, 1967. *Publications:* The Concept of a Legal System, 1970, 1980; The Authority of Law, 1979; Practical Reason and Norms, 1975, 2nd ed. 1990; The Morality of Freedom, 1986. *Contributions to:* Articles contributed to numerous magazines and journals. *Honours:* W J M Mackenzie Book Prize of the Political Studies Association of the UK, 1987; The Elaine and David Spitz Book Prize of the Conference for the Study of Political Thought, New York. Both prizes for the book The Morality of Freedom. *Membership:* Fellow, British Academy, 1987-; Honorary Member, American Acadeym of arts & Sciences, 1992; Honorary Doctor, Katolieke Universiter, Brussel, 1993. *Address:* Balliol College, Oxford OX1 3BJ, England.

READ Anthony, b. 21 Apr 1935, Staffordshire, England. Writer. m. Rosemary E Kirby, 29 Mar 1958, Great Barr, West Midlands. 2 daughters. *Education:* Central School of Speech & Drama, London, 1952-54. *Publications:* The Theatre, 1964; Operation Lucy, with David Fisher, London & USA, 1980; Colonel Z, with David Fisher, London 1984, USA 1985; The Deadly Embrace, with David Fisher, London & USA, 1988; Kristallnacht, with David Fisher, London & USA, 1989; Conspirator, with Roy Bearse, USA & London, 1991; The Fall of Berlin, with David Fisher, 1992. Also well over 100 television films, plays, serials. *Honours:* Pye Colour TV Award, 1983; Wingate Literary Prize, 1989. *Membership:* Trustee, Chairman 1981-82, Writers Guild of Great Britain. *Literary Agent:* Books, Murray Pollinger; TV & Film, Stephen Durbridge, Lemon, Unna & Durbridge Ltd. *Address:* 7 Cedar Chase, Taplow, Buckinghamshire, England.

READ Elfreida, b. 2 Oct 1920, Vladivostok, Russia. Writer. m. George J Read, 10 July 1941, 1 son, 1 daughter. *Education:* Cambridge Entrance Standard, Shanghai Public School for Girls. *Publications:* The Message of the Mask; Brothers by Choice; Days of Wonder, autobiography: Part I, A Time of Cicadas, Part II, Guns and Magnolias, Part III, Congee and Peanut Butter; Growing Up in China; Fresh Lettuce and New Faces; The Dragon and the Jadestone; The Enchanted Egg; The Spell of Chuchuchan; The Magic of Light; Magic for Granny; Kirsten and the Villains; Race Against the Dark; No One Need Ever Know. *Contributions to:* Poetry to various literary magazines. *Honours:* Canadian Centennial Contest for Children's Stories; Poetry in British Columbia; Playwriting Contest, UN International Co-op Year, Junior Literary Guild, New York; CBC Literary Contest. *Membership:* Writerws Union. *Address:* 2686 W King Edward Avenue, Vancouver, British Columbia, Canada V6L 1T6.

READ Piers Paul, b. 7 Mar 1941, Beaconsfield, England. Writer. m. Emily Albertine Boothby, 29 July 1967, 2 sons, 2 daughters. *Education:* MA, St John's College, Cambridge. *Publications:* Game in Heaven with Tussy Marx, 1966; The Junkers, 1968; Monk Dawson, 1969; The Upstart, 1973; A Married Man, 1979; The Free Frenchman, 1986; The Professor's Daughter, 1975; Polonaise, 1976; The Villa Golitsyn, 1981; A Season in the West, 1988; On The Third Day, 1990; Non-Ficiton: Alive, 1974; The Train Robbers, 1978; Quo Vadis? the subversion of the Catholic Church, 1991; Ablaze, 1993. *Contributions to:* The Spectator; The Tablet. *Honours:* FRSL; Sir Geoffrey Faber Memorial Prize, 1968; Hawthornden Prize, 1969; Somerset Maugham Award, 1969; Thomas More Award, 1976; James Tait Black Memorial Prize, 1988. *Memberships:* Society of Authors, Council Member. *Literary Agent:* Aitken and Stone. *Address:* 50 Portland Road, London W11 4LG, England.

READING Peter, b. 27 July 1946, Liverpool, England. Poet. m. Diana Gilbert, 5 Oct 1968, 1 daughter. *Education:* Alsop High School; BA, Liverpool College of Art, 1967. *Appointments:* Teacher, large comprehensive school in Liverpool; Lecturer, Department of Art History, Liverpool College of Art, 1968-70; Various jobs in Animal Feed Mill, Shropshire; Fellowship, Sunderland Polytechnic, 1981-83. *Publications:* Water and Waste, 1970; For the Municipality's Elderly, 1974; The Prison Cell and Barrel Mystery, 1976; Nothing for Anyone, 1977; Fiction, 1979; Tom o'Bedlam's Beauties, 1981; Diplopic, 1983; 5 x 5 x 5 x 5 x 5, 1983; C, 1984; Ukulele Music, 1985; Stet, 1986; Essential Reading, 1986; Final Demands, 1988; Perduta Gente, 1989; Shitheads, 1989; Evagatory, 1992; 3 in 1, 1992; Last Poems, in progress. *Honours:* Cholmondeley Award for Poetry, 1978; first Dylan Thomas Award in 1983 for Diplopic; Whitbread Award (Poetry Category), 1986; Lannan Foundation (USA) Literary Fellowship Award, 1990; Elected Fellow of the Royal Society of Literature, 1988.

RECHEIS Kathe, b. 11 Mar 1928, Engelhartszell, Austria. Freelance Writer of Children's and Young People's Literature. *Publications:* Geh heim und vergiss Alles, 1964; Professor, du siehst Gespenster, 1973; Fallensteller am Bibersee, 1972; London 13 Juli, 1974; Der weite Weg des Nataiyu, 1978; Wo die Wolfe glucklich sind, 1980; Der Weisse Wolf, 1982; Weisst du, dass die Baume reden, 1983; Lena - Unser Dorf und der Krieg, 1987; Tomasita, 1989, and others. *Honours:* Austrian State Prize for Childrens and Young Peoples literature, 1961, 1963, 1964, 1967, 1971, 1972, 1975, 1976, 1979, 1980, 1984, 1987, 1992; YBBY Certificate of Honour for Der weite Weg des Nataiyu and for Der Weisse Wolf and Lena-Unser Dorf und der Krieg. *Memberships:* Austrian Writers Association; PEN Club. *Address:* Rembrandtstrasse 1/28, A 1020 Vienna, Austria.

REDDY T Vasudeva, b. 21 Dec 1943, Mittapalem, India. Lecturer in English. m. 5 Nov 1970, 2 sons, 1 daughter. *Education:* BSc, 1963; MA, English, 1966; PhD, Englilsh, 1985; PGDTE, 1983. *Appointment:* Lecturer in English, 1966-. *Publications:* When Grief Rains (poems) 1982; The Vultures (novel) 1983; The Broken Rhythms (poems) 1987; Jane Austen, 1987; Jane Austen; Matrix of Matrimony, 1987; The Fleeting Bubbles (poems) 1989. *Contributions to:* Poems, critical articles and reviews contributed to various journals and magazines. *Honours:* Award of International Eminent POet, 1987; Hon. DLitt conferred by World Academy of Arts and Culture, Calilfornia, 1988; State Award for the Best Teacher, 1991, for University College Teachers in Andhra Pradesh, India. *Memberships:* International Poets Academy, Madras; World Poetry Society, California; American Biographical Institute, USA; Research Board of Advisors, ABI, USA; Government College Teachers Association, Andhra Pradesh, India. *Address:* Narasingapuram post, Via Chandragiri, Pin: 517 102, A.P, India.

REDGROVE Peter William, b. 2 Jan 1932. Poet; Analytical Psychologist. m. Penelope Shuttle, 1 daughter, 2 sons, 1 daughter by previous marriage. *Publications:* Poetry: The Collector, 1960; The Nature of Cold Weather, 1961; At The White Monument, 1963; The Force, 1966; Penguin Modern Poets, 11, 1968;

Work in Progress, 1969; Dr Faust's Sea Spiral Spirit, 1972; Three Pieces for Voices, 1972; The Hermaphrodite Album, (with Penelope Shuttle), 1973; Sons of My Skin: Selected Poems, 1975; From Every Chink of the Ark, 1977; Ten Poems, 1977; The Weddings at Nether Powers, 1979; The Apple-Broadcast, 1981; The Working of Water, 1984; The Man Named East, 1985; The Mudlark Poems and Grand Buveur, 1986; In the Hall of Saurians, 1987; The Moon Disposes: Poems 1954-1987, 1989; The First Earthquake, 1989; Dressed as for a Tarot Pack, 1990; Under the Reservoir, 1992; The Laborators, 1993. (Novels): In the Country of the Skin, 1973; The Terros of Dr Treviles (with Penelope Shuttle), 1974; The Glass Cottage, 1976; The Sleep of the Great Hypnotist, 1979; The God of Glass, 1979; The Beekeepers, 1980; The Facilitators, 1982; Tales From Grimm, 1989. (Plays): Miss Carstairs Dressed for Blooding, 1976; (radio) In the Country of the Skin, 1973; The Holy Sinner, 1975; Dance of the Putrefact, 1975; The God of Glass, 1977; Martyr of the Hives, 1982; Florent and the Tuxedo Millions, 1982; The Sin-Doctor, 1983; Dracula in White, 1984; The Scientists of the Strange, 1984; Time for the Cat-Scene, 1985; Trelamia, 1986; Six Tales From Grimm, 1987; (television) The Sermon, 1963; Jack Be Nimble, 1980; (Non-fiction): The Wise Wound (with Penelope Shuttle), 1978, 1986; The Black Goddess and the Sixth Sense, 1987. *Honours include:* Imperial Tobacco Award, 1978; Giles Cooper Award, 1981; Prix Italia, 1983; many other honours and awards. *Literary Agent:* David Higham Associates. *Address:* c/o David Higham Associates, 5-8 Lower John Street, Golden Square, London W1R 4HA, England.

REDMAN Joseph. *See:* **PEARCE Brian Leonard.**

REDWOOD Alec. *See:* **MILKOMANE George Alexis Milkomanovich.**

REECE Robert D, b. 25 Oct 1939, Bonham, Texas, USA. University Professor. m. Donna J Walters, 5 Jun 1965, 2 sons, 2 daughters. *Education:* BA, Baylor University, 1961; BD, Southern Baptist Theological Seminary, 1964; MA, 1966, M Phil 1968, PhD, 1969, Yale University. *Publication:* Studying People: A Primer in the Ethics of Social Research (with Harvey A Siegal) 1986. *Contributions to:* Various articles in professional journals. *Memberships:* American Academy of Religion (Chair of Medical Ethics Consultation, 1983-85); Society for Health and Human Values (Chair, Programme Directors Group, 1982-84); Society of Christian Ethics; Society for Values in Higher Education. *Address:* Department of Community Health, School of Medicine, Wright State University, P O Box 927, Dayton, OH 45401, USA.

REED Jane Barbara, b. England. Journalist. *Appointments:* Editor, Woman's Own, 1969-79; Publisher, IPC Magazines, 1979-81; Editor, Woman, 1981-83; Managing Director, Holborn Publishing, 1983-85, Managing Editor, Today, 1987-89; Director, Corporation Relations, News International, 1989-. *Publications:* Girl About Town, 1965; Kitchen Sink or Swim, Co-Author, 1982. *Contributions to:* Woman's Own; Times; Sunday Times; Guardian; Today. *Address:* 1 Virginia Street, London E1 9XY, England.

REED John (Reginald), b. 30 May 1909, Aldershot, Hants., England. Retired Schoolmaster; Music Critic. m. Edith Marion Hampton, 30 Oct 1936, 2 sons, 2 daughters. *Education:* County High School, Aldershot, 1920-27; London University, 1927-30, 1934-35, Diploma of Education, 1930, BA, Hons, English Language and Literature, 1935. *Appointment:* Guardian, Music Critic, 1974-81. *Publications:* Schubert: The Final Years, 1972; Schubert (Great Composers Series) 1978; The Schubert Song Companion, 1985; Schubert (Master Musicians Series) 1986. *Contributions to:* Numerous contributions to Music Times, Listener, and others. *Honour:* Duckles Award for best reference book on a musical topic published in 1985, by Music Library Association of America, March 1987; Honorary Member of International Franz Schubert Insitute of Vienna, 1989.

Membership: Schubert Institute (United Kingdom), Chairman 1991-. *Address:* 130, Fog Lane, Didsbury, Manchester M20 0SW, England.

REED Michael Arthur, b. 25 Apr 1930, Aylesbury, Bucks., England. University Professor. m. Gwynneth Vaughan, 1 Oct 1955, 1 son. *Education:* BA, 1954, MA, 1958, University of Birmingham; LLB, University of London, 1966; PhD, University of Leicester, 1973. *Publications:* The Buckinghamshire Landscape, 1979; The Georgian Triumph, 1983; The Age of Exuberance, 1986; The Landscape of Britain, 1990; Editions of Ipswich Probate Inventories and of Buckinghamshire Probate Inventories. *Contributions to:* Articles in The Agricultural History Review; Records of Bucks. and other journals. *Memberships:* Fellow, Royal Historical Society, 1985; Fellow, Society of Antiquaries of London, 1985. *Address:* Department of Information and Library Studies, Loughborough University, Loughborough, Leicestershire, England.

REED Simon. *See:* **DANBY Mary.**

REEDER Carolyn, b. 16 Nov 1937, Washington, DC, USA. Writer; Teacher. m. Jack Reeder, 15 Aug, 1959 1 son, 1 daughter. *Education:* BA, 1959, MEd, 1971, The American University. *Publications:* Shades of Grey, 1989, Grandpa's Mountain, 1991, and Moonshiner's Son, 1993, all historical fiction for children; adult non-fiction co-authored with husband: Shenandoah Heritage, 1978, Shenandoah Vestiges, 1980, Shenandoah Secrets, 1991. *Honours:* Scott O'Dell Award for Historical Fiction, 1989; Child Study Association Award, 1989; Jefferson Cup Award, 1990; ALA Notable Book for 1989, an Honour Book for the Jane Addam's Children's Book Award, 1989; Notable Trade Book in the Language Arts. 1989; An International Reading Association Young Adult Choice for 1991. *Address:* 7314 University Avenue, Glen Echo, MD 20812, USA.

REEDER Hubert, b. 17 Mar 1948, Plainfield, New Jersey, USA. Writer. *Education:* BS degree, 1989. *Publications:* Gates Found I, 1977; Gates Found II, 1982; Currently working on third book. *Honours:* Awards of Merit, Worlld of Poetry, 1984, 1985, 1987, 1988; Editor's Choice Award, National Library of Poetry, twice in 1989; Poet of Merit Award, American Poetry Society. *Memberships:* World of Poetry; American, Poetry Society. *Address:* PO Box 128, East Orange, NJ 07019, USA.

REEDY George Edward, b. 5 Aug 1917, East Chicago, Indiana, USA. College Professor. m. Lillian Greenwald, 22 Mar 1948 (dec.), 2 sons. *Education:* BA, University of Chicago, 1938. *Publications:* Who Will Do Our Fighting For Us?, 1969; Twilight of the Presidency, 1970, revised (Johnson to Reagan), 1987; The Presidency in Flux, 1973. Lyndon B. Johnson, A Memoir, 1982; The US Senate, Paralysis or Search for Consensus, 1986. *Contributions to:* Articles, political topics in New York Times; Washington Post; World Book Encyclopaedia Yearbook; Annals, American Academy of Political & Social Science. *Honours:* Annual Political Book Award, Washington Monthly, 1970; Knight of Golden Quill, Milwauke Press Club, 1986. *Memberships:* American Academy of Political & Social Science; American Political Science Association; American Committee on Irish Studies. *Literary Agent:* Mike Hamilburg. *Address:* 2535 North Stowell Avenue, no. 1, Milwaukee, Wisconsin 53211, USA.

REEMAN Douglas Edward (Alexander Kent), b. 15 Oct 1924, Thames Ditton, Surrey, England. Author. m. Kimberley June Jordan, 5 Oct 1985. *Publications:* A Prayer for the Ship, 1958; High Water, 1959; Send a Gunboat, 1960; Dive in the Sun, 1961; The Hostile Shore, 1962; The Last Raider, 1963; With Blood and Iron, 1964; HMS Saracen, 1965; Path of the Storm, 1966; The Deep Silence, 1967; The Pride and the Anguish, 1968; To Risks Unknown, 1969; The Greatest

Enemy, 1970; Against the Sea, 1971; Rendezvous - South Atlantic, 1972; Go In and Sink!, 1973; The Destroyers, 1974; Winged Escort, 1975; Surface with Daring, 1976; Strike from the Sea, 1978; A Ship Must Die, 1979; Torpedo Run, 1981; Badge of Glory, 1982; The First to Land, 1984; D-Day: A Personal Reminiscence, 1984; The Volunteers, 1985; The Iron Pirate, 1986; In Danger's Hour, 1988; The White Guns, 1989; Killing Ground, 1990; The Horizon, 1993. As Alexander Kent: To Glory We Steer, 1968; Form Line of Battle, 1969; Enemy in Sight!, 1970; The Flag Captain, 1971; Sloop of War, 1972; Command a King's Ship, 1974; Signal - Close Action!, 1974; Richard Bolitho - Midshipman, 1975; Passage to Mutiny, 1976; In Gallant Company, 1977; Midshipman Bolitho and the "Avenger" 1978; Captain Richard Bolitho, RN, 1978; The Inshore Squadron, 1978; Stand into Danger, 1980; A Tradition of Victory, 1981; Success to the Brave, 1983; Colours Aloft!, 1986; Honour This Day, 1987; With All Despatch, 1988; The Only Victor, 1990; The Bolitho Omnibus, 1991; Beyond the Reef, 1992; The Darkening Sea, 1993. *Contributions To:* Various journals and magazines. *Memberships:* RN Sailing Association; Member, RSPB; Hon. Member, Royal Society of Marine Artists; MTB Officers Association; Member, Garrick Club. *Literary Agent:* Caroline Dawnay, Peters, Fraser & Dunlop. *Address:* Peters, Fraser & Dunlop, The Chambers, Chelsea Harbour, London SW10 0XF, England.

REES Barbara Elizabeth, b. 9 Jan 1934, Worcester, England. Writer. m. Larry Herman, 1 Sept 1967, (div 1978), 1 daughter. *Education:* BA, Honours, English Language & Literature, University of Oxford; MA. *Appointments:* Arts Council of Great Britain Creative Writer in Residence, North London Polytechnic, 1976-78. *Publications:* Try Another Country, 3 short novels, 1969; Diminishing Circles, UK 1970, USA 1971, Netherlands 1972; Prophet of the Wind, USA 1973, UK 1975, 1976; George and Anna, 1976; The Victorian Lady, 1977; Harriet Dark, UK and USA, 1978, USA, 1980. *Contributions to:* Good Housekeeping; Melbourne Herald; Annabella; Det Nye; Woman's Own. *Honour:* Arts Council Award, 1974. *Address:* 102 Savernake Road, London NW3 2JR, England.

REES Brian, b. 20 Aug 1929, Strathfield, Sydney, Australia. Parliamentary Researcher; Writer. m. (1) Julia Birley, dec 17 Dec, 1959, (2) Juliet Akehurst, 3 Jan 1987, 2 sons, 3 daughters. *Education:* Bede Grammar School, Sunderland; First Class Historical Tripos, Parts I & II, Trinity College, Cambridge. *Appointments:* Assistant Master, Eton College, 1952-65; Headmaster, Merchant Taylors' School, 1965-73; Headmaster, Charterhouse, 1973-81; Headmaster, Rugby School, 1981-84. *Publications:* A Musical Peacemaker (Biography of Sir Edward German), 1987; ed. History and Idealism, 1990; Stowe: Story of a Public School, 1993. *Address:* 52 Spring Lane, Flore, Northants. NN7 4LS, England.

REES Helen, b. 2 Oct 1936, Washington, DC, USA. Literary Agent. 4 sons. *Education:* BA, History, George Washington University, 1959. *Appointments:* Agent for the following publications: Sandra Mackey: The Saudis, 1987; Dr Joan Borsenyko: Minding the Body, Mending the Mind, 1987; Goldwater on Goldwater, 1988; Roos, Jones, Womack: The Machine That Changed the World, 1990; Alan Dershowitz: Chitzpah, 1991. *Address:* 308 Commonwealth Avenue, Boston, MA 02115, USA.

REES-MOGG William (Baron), b. 14 July 1928, Bristol, England. Journalist. m. Gillian Shakespeare Morris, 1962, 2 sons, 3 daughters. *Education:* Balliol College, Oxford. *Appointments:* Financial Times, 1952-60, Chief Leader Writer 1955-60, Assistant Editor, 1957-60; City Editor, Sunday Times, 1960-61, Political and Economic Editor, 1961-63, Deputy Editor, 1964-67; Editor, The Times, 1967-81; Director, The Times Ltd., 1968-81; Vice Chair, BBC, 1981-86; Chairman, Arts Council, 1982-89; Chairman Broadcasting Standards Council, 1988- . *Publications:* The Reigning Error: the Crisis of World Inflation, 1974; An Humbler

Heaven, 1977; How to Buy Rare Books, 1985; Blood in the Streets, 1988; The Great Reckoning, 1991; Picnics on Vesurius, 1992. *Honours:* Hon LLD, Bath; Kt, 1981. *Memberships:* President, Oxford Union, 1951; International Committee, Pontifical Council for Culture; President, The Trollope Society. *Address:* 17 Pall Mall, London SW1, England.

REEVE F(ranklin) D(olier), b. 18 Sept 1928, Philadelphia, Pennsylvania, USA. Writer. *Education:* PhD, Columbia University, 1958. *Literary Appointments:* Professor of Letters, Wesleyan University, 1970-; Visiting Lecturer, English, Yale University, 1972-86; Visiting Professor, Columbia University, 1992. *Publications include:* The Russian Novel, 1966; In the Silent Stones, 1968; The Red Machines, 1968; Just Over the Border, 1969; The Brother, 1971; The Blue Cat, 1972; White Colors, 1973; Nightway, 1987; The White Monk, 1989; Concrete Music, 1989. Editor, Poetry Review, 1982-84. Translations, Russian Literature including two-volume Anthology of Russian Plays, 1961-63; The Russian Novel, 1966; An Arrow in the Wall, 1987; The Garden, 1990; The Trouble with Reason, 1993. *Contributions to:* Poems, essays, stories in American Poetry Review; New England Review; Yale Review; Sewanee Review; Manhattan Poetry Review; Confrontation; New Yorker; Kansas Quarterly; North American Review; Kenyon Review; Gettysburg Review; Poetry: a Magazine of Verse; New York Times Book Review. *Honours:* Literature Award, American Academy - National Institute of Arts and Letters, 1970; PEN, Syndicated Fiction Award, 1985, 1986. *Memberships:* PEN, American Centre; Poetry Society of America, Vice-President, 1982-84; Board of Directors, Poets House. *Literary Agent:* Robert Lewis. *Address:* Mount Holly, VT 05758, USA.

REEVES Patricia Houts, b. 8 Nov 1947, Columbia, Missouri, USA. Editor; Writer. m. Jerry E K Reeves, 28 June 1969, 1 son, 1 daughter. *Education:* BJ, University of Missouri, Columbia, 1969; MFA, Warren Wilson College, 1983. *Appointments:* Adjunct Teacher of English Composition and Leader of Poetry Workshop, Missouri Western State College, St Joseph, 1985; Editor of New Letters Review of Books, University of Missouri, Kansas City; Poetry workshop leader at Central Missouri State University, 1980-82; poetry reader. *Publications:* Under the name of Trish Reeves: Returning the Questions (poems) Cleveland State University Press 1988; Work represented in anthologies. *Honours:* Yaddo Fellow, 1987; Poetry Center Prize from Cleveland State University, 1988 for Returning the Question; Fellow of National Endowment for the Arts, 1988. *Address:* 6231 Glenfield Drive, Shawnee Mission, KS 66205, USA.

REGAN Dian Curtis, b. 17 May 1950, Colorado Springs, Colorado, USA. Children's Book Author. m. John Regan, 25 Aug 1979. *Education:* BS with honours, Education, University of Colorado, Boulder, 1980. *Appointments:* Speaker, numerous writers conference, USA. *Publications:* I've Got Your Number, 1986; The Perfect Age, 1987; Game of Survival, 1989; The Kissing Contest, 1990; Jilly's Ghost, 1990; Liver Cookies, 1991; The Class With The Summer Birthdays, 1991; The Curse of the Trouble Dolls, 1992; My Zombie Valentine, 1993; Princess, 1993; Cripple Creek Ghost Mine, 1993; Thirteen Days of Halloween, 1993. *Contributions to:* Assignments for Writer's Digest; Column, Byline Magazine, 5 years; Fiction, non-fiction, poetry to various children's publications. *Honours:* Children's Choice Award, 1987; Pick of the List, American Library Association, 1989; Oklahoma Cherubim Award, 1990, 1991, 1992. *Memberships:* Authors Guild; Society of Children's Book Writers; Oklahoma Writers Federation. *Literary Agent:* Curtis Brown Ltd, New York, USA.

REGINALD Robert, b. 11 Feb 1948, Fukuoka, Japan. Professor; Librarian; Publisher; Author. m. Mary Alice Wickizer, 15 Oct 1976, 1 stepson, 1 stepdaughter. *Education:* AB Hon, Gonzaga University, 1969; MS, University of Southern California, 1970. *Appointments:* Associate Editor, Forgotton Fantasy, 1970-71; Editor, Newcastle Publishing Co., 1971-; Publisher, Borgo

Press, 1975-; Editor, LTF Newsletter, 1987; Six Reprint Series. *Publications include:* Science Fiction and Fantasy Literature, 1979; Cumulative Paperback Index, 1973; Lords Temporal and Lords Spiritual, 1985; Phantasmagoria, 1976; The Holy Grail Revealed, 1982; Candle for Poland, 1982; Futurevisions, 1985; The Work of William F. Nolan, 1988; The Work of Ian Watson, 1989; Reference Guide to Science Fiction, Fantasy and Horror, 1990. *Contributions to:* 107 articles and reviews. *Honours:* Title II Fellowship, University of Southern California, 1969-70; Nomination as Finalist for Hugo Award, 1980; Choice Magazine, Book of the Year, 1980; Winner $2500 Meritorious Performance and Professional Promise Award, California State University, 1987. *Memberships include:* American Association of University Professors; Blue Earth County Historical Society; Horror Writers of America; International Association for the Fantastic in Arts; Science Fiction Writers of America. *Address:* Box 2845, San Bernardino, CA 92406, USA.

REGISTER Cheryl, b. 30 Apr 1945, Albert Lea, Minnesota. Writer and Freelance Teacher, 1980-. Married 1966-85, 2 daughters. *Education:* BA (with honours) 1967, MA (with honours) 1968, PhD (with Honours) 1973, University of Chicago. *Career:* Co-founder, organizer and workshop leader, Emma Willard Task Force on Education, Minneapolis, 1970-73; Co-ordinator of Women's Center, University of Idaho, Moscow, 1973-74; Assistant Professor of Women's Studies and Scandinavian languages and literatures, University of Minnesota - Twin Cities, Minneapolis, 1974-80; Writer and Freelance Teacher, 1980-. *Publications:* Under name Cheri Register: (co-author)Sexism in Education, 1971; Kvinnokamp och litteratur i USA och Sverige (Women's Liberation and Literature in the United States and Sweden) 1977; (Editor and contributor) A Telling Presence: Westminster Presbyterian Church 1857-1982, 1982; Mothers, Saviours, Peacemakers: Swedish Women Writers in the Twentieth Century, 1983; Living With Chronic Illness: Days of Patience and Passion, 1987; 'Are Those Kids Yours?' American Families With Children Adopted from Other Countries, 1990. *Contributions to:* Various edited volumes and to magazines. *Honour:* Jerome Foundation Travel and Study Grant, 1991. *Address:* 4226 Washburn Avenue S, Minneapolis, MN 55410, USA.

REICH Ali. *See:* **KATZ Bobbie.**

REID Christopher, b. 13 May 1949, Hong Kong. Poet; Freelance journalist. m. Lucinda Gane, 7 July 1979. *Education:* Kingswood House, Epsom, Surrey, England, 1956-62, Tonbridge School, 1962-67; Exeter College, Oxford, 1968-71, graduated 1971. *Career:* Part-time librarian, Ashmolean Classics Library; Actor; Filing-clerk; Flyman, Victoria Palace Theatre; nanny/tutor; Freelance journalist; Poet. *Publications:* Books: Arcadia, Oxford: Oxford University Press, 1979; Pea Soup, Oxford and New York, Oxford University Press, 1982; Katerina Brac, London: Faber & Faber, 1985. *Honours include:* Prudence Farmer Award, with Craig Raine, 1978 and 1980; Eric Gregory Award, Society of Authors for typescript of Arcadia, 1978; Somerset Maugham Award for Arcadia, 1980; Hawthornden Prize for Arcadia, 1981.

REID Michaela Ann (Lady), b. 14 Dec 1933. Author. m. Alexander James Reid, 15 Oct 1955. 1 son, 3 daughters. *Education:* Law Tripos, Part I, Girton College, Cambridge University. *Publications:* Ask Sir James; Sir James Reid, Personal Physician to Queen Victoria and Physician-in-Ordinary to Three Monarchs, 1987, 1989, 1990. *Address:* Lanton Tower, Jedburgh, Roxburghshire, Scotland.

REID Philip. *See:* **INGRAMS Richard.**

REID Randall Clyde, b. 4 Oct 1931, Paso Robles, California, USA. Writer; Professor of English and American Literature. 1 son, 1 daughter. *Education:* BA, San Francisco State University, 1959; MA, 1961, PhD,

1966, Stanford University. *Appointments:* Instructor in English, San Diego College, 1961-63; Acting Faculty Chairman, Deep Springs College, 1963- 65; Assistant Professor of English and Humanities, 1966-69, Associate Professor (on leave) 1969-71, University of Chicago; Director and Dean, Deep Springs College, 1969-75; Professor of English, University of Nevada, Reno, 1975-. *Publications:* The Fiction of Nathanael West, 1967; Lost and Found, 1975. *Contributions to:* Detritus, featured in New American Review 14, 1972; Stories in TriQuarterly; Story Quarterly; Carolina Quarterly; Seattle Review; Antioch Review and other publications. *Honour:* Detritus, winner in O'Henry Awards, 1973. *Address:* Department of English, University of Nevada, Reno, NV 89503, USA.

REID Victor Stafford, b. 1 May 1913, Kingston, Jamaica, West Indies. Journalist; Novelist; Biographer. m. Monica Victoria Jacobs, 10 Aug 1935, 2 sons, 2 daughters. *Appointments:* Newspaper and Magazine Editor, Jamaica. *Publications:* Novels: New Day; The Leopard; The Jamaicans; Sixty-Five; The Young Warriors; Mount Ephraim; Nanny Town; Biographies: The Horses of the Morning; About Norman Manley, National Hero of Jamaica; various novels and short stories in USA and Europe; numerous translations. *Honours:* Canada Council Fellow, 1959-60, 1960-61; Guggenheim Fellow, 1961-62; Mexican Escritores, 1962; Musgrave Gold Medal for literature; Norman Manley Award for Excellence; The Order of Jamaica. *Memberships:* Chairman, Historic Foundation Research Centre; Past Chairman, Jamaica National Trust Commission; Jamaica Library Association. *Address:* Box 129, Kingston 10, Jamaica, West Indies.

REIF Stefan Clive, b. 21 Jan 1944, Edinburgh, Scotland. Academic. m. Shulamit Stekel, 19 Sept 1967, 1 son, 1 daughter. *Education:* BA, Hons, 1964, PhD, 1969, University of London; MA, University of Cambridge, 1976. *Appointments:* Editor, Cambridge University Library's Genizah Series published by Cambridge University Press, 1978-. *Publications:* Shabbethai Sofer and his Prayer-book, 1979; Interpreting the Hebrew Bible, 1981; Published Material from the Cambridge Genizah Collections, 1988; Genizah Research after Ninety Years, 1992; Judaism and Hebrew Prayer, 1993. *Contributions to:* Over 160 articles in Hebrew and Jewish studies. *Honour:* William Lincoln Shelley Studentship of the University of London, 1967-68. *Memberships:* Jewish Historical Society of England, President 1991-92; British Association for Jewish Studies, President 1992; Hebraica Libraries Group, First Convener, 1981-84; Society for Old Testament Study, Committee 1985-89. *Address:* Taylor-Schechter Genizah Research Unit, Cambridge University Library, West Road, Cambridge CB3 9DR, England.

REIG June, b. 1 June 1933, New York, USA. Author; TV Writer-Director; Illustrator. m. Robert Maxwell, 26 Nov 1969. *Education:* BA, summa cum lauda, State University of New York, Albany, 1954; MA, Dramatic Arts, New York University, 1962. *Publications:* Diary of the Boy-King Tutankh-Amen, 1978; The Heart of Christmas NBC Special, 1965; Stuart Little, NBC TV, 1965; An Afternoon at Tanglewood, NBC TV Special, 1966; Bill Cosby and As I See It, NBC TV Special, 1969; A Day with Bill Cosby, NBC TV Special, 1971; Tut, the Boy King, NBC TV, 1977. *Contributions to:* Scholastic Magazine; Jack and Jill; American Harp Journal; New York Times Drama Section. *Honours:* Peabody, 1966; Prix Jeunesse, 1966; Emmy Nominee, 1966, 1976; American Library Association, 1967; Brotherhood Award, NCCJ, 1968; The Christopher, 1970; Ohio State, 1970; ACT Achievement, 1970. *Memberships:* Writers Guild of America; Directors Guild of America; National Academy of Television Arts and Sciences. *Address:* Bunny Chord Productions Inc, 119 W 57th St, Suite 1106, New York, NY 10019, USA.

REIN Evgeny Borisovich, b. 29 Dec 1935, St Petersburg, Russia. Writer. m. Nadejda Rein, 21 Jan 1989, 1 son. *Education:* Graduated, Mechanical

Engineer, Leningrad Technological Institute, 1959. *Publications:* Books of poems: The Names of Bridges, 1984; Shore Line, 1989; The Darkness of Mirrors, 1989; Irretrievable Day, 1991; Counter- Clockwise, 1992. *Contributions to:* Over 100 contributions to Russian, European and US magazines. *Honours:* Smena Magazine Award, 1970; Tallinn Magazine Award, 1982. *Memberships:* USSR Writers Union; Russian PEN Centre. *Address:* ulitza Kuusinena 7, apt 164, 123308 Moscow, Russia.

REISEL Vladimir, b. 19 Jan 1919, Brodzany, Czechoslovakia. Editor. m. Margita Rihova, 16 Aug 1945, 1 son, 1 daughter. *Education:* Philosophical Faculties, Prague & Bratislava Universities, 1937-42. *Literary Appointments:* Deputy Editor, Slovensky Spisovatel publishing house, 1960-72; Editor, Slovenske Pohlady, monthly review, 1972-87. *Publications:* Vidim vsetky dni a noci, 1939; Neskutocne mesto, 1943; Zrkadlo a za zrkadlom, 1945; More bez odlivu, 1960; Oci a brezy, 1972; Rozlucky, 1980; Zena a muz, 1983; Trpké plánky, 1988. Also: Poezia Laca Novomeskeho, critical essays, 1946. *Contributions to:* Numerous daily papers, literary & critical journals. *Honours:* State Prize, Slovak Socialist Republic, 1973; Artist of Merit, 1974. *Membership:* Committee, Union of Slovak Writers. *Literary Agent:* Lita, Bratislava. *Address:* Sutazna 19, 821 08 Bratislava, Czechoslovakia.

REITER David Philip, b. 30 Jan 1947, Cleveland, Ohio, USA. Publisher; Writer. m. Cherie Lorraine Reiter, 26 Apr 1992. *Education:* BA, Independent Study, University of Oregon; MA, American Literature, University of Alberta, Canada; PhD, Creative Writing, University of Denver, 1982. *Appointments:* Lecturer, Cariboo University College, Canada, 1975-84; Lecturer, University of British Columbia, 1984; Lecturer, British Columbia Institute of Technology, 1984; Lecturer, University of Canberra, Australia, 1986-90. *Publications:* The Snow in Us, 1989; Changing House, 1991; The Cave After Saltwater Tide, in press. *Contributions to:* Widely, Australian, Canadian, US and UK journals. *Honours:* Queensland Premier's Poetry Award, 1989; Imago-QUT Short Story Competition, 1990. *Literary Agent:* Debbie Golvan, Melbourne, Victoria, Australia. *Address:* 15 Gavan Street, Ashgrove, Queensland 4060, Australia.

REKAI Catherine Kati, b. 20 Oct 1921. Writer; Journalist; Broadcaster. m. John Rekai, 15 Aug 1941, 2 daughters. *Education:* Budapest, Hungary. *Publications:* The Adventures of Micky, Taggy, Puppo and Cica, and How they Discover, series of travel books for children on major cities and countries of the world, 16 titles. *Contributions to:* Columnist, Magyar Elet (Hungarian Life); Spark Magazine, performing arts in Canada magazine; Broadcaster, cultural events Chin-Radio International. *Honours:* Award for contribution to Canadian Unity, 1979; Knighthood of St. Ladislaus, 1980; Prix Saint-Exupery-Valeur Jeunesse, 1988; Rakoczi Foundation Award, 1991. *Memberships:* Writers Union of Canada, Chair External Committee; Ethnic Journalists and Writers Club, Vice President; Canadian Scene, Board of Directors, Secretary; Smile Theatre Co, Board of Directors; Performing Arts Magazine, Director. *Address:* 21 Dale Avenue, Toronto, Canada M4W 1K3.

REMEC Miha, b. 10 Aug 1928, Pluj, Yugoslavia. Journalist. m. Mira Iskra, 1 July 1970, 3 sons. *Appointments:* Editorial Staff, Daily Newspaper, Delo, 1953- . *Publications:* Novels: Solstice, 1969; Iksion, 1981; Recognition, 1980; Mana, 1985; The Big Carriage, 1986; Two Short Novels: The Hunter and the Unchaste Daughter, 1987; Dramas: The Dead Kurent, 1959; the Happy Dragons, 1963; Workshop of Clouds, 1966; The Plastionic Plague, 1982; Fairytales from the Dragon's Castle; Votlina, The Cave, (novel), 1978; 20 short stories, poems. *Contributions to:* Articles in numerous professional journals and magazines. *Honours:* Literary Award for Drama, 1950, 1976; SFera Award, for Novel, 1981; SFera Award, for Short Story, 1987. *Memberships:* Slovene Writers Association; World

Science Fiction Organization; SFera Science Fiction Club. *Literary Agent:* Ziga Leskovsek, Ljubljana, Yugoslavlia. *Address:* Pod lipami 58, Ljubljana 61000, Yugoslavia.

REMY Pierre-Jean (Jean-Pierre Angremy), b. 21 Mar 1937. Diplomat; Author. m. Odile Cail, 1963, (div 1979), 1 son, 1 daughter. *Appointments:* Served in Hong Kong, 1963; Second Secretary, Peking, 1964, London, 1966; First Secretary, London, 1968; counsellor, Ministry of Foreign Affairs, 1971; Director, programme Co-Ordination, ORTF, 1972; Cultural Counsellor, French Embassy, London, 1975-79; French Ministry of Culture, 1979-81; Consul General de France, Florence, 1985-87. *Publications:* Et Gulliver mourut de sommeil, 1961; Midi ou l'attentat, 1962; Gauguins a gogo, 1971; La sac du palais d'ete, 1971; urbanisme, 1972 une mort sale, 1973; La vie d'Adrian Putney, 1973; Ava, La mort de Floria Tosca, memoires secrets pour servir a l'histoire de ce siecle, 1974; Rever la vie, 1975; La figure dans la pierre, 1976; Chine : Un itineraire, 1977; les Enfans du parc, 1977; Si j'etais romancier, 1977; Callas, une vie, 1978; Les nouvelles aventures du Chevalier de la Barre, 1978; orient Express, 1979; Cordelia ou l'Angleterre, 1979; Don Giovanni, 1979; Pandora, 1980; Slaue pour moir le monde, 1980; Un voyage d'hiver, 1981; Don Juan, 1982; Le dernier ete, 1983; Maa Hari, 1983; La vie d'un hero, 1985; une ville immortelle 1986; Des Chatevoux Allamagne, 1987; Toscanes, 1989. *Honours:* Chevalier, Legion d'Honneur; Chevalier, Ordre national du Merite; Commander, des Arts et des Lettres. *Address:* Consulat de France, 2 Piazza Ognissanti, 50123 Florence, Italy.

RENAUD (Ernest) Hamilton Jacques, b. 10 Nov 1943. Montreal, Canada. Author; Conceptor; Writer; Teacher; Translator; Speaker. 2 sons, 1 daughter. *Appointments:* Critic and Researcher, Radio Canada, 1965-67; Reporter, Metro-Express, Montreal, 1966; Critic, Le Devoir, Montreal, 1975-78; Teacher, Creat ive Writing Workshop, Quebec University, in Montreal, 1980-89; Researcher, Senate of Canada, 1990. *Publications:* 18 titles, some of which are under pen-names including short stories, novels, poetry, short and long essays; Electrodes, Poetry, 1962; Le Cassé, stories, 1964; Clandestines, Novel, 1980; L'espace du Diable, Stories, 1989; Les Cycles du Scorpion, poetry, 1989; La Constellation Du Bouc Émissaire, a study in proto-totalitarianism, 1993; Translations in English of: Le Casse: Flat Broke and Beat, by Gerald Robitaille, 1967; Broke City, by David Homel, 1984. *Contributions to:* Nouvelles Literaires; La Presse; The Montreal Gazette; The Ottawa Citizen; Perspectives; Forces; Moebius; Parti Pris; Breves; Sexus; Nyx; L'Analyste; Liberte. *Memberships:* Spokesman and Speaker for Equality party and Political Adviser and Researcher to Equality Party's leader and elected member of Quebec National Assembly, Robert Libman, 1989. *Address:* 205 Ivy Crescent, 3, Ottawa, Ontario, K1M 1X9, Canada.

RENDELL Ruth (Barbara Vine), b. 17 Feb 1930. Crime Novelist. m. Donald Rendell, 1950, (div), remarried 1977, 1 son. *Publications include:* From Doon with Death, 1964; To Fear a Painted Devil, 1965; Vanity Dies Hard, 1966; A New Lease of Death, 1967; Wolf to the Slaughter, 1967 (televised 1987); The Secret House of Death, 1968; The Best Man to Die, 1969; A Guilty Thing Surprised, 1970; One Across Two Down, 1971; No More Dying Then, 1971; Murder Being Once Done, 1972; Some Lie and Some Die, 1973; The Face of Trespass, 1974 (televised, An Affair in Mind, 1988); Shake Hands for Ever, 1975; The Fallen Curtain (short stories), 1976; A Demon in my View, 1976; A Judgement in Stone, 1977; A Sleeping Life, 1978; Make Death Love Me, 1979; Means of Evil (short stories), 1979; The Lake of Darkness, 1980 (televised, Dead Lucky, 1988); Put on by Cunning, 1981; Master of the Moor, 1982; The Fever Tree (short stories), 1982; The Speaker of Mandarin, 1983; The Killing Doll, 1984; The Tree of Hands, 1984 (film 1989); An Unkindness of Ravens, 1985; The New Girl Friend (short stories), 1985; Live Flesh, 1986; A Dark-Adapted Eye (as Barbara Vine), 1987; Heartstones, 1987; Talking to Strange Men, 1987;

A Fatal Inversion (as Barbara Vine), 1987 (televised 1992); (ed) A Warning to the Curious - The Ghost Stories of M R James, 1987; Collected Short Stories, 1987; The House of Stairs (as Barbara Vine), 1988; The Veiled One, 1988 (televised 1989); The Bridesmaid, 1989; Ruth Rendell's Suffolk, 1989; (with Colin Ward) Undermining the Central Line, 1989; Going Wrong, 1990; Gallowglass (as Barbara Vine), 1990 (televised 1993); The Copper Peacock, 1991; King Solomon's Carpet, 1991; Kissing the Gunner's Daughter, 1992. *Honour:* Arts Council National Book Award for Genre Fiction, 1981; Crime Writers Association, Cartier Diamond Dagger Award, 1991. *Address:* Nussteads, Polstead, Suffolk, England.

RENIER Elizabeth. *See:* **BAKER Betty.**

RENO Dawn Elaine, b. 15 Apr 1953, Waltham, Massachusetts, USA. Writer. m. Robert G Reno, 25 Feb 1978, 1 daughter, 1 stepdaughter, 3 stepsons. *Education:* AA, cum laude, Liberal Arts, Bunker Hill, Community College, Boston, Massachusetts, 1976; BA, summa cum laude, Liberal Studies, Johnson State College, Johnson, Vermont, 1990. *Appointments:* Assistant Editor, Vermont Woman, 1988-91; Reporter, New England County Antiques, 1979- 86. *Publications:* Collecting Black Americana, 1986; American Indian Collectibles, 1989; American Country Collectibles, 1991; Jenny Moves, 1984; Jenny's First Friend, 1984; All That Glitters, 1992. *Contributions to:* Journals including: The Writer; Black Ethnic Collectibles; Better Homes and Gardens; Tours and Resorts; New England GetAways; Dolls; Antique Trader Weekly; Green Mountains Review; Burlington Free Press. *Honours:* Semi-finalist, Writers' Digest Contest - non-fiction, 1986; Fiction Award, Johnson State College, 1990; Fellowship at Virginia Centre for the Creative Arts, 1990. *Memberships:* League of Vermont Writers; Society of Children's Book Writers; National Writers Union. *Address:* 3280 Shingler Terrace, Deltona, FL 32738, USA.

REPKA J. *See:* **KARVAS Peter.**

REPLANSKY Naomi, b. 23 May 1918. Poet. *Education:* BA, University of California, Los Angeles, USA, 1956. *Appointments:* Poet in Residence, Pitzer College, Claremont, California, 1981. *Publications:* Ring Song, 1952; Twenty-One Poems, Old and New, 1988. *Contributions to:* Ploughshares; Missouri Review; The Nation; Feminist Studies. *Honour:* Nominated for National Book Award, 1952. *Memberships:* PEN American Center; Poetry Society of America. *Address:* 711 Amsterdam Avenue, New York, NY 10025, USA.

RESTAK Richard Martin, b. 4 Feb 1942, Wilmington, Delaware, USA. Physician; Author. m. Carolyn Serbent, 18 Oct 1968, 3 daughters. *Education:* MD. Georgetown Medical School, 1966; Trained in Neurology and Psychiatry. *Appointments:* Consultant, Encyclopedia of Bioethics, 1978; Special Contributing Editor, Science Digest, 1981-1985; Editorial Board, Integrative Psychiatry: An International Journal for the Synthesis of Medicine and Psychiatry, 1986. *Publications:* Premeditated Man: Bioethics and the Control of Future Human Life, 1975; The Brain: The Last Frontier: Explorations of the Human Mind and Our Future, 1979; The Self Seekers, 1982; The Brain, 1984; The Infant Mind, 1986; The Mind, 1988; Works in anthologies. *Contributions to:* Saturday Review; Psychology Today; Science Digest; Smithsonian Magazine; Science '82; Readers Digest; The Wilson Quarterly; Semiotica; Vogue; Publisher's Weekly; Newsday; Washington Post; Los Angeles Times; Washington Post Outlook; Washington Post Education Review; New York Times Book Review; Washington Times; New York Times; Washington Post Book World; The Sciences; Psychology Today; Zygon Journal of Religion and Science. *Honours:* Summer Fellowship, National Endowment for the Humanities, 1976; Claude Bernard Science Journalism Award, National Society for Medical Research, 1976; Distinguished Alumni Award, Gettysburg College, 1985.

Memberships: American Academy of Neurology; American Academy of Psychiatry and the Law; American Psychiatric Association; Behavioral Neurology Society; New York Academy of Sciences; Royal Society of Medicine, London, 1984; Semiotic Society of America, 1985; International Neuropsychological Society; National Book Critics Circle; International Brotherhood of Magicians; Philosophical Society of Washington; Georgetown Clinical Society, 1974-84, President 1983-84; International Platform Association. *Literary Agent:* Sterling Lord, One Madison Avenue, New York, NY, USA. *Address:* 1800 R Street NW, Suite C-3, Washington, DC 20009, USA.

REUSS-IANNI Elizabeth, b. 9 Jan 1944, New Orleans, Louisiana, USA. Anthropologist. m. Francis A J Ianni, 28 May, 1971. *Education:* BS, Political Science, Northwestern University, 1964; MA, Anthropology, New York University, 1970. *Publications:* A Family Business: Kinship and Social Control in Organized Crime (with F A J Ianni) 1972; The Crime Society (with F A J Ianni) 1979; Street Cops vs. Management Cops: The Two Cultures of Policing, 1983. *Contributions to:* Organized Crime in Encyclopaedia of Crime and Punishment, 1985. *Memberships:* American Anthropological Association; Society of Applied Anthropology; International Association on Organized Crime. *Address:* Villa L'Aquila, Clover Road, Newfoundland, NJ 07435, USA.

REUTHER David Louis, b. 2 Nov 1946, Detroit, Michigan, USA, Children's Book Publisher and Author. m. Margaret Alexander Miller, 21 July 1973, 1 son, 1 daughter. *Education:* BA, Honours, University of Michigan, Ann Arbor, 1968. *Publications:* Adult: The Hidden Game of Baseball, (Co-author), 1984; Total Baseball, 1989; The Whole Baseball catalog, 1990; Co-Editor, The Armchair Angler, 1986; The Armchair Book of Baseball, 1985; The Armchair Mountaineer, 1984; The Armchair Traveler, 1989; The Armchair Aviator, 1983; The Armchair Quarterback, 1982; Children: Fun To Go, 1982; Save-the-Animals Activity Book, 1982. *Contributions to:* The Horn Book, 1984. *Memberships:* American Library Association; Society of Children's Book Writers; Authors Guild; Children's Book Council, Board of Directors, 1985-88 and 1991-93, Treasurer, 1986, Chairman, 1993, Chairman, Book Week Committee, 1987; American Booksellers Association CBC Joint Committee, 1990-93. *Address:* 271 Central Park West, New York, NY 10024, USA.

REYES Carlos, b. 2 June 1935, Marshfield, USA. Poet; Teacher. m. Barbara Ann Hollingsworth, 13 Sept 1958, (div 1973), 1 son, 3 daughters, (2) Karen Ann Stoner, 21 May 1979 (div 1992). *Education:* BA, University of Oregon, 1961; MA, ABD, Univerity of Arizona, 1965. *Appointments:* Governor's Advisory Committee on the Arts, Oregon, 1973; Poet to the City of Portland, 1978; Poet in Residence, in various public schools in Oregon and Washington; Editor, Hubbub, 1982-90. *Publications:* The Shingle Weaver's Journal, 1980; The Prisoner, 1973; At Doolin Quay, 1982; Nightmarks, 1990. *Contributions to:* various journals and magazines. *Honours:* Oregon Arts Commission Individual Artist Fellowship, 1982; Yaddo Fellowship, 1984. *Memberships:* Board, Portland Poetry Festival Inc, 1974-84; PEN, Northwest; Co-Chair, PEN Northwest, 1992-93. *Address:* 3222 NE Schuyler, Portland, OR 97212, USA.

REYNOLDS Graham, b. 10 Jan 1914, Highgate, London, England. Writer; Art Historian. *Education:* BA Honours, Queens College, Cambridge University. *Publications:* Nicholas Hilliard and Isaac Oliver, 1947, 1971; English Portrait Miniatures, 1952, revised edition, 1988; Painters of the Victorian Scene, 1953; Catalogue of the Constable Collection, Victoria and Albert Museum, 1960, revised, 1973; Constable, The Natural Painter, 1965; Victorian Painting, 1966, revised, 1987; Turner, 1969; Concise History of Watercolour Painting, 1972; Catalogue of Portrait Miniatures, Wallace Collection, 1980; The Later Paintings and Drawings of John Constable, 2 volumes, 1984; English Watercolours, 1988; Catalogue of Portrait Minatures, Metropolitan

Museum of Art, New York, 1993. *Contributions to:* Times Literary Supplement; Burlington Magazine; Apollo; New Departures; Palindromes and Anagrams, anthology; H W Bergerson, editor, 1973. *Honours:* Mitchell Prize for The Later Paintings and Drawings of John Constable, 1984. *Literary Agent:* A M Heath & Company Limited. *Address:* The Old Manse, Bradfield St George, Bury St Edmunds, Suffolk IP30 0AZ, England.

REYNOLDS Keith Ronald (Kev Reynolds), b. 7 Dec 1943, Ingatestone, Essex, England. Author; Photojournalist; Lecturer. m. Linda Sylvia Dodsworth, 23 Sept 1967, 2 daughters. *Publications:* Walks and Climbs in the Pyrenees, 1978, 1983; Mountains of the Pyrenees, 1982; The Weald Way and Vanguard Way, 1987; Walks In The Engadine, 1988; The Valais, 1988; Walking In Kent, 1988; Classic Walks in the Pyrenees, 1989; Classic Walks in Southern England, 1989; The Jura, 1989; South Downs Way, 1989; Eye on the Hurricane, 1989; The Mountains of Europe, 1990; Visitors Guide to Kent, 1990; The Cotswold Way, 1990; Alpine Pass Route, 1990; Classic Walks in the Alps, 1991; Chamonix to Zermatt, 1991; The Bernesie Alps, 1992. *Contributions to:* The Great Outdoors; Climber and Hill Walker; Environment Now; Trail Walker; Country Walking; High. *Memberships:* Outdoor Writers' Guild. *Address:* Freshfields, Crockham Hill, Edenbridge, Kent TN8 6RT, England.

REYNOLDS Kimberley Kay Griffith, b. 8 Jan 1955, Columbus, Ohio, USA. Lecturer in English. m. Peter Lloyd Reynolds, 9 Oct 1976, 1 son, 1 daughter. *Education:* BA, summa cum laude, C W Post College, Long Island, New York, 1975; BA, 1984, MA, 1985, PhD, 1988, University of Sussex. *Publications:* Girls Only? Gender and Popular Children's Fiction 1880-1910; An Illustrated Dictionary of Art Terms. *Contributions to:* Assorted articles and chapters in academic journals; Books on the Box: The BBC Chronicles of Narnia for Critical Survey, Vol 3 No 3, 1991. *Address:* 10 Dorset Road, Lewes, East Sussex BN7 1TH, England.

REYNOLDS Pamela Christine Schrom b. 13 July 1945, Chicago, Illinois, USA. Editor. m. David R. Reynolds, 23 Aug 1969. *Education:* BA, University of Illinois, Chicago, 1967; MSc, Journalism, Medill School of Journalism, Northwestern University, 1974. *Appointments:* Assistant Editor, Selling Sporting Goods Magazine, 1974-78; Associate Editor, The Guarantor Magazine, 1978-81; Editor, PTA Today Magazine, 1981-. *Contributions to:* Chicago Daily News; Chicago Reader. *Honours:* Excellence in Educational Journalism Awards, EDPRESS, 1982, 1983, 1984, 1985, 1987, 1988. *Memberships:* Educational Press Association, Secretary, Member of Board of Directors; Society of Professional Journalists; National Association of Real Estate Editors. *Address:* c/o National PTA, 330N Wabash Avenue, Suite 2100, Chicago, IL 60611, USA.

REYNOLDS Sydney, b. 22 Jan 1939, Richmond, Surrey, England. Journalist. m. Jennifer Knapp, 26 Jan 1963, Kensington Register Office, London. 4 sons. *Literary Appointments:* Night Editor, Associate Iliffe Press, 1962-65; Sub-Editor, Daily Telegraph, 1965-84; Art Editor, Sunday Telegraph, 1984-86. *Contributions to:* The Artist; Daily Telegraph; The Lady; Scottish Field; American in Britain; Majesty; Music & Musicians; Art & Antiques; Universe; Woodworker; Melbourne Herald/Sun; Drum; Ulster Tatler; Almost every County Magazine in Britain; Sunday Times of Ceylon; Camera Weekly; Private Eye; UK Press Gazette; The Times (of Malta); Dog World; Feathered World; Morning Advertiser; The Guardian; The Stage & Television Today; What's On In London; History Today; Manchester Evening News; Cats; Western Mail; Baptist Times; PR Week; New Statesman & Society; Evening Argus (Brighton); Decanter; Grocer; Amateur Gardening; Our Dogs; Farmers Weekly; Artists & Illustrators Mag; Horse & Hound. *Address:* 113 Bridgewater Road, Berkhamsted, Hertfordshire, England.

REYNOLDS Vernon, b. 14 Dec 1935, Berlin, Germany. University Teacher. m. Frances Glover, 5 Nov 1960, 1 son, 1 daughter. *Education:* BA, Phd, London University; MA, Oxford University. *Publications:* Budongo: a forest and its chimpanzees, 1965; The Apes, 1967; The Biology of Human Action, 1976, second edition 1980; The Biology of Religion (with R Tanner) 1983. *Memberships:* Fellow, Royal Anthropological Institute; Chairman, Biosocial Society; Primate Society of Great Britain; Society for the Study of Human Biology. *Address:* Institute of Biological Anthropology, Oxford University, 58 Banbury Road, Oxford OX2 6QS, England.

RHODAS Virginia, b. Rhodes, Greece. Freelance Journalist; Writer. *Education:* Journalism, human & public relations, Eastern & Western philosophy, Argentina & Europe. *Literary Appointments:* Journalist, newspaper corrector, secretary, several magazines & journals; Director, International Poetry Letter. *Publications include:* There Will Come A Day... & Other Poems, 1968; Brother Century XXI; Open Letter to Humanity; Listen to Me, Humanity, 1985; From the Greek Nucleous... To Your Heart. Also: 6 theatre plays, short stories, essays, children's stories. Work translated into Greek, various other languages. *Contributions to:* Numerous magazines & journals, worldwide. *Honours:* Awards: Orthodox Church, Argentina (poetry, essay), 1968; World Poetry Society, 1975; Academy of Arts & Culture, 1981; Honorary Doctorate, World University, USA, 1984. *Memberships:* YWCA; Christian Committee for World Prayer; Argentine Writers Society; Latin American Regent, World Poetry International Society (WPIS). *Literary Agents:* WPIS; Gerigramme, Greece; Literary Horizon, India. *Address:* Rivadavia 2284 PB-J, 1034 Buenos Aires, Argentina.

RHODES Anthony, b. 24 Sept 1916, Plymouth, Devon, England. Writer. m. Rosaleen Forbes, 9 Apr 1956. *Education:* Royal Military Academy, Woolwich; MA, Trinity College, University of Cambridge, England; Licence et Lettres, University of Geneva, Switzerland. *Major Publications:* Sword of Bone, 1942; The Uniform, 1949; A Sabine Journey, 1952; A Ball in Venice, 1953; The General's Summer House, 1954; The Dalmation Coast, 1955; Where the Turk Trod, 1956; The Poet as Superman: A Life of Gabriele D'Annunzio, 1959; The Prophet's Carpet, 1969; Propaganda in the Second World War, 1976; Rise & Fall of Louis Renault, 1966; The Vatican in the Age of the Dictator, 1922-45, 1973; Princes of the Grape, 1970; Art Treasures of Eastern Europe, 1971; The Vatican in the Age of the Liberal Democracies, 1983; The Vatican in the Agr of the Cold War, 1992; 15 book-length translations from French, Italian and German. *Contributions to:* Encounter; Sunday Telegraph; others. *Honour:* Cavaliere Commendatore del'Ordine di San Gregorio Magno (Papal Title). *Memberships:* Society of Authors; PEN; Bucks Club; Beefsteak Club. *Literary Agent:* Anthony Sheil. *Address:* 46 Fitzjames Avenue, London W14, England.

RHODES Philip, b. 2 May 1922, Sheffield, England. Medical Practitioner; Professor, Postgraduate Medical Education; Retired. 1987. m. Elizabeth Worley, 26 Oct 1946, 3 sons, 2 daughters. *Education:* Clare College, Cambridge University, 1940-43; St Thomas's Hospital, London, 1943-46. MA (Cantab), 1946; MB,Chir (Cantab), 1946; FRCS (Eng), 1953; FRCOG, 1964; FRACMA, 1976. *Publications include:* Fluid Balance in Obstetrics, 1960; Introduction to Gynaecology & Obstetrics, 1967; Woman: A Biological Study, 1969; Reproductive Physiology, 1969; The Value of Medicine, 1976; Dr John Leake's Hospital, 1978; Letters to a Young Doctor, 1983; Outline History of Medicine, 1985; Associate Editor, The OXford Companion to Medicine, 1986. *Contributions to:* Lancet; British Medical Journal; British Journal of Obstetrics & Gynaecology; Practitioner. *Honours include:* Annual Prize, Bronte Society, 1972. *Memberships:* Medical Committee, Society of Authors; British Medical Association. *Address:* 1 Wakerley Court, Wakerley, Oakham, Leicester LE15 8PA, England.

RHODES Richard, b. 4 July 1937, Kansas City,

Kansas, USA. Writer. *Education:* BA, cum laude, Yale University, 1959. *Appointments:* Writer Trainee, Newsweek, 1959; Assistant to Policy Adviser, Radio Free Europe, New York, 1960; English Instructor, Westminster College, 1960-61; Book Editing Manager, Hallmark Cards Inc., 1962-70; Contributing Editor, Harper's, 1970-74; Freelance Writer, 1974-. *Publications:* Non-fiction: The Making of the Atomic Bomb, 1988; Looking for America, 1979; The Ozarks, 1974; The Inland Ground, 1970; Fiction: Sons of Earth, 1981; The Last Safari, 1980; Holy Secrets, 1978; The Ungodly, 1973. *Contributions to:* Numerous journals and magazines including: Playboy; Redbook; Harper's; Audience; Esquire; American Heritage; Quest. *Honours:* National Book Award in Non-fiction, National Book Critics Circle Award in Non-Fiction, 1987; Pulitzer Prize in Non-Fiction, 1988. *Memberships:* Authors Guild. *Literary Agent:* Morton L. Janklow. *Address:* c/o Morton L Janklow Associates, 598 Madison Avenue, New York, NY 10022, USA.

RHONE Trevor Dave, b. 24 Mar 1940, Kingston, Jamaica. Playwright; Director; Screenwriter. m. Camella King, 5 Mar 1974, 2 sons, 1 daughter. *Education:* Diploma Speech and Drama, Rose Bruford College of Speech and Drama, 1963. *Appointments:* Resident playwright, Barn Theatre, Kingston, 1968-75. *Publications:* Old Story Time, 1981; Two Can Play, 1984. *Honours:* Silver Musgrave Medal, Institute of Jamaica, 1972; Commander of the Order of Distinction, National Honour, Jamaica, 1980; Gold Musgrave Medal, 1988; Academy Award, Film Canada, 1989. *Literary Agent:* Yvonne Brewster, 32 Buckley Road, London NW6 7LU, England; I.C.M., New York. *Address:* 1 Haining Mews, Kingston 5, Jamaica.

RICARD Charles, b. 9 Jan 1922, Gap, France. Author. m. J. Balmens, 28 July 1951. *Education:* Professeur de Lettres. *Publications:* (Novels): Le puits, 1967; La derniere des revolutions, 1968; Le mercredi des Cendres, 1986; A propos d'un piano casse, 1977; le Pot-a-Chien, 1979; Alerte rouge aux cites soleils, 1985; Le Chemin des Oiseaux, 1991; Rédé, 1992; Les Mysteres du Villaret, 1993. (Books of Poetry): si j'avais su, 1960; Je Voudrais, 1963; Les ombres du chemin, 1964. *Contributions to:* Various journals and magazines. *Honours:* Several major prizes including: Gold Medal, International Competition of Clubs of Cote d'Azur; Gold Medal, International Competition, Lutece, 1976; Prix Diamant, 1985; Prix du Vimeu, 1986. *Memberships:* Academy of the French Provinces; Associate, Society of French Poets; Associate, Gens de Lettres de France. *Address:* 20 rue du Super-Gap, 05000 Gap, France.

RICCHIUTI Paul B(urton), b. 4 July 1925, Redford Township, Michigan, USA. Writer. *Education:* Andrews University, 1949-52; Loma Linda University, 1953. *Appointments:* Layout and Design Artist, Pacific Press Publishing Association, 1955-. *Publications:* For Children: I Found a Feather, 1967; Whose House is It?, 1967; Up in the Air, 1967; When You Open Your Bible, 1967; Jeff, 1973; Amy, 1975; Five Little Gifts, 1975; Let's Play Make Believe, 1975; My Very Best Friend, 1975; Elijah Jeremiah Phillip's Great Journey, 1975; Yankee Dan, 1976; General Lee, 1978; Mandy, 1978; Mike, 1978; Jimmy and the Great Balloon, 1978; Ellen (adult biography of Ellen G. White), 1977; End of the World Man and Other Stories, 1989; Rocky and Me, 1989; New Dog In Town, 1991. *Contributions to:* Work represented in anthologies, including: The Family Album, 1975, 1976; Articles, stories and poems to magazines including: Signs of the Times; Our Little Friend; Primary Treasurer; These Times; Adventist Review, and to newspapers. *Address:* 5702 E. Powerline, Nampa, ID 83687, USA.

RICCI Nino P, b. 23 Aug 1959, Leamington, Canada. Writer. *Education:* BA, York University, Toronto, 1981; MA, Concordia University, Montreal, 1987. *Appointments:* Concordia University, 1987- 88. *Publications:* Lives of the Saints, 1990. *Honours:* 1st Novel Award, W H Smith-Books in Canada, 1990; Governor General's Award for Fiction, Canada, 1990;

Winifred Holtby Prize, UK, 1990; Betty Trask Award, UK, 1991. *Memberships:* Writers Union of Canada; Board of Directors, Canadian Centre, International PEN. *Literary Agent:* Peter Robinson, Curtis Brown Group Ltd. *Address:* c/o Writers Union of Canada, 24 Ryerson Avenue, Toronto, Canada M5T 2P3.

RICH Frank Hart, b. 2 June 1949, Washington DC, USA. Journalist. m. Gail Winston, 1976, 2 sons. *Education:* Havard College. *Appointments:* Film Critic, Senior Editor, New Times Magazine, 1973-75; Film Critic, New York Post, 1975-77; Film and TV Critic, Time Magazine, 1977- 80; Chief Drama Critic, New York Times, 1980-. *Address:* New York Times, 229 West 43rd Street, New York, NY 10036, USA.

RICHARDS Alun, b. 27 Oct 1929, Pontypridd, Wales. Author. m. Helen Howden, 8 July 1956, 3 sons, 1 daughter. *Education:* Diploma, Social Science & Education, University of Wales. *Appointments:* Editor, Penguin Book of Welsh Short Stories and Penguin Book of Sea Stories, Volumes 1-11. *Publications:* The Elephant You Gave Me, 1963; The Home Patch, 1966; A Woman of Experience, 1969; Home to an Empty House, 1974; Ennal's Point, 1979; Dai Country, 1979; The Former Miss Merthyr Tydfil and Other Stories, 1980; Barque Whisper, 1982; Autobiography, Days of Absence, 1987. *Contributions to:* Guardian; Planet; Western Mail. *Honours:* Arts Council Prize for Collected Short Stories, 1974; Royal National Lifeboat Institution Public Relations Award, 1983; Japan Foundation Fellowship, 1984. *Memberships:* Writer Guild of Great Britain. *Literary Agent:* Harvey Unna and Stephen Durbridge Limited. *Address:* 326 Mumbles Road, Swansea SA3 5AA, Wales.

RICHARDS Denis George, b. 10 Sept 1910, London, England. Writer. m. Barbara Smethurst, 6 Jan 1940, 4 daughters. *Education:* Trinity Hall, Cambridge, 1928-31; 1st Class Hons BA, 1931; MA, 1935. *Publications:* An Illustrated History of Modern Europe, 1938; An Illustrated History of Modern Britain, 1951; Royal Air Force, 1939-45 (3 vols with H St Saunders), 1953 & 1954; Offspring of the Vic: A History of Morley College, 1958; Britain Under the Tudors and Stuarts, 1958; The Battle of Britain: The Jubliee History (with Richard Hough), 1989; The Few and the Many, 1990; Others mostly in collaboration. *Contributions to:* Books & Bookmen; Daily Telegraph Supplement; Financial Times. *Honours:* C P Robertson Memorial Trophy, 1956; OBE, 1990. *Memberships include:* PEN (Hon Treas, English Centre in 1960's); Arts Club; Society of Authors; Garrick Club. *Address:* 16 Broadlands Road, London, N6 4AN, England.

RICHARDS Gloria Delise, (nee Farnsworth), b. 13 Nov 1940, Grimethorpe, England. Teacher. m. Vaughan Richards, 27 July 1963, 1 daughter. *Education:* BA Hons, French, U C North Wales, Bangor, 1962; Diploma in Education, U C Cardiff, 1963; Licentiate of London College of Music, 1958. *Appointments:* Educational Writer, Charles Letts & Co. 1980-. *Publications:* Revise French/O Level, 1982; Objective Questions/French, 1983; Foundation Skills, French 1, 1984; 2, 1985; 3, 1986; Revise French/GCSE, 1987; Junior Cycle French: 1, 1988. *Literary Agent:* Letts Educational.

RICHARDS Hubert John, b. 25 Dec 1921, Weilderstadt, Germany. Lecturer; Writer. m. 22 Dec 1975. 1 son, 1 daughter. *Education:* STL (License in Theology), Gregorian University, Rome, Italy; LSS (License in Scripture), Biblical Institute, Rome. *Publications:* The First Christmas: What Really Happened?, 1973 (USA, 1986); The Miracles of Jesus: What Really Happened?, 1975 (USA 1986); The First Easter: What Really Happened?, 1977 (USA 1986); Death & After: What Will Really Happen?, 1979 (USA 1986); What Happens When You Pray?, 1980; Pilgrim To The Holy Land, 1985; Various Books for Children, 1986-; Focus on The Bible, 1990; The Gospel According to St Paul, 1990; God's Diary, 1991, (USA 1991); Pilgrim To Rome, 1993. *Contributions to:* Regular articles and reviews in various publications. *Membership:* Chairman, Norfolk Theological Society. *Address:* 59 Park Lane, Norwich, Norfolk NR2 3EF, England.

RICHARDS James, Sir (Jim Cladpole), b. 13 Aug 1907, London, England. Editor; Journalist; Writer; Historian. *Education:* Diploma, Architectural Association, School of Architecture, London, 1929; Associate, Royal Institute of British Architects, 1930. *Publications:* High Street, 1938; Introduction to Modern Architecture, 1940; The Castles on the Ground, 1946; The Functional Tradition, 1958; Editor, The Anti-Rationalists, 1973; Editor, Who's Who in Architecture, 1977; Eight Hundred Years of Finnish Architecture, 1978; memoirs of an Unjust Fella, 1980; Goa, 1981; National Trust Book of English Architecture, 1981; National Trust Book of Bridges. *Contributions to:* Architectural Review; Architects Journal; Times; Times Literary Supplement; Listener; New Statesman; Country Life; Editor, Architectural Review, 1937-71; Architectural Correspondent, The Times, 1947-71; Editor, European Heritage, 1974-75. *Honours include:* CBE, 1959; Bicentenary Medal, Royal Society of Arts, 1971; Knight, 1972; Honorary Fellow, American Institute of Architects, 1984; Commander, Order of the White Rose of Finland, 1985. *Literary Agent:* Curtis Brown Ltd. *Address:* 29 Fawcett Street, London, SW10, England.

RICHARDS Ronald Charles William (Allen Saddler), b. 15 Apr 1923, London, England. Writer; Journalist. *Publications:* Novels: The Great Brain Robbery, 1965; Gilt Edge, 1966; Talking Turkey, 1968; Betty, 1974. Childrens Books: The King & Queen series; Mr Wizz; Jerry and The Monsters; Jerry and the Inventions; The Relay Race; Smudger's Seaside Spectacular; Smidger's Saturday Special; Captain Cockle; Sam's Swop Shop. 24 radio plays for BBC: TV Barnet (with Doris Richards); The Concert Party (documentary); I Should Say So (radio series). Stage: Them; All Basic Comforts; Kindly Leave The Stage; King & Queen Show (for children). *Contributions to:* As Drama Critic: The Guardian; The Stage; Plays & Players; Plays International; Entertainment. Feature writer to: The Guardian; Sunday Times magazine; The Observer Magazine; Time Out; The Daily Telegraph; Daily Express; Nova; Western Morning News. Columnist For: The Western Morning News; Sunday Independent. *Membership:* Writers Guild (Chairman, Westcountry Branch 1974-87); Drama Panel, SW Arts; Editor Western Front/Westward Look (BBC Radio 3); Tutor, Arvon, Beaford. Exeter & Devon Arts Centre. *Address:* 5 St John's Hall, Station Road, Totnes, TQ9 5HW, Devon, England.

RICHARDSON Joanna, b. London, England. Biographer. *Education:* The Downs School, Seaford, Susses; MA, St Anne's College, Oxford. *Appointments:* FRSL, 1959; Member of Council, Royal Society of Literature, 1961-86. *Publications:* Fanny Brawne: a biography, 1952; Rachel, 1956; Théophile Gautier: His Life and Times, 1958; Sarah Bernhardt, 1959; Edward FitzGerald, 1960; The Disastrous Marriage: A Study of George IV and Caroline of Brunswick, 1960; Editor, FitzGerald: Selected Works, 1962; The Pre-Eminent Victorian: a Study of Tennyson, 1962; The Everlasting Spell: a Study of Keats and his Friends, 1963; Editor, Essays by Divers Hands (transactions Royal Society of Literature), 1963; Introduction to Victor Hugo: Choses Vues (The Oxford Library of French Classics), 1964; Edward Lear, 1965; George IV: A Portrait, 1966; Creevey and Greville, 1967; Princess Mathilde, 1969; Verlaine, 1971; Enid Starkie, 1973; Translator, Verlaine, Poems, 1974; Translator, Baudelaire, Poems, 1975; Victor Hugo, 1976; Zola, 1978; Keats and his Circle: an album of portraits, 1980; Paris under Siege, 1982; Colette, 1983; The Brownings, 1986; Judith Gautier, 1987; Portrait of a Bonaparte, 1987. *Contributions to:* The Times; The Times Literary Supplement; Sunday Times; Spectator; New Statesman; New York Times Book Review; Washington Post; French Studies; Bulletin; Modern Language Review. *Honours:* Chevalier de l'Ordre des Arts et des Lettres, 1987; Prix Goncourt de la biographie,

1989. *Memberships:* Fellow, Royal Society of Literature, 1959; Member, Council, RSL, 1961-86. *Literary Agent:* Curtis Brown. *Address:* c/o Curtis Brown Ltd, 162-168 Regent Street, London W1R 5TB, England.

RICHARDSON Ruth, b. 19 Dec 1951, London, England. Historian. *Education:* BA (Hons), English Literature, 1977; MA, History, 1978; DPhil, History, 1985. *Appointments:* Research Fellow, Institute of Historical Research, University of London. *Publications:* Death, Dissection and the Destitute, 1988, paperback, 1989; Contributions to books: The Nest-Egg and the Funeral - Fear of Death on the Parish among the Elderly, 1988; Why Was Death So Big in Victorian Britain?, 1989; Contributions to Journals: Orlando Curioso, 1990; Garden China, 1990; George Godwin, ou la revue d'architecture comme croisade sociale (with Robert Thorne), 1990; 'Trading assassins' and the licensing of anatomy, 1991; 'Notorious abominations': architecture and the public health in The Builder 1843-1883, 1992; Victorian Periodicals: Architecture (with Robert Thorne), 1992. *Contributions to:* With Brian Hurwitz: Jeremy Bentham's self image: an exemplary bequest for dissection, to British Medical Journal, 1987; Joseph Rogers and the reform of workhouse medicine, to British Medical Journal, 1989; Inspector General James Barry MD: putting the woman in her place, to British Medical Journal, 1989; Somnambulism, Vampirism and Suicide: The Life of Dr John Polidori, to Proceedings of the Royal College of Physicians, Edinburgh, 1991. *Honours:* Leverhulme Research Fellowship, 1992-93; Awarded Monkton Copeman Medal, Society of Apothecaries, London, 1993; Fellow, Royal Historical Society. *Memberships:* Society of Authors; Folklore Society; Trustee, Museum of Soho. *Address:* Insitute of Historical Research, University of London, London WC1E 7HU.

RICHE Pierre, b. 4 Oct 1921, Paris, France. Professor Emeritus, University of Paris X. m. Suzanne Grenier, 20 Dec 1953. *Education:* Secondary and Higher Studies, Paris; Agregé, History, 1948; Docteur es lettres, 1962. *Publications:* Education et culture dans l'Occident barbare, 1962, translated into Italian, English, Japanese; Ecoles et enseignement dans le Haut Moyen Age, 1970; La vie quotidienne dans l'Empire carolingien, 1973, translated into English, Polish, German, Japanese; Dhuoda Manuel pour mon fils (editor, translator), 1975; Les Carolingiens une famille qui fit l'Europe, 1983, translated into German and Italian, English; Gerbert d'Aurillac pape de l'an Mil, 1987, translated into Italian and Spanish; Petite vie de saint Bernard, 1989, translated into Italian and Portuguese, Corean; L'Europe barbare de 476 a 774, 1989. *Contributions to:* Le Moyen Age; Revue d'Histoire de l'Eglise de France; Notre Histoire; Histoire de l'Education; Others. *Honours:* Officier des Palmes Academiques; Prix Gobert, 1963; Prix de Courcel, 1969, 1988; Prix George Goyau, 1974. *Memberships:* Resident Member, Societe Nationale des Antiquaires de France; Board Member, Societe d'Hsitoire de France; President, Centre international de recherche et de documentation sur le monarchisme celtique; Membre de la Section á Historie Medievale et de Philologie du Comite des travaux historiques et scientifiques. *Address:* 99 rue Bobillot, Paris 75013, France.

RICHESON Cena Golder, b. 11 Apr 1941, Oregon, USA. Author; Instructor; Public Speaker. m. Jerry Richeson, 3 June 1961, 2 sons. *Education:* BA, California State University. *Appointments:* Staff, Anderson Press, 1974-77; Instructor, Shasta College, 1974-76, Liberty High School Adult Education, 1985-86. *Publications:* Love is Where You Find It; For Love's Sake; Go For Broke; Honorable Decision. *Contributions to:* numerous journals and magazines. *Honours:* Poet of the Year, J. Mark Press, 1974; Nonfiction Writing Award, Writer's Digest Annual Contest, 1976; Nonfiction Article, 3rd Place, Williamette Writers Annual Convention, 1976. *Memberships:* California Writers Club; Western Writers of America; Society of Childrens Book Writers; Zane Grey's West Society. *Address:* PO Box 268, Knightsen, CA 94548, USA.

RICHIE Donald Steiner b. 17 Apr 1924, Ohio, USA. Writer; Critic. Divorced. *Education:* Bachelor's Degree, Columbia University, New York, 1953; Presidential Citation, New York University. *Appointments:* Film Critic: Stars and Stripes 1947-49; Variety 1961-65; Japan Times 1954-69; Literary Critic: Newsweek, 1973-76; Japan Times 1973-. *Publications:* The Japanese Film: Art and Industry (with J Anderson) 1959; The Films of Akira Kurosawa, 1965; Ozu 1974; Japanese Cinema: An Introduction, 1990; The Inland Sea, 1971; Different People: Pictures of Some Japanese, 1987; Tokyo Nights, 1988; Companions of the Holiday, 1968; Zen Inklings, 1982; A Taste of Japan, 1984. *Contributions to:* Numerous magazines and journals. *Honours:* Film Day Citation, Japanese Government, 1970; National Film Critics Society, USA, 1970; Kawakita Foundation Award, 1983; Special Prize, Hawaii International Film Festival, 1986; New York University Presidential Citation, 1989; Mel Novikoff Award for Extraordinary Contribution to Film, San Francisco Film Festival, 1990. *Address:* 304 Shato Nezu, Yanaka 1, 1-18, Taito-ku, Tokyo, 110, Japan.

RICHLER Mordecai, b. 1931, Montreal, Canada. Writer. m. Florence Wood, 1960, 3 sons, 2 daughters. *Education:* Sir George Williams University; Canada Council Junior Arts Fellowship, 1959, 1960; Fellowship, Creative Writing, Guggenheim Foundation, New York, 1961; Canada Council, Senior Arts Fellowship, 1967. *Appointments:* Writer in residence, Sir George Williams University, 1968-69; Visiting Professor, Carleton University, Ottawa, 1972-74; Editorial Board, Book of the Month Club, New York, 1976. *Publications:* Novels: The Acrobats, 1954; Son of a Smaller Hero, 1955; A Choice of Enemies, 1957; The Apprenticeship of Duddy Kravitz, 1959; The Incomparable Atuk, 1963; Cocksure, 1968; St Urbain's Horseman, 1971; Images of Spain, 1978; Joshua Then and Now, 1980; Solomon Grusky was Here, 1989; Broadsides, 1991. Stories: The Street, 1972. Film Scripts: No Love for Johnny; Life at the Top; The Apprenticeship of Duddy Kravitz. TV Plays: The Trouble with Benny. Essays: Hunting Tigers Under Glass, 1969; Shovelling Trouble, 1973; Home Sweet Home, 1984; Editor, Canadian Writing Today, 1970; For Children: Jacob Two-Two Meets the Hooded Fang, 1975; The Best of Modern Humour, Editor, 1983; Solomon Guksky War Hero, 1989. *Honours:* Canadian Governor Generals Award for Fiction, 1969; Golden Bear, Berlin Film Festival, 1974. *Address:* Apartment 80C, 1321 Sherbrooke Street West, Montreal, Quebec H3G 1J4 , Canada.

RICHTER Anne, b. 25 June 1939, Brussels, Belgium. Writer; Teacher of French. Widow, 1 daughter. *Education;* Licence, Philosophy and Letters, Free University of Brussels, 1963. *Publications:* Books: Nouvelles fantastiques, Paris 1954, Brussels, 1986; Essays: Milosz, Editions Universitaires, Le Fantastique f'eminin; Anthologies: L'Allemagne fantastique, Contes fantastiques de Guy de Maupassant; Histoires de doubles et de miroirs. *Contributions to:* Literary reviews in le Magazine Litteraire; La Revue Generale; other Brussels Magazines. *Honours:* Franz Dewever Prize, Belgian Academy of French Literature & language. *Memberships:* Asrobiation of Belgian Authors; Committee Member, PEN International; Association of Literary Critics. *Address:* 93 Boulevard Louis Schmidt, bte 13, 1040 Brussels, Belgium.

RICHTER Hans Peter, b. 28 Apr 1925, Cologne, Germany. m. Elfriede Feldmann, 20 May 1952, 1 son, 3 daughters. *Education:* Universities of Cologne, Bonn, Mainz, Tubingen; Prof.Dr. rer. pol. *Publications include:* Karussell und Luftbailon (Uncle & His Merry-go-Round), 1958; Das Pferd Max (Hengist the Horse), 1959; Damals war es Friedrich (Friedrich), 1961, 40th Edition 1993, translated into 15 languages, over 4 million copies sold; Wir waren dabei, (I Was There), 1962; Saint Just, 1975; Die Zeit der jungen Soldaten (The Time of the Young Soldiers), 1980; Wissenschaft von der Wissenschaft, 1981; Translations: Montaigne, 1989; F Mein Vater, 1992. *Contributions to:* numerous magazines, journals, radio & TV. *Honours:* Jugendbuchpreis, 1961;

Auswahilliste, 1962; Cite Internationale des Arts, Paris, 1965-66; Mildred Batchelder Book Award, 1971; Best Book, Japanese Library Association. *Address:* 58 Franz-Werfel Str, D 6500 Mainz 1, Germany.

RICHTER Milan, b. 25 July 1948, Bratislava, Czechoslovakia. Writer; Translator; Diplomat. m. Adrienna Matejovova, 1 Oct 1980, 1 son, 2 daughters. *Education:* German and English Linguistics and Literature, Faculty of Philosophy, Comenius University, Bratislava, 1967-72; PhD, 1985. *Appointments:* Editor, Slovensky Spisovatel publishers, 1972-75; Editor, translations from German and Scandinavian languages, Pravda Publishing House, 1975-81; Freelance Writer and Translator, 1981-92; Head of the Slovak Embassy in Oslo, Norway, 1993; Part-time Editor, Dotyky literary magazine, 1988-89; Fulbright Research Scholar, University of California, Los Angeles, USA, 1990; Part-time Editor, Revue Svetovej Literatury, 1991. *Publications:* Poetry in Slovak language: Evening Mirrors, 1973; Whips, 1975; Pollen, 1976; The Secure Place, 1987; Roots in the Air, 1992; In German: Wurzeln in der Luft, selected poems, 1992; Translations into Slovak language: Selected poems by E Dickinson, E Hemingway, J W Goethe, Urfaust, E Lindegren, A Lundkvist, P Neruda, E Jandl, E Cardenal. *Contributions to:* London Magazine; Paris Review; Massachusetts Review; Literary Review; City Lights Review; Literary Olympians, 1992; Jacaranda Review; Akzente, Germany; Manuskripte, Austria; Anthologies in Denmark and Sweden. *Honours:* Publishers Prize for translations: Selected Poems by Artur Lundkvist, 1988, Selected Poems by Erik Lindegren, 1991; Swedish Literary Fund Award, 1991; Honorary Doctorate of Literature, World Academy of Arts and Culture, Haifa, Israel, 1992. *Memberships:* Slovak PEN Club, 1991-1992; Slovak Literary Translators Society, Secretary-General, 1990-1992. *Address:* Sidlisko 714, CS-900 42 Dunajska Luzna, Slovakia.

RICKEL Annette U, Professor of Psychology & Licensed Psychologist. *Education:* BA, Michigan State University, 1963; MA, 1965, PhD, 1972, University of Michigan. *Publications:* ed. with Gerrard M & Iscoe I, Social and Psychological Problems of Women: Prevention and Crisis Intervention, 1984; with Allen L, Preventing Maladjustment from Infancy through Adolescence, 1987; Teenage Pregnancy and Parenting, 1989. *Contributions to:* Articles in such journals as: The International Review of Education; Journal of Community Psychology; Journal of Abnormal Child Psychology; Clinical Social Work Journal; International Journal of Women's Studies; Personnel Psychology. *Honours:* Fellow, American Psychological Association, President APA Division 27 - Community Psychology, 1984-85, Secretary-Treasurer APA Division 27, 1979-82; Fellow, American Council on Education, 1990-91. *Memberships:* Society for Research in Child and Adolescent Psychopathology; International Association of Applied Psychologists; American Association for Higher Education; American Education Research Association; Psi Chi; Sigma Xi. *Address:* Wayne State University, Department of Psychology, 71 West Warren, Detroit, MI 48202, USA.

RICKFORD John R(ussell), b. 16 Sept 1949, Georgetown, Guyuana. m. Angela E Marshall, 19 July 1971, 1 son, 2 daughters. *Education:* BA (highest honours), University of California, Santa Cruz, 1971; MA 1973, PhD 1979, University of Pennsylvania. *Appointments:* Features Reporter, Sunday Graphic, Georgetown, Guyana, 1967; English Master at high school in Georgetown 1967-68; Lecturer and Reader in English, University of Guyana, Georgetown, 1974-80; Visiting Professor, 1980-81, Assistant Professor 1981-87, Associate Professor of Linguistics, 1987-, Stanford University, Stanford, California; Visiting Assistant Professor, Johns Hopkins University 1977; Member of National Science Foundation Linguistics Panel, 1986-89; Conference Co-ordinator; Member of editorial board of Camden House 1982-86 and Foris Publications, 1983-86; Full Professor of Linguistics, Stanford University, 1990-. *Publications:* (Editor and contributor) A Festival of Guyanese Word, 1976, 1978; Dimensions of Creole Continuum, 1987; Editor Board of various works including: The Carrier Pidgin, 1982-85, and International Journal of the Sociology of Language, 1987. *Contributions to:* Numerous edited volumes and of articles and reviews to scholarly journals. *Honours:* Fulbright Grant for the United States, 1968; Danforth fellow, 1971; Grants from Stanford University's Center for Research on International Studies, 1982 and Center for Research on Language and Information, 1984; Rockefeller Foundation Fellow, 1984; Grant from Pew Foundation 1985; Fellow of Center for Urban Studies, 1986; National Science Foundation Grant, 1989; Fellow, Center for Advanced Study in the Behaviorial Sciences, Stanford, 1990; Bing Fellow (for excellence in teaching and interest in pedagogy), Stanford, 1992 . *Memberships:* Numerous professional memberships. *Address:* Department of Linguistics, Stanford University, Stanford, CA 94305-2150, USA.

RIDEAMUS. *See:* **PASZKOWSKI Kazimierz Jan.**

RIDGWAY Judith Anne, b. 10 Nov 1939, Stalybridge, England. Writer. *Education:* BA, Class 11, Division 1, Keele University, 1962. *Publications:* The Vegetarian Gourmet, 1979; Salad Days, 1979; Home Preserving, 1980; The Seafood Kitchen, 1980; The Colour Book of Chocolate Cookery, 1981; Mixer, Blender, Processor Cookery, 1981; The Breville Book of Toasted Sandwiches, 1982; 101 Fun Foods to Make, 1982; Waitrose Book of Pasta, Rice and Pulses, 1982; Home Cooking for Money, 1983; Booklets: Making the Most of Rice, 1983; Making the Most of Pasta, 1983; Making the Most of Potatoes, 1983; Making the Most of Bread, 1983; Making the Most of Eggs, 1983; Making the Most of Cheese, 1983; The Little Lemon Book, 1983; Barbecues, 1983; Cooking Round the World, 1983; Cooking with German Food, 1983; The Little Bean Book, 1983; Frying Tonight, 1984; Running Your Own Wine Bar, 1984; Sprouting Beans and Seeds, 1984; Man in the Kitchen, 1984; The Little Rice Book, 1984; Successful Media Relations, 1984; Running Your Own Catering Company, 1984; Festive Occasions, 1986; The Vegetable Year, 1985; Nuts and Cereals, 1985; Cooking Without Gluten, 1986; Vegetarian Wok Cookery, 1986; Wining and Dining at Home, 1985; Cheese and Cheese Cookery, 1986; 101 Ways with Chicken Pieces, 1987; The Wine Lovers Record Book, 1988; Pocket Book of Oils, Vinegars and Seasoning, 1989; The Little Red Wine Book, 1989; The Little White Wine Book, 1989; The Vitamin and Mineral Diet Cookbook, 1990; Catering for a Wedding, 1991; Vegetarian Delights, 1992; Quick After Work Pasta Cookbook, 1993; Best Wine Buys In The High Street, 1991, 1992, 1993. *Contributions to:* New Woman; Wine Columnist. *Memberships:* Society of Authors; Guild of Food and Wine Writers; Circle of Wine Writers. *Literary Agent:* Clarissa Rushdie, A. P. Watt Ltd. *Address:* 124 Queens Court, Queensway, London, W2 4QS, England.

RIDLER Anne (Barbara), b. 30 July 1912. Author. m. Vivian Ridler, 1938, 2 sons, 2 daughters. *Education:* King's College, London. *Publications:* Poetry: Poems, 1939; A Dream Observed, 1941; The Nine Bright Shiners, 1943; The Golden Bird, 1951; A Matter of Life and Death, 1959; Selected Poems (New York), 1961; Some Time After, 1972; New and Selected Poems, 1988; (Contributor) Ten Oxford Poets, 1978; Plays: Cain, 1943; The Shadow Factory, 1946; Henry Bly and Other Plays, 1950; The Trial of Thomas Cranmer, 1956; Who is my Neighbour?, 1963; The Jesse Tree (libretto), 1972; The King of the Golden River (libretto), 1975; The Lambton Worm (libretto), 1978; A Measure of English Poetry (criticism), 1991; Translations: Italian Opera Libretti: Rosinda, 1973; Orfeo, 1975; Eritrea, 1975; Return of Ulysses, 1978; Orontea, 1979; Agrippina, 1981; Calisto, 1984; Cosi fan Tutte, 1986; Gluck's Orpheus, 1988; Don Govanni, 1990; Figaro, 1991; Coronation of Poppea, 1992; Tancredi, 1993; Biography: Olive Willis and Downe House, 1967; A Victorian Family Postbag, 1988; Editor: Shakespeare Criticism, 1919-35;

A Little Book of Modern Verse, 1941; Best Ghost Stories, 1945; Supplement to Faber Book of Modern Verse, 1951; The Image of the City and Other Essays by Charles Williams, 1958; Shakespeare Criticism 1935-60, 1963; Poems of James Thomson, 1963; Thomas Traherne, 1966; (with Christopher Bradby) Best Stories of Church and Clergy, 1966; Selected Poems of George Darley, 1979; Poems of William Austin, 1983. *Address:* 14 Stanley Road, Oxford OX4 1QZ, England.

RIDLEY Jasper Godwin, b. 25 May 1920, West Hoathly Sussex, England. Author. m. Vera Pollakova, 1 Oct 1949, 2 sons, 1 daughter. *Education:* Sorbonne Paris University, 1937; Magdalen College, Oxford University, 1938-39; Certificate of Honour, Council of Legal Education, 1945. *Publications:* Nicholas Ridley, 1957; Thomas Cranmer, 1962; John Knox, 1968; Lord Palmerston, 1970; Mary Tudor, 1973; Garibaldi, 1974; The Roundheads, 1976; Napolean III and Eugenie, 1979; The History of England, 1981; The Statesman and The Fanatic, 1982; Henry VIII, 1984; Elizabeth I, 1987; The Tudor Age, 1988; The Love Letters of Henry VIII, 1988; Maxilillian and Juárez, 1992. *Contributions to:* The Prime Ministers, 1975; Garibaldi Generale Della Liberta, 1984; English Heritage Journal, 1989. *Honours:* James Tait Black Memorial Prize, 1970. *Memberships:* English PEN (Vice-President); Fellow, Royal Society of Literature; Tunbridge Wells Writers Circle (Chairman 1988-91); Sussex Authors; Worshipful Company of Carpenters (Master 1988 & 1990). *Literary Agent:* Curtis Brown (London & New York). *Address:* 6 Oakdale Road, Tunbridge Wells, Kent, TN4 8DS, England.

RIDOUT Ronald, b. 23 July 1916, Farnham, Surrey, England. Author. m. 10 Feb 1940, 1 son, 2 daughters. *Education:* BA, Honours, Oxon. *Publications:* 509 Titles, 1st English Today, 1948; most recent: Ronald Ridout's Children's Dictionary, 1983; Now I Can Write, 1984; Now I Can Spell, 1984; Ronald Ridout's English A-Z, 1985; Getting on With Spelling, 1986; The Methuen Activity Picture Dictionary, 1987. *Membership:* Society of Authors, 1st Chairman, Educational Writers Section. *Literary Agent:* A P Watt & Co. *Address:* St Lucia, West Indies.

RIDPATH Ian, b. 1 May 1947, Ilford, Essex, England. Writer; Broadcaster. *Publications:* Over 30 books on astronomy and space, including: Worlds Beyond, 1975; Encyclopedia of Astronomy and Space, Editor, 1976; Messages From The Stars, 1978; Stars and Planets, 1978; Young Astronomer's Handbook, 1981; Hamlyn Encyclopedia of Space, 1981; Life Off Earth, 1983; Collins Guide to Stars and Planets, 1984; Gem Guide to the Night Sky, 1985; Secrets of the Sky, 1985; A Comet Called Halley, 1985; Longman Illustrated Dictionary of Astronomy and Astronautics, 1987; Monthly Sky Guide, 1987; Star Tales, 1989; Norton's Star Atlas (editor), 1989. *Address:* 48 Otho Court, Brentford Dock, Brentford, Middlesex TW8 8PY, England.

RIECAN J. *See:* **KARVAS Peter.**

RIFBJERG Klaus Thorvald, b. 15 Dec 1931, Copenhagen, Denmark. Author. m. Inge Merete Gerner, 28 May 1955, 1 son, 2 daughters. *Education:* Princeton University, 1950-51; University of Copenhagen, 1951-56. *Appointments:* Literary Critic, Information, 1955-57; Politiken, 1959-; Editor, Vindrosen, 1959-64; Literary Director, Gyldendal Publishers, 1985-92. *Publications:* Novels: Den Kroniske Uskyld, 1958; Operaelsken, 1966; Arkivet, 1967; Lonni Og Karl, 1968; Anna (Jeg) Anna, 1970; Marts 1970, 1970; Leif den Lykkelige JR, 1971; Til Spanien, 1971; Lena Jorgensen, Klintevej 4, 2650, Hvidovre, 1971; Brevet til Gerda, 1972; RR, 1972; Spinatfuglene, 1973; Dilettanterne, 1973; Du skal ikke vaere ked af det Amalia, 1974; En Hugorm i solen, 1974; Vejen ad hvilken, 1975; Tak for turen, 1975; Kiks, 1976; Tango, 1978; Dobbeltgoenger, 1978; Drengene, 1978; Joker, 1979; Voksdugshjertet, 1979; Det sorte hul, 1980; Short Stories: Og Andre Historier, 1964; Rejsende, 1969; Den Syende Jomfru, 1972; Sommer,

1974; Non-Fiction: I medgang Og Modgang, 1970; Plays: Gris Pa Gaflen, 1962; Hva' Skal Vi Lave, 1963; Udviklinger, 1965; Hvad en Mand Har brug For, 1966; Voks, 1968; Ar 1970; Narrene, 1971; Svaret Blaeser i Vinden, 1971; Det Korte af det lange, 1976; Twist, 1976; Et bortvendt ansigt, 1977; Deres majestaet!, 1977; Poems: Livsfrisen, 1979. *Honours:* Danish Dramatists, 1966; Danish Academy Award, 1966; Golden Laurels, 1967; Grand Prize, Danish Academy of Arts and Letters, 1968; Soren Gyldendal Award, 1969; Nordic Council Award 1971; Grant of Honour, Danish Writers Guild, 1973; PH Prize, 1979; Holberg Medal, 1984; H C Andersen Prize, 1987. *Membership:* Danish Academy of Arts and Letters, 1967; Professor of Statics, 1986; Doctor H C Luna University, 1992. *Address:* Kristianiagade 22, DK-2100, Copenhagen, Denmark.

RIFKIN Shepard, (Jake Logan, Dale Michaels), b. 14 Sept 1918, New York City, New York, USA. Writer; Out-of-Print Book Dealer. *Education:* City College of New York, 1936-38. *Publications:* Desire Island, 1960; What Ship? Where Bound?, 1961; LadyFingers, 1969; The Murderer Vine, 1970; McQuaid, 1974; The Snow Rattlers, 1977; McQuaid in August, 1979; Historical Westerns include: Texas, Blood Red, 1956; The Warring Breed, 1962; King Fisher's Road; Several others. *Contributions to:* Story Magazine, 1947; Atlantic First, 1961. *Membership:* Authors League. *Literary Agent:* Knox Burger, 39 1/2 Washington Sq South, New York, NY 10012, USA. *Address:* 105 Charles St, New York, NY 10014, USA.

RIGHTMIRE G Philip, b. 15 Sept 1942, Boston, Massachusetts, USA. Professor of Anthropology. m. Berit Johansson, 20 Aug 1966, 1 son, 1 daughter. *Education:* BA, Harvard University, 1964; MS, 1966, PhD, 1969, University of Wisconsin. *Appointments:* Assistant Professor, Associate Professor, Professor, State University of New York, Binghamton, New York. *Publication:* The Evolution of Homo erectus, 1990. *Contributions to:* Articles in Science; Nature; American Journal of Physical Anthropology; Journal of Human Evolution; Paleobiology; Evolutionary; Anthropology and other journals and in encyclopaediae. *Memberships:* American Association of Physical Anthropologists; Fellow, American Association for the Advancement of Science; Sigma Xi. *Address:* 4004 Fuller Hollow Road, Vestal, NY 13850, USA.

RIGONI Orlando Joseph, (Leslie Ames, Carolyn Bell, James Wesley), b. 1917, USA. Author. *Publications:* Twisted Trails; Ambuscade; Pikabo Stage; House of Haddon; Headstone for a Trailboss; As Carolyn Bell: House of Clay; Sixgun Song; Showdown at Skeleton Flat; Massacre Ranch; A Nickle's Worth of Lead; The Guns of Folly; A Close Shave at Pozo; Bullet Breed; Hunger Range; Drover Man; As Leslie Ames: The Hungry Sea; The Hidden Chapel; The Phantom Bride; Wind over the Citadel; The Big Brand; Muskeg Marshal; King's Castle; Castle on the Island; The Angry Wind; Brand of the Bow; Bride of Donnebrook; Hill of Ashes; As James Wesley: Texas Justice; Showdown at Mesa Bend; Maverick Marshal; Brand X; Four Graves to Jericho; Showdown at the MB Ranch; Diamond Range; Trail to Boothill; Bitterroot Showdown, 1985. *Address:* 2900 Dogwood Avenue, Morro Bay, CA 93442, USA.

RILEY Jocelyn Carol, b. 6 Mar 1949, Minneapolis, Minnesota, USA. Writer (fiction, non-fiction, reviews, scripts); Producer (videos, slide shows). m. Jeffrey Allen Steele, 4 Sept 1971, Northfield, Minnesota. 2 sons. *Education:* BA, English Literature, Carleton College, Northfield, 1971. *Publications:* Only My Mouth is Smiling, 1982; Crazy Quilt, 1984; Page Proof, forthcoming; Her Own Words, 1986; Belle, 1987; Zona Gale (video), 1988; Patchwork (video), 1989. *Contributions to:* Publishers Weekly; Society of Childrens Book Writers; Contemporary Literary Criticism; Writer; Book Review Digest. *Honours:* Huntington Poetry Prize, Carleton College, 1970; Best Books for Young Adults, American Library Association,

1982; Arthur Tofte Memorial Award, Council for Wisconsin Writers, 1982; Writers Cup, 1985; Finalist Award, New York Film Festival, 1987; Outstanding Achievement Award, International Association for Multi-Image, 1987; First Place Award, Council for Wisconsin Writers, 1986; Bronze Apple Award, National Educational Film & Video Festival, 1988; Award of Merit, American Association of State of Local History, 1988; Gold Medal, International Film & TV Festival of New York, 1988. *Memberships:* President, Madison Professional Chapter, 1984-85, Women in Communications; Authors Guild; President, Madison Chapter, Association for the Multi-Image, 1986-87. *Literary Agent:* Jane Gelfman, John Farquharson Ltd. *Address:* P O Box 5264, Madison, WI 53705, USA.

RILEY Samuel Gayle III, b. 8 Oct 1939, Raleigh, North Carolina, USA. University Professor. m. Mary Elaine Weisner, 14 May 1966, div. 1986, 1 son, 1 daughter. *Education:* AB, Davidson College, 1961; MBA, 1962, PhD, Mass Communication Research, 1970, University of North Carolina, Chapel Hill. *Appointments:* Assistant Professor, Journalism, Temple University, 1970-74; Associate Professor, Journalism, Georgia Southern University, 1971-81; Professor, Communication Studies, Virginia Polytechnic Institute and State University, 1981-. *Publications:* Magazines of the American South, 1986; Index to Southern Periodicals, 1986; American Magazine Journalists (Dictionary of Literary Biography), 3 vols, 1988, 1989, 1990; Index to City and Regional Magazines of the United States, 1989; Regional Interest Magazines of the United States, 1991; GR8 PL8S, 1991; Corporate Magazines of the United States, 1992; Consumer Magazines of the British Isles, 1993. *Contributions to:* Articles to scholarly journals including: American Journalism; Journalism Quarterly; American Periodicals; Mass Communications Review; Journalism History; Hundreds of articles to US newspapers and magazines; Over 100 reference book entries. *Memberships:* Association for Education in Journalism and Mass Communications; Research Society for American Periodicals; American Journalism Historians Association. *Address:* 1865 Mountainside Drive, Blacksburg, VA 24060, USA.

RINALDI Nicholas Michael, b. 2 Apr 1934, Brooklyn, New York, USA. Writer; College Professor. m. Jacqueline Tellier, 29 Aug 1959, 3 sons, 1 daughter. *Education:* AB, Classics, Shrub Oak, 1957; MA 1960, PhD 1963, English Literature, Fordham. *Appointments:* Instructor, Assistant Professor, St John's University, 1960-65; Lecturer, City University of New York, 1966; Associate Professor, Columbia University, Summer, 1966; Professor, University of Connecticut, Summer, 1972; Assistant Professor, Professor, Fairfield University, 1966-. *Publications:* The Resurrection of the Snails, 1977; We Have Lost our Fathers, 1982; The Lutwaffe in Chaos, 1985; Bridge Fall Down, novel, 1985. *Contributions to:* Yale Review; New American Review; Prairie Schooner; Carolina Quarterly. *Honours:* Joseph P Slomovich Memorial Award for Poetry, 1979; All Nations Poetry Award, 1981, 1983; AWP Award Series Publication, We Have Lost Our Fathers, 1982; New York Poetry Forum Award, 1983; Eve of St Agnes Poetry Award, 1984; Charles Angoff Literary Award, 1984. *Memberships:* Associated Writing Programme; Poetry Society of America. *Literary Agent:* International Creative Management. *Address:* 190 Brookview Avenue, Fairfield, CT 96432, USA.

RING Douglas. *See:* PRATHER Richard.

RIO-SUKAN Isabel del, b. 8 Sept 1954, Madrid, Spain. Translator; Writer; Language Consultant. m. Huseyin B Sukan, 31 July 1981, 2 daughters. *Education:* MA, Information Sciences, Madrid Central University, 1977; Incorporated Linguist, Institute of Linguists, London, 1985. *Appointments:* Broadcaster, Arts and Literary Programmes Editor, BBC Spanish Section, London, England, 1978-82; UN Supernumerary Translator, 1988-. *Publications:* BBC Get By In Spanish, 1992; Ciudad del Interior, poetry, 1993; Translations: The Secret Garden (F H Burnett), 1990; Into Cuba (P

Marshall), 1991. *Memberships:* Society of Authors, London; The Translators Association, London; Institute of Linguists; ITI; AITC; APETI; Equity. *Address:* 3 Meadow Place, Edensor Road, London W4 2SY, England.

RIOS Juan, b. 28 Sept 1914, Barranco, Lima, Peru. Poet; Dramatist; Journalist; Critic. m. Rosa Saco, 16 Sept 1946, 1 daughter. *Publications:* Cancion de Siempre, 1941; Malstrom, 1941; La Pintura Contempranea en el Peru, 1946; Teatro (I) 1961; Ayar Manko, 1963; Primera Antologia Poetica, 1981. *Honours:* National Prize, Playwriting, 1946, 1950, 1952, 1954, 1960; National Poetry Prize, 1948, 1953. *Memberships:* Writers' Fellowship, UNESCO, Europe and Egypt, 1960-61; Academia Peruana de la lengua Correspondiente a la Espanola. *Address:* Bajada de Banos 109, Barranco, Lima 04, Peru.

RIPLEY Jack. *See:* **WAINWRIGHT John.**

RIPLEY Michael David (Mike Ripley), b. 29 Sept 1952, Huddersfield, England. Chief Press Officer, The Brewers Society. m. Alyson Jane White, 8 July 1978, 2 daughters. *Education:* BA (Hons), Economic History, University of East Anglia. *Appointments:* Crime Fiction Critic, The Sunday Telegraph, 1989-91; Crime Critic, The Daily Telegraph, 1991-. *Publications:* Just Another Angel, 1988; Angel Touch, 1989; Angel Hunt, 1990; Angels in Arms, 1991; Short stories: The Body of the Beer, 1989; Smeltdown, 1990; Gold Sword, 1990. *Contributions to:* The 'Britcrit' Column in Mystery Scene, USA. *Honours:* Scholarship to public school; Runner-up, Punch Magazine Awards for funniest crime novel, 1988; Last Laugh Award, Crime Writers Association, 1989 and 1991; The Angel Literary Award For Fiction, 1990. *Memberships:* Crime Writers Association; Sisters in Crime, USA; The Dorothy L Sayers Society. *Literary Agent:* David Higham Associates. *Address:* c/o David Higham, 5-8 Lower John Street, London W1R 4HA, England.

RIPPON Angela, b. 12 Oct 1944, Plymouth, England. Television and radio presenter; Writer. m. Christopher Dare, 1967. *Education:* Grammar School, Plymouth, England. *Career:* Worked 3 years as general reporter, services correspondent and editor for local Sunday newspaper, The Independent; Reporter and Presenter, BBC Plymouth, 1966-69; Editor/Presenter/Producer, Westward Television, 1969-73; News Reporter for National News 1973-76, Newsreader for Nine O'Clock News, 1976-81, BBC; July 1981, interviewed HRH The Prince of Wales and Lady Diana Spencer on the eve of their wedding and presented live coverage of the wedding day; Joined TV-am 1982, left amid much controversy and subsequently won a court action against TV-am; Arts and Entertainment Officer, WNEV TV's Channel 7, Boston, MA, USA, 1984-85; Autumn 1989, began weekly series entitled The Health Show, which launched BBC Radio 5; Sept. 1990: Anchorwoman for LBC's 3-hour daily breakfast programme, The Angela Rippon Morning Report, reschedules as Angela Rippon's Drive Time Show in Feb 1992. *Publications:* Riding, 1980; Mark Phillips - The Man and his Horses, 1982; Angela Rippon's West Country, 1982; Vistoria Plum, 1983; In the Country, 1980; Badminton - A Celebration, 1987; Many recordings. *Honours:* Radio and Television Industries Award for Newsreader of the Year, 1976, 1977, 1978; Television Personality of the Year, 1977; Sony Award for The Health Show, 1990. *Memberships:* International Club for Women in Television, Vice-President , 1979-; Chairman, English National Ballet Association; Board Member, American College, London. *Address:* c/o International Management Group, Media House, 3 Burlington Lane, Chiswick, London W4 2TH, England.

RITCHIE Elisavietta Artamonoff, b. 29 June 1932, Kansas City, Missouri, USA. Writer; Poet; Translator; Teacher; Editor; Public Relations Specialist. m. (1) Lyell Hale Ritchie, 2 sons, 1 daughter, (2) Clyde Henri Farnsworth, 22 June 1991. *Education:* Degre Superieur, Mention Tres Bien, Sorbonne, Paris, 1951; Cornell University, 1951-53; BA, University of California, Berkeley, 1954; MA, French Literature, minor Russian Studies, American University, 1976; Advanced Russian courses, Georgetown University. *Appointments:* US Information Agency Visiting Poet: Brazil, 1972; Far East, 1977; Yugoslavia, Bulgaria, 1979; Founder, Director, The Wineberry Press, 1983-; President, Washington Writers Publishing House, 1986-89; Leader, Creative Writing Workshops. *Publications:* Timbot, 1970; Tightening The Circle Over Eel Country, 1974; A Sheath of Dreams And Other Games, 1976; Moving To Larger Quarters, 1977; Raking The Snow, 1982; The Problem With Eden, 1985; Flying Time: Stories and Half-Stories, 1992; A Wound-Up Cat and Other Bedtime Stories, 1993; Hurricane Seasons, 1993; Works in numerous anthologies. *Contributions to:* Fiction, poetry, articles, reviews, translations to: New York Times; Washington Post; Christian Science Monitor; Paris Herald Tribune; Miami Herald; Poetry; American Scholar; Ascent; Washingtonian; National Geographic; New Letters; Epoch; The Poetry Review; Many others, USA, abroad. *Honours:* New Writer's Award for Best 1st Book of Poetry, Great Lakes Colleges Association, 1975-76; Graduate Teaching Fellowship, American University; Fellow, Virginia Center for the Creative Arts; 4 times PEN Syndicated Fiction Winner; 4 Individual Artist Grants, DC Commission for the Arts. *Memberships:* Writers Center; Washington Independent Writers; PEN; Committee for Poetry in the Greater Washington Area; Amnesty International; Poetry Society of America; Poets and Writers; Environmental organisations. *Literary Agent:* Nina Graybill, Ronald Goldfarb and Associates, 918 Sixteenth St NW 400, Washington, DC 20006, USA. *Address:* 3207 Macomb Street NW, Washington, DC 20008, USA.

RITVO Harriet, b. 19 Sept 1946, Cambridge, Massachusetts, USA. Historian. *Education:* AB, 1968, PhD, 1975, Harvard University. *Appointment:* Currently, Professor of History and Writing, Massachusetts Institute of Technology. *Publications:* The Animal Estate: The English and Other Creatures in the Victorian Age; The Macropolitics of 19th-Century Literature (co-editor with Jonathan Arac). *Contributions to:* Numerous essays and reviews on 18th and 19th-Century cultural history, and on the relationship between humans and other animals. *Honour:* Whiting Writers' Award, 1990. *Memberships:* PEN American Century; National Book Critics Circle (US); American Historical Association; History of Science Society; Society for the History of Natural History. *Address:* E51 230 Massachusetts Institute of Technology, Cambridge, MA 02139, USA.

RIVARD Ken J, b. 30 June 1947, Montreal, Canada. Special Education Teacher. m. Micheline Rivard, 19 Sept 1972, 2 daughters. *Education:* BEd, University of Montreal, 1970; MEd, McGill University, 1974. *Publications:* Poetry books: Kiss Me Down To Size, 1983; Frankie's Desires, 1987; Chapbooks: Losing His Thirst, poetry, 1985; Working Stiffs, short fiction, 1990. *Contributions to:* Short fiction and poetry to: Alberta Diamond Jubilee Anthology, 1979; Lyrical Voices, USA, 1979; Alberta Poetry Yearbook; Alive; Antigonish Review; Border Crossings; Canadian Forum; Cross-Canada Writers Quarterly; Dalhousie Review; Didsbury Booster; Going for Coffee - An Anthology Of Contemporary North American Working Poems, 1981; Glass Canyons, 1985; Matrix; New Quarterly; Open Windows Anthology, 1988; Poems N' Things; Poetry Canada; Poetry Toronto; Prairie Journal of Canadian Literature; Prism International; Queen's Quarterly; Sans Crit; Small Press Lynx, 1991; Transition; Vortex; Wascana Review; Waves; Whetstone; Various other magazines and anthologies. *Memberships:* Writers Guild of Alberta; League of Canadian Poets. *Address:* 120 Whiteview Place NE, Calgary, Alberta, Canada T1Y 1R6.

RIVERO Andres, b. 18 July 1936. Writer. m. Pilar Eloisa, 19 May 1959, 3 sons. *Education:* Doctor of Literature. *Publications:* Enterrado Vivi, 1961; Cuentos Pam Entender, 1978; Recuerdos, 1979; Sorpresivemente, 1981; Somos Como Somos, 1982.

Contributions to: Several publications throughout Latin America and the United States of America. Honours: Kiwanis 1965; Club Leonistico Cubano, 1978; Cruzada Educativa, 1985; ACCA, Miami, 1990. Memberships: Poets and Writers, New York. Address: P O Box 650909, Miami, FL 33265, USA.

RIVERS Joan, b. 1935, Brooklyn, New York. American Comedienne; Actress; Recording Artist; Columnist; Playwright; Screenwriter; Author. Publications: Contemporary Theatre, Film, and Television Volume I, 1984; Current Biography, 1970; Having a Baby Can Be a Scream, 1974; The Life and Hard Times of Heidi Abromowitz : A Totally Unauthorized Biography, 1984; Enter Talking, 1986; Creator, TV Series, Husband and Wives, 1976; Author, Screenplay, The Girl Most Likely To. Contributions to: Detroit Free Press; New York Times Book Review; People; Time; Columnist, Chicago Tribune, 1973-76. Literary Agent: Bill Sammeth, Los Angeles, California. Address: c/o Richard Grant & Associates, 8500 Wilshire Boulevard, Suite 520, Beverly Hills, CA 90211, USA.

RIVET Albert Lionel Frederick, b. 30 Nov 1915, Streatham, London, England. Emeritus Professor of Roman Provincial Studies. m. Audrey Catherine Webb, 8 Apr 1947, 1 son, 1 daughter. Education: Felsted School, 1929- 34; BA, Classics 1938, MA, Classics 1946, Oriel College, Oxford. Appointments: Prep School Teacher, 1938-39; ARP 1939-40; Army 1940-46 (Ciphers 1941-46, ending as Major, Chief Cipher Officer E A Command); Bookseller 1946-51; Assistant Archaeology Officer Ordnance Survey 1951-64; Lecturer 1964, Reader 1967, Professor 1974, retired 1981, but Research Professor 1988-90, Classics Department, University of Keele. Publications: Town and Country in Roman Britain, 1958, 2nd edition 1964; The Iron Age in Northern Britain (editor and bibliography) 1966; The Roman Villa in Britain (editor and chapter) 1969; The Place-Names of Roman Britain (with C Smith) 1979; Gallia Narbonensis, 1988. Contributions to: various journals including: Antiquaries Journal; Antiquity; Archaeologia Cantiana; Archaeological Journal; Archaeological News Letter. Memberships include: The British Academy, Elected FBA 1981, British Member, Sub-Committee of Tabula Imperii Romani 1970-81, Deputy Chairman 1979-81, Chairman 1981-87; Royal Commission on the Historical Monuments of England, Commissioner 1979-85, Chairman of National Monuments Records Committee, 1981-85; Society for the Promotion of Roman Studies, Member 1964-, President 1977-80, Vice President 1976-; Society of Antiquaries of London FSA 1953-. Address: 7 Springpool, Keele, Staffordshire ST5 5BN, England.

RIVKIN J F, b. 1951, USA. Publications: Silverglass, 1986; Web of Wind, 1987; Witch of Rhostshyl, 1989; Mistress of Ambiguities, 1991; The Dreamstone, 1991. Membership: Science Fiction and Fantasy Writers of America. Address: 1430 Massachusetts Avenue, Suite 306, Cambridge, MA 02138, USA.

RIVOYRE Christine Berthe Claude Denis de, b. 29 Nov 1921. Journalist; Author. Education: University of Syracuse, USA. Appointments: Journalist, Le Monde, 1950-55; Literary Director, Marie-Claire, 1955-65; Member, haut Comite de la Langue Francaise, Conseil Superieur des Lettres, Prix Medicis Jury. Publications: L'alouette au miroir, 1956; La mandarine, 1957; La tete en fleurs, 1960; La glace a l'ananas, 1962; Les sultans, 1964; Le petit matin, 1968; Le seigneur des chevaux (with A. Kalda), 1969; Fleur d'agonie, 1970; Boy, 1973; Le voyage a l'envers, 1977; Belle alliance, 1982; Reine-Mere, 1985. Honours: Chevalier, Legion d'honneur; Chevalier, des Arts et des Lettres Prix Paul Morand, 1984; other awards. Address: Dichats Ha, Onesse Laharie, 40110, Morceux, France.

RIZKALLA John Ramsay, b. 2 Nov 1935, Manchester, England. Writer. Education: Baccalaureat Francais (1st and 2nd Part) 1952-53; BA, Hons, Manchester University, 1958. Publications: The Jericho

Garden, 1988; Contributor of short stories to: Winter's Tales 28, ed. A McLean, 1982; A Christmas Feast, ed. J Hale, 1983; BBC Radio 3, 1984; Signals, ed. A Ross, 1991. Contributions to: London Magazine; Panurge; Literary Review; New Review; Encounter; 2 Plus 2; Argo; Short Story International (US); Blackwood Magazine; Weirdbook (US). Membership: Society of Authors. Address: c/o Murray Pollinger, 222, Old Brompton Road, London SW5 0BZ, England.

RIZVI Sajid, b. 2 Feb 1949, Lucknow, India. Writer; Publisher. m. Shirley Joseph, 31 July 1975, 1 son. Education: BA, University of Karachi, 1969; Diploma in Advanced Journalism, Thomson Centre of Journalism, Cardiff, 1974. Appointments: Apprentice Proofreader, appointed in 1964 at age of 15, becoming City Editor in 1970, Morning News, English-language daily, Karachi; Executive Editor, Tehran Journal, Tehran, 1976; Chief Correspondent, United Press International (UPI), Tehran, 1977-80; UPI Chief Correspondent, Ankara, 1980; UPI Middle East Correspondent, London, 1981-84; Diplomatic Editor, Compass News Features, Luxembourg, 1984-87; Independent correspondent, 1987-, in 1987 founded the Centre for Near East, Asia and Africa Research (NEAR), which publishes Eastern Art Report, Academic File and books and pamphlets on the arts. Publications: Numerous articles on current affairs and the arts, in Morning News, Tehran Journal, in UPI international service, Compass News Features, Academic File and Eastern Art Report. Work syndicated throughout the world since joining UPI in 1977. Honours: United Press International Outstanding Coverage Award, 1979; Overseas Press Club Award, 1979; nominated for the Pulitzer Prize for Journalism, 1979. Memberships: International PEN; The Royal Society for Asian Affairs; the Indian Art Circle, London; The International Institute for Strategic Studies (IISS), London; The British Society for Middle Eastern Studies (BRISMES). Address: Centre for Near East, Asia and Africa Research (NEAR), 172 Castelnau, London SW13 9DH, England.

RIZZUTO Sharida, b. 17 July 1948, New Orleans, Louisiana, USA. Writer; Publisher. Education: Meadows-Draughon Business College, 1978; BA, University of New Orleans, 1990. Appointments: Publisher, Baker Street Publications. Publications: As publisher: Payer of Tribute (Margaret L Carter), novelette, 1989; Nocturnes (Dwight E Humphries), literary poetry chapbook, 1989; Civil Violence (Dwight E Humphries), literary poetry chpabook, 1989; Hello, Dear Heart And Other Tales of the Strange (John B Rosenman), anthology of horror stories, 1990; Dreadtime Tales (Bob Warner), anthology of horror stories, 1990. Contributions to: Drifwood weekly newspaper; National Writers Club magazine; New Orleans Chapter; Deep South Journal; Horizons West journal; Poison Pen Writers News journal; Movie Memories journal; The Haunted Journal; The Collinsport Record journal. Memberships: Mystery Writers of America; Horror Writers of America; National Writers Club; Western Writers of America; Arizona Authors Association; National Association for Independent Publishers. Literary Agent: Self. Address: PO Box 994, Metairie, LA 70004, USA.

ROBB Graham Macdonald, b. 2 June 1958, England. Academic. m. Margaret Robb, 2 May 1986. Education: BA, 1st Class Honours, 1981, Postdoctoral Research Fellow, 1987-90, Exeter College, Oxford, 1981; PGCE, Goldsmiths College, London, 1982; PhD, Vanderbilt University, Nashville, Tennessee, USA, 1986. Publications: Le Corsaire - Satan en Silhouette, 1985; Baudelaire Lectuer de Balzac, 1988; Scenes de la Vie de Boheme (editor), 1988; Baudelaire, translation, 1989. Contributions to: Times Literary Supplement; Revue d'Histoire Litteraire de la France; French Studies. Honours: British Academy Fellowship, 1987-90. Memberships: Society of Authors; Societe d'Histoire Litteraire de la France. Literary Agent: Gill Coleridge, Rogers, Coleridge and White. Address: 28 Cornwallis Road, Oxford OX4 3NP, England.

ROBBE-GRILLET Alain, b. 18 Aug 1922, Brest, France. Writer; Film-Maker; Agronomist. m. Catherine Rstakian, 1957. *Publications:* Novels: Les gommes, 1953; Le voyeur, 1955; La jalousie, 1957; Dans le labyrinthe, 1959; La maison de rendez-vous, 1965; projet pour une revolution a New York, 1970; Topologie d'une cite fantome, 1976; La belle captive, 1977; un regicide, 1978; Souvenirs du triangle d'or, 1978; Djinn, 1981; Le miroir qui revient, 1984; Angélique ou l'enchantement, 1987; Short Stories; Instantanes, 1962; Essay: Pour un nouveau roman, 1964; Films; L'annee derniere a Marienbad, 1961; Films Directed: L'immortelle, 1963; Trans-Europ-Express, 1967; L'homme qui ment, 1968; L'Eden et apres, 1970; Glissements progressifs du plaisir, 1974; Le jeu avec le feu, 1975; La belle captive, 1983. *Honours:* Chevalier, Legion d'honneur; Officier, Ordre National du Merite; prix Louis Delluc, 1963. *Memberships:* Various professional organisations. *Address:* 18 boulevard Maillot, 92200 Neuilly-sur-Seine, France.

ROBBINS Harold, b. 1916, USA. Author. m. Grace, 1 daughter. *Publications:* Never Love a Stranger, 1948; The Dream Merchants, 1949; A Stone for Danny Fisher, 1952; Never Leave Me, 1953; 79 Park Avenue, 1955; Stiletto, 1960; The Carpetbaggers, 1961; Where Love Has Gone, 1962; The Adventurers, 1966; The Inheritors, 1969; The Betsy, 1971; The Pirate, 1974; The Lonely Lady, 1976; Dreams Die First, 1977; Memories of Another Day, 1979; Goodbye Janette, 1981; Spellbinder, 1982; Descent from Xanadu, 1984; The Storyteller, 1985; The Pirhanas, 1991. *Address:* c/o c/o New English Library, 47 Bedford Square, London WC1B 3DP, England.

ROBBINS Kenneth Randall, b. 7 Jan, 1944, Georgia, USA. Professor. m. Dorothy Dodge, 14 May, 1988, 1 son, 1 daughter. *Education:* AA, Young Harris College, 1964; BSEd, Georgia Southern University, 1966; MFA, University of Georgia, 1969; PhD, Southern Illinois University-Carbondale, 1982. *Appointments:* Literary Manager, Barter Theatre, Abingdon, Virginia, 1979; Presenter, Black Hills Writers Conference, 1986-90; Programme Development, Aspen Writers Conference, 1987; Convener, Breadloaf Writers Conference, 1981-82; currently, Editor, Wayne S Knutson Dakota Playwriting Series. *Publications:* The Dallas File (play) 1982; Buttermilk Bottoms (novel) 1987. *Contributions to:* Calling the Cows (story) ND Quarterly; Dynamite Hill (play) NPR & BBC-Radio 3; The House Across the Street (story) St Andrews Review; Out of Irony (essay) Southern Quarterly; Concerning the Altered Text (essay) Theatre Topics. *Honours:* Toni Miorrison Prize for Fiction, 1986; Associated Writing Programmes Novel Award, 1986; Festival of Southern Theatre Award, 1987, 1990. *Memberships:* Dramatists Guild; Playwright's Centre (Minneapolis); The Loft, Minneapolis; American College Theatre Festival (PAC Chair, Region V); Association of Theatre in Higher Education; Society for Humanities and Technology; Southeastern Theatre Conference. *Address:* 118 Willow, Vermillion, SD 57069, USA.

ROBERSON John Royster, b. 7 Mar 1930, Roanoke, Virginia, USA. Editor; Writer. m. Charlene Grace Hale, 17 Sept 1966, 1 son, 1 daughter. *Education:* BA, 1950, MA, 1953, University of Virginia; Certificates of French Studies, 1st and 2nd Degrees, University of Grenoble, France, 1952; Diploma in Mandarin Chinese, US Army Language School, Monterey, California, 1956. *Appointments:* From Assistant to Senior Editor, Holiday, 1959-70; Copywriter, N W Ayer Advertising, 1971-76; From Associate to Senior Staff Editor, Reader's Digest Condensed Books, 1976-. *Publications:* China from Manchu to Mao 1699-1976, 1980; Japan from Shogun to Sony 1543-1984, 1985; Transforming Russia 1692-1991, 1992. *Contributions to:* Atlantic; Holiday; Reader's Digest; Studies in Bibliography; Virginia Magazine of History and Biography. *Honours:* Raven Society, University of Virginia, 1950; Rotary International Fellowship, University of Grenoble, 1951-52. *Memberships:* International House of Japan; US China People's Friendship Society; Director of Publications; Science Education Center, Fairfield County,

Connecticut. *Address:* 16 Hassake Rad, Old Greenwich, CT 06870, USA.

ROBERT Adrian. *See:* **JOHNSTON Norma.**

ROBERTS Andrew, (Roderick Logie), b. 13 Jan 1963, London. Author. *Education:* MA, 1st Class Hons, Modern History, Gonville and Caius College, Cambridge, 1985. *Publication:* The Holy Fox: A Biography of Lord Halifax. *Contributions to:* Sunday Telegraph; Spectator; Literary Review; American Spectator. *Memberships:* Beefsteak Club; UNiversity Pitt Club, Cambridge; Academy Club. *Address:* 19 Collingham Place, London SW5 0QF, England.

ROBERTS Brian, b. 1930, England. Writer. *Appointments:* Teacher of English and History, 1955-65. *Publications:* Ladies in the Veld, 1965; Cecil Rhodes and the Princess, 1969; Churchills in Africa, 1970; The Diamond Magnates, 1972; The Zulu Kings, 1974; Kimberley: Turbulent City, 1976; The Mad Bad Line: The Family of Lord Alfred Douglas, 1981; Randolph: A Study of Churchill's Son, 1984; Cecil Rhdes: Flawed Colossus, 1987; Those Bloody Women: Three Heroines of the Boer War, 1991. *Address:* North Knoll Cottage, 15 Bridge Street, Frome BA11 1BB, England.

ROBERTS Eirlys Rhiwen Cadwaladr, b. 3 Jan 1911, United Kingdom. Journalist. m. John Cullen, 1941, *Education:* Clapham High School; BA Hons, Classics, Girton College, Cambridge. *Literary Appointment:* Editor of Which? magazine, 1958-73 and Head of Research and Editorial Division, Consumers' Association. *Publication:* Consumers, 1966. *Contributions to:* Various journals and magazines. *Honours:* OBE 1971; CBE 1977. *Membership:* Royal Society of Arts. *Address:* 8, Lloyd Square, London WC1X 9BA, England.

ROBERTS Gildas Owen, b. 5 Dec 1932, Johannesburg, Souoth Africa. University Professor. m. Patricia Margaret Howe, 10 June 1963, 2 sons, 2 daughters. *Education:* Graduated, Selborne College, 1948; BA, Law, 1951, MA, 1953, BEd, 1955, STC, 1975, University of Cape Town; PhD, Ohio State University, 1966. *Publications:* Joseph of Exeter: The Iliad of Daress Phrygius, 1970; Seven Studies in English, 1971; Angels of God (novel) 1974; Chemical Eric (novel) 1974; Lotus Man (novel) 1983; Beowulf (verse translation) 1984; Gander Snatch (novel) 1991. *Contributions to:* Poems and short stories in Tickle Ace (literary magazine) and others. *Address:* English Department, Memorial University of Newfoundland, St John's, Newfoundland, Canada A1C 5S7.

ROBERTS Gillian. *See:* **GREBER Judith.**

ROBERTS I M. *See:* **ROBERTS Irene.**

ROBERTS Irene (Roberta Carr, Elizabeth Harle, I M Roberts, Ivor Roberts, Iris Rowland, Irene Shaw), b. 1925, United Kingdom. Writer. *Appointments:* Woman's Page Editor, South Hams Review, 1977-79; Tutor, Creative Writing, Kingsbridge Community College, 1978-. *Publications:* Love Song of the Sea, 1960; Squirrel Walk, 1961; The Shrine of Marigolds, 1962; Tangle of Gold Lace, 1963; Cry of the Gulls, 1963; The Whisper of Sea-Bells, 1964; Echo of Flutes, 1965; Where Flamingoes Fly, 1966; A Handful of Stars, 1967; Shadows on the Moon, 1968; Thunder Heights, 1969; Surgeon in Tibet, 1970; Birds Without Bars, 1970; The Shrine of Fire, 1970; Sister at Sea, 1971; Gull Haven, 1971; Moon over the Temple, 1972; The Golden Pagoda, 1972; Desert Nurse, 1976; Nurse in Nepal, 1976; Stars above Raffael, 1977; Hawks Barton, 1979; Symphony of Bells, 1980; Nurse Moonlight, 1980; Weave Me a Moonbeam, 1982; Jasmine for a Nurse, 1982; Sister on Leave, 1982; Nurse in the Wilderness, 1983; Moonpearl, 1986; Sea Jade, 1987; Kingdom of the Sun, 1987; Song of the Nile, 1987; Others; Juveniles: Holiday's for Hanbury, 1964; Laughing Is for Fun, 1964;

As Ivor Roberts: Jump Into Hell, 1960; Trial by Water, 1961; Green Hell, 1961; As Iris Rowland: Island in the Mist, 1962; With Fire and Flowers, 1963; Golden Flower, 1964; A Fountain of Roses, 1966; Valley of Bells, 1967; Blue Feathers, 1967; Moon over Moncrieff, 1969; Star-Drift, 1970; Rainbow River, 1970; The Wild Summer, 1970; Orange Blossom for Tara, 1971; Blossoms in the Snow, 1971; Sister Julia, 1972; Golden Bubbles, 1976; Hunter's Dawn, 1977; Golden Triangle, 1978; Forgotten Dreams, 1978; Temptation, 1983; Theresa, 1985; Others; As Roberta Carr: Red Runs the Sunset, 1963; Sea Maiden, 1965; Fire Dragon, 1967; Golden Interlude, 1970; As Elizabeth Harle: Golden Rain, 1964; Gay Rowan, 1965; Sandy, 1967; Spray of Red Roses, 1971; The Silver Summer, 1971; The Burning Flame, 1979; Come To Me Darling, 1983; As Irene Shaw: The House of Lydia, 1967; Moonstone Manor, 1968, in US Murder's Mansion, 1976; The Olive Branch, 1968; As I M Roberts: The Throne of Pharaohs, 1974; Hatshepsut, Queen of the Nile, 1976; Hour of the Tiger, 1985. *Address:* Alpha House, Higher Town, Marlborough, Kingsbridge, South Devon TQ7 3RL, England.

ROBERTS Ivor. *See:* **ROBERTS Irene.**

ROBERTS James J (Robert J Horton), b. 11 Sept 1947, Connecticut, USA. Writer. m. Naomi Ruth Nyquist, 27 Aug 1983, 2 sons, 4 daughters. *Education:* BA, Journalism, Univerity of Rhode Island, 1974. *Appointments:* Writer: Radio WK7D, 1969, Radio WNTS, 1973; Editor, WQAD TV, 1974; Editor/Anchor, WPRI TV, 1979; Managing Editor, WLOX TV, 1984; President, EduVision, 1985; Director of Public Information, Rhode Island Judiciary, 1987. *Publications:* Ernie Pyle: War Correspondent, 1974; EduVision, 1986; Hurricane, 1985; A Time to Live, A Time to Die, 1984; Hobo Trail, 1986; Economic Chaos, 1986; Blizzard, 1981; Justice For All, 1988; numerous TV Documentaries and Historical Specials. *Contributions to:* various journals and magazines. *Honours;* Numerous awards as Journalist for economic reporting, hurricane documentary, human interest work; American Bar Association, Silver Gavel Award, Justice For All, TV documentary series, 1988. *Memberships:* Sigma Delta Chi; RTNDA. *Address:* PO Box 431, Wickford, RI 02852, USA.

ROBERTS John Morris, b. 14 Apr 1928, Warden, Merton College, Oxford. m. Judith Cecilia Mary Armitage, 1964, 1 son, 2 daughters. *Education:* Taunton School; Keble College, Oxford (Scholar; Hon Fellow, 1981). *Appointments:* National Service 1949-50; Prize Fellow, Magdalen College, Oxford, 1951-53; Commonwealth Fund Fellow, Princeton and Yale, 1953-54; Merton College, Oxford: Fellow and Tutor, 1953-79 (Hon Fellow 1980-84), Acting Warden 1969-70, 1977-79, Warden 1984-; Senior Proctor, Oxford University, 1967-68, Vice-Chancellor and Professor, Southampton University, 1979-85; Member, Institute of Advanced Study, Princeton, 1960-61; Visiting Professor, University of South Carolina, 1961; Secretary of Harmsworth Trust, 1962-68; Member, Council, European University Institute, 1980-88; US/UK Education Commission (Fulbright), 1981-87; Governor of BBC, 1988-93; Board Member, British Council, 1992. *Publications:* French Revolution Documents I, 1966; Europe 1880-1945, 1967, 1990; The Mythology of the Secret Societies, 1972; The Paris Commune from the Right, 1973; Revolution and Improvement: the Western World 1775-1847, 1976; History of the World, 1976; The French Revolution, 1978; The Triumph of the West, 1985; (General Editor) Purnell's History of the 20th Century. *Contributions to:* Articles and reviews to learned journals; Editor, English Historical Review, 1967-77; Presenter, TV series, The Triumph of the West, 1985. *Honour:* Hon D Litt, Southampton University, 1987. *Memberships:* General Committee, Royal Literary Fund, 1975-; Trustee, National Portrait Gallery, 1984-; President, Council, Taunton School, 1978-88. *Address:* Merton College, Oxford OX1 4JD, England.

ROBERTS Keith John Kingston (Alistair Bevan), b. 1935, United Kingdom. Author; Freelance Graphic

Designer and Advertising Copywriter. *Appointments:* Assistant Editor, Science Fantasy, 1965-66; Assistant Editor, 1965-66, Managing Editor, 1966, Science Fiction Impulse. *Publications:* The Furies, 1966; Pavane, 1968; The Inner Wheel, 1970; Anita, 1970; The Boat of Fate, 1971; Machines and Men, 1973; The Chalk Giants, 1974; The Grain Kings, 1975; Ladies from Hell, 1979; Molly Zero, 1980; Kiteworld, 1985; Kaeti and Company, 1986; The Lordly Ones, 1986. *Address:* 23 New Street, Henley- on-Thames, Oxon RG9 2BP, England.

ROBERTS Kevin, b. 1940, Australia. Author. *Publications:* Cariboo Fishing Notes, poetry, 1973; Five poems, 1974; West Country, poetry, 1975; Deepline, poetry, 1978; S'Ney'mos, poetry, 1980; Heritage, poetry, 1981; Stonefish, poetry, 1982; Flash Harry and the Daughters of Divine Light, fiction, 1982; Black Apples, play, 1983; Nanoose Bay Suite, poetry, 1984; Picking the Morning Colour, fiction, 1985; Tears in a Glass Eye, novel, 1989; Red Centre Journal, art & poetry show, 1985. *Address:* Box 55, Lantzville, British Columbia, Canada V0R 2H0.

ROBERTS Nora, b. 10 Oct 1950. Writer. m. 6 July 1985, 2 sons. *Education:* Graduated, High School, 1968. *Publications:* Irish Thoroughbred, 1981; This Magic Moment, 1983; The MacGregors, 1985; Hot Ice, 1987; Sacred Sins, 1987; Brazen Virtue, 1988; The O'Harleys, 1988; Sweet Revenge, 1989; Public Secrets, 1990; The Calhoun Women, 1991; Genuine Lies, 1991; Carnal Innocence. 1992; Honest Illusions, 1992; Divine Evil, 1992; Private Scandals, 1993. *Honours:* Romance Writers of America (RWA), Golden Medallion, 1982, '83, '84, '86; RWA Hall of Fame, 1986; RWA Rita Award. 1990; Waldenbooks Award, 1986, '87, '89, '90, '91; B Dalton Award, 1990, 1991. *Memberships:* Romance Writers of America; Mystery Writers of America; Novelists, Inc; Crime Writers; Sisters-In-Crime. *Address:* c/o Writers House, 21 West 26th Street, New York, NY 10010, USA.

ROBERTS Selyf, b. 20 May 1912, Corwen, Gwynedd, Wales. Retired Bank Officer. m. 28 Aug 1945, 1 daughter. *Publications:* Translations into Welsh: Alice in Wonderland (abridged), 1951, (full translation), 1982; Through the Looking Glass, 1984; Essays: Deg o'r Diwedd, 1958; Mesur Byr, 1977; Hel Meddyliau, 1982; Imaginary Biography: Dr R.P. Howells, 1974; Autobiography: Tocyn Dwyffordd, 1984; Novels: Cysgod yw Arian, 1959; Helynt er hoelion, 1960; A Eilw ar Ddyfnder, 1962; Wythnos o Hydref, 1965; Ymweled ag Anwiredd, 1975; Iach o'r Cadwynau, 1977; Tebyg Nid Oes, 1981; Teulu Meima Lloyd, 1986; Gorwel Agos, 1989; Arts Council Award Winning Novel. *Contributions to:* Essays and Short Stories to: Y Llenor; yr Eurgrawn; Taliesin; Genhinen; various anthologies. *Honours:* Honorary Member, Gorsedd of Bards; Winner of Prose Medal, National Eisteddfod of Wales, Pwlheli, 1955. *Memberships:* Yr Adademi Gymreig; Chairman, Undeb Awduron Cymru (Union of Welsh Authors), 1975-86. *Address:* Hfod Las, Trefonen Road, Oswestry, Shropshire, SY11 2TW, England.

ROBERTS Thomas J, b. 10 June 1925, Omhah, Nebraska, USA. Teacher; Scholar. m. Betty Ann Nelson, 1 Dec 1951, 3 sons. *Education:* BA, Journalism, 1948, MA, English, 1952, PhD, English, Art History, 1958, University of Minnesota, Minneapolis. *Appointments:* American University in Cairo (Egypt) 1958-60, 1961-63; University of Alaska, Fairbanks, Alaska, USA, 1960-61; University of Connecticut, Storrs, Connecticut, USA, 1963-. *Publications:* When Is Something Fiction? 1972; An Aesthetics of Junk Fiction, 1990. *Contributions to:* Gold Bullet Sport, a Dime Novel by Buffalo Bill, Texas Studies in Literature and Languages, 1991. *Address:* Department of English, University of Connecticut, Storrs, CT 06269, USA.

ROBERTS Willo Davis, b. 29 May 1928, Grand Rapids, Michigan, USA. Freelance Writer. m. David Roberts, 20 May 1949, 2 sons, 2 daughters. *Publications:* 83 books including: Murder at Grand Bay,

1955; The Girl Who Wasn't There, 1957; Nurse Kay's Conquest, 1966; The Tarot Spell, 1970; King's Pawn, 1971; White Jade, 1975, Paperback Edition, 1976; 8 volumes in The Black Pearl Series, 1978-80; 8 volumes in The Black Pearl Series, 1978-80; The Search for Willie, 1980; A Long Time To Hate, 1982; Keating's Landing, 1984; The Annalise Experiment, 1985; To Share a Dream, 1986; Madawaska, 1988; Books for children and young adults: The View from the Cherry Tree, 1975; Don't Hurt Laurie, 1977; The Girl with the Silver Eyes, 1980; The Pet Sitting Peril, 1983; Eddie and the Fairy God Puppy, 1984; Baby Sitting Is A Dangerous Job, 1985; The Magic Book, 1986; Sugar Isn't Everything, 1987; Megan's Island, 1988; Nightmare, 1989; Scared Stiff, 1991; Dark Secrets, 1991. Honours: Young Hoosier Award, Evansville Book Award, Georgia Children's Book Award, Young Readers of Western Australia Award, 1977; Mark Twain Award, 1980; Mark Twain Award, Young Hoosier Award, South Carolina Children's Book Award, Nevada Young Reader's Award, 1985; Pacific Northwest Writers Achievement Award, 1986; Edgar Allen Poe Award, 1988; Numerous others. Memberships: Authors Guild; Mystery Writers of America, Founder, Northwest Seattle Chapter, Past Regional Vice-President; Society of Children's Book Writers; Seattle Freelances; Pacific Northwest Writers Conference. Literary Agent: Emilie Jacobson, Curtis Brown Ltd, New York City, New York, USA. Address: 12020 Engebretson Road, Granite Falls, WA 98252, USA.

ROBERTSON Barbara Anne, b. 1931, Canada. Biographer. Publications: The Wind Has Wings (compiled with M A Downie), 1968, Enlarged Edition, The New Wind Has Wings, 1984; Wilfrid Laurier: The Great Conciliator, 1971; The Well-Filled Cupboard (with M A Downie), 1987; Doctor-Dward and other poems for Children, (ed M A Downie), 1990; new edition, St Wilfrid Laurier: The Great Conciliator, 1991. Address: 52 Florence Street, Kingston, Ontario, Canada K7M 1Y6.

ROBERTSON Denise, b. 9 June 1933, Sunderland, England. Writer; Broadcaster. m. (1) Alexander Robertson, 19 Mar 1960, (2) John Tomlin, 3 Nov 1973, 5 sons. Publications: Year of Winter, 1986; Land of Lost Content, 1987; Blue Remembered Hills, 1987; Second Wife, 1988; None to Make You Cry, 1989; Remember the Moment, 1990. Contributions to: Numerous. Honours: Constable Fiction Trophy, 1985. Literary Agent: Carol Smith, 25 Hornton Court, East Kensington High Street, London W8 7RT, England. Address: 9 Springfield Crescent, Seaham, County Durham, England.

ROBERTSON James I, b. 18 July 1930, Danville, Virginia, USA. Professor of History. m. Elizabeth Green, 1 June 1952, Danville, Virginia. 2 sons, 1 daughter. Education: BA, Randolph-Macon College, 1954; MA, Emory University, 1955; PhD, Emory University, 1959; LittD, Randolph-Macon College, 1980. Literary Appointments: Associate Professor of History, University of Montana, 1965-67; Professor and Head, History Department, 1967-75, C P Miles Professor of History, 1976-, Virginia Polytechnic Institute and State University. Publications: The Stonewall Brigade, 1963; Civil War Books: The Civil War Letters of General Robert McAllister, 1965; A Critical Bibliography, 1965-67; Recollections of a Maryland Confederate Soldier, 1975; Four Years in the Stonewall Brigade, 1978; The 4th Virginia Infantry, 1980; Civil War Sites in Virginia: A Tour-Guide, 1982; The 18th Virginia Infantry, 1983; Tentinting Tonight: The Soldiers' View, 1984; General A P Hill, 1987; Soldiers Blue and Gray, 1988. Contributions to: More than 150 articles in Historical Journals and History Magazines. Honours: The Harry S Truman Historical Award, 1962; The Centennial Medallion of the US Civil War Centennial Commission, 1965; Phi Beta Kappa, 1967; Freeman-Nevins Award, 1981; Bruce Catton Award, 1983; William E Wine Award for Teaching Excellence, 1983; A P Andrews Memorial Award, 1985; James Robertson Award of Achievement, 1985; Jefferson Davis Medal, United Daughters of the Confederacy. Memberships: Board of

Trustees, Virginia Historical Society; Organisation of American Historians; Southern Historical Assocation; Confederate Memorial Society. Address: Department of History, Virgnia Polytechnic Institute and State University, Blacksburg, VA 24061-0117, USA.

ROBERTSON-STEPHEN. See: **ROBERT Wayne Walker.**

ROBINETTE Joseph Allen, b. 8 Feb 1939, Rockwood, Tennessee, USA. College Professor; Playwright. m. Helen M Scitz, 27 Aug 1965, 4 sons, 1 daughter. Education: BA, Carson-Newman College, 1960; MA, 1966, PhD, 1972, Southern Illinois University. Publications: The Fabulous Fable Factory, 1975; Once Upon a Shoe (play) 1979; Legend of the Sun Child (musical) 1982; Charlotte's Web (dramatization) 1983; Charlotte's Web (musical with Charles Strouse) 1989; Anne of Green Gables (dramatization) 1989; The Lion, the Witch and the Wardrobe (dramatization) 1989; The Trial of Goldilocks (operetta) 1990; Dorothy Meets Alice (musical) 1991. Contributions to: Children's Theatre News; Opera For Youth News. Honours: Charlotte Chorpennlag Cup (National Children's Playwriting Award) 1976. Memberships: American Society of Composers, Authors and Publishers; American Association for Theatre in Education; Opera for Youth; ASSITEJ. Address: Department of Speech/Theatre, Rowan State College, Glassboro, NJ 08028, USA.

ROBINS Patricia. See: **CLARK Patricia Denise.**

ROBINSON David Julien, b. 6 Aug 1930. Film Critic. Education: BA, Honours, King's College, Cambridge. Appointments: Associate Editor, Sight and Sound, and Editor, Monthly Film Bulletin, 1956-58; Programme Director, NFT, 1959; Film Critic, Financial Times, 1959-74; Editor, Contrast, 1962-63; Film Critic, The Times, 1974-. Publications: Hollywood in the Twenties, 1969; Buster Keaton, 1969; The Great Funnies, 1972; World Cinema, 1973, 2nd edition 1980 (US edition The History of World Cinema, 1974, 1980); Chaplin : the mirror of opinion, 1983; Chaplin : his life and art, 1985; Editor, Translator, Luis Bunuel (J.F. Aranda); Editor, Translator, Cinema in Revolution (anthology). Address: 96-100 New Cavendish Street, London W1M 7FA, England.

ROBINSON Ian, b. 1 July 1934, Heston, England. Writer. m. Adelheid Armbrüster, 21 Dec 1959, 1 son, 1 daughter. Education: Oriel College, University of Oxford, 1955-58; MA (Oxon). Appointments: Editor, Oasis magazine, 1969-; Publisher, Oasis Books, 1970-; Deputy Chairman, The Poetry Society of Great Britain, 1977-78. Publications: Poetry: Accidents, 1974; Three, 1978; Short Stories, 1979; Maida Vale Elegies, 1983; Journal, 1987; Fiction: Obsequies, 1979; Fugitive Aromas, 1979; Blown Footage, 1980; Dissolving Views, 1986. Contributions to: Prism International, Vancouver; The Canadian Fiction Magazine; London Magazine; Prospice; Blue Cage; Poesie Europe, Germany; Osiris, USA; 180 others. Memberships: Association of Little Presses; Society of Fulham Artists. Address: 12 Stevenage Road, London SW6 6ES, England.

ROBINSON Jancis Mary, b. 22 Apr 1950. Wine Writer & Broadcaster. m. Nicholas Laurence Lander, 1981, 1 son, 2 daughters. Education: MA, S Anne's College, Oxford, 1971. Appointments: Editor, Wine & Spirit, 1976-80; Founder, Editor, Drinker's Digest (now Which? Wine Monthly), 1977-82; Editor, Which? Wine Guide, 1980-82; Sunday Times Wine Correspondent, 1980-86; Evening Standard Wine Correspondent, 1987-88; Regular Contributor to Financial Times, 1989-; Freelance Journalism, particularly on wine, food and people, 1980-; Freelance TV and Radio Broadcasting, various subjects, 1983-; Writer, Presenter, The Wine Programme, 1983, 1985, 1987; 'Jancis Robinson Meets...', 1988; Matters of Taste, 1989-; Wine Judging & Lecturing, 1983. Publications: The Wine Book, 1979, revised edition 1983; The Great Wine Book, 1981; Masterglass, 1983, revised edition 1987; How to Choose and Enjoy Wine, 1984; Vines, Grapes and Wines, 1986; Food and Wine Adventures, 1987; The Demon Drink, 1988; Vintage Timecharts, 1989; The Oxford Companion to Wine, forthcoming. *Contributions to:* Wine Correspondent, 1980-86; Sunday Time; Evening Standard, 1987-88; Financial Times, 1989. *Honours:* Glenfiddich Trophy, 1983; Master of Wine, 1984; Andre Simon Memorial Prize, Wine Guild Award, Clicquot Book of the Year, 1986. *Membership:* Master of Wine, 1984. *Literary Agent:* Caradoc King, A P Watt Agency. *Address:* c/o A P Watt, 20 John Street, London, WC1N 2DR, England.

ROBINSON Jeffrey, b. 19 Oct 1945, New York, NY, USA. Author. m.. Aline Benayoun, 27 Mar 1985, 1 son, 1 daughter. *Education:* BS, Temple University, Philadelphia, Pennsylvania, 1967. *Publications:* Bette Davis, Her Stage and Film Career, 1983; Teamwork, 1984; The Risk Takers, 1985; Pietrov and Other Games (fiction) 1985; Minus Millionaires, 1986; The Ginger Jar (fiction) 1986; Yamani - The Inside Story, 1988; Rainier and Grace, 1989; The Risk Takers - Five Years On, 1990; The End of the American Century, 1992; The laundrymen, 1993. *Contributions to:* More than 700 articles and short stories published in major magazines and journals worldwide. *Honours:* Overseas Press Club, 1984; Benedictine - After Dinner Speaker of the Year, 1990. *Membership:* PEN. *Address:* c/o Robert Ducas, 350 Hudson Street, New York, NY 10014, USA.

ROBINSON Kim Stanley, b. 1952, USA. Author. *Appointments:* Visiting Lecturer: University of California, Davis, 1982-84, 1985; University of California, San Diego, 1982, 1985. *Publications:* The Novels of Philip K Dick, 1984; The Wild Shore, 1984; Icehenge, 1985; The Memory of Whiteness, 1985; The Planet on the Table, 1986; The Gold Coast, 1989, (Fiction). *Address:* 17811 Romelle Avenue, Santa Ana, CA 92705, USA.

ROBINSON Robert Henry, b. 17 Dec 1927, Liverpool, England. Writer and Broadcaster. m. Josephine Mary Richard, 1958. 1 son, 2 daughters. *Education:* Raynes Park Grammar School; MA, Exeter College, Oxford. *Publications:* Landscape With Dead Dons, 1956; Inside Robert Robinson, 1965; The Conspiracy, 1968; The Dog Chairman, 1982; Everyman Book of Light Verse (Editor), 1984; Bad Dreams, 1989; Perscriptions of a Pox Doctor's Clerk, 1991. TV & Radio programmes: Call My Bluff; Stop the Week; Brain of Britain; Robinson Country. *Contributions:* Times; Listener; Sunday Times. *Address:* 16 Cheyne Row, London, SW3, England.

ROBINSON Roland (Edward), b. 1912, British. *Appointments:* Member, Kirsova Ballet, 1944-47; Ballet Critic 1956-66, Book Reviewer, Sydney Morining Herald; Editor, Poetry Magazine, Sydney; President, Poetry Society of Australia. *Publications:* Beyond the Grass-Tree Spears: Verse, 1944; Lauguage of the Sand, 1948; Legend and Dreaming: Legends of the Dream-Time of the Australian Aborigines, 1952; Tumult of the Swans, 1953; The Feathered Serpent: The Mythological Genesis and Recreative Ritual of the Aboriginal Tribes of the Northern Territory of Australia, 1956; Black-Feller, White-Feller, 1958; Deep Well, 1962; The Man Who Sold His Dreaming, 1965; Aborigine Myths and Legends, 1966; Grendel, 1967; The Australian Aborigine in Colour, Wandjina: Children of the Dreamtime: Aboriginal Myths and Legends (ed), 1968; Selected Poems, 1971; The Drift of Things 1914-1952, 1973; The Shift of Sands 1952-1962, 1976; A Letter to Joan, 1978; Selected Poems, 1984; Selected Poems, 1989; The Nearest The White Man Gets, 1989. *Address:* 10 Old Main Road, Belmont North, New South Wales 2280, Australia.

ROBINSON Roxana Barry, b. 30 Nov 1946, USA. Writer. m. Hamilton Robinson, 20 Feb 1976, 1 daughter. *Education:* BA, University of Michigan, 1969. *Publications:* Summer Light, novel, UK Edition, 1987, US Edition, 1988; Georgia O'Keeffe: A Life, US Edition, 1989, UK Edition, 1990. *Contributions to:* The New

Yorker; The Southern Review; The Atlantic (US); The Fiction Magazine (UK). *Honours:* Nomination for Washington Irving Award, New York, 1987; Fellowship in Creative Writing, National Endowment for the Arts, 1987. *Membership:* PEN. *Literary Agent:* Pat Kavanagh, Peters, Dunlop and Frazer Group Ltd, London, England. *Address:* c/o Elizabeth Grossman, Sterling Lord Literistic, One Madison Avenue, New York, NY 10010, USA.

ROBINSON Sheila Mary (Sheila Radley, Hester Rowan), b. 18 Nov 1928, Cogenhoe, Northamptonshire, England. Writer. *Education:* BA, University of London. *Publications:* Death & the Maiden, 1978; The Chief Inspector's Daughter, 1981; A Talent for Destruction, 1982; Blood on the Happy Highway, 1983; Fate Worse than Death, 1985. *Agent:* Curtis Brown. *Address:* c/o Curtis Brown, 162-168 Regent Street, London W1R 5TB, England.

ROBINSON Spider, b. 1948, American. *Appointments:* Realty Editor, Long Island Commercial Review, Syosset, NY, 1972-73; Freelance Writer, 1973-; Book Reviewer, Galaxy Magazine, 1975-77. *Publications:* Telempath, 1976; Callahan's Crossing Saloon, 1977; Stardance (with Jeanne Robinson), 1979; Antinomy, 1980; Time Travelers Strictly Cash, 1981; Mindkiller, 1982; Melancholy Elephants, 1984; Night of Power, 1985; Callahan's Secre, 1986; Time Pressure, Callahan and Company, 1987.

ROCHARD Henry. *See:* **CHARLIER Henri.**

ROCHE George Charles III, b. 16 May 1935, Denver, Colorado, USA. College President. m. June Bernard, 2 sons, 2 daughters. *Education:* BS, Regis College, Colorado, 1956; MA, 1961, PhD, 1965, University of Colorado. *Publications:* The Bewildered Society, 1972; Going Home, 1986; A World Without Heroes: A Modern Tragedy, 1987; A Reason for Living, 1989; One By One, 1990. *Contributions to:* Columns in several newspapers; Human Events - the American Spectator. *Honour:* Freedom Leadership Award, Freedoms Foundation, 1972. *Memberships:* Mont Pelerin Society; The Philadelphia Society; American Association of Presidents of Independent Colleges and Universities. *Address:* Hillsdale College, Hillsdale, MI 49242, USA.

ROCHE John. *See:* **LEROI David de Roche.**

ROCHE Paul, b. 1928, British. *Appointments:* Instructor, Smith College, Northampton, MA, 1957-59; Poet-in-Residence, California Institute of the Arts, Valencia, 1972-74. *Publications:* The Rat and the Convent Dove and Other Tales and Fables, 1952; O Pale Galilean, 1954; The Oedipus Plays of Sophocles (trans), 1958; The Rank Obstinacy of Things: A Selection of Poems, Vessel of Dishonour, 1962; The Orestes Plays of Aeschylus, 1963; Prometheus Bound, by Aeschylus (trans), 1964; 22 November 1963 (The Catherisis of Anguish), 1965; Ode to the Dissolution of Morality, All Things Considered: Poems (in US as All Things Considered and Other Poems), The Love- Songs of Sappho (trans), 1966; To Tell the Truth: Poems, Te Deum for J Alfred Prufrock, Oedipus the King, 1967; 3 Plays of Plautus (trans), 1968; Philoctetes lines 676-729 by Sophocles (trans), Lament for Erica: A Poem, 1971; Three Plays of Euripides: Alcestis Medea The Bacchae (trans), Enigma Variations and ..., The Kiss, 1974; New Tales from Aesop for Reading Aloud, With Duncan Grant in Southern Turkey, 1982.

ROCKFORD E B. *See:* **BLAAS Erika B.**

ROCKWELL John (Sargent), b. 16 Sept 1940, Washington DC, USA. *Education:* BA, Harvard University, 1962; Graduate Study, University of Munich, 1962-63; MA 1964, PhD 1972, University of California. *Career:* Music critic and writer. Worked in radio and on television on opera programs and miscellaneous fereelance jobs for stations such as WHRB-Radio, Cambridge, Massachusetts, KPFA-Radio, Berkeley, California and KPED-TV, San Francsico, California, 1965-59; West Coast Correspondent, Opera News, New York, 1968-72; Music and Dance Critic, Tribune, Oakland, California, 1969; Assistant Music and Dance Critic, Los Angeles Times, Los Angeles, California, 1970-72; Freelance Music Critic, 1972-74; Staff Music Critic, 1974-, New York Times, New York City. Lecturer in cultural history at Princeton University 1977-79; lecturer in music at Brooklyn College of the City University of New York, 1980. *Publications:* (Contributor)Jim Miller (ed) The Rolling Stone Illustrated History of Rock and Roll, 1976; (with Robert Stearns) Robert Wilson: A Theater of Images, 1980; All American Music: Composition in the Late Twentieth Century, 1983; Sinatra: An American Classic (contains photographs) 1984; (Contributor and editorial adviser) Stanley Sadie and H Wiley Hitchcock (eds) New Grove Dictionary of American Music, 1986. Contributor to other volumes and to periodicals. *Honours:* German academic Exchange Fellowship, 1962-63; Woodrow Wilson Fellowship 1963-64; All American Music: Composition in the Late Twentieth Century was nominated for a 1983 National Book Critics Circle Award. *Memberships:* Music Critics Association, Treasurer 1977-81; Phi Beta Kappa. *Literary Agent:* Robert Cornfield, 145 West 79th Street, New York, NY 10024, USA. *Address:* New York Times, 229 West 43rd Street, New York, NY 10036, USA.

RODDY Lee, b. 22 Aug 1921, Marion County, Illinois, USA. Author; Lecturer. m. Cicely Price, 17 Oct 1947, 1 son, 1 daughter. *Education:* Graduated, Oakdale High School, Oakdale, California, 1940; AA, Los Angeles City College, Los Angeles, California, 1945. *Publications:* The Life and Times of Grizzly Adams (ghosted) 1977, became an NBC-TV prime time television series; The Lincoln Conspiracy (ghosted) 1977, made the New York Times best-seller list and was also a motion picture; Jesus, 1979, became a film now available in 200 languages around then world; Secret of the Shark Pit, 1988; Secret of the Sunken Sub, 1990; The Overland Escape, 1989; The Desperate Search, 1989; Danger on Thunder Mountain, 1990; Secret of the Howling Cave, 1990; The Flaming Trap, 1990; Mystery of the Phantom Gold, 1991; The Gold Train Bandits, 1992; Ghost Dog of Stoney Ridge, 1985; Dooger, Grasshopper Hound, 1985; The City Bear's Adventures, 1985; The Hair-Pulling Bear Dog, 1985; Giants on the Hill, in progress; Ladd Family Adventures, in progress. *Honours:* Twenty-nine of Lee Roddy's nearly 60 books (all published since 1974) have been best-sellers, award winners, book club selections, made into movies or television programmes; Recognised as one of 15 distinguished alumni in the 100 year history of Oakdale High School, 1992. *Memberships:* Authors League; Authors Guild of America; National Society of Children's Book Writers; Northern California Chapter, Society of Children's Book Writers. *Literary Agent:* S Rickley Christian, President of Alive Communications, Colorado Springs, CO. *Address:* P O Box 700, Penn Valley, CA 95946, USA.

RODEFER Stephen (Jean Calais). b. 20 Nov 1940, Bellaire, Ohio, USA, Writer; Lecturer. 3 sons. *Education:* BA, Amherst College, 1959- 63; MA, State University of New York at Buffalo, 1963-67; MA, San Francisco State University, 1980-81. *Appointments:* Teaching Fellow, 1963-66, Instructor, 1966-67, State University of New York at Buffalo; Assistant Professor, Co-Director of Writing Programme, University of New Mexico, 1967-71; editor, Duende Press, Placitas, New Mexico, 1972-75; Language Arts Specialist, Berkeley Unified School District, California, 1976-81; Lecturer, San Francisco State University, California, 1981-85; Curator, Archive for New Poetry, 1985-87, Lecturer in Poetry, 1985-89, University of California at San Diego; Lecturer, University of California at Berkeley, 1990-. *Publications:* The Knife, 1965; Villon, (as Jean Calais), 1976; One or Two Love Poems from the White World, 1976; The Bell Clerk's Tears Keep Flowing, 1978; Plane Debris, 1981; Four Lectures, 1982; Oriflamme Day, (Co-author Benjamin Friedlander), 1984; Safety (Translations of Sappho and the Greek Anthology), 1985; Emergency

Measures, 1987. *Contributions to:* Sulfur; Conjunctions; Temblor; Oblek; Writing; This; Sur. *Honours:* Faculty Fellowship for Poetry, Research Foundation, State University of New York at Buffalo, 1967; Co-winner, Annual Book Award for Four Lectures, American Poetry Centre, San Francisco, 1983; Public Arts Council Grant, 1987; Fund for Poetry Award, New York City, 1988. *Memberships:* American Literary Translators Association; American Association of University Professors; Poets Theatre. *Address:* 6434 Raymond Street, Oakland, CA 94611, USA.

RODGERS Carolyn M, American. *Appointment:* Former Midwest Editor, Black Dialogue, NYC. *Publications:* Paper Soul, 1968; Two Love Raps, Songs of a Blackbird, Now Ain't That Love, 1969; For H W Fuller, 1970; Long Rap/Commonly Known as a Poetic Essay, 1971; How I Got Ovah: New and Selected Poems, 1975; The Heart as Ever Green, 1978; Translation, 1980; Eden and Other Poems, 1983; A Little Lower Than the Angels, 1984. *Address:* 12750 South Sangamon, Chicago, IL 60643, USA.

RODGERS Daniel Tracy, b. 29 Sept 1942, Darby, Pennsylvania, USA. Professor of History. m. Irene Wylie Rodgers, Dec 1971, 2 sons. *Education:* AB-BSc in Engineering, Brown University, 1965; PhD History, Yale University, 1973. *Publications:* The Work Ethic in Industrial America, 1850-920, 1978; Contested Truths: Keywords in American Politics since Independence, 1987. *Contributions include:* Reviews in American History; Journal of American History. *Honours:* Frederick Jackson Turner Award of the Organization of American Historians, 1978. *Address:* Department of History, Princeton University, Princeton, NJ 08544 USA.

RODGERS Eugene, b. 22 July 1939, Brooklyn, New York, USA. Writer. m. Carol Diane Huber, 19 Mar 1977, 1 son, 1 daughter. *Education:* BS Chemistry, Villanova University, 1961; University of Wisconsin, 1961-63; MS Finance, Virginia Commonwealth University, 1991. *Publications:* Beyond the Barrier: The Story of Byrn's First Expedition to Antartica, 1990. *Honours:* Best Book in Previous Year, Virginia College Stores Association, 1991. *Literary Agent:* Scott Meredith. *Address:* 2621 Ellesmere Drive, Midlothian, VA 23113, USA.

RODGERS Mary, b. 1931, American. *Appointments:* Script Editor and Assistant to the Producer, New York Philharmonic Young People's Concerts, CBS-TV, 1957-71; Script Writer, Hunter College, Little Orchestra Society, 1958-59; Columnist (Of Two Minds), with Dorothy Rodgers, McCalls Magazine, NYC. *Publications:* Davy Jones' Locker, by Arthur Birnkrant and Waldo Salt (music and lyrics only), Three to Make Music (lyrics only), 1959; The Rotten Book, 1969; A Word to the Wives (with Dorothy Rodgers), 1970; Freaky Friday, 1972; screenplay 1977; Pinocchio (for marionettes), 1973; A Billion for Boris, 1974; The Devil and Max Devlin, 1980; Summer Switch, 1983.

RODRIGUES Santan Rosario, b. 23 Sept 1948, Goa. Public Relations Expert. m. Patricia Rodriguez, 23 Sept 1983. *Education:* MA, English Literature, Bombay University, India. *Appointments:* Founder, Editor, Kavi India poetry quarterly, 1976-83; Poetry Editor, Imprint, 1977-78; Poetry Editor, Gomantale Times, 1989-90. *Publications:* I Exist, 1976; 3 Poets, 1978; The Householder Yogi, 1982; Poems represented in: New Poetry by Indian Men; Indian English Poetry since 1950; Goan Literature. *Contributions to:* Illustrated Weekly of India; Journal of Indian Writing in English; Times of India; Gentleman; Debonair. *Honours:* Travel Grant, Sahitya Akademi, 1976-77. *Memberships:* India PEN; The Asiatic Society; Bombay English Association; Programme Director, Association of Business Communicators of India. *Address:* 7 Gautam Apts, 45-624 Kastur Park, Shimpoli Road, Borivli (W), Bombay 400092, India.

RODWAY Anne. *See:* **BRENNAN Patricia Winifred.**

ROECKER William Alan, b. 17 Jan 1942, Madison, Wisconsin, USA. Writer. m. Debbie Sue Huntsman, 31 Dec 1985. *Education:* BS, 1966, MFA, 1967, University of Oregon. *Appointments:* Assistant Editor, Northwest Review, 1967; Instructor, Associate Professor, English, University of Arizona, 1968-74; Editor, Windsport Magazine, 1981-82; Saltwater Editor, Today's Fishermen, 1985; Associate Editor, South Coast Sportfishing, 1987; Senior Editor, South Coast Sportfishing, 1988. *Publications:* Willamette, poems, 1970; Stories that Count, 1971; You Know Me, poems, 1972; Closer to the Country, poems, 1976. *Contributions to:* Numerous journals & magazines. *Honours include:* Haycox Award, 1966; Neubergr Award, 1967; Runner Up, Yale Younger Poets, 1971; NEA Award, 1973; Gray Prize, Hang Gliding Journalism, 1984. *Address:* 379 N Vulcan, Encinitas, CA 92024, USA.

ROES Nicholas A, b. 26 Dec 1952. Author; Teacher; Consultant; Speaker. m. Nancy Bennett Roes, 26 Nov 1977. *Education:* BS, College of Education, 1974, MA, College of Business and Public Management, 1983, University of Bridgeport. *Publications:* Helping Children Watch TV: America's Lowest Cost Colleges; Gambling for Fun; Pick-your-Own Farms. *Contributions to:* Columnist, Winning on Wall Street. *Honours:* Best Book Content Award, NAIP, 1988, 1989.*Memberships:* EDPRESS; MENSA; IAFP; IPA; NYDMC. *Address:* PO Box 233, Barryville, NY 12719, USA.

ROGERS Floyd. *See:* **SPENCE William John Duncan.**

ROGERS Ingrid, b. 3 May 1951, Rinteln, Federal Republic of Germany. Pastor; Teacher; Writer. m. H. Kendall Rogers, 9 June 1972, 1 son, 1 daughter. *Education:* DUEL, Sorbonne Nouvelle, Paris, France, 1971; Oxford University, England, 1972-73; Staatsexamen, 1974, PhD, 1976, Philipps University, Marburg; Doctor of Ministry Degree, Bethany Theological Seminary, 1988. *Publications:* In Search of Refuge, 1984; Peace Be Unto You, 1983; Swords into Plowshares, 1983; Tennessee Williams: A Moralist's Answer to the Perils of Life, 1976; Glimpses of Clima, 1989. *Honours:* Christopher Book Award, 1985, Angel Award of Excellence, 1985, In Search of Refuge; Fellowships from the Evangelische Studienwerk Villigst, 1971-74, 1974-76. *Address:* Manchester College, Box 64, N. Manchester, IN 46962, USA.

ROGERS Jane Rosalind, b. 21 July 1952, London, England. Novelist/Teacher. 1 son, 1 daughter. *Education:* BA Hons, English Literature, New Hall, Cambridge, 1974; Post-graduate Certificate of Education, Leicester University, 1976. *Literary Appointment:* Writer-in-Residence, Northern College, Barnsley, South Yorkshire, 1985-86; Writer-in-Residence, Sheffield Polytechnic, 1987-88; Judith E Wilson Fellow, Cambridge, 1991. *Publications:* Separate Tracks, 1983, 1984; Her Living Image, 1984, 1986; The Ice is Singing, 1987; Mr Wroe's Virgins, 1991; Screenplay: Dawn and the Candidate, 1989; BBC Serial of Mr Wroe's Virgins, 1993. *Contributions to:* Various magazines. *Honours:* North West Arts Writers' Bursary, 1984; Somerset Maugham Award for, Her Living Image, 1985. *Literary Agent:* Pat Kavanagh, The Peter Fraser Dunlop Group Ltd. *Address:* c/o Pat Kavanagh, The Peter Fraser and Dunlop Group Ltd, 5th Floor, The Chambers, Chelsea Harbour, Lots Road, London SW10 0XF, England.

ROGERS Joan Marian (North), b. 15 Feb 1920, Hendon, England, Writer. m. Professor C A Rogers, 2 daughters. *Publications:* Emperor of the Moon, 1956; The Cloud Forest, 1965; The Whirling Shapes, 1968; The Light Maze, 1972. *Contributions to:* Various magazines and journals. *Membership:* Society of Authors. *Address:* 8 Grey Close, London NW11, England.

ROGERS Linda, b. 10 Oct 1944, Port Alice, Canada.

Poet; Teacher. m. Ken Rogers, 11 June 1966, 3 sons. *Education:* MA, English Literature, University of British Columbia. *Appointments:* University of British Columbia, 1970-71; Writers Workshops, National Poets Festival, 1983-84; Creative Writing Design, University of Victoria, 1986-. *Publications:* Queens of the Next Hot Stars, 1981; I Like to Make a Mess, 1985; I Think I am Ugly, 1985; Witness, 1985; Singing Rib, 1987; Setting the Hook, 1986; Worm Sandwich, 1989; Woman at Mile 0, 1990; Children's Magic Flute, 1990; Anthology of BC Poets in French, 1990. *Contributions to:* Editor, Poetry Canada Review; Canadian Literature; Malahat Review; Vancouver Sun; Monday Magazine. *Honours:* Pat Lowther Runner Up, 1982; Cross Canada Writers Poetry Prize, 1986; Seattle Arts Council Poetry Prize, 1987; BC Writers Poetry Prize, 1988; Aya Press Poetry Prize, 1989. *Memberships:* League of Canadian Poets; Writers Union of Canada; Pen; Director, Pacific Opera Association; Vice-President, Federation of BC Writers. *Address:* 228 Douglas St, Victoria, BC, Canada.

ROGERS Michae Alan, b. 29 Nov 1950, Santa Monica, California, USA. Novelist; Journalist. *Education:* BA, Creative Writing, Stanford University, 1972. *Appointments:* Associate Editor, Rolling Stone, 1972-76; Editor-at-Large, Outside, 1976-78; Visiting Lecturer in Fiction, University of California, 1981-82; Senior Writer, Newsweek, 1983-. *Publications:* Mindfogger, 1973; Do Not Worry about the Bear, 1978; Biohazard, 1979; Silicon Valley, 1983; Forbidden Sequence, 1989. *Contributions to:* Esquire; Rolling Stone; Newsweek; Playboy; Look; Outside; Many others. *Honours:* Distinguished Science Writing Award, American Association for the Advancement of Science, 1974; Computer Press Association, 1987; Software Publishers Association, 1991. *Membership:* Authors Guild. *Literary Agent:* Gail Hochman, Brandt and Brandt, New York, USA. *Address:* c/o Newsweek, 388 Market St, Suite 1650, San Francisco, CA 94111, USA.

ROGERS Mick. *See:* **GLUT Don F.**

ROGERS Pat, b. 1938, British. *Appointments:* Fellow, Sidney Sussex College, Cambridge, 1964-69; Lecturer, King's College, University of London, 1969-73; Professor of English, University College of North Wales, Bangor, 1973-76, University of Bristol, 1977-86; DeBartolo Professor in the Liberal Arts, University of South Florida, Tampa, 1986-. *Publications:* A Tour Through Great Britain, by Daniel Defoe (ed), 1971; Grub Street: Studies in a Subculture, 1972, revised edition as Hacks and Dunces, 1980; Defoe: The Critical Heritage (ed), 1972; The Augustan Vision: An Introduction to Pope, 1976; The Eighteenth Century (ed), 1978; Henry Fielding: A Biography, Robinson Crusoe, 1979; Swift: Complete Poems (ed), Literature and Popular Culture in the Eighteenth Century, 1983; Eighteenth-Century Encounters, 1985; The Oxford Illustrated History of English Literature (ed), 1987. *Address:* Department of English, University of South Florida, Tampa, FL 33620, USA.

ROGERS Rosemary (Marina Mayson), b. 7 Dec 1932, Sri Lanka. Writer. m. (1) Summa Navaratnam, 16 Jan 1953, (div). 2 sons, 2 daughters. (2) Leroy Rogers, 1957, (div 1964). (3) Christopher M. Kadison, 1984. *Education:* BA, English, 1952. *Publications:* Sweet Savage Love, 1974; Wildest Heart, 1974; Dark Fires, 1975; Wicked Loving Lies, 1976; The Crowd Pleasers, 1978; The Insiders, 1979; Lost Love, Last Love, 1980; Love Play, 1981; Surrender to Love, 1982; The Wanton, 1984; Bound by Desire, 1988. *Contributions to:* Star Magazine; Good Housekeeping. *Memberships:* Writers Guild of America; Authors Guild. *Literary Agent:* Morton Janklow & Associates Inc. *Address:* 300 East 56th Street, Apt. 27J, New York, NY 10022, USA.

ROGERS Samuel Shepard, (Sam Shepard), b. 1943, American. Actor. *Publications:* Five Plays: Chicago, Icarus's Mother, Red Cross, Fourteen Hundred Thousand, Melodrama Play, 1967; La Turista, 1968; Operation Sidewinder, 1970; The Unseen Hand and

Other Plays, Mad Dog Blues and Other Plays, 1971; Hawk Moon, 1973; The Tooth of Crime and Geography of a Horse Dreamer, 1974; Action and the Unseen Hand, 1975; Angel City and Other Plays, 1976; Rolling Thunder Logbook, 1977, Buried Child and Other Plays, 1979, (in UK as Buried Child and Seduced and Suicide in B Flat, 1980); Four One-Act Plays, 1980; True West, Seven Plays, 1981; Motel Chronicles, 1982; Fool for Love and Other Plays, Paris Texas, 1984; A Lie of the Mind, 1985. *Address:* c/o Loris Berman, Little Theatre Building, 240 West 44th Street, New York, NY 10036, USA.

ROGGEMAN Willem Maurits, b. 9 July 1935, Brussels, Belgium. Journalist. m. 8 Jan 1975, 1 son, 1 daughter. *Education:* Economic sciences, University of Ghent. *Publications:* Poetry: Rhapsody in Blue, 1958; Baudelaire Verliefd, 1964; Memoires, 1985; Een Leegte die Verdwijnt, 1985; Al Wie Omkÿkt is Gezien, 1988. Novels: De Centauren, 1963; De Verbeelding, 1966; De belegering van een Luchtkasteel, 1990. Essays: Cesare Pavese, 1961; Beroepsgeheim, 1975. *Contributions to:* De Vlaamse Gids; Nieuw Vlaams Tijdschrift; Avenue; De Gids. *Honours:* Dirk Martensprize, 1963; Louis Paul Boon Prize, 1974; Prize, City of Brussels, 1975. *Memberships:* Vereniging van Vlaamse Letterkundigen; Secretary, Flemish PEN Centre. *Address:* Albert Heyrbautlaan 48, 1710 Dilbek, Belgium.

ROGOWSKI Ronald Lynn, b. 16 May 1944, Alliance, Nebraska, USA. Professor. *Education:* BA, 1964, University of Nebraska; PhD, Princeton University, 1970. *Publications:* Rational Legitimacy, 1974; Commerce and Coalitions, 1989. *Contributions to:* CSSH; IO; APSR. *Honours:* Franklin Burdette Award, APSA, 1988. *Memberships:* APSA, Council, 1992-93; Vice-President, 1993-. *Address:* Department of Political Science, UCLA, Los Angeles, CA 90024, USA.

ROHEN Edward (Bruton Connors). b. 10 Feb 1931, Dowlais, South Wales, Writer. m. Elizabeth Mary Jarrett, 4 Apr 1961, 1 daughter. *Education:* ATD, Cardiff College of Art, 1952. *Appointments:* served with UN in Korea, 1953-54; Permanently Commissioned Contributor, Twentieth Century Magazine, 1966-68. *Publications:* Nightpriest, 1965; Poems/Poemas, 1976; A Hundred and Nine Haiku and One Seppuku for Maria, 1987; Sonnets for Maria Marriage, 1988; Sonnets Second Sequence for Maria, 1989; Bruised Concourse, 1973; Scorpio Broadside 15, 1975. *Contributions to:* Poetry Anthologies; Poetry Wales; Anglo Welsh Review; Tribune; Irish Press; Mabon; Argot and Edge; Little Word Machine; Second Aeon; Carcanet; Poetry Nippon; Riverside Quarterly; Littack; Wormwood Review. *Memberships:* The Welsh Academy; Ex Member, Poets Society of Japan; Academician of Centro Cultural Literario e Artistico de o journal de Felgeiras, Portugal; Korean War veterans Club and Society. *Address:* 57 Kinfauns Road, Goodmayes, Ilford, Essex IG3 9QH, England.

ROHRBACH Peter Thomas (James Cody), b. 27 Feb 1926, New York City, USA. Writer. m. Sheila Sheehan, 21 Sept 1970, 1 daughter. *Education:* BA, MA, Catholic University of America. *Publications:* 16 books including: Conversation with Christ, 1981; Stagecoach East, 1983; American Issue, 1985; The Largest Event: World War II, 1993. *Contributions to:* Time-Life; Washington Star; America; Aviation News; PAMA News; AIA Journal; Various encyclopaedias. *Memberships:* Authors Guild of America; Poets, Playwrights, Editors, Essayists & Novelists; Washington Independent Writers. *Address:* 9609 Barkston Court, Potomac, Maryland 20850, USA.

ROLA Waclaw. *See:* **SADKOWSKI Waclaw.**

ROLAND Alex, b. 7 Apr 1944, Providence, Rhode Island, USA. Historian. m. 31 June 1979, 3 sons. *Education:* BS, US Naval Academy, 1966; MA, University of Hawaii, 1970; PhD, Duke University, 1974. *Publications:* Model Research: The National Advisory Committee for Aeronautics, 1985; Men in Arms: A

History of Warfare and its Interrelationships with Western Society, 1991; Underwater Warfare in the Age of Sail, 1978; Editor, A Spacefaring People: Perspectives on Early Spaceflight, 1985. *Contributions to:* Osiris; Science and Technology and Human Values; Journal of Military History. *Memberships:* Society for the History of Technology, Secretary, 1984-89; History of Science Society; Society for Military History; American Historical Association. *Address:* Department of History, Duke University, Durham, NC 27708, USA.

ROLICKI Janusz Andrzej, b. 22 Oct 1938, Wilno, Poland. Journalist; Writer. m. Ewa Stasko, 11 July 1976, 1 daughter. *Education:* MA, Warsaw University, 1962. *Appointments:* Staff, Polityka, 1961-67; Staff, Kultura, 1967-74. *Publications:* Bralem lapowki, 1966; Z syciem pod pache, 1968; Przodem do przodu, 1972; Kochana mamo wyroh mi alibi, 1976; Nie tylko bralem, 1978; Dygnitarz, 1982; adaptations for films and TV. *Contributions to:* Numerous journals and magazines. *Honours:* Boleslaw Prus Award, 1977; Drozdze Award, 1978. *Membership:* Union of Polish Writers. *Address:* Warszawa Dzika 6m 74, 00-172, Warsaw, Poland.

ROLLS Eric Charles, b. 25 Apr 1923, Grenfell, New South Wales, Australia. Author; Farmer. m. (1) Joan Stephenson, 27 Feb 1954, (dec 1985) 2 sons, 1 daughter, (2) Elaine van Kempen, 1988. *Publications:* Sheaf Tosser, 1967; They All Ran Wild, 1969; Running Wild, 1973; The River, 1974; The Green Mosaic, 1977; Miss Strawberry Verses, 1978; A Million Wild Acres, 1981; Celebration of The Senses, 1984; Doorways: A Year of the Cumberdeen Diaries, 1989; Selected Poetry, 1990; Sojourners: Flowers And The Wide Sea, 1992. *Contributions to:* The Bulletin; Overland; National Times; The Age; Sydney Morning Herald; various others *Honours include:* David Myer Trust Award for Poetry, 1968; Captain Cook Bicentennial Award for Non-Fiction, 1970; John Franklin Award, for Children's Book, 1974; Braille Book of the Year, 1975; The Age Book of the Year, 1981; Talking Book of the Year, 1982; Fellow, Australian Academy of the Humanities, 1985; Australian Creative Fellow, 1991; Member of the Order of Australia, 1991. *Memberships:* Australian Society of Authors; National Book Council. *Literary Agent:* Anthony A Williams Management Pty Ltd. 26 Cardigan Street, Stanmore, NSW 2048, Australia.

ROLOFF Michael, b. 19 Dec 1937, Berlin, Germany, US citizen, 1952-. Playwright. *Education:* BA, Haverford College, USA, 1958; MA, Stanford University, 1960. *Appointments include:* Editor, Farrar, Straus & Giroux, New York City, 1966-70; Staff, Lantz-Donadio Literary Agency, 1970-72; Senior Editor, Continuum Books, 1972-75; Publicity Manager, Urizen Books, 1975-81. *Publications:* Screenplays: Feelings, 1982; Darlings & Monsters, 1983; Graduation Party, 1984. Plays: Wolves of Wyoming, 1985; Palombe Blue, 1985; Schizzohawk, 1986. Poetry: Headshots, 1984; It Won't Grow Back, 1985. Fiction: Darlings & Monsters Quartet, 4 titles 1986-. Also numerous translations from German. *Memberships:* Executive Committee 1977-81, PEN. *Literary Agent:* Rosica Colin Ltd. *Address:* Box 6754, Malibu, California 90264, USA.

ROMANIAK Stanislaw Antoni, b. 8 May 1948, Poland. Sculptor; Writer. m. 20 June 1967, 1 daughter. *Publications:* Open Doors You Should Close, 1982; On the Crossroads, 1985; Letters to Monica, 1987; Prayerbook, 1988. *Contributions to:* Poezja; Nowy wyraz; Tygodnik Kulturalny; Odglosy. *Memberships:* Polish Writers Society; Writers Club; National Cultural Society. *Address:* ul. Nowobielanska 19, 96 100 Skierniewice, Poland.

ROMBOTIS Anastasios, (Tasos Korfis), b. 12 Oct 1929, Corfu, Greece. Vice-Admiral (retired). m. Helen Moniakis, 5 Feb 1959, 1 son, 1 daughter. *Education:* Various professional schools and academies, Hellenic War Navy, Greece and in USA; NATO Defence College, Rome, 1979-71. *Appointments:* Director, Prosperos book publishers, 1973-; Director, Anacyclisis literary magazine, 1985-90. *Publications:* Poetry: Diary I, 1963; Diary 2, 1964; Diary 3, 1968; Diarios, 1971; Handiwork, 1977; Poems, collection, 1983; Pafsi Pipa, 1987; 153 Graffiti, 1992; Prose: Journey without Polar Star, 1953; A desert house, 1973, 1978; Knowledge of the father, 1984; Essays: The poet Romos Filyras, 1974, 1992; The poet Nikos Kavadias, 1978, 1991; Glances at the poets 1920-1940, 1978; Deposits in short terms, 1982; The poet Napoleon Lapathiotis, 1985; Glances at the literature 1920-1940, 1991; Translations: Lustra (Ezra Pound), 1977; Poems (William Carlos Williams), 1979, 1989; Poems (Ezra Pound), 1981, 1987; Coexistences, 1982; The writer Stratis Doukas 1895-1936, biography, 1988. *Contributions to:* Frequently to Diagenios, 1958-80; Numerous poems, prose pieces, essays to notable magazines, Athens and other cities. *Honours:* 1st Efstathiou Award for Journey without Pole Star, The Cyprian Potters, 1952; 1st Award for The poet Nikos Kavadias, Ministry of Shipping, 1973; 2nd State Prose Award for Knowledge of the fathers, 1984. *Membership:* Society of Writers. *Address:* Alkiviadou 9, 10439 Athens, Greece.

ROME Anthony. *See:* **ALBERT Marvin H.**

ROME Tony. *See:* **ALBERT Marvin H.**

ROMER Stephen Charles Mark, b. 20 Aug 1957, Bishops Stortford, Herts, England. University Lecturer. m. Bridget Strevens, 17 July 1982, 1 son. *Education:* Radley College, 1970-74; Trinity Hall, Cambridge, English Tripos: Double First, 1975-78; Harvard University, 1978-79; British Institute, Paris, 1980-81; PhD, Cantab, May 1985. *Publications:* Idols, 1986; Plato's Ladder, 1992; The Growing Dark, 1981; Firebird 3, 1985. *Contributions to:* TLS; PN Rreview; Cambridge Quarterly; Poetry Review; New Statesman; Poetry Book Soc. Anthology, 1986, 1992; Stand, Oxford Poetry. *Honours:* Gregory Award for Poetry, 1985. *Address:* 6 rue de Verneuil, 75007 Paris, France.

ROMEU Jorge Luis, (Beltran de Quiros), b. 10 Dec 1945, Havana, Cuba. Educator; Writer. m. Zoila Barreiro, 25 July 1970, 3 sons. *Education:* Diplomas: Language, 1964, Literature, 1966, Teaching, 1970, Alliance Francaise de La Havane; Licenciado en Matematicas, University of Havana, 1973; MS, 1981, MPh, 1987, PhD, 1990, Syracuse University, USA. *Appointments:* Editor, Club Las Palmas Newsletter; Member, Collaborators Group, El Vecino, Rochester, New York; Member, Collaborators Group, AIC Newsletter, Miami, Florida; Monthly Column, Syracuse Post Standard; Radio Commentator, WAER-FM, Syracuse University Public Radio Station; Associate Professor of Statistics, State University of New York, Cortland. *Publications:* Los Unos, Los Otros y El Seibo, 1971; La Otra Cara de la Moneda, 1984; Thinking of Cuba, collection of 28 published Oped pieces on Castro's dictatorship and Latin American problems, 1992. *Contributions to:* Over 20 technical articles to statistics and engineering journals, USA, UK, Spain, Cuba; Over 70 articles, 1988-, to: Herald-American; El Nuevo Herald; The Post Standard; The Press; Cortland Standard; El Vecino; Diario Montanes; Correo Gallego. *Honours:* Mentioned as 1 of the best exiled Cuban short story writers in Seymour Menton's book Prose Fiction of the Cuban Revolution, 1975; Fulbright Scholar, 1993; Dr Nuala McGann Yearly Award, State University of New York-UUP. *Memberships:* Poets and Writers, New York; Club Las Palmas, Syracuse; Founder, Past President, Newsletter Editor; Human Rights Committee Member, American Statistical Association; Association of Cuban Engineers, Newsletter Publishing Group; Fellow, Royal Ststistical Society, UK; Operations Research Society of America; Association of Cuban-American Educators, Human Rights Committee; Activist, Of Human Rights, Washington, DC. *Address:* PO Box 6134, Syracuse, NY 13217, USA.

ROMTVEDT David William, b. 7 June 1950, Oregon, USA. Writer. m. Margo Brown, 30 May 1987. *Education:* BA, Reed College, 1972. *Appointment:* State Literature

Consultant, Wyoming, 1987. *Publications:* How Many Horses, 1988; Free and Compulsory for All, 1984; Moon, 1984; Letters from Mexico, 1987; Black Beauty and Kiev the Ukraine, 1987; Crossing the River, Poets of the Western US, 1987; A Flower Whose Name I Do Not Know, 1992; Crossing Wyoming, 1992. *Contributor to:* Paris Review; Canadian Forum; American Poetry Review; Poets and Writers Magazine. *Honours:* NEA Residency Award, 1979; NEA Fellowship, Poetry, 1987; Pushcart Prize, 1991; National Poetry Series Award, 1991. *Address:* 457 N Main, Buffalo, WY 82834, USA.

RONAY Egon, b. Pozsony, Hungary. Publisher; Journalist. m. Barbara Greenslade, 1967, 1 son (2 daughters by previous marriage). *Education:* LL.D., University of Budapest; Academy of Commerce, Budapest. *Appointments:* Trained in kitchens of family catering firm and abroad; managed 5 restaurants within family firm; emigrated from Hungary 1946; General Manager, 3 restaurants in London before opening own restaurant, The Marquee, 1952-55; Gastronomic and Good Living Columnist, Sunday Times, weekly Columnist, Eating Out, Food, Wine and Tourism, Daily Telegraph and later Sunday Telegraph, 1954-60; weekly column, The Evening News, 1968-74; Food Columnist, The Sunday Times, 1986-1991. *Publications:* Egon Ronay's Guide to Hotels and Restaurants, annually, 1956-; Egon Ronay's Just A Bite, annually, 1979-85; Egon Ronay's Pub Guide, annually, 1980-85; Egon Ronay's Guide to 500 Good Restaurants in Europe's main cities, annually, 1983-85; The Unforgettable Dishes of My Life, 1989; various other tourist guides to Britain, to ski resorts in Europe, to Scandinavian Hotels and Restaurants and to eating places in Greece. *Membership:* Academy des Gastronomes, France, 1979; Founder, President, The British Academy of Gastronomes, 1983-. *Address:* 37 Walton Street, London SW3 2HT, England.

RONDINI Adele, b. 30 Jan 1921, Italy. Headmaster, Secondary School (Retired). m. 1 Dec 1951, 2 sons. *Education:* Degree in arts; Postgraduate Qualifications in arts and French. *Appointments:* various positions, 1965-. *Publications:* Le Journal De Jean Pierre; Rimpianto a Due Voci, 1972; Fosombron Sparita, 1969; Fosombron Spareta, 1970; La tombola Di Papa (Latino), Editor, 1983. *Contributions to:* varius journals and magazines. *Honours:* Picchio d'Argento delle Monde, Rome, for Poetry, 1970; Accademia Tiberina, Roma Caripodoglio, for Poetry, 1968; 1st Prize, Poetry, G. Pascoli, 1979. *Memberships:* President, AMES, 1981-; President, Fondaz. Artistica Monassi, 1981-; President, Le Rondini Cultural Club, 1987-; Vice President, Le Migliori Mondo, Rome; Public Relations, CIAS, Rome. *Address:* Via Mondragone u/12, 00179 Rome, Italy.

ROOKE Constance, b. 14 Nov 1942, New York, New York, USA. Professor of English; Writer. m. Leon Rooke, 25 May 1969, 1 son. *Education:* BA Smith Collehe, 1964; MA, Tulane University 1966; PhD 1973, University of North Carolina at Chapel Hill. *Appointments:* Lecturer 1969-73, Assistant Professor 1973-77, Associate Professor 1977- 88, Professor of English 1988-, Director of Learning and Teaching Centre, University of Victoria, Victoria, British Columbia, Canada; Member of Canada Council's Advisory Panel on Writing and Publication. *Publications:* Reynolds Price, 1983; (ed)Night Light: Stories of Aging, 1986; Editor of Malahat Review 1983-. *Membership:* Canadian Periodical Publishers Association (member of board of directors 1986-), *Address:* Malahat Review, University of Victoria, Victoria, British Columbia, Canada V8W 2Y2.

ROOKE Daphne Marie, b. 6 Mar 1914, Boksburg, South Africa. Novelist. m. 1 June 1937, 1 daughter. *Publications:* Novels: A Grove of Fever Trees, 1950, reprint 1989; Mittee, 1951, reprint 1991; Ratoons, 1953, reprint 1990; Wizards' Country, 1957; Beti, 1959; A Lover for Estelle, 1961; The Greyling; Diamond Jo; Boy on the Mountain; Margaretha De La Porte; Juvenile books: A Horse of His Own; Double Ex. *Contributions to:* John Bull; Woman (Sydney). *Honours:* 1st Prize, APB

Novel Competition, 1946. *Address:* 54 Regatta Court, Oyster Row, Cambridge CB5 8NS, England.

ROOKE Leon, b. 11 Sept 1934, North Carolina, USA. Author. *Appointments:* Writer in Residence, University of North Carolina, 1965-66, University of Victoria, 1972-73, University of Southwest Minnesota, 1974-75; Visiting Professor, University of Victoria, 1980-81; Writer in Residence, University of Toronto, 1984-85; University of Western Ontario, 1990-91; Short-term Residencies - University of Winnipeg, University of Lethbridge, University of Toronto. *Publications:* Novels: Last One Home Sleeps in the Yellow Bed, 1968; Vault, 1974; The Broad Back of the Angel, 1977; The Love Parlour, 1977; Fat Woman, 1980; The Magician in Love, 1980; Death Suite, 1982; The Birth Control King of the Upper Volta, 1983; Shakespeare's Dog, 1983; Sing Me No Long Songs I'll Say You No Prayers, 1984; A Bolt of White Cloth, 1984; How I Saved The Province, 1990; The Happiness of Others, 1991; A Good Baby, 1991; Who Do You Love? 1992. Stage Plays: A Good Baby, 1991; The Coming, 1991; 4 others. *Contributions to:* Approximately 300 short stories in leading North American journals. *Honours:* Canada/Australia Literary Prize, 1981; Best Paperback Novel of the Year (Fat Woman), 1981; Governor General's Award (Shakespeare's Dog), 1984; Numerous short story prizes and awards; North Carolina Award for Literature, 1990. *Memberships:* PEN; Writers' Union of Canada. *Literary Agent:* Liz Darhansoff. *Address:* General Delivery, Eden Mills, Ontario, Canada, N0B 1PO.

ROOM Adrian Richard West, b. 27 Sept 1933, Melksham, England. Writer. *Education:* Honours Degree, Russian, University of Oxford, England, 1957; Diploma, Education, University of Oxford, 1958. *Major Publications include:* Place-Names of the World, 1974; Great Britain: A Background Studies English-Russian Dictionary (Russian Language), 1978; Room's Dictionary of Confusibles, 1979; Place-Name Changes since 1900, 1980; Naming Names, 1981; Room's Dictionary of Distinguishables, 1981; Dictionary of Trade Name Origins, 1982; Room's Classical Dictionary, 1983; Dictionary of Cryptic Crossword Clues, 1983; A Concise Dictionary of Modern Place-Names in Great Britain and Ireland, 1983; Guide to British Place-Names, 1985; Dictionary of Coin Names, 1987 Dictionary of Astronomical Names, 1988; Guinness Book of Numbers, 1989; Dictionary of Dedications, 1990; A Name for Your Baby, 1992; The Street Names of England, 1992; Brewer's Dictionary of Names, 1992; Corporate Eponymy, 1992; Place-Name Changes 1900-91, 1993; A Dictionary of First Names, 1993; The Naming of Animals, 1993. *Contributions to:* magazines and journals. *Memberships:* Fellow, Royal Geographical Society; Society of Authors; English Place-Name Society; American Name Society; Translators Association; Association for Language Learning; Britain-Russia Centre. *Address:* 12 High Street, St Martin's, Stamford, Lincolnshire, PE9 2LF, England.

ROONEY Lucy, b. 13 July 1926, Liverpool, England. Former Lecturer; Religious Sister of Notre Dame De Namur. *Education:* Teaching Certificate, Universities of Manchester and Liverpool; City and Guilds Advanced Handloom Weaver, 1965. *Publications:* Co-author: Mary Queen of Peace, 1984; Medjugorje Unfolds, 1986; Medjugorje Journal, 1987; Medjugorje Retreat, 1989; The Contemplative Way of Prayer, 1986; Lord Jesus Teach Me To Pray, 88; Our Lady Comes to Scottsdale, 1992. *Contributions to:* Religious journals. *Address:* 52 Warriner Gardens, London SW11 4DU, England.

ROOSE-EVANS James Humphrey, b. 11 Nov 1927. Theatre Director; Author. *Education:* MA Oxon; Ordained to the non-stipendiary priesthood of the Anglican Church 1981, (continues to earn his living as a West End theatre director and author). *Appointments:* Founded the Hampstead Theatre, 1959. Productions in the West End include: Dylan Thomas's Under Milk Wood; Oscar Wilde's An Ideal Husband; Laurie Lee's Cider With Rosie (adapted by J Roose-Evans); Noel Coward's Private Lives; Colin Spencer's Spitting Image; Jack Pulman's The Happy Apple; George Axelrod's The Seven Year Itch; Ian Curteis' A Personal Affair; 84 Charing Cross Road (adapted by J Roose-Evans from book by Helene Hanff); Hugh Whitemore's The Best of Friends; Vaclav Havel's Temptation. Founder and Artistic Director, The Bleddea Trust - Centre for Caring and the Experimental Theatre-Arts in Mid-Wales; Distinguished Visiting Fellow Ohio State University; Gian Carlo Menotti Artist-in-Residence, Charleston College, South Carolina. *Publications:* Inner Journey. Outer Journey (Rider) in America published by The Cowley Press under the title The Inner Stage; Darling Ma, letters of Joyce Grenfell, edited by J Roose-Evans, 1988; The Time of My Life, war memoirs of Joyce Grenfell, edited by J Roose-Evans, 1989; 84 Charing Cross Road, play adapted by J Roose-Evans from book by Helene Hanff; Seven children's books - a complete saga - The Adventures of Odd and Elsewhere (Andre Deutsch Ltd); London Theatre (Phaidon); Directing a Play (Studio Vista); Author: A Surprising Hunger; A Pride of Players, 1993; Play: RE:JOYCE!, an entertainment about Joyce Grenfell, for Maureen Lipman; Directed 1992 revival of Christopher Fry's Venus Observed, Chicester Festival Theatre. *Contributions to:* Reviews for Financial Times; Hampstead and Highgate Express; The Tablet. For two years wrote weekly column for Woman, entitled Something Extra; Author of a number of documentaries for BBC; Featured on television and radio. *Honours:* Nomination as Best Director of 1981 by Society of West End Theatre Managers for production of 84 Charing Cross Road; In New York received awards for Best Director and Best Play for 84, Charing Cross Road. *Membership:* The Garrick Club; The Dramatists Club. *Literary Agent:* David Higham and Associates, 5-8 Lower John Street, Godden Square, London W1. *Address:* c/o David Higham and Associates, 5-8 Lower John Street, Godden Square, London W1.

ROOT William Pitt, b. 28 Dec 1941, Austin, Minnesota, USA. Poet; Professor. m. Pamela Uschuk, 6 Nov 1988, 1 daughter. *Education:* BA, University of Washington, 1964; MFA, University of North Carolina, Greensboro, 1966; Stegman Fellow, Stanford University, 1967-68. *Appointments:* Assistant Professor, Michigan State University, 1967-68; Visiting Writer-in-Residence: University of Southwest Louisiana, 1976, Amherst College 1971, University of Montana 1978, 1980, 1982-85, Wichita State University 1976, Pacific Lutheran University 1990, Professor, Hunter College 1986-. *Publications:* Selected Odes of Pablo Nerudd, 1991; Fault Dancing, 1986; Invisible Guests, 1984; Reasons for Going It On Foot, 1981; In the World's Common Grasses, 1981; Striking the Dark Air for Music, 1973; The Storm and Other Poems, 1969; A Journey South, 1977. *Contributions to:* The Atlantic; Nation; Harpers; Poetry; New Yorker; APR; Poetry East; Triquarterly; Commonwealth. *Honours:* Academy of American Poets Prize, 1967; Borestone Mt Best Poems of the Year, 1974; Stanley Kumitz Poetry Award, 1981; Guy Owen Poetry Award, 1984; Pushcart Awards, 1977, 1980, 1985; Grants from Rockefeller 1969-70, Guggenheim 1970-71, NEA 1973-74, US/UK Exchange Artist 1978-79. *Address:* English Department, Hunter College, 695 Park Avenue, New York City, NY 10021, USA.

ROPER David, b. 30 Nov 1954, Hessle, Yorkshire, England. Critic. *Education:* MA, AKC, King's College, London. *Appointments:* Editor, Square One, 1978; Editor of, Gambit, 1978-85; Joint Editor, Platform, 1981-82; Drama Editor, Event, 1981-82; Assistant Theatre Critic, The Guardian, 1981-82; Theatre Critic, Daily Express, 1982-87; Editor, Plays and Players, 1983-84; Arts Correspondent, BBC 1987-90; Channel 4 TV, 1990-93. *Publications:* The Pineapple Dance Book, 1983; Forthcoming, The Biography of Lionel Bart. *Contributions to:* Tatler; Event; Time Out; Sunday Telegraph; Sunday Express; She. *Literary Agent:* David Higham Associates, London. *Address:* 24a Pavilion Terrace, Wood Lane, London W12, England.

ROSCA Ninotchka, b. Philippines. Writer. *Education:* AB Comparative Literature, University of the Philippines;

Graduate Studies in Khmer Civilization. *Publications:* Novels: Twice Blessed, 1992, State of War, 1988; Short Stories: Monsoon Collection, 1982, Bitter Country, 1972. *Honours:* New York Foundation for the Arts Fiction Fellowship, 1986; NYFA Fiction Fellowship, 1991. *Memberships:* Board of Directors: Pen International Women's Committee, and, Pen American Center. *Literary Agent:* Sterling Lord Literistic. *Address:* c/o Sterling Lord Literistic 1 Madison Avenue, NY 10010, USA.

ROSE Andrew Wyness, b. 11 Feb 1944, Headingley, Leeds, England. Barrister. *Education:* Trinity College, Cambridge, 1963-67; MA; LLM; Called to Bar, Gray's Inn, London, 1968. *Appointments:* Barrister, 1968-88. *Publications:* Stinie: Murder on the Common, 1985; Scandal at the Savoy, 1991. *Honours:* Shortlisted, Golden Dagger Award for Non-Fiction, Crime Writers Association, 1986. *Memberships:* Society of Authors; Crime Writers Association. *Literary Agent:* Gregory and Radice Authors Agents, London, England. *Address:* c/o Gregory and Radice Authors Agents, Riverside Studios, Crisp Road, Hammersmith, Londn W6 9RL, England.

ROSE Daniel Asa, b. 20 Nov 1949, New York City, USA. Writer. m. Laura Love, 30 Nov 1974, div. 2 sons. *Education:* AB, English, Honours, Brown University, 1971. *Appointments:* Travel Columnist, Esquire; Travel Editor, Dimension. *Publications:* Flipping for it, 1987; Small Family with Rooster, 1988; Various Screenplays, poems, stories, reviews and literary essays. *Contributions to:* Esquire; New York Times; LA Times; Partisan Review; The New Yorker; Vanity Fair; Conde Nast Traveller; North American Review; Southern Review. *Honours:* PEN Literary Award, 1987, 1988; O. Henry Prize, 1980. *Address:* 138 Bay State Road, Renoboth, MA 02769, USA.

ROSE Joel Steven, b. 1 Mar 1948, Los Angeles, California, USA. Writer. m. Catherine Texier, 2 daughters. *Education:* BA, Hobart College, 1970; MFA, Columbia University. *Publications:* Kill the Poor, novel, 1988; Between C & D, Co-editor, 1988; Love Is Strange, co-editor, 1993. *Contributions to:* New York Times; New York Newsday; Bomb; New Observations; Confrontation; Between C & D; Autremont. *Honours:* NEA Award, Fiction Writing, 1986; New York State Council on the Arts, 1986-87. *Memberships:* Poets and Writers; Co-ordinating Council of Literary Magazines; Writers Guild of America. *Literary Agent:* Michael Carlisle, William Morris Agency. *Address:* 255 East 7 Street, New York, NY 10009, USA.

ROSE Kenneth Vivian, b. 15 Nov 1924. Writer. *Education:* Repton School; Scholar, MA, New College, Oxford. *Appointments:* Assistant Master, Eton College, 1948; Editorial Staff, Daily Telegraph, 1952-60; Founder, Writer, Albany Column, Sunday Telegraph, 1961-. *Publications:* Superior Person: a Portrait of Curzon and His Circle in Late Victorian England, 1969; The Later Cecils, 1975; William Harvey: a Monograph, 1978; King George V, 1983; Kings, Queens and Courtiers: Intimate Portraits of the Royal House of Windsor, 1985. *Contributions to:* Dictionary of National Biography. *Honours:* Fellow of the Royal Society of Literature, 1976; Wolfson Award for History, 1983; Whitbread Award for Biography, 1983; Yorkshire Post Biography of the Year Award, 1984. *Address:* 38 Brunswick Gardens, London, W8 4AL, England.

ROSE Mitchell S, b. 22 Nov 1951, Pennsylvania. Literary Agent; Editor. *Education:* BA, Bard College, 1974; MFA, Goddard College, 1980. *Appointments:* Freelance Writer, 1975-80; Editor and Managing Editor for trade magazines, 1980-83; Editor, New American Library, 1983-86; Literary Agent and Editor, 1986-. *Publications:* The Victorian Fairy Tale Book, 1988; The Wizard of OZ: The Official Pictorial History, 1989; Gone With the Wind: The Definitive Illustrated History, 1989; At Dawn we Slept, 1991; Harper Dictionary of American Government and Politics, 1992; Lawrence of Arabia, 1992; Judy Garland, 1992; Healing through Nutrition, 1993; The Film Encyclopaedia, 1990; Kennedy as President, 1993; Dr Deming, 1990. *Contributions to:* Boston Phoenix. *Memberships:* Author's Guild. *Address:* The Mitchell S Rose Literary Agency, 688 Avenue of the Americas, NY, NY 10010, USA.

ROSE Richard, b. 9 Apr 1933, St Louis, Missouri, USA. Professor of Public Policy & Director, Centre for Study of Public Policy, University of Strathclyde, England. m. Rosemary J. Kenny, 14 Apr 1956, 2 sons, 1 daughter. *Education:* BA, Johns Hopkins University, USA; DPhil, Oxford University, England, 1960. *Appointments include:* Editor, Journal of Public Policy, 1985-. *Publications include:* Politics in England, 1964, 5th edition 1989; Governing Without Consensus: Irish Perspective, 1971; Electoral Behaviour, 1974; International Almanac of Electoral History, with T.T. Mackie, 1972, 1982, 1991; Problem of Party Government, 1974; Managing Presidential Objectives, 1976; Can Government Go Bankrupt?, with B.G. Peters, 1978; Do Parties Make a Difference?, 1980, 1984; Presidents & Prime Ministers, co-editor, 1980; Understanding the United Kingdom, 1982; Understanding Big Government, 1984; Nationwide Competition for Votes, 1984; Public Employment in Western Nations, 1985; Voters Begin to Choose, with d. McAllister, 1986; Ministers & Ministries, 1987; Taxation by Political Inertia, 1987; The Post Modern President, 1988; Ordinary People in Public Policy, 1989; The Loyalty of Voters (with d McAllister), 1990; Lesson Drawing in Public Policy, 1993. *Contributions to:* Times; Telegraph; New Society; Economist; Various TV stations. *Honours:* Guggenheim Fellowship, 1974; Fellow, Woodrow Wilson International Centre, Washington DC, USA, 1974; Japan Foundation Fellow, 1984; Fellow, British Academy, 1992; Honorary Foreign Member, Finnish Academy of Arts & Sciences. *Address:* CSPP, University of Strathclyde, Glasgow G1 1XH, Scotland.

ROSEN Michael Wayne (Landgrave of Hesse), b. 7 May 1946, Harrow, England. Writer; Performer. m. 30 Nov 1987, 3 sons, 2 stepdaughters. *Education:* Middlesex Hospital Medical School, 1964-65; Wadham College, Oxford, 1965- 69; National Film School, 1973-76. *Appointments:* Writer-in-Residence: Vauxhall Manor Comprehensive School, 1976-77; London Borough of Brent, 1983- 84; John Scurr Primary School, 1984-87, 1988-90; Western Australian College of Advanced Education, 1987. *Publications:* Mind Your Own Business, 1974; Quick Let's Get Out Of Here, 1983; Don't Put the Mustard in the Custard, 1984; The Kingfisher Book of Poetry, 1984; The Hypnotiser, 1988; We're Going on a Bear Hunt, 1989; You Can't Catch Me; Nasty; You're Thinking about Doughnuts; The Class 2 Monster; The Wicked Tricks of Till Owlyglass; Spollyolly Diddly Tiddlyitis. *Contributions to:* New Statesman; The Guardian; Times Educational Supplement; Jewish Socialist. *Honours:* Signal Poetry Award, 1982; The Other Award, 1984; Smarties Award, 1989. *Memberships:* Equity. *Literary Agent:* The Peters, Fraser and Dunlop Group Ltd, England. *Address:* The Peters Fraser and Dunlop Group Ltd, 5th Floor, The Chambers, Chelsea Harbour, Lots Road, London SW10 0XF, England.

ROSEN Norma, b. New York City, New York, USA. Writer. m. Robert S Eosen, 1960, 1 son, 1 daughter. *Education:* BA, Mt Holyoke College, 1946; MA, Columbia University, 1953. *Appointments:* Teacher, Creative Writing: New School, New York, 1965-69 University of Pennsylvania, 1969; Harvard University, 1971; Yale University, 1984; New York Univcersity, 1987-. *Publications:* Fiction: Joy to Levine!, 1962; Green, 1967; Touching Evil, 1969; At the Center, 1982; John and Anzia: An American Romance, 1989; Accidents of Influence: Writing as a Woman and a Jew in America, essays, 1992. *Contributions to:* Many. *Honours:* Saxton, 1960; CAPS, 1976; Bunting, 1971-73. *Memberships:* PEN; Authors Guild; Phi Beta Kappa. *Literary Agent:* Gloria Loomis. *Address:* 11 Mereland Rd, New Rochelle, NY 10804, USA.

ROSENBERG Bruce Alan, b. 27 July 1934, New York City, USA. Teacher; Writer. m. Ann Harleman, 20 June 1981, 3 sons. *Education:* BA, Hofstra University, 1955; MA, Pennsylvania State University, 1960; PhD, Ohio State University, 1965. *Publications:* The Art of the American Folk Preacher, 1970; Custer and the Epic of Defeat, 1975; The Spy Story, 1987; Ian Fleming, 1989; Can These Bones Live?, 1988; The Code of the West, 1982. *Contributions to:* Over 60 professional journals. *Honours:* James Russell Lowell Prize, 1970; Chicago Folklore Prize 1970, 1975. *Memberships:* Folklore Fellows International. *Address:* 55 Summit Avenue, Providence, RI 02906, USA.

ROSENBERG Liz, b. 3 Feb 1957, Glen Cove, New York, USA. Associate Professor of English. m. (1) John Gardner, 14 Feb 1982, (2) David Bosnick, 8 Dec 1985, 1 son. *Education:* BA, Bennington College; MA, Johns Hopkins University. *Appointments:* Amanuensis for Ved Mehta, The New York, 1977. *Publications:* Poetry: The Fire Music, 1986; Children of Pardin, 1993; Children's books: Adelaide and the Night Train, 1989; Window, Mirror Man, 1990; The Scrap Doll, 1991; Monster Mama, 1993. *Contributions to:* The New York Times; The New Yorker; The Nation; Southern Review; Poetry; Others. *Honours:* Atlantic 1st Award, 1976; Pennsylvania Council of the Arts Award, 1982; National Kelloggs Fellowship, 1982-85; Agnes Starrett Poetry Prize, 1985. *Memberships:* Association of Writers and Poets; Poets and Writers. *Address:* c/o English Department, State University of New York at Binghamton, Binghamton, NY 13902, USA.

ROSENBERG Peter Michael, b. 11 July 1958, London, England. Freelance Writer. *Education:* BSc Class 2 (ii), Applied Sciences with Social Sciences, University of Sussex, 1979. *Publications:* Novels: The Usurper (co-author), 1988; Kissing Through a Pane of Glass, 1993. *Contributions to:* Wanna Come Back To My Place, comic fiction, to Jennings Magazine, 1987; Travel articles, book reviews, 1987-91, to: Literary Review; The Adventurer; Girl About Town; Midweek; LAW Magazine; Nine to Five; TNT Magazine; Trailfinders; New Zealand News; Poetry to PEN New Poetry II; The Insufferable Being Of Lightness, New York Diary, Sharon's Secret, On Reflection, The Black Envelope, to Radio LBC, 1986-87. *Honours:* 2nd Prize, Betty Trask Award, 1992. *Literary Agent:* Christopher Little, 49 Queen Victoria Street, London EC4N 4SA, England. *Address:* 430 St Ann's Road, London N15 3JJ, England.

ROSENBLUM Martin Jack, b. 19 Aug 1946, Appleton, Wisconsin, USA. Academic Advisor; Admissions Specialist. m. Maureen Rice, 6 Sept 1970, 2 daughters. *Education:* BS, English, 1969, MA, English, 1971, PhD, Modern American Poetry, 1980, University of Wisconsin. *Appointments:* Guest Lecturer, University of East Anglia, Norwich, England, 1975; Poetry Contest Judge, University of Wisconsin, Oshkosh, 1979; Poet-in-Residence, Wisconsin Review, University of Wisconsin, Oshkosh, 1987. *Publications:* Home, 1971; On, 1972; The Werewolf Sequence, 1974; Brite Shade, 1984; Conjunction, 1987; Scattered On: Omens & Curses, 2nd edition 1987; Stone Fog, 1987; Burning Oak, 1987; Geographics, 1987; Music Lingo, 1987; Backlit Frontier, 1987; Harley-Davidson Poems, 1988; The Holy Ranger: Harley-Davidson Poems, 1989; American Outlaw Visionary, 1989; I Am The Holy Ranger, A Collection of Poems and Songs on Cassette, 1989; The Holy Ranger's Free Hand, an album of songs on CD and Cassette, 1990. *Contributions to:* Wisconsin Review; Journal of American Culture; Road Apple Review; Images; others. *Honours:* Recipient, numerous honours and awards. *Memberships:* National Rifle Association; Colt Collectors Association; Harley Owner's Group; Triumph Motorcycle Club of America. *Address:* 2521 East Stratford Court, Shorewood, WI 53211, USA.

ROSENFELD Albert Hyman, b. 31 May 1920, Philadelphia, USA. Science Writer. m. 24 Aug 1948, 1 son, 1 daughter. *Education:* BA, History & Social Science, New Mexico State University. *Appointments* include: Associate Editor, 1956-58, Senior Science Editor, 1958-60, Life; Managing Editor, Family Health 1969-71; Senior Science Editor, Saturday Review, 1973-80; Contributing Editor, Geo 1979-81, Science Digest 1980-82. *Publications include:* The Quintessence of Irving langmui, 1962; The Second Genesis: The Coming Control of Life, 1969; Prolongevity, 1976; Mind & Supermind, Editor, 1977; Science, Invention & Social Change, Editor, 1978; Responsble Parenthood, with G.W. Kliman, 1980; Prolongevity II, 1985. *Contributions to:* Life; Time; Fortune; Sports Illustrated; McCall's Redbook; Harper's; Readers Digest; Think; Saturday Review; Better Homes & Gardens; Physicians World; Horizon; Geo; Prime Time; Science Digest. *Honours include:* Aviation Space Writers Award, 1964; Westinghouse Writing Award AAAS, 1966; Lasker Award, 1967; Claude Bernard Science Journalism Award, 1974; National Magazine Award, 1975; James P. Grady Medal, American Chemical Society, 1981; Honorary DLett, New Mexico State University. *Memberships:* 3 times President, Council for the Advancement of Science Writing; National Association of Science Writers; Authors Guild. *Address:* 25 Davenport Avenue, New Rochelle, NY 10805, USA.

ROSENTHAL Barbara Ann, b. 17 Aug 1948, Bronx, New York, USA. Writer; Artist. 2 daughters. *Education:* Numerous courses, various universities and colleges; BFA, Carnegie-Mellon University, 1970; MFA, Queens College, 1975. *Appointments:* Editor-in-Chief, Patterns, 1967-70; Editor, Parsons College Faculty Affairs Committee Newsletter, 1986- 88; Adjunct Lecturer, English, The College of Staten Island (CUNY), New York City. *Publications include:* Clues to Myself, 1982; Sensations, 1984; Homo Futurus, 1986; Old Address Book, 1985; Children's Shoes, 1993; Poetry and short story anthologies: In The Round, 1990; In The West Of Ireland, 1992; Call It Courage: Women Transcending Violence, 1993. *Contributions to:* Numerous professional journals and lit-art magazines including: Feelings, 1990-91; Poetry Motel, 1993; Spit, 1990, 1993; Parting Gifts, 1993. *Honours:* Recipient, various honours and awards; Listed Writers, Poets & Writers Directory. *Literary Agent:* Gunther Stuhlmann. *Address:* 727 Avenue of the Americas, New York, NY 10010, USA.

ROSENTHAL Jack Morris, b. 8 Sept 1931. Writer. m. Maureen Lipman, 1973, 1 son, 1 daughter. *Education:* BA, English Literature & Language, Sheffield University. *Appointments:* Television: Writer of over 250 productions including: That Was the Week That Was, 1963; 150 episodes of Coronation Street, 1961-69; The Evacuees, 1975; Bar Mitzvah Boy, 1976; Ready When You Are, Mr McGill, 1976; Spend, Spend, Spend, 1977; The Knowledge, 1979; P'tang Yang Kipperbang, 1982; Mrs Capper's Birthday, 1985; London's Burning, 1986; Fools on the Hill, 1986; Day to Remember, 1986; And A Nightingale Sang, 1989; Stage: 5 plays including: Smash!, 1981; Films: 6 feature films including: Lucky Star, 1980; Yentl (co-written with Barbra Streisand), 1983; The Chain, 1985; Bye-Bye-Baby, 1992. *Publications:* Contributions to: The Television Dramatist, 1973; Anthology, First Love, 1984; numerous TV plays. *Honours:* BAFTA Writer's Award, 1976; RTS Writer's Award, 1976. *Address:* c/o Margaret Ramsay Ltd, 14A Goodwin's Court, St Martin's Lane, London WC2N 4LL, England.

ROSS Alan, b. 6 May 1922, Calcutta, India. Author; Publisher; Journalist. m. Jennifer Fry, 1949, (div 1985), 1 son. *Education:* St John's College, Oxford. *Appointments include:* Royal Navy, 1942-45; Staff, The Observer, 1950-71, toured Australia as Correspondent, with MCC 1954-55, 1962-633, South Africa 1956-57, 1964-65, West Indies, 1960-68; Editor, London Magazine, 1961-; Managing Director, London Magazine Editions (Publishers), 1965-. *Publications:* The Derelict Day, 1947; Time Was Away, 1948; The Forties, 1950; The Gulf of Pleasure, 1951; The Bandit on the Billiard Table, 1954; Something of the Sea, 1954; Australia 55, 1956, 2nd editon 1983; Abroad, Editor, 1957; Cape Summer and the Australians in England, 1957, 2nd edition 1986; To Whom It May Concern, 1958; The Onion Man, 1959; Through the Caribbean, 1960; The Cricketer's Companion, Editor, 1960; Danger on Glass Island, 1960; African Negatives, 1962; Australia, 63, 1963; West Indies at Lord's, 1963, 2nd edition 1986; North from Sicily, 1965; Poems 1942-1967, 1968; Tropical Ice, 1972; The Taj Express, 1973; Editor, London Magazine Stories 1-11, 1964-80; Editor, Living in London, 1974; Open Sea, 1975; Editor, Selected Poems of Lawrence Durrell, 1977; Death Valley and Other Poems, 1980; Editor, The Turf, 1982; Colours of War, 1983; Ranji, 1983; Editor, Living out of London, 1984; Blindfold Games, 1986; The Emissary, 1986; Coastwise Lights, 1988. *Honours:* Atlantic Award for Literature, Rockefeller Foundation, 1946; FRSL, 1971; CBE, 1982. *Address:* 4 Elm Park Lane, London SW3, England.

ROSS Angus. *See:* **GIGGAL Kenneth.**

ROSS Brian (Elliot), b. 23 Oct 1948, Chicago, Illinois, USA. News Correspondent. m. Lucinda Sanman, May 1985. *Education:* BA, University of Iowa, 1971. *Career:* National Broadcasting Company (NBC), news correspondent for affiliates KWWL-TV in Waterloo, Iowa 1971, and WCKT-TV in Miami, Florida, 1972-74 and for NBC News in Cleveland, Ohio, 1974-76 and New York, New York, 1976-. *Honours:* George Foster Peabody Broadcasting Award from the University of Georgia Henry W Grady School of Journalism and Mass Communication, 1974; Alfred I dePont-Columbia University awards from Columbia University Graduate School of Journalism, 1975, 1985 and 1986; Sigma Delta Chi Award, 1976; National Broadcasters awards 1976, 1978, 1980 and 1987; Robert F Kennedy Journalism Award from Robert F Kennedy Memorial 1979; National Emmy Awards from the National Academy of Television Arts and Sciences, 1980 and 1986; Award from Overseas Press Club, 1988. *Address:* NBC News, 30 Rockefeller Plaza, New York, NY 10020, USA.

ROSS Catherine. *See:* **BEATY Betty.**

ROSS Gary Earl, b. 12 Aug 1951, Buffalo, New York, USA. Writing Educator. m. 23 Dec. 1970, 2 sons, 1 daughter. *Education:* BA, English, 1973, MA, Humanities, 1975, University at, Buffalo. *Appointments:* Writing Educator, State University of New York Educational Opportunity Center at Buffalo, 1977-. *Publications:* Guiding the Adult Learner (editor), 1979; Developmental Perspectives (editor), 1981; Practical Considerations for Computer-Assisted Writing Instruction for Disadvantaged Learners, 1990; Teaching Creative Writing, 1990; Strategies for Addressing Technophobia in Adult Learners, 1991. *Contributions to:* Short stories to: Pure Light; Arts in Buffalo; Best for Men; EdVantage; Word Worth Anthology of Fiction; Starsong; Slipstream; A Poetry Mag; Live Writers!; Ohio Renaissance Review; Innisfree; Starsong; Gas; BFLO Journal; Artvoice; Buffalo News; BUFFALO Magazine; ELF; Poetry to: Alura; A Poetry Mag; American Poetry Anthology; Hearts on Fire; Pure Light; Homunculus; Nonfiction to: EdVantage; Development Perspectives; Spectrum; Colloquy; NEWsletter; Buffalo News. *Honours:* Hearts on Fire Award, American Poetry Association, 1983; LIFT Program Fiction Fellowship, 1989; Just Buffalo Fiction-Writer-in-Residence, 1987, 1992. *Memberships:* Just Buffalo Literary Organization; Niagara- Erie Writers, Board Chair 1987-89; United University Professions; International Society for Exploration of Teaching Alternatives. *Address:* SUNY EOC at Buffalo, 465 Washington Street, Buffalo, NY 14203, USA.

ROSS Helaine. *See:* **DANIELS Dorothy.**

ROSS Jean Munder, b. 20 June 1945, New York City, USA. Psychoanalyst. m. Katherine Wren Ball, (separated), 1 son. *Education:* BA magna cum laude, Harvard College, 1967; MA, 1973, PhD, 1974, Clinical Psychology, New York University; Certificate in Psychoanalysis, NYU Medical Centre, 1984. *Publications:* Tales of Love, Sex and Danger, 1986; The Male Paradox, 1992; The Oedipus Papers, 1988; Father and Child, 1982; New Concepts in Psychoanalytic Psychotherapy; Men and Their Psychology, 1993. *Contributions to:* New York Times; Express Magazine; Journal of American Psychoanalytic Association; The Washington Post; The American Journal of Psychiatry; American Psychological Association Monitor; Mademoiselle Magazine, among others. *Honours:* Phi Beta Kappa, 1967; Outstanding Book in Behavioural Sciences, Father and Child, 1982; Distinguished Teacher Award, 1979, 80; Peter Blos Lecturer, 1991; Rockefeller Foundation Bellagio Residency, 1993. *Memberships:* American, and International Psychoanalytic Associations; New York Psychoanalytic Society and Institute. *Literary Agent:* Suzanne Gluck, ICM 40 West 57th Street, NYC 10019, USA. *Address:* 243 West End Avenue, Suite 101, New York, NY 10023, USA.

ROSS Jonathan. *See:* **ROSSITER John.**

ROSS Leonard Q. *See:* **ROSTEN Leonard C.**

ROSS Malcolm. *See:* **ROSS-MACDONALD Malcolm John.**

ROSS Mary Adelaide Eden, b. Apr 1896, Ealing, England. m. Nicholas Ross, 1951. *Education:* Bedford College, London. *Publications:* Yellow Sands; Tomak the Sculptor; Akhnaton Verse, play; Youth of Jacob Ackmer; The Gallant Heart; Story of Alison Cleve; Song of Man; The Beacon of Memory. *Honours:* Prize Poem; Prize for Short Story, 1951. *Address:* Cobblestones, Kirkhampton, Bude, Cornwall, England.

ROSS Sinclair, b. 1908, Canadian. *Appointments:* Royal Bank of Canada, Winnipeg, 1931-42, Montreal, 1946-68. *Publications:* As for Me and My Home, 1941; The Well, 1958; The Lamp at Noon and Other Stories, 1968; Whir of Gold, 1970; Sawbones Memorial, 1974; The Race, 1982. *Address:* c/o McClelland and Stewart, 481 University Avenue, Toronto M5G 2E9, Canada.

ROSS-MACDONALD Malcolm John (Malcolm Macdonald, Malcolm Ross), b. 1932, Chipping Sodbury, Gloucestershire, England. Freelance Writer; Editor; Designer. m. Ingrid Giehr, 2 daughters. *Apppointments include:* Lektor, Folkuniversity, Sweden, 1959-61; Executive Editor, Aldus Books, 1962-65; Visiting Lecturer, Hornsey College of Art, 1966-69. *Publications:* The Big Waves, 1962; Executive Editor, Macdonald Illustrated Encyclopaedia, 10 volumes, 1962-65; Co-author, designer, Spare Part Surgery, 1968; Machines in Medicine, 1969; The Human Heart, 1970. Also numerous other titles under pen-names, including: World Wildlife Guide, 1971; Beyond the Horizon, 1971; Every Living Thing, 1973; World from Rough Stones, 1974; Origin of Johnny, 1975; Life in the Future, 1976; The Rich Are With You Always, 1976; Sons of Fortune, 1978; Abigail, 1979; Goldeneye, 1981; The Dukes, 1982; Tessa'd'Arblay, 1983; In Love & War, 1984; Mistress of Pallas, 1986; Silver Highways, 1987; Sky with Diamonds, 1988; A Notorious Woman, 1988; His Father's Son, 1989; An Innocent Women, 1989; Hell Hath No Fury, 1990; A Woman Alone, 1990; The Captain's Wives, 1991; A Woman Scorned, 1991; A Woman Possessed, 1992; All Desires Known, 1993; To the End of Her Days, 1993; Dancing on Snowflakes, 1993. *Contributions to:* Sunday Times; Times; New Scientist; Science Journal; Month; Jefferson Encyclopaedia. *Membership:* Authors Guild; Society of Authors. *Address:* c/o David Higham Ltd, 5-8 Lower John Street, London W1R 4HA, England.

ROSSI Maria Francesca, (Francesca Duranti), b. 2 Jan 1935, Genoa, Italy. Writer. m. (1) Enrico Magnani, 1956, (2) Massimo Duranti, 1970, 1 son, 1 daughter. *Education:* Laurea in Giurisprudenza, University of Pisa. *Publications:* The House on Moonlake, 1984; Happy

Ending, 1987; Effetti Personalia, 1988; Ultima Stesura, 1991; La bambina, 1976; Piazza, Mia Bella Piazza, 1978. *Contributions to:* Il Secoloxx; Il Giornale; Il Messaggero. *Honours:* Martina Franca Citta Di Milano, Bagutta, 1984; Basilicata Hemingway Campiello, 1988; Prix Lectrices d'Elle, Castglioncello, 1991. *Address:* Villa Rossi, Gattaiola, Lucca, Italy.

ROSSITER John, (Jonathan Ross), b. 1916, British. *Appointments:* Detective Chief Superintendent, Wiltshire Constabulary, 1939-69; Columnist, Wiltshire Courier, Swindon, 1963-64. *Publications:* The Blood Running Cold (as J Ross), Diminished by Death (as J Ross), 1968; Dead at First Hand (as J Ross), The Deadest Thing You Ever Saw (as J Ross), 1969; The Murder Makers, The Deadly Green, 1970; The Victims, 1971; A Rope for General Dietz, Here Lies Nancy Frail (as J Ross), 1972; The Manipulators, 1973; The Burning of Billy Toober (as J Ross), The Villains, 1974; The Golden Virgin (in US as The Deadly Gold), 1975; I Know What It's Like to Die (as J Ross), 1976; The Man Who Came Back, 1978; A Rattling of Old Bones (as J Ross), 1979; Dark Flight, Dark Blue and Dangerous (as J Ross), 1981; Death's Head (as J Ross), 1982; Dead Eye (as J Ross), 1983; Dropped Dead (as J Ross), 1984; Burial Deferred (as J Ross), 1985; Fate Accomplished (as J Ross), 1987; Sudden Departures (as J Ross), 1988; A Time For Dying (as J Ross), 1989; Daphne Dead and Done For (as J Ross), 1990; Muder de Hanged (as J Ross), 1992. *Address:* 3 Leighton Home Farm Court, Wellhead Lane, Westbury, Wilts BA13 3PT, England.

ROSSMAN Marlene Laura, b. 4 July 1954, New York City, USA. Marketing Consultant; Professor. Author; m. Elliot Silverman, 29 June 1980. *Education:* MBA, marketing, 1982; MA Linguistics, 1976; BA English, 1974. *Publications:* The International Businesswoman of the 1990s, 1990; The International Businesswoman: A Guide to success in the Global Market Place, 1986. *Contributions to:* Baylor Business Studies, 1982; American Economist; Marketing News; University of Virginia. *Memberships:* Omicron Delta Epsilon. *Address:* Rossman, Graham Associates, 17th Floor 201 E 17th Street, New York, NY 10003, USA.

ROSSNER Judith, b. 1935, American. *Publications:* To the Precipice, 1966; Nine Months in the Life of an Old Maid, 1969; Any Minute I Can Split, 1972; Looking for Mr Goodbar, 1975; Attachments, 1977; Emmeline, 1980; August, 1983; His Little Women, 1990. *Contributions to:* Stories and essays to magazines and journals. *Memberships:* Authors Guild; PEN. *Address:* c/o Wendy Weil Agency, 232 Madison Avenue, New York, NY 10016, USA.

ROSTEN Leo C (Leonard Q Ross), b. 11 Apr 1908. Author; Social Scientist. m. (1) Priscilla Ann Mead, 1935, (dec), 1 son, 2 daughters, (2) Gertrude Zimmerman, 1960. *Education:* PhD, University of Chicago; London School of Economics, Honorary Fellow, 1975. *Publications:* The Education of Hyman Kaplan, 1937; The Washington Correspondents, 1973; The Strangest Places, 1939; Hollywood: The Movie Colony, The Movie Makers, 1941; The Strangest Places, 1939; Hollywood : The Movie Colony, The Movie Makers, 1941; The Dark Corner, 1945; Editor, Guide to the Religions of America, 1957; The Return of Hyman Kaplan, 1959; Captain Newman, MD, 1961; The Story Behind the Painting, 1961; The Many Worlds, of Leo Rosten; The Leo Rosten Bedside Book, 1965; A Most Private Intrigue, 1967; The Joys of Yiddish, 1968; A Trumpet for Reason, 1970; A Most Private Intrigue, 1967; The Joys of Yiddish, 1968; A Trumpet for Reason, 1970; People I have Loved, Known or Admired, 1970; Rome Wasn't Burned in a Day, 1971; Leo Rosten's Treasury of Jewish Quotations, 1973; Dear "Herm" 1974; Editor, The Look Book, 1975; The 3,10 to Anywhere, 1976; O Kaplan! My Kaplan!, 1976; The Power of Positive Nonsense, 1977; Passions and Prejudices, 1978; Editor, Infinite Riches : Gems from a Lifetime of Reading, 1979; Silky!, 1979; King Silky!, 1980; Hooray for Yiddish!, 1983; Leo Rosten's Giant Book of Laughter, 1985; The Joys of Yinglish, 1989; Leo Roston's, Carnival of Wit, 1984.*Contributions to:*

Learned Journals. *Honours:* Grants, Rockefeller Foundation and Carnegie Corporation 1938-40; Distinguished Alumnus Award, University of Chicago, 1970; Hon. DHL, University of Rochester, 1973, Hebrew Union Theological College, 1980; many other honours and awards. *Memberships:* Various professional organisations. *Address:* 36 Sutton Place South, New York, NY 10022, USA.

ROSTENBERG Leona, b. 28 Dec 1908. Rare Book Dealer. *Education:* BA 1930; MA 1934; PhD, 1973. *Publications:* English Printing and the Graphic Arts, 1599-1700; Old and Rare: Forty years in the Book Business; Between Brands; New Thoughts on Old Books. *Honours:* American Printing History Award, 1983. *Memberships:* Printing History Association; Book Sellers Association of America; Biographical Society of America. *Address:* 40 East 88 Street, New York, NY 10128, USA.

ROSTON Murray, b. 1928, British/Israeli. *Appointments:* Professor of English Literature, Bar-Ilan University, Ramat Gan, Israel (joined faculty 1956). *Publications:* Prophet and Poet: The Bible ad the Growth of Romanticism, 1965; Biblical Drama in England from the Middle Ages to the Present Day, 1968; The Soul of Wit: A Study of John Donne, 1974; Milton and the Baroque, 1980; Sixteenth-Century English Literature, 1982; Renaissance Perspectives in Literature and the Visual Arts, 1987; Changing Perspectives in Literature and the Visual Arts (1650-1820), 1990. *Address:* 51 Katznelson Street, Kiryat Ono, Israel.

ROSZKOWSKI Janusz, b. 11 Mar 1928, Lapy, Poland. Journalist. m. Natalia Roszkowska, 1960, 1 son. *Education:* Academy of Political Sciences, Warsaw. *Appointments:* Journalist, Polish Press Agency, Warsaw, 1953-, Reporter 1953-61, Correspondent, Berlin 1961-63, Bonn 1963-67, Deputy Editor in Chief, Home Section, 1967-68, Editor in chief, Home Section 1968-71, Deputy Editor in Chief, 1969-71, Editor in Chief (acting), 1971-72, Editor in Chief, 1972-86. *Publications:* Literary Critic, regular contributions to weekly Kultura, 1967-76. *Honours:* Boleslaw Prus Award, 1st Class, 1973; Juliusz Fuczik Hon. Mdedal of International Journalist Association; Order of Banner of Labour, 2nd Class; Cross Order of Polonia Restituta. *Memberships:* Polish Workers Party, 1947-48; PZPR, 1948-90; Free Journalist, 1991; Association of Poland's Journalists; Polish Journalists Association, Vice-President of PJA; President, Polish Committee for Radio and TV, 1986-89; Polish Ambassador, Copenhagen, 1989-. *Address:* ul. Ladowa 1/3m. 14, 00-759 Warsaw, Poland.

ROTBLAT Joseph, b. 1908, British. *Appointments:* Professor 1950-76, Emeritus, Medical College of St Bartholomew's Hospital, University of London; President, Pugwash Conferences on Science and World Affairs, 1988-; Editor, Physics in Medicine and Biology, 1960-73. *Publications:* Progress in Nuclear Physics (co-author), 1950; Atomic Energy: A Survey (ed), 1954; Atoms and the Universe (with G O Jones and G J Whitrow), 1959, 1973; Radioactivity and Radioactive Substances (with Sir James Chadwick), 1961; Science and World Affairs, 1962; The Uses and Effects of Nuclear Energy (co-author), 1964; Aspects of Medical Physics (ed), 1966; Pugwash: The First Ten Years, 1967; Scientists in the Quest for Peace: A History of the Pugwash Conferences, 1972; Nuclear Reactors: To Breed or Not to Breed, 1977; Nuclear Energy and Nuclear Weapon Proliferation, 1979; Nuclear Radiation in Warfare, 1981; Scientists, the Arms Race and Disarmament, 1982; The Arms Race at a Time of Decision, 1984; Nuclear Strategy and World Security, 1985; World Peace and the Developing Countries, 1986; Strategic Defence and the Future of the Arms Race, 1987; Co-existence, Co-operation and Common Security, 1988; Verification of Arms Reductions, 1989; Global Problems and Common Security, 1989; Nuclear Proliferation: Technical and Economic Aspects, 1990; Global Security Through Co-operation, 1990; Towards A Secure World is the 21st Century, 1991; Striving for

Peace, Security and Development in the World, 1992; A Nuclear-Weapon-Free World: Desirable? Feasible?, 1993. *Honours:* CBE, 1965; Albert Einstein Peace Prize, 1992. *Address:* 8 Asmara Road, London NW2 3ST, England.

ROTH Andrew, b. 23 Apr 1919. Political Correspondent. m. Mathilda Anna Friederich, 1949, (div 1984), 1 son, 1 daughter. *Education:* BSS, City College of New York; MA, Columbia University; Harvard University. *Appointments:* Reader, City College, 1939; Research Associate, Institute of Pacific Relations, 1940; Editorial Writer, the Nation, 1945-46; Foreign Correspondent, Toronto Star Weekly, 1946-50; London Correspondent, France Observateur, Sekai, Singapore Standard, 1950-60; Political Correspondent, Manchester Evening News, 1972-84; Political Correspondent, New Statesman, 1984-; Director, Parliamentary Profiles, 1955-. *Publications:* Japan Strikes South, 1941; French Interests and Policies in the Far East, 1942; Dilemma in Japan, 1945; The Business Background of MPs, 1959, 7th edition 1980; The MP's Chart, 1967, 5th edition 1979, 6th edition 1987; Enoch Powell: Tory Tribune, 1970; Can Parliament Decide...., 1971; Heath and the Heathmen, 1972; Lord on the Board, 1972; The Prime Ministers, Volume II (Heath Chapter), 1975; Sir Harold Wilson: Yorkshire Walter Mitty, 1977; Parliamentary Profiles, Volumes I-IV, 1984-85; 2nd edition, 1988-90; New MPs of 92. 1992; Mr Nice Guy and His Chums, 1993. *Address:* 34 Somali Road, London NW2 3RL, England.

ROTH Eleanor, (Lynne Harvey), b. 19 May 1930, Brooklyn, New York, USA. Writer. m. Bernard Roth, 28 Jan 1951, 1 sons, 2 daughters. *Education:* BA, State University of New York, 1952. *Contributions to:* American, Canadian, British and Asian publications including: Air California Magazazine; Today's Family Magazine; The Christian Herald; Psychology and Successful Living; The National Enquirer; Dartmouth Chronicle; Career Worldl; Green's Fiction Magazine and Newscene; Red Star Weekly and Story World; New York State Education Magazine; Spectrum; The New England Review; Writer's Digest; The Chronicle Review; The Asian Wall Street Journal; The Asia Magazine; Uniter Press International New Service; The Straits Times; Silverkris; Galaxy; Herworld; Living Magazine; Female Magazine; The Catholic Digest; Hadassah. Short story, The Dollar, included in softcover anthology; Men's action and women's romance stories in Manhunt, Accused, Startling Mystery Stories, Galaxy, Fiction Magazine; True Story, Modern Romances. *Memberships:* The Chapel of four Chaplaris Legion of Honour. *Address:* 131 Clarendon Street, No Dartmouth, MA 02747, USA.

ROTH Lane, b. 10 Apr 1943, New York City, USA. University Professor. *Education:* BA, Sociology and Psychology, New York University, 1964; MA, 1974, PhD, 1976, Mass Communication, Florida State University. *Publications:* Film Semiotics, Metz, and Leone's Trilogy, 1983; The Power of Imagination: Archetypal Images in Science Fiction Films. *Contributions to:* Research articles in refereed scholarly journals of the humanities, philosophy, English, communication, and cinema; Chapter in scholarly book on film. *Honours:* National German Honors, 1964. *Memberships:* International Association for the Fantastic in the Arts; World Communication Association; Speech Communication Association; Science Fiction Research Association. *Address:* Communication 10050, Lamar University, Beaumont, TX 77710, USA.

ROTH Philip, b. 19 Mar 1933, Newark, New Jersey, USA. Writer. *Education:* MA, Bucknell and Chicago Universities. *Publications:* Goodbye Columbus, 1959; Novels: Letting Go, 1962; When She Was Good, 1967; Portnoy's Complaint, 1969; Our Gang, 1971; The Breast, 1972; The Great American Novel, 1973; My Life as a Man, 1974; Reading Myself and Others (essays), 1975; The Professor of Desire, 1977; The Ghost Writer, 1979; A Philip Roth Reader, 1980; Zuckerman Unbound, 1981; The Anatomy Lesson, 1983; The Prague Orgy, 1985; The Counterlife, 1986; The Facts, 1988; Deception,

1990; Patrimony, 1991. *Honours:* Guggenheim Fellowship, 1959-60; Rockefeller Grant, 1965; Ford Foundation Grant, 1966. *Membership:* National Institute of Arts and Letters. *Address:* Wylie, Aitken and Stone, 250 W 57th Street, New York, NY 10107, USA.

ROTHENBERG Jerome (Dennis), b. 11 Dec 1931, New York City, USA. Poet. m. Diane Brodatz, 25 Dec 1952, 1 son. *Education:* BA, City College, City University of New York, 1952; MA, University of Michigan, 1953. *Appointments:* Professor, English and Comparative Literature, State University of New York at Binghamton, 1986-1988; Professor, Visual Arts and Literature, University of California at San Diego, 1988-. *Publications include:* New Young German Poets, 1959; White Sun Black Sun, 1960; Sightings 1-1X, 1964; The Gorky Poems, 1966; Between, 1967; Poems 1964-67, 1968; Technicians of the Sacred 1968; Poems for the Game of Silence, 1971; Shaking the Pumpkin, 1972; America a Prophecy, 1973; Revolution of the Word, 1974; Poland/1931, 1974; A Big Jewish Book, 1977; A Seneca Journal, 1978; Vienna Blood, 1980; Pre-Faces, 1981; Symposium of the Whole, 1983; That Dada Strain, 1983; New Selected Poems, 1986; Khurbn & Other Poems, 1989; Exiled in the Word, 1989. *Contributions to:* Numerous journals and magazines. *Honours:* Longview Foundation award, 1960; Wenner Gren Foundation, 1968; Guggenheim Foundation Fellowship, 1 974; NEA Grant, 1976; Before Columbus Foundation American Book Award, 1982; New York State Writers Institute Distinguished Writer in Residence, 1986. *Memberships:* PEN International; New Wilderness Foundation. *Address:* c/o New Directions, 80 Eighth Avenue, New York, NY 10012, USA.

ROTHENSTEIN John Knewstub Maurice, (Sir), b. 11 July, 1901. Director of the Tate, 1938-64 and other Art Galleries; University Professor. *Education:* MA, Oxford University, 1927; PhD, University College, London, 1931. *Publications include:* An introduction to English Painting, 1934; Augustus John, 1944; Modern English Painters, 3 vols. 1952-74; Turner, 1960; Sickert, 1961; Paul Nash, 1961; Francis Bacon, 1967 (autobiog. in 3 vols); Summers Lease, 1965; Brave Day, Hideous Night, 1966; Time's Thievish Progress, 1970; Edward Burra, 1972; Stanley Spencer, The Man, 1979; Modern English Painters, updated edition, 1984; John Nash, 1983; Stanley Spencer, 1989. *Honours include:* Knight, 1952; CBE, 1948; Knight Commander, Order Aztec Eagle, Mexico, 1953; Honorary Fellow, Worcester College, Oxford, 1953; Fellow, University College, London, 1976-; Knight Commander, Order St Gregory the Great, 1977. *Memberships include:* Athenaum Club. *Address:* Beauforest House, Newington, Dorchester-on-Thames, Oxford OX9 8AG, England.

ROTHMAN Judith. *See:* **PETERS Maureen.**

ROUDYBUSH Alexandra, b. 14 Mar 1911, Hyres, France. Novelist. m. Franklin Roudybush, Dean of Roudybush Foreign Service School, France. *Education:* St. Paul School for Girls, London, 1924; London School of Economics, 1929. *Appointments:* Journalist, London Evening Standard, Correspondent at Washington, 1930; Time Magazine, 1931; Assistant to Drew Pierson, 1933; French News Agency, 1933; National Academy of Science, Washington DC, 1934; News and Special Events of CBS Broadcasting Company, 1935; White House Corespondent, MBC Radio, 1940-48. *Publications:* Before the Ball Was Over, 1965; Death of a Moral Person, 1967; Capital Crime, 1969; House of the Cat, 1970; A Sybarite Death, 1972; Suddenly in Paris, 1975; The Female of the Species, 1977; Bloodties, 1981; In preparation - Beyond Gehenna, a story about Armenia; Elspeth and the Cooking Fairy. *Memberships:* Crime Writers of USA; Crime Writers of UK. *Address:* Sauveterre de Rouerque, 12800, Aveyron, France.

ROUNTREE Owen. *See:* **KRAUZER Steven M.**

ROUSSEAU George S, b. 1941, American. *Appointments:* Osgood Fellow in English Literature, Princeton University, NJ, 1965-66; Instructor in English Literature, Harvard University, Cambridge, MA, 1966-68; Professor of Eighteenth-Century Studies, University of California at Los Angeles (joined faculty 1968). *Publications:* This Long Disease My Life: Alexander Pope and the Sciences (with Marjorie Hope Nicholson), 1968; John Hill's Hypochondriasis (ed), 1969; The Augustan Milieu: Essays Presented to Louis A Landa (ed with Eric Rothstein), 1970; Tobias Smollett: Bicentennial Essays Presented to Lewis M Knapp, (co-ed), 1971; Organic Form: The Life of an Idea (ed), English Poetic Satire: Wyatt to Byron (ed with Neil Rudenstine), 1972; Goldsmith: The Critical Heritage, 1974; The Renaissance Man in the 18th Century, 1978; The Ferment of Knowledge: Studies in the Historiography of Eighteenth-Century Science (ed with Roy Porter), 1980; The Letters and Papers of Sir John Hill, Tobias Smollett: Essays of Two Decades, 1982; Literature and Science (ed), 1985; Sexual Underworlds of the Enlightenment (co-ed), 1987; Exoticism and the Enlightenment (co-ed), 1988; The Languages of Psyche, 1990; Enlightenment Crossings, 1991; Perilous Enlightenment, 1991; Enlightenment Borders, 1991; Hysteria Beyond Freud, 1993. *Honour:* The Clifford Prize, 1987. *Membership:* Many International Societies in Literature, Cultural History and Medicine. *Address:* 2424 Castilian Drive, Outpost Estates, Los Angeles, CA 90068, USA.

ROVNER Anton, b. 28 June 1970, Moscow, Russia. Composer. *Education:* Piano with Phillippe Ganter, Institut International d' Etudes Musicales, Aix-en-Provence, France, 1983, 1984; Composition with Milton Babbitt, 1987-93, BMus, 1991, MMus, Composition, 1993, Juilliard School of Music, USA; Composition with Andrew Thomas, Juillard School, Pre-College Division, 1983-87; Composition with Eric Ewazen, Dobbs Ferry, New York, summer 1984; Composition Theory, IREX Arts Exchange Programme, Moscow Conservatory, 1989- 90. *Appointments:* Participant, music festivals; Director, New Music Series, series of concerts, 1991, 1992; Participant, conference on contemporary music, Nicholas Roslavetz Festival of Music, Bryansk, Russia, 1992. *Contributions to:* Article on Milton Babbitt, to Sovetskaya Muzyka, Moscow, 1991; Translations of poems by Arkady Rovner to Gnosis, New York. *Honours:* BMI Award for Student Composers, 1989. *Membership:* Artistic Council, Moscow Ensemble of Contemporary Music. *Address:* PO Box 42, Prince Street Station, New York, NY 10012, USA.

ROVNER Arkady, b. 28 Jan 1940, Odessa, Russia. Writer; Publisher; Teacher. m. Victoria Andreyeva, 5 Aug 1969, 1 son. *Education:* MA, Philosophy, Philosophy Department, 1965, Moscow University, Russia; Graduate Programme, Department of German and English, 1965-67, Moscow Pedagogical Institute, Russia; Graduate Programme, Department of Foreign Studies, American University, Washington, District of Columbia, USA, 1974-75; Doctoral studies, Department of Religion, Columbia University, 1976-87. *Appointments:* Publisher, Gnosis Press, 1978-; Instructor, Faculty member, New York University, 1981-85; Instructor, The New School, New York, 1981-. *Publications:* Gostii iz oblastii, 1975, 1991; Kalalatsy, 1980, 1990; Khod korolyom, 1989; Etagy Gadesa, 1992; The noumenal agent; The step towards Gnosis; The Russian Idea; In search of Miraculous; Principles and Applications; V F Ern; A Hermit from the Mountain Arumachala; Krishnamurti; The Third Literature (with Victoria Andreyeva); Others. *Contributions to:* Communication; Writers introduce Writers; Short Story International; City; Central Park; Another Chicago Review; Spring, Appalachian Quarterly; Science and Religion. *Honours:* Cammington Community of the Arts, USA, 1983; Mme Karolyi Foundation, Vance, France, 1984. *Membership:* American PEN Center; The Union of Russian Writers. *Address:* PO Box 42, Prince Street Station, New York, NY 10012, USA.

ROWAN Deirdre. *See:* **WILLIAMS Jeanne.**

ROWAN Hester. *See:* **ROBINSON Shelia Mary.**

ROWBOTHAM David Harold b. 27 Aug 1924, Toowoomba, Queensland, Australia. Author and Journalist. m. Ethel Jessie Matthews, 14 Jan 1952, 2 daughters. *Education:* BA, University of Queensland, 1965; MA (QUAL) 1969. *Appointments:* Honorary Visiting Professor, University of California, Berkeley, 1972; Guest Lecturer Japan-Australia Cultural Centre, Tokyo, 1974; Cultural Visitor, Italy 1976; Australian Delegate, World Congress of Poets, 1981; Cultural Visitor USA, Library of Congress, 1988; Commonwealth Literary Fund Lecturer in Australian Literature, 1956, 1961, 1964; National Book Reviewing Panel, Australian Broadcasting Commission, 1954-63; Literary Editor, Brisbane Courier-Mail, 1980-87. *Publications:* Ploughman and Poet (poems) 1954; Town and City (stories) 1956; Inland (poems) 1958; The Man in the Jungle (novel) 1964; All the Room (poems) 1964; Bungalow and Hurricane (poems) 1967; The Makers of the Ark (poems) 1970; The Pen of Feathers (poems) 1971; Mighty Like a Harp (poems) 1974; Selected Poems, 1975; Maydays (poems) 1980; New and Selected Poems now in preparation for Penguin Books. *Contributions to:* Many magazines and journals. *Honours include:* Pacific Star, World War II, 1945; Emeritus Fellow of Australian Literature (awarded by Australia Council) 1989; Second Prize for Poetry, NSW Captain Cook Bi-Centenary Celebrations Literary Competition, 1970; Grace Leven Prize, 1964; Third Prize for Poetry, Sydney Morning Herald Competition (jointly) 1949. University of Sydney Henry Lawson Prize for Poetry 1949; University of Queensland, Ford Memorial Medal for Poetry, 1948; AM (Order of Australia), Queen's Birthday Honours, 1991. *Memberships:* President, State Branch, Fellowship of Australian Writers, 1982; Founding State Vice-President (1963-72) and National Councillor since 1963, Australian Society of Authors; Reserve Member, Australian Journalists' Association; International Federation of Journalists. *Address:* 28 Percival Terrace, Holland Park, Brisbane, Queensland 4121, Australia.

ROWE William Neil, b. 4 June 1942, Newfoundland, Canada. Lawyer. m. Penelope Ayre, May 1967, 1 son, 1 daughter. *Education:* BA English, Memorial University of Newfoundland, 1962; Law School, UNB, 1964; MA Law (Hons), Oxford University, 1966. *Publications:* Novels: Clapp's Rock, 1983, Temptation of Victorgalanti, 1989; Essays: Is That You Bill?, 1989. *Memberships:* Writers Union of Canada; Writers Alliance of Newfoundland, (VP); Law Society of Newfoundland; Canadian Bar Association. *Address:* 10 Forest Road, St John's, Newfoundland, Canada A1C 2B9.

ROWETT Helen Graham Quiller, b. 30 Dec 1915, London, England. Retired Lecturer. *Education:* Girton College, Cambridge, 1935-39; BA, Natural Science, 1938; Part II, Zoology, 1939; MA, 1942. *Publications:* Guides to Dissection Parts 1-5, 1950-53, translations into Sinhalese, Spanish, Malaysian; The Rat as a Small Mammal, 1960, 3rd Edition, 1974; Guide to Dissection, 1962, Revised Edition, 1970; Histology and Embryology, 1962; Basic Anatomy and Physiology, 1959, 3rd Edition fully revised, 1988; Two Moorsway Guide, 1976, 4th edition, fully revised, 1993. *Honours:* Grisedale Research Scholarship, Manchester, 1939-40. *Memberships:* Society of Authors; Committee Member, West Country Writers; Institute of Biology; Fellow, Royal Society of Arts. *Address:* 3 Manor Park, Dousland, Yelverton, Devon PL20 6LX, England.

ROWINSKI Alexander, b. 9 Mar 1931, Poland. Author. m. Hanna Gis, 13 Sept 1975, 1 son, 1 daughter. *Education:* BA, Philosophical & Social Sciences, Warsaw University, 1953. *Appointments:* Staff, Dziennik Zachodni, 1954-57, Prawo i Zycie, 1959-70, Kultura, 1972-78; Editor in Chief, Przeglad Tygodniowy, 1982-83. *Publications:* Anioly Warszawy, 1970, 3rd edition 1974; Wstapcie do klasztoru, 1966, 2nd edition 1970; Rozkoszny Pantoffelland, 1974; Wlepszym towarzystwie, 1975; Tamci zolnierze, 1979, 2nd edition 1988; Swiat sie konczy, 1972; Spadek po synach slonca,

1987. *Contributions to:* numerous journals & magazines. *Honours:* Julian Brun's Award, 1960; Polish Journalists Association's Award, 1966; Award, Zycie Literackie, 1969; Ksawery pruszynski's Award, 1975. *Memberships:* ZAIKS; Polish Authors Association, Presidium Member. *Literary Agent:* Agencja Autorska, Warsaw. *Address:* ul. Jazgarzewska 10, 00-730 Warsaw, Poland.

ROWLAND Iris. *See:* **ROBERTS Irene.**

ROWLAND Peter Kenneth, b. 1938, British. *Appointment:* Administration Officer, London Waste Regulation Authority. *Publications:* The Last Liberal Governments: The Promised Land 1905- 1910, 1968; The Last Liberal Governments: Unfinished Business 1911-1914, 1971; Lloyd George, 1975; Macaulay's History of England in the 18th Century (ed), 1980; Macaulay's History of England from 1485 to 1685 (ed), 1985; Autobiography of Charles Dickens (ed), 1988; The Disappearance of Edwin Drood, 1991. *Address:* 18 Corbett Road, London E11 2LD, England.

ROWLAND Robin F, b. 17 June 1950, Tanga, Tanganyka Territory (now Tanzania). Writer. *Education:* Lawrence Park Collegiate, Toronto, Canada; BA, Anthropology, York University, Toronto, 1973; Bachelor of Journalism, Carleton University Ottawa, 1975. *Appointments:* Reporter, Sudbury Star, Sudbury, Ontario, Canada, 1975-76; Editor, CBC National Radio News, Toronto, 1977-80; Writer, Editor, CBC Teletext, Toronto, 1982-85; Freelance Writer, CTV National News, Toronto, 1988-. *Publications:* King of the Mob, Rocco Perri and The Women Who Ran His Rackets, 1987; Undercover: Cases of the RCMP's Most Secret Operative (with James Dubro), 1991; Radio plays: A Truthful Witness, 1985; King of the Bootleggers, 1986; Hot Coffee, 1988. *Membership:* Science Fiction and Fantasy Writers of America. *Address:* Eridani Productions, Suite 1005, 268 Poplar Plains Road, Toronto, Ontario, Canada M4V 2P2.

ROWLAND-ENTWISTLE (Arthur), Theodore (Henry), b. 30 July 1925, Clayton-le-Moors, Lancashire, England. Writer. *Education:* BA (Hons), Open University. *Publications:* Famous Composers (with J Cooke), 1974; Animal Worlds, with J Cooke, 1975; Famous Explorers, with J Cooke, 1975; Facts and Records Book of Animals, 1975; Famous Kings and Emperors, with J Cooke, 1977; The World You Never See: Insect Life, 1976; Our Earth, 1977; The Restless Earth, 1977; Exploring Animal Homes, 1978; Seashore Life (as T E Henry), 1983; Fishes (as James Hall-Clarke), 1983; Fact Book of British History, with J Cooke, 1984; Heraldry, 1984; Houses, 1985; World of Speed, 1985; Confucius, 1986; Stamps, 1986; Nebuchadnezzar, 1986; Rivers and Lakes, 1986; Focus on Rubber, 1986; Great British Architects, 1986; Great British Inventors, 1986; Great British Kings and Queens, 1986; Great British Reformers, 1986; Focus on Coal, 1987; The Royal Marines, 1987; The Secret Service, 1987; The Special Air Service, 1987; Jungles and Rainforests, 1987; Three-Dimensional Atlas of the World, 1988; Flags, 1988; Guns, 1988; Focus on Silk, 1989; Weather and Climate, 1991. *Contributions to:* Various encyclopedias and periodicals. *Memberships:* FRGS; FZS. *Literary Agent:* Rupert Crew Ltd. *Address:* West Dene, Stonestile Lane, Hastings, Sussex TN35 4PE, England.

ROYCE Kenneth. *See:* **GANDLEY Kenneth Royce.**

ROYSTER Vermont Connecticut, b. 30 Apr 1914, Raleigh, North Carolina, USA. Journalist. m. Francis Claypole, 1937, 2 daughters. *Education:* University of North Carolina; AB; LL.D. *Appointments:* Reporter, New York City News Bureau, 1936, Wall Street Journal, 1936; Washington Correspondent, Wall Street Journal, 1936-41, 1945-46, Chief Washington Correspondent, 1946-48, Editorial Writer & Colmnist, 1946-48, associate Editor 1948-51, Senior Associate Editor, 1951-58, Editor 1958-72, Contributing Editor,

Columnist, 1971-87; Senior Vice President, Dow Jonnes & Co. Inc., 1960-71, Director 1970-87. *Publications:* Journey through the Soviet Union, 1964; A Pride of Prejudices, 1967; My Own, My Country's Time (memoirs), 1983; The Essential Royster : A Half Century of a Journalist's Eye, 1985. *Honours:* Hon. Litt.D., Temple University; Hon. LHD, Elon College; Pulitzer Prize, Editorial Writing, 1953; Pulitzer Prize for Commentary, 1984; Presidential Medal of Freedom, 1986; other awards. *Memberships:* Fellow, Institute of Policy Sciences, Duke, 1973-; Pulitzer Board for Prizes in Journalism and Letters, 1968-76; President, American Society of Newspaper Editors, 1965-66. *Address:* 903 Arrowhead Road, Chapel Hill, NC 27514, USA.

ROZHDESTVENSKY Robert Ivanovich, b. 20 June 1932, Kosikha Village, USSR. Author; Poet. *Publications include:* Poetry: Flags of Spring, 1955; To My Contemporary, 1962; Radius of Action, 1965; Vera's Son, 1966; The Dedication, 1970; Requiem 1970; In All Earnestness, 1970; The Artist Aleksandra Bill, 1970; The Heart's Radar, 1971; The Return : Verse of Several Years, 1972; The Line, 1973; In the Twenty Years, 1973; Before the Holiday : Verse and Poems, 1974; Selected Works, 1974; Two Hundred and Ten Steps, 1978; The Voice of the Town, 1979; the Seventies, 1979; This is the Time, 1980; verse translated into many languages. *Honours:* Order of Red Banner; Order of Lenin; State Prize, 1979; several medals. *Address:* USSR Union of Writers, Ulitsa Vorovskogo 52, Moscow, USSR.

RU Zhi-juan, b. 13 Sept 1925, Shanghai, China. Teacher; Editor; Author. m. Wang Xiao Ping, 9 Sept 1950, 1 son, 2 daughters. *Appointments:* Vice Chairman, Chinese Writers Association, Shanghai Branch; Vice Chief Editor, Shanghai Literature. *Publications:* Short Stories: Lily Flower, 1958; Tall White Poplar, 1959; Quite Maternity Hospital, 1967; The Story Which has been Montaged It Wrong, 1978; A Path on the Prairie, 1980. Novels: She Comes from that Path, 1983; Flower Cherisher Has Gone, 1982. Plays: No 800 Locomotive Starts Off, 1951; The Soldier Without Gun, 1954. Film: If You Say You Need, 1959. Essays: Talking About My Creative Experience, 1984; Mother and Daughter Toured in America Together, 1986. *Honours:* National Best Short Story Prize, 1978. *Membership:* Chinese Writers' Association. *Address:* 675 Ju Lu Road, Shanghai, China.

RUAS Charles Edward, b. 14 Nov 1938, Tientsin, China. Author. m. Agneta Danielsson, 10 June 1967, div. 1976. 1 son. *Education:* BA, 1960, MA 1963, PhD, 1970, Princeton University; The Sorbonne, University of Paris, 1964. *Publications:* Conversations with American Writers, 1986; Entering the Dream: Lewis Carol, 1994; Trans: Michel Foucault, Death & the Labyrinth: The Life and works of Raymond Roussel, 1989; Pierre Assouline: An Artful Life: D H Kahnweiler, 1990; *Contributions to:* The New York Times; The Village Voice; The Soho News; The Paris Review. *Honours:* Best of the year, new York Time Book Review; Fulbright Lecturer, 1992; Danforth Fellow, NEA, NYSCA. *Memberships:* Pen International; Writers Room. *Literary Agent:* Irene Skolnick, Curtis Brown Association. *Address:* 347 West Broadway, NY 10013, USA.

RUBENS Bernice Ruth, b. 26 July 1928, Cardiff, Wales. Author. m. Rudi Nassauer, 1947, 2 daughters. *Education:* BA, University of Wales. *Appointments:* Author, Director, documentary films on Third World subjects. *Publications:* Novels: Set on Edge, 1960; Madame Sontsatzka, 1962; Mate in Three, 1964; The Elected Member, 1968; Sunday Best, 1970; Go Tell the Lemming, 1972; I Sent a Letter to My Love, 1974; Ponsonby Post, 1976; A Five-year Sentence, 1978; Spring Sonata, 1979; Birds of Passage, 1980; Brothers, 1982; Mr Wakefield's Crusade, 1985; Our Father, 1987; Kingdom Come; A Solitary Grie, 1991; Mother Russia, 1992; Autobiopsy, 1993. *Honours;* Booker Prize, 1970; American Blue Ribbon (documentary film), 1972; Hon D.Litt University of Wales. *Membership:* Fellow,

University College, Cardiff. *Address:* 16a Belsize Park Gardens, London, NW3 4LD, England.

RUBIN Larry Jerome, b. 14 Feb 1930, Bayonne, New Jersey, USA. Professor of English, Georgia Institute of Technology. *Education:* BA 1951, MA 1952, PhD 1956, Emory University. *Literary Appointments:* Smith-Mundt Fellow, University of Krakow, Poland, 1961-62; Fulbright Lecturer, University of Bergen, Norway, 1966-67, Free University of West Berlin, 1969-70, University of Innsbruck, Austria, 1971-72. *Publications include:* 3 books of poetry: The World's Old Way, 1963; Lanced in Light, 1967; All my Mirrors Lie, 1975; Poems in 42 Anthologies including: A Geography of Poets, 1979; The Norton Introduction to Poetry, 3rd edition, 1986. *Contributions to:* Poetry to various literary journals including: New Yorker; Poetry; Saturday Review; Yale Review; The Nation; Esquire; Transatlantic Review; London Magazine; American Scholar; Harper's Magazine; Virginia Quarterly Review; Quarterly Review of Literature; Encounter; Sewanee Review; Antioch Review; New York Quarterly; New Letters; Massachusetts Review; University of Windsor Review. *Honours:* Reynolds Lyric Award, Poetry Society of America, 1961; Literary Achievement Award, Georgia Writers Association, 1963; Sidney Lanier Award, Oglethorpe University, 1964; Georgia Poet of the Year, Dixie Council of Authors & Journalists, 1967, 1975; Kansas City Star Award, 1969; Annual Award, Poetry Society of America, 1973; Triton College All Nations Poetry Contest, 1980. *Membership:* Poetry Society of America. *Address:* Box 15014, Druid Hills Branch, Atlanta, GA 30333, USA.

RUBIN Rivka Leah Jacobs, b. 22 Feb 1952, Philadelphia, Pennsylvania, USA. Writer. m. Gerald E. Rubin, 25 Nov 1981, 1 son. *Education:* BA History 1981, MA Sociology 1982, Marshall University. *Publications:* Experimentum Crucis, 1981; The Boy From the Moon, 1985; The Milk of Paradise, 1985; Morning on Venus, 1985. *Honours:* Honourable mention for poetry, poetry manuscript, West Virginia Writers Inc, 1983; Honourable mention, Writers of the Future Contest, 1985. *Memberships:* Science Fiction Writers of America; West Virginia Sociological Association. *Address:* 1285 26th Street, Huntington, WV 25705, USA.

RUBINSTEIN Gillian Margaret, b. 29 Aug 1942, Berkhamsted, England. Author. m. Philip Rubinstein, 1973, 1 son, 2 daughters. *Education:* BA, MA, Modern Languages, Oxford University, 1961-64; Postgraduate Certificate of Education, University of London, 1972. *Publications:* Space Demons, 1986; Beyond the Labyrinth, 1988; Answers to Brut, 1988; Melanie and the Night Animal, 1988; Skymaze, 1989; Flashback, 1990; Ar Ardilla, 1991; Dog In, Cat Out, 1991; Squawk and Screech, 1991; Galax-Arena, 1992; Keep Me Company, 1992; Mr Plunkett's Pool, 1992. *Honours:* Honour Book, Australian Children's Book Council, 1987, 1989; Senior Fellowship, Australia Council, 1988, 1989-92; National Children's Book Award, 1988, 1990; New South Wales Premier's Award, 1988; Book of the Year, CBA, 1989. *Memberships:* Australian Society of Authors; National Book Council. *Literary Agent:* Australian Literary Management, Middle Park, Australia. *Address:* c/o Australian Literary Management, 2A Armstrong St, Middle Park, Victoria 3206, Australia.

RUBINSTEIN Hilary Harold, b. 24 Apr 1926, London. Literary Agent and Writer. m. Helge Kitzinger, 6 Aug 1955, 3 sons, 1 daughter. *Education:* Cheltenham College; MA, Merton College, Oxford. *Appointments:* Director, Victor Gollancz Ltd, 1953-1963; Deputy Editor, The Observer Magazine, 1964-65; Managing Director, A P Watt, 1965-1992; Managing Director, Hilary Rubinstein Books, 1992-. *Publications:* The Complete Insomniac (Cape 1974, Coronet 1976) published in the USA as Insomniacs of World Goodnight; Good Hotel Guide, founded and published annually since 1978; Editor: Hotels and Inns, 1984. *Contributions to:* Times; Guardian; Observer; New Statesman; Telegraph

Magazine; Condé Nast Traveler. *Memberships:* Literature Panel 1973-79, Literature Financial Committee, 1975-77, Arts Council; Institute of Contemporary Arts 1976-1992; Society of Authors. *Address:* 61 Clarendon Road, London W11 4JE, England.

RUDKIN James David, b. 29 June 1936, London, England. Dramatist m. Alexandra Margaret Thompson, 3 May 1967, 2 sons, 2 daughters. *Education:* King Edward's School, Birmingham, England, 1947-55; MA, St Catherine's Oxford, 1957-61. *Appointment:* Judith E Wilson Fellow, University of Cambridge, 1984. *Publications:* Afore Night Come (stage play) 1964; Ashes (stage play) 1974; Cries from Casement as his Bones are Brought to Dublin (radio play) 1974; Penda's Fen (TV film) 1975; Hippolytus, 1980 translation from Euripides; The Sons of Light (stage play) 1981; The Triumph of Death (stage play) 1981; Peer Gynt (translation from Ibsen), 1983; The Saxon Shore (stage play) 1986; Rosmersholm (translation from Ibsen) 1990; When We Dead Waken (translation from Ibsen) 1990; Broken Strings, 1992; The Lovesong of Alfred J Hitchcock, radio play, 1992. *Contributions to:* Drama; Tempo; Encounter. *Honours:* Evening Standard Most Promising Dramatist Award, 1962; John Whiting Drama Award, 1974; New York OBIE (Ashes) 1977; New York Film Festival Gold Medal (Testimony) 1987, screenplay award. *Membership:* PEN. *Literary Agent:* Margaret Ramsay Ltd. *Address:* c/o M Ramsay Ltd, 14A Goodwin's Court, London WC2N 4LL, England.

RUDMAN Mark, b. 11 Dec 1948, New York City, USA. Writer; Editor. m. Madelaine Bates, 28 Dec 1977, 1 son. *Education:* BA, New School for Social Research, 1971; Columbia University School of the Arts, 1974. *Appointments:* Editor in Chief, Perquod, 1983-. *Publications:* The Nowhere Steps, 1990; Diverse Voices, 1993; By Contraries, 1987; Robert Lowell, 1983; My Sister-Life, 1982, revised, 1992; Memories of Love: Selected Poems of Buhdan Boychuk, 1989; Rider, in progress. *Contributions to:* Best American Essays; Best American Poetry; APR; Atlantic; New Yorker; New Republic; Nation; Paris Review. *Honours:* Academy of American Poets Prize, 1972; PEN Translation Fellowship, 1976; Ingram Merrill Fellowship, 1983; New York Foundaton of the Arts 1988; Denver Quarterly Award, 1988. *Memberships:* Board of Governors, Poetry Society of America, 1985-89; PEN. *Literary Agent:* Helen Pratt. *Address:* 817 West End Avenue, New York City, NY 10025, USA.

RUDOLPH Lee, b. 28 Mar 1948. Mathematician. *Education:* BA, Princeton University, 1969; PhD, MIT, 1974. *Appointments:* Assistant Copy Editor, Standard-Times, New Bedford 1987. *Publications:* The Country Changes, 1978; Curses and Songs and Poems, 1974; Anthologies In: Contemporary Poetry, 1974; Tygers of Wrath, 1981; Contemporary New England Poetry, 1987. *Contributor To:* Kayak; Quarterly Review of Literature; Toy Sun; Counter-Measures; 17 Research articles in Mathematical Journals and Proceedings of Symposia, 1976-88; The New Yorker. *Honours:* Bain-Swigget Memorial Award, Krull Memorial Academy of American Poets, 1966-69; Book of the Month Club-College English Association, Writing Fellowship, 1969-70. *Memberships:* Past Treasurer, Alice James Poetry Cooperative; National Writers Union. *Address:* PO Box 251, Adamsville, RI 02801, USA.

RUDOMIN Esther. *See:* **HAUZIG Esther.**

RUELL Patrick. *See:* **HILL Reginald (Charles).**

RUFFIN Paul, b. 14 May 1941, Millport, Alabama, USA. Professor of English. m. Sharon Krebs, 16 June 1973, 1 son, 1 daughter. *Education:* BA 1964, MA 1968, Miss. State University; PhD, University of Southern Miss. *Appointments:* Editor, The Texas Review, 1976-. *Publications:* The Man Who would be God and other Stories; What I like about the South: Southern fiction for the Nineties; Lighting the Furnace Pilot; Our Women; The Storm Cellar; Co-author: Contemporary New England Poetry; A Sampler; Contemporary Southern Short Ficton: A Sampler; To Come up Grinning: A Tribute to George Garrett. *Contributions to:* American Way; Southern Review; Ploughshares; Alaska Quarterly Review; Michigan Quarterly Review. *Memberships:* Texas Institute of Letters; South Central Modern Language Association; Conference of College Teachers of English; Texas Association of Creative Writing Teachers. *Address:* 2014 Avenue N 1/2, Huntsville, TX 77340, USA.

RUIZ Bernardo b. 6 Oct 1953, Mexico DF. Author; Critic. m. Virginia Abrin Batule, 18 Nov 1978, 2 sons. *Education:* BA, Spanish and Latin American Literature, Universidad Nacional Autonoma de Mexico. *Appointments:* Editor, Universidad Autonoma Metropolitana, 1979; Production Manager, Premia Editora, 1982; Staff, Tiempo de Mexico, 1982; Casa del Tiempo 1983-84; Editor, Ministry of Labour, 1985-88; Advisor, National Council of Culture and Art; Advisor, Presidence of the Republic, 1990-91; Director, INBA, Centro Nacional De Informacion y Promucion De La Literatura, 1992. *Publications include:* Viene la Muerte (short stories) 1976; La otra orilla (short stories) 1980; Olvidar tu nombre (novel) 1982; Vals sin fin (short stories) 1982, revised 1986; El Tuyo, el mismo (poetry) 1986; Los caminos del hotel (fiction) 1991; Juego De Cortas (poetry), 1992. *Contributions to:* Excelsior, Revista la Universidad, Casa del Tiempo, Plural, Revista de Bellas Artes; PC Semanal; Tierro Adentro. *Honours:* Literature Scholarship, Instituto Nacional de Bellas Artes, 1973; Honorary Mention: National Essay Award Jose Revueltas, 1978. *Memberships:* Asociacion de Escritores de Mexico; Sociedad General de Escritores, Autores y Compositores de Mexico; Asociacion de Criticos de Mexico. *Address:* Arizona 94-6, Col. Napoles, Mexico DF, Mexico CP 03810.

RUKEYSER William S, b. 8 June 1939, New York, USA. Journalist. m. Elisabeth Garnett, 21 Dec 1963, 1 son, 1 daughter. *Education:* AB, Princeton University, 1961; Research Student, Christ's College, Cambridge, 1962-63. *Appointments:* Staff Reporter, Wall St. Journal, 1961-62, 1963-67; Associate Editor, 1967-71, Board of Editors, 1971-72; Managing Editor, 1980-86, Fortune Magazine; Managing Editor, Money Magazine, 1972-80; Director, International Business Development, Time Inc., 1986-88; Editor in Chief and Executive Vice President, Whittle Communications, 1988-91; Chairman and Chief Executive Officer, Whittle Books, 1991-. *Address:* Whittle Communications, 333 Main Ave, Knoxville, TN 37902, USA.

RULE Jane, b. 1931, Canadian. *Appointments:* Teacher of English, Concord Academy, MA, 1954-56; Assistant Director of International House, 1958-59; Intermittent Lecturer in English 1959-70, Visiting Lecturer in Creative Writing 1972-73, University of British Columbia, Vancouver. *Publications:* The Desert of the Heart, 1964; This Is Not You, 1970; Against the Season, 1971; Lesbian Images, 1975; Themes for Diverse Instruments, 1975; The Young in One Another's Arms, 1977; Contract with the World, 1980; Outlander, 1981; Inland Passage, A Hot-Eyed Moderate, 1985; Memory Board, 1987; After the Fire, 1989. *Address:* The Fork, Rte 1, 519 C17, Galiano, BC Canada V0N 1P0.

RUMENS Carol Ann, b. 10 Dec 1944, Forest Hill, London, England. Writer. m. 23 July 1966, 2 daughters. *Education:* BA, Honours, University of London, 1966. *Appointments:* Fellow, Royal Society of Literature, 1984. *Publications:* Unplayed Music, 1981; Star Whisper, 1983; Direct Dialling, 1985; Selected Poems, 1987; Plato Park (Novel), 1987; From Bekin to Heaven, 1989, (Poetry). *Contributions to:* Times Literary Supplement; Observer; Punch; Question; Literary Review; Poetry Review. *Honour:* Alice Hunt Bartlett Award (Jointly), 1981; Chalmondeley Award, 1984; Prudence Farmer Award, 1983. *Memberships:* International PEN; Society of Authors; Society for Cultural Relations with USSR.

Literary Agent: The Peters, Fraser and Dunlop Group Ltd. *Address:* c/o Chatto and Windus, 30 Bedford Square, London WC1, England.

RUNDLE Anne (Marianne Lamont, Alexandra Manners, Joanne Marshall and Jeanne Sanders), British. *Publications:* The Moon Marriage, 1967; Swordlight, 1968; Cuckoo at Candlemas (as J Marshall), 1968; Cat on a Broomstick (as J Marshall), The Dreaming Tower (as J Marshall), Dragonscale, 1969; Rakehell, Tamlane, Dark Changeling (as M Lamont), Green Glass Moon (as M Lamont), Flower of Silence (as J Marshall), 1970; Babylon Was Dust (as J Marshall), Bitter Bride Bed (as M Lamont), 1971; Lost Lotus, Amberwood, 1972; Widlboar Wood (as J Marshall), The Trelised Walk, Sea-Song, The Stone Maiden (as A Manners), 1973; Candles in the Wood (as A Manners), Heron Brook, Spindrift (as J Sanders), Follow a Shadow (as J Marshall), Valley of Tall Chimneys (as J Marshall), 1974; The Singing Swans (as A Manners), 1975; Judith Lammeter, 1976; Sable Hunter (in US paperback as Cardigan Square) (as A Manners), Nine Moons Wasted (as M Lamont), 1977; Grey Ghyll, The Peacock Bed (as J Marshall), Wildford's Daughter (as A Manners), 1978, in UK as The White Moths, 1979; Horns of the Moon (as M Lamont), 1979; Echoing Yesterday (as A Manners), 1981; Trilogy,Karran Kinrade (as A Manners), 1982; A Serpent's Tooth (as M Lamont), 1983; Trilogy, The Red Bird (as A Manners), Trilogy, The Gaming House (as A Manners), 1984; Moonbranches, 1986. *Address:* Cloy Cottage, Knowe Road, Brodick, Isle of Arran, Scotland.

RUNTE Hans Rainer, b. 15 Oct 1943, Brieg. Professor. m. Roseann O'Reilly, 9 Aug 1969. *Education:* MA, 1969; MPh, 1970; PhD, 1972. *Appointments:* Editor, Dalhousie French Studies, 1988. *Publications:* Li Ystoire de la male marastre, 1974; Editor: Jean Misrahi Memorial Volume, 1977; Studies on the Seven Sages of Rome, 1978; Oralité et Littérature, 1991; Co-author: The Seven Sages of Rome and the Book of Sindbad, 1984. *Contributions to:* Literary criticism in numerous professional reviews. *Memberships:* Treasurer, International Arthurian Society; International Countly Literature Society; International Comparative Literature Association. *Address:* Department of French, Dalhousie University, Halifax, Nova Scotia, Canada B3H 3J5.

RUOCCHIO Patricia Jeanne b. 18 June 1958, New Haven, Connecticut, USA. Writer. *Education:* AB, cum laude, Department of English and American Literature and Language, Harvard University, 1982. *Publications:* The National Library of Poetry Anthologies: On the Threshold of a Dream, Vol I and II, 1988, 1990; Days of Future's Past, 1989; Of Diamonds and Rust, 1989. *Contributions include:* I Feel Like I am Trapped Inside My Head, in New York Times, Mar 18, 1986; Can We Talk? in American Journal of Psychiatry, Jan 1986; The Schizophrenic Patient in Psychotherapy, translated by Praxis Der Psychotherapie und Psychosomatik, Heidelberg, Germany, The Boston Herald, December, 1982; Art and Schizophrenia in Splash Magazine of Contemporary Culture and Fashion, Feb 1988; Fighting the Fight: The Schizophrenic's Nightmare in Schizophrenia Bulletin, Vol 15, No 1, 1989; The Perils of Social Development for the Schizophrenic Patient, Hospital and Community Psychiatry, Nov 1987; How Psychotherapy Can Help the Schizophrenic Patient, Hospital and Community Psychiatry. Feb 1989; The Schizophrenic Inside, Schizophrenia Journal Vol 17, November 1991. *Honours:* December 1986,New York Times piece lead article for Hallmark Hall of Fame's Promise; Editor's Choice Awards in North American Open Poetry Contest: Endless Quest, 1988, From the Darkness, 1989, Lightness 1989; International Directory of Distinguished Leadership, 1988, 1989, 1990. *Address:* 54B Thayer Road 2, Belmont, MA 02178, USA.

RUSH Norman, b. 24 Oct 1933, San Francisco, California, USA. Writer. m. Elsa, 10 July 1955, 1 son, 1 daughter. *Education:* BA, Swarthmore College, 1956. *Career:* Part-time writer and self-employed as dealer in antiquarian books 1958-73; Instructor in English and

History and Co-Director of College A, Rockland Community College, Suffern, New York, 1973- 78; Co-Director, US Peace Corps, Botswana, Africa, 1978-83; Full-time writer 1983-. *Publications:* Whites: Stories, 1986; Mating (novel) 1991. *Contributions to:* Short stories in anthologies, including Best American Short Stories, and to periodicals. *Honours:* Short fiction selected for Best American Short Stories, 1971, 1984 and 1985; Paris Review Aga Khan Award, 1985 for Instruments of Seduction; New York Foundation for the Arts Fellowship, 1985; Grant from National Endowment for the Arts and Finalist for American Book Award, both 1986, nominated for Pulitzer Prize and recipient of Annual Literary Award from the Academy and Institute of Arts and Letters, both 1987, all for Whites; Guggenheim Fellowship 1987; National Book Award for Fiction, 1991; Finalist, National Book Critics Circle Fiction Award, 1991; Aer Lingus/Irish Times International Fiction Prize, 1992. *Membership:* American Economic Association. *Literary Agent:* Wylie, Aitken and Stone, Inc, New York. *Address:* 10 High Tor Road, New City, NY 10956, USA.

RUSHDIE (Ahmed) Salman, b. 19 June 1947, Bombay, India. Writer. m. (1) Clarissa Luard, 1976, diss. 1987, 1 son, (2) Marianne Wiggins, 1988. *Education:* MA, King's College, Cambridge. *Appointments:* Actor, Fringe Theatre, London, 1968-69; Advertising Copywriter, 1969-73; Part-time Copywriter, 1976-80. *Publications:* Grimus, 1975; Midnight's Children, 1981; Shame, 1983; The Jaguar Smile: A Nicaraguan Journey, 1987; The Satanic Verses, 1988; Haroun and the Sea of Stories, 1990; Imaginary Homelands (essays), 1991; The Wizard of Oz, 1992. TV films: The Painter and the Pest, 1985; The Riddle of Midnight, 1988. *Contributions to:* New York Times; The Guardian; Granta; New Yorker. *Honours:* Booker McConnell Prize for Fiction, 1981; Arts Council Literature Bursary, 1981; English Speaking Union Literary Award, 1981; James Tait Black Memorial Book Prize, 1981; Prix du Meilleur Livre Etranger, 1984; Nominated for Whitbread Prize, 1988. *Memberships:* PEN; Production Board, British Film Institute; Advisory Board, Institute of Contemporary Arts; Fellow, Royal Society of Literature; Executive, Camden Committee for Community Relations, 1975-82. *Address:* c/o Aitken & Stone Ltd, 29 Fernshaw Road, London SW10 0TG, England.

RUSHTON William (George), b. 1937, British. *Appointments:* Founder Editor, 1961, and Contributor, Private Eye Magazine, London; Numerous appearances on the stage, in film and as broadcaster. *Publications:* William Rushton's Dirty Book, 1964; How to Play Football: The Art of Dirty Play, 1968; The Day of the Grocer, 1971; The Geranium of Flut, 1975; Superpig, 1976; Pigsticking: A Joy of Life, 1977; The Reluctant Euro, 1980; The Filth Amendment, 1981; W G Grace's Last Case, 1984; Adam and Eve, 1985; Don't Open That Trapdoor, The Alternative Gardener, Vile Pile, Yecch!, The Flyin' Wotsit Fingy, 1986; Marylebone Versus the Rest of the World, 1987; Spy Thatcher (ed), 1987. *Address:* Wallgrave Road, London SW5, England.

RUSSELL James. *See:* **GILMAN George G.**

RUSSELL John, b. 1919, British. *Appointments:* Honorary Attache, Tate Gallery, 1940-41; served in the Ministry of Information 1941-43, the Naval Intelligence Division, Admiralty, London, 1943-46; Regular Contributor 1945-49, Art Critic 1949-74, The Sunday Times; Art Critic 1974-, Chief Art Critic 1982-, The New York Times. *Publications:* Shakespeare's Country, 1942; British Portrait Painters, 1945; Switzerland, Logan Pearsall Smith, 1950; Erich Kleiber, 1956; Paris, 1960, 1983; Seurat, Private View (with Bryan Robertson and Lord Snowdon), 1965; Max Ernst, 1967; Henry Moore, 1968; Ben Nicholson, Pop Art Redefined (with Suzi Gablik), 1969; The World of Matisse, 1970; Francis Bacon, Edouard Vuillard, 1971; The Meanings of Modern Art, 1981; New and Enlarged Edition, 1990; Reading Russell, 1989. *Address:* 166 East 61st Street, New York, NY 10021, USA.

RUSSELL John Leonard, b. 22 June 1906, Wye, Kent, England. Catholic Priest; Lecturer in Philosophy (retired). *Education:* Oundle School, 1917-25; Christ's College, Cambridge, 1925-29, 1931-35; MA, 1932; PhD, 1935. *Publications:* Science and Metaphysics, 1958; Theology of Evolution (with E Nemesszeghy), 1972. *Contributions to:* Annals of Science; British Journal for the History of Science; Heythrop Journal; Journal for the History of Astronomy; Month Nature. *Memberships:* British Society for the History of Science; British Society of the Philosophy of Science. *Address:* 114 Mount Street, London W1Y 6AH, England.

RUSSELL Martin James, b. 25 Sept 1934, Bromley, Kent, England. Writer. *Publications:* No Through Road, 1965; The Client, 1975; Mr T, 1977; Death Fuse, 1980; Backlash, 1981; The Search for Sara, 1983; A Domestic Affair, 1984; The Darker Side of Death, 1985; Prime Target, 1985; Dead Heat, 1986; The Second Time is Easy, 1987; House Arrest, 1988; Dummy Run, 1989; Mystery Lady, 1992. *Memberships:* Crime Writers' Association; Detection Club. *Literary Agent:* Curtis Brown. *Address:* 15 Breckonmead, Wanstead Road, Bromley, Kent BR1 3BW, England.

RUSSELL Paul Elliott, b. 1 July 1956, Memphis, Tennessee, USA. Novelist; College Teacher. *Education:* AB, Oberlin College, 1978; MFA, 1982, MA, 1982, PhD, 1983, Cornell University. *Appointments:* Associate Professor of English, Vassar College, 1983-. *Publications:* Boys of Life, 1991; The Salt Point, 1990. *Contributions to:* Black Warrior; Carolina Quarterly; Epoch; Southwestern; Akros Review; Swallow's Tale; Sequoia; William and Mary Review. *Literary Agent:* Harvey Klinger. *Address:* Rosendale, New York 12472, USA.

RUSSELL Ray, b. 4 Sept 1924, Chicago, Illinois, USA. Author; Editor. m. Ada Beth Stevens, 5 Sept 1950, 1 son, 1 daughter. *Education:* Chicago Conservatory; Goodman Theatre School of Drama (division of Art Institute, Chicago), *Publications:* Sardonicus, 1961; The Case Against Satan, 1962; The Little Lexicon of Love, 1966; Unholy Trinity 1967; The Colony 1969; Sagittarius 1971; Prince of Darkness 1971; Incubus 1976; Holy Horatio, 1976; Princess Pamela 1979; The Book of Hell 1980; The Devil's Mirror, 1980; The Bishop's Daughter, 1981; Haunted Castle 1985; The Night Sound (poetry) 1987; Dirty Money 1988; Stories in 100 anthologies and textbooks. *Contributions to:* The Paris Review; Verbatim; Theology Today; Ellery Queen; Fantasy and Science Fiction Magazine; Playboy (Associate Editor 1954- 55, Executive Editor 1955-60, Contributing Editor, 1968-74); Editor, The Permanent Playboy (anthology) 1959, 40 other anthologies 1960-74; Film screenplays for Warner Brothers, Universal, Columbia, MGM, Twentieth Century Fox, American International. *Honour:* Sri Chinmoy Poetry Award, 1977; World Fantasy Lifetime Achievement Award, 1991. *Literary Agent:* H N Swanson, Inc, Los Angeles. *Address:* c/o H N Swanson, Inc, 8523 Sunset Boulevard, Los Angeles, CA 90069, USA.

RUSSELL Roy, b. Blackpool, Lancashire, England. Author; Dramatist. *Publications include:* (TV Plays and Series): No Hiding Place; Fothergale; The Saint; The Troubleshooters; A Man of Our Times; Champion House; Sexton Blake; Dixon of Dock Green; Doomwatch; Crime of Passion; Crown Court; A Family at War; The Onedin Line; Intimate Strangers; A House in Regent Place, (4 plays); Tales of the Unexpected; The Woodcutter Operation; Last Video and Testament; The Irish RM; Henry's Leg; BBC Playhouse Childrens TV Dramas and Radio plays; Documentary Films: The Lonely Sea and the Sky; Prince Bernhard, Pilot Royal; Prince Charles, Pilot Royal; Stage Plays Include: The Eleventh Commandment; Books Include: A Family at War: Towards Victory, 1971. *Contributions to:* Various magazines and journals. *Honours:* Laurel Award for Distinguished Services to Writers; Writers Guild of Great Britain. *Memberships:* Writers Guild of Great Britain; Society of Authors. *Literary Agent:* Lemon, Unna and Durbridge Ltd. *Address:* c/o Lemon, Unna and Durbridge

Ltd., 24 Pottery Lane, Holland Park, London W11 4LZ, England.

RUSSELL Sharman Apt, b. 23 July 1954, California, USA. Teacher; Writer. m. Peter Russell, 24 Jan 1981, 1 son, 1 daughter. *Education:* BS, Conservation and Natural Resources, UC Berkeley; MFA English and Creative Writing, University of Montana. *Publications:* Songs of the Fluteplayer, 1991; Kill the Cowboy: A Battle of Mythology in the West, 1993; The Humpbacked Fluteplayer, 1993; Frederick Douglas, 1987; Built to Last, 1986 (co-author). *Contributions to:* Countryside; Harrowsmith; The Massachusetts Review; The North American Review; The Missouri Review; The New York Times; New Women; The Threepenny Review. *Honours:* Writers at Work Fellowship, 1989; Joseph Henry Jackson Award in Non-fiction, 1989; Essay in Pushcart Prize XV, 1990; Mountains and Plains Regional Book Award, 1992; Zia Award, NM Press Women's Award, 1992. *Memberships:* Society of Children's Book Writers; PEN West. *Literary Agent:* Felicia Eth (adult); Martha Casselman, (children's). *Address:* Rt 15 Box 2560, Mimbres, NM 88049, USA.

RUSSELL William Martin (Willy), b. 23 Aug 1947. Author. m. Ann Seagroatt, 1969, 1 son, 2 daughters. *Education:* Certificate of Education, St Katherine's College of Education, Liverpool. *Appointments:* Ladies Hairdresser, 1963-69; Teacher, 1973-74; Fellow, Creative Writing, Manchester Polytechnic, 1977-78. *Publications:* Theatre: Blind Scouse, 1971-72; When the Reds (adaptation), 1972; John, Paul, George, Ringo and Bert (musical), 1974; Breezeblock Park, 1975; One for the Road, 1976; Stags and hens, 1978; Educating Rita, 1979; Blood Brothers (musical), 1983; Our Day Out (Musical), 1983; TV Plays: King of the Castle, 1972; Death of a Young Young Man, 1972; Break In (for schools), 1974; Our Day Out, 1976; Lies (for schools), 1977; Daughter of Albion, 1978; Boy with Transistor Radio (for schools), 1979; One summer (series), 1980; Radio Play: I Read the News Today (for schools), 1979; Screenplays: Band on the Run, 1979; Educating Rita, 1981; Shirley Valentine, 1986 (stage play); several other plays included in general collections of plays, songs and poetry. *Honours:* Hon. MA, Open University; Hon. Director, Liverpool Playhouse. *Address:* c/o Margaret Ramsay Ltd, 14A Goodwin's Court, St Martin's Lane, London WC2, England.

RUSSO Albert, b. 26 Feb 1943, Kamina, Zaire. Writer. 1 son, 1 daughter. *Education:* Abschluss Diplom, Heidelberg; BSc., General Business Administration, New York University, USA. *Appointments* Member, Jury of the Prix de l'Europe (with Ionesco), 1982-. *Major Publications:* Incandescences, 1970; Eclats de malachite, 1971; La Pointe du diable, 1973; Mosaïque New Yorkaise, 1975; Your Son Leopold Princess and Gods and Triality, excerpts of which have appeared in reviews in North America, UK, India and Africa; Albert Russo anthology, 1987; Mixed Blood (novel), 1990; Le Cap des illusions (novel), 1991; Futureyes/Dans le nuit bleu-faure (poetry in English and in French), 1992; Kaleidoscope (poetry collection), 1993; Stories broadcast by the BBC World Service. *Contributions to:* Numerous professional journals. *Honours:* various awards and honours including, Willie Lee Martin Short Story Award (USA), 1987. *Memberships:* PEN; Authors Guild of America; Writers & Poets; Association of French Speaking Writers. *Address:* BP 640, 75826 Paris Cedex 17, France.

RUTSALA Vern, b. 5 Feb 1934, McCall, Idaho. USA. Writer; Teacher. m. Joan Colby, 6 May 1957, 2 sons, 1 daughter. *Education:* BA, Reed College, 1956; MFA, University of Iowa, 1960. *Publications include:* The Window, 1964; Small Songs, 1969; The Harmful State, 1971; Laments, 1975; The Journey Begins, 1976; Paragraphs, 1978; The New Life, 1978; Walking Home from the Icehouse, 1981; Backtracking, 1985; The Mystery of Lost Shoes, 1985; Ruined Cities, 1987; Selected Poems, 1991. *Contributions to:* The New Yorker; Esquire; Poetry; Hudson Review; Harpers; The Atlantic; American Poetry Review; Paris Review.

Honours: NEA Fellowship, 1974, 1979; Northwest Poetry Prize, 1976; Guggenheim Fellowship, 1982; Carolyn Kizer Poetry Prize, 1988; Master, Fellowship, Oregon Arts Commission, 1990; Hazel Hall Award, 1992; Juniper Prize, 1993. *Memberships:* PEN; Poetry Society of America. *Address:* 2404 NE 24th Avenue, Portland, OR 97212, USA.

RUTTER Michael Llewellyn, b. 15 Aug 1933, Brummanna, Lebanon. Professor, Child Psychiatry, University of London & Honorary Director, Medical Research Council, Child Psychiatry Unit. m. Marjorie Heys, 27 Dec 1958, 1 son, 2 daughters. *Education:* MB ChB, University of Birmingham Medical School, 1950-55; Academic DPM, University of London, 1961; MD, University of Birmingham, 1963; Fellow, Royal College of Psychiatrists, London, 1971; Fellow, Royal College of Physicians, London, 1972; FRS, 1987. *Publications include:* Children of Sick Parents : An Environmental & Psychiatric Study, 1966; A Neuropsychiatric Study in Childhood (co-author), 1970; Education Health & Behaviour (Editor with J Tizard & K Whitmore), 1970; The Child with Delayed Speech (Editor with J A M Martin), 1972; Helping Troubled Children, 1975; Cycles of Disadvantage, (co-author), 1976; Autism: A Reappraisal of Concepts & Treatment (Editor with E. Schopler), 1978; Changing Youth in a Changing Society, 1979; Stress, Coping & Development, (Editor with N. Garmezy), 1983; Developmental Neuropsychiatry, (Editor), 1983; Juvenile Delinquency: Trends & Perspectives (with H Giller), 1983; A Measure of Our Values: Goals & Dilemmas in the Upbringing of Children, 1983; Child & Adolescent Psychiatry: Modern Approaches, 2nd edition, (editor with L. Hersov), 1985; Depression in Young People: Developmental & Clinical Perspectives (Editor with C. Izard & P. Reed), 1986; Language Development & Disorders, (Editor with W. Yule), 1987; Treatment of Autistic Children, (co- author), 1987; Parenting Breakdown: The Making and Breaking of Intergenerational Links (Co-author), 1988; Assessment and Diagnosis in Child Psychopathology, 1988; Straight and Devious Pathways from Childhood to Adulthood, 1990; Biological Risk Factors for Psychosocial Disorders, 1991; Developing Minds: Challenge and Continuity Across the Lifespan, 1993. *Contributor to:* Numerous professional & medical/psychiatric journals. *Honours:* Nuffield Medical Travelling Fellowship, 1961-62; Belding Travelling Scholar, 1963; Goulstonian Lecturer, Royal College of Physicians, 1973; American Association on Mental Deficiency Research Award, 1975; Honorary Fellow, British Psychological Society, 1978; Rock Carling Fellow, Nuffield Provincial Hospitals Trust, 1979; Salmon Lecturer, New York, 1979 & numerous memorial lectures; Fellow, Centre for Advanced Study in the Behavioural Sciences, California, 1979-80; Honorary Doctorate, University of Leiden, Netherlands, 1985; Knight Baronet, 1992; CBE, 1985; Honorary Doctorate, University of Leiden, 1985; FRS, 1987; Foreign Associate Member, Institute of Medicine of the National Academy of Sciences, USA, 1988; Founding Member, Academia Europaea, 1988; Foreign Hon Member, American Academy of Arts and Sciences, 1989; Hon Doctorate, Catholic University, Louvain, 1990; Hon Doctor of Science, University of Birmingham, 1990; Hon Doctor of Medicine, University of Edinburgh, 1990; Foreign Associate Member, US National Academy of Education, 1990; Hon Doctor of Science, University of Chicago, 1991; Hon Doctor of Science, Unversity of Minnesota, 1993. *Address:* Dept of Child & Adolescent Psychiatry, Institute of Psychiatry, De Crespigny Park, Denmark Hill, London, SE5 8AF, England.

RUYSLINCK Ward. *See:* **DE BELSER Raymond Charles Maria.**

RUZICKA Penelope Susan, (Penny Kane), b. 23 Jan 1945, Kenya. Consultant. m. Ladislav Ruzicka, 21 Mar 1984. *Education:* MSc Economics, University of Wales, 1986. *Publications:* Womens Health: From womb to tomb, 1991; The Which? Guide to Birth Control, 1983; The Second Billion: Population and Family Planning in China, 1987; Famine in China, 1959- 61, 1988; Choice not Chance, 1978; Editor; Co-Editor: China's One Child Family, 1985; Differential Mortality, 1989; Tradition, Development and the Individual, 1986; Asking Demographic Questions, 1985. *Memberships:* International Union for the Scientific Study of Population; President, Family Planning Federation of Australia. *Literary Agent:* Bruce Hunter, David Higham Associates. *Address:* The Old School, Major's Creek near Braidwood, NSW 2622, Australia.

RYAN John Gerald Christopher b. 4 Mar 1921, Edinburgh. Artist/Writer. m. Priscilla Ann Blomfield, 3 Jan 1950, 1 son, 2 daughters. *Education:* Ampleforth College, York, 1930-40; Regent Street Polytechnic Art School, 1946-47. *Publications:* 14 children's picture books Captain Pugwash (Bodley Head and Puffins/Collins (paperback) 1956-86. Tiger Pig; 12 Noah's Ark Stories; 2 Dodo Books; Mabel and the Tower of Babel, 1990; Adventures of Sir Cumference, 1990. *Contributions to:* Eagle and Girl Magazines, Harris Tweed Extra Special Agent, 1950-60. *Membership:* Society of Authors. *Literary Agent:* Jane Gregory. *Address:* Gungarden Lodge, Rye, East Sussex TN31 7HH, England.

RYAN Nancy M, b. 13 Mar 1938, New York, USA. Spanish Teacher. *Education:* BA, Spanish and English, 1960, MA Spanish, 1966, University of New York at Albany. *Publications:* Chapbooks: Shades of Green and Darkness, 1981; Islands in a Bay, 1989 (part of anthology Timeless Shores); Past Green Edges of Realities, 1990. *Contributions to:* Poetry widely published in Midwest Poetry Review, The professional Poet, Many anthologies and poetry magazines. *Honours:* Feature Poet, Midwest Poetry Review, 1988; First Prize, Midwest Poetry Review, Oct 1985; Second Prize, Professional Poet, 1982; Many honourable mentions and certificates of merit; Honourable Mention, Chapbook Contest, New Horizons Poetry Club, 1989. *Memberships:* New Horizons Poetry Club; Papal Volunteers - Teaching Volunteer, Universidad de la Frontera, Temuco, Chile, 1964-65. *Address:* 111 Beverwyck Drive, Guilderland, NY 12084, USA.

RYBAKOV Anatoli (Naumovich), b. 1 Jan 1911, Chernigor, Russia. Author. *Education:* Graduated, Moscow Institute of Railroad Engineers, 1934. *Career:* Served Soviet Army for five years and then became full-time writer. *Publications:* Heavy Sand, Viking, 1981; Children of the Arbat, Little Brown, 1988; The Dirk, Foreign Languages Publishing House, 1956; The Bronze Bird, Foreign Languages Publishing House, 1958; Most of his works have been adapted for film and television.

RYBICKA Zofia, b. 28 Nov 1920, Klony, Poland. Writer; Critic; Translator. m. Waldemar Jerzy Rybicki, 2 Jan 1955, div. 1958. *Education:* Secondary School for Kindergarten Teachers, 1934-37; III Lyceum, 1945-46, Secondary School Certificate, 1946, Gdansk-Wrzeszcz; Graduated, Diplomatic- Consular Faculty, Academy of Political Science, Warsaw, 1950; Diploma, Organ, High Music School, 1952; MPh, Polish Philology and Literature Faculty, Warsaw University, 1953. *Appointments:* Soldier-Club Manager, Poznan, 1938-39; Typist, Lublin, 1940-44; Gestapo prisoner, 1942; Polish Army, 1944-45; Proof Reader, Press House, Gdansk, 1947-50; Grammar School Teacher, Lyceum for Kindergarten Teachers, Gdansk-Wrzeszcz, 1952-55; Editor, Ministry of National Defence Publishing House, Warsaw, 1955-75; Head, German and Scandinavian Department, Polish Publishing House, PIW, Warsaw, 1975-81. *Publications:* 48 short prose pieces translated from German into Polish including stories: Bodo Uhse: Mexikanische Erzählungen, 1960; Erika Runge: Bottroper Protokolle, 1973; Adelbert von Chamisso: Peter Schlemihls wundersame Geschichte, 1979; Hermann Hesse: Der Lateinschüler, 1979; Conrad Ferdinand Meyer: Die Hochzeit des Mönchs, 1979; Heinrich Mann: Das Herz, 1979; Friedrich Durrenmatt: Die Panne, 1979; Adolf Muschg: short stories in: U szcześcia, 1981; Robert Musil: Vereinigungen, 1982; Others; Essays, speeches, treatises of Max Horkheimer, Theodor W. Adorno, Heinrich Mann, Klaus Mann,

Thomas Mann, in: Wobe faszyzmu; 15 novels: Dieter Noll: Die Abenteuer des Werner Holt. Roman einer Jugend, 1964; Roman einer Heimkehr, 1966; Christa Wolf: Der geteilte Himmel, 1966; Kurt David: Der Schwarze Wolf, 1966; Tenggeri, Sohn des Schwarzen Wolfs, 1968; Die Uberlebende, 1975; Gerold Späth: Commedia, 1986; Others; Nicolaus v Below: Als Hitlers Adjutant, memoirs, 1990. *Contributions to:* Articles, essays, reviews to: Kultura; Wspolczesnosc; Zycie Literackie; Literatura na Swiecie; Nowe Ksiazki; Tu i Teraz; Literatura; Others. *Honours:* Silver Cross of Merit, 1975; Knight's Cross, Polonia Restituta, 1979; Medal of Victory and Freedom 1945, 1984; Other military orders. *Memberships include:* Polish Writers Union; ZAIKS; Stowarzyszenie Tlumaczy Polskich; Polish Association of Editors. *Address:* ul Stoleczna 17b m 68, 01-595 Warsaw, Poland.

RYCE-MENUHIN Joel, b. 11 June 1933, USA. Analytical Psycologist; Former International Concert Pianist. m. Yaltah Menuhin, 11 June 1960. *Education:* BMus, 1953; BSc Hons, 1976; MPhil, 1982. *Publications:* The Self in Early Childhood, 1988; Jungian Sandplay - the Wonderful Therapy, 1992. *Contributions to:* Clinical papers in Journal of Analytical Psychology, Harvest, Chiron, Free Association Journal, British Journal of Psychiatry, British Journal of Projective Psychology, Guild of Pastoral Psychology. *Memberships:* PEN; Chairman: G G Jung Analytical Psychol Club, London and, Guild of Pastoral Psychology. *Address:* 85 Canfield Gardens, London NW6 3EA, England.

RYDELL Forbes. *See:* **FORBES Deloris Stanton.**

RYDER Jonathan. *See:* **LUDLUM Robert.**

RYDER Sue. *See:* **RYDER OF WARSAW Susan Margaret.**

RYDER Susan Margaret (Baroness Ryder of Warsaw), (Sue Ryder), b. 3 July 1923, Leeds, England. Social Worker; Founder of Sue Ryder Foundation. m. Lord Cheshire of Woodhall, 5 Apr 1959, dec, 1 son, 1 daughter. *Education:* School Certificate. *Publications:* And the Morrow is Theirs, 1st autobiography; Child of My Love, 2nd autobiography, 1986; Remembrance, annual magazine of Sue Ryder Foundation. *Honours:* Order of the British Empire, 1957; Order of Polonia Restituta, 1965; Medal of Yugoslav Flag with Gold Wreath and Diploma, 1971; Companion, Order of St Michael and St George, 1976; Golden Order of Merit, Poland, 1976; Created Baroness Ryder of Warsaw in Poland and of Cavendish in the County of Suffolk, 1978; Order of Smile, Poland, 1981; Commander's Cross of the Order of Polonia Restituta and Order of Merit, Poland, 1992; Honorary LLD: Liverpool, 1973; Exeter, 1980; London, 1981; Leeds, 1984; Kent, 1986; Cambridge, 1989; Honorary DLitt, Reading, 1982. *Membership:* Special Operations Executive Club. *Address:* Sue Ryder Home, Cavendish, Sudbury, Suffolk CO10 8AY, England.

RYTKHEU Yuriy Sergeyevich, b. 8 Mar 1930, Uellen, Chukotka N.O., Magadan Region, USSR. Writer. *Education:* Leningrad University. *Publications:* Foremost Chukchi Writer; Short Stories: Friends and Comrades, People of our coast, 1953; The Sorceress of Konerga, 1960; The Saga of Chukotka, 1960; Farewell to the Gods, 1961; Nunivak, 1963; The Walrus Dissent, 1964; Blue Peppers, 1964; The Finest Ships, 1967; Dream at the Onset of Rust, 1969; Frost on the Threshold, 1970; The Harpoon Thrower, 1971; When the Whales Depart, 1976; Novels: The Magic Gauntlet, 1963; In the Vale of the Little Sunbeams, 1963; Wings Are Becoming Stronger in Flight; Dream in the Mist, 1972; White Snows, 1976; Verses: Bear Stew, 1965. *Honour:* Order of Friendship of Peoples, 1980. *Memberships:* CPSU, 1967-. *Address:* Union of Writers of the USSR, Ul. Vorovskogo 52, Moscow, USSR.

S

S Elizabeth Von. *See:* **FREEMAN Gillian.**

S H S. *See:* **SPENDER Stephen.**

SABATIER Robert, b. 17 Aug 1923, Paris, France. Writer. m. Christianne Lesparre, 1957. *Publications:* Alain et le negre, 1953; Le marchand de sable, 1954; Le gout de la cendre, 1955; Les fetes solaires, 1955; Boulevard, 1956; Canard au sang, 1958; Saint Vincent de Paul, Dedicace d'un navire, 1959; la Sainte-Farce, 1960; la mort du figuier, 1962; Dessin sur un trottoir, 1964; Les poisons delectables (poems), 1965; le Chinois d'Afrique, 1966; Dictionnaire de la mort, 1967; les chateaux de millions d'annees (poems), 1969; Les allumettes suedoises, 1969; Trois sucettes a la menthe, 1972; Noisettes sauvages, 1974; Histoire de la poesie franciase des origines a nos jours (9 volumes), 1975; Icare et autres poemes, 1976; les enfants de l'ete, 1978; Les fillettes chantantes, 1980; L'oiseau de demain, 1981; Les annees secretes de la vie d'un homme, 1984; David et Olivier, 1986; Lecture, 1987. *Address:* 64 boulevard Exelmans, 75016 Paris, France.

SABERHAGEN Fred Thomas, b. 18 May 1930, Chicago, USA. Author. m. 29 June 1968, 2 sons, 1 daughter. *Publications:* Book of Swords 1,2,3, 1983; Book of Lost Swords, 1,2,3,4,5,6, 1986; Berserker, 1967; An Old friend of the family, 1979; Dracula Tape, 1975; Empire of the East, 1979; Golden People, 1964; Brother Assassin, 1967; Broken lands, 1968; Black Mountains, 1971; Changeling Earth, 1973; Berserkers Planet, 1975; Book of saberhagen, 1975; White Bull, 1988; Veils of Azlaroc, 1978; Specimens, 1976; Mask of the Sun, 1979; Water of Thought, 1979; Thorn, 1980; Berserker wars, 1981; Earth Descended, 1981; Octagon, 1981; Dominion, 1982; Century of Progress, 1983; Berserker Blue Death, 1985; Berserker Throne, 1985; Frankenstein Papers, 1986; Berserker Attack, 1987; Pyramids, 1987; After the Fact, 1988; Love Conquers All, 1974; Holmes-Dracula File, 1978; Berserker Man, 1975; Coils, (Co-author R Zelazny), 1982. *Contributions to:* Contributor ot over 50 short stories in various science fiction magazines, popular magazines and anthologies. *Memberships:* Science Fiction Writers of America; Writers Guild. *Literary Agent:* Eleanor Wood, Spectrum Literary Agency. *Address:* c/o Spectrum Literary Agency, 432 Park Avenue South, Suite 1205, New York, NY 10016, USA.

SABLE Martin Howard, b. 1924, American. *Appointments:* Research Associate, Latin American Center, University of California, Los Angeles, 1965-68; Advisory Editor on Latin America, Encyclopedia Americana, 1967-; Associate Professor 1968-72, Professor 1972-, School of Library Science, University Wisconsin, Milwaukee; Visiting Professor, Graduate Library School, Hebrew University, Jerusalem, 1972-73. *Publications:* A Selective Bibliography in Science and Engineering, 1964; Master Directory of Latin America, 1965; Periodicals for Latin American Economic Development, Trade and Finance: An Annotated Bibliography, 1965; A Guide to Latin American Studies, UFO Guide 1947-67, 1967; Communism in Latin America, an International Bibliography: 1900-45, 1960-67, 1968; A Bio-Bibliography of the Kennedy Family, 1969; Latin American Agriculture: a Bibliography, Latin American Studies in the Non-Western World and Eastern Europe, 1970; Latin American Urbanization: A Guide to the Literature, Organiztions and Personnel, 1971; International and Area Studies Librarianship: Case Studies, 1973; The Guerrilla Movement in Latin America, an International Bibliography, 1977; Latin American Jewry: A Research Guide, Exobiology: A Research Guide, 1978; A Guide to Nonprint Materials for Latin American Studies, 1979; The Latin American Studies Directory, A Bibliography of the Future, 1981; The Protection of the Library: An International Bibliography, 1984; Industrial Espionage and Trade Secrets: An International Bibliography, 1985; Mexican and Mexica-American Agricultural Labor in the United

States: A Research Guide, 1986. *Address:* 4518 Larkin Street, Milwaukee, WI 53211, USA.

SABRE Dirk. *See:* **LAFFIN John.**

SACHS Elizabeth-Ann, b. 25 June 1946. Librarian; Journalist. *Education:* BA, 1968; MLS, 1969. *Publications:* Just Like Always, 1982; The Boy Who Ate Dog Biscuits, 1989; The Trouble with Santa, 1990; I Love You Janie Tannenbaum, 1990; A Special Kind of Friend, 1990; Kiss Me, Janie Tannenbaum, 1992. *Contributions to:* Book reviewer: New York Times Book Review; Kirkus; Features to The News-Times, Danbury, Connecticut; Editor, Kidspace, The News-Times. *Honours:* Fellow, Breadloaf Writers Conference, Middlebury, Vermont, 1982; Middlebury College Xerox Fellow, Middlebury, Connecticut, 1983. *Memberships:* American PEN; National Writers Union; Society of Children's Book Writers. *Address:* c/o Anne Borchardt Literary Agent, Georges Borchardt Inc, 136 East 57th Street, New York, NY 10022, USA.

SACHS Marilyn, b. 18 Dec 1927, USA. Writer. m. Morris Sachs, 26 Jan 1947, 1 son, 1 daughter. *Education:* BA, Hunter College, New York; MS, Library Science, Columbus University, New York. *Publications include:* Fiction: Amy Moves In, 1964; Veronica Ganz, 1968; The Bears' House, 1971; The Truth About Mary Rose, 1973; A Pocket Full of Seeds, 1973; Dorrie's Book, 1975; A Summer's Lease, 1979; Class Pictures, 1980; Call Me Ruth, 1982; Fourteen, 1983; The Fat Girl, 1984; Underdog, 1985; Baby Sister, 1986; Almost Fifteen, 1987; Fran Ellen's House, 1987; Just Like a Friend, 1989; At The Sound of the Beep, 1990; (co-editor) Big Book For Peace, 1990; Circles, 1991; What My Sister Remembered, 1992; Thirteen, Going On Seven, 1993. *Honours:* Outstanding Book of the Year, 1971; National Book Award Nominee, 1972; Austrian Children's Book Prize, 1977; School Library Journal Best Books of the Year, 1973; Silver Slate Pencil Award, 1974; Jane Addams Children's Book Award, 1974 and 1991; Garden State Children's Book Award for Younger Fiction, Association of Jewish Libraries' Award, 1983; Christopher Award, 1985. *Memberships:* Jane Austen Society, Great Britain; Jane Austin Society, North America; PEN; Authors Guild; America Civil Liberties Union. *Address:* 733 31st Avenue, San Francisco, CA 94121, USA.

SACHS Murray, b. 10 Apr 1924, Toronto, Canada. Literary Scholar; Teacher. m. Miriam Blank, 14 Sept 1961, 1 son, 1 daughter. *Education:* BA Modern Languages, University of Toronto, 1946; MA French, 1947, PhD French, 1953, Columbia University, New York, USA. *Appointments include:* Assistant Professor of Romanic Languages, Williams College, 1954-60; Professor of French and Comparative Literature, Brandeis University, 1960-, Massachusetts, USA; and others. *Publications:* The Career of Alphonse Daudet, 1965; The French Short Story in the 19th Century, 1969; Anatole France: The Short Stories, 1974; The Legacy of Flaubert in L'Hénaurme Siècle, 1984; Kamouraska in Women Writers of Quebec, 1985. *Contributions to:* Pmla; Symposium; Nineteenth Century French Studies, Modern Language Review; L'Esprit Créateur; others. *Memberships:* Modern Language Association; Modern Humanities Research Association; American Association of Teachers of French. *Honours:* Palmes Académiques (Decoration of the French Government), 1971; President, Association of Departments of Foreign Languages, 1985. *Address:* Department of Romance and Comparative Literature, Shiffman Humanities Center, Brandeis University, Waltham, MA 02254, USA.

SADDLEMYER (Eleanor) Ann, b. 28 Nov 1932, Prince Albert, Saskatchewan, Canada, Critic; Theatre Historian; Educator. *Education:* BA, 1953, Honours English Diploma, 1955, University of Saskatchewan; MA, Queen's University, 1956; PhD, Bedford College, University of London, England, 1961. *Appointments:* University of Victoria, Victoria, British Columbia, 1960-71; Victoria College, University of Toronto, 1971-;

Director, Graduate Centre for Study of Drama, University of Toronto, 1972-77, 1985-86; Berg Chair, New York University, USA, 1975; Master, Massey College, University of Toronto, 1988-; Board of Directors, Colin Smythe Publishers. *Publications:* The World of W B Yeats, 1965; In defence of Lady Gregory, Playwright, 1966; J M Synge Plays Books I and II, 1968; Lady Gregory Plays, 4 volumes, 1971; Theatre Business, 1982; The Collected Letters of J M Synge, 2 volumes, 1983-84; Synge and Modern Comedy, 1968; Letters to Molly: J M Synge to Maire O'Neill, 1971; Lady Gregory Fifty years After, 1987; Early Stages, Essays on the Theatre in Ontario 1800-1914, 1990. *Contributions to:* Co-editor, Theatre History in Canada; editorial Board, Modern drama, English Studies in Canada, Themes in Drama, Shaw, Research in the Humanities, Irish University Review. Yeats Annual, Studies in Contemporary Irish Literature, McGill English Studies in Drama. *Honours:* IODE Award, 1957; Canada Council Scholarships, 1958, 1959; Canada Council Fellowship, 1969; Guggenheim Fellowships, 1968, 1977; Fellow, Royal Society of Canada, 1976; LLD, Queen's University, 1977; Japan Society for Promotion of Science Fellowship, 1984; Province of Ontario Distinguished Service Award, 1985; Connaught Senior Research Fellowship, 1986; British Academy Rosemary Crawsnay Award, 1986; Fellow, Royal Society of Arts, 1987; DLitt, Victoria, 1989; DLitt, McGill, 1989; DLitt, Windsor, 1990. *Memberships include:* Royal Society of Canada, Executive Committee, 1987-. *Address:* Master's Lodging, Massey College, 4 Devonshire Place, Toronto, Canada M5S 2E1.

SADDLER K Allen. *See:* **RICHARDS Ronald Charles William.**

SADGROVE Sidney Henry (Lee Torrance), b. 1920, British. *Appointments:* Artist, Teacher and Writer, 1949- . *Publications:* You've Got To Do Something, 1967; A Touch of the Rabbits, The Suitability Factor, 1968; Stanislaus and the Princess, 1969; A Few Crumbs, 1971; Stanislaus and the Frog, Paradis Enow, 1972; Stanislaus and the Witch, 1973; The Link, 1975; The Bag, Half Sick of Shadows, Bleep, All in the Mind, 1977; Icary Dicary Doc, Angel, 1978; Filling, 1979; First Night, Only on Friday, 1980; Hoodunnit, 1984; Pawn en Prise, 1985; Just for Comfort, 1986; Tiger, 1987; State of Play, 1988; Warren, 1989; Dear Mrs Comfett, 1990. *Membership:* Writers Guild of Great Britain. *Address:* Pimp Barn, Withyham, Hartfield, Sussex TN7 4BB, England.

SADIE Stanley (John), b. 1930, British. *Appointments:* Professor, Trinity College of Music, 1957-65; Music Critic, The Times, 1964-81; Editor, The Musical Times, London, 1967-87; Editor, The New Grove Dictionary of Music and Musicians, 1970-. *Publications:* Handel, 1962; The Pan Book of Opera (in US as the Opera Guide), (with A Jacobs), 1964, 3rd edition, 1984; Mozart, 1965; Beethoven, 1967; Handel, 1968; Handel Concertos, 1973; New Grove Dictionary of Music and Musicians (ed), 20 volumes, 1980; Mozart, 1982; New Grove Dictionary of Musical Instruments (ed), 3 volumes, 1984; The Cambridge Music Guide (in US as Stanley Sadie's Music Guide), Mozart Symphonies, The New Grove Dictionary of American Music (ed with H Wiley Hitchcock), 4 volumes, 1986; The Brief Music Guide, 1987; The Grove Concise Dictionary of Music (ed), 1988; History of Opera (ed), 1989; Performance Practice (ed with Howard M Brown), 2 volumes, 1989; Man and Music (general ed), 8 volumes, 1989-; The New Grove Dictionary of Opera, 1992. *Address:* 12 Lyndhurst Road, London NW3 5NL, England.

SADKOWSKI Waclaw, (Waclaw Rola), b. 19 May 1932. Literary Critic; Editor; Translator. m. Danuta Sadkowski, 26 Sept 1953. *Education:* BA, MA, University of Warsaw. *Appointments:* Editor in chief, Literatura na Swiecie, 1972; President, Czytelnik, 1988-89, (publishing company); President, Literatura Swiatowa Foundation, 1990-. *Publications:* Catholic Literature in Poland, 1963; Roads and Crossroads of the Literature of the West, 1968, 1978; Circles of Community, 1972; From Conrad to Becket, 1989; James Baldwin. *Contributions to:* Tuorwsx; Polityks; Literaturature. *Honours:* Julian Brun Award, 1959. *Memberships:* PEN Club; Association Internationale des Critiques Litteraires; Societe Europeene de Culture; Union of Polish Writers. *Address:* Madalinskiego 50/52 m 18, 02-581 Warsaw, Poland.

SADLER Geoffrey Willis, (Jeff Sadler, Wes Calhoun), b. 7 Oct 1943, Mansfield Woodhouse, Nottinghamshire, England. Librarian. m. Jennifer Watkinson, 20 Nov 1965, 2 sons. *Education:* Manchester Library School, 1965-66; Associate, Library Association. *Appointments:* Librarian, Derbyshire Library Service, 1966-92; Founder, Leader, Shirebrook Writers Group, 1979-81; Assistant Local Studies Librarian, Chesterfield, 1985-; Leader, Shirebrook and District Writers Group, 1985-92. *Publications:* Arizona Blood Trail, 1981; Sonora Lode, 1982; Tamaulipas Guns, 1982; Severo Siege, 1983; Lobo Moon, 1983; Sierra Showdown, 1983; Throw of a Rope, 1984; Manhunt in Chihuahua, 1985; Return of Amarillo, 1986; Montana Mine, 1987; Saltillo Road, 1987; Chulo, 1988; Palomino Stud, 1988; At Muerto Springs, 1989; Journey to Freedom (with A Snarski), 1990; Ghost Town Guns, 1990; Texas Nighthawks, 1990; 20th Century Western Writers (editor), 1991; Shirebrook, Birth of a colliery (with E. I. Roberts), 1991; Headed North, 1992; Matamoros Mission, 1993. *Contributions to:* Native Son and other poems to Lawrence and the Real England, 1985; A Woman's Touch, short story, to A Better Mousetrap, 1988; Chulo and Pictures of Charlie, to Write First Time, 1992, (also editor). *Memberships:* Library Association; Steward, Departmental Vice-Chair, National Association of Local Government Officers; Derbyshire Chair, Shirebrook and District Local History Society. *Address:* 116 Langwith Road, Shirebrook, Mansfield, Notts NG20 8TH, England.

SADLER Jeff. *See:* **SADLER Geoffrey Willis.**

SADLER Mark. *See:* **LYNDS Dennis.**

SADOCK Eileen F (Popsy), b. 26 Sept 1927, Greensboro, USA. m. 2 May 1948, 2 sons, 1 daughter. *Education:* School of Journalism, Pennsylvania State University. *Publications:* All Newspaper Print Work, Editor, Sunday Tribune-Review Magazine, Focus. *Honours:* Keystone Press Award, 1976, 1977, 1982; American Cancer Society, 1983; Pennsylvania Womens Press Association, 3rd Place, Feature Writing, 1983, 1984, 1986, 1987; Finalist, Golden Quill, 1985, 1986. *Memberships:* Sigma Delta Chi; Pennsylvania Womens Press Association; Womens Press Club; Pittsburgh Press Club. *Address:* Tribune-Review, Cabin Hill Drive, Greensboro, PA 15601, USA.

SAFDIE Moshe b. 14 July 1938, Haifa, Israel. Architect; Writer. *Education:* B Arch (with honours) McGill University, Montreal, Quebec, Canada. *Appointments:* Van Ginkel & Associates, Architects/Planners, Montreal, Quebec, 1961-62; Louis I Kahn, Architect, Philadelphia, Pennsylvania, 1962-63; Section Head architect and planner with the Canadian Corporation for the 1967 World Exhibition, 1963-64; Private Practice, offices in Boston, Massachusetts; Montreal, Quebec; Toronto, Ontario and Jerusalem, Israel, 1964-. Academic appointments include: Professor of Architecture and Director, Desert Architecture and Environment Department, Desert Research Institute, Ben Gurion University, Israel; Director of Urban Design Programme, Professor of Architecture and Urban Design,1978-84, Ian Woodner (Studio) Professor of Architecture and Urban Design, 1984-89,Graduate School of Design, Harvard University. *Publications:* Beyond Habitat, 1970; For Everyone A Garden, 1974; Habitat Bill of Rights, Ministry of Housing, Imperial Government of Iran in collaboration with J.Ll. Sert, N Ardalan, B V Doshi and G Candilis, 1976; Form and Purpose monograph for International Design Conference in Aspen, 1980; Form and Purpose,

Houghton, Mifflin Company, 1982; The Harvard Jerusalem Studio: Urban Design for the Holy City, 1986; Beyond Habitat by Twenty Years, 1987 (revised 2nd edition); Jerusalem: The Future of the Past, 1989. Numerous papers and articles, films and exhibitions. *Honours include:* The Order of Canada; Le Prix d'excellence in Architecture of the Quebec Order of Architects; DFA (Hon) University of Victoria; Doctorate in Sciences (Hon), Laval University; Massey Medal for Architecture; LLD, (Hon) McGill University. *Memberships include:* Fellow, Royal Architectural Institute of Canada; Order of Architects of Quebec; Ontario Association of Architects; American Institute of Architects. *Address:* Moshe Safdie and Associates Inc, Architects and Planners, 100 Properzi Way, Somerville, MA 02143, USA.

SAFIRE William, b. 1929, American. *Appointments:* Reporter, New York Herald-Tribune Syndicate, 1949-51; Correspondent, WNBC- WNBT, Europe and the Middle East, 1951; Radio-TV Producer, WNBC, NYC, 1954-55; Vice-President, Tex McCrary Incorporated, 1955-60; President, Safire Public Relations, 1960-68; Special Assistant to President Nixon, 1969-73; Columnist, New York Times, WA, 1973-. *Publications:* The Relations Explosion, 1963; Plunging into Politics, 1964; Safire's Political Dictionary, 1968, 3rd edition, 1978; Before the Fall, 1975; Full Disclosure, 1977; Safire's Washington, On Language, 1980; What's the Good Word?, Good Advice (with Leonard Safir), 1982; I Stand Corrected, 1984; Take My Word For It, 1986; You Could Look It Up, 1988; Language Maven Strikes Again, 1990; Leadership (with Leonard Safir), 1990; Fumblerules, 1990; The First Dissident, 1992; Lend Me Your Ears, 1992; Good Advice On Writing (with Leonard Safir), 1992. *Address:* New York Times, 1627 Eye Street, NW, Washington DC 20006, USA.

SAFRAN Claire, b. 18 Mar 1930, New York City, New York, USA. Journalist; Author. m. John Milton Williams, 8 June 1958, 1 son. *Education:* BA cum laude, English, Brooklyn College, 1951. *Appointments:* Editor-in-Chief, TV Radio Mirror, 1961-65; Editor-in-Chief, In magazine, 1965-67; Associate Editor, Family Weekly magazine, 1967- 68; Editor-in-Chief, Coronet magazine, 1968-71; Contributing Editor, 1974-77, 1979-81, Executive Editor, 1977-78, Redbook; Roving Editor, Reader's Digest, 1983-88; Contributing Editor, Woman's Day, 1988-1991. *Publications:* New Ways to Lower Your Blood Pressure, 1984; Secret Exodus, 1987. *Contributions to:* Woman's Day; Reader's Digest; McCall's; Lear's; Parade; TV Guide; Other major magazines. *Honours:* Media Award, American Psychological Foundation, 1977; Finalist, Penney-Missouri Magazine Awards, 1977; Merit Award in Journalism, Religious Public Relations Council, 1978; Journalism Award, American Academy of Pediatrics, 1979; Odyssey Institute Media Awards, 1979, 1980, 1986; Matrix Award, Women in Communications, 1982, 1983, 1984; William Harvey Award, 1984, 1991; Journalism Award, American Academy of Family Physicians, 1984; Outstanding Magazine Article Award, American Society of Journalists and Authors, 1984. *Memberships:* American Society of Journalists and Authors, Chairperson, Professional Rights Committee. *Literary Agent:* Don Congdon Associates. *Address:* 53 Evergreen Avenue, Westport, CT 06880, USA.

SAGGS Henry William Frederick, b. 2 Dec 1920, Weeley, Essex, England, Professor of Semitic Languages. m. Joan Butterworth, 21 Sept 1946, 4 daughters. *Education:* Kings College, London, 1939-42, 1946-48; School of Oriental and African Studies, London, 1949-52; BD, 1942; MTh, 1948; MA 1950; PhD, 1953. *Appointments:* Lecturer, then Reader, in Akkadian, School of Oriental and African Studies, London, 1953-66; Professor of Semitic Languages, University College Cardiff, University of Wales, 1966-83. *Publications:* The Greatness that was Babylon, 1962, revised 1987; Everyday Life in Babylon and Assyria, 1965, 1987; The Encounter with the Divine in Mesopotamia and Israel, 1978; The Might that was Assyria, 1984; Civilization Before Greece and Rome, 1989; Abridged edition of H A Layard, Nineveh and Its Remains, 1970. *Contributions to:* Iraq; Sumer; Journal of Cuneiform Studies; Journal of Theological Studies; Archiv fuer Orientforschung; Revue d'Assyriologie; Journal of Semitic Studies; Bibliotheca Orientalis. *Memberships:* Society of Authors; Society of Antiquaries; British School of Archaeology in Iraq, Council Member; Savage Club; Royal Asiatic Society. *Address:* Eastwood, Bull Lane, Long Melford, Suffolk CO10 9EA, England.

SAHAY Akhowri Chittaranjan, b. 2 Jan 1925, Muzaffarpur, India. Poet & Writer. m. Akhowri Priyamvada, 17 June 1945, 3 sons, 1 daughter. *Education:* BA (Hons Distinction), 1945, MA, English, 1947, Patna University; MDEH, National University of Electro Homeopathy, Kanpur, 1964; PhD, English, Stanton University, New York, 1985. *Appointments:* Editor, The Nirjhar bilingual quarterly, Marwari English High School, Muzaffarpur, 1938-40; Lecturer, Head, Department of English, 1948-68, Editor, The Raka literary journal,1954-62, Rajendra College, Chapra, Bihar, 1948-68; Lecturer, Integrated Department of English, L S College, Muzaffarpur, Bihar, 1968-74; Associate Professor, English, Postgraduate Language Block, Bihar University, Muzaffarpur, 1974-85; Chief Editor, Kavita India quarterly poetry journal, 1987-. *Publications:* Hindi poetry: Van Yoothi, 1939; Van Shephali, 1941; Van Geet, 1943; Ajab Desh, 1945; Hindi short stories for children: Dick Aur Ostrich, 1946; Motilal Tota, 1948; Rani Sahiba, 1964; English poetry books: Roots and Branches, 1979; Emerald Foliage, 1981; Pink Blossoms, 1983; Golden Pollens, 1985; English prose: The Rubaiyat and Other Essays, 1980; My Interest in Occultism, 1982; Works in numerous anthologies. *Contributions to:* Numerous journals, India and abroad, including: Byword; Creative Forum; Canopy; Kavita India; Literary Endeavour; Poetry Time; Prophetic Voices; Poetry Review; Skylark; The Commonwealth Quarterly; The Poets International; The Plowman; The Quest. *Honours:* Various prizes, medals, certificates of merit, literary excellence, during school and college. *Memberships:* The Poetry Society, India; The Poetry Society, UK; PEN All-India Centre; International Writers Association; Writers Club, Madras; World Poetry Society; United Writers Association, Madras. *Address:* Kavita India House, South East Chaturbhujasthan, Muzaffarpur, Bihar 842001, India.

SAHGAL Nayantara, b. 10 May 1927, India. Writer. m. (1) 2 Jan 1949, div, 1 son, 2 daughters, (2) 17 Sept 1979. *Education:* BA, History, Wellesley College, Wellesley, Massachusetts, USA, 1947. *Appointments:* Advisory Board for English, Sahitya Academy (Indian National Academy of Letters), 1971-75; Writer-in-Residence, Southern Methodist University, Dallas, Texas, USA, 1973, 1977; Research Scholar, Radcliffe Institute, Cambridge, Massachusetts, 1976; Member, Indian delegation to the UN, 1978; Fellow, Woodrow Wilson International Center for Scholars, Washington DC, 1981-82; Fellow, National Humanities Center, North Carolinam 1983-84; Member, Jury for Commonwealth Writers Prize, 1990, 1991. *Publications:* Fiction: A Time to be Happy, 1958; This Time of Morning, 1965; Storm in Chandigarh, 1969; The Day in Shadow, 1972; A Situation in New Delhi, 1977; Rich Like Us, 1985; Plans for Departure, 1986; Mistaken Identity, 1988; Non-fiction: Prison and Chocolate Cake, 1954; From Fear Set Free, 1962; The Freedom Movement in India, 1970; Indira Gandhi: Her Road to Power, 1982. *Contributions to:* Articles and short stories, India and abroad including to: London Magazine; Vogue; The Far Eastern Economic Review; The New Republic; Cosmopolitan; Dallas Times-Herald; The Times; Christian Science Monitor. *Honours:* Sinclair Prize for Fiction (UK) for Rich Like Us, 1985; Sahitya Akademi Award for Rich Like Us, 1986; Commonwealth Writers Prize (Eurasia) for Plans for Departure, 1987; Elected Foreign Honorary Member, American Academy of Arts and Sciences, 1990. *Memberships:* Vice-President, People's Union for Civil Liberties, India, twice. *Literary Agent:* Bill Hamilton, A M Heath & Co, 79 St Martin's Lane, London WC2N 4AA, England, *Address:* 181-B Rajpur Road, Dehra Dun 248009, UP, India.

SAHLINS Marshall (David), b. 1930, American. *Appointments:* Lecturer in Anthropology, Columbia University, 1955-57; Assistant Professor 1957-61, Associate Professor 1961-64, Professor 1964-, University of Michigan, Ann Arbor; Professor of Anthropology, University of Chicago. *Publications:* Social Stratification in Polynesia, 1958; Evolution and Culture (ed with Elman R Service), 1960; Maola: Culture and Nature on a Fijian Island, 1963; Tribesmen, 1968; Stone Age Economics, 1972; The Use and Abuse of Biology: An Anthropoligical Critique of Sociobiology, 1976; Culture and Practical Reason, 1977; Historical Metaphors and Mythical Realities: Structure in the Early History of the Sandwick Islands Kingdom, 1981; Islands of History, 1985. *Address:* Department of Anthropology, University of Chicago, Chicago, IL 60637, USA.

SAIL Lawrence Richard, b. 29 Oct 1942, London, England. Poet; Writer. m. Teresa Luke, 1966, div, 1981, 1 son, 1 daughter. *Education:* Honours Degree in Modern Languages, St John's College, Oxford 1961-64. *Appointments:* Editor, South West Review, 1981-85; Chairman, The Arvon Foundation, 1990-; Programme Director, Cheltenham Festival of Literature, 1991. *Publications:* Opposite Views, 1974; The Drowned River, 1978; The Kingdom of Atlas, 1980; Collections of poems: Devotions, 1987; Aquamarine, 1988; Editor, First and Always, 1988; Out of Land: New and Selected Poems, 1992. *Contributions to:* Poetry Review; PN Review; Stand. *Honours:* Howthornden Fellowship, 1992; Arts Council Writers' Bursary, 1993. *Memberships:* Senior Common Room, St John's College, Oxford. *Address:* Richmond Villa, 7 Wonford Road, Exeter, Devon EX2 4LF, England.

SAINSBURY Maurice Joseph, b. 18 Nov 1927, Sydney, New South Wales, Australia. Psychiatrist (Consultant). m. Erna June Hoadley, 22 Aug 1953, 1 son, 2 daughters. *Education:* MB BS (Sydney), 1952; DPM, Royal College of Physicians and Surgeons, 1960; MRANZCP, 1963; FRANZCP, 1971; MRCPsych, 1971; FRCPsych, 1975; MHP, University of New South Wales, 1980. *Publications:* Key to Psychiatry, 1st Edition, 1973, 3rd Edition, 1980; Sainsbury's Key to Psychiatry (with L G Lambeth), 4th edition, 1988. *Contributions to:* Variety of articles to medical journals. *Honours:* Reserve Force Decoration (RFD), 1985; Member, Order of Australia (AM), 1987; Consultant Psychiatrist to Australian Army, 1976-1986. *Memberships:* Past President, Royal Australian And New Zealand College of Psychiatrists; President, After Care Association of New South Wales; Part-time Member, Guardianship Board, New South Wales; Part-time Member, Mental Health Review Tribunal, New South Wales; Consultant Psychiatrist to Chelmsford Royal Commission, 1988-90. *Address:* 3 Bimbil Place, Killara, New South Wales 2071, Australia.

SAINT Andrew John, b. 30 Nov 1946, Shrewsbury, England. Architectural Historian. 2 daughters. *Education:* Christ's Hospital, Horsham, 1958-64; Balliol College, Oxford; BA Lit Hum, 1969; MPhil, Warburg Institute, University of London, 1971. *Publications:* Richard Norman Shaw, 1976; The Image of the Architect, 1983; Towards A Social Architecture, 1987. *Contributions to:* Various. *Honours:* Alice Davis Hitchcock Medallion, Society of Architectural Historians, 1977, 1989. *Address:* English Heritage, London Division, Chesham House, 30 Warwick Street, London W1R 5RD, England.

SAINT Dora Jessie (Miss Read), b. 1913, United Kingdom. Novelist; Short Story and Children's Fiction Writer. *Publications:* Village School, 1955; Village Diary, 1957; Storm in the Village, 1958; Hobby Horse Cottage, 1958; Thrush Green, 1959; Fresh from the Country, 1960; Winter in Thrush Green, 1961; Miss Clare Remembers, 1962; The Market Square, 1966; The Howards of Caxley, 1967; Country Cooking, 1969; News from Thrush Green, 1970; Tyler's Row, 1972; Christmas Mouse, 1973; Battles at Thrush Green, 1975; No Holly for Miss Quinn, 1976; Village Affairs, 1977; Return to Thrush Green, 1978; The White Robin, 1979; Village

Centenary, 1980; Gossip from Thrush Green, 1981; A Fortunate Grandchild, 1982; Affairs at Thrush Green, 1983; Summer at Fairacre, 1984; At Home in Thrush Green, 1985; Time Remembered, 1986; The School at Thrush Green, 1987; The World at Thrush Green, 1988; Mrs Pringle, 1989; Friends at Thrush Green, 1990. *Address:* Strouds, Shefford Woodlands, Newbury, Berkshire RG16 7AJ, England.

SAINT JACQUES Alfred Joseph, b. 17 Sept 1956, Lausanne, Switzerland. Writer; Editor. m. Mary Lou Hurley, 9 May 1987. *Education:* BA, Communications, Fordham University, 1979. *Appointments:* Reporter: Yonkers Home News and Times, 1979, Eastside Express/Westsider, 1979; Associate Editor, Dermatology News, 1979; Editor, Special Projects, Academy Professional Information Services, 1983; Managing Editor, Immunology & Allergy Practice, 1984; Editorial Director, Medical Horizons Publishing, 1988. *Contributions to:* Respiratory Medicine Today; Truck'N Van Power; Race Car Magazine; Physician's Auto Digest; Group Practice Managed Healthcare News. *Honours:* 2nd Place, Eye on the World Photo Competition. *Memberships:* International Motor Press Association; Sports Car Club of America; Member, American Medical Writers Association; American Public Health Association; New York Academy of Sciences. *Address:* Knolls Road, Bloomingdale, NJ, USA.

SAKAMOTO Yoshikazu, b. 16 Sept 1927, USA. Professor. m. Kikuko Ono, 2 June 1956, 2 daughters. *Education:* Faculty of Law, University of Tokyo, 1951. *Publications:* International Politics in Global Perspective, 1990; The Political Analysis of Disarmament, 1988; Co-Editor: Democratizing Japan: The Allied Occupation of Japan, 1987; Editor: Strategic Doctrines and their Alternatives, 1987; Militarization and Regional Conflict, 1988. *Honours:* Fulbright Grant; Rockerfeller and Eisenhower Fellowships; The Mainichi Press National Book Award, 1976. *Memberships:* Secretary General, International Peace Research Association, 1979-83; Jury member, UNESCO Prize for Peace Education, 1984-89; American and Japanese Political Science Associations; Japanese Association of American Studies; International Peace Research Association. *Address:* 8-29-19 Shakujii-machi, Nermaku, Tokyo 177, Japan.

SAKELLARIOU Haris, b. 4 June 1923, Thavmakos Phtiotis, Greece. m. 26 Oct 1947, 1 son, 1 daughter. *Education:* University of Athens, 1964; Universite d'Aix-en-Provence, Maitrise, 1974. *Appointments:* Director, Neoellinikos Logos, 1963-; Director, Children's Literature Review, 1986-. *Publications:* Elevthera Grammata, 1945-46; Nea Estia, 1956, 1958, 1962; Philologiki Protochronia, 1984, 1986; Kimmerions Country, 1970; Anepidota (Ungiven), 1978; The Pit, (novel), 1975; The Cannibals, 1982; History of Children's Literature, 1984; Michalis Papamavros, biography, 1985; Tellos Agras and Children's literature, 1986; Modern Poetry and its Teaching Problems, 1989; Theatre of Resistance, 1989; Vatrachomyomachia (frog-mouse-war) of Homer, theatre play, 1989; Myths and Stories of Leonardo Da Vinci (translation), 1989; Spithovolakis, theatre play, 1988; 3 Collections of Poems; 2 novels; 6 essays; 3 theatre plays; 35 books for children. *Contributions to:* Nea Estia; Philologiki Protochronia; Rizospastis; Ta Nea; Ekpedeftika (educational magazine); Eleftherotipia, Vima; Kathimerini. *Honours:* Award, Kalokerinios Competition, 1961; Award, Academy of Athens, 1962; 5 Awards for Children's Books, 1962, 1965, 1967, 1976, 1983; Award, narrative from Kahtilmerini Newspaper, 1976; International Award of Children's Poetry; Gold Medal of City of Athens. *Memberships:* Greek Authors Society; Authors and Illustrators Union of Childrens Books. *Address:* 14 Thetidos St, 13122 Athens, Greece.

SAKHARNOV Svyatoslav, b. 12 Mar 1923, Artyomovsk, Ukraine. Writer; Naval Officer. m. Larisa 4 Feb 1935, 2 sons, 1 daughter. *Education:* DSc, Naval Academy of Leningrad, 1944. *Appointments:* Editor in Chief of monthly magazine, Kostyor (Campfire).

Publications: Around the World along the Seas: Children's Encyclopaedia, 1972; Selected Stories and Tales, 1987; Tales from the Travel Sack, 1979; The Horse above the City, 1990; More than 60 books in total, mostly for children, most of which have been translated into different languages. *Contributions to:* Many Soviet and foreign magazines. *Honours:* Four international awards for Children's Encyclopaedia; First Brize, Belonia Italy, 1973. *Memberships:* USSR Union of WRiters; Russian Geographic Society; Russian Historic Society. *Address:* Novorssiyskay Str 22-1-18, St Petersburg, 194018 Russia.

SAKOL Jeannie, b. 1928, American. *Publications:* What about Teen-Age Marriage?, 1961; The Inept Seducer, 1967; Gumdrop, 1972; I Was Never the Princess, 1974; New Year's Eve, 1975; Flora Sweet, 1977; All Day, All Night, All Woman, 1978; The Wonderful World of Country Music, Promise Me Romance, 1979; Hot 30, Mothers and Lovers, 1980. *Address:* 230 East 48th Street, New York, NY 10017, USA.

SAKYA Manju Ratna, b. Jan 1946, Kathmandu, Nepal. President, Nepal Journalist Association. m. Subha Luxmi Sakya, June 1967, 1 son, 1 daughter. *Appointments:* Chief Editor and Publisher, Arpan Nepali Weekly; Chief Editor: Daily News, and Commerce (English monthly). *Education:* Masters Degree in Commerce, Tribhuvan University, Nepal, 1967. *Publications:* An Approach to Nepalese Currency. Many articles on political, economical trade, commerce and business, published internationally. *Honours:* Coronation Medal, 1974; Gorkha Dashin Bahu Second Class, 1981; SAARC Medal, 1987; Government of Finland Medal, 1988. *Memberships:* Asian Mass Communication Research Informational Centre, Singapore; International Organization of Journalists, Pargue; Press Foundation of Manila; Lions Club. *Address:* PO Box No 285, Kohity Bahal, Kathmandu, Nepal.

SALCEDO Ernesto, b. 31 Jan 1931, Balinga-sag, Misamis Or. Author. m. Herminia Ocate, 8 Aug 1953, 6 sons, 2 daughters. *Education:* BSC., Elementary Education; Elementary Teachers Certificate. *Publications:* Where Did the Cross of Christ Come From, 1987; No Retreat No Surrender, 1987; The Christmas Gift of Abukay, 1986; The Unvaluable Money, 1986; The Uniform, 1980; Underwater Fire, 1981; Regina Martyrum, 1987; Mater Dolorosa, 1987; Magimar, 1985; Hara Maginda, 1984. *Contributions to:* Silaw; Bulawan; Bisaya. *Honours:* Fisla Bank, Certificate of Appreciation; Davao Savings Bank, Certificate of Appreciation; Land Bank of the Phil., Certificate of Appreciation. *Memberships:* Oro Ludabi Inc., Vice President; Metro Cagayan Ludabi, Director; Magsusulat Inc., Manila, Member; Founder, President, Barkada Inc; Founder, Executive Vice President, United Salcedo Clan. *Address:* Gumamela-Caimito St., Carmen, Cagayan de Oro 8401.

SALE Kirkpatrick, b. 1937, American. *Appointments:* Board Member, PEN American Center 1976-, Exploratory Project for Conditions of Peace 1984-, Learning Alliance 1985-; Secretary 1980-86, Co-director, 1986-, E F Schumacher Society; Contributing Editor, Nation, NYC, 1986-. *Publications:* SDS, 1973; Power Shift, 1975; Human Scale, 1980; Dwellers in the Land: The Bioregional Vision, 1985; The Conquest of Paradise: Christopher Columbus and the Columbian Legacy, 1990. *Address:* 113 West 11th Street, New York, NY 10011, USA.

SALINGER J(erome) D(avid), b. 1919, American. *Publications:* The Catcher in the Rye, 1951; Nine Stories (in UK as For Esme - With Love and Squalor and Other Stories), 1953; Franny and Zooey, 1961; Raise High the Roof Beam, Carpenters, and Seymour: An Introduction, 1963. *Address:* c/o Harold Ober Associates, 425 Madison Avenue, New York, NY 10017, USA.

SALISBURY Frank B(oyer), b. 1926, American. *Appointments:* Assistant Professor of Botany, Pomona College, Claremont, CA, 1954-55; Assistant Professor of Plant Physiology 1955-61, Professor 1961-66, Colorado State University, Fort Collins; National Science Foundation Postdoctural Fellow, Tübingen, West Germany, Innsbruck, Austria, 1962-63; Professor of Plant Physiology, 1966-, Head of Plant Science Department, 1966-70, Professor of Botany, 1968-, Utah State University, Logan; Technical Representative in Plant Physiology, US Atomic Energy Commission, 1973-74; Guest Professor, University of Innsbruck, Austria, 1983; Guest Professor, Lady Davis Fellow, Hebrew University of Jerusalem, 1983; Editor-in-Chief, Americas and Pacific Countries, Journal of Plant Physiology. *Publications:* The Flowering Process, 1963; Vascular Plants: Form and Function (with R V Parke), 1964, 1970; Truth by Reason and by Revelation, 1965; Plant Physiology (with C Ross), 1969, 3rd edition 1985, 4th edition 1991; The Biology of Flowering, 1971; Botany (with W A Jensen), 1972, 1984; The Utah UFO Display: A Biologist's Report, 1974; The Creation, 1976; Biology (co-author), 1977. *Memberships:* Various advisory boards for US National Aeronautics and Space Agency (NASA). *Address:* Plants, Soils and Biometeorology Department, Utah State University, Logan, UT 84322-4820, USA.

SALISBURY Harrison Evans, b. 14 Nov 1908. Journalist. m. (1) Mary Hollis, 1933, (div), 2 sons, (2) Charlotte Rand, 1964. *Education:* BA, University of Minnesota. *Appointments:* United Press International, 1930-48; Moscow Correspondent, New York Times, 1949-54, National Affairs Editor, 1961-63, Assistant Managing Editor, 1964-72, Associate Editor, 1972-74. *Publications:* Russia on the Way, 1946; American in Russia, 1955; The Shook-Up Generation, 1959; To Moscow - And Beyond, 1960; Moscow Journal, 1961; A New Russia?, 1962; The Northern Palmyra Affair, 1962; Orbit of China, 1967; Behind the Lines - Hanoi, 1967; The Soviet Union: The 50 Years, 1967; The 900 Days, The Siege of Leningrad, 1969; The Coming War Between Russia and China, 1970; The Many Americas Shall be One, 1971; The Eloquence of Protest, 1972; To Peking - and Beyond, 1973; The Gates of Hell, 1975; Travels Around America, 1976; Black Night, White Snow - Russia's Revolutions, 1905-1917, 1978; Without Fear or Favor: The New York Times and Its Times, 1980; China: One Hundred Years of Revolution, 1983; Journey for Our Times: A Memoir, 1983; The Long March: The Untold Story, 1985; A Time of Change: A Reporters Tale of Our Time, 1988; The Great Black Dragon Fire: A Chinese Inferno, 1989; Tianaimen Diary: 13 Days in June, 1989; The New Emperors: China in the Era of Mao & Deng, 1992; Heroes of My Time, 1993. *Honours:* Pulitzer Prize for International Correspondence, 1955; George Polk Memorial Journalism Award, 1958, 1967. *Memberships:* American Academy of Arts and Letters; American Academy of Arts and Sciences; National Institute of Arts and Letters, President 1975-76; President, Authors League, 1980-84. *Address:* c/o Curtis Brown Ltd, 10 Astor Place, New York, NY 10003, USA.

SALISBURY Joyce Ellen, b. 10 Dec 1944, Arizona, USA. Professor of History. 1 son, 1 daughter. *Education:* MA, 1975, PhD, 1981, Medieval History, Rutgers University. *Publications:* Church Fathers, Independent Virgins, 1991; Medieval Sexuality: A Research Guide, 1990; Editor: Sex in the Middle Ages, 1991; Medieval World of Nature, 1992; Beasts and Bestiality in the Middle Ages (in progress). *Contributions to:* Scholarly articles in journals such as Journal of Medieval History, Journal of Religious History, manuscripta. *Honours:* Adele Mellen Prize for Scholarship, 1985; Council for Advancement and Support of Education, Professor of the Year, Wisconsin, 1991. *Address:* Department of History, University of Wisconsin-Greenbay, Greenbay, WI 54311 USA.

SALISBURY Robert H(olt), b. 1930, American. *Appointments:* Joined faculty 1955, Chairman, Department of Political Science 1966-73, Chairman,

Center for the Study of Public Affairs 1974-76, Professor, Washington University, St Louis; Guggenheim Fellowship, 1990; Rockefeller Study Center (Bellagio) Visiting Scholar, 1990. *Publications:* Functions and Policies of American Government (co-author), 1958, 3rd edition 1967; American Government: Readings and Problems (with Eliot, Chambers and Prewitt), 1959, 1965; Democracy in the Mid-Twentieth Century (ed with Chambers), 1960, as Democracy Today, 1962; State Politics and the Public Schools (with Master and Eliot), 1964; Interest Group Politics in America, 1970; Governing America: Public Choice and Political Action, 1973; Citizen Participation in the Public Schools, 1980; Interest and Institutions, Substance and Structure in American Politics, 1992. *Membership:* Chairman, Department of Political Sciences, Washington University, 1986-92. *Address:* 337 Westgate, St Louis, MO 63130, USA.

SALKEY (Felix) Andrew (Alexander), b. 1928, Jamaican. *Appointments:* Regular outside Contributor, Interviewer and Scriptwriter, BBC External Services (Radio), London, 1952-76; English Teacher in a London Comprehensive School, 1957-59; Professor of Writing, Hampshire College, Amherst, MA, 1976-. *Publications:* A Quality of Violence, 1959; Escape to an Autumn Pavement, West Indian Stories (ed), 1960; Hurricane, 1964; Earthquake, Stories from the Caribbean (in US as Island Voices) (ed), 1965; Young Commonwealth Poets '65, 1964; Drought, The Shark Hunters, 1966; Riots, Caribbean Prose, 1967; The Late Emancipation of Jerry Stover, 1968; The Adventures of Catullus Kelly, Jonah Simpson, 1969; Havana Journal, Breaklight: Caribbean Poetry (ed), 1971; Georgetown Journal, Caribbean Essays (ed), Breaklight: An Anthology of Caribbean Poetry (in US as Breaklight: The Poetry of the Caribbean) (ed), 1972; Anancy's Score, Caribbean Essays (ed), Jamaica, 1973; Caribbean Folk Tales and Legends (ed), 1975; Come Home, Malcolm Heartland, 1976; Writing in Cuba since the Revolution(ed), 1977; In the Hills Where Her Dreams Live, 1979; The River that Disappeared, Danny Jones, Away, 1980. *Address:* Flat 8, Windsor Court, Moscow Road, Queensway, London W2, England.

SALTER Charles A, b. 12 Oct 1947, Forth Worth, Texas, USA. Research Psychologist, Army Officer. m. 13 May 1972, 1 son, 2 daughters. *Education:* BS magna cum laude, Tulane University, 1969; MA, University of Pennsylvania, 1970, PhD, 1973; MS, 1987, SD, 1989, Harvard University School of Public Health. *Appointments:* Editor, Alternative Careers for Academics Bulletin, 1978; Syndicated Columnist, Surburban Features, 1983-85; Editor, The Inn-Former Newsletter, 1989-90. *Publications:* The Professional Chef's Guide to Kitchen Management, 1985; Knight's Foodservice Dictionary, 1987; Foodservice Standards in Resorts, 1987; On the Frontlines, 1988; Getting it off, Keeping it off, 1988; Literacy and the Library, 1991; Psychology for Living, 1977; Looking Good Eating Right, 1991; The Vegetarian Teen, 1991. *Contributions to:* Scientific and trade journals and magazines. *Honours:* Phi Beta Kappa, 1969; Meritorious Service Medal, 1991. *Memberships:* American Society of Journalists and Authors; American College of Nutrition, Fellow. *Literary Agent:* Ruth Wreschner, 10 West 74th Street, NY 10023, USA. *Address:* SGRD-UAB, USA Aeromedical Research Laboratory, PO Box 577, Fort Rucker, AL 36362, USA.

SALTER James, b. 10 June 1925, USA. Writer. m. Ann Altemus, 5 June 1951 (dec 1976), 2 sons, 3 daughters. *Publications:* The Hunters, 1957; The Arm of Flesh, 1960; A Sport and a Pastime, 1967; Light Years, 1976; Sold Faces, 1980; Dusk and Other Stories, 1989. *Contributions to:* The Paris Review; Antaeus; Grand Street; Vogue; Esquire; Others. *Honours:* Grant, American Academy of Arts and Letters, 1982; PEN-Faulkner Award, 1989. *Membership:* PEN, USA. *Literary Agent:* Peter Matson, Sterling Lord Literistic, One Madison Avenue, New York, NY 10010, USA. *Address:* Mitchell Lane, Bridgehampton, NY 11932, USA.

SALTER Lionel, b. 1914, British. *Appointments:* Critic, Gramophone, 1948-; Record Critic, The Music Teacher, 1952-79; Head of Television Music, 1956-63, Head of Opera, 1963-67, Assistant Controller of Music, 1967-74, BBC, London; General Editor, BBC Music Guide, 1971-75. *Publications:* Going to a Concert, 1950; Going to the Opera, 1955; The Musician and His World, 1963; Opera Guides - Mozart (trans), 3 volumes, 1971; Music and the Twentieth Century Media (with J Bornoff), 1972; Gramophone Guide to Classical Composers, 1978. *Address:* C/o Salamander Books, 27 Old Gloucester Street, London WC1, England.

SALTER Mary D. *See:* **AINSWORTH Mary Dinsmore.**

SALTMAN Judith, b. 11 May 1947, Vancouver, Canada. Associate Professor of Children's Literature and Librarianship; Writer. m. Bill Barringer, 1 daughter. *Education:* BA 1969, BLS 1970, University of British Columbia; MA Simmons College, 1982. *Appointments:* Children's Librarian, Toronto Public Library, Toronto, Canada, 1970-72; Children's Librarian, West Vancouver Memorial Library, West Vancouver, British Columbia, 1973-79; Children's Librarian, Vancouver Public Library, 1980-83; Assistant Professor 1983-88, Associate Professor of Children's Literature and Librarianship, 1988-, University of British Columbia, Vancouver; Member, International Board on Books for Young People. *Publications:* (ed) Riverside Anthology of Children's Literature, 6th edition, 1985; Goldie and the Sea (juvenile) 1987; Modern Canadian Children's Books, 1987; The New Republic of Childhood, 1990. *Honours:* Howard V Phalin-World Book scholar of Canadian Library Association, 1981; Frances E Russell Memorial Award from Canadian section of International Board of Books for Young People, 1986. *Memberships include:* Canadian Library Association; American Library Association; Children's Literature Association. *Address:* School of Library, Archival and Information Studies, University of British Columbia, 831-1956 Main Mall, Vancouver, British Columbia, Canada V6T 1Z1.

SALTZMAN Arthur Michael, b. 10 Aug 1953, Chicago, Illinois, USA. Professor. m. Marla Jane Marantz, 26 July 1980, 1 daughter. *Education:* University of Illinois, AB, 1971; AM, 1976; PhD, 1979. *Appointments:* Teaching Fellow, University of Illinois, 1975-80; Assistant Professor, Missouri Southern State College, 1981-86; Associate Professor, 1986-92; Professor, 1992-. *Publications:* The Fiction of William Gass; Understanding Raymond Carver; Designs of Darkness in Contemporary American Fiction; The Novel in the Balance. *Contributions to:* Review of Contemoprary Fiction; Critique; Chicago Reveiw; Journal of Modern Literature; Literary Review. *Honours:* List of Excellent Teachers; Bresee Graduate Fiction Award; Phi Beta Kappa; NEH Summer Stipend; Outstanding Teachers Award. *Memberships:* Modern Language Association; PEN. *Address:* 2301 West 29th Street, Joplin, MO 64804, USA.

SALVADORI Max William (Massimo Salvadori-Paleotti), b. 1908, British/Italian. *Appointments:* With Institute of Foreign Trade, Rome, 1931-32; Farm Manager, Njoro, Kenya, 1934-37; Lecturer, University of Geneva, 1937-39; Professor, St Lawrence University, Canton, NY, 1939-41; Bennington College, VT, 1945-62; Smith College, Northampton, MA, 1947-75; with Unesco, 1948-49; NATO Secretariat, 1952-53, ENI, Rome, 1956-57; Professor, Emeritus of History, Smith College, Northampton, MA. *Publications:* L'Unita del Mediterraneo, 1931; La Penetrazione Europea in Africa, 1932; La Colonisation Europenne au Kenya, 1938; Problemi di Liberta, 1949; Resistenza ed Azione, 1951; Lettere di Giacinta Salvadori (ed), 1953; The Rise of Modern Communism, 1953, revised edition, 1975; Storia della Resistenza Italiana, 1955; Capitalismo Demoncratico, 1956; NATO, Liberal Democracy, 1957; Locke and Liberty (ed), The Economics of Freedom, 1959; Prospettive Americane, 1960; Western Roots in Europe, Cavour and the Unification of Italy, 1961; La Resistenza nell' Anconetano e nel Piceno, 1962; The American

Economic System (ed), 1963; Da Roosevelt a Kennedy, 1964; Italy, 1965; Modern Socialism, 1968; European Liberalism (ed), A Pictorial History of the Italian People, 1972; Breve Storia della Resistenza Italiana, 1974; Free Market Economics, The Liberal Heresy, 1977; L'Eresia Liberale, 2 volumes, 1984. *Address:* 36 Ward Avenue, Northampton, MA 01060, USA.

SAMADARSHI. *See:* **KRISHNASWAMY Iyenger H S.**

SAMARAKIS Antonis, b. 16 Aug 1919, Athens, Greece. Author. m. Eleni Kourebanas, 1963. *Education:* University of Athens. *Appointments:* Chief of Emeigration, Refugees and Technical Assistance Departments, Ministry of Labour, 1935-40, 1944-63; Active in Resistance Movement, World War II. *Publications:* Short Stories: Wanted: Hope, 1954; I Refuse, 1961; The Jungle, 1966; The Passport (in Nea Kimina 2), 1971; novels: Danger Signal, 1959; The Flaw, 1965; Contributions to: The Child's Song, (anthology of poems for children); works have been translated into 16 languages & frequently adapted for Cinema and TV. *Honours:* Hon. Citizen of San Francisco and New Orelans, USA; Greek National Book Award, 1962; Greek Prize of the Twelve, 1966; Grand Prix de la Litterature Policiere, France, 1970; Europalia Prize for Literature, 1982. *Memberships:* PEN; National Society of Authors; served on many humanitarian missions in many parts of the world for ILO, UNHCR, ICEM and Council of Europe. *Address:* 53 Taygetou and Ippolytu Streets, Athens, 806, Greece.

SAMBROOK Arthur James, b. 5 Sept 1931, England. Univesity Teacher. m. Patience Ann Crawford, 25 Mar 1961, 4 sons. *Education:* BA, 1955, MA 1959, Worcester College, Oxford; PhD, University of Nottingham, 1957. *Publications include:* A Poet Hidden: The Life of Richard Watson Dixon, 1833-1900, 1962; The Scribleriad 1742 & The Difference Between Verbal & Practical Virtue, 1742, Editor, 1967; James Thomson's The Seasons & The Castle of Indolence, Editor, 1972, 2nd edition 1984, 3rd edition 1987; William Cobbett an Author Guide, 1973; Pre-Raphaelitism, critical essays, editor, 1974; Editor, James Thomson's The Seasons, 1981; The Intellectual and Cultural Context of English Literature 1700-1789, 1986; Thomson 1700-1748, A Life; Biographical Critical, Biographical articles on various English writers in numerous reference books; over 100 articles & reviews in Church Quarterly Review; 18th Century Life; 18th Century Studies; English; English Language Notes; Garden History; Journal of English & German Philology; Library; Modern Language Review; Times Literary Supplement; English Miscellany; English Studies; Notes and Queries; The Scriblerian; Review of English Studies. *Contributions to:* The Rossettis and Contemporary Poets in the Sphere History of Literature, 1970, 2nd edition 1987; Pope & the Visual Arts, in Alexander Pope, Ed. Peter Dixon, 1972; Augustan Poetry, in Encyclopaedia of Literature and Criticism (ed Martin Coyle and others); Thomson Abroad: Traversing Realsm Unknown, in All Before Them (ed John McVeagh). *Address:* Dept of English, Southampton University, Hants, England.

SAMELSON William, b. 1928, American. *Appointments:* Chairman, Department of Foreign Languages, San Antonio College, TX, 1960-. *Publications:* Gerhart Herrmann Mostar: A Critical Profile, 1965; Der Sinn des Lesens (ed), 1968; All Lie in Wait, 1969; English as a Second Language: Phase One: Let's Converse, 1973; Phase Two: Let's Read, 1974, Phase Three: Let's Writer, 1975; Phase Four: Let's Continue, 1979, Phase Zero Plus: Let's Begin, 1980. *Address:* Department of Foreign Languages, San Antonio College, 1300 San Pedro Avenue, San Antonio, TX 78284, USA.

SAMPSON Anthony Terrell Seward, b. 3 Aug 1926, Durham, England. Writer. m. 31 May 1965, 1 son, 1 daughter. *Education:* Christ Church, Oxford University, 1947-50. *Appointments:* Editor, Drum Magazine, South Africa, 1951-55; Staff, Observer, 1955-66; Editorial Advisor, Brandt Commission, 1978-80; Columnist, Newsweek International, 1977-. *Publications:* Drum, 1956; Anatomy of Britain, 1962; New Europeans, 1968; The Sovereign State of ITT, 1973; The Seven Sisters, 1975; The Arms Bazaar, 1977; The Money Lenders, 1981; Black and Gold, 1987; The Midas Touch, 1989; The Essential Anatomy of Britain: New Patterns of Power in the Nineties, 1992. *Contributions to:* Numerous journals including Newsweek; New York Times; Times; Observer. *Honour:* Prix International De La Presse, Nice, 1976. *Literary Agent:* The Peters Fraser and Dunlop Group Ltd, London. *Address:* 27 Ladbroke Grove, London W11, England.

SAMPSON Edward E, b. 1934, American. *Appointments:* Profesor of Psychology, University of California, Berkeley, 1960-70; Professor of Sociology and Psychology, Clark University, Worcester, MA, 1971-82; Dean, Wright Institute, Berkeley, 1982-86; Dean, School of Social and Behavioral Science, California State University, Northridge, 1986-. *Publications:* Approaches, Contexts and Problems of Social Psychology, 1964; Student Activism and Protest, 1970; Social Psychology and Contemporary Society, 1971, 1976; Ego at the Threshold, 1975; Group Process for the Health Professions, 1978; Introducing Social Psychology, 1980; Justice and the Critique of Pure Psychology, 1983. *Address:* 55BS, California State University, Northridge, CA 91330, USA.

SAMPSON Geoffrey (Richard), b. 1944, British. Language Engineering Consultant. *Appointments:* Fellow, Queen's College, Oxford, 1969-72; Lecturer, London School of Economics, 1972-74; Lecturer, 1974-76, Reader, 1976-84, University of Lancaster; Professor of Linguistics, University of Leeds, 1985-90; Director, Centre for Advanced Software Applications, University of Sussex, 1991-. *Publications:* The Form of Language, 1975; Liberty and Language, 1979; Making Sense, Schools of Linguistics, 1980; An End to Allegiance, 1984; Writing Systems, 1985; The Computational Analysis of English (with Garside and Leech), 1987. *Address:* School of Cognitive and Computing Sciences, University of Sussex, Falmer, Brighton BN1 9QH, England.

SAMPSON Ronald Victor, b. 12 Nov 1918, St Helen's, Lancashire, England. m. 9 Jan 1943, 2 daughters. *Education:* Keble College, Oxford, 1936-39, 1946-47, 1948-51; Nuffield College, Oxford, 1950-51; MA, 1947; DPhil, 1951. *Publications:* Progress in the Age of Reason, 1957; Equality and Power, 1965, USA Edition as The Psychology of Power, Brazilian Edition as Psicanalize do Poder, Mexican Edition as Igualdad y Poder; Tolstoy: The Discovery of Peace, 1973; USA Edition as The Discovery of Peace; Chapter on Limits of Religious Thought, in 1959 - Entering an Age of Crisis, 1959. *Contributions to:* The Nation, New York; Resurgence; Peace News; The Pacifist; Academic journals; Pamphlets and translations, Housmans and Peace Pledge Union. *Membership:* PEN, English Branch. *Address:* Beechcroft, Hinton Charterhouse, Bath, Avon, England.

SAMPUTAANAE Kosu, (Kosusam-Santanna-Susampu-Santhoji), b. 3 Jan 1930, Kodihalli, Doddabaldapur Tq, Bangalore District, Karnataka, India. Civil Engineer; Poet; Retired P W D Officer. m. Prabha Samputaanae, 5 Nov 1959, 2 sons, 2 daughters. *Education:* BSc, Central College, Bangalore, 1955; BE, Civil Engineering, BMS Engineering College, Bangalore, 1959; MIE (India), Institute of Engineers, India. *Appointments:* Co-Editor: Jaycees Journal; Megha; Bhaavana; Educationist, Founder, Vittal Vihar Vidyaniketana; Philanthropist, Founder, Vittal Vihar Charitable Trust; Industrialist; Founder: Orphanage; Home for Aged; Social Worker; Publisher, KICO Prakashana; Film and Stage Actor. *Publications:* About 25 books including: Kavana Kidi, collection of poems, 1965; Goravayya, action songs for children, 1967;

Devaru Kannubittaaga, social stage play, 1976, 1982, 1991; Naadina Bhaagya, Kannada feature film (co-author of lyrics, dialogues), 1978; Saarwabhouwma Shivaji, historical stage play, 1987; Santana Kante, 1008 short poems, 1990; Altogether 3 collections of poems, 2 of community songs, 3 of action songs for children, Vichara Sahithya, 2 social stage plays, historical stage play, radio, play, radio musical feature, lyrics for documentary film, lyrics and dialogue for 3 feature films, 1 cassette recorded live, 2 discs; Editor, 1 book. *Contributions to:* Poems, short stories, articles to several special issues and periodicals; Also to All India Radio, Bangalore. *Honours:* Felicitations, 1981, 1984, several other occasions. *Memberships include:* Director, Karnataka Coop Film and Fine Arts Federation; Institute of Engineers, India; Poets International Organisation; Kannada Sahithya; Authors Guild of India; Karnata Writers Association; Karnataka B K Graduate Parishath; Founder, President, several social and literary organisations. *Address:* Vittal Vihar Charitable Trust, Phutanaybagh, Vittalnagar, Kannamangala 561203, Doddaballapur Tq, Bangalore District, Karnataka, India.

SAMS Eric, b. 3 May 1926, London, England. Civil Servant (retired). m. Enid Tidmarsh, 30 June 1952, 2 sons. *Education:* Corpus Christi, Cambridge, 1947-50; BA (1st Class Hons), 1950; PhD, 1972. *Publications:* The Songs of Hugo Wolf, 1961, 1983 and 1992; The Songs of Robert Schumann, 1969, 1975 and 1993; Brahms Songs, 1971, French translation, 1989; Shakespeare's: Edmund Ironside, 1985, 1986. *Contributions to:* Times Literary Supplement; Notes and Queries; Connotations. *Honours:* Leverhulme Grant, 1984; Honorary Patron, Songmakers Almanac, 1980; Honorary Member, Guildhall School of Music and Drama, 1983-. *Address:* 32 Arundel Avenue, Sanderstead, Surrey CR2 8BB, England.

SAMUELS Warren J(oseph), b. 1933, American. *Appointments:* Assistant Professor of Economics, University of Missouri, 1957-58, Georgia State College, Atlanta, 1958-59; Assistant Professor of Economics 1959-62, Associate Professor 1962-68, University of Miami, FL; Professor of Economics 1968-, Director of Graduate Programs, Placement Officer, Department of Economics 1969-73, Michigan State University, East Lansing; President Elect 1971-72, President 1972-73, Economics Society of Michigan; Editor, Journal of Economic Issues, 1971-81. *Publications:* The Classical Theory of Economic Policy, 1966; A Critique of Administrative Regulation of Public Utilities (ed with H M Trebing), 1972; Pareto on Policy, 1974; The Economy as a System of Power (ed), 2 volumes, 1979; Taxing and Spending Policy (co-ed), The Methodology of Economic Thought (ed), 1980; Research in the History of Economic Thought and Methodology (ed), volume 1, 1983. *Memberships:* Editorial Board, History of Political Economy, 1969-89; Public Utilities Taxation Committee, National Tax Association, 1971-73; Member of Executive Committee 1972-73, President 1981-82, History of Economics Society; President, Association for Social Economics, 1988. *Address:* 4397 Cherrywood Drive, Okemos, MI 48864, USA.

SAMUELSON Paul Anthony, b. 1915, American. *Appointments:* Assistant Professor of Economics 1940-44, Associate Professor and Staff Member, Radiation Laboratory 1944-45, Professor 1947-66, Institute Professor 1966-, Massachusetts Institution of Technology; Consultant, National Resources Planning Board, 1941-43; Professor, International Economic Relations, Fletcher School of Law and Diplomacy, Medford, MA, 1945-47; Consultant, US Treasury 1945-52, RAND Corporation, 1948-; Member, Advisory Board, National Commission on Money and Credit, 1958-60; Consultant, Council of Economic Advisors, 1960- 68. *Publications:* Foundations of Economic Analysis, 1947, 1983; Economics, 1948, 12th edition 1985; Readings on Economics (ed), 1955; Linear Programming and Economic Analysis (with R Dorfman and R M Solow), 1958; The Collected Scientific Papers of Paul A Samuelson, volumes I and II, 1966, volume III, 1972, volume IV, 1978, Vol V, 1986. *Honour:* Nobel Prize,

1970. *Address:* 75 Clairemont Road, Belmont, MA 02178, USA.

SANBORN Margaret, b. 1915, American. *Publications:* Robert E Lee, a Portrait: 1807-1861, 1966; Robert E Lee, the Complete Man: 1861-1870, 1967; The American: River of El Dorado, 1974; The Grand Tetons, 1978; Yosemite: Its Discovery, Its Wonders and Its People, 1981; Mark Twain: The Bachelor Years (biography), 1990. *Address:* 527 Northern Avenue, Mill Valley, CA 94941, USA.

SANCHEZ Sonia Benita, b. 9 Sept 1934, Birmingham, Alabama, USA. Professor of English. 2 sons, 1 daughter. *Education:* BA, 1955, Graduate Courses, 1955-57, Hunter College. *Publications:* Homegirls and Handgrenades, 1984; Under a Soprano Sky, 1987; I've Been a Woman : New and Selected Poems, 1978, 1985; Love Poems, 1975; A Blues Book for Blue Black Magical Women, 1974; Homecoming, 1969; A Sound Investment and other Stories, 1980; The Adventures of Fathead, Smallhead and Squarehead, 1973; Crisis and Culture : two Speeches by S. Sanchez, 1983; It's a New Day: Poems for Young Brothers and Sisters, 1971. *Contributions to:* American Poetry Review; Phylon; Black Scholar; Okike; African Journal of New Writing; Iowa Review. *Honours:* PEN Award, 1969; Academy of Arts and Letters, 1969; Honorary PhD, Humanities, 1972; NEA, 1977-78; Honorary Citizen, Atlanta, 1982; American Book Award, Before Columbus Foundation, 1985. *Memberships:* Poetry Society of America; Mid Atlantic Writers Association; CLA; African Heritage Studies Association; National Teachers of College English. *Address:* 407W Chelten Avenue, Philadelphia, PA 19144, USA.

SANCHEZ Thomas, b. California, USA. Writer. *Education:* MA, San Francisc State University, 1967. *Publications:* Rabbit Boss, 1973, 1989; Zoet Suit Murders, 1978, 1991; Mile Zero, 1989, 1990. *Contributions to:* Esquire Magazine; Los Angeles Times. *Honours:* Literature Fellowship, National Endowment for the Arts; Guggenheim Fellowship. *Memberships:* PEN America; Authors Guild of America. *Literary Agent:* Ester Newberg, ICM Agency, New York, USA. *Address:* Attn Ester Newberg, ICM, 40 West 57th St, New York, NY 10019, USA.

SANCHEZ-ROBAYNA, Andres. b. 17 Dec 1952, Santa Brigida, Canary Islands, Spain. Professor. m. 8 Oct 1977. *Education:* PhD, 1977. *Literary Appointments:* Literradura, 1976; Syntaxis, 1983-. *Publications:* Clima, 1978; Tinta, 1981; Museo Atlantico, 1983; Tres Estudios Sobre Gongora, 1983. Also: El Primer Alonso Quesada, 1977; Ruta, Textura, 1980; La Roca, 1984; La Luz Negra, 1985; Poemas 1970-85, 1987. *Contributions to:* Europe; Revista de Occidente, Vuelta; Syntaxis; Plural; Destino. *Honours:* Premio Nacional de Traduccion, 1983; Premio de la Critica, 1985. *Membership:* Instituto de Estudios Canarios. *Address:* Tamarco 67, 38280 Tegueste, Tenerife (Islas Canarias), Spain.

SANDELL Tom Johan Ludvig, b. 5 Feb 1936, Helsinki, Finland. Author; Literary Critic. m. Ilse Birgitta Litzen, 29 May 1956, 1 son. *Appointments:* Staff, FNA, 1956-64; Independent Critic, Hufvudstadsbladet, 1959-88. *Publications:* Just Det Dvs Livet, essays, 1978; Du, short stories, 1979; Dikter Foer medelaelders, poems, 1982; Skuggboxaren, novel, 1981; Pavlovs hundarr, novel, 1984; Traedet, novel, 1988. *Contributions to:* various journals and magazines, radio and TV. *Honours:* Finnish State Prize, 1980, 1984. *Memberships:* Finlands Svenska Foerfattarefoerening; PEN; Helsingfors Foerfattare. *Agent:* Soederstroem et Co, Helsinki. *Address:* Tolarintie 9 M 82, 00400 Helsinki 40, Finland.

SANDEN Einar, b. 8 Sept 1932, Tallinn, Estonia. Writer & Historian. *Education:* MA 1983, PhD, 1984, USA. *Appointments:* Managing Director, Owner, Boreas Publishing House, 1975; Councillor, Estonian Government in Exile, 1975-1990. *Publications:* KGB

Calling Eve, 1978; The Painter from Naissaar, 1985; Ur Eldinum Til Islands, 1988; An Estonian Saga, 1993. *Contributions to:* Editor of various Estonian periodicals. *Honours:* Distinguished Freedom Writer Poet of 1968, UPLI, Manila, The Philippines; Cultural Award, Fraternity Sakala, Toronto, 1984. *Memberships:* PEN Centre for Writers in Exile, 1954-80; Royal Society of Literature, London, 1960; Association of Estonian Writers Abroad, 1970; PEN, English, 1976, Estonian National Council, 1959; Association for the Advancement of Baltic Studies, USA, 1980; Estonian Academic Association of War History, Tallinn, 1988. *Address:* PO Box 16 225, 103 24 Stockholm 16, Sweden.

SANDERLIN David George, b. 28 June 1943, Charlotte, North Carolina, USA. College Professor of English and Humanities. m. Arnell Hecker, 21 Dec 1963, 2 sons, 2 daughters. *Education:* BA, English, UCLA, 1965; Master of Mediaeval Studies, 1968, PhD, 1969, University of Notre Dame. *Appointments:* Professor of English and Humanities, Miramar College, 1976-. *Publications:* The Mediaeval Statues of the College of Autun at the University of Paris, Notre Dame, 1971; Putting on the New Self; A Guide to Personal Development and Community Living, 1986; Writing the History Paper, 1975; Spelling for law Enforcement, 1987. *Contributions to:* Religious Studies, Journal of Religious Ethics; Carmelus, AD Newsletter, Journal of California Law Enforcement. *Honours:* Regents Scholar, University of California, 1961-62; American Philosophical Society Grant; Ranked 20 in US Men's Singles Tennis, 1968. *Memberships:* National Council of Teachers of English; California community College Humanities Association; American Alliance for Health, Physical Education, Recreation and Dance; Modern Language Association. *Address:* 1002 Pansy Way, El Caajon, CA 92019, USA.

SANDERS Bruce. *See:* **GRIBBLE Leonard (Reginald).**

SANDERS David, b. 1926, American. *Appointments:* Joined faculty 1959, Member, Department of Humanitites and Social Sciences 1959-70, Chairman of the Department 1973-77, Professor of English 1977-, Harvey Mudd College, Claremont; Chairman, Department of Humanities, Clarkson College, Potsdam, NY, 1970-73; Professor of English, Emeritus, 1991. *Publications:* John Hersey, 1967; Studies in USA (ed), 1972; John Dos Passos: A Comprehensive Bibliography, 1987; John Hersey Revisited, 1990. *Address:* 1630 Rutgers Court, Claremont, CA 91711, USA.

SANDERS Ed, b. 1939, American. *Appointments:* Editor and Publisher, Fuck You: A Magazine of the Arts, and Dick, NYC, 1962-; Organizer and Lead Singer of The Fugs, a literary-political rock group, 1964-; Professor, Free University of New York, 1965-; Owner, Peace Eye Bookstore, NYc. *Publications:* Poem from Jail, 1963; King Lord - Queen Freak, The Toe-Queen: Poems, Bugger: An Anthology (ed), Despair: Poems to Come Down By (ed), 1964; Banana: An Anthology of Banana-Erotic Poems, The Complete Sex Poems of Ed Sanders, Peace Eye, 1965, revised edition 1967; Shards of God, The Family: The Story of Charles Manson's Dune Buggy Attack Battalion, 1971; Votel (on Abbie Hoffman), 1972; Egyptian Hieroglyphics, 1973; Tales of Beatnik Glory, 1975; 20,000 AD, 1976; Fame and Love in New York, 1980; The Z-D Generation, 1982; Thirsting for Peace in a Raging Century: Selected Poems 1960-85, 1986. *Address:* c/o Station Hill Press, Station Hill Road, Barrytown, NY 12507, USA.

SANDERS James Edward, b. 1911, New Zealander. *Appointments:* Journalist, New Zealand Observer and Northland Times, 1936-39; Proprietor, James Sanders Advertising Limited, 1954-69; Columnist, Feature and Financial Writer, Wilson and Horton Limited, 1971-. *Publications:* The Time of My Life, 1967; The Green Paradise, 1971; The Shores of Wrath, 1972; Kindred of the Winds, High Hills of Gold, 1973; Our Explorers, New Zealand Victoria Cross Winners, 1974; Fire in the Forest, The Lamps of Maine, 1975; Where Lies the Land?, Desert Patrols, 1976; Chasing the Dragon, 1978; Dateline - NZPA, 1979; Frontiers of Fear, 1980; Venturer Courageous, The Colourful Colony, 1983; A Lone Patrol, 1986. *Address:* Aldergrove, 30 Nigel Road, Browns Bay, Auckland 10, New Zealand.

SANDERS Jeanee. *See:* **RUNDLE Anne.**

SANDERS Lawrence, b. 1920, USA. Author. *Education:* Graduated, Wabash College, 1940. *Career:* Served with the Marines as sergeant with a detachment aboard the battleship Iowa, 1943-46; Editor, Science and Mechanics. Now full-time writer. *Publications:* Thus Be Loved: A Book for Lovers (editor), 1966; Handbook of Creative Crafts (with Richard Carol), 1968; The Anderson Tapes, 1970; The Pleasures of Helen, 1971; Love Songs, 1972; The First Deadly Sin, 1973; The Tomorrow File, 1975; The Tangent Objective, 1976; The Second Deadly Sin, 1977; The Marlow Chronicles, 1977; The Tangent Factor, 1978; The Sixth Commandment, 1979; The Tenth Commandment, 1980; The Third Deadly Sin, 1981; The Case of Lucy Bending, 1982; The Seductions of Peter S, 1983; The Passion of Molly T, 1984; The Fourth Deadly Sin, 1985; The Loves of Harry Dancer, 1986; The Eighth Commandment, 1986; Tales of the Wolf, 1986; The Dream Lover, 1987; The Timothy Files, 1987. *Address:* c/o Putnam, 200 Madison Avenue, New York, NY 10016, USA.

SANDERS Peter Basil, b. 9 June 1938, London, England. Chief Executive, Commission for Racial Equality. m. (1) 2 sons, 1 daughter, (2) Anita Jackson, 23 Apr 1988. *Education:* Wadham College, Oxford, 1956-60, 1966-70; Honours degree in Classical Moderations and Literae Humaniores, 1960; DPhil in African History, 1970. *Publications:* Moshweshwe of Lesotho, school textbook, 1971; Lithoko: Sotho Praise Poems (edited and translated with Mosebi Damane), 1974; Moshoeshoe, Chief of the Sotho, 1975; The Simple Annals: The History of an Essex and East End Family, 1989. *Contributions to:* Articles to Journal of African History. *Address:* 5 Bentfield End Causeway, Stansted, Essex CM24 8HU, England.

SANDERSON John Michael, b. 23 Jan 1939, Glasgow, Scotland. University Reader. *Education:* MA, 1963, PhD, 1966, Queens' College Cambridge, 1957-63. *Appointments:* General Editor of Mcmillan Economic History Society Studies in Economic and Social History Series, 1992-. *Publications:* The Universities and British Industry, 1850-1970, 1972; The Universities in the 19th Century, 1975; Education Economic Change and Society in England, 1780-1870, 1983, Second Edition 1992, Japanese Edition, 1993; From Irving to Olivier, A Social History of the Acting Profession in England, 1880-1983, 1984; Educational Opportunity and Social Change in England, 1900-1980s, 1987; The Missing Stratum, the Technical School in England 1900-1960s, 1994. *Contributions to:* Economic History Review; Journal of Contemporary History; Contemporary Record; Business History; Northern History. *Membership:* Economic History Society. *Address:* School of Economic and Social Studies, University of East Anglia, Norwich, England.

SANDERSON Stewart F(orson), b. 1924, British. *Appointments:* Secretary Archivist 1952-58, Senior Research Fellow, Editor of Scottish Studies 1957-60, University of Edingburgh; Joint Secretary, Section H, British Association for the Advancement of Science, 1957-63; Lecturer in Folk Life Studies and Director of the Folk Life Survey 1960-64, Director of the Institute of Dialect and Folk Life Studies 1964-, Chairman of the School of English 1980-, University of Leeds; President, Folklore Society, 1971-73; Member of the Council, Society of Folk Life Studies, 1974-79, 1981-; Governor, British Institute of Recorded Sound, 1979-. *Publications:* Hemingway, 1961, 1970; The City of Edinburgh (with others), 1963; Studies in Folk Life (with others), 1969; The Secret Common-Wealth and A Short Treatise of Charms and Spells (ed), To Illustrate the Monuments (with others), 1976; The Linguistic Atlas of England (ed with H Orton and J Widdowson), 1978; Ernest Hemingway: For Whom the Bell Tolls, 1980. *Address:* Department of England, University of Leeds, Leeds LS2 9JT, England.

SANDFORD Jeremy. Playwright; Author; Journalist; Musician; Performer. m. (1) Nell Dunn, 1956, 3 sons, (2) Philippa Finnis, 1987. *Education:* Eton; Oxford. *Appointments:* Director, The Cyrenians; Director, Hatfield Court New Age Conference Centre; Executive, Gypsy Council; Patron: Shelter; The Simon Community; Editor, Romano Drom (Gypsy newspaper). *Publications:* Synthetic Fun, 1967; Cathy Come Home, 1967; Whelks and Chromium, 1968; Edna the Inebriated Woman, 1971; Down and Out in Britain, 1971; In Search of the Magic Mushrooms, 1972; Gypsies, 1973; Tomorrow's People, 1974; Prostitutes, 1975; Smiling David, 1975; Figures and Landscapes: The Art of Lettice Sandford, 1991; Hey Day In Hay, 1992. *Contributor to:* The Guardian; Sunday Times; Observer. *Honours:* Italia Prize, 1967; Writers Guild, Best Television Play, 1967, 1971; BECTV Best Television Play, 1967. *Memberships:* Writers Guild; ACTT; Herefordshire Traveller Support Group. *Address:* Hatfield Court, Nr Lcominster, HR6 0SD England.

SANDLIN Tim b. 10 Aug 1950, Duncan, Oklahoma, USA. Writer. *Education:* BA, Professional Writing, Journalism Department, University of Oklahoma, 1974; MFA, Creative Writing, English Department, University of North Carolina, Greensboro, 1986. *Publications:* Western Swing, Henry Holt, Inc, 1987; Sex and Sunsets, Henry Holt, Inc, 1986. *Honour:* Fellow, Wyoming Council of the Arts, 1987. *Memberships:* Emery Enoch Society; Associated Writing Programs; Poets and Writers. *Literary Agent:* Phillipa Brophy, Sterling Lord Literistic. *Address:* Box 1974, Jackson, WY 83001, USA.

SANDMAN Peter Mark, b. 18 Apr 1945. Professor; Consultant. 2 daughters. *Education:* BA, Psychology, Princeton University, USA, 1967; MA, Communication, 1968, PhD, Communication, 1971, Stanford University. *Publications include:* Where the Girls Are, 1967; Media (with David Rubin and David Sachsman), textbook, 1972, 3rd Edition, 1982; Media Casebook, 1972, 2nd Edition, 1977; Scientific and Technical Writing, 1985; Explaining Environmental Risk, 1986; Environmental Risk and the Press (with David Sachsman, Michael Greenberg and Michael Gochfeld), 1987; The Environmental News Source, 1987; Getting to Maybe, 1987; Improving Dialogue with Communities (with Billie Jo Hance and Caron Chess), 1988; Environmental Reporter's Handbook (with David Sachsman and Michael Greenberg), 1988; Risk Communication, Risk Statistics, and Risk Comparisons (eith Vincent Covello and Paul Slovic), 1988; Community Use of Quantitative Risk Assessment (with Caron Chess), 1989; Environmental Risk Communication Notebook for State Health Agencies, (ed with Alex Saville and Caron Chess) 1990; Risk Communication Activities of State Health Agencies (with Caron Chess and Kandice L. Salomone), American Journal of Public Health, 1991; Testing the Role of Technical Information in Public Risk Perception (with Branden Johnson and Paul Miller), 1992; Also numerous other publications. *Contributions to:* Numerous. *Honours:* Olive Branch Award, 1987; Special Award, Society of Professional Journalists, 1988, 1989. *Memberships:* Boards of Directors: New Jersey Environmental Lobby, 1984-1990; American Civil Liberties Union, New Jersey, 1984-87; Nuclear Dialogue Project, 1985-1990, President 1986-1990; Board of Advisiors, Environmental Scientists for Global Survival, 1988-91; American Association of University Professors; American Civil Liberties Union; Association for Education in Journalism and Mass Communication; Environmental Defense Fund; Investigative Reporters and Editors; National Association of Professional Environmenta; Communicators; Science Writing Educators Group; Society for Risk Analysis; Society of Envionmental Journalists; Society of Professional Journalists, Sigma Delta Chi. *Address:* 54 Gray Liff Road, Newton Centre, MA 02159, USA.

SANDOZ G Ellis, b. 1931, United States of America. Writer. *Publications:* Political Apocalypse: A Study of Dostoevsky's Grand Inquisitor, 1971; Conceived in Liberty, 1978; A Tide of Discontent: The 1980 Elections and Their Meaning, 1981; The Voegelinian Revolution: A Biographical Introduction, 1981; Eric Voegelin's Thought: A Critical Appraisal, 1982; Election '84; Landslide Without a Mandate?, 1985; Autobiographical Reflections, 1989; A Government of Laws: Political Theory, Religion and the American Founding, 1990; Published Essays 1966-1985, 1990; Political Sermons of the American Founding 1730-1805, 1991; Eric Voegelin's Significance for the Modern Mind, 1991; The Roots of Liberty: Magna Carta, Ancient Constitution and the Anglo-American Tradition of Rule of Law, 1992. *Address:* Department of Political Science, Louisiana State University, Baton Rouge, LA 70803, USA.

SANDY Stephen, b. 2 Aug 1934, Minneapolis, Minn, USA. *Education:* BA, Yale, 1955; MA, Harvard PhD, Harvard, 1963. *Publications:* Stresses in the Peaceable Kingdom, HM Co, 1967; Roofs, Houghton Mifflin, 1971; Riding to Greylock, Alfred A Knopf, 1983; To A Mantis, 1987; Man in the Open Air, 1988; The Epoch, 1990; Thanksgiving Over the Water, 1992; A Cloak for Hercules, verse translation, forthcoming. *Contributions to:* Agenda; American Poetry Review; The Atlantic; Harvard Magazine; Michigan Quarterly Review; Iowa Review; The New Yorker; The Paris Review; Salmagundi; Southwest Review and others. *Membership:* Poetry Society of America. *Honours:* Ingram Merrill Foundation Fellowship, 1985; Vermont Council on the Arts Fellowship, 1988; National Endowment for the Arts Fellowship, 1988. *Address:* Box 524, North Bennington, Vt 05257, USA.

SANDYS Elspeth Somerville, b. 18 Mar 1940, Timaru, New Zealand. Writer. 1 son, 1 daughter. *Education:* MA, Auckland, New Zealand; LTCL (Music); FTCL (Speech, Drama). *Publications:* Catch a Falling Star, 1978; The Broken Tree, 1981; Love and War, 1982; Finding Out, 1991. *Contributions to:* Landfall, New Zealand; PEN, England; Writer, numerous radio plays, BBC; Folio Book Society. *Membership:* Writers Guild. *Literary Agent:* Diana Tyler, MBA Literary Agents Ltd. *Address:* c/o MBA Literary Agents Ltd, 45 Fitzroy Street, London, W1P 5HR, England.

SANFORD Annette Schorre, (Anne Shore, Anne Starr, Mary Carroll, Lisa St John, Meg Dominique), b. 3 Aug 1929, Cuero, Texas, USA. Teacher; Writer. m. Lucius I Sanford, 17 Mar 1953. *Education:* BA, English, University of Texas, 1950. *Publications:* Lasting Attachments, short story collection; 25 paperback romances; Works in anthologies including: Best American Short Stories, 1979; New Stories from the South, 1988, 1989; Common Bonds, 1990. *Contributions to:* Short stories to: McCall's; Redbook; Story; American Short Fiction; North American Review; Ohio Review; Others; 1st publisher, A Child's Game, St Anthony Messenger, 1968. *Honours:* Fellowships, National Endowment for the Arts, 1974, 1988; Southwestern Booksellers Award, 1990. *Memberships:* Texas Institute of Letters; The Authors Guild Inc. *Address:* Ganado, TX 77962, USA.

SANGER Marjory Bartlett, b. 1920, United States of America. Children's Writer. *Appointments:* Chairman, Public Relations Editor, Bulletin, Massachusetts Audubon Society, Boston, 1954-57; Advisory Board, Rollins College Writers Conference, Winter Park, Florida, 1968-76. *Publications:* The Bird Watchers, 1957; Greenwood Summer, 1958; Mangrove Island, 1963; Cypress Country, 1965; World of the Great White Heron, 1967; Checkerback's Journey, 1969; Billy Bartram and His Green World, 1972; Escoffier, 1976; Forest in the Sand, 1983. *Address:* Box 957, Winter Park, FL 32790, USA.

SANJIAN Avedis K, b. 1921, United States of America. Writer (History, Literature, Medieval Paleography). *Publications:* The Armenian Communities in Syria Under Ottoman Dominion, 1965; Colophons of Armenian Manuscripts 1301-1480: A Source For Middle Eastern History, 1969; A Catalogue of Medieval Armenian Manuscripts in the United States, 1976; (with Andreas Tietze), Eremia Chelebi Kömürjian's Armeno-Turkish Poem, The Jews Bride, 1981; David Anhagt: The Invincible Philosopher, 1986; (with Thomas F Mathews) Armenian Gospel Iconography: The Tradition of the Glajor Gospel, 1991. *Memberships:* American Oriental Society; Middle East Studies Association; Society for Armenian Studies; Society for the Study of Caucasia. *Address:* 545 Muskingum Place, Pacific Palisades, CA 90272, USA.

SANTA MARIA. *See:* **POWELL-SMITH Vincent.**

SANTANNA. *See:* **SAMPUTAANAE Kosu.**

SANTHOJI. *See:* **SAMPUTAANAE Kosu.**

SANTINI Carla. *See:* **JACOBS Barbara.**

SANTINI Rosemarie, b. New York City, New York, USA. Writer. *Education:* Hunter College. *Appointments:* Senior Editor, True Story Magazine. *Publications:* Ask Me What I Want; Beansprouts; All My Children, 3 vols; Abracadabra; Forty-One Grove Street; The Sex Doctors; The Secret Fire, 1978-82; A Swell Style of Murder, 1986; The Disenchanted Diva, 1988; Blood Sisters, 1990; Private Lies, 1991. *Contributions to:* Short stories regularly to Women's World; Non-fiction to: Ladies Home Journal; Playboy Magazine; Working Woman; Regularly to Daily New Sunday Magazine; Penthouse Forum; Essence Magazine; Playbill Magazine; Weekend Magazine; Anthologies: The Dream Book; Kerouac and Friends; Side by Side: Varieties of the American Experience, 1993. *Memberships:* PEN; Mystery Writers of America; Authors Guild; Poets and Writers; Poetry Society of America; Society of American Journalists and Authors; Dramatists Guild; National Academy of TV Arts and Sciences; International Association of Crime Writers; Sisters in Crime; Novelists Inc. *Address:* c/o Pratt University, 295 Lafayette Street, New York, NY 10012, USA.

SANTOS Helen. *See:* **GRIFFITHS Helen.**

SAPERSTEIN David, b. 19 Mar 1937, Brooklyn, New York, USA. Novelist; Screenwriter; Film Director. m. Ellen-Mae Bernard, 22 June 1959, 1 son, 1 daughter. *Education:* Chemical Engineering and Chemistry, 1953-56, Film Institute, 1956-57, CCNY. *Appointments:* Assistant Professor, Film, New York University Graduate Film and TV School, 1992-93. *Publications:* Cocoon, 1985; Fatal Reunion, 1987; Metamorphosis: The Cocoon Story Continues, 1988; Red Devil, 1989. 19 screenplays. *Honours:* Writers Guild of America, Best Story For Screen Nomination, 1985. *Memberships:* Writers Guild of America; Directors Guild of America. *Literary Agent:* Susan Schulman; Motion Picture Agent: Sara Margoshes. *Address:* c/o Ebbets Field Productions, PO Box 42, Wykagyl Station, New Rochelle, NY 10804, USA.

SAPIA Yvonne, b. 10 Apr 1946, New York, New York, USA. Instructor in English and Resident Poet. *Education:* AA, Miami-Dade Community College, 1967; BA, Florida Atlantic University, 1970; MA, University of Florida, 1976; Doctoral study at Florida State University. *Appointments:* Reporter, Village Post, Miami, Florida, 1971-73; Editorial Assistant in Department of Ornamental Horticulture, University of Florida, Gainesville, 1974-76; Instructor in English and Resident Poet 1976-, Publications editor 1976-, Chairperson of Fine Arts Committee 1980-86, Lake City Community College, Lake City, Florida; Member of Fine Arts Council of Lake City, 1986-; Editorial supervisor of educational programs for Florida Horticultural Industries 1975-76; Teacher at Florida State Prisons 1977-78; Poetry Teacher at Workshops for the Elderly and for Gifted Children, 1980-82; Member of Editorial Advisory Board of Roxbury Publishing Co, gives Poetry Readings. *Publications:* (ed with Dennis McConnell) The Nurseryman's Retail Sales Handbook, 1974; (ed with McConnell) The Landscape Installation Handbook, 1975; (ed with McConnell) The Landscape Maintenance Handbook, 1976; The Fertile Crescent (poems) 1983; Valentino's Hair (poems) 1987. *Contributions to:* Work represented in anthologies, poems, articles, reviews and magazines. *Honours:* Fellow of Department of State's Division of Cultural Affairs and Florida Fine Arts Council 1981-82 and 1987-88 and National Endowment for the Arts 1986-87; Poetry Chapbook Award from Florida State University 1983 for The Fertile Crescent; Samuel French Morse Poetry Prize from Northeastern University Press, 1987 for Valentino's Hair. *Memberships:* Academy of American Poets. *Address:* Department of English, Lake City Community College, Route 3, PO Box 7, Lake City, FL 32055, USA.

SAPIRO Virginia, b. 28 Feb 1951, East Orange, New Jersey, USA. Professor. m. 30 Aug 1981, 1 son. *Education:* AB, Clark University, 1972; MA, (Political Science), University of Michigan, 1976; PhD, (Political Science), University of Michigan, 1976. *Publications:* The Political Integration of Women: Roles, Socialization, and Politics, 1983; Women in American Society: An Introduction to Women's Studies, 1990; A Vindication of Political Virtue: The Political Theory of Mary Wollstonecraft, 1992. *Contributions to:* American Political Science Review; American Journal of Political Science; British Journal of Political Science; Women and Politics; Politics and Society; Western Political Quarterly; Political Science Quarterly. *Honours:* Phi Beta Kappa, 1972; Distinguished Teaching Assistant Award, University of Michigan, 1976; Award for Best Paper on Women, Chastain Award, Southern Political Science Association, 1976; Best Paper on Women, Committee on Status of Women of the Western Political Science Association, 1978; Best Paper on Women, Sophinisba Breckinridge Award, Midwest Political Science Association, 1983; Erik Erikson Award for Early Career Contribution to Political Psychology, International Society for Political Psychology, 1986; Research Grants: Graduate Research Committee, University of Wisconsin-Madison, 1977, 1979, 1983, 1987; Spencer Foundation, 1990. *Memberships:* American Political Science Association; International Society for Political Psychology. *Address:* Department of Political Science, University of Wisconsin-Madison, Madison, WI 53706, USA.

SAPP Eva Jo Barnhill, (Jo Sapp), b. 4 Feb 1944, San Antonio, Texas, USA. Writer; Editor. m. David Paul Sapp, 1 son, 1 daughter. *Education:* BA Hons English Creative Writing, 1976, MA 1982, PhD coursework completed, 1985, University of Missouri. *Appointments:* Editorial Assistant, 1978-80, Senior Fiction Advisor, 1980-81, Associate Editor: Special Projects 1981-92, Fiction, 1986-88, all for the Missouri Review; Editorial Consultant, Cultural Plan of Action, 1987-. *Publications:* Co-Editor: The Best of the Missouri Review: Fiction 1978-90; Missouri Review Online: 1986-88; Contributor: Flash Fiction, 1992. *Contributions to:* Intro 15 & 16; Long Pond; Washington Review; Kansas Quarterly; North American Review. *Honours:* Honourable Mention, Deep South, 1981; Mckinney Prize, 1984; Editor's Book Awards Nominee, 1988; Missouri Arts Council Grant, 1988; Elmer Holmes Best Award Nominee, 1992. *Memberships:* Poets and Writers; Associated Writing Programmes; Columbia Commission on the Arts, Chair, 1988-, V-Chair, 1987-88, Secretary, 1986-87. *Literary Agent:* Barbara Hogenson at Lucy Kroll Agency. *Address:* 1025 Hickory Hill Drive, Columbia, MO 65203, USA.

SAPP Jo. *See:* **SAPP Eva Jo Barnhill.**

SARAC Roger. *See:* **CARAS Roger Andrew.**

SARAH Robyn. *See:* **BELKIN Robyn Sarah.**

SARANTI Galatia, b. 8 Nov 1920, Greece. Writer. m. Stavros Patsouris, 26 Dec 1948, 2 sons. *Education:* Law Faculty, University of Athens, 1947. *Publications:* Novels: Lilacs, 1949; The Book of Johannes and Maria, 1952; Return, 1953; Our Old House, 1959; The Limits, 1966; Cracks, 1979; The Waters of Euripoe, 1989; Short stories: Bright colours, 1962; Remember Vilna, 1972. *Contributions to:* Nea Hestia; Helliniki Ahmiozptia; Epoches; Diabazo. *Honours:* Kostas Ouranis Prize, 1953; State Prize, 1957, 1974; Academy of Athens Literature Prize, 1979. *Memberships:* National Society of Greek Writers; PEN Club. *Literary Agent:* Hestia, Solonos 60, Athens 10672, Greece. *Address:* Kallidromidy 87-89, 10683 Athens, Greece.

SARGENT Lyman Tower, b.9 Feb 1940, Rehoboth, Massachusetts, USA. Professor of Political Science. m. 1. Patricia McGinnis, 27 Dec 1961 (Divorced), 1 son; 2. Mary T Weiler, 14 Aug 1985 (Divorced). *Education:* BA, International Relations, Macalester College, 1961; MA, American Studies, 1962, PhD, Political Science, 1965, University of Minnesota. *Appointments:* University of Wyoming, 1964-65; University of Missouri - St Louis, 1965-; University of Exeter, 1978-79, 1983-84; London School of Economics, 1985-86; Editor, Utopian Studies, 1988-; Co-Editor, Syracuse University Press, Series on Utopianism and Communitarism, 1988-. *Publications:* Contemporary Political Ideologies: A Comparative Analysis, 1969, 1972, 1975, 1978, 1981, 1984, 1987, 1990, 1993; New Left Thought: An Introduction, 1972; British and American Utopian Literature 1516-1975: An Annotated Bibliography, 1979; British and American Utopian Literature, 1516-1985: An Annotated, Chronological Bibliography, 1988; Contemporary Political Ideologies: A Reader, 1990; Techniques of Political Analysis: An Introduction, 1970; Editor: IVR NORTHAM IV. Consent: Concept, Capacity, Conditions, Constraints, 1979. *Contributions to:* Minnesota Review; Minus One; Anarchy; Annals of Iowa; Futurist; Comparative Literature Studies; Political Theory; Extrapolation; Science-Fiction Studies; Personalist; Polity; History of Political Thought; Wellisan; ATQ. *Honours:* National Endowment for the Humanities Fellow 1981-82; American Council of Learned Societies, Travel Grant, 1988. *Memberships:* Society for Utopian Studies, Chair 1986-1990; Politics and Literature Group, Organizer, 1987-1992; National Historic Communal Society Association, Member, Board of Directors, 1989; Conference for the Study of Political Thought, Member at Large - USA, 1981-. *Address:* Department of Political Science, University of Missouri - St Louis, 8001 Natural Bridge Road, St Louis, MO 63121, USA.

SARGENT Pamela, b. 1948, United States of America. Author; Freelance Writer; Editor. *Publications:* Women of Wonder: Science Fiction Stories by Women About Women, 1975; More Women of Wonder: Science-Fiction Novelettes by Women about Women, 1976; Bio-Futures: Science Fiction Stories About Biological Metamorphosis, 1976; Cloned Lives, 1976; Starshadows (short stories), 1977; The New Women of Wonder: Recent Science-Fiction by Women about Women, 1978; The Sudden Star, 1979 (in United Kingdom as The White Death, 1980); Watchstar, 1980; The Golden Space, 1982; The Alien Upstairs, 1983; Earthseed, 1983; Eye of the Comet, 1984; Homesmind, 1984; Venus of Dreams, 1986; The Shore of Women, 1986; Afterlives, 1986; The Best of Pamela Sargent (short stories), 1987; Venus of Shadows, 1988; Ruler of the Sky, 1993. *Address:* Box 486, Johnson City, NY 13790, USA.

SARGESSON Jenny. *See:* **DAWSON Jennifer.**

SARICKS Ambrose, b. 1915, United States of America. Writer (History, Biography). *Publications:* A Bibliography of the Frank E. Melvin Collection of Pamphlets of the French Revelotion in the University of Kansas Libraries, 2 vols; 1960; Pierre Samuel du Pont de Nemours, 1965. *Address:* 2552 Arkansas, Lawrence, KS 66046, USA.

SARKAR Anil Kumar, b. 1 Aug 1912, India. Professor Emeritus. m. Aruna Sarkar, 1 Nov 1941, (dec), 1 son, 1 daughter. *Education:* MA 1st class, 1935, PhD, 1946, D.Litt, 1960, Patna University. *Appointments include:* Professor, Rajendra College, 1940-44; Senior Lecturer, University of Ceylon, Colombo and Peredeniya, 1944-64; Visiting Professor, University of New Mexico, Albuquerque, USA, 1964-65, Full Professor of Philosophy and West-East Philosophy, 1965-82, California State University, Hayward, USA; Research Director, Professor of Asian Studies, 1968, now Professor Emeritus, California Institute of Integral Studies, San Francisco, 1980-. *Publications:* An Outline of Whitehead's Philosophy, 1940; Changing Phases of Buddhist Thought, 1st/2nd Editions, 1968-75, 3rd Edition, 1983; Whitehead's Four Principles From West-East Perspectives, 1974; Dynamic Facets of Indian Thought, vol 1, 1980, vols 2-4, 1987-88; Experience in Change and Prospect Pathways From War To Peace, 1989; Sri Aurobindo's Vision of the Super Mind - Its Indian and Non-Indian Interpreters, 1989; Buddhism and Whitehead's Process - Philosophy, 1990; Zero - Its Role and Prospects in Indian Thought and its Impact on Post-Einsteinian Astrophysics, 1992. *Contributions to:* Indian, American and other journals. *Honours:* Research Fellow, Indian Institute of Philosophy, Amalner, Bombay, 1937-38; Research Scholar, Patna University, 1938-40; Research Professor, post-doctoral research, University College, London, 1951-52, 1958-59. *Memberships:* Life Member, Indian Philosophical Congress, Local Secretary 1954; Sectional President, 1956; General President, Plenary Session, 1975; Representative, Indian Science Congress in Ceylon; American Philosophical Association; American Association of Advancement of Science; Association for Asian Studies; Officiated at various sessions, Indian Philosophical Congress, ASPCA and Wooster Conference of Philosophy and Religion. *Address:* 818 Webster Street, Hayward, CA 94544, USA.

SARNA Jonathan D, b. 10 Jan 1955. Joseph H & Belle R Braun Professor of American Jewish History, Brandeis University. m. Ruth Langer, 8 June 1986, 1 son, 1 daughter. *Education:* BHL honours, Hebrew College, Boston, USA, 1974; BA Summa Cum Laude, Highest Honours in Judaic Studies and History, 1975, MA, Judaic Studies, 1975, Brandeis University; MA, Judaic Studies, Brandeis University, 1975; MA, History, Yale University, 1976; MPhil, History, Yale University, 1978; PhD, History, Yale University, 1979. *Appointments:* Abstracter-Consultant, ABC-CLIO, 1980-; Editor, North American Judaism section, Religious Studies Review, 1984-; Publication Committee, Jewish Publication Society, 1985-; Editorial Committee, Queen City Heritage, 1985-; Editorial Board: American Jewish History, 1988-, Religion and American Culture, 1989-; Associate Editor, American National Biography. *Publications:* Jews in New Haven (editor), 1978; Mordecai Manuel Noah: Jacksonian Politician and American Jewish Communal Leader, 1979; Jacksonian Jew: The Two Worlds of Mordecai Noah, 1981; People Walk on Their Heads: Moses Weinberger's Jews and Judaism in New York (translator, editor), 1982; Jews and the Founding of the Republic (co-editor), 1985; The American Jewish Experience: A Reader, 1986; American Synagogue History: A Bibliography and State-of-the-Field Survey (with Alexandra S Korros), 1988; American Jews and Church-State Relations: The Search for Equal Footing, pamphlet, 1989; JPS: The Americanization of Jewish Culture (A History of the Jewish Publication Society 1988-1988), 1989; The Jews of Cincinnati (with Nancy H Klein), 1989; Ethnic Diversity and Civiv Identity: Patterns of Conflict and Cohesion in Cinncinnati Since 1820, 1992; Yehude Artsot Ha-Berit, 1992; A Double Bond; The Constitutional Documents of American Jewry, forthcoming; Relgion and State in American Jewish History, forthcoming; Observing America's Jews: Selected Writing of Marshall Sklare, forthcoming Masterworks of Modern Jewish Writing (general editor), 10 vols; American Jewish Life (editor with Moses Rischin), 5 vols, forthcoming. *Contributions to:* Articles and reviews to American Jewish History; Jerusalem Post; The Principal; Canadian Jewish Historical Society

Journal; Library Journal; Judaica Book News. *Honours:* Seltzer-Brodsky Prize Essay, YIVO Institute, 1977; Nominated for National Jewish Book Award, 1981; Hebrew Free Loan Association Fellow, American Jewish Historical Society, 1974-75; Charles Andrews Fellowship, Yale University, 1976-77; Howard F Brinton Fellowship, Yale University, 1977-78; Memorial Foundation for Jewish Culture, 1977-79; American Council of Learned Socities, 1982; Lady Davis Endowment, 1986-87. *Memberships:* American Historical Association; American Jewish Historical Society; Association for Jewish Studies; Canadian Jewish Historical Society; Cincinnati Historical Society; Immigration Historical Society; Organization of American Historians; Phi Beta Kappa; Society for Historians of the Early American Republic. *Address:* Department NEJS, Brandeis University, Waltham MA 02257, USA.

SARNA Nahum Mattathias, b. 27 Mar 1923, London, England. Emeritus Professor, Biblical Studies. m. Helen Horowitz, 23 Mar 1947, 2 sons. *Education:* BA, 1944, MA, 1946, University of London; PhD, Dropsie College, Philadelphia, USA, 1955. *Appointments:* University College, London, 1946-49; Gratz College, Philadelphia, USA, 1951-57; Jewish Theological Seminary, New York, 1957-65; Faculty 1965-, Dora Golding Professor of Biblical Studies 1967-, Professor Emeritus 1985-, Brandeis University, Editor, Editorial Boards, various scholarly journals; General Editor, Jewish Publication Society Torah Commentary; Editor, Proceedings of the American Academy for Jewish Research. *Publications include:* Understanding Genesis, 1966; Exploring Exodus, 1985; Commentary of Genesis, 1989; Commentary of Exodus, 1991. *Contributions to:* Harvard Theological Review; Biblical Archaeologist; Biblical Archaeology Review; various scholarly journals. *Honours:* Award, Jewish Book Council, 1967; Senior Fellow, American Council of Learned Societies, 1971-72; Fellow, American Academy for Jewish Research, 1974-; Council, World Union of Jewish Studies, 1981-; Fellow, Institute for Advanced Studies, Hebrew University, 1982-83; Honorary Doctorates, Gratz College, 1984; Jewish Institute of Religion, 1987. *Memberships include:* Past President, Association for Jewish Studies; American Academy for Jewish Research; American Oriental Society; Israel Exploration Society; Palestine Exploration Society; World Union of Jewish Studies; Board of Advisors of the Dead Sea Scrolls Foundation. *Address:* 39 Green Park, Newton, Massachusetts, MA 02158, USA.

SARNAT Marshall, b. 1 Aug 1929, Chicago, USA. Economist. m. Carmela Shainker, 17 Jan 1956, 1 son, 1 daughter. *Education:* BA, Hebrew University, 1955; MBA, 1957; PhD, 1965, Northwestern University. *Appointments include:* Professor of Finance Hebrew University of Jerusalem. *Publications:* Development of Securities Market in Israel, 1966; Investment and Portfolio Analysis, 1972; Inflation and Capital Markets, 1978; International Finance and Trade, 1979; Saving, Investment and Capital Markets, 1982; Principles of Financial Management, 1988; Portfolio and Investment Selection, 1984; Capital Investment and Financial Decisions 4th Edition, 1990. *Contributions to:* Professional Economic and Finance Journals. *Membership:* President of European Finance Association. *Address:* Nayot 34, Jerusalem, Israel.

SARNOFF Dorothy, Communication, Speech and Image Consultant; Chairman, Speech Dynamics Inc, subsidiary of Ogilvy & Mather. *Education:* BA, Cornell University. *Career:* Former Actress, singer, sang lead in 13 operas and apppeared in 4 Broadway shows including The King & I. *Publications:* Speech Can Change Your Life, 1970; Make the Most of Your Best, 1981; Never Be Nervous Again, 1987. *Address:* Speech Dynamics Inc, 111 West 57th Street, New York, NY 10019, USA.

SARNOFF Irving, b. 5 May 1922, Brooklyn, New York, USA. Psychologist; Professor of Psychology. m. Suzanne Fischbach, 28 Nov 1946, 1 son, 1 daughter.

Education: BA, Brooklyn College, 1946; MA, 1949, PhD, 1951, University of Michigan. *Appointments:* Editorial Advisor, Encyclopaedia Britannica, 1968-. *Publications:* Personality Dynamics and Development, 1962; Society with Tears, 1966; Testing Freudian Concepts, 1971; Sexual Excitement/Sexual Peace (with Suzanne Sarnoff), 1979; Love-Centered Marriage in a Self-Centered World (with Suzanne Sarnoff), 1989. *Contributions to:* The Dialectic of Marriage (with Suzanne Sarnoff) to Psychology Today, 1989. *Honour:* Fulbright Advanced Research Scholar, University College, London, England, 1954-55. *Membership:* American Psychological Association. *Address:* 100 Bleecker Street, New York, NY 10012, USA.

SAROYAN Aram, b. 25 Sept 1943, New York City, USA Writer. m. Gailyn McClanahan, 9 Oct 1968, 1 son, 2 daughters. *Education:* University of Chicago, Illinois; New York and Columbia Universities. *Publications:* Aram Saroyan, 1968; Pages, 1969; Words and Photographs, 1970; The Street: An Auobiographical Novel, 1974; Genisis Angels: The Saga of Lew Welch and the Beat Generation, 1979; Last Rites: The Death of William Saroyan, 1982; William Saroyan, 1983; Trio: Portrait of an Intimate Friendship, 1985; The Romantic, 1988. *Contributions to:* New York Times Book Review; Nation; Village Voice; Mother Jones; Paris Review. *Honours:* Poetry Award, NEA, 1967, 1968. *Membership:* PEN Center West. *Address:* 229 Poplar Crest Avenue, Thousand Oaks, CA 91320, USA.

SARTON May, b. 3 May 1912, Wondelgem, Belgium. Writer. *Education:* High School and Latin, Cambridge, Massachusetts, USA, 1926-29; Apprentice, Eva LeGallienne's Civic Repertory Theatre, New York City, 1929-31. *Appointments:* Taught Creative Writing, Stuart School, Boston, Massachusetts, 1930-36; Scriptwriter, OWI, 1944-45; Poetry lectures, colleges nationwide, 1940-87; Briggs Copeland Instructor, Harvard College, 1950-53; Radcliffe College Seminars, 1956-58; Phi Beta Kappa Visiting Scholar, 1959-60; Lecturer, Creative Writing, Wellesley College, 1960-64; Lecturer, Breadloaf/Boulder Writers Conferences, 1951-54; Danforth Visiting Lecturer, College Arts Programme, 1960-61. *Publications:* Encounter in April, 1937; Mrs Stevens Hears the Mermaids Singing, 1965; Plant Dreaming Deep, 1968; As We Are Now, 1973; Journal of a Solitude, 1973; Collected Poems, 1974; The House By the Sea, 1977; At Seventy, 1984; The Education of Harriet Hatfield, 1989; Others. *Contributions to:* Poetry and prose to: New York Times; New York Times Book Review; Poetry; Paris Review; Cornhill; Yankee; Town and Country; Family Circle; Vogue; Country Beautiful; Reporter; The Nation; Saturday Review; New Yorker; House and Garden; Writer; Christian Science Monitor. *Honours:* Guggenheim Fellow, 1954; Phi Beta Kappa, 1955; Honorary doctorates: Russell Sage, 1959; Clark, 1975; Universities of New Hampshire, 1976 and Maine, 1981; Bates 1976, Colby, 1976; Bowdoin, 1983; Union, 1984; Bucknell, 1985; Providence, 1989; Centennary, 1990; Awards: Avon/COCOA, 1983; Fund for Human Dignity, 1984; Outstanding New England Writer, 1990. *Memberships:* Fellow, American Academy of Arts and Sciences; New England Poetry Society; Poetry Society of America; Deborah Morton Society, Westbrook (ME) College. *Literary Agent:* Timothy Seldes, Russell and Volkening, 50 West 29th Street, New York, NY 10001, USA. *Address:* Box 99, York, ME 03909, USA.

SARTORI Eva Maria, b. Subotica, Yugoslavia. Author. *Publications:* Pierre, mon amour, 1967; Wie eine Palme im Wind, 1968; Oh, diese Erbschaft, 1969; Die Rheinhagens, 1980; Spuren, die kein Wind verweht, 1981; Damals in Dahlem, 1982; Königin Luise, 1983; Der Sünder und die Heilige, 1984; Streite nicht mit dem Wind, 1985; Venedig sehen und sterben, 1986; Das Geheimnis der roten Rose, 1987; Das Schicksal stellte die Weiche, 1987; Ein Herz sucht eine Heimat, 1989; Bittere Vergangenheit, 1989; Aller Reichtum dieser Welt, 1989; Warten auf die Liebe, 1990; Und dennoch liebe ich dich, 1991 Wir wissen weder Tag noch Stunde, 1991; Der kaktuskavalier, 1993. *Contributions to:* Neue

Welt; 7 Tage; Frau aktuell; Die aktuelle; Frau mit Herz; Das Neue Blatt; TV Hören und Sehen; Romanwoche. *Honours:* Doctoral Membership, Literature, World University. *Memberships:* Freier Deutscher Autorenverband; Fellow, International Biographical Association. *Literary Agent:* Grit Peters. *Address:* Kirchenstrasse 32, D-W 84533 Stammham, Germany.

SATO Isao, b. 5 Jan 1934, Osaka, Japan. University Professor. m. Mutsuko Sato, 25 May 1963, 2 sons. *Education:* BA, 1963, MA, 1965, Meiji Gakuin University, Tokyo. *Appointments:* Professor, English and Comparative Literature, Osaka University of Arts, 1965-89; Professor, English and Comparative Literature, Faculty of International Languages and Culture, Setsunan University, Osaka, 1989-. *Publications:* English Poetry and Japanese Poets, 1973, new edition, 1983; An Essential Knowledge of English for the Japanese, 1977; John Dryden's Theory of Translation, 1980; Studies in Tsubouchi Shoyo's Acceptance of John Dryden's Literary Theory & Criticism: 2 Origins of Comparative Literature Thought in the East & West, 1981; Through a Coach Window (co-author), 1983; Record of my Autistic Son, Akashi's Growth, 1985; Story of Akashi, My Autistic Son, 1985-87; Encyclopaedia of Tsubouchi Shoyo (co-author), 1986; Annotated books: Blunden's Studies in English Literature, 1970; Dryden's Parallel of Poetry & Painting, 1970; Dryden's Essay of Dramatic Poesy, 1971; Dryden's All for Love, 1974; English Poetry and Japanese Poets, 1973, 1983, 1992; The Translation Theories of John Dryden and His Contemporary Poets, 1988. *Contributions to:* Numerous books and studies including: Tsubouchi Shoyo's Literary Indebtedness to Shakespeare and Dryden, 1986; Tsubouchi Shoyo as Pioneer in Comparative Literature in Japan, 1987; The Use of Shakespeare in Japan's Kabuki Drama, 1987; English and American Poetry and the Modern Japanese Poets, 1988; An Approach to John Dryden's Self, 1989; Study of Ohwada Takeki and His Translation of English Poems, 1990; Tsubouchi Shoyo and Lafcadio Hearn - Their Literary Intercourse and Its Meaning, 1991; Study of English History and Culture in Westminster Abbey, 1992. *Honour:* High Honours Award for paper on Education and Welfare of Autistic Children, Mayor of Osaka, Dec 1979. *Memberships:* Japan Branch, International PEN Club; International Comparative Literature Association; Historical Society of English Studies in Japan. *Address:* 4-6 Kohama-Nishi 2-chome, Suminoe-ku, Osaka 559, Japan.

SATTERTHWAIT Walter, b. 23 Mar 1946, USA. Writer. 1 daughter. *Education:* Reed College, 1969-72. *Publications:* A Flower in the Desert, 1992; Wilde West, 1991; At Ease with the Dead, 1990; Miss Lizzie, 1989; Wall of Glass, 1987; The Aegean Affair, 1981; Cocain Blues, 1980. *Contributions to:* Alfred Hitchcock's Mystery Magazine; Santa Fe Reporter. *Memberships:* Mystery Writers of America; Private Eye Writers of America. *Literary Agent:* Dominick Abel. *Address:* c/o Wind, Oranje Nassaulman 20, 1075 An Amsterdam, Netherlands.

SATTIN Anthony Neil, b. 28 June 1956, London, England. Writer. m. Sylvie Franquet, 15 Oct 1989. *Education:* BA Hons English and American Literature, Warwick University; MA Creative Writing, University of East Anglia. *Publications:* Shooting the Breeze, 1989; Lifting the Veil: British Society in Egypt, 1768-1956, 1988; Editor: Florence Nightingale's Letters from Egypt, 1849-1850, 1987; An Englishwoman in India: The Memoirs of Harriet Tytler, 1828-1858, 1986. *Contributions to:* Sunday Times; Financial Times; Conde Nast Traveler; Marie Claire; Punch. *Memberships:* Fellow, Royal Geographical Society. *Address:* c/o Curtis Brown, 162-168 Regent Street, London W1R 5TB, England.

SAUNDERS Ann Loreille (Ann Cox-Johnson), b. 23 May 1930, St John's Wood, London, England. Historian. m. Bruce Kemp Saunders, 4 June 1960, 1 son, 1 daughter (dec 1984). *Education:* Plumptre Scholar, Queen's College, London, 1946-48; BA Hons, University College, London, 1951; PhD, Leicester University, 1965. *Appointments:* Deputy Librarian, Lambeth Palace Library, London, 1952-55; Assistant Keeper, British Museum, London, 1955-56; Archivist, Marylebone Public Library, London, 1956-63; Honorary Editor, Costume Society, 1967-; Honorary Editor, London Topographical Society, 1975-. *Publications:* Regent's Park, 1969, Enlarged 2nd Edition, 1981; London, North of the Thames (Arthur Mee re-written), 1972; London, City and Westminster (Arthur Mee re-written), 1975; Art and Architecture of London, 1984, Paperback, 1988, 1992; John Bacon, R.A., 1740-1799 (as Ann Cox-Johnson); St Martin-in-the-Fields, short history and guide, 1989; The Royal Exchange, 1991; 2 solid catalogues. *Contributions to:* Articles and reviews to Burlington Magazine, Geographic Magazine, London Journal. *Honours:* Prize for Best Specialist Guide Book of the Year, British Tourist Board, 1984; Fellow of University College, London, 1992. *Memberships:* Fellow, Council Member, Society of Antiquaries; Costume Society; London Topographical Society. *Address:* 3 Meadway Gate, London NW11 7LA, England.

SAUNDERS James, b. 8 Jan 1925, Islington, London, England. Playwright. m. Audrey Cross, 1951, 2 daughters, 1 son. *Publications:* Plays: Moonshine, 1958; Alas, Poor Fred, The Ark, 1959; Committal, Barnstable, Return to a City, 1960; A Slight Accident, 1961; Double Double, 1962; Next Time I'll Sing to You, The Pedagogue, Who Was Hilary Maconochie?, 1963; A Scent of Flowers, Neighbours, 1964; Triangle, Opus, 1965; A Man's Best Friend, The Borage Pigeon Affair, 1969; After Liverpool, 1970; Games, Savoury Meringue, 1971; Hans Kohlhaas, 1972; Bye Bye Blues, 1973; The Island, 1975; Bodies, 1977; Birdsong, 1979; Fall, 1981; Emperor Waltz, 1983; Scandella, 1985; Making It Better, 1992. TV: Watch Me I'm a Bird, 1964; Bloomers, 1979 (series); TV adaptations of works by D.H. Lawrence, Henry James, H.E Bates and R.F. Delderfield; (Screenplays) Sailor's Return; The Captain's Doll. *Honours:* Arts Council of GB Drama Bursary, 1960; Evening Standard Drama Award, 1963; Writers' Guild TV Adaptation Award, 1966; Arts council Major Bursary, 1984; BBC Radio Play Award, 1986; Moliére Award (Paris), 1990. *Address:* c/o Margaret Ramsay Ltd., 14a Goodwin's Court, St Martin's Lane, London WC2, England.

SAUNDERS Louisa Ann, b. 3 Oct 1961, London, England. Journalist. m. Edward Vulliamy, 1 May 1982. *Appointments:* Features Editor, 1984, Editor, 1986-, Girl About Town. *Contributions to:* Honey; 19; Look Now. *Honours:* Runner Up, Standard/Catherine Packenham Award for Young Women Journalists, 1983. *Membership:* National Union of Journalists. *Address:* c/o Girl About Town, 141-143 Drury Lane, Covent Garden, London WC2B 5TS, England.

SAUVAIN Philip Arthur, b. 1933, British, Children's non-fiction, Environmental science/Ecology, Geography, History, Humanities (general). Freelance writer. *Appointments:* Head of Geography Department, Steyning Grammar School, Sussex, 1957-61 and Penistone Grammar School, nr Sheffield, 1961-63; Senior Lecturer in Geography, James Graham College, Leeds, 1963-68; Head of Environmental Studies Department, Charlotte Mason College of Education, Ambleside, 1968-74. *Publications include:* Exploring the World of Man, series (10 books) 1973-77; Breakaway series (8 books) 1973-76; Environment Books: First Series (4 books) 1974; Second Series (4 books) 1978; Looking Around Town and Country, 1975; A First Look at Winds (Dinosaurs, Discoveries, Ice and Snow) 5 vols, 1975-78; Imagining the Past: First Series (6 books) 1976, Second Series (6 books) 1979; Looking Back, 1977; Macmillan Local Studies Kit, 1979; Looking Around Cards, 1979; Certificate Mapwork, 1980; The British Isles, 1980; Story of Britain series (4 books) 1980; Science Discussion Pictures, 1981; Britain's Living Heritage, 1982; History of Britain (4 books) 1982; Theatre, 1983; Macmillan Junior Geography (4 books) 1983; Hulton New Geographies (5 books) 1983; History Map Books (2 books) 1983, 1985; Hulton New Histories (5 books) 1984, 1985; France and the French, 1985;

European and World History, 1815-1919, 1985; Modern World History, 1919 Onwards, 1985; How History Began, 1985; Castles and Crusaders, 1986; What to Look For (series: 4 books) 1986; British Economic and Social History, 2 vols, 1987; Exploring Energy (4 books), 1987; GCSE History Companion series (3 books), 1988; How We Build (3 books), 1989; The World of Work (3 books), 1989; Skills for Geography, 1989; Skills for Standard Grade History, 1990; Exploring the Past: Old World, 1991; Changing World, 1992; Expanding World, 1993; The Way it Works (3 books), 1991; History Detectives (3 books), 1992, 1993; Great Battles and Sieges (4 books), 1992, 1993; Breakthrough: Communications, 1992. *Address:* 70 Finborough Road, Stowmarket, Suffolk. IP14 1PU, England.

SAVA George. *See:* **MILKOMANE George Alexis Milkomanovich.**

SAVAGE Alan. *See:* **NICOLE Christopher Robin.**

SAVAGE Thomas (Tom), b. 14 July 1948, New York City, USA. Poet; Critic. *Education:* BA, English, Brooklyn College, City University of New York, 1969; Master's Degree, Columbia University School of Library Service, 1980. *Appointments:* Teaching Assistant, Naropa Institute School of Poetics, 1975; Teacher, Words, Music, Words for Poets and Composers, St Mark's Poetry Project, 1983-85; Editor, Roof magazine, 1976-78; Editor, Gandhabba magazine, 1981-. *Publications:* Poetry Books: Personalities, 1978; Slow Walse on a Glass Harmonica, 1980; Filling Spaces, 1980; Housing Preservation and Development, 1988; Processed Words. *Contributions to:* Downtown, Cover, The World, City Magazines, Transfer, The Poetry Project Newsletter, Mudfish, Appearances. *Honours:* PEN Grant, 1978; Grant from Co-ordinating Council of Literary Magazines for Gandhabba 1981-82. *Membership:* CCLM. *Address:* 622 E 11th St 14, New York, NY 10009, USA.

SAVITSKI Dmitri, (Alexandre Dimov), b. 25 Jan 1944, Moscow, USSR. Writer; journalist. *Education:* Institute Literature, Moscow, 1967-71. *Publications:* Les Hommes Double, 1979; L'Anti Guide de Moscou, 1980, 2nd Edition, 1988; Bons Baisers de Nulle Part, 1983; Valse pour K, 1984; Waltz for K, 1985; Le Theme sans Variation, forthcoming; Passe Decompose, Futur Simple, forthcoming. *Contributions to:* Liberation; Magazine Litteraire; L'Autre Journal; Emois; Others. *Memberships:* PEN Club; International Federation of Journalists. *Literary Agent:* Mary Kling, La Nouvelle Agence, 7 rue Corneille, 75006 Paris, France. *Address:* 15 bis, rue du Pot-de-fer, 75005, Paris, France.

SAVITT Sam, b. Wilkes-Barre, PA, USA. Author; Artist. m. Bette Orkin, 28 Mar 1946, 1 son, 1 daughter. *Publications include:* Midnight, 1957; Rodeo, 1963; Vicki and the Black Horse, 1964; Sam Savitts True Horse Stories, 1970; Vicki and the Brown Mare, 1976; The Dingle Ridge Fox and Other Stories, 1978; Wild Horse Running, 1973; One Horse, One Hundred Miles, One Day, 1981; A Horse to Remember, 1986. *Contributions to:* Equus Magazine; Western Horseman Magazine. *Honours:* Boys Clubs of America Book Award, 1957; Literary Guild, 1973. *Memberships:* Authors Guild; Am Academy of Equine Art; Society of Animal Artists; Society of Illustrators. *Address:* Box 302, North Salem, NY 10560, USA.

SAVLA Mavji K, b. 20 Sept 1930, Kachchh, India. Businessman. m. Sakarbai Savla, 4 Feb 1948, 3 sons, 1 daughter. *Education:* BA, Philosophy, 1966; MA, Philosophy, 1968; PhD study, 1968-74. *Publications:* Sanatan Samasyao, 1977; Yatrik-ni-Antarkatha, 1986; Gurdjieff-no-Sadhna Marg, 1986; Gurdjieff-Ek-Rahasyamay Guru, 1987; A Manifesto of Philosophy; Rajneesh Mimansa; Zen Marg; Jainagam Sutrasar; Samvad-ne; Sathwara; Bi Govind Kaha Chha Dhanji Capu Na Sanidhyama; Bhartiya Darshan. *Contributions to:* Indian Literature; Granth; Navneet Samarpan; Vichar Valonoo; Bhumiputra; Bharat Manish; Calcutta Canvas;

Others. *Honours:* Gujarat Sahitya Akademi Award for book, 1977. *Memberships:* PEN, Indian Chapter; Past President, Rotary Club, Gandhidham. *Address:* N-45 Gandhidham, Kachchh, India.

SAWASZKIEWICZ Jacek Adam, b. 10 Sept 1947, Szczecin, Poland. Author; Critic. (div), 1 daughter. *Education:* Technical School, Engineer, 1968. *Publications include:* Kronika Akaszy (Tetralogy), 1989; Stan Zagrozenia, 1989; Sukcesorzy, 1986; Na Tle Kosmicznej Otchiani, 1988; Wahdio, 1986; Czekajac, 1978; Katharsis, 1980; Mistyfikacje, 1983; Miedzy Innymi Makabra, 1985. *Contributions to:* Odjlosy; Karuzela; Nurt; Miody Technik; Donosiciel; Detektyw Dolnośląski; Erotyka; Kryminał; Karuzela; Margines; Pomorskie Skandale; Sexodrama; Skandale; Tropem zbrodni; Wszystko o Miłości - Wróżka; W Kręgu zbrodni; various magazines in Czechoslovakia; GDR; Russia; Hungary; Spain; France. *Honours:* Silver Cross of Merit, 1986; Decoration of Griffin of Pomeranian, 1980; Gold Ex-Libris, 1983, 1986; Honour Decoration for Merits of Culture Stage, 1986. *Memberships:* Polish Writers Association, Board of Control; Association of Polish Writers and Composers, Board Member; Authors and Scenic Writers Union; Club of Authors Kaw. *Literary Agent:* Authors Agency, Warsaw, Poland. *Address:* ul Kard Wyszyńskiego 16/4, 70-201 Szczecin, Poland.

SAWYER John (with Nancy Sawyer as Nancy Buckingham, John Nancy, Erica Quest), b. 1919, British, Full-time writer of historical/romance/Gothic novels. Former director of a London advertising agency. *Publications include:* All with Nancy Sawyer: (as Nancy Buckingham) The House Called Edenhythe, 1970; Return to Vienna, 1971; Quest for Alexis, 1973; Valley of the Ravens, 1973; The Jade Dragon, 1974; The Other Cathy, 1978; Vienna Summer, 1979; Marianna, 1981; (as Erica Quest) The Silver Castle, 1978; Vienna Summer, 1979; The October Cabaret, 1979; Design for Murder, 1981; (as Nancy John) The Spanish House, 1981; Tormenting Flame, 1981; To Trust Tomorrow, 1981; A Man for Always, 1981; So Many Tomorrows, 1982; Web of Passion, 1982; Outback Summer, 1982; Summer Rhapsody, 1983; Never Too Late, 1983; Make-Believe Bride, 1983; Dream of Yesterday, 1984; Window to Happiness, 1984; Night with a Stranger, 1984; Champagne Nights, 1985; Rendezvous, 1985; The Moongate Wish, 1985; Lookalike Love, 1986; Secret Love, 1986. *Address:* c/o A M Heath, 40-42 William IV Street, London WC2N 4DD, England.

SAWYER Nancy (with John Sawyer as Nancy Buckingham, Nancy John, Erica Quest), b. 1924, British, Full time writer of historical/romance/Gothic publications. Formerly medical social worker. *Publications include:* All with John Sawyer: (as Nancy Buckingham) The House Called Edenhythe, 1970; Return to Vienna, 1971; Quest for Alexis, 1973; Valley of the Ravens, 1973; The Jade Dragons, 1974; The Other Cathy, 1978; Vienna Summer, 1979; Marianna, 1981; (as Erica Quest) The Silver Castle, 1978; The October Cabaret, 1979; Design for Murder, 1981; (as Nancy John) The Spanish Houose, 1981; Tormenting Flame, 1981; To Trust Tomorrow, 1981; A Man for Always, 1981; So Many Tomorrows, 1982; Outback Summer, 1982; Web of Passion, 1982; Summer Rhapsody, 1983; Never Too Late, 1983; Make-Beliebe Bride, 1983; Dream of Yesterday, 1984; Window to Happiness, 1984; Night with a Stranger, 1984; (as Nancy John) Champagne Nights, 1985; Rendezvous, 1985; The Moongate Wish, 1985; Lookalike Love, 1986; Secret Love, 1986. *Address:* c/o A M Heath, 40-42 William IV Street, London WC2N 4DD, England.

SAWYER Roger Martyn, b. 15 Dec 1931, Stroud, Gloucestershire, England. Author. m. Diana Margaret Harte, 30 Aug 1952, 2 sons. *Education:* BA (Hons), Diploma in Education, T G James Prize for Education, University of Wales, 1952-58; PhD (History), Southampton University, 1979. *Publications:* Casement: The Flawed Hero, 1984; Slavery in the Twentieth Century, 1986; Children Enslaved, 1988; The Island From Within (ed), 1990; We are but Women, 1993.

Contributions to: Immigrants and Minorities; South. *Honour:* Airey Neave Award, 1985. *Memberships:* Society of Authors; Retired member, Incorporated Association of Preparatory Schools; Bembridge Sailing Club. *Address:* Ducie House, Darts Lane, Bembridge, Isle of Wight, PO35 5YH, England.

SAX Joseph L, b. 1936, United States of America. Writer. *Publications:* Waters and Water Rights (ed R. E. Clark), 1967; Water Law, Planning and Policy, 1968; The Environmental Crisis: Man's Struggle to Live with Himself, 1970; Defending The Environment, 1971; Mountain Without Handrails, 1980; Legal Control of Water Resources, 2nd edition, 1991. *Address:* Boalt Hall, University of California, Berkeley, CA 94720, USA.

SAXON Bill. *See:* **WALLMANN Jeffrey M.**

SAXTON Josephine Mary, b. 11 June 1935, Halifax, Yorks. Writer, Decorative Artist; Acupuncturist. (Div), 3 sons, 1 daughter. *Education:* Partly trained in Art, Biology, Psychology, Lic Ac, 1985. *Publications include:* The Travails of Jane Saint, 1984; Jane Saint and the Backlash, 1989; Queen of the States, 1985; Little Tours of Hell (short stories) 1986; The Power of Time (short stories) 1985. *Contributor to:* She; New Health; New Statesman. *Membership:* Society of Authors. *Address:* 12 Plymouth Place, Leamington Spa, Warwickshire CV31 1HN, England.

SAYLOR John Galen, b. 1902, United States of America. Writer. *Publications:* Factors Associated with Participation in Cooperative Programs of Curriculum Planning, 1941; Secondary Education: Basic Principles and Practices (with W.M. Alexander), 1950; Curriculum Planning for Better Teaching and Learning (with W.M. Alexander), 1954; Modern Secondary Education: Basic Principles and Practices (with W.M. Alexander), 1959; Curriculum Planning for Modern Schools (with W.M. Alexander), 1966; The High School:Today and Tomorrow (with W.M.Alexander), 1971; Planning Curriculum for Schools (with W.M. Alexander) (2nd Edition with W.M. Alexander and Arthur J Lewis 1981), 1974; Antecedent Developments in the Movement to Competency-based programs of Teachers Education, 1976; Who Planned the Curriculum: A Curriculum Plans Reservoir Model, with Historical Examples, 1982; A History of the Department of Secondary Education, University of Nebraska, Lincoln 1871-1980, 1982; A Saylor Lineage, 1983; A Smith Linmeage, 1985; The Gilchrist Lineage, 1987. *Address:* 3001 S. 51st Street, No. 377, Lincoln, NB 68506, USA.

SCAGLIONE Aldo, b. 10 Jan 1925, Torino, Italy. University Professor. m. Jeanne M Daman (dec 1986), 28 June 1952. *Education:* DLitt, University of Torino, Italy, 1948. *Appointments include:* University of California, Berkeley, 1952-68; University of North Carolina, 1968-87; Professor and Chairman, Department of Italian, New York University, 1987-. *Publications include:* Nature and Love in the Late Middle Ages, 1963; Ars Grammatica, 1970; The Classical Theory of Composition, 1972; The Theory of German Word Order, 1981; The Liberal Arts and the Jesuit College System, 1986; Knights at Court, 1991. *Contributions to:* Various scholarly journals. *Memberships:* Medieval Academy of America; Boccaccio Association of America, President 1980-83; American Association for Italian Studies, Honorary President 1989. *Honours:* Knighted to the Order of Merit of the Republic of Italy; Fullright Scholar, 1951; Guggenheim Fellow, 1958; Newberry Fellow, 1964; Fellow University of Wisconsin Institute for the Humanities, 1981. *Address:* 29 Washington Square West, Apartment 10B, New York 10011, USA.

SCAGNETTI Jack, b. 24 Dec 1924, Piney Fork, Ohio, USA. Literary; Talent Agent; Author. m. Doris Woolford, 19 July 1951, 1 son, 1 daughter. *Education:* Graduate, Detroit Southwestern High School. *Publications:* Life and Loves of Gable; Laurel and Hardy Scrapbook;

Intimate Life of Rudolph Valentino; Movie Stars in Bathtubs; Cars of theStars; Been Pollen: Nature's Miracle Health Food; Bicycyle Motorcross; Famous Custom and show Cars; The Joy of Walking; Co-author: Golf for Beginners; Racquetball Made Easy; Racquetball for Women. *Contributions to:* Motor Trend; Popular Hot Rodding; Golf Magazine; Golf Digest. *Memberships:* Writers Guild of America; Academy of Television Arts and Sciences. *Address:* 5330 Lankershim Blv 210, N. Hollywood, CA 91601, USA.

SCALA James, b. 16 Sept 1934, New Jersey, USA. Nutritional Biochemist. m. Nancy Peters, 15 June 1957, 2 sons, 2 daughters. *Education:* AB Columbia University; PhD, Cornell University; Postdoctoral, Harvard University. *Publications:* Making the Vitamin Connection, 1986; The Arthritis Relief Diet, 1988; The High Blood Pressure Relief Diet, 1989; Look Ten Years Younger, Feel Ten Years Better, 1990; Prescription for Longevity, 1992; If You Can't/Won't Stop Smoking, 1993. *Contributions to:* Family Circle; Alive; The Retired officer; Arizona Living; The Write News. *Memberships:* California Writers Club; British Nutrition Society; American Institute of Nutrition; American College of Nutrition. *Literary Agent:* Writers House, New York, USA. *Address:* 44 Los Arabis Circle, Lafayette, CA 94549, USA.

SCALAPINO Robert Anthony, b. 1919, United States of America. Writer. *Appointments:* Editor, Asian Survey Journal, 1962-. *Publications:* Democracy and the Party Movement in Pre-War Japan, 1953; Parties and Politics in Contemporary Japan (with J. Masumi), 1962; North Korea Today, 1964; The Japanese Communist Movement 1920-1966, 1968; Communism in Korea 2 vols (with Chong-Sik Lee), 1972; Elites in the People's Republic of China, 1972; America-Japanese Relations in a Changing Era, 1972; Asia and the Major Powers, 1972; Asia and the Road Ahead, 1975; The Foreign Policy of Modern Japan, 1977; The Early Japanese Labor Movement, 1984; Modern China and Its Revolutionary Process, vol 1 (with G.T. Yu), 1985; Major Powers Relations in Northeast Asia, 1987; The Politics of Development - Prespectives On Twentieth Century Asia, 1989; The Last Leninists: The Uncertain Future of Asia's Communist States, 1992. *Address:* Institute of East Asian Studies, University of California, Berkeley, CA 94720, USA.

SCALI John Alfred, b. 27 Apr 1918, Canton, Ohio, USA. Journalist. m. (1) Helen Lauinger Glock, 1945, 3 daughters, (2) Denise Y. St. Germain, 1973. *Education:* BS, Boston University. *Appointments:* Reporter, Boston Herald, 1942, Boston Bureau, United Press, 1942-43; Associate Press, War Correspondent, European Theatre of Operations, 1944, later Diplomatic Correspondent, Washington Bureau, 1945-61; Diplomatic Correspondent, ABC TV and Radio, Washington, 1961-71; Ambassador, Permanent Representative to UN, 1973-75; Senior Correspondent, ABC News, Washington, 1975-. *Honours:* Journalism Award, University of Southern California, 1964; Special Award, Washington Chapter, National Academy of Arts & Sciences, 1964; John Scali Award created by Washington Cahapter of AFTRA, 1964; Man of the Year Award, Journalism, Boston University, 1965; Special Award, Overseas Press Clubs, 1965; Honorary Degrees, Malone, York Colleges, 1974; Rizzuto Gold Medal Award, 1974. *Memberships:* AFTRA. *Address:* 1717 De Sales Street NW, Washington, DC 20036, USA.

SCAMMACCA Nat, b. 20 July 1924, Brooklyn, New York City, USA. Teacher; Writer. m. Nina Digiorgio, 1948, 1 son, 1 daughter. *Education:* BA, Brooklyn; MA studies, NYU; Law studies, Brooklyn Law School. *Appointments:* Editor: Terza Pagina of Trapani, 1967-92; Nuova; Antiguppo, 1970-78; Impegno 70, 1970-80; Anti, 1967; Poetry Editor, Coop Ed Antigruppo Siciliano, 1980-92; Cultural Advisor of Cross-Cultural Communications, 1980-92. *Publications:* Bye Bye America, 1986; Due Mondi, 1979; Sikano L'Amerikano, 1989; Schammachanat, 1985; Ericipeo, 1990; Antigruppo, 1975; Ombre di Luce, 1968; Glenlee, 1971; Nuove

Liriche, 1977. *Contributions to:* Epoca; Chatalaine; L'Ora; Quartiere; Akros; Antigruppo Palermo; Stroker; Tulipano Rosso. *Honours:* Ragusa Poetry Award, 1985; First Place, VII Premio Di Poesia Petrosino, 1991; Custinaci Poetry Award, 1966. *Literary Agent:* Stanley H Barkan, Cross-Cultural Communications, Merrrick, NY. *Address:* Villa Schammachata Nat, via Argenteria, Km 4 Erice-Trapani, Sicilia.

SCAMMON Richard Montgomery, b. 17 July 1915, Minneapolis, Minnesota, USA. Psephologist. m. Mary Stark Allen, 1 daughter. *Education:* BA, University of Minnesota, 1935; London School of Economics, University of London, England, 1935-36; MA, University of Michigan, 1938. *Publications:* America Votes, vols 1-18, biennially, 1955-89; America at the Polls; America at the Polls 2. *Contributions:* Various. *Memberships:* American Political Science Association; US Academy of Political Science; Cosmos Club, Washington DC; American Statistical Association. *Address:* Elections Research Center, 5508 Greystone Street, Chevy Chase, MD 20815, USA.

SCANNELL Vernon, b. 23 Jan 1922, Spilsby, Lincolnshire. Author. m. 4 Oct 1954, 3 sons, 2 daughters. *Appointments:* Writer in Residence, Berinsfield, Oxon, 1975-76; Visiting Poet, Shrewsbury school, 1973- 75; Poet in Residence, King's School, Canterbury, 1979. *Publications:* New & Collected Poems, 1980; The Tiger & the Rose, Autobiography, 1971; Ring of Truth, Novel, 1983; Argument of Kings, Autobiography, 1987; Funeral Games, 1987; Winterlude, 1983; The Fight, 1952; The Wound & The Scar, 1953; The Face of the Enemy, 1960; The Dividing Night, 1962; The Big Time, 1967; Soldiering On, 1989, (Poetry); A Time For Fires (poetry), 1991; Drums of Morning, Growing Up in the 30's (autobiography), 1992. *Contributions to:* The Listener; The Observer; Sunday Times; Encounter; London Magazine; TLS; American Scholar; Yale Literary Magazine. *Honours:* Heinmann Award for Literature, 1960; Cholmondoley Poetry Prize, 1974. *Memberships:* Fellow, Royal Society of Literature, 1961. *Address:* 51 North Street, Otley, West Yorkshire, LS21 1AH, England.

SCARBOROUGH William Kauffman, b. 17 Jan 1933, Baltimore, Maryland, USA. University Professor; Historian. m. Patricia Estelle Carruthers, 16 Jan 1954, 1 son, 1 daughter. *Education:* AB, 1954, PhD, 1962, University of North Carolina; MA, Cornell University, 1957. *Publications:* The Overseer: Plantation Management in the Old South, 1966; Reprinted, 1984; The Diary of Edmund Ruffin, 3 vols, 1972-1989; Heartland of the Cotton Kingdom, in A History of Mississippi, 1973; Slavery - The White Man's Burden, in Pespectives and Irony in American Slavery, 1976; Science on the Plantation, in Science and Medicine in the Old South, 1989. *Contributions to:* Agricultural History, 1964; Civil War Times Illustrated, 1976; Virginia Magazine of History and Biography, 1989. *Honours:* Phi Beta Kappa, 1953; President, Mississippi Historical Society, 1979-80; Jules and Frances Landry Award for The Diary of Edmund Ruffin, Vols I-III, Louisiana State University Press, 1989. *Memberships:* American Historical Association; Organization of American Historians; Southern Historical Association; Agricultural History Society; Mississippi Historical Society. *Address:* Department of History, University of Southern Mississippi, Southern Station, Box 5047, Hattiesburg, MS 39406, USA.

SCARDINO Albert James, b. 22 Sept 1948, Baltimore, Missouri, USA. Independent Journalist. m. Marjorie Beth Morris, 19 Apr 1974, 2 sons, 1 daughter. *Education:* BA, Columbia University, 1970; MJ, University of California, 1976. *Appointments:* Staff, Associated Press, 1971; Editor, Georgia Gazette, Savannah, Georgia, 1978-85; Correspondent, New York Times, 1985-89; Press Secretary, Mayor Of the City of New York, 1990-91. *Publication:* Guale, 1976, documentary film. *Contributions to:* Columbia Journalism Review. *Honours:* Golden Quill for Editorial Writing, International Society of Weekly Newspaper

Editors, 1982; Pulitzer Prize for Editorial Writing, 1984. *Memberships:* Sigma Delta Chi, President, Chapter, 1982. *Literary Agent:* Wylie, Aitkin & Stone. *Address:* 2 Rutherford Place, New York, NY 10003, USA.

SCARF Maggie (Margaret), b. 13 May 1932, Philadelphia, Pennsylvania, USA. Writer. m. Herbert Eli Scarf, 28 June 1953, 3 daughters. *Education:* BA, South Connecticut State University, 1989. *Appointments:* Contributing Editor, The New Republic, 1975-; Writer-in-Residence, Jonathan Edwards College, Yale University, New Haven, Connecticut, 1979-. *Publications:* Body, Mind, Behavior, 1976; Unfinished Business, 1980; Intimate Partners, 1987. *Contributions to:* (1)The New York Times Magazine; Psychology Today; Atlantic Monthly; New Republic; Self; Cosmopolitan. *Honours:* Ford Foundation Fellow, 1973-74; Nieman Fellow, Harvard, 1975-76; Fellow, Center for Advanced Study, Stanford, 1977-78, 1985- 86; Alicia Patterson Fellow, 1978-79. *Memberships:* PEN; Elizabethan Club, Yale University; Connecticut Society of Psychoanalytic Psychologists. *Literary Agent:* Janklow and Nesbit. *Address:* Jonathan Edwards College, Yale University, 68 High Street, New Haven, CT 06517, USA.

SCARFE Norman, b.1 May 1923, Felixstowe, Suffolk, England. *Education:* MA Hons, History, Oxford, 1949. *Appointments:* Chairman of East Anglia Studies, University of East Anglia; Founder, Honorary General Editor, Suffolk Records Society, 1958-92. *Publications:* Suffolk, 1960, 1988; Essex, 1968, 1982; Cambridgeshire, 1983; The Suffolk Landscape, 1972, 1987; Suffolk in the Middle Ages, 1986; Assault Division, 1947; A Frenchman's Year in Suffolk, 1784, 1988; The La Rochefoucauld Tour of England in 1785, (in progress). *Contributions to:* Proceedings; Suffolk Institute of Archaeology; Aldeburgh Festival annual Programme Hook; Country Life; Textile History. *Honours:* Hon DLitt, University of East Anglia, 1989. *Memberships:* International PEN: Founder Chairman, Suffolk Book League, 1982-; Fellow, Society of Antiquaries. *Literary Agent:* John Welch, Milton House, Cambridge, CB4 6AD, England. *Address:* The Garden Cottage, 3 Burkitt Road, Woodbridge, Suffolk IP12 4JJ, England.

SCARFE Wendy Elizabeth, b. 1933, Australia. Author; Poet. *Publications:* Shadow and Flowers (poetry), 1974, 1984; The Lotus Throne (novel), 1976; Neither Here Nor There (novel), 1984; Laura My Alter Ego (novel), 1988; Laura My Alter Ego (novel), 1988; The Day They Shot Edward (novel), 1991; NWith Allan John Scarfe: A Mouthful of Petals, 1967; Tiger on a Rein, 1969; People of India, 1972; The Black Australians, 1974; Victims or Bludgers? Case Studies in Poverty in Australia, 1974; J.P., His Biography, 1975; Victims or Bludgers? A Poverty Inquiry for Schools, 1981; Labor's Titan: The Story of Percy Brookfield 1878-1921, 1983; All That Grief (with Allan Scarfe), 1992; In Progess: Miranda Finds Helios (novel) and No Taste For Carnage (biography with Allan Scarfe). *Honours:* with Allan Scarfe Australia Council Literature Board Special Purpose Writers Grant, 1980 & 1988. *Memberships:* Fellowship of Australian Writers; Melbourne Writers' Centre. *Address:* 8 Bostock Street, Warrnambool, Victoria 3280, Australia.

SCARGILL David Ian, b. 1935, Writer. *Publications:* Economic Geography of France, 1968; The Dordogne Region of France, 1974; The Form of Cities, 1979; Oxford and Its Countryside (with A.G. Crosby), 1982; Urban France, 1983. *Address:* St. Edmund Hall, Oxford, England.

SCARR(-SALAPATEK) Sandra (Wood), b. 8 Aug 1936, Washington DC, USA. Professor of Psychology. m. 1. Harry Alan Scarr, 1961 (marriage ended), 2. Philip H Salapatek, 1971; 1 son, 3 daughters. *Education:* AB (with honours) Vassar College, 1958; AM (with distinction) 1963, PhD 1965, Harvard University. *Appointments:* Case Aide, Family and Child Service of Omaha, Nebraska, 1958-59; Research Assistant at

Laboratory of Socio-Environmental Studies, National Institute of Mental Health, Bethesda, Maryland, 1959-60; Instructor 1964-65, Assistant Professor of Child Studies 1965-66, University of Maryland at College Park; Visiting Lecturer 1966-67, Lecturer 1967-68, Assistant Professor 1968-70, Associate Professor of Education Psychology, 1970-71, Acting Director, William T Carter Foundation for Child Development, 1967-70, University of Pennsylvania, Philadelphia; Associate Professor 1971-74, Professor of Child Development 1974-77, University of Minnesota-Twin Cities, Minneapolis; Professor of Psychology 1977-83, Yale University, New Haven, Connecticut; Commonwealth Professor of Psychology, 1983-, Chairman of Department 1984-87 fellow at Centre for Advanced Study, 1983-84, University of Virginia, Charlottesville; Visiting Associate Professor at Bryn Mawr College, 1969; Fellow at Center for Advanced Studies in the Behavioral Sciences, Stanford, California, 1976-77; Editor, Current Directions in Psychological Science, a journal of the Cambridge University Press. Member of various boards of directors. *Publications include:* (with husband Philip H Salapatek), Socialization, 1973; (ed with F D Horowitz, E M Hetherington and G Siegel and contributor) Review of Child Development Research, Vol IV 1975; Race, Social Class and Individual Differences in IQ: New Studies of Old Issues, 1981; Child Care, 1984; Mother Care/Other Care, 1984, revised edition 1985; (with James Vander Zanden) Understanding Psychology, , 4th ed 1984, 5th ed 1987; (with Ann Levine and R A Weinberg) Understanding Development, 1986; (with Judy Dunn) Mother Care/Other Care: Dilemma in Britain, 1987. *Contributions to:* numerous edited volumes. *Honours:* National Book Award from American Psychological Association, 1985 for Mother Care/Other Care. *Memberships:* Member of numerous professional associations including the American Academy of Arts and Sciences, 1990. *Address:* Department of Psychology, University of Virginia, Charlottesville, VA 22903, USA.

SCARRY Richard, b.1919, United States of America. Children's Writer. *Publications:* Tinker and Tanker series, 7 vols, 1960-78; Best Ever series, 7 vols, 1963-79; Busy, Busy World, 1965; Storybook Dictionary, 1966; What Do People Do All Day, 1968; Look and Learn Library, 1971; Great Big Air Book, 1971; ABC Workbook, 1971; Funniest Storybook Ever, 1972; Great Big Mystery Book, 1972; Please and Thank You Book, 1973; Find Your ABC's, 1973; Cars and Trucks and Things That Go, 1974; Animal Nursery Tales, 1975; Look-Look Books, 1976; Color Books, 1976; Early Words, 1976; Busiest People Ever, 1976; Best Make-It Book Ever, 1977; Postman Pig, 1978; Toy Book, 1978; Lowly Worm series, 1979; Easy to Read Books, 1981. *Address:* Schwyzerhus, 3780 Gstaad, Switzerland.

SCHAEFFER Boguslaw, b. 6 June 1929, Lwow, Poland. Composer; Playwright. m. Mieczyslawa Hanuszewska, 1953, 1 son. *Education:* PhD, Jagiellonian University, Cracow, 1970. *Appointments Include:* Associate Professor, State Higher School of Music, Cracow, 1963-; Chief Editor, Forum Musicum 1967-; Professor, Academy of Music, Cracow, Poland, 1985-; Professor, Mozarteum, Salzburg, 1986-. *Publications:* New Music, Problems of Contemporary Technique in Composing, 1958; Classics of Dodecaphonic Music, 1964; Lexicon of 20th Century Composers, 1965; In the Sphere of New Music, 1967; Introduction to Composition (in English), 1975; Story of Music, 1980; Composers of the 20th Century, 2 volumes. Theatrical pieces: Scenario for an inexisting, but possible instrumental actor, 1963; Audiences I-V for actors, 1964; Quartet for fouur actors, 1966; Scenario for three actors, 1970; The Darknesses, 1980; The Dawn, 1981; The Sins of Old Age, 1985; Katcho, 1988; The Actor, 1989; The Rehearsals, 1990; The Séance, 1990; The Break of Day, 1990. *Honours:* G. Fiteberg Prize, 1959, 1960, 1964; A. Malawski Prize, 1962; Minister of Culture and Arts Prize, 1971, 1980; Union of Polish Composers Prize, 1977; Theatre Prize, 1987. *Address:* Osiedle Kolorowe 4, 31-938 Cracow, Poland.

SCHALK Adolph F(rancis), b. 1923, United States of America. Writer. *Appointments:* Editor, Today Magazine, Chicago, 1951-55; Editor, The Bridge, Hamburg, West Germany, 1957-62. *Publications:* Eyes On Modern World, 1964; The Germans, 1971, 1972; Germans in America, 1973. *Address:* CH 6579 Indemini, Ticino, Switzerland.

SCHAMA Simon, b. 13 Feb 1945, London, England. Historian; Writer. m. 2 children. *Education:* BA, 1966, MA, 1969 (History), Cambridge University. *Appointments include:* Professor, Harvard University, 1980-; Senior Associate, Harvard's Center for European Studies. *Publications:* Patriots and Liberators: Revolution in the Netherlands 1780-1813, 1977; Two Rothschilds and the Land of Israel, 1979; The Embarrassment of Riches: An Interpretation of Dutch Culture in the Golden Age, 1987; Citizens: A Chronicle of the French Revolution, 1989. *Honours:* For Patriots and Liberators: Recipient of Wolfson Prize for History, 1977, Leo Gersoy Memorial Prize, American Historical Association, 1978; For Citizens: New York Times Bestseller List, 1989. *Address:* Lexington, Massachussets, USA.

SCHANBERG Sydney H., b. 17 Jan 1934, Clinton, Massachusetts, USA. Journalist. (div), 2 daughters. *Education:* BA, Harvard, 1955. *Literary Appointments:* Joined New York Times, 1959: Reporter, 1960; Bureau chief, Albany, New York 1967-69, New Delhi, India 1969-73; Southeast Asia correspondent, Singapore, 1973-75; Metropolitan editor, 1977-80; Columnist, 1981-85; Columnist/associate editor, New York Newsday, 1986-. *Publications include:* The Death & Life of Dith Pran, 1985. *Honours:* Page One Award, Foreign Reporting, 1972; Overseas Press Club Awards, Foreign Reporting 1972, Foreign Photography 1974; George Polk Memorial Award, Foreign Reporting, 1972; Special George Polk Award, coverage, Fall of Phnom Penh, 1975; Bob Considine Memorial Award, 1975; Pulitzer Prize, 1975; Front Page Award, Newspaper Guild, 1975; Sigma Delta Chi Award, Distinguished Service in Journalism, 1975. *Address:* c/o New York Newsday, 2 Park Avenue, New York, NY 10016, USA.

SCHAPSMEIER Edward Lewis, b. 8 Feb 1927, Iowa, USA. History Professor. m. Lee Love, 22 Nov 1984, 2 sons, 3 daughters. *Education:* BA, Concordia College, 1949; MA, University of Nebraska, 1952; PhD, University of Southern California, 1966. *Publications:* Gerald R. Ford's Date with Destiny, 1989; Biography of Henry A. Wallace, 2 vols., 1968, 1970; Dirksen of Illinois: Senatorial Statesman, 1985; Political Parties and Civic Action Groups, 1981; Ezra Taft Benson: Eisenhower Years, 1975; Encyclopedia of Agricultural History, 1976; Walter Lippmann: Philosopher-Journalist, 1969; Abundant Harvests: The Story of American Literature, 1973. *Contributions to:* Journal of American History; Journal of Illinois History; Agriculture History; The Historian; Journal of the West; Ohio History. *Honours:* Distinguished Professor of History, Illinois State University, 1984. *Memberships:* American Historical Association; Organization of American Historians; Agricultural History Society; Illinois State Historical Society. *Address:* 3103 Winchester Drive, Bloomington, Illinois 61704, USA.

SCHAPSMEIER Frederick H., b. 8 Feb 1927, Council Bluff, Iowa, USA. Historian. m. Mary Schmidt, 18 June 1976, 2 sons, 1 daughter. *Education:* BS, Concordia College, 1949; MS, Nebraska University, 1952; PhD, University of Southern California, 1965. *Publications include:* Henry A. Wallace: Agrarian Years, 1968; Walter Lippmann: Philosopher-Journalist, 1969; Henry A. Wallace: War Years, 1970; Ezra Taft Benson & the Politics of Agriculture, 1975; Encyclopaedia of American Agriculture, 1976; Agriculture & the West, 1979; Dictionary of Political Parties, 1981; Everett M Dirksen: Senatorial Statesman, 1984; Gerald R Ford's Date With Destiny: A Political Biography, 1990. *Contributions to:* Agricultural History; Historian; Illinois State Historical Journal; Journal of the West; Annals of Iowa; Nebraska Historical Journal; Social Studies; Social Science;

Forum. *Honours:* Harry E. Pratt Award, best article, Illinois Historical Society, 1977; Award, outstanding reference book, American Library Association, 1981; 1st John McN.Rosebush University Professorship, 1983. *Memberships:* American Historical Association; Organisation of American Historians; Western Historical Association; Society for Study of American Foreign Relations. *Address:* 624 Jackson Street, Oshkosh, Wisconsin 54901, USA.

SCHEFFER Victor B(lanchard), b. 1906, United States of America. Writer. *Publications:* The Year of the Whale, 1969; The Year of the Seal, 1970; The Seeing Eye, 1971; A Voice for Wildlife, 1974; A Natural History of Marine Mammals, 1976; Adventures of a Zoologist, 1980; The Amazing Sea Otter, 1981; Spires of Form, 1983; The Shaping of Environmentalism in America, 1991. *Address:* 14806 S.E. 54th Street, Bellevue,WA 98006, USA.

SCHEIBER Harry N, b. 1935, United States of America. Writer; Associate Dean and Professor of Law; Chair of Jurisprudence and Social Policy, University of California, Berkeley. *Appointments:* Co-Editor, History of American Economy Series, Johnson Reprint; Member of Editorial Boards, Publius: Journal of Federalism, Review's in American History; Founding director, Berkeley Seminar on Federalism 1986-; Academic Director, National Endowment of the Humanites Institute on Constitutionalism, University of California, Berkeley, 1987-90; Co-ordinator for Marine Affairs, California Sea Grant College Program; Academic Chair for history and civics, National Assessment of Educational Progress, 1986-88. *Publications:* The Wilson Administration and Civil Liberties, 1960; United States Economic History, 1964; Co-Author, America: Purpose and Power, 1965; The Condition of American Federalism, 1966; Co-Author and Editor, The Frontier in American Development, 1969; The Old Northwest, 1969; Ohio Canal Era, 1820-1861, 1969, 2nd edition 1987; Black Labor in America (with J. Scheiber), 1970; Co-Author, Law in American History, 1972; Agriculture in the Development of the Far West, 1975; Co-Author, American Economic History, 1976; Co-editor, American Law and the Constitutional Order, 1978, 1990; editor, Perspectives on Federalism, 1987; Co-editor and contributing author, Power Divided, 1989. *Honours:* Guggenheim Fellow, 1967, 1989; Fellow, Center for Advanced Study in Behaviourial. Science, 1966, 1971; Distinguished Fulbright Lecturer (Australia), 1984; Fellow, National Endowment for the Humanities, 1986; Fellow, University of California Humanities Research Institute, 1989. *Address:* School of Law, University of California, Berkeley, CA 94708, USA.

SCHEIN M V. *See:* DIMEN Muriel Vera.

SCHELL Jonathan Edward, b. 1943, United States of America. Writer. *Appointments:* Staff Writer, The New Yorker Magazine; Columnist, New York Newsday, 1990- . *Publications:* The Village of Ben Sue, 1967; The Military Half, 1968; The Time of Illusion, 1975; The Fate of the Earth, 1982; The Abolition, 1984; History in Sherman Park, 1987; The Real War, 1988; Observing the Nixon Years, 1989. *Address:* 108 Reade Street, New York, NY 10013, USA.

SCHELL Orville Hickok, b. 20 May 1940, New York City, New York, USA. Writer. 1 son. *Education:* BA magna cum laude, Harvard College; MA, PhD (ABD), University of California, Berkeley. *Publications:* Discos and Democracy: China in the Throes of Reform; To Get Rich Is Glorious - China in the 1980s; Watch Out for the Foreign Guests: China Confronts the West; Modern Meat. *Contributions to:* New Yorker; Atlantic Monthly; New York Times Magazine; Rolling Stone. *Honours:* Alice Patterson Fellowship, 1981; MacDowell Colony Fellow, 1984, 1987; John Simon Guggenheim Fellow, 1989-90. *Memberships:* PEN; Authors Guild. *Literary Agent:* Amanda Urban, ICM. *Address:* 40 W 57th Street, New York, NY 10019, USA.

SCHELLENBERG James Arthur, b. 7 June 1932, Vinland, Kansas, USA. Social Scientist. m. 28 Dec 1974, 3 sons, 1 daughter. *Education:* AB, Baker University, 1954; MA, 1955, PhD, 1959, University of Kansas. *Publications:* An Introduction to Social Psychology, 1970, Revised Edition, 1974; Masters of Social Psychology, 1978, with subsequent Swedish, Spanish, Japanese and Malay Editions; The Science of Conflict, 1982; Conflict Between Communities, 1987; Primitive Games, 1990. *Address:* 124 Madison Boulevard, Terre Haute, IN 47803, USA.

SCHELLING Thomas Crombie, b. 14 Apr 1921, Oakland, California, USA. Professor. m. Corinne Saposs, 13 Sept 1947, 4 sons. *Education:* BA, University of California, Berkeley, 1944; PhD, Economics, Harvard University, 1951. *Publications:* National Income Behavior, 1951; International Economics, 1958; Strategy of Conflict, 1960; Arms and Influence, 1967; Micromotives and Macrobehavior, 1978; Choice and Consequence, 1984. *Contributions to:* Numerous journals, magazines and newspapers. *Honours:* Frank E Seidman Distinguished Award in Political Economy, 1977; Distinguished Fellow, American Economic Association, 1986. *Memberships:* American Economic Association, President 1991; National Academy of Sciences; American Academy of Arts and Sciences. *Address:* Department of Economics, University of Maryland, College Park, MD 20742, USA.

SCHENK Joyce, b. 19 June 1937, New York, USA. Associate Professor, El Camino College; Writer. *Education:* BA, Hunter College, 1966; MA, English Literature, Boston University, 1968. *Publications:* Caves of Darkness, 1977; The Promise Ring, 1979; Time to Choose, with Carl Green, 1981; Run from Danger, 1981; Andrea, 1982; Color it Love, 1983; Blues for Cassandra, 1984; Love Vote, 1984; Madly in Love, 1985; Seaside Heights, with Harriette Abels, 1985; Love Contest, 1985. *Honours:* Winner, best young adult novel 1982, Finalist, best novel, 1984, Romance Writers of America. *Memberships:* PEN; Society of Children's Bookwriters; Phi Beta Kappa. *Literary Agent:* Maryanne Colas, 229 East 79th Street, New York 10021. *Address:* 20455 Anza Avenue no.53, Torrance, California 90503, USA.

SCHENKAR Joan Marlene, b. 15 Aug 1946, Seattle, Washington, USA. Playwright. *Education:* BA Bennington College; MA University of California and SUNY; ABD, SUNY, Stony Brook. *Publications:* Signs of Life; Cabin Fever; The Universal Wolf, 1991; Family Pride in the 50's, 1992; The Last of Hitler; Produced Plays: Signs of Life; Cabin Fever; The Lodger; Mr Monster; Bucks and Does; Fire in the Future; Family Pride in the 50's; Between the Acts; Muder in the Kitchen; The Last of Hitler; The Universal Wolf. *Contributions to:* TDR; Theatre Journal Quarterly; Modern Drama; Women and Performance; Michigan Quarterly Reviews; Studies in American Drama; Alternative Theatrales; Feminist Revisions. *Honours:* 33 grants, fellowships and awards from North American foundations and granting agencies including 7 National Endowment for the Arts Fellowships. *Memberships:* The Bronte Society; PEN American Centre; The Dramatists' Guild; Societe des Auteurs et Compositerus Dramatiques; The Women's Project; The League of Professional Theatre Women. *Address:* PO Box 814, North Bennington, VT 05257, USA.

SCHEPISI Frederic Alan, b. 26 Dec 1939, Melbourne, Australia. Film Writer; Director. m. (1) Joan Mary Ford, 1960, (2) Rhonda Elizabeth Finlayson, 1973, 3 sons, 4 daughters. (3) Mary Rubin, 1984. *Appointments:* TV production Manager, Patron Advisory Service, Melbourne, 1961-64; Victorian Manager Cinesound Productions, Melbourne, 1964-66; Managing Director, The Film House, Melbourne, 1964-66, Governing Chairman, 1979-. *Publications:* Films: The Devil's Playground, 1975; The Chant of Jimmie Blacksmith, 1978; Barbarosa, 1981; Iceman, 1983; Plenty, 1984-85; Roxanne, 1986; Evil Angels, 1987. *Honours:* Australian Film Awards, Best Film, The Devil's Playground, 1975; Australian Film Awards, Best Film,

Best Achievement in Direction, Best Screenplay adapted from another source and The AFI Members Prize Special Award, for Evil Angels, 1989. *Address:* 159 Eastern Road, South Melbourne, VIC, Australia.

SCHEVILL James (Erwin), b. 1920, United States of America. Author; Poet; Playwright. *Publications:* Tensions (poetry), 1947; The American Fantasies (poetry), 1951; Sherwood Anderson: His Life and Work, 1951; High Sinners, Low Angels, 1953; The Right to Greet (Poetry), 1956; The Roaring Market and the Silent Tomb (biography), 1956; Edited Six Historians, by Ferdinand Schevill, 1986; Selected Poems 1945-1959, 1959; Voices of Mass and Capital A, 1962; Private Dooms and Public Destinations: Poems 1945-1962, 1962; The Master, 1963; The Stalingrad Elegies (poetry), 1964; The Black President, 1965; Release (poetry), 1968; Violence and Glory: Poems 1962- 1968, 1969; Lovecraft's Follies (play), 1971; Breakout! In Search of New Theatrical Environments, 1972; The Buddhist Car and Other Characters (poetry), 1973; Pursuing Elegy, 1974; Cathedral of Ice, 1975; The Arena of Ants (novel), 1977; The Mavan Poems, 1978; Fire of Eyes: A Guatemalan Sequence, 1979; Edison's Dream, 1982; The American Fantasies: Collected Poems 1945-1982, 1983; The Invisible Volcano (poem), 1985; Oppenheimer's Chair (play), 1985; Collected Short Plays, 1986; Ambiguous Dancers of Fame: Collected Poems 1945-1986, 1987; Bern Porter: A Personal Biography, 1993; Five Plays, 1993. *Honour:* Literary Award, American Academy & Institute of Arts & Letters, New York, 1991. *Literary Agent:* Helen Merrill, 435 W. 23 St, Suite 1A, New York, NY 10011, USA. *Address:* 1309 Oxford Street, Berkeley, CA 94709, USA.

SCHICKEL Richard, b. 1933, United States of America. Writer (Television). *Appointments:* Senior Editor, Look Magazine, 1956-60; Senior Editor, Show Magazine, 1960-63; Film Critic, Life Magazine, 1965-73; Film Critic, Time Magazine, 1973-. *Publications:* The World of Varnegie Hall, 1960; The Stars, 1962; Movies: The History of an Art and an Institution, 1974; The Gentle Knight, 1964; The Disney Version, 1968; The World of Goya, 1968; Second Sight: Notes on Some Movies, 1972; His Picture in the Paper, 1974; The Men Who made the Movies, 1974; The Platinum Years, 1974; The Fairbanks Album, 1975; The World of Tennis, 1975; Another I, Another You, 1978; Singled Out, 1981; Cary Grant: A Celebration, 1983; D.W. Griffith: An American Life, 1984; Intimate Strangers: The Culture of Celebrity, 1985; James Cagney: A Celebration, 1985. *Address:* 311 E. 83rd Street, New York, NY 10028, USA.

SCHILPP Paul Arthur, b. German, 1897, American. Philosophy, Theology/Religion. *Appointments:* Emeritus Professor of Philosophy, Northwestern University, Evanston, Illinois, since 1965, (Lecturer Associate Professor and Professor of Philosophy 1936-65); Professor Emeritus, Southern Illinois University, Carbondale, since 1980 (Visiting Distinguished Research Professor 1965-82). Adjunct Professor of Philosophy, University of California at Santa Barbara, since 1982. Professor of Psychology, Bible and Religious Education, University of Puget Sound, Washington, 1922-23; Associate Professor of Philosophy, University of the Pacific, San Jose, California, 1923-24; Professor of Philosophy, 1924-34 and Associate Professor of German, 1935-36, University of the Pacific, Stockton, California. Founder President and Ed., Library of Living Philosophers, 1938-81. *Publications:* Do We Need a New Religion?, 1929; (ed.) Higher Education Faces the Future, 1930; (ed.) College of the Pacific Publications in Philosophy, 3 vols., 1932-34; Kant's Pre-Critical Ethics, 1938; The Quest for Religious Realism; Some Paradoxes of Religion, 1938; (ed.) Philosophy of John Dewey, 1939; (ed.) Philosophy of George Santayana, 1940; (ed.) Theology and Modern Life, 1940; (ed.) Philosophy of Alfred North Whitehead, 1941; (ed.) Philosophy of G.E. Moore, 1942; (ed.) Philosophy of Bertrand Russell, 1944; (ed.) Philosophy of Ernst Cassirer, 1949; (ed.) Albert Einstein: Philosopher-Scientist, 1949; (ed.) Philosophy of Sarvepalli Radhakrishnan, 1952; Human Nature and Progress,

1954; (ed.) Philosophy of Karl Jaspers, 1957; (ed.) Philosophy of C.D. Broad, 1959; (ed.) Philosophy of Rudolf Carnap, 1963; The Crisis in Science and Education, 1963; (ed.) Philosophy of Karl Popper, 1974; Philosophy of Brand Blanshard, 1980; The Philosophy of Jean-Paul Sartre, 1981; (ed. with Lewis E. Hahn) The Philosophy of Gabriel Marcel, 1984.

SCHINTO Jeanne, b. 19 Dec 1951, Greenwich, Connecticut, USA. Writer. m. Robert J Frishman, 22 Dec 1973. *Education:* BA George Washington University, 1973; MA Johns Hopkins University, 1981. *Publications:* Shadow Bands, 1988; Children of Men, 1991; Editor, The Literary Dog, 1990. *Literary Agent:* Faith Hornby Hamlin, Sanford J Greenburger Associates. *Address:* 173 Prospect Street, Lawrence, MA 01841, USA.

SCHLAFLY Phyllis Stewart, b. 15 Aug 1924, St Louis, USA. Author; Lawyer. m. Fred Schlafly, 20 Oct 1949, 4 sons, 2 daughters. *Education:* BA, Washington University, 1944; MA, Harvard University, 1945; LLD, Niagara University, 1976; JD, Washington University Law School 1978. *Appointment:* Syndicated Colmnist, Copley News Service, 1976-. *Publications:* A Choice Not an Echo, 1964; The Gravediggers, 1964; Strike from Space, 1965; Safe Not Sorry, 1967; The Betrayers, 1968; Mindszenty the Man, 1972; Kissinger on the Couch, 1975; Ambush at Vladivostok, 1976; The Power of the Positive Woman, 1977; Editor: Child Abuse in the Classroom, 1984; Pornography's Victims, 1987; Equal Pay for Unequal Work, 1984; Who Will Rock the Cradle?, 1989. *Contributions to:* Numerous journals and magazines; Broadcaster, Commentator. *Honours:* DAR, various offices including Chairman, National Defence 1977-80, 1983-; American, Illinois Bar Associations; Phi Beta Kappa; Pi Sigma Alpha. *Memberships:* 10 Honour Awards, Freedoms Foundation; Named Woman of Achievement in Public Affairs; One of Ten Most Admired Women in World Good Housekeeping Poll, 1977-; many others. *Address:* 68 Fairmount, Alton, IL 62002, USA.

SCHLEIN Miriam, American. Writer of children's fiction, children's non-fiction. *Publications include:* Big Talk, 1955; Lazy Day, 1955; Henry's Ride, 1956; Deer in the Snow, 1956; Something for Now, Something for Later, 1956; Little Rabbit, The High Jumper, 1957; Amazing Mr Pelgrew, 1957; The Big Cheese, 1958; The Bumblebee's Secret, 1958; Home, The Tale of a Mouse, 1958; Herman McGregor's World, 1958; Kittens, Cubs and Babies, 1959; The Fisherman's Day, 1959; My Family, 1960; The Sun, The Wind, The Sea and the Rain, 1960; Laurie's New Brother, 1961; Amuny, Boy of Old Egypt, 1961; The Pile of Junk, 1962; Snow Time, 1962; The Snake in the Carpool, 1963; The Way Mothers Are, 1963; Who?...1963; The Big Green Thing, 1963; Big Lion, Little Lion, 1964; Billy, The Littlest One, 1966; The Best Place, 1968; My House, 1971; Moon-Months and Sun-Days, 1972; Juju Sheep and the Python's Moonstone, and Other Moon Stories from Different Times and Different Places, 1973; The Rabbit's World, 1973; What's Wrong with Being a Skunk? 1974; The Girl Who Would Rather Climb Trees, 1975; Metric: The Modern Way to Measure, 1975; Bobo the Troublemaker, 1976; Giraffe, The Silent Giant, 1976; I, Tut, 1978; On the Track of the Mystery Animal, 1978; Snake Fights, Rabbit Fights and More, 1979; Lucky Porcupine, 1980; Antarctica, the Great White Continent, 1980; Billions of Bats, 1982; Project Panda Watch, 1984; The Dangerous Life of the Sea Horse, 1986; What the Elephant Was, 1986. *Membership:* Past President, Forum of Writers for Young People. *Address:* 19 E 95th Street, New York, NY 10028, USA.

SCHLESINGER Arthur, JR., b. 15 Oct 1917, Columbus, Ohio, USA. Writer; Educator. m. (1) Marian Cannon, 1940, div. 1970, 2 sons, 2 daughters, (2) Alexandra Emmet, 1971, 1 son. *Education:* Harvard University; Peterhouse, Cambridge, England. *Publications:* Orestes A Brownson: A Pilgrim's Progress, 1939; The Age of Jackson, 1945; The Vital Center (English title The Politics of Freedom), 1949; The General and the President (with R H Revere), 1951; The Age of Roosevelt: Volume I, The Crisis of the Old Order, 1957, Volume II, The Coming of the New Deal, 1958, Volume III, The Politics of Upheaval, 1960; Kennedy or Nixon, 1960; The Politics of Hope, 1963; Paths of American Thought (editor with Morton White), 1963; A Thousand Days: John F Kennedy in the White House, 1965; The Bitter Heritage: Vietnam and American Democracy, 1941-1966, 1967; The Crisis of Confidence, 1969; History of American Presidential Elections (editor with F L Israel), 1971; The Imperial Presidency, 1973; Robert Kennedy and His Times, 1978; Cycles of American History, 1986; The Misuniting of America, 1992. *Contributions to:* Various magazines and newspapers. *Honours include:* Honorary D.Litt, University of Oxford, 1987; and honorary degrees from many other universities and colleges; Pulitzer Prize for History, 1946, for biography, 1960. *Address:* City University of New York, 33 West 42nd Street, New York, NY 10036, USA.

SCHLOSSMAN Beryl, b. New York, USA. Teacher of Literature. *Education:* PhD, University of Paris, 1981; PhD, Johns Hopkins University, 1987. *Publications:* The Orient of Style, 1991; Joyce's Catholic Comedy of Language, 1985. *Contributions to:* MLN; Comparitio; Tel Quel; James Joyce Quarterly; Revue des Lettres Modernes; Symposium Wunderblock. *Honours:* Fulbright 1976; PHi Beta Kappa 1976; Newcombe Fellowship, 1985; Mellon Fellowship, 1988. *Memberships:* Modern Language Association. *Address:* Department of Modern Languages, Carnegie Mellon University, Pittsburgh, PA 15213, USA.

SCHMANDT Henry J, b. 1918, United States of America. Writer (Politics). *Publications:* History of Political Philosophy, 1960; Exploring the Metropolitan Community (with J. Bollens), 1961; Metropolitan Reform in St. Louis (with P. Stenibicker and G. Wendel), 1961; Milwaukee Metropolitan Study Commission, 1965; Courts in the American Political System, 1968; Power, Poverty and Urban Life (with W. Bloomberg), 1968; The Quality of Urban Life (with W. Bloomberg), 1969; Milwaukee: A Contemporary Urban Profile (with D. Vogel and J. Goldbach), 1971; The Metropolis: Its People, Politics and Economic Life, 3rd Edition (with J. Bollens), 1975; Federal Aid to St Louis (with G.D. Wendel), 1983.

SCHMEISER Douglas A, b. 22 May 1934, Bruno, Saskatchewan, Canada. Professor of Law. m. Irene Ositis, 6 Dec 1980, 4 sons, 2 daughters. *Education:* BA, 1954, LLB, 1956, University of Saskatchewan; LLM, 1958, SJD, 1963, University of Michigan, USA. *Publications:* Civil Liberties in Canada, 1964; Canadian Criminal Law, 1966, 1973, 1977, 1981, 1985; Cases on Canadian Civil Liberties, 1971; The Native Offender and the Law, 1974. *Contributions to:* Various articles and chapters to books, dealing primarily with Constitutional Law, Human Rights, and Criminal Law. *Honour:* Queen's Counsel, 1982. *Memberships:* Former Director and President, Canadian Association of Law Teachers; Former Director and President, Saskatoon Bar Association; Law Society of Saskatchewan; Law Reform Commission of Saskatchewan, Chairman 1982-87; Advisory Academic Panel, Canada Council, 1971-74; Council Member, Canadian Human Rights Foundation; Director, former President and Campaign Chairman, Saskatoon United Way. *Address:* College of Law, University of Saskatchewan, Saskatoon, Saskatchewan, Canada S7N 0W0.

SCHMIDHUBER Guillermo, b. 27 Oct 1943, Mexico City, Mexico. Playwright; Museum Director. m. Olga Martha Pena, 10 Sept 1977. 1 son, 2 daughters. *Education:* BSc, Chemistry, 1968; MBA, Organisational Behaviour, 1971; MA, Spanish Literature, 1987; PhD, University of Cincinnati, 1989. *Publications:* 21 plays including: The Human Cathedral, 1974; The Useless Heroes, 1979; The Heirs of Segismund, 1980; Quartet of my People, collection, short plays, 1984; the Day Mona Lisa Stopped Smiling, 1985; In the Lands of Columbus, 1987. Also: The Parable of the Evil Inn, 1969; Our Lord Quetzalcoatl, 1974; We All Are King Lear,

1979; Lacandonia, 1982; Instant Happiness, 1983; The Cyclop, 1987; The 5th Trip of Columbus, 1987; The Armour of Our Grandmothers, 1990. Editor: The Second Celestina, 1990; Mexican Theatre 1923-38, 1990. *Contributions to:* Mexican newspapers: El Porvenir; Excelsior. American journals: LATR; Estreno. Mexican journals; Repertoro; la Cabra UNAM; Tierra Adentro INBA; Revista Iberoamericana; Lira. *Honours:* Nezahualcoyotl Award, Mexican Writers Guild (SOGEM), 1978; National Drama Award, Fine Arts Institute, Mexico, 1980; Letras de Oro Award, University of Miami, USA, 1987; 17 recognitions in Spain, Venezuela and Mexico. *Memberships:* Mexican Writers Guild; PROTEAC Theatre Guild, Mexico; PEN Club of Mexico; Executive, CIMUSET-ICOM, UNESCO, 1980-86; Arts Council, Nuevo Leon, Mexico, 1980-86; Board Member, Alfa Cultural Centre, Mexico, 1978-86. *Address:* Modern Languages, University of Louisville, Louisville, KY 40292, USA.

SCHMIDMAN Jo Ann, b. 18 Apr 1948, Omaha, Nebraska, USA. Theatre Director; Playwright. *Education includes:* BFA, Boston University, 1970. *Appointments include:* Producing Artistic Director, Omaha Magic Theatre, 1968-; Artist-in-Schools, performing arts & poetry, Nebraska Arts Council. *Publications include:* Plays, This Sleep Among Women, 1974, Running Gag, 1980, in High Energy Musicals from the Omaha Magic Theatre; Astro Bride, 1985; Velveeta Meltdown, 1985; Co-Editor (with M. Terry & S. Kimberlain) Right Blain Vacation Photos, new plays and production photographs From The Omaha Magic Theatre, 1972-92; Plays produced (unpublished) include: This Sleep Among Women, 1978; Change Yer Image, 1981; Aliens Under Glass, 1982; Watch Where We Walk, 1983; X-Rayed-late: E-Motion in Action, with M. Terry, 1984; Walking Through Walls, with Megan Terry, 1987; Sea of Forms, with M. Terry, 1987; Body Leaks, 1990, Sound Fields, (with M. Terry & S. Kimberlain, 1192. *Honours include:* Numerous Awards, Citations. *Memberships include:* Reporter, Theatre Programme 1980-81, Opera-Musical Theatre Programme 1982, Member, Artistic Advancement Committee, Japanese American Committee 1987-, National Endowment for the Arts. *Address:* 2309 Hanscom Boulevard, Omaha, Nebraska 68105, USA.

SCHMIDT Michael, b. 2 Mar 1947, Mexico City, Mexico. Poet; Publisher. m. Claire Harman, 1979, 1 son, 1 daughter. *Education:* The Hill School, USA; Christ's Hospital, England; Harvard University 1966; BA, Wadham College, Oxford, England, 1969. *Contributions to:* (ed), the Oxford Undergraduate magazine, Carcanet, during student years, and founded Carcanet Press during his last year at Oxford. Carcanet Press began with the publication of a number of small poetry pamphlets, greatly expanded and moved to Manchester in 1972; Appointed Special Lecturer in Poetry, University of Manchester, 1972; Carcanet now considered a Primary publisher of poetry in Britain. Founded magazine, P N Review, 1972, which he continues to edit. *Publications:* Black Buildings, 1969; Bedlam and the Oakwood, 1970; Desert of the Lions, 1972; It Was My Tree, 1972; My Brother Gloucester, 1976; A Change of Affairs, 1978; An Introduction to Fifty Modern British Poets, 1979, republished as A Reader's Guide to Fifty Modern British Poets, 1979; An Introduction to Fifty British Poets 1300-1900, 1979, republished as A Reader's Guide to Fifty British Poets, 1300-1900, 1979; Tyhe Colonist, 1980, republished as Green Island, 1982; Choosing a Guest: New and Selected Poems, 1983. Other works: British Poetry Since 1960, edited by Schmidt and Grevel Lindop, 1972; Flower and Song Poems of the Aztec Peoples, translated, with an introduction by Schmidt and Edward Kissam, 1977; British Poetry Since 1970, edited by Schmidt and Peter Jones, Manchester: Carcanet Press, 1980; New York: Persea, 1980; The Love of Strangers, 1989, (Poetry).

SCHMIDT Stanley Albert, b. 7 Mar 1944, Cincinnati, Ohio, USA. Editor. m. Joyce Mary Tokarz, 9 June 1979, Shelby, Ohio. *Education:* BS, University of Cincinnati, Ohio, 1966; MA 1968, PhD 1969, Case Western

Reserve University. *Literary Appointments:* Editor, Analog Science Fiction/Science Fact, 1978-. *Publications:* Newton and the Quasi-Apple, 1975; The Sins Of The Fathers, 1976; Lifeboat Earth, 1978; TweedLloop, 1986. *Contributions to:* Analog Science Fiction/Science Fact, short stories, articles and serialised novels; Isaac Asimov's Science Fiction Magazine; The Magazine of Fantasy and Science Fiction; Rod Serling's The Twilight Zone; Rigel; Camping Journal; Writers Market. *Membership:* Science Fiction Writers of America. *Literary Agent:* Scott Meredith Literary Agency. *Address:* c/o Analaog, 380 Lexington Avenue, New York City, NY 10017, USA.

SCHMIDT Werner H, b. 9 June 1935, Mulheim, Ruhr, Germany. Professor. m. Waltraud Schmidt, 20 Apr 1965, 1 son, 1 daughter. *Education:* Theologiestudium i marburg, Gottingen, Berlin, 1955-60; Promotion Dr Theol, and der Kirchlichen Hochschule Berlin, 1960; Wiss Assistent, 1962-64; Privatdozent an der Universitat Mainz, 1964-66. *Appointments:* Professor: University of Wien, 1966-1969, University of Kiel, 1969-1969; University of Marburg, 1979-1984; University of Bonn, 1984-. *Publications include:* Konigtum Gottes in Ugarit und Israel, BZAW 80, 1961, 1966; Die Schopfungsgeschichte der Priesterschrift, WMANT 17, 1964, 1974; Alttestamentlicher Glaube in seiner Geschichte, 1968, 1990; Wörterbuch zur Bibel (with G. Delling), 1971, 3ed edition 1981; Zukunftsgewißheit und Gegenwartskritik, 1973; Einführung in das Alte Testament, 1979, 4th edition 1989, in English 2nd edition 1990; Zukunft und Hoffnung (with J Becker), 1981; Exodus, Snai und Mose, 1983, 2nd edition 1990; The Faith of the Old Testament, 1983, 1986, in Japanese, 1985; Exodus: Biblischer Kommentar II/1, 1988; Altes Testament: Grundkurs THeologie I, 1989; Die Zehn Gebote im Rahmen alttestamentlicher Ethik, (with H Delkurt & A. Graupner), 1993. *Address:* Evangelisch-Theologisches Seminar der Universitat Abt. fur Altes Testament, Am Hof 1, D-5300 Bonn 1, Germany.

SCHMIDT-NIELSEN Knut, b. 24 Sept 1915, Norway. Scientist; Writer. *Education:* DrPhil, Copenhagen, 1946; DrMed, honoris causa, Lund, Sweden, 1983. *Literary Appointments:* Editor and Editorial Boards of numerous Scientific Journals. *Publications:* Animal Physiology, 1975, 4th edition, 1990; Scaling: Why is Animal Size So Important, 1984; How Animals Work, 1972; Desert Animals, 1964. *Contributions to:* More than 200. *Memberships:* Royal Society, London; National Academy of Sciences, USA; Academie des Sciences, Paris. *Address:* Department of Zoology, Duke University, Durham, NC 27706, USA.

SCHMOKEL Wolfe William, b. 25 July 1933, Waldenburg, Germany. Professor Emeritus. m. (1) 2 sons, 2 daughters, (2)Kay hester Barbour, 27 Dec 1984. *Education:* BA, University of Maryland, 1957; MA, 1958, PhD, 1962, Yale University. *Publications:* Dream of Empire, 1964; The Living Past (with A J Andrea), 1975; Annual articles on Germany in World Topics Yearbook, 1968-88. *Contributions to:* Numerous articles and reviews in: American Historical Review; International Journal of African Historical Studies; History. *Honours:* Alexander von Humboldt Fellow, 1969; Distinguished Alumnus Award, University of Maryland, 1982. *Memberships:* Liberian Studies Association, Vice-President 1974, President 1980. *Address:* 23 Olde Orchard Lane, Shelburne, VT 05482, USA.

SCHMOOKLER Andrew Bard, b. 19 Apr 1946, Long Branch, New Jersey, USA. Writer; Speaker; Consultant. m. 28 Sept 1986, 2 sons, 1 daughter. *Education:* BA summa cum laude, harvard College, 1967; PhD, Theological Union and University of California, 1977. *Publications:* The Parable of the Tribes: THe Problem of Power in Social Evolution, 1984; Out of Weakness: Healing the Wounds that Drive us to War, 1988; Sowings and Reapings: The Cycling of Good and Evil in the Human Systgem, 1989; The Illusion of Choice: How the Market Economy Shapes our Destiny, 1992; Fools Gold: The Fate of Values in a World of Goods,

1993. *Contributions to:* Harpers; The Futurist; The Christian Science Monitor; New York Times; Los Angeles Times. *Honours:* Erik H Erickson Prize, International Society for Political Psychology, 1984; Featuresin Esquire Register as, One of the Men and Women Under Forty who are Changing the Nation, 1985. *Address:* Route 2/Box 200T, Broadway, VA 22815, USA.

SCHNAPPER Dominique Aron, b. 9 Nov 1934. Director of Studies. m. Antoine Schnapper, 28 Nov 1958, 1 son, 2 daughters. *Education:* IEP, 1957; Doctorate, Sorbonne, 1967; Doctorat d'Etat, 1979. *Appointments:* Director of Studies, Ecole des Hautes Etudes en Sciences Sociales, Paris. *Publications:* L'Italie Rouge et Noire, 1971; Juifs et Israelites, 1980; L'epreuve du chomage, 1981; La France de l'integration, 1991; L'Europe des immigres, 1992. *Memberships:* Societe Francaise de Sociologie; Societe Francaise de Sciences Politiques; Society of Friends of Raymond Aron. *Address:* 75 Bd Saint-Michel, 75005 Paris, France.

SCHNEEBAUM Tobias, b.25 Mar 1922, Writer/Lecturer. *Education:* BA, City College of New York, 1942; MA, Cultural Anthropology, Goddard College, 1977. *Publications:* Keep the River on Your Right, 1969; Wild Man, 1979; Life with the Asmat, 1981; Asmat Images, 1985; Where the Spirits Dwell, 1988; Embodied Spirits, 1990. *Contributions to:* Pacific Arts (about 10 articles); 4 articles in The New York Native; The Asmat, in Louisiaa Revy, Copenhagen, 1991. *Honours:* Fulbright Fellowship, 1955; CAPS Grant, 1974; JDR 3rd Fund Grant, 1975, 1978; Ingram Merrill Foundation, 1982, 1989; Ludwig Vogelstein Foundation, 1985. *Memberships:* PEN; Explorers Club. *Literary Agent:* Don Congdon, Don Congdon Associates Inc. *Address:* 463 West Street, 410A, New York, NY 10014, USA.

SCHOEMPERLEN Diane Mavis, b. 9 July 1954, Thunder Bay, Ontario, Canada. Writer; Teacher. 1 son. *Education:* BA English, Lakehead University, Ontario, 1976. *Appointments:* Teacher: Kingston School of Writing, Queens University, Ontario, 1986-91; St Lawrence College, Kingston, 1978-; University of Toronto Summer Writers' Workshop, 1992. *Publications:* Double Exposures, 1984; Frogs and Other Stories, 1986; Hockey Night in Canada, 1987; The Man of my Dreams, 1990; Hockey Night in Canada and other Stories, 1991. *Contributions include:* 87 and 90 Best Canadian Stories; Macmillan Anthology 1 & 3; Oxford Canadian Short Stories. *Honours:* WGA Award for Short Fiction, 1987; Silver National magazine Award, 1989; The Man of my Dreams shortlisted for Governor General's Award and Trillium Award. *Memberships:* Writer's Union of Canada. *Literary Agent:* Bella Pomer, Toronto, Ontario. *Address:* 32 Dunlop Street, Kingston, Ontario Canada K7L 1L2.

SCHOENBERGER Nancy, b. 3 Dec 1950, Oakland, California, USA. Programme Director and Workshop Instructor; Writer. *Education:* BA 1972, MA 1974, Louisiana State University; MFA, Columbia University, 1981. *Appointments:* Programme Director and Workshop Instructor, Avademy of American Poets, New York, 1983-; Associate Professor in School of the Arts at Columbia University, spring 1988. *Publications:* The Taxidermist's Daughter (poems) 1979; Girl on a White Porch (poems) 1987. *Contributions to:* poems in magazines, including New Yorker; Antaeus; Antioch Review; Columbia; Southern Review and Poetry. *Honours:* Resident at Centrum, 1981; Rockefeller Conference and Study Center, Bellagio, Italy, 1985 and MacDowell Colony, 1987; Mary Carolyn Davies Memorial Prize from Poetry Society of America, 1984, for a lyric poem; Grant from National Endowment for the Arts, 1984; Editor's Choice Award from Columbia, 1985 for the poem, Easy the Life of the Mouth; Richard Hugo Memorial Award from Cutbank, 1985 for the poem Girl on a White Porch; Devins Award from University of Missouri Press, 1987 for the book Girl on a White Porch. *Membership:* Poetry Society of America. *Address:* Academy of American Poets, 177 East 87th Street, New York, NY 10128, USA.

SCHOENEWOLF Gerald Frederick, b. 23 Sept 1941, Fredericksburg, Texas, USA. Psychoanalyst; Writer. m. (1) Carol Slater, 1964-1969, 1 daughter, (2) Theresa Lamb, 1979-84. *Education:* BA, Goddard College, Plainfield, Vermont; MA, California State University, Dominguez Hills; PhD, The Union Institute, Cincinnati, Ohio. *Publications:* 101 Common Therapeutic Blinders (with R Robertiello), 1987; 101 Therapeutic Successes, 1989; Sexual Animosity between Men and Women, 1989; Turning Points in Analytic Therapy: The Classic Cases, 1990; Turning Points in Analytic Therapy: From Winnicott to Kernberg, 1990; The Art of Hating, 1991; Jennifer and Her Selves, 1991. *Contributions to:* Numerous papers and short stories to various publications. *Memberships:* American Psychological Association; American Academy of Psychotherapists. *Literary Agent:* Don Congdon. *Address:* 332 East 18th Street, New York, NY 10003, USA.

SCHOENFELD Maxwell Philip, b. 1936, United States of America. Author. *Publications:* The Restored House of Lords, 1967; The War Minstry of Winston Churchill, 1972; Sir Winston Churchill: His Life and Times, 1973, 1986; Fort de la Presqu'ile, 1979; Charles Vernon Gridley: A Naval Career, 1983. *Address:* Department of History, University of Wisconsin, Eau Claire, WI 54701, USA.

SCHOENHERR Richard Anthony, b. 1935, United States of America. Writer (Sociology). *Publications:* The Structure of Organizations (with Peter M. Blau), 1971; Co-Author, Catholic Priest in the United States: Sociological Investigations, 1972; Co-Author, The Political Economy of Diocesan Advisory Councils, 1980; From the Second Vatican to the Second Millennium: Decline and Change in the U.S. Catholic Church, 1981. *Address:* Department of Sociology, 3454 Social Science Building, University of Wisconsin, Madison, WI 53706, USA.

SCHOEPFER Virginia B, b. 1934, United States of America. Writer. *Publications:* Desk Companion for Legal Secretaries; Stenospeed for the Legal Secretary; Legal Secretarial Typewriting and Dictation Course; Legal Glossary; Edited, River of Miracles, by G.R. Schoepfer, 1978. *Address:* 268 Kentwood Blvd, Brick Town, NJ 08724, USA.

SCHOFIELD Carey. *See:* SCHOFIELD Caroline Monica Elizabeth Ann.

SCHOFIELD Caroline, (Carey Schofield), b. 29 Dec 1953, Surrey, England. Writer. m. Laurence King, 14 June 1985. *Education:* BA Cantab, 1976. *Publications:* Inside the Soviet Army, 1991; Russia at War, 1987; Jagger, 1984; Mesrine, 1980. *Contributions to:* Various Publications. *Memberships:* International Institute of Strategic Studies; Royal United Services Institute. *Address:* 6 St Martins Road, London SW9, England.

SCHOFIELD Michael, b. 1919. Sociologist and Writer. *Publications:* The Sexual Behavior of Young People, 1965; The Sociological Aspects of Homosexuality, 1965; Society and the Young School Leaver, 1967; Drugs and Civil Liberties, 1968; Social Research, 1969; Co-Author, Behind the Drug Scene, 1970; The Strange Case of Pot, 1971; Co-Author, The Rights of Children, 1972; The Sexual Behaviour of Young Adults, 1973; Promiscuity, 1976; The Sexual Containment Act, 1978. *Address:* 28 Lyndhurst Gardens, London, NW3 5NW, England.

SCHOFIELD Paul. *See:* TUBB E C.

SCHOFIELD William Greenough, b. 13 June 1909, Providence, Rhode Island, USA. Author. m. 21 Nov 1934, 2 sons, 1 daughter. *Appointments:* Feature Writer, Providence Journal, 1936-40; Chief Editorial Writer, Columnist, Foreign Correspondent, Boston Traveler, 1940-67; Manager, Editorial Services, Raytheon Co., 1967-70; Director, Public Information Consultant, Public Affairs, Publications Editor, Boston University, 1970-79. *Publications:* Ashes in the Wilderness, 1942; The Cat in the Convoy, 1946; Payoff in Black, 1947; The Deer Cry, 1948; Seek for a Hero, 1956; Sidewalk Statesman, 1959; Destroyers - 60 Years, 1962; Treason Trail, 1964; Eastward the Convoys, 1966; Freedom by the Bay, 1974; Frogmen - First Battles, 1987; others. *Contributions To:* Readers Digest; Catholic Digest; Redbook; Skipper; Information; Boston Sunday Herald. *Honour:* Achievement Award, US Dept. of Interior, 1976. *Address:* 16 Hunnewell Circle, Newton, MA 02158, USA.

SCHOLEFIELD Alan (Lee Jordan), b. 1931, South Africa. Author. *Appointment:* Foreign Staff, Sydney Morning Herald and Defence Correspondent, The Scotsman. *Publications:* As Alan Scholefield: A View of Vultures, 1966; Great Elephant, 1967; The Eagles of Malice, 1968; Wild Dog Running, 1970; The Young Masters; The Hammer of God; Lion in the Evening; The Alpha Raid, Venom; Point of Honour; Berlin Blind; The Stone Flower; The Sea Cave; Fire in the Ice; King of the Golden Valley; The Last Safari; The Lost Giants; Loyalties; Dirty Weekend; Thief Taker; Night Child; Never die in January; Threats & Menaces; The Dark Kingdoms (history); Chaka (screenplay); Treasure Island (stage adaptation); My Friend Angelo (TV movie); River Horse Lake (TV series); Sea Tiger (TV series). As Lee Jordan: Cat's Eyes; Criss Cross; The Deadly Side of the Square; The Toy Cupboard; Chain Reaction. *Address:* c/o Elaine Greene Limited, 37 Goldhawk Road, London W8 8QQ, England.

SCHOLEY Arthur (Edward), b. 1932. Children's Writer; Playwright. *Publications:* The Song of Caedmon (with Donald Swann), 1971; Christmas Plays and Ideas for Worship, 1973; The Discontented Dervishes, 1977; Sallinka and the Golden Bird, 1978; Twelve Tales for a Christmas Night, 1978; Wacky and His Fuddlejig (with Donald Swann), 1978; Singalive (with Donald Swann), 1978; Herod and the Rooster (with Ronald Chamberlain), 1979; The Dickens Christmas Carol Show, 1979; Baboushka (with Donald Swann), 1979; Candletree (with Donald Swann), 1981; Five Plays for Christmas, 1981; Four Plays about People, 1983; Martin the Cobbler, 1983; The Hosanna Kids, 1985; Make a Model Christmas Crib, 1988; Who'll Be Brother Donkey?, 1990. *Address:* 1 Cranbourne Road, London, N10 2BT, England.

SCHOM Alan, b. 9 May 1937, Starling, Illinois, USA. Historian; Author. div. 2 daughters. *Education:* AB History, University of California; PhD, French Colonial History, Durhan University. *Publications:* Lyautey in Morocco, Protectorate Administration, 1912-1925, 1970; Emile Zola, A Biography, 1987; Trafalgar Countdown to Battle, 1803-1805, 1990; One Hundred Days, Napoleon's Road to Waterloo, 1992. *Contributions to:* American Historical Review, Midstream, US Naval Proceedings. *Honours:* Fellow, Hoover Institution, 1982; US National Book Award Nomination, 1991. *Memberships:* President, Founder, French Colonial Historical Society, 1974-76. *Literary Agent:* James Trupin, JET Associates, 124 East 84th St, NY 10028, USA. *Address:* 135 North Clark Drive, Beverly Hills, CA 90211, USA.

SCHONBERG Harold C, b. 1915, United States of America. Writer. *Appointments:* Associate Editor, American Music Lover,1946-48; Music Critic, New York Sun, 1946-50; Contributing Editor, Record Columnist, Musical Courier, 1948-52; Columnist, The Gramophone, London, 1948-60; Music and Record Critic, 1950-60, Senior Music Critic, 1960-, The New York Times. *Publications:* The Guide to Long-Playing Records: Chamber and Solo Instrument Music, 1955; The Collector's Chopin and Schumann, 1959; The Great Pianists, 1963; The Great Conductors, 1967; Lives of the Great Composers, 1970; Grandmasters of Chess, 1973; Facing the Music, 1981; The Glorious Ones: Classical Music's Legendary Performers, 1985.

Address: New York Times, 229 W. 43rd Street, New York, NY 10036, USA.

SCHOONOVER Jason Brooke Rivers Morgan, b. 14 Sept 1946, Saskatchewan, Canada. Writer. *Education:* BA English, Simon Fraser University, 1970. *Publications:* The Bangkok Collection, 1988; Thai Gold, 1989. *Memberships:* Fellow, The Explorers Club, New York; Foreign Correspondents Club of Thailand. *Address:* 720 University Drive, Saskatoon, Sask, Canada S7N 0J4.

SCHOTTER Roni, b. 9 May 1946, New York City, New York, USA. Writer of Children's Books. m. Richard Schotter, 16 June 1968, 1 son. *Education:* BA, English Literature, New York University, 1968. *Publications:* A Matter of Time, 1979; Northern Fried Chicken, 1983; Rhoda, Straight and True, 1986; Efan, The Great, 1986; Captain Snapon and The Children of Vinegar Lane, 1989; Bunny's Night Out, 1989; Hanukkah!, 1990; Warm at Home, 1993. *Contributions to:* Something Beyond Reason, to New Voices, 1976; Seeley Street, to Confrontation, 1981. *Honours:* Emmy Award, 1981; Parents Choice Award, 1989; National Council of Teachers of English Award, 1990; National Jewish Book Award, 1991. *Memberships:* Society of Children's Book Writers; Bank Street Professional Writers Lab. *Literary Agent:* Susan Cohen, Writers House, New York, USA. *Address:* c/o Susan Cohen, 21 West 26th St, New York, NY 10010, USA.

SCHOULTZ Solveig von, b. 5 Aug 1907, Borga, Finland. Author. m. Erik Bergman, 7 July 1961, Aarhus. *Education:* Teacher's Qualification. *Publications:* Poetry: Eko av ett rop, 1946; Natet, 1956; Sank ditt ljus, 1963; De fyra flojtspelarna, 1975; Bortom traden hors havet, 1980; En enda minut, 1981; Vattenhjulet, 1986; Alla Träd Hantar fäglar, 1988; Ett sätt att räkna tiden, 1989. Short Novels: Ingenting ovanligt, 1948; Narmare nagon, 1951; Den blomstertid, 1958; Aven dina Kameler, 1965; Rymdbruden, 1970; Somliga mornar, 1976; Kolteckning, ofullbordad, 1983; Ingen dag forgaves, 1984; Nästa dag, 1991; Längs vattenbrynet, 1992. Plays for TV & Radio. *Honours:* The State Literary Prize, 1953, 1957, 1959, 1982; Svenska Litteratursall Lskapets Prize, 1959, 1981; Svenska Akademiens Literary Prize, 1972; The Church's Literary Prize, 1981; Edith Sodergran Prize, 1984; The Bellman Prize, 1986; Nils Ferlins Prize, 1988; Honorary Member, Svenska Litteratursall Liskapet, 1976; Pro Finlandia Medal, 1980; PhD, honouris causa, 1986. *Memberships:* PEN Club; Board Member, Finland's Svenska fort fattareforening, 1947-69, 1982-. *Address:* Berggatan 22C, Helsinki 10, Finland.

SCHRAG Peter, b. 1931, United States of America. Writer (Education, Politics, Education). *Appointments:* Reporter, El Paso Herald Post, Texas, 1953-55; Assistant Secretary, Amherst College, Massachusetts, 1955-66; Associate Education Editor, 1966-68, Executive Editor, 1968-73, Saturday Review, New York City; Editor, Change, New York City, 1969-70; Editor, Editorial page Sacramento Bee, 1978-; Lecturer, University of Massachusetts, 1970-72; University of California, Berkeley, 1990-. *Publications:* Voices in the Classroom, 1965; Village School Downtown, 1967; Out of Place in America, 1970; The Decline of the WASP (in United Kingdom as The Vanishing American), 1972; The End of the American Future, 1973; Test of Loyalty, 1974; The Myth of the Hyperative Child (with Diane Divoky), 1975; Mind Control, 1978. *Address:* Sacramento Bee, 21st and Q Sts., Sacramento, CA 95816, USA.

SCHRAMM David Norman, b. 25 Oct 1945, St Louis, Missouri, USA. Professor of Astrophysics. m. Judith Jane Gibson, 20 June 1986, 2 sons. *Education:* SB Physics, Mass. Institute of Technology, 1967; PhD Physics, California Institute of Technology, 1971. *Appointments:* Editorial Commission, Ann. Rev. of Nucl. Science, 1976-80; Associate Editor, American Journal of Physics, 1978-81; Editor, Theoretical Astrophysics Series, University of Chicago Press, 1981-; Columnist, Outside Magazine, 1979- ; Astrophysics Editor, Physics Reports, 1981-; Correspondent, Comments on Nuclear and Particle Physics, 1984-; Associate Editor, Particle World, 1990-. *Publications:* Co-author: From Quarks to the Cosmos: Tools of Discovery, 1989; The Shadows of Creation: Dark matter and the Structure of the Universe, 1991. *Honours:* Richtmeyer Memorial Award Lecturer, American Association of Physics Teachers, 1984; Alexander von Humbolds Award, 1986; Einstein medal, Eotovos University, Hungary, 1989; Lilienfeld Award, American Physical Society, 1993. *Memberships:* National Academy of Sciences, Chair Astrophysics Panel, 1989-; American Physics Society, Fellow, 1975-; American Astronomical Society, Executive Commission, 1977-78; Secretary, Treasurer, 1979-82; The Meteoritical Society, Fellow, 1981-; International Astronomical Union, 1973-. *Literary Agent:* John Brockman Associates Inc. *Address:* University of Chicago, 5640 South Ellis Avenue, AAC 140 , Chicago, IL 60637, USA.

SCHRAMM Werner, b.28 Apr 1926, Hohenlockstedt, Germany. Author; Painter. *Education:* Teacher Training Institute; Langemarck Studies (Wounded during World War II). *Publications:* Stefan Zweig, 1961; Im Malstrom der Zeit: Eine Darstellung des dichterischen Lebenswerkes von Lee van Dovski, 1976; Hugo Wolfgang Philipp im Spiegel der Nachwelt: Philipp als Romancier, 1979; Das antike Drama 'Die Bacchantinnen' in der Neugestaltung durch H Wolfgang Philipp, 1980; Hugo Wolfgang Philipps Tragikomodie 'Der Clown Gottes', 1983; Moderner deutscher Roman, 1983; Stefan Zweig: Bildnis eines genialen Charakters, 1984. *Honours include:* Deutsche Sprache und Literatur, 1963; Lee van Dovski's Magnum Opus, Genie und Eros, 1978; Donald A Prater's Stefan Zweig, Autoren im Exil, 1981; Büttel an der Elbe, 1989. *Memberships:* American Biographical Institute Research Association's Board of Governors, 1989; Fellowship of the International Biographical Association, 1989. *Address:* Eckenerweg 8, D-221 Itzehoe, Germany.

SCHRANK Jeffrey, b. 1944, United States of America. Writer. *Appointment:* Editor, Media Mix Newsletter, 1968. *Publications:* Interpersonal Communication (audio tape series), 1971; Teaching Human Beings: 101 Subversive Activities for the Classroom, 1972; Freedom: Now and When?, 1972; Feelings: Exploring Inner Space, 1973; The Seed Catalog: Teaching/Learning Resource Guide, 1974; Deception Detection: An Educator's Guide to the Art of Insight, 1975; Understanding Mass Media, 1975; Guide to the Short Film, 1978; Snap, Crackle and Popular Taste, 1978; Snap Crackle and Write, 1979; Guide to Checking and Savings Accounts, 1979. *Address:* c/o American Photographic Book Publishing Co., 1 Astor Plaza, 1515 Broadway, New York, NY 10036, USA.

SCHREIBER Hermann O L (Lujo Bassermann), b. 1920, Austria. Author. *Publications:* Vanished Cities, 1957; Merchants, Pilgrims and Highwaymen, 1961; Teuton and Slav, 1963; As Lujo Bassermann: The Oldest Profession; Paris; Captain Carpfanger; Marco Polo; Die Provence; Die Hunnen; Das Schiff aus Stein; Marie Antoinette (biography), 1988; Die Belle Epoque, 1990; Dictionary of Discoveries, 1992. *Memberships:* International PEN-Club, Austrian Center. *Literary Agent:* AVA-GmbH, Seeblickstraße 46, D-8036 Herrsching 2, Germany. *Address:* Schleißheimer Str 274/VIII, D-80809 Munich 40, Germany.

SCHREINER Samuel Agnew Jr, b. 6 June 1921, Mt Lebanon, Pennsylvania, USA. Author. m. Doris Moon, 22 Sept 1945, 2 daughter. *Education:* AB , Princeton University, USA, 1942; Summa Cum Laude. *Publications:* Thine Is The Glory, 1975; The Condensed World of the Reader's Digest, 1977; Pleasant Places, 1977; Angelica, 1978; The Possessors and the Possessed, 1980; The Van Alens, 1981; A Place Called Princeton, 1984; The Trials of Mrs Lincoln, 1987; Cycles, 1990; Mayday! Mayday!, 1990. *Contributions to:* Reader's Digest; Woman's Day; McCalls, Redbook, Parade. *Literary Agent:* Harold Ober Associates.

Address: 111 Old Kings Highway South, Darien, Ct 06820, USA.

SCHRODER Friedrich. *See:* **BABINECZ Friedrich Karl.**

SCHROEDER Andreas Peter, b. 26 Nov 1946, Hoheneggelsen, Germany. Writer; Journalist; Editor; Translator. *Education:* BA, 1969, MA, Creative Writing, Comparative Literature, 1971, University of British Columbia, Canada. *Appointments:* Literary Critic, Columnist, The Vancouver Province Newspaper, 1968-73; Founding Editor, Contemporary Literature in Translation Magazine, 1969-80; Editor, Poetry Canada, 1970-71; Associate Editor, Canadian Fiction Magazine, 1971-73; Teaching Creative Writing; 7 Writer-in-Residence appointments. *Publications:* Poetry: The Ozone Minotaur, 1969; File of Uncertainties, 1971; Universe, 1971; The Late Man, modern parables, 1972; Shaking It Rough, memoir, 1976; Toccata in D, micronovel, 1984; Dust-Ship Glory, novel, 1986; Word for Word: The Business of Writing in Alberta, 1989; The Mennonites: A History of their Experience in Canada, 1990; The Eleventh Commandment, short story translations (with Jack Thiessen), 1990; Parent to Parent: A History of Child-rearing in Canada (with Sharon Brown), 1991; Editor: Contemporary Poetry of British Columbia (with J M Yates), vols I, II, 1970, 1972; Volvox: Poetry from the Unofficial Languages of Canada (with Lillard and Yates), 1971; Stories From Pacific and Arctic Canada (with Rudy Wiebe), 1974; Words From Inside, prison anthology, 1976, 1977, 1980; Carved From Wood: Mission, BC 1861-92 (history); Translations, screen and radio plays; Poems and short stories in many anthologies. *Contributions to:* Hundreds of articles and columns in most of Canada's major newspapers and magazines; Numerous literary magazines. *Honours include:* Woodward Memorial Award for Prose, 1969; Finalist, Governor-Generalis Award, Non-Fiction, 1977; Finalist, Sealbooks First Novel Award, 1984; Grants: National Film Board, 1970; Leon Koerner Foundation, 1974; Investigative Journalism Award, Canadian Association of Journalists, 1991. *Memberships:* PEN; Writers Union of Canada, Past Chairman; League of Canadian Poets; Canadian Periodical Publishers Association; Saskatchewan Writers Guild; Federation of British Columbia Writers; Manitoba Writers Guild; ACTRA; Periodical Writers Association, Canada; Public Lending Right Commission, Canada, Past Chairman. *Literary Agent:* Peter Livingstone Associates. *Address:* 9564 Erickson St, RR5, Mission, British Columbia, Canada V2V 5X4.

SCHUCHMAN Joan. *See:* **FEINBERG Joan Miriam.**

SCHUDSON Charles Benjamin, b. 30 Jan 1950, Milwaukee, Wisconsin, USA. Judge. *Education:* BA Dartmouth College, 1972; JD, University of Wisconsin Law School, 1974. *Publications:* Co-author: On Trial: America's Courts and Their Treatment of Sexually Abused Children, 1989, 1991; Nailing an Omlette to the Wall: Prosecuting Nursing Home Homicide, 1984-. *Contributions to:* 15 published articles in various newspapers, magazines and professional journals. *Address:* Wisconsin Court of Appeals, 633 W Wisconsin Avenue, Milwaukee, WI 53203, USA.

SCHUH George Edward, b. 1930, United States of America. Writer (Agriculture, Forestry). *Publications:* The Agriculture Development of Brazil, 1971; Research on Agricultural Development in Brazil, 1972; Co-Author, The Development of Sao Paulo Agriculture, 1973; Costs and Benefits of Agricultural Research (with H Tollini), 1979; Food and Development in the Pacific Basin (with J. McCoy), 1985. *Address:* The World Bank, 1818 H Street, Washington DC 20433, USA.

SCHUL Bill D, b. 16 Mar. 1928, Winfield, Kansas, USA. Social Psychologist. m. Virginia Dubose, 3 June 1952, 1 son, 1 daughter. *Education:* BA, 1952; MA, 1954; PhD, 1976. *Publications:* Hear Me, Barabas, 1969; How to Be an Effective Group Leader, 1975; The Secret Power of Pyramids, 1975; The Psychic Power of Pyramids, 1976; The Psychic Power of Animals, 1977; Psychic Frontiers of Medicine, 1977; Pyramids and the Second Reality, 1978; Let Me Do This Thing, 1986; The New Reality, 1986; The Immortality of Animals, 1990. *Contributions to:* Over 200 magazines & Journals. *Honours:* American Freedoms Foundation Award for Editorials, 1967; John H. McBinnes Award for Non-fiction, 1972. *Literary Agent:* Richard Curtis, Richard Curtis Agency. *Address:* RR No 3, Box 33, Winfield, KS 67156, USA.

SCHULLER Gunther, b. 1925, United States of America. Writer (Music). *Appointments:* Publisher, Editor, Margun Music Inc, Newton Centre, Massachussetts; Producer, G M Recordings Inc, Newton Centre, Massachussetts. *Publications:* Horn Technique, 1962; Early Jazz: Its Roots and Musical Development, 1968; Musings, 1985; The Swing Era, 1988. *Membership:* American Academy of Arts and Letters, 1977; President, New England Conservatory of Music, Boston, 1967-77. *Address:* 167 Dudley Road, Newton Centre, MA 02159, USA.

SCHULLER Robert H(arold), b. 1926, American, Administration/Management, Human relations, Psychology, Theology/Religion. *Appointments:* Founder and Senior Pastor, Crystal Cathedral of the Reformed Church in America, formerly Garden Grove Community Church, California, 1955-. President, Board of Directors, Christian Counseling Service Inc, 1969-; Founder and featured Pastor, Hour of Power, national television Programme, 1970-; Founder and President, Robert Schuller Institute for Successful Church Leadership, 1970-; Member, Board of Directors, Religion in American Life, 1975-; Pastor, Ivanhoe Church, Illinois, 1950-55. *Publications:* God's Way to the Good Life, 1963; Your Future Is Your Friend, 1964; Move Ahead with Possibility Thinking, 1967; Self-Love: The Dynamic Force of Success, 1969; Power Ideas for a Happy Family, 1972; You Can Become the Person You Want to Be, 1973; The Greatest Possibility Thinker That Ever Lived, 1973; Your Church Has Real Possibilities, 1974; Love or Loneliness: You decide, 1974; Reach Out for New Life, 1977; Peace of Mind Through Possibility Thinking, 1977; It's Possible, 1978; The Courage of Carol, 1978; Turn Your Stress into Strength, 1978; Bloom, Where You Are Planted, 1978; Positive Prayers, 1978; The Peak to Peek Principle, 1980; Self-Esteem: The New Reformation, 1982; Tough Times Never Last, But Tough People Do! 1983; Tough Minded Faith for Tender Hearted People, 1984; The Be-Happy Attitudes, 1985; The Power of Being Debt Free, 1985; Be Happy You Are Loved, 1986; Success Is Never Ending, Failure Is Never Final, 1987. *Address:* 12141 Lewis Street, Garden Grove, CA 92640, USA.

SCHULMAN J.(oseph) Neil, b. 16 Apr 1953, New York City, USA. Writer; Author; Producer. m. Kate O'Neal, 20 July 1985. *Appointments:* Managing Editor, New Libertarian Notes, 1972; Executive Editor, New Libertarian Weekly, 1976; Assistant Editor, New Libertarian, 1984. *Publications:* Alongside Night, 1979; The Rainbow Cadenza, 1983; Toward a Natural Rights Theory of Logoright, 1984; Profile in Silver, Teleplay, broadcast as episode of CBS TV's The Twilight Zone, 1986; The Musician, Radio Drama, 1980. *Contributions to:* Los Angeles Times; San Antonio Light; New Libertarian. *Honour:* Prometheus Award, Libertarian Futurist Society, 1984. *Memberships:* Writers Guild of America; Science Fiction Writers of America; Los Angeles Science Fantasy Society; C S Lewis Society. *Literary Agent:* Joel Gotler, Los Angeles, USA.

SCHULTZ John, b. 28 July 1932, Columbia, Missouri, USA. Writer; Teacher. m. Anne Gillian Bray, 10 Dec 1962, div, Nov 1975; (2) Betty E Shiflett, 9 May 1992. 1 son, 1 daughter. *Appointments:* Head, Master of Fine Arts in Creative Writing, Columbia College, Chicago, 1990-; Head, Master in Teaching of Writing, 1983-, and Chair, Fiction Writing Department, Columbia College,

Chicago, 1967-. *Publications:* The Tongues of Men, 1969; Custom, 3x3 and 4xY, 1962-67; No One Was Killed, 1969; Motion Will be Denied, 1972; Writing From Start to Finish, 1982, 1990; The Chicago Conspiracy Trial, 1993. *Contributions to:* The Georgia Review. *Honours:* Editor, F Magazine; Originator and developer of the Story Workshop Method. *Memberships:* MLA; AWP; NCTE: CCCC. *Literary Agent:* Jeff Herman. *Address:* 1405 W. Belle Plaine, Chicago, IL 60613, USA.

SCHULZ Charles (Monroe), b. 1922. United States of America. Writer. *Appointments:* Created syndicated strip cartoon, Peanuts, 1950 (since 1952, more than 110 titles based on strip reprints, TV Programmes, Feature Films. *Publications:* Peanuts, 1952; More Peanuts, 1954; Good Grief, More Peanuts, 1956; Good of Charlie Brown, 1962; Snoopy. 1962; You're Out of Your Mind, Charlie Brown, 1962; But We Love You Charlie Brown, 1962; Peanuts, Revisited, 1962; Go Fly a Kite, Charlie Brown, 1962; Peanuts Every Sunday, 1962; You Can Do It, Charlie Brown, 1962; Happiness Is a Warm Puppy, 1962; Love Is Walking Hand in Hand, 1965; A Charlie Brown Christmas, 1965; You Need Help, Charlie Brown, 1966; Charlie Brown's All-Stars, 1966; You've Had It, Charlie Brown, 1969; Peanuts Jubilee: Thee Art of Charles Schulz, 1975; Speak Softly and Carry a Beagle, 1975; Charlie Brown's Super Book of Things to Do and Collect, 1975; By My Valentine, Charlie Brown, 1976; It's a Mystery, Charlie Brown, 1976; He's Your Dog, Charlie Brown, 1977; Hooray for You, Charlie Brown, 1977; Play Ball, Snoopy, 1978; Race for Your Life, Charlie Brown, 1978. *Address:* Snoopy Place, Santa Rosa, CA 95401, USA.

SCHULZ Max Frederick, b. 1923, United States of America. Writer. *Appointments:* Professor of English, 1963-, Chairman, 1968-80, University of Southern California, Los Angeles; Associate Editor, Critique Magazine, 1971-85. *Publications:* The Poetic Voices of Coleridge, 1963, revised edition, 1965; Essays in American and English Literature, Presented to Bruce Robert McElderry Jr., 1967; Radical Sophistication: Studies in Contemporary Jewish-American Novelists, 1969; Bruce Jay Friedman, 1973; Black Humor Fiction of the Sixties: A Pluralistic Definition of Man and His World, 1973; Paradise Preserved: Recreations of Eden in 18th and 19th Century England, 1985; The Muses of John Barth: Tradition and Metafiction from Lost in the Funhouse to the Tidewater Tales, 1990. *Address:* Department of English, University of Southern California, Los Angeles, CA 90089, USA.

SCHULZE Kenneth Willard, b. 18 Apr 1951, Lakewood, Ohio, USA. Writer. *Education:* BA, cum laude, University of Michigan, 1973. *Appointments:* Panelist; Earthcon, 1985, WorldCon, 1986, WindyCon, 1987, Marcon, 1987; Instructor, Western Reserve Writers Conference, 1987. *Publications:* Starlet Falls, 1982; Reunion, 1985; Redmond, 1986; Theone, 1987; King of Constellations, 1987; Artificial Satellites, 1987; Night Vision, 1987; Why Buy a Telescope?, 1987. *Contributions to:* Interdemensional Journal; Horizons Beyond; Science Fiction Chronicle; Chicago Sheet. *Honours:* 2nd Prize, Writers of the Future Contest, 1985; Finalist, Katherine Anne Porter Prize for Fiction, 1985.

SCHUNCKE Michael, b. 8 May 1929, Dresden Blasewitz, Germany. Special Teacher; Author; Consultant. m. Dorothea Czibulinski-Dressler, 22 Dec 1956, 2 daughters. *Education:* Theory of Music with Professor Otto Schaefer, 1945-49; Advertising, Academy Mannheim, 1953-54; Seminars in writing, advertising and marketing. *Appointments:* Vice Chairman, Poetical Ludwig-Finckh-Freundeskreis Gaienhofen, 1989-. *Publications:* Wanderer ZZwischen 2 Welten, 1975; Sprecht die Sprache der Adressaten, 1982; Schlüsselworte erfolgricher Anzeigen, 2 Auft, 1986; Praktische Werbehilfe, 1987; Many articles for advertising and music-hisotyr; Sammelbände der Robert-Schumann-Ges Zwickau, 1961-66; Catalogue for Exhibition, Ludwig Schuncke and Musikerfamilie Schuncke, 1984. *Contributions to:* Ein unbek Mendelssohn-Bilden v J P Lyses/Max F Schneider

Basel, 1958; Werbeforschung und praxis, 1985 & 1991; Histories of Corporates; Newsletter of the Rachmaninoff Society, 1992; Aufsatze in Muttersprache; Das System der Text-CI, 1991, among others. *Honours:* Goldene Hans Buchholz Medaille, 1974. *Memberships:* Gesellschaft fur Deutsche Sprache; Poetical Ludwig-Finckh-Freundeskreis Gaienhofen; Robert Schumann Gesellschaft; Mendelssohn Gesellschaft. *Address:* Heschmattweg 11, D-7570 Baden Baden, Germany.

SCHUSKY Ernest L., b. 1931, United States of America. Writer. *Publications:* A Manual for the Analysis of Kinship, 1964, 1972; Introducing Culture (with T.P. Culbert), 1967, 4th edition, 1987; The Right to Be Indian, 1970; Variation in Kinship, 1973; The Study of Cultural Anthropology, 1975; The Forgotten Sioux, 1975; The Political Organization of Native North Americans, 1980; Introduction to Social Science, 1981; Culture and Agriculture, 1989l; Ancient Spender of Prehistoric Cahokia, 1992. *Address:* 412 Willowbrook, Collinsville, IL 62234, USA.

SCHUTZ William C., b. 1925, United States of America. Writer. *Publications:* A Three Dimensional Theory of Interpersonal Behavior, 1958 (reissued as The Interpersonal Underworld); Joy, 1967; Here Comes Everbody, 1971; Elements of Encounter, 1973; Body Fantasy, 1977; Leaders of Schools, 1977; Profound Simplicity, 1979; The Truth Option, 1984.

SCHUYLER Doris Elmendorf, b. 26 Apr 1920, Amsterdam, New York, USA. Author. m. Wiliam R Schuyler Sr, 26 Jan 1941, 3 sons. *Education:* Graduate, Eleanor School, University of Buffalo; New York State Teacher's License; Graduate of American Conservatory of Music. *Appointments:* Taught for 25 Years in Amsterdam, NY, USA; Taught for 5 years in Broadalbin; Officer in Canal Side Publishers, Frakfort, NY, USA. *Publications:* The Adirondack Princess 1982; Aunt Cad, 1984; Butlerbury 1985; Adirondack Princess, Book II, 1990. *Memberships:* American Poets and Writers; International Women's Writing Guild. *Address:* Schuyler Hall RD 3, Frankfort, NY 13340, USA.

SCHUYLER James Marcus, b.1923, United States of America. Author; Playwright; Poet. *Publications:* Alfred and Guinevere, 1958; Salute, 1960; Unpacking the Black Trunk (with Kenward Elmslie), 1965; May 24th or So, 1966; A Nest of Ninnies, 1969; Freely Espousing: Poems, 1969; The Crystal Lithium, 1972; Penguin Modern Poets 24 (with Kenneth Koch and K. Elmslie), 1973; Hymn to Life: Poems, 1974; The Fireproof Floors of Witley Court, 1976; The Home Book: Prose and Poems, 1977; What's for Dinner?, 1978; The Morning of the Poem (poetry), 1980; A Few Days, 1985. *Address:* c/o Maxine Groffsky, 2 Fifth Avenue, New York, NY 10011, USA.

SCHUYLER Keith C., b. 1919, United States of America. Writer. *Appointments include:* Columnist, Berwick Enterprise, Press Enterprise, 1938-1991; Columnist, Veterans of Foreign Wars Magazine, 1952-80; Columnist, Pennsylvania Game News, 1963-. *Publications:* Lures - The Guide to Sport Fishing, 1955; Elusive Horizons, 1969; Archery - From Golds to Big Game, 1970; Bow Hunting for Big Game, 1974; A Last Time to Listen, 1977; Fly Rod Fishing, 1979. *Address:* Box 3094, R.D. 3, Berwick, PA 18603, USA.

SCHWANDT Stephen (William), b. 5 Apr 1947, Chippewa Falls, Wisconsin, USA. Educator. m. Karen Sambo, 13 June 1970, 2 sons. *Education:* BA, Valparaiso University, 1969; BS, St Cloud State University, 1972; MA, University of Minnesota - Twin Cities, 1972. *Appointments:* Teacher of Composition and American Literature, Irondale High School, New Brighton, Minnesota, 1974-; Instructor at Concordia College, St Paul, Minnesota, 1975-80 and Normandale Community College, 1983-. *Publications:* The Last Goodie, 1985; A Risky Game, 1986; Holding Steady, 1988; Guilt Trip, 1990; Funnybone, 1992. *Contributions* to: Various newspapers. *Memberships:* National Education Association; Authors Guild; Book Critics Circle; National Council for Teachers of English; The Loft. *Literary Agent:* Marilyn Marlow, Curtis Brown Ltd, New York. *Address:* Marilyn Marlow, Curtis Brown Ltd, 10 Astor Place, New York, NY 10003, USA.

SCHWARTZ Eli, b. 1921, United States of America. Writer. *Publications:* Co-Author, Study of the Probable Effects of a Move Toward Land Value Taxation in the City of Bethlehem, 1958; Corporation Finance, 1962; Editor and Co-Author with J.R. Aronson, Management Policies in Land Government Finance, 1975, 1981, 1987; Trouble in Eden: A Comparison of the British and Swedish Economicies, 1980. *Address:* Rauch Bus Center, 37, Lehigh University, Bethlehem, PA 18015, USA.

SCHWARTZ Elliott S, b. 19 Jan 1936, Brooklyn, New York, USA. Composer; Professor. m. Dorothy Feldman, 26 June 1960, 1 son, 1 daughter. *Education:* AB, Columbia College, 1957; MA, EdDm Columbia University, 1962; Composition study with Otto Luening, Jack Beeson and Paul Creston. Piano study with Alton Jones, Thomas Richner. *Appointments:* University of Massachusetts, 1960-64; Bowdoin College 1964-1991; Visiting Professor, The Ohio State University, 1985-86, spring term 1989, 90, 91; Visiting fellowships and extended residencies at the University of California, San Diego (Center for Music Experiment), University of California, Santa Barbara (College of Creative Studies), Trinity College of Music, London, Cambridge University (Robinson College). *Publications:* Electronic Music: A Listener's Guide, 1973, revised 1985; The Symphonies of Ralph Vaughan Williams, 1965; Contemporary Composers on Contemporary Music, 1967; Music: A Listener's Guide, 1982; Music Since 1945, 1993. *Contributions to:* Many essays, reviews for The Musical Quarterly, Musical America, Perspectives of New Music, Music and Musicians, NOTES, Music Educators Journal, Nutida Musik, Contact. *Honours:* Gaudeamus Prize (Netherlands) 1970; Maine State Award in the Arts and Humanities, 1970; National Endowment for the Arts Composition Grants 1975-83; Rockefeller Foundation Bellagio Residency, 1980 and 1989. *Memberships:* President, College Music Society; Former Vice President, American Music Center; Former National Chair, American Society of University Composers. *Address:* 11 Highview Road, PO Box 451, South Freeport, ME 04078, USA.

SCHWARTZ John Burnham, b. 8 May 1965, New York, USA. Writer. *Education:* BA, East Asian Studies, Harvard University, 1987. *Publications:* Bicycle Days, novel, 1989. *Contributions to:* New York Times Book Review, New York Times. *Memberships:* Writers Guild. *Literary Agent:* Amanda Urban, International Creative Management. *Address:* 2 Mason Street, Cambridge, MA 02138, USA.

SCHWARTZ Lynne Sharon, b. 1939, United States of America. Author; Full Time Writer. *Publications:* Rough Strife (novel), 1980; Balancing Acts (novel), 1981; Disturbances in the Field (novel), 1983; Acquainted with the Night (stories), 1984; We Are Talking about Homes (stories), 1985; The Melting Pot and Other Subversive Stories, 1987; Leaving Brooklyn, 1989. *Honours:* National Endownment for the Arts Fellowship, 1984; Guggenheim Fellowship, 1985; New York State Foundation for the Arts Fellowship, 1986. *Memberships:* PEN American Centre; Authors Guild; National Book Critics Circle; National Writers Union. *Literary Agent:* Amanda Urban, ICM. *Address:* c/o Amanda Urban, ICM, 40 W 57th Street, NY 10019, USA.

SCHWARTZ Mildred Anne, b. 1932, Canada. Writer (Politics, Government, Sociology, Race Relations). *Publications:* Trends in White Attitudes Toward Negroes, 1966; Public Opinion and Canadian Identity, 1967; Co-Author, Political Parties and the Canadian Social Structure, 1967; Politics and Territory, 1974; Co-Author, Canadian Political Parties: Origin, Character, Impact,

1975; The Environment for Policy-Making in Canada and the United States, 1981; A Sociological Perspective on Politics, 1990; The Party Network: The Robust Organization of Illinois Republicans, 1990. *Address:* 1007 W Harrison St, University of Illinois at Chicago, Chicago, IL 60607, USA.

SCHWARTZ Ros, b. 24 Oct 1952, London, England. Translator. Partner, Andrew Cowen, 1 son, 1 daughter. *Education:* Licence-ès- lettres, Universite de Paris VIII, 1978. *Publications:* Translations: I Didn't Say Goodbye (Claudine Vegh), 1984; The Blue Bicycle (Regine Deforges), 1985; Black Docker (Ousmane Sembene), 1987; Desperate Spring (Fettouma Tovati), 1987; The Net (Ilie Nastase), 1987; Cuisine Extraordinaire, 1988; Return to Beirut (Andree Chedid), 1989; Women in Evidence (Sebastien Japrisot), 1990; Dining with Proust (Anne Borel), 1992; The Dragon Book (Ciruelo), 1992. *Memberships:* Translators Association, Chairwoman 1991-92; Society of Authors; Institute of Translation and Interpreting; Women in Publishing. *Address:* 34 Uplands Road, London N8 9NL, England.

SCHWARTZ Sheila, b. 15 Mar 1936, New York, USA. Professor; Author; Lecturer, div. 1 son, 1 daughter (1 dec). *Education:* BA, Adelphi University; MA Teachers College, Columbia; EdD, New York University. *Publications:* How People Lived in Ancient Greece and Rome, 1967; How People Lived in Mexico, 1969; Teaching the Humanities, 1970; Earth in Transit, 1977; Like Mother, Like me, 1978; Growing Up Guilty, 1978; Teaching Adolescent Literature, 1979; The Solid Gold Circle, 1980; One day You'll Go, 1981; Jealousy, 1982; The Hollywood Writers' Wars, 1982; Bigger is Better, 1987; Sorority, 1987; The Most Popular Girl, 1987. *Contributions to:* Writing In America, 1989. *Honours:* Excellence in Letters, New York State, 1979; Excellence in Teaching, New York State, 1979; Annual award of Adolescent Literature Association for Contribution to the Field, 1981; Fulbright Fellow, University College, Cork, Republic of Ireland. *Literary Agent:* Harvey Knlinger. *Address:* State University College, New Paltz, NY 12561, USA.

SCHWARTZ Stephan Andrew, b. 10 Jan 1942, Cincinnati, Ohio, USA. Writer; Researcher; Businessman. m. (1) 1 daughter, (2) Hayden Oliver Gates, 1 step-daughter. *Education:* Humanities, University of Virginia. *Appointments:* Editor, Subtle Energies. *Publications include:* The Secret Vaults of Time, 1978; The Alexandria Project, 1983; Television Writing: Project Deep Quest, The Alexandria Project, Small World, Master of The House, Conversations at the Smithsonian; Psychic Detectives; Report from the Unknown. *Contributions to:* Stories from Omni, 1984; Psychic Detectives, 1985; The Millennium Agenda: Visions of a Multi-racial America; Within Your Lifetime; Washington Post, Omni, Harpers, The Washingtonian, Venture Inward. *Memberships:* Senior Fellow, Philosophical Research Society; Fellow Royal Geographical Society; Explorer's Club of New York; Past President and founding member, Society for the Anthropology of Consciousness; Society for Historic Archaeology; Society of Underwater Archaeology; Associate, Parapsychology Association; Board, International Society for Subtle Energies and Energy Medicine; Board, California USSR Trade Association Director, World Children's (Organ) Transplant Fund. *Literary Agent:* ICM. *Address:* 4470-107 Sunset Blvd No 339, Los Angeles, CA 90027, USA.

SCHWARTZ Susan Martha, b. 31 Dec 1949, Youngstown, Ohio, USA. Writer; Editor. *Education:* BA, Mount Holyoke College, 1972; MA, 1973, PhD, 1977, Howard University. *Appointments:* Fellow, Radcliffe Institute 1973; Medieval Academy 1976. *Publications:* White Wing, (co-author), 1985; Byzantium's Crown, 1987; The Woman of Flowers, 1987; Silk Roads & Shadows, 1988; Arabesques, 1988. Numerous short stories. *Contributions to:* New York Times; Washington Post; Vogue; Writers Digest; Cleveland Plain Dealer; Analog; Amazing; Various anthologies. *Honours:* Phi Beta Kappa, 1972; Finalist World Fantasy Award, 1983;

Compton Crook Award, 1985. *Membership:* Science Fiction Writers of America. *Literary Agent:* Richard Curtis.

SCHWARZ Daniel Roger, b. 12 May 1941, Rockville Centre, New York, USA. Professor of English. 2 sons. *Education:* BA Union College, 1963; MA 1965, Phd 1968, Brown University. *Appointments:* Assistant, Associate, and full Professor, Cornell University, 1968-; Distinguished Visiting Cooper Professor, University of Arkansas at Little Rock, 1988; Citizen's Chair in Literature, University of Hawaii, 1992-93. *Publications:* Narrative and Representation in the Poetry of Wallace Stevens, 1993; The Case for a Humanistic Poetics, 1991; Reading Joyce's Heritage, 1987; The Humanistic Heratage: Critical Theories of the English Novel from James to Hillis Miller, 1986; Conrad: The Later Fiction, 1983; Disraeli's Fiction, 1979; The Transformation of the English Novel, 1890-1930, 1989; Conrad: Almayer's Folly to Under Western Eyes, 1980. *Contributions to:* Modern Fiction Studies, 19th Century Fiction, JEGP, James Joyce Quarterly, Studies in the Novel, Sewanee Review, Diacritics, Novel, University of Toronto Quarterly. *Honours:* Nine NEH Summer Seminars for College and High School Teachers, 1984-1993; American Philosophical Society Grant, 1981. *Memberships:* International Association of University Professors of English. *Address:* Department of English, 304 Rockefeller Hall, Cornell University, Ithca NY 14853, USA.

SCHWARZ Henry G, b. 1928, United States of America. Writer (History, Politics, Government). *Publications:* China: Three Facets of a Giant, 1966; Liu Shao-ch'i and People's War, 1969; Chinese Policies Toward Minorities, 1971; Mongolian Short Stories, 1974; Bibliotheca Mongolica, Part 1, 1978; The Minorities of Northern China, 1984. *Address:* Center for East Asian Studies, Western Washington University, Bellingham, WA 98225-9056, USA.

SCHWERIN Doris Belle, b. 24 June 1922, Peabody, Massachusetts, USA. Author; Composer. m. Jules V Schwerin, 2 Mar 1946, 1 son. *Education:* Boston University; New England Conservatory of Music; Diploma, Juilliard School of Music, 1943; Student of George Antheil and Stefan Wolpe. *Publications:* Diary of a Pigeon Watcher, 1976; Leanna, novel in 6 movements, 1978; The Tomorrow Book, children's book, 1984; Rainbow Walkers, 1986, UK Edition as The Missing Years; The Tree That Cried, children's book, 1988; Cat and I, memoir, 1990. *Contributions to:* MS Magazine. *Honours:* Charles Sergal National Play Award, University of Chicago, 1971. *Memberships:* PEN; Association of American Composers, Authors and Publishers; Authors Guild; Authors League. *Literary Agent:* Nancy Coffey, Jay Garon-Brooke Associates. *Address:* 317 West 83rd Street, New York, NY 10024, USA.

SCHWERNER Armand, b. 1927, Antwerp, Belgium. Writer; Poet; Translator; Musician. *Education:* Cornell University, USA; University of Geneva, Switzerland; BA, French, French Literature, MA, English, Comparative Literature, Graduate study, Department of Anthropology, Columbia University, USA. *Appointments:* Professor, Department of English, Speech and World Literature, College of Staten Island, New York, USA. *Publications:* The Lightfall, 1963; The Domesday Dictionary (with D Kaplan), 1963; (if personal), 1968; The Tablets I-VIII, 1968; Seaweed, 1969; The Tablets I-XV, 1971; The Bacchae Sonnets, 1974; The Tablets I-XVIII, audiotape, 1974; Redspell, from the American Indian, 1975; Tablets XVI, XVII, VXIII and other poems, 1975; Bacchae Sonnets, 1977; the work, the joy and the triumph of the will, 1978; Philoctetes, translation from Sophocles, stereo cassette, 1978; Sound of the River Naranjana and The Tablets I-XXIV, 1983; Tablets I-XXVI, 1989; Works including translations, in numerous anthologies. *Honours:* Faculty Research Fellowship, State University of New York, summers 1970, 1972; Faculty Research Fellowship, City University of New York, summer 1971; Creative Writing Fellowship, National Endowment for the Arts, 1973, 1979, 1987; Creative Writing Fellowship, Creative Artists Public Service Programme, 1973, 1975; National Endowment for the Humanities Summer Seminar, Princeton University, 1978, Fordham University, New York, 1981, Columbia University, Paris, France, 1985; Creative Incentive Fellowship, Professional Staff Congress-City University of New York, 1986, 1992; Grant for Poetry, Greater New York Arts Development Fund, 1987; Grant for Contribution to Contemporary Poetry, 1991. *Address:* 20 Bay Street Landing B-3C, Staten Island, NY 10301, USA.

SCIARRILLO Carmen Francisca Maria Vivern, b. 8 July 1919. Author; Piano Teacher. *Publications:* La Educacion Musical En La Escuela Primaria, 1964; Cuentos Musicales Escenificados, 1965; Marcha Para Mi Escuela, La Escarapela, 1967; Cinco Canciones Para Jardin de Infantes, 1969; Canciones para Mi Escuela, 1970; Cancionero Didactico Escolar, 1970; Comedias Musicales Escolares, 1972; La Educacion Musical En La Escuela Primaria, 1979. *Honours:* Ten Confs. by LRA Radio Nacional; Narrator and Coordinator, Firsts Musical Educational Congress at the Medical University, 1970. *Literary Agent:* Rogelio Sciarrillo. *Address:* Ignacio Fermin Rodriguez 2427, Capital Federal CP 1406, Buenos Aires, Argentina.

SCOTT Alexander, b. 1920. Writer; Playwright; Poet. *Appointments Include:* Editor, Northeast Review, 1945-46, Scots Review, 1950-51, Satire Review, Edinburgh, 1954-57; General Editor, The Scottish Library, Calder and Boyars, Publishers, London, 1968-71. *Publications:* Prometheus 48, 1948; The Latest in Elegies, 1949; Selected Poems, 1950; Selected Poems of William Jeffrey, 1951; The Poems of Alexander Scott 1530-1952, 1952; Untrue Thomas, 1952; Mouth Music: Poems and Diversions, 1954; Right Royal, 1954; Shetland Yarn, 1954; Tam O'Shanter's Tryst, 1955; Diaries of a Dying Man, by William Soutar, 1955; The last Time I Saw Paris, 1957; Truth to Tell, 1958; Still Life: William Soutar 1898-1943, 1958; Cantrips, 1968; Contemporary Scottish Verse (with N. MacCaig), 1970; Greek Fire, 1971; Double Agent, 1972; The MacDonald Makars 1923-1972, 1972; The Hugh MacDiarmid Anthology: Poems in Scots and English (with M. Grieve), 1972; Neil M. Gunn: The Man and the Writer (with D. Gifford), 1973; Selected Poems 1943-1974, 1975; Modern Scots Verse, 1978; Poems in Scots, 1978; Scotch Passion,1982; New Writing Scotland 2(with James Aitchson), 1984; Voices of Our Kind: Scottish Poetry 1920-1985, 1985.

SCOTT Arthur Finley, b. 30 Nov. 1907, Kronstad, Orange Free State, Republic of South Africa. Teacher; Author. m. (1) Margaret Ida Scott, June 1935, (dec), (2) Margaret Clare Scott, Jan 1954, (dec), 2 daughters. *Education:* Emmanuel College, Cambridge, England; BA, 1930, MA, 1934, Cambridge University; Graduate study, Education, Oxford University, 1930. *Appointments:* Senior Master, English: Oakham School, 1930-33, Taunton School, 1933-43; Headmaster, Kettering Grammar School, 1943-51; Senior Lecturer, English, Borough Road College of Education, London, 1952-73; University Teacher, London University, 1968-73; Reader of English educational publications, MacMillan, Harrap, Heinemann, Cambridge University Press; Director, Scott and Finley Limited. *Publications:* Over 130 books including: Meaning and Style, 1938; New Reading, 10 books, 1956-60; Parrish Poetry Books, 4 books, 1958-59; The Craft of Prose, 1963; Current Literary Terms: Dictionary of Their Origin and Use, 1965; New Horizons (with N K Aggarwala), 10 books, 1968-71; The Stuart Age, 1974; Who's Who in Chaucer, 1974; The Roman Age, 1977; The Saxon Age, 1979; Early Hanoverian Age, 1980; America Grows, 1982; What Fire Kindles Genius, 1982; What Makes a Prose Genius, 1983. *Honours:* Exhibition, Arthur Finley Scott Collection of Books held at University of Southern Mississippi, 1968, 1969; Life Fellow, International Biographical Association. *Memberships:* Royal Society of Literature; Society of Authors; Life Member, National Book League; Past Chairman, Kettering Three Arts Society. *Address:* 59

Syon Park Gardens, Isleworth, Middlesex TW7 5NE, England.

SCOTT Bill (William Neville Scott), b. 1923, Australia. Author. *Publications:* Focus on Judith Wright, 1967; Some People (short stories), 1968; Brother and Brother (verse), 1972; The Continual Singing: An Anthology of World Poetry, 1973; Portrait of Brisbane, 1976; The Complete Book of Australian Folklore, 1976; Bushranger Ballads, 1976; My Uncle Arch and Other People (short stories), 1977; Boori (children's fiction), 1978; Tough in the Old Days (autobiography), 1979; Ned Kelly After a Century of Acrimony (with John Meredith), 1980; The Second Penguin Australian Songbook, 1980; Darkness Under the Hills (childrens fiction), 1980; Reading 360 series (The Blooming Queensland Side, On the Shores of Botany Bay, The Golden West, Bound for South Australia, Upon Van Diemen's Land, The Victorian Bunyip), 6 vols, 1981; Australian Bushrangers, 1983; Reading 360 series, 6 vols, 1983; Penguin Book of Australian Humorous Verse, 1984; Shadows Among the Leaves (children's fiction), 1984; The Long and the Short and the Tall (folklore) 1985; Following The Gold (poems for children), 1989; Many Kinds Of Magic (short stories), 1990. *Honours:* Awarded Medal of the Order of Australia, for work as a folklorist, 1992. *Address:* 157 Pratten Street, Warwick Qld 4370, Australia.

SCOTT Christopher, b. 1930. Writer. *Publications:* (all with Amoret Scott) A-Z of Antique Collecting, 1963; Collecting Bygones, 1964; Dummy Board Figures, 1966; Tobacco and the Collector, 1966; Collecting, 1967; Antiques as an Investment, 1967; Discovering Staffordshire Figures, 1969; Discovering Smoking Antiques, 1970; Treasure in Your Attic, 1971; Discovering Stately Homes, 1973; Wellington, 1973; Smoking Antiques, 1981; Staffordshire Figures, 1986.

SCOTT David Aubrey (Sir), b. 3 Aug 1919, London, England. Retired Diplomat. m. 21 Jan 1941, 2 sons, 1 daughter. *Education:* Charterhouse, 1933-38; Mining Engineering, Birmingham University, 1938-39. *Appointments:* Leader Writer, Egyptian Gazette, 1946-47; Correspondent, The Aeroplane, 1946-47. *Publication:* Ambassador in Black and White, 1981. *Contributions to:* Occasional. *Honour:* GCMG, 1979. *Memberships:* PEN, 1981-86; Royal Overseas League, Chairman 1981-86. *Literary Agent:* Peterborough Literary Agency (now defunct). *Address:* Wayside, Moushill Lane, Milford, Surrey GU8 5BQ, England.

SCOTT Dick, b. 17 Nov 1923, New Zealand. Writer. 2 sons, 3 daughters. *Education:* Diploma in Agriculture, Massey College, 1943. *Appointments:* Member, Literary Fund, Queen Elizabeth II Arts Council of New Zealand, 1988-90. *Publications:* 151 Days, 1952; The Parihaka Story, 1954; In Old Mt Albert, 1961; Inheritors of a Dream, 1962; Winemakers of New Zealand, 1964; Ask That Mountain, 1975; Fire on the Clay, 1979; Seven Lives on Salt River, 1987; Years of the Pooh-Bah, 1991. *Contributions to:* Columnist, New Zealand Listener, 1970-73. *Honours:* New Zealand Book Award, 1988; J M Sherrard History Prize, 1989. *Membership:* PEN New Zealand Inc, Past President. *Address:* 3 Pencarrow Ave, Mt Eden, Auckland 3, New Zealand.

SCOTT Donald Fletcher, b. 29 Nov 1930, Norfolk, England. Medical Consultant. m. Adrienne Mary Moffett, 2 Sept 1967 (dec 1992), 1 son, 1 daughter. *Education:* MB, ChB, Edinburgh University, Scotland, 1951-57; DPM, London University, 1965; FRCP, Royal College of Physicians, London, 1979. *Publications:* About Epilepsy, 1969; Fire and Fire Raisers, 1974; Understanding EEG, 1975; Coping with Suicide, 1989; Beating Job Burnout, 1989; The History of Epileptic Therapy, 1992. *Contributions to:* Over 100 articles mainly to medical/ psychological journals. *Memberships:* Electro-Encephalogram Society, former Meeting Secretary; Association of British Neurologists; Association of British Clinical Neurophysiology; British Society of Clinical Neurophysiology; Association of British

Neurologists. *Address:* Department of Clinical Neurophysiology, London Independent Hospital, Beaumont Square, London E1 4NL, England.

SCOTT Gail, b. Ottawa, Canada. Writer. 1 daughter. *Appointments:* Writer in Residence, Concordia University, Montreal, 1991-92; Writing Instructor, 1981-90; Journalist, Montreal Gazette, The Globe and Mail, Toronto, 1970-79. *Publications:* Heroine, 1987; Spaces like Stairs, 1989; Spare Parts, 1982; La Theorie, un Dimanche, 1988; Serious Hysterics, 1992; Resurgences, 1992. *Contributions to:* Critical journals, Spirale, and Tessera, (Founding Editor). *Memberships:* Writer's Union of Canada; L'Union Des Ecrivains Quebecois. *Address:* c/o Coach House Press, 401 near Huron Street, Toronto, Canada M5S 2Q5.

SCOTT Jane. *See:* **MCELFRESH (Elizabeth) Adeline.**

SCOTT Jay, b. 4 Oct 1949, Lincoln, Nebraska, USA. Journalist; Film Critic. m. Mary Blakeley, 5 Oct 1968. *Education:* University of New Mexico, 1968-70. *Publications:* Midnight Matinees, 1986, also US, 1987. *Contributions to:* American Film; Premiere; Chateline, book editor; Christopher Street; Canadian Art, Contributing Editor. *Honours:* Silver Gavel, Investigative Reporting, American Bar Association, 1975; National Newspaper Award, Criticism, 1975, 1981, 1984; National Magazine Award,, Food Criticism, 1987. *Memberships:* Casey House Hospice, Board of Directors. *Literary Agent:* Sallie Gouverneur.

SCOTT Jeffrey Alan, b. 7 May 1952, Los Angeles, California, USA. Motion Picture, TV Writer. m. Sonya Kroch, 13 Aug 1978, 1 daughter. *Education:* Bachelor of Fine Arts, UCLA, 1974. *Appointments:* Marvel Productions, Head Writer, 1984; Stephen J Cannell Productions, Executive Producer, 1986. *Publications:* Jim Hensons Muppet Babies; Super Friends; Pac Man; James Bond, Junior; Starchaser. *Honours:* 3 Emmy Award; Humanitas Prize. *Memberships:* Writers Guild of America; Academy of Television Arts & Sciences. *Literary Agent:* Chris Barrett, Metropolitan Talent Agency, Beverly Hills, CA. *Address:* c/o Metropolitan Talent Agency, 9320 Wilshire Boulevard, Beverly Hills, CA 90212, USA.

SCOTT John Peter, b. 8 Apr 1949, London, England. University Teacher. m. Jill Wheatley, 4 Sept 1971, 1 son, 1 daughter. *Education:* Kingston College of Technology, 1968-71; BSc (Soc) (Lond), 1971; London School of Economics, 1971-72; PhD (Strathclyde), 1976. *Appointments:* Lecturer in Sociology, University of Strathclyde, Scotland, 1972-76; Lecturer in Sociology, 1976-87, Reader in Sociology, 1987-91, Professor of Sociology, 1991-, University of Leicester, England; Editor, Network newsletter, British Sociological Association, 1985-89; Editor, Sociology Review (Formerly Social Studies Review), Review, 1986-. *Publications:* Corporations, Classes and Capitalism, 1979, 2nd Edition, 1985; The Upper Classes, 1982; The Anatomy of Scottish Capital (with M Hughes), 1982; Directors of Industry (with C Griff), 1984; Networks of Corporate Power (joint editor), 1985; Capitalist Property and Financial Power, 1986; A Matter of Record, 1990; The Sociology of Elites (3 volumes, editor), 1990; Who Rules Britain, 1991; Social Network Analysis, 1992. *Contributions to:* Numerous articles for professional journals and magazines. *Membership:* Chairperson, General Secretary, British Sociological Association. *Address:* Department of Sociology, University of Leicester, Leicester LE1 7RH, England.

SCOTT Jonathan Henry, b. 22 Jan 1958, Auckland, New Zealand. Historian. *Education:* BA, 1980, BA Hons, 1981, Victoria University of Wellington, New Zealand; PhD, Cambridge, 1986. *Publications:* Algernon Sidney and the English Republic, 1623-1677, 1988; Algernon Sidney and the Restoration Crisis, 1677-1683, 1991. *Contributions to:* Historical Journal, 1988; The Politics of Religion in Retsoration England, 1990; Contributor of poetry to literary journals, 1984-86. *Address:* Downing College, Cambridge CB2 1DQ, England.

SCOTT Melissa Elaine, b. 7 Aug 1960, Little Rock, Arkansas, USA. *Education:* AB, magna cum laude, History, Harvard College, 1981. *Publications:* The Game Beyond, 1984; Five-Twelfths of Heaven, 1985; Silence in Solitude, 1986; A Choice of Destinies, 1986; The Kindly Ones, 1987; The Empress of Earth, 1987. *Honour:* John W Campbell Award for Best New Writer, 1986. *Memberships:* Science Fiction Writers of America; Authors Guild; Harvard Club, Boston. *Literary Agent:* Ashley D. Grayson.

SCOTT Nathan A, Jr. b. 1925, American, Writer on Literature, Philosophy, Theology/Religion. William R Kenan Jr, Professor Emeritus of Religious Studies and Professor Emeritus of English, University of Virginia, Charlottesville, 1976-. Advisory Editor, Literature and Theology, Religion and Literature, Callaloo, and Religion and Intellectual Life. *Appointments:* Associate Professor of Humanities, Howard University, Washington DC, 1948-55; Shailer Mathews Professor of Theology and Literature and Co-Editor, The Journal of Religion, University of Chicago, 1955-76; Fellow, School of Letters, Indiana University, Bloomington, 1965-72. *Publications include:* (ed)The Climate of Faith in Modern Literature, 1964; Samuel Beckett, 1965; (ed)Four Ways of Modern Poetry, 1965; (ed)Man in the Modern Theatre, 1965; The Broken Center: Studies in the Theological Horizon of Modern Literature, 1966; Ernest Hemingway, 1966; (ed)The Modern Vision of Death, 1967; (ed) Adversity and Grace: Studies in Recent American Literature, 1968; Craters of the Spirit: Studies in the Modern Novel, 1968; Negative Capability: Studies in the New Literature and the Religious Situation, 1969; The Unquiet Vision: Mirrors of Man in Existentialism, 1969; Nathaniel West, 1971; The Wild Prayer of Longing: Poetry and the Sacred, 1971; Three American Moralists: Mailer, Bellow, Trilling, 1973; (ed) The Legacy of Reinhold Niebuhr, 1975; The Poetry of Civic Virtue: Eliot, Malraux, Auden, 1976; Mirrors of Man in Existenialism, 1978; The Poetics of Belief: Studies in Coleridge, Arnold, Pater, Santayana, Stevens and Heidegger, 1985; Visions of Presence in Modern American Poetry, 1993. *Address:* Department of Religious Studies, University of Virginia, Charlottesville, VA 22903, USA.

SCOTT Roney. *See:* **GAULT William Campbell.**

SCOTT Rosie, b. 22 Mar 1948, New Zealand. Writer. m. 28 Nov 1987, 2 daughters. *Education:* MA Hons, English, 1968; Graduate Diploma, Drama, 1984. *Appointments:* Member, Queensland Literary Board, 1991-92. *Publications:* Flesh and Blood, poetry, 1984; Queen of Love, stories, 1989; Novels: Glory Days, 1988; Nights with Grace, 1990; Feral City, 1992; Lives on fire, 1993. *Contributions to:* Literary essays, poems, stories to: Rolling Stone; Metro; Island; Australian Book Review; 24 Hours; Australian Author. *Honours:* Sunday Times Bruce Mason Award for play Say Thank You to the Lady, 1986; Glory Days shortlisted, National Book Award, 1988; Australian Writers Fellowship, Category A, 1992. *Memberships:* PEN New Zealand; Australian Society of Authors. *Literary Agent:* Margaret Connelly, Paddington, Australia. *Address:* c/o Margaret Connelly, 37 Ormond St, Paddington, New South Wales 2021, Australia.

SCOTT Roy Vernon, b. 1927, United States of America. Writer. *Publications:* The Agrarian Movement in Illinois 1880-1896, 1962; The Reluctant Farmer: The Rise of Agricultural Extension to 1914, 1970; The Public Career of Cully A. Cobb: A Study in Agricultural Leadership (with J.G. Shoalmire), 1973; Southern Agriculture Since the Civil War (with George L. Robson Jr.), 1979; Railroad Development Programs in the Twentieth Century, 1985; The Great Northern Railway: A History (with R W Hidy and others), 1988; Eugene Beverly Ferris and Agricultural Science in the Lower South, 1991. *Address:* Department of History,

Mississippi State University, Mississippi State, MI 39762, USA.

SCOTT Sally Elisabeth, b. 30 May 1948, London, England. Writer; Illustrator. *Education:* BA Hons, Philosophy and English Literature, York University, 1970. *Publications:* The Magic Horse, 1985, The Three Wonderful Beggars, 1987, The Elf-King's Bride, 1981, all self-illustrated; Illustrator, Tales and Legends of India. *Memberships:* Society of Authors. *Literary Agent:* Bruce Hunter, David Higham Associates Ltd. *Address:* c/o Bruce Hunter, David Higham Associates Ltd, 5-8 Lower John Street, Golden Square, London WC1R 4HA, England.

SCOTT Tom, b. 1918. Poet; Childrens Writer. *Appointment:* Former Editor, Scottish Literature Series, Pergamon Press, Oxford. *Publications:* Seven Poems of Maister Francis Vilton, 1953; An Ode til New Jerusalem, 1956; The Ship and the Poems, 1963; A Possible Solution to the Scotch Question, 1963; Dunbar: A Critical Exposition of the Poems, 1966; The Oxford Book of Scottish Verse (with J. MacQueen), 1966; Late Medieval Scots Poetry: A Selection from the Makars and Their Heirs down to 1610, 1967; At the Shrine of the Unkent Sodger: A Poem for Recitation, 1968; Tales of King Robert the Bruce, 1969; The Penguin Book of Scottish Verse, 1970; Brand the Builder, 1975; The Tree, 1977; Tales of Sir William Wallace, 1981; The Dirty Business, 1986. *Address:* Duddington Park, Edinburgh 15, Scotland.

SCOTT TANNER Amoret, b. 27 Mar 1930, Vancouver, British Columbia, Canada. Social Historian. m. Ralph Tanner, 24 Aug 1985. *Publications:* Hedgerow Harvest, 1979; Parrots, 1982; With Christopher Scott: Collecting Bygones, 1964; Tobacco and the Collector, 1966; Dummy Board Figures, 1966; Discovering Smoking Antiques, 1970, 1981; Discovering Stately Homes, 1973, 1981, 1989. *Contributions to:* Regularly to the Saturday Book; Country Life; Antique Collector. *Memberships:* Founder Member, Member of Council, Ephemera Society; Trustee, Foundation for Ephemera Studies. *Address:* The Footprint, Padworth Common, Reading, RG7 4QG, England.

SCOTT-STOKES Natascha, (Norton), b. 11 Apr 1962, Munich, Germany. Travel Writer. m. Benoit LeBlanc, 27 Feb 1992. *Education:* BA Hons Humanities, Middlesex Polytechnic; MA Latin American Studies, University of London. *Appointments:* Associate Editor, Writer's Newsletter, 1989-90. *Publications:* An Amazon and a Donkey, 1991; Co-author: Germany: The Rough Guide, 1989; The Cadogan Guide to Central America, 1992; The Amber Trail, 1993. *Contributions to:* The Lima Times; Writers' Newsletter. *Memberships:* Writer's Guild of Great Britain; PEN English Centre; Fellow, Royal Geographical Society. *Address:* 55 Leconfield Road, London N5 2RZ, England.

SCOVILLE James Griffin, b. 1940, United States of America. Writer (Economics, Industrial Relations). *Publications:* The Job Content of the U.S. Economy 1940-70, 1969; Perspectives on Poverty and Income Distribution, 1971; Manpower and Occupational Analysis: Concepts and Measurements, 1972; The International Labor Movement in Transition, 1973; Status Influences in Third World Labor Markets - Caste, Gender and Custom, 1991. *Address:* 4849 Girard Avenue S, Minneapolis, MN 55409, USA.

SCRUTON Roger V, b. 27 Feb 1944, Burlingthorpe, England. Professor of Philosophy, Boston University. *Education:* BA, Philosophy 1965, PhD 1972, Jesus College, Cambridge. *Literary Appointment:* Editor, Salisbury Review, 1982-. *Publications:* The Meaning of Conservatism, 1980; The Aesthetics of Architecture, 1979; A Dictionary of Political Thought, 1982; Fortnight's Anger, 1981; The Aesthetic Understanding, 1983; Sexual Desire, 1986; Art and Imagination, 1974; Politics of Culture, 1981; Short History of Modern

Philosophy, 1981; Thinkers of The New Left, 1986; A Land Held Hostage, 1987; Untimely Tracts, 1987; The Philosopher on Dove Beach, 1990; Francesca, 1991; A Dove Descending and other Stories, 1991; Conservative Texts: an anthology, 1992; Xanthippic Dialogues, 1993. *Contributions to:* Times; Times Literary Supplement; Spectator; Guardian; Field; Salisbury Review; Encounter. *Literary Agent:* Curtis Brown. *Address:* 5 Trenchard Road, Stanton Fitzwarren, Wilts, England.

SCUDAMORE Pauline, b. 14 Nov 1936, Leeds, England. m. James Scudamore, 14 Dec 1959, 3 sons. *Education:* BA Hons, Thames Polytechnic, 1979. *Publications:* Spike Milligan, A Biography, 1986, 1987, 1989; Dear Robert/Dear Spike, 1991. *Literary Agent:* A P Watts. *Address:* 8 Upper Cheyne Row, Chelsea, London SW3 5JN, England.

SCULLY James (Joseph Patrick), b. 23 Feb 1937, New Haven, Connecticut, USA. Teacher. m. Arlene Marie Steeves, 10 Sept 1960, 2 sons, 1 daughter. *Education:* BA 1959, PhD 1964, University of Connecticut. *Publications include:* The Marches, 1967; Avenue of the Americas, 1971; Santiago Poems, 1975; Scrap Book, 1977; May Day, 1980; Apollo Helmet, 1983. Also: Editor, Modern Poetics, 1965. Translations: Aeschylus' Prometheus Bound, with C.J.Herington, 1975; Quechua Peoples Poetry, with M.A.Proser, 1977; Teresa de Jesus' De Repente/All of a Sudden, with Proser & A. Scully, 1979; Line Break: Poetry as Social Practice, 1988. *Contributions to:* Critical Quarterly; Leviathan; Massachusetts Review; Arion; Praxis; New Yorker; Minnesota Review; Literatura Chilena en el Exilio; Harvard Magazine; Poetry Review; Compages; Alcatraz. *Honours:* Fellowship, Ingram Merrill Foundation, 1962-63; Lamont Poetry Award, 1967; Guggenheim Fellowship, 1973-74; Contributors' Prize, Far Point, 1969; Jenny Traine Memorial Award, Massachusetts Review, 1971; Fellowship, National Endowment for Arts, 1976-77; Translation Award, Islands & Continents, 1980; Award, Bookcover Design, Bookbuilders of Boston, 1983. *Memberships:* PEN; Poetry Society of America. *Address:* 250 Lewiston Avenue, Willimantic, Connecticut 06226, USA.

SCUPHAM John Peter, b. 24 Feb 1933. Writer. m. Carola Nance Braunholtz, 10 Aug 1957, 3 sons, 1 daughter. *Education:* The Perse School, Cambridge; Hons degree in English, Emmanuel College, Cambridge. *Literary Appointment:* Proprietor and Founder of The Mandeville Press. *Publications include:* Prehistories, 1975; The Hinterland, 1977; Summer Palaces, 1980; Winter Quarters, 1983; Out Late, 1986; The Air Show, 1988; Selected Poems, 1991. *Membership:* Fellow, Royal Society of Literature. *Address:* 2, Taylors Hill, Hitchin, Herts SG4 9AD, England.

SE Nan. *See:* KUO Nancy.

SEABORG Glenn (Theodore), b. 1912, United States of America. Writer (Chemistry). *Publications:* The Chemistry of the Actinide Elements, 1958; The Transuranium Elements, 1958; Elements of the Universe, 1958; Man-Made Transuranium Elements, 1963; Education and the Atom, 1964; The Nuclear Properties of the Heavy Elements, 1964; Oppenheimer, 1969; Man and Atom, 1971; Nuclear Milestones, 1972; Transuranium Elements: Products of Modern Alchemy, 1978; Kennedy, Khrushchev and the Test Ban, 1981; Nuclear Chemistry, 1982; Stemming the Tide: arms control Johnson years, 1987. *Honour:* Recipient, Nobel Prize for Chemistry, 1951. *Address:* Lawrence Berkeley Laboratory, University of California, Berkeley, CA 94720, USA.

SEABROOK Jeremy, b. 1939. Writer (Sociology). *Appointments:* Dramatist, mainly in collaboration with Michael O'Neill. *Publications:* The Unprivledged: A Hundred Years of Family Life and Tradition in a Working Class Street, 1967; City Close-Up,1971; The Everlasting Feast, 1974; A Lasting Relationship: Homosexuals and Society, 1976; What Went Wrong? Working People and the Ideals of the Labour Movement, 1978; Mother and Son: An Autobiography, 1980; Working Class Childhood, 1982; A World Still to Win: The Reconstruction of the Post War Working Class, 1985; Landscapes of Poverty, 1985; Life and Labour in a Bombay Slum, 1987. *Address:* c/o Curtis Brown, 162-168 Regent Street, London, W1R 5TB, England.

SEAGER Ralph William b. 3 Nov 1911, Geneva, New York, USA. Writer. m. Ruth M Lovejoy, 1932, 3 sons. *Education:* Graduated from Penn Yan Academy, 1928; Studied basic and advance verse, University of California at Berkeley, 1950-51; Studied with Pulitzer Poet Robert Peter Tristram Coffin at University of New Hampshire Writers' Conference, 1954 and John Holmes, Harvard Phi Beta Kappa Poet, 1956; Litt D, Keuka College 1970; Professor Emeritus, 1977. *Appointments:* Assistant Professor of English, Keuka College, teaching a creative course in Verse Writing since 1960; Served with United States Navy in the South Pacific campaigns during World War II. *Publications include:* Books of Verse: Songs from a Willow Whistle, 1956; Beyond the Green Gate, 1958; Christmas Chimes in Rhyme, 1962; Cup, Flagon and Fountain, 1965; A Choice of Dreams, 1970; Wheatfields and Vineyards, 1975; The Manger Mouse and Other Christmas Poems, 1977; Hiding in Plain Sight, 1982; The Love Tree, 1985; The First Quartet (with 3 other poets), 1988; Books in prose: The Sound of an Echo, 1963; Little Yates and the United States, 1976; The First Baptist Church - One Hundred Fifty Years (co-author) 1980. *Contributions to:* Poems in publications including The Saturday Evening Post, New York Times, Ladies' Home Journal. Director or instructor of numerous poetry workshops. *Address:* 311 Keuka Street, Penn Yan, NY 14527, USA.

SEAGRAVE Sterling, b. 15 Apr 1937, USA. Writer. m. (1) Wendy Law-Yone, 1967, (2) Peggy Sawyer, 1982, 1 son, 1 daughter. *Education:* In India, USA, Latin-America. *Publications:* Yellow Rain, 1981; Soldiers of Fortune, 1981; The Soong Dynasty, 1985; The Marcos Dynasty, 1988; Dragon Lady, 1992. *Contributions to:* Atlantic; Far Eastern Economic Review; Esquire; Time; Smithsonian. *Membership:* Authors Guild. *Literary Agents:* Robert Gottlieb (New York), Lavinia Trevor (UK), William Morris Agency. *Address:* c/o William Morris Agency, 31 Soho Sq, London W1V 5DG, England.

SEAL Basil. *See:* BARNES Julian Patrick.

SEALEY Leonard George William, b.7 May 1923, London, England. Educational Author, Consultant. m. (1) Joan Hearn, Mar. 1944, dec., (2) Nancy Verre, August 1972. 5 Sons. *Education:* Teachers Certificate, Peterborough College, England; DipED, MEd, University of Leicester. *Publications:* The Creative use of Mathematics, 1961; Communication and Learning (co-author), 1962; Exploring Language, 1968; Basic Skills in Learning, 1970; Introducing Mathematics, 1970; The Lively Readers, 1973; Our World Encyclopedia (Editor), 1974; Open Education, 1977; Children's Writing, 1979. *Memberships:* Fellow of the Royal Society of Arts; Phi Delta Kappa (Harvard Chapter Honorary). *Address:* 136 Sandwich Road, Plymouth, MA 02360, USA.

SEALTS Merton M. Jr. b. 8 Dec 1915, United States of America. Writer. *Publications:* Melville as Lecturer, 1957; Billy Budd, Sailor by Herman Melville (with H Hayford), 1962; The Journals and Miscellaneous Notebooks of Ralph Waldo Emerson 1835-1838, vol V, 1965; Melville's Reading, 1966, 1988; Emerson's Nature: Origin, Growth, Meaning (with A.R. Ferguson), 1969, 1979; The Journals and Miscellaneous Notebooks of Ralph Waldo Emerson 1847-1848, Vol X, 1973; The Early Lives of Melville: Nineteenth Century Biographical Sketches and Their Authors, 1974; Pursuing Melville, 1940-1980: Chapters and Essays, 1982; Emerson on the Scholar, 1992. *Address:* 6209 Mineral Point Road, Apt. 1106/08, Madison, WI 53705-4537, USA.

SEARE Nicholas. *See:* **WHITAKER Rodney William.**

SEARLE Ronald (William Fordham), b. 1920. *Publications:* Forty Drawings, 1946; Le Nouveau Ballet Anglais, 1947; Hurrah for St. Trinian's, 1948; The Female Approach, 1949; Back to the Slaughterhouse, 1951; Souls in Torment, 1953; Rake's Progress, 1955; Merry England, 1956; Which Way Did He Go, 1961; Searle in the Sixties, 1965; From Frozen North to Filthy Lucre, 1964; Pardong M'sieur, 1965; Searle's, 1969; Hommage a Toulouse Lautrec, 1969; Secret Sketchbook, 1970; The Addict, 1971; More Cats, 1975; Drawings from Gilbert and Sullivan, 1975; The Zodiac, 1977; Ronald Searle, 1978; The King of Beasts, 1980; The Big Fat Cat Book, 1982; Winespeak, 1983; Ronald Searle in Perspective, 1984; Ronald Searle's Golden Oldies, 1985; To the Kwai-and Back, 1986; Something in the Cellar, 1986; Slightly Foxed - but still desirable, 1989. *Address:* c/o Tessa Sayle, 11 Jubilee Place, London, SW3 3TE, England.

SEARLS Hank H, b. 10 Aug 1922, San Francisco, California, USA. Author. m. Berna Ann Cooper, 12 Dec 1959, 2 sons, 1 daughter. *Education:* BS, US Naval Academy; University of California, Berkeley. *Publications include:* Overboard; Sounding; Crowded Sky; Kataki; Jaws 2; Young Joe, The Forgotten Kennedy; Big X; Pilgrim Project; The Penetrators; The Hero Ship; The Lost Prince; Young Joe; Pentagon; Firewind; Blood Song; Jaws the Revenge. *Memberships:* Authors Guild; Writers Guild West. *Literary Agent:* Scott Meredith, USA. *Address:* c/o Scott Meredith Agency, 845 3rd Avenue, New York, NY 10022, USA.

SEARS David O'Keefe, b. 1935, United States of America. Writer (Politics, Psychology). *Publications:* Public Opinion (with R.E. Lane), 1964; Social Psychology (with J.M. Freedman and J.M. Carlsmith), 1970; Readings in Social Psychology (with Freedman and Carlsmith), 1971; The Politics of Violence (with J.B. McConahay), 1973; Tax Revolt (with J. Citrin), 1982. *Address:* Department of Psychology, University of California, Los Angeles, CA 90024, USA.

SEATS Dolores, b. 1 Oct 1928, Urbana, Illinois, USA. Businesswomen (retired). m. Lloyd Seats, 2 Nov 1947, 1 son, 1 daughter. *Education:* Glendale Community College, Arizona, 1981-82; Extension course in Poetry, Arizona State University, 1983. *Literary Appointments:* Co-Chairman, Writers' Workshop, 1967, Chairman, Poetry Workshop, 1979, Phoenix Writers Club; Newsletter Editor, Phoenix Poetry Society, 1979; ASPS State Historian, 1987 & 1988. *Publications:* Birds-Eye View (book), 1986; Anthologies: Melodies of a Jade Harp, 1968; Ballet on the Wind, 1969; Sing Naked Spirit, 1970; Phoenix Writers Club Anthology, 1979, 1980; Cactus Jelly, 1981; Caliche Footprints, 1981; The Arizona Anthem, 1982; Poetry for Children, 1984; Desert Moods, 1986. *Contributions to:* Maryvale Star, 1965; The Lark, 1966; Clubwoman Magazine, 1967; The Swordsman Review, 1967, 1968; American Bard, 1968; Prairie Poet, 1968; Encore, 1968, 1969; Mushrooms and Berries, 1968; Angel Hour, 1968; United Poet, 1969; Maryvale Sun, 1969; Southwest Breeze, 1970; Poet International, 1970; The Arizona Republic, 1973, 1983; The Traveler, 1983. *Honours:* Certificate for Poetry Advancement, 1970; Member of Year Plaque, Phoenix Poetry Society, 1978; 6 Gil Handegard State Poetry Awards, 1982; Honourable Mention, 1980, 2nd place, 1982, 1st Honourable Mention, 1983, 2nd Honourable Mention, 1984; NFSPS Contests; 3rd Place, Juvenile Prose Contest, 1983, 3rd Place, Poetry Contest, 1986, Phoenix Writers Club. *Memberships:* Phoenix Poetry Society (Chairman, National Poetry Contest, 1979, Recording/ Corresponding Secretary, 1981 Nominating Committee, 1987); National League of American Pen Women (Telephone Committee, 1987); Arizona State Poetry Society (State Historian 1987); Phoenix Writers Club; Academy of American Poets; World Poetry Society Intercontinental. *Address:* 7010 West Campbell Avenue, Phoenix, AZ 85033, USA.

SEBASTIAN Lee. *See:* **SILVERBERG Robert.**

SEBESTYEN Ouida, b. 13 Feb 1924, Texas, USA. Children's Fiction Writer. 1 son. *Publications:* Words by Heart, 1979; Far from Home, 1980; IOU's, 1982; On Fire, 1985; The Girl in the Box, 1989. *Contributions to:* ALAN Review, National Council of Teachers of English; short stories, various US magazines & anthologies. *Honours:* Children's Book Award, International Reading Association, 1979; American Book Award, children's fiction, 1982; Silver Pencil Award, Holland, 1984. *Address:* 115 S 36th Street, Boulder, CO 80303, USA.

SEBLEY Frances Rae (Rae Jeffs), b. 1921, British. *Appointments:* Publicity Manager for the Hutchinson Group, 1957-64; Publisher's Reader, Hutchinson and Company, London, 1964-; Copy Writer, Heron Books, 1966-69. *Publications:* Brendan Behan's Island (ed), 1962; Hold Your Hour and Have Another (ed), 1963; Brendan Behan's New York (ed), 1964; Confessions of An Irish Rebel (with Brendan Behan), 1965; The Scarperer (ed), Brendan Behan: Man and Showman, 1966. *Address:* Rotherfield Farmhouse, Newick, Lewes, Sussex, England.

SEDERBERG Arelo (Charles), b. 1931, United States of America. Author. *Appointments include:* Reporter, Los Angeles Mirror, 1954-63; Financial Writer, Los Angeles Times, 1963-70; Public Relations Executive, Carl Byoir and Associates, Inc. Los Angeles and Las Vegas, 1970-78; Assistant Managing Editor, Los Angeles Herald-Examiner. *Publications:* The Stock Market Investment Club Handbook, 1971; A Collection for J.L., 1973, in paperback as How to Kidnap a Millionaire, 1974; Sixty Hours of Darkness, 1974; Casino, 1977; Breedlove, 1979; The Power Players, 1980; Hollywood Graffiti, 1986. *Address:* 447 W. Duarte Road, No. 6, Arcadia, CA 91006, USA.

SEDLEY Kate. *See:* **CLARKE Brenda.**

SEE Carolyn (Monica Highland), b. 13 Jan 1934, California, USA. Writer. m. (1) Richard See, 18 Feb 1954, (2) Tom Stark, 30 Apr 1960. 2 daughters. *Education:* PhD, University of California, Los Angeles (UCLA), 1953. *Appointments include:* Professor of English, UCLA. *Publications include:* The Rest is Done with Mirrors, 1970; Blue Money, 1974; Mothers, Daughters, 1977; Rhine Maidens, 1980; Golden Days, 1985; When Knaves Meet, 1988; The Mirrored Ball in the Hollywood Dance Hall, 1988; Making History, 1991. As Monica Highland: Lotus Land, 1983; 1-10 Shanghai Road, 1985; Greetings From Southern California, 1987; Precious Cargo, 1990; Two Schools of Thought (with John Espey), 1991. *Contributions to:* Esquire; McCalls; Atlantic; Sports Illustrated; California Magazine; Contributing editor, book reviews, Los Angeles Times. *Honours:* Samuel Goldwyn Award, 1963; Sidney Hillman Award, 1969; Grant, National Endowment for the Arts, 1974; Bread and Roses Award, National Womens Political Caucus, 1988; Vesta Award, 1989; Guggenheim Fellowship in Fiction, 1989. *Literary Agent:* Elaine Markson. *Address:* PO Box 107, Topanga, California 90290, USA.

SEED Cecile Eugenie (Jenny Seed), b. 18 May 1930, Cape Town, South Africa. Author. m. Edward (Ted) Robert Seed, 31 Oct 1953, 3 sons, 1 daughter. *Publications:* The Great Thirst, 1985; The Great Elephant, 1985; Place Among the Stones, 1987; Hurry, Hurry, Sibusiso, 1988; The Broken Spear, 1989; The Prince of the Bay, 1989; The Big Pumpkin, 1990. *Honours:* MER Award for Place Among the Stones, 1987; Runner-up, Noma Award, for Ntombi's Song. *Address:* 10 Pioneer Crescent, Northdene, Natal 4093, South Africa.

SEED Jenny. *See:* **SEED Cecile Eugenie.**

SEELYE John Douglas, b. 1931, United States of America. Author. *Appointments include:* Contributing Editor, New Republic, Washington, DC, 1971-79; Editorial Board, American Literature, Durham, NC, 1874-78; Consulting Editor, Penguin Books, London, 1979-. *Publications:* Arthur Gordon Pym, Benito Cereno and Related Writings, 1967; Etchings of a Whaling Cruise, by J.Ross Browne, 1968; The True Adventures of Huckleberry Finn, as told by John Seelye, 1970; Melville: The Ironic Diagram, 1970; The Kid, 1972; Dirty Tricks, or Nick Noxin's natural Nobility, 1974; Prophetic Waters: The River in Early American Life and Literature, 1977; Mark Twain in the Movies: A Meditation with Pictures, 1977; Beautiful Machine, 1991. *Address:* Department of English, University of Florida, Gainesville, FL 32611-2036, USA.

SEFTON Catherine. *See:* **WADDELL Martin**.

SEGAL Erich, b. Brooklyn, New York, USA, 1937. Classicist; Author. m. 1 daughter. *Education:* PhD, Harvard University, 1964. *Appointments:* Teaching, Harvard University; Several positions including Professor of Classics, Yale University, 1964-87; Visiting Professor of Classics, Princeton University and University of Munich, Federal Republic of Germany; Currently Fellow, Wolfson College, Oxford, England. *Publications:* Novels: Love Story, 1970; Oliver's Story, 1977; Man, Woman and Child; The Class, 1985; Doctors, 1988; Acts of Faith, 1992; Screenplays including Yellow Submarine; Academic books including: Roman Laughter: The Comedy Of Plautus, 1987. *Honours:* Golden Globe Award and Oscar nomination for screenplay of Love Story; 2 international literary prizes for The Class; Guggenheim Award for classical scholarship.

SEGAL Lore, b. 8 Mar 1928, Vienna, Austria. Writer. m. David I. Segal, 3 Nov 1960, dec., 1 son, 1 daughter. *Education:* BA, English, Bedford College, University of London, England, 1948. *Appointments:* Professor, Writing Division, School of Arts, Columbia University, Princeton University, Sarah Lawrence College, Bennington College, USA; Professor of English, University of Illinois, Chicago, Illinois; The Ohio State University. *Publications:* Novels: Other People's Houses, 1964; Lucinella, 1976; Her First American, 1985; Children's books: Tell Me A Mitzi, 1970; All the Way Home, 1973; Tell Me A Trudy, 1977; The Story of Mrs Brubeck and How She Looked for Trouble and Where She Found Him, 1981; The Story of Mrs Lovewright and Purrless Her Cat, 1985; Translations: Gallows Songs (with W D Snodgrass), 1968; The Juniper Tree and Other Tales from Grimm, 1973; The Book of Adam to Moses; The Story of King Soul and King David. *Contributions to:* Short stories and articles to: New York Times Book Review; Partisan Review; New Republic; The New Yorker; Others. *Honours:* Guggenheim Fellow, 1965-66; Grantee, Council of Arts and Humanities, 1968- 69; Grantee, Artists Public Service, 1970-71; Grantee, CAPS, 1975; Grantee, National Endowment for the Arts, 1982; Grantee, National Endowment for the Humanities, 1983; Academy of Arts and Letters Award, 1986. *Address:* 280 Riverside Drive, New York, NY 10025, USA.

SEGAL Ronald Michael, b.14 July 1932, Cape Town, South Africa. Author. m. Susan Wolff, 17 July 1962, 1 son, 2 daughters. *Education:* BA, University of Cape Town, 1951; BA, Cantab, 1954; Philip Francis Du Pont Fellowship, University of Virginia, 1955; Visiting Fellow, Center for Study of Democratic Institutions, Santa Barbara, 1973. *Literary Appointments:* Founding Editor, Penguin African Library, 1961-84; Pluto Crime Fiction 1983-86. *Publications include:* Into Exile, 1963; The Crisis of India, 1965; The Race War, 1966; America's Receding Future, 1968; The Tragedy of Leon Trotsky, 1979; The State of the World Atlas, 1981. *Contributions to:* Publisher and Editor, Africa South 1956-60; Africa South in Exile 1960-61. *Literary Agent:* Deborah Rogers. *Address:* Old Manor House, Walton-on-Thames, Surrey KT12 2NZ, England.

SEGAL Stanley Solomon, b. 9 Nov 1919, London, England. Educator. m. Tamar Shuster, 29 Apr 1945, 1 son, 1 daughter. *Education:* Certificate in Education, Goldsmiths College, University of London, 1950; Diploma in Education of Handicapped Pupils, Institute of Education, London, 1954; Masters Degreee in Education, University of Leicester, School of Education, 1970; Appointed Professor of Special Education, Bulmershe College of Higher Education, 1981. *Literary Appointments:* Honorary Editor, Forward Trends in the Treatment of the Backward Child, 1954-74; Honorary Editor, British Journal of Special Education, 1974-. *Publications:* No Child is Ineducable, 1967, 1974; Teaching Backward Pupils, 1963; Eleven-Plus Rejects? 1961; Backward Pupils in the USSR, 1965; From Care to Education, 1970; Society and Mental Handicap, 1984; The Space Age Readers 1963; The Working World Series 1965; The Creative Arts in the Development of People with Mental Handicaps, 1990. *Contributions to:* Times Educational Supplement, Teachers World, The Teacher, Parents Voice, Mental Health. *Honour:* OBE for Services to the Education of Handicapped Children. *Memberships:* Life President, National Council for Special Education, Magistrates Association, Association of Professions for the Mentally Handicapped (former Chairman). *Address:* 11 Ravensdale Avenue, Finchley, London N12 9HP, England.

SEGHERS Greta Irene Pieter, b. 11 Feb 1942, Beveren, Waas, Belgium. Writer; History Teacher. m. Ludo De Cock, 12 July 1966, 1 son, 1 daughter. *Education:* Secondary Teacher Training, Dutch, History. *Appointments:* Member, Editorial Staff, Dietsche Warande en Belfort, 1984; Member, Literary Commission, East Flanders, 1991. *Publications:* Het blauwe meisje, stories, 1980; Wat ge leest en schrijft, dat zijt ge zelf, essay, 1985; Het eigenzinnige leven van Angèle Manteau, biography, 1992; Novels: Afkeer van Faulkner, 1977; Omtrent de man die wederkwam, 1978; Ontregeling en Misverstand, 1983; De zijpaden van het paradijs, 1988; Hoe moordend is mijn school, 1990. *Contributions to:* Interviews to magazines including: Knack; Intermediair; Short stories to: Dietsche Warande en Belfort; Kreqtief; Others. *Honours:* Best Debut Prize, 1977; Yang Prize, 1977; Prize, 1983, Honourable Mention, 1985, Province of East Flanders. *Membership:* Dietsche Warande en Belfort. *Address:* Tuinlaan 14, 9120 Vrasene, Belgium.

SEIDEL George Joseph, b. 1932, United States of America. Writer (Philosophy). *Publications:* Martin Heidegger and the Pre-Socratics: An Introduction to His Thought, 1964; Crisis of Creativity, 1966; A Contemporary Approach to Classical Metaphysics, 1969; Being, Nothing and God: A Philosophy of Appearance, 1970; Activity and Ground: Fichte, Scheling and Hegel, 1976. *Address:* St. Martin's College, Lacey, WA 98503, USA.

SEIDEL Kathleen Gilles, b. 20 Oct 1951, Lawrence, Kansas, USA. Writer. m. Larry R Seidel, 14 Apr 1973, 2 daughters. *Education:* AB, University of Chicago, 1973; MA, Johns Hopkins University, 1975; PhD, Johns Hopkins University, 1978. *Publications:* The Same Last Name, 1983; A Risk Worth Taking, 1983; Mirrors and Mistakes, 1984; After All These Years, 1984; When Love Isn't Enough, 1984; Don't Forget to Smile, 1986; Maybe This Time, 1990. *Honours:* Romantic Times, Best Harlequin American Romance, 1983; Romance Writers of America, Best Non-Series Romance, 1984. *Memberships:* Romance Writers of America; Washington Romance Writers, Chairman, 1983-85. *Literary Agent:* Adele Leone. *Address:* c/o The Adele Leone Agency, 26 Nantucket Place, Scarsdale, NY 10583, USA.

SEIDLER Ann, b. 1925, American. Writer; Author. *Appointments:* Associate Professor of Speech, Montclair State College, Upper Montclair, New Jersey since 1967; Teacher of Speech and Drama, Punahau School, Honolulu, Hawaii, 1946-47; Speech Consultant to National Hospital for Speech Disorders, NYC, 1949-51; Mountainside Hospital, New Jersey, 1953-54, and

Cedar Grove Board of Education, New Jersey, 1954-62. *Publications:* (All with J. Slepian unless otherwise noted), Magic Arthur and the Giant, 1964; Alfie and the Dream Machine, 1964; Mr Sipple and the Naughty Princes, 1964; Lester and the Sea Master, 1964; The Best Invention of All, 1967; The Silly Listening Book, 1967; Ding Dong Bing Bong, 1964; The Hungry Thing, 1967; An Ear Is to Hear, 1967; Bendemolena, 1967 (co-author); Make Yourself Clear, 1974; The Cat That Wore a Pot on Her Head, 1981

SEIDMAN Hugh, b. 1 Aug 1940, USA. Poet. *Education:* Massachusetts Institute of technology, 1957; BS, cum laude, Polytechnic Institute of Brooklyn, 1961; MS, University of Minnesota, 1964; MFA, with Distinction, Columbia University, 1969. *Appointments include:* Teacher of poetry for workshops, lectures and courses including: Visiting Poet, Writer's Voice, New York City, 1988; Faculty Member, New School for Social Research, 1976-. *Publications:* People Live, They Have Lives, 1992; Throne/Falcon/Eye, 1982; Blood Lord, 1974; Collecting Evidence, 1970. *Honours:* New York Foundation for the Arts, Poetry Fellowship, 1990; National Endowment for the Arts, Creative Writing Fellowship, 1972, 1985; Writers Digest, Poetry Prize, 1982; Resident Fellow, Yaddo, 1972, 1976, 1988; Resident Fellow, MacDowell Colony, 1974, 1975, 1989; Poetry Grant, Creative Artists Public Service Programme, 1971; Discovery Grant, National Endowment for the Arts, 1970; Yale Series of Younger Poets Prize, for Collecting Evidence, 1969. *Memberships include:* American PEN; Poetry Society of America; Authors Guild; Authors League; Board Member, Millay Colony for the Arts, 1975-79; Maryland Arts Council, Panelist, 1978; Massachusetts Council on the Arts, Panelist, 1977; Reviewer, New York Times Book Review, 1975-85. *Address:* 463 West Street, New York, NY 10014, USA.

SEIFMAN Eli, b. 4 Aug 1936, New York, USA. Professor of Social Sciences. *Education:* BA 1957, MS 1959, Queens College, City University of New York; PhD, New York University, 1965. *Publications:* History of New York State Colonization Society, 1966. Social Studies: Structure, Models & Strategies, 1969; Teacher's Handbook, 1971; Towards a New World Outlook, 1976; Education & Socialization Modernization, 1987; *Contributions to:* Asian Affairs; Asian Thought & Society; American Journal of Chinese Medicine; History of Education Quarterly; Social Education; Pennsylvania History; Teaching History; Liberian Studies Journal. *Honours:* Phi Beta Kappa, 1956; Phi Alpha Theta, 1956; Kappa Delta Pie, 1963; Book Award, Phi Lamda Theta, 1973. *Memberships:* American Historical Association; Royal Society for Asian Affairs; National Council for Social Studies; Historical Association. *Address:* Social Sciences Interdisciplinary Programme, State University of New York, Stony Brook, New York 11794, USA.

SEIP Heige Lunde, b. 5 Mar 1919. m. Therese Holth, 1943, 3 daughters. *Education:* Oslo, Harvard, USA and Cambridge Universities. *Appointments:* Assistant, Oslo University, 1939; Statistical Secretary, Norwegian Leather Board, 1941; Consultant, Rieber & Co, 1942; Ministry of Finance, 1945; Division Head, Ministry of Commerce, 1948; Division Head, Central Bureau of Statistics, Oslo, 1952; Editor in Chief, Dagladet 1954-65; MP 1954-61 and 1965-73; Minister of Labour and Local Government, 1965-70; Chairman of the Storting (Parliamentary) Committee on Foreign Policy and Constitutional Matters, 1970-73; Secretary General of the Nordic Council, 1973-77; Chief Editor of the Norwegian Journal of Commerce and Shipping, 1977-880; Norwegian Data Protection Commissioner, 1980-89; Elected Data Commissioner of the Council of Europe, Strasbourg, 1989-. *Publications:* Kommunenes O/konomi, 1949; Numerous articles in books, periodicals and daily papers. *Memberships:* Nordic Council, 1958-61 and 1966-73; Nordic Cultural Commission, 1955-61; Chairman, Liberal Party, 1970-72 and New Liberal Party, 1972-73. *Honours:* Commander Cross of Saint Olav's Order.

SELBOURNE David, b. 1937. Writer; Playwright. *Publications:* The Play of William Cooper and Edmund Dew-Nevett, 1968; The Two Backed Beast, 1969; Dorabella, 1970; Samson and Alison Mary Fagan, 1971; The Damned, 1971; Class Play, 1973; Brook's Dream: The Politics of Theatre, 1974; What's Acting? and Think of a Story, Quickly!, 1977; An Eye to India, 1977; An Eye to China, 1978; Through the Indian Looking Glass, 1982; The Making of a Midsummer Night's Dream, 1983; Against Socialist Illusion: A Radical Argument, 1985; In Theory and In Practice: Essays on the Politics of Jayaprakash Narayan, 1986; Left Behind: Journeys into British Politics, 1987; A Doctor's Life: The Diaries of Hugh Selbourne MD 1960-63, 1989; Death of the Dark Hero: Eastern Europe 1987-90, 1990; The Spirit of the Age, 1993; Not an Englishman: Conversations with Lord Goodman, 1993. *Address:* c/o Ed Victor, 162 Wardour Street, London W1, England.

SELBY Stephen, b. 5 June 1952, Darley Dale, Derbyshire, England. Playwright. m. Ann Spence, 6 Mar 1982, 1 daughter. *Education:* Social Science & Philosophy. *Appointments:* Writer, Director, Producer, Noc On Theatre, 1987-; Writer, Director, Producer, Hurdles of Time Theatre, 1991-. *Publications:* Better Looking Corpes; Contentious Work; Archie Pearson The one Legged Shoemaker; Eviction; Cuts; Nottingham By The Sea; Hurdles of Time; Erewash Giants, 1993. *Memberships:* Theatre Writers Union. *Literary Agent:* Hurdles of Time. *Address:* 53 Percival Road, Sherwood, Nottingham NG5 2FA, England.

SELDES George, b. 1890. United States of America. Writer; Journalist. *Appointments:* Reporter, Pittsburgh Leader, PA, 1909-10; Night Editor, Pittsburgh Post, PA, 1910-16; Managing Editor, Pulitzer's Weekly, NYC, 1916; War Correspondence, American Expeditionary Force, 1918-19; Head, Berlin Bureau,1920-27, Rome Branch, 1925, Chicago Tribune; In Fact (weekly newsletter), 1940-50. *Publications:* You Can't Print That (in United Kingdom as The Truth Behind the News), 1929; Can These Things Be?, 1931; World Panorama, 1933; The Vatican Yesterday, Today, Tomorrow, 1934; Iron, Blood and Profits, 1934; Sawdust Caesar, 1935; Lords of the Press, 1938; You Can't Do That, 1938; The Catholic Crisis, 1940; Witch Hunt, 1940; The Facts Are....., 1942; Facts and Fascism, 1943; 1000 Americans, 1947; The People Don't Know, 1949; Tell the Truth and Run, 1953; Compiler and editor, The Great Quotations, 1961; Never Tire of Protesting, 1968; Even the Gods Cannot Change History, 1976; The Great Thoughts, 1985; Witness To A Century, 1987. *Address:* RD 1, Box 127, Windsor, VT 05089, USA.

SELLIN Eric, b. 7 Nov 1933, Philadelphia, Pennsylvania, USA. m. 25 Jan 1958, 2 sons. *Education:* BA 1955, MA 1958, PhD, French, 1965, University of Pennsylvania. *Appointments include:* Editor, Pennsylvania Literary Review 1954-55, CELFAN Review 1981, Africana Journal 1983-87; Lecturer, Creative Writing, University of Pennsylvania, 1960-62; Professor, French Literature, Temple University, 1965-. *Publications include:* Night Voyage, 1964; Dramatic Concepts of Antonin Artaud, 1968; Borne Kilometrique, 1973; Inner Game of Soccer, 1976; Soccer Basics, 1977; Nightfall over Lubumbashi, 1983; Crepuscule prolonge a El-Biar, 1983; Night Foundering, 1985. *Contributions to:* Several hundred poems, translations, critical essays in journals, newspapers & anthologies. *Honours:* Phi Beta Kappa, 1955; Burr Book Prize, 1954; Cape Rock Quarterly Prize Poet; Fulbright-Hays senior lecturer, Algiers 1968-69, Senegal 1978-79; Senior fellowship, National Endowment for Humanities, 1973-74; Fulbright-Hays Senior Research Award, Morocco, 1988-89. *Memberships:* Modern Language Association of America; African Literature Association; Association for Study of Dada & Surrealism. *Address:* 312 Kent Road, Bala-Cynwyd, Pennsylvania 19004, USA.

SELLMAN Roger Raymond, b. 24 Sept 1915, London, England. Schoolmaster; Lecturer; Devon County Inspector of Schools (Retired). m. Minnie Coutts, 10 Aug 1938. *Education:* MA, Dip Ed, Oxford University;

PhD, Exeter University. *Publications:* Methuen's Outline Series : Castles and Fortresses 1954; The Crusades, 1955; Roman Britain, 1956; English Churches, 1956; The Vikings, 1957; Elizabethan Seamen, 1957; Prehistoric Britain, 1958; Civil War and Commonwealth, 1958; The Anglo Saxons, 1959; Ancient Egypt, 1960; Norman England, 1960; Medieval English Warfare, 1960; The First World War, 1961; The Second World War, 1964; Garibaldi and the Unification of Italy, 1973; Bismarck and the Unification of Germany, 1973; The Prairies, 1974; Historical Atlases and Textbooks: Outline Atlas of Eastern History, 1954; Outline Atlas of World History, 1970; Modern World History, 1972; Sudents Atlas of Modern History, 1973; Historical Atlas for First Examinations, 1973; Modern British Economic and Social History, 1973; Modern European History, 1974; Local History : Illustrations of Dorset History, 1960; Illustrations of Devon History, 1962; Devon Village Schools in the Nineteenth Century, 1968; Aspects of Devon History, 1985. *Contributions to:* The Victorian Contryside, 1981; The Devon Historian; Devon and Cornwall Notes and Queries. *Address:* Pound Down Corner, Whitestone, Exeter EX4 2HP, England.

SELTZER Joanne, b. 21 Nov 1929, Detroit, Michigan, USA. Poet; Writer. m. Stanley Seltzer, 10 Feb 1951, 1 son, 3 daughters. *Education:* BA, University of Michigan; MA, College of Saint Rose. *Publication:* Adirondack Lake Poems, 1985; Suburban Landscape, 1988; Inside Invisible Walls, 1989. *Contributions to:* Blueline; Waterways; The Village Voice; Small Press Review; Minnesota Review; Studia Mystica; Glens Falls Review; Poetry Now; Primavera; Earth's Daughters; The Greenfield Review; Calliope. *Honours:* Winner, Fifth Annual All Nations Contest, 1978; Honourable Mention, Robert Browning Award, World Order of Narrative Poets, 1984; 1st Place Tie, 2nd Place Tie, 2 Honourable Mentions, World Order of Narrative Poets Contest, 1986; Residency, Ragdale Foundation, 1988; World Order of Narrative Poets: 2 second place ties, 2 third place ties and 4 Honourable Mentions, 1988. *Memberships:* The Poetry Society of America; Associated Writing Programs; International Women's Writing Guild; American Literary Translators Association. *Address:* 2481 McGovern Drive, Schenectady, NY 12309, USA.

SELTZER Richard Warren Jr, b. 23 Feb 1946, Clarksville, Tennessee, USA. Writer. m. Barbara Hartley, 28 July 1973, 3 sons, 1 daughter. *Education:* BA English, Yale University, New Haven, CT, 1969; MA Comparative Literature, University of Mass., Amherst, 1972. *Publications:* The Lizard of Oz, 1974; The Name of Hero, 1981; Now and Then, 1976; Rights Crossing, 1977. *Contributions to:* What's the Word For...?, 1990; New York Medical Journal, 1989; Aspect, 1975. *Memberships:* Society of Children's Book Authors; International Association of Business Communications. *Address:* P Box 161, West Roxbury, MA 02132, USA.

SEMMLER Clement William, b. 23 Dec 1914, Eastern Well, S.A. Broadcaster; Writer. m. (div) 1 son, 1 daughter, m. Catherine Helena Wilson, 20 Dec 1974, 1 daughter. *Education:* MA, Adelaide University, 1938; D. Litt, University of New England, Armidale, 1968; Fellow, College of Fine Arts, University of NSW. *Publications:* The Banjo of the Bush, 1966; The ABC - Aunt Sally and Sacred Cow, 1981; Twentieth Century Australian Literay Criticism, (editor), 1967; Douglas Stewart, (critical study), 1974; The War Diaries of Kenneth Slessor, 1985; The War Despatches of Kenneth Slessor, 1987; For the Uncanny Man, (essays), 1963; Literary Australia, (editor), 1965; Kenneth Slessor, 1966; The Art of Brian James; 1972; Barcroft Boake, 1965; A Frank Hardy Swag, (editor), 1982; The War Diaries of Kenneth Slessor, 1985; The War Despatches of Kenneth Slessor, 1987; Pictures on the Margin (memoirs), 1991; AB 'Banjo' Paterson: Bush Ballads, Poems, Stories and Journalism (editor). *Contributions to:* The Bulletin; Quadrant; Book reviewer, The Australian; The Courier Mail. *Honours:* OBE, 1972; AM, 1988. *Membership:* Consulting Editor, Poetry Australia. *Address:* The Croft, St Clair Street, Bowral, NSW Australia 2576.

SENDAK Maurice Bernard, b. 10 June 1928. Writer, Illustrater of Children's Books; Theatrical Designer. *Publications:* Kenny's Window, 1956; Very Far Away, 1957; The Sign on Rosie's Door, 1960; Nutshell Library Set, 1962; Where the Wild Things Are, 1963; Higglety Pigglety Pop!, 1967; Hector Protector, 1967; In the Night Kitchen, 1971; (with Charlotte Zolotow) Rabbit and the Lovely Present, 1971; Pictures, 1972; Maxfield Parrish Poster Book, 1974; (with Matthelo Margolis) Some Swell Pup, 1976; Charlotte and the White Horse, 1977; Editor, Disney Poster Book, 1977; Seven Little Monsters, 1977; (with Doris Orgel) Sarah's Room, 1977; Very Far Away, 1978; Outside over There, 1981; (with Frank Corsaro), The Love for Three Oranges, 1984; (with Ralph Manheim) Nutcracker, 1984; Dear Mili, 1988; Caldecott and Company (essays), 1989; Stage Designs for The Magic Flute, Houston, 1980, The Cunning Little Vixen, New York, 1981, The Love of Three Oranges, Glyndebourne, 1982, Where The Wild Things Are, 1984. *Address:* c/o Harper & Row, 10 East 53rd Street, New York, NY 10022, USA.

SENGUPTA Preety, b. 17 May 1944, Lahmedabad, India. Traveller by Religion; Writer; Poet. m. Chandan Sengupta, 21 June 1975. *Education:* Masters in English Literature. *Appointments:* Teacher English Literature, India, 1968; Secretary of Tagoe Society, NY, 1973-80. *Publications:* Poorva; Dikdigant; Khandit Aakash; Sooraj Sanĝe Dakshin Panthe; Gha Thi Door na Gha; Antim Kslitijo; Dhaval Aalok Dliaval Andhar; O Juliet; Joy of Travelling Alone. *Contributions to:* Kuma; Nireekshak; Kavita; Kavilok; Janmabhoomi Pravasi; Gujarat Mitra; Pen India; Skylark; Indian Express. *Honours:* Highest Literary Award in Gujarat. *Memberships:* Poetry Society of America; Pen of India. *Address:* 15 Stewart Place, White Plains, NY 10603, USA.

SENNETT Richard, b. 1 Jan 1943, Chicago, Illinois, USA, Professor; Writer. *Education:* BA, summa cum laude, University of Chicago, 1964; PhD, Harvard University, 1969. *Appointment:* Vice President, Penn American Centre, 1978-82. *Publications:* Palais-Royal, 1986; Fall of Public Man, 1977; Authority, 1980; Hidden Injuries of Class, 1972; An Evening of Brahms, 1984; The Uses of Disorder, 1970; Families Against the City, 1970; The Frog Who Dared to Croak, 1982; Conscience of the Eye, 1990. *Contributions to:* New Yorker; Times Literary Supplement; New York Review of Books; Telquel; The Spectator; Corrierer delle Serre. *Honours:* Guggenheim Foundation, 1973; Ingram-Merril Award for Fiction, 1984. *Memberships:* Penn American Centre, 1977-, Vice President, 1978-82. *Literary Agent:* Lynn Nesbit. *Address:* 44 Washington Square Mews, New York, NY 10003, USA.

SEQUEIRA Isaac J. F, b. 5 Jan 1930, Hyderabad, India. University Professor. *Education:* BA 1955; MA 1958; PhD, 1970, Utah. *Publications:* The Theme of Initiation in Modern American Fiction, 1975; A Manifesto for Humour, 1985; Popular Culture: East and West, 1991; Studies in American Literature, 1991; Viewpoints USA, 1992. *Contributions to:* Research journals in USA, Korea and India. *Honours:* Seaton Scholar, 1947; Fulbright Smith-Mundt Fellow, 1966; American Council of Learned Societies Fellow, 1979; UGC National Lecturer, 1983, Professor Emeritus, 1991. *Memberships:* Modern Language Association, USA; Indian Association of American Studies; American Studies Association, USA; President: Poetry Society, 1975-80, Dramatic Circle, 1980-, Hyderabad. *Address:* Senior Academic Fellow, American Studies Research Centre, ASRC Hyderabad 500007, AP India.

SERLING Robert J, b. 1918, United States of America. Author. *Publications:* The Probable Cause, 1960; The Electra Story, 1962; The Left Seat, 1964; The President's Plane Is Missing, 1967; The Newsman and Air Accidents, 1967; Loud and Clear, 1969; She'll Never Get Off the Ground, 1971; Ceiling Unlimited, 1973; The Only Way to Fly: The Story of Western Airlines, 1976; McDermott's Sky, 1977; Wings, 1978; From the Captain to the Colonel, 1980; The Jet Age, 1982; Eagle: The History of American Airlines, 1985;

Air Force 1 is Haunted, 1985. *Address:* c/o Doubleday & Co. Inc., 245 Park Avenue, New York, NY 10017, USA.

SERRAILLIER Ian (Lucien), b. 1912, British, Writer of children's fiction, poetry, children's non-fiction. *Publications:* (co-author) Three New Poets, 1942; The Weaver Birds, 1944; Thomas and the Sparrow, 1946, 1951; They Raced for Treasure, 1946, as Treasure Ahead, 1954; Flight to Adventure, 1947, as Mountain Rescue 1955; Captain Bounsaboard and the Pirates, 1949; The Monster Horse, 1950; There's No Escape, 1950, 1973; The Ballad of Kon-Tiki, 1952; Belinda and the Swans, 1952; Jungle Adventure, 1953, 1956; The Adventures of Dick Varley, 1954, 1956; Beowulf the Warrior, 1954; Making Good, 1955, 1956; Everest Climbed, 1955; Guns in the Wild, 1956; The Silver Sword, 1956, reissued in US as Escape from Warsaw, 1963; Katy at Home, 1957; Poems and Pictures, 1958; (co-author) A Puffin Quartet of Poets, 1958, revised edition, 1964; Katy at School, 1959; The Ivory Horn, 1960, 1962; The Gorgon's Head, 1961; The Windmill Book of Ballads, 1962; The Way of Danger, 1962, 1965; Happily Ever After, 1963; The Clashing Rocks, 1963, 1971; The Midnight Thief, 1963; The Enchanted Island, 1964 (in US as Murder in Dunsinane, 1967); The Cave of Death, 1965; Fight for Freedom, 1965; Ahmet the Woodseller, 1965; A Fall From the Sky, 1966; The Challenge of the Green Knight, 1966; Robin in the Greenwood, 1967, in USA; Chaucer and his World, 1967; The Turtle Drum, 1967, 1968; Havelok the Dane, (USA 1967), in UK as Havelok the Warrior, 1968; Robin and His Merry Men, 1969 (USA 1970); The Tale of Three Landlubbers, 1970 (USA 1971); Heracles the Strong (USA), 1970; The Ballad of St Simeon, 1970; A Pride of Lions, 1971; The Bishop and the Devil, 1971; Have You Got Your Ticket? 1972; Marko's Wedding, 1972; I'll Tell You a Tale, 1973, 1976; Pop Festival, 1973; Suppose You Met a Witch (USA), 1974; The Robin and the Wren, 1974; How Happily She Laughs, 1976; The Sun Goes Free, 1977; The Road to Canterbury, 1979; All Change at Singleton, 1979; (co-author) Goodwood Country in Old Photographs, 1987. *Address:* Singleton, Chichester, Sussex, England.

SERRANO Miguel Juaquin Diego del Carmen, b. 10 Sept 1917, Santiago, Chile. Weiter; Retired Ambassador. m. Carmen Rosselot Bourdie, 1944, 2 sons, 1 daughter. *Education:* Internado Nacional Barros Arana, 1929- 34. *Publications:* C G Jung and Hermann Hesse, A Record of two Friendships, 1966; The Serpent of Paradise, 1963; Nos Book of Ressurrection, 1984; El/Ella Book of Magic Love, 1972; The Ultimate Flower, 1970; The Visits of the Queen of Sheba, 1972; Ni por mar ni por tierra, 1950; Nietzsche y el eterno Retorno, 1974. *Contributions to:* El Mercurio; La Prensa de Buenos Aires; The Hindustan Times Weekly. *Honours:* Municipalidad de Santiago, 1953. *Literary Agent:* Mohrbooks Rainer Heuman, Kloshachstr, 110 8032, Zurich; Brondt & Brondt 1501 Broadway, NY 10036. *Address:* Casilla 3540, Correo Central, Santiago, Chile.

SERVADIO Gaia Cecilia, b. 13 Sept 1938, Padoua. Writer; Journalist. 2 sons, 1 daughter. *Education:* St Martin's School of Art, London, England; National Diploma, Graphic Art. *Appointments:* Associazione Italiana Lecturer, 1970; Manchester Museum Lecture, 1982; Consultant Editor, Editore, Italy, 1987; Director of Debates and Literary Talks, Accademia Italiana, 1988-89. *Publications:* Melinda, 1968; Don Juan/Salome, 1969; Il Metodo, 1970; Mafioso, 1972; A Siberian Encounter, 1973; Luchino Visconti a Biography, 1985; A Profile of a Mafia Boss; Insider Outsider, 1986; To a Diffferent World; La donna nel Rinascimento; Il Lamento di Arianna, 1987; Una infanzia diversa, 1988; La storia di R, 1990; La Vallata, 1991. *Contributions to:* Arts Correspondent: Il Corriere della Sera. *Honour:* Cavaliere Ufficiale della Republica Italiana, 1980. *Memberships:* Society of Authors; Foreign Press Association, Vice President 1974-79; London Symphony Orchestra, Executive Committee, 1980-87; Mahler Festival, 1982-83. *Literay Agent:* Artellus, 30 Donet House, Gloucester Place, London NW1 5AD, England.

Address: 31 Bloomfield Terrace, London SW1 W8PQ, England.

SERVICE Alastair Stanley Douglas, b. 8 May 1933. m. (1) Louisa Anne Hemming, 28 Feb 1959, div 1983, 1 son, 1 daughter; (2) Zandria Madeleine Pauncefort, 21 Feb 1992. *Education:* Modern History, Queen's College, Oxford 1953-55. *Publications:* Edwardian Architecture, 1977; Architects of London: 1066 to Today, 1979; Anglo-Saxon and Norman Buildings - A Guide, 1981; The Megaliths of Europe - A Guide, 1979; Lost Worlds, 1980; Edwardian Interiors, 1981; London, 1900, 1978; A Birth Control Plan for Britain, 1972; Victorian/Edwardian Hampstead, 1990; Edwardian Architecture and its Origins, 1975; Standing Stones of Europe: the great Neolithic monuments, 1993. *Contributions to:* The Guardian; Architectural Review; New Statesman; Architects Journal. *Memberships:* Society of Architectural Historians of GB; The Victorian Society; Family Planning Association, National Chairmam, 1975-80; Health Education Authority, V-Chairman, 1978-89-; Wessex Region Health Authority, V-Chairman, 1992-; Wiltshire & Bath Health Commission, Chairman 1993-. *Literary Agent:* Caroline Dawnay, peters, Fraser and Dunlop. *Address:* Swan House, Avebury, Wilts SN8 1RA, England.

SETH-SMITH Leslie James (James Brabazon), b. 1923, United Kingdom. Freelance Film and Television Writer and Producer. *Appointments:* Actor, 1946-54; Advertising Copywriter, 1954-58; Story Editor, 1963-68; Drama Director, 1969, BBC Television; Drama Producer, Granada Television Ltd, 1970-74, 1978-82; Drama Producer, London Weekend Television Ltd, 1976-77. *Publications:* People of Nowhere, play, 1959; Albert Schweitzer, 1975; Dorothy L Sayers, 1981. *Address:* 36 Kingswood Road, Chiswick, London W4 5ET, England.

SETHI Robbie Clipper, b. 13 Aug 1951, Camden, New Jersey, USA. Professor. m. Davinder Pal Singh Sethi, 24 Oct 1976, 1 son. *Education:* Ba English and Slavic Languages and Literatures, Indiana University, 1973; MA Comparative Literature, University of Califronia, 1975; PhD, 1981. *Appointments:* Assistant Professor of English, Creative Writing, 1986- 88; Associate Professor of English, (Creative Writing Literature and Russian), 1988-. *Contributions to:* Atlantic, 1991; Mademoiselle, 1987; Grazia, 1987; The Literary Review, 1988; Crescent Review, 1987; Boulevard, 1987; Alaska Quarterly Review, 1992; USI Worksheets, 1992; Ascent, 1992; California Quarterly, 1992; The New Review, 1992; Massachusetts Review, 1993; Russian Literature, 1983. *Honours:* Phi Beta Kappa; National Defense Fellowship, 1982; New Jersey State Council on the Arts Fellowships, 1987, 1991. *Memberships:* New Jersey College English Association, Trustee, 1987-91; Northeast Modern Language Association; Associated Writing Programs. *Literary Agent:* Kimberly Witherspoon, Witherspoon & Chernoff Assoc. *Address:* English Department, Rider College, 2083 Lawrenceville Road, Lawrenville, NJ 08648, USA.

SEVERANCE Carol Ann Wilcox, b. 15 Feb 1944, USA. Writer. m. Craig J Severance, 1968, 1 son, 1 daughter. *Education:* BA Art, 1966; MA Journalism, 1975. *Publications:* Reefsong, 1991; Demon Drums: Book One of Island Warrior Trilogy, 1992; Storm Caller: Bok Two of Island Warrior Trilogy, 1993; Sorcerous Sea: Book Three of Island Warrior Trilogy, 1993; Day of Strange Fortune, in Magic in Ithkar, 1987; Isle of Illusion, in Tales of the Witch World, Vol 1, 1987; Whispering Cane, in Tales of the Witch World, Vol 3, 1990. *Contributions to:* Dragon Magazine, 1988. *Honours:* Grand Prize, Hilo Community Players Playwriting Contest, 1989; Compton Crook/Stephen Tall Memorial Award for Best First Novel, 1991. *Memberships:* Science Fiction and Fantasy Writers of American; Clarion West. *Address:* Hilo, HI 96720, USA.

SEVERIN Giles Timothy, b. 25 Sept 1940, Jorhat, Assam. Author. *Publications:* Tracking Marco Polo,

1964; Explorers of the Mississippi, 1967; The Brendan Voyage, 1978; The Sinbad Voyage, 1982; The Jason Voyage, 1985; The Ulysses Voyage, 1987; The Golden Antilles; Vanishing Primitive Man; The African Adventure; The Oriental Adventure; Crusader, 1989; In Search of Genghis Khan, 1991. *Honours:* Book of the Sea Award, 1979, 1983; Thomas Cook Book Prize, 1984; Founders Medal, Royal Geographical Society, 1986; Livingstone Medal, Royal Scottish Geographical Society. *Literary Agent:* Anthony Shiel Associates, London. *Address:* The Moorings, Courtmacsherry, Co Cork, Ireland.

SEWART Alan (Padder Nash), b. 26 Aug 1928, Bolton, Lancashire, England. Writer. m. Dorothy Teresa Humphreys, 13 Oct 1962, 2 sons, 1 daughter. *Education:* LLB, University of London. *Publications include:* Tough Tontine, 1978; A Ribbon for My Repute, 1978; The Salome Syndrome, 1979; The Women of Morning, 1980; In That Rich Earth, 1981; Smoker's Cough, 1982; Death Game - Five Players, 1982; If I Should Die, 1983; Dead Man Drifting, 1984; The Educating of Quinton Quinn, 1984. Non-fiction: Murder in Lancashire, 1988; Leisure Guides, Lancashire (with Dorothy Sewart), 1989. As Alan Sewart Well: Mr Crumblestone's Eden, 1980; Where Lionel Lies, 1984; Candice is Dead, 1984, As Padder Nash: Grass, 1983; Coup de Grass, 1983; Wayward Seeds of Grass, 1983; Grass and Supergrass, 1984. Others in press. *Contributions to:* Police Review. *Membership:* Crime Writers Association. *Address:* 7 Knott Lane, Easingwold, York YO6 3LX, England.

SEWELL Brocard, b. 30 July 1912, Bangkok, Thailand. Clerk in Holy Orders. *Education:* Weymouth College, Dorset, England, 1922-28; Theological Colleges: St Edmund's, Ware, England; Liege, Belgium, Rome, Italy, 1950-54. *Appointments:* Editorial Assistant, G K's Weekly, England, 1928-31; Editorial Assistant, St Dominic's Press, Ditchling, 1932-37; Editor, The Aylesford Review, 1955-68; Director, St Albert's Press, Aylesford, 1955- 68; Editor, The Antigonish Review, Canada, 1969-72. *Publications:* My Dear Time's Waste, autobiography, 1966; Footnote to the Nineties, 1966; The Vatican Oracle, critique of the Papacy, 1970; Cecil Chesterton, 1975; Olive Custance, her life and work, 1975; Three Private Presses, printing history, 1979; Like Black Swans, some people and themes, 1982; In the Dorian Mode: A Life of John Gray, 1983; Cancel All Our Vows, biography of J Gardner, 1988; G K's Weekly: An Appraisal, 1990. *Contributions to:* G K's Weekly; Blackfriars; The Tablet; Aylesford Review; Antigonish Review; Lodestar. *Honour:* The Mrs Anne Radcliffe Award, The Dracula Society, Los Angeles, 1966. *Memberships:* Vice-President, The Henry Williamson Society; The Sheila Kaye-Smith Society; Royal Society of Arts. *Address:* Whitefriars, Tanners Street, Faversham, Kent ME13 7JW, England.

SEWELL Elizabeth, b. 9 Mar 1919, Coonoor, India. Writer; Lecturer. *Education:* Cambridge University, BA, 1942; MA, 1945; PhD, 1949. *Publications:* The Orphic Voice; The Field of Nonsense; Paul Valery: The Mind in the Mirror; An Idea; The Structure of Poetry; The Dividing of Time; The Singular Hope; Now Bless Thyself. *Contributions to:* USA, Canada, England, France, Austria, Netherlands. *Honours:* Honorary Degree, Various American Colleges & Universities; National Award; Zoe Kincaid Brookman Award. *Memberships:* PEN; Lewis Carroll Society of North America; National Writers Union; North Carolina Writers Network. *Literary Agent:* Harold Ober Associates Inc, New York. *Address:* 854 West Bessemer Avenue, Greensboro, NC 27408, USA.

SEYERSTED Per, b. 18 May 1921, Oslo, Norway. University Professor. *Education:* MA, Harvard, USA, 1959; Dr philos, Oslo, 1969. *Appointments:* Chair, American Literature, University of Oslo, 1973-1991; Member, Editorial Committee, Norway-America Association Yearbook, 1980-; Associate Editor, Southern Studies, 1980-; Associate Editor, Studies in American Fiction, 1985-. *Publications:* Gilgamesj, 1967, 1979, 1988; Kate Chopin: A Critical Biography, 1969,

1980, 1990; The Complete Works of Kate Chopin (editor), 1969, 1981; A Kate Chopin Miscellany (editor), 1979; Leslie Marmon Silko, 1980; Scando-Americana: Papers on Scandinavian Emigration to the United States (editor), 1980; Dakky Kiaer (editor), 1980; From Norwegian Romantic to American Realist: Studies in the Life and Writings of Hjalmar Hjorth Boyesen, 1984; The Artic: Canada and the Nordic Countries (editor), 1991. *Contributions to:* Some 40 articles to 25 journals including The Indian in Knickerbocker's New Amsterdam, in the Indian Historian, 1974. *Honours:* Fellow, American Council of Learned Societies, 1964-66; Fellow, Norwegian Research Council for Science and Letters, 1966-69. *Memberships:* Norsk faglitteraer forfatterforening; Modern Languauge Association; Elected Member, Norwegian Academy for Science and Letters, Chairman, Literature Section; Nordic Association for American Studies, President 1973-79; Nordic Association for Canadian Studies, Vice President, 1984-93. *Address:* Department of British and American Studies, University of Oslo, PB 1003, Norway.

SEYMOUR-SMITH Martin, b. 1928, United Kingdom. Author. *Appointments:* Schoolmaster, 1954-60; Editorial Assistant, The London Magazine, 1955-56; Poetry Editor, Truth magazine, London, 1955-57, The Scotsman, Edinburgh, 1964-66; Literary Adviser, Hodder & Stoughton, London, 1963-65; General Editor, Gollancz Classics series, Victor Gollancz Ltd, London, 1967-69. *Publications:* Poems (with R Taylor and T Hards), 1952; (Poems), 1953; Poetry from Oxford (editor), 1953; All Devils Fading, 1954; Robert Graves, 1956, 1970; Shakespeare's Sonnets (editor), 1963; Tea with Miss Stockport: 24 Poems, 1963; A Cupful of Tears: Sixteen Victorian Novelettes (editor), 1965; Bluff Your Way in Literature, 1966, 1972; Every Man in His Humour, by Ben Jonson (editor), 1966, 1983; A New Canon of English Poetry (edited with J Reeves), 1967; Fallen Women: A Sceptical Inquiry into the Treatment of Prostitutes, Their Clients, and Their Pimps in Literature, 1969; Poets Through Their Letters, 1969; The Poems of Andrew Marvell (edited with J Reeves), 1969; Longer Elizabethan Poems (editor), 1970; Inside Poetry (with J Reeves), 1970; Reminiscences of Norma: Poems 1963-1970, 1971; Guide to Modern World Literature, in US Funk and Wagnalls' Guide to World Literature, 1973, 3rd rewritten edition as Macmillan Guide to Modern World Literature, 1986; Sex and Society, 1975; Who's Who in Twentieth-Century Literature, 1976; The English Sermon 1550-1650 (editor), 1976; Selected Poems, by Walt Whitman (editor), 1976; The Mayor of Casterbridge, by Thomas Hardy (editor), 1979; Fifty European Novels, 1979; Novels and Novelists, 1980; The New Astrologer, 1981; Robert Graves: His Life and Work, 1982; Nostromo, by Conrad (editor), 1983; The Nigger of the Harcissus, (editor), 1990; The Secret Agent, by Conrad (editor), 1984; Rudyard Kipling, 1989, revised, 1990; The Dent Dictionary of Literary Characters 1991; From Bad to Verse (editor), 1992; Handy, 1993. *Address:* 36 Holliers Hill, Bexhill-on-Sea, Sussex TN40 2DD, England.

SFAELLOU Calliope, b. 26 Nov 1912, Alexandria, Egypt. Journalist; Author. *Publications:* Novels: Memories of a Cat, 1971; The King and the Shepherd, 1967; For his Father, 1981; The Lion Cub, 1966; The Treasure of Nafpoctos, 1976; Children of the Resistance, 1979; (Stories) Symbols and Facts, 1977; Essays: Cavafi the Greek, 1978; The Ode to the Lost Lieutenant of Elytis, 1983; The Woman in The Works of Carcavitsa, 1981. *Contributions to:* many magazines and journals including: Estia; Woman. *Honours:* Awards, Literary Company of Women, 1966, 1968; Circle of Childen's Books Awards, 1971, 1978, 1979; IBBY, 1971. *Memberships:* National Society of Literature; Circle of Childrens Books; Union of Journalists. *Address:* Valtetsiou Street No. 40, Athens 106-81, Greece.

SH Shani. See: SHRIRA Shoshaira.

SHAABAN Bouthaina, b. 1 Apr 1953, Syria. University Professor. m. Khalil Jawad, 2 Sept 1981, 2 daughters. *Education:* BA, English Literature, Damascus

University, Syria, 1975; MA, English Literature, Warwick University, England, 1978; PhD, English Literature, Warwick University, England, 1982. *Appointments:* Lecturer, Constantine University, Algeria, 1982-84; Damascus University, Syria, 1985-90; Fullbright Professor, Duke University, USA, 1990-91; Associate Professor, Damascus University, Syria, 1991-. *Publications:* Both Right and Left-Handed, Arab Women Talk About Their Lives, London, 1988, USA, 1991; Poetry and Politics; Shelly and the Charvist Movement, (Arabic), Dartalas, Damascus, 1993. *Contributions to:* Keats-Shelly, Journal; Al maw Kif Al Adabi; Al Nashir al-Arabi. *Honours:* Fulbright, Duke University, 1990-91; Rockefeller, Rice University, 1992-93. *Memberships:* Keats-Shelley Society; FIT, Arab Writers Union. *Address:* Arab Writers Union, Damascus, PO Box 3230, Syria.

SHAFFER Karen Alice, b. 12 Oct 1947, Dayton, Ohio, USA. Lawyer; Writer; Educator. *Education:* BA, International Relations, 1969, JD, 1972, International Relations, 1969. *Publications:* Maud Powell, Pioneer American Violinist, 1988. *Contributions to:* The New Grove Dictionary of American Music; Journal of Violin Society of America, 1987; The Strad. *Memberships:* DC and Virginia Bars; National Academy of Science's Committee on the Disposal of Excess Spoil, 1980-81; American Bar Association; Founder & President, The Maud Powell Foundation, 1986-; Co-Founder, The Writer's Workshop, 1992-. *Address:* 5333 N 26th Street, Arlington, VA 22207, USA.

SHAFFER Peter Levin (Peter Anthony), b. 15 May 1926, Liverpool, England. Playwright. *Education:* BA, Trinity College, Cambridge, 1947-50. *Appointments:* With Acquisition Department, New York Public Library, 1951-54; Boose & Hawkes, Music Publishers, 1954-55; Literary Critic, Truth, 1956-57; Music Critic, Time and Tide, 1961-62. *Publications:* Plays: Five Finger Exercise, 1958; The Private Ear and The Public Eye, 1962; The Royal Hunt of the Sun, 1964; Black Comedy, 1965; White Lies, 1967; Shrivings, 1970; Equus, 1973; Amadeus, 1979; The Collected Plays of Peter Shaffer, 1982; Yonadab, 1985; Lettice and Lovage, 1987; Whom Do I Have The Honour of Addressing radio play, 1990; The Gift of Gorgon, 1992. *Honours:* Standard Drama Award, 1958, 1979; Antoinette Perry Award, 1975, 1981; New York Drama Critics Award, 1960, 1975; Academy Award (Oscar), 1984; CBE, 1987; Hamburg Shakespeare Prize, 1987; William Inge Award for Distinguished Contribution to American Theatre, 1992. *Address:* c/o London Management, 235 Regent Street, London, W1A 2JT, England.

SHAH Idries, b. 16 June 1924, Author. *Appointments:* Director, Institute for Cultural Research, 1966; Adviser, Harcourt Brace Jovanovich publishers, USA, 1975-79. *Publications include:* Oriental Magic, 1956; Destination Mecca, 1957; The Sufis, 1964; Exploits of the Incomparable Mulls Nasrudin, 1966; Tales of the Dervishes, 1967; Caravan of Dreams, 1968; The Book of the Book, 1969; The Dermis Probe, 1970; Ten Texts, 1971; The Magic Monastery, 1972; Subtleties of the Inimitable Mulla Nasrudin, 1973; The Elephant in the Dark, 1974; Neglected Aspects of Sufi Study, 1977; The Hundred Tales of Wisdom, 1978; World Tales, 1979; Letters and Lectures, 1981; Seeker After Truth, 1982; Kara Kush, 1986; Darkest England, 1987. *Honours:* 5 First Prizes, UNESCO World Book Year, 1972; Gold Medal, Distinguished Services to Poetry, 1973; Award for Outstanding Contributions to Human Thought, USA, 1975. *Memberships:* Society of Authors; PEN; London Authors Club. *Literary Agent:* A P Watt Limited; Jonathan Clowes Limited. *Address:* P O Box 457, London NW2 4BR, England.

SHAH Tahir, b. 16 Nov 1966, London, England. Author. *Education:* BA International Relations, US International University. *Publications:* Monographs: The Development and Collapse of Gond Society; Secret Societies of Sierra Leone; Mariscos and the Demise of the Arab Empire in Spain; Private International Law: The Conflict of Law; Macumba: African-based religions in South America; The Ainu: First People of Japan; The Kafirs of Kafiristan; The Celtic Druids. *Contributions to:* International Press. *Literary Agent:* Curtis Brown. *Address:* PO Box 2227, London NW2 3BP, England.

SHAHEEN Jack G, b. 21 Sept 1935, Pittsburgh, Pennsylvania, USA. Professor; Journalist. m. Bernice Marie, 22 Jan 1966, 1 son, 1 daughter. *Education:* BFA, Carnegie Institute of Technology, 1957; MA Pennsylvania State University, 1964; PhD University of Missouri, 1967. *Appointments:* Reporter, KMOU-TV, 1968; Arts Critic, WSIE Radio, 1970- 85. *Publications:* The TV Arab, 1984; Nuclear War Films, 1978. *Contributions to:* The Wall Street Journal, Newsweek; The Washington Post; The Los Angeles Time; Journal of Popular Film and Television; Journal of Popular Culture; The Television Quarterly. *Honours:* Outstanding book of the year, Choice Magazine, 1984; Scholar-Diplomat, Department ofState, 1978; Fulbright Scholar, 1974, 1981. *Literary Agent:* James C G Conniff, Megadot. *Address:* 1526 Weber Lane Edwardsville, IL, 62025, USA.

SHAHI Akhilesh Kumar, b. 16 Sept 1943, Tari, Behar, India. Writer; Journalist; Publisher. m. Jyoti Shahi, 3 Feb 1991, 1 son. *Appointments:* Editor, Roti, 1965-66; Founder, Managing Editor, Press Service of India, Patna, 1970-. *Publications:* Hindi novels: Zinda Murda, 1964-65; Chameli Ke Phool, 1969; Dekha Desh Samovcha, 1973; Meenpash, 1975; Poetry: Krantigeet, 1972; Shahika, 1973; Thirty Love Poems, 1985; The Autobiography of an Empress, 1992; Krasti Korisi Hos, 1972; Living Like a Muslim, narrative, 1973; Netaji Mare Gaye, biography, 1973; Several tracts, Revolutionary Papers; Others. *Contributions to:* Several publications. *Memberships:* Life Member: PEN All India Centre; Indian Institute of Public Administration; Youth Hostel Association of India. *Address:* 6C Rajendra Nagar, Patna 800016, India.

SHAIN Merle, b. 14 Oct 1935, Toronto, Canada. Writer. 1 son. *Education:* BA1957, BSW 1959, University of Toronto. *Publications:* Some Men are More Perfect than Others, 1973; When Lovers Are Friends, 1978; Hearts that We Broke Long Ago, 1983; Courage My Love, 1988. *Contributions to:* Columnist for The Sun; Feature Writer, Toronto Telegram; Associated Editor, Chatelaine Magazine; Book Critic, Globe Mail. *Honours:* Trustee, National Film Board, 1981-. *Memberships:* ACTRA; Writers Guild of Canada; Writers Union of Canada. *Address:* 50 Chestnut Park Road, Toronto, Ontario, M4W 1W8, Canada.

SHAIN Yossi, b. 21 Sept 1956, Israel. Professor of Political Science. m. Nancy Schnog, 7 June 1987, 1 son. *Education:* BA, 1981, MA, 1983, Tel Aviv University; MPhil and MA, 1985, PhD, 1988, Yale University. *Publications:* Frontier of Loyalty, 1989; Governments in Exile in Contemporary World Politics, 1991. *Contributions to:* Government and Opposition, Comparative Politics, Journal of Democracy, Co-Existance Conflict, Journal of Political Science. *Honours:* Danish Government Special Award, 1982; Yale Award, 1986; Breadly Foundation, 1988; Israeli Distinguished Scholar, 1989; Helen Dwight Reed Award, American Political Science Association, 1989; International Fulbright, 1992. *Memberships:* American and International Political Science Associations; International Studies Association. *Address:* Tel Aviv University, Department of Political Science, Ramat Aviv, Israel.

SHAMIR Moshe, b. 15 Sept 1921, Safed, Israel. Author. m. Zvia Frumkin, 6 June 1946, 1 son, 2 daughters. *Appointments:* Founder, First Editor, Bamachane, Israel Army Weekly, 1948; Editor, Maariv Daily Papers, Literary Supplement, 1973-77. *Publications:* He Walked in the Fields, 1948; With His Own Hands, 1952; The King of Flesh & Blood, 1954; From a Different Yard, 1973; The Bridal Veil, 1986; My Life with Ishmael (non-fiction), 1968; Under the Sun, 1950; David's Stranger, 1956; That You Are Naked,

1958; The Border, 1963; Far From Rubies, a 3 volume trilogy novel, 1973, 1984, and 1991; 5 volumes of collected essays; Plays: 15 full length, 6 one-act (all performed). *Contributions to:* various literary magazines and journals. *Honours:* Ussishkin Prize, 1948; Brenner Prize, 1953; Bialik Prize, 1955; Newman Prize, 1981; Baratz-Govinska Prize for Drama, 1982; Israel's Prize for Literature, 1988. *Memberships:* Hebrew Writers Association; ACUM. *Address:* 3 Rosanis Street, Tel Aviv 69018, Israel.

SHANE John. *See:* **DURST Paul.**

SHANKARANARAYANA RAO Kydala Ramaswamy, b. 23 June 1941, Bangalore, India. Joint Labour Commissioner. m. S Pramila, 31 May 1972, 1 daughter. *Education:* Karnataha University, 1966; Calcutta University, 1977; Bangalore University, 1980; Mysore University, 1984. *Appointments:* indian Air Force, Civilian store Keeper, 1960-70; Department of Labour Government of Karnataha, 1970-. *Publications:* Udyoga Mathu Vrithi Kushalatheya Abhividdhi; Editorial Board Member for Badaganadu Brahmanara Itihasa. *Contributions to:* Mythic Society Journal. *Memberships:* Kannada Sahilya Parishath; Karnataka Lekhakara Sangha; Bangalore Gayana Samaja; Malleswaram Sangetha Sabha. *Address:* 21/3 4th Cross Magadi Road, Bangalore 500023, Karnataka State, India.

SHANNON Doris, b. 7 Aug 1924, Elmira, New York, USA. Housewife. m. 1 Aug 1947, 2 daughters. *Education:* Graduate, Napanee Collegiate Institute. *Publications:* Hawthorn Hill, 1976; Cain's Daughters, 1978; Beyond the Shining Mountains, 1979; The Punishment, 1980; Little Girls Lost, 1983; Family Money, 1984; Series of mysteries featuring Robert Forsythe (as E X Giroux) including: A Death for a Dreamer, 1989; A Death for a Double, 1990. *Address:* 10580 154A Street, Lunrey, British Columbia, Canada V3R 8N4.

SHAPIRO Harvey, b. 27 Jan 1924, Chicago, Illinois, USA. Poet; Journalist. m. Edna Kaufman, 23 July 1953, 2 sons. *Education:* BA, Yale University, 1947; MA, Columbia University, 1949. *Publications:* Poetry: The Eye, 1953; Mountain, Fire, Thornbush, 1961; Battle Report, 1966; This World, 1971; Lauds & Nightsounds, 1978; The Light Holds, 1984; National Cold Storage Company: New Selected poems, 1988. *Address:* 43 Pierrepont Street, Brooklyn, NY 11201, USA.

SHAPIRO Karl, b. 10 Nov 1913, Baltimore, Maryland, USA, Poet. m. (1) Evelyn Katz, 1945, (div 1967), (2) Teri Kovach, 1967, (3) Sophie Wilkins, 1985. *Education:* University of Virginia, 1932-33; Johns Hopkins University, 1937-39; Pratt Library School, Baltimore, 1940. *Appointments:* Consultant in Poetry, Library of Congress, 1946-47; Associate Professor of English, Johns Hopkins University, 1947-50; Lecturer, Salzburg Seminary in American Studies, 1952; Editor, Poetry Chicago, 1950-1955; Visiting Professor of English, University of California, Berkeley and Davis and University of Indiana, Bloomington, 1955-57; Professor of English, University of Nebraska, 1956-66; Editor, Prairie Schooner, 1956-66; Professor of English, University of Illinois, Chicago Circle, 1966-68; Professor of English, University of California, Davis, 1968-; Editorial Board, The California Quarterly, 1971-. *Publications include:* Poems, 1935; Five Young American Poets, 1941; V-Letter and Other Poems, 1944; Essay on Rime, 1945; Trial of a Poet and Other Poems, 1947; Poems 1940-1953, 1953; Poems of a Jew, 1958; The Bourgeois Poet, 1964; To Abolish Children and Other Essays, 1968; White-Haired Lover, 1968; Edsel, 1971; Love and War/Art and God, 1984; New and Selected Poems 1940-1986, 1987; The Younger Son, memoir, 1988; Reports of My Death, memoir, 1990. *Contributions to:* Numerous anthologies. magazines and journals. *Honours include:* Levinson Prize, Poetry Magazine, 1943; Pulitzer Prize for Poetry, 1945; Guggenheim Fellow, 1945-46; Eunice Tietjens Memorial Prize, Poetry magazine, 1961; Bollingen Prize

for Poetry, 1969; Hart Crane Memorial Poetry Contest, 1976. *Address:* 211 West 106 Street 11-C, New York, NY 10025, USA.

SHARAT Chandra G S, (Jean Parker), b. 3 May 1938, India. Professor of English and Creative Writing. m. Jane Ronnermann, 1966, 1 son, 2 daughters. *Education:* AB, LLB, University of Mysore, India; MS, SUNY, NY; LLM, University of Toronto, Canada; MFA, University of Iowa, USA. *Appointments:* Editor: Kamadhenu, 1970-75; South Asian Review, 1989-; Consultant, Centre for Research in New Literatures in English, Flinders University, Australia. *Publications:* Immigrants of Loss, 1992; Heirloom, 1982; Once or Twice, 1974; April in Nanjangud, 1971; The Ghost of Meaning, 1978; Bharata natyam Dancer, 1968. *Contributions to:* London Magazine, Stand, Encounter, Outposts, New Welsh Review, New York Quarterly, Poetry, Iowa Review, Poet and Critic, Poetry Australia, Paris Review. *Honours:* NEH Fellow, 1981; Florida State Poetry Award, 1980; Distinguished Visiting Professor, Poetry/Fiction, Purdue University, 1985, University of Hawaii, 1987. *Memberships:* Modern language Association; Associated Writing Programme; South Asian Language Association. *Address:* Department of English, University of Missouri, Kansas City, MO 64110, USA.

SHARKEY Jack (Rick Abbot, Monk Ferris, Mike Johnson, Mark Chandler), b. 6 May 1931, Chicago, Illinois, USA, Author; Playwright; Lyricist; Composer. m. Patricia Walsh, 14 July 1962, 1 son 3 daughters. *Education:* BA, English and Creative Writing, St Mary's College, Winona, Minnesota, 1953. *Publications:* Several hundred short stories, 7 novels and about 78 published plays. As Jack Sharkey writes broad comedies and thrillers, as Rick Abbot writes subtle comedies and musicals; as Monk Ferris writes zany comedies and musicals; as Mike Johnson writes terrifying thrillers; as Mark Chandler writes silly thrillers. Works include: Death for Auld Lang Syne (novel); While the Lights Were Out (mystery-comedy); The Perfect Murder (thriller) as Mike Johnson; Dracula: The Musical? (musical) as Rick Abbot; Hamlet, Cha-Cha-Cha! (musical) as Monk Ferris; The Premature Corpse (thriller) as Mike Johnson; I Shot My Rich Aunt (silly thriller) as Mark Chandler. *Contributions to:* Wide variety of short stories, humour pieces and comical essays in every level of magazine in the USA. *Honours:* Best Editorial of 1967 awarded by American Association of Industrial Editors for an editorial entitled Stop or I'll Shoot, Unless We're in a Hospital Zone. *Memberships:* Dramatists Guild; Writers League of America; Nu Delta Chapter of Alpha Psi Omega Dramatic Fraternity. *Literary Agent:* M Abbott Van Nostrand of Samuel French, Inc. *Address:* Southern California, USA.

SHARKEY Olive Margaret, b. 18 Dec 1954, Westmeath. Retired Public Servant. m. Denis J Shakey, 29 Aug 1979. *Education:* Loreto College, Mulligar; Qualified Architect's Technician. *Appointments:* Co-Owner, Magpie Publications. *Publications:* Old Days, Old Ways, 1985; Nature Spy, 1989; Country Cameos, 1989; Forthcoming: History of the Diocise of Meath. *Contributions to:* Ireland's Eye; Irish Farmers Monthly; Irish Arts Review; Irish Roots. *Honours:* Irish Book Award, 1985; Nominated in Best Children's Category Award, IBA, 1989. *Address:* Mullingar, Co. Westmeath, Ireland.

SHARMA Sita Sharan, b. 26 Mar 1931, Shamhu, Begusarai, India. Sarvodaya Worker. m. Sharada, 26 Feb 1970, 1 son. *Education:* Studied under Bhoodan Movement Leader Acharya Vinoba Bhave. *Publications:* Acharya Sri Tulasi Jaise Main Samajha; Ram Kathaki Parampara Main AgniPariksha; Bihar Ki Jhanki; Triloohan Kavita; Shakto Pooja; Prerak Kathaye; Manas Marmonk; Karnataka Ki Jhanki. *Contributions to:* Hindi Articles in Many Weeklies & Souvenirs. *Honours:* Lal Bahadur Sastrys award; Anuvrat Pravartak Award. *Memberships include:* Authors uild of India; Poet International Organisation; Daxina Bharath Hindi Prachara Sabha; Bharatiya Sanskriti Vidya Pith; State

Sarvodaya Mandela. *Address:* 19 Vallabha Niketan, Kumara Park East, Bangalore 560001, India.

SHARMA Vera, b. 10 Feb 1926, Bombay, India. Writer; House Wife. m. 10 Mar 1949, 1 daughter. *Publications:* Random Thoughts; The Unrepentant & Othe Stories; The Early Bird & Othe One Act plays; The Hermaphroditc & Other Indian Poems; The Blind Musician; Naina & Other Indian Stories; The Chameleon & Six Other Radio Plays. *Contributions to:* Illustrated Weekly of india; PEN Journal; Debonair; MAFIL; Kunnapipi. *Honours:* Prizes, National Newspaper Competitions; Free Press Jounral; Bharat Jyoti; Deccan Herald. *Memberships:* PEN Bombay; Asiatic Society of Bombay. *Address:* 106, 6th Road, Tilaknagar, Goregaon W, Bombay, India.

SHARMAT Marjorie Weinman, (Wendy Andrews) b. 1928, American. Writer. *Publications:* Rex, 1967; Goodnight Andrew, Goodnight Craig, 1969; Gladys Told Me to Meet Her Here, 1970; A Hot Thirsty Day, 1971; 51 Sycamore Lane, 1971; Getting Something on Maggie Marmestein, 1971; A Visit with Rosalind, 1972; Nate the Great, series, 8 vols., 1972-85; Sophie and Gussie, 1973; Morris Brooksdie, A Dog, 1973; Morris Brookside is Missing, 1974; I Want Mama, 1974; I'm Not Oscar's Friend Anymore, 1975; Burton and Dudley, 1975; The Lancelot Closes at Five, 1976; The Trip and Other Sophie and Gussie Stories, 1976; Mooch the Messy, 1976; Edgemont, 1977; I'm Terrific, 1977; I Don't Care, 1977; (with others) Just for Fun, 1977; A Big Fat Enormous Lie, 1978; Thornton the Worrier, 1978; Mitchell is Moving, 1978; Mooch the Messy Meets Prudence the Neat, 1979; Scarlet Monster Lives Here, 1979; Mr Jameson and Mr Phillips, 1979; Uncle Boris and Maude, 1979; The 329th Friend, 1979; (with Mitchell Sharmat) I Am Not a Pest, 1979; Octavia Told Me a Secret, 1979; Say Hello, Vanessa, 1979; Griselda's New Year, 1979; The Trolls of 12th Street, 1979; Little Devil Gets Sick, 1980; 1979; What Are We Going to Do About Andrew?, 1980; Sometimes Mama and Papa Fight, 1980; Taking Care of Melvin, 1980; Gila Monsters Meet You at the Airport, 1980; Grumley the Grouch, 1980; (with Mitchell Sharmat) The Day I Was Born, 1980; Twitchell the Wishful, 1981; Chasing After Annie, 1981; Rollo and Juliet Forever!, 1981; The Sign, 1981; Lucretia the Unbearable, 1981; The Best Valentine in the World, 1982; Two Ghosts on a Beach, 1982; Mysteriously Yours, Maggia Marmestein, 1982; Square Pegs, (adaptation of CBS-TV sit-comm), 1982; Frizzy the Fearful, 1983; I Saw Him First, 1983; How to Meet a Gorgeous Guy, 1983; Rich Mitch, 1983; The Story of Bently Beaver, 1984; Bartholomew the Bossy, 1984; How to Meet a Gorgeous Girl, 1984; Sasha the Silly, 1984; He Noticed I'm Alive...and Other Hopeful Signs, 1984; (as Wendy Andrews) Vacation Fever!, 1984; (as Wendy Andrews) Supergirl, 1984; My Mother Never Listens to Me, 1984; Two Guys Noticed Me...and Other Miracles, 1985; Attila the Angry, 1985; (as Wendy Andrews) Are We There yet?, 1985; How to Have a Gorgeous Wedding, 1985; Get Rich Mitch! 1985; The Son of the Slime, Who Ate Cleveland, 1985; One Terrific Thanksgiving, 1985; Helga High-Up, 1986; Hurray for Mother's Day!, 1986; Who,s Afraid of Ernestine?, 1986; Marjorie Sharmat's Sorority Sisters, 4 vols., 1986.

SHAROUNI Youssuf Al, b. 14 Oct 1924, Menuf, Egypt. Ministry of Information. m. Nargis S Basta, 2 Oct 1952, 1 son, 1 daughter. *Education:* BA, Cairo University. *Appointments:* Under-secretary, High Council of Culture, 1978-83; Editorial Board: Al Magallah, 1963-66, Al Magalla, 1963- 66, (monthlies); Professor for Postgraduate Courses, Cairo University, 1979- 81; Editori *Publications:* The Five Lovers; A Message to a Woman; The Last Eve; Studies on Love and Friendship in Arabic Tradition. *Contributions to:* Al Adib; Al Adab; Al Arabi; Al Muntada; Al Ahram; Abd'a. *Honours:* Egyptian State Prizes in Short Story, 1970, and Literary Studies, 1978, categories; First Grade Order of Science and Arts, Arab Republic of Egype, 1970; Order of the Republic, 1978; Fellow: German Academic Exchange Service, Free University of Berlin, 1976, Netherlands Organisaton for Advancement of Pure

Research, 1981-82. *Memberships:* Story CLub, Cairo; Board, 1970-73; Writers' Union, Cairo; Pen Club; Fiction Committee at High Council of Culture, 1963-83. *Address:* Ministry of Information, PO Box 600 Muscat, Sultanate of Oman.

SHARP Ronald Alan, b. 19 Oct 1945, Cleveland, Ohio, USA. Professor of English. m. Inese Brutans, 22 June 1968. 2 sons. *Education:* BA, Kalamazoo College, 1967; MA, University of Michigan, 1968; PhD, University of Virginia, 1974. *Appointments include:* John Crowe Ransom Professor of English, Kenyon College, 1985-; Founding Co-editor, Kenyon Review, 1978-82. *Publications:* Keats, Skepticism and the Religion of Beauty, 1979; Friendship and Literature: Spirit and Form, 1986; The Norton Book of Friendship, 1991; Reading George Steiner, 1994; Three Short Plays of Federico Garcia Lorca, 1979. *Contributions to:* New Literary History, American Literature, Modern Philology, Kenyon Review, Keats-Shelly Journal. *Honours:* Fellow: English Speaking Union, National Humanities Center, National Endowment for Humanities, American Council of Learned Societies. *Memberships:* Modern Language Association of America; Keats-Shelly Association of America; Wordsworth-Coleridge Association; Ohio College English Group. *Literary Agent:* Timothy Seldes at Russell & Volkening. *Address:* Department of English, Kenyon College, Gambier, OH 43022, USA.

SHARPE Kevin Michael, b. 26 Jan 1949, Kent, England. University Reader. *Education:* BA, Oxford, 1971; MA, 1975; D Phil, 1975. *Appointments:* Fellow, Oriel College, Oxford, 1974-78; Lecturer, Christ Church, Oxford, 1976-78; Lecturer, Senior Lecturer, Reader, University of Southampton, 1979-. *Publications:* The Personal Rule of Charles I; Criticism and Compliment; Politics and Ideas in Early Stuart England; Sir Robert Cotton; Faction and Parliament; Politics of Discourse; Culture and Politics in Early Stuart England. *Contributions to:* Sunday Times; Spectator; TLS; History Today; New York Review. *Honours:* Royal Historical Society Whitfield Prize; Visiting Fellowships: Fulbright; Institute for Advanced Study, Princeton; Stanford Humanities Center, Australian National University; Huntingdon Library; California Institue of Technology. *Memberships:* Royal History Society Fellow; Associate Members Institute for Advanced Study Princeton. *Literary Agent:* Curtis Brown. *Address:* 97 Livingstone Road, Portswood, Southampton, SO2 1DG, England.

SHARPE Thomas Ridley (Tom), b. 30 Mar 1928, London, England. Author. m. Nancy Anne Looper, 6 Aug 1969. 3 daughters. *Education:* Lancing College, 1942-46; Pembroke College, Cambridge, 1948-51. *Publications:* Riotous Assembly, 1971; Indecent Exposure, 1973; Porterhouse Blue, 1974; Blott on the Landscape, 1975; Wilt, 1976; The Great Pursuit, 1977; The Throwback, 1978; The Wilt Alternative, 1979; Ancestral Vices, 1980; Vintage Stuff, 1982; Wilt on High, 1984. *Contributions to:* Numerous magazines and journals. *Honours:* Laureat Le Grand Prix De L'Humour Noir, Paris, 1986; Le Legion De L'Humour, Aphia, Paris, 1986. *Membership:* The Society of Authors. *Literary Agent:* Richard Scott Simon. *Address:* 38 Tunwells Lane, Great Shelford, Cambridge CB2 5LT, England.

SHAVELSON Melville, b. 1 Apr 1917, New York City, USA. Writer; Director. m. Lucille T Myers, 2 Nov 1938, 1 son, 1 daughter. *Education:* AB, Cornell University, 1937. *Appointments:* Writer, Bob Hope Pepsodent Show, NBC Radio, 1938-43. *Publications:* Screenplays Including: The Princess and the Pirate, 1944; Wonder Man, 1944; Room for One More, 1951; I'll See You in My Dreams, 1952; Writer, Director: The Seven Little Foys, 1954; Beau James, 1956; Houseboat, 1957; The Five Pennies, 1958; It Started in Naples, 1959; On the Double, 1960; Yours, Mine and Ours, 1968; The War Between Men and Women, 1972; The Legend of Valentino, 1975; Deceptions, 1985; Writer, Director, Producer: The Pigeon That Took Rome, 1962; A New Kind of Love, 1963; Cast a Giant Shadow, 1966; Mixed Company, 1974; The Great Houdinis, 1976; Ike, 1979; Author, Broadway Musical, Jimmy, 1969; Books: How to Make a Jewish Movie, 1970; Lualda, 1975; The Great Houdinis, 1976; The Eleventh Commandment, 1977; Ike, 1979; Don't Shoot It's Only Me, 1990. *Honours include:* President, Writers Guild of America, West 1969-71, 1979-81, 1985-87; Academy Award Screenplay Nominations, 1955, 1958; Screenwriters Guild Award, 1959; Christopher Award, 1959; Screenwriters Award Nominations, 1952, 1958, 1959, 1962, 1968, 1972, 1975; Screen Writers Award, Best Written American Musical, 1959; Award of Merit, United Jewish Appeal, 1966; Writers Guild Laurel Award; Writers Guild Valentine Davies Award. *Address:* 11947 Sunshine Terr, Studio City, CA 91604, USA.

SHAVER Philip Robert, b. 7 Sept 1944, Iowa City, USA. Professor of Psychology. *Education:* BA, Wesleyan , 1966; PhD, Social Psychology, University of Michigan, 1971. *Appointments:* Editorial Board, Journal of Social and Personal Relationships, 1988-. *Publications:* In Search of Intimacy, 1982; Review of Personality and Social Psychology, 1983, 1984, 1985, 1987; Measures of Personality and Social Psychological Attitudes, 1991. *Contributions to:* Journal of Personality Assessment, Psychological Inquiry, Personality and Social Psychology Bulletin; Journal of Social and Clinical Psychology. *Honours:* National Merit Scholarship; Phi Beta Kappa; Nominated for awards, Iowa Network on Personal Relationships and International Society for the Study of Personal Relationships; *Memberships:* American Psychological Society; American and Eastern Psychological Associations; Society for the Psychological Study of Social Issues; International Society for Research on Emotion. *Address:* Department of Psychology, University of California, Davis, CA 95616, USA.

SHAW Alison Jane, b. 16 Oct 1957, Hertfordshire, England. Social Anthropologist. m. Jonathan Flint, 21 June 1980, 1 son, 2 daughters. *Education:* BA Human Sciences, Wadham College, Oxford, 1976; DPhil, Social Anthropology, 1984. *Publications:* A Pakistani Community in Britain, 1988; Get by in Hindi and Urdu, 1989; Teacher's Guide for a new course in Urdu and Spoken Hindi, part 1, 1991. *Address:* 21 Kingston Road, Oxford, OX2 6RQ, England.

SHAW Brian. *See:* TUBB E C.

SHAW Bynum (Gillette), b. 10 July 1923, Alamance County, North Carolina, USA. Professor of Journalism. m. (1) Louise N Brantley (dec), 30 Aug 1948, (2) Emily P Crandall, (dec), 19 June 1982, (3) Charlotte E Reeder, 26 Nov 1986; 2 daughters. *Education:* BA, Wake Forest College, 1951. *Publications:* The Sound of Small Hammer, 1962; The Nazi Hunter, 1968; Divided We Stand, The Baptists in American Life, 1974; Days of Power, Nights of Fear, 1980; W W Holden: A Political Biography (with Edgar E Folk), 1982; Days of Power, Nights of Fear (novel), 1980; The History of Wake Forest College, Vol IV, 1988; Oh, Promised Land!, 1992. *Contributions to:* Esquire; New Republic; Moneysworth; New York Times; The Baltimore Sun. *Honour:* Sir Walter Raleigh Award in Fiction, 1969. *Memberships:* North Carolina Writers Conference, Chairman, 1972. *Literary Agent:* Scott Meredith. *Address:* 2700 Speas Road, Winston-Salem, NC 27106, USA.

SHAW Felicity (Ann Morice), b. 1918. Author. *Publications:* As Felicity Shaw: The Happy Exiles, 1956; Sun Trap, 1958; Mystery Novels as Anne Morice: Death in the Grand Manor, 1970; Murder in Married Life, 1971; Death of a Gay Dog, 1971; Murder on French Leave, 1972; Death and the Dutiful Daughter, 1973; Death of a Heavenly Twin, 1974; Killing with Kindness, 1974; Nursery Tea and Poison, 1975; Death of a Wedding Guest, 1976; Murder in Mimicry, 1977; Scared to Death, 1977; Murder by Proxy, 1978; Murder in Outline, 1979; The Hen in Her Death, 1980; Hollow Vengeance, 1982; Sleep of Death, 1982; Murder Post-Dated, 1983; Getting Away with Murder?, 1984; Dead on Cue, 1985; Publish and Be Killed, 1986; Treble

Exposure, 1987. *Address:* 41 Hambledon Village, Henley-on-Thames, Oxon, England.

SHAW Irene. *See:* **ROBERTS Irene.**

SHAW Robert (Bob), b. 31 Dec 1931, Belfast, Northern Ireland. Author. m. Sarah Gourley, 3 July 1954, 1 son, 2 daughters. *Education:* College of Technology, Belfast. *Publications:* Novels: Night Walk, 1967; The Two-Timers, 1968; Shadow of Heaven, 1969; The Palace of Eternity; One Million Tomorrows, 1970; Ground Zero, 1971; Other Days, Other Eyes, 1972; Orbitsville, 1975; A Wreath of Stars, 1976; Medusa's Children, 1977; Who Goes Here, 1977; Ship of Strangers, 1978; Vertigo, 1978; The Ceres Solution, 1981; Orbitsville Departure, 1983; Fire Pattern, 1984; The Ragged Astronauts, 1986; The Wooden Spaceships, 1988; Killer Planet, 1989; The Fugitive Worlds, 1989; Orbitsville Judgement, 1990; Warrn Peace, 1993. Short story collections: Tomorrow Lies in Ambush, 1973; Cosmic Kaleidoscope, 1976; A Better Mantrap, 1981; Dark Night in Toyland, 1989; Non-Fiction: How To Write Science Fiction, 1993. *Contributions to:* About 70 short stories to science fiction magazines, UK and USA. *Honours:* British Science Fiction Awards: Best Novel, 1976, Best Novel, 1987, Best Short Story, 1989. *Membership:* Science Fiction Writers of America. *Literary Agent:* E J Carnell Literary Agency, Bishop's Stortford, England. *Address:* 66 Knutsford Road, Grappenhall, Warrington, Cheshire, England.

SHAW Ronnie Glen, b. 26 Aug 1958, Fort Worth, Texas, USA. Managing Editor; Choral Journal. m. Laquita Jenise Fisher, 10 Aug. 1985. *Education:* BM, Hardin-Simmons University, Abilene, Texas, USA. *Appointments:* Managing Editor, The Choral Journal. *Memberships:* Educational Press Associates of America, New Jersey.

SHEAFFER Louis, b. 1912, United States of America. Writer. *Appointments include:* Theatre Critic, Brooklyn Eagle, 1949-55. *Publications:* O'Neill, Son and Playwright, 1968; O'Neill, Son And Artist. *Honour:* Pulitzer Prize for Biography, 1973. *Address:* c/o Little, Brown & Co., 34 Beacon Street, Boston, MA 02106, USA.

SHECKLEY Robert, b. 1928, United States of America. Author. *Publications Include:* Untouched by Human Hands (short stories), 1954; Citizen in Space (short stories), 1955; Pilgrimage to Earth (short stories), 1957; Immortality Delivered, 1958; as Immortality Inc., 1959; Store of Infinity (short stories), 1960; The Status Civilization, 1960; Notions, Unlimited (short stories), 1960; Calibre 50 (suspense), 1961; Dead Run (suspense), 1961; Live Gold (suspense), 1962; The Man in the Water (suspense), 1962; Journey Beyond Tomorrow, 1962 (in United Kingdom as Journey of Joenes, 1978); Shards of Space (short stories), 1962; White Death (suspense), 1963; The Game of X (suspense), 1965; In a Land of Clear Colors, 1974; Crompton Divided (in United Kingdom as The Alchemical Marriage of Alistair Crompton), 1978; The Wonderful World of Rober Sheckley (short stories), 1979; Victim Prime, 1987; Hunter/Victim, 1988; The Draconian Alternative, 1988. *Address:* c/o Marty Shapiro, Shapiro Lichtman Talent, 8827 Beverly Boulevard, Los Angeles, CA 90048, USA.

SHEED Wilfrid John Joseph, MA, b. 27 Dec. 1930, London, England (now US citizen). Author. m. Miriam Ungerer, 1 son, 2 daughters. *Education:* Lincoln College, Oxford University. *Appointments include:* Film reviewer 1959-61, associate editor 1959-66, Jubilee magazine; Drama critic, former book editor, Commonwealth magazine, New York; Film critic, Esquire magazine, 1967-69; Visiting Professor, Princeton University, 1970-71; Judge, editorial board member, Book of the Month Club, 1972-. *Publications:* A Middle Class Education, 1961; The Hack, 1963; Square's Progress, 1965; Office Politics, 1966; The Blacking Factory, 1968; Max

Jamison, 1970; The Morning After, 1971; People Will Always Be Kind, 1973; Three Mobs: Labor, Church & Mafia, 1974; Transatlantic Blues, 1978; The Good Word, 1979; Clare Boothe Luce, 1982; Frank & Maisie, 1985; editor, G.K.. Chesterton's Essays & Poems, 1957; 16 Short Novels, 1986; The Boys of Winter, 1988. *Contributions to:* Popular magazines. *Honour:* Guggenheim Fellow, 1971-72. *Membership:* PEN Club. *Address:* Sag Harbor, New York, NY 11963, USA.

SHEEHAN Susan, b. 1937, United States of America. Writer (Social Sciences). *Appointments:* Editorial Assistant, Esquire-Coronet Magazines, 1959-60; Staff Writer, New Yorker Magazine, 1961-. *Publications:* Ten Vietnamese, 1967; A Welfare Mother, 1976; A Prison and a Prisoner, 1978; Is There No Place on Earth for Me? 1982; Kate Quinton's Days, 1984; A Missing Piece, 1986. *Honour:* Pulitzer Prize. *Literary Agent:* Robert Lescher. *Address:* c/o New Yorker, 20 W 43rd Street, New York, NY 10036, USA.

SHEFFIELD Charles, Author. *Publications:* Sight of Proteus, 1978; The Web Betwen the Worlds, 1979; Vectors, 1980; Hidden Variables, 1981; Earthwatch: A Survey of the World from Space, 1981; Commercial Operations in Space 1980-2000 (with John L. McLusas), 1981; The Selkie (novel with David F. Bischoff), 1982; My Brother's Keeper, 1982; Erasmus Magister, 1982; Man on Earth (non-fiction), 1983; The McAndrew Chronicles, 1983; Space Careers (with Carol Rosin), 1984; Between the Strokes of Night, 1985. *Memberships:* Vice President, Earth Satellite Corporation; President, Science Fiction Writers of America; Formerly President, American Astronautical Society. *Address:* 6812 Wilson Lane, Bethesda, MD 20817, USA.

SHELBOURNE Cecily. *See:* **EBEL Suzanne.**

SHELBY Graham. Writer. *Publications:* The Knights of Dark Renown, 1969; The Kings of Vain Intent, 1970; The Villains of the Piece, 1972; The Devil is Loose, 1973; The Wolf at the Door, 1975; The Cannaways, 1978; The Cannaway Concern, 1980; The Edge of the Blade, 1986; Demand the World, 1990. *Literary Agent:* A.P. Watt Ltd, 20 John Street, London WC1N 2DR, England.

SHELDON Ann. *See:* **WAGNER Sharon Blythe.**

SHELDON Caroline Mary, b. 25 Apr 1954, Oxford, England. Literary Agent. *Education:* BA Hons History, Exeter University. *Memberships:* Association of Authors Agents; Children's Book Circle. *Address:* 71 Hillgate Place, London W8 7SS, England.

SHELDON John. *See:* **BLOCH Robert.**

SHELDON Lee. *See:* **LEE Wayne C.**

SHELDON Roy. *See:* **TUBB E C.**

SHELDON Scott. *See:* **WALLMANN Jeffrey M.**

SHELDON Sidney, b. 1917, United States of America. Author; Playwright. *Appointments Include:* Television Show Creator, Producer, Writer, 1963-. *Publications:* The Merry Widow (operetta, adaptor with Ben Roberts), 1943; Jackpot, 1944; Dream with Music, 1944; Alice in Arms, 1945; The Batchelor and the Bobby Soxer (screenplay), 1947; Easterparade (screenplay, with Albert Hackett and Frances Goodrich), 1948; Annie get Your Gun (screenplay), 1950; Rich, Young and Pretty (screenplay), 1951; Dream Wife, 1953; Anything Goes (screenplay), 1956; Never Too Young, 1956; The Buster Keaton Story (screenplay), 1957; Redhead, 1959; Roman Candle, 1960; Billy Rose's Jumbo (screenplay), 1962; The Naked Face (novel), 1970; The Other Side of Midnight, 1974; Bloodline, 1977; Rage of Angels, 1980; The Master of the Game, 1982; If Tomorrow

Comes, 1985; Windmills of the Gods, 1987; The Sands of Time, 1988; Memories of Midnight, 1990; The Doomsday Conspiracy, 1991; The Stars Shine Down, 1992. *Address:* c/o Press Relations, William Morrow, 1305 Avenue of the Americas, New York, NY 10019, USA.

SHELTON Mark Logan, b. 19 May 1958, Chicago, Illinois, USA. Writer. m. Eve Shelnutt, 29 May 1982. *Education:* AB, Western Michigan University, 1980; MFA, University of Pittsburgh, 1982. *Publications:* Working in a Very Small Place, 1989, 1990, 1991. *Contributions to:* Ohio, Pittsburgh, Milwaukee Journals; Columbus Dispatch, Library Journal. *Honours:* Best Sports Stories, Sport News; A Dozen Sigma Delta Chi Awards. *Memberships:* Judge, Ohioana Library Association Book Awards, 1990-. *Literary Agent:* Tim Seldes, Russell and Volkening, 50W 29th St, NY 10001, USA. *Address:* 2 South Congress, Suite 17, Athens, OH 45701, USA.

SHEN Tong, b. 30 July 1968, China. Student. *Education:* BA Brandeis University, 1991; Hon PhD, St Ambrowse University, 1991; PhD Candidate, Boston University, 1991-. *Publications:* Almost a Revolution, 1990, 1991, 1992. *Contributions to:* Christian Science Monitor, San Francisco Chronicle. *Membership:* Chairman, Democracy for China Fund. *Literary Agent:* Tom Woen, Williams Morris Agency. *Address:* Democracy for China Fund, Newton, MA 02166, USA.

SHENKER Israel, b. 1925, USA. Journalist. *Appointments:* Correspondent, Time Magazine, New York City, 1949-68; Reporter, New York Times, New York City, 1968-. *Publications:* As Good as Golda (edited with M Shenker), 1970; Words and Their Masters, 1974; Zero Mostel's Book of Villains (with Zero Mostel), 1977; Nothing Is Sacred, 1979; In the Footsteps of Johnson and Boswell, 1984; Coat of Many Colors, 1985. *Address:* c/o New York Times, 229 West 43rd Sreet, New York, NY 10036, USA.

SHEPARD Sam. *See:* **ROGERS Samuel Shepard.**

SHEPHERD Mark, b. 19 Sept 1961, Tampa, Florida, USA. *Appointments:* Assistant Editor, Tulsa Week Magazine, 1987. *Publications:* Wheels of Fire, 1992; Prison of Souls, 1993. *Memberships:* Science Fiction and Fantasy Writers of America; American MENSA Ltd. *Address:* PO Box 8309, Tulsa, OK 74101, USA.

SHEPHERD Michael. *See:* **LUDLUM Robert.**

SHEPHERD Robert James, b. 14 Feb 1949, Solihull, Warwickshire, England. Author; journalist; TV Producer; Director. *Education:* Tudor Grange, GS Solihull, 1960-67; University of Kent, BA, MA, 1968-72. *Appointments:* Leader and Features Writer, Investors Chronicle, 1983; Editorial Team, Producer, A Week in Politics, 1983-88; Parliamentary Lobby Correspondent, 1984-87; Producer, documentaries, Democracy in Danger, All the Presidency Men, 1992. *Publications:* The Power Brokers, 1991; Irelands Fate, 1990; A Class Divided, 1988; Public Opinion and European Integration, 1975. *Contributions to:* Political Quarterly; New Statesman; Investors Chronicle; Marxism Today; The Guardian; The Times; The Irish Independent; The Sunday Press; Ireland of the Welcomes. *Memberships:* Society of Authors; International PEN; National Union of Journalists; BECTU. *Literary Agent:* Michael Shaw, Curtis Brown. *Address:* c/o Michael Shaw, Curtis Brown, 162-8 Regent Street, London W1R 5TB, England.

SHEPPARD David, (Rt Rev), b. 6 Mar 1929, Reigate, Surrey, England. Bishop. m. Grace Isaac, 19 June 1957, Lindfield. 1 daughter. *Education:* MA, Trinity Hall, Cambridge University. *Publications:* Parson's Pitch, 1964; Built as a City, 1974; Bias to the Poor, 1983; Better Together (with Archbishop Derek Worlock), 1988; With Christ in the Wilderness (with Archbishop Derek

Worlock), 1990. *Contributions to:* Woman's Own, columnist, 1957-74; Occasional contributor to various other publications. *Honours:* Honorary LLD, Liverpool University, 1981; Honorary DTech, Liverpool Polytechnic, 1987; Hon Doctorate, Cambridge University. *Address:* Bishop's Lodge, Woolton Park, Liverpool L25 6DT, England.

SHER Steven Jay, b. 28 Sept 1949, USA. Writer. m. Nancy Green, 11 March 1978, 1 son, 1 daughter. *Education:* BA, CCNY, 1970; MA, University of Iowa, 1972; MFA, Brooklyn College, 1978. *Appointments:* Director, Creative Writing, Spalding University, 1979-81; Oregon State University, 1981- 86; University of North Carolina, Wilmington, 1986-89. *Publications:* Man with a Thousand Eyes and Other Stories, 1989; Trolley Lives, 1985; Caught in the Revolving Door, 1980; Persnickety, 1979; Nickelodeon, 1978. *Contributions to:* Blood to Remember: American Poets on the Holocaust, 1991; The Anthology of Magazine Verse and Year Book of American Poetry. *Honours:* All Nations Poetry Contest, 1977; Weymouth Centre Residency, 1988; North Carolina Writers Network Writers and Readers Series Competition, 1989. *Memberships:* Academy of American Poets; AWP; Poetry Society of America; Poets and Writers. *Address:* 3930 N W Witham Hill Dr C-26, Corvallis, OR 97330, USA.

SHERATON Mimi, b. 10 Feb 1926, Brooklyn, New York, USA. Food Critic. m. 1. William Sheraton, 20 Aug 1945 (div 1954), 2. Richard Falcone, 30 July 1955, 1 son. *Education:* BS, New York University, 1947. *Appointments:* Food and Home Furnishing Editor, Seventeen, New York, 1947-53; Managing Editor of Supplement Division, House Beautiful, New York City, 1954-56; Freelance writer 1956-69; Food Critic, New York, New York City, 1967-75; Food Critic, New York Times, 1975-83; Food Critic, Time, New York City, 1984-; Publisher of newsletter Mimi Sheraton's Taste; consultant on folk art exhibitions. *Publications:* Visions of Sugar Plums, 1968; From My Mother's Kitchen, 1979; Mimi Sheraton's New York Times Guide to New Restaurants, 1983; (with Alan King) Is Salami and Eggs Better Than Sex? 1985; Mimi Sheraton's Favorite New York Restaurants, 1986, 1989; The Seducer's Cookbook, 1962; City Portraits, 1963; The German Cookbook, 1965. *Contributions to:* magazines, including Conde Nast Traveler and Town and Country. *Honours:* Penney Missouri Award from school of Journalism at University of Missouri, Columbia, 1974 for articles in New York magazine; Front Page Award from Newswomen's Club of New York, 1977 for New York Times article on nitrites in meats. *Address:* PO Box 1396. Old Chelsea Station, New York, NY 10011, USA.

SHERIDAN Lee. *See:* **LEE Elsie.**

SHERMAN Dan. *See:* **SHERMAN Daniel M.**

SHERMAN Daniel M, (Dan Sherman), b. 31 July 1950, Los Angeles, California. Author. m. Alarie Manon, 25 Apr 1983. *Education:* BA English Literature, California State University. *Publications:* The Dynasty of Spies; the Man Who loved Mata Hari; The Prince of Berlin; The White Mandarin; The Traitor; The Mole; King Jaguar; Riddle; The Glory Trap. *Memberships:* Author's Guild; PEN. *Literary Agent:* Richard Curtis. *Address:* 4440 Ambrose Avenue, Los Angeles, CA 90027, USA.

SHERMAN Eileen Bluestone, b. 15 May 1951, Atlantic City, USA. Author; Playwright; Lyricist; Instructor; Lecturer. m. Neal Jonathan Sherman, 10 June 1973, 1 son, 1 daughter. *Education:* BA, Theatre Arts, English, Finch College, New York, 1973; MA, Theatre Arts, State University of New York, Albany, 1976. *Publications:* The Odd Potato, 1984; Monday in Odessa, 1986; Independence Avenue, 1990. Musical Plays produced: Me, Myself and I; The Odd Potato; Rotten Apples; The Sabbath Peddler; Independence Avenue. Dramatic Play produced: Monday in Odessa.

Scriptwriter: The Magic Door, TV series, 1987-.*Honours:* Monday in Odessa, Outstanding Social Studies Trade Book, 1986, Children's Book Council; National Jewish Book Award, Childrens Literature, 1986; Emmy Award, Best Children's Special, Nothing is Simple, (co-writer), 1988; Emmy Award, Best Children's Special, The Odd Potato, 1989; The Teacher's Choice Award, International Reading Association for Independance Avenue, 1991 . *Memberships:* Authors Guild Inc.; Society of Childrens Book Writers; National League of American Pen Women; The Dramatists Guild. *Address:* 10720 Horton, Overland Park, KS 66211, USA.

SHERMAN Josepha, b. New York City, USA. Writer, Editor. *Education:* MA, Hunter College. *Publications:* Castle of Deception; Child of Faerie, Child of Earth; A Sampler of Jewish American Folklore; The Horse of Flame; The Shining Falcon; Indian Tribes of North America; Vassilisa The Wise; Swept Away; The Dark Gods. *Contributions to:* Numerous. *Honours:* Compton Crook Award; Nominee Nebula Award. *Memberships:* Authors Guild; Science Fiction and Fantasy Writers of America; Society of Childrens Book Writers; American Folklore Society. *Address:* PO Box 1403, Riverdale, NY 10471, USA.

SHERRIN Edward George (Ned), b. 18 Feb 1931, Lowham, Somerset, England. Director; Producer; Presenter; Writer. *Education:* MA, Oxford University; Barrister-at-Law. *Publications:* Cindy-Ella (with Caryl Brahms), 1962; Rappel (with C B), 1964; Benbow Was His Name (with C B), 1967; Ooh La La (with C B), 1973; After You Mr Feydeau (with C B), 1975; A Small thing Like an Earthquake, 1983; Song By Song (with C B), 1984; Cutting Edge, 1984; 1956 and All That (with Neil Shand), 1984; The Metropolitan Mikado (with Alistair Beaton), 1985; Too Dirty for the Windmill (with C B), 1986; Loose Ends, 1990; Theatrical Anecdotes, 1991. *Literary Agent:* Margaret Ramsey. *Address:* c/o Margaret Ramsey, 14A Goodwin's Court, St Martin's Lane, London WC3, England.

SHERRY Sylvia, b. United Kingdom. Author; Former Educator. *Publications:* Street of the Small Night Market, 1966; Frog in a Coconut Shell, 1967; A Pair of Jesus Boots, 1969; The Loss of the Night Wind, 1970; Snake in the Old Hut, 1972; Dark River, Dark Mountain, 1974; Mat, The Little Monkey, 1977; Girl in a Blue Shawl, for adults, 1978; South of Red River, for adults, 1981; A Pair of Desert-Wellies, for children, 1985.

SHERWIN Byron Lee, b. 18 Feb 1946, New York, USA. Professor. m. 24 Dec 1972, 1 son. *Education:* BS Columbia University, 1966; MA New York University, 1969; BHL, MHL, Rabbinic Ordination Jewish Theological Seminary of America, 1966, 1970; PhD, University of Chicago, 1978. *Publications:* Mystical Theology and Social Dissent, 1982; In Partnership with God, 1990; No Religion is an Island, 1991; Toward a Jewish THeology, 1992; Judaism, 1978; Encountering the Holocaust, 1979; Abraham Joshua Heschel, 1979; Golem Legend, 1985; How to be a Jew: Ethical Teachings of Judaism, 1992. *Contributions to:* More than 100 articles and monographs in English, Hebrew and Polish journals. *Memberships:* Founding President, Midwest Jewish Studies Association. *Honour:* Man of Reconciliation, Polich Council of Thristians and Jews, 1992. *Address:* 618 S Michigan Avenue, Chicago, IL 60605, USA.

SHIELDS Carol, b. 2 June 1935, USA. Writer; Teacher. m. Donald Shields, 20 July 1957, 1 son, 4 daughters. *Education:* Hanover College, BA, 1957; University of Ottawa, MA, 1975. *Publications:* The Republic of Love; Swann; Various Miracles; The Orange Fish; Small Ceremonies; The Box Garden; Happenstance; A Fairly Conventional Woman; Others; Intersect; Comins to Canada; Departures and Arrivals; Thirteen Hands. *Honours:* Canadian Authors Award; Arthur Ellis award; Marion Engel award. *Memberships:* The Writers Union of Canada; PEN. *Literary Agent:* Bella

Pomer. *Address:* 701-237 Wellington Cr, Winnipeg, Monitoba, Canada R3M 0A1.

SHIELDS Carol Ann, b. 2 June 1935, Oak Park, Illinois, USA, Writer; Professor, m. Donald Hush Shields, 20 July 1957, 1 son, 4 daughters. *Education:* BA, Hanover College, 1957; MA, University of Ottawa, Canada, 1975. *Appointments:* Professor, 1976-77, Writer-in-Residence, 1989, University if Ottawa; Professor, University of British Columbia, 1978- 79; Professor, University of Manitoba, 1980-; Writer-in-Residence, University of Winnipeg, 1987. *Publications:* Others, 1972; Intersect, 1974; Small Cermonies, 1976; The Box Garden, 1977; Happenstance, 1980; A Fairly Conventional Woman, 1982; Various Miracles, short stories, 1985; Swann: A Mystery, 1987; The Orange Fish, 1989; The Republic of Love, 1992. *Contributions to:* Numerous Canadian Magazines and Journals. *Honours:* CBC Prize, Poetry, 1965; Canadian Authors Association Award, 1976; Canadian Authors Association Prize, 1977; CBC Drama Prize, 1983; CBC Short Story Prize, 1984; National Magazine Award, 1985; Governor General's Award, Shortlist, 1987; Canadian Crimewriters Award, 1987. *Memberships:* Writers Union of Canada; Manitoba Writers Guild. *Literary Agent:* Bella Pomer. *Address:* 701-237 Wellington Crescent, Winnipeg, Manitoba, Canada R3M 0A1.

SHIELDS Michael Joseph, b. 29 Oct 1938. Writer; Translator; Poet. *Appointments include:* Associate Editor, Here Now, 1970-73; Editor, Orbis Magazine, 1980-; Editor, Professional Translator and Interpreter, 1989-; Consultant Editor, International Authors and Writers Who's Who and Who's Who of Poetry. *Publications:* Poetry: Helix, 1970. Translations: Superfine Particle Technology by Ichinose et al, 1991; Offshore Structures Vol I by Clauss et al, 1991; Submarines of the US Navy by Terzibaschitsch, 1991; Dubbel, Engineers Handbook, 1992. *Contributions to:* Collins English Dictionary; Outposts; Littack; The Writer; New Headland; Poetry Nottingham; Readers Digest; Weekend; Writers News; The Publisher. *Honours:* George Eliot Fellowship Trophy, NFA, 1975, 1977, 1979; John Masefield Award, World Order of Narrative Poets, 1987. *Memberships:* Society of Authors; Fellow, Institute of Information Scientists; Chairman, Translators Association 1984-85; Institute of Translating and Interpreting; Club: Royal Over-Seas League. *Address:* 199 The Long Shoot, Nuneaton, Warwickshire CV11 6JQ, England.

SHIHWARG Joan Olivia, (Wyndham), b. 11 Oct 1921, London, England. m. Alexander Shihwarg, 2 June 1950, 2 daughters. *Education:* Holy Child Convent, Hastings, England, 1929-1936. *Publications:* Love Lessons, 1985; Love is Blue, 1986; Anything Once, 1992. *Contributions to:* Now Magazine; Tatler; Harpers Queen. *Honours:* Prix Literaire, Elle Magazine, 1990.*Memberships:* Chelsea Arts CLub. *Literary Agent:* Pat Kavanagh, AD Peters. *Address:* 429 Fulham Road, SW10 9TX, London, England.

SHILLINGSBURG Miriam Jones, b. 5 Oct 1943, Baltimore, Maryland, USA. Professor of English. m. Peter L. Shillingsburg, 21 Nov 1967, 3 sons, 2 daughters. *Education:* BA, Mars Hill College, 1964; MA, University of South Carolina, 1966; PhD, 1969. *Publications:* At Home Abroad: Mark Twain in Australasia, 1988; Irving's Conquest of Granada, 1988. *Contributions to:* Atlanta Historical Journal, North Carolina Folklore, Appalachian Journal, Southern Literary Journal; Mark Twain Journal; Georgia Review; Australasian Journal of American Studies. *Honours:* National Endowment for the Humanities Awards, 1978, 1982; Phi Kappa Phi. *Memberships:* South Atlantic, and South Central Modern Language Associations; Society for the Study of Southern Literature. *Address:* Box BQ, Mississippi State, MS 39762, USA.

SHINDLER Colin, b. 3 Sept 1946, Hackney, London, England. Editor; Lecturer. m. Jean Pollock, 27 Oct 1976,

1 son, 3 daughters. *Education:* BSc Hons Chemistry; MSc Inorganic Macromolecules. *Appointments:* Editor, Jews n the USSR, 1972-75; Editor, The Jewish Quarterly, 1985-. *Publications:* Exit Visa: Detente Humanrights and Jewish Emigration Movement in the USSR, 1978; Ploughshares into Swords: Israel's Jews in the Shadow of the Intifada, 1991. *Contributions to:* New Statesman; Fortnight; Guardian; Independent; Geographical Magazine. *Address:* c/o Jewish Quarterly, PO Box 1148, London NW5 2AZ, England.

SHINICHI Kano. *See:* **JACKSON G Mark.**

SHIPMAN David, b. 4 Nov 1932, Norwich, England. Writer. *Education:* Merton College, Oxford. *Publications include:* Great Movie Stars: Golden Years, 1970, revised, updated, 1979, 1989; Great Movie Stars: International Years, 1972, revised, updated, 1980, 1989; Brando, monograph, 1974, full-length biography retitled Marlon Brando, 1989; Story of Cinema, 2 Volumes, UK 1982, 1984, 1 Volume US 1984; Good Film & Video Guide, 1984, revised and expanded 1986; Pictorial History of Science Fiction Films, 1985; Caught in the Act: Sex & Eroticism in the Cinema, 1985; Movie Talk: Who Said What About Whom In The Movies, 1989; The Great Movie Stars: The Independent Years, 1991; Judy Garland, 1992; Conema: The First Hundred Years, 1993. *Contributions to:* Films & Filming; Radio Times; Independent; Contemporary Review. *Membership:* British Film Institute, Consultant, 1989. *Literary Agent:* Frances Kelly. *Address:* c/o The Frances Kelly Agency, 111 Clifton-upon-Thames, Surrey KY2 6PL, England.

SHIRER William L(awrence), b. 1904, USA. Author; Former Journalist. *Appointments:* Foreign Correspondent for US newspapers in Europe, India and Near East, 1925-45; Columnist, New York Herald Tribune, 1942-48. *Publications:* Berlin Diary, 1941; End of a Berlin Diary, 1947; Midcentury Journey, 1952; The Challenge of Scandinavia, 1955; The Consul's Wife, 1956; The Rise and Fall of the Third Reich, 1960; The Rise and Fall of Adolf Hitler, 1961; The Sinking of the Bismarck, 1962; The Collapse of the Third Republic: An Enquiry into the Fall of France in 1940, 1969; 20th Century Journey: A Memory of a Life and the Times, vol I, The Start, 1976, vol II, The Nightmare Years, 1930-1940, 1984; Gandhi: A Memoir, 1980; Native's Return, 1945-1988, Vol III, 1990. *Address:* PO Box 487, Lenox, MA 01240, USA.

SHIRLEY John, b. 10 Feb 1953, Houoston, Texas, USA. Writer. m.1. Alexandra Allinne (div 1985) twin sons, 2. Kathy Woods, 18 Apr 1986, 1 son. *Education:* Self-educated. *Publications:* City Come A-Walkin' (fantasy novel), 1980; The Brigade (suspense thriller), 1981; Cellars (horror), 1982; Eclipse (political science fiction thriller), 1987; A Splendid Chaos (science fiction allegory), 1988; Heat Seeker (stories), 1988; In Darkness Waiting, 1988; Eclipse Penumbra (science fiction thriller), 1988; Eclipse Shattered, 1989. *Literary Agent:* Martha Millard, Brookline, Massachusetts, USA. *Address:* c/o Martha Millard, 21 Kilsyth Road, Brookline, MA 02146, USA.

SHIRREFFS Gordon Donald (Gordon Donalds, Jackson Flynn, Stewart Gordon, Art Maclean), b. 1914, USA. Author. *Publications:* Rio Bravo, 1956; Code of the Gun, 1956; Arizona Justice, 1956; Range Rebel, 1956; Fort Vengeance, 1957; Gunswift (as Stewart Gordon), 1957; Bugles on the Prairie, 1957; Massacre Creek, 1957; Son of the Thunder People, 1957; Top Gun (as Gordon Donalds), 1957; Shadow Valley, 1958; Ambush on the Mesa, 1958; Swiftwagon, 1958; Last Train from Gun Hill, 1958; The Brave Rifles, 1959; The Lonely Gun, 1959; Roanoke Raiders, 1959; Fort Suicide, 1959; Trail's End, 1959; Shadow of a Gunman, 1959; Renegade Lawman, 1959; Apache Butte, 1960; They Met Danger, 1960; The Mosquito Fleet, 1961; The Rebel Trumpet, 1961; The Proud Gun, 1961; Hangin' Pards, 1961; Ride a Lone Trail, 1961; The Gray Sea Raiders, 1961; Powder Boy of the Monitor, 1961; The Valiant Bugles, 1962; Tumbleweed Trigger, 1962; The Haunted

Treasure of the Espectros, 1962; Voice of the Gun, 1962; Rio Desperado, 1962; Action Front, 1962; The Border Guidon, 1962; Mystery of Lost Canyon, 1963; Slaughter at Broken Bow, 1963; The Cold Seas Beyond, 1963; The Secret of the Spanish Desert, 1964; Quicktrigger, 1964; Too Tough to Die, 1964; The Nevada Gun, 1964; The Hostile Beaches, 1964; The Hidden Rider of Dark Mountain, 1964; Blood Justice, 1964; Judas Gun, 1964; Gunslingers Three, 1964; Last Man Alive, 1964; Now He Is Legend, 1965; The Lone Rifle, 1965; The Enemy Seas, 1965; Barranca, 1965; The Bolo Battalion, 1966; Southwest Drifter, 1967; The Godless Breed, 1968; The Killer Sea, 1968; Five Graves to Boothill, 1968; The Mystery of the Lost Cliffdwelling, 1968; Torpedoes Away, 1969; Showdown in Sonora, 1969; Jack of Spades, 1970; The Manhunter, 1970; Brasada, 1972; Bowman's Kid, 1973; Renegade's Trail, 1974; Shootout (as Jackson Flynn), 1974; Apache Hunter, 1975; The Marauders, 1977; Rio Diablo, 1977; Legend of the Damned, 1977; Captain Cutlass, 1978; Calgaich, The Swordsman, 1980; The Untamed Breed, 1981; Showdown in Sonora, 1981; Bold Legend, 1982. *Address:* 17427 San Jose Street, Granada Hills, CA 91344, USA.

SHOESMITH Kathleen A, b. 1938, United Kingdom. Teacher; Writer. *Appointments:* Teacher, West Riding County Council, 1958-. *Publications:* Three Poems for Children, 1965; Playtime Stories, 6 titles, 1966; Judy Stories, 4 titles, 1967; Easy to Read, 6 titles, 1967; How Do They Grow, 4 titles, 1967; Jack O'Lantern, 1969; Cloud Over Calderwood, 1969; Do You Know About, 4 titles, 1970; The Tides of Tremmanion, 1970; Mallory's Luck, 1971; Return of the Royalist, 1971; Reluctant Puritan, 1972; Do You Know About, 12 titles, 1972-73; Use Your Senses, 5 titles, 1973; The Highwayman's Daughter, 1973; Belltower, 1973; The Black Domino, 1975; Elusive Legacy, 1976; The Miser's Ward, 1977; Smuggler's Haunt, 1978; Guardian at the Gate, 1979; Brackenthorpe, 1980; Autumn Escapade, 1981; Rustic Vineyard, 1982; A Minor Bequest, 1984. *Address:* 351 Fell Lane, Keighley, West Yorks, England.

SHOR Ira Neil, b. 2 June 1945. Professor of English. m. Sarah Benesch, 11 Oct 1990. *Education:* BA, 1966, MA, 1968, University of Michigan, 1966; PhD, 1971, University of Wisconsin. *Publications:* Empowering Education, 1992; Critical Teaching and Everyday Life, 1987; A Pedagogy for Liberation, 1986; Freire for the Classroom, 1987; Culture Wars: School and Society in the Conservative Restoration, 1969-91, 1992. *Contributions to:* Harvard Educational Review, College English, Journal of Education. *Honours:* Fellowships, 1966, 1982, 1983; Chancellor's Scholar, City University of NY, 1985. *Address:* English Doctoral Programme, City University of New York, 33 West 42nd Street, NY 10036, USA.

SHORE Anne. *See:* **SANFORD Annett Schorre.**

SHORROCKS Graham, b. 14 June 1948. Associate Professor. *Education:* BA, University of Birmingham, 1970; PGC, 1971; MA, University of Sheffield, 1973; PhD, 1981. *Appointments:* School Teacher, 1974-85; Assistant Professor, Memorial University of Newfoundland, 1986-90; Associate Professor, 1990-. *Publication:* A Grammar of the Dialect of Farnworth and District. *Contributions to:* Numerous Scholarly Journals. *Honours:* Edgar Allen Scholar; Various Grants; Guest of the Academy of Finland, 1993; The Bergen Exchange Fellow, 1994. *Membership:* English National Committee, European Linquistic Atlas; Editorial Board, European Lingustic Atlas, 1993. *Address:* Department of English Language & Literature, Memorial University of Newfoundland, St John's, Newfoundland, Canada A1B 3X9.

SHORT Brian Michael, b. 27 Feb 1944, Canterbury, Kent, England. University Senior Lecturer. m. (1) 2 sons, (2) Valerie, 17 Dec 1979, 1 son. *Education:* North Western Polytechnic, 1963-66; PhD, University of london, 1966-73. *Publications:* The South East From

AD100; The English Rural Community. *Contributions to:* Many inc. Agricultural History Review; Journal of Peasant Studies; Sussex Archaeological Collections. *Memberships:* Institute of British Geographers; Agricultural History Society; Sussex Archeaological Society. *Address:* CCS, Arts B, University of Sussex, Falmer, Brighton, BN1 9QN, England.

SHORT Philip, b. 1945, United Kingdom. BBC Chief Correspondent. *Appointments:* Freelance Correspondent: Malawi, 1967-70; Uganda, 1971-73; Moscow Correspondent, 1974-76, Peking Correspondent, 1977-81, Chief of BBC Paris Bureau, 1981-1990; Far East Correspondent (based in Tokyo), 1990-. *Publications:* Banda, 1974; The Dragon and the Bear, 1982. *Address:* c/o Lloyds Bank, PO Box 770, St Hellier, Jersey, Channel Islands.

SHRAPNEL Norman, b 5 Oct 1912, Grimsby, England. Journalist; Critic. *Publications:* A View of the Thames, 1977; The Performers: Politics as Theatre, 1978; The Seventies: Britain's Inward March, 1980. *Contributions to:* The Guardian; Times Literary Supplement. *Honours:* Recipient, Pol. Writer of the Year Award, 1969. *Address:* 27A Shooters Hill Rd, Blackheath, London SE3, England.

SHREEVE James Marion, b. 26 Feb 1951, Ohio, USA. Writer. m. Christine Kuethe, 8 June 1985, 1 daughter, 1 stepson, 1 stepdaughter. *Education:* BA Brown University, 1973; MFA, University of Iowa, 1979. *Publications:* Lucy's Child, Co-author), 1989; Nature: The Other Earthlings, 1987; The Sex Token, 1976. *Contributions to:* Discover, MD, Science 8, Science Illustrated, Smithsonian. *Literary Agent:* Victoria Pryor, Arcadia Ltd. *Address:* 10549 St Paul Street, Kensington, Maryland 20895, USA.

SHRIMSLEY Bernard, b. 1931, United Kingdom. Newspaper Editor. m. Norma Jessie Alexandra Porter, 1952, 1 daughter. *Appointments:* Assistant Editor, Daily Mirror, London, 1964-68; Editor, Liverpool Daily Post, 1968-69; Deputy Editor, 1969-72, Editor, 1972-75, The Sun, London; Editor, News of the World, London, 1975-80; Editor, The Mail on Sunday, London, 1982; Associate Editor, Daily Express, London, 1983-; British Press Awards judge, 1989-91; Vice Chairman, British Press Council, 1989-90. *Publications:* The Candidates, 1968; Lion Rampant, 1984. *Membership:* Society of Authors. *Literary Agent:* John Farquharson Ltd, England. *Address:* Daily Express, Ludgate House, 245 Blackfriars Road, London SE1 9UX, England.

SHRIRA Shoshana, (Sh Shani Sh. Sh. Sh.), b. 10 Feb 1917, Poland. Writer. m. Ariel Kohn, 15 May 1941, 1 daughter. *Education:* English Diploma, London University; Phonetics, Institute of Education, London. *Publications:* The Green River, 1947; Bread of the Beloved, 1958; The Gates of Gaze, 1960; For Whom for Whom for Whom, 1971; Thanks to the Fig Trees, 1972; The Yellow Bachelors, 1979; Translations from English to Hebrew. *Contributions to:* Critic: Children of the Ran; Critic: Literary Theatrical Criticism; Playing the Violin. *Honours:* Prizes for Literature, 1960, 1958, 1972. *Memberships:* Hebrew Writer Association; PEN International; Hebrew Journalists Association; Writers and Artists Akum Association. *Address:* 9 Bezalel St, Tel Aviv, Israel.

SHUBIN Seymour, b. 14 Sept 1921, Philadelphia, USA. Author. m. Gloria Amet, 27 Aug 1957, 1 son, 1 daughter. *Education:* BA, Temple University. *Appointments:* Managing Editor: Official Detective Stories Magazine; Psychiatric Reporter. *Publications:* Anyone's My Name, 1953; Manta, 1958; Wellville, USA, 1961; The Captain, 1982; Holy Secrets, 1984; Voices, 1985; Never Quite Dead, 1989. *Contributions to:* Saturday Evening Post; Reader's Digest; Redbook; Family Circle; Story; Ellery Queen's Mystery Magazine; Emergency Medicine; Official Detective Stories Magazine; Perspectives in Biology and Medicine;

numerous others. *Honours:* Jesse H Neal Award, 1978; Edgar Allan Poe Special Edgar Award, 1983; Special Citation for Fiction Athenaem, 1984; Fellowship in Literature, Pennsylvania Council on the Arts. *Memberships:* Poets Playwrights Editors Essayists and Novelists American Centre; American Society of Journalists and Authors; Mystery Writers of America; Authors Guild. *Address:* 122 Harrogate Road, Wynnewood, PA 19096, USA.

SHUKMAN Harold b. 23 Mar 1931. University Teacher of Modern Russian History. m. (1) Ann King Farlow 1956, (div. 1970), 2 sons, 1 daughter, (2) Barbara King Farlow. *Education:* BA Hons, Nottingham, 1956; DPhil, 1961; MA, 1961, Oxford. *Publications:* Lenin and the Russian Revolution, 1977; Blackwells Encyclopedia of the Russian Revolution, 1988; Andrei Gromyko Memories, (editor and translator), 1989; Children of the Arbat, (translator), 1988; Heavy Sand, (translator), 1981; Triumph and Tradgedy: Stalin (editor & translator), 1991, Stalin's Generals (editor). *Contributions to:* Commentary; TLS; THES; Independent; Times; English Historical Review; Economist; Soviet (East European) Jewish Affairs. *Memberships:* Authors Society; Translators Association; Royal Historical Society, Fellow. *Address:* St. Antony's College, Oxford OX2 6JF, England.

SHULER Linda Lay, b. 12 Dec 1925, Los Angeles, California, USA. novelist. m. 7 Sept 1945, 2 sons, 2 daughters. *Education:* English Honours, Manual Arts High School; University of California at Los Angeles. *Publications:* She who Remembers, 1988; Voice of the Eagle, 1992. *Contributions to:* British Screen Writer's Digest. *Honours:* Distinguished Award, Texas Safety Association, 65. *Memberships:* The Author's Guild; Circuit Writers of Brownwood; Oregon Writer's Colony; National Safety Council, Chicago; Business and Professional Women's Club, Dallas. *Literary Agent:* Jean V Naggar, New York. *Address:* 2400 Bonita, Brownwood, Texas, 76801, USA.

SHULMAN Alix Kates, b. 17 Aug 1932, Cleveland, Ohio, USA. 1 son, 1 daughter. *Education:* BA Case Western Reserve, 1953; MA Humanities, NY University, 1978. *Appointments:* Graduate Writing Programme, NY University, 1981-84; Writing Workshops, Yale, Newhave, CT, 1979-81. Visiting Writer in Residence, Ohio State University, Columbus, 1987; Citizens chair, University of Hawaii at Manoa, Honolulu, 1991-92. *Publications:* Memoirs of an Ex-Prom Queen, 1972; Burning Questions, 1978; On the Stroll, 1981; In Every Women's Life..., 1987; Red Emma Speaks; To the Barricades, 1971; Basley on the Number Life, 1970; Finders Keepers, 1971; Awake and Asleep, 1971. *Contributions to:* Atlantic Monthly; Village Voice; New York Times Book Review; Redbook; Feminist Studies; Cosmopolitan; Life. *Honours:* Fiction Grant, National Endowment for the Arts, 1983; American Academy in Rome Visiting Artist, 1982; DE Witt Wallace Reders Digest Fellow, 1979. *Memberships:* PEN American Centre, Executive Board, 1976- 91, VP, 1982, 1983; Authors Guild; National Writers Union. *Literary Agent:* Amanda Urban, ICM.

SCUMSKY Zena. *See:* **COLLIER Zena.**

SHUPE Anson. *See:* **SHUPE Anson David Jr.**

SHUPE Anson David Jr, (Anson Shupe), b. 21 Jan 1948, Buffalo, New York, USA. Sociology Professor. m. Janet ANn Klickua, 27 June 1970. 1 son, 1 daughter. *Education:* BA, College of Wooster, Ohio, 1970; MA, 1972, PhD, 1975, Indiana University. *Publications:* The Darker Side of Virtue, 1991; The Morman Corporate Empire, 1985; The Family Secret, 1983; Strange Gods, 1981; Moonies in America, 1979; The New Vigilantes, 1980; Co- editor: The Politics of Religion and Social Change; Secularization and Fundamentalism Reconsidered. *Contributions to:* The Wall Street Journal; GEO; The Christian Century; Religious Broadcasting;

Fort Worth Star Telegram; Dallas Morning News; Ft Wayne Journal; Gazette. *Memberships:* American Sociological Association; Association for the Sociology of Religion; Society for the Scientific Study of Religion; Religious Research Association. *Literary Agent:* Jeffrey H Harman, The Jeff Harman Agency, 500 Greenwich Street, Suite 5016, NY 10013, USA. *Address:* Sociology & Anthropology Department, Indiana/Purdue University, Fort Wayne, IN 46805, USA.

SHUSTERMAN Richard Mark, b. 3 Dec 1949. Philosopher. m. Rivka Nahmani, 16 Aug 1970, 2 sons, 1 daughter. *Education:* BA, Hebrew University, 1971; MA, 1973; PhD, St Johns College, Oxford University, 1979. *Publications:* Pragmatist Aesthetius; The Interpretire Turn; Analytic Aesthetics; T S Eliot and the philosophy of Criticism; The object of Literary Criticism. *Contributions to:* British Journal of Aesthetic; New Literary History; Poetics Today; Philosophical Quarterly; Critique; Journal of Aesthetics. *Honours:* NEH Fellowship. *Memberships:* American Philosophical Assocation; British Society of Aesthetics; American Society for Aesthetics. *Address:* 1810 Hemlock Circle, Abington, PA 19001, USA.

SHUTTLE Penelope Diane, b. 12 May 1947, Staines, Middlesex, England. Writer. m. Peter Redgrove, 16 Sept 1980, 1 daughter. *Publications:* Novels: An Excusable Vengeance, 1967; All The Usual Hours of Sleeping, 1969; Wailing Monkey Embracing A Tree, 1974; Rainsplitter In The Zodiac Garden, 1976; The Mirror Of The Giant, 1979; (with Peter Redgrove) The Terrors Of Dr Treviles, 1974; The Glass Cottage, 1976. Poetry Collections: The Orchard Upstairs, 1980; The Child-Stealer, 1983; The Lion From Rio, 1986; Adventures With My Horse, 1988; The Hermaphrodite Album (with Peter Redgrove), 1973; Taxing The Rain, 1992. Psychology and Sociology: The Wise Wound: Menstruation and Everywoman (with Peter Redgrove), 1978, updated 1986, 1989, 1990. Numerous pamphlet collections, broadsheets, radio dramas, recordings, readings and television feature. *Contributions to:* Times Literary Supplement; Encounter; Outposts; The Aylesford Review; The Poetry Review; Pequod; Poetry Book Society Xmas Supplements, 1978, 1980 and 1981; Poetry Australia; Poetry Southwest; Poetry Chicago; The Literary Review; The Manhattan Review; Stand; Poetry Book Society Anthology 1987/8. *Honours:* Joint 3rd prize, Radio Times Drama Bursaries Competition, 1974; 3 Arts Council Awards, 1969, 1972 and 1985; Greenwood Poetry Prize, 1972; E C Gregory Award for Poetry, 1974. *Address:* c/o David Higham Ass Ltd., 5-8 Lower John Street, London W1R 4HA, England.

SHUTTLEWORTH Christine Maria, b. 31 Oct 1939, Cambridge, England. Indexer; Editor; Translator. m. Frank Shuttleworth, 18 Jan 1981, 1 daughter. *Education:* BA, 1961. *Publications:* English Version of Fanny von Arnstein. *Contributions to:* Country Life; Art & Antiques Weekly; Antiques & Art Monitor. *Memberships:* Society of Authors; Translators Association; Society of Indexers; Society of Freelance Editors & Proofreaders. *Address:* Flat 1, 25 St Stephen's Avenue, London W12 8JB.

SHVARTS Elena, b. 17 May 1948, Leningrad, USSR. Writer. m. Michael Sheinker, 1986. *Education:* Leningrad Theatre Institute, 1971. *Publications:* Trudy i Dni Monghim Lavinii; Tanzujuschij David; Poems; Stihotvocemja. *Honours:* Andrej Belgi Award: Prize of Magazine Junost. *Membership:* Union of Writers. *Address:* 5 jg Krasmarmejskaja, 30, 3, 198052 St Petersburg, Russia.

SICHOL Marcia Winifred, b. 17 Oct 1940, Lewiston, Maine, USA. Planning Director; Lecturer. *Education:* BA magna cum laude, Humanities, Villanova , 1969; MA 1977, PHd, 1984, Philosophy, Georgetown University. *Publications:* Book, The Making of a Nuclear Peace: The Task of Today's Just War Theorists, 1989. *Contributions to:* Thought, Fordham University Journal, 1992. *Honours:* Hubert Humphrey Fellowship, arms control and disarment, 1983-84. *Memberships:* Society of Holy Child Jesus; Trustee, Rosemont College; Society of Christian Ethics. *Hobbies:* Geology; Astronomy; Musical Skiing; Snorkelling. *Address:* 460 Shadeland Avenue, Drexel Hill, PA 19026, USA.

SICK Gary Gordon, b. 4 Apr 1935, Kansas, USA. Writer; Consultant. m. Karlan Kay Ison, 18 June 1960, 1 son, 1 daughter. *Appointments:* BA French Literature, University of Kansas, 1957; MS, International Affairs, George Washington University, 1970; PhD, Political Science, Columbia University, NY, 1973. *Publications:* October Surprise; America's Hostages in Iran and the Election of Ronald Regan, 1991; ALI Fall Down: America's Tragic Encounter with Iran, 1985. *Contributions to:* New York Times and other major newspapers; Ethics and International Affairs; Middle East Journal; SAIS Review. *Honours:* 20th Century Fund Book Grant, 1989-90. *Memberships:* Authors Guild and Authors League of America; Founding member and Associate Chairman, Columbia University Seminar on the Middle East, New York; Chirman, Middle East Watch; Board, Middle East Institute, Washington; Editorial Board, Middle East Journal; The Council of Foreign Relations, New York; International Institute for Strategic Studies, London; *Literary Agent:* James Stein, William Morris Agency. *Address:* 395 Riverside Drive, New York, NY 10025, USA.

SIEGEL Lee, b. 22 July 1945, Los Angeles, California, USA . Professor of English. 1 son. *Education:* BA, University of California, Berkeley, 1967; MFA, Columbia University, 1969; D Phil, Oxford University, 1975. *Appointments:* Instructor in English, Western Washington University, Bellingham, 1969-72; Professor of English, University of Hawaii at Manoa, Honolulu, 1976-, Chairman of Graduate Program; Guest Lecturer at Oriental Institute, Oxford University 1985 and College de France 1985. *Publications:* Vivisections (drawings and poems) 1973; Sacred and Profane Love in Indian Traditions, 1979; (with Jagdish Sharma) Dreams in the Sramanic Traditions, 1980; Fires of Love, Waters of Peace: Passion and Renunciation in Indian Culture, 1983; Laughing Matters: Satire and Humor in India, 1987; Sweet Nothings (translation of the Amarusataka) 1988; Author and director of Mask and Mystery, a television series produced at Media Center, University of Hawaii at Manoa, 1978. Contributor to Encyclopaedia of Religion. *Contributions to:* articles and reviews to history, religion and philosophy journals and to newspapers. *Honours:* Senior Fellow of American Institute of Indian Studies and Smithsonian Institution, 1979, 1983 and 1987; Grants from Center for Asian and Pacific Studies, 1981 and American Council of Learned Societies and Social Science Research Council, 1982, 1985 and 1987; Presidential Award for Excellence in Teaching from the University of Hawaii, 1986. *Memberships:* International Brotherhood of Magicians; Society of American Magicians; Society of Indian Magicians. *Address:* Department of Religion, University of Hawaii at Manoa, 2500 Campus Road, Honolulu, HI 96822, USA.

SIEGEL Robert Harold, b. 18 Aug 1939, Illinois, USA. Professor of English. m. 19 Aug 1961, 3 daughters. *Education:* BA, Wheaton College, 1961; MA John Hopkins University, 1962; PhD English, Harvard University, 1968. *Appointments include:* Assistant Professor, 1976-79, Associate Professor, 1979-83, Professor of English, 1983-, University of Wisconsin, Milwaukee. *Publications:* Poetry: In a Pig's Eye, 1980; The Beasts an the Elders, 1973; Fiction: The Ice at the End of the World, 1993; White Whale: A novel, 1991; Whalesong: A Novel, 1991; The Kingdom of Wundle, 1982; Alpha Centauri, 1982. *Contributions to:* Atlantic Monthly; The Poetry Anthology; New York Quarterly; Midwest Review; Carolina Quarterly; Beloit Poetry Journal. *Honours:* Sabbatical Grant and Research Grant, University of Wisconsin; National Endowment for the Arts Creative Writing Fellowship; Ingram Merrill Foundation Award for Writing Poetry, 1979. *Literary Agent:* Marian Young. *Address:* Department of English,

University of Wisconsin-Milwaukee, Milwaukee WI 53201, USA.

SIEPMANN Mary Aline (Mary Wesley), b. 24 June 1912. Writer. m. (1) 2nd Baron Swinfen, 1937 (diss 1945), 2 sons, (2) Eric Siepmann, 1952 (d 1970), 1 son. *Education:* LSE. *Publications:* Speaking Terms (for children), 1968; The Sixth Seal (for children), 1968; Haphazard House (for children), 1983; Jumping the Queue, 1983; The Camomile Lawn, 1984; Harnessing Peacocks, 1985; The Vacillations of Poppy Carew, 1986; Not That Sort of Girl, 1987; Second Fiddle, 1988; A Sensible Life, 1990; A Dubious Legacy, 1992. *Address:* c/o Transworld Publishers, 61-63 Uxbridge Road, London W5 5SA, England.

SIGAL Clancy, b. 1926, USA. Novelist. *Publications:* Weekend in Dinlock, 1960; Going Away: A Report, A Memoir, 1963; Zone of the Interior, 1976. *Address:* c/o Jonathan Cape, 30 Bedford Square, London WC1B 3EL, England.

SIKULA Vincent, b. 19 Oct 1936, Dubova, Czechoslovakia. Editor. m. Anna, 6 Aug 1983, 1 son, 3 daughters. *Publications:* With Rozarka, 1966; Vacations with Oncle Rafael, 1966; Masters, 1976; Geranium, 1977; Vilma, 1979; George, grees George, 1979. *Contributions to:* Numerous professional journals. *Honours:* Award, Pen Club, 1966; Awards, Publishing House Slovensky Spisvatel, 1964, 1979; Award, Union of Czechoslovak Writers, 1966; Award, Publishing House Smena, 1966; Award, Union of Slovak Writers, 1968; Award, Franvo Krála, 1975. *Membership:* Union of Slovak Writers. *Address:* Palckeho 20, 81102 Bratislava, Czechoslovakia.

SILBER Joan Karen, b. 14 June 1945, Milburn, New York, USA. Novelist. *Education:* BA, Sarah Lawrence College, 1967; MA, New York University, 1979. *Appointments:* Writing Faculty, Sarah Lawrence College, 1985-; Warren Wilson MFA Program for Writers, 1986-; The Poetry Centre of the 92nd Street Y, 1987-; University of Utah, 1988. *Publications:* Household Words, 1980; In the City, 1987. *Contributions to:* Book Reviews for New York Times Book Review, Ms, Newsday, Washington Post, Village Voice; short stories in Paris Review, Redbook. *Honours:* Ernest Hemingway Award, 1981; Guggenheim Fellowship, 1984-85; New York Foundation for the Arts, 1986; NEA, 1986. *Memberships:* PEN; Authors League; Poets & Writers. *Literary Agent:* Amanda Urban, ICM, New York, USA. *Address:* 43 Bond St, New York, NY 10012, USA.

SILBERMAN James Henry, b. 21 Mar 1927, Boston, Massachusetts, USA. Editor; Publisher. m. (1) 1 son, 1 daughter, (2) Selma Shapiro, 26 Aug 1986. *Education:* AB, Harvard University, 1950. *Appointments:* Assistant to Publisher, Writer Inc, 1950-51; Assistant to Advertising Manager, Little, Brown and Co, 1951-53; Publicity Director, 1953-55, Editor, 1954-55, Executive Editor, 1955-59, Vice-President, Editor-in-Chief, 1959-63, Dial Press Inc; Editor, The Dial, 1959-62; Senior Editor, 1963-65, Executive Editor, 1965-66, Executive Editor, Vice-President, 1966-68, Vice-President, Editor-in-Chief, 1968-76, Publisher, 1975-76, Random House Inc, New York City; President, Editor-in-Chief, Summit Books Division, Simon & Schuster, New York City, 1976-91; Vice-President, Senior Editor, Little Brown & Co, 1991-; Member, Advisory Committee, George Polk Memorial Awards, 1980-; Judge, 1st Novel, American Book Awards, 1982. *Memberships:* PEN; Association of American Publishers, Freedom to Read Committee 1971-80, Freedom to Publish Committee 1982; Book Table; Publishers Lunch Club; Board of Directors, Corporation of Yaddo, Board of Directors, 1987-; Executive Committee, 1989-; Harvard (NYC); Century Association. *Address:* Little Brown and Company, 1271 Avenue of the Americas, New York, NY 10020, USA.

SILKIN Jon, b. 2 Dec 1930, London, England. Poet; Critic; Editor. m. Lorna Tracy. 3 sons (1 dec), 1 daughter.

Education: Degree in English, 1962. *Literary Appointments:* Journalist, 1947; Visiting Poet, University of Iowa, 1968, 1991; Distinguished Writer-in-Residence, The American University, 1989; University of Tsukuba, 1991-. *Publications include:* The Peaceable Kingdom, 1954, 1975; The Two Freedoms, 1958; The Re-ordering of the Stones, 1961; Nature with Man, 1965; Poems New and Selected, 1966; Amana Grass, 1971; Out of Battle: Criticism of Poets of World War I, 1972-1987; Poetry of the Committed Individual: anthology of poetry from Stand, 1973; The Principle of Water, 1974; The Little Time-Keeper, 1976; Editor, The Penguin Book of First World War Poetry, 1979; The Psalms with their Spoils, 1980; Selected Poems, 1980, englarged edition, 1988; Gurney: a play in verse, 1985; Editor, The War Poems of Wilfred Owen, 1985; Editor with Jon Glover, The Penguin Book of First World War Prose, 1989; The Ship's Pasture (Poems), 1986; The first twenty-four years, Contemporary Authors Biography Series, Volume 5, 1987; Natan Zach, Against Parting translation, 1967; The Lens-breakers, 1992. *Honours:* Geoffrey Faber Memorial Prize for Nature with Man, 1966; Awarded Gregory Fellowship in Poetry, University of Leeds, 1958; Visiting Poet, Mishkenot Sha'ananim, Jerusalem, 1980; Bingham Poet, University of Louisville, USA, 1981; Elliston Poet, University of Cincinnati, 1983; Visiting Poet, yearly festival, University of Notre Dame, 1985; Fellow, Royal Society of Literature; Visiting Poet, Writers' Conference, University of North Alabama, 1987. *Memberships:* Literary Fellow, Dumfries & Galloway Arts Association. *Literary Agent:* Laurence Pollinger. *Address:* 19 Haldane Terrace, Newcastle Upon Tyne NE2 3AN, England.

SILLITOE Alan, b. 1928, United Kingdom. Author. *Publications:* Saturday Night and Sunday Morning, 1958; The Loneliness of the Long Distance Runner, 1959; The General, 1960; Key to the Door, 1961; The Ragman's Daughter, 1963; Road to Volgograd, 1964; A Falling Out of Love, Poems, 1964; The Death of William Posters, 1965; A Tree on Fire, 1967; The City Adventures of Marmalade Jim, 1967 (for children); Love in the Environs of Voronezh, (poems), 1968; Guzman, Go Home, 1968; All Citizens are Soldiers, Play, with Ruth Fainlight, 1969; A Start in Life, 1970; Travels in Hihilon, 1971; Raw Material, 1972; Men Women and Children, 1973; The Flame of Life, 1974; Mountains and Caverns, Selected Essays, 1975; The Widower's Son, 1976; Big John and the Stars (for children) 1977; Three Plays, 1978; Snow on the Side of Lucifer, 1979; the Storyteller, 1979; Marmalade Jim at the Farm (for children) 1980; The Second Chance, 1981; Her Victory, 1982; The Saxon Shore Way, with Fay Godwin, 1983; The Lost Flying Boat, 1983; Sun Before Departure, poems, 1984; Down From the Hill, 1984; Marmalade Jim and the Fox, (for children) 1985; Life Goes On, 1985; Tides and Stone Walls, poems, 1986; Nottinghamshire, with D. Sillitoe, 1987; Out of the Whirlpool, 1987; The Open Door, 1988; Last Loves, 1990; Leonard's War, 1991. *Address:* c/o Savage Club, 9 Fitzmaurice Place, London SW1, England.

SILLS Leslie Elka, b. 26 Jan 1948, Brooklyn, New York, USA. Artist; Author; Lecturer. m. Robert J Oresick, 9 July 1978, 1 son. *Education:* BA Psychology, Boston University, 1969; School of the Museum of Fine Arts, Boston, MA, 1970-73. *Publications:* Inspirations: Stories about Women Artists, 1989; Visions: Stories About Women Artists, 1993; Pilgrims and Pioneers: New England Women in the Arts, 1987. *Contributions to:* School Arts Magazine; Sojourner. *Honours:* Notable Book Award, American Library Association, 1989; Booklist's Editors' Choice, 1989; Best 10 Books for Children, Parenting Magazine, 1989; Recommended List, Biographies for children, 1991. *Memberships:* New England Authors and Illustrators of Children's Books; Natonal Women's Caucus for Art, Boston, Co-Chair, 1984-85. *Literary Agent:* Marie Brown, Marie Brown Associates, NYC, USA. *Address:* 38 St Paul Street, Brookline, MA 02146, USA.

SILLS-DOCHERTY Jonathon John (John Docherty), b. 7 Jan 1941, Bowden, Cheshire, England.

Humorous Writer, Lyricist & Poet. *Education:* Fielden Park College, West Didsbury, Manchester, 1977; Poetry Workshop 1981, Extramural Department 1986-87, University of Manchester. *Appointments include:* Editor, Guardian Society, 1974; Reporter, Dun & Bradstreet, 1975; Proof reader, sub-editor, biography compiler, Odd Fellow Magazine. *Publications include:* A Walk Around the City & Other Groans, 1969, revised 1973; Words on Paper, 1977; From Bottoms to Tops & Back Again, 1977, limited edition 1987; Ballads of Fantasy & Reality, 1982; Ballads of Ecstasy & Perspicacity, 1987; Ballads of North West John (plus cassette tape), 1987. *Contributions to:* News/Views, House Journal, Mappin & Webb; Sunday Times; Sunday Telegraph; Manchester Evening News; Stretford & Urmston Journal; Daily Mail; Star; Artful Reporter; What's On In Hulme; Dun & Bradstreet Report Magzine; Radio Manchester. *Honours:* North West Arts Poetry Award, 1978; Double prizewinner, Tribute for St George's Day, Granada TV, 1978; Various other prizes, awards, including most prolific letter writer to Manchester Evening News. *Memberships include:* Turner Society; Court School of Dancing; Independent Order of Odd Fellows; Friend, North West Arts, Manchester City Art Gallery; Authors North. *Address:* 43 Cornbrook Park Road, Old Trafford, Manchester M15 4EH, England.

SILMAN Roberta, b. 29 Dec. 1934, New York, USA. Writer. m. Robert Silman, 14 June 1956. *Education:* BA, English Literature, Cornell University, 1956; MFA, Writing, Sarah Lawrence College, 1975. *Publications:* Somebody Else's Child, 1976; Blood Relations, 1977; Boundaries, 1979, UK 1980; The Dream Dredger, 1986; Beginning the World Again, 1990. *Contributions to:* Numerous magazines in USA and UK including: Atlantic monthly; New Yorker; McCall's Redbook; Family Circle; Hadassah. *Honours:* Child Study Association, Award for Best Children's Book (Somebody Else's Child), 1976; Honourable Mention, Hemingway Award, 1978, Janet Kafka Prize, 1978, 1980; Guggenheim Fellowship, 1979; NEA, Fellowship, 1983; National Magazine Award, Fiction, 1984; PEN Syndicated Fiction Project Award, 1983-84. *Memberships:* PEN (Freedom to Write Committee); Authors Guild; Poets and Writers; Phi Beta Kappa. *Agent:* Philippa Brophy, Sterling Lord Literistic. *Address:* 18 Larchmont Street, Ardsley, NY 10502, USA.

SILVER Alfred. *See:* SILVER Robert Leslie.

SILVER Richard. *See:* BULMER Henry Kenneth.

SILVER Robert Leslie, (Alfred Silver), b. 13 Mar 1951, Brandon, Manitoba, Canada. Writer. m. Jane Buss, 24 Apr 1989. *Publications:* Lord of the Plains; Red River story; Where the Ghost Horse Runs; A Savage Place; Good Time Charlies Back In Town Again. *Literary Agent:* Mitch Douglas ICM. *Address:* Rural route 1, Ellershouse, Nova Scotia, Canada BON 1LO.

SILVERBERG Robert (Walker Chapman, Walter Drummond, Ivar Jorgenson, Calvin Knox, Calvin M Knox, David Osborne, Robert Randall, Lee Sebastian), b. 1935. American, Full-time writer of Science fiction/Fantasy, Children's fiction, Children;s non-fiction, History, Sciences, Biography. *Publications:* Science fiction includes: The Stochastic Man, 1975; Shadrach in the Furnace, 1976; The Shores of Tomorrow (short stories), 1976; The Best of Robert Silverberg (short stories) 1976; Capricorn Games (short stories) 1976; The Songs of Summer (short stories) 1979; Lord Valentine's Castle, 1980; Majipoor Chronicles, 1982; World of a Thousand Colours (short stories) 1982; Valentine Pontifex, 1983; Land of Darkness, 1983; The Conglomeroid Cocktail Party, 1984; Tom O'Bedlam, 1985; Sailing to Byzantium, 1985; Star of the Gypsies, 1986; Beyond the Safe Zone (stories) 1986; other publications include: (ed)The Androids Are Coming, 1979; (ed)Lost Worlds, Unknown Horizons, 1979; (ed)Edge of Space, 1979; (ed with Martin H Greenberg and Joseph D Olander) Car Sinister, 1979; (ed with Martin H Greenberg and Joseph D Olander) Dawn of Time: Prehistory Through Science Fiction,

1979; (ed) The Best of New Dimensions, 1979; (ed with Martin H Greenberg) The Arbor House Treasury of Modern Science Fiction, 1980; (ed with Martin Greenberg) The Arbor House Treasury of Great Science Fiction Short Novels, 1980; (ed with Martin H Greenberg) The Arbor House Treasury of Science Fiction Masterpieces, 1983; (ed with Martin H Greenberg) The Time Travelers: A Science Fiction Quartet, 1985.

SILVERMAN-WEINREICH Beatrice. *See:* WEINREICH Beatrice.

SILVERSTEIN Herma, b. 21 Feb 1945, Fort Worth, Texas, USA. Author, Children's & Young Adult Books. (div), 2 sons. *Education:* BA, Spanish, Sophie Newcomb College, Tulane University, 1967. *Literary Appointments:* Panellist, International Reading Association, 1987; Faculty, writers' workshops, Highlights for Children Magazine, 1987; Speaker, schools & libraries. *Publications include:* Children's books: Anti-Semitism: A Modern Perspective, with Caroline Arnold, 1985; Mary Lou Retton & the New Gymnasts, 1985; Scream Machines: Roller Coasters Past, Present & Future, 1986; Hoaxes That Made Headlines, with C. Arnold, 1986; Mad Mad Monday, 1988; David Ben-Gurion, biography, 1988; Spies Among Us: Truth About Modern Espionage, 1988; Teenage Pregnancy, 1988. *Contributions to:* Highlights for Children; The Friend; Bulletin, Society of Childrens Book Writers. *Honour:* Authors Award, Highlights for Children, article on Mother Teresa, 1983. *Memberships:* Society of Childrens Book Writers; Southern California Council on Literature for Children & Young People; Womens Writers West. *Literary Agent:* Andrea Brown. *Address:* 509 14th Street, Santa Monica, California 90402, USA.

SILVERSTEIN Shel(by), b. 1932, USA. Author; Cartoonist; Composer; Songwriter. *Appointments:* Freelance Writer and Cartoonist for Playboy, Chicago, and other magazines. *Publications:* Now Here's My Plan: A Book of Futilities, drawings, 1960; Uncle Shelby's ABZ Book: Primer for Tender Young Minds, children fiction, 1961; Playboy's Teevee Jeebies, drawings, 1963; Uncle Shelby's Story of Lafcadio, The Lion Who Shot Back, children's fiction, 1963; Who Wants a Cheap Rhinoceros, children's fiction, 1964; The Giving Tree, children's fiction, 1964; Uncle Shelby's A Giraffe and A Half, children's verse, 1964; Uncle Shelby's Zoo: Don't Bump the Glump, children's verse, 1964; More Playboy Teevee Jeebies, drawings, 1965; Where the Sidewalk Ends: The Poems and Drawings of Shel Silverstein, children's verse, 1974; The Missing Piece, children's fiction, 1976; Different Dances, drawings, 1979; The Missing Piece Meets the Big O, children's fiction, 1981; A Light in the Attic: Poems and Drawings, children's verse, 1981. *Address:* c/o Harper Collins, 10 East 53rd Street, New York, NY 10022, USA.

SILVESTER Peter P, b. 25 Jan 1935. Engineer. m. Elizabeth V Placek, 1958. *Education:* BSEE, Carneigie Institute of Technology, 1956; MASc, University of Toronto, 1958; PhD, McGill University, 1964. *Publications:* Data structures for Engineering Software; Finite Elements for Electrical Engineers; Computer Aided Design in Magnetics; The Unix System Guidebook; Finite Elements in Electrical and Magnetic Field Problems; Computer Engineering. *Contributions to:* Numerous. *Memberships:* IEEE; NYAS; Royal Photographic Society. *Address:* Department of Electrical Engineering, McGill University, 3480 University Street, Montreal, Canada H3A 2A7.

SILVIS Randall Glenn, b. 15 July 1950, Rimersburg, Pennsylvania, USA. Novelist; Playwright. m. Rita Lynne McCanna, 25 Sept 1982, 2 sons. *Education:* Clarion University, BS, 1973; Indiana University, MEd, 1976. *Appointments:* James Thurber Writer in Residence, Thurber House, Columbus, 1989; Mercyhurst College, Pennsylvania, 1989-90; Ohio State University, 1991,1992. *Publications:* The Luckiest Man in the World; Excelsior; An Occasional Hell; Under the

Rainbow; Driven to Acts of Kindness. *Contributions to:* Prism International; Manoa; Destination Discovery; Pittsburgh Magazine. *Honours:* National Endowment for the Arts Fellowship; Drue Heinz Literature Prize; National Playwright Showcase Award; Fulbright Senior Scholar Research Grant; James Thurber Writer in Residence. *Address:* PO Box 297, St Petersburg, PA 16054, USA.

SIMECKA Martin M. *See:* SIMECKA Milan.

SIMECKA Milan, (Martin M Simecka), b. 3 Nov 1957, Bratiscava. Writer. m. Marta Simecjova, 7 July 1985, 1 son, 1 daughter. *Education:* Private Education. *Publications:* L'Annee De Chien; The Genie; Luminous Signals. *Contributions to:* Lettre International; Liber; Uncaptive Minds; Literarni Noviny; Slovenske Pohcady. *Honours:* Award of Jiri Orten; The Pegasus Prize. *Memberships:* Community of Writers in Slovakia; Slovak Centre of PEN. *Literary Agent:* Aura Pont. *Address:* Na UVrati 35, 82104 Brajislava, Czechoslovakia.

SIMIONESCU Mircea Horia, b. 23 Jan 1928, Tirgoviste, Romania. Writer. m. Teodora Dinca, 26 Feb 1953, 2 daughters. *Education:* BA, Literature, Bucharest University, 1964. *Publications:* The Well Tempered Ingenious Man, 4 volumes, 1969, 1970, 1980, 1983; After 1900, About Noon, 1974; Ganymede's Kidnapping, 1975; Endless Dangers, 1978; Advice for the Dauphin, 1979; Ulysse and the Shadow, 1982; The Banquet, 1982; The Cutaway, 1984; Sale by Auction, 1985; Three Looking Glasses, 1987; The Siege of the Common Place, 1988; The Angel with an Apron, 1992. *Contributions to:* various magazines and journals, Radio & TV programmes in Romania; PEN Club. *Honours:* Prize, for Prose, Romanian Academy, 1976; Prize for Prose, Writers Union of Romania, 1974. *Memberships:* Writers Union of Romania; Journalists Union of Romania. *Address:* 3 Belgrad Str, Bucharest, CD 71248, Romania.

SIMKIN Tom, b. 11 Nov 1933, Auburn, New York, USA. Geologist. m. Sharon Russell, 3 July 1965, 1 son, 1 daughter. *Education:* BS Swarthmore College, 1955; MSE, 1960, PhD, 1965, Princeton University. *Publications:* Volcanoes of the World, 1981; Krakatau 1883: The Volcanic Eruption and its Effects, 1983; Global Volcanism, 1975-85, 1989; Volcano Letter, 1987. *Contributions to:* Various scientific journals. *Honours:* Choice Outstanding Academic Book Award, 1984. *Memberships:* International Association of Volcanology, Editor: Catalog and Active Volcanoes; Geological Society of Washington, President, 1990; Charles Darwin Foundation for Galapagos Isles, Sec for Americas, 1970-90; American Geophysical Union, 1972-. *Address:* Smithsonian Institution, National Museum of National History MS119, Washington DC 20560, USA.

SIMMERMAN Jim, b. 5 Mar 1952, Denver, Colorado, USA. English Professor; Poet. *Education:* BS, Education 1973, MA, English 1976, University of Missouri; MFA, Creative Writing, University of Iowa, 1980. *Appointments include:* Member, Literary Panel 1984, 1986, Literary Grants Panel 1987, Arizona Commission on the Arts; Editorial Board member, Pushcart Prize series, 1985-. *Publications:* Home, 1983; Bad Weather, 1987; Once Out Of Nature, 1989. Numerous poems. *Contributions to:* Literary journals & anthologies (poetry) including: Antaeus; Bread Loaf Anthology of Contemporary American Poetry; Anthology of Magazine Verse; Poetry; Missouri Review; Western Humanities Review. *Honours:* Poetry Fellowships 1983, 1987, Arizona Commission on the Arts; Creative Writing Fellowship Grant, National Endowment for the Arts, 1984; Poetry Fellowship, Fine Arts Work Centre, 1984; Pushcart Writers Choice Selection, 1984; Pushcart Prize, 1985. *Memberships:* Associated Writing Programmes; Poets & Writers Inc. *Address:* c/o English Department, Box 6032, Northern Arizona University, Flagstaff, AZ 86011, USA.

SIMMONS Jack b.30 Aug 1915, Isleworth, Middlesex, England. Retired Professor; Writer. *Education:* Westminster School, 1928-33; BA, MA, Christ Church, Oxford, 1933-37. *Appointments:* Professor of History, University of Leicester, 1947-75. *Publications include:* The Railways of Britain, 1961, 3rd edition 1986; The Railway in Town and Country, 1986; Southey, 1945; New University, 1958; Leicester Past and Present (2 vols) 1974; The Victorian Railway, 1991; Railways: an Anthology, 1991. *Membership:* FSA (London). *Literary Agent:* David Higham Associates Ltd, London. *Address:* Flat 6, 36 Victoria Park Road, Leicester LE2 1XB, England.

SIMMONS James Stewart Alexander (Stanley Cromie, Derek Montgomery), b. 14 Feb 1933, Londonderry, Northern Ireland. Writer. m. (1) Laura Stinson, (2) Imelda Foley, 1 son, 5 daughters. *Education:* BA, Honours, Leeds University, 1958. *Appointments:* Lecturer, English, Ahmadu Bello University, Nigeria, 1963-67; Lecturer senior Lecturer, English, Chairman, Dept. of English, 1968- 83, University of Ulster. *Publications Include:* Late but in Ernest, 1967; In the Wilderness, 1969; Energy to Burn, 1971; The Long Summer Still to Come, 1973; West Strand Visions, 1976; Judy Garland and the Cold War, 1976; The Selected James simmons, 1978; Constantly Singing, 1981; Plays: An Exercise in dying, 1970; Black Eye, 1975; The Death of Herakles, 1978; Anthologies: Editor, Out on the Edge, 1958; New Poems from Ulster, 1971; Ten Irish Poets, 1974; Soundings 3, 1976; From the Irish, 1985; Poems, 1956-86, 1986; various recordings and settings of poems; LP, The Rostrevor Sessions, 1987; Critical Book, Sean O'Casey, 1983. *Contributions to:* numerous professional journals. *Honours:* Gregory Award; Cholmondelly Award; Subject of BBC TV Programme, 1976; Medal for Literature, Irish Book Awards, 1987. *Address:* 134 My Lady's Road, Belfast BT6 8FE, Ireland.

SIMMONS Michael, b. 17 Oct 1935, England. Journalist. m. Angela Thomson, 20 Apr 1963, 2 sons. *Education:* BA Hons, Manchester, 1960. *Appointments:* Political Correspondent, Glasgow Herald, 1964-67; East Europe Correspondent, Financial Times, 1968-72; Third World Editor, 1978-81, East Europe Editor, 1983-89, Diplomatic Correspondent, 1989-92, Community Affairs Correspondent, 1993, Guardian. *Publications:* Berlin: Dispossessed City, 1988; The Unloved country: Portrait of East Germany, 1989; Reluctant President: A political Life of Vaclav Havel, 1991; Voices from the South, 1983, (co-editor). *Contributions to:* Various magazines, newspapers and journals. *Memberships:* Society of Authors; Trinity Cricket Club. *Literary Agent:* Tessa Sayle, London SW3 3TG, England. *Address:* The Guardian, London EC1R 3ER, England.

SIMMS Suzanne. *See:* **GUNTRUM Suzanne Simmons.**

SIMON Claude, b. 10 Oct 1913, Madagascar. Writer. *Education:* College Stanislas, Paris. *Publications:* Le tricheur, 1945; La corde raide, 1947; Gulliver, 1952; Le sacre du printemps, 1954; le vent, 1957; L'herbe, 1958; la route des Flandres, 1960; Le palace, 1962; Histoire, 1967; La bataille de Pharsale, 1969; Orion aveugle, 1970; les corps conducteurs, 1971; Tryptyque, 1973; Lecon de choses, 1975; les Georgiques, 1981; La chevelure de Bérénice, 1984; Discours de Stockholm, 1986; L'invitation, 1987; L'acacia, 1989; The Georgies, 1989. *Honours:* Prix de l'Express for La Route des Flandres, 1960; Prix Medicis for Histoire, 1967; Doctor (honoris causa), University of East Anglia, Norwich, England, 1973; Nobel Prize for Literature, 1985; Doctor (honoris causa), Univesity of Bologna, 1989; Grand Croix Ordre National du Mérite, 1990. *Address:* Editions de Minuit, 7 rue Bernard-Palissy, 75006 Paris, France.

SIMON Karl Gunter, b. 9 Feb 1933, Ludwigshafen, Germany. Journalist. *Education:* Studies, romance languages, journalism; PhD, Free University, Berlin. *Major Publications:* Jean Cocteau, 1958; Pantomime, 1960; Die Kronprinzen, 1969; Millionendiener, 1973; Islam, 1988. Comedies & Musicals with brother, Saul Simon. *Contributions to:* Stern; Geo; Playboy; Theatre Heute; etc. Radio, Television Broadcasts, Journalistic works, especially in France, Spain, South America & Arab countries. *Address:* PO Box 9, Dilsberg bei Heidelberg, D-6903, Germany.

SIMON Neil b. 4 July 1927, New York, New York, USA, Playwright. m. 1. Joan Baim, 1953 (dec); 2. Marsha Mason, 1973 (divorced); 3. Diane Lander, 1987. *Education:* New York University, 1946; Hon Doctorate of Humane Letters, Hofstra University, 1981. *Publications:* Plays: Come Blow Your Horn, 1961; Little Me, 1962; Barefoot in the Park, 1963; The Odd Couple, 1965; Sweet Charity, 1966; The Star-Spangled Girl;, 1966; Plaza Suite, 1968; Promises, Promises, 1968; Last of the Red Hot lovers, 1969; The Gingerbread Lady, 1970; The Prisoner of Second Avenue, 1971; The Sunshine Boys, 1972; The Good Doctor, 1973; God's Favorite, 1974; California Suite, 1976; Chapter Two, 1977; They're Playing Our Song, 1979; I Ought to be in Pictures, 1980; Fools, 1981; Little Me, (revised version) 1982; Brighton Beach Memoirs, 1983; Biloxi Blues, 1985; The Odd Couple (female version) 1985; Broadway Bound, 1986; Rumors 1988; Lost in Yonkers, 1991; Jake's Women, 1992; The Goodbye Girl, 1993. Screenplays: After the Fox, 1966; Barefoot in the Park, 1967; The Odd Couple, 1968; The Out-of-Towners, 1970; Plaza Suite, 1971; Last of the Red Hot Lovers, 1972; The Heartbreak Kid, 1973; The Prisoner of Second Avenue, 1975; The Sunshine Boys, 1975; Murder by Death 1976; The Goodbye Girl, 1977; The Cheap Detective, 1978; California Suite, 1978; Chapter Two, 1979; Seems Like Old Times, 1980; Only When I Laugh, 1981; I Ought to be in Pictures, 1982; Max Dugan Returns, 1983; Lonely Guy (Adaptation) 1984; The Slugger's Wife, 1984; Brighton Beach Memoirs, 1986; Biloxi Blues, 1988; The Marrying Man, 1991; Broadway Bound, 1992; (television motion picture), Lost in Yonkers, 1993. Other motion pictures based on stage plays: Come Blow Your Horn, 1963; Sweet Charity, 1969; The Star-Spangled Girl, 1971. Books: Three omnibus collections of Neil Simon's plays: The Comedy of Neil Simon, 1971, The Collected Plays of Neil Simon, Vol II, 1979, and The Collected Plays of Neil Simon, Vol III, 1991; individual plays also published separately. Various television shows. *Honours include:* Pulitzer Prize for Drama: Lost in Yonkers, 1991; Emmy award for the Sid Cæsar Show 1957, the Phil Silvers Show, 1959; Tony award for The Odd Couple, 1965, Biloxi Blues (Best Play) 1985; Lost in Yonkers: (Best Play), 1991; Various Tony award nominations; Writers Guild screen award for The Odd Couple, 1969, The Out-of-Towners, 1971; American Comedy Award for Lifetime Achievement, 1989; Writers Guild screen award nominations for Barefoot in the Park, 1967; Oscar Nomination for The Odd Couple, 1969; Evening Standard award, 1967; Sam S Shubert Foundation Award, 1968; Writers Guild Laurel Award, 1979. *Memberships:* The Dramatists Guild; Writers Guild of America. *Address:* c/o G DaSilva, 10100 Santa Monica Blvd, 400, Los Angeles, CA 90067, USA.

SIMON Robert. *See:* **MUSTO Barry.**

SIMON Sheldon Weiss, b. 31 Jan 1937, USA. Professor of International Politics. m. Charlann Scheid, 23 Apr 1962, 1 son. *Education:* BA, University of Minnesota, 1958; MA, Princeton University, 1960; PhD, University of Minnesota, 1964. *Appointments:* Assistant Professor through to Professor, University of Kentucky, 1966-75; Professor, Arizona State University, 1975-; Chairman, Political Science, ASU, 1975-79, Director, Center for Asian Studies, ASU, 1980-88; Visiting Professor, University of British Columbia, 1972-73, 1979-80; Visiting Professor, Carleton University, 1976; Visiting Professor, Montrey Institute of International Studies, 1988; Visiting Professor, Americann Graduate School of International Management, 1991-92. *Publications:* East Asian Security in the Post-Cold War Era, 1993; The Future of Asian-Pacific Security Collaboration, 1988; The Asean States and Regional

Security, 1982; The Military and Security in the Third World, 1976; War and Politics in Cambodia, 1974; Asian Neutralism and US Policy, 1975; The Broken Triangle: Peking, Djakarta and the PKI, 1969. *Contributions to:* Research papers in Asian Survey, Pacific Affairs, Problems of Communism, Third World Quarterly, Journal of International Affairs, Journal of Northeast Asian Studies, Australian Outlook, New Zealand International Review, Indochina Issues. *Honours:* Phi Beta Kappa 1957; Phi Kappa Phi outstanding professor, 1985; Military Book Club selection 1976 for The Military and Security in the Third World. *Memberships:* American Political Science Association; International Studies Association; Association for Asian Studies. *Address:* Department of Political Science, Arizona State University, Tempe, AZ 85287, USA.

SIMON Werner, b. 5 June 1914, Bremen, Germany. Psychiatrist. m. Elizabeth Strawn, 24 Apr 1939. *Education:* Medical Schools, University of Frankfurt, Germany, 1932-36; MD Degree, University of Bern, Switzerland, 1937. *Appointments:* Chief of Psychiatry, Veterans Administration Medical Center, Minneapolis, 1948-71; Consultant, Hennepia County Medical Center, Minneapolis, 1971-; Emeritus Professor of Psychiatry, University of Minnesota Medical School. *Publications include:* Differential Treatment and Prognosis in Schizophrenia, 1959; Suicide Among Physicians, 1989; The Veterans Administration Center Develops - in Minnesota Psychiatry Evolves-Bernstein, 1989; Chapters in several books, over 55 papers in professional journals. *Memberships:* Minnesota Psychiatric Society, President 1967- 69; American Psychiatric Association, Life Fellow; American College of Physicians, Fellow; International Association for Suicide Prevention; Minnesota Society of Neurological Sciences. *Address:* 8915 River Ridge Road, Minneapolis, MN 55425, USA.

SIMONSUURI Kirsti Katariina, b. 26 Dec 1945, Helsinki, Finland. Professor; Writer; Poet. *Education:* BA, 1968, MA Honours, 1971, University of Helsinki; PhD, University of Cambridge, England, 1977. *Appointments:* Professor, Literature, University of Oulu, 1978-81; Senior Research Fellow, Academy of Finland, 1981-; Visiting Scholar, Harvard University, USA, 1984-86; Visiting Professor, Columbia University, USA, 1986-88. *Publications:* Homer's Original Genius, 1979; Murattikaide, Poems, 1980; Pohjoinen Yokirja, Prose, 1981; Tuntemeton Tekija, Poems, 1982; Europan Ryosto, Poems, 1984; Paholaispoika, Novel, 1986; Enchanting Beasts (translation), 1991; other poetry and prose. *Contributions to:* World Literature Today; Ploughshares; Horen; Diavaso. *Honours:* J.H. Erkko Award for best 1st Book, 1980; British Academy Wolfson Fellowship Award, 1981; Fulbright Postdoctoral Fellowship, 1984. *Literary Agent:* Kirjay htyma Oy, Helsinki. *Address:* 67A Sands Point Road, Port Washington, NY 11050, USA.

SIMPSON Alan, b. 27 Nov 1929. Author; Scriptwriter. m. Kathleen Phillips, 1958, (dec 1978). *Publications:* Author, Scriptwriter, (with Ray Galton), 1951-; Hancock's Half Hour, 1954-61; Comedy Playhouse, 1962-63; Steptoe and Son, 1962-74 (Translated into Dutch, Scandinavian and USA); Galton-Simpson Comedy, 1969; Clochemerle, 1971; Casanova '74, 1974; Dawson's Weekly, 1975; The Galton and Simpson Playhouse, 1976-77; Films: The Rebel, 1960; The Bargee, 1961; The Wrong Arm of the Law, 1963; The Spy with a Cold Nose, 1966; Loot, 1969; Steptoe and Son, 1971; Steptoe and Son Ride Again, 1973; Den Siste Fleksnes, 1974; Skraphandlarne, 1975; Theatre: Way Out in Piccadilly, 1966; The Wind in the Sassafras Trees, 1968; Albert och Herbert, 1981; Fleksnes, 1983; Mordet pa Skolgatan 15, 1984; (Books)Hancock, 1961; Steptoe and Son, 1963; The Reunion and Other Plays, 1966; Hancock Scripts, 1974; The Best of Hancock, 1986. *Honours:* Scriptwritrs of the Year, Guild of TV Producers and Directors, 1959; Best TV Comedy Series, Steptoe and Son, 1962, 1963, 1964, 1965, Screenwriters Guild; John Logie Baird Award, 1964; Best Comedy Series, Dutch TV, 1966; Best Comedy Screenplay, Screenwriters Guild, 1972. *Address:* c/o

Tessa Le Bars Management, 18 Queen Anne Street, London W1M 9LB, England.

SIMPSON Dorothy (Preece), b. 1933, United Kingdom. Author. *Appointments:* Teacher of English and French; Dartford Grammar School for Girls, Kent, 1955-59; Erith Grammar School, Kent, 1959-61; Teacher of English, Senacre School, Maidstone, Kent, 1961-62. *Publications:* Harbingers of Fear, 1977; The Night She Died, 1981; Six Feet Under, 1982; Puppet for a Corpse, 1983; Close Her Eyes, 1984; Last Seen Alive, 1985; Dead on Arrival, 1986; Element of Doubt, 1987; Suspicious Death, 1988; Dead by Morning, 1989; Doomed to Die, 1991; Wake the Dead, 1992. *Honour:* Silver Dagger Award for Last Seen Alive, 1985. *Literary Agent:* Curtis Brown, England. *Address:* c/o Anne McDermid, Curtis Brown, 162-168 Regent Street, London W1R 5TA, England.

SIMPSON John Cody Fidler, 9 Aug. 1944, Cleveleys, England. Television Journalist. m. Diane Jean Petteys, 14 Aug 1965 (now separated), 2 daughters. *Education:* MA, Magdalene College, Cambridge, 1963-66. *Literary Appointments:* Editor, Granta, 1965; Trainee, sub-editor, producer, reporter, BBC Radio News, 1966-72; BBC correspondent in Dublin 1972, Brussels 1975, Johannesburg 1977; Political editor, 1980; Diplomatic Editor, BBC TV, 1982-88; Foreign Affairs Editor, BBC TV & Radio, 1988-; Contributing Editor, The Spectatoe, 1990-. *Publications:* The Best of Granta, 1967; Moscow Requiem, novel, 1981; A Fine & Private Place, novel, 1983; The Disappeared, 1985; Behind Iranian Lines, 1988; Despatches from the Barricades, 1990; From the House of War: Baghdad and the Gulf, 1991; The Darkness Crumbles: the death of Communism, 1992; In The Forests of The Night: Encounters with Terrorists, Drugs-Runners and Oppressors in Peru, 1993. *Contributions to:* Articles, reviews: The Listener; Harper's; Granta; The Spectator. *Honour:* CBE, 1991. *Membership:* Athenaeum; Chelsea Arts Club. *Literary Agent:* Jacintha Alexander Associates. *Address:* c/o BBC Television News, Television Centre, Wood Lane, London W12, England.

SIMPSON Louis Aston Marantz, b. 27 Mar 1923, Jamaica, West Indies. Writer; Teacher. m. (1) Jeanne Rogers, 1949, (div 1954), 1 son, (2) Dorothy Roochvarg, 1955, (div 1979), 2 sons, 1 daughter, (3) Miriam Bachner, 1985. *Education:* Columbia University, New York. *Appointments:* Editor, Bobbs-Merrill Publishing Co., New York, 1950-55; Instructor, Assistant Professor, Columbia University, 1955-59; Professor, University of California, Berkeley, 1959-67, State University of New York, Stony Brook, 1967-93. *Publications:* Poetry: The Arrivistes: Poems 1940-49, 1949; Good News of Death and Other Poems, 1955; The New Poets of England and America, Editor, 1957; A Dream of Governors, 1959; At the End of the Open Road, 1963; Selected Poems, 1965; Adventures of the Letter I, 1971; Searching for the Ox, 1976; Caviare at the Funeral, 1980; People Live Here: Selected Poems, 1949-83; The Best Hour of the Night, 1983; Collected Poems, 1988; In the Room We Share, 1990. Prose: James Hogg: a Critical Study, 1962; Riveside Drive, 1962; An Introduction to Poetry, Editor, 1967; North of Jamaica, 1971; Three on the Tower: the Lives and Works of Exra Pound T.S. Eliot and William Carlos Williams, 1975; A Revolution in Taste, 1978; A Company of Poets, 1981; The Character of the Poet, 1986; Selected Prose, 1989. *Address:* 186 Old Field Road, Setauket, NY 11733, USA.

SIMPSON Matt. *See:* SIMPSON Matthew William.

SIMPSON Matthew William, (Matt Simpson), b. 13 May 1936, Lancs, England. Lecturer; Writer. m. Monika Ingrid Weydert, 13 Dec 1962, 1 son, 1 daughter. *Education:* Cambrige University, 1955-58; Liverpool University, 1958-59. *Appointments:* Literature Panel of Meryside Arts Association, 1970-75; Chairman, Executors of the Widows Project, 1980-. *Publications:* An Elegy for the Galosherman, 1990; Making Arrangements, 1982; The Pig's Thermal Underwear,

1992. *Contributions to:* Major UK journals and magazines; Reviews and criticisms and poetry for children in a number of anthologies. *Memberships:* Poetry Society of Great Britain. *Address:* 29 Boundary Drive, Liverpool L25 OQB, England.

SIMPSON N(orman) F(rederick), b. 1919, United Kingdom. Author. *Appointments:* Teacher, City of Westminster College, London, and Extramural Lecturer, 1946-62; Literary Manager, Royal Court Theatre, London, 1976-78. *Publications:* The Hole, 1958; One Way Pendulum, 1960; The Form, 1961; The Hole and Other Plays and Sketches, 1964; The Cresta Run, 1966; Some Tall Tinkles: Television Plays, 1968; Was He Anyone, 1973; Harry Bleachbaker, novel, 1974, US Edition Man Overboard, 1976; Inner Voices, 1983. *Literary Agent:* Deborah Rogers Ltd, England. *Address:* c/o Deborah Rogers Ltd, 49 Blenheim Crescent, London W11 2EF, England.

SIMPSON Ronald Albert, b. 1 Feb 1929, Melbourne, Victoria, Australia; Senior Lecturer, retired 1987; Poet; Poetry Editor, m. Pamela Bowles, 27 Aug 1955, 1 son, 1 daughter. *Education:* Trained Primary Teacher's Certificate. 1951; Associate Diploma in Fine Art, Royal Melbourne Institute of Technology, 1966. *Appointments:* Teacher, Junior and Secondary Schools, Australia and England, 1951-68; Lecturer, Senior Lecturer, The Chisholm Institute of Technology, Melbourne, Victoria, 1968-87. *Publications:* The Walk Along the Beach, 1960; This Real Pompeii, 1964; After the Assassination, 1968; Diver, 1972; Poems from Murrumbeena, 1976; The Forbidden City, 1979; Editor, Poems from the Age, 1979; Selected Poems, 1981; Words for a Journey, 1986; Dancing Table, 1992; Poetry Editor, The Age. *Honours:* The Australia Council for Travel, 1977, Category A Fellowship to write poetry, 1987; FAW Christopher Brennan Award, 1992. *Membership:* Australian Society of Authors. *Address:* 29 Omama Road, Murrumbeena, Melbourne, Victoria 3163, Australia.

SIMS George Frederick Robert b. 3 Aug 1923, Hammersmith, London, England. Rare Book Dealer & Author. m. Beryl Simcock, 2 sons, 1 daughter. *Education:* Lower School of John Lyon, Harrow, 1934-40. *Publications:* The Terrible Door, 1964; Sleep No More, 1966; The Last Best Friend, 1967; The Sand Dollar, 1969; Deadhand, 1971; Hunters Point, 1973; The End of the Web, 1976; Rex Mundi, 1978; Who Is Cato? 1981; The Keys of Death, 1982; Coat of Arms, 1984; The Rare Book Game, 1985; More of The Rare Book Game, 1988; Last of The Rar Book Game, 1990; The Despain Papers, 1992. *Contributions to:* Black Mask; Saturday Book; London Magazine; American Book Collector; Book Collector; Antiquarian Book Monthly Review. *Memberships:* Crime Writers Association; The Detection Club. *Address:* Peacocks, Hurst, Reading, Berkshire RG10 ODR, England.

SINCLAIR Andrew Annandale, b. 21 Jan 1935, Oxford, England, Writer; Historian. m. Sonia Melchett, 25 July 1984, 2 sons. *Education:* Major Scholar, BA, PhD, Trinity College, Cambridge, 1955-59; Harkness Fellow, Harvard University, USA 1959-61; ACLS Fellow, Stanford University, 1964-65. *Appointments:* Founding Fellow, Churchill College, 1961-63; Lecturer, University College, London, 1966-68; Publisher, Lorrimer Publishing, 1968-89. *Publications:* The Breaking of Bumbo, 1959; My Friend Judas, 1959; Prohibition: The Era of Excess, 1961; Gog, 1967; Magog, 1972; Jack: A Biography of Jack London, 1977; The Other Victoria, 1981; King Ludd, 1988; War Like a Wasp, 1989; The War Decade: an anthology of the 1940's, 1989; The Need tio Give, 1990; The Far Corners of the Earth, 1991; The Naked Savage, 1991; The Strength of the Hills, 1992; The Sword and the Grail, 1992; Francis Bacon: His Life & Violent Times, 1993. *Contributions to:* The Sunday Times; The Times; The New York Times; Atlantic Monthly. *Honours:* Somerset Maugham Prize, 1967; Venice Film festival Award, 1971. *Memberships:* Fellow, Society of American Historians, 1970; Fellow, Royal

Literary Society, 1968. *Literary Agent:* Aitken & Stone. *Address:* 16 Tite Street, London SW3 4HZ, England.

SINCLAIR Carol Louise, b. 20 Dec 1955, Edmonton, Canada. Playwright. *Education:* Carnosun College, 1977. *Appointments:* Writer in Residence, Mulgrave Road Co-Op Theatre, 1986; Writer for CBC Radio Drama in Halifax; Freelance Contributor, 1983-87. *Publications:* Idyll Gossip, 1987; The Summer of the Handley Page, 1987; A Child is Crying on the Stairs, 1986; Occupational Hazards, 1985; Presents, 1984; The Night Before, 1983; Writer, in Collectives of many new plays, 1978-87. *Contributions to:* Canadian Theatre Review, 1986; Sociology, Nova Scotia, 1986. *Honour:* Edmonton Journal, Fiction Writing Award, 1981. *Memberships:* Playwrights Union of Canada, 1987; Dramatists Co-Op of Nova Scotia; Actors Equity Association of Canada; ACTRA. *Literary Agent:* Christopher Banks & Associates, Toronto. *Address:* 2125 Brunswick Street, Halifax, Nova Scotia B3K 2Y4.

SINCLAIR Clive John, b. 19 Feb 1948. Writer. m. Fran Redhouse, 2 Nov 1979, 1 son. *Education:* BA 1969, PhD, 1983, University of East Anglia; Graduate Student, University of California, Santa Cruz. *Appointments:* Literary Editor, Jewish Chronicle, 1983-87. *Publications:* Hearts of Gold, 1979; Bedbugs, 1982; Blood Libels, 1985; Cosmetic Effects, 1989; Augustus Rex, 1992; Bibliosexuality, 1973; The Brothers singer, 1983; Diaspora Bules, 1987; For Good or Evil, Collected Stories, 1991. *Contributions to:* TLS; The Independent; The Sunday Times. *Honours:* Bicentennial Arts Fellow, 1980; Somerset Maughan Award, 1981. *Literary Agent:* Deborah Rogers. *Address:* c/o 20 Powis Mews, London W11 1UN, England.

SINCLAIR James. *See:* **STAPLES Reginald Thomas.**

SINCLAIR Olga Ellen (Ellen Clare, Olga Daniels), b. 23 Jan 1923, Norfolk, England. Writer. m. Stanley George Sinclair, 1 Apr 1945, 3 sons. *Publications:* Gypsies, 1967; Hearts By the Tower, 1968; Bitter Sweet Summer, 1970; Dancing in Britain, 1970; Children's Games, 1972; Toys, 1974; My Dear Fugitive, 1976; Never Fall in Love, 1977; Master of Melthorpe, 1979; Gypsy Girl, 1981; Ripening Vine, 1981; (as Olga Daniels) The Gretna Bride, 1985; When Wherries Sailed By, 1987; (as Olga Daniels) Lord of Leet Castle, 1984; The Bride from Faraway, 1987; The Untamed Bride, 1988; Gretna Green: A Romantic History, 1989; (as Olga Daniels) The Arrogant Cavalier. *Memberships:* Society of Authors; Romantic Novelists Association; Society of Women and Journalists; Vice President, Norwich Writers' Circle. *Address:* Dove House Farm, Potter Heigham, Norfolk NR29 5LJ, England.

SINCLAIR Sonia Elizabeth (Sonia Graham, Sonia Melchett), b. 6 Sept 1928, Nainital, India. Writer. m. (1) Julian Mond, Lord Melchett (dec June 1973), 1 son, 2 daughters, (2) Andrew Sinclair, 1984. *Education:* Attended Royal School, Bath and Queen's Secretarial College, Windsor, England. *Appointments:* Writer; Member of Board of Directors, English Stage Company and The Royal National Theatre. *Publications:* (as Sonia Graham) Tell Me Honestly (nonfiction) 1964; (as Sonia Melchett) Someone is Missing (nonfiction) 1987; (as Sonia Melchett) Passionate Guests - Five Contemporary Women Travellers, 1989. *Contributions to:* Periodicals, including Vogue, Harper's & Queen, Tatler, Portraits and Marie-Clare. *Address:* 16 Tite Street, London SW3 4HZ, England.

SINDEN Donald, b.9 Oct 1923, Plymouth, England. Actor. m. Diana Mahony, 3 May 1948, 2 sons. *Publications:* A Touch of the Memoirs, 1982; Laughter in teh Second Act, 1985; Editor, Everyman Book of Theatrical Anecdotes, 1987. *Honours:* Commander, Order of the British Empire, 1979. *Memberships include:* Council, 1966-77, British Actors Equity Association; Fellow, 1966-, Council 1972, Royal Society of Arts; Arts

Council Drama Panel, 1973-77; Council, London Academy of Music and Dramatic Art, 1976- ; Arts Counci of Great Britain, 1982-86; Chairman, British Theatre Museum Association, 1971-77; VP, London Appreciation Society, 1960-; Pesident, Federation of Playgoers Societies, 1968-; President, Royal General Theatrical Fund, 1986-. *Literary Agent:* Richard Scott Simon. *Address:* c/o Richard Scott Simon, 32 College Cross, London N1, England.

SINGAL Daniel Joseph, b. 17 Nov, 1944, Boston, MA, USA. Historian. m. Sarah Fonda Snell, 24 June 1969, 2 daughters. *Education:* BA Harvard College, 1966; MA, 1967, Phd, 1976, Columbia University. *Publications:* The War Within: From Victorian to Modernist Thought in the South, 1919-1945, 1982; Editor: Modernist Culture in America, 1991; The Other Crisis in American Education, 1992; Beyond Consensus: Richard Hofstadter and American Historigraphy, 1984. *Honours:* Charlew W Ramsdell Award, 1981; Ralph Waldo Emerson Award, 1983; John Simon Guggenheim Foundation Fellowship, 1984-85; George A And Eliza Gardner Foundation Fellowship, 1988- 89. *Memberships:* American Historical Association; Organization of American Historians; Southern Intellectual History Circle. *Address:* 7 Arlington Drive, Pittsford, NY 14534, USA.

SINGER Adam. *See:* **KARP David.**

SINGER Frieda, b. 4 June 1938, New York City, USA. Poet; Editor; Teacher. m. Morris Shapiro, 25 June 1978, 2 stepdaughters. *Education:* MA, City College of New York, 1985. *Publications;* Daughters in High School, 1974-75; 100 Tested Books for Reluctant Readers, 1967, 1972 (Book Reviews). *Contributions to:* Various poetry journals and magazines. *Honours:* New York Poetry Forum Poet of Year, 1981; Shelley Society 10th Anniversary Award, 1983; Irma Rhodes Award, 1984; Composer, Authors, Artists of America Award, 1986; Florida Freelance Writers Association Award, 1986; World Order of Narrative Poets Awards in Dramatic Monologue, 1986; Florida Freelance Writers Award, 1st Place, 1987; Finalist, Eve of St Agnes Award, 1987. *Memberships:* Poetry Society of America; Authors League; Authors Guild; Shelley Society. *Address:* 161-08 Jewel Avenue, Flushing, NY 11365, USA.

SINGER June Flaum, b. 17 Jan 1932, Jersey City, New Jersey, USA. Writer. m. Joseph Singer, 7 Sept 1950, 1 son, 3 daughters. *Education:* Ohio State University, Columbus, 1948-50. *Publications:* The Bluffer's Guide to Interior Decorating, 1972; The Bluffer's Guide to Antiques (American editor), 1972; The Debutantes, 1981; Star Dreams, 1982; The Movie Set, 1984; The Markoff Women, 1986; The President's Women, 1988; Sex in the Afternoon, 1990; Till the End of Time, 1991; Brilliant Divorces, 1992. *Memberships:* The Southern California Society of Women Writers; PEN West; Authors Guild. *Literary Agent:* Roslyn Targ. *Address:* 780 Stone Canyon Rd, Bel-Air, CA 90077, USA.

SINGER Kurt Deutsch, b. 10 Aug 1911, Vienna, Austria. News Commentator; Author. m. (1) Hilda Tradelius, 23 Dec 1932, 1 son, 1 daughter, (2) Jane Sherrod, 1955 (dec 1985), (3) Katherine Han, 1985. *Publications:* The Coming War, 1934; Germany's Secret Service in Central America, 1943; Spies and Saboteurs in Argentina, 1943; Duel for the Northland, 1943; White Book of the Church of Norway, 1944; Spies and Traitors of World War II, 1945; Who are the Communists in America, 1948; 3000 Years of Espionage, 1951; World's Greatest Women Spies, 1952; Kippie the Cow (juvenile), 1952; Gentlemen Spies, 1953; The Man in the Trojan Horse, 1954; World's Best Spy Stories, 1954; Charles Laughton Story (adapted TV, motion pictures), 1954; Spy Stories and Asia, 1955; More Spy Stories(1955; My Greatest Crime Story, 1956; My Most Famous Case, 1957; The Danny Kaye Saga; My Strangest Case, 1958; Spy Omnibus, 1959; Spies for Democracy, 1960; Crime Omnibus Spies Who Changed History, 1961;

Hemmingway-Life and Death of a Giant, 1961; True Adventures in Crime; Dr Albert Schweitzer, Medical Missionary, 1962; Kurt Lyndon Baines Johnson - Man of Reason, 1964; Ho-i-man (juvenile), 1965; Kurt Singer's Ghost Omnibus, 1965; Kurt Singer's Horror Ominbus, The World's Greatest Stories of the Occult, The Unearthly, 1965; Mata Hari: Goddess of Sin, 1965; Lyndon Johnson - From Kennedy to Vietnam, 1966; Weird Tales Anthology, 1966; I Can't Sleep at Night, 1966; Weird Tales of Supernatural, 1967; Tales of Terror, 1967; Famous Short Stories, 1967; Folktales of the South Pacific, 1967; Tales of the Uncanny, 1968; Bloch and Bradbury, 1969; Folktales of Mexico, 1969; Tales of the Unknown, 1970; Tales of the Macabre, 1971; Solve a Crime, 1972; More Solve a Crime, 1974; Dictionary of Home Repair, 1980; Target Horro Books, volume 1-4, 1985-86; I Spied and Survived, memoir, 1988. *Contributions to:* articles, newspapers and popular magazines. *Address:* c/o Singer Media Corp, Seaview Business Park, 1030 Calle Cordillera, Unit 106, San Clemente, CA 92672, USA.

SINGER Marilyn, b. New York City, USA. Writer. m. Steven Aronson, 31 July 1971. *Education:* BA, Queens College, 1969; MA, NYU, 1979. *Publications:* It Cant Hurt Forever; Tarantules on the Brain; The Course of True Love Never Did Run Smooth; Ghost Host; Turtle in July; Several Kinds of Silence; Horsemaster. *Contributions to:* Yes; Encore; Corduroy; The Archer. *Honours:* Childrens Choice Award; Parents Choice Award; American Library Association Best Book Award; Maud Hartlovelace Award; NCTE Award; The New York Times Best Illustrated Childrens Book of 1989. *Memberships:* Authors Guild; PEN American Centre; Society of Childrens Book Writers and Illustrators. *Literary Agent:* Marilyn Malin, Foreign Rights Only. *Address:* 42 Berkeley Place, Brooklyn, NY 11217, USA.

SINGER Oscar, b. 20 Sept 1920, Chicago, Illinois, USA. Meteorologist. *Education:* BS, Meteorology, University of Chicago, 1946; Graduate Training, University of California. *Publications:* Singer's Lock: The Revolution in the Understanding of Weather, 1983. *Contributions to:* Sole Author, Publisher, Bible of Weather Forecasting, 1984-. *Address:* 1540 Rollins Drive, Los Angeles, CA 90063, USA.

SINGER Sarah Beth, b. 4 July 1915, USA. Poet. m. 23 Nov 1938, 1 son, 1 daughter. *Education:* BA, 1934; Graduate courses, 1960-64. *Appointments:* Consulting Editor, Poet Lore, 1976-81. *Publications:* After the Beginning, 1975; Of Love and shoes, 1987; The Gathering, 1992. *Contributions to:* New York times; Poet Lore; Yankee; McCall's : The Lyric; Voices. *Honours include:* Biennial Poetry Award, Seattle NLAPQ, 1988; Washington Poets Association Award, 1989; Structured Verse Award, Oregon NLSPQ, 1990; Haiku Award, Brussels Sprout Magazine, 1992. *Memberships:* Poetry Society of American: VP, 1974-78, Executive Director, PSA Long Island, 1979-83; National League of American Penwomen: Secretary, Seattle Branch, 1990-92, Pers, 1992. *Address:* 2360 43rd Avenue East, Seattle, WA 98112, USA.

SINGH Charu Sheel, b. 15 May 1955, UP, India. Teacher. m. Maya, 6 June 1987, 1 son. *Education:* BA, 1974; MA, 1976; PhD, 1978. *Appointments:* Lecturer, MBS College Gangapur, 1977-79; Lecturer, Kashi Vidyapith University, 1979-91; Reader, 1991-. *Publications:* The Chariot of Fire; Auguries of Evocation; Contemporary Literary Theory; Literary Thory: Possibilities and Limits; Three Collections of poems; Confederate Gestures; Self Reflexive Materiality; Concentric Imagination. *Contributions to:* The Literary Criterion; Journal of Literary Criticism; Modern Language Review; Years Work in English Studies. *Honours:* British Council Fellowship; Prestigious University Grants; Fellowship Indian Institute of Advanced Study Shimla. *Memberships:* Journal of Indian Writing in English; American Studies Research Centre; Indian PEN. *Address:* 36 Brahmanand Nagar, Ext 1, Durga Kund, Varanasi 221005, India.

SINGH Darshan, b. 14 Sept 1921, India. Spiritual Master, Leader, Sawan Kirpal Ruhani Mission; Poet; Author. m. Harbhajan Kaur, 20 Aug 1943, 2 sons. *Education:* BA, Honours, Government College, Punjab University, Lahore, 1941. *Publications:* Talash-e-Noor, 1965; Mazil-e- Noor, 1969; Secret of Secrets : Spiritual Discourses, 1978; Spiritual Awakening, 1982; A Tear and a Star, Poetry, 1986; Cry of the Soul, poetry, 1977; Challenge of Inner Space, 1984; Meaning of Christ, 1985; Soulergy : Source of All Energy, 1987; Ambassadors of Peace, 1987. *Contributions to:* Numerous professional journals and magazines worldwide. *Honours include:* Urdu Academy Award for Poetry, 1969. *Memberships:* Secretary, Bazame-Adab; Joint Secretary, Halqa-e-Arbab-e-Fikr. *Address:* Kirpal Ashram, 2 Canal Road, Vijay nagar, Delhi 110009, India.

SINGH Gurcharan, b. 8 Feb 1917, India. Author. m. 12 Feb 1942, 3 sons, 1 daughter. *Education:* MA, English, 1940; MA, Punjabi, 1953; Phd, 1964. *Appointments:* Editor, Daily Ranjit, Lahore, 1945, Khalsasewata, Amritsar, 1945; Publicity Officer, PEPSU, 1949; Agricultural publicity Officer, nabha, 1950; Editor, Kheti Bare, Nabha, 1951; Lecturer, Mohindih College, 1954; Reader, Punjabi University, 1966; Chairman, PreSchool Education Board, 1972. *Publications:* Wagdi Si Ravi, 1950; Wan te Karie, 1946; Dharti Da Sandhur, 1977; Sunam Da Surna Shahid, 1977; Behi Sharab, 1987; Three volumes of Punjabi short stories; 3 collections of one act plays; 20 books of poems; etc. *Contributions to:* various journals and magazines. *Honours:* Pepsu state Award, 1951, 1952; Punjab State Award, 1963; Government of India Award, 1963; Bal Sahit Abademy Award, 1963; Indian Writers Union Award, 1985; Congress Centenary award, 1985; many other honours and awards. *Memberships include:* President, Punjabi Kala Sansar; Shiromany Kav te Kala-Manoh, Vice President; Punjabi Sahit Abademy; Indian Writers Union. *Address:* 35/9A Chandigarh, India.

SINGH Ram Krishna Singh, b. 31 Dec 1950, Varanasi, India. Teacher. m. Durga, 1 Mar 1978. 1 son, 1 daughter. *Education:* BA University of Gorakhpur, 1970; MA Banares Hindu University, 1972, PhD English, Kashi Vidyapith, 1981. *Appointments:* Guest Editor, Language Forum, New Delhi, 1986; Board of Advisors, Canopy, 1986-; Co-editor, Creative Forum, 1988-; Advisory Council, Poecrit, 1991-. *Appointments:* Professor and Head, Dept of HSS, Indian School of Mines. *Publications:* Savitri: A Spiritual Epic, 1984; My Silence, 1985; Using Contemporary English Idoms, 1985-86; Indian English Writing, 1981-85, Edited, 1987; Using English in Science and Technology, 1988; Music Must Sound, 1990; Krishna Srinivas: The Poet of Inner Aspiration, 1984; Memories Unmemoried, 1988; Flight of Poenix, 1990; Recent Indian English Poets: Expressions and Beliefs, edited 1992, I Do Not Question, 1993. *Contributions to:* Indian Journal of English Studies; Littcrit; The Literary Endeavour; Language Forum; Journal of Indian Writing in English. *Honours:* Hon DLitt, World Academy of Arts and Culture, 1984; Certificate of Excellencs, International Writers and Astists Association, 1987, 1988; International Eminent Poet and Fellowship of International Poets Academy, Madras, 1987. *Memberships include:* International Writers and Artists Association; World Poetry Society Intercontinent; International Poets Academy, Madras; International Association of Teachers of English as a Foreign Language, UK. *Literary Agent:* Dhanbad Chapter of SID, Rome. *Address:* Type C-1 Indian School of Mines, Dhanbad 826004, India.

SINOU Kira, b. 12 Mar 1923, Rostov, USSR. Writer; Translator. m. 5 Feb 1961, 1 son. *Education:* Certificate of German Gymnasium Thessaloniki, 1942; Certificate, Proficiency in English, University of Cambridge, 1950; Diploma, School of Tourist Guides, 1957. *Appointments:* Rodi, Children's Periodical, 1977-82; Kifissos, 1987-. *Publications:* The Country of the Mammoths, 1977; Mystery of the Old Mansion, 1978; The End of the Monsters, 1980; The Great Experiment, 1981; The Town of Saint Demetrious, 1982; The Monkey's Diamonds, 1983; The Hand in the Deep, 1986; A Ray of Light,

1986; Meeting in Delphi, 1987; The Contract of the Old House, 1988; The Last King of Atlantis, 1990; Translated 70 books from 4 languages. *Contributions to:* Rodi; Kifissos; Nea Skepsis. *Honours:* Prize, Delphisch Amphictionies Society, 1975; Prize, Association des Gens de Lettres Hellenes, 1985; IBBY Certificate of Honour, 1985; Prize, Women Literary Club, 1985; Prize, Federation Helleniques des Activites Subaquatiques, 1986; Lista d'Onore per la Narrativa, University di Padova, 1987; Prize Association des Ecrivains de Tourisme; Prize Association des Gens de Lettres Hellenes, 1988; Prize, Women Literary Club, 1988; Diploma of Honour for Translation from Russian of VAAP, 1987; IBBY Certificate of Honour, 1990. *Memberships:* Association des Gens de Lettres Hellenes; Circle of Greek Childrens' Books; Association of Translators of Literature. *Address:* 21 Ekalis Str., 145-64 Kifissia, Athens, Greece.

SIROF Harriet Toby, b. 18 Oct 1930, New York City, USA. Writer; Teacher. m. 18 June 1949, 1 son, 1 daughter. *Education:* BA, New School for Social Research, 1962. *Publications:* The Real World, 1985; Anything You Can Do, 1986; That Certain Smile, 1981; Save the Dam!, 1981; The Junior Encyclopedia of Israel, 1980 The IF Machine, 1978; A New-Fashioned Love Story, 1977. *Contributor to:* Colorado Review; Descent; Inlet; Maine Review; North American Review; New Orleans Review; Sam Houston Review; San Jose Studies; Woman; Voices of Brooklyn. *Honours:* Junior literary Guild Selection of The Real World, 1985. *Membership:* Authors Guild. *Literary Agent:* Greenburger Associates. *Address:* 792 East 21 Street, Brooklyn, NY 11210, USA.

SISLER Harry Hall, b. 13 Mar 1917. Chemist; Educator; Dean Emeritus, Graduate School of University of Flordia. m. (1) Helen E. Shaver, 29 June 1940, 2 sons, 2 daughters, (2) Hannelore L Wass, 13 Apr 1978. *Education:* BSc. Honours, Ohio State University, 1936; MSc, Chemistry, 1937; PhD, 1939, University of Illinois. *Appointments:* Board of Publication, Journal of Chemical Education, 156-58; Editor, Reinhold Publication Corp., 1958-78; Assistant to Editor, Death Studies, 1978-; Consulting Editor, Dowden, Hutchinson and Ross, 1971-78. *Publications include:* Chemistry - A Systematic Approach, 1980; Electronic Structure, Properties and the Periodic Law, 1963; Chemistry in Non-Aqueous Solvents, 1961; The Chloramination Reaction, 1977; Of Outer and Inner Space, (poems), 1980; Starlight, (poems), 1976; Earth, Air, Fire and Water, (poems), 1989, numerous others. *Contributions to:* Over 200 articles in major scientific and scholarly journals. *Honours:* Florida ACS Section Outstanding Southeastern Chemist Award, 1960; ACS Southern Chemist Award, 1969; ACS James Flack Norris Award in Chemical Education, 1979; Royal Order of the North Star from the King of Sweden; Honorary Doctorate, University of Poznan, Poland, 1977; Centennial Achievement Award, Ohio State University, 1970. *Memberships:* Phi Beta Kappa; Sigma Xi; American Chemical Society. *Address:* 6014 NW 54th Way, Gainesville, FL 32606, USA.

SISSON Charles Hubert, b. 22 Apr 1914, Bristol, England, retired Civil Servant. m. Nora Gilbertson, 19 Aug 1937 2 daughters. *Education:* BA, 1st Class Honours, University of Bristol, 1931-34; Postgraduate studies, Berlin and Paris, 1934-36. *Publications:* The Spirit of British Administration, 1959; Christopher Homm, 1965; Art and Action, 1965; Essays, 1967; David Hume, 1976; The Avoidance of Literature; 1978; The Divine Comedy of Dante, 1980; Collected Poems, 1984; On The Lookout, 1989; An Asiatic Romance, 1953; In The Trojan Ditch, 1974; Anglican Essays, 1983; In Two Minds, 1990; Jeremy Taylor: Selected Writings, 1990; English Perspectives, 1992; Verse translations of Catullus, Lucretius, Virgil, Du bellay, Racine. *Contributions to:* Agenda; London Magazine; London Review of Books; New Criterion, New York; New York Times review of Books; PN Reviewp; Spectator; Times Literary Supplement. *Honours:* FRSL, 1975; Honorary DLitt, Bristol, 1980. *Literary Agent:* Laurence Pollinger

Limited. *Address:* Moorfield Cottage, The Hill, Langport, Somerset TA10 9PU, England.

SISSON Rosemary Anne, b. 13 Oct 1923, London, England. Writer. *Education:* BA, Honours, UCL; Mlit, Newnham College, Cambridge University. *Appointments:* Junior Lecturer, University of Wisconsin, 1949-50; Lecturer, University College, London, 1950-53; Lecturer, University of Birmingham, 1953-54; Dramatic Critic, Stratford-upon-Avon Herald, 1954-57. *Publications:* The Bretts, 1987; Beneath the Visiting Moon, 1986; Bury Love Deep, 1985; The Manions of America, 1981; The Queen and the Welshman, 1979; The Stratford Story, 1975; The Exciseman, 1972; The Killer of Horseman's Flats, 1973; Escape from the Dark, 1976; The Queen and the Welshman, 1979; The Manions of America, 1982; Bury Love Deep, 1985; Beneath the Visiting Moon, 1986; The Bretts, 1987; The Young Indiana Jones Chronicles, 1993-. *Contributions to:* numerous magazines and journals. *Honours:* Writers Guild of Great Britain, Laurel Award for services to Writers. *Memberships:* Co-chair, The Writers Guild of Great Britain; Writers Guild of America; BAFTA; Dramatists' Club; Academy Club. *Literary Agent:* Andrew Mann Limited. *Address:* 167 New King's Road, Parson's Green, London SW6, England.

SITWELL Pauline, Artist; Poet; Dancer. *Education:* St Johns Wood School of Art, UK, 1930; Royal Academy Schools of Art, 1933-37. *Publication:* Green Song, 1979. *Contributions to:* various publications, exhibitions and One Man Shows; Poetry Recitals & public speaking. *Honours:* Laureat, Paris Salon de Printemps; Green Song, National Book League Choice, 1981; Green Song in the Museum of the Book, The Hague, Holland. *Memberships:* SWE; various exhibiting Associations. *Address:* 46 Porchester Road, Bayswater, London W2, England.

SIZER John b. 14 Sept 1938, Grimsby, England. University Professor. m. 1965, 3 sons. *Education:* BA, Nottingham University 1961- 64; D Litt, Loughborough University of Technology, 1989; FCMA; FBIM; FRSA. *Publications:* An Insight into Management Accounting, 1969, 1979, and 1989; Perspectives in Management Accounting, 1981; A Casebook of British Management Accounting Vol I and Vol II, 1984 and 1985; Institutional Responses to Financial Reductions in University Sector, DES 1987. *Contributions to:* Numerous articles in Accounting, Management and Higher Education journals. *Honour:* CBE 1989. *Membership:* Fellow, Chartered Institute of Management Accountants. *Address:* Scottish Higher Education Funding Council, Donaldson House, 97 Haymarket Terrace, Edinburgh EH12 5HD.

SKALA Ivan (b. as Karel Hell), b. 6 Oct 1922, Czechoslovakia. Poet. *Appointments Include:* Director, Mlada Fonta Publishing House, Prague, 1967-68; Deputy to House of the People, Federal Association of CSSR 1969-71; Director, Ceskoslovensky spisovatel Publishing House, Prague, 1970-82. *Publications:* Collections of Poems: Kresadlo, 1946; Pres Prah, 1948; Maj zeme, 1950; Fronja je vsude, 1951; A Cokoliv se stane, 1957; Ranni vlak nadeje, 1958; Zdravim vas okna, 1962; Blankytny kalendar, 1963; Posel Prichazi pesky, 1968; Ctyri basne o smrti a strom, 1969; Co si beru na cestu, 1975; Zizen, Ci je jaro, 1976; Osudova, 1978; Ohen specha, 1979; Okno dokoran, 1981; selection from his works as a publicist: Kontinuita 1, 2, 1980. *Honours;* Klement Gottwald State Prize, 1959, 1983; Artist of Merit, 1974; National Artist, 1979; Order of Labour, 1982; World Peace Council Medal, 1982. *Memberships:* Union of Czech Writers, Deputy Chairman, 1977-82, Chairman, 1982- ; many other professional organisations. *Address:* Svaz cs. spisovatelu, narodni tr. 11, Prague 1, Czechoslovakia.

SKALDASPILLIR Sigfriouv. *See:* **BROXON Mildred Downey.**

SKARSAUNE Oskar, b. 2 July 1946, Trondheim, Norway. Professor. m. Karin, 4 Aug 1973, 2 sons, 1 daughter. *Education:* Free Faculty of Theology, Oslo, 1972; Doctor of Teology, University of Oslo, 1982. *Appointments:* Co Editor, Luthersk Kirketidende, 1985-. *Publications:* The Proof from Prophecy; Incarnation, Myth or Fact; Da Suriften Ble Apnet; Fra Jerusalem Til Rom Og B. *Contributions to:* Several Articles. *Address:* PO Box 27, Bekkelaget, 0137 Oslo, Norway.

SKEGGS Douglas b. 23 Jan 1952, Winchester, England. Author and Art Historian. m. Imogen Feilden, 24 July 1982. *Education:* Harrow School; MA (Cantab) Magdalene College, Cambridge. *Publications:* River of Light, 1987; The Estuary Pilgrim, 1989; The Talinin Madonna, 1991. *Literary Agent:* Shiel Land Associates. *Address:* 22 Stonor Road, London W14 8RZ, England.

SKELTON Geoffrey David, b. 11 May 1916, Springs, South Africa. Writer; Translator. m. Gertrude Klebac, 4 Sept 1947, 2 sons. *Education:* Plymouth College, City of London School, 1927-34. *Appointments:* BBC, England, 1956-67. *Publications:* Wagner at Bayreuth, 1965, 1976; Wieland Wagner, 1971; Paul Hindemith, 1975; Richard and Cosima Wagner, 1982; Wagner in Thought and Practice, essays, 1991; Translations from German: The Marat-Sade, play by Peter Weiss (with Adrian Mitchell), 1964; Cosima Wagner's Diaries, 1978, 1980; Works by Max Frisch, Friedrich Heer, Günter Herburger, Robert Lucas; Training Ground, novel by Siegfried Lenz, 1991. *Honours:* American PEN Prize for Translation (with Adrian Mitchell) for Marat-Sade, 1967; Schlegel-Tieck Translation Prize for Frieda Lawrence by Robert Lucas, 1973, for Training Ground, 1992; Yorkshire Post Music Award for Paul Hindemith, 1975. *Memberships:* Radiowriters Association, Executive Committee 1969-72; Translators Association, Executive Committee 1972-74, 1979- 81, Chairman 1974. *Literary Agent:* David Higham Associates. *Address:* 49 Downside, Shoreham, West Sussex BN43 6HF, England.

SKELTON Peter, b. 29 Dec 1929, Amsterdam, Netherlands. Author. m. Lady Doreen Fox-Strangways, 23 Sept 1959, 1 daughter. *Education:* Tripos, Law & Economics, Cambridge University. *Appointments:* Publishers Reader; Art Editor; Magazine Editor; General Production Editor, Sunday Times Newspaper Group, Founder, Sunday Times Magazine, 1952; Film Script Writer. *Publications include:* The Charm of Hours, 1954; Animals All, 1956; All About Paris, Paris By Night, 1959; The Promise of Days, 1962; The Room of Overnight (Play), 1963; The Blossom of Months (novel, 5 volumes), 1973; Tiger Kub & The Royal Jewel, 1983; The Flowering of Seasons, 1985. *Contributions to:* Daily Telegraph (book reviews); Sunday Times (science fiction); News of the World (features as Edward Trevor); Holland Herald (features); Daily Express (contributor to William Hickey Column). *Honours:* Fellow, International Institute of Arts & Letters, 1962; KLM Golden Anniversary Award, 1969. *Membership:* South Devon Literary Society, (Honorary Secretary). *Address:* St Anthony, Higher Woodfield, Torquay, Devon, England.

SKELTON Robin, b. 12 Oct 1925. Author; Professor of English. m. Sylvia Mary Jarrett, 1957, 1 son, 2 daughtes. *Education:* BA, 1950, MA, 1951, University of Leeds. *Appointments include:* RAF Service, 1944-47; Assistant Lecturer, English, 1951, Lecturer, 1954, University of Manchester; Examiner, NUJMB, 1954-58; Chairman, Examiners, English 'O' Level, 1958-60; Co-Founder, Chairman, Peterloo Group, Manchester, 1957-60; Founding Member, Honorary Secretary, Manchester Institute of Contemporary Arts, 1960-63; Centenary Lecturer, University of Massachusetts, USA, 1962-63; General Editor, OUP Edition of Works of J.M. Synge, 1962-68; Associate Professor, English, 1963-66, Professor, 1966-, Chairman, Creative Writing, 1973-76, University of Victoria, British Columbia. *Publications include:* Poetry: Patmos and Other Poems, 1955; Third Day Lucky, 1958; Two Ballads of the Muse, 1960; Begging the Dialect, 1960; The Dark Window, 1962; A Valedictory Poem, 1963; An Irish Gathering, 1964;

A Ballad of Billy Barker, 1965; Inscriptions, 1967; Because of This, 1968; The Hold of Our Hands, 1968; Selected Poems, 1947-67, 1968; An Irish Album, 1969; Georges Zuk, Selected Verse, 1969; The Hunting Dark, 1971; Two Hundred Poems from the Greek Anthology, 1971; Three for Herself, 1972; Country Songs, 1973; Timelight, 1974; Because of Love, 1977; Landmarks, 1979; Collected Shorter Poems, 1947-77, 1981; Limits, 1981; De Nihilo, 1982; Zuk, 1982; Wordsong, 1983; Distances, 1985; (Prose): John Ruskin: the Final Years, 1955; The Poetic Pattern, 1956; Cavalier Poets, 1960; Poetry (Teach Yourself Series), 1963; The Writings of J.M. Synge, 1971; J.M. Synge and his World, 1971; The Practice of Poetry, 1971; J.M. Synge (Irish Writers Series), 1972; Poetic Truth, 1978; Spellcraft, 1978; The Call It The Cariboo, 1980; Talismanic Magic, 1985; (Fiction) The Man Who Sang in His Sleep, 1984; (Drama): The Paper Cage, 1982; numerous edited texts and anthologies. *Address:* 1255 Victoria Avenue, Victoria, BC V8S 4PE, Canada.

SKENE Anthony, b. England. Television Playwright. *Television Plays include:* Square on the Hypotenuse; What's In It For Me?; A Walk Through the Forest; Blunt Instrument; I Thought They Died Years Ago; A Gift of Tongues. *Contributions to:* Numerous television series including: The Prisoner; The Name of the Game; Upstairs, Downstairs. *Address:* 5a Furlong Road, London N7 8LS, England.

SKINNER June O'Grady (A Carleon, Rohan O'Grady), b. 1922, Canada. Freelance Writer (Historical/Gothic/Romance). *Publications:* O'Houlihan's Jest: A Lament for the Irish, 1961; Pippin's Journal; or Rosemary Is For Remembrance, 1962 (in USA paperback as Master of Montrolfe Hall, 1965, as Curse of the Montrolfes, 1983); Let's Kill Uncle, 1963; Bleak November, 1970; As A Carleon: The May Spoon, 1981. *Address:* 1243 River Drive, Port Coquitlam, BC, Canada V3E 1N7.

SLADE Bernard, b. 2 May 1930, Ontario, Canada. Playwright; Screenwriter. m. 25 July 1953, 1 son, 1 daughter. *Appointments:* Story Editor, Bewitched, TV Series, 1965; Love on a Rooftop, TV Series, 1966. *Publications include:* Broadway plays: Same Time Next Year, 1975; Tribute, 1978; Romantic Comedy, 1980; Special Occasions, 1981. Other published plays: Fatal Attraction, (London West End), 1985; An Act of the Imagination, (play), 1987; Fling, (play), 1979; Return Engagements, (play), 1988; Creator of TV Series, Love on a Rooftop; The Flying Nun; The Partridge Family; The Girl with Something Extra. *Contributions to:* Contemporary Authors; Critical Survey of Drama. *Honours:* Drama Desk Award for Best Play, 1975; Antoinette Perry Nomination, Best Play, 1975; Academy Award Nomination, Best Screenplay, 1978. *Memberships:* Writers Guild of America; Dramatists Guild of America; Society of Authors and Artists (France); Academy of Notion Picture Arts and Sciences. *Literary Agent:* Jack Hutto. *Address:* 405 West 23rd Street, New York 10011, USA.

SLADE Jack. *See:* **GERMANO Peter B.**

SLADE Peter b.7 Nov 1912, Fleet, Hampshire, England. Actor, Director, Drama Advisor, Drama Therapist. m. 25 Nov 1939, 2 daughters. *Education:* Public School, Lancing, 1926-30; Central School of Speech and Drama, 1st Class Certificate in Acting, 1933-34. *Publications:* Child Drama, 1954; Introduction to Child Drama, 1958; Experience of Spontaneity, 1968; Natural Dance, 1977; Contribution to Drama in Therapy, Vol 1, New York, 1981; Education pamphlets published by the Educational Drama Association. *Contributions to:* Athene Arts; Guild of Pastoral Psychology; Educational Drama Association. *Honour:* The Queen's Silver Jubilee Medal, 1977. *Memberships:* Director, 1948-77, President 1977-, Educational Drama Association; Patron Institute of Dramatherapy; President, North Cotswold Arts Association. *Address:*

Swingletrees, Park Crescent, Stow-on-the-Wold, Cheltenham, Gloucestershire GL54 1DT, England.

SLADE Quilla. *See:* **LEWIS-SMITH Anne Elizabeth.**

SLATER Ian David, b. 1 Dec 1941, Queensland, Australia. Author; Lecturer; Editor. m. Marian Ella Wray Johnston, 18 Dec 1968, 1 son, 1 daughter. *Education:* BA, University of British Columbia, 1972; MA, 1972; PhD, 1977. *Appointments:* Visiting Lecturer, University of Ljubljana, 1984; Writer in Residence, Simon, Fraser University, 1986; Writer in Residence, Sechelt & Festival of the Arts, 1988. *Publications:* Orwell - The Road to Airstrip One; Firespill; Sea Gold; Air Glow Red; World War III series, Deep Chill; Storm. *Honours:* Royal Institute Scholarship; Mark Eastman United Nations Award. *Memberships:* Writers Union of Canada; Authors Guild of America; LBC Faculty Club; Sir Winston Churchill Society. *Literary Agent:* Mr Henry DuNow. *Address:* 4074 West 17th Ave, Vancouver, BC, Canada V6S 1A6.

SLATTA Richard Wayne, b. 22 Oct 1947, North Dakota, USA. Professor of History. m. Maxine P Atkinson, 15 June 1983, 1 son. *Education:* BA cum laude, Pacific Lutheran University, 1969; MA Portland State University, 1974; PhD History, University of Texas at Austin, 1980. *Contributions to:* The Futurist, 1987; Family Computing, 1986; Criminal Justice History: An International Review, 1990; Social Science Computer Review. *Honours:* Western Heritage Award for Nonfiction, National Cowboy Hall of Fame, 1991; Hubert Herring Book Prize, 1984. *Memberships:* American Historical Association; Conference on Latin American History; Western History Association. *Address:* History Department, North Carolina State University, Raleigh NC 27695, USA.

SLATZER Robert (Franklin), b. 1927, USA. Author; Film Producer. *Appointments:* Producer, Columbia Pictures Corporation, Hollywood, California, 1948, 1969-74; Screenwriter, RKO Radio Pictures, 1949; Screenwriter, Director, Monogram Studios, 1949-50; Screenwriter, Director, Paramount Pictures Corporation, Hollywood, 1951-53; Executive Producer, Television Series, Republic Studios, 1953-54; Executive Producer, Jaguar Pictures Corporation, Hollywood, 1959-; President, Slatzer Oil and Gas Co, 1960-63; Member, Board of Directors, United Mining and Milling Corporation, 1967-69; Director, National Academy of TV Arts and Sciences, 1972; Board Director, Millionaire's Club, 1977. *Publications:* The Hellcats, 1968; Cowboy and the Heiress, 1970; The Young Wildcats, 1971; Campaign Girl, 1972; The Punishment Pawn, 1973; The Life and Curious Death of Marilyn Monroe, 1974; Duke of Thieves, 1976; Daphne, 1978; Bing Crosby: The Hollow Man, 1981; Duke: The Life and Times of John Wayne, 1986. *Address:* PO Box 1075, Hollywood, CA 90078, USA.

SLAUGHTER Carolyn b.7 Jan 1947, New Delhi, India. Novelist; Critic. m. Kemp Battle, 5 May 1984, 2 sons, 2 daughters. *Publications:* Dreams of the Kalahari, 1981 UK, 1987 USA; The Innocents, 1986; The Banquet, 1983; A Perfect Woman, 1984; The Widow, 1989; The Story of the Weasel (Relations US) 1976; Magdalene, 1978; Columba, 1978; Heart of the River, 1983. *Honours:* Geoffrey Faber Memorial Prize, 1976; Arts Council Award, 1984. *Memberships:* PEN Executive Committee. *Literary Agent:* Anthony Sheil - UK; Charlotte Sheedy - USA. *Address:* 2805 Main Street, Lawrenceville, NJ 08648, USA.

SLAUGHTER Frank Gill (C V Terry), b. 25 Feb 1908, Washington, USA. Novelist; Physician; Surgeon. m. Jane Mundy, 1933, 2 sons. *Education:* AB, Duke University; MD, Johns Hopkins. *Publications:* That None Should Die, 1941; Spencer Brade, MD, 1942; Air Surgeon, 1943; Battle Surgeon, 1944; A Touch of Glory, 1945; In a Dark Garden, 1946; The New Science of Surgery, 1946; The Golden Isle, 1947; Sangaree, 1948;

Medicine for Moderns, 1948; Divine Mistress, 1949; The Stubborn Heart, 1950; Immortal Magyar, 1950; Fort Everglades, 1951; The Road to Bithynia, 1951; East Side General, 1952; The Galilieans, 1953; Storm Haven, 1953; The Song of Ruth, 1954; Apalachee Gold, 1954; The Healer, 1955; Flight from Natchez, 1955; The Scarlet Cord, 1956; The Warrior, 1956; Sword and Scalpel, 1957; The Mapmaker, 1957; Daybreak, 1958; The Thorn of Arimathea, 1958; The Crown and the Cross, 1959; Lorena, 1959; The Land and the Promise, 1960; Pilgrims in Paradise, 1960; Epidemic, 1961; The Curse of Jezebel, 1961; David : Warrior and King, 1962; Tomorrow's Miracle, 1962; Devil's Harvest, 1963; Upon This Rock, 1963; A Savage Place, 1964; The Purple Quest, 1965; Constantine : The Miracle of the Flaming Cross, 1965; Surgeon, USA, 1966; God's Warrior, 1967; Doctor's Wives, 1967; The Sins of Herod, 1968; Surgeon's Choice, 1969; Countdown, 1970; Code Five, 1971; Convention, MD, 1972; Life Blood, 1974; Stonewall Brigade, 1975; Plague Ship, 1977; Devil's Gamble, 1978; The Passionate Rebel, 1979; Gospel Fever, 1980; Doctor's Daughters, 1981; Doctors At Risk, 1983; No Greater Love, 1985; Transplant, 1986. *Address:* 5051 Yacht Club Road, Jacksonville, FL 32210, USA.

SLAVITT David Rytman (Henry Sutton), b. 1935, USA. Novelist; Short Story Writer; Poet. *Appointments:* Associate Editor, Newsweek Magazine, 1958- 65; Associate Professor of English, Temple University, Philadelphia, Pennsylvania, 1978-80; Lecturer in English, Columbia University, New York City, 1985-. *Publications:* Suits for the Dead, 1961; The Carnivore, 1965; Rochelle, or Virtue Rewarded, 1966; The Exhibitionist (as Henry Sutton), 1967; Feel Free, 1968; The Voyeur (as Henry Sutton), 1969; Day Sailing, 1969; Anagrams, 1970; Vector (as Henry Sutton), 1970; The Eclogues of Virgil, translation, 1971; Child's Play, 1972; ABCD, 1972; The Eclogues and the Georgics of Virgil, translation, 1972; The Liberated (as Henry Sutton), 1973; The Outer Mongolian, 1973; The Killing of the King, 1974; Vital Signs, 1975; Essentials of Social Psychology (with P Secord and C Backman), 1976; King of Hearts, 1976; Jo Stern, 1978; The Sacrifice, 1978; Rounding the Horn, 1978; The Idol, 1979; Dozens, 1981; Ringer, 1982; Big Nose, 1983; Alice at 80, 1984; The Elegies to Delia of Albius Tibullus, 1985; Secrets (with Bill Adler), 1985; The Walls of Thebes, 1985; The Agent (with Bill Adler), 1986. *Literary Agent:* William Morris Agency, USA. *Address:* c/o William Morris Agency, 1350 Avenue of the Americas, New York, NY 10019, USA.

SLESAR Henry (O H Leslie), b. 1927, USA. Author; Dramatist. *Appointments:* Headwriter, Somerset, NBC, 1971-73; The Edge of Night, 1968-83, and Capitol, TV series, 1984-86. *Publications:* The Grey Flannel Shroud, 1959; Enter Murderers, 1960; Clean Crimes and Neat Murders, stories, 1960; A Crime for Mothers and Others, stories, 1961; The Bridge of Lions, 1963; Two on a Guillotine, screenplay, 1968; The Seventh Mask, 1969; The Thing at the Door, 1974; Murders Most Macabre, stories, 1987; Death on Television, stories, 1989. *Address:* 125 East 72nd Street, New York, NY 10021, USA.

SLIDE Anthony Clifford, b. 7 Nov 1944, Birmingham, England. Film Historian, archivist. *Appointments:* Editor, Filmmakers, 1982- *Publications include:* The American Film Industry: A Historical Dictionary, 1986; Early American Cinema, 1970; Early Women Directors, 1977; The Big V: A History of the Vitagraph Company, 1987; The Vaudevillians, 1981; Silent Portraits, 1990; book review column, Classic Images, 1989-; Nitrate Won't Wait: A History of Film Preservation in The United States, 1992; Before Video: A History of The Non-Theatrical Film, 1992; Gay and Lesbian Characters and Themes in Mystery Novels, 1993. *Honours:* The American Film Industry: A Historical Dictionary, named Outstanding Reference of the Year, American Library Association; Honorary Doctor of Letters, Bowling Green University, 1990. *Address:* 4118 Rhodes Avenue, Studio City, CA 91604, USA.

SLOAN Carolyn. *See:* **HOLLIS Carolyn Sloan.**

SLOMAN Anne, b. 24 Apr 1944, London, England. Journalist. m. Martyn Sloman, 22 Apr 1972, 2 sons. *Education:* BA, Honours, Politics, Philosophy and Economics, St Hilda's College, Oxford University, 1963-66. *Appointments:* Radio Producer 1967-72, TV Producer, 1972-73, Senior Producer, Radio, Current Affairs, Executive Producer, General Election and US Presidential Results Coverage, 1973-81, Assistant Editor, Today Programme, 1981-82, Editor, Special Current Affairs, 1983-, BBC. *Publications:* Co-Author: British Political Facts 1900-79, 1980; No Minister, 1982; But Chancellor, 1983; With Respect Ambassador, 1985; The Thatcher Phenomenon, 1986. *Honours:* Award, Outstanding Programme Contribution, Broadcasting Guild of Journalists; Broadcasting Press Guild Radio Award, Outstanding Programme: The Thatcher Phenomenon, 1985; Outstading Contribution: My Country Right or Wrong, 1988. *Address:* 29 Church Crescent, London N10, England.

SLYK Marek, b. 14 Nov 1953, Warsaw, Poland. Writer. m. Magdelena, 3 Nov 1981, 1 son. *Appointments:* Jankowo Dolne, 1979; Zaborow, 1981. *Publications:* Trilogy: In a Borsch of Adventures, 1980; In a Broth of Complications, 1982; In a Barlye Soup of Conclusions, 1986; Game for a Super Brain, 1982. *Contributions to:* Szpilki; Rzeczywistosc; Walka Mlodych; Razem; Nurt; Zycie Literackie; Poezja. *Honour:* Wilhelm Mach's Award, 1980. *Membership:* Zwiazek Literatow Polskich. *Address:* Wiolinowa Str. 8/40, 02-789 Warsaw, Poland.

SMALL Ernest. *See:* **LENT Blair.**

SMALLEY Stephen Stewart, b. 11 May 1931, London, England. Clerk in Holy Orders. m. Susan Jane Paterson, 13 July 1974. *Education:* BA, 1955, MA 1958, PhD, 1979, Jesus College, Cambridge; BD 1957, Eden Theological Seminary, USA; Deacon 1958, Priest 1959, Ridley Hall, Cambridge. *Appointments:* Assistant Curate, St Paul's, Portman Square, London, 1958-60; Chaplain, Peterhouse, Cambridge, 1960-63, Acting Dean, 1962-63; Lecturer and Senior Lecturer, University of Ibadan, Nigeria, 1963-69; Lecturer and Senior Lecturer, University of Manchester, 1970-77, also Warden of St Anselm Hall, 1972-77; Canon Residentiary and Precentor of Coventry Cathedral, 1977-86, Vice-Provost 1986; Dean, Chester Cathedral, 1987-. *Publications:* John: Evangelist and Interpreter, 1978; 1,2,3 John, 1984; The Spirit's Power, 1972; (Ed)Christ and Spirit in the New Testament, 1973. *Contributions to:* Numerous articles and reviews in learned journals, including Journal of Theological Studies, New Testament Studies, Journal of Biblical Literature, Expository Times, Novum Testamentum. *Honours:* Foundation and Lady Kay Scholar, Jesus College, Cambridge, 1948, 1955; Select Preacher, University of Cambridge, 1963-64; Manson Memorial Lecturer, University of Manchester, 1986; Member, Archbishops' Doctrine Commission of the Church of England, 1981-86. *Memberships:* Studiorum Novi Testamenti Societas; Chester City Club. *Address:* The Deanery, 7, Abbey Street, Chester CH1 2JF, England.

SMARANDACHE Florentin, b. 10 Dec 1954, Balcesto, Vilcea, Romania. Software Engineer; Writer. *Education:* MA, Faculty of Mathematics and Computer Science, University of Craiova. *Publications:* Books written in Romanian: Formule Pentru Spirit (Formulas for the Spirit) (poems), 1981; Culegere de Exercitii Poetice (Collection of Poetical Exercises), Editor El Kitab, 1982; Legi de Compozitie Interna. Poeme Cu...Probleme! (Laws of Internal Composition. Poems with...Problems!) Editor El Kitab, 1982; Sentimente Fabricate in Laborator (Feelings Made in Laboratory) (poems) Editor El Kitab, 1984; Strain de Cauza (Out in Left Field) (sketch), 1990; America - Paradisul diavolului, 1992; Books in French: Le Sens du Non-Sens (The Sense of Non-sense), 1983, 84; Anti-Chanbres, Anti-Poesies, Bizarreries (Ante-Rooms, Ante-Poems, Wiersnesses), Editor Claude Le

Roy, 1989; Books in English: Nonpoems, 1990; Circles of Light Dark Snow, 1992; Anthologies: Ora Planetei (Planet Time), 1980; Clair de Signes (Clear Signs), 1989; Cristal (Crystal), 1990; Anthology of the Paradoxist Literary Movement, 1993. *Contributions to:* Literary Magazines in Romania, France, England, United States of America, Japan. *Memberships:* US Mathematical Association; Romania Mathematical Association; Reviewer to Zentralblatt fur Mathematik, West Germany. *Address:* PO Box 42561, Phoenix, AZ 85080, USA.

SMEDS Dave, b. 23 Feb 1955, Reedley, California, USA. Author. m. Connie Willeford, 26 June 1982, 1 daughter, 1 son. *Education:* BA, English, Psychology, Sonoma State University. *Publications:* The Sorcery Within, 1985; The Schemes of Dragons, 1989; Piper in the Night, forthcoming. *Contributions to:* Isaac Asimov's Science Fiction Magazine; Lui; Mayfair; The Magazine of Fantasy and Science Fiction. Inside Karate; Anthologies include: Dragons of Light, 1980; Far Frontiers, Volume 6, 1986; In the Field of Fire, 1987; Full Spectrum 4, Sword & Sorceress 4, 1987. *Memberships:* Science Fiction Writers of America; Author's Guild. *Address:* 164 Jack London Drive, Santa Rosa, CA 95409, USA.

SMEED Frances. *See:* **LASKY Jesse Louis.**

SMEED John William, b. 21 Feb 1926, London, England. Emeritus Professor in German. m. Gay Jones, 24 Mar 1952. *Education:* BA, MA, PhD, University of Wales. *Publications:* Jean Paul's Dreams, 1966; Faust in Literature, 1975; The Theophrastan Character, 1985; German Song and its Poetry, 1987; Don Juan Variations on a Theme, 1990; Famour Poets, neglected Composers, Songs to Lyrics by Goethe, Heine, mörike and others, 1992. *Contributions to:* Literary Periodicals in England, Germany and USA. *Honours:* University of Wales Fellowship, 1953; Leverhulme Research Fellowship, 1983. *Address:* 53 Claypath, Durham DH1 1QS, England.

SMELSER Neil Joseph, b. 22 July 1930, Missouri, USA. University Professor of Sociology. m. (1) Helen Margolis, 10 June 1954, div, 1965; (2) Sharin Hubbert, 20 Oct 1967, 2 sons, 2 daughters. *Education:* BA 1952, PhD, 1958, Harvard University; BA 1954, MA, 1959, Oxford University; Graduate, San Francisco Psychoanlaytic Institute, 1971. *Publications:* Economy and Soiciety, 1956; Social Change inthe Industrial Revolution, 1959; Theory of Collective Behaviour, 1962; The Sociology of Economic Life, 1962, 1973; Sociology, 1981, 1984, 1987. 1991; Handbook of Sociology, editor, 1988; Social Paralysis and Social Change, 1991. *Contributions to:* American Behavioural Scientist; American Sociologist. *Honours:* Rhodes Scholar, 1952-54; Junior Fellow, Society of Fellows, 1955-58; Fellow, AAAS, 1968. *Memberships:* American Philosophical Society, 1976; VP, Association Sociological Association, 1973; International Sociological Association, VP, 1990-94. *Address:* Department of Sociology, University of California, Berkeley, CA 94720, USA.

SMILEY Jane, Distinguised Professor, Liberal Arts and Sciences, English Department. *Education:* MA, University of Iowa, 1975; MFA, University of Iowa, 1976; PhD, University of Iowa, 1978, dissertation: Harms and Fears (Short Stories). *Appointments include:* Graduate Teaching Assistant, Core Literature Program, University of Iowa, 1974-76, 1977-78; Adjunct Assistant Professor, Saturday and Evening Class Program, University of Iowa, 1980; Visiting Assistant Professor, Writer's Workshop, University of Iowa, 1981; Assistant Professor, Member of Graduate Faculty, University of Iowa State University, 1981-84; Full Professor, Iowa State University, 1989-; Distinguished Professor, Iowa State University, 1992-. *Publications include:* At Paradise Gate (novel), 1981; The Age of Grief, A Novella and Stories, 1988; Craftspeople of the Catskills, (nonfiction), 1987; Ordinary Love and Good Will, 1989; A Thousand Acres, 1991. *Contributions to:* Book reviews for: New York Times; Washington Post; Vogue; Washington Times; Chicago Tribune; Boston Globe; 3 new ones this year in New York Times. *Honours include:* Los Angeles Times, Fiction Prize, A Thousand Acres, 1992; National Book Critic's Circle Award, A Thousand Acres, 1992; Ambassador Prize ofthe English Speaking Union, A Thousand Acres, 1992; The Heartland Award of the Chicago Tribune, A Thousand Acres, 1992; Pulitzer Prize for Fiction, A Thousand Acres, 1992. *Memberships:* Review Committee, 1988, 1990; Vice-Provost, Research Search Committee; Member, Faculty Senate; Member, Graduate Committee. *Address:* 301 Ross Hall, Iowa State University, Ames, IA 50011, USA.

SMIRNOV Igor Pavlovich, b. 19 May 1941, Leningrad, Russia. Professor of Russian Literature. m. Johanna Renate Luise Elisabeth Döring- Smirnov, 16 July 1979. *Education:* MA, Leningrad State University, 1963; Dr Phil Sci, Insitute of Russian Literature, Leningrad, 1967. *Appointments:* Editorial Board, Elementa, Journal of Slavic Studies and Comparative Cultural Semiotics, Los Angeles, 1992; New Literary Review, Moscow, 1992. *Publications:* Meaning in Art and the Evolution of Poetic Systems, 1977; The Emergence of the Inter-text, 1985; Towards a Theory of Literature, 1987; Being and Creating, 1990; An Old Russian Culture, Russian National Speciality and the Logic of History, 1991. *Contributions to:* Russian Literature; Winer Slawistischer Almanach. *Address:* Guerickestr 35, 8 Munchen 40, Germany.

SMITH A C H, b. 31 Oct 1935, Kew, England. Writer. *Education:* MA, Cambridge University. *Publications:* The Crowd, 1965; Zero Summer, 1971; Orghast at Persepolis, 1972; Paper Voices, 1975; Treatment, 1976; The Jericho Gun, 1977; Edward and Mrs Simpson, 1978; Extra Cover, 1981; The Dark Crystal, 1982; Wagner, 1983; Sebastian the Navigator, 1985; Lady Jane, 1985; Labyrinth, 1986. *Contributions to:* New Society; Transatlantic Review; Listener; Times; Telegraph Magazine; Sunday Times; Observer; BBC and ITV. *Honours;* Writing Awards, Arts Council, 1970-71, 1974-75, 1980. *Memberships:* Writers Guild of Great Britain; Literary Advisory Panel, Southwest Arts, 1972-75; Director, Cheltenham Festival of Literature, 1978-79; Executive, Playwrights Company, 1979-83. *Literary Agent:* Aitken and Stone. *Address:* 21 West Shrubbery, Bristol BS6 6TA, England.

SMITH Alfred G b.20 Aug 1921, The Hague, Netherlands. Anthropologist. m. Britta H Bonazzi, 30 May 1946. *Education:* BA, University of Michigan, 1943; Graduate Study and Certification, Oriental Languages, Princeton University; Graduate Study, Malay, Yale University, 1943; MA 1947, PhD 1956, Anthropology, University of Wisconsin. *Appointments:* Consulting and Contributing Editor and Member of Editorial Board, Journal of Communication, 1973; Editorial Board, Communication and Information Science, 1977; Editorial Board, Information and Behaviour, 1983; and formerly about 12 other journals. *Publications:* Communication and Culture, 1966 Spanish editions 1972 and 1976; Communication and Status, 1966, reprinted by US Navy, 1982; Cognitive Styles in Law Schools, 1979; series of Linguistic Analyses: Gamwoelhaelhi Ishilh Weleeya (Woleal); Ki Luwn Specl Kosrao (Kushien). Contributions to: Land Economics; Collier's Encyclopaedia; American Anthropologist; Current Anthropology. *Honours:* American Council of Learned Societies, Fellow, 1942; More than 20 grants from National Science Foundation, Georgia Department of Public Health, Oregon Governors Committee on Children and Youth. *Memberships:* Phi Kappa Phi; Alpha Kappa Delta; Sigma Xi; International Communication Association, President 1973-74; American Anthropological Association, Fellow; American Association for Advancement of Science, Fellow. *Address:* 1801 Lavaca, Austin, TX 78701, USA.

SMITH Badley F, b. 5 Oct 1931, Seattle, USA. Writer; Teacher. m. 31 Dec 1983, 2 daughters. *Education:* BA, 1957; MA, 1960, University of California, Berkeley. *Publications:* Reaching Judgement at Nuremberg, 1977;

The Shadow Warriors, 1983; Himmler Geheimreden, 1974; Operation Sunrise, (with Elena Agarossi), 1979; The War's Long Shadow, 1986; Adolf Hitler, his Family, Childhood, and Youth, 1967; The Road to Nuremberg, 1981; The American Road to Nuremberg, 1981; The Ultra-Magic Deals and the Special Relatioships, 1940-46, 1992-93 (Presido US & Airline UK). *Contributions to:* Encounter; Los Angeles Times; The Independent; The Washington Post; The American Review; Vierteljahrshefte fu Zeigeschiechte. *Honours:* Shortlisted for Los Angeles Times Book of the Year, 1981; Observer Book of the Year, 1977. *Memberships:* Phi Beta Kappa; Authors Guild. *Address:* 104 Regents Park Road, London NW1 8UG, England.

SMITH Barbara Herrnstein, b. 6 Aug 1932, New York, USA. Educator. m. (1) R J Herrnstein, 28 May 1951 (div 1961), (2) T H Smith, 21 Feb 1964, (div 1974), 2 daughters. *Education:* BA 1954, MA 1955, PhD, English and American Literature, 1965, Brandeis University. *Appointments:* Faculty, Literature and Language, bennington Colege, 1961-73; Communications, English and Communications, Comparative Literature and Literary Theory, University of Pennsylvania, 1973-87; Professor of Comparative Literature and English, Duke University, 1987-; Northrop Frye Chair in Lit Theory, University of Toronto, 1990. *Publications:* Contingencies of Value: Alternative Perspectives for Critical Theory, 1988; On the Margins of Discourse: The Relation of Literature to Language, 1978; Poetic Closure: A Study of How Poems End, 1968; The Politics of Liberal Education, co-editor, 1991. *Contributions to:* Critical Inquiry; South Atlantic Quarterly; University of Toronto; Cardozo Law Review; Annals of Scholarship. *Honours include:* Christian Gauss Award, 1968; Explicator Award, 1968; Fellowship, National Endowment for the Humanities, 1970-71; Guggenheim Fellowship, 1977-78; Rockefeller foundaiton Fellowship, 1981; Fellow, Centre for Advanced Study in Behavioral Sciences, Stanford University, 1985-86; Distinguished Professor, Duke University, 1987; National Humanities Center, 1992; Davis Center, Princeton, 1993. *Memberships include:* President, Academy of Literary Studies, 1983-84; President, Society for Critical Exchange, 1986-89; American Comparative Literature Association; Supervisor/Trustee, The English Institute, 1978-93; President, Modern Language Association of America, 1988; AAAS. *Address:* 325 Allen Building, Box 90015, Duke University, Durham NC 27706, USA.

SMITH Bernard William, b. 3 Oct 1916, Sydney, New South Wales, Australia. Art Historian and Critic. m. Kate Beatrice Hartley Challis, 16 May 1941, 1 son, 1 daughter. *Education:* BA, Sydney University, 1952; Warburg Institute, London, England, 1948-50; PhD, Australian National University, 1956. *Appointments:* Category A Literary Fellowship, Australia Council, 1990-91. *Publications:* Place, Taste and Tradition, 1945; European Vision and the South Pacific, 1960; Australian Painting, 1962; The Architectural Character of Glebe, Sydney (with K Smith), 1973; Documents on Art and Taste in Australia, 1975; The Boy Adeodatus, 1984; The Art of Captain Cook's Voyages (with R Joppien), 3 vols, 1985-87; The Death of the Artist as Hero, 1988; The Critic as Advocate, 1989; Imagining the Pacific, 1992. *Contributions to:* Journal of the Warburg and Courtauld Institutes, Modern Painters (London); Meanjin, Scripsi, Australian Society. *Honours:* Co-Recipient, Ernest Scott Prize for History, Melbourne, 1962; Henry Lawson Prize for Poetry, 1964; Honorary LittD, University of Melbourne, 1976; Australian National Book Council Prize, The Nettie Palmer Prize for Non-Fiction, and the Talking Book Award, all for The Boy Adeodatus, 1984. *Memberships:* Australian Society of Authors; Australian Academy of the Humanities, President 1977-80; Australian Humanities Research Council, 1956-69, Secretary 1962-65; Fellow, Society of Antiquaries; UNESCO Committee for Letters, Australia, 1963-69. *Address:* 168 Nicholson Street, Fitzroy, Victoria 3065, Australia.

SMITH Brian Roger, b. 29 May 1939, Montreal, Canada. Business consultant. m. Myrna M Milani, 3 Mar 1985, 1 son, 2 daughters. *Education:* BSc Mechanical Engineering, Northeastern University, Boston, 1962; MBA, University of Pittsburgh, 1963. *Publications:* The Country Consultant, 1983; A Primer of Rotational Physics, 1985; How to become successfully self- employed, 1991; The Principles of Energy, 1986; The Small computer in small Business, 1981; How to Prosper in you Own Business, 1981; Word Processing, 1983; Soft Words for a Hard Technology, 1987; Buying Your Own Small Business, 1988; Buying a Franchise, 1989; Computers in Veterinary Medicine, 1986. *Contributions to:* Business and scientific journals and newsletters. *Address:* HC60 Box 40, Charlestown, NH 03603, USA.

SMITH Bryan. *See:* **KNOTT William Cecil.**

SMITH C Busby. *See:* **SMITH John.**

SMITH Charles William, b. 20 Mar 1940. Teacher; Writer. 1 son, 1 daughter. *Education:* BA, North Texas State University, 1964; MA, Northern Illinois University, 1967. *Appointments:* Instructor, Drury College and Southwest Missouri State University, 1966-74; Film Critic, Feature Writer, Dallas Times Herald, 1978-80; Lecturer, SMU, 1980-86; Associate Professor, 1986-88; Professor, 1988-91. *Publications:* Stort Stories inc. Hugo Molder and the Symbol of Misplaced Persons Everywhere; The Jailbird Game; Fool and Pathfinder; A Letter From the Horse Latitudes; Witnesses; book. Thin Men of Haddam; Country Music; The Vestal Virgin Room; Buffalo Nickel; Will They Love Me When I Leave?; Uncle Dad. *Honours:* The Southwestern Library Association Award; Jesse H Jones award; Dobie Paisano Fellowship; National Endowment for the Arts Creative writing Fellowship; Charles Green award; Special Merit Award; Frank O'Connor Memorial award; John H mcGinnis Award; Pushcart Prize Nomination; Best Non Fiction Award. *Memberships:* The Authors Guild; Writers Guild; Texas Institute of Letters; Pen. *Literary Agent:* Elaine Markson Agency, 44 Greenwich Avenue, NY 10011, USA. *Address:* 5555 Goodwin, Dallas, TX 75206, USA.

SMITH Clara May Freeman b. 28 Aug 1912, Flushing, Michigan, USA. Teacher. m. Russell Frederick Smith, 21 Dec 1952, 1 stepson, 2 stepdaughters. *Education:* BS, Eastern Michigan University, 1939; MA, Northwestern University, 1942; PhD, University of Michigan, 1962; 60 hours of Engineering, Michigan State College, 1943. Correspondence Course, Newspaper Institute of America, Mamaroneck, New York, 1983-85, Certificate in Journalism. *Appointments:* Nursery School King's Daughters, Flint, Michigan, 1931; Kent Rural School. Genesee County, 1933-34; Teacher, Lansing Public Schools, 1936-42; National College of Education, 1943-45; Central Washington State College, 1945. *Publications:* A History of Lincoln Consolidated Training School and its Contributions to the Improvement of Rural Education, 1962; A Brief Biography of Alfred Hitchcock (unpublished) 1985. *Memberships:* Life Member, Michigan Education Association; Life Member, National Education Association; Ann Arbor Teachers Club; Northwestern University Alumni Association; Eastern Michigan University Alumni Association. *Address:* Eastern Michigan University Library, Ypsilanti, MI 48197, USA.

SMITH Dean Wesley, b. 10 Nov 1950, Boise, Idaho, USA. Fiction Writer. *Education:* BArch, University of Idaho. *Literary Appointments:* Clarion Science Fiction Writers Workshop, 1982; Taos Experimental Writers of the Future Workshop, 1986; Editor, Pulphouse Reports. *Publications:* Short stories including: One Last Dance; Flawless Execution; Starship Shirley; Plane Crash Love; Jukebox Man. Novel: Laying The Music To Rest, 1989. Over 30 poems. *Honours:* Finalist, Writers of the Future Contest, 1985; Winner, World Fantasy Award, 1989; Stokes Finalist, Best First Novel, 1989; Hugo Nominee, Editor Best Nonfiction, 1990. *Membership:* Science Fiction Writers of America. *Literary Agent:* Marilee

Hiefez, Writers House Inc. *Address:* Box 11192, Eugene, OR 97440, USA.

SMITH Delia, Cookery Writer and Broadcaster. m. Michael Wynn Jones. *Appointments:* Several BBC TV Series; Cookery Writer, Evening Standard, later the Standard, 1972-85; Columnist, Radio Times. *Publications:* How to Cheat at Cooking, 1973; Country Fare, 1973; Recipes from Country Inns and Restaurants, 1973; Family Fare, book 1, 1973; book 2, 1974; Evening Standard Cook Book, 1974; Country Recipes from "Look East" 1975; More Country Recipes from "Look East" 1976; Frugal Food, 1976; Book of Cakes, 1977; Recipes from "Look East" 1977; Food for Our Times, 1978; Cookery Course, part 1, 1978, part 2, 1979, part 3, 1981; The Complete Cookery Course, 1982; A Feast for Lent, 1983; A Feast for Advent, 1983; One is Fun, 1985; Editor, Food Aid Cookery Book, 1986; A Journey into God, 1988; Delia Smith's Christmas, 1990. *Address:* c/o BBC Publications, Woodlands, 80 Wood Lane, London W12 0TT, England.

SMITH Dudley (Sir), b. 14 Nov 1926, Cambridge, England. Member of Parliament. m. 1st marriage dissolved, 1 son, 2 daughters, (2) Catherine Amos, 1976. *Appointments:* worked for various provincial and national newspapers as journalist and senior executive, 1943-66; Assistant News Editor, Sunday Express, 1953-59; Divisional Director, Beecham Group, 1966-70; Member of Parliament. *Publications include:* Harold Wilson: A Critical Biography, 1964; They Also Served, 1945. *Honours:* Kt, 1983; D.L., 1989. *Memberships:* Secretary General, European Democratic Group, Council of Europen, 1985; Chairman, United and Cecil Club, 1975-80. *Address:* Church Farm, Weston under Wetherley, Nr. Leamington Spa, Warwickshire, England.

SMITH Emma, b. 21 Aug 1923, Newquay, Cornwall, England. Writer. m. Richard Llewellyn Stewart-Jones (dec 1957), 31 Jan 1951, 1 son, 1 daughter. *Publications:* Maiden's Trip, 1948; The Far Cry, 1949; Emily, 1959; Out of Hand, 1963; Emily's Voyage, 1966; No Way of Telling, 1972; The Opportunity of a Lifetime, 1978. *Contributions to:* Various magazines. *Honours:* Atlantic Award, short stories, 1948; John Llewellyn Thys Memorial Prize, 1948; James Tait Black Memorial Prize, 1949. *Literary Agent:* Curtis Brown. *Address:* c/o Curtis Brown, 162-168 Regent Street, London W1R 5TB, England.

SMITH Frederick E(screet), (David Farrell), b. 4 Apr 1922, Hull, Yorkshire, England, Author; Playwright. m. Shelagh McGrath, 11 July 1945, 2 sons. *Publications include:* 633 Squadron, 1956; A Killing for the Hawks, 1967; The Tormented, 1970; The Obsession, 1984; Laws Be Their Enemy, 1954; Rage of the Innocent, 1986; Of Masks and Minds, 1954; Lydia Trendennis, 1958; The Sin and the Sinners, 1958; The Grotto of Tiberius, 1962; The Devil Behind Me, 1962; The Storm Knight, 1968; The Wider Sea of Love, 1969; Waterloo, 1970; Saffron's war, 1972; Saffron's Army, 1973; 633 Squadron Operation Rhine Maiden, 1984, and 4 additional sequels; A Meeting of Stars, 1987; A Clash of Stars, 1987; In Presence of My Foes, 1988; Years of the Fury, 1989. *Contributions to:* Magazines in 20 countries. *Honours:* Mark Twain Literary Award for novel, A Killing for the hawks, 1967; 633 Squadron: Operation Crisis, 1993. *Memberships;* Crime Writers Association; Writers Guild of Great Britain. *Address:* 3 Hathaway Road, Southbourne, Bournemouth, Dorset BH6 3HH, England.

SMITH George Henry (Jan Hudson, Jerry Jason, Diana Summers), b. 1922, USA. Freelance Writer. *Publications:* Satan's Daughter, 1961; 1976: Year of Terror, 1961; Scourge of the Blood Cult, 1961; The Coming of the Rats, 1961; Doomsday Wing, 1963; A Place Called Hell (with M Jane Deer Smith under joint pseudonym M J Deer), romance, 1963; Flames of Desire (with M Jane Deer Smith as M J Deer), 1963; The Unending Night, 1964; The Forgotten Planet, 1965; The Psycho Makers (as Jerry Jason), 1965; The Four Day Weekend, 1966; Druid's World, 1967; The Hell's Angels (as Jan Hudson), non-fiction, 1967, UK Edition The New Barbarians, 1973; The People in the Saucers (as Jan Hudson), non-fiction, 1967; Who Is Ronald Reagan, biography, 1968; Kar Kaballa, 1969; Witch Queen of Lochlann, 1969; Martin Luther King, Jr, biography, 1971; Bikers at War, non-fiction, 1976; The Second War of the Worlds, 1978; The Island Snatchers, 1978; Wild Is the Heart (as Diana Summers), romance, 1978; Love's Wicked Ways (as Diana Summers), romance, 1979; The Devil's Breed, 1979; The Rogues, 1980; The Firebrands, 1980; Fallen Angel (as Diana Summers), 1981; Louisana (as Diana Summers), 1984; The Emperor's Lady (as Diana Summers), 1984.

SMITH Gregory Blake, b. 24 July 1951, Torrington, Connecticut, USA. Novelist; College Professor. 1 son. *Education:* AB, Bowdoin College, 1975; MA, Boston University, 1981; MFA, University of Iowa, 1983. *Publications:* Novels: The Devil in the Dooryard, 1986; The Last Shakeress, 1991. *Honours:* Stegner Fellowship, Stanford University, 1985; National Endowment for the Arts Fellow, 1988. *Literary Agent:* Paula Diamond. *Address:* Department of English, Carleton College, Northfield, MN 55057, USA.

SMITH Howard Everett Jr, b. 18 Nov 1927, Gloucester, Massachusetts, USA. Writer. m. Louanne Norris, 1 June 1953, 1 son, 1 daughter. *Education:* Carmel Union High School, Carmel, California, 1941-46; University of California, Berkeley, California, 1948; BA, Colorado College, Colorado Springs, Colorado, 1946-47, 1948-52. *Appointments:* Editor, Basic Books, New York, New York, 1962; Editor, McGraw Hill Book Co, New York, 1967-75. *Publications include:* Daring the Unknown: A History of NASA, 1987; Small Worlds; Communities of Living Things, 1987; A Naturalist's Guide to the Year, 1985; The Complete Beginner's Guidfe to Mountain Climbing, 1977; Killer Weather, 1982; From Under the Earth: America's Metals, Fuels and Minerals, 1967. *Contributions to:* The Art of Mary Bavermeister in Art and Artists, London. *Honours:* NSTA-CBC Outstanding Science Trade Books for Children, 1979, 1987; NCSS-CBC Notable Children's Trade Books in the Field of Social Studies, 1974; Teenage Showcase, New York, Public Library, 1982, 1986, 1987; Something About the Authors, Gale Research, 1984. *Literary Agent:* Fon Congdon. *Address:* 128 Willow Street, Apt 2C, Brooklyn, NY 11201, USA.

SMITH Howard Kingsbury, b. 12 May 1914, Ferriday, Louisiana, USA. TV News Journalist; Commentator. *Education:* BA, Tulane University, Berlin, 1936; Merton College, Oxford, 1937-39. *Publications:* Last Train from Berlin; The State of Europe; Washington DC. *Memberships:* Sigma Delta Chi; Overseas Press Club; AFTRA. *Address:* 6750 Brooks Lane, Bethesda, MD 20816, USA.

SMITH Iain Crichton, b. 1 Jan 1928, Glasgow, Scotland, Writer. m. 16 July 1977, 2 stepsons. *Education:* MA, Honours, English, Aberdeen University, 1949; D.Litt, Aberdeen University, 1988. *Publications include:* Thistles and Roses (poems), 1961; The Law and the Grace (poems), 1965; Consider the Lilies (novel), 1968; The Last Summer (novel), 1969; The Black and the Red (short stories), 1973; On the Island (short stories), 1974; The Hermit and Other Stories, 1977; Selected Poems, 1982; A Life (poems), 1985; The Village and Other Poems, 1989; Collected Poems, 1992; Bibliography of Iain Crichton Smith by Grant Wilson, 1988; Mirror and Marble - The Poetry of Iain Crichton Smith by Carol Gow, 1992; Critical Essays on Iain Crichton Smith, 1992. *Contributions to:* Spectator; The Literary Review; Times Literary Supplement; BBC; Encounter; Poetry Review; New Statesman. *Honours:* 8 Scottish Arts Council Awards; LLD, Dundee University; DLitt, Glasgow University; OBE; FRLS; Saltire Award for Scottish Book of the Year awarded to Collected Poems, 1992. *Memberships:* Scottish Arts Council, 1985-88; Scottish Arts Council Literary Committee, 1984-. *Address:* Tigh Na Fuaran, Taynuilt, Argyll, Scotland.

SMITH Joan, ·b. 1938, USA. Author. *Publications:* An Affair of the Heart, 1977; Escapade, 1977; La Comtesse, 1978; Imprudent Lady, 1978; Dame Durden's Daughter, 1978; Aunt Sophie's Diamonds, 1979; Flowers of Eden, 1979; Sweet and Twenty, 1979; Talk of the Town, 1979; Aurora, 1980; Babe, 1980; Endure My Heart, 1980; Lace for Milady, 1980; Delsie, 1981; Lover's Vows, 1981; Love's Way, 1982; Reluctant Bride, 1982; Reprise, 1982; Wiles of a Stranger, 1982; Prelude to Love, 1983; Grandmother's Donkey, 1983; Grandmother's Secret, 1983; Royal Rebels, 1985; Midnight Masquerade, 1985; The Devious Duchess, 1985; True Lady, 1986; Bath Belles, 1986; A Country Wooing, 1987. *Literary Agent:* Fawcett, USA. *Address:* c/o Fawcett, 1515 Broadway, New York, NY 10036, USA.

SMITH John (C Busby Smith), b. 1924, United Kingdom. Author. *Appointments:* Director, 1946-58, Managing Director, 1959-71, Christy and Moore Ltd, literary agents, London; Editor, Poetry Review, London, 1962-65. *Publications:* Gates of Beauty and Death: Poems (as C Busby Smith), 1948; The Dark Side of Love, 1952; The Birth of Venus: Poems, 1954; The Mask of Glory, 1956; Mr Smith's Apocalypse: A Jazz Cantata, 1957; Excursus in Autumn, 1958; The Pattern of Poetry (edited with W Seymour), 1963; A Discreet Immorality, 1965; My Kind of Verse (editor), 1965; Modern Love Poems (editor), 1966; Five Songs of Resurrection, 1967; Four Ritual Dances, 1968; Happy Christmas (edited with W Seymour), 1968; Jan Le Witt: An Appreciation of His Work (with H Read and J Casson), 1971; The Broken Fiddlestick, 1971; The Early Bird and the Worm, 1972; Entering Rooms, 1973; My Kind of Rhymes (editor), 1973; The Arts Betrayed, 1978; A Landscape of My Own: Selected Poems 1948- 1982, 1982; Songs for Simpletons, 1984. *Address:* 3 Adelaide Court, Hove, Sussex, England.

SMITH Julie, Annapolis, Maryland, USA. Writer. *Education:* BA, University of Mississippi, 1965. *Publications:* 5 Novels: Death Turns a Trick, 1982; The Sourdough Wars, 1984; True-Life Adventure, 1985; Tourist Trap, 1986; Huckleberry Fiend, 1987. *Memberships:* Mystery Writers of America; Red Headed League; Private Eye Writers of America. *Literary Agent:* Charlotte Sheedy. *Address:* c/o Charlotte Sheedy Agency, 145 W 86th St., New York, NY 10024, USA.

SMITH Kay Nolte, b. 4 July 1932, Eveleth, Minnesota, USA. Author. m. Phillip J. Smith, 30 May 1958. *Education:* BA, University of Minnesota, 1952; MA, University of Utah, 1955. *Publications:* The Watcher, 1980, UK Edition, 1981; Catching Fire, 1982; Mindspell, 1983, UK Edition, 1984; Elegy for a Soprano, 1985, UK Edition, 1986; Country of the Heart, 1987, UK Edition, 1987; Translation of Edmond Rostand's Chantecler, 1987, UK Edition, 1987; A Tale of the Wind, 1991, UK edition, 1991. *Contributions to:* Vogue; Opera News; American Baby; The Objectivist; Others. *Honour:* Edgar Allan Poe Award for Best First Novel for The Watcher, Mystery Writers of America, 1981. *Memberships:* Authors Guild; Phi Beta Kappa; Actors Equity Association. *Literary Agent:* Meredith Bernstein. *Address:* 73 Hope Road, Tinton Falls, NJ 07724, USA.

SMITH Ken, b. 4 Dec 1938. Writer. m. Judi Benson, 6 July 1981, 2 sons, 2 daughters. *Education:* BA, Leeds University. *Appointments:* Writer in Residence, Clark University, Worcester, Mass, USA, 1972-73; Leeds University, Leeds, England, 1976-78; Kingston Polytechnic, Surrey, 1979-81; H.M.P. Wormwood Scrubs, 1985-87. *Publications:*The Pity, 1973; Work, Distances, 1973; The Poet Reclining, 1982; Chinese Whispers, 1987; Terra, 1987; Wormwood, 1988; Inside Time, 1989; The Heart, The Border, 1990; Berlin: Coming in From the Cold, 1990; Tender to the Queen of Spain. *Contributions to:* various publications. *Honours:* Gregory Award, 1964; Arts Council Bursary, 1974; Arts Council Award, 1988. *Literary Agent:* Mic Cheetham. *Address:* Anthony Sheils Associates, 43 Doughty Street, London WC1N 2LF, England.

SMITH Kenneth Roger, (Ken Smith), b. 14 Apr 1944. Writer; Professor. m. 14 July 1992, 3 sons, 1 daughter. *Education:* BA, University of Arizona, 1976; MFA, 1980. *Appointments:* Fiction Editor, The Poetry Miscellany, 1986-. *Publications:* Decoys and Other Stories; Angels and Others. Contributions to: The Atlantic; Sonora Review; Triquarterly; Crazyhorse. *Honours:* Arizona Commission on the Arts Fellowship; PEN Fiction award; John Gardner Fellowship; Kentucy Arts Council Fellowship. *Membership:* Associated Writing Program. *Literary Agent:* Ms Jean V Naggar. *Address:* Rt 10, Box 1006, Ringgold, GA 30736, USA.

SMITH L Neil, b. USA. Science Fiction Writer. *Publications:* Their Majesties' Buccaneers, 1981; The Venus Belt, 1981; The Nagasaki Vector, 1983; Lando Calrissian and the Flamewind of Oseon, 1983; Lando Calrissian and the Mindharp of Sharu, 1983; Lando Calrissian and the Starcave of ThonBoka, 1983; Tom Paine Maru, 1984; The Crystal Empire, 1986.

SMITH Lacey Baldwin, b. 1922, USA. Professor of English History, Northwestern University. *Publications:* Tudor Prelates and Politics, 1953; A Tudor Tragedy: The Life and Times of Catherine Howard, 1961; This Realm of England 1399-1689, 1966, 3rd Edition, 1975; The Elizabethan Epic, US Edition The Elizabethan World, 1966; The Spanish Armada (with Jay Williams), 1966; Henry VII: The Mask of Royalty, 1971; Elizabeth Tudor: Portrait of a Queen, 1975; Essentials of World History, 1979. *Address:* Department of History, Northwestern University, Evanston, IL 60201, USA.

SMITH Lew. *See:* FLOREN Lee.

SMITH Mark Richard, b. 1935, American. Writer Novels/Short stories. *Appointments:* Professor of English, University of New Hampshire. *Publications:* Toyland, 1965; The Middleman, 1967; The Death of the Detective, 1974; The Moon Lamp, 1976; The Delphinium Girl, 1980; Doctor Blues, 1983; Smoke Street, 1984. *Honours:* Rockefeller Grant, 1965; Guggenheim Fellowship, 1968; Ingram Merrill Grant, 1975; NEA Grant, 1976; Senior Fulbright Fellowship to Yugoslavia, 1985. *Membership:* Board Member, AWP. *Literary Agent:* Harriet Wasserman. *Address:* English Dept, Hamilton-Smith, UNH, Durham, NH 03824, USA.

SMITH Martin Cruz (Nick Carter, Jake Logan, Martin Quinn, Simon Quinn), b. 3 Nov. 1942, Reading, PA, United States of America. Author. m. Emily Arnold, 1 son, 2 daughters. *Publications include:* Gypsy in Amber, 1971; Canto for a Gypsy, 1972; Nightwing, 1977; Gorky Park, 1981; Stallion Gate, 1986; Polar Star, 1989; Red Square, 1992. *Honours:* New York Times Bestseller Charts, 1989 (with Polar Star). *Address:* Mill Valley, California, USA.

SMITH Michael, b. England. Writer; Broadcaster; Lecturer. *Literary Appointment:* Contributor (contracted), Bon Appetit Section, Homes and Gardens. *Publications:* Fine English Cookery, 1973; 4th reprint, 1983; Best of British Cookware, 1975; Cooking with Michael Smith, 1981, rerptined 1983; The Homes and Gardens Cookbook, 1983; A Cook's Tour of Britain, 1984; New English Cookery, 1985; Michael Smith Entertains, 1986; Michael Smith's Afternoon Tea Book, 1986; The Handbook for Hosts, 1987; The Glyndebourne Picnic Book, 1988; BBC Publications: Grace and Flavour, 1976; More Grace and Flavour, 1977; Grace and Flavour a la Mode, 1978; The Book of Sandwiches, 1979; The Saucy Cookbook, 1980; A Fine Kettle of Fish, 1981; Just Desserts, 1982; The Collected Recipes of Michael Smith from Pebble Mill, 1982; reprinted, 1984; Amazing Grace and Flavour, 1983; Naughty But Nice, 1983; Others; Various Television films. *Contributions to:* Cookery Correspondent, The Daily Telegraph, 1986-. *Honours:* Glenfiddich Cookery Book Award, 1982-83; Glenfiddich Trophy for person contributing most to food and wine in Britain, 1982; Sunday Times Best Seller List, 1976; 1982, 1983 (2 books). *Membership:* Guild of Food Writers. *Literary Agent:* David Higham Associates, 5-8 Lower John Street, London, W1R 4HA, England. *Address:* 4 Woodside Road, Kingston-upon-Thames, KT2 5AT, England.

SMITH Moe Sherrard, (Tyler Maddison), b. 22 June 1939, Leeds, England. Author; Journalist; Adjudicator; Literary Agent. m. Thomas Maddison Smith, 14 Mar 1962. *Appointments:* Freelance Author, 1960-; Editor, Driving Mirror Magazine, 1975-84; Scribe Magazine, 1975-78; Pocklington Post, 1988-90; Principal, Writing Tutorial, 1975-; Managing Editor. *Publications:* Write A Successful Novel; Cold Blast of Winter; Rubbings; Wholly Love; Yorkshire Air Museum Guide Book. *Contributions to:* Numerous. *Honours:* Numerous Competitions. *Memberships:* Various Writers Groups and Committees; Magistrates Association. *Literary Agent:* Sherrard Smith Associates, Garthend House, Millington. *Address:* Garthend House, Millington, York, YO4 2TX, England.

SMITH Page, b. 1917, USA. Professor Emeritus; Writer. *Appointments:* Fellow, Institute of Early American History and Culture, 1951-53; Assistant to Professor, University of California, Los Angeles, 1953-64; Provost, 1964-70, Professor, 1970-73, Professor Emeritus of Historical Studies, 1973, Cowell College, University of California, Santa Cruz. *Publications:* James Wilson, Founding Father, 1956; John Adams, 1962; The Historian and History, 1964; As a City Upon a Hill: The Town in American History, 1966; Daughters of the Promised Land: Women in American History, 1970; Jefferson, 1976; A New Age Now Begins: A People's History of the American Revolution, 1976; The Chicken Book (co-author), 1976; A Letter from My Father, 1976; The Religious Origins of the American Revolution (editor), 1976; The Constitution: A Documentary and Narrative History, 1978; The Shaping of America, 1980; The Nation Comes of Age, 1981; Trial by Fire: The Civil War and Reconstruction, 1982; The Rise of Industrial America, Vol 6, People's History of US, 1984; America Enters the World, 1985, vols III, IV, V, VI and VII of A People's History of the United States; Dissenting Opinions, 1984; Redeeming the Time, vol VIII, People's History of the United States, 1987; Killing the Spirit: Higher Education in the United States, 1990. *Address:* 235 Pine Flat Road, Santa Cruz, CA 95060, USA.

SMITH Patrick D, b. 8 Oct 1927, Mendenhall, Mississippi. Writer; Lecturer. m. Iris Doty, 1 Aug 1948, 1 son, 1 daughter. *Education:* BA, University of Mississippi, 1947; MA, 1959. *Appointments:* Director, Public Relations, Hinds Community College, 1959-62; Director, Public Information, University of Mississippi, 1962-66; Director College Relations, Brevard Community college, 1966-88. *Publications:* Novels; A Land Remebered; Allapattah; Angel City; Forever Island; The River Is Home; The Beginning. *Contributions to:* More Than 1000. *Honours:* Tebeay Prize; Outstanding Author Award; Outstanding Florida Author Award; Best Writier Award; Toastmasters International Communication Achievement Award; Environmental Writers award; Medal of Honor. *Memberships:* Space Coast Writers Guild; Authors Guild; Poets & Writers. *Address:* 1370 Island Drive, Merritt Island, FL 32952, USA.

SMITH Peter Charles Horstead, b. 1940, United Kingdom. Author. *Appointments:* Editor, Photo Precision Ltd, printers and publishers, 1972-75. *Publications:* Destroyer Leader, 1968; Task Force 57, 1969; Pedestal, 1970, 2nd Edition, 1987; Stuka at War, 1970, 2nd Edition, 1980; Hard Lying, 1971; British Battle Cruisers, 1972; War in the Aegean (with Edwin Walker), 1974; Heritage of the Sea, 1974; Royal Navy Ships' Badges, 1974; The Haunted Sea (editor), 1974; Battles of the Malta Striking Forces (with Edwin Walker), 1974; Destroyer Action (editor and contributor), 1974; R A F Squadron Badges, 1974; The Story of the Torpedo Bomber, 1974; Per Mare Per Terram: A History of the Royal Marines, 1974; Arctic Victory, 1975; The Battle of Midway, 1976; Fighting Flotilla, 1976; Undesirable Properties (editor and contributor), 1977; The Great Ships Pass, 1977; Hit First, Hit Hard, 1979; The Phantom Coach (editor and contributor), 1979; Action Imminent, 1980; Haunted Shores (editor and contributor), 1980; Impact: The Dive Bomber Pilots Speak, 1981; Cruisers in Action (with J R Dominy), 1981; Dive Bomber, 1982; Rendezvous Skerki Bank, fiction, 1982; Hold the Narrow Sea, 1984; Uninvited Guests, 1984; H M S Wild Swan, 1985; Into the Assault, 1985; Vengeance, 1986; Jungle Dive Bombers at War, 1987; Victoria's Victories, 1987; Dive Bombers in Action, 1988; The Royal Marines, A Pictorial History (with Derek Oakley), 1988; Battleship Royal Sovereign, 1988; Stuka Squadron, 1990; Close Air Support, 1990. *Contributions to:* Cambridgeshire Life; Warship International (USA); Mariners Mirror; The Army Quarterly; Navy International; War Monthly; Fly Past; World War Investigator; Images of War; World War II (USA); Military History (USA); In Flight (USA); Defense Update (USA). *Honour:* Royal Marines Historical Society Award for 1987/88. *Memberships:* The Society of Authors, London; The Royal Marines Historical Society, Eastney; The American Aviation Historical Society. *Address:* Foxden, 12 Brooklands Road, Riseley, Bedford MK44 1EE, England.

SMITH Ralph Bernard, b.9 May 1939, Bingley, England. University Professor. *Education:* Burnley Grammar School, Lancashire 1950-56; BA 1959, PhD 1963, University of Leeds. *Appointments:* Lecturer, then Reader in the History of South East Asia, School of Oriental and African Studies, University of London, 1962-88; Professor of the International History of Asia, School of Oriental and African Studies, University of London, 1989-. *Publications:* Land and Politics in the England of Henry VIII, 1970; Vietnam and the West, 1968, 1971; An International History of the Vietnam War: Vol I 1983, Vol II 1985, Vol III, 1991. *Contributions to:* Articles in learned journals (Fields of History, Asian Studies); Book reviews in various periodicals. *Address:* School of Oriental and African Studies, Russell Square. London WC1, England.

SMITH Robert Edward, b. 10 Mar 1943, Holyoke, Massachusetts, USA. Professor. m. Pauletta Verett, 28 July 1968. *Education:* BA, Harding University, 1964; MFA, University of Oregon, 1966; PhD, University of Missouri Columbia, 1969. *Publications:* Principles of Human Communication; The Gift Horses Mouth; Janice, Bobby and Sarah; Cyrano of the Hill Country. *Contributions to:* Karamu; Descant; Four Quarters; Tales; Texas Review. *Honours:* Writer in Residence, Amerika Haus. *Memberships:* Texas Creative Writing Association; Speech Communication Association; Central States Communication Association. *Literary Agent:* Nat Sobel and Associates. *Address:* 520 Terry Lane, West Lafayette, IN 47906, USA.

SMITH Sarah W R, b, 9 Dec 1947, Boston, Massachusetts, USA. Writer. m. Frederick S Perry, 26 Aug 1979, 1 son, 1 daughter. *Education:* BA, Radcliffe College, 1968; University of London, 1968-69; PhD, Harvard University, 1975. *Appointments:* Assistant Professor, Northeastern University, 1975-76; Assistant Professor, Medford, MA, 1976-82. *Publications:* The Vanished Child; King of Space; Samuel Richardson; Future Boston; Macintosh Common Lisp. *Contributions to:* Numerous. *Honours:* Fulbright; Harvard Graduate Prize Fellow; Bowdoin Prize; Mellon Fellow. *Memberships:* Science Fiction Writers of America; Signet Society; Boston Computor Society. *Literary Agent:* Jane Otte, The Otte Company. *Address:* 32 Bowker Street, Brookline, MA 02146, USA.

SMITH Terence Fitzgerald, b. 18 Nov 1938, Philadelphia, USA. Journalist. 1 son, 1 daughter. *Education:* BA, University of Notre Dame. *Publications:* No Hiding Place, 1981; About Men, 1987, Contributor. *Contributions to:* New York Times Magazine; Esquire; Harper's; Saturday Review; New Republic. *Honours:* Pulitzer Nominations; Emmy Award, The Nightmare Next Door, 1989. *Address:* c/o CBS News, 2020 M St. NW, Washington, DC 20015, USA.

SMITH Wilbur Addison, b. 9 Jan 1933, Zambia. Author. 2 sons, 1 daughter. *Education:* BCom, Rhodes University, 1953. *Publications include:* The Courtney novels, 6 volumes 1964-87; When the Lion Feeds; The Sound of Thunder; A Sparrow Falls; The Burning Shore; Power of the Sword; Rage. The Ballantyne novels, 4 volumes 1980-84: A Falcon Flies; Men of Men; The Angels Weep; The Leopard Hunts in Darkness. Also: The Dark of the Sun, 1965; Shout at the Devil, 1968; Gold Mine, 1970; Diamond Hunters, 1971; The Sunbird, 1972; Eagle in the Sky, 1974; The Eye of the Tiger, 1975; Cry Wolf, 1976; Hungry as the Sea, 1978; Wild Justice, 1979; A Time to Die; Golden Fox, 1990; Elephant Song, 1991. 23 books total. *Contributions to:* Numerous journals & magazines. *Literary Agent:* Charles Pick. *Address:* c/o Charles Pick, Flat 3, 3 Bryanston Place, London W1H 7FN, England.

SMITH Wilma Janice b. 15 Aug 1926, Aryor, Oklahoma, USA, Writer; Publicist. m. Merle Thomas Smith, 30 Apr 1948. *Education:* Oklahoma A&M, 1946; Courses at Tulsa; Graduate, Oklahoma School of Business Accountacy Law and Finance, Tulsa, 1947; Adult education classes. *Appointments:* Academy of Country Music, Hollywood, California, 1974-78; Contributing Editor, Nashville Star reporter, 1976-78; Columnist, Country Music Review, 1977-80; Publicist, Photographer, Lerner Publications, On-staff, PAG (All Music magazine), 1989-. *Publications:* Black Stars of Country Music, 1977; My Story, 1982; Elvis, Saint or Sinner, 1980; Greatest Show on Earth, 1979; Liner Notes on Patsy Montana album, with Waylon Jennings, 1983; Freddie Hart's Fan Club, staff-writer, 1974-79. *Contributions to:* numerous articles, biographies, book and record reviews and photographs in magazines, journals and newspapers. *Honours:* Finalist, Writers Digest; Articles Division, 1981; Winner, Safety Doodles Contests, OK City;s major Opaper, 1972; Winner, Children's Contests, various papers and Wee Wisdom magazine, 1938-78; Guest on Turner Cable TV, 1981; Channel 9 TV, 1989; Guest DJ on numerous radio stations, 1974-83. *Memberships:* Academy of Country Music, 2 term Secretary, 1975-78; CCMA, Los Angeles Branch, former Greater Los Angeles; Press Club; Academy of Country Music, Hollywood; Country Music Society of America. *Literary Agent:* Oceanic Press. *Address:* RAG (All Music magazine) PO Box 24308, Ft Lauderdale, FL 33302, USA.

SMITH Z Z. *See:* **WESTHEIMER David.**

SMITHER Elizabeth Edwina, b. 15 Sept 1941, New Plymouth, New Zealand, Writer. m. Michael Duncan Smither, 31 Aug 1963, 2 sons, 1 daughter. *Education:* Extra-mural studies, Victoria University and Massey University, 1959-60; Graduate, New Zealand Library School, 1962. *Appointment:* New Zealand Literary Fund Advisory Committee, 1988-. *Publications:* Here Come the Clouds, 1975; You're Very Seductive William Carlos Williams, 1978; The Sarah Train, 1980; The Legend of Marcello Mastroianni's Wife, 1981; Casanova's Ankle, 1981; First Blood, 1983; Shakespeare Virgins, 1985; Professor Musgrove's Canary, 1985; Brother Love Sister Love, 1986; A Pattern of Marching, 1989. *Contributions to:* PN Review; TLS; The London Magazine; New Poetry; Poetry Review; Poetry Now; Encounter; Westerly; Meanjin; Landfall; NZ Listener; Poetry Australia; Verse; Numbers. *Honours:* Writing Bursary, 1977; Freda Buckland Award, 1983; Auckland University Literary Fellowship, 1984; Scholarship in Letters, 1987; Literary Fund Travel Bursary, 1988; Lilian Ida Smith Award, 1989. *Memberships:* Amnesty International; PEN NZ. *Address:* 19-A Mt View Place, New Plymouth, New Zealand.

SMITHYMAN Kendrick, b. 9 Oct 1922. m. (1) Mary Stanley Smithyman, (dec 1980), 3 sons, (2) Margaret Ann Edgcumbe, 1981. *Education:* Seddon Memorial Technical College, Auckland; Auckland Teachers College; Auckland University College. *Appointments:* Visiting Fellow, Commonwealth Literature, University of Leeds, England, 1969. *Publications:* Seven Sonnets, 1946; The Blind Mountain, 1951; The Gay Trapeze,

1955; The Night Shift: Poems on Aspects of Love, (co-author), 1957; Inheritance, 1962; Flying to Palmerston, 1968; Eathquake Weather, 1974; The Seal in the Dolphin Pool, 1974; Dwarf with a Billiard Cue, 1978; Stories about Wooden Keyboards, 1985; Are You Going to the Pictures?, 1987; Selected Poems, 1989; Auto/ Biographies, 1992. Editor: Novels by William Satchell, 1971, 1985, short stories by Greville Texidor, 1987. *Contributions to:* Academic Journals; Anthologies including: A Book of New Zealand Verse, 1951; An Anthology of New Zealand Verse, 1966; Poems of Today, 1967; Poetry New Zealand, 1971-; Fifteen Contemporary New Zealand Poets, 1980; Oxford Book of Contemporary New Zealand Poetry, 1982; Penguin Book of New Zealand Verse, 1985; Penguin Book of Contemporary New Zealand Verse, 1989. *Honour:* D Litt, University of Auckland, 1986. *Address:* 66 Alton Avenue, Northcote, Auckland, New Zealand.

SMITTEN Richard, b. 22 Apr 1940. 1 daughter. *Education:* BA, University of Western Ontario. *Appointments:* Marketing Manager, Vick Chemcal Company; Executive Vice President MTS International. *Publications:* Twice Killed; The Man Who Made It Snow; The Godmother; Legal Tender; The Bank of Death; Captial Crimes; Hard Evidence; Kathy: A Case of Nymphomania; Several Film Projects. *Address:* 3675 Skyline Dr, Jensen Beach, FL 34957, USA.

SMUCKER Barbara C, b. 1 Sept 1915, Newton, Kansas, USA. Writer; Librarian. m. 21 Jan 1939, 2 sons, 1 daughter. *Education:* BS, Kansas State University, 1936. *Publications:* Henry's Red Sea, 1955; Cherokee Run, 1957; Wigwam in the City, 1966; Underground to Canada, 1977; Days of Terror, 1979; Amish Adventure, 1983; Incredible Jumbo, 1990; Garth and the Mermaid, 1992. *Contributions to:* Autobiography, to Something About the Author, 1991; Essay on writing historical fiction, to Writers on Writing: A Guide to Writing and Illustrating Children's Books; My adventure with Time Travel, to Canadian Children's Literature; Books translated into French, German, Spanish, Dutch, Danish, Swedish, Japanese, Italian, Chinese. *Honours:* Best Children's Book, Canada Council, 1979; Ruth Schwartz Award for Children's Book, 1980; LLD honoris causa, University of Waterloo, 1986; DHL, Bluffton College, 1988; Vicky Metcalf Award for Body of Works, 1988; Review of Jacob's Little Giant, Times Literary Supplement, 1988; 2-column review of Incredible Jumbo, New York Times, 1991; Purchase of broadcasting rights to Underground to Canada, BBC Radio, 1992; Film Rights purchased by Atlantis Films for Television, 1993. *Memberships:* Canada Society of Children's Authors, Illustrators and Performers; The Children's Reading Round Table of Chicago; Writers Union of Canada; American Association of University Women; Canadian Association of University Women; Senior Fellow, Renison College, University of Waterloo, Ontario. *Address:* 20 Pinebrook Dr, Bluffton, OH 45817, USA.

SMYLLIE J S. *See:* **SMYLLIE James Stuart.**

SMYLLIE James Stuart, (J S Smyllie), b. 21 Nov 1955, Wilmslow, Cheshire, England. m. Kate Cargin, 17 Dec 1989, 1 son, 1 daughter. *Education:* Degree, English Literature, University College of Swansea, 1974-77; Advanced Certificate in Drama, Welsh College of Music and Drama, 1977-78. *Publications:* The Firth Sun, novel, 1990. Poems in magazines and anthologies. *Address:* 40 Walford Road, London N16 8ED, England.

SNELLGROVE Laurence Ernest, b. 1928, United Kingdom. Author. *Publications:* From Kitty Hawk to Outer Space, 1960; From Steamcarts to Minicars, 1961; From Coracles to Cunarders, 1962; From Rocket to Railcar, 1963; Suffragettes and Votes for Women, 1964; Franco and Spanish Civil War, 1965; Modern World since 1870, 1968, 2nd Edition, 1981; The Ancient World (with R J Cootes), 1970; Hitler, 1971; Second World War, 1971; Early Modern Age, 1972; Mainstream English (with J R C Yglesias), 5 vols, 1974; Picture the

Past, 5 vols, 1978; Wide Range Histories, 1978; History Around You (with David Thornton), 4 vols, 1982-83; Modern World, 1984; Britain since 1700, 1985; Storyline Histories, 4 vols, 1986. *Address:* 23 Harvest Hill, East Grinstead, Sussex, England.

SNIDER Ruth. *See:* **HOEPPNER Iona Ruth.**

SNILLOC MIT. *See:* **COLLINS Timothy Maurice.**

SNODGRASS W D (S S Gardens, Will McConnell, Kozma Prutkov), b. 5 Jan 1926, USA. Poet; Professor. m. (3) Kathleen Brown, 20 June 1985, 1 son, 2 daughters, previous marriages. *Education:* BA 1949, MA 1951, MFA 1953, State University of Iowa. *Appointments include:* English Departments, Cornell, Rochester, Wayne State, Syracuse Universities, 1955-77; Distinguished Visiting Professor, Old Dominion University 1978-79, University of Delaware 1979-, (title now Distinguished Professor of Creative Writing & Contemporary Poetry). *Publications include:* Poems: Heart's Needle, 1959; After Experience, 1967; Remains, as S.S. Gardons 1970, as W.D. Snodgrass 1985; The Fuehrer Bunker, cycle of poems-in-progress, 1977; If Birds Build With Your Hair, 1979; D.D. Byrde Calling Jennie Wrenne, 1984; A Colored Poem, 1986; The House the Poet Built, 1986; A Locked House, 1986; The Kinder Capers, 1986; Selected Poems, 1957-87, 1987; W D's Midnight Carnival, 1988; The Death of Cock Robin, 1989. Also critical essays, translations of songs. *Honours:* Numerous awards & grants including: Ingram-Merrill Award, 1958; Hudson Review Fellowship, 1958-59; Longview Literary Award, 1959; Grant, National Institute of Arts & Letters, 1960; Pulitzer Prize, 1960; Guinness Poetry Award, UK, 1961; Grant, National Council of the Arts, 1966-67; Guggenheim Fellowship, 1972-73; Centennial Medal, Government of Romania, 1977. *Address:* Department of English, University of Delaware, Newark, DE 19711, USA.

SNOW Michael R b. 21 May 1949, Los Angeles, USA, Journalist; Author. *Education:* Bachelors degree, California State University, Northridge, 1971; Masters degree, Honours, University of California at Los Angeoles, 1973; University of California at Santa Barbara. *Publications:* Chimerunga, 1980; A Reed in the Wind, 1984. *Contributions to:* New York Times; Time; Newsweek; Far Eastern Economic Review. *Honours:* University of California, Los Angeles, Honours for articles. *Memberships:* Foreign Correspondents Club; Sigma Delta Chi. *Address:* PO Box 30151, Charlotte, NC 28230, USA.

SNOWMAN Daniel, b.4 Nov 1938. BBC Producer. m. Janet Linda Levison, 1 son, 1 daughter. *Education:* BA (Double First Class) History, Cambridge, 1961; MA, Government, Cornell University, New York, USA. 1963. *Appointments:* Lecturer in History and American Studies, University of Sussex, 1963-67; BBC Producer 1967-; currently Chief Producer, BBC Radio Features and Arts; Visiting Professor of History, California State University, 1972-73. *Publications:* America Since 1920; 1968; Eleanor Roosevelt, 1970; Kissing Cousins (British and American Culture) 1977; If I Had Been....Ten Historical Fantasies, 1979; The Amadeus Quartet, 1981; The World of Placido Domingo, 1985; Beyond the Tunnel of History, 1990; Pole Positions: The Polar Regions and the Future of Planet, 1993. *Contributions to:* Numerous chapters in books and articles and reviews. *Memberships:* Regular singer with London Philharmonic Choir 1967-, former Chairman. *Literary Agent:* Dinah Wiener, 27 Arlington Road, London NW1 7ER. *Address:* 47 Wood Lane, Highgate, London N6 5UD, England.

SNYDAL James Matthew, b. 6 May 1949, Williston, North Dakota, USA. Writer. m. Kathryn Church, 25 July 1970. *Education:* BA, University of Washington, Seattle, 1971. *Publications:* Numerous poems including: City Life Along the Home Front, 1942 in Poem The Nukes, 1983, in Alternatives: An American Poetry Anthology,

1988, in The New Poet's Anthology, 1987; Empire of Light, On May 4 1985, the Fifteenth Anniversary of My Antiwar Demonstration Arrest, February 5 1989, On Bainbridge Island in American Poetry Confronts The 1990s, Overgrowth Was Not Permitted To Proceed! in Poems From The Earth: On Nature and the Environment. *Contributions to:* Inscape; The Pawn Review; Big Moon; Permafrost; University of Windsor Review; Pacific; Poetry Seattle; Vegetable Box; Yakima; Maniac; Poetry Now; Snowy Egret; Matrix; West Hills Review; Fine Madness. *Address:* 11034 Old Creosote Hill Road, Bainbridge Island, WA 98110, USA.

SNYDER Don J, b.11 Aug 1950, Pennsylvania, USA. Writer. m. Colleen McQuinn, 14 Dec 1987, 1 son 2 daughters. *Education:* BA, English Literature, Colby College, 1972; MFA, Fiction Writing, The Iowa Writers Workshop, 1987. *Publications:* A Soldier's Disgrace, 1987; Veterans Park, 1987; From the Point, 1988. *Contributions to:* Yankee Magazine; The Boston Globe Sunday Magazine; Northeast Magazine. *Honours:* Teaching Writing Fellowship from the Iowa Writers Workshop, 1987; A James Michener Fellowship, 1988. *Literary Agent:* The Elaine Markson Agency. *Address:* English Department, Colgate University, Hamilton, NY 13346, USA.

SNYDER Francis Gregory, b. 26 June 1942, Madison, Wisconsin, USA. Law Professor. m. Sian Miles, 20 Aug 1967, 1 son. *Education:* BA, Yale 1964; Fulbright Scholar, Institut d'Etudes Politiques de Paris 1964-65; JD, Harvard Law School, 1968; Certificat de Droit et Economie des Pays d'Afrique,1969; Doctorat de Specialite, 1973, Universite de Paris I; US Attorney, MA, 1968. *Publications:* European Community Law, 2 vols, 1993; New Directions in European Community Law, 1990; Law of the Common Agricultural Policy, 1985; International Law of Development, (co-editor), 1987; The Political Economy, (co-editor), 1987; Capitalism and Legal Change, 1981; One-Party Government in Mali, 1965; Labour, Law and Crime, (co-editor), 1987; Policing and Prosecution in Britian 1750-1850, (co-editor), 1989; Law and Population in Senegal, 1977. *Contributions to:* Over 50 articles and 100 reviews to various journals. *Honours include:* Officier dans l'Ordre des Palmes Academiques, 1988; Research Associate International Development Research Center, 1978. *Memberships include:* Law and Society Association. *Address:* Department of Law, European University Institute, Badia Fiesolana 150016, San Domenica di Fiesole (Fi), Italy.

SNYDER Zilpha Keatley, b. 11 May 1927, California, USA. Writer. m. 18 June 1950, 2 sons, 1 daughter. *Education:* BA, Whittier College, 1948. *Publications:* Season of Ponies, 1964; The Velvet Room, 1965; Black and Blue Magic, 1966; The Egypt Game, 1967; The Changeling, 1970; The Headless Cupid, 1971; The Witches of Worm, 1972; The Princess and the Giants, 1973; The Truth About Stone Hollow, 1974; The Famous Stanley Kidnapping Case, 1979; Blair's Nightmare, 1984; The Changing Maze, 1985; And Condors Danced, 1987; Squeak Saves the Day and Other Tooley Tales, 1988; Janie's Private Eyes, 1989; Libby on Wednesday, 1990; Song of the Gargoyle, 1991; Fool's Gold, 1993; numerous others. *Honours include:* 3 Newbery Honor Books; 1st prize, Spring Book Festival, 1967; Lewis Carroll Shelf Award; George C Stone Recognition of Merit, 1973; American Library Association Notable Book, 1984; American Library Association Notable Book; Hans Christian Andersen International Honours List; Christopher Medal; William Allen White Award; Nominee, National Book Award. *Memberships:* Author's Guild; Society of Childrens Book Writers; United States Board on Books for Young People. *Address:* 52 Miller Ave, Mill Valley, CA 94941, USA.

SOBER Elliott, b. 6 June 1948, Baltimore, Maryland, USA. Professor of Philosophy. *Education:* MA University of Pennsylvania, 1969; PhD, Harvard, 1974. *Publications:* Reconstructing the Past, 1988; Core Question in Philosophy, 1990; Nature of Selection, 1989; Philosophy of Biology, 1992. *Honours:* Lakatos

Award, 1991; Spencer Lecture, Oxford University, 1988; Guggenheim Fellow, 1980. *Memberships:* APA; PSA. *Address:* Dept of Philosophy, 5173 White Hall, Univ of Wisconsin- Madison, Madison, WI 53706, USA.

SOBOL Donald J, b. 4 Oct 1924, New York, USA. Author. m. Rose Tiplitz, 14 Aug 1955, 3 sons, 1 daughter. *Education:* BA, English Literature, Oberlin College. *Publications:* About 65 books, translations into 13 languages. *Contributions to:* numerous magazines & journals. *Memberships:* Authors League of America; Mystery Writers. *Literary Agent:* McIntosh & Otis. *Address:* c/o McIntosh & Otis, 310 Madison Avenue, New York, NY 10017, USA.

SOCOLOFSKY Homer Edward b. 20 May 1922, Tampa, Kansas, USA. Emeritus Professor of History. m. Helen Margot Wright, 23 Nov. 1946, 4 sons, 2 daughters. *Education:* BS, 1944, MS 1947, Kansas State University; PhD, University of Missouri, 1954. *Appointments:* History Editor, Kansas Quarterly, 1969-92; Book Review Editor, Journal of the West, 1978-. *Publications:* Arthur Capper, Publisher, Politician, Philanthropist, 1962; Historical Atlas of Kansas (with Huber Self), 1972, 1989; Landlord William Scully, 1979; The Presidency of Benjamin Harrison, 1987 (with Allan Spetter); Governors of Kansas, 1990. *Contributions to:* Over 40 articles in journals and anthologies. *Honours:* RS: Award of Merit, American Academy for State and Local History, 1963; Westerners international Co-Founder Award, 1973; Edgar Langsdorf Award for Excellence in Writing, 1983. *Memberships:* President 1975-76, Board of Directors, Executive Committee, Kansas State Historical Society; President 1969, Agricultural History Society; Executive Council, 1979-81, Western History Association. *Address:* Dept. of History, Kansas State University, Manhattan, KS 66506, USA.

SOHL Gerald A (Nathan Butler, Roberta Jean Mountjoy, Jerry Sohl, Sean Mei Sullivan), b. 13 Dec 1913, Los Angeles, California, USA. Author; Screenwriter. m. Jean Gordon, 28 Oct 1943, 1 son, 2 daughters. *Education:* 2 years' college. *Publications:* As Jerry Sohl: Death Sleep, 1983; I, Aleppo, 1976; Underhanded Bridge, 1975; Underhanded Chess, 1973; The Spun Sugar Hole, 1971; Night Slaves, 1963; The Odious Ones, 1959; The Time Dissolver, 1957; The Altered Ego, 1954; The Haploids, 1952. Also various other novels as Roberta Jean Mountjoy, Nathan Butler, Sean Mei Sullivan. Staff writer, TV programmes including Star Trek, Alfred Hitchcock Presents, The New Breed; Episodes, various other programmes. Filmscripts including: 12 Hours to Kill; Die, Monster, Die; Night Slaves. *Contributions to:* Playboy; Galaxy; If; Magazine of Fantasy & Science Fiction; Science Fiction Adventures; Imagination; Space; Infinity; Various anthologies. *Memberships:* Charter member, Science Fiction Writers of America; Writers Guild of America (West); Authors Guild; Authors League. *Literary Agent:* Scott Meredith Literary Agency, 845 Third Ave., New York. *Address:* 3020 Ash Court, Thousand Oaks, California 91360, USA.

SOHL Jerry. *See:* SOHL Gerald A.

SOLLOV Jacques, b. 3 Aug 1935, Cornwall, Canada. US Citizen. Realtor. *Publications:* The Temple of Love, 1979; Reborn Again in the Kingdom, 1982; Gold of the Stars, 1983. *Contributions to:* Our World's Most Beloved Poems Anthology, 1984; numerous Journals & Magazines. *Honours include:* Recipient, Silver Medal & Diploma, Universal Academy, Switzerland, 1983; Golden Poet Award, 1985, Silver Poet Award, 1986, World of Poetry, California, USA; Confederation of Chivalry, Diploma of Life Membership of Merit, 1990; World Parliament Grand Council CoC Decree of Nomination, 1990; Orddre Souverain et Militarie de la milice du Saint Sepulcre, 1990; Maison Internatioale des Intellectuals Akademie MIDI, 1992. *Memberships:* Authors Guild of America; Poets & Writers Inc.; American Film Institute; International Traders;

American Entrepreneurs Association; Smithsonian Institution; National Association of Realtors; The Academy of American Poets. *Address:* Box 1332 Dept S-0111, Lowell, MA 01853, USA.

SOLOMAN Barbara Probst, b. 3 Dec 1929, New York City, USA. Writer. m. Harold William Soloman, 21 Dec 1952, 2 daughters. *Education:* Sorbonne, Paris, 1948-51; BS, Columbia University, 1960. *Publications:* The Beat of Life; Arriving Where We Started; Operation Ogro; Short Flight; Horse Trading and Ecstasy; Smart Heart In The City. *Contributions to:* The New York Times; Harpers NY Review of Books; Washington Post; Pen, Authors League. *Honours:* Pablo de Olauide Barcelona Prize. *Literary Agent:* Eugene Winick, Mackintosh E, Otis.

SOLOMON Deborah, b. 9 Aug 1957, New York, USA. Writer; Art Critic. m. Kent Sepkowitz, 23 Sept 1989, 1 son. *Education:* BA, Cornell University, 1979; Masters of Journalism, Columbia University, 1980. *Publications:* Jackson Pollock: A Biography, 1987. *Contributions to:* The New York Times Magazine. *Literary Agent:* Kathy Robbins. *Address:* 15 West 81st Street, New York, NY 10024, USA.

SOLOMON Goody L, b. 1 June 1929, Brooklyn, New York, USA. Syndicated Newspaper Columnist/ Consumer Writer; Author; Educator. *Education:* BA, Brooklyn College, 1950; MA, New York University, 1955. *Appointments include:* Executive Editor, Food, Nutrition Health News Service, 1992; Editor, Food & Drug Letter, bi-weekly newsletter, 1986-92; Former editor, Nutrition Policy, monthly newspaper. *Publications include:* Radical Consumer's Handbook, 1972. *Contributions to:* Washington Star; Money; Womens World; Changing Times; Barron's Weekly; Ladies Home Journal; Redbook; Stores; Modern Textiles; US Consumer; Family Circle; Washington Women; Gannet News Service. *Honours:* Writing awards, National Federation of Press Women, 1975-78; Special citation, consumer reporting, National Press Club, 1980, 1988; 1st place, 2 categories, Capitol Press Women, 1984, 1988, 1990, 1991. *Memberships:* American Society of Journalists & Authors; Society of Professional Journalists; American Newspaper Womens Club; Capitol Press Women. *Address:* 1712 Taylor Street NW, Washington DC 20011, USA.

SOLOMON Henry A, b. 16 Jan 1937, New York City, USA. Physician. m. Carol Ann Batchelor, 25 May 1961, 2 daughters. *Education:* AB, Columbia College, NY, 1958; MD, Columbia University, 1962.. *Appointments:* Editor in Chief and Publisher: Cardiology Update, 1976-78; Editor in Chief, Heart Health, 1985; Chairmn of Editorial Board, Masters in Cardiology, 1986-; Columnist, Tampa Tribune, 1989-. *Publications:* The Exercise Myth, 1984. *Contributions to:* Cardiovascular Reviews and Reports; The Sciences; American Journal of Medicine. *Memberships:* Fellow: American College of Cardiology and Physicians. *Address:* 3 East 71 Street, New York, NY 10021, USA.

SOLZHENITSYN Aleksandr Isayevich, b. 11 Dec 1918. Writer. m. (1) Natalya Reshetovskaya, div 1970, (2) Natalya Svetlova, 3 sons. *Publications:* One Day in the Life of Ivan Denisovich, 1962, (film 1971); Matryona's Home and An Incident at Krechetovka Station, 1963; For the Good of the Cause, 1964; The First Circle, 1968; Cancer Ward, 1968; The Easter Procession, The Love Girl, Innocent, 1969; Collected Works, 6 volumes, 1969, 1970; Stories and Prose Poems, 1971; August 1914, 1971; The Gulag Archipelago, Volume I, 1973, Volume II, 1974, Volume III, 1976; Letter to Soviet Leaders, 1974; Peace and Aggression, 1974; Quiet Flows the Don : the Enigma of a Novel, 1974; Candle in the Wind (play); The Oak and the Calf : Sketches of Literary Life in the Soviet Union, 1975; The Nobel Prize Lecture, 1975; Lenin in Zurich, 1975; Detente, with others, 1976; Prussian Nights, poem, translated by Robert Conquest, 1977; Collected Works, 1978-; Victory Celebrations, Prisoners (play), 1983; October 1916, 1985. *Honours:* Prix u

Meilleur Livre Etranger, France, 1969; Nobel Prize for Literature, 1970; Templeton Prize, 1983. *Address:* c/o Harper and Row Inc., 10 East 53rd Street, New York, NY 10022, USA.

SOMAIN Jean-Francois. *See:* **SOMCYNSKY** Jean-Francois.

SOMCYNSKY Jean-Francois (Jean-François Somain), b. 20 Apr 1943, Paris, France. Author; Diplomat. m. Micheline Beaudry-Somcynsky, 22 Aug 1968. *Education:* MA, Economics, University of Ottawa, 1970. *Publications:* Sortir du piège, 1988; Les visiteurs du pôle Nord, 1987; La frontiere du milieu, 1983; Vingt minutes d'amour, 1983; Peut-être à Tokyo, 1981; La planète amoureuse, 1982; Un tango fictif, 1986; Les grimaces, 1975; Vivre en beauté, short stories, 1989; Dernier départ, novel, 1989. *Contributions to:* 30 short stories & poetry in Canadian and French magazines and 5 anthologies. *Honours:* Prix International Solaris de Science-fiction, 1982; Two Prix Boreal for best short stories, 1982; prix littéraire Esso du Cercle du Livre de France, 1983; prix Louis-Hémon de l'Académie du Languedoc, 1987. *Memberships:* Union des écrivains quebécois; Professional Association of Foreign Service Officers. *Address:* 5 Putman Avenue, Ottawa, Ontario, Canada K1M 1Y8.

SOMERS Suzanne. *See:* **DANIELS** Dorothy.

SOMERSET FRY Peter George Robin Plantagenet, b. 3 Jan 1931, England. Author; Journalist. m. (1) Daphne Diana Elizabeth Caroline Yorke, 1958 (dec. 1961), (2) Hon Mrs Leri Butler, 1961 (div. 1973), (3) Pamela Fiona Ileene Whitcombe, 1974. *Education:* Lancing College; St Thomas's Hospital Medical School, London; St Catherine's College, Oxford. *Appointments include:* Editorial staffs: Atomics & Nuclear Energy 1957-58, Tatler & Bystander 1958; Information Officer, Ministry of Public Buildings & Works, 1967-70; Head of Information at COSIRA, 1970-74; Editor of Books, HM Stationery Office, 1975-80; General editor, Macmillan History in Pictures series, 1977-. *Publications include:* Mysteries of History, 1957; The Cankered Rose, 1959; Rulers of Britain, 1967, 3rd edition 1973; They Made History, 1971, 1973; The World of Antiques, 1970, 4th edition 1972; Antique Furniture, 1971, 1972; Children's History of the World, 1972, 11th edition 1987; Zebra Book of Famous Men, 1972; Zebra Book of Famous Women, 1972; Collecting Inexpensive Antiques, 1973, 5th edition 1980; British Medieval Castles, 1974; Great Caesar, 1974; 1000 Great Lives, 1975, 9th edition 1987; 2000 years of British Life, 1976; Chequers: The Country Home of Britain's Prime Ministers, official history, 1977; 3,000 Questions & Answers, 1977, 12th edition 1984; Boudicca, 1978; The David & Charles Book of Castles, 1980; Beautiful Britain, 1981; Great Cathedrals, 1982; The History of Scotland (with Fiona Somerst Fry), 1982, 1985 and 1992; Rebellion Against Rome, 1982; Roman Britain: History & Sites, 1984; 3,000 More Questions & Answers, 1984; Antiques, 1984; Junior Illustrated Dictionary, 1987; A History of Ireland (with Fiona Somerst Fry), 1988, 1991; Castles of the British Isles, 1990; The Tower of London, 1990; Kings & Queens of England and Scotland, 1990, 1991, 1992. *Memberships include:* Council, East Anglian Writers, 1977-82; Senior member Wolfson College, Cambridge since 1980; Co-founder, Congress of Independent Archaeologists, 1985; Eastern Region Manager, Charities Aid Foundation, 1987-1991; Antique Furniture Consultant, Christchurch Mansion, Ipswich Museum since 1987. *Address:* Wood Cottage, Wattisfield, Bury St Edmunds, Suffolk IP22 1NE, England.

SOMLYÓ György, b. 28 Nov 1920, Balatonboglar, Hungary, Writer; Magazine Director. div, 1 son. *Education:* Budapest University, 1945- 46; Sorbonne, Paris, France, 1947-48. *Appointments:* Director, Literary section, Radio Budapest, 1954-55; Secretary, International Poetry Meeting, days of Poetry in Budapest, 1966, 1970; Director, magazine Arion, 1966-. *Publications:* Arion's Canto: Stone Cercles, collected poems 1-2, 1978; Phyloctetes's Blessing, essay, 1980; Shadow Play, novel, 1977; The Rampe, novel, 1984; The Trip, French Poetry from Baudelaire To..., translation, 1984; Parisiens, 1987; Beyond Myself, Selected Poems, 1988; Palimpsest, poems, 1990; Talisman, 101 Sonnets, 1990; Two-Step in Paris, novel, 1990. *Contributions to:* Hungarian Literary Reviews, 1939-; French literary magazines including: La Nouvelle Revue Française; Po&sie; Action Poetique; Europe. *Honours:* Jozsef Attila Prize, 1950, 1951, 1954, 1966; Officier de l'Ordre des Arts et Lettres, France, 1984; Dery Tibor Prize, 1987; Soros Foundative Kassák Prize, 1992. *Memberships:* Hungarian Siécheuyi Academie of Arts and Letters; Hungarian PEN, Vice President; Hungarian-French Society, Vice President; Academie Mallarme, Paris, Corresponding Member; French Poetry magazine Po&sie, Board Member. *Address:* Irinyi J ul 39, Budapest H-1111, Hungary.

SOMMERS Robert Thomas, b. 6 Aug 1926, Baltimore, Maryland, USA. m. Helen Louise Ray, 19 Oct 1952, 1 son, 1 daughter. *Education:* BS, University of Maryland, College Park, 1950. *Publication:* The U.S. Open: Golf's Ultimate Challenge, 1986. *Membership:* Author's Guild. *Literary Agent:* Kenneth Bowden.

SONENBERG Maya, b. 24 Feb 1960, New York City, USA. Writer; Professor. *Education:* MA Graduate Writing Programme, Brown University, 1984; BA, Wesleyan University, 1982. *Appointments:* English Department: Instructor, Sonoma State University, 1986, Lecturer, Chabot College, 1989-90, Assistant Professor, Oregon State University, 1990-. *Publications:* Cartographies, 1989. *Contributions to:* The Writer; Grand Street; Chelsea; The Cream City Review; Columbia; Gargoyle. *Honours:* McDowell Colony Fellow, 1987; Drue Heinz Literature Prize, 1989; Centre for the Humanities Faculty Fellow, Oregon State University, 1992-93. *Memberships:* Associate Writing Programmes; Modern Language Association. *Address:* English Department, Moreland Hall 238, Oregon State University, Corvallis OR 97331, USA.

SONO Ayako. *See:* **MIURA Chizuko.**

SOREL Julia. *See:* **DREXTER Rosalyn.**

SORENSEN Knud, b. 10 Mar 1928, Hjorring, Denmark. Writer. m. Anne Marie Dybro Jorgensen, 4 July 1950, 2 sons. *Education:* Graduate Royal Vet and Agricultural University of Copenhagen, 1952. *Publications:* Revolutionen i Toving, 1972; Bondeslutspil, 1980; St St Blicher Digterog Samfordsborger, 1984; Historier fra engang, 1989; Naboskab, 1991; Sandemoses ryg, 1992; Den Rode Kaffekande. Smaborgerlige digte, 1965; Slutsedlen, 1977; Beretninger fra en dansk udkant, 1978; Historie om Martin, 1979; Hvad skal vi med solnedgangen (digte), 1977; Marginaljord (noveller), 1987; Danmark mellem land og by, 1988. *Contributions to:* Hvedekorn; Chancen; Kritik; Fredag; Aktuelt; Jyllands-Posten. *Honours:* Otto Rung 1978; Kaj Hoffmann, 1981; Prize, 1982, Culturel Fund of Danish Agriculture, 1984; Oehlenschlager, 1986; Life- time State Grant, 1988; Gelsted, 1988; Morten Nielsen, 1991; Drassovs legat, 1993. *Memberships:* International PEN: The Danish Writer's Union; Autorenkreis Plesse. *Address:* Skjelholmvej 2, DK 7900 Nykobing Mors, Denmark.

SORENSEN Villy, b. 13 Jan 1929, Frederiksberg, Denmark. Writer. *Education:* Philosophical And Philological Studies in Copenhagen, Freiburg, Germany. *Publications:* Strange Stories; Harmless Tales; Tutelary Tales; Seneca, the Humanist at the Court of Nero; Another Metamorphosis; Four Biblical Tales; The Downfall of the Gods. *Honours:* Prize of the Danish Academy; Henrik Steffens Preis; The Nordic Prize of the Swedish Academy. *Memberships:* The Danish

Academy. *Address:* Skovvej 6, DK 2930 Klampenborg, Denmark.

SORESTAD Glen Allan, b. 21 May 1937, Vancouver, Canada. Writer. m. Sonia Diane Talpash, 17 Sept 1960, 3 sons, 1 daughter. *Education:* University of Saskatchewan, 1963; Master of Education, 1976. *Publications:* Prairie Pub Poems; Ancestral Dances; Jan Lake Poems; Air Canada Owls; West Into Night. *Contributions to:* Numerous. *Honours:* Hilroy Fellowship; Founder Award. *Memberships:* The Saskatchewan Writers Guild; League of Canadian Poets; Writers Union of Canada; International PEN. *Address:* 668 East Place, Saskatoon, Sask, Canada S7J 2Z5.

SORRENTINO Gilbert, b. 1929, USA. Professor of English; Novelist; Short Story Writer; Poet. *Publications:* Editor, Publisher, Neon magazine, New York City, 1956-60; Editor, Grove Press, New York City, 1965-70; Currently Professor of English, Stanford University, California. *Publications:* The Darkness Surrounds Us, 1960; Black and White, 1964; The Sky Changes, novel, 1966; The Perfect Fiction, 1969; Steelwork, novel, 1970; Corrosive Sublimate, 1971; Imaginative Qualities of Actual Things, novel, 1971; Splendide-Hotel, 1973; Flawless Play Restored: The Masque of Fungo, 1974; Elegiacs of Sulpicia, 1977; The Orangery, 1978; Mulligan Stew, novel, 1979; Aberration of Starlight, novel, 1980; Crystal Vision, novel, 1981; Selected Poems 1958-80, 1981; Blue Pastoral, novel, 1983; Something Said, critical essays, 1984; Odd Number, novel, 1985; Rose Theatre, novel, 1987; Misterioso, novel, 1989; novel, Under The Shadow, 1991. *Address:* Department of English, Stanford University, Stanford, CA 94305, USA.

SOSKIN V H. *See:* **ELLISON Virginia Howell.**

SOULE Gardner, b. 16 Dec 1913, Paris, Texas, USA. Author. m. Janie Lee McDowell, 20 Sept 1940. *Education:* BA, Rice University, 1933; BSc., 1935, MSc., 1936, Columbia Univerity. *Appointments:* Associated Press, 1936-41; US Naval Reserve, 1942-45; Managing Editor, Better Homes & Gardens, 1945-50. *Publications:* UFO's and IFO's, 1967; Trail of the Abominable Snowman, 1965; The Ocean Adventure, 1966; The Maybe Monsters, 1963; The Mystery Monsters, 1965; Tomorrow's World of Science, 1963; Wide Ocean, 1970, British Edition 1974; Men Who Dared the Sea, 1976, German Edition, 1978; The Long Trail, How Cowboys and Longhorns Opened the West, 1976; Mystery Monsters of the Deep, 1981; Mystery Creatures of the Jungle, 1982; Antarctica, 1985; Christopher Columbus, 1989; Books translated into Spanish, Japanese, Thai, three languages in India. *Contributions to:* Popular Science Monthly; United Features; London Express Syndicate; Boy's Life; Illustrated London News. *Honours:* Navy League Commendation, 1956. *Memberships:* Sigma Delta Chi; Columbia University Club. *Address:* Apt. 53, 517 West 113th Street, New York, NY 10025, USA.

SOULE Maris Anne, b. 19 June 1939, Oakland, California, USA. Writer; Teacher. m. William L Soule, 11 May 1968, 1 son, 1 daughter. *Education:* BA, University of California, Davis, 1961; Secondary Teaching Credential, University of California, Berkeley. *Publications:* A Winning Combination, 1987; Sounds Like Love, 1986; Lost and Found, 1985; No Room for Love, 1984; First Impressions, 1983; The Best of Everything, 1988; The Law of Nature, 1988; Storybook Hero, 1989; Jared's Lady, 1991. *Memberships:* Romance Writers of America Inc; Mid-Michigan Chapter, RWA, Inc, Chapter Adviser; Member, Novelists Inc. *Literary Agent:* Denise Marcil Literary Agency, New York. *Address:* RR 1, Box 173B, Fulton, MI 49052, USA.

SOURELI-GRIGORIADOU Galatia, b. 18 June 1930, Kavala, Greece. Author. m. 1951, 2 sons, 2 daughters. *Education:* School of Social Service, 1950; School of Journalism, 1954. *Appointments:* Radio, TV,

various magazines and newspapers, 1960-88. *Publications:* The Sparrow with the Red Coat, 1971; It Matters to Me, 1969; The Moon the Stamp and Me, 1987; The St Bernards' Dogs, 1985; Game Without Rules, 1982; Alex and the Wooden Horse, 1974; Memories from Smyrnx, 1986; Together with the Wind, 1984; Kottas, 1970; The Roots of Freedom, 1970; Rigas Fereos, 1975; Katerina, 1970; Fourfouris, 1973; The Twelve Moons, 1974; Africa Good-Day, 1975. *Contributor To:* magazines & journals. *Honours:* Athens Academy Award, 1980; Listed in Andersen's Award List, 1981; European Award, Best Writer in Europe, 1971; numerous other honours and awards. *Memberships:* National Society of Greek Authors and Writers; Circle of the Greek Childrens Book. *Address:* Ahamon 37 Kilissix, TK 14561, Athens, Greece.

SOURITZ Elizabeth, b. 25 Feb 1923, Berlin, Germany. Ballet Historian. m. Vladimir Varkovitsky, 4 Sept 1948, dec 1974, 1 daughter. *Education:* Graduate, State Institute of Theatre Art, 1949; Candidate in Arts Degree, Institute of Research in Arts, Moscow, 1976. *Publications:* Soviet Choreographers in the 1920s, 1979, 1990. *Contributions to:* Soviet ballet; Ballet Review; Dance Research Journal; World Ballet and Dance; La Danza Italiana. *Honours:* The de la Torre Bueno Prize, Dance Perspectives Foundation, USA, 1991. *Memberships:* Union of Theatre Workers of the USSR; Assocation Européenne des Historiens de la danse. *Address:* Victorenco Street 2/1 Apt 79, Moscow 125167, Russia.

SOUSTER Raymond (John Holmes, Raymond Holmes), b. 1921, Canada. Author; Banker (retired). *Publications:* When We are Young, 1946; Go to Sleep World, 1947; The Winter of Time (as Raymond Holmes), 1949; Selected Poems, 1956; A Local Pride, 1962; Place of Meeting, 1962; The Colour of the Times, 1964; Ten Elephants on Yonge Street, 1965; As Is, 1967; New Wave Canada (editor), 1966; Lost and Found, 1968; So Far So Good, 1969; Generation Now (edited with R Woollatt), 1970; Made in Canada (edited with D Lochhead), 1970; The Years, 1971; Selected Poems, 1972; On Target (as John Holmes), 1972; 100 Poems of 19th Century Canada (edited with D Lochhead), 1974; Change Up, 1974; Sights and Sounds (edited with R Wollatt), 1974; These Loved, These Hated Lands (edited with R Woollatt), 1974; Double Header, 1975; Rain Check, 1975; Extra Innings, 1977; Vapour and Blue: The Poetry of W W Campbell (editor), 1978; Hanging In: New Poems, 1979; Comfort of the Fields: The Best-Known Poems of Archibald Lampman (editor), 1979; Collected Poems, 7 vols, 1980-88; Going the Distance: New Poems 1979-82, 1983; Powassan's Drum: Selected Poems of Duncan Campbell Scott (edited with Douglas Lochhead), 1983; Queen City, Toronto in Poems and Pictures (with Bill Brooks), 1984; Jubilee of Death: The Raid on Dieppe, 1984; Windflower: The Selected Poems of Bliss Carman (edited with Douglas Lochhead), 1986; It Takes All Kinds: New Poems, 1986; The Eyes of Love, 1987; Asking for More, 1988; Collected Poems of Raymond Souster, Vol 6, 1988; Running Out The Clock, 1991; Collected Poems of Raymond Souster, volume 7, 1992; Riding The Long Black Horse, 1993; Old Bank Notes, 1993. *Honours:* Governor General's Award for Poetry in English, 1964; President's Medal, University of Western Ontario, 1967; Centennial Medal, 1967; Canadian Silver Jubliee Medal, 1977; City of Toronto Book Award, 1979. *Memberships:* Founding & Life Member, League of Canadian Poets; President & Chairman, 1968-1972. *Address:* 39 Baby Point Road, Toronto, Ontario, Canada M6S 2G2.

SOUTHALL Ivan Francis, b. 8 June 1921, Melbourne, Australia. Writer. m. (1) Joy Blackburn, 8 Sept 1945 (div.), 1 son, 3 daughters, (2) Susan Westerlund Stanton, 11 Nov 1976. *Appointments include:* Whitall Poetry & Literature Lecturer, Library of Congress, USA, 1973; May Hill Arbuthnot Honour Lecturer, University of Washington, USA, 1974; Writer-in-residence, Macquarie University, Sydney, 1979. *Publications include:* Softly Tread the Brave, 1960; Hills End, 1962; Ash Road, 1965; To the Wild Sky, 1967; Let the Balloon

Go, 1968; Josh, 1971. Also: They Shall Not Pass Unseen, 1956; Bread & Honey, 1970; Head in the Clouds, 1972; Matt & Jo, 1973; What About Tomorrow, 1977; City Out of Sight, 1984; Christmas in the Tree, 1985; Rachel, 1986; Blackbird, 1988. *Contributions to:* Numerous magazines & journals. *Honours include:* Australian Children's Book of Year, 1966, 1968, 1971, 1976; Australian Picture Book of Year, 1969; Children's Welfare & Culture Encouragement Award, Japan, 1969; Carnegie Medal, 1971; Zilver Griffel, Holland, 1972; Australian Writers Award, 1974; Order of Australia (AM), 1981; Adelaide Festival National Children's Book Award, 1986. *Membership:* Committee of Management 1980-81, Australian Society of Authors. *Address:* PO Box 25, Healesville, Victoria 3777, Australia.

SOUTHAM B(rian) C(harles), b. 1931, United Kingdom. Publisher. *Appointments:* Lecturer in English Literature, University of London, 1961-63; Currently Publisher, The Athlone Press, London. *Publications:* Volume the Second (editor), 1963; Jane Austen's Literary Manuscripts, 1964; Selected Poems of Lord Tennyson (editor), 1964; Jane Austen: The Critical Heritage (editor), 2 vols, 1966, 87; Critical Essays on Jane Austen (editor), 1968; Minor Works of Jane Austen (edited with R W Chapman), 1969; A Student's Guide to the Selected Works of T S Eliot, 1969, 5th edition 1988; Tennyson, 1971; Jane Austen (editor), 1975; Jane Austen: Northanger Abbey and Persuasion (editor), 1976; Jane Austen: Sense and Sensibility, Pride and Prejudice, and Mansfield Park (editor), casebooks, 3 vols, 1976; T S Eliot (editor), casebook, 1978; Sir Charles Grandison (editor), 1981. *Membership:* Chairman, Jane Austen Society. *Address:* 3 West Heath Drive, London NW11, England.

SOUTHERN Terry (Maxwell Kenton), b. 1924, USA. Author. *Publications:* Candy Kisses (with D Burnett), screenplay, 1955; Flash and Filigree, 1958; Candy (as Maxwell Kenton with Mason Hoffenberg), 1958, under real names, 1964; The Magic Christian, 1959, screenplay, 1971; Writers in Revolt (co-editor), 1963; Dr Strangelove (with S Kubrick), screenplay, 1964; The Loved One (with Christopher Isherwood), screenplay, 1965; The Journal of The Loved Ones: The Production Log of a Motion Picture, 1965; The Cincinnati Kid (with Ring Lardner Jr), screenplay, 1966; Barbarella, screenplay, 1967; Red-Dirt Marijuana and Other Tales, short stories, 1967; Easy Rider, screenplay, 1968; End of the Road, screenplay, 1969; Blue Movie, 1970; The Rolling Stones on Tour, 1978. *Address:* R F D, East Canaan, CT 06024, USA.

SOYINKA Olukayode Adedeji, (Kayode), b. 15 Dec 1957, Ibadan, Nigeria. Journalist. m. Titilope Oluwadamilola Odugbesan, 15 Oct 1983, 1 son, 1 daughter. *Education:* Diploma in Journalism, College of Journalism, Fleet Street, London, 1980; BA International Relations, US International University, Watford, England, 1986; MA International Journalism, The City University, London, 1989. *Appointments:* Reporter: Daily Sketch, Ibadan, 1976-78; London Correspondent, 1978-80; London Correspondent, National Concord, Lagos, 1980- 83; General Editor, Africa Now, London, 1984-85; London Bureau Chief, Newswatch, Lagos, 1985-. *Publications:* Diplomatic Baggage: The Dikko Story, 1993. *Contributions to:* Newswatch - Nigeria's Weekly news Magazine; The Guardian, London; The Independent, London *Honours:* Hon Harry Brittain Fellow, Commonwealth Press Union, 1979; Visiting Scholar, Wolfson College, Cambridge, 1990; Fellow, 21st Century Trust, Worcester College, Oxford, 1991. *Memberships:* Commonwealth Journalists Association; Commonwealth NGO Forum, 1991; Commonwealth Human Rights Intiative; Royal Institute of International Affairs; Royal African Society; The Press Club, London. *Literary Agent:* Jeffrey Simmons, 10 Lowndes Square, Londn SW1X 9HA, England. *Address:* 3 Tithe Walk, Mill Hill, London NW7 2PY, England.

SPACH John Thom, b. 5 Mar 1928, Winston Salem, North Carolina, USA. Writer. *Education:* BA, Duke University, 1955; Counter Intelligence Corps, US Army, 1952. *Publications:* Time Out From Texas; Dictionary of NC Biographies. *Contributions to:* The Saturday Evening Post; Far West; Grit; Readers Digest; Confederate Veteran. *Memberships:* Wachovia Historical Society; Historic District Commission; Poets & Writers; NC Writers Conference. *Address:* PO Box 11408, Winston Salem, NC 27116, USA.

SPACHE George Daniel, b. 22 Feb 1909, New York, USA. Psychologist; Reading Specialist. m. Evelyn B. Schoonover, 28 Oct 1968, 1 son, 4 daughters. *Education:* BS, 1933; MA, 1934; PhD, 1937, School of Education, New York University. *Publications include:* Good Books for Poor Readers, 1954; Resources in Teaching Reading, 1955; Faster Reading for Business, 1958; Toward Better Reading, 1963; Good Reading for Poor Readers, 10th Edition, 1978; Reading in the Elementary School, 5th edition, 1985; Art of Efficient Reading, 4th edition, 1988; Vision and School Success (with Lillian B Nindo and Lois B Hinds, 1990; various case studies, papers and articles in professional journals. *Honours:* Service Award, 1934; Apollo Award, 1961; Citation of Merit, 1980; Oscar J Causey Award, 1969. *Memberships:* National Association for Remedial Teaching, President 1954; Board of Directors International Reading Association, President 1958; Board of Directors, 1960, S W Reading Conference; President National Reading Conference, 1961-64; Board of Directors, American Reading Forum, 1984. *Address:* 4042 Wilshire Circle E, Sanasota, FL 34238, USA.

SPACKS Patricia Meyer, b. 1929, USA. Professor of English. *Appointments:* Instructor in English, Indiana University, Bloomington, 1954-56; Instructor in Humanities, University of Florida, 1958-59; Instructor, 1959-61, Assistant Professor, 1961-63, Associate Professor, 1965-68, Professor of English, 1968-79, Wellesley College, Massachusetts; Professor of English, 1979-89, Chairman, Department of English, 1985-88, Yale University, New Haven, Connecticut; Edgar F Shannon Professor of English, University of Virginia, 1989-; Chairman, Department of English, 1991-. *Publications:* The Varied God, 1959; The Insistence of Horror, 1962; 18th Century Poetry (editor), 1964; John Gay, 1965; Poetry of Vision, 1967; Late Augustan Prose (editor), 1971; An Argument of Images, 1971; Late Augustan Poetry (editor), 1973; The Female Imagination, 1975; Imagining a Self, 1976; Contemporary Women Novelists, 1977; The Adolescent Idea, 1981; Gossip, 1985; Desire and Truth, 1990. *Membership:* A SECS, Modern Language Assoc, 2nd VP, 1992, 1st VP, 1993, President, 1994. *Address:* Department of English, University of Virginia, Charlottesville, VA 22903, USA.

SPAHNI Jean Christian, b. 7 Nov 1923, Geneva, Switzerland. Archeologist; Ethnologist. *Education:* University of Vieena; University of Grenada. *Appointments:* Professor, University in Archeology and Ethnology. *Publications:* L'Alpujarra; Itineraire; Les Indiens des Andes; La route des épices; Le Defi Indien; Others inc,Die Anden; L'Amerique centrale; Les Indiens d'Amerique du Sud. *Contributions to:* Some Newspapers and Magazines, Switzerland & France. *Honours:* First International Prize; Prize Broquette Gonin; Prize Alpes Jura. *Memberships:* Société suisse des Ecrivains; Société Genevoise des Ecrivains.

SPALDING Frances, b. 16 July 1950. Writer. m. 24 Apr 1974. dis 1991, 1 son. *Education:* BA Hons, University of Nottingham, 1972; PhD, 1978. *Publications:* Roger Fry: Art and Life, 1980; Vanessa Bell, 1983; Stevie Smith: A Critical Biography, 1986; British Art Since 1990, 1986; Dance till the Stars Come Down: A Life of John Minton, 1991; Magnificent Dreams: Burne Jones and the Late Victorians, 1978; Whistler, 1979; Dictionary of 20th Century British Painters and Sculptors, 1990; Paper Dart: A Selection of Virginia Wolf's Letters, 1991. *Contributions to:* TLS; TES; The Sunday Times; The Spectator; Burlington Magazine. *Honours:* FRSL, 1984. *Memberships:* PEN; Society of Authors. *Literary Agent:* Gill Coleridge.

Address: c/o Coleridge & Rogers, 20 Powis Mews, London W11 1JN, England.

SPARK David Brian, b. 5 Oct 1930, Darlington, England. Journalist. m. 20 Sept 1958, 1 son, 1 daughter. *Education:* MA Modern Languages, Trinity Hall, Cambridge, 1948-51. *Appointments:* Assistant Editor, The Northern Echo, 1965-66; Leadwriter, Westminister Press, 1967-86; Editor, National Press Agency, 1972-82; Assistant London Editor, Westminister Press, 1982-86; Editor Commonwealth Journalists Association Newsletter, 1986-. *Publications:* Practical Newspaper Reporting, 1966, 1993; Who to Ask about Developing Countries, 1992. *Contributions to:* Financial Times; The Independent. *Memberships:* Commonwealth Journalists Association. *Address:* 47 Seagry Road, Wanstead, London E11 2NH, England.bblank

SPARK Muriel Sarah, b. Edinburgh, Scotland. Writer. m. S O Spark, 1937, marriage dissolved, 1 son. *Appointments:* Political Intelligence Department, British Foreign Office, World War II; General Secretary, Poetry Society, Editor, Poetry Review, London, 1947-49. *Publications include:* The Comforters, 1957; Robinson, 1958; The Bacchelors, 1960; The Prime of Miss Jean Brodie, 1961 (adapted to stage 1966, filmed 1969, and BBC TV 1978); The Mandelbaum Gate, 1965; The Stories of Muriel Spark, 1987; A Far Cry From Kensington, 1989; Symposium, 1990; Curriculum Vitae, 1992; The Essence of the Brontes, 1993; The French Window and The Small Telephone (for children), 1993; Omnibus I, 1993; Omnibus II, 1993. *Honours:* The Observer Story Prize, 1951; Italia Prize for Radio Drama, 1962; James Tait Black Memorial Prize, 1966; Hon DLitt, University of Strathclyde, Glasgow, 1971; OBE; Prix du Meilleur Recueil de Nouvelles Etrangeres Fondation FNAC, 1987; Scottish Book of the Year, The Saltire Society and the Royal Bank of Scotland, 1987; Hon D Litt, University of Edinburgh, 1989; C.Litt, 1991, Ingersoll Foundation; T S Eliot Award, 1992. *Membership:* Honorary Member, American Academy, 1978. *Address:* c/o David Higham Associates Ltd, 5-8 Lower John Street, Golden Square, London WIR 4HA, England.

SPARSHOTT Francis Edward, b. 19 May 1926, Chatham, England. University Teacher; Author. m. Kathleen Elizabeth Vaughan, 7 Feb 1953, 1 daughter. *Education:* King's School, Rochester; Corpus Christi College, Oxford, 1943-44, 1947-50; BA, MA, 1950. *Publications:* An Enquiry into Goodness, 1958; The Structure of Aesthetics, 1963; A Divided Voice, poems, 1965; The Concept of Criticism, 1967; A Cardboard Garage, poems, 1968; Looking for Philosophy, 1972; The Naming of the Beasts, poems, 1979; The Rainy Hills, poems, 1979; The Theory of the Arts, 1982; The Hanging Gardens of Etobicoke, poems, 1983; Storms and Screens, poems, 1987; Off the Ground, 1988; Sculling to Byzantium, poems, 1989. *Contributions to:* Numerous. *Honour:* 1st Prize for Poetry, CBC Literary Competition, 1981. *Memberships:* League of Canadian Poets, President 1977-79; PEN International, Canadian Centre; Canadian Philosophical Association, President 1975-76; American Society for Aesthetics, President 1981-82. *Address:* 50 Crescentwood Road, Scarborough, Ontario, Canada M1N 1E4.

SPÈDE Lucie Rosa Judith, b. 27 Sept 1936, Brussels, Belgium. Advertising Copywriter; translator; Author; Journalist. Divorced, 2 sons, 1 daughter. *Publications:* La Savourante, 1978; Furies Douces, 1984; Inventaire, 1974; Volte-Face, 1973; Comme on plonge en la Mer, 1984; Eves, 1986; Radio Play Portes 1981; Contes pour petits et grands, for Radio 4 Internationpale; Translator, C. Friedrich's Book, Federalism in Theory and in Practise. *Contributions to:* various journals and magazines for adults and children. *Honours:* Prix Rene Lyr, 1979; Prix Louis Delattre, 1980; Prix des Dramatiques de la Radio-Télévision Belge, 1980; Prix de la Louve, 1983; Prix René Gerbeault, 1985; Prix Robert Goffin, 1986. *Memberships:* PEN; Association of Belgian Authors; Royal Association of Walloon Authors. *Address:* Rue

Theodore Decuyper 161, b. 42, B 1200 Brussels, Belgium.

SPEED Carol. *See:* **BENNETT-SPEED Carolyn.**

SPEIGHT Johnny, b. 2 June 1920, England. Writer. m. Constance Beatrice Barrett, 1956, 2 sons, 1 daughter. Has written for (television): Arthur Haynes Show; Morcambe & Wise Show; Peter Sellers; Till Death Us Do Part; The Lady Is A Tramp; In Sickness & in Health, with Ray Galton; Tea Ladies, 1979; Spooner's Patch. Plays: Compartment; Playmates; Salesman; Knackers Yard; If There Weren't Any Blacks You Would Have To Invent Them. *Publications:* It Stands to Reason, 1974; The Thoughts of Chairman Alf, 1974; Various scripts. *Honours:* Screenwriters Guild Awards, 1962, 1966, 1967, 1968; Pye TV Award, 1982; Prague Festival Award, 1969; Evening Standard Drama Award, best comedy, 1969. *Address:* Fouracres, Heronsgate, Chorleywood, Herts, England.

SPENCE Bill. *See:* **SPENCE William John Duncan.**

SPENCE William John Duncan (Jessica Blair, Jim Bowden, Kirk Ford, Floyd Rogers, Bill Spence), b. 20 Apr 1923, Middlesbrough, England. Author. m. Joan Mary Rhoda Ludley, 8 Sept 1944. 1 son, 3 daughters. *Education:* St Mary's Teachers Training College, 1940-42. *Publications:* Harpooned, 1981; Romantic Rydale (with Joan Spence), 1977, 1987; The Medieval Monasteries of Yorkshire (with Joan Spence), 1981; 36 Westerns (by Jim Bowden, Floyd Rogers, Kirk Ford); 3 War Novels; 1 Romance; Stories from Yorkshire Monasteries (with Joan Spence), 1992; 2 historical Sagas (by Jessica Blair), 1993; AA Leisure Guide North York Moors (co-author). *Contributions to:* Yorkshire Gazette & Herald; Writing manuals for the Writing School. *Memberships:* Society of Authors; Whitby Literary and Philosophical Society; Hakluyt Society. *Address:* Post Office, Ampleforth College, York YO6 4EZ, England.

SPENCER Colin b.17 July 1933, London, England. Writer; Novelist; Playwright. m. Gillian Chapman, 2 Oct 1959, 1 son. *Education:* Selhurst Grammar School; Brighton Art College. *Publications:* Novels: An Absurd Affair; Anarchists in Love; Poppy, Mandragora and the New Sex; The Tyranny of Love; Lovers in War; Panic; How the Greeks Kidnapped Mrs Nixon; Asylum; The Victims of Love. Non-Fiction: Reports from Behind with Chris Barias; Which of Us Two?; The Heretic's Feast - A History of Vegeterianism; Plays: The Ballad of the False Barman; Spitting Image; The Trial of St George; The Sphinx Mother; Why Mrs Neustadter Always Loses; Keep It In the Family; Flossie (Granada Television). Cookery Books: The Vegetarians' Healthy Diet Book; Gourmet Cooking for Vegetarians; Colin Spencer's Vegetarian/Wholefood Cookbook; Al Fresco; Feast for Health; Mediterranean Vegetarian Cooking; The Romantic Vegetarian; The Adventurous Vegetarian; Vegetable Pleasures. *Contributions to:* The Guardian, The Sunday Times; Cosmopolitan; Country Living; The Observer; The Daily and Sunday Telegraph; Taste; The New Statesman. *Honour:* The Glenfiddich Awards, 1989 Food Writer of the Year. *Memberships:* The Guild of Food Writers, Chairman 1988-90; The Writers Guild of Great Britain, Chairman 1982. *Literary Agent:* Richard Scott Simon Limited. *Address:* Two Heath Cottages, Tunstall, Woodbridge, Suffolk IP12 2HQ, England.

SPENCER Elizabeth, b. Carrollton, Mississippi, USA. Fiction Writer. m. John Arthur Rusher, 29 Sept 1956. *Education:* AB, cum laude, Belhaven College; MA Vanderbilt University. *Appointments:* Instructor, Northwest Mississippi Junior College, Senatobia, 1943-44; Ward-Belmont School, Nashville, 1944-45; Instructor, University of Mississippi, 1948-51, 1952-53; Visiting Professor of Creative Writing, Concordia University, Montreal, Canada, 1976-77; Writer-in-Residence, Adjunct Professor, 1977-86; Visiting Professor, University of North Carolina at Chapel Hill,

1986-1992. *Publications:* The Light in the Piazza, 1960; The Voice at the Back Door, 1956; The Stories of Elizabeth Spencer, 1981; Jack of Diamonds, 1988; The Salt Line, 1984; Fire in the Morning, 1948; This Crooked Way, 1952; The Snare, 1972; Ship Island and Other Stories, 1968; No Place for an Angel, 1967; For Lease or Sale, drama, 1989; The Night Travellers, 1991. *Contributions to:* The New Yorker; The Atlantic; Southern Review; Kenyon Review. *Honours:* Recognition Award, American Academy of Arts and Letters, 1952; Guggenheim Fellowship, 1953; 1st Rosenthal Award, American Academy of Arts and Letters, 1957; Kenyon Review Fiction Fellowship, 19056-57; McGraw-Hill Fiction Award, 1960; Donelly Fellowship, Bryn Mawr College, 1962; Bellman Award, 1968; National Endowment for the Arts Fellowship, 1983; Award of Merit Medal, American Academy, 1983; Election to the Institute, 1985; National Endowment for the Arts Senior Fellowship in Literature Grant, 1988; Charter member, Fellowship of Southern Writers, 1987, elected vice chancellor, 1993; Honorary Degrees from Rhodes University, Memphis, and University of the South Concordia University. *Memberships:* PEN Canadian, 1960-86; American PEN, 1986-; Authors Guild, Programme Chairman, Canadian PEN, 1980-83, Vice President, 1983-86. *Literary Agent:* Virginia Barber, 383 West 21st Streets, New York, NY 10011, USA. *Address:* 402 Longleaf Drive, Chapel Hill, NC 27514, USA.

SPENCER Ross H, b. 1921, USA. Author. *Publications:* The Data Caper, 1978; The Reggis Arms Caper, 1979; The Stranger City Caper, 1980; The Abu Wahab Caper, 1980; The Radish River Caper, 1981; Echoes of Zero, 1981; The Missing Bishop, 1985; Monastery Nightmare, 1986; Kirby's Last Circus, 1987; Death Wore Gloves, 1987. *Address:* 551 North Dunlap Avenue, Youngstown, OH 44509, USA.

SPENCER Scott, b. USA. Author. *Publications:* Last Night at the Brain Thieves Ball, 1973; Preservation Hall, 1976; Endless Love, 1979; Waking the Dead, 1986. *Address:* c/o ICN, 40 West 57th Street, New York, NY 10019, USA.

SPENCER William, b. 1 June 1922, Erie, Pennsylvnia, USA. Writer; University Professor. m. Elizabeth Bouvier, 18 May 1969, 1 son, 2 daughters. *Education:* AB, Princeton University, 1948; AM, Duke University, 1950; PhD, International Relations, American Univerity, 1965. *Appointments:* English Instructor, St Lawrence University, 1950; Fellow, US Information Agency, Turkey, 1953; Assistant Editor, Middle East Journal, 1956; Professor Florida State University, 1968-80. *Publications:* Political Evolution in the Middle East, 1962; The Land and People of Turkey, 1970, 1972, 1988; Algiers in the Age of the Corsairs, 1976; Historical Dictionary of Morocco, 1980; The Islamic States in Conflict, 1983; Global Studies: The Middle East 1985, 1988, 1990; The Challenge of World Hunger, 1990. *Contributions to:* Travel; Landscape; Africa Report; Mideast; Middle East Journal; Venture; New York Times Travel; Regular Book Reviewer, various journals, many years. *Honour:* Carnegie and Lippincott Literary Awards, 1960. *Address:* PO Box 1702, Suite 52, Gainesville, FL 32602, USA.

SPENDER Stephen Harold Sir (S H S), b. 1909, United Kingdom. Author; Poet; Professor Emeritus. *Appointments:* Editor, Horizon, London, 1939- 41; Co-Editor, 1953-66, Corresponding Editor, 1966-67, Encounter, London; Consultant, Poetry in English, Library of Congress, Washington DC, USA, 1965- 66; Professor of English Literature, 1970-77, Emeritus Professor, 1977-, University College, London, England. *Publications:* Various, 1928-49; To the Island, 1951; World Within World: The Autobiography of Stephen Spender, 1951; Europe in Photographs, 1951; Shelley, 1952; Learning Laughter (on Israel), 1952; The Creative Element: A Study of Vision, Despair, and Orthodoxy among Some Modern Writers, 1953; Sirmione Peninsula, 1954; Collected Poems 1928-1953, 1955, 1928-1985, 1986; The Making of a Poem, essays, 1955;

Mary Stuart, adaptation of play by Schiller, 1957; Inscriptions, 1958; Lulu, adaptation of play by Frank Wedekind, 1958; Engaged in Writing, and The Fool and the Princess, short stories, 1958; The Imagination in the Modern World: Three Lectures, 1962; Rasputin's End, 1963; The Struggle of the Modern, 1963; Selected Poems, 1964; Ghika: Paintings, Drawings, Sculpture (with P Fermor), 1964; The Magic Flute: Retold, 1966; Chaos and Control in Poetry, 1966; The Year of the Young Rebels, 1969; The Generous Days: Ten Poems, 1969, augmented edition, The Generous Days, 1971; Descartes, 1970; Art Student, 1970; Penguin Modern Poets 20 (with John Heath-Stubbs and F T Prince), 1971; Love-Hate Relations: A Study of Anglo-American Sensibilities, 1974; W H Auden: A Tribute, 1975; Eliot, 1975; The Thirties and After, 1978; Recent Poems, 1978; Venice (with Fulvio Roiter), 1979; America Observed (with Paul Hogarth), 1979; Letters to Christopher: Stephen Spender's Letters to Christopher Isherwood 1929-1939, 1980; China Diary (with David Hockney), 1982; Rasputin's End, libretto, 1983; Oedipus Trilogy, 1985; Journals 1939-1983. 1985; In Irina's Garden, 1986; The Temple, 1988; (et al) The Forward Book of Poetry, 1992. *Honours:* CBE, 1962; CLitt, 1977; FRSL; Kt, 1983. *Memberships:* President, English Centre, PEN, 1975-. *Address:* 15 Loudoun Road, London NW8, England.

SPERBER A(nn) M, b. Vienna, Austria. Writer. *Education:* Attended Julliard School of Music, 1947-52; BA, Barnard College, 1956. *Appointments:* Senior Editor, G P Putnam's Sons, New York, New York, 1963-68; Senior Editor, McGraw-Hill Book Co, New York, New York, 1968-70; Writer, c. 1974-; Consultant to Alfred A Knopf Inc; Member of Executive Council of the New York City Opera Guild (past president), and of the Board of Managers of the Women's National Book Association, 1969. *Publications:* Murrow: His Life and Times, Freundlich Books, 1986. *Contributions to:* Articles and reviews to newspapers and periodicals, including New York Newsday, New York Times Book Review, Opera News, and the American Record Guide. *Honours:* Fulbright Fellow at Freie Universitaet Berlin, 1956- 57; Murrow: His Life and Times was named a 1986 Notable Book of the Year by the New York Times; also Book-of-the-Month Club selection. *Membership:* Authors Guild. *Literary Agency:* William Morris Agency, New York. *Address:* c/o William Morris Agency, 1350 Avenue of the Americas, New York, NY 10019, USA.

SPIEL Hilde (Maria), (Mrs Flesch von Brunningen), b. 19 Oct 1911, Vienna, Austria. Writer. m. (1) Peter de Mendelssohn, 1936, (2) Hans Flesch von Brunningen, 1971. 1 son, 1 daughter. *Education:* Dr Phil. University of Vienna; Hon. Professor, State of Austria. *Publications:* Flue and Drums, novel, 1939; The Darkened Room, novel, 1961; Fahby von Arnstein, biography, 1962; Vienna's Golden Autumn, 1987; 4 other novels; six collections of essays; 1 volume of short stories; 1 book on Vienna and contributions to anthologies in English (Gustav Mahler in Vienna, Genius in the Drawing Room etc). *Contributions to:* From 1944-50, The New Statesman; Vienna cultural correspondent to the Manchester Guardian, 1963-66; Suddeutsche Zeitung from London and to Frankfurter Allgemeine and Weltwoche from Vienna. *Honours include:* Great Cross of Merit, Federal German Republic, et al; Julius Reich Prize, City of Vienna, 1933; Salzburg Critics' Prize, 1970; Jon H Merck-Prize of German Academy, Darmstadt, 1981; Poeter Rosegger-Prize of Province of Styria, 1986; Ernst R Curtius-Prize for Essays, 1986. *Memberships:* International PEN; German Academy for Language and Poetry, Darmstadt; Bavarian Academy of Arts. *Address:* Cottagegasse 65/2/3, 1190 Vienna, Austria.

SPIERENBURG Pieter Cornelis, b. 2 June 1948, Haarlem, Netherlands. Historian. *Education:* Dissertation, University of Amsterdam, 1978. *Publications:* The Spectacle of Suffering; The Broken Spell; The Prison Experience. *Contributions to:* Social Science History; Journal of Social History. *Memberships:* Secretary, International Association for the History of Crime and Criminal Justice. *Address:*

Erasmus University, Department of History, PO Box 1738, 3000 Dr Rotterdam, Netherlands.

SPILLEBEEN Willy Frans, b. 30 Dec 1932, Westroxebehe, belgium. Professor. m. Zulma Denys, 9 July 1958, 2 sons, 2 daughters. *Education:* Greek Latin Humanities. *Publications:* Dooinsoosjis Lowen; Aencas of De Levenszies Von Eln Man; De Aurncaine Jesuiet; Cortes of De Val; Steen Ves Auxtoots. *Contributions to:* most Literary Magazines of Flanders. *Honours:* First Flemish Writer in Residence. *Memberships include:* PEN; Vercniging Auteurs en Vertales. *Address:* Sluijenkaai 77, 8930 Meuen, Belgium.

SPILLEMAECKERS Werner Lodewijk, b. 3 Dec 1936, Antwerp, Belgium. Author. *Education:* BA, History, 1965. *Appointments:* Founder, Editor, Mandragora, 1954, Artisjok, 1968-69, Editor, Diogenes, 1984-. *Publications:* Ik ben Berlijn, 1961; Tekst in Tekst Asbest, 1964; Fuga Magister, 1970; Veranda, 1974; Blad na Blad, 1983; Vanaf Alfa, 1970; Verzamelde Gedichten 1954-1974, 1974. *Contributions to:* Mandragora; Frontaal; De Tafelronde; Artisjok; Album Poëziemarkt Wetteren Nieuw Vlaams Tijdschrift; Diogenes; Avenue. *Honours:* Signaal Prize, 1969; Trap Prize, 1975; Kt, Order of the Crown, 1975; Kt, Leopold Order, 1980; Officer, Order of the Crown, 1985. *Memberships:* Vereniging van Vlaamse Letterkundigen; Belgian PEN; MENSA; Intertel. *Address:* Molenstraat 57, B 2018 Antwerp, Belgium.

SPILMAN Richard Stuart, b. 5 Nov 1946, Bloomington, Illinois, USA. Professor. m. Joan Heck, 21 June 1986, 2 daughters. *Education:* BA Illinois Wesleyan University, 1968; MA San Francisco State University, 1972; PhD, State University of New York, 1982. *Publications:* Hot Fudge, 1990. *Contributions to:* MSS: Quarterly West; The George Mason Review, Shane Painter; Triquarterly; Anthologies in Editor's Choice. *Honours:* Quarterly West Novella Award, 1983; West Virgina Writer's Short Story Competition Awards, 1984, 1987; Marshall University Meet the Scholar Award, 1990. *Literary Agent:* Jane Gelfman of John Farquharson Ltd. *Address:* Rt 2 Box 252, Milton, WV 25541, USA.

SPINK Reginald (William), b. 9 Dec 1905, York, England. Journalist; Translator. *Publications include:* Land and People of Denmark, 1953; Fairy Tales of Denmark, retellings, 1961; The Young Hans Andersen, 1962; Hans Christian Andersen and His World, 1972; Hans Christian Andersen: The Man and His Work, 1972; 40 Aar efter, memoirs, 1983; England bygger op (with Jens Otto Krag), 1947, Swedish Edition, 1948. Translations include: Ludvig Holberg, 3 Comedies; Carl Nielsen, My Childhood, Living Music; Palle Lauring, The Roman, Land of the Tollund Man; Poul Borchsenius, Behind the Wall; Hans Christian Andersen, Fairy Tales and Stories; Bengt Danielsson, Gauguin in the South Seas. *Contributions to:* Several leading journals. *Honours:* Knight's Cross, Danish Order of Dannebrog, 1966; Ebbe Munck Memorial Award, 1983. *Memberships:* Society of Authors; Executive, Translators Association. *Address:* 6 Deane Way, Eastcote, Ruislip, Middlesex HA4 8SU, England.

SPINRAD Norman, b. 1940, USA. Writer. *Publications:* The Solarians, 1966; Agent of Chaos, 1967; The Men in the Jungle, 1967; Bug Jack Barron, 1969; Fragments of America, 1970; The Last Hurrah of the Golden Horde, 1970; The New Tomorrows (editor), 1971; The Iron Dream, 1972; Modern Science Fiction (editor), 1974; Passing Through the Flame, 1975; No Direction Home, 1975; A World Between, 1979; Songs from the Stars, 1980; The Mind Game, 1980; The Void Captain's Tale, 1983; Staying Alive: A Writer's Guide, 1983; Child of Fortune, 1985.

SPITZER Lyman Jr, b. 26 June 1914, Toledo, Ohio, USA. Astrophysicist. m. Doreen D. Canaday, 29 June 1940, 1 son, 3 daughters. *Education:* AB, Yale University, 1935; MA, 1937; PhD, 1938, Princeton University. *Publications include:* Physics of Sound in the Sea, (editor), 1946; Physics of Fully Ionized Gases, 1962; Diffuse Matter in Space, 1968; Physical Processes in the Interstellar Medium, 1978; Searching Between the Stars, 1982; Dynamical Evolution of Globular Clusters, 1987. *Contributions to:* Astrophysical Journal; Physical Review; Monthly Notices of the Royal Astronomical Society; Physics of Fluids; Physica Scripta. *Honours:* Rittenhouse Medal, Franklin Institute, 1957; Bruce Gold Medal, Astronomical Society of the Pacific, 1973; Henry Draper Medal, National Academy of Sciences, 1974;Karl Schwarzchild Medal, Astronomiche Gesellschhaft, 1975; James Clark Maxwell Prize, American Physical Society, 1975; Gold Medal, Royal Astronomical Socety, 1978; Jules Janssen Medal, Société Astronomique de France, 1980; National Medal of Science, 1980; Crafoord Prize, Royal Swedish Academy of Sciences, 1985; James Madison Medal, Princeton University, 1989; Franklin Medal, American Philosophical Society, 1991. *Memberships:* National Academy of Science; American Philosophical Society; American Academy of Arts and Sciences; Royal Society, London (Foreign member); Société Royale des Sciences, Liegé (Correspondent); Royal Astronomical Society, London (Associate); American Astronomical Society, President 1958-60; American Physical Society. *Address:* Princeton University Observatory, Peyton Hall, Princeton, NJ 08544, USA.

SPIVACK Charlotte, b. 23 July 1926, Schoharie, NY, USA. University Professor. m. Bernard Spivack, 17 Oct 1956, 1 son, 1 daughter. *Education:* BA, State University of New York at Albany, 1947; MA, Cornell University, 1948; PhD, University of Missouri, 1954. *Publications:* George Chapman, 1967; The Comedy of Evil on Shakespeares's Stage, 1968; Ursula K. Le Guin, 1984; Merlin's Daughters, 1987; Merlin vs. Faust, 1992. *Contributions to:* Centennial Reivew; Bucknell Reivew; Medieval and Renaissance Drama in England. *Honours:* AAUW Fellowship, 1959; Massachusetts Professor of the Year, 1988. *Memberships:* International Association of the Fantastic in the Arts; Modern Language Association; Dante Society; Mythopoeic Society. *Address:* English Department, University of Massachusetts, Amherst, MA 01003, USA.

SPOTO, Donald, b. 28 June 1941, New Rochelle, USA. Writer. *Education:* AB, Iona College, 1963; MA, 1966, PhD, 1970, Fordham University. *Appointments:* Contributing Editor, Audio Magazine, 1974-. *Publications:* The Art of Alfred Hitchcock, 1976; Camerado, 1978; The Dark Side of Genius : The Life of Alfred Hitchcock, 1983; The Kindness of Strangers : The Life of Tennessee Williams, 1985; Falling in Love Again : Marlene Dietrich, 1985; Lenya : A Life, 1988, (Biography); Stanley Kramer, Film Maker, 1978. *Contributions to:* Audio; Video; New York Times; Notre Dame Journal. *Honours:* Edgar Award, 1983; Annual Lecturer, British Film Institute, London, American Film Institute. *Memberships:* Authors Guild; Writers Guild of America. *Literary Agent:* Elaine Markson, New York. *Address:* c/o Little, Brown and Co., 34 Beacon Street, Boston, MA 02106, USA.

SPRAGUE Irvine H, b. 4 July 1921, San Francisco, USA. Government. m. Margery Craw, 3 Nov 1941, 2 sons, 1 daughter. *Education:* Graduate: English, Stochton College: Economics, College of the Pacific; Business, Harvard AMP; Also attended George Washington, (Law); and Indiana University, (Engineering). *Publications:* Bailout, An Insiders Account of Bank Failures and Rescues, 1986. *Literary Agent:* ICM. *Address:* 962 Millwood Lane, Great Fall, VA 22066, USA.

SPRAGUE William Leigh, b. 28 July 1938, Weatherford, Oklahoma, USA. Minister; Writer-Editor-Publisher. *Education:* BA 1960, Phillips University, Enid, Oklahoma, Bachelor of Divinity, (Graduate degree), 1964; The Graduate Seminary, Phillips University, Enid, Oklahoma; Master of Sacred Theology, Boston University School of Theology, Boston, Massachusetts,

1966. *Literary Appointment:* Member, Zollars Literary Society, Phillips University, 1960. *Publications:* Shirt-Sleeve Ministries: Christian Laity In Action (Editor), 1981; Our Christian Church Heritage: Journeying in Faith (A Resource Book for Lay Persons), Editor, 1979; Chapter (Session) 2 in General Program Book, CMF/CWF Lay Studies 1981-1982; Chapter 8 in Put Love First: CMF/CWF General Programs, Co-Author, 1982-83; Chapter 9 in Put Love First: CMF/CWF General Programs, Co-Author, 1982-83. *Contributions to:* The Bugle; The Haymaker; Children Limited; The New Hampshire Churchman; The Ecumenical Council on Alcohol Programs; The Disciple Chaplain; The Disciple; Vanguard; Ministers Bulletin; The Christian Home; JED Share. *Honours:* Outstanding Student in Pastoral Psychology and Counseling, The Graduate Seminary, Phillips University, 1961. *Membership:* Zollars, Phillips University. *Address:* 1135 Aqua Vista Drive, Indianapolis, IN 46229, USA.

SPRIGEL Oliver. See: BARBET Pierre Claude Avice.

SPRIGGE Timothy Lauro Squire, b. 14 Jan 1932, London, England. University Professor. m. Giglia Gordon, 4 Apr 1959, 1 son, 2 daughters. *Education:* BA, 1955; MA; PhD, 1961, Cantab. *Appointments:* Editorial board, Journal of Applied Philosophy; Philosophical Quarterly; The Journal of Speculative Philosophy; Studia Spinozana. *Publications:* The Correspondence of Jeremy Benthan, 1968; Facts, Words and Beliefs, 1970; Santayana: An Examination of his Philosophy, 1974; The Vindication of Absolute Idealism, 1983; Theories of Existence, 1984; The Rational Foundation of Ethics, 1987. *Contributions to:* Various professional journals, including Mind; Philosophy; Inquiry; Journal of Applied Philosophy; Utilitas. *Memberships:* Mind Association; Scots Philosopohical Club. *Address:* David Hume Tower, University of Edinburgh, George Square, Edinburgh EH8 9JX, Scotland.

SPRING Michael, b. 14 Oct 1941, New York City, USA. Editor; Writer. (div). 2 sons. *Education:* BA, Haverford College, Haverford, Pennsylvania, 1964; MA, English Literature, Columbia University, 1970. *Publications:* Great Weekend Escape Book, 3rd edition, 1987, 4th edition, 1990; Great European Itineraries, 1987; American Way of Working, (editor), 1980;A Student's Guide to Julius Ceasar, 1984; Editor, 50 volumes, Barron's Book Notes series, 1984; Vice President and Editorial Director, Fodor's Travel Publications, 140 titles; Contributing editor, Conde Nast's Traveler magazine. *Contributions to:* Travel & Leisure; Signature; Modern Bride and numerous others. *Honours:* Distinguished Achievement Award in Educational Journalism, Educational Press Association of America, 1987. *Address:* c/o Random House, 201 East 50th Street, New York, NY 10022, USA.

SPRINGER Nancy, b. 5 July 1948, New Jersey, USA. Novelist. m. Joel H. Springer, 13 Sept 1969, 1 son, 1 daughter. *Education:* BA, English Literature, Gettysburg College, 1970. *Appointments:* Personal Development Plan Instructor, University of Pittsburg, 1983-85; Leisure Learning Instructor, York College, Pennsylvania, 1986-. *Publications:* The White Hart, 1979; The Silver Sun, 1980; The Black Beast, 1982; The Sable Moon, 1981; The Golden Swan, 1983; Wings of Flame, 1985; Chains of Gold, 1986; A Horse to Love (Juvenile), 1987; Madbond, 1987; Chance and Other Gestures of the Hand of Fate, 1987; The Hex Witch of Seldom, 1988; Not on a White Horse (juvenile), 1988; Apocalyypse, 1989; They're All Named Wildfire (juvenile), 1989; Red Wizard (juvenile), 1990; Colt, (juvenile), 1991; The Friendship Song (juvenile), 1992. *Contributions to:* journals and magazines. *Honours:* Phi Beta Kappa, 1970; Rhysling Nominee, 1983; Nominee, Short Story Category, Nebula Award, 1986; Distinguished Alumna, Gettysburg College, 1987. *Memberships:* Science Fiction Writers of America; Society of Children's Book Writers; Poets & Writers Inc; Central Pennsylvania Writers' Organization; Board Member, Children's Literature Council of Pennsylvania;

Board member, Pennwriters. *Literary Agent:* Jean V Naggar. *Address:* c/o Virginia Kidd Agency, Box 278, 538 E Harford St, Milford, PA 18337, USA.

SPRINKLE Patricia Houck, b. 13 Nov 1943, West Virginia, USA. Writer. m. Robert William Sprinkle, 12 Sept 1970, 2 sons. *Education:* AB Vassar College, 1965. *Appointments:* Managing Editor, United Pub. Co. Atlanta, 1967-68; Director of PR, Kendall College, 1970; Staff Writer, Presbyterian Church, 1968-70, 1971-73. *Publications:* Hunger: Understanding the Crisis through games, 1980; Murder at Markham, 1988; Murder in the Charleston Manner, 1990; Murder on Peachtree Street, 1991; Somebody's Dead in Snellville, 1992; Death of a Dunwoody Matron, 1993; Women Who Do too much: Stress and the Myth of the Superwoman, 1992; Do I Have To? What to do about Children Who Do Too Little Around the House, 1993; In God's Image: Meditation for the New Mother, 1988; Housewarmings: For those who make a House a Home, 1992. *Contributions include:* Guideposts; Jack and Jill; Presbyterian Survey. *Memberships:* Penwomen; Sisters in Crime; Mystery Writers of America. *Literary Agent:* Dominick Abel. *Address:* 1557 Fearn Way, Mobile, AL 36604, USA.

SPURLING Hilary, b. 25 Dec 1940, Stockport, Cheshire, England. Writer. m. 4 Apr 1961, 2 sons, 1 daughter. *Education:* BA Oxon. *Literary Appointment:* Theatre Critic, Literary Editor, The Spectator, 1964-70. *Publications:* Ivy When Young (The Early Life of I. Compton-Burnett, 1884-1919), 1974; Elinor Fettiplace's Receipt Book, 1986; Handbook to A Powell's Music of Time, 1977; Secrets of A Woman's Heart (the later life of I Compton-Burnett), 1984; Paul Scott, A Life, 1990. *Honours:* Duff Cooper Prize, 1984; Joint Recipient, Heinemann Award, 1984. *Literary Agent:* David Higham. *Address:* c/o David Higham, 5-8 Lower John Street, Golden Square, London, W1R 4HA, England.

SPURLING John Antony b. 17 July 1936, Kisumu, Kenya. Writer. m. Hilary Spurling, 4 Apr 1961, 2 sons 1 daughter. *Education:* Dragon School, Oxford; Marlborough College, Wilts; BA, St John's College, Oxford, 1960. *Literary Appointment:* Henfield Writing Fellow, University of East Anglia, 1973. *Publications:* MacRune's Guevara (play) 1969; In the Heart of the British Museum (play) 1972; Shades of Heathcliff (play) 1975; The British Empire part one (play) 1982; The Ragged End (novel) 1989; Beckett the Playwright (with John Fletcher) 1972, 3rd edition 1985; Grahame Greene, 1983. *Contributions to:* Art critic of The New Statesman, 1976-88; Freelance contributor at various times to The Spectator, The Times, The Sunday Times, The Observer, The Independent, Modern Painters; TLS, The Guardians, The Daily Telegraph. *Literary Agent:* Patricia Macnaughton, MLR, 200 Fulham Road, London SW10 9PN. *Address:* c/o Patricia Macnaughton, MLR, 200 Fulham Road, London SW10 9PN, England.

SRIVASTAVA Ramesh Kumar, b. 2 Jan 1940, Banpur, India. m. Usha Rani Srivastava, 27 June 1959, 2 sons. *Education:* BA 1957; MA 1961; PhD, 1972. *Appointments:* Editor, The Summit, 1970-72; Associate Editor, 1976-88, Editor, 1988-93, The Punjab Journal of English Studies. *Publications:* Neema - a novel, 1986; Six Indian Novelists in English, 1987; Games they play and other Stories, 1989; Love and Animality: Stories 1984; Cooperative Colony: Stories, 1985. *Contributions to:* Art of Living; The Sunday Tribune; Indian Book Chronicle; Indian Express; Games they Play and Other Stories. *Honours:* Fulbright Fellowship, 1969; Senior Fulbright Grant, 1984. *Memberships:* Authors Guild of India; Indian PEN: Modern Language Association. *Address:* B-16 Guru Nanak Dev University, Amritsar 143005, India.

SSUJEN. *See:* **KUO Nancy.**

ST AUBIN DE TERAN Lisa, b. 2 Oct 1953, London, England. m. (1) Jaime Teran, Oct 1970 (div 1981), 1 daughter, (2) George MacBeth, Mar 1981 (div 1986), 1 son. *Education:* Attended school in London. *Career:* Farmer of sugar cane, avocados, pears and sheep in Venezuela 1972-78; Writer 1972-. *Publications:* The Streak (poetry) 1980; Keepers of the House (novel) 1982, published as The Long Way Home, 1983; The Slow Train to Milan (novel) 1983; The Tiger (novel) 1984, 1985; The High Place (poems) 1985; The Bay of Silence (novel) 1986; Black Idol (novel) 1987; Off the Rails (memoir) 1989; The Marble Mountain and Other Stories, 1989; Nocturne, 1992. *Honours:* Somerset Maugham Award, from the Society of Authors, The Long Way Home, John Llewellyn Rhys Memorial Prize, Book Trust for Slow Train to Milan and Eric Gregory Award, the Society of Authors for poetry, all 1983. *Membership:* Royal Society of Literature (Fellow). *Literary Agent:* A M Heath, 79 St Martins Lane, London WC2N 4AA, England. *Address:* 7 Canynge Square Clifton Bristol England.

ST AUBYN Giles R (The Hon), b. 11 Mar 1925, London, England. Writer. *Education:* Wellington College; MA, Trinity College, Oxford University. *Publications:* Lord Macaulay, 1952; A Victorian Eminence, 1957; The Art of Argument, 1957; The Royal George, 1963; A World to Win, 1968; Infamous Victorians, 1971; Edward VII, Prince and King, 1979; The Year of Three Kings 1483, 1983; Queen Victoria: A Portrait, 1991. *Honour:* LVO. *Memberships:* Fellow, Royal Society of Literature; Society of Authors. *Address:* Cornwall Lodge, Cambridge Park, St Peter Port, Guernsey, Channel Islands.

ST CLAIR Elizabeth. *See:* **COHEN Susan.**

ST CLAIR Margaret, b. 17 Feb 1911, Kansas, USA. Writer. m. Eric St Clair, 25 May 1932, Berkeley. *Education:* MA, Greek, University of California, 1934. *Publications:* Agent of the Unknown, 1956; The Green Queen, 1956; The Games of Neith, 1960; Sign of the Labrys, 1963; Message from the Eocene, 1964; The Worlds of Futurity, 1964; The Dolphins of Altair, 1967; The Shadow People, 1969; The Dancers of Noyo, 1973; Change the Sky & Other Stories, 1974; The Best of Margaret St Clair, 1985; The Lack of Teddy Bears (autobiography), 1989. *Contributions to:* More than 100 pieces of short fiction published in various journals and magazines. *Memberships:* Former Member, Authors League of America; Science Fiction Writers of America. *Literary Agent:* Julie Fallowfield, McIntosh & Otis, New York City. *Address:* 684 Benicia Drive, No 44, Santa Rosa, CA 95409, USA.

ST CLAIR William, b. 7 Dec 1937, London, England. Author; Under-Secretary, Her Majesty's Treasury. 2 daughters. *Education:* St Johns College, Oxford, 1956-60; Fellow, All Souls College, Oxford, 1992, Visiting Fellow, 1981-82; Fellow, Huntington Library, 1985. *Publications:* Lord Elgin and the Marbles, 1967, revised 1983; That Greece Might Still Be Free, 1972; Trelawny, 1978; The Godwins and the Shelleys: The Biography of a Family, 1989; Policy Evaluation, A Guide for Managers, 1988; Executive Agencies, A Guide to Setting Targets and Judging Performance, 1992; Consultant to OECD, 1992-; Reviews regularly for Financial Times and other journals. *Honours:* Heinemann Prize, Royal Society of Literature, 1973; Time Life Prize and Macmillan Silver Pen for non-fiction, 1990. *Memberships:* International President, Byron Society; Fellow, British Academy; Fellow, Royal Society of Literature; Executive Committee of English Centre of International PEN; Chairman, Writers-in-Prison Committee. *Literary Agent:* Deborah Rogers. *Address:* 52 Eaton Place, London SW1, England.

ST CRISPIAN Crispin De. *See:* **WAUGH Auberon Alexander.**

ST CYR Napoleon, b. 8 May 1924, Franklin, New Hampshire, USA. Editor; Publisher. *Education:* BA, University of New Hampshire; MA, Certificate of Advanced Study, Fairfield University. *Appointments:* Editor, The Small Pond Magazine of Literature, 1969-; Literary Advisor, Stratford Cultural Commission, 1975-80; One of Final Judges in poetry and history, National Book Awards; Advisory Board of Consultants, Small Press Review of Books, 1985-; Poetry Editor, Cider Mill Press. *Publications:* Pebble Ring, 1966, (poems); Stones Unturned, 1967 (poems). *Contributions to:* Over 60 journals in the form of poetry, including Editor's Line, The Small Pond Magazine of Literature, 1969-. *Honour:* Sherrard Short Story Prize/Honours Convocation, University of New Hampshire. *Memberships:* Academy of American Poets; CLMP; Life member Stratford Library Board, Chair Book Committee, intermittently, 1975-, 1984-; Past President Halsey International Scholarship Program, University of Bridgeport, French Committee, Red Cross Board of Directors, Stratford Chapter, 1985-89. *Address:* PO Box 664, Stratford, CT 06497, USA.

ST DAWN Grace Galasso (Her Excellency), Poet; Speaker. *Education:* Hon Doctorates: of Humane Letters, University Libre; of Literature, Republic of China; of Divinity, Universal Orthodox College; PhD, National Academy of Management, Republic of China; The World Academy of Arts and Culture. *Appointments:* National Advisor, American Biographical Research Institute. *Publications include:* The Gift of Peace; God Gave me His Peace; Trust God - Love God. *Honours include:* Poet Laureate of Spiritual Revelation; American Poet of Bi-Centennial Distinction; Dame of High Grace of the Knights of Malta, L F; World Decoration of Excellence, ABI; American Biographical Institute Gold Commemortative Medal of Honor; Historical Preservations of American Biographee of the Year, 1986; World Poet Resource Center Award; Golden Poet Award; Silver Award; National Library of Poetry, Editors Choice Award; ABI, Woman of the Year, 1990. *Memberships include:* American Biographical Research Institute, Life Fellow; International Life Fellow, Platform Association; United Poets Laureate International (Laurel Wreath) Poet Laureate of Spiritual Revelation; International Biographical Centre, Life Fellow. *Address:* 340 Elliot Place, Paramus, NJ 07652, USA.

ST GEORGE Judith, b. 26 Feb 1931, Westfield, New Jersey, USA, Writer. m. David St George, 5 June 1954, 3 sons, 1 daughter. *Education:* BA, Smith College, 1952. *Appointment:* Teacher, Rutgers University Extension Division, Writing for Children, 1980-83. *Publications:* The Brooklyn Bridge: They Said It Couldn't Be Built, 1982; The Mount Rushmore Story, 1985; What's Happening to My Junior Year?, 1986; Who's Scared? Not Me!, 1987; Panama Canal: Gateway to the World, 1989; The White House: Cornerstone of a Nation, 1990; Mason and Difon's Line of Fine, 1991; Dear Dr Bill . . . Your Friend, Helen Keller, 1992. *Honours:* M Haunted, New York Times Best Mystery of 1980; Brooklyn Bridge, American Book Honor Award; ALA Notable Book; New York Academy of Sciences Award; The Mt Rushmore Story, Christopher Award, ALA Notable Book; Panama Canal, Society of Children's Book Writers, Golden Kite Non-Fiction Award, ALA Notable Book. *Memberships:* Authorws Guild; Society of Children's Book Writers; Rutgers University Advisory Council on Children's Literature; Delegate, White House Conference on Libraries, 1979; Commissioner, Brooklyn Bridge Centennial Commission, 1983. *Literary Agent:* Marilyn Marlow. *Address:* 290 Roseland Avenue, Essex Fells, NJ 07021, USA.

ST GERMAIN Gregory. *See:* **WALLMANN Jeffrey M.**

ST JOHN Bruce (Carlisle), b. 1923, Barbadian. *Appointments:* Assistant Master, St Giles' Boys' School, 1942-44, Combermere School, 1944-64; Lecturer 1964-75, Senior Lecturer in Spanish 1976-, University of the West Indies, Bridgetown; Editor, Ascent Series of Poetry Chap-Books, 1982. *Publications:* The Foetus Pains, The Foetus Pleasures, 1972; Bruce St John at Kairi House, 1974, 1975; Joyce and Eros and Varia, 1976; The Vests, Aftermath: An Anthology (ed), 1977; Por el Mar de las Antillas: A Spanish Course for Caribbean Secondary Schools, 4 volumes, 1979; Caribanthology (ed), 1981; Bumbatuk 1, 1982.

Membership: National Council for Arts and Culture, Barbados. *Address:* PO Box 64, Bridgetown, Barbados.

ST JOHN David. *See:* **HUNT E(verette) Howard.**

ST JOHN Leonie. *See:* **BAYER William.**

ST JOHN Lisa. *See:* **SANFORD Annette Schorre.**

ST JOHN Lucia. *See:* **DIORIO Mary Ann Lucia.**

ST JOHN Nicole. *See:* **JOHNSTONE Norma.**

ST JOHN Patricia Mary, b. 5 Apr 1919, St Leonards, Sussex, England. *Appointment:* Missionary Nurse in Morocco, 1949-76. *Publications:* Tanglewood Secret, 1948; Treasures of the Snow, 1950; Star of Light, 1953; Four Candles, Poems, 1956; Harold St John, 1960; A Missionary Muses on the Creed, 1961; Hudson Pope, 1962; Rainbow Garden, 1963; Missing the Way, 1966; Twice Freed, 1968; Breath of Life, 1970; Man of Two Worlds, 1972; The Mystery of Pheasant Cottage, 1978; Where the River Begins, 1981; Nothing Else Matters (in US as If You Love Me), 1982; Would You Believe It?, The Victor (in US as The Runaway, 1983; The Other Kitten, 1984; Friska My Friend, 1985; I Needed a Neighbour, 1988; Until the Day Breaks, 1990. *Contributions to:* Good Housekeeping; Witness; Christian Herald. *Honours:* Eisteddfod Poetry Prize, 1935; Book of the Month, Switzerland, 1953; Christian Novel of the Year, Publishers Conference, 1984. *Address:* 10 Preston Close, Canley, Coventry, England.

ST JOHN-STEVAS Norman (Anthony Francis), b. 1929, British, Law Biography, Conservative M.P.(UK) for Chelmsford Essex 1964-87. *Appointments:* Called to the Bar, Middle Temple, London, 1952; Lecturer, Southampton University, 1952-53; King's College, University of London, 1953-56; Tutor in Jurisprudence, Christ Church, 1953-55, Merton College, 1955-57; Oxford; Fellow, Yale University, New Have, CT, 1957; Legal and Political Correspondent, The Economist, 1959-64; Conservative MP (UK) for Chelmsford, Essex, 1964-87, Chancellor of the Duchy of Lancaster, Leader of the house of Commons, Minister for the Arts, 1979-81. *Publications:* Obscenity and the Law, 1956; Walter Bagehot, 1959; Life, Death and the Law, 1961; The Right to Life, 1963; Law and Morals, 1964; Walter Bagehot: The Works (ed), 11 volumes, 1966-78; The Agonising Choice, 1971; Pope John Paul II: His Travels and Mission, 1982; The Two Cities, 1984. *Contributions to:* Critical Quarterly; Modern Law Review; Criminal Law Review; Law and Contemporary Problems; Twentieth Century; Times Literary Supplement; Dublin Review. *Honours:* FRSL, 1966; PC, 1979; Life Peerage, 1987. *Address:* 34 Montpelier Square, London SW1, England.

ST OMER Garth, West Indian. *Publications:* A Room on the Hill, Shades of Grey, 1968; Nor Any Country, 1969; J Black Bam and the Masquerardes, 1972; The Lights on the Hill, 1985. *Address:* c/o Faber and Faber Limited, 3 Queen Square, London WC1N 3AU, England.

STACEY Nicholas Anthony Howard Industrialist. m. Marianne Louise Ehrhardt. *Education:* Fellow, Chartered Institute of Secretaries (FCIS); B Com. *Publications:* English Accountancy: A Study in Social and Economic History, 1954; Changing Patterns of Distribution, 1958; Industrial Market Research, 1960; Mergers in Modern Business, 1970; Living in an Alibi Society, 1989. *Contributions to:* Financial Times; Times; Guardian; Government and Opposition. *Memberships:* Reform Club; Chelsea Arts Club (Honorary Member). *Literary Agent:* Anne Dewe, Andrew Mann Ltd, 10 Old Compton Street, London W1V 5PH. *Address:* c/o Reform Club, Pall Mall, London SW1Y 5EW, England.

STACEY Tom, b. 11 Jan 1930, Bletchingley, England. Author. *Education:* Oxford University. *Publications:* The Hostile Sun, 1953; The Brothers M, 1960; Summons to Ruwenzori, 1964; Today's World, 1968; The Living and the Dying, 1975; The Pandemonium, 1979; The Worm in the Rose, 1985; Deadline, 1988; Bodies and Souls, 1989; Decline, 1991. *Contributions to:* Numerous journals. *Honours:* John Llewellyn Rhys Memorial Prize, 1954; Granada Award, 1961; Fellow, Royal Society of Literature, 1977. *Literary Agent:* Jacintha Alexander. *Address:* 128 Kensington Church Street, London W8, England.

STACK George Joseph b. New York, New York, USA. Professor of Philosophy. m. Claire A Avena, 8 Sept 1962 (deceased 1985), 1 son, 1 daughter. *Education:* BA, Social Science, Pace University, New York, 1960; MA, Philosophy, 1962, PhD, Philosophy, 1964, Pennsylvania State University, State College. *Publications:* Kierkegaard's Existential Ethics, 1977; Kierkegaard's Existential Ethics (Japanese translation) 1985, UK 1992; Berkeley's Analysis of Perception, Mouton and Co 1970, Humanities Press 1972, Peter Lang, 1992; On Kierkegaard: Philosophical Fragments, Fini Lokkes Vorlag, Copenhagen, 1976, Humanities Press, 1976; Sartre's Philosophy of Social Existence, 1978; Lange and Nietzsche (selected as an important recent work in Philosophy, published between 1982-86 in English, by the Philosophy Documentation Center in 1991), 1983; Nietzsche and Emerson, 1992. *Contributions to:* Over 310 articles and reviews published in professional journals. *Memberships:* American Philosophical Association; Society for the Advancement of American Philosophy; North American Nietzsche Society. *Address:* Department of Philosophy, 139 FOB, SUNY-Brockport, Brockport, NY 14420, USA.

STADTLER Beatrice, b. 26 June 1921, Cleveland, Ohio, USA. Educator; Writer. m. Oscar Stadtler, 31 Jan 1945, 1 son, 2 daughters. *Education:* Diploma, Sunday School Teachers, 1957; Bachelor, Judaic Studies, 1971; MSc., Religious Education, 1983; Master of Jewish Studies, 1988. *Appointments:* Weekly Column, Cleveland Jewish News for Youth, 1962; Weekly Column, Boston Jewish Advocate, 1975. *Publications:* Once Upon a Jewish Holiday, 1965; The Adventures of Gluckel of Hamein, 1967; Personalities of the American Jewish Labor Movement, 1968; The Story of Dona Gracia Mendes, 1969; The Holocaust: A History of Courage and Resistance, 1975; Significant Lives, 1976; Rescue from the Sky, translated into Hebrew, 1978; Chapters In: The Holocaust, 1976, and Genocide; A Search for Conscience; Chapter: Anthology on Armed Jewish Resistance during the Holocaust, 1939-1945; Chapter, The Second Jewish Catalog, Heranca Judaica. *Contributions to:* World Over; Davka; Jewish Education; Young Judaean, Shofar; Olomeinu; Update; Outlook; Our Age; Keeping Posted; Israel Philatelist, Judaica Journal; Jewish Digest. *Honours:* Jewish Book Council Award for best Jewish Juvenile in America, for The Holocaust, 1975; Jewish Library Association of Great Cleveland, Citation, 1975. *Memberships:* Ohio State Holocaust Education Committee; United States Holocaust Memorial Council, Education Committee; Ohioana Library Association. *Address:* 24355 Tunbridge Lane, Beachwood, OH 44122, USA.

STAFFORD Fiona Jane, b. 27 July 1960, Lincoln, England. English Lecturer. m. Malcolm Sparkes, 2 Apr 1988, 1 son. *Education:* BA English Literature, Leicester University, 1981; MPhil, English Romantic Studies, 1983, DPhil, 1986, Oxon. *Publications:* The Sublime Savage: James Macpherson and the Poems of Ossian, 1988. *Contributions include:* Various articles and book reviews in a variety of magazines and journals and books. *Address:* Somerville College, Oxford, England.

STAHL Hilda Ann, b. 13 Sept 1938, Chadron, Nebraska, USA. Author, Children's Books, Romances. m. Norman Stahl, 1 Aug 1959, 4 sons, 3 daughters. *Education:* Normal degree, Teachers College, Wayne, Nebraska, 1956; Diploma, Famous Writers School, 1967; Diploma, Writers Digest School, 1978. *Publications include:* 18 volumes, Elizabeth Gail series, 1979-84; 7 volumes, Tina series, 1980-82; 14 volumes

Teddy Jo series, 1982-86; 6 volumes, Tyler Twins series, 1986-88; 5 volumes, Wren House Mysteries series, 1986-87; 5 volumes Prairie Family Adventure Series, 1989-; 3 volumes Super JAM Series, 1989-; 4 volumes Amber Ainslie Detective Series, 1989-; Gently Touch Sheela Jenkins, 1989. *Contributions to:* Numerous publications, religious & educational. *Honour:* Silver Angel Award, for Sadie Rose and the Daring Escape. *Memberships:* Society of Children's Book Writers; Romance Writers of America. *Address:* 5891 Wood School Road, Freeport, MI 49325, USA.

STAICAR Thomas Edward, b. 30 May 1946, Detroit, Michigan, USA. Writer. m. 27 Apr 1975. *Education:* BA, Political Science, Wayne State University. *Appointments:* Science Fiction General Editor, Frederick Ungar Publishing Co., 1980-82; Book Review Columnist, Amazing Stories Magazine, 1979-82, Fantastic Stories Magazine, 1982. *Major Publications:* Fritz Leiber, 1983; Critical Encounters II (essays) Editor, 1982; The Feminine Eye (essays), Editor, 1982. *Contributions to:* New Magazine Review; Science Fiction Review; SF & Fantasy Book Review; New England Senior Citizen; Ann Arbor News; Twilight Zone magazine; others. *Address:* 2109 Medford Road, Apt 34, Ann Arbor, MI 48104, USA.

STAINES David, b. 8 Aug 1946, Toronto, Ontario, Canada. Educator; Writer. *Education:* BA, University of Toronto, 1967; AM, 1968, PhD, 1973, Harvard University. *Appointments:* Assistant Professor of English, Harvard University, 1973-78; Honarary Research Fellow, University College London, 1977-78; Associate Professor, 1978-85, Professor of English, 1985-, University of Ottawa, Five College Professor of Canadian Studies, Smith College, 1982-84. *Publications:* Editor: The Canadian Imagination: Dimensions of a Literary Culture, 1977; Stephen Leacock: A Reappraisal, 1986; The Forty-ninth and Other Parallels: Contemporary Canadian Perspectives, 1986; Author: Tennyson's Camelot: The Idylls of the King and Its Medieval Sources, 1982; Translator: The Complete Romances of Chretien de Troyes, 1990. *Contributions to:* Studies in Philology; Modern Language Review; Speculum; and many others. *Honours:* Fellowships: National Endowment for the Humanities, 1977-78; Huntington Library, 1979; Newberry Library, 1980; Social Sciences and Humanities Research Council of Canada, 1986-87. *Memberships include:* Executive Committee, International Arthurian Society, 1991-94; Standing Committee, Medieval Academy of America. VP, Association for Canadian and Quebec Literatures, 1988-1990; Modern Language Association. *Address:* Department of English, University of Ottawa, Ottawa, Ontario, Canada K1N 6N5.

STAINES Trevor. *See:* **BRUNNER John Kilian Houston.**

STALLWORTHY Jon, b. 18 Jan 1935, London, England. Poet. m. Gillian Waldock, 25 June 1960, 3 children. *Education:* Dragon School, Oxford, 1940-48; Rugby School, Warwickshire, 1948-53; Served as Lieutenant in Oxfordshire and Buckinghamshire Light Infantry, seconded to the Royal West African Frontier Force; Served for fifteen months in Nigeria, 1954-55; BA 1958, B Litt 1961, Magdalen College, Oxford. *Appointments:* Editor, Oxford University Press, London, 1959-71; Editor for Clarendon Press, Oxford, 1974-77; Deputy Academic Publisher, Oxford University Press, Oxford, 1972-77; Visiting Fellow, All Souls College, Oxford, 1971-72; John Wendell Anderson Professor of English Literature, Cornell University, Ithaca, New York, USA, 1977-86; Reader in English Literature, Oxford University, 1988-92; Professor of English Literature, Oxford University, 1992-. *Publications:* Books: The Earthly Paradise, 1958; The Astronomy of Love, 1961; Between the Lines: Yeats's Poetry in the Making, 1963; Out of Bounds, 1963; The Almond Tree, 1967; A Day in the City, 1967; Vision and Revision in Yeats's Last Poems, 1969; Root and Branch, London: 1969, New York: 1969; Positives, 1969; A Dinner of Herbs, 1970; Hand in Hand, London: 1974, New York: 1974; The

Apple Barrel: Selected Poems 1955-63, 1974; Wilfred Owen: A Biography, London: 1974, New York: 1975; Poets of the First World War, 1974; A Familiar Tree, London: 1978, New York: 1978. Other works include: Boris Pasternak, Selected Poems, translated by Stallworthy and France, 1982; The Complete Poems and Fragments of Wilfred Owen, edited by Stallworthy, 1983; The Oxford Book of War Poetry, edited by Stallworthy, 1984; The Poems of Wilfred Owen, edited by Stallworthy, 1985; First Lines: poems written in youth from Herbert to Heaney, 1987; Henry Reed: collected poems, 1991. *Memberships:* FRSL; FBA. *Address:* Wolfson College, Oxford OX2 6UD, England.

STAMBLER Irwin, b. 20 Nov 1924, USA. Author; Editor; Publisher. m. Constance Gay, 5 Nov 1950, 2 sons, 2 daughters. *Education:* BS, MS, New York University College of Engineering. *Publications:* over 50 books published including: Ocean Liners of the Air, 1969; Encyclopedia of Folk, Country & Western Music, 1969; Guitar Years: Pop Music from Country & Western to Hard Rock, 1970; Great Moments in Stock Car Racing, 1971; Golden Guitars, Story of Country Music, 1971; Revolution in Light: Losers and Holography, 1972; Unusual Automobiles of Today and Tomorrow, 1972; Shorelines of America, 1972; Speed Kings: World's Fastest Humans, 1973; Women in Sports, 1974; Encyclopedia of Pop, Rock & Soul, 1974; Supercars and the Men Who Drive Them, 1976; Bill Walton, Super Center, 1976; Here Come the Funny Cars, 1976; Minibikes and Small Cycles, 1977; Encyclopaedia of Pop, Rock & Soul, 1977; Top Fuelers, Drag Racing Royalty, 1978; Racing the Sprint Cars, 1979; Dream Machines: Vans & Pickups, 1980; Encyclopedia of Folk, Country & Western Music, 1983; New Edition Encyclopaedia of Pop, Rock & Soul, 1989, updated 1990; Book of the Month Club selection; Forthcoming: 2 volume edition, Encyclopedia of Folk, Country and Western. *Contributions to:* various journals and magazines. *Honour:* Encyclopedia of Folk, Country & Western Music named one of the Reference Works of the Year by Library Journal. *Memberships:* Aviation/Space Writers Association; Country Music Association. *Address:* 205 S Beverly Drive, Ste 208, Beverly Hills, CA 90212, USA.

STAMEY Sara (Lucinda), b. 23 Jan 1953, Bellingham, Washington, USA. Writer; Teacher. m. Jesse Berst, Feb 1976 (div 1979). *Education:* Attended University of Puget Sound, 1971-73; BA, Magna cum laude, Western Washington University, 1981, graduate study 1988-. *Appointments:* Nuclear reactor control operator in hanford, Washington and San Onofre, California, 1974-78; scuba diving instructor in Mediterranean. the Virgin Islands and Honduras, 1982-87; writer 1987-. Teacher of English composition. *Publications:* Wild Card Run (science fiction novel), Berkley Publishing, 1987; Win, Lose, Draw (science fiction novel) Berkley Publishing, 1988; Double Blind (science fiction novel) Berkley Publishing, 1989. *Memberships:* Science Fiction Writers of America, Pacific Northwest Writers Conference. *Literary Agent:* Merilee Heifetz, Writer's House, 21 West 16th Street, New York, NY 10010, USA. *Address:* 324 North State Street, No 1, Bellingham, WA 98225, USA.

STAMP Robert Miles, b. 11 Feb 1937, Toronto, Canada. Writer; Bookseller. m. Arlene Louise Smith, 27 Aug 1960. 1 son, 1 daughter. *Education:* BA, History 1959, PhD, History 1970, University of Western Ontario; MA, History, University of Toronto, 1962. *Publications:* The Schools of Ontario 1876-1976, 1982; The World of Tomorrow, 1986; QEW: Canada's First Super Highway, 1987; Kings, Queens and Canadians, 1987; Royal Rebels, 1988; Riding The Radials, 1989; Early Days in Richmond Hill, 1991; Bridging the Burder, 1992. *Address:* 866 Palmerston Ave, Toronto, Canada M6G 2S2.

STAMPER Alex. *See:* **KENT Arthur.**

STANFILL Dorothy McMahen, b. 22 Dec 1911, Stanton, Texas, USA. Freelance Writer, retired. m.

Charles Tillman Stanfill, 21 June 1941, dec, 1 son. *Education:* BA, 1962. *Appointments:* Fiction Editor, Old Hickory Review, 1969. *Publications:* Kaiharine And The Quarter Mile Drag; Goodbye Ocie May. *Contributions to:* Numerous inc. Texas Review; Mississippi Review; Delta Scene; Southern Review; South & West; New Writers; Pen Women Magazine. *Honours:* 2 First Places, Deep South Writers Conference; Numerous State & National Prizes. *Memberships:* ASPW; Jackson Writers Group. *Literary Agent:* Diane Cleaver, Nat Sohel. *Address:* 1585 Hollywood Drive, Apt B-10, Jackson, TX 38305, USA.

STANGL Jean, b. 14 May 1928, Missouri, USA. Author; Teacher. m. Herbert Stangl, 14 Aug 1946, 3 sons. *Education:* Master Early Childhood, 1977; BA Human Development, 1975; Community College, Adult Education Credential. *Publications:* Paper Stories; Crystals and Crystal Gardens; Tools of Science; H2O Science; Story Sparklers. *Contributions to:* Numerous. *Honours:* International Reading Association, Literacy award; Honorary Life Member Parent/Teacher Association. *Memberships:* Ventura County Reading Association; Society of Childrens Book Writers; National Association for the Education of Young Children; Beatrix Potter Society. *Address:* 1658 Calle La Cumbre, Camarillo, CA 93010, USA.

STANLEY Bennett. *See:* **HOUGH Stanley Bennett.**

STANSFIELD Anne. *See:* **COFFMAN Virginia (Edith).**

STANSKY Peter David Lyman b. 18 Jan 1932, New York City, USA. Teacher; Writer. *Education:* BA, Yale University, 1953; BA 1955, MA 1959, King's College, Cambridge; PhD, Harvard University, 1961. *Publications:* Ambitions and Strategies, 1964; with W Abrahams, Journey to the Frontier, 1966; with W Abrahams, Orwell: the Transformation, 1979; Redesigning the World, 1985; with W Abrahams, The Unknown Orwell, 1972; William Gladstone, 1979; William Morris, 1983. *Contributions to:* Numerous journals and magazines. *Honours:* D L (Hon) Wittenburg University, 1984; Fellow, American Academy of Arts and Sciences; Guggenheim Fellowships 1966-67, 1973-74; NEH Senior Fellowship 1983; ACLS Fellowship, 1978-79. *Memberships:* President, North American Conference on British Studies; President, Pacific Coast Branch, American Historical Association; Victorian Society; Fellow, Royal Historical Society; Century Association, New York. *Literary Agent:* Lois Wallace. *Address:* 375 Pinehill Road, Hillsborough, CA 94010, USA.

STANTON Vance. *See:* **AVALLONE Michael.**

STAPLES Reginald Thomas (Robin Brewster, James Sinclair, Robert Tyler Stevens), b. 26 Nov 1911, London, England. Company Director. m. Florence Anne Hume, 12 June 1937, 1 son. *Education:* West Square Grammar School, 1923-28. *Publications include:* The Summer Day is Done; Appointments in Sarajevo; The Fields of Yesterday; Shadows in the Afternoon; Warrior Queen; Down Lambeth Way; Flight From Bucharest; Women of Cordova; The Professional Gentleman; The Hostage. *Memberships:* Society of Authors; The Brevet Flying Club. *Literary Agent:* Sheila Watson (Watson, Little Ltd). *Address:* Wenvoe, Dome Hill, Caterham, Surrey CR3 6EB, England.

STARER Robert, b. 8 Jan 1924, Vienna, Austria. Composer. m. Johanna Herz, 27 Mar 1942, 1 son. *Education:* State Academy Vienna, 1937-38; Jerusalem Conservatoire, 1938-43; Juilliard School, 1947-49. *Publications:* Rhythmic Training; Continuo a Life of Music. *Contributions to:* New Yorker; Musical America; New York Times; London Times. *Honours:* Guggenheim Fellowship, 1957, 1964; American Academy Institute of Arts and Letters. *Membership:* ASCAP. *Literary*

Agent: John Hawkins. *Address:* PO Box 946, Woodstock, NY 12498, USA.

STARK Joshua. *See:* **OLSEN Theodore Victor.**

STARK Richard. *See:* **WESTLAKE Donald E.**

STARKE Roland Adrian Malan, Novelist; Playwright; Screenwriter. *Publications:* Freedom Ceremony; Something Soft; I Never Touched You; The 14; Goodbye, Mr Chips, Stage Musical Adaptation, with Leslie Bricusse; Girlie; The Towers Open Fire. *Honours:* Golden Bear, Best Screenplay for film The 14. *Membership:* Writers' Guild. *Address:* c/o The Peter Fraser and Dunlop Group Ltd, 503/4 The Chambers, Chelsea Harbour, Lots Road, London SW10 0XF, England.

STARNES John Kennett, b. 5 Feb 1918, Montreal, Canada. Retired Diplomat. m. Helen Gordon Robinson, 10 May 1941, 2 sons. *Education:* Institute Sillig, Switzerland, 1935-36; University of Munich, Germany, 1936; Bishops University, BA, 1939. *Appointments:* Personal Assistant, Ottawa, 1945-48; Advisor, Canadian Delegation, 1948-50; Head, 1950-53; Counsellor, Canadian Embassy, 1953-56; Head of Defence Liaison, 1958-62; Ambassador to Federal Republic of Germany, 1962-66; Ambassador United Arab Republic, 1966-67; Assistant Undersecretary, State For External affairs, 1967-70; Director General, RCMP Security Service, 1970-73; Member Council, International Institute for Strategic Studies, 1977-85. *Publications:* Deep Sleepers, 1981; Scarab, 1982; Orions Belt, 1983; The Cornish Hug, 1985; Albric's Cloak - With a Publisher, 1986; Film & TV rights to first three books sold 1983. *Contributions to:* Numerous. *Honours:* Centennial Medal; DCL. *Memberships:* Writers' Union of Canada; 1155 (London); Canadian Institute of Strategic Studies; Canadian Institute of International Affairs; Board of Directors, The Canadian Writers Foundation; National Geographic Society. *Literary Agent:* Larry Hoffman, Toronto. *Address:* Apt 9 100, Rideau Terrace, Ottawa, Ontario, Canada K1M 0Z2.

STAROBINSKI Jean, b. 17 Nov 1920, Geneva, Switzerland. Writer. m. Jacqueline Sirman, 15 August, 1954, 3 sons. *Education:* PhD, Geneva, 1958; MD, Lausanne, 1960. *Publications:* Jean Jacques Rousseau: La Transparence et L'Obstacle, 1957; La Relation Critique, 1970; 1789: Les Emblemes de la Raison; Montaigne en Mouvement, 1983; Le Remede Dans le Mal, 1989. *Contributions to:* Le Monde, Magazine Litteraire, TLS, New York Book Review; Hudson Review, La Repubblica, Leggere, NZZ, FAZ. *Honours:* Cheval, Legion D'Honneur, 1980; AAAS; British Acadmy; Prix Europeene de l'Essai, 1983; Balzan Prize, 1984; Prix de Monaco, 1988. *Memberships:* President, Societe J J Rousseau, Geneva; President, Recontres Intern. de *Address:* Universite de Geneve, CH-1211, Geneva, Switzerland.

STARR Anne. *See:* **SANFORD Annette Schorre.**

STATHAM Frances Patton, b. York County, South Carolina, USA. Author; Musician; Artist; Lecturer. 2 sons, 1 daughter. *Education:* BS, magna cum laude, double major in voice and music education, Winthrop College; MFA, voice, University of Georgia; Honorary Doctorate, World University; further voice and opera study, Dr Ernesto Vinci, Royal Conservatory of Canada, Ralph Errolle, Rosa Simmons; Six years art study, Decatur Art Centre. *Career:* Author under contract: Random House/Ballantine, New York; Pan Ltd, London; Peruzzo Editor, Milan; Lucce Verlag, Bergisch Gladbach; Contributing Editor, Go Magazine, Atlanta; Past Choral Music Teacher, Winston-Salem, North Carolina City Schools and Dekalb County, Georgia Schools. *Honours:* Georgia Author of the Year, 1978, 1979, 1984; Many First Prizes in national competitions for novels, journalism, non-fiction and oil paintings; Frank Stiepitz Memorial Award, original music composition; IBC Medal of Congress, 1985; Bar 1987; Over 100 recent television and radio appearances; Slected as 1983 Image Maker, Atlanta Professional Women's Directory; Outstanding Alumna, 1980, Rock Hill, South Carolina High School Yearbook; Chosen Outstanding Volunteer in Community Service Volunteer, Dekalb; Valedictorian, 14 Certificates of Merit, 6 First Place State Awards in English, French, Drama, Voice, Solo Piano and Duet, Rock Hill South Carolina High School, Salutatorian, Winthrop College with Academic Honours. *Publications:* Novels: Bright Sun, Dark Moon, 1975; Flame of New Orleans, 1977; Jasmine Moon, 1978; Daughters of the Summer Storm, 1979; Phoenix Rising, 1983; From Love's Ashes, 1984; On Wings of Fire, 1985; To Face the Sun, 1986; The Roswell Women, 1987; The Roswell Legacy, 1988; various magazine articles, programme notes. *Memberships include:* Board of Trustees, Dixie Council of Authors and Journalists, Inc; Board of Directors, Dekalb Council of the Arts; Board of Directors and Past-President, Rabun Gap-Nacochee Guild; President, Georgia Branch, National League of American Pen Women, Inc; Authors Guild; Authors League of America, and many other professional, academic and community memberships. *Address:* PO Box 29892, Atlanta, GA 30359, USA.

STAVE Bruce M(artin) b. 17 May 1937, New York City, USA. Historian. m. Sondra T Astor, 16 June 1961, 1 son. *Education:* AB, Columbia College, 1959; MA, Columbia University, 1961; PhD, University of Pittsburgh, 1966. *Appointments:* Professor 1975; Director, Center for Oral History, 1981-, Chairman, Department of History 1985-, University of Connecticut. *Publications:* The New Deal and the Last Hurrah, 1970; Urban Bosses, Machines and Progressive Reformers, 1972, 1984; The Discontented Society, co-editor, 1972; Socialism in the Cities, contributing editor, 1975; The Making of Urban History, 1977; Modern Industrial Cities, 1981; Talking About Connecticut, 1985, 1990; Mills & Meadows: A Pictorial History of Northeast Connecticut, co-author, 1991. *Contributions to:* Journal of Urban History; Americana Magazine; International Journal of Oral History. *Honours:* Harvey Kantor Memorial Award for Significant Work in Oral History, New England Association of Oral History, 1977; Fulbright Professorships, India 1968-69, Australia, New Zealand, Philippines 1977, People's Republic of China, 1984; NEH Fellow, 1974. *Memberships:* Connecticut Academy of Arts and Sciences; Vice President, President Elect, New England Historical Association; President, New England Association of Oral History; President and Founder, Connecticut Co-ordinating Committee for Promotion of History; Oral History Association; Board of Directors, Urban History Association, 1989-92; American Historical Association; Organization of American Historians, Immigration History Society. *Address:* 200 Broad Way, Coventry, CT 06238, USA.

STEAD C(hristian) K(arlson), b. 1932, New Zealand. Author; University Educator. *Appointments:* Lecturer in Literature, University of New England, New South Wales, Australia, 1956-57; Faculty Member, 1960-86, Professor of English, 1969-86, Auckland University, New Zealand; Chairman, New Zealand Literary Fund, 1973-75. *Publications:* Whether the Will Is Free: Poems 1954-62, 1964; The New Poetic: Yeats to Eliot, 1964; New Zealand Short Stories: Second Series (editor), 1966; Smith's Dream, novel, 1971; Measure for Measure: A Casebook (editor), 1971; Crossing the Bar, 1972; Selected Letters and Journals of Katherine Mansfield (editor), 1973; Quesada: Poems 1972-74, 1975; Walking Westward, 1978; Five for the Symbol, short stories, 1981; In the Glass Case: Essays on New Zealand Literature, 1981; Collected Stories of Maurice Duggan (editor), 1981; Geographies, 1982; Poems of a Decade, 1983; Paris, 1984; All Visitors Ashore, novel, 1984; Pound, Yeats, Eliot, and the Modernist Movement, 1986; The Death of the Body, novel, 1986. *Address:* 37 Tohunga Crescent, Parnell, Auckland 1, New Zealand.

STEADMAN Mark Sidney, b. 2 July 1930, Statesboro, Georgia, USA. College Professor. m. Joan Marie Anderson, 29 Mar 1952, 3 sons. *Education:*

Emory University, BA, 1951; Florida State University, MA, 1956; PhD, 1963. *Appointments:* Writer in Residence, Clemson University, 1980. *Publications:* McAfee County; A Lions Share; Angel Child; Bang Up Season. *Contributions to:* Southern Review; South Carolina Review; Kennesaw Review; Nova. *Honours:* Winthrop Fiction Award; NEA creative Writing Fellowship. *Memberships:* South carolina Writers Workshop; South Atlantic Modern Language Association. *Literary Agent:* Lois Wallace. *Address:* 450 Pin du Lac Drive, Central, SC 29630, USA.

STEBEL Sidney Leo, (Leo Bergson: Steve Toron), b. 28 June 1923, Iowa, USA. Writer. m. Jan Mary Dingler, 10 Sept 1954, 1 daughter. *Education:* BA English Literature, University of Southern California, 1949. *Appointments:* Adjunct Professor, Masters of Professional Writing, USC, 1991. *Publications:* The Collaborator, 1968; The Vorovich Affair, 1975; The Shoe Leather Treatment, 1983; Spring Thaw, 1989; The Boss's Wife, 1992; The Widowmaster, 1967; Main Street, 1971. *Contributions to:* West Magazine; Air Mail; Botteghe Obscure; Story Magazine; Connoiseur's World; Architectural Digest; Calendar; LA Times; Sunday Book Review. *Honours:* International Secretary, PEN Centre, USA West. *Memberships:* Writers Guild of America West; Australian Writers Guild. *Literary Agent:* Don Congdon, New York City. *Address:* 1963 Mandeville Canyon Road, Los Angeles, CA 90040, USA.

STEEL Ronald, b. 25 Mar 1931, USA. Writer; Professor. *Education:* BA, Northwestern University, 1953; MA, Harvard University, 1955. *Publications:* Walter Lippmann and the American Century, 1980; Imperialists and Other Heroes, 1971; Pax Americana, 1967; The End of Alliance : America & the Future of Europe, 1964. *Contributions to:* New York Review of Books; New Republic. *Honours:* Sidney Hillman Prize, 1967; National Book critics Circle Award, 1980; Bancroft Prize, 1980; American Book Award, 1981; Los Angeles Times Book Prize, 1980; Washington Monthly Book Prize, 1981. *Memberships:* Council on Foreign Relations; Society of American Historians; American Historical Association. *Literary Agent:* Morton Janklow, New York. Address: School of International Relations, University of Southern California, Los Angeles, CA 90089, USA.

STEELE Danielle. Author. m. 9 children. *Publications:* 33 novels including: Daddy, 1989; Zoya, 1989; Heartbeat, 1991; No Greater Love, 1991; Jewels, 1992. 1 non-fictional work: Having A Baby, 1984. 8 children's books and 1 poetry book. *Address:* USA.

STEELE Mary Q(uintard) Govan (Wilson Gage), b. 1922, USA. Author. *Publications:* Secret of Fiery Gorge (as Wilson Gage), 1960; A Wild Goose Tale (as Wilson Gage), 1961; Dan and the Miranda (as Wilson Gage), 1962; Big Blue Island (as Wilson Gage), 1964; Miss Osborne - the Mop (as Wilson Gage), 1965; Ghost of Fire Owl Farm (as Wilson Gage), 1966; Journey Outside, 1969; Mike's Toads (as Wilson Gage), 1970; The Living Year, 1972; The First of the Penguins, 1983; The Eye in the Forest (with W O Steele), 1975; Because of the Sand Witches There, 1975; The True Men, 1976; Squash Pie (as Wilson Gage), 1976; Down in the Boondocks (as Wilson Gage), 1977; The Fifth Day (editor), 1978; The Owl's Kiss, 1978; Wish, Come True, 1979; Mrs Gaddy and the Ghost (as Wilson Gage), 1979; The Life (and Death) of Sarah Elizabeth Harwood, 1980; Cully Cully and the Bear (as Wilson Gage), 1982; The Crow and Mrs Gaddy (as Wilson Gage), 1984; Mrs Gaddy and the Fast Growing Vine (as Wilson Gage), 1985. *Literary Agent:* Greenwillow, Morrow, USA. *Address:* c/o Greenwillow, Morrow, 105 Madison Avenue, New York, NY 10016, USA.

STEELE Timothy Reid, b.22 Jan 1948, Burlington, Vermont, USA. Writer; Teacher. m. Victoria Lee Erpelding, 14 Jan 1979. *Education:* BA, Stanford University, 1970; PhD, Brandeis University, 1977. *Appointments:* Jones Lecturer in Poetry, Stanford

University, 1975-77; Lecturer in English, University of California at Los Angeles, 1977-83; Lecturer in English, University of California at Santa Barbara, 1986; Professor in English, California State University, Los Angeles, 1987-. *Publications:* Sapphics Against Anger and Other Poems, 1986; Uncertainties and Rest, 1979; Missing Measures: Modern Poetry and the Revolt Against Meter, 1990. The Prudent Heart, 1983; Nine Poems 1984; On Harmony 1984; Short Subjects. 1985; Beatitudes, 1988. *Contributions to:* Poetry; Paris Review; New Criterion, Threepenny Review in USA; Numbers; PN Review; The Spectator in UK. *Honours:* Stegner Fellowship in Poetry, 1972-73; Guggenheim Fellowship, 1984-85; Peter IB Lavan Younger Poet Award, Academy of American Poets, 1986. *Memberships:* Academy of American Poets; Modern Language Association. *Address:* 1801 Preuss Road, Los Angeles, CA 90035, USA.

STEFFLER John Earl, b. 13 Nov 1947, Toronto, Canada. Writer; Professor. m. Shawn O'Hagan, 30 May 1970, 1 son, 1 daughter. *Education:* MA, University of Guelph, 1974; BA, University of Toronto, 1971. *Publications:* An Explanation of Yellow; The Grey Islands; The Wreckage of Play; The Afterlife of George Cartwright; Flights of Magic. *Contributions to:* Malahat Review; Canadian Literature; Event; Poetry Canada; Queens Quarterly; Descant; Orbis; Fiddlehead. *Honours:* Norma Epstein Prize; Canada Council Award; Ontario Arts Council And Newfoundland Arts Council Award. *Memberships:* League of Canadian Poets; PEN; Writers Alliance of Newfoundland & Labrador. *Literary Agent:* Susan Schulman, 454 West 44th Street, New York, NY 10036, USA. *Address:* Department of English, Sir Wilfred Grenfell College, Memorial University of New Foundland, Corner Brook, NF, Canada A2H 6P9.

STEGNER Wallace (Earle), b. 1909, USA. Author; Former Professor. *Appointments:* Instructor: Augustana College, Rock Island, Illinois, 1934; University of Utah, Salt Lake City, 1934-37; University of Wisconsin, Madison, 1937-39; Faculty Instructor, Harvard University, Cambridge, Massachusetts, 1939-45; Professor of English, 1945-69, Jackson Eli Reynolds Professor of the Humanities, 1969-71, Stanford University, Stanford, California; Honorary Consultant, Library of Congress, 1973-77. *Publications:* Remembering Laughter, 1937; The Potter's House, 1938; On a Darkling Plain, 1940; Fire and Ice, 1941; Mormon Country, 1942; The Big Rock Candy Mountain, 1943; One Nation (co-author), 1945; Second Growth, 1947; The Women on the Wall, 1950; The Preacher and the Slave, 1950, reissued as Joe Hill: A Biographical Novel, 1969; Beyond the Hundredth Meridian, 1954; The City of the Living, 1956; A Shooting Star, 1961; Wolf Willow, 1962; The Gathering of Zion, 1964; All the Little Live Things, 1967; The Sound of Mountain Water, 1969; Angle of Repose, 1971; The Uneasy Chair, 1974; The Spectator Bird, 1976; Recapitulation, 1979; American Places (with Page Stegner), 1981; One Way to Spell Man, 1982; Crossing to Safety, 1987; Collected Stories, 1990; Where the Bluebird Sings to the Lemonade Springs, 1992. *Honours:* Pulitzer Prize, 1972; National Book Award, 1977. *Memberships:* American Academy and Institute of Arts and Letters; American Academy of Arts and Sciences; Phi Beta Kappa; Society of American Histories. *Literary Agent:* Brandt and Brandt, No1 Broadway, NYC 10036, USA. *Address:* 13456 South Fork Lane, Los Altos Hills, CA 94022, USA.

STEIN Peter Gonville, b. 29 May 1926, Liverpool, England. Professor of Law. m. Anne M Howard, 16 Aug 1978, 3 daughters by previous marriage. *Education:* BA 1949, LLB 1950, Gonville and Caius College, Cambridge; University of Pavia 1951-52; Admitted as Solicitor, 1951. *Appointments:* Regius Professor of Civil Law at the University of Cambridge 1968-93; Professor of Jurisprudence, University of Aberdeen, 1956-68. *Publications:* Regulae iuris: from juristic rules to legal maxims, 1966; Legal Values in Western Society (with J Shand) 1974, Italian translation 1981; Legal Evolution: the story of an idea, 1980, Japanese translation 1989; Legal Institutions: the development of dispute settlement, 1984, Italian translation, 1987; The Character and Influence of the Roman Civil Law: historical essays, 1988; The Teaching of Roman Law in Twelfth Century England (with F de Zulueta), 1990. *Honours:* Fellow, British Academy, 1974; Hon Dr iuris, Gottingen University, 1980; Foreign Fellow, Italian National Academy (Lincei) 1987; Hon Dott. Giur. Ferrara University, 1991; Q.C. (Hon), 1993. *Memberships:* Vice-President, Selden Society, 1984-87; President, Society of Public Teachers of Law, 1980-81; Belgian National Academy, 1991. *Address:* Queen's College, Cambridge CB3 9ET, England.

STEIN Sol, b. 1926, USA. Author; Publisher. *Appointments:* Lecturer, Social Studies, City College, New York City, 1948-51; Editor, Voice of America, US State Deaprtment, 1951-53; Consultant, Harcourt Bruce Jovanovich, New York City, 1958-69; Lecturer, Columbia University, New York City, 1958-60; Executive Vice-President, Mid-Century Book Society, 1959-62; President, Stein & Day, publishers, Briarcliff Manor, New York, 1962-. *Publications:* The Illegitimist, play, 1953; A Shadow of My Enemy, play, 1957; The Husband, 1969; The Magician, 1971; Living Room, 1974; The Childkeeper, 1975; Other People, 1979; The Resort, 1980; The Touch of Treason, 1985.

STEINBACH Meredith Lynn, b. 18 Mar 1949, Ames, Iowa, USA. Novelist; Professor. m. Charles Ossian Hartman, 5 May 1979 (div 1991), 1 son. *Education:* BGS, 1973, MFA, 1976, University of Iowa. *Appointments:* Teaching Fellow, University of Iowa, 1975-76; Writer in Residence, Antioch College, 1976-77; Lecturer, Fiction, Northwestern University, 1977-79; Visiting Assistant Professor, University of Washington, 1979-82; Bunting Fellow, Radcliffe-Harvard, 1982-83; Assistant Professor, Brown University, 1983-; Associate Professor, Brown University. *Publications:* Novels: Zara, 1982; Here Lies The Water, 1990; The Birth of The World As We Know It, (forthcoming). Short stories: Reliable Light, 1990. *Contributions to:* Tri-Quarterly Magazine; Antaeus; Massachusetts Review; Antioch Review; South West Review; Black Warrior Review. *Honours:* Pushcart Prize, Best of the Small Presses, 1977; Fellow NEA, (National Endowment fore the Arts), 1978; Bunting Fellow, Bunting Summer Fellow, Mary Ingraham Bunting Institute, Radcliffe College, Harvard, 1982-83; Rhode Island Artists Fellowship, 1986-87; O Henry Award, 1990. *Memberships:* PEN; Associated Writing Programme. *Address:* Dept. of English, Brown University, Box 1852, Providence, RI 02912, USA.

STEINEM Gloria, b. 25 Mar 1934, USA. Writer; Journalist; Feminist. *Education:* Smith College; Chester-Bowles Asian Fellow, India, 1957-58. *Appointments:* Co-director, Indian Research Service, Massachusetts/ New York, 1959-60; Editorial assistant, contributing editor, freelance writer, various national & New York publications, 1960-; Co-founder, New York Magazine 1968, Ms Magazine 1971 (columnist 1980-); Active, various civil rights, peace campaigns. *Publications:* The Thousand Indias, 1957; The Beach Book, 1963; Marilyn, 1986. *Contributions to:* Various anthologies. *Honours:* Penney-Missouri Journalism Award, 1970; Ohio Governor's Award for Journalism, 1972; Woman of the Year, McCall's Magazine, 1972; Fellow, Woodrow Wilson International Centre for Scholars, 1977. *Address:* c/o Ms Magazine, 119 West 40th Street, New York, NY 10018, USA.

STEINER George, b. 23 Apr 1929, Paris, France (American citizen). Writer; Scholar. m. Zara Shakow, 1955, 1 son, 1 daughter. *Education:* Universities of Paris & Chicago; Harvard University; Balliol College, Oxford, UK. *Appointments include:* Editorial staff, The Economist, London, 1952-56; Fellow, Director of English Studies 1961-69, Extraordinry Fellow 1969-, Churchill College, Cambridge, UK; Visiting Professor, New York University 1966-67, Yale University 1970-71; Professor of English & Comparative Literature, University of Geneva, Switzerland, 1974-; Lecturer, worldwide. *Publications include:* Tolstoy or Dostoevsky, 1959; The Death of Tragedy, 1961; Anno Domini: Three Stories,

1964; Editor, Penguin Book of Modern Verse, translation, 1967; Language & Silence, 1967; Extraterritorial, 1971; In Bluebeard's Castle, 1971; The Sporting Scene: White Knights in Reykjavik, 1973; Field of Force, 1974; Nostalgia for the Absolute (Massey Lectures), 1974; After Babel, 1975; Heidegger, 1978; On Difficulty & Other Essays, 1978; The Portage of A.H. to San Cristobal, 1981; Antigones, 1984; George Steiner: A Reader, 1984; Real Presences, in there anything in what we say? 1989; Proofs and Three Parables, 1992. *Honours include:* O Henry Short Story Award, 1958; FRSL, 1964; Zabel Award of National Institute of Arts and Letters of the USA, 1970; Guggenheim Fellowship. 1971-72; Faulkner Stripend for Fiction, PEN, 1983; Hon DLitt; Winner, Macmillan Silver Pen Award for Fiction, Proofs and Three Parables, 1993. *Address:* 32 Barrow Road, Cambridge, England.

STEINHARDT Nancy R Shatzman, b. 14 July 1954, St Louis, MO, USA. Art Historian. m. Paul Joseph Steinhardt, 1 July 1979, 3 sons. *Education:* AB Washington University, 1974; AM, 1975, PhD, 1981, Harvard. *Publications:* Chinese Imperial City Planning, 1990; Chinese Traditional Architecture, 1984. *Contributions to:* More than 20 scholarly articles and 10 reviews. *Memberships:* College Art Association; Association for Asian Studies; Society of Architectural Historians. *Address:* Department of Asian and Middle Eastern Studies, University of Pennsylvania, Philadelphia, PA 19104, USA.

STEINKE Ann E, b. 5 Nov 1946, River Falls, Wisconsin, USA. Writer. m. William P Steinke, 28 Oct 1967, Penn Yan, New York. 1 son, 1 daughter. *Major Publications:* An Ocean of Love, (as E Reynolds), 1982; The Rare Gem (as A Williams), 1982; Love for the Taking, (as B Christopher), 1983; Sailboat Summer, 1983; Jeff's New Girl, 1984; The Perfect Boy (as E Reynolds), 1986; Stolen Kisses, (as E Reynolds), 1986; Taking Risks, (as E Reynolds), 1986; Rivals, 1986; Stealing Secrets, 1986; Falling in Love, 1987; Saying No, 1987; Marie Curie, A Biography, 1987. *Membership:* Charter Member of Romance Writers of America, 1982-. *Literary Agent:* Denise Marcil, New York. *Address:* 17 Sutton Park Road, Poughkeepsie, NY 12603, USA.

STEINMETZ Leon, b. 10 Oct 1944, Russia. Writer; Painter. m. Inga Karetnikova, 23 Dec 1963, 1 stepson. *Education:* Moscow Academy of Arts School. *Appointments:* Visiting Professor, Williams College, 1981; Massachusetts College of Art, 1982-; Harvard University, 1983-; Wellesley College, 1983. *Publications:* Hans Clodhopper; The story of Ricky the Royal Dwarf; Clocks in the Woods; Pip Stories; Mexico According to Eiseustein; Old Dog Sirko; Stumpy; The Long Day of the Giants. *Contributions to:* National Review; Commentary; Webster Review; Chronicles. *Honours:* Biennale of European Artists and Sculptors; Childrens Reading Round Table Book Award; Bread Loaf Writers Conference Award. *Memberships:* The Rockford Institute, Rockford. *Literary Agent:* Mitchell Rose Literary Agency, 688 Avenue of the Americas, Suite 302, New York, NY 10010. *Address:* Cambridge, Massachusetts 02138, USA.

STEINMETZ S J Paul Bernard, b. 10 July 1928, St Louis, Missouri, USA. Associate Pastor, Catholic Priest of the Society of Jesus. *Education:* BA Philosophy and Letters, St Louis University, 1954; MLitt, Religious Studies, University of Aberdeen, Scotland, 1956; PhD Anthropology of Religion, University of Stockholm, Sweden, 1980. *Publications:* Meditation with Native Americans: Lakota Spirituality, 1984; Pipe, Bible and Peyote Among the Oglala Lakota: A Study of Religious Identity, 1990. *Contributions to:* American Indian Culture and Research Journal. *Address:* St Rita Catholic Church, 13645 Paddock Drive, West Palm Beach, FL 33414, USA.

STEPHAN John Jason, b. 8 Mar 1941, Chicago, Illinois, USA. Professor; Historian. m. 22 June 1963. *Education:* BA, 1963, MA, 1964, Harvard University; PhD, University of London, England, 1969. *Appointments:* Far Eastern Editor, Harvard Review, 1962; Visiting Fellow, St Antony's College, Oxford, 1977; Editorial Board, University of Hawaii Press, 1980-1992; Visiting Professor of History, Stanford University, 1986; Research Fellow, Kennan Institute of Advanced Russian Studies, 1987; Editor, Encyclopedia of Siberia, 1988-. *Publications:* Sakhalin: A History, 1971; The Kuril Islands: Russo-Japanese Frontier in the Pacific, 1974; The Russian Fascists, 1978; Hawaii under the Rising Sun, 1984; Soviet-American Horizons in the Pacific, with V.P. Chichkanov, 1986; The Russian Far East: A History, 1993. *Contributions to:* Modern Asian Studies; American Historical Review; Pacific Affairs; Pacific Community; Journal for Asian Studies; New York Times; Siberica; Pacifica; Australian Slavic and E European Studies. *Honours:* Fulbright Fellowship, 1967-68; Japan culture Translation Prize, 1973; Japan Foundation Fellowship, 1977; Sanwa Distinguished Scholar, Fletcher School of Law & Diplomacy, Tufts University, 1989; Distinguished Invited Speaker, Canadian historical Association, 1990. *Memberships:* Authors Guild; PEN; International House of Japan, Life Member; American Association for the Advancement of Slavic Studies, Life Member; American Historical Association; Canadian Historical Association. *Literary Agent:* John Hawkins & Associates, New York, USA. *Address:* Dept of History, University of Hawaii, 2530 Dole Street, Honolulu, HI 96822, USA.

STEPHEN George Martin, (Martin Stephen), b. 18 July 1949, England. Headmaster and Author. m. Jennifer Elaine Fisher, 21 July 1971. 3 sons. *Education:* BA English and History, University of Leeds, 1970; DipEd, 1971, PhD, 1976, both with distinctions, University of Sheffield. *Publications:* The Best of Saki Short Stories, 1993; The Great War and Modern Myth, 1993; Never Such Innocence, 1988; The Fighting Admirals, 1991; Sea Battles in Close Up, 1986; English Literature, 1991; British War Ship Designs since 1906, 1984; An Introductory Guide to English Literature, 1989; Studying Shakespeare, 1989. *Contributions to:* The Daily Telegraph; Conference, Agenda, The Times Literary Supplement, The Times Higher Education Supplement, Naval Review. *Memberships:* Associate Member of the Room, Gonville and Caius; Nautical Research Society; Naval Review; East India Club; Economics Research Council. *Address:* 80 Glege Road, Cambridge, CB1 4SZ, England.

STEPHEN Martin. *See:* **STEPHEN George Martin.**

STEPHEN-DE WINTERS Danielle. *See:* **TIMSON Keith.**

STEPHENS Blythe. *See:* **WAGNER Sharon Blythe.**

STEPHENS Casey. *See:* **WAGNER Sharon Blythe.**

STEPHENS Michael Gregory, b. 4 Mar 1946. Writer. 1 daughter. *Education:* City College of New York, BA, MA, 1976; Yale University, MFA, 1979. *Appointments:* Columbia University, Lecturer, 1977-91; Fordham University, Assistant Professor, 1979-85; Princeton University, Lecturer, 1987-91; New York University, Lecturer, 1989-91. *Publications:* Seasons at Coole; Lost in Seoul; Shipping Out; Jigs and Reels; Circles End. *Contributions to:* Ontario Review; Paris Review; Fiction; Fiction International; Ohio Review; Peguod; NY Times; Washington Post; Rolling stone; Village Voice; Baltimore Sun; International Herald Tribune. *Membership:* PEN. *Address:* c/o Spuyten Duyvil Press, Box 1852, New York, NY 10025, USA.

STEPHENS Reed. *See:* **DONALDSON Stephen R.**

STEPHENSON Hugh, b. 18 July 1938, England. Writer; Journalist; Teacher. m. Auriol Stevens, 1962, 2 sons, 1 daughter. *Education:* BA, New College, Oxford; University of California, Berkeley, USA. *Appointments* *include:* HM Diplomatic Service, 1964-69; Staff, The Times, 1968; Editor, The Times Business News, 1972-81; Editor, New Statesman, 1982-86; Professor of Journalism, City University, 1986-. *Publications:* The Coming Clash, 1972; Mrs Thatcher's First Year, 1980; Claret and Chips, 1982. *Honour:* President, Oxford Union, 1962. *Memberships include:* Committee to Review Functioning of Financial Institutions, 1977-80. *Address:* Graduate Centre for Journalism, 223-227 St John Street, London EC1, England.

STERLING Bruce, b. 1954, USA. Science Fiction Writer. *Publications:* Involution Ocean, 1977; The Artificial Kid, 1980; Schismatrix, 1985; Mirrorshades (editor), 1986. *Address:* 809-C West 12th Street, Austin, TX 78701, USA.

STERLING Maria Sandra. *See:* **FLOREN Lee.**

STERN Michael, b. 3 Aug 1910. Author; Journalist; Film Producer. 1 son, 1 daughter. *Education:* BS, Journalism, Syracuse University. *Appointments:* Reporter: Syracuse (NY) Journal, Middletown (NY) Times Herald, New York Journal; Staff Writer, MacFadden Publications; War Correspondent, Fawcett Publications; Chief European Correspondent, Fawcett Publications. *Publications:* An American in Rome, 1964; No Innocence Abroad, 1954; Flight from Terror, 1942; Into the Jaws of Death, 1944; Farouk, 1968; The White Ticket, 1938; Editor, Publisher, La Scienza Illustrata; (Films) Satyricon; The Heroes; The Rover; Love - The Italian Way; Marathon. *Contributions to:* about 1,000 major magazine articles. *Honours:* Best 100 Stories of World War II; Syracuse University, Man of the Year, 1986. *Memberships:* Board of Governors, Intrepid Sea-Air-Space Museum, New York City; Overseas Press Club of America. *Literary Agent:* Ms. Rosalind Cole, New York, USA. *Address:* Via Zandonai 95, Rome, Italy, 00194.

STERN Richard G, b. 25 Feb 1928, New York City, USA. Writer; Professor. m. (1) Gay Clark, (2) Alane Rollings, 3 sons, 1 daughter. *Education:* BA, University of North Carolina; MA, Harvard University; PhD, University of Iowa. *Publications:* Golk, 1960, reissued 1987; In Any Case, 1962, reissued 1981; Stitch, 1965, reissued 1986; Other Men's Daughter, 1973; A Father's Words, 1986; Noble RoT Stories, 1949-89; Europe, or Up & Down with Baggish and Schreiber, 1961; One Person and Another, 1993. *Contributions to:* Numerous journals and magazines, worldwide. *Honours:* Longwood, 1954; American Academy Arts & Letters, 1968; Friends of Literature, 1968; Sandburg, 1979; Award of Merit for the Novel, 1985. *Address:* 1050 E 59th St., Chicago, IL 60637, USA.

STERN Richard Martin, b. 17 Mar 1915, Fresno, California, USA. Writer. m. Dorothy Helen Atherton, 20 Dec 1937, 1 daughter (adopted). *Education:* Harvard College, 1933-36. *Appointments include:* Editorial Board, The Writer, 1976-. *Publications:* Bright Road to Fear, 1958; Search for Tabatha Carr, 1960; These Unlucky Deeds, 1960; High Hazard, 1962; Cry Havoc, 1963; Right Hand Opposite, 1963; I Hide, We Seek, 1964; The Kessler Legacy, 1967; Brood of Eagles, 1969; Merry Go Round, 1969; Manuscript For Murder, 1970; Murder in the Walls, 1971; Stanfield Harvest, 1972; Death in the Snow, 1973; The Tower, 1973; Power, 1974; The Will, 1976; Snowbound Six, 1977; Flood, 1979; The Big Bridge, 1982; Wildfire, 1985; Tsunami, 1988; Tangled Murders, 1989; You Don't Need An Enemy, 1989; Missing Man, 1990; Interloper, 1990. *Contributions to:* Short stories, serials to national magazines, 1942-69, including: Saturday Evening Post; Colliers; Good Housekeeping; Cosmopolitan; McCalls; Redbook; American Liberty. *Honour:* Edgar Award, Mystery Writers of America, 1958. *Memberships:* Past president, Mystery Writers of America; Crime Writers Association, UK; Authors Guild, USA. *Literary Agent:* Brandt & Brandt, 1501 Broadway, New York, NY 10036. *Address:* Route 9, Box 55, Santa Fe, New Mexico 87505, USA.

STERN Steve, b. 21 Dec 1947, Memphis, Tennessee, USA. Fiction Writer; Teacher. *Education:* BA, Rhodes College, 1970; MFA, University of Arkansas, 1977. *Appointments:* Lecturer, University of Wisconsin at Madison, 1987; Lecturer, Skidmore College, 1988, 1990-92; Writer-in-Residence, West Side YMCA Writer's Voice Community, 1988 and Lake George Arts Project, 1989. *Publications:* Isaac and the Undertaker's Daughter, 1983; The Moon and Ruben Shein, 1984; Mickey and the Golem (for children), 1986; Lazar Malking Enters Heaven, 1987; Hershel and the Beast (for children), 1987; Harry Kaplan's Adventures Underground, 1991; A Plague of Dreamers (3 novellas), forthcoming. *Contributions to:* Epoch; Eureka Review; Nimrod; Southern Magazine and anthologies. *Honours:* John Gould Fletcher Award, 1976; O Henry Prize, 1981; Pushcart Writer's Choice Award, 1984; Edward Lewis Wallant Award, 1987. *Literary Agent:* Liz Darhansoff. *Address:* 13 1/2 Jumel Place, Saratoga Springs, NY 12866, USA.

STERN Stuart. *See:* **RAE Hugh Crawford.**

STERNBERG Robert J, b. 8 Dec 1949, Newark, New Jersey, USA. Psychology Educator. m. Alejandra Campos, 11 Aug 1991, 1 son, 1 daughter. *Education:* BA summa cum laude, Yale University, 1972; PhD, Stanford University, 1975. *Literary Appointments:* Associate Editor, Intelligence, 1977-82; Associate Editor, Child Development, 1981-84; Consulting Editor, Memory & Cognition, 1979-81; Journal of Educational Psychology, 1979-81; American Journal of Psychology, 1979-81 and 1989-; Human Intelligence International Newsletter, 1979-89; Roeper Review, 1984-90; Journal of Experimental Psychology: General, 1985-88; Cognitive Development, 1986-90; Developmental Review, 1986-90; Psychological Review, 1989-90; Journal of Personality and Social Psychology, 1989; Editor, Psychological Bulletin, 1991-. *Publications:* Beyond IQ: A Triarchic Theory of Human Intelligence, 1985; Intelligence Applied: Understanding Your Intellectual Skills, 1986; Practical Intelligence: Nature and Origins of Competence in the Everyday World (edited with Richard K Wagner), 1986; The Triangle of Love, 1987; The Triarchic Mind, 1988; The Nature of Creativity (editor), 1988; Metaphors of Mind: Conceptions of the Nature of Intelligence, 1990. *Contributions to:* Phi Delta Kappan, 1990; Educational Leadership, 1990; Journal of Reading, 1991; Human Development, 1991. *Honours include:* Distinguished Scientific Award for an Early Career Contribution to Psychology of the APA, 1981; Boyd R McCandless Young Scientist Award, APA (Div 7), 1982; Fellow, American Psychological Association, 1983; Distinguished Scholar Award, National Association for Gifted Children, 1985; Research Review Award, American Educational Research Association (co-recipient), 1986; Outstanding Book Award, American Educational Research Association, 1987; Mensa Education and Research Foundation (MERF) Award for Excellence, 1989. *Memberships include:* Fellow, American Psychological Association; Fellow, American Psychological Society; American Association for the Advancement of Science; American Educational Research Association; Society for Research in Child Development. *Address:* Department of Psychology, Yale University, Box 11A Yale Station, New Haven, CT 06520, USA.

STERNLICHT Sanford, b. 20 Sept 1931, New York, New York, USA, University Professor. m. Dorothy Hilkert, 6 June 1956, (dec 1977), 2 sons. *Education:* BS, State University of New York at Oswego, 1953; MA, Colgate University, 1955; PhD, Syracuse University, 1962. *Publications:* Gulls way, 1961; Love in Pompeii, 1967; McKinley's Bulldog, 1977; USF Constellation: Yankee Race Horses, 1981; John Webster's Imagery and the Western Canon, 1972; The Black devil of the bayous, 1971; John Masefield, 1977; C S Forester, 1981; Padraic Colum, 1985; R F Delderfield, 1988; John Galsworthy, 1987. *Contributions to:* 300 articles, poems, stories in US, UK, Canadian and Belgian publications. *Honour:* Poetry Society of America Fellow, 1965. *Memberships:*

PEN; Modern Language Association. *Address:* 126 Dorset Road, Syracuse, NY 13210, USA.

STETSON Ernest Kent, b. 5 July 1948, Charlottetown, Prince Edward Island, Canada. Playwright. *Education:* BA (Hons) Prince of Wales College. *Literary Appointment:* Playwright in Residence, 1987-88, Neptune Theatre, Halifax, Nova Scotia, Canada. *Publications:* Drama, Radio: Jonah's Eye, 1987; Master of the Phantom, 1987. Stage: Warm Win in China, 1987; As I Am, 1986; Woodlot Rap!, 1984; Queen of the Cadillac, 1987- 88. Television: Chapell's Diary, 1974; Fog Magic, 1975; Island Folk, 1974; After the Season, 1967. Films: Clockworks, 1982; Beggarman, 1980; Walter Shaw, 1974; P.L.F., 1984; The Bell Ringers, 1982. *Honours:* CBC Film and Television Archives; Canada Council Archives; National Film Board Archives. *Memberships:* Association for Canadian Studies; A.C.T.R.A.(Past President, Maritime Branch; Playwright's Union of Canada (Editorial Board); Actor's Equity; Director's Guild of Canada. *Literary Agent:* Ralph Zimmerman, Great North Artist Management. *Address:* 5769 Southwood Drive, Halifax, Nova Scotia, Canada B3H 1E6.

STEVENS Andy. *See:* **DANBY Mary.**

STEVENS Art, b. 17 July 1935. Public Relations. m. 19 Mar 1972. *Education:* BA Degree, City College, New York. *Publications:* The Persuasion Explosion, 1986. *Contributions to:* Harvard Business Review, Public Relations Journal, Nation's Business, New York Times. *Memberships:* New Jersey Press Association; Public Relations Society of America; Counsellors Academy, Chairman Ethics Committee; Professional Communicators of NY, President. *Address:* 201 East 21 Steeet, New York, NY 10010, USA.

STEVENS Blaise. *See:* **Whittington Harry.**

STEVENS Bryna, b. 22 Oct 1924. Piano Teacher; Writer. div. 2 sons, 1 daughter. *Education:* BMus, University of Wisconsin. *Publications:* Frank Thompson: Her Civil War Story, 1992; Handel and the Famous Sword Swallower of Halle, 1990; Deborah Sampson goes to War, 1984; Ben Franklin's Armonica, 1983; Borrowed Fathers and Other Fables; The Harbor Book. *Contributions to:* Music Journal Clavier, American Music Teacher, Bravo Carnegie Hall. *Honours:* Area Writers Contest; Virginia Historical Association Honour award. *Address:* 491-31st Avenue 304, San Francisco, CA 94121, USA.

STEVENS Carl. *See:* **OBSTFELD Raymond.**

STEVENS Graeme Roy, b. 17 July 1932, Lower Hutt, New Zealand. Palaeontologist. m. Diane Louise Morton Ollivier, 20 Oct 1962, 2 sons, 1 daughter. *Education:* BSc., 1954, MSc., 1st Class, 1956, University of New Zealand; PhD, University of Cambridge, England, 1960; Fellowship, Royal Society of New Zealand, 1976. *Appointments:* UNESCO Sub Commission for the Natural Sciences, 1976; Advisory Committee on Adult Education, 1979; Book Resources Panel, National Library of New Zealand, 1981. *Publications:* Rugged Landscape, 1974; Geology of the Tararuas, 1975; New Zealand Adrift, 1980; Lands in Collision, 1985; Geology of New Zealand, 1978; Prehistoric New Zealand, 1988; 138 scientific papers. *Contributions to:* various professional journals. *Honours:* Hamilton Prize, Royal Society of New Zealand, 1959; McKay Hammer Geological Society of New Zealand, 1956; Wattie Book of the Year Award, (non-fiction) 1974, 1980; Doctor of Science, Victoria University of Wellington, 1989. *Memberships:* Royal Society of New Zealand, Home Secretary; Geological Society of New Zealand, Publisher. *Address:* 19A Wairere Road, Belmont, Lower Hutt, New Zealand.

STEVENS John. *See:* **TUBB E C.**

STEVENS Robert Tyler. *See:* **STAPLES Reginald Thomas.**

STEVENS William Christopher. *See:* **ALLEN Stephen Valentine.**

STEVENSON Anne Katharine, b. 3 Jan 1933, Cambridge, England. Writer; Poet. m. (4) Peter David Lucas. 2 sons, 1 daughter. *Education:* BA, MA, University of Michigan, USA. *Literary Appointments:* Compton Fellow in Writing, University of Dundee, 1973-75; Fellow, Lady Margaret Hall, Oxford, 1975-77; Fellow in Writing, Balmersh College, Reading, 1977-78; Northern Arts Literary Fellow, Newcastle, Durham, 1981-82, 1984-85; Writer in Residence, University of Edinburgh, 1987-88. *Publications:* Living in America (poems), 1965; Elizabeth Bishop (criticism), 1966; Reversals (poems), 1969; Correspondences (poems), 1974; Travelling Behind Glass (selected poems), 1974; Enough of Green (poems), 1977; Minute by Glass Minute (poems), 1982; The Fiction-Makers (poems), 1985; Selected Poems, 1987; Bitter Fame: A Life of Sylvia Plath, 1989; The Other House (poems), 1990; Four and a Half Dancing Men (poems), 1993. *Contributions to:* The Listener; The TLS; The New Yorker; Encounter; The New Statesman; Stand; Pn Review; Poetry Review; Poetry Chicago; Outposts; Other Poetry; Country Life; The Scotsman; Poetry Reviewer for The Listener, 1973-75; Arts North, 1984-85; Reviews in TLS and New York Times. *Honours:* Hopwood Awards, University of Michigan, 1952, 1954; Scottish Arts Award for Poetry, 1975; Poetry Book Society Recommendation for Minute by Glass Minute, 1982; Poetry Book Society Choice for The Fiction Makers, 1985; University of Michigan's Athena (Alumae) Award, 1990. *Memberships:* FRSA; Advisory Panel, Arts Council of Great Britain (Literature), 1983-85. *Address:* 9 Coton Road, Grantchester, Cambridge, CB3 9NH, England.

STEVENSON David, b. 30 Apr 1942. University Professor. m. Wendy McLeod, 2 sons. *Education:* BA, Dublin, 1966; PhD, 1970, D Litt., 1989, Glasgow. *Appointments:* Editor, Northern Scotland, 1980-90. *Publications include:* The Scottish Revolution, 1973; Revolution and Counter-Revolution in Scotland, 1977; Alasdair Maccolla and The Highalnd Problem, 1980; Scottish Covenanters and Irish Confederates, 1981; The Origins of Freemasonry, 1988; The First Freemason, 1988; *Contributions to:* many historical journals. *Memberships:* Scottish History Society, Honorary Secretary 1976-84; Fellow, Royal Society of Edinburgh, Royal Historical Society, Society of Antiquaries of Scotland. *Address:* Department of Scottish History, University of St. Andrews, St. Andrews KY16 9AL, Scotland.

STEVENSON Florence (Zandra Colt, Lucia Curzon, Zabrina Faire, Ellen Fitzgerald, Pamela Frazier), Author. *Appointments:* Columnist, Mirror newspaper, Los Angeles, California, 1949-50; Editorial Assistant, Mademoiselle, New York City, 1956-57; Press Assistant, James D Proctor, 1957-58; Assistant Editor, 1959-60, Contributing Editor, 1960-70, Opera News, New York City; Columnist, Opera Boutique (Metropolitan Program), Things of Beauty (Lincoln Center Program), New York City; Associate Editor, FM Guide, New York City, 1964-65; Contributing Editor: Weight Watchers, 1968-75, New Ingenue, 1974-75, New York City. *Publications:* The Story of Aida, Based on the Opera by Giuseppe Verdi, juvenile, 1965; Ophelia, 1968; Feast of Eggshells, 1970; The Curse of the Concullens, 1970; The Witching Hour, 1971; Where Satan Dwells, 1971; Bianca (with Patricia Hagan Murray), 1973; Kilmeny in the Dark Wood, 1973; Altar of Evil, 1973; The Mistress of Devil's Manor, 1973; The Sorcerer of the Castle, 1974; Dark Odyssey, 1974; The Ides of November, 1975; A Shadow on the House, 1975; Witch's Crossing, 1975; The Silent Watcher, 1975; A Darkness on the Stairs, 1976; The House at Luxor, 1976; Dark Encounter, 1977; The Horror from the Tombs, 1977; Call Me Counselor (with Sara Hulbert), non-fiction, 1977; Julie, 1978; The Golden Galatea, 1979; The Moonlight Variations, 1981; The Household, 1988; As Zabrina Faire: Lady Blue,

1979; The Midnight Match, 1979; The Romany Rebel, 1979; Enchanting Jenny, 1979; Wicked Cousin, 1980; Athena's Arts, 1980; Bold Pursuit, 1980; Pretender to Love, 1981; Pretty Kitty, 1981; Tiffany's True Love, 1981; As Lucia Curzon: The Chadbourne Luck, 1981; Adverse Alliance, 1981; The Mourning Bride, 1982; Queen of Hearts, 1982; The Dashing Guardian, 1983; As Zandra Colt: The Cactus Rose, 1982; The Splendid Savage, 1983; As Ellen Fitzgerald: A Novel Alliance, 1984; Lord Caliban, 1985; The Irish Heiress, 1985; Rogue's Bride, 1985; The Dangerous Dr Langhorne, 1985; The Forgotten Marriage, 1986; Lessons in Love, 1986; The Heirs of Bellair, 1986; Venetian Masquerade, 1987; A Streak of Luck, 1987; Romany Summer, 1988; As Pamela Frazier: The Virtuous Mistress, 1988. *Address:* 227 East 57th Street, New York, NY 10022, USA.

STEVENSON John (Mark Denning), b. 8 May 1926, London, England. Freelance Novelist; Columnist. m. Alison, 1951, div. *Appointments:* Fiction Editor, 1981-82; Book Review Columnist, Mystery News, 1982-90; Instructor of crime and suspense and advanced novel writing, Writer's Digest Schools, 1989-. *Publications:* Writing Commercial Fiction, 1983; Ransom, 1989; Din of Inequity, 1983; Merchant of Menace, 1980; Beyond the Prize, 1978; Die Fast, Die Happy, 1976; Shades of Gray, 1976; 20 novels of suspense, mystery and adventure under a variety of pseudonyms; 2 non-fiction books; numerous short stories. *Contributions to:* numerous journals and magazines. *Honour:* 4th Prize, Crime Writers International Congress, Stockholm, 1981. *Memberships:* Regional Vice President Mystery Writers of America, 1984, 1985; International Association of Crime Writers. *Address:* 2005 Ivar Ave., No. 3, Los Angeles, CA 90068, USA.

STEVENSON Randall William, b. 25 June 1953. University Lecturer. m. Sarah Carpenter, 18 Sept 1981, 2 sons, 1 daughter. *Education:* MA 1st Class Honours, University of Edinburgh, 1975; MLitt, University of Oxford, 1978. *Appointments:* Lecturer, Women Teachers' College, Birnin-Kebbi, North West State, Nigeria, 1975-76; Lecturer, Department of English Literature, University of Edinburgh, 1978-. *Publications:* The British Novel since the Thirties, 1986; Modernist Fiction, 1992; The Twentieth-Century Novel in Britain, 1993; Articles/chapters for essay collections in Harold Pinter, 1985, The History of Scottish Literature, 1988, Postmodernist Fiction, 1990; 3 volumes in York Notes Series of study guides to English Literature; The British Novel in the Twentieth Century: An Introductory Bibliography, 1988. *Contributions to:* Theatre reviews and book reviews for: Times Literary Supplement; The Independent; BBC radio and TV. *Membership:* Wyndham Lewis Society. *Address:* 134 Craiglea Drive, Edinburgh, Scotland.

STEWART Bruce Robert, b. 4 Sept 1927, Auckland, New Zealand. Writer. m. Ellen Noonan, 16 Oct 1950, Sydney, Australia. 3 sons, 3 daughters. *Education:* BA, Auckland. *Publications include:* A Disorderly Girl, 1980; The Turning Tide, 1980; The Hot and Copper Sky, 1982; The Hallelujah Boy, play; Shadow of a Pale Horse, play; The Devil, Makes Sunday, television play; Jungle, Juice, The Sin Shifter, Old Man March is Dead, A Laugh at the Dark Question, The Daedalus Equations, television plays; Stars in My Hair, radioplay; Hector's Fixed Idea, radioplay; Me and My Shadow, radioplay, 1988; The Dog That Went to War, TV mini-series, 1989. *Contributions to:* Film Criticism, The Month, 1970-80; Reviews and Criticisms in publications including: The New Stateman; Times Literary Supplement; The Tablet. *Honours:* Edgar Allen Poe Award, USA, 1963; Charles Henry Foyle Award, UK, 1968. *Memberships:* Writers Guild of Great Britain; Writers Guild of Australia; British Film Institute; Co-Chairman, WGGB, 1978-80. *Literary Agent:* Harvey Unna. *Address:* c/o Harvey Unna, 24 Pottery Lane, Holland Park, London W11, England.

STEWART Fred M(ustard), b. 1936, USA. Author. *Publications:* The Mephisto Waltz, 1969; The Methuselah Enzyme, 1970; Lady Darlington, 1971; The Mannings, 1973; Star Child, 1974; Six Weeks, 1976;

A Rage Against, Heaven, 1978; Century, 1981; Ellis Island, 1983; The Titan, 1985. *Literary Agent:* William Morris Agency, USA. *Address:* c/o William Morris Agency, 1350 Avenue of the Americas, New York, NY 10019, USA.

STEWART Kaye. *See:* **HOWE Doris Kathleen.**

STEWART Leslie, b. 23 May 1949, Benghazi, Libya. Scriptwriter; Director; Author. 1 son. *Education:* St Edward's College, Malta. *Publications:* Two of Us (novel), 1989; Three Minute Heroes (screenplay), 1985; 1984; Good Neighbours (play), 1987; Wide Games (play), 1987. TV Films and Plays: Three Minute Heroes, 1982; Wide Games, 1984; The Amazing Miss Stella Estelle, 1984; Good Neighbours, 1984; Space Station: Milton Keynes, 1985; The Little Match Girl, 1986; Janna, Where Are You?, 1987; Boogie Outlaws (TV serial), 1987; QPR Askey is Dead, 1988; Two of Us, 1988; That Green Stuff, 1990. Radio: The Key To My Father's House, 1992. Stage: Shoot-Up At Elbow Creek (musical), 1976; The Little Match Girl (musical), 1977; The Soldier (play), 1983. Directed: Space Station: Milton Keynes (with Colin Rogers, TV film), 1985; That Green Stuff (TV film), 1990. *Honours:* Emmy Nomination, 1987; Ivor Novello Award, 1988. *Membership:* Writers Guild of Great Britain; British Academy of Film and Television Arts. *Agent:* Jane Annakin, William Morris Agency (UK) Ltd. *Address:* York Villa, Station Road, Haddenham, Cambridgeshire CB6 3XD, England.

STEWART Mary Florence Elinor, b. 17 Sept 1916, Sunderland. Writer. m. Frederick Henry Stewart, 24 Sept 1945. *Education:* BA, 1938; DipEd, 1939; MA, 1941, Durham University. *Publications:* Madam, Will You Talk?, 1954; Thunder on the Right, 1957; My Brother Michael, 1959; The Moonspinners, 1962; The Crystal Cave, 1970; The Little Broomstick, 1971; Touch Not The Cat, 1976; A Walk in Wolf Wood, 1970; Thornyhold, 1988; Frost on the Window and Other Poems, 1990; Stormy Petrel, 1991. *Contributions to:* Many articles to various magazines. *Honours:* Frederick Niven Prize; Scottish Arts Council Award; Honorary Fellow Newnham College, Cambridge. *Memberships:* PEN; New Club. *Address:* 79 Morningside Park, Edinburgh EH10 5EZ, Scotland.

STICKLAND Caroline Amanda, b. 10 Oct 1955, Germany. Writer. m. William Stickland, 3 Aug 1974, 1 daughter. *Education:* BA Hons English and American Literature, University of East Anglia, 1977. *Publications:* The Standing Hills, 1986; A House of Clay, 1988; The Darkness of Corn, 1990. *Honours:* Betty Trask Award, 1985. *Memberships:* Society of Authors, Mrs Gaskell Society, Jane Austen Society. *Address:* 81 Crock Lane, Bothenhampton, Bridport, Dorset, DT6 4DQ, England.

STICKLAND Eugene Gordon, b. 24 Sept 1956, Regina, Canada. Communications Consultant. *Education:* BA, Honours, English, University of Regina, 1980; MFA, Theatre, York University, Toronto, 1984. *Appointments:* Playwright in Residence/Co-Artistic Director, ACT I.V. Theatre Co., Toronto, 1984-. *Publications:* Victoria & Elvis, 1987; Darkness on the Edge of Town, 1987; Quartet, 1985; The Family, 1984. *Honour:* Canada Council Grant, 1986. *Membership:* Playwrights Union of Canada. *Address:* 8 Pinewood Avenue, Apt. 10, Toronto, Ontario, Canada M6C 2V1.

STILES Martha Bennett, b. 30 Mar 1933, Writer. m. Martin Stiles, 18 Sept 1954, 1 son. *Education:* BS, University of Michigan, 1954. *Publications:* Darkness Over the Land, 1966; Sarah the Dragon Lady, 1986; Kate of Still Waters, 1990; The Star in the Forest, 1977; The Strange House at Newburyport, 1963. *Contributions to:* Winter Love Story; Tri Quarterly; Wolfe County Tri Quarterly; The Harvesters; New Orleans Review; The Pastoral Life; Virginia Quarterly. *Honours include:* Society of Children's Bookwriters Grant, 1988; Professional Assistance Award, Kentucky Arts Council, 1990. *Memberships:* Paris Arts Club; King Library

Associates. *Literary Agent:* Jean Naggar. *Address:* 861 Hume-Bedford Road, Paris, KY 40361, USA.

STILLINGER Jack, b. 1931, USA. Professor of English. *Appointments:* Assistant Professor, 1958-61, Associate Professor, 1961-64, Professor of English, 1964-, University of Illinois, Urbana-Champaign. *Publications:* The Early Draft of John Stuart Mill's Autobiography (editor), 1961; Anthony Munday's Zelauto (editor), 1963; William Wordsworth: Selected Poems and Prefaces (editor), 1965; The Letters of Charles Armitage Brown (editor), 1966; Twentieth Century Interpretations of Keats's Odes (editor), 1968; John Stuart Mill: Autobiography (editor), 1969; John Stuart Mill: Autobiography and Other Writings (editor), 1969; The Hoodwinking of Madeleine and Other Essays on Keats's Poems, 1971; The Texts of Keats's Poems, 1974; The Poems of John Keats, 1978; Mill's Autobiography, and Literary Essays (editor), 1981; Keats's Complete Poems, 1982; John Keats: Poetry Manuscripts at Harvard, 1990; Multiple Authorship and the Myth of Solitary Genius, 1991. *Address:* English Building, University of Illinois, Urbana, 608 S Wright Street, IL 61801, USA.

STINE George Harry (Lee Correy), b. 26 Mar 1928, Philadelphia, Pennsylvania, USA, Consulting Engineer; Author. m. Barbara A Kauth, 10 June 1952, 1 son, 2 daughters. *Education:* BA, Physics, Colorado College, Colorado Springs, 1952. *Publications include:* Starship Through Space, 1954; Contraband Rocket, 1956; Earth Satellites and the Race for Space Superiority, 1957; The Handbook of Model Rocketry, 1965, 1967, 1969, 1976, 1983; The Lionel Train and Accessory manual, 1971; The New Model Rocketry manual, 1977; Shuttle into Space, 1978; Star Driver, 1980; Space Doctor, 1981, 1985; Confrontation in Space, 1981; The Silicon Gods, 1984; Bits, Bytes, Bauds and Brains, the Untold Story of the Computer revolution, 1984; A Matter of Metalaw, 1986; The Corporate Survivors, 1986; Thirty Years of Model Rocketry, 1988; Warbots, 1988; Warbots 2, Operations Steel Band, 1988' Warbots 3, The Bastaard Rebellion, 1988; Warbots 4, Sierra Madre, 1988; Warbots 5, Operation High Dragon, 1989; Warbots 6, The Lost Battalion, 1989; Warbots 7, Operation Iron Fist, 1989; Warbots 8, Force of Arms, 1990; Warbots 9, Blood Siege, 1990; Warbots 10, Guts and Glory, 1991; ICBM, The Making of the Weapon That Changed the World, 1991; Warbots 11, Warrior Shield, 1992; Warbots 12, Judgesment Day, 1992; The Quest Model Rocket Design Handbook, 1991; StarSea Invaders 1: First Action, 1993; Forthcoming: StarSea Invaders 2: Second Contact; The Handbook of Model Rocketry, sixth edition; Various television and motion picture scripts. *Contributions to:* Numerous articles in various magazines and journals including American Modeler, Space Journal, American Way; AIAA Student Journal; American Spacemodeling; Model Rocket News. *Address:* 2419 West Saint Moritz Lane, Phoenix, AZ 85023, USA.

STINSON Kathy, b. 22 Apr 1952, Toronto, Canada. Childrens Author. 1 son, 1 daughter. *Appointments:* Writer in the Library, East York Public Library System, 1989. *Publications:* Red is Best; Big or Little; The Bare Naked Book; Who Is Sleepin In Auntys Bed; Fish House Secrets; Others inc. Mom & Dad Don't Live together Any More; Stevens Baseball Mitt. *Honours:* IODE Award. *Memberships:* CANSCAIP; The Writers Union of Canada. *Address:* 49 Blantyre Avenue, Scarborough, Ontario, Canada M1N 2R3.

STIRLING Jessica. *See:* **RAE Hugh Crawford.**

STIRLING Stephen Michael, b. 30 Sept 1953, Metz, France. Novelist. m. 15 Apr 1988. *Education:* BA, Carleton University, 1976; LLB, Osgoode Hall, 1979. *Publications:* Marching Through Georgia; The Cage; Under The Yoke; The Stone Dogs; Snow Brother; Go Tell The Spartons; The Ship Who Fought; The General; The Childrens Hour. *Contributions to:* The Women Warrior. *Memberships:* Science Fiction Writers of

STIVENS Dal(las George), b. 1911, Australia. Author. *Appointments:* Australian Department of Information, 1944-50; Press Officer, Australia House, London, England, 1949-50; Foundation President, 1963-64, Vice-President, 1964-66, President, 1967-73, Australian Society of Authors; Chairman, Literary Committee, Captain Cook Bicentenary Celebrations, 1969-70; Member, New South Wales Advisory Committee, ABC, 1971-73. *Publications:* The Tramp and Other Stories, 1936; The Courtship of Uncle Henry: Short Stories, 1946; The Gambling Ghost and Other Stories, 1946; Jimmy Brockett: Portrait of a Notable Australian, 1951; Ironbark Bill, 1955; The Wide Arch, 1958; Coast to Coast: Australian Stories, 1957-58 (editor), 1959; A Guide to Book Contracts (with B Jefferis), 1967; Three Persons Make a Tiger, 1968; A Horse of Air, 1970; The Incredible Egg: A Billion Year Journey, 1974; The Unicorn and Other Tales, 1976; The Bushranger, 1979; The Demon Bowler and Other Cricket Stories, 1979; The Portable Dal Stivens, 1982. *Address:* 5 Middle Harbour Road, Lindfield, New South Wales 2070, Australia.

STOCK Catherine Julia, b. 26 Nov 1952, Stockholm, Sweden. Writer; Illustrator; Designer. *Education:* BAFA, University of Capetown, 1974; PGCE, London Univeristy Institute of Education, 1976; MS, Pratt Institute, 1978. *Publications include:* Author/Illustrator: 15 Books; Illustrator Only: 44 Books; A Christmas Angel Collection, 1978; Emma's Dragon Hunt, 1984; Sampson the Christmas Cat, 1984; Sophie's Bucket, 1985; Sophie's Knapsack, 1988; Alexander's Midnight Snack, 1988; Mr Meredith, 1989; The Copycat, 1989; Armien's Fishing Trip, 1990; Halloween Monser, 1990; Secret Valentine, 1991; Mara in the Morning, 1991; Eddie's Friend, Boodles, 1992; An Island Christmas, 1992; The Willow Umbrella, 1993; Snowed In, 1993; Forthcoming: By Dawn's Early Light; Tap-Tap; Untitled Greek Story; A Very Important Day; Illustrator, 25 other books. *Contributions to:* The New York Times; The New Yorker; The Argus; Fair Lady; Cricket; Ladybug; Fukutaki Magazine; Learningland. *Honour:* Christopher Award, 1984. *Address:* 17 East 96th St., New York, NY 10128, USA.

STODDARD Alan b. 22 Aug 1915, Hale, Cheshire, England. Medical Practitioner. m. Joan Stoddard, 25 Mar 1937, 2 sons, 4 daughters. *Education:* DO, MB BS, D Phys Med, British School of Osteopathy 1931- 35, Kings College Hospital, 1937-42. *Publications:* Manual pf Osteopathic Technique, 1959, 1962, 1980, 1987 (published in five languages); Manual of Osteopathic Practice, 1969, 1983, 1986; The Back, Relief from Pain, 1979 (published in eight languages). *Contributions to:* Manipulative Procedures in the Treatment of Intervertebral Disc Lesions, British Jounral of Physical Medicine, 1951; Scheuermann's Disease or Spinal Osteochondrosis, Journal of Bone Joint Surgery, Feb 1979, Vol 61B. *Memberships:* Honorary Member, Swedish Society for Manual Medicine; Honorary Member, German Society for Manual Medicine; Register of Osteopaths. *Address:* The Anchorage, Spinney Lane, Itchener, Chichester, Sussex PO20 7DJ, England.

STODDARD Robert Hugh, b. 29 Aug 1928, Auburn, Nebraska, USA. Professor. m. Sara E Salisbury, 10 Dec 1955. 2 sons, 1 daughter. *Education:* BA, Nebraska Wesleyan University, 1950; MA, University of Nebraska, 1960; PhD, University of Iowa, 1966. *Publications:* Human Geography: People Places and Cultures, 1989; Field Techniques and Research Methods in Geography, 1982. *Contributions to:* Characteristics of Buddhist Pilgramages in Sri Lanka; The Location of Holy Sites in India. *Address:* 1131 Carlos Drive, Lincoln , NE 68505, USA.

STOECKLE John Duane, b. 17 Aug 1922, Michigan, USA. Professor of Medicine. m. Alice Agusta Young,

27 Mar 1948, 4 sons. *Education:* BS, Antioch College, 1944; MD, Harvard Medical School, 1948. *Publications:* Plain Pictures of Plain Doctoring, co-author, 1985; Encounter of Patients and Doctors, 1987; The Clinical Encounter, 1989, co-author: Collected Works of R C Cabot, 1977. *Contributions include:* Some 150 articles, reviews, and research reports. *Honours:* Glazer Award, Social General Internal Medicine. *Memberships:* Society of General Internal Medicine; American College of Physicians; American Psychosomatic Society; American Sociological Association; President, Roxbury Clinical Record Club, Pres, 1989-92. *Address:* Massachusetts General Hospital, Boston, MA 02114, USA.

STOKER Alan. *See:* **EVANS Alan.**

STOLOFF Carolyn, b. 14 Jan 1927. Poet; Painter; Teacher. *Education:* Distinction Literature and Fine Arts, Dalton School; University of Illinois; BS Painting, Columbia School of General Studies; Art Studies, Xavier Gonzalez, Eric Isenburger, Hans Hofmann; Poetry Study, Workshops with Stanley Kunitz. *Appointments:* Teaching: Manhattanville College, 1957-74; Painting and Drawing, 1957-74; Chairman of Art History and Studio Art, 1960-65; Seminar in Creative Writing, Poetry, 1969-74; Discussion Group, Women's House of Detention, 1971-72;English and Creative Writing, Baird House, 1973; Visiting Writer: Stephens College, 1975, Hamilton College, 1985, Summer Writers Workshop, University of Rochester, 1985; Poets in Public Service, 1989-. *Publications:* Stepping Out, 1971; Dying to Survive, 1973; In the Red Meadow, 1973; Lighter-than-Night Verse, 1977; Swiftly Now, 1982; A Spool of Blue, New and Selected Poems, 1983; You Came To Meet Someone Else, 1993. *Contributions to:* Numerous magazines and anthologies including, The New Yorker, Chelsea, Caliban, Partisan Review, Poetry Northwest, New Yorker Book of Poems, Alcatraz, New Directions 53, Rising Tides. *Honours include:* MacDowell Colony Residence Grants, 1961, 1962, 1970, 1976; Helene Wurlitzer Foundation, New Mexico, 1972, 1973, 1974; Robert Philipp Memorial Award; National Council on the Arts Award for achievement, 1968. *Address:* 24 West 8th Street, New York, NY 10011, USA.

STOLZ Mary (Slattery), b. 1920, USA. Author. *Publications:* To Tell Your Love, 1950; The Organdy Cupeakes, 1951; The Sea Gulls Woke Me, 1951; The Leftover Elf, 1952; In a Mirror, 1953; Ready or Not, 1953; Truth and Consequence, 1953; Pray Love, Remember, 1954; Two by Two, 1954, as A Love or a Season, 1964; Rosemary, 1955; Hospital Zone, 1956; The Day and the Way We Met, 1956; Good-bye My Shadow, 1957; Because of Madeline, 1957; And Love Replied, 1958; Second Nature, 1958; Emmett's Pig, 1959; Some Merry-Go-Round Music, 1959; The Beautiful Friend and Other Stories, 1960; A Dog on Barkham Street, 1960; Belling the Tiger, 1961; Wait for Me, Michael, 1961; The Great Rebellion, 1961; Fredou, 1962; Pigeon Flight, 1962; Siri, The Conquistador, 1963; The Bully of Barkham Street, 1963; Who Wants Music on Monday, 1963; The Mystery of the Woods, 1964; The Noonday Friends, 1965; Maximilian's World, 1966; A Wonderful, Terrible Time, 1967; Say Something, 1968; The Dragons of the Queen, 1969; The Story of a Singular Hen and Her Peculiar Children, 1969; Juan, 1970; By the Highway Home, 1971; Leap Before You Look, 1972; Lands End, 1973; The Edge of Next Year, 1974; Cat in the Mirror, 1975; Ferris Wheel, 1977; Cider Days, 1978; Go and Catch a Flying Fish, 1979; What Time of Night Is It, 1981; Cat Walk, 1983; Quentin Corn, 1985; Explorer of Barkham Street, 1985; Night of Ghosts and Hermits, 1985; The Cuckoo Clock, 1986; Ivy Larkin, 1986; The Scarecrows and Their Child, 1987; Zekmet the Stone Carver, 1988; Storm in the Night, 1988; King Emmett II, 1990; Go Fish, 1991; Bartholomew Fair, 1991; Stealing Home, 1992. *Literary Agent:* Roslyn Targ, Literary Agency, 105 West 13th St, NYC 10011, USA. *Address:* PO Box 82, Longboat Key, FL 34228, USA.

STONE Elaine Murray, b. 22 Jan 1922, New York,

USA. m. F Courtney Stone, 30 May 1944, dec, 3 daughters. *Education:* Julliard School of Music, 1939-41; BA Music, NY College of Music, 1943; Licentiate in Organ, Trinity College of Music, London, 1947; Hon Doctorate in Communication, World University, 1984. *Appointments:* Editor in Chief, Cass Inc, Florida, 1970-72; Spot Writer, WTAI AM-FM Florida, 1972-77; Writer Producer: Countdown, Channel 39, Dallas, 1978-81, Focus on History, Channel 19, Florida, 1982-93. *Publications:* Uganda: Fire and Blood, 1977; The Taming of the Tongue, 1954; Christopher Columbus, His Worlds, His Faith His Adventures, 1991; Brevard County: From Cape of the Canes to Space Coast, 1988; Love One Another, 1957; Elizabeth Bayley Seton: An American Saint, 1993. *Contributions to:* Indian River Life, Florida Catholic, Central Florida Life, Melbourne Times, Callings, New York Herald Tribune, among others. *Honours include:* Author of the Year, Florida Space Coast Writer's Guild, 1992; First Place for Short Story, Texas Penwomen, 1977; First Place, Children's Book, Washington, 1992. *Memberships include:* President, Pen Women, Dallas Branch, 1980; VP, Space Coast Writer's Guild; Women in Communication; American Association of University Women; American Society of Composers, Authors and Publishers, NYC. *Literary Agent:* Canadian Literary Associates, Edmonton, Alberta, Canada. *Address:* 1945 Pineapple Avenue, Melbourne, FL 32935, USA.

STONE Gayle Hallenbeck, b. 23 June 1945, Omaha, Nebraska, USA. Author; Editor. m. Dennis Lynds, 14 Feb 1986, 1 son, 1 daughter. *Education:* BA, University of Iowa, 1967. *Publications:* Intimacy, (co-author) 1986; Day of the Mahdi, 1984; The Mayan Connection, 1984; Pursuit of the Eagle, 1985; White Death, 1985; The Execution Exchange, 1985; The Dying Place (retitled Moving Target), 1988; Blood Fever, 1988; Rough Stuff, 1988; Reel Trouble, 1989. *Contributions to:* Assistant Editor, Santa Barbara Magazine, 1983-86; Editor, Santa Barbara Magazine, 1986; Editor, Prime Real Estate Magazine, 1987-88. *Literary Agent:* Agnes Birnbaum, Bleecker Street Associates, New York, USA. *Address:* 12 St Anne Drive, Santa Barbara, CA 93109, USA.

STONE Gerald Charles, b. 22 Aug 1932, Surbiton, Surrey, England. University Lecturer. m. Vera Fedorovna Konnova, 10 Apr 1974, 2 sons, 2 daughters. *Education:* BA, London University, School of Slavonic & East European Studies, 1964; PhD, London University, School of Slavonic & East European Studies, 1969. *Publications:* The Smallest Slavonic Nation: The Sorbs of Lusatia. 1972; The Russian Language Since the Revolution (with Bernard Comrie), 1978; An Introduction to Polish, 1980, 2nd Edition, 1992; The Formation of the Slavonic Literary Languages, (edited with Dean Worth), 1985, Oxford Slavonic Papers (editor since 1982). *Memberships:* The Philological Society, Member of Council 1981-86; The Society for Slovene Studies. *Address:* 6 Lathbury Road, Oxford OX2 7AU, England.

STONE Harry, b. 1 Feb 1926, New York, USA. Professor of English. m. Esther M Brucker, 1 July 1952, 1 son. *Education:* BA, 1946; MA 1950, PhD, 1955, University of California at Los Angeles. *Appointments:* Associate in English, 1953-55, Visiting Assistant Professor of English, 1956, UCLA; Asst Professor or English, Northwestern University, 1955-60; Asstant Professor, 1960-63, Associate Professor, 1963-66, Professor, 1966-, California State University, Northridge. *Publications:* The Uncollected Writings of Charles Dickens, 1968; Dickens and the Invisible World 1979; George Silverman's Explanation, 1984; Dickens' Working Notes for His Novels, 1987. *Honours:* Guggenheim Fellow, 1968-69; National Endowment for the Humanities Senior Fellow, 1976-77; President's Prizes, CSUN, 1980, 1987; 39th Annual Chicago Book Show Award, 1988. *Memberships include:* Dickens Fellowship, London; Dickens Society USA; International Association of University Professors of English; Modern Language Association. *Address:* Department of English, California State University, Northridge, CA 91330, USA.

STONE Joan Elizabeth, b. 22 Oct 1930, Port Angeles,

Washington, USA. Professor of English. 4 sons, 1 daughter. *Education:* BA, 1970, MA, 1974, PhD, 1976, University of Washington. *Appointments:* Poet in Residence, The Colorado College, 1979-; Associate Professor of English, University of Washington, 1975; Visiting Professor of Poetry, University of Montano, 1974. *Publications:* A Letter to Myself to Water, 1981; Our Lady of the Harbor, 1986; The Swimmer and Other Poems, 1975; Alba, 1976. *Contributions to:* Yale Review; Poetry Northwest' Seattle Review; New American and Canadian Poetry; Kansas Quarterly; The Southern Poetry Review; Texas Quarterly; Beloit Poetry Journal. *Honours:* Borestone Mountain Awards, Best Poems, 1973, 1974; Academy of American Poets Award, University of Washington, 1969, 1970, 1972. *Address:* 312 E. Yampa Street, Colorado Springs, CO 80903, USA.

STONE Patricia, Anne, b. 21 May 1952, Oshawa, Ontario, Canada. Writer; Teacher. m. Robert Johnston, 16 Feb 1991. *Education:* BA, University of Western Ontario; BEd; MA, Simon Fraser University; MA, Concordia University. *Publication:* Close Calls. *Contributions to:* Room of One's Own; Event; Writing Magazine; Matrix; White Wall Review; The New Quarterly; The Antigonish Review; The University of Windsor Review; The Wascana Review. *Honours:* 1st Prize, Cross-Canada Writers Quarterly; Appeared McClelland & Stewarts Journey Prize Anthology. *Address:* c/o Cormorant Books, RR1 Dunvegan, Ontario, Canada K0C 1J0.

STONE Peter, b. 27 Feb 1930, Los Angeles, California, USA. Playwright; Screenwriter. m. Mary O'Hanley, 17 Feb 1961. *Education:* BA, 1951, DLitt, 1971, Bard College, Annandale-on-Hudson, New York; MFA, Yale University, New Haven, Connecticut, 1953. *Publications:* Broadway musicals: Kean, 1961; Skyscraper, 1965; 1776, 1969; Two By Two, 1970; Sugar, 1972; Woman of the Year, 1981; My One and Only, 1983; Grand Hotel, 1989; Will Rogers Follies, 1991; Films: Charade, 1963; Father Goose, 1964; Mirage, 1964; Arabesque, 1965; Sweet Charity, 1968; Taking of Pelham 1-2-3, 1974; Who's Killing the Great Chefs of Europe, 1978. *Honours:* Emmy Award, TV, for Defenders, 1962; Academy Award for Father Goose, 1964; Edgar Award for Charade, Mystery Writers of America, 1964; Tony Award, New York Drama Critics Award and Drama Desk Award for 1776, 1969; Will Rogers Follies, 1991; London Theatre Critics Award for 1776, 1970; Christopher Award for 1776, 1972; Tony Award for Woman of the Year, 1981. *Memberships:* President, Dramatists Guild of America; Authors League of America; Academy of Motion Picture Arts and Sciences; Writers Guild of America. *Literary Agent:* Sam Cohn, ICM, New York City, USA. *Address:* 160 East 71st Street, New York, NY 10021, USA.

STONE Robert (Anthony), b. 1937, USA. Author; Educator. *Appointments:* Editorial Assistant, New York Daily News, 1958-60; Writer-in-Residence, Princeton University, New Jersey, 1971-72, 1985; Taught: Amherst College, Massachusetts, 1972-75, 1977-78; Stanford University, California, 1979; University of Hawaii, Manoa, 1979-80; Harvard University, Cambridge, Massachusetts, 1981; University of California, Irvine, 1982; New York University, 1983-84; University of California, San Diego, 1985. *Publications:* A Hall of Mirrors, 1967; Dog Soldiers, 1974; Who'll Stop the Rain (with Judith Rascoe), screenplay, 1978; A Flag for Sunrise, 1981; Children of Light, 1986; Outerbridge Reach, 1992. *Honours:* Mildred and Harold Strauss Living, American Academy and Institute of Arts and Letters, 1988-92. *Memberships:* Chairman, PEN/Faulkner Foundation; Vice President, PEN American Center. *Literary Agent:* Candida Donadio, Donadio & Ashworth. *Address:* c/o Candida Donadio, Donadio & Ashworth, 231 West 22nd Street, New York, NY 10011, USA.

STONG Pat. *See:* **HOUGH Richard Alexander.**

STOPPARD Miriam, b. 12 May 1937. Writer; Broadcaster. m. Tom Stoppard, 1972 (diss 1992), 2 sons, 2 stepsons. *Education:* Royal Free Hospital School of Medicine, University of London; King's College Medical School, University of Durham, Newcastle-upon-Tyne; MB BS Durham, 1961; House Surgeon, 1961, House Physician, 1962, Senior House Officer in Medicine, 1962-63, Royal Victoria Infirmary, King's College Hospital, Newcastle-upon-Tyne; Research Fellow, Department of Chemical Pathology, 1963-65, Registrar in Dermatology, 1965-66, Senior Registrar in Dermatology, 1966-68, University of Bristol; MRCP, 1964; MD Newcastle, 1966. *Appointments:* TV series: Where There's Life, 1981-; Baby and Co, 1984-; Woman to Woman, 1985-; Miriam Stoppard's Health and Beauty Show, 1988-. *Publications:* Miriam Stoppard's Book of Baby Care, 1977; My Medical School (contributor), 1978; Miriam Stoppard's Book of Health Care, 1979; The Face and Body Book, 1980; Everywoman's Lifeguide, 1982; Your Baby, 1982; Fifty Plus Lifeguide, 1982; Your Growing Child, 1983; Baby Care Book, 1983; Pregnancy and Birth Book, 1984; Baby and Child Medical Handbook, 1986; Everygirl's Lifeguide, 1987; Feeding Your Family, 1987; Miriam Stoppard's Health and Beauty Book, 1988; Every Woman's Medical Handbook, 1988; Lose 7lb in 7 Days, 1990; Test Your Child, 1991; The Magic of Sex, 1991; Conception, Pregnancy & Birth, 1993. *Contributions to:* Over 40 to medical journals. *Honours:* State Scholarship, 1955; Medical Research Scholarship, 1963-65. *Memberships:* Dermatology and Endocrinology Sections, Royal Society of Medicine; Heberden Society; British Association of Rheumatology and Rehabilitation. *Address:* Iver Grove, Iver, Bucks, England.

STOPPARD Tom, b. (as Thomas Straussler) 3 July 1937, Zlin, Czechoslovakia (now British citizen). Writer. m. (1) Jose Ingle, 1965 (div. 1972), 2 sons, (2) Dr Miriam Moore-Robinson, 1972, 2 sons. *Education:* Grammar school, Yorkshire, UK. *Appointments include:* Journalist, Bristol, 1954-60; Freelance journalist, London, 1960-64. *Publications:* Plays: Rosencrantz & Guildenstern Are Dead, 1967; The Real Inspector Hound, 1968; Enter a Free Man, 1968; After Magritte, 1970; Dogg's Our Pet, 1972; Jumpers, 1972; Travesties, 1975; Dirty Linen, 1976; New-Found-Land, 1976; Every Good Boy Deserves Favour (music, Andre Previn), 1978; Night & Day, 1978; Dogg's Hamlet, Cahoots Macbeth, 1979; Undiscovered Country, 1980; On the Razzle, 1981; The Real Thing, 1982; Rough Crossing, 1984; Dalliance (adaptation, Schnitzler's Liebelei), 1986; Hapgood (Aldwych Theatre) 1988; The Love for Three Oranges (English Libretto for Prokofiev's opera) Glyndebourne, 1983; Largo Desolato (adaptation of Vaclev Havel) 1987; Tango (adaptation Mrowzek) RSC 1966; The House of Bernard Alba (Greenwich) 1973; (English version of Lorca play not published). Film scripts: Empire of the Sun, 1987; Russia House, 1989; Largo Desolato by Vaclav Havel (trans), 1987; Hapgood, 1988; In the Native State, 1991; Billy Bathgate, 1990; Rosencrantl & Guildenstern Are Dead (also directed), 1990; Stage: Arcadia, Royal National Theatre, 1993. Also Radio plays, screenplays, television plays. Novel, short stories. *Honours include:* Honorary degrees, various universities; John Whiting Award, Arts Council, 1967; New York Drama Critics Award, best play, 1968; Antonette Perry Tony Award, 1968, 1976; 1984; Evening Standard Awards, 1967, 1972, 1978, 1982; Italia Prize, radio drama, 1968; Shaakespeare Prize, 1979. *Memberships include:* Committee of the Free World, 1981-. *Address:* c/o The Peters Fraser & Dunlop Group Ltd, 503/4 The Chambers, Chelsea Harbour, Lots Road, London SW10 0XF, England.

STOREY Anthony, b. 1928, United Kingdom. Author; Psychology Tutor, Cambridge University. *Publications:* Jesus Iscariot, 1967; Graceless Go I, novel, 1969, screenplay, 1973, television play (with L Hughes), 1974; The Rector, 1970; The Plumed Serpent, screenplay, 1971; Platinum Jag: A Psycho-Thriller, 1972; The Centre Holds, 1973; Zulu Dawn, screenplay, 1974; Platinum Ass, 1975; Brothers Keepers, 1975; Stanley Baker, biography, 1978; The Saviour, 1979; On Becoming a Virgin, 1985. *Address:* Beyton Cottage, Beyton, Bury St Edmunds, Suffolk, England.

STOREY David Malcolm, b. 13 July 1933, Wakefield, Yorkshire, England. Author; Playwright. m. Barbara Hamilton, 1956, 2 sons, 2 daughters. *Education:* Wakefield College of Art; Slade School of Art. *Publications:* Novels: This Sporting Life, 1960; Flight into Camden, 1960; Radcliffe, 1963; Pasmore, 1972; A Temporary Life, 1973; Saville, 1976; A Prodigal Child, 1982; Present Times, 1984. Plays: The Restoration of Arnold Middleton, 1967; In Celebration (also film), 1969; The Contractor, 1969; Home, 1970; The Changing Room, 1971; Cromwell, 1973; The Farm, 1973; Life Class, 1974; Night, 1976; Mother's Day, 1976; Sisters, 1978; Dreams of Leaving, 1979; Early Days, 1980; Storey's Lives: Poems 1951-1991, 1992. *Honours:* Numerous litarary awards & prizes, UK, USA; Fellow, University College, London, 1974. *Address:* c/o Jonathan Cape Ltd, Random Century House, 20 Vauxhall Bridge Road, London SW1V 2SA, England.

STOREY Douglas Reginald, b. 15 May 1945, Salisbury, Wiltshire, England. Literary Agent. 1 son, 1 daughter. *Education:* BA University of Dalaware, 1967; MS 1972, MSIA, 1972, Purdue University. *Literary Agent:* The Catalog Literary Agency. *Address:* The Catalog Literary Agency, PO Box 2964, Vancouver, WA 98668, USA.

STOREY Edward, b. 1930, United Kingdom. Writer. *Appointments:* Formerly Lecturer, Adult Education Centre, Peterborough; Member, Literature Panel, Eastern Arts Association, 1970-. *Publications:* North Bank Night, 1969; Portrait of the Fen Country, 1970, 2nd Edition, 1982; A Man in Winter, 1972; Four Seasons in Three Countries, 1974; Katharine of Aragon, libretto; The Solitary Landscape, 1975; Call It a Summer Country, 1978; The Dark Music, 1979; Old Scarlet, libretto, 1981; A Right to Song: The Life of John Clare, 1982; Spirit of the Fens, 1985. *Literary Agent:* David Higham Associates Ltd, England. *Address:* c/o David Higham Associates Ltd, 5 Lower John Street, London W1R 4HA, England.

STORM Christopher. *See:* **OLSEN Theodore Victor.**

STORR (Charles) Anthony, b. 18 May 1920, Bentley, England. Psychiatrist; Author. m. 1. Catherine Cole, 6 Feb 1942, 3 daughters, 2. Catherine Barton, 9 Oct 1970. *Education:* Winchester College; MB BChir, Cantab, 1944, MA Cantab, 1946, Christ's College, Cambridge; Westminster Hospital FRCP (London) 1975; FRCPsych, 1972. *Publications:* The Integrity of the Personality, 1960; Sexual Deviation, 1964; Human Aggression 1968; Human Destructiveness, 1972; The Dynamics of Creation, 1972; Jung, 1973; The Art of Psychotherapy, 1979; The Essential Jung, 1983; Solitude: A Return to the Self), 1988; Churchill's Black Dog and Other Phenomena of the Human Mind (USA, Churchill's Black Dog, Kafka's Mice and Other Phenomena of the Human Mind), 1989; Freud 1989; Music and the Mind, 1992. *Contributions to:* Reviews for New York Times, Washington Post, The Independent, The Spectator, Times Literary Supplement. *Honour:* Fellow, Royal Society of Literature, 1990; Hon Fellow, Royal College of Psychiatrists, 1993. *Membership:* Fellow, Green College, Oxford, 1979, Emeritus 1984. *Literary Agent:* The Peters, Fraser and Dunlop Group Ltd. *Address:* 45 Chalfont Road, Oxford, OX2 6TJ, England.

STORR Catherine (Lady Balogh), b. 1913, United Kingdom. Novelist; Short Story Writer; Children's Fiction Writer; Former Psychiatrist. *Appointment:* Assistant Editor, Penguin Books, London, 1966-70. *Publications:* Clever Polly series, 5 vols, 1952-80; Stories for Jane, 1952; Marianne Dreams, 1958; Marianne and Mark, 1959; Robin, 1962; Flax into Gold, libretto, 1964; Lucy, 1964; The Catchpole Story, 1965; Rufus, 1969; Puss and the Cat, 1969; Thursday, 1971; Kate and the Island, 1972; Black God, White God, 1972; Children's Literature (editor), 1973; The Chinese Egg, 1975; The Painter and the Fish, 1975; Unnatural Fathers, 1976; The Story of the Terrible Scar, 1976; Tales from the Psychiatrist's couch, short stories, 1977; Winter's End, 1978; Vicky,

1981; The Bugbear, 1981; February Yowler, 1982; The Castle Boy, 1983; Two's Company, 1984. *Address:* Flat 5, 12 Frognal Gardens, London NW3, England.

STOTT Richard Keith, b. 17 Aug 1943, Oxford, England. Editor. m. Penelope Anne Scragg, 18 Apr 1970, 1 son, 2 daughters. *Appointments:* Features Editor, 1979, Assistant Editor, 1981, Editor, 1985-, Daily Mirror; Editor, The People, 1984. *Honour:* British Press Awards, Reporter of the Year, 1977. *Address:* Daily Mirror, 33 Holborn Circus, London EC1P 1DQ, England.

STOUT William, b. 18 Sept 1949, Salt Lake City, Utah, USA. Artist; Writer; Art Director. m. Mary Kent Wilson, 21 June 1982, 2 sons. *Education:* BA, Chouinard Art Institute (now California Institute of the Arts), 1971. *Appointments:* Artist and writer; Art Director of Bomp, 1976-77, and Varese-Sarabande Records, 1978-. *Publications:* The Dinosaurs: A Fantastic New View of a Lost Era, 1981; The Little Blue Brontosaurus (children's book) self-illustrated, 1983; (Illustrator) Ray Bradbury, Dinosaur Tales, 1983. Screenplays including The Warrior and the Sorceress, 1984, re-released as Kain of Dark Planet; Conan the Buccaneer; Spawn of the Dead and Natural History Project. *Honours:* Inkpot Award, 1978; Children's Choice Award, 1985 for The Little Blue Brontosaurus. *Memberships:* Comic Art Professional Society (Founding Member of Board of Directors, 1977-81; President 1986-87), American Film Institute, National Geographic Society, Audubon Society, Oceanic Society, Sierra Club, Smithsonian Institution, American Museum of Natural History, Greater Los Angeles Zoo Association. *Address:* 1468 Loma Vista Street, Pasadena, CA 91104, USA.

STOW (Julian) Randolph, b. 28 Nov 1935, Geraldton, Western Australia. Writer. *Education:* University of Western Australia. *Appointments include:* Lecturer, English Literature, University of Leeds, UK 1962, University of Western Australia 1963-64; Lecturer, English & Commonwealth Literature, University of Leeds, 1968-69. *Publications:* Poems: Outrider, 1962; A Counterfeit Silence, 1969. Novels: To the Islands, 1958, 1981; Tourmaline, 1963; The Merry-go-round in the Sea, 1965; Visitants, 1979. The Girl Green as Elderflower, 1980; The Suburbs of Hell, 1984. Music theatre: 8 Songs for a Mad King, with Peter Maxwell Davies, 1969; Miss Donnithorne's Maggot, with P M Davies, 1974. For children: Midnite, 1967. *Honours:* Harkness Fellow, USA, 1964-66; Miles Franklin Award, 1958; Britannica Australia Award, 1966; Patrick White Award, 1979. *Address:* c/o Richard Scott Simon Ltd, 43 Doughty Street, London WC1N 2LF, England.

STRANDBERG Keith William, b. 21 Aug 1957, Toledo, Ohio, USA. Professional Writer. m. Carol Anne Hartman, 25 Sept 1982, 2 sons. *Education:* BA, Chinese Language & Literature, 1979; BA, Physical Education, 1979. *Publications:* No Retreat, No Surrender, (feature film), 1986; Raging Thunder, 1987, (feature film); Stir Fry Cooking, 1985; Blood Brothers (film), 1989; The King of the Kickboxers (film), 1990; American Shaolin (film), 1991; Self Defense Choices for Women (video), 1992. *Contributions To:* Travel & Leisure; Rider; D & B Reports; Far East Traveler; Baby Talk; The China Business Review; American Motor Cyclist; Black Belt; Child Life; Motorworld. *Memberships:* National Writer's Club; National Martial Arts Advisory Board. *Literary Agent:* Shirley Strick, Los Angeles. *Address:* 3634 Peregrine Circle, Mountville, PA 17554, USA.

STRANGE James Francis, b.2 Feb 1938, Pampa, Texas, USA. Dean & University Professor. m. Lillian Carolyn Midkiff, 19 Aug 1960, 1 son, 3 daughters. *Education:* BA, Rice University, 1959; M. Div., 1964, Yale Divinity School; PhD, Drew University, 1970. *Appointments:* Editorial Board: Annual Series, American Schools of Oriental Research, 1980, Biblical Archaeology Review, 1983. *Publications:* Archaeology, The Rabbis, and Early Christianity, 1981, co-author; Excavations at Ancient Meiron, 1981, co-author; Ancient Synagogue Excavations at Khirbet Shema,

Israel, 1970-72, 1976, co author; Revision and Editing, Discovering the Biblical World, by H.T. Frank, 1987. *Contributions to:* Professional journals. *Honour:* Phi Kappa Phi, 1984. *Memberships:* American Schools of Oriental Research, Chairman Committee for Computer Archaeology; Trustee, 1985-89, Israel Exploration Society; Society for Biblical Literature. *Address:* 9712 Woodland Ridge Drive, Tampa, FL 33637, USA.

STRANGER Joyce. *See:* **WILSON Joyce Muriel.**

STRATTON Rebecca (Lucy Gillen), b. United Kingdom. Full-time Writer. *Publications:* As Lucy Gillen: The Ross Inheritance, 1969; The Silver Fishes, 1969; Heir to Glen Ghyll, 1970; Doctor Toby, 1970; The Whispering Sea, 1971; Winter at Cray, 1971; A Time Remembered, 1971; The Pretty Witch, 1971; Dangerous Stranger, 1972; Glen of Sighs, 1972; Means to an End, 1972; The Changing Years, 1972; Painted Wings, 1972; The Pengelly Jade, 1972; The Runaway Bridge, 1972; An Echo of Spring, 1973; Moment of Truth, 1973; A Touch of Honey, 1973; Gentle Tyrant, 1973; A Handful of Stars, 1973; The Stairway to Enchantment, 1973; Come, Walk with Me, 1974; Web of Silver, 1974; All the Summer Long, 1975; Return to Deepwater, 1975; The Hungry Tide, 1976; The House of Kingdom, 1976; Master of Ben Ross, 1977; Back of Beyond, 1978; Heron's Point, 1978; Hepburn's Quay, 1979; The Storm Eagle, 1980; Others; As Rebecca Stratton: The Golden Madonna, 1973; The Bride of Romano, 1973; Castles in Spain, 1974; The Yellow Moon, 1974; Island of Darkness, 1974; Autumn Concerto, 1974; The Flight of the Hawk, 1974; Run from the Wind, 1974; Fairwinds, 1974; The Warm Wind of Farik, 1975; Firebird, 1975; The Fire and the Fury, 1975; The Goddess of Mavisu, 1975; Isle of the Golden Drum, 1975; Moon Tide, 1975; The White Dolphin, 1976; Proud Stranger, 1976; The Road to Gafas, 1976; Gemini Child, 1976; Chateau d'Armor, 1976; Dream of Winter, 1977; Girl in a White Hat, 1977; Spindrift, 1977; More Than a Dream, 1977; Lost Heritage, 1978; Image of Love, 1978; Bargain for Paradise, 1978; The Corsican Bandit, 1978; The Eagle of the Vincella, 1978; Inherit the Sun, 1978; The Sign of the Ram, 1978; The Velvet Glove, 1978; Close to the Heart, 1979; Lark in an Alien Sky, 1979; The Tears of Venus, 1979; Trader's Cay, 1980; The Leo Man, 1980; The Inherited Bride, 1980; Apollo's Daughter, 1980; The Black Invader, 1981; Black Enigma, 1981; The Silken Cage, 1981. *Address:* c/o Mills and Boon Ltd, 15-16 Brooks Mews, London W1A 1DR, England.

STRATTON Thomas. *See:* **DE-WEESE Gene Thomas Eugene.**

STRAUB Gerard Thomas, b. 31 Mar 1947, Brooklyn, New York, USA. Writer. m. 2. Kathleen Grosso, 11 July 1986, 1 daughter. *Appointments:* Executive, Columbia Broadcasting System, Inc, New York, New York, 1964-78; Producer of The 700 Club and creator of soap opera, Another Life, Christian Broadcasting Network, Virginia Beach, Virginia, 1978-80; Associate Producer, General Hospital, American Broadcasting Companies, Inc, Hollywood, California, 1980-81; Executive Producer, The Doctors, National Broadcasting Company, Inc, New York City, 1982; Producer of You Are the Jury, Dick Clark Productions, Burbank, California, 1983; Independent Television Director and free-lance writer, San Francisco, California and New York City, 1983-86; Supervising Producer of Capitol, John Conboy Productions, Hollywood, 1986-87; Free-lance writer, 1987-. *Publications:* Salvation for Sale: An Insider's View of Pat Robertson's Ministry, 1986, revised paperback edition, 1988; God Said What?. *Literary Agent:* Jay Garon, Jay Garon-Brooke Associates, Inc, New York. *Address:* c/o Jay Garon, Jay Garon-Brooke Associates, Inc, 415 Central Park W, New York, NY 10025, USA.

STRAUB Peter Francis b. 2 Mar 1943, Milwaukee, Wisconsin, USA. Novelist. m. 27 Aug 1966. *Education:* BA, University of Wisconsin, 1965; MA, Columbia University, 1966. *Publications:* Open Air (poetry), 1972;

Marriage, 1973; Julia, 1975; If You Could See Me Now, 1977; Ghost Story, 1979; Shadowland, 1980; Floating Dragon, 1983; The Talisman (with Stephen King), 1984; Koko, 1988; Mystery, 1989; Houses Without Doors, 1990; The Throat, 1992. *Contributions to:* Reviews to TLS; New Statesman; Washington Post. *Honours:* British Fantasy Award, August Derleth Award for Floating Dragon, 1983; World Fantasy Award, Best Novel for Koko, 1988. *Memberships:* PEN; Author's League; Author's Guild. *Literary Agent:* Robert J Schuster. *Address:* 53 W 85th Street, New York, NY 10024, USA.

STRAUBING Harold Elk, b. 19 Feb 1918, New York, New York, USA. Writer. m. Helen Mozlin, 13 Mar 1943, 1 daughter. *Education:* BA, Long Island University, 1940. *Appointments:* Artist and writer, Fleischer Studios, Miami, Florida, 1940-42; US Army, wrote animated cartoon series, Snafu, 1942-45; Goodman Publications, Comic Books editor, 1945-47; Comics Editor of the newspaper and its syndicate, New York Herald Tribune, New York, 1947-51; Comics Editor, Associated Press News-features, 1951-52; Editor, Lev Gleason Publications, 1952-54; Magazine Editor, Crestwood Publishing Company, New York, 1954-61; Executive Editor, General Manager, American Art Enterprises, Inc, North Hollywood, California, 1961-75; Executive Editor, Chatsworth Enterprises, Inc, Chatsworth, California, 1975-82; Writer 1982-; Producer and director of radio dramas, Chairman of Board of Directors of Oceanside Community Theatre, Oceanside, New York. *Publications:* Little Girl with Red Nails (3-act play) readings of script given in New York in 1961; Target Number One (novel) 1983; Civil War - Eyewitness Reports, 1985, reprinted as The Fateful Lightning, 1987; The Last Magnificent War, 1988 to be issued as an oral reading by Books on Tape, Autumn 1990; Bandages, Bullets and Beans, to be published, Autumn 1990; A Touch of War, 1991; In Hospital and Camp, 1993; Forthcoming: Motion Pictures Finds It's Voice; Devil Clan. *Honour:* Fletcher Pratt Award for nomination from Civil War Round table of New York, 1985 for Civil War: Eyewitness Reports. *Memberships:* Writers Guild of America West; Mystery Writers of America. *Address:* 5336 Corteen Place 1, North Hollywood, CA 91607, USA.

STRAUS Dennis David, (Ascher/Straus), b. New York. Writer. *Education:* MA, Columbia University. *Publications:* Letter to an Unknown Woman; The Menaced Assassin; Red Moon/Red Lake; The Other Planet; The Menaced Assassin. *Contributions to:* Chicago Review; Paris Review; Epoch; Top Stories; Chelsea; Exile; Calyx; Zone. *Honours:* Panache Experimental Fiction Prize; Pushart Prize; Caps Fellowship. *Address:* PO Box 176, Rockaway Park, NY 11694, USA.

STRAUS Dorothea, b. 1916, USA. Author. *Publications:* Thresholds, 1971; Showcases, memoirs, 1974; Palaces and Prisons, 1976; Under the Canopy, 1982; The Birthmark, 1987. *Address:* 160 East 65th Street, New York, NY 10021, USA.

STRAUS ASCHER. *See:* **STRAUS Dennis David & ASCHER Shelia.**

STRAUSS Botho, b. 1944, near Leipzig, Germany. Playwright; Novelist. *Publications:* Plays include: Die Hypochonder; Trilogie des Wiedersehens; Gross und Klein an der Park; etc. Novels: Die Widmung, 1979; Rumor, 1980; Paare, Passanten, 1981; Der Junge Mann, 1984. *Honours:* Hannover Dramaturgie Award, 1971; Mulheimer Drama Prize, 1982. *Address:* Keithstrasse 8, 1000 Berlin 30, Germany.

STRAWSON Galen John, b. 5 Feb 1952, Oxford, England. Philsopher. m. Jose Said, 20 July 1974, 1 son, 2 daughter. *Education:* BA Philosophy, 1973, MA 1977, Cambridge; BPhil, 1977, DPhil, 1983, Oxford. *Appointments:* Assistant Editor, 1978-87, Consultant 1987-, Times Literary Supplement, London.

Publications: Freedom and Belief, 1986; The Secret Connection, 1989. *Contributions to:* TLS; Sunday Times; Observer; London Review of Books; Independent on Sunday; Mind; American Philosophical Quarterly; Inquiry. *Honours:* R A Nicholson Prize for Islamic Studies, Cambridge, 1971; T H Green Prize for Moral Philosophy, Oxford, 1983; Fellow, Jesus College, Oxford. *Membership:* Mind Association. *Address:* Jesus College, Oxford OX1 3DW, England.

STREET Pamela, b. 3 Mar 1921, Wilton, Wiltshire, England. Writer. (div). 1 daughter. *Education:* The Godolphin School, Salisbury, 1930-1938; Salisbury & South Wiltshire College of Further Education, 1967-69. *Publications:* My Father, A G Street, 1969, reprinted 3 times, Second edition, 1984; The Illustrated Portrait of Wiltshire, 1986; Arthur Bryant-Portrait of a Historian, 1979; Light of Evening, 1981; The Stepsisters, 1982; Morning Glory, 1982; Portrait of Rose, 1986; Personal Relations, 1987; The Mill-Race Quartet, 1988; The Timeless Moment, 1988; Mr Brown & Prudence (radio story), 1988; The Beneficiaries, 1989; Doubtful Company, 1990; Guilty Parties, 1991; Late Harvest, 1991; The Colonel's Son, 1992. *Contributions to:* The Field; Punch; The Farmers Weekly; The Sunday Times; The Lady. *Address:* Flat 5, 47 South Street, London W1Y 5PD, England.

STRESHINSKY Shirley, b. 7 Oct 1934, Alton, Illinois, USA. Writer. m. Ted Streshinsky, 16 June 1966, 1 son, 1 daughter. *Education:* BA, University of Illinois. *Publications:* And I Alone Survived, 1978; Hers The Kingdom, 1981; A Time Between, 1984; Gift of the Golden Mountain, 1988. *Contributions to:* Over 100 articles in journals and magazines including: Redbook; Ms; Glamour; Ladies Home Journal; McCalls. *Honours:* Best Human Interest Article, Society Magazine Writers Association, 1968; Educational Press Award, 1968. *Membership:* Authors Guild. *Literary Agent:* Claire Smith, Harold Ober Associates, New York. *Address:* PO Box 674, Berkeley, CA 94701, USA.

STRICKLAND Margot Teresa, b. 5 Mar 1937, Madrid, Spain. m. A.H. Strickland. 2 children. *Publications:* The Byron Women, 1975; Angela Thirkell: Portrait of a Lady Novelist, 1977; Memoirs of Sir Sydney Stadler of El Salvador (editor); Moura: Her Autobiography, 1991. *Contributions to:* The Times; Country Life; Literary Review; The Byron Journal; Woman's Realm; Guns Review; The Lady; Former Editor, Primer East Angles. *Memberships:* The Byron Society; Friend, Historic Houses Association; Royal Norfolk Agricultural Association; Irish Georgian Society. *Address:* 10 Redenhall Road, Harleston, Norfolk IP20 9EN, England.

STROM Robert Duane, b. 21 Jan 1935, Chicago, Illinois, USA. Professor. m. Shirley Kaye Mills, Apr 1962, 2 sons. *Education:* BS, Macalester College, 1958; MA, University of Minnesota, 1959; PhD, University of Michigan, 1962. *Publications:* Teaching in the Slum School, 1965; Psychology for the Classroom, 1969; Teachers and the Learning Process, 1971; Education for Affective Achievement (with E P Torrance), 1973; Values and Human Development, 1973; Learning Processes, 1976; Parent and Child Development, 1978; Growing Through Play: Parents and Children, 1981; Educational Psychology, 1982; Human Development and Learning, 1989. *Contributions to:* Over 150 articles to journals of education, psychology, educational research, aging and human development, child development, creativity and exceptional children. *Honours:* NATO Scholar, University of Ankara, Turkey, 1967; Fulbright Scholar, Canberra, Australia, 1975; Fulbright Scholar, University of Stockholm, Sweden, 1985. *Membership:* American Psychological Association. *Address:* Arizona State University, Tempe, AZ 85287, USA.

STROM-PAIKIN Joyce Elizabeth, b. 25 Oct 1946, Syracuse, New York, USA. Medical Psychotherapist; Nurse Clinician. m. 26 June 1982, 1 son. *Education:* AAS, Nursing, 1976; BS, Community Psychology, 1978; MS, Counselling Psychology, 1980. *Publications:* Silent Thoughts in Courtroom QU6, 1983; The Gift of Life, 1984; The Near Death Experience, 1986; A New Breed of Gypsies, 1979; Giving the Gift of Life, 1983; Feiru, My Iranian Sister, 1979; 2 novels: Medical Treason, & Through the Light; Non-Fiction: Psycho Awareness; Stress Management; Messiahs of Modern Day Medicine. *Contributions to:* numerous professional journals. *Honours:* Writers Digest Winner, 1981; Writers Instructor, American Psychological Association, Midwinter Convention, 1987. *Memberships:* American Psychological Association; American Nursing Association; President, South Florida Nurse Educators Inc., 1984. *Address:* 6112 NW 1st Street, Margate, FL 33063, USA.

STRONG Eithne, b. 28 Feb 1923, W. Limerick, Ireland. Writer. m. Rupert Strong, 1943, 2 sons, 7 daughters. *Education:* BA, H.Dip.Ed., Trinity College, Dublin. *Publications:* Sarah, in Passing; Flesh - The Greatest Sin; Songs of Living; Degrees of Kindred; Patterns; Cirt Oibre; Fuil agus Fallaí; My Darling Neighbour; Aoife faoi Ghlas (poetry in Irish), 1990; An Sagart Pine (poetry in Irish), 1990; Let Live (poetry in English), 1990. *Contributions to:* numerous journals and magazines. *Honour:* PEN, short story Prize, 1986. *Memberships:* several professional bodies including: Poetry Ireland; PEN; Irish Writers' Union. *Address:* 17 Eaton Square, Monkstown, Co. Dublin, Ireland.

STRONG Jonathan, b. 13 Aug 1944, Evanston, Illinois, USA. Novelist. Teacher. *Education:* BA, Harvard University, 1969. *Publications:* Secred Words, 1992; Elsewhere, 1985; Ourselves, 1971; Tike, 1969; Companion Pieces, 1993; An Untold Tale (novel), 1993; Forthcoming: Offspring (novel). *Contributions to:* Partisan Review; Triquarterly; Shenandoah; Esquire; Transatlantic Review. *Honours:* Rosenthal Award, 1970; O Henry Story Award, 1967, 1970; National Endowment for the Arts Award, 1986. *Memberships:* New England Gilbert and Sullivan Society' Sir Arthur Sullivan Society. *Address:* English Department, Turfs University, Medford, MA 02155, USA.

STRONG June (Sara Greene), b. 17 Mar 1928, Vermont, USA. Writer. m. Donald W Strong, 14 Sept 1947, 3 sons, 2 daughters. *Education:* Attended Atlantic Union College 1945-46, and Burlington Business College, 1946-47. *Appointments:* Secretary in Batavia, New York, 1947-49 and 1950-52; Writer. *Publications:* Journal of a Happy Woman, 1973; Mindy, 1977; Project Sunlight, 1980; A Little Journey, 1984; Song of Eve, 1987; Why Are We Running? *Contributions to:* Author of monthly column in Signs of the Times, 1974-87. Contributor to magazines, sometimes under pseudonym Sara Greene. *Membership:* Writers Workshop. *Address:* 8507 Prole Road, Batavia, NY 14020, USA.

STRONG Roy (Colin) (Sir), b. 1935, United Kingdom. Author. *Appointments:* Assistant Keeper, 1959-67, Director, Keeper, Secretary, 1967-73, National Portrait Gallery, London; Museum Director, Victoria and Albert Museum, 1974-87. *Publications including:* Portraits of Queen Elizabeth I, 1963; Leicester's Triumph (with J A Van Dorsten), 1964; Holbein and Henry VIII, 1967; Tudor and Jacobean Portraits, 1969; The English Icon, 1969; Elizabeth R (with J T Oman), 1971; Van Dyck, Charles I on Horseback, 1972; Mary Queen of Scots (with J T Oman), 1972; Inigo Jones: The Theatre of the Stuart Court (with S Orgel), 1973; Splendour at Court, 1973; An Early Victorian Album: The Hill/Adamson Collection, 1974; Nicholas Hilliard, 1975; The Cult of Elizabeth: Elizabeth Portraiture and Pageantry, 1977; When Did You Last See Your Father, The Victorian Painter and British History, 1978; The Renaissance Garden in England, 1979; Britannia Triumphans: Inigo Jones, Rubens, and Whitehall Palace, 1980; The English Miniature (co-author), 1981; Designing for the Dancer (contrib), 1981; The English Year (with J T Oman), 1982; The New Pelican Guide to English Literature (co-author), 1982; The English Renaissance Miniature, 1983; Artists of the Tudor Court Catalogue (with J Murrell), 1983;

Art and Power, 1984; Glyndebourne: A Celebration (co-author), 1984; Strong Points, 1985; Henry, Prince of Wales and England's Lost Renaissance, 1986; Creating Small Gardens, 1986; Gloriana: Portraits of Queen Elizabeth I, 1987; A Small Garden Designer's Handbook, 1987; Cecil Benton, The Royal Portraits, 1988; Creating Small Formal Gardens, 1989; Sidney's Achievements (contrib), 1990; England and Me Continental Renaissance (co-author), 1990; Lost Treasures of Britain, 1990; The Garden Trellis, 1991; Small Period Gardens, 1992; The Royal Gardens, 1992. Contribution to: The Art of The Emblem, 1993. Literary Agent: Felicity Bryon. Address: The Laskett Much Birch, Herefords, HR2 8HZ, England.

STROUD Drew McCord, b. 3 Sept 1944, Phoenix, Arizona, USA. Writer. Education: BA, English, cum laude, Harvard University, 1966; MA, Hispanic Studies, University of Arizona, 1986. Appointments: Editor, Prentice-Hall, 1967- 68, Holt, Rinehart & Winston 1970-73, Harper & Row 1973, Charles E. Tuttle Co., 1976-77, Kodansha International, 1977-80, Past-Director, International Promotion; Editor-in-Chief, Saru Press International, 1980-; Adjunct Instuctor of English and Spanish (Literature and Creative Writing), Temple University, Japan, 1987. Publications: The Majority Minority, 1973; Lines Drawn Towards, 1980; Poamorio, 1985; Hospitality of Circumstance, 1988. Contributions to: New Republic; Mediterranean Review; Expatriate Review; Christopher Street; Tokyo Journal; Japan Quarterly; The Magazine; Musashino Joshi Daigaku Eibun Gakkai; Musashino Joshi Daigaku Kiyoo. Honours: Grand Prize, Tokyo English Literature Society, 1982; Grant for Translation, Witter Bynner Foundation for Poetry, 1983. Memberships: Poetry Society of America; Academy of American Poets; Tokyo English Literature Society; Asiatic Society of Japan; American Association of Teachers of Spanish & Portuguese. Address: Temple University Japan, 1-16-7 Kami Ochiai, Shinjuku-ku, Tokyo 161, Japan.

STROUD Patricia Tyson, b. 22 Dec 1932, Philadelphia, Pennsylvania, USA. Writer. m. (1) Noel Tyson, 1956, dec. 1982, 2 sons, 1 daughter, (2) Morris Stroud III, 1989, dec. 1990, (3) Alexander McCurdy III, 1991. Education: BA, Smith College, 1955. Publications: Thomas Say: New World Naturalist, 1992. Contributions to: Frontiers, annual magazine of Academy of Natural Sciences of Philadelphia. Address: 613 Maplewood Road, Wayne, PA 19087, USA.

STRUTTON Bill, b. 23 Feb 1918, Moonta, South Australia, Australia. Writer. m. Virginia Bolt, 18 Apr 1970, 1 son, 2 daughters. Education: South Australian Country Studentship, Kadina Memorial High School, 1932; Adelaide, 1933-35. Appointments: Feature Writer, Australian Consolidated Press, 1945-58. Publications: A Jury of Angels, 1957; The Secret Invaders (with Michael Pearson), 1959; Island of Terrible Friends, 1961; Dr Who and the Zarbi, 1965; The Carpaccio Caper, 1973; Many screenplays for popular TV series, Britain, USA and Australia, 1958-75. Memberships: Crimewriters Association; Writers Guild of Great Britain. Literary Agent: David Higham Associates, Lower John Street, London, England. Address: Federico Marti Carreras 2, 17200 Palafrugell, (Gerona), Spain.

STUART Clay. See: WHITTINGTON Harry.

STUART Sidney. See: AVALLONE Michael.

STUBBS Harry Clement (Hal Clement), b. 1922, USA. Appointments: Science Teacher, Milton Academy, MA, 1949-87. Publications: Needle, 1951; Iceworld, 1953; Mission of Gravity, 1954; The Ranger Boys in Space, 1956; as From Outer Space, Cycle of Fire, 1957; Some Notes on Xi Bootis, 1960; Close to Critical, 1964; Natives of Space, 1965; Small Changes, as Space Lash, 1969; First Flights to the Moon (ed), 1970; The Moon by George Gamow (ed), Star Light, 1971; Ocean on Top,

1973; Left of Africa, 1976; Through the Eye of the Needle, 1978; The Best of Hal Clement, 1979; Nitrogen Fix, 1982; Still River, 1987. Address: 12 Thompson Lane, Milton, MA 02186, USA.

STUBBS Jean, b. 23 Oct 1926, Denton, Lancashire, England, Author. m. (1) Peter Stubbs, 1 May 1948, 1 son, 1 daughter, (2) Roy Oliver, 5 Aug 1980. Education: Manchester School of Art, 1944-47; Diploma, Loreburn Secretarial College, Manchester, 1947. Appointment: Writer-in-Residence for Avon, 1984. Publications: The Rose Grower, 1962; The Travellers, 1963; Hanrahan's Colony, 1964; The Straw Crown, 1966; My Grand Enemy, 1967; The Passing Star, 1970; The Case of Kitty Ogilvie, 1970; An Unknown Welshman, 1972; Dear Laura, 1973; The Painted Face, 1974; The Golden Crucible, 1976; Kit's Hill, 1979; The Ironmaster, 1981; The Vivian Inheritance, 1982; The Northern Correspondent, 1984; 100 Years Aroung the Lizard, 1985; Great Houses of Cornwall, 1987; A Lasting Spring, 1987; Like We Used to Be, 1989; Summer Secrets, 1990. Contributions to: Stories in: Winter's Tales; Winter's Crimes; Ghost Books; Penguin Modern Stories; Reviewed for Books and Bookmen 1965-76; Women's magazines; Copywriter, Henry Melland, Industrial Publishers, 1964-66. Honours:Tom Gallon Trust Award for short story writing, 1964; Daughter of Mark Twain, 1973. Memberships: PEN; Society of Women Writers and Journalists; Detection Club; Crime Writers Association, former committee member; Lancashire Writers Association; West Country Writers. Literary Agent: Jennifer Kavanagh, 39 Camden Park Road, London NW1 9AX, England. Address: Trewin, Nancegollan, Helston, Cornwall TR13 0AJ, England.

STUDDY-CLIFT Pat. See: CLIFT Patricia Elizabeth.

STUDER Constance Elaine Browne, b. 4 Dec 1942, Lodi, Ohio, USA. Professional Writer-Poet; Registered Nurse. (div), 1 son. Education: Nursing Diploma, Toledo Hospital School of Nursing, 1963; BA, Illinois College, 1971; MA, English Literature, Creative Writing, University of Colorado, Boulder, 1980. Appointments: Teaching Assistant, 1978-79, Taught Introduction to Creative Writing, 1978-80, University of Colorado; Artist-in-Residence, Poetry, Rocky Mountain Womens Institute, 1987. Publications: Toward Solomon's Mountan, 1986; Wingbone : Poetry from Colorado, 1986; Hyperion : Black Sun, New Moon, 1980; Womanthology, 1977. Contributions to: Room of our Own; Eleventh Muse; Kaleidoscope. Honours: Ann Woodbury Hafen Prize, 1977; Finalist, Nimrod Poetry Contest, 1986; 3rd Place, International Kaleidoscope Poetry Contest, 1986; Winner, Embers Poetry Contest, Winter, 1986; Winner, Artist-in-Residence Associateship, Poetry, Rocky Mountain Women's Institute, 1987. Address: 4518 Aberdeen Place, Boulder, CO 80301, USA.

STUEWE Paul William, b. 5 Oct 1943, Rochester, New York, USA. Editor; Writer. m. Deanna Groetzinger, 30 Aug 1976, 1 son, 2 daughters. Education: BA, Columbia University, 1965; MA, University of Toronto, 1993. Appointments: Contributing Editor, Quill & Quire, 1979-90; Editor, Books in Canada, 1990-. Publications: Dont Deal Five Deuces; The Storms Below; Hugh Garners Life And Works; Clearing the Ground. Contributions to: Too Numerous. Honours: Shortlisted, City of Toronto Book Award. Memberships: Canadian Society of Magazine Editors. Address: 149 Essex Street, Toronto, Canada M6G 1T6.

STURMAN John Rollin, b. 15 May 1952, New York City, USA. Editor. Education: BA, Columbia College, New York, 1973; MA, University of North Carolina, 1975. Publications: The Bedside, Bathtub and Armchair Companion to Agatha Christie, 1979; Roadside Food, 1986; Chae's Medieval Tales, 1987; DuMont Guide to Paris and Ile de France, 1985; DuMont Guide to French Riviera, 1988; DuMont Guide to Loire Valley, 1986. Contributions to: Art News; East Village Eye. Honour: Seymour Vrick Memorial Prize, Playwriting, 1973.

Address: P O Box 20135, London Terrace Station, New York, NY 10011, USA.

STYLES Frank Showell (Glyn Carr), b. 14 Mar 1908, England. Author. m. Kathleen Jane Humphreys, 1954, 1 son, 2 daughters. *Appointments include:* Royal Navy, 1939-46 (retired as Commander); Professional author, 1946-76; Led 2 private Arctic expeditions 1952-53, Himalayan expedition 1954. *Publications:* Mystery novels include: Death Under Snowdon, 1952; A Corpse at Camp Two, 1954; Murder of an Owl, 1956; The Ice Axe Murders, 1958; Swing Away, Climber, 1959; Holiday With Murder, 1960; Death Finds a Foothold, 1961; Lewker in Norway, 1963; Death of a Weirdy, 1965; Lewker in Tirol, 1967; Fat Man's Agony, 1969. Other novels include: Number Two-Ninety, 1966 (in US as Confederate Raider, 1967); A Tent on Top, 1971; Vincey Joe at Quiberon, 1971; Admiral of England, 1973; A Sword for Mr Fitton, 1975; Mr Fitton's Commission, 1977; The Baltic Convoy, 1979; A Kiss for Captain Hardy, 1979; Centurion Comes Home, 1980; The Quarterdeck Ladder, 1982; Seven-Gun Broadside, 1982; The Malta Frigate, 1983; Mutiny in the Caribbean, 1984; The Lee Shore, 1985; Gun-Brig Captain, 1987; HMS Cracker, 1988; Nelson's Midshipman, 1990; Nelson's Midshipman, 1990; A Ship for Mr Fitton, 1991; The Independent Cruise, 1992; Mr Fitton's Prize, 1993. Other works include: First on the Summits, 1970; First Up Everest, 1970; The Forbidden Frontiers: A Survey of India from 1765 to 1949, 1970; Welsh Walks and Legends, 1972; Snowdon Range, 1973; The Mountains of North Wales, 1973; Glyder Range, 1974; Backpacking: A Comprehensive Guide, 1976; Backpacking in the Alps and Pyrenees, 1976; Backpacking in Wales, 1977; Welsh Walks and Legends: South Wales, 1977. *Honour:* Fellow, Royal Geographic Society, 1954. *Address:* Trwyn Cae Iago, Borth-y-Gest, Porthmadog, Gwynedd LL49 9TW, Wales.

STYRON William (Clark) Jr, b. 11 June 1925, Newport News, Virginia, USA, Writer. m. Rose Burgunder, 4 May 1953, 1 son, 3 daughters. *Education:* LLD, Davidson College, 1942-43; AB, LLD, Duke University, 1943-47. *Publications:* Lie Down in Darkness, 1951; The Long March, 1953; Set This House on Fire, 1960; The Confessions of Nat Turner, 1967; Sophie's Choice, 1979 This Quiet Dust, 1982; Darkness Visible, 1990. *Contributions to:* Articles, essays and reviews to numerous journals. *Honours:* Pulitzer Prize, 1968; American Book Award, 1980; Prix Mondial Cino del Duca, 1985; Commandeur Ordre des Arts et des lettres, 1985; Edward MacDowell Medal, 1988; decorated Commandeur Legion d'Honneur, France, 1988; Elmer Holmes Bobst Award for fiction, 1989. *Memberships:* Honorary member, Academie Goncourt, France; American Academy of Arts and Sciences; American Academy of Arts and letters. *Literary Agent:* Don Congdon, 156 Fifth Avenue, New York, NY 10010, USA. *Address:* 12 Rucum Road, Roxbury, CT 06783, USA.

SUBBA RAO Ch V. *See:* **SUBBA RAO Chamarty Venkata.**

SUBBA RAO Chamarty Venkata, (Ch. V. Subba Rao), b. 1 July 1942, India. Journalist. m. Padmavati Devi, 25 Feb 1965, 1 son, 3 daughters. *Education:* BA, 1978. *Publications:* Mana Jetaji, 1989; Number of articles on various social matters concerning humanity. *Memberships:* VP, Society of University Love, India; Small and Medium Newspapers Federation. *Address:* Indo-British Friendship Society (CHQ), 23-34-1 Mannepallivari Street, Laxminagar, Vijayawada 520011, India.

SUBRAHMANYAM T S, b. 25 June 1930, Mysore City, India. m. T S Nagalakshmi, 19 June 1964, 1 son, 1 daughter. *Education:* BA, Mysore University, 1950; B Cum, 19652. *Appointments:* Secretary, Mythic Society, 1966-69; General Secretary, Karnataka Writers Association, 1959-; Vice President, Mysore Civic And Progressive Association, 1985-. *Publications:* An

Ireekshitha; Gubbi Veeranni; Ocadani; Shradhanjaci; Dhwani Prathi DWani. *Contributions to:* Jana Pragath; prajamatha; Vidyarthi; Koravanji; JMS. *Memberships:* PEN; Kannada Sahitya Parishat; Gandhi Sahity Sanga; BM SRI; Ganakala Parisht; GUPA. *Address:* 144 II Main AG's Colony, Ananda Nagar, Bangalore 560024, India.

SUBRAMAN Belinda (Mary Bumgarer), *Education:* BA, Regents College, New York, 1987; MA, California State University, 1990. *Appointments:* Poetry Editor, Gypsy Magazine and Vergin Press, 1983-. *Publications:* Poetry Books: Skin Divers, (co-author Lyn Lifshin), 1988; Halloween, 1989; Fighting Woman, 1986; Heather and Mace, 1985; The Jesuit Poems, 1989; Nurnberg Poems, 1983; Eye of the Beast, 1986; Snow Summits, 1988; In the Sun He Dreams His Playmate, 1987; Body Parts, 1987. *Contributions to:* The Baltimore Sun; Puerto del Sol; Genre; Open; Rio Grande Review; Slipstream; Amelia; Bogg; Samisdat; Gargoyle; Second Coming; The Plough. *Address:* PO Box 370322, El Paso, TX 79937, USA.

SUCKIEL Ellen Kappy, b. 15 June 1943. University Professor. m. Joseph W Suckiel, 23 June 1973. *Education:* AB Douglass College, 1965; MA 1968, PhD, 1972, University of Wisconsin, Madison. *Publications:* The Pragmatic Philosophy of William James, 1982. *Contributions to:* A variety of philosophy journals. *Memberships:* American Philosophical Association; Society for the Advancement of American Philosophy. *Address:* Stevenson College, University of California, Santa Cruz, CA 95064, USA.

SUDAMA Bhikkhoo. *See:* **GOKANI Pushkar Haridas.**

SUGIMOTO Yoshio, b. 7 Dec 1939, Japan. University Professor. m. Machiko Satow, 19 June 1966, 1 son, 2 daughters. *Education:* Political Science, Kyoto University, 1964; PhD Sociology, University of Pittsburgh, 1973. *Publications:* Popular Disturbance in Postwar Japan, 1981; Images of Japanese Society, 1986; Democracy in Contemporary Japan, 1986; The Japanese Trajectory, 1988; Constructs for Understanding Japan, 1989; The MFP Debate, 1990. *Honours:* Japan Intercultural Publications Award, 1987. *Memberships:* Fellow, Australian Academy of the Humanities. *Address:* Department of Sociology, La Trobe University, Bundoora, Melbourne, Victoria 3083, Australia.

SUKENICK Ronald, b. 1932, USA. Professor of English; Writer. *Appointments:* Lecturer, Brandeis University, Waltham, Massachusetts, 1956-57; Lecturer, Hofstra University, Hempstead, New York, 1961-62; Part-time Teacher, 1963-66; Assistant Professor of English, City College of New York, 1966-67; Assistant Professor of English, Sarah Lawrence College, Bronxville, New York, 1968-69; Writer-in-Residence, Cornell University, Ithaca, New York, 1969-70; Writer-in-Residence, University of California, Irvine, 1970-72; Professor of English, 1975-, Director of Writing Programme, 1975-77, University of Colorado, Boulder; Founding Member, Fiction Collective; Chairman, Coordinating Council of Literary Magazines, 1975-77; Advisory Committee, PMLA, 1987-90; Co-Director, Fiction Collective Two; Publisher, American Book Review; Editor, Black Ice; Director, English Department Publications Center of University of Colorado, Boulder, USA. *Publications:* Wallace Stevens: Musing the Obscure, 1967; Up, 1968; The Death of the Novel and Other Stories, 1969; Out, 1973; 98.6, 1975; Long Talking Bad Conditions Blues, 1979; In Form: Digressions on the Act of Fiction, 1985; Blown Away, 1985; The Endless Short Story, 1986; Down and In, 1987. *Honours:* Fulbright Fellowship, 1958; Guggenheim Fellowship, 1977; National Endowment for the Arts Fellowship, 1980 and 1989; CCLM Award for Editorial Excellence, 1985; Western Book Award for Publishing, 1985; American Book Award, 1988. *Memberships:* National Book Critics Circle; PEN American Center. *Literary Agent:* Gene Winick, McIntish

& Otis. *Address:* Department of English, University of Colorado, Boulder, CO 80309, USA.

SUKOSD Mihaly, b. 4 Oct 1933, Budapest, Hungary. Writer; Journalist. div. 2 sons. *Education:* MA, PhD, Budapest ELTE University. *Publications:* 26 published books including novels, short stories, literary and sociological essays. *Contributions to:* German, English and American papers. *Honours:* Hungarian Literary Prizes. *Memberships:* Numerous professional bodies all over the world including International PEN CLub. *Address:* 1111 Egry J u 36, Budapest, Hungary.

SULIMA-KAMIMINSKI Jerzy, b.20 Sept 1928, Bydgoszcz, Poland. Writer. m. Irena, 8 Jan 1952, 1 daughter. *Education:* State Technical School, State Engineering School in Bydgoszcz. *Appointment:* Polish Radio and TV in Bydgoszcz, 1955-90 (retired August 1990). *Publications:* The Hat with Veil, 1964; My Mother's Home, 1970; The Subfeorile State, 1972; A Captive Flight 1974; The Paradise with Eve, 1982; Queen Jadwiga Bridge (trilogy 1981-88; Someone with the Mistletoe Spring, 1968; The Empties 1976; Cimelium, Radio Plays, 1978; The Patriarch 1982; The Three Ledged Man, 1979; Where Are Your running Horses? a story for children, 1989; A Ticket to Singapur, a radio novel, 1989; A Ticket to Singapore, 1991. *Contributions to:* The Pomorze, The Dialog, The Teatr Polskiego Radia, The Zycie Literackie, Miesiecznik Literacki. *Honours:* Annual Literary Award, Chairman of the Polish Radio and TV Committee, 1987, series of regional literary awards. *Membership:* Polish Writers Association, Vice-Chairman of Polish Radio Literary Section, 1958-63. *Address:* ul Poziomkowa 4, 85-343 Bydgoszcz, Poland.

SULITZER Paul-Loup, b. 22 July 1946, Paris, France. Investor, Financial Counselor and International Consultant; Writer. m. 1. Lyne Chardonnet, 1968, (div 1970); 2. Magali Colcanap, 24 Mar 1973 (div), 1 daughter. *Education:* Attended schools in Paris, France. *Appointments:* Labourer in Spain, Kibbutz Worker in Israel and Movie Assistant, 1959-64; Founder and Chief Executive Officer of a Key Ring Collector's Club in France, 1965-67; Designer of Novelties and Founder of a French Company that imported gadgets from Hong Kong, 1967-68; Investor, Financial Counselor and International Consultant, early 1970s-; Writer 1979-. *Publications:* Money, Denoel, 1980, translation by Susan Wald published as Money, Lyle Stuart, 1985; Cash! Denoel, 1981, translation by Susan Wald published as Cash, Lyle Stuart, 1986; Fortune, Denoel, 1982, translation published as Fortune, Lyle Stuart, 1986; Le Roi vert, Edition No 1/Stock 1983, translation by Denise Roab Jacobs, published as The Green King (Literary Guild alternate selection) Lyle Stuart, 1984;Popov, Edition No 1/Orban, 1984; Hannah, Edition No 1/Stock, 1984; Duel a Dallas, Edition No 1, 1984. *Membership:* International Safari Club and Hunting Association. *Address:* 5 Square des Ecrivains Combattants, F-75116, Paris, France.

SULKIN Sidney, b. 2 Feb 1918, Boston, Massachusetts, USA. Writer; Journalist. m. Naomi A Levenson, 1950, 1 son. *Education:* Boston Public Latin SChool, 1935; AB, harvard College, 1939. *Appointments:* Chief, Washington Bureau, Voice of America, 1949-53; Editorial Director, national Issues Committee, 1953-55; Assoicate Editor, Changing Times Magazine, 1955, Senior Education Editor, 1956-76,Editor, 1976-82. *Publications:* The Family Man, 1962; The Secret Seed, 1982; Gate of the Luns, 1982; Matthew the Young King, 1943 (co-translator from Polish); Complete Planning for College, 1962; For Your Freedom and Ours, 1972 (co-editor). *Contributions to:* Kenyon Review, Sewanee Review, Virginia Quarterly, Tri Quarterly, North America Review; Harpers; Tribune. *Honours:* Best American Short Stories, 1948; O Henry Prize Stories, 1948; Fiction of the 1980's, 1982. *Memberships:* PEN; Writers Watch, Past President; Poetry Society of American; Dramatists Guild; Author's Guild; National Press Club. *Address:* 5012 Elsmere Place, Bethesda, MD 20814, USA.

SULLIVAN Matthew Barry, b. 7 June 1915, Toronto, Canada. Writer. m. Elizabeth Margaret Bayley, 7 Oct 1947, 4 sons, 2 daughters. *Education:* Modern History Degree, Hons, New College, Oxford, 1938. *Publications:* Fibre, 1946; Mount Athos, the Call from Sleep, 1961, translation; Adam Unbound, 1969; Thresholds of Peace: German Prisoners and the People of Britain, 1944-48, 1979; Groundwork for Caring, 1983; Living Religion in Subud, 1991; The Second Country of Loving, 1993. *Honours:* Order of Merit, Germany, 1983. *Address:* Nine Elms, Jordans, Beaconsfield, Bucks HP9 2SP, England.

SULLIVAN Sean Mei. *See:* **SOHL Gerald A.**

SULLIVAN Thomas William, b. 20 Nov 1940, Highland Park, Michigan, USA. Author; Teacher. 1 son, 1 daughter. *Education:* BA, 1964. *Publications:* Diapason, 1978; The Phases of Harry Moon, 1988; Born Burning, 1989; Drummers on Glass, 1991; Approx 50 short stories published. *Contributions to:* Over 30 articles in magazines including: Omni; Best of Omni; Twilight Zone; Michigan Magazine. *Honours:* Pushcart Nomination, 1985; Cash Awards, Hemingway Days Festival Literary Contest, 1985, DADA Literary Contest, 1985, 1987; Nebula Award Nomination, 1987; Pulitzer Prize Nomination, 1989. *Memberships:* SFWA; MENSA; Literary Guild; Society of the Black Bull; Arcadia Mixture. *Literary Agent:* Peekner Literary Agency. *Address:* 17376 Catalpa, Lathrup Village, MI 48076, USA.

SULLIVAN Walter Seager, b. 12 Jan 1918, New York, USA. Journalist; Author. m. Mary E. Barrett, 1950, 1 son, 2 daughters. *Education:* Yale University. *Appointments include:* New York Times, 1940-; (US Navy 1940-46). Positions as: Foreign correspondent, Far East, 1948-50; United Nations, 1950-52; Germany & Berlin, 1952-56; US Antarctic Expeditions 1946-47, 1954-55, 1956-57, 1976, 1991; Science news editor, 1960-63; Science editor, 1964-87. Governor, Arctic Institute of North America, 1959-66; Councillor, American Geographical Society, 1959-81. *Publications include:* Quest for a Continent, 1957; White Land of Adventure, 1957; Assault on the Unknown, 1961; We Are Not Alone, 1964; Continents in Motion, 1974; Black Holes: The Edge of Space, The End of Time, 1979; Landprints, 1984. *Honours include:* Public Welfare Medal, National Academy of Sciences, Public Service Award, National Science Foundation, John Wesley Powell Award, US Geological Survey Fellow, Westinghouse Award 1963, 1968, 1972, American Association for Advancement of Science; Honorary degrees, various universities; International Non-Fiction Book Prize, Frankfurt, 1965; American Institute Physics/ US Steel Foundation Award, Physics & Astronomy, 1969; Science-in-Society Journalism Award, National Association of Science Writers, 1976. *Address:* New York Times, Times Square, New York, NY 10036, USA.

SULLOWAY Frank Jones, b. 2 Feb 1947, Concord, New Hampshire, USA. Historian of Science. *Education:* AB summa cum laude, 1969, AM, History of Science, 1971, PhD, 1978, Harvard University. *Publications:* Freud, Biologist of the Mind, 1979; Darwin and his Finches, 1982; Freud and Biology: The Hidden Lagacy, 1982; Darwin's Conversion, 1982; Darwin and the Galapagos, 1984; Darwin's Early Intellectual Development, 1985; Reassessing Freud's Case Histories, 1991. *Honours:* Pfizer Award, History of Science Society, 1980; MacArthur Foundation Fellowship, 1984-89. *Memberships:* Fellow, American Association for the Advancement of Science: Electorate Nominating Committee, Section on the History and Philosophy of Science, 1988-91; History of Science Society, Finance and Development Committees. *Address:* Massachusetts Institute of Technology, Programme in Science, Technology and Society, Bldg E51-128, Cambridge, MA 02139, USA.

SUMAN. *See:* **VAISHAMPAYAN A.**

SUMMERFOREST Ivy B. *See:* **KIRKUP James.**

SUMMERS Anthony (Bruce), b. 21 Dec 1942, UK. Author; Journalist. m. (4) 27 June 1992. *Education:* BA, Modern Languages, New College, Oxford, 1964. *Appointments:* Researcher, World in Action programme, Granada-TV, 1963; Newsreader, Writer, Swiss Broadcasting Corporation, 1964-65; Scriptwriter, BBC-TV News, 1965; Senior Film Producer, BBC-TV Current Affairs Programmes, 1965-73. *Publications:* The File on the Tsar (with Tom Mangold), 1976; Conspiracy (Who Killed President Kennedy), 1980; Goddess: The Secret Lives of Marilyn Monroe, 1985; Honeytrap: The Secret Worlds of Stephen Ward (with Stephen Dorril), 1987. *Contributions to:* Sunday Times; Observer; Independent. *Honour:* Golden Dagger, Crime Writers Association for Best Non-Fiction, 1980. *Memberships:* PEN; Authors Guild. *Literary Agent:* Sterling Lord Literistic Inc (New York City). *Address:* One Madison Avenue, New York City, NY 10010, USA.

SUMMERS Diana. *See:* **SMITH George H.**

SUMMERS Essie. *See:* **FLETT Ethel.**

SUMMERS Judith (Anne), b. 1953, United Kingdom. Full-time Writer. *Appointments:* Freelance London Tourist Guide/Lecturer, 1976-85; Assistant Film Editor, BBC Television, London, 1978-81. *Publications:* Dear Sister, 1985; I, Gloria Gold, 1988. *Literary Agent:* Toby Eady Associates, England. *Address:* c/o Toby Eady Associates, 5 Gledhow Gardens, London SW5 0BL, England.

SUMMERS Merna, b. 22 Mar 1933, Mannville, Alberta, Canada. *Appointments include:* Writer in Residence: University of Alberta, 1991-92; Winnipeg Public Library, 1990-91; St Albert Public Library, 1989. *Publications:* The Skating Party, 1974; Calling Home, 1982; North of the Battle, 1988. *Contributions to:* Anthologies: The Best of ALberta; ALberta Bound; Horizon; In Jeopardy; Western Moods; The Old Dance; West of Fiction; New Worlds; Prose for Discussion; Double Bond; Your VOice and Mind; 73 New Canadian Stories; Reviews for: Toronto Globe and Mail, CBC Sunday Morning, The Candiaian Forum; Books in Canada; The Edmonton Journal; Newest Review; Dandelion magazine; Calgary Herald. *Honours:* Marian Engel Award, 1989; Kathering Anne Porter Prize for Fiction, 1979; Writers' Guild of Alberta Award, 1983; Georges Bugnet Award for Short Fiction, 1983; Grants from, Alberta Foundation for Literary Arts and the Ontario Arts Council. *Memberships include:* Canada Council Writing and Publishing Advisory Committee, 1987-90; International PEN; Children's Literature Roundtable. *Address:* 11455 41st Ave, No 201, Edmonton, Alberta, Canada T6J 0T9.

SUMMERSON John Newenham (Sir), b. 25 Nov 1904, Darlington, England. Architectural Historian. m. Elizabeth Hepworth, 29 Mar 1938, 3 sons. *Education:* Harrow, 1918-22; University College, London, 1922-27; BA (Arch); ARIBA. *Publications:* John Nash, Architect to King George IV, 1935; Georgian London, 1945, 1970; Heavenly Mansions, essays, 1949; Architecture in Britain 1530-1830, 1953, 8th Edition, 1991; Sir John Soane, 1955; The Classical Language of Architecture, 1964, 1980; The Book of John Thorpe, 1966; Inigo Jones, 1966; History of the King's Works (co-author), Vol III, 1976; Vol IV, 1982; The Unromantic Castle, essays, 1990. *Contributions to:* Many articles and reviews in: Times Literary Supplement; Architectural Review; New Statesman; The Listener. *Honours:* CBE, 1952; FBA, 1954; Knight, 1958; Companion of Honour, 1986; Royal Gold Medal Architecture, 1976; Honorary DLitt: Leicester, 1959; Oxford, 1963; Hull, 1971; Newcastle, 1973; Honorary DSc, Edinburgh, 1968; Honorary Fellow, Trinity Hall, Cambridge. *Memberships:* Royal Institute of British Architects; Architecture Association, Council Member 1940-45. *Literary Agent:* Curtis Brown. *Address:* 1 Eton Villas, London NW3 4OX, England.

SUMONY PAPP Zoltan, (Sumonyi Zoltan), b. 5 Feb 1942, Szatmarnemeti. Teacher; Radio Producer. m. Judit Kovacs, 21 July, 1964, 2 sons. *Education:* MA, Hungarian and Russian Literature and Linguistics, 1966. *Publications:* The Portrait is complete, 1977; It is still Summer in Pest, 1983; Selected Poems, 1986; Pazmany, 1979; Istvan VAS, 1982. *Contributions to:* Life and Literature; Glance; Things. *Honours:* Robert Graves Award, 1978; Selected Poems Award, 1988. *Memberships:* Hungarian Author's Guild; Hungarian PEN; Batthyany Society. *Literary Agent:* Artisjus, Hungarian Copyright Office. *Address:* Hungarian Radio, Drama Department, Budapest H-1800, Hungary.bblank

SUNDARAM P S, b. 1 Jan 1910, Tanjore, India. Professor, Retired. m. Padma Hatikudu, 23 Aug 1937, 1 son, 1 daughter. *Education:* MA, Mashas University, 1930; MA, Oxford University, 1934. *Appointments:* Professor, DAV College, Lahore, 1935; Ravenshaw College, Cuttack, 1938; Principal, FM college, 1950; Member, Public Service Commission, Orissa, 1953; Principal, Bareilly College, 1959; Director, Maharajas College, Jaipur, 1964; Professor, Rajasthan University, 1968. *Publications:* Poems of Snbramaria Bharati; Poems of Andal; The Kuml; Karnba Ramayanam; R K Narayan. *Contributions to:* The Quest; The New Quest; Triverni; Indian Literature; Journal of the Rajasthan University. *Memberships:* All Indian English Teachers Conference. *Address:* B14 Atandra, 15 Triumalai Road, Madras, 600017, India.

SUNDERLAND Eric, b. 18 Mar 1930, Ammanford, Dyfed, Wales. University College, Bangor, Principal and Vice-Chancellor, University of Wales. m. 19 Oct 1957, 2 daughters. *Education:* BA Class I, Geography with Anthropology, University of Wales; MA Anthropology (by thesis), University of Wales; PhD in Anthropology (by thesis), University College, London. *Publications:* Elements of Human and Social Geography; some anthropological perspectives, 1973; Genetic Variation in Britain (co-editor), 1973; The operation of Intelligence: biological pre-conditions for the operation of intelligence (co-editor), 1980; Genetic and Population Studies in Wales (co-editor), 1986. *Contributions to:* About 80 papers to journals; About 50 book reviews. *Honours:* Fellow, Institute of Biology, 1975; Hardlicka Medal for Anthropological Research, 1976; Honorary Fellow and Gorjanovic-Krambergeri Medal, Croatian Anthropological Society, 1985; Created Honorary Member of the Gorsedd of Bards, Royal National Eisteddfod of Wales, Rhyl, 1985; Welsh Supernumerary Fellow, Jesus College, Oxford, 1987-1988; President, Royal Anthropological Institute, London, 1989-1991, 1992-1993. *Memberships:* Secretary-General, International Union of Anthropological and Ethnological Sciences, 1978-; Royal Anthropological Institute; The Athenaeum. *Address:* Bryn, Ffriddoedd Road, Bangor, Gwynedd LL57 2EH, Wales, UK.

SUSAMPU. *See:* **SAMPUTAANAE Kosu.**

SUTCLIFF Rosemary, b. 14 Dec 1920, Surrey, England, Writer. *Education:* Bideford School of Art. *Publications include:* The Eagle of the Ninth, 1954; The Lantern Bearers, 1959; Frontier Wolf, 1980; Bonnie Dundee, 1984; Sword at Sunset, 1962; Blood and Sand, 1988; The Shining Company, 1990; Author of over 40 books for children and young adults and 5 for adults. *Honours:* Carnegie Award, 1959; OBE for Services to Children's Literature, 1975. *Membership:* Royal Society of Literature. *Literary Agent:* Murray Polinger. *Address:* Swallowshaw, Walberton, Arundel, Sussex BN18 0PQ, England.

SUTHERLAND Margaret, b. 16 Sept 1941, Auckland, New Zealand. Author. Married, 2 sons, 1 daughter. *Education:* Registered Nurse. *Appointments:* Literary Fellow, Auckland University, 1981; Scholarship in Letters, New Zealand Government, 1984; Australia Council Writers Fellowship, 1992. *Publications:* The Fledgling, 1974; The Love Contract, 1976; Getting Through, 1977, (USA, Dark Places, Deep Regions, 1980); The Fringe of Heaven, 1984; The City Far From Home,

1992. Childrens Books: Hello I'm Karen, 1974. *Contributions to:* Literary & Popular New Zealand Magazines and Journals. *Honours:* Katherine Mansfield Short Story Award; Scholarship in Letters, New Zealand, 1981. *Membership:* Federation of Australian Writers. *Address:* 10 Council Street, Speers point, NSW 2284, Australia.

SUTHERLAND SMITH Beverley Margaret b. 1 July 1935, Australia. Writer. (div), 2 sons, 2 daughters. *Publications include:* A Taste for All Seasons, 1975 revised 1991; A Taste of Class, 1980; A Taste in Time, 1981; Chocolates and Petit Fours, 1987; Gourmet Gifts, 1985; Delicious Desserts, 1989; Oriental Cookbook, 1990. *Contributions to:* Gourmet Magazine; Epicurean Magazine; The Age; Australian Wine Club Magazine; Golden Wings; German Geographical Magazine. *Memberships:* International Association of Culinary Professionals; Ladies Wine and Food Society of Melbourne; Chaine des Rotisseurs; Wine Press Club; Amities Gastronomiques Internationales. *Literary Agent:* Curtis Brown (Australia and USA). *Address:* 29 Regent Street, Mount Waverley, 3149 Melbourne, Victoria, Australia.

SÜTO András, b. 17 June 1927, Pusztakamarás, Transylvania, Romania (Hungarian ethnic origin). Writer; Journalist. m. Eva Szabo, 1949, 2 children. *Appointments include:* Journalist, Vilagossag daily newspaper, Kolozsvár; Contributor, later editor-in-chief, Falvak Népe, 1949-54; Deputy chief editor, Igaz Szo literary monthly, Marosvásárhely, Tirgu Mures, 1955-57; Chief editor, Uj Elet, pictorial, Marosvásárhely, 1957-1989; Vice president, Writers Federation, Socialist Republic of Romania, 1973-81. *Publications include:* Emberek indulnak, short stories, 1953; Félrejaro Salamon, short novel, 1956; Anyam könnyu álmot iger, novel, 1970; Rigó és apostol, essays, travelogue, 1970; Engedjétek hozzam jönni a szavakat, novel, 1977; Az Idö Markában, essays, 1984. Dramatic works: Tékozló szerelem, play, 1963; Pompás Gedeon, play, 1968; Egy lócsiszár virágvasarnápja, 1978; Csillag a máglyán, 1978; Cain & Abel, 1978; A szuzai menyegzö, 1981; Advent a Hargitán, 1987; Az Álomkommandé; Books translated into Romanian, German, Russian, Bulgarian, Slovak, Ukrainian; Plays performed, Budapest, Bucharest, Cluj, Novi-Sad, Zagreb, Bratislva, New York. *Honours:* State Prize, Literature, Romania, 1953, 1954; Herder Prize, Vienna, Austria, 1979; Kossuth Prize, 1992. *Address:* Tirgu Mures, Marosvasarhely, Str.Marasti Nr.36, Romania.

SUTTON Henry. *See:* **SLAVITT David.**

SUTTON Remar Marion, b. 11 May 1941, Swainsboro, Georgia, USA. Author; Syndicated Columnist. *Publications:* Mysteries: Long Lines, 1989; Boiling Rock, 1991; Non-fiction: Don't Get Taken Every Time, 1986; Body Worry, 1988; The Common Book, 1991; Knowing Yourself. *Contributions to:* Contributing editor, American Health magazine; Features to: Sports Illustrated; Readers Digest. *Honours:* Long Lines selected by Book-of-the-Month Club and Mysterious Book Club. *Membership:* Mystery Writers of America. *Literary Agent:* Red Boates Agency. *Address:* 603 West Sandtown Road SW, Marietta, GA 30064, USA.

SUTTON Scott Elder, b. 6 Sept 1952, Santa Monica, California, USA. Artist; Children's Book Author, Illustrator, Publisher. m. Susan Catherine Conley, 1 Apr 1979. *Education:* Private Tutoring, all aspects of publications under Thomas Morgan, 5 years. *Publications:* The Wizard Tells a Story Series No. 1, The Family of Ree, 1986; No.2 Oh No! More Wizared Lessons!, 1986; No.3, The Secret of GorBee Grotto, 1987; No.4, More Altitude, Quick, 1988; No.5, Look At The Size Of That Long-Legged Ploot, 1990; Illustrations for the book, The Way to Happiness, 1984; Illustrations for Art Text, The Basics of Creativity and the Arts, 1971, 1975; No.6, The Legend of Snow Pookas, 1991. *Contributions to:* Centerpost Magazine, 1971-76; Celebrity Magazine, 1984. *Honour:* The Way to

Happiness Foundation and Concerned Business Men of America, Set A Good Example Award, 1987. *Memberships:* Society of Children's Book Writers; The Way to Happiness Foundation; Founder, former Director, Celebrity Centre Los Angeles Visual Artists Association. *Address:* Sutton Publications Inc., 14252 Culver Drive, Suite A644, Irvine, CA 92714, USA.

SUTTON Shaun Alfred Graham, b. 14 Oct 1919, England. Stage and Television director, producer & writer. m. Barbara Leslie, 1948, 1 son, 3 daughters. *Education:* Latymer Upper School; Embassy School of Acting, London. *Appointments include:* Stage Manager, London Theatres, 1938-40; Royal Navy 1940-46; Director, Buxton Repertory Theatre, Embassy Theatre, 1947-51; Director, On Monday Next, Comedy Theatre, 1949; Entered BBC TV service, 1952, produced & wrote many children's TV plays & serials; Directed television series including Z Cars, Softly Softly, Sherlock Holmes, Kipling, Detective; Head, BBC Drama Serials Department, 1966-68; Head of BBC TV Drama Group, 1969-81; Producer, Shakespeare series, 1981-1984; Theatre Night series, 1984-89. *Publications:* A Christmas Carol (stage adaptation), 1949; Queen's Champion, children's novel, 1961; The Largest Theatre in the World, 1982. *Honours:* OBE, 1979; Fellow, Royal TV Society; Director, Prime Time Television; OBE, 1979. *Membership:* BAFTA. *Address:* 15 Corringham Court, Corringham Road, London NW11 7BY, England.

SWAIM Alice Mackenzie, b. 5 June 1911, Craigdam, Scotland. Writer; Consultant; Contest Judge. m. William Thomas Swaim, 27 Dec 1932, 2 daughters. *Education:* BA, Wilson College, 1932. *Appointments:* Newspaper Columnist, Cornucopia, Tejas, Carlisle, Pennsylvania Evening Sentinel, 1953-70; National Contest Judge, 1954-85; Newspaper Columnist, Touchstone, New Hampshire, 1970-85; Poetry Therapy Consultant 1971-75; Public Relations Director, 2nd World Congress of Poets; Writer, Concordia Greeting Card Company, 1981-82. *Publications:* Let The Deep Song Rise, 1952; Up To The Stars, 1954; Sunshine in a Thimble, 1958; Crickets are Crying Autumn, 1960; The Gentle Dragon, 1962; Pennyslvania Profile, 1966; Scented Honeysuckle Days, 1966; Here On The Threshhold, 1966; Beneath a Dancing Star (Italy), 1968; Beyond My Catnip Garden, 1970; And Miles to go, 1981; Unicorn and thistle, 1981; Children in summer, 1983; As wrens sing madringals, 1987; Horizon - makers, 1991; Beneath a dancing star, 1991; 5 brochures, 1974-80; And Miles to Go, 1981; Unicorn and Thistle, 1982; Children in Summer, 1983. *Contributions to:* Radio programmes in USA, Canada, Germany, UK; numerous poems published. *Honours include:* Over 800 Awards and Citations including Medals from Philippines, Italy and USA; American Heritage Award, JFK Library for Minorities, 1974; 1st Prize, Writer's Digest Contest, 1988. *Memberships:* Poetry Society of America; Academy of American Poets; National Federation of State Poetry Societies; Marketing Editor, Poetry Society of New Hampshire; Poetry Society of Pennsylvania, Kentucky and California. *Address:* 322 North Second Street Apt. 1606, Harrisburg, PA 17101, USA.

SWAN Gladys, b. 15 Oct 1934, New York City, USA. Writer. m. 9 Sept 1955, 2 daughters. *Education:* BA, Western New Mexico University, 1954; MA, Claremont Graduate School. *Appointments:* Distinguished Visiting Writer in Residence, University of Texas, El Paso, 1984-85; Visiting Professor, Ohio University, 1986-87; Associate Professor, University of Missouri, 1987-. *Publications:* On the Edge of the Desert (short stories), 1979; Carnival for the Gods (novel), 1986; Of Memory and Desire (short stories), 1989. *Contributions to:* 25 short stories to various magazines including: Sewanee Review; Virginia Quarterly Review; Writer' Forum; Ohio Review; Mid- American Review, Kenyon Review, Manoa. *Honour:* Fulbright Fellowship, Writer-in-Residence, Yugoslavia, 1988. *Memberships:* Associated Writing Programmes; PEN American Center. *Address:* 2601 Lynwood Dr., Columbia, MO 65203, USA.

SWANTON Ernest William, b. 11 Feb 1907, London,

England. Author. m. Ann Marion Carbutt, 11 Feb 1958. *Education:* Cranleigh School, 1921- 24. *Appointments:* Evening Standard Staff, 1927-39; Daily Telegraph Staff, 1946-75; Editorial Director, The Cricketer, 1965-89. *Publications:* History of Cricket, 1938-1962, with H S Altham, 1962; Barclays World of Cricket, 1st Edition, 1966, 2nd Edition, 1980, 3rd Edition, 1986; As I Said at the Time, 1983; Essential E W Swanton, 1990. *Contributions to:* The Cricketer. *Honours:* OBE, 1965; Appointed Life Vice-President, MCC. *Literary Agent:* Curtis Brown; John Farquharson. *Address:* Delf House, Sandwich, Kent CT13 9HB, England.

SWARD Robert Stuart, b. 23 June 1933, Chicago, Illinois, USA, University Professor; Writer, 2 sons, 3 daughters. *Education:* BA, Honours, University of Illinois, 1956; MA, University of Iowa, 1958; Postgraduate Work, University of Bristol, England, 1960-61; Middlebury College, Vermont, USA, 1959-60. *Appointments:* Poet-in-Residence, Cornell University, 1962-64; Poet-in-Residence, University of Victoria, British Columbia, Canada, 1969-73; Visiting Writer, University of California Extension, Santa Cruz, 1986-; Writer-in-Residence, Aspen Writers Conference, 1968; Writer-in-Residence, Foothill Writers Conference, summer, 1988-; Canada Council Fellowship; Exploration Grant; Writer, Writing Programme, Language Arts Department, Cabrillo College, 1989-; Poet-in-residence, University of California, Santa Criz, 1987-. *Publications include:* Uncle Dog and Other Poems, 1962; Kissing the Dancer and Other Poems, 1964; Thousand-Year-Old Fiancee, 1965; Horgbortom Stringbottom, 1970; Hannah's Cartoon, 1970; Quroum/Noah, 1970; Half a Life's History: Poems New and Selected, 1983; Poet Santa Cruz, 1985; Five Iowa Poems and One Iowa Print, 1975; Honey Bear on Lasqueti Island, 1978; The Three Roberts, (Co-authors Robert Zend and Robert Priest), 1985; Four Incarnations, New & Selected Poems, 1957-1991: Golden Oldies and New Releases, 1991. *Contributions to:* The New Yorker; Poetry, Chicago; Transatlantic Review; The Paris Review; Tri-Quarterly; Chicago Review; New York Times; Antioch Review; Poetry Northwest; The Nation. *Honours:* Fulbright Fellowship, 1960-61; Guggenheim Fellowship, 1965-66; D H Lawrence Fellowship, 1966; McDowell Colony Fellowship, 1959-80s; Montalvo Literary Arts Award, Biennial Poetry Competition; Djerassi Foundation Residency, 1990. *Memberships:* Writers Union of Canada, Newsletter Committee Chairman; League of Canadian Poets; National Writers Union USA. *Address:* PO Box 7062, Santa Cruz, CA 95061, USA.

SWARTHOUT Glendon, b. 1918, American. *Appointments:* Associate Professor of English, Michigan State University, East Lansing, 1951-59; Lecturer, Arizona State University, Tempe, 1959-62. *Publications:* Willow Run, 1943; They Came to Cordura, 1958; Where the Boys Are, 1960; Welcome to Thebes, 1962; The Ghost and the Magis Saber (with K Swarthout), 1963; The Cadillac Cowboys, 1964; Whichaway (with K Swarthout), The Eagle and the Iron Cross, 1966; Loveland, 1968; The Button Boat (with K Swarthout), 1969; Bless the Beasts and Children, 1970; TV Thompson (with K Swarthout), The Tin Lizzie Troop, 1972; Luck and Pluck, 1973; The Shootist, Whales to See the (with K Swarthout), 1975; The Melodeon, 1977; Skeletons, 1979; Cadbury's Coffin (with K Swarthout), 1982; The Old Colts, 1985. *Address:* 5045 Tamanar Way, Scottsdale, AZ 85253, USA.

SWARTZ Jon David, b. 28 Dec 1934, Houston, Texas, USA. Psychologist; Professor; University Administrator. m. Carol Joseph Hampton, 20 Oct 1966, 2 sons, 1 daughter. *Education:* BA, 1956, MA, 1961, PhD, 1969, Senior Postdoctoral Fellowship in Community Psychology and Community Mental Health, Counseling-Psychological Services Center and Hogg Foundation for Mental Health, 1973-74, University of Texas, Austin. *Publications:* Inkblot Perception and Personality (with W H Holtzman), 1961; Mental Retardation (with C C Cleland), 1969; Administrative Issues in Institutions for the Mentally Retarded, 1972; Multihandicapped Mentally Retarded, 1973; Personality Development in Two Cultures (with W H Holtzman), 1975; Profound Mental Retardation (with C C Cleland), 1976; The Profoundly Mentally Retarded (editor), 1978; Exceptionalities Through the Lifespan (with C C Cleland), 1982; Holtzman Inkblot Technique, 1956-1982, 4th edition, 1983; Jesse Daniel Ames: An Exhibition at Southwestern University, 1986; HIT: An Annotated Bibliography (Supplement), 1988; Clara Harmon Lewis Collection, 1989; Other separate works. *Contributions to:* Over 350 articles and reviews in over 100 journals and magazines. *Honours include:* Psi Chi, 1959; US Office of Education Fellow, 1964-66; Franklin Gilliam Prize, 1965; Mu Alpha Nu, 1965; Phi Kappa Phi, 1967; Sigma Xi, 1968; Spencer Fellow, National Academy of Education, 1972-74; Postdoctoral Fellow, 1973-74; Delta Tau Kappa, 1976; Phi Delta Kappa, 1980; Faculty Fellowship Award, 1981. *Memberships:* San Gabriel Writers League; Fellow, American Psychological Society; Fellow, American Association for the Advancement of Science; Fellow, Society for Personality Assessment; American Library Association; Southwestern Psychological Association; American Academy on Mental Retardation; Board Member, Western Research Conference on Mental Retardation. *Address:* 1401 East 18th Street, Georgetown, TX 78626, USA.

SWEARER Donald Keeney, b. 2 Aug 1934, Wichita, Kansas, USA. College Professor of Religion. m. 17 June 1964, 1 son, 1 daughter. *Education:* AB cum laude, 1956, MA, 1965, PhD, 1967, Princeton University, New Jersey. *Publications:* Buddhism in Transition, 1970; Secrets of the Lotus, 1971; Wat Haripunjaya: The Royal Temple of the Buddha's Relic, 1976; Dialogue, the Key to Understanding Other Religions, 1977; Buddhism, 1977; Buddhism and Society in Southeast Asia, 1981; For the Sake of the World. The Spirit of Buddhist and Christian Monasticism, 1989; Me-and- Mine. Selected Essays of Bhikkhu Buddhadasa, 1989. *Contributions to:* Journal of the American Academy of Religion; Journal of Religious Ethics; Philosophy East and West; Journal of Ecumenical Studies; Journal of the Siam Society; Religious Studies Review. *Honours:* Phi Beta Kappa, 1956; Kent Fellow, 1964-65; Asian Religions Fellowship, Society for Religion in Higher Education, 1967-68; Senior Fellowship, National Endowment for the Humanities, 1972-73; Humanities Fellowship, Rockefeller Foundation, 1985-86; Senior Research Fellowship, Fulbright (CIES), 1989-90. *Memberships:* American Academy of Religion, Vice-President, Mid-Atlantic Region, 1971-72; Association for Asian Studies, Board of Directors, SE Asia Council, 1977-780; American Society for the Study of Religion; Society for Buddhist-Christian Studies. *Address:* 109 Columbia Avenue, Swarthmore, PA 19081, USA.

SWEDE George, b. 20 Nov 1940, Riga, Latvia. Writer; Professor. m. Anita Krumins, 23 July 1974, 2 sons. *Education:* BA, University of British Columbia, 1964; MA, Dalhousie University, 1965. *Appointments:* Director, Poetry and Things, 1969-71; Poetry Editor, Poetry Toronto, 1980-81; Reviews and Poetry Editor, Writers' Quarterly, 1982-88; Judge, Japan Air Lines Haiku Contest, 1987 and 1990; Poetry Editor, Writers' Magazine, 1988-90; Judge, Haiku Society of American Henderson Award, 1989; Mirrors, International Tanka Awards, 1991. *Publications include:* Poetry: Tell-Tale Feathers, 1978; Endless Jigsaw, 1978; Canadian Haiku Anthology (editor), 1979; Wingbeats, 1979; A Snowman, Headless, 1979; As Far As The Sea Can Eye, 1979; This Morning's Mockingbird, 1980; Eye To Eye With A Frog, 1981; All Of Her Shadows, 1982; Tick Bird, 1983; Frozen Breaths, 1983; I Throw Stones At The Mountain, 1988; Flaking Paint, 1983; Night Tides, 1984; Bifids, 1984; Time is Flies, 1984; The Space Between (with LeRoy Gorman & Eric Amann), 1986; High Wire Spider, 1986; Multiple Personality, 1987; Where Even The Factories Have Lawns (with John Curry), 1988; Leaping Lizard, 1988; Holes in my Cage, 1989; The Universe Is One Poem (editor), 1990; I Want To Lasso Time, 1991; Leaving My Loneliness, 1992. Essays: The Modern English Haiku, 1981. Fiction: Moonlit Gold Dust, 1979; Quillby, The Porcupine Who Lost His Quills (with Anita Krumins), 1980; Missing

Heirloom, 1980; Seaside Burglaries, 1981; Downhill Theft, 1982; Undertow, 1982; Dudley and the Birdman, 1985; Dudley and the Christmas Thief, 1986. *Contributions to:* Poetry, short stories and articles in over 125 different magazines around the world. *Honours:* Haiku Society of America Book Award, 1980; High/Coo Press Chapbook Competition Winner, 1982; Museum of Haiku Literature Award, 1983, 1985, 1993; Canadian Children's Book Centre Our Choice Award, 1984, 1985, 1987, 1991 and 1992. *Memberships:* League of Canadian Poets; The Writers Union of Canada; PEN; Haiku Canada, co-founder 1977; Haiku Society of America; Canadian Society for Authors, Illustrators and Performers; Canadian Authors Association. *Address:* Box 279, Station P, Toronto, Canada M5S 2S8.

SWEENY Mary K, b. 4 Dec 1923, Cleveland, Ohio, USA. Librarian. m. 23 Apr 1949, 1 son, 1 daughter. *Education:* BA, Notre Dame College, 1944; MSLS, Western Reserve University, 1966; MA, John Carroll University, 1984. *Appointments:* Librarian, John Carroll University, University Heights, Ohio. *Publications:* Walker Percy and the Postmodern World, 1987. *Contributions to:* Book reviews; Poetry. *Address:* c/o John Carroll University Library, University Heights, OH 44118, USA.

SWENSEN Cole, b. 22 Oct 1955, San Francisco, USA. Teacher. *Education:* BA Creative Writing, 1980, MA, 1983, San Francisto State University; ABD Comparative Literature, University of California, 1992. *Publications:* Park, 1991; New Math, 1983; It's Alive She Says, 1984; Given, 1986; It's Like You Never Left, 1983. *Contributions to:* Anthologies: under 35: The New Generation of American Poets; Journals: Avec, Five Fingers Review, Zyzzyva, The Quarterly. *Honours:* Marin Arts Council Creative Advancement Grant, 1987; National Poetry Series, 1987; Shifting Foundation Grand, 1989. *Memberships:* Marin Poetry Centre, Pres, 1985-87. *Address:* PO Box 927, Fairfax, CA 94978, USA.

SWETENHAM Violet Hilda (Violet Hilda Drummond), b. 30 July 1911, London, UK. Author; Illustrator; Artist. m. Anthony Swetenham, 28 Feb 1948, 1 son. *Appointment:* Chairman, V H Drummond Productions. *Publications:* Mrs Easter & the Storks, 1957; The Flying Postman, 1964; Phewtus the Squirrel, 1939, 3rd edition 1987; Little Laura series, 1961-62; Mrs Easter's Parasol, 1944; Miss Anna Truly, 1945. All illustrated by author. *Contributions to:* Punch. *Honour:* Kate Greenaway Award, 1958. *Literary Agent:* Diana Lady Avebury, Strathmore Literary Agency. *Address:* 24 Norfolk Road, London NW8 6HG.

SWETZ Frank Joseph, b. 7 July 1937, New York City, USA. University Professor. *Education:* BA Marist College, 1962; MA Fordham University, 1963; DED, Columbia University, 1972; Dip (Supervision), 1969. *Publications:* Mathematics Education i China, 1974; Was Pythagoras Chinese?, 1977; Socialist Mathematics Education, 1979; Capitalism and Arithmetic, 1987; The Sea Island Mathematical Manual, 1992; From Five Fingers to Infinity, 1993; Mathematical Modelling in School Curriculum, 1991. *Contributions to:* Mathematics Teacher; American Mathematical Monthly; Historia Mathematics; Journal of Developing Areas; Science Teacher; USA Today; Physics Teacher; Educational Studies in Mathematics; Curriculum Review. *Honours:* Edpress Awards, 1971, 1984; Fulbright Asean Research Fellowship, 1985; Outstanding Research Awards Penn State University, 1986, 1989. *Memberships:* National Council of Teachers of Mathematics; PA Council Teachers of Mathematics; International Study Group on History of Pedagogy of Mathematics. *Address:* 616 Sandra Avenue, Harrisburg, PA 17109, USA.

SWIFT Graham Colin, b. 4 May 1949, London, England. Author. *Publications:* The Sweet Shop Owner, 1980; Shuttlecock, 1981; Learning to Swim and Other Stories, 1982; Waterland, 1983; The Magic Wheel (edited with David Profumo), 1986; Out of this World,

1988; Ever After, 1992. *Honours:* Nominated for Booker Prize, 1983; Geoffrey Faber Memorial Prize, 1983; Guardian Fiction Award, 1983; Royal Society of Literature Winifred Holtby Award, 1983; Premio Grinzane Cavour, Italy, 1987. *Literary Agent:* A.P. Watt Ltd. *Address:* 20 John Street, London WC1N 2DR, England.

SWINBURNE Richard Granville, b. 26 Dec 1934, Smethwick, Staffordshire, England. University Teacher. m. Monica Holmstrom, 1960 (separated 1960), 2 daughters. *Education:* BA, 1957; B.Phil, 1959; DpTheol, 1960; MA, 1961, University of Oxford. *Publications:* Space and Time, 1968, 2nd edition, 1981; The Coherence of Theism, 1977, rev ed, 1993; The Existence of God, 1979, rev ed, 1991; Faith and Reason, 1981; The Evolution of the Soul, 1986; Responsiblity and Atonement, 1989; The Concept of Miracle, 1971; An Introduction to Confirmation Theory, 1973; Personal Identity, (with S. Shoemaker), 1984; The Evolution of the Soul, 1986; Responsibility and Atonement, 1989; Revelation, 1992. *Contributions to:* Many philosophical journals. *Address:* Oriel College, Oxford OX1 4EW, England.

SWINDELLS Philip Roy, b. 10 Sept 1945, Cambridge, England. Garden Curator. m. Hazel Mary White, 30 Sept 1972, 4 sons, 1 daughter. *Education:* University of Cambridge Botanic Garden. *Literary Appointments:* Editor, Journal of the International Waterlily Society; Editor, Journal of the International Association of Botanic Gardens (European/Mediterranean Division). *Publications:* Ferns for Garden and Greenhouse, 1971; Water Gardening, 1975; Making the Most of Water Gardening, 1980; Aquatic Plants, 1982; Waterlilies, 1983; The Water Gardener's Handbook, 1984; Water Gardening, 1985; Ward Lock Book of the Water Garden, 1985; Cottage Gardening, 1986; Bulbs for all Seasons, 1987; Harlow Car Book of Herb Gardening, 1987; At The Waters Edge, 1988; Primulas, 1989; The Complete Book of the Water Garden (with David Macon), 1989. *Contributions to:* many journals and magazines including: Horticulture Week; Garden News; Flower Specialist of Garden Answers; Gardening Correspondent: Lancashire Life, The Northern Echo, Yorkshire Evening Post, Derbyshire Life, Staffordshire Life. *Honours:* Churchill Fellowship, 1983; Nuffield Scholarship, 1985; Geest Garden Writer of the Year Gold Award, 1985; Garden Writers' of America Quill and Trowel Award, (Radio), 1986; Jiffy 7 Writers Contest Winner, 1986; Professional Plant Growers Association International Garden Writers Award for Magazine Writing, 1988; Award, Newspaper Journalism, 1988. *Memberships:* Northern Region, Institue of Scientific and Technical Communicators; Garden Writers' Association of America; Fellow, Linnean Society of London; Former Chairman, Northern Region Institute of Horticulture. *Address:* Wycliffe Hall Botanical Gardens, Barnard Castle, Co Durham, DL12 9TS, England.

SYLVESTER Doreen Rosalie Mammatt, b. 21 Jan 1947, Brigg, Lincolnshire, England. Freelance Artist. m. R J Sylvester, 10 July 1983. *Education:* Diploma, London Art College, (Press Art, Cartooning). *Appointments:* Founder, Fellow, International Poetry Society. *Publications:* Anthologies, Poetry, Poetry Magazine, Lincolnshire Life: The Small Poetry magazines, 1979; Mitre press Anthologies. *Honours:* International Poetry Day, 2nd Place, 1967; Runner-up, Arnold Vincent Bowen Competition, 1981. *Memberships:* Fellow, Poetry in Orbis Magazine. *Address:* Reedbank, 78 Stather Road, Burton-Upon-Stather, Nr Scunthorpe, South Humberside, DN15 9DH, England.

SYMONS Julian Gustave, b. 30 May 1912, England. Author. m. Kathleen Clark, 1941, 1 son, 1 daughter (dec). *Publications include:* Confusions About X, 1938; The Second Man, 1944; A.J.A. Symons, 1950; Charles Dickens, 1951; The General Strike, 1957; A Reasonable Doubt, 1960; The Detective Story in Britain, 1962; Buller's Campaign, 1963; Critical Occasions, 1966; Picture History of Crime & Detection, 1966; Bloody

Murder: From the Detective Story to the Crime Novel, a History, 1972, 1985; Notes From Another Country, 1972; The Hungry Thirties, 1976; Conan Doyle, 1979; The Great Detectives, 1981; Critical Observations, 1981. Editor, various anthologies, etc. Author, 27 crime novels, several television plays. *Honours include:* CWA Critics Award, 1957; MWA Edgar Allan Poe Award, 1960, 1972; Fellow, Royal Society of Literature, 1975. *Memberships include:* Chairman, Crime Writers Association, 1958-59; Committee of Management, Society of Authors, 1970-71; Grand Master MWA, 1982; President, Detection Club, 1976-85. *Address:* Groton House, 330 Dover Road, Walmer, Deal, Kent CT14 7NX, England.

SYROP Konrad, b. 9 Aug 1914, Vienna, Austria. Writer; Broadcaster; Translator. m. Dr Sara Joelson, 6 Apr 1940, 1 son, 3 daughters. *Education:* Universities of Krakow and Warsaw; Institute Francais, Warsaw. *Appointments:* BBC World Service, Feature Writer, Editor, 1939-74. *Publications:* Spring in October; Poland Between The Hammer & The Sickle; Poland In Perspective; Radio Play, The White Divorce. *Contributions to:* The Guardian; The Times; The Times Literary Supplement; The Author. *Honours:* OBE. *Memberships:* Society of Authors; Authors Licensing Copyright Society. *Literary Agent:* Watson, Little Limited. *Address:* 7 Great Spilmans, Dulwich, London SE22 8SZ, England.

SZABLYA Helen Mary b. 6 Sept 1934, Budapest, Hungary, Writer; Columnist; Lecturer; Translator. m. Dr John F Szablya, 12 June 1951, 3 sons, 4 daughters. *Education:* BA, with Distinction, Foreign Language and Literature, Washington State University, USA, 1976; Diploma (Ex MBA), Sales and Marketing Management, University of British Columbia, 1962. *Appointments:* Freelance Writer, Lecturer, Translator, 1967-; Columnist, Catholic News, Trinidad, West Indies, 1980-1991; Adult Educator, TELOS, Bellevue, (Washington) Community College, 1987-89; Pullman, Spokane Community College, 1976-80; Faculty Christian Writers Conference, Seattle Pacific University, 1983-1990; Faculty, Pacific Northwest Writers Conference, 1987, 1989; Executive Director, Eclectic Union Theater, 1986-; Inquiring Mind Lecturer, Washington Commission for the Humanities, 1987-89; Project Director, Major Grant, Washington Commission for the Humanities, Hungary Remembered, 1985-87. *Publications:* Hungary Remembered (Co-author), in English and Hungarian; Otvenhatos Cserkeszcsapat, 1986; Mind Twisters, 1987; Turning Oral Histories into Dramas/Grant Proposal Writing, one-day workshop, American Translators Association, National Conference, 1989. *Contributions to:* Many popular and religious articles in magazines and journals. *Honours include:* Washington Press Association Professional Excellence Awards, 1983, 1987, 1988, 1989, 1990, 1991, 1992; 1st Prize for editorial, 1988, President's Award for best affiliate president, 1988, National Federation of Press Women; Professional Excellence Award for Editorial, Society for Professional Journalists, 1989; Community Woman of the Year, 1990, American Business Women's Association; Honorary Consul of the Republic of Hungary, 1993, Seattle for the Pacific NW of USA. *Memberships include:* Authors Guild; National Writers Club, Professional member; American Translators Association, Publicity Chair for Seattle National Conference; International PEN Club; Hungarian PEN Club. *Address:* 4416 134th Place SE, Bellevue, WA 98006, USA.

SZABO Arpad K, b. 16 Oct 1913, Budapest, Hungary. Professor. m. 23 Feb 1951, 2 sons, 2 daughters. *Education:* PhD, 1935. *Publications:* Anfänge der griechischeu Mathematik; The Beginnings of Greek Math; Les Débuts des Math Grecques; Enklima Athen; Les débuts de l'Astronomie. *Memberships:* Hungarian Academy of Science. *Address:* Pasoreti ut 60/A, 102 Budapest, Hungary.

SZABO Istvan, b. 18 Feb 1938, Hungary. Film Director; Scenario Author. m. Vera Gyurey. *Education:*

Budapest Academy of Theatre & Film Arts. *Appointments include:* Leading member, Hungarian Film Studios; Tutor, College of Theatre & Film Arts, Budapest, Deutsche Film- und Fernsehakademie, West Berlin. Numerous productions, films, plays, documentaries, television. *Honours include:* Bela Balazs Prize, 1967; Kossuth Prize; Grand Prix, Oberhausen, 1971, 1977; Grand Prix, Locarno, 1973; Silver Bear of Berlin, Academy Award nomination, 1981; Academy Award, David di Donatello Prize (Italy), Italian Critics' Prize, UK Critics' Prize, 1982; BAFTA Award, 1986; Akademy Award Nomination, 1985, 1988; Silver Bear of Berlin, 1992; European Script Writer of the Year, 1992. *Memberships:* Academy of Motion Picture Arts & Sciences; Akademie der Kunste, Berlin. *Address:* Objektiv Film Studio-MAFILM, 1149 Budapest, Lumumba utca 174, Hungary.

SZABO Magda, b. 5 Oct 1917, Hungary. Author. m. Tibor Szobotka, 1948. *Education:* Graduated as teacher, 1940; Dr. phil. of Classical Philology. *Appointments:* Teacher, secondary schools, 1940-44, 1950-59. Started literary career as poet, has since written novels, plays, radio dramas, essays, film scripts. Works translated, 26 languages including English, French, German, Italian, Russian, Polish, Swedish. *Publications:* Neszek (Noises), poems; Okut (Old Well), autobiography. Children's novels: Szigetkek (Blue Island); Tunder Lala (Lala the Fairy); Abigel (Abigail). Novels: Az oz (The Fawn); Fresko (Fresco); Disznotor (Night of Pig Killing); Pilatus (Pilate); A Danaida (The Danaid); Mozes 1.22 (Genesis 1.22); Katalin utca (Kathleen Street); A szemlelok (The Onlookers); Regimodi tortenet (Old-fashioned Story); Az ajso (The Door). Plays: Az a Szep Fenyes Nap (That Bright Beautiful Day); A Merani Fiu (The Boy of Merano); A Csata (The Battle), 1982; Bela Kiraly (King Bela); A Macskak Szerdaha (The Wednesday of the Cats), 1985. *Honours:* Jozsef Attila Prize, 1959, 1972; Kossuth Prize, 1978. *Membership:* Academy of Sciences of Europe. *Address:* H-1026 Budapest II, Julia-utca 3, Hungary.

SZASZ Imre, b. 19 Mar 1927, Budapest, Hungary. Writer and Translator. m. Elizabeth Windsor, 23 Sept 1965, 2 daughters. *Education:* Degree, English and Hungarian Literature, Budapest University, 1945-50. *Appointments:* Publishing House Editor, 1949-689; Literary Editor of Cultural Weekly in Budapest, 1968-90; General Secretary, Hungarian PEN Centre, 1989-. *Publications:* Come at Nine, 1969; Menesi Street, 1986; One Went Hunting 1985; This is the way the world Ends, 1986; Dry Martini, 1973. *Contributions to:* Magazines and journals. *Honours:* Jozef Attila Award, 1954, 1989; Book of the Year, 1989. *Memberships:* Hungarian Writer's Union; Hungarian PEN Centre; Hungarian Journalists' Union. *Address:* Szeher ut 82, Budapest 1021, Hungary.

SZASZ Thomas Stephen, b. 15 Apr 1920, Budapest, Hungary, Psychiatrist. m. 1951, (div), 1 daughter. *Education:* AB, Honours, 1941, MD, 1944, University of Cincinnati, USA; Diplomate, National Board of Medical Examiners, 1945; Diploma, Chicago Institute for Psychoanalysis, 1950; Diplomate in psychiatry, American Board of Psychiatry and Neurology, 1951; Various Internships and Residencies. *Appointments include:* Professor of Psychiatry, State University of New York, Health Science Centre, Syracuse, 1956-; Visiting Professor, New Mexico State University, Las Cruces, New Mexico, 1981; Adjunct Scholar, The Cato Institute, 1985-. *Publications include:* The Myth of Mental Illness, 1961; The Manufacture of Madness, 1970; Ceremonial Chemistry, 1974; Pain and Pleasure: A Study of Bodily Feelings, 1957, 1975; Psychiatric Justice, 1965, 1988; Ideology and Insanity, Essays on the Psychiatric Dehumanization of Man, 1970; The Second Sin, 1973; Heresies, 1976; Schizophrenia: The Sacred Symbol of Psychiatry, 1976, 1988; The Theology of Medicine: The Political-Philosophical Foundations of Medical Ethics, 1977, 1988; Sex by Prescription, 1980; Insanity: The Idea and Its Consequences, 1987; The Untamed Tongue: A Dissenting Dictionary. *Contributions to:* Approximately 500 articles, book chapters, book reviews and newspaper columns. *Honours:* Recipient of numerous awards for professional services. *Memberships:* Numerous including: Life Fellow, American psychiatric Association; Fellow, International Academy of Forensic Psychology. *Literary Agent:* McIntosh and Otis Incorporated, New York, USA.

SZAVAI Geza, b. 4 Dec 1950, Kusmod, Hungary. Editor. m. Ilona Simon, 4 Jan 1974, 1 daughter. *Education:* Philosophy Degree, State University, 1973; Postgraduate school for Journalists, 1977. *Appointments:* Editor: A Het, 1978-89, Datum, 1990-91, Uj Magyarorszag, 1991-; Vice- Editor in Chief: Magyarok Vilaglapja, 1992-. *Publications:* Promenade on gramaphone music, 1985; The Supervisor, 1987; Post Lude, 1991; Essay on children's thinking, 1983; Stories, 1982; Thought and Literature, 1980; Essays, 1981; Mr Bergum, the great detective, (four volumes). *Memberships:* Hungarian Writers' Society; Society of Hungarian Journalists. *Address:* Kiskorona u 2, 1036 Budapest, Hungary.

SZENTMIHALYI SZABO Peter, b. 8 Jan 1945, Budapest, Hungary. Author; Editor. m. Edith Kundl, 1 Sept 1966, 1 son, 1 daughter. *Education:* MA, University of Budapest, 1969. *Appointments:* Editor, Szepirodalmi Publishing House, Budapest, 1979-; Editor, Galaktika Science Fiction Monthly, 1985-. *Publications:* Avarok Gyuruje, 1980; Gellert, 1982; A Latoes a Vak, 1984; Edua Es Kun Laszlo, 1986; A Sebezhetetlen, 1978; A Tokeletes Valtozat, 1984; 8 collections of poems; novels; literary biography; essays; plays. *Contributions to:* Numerous magazines & journals. *Honour:* Attila Joszef Literary Prize, 1983. *Memberships:* Hungarian Writers Union; Hungarian Pen Club; World Science Fiction; SFWA. *Address:* PB8, 1311 Budapest, Hungary.

SZIRTES George Nicholas, b. 29 Nov 1948, Budapest, Hungary. Poet. m. Clarissa Upchurch, 11 July 1970, 1 son, 1 daughter. *Education:* BA, (First Hons), Fine Art, Leeds College of Art, UK. *Publications:* The Slant Door, 1979; November & May, 1981; The Kissing Place, 1982; Short Wave, 1984; The Photographer in Winter, 1986; Metro, 1988; Selected Poems, Hungary 1987; Bridge Passages, 1991. Translation: Imre Madach's Tragedy of Man, from Hungarian, 1987. *Contributions to:* Numerous journals & magazines. *Honours:* Faber Memorial Prize, 1980; Arts Council Bursary, 1984; British Council Fellowship, 1985; Cholmondeley Award, 1987. *Memberships:* Fellow, Royal Society of Literature; PEN. *Address:* 20 Old Park Road, Hitchin, Hertfordshire SG5 2JR, England.

SZKAROSI Endre, b. 28 May 1952, Budapest, Hungary. Poet; University Professor. m. Athena Hadzopulu, 21 Sept 1974, 2 daughters. *Education:* Hungarian Language & Literature, 1977; PhD, Italian Literature, 1985. *Appointments:* Editor, Mozgo Vilag, 1978-83; Editor in Chief, Uj Holgyfutar, 1986-; Editor, Szkarosi Hangado, 1992-. *Publications:* Unknown Monologues; Works in Ventilation; The Wind Rises. *Contributions to:* Inter; Poesia; Atelier Magyar Muhely; Bollettario; Tamtam; Baobab; Hangar; Testo. *Honour:* Kassak Award. *Memberships:* Association of Hungarian Writers; Uj Holgyfutar Association; AILC; AISLLI; International Association of Hungarian Philology. *Address:* VACI UT 34, H-1132 Budapest, Hungary.

SZUCSANY Desiree, b. 14 Feb 1955, Montreal, Canada. Writer. m. Denis Keil, 14 Oct 1987. *Education:* University of Madrid, 1974; University of Montréal, 1975; College du Vieux Montréal, 1973. *Appointments:* Reporter, Translator. *Publications:* La Chasse Gardee; Le Violon; La Passe; L Aveugle; Les Filets. *Contributions to:* Le Masque d Agonie; Feminin Pluiel; La Valise; La Vie en Rose; Writ Magazine. *Address:* CP 494, 336 Rue De La Care, Lac Carre, Quebec, Canada J0T 1J0.

T

TA Tai Van, b. 16 Apr 1938, Vietnam. Legal Scholar and Attorney. m. Lien-Nhu Tran, 26 Oct 1967, 1 son, 3 daughters. *Education:* LLB, Saigon University Law School, 1960; MA, PhD, Government and Foreign Affairs, University of Virginia, 19645; LLM, Harvard Law School, 1985. *Publications:* The Vietnamese Tradition of Human Rights, 1988; Co- author: Investment Law and Practice in Vietnam, 1990; The Le Code: Law in Traditional Vietnam, 1987; The Laws of Southeast Asia, 1986; Law and the State in Traditional East Asia, 1986. *Contributions to:* American Journal of Comparative Law, Journal of Asian History, Asian Thought and Society, UNHCR Refugee Abstracts, Vietnam Forum. *Honours:* Fulbright, 1960; US Agency for International Development, 1962; Asia Foundaton, 1971; Ford Foundation, 1975, 1978. *Memberships:* Massachusetts Bar Association; Association of Asian Studies; American Political Science Association; Vietnam Council on Foreign Relations. *Address:* Harvard Law School, Pound Hall 423, Cambridge, MA 02138, USA.

TABARD Peter. *See:* **BLAKE Leslie James.**

TABOR Stephen Randall, b. 2 Jan 1951, Oakland, California, USA. Librarian. *Education:* MLS, UCLA, 1977; BA, Pomona College, 1973. *Publications:* Sylvia Plath: An Analytical Bibliography, 1987; Ted Hughes: A Bibliography, 1946-80, 1983, co-author. *Contributions to:* Sound Post. *Honours:* Besterman Medal. *Memberships:* Bibliographical Society, Bibliographical Societies of America and of the University of Virginia. *Address:* 2315 14th Street No. 10, Santa Monica, CA 90405, USA.

TABORSKI Boleslaw, b. 7 May 1927, Torun, Poland. Writer; Translator; Broadcaster. m. Halina Junghertz, 20 June 1959, 1 daughter. *Education:* BA, MA, Bristol University. *Publications:* (Poetry) Times of Passing, 1957; Grains of Night, 1958; Crossing the Border, 1962; Lesson Continuing, 1967; Voice of Silence, 1969; Selected Poems, 1973; Web of Words, 1977; For the Witnesses, 1978; Observer of Shadows, 1979; Love, 1980; A Stranger's Present, 1983; Art, 1985; The Stillness of Grass, 1986; Life and Death, 1988; Politics, 1990; Shakespeare, 1990; Goodbye Nonsense, 1991. Criticism: New Elizabethan Theatre, 1967; Polish Plays in English Translations, 1968; Byron and the Theatre, 1972; The Inner Plays of Karol Wojtyla, 1989. Co-Author: Crowell's Handbook of Contemporary Drama, 1971; Polish Plays in Translation, 1983; Major Translations into English of works by Jan Kott, Wiktor Woroszylski, Karol Wojtyla, Stanislava Przybyszewska and others; Translations into Polish of works by Graham Greene, Robert Graves, Harold Pinter, Robert Lowell and others. *Contributions to:* Oxford Companion to the Theatre, 1957; Gambit; Stand; Theatre Research; Theatre Quarterly; Miesiecznik Literacki; Tulane Drama Review; Slavic and East European Arts; Polish Review; Kultura, France; Dialog, Teatr, Wiez, Zycie Literackie, Tygodnik Powszelhny, Literatura, Poezja, Twor Czosc. *Honours:* Polish Writers Association Abroad Award, 1954; Jurzykowski Foundation Award, New York, 1968; Merit for Polish Culture Badge and Diploma, Warsaw, Poland, 1970; Koscielski Foundation Award, Geneva, Switzerland, 1977; SI Witkiewicz ITI Award, Warsaw, 1988; ZAIKS, Translation Award, Warsaw, 1990. *Memberships:* Honorary Committee Leon Schiller Foundation, 1987-; Association of Authors, ZAIKS, 1985-; Council Gallery in the Provinces Foundation, Lublin, Poland, 1990-; ZAIKS Associaion of Authors, Warsaw, 1985; Association of Polish Writers, Warsaw, 1991-; World Association of Polish Home Army (AK), Ex-Serviceman, Warsaw, 1992-. *Address:* 66 Esmond Road, Bedford Park, London W4 1JF, England.

TADEUSZ Rozewicz, b. 9 Oct 1921, Radomsko, Poland. Poet; Playwright. m. Wiestawa Koztowska, 1949. *Education:* University of Cracow. *Publications include:* Face of Anxiety; Conversation with the Prince; The Green Rose; The Card Index; The Witnesses; White Marriage; The Trap. *Contributions to:* various journals.

Honours: State Prize, Poetry, 1955, 1956; Literary Prize, City of Cracow, 1959; Prize, Minister of Culture and Art, 1962; State Prize, 1st Class, 1966; Prize, Minister of Foreign Affairs, 1974, 1987; Austrian National Prize, European Literature, 1982. *Memberships:* Bavarian Academy of Fine Arts, Munich; Academy of Fine Arts of GDR, Berlin. *Address:* ul. Januszowicka 13 m 14, 53-136 Wroclaw, Poland.

TAFT John Thomas, b. 7 July 1950, Dublin, Ireland. Historian and Television Producer. m. Chirstine Rinehart Jordan, 28 June 1990, 1 son, 1 stepdaughter. *Education:* MA, International Studies, Johns Hopkins University, 1981; BA, Yale University, 1972; BA, University College, Oxford, 1974, MA, 1979. *Appointments include:* Part-time Writer for the New Republic, 1976-8 Washington Editor, Harpers magazine, 1987-89. *Publications:* American Power: The Rise and Decline of US Globalism, 1989; Mayday at Yale: A Case Study in Student Radicalism, 1976. *Contributions to:* The New Republic; The Listener; The Journal of Popular Film and Television. *Memberships:* Manuscript Society, Aurelian Honor Society; Elizabethan Club, at Yale University; Bishop Stubbs Society, Oxford University; The Authors Guild; 1925 F Street Club, Washington DC. *Literary Agent:* Ronald Goldfarb, Washington DC, USA. *Address:* 1526 34th St NW, Washington, DC 20007, USA.

TAGLIABUE John, b. 1 July 1923, Cantu, Italy. College Teacher. m. Grace Ten Eyck, 11 Sept 1946. 2 daughters. *Education:* BA 1944, MA 1945, and advanced Graduate Work, 1947-48, Columbia, New York City. *Literary Appointments:* Professor, English Department, Bates College, Maine; Fulbright Lecturer, University of Indonesia, 1993. *Publications:* The Great Day, 1984; The Doorless Door, 1970; The Buddha Uproar, 1970; A Japanese Journal, 1966; Poems, 1959. *Contributions to:* More than 1500 poems published in magazines including: The Atlantic Monthly; Chelsea; Centennial Review; Carolina Quarterly; Chicago Review; Epoch; Greenfield Review; Hudson Review; Harpers; Kayak; Kenyon Review; Literature East and West; Massachusetts Review; New York Quarterly; The Nation; Northeast; Poetry (Chicago); Poetry Northwest. *Honours:* Bellagio Writing Grant; Karolyi Foundation Writing Grant; Fulbright Lecturer, 1950-52, University of Pisa, 1958-60, Tokyo University; 1984, Fudan University, People's Republic of China. *Memberships:* PEN; Academy of American Poets; Main Writers and Publ. Alliance; Poetry Society of America. *Address:* 12 Abbott Street, Lewiston, ME 04240, USA.

TAIBO Paco Ignacio, b. 11 Jan 1949, Gijon, Spain. Writer. m. Paloma Saiz, 1 daughter. *Appointments:* Director, Etiqueta Hegra and Biblioteca Policiaca, Mystery Series in Spanish and Mexican. *Publications:* 24 books, 7 mystery novels, 1 short story, including: Dias de Combate, 1976; Cosa facil, 1977; No habra final feliz, 1981; Sombra de la sombra, 1986; Algunas nubes, 1985; Bolshovikis, 1986; De paso, 1986; Dona Eustolia blandio el cuchillo cebollero, 1984; Irapuato mi amor, 1984; La vida misma, 1987; Arcangeles, 1988; El socialismo en un solo puerto, 1983. *Honours:* Premio Grijalbo Novela, 1982; Cafe Gijon, 1986; Premio Nacional Historia INAH, 1986. *Memberships:* PEN; Asociacion Internacional de Escritores Policiscos; Mystery Writers of America. *Address:* Benjamin Hill 242-4, Colonia Condesa, Mexico DF, Mexico.

TAIT Arch, b. 6 June 1943, Glasgow, Scotland. Translator; University Lecturer. *Education:* Trinity Hall, Cambridge, MA, 1966; PhD, 1971. *Appointments:* Lecturer, University of East Anglia, 1970; Lecturer, University of Birmingham 1983; UK Editor, Glas: New Russian Writing, 1991-. *Publications:* Lunacharsky, The Poet Commissar; Translations: The Russian Style, 1991; Is Comrade Bulgakov Dead? 1993. *Memberships:* Translators Association; Society of Authors; British Association for Slavonic and East European Studies. *Address:* Department of Russian Literature, University of Birmingham, B15 2TT, England.

TAKAMURA Hiromasa, b. 4 Apr 1943, Japan. Professor of English. m. Eiko Numata, 15 Oct 1972. 1 daughter. *Education:* MA, Kansai University, Osaka, Japan, 1968. *Appointments:* Professor of English, Ohatani Women's University, 1984-. *Publications:* Steinbeck and Drama, 1990; Canadian Folktales, 1991; A Study Guide to Steinbeck's The Long Valley, 1992; Steinbeck and River, 1992; Steinbeck and his Dramatic World, 1992. *Memberships:* Advisory Board, The Steinbeck Quarterly; International John Steinbeck Society; John Steinbeck Society of Japan. *Address:* 10-22 Yamatecho, Tondabayashi, Osaka 584, Japan.

TAKI. *See:* **THEODORACOPULOS Peter.**

TAKIS Theodoropoulos, b. 28 Mar 1954, Athens, Greece. Novelist. m. Danai-Victoria Mitsotakis, 25 Sept 1982. *Education:* Licence Lettres, Paris, 1978; Maitrise Theatre, Paris, 1979; DEA Social Anthropology in Paris, 1980. *Publications:* The Absolute Landscape, 1991; Nights in Arcadia, 1987; The Whisper of Persephone, 1985. *Contributions to:* Numerous newspapers and magazines. *Memberships:* Union of Greek Writers. *Literary Agent:* Estia Co 60, Solonos St, 106 72, Athens, Greece. *Address:* 49 Eleftherotrias St, 145 63 Kifissia, Greece.

TALAMANTES Florence Williams, b. 15 Aug 1931, Alliance, Ohio, USA. University Educator. m. Eduardo Talamantes, 1970. *Education:* BA magna cum laude, Spanish, Mt Union College, 1954; MA, Spanish, 1956, PhD, Spanish, 1961, University of Cincinnati; Graduate study, Indiana University, 1957-58. *Appointments:* Teacher, Spanish, English: Windham, Ohio, 1954-55; Cincinnati, Ohio, 1956-57; Assistant Professor, Spanish, Lake Forest College, Lake Forest, Illinois, 1961-62; Assistant Professor, 1962-67, Associate Professor, Spanish, 1967-, San Diego State University, San Diego, California; Editorial Board Member, 1972-74, Acting Editor, 1973, Co-Editor, 1975-, Virginia Woolf Quarterly. *Publications:* Alfonsina Storni: Argentina's Feminist Poet, 1975; Nikola Vaptsarov: Selected Poems translated into Spanish with Gilberto Garcia-Pena, Preface by Camilo Jose Cela, 1991; Editor, author of introduction: Jose Marie de Pereda's Don Gonzalo Gonzalez de la Gonzalera, 1972; Jose Maria de Pereda: Selections from Sotileza and Penas Arriba, 1978; Editor, translator: Alfonsina Storni: Poemas de Amor, 1977; Ramon Sender: Selecciones de Poesia Lirica y Aforistica, 1979; Translator, author of introduction, Ulyses Petit de Murat: Selected Poems; Film and TV scripts. *Contributions to:* Articles and book reviews to: Virginia Woolf Quarterly; Mosaic; Polish Review; Others. *Honours:* Taft Fellowship, University of Cincinnati, 1955-56; Faculty Research Grant, San Diego State University, 1974; Affirmative Action Faculty Development Programme Grant, 1985; Support Grant for Faculty Research, 1985. *Memberships:* Modern Language Association of America; American Association of Teachers of Spanish and Portuguese; American Federation of Teachers; National Organization for Women; Alpha Mu Gamma; Sigma Delta Pi. *Address:* Department of Spanish, San Diego State University, San Diego, CA 92182, USA.

TALBOT Michael, b. 4 Jan 1943, Luton, Bedfordshire, England. Professor of Music. m. Shirley Mashiane 26 Sept 1970, 1 son, 1 daughter. *Education:* ARCM, Royal College of Music, London, 1960-61; BA, 1964, BMus, 1965, PhD, 1969, Clare College, Cambridge. *Publications:* Vivaldi, 1978; Tomaso Albinoni: The Venetian Composer and his World, 1990; Antonio Vivaldi: A Guide to Research, 1988. *Contributions to:* Music and Letters; Journal of the Royal Musical Association; Music Review, Rivista Italiana de Musicologia; Informazioni e Studi Vivaldiani. *Honours:* Cavaliere del, ordine al merite della Repubblica Italiana, 1980; FBA, 1990. *Memberships:* Ateneo Veneto, Corresponding Fellow; Fellow, British Academy. *Address:* 36 Montclair Drive, Liverpool L18 OHA, England.

TALBOT Norman Clare, b. 14 Sept 1936, Gislingham, Suffolk, England. University Professor; Poet. m. 17 Aug 1960. 1 son, 2 daughters. *Education:* BA, 1st class English, Durham University, Hatfield College, 1956-59; PhD, American Lit., Leeds University, 1959-62. *Literary Appointments:* Lecturer in English, 1962, Senior Lecturer, 1968, Associate Professor, 1973-, Newcastle University College, University of New South Wales, since 1965 this became, University of Newcastle, New South Wales, Australia. Fellow, American Council of Learned Societies, 1967-68. *Publications:* The Major Poems of John Keats (criticism), 1967; Poems for a Female Universe, 1968; Son of a Female University, 1972 (poetry); The Fishing Boy (illus. Montefiore), 1975 (poetry); Find the Lady, 1978 (poetry); A Glossary of Poetic Terms, 1980, reprinted 1982, 85, 87, 1989; Where Two Rivers Meet, 1981 (poetry); The Kelly Haiku, 1985 (poetry); Contrary Modes (editor) 1985; Another Site to be Mined: New South Wales Anthology (editor), 1986; Spelling English in Australia (with Nicholas Talbot), 1989; Wearing the Heterocom: An Anthology of Narrative Poetry (ed), 1989. *Contributions to:* Numerous magazines including: Poetry Australia; Makar; Southern Review; Meanjin; Quadrant; New Poetry; Westerly; Northern Perspective; Southerly; The Newcastle Herald; The Australian; The Age; The Sydney Morning Herald; Aspect. *Honours:* E C Gregory Memorial Award for Poetry, 1965; ACLS Fellowship, 1967-68; Visiting Professorships at the Universities of East Anglia, 1975-76; Aarhus, 1976; Eugene, 1983; Leicester, 1984; Oxford, Linacre College, 1987-88. *Memberships:* William Morris Society; ex-President, Australian Victorian Studies Association; ex-Councillor, Australasian Universities Lang & Lit Association; Federation of Australian Universities Staffs Associations. *Address:* Department of English, University of Newcastle, NSW 2308, Australia.

TAMARI Moshe, b. 20 May 1910, Warkowicze, Poland (now Ukraine). Editor, Books/Periodicals. m. Miriam Gefel, 31 Dec 1937, 1 son, 1 daughter. *Education:* Biblical & Literary Studies, 1920-28; DLit, World University, USA, 1989. *Appointments include:* Parliamentary Secretary, 1952; Control Commission, Hebrew Writers Association, 1954, 1958; Judges Committee, Acum-Association of Writers, Composers and Editors of Music, 1958; Editorial Secretary, Hapoel Hazair Weekly; Column of Literary Criticisms, Davar. *Publications include:* Poetry, 1928-34; Days Gone By - Bible Miniatures, 1972, 1984, 1986; Prose: Voice of Life, 1941; In Vain, 1944; From Scene to Scene, 1951; Blossoming Orange Groves (translated in Arabic), 1968; Essays: Two Brazilian Books, 1963; The Mirror of our Conscience, 1984; An Historical Illumination on Bible Miniatures, 1989; Ancient Foundations of Middle Eastern Culture, 1990. *Contributions to:* various journals, including Davar; Moznayim; Gilionoth; Gazith. *Honour:* Grant, Lamdan Promotion Fund, 1961. *Memberships include:* Hebrew Writers Association; Acum; P.E.N; LFWLA. *Literary Agent:* Book Publishers Association of Israel. *Address:* 4 Pineless Street, P.O. Box 21488, Tel Aviv 62265, Israel.

TAMARKIN Jeffrey Mitchell, b. 15 Oct 1952. Editor Goldmine Magazine. *Education:* BA, San Francisco State University, 1977. *Publications:* Billy Joel - From Hicksville to Hitsville; over 1000 articles on Popular Music. *Contributions to:* Goldmine Magazine; Pulse Magazine; New Music Report; Music Alive; Billboard; Relix; NY Tribune; Vegetarian Times and others. *Membership:* Nominating Committee, Rock and Roll Hall of Fame. *Address:* PO Box 497, Hoboken, NJ 07030, USA.

TAMBLING Jeremy Charles Richard, b.18 Feb 1948. University Lecturer. m. Pauline Ann Dorling, 18 Dec 1976, 1 daughter. *Education:* Dulwich College, 1957-66; BA Hons, Upper Second, York University, 1966-69; M Phil, Nottingham University, 1969-71; PhD, Essex University, 1982-84. *Publications:* Opera, Ideology and Film, 1987; Dante and Difference, 1988; What is Literary Language? 1988; Confession: Sexuality, Sin, the Subject, 1990. *Contributions to:* New

Universities Quarterly; Essays in Criticism. *Address:* 2, Clapham Mansions, Nightingale Lane, London SW4 9AQ, England.

TAMES Richard Lawrence (James Lawrence), b. 1946, British. *Appointments:* Sixth Form Master, Haberdashers' Aske's School, Elstree, Hertfordshire, 1967-70; Lecturer, Chiswick Polytechnic, London, 1970-71; Secretary to the Council, Hansard Society, 1973-74; joined faculty 1975, Head of External Services, School of Oriental and African Studies 1984-90, University of London; Consultant (Education/Training/Publications) University Consultants (Japan) Ltd. *Publications:* Economy and Society in 19th Century Britain, William Morris, Isambard Kingdom Brunel, 1972; The Conquest of South America, 1974; Modern France: State and Society, Japan Today, 1976; The World of Islam: A Teacher's Handbook, 1977; China Today, People Power and Politics, The Japan Handbook: A Guide for Teachers, 1978; The Arab World Today, 1980; India in the 20th Century, Japan in the Twentieth Century, Emergent Nations, Journey into Japan, Servant of the Shogun, 1981; Approaches to Islam, The Muslim World, Case Studies in Development, The Japanese, 1982; Makers of Modern Britain, Growing Up in the 1960s, 1983; The Great War, Victorian London, Britain and the World in the 20th Century, 1984; Nazi Germany, Dictionaries of Religion: Islam, 1985; Radicals, Railways and Reform: Britain 1815-51, 1986; Exploring Other Civilizations, Planters Pilgrims and Puritans, 1987; The American West; Passport to Japan 1988 Let's Go to Lebanon; Let's Go to Libya; Let's Go to Iran; Let's Go to Iraq; Japan Since 1945; Anne Frank; Helen Keller; Amelia Earhart; Florence Nightingale; Marie Curie; Mother Teresa 1989; The First Day of the Somme; Alexander Flemming; Louis Pasteur; The Wright Brothers; Thomas Edison; Alexander Graham Bell; Guglielmo Marconi; The 1950's; The 1980's; 1990 Journey Through Japan; Journey Through Canada; The 1930's; The 1920's; Nelson Mandela; Wolfgang Amaedua Mozart; Ludwig van Beethoven; Giuseppe Verdi; Fryderyk Chopin; Wilhelm Richard Wagner; Peter Tchaikovsky. *Address:* 76 Regent Square, Bruce Road, Bow, London E3 3HW, England.

TAMMEUS William D, b. 18 Jan 1945, Woodstock, Illinois, USA. Journalist. m. Marcia A. Bloom, 21 Sept 1968, 2 daughters. *Education:* BJ, University of Missouri, 1967; University of Rochester, 1967-69. *Appointments:* Reporter, Rochester (NY) Times-Union, 1967-70; Reporter, 1970-77, Columnist, 1977-, Kansas City Star; Commentator, KCPT TV, Kansas City, 1979-1990. *Contributions to:* Contributing Editor, Missouri Life Magazine, 1980-81; Writing syndicated by New York Times News Service, 1989-. *Honours:* Member of the Kansas City Star Staff that won the Pulitzer Prize for Local Reporting, 1982; Humor Writing Award, National Society of Newspaper Columnists, 1989, 1992. *Memberships:* Society of Professional Journalists, Sigma Delta Chi; National Society of Newspaper Columnists, President, 1992-. *Address:* 409 E. 65th Terrace, Kansas City, MO 64131, USA.

TANG Victor, b. 12 April 1942, China. Business Executive, IBM. m. Wendy Chu, 3 June 1968, 1 son, 2 daughters. *Education:* BSEE, Purdue University, USA, 1963; MS, Mathematical Physics, 1965; Advanced Research and Studies, Pennsylvania State University, 1967-69; MBA, Columbia University, 1983. *Publications:* Digital Private Branch Exchanges (PBX), Chapter 6, 1989; The Silverlake Project, 1992; Competitive Marketing, Part I and II (with Philip Kotler), 1993. *Contributions to:* Methodology and Declarative Language for Displays, 1975; Traffic Management in VTAM-NCP Network, 1977; Flat Panel Displays, 1984; ISDN - New Vistas in Information Processing, 1987; ISDN - Strategic Analysis, 1989; AS-400 New Product Launch Process, 1992; Organizational Implications of EIS, 1992. *Memberships:* Eta Kappa Nu, Electrical Engineering Honour Society; Pi Mu Epsilon, Mathematics Honour Society; Beta Gamma Sigma, Business Honour Society; Sigma Pi Sigma, Physics

Honour Society. *Address:* 55 Deerfield Lane South, Pleasantville, NY 10570, USA.

TANGYE Derek, Writer, m. Jeannie. *Education:* Harrow. *Appointments:* Worked as journalist on national newspapers. During WWII and afterwards was member of MI5. Left London and moved to Minack, a deserted cottage in Mount's Bay, Cornwall to establish a flower farm. *Publications:* Series of bestsellers about Life on the Flower Farm include: A Gull on the Roof; The Cherry Tree; Jeannie. *Address:* Minack, Mount's Bay, Cornwall, England.

TANNER John Ian, b. 2 Jan 1927, London, England. Museum Director. m. April Rothery, 1953, 1 daughter. *Education:* City of London Library School; Universities of London, Nottingham (MA, PhD), Oxford (MA). *Appointments include:* Founding Director: Royal Air Force Museum, 1963-; Battle of Britain Museum, 1978-; Cosford Aero-Space Museum, 1978-; Bomber Command Museum, 1982-. Honorary Archivist 1980-, Senior Research Fellow 1982-, Pembroke College, Oxford. *Publications include:* Editor, List of Cranwell Graduates, 2nd edition 1963; Co-author, Encyclopaedic Dictionary of Heraldry, 1968; How to Trace Your Ancestors, 1971; Man in Flight, limited edition, 1973; Royal Air Force Museum: 100 Years of Aviation History, 1973; Co-author, Badges & Insignia of British Armed Services, 1974; Charles I, 1974; Who's Famous in Your Family: Reader's Digest Guide to Genealogy, 1975, 1979; Wings of the Eagle, exhibition catalogue, 1976; Editor, They Fell in the Battle, limited edition, 1980; Sir William Rothenstein: RAF Museum exhibition catalogue, 1985; Editor, RAF Museum Publications series, 10 volumes; General editor, Museums & Libraries, international series; Studies in Air History. *Contributions to:* Reviews, articles in professional journals. *Honours:* Numerous honours & awards including CBE, 1979. *Memberships include:* Advisory Council, Institute of Heraldic & Genealogical Studies; Chairman, International Air Museum Committee; Vice President, Guild of Aviation Artists, Croydon Museum Society; Trustee, Manchester Air & Space Museum. *Address:* Flat One, 57 Drayton Gardens, London SW10 9RU, England.

TANNER Tony, b. 1935, British. *Appointments:* Fellow, King's College, Cambridge, 1964-; Reader in the Faculty of English, Cambridge University, 1984-; Professor of English and American Literature, 1989-. *Publications:* Conrad: Lord Jim, 1963; The Reign of Wonder: Naivety and Reality in American Literature, Saul Bellow, 1965; Mansfield Park, by Jane Austin (ed), 1966; Henry James: Modern Judgements (ed), Hawthorne by Henry James (ed), 1968; City of Words: American Fiction 1950-1970, 1971; Adultery in the Novel: Contact and Transgression, 1980; Jane Austen, 1986. *Address:* King's College, Cambridge, England.

TANSKA Natalie, (Natasa Tanska, Jana Dankova), b. 30 Dec 1929, Praha. Czechoslovakia. Writer. m. Jan Valek, 20 Oct 1960. *Education:* Academy of Performing Arts, Czechoslovakia, 1954. *Appointments:* Theatre Critic, Cultural Life, 1956-63; Script Writer, Film Studios Koliba, 1965-68. *Publications:* The Duel; An English Lesson; Fluff and Muff; The Postscripts; Wont You Get Lost in a Crowds; Shop No. 004; Men Women Dictionary. *Contributions to:* Cultural Life; Mlada Fronta; Mona. *Honours:* Frano Kral Award; Award for the Best Radio Play; Publishers Award for the Best Book; Three Roses Award. *Membership:* PEN. *Address:* Vikova 7, Praha 4 post Code 140 00, Czech Republic.

TANSKA Natasa. *See:* **TANSKA Natalie.**

TANTIMEDH Adisakdi, b. 4 Nov 1967, Singapore. Author. *Education:* BA, English Literature and Creative Writing, Bennington College, USA, 1988. *Publications:* After the Beep; BBC Young Playwrights Festival, 1988; John Wayne and His Belly, 1989; Devils in the Glass, 1990. *Contributions to:* Flypost (weekly music listings magazine). *Membership:* Writers' Guild of Great Britain. *Address:* Flat 1, Empire House, Thurloe Place, London SW7 2RU, England.

TARGAN Barry, b. 30 Nov 1932, Atlantic City, New Jersey, USA. Professor. m. Arleen Shanken, 9 Mar 1958, 2 sons. *Education:* Rutgers University, BA, 1954; University of Chicago, MA, 1956; Brandeis University, PhD, 1962. *Publications:* Harry Belten and the Mendelssohn Violin Concerto; Surviving Adverse Seasons; Kingdoms; Falling Free; The Tangerine Tango Equation. *Contributions to:* Sewanee Review; Salmagundi; Esquire; Georgia Review. *Honours:* University of Iowa, School of Letters Award; Saxifrage Award; Associated Writing Programs Award. *Literary Agent:* Nat Sobel. *Address:* RD2 Box 194C, Greenwich, NY 12834, USA.

TARRANT John. *See:* **EGLETON Clive Frederick William.**

TART Indrek (Julius Ürt), b. 2 May 1946, Tallinn, Estonia. Physicist; Poet; Literary Critic. m. Aili Aarelaid Tart, 7 Feb 1980, 1 son, 1 daughter. *Education:* Graduated with Silver Medal, Tallinn Secondary School No 4; Graduated as Physicist with praise, Tartu University. *Appointments:* Institute of Cybernetics, 1969-80; Institute of Chemical Physics and Biophysics, Estonian Academy of Sciences, 1980-1992; Tallinn Pedagogical University, 1992-; Estonian National Commission for UNESCO, Director of Information, 1992-; Chairman, Young Writers Tallinn Branch, Estonian Writers Union, 1978-83. *Publications:* Poetry books: Haljendav ruumala (Greening Space), 1981; Väike luuletaja ja teised (The Little Poet and the Others), 1993; in anthologies: Kôik siin maailmas (All in This World), Estonian Haiku's Anthology, 1980; Eesti Luule aastaraamat (Year book of Estonian Poetry), 86; 87; 88-89; 1987; 1989; 1990; Translations into Estonian: Poems of William Carlos Williams, Adrienne Rich, Norman Dubie, Raymond Carver, Charles Tomlinson, R.S Thomas, Iain Crichton Smith in newspapers, 1989-92. *Contributions to:* Looming (Creation); Keel ja Kirjandus (Language and Literature); Noorus (Youth). *Honour:* Honorary Fellow in Writing, University of Iowa. *Membership:* Member, Estonian Writers' Union, 1991-. *Address:* Kurni 17-1, Tallinn-16, EE0016, Estonia.

TATE Joan, b. 1922. Freelance Writer; Translator; Publishers Reader. *Publications:* Jenny, 1964; The Crane, 1964; The Rabbit Boy, 1964; Coal Hoppy, 1964; Next Doors, 1964; Silver Grill, 1965; Picture Charlies, 1965; Lucy, 1965; The Tree (in US as Tina and David), 1966; The Holiday, 1966; Tad, 1966; Bill, 1966; Mrs Jenny, 1966; Bits and Pieces, 1966; The New House, 1967; The Soap Box Car, 1967; The Old Car, 1967; The Great Birds, 1967; The Circus, 1967; Letters to Chris, 1967; Wild Martin, 1967; Luke's Garden, 1967, augmented version, 1976; Sam and Me, 1968; Out of the Sun, 1969; Whizz Kid (in US as An Unusual Kind of Girl), 1969; The Train, 1969; The Letter, 1969; Puddle's Tiger, 1969; The Caravan, 1969; Edward and the Uncles, 1969; The Secret, 1969; Lucy, 1969; The Next, 1969; The Cheapjack Man, 1969; The Gobbleydock, 1969; The Tree House, 1969; The Ball, 1969; Going Up, vol I 1969, vol II, 1971, vol III 19074; Clipper, 1969; Ring on My Finger, 1971; The Long Road Home, 1971; Gramp, 1971; Wild Boy, 1972; Wump Day, 1972; Dad's Camel, 1972; Your Town, 1972; Jock and the Rock Cakes, 1973; Grandpa and My Little Sister, 1973; Taxi!, 1973; Night Out, 1973; The Match, 1973; Dinah, 1973; The Man Who Rang the Bell, 1973; Journal for One, 1973; Ben and Annie, 1973; Ginger Mick, 1974; The Runners, 1974; The Living River, 1974; Dirty Dan, 1974; Sandy's Trumpet, 1974; Your Dog, 1975; Disco Books, 8 vols 1975; The House That Jack Built, 1976; The New House, 1976; Crow and the Brown Boy, 1976; Polly and the Barrow Boy, 1976; Billoggs, 1976; You Can't Explain Everthing, 1976; See You and Other Stories, 1977; On Your Own, 1977; Cat Country, 1979; Helter Skelter (poems), 1979; Turn Again Whittington, 1980; Safari, 1980; Panda Car, 1980; Clee and Nibs,

1990; Dad's Camel, 1990. *Address:* 7 College Hill, Shrewsbury SY1 1LZ, England.

TATTERSALL Laura Catherine Mary, b. 25 Nov 1922, Citta di Castello, Italy. Author. m. R. Tattersall, 10 Oct 1946, dec. 1965, 1 son, 1 daughter. *Education:* School Teaching Certificate, Maturita Magistrale, Italy, 1939; Higher School Teaching Certificate, Maturita Scientifica, 1941. *Publication:* A Siren in the Dining Room, book. *Address:* 23 Wyreside Drive, Hambleton, Poulton-Le-Fylde, Lancs FY6 9DP, England.

TAUBMAN Jane A, b. 23 Oct 1942, Professor of Russian. m. William C Taubman, 1 son, 1 daughter. *Education:* BA, magna cum laude, Russian History and Literature, Radcliffe College, 1964; MA 1968, PhD, 1972, Yale University. *Publications:* A Life through Poetry: Marina Tsvetaeva's Lyric Diary, 1989; Mosccow Spring (co-author), 1989. *Contributions to:* Russian Review, 1993; Literaturnoe Obozrenie, 1992; Proceedings of the Lausanne Symposium on Maria Tsvetaeva, 1991; The Boston Globe; Vecherniaia Odessa, 1990; Russian Literature Triquarterly, 1974. *Honours include:* IREX Grant, 1988; American Philosophical Society Grant, 1975; National Defence Title VI Fellowshps, 1965-68; Woodrow Wilson Fellow, 1964-65. *Memberships:* American Association for the Advancement of Slavic Studies; American Association of Teachers of Slavic and East European Languages; American Council of Teechers of Russian; Modern Language Association; American Association of University Professors. *Address:* Department of Russian, PO Box 2260, Amherst College, Amherst, MA 01002, USA.

TAVIRA Luis de, b. 1 Sept 1948, Mexico. Playwriter; Theatre Director. 3 sons. *Education:* Licentiate, Literature and Dramatic Arts, UNAM, 1972; Master of Philosophy, Instituto Libre de Filosofia, Mexico, 1976. *Appointments:* Director, Centro Universitario de Teatro, UNAM, 1978-82; Director, Centro de Experimentacion Teatral, INBA, Mexico, 1985-90; Director, Casa del Teatro, AC Mexico, 1990-. *Publications:* Poetry: Coloquio con la Soledad, 1972; La Tarde y el rio, 1978; Tarde Perpetua, 1992; Dramas: La Sombra del Caudillo, 1982; Lances de amor, 1984; La Pasion de Pentesilea, 1988; Zozobra, 1990; La Septima Morada, 1991; Novedad de la Patria, play, 1984. *Contributions to:* Weekly column Proscenio, to La Jornada Semanal, Sunday edition of journal La Jornada; Process review. *Honours:* Best Play, AMCT, Mexico, 1985; Best Mise en scene, Festival of Theater of Americas, Montreal, 1985. *Membership:* International Association of Critics and Theatrologists. *Address:* Ofiuco 59, Prados de Coyoacan, Mexico DF, Mexico CP 04810.

TAYLOR Allegra, b. 23 Dec 1940. Writer. m. Richard Taylor, 16 Aug 1958, 3 sons, 3 daughters. *Education:* BEd, University of London, 1974. *Publications:* I Fly Out With Bright Feathers; Acquainted with The Night; Prostitution, Whats Love Got To Do With It; Healing Hands; Older Than Time; Tal Nivs Kibbutz. *Contributions to:* Annabel; She; Women; Womens Own; Illustrated London News; Africa Today; 19; The Times; The Guardian. *Literary Agent:* Toby Eady. *Address:* 6 Amyand Park Gardens, Twickenham, Middlesex, TW1 3HS, England.

TAYLOR Andrew John Robert, b. 14 Oct 1951. Writer. m. Caroline Jane Silverwood, 8 Sept 1979, 1 son, 1 daughter. *Publications:* Caroline Minuscule, 1982; Waiting for the End of the World, 1984; Our Fathers' Lies, 1985; An Old School Tie, 1986; Freelance Death, 1987; The Second Midnight, 1987, USA, UK, 1988; Blacklist, 1988; Toyshop, 1990. Childrens Books: as John Robert Taylor, Hairline Cracks, 1988; The Private Nose, 1989; Snapshot, 1989; Double Exposure, 1990; Blood Relation, 1990; The Raven on the Water, 1991; The Sleeping Policeman, 1992; The Barred Window, 1993; Odd Man Out, 1993; For Children: Negative Image, 1992. *Honours:* Caroline Minuscule, winner of the 1982 John Creasey Award of the Crime

Writers Association and shortlisted for an Edgar by the Mystery Writers of America; Our Fathers' Lies, shortlisted for the 1985 Gold Dagger of the Crime Writers Association. *Membership:* Society of Authors. *Literary Agent:* Richard Scott Simon. *Address:* c/o Richard Scott Simon Ltd., 43 Doughty Street, London WC1N 2LF, England.

TAYLOR Andrew McDonald, b. 19 Mar 1940, Warrnambool, Australia. Professor of English. m. Beate Josephi, 1981. 1 son, 1 daughter. *Education:* MA, Hons, Melbourne Univ, 1971. *Literary Appointments:* Member, Literature Board of The Australia Council, 1978-81; Chair, Writers' Week of Adelaide Festival of Arts, 1980 & 1982; Member, South Australian Arts Finance Advisory Committee, 1988-1991. *Publications:* Miracles of Disbelief, 1985 (translations of Poetry with Beate Josephi); Travelling (Poems), 1986; Reading Australian Poetry (Criticism), 1987; Selected Poems 1960-85, 1988; Folds In The Map (Poems), 1991. *Contributions to:* Australia, USA, Britain, Europe, India (Poetry and Criticism), and others. *Honours:* A.M. (Member of The Order of Australia), 1990. *Memberships:* Australian Society of Authors, Management Committee, 1984-86, 1993; PEN International; Australian Society of Authors, Association for the Study of Australian Literature, European Association for the Study of Australia. *Address:* English Department, Edith Cowan University, Mount Lawley, Western Australia 6050.

TAYLOR Beverly White, b. 30 Mar 1947, Mississippi, USA. University Professor. *Education:* BAE, University of Mississippi, 1969; MA, 1970, PhD, 1977, Duke University. *Appointments:* Assistant Professor of English, 1977-84, Associate Professor, 1984-92, Professor, 1992-, University of North Carolina at Chapel Hill. *Publications:* The Return of King Arthur, 1983; Arthurian Legend and Literature, 1984; Francis Thompson, 1987; The Cast of Consciousness, 1987; Gender and Discourse in Victorian Literature and Art, 1992. *Contributions to:* Periodicals and encyclopaedias on 19th century and Arthurian literature. *Memberships:* Victorians Institute, President, 1989-90, VP, 1987-88, Secretary, 1985-86; Tennyson Society; Browning Institute; Modern Language Association; International Arthurian Society. *Address:* Department of English, University of NC, Chapel Hill, NC 27599, USA.

TAYLOR Elisabeth Dewar, (Elisabeth McNeill), b. 25 Apr 1931, Fife, Scotland. Writer. m. Adam Taylor, 30 Oct 1956, 1 son, 3 daughters. *Education:* MA Hons, History, Aberdeen University. *Publications:* Shanghai Emerald; Woman of Gallantry; Lark Returning; Mistress of Green Tree Mill; Perseverane Place; St James' Fair; Livingwith Loss; The Writing Business; Living Alone. *Contributions to:* Numerous magazines and newspapers. *Memberships:* Society of Authors; NUJ. *Literary Agent:* Sarah Odedina. *Address:* Cairnhill, Newstead, Melrose TD6 9DX, Scotland.

TAYLOR H Baldwin. *See:* **WAUGH Hilary Baldwin.**

TAYLOR Henry, b. 1942, American. *Appointments:* Instructor in English, Roanoke College, 1966-68; Assistant Professor of English, University of Utah, Salt Lake City, 1968-71; Director, University of Utah Writers' Conference, 1969-72; Associate Professor 1971-76, Professor of Literature 1976-, Co-Director of the MFA Program in Creative Writing 1982-, Director of American Studies Program 1983-85, American University, DC; Writer- in-Residence, Hollins College, Virginia, 1978. *Publications:* The Horse Show at Midnight, 1966; Breakings, 1971; An Afternoon of Pocket Billiards, Poetry: Points of Departure (author and ed), 1974; The Water of Light: An Anthology in Honor of Brewster Ghiselin, 1976; Desperado, 1979; The Children of Herakles, translated from Euripedes' Herakleidai (trans with Robert Brooks), 1981; The Flying Change, 1985; Compulsory Figures: Essays on Recent American Poets, 1992. *Honour:* Pulitzer Prize. *Address:* Box 85, Lincoln, VA 22078, USA.

TAYLOR Janelle. *See:* **TAYLOR Janelle Diane Williams.**

TAYLOR Janelle Diane Williams, (Janelle Taylor), b. 28 June 1944, Georgia, USA. Author; Lecturer. m. Michael Howard Taylor, 8 Apr 1965. 2 daughters. *Education:* Medical Research Technologist Training, Medical College of Georgia, 1977-79; Agusta College, 1980-81. *Publications include:* Wild is my love, 1987; Fortune's Flames, 1988; Passions Wild and Free, 1988; Wild, Swéet Promise, 1989; Kiss of the Night Wind, 1989; Follow the Wind, 1990; Forever Ecstasy, 1991; Promise me Forever, 1991; Stardust and Shadows, 1992; Dangerous Deceptions, 1992. *Contributions to:* Romantic Times; Fiction Writer's Monthly; Dictaphone Bulletin; RWA Report; RWA Self Promotion Handbook; Galley; Secneand Sequel; Love Line. *Honours include:* Board of Directors for Jo Beth Williams Romance Screenplay Award; Romantic Times Writers Hall of Fame, 1987. Finalist: Romantic Times REviews Choice Award, 1986; RWA Best Single Title Novel Award, 1986; Best Mainstream Novel Maggie Award, 1989; Best Historical Novel Maggie Award, 1991. *Memberships:* Novelists Inc; Romance Writers of America; Western Writers of America; Agusta Author's Club; GA Romance Writers; Authors League, Guild of America; First Baptist Church of Agusta; ABI Research Board of Advisors; Cowboy Hall of Fame. *Literary Agent:* Adele Leone Agency. *Address:* PO Box 211646, Martinez, GA 30917, USA.

TAYLOR John Gerald, b. 18 Aug 1931, Hayes, Kent, England. Scientist. 2 sons, 3 daughters. *Education:* BSc, London, 1950, 1952; BA, Cantab, 1953; MA, Cantab, 1955; PhD, Cantab, 1956, Christs College, University of Cambridge. *Publications include:* Black Holes: The End of the Universe, 1973; Superminds, 1975; The Shape of Minds to Come, 1971; The New Phsyics, 1972; Science and the Supernatural, 1980; The Horizons of Knowledge, 1982; Special Relativity, 1975; Quantum Mechanics, 1969; Finite Superstrings, 1992. *Contributions to:* Science Journal; Vogue; Physical Review; Physics Bulletin; Journal of Mathematical Physics; many BBC Radio and TV Programmes. *Memberships:* Mathematical Physics Group, Chairman; Institute of Physics, Vice Chairman 1988-; British Neural Network Society, Convenor; Cambridge Philosophy Society, Fellow; Neural Network Society. *Address:* 33 Meredyth Road, Barnes, London SW13 ODS, England.

TAYLOR John Laverack, b. 25 May 1937, England. College Principal; Bramley Professor of Educational Development. m. Jennifer Margaret Green, 21 Sept 1981, 1 son, 2 daughters. *Education:* DipArch, Leeds, 1960; MSc, Urban Design, Education and City Planning, Columbia, USA, 1963; PhD, Instructional Planning Systems, Sheffield, England, 1969. *Appointment:* Editor, Salzburgh Journal of Urban Planning and Development, 1970-76. *Publications:* Simulation in the Classroom, 1974; Learning and the Silmulation Game, 1978; Instructional Planning Systems, 1971; Guide on Simulation and Gaming for Environmental Education, 1984; Planning for Urban Growth, 1972; Instructional Simulation Systems in Higher Education, 1971; Feedback on Instructional Simulations Systems, 1972. *Contributions to:* Over 80 articles and papers in various journals, including Architectural Design; Architects Journal; Bau; Building; Built Environment; Ekistics; Local Government Chronicle; RIBA Journal; RTPI Journal. *Honours:* Fulbright Fellow, 1962-64; ESU Columbia University Fellow, 1962-64; Salzburg Fellow, 1065-66; Nuffield Social Science Fellow, 1968-74; Various visiting Professorships in Australia, Canada, Cyprus; OBE, 1990. *Memberships:* Standing Conference of College Principals, Chairman 1986-89; Freeman of the City of London. *Address:* Principal's Lodge, Bretton Hall, West Bretton, Wakefield, West Yorkshire WF4 4LG, England.

TAYLOR John Russell, b. 1935, United Kingdom. Writer; Critic. *Appointments:* Film Critic, 1962-72, Art Critic, 1978-, The Times, London; Professor, Cinema Division, University of Southern California, USA, 1972-

78; Editor, Films and Filming, 1983-90. *Publications:* Joseph L Mankewicz: An Index, 1960; Anger and After: A Guide to the New British Drama, US Edition The Angry Theatre, 1962, 1969; Anatomy of a Television Play, 1962; Cinema Eye, Cinema Ear: Some Key Film-Makers of the 60s, 1964; Three Plays of John Arden (editor), 1964; New English Dramatists 8 (editor), 1965; Penguin Dictionary of the Theatre, 1966; The Art Nouveau Book in Britain, 1966; Art in London: A Guide, 1966; The Rise and Fall of the Well-Made Play, 1967; The Publications of T N Foulis, 1967; Look Back in Anger: A Casebook, 1968; The Art Dealers, 1969; Harold Pinter, 1969; The Playwrights Speak (editor), 1969; The Hollywood Musical, 1971; The Second Wave: British Dramatists for the Seventies, 1971; The Pleasure Dome: Collected Film Criticism of Graham Greene (editor), 1972; David Storey, 1974; Fifty Superstars, 1974; Masterworks of British Cinema (editor), 1974; Peter Shaffer, 1975; Directors and Directions: Cinema for the Seventies, 1975; Hitch: The Life and Times of Alfred Hitchcock, 1978; Impressionism, 1981; Strangers in Paradise: The Hollywood Emigres 1933-1950, 1982; Ingrid Bergman, 1983; Alec Guinness: A Celebration, 1984; Vivien Leigh, 1984; Hollywood 1940s, 1985; Portraits of the British Cinema, 1985; Orson Welles, 1986; Edward Wolfe, 1986; Great Movie Moments, 1987; Post-War Friends, 1987; Robin Tanner, 1989; Impressionist Dreams, 1990; Bernard Meninsky, 1990; Liz Taylor, 1991; Ricardo Cinalli, 1993; Igor Mitoraj, 1993; Muriel Pemberton: Art and Fashion, 1993; Forthcoming: Monet: Artist in Context. *Memberships:* Private Libraries Association, President, 1956-89. *Address:* The Times, 1 Pennington Street, London E1 9XN, England.

TAYLOR John Vernon, b. 11 Sept 1914, Cambridge, England. Retired Bishop. m. Peggy Wright, 5 Oct 1940, Oxford, 1 son, 2 daughters. *Education:* MA, Trinity College, Cambridge University; MA, St Catherines, Oxford University; Dip.Ed., London University Institute of Education. *Publications:* Christianity and politics in Africa, 1955; The Growth of the Church in Buganda, 1958; The Primal Vision, 1963; The Go-Between Goti, 1972; Enough is Enough, 1975; Weep Not for Me, 1985; A Matter of Life and Death, 1986; A Christmas Sequence and Other Poems, 1989; Kingdom Come, 1989; The Christlike God, 1992. *Honours:* Honorary Doctor of Divinity, Toronto, 1983; Collins Religious Book Prize, 1984; Hon. Fellow, New College & Magdalen College, Oxford, 1986; Trinity College, Cambridge, 1987; Hon Doctor of Literature (CNNA), King ALfred's College, Winchester, 1991. *Address:* 65 Aston Street, Oxford, OX4 1EW, England.

TAYLOR John William Ransom, Dr, b. 8 June 1922, England. Author; Editor. m. Doris Alice Haddrick, 1946, 1 son, 1 daughter. *Appointments include:* Editor, contributing editor, correspondent, various journals, aircraft/aviation. Editor-in-Chief (formerly editor & compiler), Jane's All the World's Aircraft, 1959-. *Publications include:* Spitfire, 1946; Aircraft Annual, 1949-75; Civil Aircraft Markings, 1950-78; Military Aircraft Recognition, 1953-79; Science in the Atomic Age, 1956; Jane's All the World's Aircraft, 1956-; Royal Air Force, 1957; Russian Aircraft, 1957; US Military Aircraft, 1959; Combat Aircraft of the World, 1969; Pictorial History of Royal Air Force, 3 volumes, 1968-71, 1980; Aircraft Aircraft, 1967, 4th edition 1974; Encyclopaedia of World Aircraft, 1966; Rockets & Missiles, 1971; Civil Aircraft of the World, 1970-79; British Civil Aircraft Register, 1971; History of Aviation, with K.Munson, 1973, 1978; Jane's Aircraft Pocket Books, 1973-; Jets, 1976; Helicopters of the World, 1976-79; Aircraft, Strategy and Operations of the Soviet Air Force, 1986; CFS-Birthplace of Air Power, 1987; Soviet Wings, 1991. *Honours include:* FRAeS; FRHistS; AFAIAA; Freeman and Liveryman, Guild of Air Pilots & Air Navigators, 1983; Freedom of the City of London, 1987; C.P. Robertson Memorial Trophy, 1959; Certificate of Honour, Commission of Bibliography, History & Arts, Aero Club de France, 1971; Order of Merit, World Aerospace Education Organisation, 1981. *Address:* 36 Alexandra Drive, Surbiton, Surrey KT5 9AF, England.

TAYLOR (HOUGH) Judy, (Julia Marie), b. 12 Aug 1932, Wales. Writer. m. Richard Hough, 1980. *Appointments include:* Joined The Bodley Head publishers, 1951, specialising in children's books; Director, Bodley Head Ltd 1967-84; Chatto, Bodley Head & Jonathan Cape Ltd 1973-80, Chatto, Bodley Head & Jonathan Cape Australia Pty Ltd, 1977-80. Consultant to Penguin (formerly to Frederick Warne) on Beatrix Potter, 1981-87. *Publications:* Sophie & Jack, 1982; Sophie & Jack Help Out, 1983; My First Year: A Beatrix Potter Baby Book, 1983; Sophie & Jack in the Snow, 1984; Beatrix Potter: Artist, Storyteller & Countrywoman, 1986; Dudley & the Monster, 1986; Dudley Goes Flying, 1986; Dudley in a Jam, 1986; Dudley & the Strawberry Shake, 1986; That Naughty Rabbit: Beatrix Potter and Peter Rabbit, 1987; Beatrix Potter, 1866-1943: The Artist and her World (part-author with three others), 1987; Beatrix Potter's Letters: A Selection, 1989; (ed) Letters to Children from Beatrix Potter, 1992; So I Shall Tell You a Story, 1993. *Contributions to:* Numerous professional journals. *Honour:* MBE, 1971. *Memberships include:* Publishers Association Council, 1972-78; Book Development Council, 1973-76; Unicef International Art Committee, 1968-70, 1976, 1982-83; UK Unicef Greetings Card Committee, 1982-85; Beatrix Potter Society, Chair, 1990. *Address:* 31 Meadowbank, Primrose Hill Road, London NW3 1AY, England.

TAYLOR Kamala (Kamala Markandaya), Writer. m. 1 child. *Publications:* Nectar in a Sieve, 1955; Some Inner Fury, 1956; A Silence of Desire, 1961; Possession, 1964; A Handfull of Rice, 1968; The Coffer Dams, 1969; The Nowhere Man, 1973; Two Virgins, 1974; The Golden Honeycomb, 1977; Pleasure City, 1982. *Address:* Markandaya Ltd, c/o Norman Alexander & Co, 19 Bolton Street, London W1, England.

TAYLOR Laurie Aylma, b. 3 Sept 1939, Tappan, New York, USA. Writer. m. Allen Sparer, 17 July 1971, 2 daughters. *Education:* BA, Ohio Wesleyan University, 1960. *Publications:* Footnote to Murder; Only Half a Hoax; Deadly Objectives; Shed Light on Death; The Blossom of Erda; Changing the Past; Love of Money; Poetic Justice; A Murder Waiting to Happen. *Contributions to:* Several. *Honours:* Minnesota Voices Project; Lois Phillips Hudson Prize. *Memberships:* Poets & Writers; Mystery Writers of America; Science Fiction and Fantasy writers of America. *Literary Agent:* Frances Collin. *Address:* 4000 York Avenue South, Minneapolis, MN 55410, USA.

TAYLOR Stephen, b. 10 Apr 1948, Cape Town, South Africa. Journalist. m. Caroline Bowring, 1 son, 1 daughter. *Appointments:* Foreign Correspondent, The Times, London, 1980-87. *Publications:* The Mighty Nimrod, 1989.*Contributions to:* Reports for The Observer, London; The Economist, London, from Zimbabwe and South Africa. *Literary Agent:* Brian Stone, 29 Fernshaw Rd, London SW10. *Address:* 9 Dorset Road, Windsor, Berks, SL4 3BA.

TAYLOR Theodore Langhans, b. 23 June 1921, Statesville, North Carolina, USA. Writer. m. (1) Gwen Goodwin, 25 Oct 1946, 2 sons, 1 daughter, (2) Flora Gray, 18 Apr 1982. *Publications:* The Magnificent Mitscher, 1954; Fire on the Beaches, 1957; The Cay, 1968; The Children's War, 1971; The Maldonado Miracle 1973; Teetoncey, 1974; Jule 1979; The Trouble with Tuck, 1981; Battle of the Midway Island, 1982; HMS Hood vs Bismarck, 1983; Battle in the English Channel, 1984; Sweet Friday Island, 1984; The Cats of Shambala, 1985; Walking Up a Rainbow, 1986; The Stalker, 1987; The Hostage, 1988; Sniper, Monocolo, 1989; Tuck Triumphant, 1990; The Weirdo, 1991; Maria, 1992; To Kill The Leopard, 1993. *Contributions to:* Saturday Evening Post; McCall's; Ladies Home Journal; Saturday Review of Literature; Argosy. *Honours:* Lewis Carroll Shelf Award; Jane Addams Peace & Freedom Foundation Award; Western Writers of America Award; George G. Stone Center Award; Edgar Allan poe Award; International Association of School Librarians Award. *Literary Agent:* Gloria Loomis, Watkins-Loomis, New

York City. *Address:* 1856 Catalina Street, Laguna Beach, CA 92651, USA.

TAYLOR William, b. 11 Oct 1938, Wellington, New Zealand. Writer. m. Delia Wellington, 16 Jan 1965, div 1976, 2 sons. *Appointments:* Childrens Writing Fellowship, Palmerston North College of Education, 1992. *Publications:* Pack Up Pick Up & Off; Possum Perkins; My Summer of the Lions; Shooting Through; The Worst Soccer Team Ever; Break A Leg; Making Big Bucks; Fast Times at Greenhill High; The Kidnap of Jessie Parker; I Hate My Brother Maxwell Potter; The porter Brothers; Agnes The Sheep; Supermum & Spike the Dog; Knitwits; Beth & Bruno. *Honours:* New Zealand Library Association, Esther Glen Medal. *Address:* Kaitieke Road, RD2 Owhango, King Country, New Zealand.

TAYLOR William Ewart Jr, b. 21 Nov 1927, Toronto, Ontario, Canada. Archaeologist. m. Joan Elliott, 12 Sept 1952, 1 son, 2 daughters. *Education:* BA, Hons, University of Toronto, 1951; AM, University of Illinois, 1952; PhD, University of Michigan, 1965. *Appointments:* Arctic Archaeologist, 1956-60, Chief of Archaeology Division, 1960-67, Director of Human History Branch, 1967-68, National Museums of Canada, Ottawa, Ontario; Director, National Museum of Man, Ottawa, 1967-83; President, Social Science and Humanities Research Council of Canada, Ottawa, 1982-88; Writer; Conducted arctic field research 1950-65, 1988-90; Visiting Professor at University of Alaska, 1966, Ashley Fellow, Trent University, 1989. *Publications:* (General editor) The Arctic World, Sierra Books, 1985; Author of four books in arctic prehistory. *Contributions to:* Nearly 100 articles to archaeology, native art and museology journals. *Honours:* LLD from University of Calgary, 1975; Centennial Medal from Royal Society of Canada, 1982; D Litt from University of Newfoundland, 1983; Fiftieth Anniversary Award from Society for American Archaeology, 1985; Queen's Jubilee Medal; Bicentennial Medal from Society of Antiquaries of Scotland. *Memberships:* International Union of Anthropological and Ethnological Sciences; International Union of Prehistoric and Protohistoric Sciences (Permanent Council); Arctic Institute of North America (Fellow); Royal Society of Canada (Fellow); American Anthropological Association (Fellow); American Association for the Advancement of Science; National Press Club; Royal Anthropological Institute (Fellow); Royal Geographical Society (Fellow); Society of Antiquaries of Scotland (Honorary Fellow); Sigma Xi. *Address:* 509 Piccadilly Ave, Ottawa, Ontario Canada K1Y 0H7.

TAYLOR-MARTIN Patrick, b. 1 Aug 1953, England. Writer. *Education:* BA Hons History, University of Hull. *Publications:* John Betjeman: His Life and Work, 1983; Osbert Sitwell's Left Hand! Right Hand!, 1984. *Contributions to:* Books and Bookmen; Listener; Spectator; Sunday Times; Literary Review. *Memberships:* PEN. *Address:* Lumford House, Old Lumford, Bakewell, Derbyshire DE4 1GG, England.

TEBBEL John, b. 16 Nov 1912, Boynce City, USA. Writer; Retired Professor. m. 29 Apr 1939, 1 daughter. *Education:* BA, 1935, Litt.D, Hon., 1948, Central Michigan University; MS, Columbia University. *Publications:* The Life and Good Times of William Randolph Hearst, 1952; George Horace Lorimer and the Saturday Evening Posts, 1952; History of Book Publishing in the United States, Volumes I, IV, 1972-81; The Media in America, 1974; The Press and the Presidency, 1985; Between Covers, 1987; The Magazine in America, 1991, over 40 others. *Contributions to:* over 500 articles in national magazines & professional journals. *Honours:* Graduate, School of Journalism, Columbia University, 50th Anniversary Awards, 1963; Alumni award, 1975; Publishing Hall of Fame, 1985. *Memberships:* Society of Professional Journalists; Authors Guild. *Literary Agent:* William B Goodman. *Address:* 4033 The Forest AT Duke, 2701 Pickett Road, Durham, NC 27705, USA.

TEBBIT Norman, b. 1931, Ponders End, North London, England. Member of Parliament; Journalist. m. Margaret Elizabeth Daines, 1956, 2 sons, 1 daughter. *Appointments include:* Embarked in Career, Journalism, 1947; Served RAF, Qualified Pilot, 1949-51; Publishing, Advertising, 1951-53; Civil Airline Pilot, 1953-70; Minister of State, Department of Employment, 1972-73; Parliament Under Secretary of State, Department of Trade, 1978-81; Minister of State, Department of Industry, 1981; Secretary of State, for Employment, 1981-83; Conservative Party, 1985-87; Director, J.C. Bamford Excavaters, 1987-91; Co-Presenter, Target, SKY TV, 1989-. *Publications:* Upwardly Mobile, autobiography, 1989; Unfinished Business, 1991. *Honour:* Life Peer, 1992. *Memberships:* Aviation Committee; Secretary, House of Commons New Town Members Committee. *Address:* c/o 34 Thomas More House, Barbican, London EC2Y 8BT, England.

TELFER Tracie. *See:* **CHAPLIN Jenny.**

TEMKO Allan Bernard, b. 4 Feb 1924. Writer; Teacher. m. Elizabeth Ostroff, 1 July 1950, 1 son, 1 daughter. *Education:* AB, Columbia, 1947; Univerity of California, Berkeley, 1949-51; Sorbonne, 1948-49, 1951-52. *Appointments:* Architecture Critic, San Francisco Chronicle, 1961-; Art Editor, 1979-82. *Publications:* Notre Dame of Paris; Eero Saarinen; No Way to Build A Ballpark. *Contributions to:* The New Yorker; Harpers; Horizon; New York Times; Washington Post. *Honours include:* Gold Medal; Commonwealth Club of California; Journalism Award; Silver Spur Award; Manufactures Hanover Art World Award; Critics Award; Professional Achievement Award; Pulitzer Prize; Fellowships & Grants. *Literary Agent:* Fifi Oscard, New York City. *Address:* c/o San Francisco Chronicle, 901 Mission Street, San Francisco, CA 94103, USA.

TEMPEST Victor. *See:* **Philipp Eliot Elias.**

TEMPLE Ann. *See:* **MORTIMER Penelope (Ruth).**

TEMPLE Dan. *See:* **NEWTON Dwight Bennett.**

TEMPLE Nigel Hal Longdale b. 21 Jan 1926, England. Painter; Architectural Historian; Lecturer. m. Judith Tattersill, 1 son, 1 daughter. *Education:* National Diploma in Design, 1951; Art Teachers Diploma, Sheffield, 1953; MLitt. Architecture, Bristol, 1978; PhD, Keele, 1985. *Publications include:* Farnham Inheritance, 1956, 1965; Farnham Buildings and People, 1963, 1973; Looking at Things, 1968; Seen and Not Heard, 1970; John Nash and the Village Picturesque, 1979; Blaise Hamlet (a brief guide), 1986. *Contributions to:* Country Life; Journal of Garden History; Architectural Review; Garden History; Georgian Group Journal, and others. *Honours:* Fellow, National Society for Art Education, 1964; Companion of the Guild of St. George. *Memberships:* Royal West of England Academy (RWA); Garden History Society, Council Member; Cheltenham Group of Artists. *Address:* 4 Wendover Gardens, Christchurch Road, Cheltenham, Gloucestershire GL50 2PA, England.

TEMPLE Paul. *See:* **DURBRIDGE Francis Henry.**

TEMPLE (Robert) Philip, b. 20 Mar 1939, Yorkshire, England, Author. m. Daphne Evelyn Keen, 12 June 1965, 1 son, 1 daughter. *Appointments:* Katherine Mansfield Memorial Fellowship, Menton, France, 1979; Robert Burns Fellowship, University of Otago, Dunedin, New Zealand, 1980; Berliner Kunstlerprogramm Fellowship, West Berlin, 1987. *Publications:* Beak of the Moon, 1981; New Zealand Explorers, 1985; Ways to the Wilderness, 1977; Kakapo, 1988; Sam, 1984; The World at Their Feet, 1969; Dark of the Moon, 1993; The Explorer; Stations; Moa; Legend of the Kea; walking Track Guide Series; Author of 5 photographic books and 3 other non-fiction books. *Contributions to:* Associate Editor, Landfall, 1972-75. *Honours:* Wattie Award,

1970; New Zealand Literary Fund Grants and Busaries, 1972, 1976, 1986, 1987, 1991, 1992. *Memberships:* PEN, New Zealand Centre, 1970-; PEN representative, New Zealand Authors Advisory Committee, 1986-88; New Zealand Writers Guild, 1981-; New Zealand Alpine Club, 1960-86, 1993. Editor; New Zealand Alpine Journal, 1968-70, 1973. *Literary Agent:* John Johnson Limited, London, England. *Address:*147a Tomahawk Road, Dunedin, New Zealand.

TEMPLETON Fiona, b. 23 Dec 1951, Scotland. Writer; Director; Performer. *Education:* MA Hons French/Spanish, Edinburgh University, 1973; Auditrice Libre, Aix- en-Provence University, 1971-72; MA Poetics, New York University, 1985. *Publications:* London, 1984 (poem); Elements of Performance Art (theory & textbook), 1976; Performance pieces produced include: Thought/Death, 1980; Cupid and Psyche, 1981; There Was Absent Achilles, 1982; The Seven Deadly Jealousies, 1982; Under Paper Spells, 1982; Defense, 1982; Against Agreement, 1982; Experiments in the Destruction of Time, 1983; Five Hard Pieces including The New Three Act Piece, 1983; Out of the Mouths, 1984; A/Version, 1985; Only You, 1986; The Future, 1987; Are you Back? 1987; You - The City (play), produced, 1988, published, 1990; Delirum of Interpretations, 1991. *Contributions to:* Boundary 2; Pessimistic Labor 2; Poetics Journal 5; JAA 6; ABC No Rio; Appearances; Sun & Moon 11; Wallpaper 5/6; Musics 9; Partisan Review 2; Poetry Project Newsletter, 3/91; Big Allis 1, 5; Blatant Artifice 2/3; Motel 7; Writing, Raddle Moon 12, Conjunctions 20. *Honours:* Foundation for Contemporary Performance Arts Grant, 1987; New York State Council on the Arts Individual Artists' Project Grant, 1988; National Endowment for the Arts Interarts Grant, 1987-88; Art Matters Award, 1988; New York Foundation for the Arts Fellowship, Interarts 1985, 1989; Jerome Fund for Performance Art Award, 1984; PEN Writers Grant, 1985; National Endowment for the Arts Visual Arts (New Genres) Fellowship, 1983; Abendzeitung (Munich) Stern Des Jahres, Award for Theatre, 1991. *Address:* c/o Downtown Arts, 280 Broadway, Room 412, New York, NY 10007, USA.

TENE Benjamin, b. 10 Dec 1914, Warsaw, Poland. Writer. m. Sarah, 1937, 1 son, 1 daughter. *Appointment:* Editor, Michmar L'iladim. *Publications:* Mehora, 1939; Massa Begalil, 1941; Beheret hadwai, 1945; Tmolim Al Hasaf, 1947; Hazamir, 1963; Shirim Upoemot, 1967; Ktsir Hapele, (for children), 1957; Translation Poems and Ballads by Itzik Manger; Mizmor Lehag, (for childen), 1973; Prose Books; In the Shade of the Chestnut Tree, 1973; Schoolboys Before the Storm, 1976; The Story of Mor, 1977; City of My Youth, 1979; A Friend in Need, 1981; The Third Courtyard, 1982. *Honours:* Alfred Jurzykowski Foundation Award, 1970; Zew Award, 1974; Lamdan Award, 1980; Zew Award, 1981; Itzik Manger Award, 1987. *Memberships:* Association of Hebrew Writers in Israel. *Address:* Karni 8, 69025 Tel Aviv, Israel.

TENNANT Emma Christina (Catherine Aydy), b. 20 Oct 1937, London, England. Author. 1 son, 2 daughters. *Publications:* Hotel De Dream, 1976; The Bad Sister, 1978; The Adventures of Robina, 1985; Woman Beware Woman, 1983; The Colour of Rain, 1963; Queen of Stones; Alice Fell; Wild Nights, 1979; The Crack, 1973; The Last of the Country House Murders, 1975; Black Marina, 1984; Adventures of Robina, 1986; The House of Hospitalities, 1987; A Wedding of Cousins, 1988; The Bad Sister, 1989; Sisters & Strangers, 1990; Faustine, 1991; Rag Rugs of England & America, 1992; The ABC of Writing, 1992. *Contributions to:* London Review of Books. *Memberships:* Fellow, Royal Society of Literature. *Literary Agent:* The Peters Fraser and Dunlop Group Ltd. *Address:* c/o The Peters Fraser and Dunlop Group Ltd, 503/4 The Chambers, Chelsea Harbour, London SW10 0XF, England.

TERAHATA Jun. *See:* **KIRKUP James.**

TERLECKI Tymon Tadeusz Julian, b. 10 Aug 1905, Poland. Writer; Professor Emeritus. m. (1) Antonia Kopczynska, 1946, dec 1983; (2) Nina Taylor, 1987. *Education:* PhD, King John Casimir University, 1932. *Appointments:* Editor of Teatr, 1936-39; Scena Polska, 1936-38; Wiedza o Teatrze, 1938-39; Co-editor, Zycie Sztuki, 1932-35, 1938-39; Co-Founder and Editor, Polska Walczaca, 1939-49; Editorial Advisor, Polish Review, New York. *Publications:* Rodwood poetycki Ryszarda Berwinskiego, 1937; Krytyka Personalistyczna, 1957; Egzystencjalizm chrzescijanski, 1958; Pani Helena, 1962; Stanistaw Wyspianski, 1983; Rzeczy teatralne, 1984; Szukanie Rownowagi, 1985; Londyn-Paryz, 1987. *Contributions to:* Kultura (Paris) and many Polisy periodicals. *Honours:* Theatrical Book of the year, 1985; Stanislaw Vincenz Prize, 1985; Radziszewski Prize, Catholic University of Lublin, 1990; Hon Doctorate, University of Wroclaw, 1990. *Memberships:* Polish Hist-Lit Society of Paris, 1950; Co-founder, Chm, 1955-59, 1965-66, Union of Polish Writers Abroad; Co-Founder of Association of Polish Writers; Polish Society of Arts and Sciences Abroad, 1952-; Polish Institute of Arts and Sciences of America. *Address:* 325 Woodstock Road, Oxford OX2 7NX, England.

TERLECKI Wladyslaw Lech, b. 18 May 1933, Czestochowa, Poland. Writer. m. Lucyna Basaj, 1955, 1 son, 1 daughter. *Education:* University of Wroclaw. *Appointments:* Staff: Wspolczesnosc, 1958-65, Polish Radio (Drama Section), 1965-70. *Publications:* Black Romancy, 1974; Two Heads of a Bird, 1970; Rest After the Race, 1975; The Forest Grows, 1977; Tea with the Man Who is Not Here, 1976; Pismak, 1984; Cobble Stones, 1956; Fire, 1962; The Conspiracy, 1966; High Season, 1966; The Wormwood Star, 1968; Pilgrims, 1972; Return from Clarskoe Selo, 1973; numerous films scripts, theatre plays. *Honours:* Koscielski Prize, switzerland, 1973; ODRA Award, 1978; Literatura Award, 1981; Teatr Polski Drama Award, 1987. *Memberships:* PEN; Polish Film-makers Union. *Address:* Ul. Mazurska 1, 05-806 Komorow, Poland.

TERRAINE John Alfred, b. 15 Jan 1921, London, England. Author. m. 27 Nov 1945, 1 daughter. *Education:* Keble College, Oxford. *Publications:* Mons : The Retreat to Victory, 1960; Douglas Haig : The Educated Soldier, 1963; The Great War, An Illustrated History, 1964; The Western Front, 1964; General Jack's Diary, Editor, 1964; The Life and Times of Lord Mountbatten, 1968; Impacts of War, 1914 and 1918, 1970; The Mighty Continent, 1974; Trafalgar, 1976; To Win a War : 1918 The Year of Victory, 1978; The Road to Passchendaele, 1977; The Smoke and the Fire: Myths and Anti-Myths of War 1861-1945, 1980; The Right of the Line : The Royal Air Force in the European War, 1939-45, 1985; White Heat : The New Warfare 1914-1918, 1982; Business in Great Waters: the U-Boat Wars 1916-1945, 1989. *Contributions to:* various professional journals. *Honours:* Royal United Services Institute Cheaney Gold Medal; Yorkshire Post Book of the Year, 1985; Air Public Relations Association Award, 1985; Honorary Fellow, Keble College, Oxford, 1986; Fellow, Royal Historical Society, 1986. *Memberships:* Society of Authors; Royal United Institute; many other organisations. *Address:* 74 Kensington Park Road, London W11 2PL, England.

TERRIS Susan, b. 5 June 1937, St Louis, USA. Author. m. David Warren Terris, 1958, 2 sons, 1 daughter. *Education:* BA, English, Wellesley College, 1959; MA, English Literature, San Francisco State University, 1966. *Publications:* The Upstairs Witch and the Downstairs Witch, 1970; The Backwards Boots, 1971; The Drowning Boy, 1972; On Fire, 1972; Pickle, 1973; Plague of Frogs, 1973; Whirling Rainbows, 1974; Tucker and the Horse Thief, 1974; The Pencil Families, 1975; Amanda, The Panda, and the Redhead, 1975; The Chicken Pox Papers, 1976; No Boys Allowed, 1976; Two P's in a Pod, 1977; Stage Brat, 1980; No Scarlet Ribbons, 1981; Wings and Roots, 1982; Octopus Pie, 1983; Baby-Snatcher, 1984; The Latchkey Kids, 1986;

Nell's Quilt, 1987; Author! Author! 1990. *Address:* 11 Jordan Avenue, San Francisco, CA 94118, USA.

TERRY C V. *See:* **SLAUGHTER Frank Gill.**

TERRY Carolyn Mary, b. 18 June 1940, Bristol, England. Writer. m. Roy Terry, 1969. *Publications:* King of Diamonds, 1983; The Fortune Seekers, 1985. *Membership:* Society of Authors. *Literary Agent:* Christopher Little. *Address:* c/o Christopher Little Literary Agency, 49 Queen Victoria Street, London EC4N 4SA, England.

TERRY Megan, b. 22 July 1932, Seattle, Washington, USA. Playwright. *Education:* BEd, University of Washington; Graduate work, University of Alberta and Banff School of Fine Arts, Canada. *Literary Appointment:* Playwright-in-Residence, Omaha Magic Theatre, Omaha, Nebraska, USA. *Publications:* Writer of over 60 plays including: American King's English for Queens; Approaching Simone; Babes in the Bighouse; Calm Down Mother; Comings and Goings; Couplings and Groupings; Ex-Miss Copper Queen on a Set of Pills; Fifteen Million Fifteen Year-Olds; The Gloaming, Oh My Darling; Hothouse; Keep Tightly Closed in a Cool Dry Place; Kegger; The Magic Realists; Massachusetts Trust; Megan Terry's Home: Or Future Soap; The People VS Ranchman; The Pioneer; Pro Game; Sanibel and Captiva; Viet Rock, Walking Through Walls. *Contributions to:* Performing Arts Journal; The New York Times; The Southwestern Review; the Drama Review; Notable American Women. *Honours:* Obie Award for best Play, 1970; Dramatists Guild Annual Award, 1983; Rockefeller Fellowship; Guggenheim Fellowship; Nebraska Poet Laureate Nomination; Stanley Drama Award; 2 Grants from the Office of Advanced Drama Research, University of Minnesota; 2 Rockefeller Grants; New York State CAPS Fellowship; ABC Fellowship, Writing for the Camera, Yale; Literature Fellowship, National Endowment for the Arts. *Literary Agent:* Elisabeth Marton. *Address:* c/o Elisabeth Marton, 96 Fifth Avenue, New York, NY 10011, USA.

TERRY Walter, b. 18 Aug 1924, Birmingham, England. Journalist. m. Mavis Landen, 24 Mar 1950, 1 son, 1 daughter. *Appointments:* Glossop Chronicle, 1943; Derby Evening Telegraph, 1947; Nottingham Journal, 1948; Daily Mail, Manchester, 1949; Daily Mail, Parliamentary Staff, 1955, Political Correspondent, 1959, Political Editor, 1965, Washington Correspondent, 1969, Deputy Editor, 1970-71, Political Editor, 1971-73; Political Editor, Daily Express, 1973-75; Political Editor, The Sun, 1978-83. *Address:* St Germans House, Eliot Place, London, SE3 0QL, England.

TERRY William. *See:* **GILMAN George G.**

TERSON Peter. *See:* **PATTERSON Peter.**

TERZIAN Pierre, b. 10 Nov 1948, Lebanon. Journalist; University Teacher. m. Manik Yaghobian, 1984, 1 son. *Education:* PhD, Sorbonne University, Paris, 1980. *Publications:* OPEC, The Inside Story; prices and Contracts for Oil in the Middle East. *Contributions to:* Le Monde; Financial Times; petro Money Report; Petrostrategies; Opec Bulletin. *Address:* 4 Rue Bocelitte, 75014 Paris, France.

THAYER Geraldine. *See:* **DANIELS Dorothy.**

THEAKSTON Kevin, b. 16 Feb 1958, England. University Lecturer. m. Breda Finegan, 20 Aug 1982, 2 sons, 1 daughter dec. *Education:* BSc Econ, London School of Economics, 1982; PhD, 1985; Kennedy Scholar, Harvard University, 1982-83. *Publications:* Junior Ministers in British Government, 1987; The Labour Party and Whitehall, 1992. *Contributions to:* Public Administration, Political Quarterly, Contemporary Record and other academic journals. *Memberships:*

Royal Institute of Public Administration. *Address:* Department of Politics, University of Leeds, Leeds LS2 9JJ, England.

THELLE Notto Reidar, b. 19 Mar 1941, Hong Kong. Professor of Theology. m. Mona Irene Ramstad, 2 sons, 3 daughters. *Education:* Candidate of Theology, 1965, Degree in Practical Theology, 1966, DTheol, 1982, Oslo University. *Appointments:* Missionary in Japan, 1969-1985; Associate Director, The Centre for Th Study of Japanese Religions in Kyoto. *Publications:* Buddhism and Christianity in Japan: From Conflict to Dialogue, 1854-1899, 1987; Norwegian Books: Who Can Stop The Wind?, 1991; The Human and the Mystery, 1992. *Contributions to:* Japanese Religions; Japan Christian Quarterly; Cross Currents; Inter-religio; Update; Japan Missionary Bulletin; International Bulletin of Mission Studies; Current Dialogue. *Address:* Nordengveien 29, 0755 Oslo 7, Norway.

THELWELL Norman, b. 3 May 1923, Birkenhead, Cheshire, England. Artist; Writer; Cartoonist. m. 11 Apr 1949, 1 son, 1 daughter. *Education:* NDA, ATD, Liverpool College of Art, 1947-50. *Appointments:* Art Teacher, Wolverhampton College of Art, 1950-57. *Publications:* Angels on Horseback, 1957; Thelwell Country, 1959; A Place of Your Own, 1960; Thelwell in Orbit, 1961; A Leg at Each Corner, 1962; The Penguin Thelwell, 1963; Top Dog, 1964; Thelwell's Riding Academy, 1965; Drawing Ponies, 1966; Up the Garden Path, 1967; The Compleat Tangler, 1967; The Thelwell Book of Leisure, 1968; This Desirable Plot, 1970; The Effluent Society, 1971; Penelope, 1972; Three Sheets in the Wind, 1973; Belt Up, 1975; Thelwell Goes West, 1976; Thelwell's Brat Race, 1978; A Plank Bridge by a Pool, 1979; Thelwell's Gymkhana, 1980; Pony Calvelcade, 1981; A Mill Stone Round My Neck, 1982; Some Damn Fool's Signed the Rubens Again, 1983; Magnificat, 1984; Thelwell's Sporting Prints, 1985; Wrestling with a Pencil, 1986; Play it as it Lies, 1987; Penelope Rides Again, 1988; The Cat's Pyjamas, 1992. *Contributions to:* Punch, 1952-77; Cartoonist for News Chronicle, 1956-60, Sunday Dispatch, 1960-62, Sunday Express, 1962-72; numerous other journals and magazines. *Literary Agent:* Momentum Licensing Ltd., London. *Address:* Herons Mead, Timsbury, Romsey, Hampshire, SO51 0NE, England.

THEODORACOPULOS Peter (Taki), b. 1937, Athens, Greece. Journalist. *Appointments:* War Correspondent; Columnist, High Life, Spectator, 1977-. *Publications:* Nothing To Declare: A Memoir; High Life, 1989, (Autobiography). *Contributions to:* Esquire; Vanity Fair; Interviews. *Honours:* Represented Greece, Davis Cup and as Skier in Winter Olympics; Captain, Greek Karate Team.

THEODOROPOULOS Takis, b. 28 Mar 1954, Athens, Greece. Novelist. m. Danai Victoria Mitsotakis, 25 Sept 1982, 1 daughter. *Education:* Licence/Letters, Paris, 1978; Maitrise, Theatre, Paris, 1979; DEA, Social Anthropology, Paris, 1980. *Publications:* The Absolute Landscape; Nights in Arcadia; The Whisper of Persephone. *Contributions to:* Numerous. *Membership:* Union of Greek Writers. *Literary Agent:* Estia Co., 60 Solonos Street, 106 72 Athens. *Address:* 49 Eleftherotrias Street, 145 63 Kifissia, Greece.

THEROUX Paul Edward, b. 10 Apr 1941, USA. Writer. m. Anne Castle, 1967, 2 sons. *Education:* BA, University of Massachusetts. *Appointments include:* Lecturer, various universities. *Publications:* Novels: Waldo, 1967; Fong & the Indians, 1968; Murder in Mount Holly, 1969; Girls at Play, 1969; Jungle Lovers, 1971; Sinning with Annie, 1972; Saint Jack, 1973 (film, 1979); The Family Arsenal, 1976; The Consul's File, 1979; Picture Palace, 1978; London Snow, 1980; World's End, 1980; The Mosquito Coast, 1981, (film 1986); The London Embassy, 1982; Doctor Slaughter, 1984, (film 1986); O-Zone, 1986; My Secret History, 1989; Chicago Loop, 1990; Doctor de Marr, 1990. Criticism: V.S. Naipaul, 1972. Travel: The Great Railway

Bazaar, 1975; The Old Patagonian Express, 1979; The Kingdom by the Sea, 1983; Sailing Through China, 1983; Sunrise with Seamonsters: Travels & Discoveries 1964-84, 1985; The Imperial Way, 1985; Riding the Iron Rooster, 1988; Traveling the World, 1990; Happy Isles of Oceania, 1992. *Honours:* Honorary degrees, USA; Whitbread Award, 1978; James Tait Black Award, 1982; Yorkshire Post Best Novel, 1982; Thomas Cook Travel Book Prize, 1989; Hon DLitt (Tufts University, 1985; University of Massachusetts, 1988). *Address:* c/o Hamish Hamilton Ltd, 27 Wrights Lane, London W8 5TZ, England.

THERRIAULT Daniel, b. 16 May 1953, Chicago, USA. Dramatist. m. Alison Mackenzie, 8 Apr 1983, 1 son, 1 daughter. *Education:* BA, Theatre, Niles College, Loyola University, 1975. *Publications:* Battery, 1983, 2nd edition 1987; Floor Above the Roof, 1984; The White Death, 1989; The Hitch (radio drama), broadcast US, Germany, 1992. *Honours:* Drama-Logue Award for Writing, Los Angeles, 1983, 1987; Winner in Play Expo, Chicago, 1987; American Exchange Writer to Ireland, 1987; New Dramatists, New York City; Sundance Institute 1988; McKnight Fellowship, 1991-92. *Membership:* Dramatists Guild. *Literary Agent:* Ms Leah Schmidt, Curtis Brown, London, England. *Address:* 60 Clark Street Brooklyn Heights, NY 11201, USA.

THIELE Colin Milton, b. 16 Nov 1920, Eudunda, South Australia. Author. m. Rhonda Gladys Gill, 17 Mar 1945, 2 daughters. *Education:* BA, Dip.Ed, Dip.T, University of Adelaide. *Publications:* 90 books including: The Sun On The Stubble; Storm Boy; Blue Fin; The Fire in the Stone; Seashores and Shadows. *Contributions to:* Meanjin; The Australian; The Australiam Author; The Sydney Morning Herald; The Adelaide Advertiser. *Honours:* Companion of the Order of Australia; Grace Levin Poetry Prize; Austrian State Prize; Australian Childrens Book of the Year Award; Netherlands Silver Pencil Award. *Memberships:* Australian Society of Authors; Australian College of Education. *Address:* 24 Woodhouse Crescent, Wattle Park, South Australia 5066, Australia.

THIRY August, b. 24 Apr 1948, Grazen, Belgium. Professor. m. Simonne Rutten, 28 July 1972, 2 daughters. *Education:* Master of arts, Germanic Languages, 1972; Slavonic Languages, Russian, 1975. *Appointments:* Editor, Cultural Magazine, 1976-82; Reviewer Russian Literature, 1990-. *Publications:* Het Paustovski Syndroom; Onder Assistenten; Russische Literatuur in de zoste Eeuw; Montagne Russe. *Contributions to:* Jeugd & Cultuur; Kreatief; Argus; Dietsche Warande; Nieuw Wereldtýdschrift; Slavica Gandensia. *Honours:* De Brakke Hond Story Award; Guido Gezelle Novel Award. *Literary Agent:* Deflo Lionel. *Address:* Dorenstraat 196, 3020 Herent, Belgium.

THISTLETHWAITE Frank, b. 24 July 1915. Emeritus Professor. m. Jane Hosford, 1940, 2 sons (1 dec), 3 daughters. *Education:* Exhibitioner and Scholar, St John's College, Cambridge; BA 1st class honours, History and English Literature, 1938; Commonwealth Fund Fellow, University of Minnesota, 1938-40; MA (Cantab), 1941. *Appointments include:* Editor, The Cambridge Review, 1937; British Press Service, New York, USA, 1940-41; Various university teaching positions; Founding Vice-Chancellor, 1961-80, Emeritus Professor, 1980-, University of East Anglia, Norwich; Visiting Scholar, various American universities. *Publications:* The Great Experiment: An Introduction to the History of the American People, 1955; The Anglo-American Connection in the Early Nineteenth Century, 1958; Dorset Pilgrims, 1989; Chapters in New Cambridge Modern History, New Universities in the Modern World. *Contributions to:* Historical journals. *Honours:* Honorary Fellow RIBA, St John's College, Cambridge, 1974; Honorary Professor of History, University of Mauritius, 1981; Honorary LHD, Colorado, 1972; Honorary DCL, East Anglia, 1980; CBE, 1979. *Memberships include:* Founding Chairman, British Association of American Studies; Fellow, Royal

Historical Society. *Address:* 15 Park Parade, Cambridge CB5 8AL, England.

THOM James Alexander, b. 28 May 1933, Gosport, Indiana, USA. Novelist. m. Dark Rain, 20 May 1990. *Education:* AB, Butler University, Indianapolis, Ind, 1961. *Appointments:* Reporter & Columnist, The Indianapolis Star, 1961-1967; Lecturer in Journalism, Indiana University, 1978-1980. *Publications include:* Spectator Sport, 1978; Long Knife, 1979; Follow the River, 1981; From Sea to Shinging Sea, 1984; Staying Out of Hell, 1985; Panther in the Sky, 1989. *Contributions to:* National Geographic; Readers Digest; Washington Post Book World and others. *Memberships:* Authors Guild; Western Writers of America. *Literary Agent:* Mitch Douglas, International Creative Management, NY. *Address:* 10061 West Stogsdill Road, Bloomington, IN 47404, USA.

THOMANECK Jurgen Karl Albert, b. 12 June 1941, Stettin. University Professor. m. Euinevere Ronald, 3 Aug 1964, 2 daughters. *Education:* Universities of Kiel, Tubingen, Aberdeen, Aberdeen College of Education. *Publications:* Police and Public Order in Europe, 1985; The German Democratic Republic, 1989; Plenzdorf's Die Neuen Leiden des jungen W, 1991; Deutsches Abiturienten Lesikon, 1974; Fremdsprachenunterricht und Soziolonguistik, 1981. *Contributions to:* Learned journals. *Memberships:* FRSA. *Address:* 17 Elm Place, Aberdeen AB2 3SN, Scotland.

THOMAS G K. *See:* **DAVIES Leslie Purnell.**

THOMAS Audrey Grace, b. 17 Nov 1935, Binghamton, New York, USA. Writer. m. Ian Thomas 1958, (div 1978). 3 daughters. *Education:* BA, English, Smith College, 1957; MA, English, University of British Columbia, 1963. *Appointments:* Visiting Assistant Professor, Creative Writing, Concordia University, 1978; Visiting Professor, Creative Writing, University of Victoria, 1978-79; Writer-in-Residence, Simon Fraser University, 1981-82; Senior Fellow, Edinburgh; Writer-in-Resident, University of Ottawa, 1987; Visiting Professor, Spring Term, Univerity of Victoria, BC, 1992. *Publications:* Ten Green Bottles, 1967; Mrs Blood, 1970; Munchmeyer and Prospero on the Island, 1972; Songs My Mother Taught Me, 1973; Blown Figures, 1974; Ladies and Escorts, 1977; Latakia, 1979; Real Mothers, 1981; Two in the Bush and Other Stories, 1982; Intertidal Life, 1984; Goodbye Harold, Good Luck, 1986; 13 Radio Dramas. *Contributions to:* Many stories have appeared in: The Atlantic; Saturday Night; Toronto Life; The Capilano Review; Fiddlehead; Interface. *Honours:* 2nd Prize, National Magazine Awards, Fiction, 1980; 2nd Prize, CBC Literary Competition, Fiction, 1980; 2nd Prize, CBC Literary Competition, Memoirs, 1981; 2nd Prize, Chatelaine Fiction Competition, 1981; Canada Council Arts Grant "A", 1991; Ethel Wilson Award, 1991. *Memberships:* PEN; Writers Union of Canada; Member of ACTRA. *Address:* The Writers Union of Canada, 24 Ryelson Ave, Toronto, Ontario, M5T 2P3 Canada.

THOMAS Craig (David Grant), b. 1942, Cardiff, Wales. Novelist. m. *Education:* MA, University College, Cardiff, 1967. *Publications:* Rat Trap; Firefox; Wolfsbane; Snow Falcon; Emerald Decision (as David Grant); Moscow 5000 (as David Grant); Sea Leopard; Jade Tiger; Firefox Down; The Bear's Tears; Winter Hawk; All the Grey Cats, 1989; The Last Raven. *Address:* Nr Lichfield, Staffordshire, England.

THOMAS David Arthur, b. 6 Feb 1925, Wanstead, England. Retired Marketing Executive. m. Joyce Irene Petty, 3 Apr 1948, 1 daughter. *Education:* Leyton County High School, 1936-41; Northampton Polytechnic, 1948-53. *Publications:* With Ensigns Flying, 1958; Submarine Victory, 1961; Battle of the Java Sea, 1968; Crete 1941: The Battle at Sea, in US Nazi Victory, 1972; Japan's War at Sea, 1978; Royal Admirals, 1982; Compton Mackenzie: A Bibliography, 1986; Companion to the

Royal Navy, 1988; Illustrated Armada Handbook, 1988; The Atlantic Star, 1990; Christopher Columbus, Master of the Atlantic, 1991. *Membership:* Fellow, Royal Society of Arts. *Literary Agent:* A M Heath & Co Ltd. *Address:* Cedar Lodge, Church Lane, Sheering, Bishop's Stortford, Herts, England.

THOMAS David Hurst, b. 27 May 1945, California, USA. Curator. m. Lorann S.A. Pendleton, 25 Aug 1985. 1 son. *Education:* BA,1967, MA, 1968, PhD, 1971, Anthroplogy, University of California, Davis. *Appointments include:* Associate Editor, Cambridge University Press; Cheif Editorial Advisor, Archaeology for American Anthropologist; General Editor, Archaeology and History of the Spanish Borderlands, The North American Indian, Columbian Consequences. *Publications include:* Archaeology, 1979, 1989; Archaeology: Down to Earth, 1991; St. Catherines: An Island in Time, 1988; Refiguring Anthrolpogy, 1976; Figuring Anthropology, 1986; Predicting the Past, 1974; The Archaeology of Monitor Valley, 3 vol., 1983, 1983, 1988; The Archaeology of St. Catherines Island, 5 vol. 1978, 1979, 1982, 1986, 1987; The Archaeology of Hidden Cave, 1985. *Contributions to:* various journals. *Honours:* Founding Trustee, Vice Chairman of the Board National Museum of the American Indian; National Academy of Sciences, 1989; Council of The International Union of Prehistoric and Protohistoric Sciences. *Memberships include:* Executive Committee, Society for American Archaeology; Overseers' Committee to Visit Peabody Museums, Harvard University; Acting Director, Museum Studies Program, New York University. *Address:* Department of Anthroplogy, American Museum of Natural History, Central Park West 79th Street, New York, NY 10024, USA.

THOMAS Denis, b. 23 July 1922, London, England. Author; Journalist, m. Joyce Betts, 10 Jan 1951, 4 sons. *Education:* BA, Honours, St Edmund hall, Oxford, 1946-49. *Publications:* Thomas Churchyard of Woodbridge, 1966; The Visible Persuaders, editor, 1969; The Mind of Economic Man, editor, 1970; Picasso and His Art, 1975; The Face of Christ, 1979; Dictionary of Fine Arts, 1981; Rowland Hilder's England, 1986; The Age of the Impressionists, 1987; Rowland Hilder Country, in collaboration with the artist, 1987. *Contributions to:* Connoisseur; Antique Collector; Observer; The Listener. *Memberships:* Society of Authors; Association of Art Historians. *Address:* Coach House, Oakwood Close, Chislehurst, Kent, England.

THOMAS Donald Michael, b. 27 Jan 1935, Redruth, Cornwall, England. Poet; Novelist. 2 sons, 1 daughter. *Education:* BA, 1st Class Honours English, MA, New College, Oxford. *Appointments include:* School teacher, 1959-63; Lecturer, Hereford College of Education, 1964-78. *Publications:* Poetry: Penguin Modern Poets 11, 1968; Two Voices, 1968; Logan Stone, 1971; Love & Other Deaths, 1975; The Honeymoon Voyage, 1978; Dreaming in Bronze, 1981; Selected Poems, 1983; Puberty Tree, 1992. Novels: The Flute Player, 1979; Birthstone, 1980; The White Hotel, 1981; Ararat, 1983; Swallow, 1984; Sphinx, 1986; Summit, 1987. Translations: Requiem, and Poem Without a Hero, Akhmatova, 1976; Way of All the Earth, Akhmatova, 1979; Bronze Horseman, Pushkin, 1982; Fiction: Lying Together, 1990; Flying into Love, 1992. *Address:* The Coach House, Rashleigh Vale, Tregolls Road, Truro, TR1 1TJ, England.

THOMAS Elizabeth Marshall, b. 13 Sept 1931, Boston, Massachusetts, USA. m. 14 Jan 1956, 1 son, 1 daughter. *Education:* AB, RADcliffe, 1954. *Publications:* The Harmless People, 1959; Warrior Herdsmen, 1966; Reindeer Moon, 1987; The Animal Wife, 1990; The Old Way, 1990; The Hill People, 1953; The Hidden Life of Dogs, 1993. *Contributions to:* Behavioural Ecology and Sociobiology; Studying War: Anthropological Perspectives. *Honours:* Doctorate of Letters (Hon), Franklin Pierce College, 1992; Radcliffe Alumnae Recognition Award, 1989; PEN Hemingway Citation, 1988; Brandeis Creative Arts Award, 1968. *Memberships:* PEN: Authors Guild; Author's League;

Society of Women Geographers. *Literary Agent:* John Taylor Williams at Palmer and Dodge. *Address:* 80 East Mountain Road, Peterbrough, NH 03458, USA.

THOMAS Franklin Richard, b. 1 Aug 1940, Indiana, USA. Professor. m. Sharon Kay Myers, 2 June 1962, 1 son, 1 daughter. *Education:* AB, MA, Purdue University; PhD, Indiana University, 1970. *Appointments:* Purdue University, 1969-70; Professor, Michigan State University, 1971-; Research Associate, Indiana University, 1978-79. *Publications:* Poetry: Fat Grass, 1970; Frog Praises Night, 1980; Alive With You This Day, 1980; The Landlocked Heart: Poems from Indiana, 1980; Heart Climbing Stairs, 1986; Corolla, Stamen, & Style, 1986; The Whole Mustery of the Bregn, 1989. Scholarship: The Literary Admirers of Alfred Stieglitz, 1983; Americans in Denmark, 1989; Novel: Prisim: The Journal of John Fish, 1992. *Contributions to:* numerous journals and magazines. *Honours:* several including: MacDowell Colony Fellowship; Fulbright Teaching Awards to Denmark, 1974-75, 1985-86; Michigan Council for the Arts Award for Poetry, 1990. *Address:* Dept. of American Thought & Language, Michigan State University, E. Lansing, MI 48824, USA.

THOMAS Gordon, b. 21 Feb 1933, England. Author; Journalist; Screenwriter; Film Director; Producer. m. Edith Kraner, 2 sons, 3 daughters. *Education:* Cairo High School for Boys; Bedford School. *Appointments:* Foreign Correspondent, London Daily and Express and Sunday Express, Middle East, Algeria, Cyprus, Kenya, Uganda, 1955-60; Writer, Director, Producer, British Broadcasting Corporation, Federal Republic of Germany, South and North Africa, USA, Canada, 1961-69; New Features Correspondent, The Press Association, London, 1984-; Contributing Correspondent: Toronto Globe and Mail, 1982-84; Sunday Star, Toronto Star, 1984-. *Publications:* Descent into Danger, 1954; Physician Extraordinary, 1955; Bed of Nails, 1956; Heroes of the Royal Air Force, 1956; Miracle of Surgery, 1957; The National Health Service and You, 1958; The Parents Home Doctor, 1959, 4th Edition, 1971; The Day the World Ended, 1965; Earthquake, 1966; Shipwreck, 1968; The Strange Fate of the Morro Castle, 1968; Voyage of the Damned, 1970; Guernica: The Crucible of World War Two, 1973; Issels: The Biography of a Doctor, 1975; Ruin From the Air, 1977; Enola Gray, 1977; The Day the Bubble Burst, 1979; Trauma, 1981; The Year of Armageddon, 1984; The Operation, 1985; Desire and Denial, 1986; The Trial, 1987; Journey into Madness, 1988; Enslaved, 1989; Chaos Under Heaven, 1990; Films: Voyage of the Damned, 1974; Time Ran Out, 1976; A Bit of an Experience, 1978; The Heart Man, 1979; Go Climb a Mountain, 1980; The Day the Bubble Burst, 1980; Chaos Under Heaven, 1990; Godless, 1992. *Honours:* Jury's Prize and Critics Prize, Monte Carlo Film Festival, 1979; Award for Historical Reportage, Mark Twain Society, 1980, 1983, 1985. *Membership:* Institute of Journalists, London. *Literary Agent:* Russel Galen, Scott Meredity Literary Agency. *Address:* 845 Third Avenue, New York, NY 10022, USA.

THOMAS Gwyn, b. 2 Sept 1936, Blaenau Ffestiniog, Wales. University Professor. m. 11 July 1964, 2 sons, 1 daughter. *Education:* BA 1957, MA 1961, University College of North Wales, Bangor; D.Phil. (Oxon) 1966. *Publications include:* In Welsh: Y Bardd Cwsg a'i Gefndir, 1971; Y Traddodiad Barddol, 1977; Ysgyrion Gwaed, poetry, 1967; Y Pethau Diwethaf a Phethau Eraill, poetry, 1975; Enw'r Gair, poetry, 1972. Also: Living a Life, poems in English, 1982; Tales from the Mabinogion, with K. Crossley-Holland, 1984; Co-editor, Presenting Saunders Lewis, 1973; Editor, translations into Welsh, plays in World Drama series. *Contributions to:* Various articles, Welsh literature, literature in general. *Honours:* Sir Ellis Griffith Memorial Prize, 1973; Literary prizes, Welsh Arts Council, 1968, 1973, 1977, 1978. *Membership:* Secretary, Vice Chairman, Yr Academi Gymreig. *Address:* 17 Lon y Bryn, Bangor, Gwynedd LL57 2LD, Wales.

THOMAS Henri, b. 7 Dec 1912, Anglemont, Vosges, France. Writer; Poet. m. Jacqueline le Beguec, 1957,

1 daughter. *Education:* Strasbourg University. *Appointments include:* Programme assistant, BBC French Section, 1947-58; Lecturer, French, Brandeis University, USA, 1956-60; In charge, German Department, Gallimard's Publishing House, 1960-. *Publications:* Poetry: Travaux D'Aveugle, 1941; Signe De Vie, 1944; Le Monde Absent, 1947; Nul Desordre, 1950; Sousle Lien Du Temps, 1963; A Quoi Tu Penses, 1979; Joueur Surpris, 1982; Poesies Completes, 1970; Trezeaux, 1989. Novels: Le Seau a Charbon, 1940; Le Precepteur, 1942; Lavie Ensemble, 1943; Les Déserteurs, 1951; La Nuit De Londres, 1956; La Dernière Année, 1960; John Perkins, 1960; Le Promontoire, 1961; Le Parjure, 1964; La Relique, 1969; Le Croc Des Chiffonniers, 1985; Une Saison Volée, 1986; Une Détour Par La Vie, 1988; Le Gouvernement Provisoire, 1989; Le Goût De L'Eternel, 1990; Al-Je One Patrie, 1991; Le Cinema Dans La Grange, 1992; Le Poison Des Images, 1993. Short Stories: La Cible, 1956; Histoire De Pierrot Et Quelques Autres, 1960; Les Tours De Notre-Dame, 1979. Essays: Sous Le Lien Du Temps, 1963; Sainte-Jeunesse, 1972; Le Migrateur, 1983; Le Tableau D'Avancement, 1983. Critic: La Chasse Aux Trésors, 1961; Tristan Le Dépossedé, 1978; La Chasse Aux Tresors II, 1992. Translations: Gorthe; Sttifter; Jungen; Shakespeare; Pushkin; Melville; Mosley; Kleist; Brentano; Arnim. *Honours:* Prix Medicis, 1960; Prix Femina, 1961; Prix des Sept; Prix Valery Larbaud, 1970; Chevalier, Legion d'honneur. *Address:* Editions Gallimard, 5 rue Sebastien-Bottin, 75007 Paris, France.

THOMAS Hugh. (Lord Thomas of Swynnerton). b. 1931. British. Writer. *Appointments:* Chairman, Centre for Policy Studies, 1979-1990; Professor of History, University of Reading, 1965-75. *Publications:* The World's Game (novel), 1957; The Oxygen Age (novel), 1958; (ed.) The Establishment (essays), 1959; Assult at Arms (political text), 1960; The Spain Civil War, 1961, 1977; The Story of Sandhurst, 1961; The Suez Affair, 1967; (ed.) Crisis in the Civil Service, 1968; Cuba; or, The Pursuit of Freedom, 1971; (ed.) The Selected Writings of José Antonio Primo de Rivera, 1972; Goya and the Third of May 1808 (art history), 1972; John Strachey, 1973; An Unfinished History of the World, 1979, 1982; The Case for the Round Reading Room, 1983; Havannah (novel), 1984; Armed Truce, 1986; Madrid: a Travellers Companion, 1989; Klara, novel, 1989.

THOMAS Lee. *See:* FLOREN Lee.

THOMAS Leslie John, b. 22 Mar 1931, Newport, Gwent, Wales. Author. m. (2) Diana Miles, 11 Nov 1970, 1 son (2 sons, 1 daughter from previous marriage). *Education:* Various Schools: Wales and London; Dr. Barnardo's, Kingston, Surrey, 1944-46; Kingston Technical College; SW Essex Technical College, London. *Appointments:* Journalist, London Evening News, 1955-65. *Publications:* Novels: The Virgin Soldiers, 1965; Tropic of Ruislip, 1974; The Magic Army, 1981; The Dearest and the Best, 1984; Goodnight and Loving, 1986; Orders For New York, 1989. Autobiographies: This Time Next Week, 1964; In My Wildest Dreams, 1986. Travel Books: Some Lovely Islands, 1968; The Hidden Places of Britain, 1981; My World of Islands, 1993; The Loves and Journeys of Revolving Jones, 1991; Arrivals and Departures, 1992. TV Plays, Documentaries. *Contributions to:* Numerous magazines. *Memberships:* MCC; The Society of Authors; PEN; The Lords Taverners. *Literary Agent:* Diana Thomas, The Walton Canonry, The Close, Salisbury, Wiltshire, England. *Address:* The Walton Canonry, The Close, Salisbury, Wilts, England.

THOMAS Ronald Stuart, b. 1913. Clergyman (Retired); Poet. m. Mildred E. Eldridge, 1 son. *Education:* University of Wales and St Michael's College, Llandâf; Ordained Deacon 1936, Priest 1937. *Appointments:* Curate of Chirk, 1936-40, of Hanmer 1940-42; Rector, Manafon, 1942-54; Vicar, St Michael's, Eglwysfach, 1954-68, of St Hywyn, Aberdaron 1968-78; Rector of Rhiw with Llanfaelrhys, 1973-78. *Publications:* Stones of the Field (privately published), 1947; Song at the Years Turning, 1955; Poetry for Supper, 1958; Tares, 1961;

The Bread of Truth, 1963; Pietà, 1966; Not That He Brought Flowers, 1968; H'm, 1972; Selected Poems 1946-1968, 1974; Laboratories of the Spirit, 1975; Frequencies, 1978; Between Here and Now, 1981; Later Poems, 1972-82, 1983; Experimenting with an Amen, 1986; Welsh Airs, 1987; Counterpoint, 1990. *Honours:* Heinemann Award, Royal Society of Literature, 1955; Sovereign's Gold Medal for Poetry, 1964; Cholmondeley Award, 1978. *Address:* Sarn Y-Plas, Y Rhiw, Pwllheli, Wales.

THOMAS Rosanne Daryl, (Prince Charming), b. 25 Feb 1956, USA. Writer. m. R B Cohn, 4 May 1986, 1 daughter. *Education:* MFA, Columbia University. *Appointments:* Teacher, Comic Fiction Workshop, Writers Voice, NY, 1989, 1990. *Publications:* Complications; The Angel Carver. *Contributions to:* Cosmopolitan. *Memberships:* Authors Guild. *Literary Agent:* Emma Sweeney, Curtis Brown Limited, USA. *Address:* c/o Emma Sweeney, Curtis Brown Limited, 10 Astor Place, New York, NY 10003, USA.

THOMAS Rosie, British, Novelist. *Publications:* Celebration, Fontana, 1982; Love's Choice, Avon, 1982; Follies, 1983. Sunrise, 1984; The White Dove, 1986; Strangers, 1987; Bad Girls, Good Women. *Honours:* Romantic Novel of the Year Award for Sunrise, 1984; The White Dove was a Literary Guild dual main selection.

THOMAS Victoria. *See:* DE-WEESE Gene Thomas Eugene.

THOMPSON Ernest Victor, b. 14 July 1931, London, England. Author. m. Celia Carole Burton, 11 Sept 1972, 2 sons. *Publications:* Chase the Wind, 1977; Harvest of the Sun, 1978; The Music Makers, 1979; Ben Restallick, 1980; The Dream Traders, 1981; Singing Spears, 1982; The Restless Sea, 1983; Cry Once Alone, 1984; Polrudden, 1985; The Stricken Land, 1986; Becky, 1988; various books on Cornish & West Country subjects. *Contributions to:* Approximately 200 short stories. *Honour:* Best Historical Novel, 1976. *Memberships:* Society of Authors; West of England Writers' Club; President, Mevagissey Inshore Rescue Boat; Patron, Cornwall Drama Association; Vice Patron, Mevagissey Male Choir. *Address:* Parc Franton, Pentewan, St Austell, Cornwall, England.

THOMPSON Jean Louise, b. 1 Mar 1950, Chicago, Illinois, USA. Writer. *Education:* MFA, Bowling Green State University, 1973; BA, University of Illinois, 1971. *Appointments:* Graduate Assistant, Bowling Green State University, 1971-73; Professor, University of Illinois, 1973-; Warren Wilson College, 1988; Distinguished Visiting Writer, Wichita State University, 1991. *Publications:* The Woman Driver; Little Face and Othe Stories; My Wisdom; The Gasoline Wars. *Contributions to:* Numerous inc, The New Yorker; Indiana Review; Carolina Quarterly; Epoch; Mademoiselle; Southewest Review; Descant; Fiction International; Best American Short Stories. *Honours:* Flannery O'Connor Award; Reader, Associated WQriting Programs Novel Contest; Guggenheim Fellow; McGinnis Memorial Award; National Endowment for the Arts Fellowship; Canarad Fellow. *Literary Agent:* David Black. *Address:* 203 Smith Road, Urbana, IL 61801, USA.

THOMPSON John William McWean (Peter Quince), b. 12 June 1920, York, England. Journalist. m. Cynthia Ledsham, 12 July 1947, 1 son, 1 daughter. *Literary Appointments:* Deputy Editor, The Spectator, 1964-70; Editor, The Sunday Telegraph, 1976-86. *Publication:* Country Life, 1975. *Contributions to:* Numerous Journals and Magazines. *Honour:* CBE, 1986. *Address:* Corner Cottage, Burnham Norton, King's Lynn, Norfolk, PE31 8DS, England.

THOMPSON Michael Welman, b. 13 Aug 1928, London, England. Archaeologist; Architectural

Historian. m. Ann E Crockatt, 10 Oct 1964. 1 daughter. *Education:* MA 1952, PhD 1953, Pembroke College, Cambridge. *Publications:* Russian Translation, Frozen Tombs of Siberia, 1970; Ruins-Their Preservation & Display, 1981; General Pitt-Rivers-Evolution & Archaeology In The 19th Century; Edited, The Journals of Sir Richard Colt Hoare, 1984; The Decline of The Castle, 1988; The Rise of The Castle, 1991; Translation from Russian, Archaeology In The USSR, 1961; Novgorod The Great, Excavations 1951-62, 1967; The Cambridge Antiquarian Society 1840-1990, 1990. *Contributions to:* Numerous to journals and a number of guidebooks to ancient monuments for HMSO. *Memberships:* Fellow, Society of Antiquaries; President, Society for Medieval Archaeology; President, Cambridge Antiquarian Society, 1990-92. *Address:* 2 Offa Lea, Newton, Cambridge CB2 5PW, England.

THOMPSON Vivian L, b. 7 Jan 1911, Author; Playwright; Former Teacher. m. Daniel Thompson, 17 Mar 1951. *Education:* BS, 1939, MA, 1943, Teachers College, Columbia University, New York City; Maren Elwood School of Professional Writing, Hollywood, California, 1948; private study in Juvenile Fiction with Odessa Davenport, Hollywood, 1949. *Appointments:* Member of Library Advisory Commission, Hawaii island, 1960-67; delegate to Governor's Library Convention, Honolulu, 1966. *Publications:* Hawaiian Myths of Earth, Sea and Sky, 1966, 1988; Hawaiian Legends of Tricksters and Riddlers, 1969, 1990; Hawaiian Tales of Heroes and Champions, 1971, 1986; Aukele the Fearless, 1972, 1992; Maui-Full-of-tricks, 1970; Keola's Hawaiian Donkey, 1966; Camp-in-the-Yard, 1961; Kimo Makes Music, 1962; Sad Day, Glad Day, 1962; Faraway Friends, 1963; Kawelo Roding Chief, 1991; Tatsinda, A Fairy Tale Musical, 1991; 3 published plays and 8 produced plays. *Contributions to:* Junior Red Cross News; News Explorer; News Trails; Highlights for Children; Humpty Dumpty's Magazine; Young Keyboard Junior. *Honours:* Camp-in-the-Yard Junior Literary Guild Selection, 1961; Sad Day, Glad Day, Citation from New Jersey Association of Teachers of English, 1963; Outstanding Achievement award for contribution to the Arts. Hawaii Island YWCA, 1984. *Memberships:* Society of Children's Book Writers; Literacy Volunteers of America; Dr Grummond Collection of Children's Books, McLain Library, University of Southern Mississippi. *Address:* 936 Kumukoa Street, Hilo, HI 96720, USA.

THOMSON David, b. 1914, British. *Publications:* The People of the Sea, 1954, 1965; Daniel, 1962; Break in the Sun, 1965; Danny Fox, 1966; Danny Fox Meets a Stranger, 1968; The Leaping Hare (with G E Evans), 1972; Woodbrook, 1974; Danny Fox at the Palace, 1976; The Irish Journals of Elizabeth Smith 1840-1850 (ed), 1980; Dandiprat's Days, In Camden Town, 1983; Ronan and Other Stories, 1984; Nairn in Darkness and Light, 1987. *Address:* 22 Regent's Park Terrace, London NW1, England.

THOMSON Derick S, (MacThómais Ruaraidh), b. 5 Aug 1921. Emeritus University Professor. m. 1952, 5 sons, 1 daughter. *Education:* MA Aberdeen, 1947; BA CAntab, 1948; DLit Hon, University of Wales, 1987; FRSE, 1977; FBA, 1992. *Appointments:* Editor, Gaim Quarterly, 1952-. *Publications:* Introduction to Gaelic Poetry, 1974, 1990; The Gaelic Sources of Macpherson's Ossian, 1952; The Companion to Gaelic Scotland, 1983, 1987; European Poetry in Gaelic, 1990; The MacDiarmid MS Anthology, 1992; Collected Poems: Creachadh Na Clàrsaich (Plundering the Harp), 1982. *Contributions to:* Scottish Gaelic Studies; Scottish Studies; Gairm; Lines; Chapman; Stand; Studia Celtica. *Honours:* Ossian Prize, FVS Foundation, Hamburg, 1974. *Memberships:* Saltire Literary Award Jury, 1983-; MacVitie Literary Award, 1987-89; Scottish Gaelic Texts Society, (President); Gaelic Books Council, Chairman, 1968-91. *Address:* 263 Fenwick Road, Giffnock, Glasgow G46 6JX, Scotland.

THOMSON Edward. *See:* **TUBB E C.**

THOMSON Elizabeth (Liz) Mary, b. 12 Sept 1957, London, England, Writer; Editor. *Education:* BA, Honours, Music, University of Liverpool, 1976-79. *Publications:* The Lennon Companion, (Co-author, David Gutman), 1987; The Dylan Companion, (Co-author, with David Gutman), 1991; Conclusions on the Wall: New Essays on Bob Dylan, 1980; Folk Songs and Dances of England/Folk Songs and Dances of Scotland, (Arranger), 1982. *Contributions to:* Woman's Journal; New Statesman & Society; Melody Maker; Books and Bookmen; The Listener; The Times; The Standard; Staff Writer, Publishing News, Books; Numerous radio appearances for BBC and IBA. *Memberships:* Society of Authors; National Union of Journalists; International Association for the Study of Popular Music; Charter 88; Greenpeace. *Address:* 24 Grosvenor Park Road, Walthamstow, London E17 9PG, England.

THOMSON June Valerie, b. 24 June 1930, Sandgate, Kent. Writer. (div). 2 sons. *Education:* BA (Hons), English, Bedford College, University of London. *Publications include:* Not One of Us, 1972; A Question of Identity, 1978; Deadly Relations, 1979; Shadow of a Doubt, 1981; To Make a Killing, 1982; A Dying Fall, 1985; No Flowers by Request, 1987; Rosemary for Remembrance, 1988; The Spoils of Time, 1989; Past Reckoning, 1990; several short stories to various magazines. *Honours:* Prix du Roman d'Aventures, France, 1983. *Memberships:* Crime Writers' Association; Detection Club. *Literary Agent:* Michael Shaw, Curtis Brown & Associates, 162-168 Regent Street, London W1R 5TB, England. *Address:* 177 Verulam Road, St. Albans, Hertfordshire AL3 4DW, England.

THORBURN James Alexander, b. 24 Aug 1923. Martins Ferry, Ohio, USA. Professor of English (retired). m. (1) Lois McElroy, 3 July 1954, 1 son, 1 daughter, (2) June Yingling, 18 Apr 1981. *Education:* BA 1949, MA 1951, Ohio State Univesity; PhD, Linguistics, Louisiana State University, 1977. *Appointments include:* Head, English, Sheridan Rural Agricultural School, Michigan; Instructor, English, University of Missouri, Monmouth College, Illinois, Texas Western College; Instructor, English, In Charge, English, University of Missouri, St Louis; Instructor, English, Louisiana State University, 1961-70; Professor, English & Linguistics, Southeastern Louisiana University, 1970-89. *Contributions to:* Book Review Editor, Experiment; Editor, Valedictory Issue of Innisfree; Articles in numerous periodicals & anthologies including: National Poetry Anthology; Spring Anthology; Ardentia Verba; Laudamus Te; Poetry Dial Anthology; Prairie Poet; Poetry Digest; Writers Digest; Cardinal Poetry Quarterly; Poet Lore; Translator, several old Portuguese & old Provencal lyrics into modern English verse, Beowulf into modern English verse. *Honours:* La Sociedad Nacional Hispánica, Sigma Delta Pi; Phi Mu Alpha Sinfonia; The Honor Society of Phi Kappa Phi; Professor Emeritus of English & Linguistics, Louisiana Board of Trustees for State Colleges & Universities, & Southeastern Louisiana University, 1989. *Memberships:* Numerous professional organisations including: Avalon World Arts Academy; Life Member, Modern Language Association; Lingustic Association of the South and Southwest; Southern Conference on Lingusitics; American Dialect Society; Conference on Christianity and Literature. *Address:* 739 Southeastern Louisiana University, Hammond, LA 70402, USA.

THORNE Nicola. *See:* **ELLERBECK Rosemary.**

THORNTON Michael b. 6 Jan 1941, Pinkneys Green, Berkshire, England. Author; Journalist. *Education:* Studied Modern History at King's College, University of London, 1960-63. *Appointments:* Edited historical review, The Trumpet, at King's College, University of London, 1962- 63; Film and Drama Critic, Sunday Express, London, 1964-67; Special Features Writer, Sunday Express, London, 1969-76; Show Business editor and columnist, What's On in London, London 1976-77. *Publications:* Gilbert Harding, by his Friends, 1961; Jessie Matthews: A Biography, 1974, revised edition 1975; Forget Not (with Margaret, Duchess of Argyll) 1975; Royal Feud: The Queen Mother and the Duchess of Windsor, 1985; Royal Feud: The Dark Side of the Love Stody of the Century (revised) 1985. Royal Feud (revised paperback) London 1986; Royal Feud, New York, 1987; Argyll versus Argyll, 1992. *Contributions to:* The Times, London; the Daily Express, London; the Evening Standard, London, The Observer, London; The Stage, London; Royalty Monthly, London; The Guardian, London; The Independent on Sunday, London; The Sunday Times, London; The Literary review, London; The Dicitonary of National Biography, 1992; the Daily News, New York City; New York Post. *Literary Agent:* Mrs Dinah Wiener, Dinah Wiener Ltd, 27 Arlington Road, London NW1 7ER. *Address:* Apartado de Correos 426, 07700 Mahon, Menorca, Islas Baleares, Spain.

THORP Roderick b. 1 Sept 1936, NYC, America. Writer; Author. *Education:* BA, CCNY, 1957. *Appointments:* Associate Professor of Literature, Ramapo College, New Jersey, 1971-76. *Publications:* Into the Forest, 1961; The Detective, 1966; Dionysus, 1969; (with Robert Blake) The Music of Their Laughter, 1970; (with Robert Blake) Wives, 1971; Slaves, 1972; The Circle of Love, 1974; Westfield, 1978; Nothing Lasts Forever (Die Hard), 1979; Rainbow Drive, 1986. *Honour:* Theodore Goodman Memorial Short Story Award, 1957. *Literary Agent:* Theron Raines.

THORPE David Richard, b. 12 Mar 1943, Schoolmaster & Political Biographer. *Education:* BA Hons, 1965, MA, 1969, Selwyn college, Cambridge. *Publications:* Selwyn Lloyd, 1989; The Uncrowned Prime Ministers: A Study of Sir Austen Chamberlain, Lord Curzon and Lord Butler, 1980. *Contributions to:* The Blackwell Biographical Dictionary of British Political Life in the 20th Century, 1990. *Memberships:* Johnson Club; United Oxford and Cambridge University Club. *Address:* Brooke Hall, Charterhouse, Godalming, Surrey GU7 2DS, England.

THORPE Dobbin. *See:* DISCH Thomas Michael.

THORPE-CLARK Mavis (Mavis Latham), b. Australia. Children's Writer. *Publications:* Hatherly's First Fifteen, 1930; Dark Pool Island, 1949; Missing Gold, 1949; The Twins from Timber Creek, 1949; Home Again at Timber Creek, 1950; Jingaroo, 1951; The Brown Land was Green, 1956; Gully of Gold, 1958; Pony from Tarella, 1959; John Batman (as Mavis Latham), 1962; Fishing (as Mavis Latham), 1963; They Came South, 1963; Pastor Doug, 1965, 2nd Edition, 1972; The Min-Min, 1966; Blue Above the Trees, 1967; Spark of Opal, 1968; A Pack Tracker, 1968; Opal Mining, 1969; Nowhere to Hide, 1969; Iron Mountain, 1970; Strolling Players, 1972; New Golden Mountain, US Edition If the Earth Falls In, 1973; Wildlife, 1973; The Sky Is Free, 1974; The Hundred Islands, 1976; Spanish Queen, 1977; The Boy from Cumeroogunga, 1979; The Lilly-Pilly, 1979; A Stranger Came to the Mine, 1980; Solomon's Child, 1982; Young and Brave, 1984; No Mean Destiny: History of the War Widows' Guild, Australia, 1986; Soft Shoe, 1988. *Address:* 1/22 Rochester Rd, Canterbury, 3126, Australia.

THRING Meredith Woodridge, b. 17 Dec 1915, Melbourne, Australia. Professor of Engineering. m. 14 Dec 1940, 2 sons, 1 daughter. *Education:* BA Physics, First Class Hons, Trinity College Cambridge, 1937; ScD, Cambridge, 1964. *Publications:* The Engineer's Conscience, 1980; Man, Machines and Tomorrow, 1973; How to Invent, 1977; Machines: Master or Slaves of Man?, 1973; Robots and Telechirs, 1983. *Contributions:* More than 150 scientific and technical articles. *Memberships:* FEng; FIEE; FIMechE; FInstPhys; FICHEME: SFInstE, President, 1962-63. *Address:* Bell Farm, Brundish, Suffolk IP13 8BL, England.

THUBRON Colin Gerald Dryden, b. 14 June 1939, London, England. Writer. *Education:* Eton College, 1953-57. *Appointments:* Editorial Staff, Hutchinson &

Company Limited, London, 1959-62; Freelance Filmmaker, British Broadcasting Corporation Television, London, 1963-64; Editorial Staff, Macmillan Company, New York, 1964-65. *Publications:* Mirror To Damascus, 1967; The Hills of Adonis: A Quest in Lebanon, 1968; Jerusalem, 1969; Journey Into Cyprus, 1975; The God In The Mountain, novel, 1977; Emperor, novel, 1978; The Venetians, 1980; The Ancient Mariners, 1981; The Royal Opera House Covent Garden, 1982; Among The Russians, 1983; A Cruel Madness, 1984; Behind The Wall: A Journey Through China, 1987; Falling, 1989; Turning Back The Sun, 1991. *Contributions to:* Times; Times Literary Supplement; Independent; Sunday Times; Sunday Telegraph; New York Times; Granta. *Honours:* Fellow, Royal Society of Literature, 1969; Silver Pen Award, 1985; Thomas Cook Award, 1988; Hawthornden Prize, 1989. *Memberships:* Royal Society of Literature; PEN. *Literary Agent:* Gillow Aitken & Stone. *Address:* Garden Cottage, 27 St Ann's Villas, London W11 4RT, England.

THUM Marcella, b. St Louis, Missouri, USA. Author. *Education:* MA, Webster College, St Louis, Missouri; MLA, University of California, Berkeley, USA. *Publications:* Mystery at Crane's Landing, 1964; The Persuaders: Propaganda in War & Peace, 1972; Exploring Black America, 1975; Exploring Literary America, 1979; Exploring Military America, 1982; Airlift: The Story of Military Airlift Command, 1986; USA Guide to Black America, 1991; The White Rose, 1980; Blazing Star, 1983; Jasmine, 1984; Wild Laurel, 1985; Margarite, 1986; Mistree of Paradise, 1988; Thorn Trees, 1990. *Honours:* several awards for books. *Memberships:* St Louis Writers Guild, past President; Missouri Writers Guild; Romance Writers of America. *Literary Agent:* Eleanor Woods. *Address:* 6507 Gramond Drive, St Louis, MO 63123, USA.

THURSTON Carol M, b. 18 Sept Chicago, Illinois, USA. Author; Market Research Consultant. m. G. B. Thurston, 1 son, 1 daughter. *Education:* MA, Communication, 1975, PhD, Communication, 1979, University of Texas at Austin. *Publications:* Case Studies in Institutional Licensee Management, nonfiction, 1980; The Romance Revolution, nonfiction, 1987; Flair, novel, 1987, UK, 1987, 1989; Current Affairs, novel, 1989. *Contributions to:* Psychology Today; The Progressive; Christian Science Monitor newspaper; Journalism Quarterly; Journal of Communication; Numerous other scholarly journals. *Literary Agent:* Robin Rue, Anita Diamant Literary Agency, New York City, USA. *Address:* 1000 Madrone Road, Austin, TX 78746, USA.

THWAITE Anthony Simon, b. 23 June 1930, Chester, England. Writer. m. Ann Harrop, 4 Aug 1955, 4 daughters. *Education:* Kingswood School, Bath, 1944-49; Major Open Scholar, Christ Church, Oxford; BA, 1955; MA, 1959. *Appointments:* Literary Editor, The Listener, 1962-65; Literary Editor, New Statesman, 1968-72; Co-Editor, Encounter, 1973-85. *Publications:* Twentieth Century English Poetry, 1978; Six Centuries of Verse, 1984; Poems 1953-1988, 1989; Co-Editor, Penguin Book of Japanese Verse, 1964, latest reprint, 1987; Editor, Philip Larkin: Collected Poems, 1988; Selected Letters of Phillip Larkin: 1940-1925, 1992. *Contributions to:* Numerous. *Honours:* Richard Hillary Memorial Prize, 1968; Cholmondeley Award, 1983; Honorary DLitt, University of Hull, 1989; OBE, 1990; Honorary Fellow, Westminster College, Oxford, 1990. *Memberships:* Society of Authors, Former Member of Committee of Management; Fellow, Former Council Member, Royal Society of Literature. *Literary Agent:* Curtis Brown. *Address:* The Mill House, Low Tharston, Norfolk, England.

THYAGARAJAN Jagadisan. *See:* **ASHOKAMITRAN.**

TIBBER Robert. *See:* **FRIEDMAN Eve Rosemary.**

TIBBER Rosemary. *See:* **FRIEDMAN Eve Rosemary.**

TICKLE Phyllis A, b. 12 Mar 1934, Johnson City, Tennessee, USA. Writer. m. Dr Samuel M. Tickle, 17 June 1955, 3 sons, 4 daughters. *Education:* BA, East Tennessee State University; MA, Furman University. *Appointments:* Poet-in-Residence, Memphis Brooks Museum, 1977-85; Director, St Lukes Press, 1975-89; Director, Trade Publishing Group, The Wimmer Companies, 1989; Director Emeritus, 1992-; Religion Editor, Publishers Weekly, 1992-. *Publications:* The Story of Two Johns, 1976; American Genesis, 1976; On Beyong Koch, 1981; The City Essays, 1983; Selections, 1984; What the Heart Already Knows, 1985; Final Sanity, 1987; Ordinary Time, 1988; The Tickle Papers, 1989. *Contributions to:* The Episcopalian; The Tennessee Churchman; The Dixie Flyer; The Feminist Digest; 365 Meditations For Women, 1989; Disciplines, 1989. *Honour:* Individual Artists Fellowship in Literature, 1983. *Memberships:* Vice President, President, Tennessee Literary Arts Association; Chair, Publishers Association of the South. *Literary Agent:* Mary Jane Ross. *Address:* 3522 Lucy Road South, Lucy Community, Millington, TN 38053, USA.

TIEDE Tom, b. 24 Feb 1937, USA. Journalist; Author. *Education:* BA, Washington State University, 1959. *Appointments:* Instructor, Lecturer in Field, 1965-; Currently, Senior Editor, National Correspondent, Newspaper Enterprise Association, the Scripps-Howard Syndicate. *Publications:* Your Men at War, 1966; Coward, 1968; Calley: Soldier or Killer?, 1970; Welcome to Washington, Mr Witherspoon, 1982; The Great Whale Rescue, 1986. *Honours:* Ernie Pyle Memorial Award for War Reporting; National Headliners Award for Feature Writing; Freedom's Foundaion Award; George Washington Meadle. *Address:* Publicity Division, UME, 200 Park Avenue, New York City, NY 10166, USA.

TIGAR Chad. *See:* **LEVI Peter.**

TIGHE Carl, b. 26 Apr 1950, Birmingham, England. Writer. *Education:* BA Hons English, 1973, MA 1974, University College, Swansea; PDESL, Leeds University, 1979. *Appointments:* Script Reader, BBC Wales Radio and TV, 1985-87. *Publications:* Little Jack Horner, 1985; Bakn!, 1986; Gdansk: National identity in the Polish-German Borderlands, 1990; Rejoice! And Other Stories, 1992; Anthology contributions to: The Best Short Stories of 1989; Minerva Book of Short Stories; Poetry Street 2. *Contributions to:* Planet; Ambit; 20/20; Literary Review; Margin; Poetry Wales; The Works; Passport; Literature and History; Monthly Review; Journal of European Studies. *Honours:* All London Drama Prize, 1987; Welsh Arts Council Literary Bursary, 1983; British Council Travel Bursary, 1990. *Memberships:* PEN; Writer's Guild; Welsh Union of Writers; Welsh Academy. *Literary Agent:* Giles Gordon, Shieland Associates. *Address:* 36 Oak Road, Withington, Manchester M20 9DA, England.

TILLMAN Barrett, b. 24 Dec 1948, Pendleton, Oregon, USA. Author. *Education:* Oregon State University, 1967-68; BS Journalism, University of Oregon, 1971. *Appointments:* Editorial Committee, American Aviation? Historical Society, 1971-77; Founder, Publisher, Champlin Musuem Press, 1982-87; Managing Editor, The Hook Magazine, 1986-89. *Publications:* Warriors, 1990; On Yankee Station, 1987; The Dauntless Dive Bomber of WWII, 1976; Hellcat: The F6F in WWII, 1979; Corsair: The F4U in WWII and Korea, 1979; AVenger at War, 1979. *Contributions to:* Naval Institute Proceedings, Naval History, The Hook, Soldier of Fortune, USAF Fighter Weapons Review, Wings, Airpower, Air Progress, American Aviaion Historical Society Journal. *Honours:* Outstanding Contributor's Award, AAHS Journal, 1976; USAF

Historical Foundation Writing Award, 1981; North American Society of Oceanic History, 1987. *Memberships:* Founder, Conference of Historic Aviation Writers; Life Member, US Naval Institute; Tailhook Association; Association of Naval Aviation. *Literary Agent:* Robert Gottlieb, William Morris Agency, New York. *Address:* Box 567, Athena, OR 97813, USA.

TIMM Uwe, b. 30 Mar 1940, Hamburg, Germany. Writer. m. Dagmar Ploetz, 13 Nov 1969, 1 son, 3 daughters. *Education:* PhD, Munchen and Paris. *Appointments:* Editor, Autoren Editoon, 1972-82. *Publications:* Heisser Sommer, 1974; Morenga, 1978; Der Mann auf dem Hochrad, 1984; Der Schlangenbaum, 1986; The Snaketree, 1988; Kopfjager, 1992; Headhunter, 1993. *Honours:* Munchen Literaturpreis, 1990; Deutscher Kinderbuchpreis, 1990. *Memberships:* PEN. *Literary Agent:* Kiepeuheuer Witsch, Koln, Germany. *Address:* Oettingenstr 46, D-8000 Munchen 22, Germany.

TIMPERLEY Rosemary Kenyon, b. 1920, British. *Appointment:* Editor, Ghost Books, Barrie and Jenkins Limited, London, 1969-73. *Publications:* The Listening Child, A Dread of Burning, Web of Scandal, The Fairy Doll, Shadow of a Woman, 1955; Dreamers in the Dark, The Velvet Smile, Yesterday's Voices, Across a Crowded Room, Twilight Bar, The Bitter Friendship, Let Me Go, 1962; Broken Circle, 1963; The Veiled Heart, Devil's Paradise, 1964; The Suffering Tree, They Met in Moscow, 1965; Forgive Me, Blind Alley, 1966; My Room in Rome, Lights on the Hill, 1967; The Washers-up, The Cat-walk, 1968; The Tragedy Business, Rome with Mrs Evening, 1969; Fifth, Sixth, Seventh, Eighth and Ninth Ghost Books (ed), 1969-73; Doctor Z, The Mask-shop, 1970; House of Secrets, Walk to San Michele, The Summer Visitors, 1971; The Passionate Marriage, The Long Black Dress, 1972; Shadows in the Park, Journey with Doctor Godley, The Echo-game, 1973; Juliet, The White Zig- Zag, 1974; The Egyptian Woman, The Private Prisoners, 1975; The Devil of the Lake, The Phantom Husband, 1976; The Stranger, The Man with the Beard, 1977; The Nameless One, Syrilla Black, Suspicion, 1978; Chidori's Room, 1983; The Office Party and After, 1984; Love and Death, 1985; Tunnel of Shadows, The Wife's Tale, 1986. *Address:* 21 Ellerker Gardens, Richmond, Surrey TW10 6AA, England.

TIMSON Keith Stephen (Danielle De Winters), b. 4 Feb 1945, London, England. Author. m. Julia Fitzgerald, 1981, 1 son, 1 daughter. *Publications:* On A Far Magic Shore, 1989; The Dark Eternal Forest, 1990; Passionate Rebel, as Danielle de Winters, 1981. *Contributions to:* Irregular Reviewer, Romantic Times, USA & others; Lecturer on Fantasy & other aspects of writing. *Memberships:* British Fantasy Association; British Science Fiction Association. *Literary Agent:* Shelley Power, INPRA. *Address:* 4 Lansdowne Grove, Hough Green, Chester CH4 8LD, England.

TINDALL Gillian Elizabeth, b. 4 May 1938. Novelist; Biographer; Historian. m. Richard G. Landown, 1 son. *Education:* BA, 1st Class, MA, University of Oxford. *Publications:* Novels: No Name in the Street, 1959; The Water and the Sound, 1961; The Edge of the Paper, 1963; The Youngest, 1967; Someone Else, 1969, 1975; Fly Away Home, 1971; The Traveller and His Child, 1975; The Intruder, 1979; Looking Foreward, 1983; To the City, 1987; Give Them All My Love, 1989. Short Stories: Dances of Death, 1973; The China Egg and Other Stories, 1981. Biography: The Born Exile on George Gissing, 1974. Non-Fiction: A Handbook on Witchcraft, 1965; The Fields Beneath, 1977; City of Gold: The Biography of Bombay, 1981; Rosamond Lehmann, a Appreciation, 1985. *Contributions to:* Encounter; The Observer; Guardian; New Statesman; Evening Standard, 1973-; The Times, 1983-; The Independent, 1987-. *Honours:* Somerset Maugham Award for Fly Away Home, 1972. *Address:* c/o Curtis Brown Limited, 162-168 Regent Street, London W1, England.

TINER Ralph William, b. 25 Oct 1948, Stuttgart, Germany. Wetland Ecologist. m. Barbara Jongbloed, 24 May 1986, 1 son, 1 daughter. *Education:* BA Zoology, University of Connecticut, 1970; MS Marine Biology, University of Connecticut, 1974; MPA, Harvard University, 1981. *Publications:* A Field Guide to Coastal Wetland Plants of the Northeastern United States; Field Guide to Nontidal Wetland Identification, 1988, 1987; Field Guide to Coastal Wetland Plants of the Southeastern United States, 1992; Wetlands of the United States: Current Status and Recent Trends, 1984; Wetlands of New Jersey, 1985; Wetlands of Rhode Island, 1989; Wetlands of Delaware, 1985; Hydric Soils of New England, 1989; Pennsylvania's Wetlands: Current Status and Recent Trends, 1990. *Contributions to:* Bioscience; First Ecology and Management. *Honours:* Blue Pencil Award, 1989. *Address:* 83 North Main Street, Sherborn, MA 01770, USA.

TINNISWOOD Peter, b. 1936, British. Former journalist with Sheffield Star, Sheffield Telegraph, Liverpool Daily Post and Western Mail. *Publications:* A Touch of Daniel, 1969; Mog, 1970; I Didn't Know You Cared, 1973; Except You're A Bird, The Stirk of Stirk, 1974; Tales (and More Tales) from a Long Room, 2 volumes, 1981-82; Shemerelda, 1981; The Homes Front, 1982; The Brigadier Down Under, 1983; The Brigadier in Season, 1984; Call It a Canary, 1985; Stage Plays: Wilfred; The Day War Broke Out; You Should See Us Now; At The End of The Day; The Village Fete: The Brigadier and Uncle Mort; Napoli Milionaria (Adaption of Eduardo De Filippo's play at Royal National Theatre) and radio and television plays. *Honours:* Best First Novel of The Year, 1969; Book of the Month Choice, 1969; Winfred Holiby Award FRLS, 1974; Welsh Arts Council Best Novel of the Year, 1974; Sony Award for Radio, 1987; Giles Cooper Award, 1987; Writer's Guild Comedy Award, 1991. *Membership:* Fellow of Royal Society of Literature. *Literary Agent:* Jonathan Clowes Agency, Ironbride Bridge House, Bridge Approach, London NW1 8BD. *Address:* c/o Jonathan Clowes Agency, Ironbride Bridge House, Bridge Approach, London NW1 8BD, England.

TINTNER Adeline Ruth, b. 2 Feb 1912, New York City, New York, USA. m. Henry D Janowitz, 2 daughters. *Education:* BA Barnard College, Columbia University, 1932; MA Columbia University, 1933. *Appointments:* Editorial Board; The Henry James Review, 1979-; The Advisory board, Journal of Pre-Raphaelite Studies, 1979. *Publications:* The Museum World of Henry James, 1986; The Book World of Henry James, 1987; The Pop World of Henry James, 1989; The Cosmopolitan World of Henry James, 1991; The Library of Henry James 1987, co-author; Henry James and the Lust of the Eyes: Thirteen Artists in his Work, 1993. *Contributions to:* PMLA; MFS; 19th Century Literature, 20th Century Literature, American Literature, Edith Wheton Memo. *Honours:* Carnegie Fellow, Courtauld Institute, 1934. *Memberships:* The Henry James Society, President, 1986-87; The Society for the Study of Naudtine Technique, Founding member, 1985. *Address:* 180 East End Avenue Apt 4F, New York, NY 10128, USA.

TIPTON David John b. 28 Apr 1934, Birmingham, England. Author. Married twice, (div). 2 sons, 3 daughters. *Education:* King Edward's School, Birmingham, 1945-52; Saltley College, Birmingham, 1957-59; Essex University, 1976-77. *Appointments:* Editor, Rivelin Press, 1974- 84; Editor, Redbeck Press, 1984-. *Publications:* Poetry: Millstone Grit, 1972; Wars of the Roses, 1984; Nomads and Settlers, 1980; Peru The New Poetry (Translations 1970 and 1977); Biography Fiction: Atahualpa, 1976, Freak Summer, 1984. *Contributions to:* Ambit; London Magazine; Stand; Poetry Review; Poetry (Chicago); Evergreen Review; Twentieth Century; Tribune; Outposts. *Literary Agent:* Jeffrey Simmonds. *Address:* 24 Aireville Road, Frizinghall, Bradford BD9 4HH, Yorkshire, England.

TIRBUTT Honoris, (Emma Page). Author. *Publications:* In Loving Memory, 1970; Family and Friends, 1972; A Fortnight by the Sea (in United States

of America as Add a Pinch of Cyanide), 1973; Element of Chance, 1975; Every Second Thursday, 1981; Last Walk Home, 1982; Cold Light of Day, 1983; Scent of Death, 1985; Final Moments, 1987; A Violent End, 1988; Deadlock, 1991. *Address:* c/o The Crime Club, Harper Collins Publishers, 77-85 Fulham Palace Road, London, W6 8JB, England.

TITUNIK Irwin Robert, b. 8 June 1929, New York City, New York, USA. Professor of Slavic Languages and Literatures. (div), 3 daughters. *Education:* BA, Classical Languages, 1953, MA, Slavic Languages and Literatures, 1956, PhD, Slavic Languages and Literatures, 1963, University of California, Berkeley. *Appointments:* Professor of Slavic Languages and Literatures, University of Michigan, Ann Arbor, 1959- . *Publications:* Translator: P V Annenkov's The Extraordinary Decade, 1968; V N Volosinov's Marxism and the Philosophy of Language, 2nd Edition, 1986; V N Volosinov's Freudianism (A Critical Sketch), 2nd Edition, 1987. *Contributions to:* Numerous specialised scholarly articles. *Address:* Department of Slavic Languages and Literatures, University of Michigan, Ann Arbor, MI 48109, USA.

TOBIAS-TURNER Bessye, b. 10 Oct 1917, Liberty, Mississippi, USA. Poet; Lecturer; Retired Educator. *Education:* AB, English, Rust College; MA, English, MA Speech, Columbia University; PhD, Literature, World University. *Appointments:* Honorary Vice President, Centro Studi Scambi International; Special Guest Poet, Asian Poets Conference, Japan, 1984; Librae Foundation for the Arts and Culture, Director General, 1990; Charter Member, International POetry Society, USA, 1991. *Publications:* La Librae: Anthology of Poetry for Living, 1968; Peace & Love, 1972; Laurel Leaves for Bess, 1977. *Contributions to:* Anthologies: Tokyo, Japan, 1980, 1984; Seole, Korea, 1979; Teipei, Taiwan, 1988; Bangkok, Thailand, 1989; USA; Academia d'Europo, 1984, 1985, 1989, 1990; World Congress of Poets, Poets Conferences Worldwide. *Honours include:* Clover International Poetry Association, Certificate, Award, 1976; Poet Laureate International, 1977; Grand Prix Mediterranee, Academia d'Europa, 1983, 1934; Star of Poetry, 1984; Special Guest Poet, APC, 1984; Grand Prix Etoiles D'Europa, Academia d'Europa, 1986; Grand Prix Etoiles Mediterranee d'Europa, 1989. *Memberships:* Centro Studi e Scambi Internazionali; New York Poetry Forum; Attended World Congress of Poets, 1976, 1979, 1981; International Poets Conference, 1980; WCP World Academy of Arts and Culture, Bangkok, Thailand, 1988; Associate Member, the Academy of American Poets, 1987, 1988, 1989. *Address:* 829 Wall Street, McComb, MS 39698, USA.

TOCH Henry, b. 15 Aug 1923. Tax Consultant. m. Margaret Schwarz, 3 Apr 1958. *Education:* Bachelor of Commerce, 2nd Class Honours (Upper Division), London School of Economics and Political Science, University of London, 1950. *Publications:* How to Pay Less Income Tax, 1958, 4 editions, re-issued, 1986; Tax Saving for Businessmen, 1960, 3 editions; Income Tax, handbook, 1966, 14 editions; Economics for Professional Studies, 1974, 3 editions; How to Survive Inflation, 1977; How to Pass Examinations in Taxation, 1979; Cases in Income Tax Law, 1981; Essentials of British Constitution and Government, 1983; Taxation Made Simple, 1985, 2 editions. *Contributions to:* Cooperative News for over 15 years; Journal of Business Law; Monthly column, Law for Business. *Memberships:* The Financial Intermediaries Manager and Brokers Regulatory Association. *Address:* Candida, 49 hawkshead Lane, North Mymms, Hatfield, Herts AL9 7TD, England.

TODD Paul. *See:* POSNER Richard.

TODD R Larry, b. 14 Mar 1952, Seattle, Washington, USA. Professor of Music. m. Karin A Yoch, 18 Nov 1988. *Education:* BA summa cum laude, 1974, MPh, 1977, PhD, Music History, 1979, Yale University. *Publications:* Mendelssohn and his World, (ed), 1991; Mendelssohn

Studies, (ed), 1992; Perspectives on Mozart Performance, 1991, co-editor: 19th Century Piano Music, (ed), 1990; Mendelssohn and Schumann Essays, 1984, co-editor. *Contributions to:* The Musical Quarterly; 19th Century Music; The Music Review; Music and Letters; Musical Times; Organ Yearbook. *Memberships:* American Musicological Society, Board, 1986-87; International Mendelssohn Stiftung. *Address:* PO Box 90665 College Station, Dept of Music, Duke University, Durham, NC 27708, USA.

TOFFLER Alvin, b. 4 Oct 1928, New York City, USA. Author. m. Adelaide Elizabeth (Heidi) Farrell Toffler, 29 Apr 1950, 1 daughter. *Education:* BA, New York University. *Literary Appointment:* Associate editor, Fortune Magazine, 1959-61. *Publications:* (Mostly in collaboration with Heidi Farrell): Future Shock, 1970; The Third Wave, 1980; Previews & Premises, 1983; The Adaptive Corporation, 1984; The Culture Consumers, 1964. Editor: Learning for Tomorrow, 1973; The Futurists, 1972. *Contributions to:* New York Times Magazine; Annals, American Academy of Political & Social Science; Observer, UK; Sunday Times, UK; Christian Science Monitor; Nouvelle Observateur; Nouvelle Economiste; Washington Post; Wall Street Journal; Readers Digest; Technology & Culture; Playboy; Horizon; Nation; New Republic. *Honours:* Prix de Meilleur Livre Etranger, 1971; McKinsey Foundation Book Award, 1970; Author of Year, American Society of Journalits & Authors; 6 Honorary Degrees; Officier de l'Ordre des Arts et Sciences; Fellow, American Association for Advancement of Science; Centennial Award, Institute of Electrical & Electronics Engineers; Medal, President of Italy. *Memberships include:* PEN; Authors League; American Society of Journalists & Authors; World Future Studies Federation; International Institute for Strategic Studies; Former Trustee, Antioch University. *Literary Agent:* Curtis Brown Ltd. *Address:* c/o Curtis Brown Ltd, 10 Astor Place, New York, NY 10003, USA.

TOFT (Eric) John, b. 1933, British. *Appointments:* Lecturer, Malayan Teachers College, 1961-64; Lecturer, Brighton Polytechnic, 1965-. *Publications:* The Bargees, 1969; The Wedge, 1971; The House of the Arousing, 1973; The Underground Tree, 1978; The Dew, 1981. *Address:* 1 Clarendon Terrace, Brighton, Sussex, England.

TOKMAKOFF George, b. 9 July 1928, Tientsin, China. Professor of History. m. Erika Berzewski, 31 Aug 1959. *Education:* BA 1952, MA 1957, University of Washington, Seattle; PhD, London University, England, 1963. *Publications:* P.A Stolypin and the Third Duma, 1981. *Contributions to:* Russian Review; Slavic Review; Slavonic and East European Review. *Honours:* NEH Senior Scholar Award, 1971; Phi Kappa Phi Outstanding Faculty Award, 1975. *Memberships:* The American Association for the Advancement of Slavic Studies. *Address:* 4837 Foster Way, Carmichael, CA 95608, USA.

TOLAN Stephanie Sue, b. 25 Oct 1942, Canton, Ohio. USA. Writer; Consultant. m. Robert Warren Tolan, 19 Dec 1964, 1 son, 3 stepsons. *Education:* BA, Purdue University, 1964; MA, 1967. *Publications:* A Good Courage; Plague Year; Marcy Hooper & The greater Treasure in the World; Sophie and the Sidewalk Man; The Witch of Mapple Park; Grandpa And Me; The Last of eden. *Contributions to:* The Advocate; Horn Book; Gifted Child Monthly; Roeper Review; Understanding Our Gifted; The New Advocate; The Bookmark; The Hollingworth Centre Newsletter. *Honours:* Individual Artist Grants; Albany, NY Author of the Year; Various Novels Nominated for State Awards. *Memberships:* Authors Guild; Society of Childrens Book Writers; Childrens Book Guild. *Literary Agent:* Marilyn Marlow, Curtis Brown Limited. *Address:* 300 EN Broadway, Columbus, Oh 43214, USA.

TOLES Thomas G, b. 10 Oct 1951, Buffalo, New York, USA. Editorial Cartoonist. m. Gretchen Saarnijoki,

26 May 1973, 2 children. *Education:* BA, State University of New York at Buffalo, 1973. *Appointments:* Staff Artist, 1973-80, Graphics Designer 1980, Editorial Cartoonist 1980-82, Buffalo Courier-Express, Buffalo, New York; EDitorial Cartoonist, Buffalo News, Buffalo, 1982-. *Publications:* Under name of Tom Toles: The Taxpayer's New Clothes (editorial cartoons) foreword by Jeff Macnelly, Andrews, Mcmeel and Parker, 1985; Mr. Gazoo: A Cartoon History of the Reagan Era, Pantheon, 1987. Cartoons distributed by Universal Press Syndicate, 1982-. *Honours:* Twenty Page One Awards from Buffalo Newspaper Guild, 1973-82; George W Thorn Award from University of Buffalo Alumni Association, 1983; First Place Award in John Fischetti Editorial Cartoonist Competition, 1984; Golden Apple Award for Excellence in Educational Journalism from New York State United Teachers, 1984; Pulitzer Prize nomination, 1985; Pulitzer Prize for Editorial Cartooning, 1990. *Literary Agent:* Universal Press Syndicate, 4400 Johnson Drive, Fairway, KS 66205, USA. *Address:* 1 News Plaza, Buffalo, NY 14240, USA.

TOLGYESSY Juraj, b. 27 Jan 1931, Dun Streda, SR. Professor. m. Eva Cicha, 8 Aug 1967, 1 son, 2 daughters. *Education:* Slovak Technical University, 1953; Chemicotechnological University, PhD, 1959; Lomonosov State University, DSc, 1968; Slovak Technical University, 1972. *Appointments:* Founder & Editor, Journal of Radioanalytical and Nuclear Chemistry, 1967-. *Publications:* Radiometric Titrations; Isotope Dilution Analysis; Nuclear Analytical Chemistry; Emanation Thermal Analysis; Radionuclide X ray Fluorescence Analysis of Environmental Samples; Other inc. Chemistry and Biology of Water Air and Soil. *Honours:* Slovak Academy of Sciences Prize; Hungarian Academy of Sciences Award. *Address:* Radlinskeho 9, 812 37 Bratislava, SR.

TOLLEY Arnold Trevor, b. 15 May 1927, Burmingham, England. Professor. m. Glenda Mary Tolley, 10 June 1974. *Education:* Queen's College, Oxford, 1948-51. *Publications:* The Poetry of the Thirties, 1975; the Poetry of the Forties, 1985; My Proper Ground, 1991; John Leamann: A tribute, 1987; The Early Published Poems of Stephen Spender: A Chronology, 1967. *Contributions to:* Aquarius (Guest Editor, 1987). *Honours:* Ontario Arts Council Works in Progress Competition, 1985. *Address:* RR No 2, Williamsburg, Ontario, Canada K0C 2H0.

TOMALIN Ruth (Ruth Leaver), b. Bessborough Gardens, Co Kilkenny, Republic of Ireland. Writer. m. (1) 1942, 1 son, (2) 1971. *Education:* Chichester High School, Sussex, England. *Appointments:* Staff Reporter, Evening News, Portsmouth and subsequently various other newspapers, 1942-64; Press Reporter, London Courts, 1964-. *Publications:* Verse: Threnody for Dormice, 1947; Deer's Cry, 1952; Novels: The Garden House, 1964; The Spring House, 1968; Away to the West, 1972; Long Since, 1989; For children: The Sea Mice, 1962; A Green Wishbone, 1975; A Stranger Thing, 1975; Gone Away, 1979; W H Hudson, biography, 1982; A Summer Ghost, 1986; Another Day, 1988. *Address:* c/o Barclays Bank, 15 Langham Place, London W1, England.

TOMASZEWSKA Marta, b. 10 Apr 1933, Warsaw, Poland. Author. *Education:* MA, University of Warsaw, 1956. *Appointments:* Reporter, Swiat Mlodych, 1950-52; Editor, Cultural Section, Walka Mlodych, 1956-8; Motywy 1961-67; Author, 1967-. *Publications:* Zorro Put On Your Glasses, 1974; Tapatiki, Cycle Volumes I-IV, 1974-84; The Wig, 1974; Night After the Day of Love, 1977; Seprente in Paradise, 1978; The Giant in the Pirates Cavern, or Mystery of Fourthwall, 1986; The Travel to Om Land, 1979; The Queen of Invisible Riders, 1988; The Tapatiki's Expedition, musical play, 1982; Tetraktys, 1991, some 30 other novels. *Contributions to:* Fantasy, Fantastyka, Fantazia. *Honours:* Polish Prime Minister's Award, 1981; Eagle's Pen, Young Readers Award, 1986; Cross Polonia Restituta Order, 1986; XII Premio Europeo Di Litteratura Giuvanile-Lista D'Onoren Arrativa for The Queen of Invisible Riders, 1988; Ibby awards a Certificate of Honour for Writing The Giant in The Pirates Cavern, Mystery of Fourthwall, 1988. *Memberships:* ZAIKS, 1967; Polish Writers Union, 1969. *Address:* Natolinska 3 m 64, Warsaw 00-562, Poland.

TOMKIEL Judith Irene, b. 4 Nov 1949, St Louis, Missouri, USA. Writer; Company Owner. m. William George Tomkiel, 15 Dec 1972, 3 sons, 2 daughters. *Education:* Institute of Childrens Literature. *Appointments:* Writer, Owner, Idea Shoppe, 1985-. *Publications:* (Poetry) Sonny Boy, 1983; Christopher, 1983; Life's Circle, 1983; Snack Time, 1984; My Son, 1985; Writer's Rights, 1985; Whose Son?, 1985; One Family, 1985; The Second Birthday Gone, 1986; To Daddy with Love, 1986; Mother's Thoughts, 1987; Time Spent, 1987; My Child, 1987. *Contributions to:* various journals and magazines. *Honours:* Golden Poet Award, 1987; 3rd Prize Poetry Award, 1983. *Memberships:* National Writers Club; National Association for Female Executives; Mail Order Business Board; Publishers Association of North America. *Address:* 13351 Hale Ave., Garden Grove, CA 92644, USA.

TOMLINSON Charles, b. 8 Jan 1927, Stoke-on-Trent, England. Professor, English Literature. *Education:* BA, Queens' College, University of Cambridge; MA, University of London. *Publications:* Poems: The Necklace, 1955, 1966; Seeing is Believing, 1958; Versions from Tyutchev (with H. Gifford), 1960; A Peopled Landscape, 1963; Castilian Ilexes (with H. Gifford), 1963; American Scenes, 1966; The Way of a World, 1969; Poems (with A Clarke & T Connor), 1964; Poems (with A Brownjohn & M Hamburger), 1969; The Poem as Initiation, 1968; Renga (with O. Paz), 1971, 1972, 1979, 1983; Words & Images, 1972; Written on Water, 1972; The Way In, 1974; Selected Poems, 1951-74, 1978; The Shaft, 1978; Air Born/Hijos del Aire (with O Paz), 1979; The Flood, 1981; Translations, 1983; Notes from New York, 1984; Eden, 1985; Collected Poems, 1985; The Return, 1987; Collected Poems (enlarged), 1987; Annunciations, 1989; Selected Poems, 1989; Poems, The Door in the Wall, 1992; Prose: In Black and White, 1976; Some Americans: A Literary Memoir, 1981; Poetry & Metamorphosis (The Clark Lectures), 1983; Editor, The Oxford Book of Verse in English Translation, 1980; George Oppen: Selected poems, 1990; Eros Englished, erotic poems from the Greek & Latin, 1991; also essays on Marianne Moore & William Carlos Williams, Poetry of Williams & Octavio Paz. *Honours:* Fellow, Royal Society of Literature; D.H. Lawrence Fellowship, University of New Mexico, USA, 1963; National Translation Centre Award, University of Texas, 1968; Cheltenham Poetry Prize, 1976; Honorary Fellow, Queens' College, Cambridge, 1976; Arts Council Travelling Exhibition, The Graphics & Poetry of Charles Tomlinson, 1978-81; Chlmondeley Award for Poetry, 1979; Honorary D.Litt, University of Keele, 1981, Colgate University, 1981, New Mexico, 1986; Honorary Professor, University of Keele, 1989; Honorary Fellow, Royal Holloway & Bedford New College, University of London, 1990; Cittadella European Poetry Prize, 1991; Bennett Award for Poetry, New York, 1993. *Address:* Dept. of English, University of Bristol, Bristol BS8 1HY, England.

TOMLINSON Gerald, b. 24 Jan 1933, Elmira, New York, USA. Writer; Editor; Publisher. m. (Mary) Alexis Usakowski, 19 Aug 1966, 2 sons. *Education:* BA, Marietta College, Marietta, Ohio, 1955; Columbia Law School, New York City, 1959-60. *Appointments:* Associate Editor, Business and Professional Books, Prentice Hall, 1960-63; Associate Editor, School Department, Harcourt Brace Jovanovich, 1963-66; Senior Editor, English Department, Holt, Rinehart and Winston, 1966-69; Executive Editor, K-12 English, Silver Burdett and Ginn, 1969-82; Publisher, Home Run Press, 1985-. *Publications:* On a Field of Black, novel, 1980; School Administrator's Complete Letter Book, 1984; Heath Grammar and Composition (contributing writer), 1986; Managing Smart (co-author), 1987; The Baseball Research Handbook, 1987; Accountant's Complete Model Letter Book (co-author), 1987; Prentice Hall Literature 11-12 (contributing writer), 1989;

Speaker's Treasury of Political Stories, Anecdotes, and Humor, 1990; Speaker's Treasury of Sports Anecdotes, Stories, and Humor, 1990. *Contributions to:* 23 mystery short stories in: Ellery Queen's Mystery Magazine; Alfred Hitchcock's Mystery Magazine; Mike Shayne Mystery Magazine; Mystery Monthly; 6 articles to: The National Pastime; Baseball Research Journal; other Sports magazines. *Honours:* Best Detective Stories of the Year, E.P. Dutton, 1976; Mystery Writers of America Annual Anthologies, 5 appearances, 1977-87. *Memberships:* Mystery Writers of America; Society for American Baseball Research; National Council of Teachers of English; New Jersey Historical Society. *Address:* 19 Harbor Drive, Lake Hopatcong, NJ 07849, USA.

TOMLINSON Mary Teresa, b. 15 Aug 1935, England. Journalist; Public Relations/Lecturer; Specialist in E C Affairs & Tourism. m. Noel Tomlinson, 15 Aug 1959, 1 son, 1 daughter. *Education:* English, Accountancy & Economics Diploma; School of Economics, 1952-54; School of Drama & Music; School of Art, 1955-56. *Appointments:* Partner, Ays Press & Public Relations. *Publications include:* Wool on the Back, (co-author Peter Taylor), 1987; Around the World in Cookery & Cakes, 1980. *Contributions to:* Lady; Nursery World; Devon Life; RAF News; Cotswold Life; Sunday Times; Times; Debretts, 'Best of Britain', 1990; Hollis Europe. *Memberships:* Society of Women Writers and Journalists; Institute of Journalists. *Address:* Mayfield Cottage, Ebrington, nr. Chipping, Campden, Glos. GL55 6NQ, England.

TOOMBS Jane Ellen, b. 27 Dec 1926, California, USA. Writer; Registered Nurse. m. (1) 2 sons, 3 daughters, (2) John Toombs, 2 Mar 1972. *Education:* Registered Nurse, 1949. *Publications:* Destiny's Bride (as Diana Stuart), 1978; Chippewa Daughter, 1982; Arapaho Spirit, 1983; The Scots, 1984; Leader of the Pack (as Diana Stuart), 1985; Doctors and Lovers, 1989; Riverboat Rogue, 1990. *Honour:* Silver Rose Award, Romance Writers of America. *Memberships:* Charter Member, Romance Writers of America, Treasurer and Past Advisor of Hudson Valley Chapter; Science Fiction Writers of America. *Literary Agent:* Maureen Walters, Curtis Brown Ltd. *Address:* 14 Roe Avenue, Cornwall-on-Hudson, NY 12520, USA.

TOONA Elin-Kai, b. 12 July 1937, Tallinn, Estonia. Freelance Writer. m. Donald Frederick Gottschalk, 9 Oct 1967, 1 son. *Publications:* Puuingel, 1965; Lotukata, 1968; Sipelgas Sinise Kausi All, 1973; In Search of Coffee Mountains, US Edition, 1977, UK Edition, 1979; Lady Cavaliers, 1977; Pictures, and DP Camp Child, poetry in Visions, 1988; Kalevikula Viimne Tütar (Estonian novel published in Sweden), 1988; Kolm Valget Tuvi (novel published in Lund, Sweden), 1992. Radio plays: The Amateurs, 1967; When All the Trees were Bread and Cheese, 1970; The Square, 1971. *Contributions to:* Regular column for The Coastal Illustrated, St Simons Island, Georgia, 1974-75; Coastal Quarterly, Georgia; Indian River Life, Florida; Lady's Circle, New York; Talent Magazine, International Platform Association; St Petersburg Times, Florida; New Writers Magazette, Florida; Storyteller Magazine; Eesti Haal, London; Vaba Eesti Sona, New York; Tulimuld, Sweden; Mana, Canada/USA; Triinu; Scripts/contributions to Radio Liberty, Voice of America. *Honours:* 1st Prize for Young Estonian Writers in England, 1952; Certificate of Merit for short story The Old Farm, Storyteller Magazine, London, 1962; 1st Prize for Short Story Competition 13, Writer's Review, London, 1966; The H Visnapuu Literary Award for Estonians for novel Puuingel, World Association of Estonians, 1966; Ennu Literary Prize for juvenile novel Lotukata, Estonians, USA, 1968; Certificate of Commendation for The Square, Golden Windmill Radio Drama Contest, Radio Nederland Wereldomroep, 1971; 1st prize for Photo Turks in a Field, National Examiner Contest, 1983; 1st Prize, Florida State Award for Non-Fiction and 2nd Prize, Florida State Award for Photo Journalism, National League of American Pen Women, 1985; Honourable Mention for short stories Sand Prints and When Butterflies Pass Over, Short Story Contest, National League of American Women, 1988; Lauri Literary Prize for Estonian Novel, Kolm Valget Tuvi, 1993. *Memberships:* International PEN, Estonian Branch; All Estonian Literary Associations Worldwide; Fellow, International Biographical Association; National League of American Pen Women; International Platform Association. *Address:* 27554 US 19N, 37 Clearwater, FL 34621, USA.

TOPOL Edward, b. 8 Oct 1938, Baku, Russia. Author; Screenwriter. m. Emilia Topol, 1984-1989, 1 daughter. *Education:* Graduate, All Union University of Cinematography, Screenwriter's Department, Moscow, 1965; Master in Screen and Playwriting. *Appointments:* Special Reporter, Bakuworker, Literary Gazetta, Russia, 1959-67. *Publications:* Red Square, 1983; Deadly Games, 1984; Submarine U-137, 1985; Red Snow, 1986; Russian Seven, 1990; Tomorrow in Russia, 1990; Kremlin Wife, 1989; Moscow Flight, 1992; Love-Kike, 1992; Motion Pictures: The Errors of Youth; Long Winter; The Sea of Our Hope; Discovery; Ship's Boy of the North Fleet; The Love of the First Signt; The Adolescents. *Honours:* Red Carnation Award for Best Movie Script, 1974; Boris Smolak Award for Best Magazine Article, 1980. *Memberships:* Writers Guild of America. *Literary Agent:* Peter Lampack Agency. *Address:* c/o Peter Lampack Agency, 551 Fifth Avenue, Suite 2015, New York, NY 10019, USA.

TOPPING Frank, b. 30 Mar 1937, Birkenhead, Cheshire, England. Author and Broadcaster. m. June Berry, 15 Apr 1958, 2 sons, 1 daughter. *Education:* St. Anselm's College (Irish Christian Brothers Grammar School); North West School of Speech and Drama; Wesley Theological College, Bristol. *Literary Appointments:* BBC Short Story Editor; Producer and Editor of various programmes, 1970-80. *Publications:* Lord of The Morning, 1977; Lord of The Evening, 1979; Lord of My Days, 1980; Working at Prayer, 1981; Lord of Life, 1982; The Words of Christ: Forty Meditations 1983; God Bless You, Spoonbill, 1984; Lord of Time, 1985; An Impossible God, 1985; Wings of The Morning, 1987; Act Your Aye, 1989; Laughing in my Sleep, autobiography, 1993; Co-Author with Donald Swann of West End Show, Swann With Topping, 1980. *Contributions to:* Weekly and Monthly contributor to a variety of BBC Radio Programmes written and presented a considerable number of TV Programmes for both BBC and ITV; variety of Religious Newspapers and Magazines. *Honours:* Grace Wyndham Goldie UNDA Dove Award, 1975; for Radio Play, On The Hill. *Memberships:* Patron of Group 81; A Drama Society specialising in religious plays performed in churches and cathedrals. *Memberships:* The Naval Club; Hurst Castle Sailing Club. *Literary Agent:* Curtis Brown. *Address:* Osborn House, Kent College, Pembury, Tunbridge Wells, Kent, TN2 4AX, England.

TORDAY Ursula (Paula Allardyce, Charity Blackstock, Lee Blackstock, Charlotte Keppel), British, Writer- Mystery/Crime/Suspense, Historical/ Romance/Gothic. *Publications include:* As Paula Allardyce: The Moonlighter, 1966, in US as Gentleman Rogue, 1975; Party in Dolly Creek, in US as The Widow, 1967; Six Passengers for the Sweet Bird, 1967; Waiting at the Church, 1986, in US as Emily, 1976; The Melon in the Cornfield, in US as The Lemmings, 1969; The Ghost of Archie Gilroy, 1970, in US as Shadowed Love, 1977; The Daughter, 1970; The Encounter, 1971; The Jungle, 1972; The Lonely Strangers, 1972; Miss Jonas's Boy, 1972, in US as Eliza, 1975; The Gentle Sex, 1974, in US as The Carradine Affair, 1976; As Charlotte Keppel: Madam You Must Die, 1974, in US as Loving Sands, Deadly Sands, 1975; People in Glass Houses, 1975; Ghost Town, 1976; My Name is Clary Brown, 1976, in US as When I Say Goodbye, I'm Clary Brown, 1977; I Met Murder on the Way, in US as The Short Front, 1977; As Paula Allardyce: Miss Philadelphia Smith, 1977; Haunting Me, 1978; Miss Charley, 1979; The Rogue's Lady, 1979; With Fondest Thoughts, 1980; The Vixen's Revenge, 1980; As Charlotte Keppel: I Could Be Good to You, 1980; The Villains, 1980; Dream

Towers, 1981; The Ghosts of Fontenoy, 1981. *Address:* 23 Montagu Mansions, London W1H 1LD, England.

TORON Steve. *See:* **STEBEL Sidney Leo.**

TORRANCE Lee. *See:* **SADGROVE Sidney Henry.**

TORRANCE Thomas Forsyth, b. 30 Aug 1913, Chengdu, China. Minister of Religion; Professor of Theology. m. Margaret Edith Spear, 2 Oct 1946, 2 sons, 1 daughter. *Education:* MA, 1934; BR, 1937; DrTheol, 1946; D.Litt, 1971; FRS (Edinburgh), 1979; FBA (London), 1982. *Appointments:* Founder, Editor, The Scottish Journal of Theology, 1948-88. *Publications:* The Doctrine of Grace, 1949; Calvin's Doctrine of Man, 1949; Kingdom and Church, 1956; Conflict and Agreement in the Church, 2 vols, 1959-60; Theology in Reconstruction, 1965; Theological Science, 1969; God and Rationality, 1971; Theology in Reconciliation, 1975; Space, Time and Resurrection, 1976; Space, Time and Incarnation, 1979; The Ground and Grammar of Theology, 1980; Christian Theology and Scientific Culture, 1980; Divine and Contingent Order, 1981; Reality and Scientific Theology, 1984; The Trinitarian Faith, 1988; The Humanities of John Calvin, 1987; Karl Barth, Biblical and Evangelical Theologian, 1990; The Christian Frame of Mind, Reason, Order and Openness in Theology and Natural Science, 1989; Royal Priesthood, 1993; Divine Meaning. Studies in Patristic Hermeneutics, 1993; Trinitarian Perspectives. Toward Doctrinal Agreement, 1993; (ed) Theological Dialogue between Orthodox and Reformed Churches, 1993; Senso del divino e scienza moderna, 1992. *Contributions to:* Numerous. *Honours:* Honorary doctorates: DD, Montreal, 1950; DrTheol, Geneva and Paris, 1959; DD, St Andrews, 1960; DrTeol, Oslo, 1961; DSc, Heriott-Watt University, Edinburgh, 1983; DrTheol, Debrecen, Hungary, 1989; Appointed Moderator, General Assembly of the Church of Scotland, 1976-77. *Memberships:* International Academy of Religious Sciences, President 1972-81; International Academy of the Philosophy of Sciences; Royal Society of Edinburgh, Committee Member 1985; British Academy; Center of Theological Inquiry, Princeton, USA. *Address:* 37 Braid Farm Road, Edinburgh EH10 6LE, Scotland.

TORRES Tereska. *See:* **LEVIN Torres.**

TORSNEY Cheryl B, b. 8 Sept 1955, Ohio, USA. English Professor. m. Jack R Torsney Jr, 10 Aug 1974, 2 sons. *Education:* BA English and French, Allegheny College, 1977; MA English, Louisiana State University, 1979; PhD, English, University of Florida, 1982. *Appointments:* Lecturer, American Literature, University de Savoie, France, 1982-83; Assistant Professor of English, Delta State University, Mississippi, 1983-85; Assistant then Associate Professor of English, West Virginia University, 1985-. *Publications:* Constance Fenimore Woolson: The Grief of Artistry, 1989; Critical Essays on Constance Fenimore Woolson, 1992. *Contributions:* Numerous articles on American writers, especially Henry James. Other essays on feminist literary theory and quilting. *Honours:* Fulbright Lecturer: Universite de Savoie, 1982-83, University of Utrecht, 1989; American Council of Lerned Societies Fellow, 1985. *Memberships:* Modern Language Association; South Atlantic Modern Language Association; Midwest Modern Language Association; Henry James Society. *Address:* 536 Monongalia Avenue, Morgantown, WV 26505, USA.

TOSTESON Heather b. 7 Nov 1950, New York, New York, USA. Author; Editor; Teacher. 1 son. *Education:* BA, Sarah Lawrence College, 1971; MFA, University of North Carolina, Greensboro, 1977; PhD, Ohio University, 1982. *Appointments:* Associate in Medicine (Epidemiology), Channing Laboratory, Harvard Medical School. *Publications:* Hurricane, short story, 1984; Evelyn May, short story, 1984; Launcelot, short story, 1988; Maids, essay, 1987; Woman Devoured by Fishes, poem, 1990; Il N'est Pire Aveugle, poem, 1989.

Contributions to: Short fiction in Four Quarters; Poetry in Northwest Review, Zone 3, Mid-American Review; Cardinal; Fine Madness. *Honours:* Writing Fellowship, Yaddo, 1984; Writing Fellowship, Virginia Centre for the Creative Arts, 1985; Writing Fellowship, The McDowell Colony, 1986; Writing Fellowship, Yaddo, 1990. *Literary Agent:* Jonathon Dolger. *Address:* c/o Jonathon Dolger Agency, 49 East 96th Street 9B, New York, NY 10128, USA.

TOTH Endre, b. 17 Nov 1914, Debrecen, Hungary. Writer. 1 son, 2 daughters. *Appointments:* Editor, Alfold Literary Monthly. *Publications:* Alone in the Crowd; Neither Outside nor Inside; Song of the Well; I Paid for Everything In Life Size; Confidential Confession; Our Contemporaries, Our Friends. *Contributions to:* Válasz; Kelet Nepe; Diarium; Protestans Szemle; Kortárs. *Honours:* Hsokonai Prize; József Attila Prize. *Memberships:* Hungarian Writers Association; Society of Zsigmond Móricz. *Address:* Egyetem Sugarut 54/a, 4027 Debrecen, Hungary.

TOURNIER Michel Edouard, b. 19 Dec 1924, Paris, France. Author. *Literary Appointment:* Editions Gallimard, Paris. *Publications:* Friday or the other Island, 1969; The Erl King (The Ogre), 1972; Gemini, 1981; The Four Wise Men, 1982; The Fetishist, 1984; Gilles & Jeanne, 1987; The Golden Droplet, 1987. *Honours:* Grand Prix du Roman, Academie Francaise, 1967; Prix Goncourt, 1970. *Memberships:* Academie Goncourt, France; Akademie der Kunste, Berlin, Germany. *Address:* 78460 Choisel, Chevreuse, France.

TOWNSEND Joan, b. 23 May 1913, Darwen, Lancashire, England. Freelance Writer. *Publications:* Summat From Home, 1964; Nowt So Queer, 1969; Lancashire Evergreen, 1969; Twixt Thee and Me, 1973; Mermaids Moon, 1975. *Contributions to:* Lancashire Life; BBC. *Honours:* Lancashire Authors' Association Awards, 1938, 1946, 1947, 1948, 1952, 1953, 1959, 1972; Writer of the Year, 1972; IWWP Awards 1972 and 1974; 1st prizes for dialect poems and prose, 1978; LAA Awards, 1982, 1983; Writer of the Year, 1983. *Memberships:* Lancashire Dialect Society; Preston Poets' Society, Hon Life Member; FRSA; Lancashire Authors' Association, Vice President; Great Harwood Male Voice Choir, President; Romatic Novelists' Association. *Address:* Stoops Farm, Great Harwood, Nr Blackburn, Lancashire, England.

TOWNSEND John Rowe, b. 10 May 1922. Author. m. Vera Lancaster 3 July 1948, (dec 1973), 1 son 2 daughters. *Education:* Leeds Grammar School; MA, Cambridge University. *Publications:* Gumble's Yard, 1961; The Intruder 1969; Noah's Castle, 1974; The Islanders, 1981; The Invaders, 1992; Written for Children (History of Children's Literature) 5th edition 1990. *Honours:* Silver Pen Award, International PEN, 1970; Boston Globe/ Horn Book Award, 1970; Edgar Award, Mystery Writers of America, 1970; Christopher Award, 1981. *Memberships:* Society of Authors, former member of Management Committee and Chairman, Children's Writers Group. *Address:* 72 Water Lane, Histon, Cambridge CB4 4LR, England.

TOWNSEND Peter Wooldridge, b. 22 Nov 1914, Rangoon, Burma. Author. m. Marie Luce Jamagne, 21 Dec 1959, 1 son, 2 daughters (2 sons from 1st marriage). *Education:* Haileybury; Royal Air Force College, 1933-35; Royal Air Force Staff College, 1942-43. *Publications:* Earth my Friend, 1960; Duel of Eagles, 1970; The Last Emperor, 1975; Time & Chance (Autobiography), 1978; The Smallest Pawns in the Game, 1979-80; The Girl in the White Ship, 1982; The Postman of Nagasaki, 1984; Duel in the Dark, 1986; *Contributions to:* Daily Telegraph; Daily Mail; Daily Express; Sunday Express; Paris Match; Journal du Dimanche; Le Figaro; Le Figaro Litteraire; Madame Figaro; Le Temps Retrouvé. *Address:* La Mare aux Oiseaux, 78610 Saint Léger-en-Yvelines, France.

TOWNSEND Sue, b. 4 Feb 1946, Leicester, England. Author. *Publications:* The Secret Diary of Adrian Mole Aged Thirteen and Three-Quarters, 1982; The Growing Pain of Adrian Mole, 1984; The Diaries of Adrian Mole (combined volume issued in the United States of America), 1986; Bazaar and Rummage, Groping for Words, Womberang: Three Plays, 1984; True Confessions of Adrian Albert Mole; Mr Bevan's Dream, 1989; Ten Tiny Finger, Nine Tiny Toes (play), 1989; Adrian Mole From Minor to Major, 1991; The Queen and I, 1992. *Contributions to:* London Times; New Statesman; Observer. *Memberships:* Writers Guild; PEN. *Literary Agent:* Giles Gordon, c/o Land Shell Agency, 43 Doughty Street, London. *Address:* c/o Giles Gorden Agency, 43 Doughty Street, London, England.

TOWNSEND Thomas L, (Tom Townsend), b. 1 Jan 1944, Illinois, USA. Novelist. m. Janet L Simpson, 17 Apr 1965, 1 Department. *Education:* Arkansas Military Academy. *Publications:* Texas Terasure Coast, 1978; Where the Pirates Are, 1985; Trader Wooly, 1987; Trader Wooly and the Terrorists, 1988; Queen of the Wind, 1989; Trader Wooly and the Ghost in the Colonel's Jeep, 1991; The Holligans, 1991; Battle of Galveston, 1990; Bubba's Truck, 1992. *Honours:* Friend of American Writers Award, 1986; Texas Blue Bonnet Master List, 1986; Silver Award, Best Children's Video, Houston International Film Festival, 1986. *Address:* PO Box 905, Kemah, TX 77565, USA.

TOWNSEND Tom. *See:* **TOWNSEND Thomas L.**

TOYNBEE Polly, b. 27 Dec 1946, England. Journalist; Writer. m. Peter Jenkins, 1970, 1 son, 2 daughters, 1 step-daughter. *Education:* St Anne's College, Oxford. *Literary Appointments:* Reporter, The Observer, 1968-71; Editor, Washington Monthly, USA, 1972-73; Feature writer, Observer, 1974-76; Columnist, The Guardian, 1977-88; BBC Social Affairs Editor, 1988-. *Publications:* Leftovers, 1966; A Working Life, 1970, 1972; Hospital, 1977, 1979; The Way We Live Now, 1981; Lost Children, 1985. *Honours:* Catherine Pakenham Award for Journalism, 1975; British Press Awards, 1977, 1982. *Address:* 1 Crescent Grove, London SW4, England.

TRAAT Mats, b. 23 Nov 1936, Arula, Estonia. Writer. m. Victoria Viir, 13 May 1970, 1 daughter. *Education:* Gorki Literary Institute, Moscow. *Publications:* Poetry: Angular Songs, 1962; Knolly Land, 1964; Lanterns in the Fog, 1968; Cardinal Points, 1970; Sketches Intended for Starting a Fire, 1971; Late Lambs, 1976; Time of Open Lands, 1977; September Fugue, 1980; Autumn Hope, 1986; Frost Flowers, 1989. Novels: Dance around a Locomobile, 1971; A Landscape with an Apple Tree and a Diary Chimney, 1973; Pommer's Orchard, 1974; Coffee Beans, 1974; Inger, 1975; Trees - They Were Tender Brothers, 1979; Suspension Bridge, 1980; Pasque Flower - A Remedy for Melancholy, 1982; I Walk Alone, 1985; Go Up To The Hills, 1987; The Dead Knot, 1989; The Power of Love, 1989 (all written in Estonian). *Honours;* Literary Prize by the collective farm named after Ed Vilde, 1967, 1971, 1980; Soviet Estonian Prize, 1972; Fr Tuglas Prize, 1975; Juhan Smuul Prize, 1977; Literary Prize by collective farm named after A H Tammsaare, 1983; Merited Writer of the Estonian SSR, 1977. *Membership:* Writers' Union of Estonia. *Address:* Tallinn 200010 Oru 16, Estonia, USSR.

TRACEY Hugh. *See:* **EVANS Stuart.**

TRAFFORD Ian Colton, b. 8 July 1928, England. Publisher. m. (1) Nella Georgara, 1949 (div 1964), 1 daughter, (2) Jacqueline Carole Trenque, 1972. *Education:* St John's College, Oxford. *Appointments:* Feature writer, Industrial Correspondent, Financial Times, 1951-58; UK Correspondent, Barrons Weekly, New York, 1954-60; Director 1958-71, Managing Director 1966-71, Industrial & Trade Fairs Holdings Ltd; Director-General British Trade Fairs in Peking 1964, Moscow 1966, Bucharest 1968, Sao Paulo 1969,

Buenos Aires 1970; Managing Director, Economist newspaper, 1971-81; Chairman, Economist Intelligence Unit, 1971-79; Publisher, The Times Supplements, 1981-; Deputy Chairman, Times Books Ltd, 1981-85. *Honour:* OBE, services to exports, 1967. *Address:* Grafton House, Westhall Road, Warlingham, Surrey CR6 9HF, England.

TRALINS S(andor) Robert (Ray Z Bixby, Norman A King, Alfred D Laurance, Keith Miles, Sean O'Shea, Rex O'Toole, Cynthia Sydney, Leland Tracy, Bob Tralins, Robert S Tralins, Richard Trainor, Ruy Traube, Dorothy Verdon), b. 1926, American, Writer of Novels/Short stories, Plays/Screenplays, Psychology, Supernatural/Occult topics. *Publications include:* as Ruy Traube: The Seduction Art, 1967; Memoirs of a Beach Boy Lover, 1967; Uninhibited, 1968; Sex Cultists, 1969; (as Ray Z Bixby) Rites of Lust, 1967; as Rex O'Toole: Cheating and Infidelity, 1968; Confessions of an Exhibitionist, 1968; Gigolos, 1969; The Mind Code, 1969; Ba Black Brute, 1969; Slave's Revenge, 1969; Clairvoyance in Women, 1969; ESP Forewarnings, 1969; Weird People of the Unknown, 1969; Children of the Supernatural, 1969; Panther John, 1970; Black Pirate, 1970; The Hidden Spectre, 1970; Ghoul Lover, 1971; (as Richard Trainor) Yum-Yum Girl, 1968; (as Sean O'Shea) The Topless Kitties, 1968; Clairvoyant Strangers, 1968; Runaway Slave, 1968; (as Alfred D Laurance) Homer Pickle the Greatest, 1971; Clairvoyant Women, 1972; Supernatural Strangers, 1972; Supernatural Warnings, 1973; (as Keith Miles) Dragon's Teeth, 1973; Android Armageddon, 1974; Illegal Tender (screenplay) 1975; Buried Alive, 1977.

TRANTER John E, b. 1943, Cooma, New South Wales, Australia. Poet; Writer. m., 2 children. *Literary Appointments include:* Senior editor, Education Division, Angus & Robertson, based Singapore, 1971-73; Associate editor, various magazines including Transit, Aspect Art & Literature, New Poetry, Poetry Australia; Publisher, Transit Poetry, 1981-83; Writer-in-residence, NSW Institute of Technology 1983, Macquarie University 1985, Australian National University, 1987; Various radio & TV appointments; Teacher, creative writing. *Publications include:* Poetry: Parallax, 1970; Red Movie, 1972; The Blast Area, 1974; The Alphabet Murders, 1975; Crying in Early Infancy: 100 Sonnets, 1977; Dazed in the Ladies Lounge, 1979; Selected Poems, 1982; Under Berlin : New Poems, 1988. Also: Editor, compiler, critical introduction, New Australian Poetry, 1979; Critical articles; Radio scripts, mainly literary topics; Articles & reviews; Co- translator, Recent German Poetry, 1977. *Contributions to:* Numerous newspapers, journals & magazines; Radio. *Honours:* 8 Writing Fellowships, Literature Board, Australia Council, 1974-86; Visiting Fellow, Faculty of Arts, Australian National University, 1981: Reading Tours of North America and Europe, supported by Literature Board, Australia Council/Australian Department of Foreign Affairs, 1985 and 1986. *Address:* c/o Literary Arts Board, Australia Council, PO Box 302, North Sydney 2060, Australia.

TRANTER Nigel Godwin (Nye Tregold), b. 23 Nov 1909, Glasgow, Scotland. Author and Novelist. m. May Jean Campbell Grieve, 11 July 1933, 1 son (dec), 1 daughter. *Appointments:* Writer of historical, romance, Gothic, Western, Adventure fiction and children's fiction. Also wrote western novels under name of Nye Tredgold. Full- time writer. lecturer and broadcaster 1946-; Accountant and inspector, family insurance company, Edinburgh, 1929-39; President of PEN, Scottish Centre, 1962-66, now Honorary President; Chairman, Society of Authors, 1966-72; Chairman, National Forth Road Bridge Committee, 1953-57; Vice-President, Scottish Teachers of History Association, 1990. *Publications:* Numerous titles, the most recent being: Robert the Bruce (trilogy): The Steps to the Empty Throne, 1969, The Path of the Hero King, 1970, The Price of the King's Peace, 1971; The Queen's Scotland (non-fiction) 4 vol 1971-77; Portrait of the Border Country (non-fiction) 1972; The Wisest Fool, 1974; The Wallace, 1975; Stewart Trilogy: Lords of Misrule, 1976,

A Folly of Princes, 1977, The Captive Crown, 1977; Macbeth the King, 1978; Margaret the Queen, 1979; Portrait of the Lothians (non-fiction) 1979; David the Prince, 1980; True Thomas, 1981; Nigel Tranter's Scotland: A Very Personal View, 1981; The Patriot, 1982; Lord of the Isles, 1983; Unicorn Rampant, 1984; The Riven Realm, 1984; James, By the Grace of God, 1985; Rough Wooing, 1986; The Fortified House in Scotland (5 vols), 1962-1986; Columba: The Story of Scotland (non-fiction) 1987; Cache Down, 1987; Flowers of Chivalry, 1988; Mail Royal, 1989; Warden of the Queen's March, 1989; Crusader, 1991; Kenneth, 1990; Footbridge to Enchantment, 1992; Children of The Mist, 1992; Druid Sacrifice, 1993; Forthcoming: Tapestry of The Boar. *Honours:* Honorary DLitt, Strathclyde; Honorary MA, Edinburgh; OBE, 1983; Scot of The Year, 1991; Hon President, Saltire Society. *Address:* Quarry House, Aberlady, East Lothian, EH32 0QB, Scotland.

TRAPIDO Barbara. *See:* **TRAPIDO Barbara Louise.**

TRAPIDO Barbara Louise, (Barbara Trapido), b. 5 Nov 1941, Cape Town, South Africa. Writer. m. Stanley Trapido, 29 Apr 1963, 1 son, 1 daughter. *Education:* BA Hons, English; Postgraduate Certificate, London. *Publications:* Brother of the more Famous Jack, 1982; Noah's Ark, 1985; Temples of Delight, 1990. *Contributions to:* Spectator, Sunday Telegraph, Sunday Times. *Honours:* Whitbread Award, 1982; Shortlisted for Sunday Express Book of the Year Award, 1990. *Literary Agent:* Felicity Bryan. *Address:* c/o Felicity Bryan, 2a North Parade, Oxford OX2 6PE, England.

TRAVIS Frederick Francis, b. 10 Nov 1942, Brookhaven, Mississippi, USA. Historian; Academic Dean. m. Alix Gregory Hallman, 15 May 1971, 2 daughters. *Education:* BS 1965, MA 1967, University of Mississippi; PhD, Emory University, 1974. *Publications:* George Kennan and the American-Russian Relationship, 1865-1924, 1990. *Contributions to:* Philippine Studies; Russian Review; Kabar Seburung; Slavic and European Education Review; Journal of American History. *Memberships:* American Historical Association; American Association for the Advancement of Slavic Studies; Society for Historians of American Foreign Relations; Ohio Academy of History; American Conference of Academic Deans; American Association of Higher Education. *Address:* 2318 Coventry Road, Cleveland Heights, OH 44118, USA.

TRAVIS Millicent Elizabeth. *See:* **LANE M Travis.**

TREADWAY John David, b. 30 June 1950, San Bernardino, California, USA. Professor of History. m. Sandra Gioia, 4 Sept 1976, 1 daughter. *Education:* BA summa cum laude 1972, Florida State University; PhD 1980, University of Virginia. *Publications:* The Falcon and the Eagle: Montenegro and Austria-Hungary, 1908-1914, 1983; The Soviet Union under Gorbachev: Assessing the First Year, 1987; Editor: Indiana Slavic Studies/Balkanistica, 1991-93. *Contributions to:* Articles: Evangelische Kommentare, 1985; Book of Days, 1987, 1988; Read More About It, 1989; Woodrow Wilson Centre Occasional Papers, 1991; Serbian Studies, 1992; Reviews: American Historical Review; Choice; Historian; Slavic Review; Serbian Studies. *Honours:* Fulbright Awards, Germany 1985, Yugoslavia 1990; Virginia Outstanding Faculty Award, 1993; University of Richmond Distinguished Educator Award, 1985, 1988, 1991. *Memberships:* American Historical Association; American Association for the Advancement of Slavic Studies; American Association for Southeast European Studies; North American Society for Serbian Studies; Virginia Historical Society. *Address:* History Department, University of Richmond, VA 23173, USA.

TREANOR Oliver, b. 1 May 1949, Warrenpoint. Northern Island. Catholic Priest. *Education:* Queen's University, Belfast 1968- 74; BA (Hons) PGCE; Dip Phil; STB 1977, STL 1979, STD 1984, Pont Universita

Gregoriana, Roma. *Publication:* Mother of the Redeemer, Mother of the Redeemed, 1988. *Contributions to:* Observatore Romano, Vatican City; Priests and People, Durham,England; Theology Digest, USA; Religious Life Review, Dublin. *Address:* St Malachy's College, Belfast BT15 2AE, N Ireland.

TREASE (Robert) Geoffrey, b. 11 Aug 1909, Nottingham, England. Author. m. Marian Granger Boyer, 11 Aug 1933. 1 daughter. *Education:* Open Scholar in Classics, Queen's College, Oxford, 1928-29. *Publications:* 104 books including: Tales Out of School, 1948; A Whiff of Burnt Boats: An Early Autobiography, 1971; Laughter at the Door: A Continued Autobiography, 1974; Bows Against the Barons, 1934; Cue for Treason, 1940; No Boats on Bannermere, 1949; Tomorrow is a Stranger, 1987; The Arpino Assignment, 1988; A Flight of Angels, 1988; Shadow Under the Sea, 1990; Calabrian Quest, 1990; Aunt Augusta's Elephant, 1991; Song For a Tattered Flag, 1992; Fire on the Wind, 1993. *Contributions to:* Daily Telegraph; Times Literary Supplement; Times Educational Supplement; The Author. *Honours:* Welwyn Theatre Festival, New Play Prize for After the Tempest, 1938; New York Herald Tribune's Award for This Is Your Century, Book Festival, 1966; FRSL, 1979. *Memberships:* Society of Authors, Chairman 1972-73, Member of Council, 1973-; Fellow, Royal Society of Literature; PEN. *Literary Agent:* Murray Pollinger, London, England. *Address:* 1 Yomede Park, Newbridge Road, Bath BA1 3LS, England.

TREAT Jessica Thayer, b. 18 Aug 1958, Moncton, NB, Canada. Writer; Teacher. *Education:* MFA, Brooklyn College, 1989; BA, The Evergreen State College, 1981. *Publications:* A Robber in the House; Word of Mouth, vols I & II. *Contributions to:* American Literary Review; Alaska Quarterly Review; Black Warrior Review. *Memberships:* American Poets and Fiction Writers; The Associated Writing Programs; International Womens Writing Guild. *Address:* PO Box 157, Amenia, NY 12501, USA.

TREAT Lawrence, b. 21 Dec 1903, New York City, USA. Writer. m. 7 May 1943. *Education:* AB, Dartmouth College, 1924; LLB, Columbia Law School, 1927. *Publications:* V as in Victim, 1945; Big Shot, 1951; Venus Unarmed, 1961; P as in Police, 1970; Lady Drop Dead, 1960; H as in Haunted, 1946; 20 other books; Originator of Pictorial Crime Puzzles: Bringing Sherlock Home, 1935; Crime and Puzzlement, 1981; Crime and Puzzlement 2, 1982; Crime and Puzzlement 3, 1988; You're the Detective, 1983; Cluedo Armchair Detective, 1983; Crime & Puzzlement, My Cousin Phoebe, 1991. *Contributions to:* Numerous journals including: Ellery Queen's Mystery Magazine; Hitchcock Mystery Magazine; The Saint; Redbook. *Honours:* Edgar Allan Poe Award, 1965, 1979; Short Story Award, International Crime Writers Convention, 1981; Special Edgar Allan Poe Award, TV Alfred Hitchcock Hour. *Memberships:* Mystery Writer of America, Past President, Director, Treasurer, Founder; Boston Authors Club. *Literary Agent:* Vicky Bijur. *Address:* c/o Vicky Bijur, 333 West End Ave, New York, NY 10023, USA.

TREGLOWN Jeremy Dickinson, b. 24 May 1946, Anglesey, North Wales. Editor; Critic. m. (1) Rona Bower, 1970, 1 son, 2 daughters, (div), 1982, (2) Holly Eley Urquhart, 1984. *Education:* B.Litt., MA, Oxon; PhD, London. *Appointments:* Lecturer, English, Lincoln College, Oxford, 1974-77; University College, London, 1977-80; Assistant Editor, 1980-82, Editor, 1982-, Times Literary Supplement. *Publications:* Editor, Letters of John Wilmot, Earl of Rochester, 1980; Editor, Spirit of Wit: Reassessments of Rochester, 1982; Introduction, R.L. Stevenson, In the South Seas, 1986; Sel, and Introduction, The Lantern Bearers: Essays by Robert Louis Stevenson, 1987. *Contributions to:* numerous magazines & journals. *Memberships:* Council, Royal Society of Literature. *Literary Agent:* The Peters Fraser and Dunlop Group Ltd. *Address:* 102 Severnake Road, London NW3, England.

TREGOLD Nye. *See:* **TRANTER Nigel.**

TREHEARNE Elizabeth. *See:* **MAXWELL Particia Anne.**

TRELFORD Donald Gilchrist, b. 9 Nov 1937, Coventry, England. Journalist. m. (1) Janice Ingram, 1963, 2 sons, 1 daughter, (2) Katherine Louise Mark, 1978, 1 daughter. *Education:* MA, Selwyn College, Cambridge. *Appointments:* Pilot Officer, RAF, 1956-58; Staff, Newspapers in Coventry and Sheffield, 1961-63; Editor, Times of Malawi and Correspondent in Africa, The Times, Observer, BBC, 1963-66; Joined Observer as Deputy News Editor, 1966, Assistant Managing Editor 1968, deputy Editor 1969-75, Director and Editor, 1976-. *Publications:* Siege; County; Champions; Sunday Best; Snookered, 1985; Child or Change (with Gary Kasparov), 1988; Len Hutton Remembered, 1992. *Contributions to:* The Queen Observed, 1986; Saturday's Boys, 1990. *Honours:* Editor, Newspaper of the Year, Granada TV Press Awards, 1982; Commended, International Editor of the Year, 1984. *Memberships:* British Executive Committee, International Press Institute, 1976-; Fellow, Royal Society of Arts, 1988. *Address:* The Observer, Chelsea Bridge House, Queenstown Road, London SW8 4NN, England.

TREMAIN Rose, b. 2 Aug 1943, London, UK. Writer. m. Jonathan Dudley, 2 Aug. 1982, (diss 1991), 1 daughter. *Education:* Diploma, French Language, Sorbonne, Paris, 1962; BA Honours, University of East Anglia, 1967. *Appointments include:* Co-tutor, University of East Anglia Creative Writing Course, 1983-. *Publications:* Freedom for Women, 1971; Stalin: An Illustrated Biography, 1974; Sadler's Birthday, 1976; Letter to Sister Benedicta, 1979; The Cupboard, 1981; The Colonel's Daughter and Other Stories, 1984; The Swimming Pool Season, 1985; Journey to the Volcano (children's novel), 1985; The Garden of the Villa Mollini, 1987; Restoration, 1989; Sacred Country, 1992. *Contributions to:* Short stories: Grand Street (USA); Paris Review (USA); Listener; Granta; Critical Quarterly; Woman's Journal. *Honours:* Listed 1 of 20 best young British novelists, 1983; Dylan Thomas Short Story Award, 1984; Giles Cooper Award, 1985; Angel Literary Award, 1985; Sunday Express, Book of the Year, 1989. *Membership:* Royal Society of Literature. *Literary Agent:* Richard Simon, 43 Doughty Street, London, WC1N 2LF, England. *Address:* c/o Richard Simon, 32 College Cross, London, N1 1PR, England.

TREMBLAY Gail Elizabeth, b. 15 Dec 1945, Buffalo, New York, USA. Poet; Artist; Faculty Member, The Evergreen State College. *Education:* BA, Drama, University of New Hampshire, 1967; MFA, Creative Writing, University of Oregon, 1969. *Publications:* Night Gives Woman the Word, 1979; Talking to the Grandfathers, 1980; Indian Singing in 20th Century America, 1990. *Contributions to:* Wooster Review; Denver Quarterly; Calyx; Northwest Review; Maize. *Honour:* Alfred E Richards Poetry Prize, 1967. *Memberships:* Board Member, Women's Caucus for Art; President of the Board, Indian Youth of America. *Address:* Library 2102, The Evergreen State College, Olympia, WA 98505, USA.

TREMBLAY Mildred Maria, b. 21 June 1925, Kenora, Ontario, Canada. Fiction Writer. m. Ross E Tremblay, 22 July 1947, 6 daughters. *Education:* Grade 11, Kenora High School. *Publication:* Dark Forms Gliding, 1988. *Contributions to:* Canadian Fiction Magazine; Writers Quarterly; Other literary magazines. *Honours:* Pacific Northwest Short Fiction Award, 1982; Canadian Authors Poetry Award - 1st, 1983; BC Federation of Writers Literary Rites Award-1st, 1988. *Memberships:* Nanaimo Writers' Group, Co-Founder; BC Federation of Writers. *Address:* 1643 Sheriff Way, Nanaimo, British Columbia, Canada V9T 4A4.

TREMLETT George William, b. 5 Sept 1939, England. Author; Journalist; Bookseller. m. Jane Mitchell, 1971,

3 sons. *Publications:* 17 biographies of Rock Musicians, published many different countries, 1974-77; Living Cities, 1979; Homeless but for St Mungo's, 1989; Rock Gold, 1990; Dylan Thomas: in the mercy of the means, 1991. *Honour:* OBE, community & local government work, 1981. *Memberships include:* Advisory panel, BBC Community Programme Unit, 1985-. *Address:* Corran House, Laugharne, Carmarthen, Dyfed SA33 4SJ, Wales.

TRENHAILE John Stevens, b. 1949, British. *Publications:* Kyril, 1981; A View from the Square, 1983; Nocturne for the General, 1985; The Mahjong Spies, 1986; The Gates of Exquisite View, 1987; The Scroll of Benevolence, 1988; Kyrsalis, 1989; Acts of Betrayal, 1990; Blood Rules, 1991; The Tiger of Desire, 1992. *Address:* c/o Blake Friedman, Literary agents, 37-41 Gower Street, London WC1E 6HH, England.

TRENTON Gail. *See:* **GRANT Neil David Mountfield**

TRESILLIAN Richard. *See:* **ELLIS Royston.**

TRESSELT Alvin, b. 1916, USA. Author; Educator. *Appointments:* Display Designer, Advertising Copywriter, B Altman Co, New York City, 1946-52; Editor, Humpty Dumpty's Magazine, New York City, 1952-65; Editor, 1965-67, Executive Editor, Vice-President, 1967-74, Parents' Magazine Press, New York City; Instructor, Faculty Dean, Institute of Children's Literature, Redding Ridge, Connecticut, 1974-. *Publications:* Rain Drop Splash, 1946; White Snow Bright Snow, 1947; Johnny Maple-Leaf, 1948; The Wind and Peter, 1948; Bonnie Bess: The Weathervane Horse, 1949; Sun Up, 1949; Little Lost Squirrel, 1950; Follow the Wind, 1950; Hi, Mr Robin, 1950; Autumn Harvest, 1951; A Day with Daddy, 1953; Follow the Road, 1953; I Saw the Sea Come In, 1954; Wake Up Farm, 1955; Wake Up City, 1957; The Rabbit Story, 1957; The Frog in the Wall, 1958; The Smallest Elephant in the World, 1959; Timothy Robin Climbs the Mountain, 1960; An Elephant is not a Cat, 1962; Under the Trees and Through the Grass, ecology, 1962; The Mitten: An Old Ukrainian Folktale, 1964; How Far Is Far, science, 1964; Hide and Seek Fog, 1965; The Old Man and the Tiger, 1965; A Thousand Lights and Fireflies, 1965; The World in the Candy Egg, 1967; The Tears of the Dragon, 1967; Legend of the Willow Plate (with Nancy Cleaver), 1968; The Crane Maiden, 1968; Helpful Mr Bear, 1968; Ma Lien and the Magic Brush, 1968; The Fox Who Traveled, 1968; It's Time Now, 1969; How Rabbit Tricked His Friends, 1969; The Rolling Rice Ball, 1969; The Fisherman under the Sea, 1969; The Land of Lost Buttons, 1970; Eleven Hungry Cats, 1970; Gengoroh and the Thunder God, 1970; The Beaver Pond, ecology, 1970; A Sparrow's Magic, 1970; The Hare and the Bear and Other Stories, 1971; Stories from the Bible, 1971; Ogre and His Bride, 1971; Lum Fu and the Golden Mountain, 1971; The Little Mouse Who Tarried, 1971; Wonder Fish from the Sea, 1971; The Dead Tree, ecology, 1972; The Little Green Man, 1972; The Nutcracker, 1974; What Did You Leave Behind, 1978. *Address:* 53 Dorethy Road, West Redding, CT 06896, USA.

TREVANIAN. *See:* **WHITAKER Rodney William.**

TREVELYAN (Walter) Raleigh, b. 6 July 1923, Port Blair, Andaman Islands. Author. *Education:* Winchester College, 1937-42. *Literary Appointments:* Publisher 1948-88 with Collins, Hutchinson, Michael Joseph (13 years Editorial Director), Hamish Hamilton, Jonathan Cape, Bloomsbury. *Publications:* The Fortress, 1956; A Hermit Disclosed, 1960; The Big Tomato, 1966; Princes Under the Volcano 1972; The Shadow of Vesuvius, 1976; A Pre-Raphaelite Circle, 1978; Rome '44, 1982; Shades of the Alhambra, 1984; The Golden Oriole, 1987; 1 La Storia dei Whitaker, 1989; Grand Dukes and Diamonds, 1991; Editor of Italian Short Stories: Penguin Parallel Texts, 1965. *Contributions to:* Apollo;

Connoisseur; Harpers Queen; John Ryland's Bulletin and has reviewed in most leading daily and Sunday papers. *Honour:* John Florio Prize 1967 for Italian Translation (The Outlaws by Luigi Meneghello). *Memberships:* PEN (committee), Fellow; Royal Society of Literature (Member of Council); Brooks's Fellow Groucho Club; Chairman, Anglo-Italian Society for Protection of Animals. *Literary Agent:* A M Heath, 79 St Martin's Lane, London WC2N 4AA. *Address:* 18 Hertford Street, London W1Y 7DB; St Cadix, St Veep, Lostwithiel, Cornwall, PL22 0PB, England.

TREVOR Meriol, b. 15 Apr 1919, London, England. Author. *Education:* BA, St Hugh's College, Oxford, 1942. *Publications:* Newman: The Pillar of the Cloud, Newman: Light in Winter, 2 volumes, 1962; Pope John, 1967; The Arnolds, 1973; The City and the World, 1970; The Golden Palaces, 1985; James II : The Shadow of a Crown, 1988; 16 historical novels, 1956-; 2 biographical books; 12 books for older children, 1949-66. *Contributions to:* Reviewer for Times Literary Supplement, 1960's, 1970's. *Honours:* James Tait Black Memorial Prize, 1962; Elected Fellow, Royal Society of Literature, 1967. *Address:* 41 Fitzroy House, Pulteney Street, Bath BA2 4DW, England.

TREVOR William. *See:* **COX William Trevor.**

TRIER MORCH Dea, b. 9 Dec 1941, Copenhagen, Denmark. Writer; Graphic Artist. m. Troels Trier, 1 son, 2 daughters. *Education:* Graduated, The Royal Academy of Fine Arts, Copenhagen, 1964; Postgraduate studies, Academies of Fine Arts, Warsaw, Cracow, Belgrade, Leningrad and Prague, 1964-67. *Appointments:* Chairman, Danish Writers Association, 1990-1991. *Publications:* Sorgmunter socialisme, 1968; Polen, 1970; Vinterborn, 1976, translated into 22 languages; En Trekant, 1977; Ind i verden, 1977; Kastaniealleen, 1978; Den Indre By, 1980; Aftenstjernen, 1982; Morgengaven, 1984; Da jeg opdages Amerika, 1986; Skibet i flasken, 1988; Barnet uden navn, 1990; Pengene og livet, 1990; Landskab i to eteger, 1992. *Honours:* Elected Danish Author of the Year, 1977; Awarded Government Stipend for life, 1985; The Hvass Foundation, 1985; Peter Sabroe Children's Prize, 1987; Tagea Brandt Travel Fellowship, 1988. *Memberships:* PEN Club, Denmark; Union of Danish Graphic Artists; The Danish Fiction Writers Association. *Literary Agent:* Gyldendal Publishing, Copenhagen, Denmark. *Address:* Jens Juels Gade 7, 2100 Copenhagen O, Denmark.

TRIGGER Bruce Graham, b. 18 June 1937, Cambridge, Ontario, Canada. Professor of Anthropology. m. Barbara Marian Welch, 7 Dec 1968, 2 daughters. *Education:* BA, University of Toronto, 1959; PhD, Yale University, 1964. *Appointments:* Assistant Professor, Northwestern University, 1963-64; Assistant Professor, 1964-67, Associate Professor 1967- 69, Professor 1969-, McGill University. *Publications:* History and Settlement in Lower Nubia, 1965; The Huron: Farmers of the North, 1969, revised 1990; The Children of Aataentsic, 1976, revised 1987; Time and Traditions, 1978; Vol ed Handbook of North American Indians, Vol 15, Northeast 1978; Natives and Newcomers, 1985; The History of Archaeological Thought, 1989; Late Nubian Settlement at Arminna West, 1967; Beyond History, 1968; Cartier's Hochelaga and the Dawson Site, 1972; Nubia Under the Pharaohs, 1976; Gordon Childe, 1980. *Contributions to:* Antiquity; American Antiquity; World Archaeology; Man. Editor, Native and Northern Series, McGill-Queen's University Press. *Honours:* Canadian Silver Jubilee Medal, 1977; Cornplanter Medal, 1979; Innis-Gerin Medal, Royal Society of Canada, 1985; DSc, hc University of New Brunswick, 1987; John Porter Prize, 1988; DLitt, University of Waterloo, 1990; Prix du Québec, 1991. *Memberships:* Various professional organizations *Address:* Department of Anthropology, McGill University, 855 Sherbrooke Street West, Montreal, Quebec, Canada H3A 2T7.

TRILLIN Calvin, b. 5 Dec 1935, Kansas City, Missouri, USA. m. Alice Stewart Trillin, 2 daughters. *Education:*

BA, Yale College, 1957; Beloit College; Albertus Magnus College. *Appointments:* Staff Writer, The New Yorker, 1963-; Columnist, King Features Syndicate, 1986-. *Publications:* An Education in Georgia; Barnett Frummer is an Unbloomed Flower. *Contributions to:* Numerous inc. US Journal; New Yorker; American Friend; Runestruck; The New Yorker; Harpers; NY Times Sunday Magazine; Life; Time; Esquire; Travel & Leisure. *Memberships:* PEN American Centre. *Literary Agent:* Robert Lescher, 67 Irving Placle, NYC 10003. *Address:* c/o The New Yorker, 20 West 43, New York, NY 10036, USA.

TRIMBLE Barbara Margaret, (Margaret Blake, B M Gill), b. 1921, British. *Appointments:* Clerk/Typist; School Teacher; Chiropodist; Full-time Writer. *Publications:* as Margaret Blake - Stranger at the Door, 1967; Bright Sun, Dark Shadow, 1968; The Rare and the Lovely, 1969; The Elusive Exile, 1971; Flight from Fear, Courier to Danger, 1973; Apple of Discord, 1975; Walk Softly and Beware, 1977; as B M Gill - Target Westminster, 1977; Death Drop, 1979; Victims (in US as Suspect), 1981; The Twelfth Juror, 1984; Seminar for Murder, 1985; Nursery Games, 1986. *Address:* C/o Patricia Robertson, 87 Caledonian Road, London N1 9BT, England.

TRIMMER Eric, b. 11 June 1923, Physician. m. Marjorie Rudge, 5 June 1948, 1 son, 1 daughter. *Education:* King's College; Westminster Hospital, London; MB; MRCGP. *Appointments:* Advisor, Readers Digest, 1957; Medical Editor, Medical News, 1960-70; Editorial Director, Medical Tribune, 1970-80; Editor, British Journal of Clinic Practice, 1980-. *Publications:* Femina, 1966; Dictionary of Sex, 1977; Textbook of Sexual Medicine, 1978; Complete Book of Slimming and Diets, 1981; Ten Day Relaxation Plan, 1984; Magic of Magnesium, 1987. *Contributions to:* Numerous. *Honours:* Honorary Member, Medical Journalists Association. *Membership:* Former Member, Society of Authors, Medical Group Committee; Fellow, Royal Society of Medicine, former Committee Member, Section of Medical History. *Address:* Yew Tree Lodge, Love Lane, Bembridge, Isle of Wight PO35 5RY, England.

TRIPP Miles Barton (John Michael Brett, Michael Brett). b. 5 May 1923, Ganwick Corner. Writer. *Publications include:* The Eighth Passenger, 1969; Kilo Forty 1963; A Man Without Friends, 1970; High Heels 1980; A Charmed Death, 1984; Death of a Man-Tamer, 1987; The Frightened Wife, 1987; The Cords of Vanity, 1989; Video Vengeance, 1990. *Memberships:* Society of Authors; Crime Writers Association, Chairman 1968-69; Detection Club. *Literary Agent:* The Peters Fraser and Dunlop Group Ltd. *Address:* The Peters Fraser and Dunlop Group Ltd, 5th Floor, The Chambers, Chelsea Harbour, Lots Road, London SW10 OXF, England.

TRISTRAM Uvedale Francis Barrington, b. 20 Mar 1915. Journalist. m. Elizabeth Frances Eden-Pearson, 8 Sept 1939, 1 daughter. *Appointments:* Morning Post; Assistant Editor, Aeropilot; Managing Editor, Hulton Publications, 1960-61; Editorial Manager, Longacre Press, 1961- 62; Director of Information and Broadcasting, Basutoland, 1962-67; Director of Information, UK Freedom from Hunger Campaign, 1967-73; Founder Editor, World Hunger. *Publications:* Adventure in Oil, 1958; John Fisher; Basutoland, 1961. *Contributions to:* Sunday Telegraph; Time & Tide; Tablet; Universe; Catholic Herald; Commercial Times. *Honours:* Rics Award, Best Property Column in Weekly Paper, 1988, 1991; ISVA Provincial Property of The Year, 1990. *Memberships:* Master of the Keys, Guild of Catholic Writers, 1987-1991; Deputy Master, 1991-; Insitute of Journalists. *Address:* 19 Mallards' Reach, Weybridge, Surrey KT13 9HQ, England.

TROJAN Judith Lynn, b. 7 July 1947, New Jersey, USA. Editor in Chief; Film Video Critic. *Education:* BA 1969, Fairleigh Dickinson University; MA Cinema Studies 1972, New York University. *Appointments:* Copywriter, WMTR Radio, New Jersey 1969-70;

Editorial Coordinator, Educational Film Library Association 1972-88; Contributing Editor, Media & Methods 1976-80; Managing Editor 1972-82, Senior Editor 1982-84, Editor in Chief 1984-88, Sightlines; Film & TV Columnist, Wilson Library Bulletin 1980- 89; Film and Broadcasting Officer 1989-90, US Catholic Conference, Office for Film & Broadcasting; Film & TV Reviews Service Coordinator 1988, US Catholic Conference; Promotion & Marketing Manager, The Cinema Guild 1990-91; Contributing Writer, New Directions for Women 1991-1992. *Publications include:* 16mm Distribution, 1977; American Family Life Films, 1981; American Families in Transition, 1980; Aging: A Filmography, 1974. *Contributions include:* Film, TV and Video reviews for US Catholic Conference were syndicated by the Catholic News Service to over 150 newspapers (Catholic) in the US and Canada; Also served publications, broadcasters and secular news agencies in 40 other countries and Vatican radio; Contributed over 100 critical annotations of multicultural videos published as part of book, Mediating History: The MAP Guide to Independent Video by and about African American, Asian American, Latino and Native American People, 1992. *Memberships:* Edpress; Association of Independent Video & Filmmakers; New York Film/Video Council; The National Association for Female Executives. *Address:* 17 Cottage Lane, Clifton, NJ 07012, USA.

TROLLOPE Joanna. *See:* **PETER Joanna.**

TRONSKI Bronislaw, b. 23 Sept 1921, Wilno, Poland. Journalist; Writer. m. Janina Zajacowna, 3 July 1980, 1 son, 1 daughter. *Education:* MA, Law, Jagielloniau University, Krakow, 1949; Academy of Political Sciences, 1946-48. *Appointments:* Staff: Socjalistyczna Agencja Prasowa, 1946-48; Agencja Robotnicza, 1948-64; Staff, Polska Agencja Prasowa, 1964; Foreign Correspondent, Far East, 1959-60, Balkan Countries, 1972-76, Algiers and Tunisia, 1980-82, Special Correspondent, European Countries. *Publications:* Tedy przeszta Smierc, 1957; Na Dachu Swiata, 1961; Stonce Nad Stara Planina, 1979; W Cieniu Nadziei, 1980; Turcja Bez Tajemnic, 1981; Algierskie Osobliwosci, 1984; Test Pan Wolny, 1987; Tanczacy prezydent, 1988; Mozaika śródziemnomorska, 1988; Smak ziemi obiecanej, 1990; Stambul, 1992; Translations of Dramas. *Contributions to:* Numerous journals and magazines. *Honours:* Award, President of Polish Parliament; Award, Parliament Reporters Club, 1965, 1966; Award, Publishing Company, Epoka, 1979; Award, Bulgarian Journalist Association Golden Pen, 1976; Award, Polonia Club, Polish Journalist Association, 1985; Award: Weekly, Kultura, 1988; Award: Counsel Fund of Literature, 1988; Award: Club of International Published, 1990; many others. *Memberships:* Polish Writers Association; Polish Journalists Association; Authors and Composers Association; Vice President, Union of Warsaw Insurgent, 1991-. *Address:* Rakowiecka Street 33 App. 30, 02-519 Warsaw, Poland.

TROTMAN Jack, (John Penn), Canadian. *Appointments:* British Army Intelligence Corps Officer, 1940-46; Foreign Office, 1946-48; Joint Intelligence Bureau, Ottawa, 1949-65; Canadian Department of National Defence, 1965-73; NATO International Staff, Paris, 1973-77; President, National Trust for Jersey, Channel Islands, 1984-87, 1990-92. *Publications:* Notice of Death (in US as An Ad for Murder), 1982; Deceitful Death (in US as Stag-Dinner Death), A Will to Kill, 1983; Mortal Term, 1984; A Deadly Sickness, 1985; Unto the Grave, Barren Revenge, 1986; Accident Prone, 1987; Outrageous Exposures, 1988; A Feast of Death, 1989; A Killing to Hide, 1990; A Knife Ill-Used, 1991; Death's Long Shadow, 1991; A Legacy of Death, 1992; A Haven of Danger, 1993. *Address:* c/o Murray Pollinger, 222 Old Brompton Road, London SW5 0BZ, England.

TROUBETZKOY Dorothy Livingston Ulrich, (Ulrich Troubetzkoy), b. Hartford, Connecticut, USA. Writer; Editor. m. Prince Serge Troubetzkoy, 25 Dec 1941. 1 son, 2 daughters. *Education:* BA, University of Chicago;

Graduate study, Columbia University. *Literary Appointments:* Feature writer, columnist, Richmond Times Dispatch, 1950-56; Assistant Editor, Virginia Wildlife, 1953-56; Director, Information & Research, City of Richmond, 1956-58; Editor, Virginia Cavalcade, 1959-63; Editor, The Independent Virginian, 1971-. *Publications:* Out of the Wilderness, 1957; Richmond, City of Churches, 1957; Bluebonnets and Blood, 1968; Sagamore Creek, 1969; The Petrarch Beat, 1979; Poems from Korea, 1980, 1982; Love in the Rain, 1986; Where is Christmas? 1967; The Time We Drove aAll Night (Golden Eagle Prize), 1988; Editor of 2 books. *Contributions to:* Numerous magazines and journals including Saturday Review; Ladies' Home Journal; Texas Quarterly; Crosscurrents; Manhattan Poetry Review; Virginia Quarterly Review; New York Times. *Honours:* Recipient of numerous awards including: 11 Poetry Society of America Awards, 1955-80's; 4 collections published as winners open national competitions between 1957-88; Freedoms Foundation George Washington Honor Medal, 1961; Virginia Cultural Laureates Medal in American Literature, 1981; W H Auden Prize, 1984; Francois Villon Award, 1986; International Narrative Prize, 1983; Mark Twain Prize, 1983; Mozart Prize, 1984; Leache Foundation Prize, 1986; Mississippi Valley Prize, 1987; DRAPA, 1987; Norma Farber Prize, 1988 and many others. *Memberships:* Poetry Society of America; New England Poetry Club; Virginia Writers Club; National Federation of Press Women, President 1967-69; National Press Club. *Address:* 2223 Grove Avenue, Richmond, Virginia, 23220, USA.

TROW George W S, b. 28 Sept 1943, Greenwich, Connecticut, USA. *Education:* AB, Harvard University, 1965. *Appointment:* Staff Writer, New Yorker, New York City, 1966-. *Publications:* Prairie Avenue (three-act play) first produced Off-Broadway at the South Street Theatre, April 1979; The Tennis Game (three-act play) first produced Off-Broadway at Theatre of the Open Eye, Feb 1978; Dramatists Play Service, 1979; Elizabeth Dead (one-act play) first produced in New York City at the Cubiculo Theatre. Nov 1980; Bullies (collection of stories) Little, Brown, 1980; Within the Context of No Context (nonfiction essays; contains Within the Context of No Context and Within That Context, One Style) Boston, 1981; The City in the Mist (novel) Little, Brown, 1984. *Contributions to:* Periodicals, including New Yorker and Harper's. *Honours:* Jean Stein Award from the American Academy and Institute of Arts and Letters, 1986, for essays, Within the Context of No Context and The Harvard Black Rock Forest and for novel, The City in the Mist. *Literary Agent:* Jawklow & Nesbit, 598 Madison Ave, NY 10022, USA. *Address:* c/o New Yorker, 20 West 43rd Street, New York, NY 10036, USA.

TROY Katherine. *See:* **BUXTON Anne.**

TRUCK Robert-Paul (Count), b. 3 May 1917, Calais, France. Writer (Poet and Historian). m. Jeanne Brogniart, 24 July 1942, 1 daughter. *Education:* Baccalaureat, 1935; French Naval School, 1938; Naval Officer, 1939. *Appointments:* Poet, 1938; Art Critic, 1940; Lecturer, 1948; Literary Critic, 1966; Historian, 1975. *Publications:* Heures folles, poems, 1938; Au bord de la nuit, poems, 1948; Intersignes, poems, 1953; Medecins de la honte (with Betty Truck), 1975; Mengele, l'ange de la mort (with Betty Truck), 1976; Vertiges, poems, 1989; 1492-1992, 1991; Poems in anthologies: les Poetes de la Vie, Les Poetes de la Mer, Carterie Poetique, 1984; Flammes Vives. *Contributions to:* Les Cahiers du Nord; Maintenant; Quo Vadis; Points et Contrepoints; Elysees-Jonchere; Nostra; Historia; Life; L'Eco del Popolo; Washington Post, Les Poètes et l'Amerique. *Honours:* Master of the Intellectual Elite, Milan, Italy, 1953; Diploma of Honour, Relations Latines, Milan, 1954; Selection Diploma, Academic Institute of Paris, 1981; Diploma of Honour, La Gloire International Prize, Rome, Italy, 1982; Certificate of Merit, Men of Achievement, 1982; Diploma di Benemerenza, 1983; Targa d'Onore, 1983; Gold Palms, 1984; Leonardo da Vinci International Academy, Rome; Doctor of Literature (Honoris Causa), The Marquis Giuseppe Scicluna (1855-

1907) International University Foundation, Delaware, USA, 1987; Commemorative Medal of Honor, American Biographical Institute, 1987; Bronze Medal with collar Ribbon Award, Albert Einstein Academy, Missouri, USA, 1989. *Memberships:* Fellow, International Academy of Poets, Cambridge, England; Fellow, World Literary Academy, Cambridge; Titular Member, Leonardo da Vinci International Academy; Academic Institute of Paris; Society of French Poets. *Address:* Varouna, 49 Rue de Lhomel, 62600 Berck-Plage, France.

TRUEHEART Charles, b. 5 Sept 1951, Washington, USA. Journalist. *Education:* AB, Amherst College, 1973. *Appointments:* Book Review Editor, Greensboro Daily News, 1973-78; Book Review Editor, Baltimore News American, 1978-81; West Coast Correspondent, Publishers Weekly, 1982-83; Magazine Columnist, USA Today, 1982-86; Literary Correspondent, & Magazine Columnist, The Washington Post, 1986-. *Publication:* Kyrie : Letters to a Friend, 1971. *Contributions to:* numerous journals & magazines. *Membership:* National Book Critics Circle. *Literary Agent:* Raphael Sagalyn. *Address:* 1351 28th Street NW, Washington, DC 20007, USA.

TRUMAN Jill, b. 12 June 1934, Enfield, Middlesex, England. Teacher; Writer. m. Tony Truman 31 Mar 1956, dec 1975, 1 son, 3 daughters. *Education:* BA English Literature 1955; Postgraduate Certificate in Drama 1979. *Publications:* Book, Letter to My Husband, 1988; Theatre, The Web, 1991; Radio plays (BBC radio 4 & 5), Letter to My Husband, 1986; Gone Out-Back Soon, 1988; Travels in West Africa, 1990; Flit, 1992. *Contribution:* Letter to My Husband serialised in magazines in UK, US, Australia and Belgium. *Honour:* New London Radio Playwrights Festival 1992, Special Commendation (for Women's Radio Group) for facilitating Nine Lives. *Membership:* Writers' Guild of Great Britain. *Literary Agent:* June Hall. *Address:* 34 Wellington Park, Clifton, Bristol BS8 2UW, England.

TRUSSELL Donna, b. 11 Aug 1953, Dallas, Texas, USA. m. 14 May 1977. *Education:* BA 1986, University of Missouri. *Appointments:* Teacher, Young Writers Conference, 1990-; Film Columnist, The New Times, 1991-. *Publications:* Fishbone, TriQuarterly, 1989; Fishbone anthologized in Triquarterly's Fiction of the Eighties and in Algonquin's New Stories from the South, The Year's Best 1990. *Contributions to:* Triquarterly; Poetry; The Kansas City Star Magazine; and others. *Honours:* Finalist, Best American Short Stories, 1989; David Sokolov Scholar in Fiction at Bread Loaf Writers' Conference 1989. *Memberships:* Last Chance Writers, Co-Founder; Phi Kappa Phi Honour Society 1986. *Address:* ssa 007520 Briar, Prairie Village, KS 66208, USA.

TRYON Thomas, b. 1926, American. Actor and Freelance Writer. *Publications:* The Other, 1971; Harvest Home, 1974; Lady, 1975; Crowned Heads, 1976; Other, 1978; All That Glitters: Five Novellas, 1986; Night of the Moonbow, 1988; The Wings of the Morning, 1990; In The Fire of Spring, 1992; The Adventures of Opal and Cupid, 1992. *Address:* c/o Alfred A Knopf Incorporated, 201 East 50th Street, New York, NY 10022, USA.

TSAI Shih-shan Henry, b. 1 Feb 1940, Chia-yi, Taiwan. History Professor. m. Dr Hsiu-chuan Sonia Tsai, 29 Mar 1971, 1 son, 1 daughter. *Education:* BA English Literature 1962, National Taiwan Normal University; MA History 1967, PhD History 1970, University of Oregon, USA. *Appointments:* Visiting Associate Professor, National Taiwan University 1970-71; Assistant Professor 1971-76, Associate Professor 1976-83, University Arkansas; Visiting Associate Professor, UCLA, USA 1979; Visiting Associate Professor, University California, USA 1981; Professor, University of Arkansas, USA 1983-. *Publications:* Western Historiography, 1975, 3rd ed in paperback 1985; China and the Overseas Chinese in the United States, 1868-1911, 1983; The Chinese Experience in America, 1986;

Article, The Supply and Demand of Ming Eunuchs, 1992. *Contributions to:* The Historian; The American Studies; The Amerasia Journal; The Pacific Review; The Californians; Asian Profile; Overseas Chinese Studies; International Migration Review; Journal of American Ethnic History; Journal of Asian History. *Honours:* Postdoctoral Fellowship, Institute of American Culture, UCLA; Grants from such organisations as Academia Sinica, South Seas Society of Singapore and Arkansas Endowment for the Humanities. *Memberships:* Chinese Historical Association; Asian Studies Association; South Seas Society of Singapore; Association for Asian American Studies. *Address:* 2105 Austin Drive, Fayetteville, AR 72703, USA.

TSURUMI Shunsuke, b. 25 June 1922. Writer. m. Sadako Yokoyama, 11 Nov 1960, 1 son. *Education:* BS, Harvard College, USA. *Publications:* Marginal Arts, 1967; Studies on Forced Conversion, 1976; Collected Works, 5 volumes, 1976; An Intellectual History of Wartime Japan, 1982; A Cultural History of Post-War Japan, 1983; A Biography of Stripper God, 1991; Collected Works, 12 volumes, 1992. *Honours:* Takano Choei Prize, 1976; Osaragi Jiro Prize, 1982; Japan Mystery Writers Club Prize, 1989. *Memberships:* Japan PEN Club; Society for the Science of Thought; Society for the Study of Contemporary Mores. *Address:* 230-99 Nagatanicho, Iwakura, Sakyoku, Kyoto, Japan.

TSURUTANI Hisashi, b. 3 May 1925, Japan. Professor of American Studies. m. Miyo Okamoto, 22 Dec 1963, 1 son, 2 daughters. *Education:* Graduated 1952, Kyushu University; MA American Studies, University of Wyoming. *Publications:* The Necessary Earth, translation, 1960; The American Western Novel, translation, 1984; The Japanese and the Opening of the American West, 1989; The American History and the American Cowboy, 1989; Miscellaneous Stories of the American West, 1990; Way Out West, 1991. *Contributions to:* Asahi Newspaper; Tokyo Newspaper; Esquire. *Memberships:* Japanese Association for American Studies; International John Steinbeck Society. *Address:* 3-33-23-403 Kasuga-cho, Nerima-ku, Tokyo 176, Japan.

TSUTAKOS Panayotis, b. 19 Feb 1920, Piraeus, Greece. Journalist. m. Dimitra Liakakos, 10 Oct 1952, 2 sons, 1 daughter. *Publications:* (Poetry): Nostalgic Harmonies, 1939; Open Windows, 1940; Bitter Earth, 1953; Holly Bread of Love, 1970, 2nd edition 1986; This is the Polytechnic School, 1974; 2651 Memory of a Tyranny, 1976; This World, 1977; Blood Circle, 1978; Roll Call, 1979; Margarita of Combat, 1981; Peace, 1982; 15 Akakion Str., 1983; Letters to Alexander, 1984; Avis Amoris, 1985; Counsuello, 1987; (Novel)The Anonimous, 1964; (Historical)The History of Keratsini from Ancient Times till Nowadays, 3 volumes, 1986. *Contributions to:* various professional journals. *Honours:* Medal, Allied Staff of Middle East; Medal, National Resistance, Ministry of National Defence; 2nd World Award of Poetry, Italy, 1985; Prize of Peace & Friendship, Ipektsi, Turkey, 1986; Silver Plate of Keratsini Municipality; Greek Republic's Honour Pension for his contribution to Greek Literature. *Memberships:* Greek Authors Society; Literature and Arts Society of Piraeus. *Address:* Kalanzaku 14, Keratsini 18756, Greece.

TSUYUKI Shigeru. *See:* **KIRKUP James.**

TUBB E(dwin) C(harles) (Chuck Adams, Jud Cary, J F Clarkson, James S Farrow, James R Fenner, Charles S Graham, Charles Grey, Volsted Gridban, Alan Guthrie, George Holt, Gill Hunt, E F Jackson, Gregory Kern, King Lang, Mike Lantry, P Lawrence, Chet Lawson, Arthur MacLean, Carl Maddox, M L Powers, Paul Schofield, Brian Shaw, Roy Sheldon, John Stevens, Edward Thomson, Douglas West, Eric Wilding), b. 15 Oct 1919, London, England. Writer. *Literary Appointment:* Editor, Authentic Science Fiction magazine, London, 1956-57. *Publications include:* Over 100 under various pseudonyms: Science Fiction/

Fantasy: Saturn Patrol, 1951; Argentis, 1952; Planetoid Disposals Ltd, 1953; The Living World, 1954; Alien Dust, 1955; The Space-born, 1956; Touch of Evil, 1959; Moon Base, 1964; Ten From Tomorrow, short stories, 1966; Death Is A Dream, 1967; C O D Mars, 1968; STAR Flight, 1969; The Jester at Scar, 1970; Lallia, 1971; Century of the Manikin, 1972; Mayenne, 1973; Veruchia, 1973; Zenya, 1974; Atilus the Slave, 1975; Jack of Swords, 1976; Haven of Darkness, 1977; Incident on Ath, 1978; Stellar Assignment, 1979; The Luck Machine, 1980. Suspense and Western novels: The Fighting Fury, 1955; Scourge of the South, 1956; Wagon Trail, 1957; Target Death, 1961; Too Tough To Handle, 1962; Airbourne Commando, 1963; The Quillian Sector, 1978; Web of Sand, 1979; Iduna's Universe, 1979; The Terra Data, 1980; World of Promise, 1980; Nectar of Heaven, 1981; The Terridae, 1981; The Coming Event, 1982; Earth is Heaven, 1982; Melome, 1983; Stardeath, 1983; Angado, 1984; Symbol of Terra, 1984; The Temple of Truth, 1985. *Contributions to:* 230 stories to magazines and journals. *Literary Agent:* Carnell Literary Agency. *Address:* 67 Houston Road, London SE23 2RL, England.

TUCKER Edward Llewellyn, b. 19 Nov 1921, Crewe, Virginia, USA. Professor. *Education:* BA, Roanoke College, 1946; MA, Columbia University, 1947; PhD, University of Georgia, 1957. *Appointments:* Instructor, Roanoke College, 1947-52; Assistant Professor, University of Richmond, 1957-60; Assistant Professor, Virginia Tech, 1960-66; Associate Professor, 1966-86; Professor, Virginia Tech, 1986-. *Publications:* Richard Henry Wilde, Life and Selected Poems; The Shaping of Longfellows John Endicott; Vocabulary Power. *Honours:* The Shaping of Longfellows John Endicott. *Memberships:* Melus; Sherwood Anderson Society; John Steinbeck Society; MLA; SAMLA. *Address:* 508 College View Drive, Blacksburg, VA 24060, USA.

TUCKER Eva Marie, b. 18 Apr 1929, Berlin, Germany. Writer. m. 11 Mar 1950 (widowed 1987), 3 daughters. *Education:* BA Hons German & English, University of London. *Appointments:* C Day Lewis Writing Fellow, Vauxhall Manor School, London 1978-79; Hawthornden Writing Fellowship, 1991. *Publications:* Contact, novel, 1966; Drowning, novel, 1969; Radetzkymarch by Joseph Roth, translation, 1974. *Contributions to:* BBC Radio 3 & 4; Encounter; London Magazine; Woman's Journal; Vogue; Harpers; Spectator; Listener; PEN International. *Memberships:* English PEN; Turner Society. *Address:* 63B Belsize Park Gardens, London NW3 4JN, England.

TUCKER Helen, b. 1926, American. *Appointments:* Reporter, Times-News, Burlington, 1946-47, Times-News, Twin Falls, 1948-49, Statesman, Boise, 1950-51, Raleigh Times, 1955-57; Continuity Writer, Radio KDYL, Salt Lake City, UT, 1952-53; Continuity Supervisor, Radio WPTF, Raleigh, 1953-55; Editorial Assistant, Columbia University Press, 1959-60; Director of Publicity and Publications, North Carolina Museum of Art, Raleigh, 1967-70. *Publications:* The Sound of Summer Voices, 1969; The Guilt of August Fielding, 1971; No Need of Glory, 1972; The Virgin of Lontano, 1973; A Strange and Ill-Starred Marriage, 1978; A Reason for Rivalry, 1979; A Mistress to the Regent, An Infamous Attachement, The Halverton Scandal, 1980; A Wedding Day Deception, 1981; The Double Dealers, Season of Dishonor, 1982; Ardent Vows, 1983; Bound by Honor, 1984; The Lady's Fancy, 1991; Bold Impostor, 1991. *Honours:* First Woman to receive the Distinguished Alumni Award, Wake Forest University, 1971; Franklin County Artist of the Year Award, 1992. *Literary Agent:* Don Congdon Associates Inc, 156 Fifth Avenue, New York, NY 10010, USA. *Address:* 2930 Hostetler Street, Raleigh, NC 27609, USA.

TUCKER Martin, b. 8 Feb 1928, Philadelphia, Pennsylvania, USA. Author; Professor of English. *Education:* BA, New York University, 1949; Ma, University of Arizona, 1954; PhD, New York University, 1963. *Literary Appointments:* Editor, Confrontation magazine, 1970-; Executive Board, PEN American

Center, 1973-; Governing Board, Poetry Society of America, 1984-1988. *Publications:* Joseph Conrad, 1976; Africa in Modern Literature, 1967; Homes of Locks and Mysteries, 1982 (poems); Ed: The Critical Temper, Vols I-IV 1970-89; Ed: Modern British Literature, Vols I-IV 1967-76. *Contributions to:* New York Times Book Review; The Nation; The New Republic; The Saturday Review; Research in African Literature. *Honours:* NEA/Co-ordinating Council and Literary Magazine Award for Editorial Distinction on Confrontation, 1976, 1984; English-Speaking Union Award, 1982. *Memberships:* PEN; Poetry Society of America; Authors Guild; National Book Critics Circle; African Literature Association; Modern Language Association; African Studies Association; Phi Beta Kappa. *Address:* 90-A Dosoris Lane, Glen Cove, NY 11542, USA.

TUCKMAN Bruce W, b. 24 Nov 1938, New York, USA. College Professor. m. Darby Goodwin, 26 July 1980, 1 son, 1 daughter. *Education:* BS, Psychology, Rensselaer Polytechnic Institute, 1960; MA, Psychology, 1962, PhD, Psychology, 1963, Princeton University. *Appointments:* Research Associate, Princeton University, 1963; Adjunct Professor, University College, University of Maryland, 1963-65; Research Psychologist, Naval Medical Research Institute, Bethesda, Maryland, 1963-65; Associate Professor of Education, 1965-70, Professor of Education, 1970-78, Rutgers University; Director of Research, Graduate School of Education, Rutgers University, 1975-78; Dean, School of Education, Baruch College of The City University of New York, 1978-82; Senior Research Fellow, Center for Advanced Study in Education, City University of New York, 1982-83; Dean, 1983-85, Professor 1985-, College of Education, The Florida State University. Consulting Editor, Journal of Experimental Education, 1987-; Contributing Editor and Columnist, Educational Technology Magazine, 1981-. *Publications:* Conducting Educational Research, 1972, 1978, 1988; Evaluating Instructional Programs, 1979, 1985; Testing for Teachers, 1975, 1988; Effective College Management, 1987; Analyzing and Designing Educational Research, 1985; Preparing to Teach the Disadvantaged, 1969; Long Road to Boston (novel) 1988; Educational Psychology, 1992. *Contributions to:* Runner's World; Phi Delta Kappan Journal of Educational Psychology; American Education Research Journal; Journal of Educational Research. *Honours:* National Institute of Mental Health Fellowship, 1961-63; New Jersey Association of English Teachers Author's Award, 1969; Phi Delta Kappa Research Award, 1973; Outstanding Teaching Award, 1993. *Memberships:* Fellow, American Psychological Association; American Educational Research Association; Gulf Winds Track Club. *Address:* Department of Educational Research. B-197, Florida State University, Tallahassee, FL 32306, USA.

TUDOR Andrew Frank, b. 19 Nov 1942, Edinburgh, Scotland. University Lecturer. *Education:* BA, Sociology, 1965. *Publications:* Theories of Film, 1973; Image and Influence, 1974; Beyond Empiricism, 1982; Monsters and Mad Scientists, 1989. *Contributions to:* Film Critic for New Society, 1975-82. *Address:* Department of Sociology, University of York, Heslington, York YO1 5DD, England.

TUDOR-CRAIG Pamela. *See:* **TUDOR-CRAIG (WEDGWOOD) Pamela Wynn.**

TUDOR-CRAIG (WEDGWOOD) Pamela Wynn, (Pamela Tudor-Craig), b. 26 June 1928, London, England. Art Historian. m. (1) Algernon James Riccarton Tudor-Craig, 27 July 1956, dec 1969, 1 daughter, (2) Sir John Wedgwood, 1 May 1982-1989. *Education:* 1st Class Honours degree 1949, PhD 1952, Courtauld Institute, University of London. *Appointments:* Taught at numerous American Colleges with Houses in England, currently Grinnell, London. *Publications:* Richard III, 1973; Secret Life of Paintings, co-author, 1986; Bells Guide to Westminster Abbey, co-author, 1986; Age of Chivalry, Royal Academy, Contbr 1987;

Exeter Cathedral, 1991; Anglo-Saxon Wall paintings, 1991; Television: Own Series, The Secret Life of Paintings, 1986; . *Contributions to:* Arts Page of the Church Times 1988-; Harlaxton Medieval Studies, 3 issues; Anglo Saxon England; British Archaeological Journal; Royal Archaeology Journal; and others. *Honour:* Honorary Doctor of Humanities, William Jewell College, 1983. *Membership:* Fellow, Society of Antiquaries 1958-, Council 1989-92; Committees for the Care of Churches and Cathedrals; Cathedrals Advisory Commission, 1975-90; Chairman, Wall Paintings Committee; Fabric Committee for Westminister Abbey. *Address:* Home Farm, Leighton Bromswold, Nr Huntingdon PE18 0SL, England.

TUFTE Virginia James, Professor; Author. *Education:* AB, University of Nebraska; MA and PhD, University of California at Los Angeles. *Appointments:* Professor, English Renaissance Literature and Milton, University of Southern California, 1964-89, Emeritus Professor, 1989-. *Publications:* The Poetry of Marriage: the Epithalamium in Europe, 1970; High Wedlock Then Be Honored, 1970 (editor); Grammar as Style, 1971; Changing Images of the Family (editor with Barbara Myerhoff) 1979. *Contributions to:* Essays on Illustrations as Interpretations of Milton's Paradise Lost in Milton Quarterly, Mosaic and elsewhere, 1986-90. *Honour:* Phi Beta Kappa. *Memberships:* Modern Language Association of America; Renaissance Society of America; Former President of Renaissance Conference of Southern California; American Association of University Professors. *Address:* Department of English, University of Southern California, Los Angeles, CA 90089, USA.

TUFTY Barbara Jean, b. 28 Dec 1923, Iowa City, Iowa, USA. Conservation Writer and Editor. m. Harold G. Tufty, 29 Dec 1948, 2 sons, 1 daughter. *Education:* BA, Botany, Duke University; Postgraduate classes, New School for Social Research, New York City, 1946; Sorbonne, Paris, France, 1948; University of Colorado, 1949, 1950, 1951. *Appointments:* Editor, Union Carbide and Carbon Corporation, 1945-47; Information Writer, University of Colorado Extension Center, 1949-51; Editor, Freelance Writer, Tufty Associates; Science Writer, Science Service, 1948-72; Science Writer, National Academy of Sciences, 1970-72; Editor, National Science Foundation, 1972-84; Conservation Writer and Editor, Audubon Naturalist Society, 1986-. *Publications:* 1001 Questions Answered About Natural Land Disasters, 1969, paperback, 1978; 1001 Questions Answered About Storms, 1970, paperback, 1986; Cells, Units of Life, 1973; Crafts in the Ivory Coast, translation, French to English, 1963. *Contributions to:* Books: Science Year Encyclopedia, 1970; Women in Science, 1979; Book of Biology, 1985; The Atlantic Naturalist; Mosaic Magazine; Science News Letter; Bombay Natural History Society Journal; Coal Age; Iron Age. *Honours:* Chi Delta Phi, 1945; Honorary Life Member (1st Woman), Bombay Natural History Society, 1960; Thomas Honourable Mention Writing Award, 1972; Catherine O'Brien Honourable Mention Writing Award, 1972. *Memberships include:* Washington Independent Writers; National Association of Science Writers; The Nature Conservancy; American Association for Advancement of Science; New York Academy of Sciences. *Address:* 3812 Livingston Street NW, Washington, DC 20015, USA.

TUGENDHAT Julia. *See:* **DOBSON Julia Lissant.**

TULLY William Mark, b. 24 Aug 1935, Calcutta, India. Journalist. m. Margaret Tully, 13 Aug 1960, 2 sons, 2 daughters. *Education:* Malborough College, 1949-53; Trinity Hall, Cambridge, 1956-59. *Publications:* Amritsar Mrs Gandhis Last Battle; Raj to Rajiv; No Full Stops in India. *Honours:* OBE; Bafta Dimbleby; Broadcasting Press Guild; Padmashri. *Literary Agent:* Gill Coleridge. *Address:* 1 Nizamuddin East, New Delhi 110013, India.

TUOHY John Francis (Frank), b. 2 May 1925, Uckfield, Sussex, England. *Education:* MA, Honours,

King's College, Cambridge, 1946. *Publications:* The Animal Game, 1957; The Warm Nights of January, 1960; The Ice Saints, 1964; Collected Stories, 1984; Portugal, 1970; W.B. Yeats, 1976. *Contributions to:* numerous magazines & journals. *Honours:* Katherine Mansfield Prize, 1960; James Tait Black Memorial Prize, 1964; Geoffrey Faber Memorial Prize, 1964; William Heinemann award, 1978. *Memberships:* PEN; Society of Authors. *Literary Agent:* The Peters Fraser and Dunlop Group Ltd. *Address:* Shatwell Cottage, Yarlington, Nr Wincanton, Somerset, BA9 8DL, England.

TURCO Richard Peter, b. 9 Mar 1943, New York City, USA. Atmospheric Scientist; Professor. m. Linda Stevenson Newman, 27 July 1991. *Education:* BS EE 1965, Rutgers University; PhD EE & Physics 1971, University of Illinois. *Appointments:* Associate Editor, Journal of Geophysical Research, 1993. *Publications:* The Environmental Consequences of Nuclear War, co-author, 1986; A Path Where No Man Thought: Nuclear Winter and the End of the Arms Race, co-author, 1990. *Contributions to:* Over 170 articles to Parade; Scientific America; Nature; Science; Newton. *Honours:* Leo Szilard Prize, Physics in the Public Interest, 1985; MacArthur Fellowship 1986; NASA's H Julian Allen Award 1988; UCLA Faculty Research Lectureship 1992. *Memberships:* American Geophysical Union, President Atmospheric Sciences Section; Sigma Xi. *Literary Agent:* Scott Meredith, New York. *Address:* Department of Atmospheric Sciences, University of California, Los Angeles, CA 90024, USA.

TURK Frances Mary, b. 14 Apr 1915, Huntingdon, England. Novelist. *Publications include:* Numerous books including: Paddy O'Shea, 1937; The Precious Hours, 1938; Paradise Street, 1939; Lovable Clown, 1941; Angel Hill, 1942; The Five Grey Geese, 1944; Salutation, 1949; The Small House at Ickley, 1951; The Gentle Flowers, 1952; The Dark Wood, 1954; The Glory and the Dream, 1955; Dinny Lightfoot, 1956; No Through Road, 1957; The White Swan, 1958; The Secret Places, 1961; The Guarded Heart, 1964; Legacy of Love, 1967; Fair Recompense, 1969; Goddess of Threads, 1975; A Visit to Marchmont, 1977; Candle Corner, 1986. *Contributions to:* The Writer; Woman's Way; Land Girl; Home & Country; Cambridgeshire Life; Beds & Northants Life; Sunday Companion; Peterborough Evening Telegraph; many other journals. *Memberships:* Romantic Novelists Association; many other professional organisations. *Address:* Hillrise, Brampton Road, Buckden, Huntingdon PE18 9UJH, England.

TURNBULL Gael Lundin, b. 7 Apr 1928, Edinburgh, Scotland. Writer; Former Medical Practitioner. m. (1) Jonnie May Draper, 1952, 3 daughters, (2) Pamela Jill Iles, 1983. *Education:* BA, Cambridge University, England, 1948; MD, University of Pennsylvania, USA, 1951. *Publications:* A Trampoline, 1968; Scantlings, 1970; A Gathering of Poems: 1950-1980, 1983; A Year and a Day, 1985; A Winter Journey, 1987; While Breath Persist, (Canada), 1992; numerous collections since 1954. *Contributions to:* Numerous journals and magazines. *Honour:* Alice Hunt Bartlett Award, Poetry Society of London, 1969. *Address:* 12 Strathearn Place, Edinburgh EH9 2AL, Scotland.

TURNER Alberta Tucker, b. 22 Oct 1919, New York City, USA. Poet; Professor. m. 9 Apr 1943, 1 son, 1 daughter. *Education:* BA, Hunter College, 1940; MA, Wellesley College, 1941; PhD, Ohio State University, 1946. *Appointments:* Director, Cleveland State University Poetry Centre, 1964-1990; Associate Editor, Field: Contemporary Poetry & Poetics, 1969-; Professor, English, Cleveland State University, 1978-1990; Responses To Poetry, 1990. *Publications:* 50 Contemporary Poets : The Creative Process, 1977; 45 Contemporary Poems : the Creative Process, 1985; To Make a Poem, 1982; Poets Teaching, 1980; A Belfry of Knees, 1983; Lid and Sppon, 1977; Learning to Count, 1974. *Contributions include:* Stand; Poetry; Prairie Schooner; Missouri Review; Atlantic Monthly; Poetry Now. *Honours:* Ohio Arts council Grant for Poetry, 1980; Cleveland Artists Prize for Literature, 1985; Ohioana Award for Poetry, 1986; Governor's Award for the Arts, in Education, 1988. *Memberships:* PEN; Milton Society of America. *Address:* 482 Caskey Court, Oberlin, OH 44074, USA.

TURNER Frederick, b. 19 Nov 1943, East Haddon, Northamptonshire, England. Professor of Humanities; Writer. m. Mei Lin Chang, 25 June 1966, 2 sons. *Education:* Christ Church, Oxford University 1962-67; BA, 1965, MA, 1967, BLitt, 1967, English Language and Literature, Oxford. *Appointments:* Assistant Professor of English, University of California, Santa Barbara, USA, 1967-72; Associate Professor of English, Kenyon College, 1972-85; Editor, Kenyon Review, 1978-83; Visiting Professor of English, University of Exeter, England, 1984-85; Founders Professor of Arts and Humanities, University of Texas at Dallas, Richardson, USA, 1985-. *Publications:* Shakespeare and the Nature of Time, 1971; Between Two Lives, 1972; A Double Shadow, 1978; Counter-Terra, 1978; The Return, 1979; The New World, 1985; The Garden, 1985; Natural Classicism, 1986; Genesis: an Epic Poem, 1988; Rebirth of Value, 1991; Tempest, Flute and Oz, 1991; Beauty, 1991; Foaming Sky: the Major Poems of Miklos Radnoti (translation with Zsuzsanna Ozsvath), 1992. *Contributions to:* Essays in Harper's; Poetry; New Literary History. Poems in Poetry; Southern Review; Poetry Nation Review. Translations in New Hungarian Quarterly; Partisan Review. *Honours:* Ohioana Prize for Editorial Excellence, 1980; Djerassi Foundation Grant and Residency, 1981; Levinson Poetry Prize, 1983; Missouri Review Essay Prize, 1986; PEN Golden Oen Award, 1992. *Memberships:* PEN; Modern Language Association. *Address:* 2668 Aster Drive, Richardson, TX 75082, USA.

TURNER George (Reginald), b. 1916, Australian. *Appointments:* Employment Officer, Commonwealth Employment Service, Melbourne, 1945-49, Wangaratta, Victoria, 1949-50; Textile Technician, Bruck Mill, Wangaratta, 1951-64; Senior Employment Officer, Volkswagen Limited, Melbourne, 1964-67. *Publications:* Young Man of Talent, 1959; A Stranger and Afraid, 1961; The Cupboard under the Stairs, 1962; A Waste of Shame, 1965; The Lame Dog Man, 1967; The View from the Edge (ed), 1977; Beloved Son, Transit of Cassidy, 1978; Vaneglory, 1982; Yesterday's Men, 1983; In the Heart or In the Head, 1984; The Sea and Summer, 1987; A Pursuit of Miracles, 1990; Brain Child, 1991; The Destiny Makes, 1993. *Honours:* Miles Franklin Award, 1962; Arthur C Clarke Award, 1987. *Membership:* Australian Society of Authors. *Literary Agent:* Cherry Weiner, 28 Kipling Way, Manalapan, NJ 07726, USA. *Address:* 4/296 Inkerman Street, East St Kilda, Victoria 3183, Australia.

TURNER George William, b. 26 Oct 1921, Dannevirke, New Zealand. University Teacher (retired). m. Beryl Horrobin, 18 Apr 1949, 2 sons. *Education:* BA (NZ), 1944; MA (NZ), 1948; Diploma, New Zealand Library School, 1948; Diploma in English Linguistic Studies, University College, London, England, 1964. *Appointments:* Tutor and Lecturer, University of Canterbury, New Zealand, 1955-64; Reader, University of Adelaide, 1965-86. *Publications:* The English Language in Australia and New Zealand, 1966, 2nd Edition, 1972; Good Australian English (editor), 1972; Stylistics, 1973; Australian Pocket Oxford Dictioary, 2nd Edition (editor), 1984; Australian Concise Oxford Dictionary (editor), 1986; The Australian Oxford Paperback Dictionary (co-editor with Beryl Turner), 1989. *Contributions to:* The Verses in Gunnlaugs saga Ormstungu in the Journal of English and Germanic Phiology, 1977; The language of literature in Beitrage zur Phonetik und Linguistik, 1986. *Honours:* Fellow, Australian Academy of the Humanities, 1974; Festschrift: Lexicographical and linguistic studies, edited by T L and Jill Burton, D S Brewer, 1988. *Address:* 3 Marola Avenue, Rostrevor, SA 5073, Australia.

TURNER Len. *See:* **FLOREN Lee**.

TURNER Lloyd Charles, b. 2 Oct 1938, Australia. Journalist; Editor. m. (1) Rosemary Munday, 1961 (div 1966), (2) Jennifer Anne Cox (div 1972), (3) Jill Marguerite King, 1973. *Appointments include:* Cadet journalist 1956, Chief Crime Reporter 1960, Features Editor 1961, Picture Editor 1962, Assistant Editor 1964, Newcastle Morning Herald, Australia; Industrial correspondent, Manchester Evening News, UK, 1968; Sub-Editor 1968, Assistant Chief Sub-Editor 1974, Deputy Chief Sub-Editor 1975, Assistant Night Editor 1976, Deputy Night Editor 1977, Night Editor 1979, Daily Express; Editor, Daily Star, 1980-. *Honour:* CPU Scholar, 1966. *Memberships:* President, Australian Journalists Association (Provincial), 1962-65; Chairman (Father), Daily Express/Sunday Express NUJ Chapel, 1969-74. *Address:* 121 Fleet Street, London EC4P 4JT, England.

TURNER Mary. *See:* **LAMBOT Isobel Mary.**

TURNER Philip William (Stephen Chance), b. 3 Dec 1925, Rossland, British Columbia, Canada. Writer; Dramatist. m. Margaret Diana Samson, 23 Sept 1950, 2 sons, 1 daughter. *Education:* BA/MA, English Language & Literature, Oxford University, 1946. *Publications:* The Bible Story, 1968; The Grange at High Force, 1965; Septimus & the Danedyke Mystery, 1973; The Candlemass Treasure, 1988. Plays: Christ in the Concrete City, 1956, 1965; How Many Miles to Bethlehem?, 1987. *Honour:* Carnegie Medal, 1965. *Literary Agent:* Watson Little, London, England. *Address:* St Francis, 181 West Malvern Road, Malvern, Worcs, England.

TURNER WARD Douglas, b. 5 May 1930, Burnside, Louisiana, USA. Dramatist. m. Diana Hoyt Powell, 1966, 2 children. *Publications:* Books: Happy Ending and Day of Absence, 1966; The Reckoning, 1970; Brotherhood, 1970; Play Productions: Happy Ending & Day of Absence, 1965; The Reckoning, 1969; Brotherhood and Day of Absence, 1970; The Redeemer, 1979. *Contributions to:* various journals and magazines. *Memberships:* various professional organisations. *Address:* The Negro Ensemble Company, 1560 Broadway, Suite 409, New York City, NY 10036, USA.

TURNILL Reginald, b. 12 May 1915, Dover, England. Writer; Broadcaster. m. 10 Sept 1938, 2 sons. *Education:* As Fleet Street reporter. *Appointments:* Reporter, Industrial Correspondent, Press Association, London, 1930-56; Industrial Correspondent, 1956-58, Aerospace and Defence Correspondent, 1958-75, British Broadcasting Corporation. *Publications:* The Language of Space, 1970; Observer's Book of Manned Spaceflight, 1972, 1975, 1978; Observer's Unmanned Spaceflight, 1974; Observer's Spaceflight Directory, 1978; Space Age, 1980; Jane's Spaceflight Directory, 1984, 1986, 1987, 1988; Space Technology International (editor), 1989, 1990, 1991, 1992; World Aerospace Development, 1993; Celebrating Concorde, 1993. *Contributions to:* Zodiac; Executive Travel; Aerospace; Aviation Week; Space Technology. *Memberships:* Fellow, British Interplanetary Society; Associate, Royal Aeronautical Society. *Address:* Somerville Lodge, Hillside, Sandgate, Kent CT20 3DB, England.

TUSIANI Joseph, b. 14 Jan 1924, San Marco in Lamis, Foggia, Italy. University Professor. *Education:* D.Lit., University of Naples, Italy and College of Mount St Vincent, USA. *Publications Include:* The Complete Poems of Michelangelo, 1960; Envoy from Heaven, 1965; Tasso's Jerusalem Delivered, 1970; Gente Mia and Other Poems, 1978; Rosa Rosarum, poems in Latin, 1984; In Exilio Rerum, in Latin, 1985. *Contributions to:* Numerous journals including: New York Times; New Yorker; Catholic World; Sign; Spirit; Classical Outlook; La parola. *Honours:* Greenwood Prize, Poetry society of England, 1956; Alice Fay di Castagnola Award, Poetry Society of America, 1969; Spirit Gold Medal, Catholic Poetry Society of America. *Memberships:* Past Vice President, Poetry Society of America; Past Director, Catholic Poetry Society of America. *Address;* 2140 Tomlinson Avenue, Bronx, NY 10461, USA.

TUSKA Jon, b. 30 Apr 1942, Milwaukee, Wisconsin, USA. m. Vicki Lee Piekarski, 24 May 1980, 1 daughter. *Education:* Marquette University, 1966. *Appointments include:* Founded Sales Consultants, Milwaukee, 1968; Founded Sales Consultants, Madison, 1969; OWner, Operator, Personnel Consultants, Wisonsin; Founder, Golden West Literary Agency, Portland. *Publications:* The Filming of the West; Billy the Kid; Encyclopedia of Frontier and Western Fiction; The American West in Fiction; The American West in Film. *Contributions to:* Ovation; Classical; Fanfare; West Coast Review of Books; Portland Business Journal; Mystery Scene. *Literary Agent:* Golden West Literary Agency. *Address:* 2327 SE Salmon Street, Portland, OR 97214, USA.

TUTTLE Lisa, b. 16 Sept 1952, Houston, Texas, USA. Writer. *Education:* BA, Syracuse University, 1973. *Publications:* Windhaven, (novel, with George R R Martin), 1981; Familiar Spirit, novel, 1983; Catwitch, (with Una Woodruff), 1983; Children's Literary Houses, with Rosalind Ashe, 1984; Encyclopedia of Feminism, 1986; A Nest of Nightmares, 1986, A Spaceship Built of Stone & Other Stories, 1987, short stories; Gabriel, novel, 1987; Heroines: Women Inspired by Women, 1988; Lost Futures, novel, 1992; Memories of The Body, short stories, 1992. *Contributions include:* TV Critic, Austin American Statesman, 1975-79; City Limits; Time Out; Fiction Magazine. *Honour:* John W. Campbell Award for Best New Writer, 1974. *Literary Agent:* Caradoc King, A P Watt Ltd. *Address:* c/o A P Watt Ltd, 20 John Street, London WC1N 2DL, England.

TUTTLE William McCullough, b. 7 Oct 1937. Professor of History. m. Linda L Stumpp, 12 Dec 1959 (now divorced), 2 sons, 1 daughter. *Education:* BA Denison University, 1959; MA, University of Wisconsin, 1964; PhD, University of Wisconsin, 1967. *Appointments:* Assistant Professor 1967- 70, Associate Professor 1970-75, University of Kansas; Senior Fellow in Southern and Negro History, Johns Hopkins University, 1969-70; Research Fellow, Harvard University, 1972-73; Professor of History, University of Kansas, 1975-; Visiting Professor, USC, 1980; Intra-University Professor, University of Kansas, 1982-83; Associate Fellow, Stanford Humanities Center, 1983-84; Research Associate, University of California, Berkeley, 1986-88. *Publications:* Race Riot: Chicago in the Red Sumer of 1919, 1970; W E B DuBois, 1973; Co-author, Plain Folk, 1982; Co-author, A People & a Nation, 1982, 1986, 1990; Daddy's Gone to War: The Second World War in the Livse of America's Children, 1993. *Contributions to:* Journal of American History, American Studies, Labor History, Technology and Culture and other journals. *Honours:* National Endowment for the Humanities, Younger Humanist Fellowship, 1972-73; Award of Merit, American Association for State and Local History, 1972; Guggenheim Fellowship, 1975-76; Evans Grant 1975-76; Beveridge Grant, 1982; Fellowship for Independent Study and Research, 1983-84; National Endowment for the Humanities, Projects Research Grant, 1986-89, Hall Humanities Research Fellow, 1990. *Memberships:* Society of American Historians; American Historical Association; Organization of American Historians (Nominating Board 1979-81). *Address:* 21 Winona Avenue, Lawrence, KS 66046, USA.

TWEEDIE Jill Sheila, b. 1936, UK. Author; Journalist; Scriptwriter. m. (1) Count Bela Cziraky, 1954, 1 son, 1 daughter, (2) Robert d'Ancona, 1963, 1 son, (3) Alan Brien, 1973. *Appointments include:* Columnist, Guardian newspaper, 1969-; Freelance writer, press, radio, television. *Publications include:* In the Name of Love, 1979; It's Only Me, 1980; Letters from a Faint-Hearted Feminist, 1982; More From Martha, 1983; Bliss, novel, 1984; Internal Affairs, novel, 1986. *Contributions to:* Various European & American anthologies. *Honours:* Woman Journalist of the Year, IPC National Press Awards, 1971; Granda TV Award, 1972. *Address:* 15

Marlborough Yard, Marlborough Road, London N19 4ND, England.

TWINING William Lawrence, b. 22 Sept 1934, Kampala. Professor of Law. m. Penelope Elizabeth Hall-Morris, 31 Aug 1957, 1 son, 1 daughter. *Education:* BA 1955, MA 1960, DCL 1990, Brasenose College, Oxford; JD 1958, University of Chicago; LLD (Hon) 1980, University of Victoria, BC. *Appointments:* Editor, Law in Context series 1965-; Editor, Jurists series 1979-. *Publications include:* Karl Llewellyn and the Realist Movement, 1973, 1985; Law Publishing and Legal Information, co-author, 1981; How to Do Things With Rules, co-author, 3rd edn 1991; Theories of Evidence: Bentham and Wigmore, 1985; Legal Theory and Common Law, ed 1986; Access to Legal Education and the Legal Profession, co-ed, 1989; Learning Lawyers' Skills, co-ed, 1989; Rethinking Evidence, 1990; Analysis of Evidence, co- author, 1991; Evidence and Proof, co-editor, 1992. *Contributions to:* Numerous journals. *Honour:* LLD (Hon) University of Victoria, BC 1980. *Memberships:* President, Society of Public Teachers of Law 1978-79; Chairman, Commonwealth Legal Education Association 1983-; President, UK Association for Legal and Social Philosophy 1981-83. *Address:* Faculty of Laws, University College, Endsleigh Gardens, London WC1H 0EG, England.

TWISK Russell Godfrey, b. 24 Aug 1941, London, England. Editor. m. 22 May 1965, 2 daughters. *Education:* Salesian College, Farnborough. *Literary Appointments:* Staff, Harmsworth Press, 1960-62; Sub-Editor, Sphere, 1962-66; Joined BBC, 1966, Deputy Editor, Radio Times, 1969-75, Editor, BBC Special Publications, 1975-81, Editor, The Listener, 1981-87; Editor-in-Chief, reader's Digest, 1987-; Radio Critic, The Observer, 1989-. *Contributions to:* Numerous journals, magazines and newspapers. *Memberships:* Vice-President, The Media Society, 1990-; Chairman, The British Society of Magazine Editors, 1990. *Literary Agent:* The Carol Smith Literary Agency. *Address:* 20 Elm Grove Road, Ealing, London, W5 3JJ, England.

TWUM Michael Kyei b. 30 Apr 1954. Writer; Poet. m. Maureen Twum, 22 Aug 1986, 1 son. *Education:* Diploma in Accountancy, Modern School of Commerce, Ghana, 1974; Course Professeur Marie, France, 1981; University of Bonn, W. Germany, 1981. *Appointments:* Lifetime Deputy Governor, ABIRA, USA, 1987. *Publications include:* Golden Poems from Africa, 1982; Beyond Expectations, 1983; Great Adventures of an African, 1983. *Contributions to:* Several magazines and newspapers, including New York Times. *Honours:* Silver Medal, 1985; Gold Medal, 1987, ABI, USA; Certificates, IBC, England. *Memberships:* National Association of Writers, Ghana; World Institute of Achievement, Fellow, IBC, Life Patron; PEN International; Member, World Institute of Achievement, USA, 1986. *Literary Agent:* Vantage Press, New York. *Address:* 78 Acacia Road, Mitcham, Surrey CR4 1ST, England.

TYLER Anne, b. 1941, American. *Publications:* If Morning Ever Comes, 1964; The Tin Can Tree, 1965; A Slipping Down Life, 1970; The Clock Winder, 1972; Celestial Navigation, 1974; Searching for Caleb, 1976; Earthly Possessions, 1977; Morgan's Passing, 1980; Dinner at the Homesick Restaurant, 1982; The Best American Short Stories 1983 (ed with Shannon Ravenel), 1983; The Accidental Tourist, 1985. *Address:* 222 Tunbridge Road, Baltimore, MD 21212, USA.

TYLER-WHITTLE Michael, (Tyler Whittle and Mark Oliver), b. 1927. Essayist, Literary Critic, Historian, Biographer, Novelist, Writer of Children's fiction and non-fiction, Broadcaster on both Radio and Television. *Publications:* (As Tyler Whittle): Spades and Feathers, 1954; The Runners of Orford, 1955; Castle Lizard, 1956; The Bullhead; Five Spinning Tops of Naples, 1964; Some Ancient Gentlemen, 1968; Common or Garden, 1970; The Last Plantagenet, 1970; The Plant Hunters, 1971; The Young Victoria, 1971; The Birth of Greece, 1972; Albert's Victoria, 1972; The World of Classical Greece,

1973; Royal and Republican Rome, 1974; Imperial Rome, 1974; The Widow of Windsor, 1974; Bertie, 1974; Edward, 1975; The Last Kaiser, 1976; Curtis' Wunderwelt der Blumen, 1979; Vicoria and Albert, 1980; Curtis's Flower Garden Displayed, 1981; The House of Flavell, 1981; Solid Joys and Lasting Treasure, 1985; (As Mark Oliver): A Roll of Thunder, 1960; Luke Benedict, 1961; Feet of Bronze, 1962; Young Plants and Polished Corners, 1963; Co-Author: Heroes of our Time, 1959; Tales of Many Lands, 1960. *Address:* c/o Curtis Brown Ltd., 162-168 Regent Street, London W1R 5TA, England.

TYSON Remer Hoyt, b. 2 July 1934, Statesboro, Georgia, USA. Journalist. m. Virginia Curtin Knight, 18 Feb 1984, 1 son, 1 daughter. *Education:* Georgia Teacher College 1952-54; University of Georgia 1954-56; Art degree, Harvard University, Nieman Fellow 1967-68; Harvard Business School 1981. *Publication:* They Love a Man in the Country, 1988. *Memberships:* Foreign Correspondents Association of Southern Africa; East Africa Foreifn Correspondents Association. *Address:* 3 Woking Drive, Northwood, Mt Pleasant, Harare, Zimbabwe.

U

UECKERT Charlotte b. 22 July 1944, Oldenburg, Germany. Writer. m. (1) Hans Ueckert, 3 Mar 1967, (2) Wulf Hilbert, 17 May 1982, 1 son. *Education:* Diploma as Librarian, 1972; Magister Artium, Literature and Psychology, 1981. *Appointments:* Taught Creative-Writing Courses at various academies 1981-; Assistant Professor for Litertature, 1986-1991. *Publications:* Als wär ich hier nicht fremd (poems) 1979, 1983; Den Jaguarschrei üben (poems) 1988; Finnisch singen (Lyrical prose) 1989; Kein Horizont zu weit (poems), 1991; editor of a number of books; numerous contributions to anthologies. *Contributions to:* Deutsches Allgemeines Sonntagsblatt; Neue Deutsche Hefte, various radio stations. *Honour:* Residence - Scholarship, Italy 1989. *Memberships:* Literaturhaus Hamburg; Society for Exile Studies; GEDOK; Association of German Writers. *Address:* Beerenwinkel 5, 20359 Hamburg, Germany.

UFLIAND Vladimir Iosiphovitch, b. 22 Jan 1937, St Petersburg, Russia. Poet; Writer; Playwrighter. m. (2) 22 June 1977, 1 son. *Publications:* Texts; Detailed Anticipation; Rhymed Nonsense. *Contributions to:* Continent; La Pensee Russe; Panorama; Aurora; Solo. *Honours:* Prize of Russian Poetry Foundation. *Memberships:* Union of Russian Authors; Union of St Petersburg Writers; Pen Club Francais. *Address:* Furshtadskaya 23, Ap 18, St Petersburg, 191028 Russia.

UHNAK Dorothy, b. 1933, American. *Appointment:* Detective, NYC Transit Police Department, 1953-67. *Publications:* Policewoman, 1964; The Bait, 1968; The Witness, 1969; The Ledger, 1970; Law and Order, 1973; The Investigation, 1977; False Witness, 1981; Victims, 1985. *Address:* c/o Simon and Schuster Incorporated, 1230 Sixth Avenue, New York, NY 10020, USA.

UHRY Alfred Fox, b. 3 Dec 1936, Atlanta, Georgia, USA. Playwright; Screenwriter. m. Joanna Kellogg, 13 June 1959, 4 daughters. *Education:* BA 1958, Brown University, Providence, Rhode Island. *Publications:* The Rubber Bridegroom, musical comedy, 1975; Mystic Pizza, film, 1987; Driving Miss Daisy, play 1988, film 1989; Rich in Love, film, 1992. *Honours:* Tony Nomination 1975; Politzer Prize for Drama 1988; Outer Critics Circle Award 1988; Writers Guild Award 1989; Academy Award 1989; Nomination for British Academy Award 1990. *Memberships:* President, Dramatlst Guild Foundation 1991-; Dramatist Guild Council 1988- ; Board Member, Dramatists Play Service 1991-. *Literary Agent:* Flora Roberts. *Address:* c/o Flora Roberts Inc, 157 West 57th Street, New York, NY 10019, USA.

UJORANAF (A)llyich. *See:* PAJOR John Joseph.

ULAM Adam Bruno b. 8 Apr 1922, Lwow, Poland. Professor and Director, Russian Research Center, Harvard University. 2 sons. *Education:* AB, Brown University, 1943; PhD, Harvard University, 1947. *Publications:* Stalin: The Man and His Era (revised edition 1989); Expansion and Co-existence, 1968; The Bolsheviks, 1965; The Kirov Affair (novel) 1988; The Unfinished Revolution, 1960; A History of Soviet Russia, 1980. *Contributions to:* Los Angeles Times, New York Times, the international press; Magazines such as Commentary, The New Republic. *Honour:* Honorary LLD, Brown University. *Memberships:* American Philosophical Society; American Academy of Arts and Sciences. *Literary Agent:* Julian Bach. *Address:* Russian Research Center, Harvard University, 1737 Cambridge Street, Cambridge, MA 02138, USA.

ULRICH Betty Garton, b. 28 Oct 1919, Indianapolis, Indiana, USA. Writer. m. Reverend Louis E Ulrich, 5 Jan 1946, 3 sons, 2 daughters. *Education:* BS, Education. *Publications:* Away We Go, 1970; Every Day With God, 1972, re-issued in paper-back, 1980, translated into 4 foreign languages; Rooted in the Sky: A Faith To Cope With Cancer, 1989. *Contributor to:* Co-Founder, associate Editor, Inkling Literary Journal (now known as Writers' Journal); Articles, short stories, poems in over 30 publications including Christian Herald; Eternity; Scope; The Lutheran; Reader's Digest; Redbook; Guideposts, Lighthouse. *Membership:* Wisconsin Regional Writers Association. *Address:* PO Box 265, Stone Lake, WI 54876, USA.

UNCLE JACK. *See:* COWLES Ernest John Robert.

UNDERHILL Charles. *See:* HILL Reginald (Charles).

UNDERWOOD Michael. *See:* EVELYN John Michael.

UNDERWOOD Michael, b. 2 June 1916, Worthing, Sussex, England. Barrister, Government Legal Service. *Education:* MA, University of Oxford. *Publications include:* Over 40 crime novels, 1954-. *Memberships:* Detection Club; Past Chairman, Crime Writers Association. *Address:* 100 Ashdown, Eaton Road, Hove, Sussex BN3 3AR, England.

UNDERWOOD Peter, b. 16 May 1923, Letchworth Garden City, England. Author. m. Joyce Elizabeth Davey, 15 July 1944, 1 son, 1 daughter. *Appointments include:* With J.M. Dent, publishers, over 25 years. Also book reviewer for: Publisher; Books & Bookmen; Two Worlds; Society for Psychical Research; Ghost Club. *Publications include:* Gazetteer of British Ghosts, 1971; Into the Occult, 1972; Host of Hauntings, 1973; Gazetteer of Scottish & Irish Ghosts, 1973; Haunted London, 1973; Ghosts of Borley, with Dr P. Tabori, 1975; Deeper into the Occult, 1975; Vampire's Bedside Companion, 1975; Lives to Remember: Casebook on Reincarnation, with Leonard Wilder, 1975; Dictionary of Supernatural, 1978; Ghosts of Wales, 1978; Hauntings: New Light on 10 Famous Cases, 1977; Ghost Hunter's Handbook, 1980; Complete Book of Dowsing & Divining, 1980; Ghosts of Devon, 1982; Ghosts of Cornwall, 1983; This Haunted Isle: Ghosts & Legends of Britain's Historic Buildings, 1984; Ghost Hunters, 1985; Ghost Hunters Guide, 1987; Queen Victoria's Other World, 1987; Exorcism!, 1990. Also autobiography, No Common Task: Autobiography of a Ghost Hunter, 1983. Biographies, Boris Karloff 1972, Danny La Rue 1974. *Contributions to:* Publisher; Local Government Chronicle; Psychic Researcher; Sunday Times Magazine. *Memberships:* Society of Authors; President, Ghost Club; International PEN; Unitarian Society for Psychical Studies; International Ghost Society. *Literary Agent:* Andrew Hewson, John Johnson Ltd. *Address:* c/o Savage Club, Fitzmaurice Place, Berkeley Square, London W1, England.

UNGER Barbara, b. 2 Oct 1932, New York City, New York, USA. College Professor. m. (1) 2 daughters, (2) Theodore Sakano, 31 July 1986. *Education:* BA, MA, City College of New York. *Appointments:* Professor, Rockland Community College, Suffern, 1969-. *Publications:* Dying for Uncle Ray; Blue Depression Glass; Learning to Foxtrot; Inside the Wind; Basement; The Man Who Burned Money. *Contributions to:* Massachusetts Review; The Nation Beloit Poetry Journal; Midstream; Kansas Quarterly; Carolina Quarterly; Southern Humanities Review. *Honours:* NEH Fellow; National Poetry Award; Goodman Award; Judah Magnes Award; Roberts Writing Award; John Williams Harrative Poetry Award. *Memberships:* AWP; PSA. *Address:* 101 Parkside Drive, Suffern, NY 10901, USA.

UNGER Douglas Arthur, b. 27 June 1952, Moscow, Idaho, USA. Writer, Professor. m. Amy Burk, 10 May 1980, 1 daughter. *Education:* BA, University of Chicago, USA, 1973; MFA, University of Iowa, 1977. *Appointment:* Syracuse University, Associate Professor of Creative Writing. *Publications:* Leaving the Land, 1984; El Yanqui, 1986; The Turkey War, 1988. *Contributions to:* New York Times; LA Times; Vogue; Boston Globe; also to broadcasting. *Honours:* Society of Midland Authors Award, 1984; A.L.A. notable book,

1984; Ernest Hemingway Citation, 1985; Guggenheion Fellowship, 1985; Finalist, Pultizer Prize, 1985. *Literary Agent:* Amanda Urban, I.C.M., New York. *Address:* Department of English, Syracuse University, Syracuse, NY 13244, USA.

UNGER J Marshal, Professor of Japanese. *Education:* AB 1969, AM 1971 University of Chicago, Far Eastern Languages and Civilisations; MA 1973, PhD 1975, Yale University, Linguistics. *Publications:* The Fifth Generation Fallacy: Why Japan is Betting Its Future on Artificial Intelligence, 1987; Sixteen chapters and essays in anthologies including: Language Engineering versus Machine Engineering: A Linguist's view of the Character Input Problem, 1989; Japanese and That Other Altaic Languages?, 1990; Summary Report of the Altaic Panel, 1990; Kanji to arufabetto no yomikaki noryoku, 1990; 21 articles in professional journals; Eight book reviews including: The Phonology of Eighth-Century Japanese, 1981; A History of Writing in Japan, 1991. *Honours:* 8 major postdoctoral grants including support from the Control Data Corporation 1980-82, the Japan Foundation 1985 and the National Museum of Ethnology, Suita, Osaka, Japan 1991. *Memberships:* Chair, Curriculum Guidelines Taskforce; Educational Testing Service Committee of Examiners. *Address:* Department of Hebrew and East Asian Languages and Literatures, University of Maryland, College Park, MD 20742, USA.

UNGER Michael Ronald, b. 8 Dec 1943, Surrey, England. m. Eunice Dickens, 20 Aug 1966, 1 son, 1 daughter (dec). *Appointments:* Editor, Manchester Evening News, Director, Guardian & Manchester Evening News PLC; Trustee, The Scott Trust. *Publication:* The Memoirs of Bridget Hitler. *Address:* 164 Deansgate, Manchester, England.

UNSWORTH Barry Forster, b. 10 Aug 1930, County Durham, England, novelist. *Education:* BA, English Literature, Manchester Univesity, 1948-51. *Appointments:* Arts Council Creative Writing fellowship, Charlotte Mason College, Ambleside, Cumbria, 1978-79; Literary fellow, Universities of Durham and Newcastle, 1982-84; Writer-in-Residence, Liverpool University, 1984-85; Writer-in-Residence, Lund University, Sweden, 1988. *Publications:* Mooncranker's Gift, 1973; Pascali's Island, 1980; Stone Virgin, 1985; Sugar and Rum, 1988; The Partnership, 1966; The Hide, 1970; The Greeks Have A Word For It, 1967; The Big Day, 1976; The Rage of the Vulture, 1983; Sacred Hunger, 1992. *Contributions to:* Numerous magazines and journals. *Honours:* Heinemann Prize, 1973; Joint Winner, Booker Prize, 1992. *Membership:* Fellow, Royal Society of Literature. *Literary Agent:* Giles Gordon, Anthony Sheil Associates. *Address:* Lauranpolku 1 a 35, 01360 Vantaa 36, Finland.

UPDIKE John Hoyer, b. 18 Mar 1932, USA. Writer. m. (1) Mary Pennington 1953, (2) Martha Bernhard, 1977, 2 sons, 2 daughters. *Appointments:* Reporter, New Yorker, 1955-57. *Publications:* The Carpentered Hen, 1958; The Poorhouse Fair, 1959; The Same Door, 1959; Rabbit, Run, 1960; Pigeon Feathers and Other Stories, 1962; The Centaur, 1963; Telephone Poles and Other Poems, 1969; Bech: A Book, 1970; Rabbit Redux, 1972; Museums and Women and Other Stories, 1972; Buchanan Dying, 1974; A Month of Sundays, 1975; Picked up pieces, 1976; Marry Me, 1976; The Coup, 1978; Tossing and Turning, 1978; Problems, 1979; Your Lover Just Called, 1980; Rabbit is Rich, 1981; Bech is Back, 1982; hugging the Shore, 1984; The Year's Best American Short Stories, 1985; Roger's Version, 1986; Trust Me, 1987; S, 1988; Self Consciousness, 1989; Just Looking, 1989; Rabbit at Rest, 1991; Momories of the Ford Administration, 1993. *Honours:* Rosenthal Award, 1960; National Book Award, 1963; O'Henry Story Award, 1967; US National Book Critics Circle Award, 1982, 1984; American Book Award, 1982; Pulitzer Prize, 1982, 1991. *Address:* Beverly Farms, MA 01915, USA.

UPSHALL Helen Ruby, (Helen Beaumont, Susannah Curtis), b. 19 Feb 1926, Bournemouth, England. Author. m. Frederick Upshall, 31 May 1952, 1 son. *Publications:* Tears Won't Set You Free, 1977; Appointment to Remember, 1978; Surgeon, RN, 1979; Doctor's Prize, 1979; Surgeon's Challenge, 1980; Doctor's Decree, 1982; Nurse in Bermuda, 1984; Sister Stephanie's Ward, 1984; Candles for the Surgeon, 1984; Doctor from the Past, 1986; Crusading Consultant, 1987; New England Nurse, 1988; Love Is The Cure, 1988; A House Full Of Women, 1990; The Strawberry Girl, 1993; Under the pen-name of Susannah Curtis: The Monk's Retreat, 1973; Time-honoured Vows, 1985; Inherit the Wind, 1987; The Sad and Happy Years, 1987; Love is my Reason, 1988; Under the pen- name of Helen Beaumont: Whisper to the Waves, 1981; Alpine Passion, 1982. *Contributions to:* My Story Magazine; Serial in Daily Star, 1984; My Weekly; Evening News; Woman's Weekly Library. *Memberships:* Society of Women Writer's and Journalists; Romantic Novelist's Association. *Literary Agent:* Judith Murdoch. *Address:* "Stephanie" 14 Comley Road, Moordown, Bournemouth, Dorset BH9 2ST, England.

UPTON Dell, b. 24 June 1949, USA. Professor. m. Karen Kevorkian, 21 Dec 1982, 1 son, 3 daughters. *Education:* BA History & English 1970, Colgate University; MA American Civilisation 1975, PhD American Civilisation 1980, Brown University. *Appointments:* Assistant Professor, Case Western Reserve University 1982-83; Assistant, Associate, Full Professor, University California at Berkeley 1983-. *Publications:* Holy things and profane: Anglican parish churches in colonial Virginia, 1986; America's architectural roots: ethnic groups that built America, 1986; Common Places: readings in American vernacular architecture, co-author, 1986. *Contributions:* Pattern books and professionalism, in Winterthur Portfolio, 1984; White and black landscapes, in Places, 1985; Architectural history or landscape history?, in Journal of Architectural Education, 1991. *Honours:* Alice Davis Hitchcock book award, 1987; John Hope Franklin publication prize, 1987; Abbott Lowell Cummings prize, 1987; Rachal prize, 1988; Getty Senior Research Grant, 1990; Guggenheim Fellowship, 1990. *Memberships:* Vernacular Architecture Forum, Editor 1979-89; Society of Architectural Historians, Director 1985-88; American Historical Association; American Studies Association; Organisation of American Historians. *Address:* 1910 Sacramento Street, Berkeley, CA 94702, USA.

URE Jean Ann, b. 1 Jan 1943, Caterham, Surrey, England. Writer. m. Leonard Gregory, 12 Aug 1967. *Education:* Webber Douglas Academy of Dramatic Art, 1965-66. *Publications:* See You Thursday, 1981; A Proper Little Nooryeff, 1982; If It Weren't For Sebastian, 1982; Hi There, Supermouse, 1983; The You-Two, 1984; One Green Leaf, 1987; Play Nimrod For Him, 1990; Plague 99, 1989. *Honour:* Lancs Book Award 1989. *Membership:* Society of Authors. *Literary Agent:* Maggie Noach, 21 Redan Street, London W14 0AB. *Address:* 88 Southbridge Road, Croydon CR0 1AF, England.

URIS Leon Marcus, b. 3 Aug 1924, Baltimore, USA. Writer. m. (1) Betty Beck, 1945, 2 sons, 1 daughter, (2) Jill Peabody, 1971. *Publications:* Battle Cry, 1953 (novel and screenplay); The Angry Hills, 1955; Exodus, 1957; Mila, 18, 1960; Gunfight at the OK Corral (screenplay); Armageddon, 1964; Topaz, 1967; QB VII, 1970; Trinity, 1976; Ireland : A Terrible Beauty (with Jill Uris), 1976; The Haj, 1984; with others, Exodus Revisited (Photo Essay), 1959; Mitla Pass, 1989. *Address:* c/o Doubleday Publishing Co. Inc., 245 Park Avenue, NY 11530, USA.

URQUHART Fred(erick Burrows), b. 12 July 1912. Writer. *Appointments:* Reader for a London literary agency, 1947-51, and for MGM 1951-54; London Scout for Walt Disney Productions, 1959-60; Former Reader for Cassell Co and J M Dent & Sons, publishers, London. *Publications:* Time Will Knit, 1938; I Fell for a Sailor and Other Stories, 1940; The Clouds Are Big With Mercy, 1946; Selected Stories 1946; (ed with J Maurice Lindsay) No Scottish Twilight; New Scottish Stories 1947; The Last GI Bride Wore Tartan: A Novella and some short stories 1948; The Year of the Short Corn and Other Stories, 1949; The Ferret Was Abraham's Daughter, 1949; The Last Sister and Other Stories, 1950; Jezebel's Dust, 1951; The Laundry Girl and the Pole: Selected Stories, 1955; (ed) WSC: A Cartoon Biography, 1955; (ed) Great True War Adventures, 1956; (ed) Scottish Short Stories, 1957; (ed) Men at War: The Best War Stories of All Time, 1957; (ed) Great True Escape Stories, 1958; (ed) The Cassell Miscellany, 1848-1958, 1958; Scotland in Colour, 1961; The Dying Stallion and Other Stories, 1967; The Ploughing Match and Other Stories, 1968; (co-ed) Modern Scottish Short Stories, 1978; Palace of Green Days, 1979; Proud Lady in a Cage, 1980; A Diver in China Seas and Other Stories, 1980; (ed) The Book of Horses, 1981; Seven Ghosts in Search, 1983; Full Score, 1989. *Address:* Spring Garden Cottage, Fairwarp, Uckfield, Sussex, England.

URQUHART Jane, b. 21 June 1949, Canada. Writer. m. (1) Paul Brian Keele, 6 Jan 1969, (2) Tony Urquhart, 5 May 1976, 1 daughter. *Education:* BA, University Guelph, Canada. *Appointments:* Writer in Residence: University of Ottawa, Ottawa, Canada, 1990; Memorial University, St John's, Newfoundland, 1992. *Publications:* The Whirlpool, 1986; Storm Glass, 1987; Changing Heaven, 1990; also: False Shuffles, 1982; The Little Flowers of Madame de Montespan, 1984; Forthcoming: Away (novel). *Contributions to:* Brick Magazine; The Globe and Mail Book Pages; Quill and Quire; Malahat Review. *Honour:* Short listed for Seal First Novel Award, Le Prix de Meilleur Livre Étranger, France, 1992. *Memberships:* Writer's Union of Canada; PEN International. *Literary Agent:* Ellen Levine Literary Agency, Inc, New York. *Address:* c/o Ellen Levine Literary Agency, 15 East 26th Street, Suite 1801 New York, NY, USA.

URSELI Geoffrey Barry, b. 14 Mar 1943, Moose Jaw, Saskatchewan, Canada. Writer; Editor. m. Barbara Davies, 8 July 1967. *Education:* BA, University of Manitoba, 1965; MA, 1966; PhD, University of London, 1973. *Appointments:* Writer in Residence, Saskatoon Public Library, 1984-85; Winnipeg Public Library, 1989-90; Editor, Grain, 1990. *Publications:* Way Out West; The Look Out Tower; Perdue; Trap Lines; Saskatoon Pie; The Running of the Deer. *Contributions to:* This Magazine; Saturday Night; Canadian Forum; Quarry; Border Crossings; Canadian Fiction magazine; NeWest Review; Western People. *Honours:* Clifford E Lee National Playwriting Award; Special Commendation in Commonwealth Poetry Prize; Books in Canada First Novel Award. *Memberships:* PEN; Writers Union of Canada; Playwright's Union of Canada; Saskatchewan Writers Guild; Sk Playwrights Centre. *Address:* c/o Coteau Books, 401-2206 Dewdney Avenue, Regina, Saskatchewan, Canada S4R 1H3.

USCHUK Pamela Marie, b. 10 June 1948, Lansing, Michigan, USA. Poet; Professor. m. William Pitt Root, 6 Nov 1987. *Education:* BA, English cum laude, Central Michigan University, 1970; MFA, Fiction and Poetry, University of Montana, 1986. *Publications:* Light From Dead Years, 1981; Loving The Outlaw, 1984; Meditations Beside Kootenai Creek, 1985; Waiting For Rain 1987; Without Birds, Without Flowers, Without Trees, 1991. *Contributions to:* Various journals. *Honours:* Recipient of numerous honours and awards for professional services including: Ascent Poetry Award, 1989; Flume Press Chapbook Competition, 1990; The Iris Poetry Prize, 1991; The King's English Poetry Prize, 1991. *Memberships:* Associated Writing Programs, 1986-; Poets and Writers, 1987-; Native American Languages Institute, 1985. *Address:* 274 Red Mills Road, Wallkill, New York, NY 12589, USA.

USHAKOVA Elena. *See:* **NEVZGLIADOVA Elena Vseuolodovna.**

USHER George, b. 15 Mar 1930. Clerk in Holy Orders. m. Margaret Helen Dillon, 24 Aug 1957, 2 sons, 2 daughters. *Education:* BSc (Wales), 1951; DipAgricSc (Cantab), 1952; DTA (Trin), 1953. *Publications:* GCE Model Answers - Biology O Level, 1962; Text Book of Practical Biology, 1965; Dictionary of Botany, 1966; An Introduction to Viruses, 1970; Dictionary of Plants Used by Man, 1974; Human and Social Biology, 1977; GCE Model Answers - Biology A Level, 1978; Chemistry for O Level, 1980; Objective Tests in Certificate Biology, 1981; Dictionary of the Christian Church, in press; Dictionary of Hymns, Their Tunes and Sources, in preparation. *Address:* St Mary's Rectory, Credenhill, Hereford HR4 7DL, England.

USHERWOOD Elizabeth Ada, b. 10 July 1923. Author. m. Stephen Dean Usherwood, 24 Oct 1970. *Publications:* Visit Some London Catholic Churches, 1982; The Counter-Armada 1596, 1983; We Die for the Old Religion, 1987; Women First, 1989; A Saint In The Family, 1992. *Contributions to:* The Universe; Catholic Herald; other papers and periodicles. *Address:* 24 St Mary's Grove, London N1 2NT, England.

USTINOV Peter (Sir), b. 16 Apr 1921, London, England. Actor; Producer; Director; Novelist; Playwright. m. (3) Hélene Du Lau D'Allemans, 1972, 1 daughter by 1st marriage, 1 son, 2 daughters by 2nd marriage. *Education:* London Theatre School. *Publications:* Novels: The Disinformer, 1989; The Old Man and Mr Smith, 1990. Plays include: Romanoff and Juliet, 1956; Photo Finish, 1962; The Life in My Hands, 1964; Half Way Up the Tree, 1967; Overheard, 1981; Beethoven's Tenth, 1983; Dear Me, Autobiography, 1977; My Russia, non-fiction, 1983; Ustinov in Russia, non.fiction, 1987; Films include: The Way Ahead (with Eric Ambler), 1942-43; School for Secrets, 1946; Vice Versa, 1947; Privat Angelo, 1949; Romanoff and Juliett, 1961; Billy Budd (in collaboration with DeWitt Bodeen), 1962-63; The Lady L (with Carlo Ponti), 1964; Hot Millions (in collaboration with Ira Wallach), 1968; Memed, My Hawk, 1982; The French Revolution, 1989; Ustinov at-Large (compilation of articles in The European), 1991. *Contributions to:* various magazines and journals. *Honours:* New York Drama Critics Award, 1953; Evening Standard Award, 1957; Benjamin Franklin Medal, Royal Society of Arts, 1957; Honorary Doctor of Music, Cleveland Institute of Music, 1967; Rector, University of Dundee, 1968, Honorary Doctor of Law, 1969; Honorary Doctor of Laws, La Salle College, Philadelphia, 1971; Hon. Doctor of Letters, University of Lancaster, 1972; Rector, University of Dundee, 1971-73; CBE, 1975; UNICEF Award, 1978; Prix De La Butte, 1979; Variety Club of Gt. Britain Best Actor, 1979; Honorary Doctorate, University of Toronto, 1984; Commandeur Des Arts et Des Lettres, 1985; Order of Istiglal, 1987; Order of the Yugoslav Flag; Elected to Academy of Fine Arts, 1988; Hon Dc, Humane Letters, Georgetown University, Washington DC, 1988; Knighted, 1990; Gold Medal of the City of Athens, 1990; Medal of the Greek Red Cross, 1990; Honorary Doctorate of Laws, University of Ottawa, 1991; Medal of honour, Charles University, Prague, 1991; Honorary Dcotorate of Letters, University of Durham, 1992; Chancellor, University of Durham, 1992; President, World Federalist Movement, 1992; Britannia Award, British Academy of Film and Television Arts, Los Angeles Branch, 1992. *Address:* c/o William Morris Agency UK, 31-32 Soho Square, London W1V 5DG, England.

UTLEY Robert Marshall, b. 31 Oct 1929, Bauxite, Arkansas, USA. Historian. m. (1) Lucille Dorsey, 5 May 1956, 2 sons, (2) Melody Webb, 12 Nov 1980. *Education:* BA, Purdue University, 1951; MA, Indiana University, 1952. *Publications:* Custer and the Great Controversy, 1962; The Last Days of the Sioux Nation, 1963; Frontiersmen in Blue: The US Army and the Indian 1846-65, 1967; Frontier Regulars: The US Army and the Indian 1866-91, 1973; The American Heritage History of the Indian Wars (with Wilcomb Washburn), 1977; The Indian Frontier of the American West, 1846-91, 1984; High Noon in Lincoln: Violence on the Western Frontier, 1987; Cavalier in Buckskin: George Armstrong

Custer and the Western Military Frontier, 1988; Billy the Kid: A Short and Violent Life, 1989. *Honours:* Buffalo Award for Last Days of the Sioux Nation, New York Westerners, 1964; Wrangler Award for High Noon in Lincoln, 1988, Wrangler Award for Cavalier in Buckskin, 1989, National Cowboy Hall of Fame; Western History Association Prize for Distinguished Published Writings, 1988; Honorary LittD, Purdue University, 1974, University of New Mexico, 1976, Indiana University, 1983. *Membership:* Western History Association, President 1967-68. *Literary Agent:* Carl Brandt. *Address:* PO Box 744, Dripping Springs, TX 78620, USA.

UTTAMCHANDANISUNDRI ASSANDAS Sugni-Sundri, b. 28 Sept 1924, Pakistan. Writer. m. 14 Nov 1947, 2 daughters. *Education:* BA, Benares University; MA, Karvey University, Bombay. *Publications:* Kirandar Devaroon, 1953; Preetpurani-Reet Nivali, 1956; Five short Story Collections, 1965-85; Amar Sade Piya; Nai Sabhiyta jo darshan; Bharat Rus Ba Bahheli, 1975; Radio Dramas; short stories. *Contributions to:* Nai Duniya; Hindwas; Alka; Moomal. *Honours:* 1st Prize, Short Story Competitions, 1952, 1954, 1960; 1st Prize, for Novel, 1962; Government of India's Prize; Recipient, many other honours and awards. *Memberships:* President, Literary Sessions, Akhil Bharat Sindhi Sohidya Sancha, 1970; Founder, President, Sindhu Nari Sabha and Sindha Bal Mandir, 1966-. *Address:* B9 Floreana, miraway Society, Sitladevi Road, Malin, Bombay 40016, India.

V

VACHASPATI. See: **BHARATI S.**

VACHSS Andrew Henry b. 19 Oct 1942, New York City, New York, USA. Attorney at Law, Consultant, Writer. *Education:* BA, Case Western Reserve University, 1965; JD, magna cum laude, New England School of Law, 1975. *Appointments include:* Director, Libra Inc, Massachusetts, 1971; Deputy-Director, Medfield-Norfolk Prison Project, Massachusetts, 1971-72; Director, Intensive Treatment Unit (ANDROS II) Massachusetts, 1972-73; Project Director, Department of Youth Services, Massachusetts, 1972-73; Planner Analyst, Crime Control Co-ordinator's Office, New York, 1974-75; Director, Advocacy Associates, New York and New Jersey, 1973-75; Director, Juvenile Justice Planning Project, New York City, 1975-85; Adjunct Professor, College of New Resources, New York City, 1980-81; Attorney, Private Practice, New York City, 1976-; Numerous consultancy appointments. *Publications:* Non-fiction: The Life-Style Violent Juvenile: The Secure Treatment Approach, 1979; The Child Abuse-Delinquency Connection - A Lawyer's View, 1989. Novels: Flood, DIF 1986, Pocketbooks 1986; Strega, 1987, NAL 1988; Blue Belle, 1988, NAL 1990; Hard Candy, 1989, NAL 1990; Blossom, 1990, Ivy, 1991; Sacrifice, 1991, Ivy 1992; Shella, 1993; Short Stories: Warlord, New Mystery 1, 1991; Anytime I Want, Invitation to Murder, 1992; Born Bad, Ellery Queen's Mystery Magazine, 1992; Stone Magic, Narrow Houses, 1992. *Contributions to:* Numerous articles and short stories contributed to magazines and anthologies. *Honours:* The Grand Prix de Litterature Policiere, 1988 for Strega; The Falcon Award, 1988, Maltese Falcon Society of Japan for Strega; The Deutschen Krimi Preis 1989 for Flood. *Memberships:* PEN American Centre; National Association of Counsel for Children; American Society of Criminology; American Professional Society on the Abuse of Children. *Address:* 299 Broadway, Suite 1803, New York City, NY 10007, USA.

VAFOPOULOS George Thomas, b. 6 Sept 1903, Gevgeli, former Yugoslavia. Creative Writer; Librarian. m. Anastasia Yera Copoulou, 2 Sept 1946. *Education:* Mathematics, University of Athens 1922-26; Philosophy and Literature, Aristotelian University of Thessaloniki, Greece 1927-30. *Appointments:* Editor, literary periodical Macedonian Letters 1922-24; General Secretary, Thessaloniki City Council 1932-38; Founder and Director, Municipal Library of Thessaloniki 1938-63. *Publications:* 12 volumes poetry including: The New Satiric Exercises, 1975; The Sequel, 1977; Poems, 1978; The End, 1985; Complete Poems, 1990; 5 volumes essays including: The Theatre 1924-74, 1988; The Legend of Byron, 1988; Plays: Esther; The Awakening, 1990; Short Story, Annika's violin, 1989; 5 volumes of autobiography, 1970-91. *Honours:* First State Prize for poetry 1966; Poetry Prize of Athens Academy 1972; Honorary award bestowed by the City of Thessaloniki for entire literary work 1980; Corresponding member of the Athens Academy 1980; Together with wife Anastasia, awarded honorary diploma and the City Silver medal for their creation of Vafopoulio Cultural Centre 1983; Gold Medal awarded by Institute of Macedonian Studies 1985; Honorary Doctorate of School of Philosophy of the Aristotelian University of Thessaloniki 1988. *Memberships:* National Association of Greek Writers; Association of Thessaloniki Literary Writers; Institute of Macedonian Studies; Member and Secretary of Board, Northern Greece State Theatre 1964-67. *Hobbies:* World literature; Philosophy; Theatre; Classical music; Travelling. *Address:* 21 Megalou Alexandrou Avenue, 54640 Thessaloniki, Greece.

VAIL Peter, b. 29 Sept 1949, Riga, USSR. Essayist; Critic; Journalist. m. Elvira Tseytlin, 15 Sept 1991. *Education:* Moscow Polygraphical Institute, Diploma Editor 1976. *Appointments:* Editor, Sovetskaya Molodezh, Riga 1974-77; Editor, Novor Russuoge Slovo, New York 1978-80; Editor, Novy Americanets, New York 1980-83; Seven Days, New York 1983-87; Editor, Radio Liberty 1988-. *Publications:* Co-Author: Russian Prose Today, 1982; Paradise Lost, Self Portrait of Russian Emigration, 1983; Russian Cuisine in Exile, 1987; 60's, The World of Russian People, 1987; Russian Speech, 1990; Americana, 1992. *Contributions to:* Many publications. *Membership:* AAASS, American Association of Advanced Slavic Studies. *Address:* 461 Ft Washington Avenue 5, New York, NY 10033, USA.

VAISHAMPAYAN A, (Suman), b. 11 Jan 1954, Muzaffarpur, India. Associate Professor Genetics. m. Dr Mrs Anupama Sahay, 21 Nov 1979, 3 daughters. *Education:* MSc First Class in Botany 1974; PhD Botany 1978, Banaras Hindu University, India; Special training abroad, University of Maryland, USA, on Preservation of Genetically Engineered Microorganisms 1988. *Appointments:* Widely lectured and published in Standard Scientific World Conferences in Genetics, Microbiology, Physiology, Biochemistry, Phycology and Biological Nitrogen Fixation in a number of Universities and Research Laboratories in USA, UK, Thailand and elsewhere 1978-. *Publications:* Genetic dissections in cyanobacteria; Molecular biology of Azolla-Anabaena symbiosis; Cyanobacteria: a gene bank for herbicide-resistance; Genetics of nitrogen fixation and its regulation; Pesticides in relation to the nitrogen-fixing apparatus; Genetics engineering for the nitrogen fixation genes; Genetic recombination for pesticide-resistance markers in cyanobacteria; Cyanobacteria as a bio N fertilizer. *Contributions to:* Over 100 substantial research papers and review articles in leading most World Journals of Biological Sciences in USA, UK, Japan, Egypt, Australia; Widely referred and cited in Journals like Nature and Science. *Honours:* Recipient of financial assistance under the Indian National Science Academy-Young Scientist Category for deliberations in USA and UK in 1988; Recipient of a large number of Research Fellowships and Associateships from all top rank Government agencies in India, including Scientist A and B Awards of the University Grabts Commission, India. *Memberships:* International Union of Biological Sciences, Paris; Indian Society of Genetics and Plant Breeding; Environmental Mutagen Society of India, BARC, Bombay; Secretary, Genetics Club, Banaras Hindu University; Association Young Scientists in India; Association Microbiologists in India; World Federation for Culture Collections: Microbial Gene Pool, England; Associated with All-India Co-ordinated Project on Biological Nitrogen Fixation, ICAR, Government of India. *Address:* Department of Genetics and Plant Breeding, Institute of Agricultural Sciences, Banaras Hindu University, Varanasi-221005, India.

VAIZEY Alandra Marina (Lady), b. 16 Jan 1938, Art Critic, m. Lord Vaizey, 1961, (dec 1984), 2 sons, 1 daughter. *Education:* BA, Medieval History and Literature, Harvard University, USA; BA, MA, Girton College, Cambridge University, England. *Appointments:* Art Critic, Financial Times, 1970- 74; Dance Critic, Now!, 1979-81; Member, Arts Council, 1976-78, Art Panel, 1973-78, deputy chairman, 1976-78; Advisory Committee, DoE, 1975-81; Paintings for hospitals, 1974-; Committee, Contemporary Art Society, 1975-79, 1980-; History of Art and Complementary Studies Board, CNAA, 1978-82; Photography Board, CNAA, 1979-81; Fine Art Board, CNAA, 1980-83; Passenger Services Subcommittee, Heathrow Airport, 1979-83; Fine Arts Advisory Committee, British Council, 1987-; Trustee, National Museums and Galleries on Merseyside, 1986-; Trustee, Geffrye Museum, London 1990-; Executive Director, Mitchell Prize for the History of Art, 1976-87; Editorial Director, National Art Collections Fund, 1991-. *Publications:* 100 Masterpieces of Art, 1979; Andrew Wyeth, 1980; The Artist as Photographer, 1982; Peter Blake, 1985; Christo, 1990. *Contributions to:* Contribuor of articles in periodicals, anthologies, exhibition catalogues. *Memberships:* Governor, Camberwell College of Arts and Crafts, 1971-82; Bath Academy of Art, Corsham, 1979-81; Crafts Council, 1988-. *Address:* 24 Heathfield Terrace, London W4 4JE, England.

VAL. *See:* WILLIS Valerie Joan.

VALDAR Colin Gordon, b. 18 Dec 1918, England. Journalist; Consultant Editor. m. (1) Evelyn Margaret Barriff, 1940 (div), 2 sons, (2) Jill Davis. *Appointments include:* Freelance journalist, 1936-39; Successively production editor, features editor, assistant editor, Sunday Pictorial, 1942-46; Features editor 1946-51, assistant editor 1951-53, Daily Express; Editor, Sunday Pictorial, 1953-59; Editor, Daily Sketch, 1959-62; Director, Sunday Pictorial Newspapers Ltd, 1957-59; Director, Daily Sketch & Daily Graphic Ltd, 1959-62; Chairman, Bouverie Publishing Company, 1964-83. Founded UK Press Gazette, 1965. *Address:* 2A Ratcliffe Wharf, 18-22 Narrow Street, London E14 8DQ, England.

VALEK Miroslav, b. 17 July 1927, Trnava, Czechoslovakia. Poet; Politician. *Education:* College of Economics, Bratislava. *Appointments Include:* Minister of Culture, Slovak Socialist Republic, 1969-; Deputy Chair, Slovak Central Committee, Czechoslovak-Soviet Friendship Society, 1969-82; Member, Central Committee, President, National Front, 1971-76; member, Central Committee, Comunist Party of Czechoslovakia, 1971-; Deputy Slovak National Council, 1976. *Publications:* Collections of poems, selected articles, and interviews, translations of Russian, French and Polish Poetry. *Honours:* Klement Gottwald State Prize, 1966; Bedrich Smetana Medal, 1974; Title Artist of Merit, 1975; National Artist, 1977; Order of Labour, 1977; Literary Prize, Sofia 1983, Bulgaria, 1984. *Address:* Communist Party of Czechoslovakia, Nabr. Ludvika Svobody 12, Prague, Czechoslovakia.

VALENCAK Hannelore, b. 23 Jan 1929, Donawitz, Austria. Writer. m. (2) Viktor Mayer, 28 Apr 1962, 1 son. *Education:* PhD, Physics, University of Graz, Styria, Austria. *Publications:* Novels: Die Hohlen Noahs, 1961; Ein Fremder Garten, 1964, 1970; Zuflucht hinter der Zeit, 1967, 1977; Vohof der Wirklichkeit, 1972; Das magische Tagebuch, 1981; various short stories, poetry & books for young people. *Contributions to:* Neue Deutsche Hefte; Literatur und Kritik; Dimension, USA; others. *Honours:* National Advancement Award, 1957; Peter Rosegger Prize, Styrian Regional Government, 1966; Austrian Children's Book Prize, 1977; Amade Prize, Monaco, 1978; various other awards. *Memberships:* Austrian PEN Club; Austrian Writers Union; Styrian Writers Union; Podium. *Address:* Schwarzspanierstrasse 15/2/8, A-1090 Vienna, Austria.

VALENSTEIN Elliot S, b. 9 Dec 1923. Psychologist; Neuroscientist. m. Thelma Lewis, 15 June 1947, 2 sons. *Education:* BS 1949, Citu University of New York; MA 1952, PhD 1954, University of Kansas. *Publications:* Brain Control, 1973; Brain Stimulation and Motivation, 1973; The Psychosurgery Debate, 1980; Great and Desperate Cures, 1986; 150 articles in professional journals; 30 book chapters. *Contributions to:* Michigan Quarterly; Science; Psychology Today; Brain Research; and others. *Honours:* Award for Outstanding Achievement in published works; Elected Foreign Member of the Academy of Science of Mexico; Kenneth Craik Research Award, Cambridge University; Outstanding Achievement in Psychology, City University of New York; Phi Beta Kappa. *Memberships:* International Brain Research Organisation; American Psychological Association; American Psychological Society; Society for Neurosciences. *Address:* Neuroscience Laboratory, 1103 E Huron, University of Michigan, Ann Arbor, MI 48109, USA.

VALENTINE Alec. *See:* ISAACS Alan.

VALENTINE James William, b. 10 Nov 1926, California, USA. Professor; Author. m. Diane Mondragon, 16 Mar 1988. *Education:* BA 1951, Philipps University, Enid, Oklahoma; MA 1954, PhD 1958, UCLA, Los Angeles. *Publications:* Evolutionary Palaeocology of the Marine Environment, 1973; Evolution, 1977;

Evolving, 1979; Phanerozoic Diversity Patterns, 1985, editor. *Contributions to:* Over 200 scientific articles. *Memberships:* National Academy of Sciences; American Academy of Arts and Sciences, Fellow; Paleontological Society, President 1974-75. *Address:* 1351 Glendale Avenue, Berkeley, CA 94708, USA.

VALERIO Anthony, b. 13 May 1940, USA. Author. 1 son, 2 daughters. *Education:* BA, Columbia College, 1962. *Appointments:* Book Editor, Major Publishing Houses, 1966-72; Instructor of writing, 1986-88. *Publications:* Bart; Valentino and the Great Italians; The Mediterranean Runs Through Brooklyn. *Contributions to:* Paris Review; Philadelphia Magazine; Patterson Review; Anthologies; Dream Streets. *Memberships:* PEN. *Literary Agent:* Susan Zeckendorf, New York City. *Address:* 106 Charles Street, 14, New York, NY 120014, USA.

VALERY Anne, b. 24 Feb 1926, London, England. Writer. *Education:* Badminton School, Bristol. *Appointments:* Lecturer on writing for television, Royal Television Society, London 1980s; Guest Lecturer, Avon Foundation 1990s. *Publications:* Bar on Von Kodak, Shirley Temple and Me; The Edge of a Smile, 1980s; Talking About the War, 1991; Theatre: Passing Out Parade, Greenwich Theatre, London, published by French; Over 50 television plays including award winning Tenko. *Contributions to:* The Radio Times; The Observer. *Honours:* Baron Von Kodak, Shirley Temple and Me, book of the month, Telegraph Supplement; Tenko, runner up in best series of the year. *Memberships:* PEN; Executive Committee, The Writers Guild of Great Britain, Chair Censorship Committee. *Literary Agent:* Linda Seifert Associates. *Address:* 5 Abbot's Place, London NW6 4NP, England.

VALERY Dawn. *See:* LOWE-WATSON Dawn.

VALGARDSON William Dempsey, b. 7 May 1939, Winnipeg, Canada. Writer; Professor. div, 1 son, 1 daughter. *Education:* BA, United College, 1961; BEd, University of Manitoba, 1966; MFA, University of Iowa, 1969. *Appointments:* Associate Professor, 1970-74; Professor, University of Victoria, 1974-. *Publications:* Bloodflowers; God Is Not A Fish; Gentle Sinners; What Cant Bechanged ShoudInt be Mourned; The Girl with the Buttichelli Face; Red Dust; The Carpenter of Dreams; In The Gutting Shed. *Contributions to:* The Saturday Evening Post; Readers Digest; TV Guide; The Globe and Mail; The Time Colonist; EnRoute. *Honours:* Presidents Medal; First Prize CBC Annual Literary Competition; First Novel Award; CAA Silver Medal. *Memberships:* CACLALS; ACTRA; The Writers Union of Canada; PWAC. *Literary Agent:* Denise Bukowski. *Address:* 1908 Waterloo Road, Victoria, BC, Canada V8P 1J3.

VALIN Jonathan (Louis), b. 1947, American. *Appointments:* Lecturer in English, University of Cincinnati, 1974-76, Washington University, 1976-79; Freelance Writer, 1979-. *Publications:* The Lime Pit, Final Notice, 1980; Dead Letter, 1981; Day of Wrath, 1982; Natural Causes, 1983; Life's Work, 1986; Fire Lake, 1987. *Address:* C/o Dominick Abel Literacy Agency, 498 West End Avenue, New York, NY 10024, USA.

VALLBONA (Rothe) de Rima Gretchen, b. 15 Mar 1931, San José, Costa Rica. Professor; Author. m. Carlos Vallbona, 26 Dec 1956, 1 son, 3 daughters. *Education:* BA, BS, Colegio Superior de Senoritas, San Jose, 1948; MA, University of Costa Rica, 1962; DML, Middlebury College, 1981. *Appointments:* Professor, Hispanic Literature, Liceo J.J. Vargas Calvo, Costa Rica, 1955-56, University of St Thomas, Houston, 1964-; Member, Editorial Board: Letras Femeninas, 1975-; Alba de America, 1981-, Foro Literario, 1979-; Co-Director, Foro, 1984-89; Contributing Editor, The America's Review, 1989-. *Publications:* Noche en vela, 1968; Polvo del camino, 1971; Yolanda Oreamuno, 1972; la obra en prosa de Eunice Odio, 1981; Mujeres y agonias, 1982;

Las sombras que perseguimos, 1983; La Salamandra rosada, 1979; Cosecha de pecadores, 1988; El aréngel del perdón, 1990; Mundo demonio y mujer, 1991; Los infiernos de la mujer y algo mas, 1992; Vida i sucesos de la Morja Alférez, 1992. *Contributions to:* Articles, poems & short stories in Spanish, French, English and Portuguese in various professional journals and magazines. *Honours:* Aquileo J. Echeverria Costa Rican Novel Prize, 1968; Agripina Montes del Valle Novel Prize, Colombia, 1978; Jorge Luis Borges Short Story Prize, Argentina, 1977; Literary Award, Southwest Conference of Latin American Studies, 1982; Ancora Literary award, Costa Rica, 1984; El Lazo de la Dama de la Orden del Mérito Civil, condecorated by His Royal Majesty D Juan King Carlos I of Spain, 1988; Cullen Foundation Professor of Spainsh, 1989. *Memberships:* Comunidad de Escritores Latinoamericanos de Costa Rica; Asociacion de Literatura Femenina Hispanica; National Writrs Club; Cultural Sectrary, Instituto Literario y Cultural Hispanico; and others. *Agent:* Dr Nick Kanellos, Arte Publico Pres. *Address:* University of St Thomas, 3800 Montrose Blvd., Houston, TX 77006, USA.

VALTINOS Thanassis, b. 16 Dec 1932, Arcadia, Greece. Writer; Screenplay Writer. 1 daughter. *Education:* Cinematography Studies, Athens, 1950-53. *Publications:* The Book of the Days of Andreas Kordopatis, 1972; The Descent of the Nine, 1978; Three Greek One-Act Plays, a novel, 1978; Deep Blue Almost Black, 1985; Data on the Decade of the Sixties, 1989; Woodcock Feathers, 1992; You Will Find My Bones in the Rain, 1992. *Contributions to:* I Lexi, Greece; To Thendro, Greece; Akzente, Germany; Le Monde, France; To Tram, Greece; Shenandoah, USA; Meanjin, Australia. *Honours:* Screen Play Prize, Cannes Film Festival, 1984; Greek State Prize for Literature, 1989. *Memberships:* President, Greek Society of Writers; International Theatre Institute; Greek Society of Playwrights; The European Academy of Science and Arts (Academia Scientiarum et Artium Europaea). *Address:* Astydamantos 66-68, Athens 11634, Greece.

VAMOS Miklos, b. 29 Jan 1950, Budapest, Hungary. Writer. m. Judit Pataki, 5 Nov 1972, 1 daughter. *Education:* Law degree 1975. *Publications:* Somebody Else, stories, 1981; Sing a Song, novel, 1983; Protest Song, novel, 1986; Oy, novel, 1988; The New York-Budapest Subway, novel, 1993; Several full length plays and scripts of Hungarian films. *Contributions to:* Columnist of Elet Es Irodalom 1989-; Correspondent to The Nation, weekly, USA. *Honours:* Award of the Hungarian Youth Association, 1983; Award of the Critics, 1984, 1977; Jozsef Attica Award, 1984. *Memberships:* PEN Club; Hungarian Writers' Association; Hungarian Journalists' Association. *Literary Agent:* Artisjus, Budapest. *Address:* Pozsonyi ut 38, BP 1137, Hungary.

VAN CAMP Gaston, b. 5 Feb 1939, Beerzel, Belgium. Teacher; Writer. m. (1) 1963, (2) Marie-José Reynders, 1989, 4 sons, 3 daughters. *Publications:* Ik Ben Harry Van De Achterbuurt; De Kracht Van Marrakesh; Tot Aan De brug Naar Nergens; Kruismoordraasel; Grafikos. *Address:* Houwstraat 12, B-2580 Putte, Belgium.

VAN COTT Laurence. *See:* NIVEN Larry.

VAN DE LAAR Waltherus Antonius Bernardinus, (Victor Vroomkoning), b. 6 Oct 1938, Boxtel, Netherlands. Teacher; Poet. m. Inge Gorris, 22 Jan 1968, 1 son, 1 daughter. *Education:* Master's degree, Dutch Linguistics and Literature, 1978. *Appointments:* Contact publishing house, Amsterdam, 1966-67; Teacher, Interstudie teacher's training college, Arnhem, 1977-83; Co-Writer, Kritisch Literatuur Lexicon reference book for literature, 1981-. *Publications:* De einders tegemoet, 1983; De laatste dingen, 1983; Circuit des souvenirs, 1984; Klein museum, 1987; Groesbeek, Tijdrit, 1989; Echo van een echo, 1990; Oud zeer, 1993. *Contributions to:* Avenue; Bzzlletin; Tirade; De Tweede Ronde; Maatstaf; Preludium; Parmentier; Dietsche

Warande and Belfort; Yang; Kreatief; Poeziekrant; Nieuw Wereldtijdschrift. *Honours:* Pablo Neruda Prize, 1983. *Memberships:* Lira; Former Member, Literair Cafe Nijmegen. *Address:* Aldenhof 70-17, 6537 DZ Nijmegen, Netherlands.

VAN DE POL Lotte Constance, b. 11 May 1949, Enschede, Netherlands. Historian. m. Egmond Elbers, 15 Mar 1985, 2 daughters. *Education:* MA History and English 1977, University of Amsterdam. *Appointments:* Teacher of History, Hervormd Lyceum, Amsterdam 1977-78; Rijks Pedagogische Academie (Teacher Training College), Amersfoort 1977-81; Research Fellow, Department of History, Erasmus University, Rotterdam 1982-88. *Publications:* Books: Daar was laatst een meisje loos. Nederlandse vrouwen als matrozen en soldaten. Een historisch onderzoek, co-author, 1981; F. L. Kersteman, De Bredasche Heldinne, co-author, 1988; The tradition of female transvestism in early modern Europe, co-author, 1989; Vrouwen in mannenkleren. De geschiedenis van een tegendraadse traditie. Europa 1500-1800, co-author, 1989, 2nd ed 1991; Frauen in Mannerkleidern. Weibliche Transvestiten und ihre Geschichte, co-author, 1990; Several articles in professional journals including: Republican heroines: cross-dressing women in the French Revolutionary armies, co-author, 1989; Women and political culture in the Dutch Revolutions 1780-1800, co-author, 1990. *Address:* Jan van Scorelstraat 127, 3583 CM Utrecht, The Netherlands.

VAN DER POST Laurens Jan, (Sir) b. 13 Dec 1906, Philippolis, South Africa. Writer; Explorer. m. (1) Marjorie Wendt 1929, div 1947, 1 son (dec), 1 daughter, (2) Ingaret Giffard 1949. *Publications:* In a Province, 1934; Venture to the Interior, A Bar of Shadow, 1952; The Face Beside the Fire, 1953; Flamingo Feather, The Dark Eye in Africa, 1955; The Lost World of the Kalahari, 1958; The Heart of the Hunter, 1961; The Seed and the Sower, 1962; Journey into Russia, 1964; A Portrait of All the Russias, 1967; The Hunter and the Whale, 1967; A Portrait of Japan, 1968; The Night of the New Moon, 1970; A Story Like the Wind, 1972; A Far Off Place, 1974; A Mantis Carol, 1975; Jung and the Story of our Time, 1976; First Catch Your Eland : A Taste of Africa, 1977; Yet Being Someone Other, 1982; Testament to the Bushmen (with Jane Taylor), 1984; A Walk with a White Bushman : Laurens van der Post in Conversation with Jean-Marc Pottiez, 1986; About Blady, 1991.

VAN DER VAT Dan, b. 28 Oct 1939, Alkmaar, The Netherlands. Author & Journalist. m. Christine Mary Ellis, 1962, 2 daughters. *Education:* BA, honours, Classics, University of Durham, England, 1960. *Appointments:* The Journals, Newcastle Upon Tyne, 1960; Daily Mail, 1963; The Sunday Times, 1965; The Times, 1967, including ten years as foreign correspondent; The Guardian, 1982-88, Chief Foreign Leader-Writer; Full-time author, 1988-. *Publications:* The Grand Scuttle, 1982; The Last Corsair, 1983; Gentlemen of War, 1984; The Ship That Changed the World, 1985; The Atlantic Campaign, 1939-1945, 1988; The Pacific Campaign, 1941-45, 1991; Freedom was Never like This: a winter's journey in east Germany, 1991. *Contributions to:* Newspapers, magazines, radio and TV. *Honours:* Best First Work Award, Yorkshire Post, 1982; Best Book of the Sea Award, 1983, King George's Fund for Sailors, 1983. *Memberships:* Society of Authors; London Library. *Literary Agent:* Michael Shaw, Curtis Brown, 162 Regent Street, London W1R 5TA. *Address:* c/o Curtis Brown, 162 Regent Street, London W1R 5TA, England.

VAN DER WEE Herman, b. 10 July 1928, Lier. Professor of Social and Economic History. m. Monique Verbreyt, 27 Feb 1954, 1 son, 1 daughter. *Education:* BA Philosophy 1949, LLD 1950, Licentiaat Political and Social Sciences (MA status) 1951, Doctor in Historical Sciences 1963, KU Leuven, Belgium; Graduate Studies, Sorbonne, Paris, France and London School of Economics, UK. *Publications:* Prix et salaires, Manuel méthodologique, 1956; The Growth of the Antwerp market and the European Economy (14th-16th centuries), 3 vol, 1963; La Banque Nationale de Belgique et la politique monétaire entre les deux guerres, 1975; Prosperity and Upheaval, The World Economy, 1945-1980, 1987, several translations; Histoire economique mondiale, 1945-1990, 1991; Banking in Europe (Middle Ages-Early Modern and Modern Times), 1992. *Contributions to:* Annales (Economies, Sociétés, Civilisations); Vierteljahrschrift fur Sozial-und Wirtschaftsgeschichte; The Business History Review; The Economic History Review; Journal of European Economic History; Bijdragen tot de Geschiedenis. *Honours:* De Stassart Prize for national history (1961-1967) of the Royal Academy of Belgium, 1968; Fulbright-Hayes Award, 1975, 1981; Quinquennial Solvay prize for the Social Sciences (1976-1980) by the National Foundation of Scientific Research of Belgium, 1981; Amsterdam Prize for the Historical Sciences by the Royal Academy of the Netherlands, 1992. *Memberships:* Foundation Member of Academia Europeae (Cambridge, Great Britain) and Member of the Council 1987-90; Chairman of the Advisory Council of the West European Programme at the Wilson International Centre for Scholars, Washington DC 1986-; President, Advisory Council of Leuven Institute for Central and East European Studies; President of Board of Trustees of Leuven University Press, 1990-; President, International Economic History Association 1986-90; Royal Academy of Belgium, Class of Arts 1972-; Corresponding Fellow, British Academy and Royal Academy of the Netherlands; External Member of Research Council of European University Institute of Florence. *Address:* Centrum voor Economische Stüdien, E Van Evenstraat 2B, 3000 Leuven, Belgium.

VAN DINE Alan Charles, b. 12 Jan 1933, Ford City, Pennsylvania, USA. Writer; Consultant; Advertising Executive. m. (1) 2 sons, 2 daughters, (2) Holly Shefler Van Dine, 23 Apr 1977. *Education:* BA, Duquesne University, Pittsburgh, Pennsylvania, 1955; Postgraduate courses, University of Pittsburgh, Pennsylvania, 1968-71. *Appointments:* Editor, East Liberty Tribune, 1955; Editor, Mt Lebanon News, 1956-58; Editorial Director, Pittsburgh Suburban Newspaper Group, 1958-61; Associate Creative Director, BBD&O International, 1961-70; President, Van Dine Horton Advertising, 1971-89; Member, Advisory Council, International Poetry Forum, 1969-80; Chairman, Van Dine, Humphrey Advertising Agency, Pittsburgh, Pennsylvania. *Publications:* Can You Imagine, children's book, 1967; Moth Meats, poetry, 1970; Unconventional Builders, book on architecture, 1977; The Encyclopedia of Advertising, satire, 1987. Included in anthologies: The Bedside Phoenix Nest, 1965; Reading Writing Workshop, textbook, 1968. *Contributions to:* Numerous magazines including: Saturday Review (essays and verses); McCall's; Parents' Magazine (articles); Family Digest; Pennsylvania Illustrated. *Honours:* Numerous awards, New York Art Directors Society and Business and Professional Advertising Association, 1964-. *Memberships:* Advisory Council, International Poetry Forum, 1969-80; American Association of Advertising Agencies; Pittsburgh Advertising Management Association. *Address:* 322 Boulevard of the Allies, Pittsburgh, PA 15222, USA.

VAN DYK Wilmer Gerald, (Jere), b. 14 Dec 1945, Vancouver, Washington, USA. Writer; Journalist. *Education:* BS Political Sciences, University of Oregon; L'Institut d'Etudes Politiques, Paris (CEP). *Publications:* Runners Guide to Europe, 1979; In Afghanistan, 1983; Long Journey of the Brahmaputran, 1988; Long Journey of the Pacific Salmon, 1990; Travel in the Rain Forest, 1990; Growing Up in East Harlem, 1990. *Honour:* Politzer Prize nomination 1981-82, New York Times Series, 6- part, on Afghanistan. *Address:* 301 East 63rd Street, New York, NY 10021, USA.

VAN HELLER Marcus. *See:* **ZACHARY Hugh.**

VAN NOORD Frits. *See:* **DROSTE Flip G.**

VAN OVER Raymond, b. 29 June 1934, Inwood, Long Island, New York, USA. Writer. Appointments: Editor, Garret/Helix Press, 1962-65; International Journal of Parapsychology, 1965-1968; Film, Story editor, 20th Century Fox, Columbia Pics, 1968-72; Book Reviewer, Book of the Month Club, 1970-71; Staff writer, Governor Nelson Rockefeller's Commission to Preserve the Adirondacks, 1972-72. *Publications include:* Explorer of the Mind, 1967; I Ching, 1971; A Treasury of Chinese Literature, 1972; Psychology and Extrasensory Perception, 1972; Unfinished Man, 1972; The Chinese Mystics, 1973; Taoist Tales, 1973; Eastern Mysticism, 2 volumes, 1977; Total Meditation, 1973; Sun Songs, 1980; Ecstasy: The Perilous Journey; Smearing the Ghost's Face with Ink, 1983; Monsters You Never Heard of, 1983; Screenwriter, documentaries, 1983; Khomeini, A Biography, 1985; Crack in the Well, 1988; The Burial Ground, 1988; The Twelfth Child, 1990; Whisper, 1991; In A Father's Rage, 1991. *Contributions to:* Various journals & magazines. *Memberships:* Author's Guild; United Nations, NGO, Global Education Motivators; Voting Member American Society for Psychical Research. *Literary Agent:* Elizabeth Backman & Co. *Address:* 2905 Rittenhouse Street, NW, Washington, DC 20015, USA.

VAN SCYOC Sydney Joyce, b. 27 July 1939, Mt. Vernon, Indiana, USA. Writer. m. Jim R Van Scyoc, 23 June 1957, 1 son, 1 daughter. *Education:* Colleges in Florida, Hawaii, & California. *Publications:* Saltflower, 1971; Assignment: Nor'Dyren, 1973; Starmother, 1976; Cloudcry, 1977; Sunwaifs, 1981; Dark Child, 1982; Blue Song, 1983; Star Silk, 1984; Downtide, 1987; Feather Stroke, 1988. *Contributions to:* numerous short fiction to Galaxy; If; Worlds of Tomorrow; Fantasy & Science Fiction; Analog; Asimov's Magazine. *Address:* 2636 East Ave., Hayward, CA 94541, USA.

VAN STEENBERGHEN Fernand, b. 13 Feb 1904, Brussels. Catholic Priest; Honorary Professor, University of Louvain. *Education:* Dr Philosophy 1923, Baccalaureate in Theology 1928, Mathe-Agrege en Philosophie 1931, Louvain. *Publications:* Dieu cache, 1966, English translation, Hidden God, 1966; Aristotle in the West, 2nd ed 1970; Le Thomisme, 1983, 2nd ed 1992; Philosophie fondamentale, 2nd ed 1991; Etudes philosophiques, 3rd ed 1991; Etudes religieuses, 1991; La philosophie au XIIIe siecle, 2nd ed 1991. *Contributions to:* Revue Philosophique de Louvain. *Honours:* Docteur h.c. University of Salzburg, Austria 1972, University of Washington, The Catholic University of America, 1978; Aquinas Medal, 1978. *Memberships:* Société Philosophique de Louvain; Société Internationale pour l'Etude de la Philosophie Médiévale. *Address:* Rue Vanderborght, 205, B-1090 Brussels, Belgium.

VAN VEGHEL Lawrence, b. 28 July 1947. Writer; Compressor Engineering Tech. *Education:* Milwaukee Institute of Technology, 1969. *Appointments:* Wisconsin Editor, 1975; Contributing Writer, Badger Sportsman, 1975; Field Editor, Wood & Waters, 1983; Media Director, Wisconsin Counci of Sport Fishing Organizations, 1989. *Publications:* Over 800. *Contributions to:* The Milwaukee Journal; Above the Bridge; Outdoor Beacon; Midwest Outdoors; Badger Sportsman; Walleye Magazine; Outdoors Unlimited. *Memberships:* Outdoor Writers Association of America; Association of great Lakes Outdoor Writers; Wisconsin Regional Writers Association; Wisconson Fishing Club, Secretary; Wisconsin Outdoor Communicators Association; Writer's Ink, Vice-President; Raconteurs, Inc, board member; National Writers Club. *Address:* 5557 So, Disch Avenue, Cudahy, WI 53110, USA.

VANCAENEGHEM Stef, b. 15 Feb 1950, Gent, Belgium. Reporter. m. Lieve Devacht, 12 May 1973, 2 sons, 1 daughter. *Appointments:* Reporter, Belgium Business Magazine, 1970-73; Spectator Magazine, 1974-84; Het volk, 1985-. *Publications:* Zonde Van Nini; Bal Masque; Madame Valentine; een En Al Begeerte. *Contributions to:* TV; Radio; Newspaper Het Volk.

Literary Agent: Manteau, Isabeela Li 76, Belgium. *Address:* Broeckestraat 116, 9600 Ronse, Belgium.

VANCE Eugene, b. 14 Apr 1934, Cambridge, Massachusetts, USA. Writer. m. Christie McDonald, 11 June 1965 (div June 1985) 2 sons. *Education:* BA, Dartmouth College, 1957; MA, 1958, PhD 1964, Cornell University. *Appointments:* Instructor 1962-66, Assistant Professor of English and French, 1966-69, Yale University, New Haven, Connecticut; Associate Professor 1969-75, Professor of Comparative Literature, 1975-84, Chairperson of Program or Comparative Literature, 1969-74, Universite de Montreal, Montreal, Quebec; Professor of French and Comparative Literature, 1984-, Director of Program of Comparative Literature, 1985-, member of Classical Studies Program and Literature and Religion Program, Emory University, Atlanta, Georgia; Visiting Professor to numerous universities in Canada, USA, Israel, Italy, South Africa, Switzerland. *Publications:* Reading the Song of Roland, 1970; (Editor)Language as Action, 1970; (Editor with Lucie Brind'Amour) Archeologie du signe (The Archeology of the Sign) 1983; Marvelous Signals: Poetics and Sign Theory in the Middle Ages, 1986; From Tropic to Tale: Logic and Narrativity in the Middle Ages, 1987; Principal editor of monograph series. *Contributions to:* many edited volumes. *Honours:* Morse fellow at Yale University, 1966-67; Fellow of Canada Council at Oxford University, 1974-75; Fellow of Social Science and Humanities Research Council of Canada, 1981-82; Research fellow, Newberry Library, 1989. *Memberships:* Modern Language Association of America; Medieval Academy; Canadian Association of Comparative Literature; Societe Rencesvals. *Address:* 447 Emory Drive, Atlanta, GA 30307, USA.

VANCE Jack. *See:* **VANCE John Holbrook.**

VANCE John Holbrook (Peter Held, Jack Holbrook, John Holbrook, Jack Vance, Alan Wade), b. 1916, USA. Author. *Appointments:* Scriptwriter for Captain Video programme. *Publications:* The Dying Earth, 1950; The Space Pirate, 1953, as The Five Gold Bands, 1963; Vandals of the Void, 1953; To Live Forever, 1956; Isle of Peril (as Alan Wade), 1957; Big Planet, 1959; Slaves of the Klau, 1959; Take My Face (as Peter Held), 1959; The Man in the Cage, 1960; The Dragon Masters, 1963; Demon Prince Series: The Star King, The Killing Machine, The Palace of Love, The Face, The Book of Dreams, 1963-81; The Houses of Iszm, 1964; Son of the Tree, 1964; Future Tense, 1964; Monsters in Orbit, 1965; The World Between, and Other Stories, 1965; The Blue World, 1966; The Brains of Earth, 1966; The Languages of Pao, 1966; Many Worlds of Magnus Ridolph, 1966; Eye of the Overworld, 1966; The Fox Valley Murders, 1966; The Pleasant Grove Murders, 1967; The Last Castle, 1967; Planet of Adventure No 1: City of the Church, 1968; The Deadly Isles, 1969; Planet of Adventure No 2: The Servants of the Wankh, 1969; Eight Fantasms and Magics: A Science Fiction Adventure, 1969; Planet of Adventure No 3: The Dirdir, 1969; Emphyrio, 1969; Planet of Adventure No 4: The Pnume, 1970; The Durdane Trilogy: The Anome, The Brave Free Men, The Asutra, 1973-74; The Alastor Series: Trullion 2262, Marune 933, Wyst 1716, 1973-78; Bad Ronald, 1973; The Worlds of Jack Vance, 1976; Green Magic, 1979; The House on Lily Street, 1979; The View from Chickweed's Window, 1979; Lyonesse I, 1983; Cugel's Saga, 1983; Rhialto the Marvellous, 1984; Lyonesse II: The Green Pearl, 1985; The Cadwal Chronicles I: Araminta Station, 1987. *Address:* 6383 Valley View Road, Oakland, CA 94611, USA.

VANCE William L, b. 19 Apr 1934. Educator; Writer. *Education:* AB 1956, Oberlin College, Ohio; MA English Language and Literature 1957, PhD English Language and Literature 1962, University of Michigan, Ann Arbor. *Appointments:* Boston University, Assistant Professor of English 1962-67, Associate Professor of English 1967-73, Professor of English 1973-. *Publications:* America's Rome, vol 1: Classical Rome, 1989; America's Rome, vol 2: Catholicism and Contemporary Rome, 1989; American Literature, 2 vols, co-editor, 1970; The

Faber Book of America, co-editor, 1992; Immaginari a confronto, co-editor, 1993. *Contributions to:* Numerous contributions to scholarly journals and to exhibition catalogues. *Honours:* Senior Writing Prize, Oberlin's, 1956; Ralph Waldo Emerson (Phi Beta Kappa) Prize, 1990; Association of American Publishing Prize, 1989; John Simon Guggenheim Fellowship, 1990-91; National Book Critic's Circle Award Nomination, 1990; LLD (Hon) University of South Dakota, 1992. *Membership:* American Literature Section of Modern Language Association of America. *Address:* 255 Beacon Street, Boston, MA 02116, USA.

VANDERBILT Arthur T II b. 20 Feb 1950. Attorney. *Education:* BA, Wesleyan Unviersity, 1972; Juris Doctor, University of Virginia School of Law, 1975. *Publications:* Fortunes Children: The Fall of the House of Vanderbilt, 1989; Treasure Week: The Fortunes and Fate of the Pirate Ship Whydah, 1986; Law School: Briefing for a Legal Education, 1981; Changing Law: A Biography of Arthur T. Vanderbilt, 1976. *Honour:* Scribes Award, 1976. *Memberships:* Authors Guild; National Writers Union. *Literary Agent:* Robert Lescher, Lescher and Lescher Ltd., *Address:* 67 Irvins Place, New York, NY 10003, USA.

VANDERHAAR Gerard A, b. 15 Aug 1931, Louisville, Kentucky, USA. Professor. m. Janice Marie Searles, 22 Dec 1969. *Education:* BA 1954, Providence College; STD 1965, University of St Thomas, Rome. *Appointments:* Taught on faculties of St John's University, New York 1964-65, Providence College 1965-68, Wesleyan University 1968-69, Christian Brothers University 1971-. *Publications:* A New Vision and a New Will for Memphis, 1974; Christians and Nonviolence in the Nuclear Age, 1982; Enemies and How to Love Them, 1985; Way of Peace: A Guide to Nonviolence, Co-Editor, 1987; The Philippines: Agony and Hope, Co-Author, 1989; Active Nonviolence: A Way of Personal Peace, 1990; Booklets: Nonviolence, Theory and Practice, 1980; Nonviolence in Christian Tradition, 1983. *Contributions to:* Articles in Encyclopaedia of World Biography; Fellowship; Cross Currents; The Wesleyan Public Affairs Review; Pax Christi; The Encyclopaedic Dictionary of Religion; Pro Mundi Vita; and others. *Honours:* Outstanding Educators of America, 1971; Distinguished Service Award, United Nations Association, 1981; Catholic Press Association Book Award for Spirituality, 1991. *Memberships:* American Academy of Religion; American Association of University Professors; Pax Christi; National Conference of Christians and Jews; Fellowship of Reconciliation; War Resisters League. *Address:* Christian Brothers University, 650 East Parkway South, Memphis, TN 38104, USA.

VANDERHAEGHE Guy Clarence, b. 5 Apr 1951, Esterhazy, Canada. Writer. m. Margaret Elizabeth Nagel, 2 Sept 1972. *Education:* BA, 1971; BA, Hons.Dip, 1972; MA, 1975; BEd, 1978. *Appointments:* Writer- in-Residence, Saskatoon Public Library, 1983-84; Writer-in-Residence, University of Ottawa, 1985; Visiting Professor, Creative Writing, University of Ottawa, 1985-86. *Publications:* Man Descending, 1982; The Trouble with Heroes, 1983; My Present Age, 1984. *Contributor to:* London Magazine; London Review of Books; Fiction Magazine; Saturday Night. *Honours:* Annual Contributor's Prize, Canadian Fiction Magazine, 1980; Governor-General's Prize for Fiction, Canada, 1982; Geoffrey Faber Memorial Prize, Britain, 1987. *Memberships:* Writers Union of Canada; Saskatchwan Writers' Guild; Authors Guild of America. *Literary Agent:* Curtis Brown. *Address:* c/o Writers' Union of Canada, 24 Ryerson Avenue, Toronto, Ontario, Canada M5T 2P3.

VANDIEVOET Jacques F G. *See:* **ORIOL Jacques.**

VANDIVER Frank Everson, b. 9 Dec 1925, Austin, Texas, USA. Director, Defense Studies Institute, Texas A&M University. m. (1) Carol Sue Smith (dec 1979), 1 son, 2 daughters, (2) Renée Aubry, 21 Mar 1980. *Education:* MA, University of Texas, 1949; PhD, Tulane

University, 1951; MA by Decree, Oxford University, 1963; DH, Austin College (Hon) 1977; DHL, Lincoln College (Hon), 1989. *Appointments:* Harmsworth Professor, Oxford University, 1963-64; Acting President, Rice University, 1969-70; Visiting Professor, Military History, US Military Academy, 1973-74; President, North Texas State University, 1980-81; President, Texas A & M University, 1981-88. *Publications include:* Ploughshares into Swords: Josiah Gorgas & Confederate Ordnance, 1952; Rebel Brass; The Confederate Command System, 1956; Mighty Stonewall, 1957; Jubal's Raid: General Early's Famous Attack on Washington in 1864, 1960; Fields of Glory: A Pictorial Narrative of American Wars, 1960; Basic History of the Confederacy, 1962; John J.Pershing, 1967; Their Tattered Flags: The Epic of the Confederacy, 1970; Black Jack: The Life & Times of John J.Pershing, 1977. Editor: Civil War Diary of General Josiah Gorgas, 1947; Confederate Blockade-Running Through Bermuda, 1981-1865, 1947; Proceedings, Congress of the Confederate States of America, 3 volumes, 1953, 1959; Joseph E.Johnston's Narrative of Military Operations, 1959; Jubal A.Early's War Memoirs, 1960; The Idea of the South, 1964; Blood Brothers; A Short History of the Civil War, 1992. *Contributions to:* Books: The American Tragedy: Civil War in Retrospect, 1959; Lincoln for the Ages, 1960; American People's Encyclopaedia, 1952; Encyclopaedia Americana, 1960, 1963, 1967; Encyclopaedia Britannica, 1963; Encyclopaedia of World Biography, 1972; Numerous historical journals, reviews. *Honours include:* Carr P.Collins Prize, Texas Institute of Letters, 1958; Harry S.Truman Award, Kansas City Civil War Round Table, 1966; Jefferson Davis Award, Confederate Memorial Literary Society, 1971; Fletcher Pratt Award, New York Civil War Round Table, 1971; Regent's Award, Lincoln Academy, Illinois, 1973; George R.Brown Award, Rice University, 1985, 1978; Fulbright- Hays Lectureship, Italy, Council for International Exchange of Scholars, 1976, 1979; Finalist, National Book Awards, 1978; Best Book Award, non-fiction, Editors of Texas Books in Review, 1978; Americanism Award, Sons of American Revolution, 1974. Numerous fellowships, grants. *Memberships:* Offices, various educational & historical associations. *Address:* PO Box 10600, College Station, TX 77842-0600, USA.

VANE Brett. *See:* **KENT Athur.**

VANSITTART Peter, b. 1920, British. *Publications:* I Am the World, 1942; Enemies, 1947; The Overseer, 1949; Broken Canes, 1950; A Verdict of Treason, 1952; A Little Madness, 1953; The Game and the Ground, 1956; Orders of Chivalry, 1958; The Tournament, 1959; A Sort of Forgetting, 1960; Carolina, 1961; Sources of Unrest, 1962; The Friends of God, 1963; The Siege, The Lost Lands, 1964; The Dark Tower, 1965; The Shadow Land, 1967; The Story Teller, 1968; Green Knights Black Angels, Pastimes of a Red Summer, 1969; Landlord, 1970; Vladivostok: Figures in Laughter, 1972; Marlborough House School, Worlds and Underworlds, 1974; Quintet, 1976; Lancelot, Flakes of History, 1978; Harry, The Death of Robin Hood, 1980; Voices from the Great War, 1981; Three Six Seven, 1982; Voices 1870-1914, John Masefield's Letters from the Front, 1984; Aspects of Feeling, Paths from a White Horse, The Ancient Mariner and the Old Sailor, 1985; Happy & Glorious, 1987; Parsifal, 1988; Voices of the Revolution, 1989; The Wall, 1990; A Choice of Murder, 1992; London, 1992. *Memberships:* F.R.S.L. *Literary Agent:* Anthony Sheil. *Address:* 9 Upper Park Road, Hampstead, London NW3, England.

VAPURU. *See:* **PASZKOWSKI Kazimierz Jan.**

VARDRE Leslie. *See:* **DAVIES Leslie Purnell.**

VARE Ethlie Ann, b. 8 Mar 1953, Montreal. Journalist; Author. 1 son. *Education:* BA World Literature 1972, University of California at Santa Barbara. *Appointments:* Columnist, United Media 1980-90; Exec Editor, Rock 1983-86; Pop Editor, Goldmine

1984-85; Cont Ed, RTZ Countdown 1990-92. *Publications:* Stevie Nicks, 1985; Ozzy Osbourne, 1986; Mothers of Invention, 1988; Adventurous Spirit, 1992. *Contributions to:* Hollywood Reporter; Billboard; NY Times; Elle; others. *Honours:* Western Magazine Publishers Maggie Award for Editorial Content, Rock Magazine, 1984; American Library Association Award, Best Books for Young Adults, Mothers of Invention, 1988. *Membership:* Los Angeles Women in Music, Past President. *Literary Agent:* Madeleine Morel, books; Leslie Kallen, screenplays. *Address:* 8306 Wilshire Boulevard 6005, Beverly Hills, CA 90211, USA.

VARIA Radu, b. 21 May 1940, Iassy, Romania. Art Historian; Author. *Education:* Literature and Aesthetics 1964, University of Bucharest; PhD in Art History, University of Paris. *Appointments:* President, The Constantin Brancusi International Foundation, New York 1991. *Publications:* Brancusi, New York 1986, Paris 1989; Tokyo, 1993. *Honour:* The Romanian Academy Award, 1991. *Address:* 350 E 57. Suite 8A, New York, NY 10022, USA.

VARNEY Philip Allen, b. 3 Dec 1943, Evanston, Illinois, USA. Author. 1 daughter. *Education:* BEd 1965, MEd 1971, University of Arizona. *Publications:* Arizona's Best Ghost Towns, 1980; New Mexico's Best Ghost Towns, 1987; Southern California's Best Ghost Towns, 1990; Bike Tours in Southern Arizona, 1991. *Contributions to:* Arizona Highways Magazine. *Address:* 4764 E 10th Street, Tucson, AZ 85711, USA.

VARVERIS Yannis, b, 25 Nov 1955. Writer. m. 6 Oct 1982, 1 son. *Education:* University of Athens; Sorbonne III, Paris. *Publications:* In Imagination and Reason; The Leak; Invalids of War; Death Extends; Bottoms Piano. *Contributions to:* Numerous. *Memberships:* society of Writers; Greek Union of Theatrical Critics; Greek ITI. *Address:* 51 Omirou Str, 10672 Athens, Greece.

VAS DIAS Robert, b. 19 Jan 1931, London, England. Writer. m. divorced, 1 son. *Education:* BA, Honours, Grinnell College, Iowa; Graduate Study, Columbia University, New York. *Appointments:* Director, Aspen Writers' Workshop, Aspen, Colorado, 1964-67; Poet-in-Residence, Thomas Jefferson College, Allendale, Michigan, 1971-74; Editor, Publisher, Permanent Press, 1972-; General Secretary, Poetry Society, and Director, National Poetry Centre, London, 1975-78; Joint Editor, Ninth Decade (International Literary Journal), 1983-; Contributing Editor, High Plains Literary Review; Adviser, Contemporary Poets. *Publications:* Editor: Inside Outer Space: New Poems of the Space Age, 1970; Speech Acts and Happenings, poems, 1972; Making Faces, poems, 1975; Poems Beginning: The World, 1979. *Contributions to:* Chelsea; Choice; Encounter; Maps; Mulch; The Nation; The New Yorker; Partisan Review; Poetry (Chicago); Poetry Review; Stony Brook; Sumac; American Book Review; Margin; Oasis. *Honours:* CAPS Fellowship in Poetry, New York State Council on Arts, 1975; C. Day Lewis Fellowship in Poetry, Greater London Arts Association, 1980. *Address:* 5 B Compton Avenue, Canonbury, London N1 2XD, England.

VASILIU Emanuel, b. 7 Sept 1929, Chisinau, Moldova. Professor General Linguistics and Romanian. m. Maria-Laura Stoka, 1 Aug 1952. *Education:* Graduate of Faculty of Philology 1952, PhD 1956, Doctor Docent 1969, Bucharest University. *Appointments:* Lecturer at Faculty of Philology 1956, Associate Professor 1968, Full Professor, Faculty of Romanian Language and Literature 1970, Bucharest University; Researcher 1951-53, Scientific Secretary 1956-60, Institute of Linguistics of Romanian Academy; Researcher, Centre for Phonetic and Dialectal Researches 1960-65; Dean of Faculty of Letters of Bucharest University 1990-92; Director, Al Rosetti Institute of Phonetics and Dialectology, Romanian Academy 1990-. *Publications include:* Romanian Phonology, 1965; Historical Phonology of the Dacoromanian Dialects, 1968; The

Transformational Syntax of Romanian, co-author, 1972; Outline of a Semantic Theory of Kernel Sentences, 1972; Logic Preliminaries to the Semantics of Compound Sentences, 1978; Meaning, Analyticity, Knowledge, 1984; Introduction to Text Theory, 1990; Introduction to Language Theory, 1992. *Contributions to:* Studies and papers published in Romanian and foreign journals. *Honours:* State Award, Second Class, 1953; B P Hasdeu Award of the Romanian Academy, 1960. *Memberships:* Correspondent Member 1991, Full Member 1992, Romanian Academy; International Permanent Committee of Linguists (CIPL) 1977-87; Societas Linguistica Europaea, 1976-80 Nominations Committee; International Pragmatic Association , member of the Consultative Committee 1985-; Romanian Society of Romance Linguistics; Romanian Society of Linguistics; International Association of Phonetic Sciences. *Address:* Intrarea Lucaci 3, 74111 Bucharest, Romanian.

VASSILIADES-ROKOU Mapia, b. 25 Mar 1931, Chios, Greece. Housewife, Writer. m. George, 7 Dec 1951. 1 son, 1 daughter. *Education:* High School. *Publications:* Feelings and Thoughts, 1989; Stalagmites, 1990; Unfailing Friendship (poems), 1990; Immortal Memories, Wise Proverbs (stories), 1991; Mosaics and Bruches, 1992. *Contributions to:* NEA Skepsi; Psara; Chiaki; Filologiki Epitheorisi; Akropolis; Eleftheros; Eleftheri Ora; Chiaki Foni; Proodos; Chiakos Laos. *Honours:* Prize, Poetic Games Delfi (PEL) 1st Poetry Prize; 2nd Novel Prize (PEL) 1989; 2nd Poetry Prize, Pneumatikis Estias Moschatou, 1989; 1st Prize Poetry PEL 1990; 1st Poetry Prize Cultural Agency, Johannesburg, 1990-; 1st Prize, Literary Society Parnassos, for Mosaics and Bruches, 1992. *Membership:* PEL (Panellinia Enosi Logotechnon). *Literary Agent:* Cultural Agency, Johannesburg. *Address:* 17 Anastasaki Street, 157-72, Zografou, Athens, Greece.

VAUGHN Phoebe Juanita Fitzgerald, b. 9 Mar 1939, Portsmouth, Virginia, USA. Licensed Pratical Nurse; Greyhound Fancier; Lyricist; Poet. m. 8 Dec 1956, 2 sons. *Education:* Practical Nurse graduate, 1962 (M M Washington) Miami-Dade Community College, 1979-84 (medically related subjects) no degree. *Publications:* World of Poetry Anthology, 1981, 82, 87. 88. 89; The National Library of Poetry Anthology, 1987; The North American Poetry Review, 1986; American Poetry Association 1986; The Cambridge Collection Anthology 1987; Chapel Recording Co & gospel Recording Co, 1986, 87 and 88; Sunrise Recording Company, 1988 & 1989, and others. *Honours:* 1983-90 Honorable Mentions, World of Poetry; 1987-90 Golden Poet Award, World of Poetry; 1988 Exceptional Artistry and Creativity Award, Library of Poetry; 1986 Lyricist Award for Merit (Talent and Associated Companies). *Memberships:* National Writers Club, Aurora, Colorado; National Greyhound Association, Abilene, Kansas; Cultural Alliance of Greater Washington, DC; Song Writers Association of Washington; National Writers Club, Aurora, Colorado. *Address:* P O Box 7268 Silver Spring, MD 20907, USA.

VAZQUEZ DIAZ Rene, b. 7 Sept 1952, Caibarien, Cuba. Writer; Translator. *Education:* Degree, Polish Language, University of Lodz, Poland; Degree, Swedish Language, University of Lund, Sweden. *Appointment:* Review Writer, Swedish Journal, Sydsvenska Dagbladet. *Publications:* Trovador Americano, poems, 1978; La Precocidad de los Tiempos, short stories, 1982; Tambor de Medianoche, poems, 1983; La Era Imaginaria, novel, 1986; translations, several Swedish books into Spanish. *Contributions to:* In Sweden: (Journals) Sydsvendska Dagladet; (Magazines) Bonniers Litterara Magazine; Artes, Fenix, Rallarros; Bra Lyrik; Attiotal; In Spain: Hora de Poesia. *Honours:* Fellowships from Swedish Union of Writers, 1980, 1982, 1983, 1984-89. *Memberships:* Swedish Union of Writers; Swedish Pen Club. *Address:* Albert Bonniers Forlag, Box 3159, 103-63 Stockholm, Sweden.

VEGE Nageswara Rao, b. 18 Jan 1932, Peda

Avutapalli, India. Physician and Surgeon. *Education:* BA, Economics, Andhra University, Nellore, India; MD, Medicine and Surgery, Parma University, Italy. *Publications:* Poetry: Life and Love, 1965; The Light of Asoka, foreword by Bertrand Russell, 1970; Peace and Love, 1981; Socialism (drama), 1983; Poetry in Italian: Aurora, 1961; Pace e Vita, 1963; Santi Priya, 1966; Sorrisi e Lacrime, 1970; Il Canto dell'Universo, 1979; A-Z dell'Amore, 1981; Pace e Amore, 1981; Templi trascurati, 1983; Socialismo, 1985; Amare l'Amore, 1989; The Best of Vege, 1992, Editions Best-Seller; 100 Opinions of Great Men on Life, 1992, Editions Best-Seller, 1992. *Contributions to:* International Herald Tribune; Indian Express; Paris France; Epoca; Espresso; Various English and Italian newspapers, Milan, Paris and Rome. *Honours:* Member, Imperial Academy of San Cirillo, Rome; Member, Tiberian Academy, Rome; Member, Academy of San Marco, Naples; Member, Citta di Boretto Academy, Italy; Member, Accademia d'Europa; Member, Burchhardt Academy; Gold Medal, National Competition of Poetry, Bergamo, Italy; Gold Plaque, Poet of the Year, World Peace Foundation, Rome; Gold Medal, Diploma of Award, International Competition of Poetry, Columbian Trophy, St Louis, USA, 1980; Il Grifone, Rapallo, 1980; Guiseppe Ungaretti Award, Rome, 1982; Oscar Mondiale, 1982; Grand Prix Mediterranee, European Parliament, 1982; Galilei Award, Italy, 1983; Schiller Award, Zurich, Switzerland, 1985; Greenwood Poetry Forum Award, Washington DC, USA, 1985; Fraternita nell'Arte, Livorno, 1987; Gold Medal Natale Agropolese, Italy, 1988; Italian Republic President Award, 1990; La Ballata Award, Liverno, 1991; Guiseppe Ungaretti Award, Napoli, 1991; San Valentino Award, Terni, Italy, 1991; Viareggio Award, 1992. *Memberships:* International PEN Club; World Doctors Writers Association; Italian Writers Association; Swiss Writers Association; Scrittori della Svizzera Italiana; Founder President of the World Culture Organization. *Address:* 6516 Gerra Piano-Ti, Switzerland.

VEIGL Ferdinand, (Svetloslav Veigl), b. 24 Dec 1915, Hornany, Slovakia. Roman Catholic Priest. *Education:* Religious Faculty, 1940; Philosophical Faculty, 1945; PhD, 1946. *Appointments:* Poet, 1938. *Publications:* Cestami Vetrov; Vystup na horu Tábor; Kvety na troskách; Volanie z dialky; Láska Smrt; Pred ruzou stojim nemy; Jemu Jediné; Hladanie Svetla; Zlatý Klúc. *Contributions to:* Slovenske Pohlady; Romboid; Literarn tyzdennik; Katolicke Noviny; Box. *Memberships:* Directorales Membership of Slovakian Writers Union. *Address:* 925 24 Kralova, Pri senci, Slovakia.

VEIGL Svetloslav. *See:* **VEIGL Ferdinard.**

VENDLER Helen (Hennessy), b. 1933, American. *Appointments:* Instructor, Cornell University, Ithaca, NY, 1960-63; Lecturer, Swarthmore College and Haverford College, Pennsylvania, 1963-64; Assistant Professor, Smith College, Northampton, 1964-66; Associate Professor 1966-68, Professor 1968-85, Boston University; Kenan Professor of English, Harvard University, Cambridge, MA, 1985-; Porter University Professor, 1990-. *Publications:* Yeats's Vision and the Later Plays, 1963; On Extended Wings: Wallace Stevens' Longer Poems, 1969; The Poetry of George Herbert, 1975; Part of Nature, Part of Us: Modern American Poets, 1981; The Odes of John Keats, 1983; Wallace Stevens: Words Chosen Out of Desire, 1984; The Harvard Book of Contemporary American Poetry (ed), 1986; The Music of What Happens, 1988. *Honours:* ACLS, Guggenheim and NEH Fellowships. *Memberships:* MLA, President, 1980; American Academy of Arts and Sciences, Vice President, 1992-. *Address:* Department of English, Harvard University, Cambridge, MA 02138, USA.

VERDUIN John Richard, Jr, b. 6 July 1931, Muskegon, Michigan, USA. University Professor. m. Janet M. Falk, 26 Jan 1963, 1 son, 1 daughter. *Education:* BS, Science, University of Albuquerque, 1954; MA, Education Administration, 1959, PhD, Curriculum, 1962, Michigan State University.

Publications: Cooperative Curriculum Improvement, 1967; Conceptual Models in Teacher Education, 1967; Adults Teaching Adults, 1977; The Adult Educator, 1979; Curriculum Building for Adult Learning, 1980; The Lifelong Learning Experience, 1986; Adults and Their Leisure, 1984; Handbook for Differential Education for the Gifted, 1986; Differentielle Erziehung Besonders Begabter, 1989; Distance Education: The Foundation of Effective Practice, 1991. *Contributions to:* Lifelong Learning; Leisure Quarterly; Gifted Education Press Newsletter; Dialogue on Aging; Science Education; NAPCAE Exchange; Illinois Career Education Journal. *Memberships:* American Association for Supervision and Curriculum Development; IACEA; Phi Delta Kappa. *Address:* 107 North Lark Lane, Carbondale, IL 62901, USA.

VERHELST Peter Roger Arthur Marcel, b. 28 Jan 1962, Brugge, Belgium. m. Katrien Haesaert, 12 July 1986, 1 daughter. *Appointments:* Editor, Dietsche Warande en Belfort. *Publications:* Master; Witte Bloemen; Angel; Obsidiaan; Otto. *Honours:* George Orwell Literatuurprys; Yang Literatuuprys; Paul Sndekprijs. *Address:* s Gravenstraat 54, 9810 Nazareth, Belgium.

VERHENNE Jan Frans, (Bouts Axel), b. 2 May 1938, Belgium. Corporate Vice-President. m. Ghislaine Devos, 23 Mar 1964, 1 son, 1 daughter. *Education includes:* PhD, Chemistry, University of Louvain. *Publications:* Martin en Martins, 1981; De Glazen Deur, 1983; De Derde Dag, 1984; Een Bijzonder Oordeel, 1985; Scherven, 1987; Voor het Geval Dat, 1987; Dood in Arles, 1988; Trits, 1989; Rose de Provence, 1992; Woelwater, 1993. *Honours:* Literary Debut Prize, 1982; West Flanders Literary Award, 1985. *Literary Agent:* Manteau, Antwerp, Belgium. *Address:* Open Veld 16, B-8500 Kortrijk, Belgium.

VERMA Daya Nand, b. 12 Dec 1930, Multan City. Author; Palmist. m. 28 Jan 1951, 1 daughter. *Publications:* Yaun Vyavhar Anusheelan; Zindabad Murdabad; Pashchim Ke Teen Rang; Kam Bhav Ki Nayee Vyakhya; Palmistry Ke Goorh Rahsya; Mansik Saphalta; Hum Sab Aur Voh; Dhyan Yoga; Palmistry Ke anubhoot Prayog. *Contributions to:* Gyanodya; Hamara Mun; Prakashit Man. *Honours:* Literary Award; Honoured Vishva Yoga Conference. *Memberships:* Authors Guild of India; Film Writers Association; Bhartiya Lekhak Sangathan; PEN; Akhil Bhartiya Hindi Prakashak Sangh; Creater Kailash Residents Association. *Address:* W-21 Greater Kailash 1, New Delhi 110048, India.

VERMEIREN Kocn, b. 18 Dec 1953, Antwerp, Belgium. *Education:* Study Germanic Philology, 1978; Doctor of Litterature & Philosophy, 1984. *Appointments:* Teacher, Writers Academy of Antwerp. *Publications:* Hermans and Wittgenstein; De Vrolijke Eenzaamheid; Schaduwen; Dood Spoor; De Droomexpres; De Kus Van Selena; Herr Ludwig; Die geh op de heuvel. *Contributions to:* Numerous. *Honours:* ANV Visser Neerlandia Award; August Beernaert Award. *Address:* Visbeekbaan 32, 2275 Wechelderzande, Belgium.

VERMES Geza, b. 22 June 1924, Mako, Hungary. Professor Emeritus of Jewish Studies, University of Oxford. m. Pamela Curle (nee Hobson), 12 May 1958. *Education:* Universities of Budapest and Louvain, 1945-52; Lic in Oriental History and Philology; DTheol; MA (Oxford); DLitt (Oxford); Honorary D.D. Edinburgh, 1989; Durham, 1990. *Appointments:* Editor, Journal of Jewish Studies, 1971-; Director of the Forum for Qumran Research, Oxford Centre for Hebrew Studies, 1987-. *Publications:* Scripture and Tradition in Judaism, 1961, 1973; The Dead Sea Scrolls in English, 1962, 1975, 1987; Jesus the Jew, 1973, 1981; Postbiblical Jewish Studies, 1975; The Dead Sea Scrolls - Qumran in Perspective, 1977; Jesus and the World of Judaism, 1982; The Religion of Jesus the Jew; Joint editor/reviser, The History of the Jewish People in the Age of Jesus Christ by E Schuerer, 3 vols, 1973-87; Joint author, The Essenes According to the Classical Sources,

1989. *Contributions to:* Journal of Jewish Studies; Journal of Semitic Studies; Jewish Chronicle; The Times; TLS. *Memberships:* Fellow, British Academy; British Association for Jewish Studies, President, 1975, 1988; European Association for Jewish Studies, President 1981-84. *Address:* West Wood Cottage, Foxcombe Lane, Boars Hill, Oxford OX1 5DH, England.

VERMILYA Claire (Szala) b. 12 Dec 1919, Michigan, USA, Cosmetologist, m. Harlan Eugene Vermilya, 29 July 1940, (dec 12 July 1968), 2 sons, 1 daughter (dec). *Education:* Graduate, Alpena Michigan Academy of Cosmetology, 1938; State Board Examinations with honours, State License to practice. *Publication:* Bootlegger's Daughter, Reflections by Claire Vermilya. *Contributions to:* Letters to the Editor. *Memberships:* National Hairdressers and Cosmetologists Association; US Affiliate, Confederation Internationale de la Coiffure; International Star Registry. *Address:* Rt 3 Box 1565, 210 Spruce Street, Onaway, MI 49765, USA.

VERNEY Michael Palmer, b. 17 Feb 1923, Gloucester, England. Chartered Civil Engineer. m. Dora Reader, 20 Nov 1948, 2 sons. *Education:* Civil Engineering Trainee 1940-44. *Publications:* Amateur Boat Building, 1948; Lifeboat into Yacht, 1950; Practical Conversions and Yacht Repairs, 1951; Building Chine Boats, 1960, 1990; Umbau von Booten selbst gemacht, 1961; Complete Amateur Boat Building, 1969, 1990; Boat Maintenance, 1970; Boat Repairs and Conversions, 1979; The Care and Repair of Hulls, 1979; The Compleat Book of Yacht Care, 1986; Das grobe Buch der Boots pflege, 1988. *Contributions to:* 150 illustrated articles in magazines including: Yachting Monthly; The Helmsman; Sunday Times; Yachting World; Light Steam Power. *Membership:* Institution of Civil Engineers. *Address:* 36 The Parkway, Rustington, West Sussex BN16 2BU, England.

VESETH Michael, b. 4 Nov 1949, Tacoma, Washington, USA. Economics Professor. m. Sue Trbovich, 24 July 1976. *Education:* BA Maths and Economics 1972, University of Puget Sound; MS Economics 1974, PhD Economics 1975, Purdue University. *Appointments:* Editorial Board, Puget Sound Magazine 1991-; Director, Poltcal Economy Program, 1992-. *Publications:* Introductory Economics, 1981; Public Finance, 1984; Introductory Macroeconomics, 1984; Economics: Cost and Choice, 1987; Mountains of Debt, 1990. *Honours:* Mattersdorf Award 1974; Mortar Board Outstanding Professor 1987; Burlington Northern Award, 1988; Regester Lecturer 1991. *Memberships:* American Economic Association; National Tax Association. *Address:* ssa 00Economics Department, University of Puget Sound, Tacoma, WA 98416, USA.

VESTER Frederic, b. 23 Nov 1925, Saarbrucken, Germany. Biochemist. m. Anne Pillong, 2 Feb 1950, 1 son, 2 daughters. *Education:* Science Degree, Paris University; Doctorate in Natural Sciences, Hamburg University, 1953; University Teaching Qualification, 1979. *Publications:* Denken, Lernen, Vergessen, 1978; Neuland des Denkens, 1984; Unsere Welt-ein vernetztes System, 1983; Phaenomen Stress, 1978; Bilanz einer Ver(w)irrung, 1986; Januskopf Landwirtschaft, 1986; Krebs-fehlgesteuertes Leben, 1977; Ein Baum ist mehr als ein Baum, 1985; Wasser-Leben, 1987, 1985; Auslakrt Zukunlt, 1991. *Contributions to:* About 200 articles in professional journals, most recent: Technische Rundschau; Management Wissen. *Honours:* Adolf-Grimme Prize, 1974; German Environment Protection Medal, 1975; Deutscher Umwelthilfe Authors Prize, 1979; Emmy und Karl Kaus-Preis, 1982; Philip Morris Research Prize, 1984; Essen City Prize for Journalism, 1984; Bayerische Umweltmedaille, 1992. *Memberships:* FBS; ASIM; GEK; DEG. *Address:* Studiengruppe fur Biologie und Umwelt GmbH, Nussbaumstr. 14, 8000 Munich, Germany.

VICARION Count Palmiro. *See:* **LOGUE Christopher.**

VICHARAPRIYA. *See:* **KRISHASWAMY Iyenger H S.**

VICKERS Hugo, b. 12 Nov 1951. Writer; Editorial Consultant. *Education:* Eton; Strasbourg University. *Appointments:* Editorial Consultant with Burke's Peerage 1971-73; Director, Burke's Peerage 1974-79; Editor, Cocktails and Laughter, 1983; Lectured in England, Italy, Ireland and Australia, usually about Cecil Beaton, sometimes Vivien Leigh, Gladys, Duchess of Marlborough, and the Royal Family; Broadcaster on tv and radio 1973-; Writes obituaries. *Publications:* Gladys, Duchess of Marlborough, UK 1979, USA 1980; We Want the Queen, 1977; Debrett's Book of the Royal Wedding, 1981; Cecil Beaton: The Authorised Biography, 1985; Vivien Leigh, 1988, 1989. *Contributions to:* Burke's Guide to the Royal Family, 1973; Burke's Royal Families of the World, 1977; Burke's Guide to the British Monarchy, 1977; Book Reviewer for The Times 1980-91; Contributed reviews to other publications; Contributed to Daily Mail Year Book 1975-91; Occasional articles on variety of topics in Sunday Telegraph, Observer, Harper's and Queen, The Tatler, The Architectural Digest and others. *Memberships include:* Lay Steward of St George's Chapel, Windsor Castle 1970-; Festival Marshal of the Windsor Festival 1974- 80; Executive Committee, Commemorative Collectors' Society 1975-; Queen's Birthday Committee 1986; Organising Committee of Cecil Beaton's Retrospective Exhibition, Barbican Art Gallery 1986. *Hobbies:* Traveller; Diarist; Photographer; Collecting press cuttings of the Royal Family. *Address:* 62 Lexham Gardens, London W8 5JA, England.

VIDAL Gore (Edgar Box), b. 3 Oct 1925. Writer. *Publications:* Novels: Williwaw, 1946; In a Yellow Wood, 1947; The City and the Pillar, 1948; The Season of Comfort, 1949; A search for the King, 1950; Dark Green, Bright Red, 1950; The Judgement of Paris, 1952; Messiah, 1954; Julian, 1964; Washington DC 1967; Myra Breckinridge, 1968; Two Sisters, 1970; Burr, 1972; Myron, 1974; 1876, 1976; Kalki, 1978; Creation, 1980; Duluth, 1983; Short Stories: A Thirsty Evil, 1956; Hollywood, 1989; Plays: Visit to a Small Planet, 1956; The Best Man, 1960; Romulus, 1962; Weekend, 1968; An Evening with Richard Nixon, 1972; Screening History, 1992; Travel: Vidal in Venice, 1986; Film Scripts and Adaptations: Wedding Breakfast; I Accuse; Ben Hur; Suddenly Last Summer; The Best Man; Caligula; Dress Gray; Essays: Rocking the Boat, 1963; Reflections upon a Sinking Ship, 1969; Homage to Daniel Shays, 1972; Matters of Fact and Fiction; Live from Golgothan, 1992. *Contributions To:* Partisan Review; the Nation; new York Review of Books; Esquire. *Address:* c/o Random House, 201 East 50th Street, New York, NY 10022, USA.

VIDOR Miklos Janos (Nicholas John), b. 22 May 1923, Budapest, Hungary. Writer. m. 22 Aug 1972. *Education:* Doctor of German and Hungarian Literature and Aesthetics, 1947. *Appointments:* Freelance Writer. *Publications:* Poetry: On the Border, 1947; Monologue, 1957; Empty Season, 1966; Meeting, 1986; novels: Tiderace, 1954; Strangers 1958; Pawn on the Chessboard, 1968; Hurt People, 1973; Challenge, 1975; Just One Day More, 1981; The Death and Resurrection of the Back, 1991; Short Stories: Guests of Baucis, 1963; Voluntary Shipwrecked Persons, 1974; Cadet with Mandoline, 1981; Ensign with Mandoline, 1986; Five Volumes of Lyrics. *Contributions to:* Nagyvilag; Liget; Magyar Nemzet. *Honours:* Jozsef Attila Prize, 1955. *Memberships:* Hungarian Art Foundation; Union of Hungarian Writers; PEN. *Literary Agent* Artisjus, 1051 Budapest, Vörösmarty-ter 1. *Address:* 17. Puskin-u, H.1088 Budapest, Hungary.

VIERECK Peter, b. 5 Aug 1916, New York, USA. Poet; Historian; Dramatist. m. (1) Anya de Markov, 1945 (div 1970), 1 son, 1 daughter, (2) Betty Martin Falkenberg, 1972. *Education:* Harvard University; Christ Church, Oxford. *Publications:* Metapolitics - From the Romantics to Hitler, 1941; Terror and Decorum (poems), 1948; Who Killed the Universe?, 1948; Conservation Revisited - The Revolt Against Revolt 1815-1849, 1949;

Strike Through the Mask: New Lyrical Poems, 1950; The First Morning: New Poems, 1952; Shame and Glory of the Intellectuals, 1953; Dream and Responsibility: The Tension Between Poetry and Society, 1953; The Unadjusted Man: a New Hero for Americans, 1956; Conservatism: From John Adams to Churchill, 1956; The Persimmon Tree (poems), 1956; The Tree Witch: A Poem and Play, 1961; Metapolitics: The Roots of the Nazi Mind, 1961; Conservatism Revisited and the New Conservatism: What Went Wrong?, 1962; New and Selected Poems, 1967; Soviet Policy Making, 1967; Outside Looking In, 1972; A Question of Quality, 1976; Archer in the Marrow (poems), 1986. *Contributions to:* Numerous articles in professional journals. *Honours:* Pulitzer Prize for Poetry, 1949; Sadin Poetry Prize, New York Quarterly, 1977; Guggenheim Fellow, Rome, 1949-50. *Address:* Mount Holyoke College, South Hadley, MA 01075, USA.

VIERROS Tuure Johannes, b. 20 Dec 1927, Kankaanpaa, Finland. Senior Teacher. m. Enni Luodetlahti, 22 June 1952. 4 sons, 1 daughter. *Education:* Candidate of Philosophy, University of Helsinki, 1952. *Publications include:* (Novels) Loukkauskivet, 1959; Laivurinsolmu, 1961; Harjahirsi, 1963; Porilaiseni, 1965; Lahella kuolon rantaa, 1967; Harhaoppinen piispa, 1968; Maa oli minuun tyytyvainen, 1971; Komeetta, 1972; Tarton tanssi, 1974; The Kankaanpaa Quartet (Taivaassa torpan maa, 1976; Kultasantainen raitti, 1977; Valhetta kaikki totuus, 1979; Ei saavu satamaan, 1981); Samum, 1983; Majesteettirikos, 1988; Julmat jumalat, 1990 (essays); Jkuinen Kaupunki, 1991. Various textbooks. approx. 30 volumes. *Contributions to:* Various journals and magazines. *Honours:* R SVR, 1986; Nortamo-Prize of Satakunnan Kirjallinen Kerho, 1966; Literary Prize of Pori Town, 1960, 1962; Honour-Prize of Uusi Kirjakerho, 1982; First Prize in Literary Game of Kalevala Festival year, 1985; Literary Prize of Suomon Maakuntakirjailijat, 1992. *Memberships:* Finnish Society of Authors, 1962-; PEN, 1965-; Chairman, Authors in Helsinki, 1970-71. *Literary Agent:* Kirjayhtyma. *Address:* Untuvaisentie 7 G 94, 00820 Helsinki, Finland.

VIERTEL Joseph, b. 1915, American. *Appointment:* President, Presidential Realty Corporation. *Publications:* So Proudly We Hail, 1936; The Last Temptation, 1955; To Love and Corrupt, 1962; Monkey on a Strong, 1968; Life Lines, 1982.

VILLA-GILBERT Mariana Soledad Magdalena, b. 21 Feb 1937, Croydon, England. Writer. *Education:* Various schools including Newbury High School, Berkshire. *Publications:* Mrs Galbraith's Air, 1963; My Love All Dressed in White, 1964; Mrs Cantello, 1966; A Jingle Jangle Song, 1968; The Others, 1970; Manuela - A Modern Myth, 1973; The Sun in Horus, 1986. *Address:* 28 St Martin's Road, Canterbury, Kent CT1 1QW, England.

VINAS David, b. 28 July 1927, Buenos Aires, Argentina. Professor. (div), 1 son, 2 daughters. *Education:* Arts Degree, National University of Buenos Aires; Doctorate (Arts) Autonoma, Madrid, Spain. *Appointments:* El Periodista, de Buenos Aires, 1984; Plural de Mexico, 1981. *Publications:* Novels: Los duenos de la tierra, 1959; Hobes de a caballo, 1967; Jauria, 1973; Cuerpo a cuerpo, 1979; Theatre: Tupac-Amaru, 1974; Dorrego, 1987; Essays: De Sarmiento a Cortazar, 1975; Indios, ejercito y frontera, 1983; Anarquistas en America Latina, 1985. *Contributions to:* Les Temps Modernes; El Pais; la Settimana; Autrement. *Honours:* Prize, Casa de las Americas, La Habana, Cuba, 1967; prize, National Theatre, Argentina, 1973. *Memberships:* Argentian Society of Writers; PEN; Playwrights of Argentina. *Literary Agent:* Jorge Timossi, Havana, Cuba. *Address:* Cordoba 1646, Buenos Aires, Argentina.

VINCENT Gabrielle, b. Brussels, Belgium. Illustrator and Author (Children's Books); Painter. *Publications:* Illustrator and author (English translation titles included): Ernest et Celestine ont perdu Simeon, 1981, Ernest and Celestine, 1982; Ernest et Celestine, musiciens des rues, 1981, Bravo, Ernest and Celestine, 1982; Ernest et Celestine vont pique- niquer, 1982, Ernest and Celestine's Picnic, 1982; Ernest et Celestine chez le photographe, 1982, Smile, Ernest and Celestine, 1982; Le Patchwork, 1982; Ernest and Celestine's Patchwork Quilt, 1982; La Tasse cassee, 1982, Breakfast Time, Ernest and Celestine, 1985; Noel chez Ernest et Celestine, 1983, Merry Christmas, Ernest and Celestine, 1984; Ernest et Celestine au musee, 1985, Where Are You, Ernest and Celestine, 1986. *Address:* Brussels, Belgium.

VINCENT John James, b. 29 Dec 1929, Sunderland, England. Methodist Minister. m. Grace Johnston Stafford, 4 Dec 1958, 2 sons, 1 daughter. *Education:* BD, Richmond College, London University, 1954; STM, Drew University, 1955; DrTheol, Basel University, Switzerland, 1960; Ordained, Methodist Church, 1956. *Appointments:* Director, Urban Theology Unit, 1969-; Editor, New City Journal, 1971-; Adjunct Professor, New York Theological Seminary, 1979-87; Honorary Lecturer, Sheffield University, 1990-. *Publications:* Christ in a Nuclear World, 1962; Christ and Methodism, 1964; Christian Nuclear Perspective, 1964; Here I Stand, 1967; Secular Christ, 1968; The Race Race, 1970; The Jesus Thing, 1973; Stirrings: Essays Christian and Radical, 1975; Alternative Church, 1976; Disciple and Lord, 1976; Starting all over again, 1981; Into the City, 1982; OK Let's Be Methodists, 1984; Radical Jesus, 1986; Mark at Work, 1986; Britain in the 90's, 1989; Discipleship in the 90's, 1991; Liberation Theology from the Inner City, 1992; A Petition of Distress from the Cities, 1993; A British Liberation Theology, forthcoming. *Memberships:* Elected Member, Studiorum Novi Testamenti Societas, 1961; Chairman, Alliance of Radical Methodists, 1971-74; Founder Member, Leader, Ashram Community. *Address:* 178 Abbeyfield Road, Sheffield S4 7AY, England.

VINE Barbara. *See:* RENDELL Ruth.

VINE Janet, b. 6 Apr 1937, Albany, New York, USA. Teacher; Freelance Writer. *Education:* BA, Syracuse University, 1959; MA, State University of New York, Albany, 1964. *Publications:* English, A Comprehensive Review, 1982, 1986; Discovering Literature, Reading Guide & Review, 1968; Exploring Literature, Reading Guide & Review, 1968. *Contributions to:* Children's Periodicals of the United States, 1984; articles in Women's World; New York Alive; Off Duty; Sports Parade; Outside; The Best Report; The Lion; Pegasus; The Golden Falcon. *Honours:* Phi Kappa Phi, 1959; Eta Pi Upsilon, 1959; Winner, Writers Digest poetry contest, 1978. *Memberships:* National League of American Pen Women, Western New York Branch President; State Treasurer; Association of Professional Women Writers; The Write People; Write Associates; American Federation of Teachers; New York State United Teachers; Kenmore Teachers Association; National Council of Teachers of English.

VINGE Joan (Carol) D(ennison), b. 1948, American. *Appointment:* Salvage Archaeologist, San Diego Company, 1971. *Publications:* The Outcases of Heaven Belt, Fireship, 1978; Eyes of Amber and Other Stories, 1979; The Snow Queen, Binary Star 4 (ed with Steven G Sprukill), 1980; Psion, 1982; World's End, 1984; Phoenix in the Ashes, Ladyhawke, 1985; Catspaw, 1988. *Address:* 26 Douglas Road, Chappaqua, NY 10514, USA.

VINGE Vernor Steffen, b. 2 Oct 1944, Waukesha, Wisconsin, USA. Writer; Teacher. *Education:* PhD, Mathematics, University of California, San Diego. *Publications:* True Names; Marooned in Real Time; Peace War; Threats and Other Promises; Witling; Tatja Grimm's World. *Literary Agent:* Sharon Jarvis, 260 Willard Avenue, Staten Island, NY 10314, USA. *Address:* Department of Mathematical Sciences, San Diego State University, San Diego, CA 92182, USA.

VINSON Rex Thomas (Vincent King), b. 1935, United Kingdom. Painter; Printmaker; Freelance Writer; Art Teacher. *Publications:* Light a Last Candle, 1969; Another End, 1971; Candy Man, 1971; Time Snake and Superclown. 1976. *Literary Agent:* Carnell Literary Agency, England. *Address:* c/o Pamela Buckmaster, Carnell Literary Agency, Danescroft, Goose Lane, Little Hallingbury, Herts CM22 7RG, England.

VISSER Margaret, b. 11 May 1940, South Africa. Writer; Lecturer; Broadcaster. m. Colin Wills Visser, 9 June 1962, 1 son, 1 daughter. *Education:* BA Hons Classics 1970, MA Greek 1973, PhD Classics 1980, University of Toronto. *Appointments:* Lecturer, Course Director, Classics, York University, Toronto 1982-. *Publications:* Much Depends on Dinner, 1986; The Rituals of Dinner, 1991. *Contributions to:* Various classics journals; Monthly column entitled The Way We Are, Saturday Night magazine 1988-. *Honour:* Glenfiddich Award, Food Book of the Year 1990; International Association of Culinary Professionals' Literary Food Writing Award, 1991; Jane Grigson Prize, 1991.

VISWANATHAN Subrahmanyam, b. 23 Oct 1933, Sholavandan, Tamil Nadu, India. Professor of English. m. Nirmala Nilakantan, 26 June 1960, 1 daughter. *Education:* BA 1953, MA 1958, University of Madras; PhD 1977, Sri Venkateswara University, Tirupati, India. *Appointments:* Lecturer in English Literature, Sri Venkateswara University 1959-77; Reader in English 1977-82, Professor of English 1982-, University of Hyderabad. *Publications:* The Shakespeare Play as Poem, 1980; On Shakespeare's Dramaturgy, 1992; Co-Editor, Shakespeare in India, 1987; Co-Editor, Critical Essays, 1982. *Contributions to:* Learned journals and collections of essays and papers, about 50. *Honour:* The Indian UGC National Lecturer in English Literature 1986-87. *Address:* A-14, Staff Quarters, University of Hyderabad, Hyderabad 500134, India.

VITZ Robert Carl, b. 26 Dec 1938, Minneapolis, USA. Professor. m. Margaret Markel, 13 June 1964, 2 sons, 1 daughter. *Education:* DePauw University, BA, 1960; Miami University, MA, 1967; University of North Carolina, PhD, 1971. *Appointments:* Purdue University, Assistant Professor, 1971-72; Northern Kentucky University, Professor, 1972- *Publications:* The Queen and the Arts; Painters of Reform. *Contributions to:* Queen City Heritage; New York History; The Old Northwest; Filson Club Quarterly. *Honour:* Post Corbett Award. *Memberships:* The Literary Club; Organization of American Historians; Cincinnati Historical Society. *Address:* 43E Vernon Ln, Ft Thomas, KY 41075, USA.

VIVIAN Daisy. *See:* KENYON Bruce Guy.

VIZINCZEY Stephen, b. 12 May 1933, Kaloz, Hungary. Writer. m. Sept 1963, 3 daughters. *Education:* University of Budapest, 1949-50; Academy of Theatre Arts, Budapest, 1951-56. *Appointment:* Editor, Exchange magazine, 1960-61; Producer, Canadian Broadcasting Corporation, 1962-65. *Publications:* In Praise of Older Women, 1965; The Rules of Chaos, 1969; An Innocent Millionaire, 1983; Truth and Lies in Literature, 1986; The Man with the Magic Touch, 1993. *Contributions to:* Currently: Observer; ABC. *Memberships:* PEN; The Writers' Guild of Great Britain. *Address:* 70 Coleherne Court, Old Brompton Road, London SW5 0EF, England.

VLACH John Michael, b. 21 June 1948, Honolulu, Hawaii. Folklorist. m. Beverly Wood Brannan, 14 Feb 1984, 2 daughters. *Education:* BA American History and Literature 1970, University of California at Davis; MA, PhD in Folklore 1972, 1975 from Indiana University. *Publications:* The Afro-American Tradition in Decorative Arts, 1978; Charleston Blacksmith, 1981; Common Places, Co-Author, 1986; Plain Painters: Making Sense of American Folk Art, 1988; By the Work of Their Hands, 1992. *Contributions to:* Numerous articles and reviews to: Journal of American Folklore; Western Folklore; American Studies International. *Honour:* National Endowment for the Humanities Fellow at the Winterthur Museum. *Memberships:* American Folklore Society, Executive Board; Vernacular Architecture Forum, Board of Directors; Pioneer America Society, Board of Directors. *Address:* American Studies Programme, The George Washington University, Washington DC 20052, USA.

VLAD, Alexandru, b. 31 July 1950, Romania. Author. m. Maria Vlad, 4 Mar 1985, 2 sons. *Education;* BA, English Literature & Language, Cluj-Napoca University. *Publications:* The Giffin's Wing, 1981; The Way to the South Pole, 1985; In the Cold of the Summer, 1985; Joseph Conrad - The Duel, translation, preface, (1989); W H Hudson Green Mansions, translation, 1992. *Contributions to:* Steaua; Vatra; Amfiteatru; Astra; Tribuna. *Honour:* Union of Writer's Prize for First Book, 1981. *Membership:* Union of Writers. *Address:* Str. lugoslaviei Nr. 72 Bl. B4 Ap. 23, 3400 Cluj-Napoca, Romania.

VLAVIANOS Haris, b. 18 June 1957, Athens, Greece. Professor. m. Catherine Schina, 1 Feb 1990, 1 son. *Education:* BSc, University of Bristol, 1979; M Phil, University of Oxford, 1984; D Phil, 1988. *Appointments:* Editor, Nefeli Publishers, 1989; Editor, Poetry, Quarterly Journal of Modern Poetry, 1992. *Publications:* In a Manner of Speaking; Refutation; The Nostalgia of the Skies; Translations into Greek: Walt Whitman; Ezra Pound; Wallace Stevens; John Asbery. *Contributions to:* Numerous. *Honours:* Poetry Award of the Hellenic Foundation of Great Britain. *Memberships:* Society of Greek Writers. *Address:* Stratigou Dagli 136, Athens 11145, Greece.

VOGASSARIS Angelo-Eftihios (Felix), b. 6 May 1935, Piraeus, Greece. Educator; Writer. div. *Education:* Degree in Philosophy and Greek Literature, University of Athens; Diploma, Germanistics, Munich Greman Academy; Diploma, English, French. *Appointments:* Editor, Writer, Common Market News, Ionian and Popular Bank of Greece, to 1977; Ex-Director, Experimental Evening High School; High School Teacher, Greek Literature; Pedagogy Advisor. *Publications:* A Man, A Life, A Death, Costas Cariotakis, 1968, 2nd Edition, 1969; The Poet Andrea Calvos, 1968; Andrea Calvos, Poet of Virtue, Patriotism and Liberty, essay, 1970; Dionyssios Solomos and Liberty, essay, 1972; Windspeed Eight to Ten Beaufort, novel, 1974; Nicolas Kavvadias (Marabu): The Poet of the far seaways, 1979; The Ghost of Che Guevara, 2 novels, 1982; Paul Nor (Nicolas Nicolaides) (The satirical, the lyrical, the theatrical, the antifascist), essay, 1985; Harry's Night Encounter in Aphrodite Street, novel, 1988-89; Forthcoming: In the Land of Portugal; The Monkey's Love, contemporary tragedy; The Star, tragi-comedy; Fury and Disgust of Citizen 'A' tragi-comedy; Poetry: Languor; Silence...Better Silence (In memory of the 40 years anniversary of the Spanish writer Federico Garcia Lorca), 1977; Memory of Bobby Sads Who Died in the Maze Prison, 1984; The Fury and Loneliness Monologue of Citizen 'A' 1992; Radio plays include: George Gershwin's Life; Al Johnson's Life; Cole Porter's Life; Voyage to Tilsit; The death of a salesman, radio version; Madness on mountains. *Contributions to:* Prose to newspapers and magazines. *Memberships:* Association of Greek Writers; President, Piraeus Literary and Arts Society; Represented Greek writers in poetry and literature, international meetings, most European countries, USA, USSR. *Address:* 1-3 Aristotelous str, GR 18535 Piraeus, Greece.

VOGEL Steven James, b. 10 Dec 1946, Pontiac, Illinois, USA. Broadcaster; Writer. m. Mary L Koopman, 25 Aug 1973, 2 sons, 1 daughter. *Education:* BA Political Science, Illinois Wesleyan University; MS Journalism, Northwestern University. *Publication:* Reasonable Doubt, 1989. *Contributions to:* Various professional publications. *Memberships:* Radio-Television News Directors Association; Illinois News Broadcasters Association. *Literary Agent:* Clyde Taylor; Curtis Brown

Ltd. *Address:* 9 Kensington Circle, Bloomington, IL 61704, USA.

VOIGT Ellen Bryant, b. 9 May 1943, Danville, Virginia, USA. Poet; Teacher. m. Francis G W Voigt, 5 Sept 1965, 1 son, 1 daughter. *Education:* BA, Converse College, Spartanburg, South Carolina, 1964; MFA, University of Iowa, Iowa City, Indiana, 1966. *Appointments:* Faculty Member: Iowa Wesleyan College, 1966-69, Goddard College 1969-79, Massachusetts Institute of Technology, 1979-82, Warren Wilson College, 1981-; Participant: Indiana, Tucson, Napa Valley, Catskills and Breadloaf Writers' Conferences. *Publications:* The Lotus Flowers, 1987; The Forces of Plenty, 1983; Claiming Kin, 1976. *Contributions to:* New Yorker; Atlantic; American Poetry Review; Antioch Review; Partisan Review; Pequod; Ploughshares; Georgia Review; Ohio Review; Poetry; New Republic. *Honours:* Fellowship, National Endowment for the Arts, 1975; Fellowship, Guggenheim Foundation, 1978. *Address:* Box 16, Marshfield, VT 05658, USA.

VON ECKARDT Wolf, b. 6 Mar 1918, Berlin, Germany. Author. m. Nina French Frazier, 14 Feb 1937, 2 daughters from previous marriage. *Publications:* A Place to Live, the Crisis of the Critics, 1967; Bertolt Brecht's Berlin, with Sander Gilman, 1975; Oscar Wilde's London, with Sander Gilman, 1987; Back to the Drawing Board, 1979; Please Write, 1988; Live the Good Life : Creating Community Through Art, 1982; Eric Mendelsohn, 1960; The Challenge of Megalopolis, 1964. *Contributions to:* Harpers; New Republic; Architecture; Horizon; National Geographic; Travel & Leisure; Washington Post. *Honours:* Doctorate of Humane Letters, Maryland Institute of Arts; The Tapiola (Finland) Medal for Contribution to Community Planning; Architecture Critic's Medal, American Institute of Architects. *Memberships:* American Institute of Architecture; Society of Architectural Historians. *Address:* 2014 Hillyer Place, NW, Washington, DC 20009, USA.

VON STACKELBERG Peter, b. 28 Oct 1953, Elk Point, Alberta, Canada. Writer. m. 20 July 1974, 1 son, 2 daughters. *Education:* Journalism, Ryerson Polytechnical Institute, Toronto, 1971-74. *Appointments:* Staff writer, Grande Prairie (Alberta) Herald-Tribune 1975-79, The Leader-Post, Regina, Saskatchewan 1979-81, Edmonton (Alberta) Journal 1981-82; Freelance writer, 1983-. *Contributions to:* Wide variety of magazines including: Maclean's; En Route; Edmonton Magazine; Omni; PC World; Info Age; PC World Canada; Electronic Times; Office Mangement & Automation; Quest; PC Magazine. *Honour:* Citation, Roland Michener Award, public service in Canadian journalism, 1981. *Memberships:* Lakeland College Literary Arts Advisory Committee; Copyright Committee Chairman, Periodical Writers Association of Canada; Canadian Science Writers Association; Centre for Investigative Journalism. *Address:* 9302-168 Street, Edmonton, Alberta, Canada T5R 2W2.

VON TROTTA Margarethe, b. 21 Feb 1942, Berlin, German. Screen writer and director. m. (2) Volker Schloendorff, 1 son from first marriage. *Career:* Screenwriter and director of motion pictures; Actress in stage productions during 1960s and, subsequently, in television productions and in motion pictures, including Gods of the Plague, 1969, A Free Woman, 1972 and Coup de Grace, 1977. *Publications:* Screenplays and director: Schwestern: oder, Die Balance des Gluecks (Bioskop-Film, 1979; released in the United States as Sisters or The Balance of Happiness, Cinema 5, 1982), Fischer Yaschenbuch Verlag, 1979; Die bleierne Zeit (The Leaden Time), Bioskop-Film, 1981; released in the United States as Marianne and Juliane, New Yorker Films, 1982 (released in England as The German Sisters); Heller Wahn (Bioskop- Film/Les Films du Losage/West Deutscher Rundfunk, 1983; released in the United States as Sheer Madness, R5/S8, 1985; (released in England as Friends and Husbands) Fischer Taschenbuch

Verlag, 1981; Rosa Luxemburg (Bioskop-Film/Pro- ject Film/Filmverlag der Autoren Regina Ziegler Film/Baren Film/WDR, 1986; released in the United States by New Yorker Films, 1987) F Greno, 1986. Also other screenplays. *Honours:* Golden Lion from Venice Film Festival, 1981, for Marianne and Juliane. *Address:* c/o German Film and Television Academy, Pommernallee 1, 1 Berlin 19, Germany.

VON ZWECK Dina, b. 16 Oct 1933, New York City, New York, USA. Writer; Artist. 2 sons, 1 daughter. *Publications:* American Victorian (co-author), 1984; Sam Shepard's Dog, 1984; Halloween and Other Poems, 1985; Venus Unbound, 1989; Children's books include: I Am Dreaming; All About Me; Make Zoup; Questions, Questions, Questions; Imagine That; Creative Writing for Kids; Adult short stories in Helicon Nine Reader, 1990. *Contributions to:* New Letters; Helicon Nine. *Honours:* Massachusetts Council-on-the- Arts Grant for poetry, 1984; Altos de Chavon Artist-in-Residence, Dominican Republic to complete novel Dominga y El Rio Hablando, 1989. *Memberships:* PEN America; Poets and Writers; Artists Equity. *Address:* PO Box 171, Peck Slip Station, New York, NY 10272, USA.

VONNEGUT Kurt, b. 11 Nov 1922, USA. Author. m. Jane Marie Cox, 1 Sept. 1945, (div 1979), 1 son, 2 daughters, adopted 3 nephews, (2) Jill Krementz, 1979. *Publications:* Novels: Player Piano, 1951; Sirens of Titan, 1959; Mother Night, 1961; Cat's Cradle, 1963; God Bless You, Mr Rosewater, 1964; Story Collection, Welcome to the Monkey House, 1968; Slaughterhouse Five, 1969; Play, Happy Birthday, Wanda June, 1970; TV Script, Between Time & Timbuktu or Prometheus 5, 1972; Deadeye Dick, 1982; Galapagos, 1985; Bluebeard, 1987; Hocus Pocus, 1990; Fates Worse Than Death (essays and speeches), 1991. *Contributions to:* various journals and magazines. *Membership:* National Institute Arts and Letters. *Address:* Donald C Farber, 99 Park Ave., New York, NY 10016, USA.

VOTH Alden H, b. 4 May 1926, Goessel, Kansas, USA. University Professor. m. 18 Aug 1956, 1 son, 1 daughter. *Education:* BA Economics 1950, Bethel College; MS Economics 1953, Iowa State University; PhD International Relations 1959, University of Chicago. *Appointments:* Upland College, Upland, California 1960-63; San Jose State University 1963-91; American University in Cairo (2 year leave-of-absence from San Jose State University) 1965-67. *Publications:* Moscow Abandons Israel for the Arabs, 1980; The Kissinger Legacy: American Middle East Policy, 1984. *Contributions to:* Vietnam: Studying a Major Controversy, Journal of Conflict Resolution, 1967; Portugal in Africa: Angola and Mozambique, Contemporary Review, 1968; The Moral Dimension of International Relations, Rocky Mountain Social Science Journal, 1972. *Honours:* Wall Street Journal Award, 1950; Excellence in Teaching Award, American University in Cairo, 1967; Most Influential Professor Award, SJSU, 1987, 1989 & 1991; Research Grant for the study of African politics, AUC, 1966; Fellow, National Council on US-Arab Relations, 3-week guest of the Iraqi and UAE governments, 1990. *Memberships:* Pomona Valley American Association for the United Nations, member of the Board of Trustees 1961-63; International Studies Association; American Political Science Association; Western Political Science Association. *Address:* 1385 Kimberly Drive, San Jose, CA 95118, USA.

VOYLE Mary. *See:* **MANNING Rosemary.**

VROOMKONING Victor. *See:* **VAN DE LAAR Waltherus Antonius Bernardinus.**

VUONG Lynette Dyer, b. 20 June 1938, Owosso, Michigan, USA. Author-Lecturer. m. Ti Quang Vuong, 9 Jan 1962, 2 sons, 2 daughters. *Education:* University of Wisconsin, Milwaukee, 1958-61; Graduated, Registered Nurse, Milwaukee County Hospital School of Nursing, 1959, University of Houston, 1992-. *Publications:* The Brocaded Slipper and Other Vietnamese Tales, 1982; A Friend for Carlita, 1989; The Golden Carp and Other Tales from Vietnam, 1993; Sky Legends of Vietnam, 1993. *Contributions to:* Highlights For Children; Guide; Trails; Reflection; Face-To-Face; Venture; Discoveries; Straight; In Touch; Davis Nursing Survey; Hi-Call; Teens Today; Romance Writers Report; Contact; Family and Friends; Partners; Bread for Children; Between Times. *Honours:* Texas Bluebonnet Award List Title (The Brocaded Slipper), 1984; Georgia Children's Book Award Nominee, The Brocaded Slipper, 1985; Romance Writers of America Golden Heart Award, 1st Place in Mainstream Division, The Shadow of The Sickle, unpublished manuscript; Catholic Library Association's Ann Martin Book Award, 1991. *Memberships:* Associated Authors of Children's Literature, Houston (past President); Romance Writers of America; Society of Children's Book Writers; Golden Key National Honor Society, Classical Association of Houston. *Literary Agent:* Gary L Hegler Literary Agency, 17629 El Camino Real, Houston, TX 77058, USA. *Address:* 15211 Morning Dove Drive, Humble, TX 77396, USA.

W

WACHTEL Albert, b. 20 Dec 1939, Queens, New York, USA. Professor of English. m. Sydelle Farber Zetkin, 1958, 3 sons, 4 daughters. *Education:* BA 1960, Queens College; PhD 1968, State University of New York at Buffalo. *Appointments:* Professor of English and Creative Writing, Pitzer College 1974-. *Publications:* The Cracked Looking Glass, 1992; Co-Editor, Modernism: Challenges and Perspectives, 1986. *Contributions to:* On Analogical Action, JAAC, 1963; The Burden, Spectrum, 1971; Detroit and Hong Kong, The Grain, 1975; A Clean Slate, Moment, 1976; Cradle and All, The Southern Review, 1982; Why Learn? Why Live?, LA Times, 1988; Damage Control in the Middle East, Midstream, 1992; Open Forum, San Francisco Chronicle, 1993. *Honours:* National Defense Education Act Fellow, 1960-63; Fellow, Creative Arts Institute, 1970; Danforth Associate, 1978; NEH Fellow, 1986. *Memberships:* MLA; James Joyce Foundation. *Address:* Pitzer College, The Claremont Colleges, Claremont, CA 91711, USA.

WADDELL Evelyn Margaret (Lyn Cook), b. 4 May 1918, Weston, Ontario, Canada. Children's Librarian. m. Robb John Waddell, 19 Sept 1949, 1 son, 1 daughter. *Education:* BA English Language & Literature, BLS, University of Toronto. *Publications:* All as Lyn Cook: The Bells on Finland Street, 1950; The Little Magic Fiddler, 1951; Rebel on the Trail, 1953; Jady and the General, 1955; Pegeen and the Pilgrim, 1957; The Road to Kip's Cove, 1961; Samantha's Secret Room, 1963; The Brownie Handbook for Canada, 1965; The Secret of Willow Castle, 1966; The Magical Miss Mittens, 1970; Toys from the Sky, 1972; Jolly Jean-Pierre, 1973; If I Were All These, 1974; A Treasure for Tony, 1980; The Magic Pony, 1981; Sea Dreams, 1981; The Hiding Place (historical novel for young people), 1990; A Canadian ABC (poetry with art by Thoreau MacDonald), 1990. *Honours:* Honorary Member, Academy of Canadian Writers, Vicky Metcalf Award, 1978. *Memberships:* Writers Union of Canada; Canadian Society of Children's Authors, Illustrators and Performers. *Address:* 72 Cedarbrae Blvd., Scarborough, Ontario, Canada M1J 2K5.

WADDELL Martin (Catherine Sefton). b. 1941, Irish, Full-time writer of novels/short stories, children's fiction. m. Rosaleen Carragher, Dec 1969, 3 sons. *Publications:* as Catherine Sefton: In a Blue Velvet Dress, 1972; The Sleepers on the Hill, 1973; The Backhouse Ghosts, 1974, in USA as The Haunting of Ellen, 1975; The Ghost and Bertie Boggin, 1980; Emer's Ghost, 1981; A Puff of Smoke, 1982; The Emma Dilemma, 1982; Island of the Strangers, 1982; My Gang, 1984; The Blue Misty Monsters, 1985; The Ghost Girl, 1985; Shadows on the Lake, 1985. Shorter texts: A Puff of Smoke; My Gang; The Haunted Schoolbag; The Finn Gang; The Ghost Ship, 1985; Flying Sam, 1986; The Day The Smells Went Wrong; The Boggart in the Barrel; Haroace the ghost; The Ghosts of Cobweb; The Ghosts of Cobweb and the Skully Bones Mystery; The Ghost Family Robinson; The Ghost Family Robinson at the Seaside. For Older Readers: Starry Night, 1986; Frankie's Story; The Beat of The Drum; Along a Lonely Roadl The Cast Off. Children's fiction as Martin Waddell: Ernie's Chemistry Set (Flying Trousers) 2 vols, 1978; Napper Goes for Goal (Strikes Again) 2 vols, 1981; The Great Green Mouse Disaster, 1981; Harriet and the Crocodiles (Haunted School, Robot, Flying Teachers), 4 vols 1982-87; The House under the Stairs, 1983; Solve It Yourself Mysteries: The Mystery Squad and the Dead Man's Message (the Artful Dodger, the Whistling Thief, Mr. Midnight, the Creeping Castle, the Candid Camera, the Robot's Revenge, the Cannonball Kid) 8 vols, 1983-86; Going West, 1983; Big Bad Bertie, 1984; Napper's Golden Goals, 1984; The Budgie Said GRRR, 1985; The School Reporter's Notebook, 1985; Owl and Billy, 1986; The Day It Rained Elephants, 1986; Our Wild Weekend, 1986; Little Dracula's First Bite (Christmas, at the Seaside, Goes to School) 4 vols, 1986-87; The Tough Princess, 1986; Owl and Billy and the Space Days, 1987; The Tall Story of Wilbur Small, 1987; The Park in the Dark, 1989; Judy the Bad Fairy, 1989; Once There were

Giants, 1989; Amy Said, 1990; Rosie's Babies, 1990; My Great Grandpa, 1990; We Love Them, 1990; The Hidden House, 1990. Novels as Martin Waddell: Otley, 1966; Otley Pursued (Forever, Victorious) 3 vols, 1967-69; Come Back When I'm Sober, 1969; A Little Bit British, Being the Diary of an Ulsterman, 1970, other - (ed)A Tale to Tell, 1982; Can't You Sleep Little Bear; Let's Go Home Little Bear; Farmer Duck. *Address:* c/o Murray Pollinger, 222 Old Brompton Road, London SW5 0BZ.

WADDEN Marie T, b. 2 Mar 1955, St John's, Newfoundland, Canada. Journalist. *Education:* BA Hons History, Memorial University of Newfoundland and Labrador, St John's Newfoundland; MA Journalism, University of Western Ontario, London, Ontario. *Publications:* Nitassinan: The Innu Struggle to Reclaim their Homeland, 1991; Film, Hunters and Bombers, 1990. *Contributions to:* Harrowsmith Magazine; Arctic Circle magazine; Globe and Mail newspaper; Toronto Star; Montreal Gazette; This Magazine; Atlantic Insight magazine. *Honours:* National Journalism Award, 1985; Atlantic Canada's Film and Video Awards, Best Documentary Film Award, Mannheim International Film Festival, 1991; Newfoundland and Labrador Arts and Letters Competition, 1st Prize non-fiction, 1990; National Distinction the Edna Staebler Award for creative non fiction, 1992. *Memberships:* Readings Committee Chair, Newfoundland Writers Alliance; Writers Alliance of Newfoundland and Labrador; National Radio Producers Association. *Address:* 192 Old Topsail Road, St John's, Newfoundland, Canada A1E 2B1.

WADDINGTON-FEATHER John Joseph, b. 10 July 1933, Keighley, Yorkshire, England. Anglican Priest; Publisher. m. Sheila Mary Booker, 23 July 1960, 3 daughters. *Education:* BA, English, Leeds University. *Appointment:* Co-Editor, Orbis, 1971-80. *Publications:* Yorkshire Dialect, 1969; Garlic Lane, 1970; Easy Street, 1971; One Man's Road, 1979; Quill's Adventures in the Great Beyond, 1980; Tall Tales from Yukon, 1983; Khartoum Trilogy, 1985; Quill's Adventures in Wasteland, 1986; Quill's Adventures in Grozzieland, 1988. *Contributions to:* Various journals and magazines. *Honours:* Bronte Society Prize, 1963; Cyril Hodges Poetry Award, 1976. *Memberships:* Yorkshire Dialect Society, Secretary, Editor; Bronte Society; Independent Publishers Guild; Fellow, Royal Society of Arts, 1989. *Address:* Fair View, Old Coppice, Lyth Bank, Shrewsbury, Shropshire, SY3 0BW, England.

WADDINGTON Miriam (E B Merritt), b. 23 Dec 1917, Winnipeg, Canada. Writer, University Teacher. (div), 2 sons. *Education:* MSW, Social Work, MA, English, 2 honorary doctorates (DLitt). *Appointments:* Caseworker in child guidance clinics, hospitals, prisons, family and children's agencies in Toronto and Montreal; Teacher of Social Work; Senior Scholar and Professor of English Literature at York University, Toronto; Writer-in-Residence, Windsor Public Library 1983; Advisory Editor, Journal of the Otto Rank Association, 1973-83; Writer in Residence, University of Ottawa, 1974; Writer in Residence, Toronto Metro Library June-Dec 1986. *Publications:* 12 Books of Poetry including: Driving Home, 1972; The Price of Gold 1976; Mister Never 1978; The Visitants 1981; Collected Poems 1986; The Last Landscape, 1992. Author of a critical study of A M Klein, edited work of Canadian critic John Sutherland as well as The Collected Poems of A M Klein; Summer at Lonely Beach (stories) 1982; Apartment Seven: Essays New and Selected, 1989; Canadian Jewish Stories (edited with an introduction), 1990. *Contributions to:* Dozens of critical articles, reviews, and short stories in various journals. *Honours:* Driving Home won the J I Segal prize in 1972; Collected Poems won the J I Segal prize in 1987; 3 times recipient of Senior Writing Fellowships from the Canada Council. *Address:* 625 West 27th Ave, Vancouver, BC, Canada V5Z 4H7.

WADDINGTON Raymond Bruce, b. 27 Sept 1935, Santa Barbara, California, USA. Professor of English Literature. m. Kathleen Martha Ward, 11 Oct 1985, 2

sons. *Education:* BA, Stanford University, 1957; PhD, Rice University, 1963. *Appointments:* Editorial Board, Sixteenth Century Journal, 1975-; Editorial Board, Literary Monographs, 1975-77; Editor, Garland Studies in the Renaissance, Garland Publishing Inc, 1989-. *Publications:* The Mind's Empire, 1974; The Rhetoric of Renaissance Poetry (co-editor), 1974; The Age of Milton (co-editor), 1980. *Contributions to:* Numerous essays to scholarly journals. *Honours:* Postdoctoral Fellow in Humanities, Johns Hopkins University, 1965-66; Fellow, Institute for Research in Humanities, 1971-72; Guggenheim Fellow, 1972-73; Newberry Library-NEH Fellow, 1978; NEH Fellow, 1983. *Memberships:* President, Sixteenth Century Studies Conference, 1985; Executive Committee, Milton Society of America, 1983-85; Renaissance Society of America. *Address:* 39 Pershing Avenue, Woodland, CA 95695, USA.

WADE Alan. *See:* **VANCE John Holbrook.**

WADE David, b. 1929, British. *Appointments:* Radio Critic, The Listener, 1965-67, The Times, 1967-89. *Publications:* Trying to Connect You; The Cooker; The Guthrie Process; The Gold Spinners; Three Blows in Anger; The Ogden File; The Carpet Maker of Samarkand; The Nightingale; Summer of'39; The Facts of Life; A Rather Nasty Crack; On Detachment; The Tree of Strife; Power of Attorney Alexander. *Address:* Willow Cottage, Stockland, Green Road, South Borough, Kent TN3 0TL, England.

WADE Edwin L, b. 1 July 1947, Inyokern, California, USA. Art Curator. m. *Education:* BA, California State University, Fullerton, 1969; MA, 1973, PhD, 1976, University of Washington, Seattle. *Publications:* America's Great Lost Expedition, 1981; Magic Images, 1981; Historic Hopi Ceramics, 1981; As in a Vision: Masterworks of American Indian Art, 1983; Indianische Kunst im 20 Jahrhundert, 1984, Revised English Edition One Hundred Years of Native American Art; The Arts of the North American Indian, 1986. *Contributions to:* Articles to periodicals. *Honours:* Western Heritage Wrangler Award for The Arts of the North American Indian, National Cowboy Hall of Fame, 1986; Governor's Arts Award for exhibition What Is Native American Art, 1986. *Address:* Philbrook Museum of Art, 2727 South Rockford Road, Tulsa, OK 74114, USA.

WADMAN Anne Sijbe, b. 30 Nov 1919, Langweer, Netherlands. Educator. *Education:* D.Litt, University of Amsterdam, 1955. *Publications Include:* Handdruk en Handgemeeen, Handshakes and Close Quarters, essays and criticism, 1965; Yn'e lyts loege, In a Hole, 1960; Kûgels foar in labbekak, Bullets for a Coward, novel, 1964; By de duvel to bycht, Gone to the Wrong Shop, 1966; De feestgongers, the Merry-Makers, 1968; It rammeljen van de pels, It's of No Use, 1970; Yn Adams harnas, In Adams Armour, 1982; De verkrachting, The Rape, 1984; Tinke oan alde tiden, Thinking About Olden Times, 1985; 16 deiboek, 1936, 16 Diary 1936, 1985; In bolle yn'e reak, A Brute, 1986; De terechtstelling, The Execution, 1987; De frou yn e flesse, The Women in the Bottle, 1988; Veel meer dan tien geboden, Much More Than Ten Commandments, 1989; It Kritys Karwei, The Critical Job, 1989. *Honours:* Gysbert Japiks prise for Frisian Literature, 1951 and 1989. *Memberships:* Dutch Centre, PEN. *Address:* Esdoorniaan 2, 8603 CA Sneek, Friesland, The Netherlands.

WAELTI-WALTERS Jennifer Rose, b. Wolverhampton, England. Professor of French and Women's Studies. *Education:* BA Hons, 1964, PhD, 1968, University of London; Licence-es-Lettres, Universite de Lille, France,1965. *Publications:* Alchimie et litterature (Butor), 1975; J M G Le Clézio, 1977; Michel Butor, a view of his World and a Panorama of his Work, 1977; Icare ou l'evasion impossible (J M G Le Clezio), 1981; Fairytales and the Female Imagination, 1982; Jeanne Hyvrad (with M Verthuy), 1989; Feminist Novelists of the Belle Epoque, 1991; Michel Butor, 1992. *Contributions to:* Numerous magazines and journals. *Honours:* APFUCC Prize, Best Book of Literary Criticism

in French, 1989. *Memberships:* Canadian Research Institute for the Advancement of Women; Canadian Women's Studies Association; Association des Professeurs de Francais des Universites et Colleges Canadiens. *Address:* Women's Studies, University of Victoria, Victoria, British Columbia, Canada V8W 3P4.

WAGMAN Robert J, b. 11 Nov 1942, Chicago, Illinois, USA. Journalist. *Education:* AB; MA; JD; St Louis University. *Appointment:* Syndicated Columnist, Newspaper Enterprise Association. *Publications:* Humbert Humphrey : The Man and His Dream, 1978; The Tax Revolt, 1980; Hostage, 1980; Asbestos : the Silent Killer, 1981; Lord's Justice, 1985; Instant Millionaires, 1987; The Nazi Hunters, 1988. *Contributions to:* Various magazines & journals. *Honour:* Thomas J Stokes Award for National Environmental Writing, 1978. *Memberships:* National Press Club; White House Correspondents Association. *Address:* Suite 610, 1110 Vermont Avenue NW, Washington, DC 20005, USA.

WAGNER Sharon Blythe (M E Cooper, Ann Sheldon, Blythe Stephens, Casey Stephens), b. 1936, American. *Publications:* Prairie Wind, 1967; Dude Ranch Mystery, 1968; Curse of Still Valley, 1969; Country of the Wolf, Maridu, 1970; Circle of Evil, Gypsy from Nowhere, Winter Evil, Moonwind, 1971; House of Shadows, Shadow on the Sun (with B Casey), Legacy of Loneliness, Cove in Darkness (with B Casey), 1972; Cry of the Cat, Haitian Legacy (with B Casey), Wind of Bitterness (with B Casey), Gypsy and Nimblefoot, 1973; Satan's Acres, Shades of Evil, Colors of Death, Havenhurst, Roses from Yesterday, Dark Waters of Death, Dark Side of Paradise, The Turquoise Talisman, Dark Sun at Midnight (with B Casey), 1974; Echoes of an Ancient (with B Casey), Bride of the Dullahan (with B Casey), 1976; Shadow of Her Eyes, Haunted Honeymoon, Love's Broken Promises (with B Casey), 1979; Gypsy and the Moonstone Stallion, House of Doom House of Desire, Secrets, Embraces, Porterfield Legacy (as Casey Stephens), The Shadows of Fieldcrest Manor (as Casey Stephens), 1980; The Chadwicks of Arizona, Charade of Love, 1981; New Dreams for Kendra, Jacquelle's Shadow, Journey to Paradise, 1982; Tour of Love, 1983; Strangers Who Love, 1983; Change Partners, 1983; House of the Hill, 1988; Lost Lilacs of Latimer House, 1990. As Ann Sheldon: Haunted Valley, 1982; Secret of the Old Sleigh, 1983; Emperor's Pony, 1983; Phantom of Dark Oaks, 1983. As M E Cooper: Picture Perfect, 1986. As Blythe Stephens: Rainbow Days, 1989; Gift of Mischief, 1991; Wake To Darkness, 1992. *Memberships:* Romance Writers of America; Mystery Writers of America; Novelists Inc. *Literary Agent:* The Martell Agency. *Address:* 2137 East Bramble Avenue, Mesa, AZ 85204, USA.

WAGNER-MARTIN Linda C, b. 1936, American. *Appointments:* Former Teacher, Wayne State University, Detroit; Bowling Green State University, Ohio; Michigan State University, East Lansing; Hanes Professor of English and Comparative Literature, University of North Carolina, Chapel Hill, NC; Editor, The Centennial Review. *Publications:* The Poems of William Carlos Williams, 1964; Denise Levertov, Intaglios, 1967; The Prose of William Carlos Williams, 1970; Phyllis McGinley, 1971; William Faulkner: Four Decades of Criticism (ed), 1973; T S Eliot (ed), Ernest Hemingway: Five Decades of Criticism (ed), 1974; Hemingway and Faulkner: Inventors/Masters, 1975; Introducing Poems (with C David Mead), 1976; Ernest Hemingway: A Reference Guide, Robert Frost: The Critical Heritage, Speaking Straight Ahead: Interviews with William Carlos Williams, 1977; William Carlos Williams: A Reference Guide, 1978; Dos Passos: Artist as American, Joyce Carol Oates: Critical Essays (ed), 1979; American Modern, 1980; Songs for Isadora, 1981; Ellen Glasgow: Beyond Convention, 1982; Sylvia Plath: Critical Essays (ed), 1984; Sylvia Plath: A Biography, 1987; New Essays on The Sun Also Rises (ed), Ernest Hemingway: Six Decades of Criticism (ed), 1987; Sylvia Plath: The Critical Hertiage (ed), 1988; Anne Sexton: Critical Essays (ed), The Modern American Novel, 1914-1945, 1989;

Wharton's: The House of Mirth, A Novel of Admonition, 1990; Denise Leverton: Critical Essays (ed), 1990. *Address:* Department of English, University of North Carolina, Chapel Hill, NC 27514, USA.

WAH Frederick James, b. 23 Jan 1939, Swift Current, Saskatchewan. Writer. m. Pauline Butling, 1962, 2 daughters. *Education:* Studied music and English literature, University of British Columbia, 1960s; Graduate work in literature and linguistics, University of New Mexico, Albuquerque; Masters degree 1967, State University of New York at Buffalo. *Appointments:* Founding Editor, TISH, poetry newsletter; Editor, Sum magazine; Co-editor, Niagara Frontier Review and The Magazine of Further Studies; Editor, Scree; Contributing Editor, Open Letter; Teacher, Selkirk College; Founding Coordinator of writing programme at David Thompson University Centre; Teacher, English Literature and Creative Writing, University of Calgary. *Publications:* Lardeau, 1965; Mountain, 1967; Among, 1972; Tree, 1972; Earth, 1974; Pictograms from the Interior of BC, 1975; Loki is Buried at Smoky Creek: Selected Poetry, 1980; Owners Manual, 1981; Breathin' My Name With a Sigh, 1981; Grasp the Sparrow's Tail, 1982; Waiting for Saskatchewan, 1985; Rooftops, 1987, 1988; Music at the Heart of Thinking, 1987; Limestone Lakes Utaniki, 1989; So Far, 1991. *Honour:* Governor-General's Award for Waiting for Saskatchewan 1986. *Address:* 2707 Chalice Road NW, Calgary, Alberta, Canada T2L 1C7.

WAHL Jan, b. 1933. American, Writer of children's fiction, plays/screenplays, poetry. Secretary to Isak Dinesen, Denmark,, 1957-58. *Publications include:* Crazy Brobobalou, 1973; The Five in the Forest, 1974; Pleasant Fieldmouse's Halloween Party, 1974; Mooga Mega Mekki, 1974; Jeremiah Knucklebones, 1974; The Muffletump Storybook, 1975; The Clumpets Go Sailing, 1975; The Bear, The Wolf and the Mouse, 1975; The Screeching Door or, What Happened at the Elephant Hotel, 1975; The Muffletumps' Christmas Party, 1975; The Woman With the Eggs, 1975; Follow Me, Cried Bee, 1976; Great-Grandmother Cat Tales, 1976; Grandpa's Indian Summer, 1976; The Pleasant Fieldmouse Storybook, 1977; Doctor Rabbit's Foundling, 1977; Frankenstein's Dog, 1977; The Muffletumps' Halloween Scare, 1977; Pleasant Fieldmouse's Valentine Trick, 1978; Youth's Magic Horn, 1978; Drakestail, 1978; Who Will Believe Tim Kitten? 1978; The Tenny Tiny Witches, 1979; Sylvester Bear Overslept, 1979; Needle Noodle, 1979; Doctor Rabbit's Lost Scout, 1979; Old Hippo's Easter Egg, 1980; Button Eye's Orange, 1980; The Cucumber Princess, 1981; The Little Blind Goat, 1981; Grandpa Gus's Birthday Cake, 1981; Tiger Watch, 1982; The Pipkins Go Camping, 1982; Small One, 1983; Peter and the Troll Baby, 1983; More Room for the Pipkins, 1983; Humphrey's Bear, 1983; So Many Racoons, 1985; The Toy Circus, 1986. *Address:* Aptdo, Postal 33, San Miguel Allende, Mexico.

WAILEY Anthony Paul, b. 3 Dec 1947, Liverpool, England. Writer; Teacher. *Education:* Diploma in History, Ruskin College, Oxford, 1975; BA, University of Exeter, 1977; PhD. University of Liverpool, 1980. *Appointments:* English Teacher, Barcelona, Spain, 1970-72; Part-time Adult Education Teacher, City Literary Institute, London, England. *Publications:* Contribution to book Merseyside in Crisis, 1980; Living the Fishing (as Tony Wailey with Paul Thompson and Trevor Lummis), 1983; The Balance of Strange Times; The Difficult Match, 1990; The Western Approaches, 1993. *Contributions to:* Periodicals including: Footsteps; History Workshop; Record. *Honour:* Recipient of State Mature Scholarship, 1975. *Membership:* Liverpool Football Supporters Club. *Address:* 91 Alderney Street, Pimlico, London SW1, England.

WAIN John Barrington, b. 14 Mar 1925, Stoke on Trent, England. Writer. m. (1) Eirian James, 1960 (dec 1988), 3 sons, (2) Patricia Adams, 1989. *Education:* St John's College, Oxford. *Appointments:* Lecturer, English Literature, University of Reading, 1947-55; Freelance Writer, Literary Critic, 1955-. *Publications:* Poetry: Mixed Feelings, 1951; A Word Carved on a Sill, 1956; Weep

Before God, 1961; Wildtrack, 1965; Letters to Five Artists, 1969; The Shape of Feng, 1972; Feng, 1975; Poems 1949-1979, 1981; Open Country, 1987; Novels: Hurry on Down, 1953; Living in the Present, 1955; The Contenders, 1958; A Travelling Woman, 1959; Strike the Father Dead, 1962; The Young Visitors, 1965; The Smaller Sky, 1967; A Winter in the Hills, 1970; The Pardoner's Tale, 1978; Lizzie's Floating Shop, 1981; Young Shoulders, 1982; Where the Rivers Meet, 1988; Stories: Nuncle and other Stories, 1960; Death of the Hind Legs, 1966; The Life Guard, 1971; Plays: Harry in the Night, 1975; Frank, 1982; Non-fiction: Preliminary Essays, 1957; Sprightly Running (autobiography), 1962; Essays on Literature and Ideas, 1963; The Living World of Shakespeare, 1964; A House for the Truth, 1972; Samuel Johnson, 1974, new edition, 1988; Professing Poetry, 1977; Dear Shadows, Portraits from memory, (memoirs), 1986; Editor: Johnson as Critic, 1974; Johnson on Johnson, 1976; An Edmund Wilson Celebration, 1978; Everyman's Book of English Verse, 1981; Oxford Library of English Poetry, 1986. *Honours Include:* 1st Holder, Fellowship in Creative Arts, Brasenose College, Oxford University, 1971-72; James Tait Black Memorial Prize, 1974; Heinemann Award, 1975; Whitbread Award, 1982; Hon. DLitt, Keele, 1985; Hon.D.Litt, Loughborough, 1985; FRSL, 1960 (resigned 1961). *Address:* c/o Curtis Brown Ltd, 164-168 Regent Street, London, W1R 5TB, England.

WAINWRIGHT Geoffrey, b. 16 July 1939, Yorkshire, England. Theologian (Professor of Systematic Theology); Minister, Methodist Church. m. Margaret Wiles, 20 Apr 1965, 1 son, 2 daughters. *Education:* BA, 1960, MA, 1964, BD, 1972, DD, 1987, Cambridge University; DrTheol, Geneva University, 1969. *Appointments:* Editor, Studia Liturgica, 1974-87; Co-Editor, Dictionary of the Ecumenical Movement, World Council of Churches, Geneva, Switzerland, 1991. *Publications:* Christian Initiation, 1969; Eucharist & Eschatology, 1971, 1981; The Study of Liturgy (co-editor), 1978, 1992; Doxology, 1980; The Ecumenical Moment, 1983; The Study of Spirituality (co-editor), 1986; On Wesley and Calvin, 1987; Keeping the Faith - Essays to Mark the Centenary of Lux Mundi (editor), 1989. *Contributions to:* Numerous articles to dictionaries, encyclopedias and theological journals. *Honours:* Numerous named lectureships throughout the world. *Memberships:* Societas Liturgica, President 1983-85; Chairman, International Dialogue between World Methodist Council and Roman Catholic Church; Faith and Order Commission, World Council of Churches; Secretary, American Theological Society. *Address:* The Divinity School, Duke University, Durham, NC 27708, USA.

WAINWRIGHT Jeffrey, b. 19 Feb 1944, Stoke-on-Trent, England. Poet; Critic. Married, 2 children. *Education:* BA, 1965, MA 1967, University of Leeds. *Appointments:* Lecturer, University of Wales, Aberystwyth, 1967-72, except Visiting Lecturer, Long Island University 1970- 71; Senior Lecturer in English, Manchester Polytechnic, 1972-. *Publications:* Books: The Important Man, 1970; Heart's Desire, 1978; Selected Poems, 1985; Other publications: Poetry by Wainwright included in:Jon Silkin ed, Poetry of the Committed Individual, 1972; Poetry Introduction 3, 1975; Michael Schmidt and Peter Jones (eds)British Poetry Since 1970, 1980; Blake Morrison and Andrew Motion (eds) The Penguin Book of Contemporary British Poetry, 1982; Schmidt (ed) Some Contemporary Poets of Britain and Ireland, 1983; Peter Robinson (ed) Geoffrey Hill: Essays on His Work, 1985. *Contributions to:* Various periodicals including: Stand; Agenda; PN Review; Poetry Review.

WAINWRIGHT John (Jack Ripley), b. 25 Feb 1921, Leeds, England. m. Avis Wrathmell, 7 July 1941, Huddersfield. *Education:* LLB. *Publications include:* Death in a Sleeping City, 1965; The Last Buccaneer, 1971; Death of a Big Man, 1975; Landscape with Violence, 1975; The Bastard, 1976; The Jury People, 1978; Tail-End Charlie, 1978; Brainwash, 1979; Blayde R.I.P., 1982; Cul-de-Sac, 1983; The Forest, 1984; The Ride, 1984; approximately 80 other crime novels, short stories. *Contributions to:* Northern Echo; Police Review. *Membership:* Detection Club. *Literary Agent:* Campbell Thomson & McLaughlin Ltd. *Address:* 67 Albany Road, Ansdell, Lytham St Annes, Lancashire FY8 4AT, England.

WAITE Peter Busby, b. 12 July 1922, Toronto, Ontario, Canada. Professor of History. m. Masha Maria Gropuzzo, 22 Aug 1958. *Education:* BA (Hons), 1948, MA, 1950, University of British Columbia; PhD, University of Toronto, 1954. *Publications:* The Life and Times of Confederation, 1864-1867, 1962; Canada 1874-1896, 1971; John A. Macdonald, his life and world, 1975; The man from Halifax: Sir John Thompson, Prime Minister, 1985; Lord of Point Grey: Larry MacKenzie of UBC, 1987; Between three oceans: challenges of a continental destiny, 1940-1900, Chapter IV, Illustrated History of Canada, 1988. *Contributions to:* Some 55 articles to numerous magazines and journals. *Honours:* Fellow, Royal Society of Canada, 1972; Runner-up, Governor-General's Gold Medal Prize, 1985; Lieutenant-Governor's Medal for Lord of Point Grey, British Columbia, 1987. *Memberships:* President, Canadian Historical Association, 1968-69; Chairman, Humanities Research Council, 1968-70; Chairman, Aid to Publications Committee, Social Science Federation, 1987-89. *Address:* 960 Ritchie Drive, Halifax, Nova Scotia, Canada B3H 3P5.

WAKEMAN Carolyn, b. 11 Oct 1943, Connecticut, USA. Writer. m. 2. Frederic Wakeman Jr, 31 Dec 1974, 1 son, 1 daughter. *Education:* AB, cum laude, Pembroke College (now Brown University), 1964; AM 1968, PhD 1980, Washington University. *Appointments:* English Teacher, Hope High School, Providence, Rhode Island, 1964-66; Teaching Associate in English Composition, University of California, Berkeley, 1974-80; Assistant Professor of English Literature, 1980-82 and 1985-86, Beijing University of Foreign Studies, Beijing, China; Research Associate at Center for Chinese Studies, University of California, Berkeley, 1986-87. *Publications:* (Editor with husband, Frederic Wakeman Jr) Conflict and Control in Late Imperial China, 1975; (with Yue Daiyun)To the Storm: The Odyssey of a Revolutionary Chinese Woman (autobiography) 1985. *Contributions to:* Articles to Journal of Asian Studies, Shakespeare Quarterly, and Foreign Literature (China), and book reviews to New York Times, Los Angeles Times and San Francisco Chronicle. *Honours:* Award from Bat Area Book Reviewers Association, 1986 for To the Storm. *Memberships:* Association of Asian Studies, Columbia University Modern History Seminar. *Address:* New York, New York, USA.

WAKEMAN Evans. *See:* **WAKEMAN Frederic Evans.**

WAKEMAN Frederic Evans (Evans Wakeman), b. 12 Dec 1937, Kansas City, USA. Professor. div, 2 sons, 1 daughter. *Education:* BA, Harvard College, 1959; MA, 1962, PhD, 1965, University of California, Berkeley. *Appointments:* Editorial Advisor, Modern Asian Studies, 1980-81; Editorial Advisory Board, American Historical Review, 1981; President, Social Science Research Council, 1986-89; President American Historical Association, 1992; Haas Professor of Asian Studies, Berkeley, 1989-. *Publications:* Strangers at the Gate: Social Disorder in South China, 1839-1861, 1966; Nothing Concealed: Essays in Honor of Liu Yu-Yun, 1970; Co-Editor, Conflict & Control in Late Imperial China, 1975; History and Will, 1976; The Great Enterprise: The Manchu Reconstruction of Imperial Order in Seventeenth Century China, 1985, 2 volumes; co-editor, Shanghai Sojourners, 1992. *Contributions to:* The China Quarterly; Journal of Asian Studies. *Honours:* History and Will, nominated for National Book Award, 1974; The Great Enterprise, Winner, Levenson Prize, 1986; The Great Enterprise, Winner, Lilienthal Award. *Memberships:* American Historical Association; Association for Asian Studies; American Academy of Arts & Sciences. *Address:* Institute of East Asian Studies, University of California, Berkeley CA 94720, USA.

WAKEMAN John, b. 29 Sept 1928, London, England. Editor; Writer. m. Hilary Paulett, 15 Mar 1957, 4 sons, 1 daughter. *Education:* Associate, British Library Association, 1950; BA in English and American Literature, with 1st Class Honours, University of East Anglia, Norwich, 1989; MA, University of East Anglia, 1990. *Publications:* A Room for Doubt, poems, 1985. Editor: Wilson Library Bulletin, New York, 1959-1961; World Authors: 1950-1970, 1975; World Authors: 1970-1975, 1980; World Film Directors (2 vols) 1987 and 1988. The Rialto, poetry magazine (with Michael Mackmin), 1985-; The Beach Hut (TV play), 1987. *Contributions to:* Poems, essays and reviews in: Ambit; Encounter; London Magazine; New Statesman; New York Times; New York Times Book Review; Observer; Poetry (Chicago); Times (London); Times Literary Supplement; Punch. *Honours:* World Film Directors selected by Library Journal as 1 of Best Reference Books of 1988 and by Choice as 1 of Outstanding Academic Books of 1989; Eastern Arts Travel Bursary (to Mexico), 1991; Hawthornden Fellowship, 1992. *Address:* 32 Grosvenor Road, Norwich, Norfolk NR2 2PZ, England.

WALD Richard C, b. New York, USA. Journalist. m. Edith May Leslie, 1953, 2 sons, 1 daughter. *Education:* Columbia University; Clare College, Cambridge. *Appointments:* Reporter, later Managing Editor, Herald Tribune 1955-66; Assistant Managing Editor, Washington Post, 1967; Executive Vice President, Whitney Communications Corporation, New York, 1968-; Vice President, News, NBC, President 1968-78; Senior Vice President, ABC News, 1978-; Chair, Columbia Spectator; Board of Directors, Associated Press, Worldwide TV News. *Address:* 47 West 66th Street, New York, NY 10023, USA.

WALDEN (Alastair) Brian, b. 8 July 1932. Broadcaster; Journalist. m. Hazel Downes, 1 son, 3 sons from former marriages. *Education:* Queens College, and Nuffield College, Oxford. *Appointments:* University Lecturer; MP for Birmingham All Saints 1964-74, Birmingham Ladywood 1974-77, Labour; TV Presenter, Weekend World (London Weekend TV) 1977-86; Member, West Midland Board, Central Independent TV 1982-84; Columnist, London Standard, 1983-86; Thomson Regional Newspapers, 1983-86; Columnist, Sunday Times, 1986-; The Walden Interviews, 1990. *Honours:* Shell International Award, 1982; BAFTA Richard Dimbleby Award, 1985; Aims of Industry Special Free Enterprise Award, 1990; TV Times Favourite TV Current Affairs Personality, 1990; Television and Radio Industries Club ITV Personality of the Year, 1991. *Address:* Landfall, Fort Road, St Peter Port, Guernsey, Channel Islands.

WALDENFELS Hans, b. 20 Oct 1931, Essen, Ruhr. University Professor. *Education:* Lic phil 1956 Pullach, Munchen; Lic theol 1964 Sophia University, Tokyo; Dr theol 1968 Gregoriana Rome; Dr theol habil 1976 Wurzburg University; Joined Societas Jesu 1951; Ordained Roman Catholic Priest 1963. *Publications:* Faszination des Buddhismus, 1982; Kontextuelle Fundamentaltheologie, 2 ed, 1988, also in French, Polish, Italian and Spanish; An der Grenze des Denkbaren, 1988; Lexikon der Religionen (Hg) 1988; Begegnung der Religionen, 2 ed, 1990. *Memberships:* Internationales Institut fur missionswissenschaftliche Forschungen, Chairman 1978-; International Association for Mission Studies; Deutsche Vereinigung fur Religionsgeschichte; Invited member, Deutsche Gesellschaft fur Missioswissenschaft; Rotary Club. *Address:* Grenzweg 2, D-4000 Dusseldorf 31, Germany.

WALDMAN Jules Lloyd, b. 4 Dec 1912, New York, USA. Publisher; Editor. m. Agnes Tolnay, 24 Sept 1949, 1 son, 1 daughter. *Education:* BA, Columbia University, 1932; Postgraduate studies, Columbia University, 1934. *Appointments:* Associate Editor, Columbia Review, 1931-32; Contributing Editor, Columbia Spectator, 1932; Editor, Caracas Daily Journal, 1945-80; Correspondent: The New York Times, 1945-70, Time Magazine, 1945-51; Editor, Clave Magazine, 1950-60; Professor of Journalism, Universidad Central de

Venezuela, 1947-51. *Publications:* Report on Venezuela, 1985; Speaking of Venezuela, 1946. *Contributions To:* New Republic; Harpers; New York Times; Time Magazine; many daily newspapers in New York, and Caracas. *Honours:* Municipal Newspaper Prize, Caracas, 1947; National Newspaper Prize, Venezuela, 1948; Order of Merit, 1958; Order of Andres Bello, 1965; Order of Francisco Miranda, 1968; Order of Simon Bolivar, 1985. *Memberships:* Interamerican Press Association; Overseas Press Club, President, Caracas Chapter; Venezuela Press Association, Vice President; Bloque de Prensa Venezolano, Vice President. *Address:* The Daily Journal, Apartado 1408, Caracas, Venezuela.

WALDROP Rosmarie, b. 24 Aug 1935, Kitzingen/Main, Germany. Writer; Translator; Editor. m. 21 Jan 1959. *Education:* Undergraduate studies, Universities of Wurzburg, Freiburg and Aix-Marseille; MA, 1960, PhD, 1966, University of Michigan, USA. *Appointments:* Editor, Publisher, Burning Deck Press, USA, 1963-; Wesleyan University, 1964-70; SMU, 1977; Brown University, 1977-78, 1983, 1990-91; Tufts University, 1978-81. *Publications:* The Road is Everywhere or Stop This Body, 1978; Streets Enough to Welcome Snow, poems, 1986; The Reproduction of Profiles, poems, 1987; The Hanky of Pippin's Daughter, novel; A Form/of Taking/ It All, novella, 1990; The Book of Questions by Edmond Jabes (translator), 7 vols bound as 4, 1976-84. *Contributions to:* Conjunctions; Sulfur; Oblek; Denver Quarterly; Temblor. *Honours:* Major Hopwood Award in Poetry, 1963; Howard Fellowship, 1974-75; Columbia Translation Center Award, 1978; NEA Fellowship in Poetry, 1980; Rhode Island Governor's Arts Award, 1988. *Membership:* PEN. *Address:* 71 Elmgrove Avenue, Providence, RI 02906, USA.

WALES Robert, b. 12 July 1933, Greenock, Scotland. Writer. m. (1) Joan Marie Austin, 1947, 3 daughters, 2 sons, (2) Susan Clare Richardson, 1970, 1 son. *Publications:* The Cell, 1971; 'Harry' 1985; The Navigator, 1989. Also: Films, television & theatre plays, TV series, short stories. *Memberships:* Chairman, Broadcasting Committee 1978-80, Society of Authors; Writers Guild, UK & Australia. *Literary Agent:* Peters Fraser & Dunlop, The Chambers, Chelsea Harbour, London SW10. *Address:* 2 Thorne Street, Barnes, London SW13 0PR.

WALKER Alexander, b. 22 Mar 1930, Portadown, Northern Ireland. Journalist; Film Critic. *Education:* BA, Queen's University, Belfast; College d'Europe, Bruges, Belgium; University of Michigan, USA. *Appointments include:* Lecturer, University of Michigan, 1952-54; Features editor, Birmingham Gazette, UK, 1954-56; Leader writer, film critic, Birmingham Post, 1956-59; Journalist, Film Critic, Evening Standard, 1960-; Columnist, Vogue magazine, 1974-1986; Frequent broadcaster; Author, TV series; Author, co-producer, TV programmes on History of Hollywood, Garbo, Chaplin. *Publications include:* The Celluloid Sacrifice: Aspects of Sex in the Movies, 1966; Stardom: The Hollywood Phenomenon, 1970; Rudolph Valentino, 1976; Double Takes: Notes & Afterthoughts on the Movies 1956-76, 1977; Garbo, 1980; Peter Sellers: Authorised Biography, 1981; Joan Crawford, 1983; Dietrich, 1984; National Heroes: British Cinema Industry in the 70's & 80's, 1985; Bette Davis, 1986; Vivien: The Life of Vivien Leigh, 1987; It's only a Movie, Ingrid: Encounters on and off the Screen, 1988; Elizabeth: The life of Elizabeth Taylor, 1990; Zinnemann (CLB Fred Zinnemenn), 1991; Fatal Charm: The life of Rex Harrison, 1992. *Contributions to:* Encounter; Various other British & foreign publications. *Honours:* Critic of the Year 1970, 1974, commended 1985, British Press Awards; Chevalier de l'Ordre des Arts et des Lettres, 1981; Award of Golden Eagle, Philippines, services to international cinema, 1982. *Memberships:* British Screen Advisory Council, 1977-1992; Governor, British Film Institute, 1989-. *Address:* 1 Marlborough, 38-40 Maida Vale, London W9 1RW, England.

WALKER Alice Malsenior, b. Feb 1944, Eatonton, Georgia. Writer. 1 daughter. *Education:* AB, Sarah Lawrence College, 1963-65. *Appointments:* Publisher, Wild Trees Press, 1984-88; Consultant to Quincy Jones and Steven Speilburg on the film, The Color Purple, 1985. *Publications:* Once, 1968; The Third Life of Grange Copeland, 1970; To Hell With Dying, 1988; The Temple of My Familiar, 1989. *Contributions to:* Various journals. *Memberships:* Authors Guild; PEN; Board of Trustees, Sarah Lawrence College, 1971-73. *Honours:* Recipient of numerous honours and awards for professional services.

WALKER Andrew Norman, b. 19 May 1926, Looe, Cornwall, England. Retired BBC Journalist. m. Avril Anne Elizabeth Dooley, 20 June 1956, 2 sons, 2 daughters. *Publications:* The Modern Commonwealth, 1975; The Commonwealth: a new look, 1978; A Skyful of Freedom, 1992. *Contributions to:* Occasional articles in Jane's Defence Weekly; Commonwealth Magazine. *Membership:* Diplomatic and Commonwealth Writers of Britain, Past President; Commonwealth Journalists Association. *Address:* 9 Chartwell Court, Brighton, East Sussex BN1 2EW, England.

WALKER Clive Phillip, b. England. University Lecturer. *Education:* LLB; PhD; Solicitor. *Publications:* Political Violence and the Law in Ireland, 1989; The Prevention of Terrorism in British Law, 2nd ed 1992. *Contributions to:* Many professional publications. *Address:* Centre for Criminal Justice Studies, University of Leeds, Leeds LS2 9JT, England.

WALKER David Maxwell, b. 9 Apr 1920, Glasgow, Scotland. University Professor, retired. m. Margaret Knox, 1 Sept 1954. *Education:* MA, 1946, LLB, 1948, LLD, 1985, Glasgow University; PhD, 1952, LLD, 1960, Edinburgh University; LLB, 1957, LLD, 1968, London University. *Publications:* The Oxford Companion to Law, 1980; Principles of Scottish Private Law, 4 vols, 4th Edition, 1988; Law of Delict in Scotland, 2nd Edition, 1981; Law of Contracts in Scotland, 2nd Edition, 1985; Law of Civil Remedies in Scotland, 1974; The Scottish Jurists, 1985; Law of Prescription and Limitation in Scotland, 4th Edition, 1990; Stair's Institutions of the Law of Scotland (editor), 1981. *Contributions to:* Numerous, mostly to Juridical Review and Scots Law Times. *Honours:* Honorary LLD (Edinburgh), 1974; Fellow, British Academy, 1976; Fellow, Royal Society of Edinburgh, 1980, Vice-President, 1985-88; CBE, 1986. *Memberships:* Faculty of Advocates; Honourable Society of the Middle Temple; Stair Society; Scottish History Society; Society of Antiquaries in Scotland. *Address:* 1 Beaumont Gate, Glasgow G12 9EE, Scotland.

WALKER Geoffrey De Quincey, b. 27 Oct 1940, Waratah, NSW, Australia. Professor of Law. m. Patricia Mary Kehoe, 7 Dec 1990. *Education:* LLB 1962, Sydney; LLM 1963, SJD 1966, Pennsylvania. *Publications:* Australian Monopoly Law, 1967; Initiative and Referendum: The People's Law, 1987; The Rule of Law: Foundation of Constitutional Democracy, 1988. *Contributions to:* Over 60 articles in legal, economic and related journals. *Honour:* Gowen Fellow, University of Pennsylvania, 1966. *Address:* T C Beirne School of Law, University of Queensland, Queensland 4072, Australia.

WALKER Harry. *See:* WAUGH Hilary Baldwin.

WALKER Kenneth Roland, *Education:* BA, History, English, Goshen College, 1949; MA, American and European History, 1950, PhD, History, Political Theory and Comparative Government, 1952, Indiana University; MEd, Education Administration, University of Arkansas, 1964; MEd, Social Studies, Arkansas Tech University, 1978. *Publications:* The Month of Assassination, September 1901, 1952; Days the Presidents Died, 1966; A History of the Middle West, 1972; History of the First United Methodist Church, Russellville, Arkansas, 1783-1984, 1984; Revised Edition 1783-1992, 1993; History of Arkansas Tech University, 1909, 1990. *Contributions* *to:* The Growing Political Significance of the United States Midwest in 1901 to Northwest Ohio Quarterly, A Journal of History and Civilization, 1957; Missouri: A Southern or Midwestern State, Arkansas Academy of Science, 1961; Distinctively American: A Glimpse of Midwestern Culture in 1901, Northwest Ohio Quarterly: A Journal of History and Civilization, 1962. *Honour:* Air Force Commendation Medal for instruction at Air Force Academy. *Memberships:* Phi Delta Kappa; Organization of American Historians; Phi Alpha Theta; Arkansas Department of Higher Education, Vice-President and President 1964-66; Reserve Officers Association; Arkansas Council of Social Studies, Vice-President 1965-67; Arkansas College History Teachers. *Address:* Social Sciences and Philosophy Department, Arkansas Tech University, Russellville, AR 72801, USA.

WALKER Lou Ann, b. 9 Dec 1952, Hartford City, Indiana, USA. Writer. m. Speed Vogel, 8 Sept 1986, 1 daughter. *Education:* Attended Ball State University, 1971-73; Degree in French Language and Literature, University of Besancon, 1975; BA, Harvard University, 1976. *Appointments:* Reporter, Indianapolis News, 1976; Assistant to Executive Editor, New York (magazine) New York, 1976-77; Associate Editor, Esquire, New York City, 1976-78; Assistant to Executive Editor, Cosmopolitan, New York City, 1979-80; Associate Editor, Diversion (magazine) New York City, 1980-81; Editor, Direct (magazine) New York City, 1981-82; Sign language interpreter for New York Society for the Deaf; Consultant on special project for handicapped people for Museum of Modern Art, 1980-85; Consultant to Broadway's Theater Development Fund and sign language advisor on many Broadway shows, 1984-; Contributing Editor, New York Woman, 1990-92. *Publications:* Amy: The Story of a Deaf Child, photographs by Michael Abramson, 1985; A Loss for Words: The Story of Deafness in a Family (autobiography) 1986; Hand, Heart and Mind, 1993. *Contributions to:* Esquire; The New York Times Magazine; New York Woman; Life. *Honours:* Rockefeller Foundation Humanities Fellowship, 1982-83; Rockefeller Foundation Grant, 1983-84; Christopher Award for A Loss for Words, 1987; National Endowment for the Arts Creative Writing Grant, 1988. *Membership:* Authors Guild. *Literary Agent:* Liz Darhansoff. *Address:* c/o Darhansoff & Verrill, 1220 Park Avenue, New York, NY 10128, USA.

WALKER Mary Alexander, b. 24 Sept 1927, Beaumont, Texas, USA. Author; Educator. m. Tommy Ross Walker, 23 Dec 1952, 3 sons. *Education:* BA, Texas Women's University; MA, San Francisco State University; Hans Hofmann School of Painting; San Francisco Academy of Art. *Appointments:* Editor, Norcal Newsletter, Mystery Writers of America, 1984-85; Lecturer, University of San Francisco, 1983-. *Publications:* Year of the Cafeteria, 1971; Maggot, 1980; To Catch a Zombi, 1979; Maeve's Daughters, forthcoming; The Princess with 28 Heads, play; The Pied Piper; Has had numerous short stories appear in magazines and books. *Contributions to:* Arizona Author's Literary magazine. *Honours:* Award, Short Stories, Northwest Writers Conference, 1976, 1979; Fellowship, Breadloaf Writers Conference, 1972; Award, Norcal Conference, Mystery Writers of America, 1983; Judge, Texas Circuit, Austin Authors, 1986; Judge, Edgar Allan Poe Award, Mystery Writers of America, 1987. *Memberships:* Society of Children's Book Writers; National Board, Mystery Writers of American, 1987. *Literary Agent:* Anita Diament Literary Agency, New York City, USA. *Address:* 22 Corte Lodato, Greenbrae, CA, 94904, USA.

WALKER Robert Wayne (Geoffry Cain, Stephen Robertson), b. 17 Nov 1948, Corinth, Mississippi. USA. Novelist. m. Cheryl A. Ernst, 8 Sept 1967, 1 son. *Education:* BS, 1971, MS, 1972, Northwestern University. *Publications:* As Robert Walker: Sub-Zero, 1979; Brain Watch, 1985; Salem's Child, 1987; Aftershock, 1987; Disembodied, 1988; Dead Man's Float, 1988; Razor's Edge, 1989; Burning Obsession, 1990; Dying Breath, 1990; Killer Instinct, 1992; Fatal

Instinct, 1993; Savage Instinct, forthcoming; Daniel Webster Jackson & The Wrongway Railway, 1982; Search for the Nile, 1986; As Glenn Hale: Dr O, 1991; As Stephen Robertson: Decoy Bk 1 & 2, 1989; Decoy Bk 3, 1990; The Handyman, 1990; As Geoffrey Caine: Curse of the Vampire, 1991; Wake of the Werewolf, 1991; Legion of the Dead, 1992. *Memberships:* Horror Writers of America; Mystery Writers of America. *Agent:* Acton, Dystel, Leone & Jaffe, New York. *Address:* 928 Broadway, New York, NY 10010, USA.

WALKER Sheila Suzanne, b. 5 Nov 1944, Jersey City, Jersey, USA. Anthropologist; University Professor. *Education:* African Politics, Institute d'Etudes Politiques, Paris and African Ethnology and Sociology, Sorbonne, 1964-65; BA cum laude, Political Science, Bryn Mawr College, 1966; MA, 1969, PhD, Anthropology, 1976, University of Chicago. *Publications:* Ceremonial Spirit Possession in Africa and Afro-America, 1972; African Christianity: Patterns of Religious Continuity (edited with George Bond and Walton Johnson), 1979; The Religious Revolution in the Ivory Coast: The Prophet Harris and the Harrist Church, 1983. *Contributions to:* Patterns of Prejudice; Journal of African Studies; Anthropology and Education Quarterly; Ethiopiques: Revue de Culture Negro-Africaine; The Black Scholar; Journal of African Studies; Black Art: An International Quarterly; A Scholarly Journal on Black Women; Essence; The Black Collegian; Center for Southern Folklore Newsletter; Genetic Dancers; Emerge Magazine; Many others including books. *Literary Agent:* Marie Brwn, Marie Brown Associates, New York, USA. *Address:* Center for African and Afro-American Studies, University of Texas, Austin, TX 78705, USA.

WALKER Ted, b. 28 Nov 1934, Writer. m. (1) Lorna Ruth Benfell, 11 Aug 1956 (dec Apr 1987), 2 sons, 2 daughters, (2) Audrey Joan Hicks, 8 July 1988. *Education:* St John's College, Cambridge. *Appointments:* Chairman of Judges' Panel, Cholmondeley Award for Poetry, 1974-1990. *Publications:* Fox on a Barn Door, 1965; The Solitaries, 1967; The Night Bathers, 1970; Gloves to the Hangman, 1973; Burning the Ivy, 1978; The High Path, autobiography, 1982; You've Never Heard Me Sing, 1985; In Spain, 1987; Hands at a Live Fire, 1987; The Last of England, 1992. *Contributions to:* The New Yorker; The New Statesman; The Times Literary Supplement; The Listener; The Atlantic Monthly; The London Magazine; The Observer; Encounter; The Poetry review; Sunday telegraph. *Honours:* The Eric Gregory Award, 1964; The Cholmondeley Award, 1966; The Alice Hunt Bartlett Award, 1969; The Society of Authors Travel Bursary, 1978; The Ackerley Award for Literary Autobiograhy, 1982. *Membership:* Fellow, Royal Society of Literature. *Literary Agent:* David Higham Associates Limited, Golden Square, London, England. *Address:* Argyll House, The Square, Eastergate, Chichester, West Sussex PO20 6UP, England.

WALKER Wilbert Lee, b. 22 July 1925, Durham, NC, USA. Retired Public Administrator. m. Grace Clayborne, 15 June 1951, 1 son. *Education:* BA, Morgan State University, 1950; MSW, Social Work, Howard University, Washington DC, 1954. *Publications:* The Deputy's Dilemma, 1987; Servants of All, 1982; Stalemate at Panmunjon, 1980; The Pride of our Hearts, 1978; We are Men, 1972. *Honours:* Trinity Presbyterian Church Literary Award, 1978; Alpha Phi Alpha Literary Award, 1979. *Memberships include:* Mid Atlantic Writers Association; Committee of Small Magazines, Editors and Publishers; National Assocation of Social Workers, life member; Delta Lambda Chapter, Alpha Phi Alpha Fraternity, Past-President. *Address:* PO Box 18625, Baltimore, MD 21216, USA.

WALL Ethan. *See:* **HOLMES Bryan John.**

WALL Geoffrey. *See:* **CHADWICK Geoffrey.**

WALL Mervyn, b. 23 Aug 1908, Dublin, Ireland.

Retired Chief Executive of Irish Arts Council. m. Fanny Feehan, 25 Apr 1950, 1 son, 3 daughters. *Education:* BA, National University of Ireland, 1928. *Appointments:* Civil Servant, 1934-48; Programme Officer, Radio Eireann, 1948-57; Irish Arts Council, Chief Executive, 1957-75; Book Reviewer, Radio Critic, Radio Broadcaster. *Publications:* The Unfortunate Fursey, 1946; The Return of Fursey, 1948; Leaves for the Burning, 1952; No Trophies Raise, 1956; Forty Foot Gentlemen Only 1962; A Flutter of Wings (short stories), 1974; Hermitage, 1982; The Garden of Echoes, 1988. Plays: Alarm Among the Clerks, 1937; The Lady in the Twilight, 1941. *Contributions to:* Journals in Ireland, Britain and USA. *Honours:* Best European Novel of the Year, Copenhagen, Denmark, 1952. *Memberships:* Irish Academy of Letters, Treasurer and Secretary 1968-76, President 1976-78; Aosdana, 1985-; Irish Hellenic Society; President, Irish Writers Union, 1990-. *Address:* 16 Castlepark Road, Sandycove, Dun Laoghaire, Co Dublin, Ireland.

WALLACE Betty Frances, b. 28 June 1926, Gastonia, North Carolina, USA. Retired teacher/educator; Librarian. m. William Andrew Wallace Jr, 4 Sept 1948, 1 son, 2 daughters. *Education:* BFA Degree, Painting, University of Georgia, 1948; Post graduate study, Georgia State University, 1967-69, 1972-73; Tift College, 1976; Elementary Certification, Art Certification, Georgia State University, 1976; Teacher of Gifted Certification, West Georgia College, 1981. *Publications:* Through a Time Sieve, 1984; With Wings Afire, 1990; Poems include, The Bayeaux Tapestry, 1980; House of the Muses, 1980; The Io Moth, 1983; Retreat without Maximilian, 1983; Ballade for the Lady, 1984; Posture of Sleep, 1988. *Contributions to:* New York Herald Tribune; American Bard; The Writer; Poetry Scope; North American Mentor; Hampton News; Anthologies, Georgia State Poetry Society; American Poetry Anthology; New Worlds Unlimited. *Honours include:* New York Poetry Forum, Villanelle, 1983; Daniel Whitehead Hicky National Awards, 1983, 1988; Author of Year in Poetry, 1985; Free Verse, Nevada State Poetry Society, 1987; Yearbook Dedication, HAWKS, 1986; Teacher of Year, 1987; Blue Ribbon Award, Southern Poetry Association, 1989. *Memberships include:* Georgia State Poetry Society, Charter Member; Southern Poetry Association; American Association of University Women; National Geographics Association. *Address:* 30 Woodlawn Avenue, Hampton, GA 30228, USA.

WALLACE David Foster, b. 21 Feb 1962, USA. Fiction Writer. *Education:* AB summa cum laude, Amherst College, 1985; MFA, University of Arizona, 1987. *Publications:* Signifying Rappers, non-fiction, 1990; Girl With Curious Hair, stories, 1991; The Broom of the System, novel, 1993. *Contributions to:* Harper's; Playboy; Grand Street; The Paris Review; Fiction; Fiction International; Harvard Review. *Honours:* Whiting Writers Award, 1987; O Henry Award, 1989; National Endowment for the Arts, 1989; New Voices Fiction Award, 1991; Best American Short Stories, 1992. *Membership:* The Authors Guild. *Literary Agent:* Frederick Hill Associates, San Francisco, USA. *Address:* c/o Frederick Hill Associates, 1842 Union St, San Francisco, CA 94123, USA.

WALLACE Ian Robert, b. 31 Mar 1950, Ontario, Canada. Author; Illustrator. *Education:* Ontario College of Art, 1969-73, 1973-74. *Publications:* Julie News 1974; The Sandwich, co-author, 1975; The Christmas Tree House, 1976; Chin Chiang and the Dragon's Dance, 1984; Very Last First Time, 1985, Illustrator; The Sparrow's Song, 1986; Morgan the Magnificent, 1987; Architect of the Moon, 1988, Illustrator, 1988; The Name of the Tree, Illustrator. *Contributions to:* Quill & Quire. *Honours:* Runner Up, City of Toronto Book Awards, 1976; IODE Book Award, 1985; Canadian Library Association's Amelia Francis Howard-Gibbon Award, 1985; Ibby Honour Book, 1986; ALA Notable Book, 1986; White Raven Book, Bologna Children's Book Fair, 1987. *Memberships:* Writers Union; The Authors Guild.

Address: 184 Major Street, Toronto, Ontario, Canada M5S 2L3.

WALLACE Ronald William, b. 18 Feb 1945, Cedar Rapids, Iowa, USA. Poet; Professor of English. m. Margaret Elizabeth McCreight, 3 Aug 1968, 2 daughters. *Education:* BA, College of Wooster, 1967; MA, 1968, PhD, 1971, University of Michigan. *Appointments:* Director of Creative Writing, University of Wisconsin, Madison, 1975-; Series Editor, Brittingham Prize in Poetry, 1985-; Director, Wisconsin Institute for Creative Writing, 1986-. *Publications:* Henry James and the Comic Form, 1975; Installing the Bees, 1977; Cucumbers, 1977; The Last Laugh, 1979; The Facts of Life, 1979; Plums, Stones, Kisses and Hooks, 1981; Tunes for Bears to Dance to, 1983; God Be With The Clown, 1984; The Owl in the Kitchen, 1985; People and Dog in the Sun, 1987; Vital Signs, 1989. *Contributions to:* The New Yorker; The Atlantic; The Nation; Poetry; Southern Review; Poetry Northwest; Prairie Schooner; Georgia Review; American Scholar; Others. *Honours:* Hopwood Award for Poetry, 1970; Council for Wisconsin Writers Awards, 1978, 1979, 1984, 1985, 1986, 1988; Helen Bullis Prize in Poetry, 1985; Robert E Gard Award for Excellence in Poetry, 1990. *Memberships:* Poets and Writers; Associated Writing Programs. *Address:* Department of English, University of Wisconsin, Madison, WI 53706, USA.

WALLER Jane Ashton, b. 19 May 1944, Aylesbury, Bucks, England. Writer; Ceramist. m. Michael Vaughan-Rees, 11 June 1982. *Education:* Pre-Diploma Year, Oxford Art College 1962-63; Structured Ceramics Course, Sir John Cas College 1966-69; MA 1982, Royal College of Art; BA 1985, Hornsey Art College. *Publications:* A Stitch in Time, 1972; Some Things for the Children, 1974; Some 'Dinosaur Poems' for Children. 1975; A Man's Book, 1977; Some 'Bedtime Tales' for Children, 1978; Some 'Bedtime Stories' for Children, 1980; Happy Day Stories for Children, 1980; The Thirties Family Knitting Book, 1981; Below the Green Pond, 1982; The Man's Knitting Book, 1984; Women in Wartime, Co-Author, 1987; Women in Uniform, Co-Author, 1989; Handbuilt Ceramics, 1990; Blitz, The Civilian War 1940-45, Co-Author, 1990. *Contributions to:* Ceramic Review. *Honour:* The Herbert Read Literary Award for The War of the Weather, 1981, RCA. *Literary Agent:* Mike Shaw, Curtis Brown. *Address:* 22 Roupell Street, Waterloo, London SE1 8SP, England.

WALLER John Stanier (Sir), b. 27 July 1917, England. Author; Poet; Journalist. m. Anne Eileen Mileham, 1974. *Education:* BA, English Language & Literature, 1939, Worcester College, Oxford; OU DipEd, Teaching, 1940. *Literary Appointments include:* Founder-editor, Kingdom Come, quarterly, 1st new literary mgazine of war, 1939-41; Features editor, British Ministry of Information, Middle East, 1943-45; Chief press officer, British Embassy, Baghdad, 1945; News & features editor, MIME, Cairo, 1945-46; Dramatic critic, Cairo weekly, The Sphinx, 1943-46; Lecturer, tutor, English & English Literature, Carlisle & Gregson (Jimmy's) Ltd, 1953-54; Information officer, Overseas Press Services Division, Central Office of Information, 1954-59; Director, Literature Ltd 1940-42, Richard Congreve Ltd 1948-50. *Publications:* The Confessions of Peter Pan, 1941; Fortunate Hamlet, 1941; Spring Legend, 1942; The Merry Ghosts, 1946; Middle East Anthology, editor, 1946; Crusade, 1946; the Kiss of Stars, 1948; Collected Poems of Keith Douglas, editor, 1951, 1966; Shaggy Dog, 1953; Alamein to Zem Zem by Keith Douglas, editor, 1966; Goldenhair & the Two Black Hawks, 1971; Return to Oasis, co-editor, 1980. *Contributions to:* Numerous anthologies & periodicals, UK & abroad. *Honours:* Greenwood Award, poetry, 1947; Keats Prize, 1974; Fellow, Royal Society of Literature, 1948. *Memberships include:* Founder member, Salamander Society of Poets, Cairo, 1942. *Address:* Winchcombe, 37A Maderia Road, Ventnor, Isle of White PO38 1TQ.

WALLMANN Jeffrey Miner (Nick Carter, R Vaan Corne, Leon Da Silva, Amanda Hart Douglas, Wesley

Ellis, William Jeffrey, Richard Mountbetten, Bill Saxon, Scott Sheldon, Gregory St Germain, Carole Wilson), b. 1941, Seattle, Washington, USA. Novelist. *Education:* BS, Portland State University, 1963. *Publications:* Over 100 novels, numerous novelettes, short stories and articles including: The Spiral Web, 1969; Judas Cross, 1974; Clean Sweep,. 1976; Deathrek (Science Fiction), 1980; The Blood and The Passion, 1980; Brand of the Damned, 1981; The Manipulator, 1982; Return to Canta Lupe, 1983; The Celluloid Kid, 1984; Business Basic for Bunglers, 1984; (as Richard Mountbetten) Spell of the Beast, 1969; (as R Van Corne) The Desolate Cove, 1970; (as Carole Wilson) Karen & Mother, 1971; (as Bill Saxon) The Terrorists, 1972; Junkyard Rape, 1973; (as Nick Carter) Hour of the Wolf, (award), 1973; Ice Trap Terror (award), 1974; (as Leon DaSilva) (non-Fiction) Green Hell, 1976; Angolan Breakout, 1976; (as Scott Sheldon) The Ikon, 1977; (as Amanda Hart Douglass) Jamaica, 1978; (as Gregory St Germain) Resistance No 1, Night & Fog, 1982; Resistance No 2, Magyar Massacre, 1983; (as Wesley Ellis) Many of the Lonestar Western Series; (as William Jeffery with Bill Pronzini) Duel at Gold Buttes, 1980; Border Fever, 1982; Day of the Moon, 1983; Lonestar on the Treachery Trail, 1982; Longarm and the Lonestar Showdown, 1986; Trailsman 58; Slaughter Express, 1986; numerous others in Trailsman series; also many other pseudonyms and titles. *Contributions to:* Articles and short stories to Argosy; Ellery Queen's Mystery Mag; Alfred Hitchcock's Mystery Mag; Mike Shayne's Mystery Mag; Zane Grey Western; Venture Oui; TV Guide. *Memberships:* Mystery Writers of America; Science Fiction Writers of America; Western Writers America; Crime Writers Association; Nevada World Trade Council. *Literary Agent:* Joe Elder. *Address:* c/o Joe Elder, PO Box 298, Warwick, New York, USA.

WALLS Ian Gascoigne, b. 28 Apr 1922, Yoker, Glasgow, Scotland. Horticulturist. m. Eleanora McIntosh McCaig, 11 Aug 1947, 2 daughters. *Education:* College Diploma in Horticulture, West of Scotland Agricultural College, 1949; National Diploma in Horticulture, 1959. *Publications:* Gardening Month by Month, 1962; Creating Your Garden, 1967; The Lady Gardener, 1968; Greenhouse Gardening, 1970; Complete Book of the Greenhouse, 1973, 1979, 1983, 1988, 1993; Tomato Growing Today, 1972, 1977; A-Z of Garden Pests and Problems, 1979; Modern Greenhouse Methods, Flowers, Vol 1, 1984, Vegetables, Vol 2, 1984; Profit from Growing Vegetables, Fruits and Flowers, 1988; Simple Tomato Growing, 1988; Simple Vegetable Growing, 1988; Growing Tomatoes, 1989; Making Your Garden Pay; Low Cost Gardening, 1992. Hydroponics, UK reissue; Bowling Green Care and Maintenance. *Contributions to:* Scottish Farmer; The Grower; Horticultural Product News; Amateur Gardening; The Greenock Telegraph. *Memberships:* Glasgow Wheelers CC (TSB); Life Member, Milngavie Horticultural Society. *Literary Agent:* Robert Crewe Ltd, Kings Mews, London, England. *Address:* 17 Dougalston Avenue, Milngavie, Glasgow G62 6AP, Scotland.

WALMSLEY Tom, b. 13 Dec 1948, Liverpool, Lancashire, England, emmigrated to Canada 30 Nov 1953. Playwright; Poet. m. (1) Marie Smith, Feb 1968 (div Jan 1969), (2) Brenda Hilimoniuk, 30 Jan 1976 (div Dec 1976), (3) Diana Clifford, 20 June 1987. *Appointments:* Worked odd jobs, including cleaning herring, selling newspapers and doing carpet factory work; worked on assembly line at General Motors, 1968-69; heroin addict and thief 1971-74; Pulp Press, Vancouver, British Columbia, editor 1974-79; writer 1975-. *Publications include:* Doctor Tin (novel) 1979; Something Red (two-act play; first produced in Vancouver at the New Play Center, Sept 2, 1978), 1980; (with Dolly Reisman) Mr. Nice Guy (two-act play) first produced in Toronto at Toronto Free Theatre, Apr 3, 1986; Getting Wrecked (one-act juvenile play, first produced in Toronto at the Theatre Direct, Apr 12 1985) published in Your Voice and Mine 1, Joan Green, editor, Holt, 1987; White Boys (two-act play; first produced in Toronto at the Tarragon Theatre, Mar 13, 1982) Playwrights Canada, 1988; White Boys (film) Alternative Pictures, 1989. *Honours:* Award from Pulp Press, 1978,

for Doctor Tin; co-winner of the Floyd S Chalmers Canadian Play Award from the Ontario Arts Council, 1983 for White Boys. *Membership:* Playwrights Union of Canada.

WALSER Martin, b. 24 Mar 1927, Wasserburg, Federal Republic of Germany. Writer. *Education:* Theological-Philosophical College, Regensburg; PhD, University of Tubingen. *Publications:* Ehen in Philippsburg, 1957; Halbzeit, 1960; Das Einhorn, 1966; Fiction, 1970; Die Gallistl'sche Krankheit, 1972; Der Sturz, 1973; Jenseits de Liebe, 1976; Ein fliehendes pferd, 1978; Seelenarbeit, 1979; Das Schwanenhaus, 1980; Brief on Lord Liszt, 1982; Messmers Gedanken, 1985; Brandung, 1985; Jagd, 1988; Die Veri teidigung derkindheit, 1991. *Honours:* Grp 47 Prize, 1955; Hermann Hesse Prize, 1957; Gerhart Hauptmann, 1962; Schiller Prize, 1965; Georg Buechner Prize, 1981. *Memberships:* German Academy for Language and Literature; Association German Writers; PEN Club; Academy of Arts, Berlin. *Address:* 777 Uberlingen-Nussdorf, Zum Hecht 36, Federal German Republic.

WALSH George William, b. 16 Jan 1931, New York, USA. Editor; Author. m. 29 May 1961, 1 son, 1 daughter. *Education:* BS, Fordham University, 1952; MS, Columbia Graduate School of Journalism, 1953. *Appointments:* Editor, Reporter, Cape Cod Standard Times, Hyannis, 1955; Communications Specialist, IBM, New York City, 1955-58; Editorial Trainee, Time Inc., 1958-59; Writer-Reporter, Sports Illustrated, 1959-62; Book Editor, 1962-65, Managing Editor, 1965-74, Cosmpolitan; Editor in Chief, Vice President, Ballantine Books, 1974-79; Editor in Chief, Vice President, Macmillan Publishing Co., New York City, 1979-85; Publishing consultant, 1985-. *Publications:* Gentlemen Jimmy Walker, 1974; Public Enemies : The Mayor, the Mob and the Crime that Was, 1979. *Contributions to:* numerous magazines. *Membership:* Association of American Publishers. *Address:* 597 Fourth St., Brooklyn, NY 11215, USA.

WALSH John Evangelist, b. 27 Dec 1927, New York City, USA. Author. *Education:* Iona College, New Rochelle, NY. *Publications:* The Shroud, 1963; Strange Harp, 1967; Poe the Detective, 1968; Letters of Francis Thompson, 1969; Hidden Life of Emily Dickinson, 1971; One Day at Kitty Hawk, 1975; Night on Fire, 1978; Plumes in the Dust, 1980; Bones of St Peter, 1982; Into My Own, 1988; The Man Who Buried Jesus (novel), 1989; This Brief Tragedy, 1990. *Honour:* Edgar Award, best fact-crime book, Mystery Writers of America, 1968. *Literary Agent:* Julian Bach. *Address:* c/o Julian Bach, 747 3rd Avenue, New York City, USA.

WALSH Sheila, (Sophie Leyton), b. 1928. Writer. *Publications:* The Golden Songbird, 1975; Madalena, 1976; The Sergeant Major's Daughter, 1977; A Fine Silk Purse, 1978, in US as Lord Gilmore's Bride, 1979; The Incomparable Miss Brady, 1980; (as Sophie Leyton) Lady Cecily's Dilemma, 1980, in US as The Pink Parasol, 1985; The Rose Domino, 1981; A Highly Respectable Marriage, 1983; The Runaway Bride, 1984; Cousins of a Kind, in US as The Diamond Waterfall, 1985; The Incorigible Rake, 1985; Improper Acquaintances, 1986; An Insubstantial Pageant, in US as The Wary Widow, 1986; Bath Intrigue, 1986; Lady Aurelia's Bequest, 1987; Minerva's Marquis, 1988; The Nabob, 1989-90; A Woman of Little Importance, 1991; Until Tomorrow, 1993. *Memberships:* Historical/Romance Secretary, Romantic Novelists Association, Chairman 1985-87, currently Vice President. *Literary Agent:* Mary Irvine, 11 Upland Park Road, Oxford, England. *Address:* 35 Coudray Rd, Southport, Merseyside, PR9 9NL, England.

WALSHE Aubrey Peter, b. 12 Jan 1934, Johannesburg, South Africa. Professor Political Science. m. Catherine Ann Pettifer, 26 Jan 1957, 1 son, 3 daughters. *Education:* BA Hons Oxford 1956, Wadham College; DPhil Oxford 1968, St Antonys College. *Appointments:* Lecturer, University of Lesotho 1959-62; Professor, University of Notre Dame, Indiana, USA 1967-. *Publications:* The Rise of African Nationalism in South Africa, 1971; Black Nationalism in South Africa, 1974; Church versus State in South Africa, 1983; Southern Africa, Cambridge History of Africa, vol 7, ch 11, 1986. *Contributions to:* Journal of Modern African Studies; Journal of Church and State; Cross Currents; The Review of Politics; New York Times; Journal of African History; Transafrica Forum; Christianity and Crisis; and others. *Literary Agent:* Christopher Hurst, London. *Address:* Department of Government, University of Notre Dame, Notre Dame, IN 46556, USA.

WALTER Richard, b. 11 July 1944, New York, USA. Writer; Educator. m. Patricia Sandgrund, 18 June 1967, 1 son, 1 daughter. *Education:* BA History 1965, Harpur College, State University of New York; MS Communications 1966, Newhouse School of Public Communications, Syracuse University; Post Graduate Study, Department of Cinema, University of Southern California 1967- 70. *Appointments:* Professor and Screenwriting Chairman, Department of Film and Television, University of California at Los Angeles 1977- . *Publications:* Barry and the Persuasions, 1976; Screenwriting - The Art, Craft and Business of Film and Television Writing, 1988; Screenplays: Group Marriage; Return of Zorro; Dynamite Lady; Mrs Charlie; Split; Young Love; Marked Man; Jackie Whitefish. *Contributions to:* Asian Wall Street Journal; Los Angeles Times; Los Angeles Herald Examiner. *Memberships:* Writers Guild of America; PEN Centre West; University Film and Video Association. *Literary Agent:* Henry Dunow at Harold Ober Associates, NYC. *Address:* Department of Film and Television, University of California at Los Angeles, Los Angeles, CA 90024, USA.

WALTERS David Gareth, b. 1 Jan 1948, Neath, West Glamorgan. University Lecturer; Professor. m. Christine Ellen Knott, 14 Dec 1973, 1 son, 1 daughter. *Education:* BA Hons 1969, PhD 1974, University College, Cardiff. *Appointments:* Temporary Lecturer, University of Leeds 1972- 73; Lecturer in Hispanic Studies, University of Glasgow 1973-; Senior Lecturer 1989, Titular Professor 1991-. *Publications:* Francisco de Quevedo, Love Poet, 1985; The Poetry of Francisco de Aldana, 1988; Francisco de Quevedo: Poems to Lisi, 1988. *Contributions to:* Articles and reviews to miscellaneous journals on Hispanic literature including: Bulletin of Hispanic Studies; Modern Language Review; Journal of Hispanic Philology and European Journals. *Memberships:* Association of Hispanists of Britain and Ireland, Section Convenor 1985-88; Asociacion Internacional Siglo de Oro. *Address:* Department of Hispanic Studies, Hetherington Building, The University, Glasgow G12 8QQ, Scotland.

WALTON John Kimmons, b. 18 Nov 1948, Chesterfield, England. University Teacher. *Education:* BA Modern History 1970, Merton College, Oxford; PhD 1974, University of Lancaster. *Appointments:* Lecturer in History 1974-86, Senior Lecturer 1986-89, Reader in Modern Social History 1989-, University of Lancaster. *Publications:* The Blackpool Landlady, 1978; The English Seaside Resort 1750-1914, 1983; Lancashire: A Social History 1558-1939, 1987; The National Trust Guide to Late Georgian & Victorian Britain, 1989; Fish & Chips & the British Working Class, 1992; Several co- Authored or Co-Edited books, and Lancaster Pamphlets on the Second Reform Act, 1987, Disraeli, 1990. *Contributions to:* Numerous academic articles (about 20) and chapters and contributions to Open University Television Programmes. *Memberships:* FRHist Soc; Publications Sub-Committee, The Chetham Society. *Address:* Department of History, Furness College, University of Lancaster, Lancaster LA1 4YG, England.

WALTON Kendall L, b. 12 Sept 1939, Garden City, Kansas, USA. Professor of Philosophy. m. Susan Pratt Walton, 2 sons. *Education:* Fresno State University, 1957-59; BA, Philosophy, University of California, Berkeley, 1961; Doctoral study, 1961-65, PhD, Philosophy, 1967, Cornell University. *Publications:* Mimesis as Make-Believe: On the Foundations of the Representational Arts. *Contributions to:* Transparent Pictures: On the Nature of Photographic Realism, to Critical Inquiry, 1984. *Memberships:* American Philosophical Association; American Society for Aesthetics. *Address:* Department of Philosophy, 2205 Angell Hall, University of Michigan, Ann Arbor, MI 48109, USA.

WALVIN James, b.2 Jan 1942, Manchester, England. Historian. m. Jennifer, 2 sons. *Education:* BA, Keele University, 1964; MA, McMaster University, 1965; D Phil, York University 1970. *Publications:* Black- White, The Negro and English Society, 1973; The People's Game, Social History of Football, 1975; Victorian Values, 1987; A Child's World, A Social History of English Childhood, 1982; Slavery and The Slave Trade, 1983; England, Slaves and Freedom, 1986. *Honour:* Martin Luther King Memorial Prize (for Black-White) 1974. *Membership:* Royal Historical Society. *Literary Agent:* The Peters, Fraser and Dunlop Group Ltd. *Address:* Department of History, University of York, Heslington, York YO1 5DD, England.

WAMBAUGH Joseph, b. 22 Jan 1937, Penna, USA. Author. m. 26 Nov 1955, 1 son, 1 daughter. *Education:* BA; MA, California State University, Los Angeles. *Publications:* The Onion Field, 1973; The Choirboys, 1975; The Glitter Dome, 1981; The Delta Star, 1983; Lines and Shadows, 1984; The Secrets of Harry Bright, 1985; Echoes in the Darkness, 1987; The Blooding, 1989; The Golden Orange, 1990. *Address:* c/o Wm. Morrow and Co., 105 Madison Avenue, New York, NY 10016, USA.

WANDOR Michelene Dinah, b. 20 Apr 1940, London. Writer m. Edward Victor, 1963, Divorced 1975, 2 sons. *Education:* BA Hons, English, Newnham College, Cambridge; MA, Sociology of Literature, University of Essex, 1976. *Literary Appointment:* Poetry Editor, Time Out, 1971-82. *Publications include:* Carry on Understudies, Methuen 1981, Routledge 1986; Look Back in Gender, 1987; Gardens of Eden (selected poems) 1990; Five Plays, 1984; Guests in the Body (stories) 1987. *Contributions to:* Regular reviewer for The Listener, The Sunday Times. *Honour:* International Emmy for the film The Belle of Amherst, about Emily Dickinson, adapted from William Luce play: 1987 (Thames Television). *Membership:* Writers' Guild. *Address:* 71 Belsize Lane, London NW3 5AU, England.

WANG Yuan Jian, b. 1 Mar 1929, China. m. 6 Dec 1952, 3 daughters. *Education:* BA; College Graduation Diploma. *Appointments:* Dean of Literature, P.L.A. Arts College. *Publications:* The Party Membership Dues, short stories, 1956; Posterity, 1958; Common Labourers, 1959; Selected Short Stores and Novels by Wang Yuan Jian, 1985; The Shining Red Star, 1975; Crossing the Shui River for Four Times; The Grass Land. *Contributions to:* various journals, newspapers and magazines. *Honours:* The Party Membership Dues, awarded Best Novel of the Nation, 1956; Short Story Footprints, National Award for Best Short Stories, 1978; many other honours and awards. *Memberships:* Director, Chinese Writers Association; Director, Chinese Film Actors Association; Vice Chairman, Chinese Children's Film Academy. *Address:* Literature and Arts Dept., P.L.A Arts College, Wei Gong Chen, Haidian District, Beijing, China.

WARD Geoffrey C, b. 30 Nov 1940, Newark, Ohio, USA. Writer. m. Diane Raines Keim, 26 Nov 1983, 2 sons, 1 daughter. *Education:* BA, Oberlin College, 1962. *Literary Appointments:* Editor, Audience magazine 1970-73; American Heritage magazine 1977-82. Co-founder, Contemporary Photographer. *Publications include:* The Maharajahs, 1983; Before the Trumpet: Young Franklin Roosevelt 1882-1905, 1985; A First-Class Temperament: The Emergence of Franklin Roosevelt, 1989. Also: Scripts, several television documentaries including: Statue of Liberty, 1985; Huey Long, 1985; Thomas Hart Benton, 1988; The Civil War, 1990. *Contributions to:* Numerous magazines & journals. Columnist, American Heritage magazine; Frequent Book Reviewer, various publications including

New York Times. *Honours:* Academy Award nominee, Best Documentary, 1985; Inclusion, Best American Essays of 1987; Christopher Award, film script, 1986. *Memberships:* Society of American Historians; Authors Guild. *Literary Agent:* Carl Brandt. *Address:* 1 West 85th Street, Apt. 10E, New York, NY 10024, USA.

WARD John Hood, b. 16 Dec 1915, Newcastle-upon-Tyne, England. Former Senior Principal, Civil Service. m. Gladys Hilda Thorogood, 27 July 1940, Great Crosby. 1 son, 2 daughters. *Education:* Royal Grammar School, Newcastle-upon-Tyne. *Publications:* A Late Harvest, 1982; The Dark Sea, 1983; A Kind of Likeness, 1985; The Wrong Side of Glory, 1986; A Song At Twilight, 1989; Grandfather Best and The Protestant Work Ethic, 1991. *Contributions to:* Over 100 short stories, 200 poems, various commercial and literary magazines, commercial radio and BBC radio. *Honours:* Imperial Service Order, 1977; City of Westminster Arts Council Poetry Prize, 1977; Wharfedale Music Festival Open Poetry Prize, 1978; Society of Civil Service Authors Jubilee Open Short Story Prize, 1985; Winner, Bury Open Poetry Competition, 1987; H E Bates Short Story Prize, 1988; High Peak Community Writers Open Poetry Competition, 1988, 1989, and Open Short Story Competition, 1989; West Sussex Writers Club Open Short Story Competition First Prize, 1991. *Membership:* Society of Civil Service Authors. *Address:* 42 Seal Road, Bramhall, Stockport, Cheshire SK7 2JS, England.

WARD John Powell, b. 28 Nov 1937, Felixtowe, England. University Lecturer. m. Sarah Woodfull Rogers, 16 Jan 1965, 2 sons. *Education:* BA, Toronto, 1959; BA, 1961, MA, 1969, Cambridge; MSc.(Econ) Wales, 1969. *Appointment:* Editor, Poetry Wales, 1975-80. *Publications:* To Get Clear (poems), 1981; The Clearing (poems), 1984; Poetry and the Sociological Idea, 1981; Wordsworth's Language of Men, 1984; Raymond Williams, 1981; The Poetry of R.S. Thomas, 1986; The English Line, 1991; As You Like It, 1992; Thomas Hardy's Poetry, 1992; The Other Man (poems), 1972; From Alphabet to Logos, (Experimental Poetry), 1972; To Get Clear (poems), 1981; The Clearing (poems), 1984; A Certain Marvellous Thing (poems), 1993. *Contributions to:* Times Literary Supplement; Times Higher Education Supplement; Encounter; Critical Quarterly; Sociology; Poetry (Chicago); Poetry Review; Poetry Nation Review; Poetry Wales; Anglo-Welsh Review; Human Studies, USA; Victorian Studies, USA; Poetry Australia. *Honours:* Welsh Arts Council Literature Prize, 1981, Poetry Prize, 1984. *Memberships:* Welsh Academy; Poetry Society of Great Britain. *Address:* Court Lodge, Horton Kirby, Dartford, Kent DA4 9BN, England.

WARD Norman McQueen, b. 10 May 1918, Hamilton, Ontario. University Professor; Writer. m. Elizabeth Davis, 11 Sept 1943, 4 sons, 2 daughters. *Education;* BA, 1941; MA 1943; Phd, 1949. *Publications:* Mice in the Beer, 1960, 1970, 1986; Government of Canada, 6th Edition 1987; The Fully Processed Cheese, 1964; Her Majesty's Mice, 1977; several academic monographs including: The Public Purse, 1962, 1964. *Contributions to:* Numerous journals and magazines. *Honours:* Officer, Order of Canada; President's Medal, University of Western Ontario, 1952; Leacock Medal, for Humour; LLD, McMaster University, 1974, Queen's University, 1977; Fellow, Royal Society of Canada, 1974; Recipient of Festschrift: The Canadian House of Commons: Essays in Honour of Norman Ward, 1985. *Memberships:* Canada Council, 1974-80; Canadian Political Science Association; Writers Union of Canada; Hon Life Member, Saskatchewan Writers' Guild. *Address:* 412 Albert Avenue, Saskatoon, Canada, S7N 1G3.

WARD Philip, b. 10 Feb 1938, Harrow, England. Chartered Librarian, now Professional Writer. m. 4 Apr 1964, 2 daughters. *Education:* University for Foreigners, Perugia; Coimbra University. *Appointments:* Editor, The Private Library, 1958-64; Co-ordinator, Library Services, Tripoli, Libya, 1963-71; Director, National Library Services, UNESCO-UNDP, Jakarta, Indonesia, 1973-74.

Publications include: The Oxford Companion to Spanish Literature, 1978; Lost Songs (poems) 1981; A Dictionary of Common Fallacies, 1978-80; A Lifetime's Reading, 1983; Forgotten Games (novel) 1984; Japanese Capitals, 1985; Travels in Oman, 1987; Wight Magic, 1990; Bulgaria, 1990; Bulgarian Voices, 1992; Sofia Portrait of a City. *Honours:* Fellow, Royal Geographical Society; Fellow, Royal Society of Arts; Guinness Poetry Award, 1959; 1st Prize, International Travel Writers' Competition, 1990. *Membership:* Private Libraries Association (Founder, former Hon Secretary). *Address:* c/o Oxford University Press, Walton Street, Oxford OX2 6DP, England.

WARD-THOMAS Evelyn Bridget Patricia (Evelyn Anthony), b. 1928. Author. *Publications:* Imperial Highness (in USA as Rebel Princess), 1953; Curse Not the King (in USA as Royal Intrigue), 1954; Far Flies the Eagle, 1955; Anne Boleyn, 1957; Victoria and Albert, 1958, as Victoria, 1959; Elizabeth (in USA as All the Queen's Men), 1960; Charles the King, 1961; Clandara, 1963; The Heiress (in USA as The French Bride), 1964; Valentina, 1966; The Rendezvous, 1967; Anne of Austria (in USA as The Cardinal and the Queen), 1968; The Legend, 1969; The Assasin, 1970; The Tamarind Seed, 1971; The Poellenberg Inheritance, 1972; The Occupying Power (in USA as Stranger at the Gates), 1973; The Malaspiga Exit (in USA as Mission to Malaspiga), 1974; The Persian Ransom (in USA as The Persian Price), 1975; The Silver Falcon, 1977; The Return, 1978; The Grave of Truth, 1979 (in USA as The Janus Imperative, 1980); The Defector, 1980; The Avenue of the Dead, 1981; Albatross, 1982; The Company of Saints, 1983; Voices on the Wind, 1985; No Enemy But Time (in USA as A Place to Hide), 1987; The Scarlet Thread, 1989; The Relic, 1991. *Address:* Horham Hall, Thaxted, Essex, England.

WARDLE (John) Irving, b. 20 July 1929, England. Drama critic. m. (1) Joan Notkin, 1958 (div), (2) Fay Crowder, 1963 (div), 2 sons, (3) Elizabeth Grist, 1975, 1 son, 1 daughter. *Education:* BA, Wadham College, Oxford; ARCM, Royal College of Music. *Appointments:* Joined Times Educational Supplement as sub-editor, 1956; Deputy theatre critic, Observer, 1960; Editor, Gambit, 1973-75; Drama critic, The Times, 1963-; Theatre Critic, The Independent on Sunday, 1989. *Publications:* The Theatres of George Devine, biography, 1978. Play, The Houseboy, produced Open Space Theatre 1974, ITV 1982; Theatre Criticism, 1992. *Address:* 51 Richmond Road, New Barnet, Herts, England.

WARE Wallace. *See:* **KARP David.**

WARK Wesley K, b. 31 Dec 1952, Edmonton, Canada. Historian. m. Professor Christine Bold, 1 son. *Education:* BA 1975, 1975; MA 1977, Cambridge; PhD 1984, London School of Economics. *Publications:* The Ultimate Enemy: British Intelligence and Nazi Germany 1933-1937, 1985; Spy Fiction, Spy Films and Real Intelligence, 1991; Security and Intelligence in a Changing World, Co-Author, 1991. *Contributions to:* Numerous articles for historical journals on British, Canadian and US Intelligence. *Honour:* Best Book Award, National Intelligence Study Centre, Washington DC, 1985 for The Ultimate Enemy; Arthur Ellis Award for Spy Ficiton, Spy Films and Real Intelligence, Crime Writers Association of Canada. *Memberships:* Canadian Association for Security and Intelligence Studies; British Study Group on Intelligence. *Address:* Department of History, University of Toronto, Toronto, Canada M5S 1A1.

WARMINGTON William Allan b. 1922. Retired Lecturer. m. Chairman Wind, 1951, 2 sons. *Education:* BA. University of Bristol. *Publications:* A West African Trade Union; Organizational Behaviour and Performance, (co-author); Studies in Industrialization, (with F.A. Wells); Plantation and Village in the Cameroons, (co-author). *Contributions to:* Journal of Management Studies; Personnel Review, and others.

Address: Westington Corner, Chipping Campden, Gloucestershire, England.

WARNER Debora Cassie Sperling, (Cass Warner Sperling), b. 8 Mar 1948, Hollywood, California, USA. Writer; Producer. 2 sons, 2 daughters. *Education:* Stephens College, 1964-65. *Publications:* The Second Dynamic Book - compilation of the works of L Ron Hubbard, 1981; Hollywood Be Thy Name: The Inside Story of the Warner Bros, 1993. *Memberships:* Founding Member, Earth Communications Office; Greenpeace; Sierra Club; American Civil Liberties. *Literary Agent:* Natasha Kern, Portland, USA. *Address:* c/o Natasha Kern Literary Agency, PO Box 2908, Portland, OR 97208, USA.

WARNER Francis (Robert Le Plastrier), b. 21 Oct 1937, Bishopthorpe, Yorkshire, England. Poet; Dramatist; Vice-Master of St Peter's College, Oxford. m. (1) Mary Hall, 1958 (div. 1972), 2 daughters, (2) Penelope Anne Davis, 1983, 1 daughter, 1 son. *Education:* Christ's Hospital, London College of Music; BA, MA, St Catharine's College, Cambridge. *Appointments include:* Fellow & Tutor, St Peter's College Oxford/University Lecturer (CUF), 1965-, Vice-Master of St. Peter's College, Oxford, 1987-. Pro Senior Proctor, University of Oxford, 1989-90. *Publications include:* Poetry: Perennia, 1962; Early Poems, 1964; Experimental Sonnets, 1965; Madrigals, 1967; The Poetry of Francis Warner, USA, 1970; Lucca Quartet, 1975; Morning Vespers, 1980; Spring Harvest, 1981; Epithalamium, 1983; Collected Poems 1960-84, 1985. Plays: Maquettes, trilogy of one-act plays, 1972; Requiem: Part 1, Lying Figures 1972, Part 2, Killing Time 1976, Part 3, Meeting Ends 1974; A Conception of Love, 1978; Light Shadows, 1980; Moving Reflections, 1983; Living Creation, 1985; Healing Nature, 1987; Byzantium, 1990; Virgil and Caesar, 1992. Editor, various other publications. *Contributions to:* Various anthologies, journals. *Honour:* Messing International Award, distinguished contributions to literature, 1972. *Address:* St Peter's College, Oxford OX1 2DL, England.

WARNER Marina Sarah, b. 9 Nov 1946, London, England. Writer. m. (1) William Shawcross, 1971-80, 1 son, (2) John Dewe Mathews, 1981. *Education:* MA, Oxford. *Publications:* The Dragon Empress, 1972; Alone of all Her Sex: The Myth and the Cult of the Virgin Mary, 1976; In a Dark Wood, novel, 1977; Joan of Arc: The Image of Female Heroism, 1981; The Skating Party, novel, 1985; Monuments & Maidens: The Allegory of the Female Form, 1986; The Lost Father, novel, 1988; Into the Dangerous World, (pamphlet), 1989; Indigo, (novel), 1992; The Mermaids in the Basement, (short stories), 1993; Childrens Books: Catalogue Essays, short stories. *Contributions to:* Book Reviewer: Sunday Times, 1980-86; Arts Reviewer, The Independent, 1986-; Contributing Editor, Connoisseur, 1984-86; Times Literary Supplement; The Listener; New Statesman. *Honours:* Young Writer of the Year, 1969; Fawcett Prize, 1986; Commonwealth Writers Prize (Eurasia), 1989. *Memberships:* Getty Scholar, 1987-88; Fellow, Royal Society of Literature; Visting Fellow, British Film Institute, 1992; Reilt Lecturer, 1993. *Literary Agent:* The Peters, Fraser & Dunlop Group Ltd. *Address:* c/o The Peters, Fraser & Dunlop Group Ltd, 5th Floor, The Chambers, Chelsea Harbour, Lots Road, London SW10 OXF, England.

WARNER Philip A W, b. 19 May 1914, Warwickshire, England. Author. 2 sons, 1 daughter. *Education:* MA (Cantab). *Publications:* Siege of The Middle Ages, 1968; The Medieval Castle 1971; The SAS, 1971; The Crimean War, 1972; Distant Battle, 1973; British Battlefields : the South, the Midlands, the North, Scotland and the Borders, 1973; Dervish, 1973; The Soldier, 1975; Stories of Famous Regiments, 1975; The Battle of Loos, 1976; The Fields of War, 1977; The Best of British Pluck, 1976; Panzer, 1977; The Best of Chums, 1978; The Zeebrugge Raid, 1978; Alamein, 1979; Famous Welsh Battles, 1979; The D Day Landings, 1980; Invasion Road, 1981; Auchinleck, 1981; Phantom, 1982; The SBS,

1983; Horrocks, 1984; The British Cavalry, 1984; Kitchener, 1985; The Secret Forces of World War II, 1985; Passchendaele, 1987; Firepower, 1988; World War II: The Untold Story, 1988; The Vital Link, 1989; The Harlequins, 1991; The Great British Soldier, 1992. *Contributor To:* Reviews for: Daily Telegraph; Spectator; Times Literary Supplement. *Agent:* J. Reynolds. *Address:* c/o J Reynolds Associates, Westbury Mill, Near Bruckley, Northants NN13 5JS, England.

WARNER Val, b. 15 Jan 1946, Middlesex, England. Writer. *Education:* BA Hons Modern History 1968, Somerville College, Oxford. *Appointments:* Freelance Copyeditor 1972-77. *Publications:* Under the Penthouse, 1973; Before Lunch, 1986; Translation, The Centenary Corbière (translations of Tristan Corbière), 1975; Editor, Collected Poems & Prose of Charlotte Mew, 1981, 1982; These Yellow Photos, pamphlet, 1971. *Contributions to:* Poems: Encounter; Tribune; The Scotsman; Poetry Review; Ambit; Poetry Wales; Lines Review; Critical Quarterly; PN Review; Antaeus, USA; Cencrastus; Other Poetry; Outposts; Pequod, USA; Green River Review, USA; Verse; Chapman; Gairfish; The Honest Ulsterman; New Writing Scotland; and others. *Honours:* Gregory Award for Poetry, 1975; Writer- in-Residence: University College of Swansea, Wales, 1977-78; University of Dundee, Scotland 1979-81. *Membership:* PEN. *Address:* Carcanet Press Ltd, 208-212 Corn Exchange Buildings, Manchester M4 3BQ, England.

WARNER SPERLING Cass. *See:* **WARNER (SPERLING) Debora Cassie.**

WARTOFSKY Victor b. 15 June 1931, New York, USA. Writer. m. Tamar Chachik, 1957, 1 son, 2 daughters. *Education:* BA, Journalism. *Publications:* Mr Double and Other Stories; Meeting the Pieman; Year of the Yahoo; The Passage; Prescription for Justice; Terminal Justice; Screenplays: Death be my Destiny; The Hellbox; Feathers. *Contributions to:* USIA America; Fifty Plus; Macabre; Quartet; True. *Address:* 8507 Wild Olive Drive, Potomac, MD 20854, USA.

WARZECHA Andrzej, b. 1 Oct 1946, Poland. Journalist; Art Critic. m. Hanna Jedrzejczyk, 3 Mar 1973, 1 son. *Education:* MA, 1975. *Appointments:* Dziennik Polski, 1975-. *Publications:* 6 Poetry Collections: White Passport, 1975; A Family TV Set, 1977; Foreign Body, 1979; Fen-Fire, 1981; Money for the Dead, 1987; Devil's Circle, 1986; A Winter Walk, 1987; At the Family's Table, 1991; The Short Poem About the Eternal Love, 1992. *Contributions to:* Numerous journals and magazines including: Literatura; Zycie Literackie; Poezja; Kultura; Lektura. *Honours:* Stanislaw Pietak Literary Award, 1981. *Memberships:* Tylicz, 1969-75; Society of Polish Writers, member Krakow Board; Polish Journalists' Association. *Address:* ul Teligi 12/52, 30-835 Krakow, Poland.

WASSERFALL Adel, (Adel Pryor), b. 2 Dec 1918, Haugesund, Norway. Writer; Housewife. m. *Education:* High School, 3 1/2 years, including Cape Technical College, South Africa. *Publications:* Novels: Tangled Paths, 1959; Clouded Glass, 1961; Hidden Fire, 1962; Out of the Night, 1963, 3rd Edition, 1971; Hearts in Conflict, 1965; Forgotten Yesterday, 1966; Valley of Desire, 1967; Sound of the Sea, 1968, Norwegian Edition, 1975; Free of a Dream, 1969, German Edition, 1973; Her Secret Fear, 1971; A Norwegian Romance, 1976; All Is Not Gold, 1979; Flame of Jealousy. *Honours:* English Composition Prize, 1934; Sir William Thorne Award, Distinction in English, Cape Technical College, 1937; Short Story Contest Award, 1946. *Address:* 8 Iona St, Milnerton 7441, Cape, South Africa.

WASSERSTEIN Wendy, b. Brooklyn, USA. Dramatist. *Education:* BA, Mount Holyoke College; MFA, Yale School of Drama. *Appointments:* Teacher, Columbia University and New York University; served as Contributing Editor, New York Woman magazine;

Currently Contributing Editor, Harper's Bazaar. *Creative Works:* Plays include: The Sisters Rosensweig; The Heidi Chronicles; Isn't It Romantic; Uncommon Women and Others, 1978; Any Woman Can't; Montpelier Pa-Zazz; Miami; Drive, She Said; Adapted, John Cheever's The Sorrows of Gin; Author: Bachelor Girls, essays; The Heidi Chronicles and Other Plays. *Honours:* Awards in 1988 for play The Heidi Chronicles: Pulitzer Prize, The New York Drama Critics Circle Prize, The Drama Desk Award, The Outer Critics Circle Award, the Susan Smith Blckburn Prize, Tony Award; Honorary Doctorate, Mt Holyoke College. *Memberships:* Council, Dramatists Guild; Board, British American Arts Association; Playwrights Horizons' Artistic Board. *Address:* Royce Carlton Inc, 866 United Nations Plaza, Suite 4030, New York, NY 10017, USA.

WATERHOUSE Keith Spencer (Herald Froy, Lee Gibb), b. 6 Feb 1929, Leeds, Yorkshire, England. Writer. 1 son, 2 daughters. *Education:* Osmondthorpe Council School, Leeds. *Literary Appointments:* Journalist, Leeds and London, 1950-; Columnist with Daily Mirror, 1970-86, and Daily Mail 1986-; Contributor to Punch 1966-88. *Publications:* Novels: There is a Happy Land, 1957; Billy Liar 1959; Jubb 1963; The Bucket Shop 1968; Billy Liar on the Moon 1975; Office Life 1978; Maggie Muggins 1981; In the Wood 1983; Thinks 1984; Our Song 1988; Bimbo 1990; Unsweet Charity, 1992; General: The Passing of the Third Floor Buck 1974; Mondays, Thursdays 1976; Rhubarb, Rhubarb and Other Noises 1979; Fanny Peculiar 1983; Mrs Pooter's Diary 1983; Waterhouse at Large 1985; The Collected Letters of a Nobody 1986; The Theory and Practice of Lunch 1986; The Theory and Practice of Travel 1988; Waterhouse on Newspaper Style 1989, previously published as Daily Mirror Style; English Our English, 1991; Sharon and Tracy and the Rest, 1992. Cafe Royal: 90 Years of Bohemia (with Guy Deghy) 1955. Writer's Theatre (editor with Willis Hall) 1967; With Willis Hall: The Television Adventures (and More Television Adventures) of Worzel Gummidge, 2 vols, 1979; Worzel Gummidge's Television Adventures 1981; Worzel Gummidge at the Fair, 1980; Worzel Gummidge Goes to the Seaside 1980; The Trials of Worzel Gummidge, 1980; Worzel's Birthday 1981; New Television Adventures of Worzel Gumidge and Aunt Sally, 1981; Worzel Gummidge and Aunt Sally 1982; The Irish Adventures of Worzel Gummidge 1984; Worzel Gummidge Down Under 1987; Screenplays with Willis Hall include: Whistle Down the Wind 1961, The Valiant 1962, Billy Liar 1963, A Kind of Loving 1963. West Elevan 1963, Pretty Polly 1967, Lock Up Your Daughters 1969; Television films: Happy Moorings 1963. How Many Angels 1964, The Warmonger 1970, Charlie Muffin 1979, This Office Life 1984, The Great Paper Chase 1986. Series: The Upchat Line 1977, The Upchat Connection 1978, West End Tales 1981, The Happy Apple 1983, Charters and Caldicott 1984, Queenie's Castle 1970, Budgie 1971-72, The Upper Crusts 1973, Billy Liar 1973-74, Worzel Gummidge 1979-. Radio Plays: The Town That Wouldn't Vote, 1951; There is a Happy Land, 1962; The Woollen Bank Forgeries 1964; The Last Phone-In, 1976; The Big Broadcast of 1922, 1979; Plays include: with Willis Hall: Billy Liar 1960; Celebration: The Wedding and the Funeral, 1961; The Card 1973; Solo work for the theatre: Mr and Mrs Nobody, 1986, Jeffrey Bernard is Unwell, 1989, Bookends 1990. *Honours:* Granada Columnist of the Year Award, 1970; IPC Descriptive Writer of the Year Award, 1970; IPC Columnist of the Year Award, 1973; Granda Special Quarter Century Award, 1982; British Press Awards Columnist of the Year, 1978, 1991; CBE 1991; Hon Fellow, Leeds Polytechnic, 1991. *Memberships:* PEN; Chelsea Arts; Saville Club; Garrick. *Literary Agent:* David Higham Associates, 5-8 Lower John Street, London W1; Theatrical Agent: London Management Ltd, 2-4 Noel Street, London W1. *Address:* 29 Kenway Road, London SW5 ORP, England.

WATERS John (M), b. 1946, Baltimore, Maryland, USA. Filmmaker; Author. *Publications:* Books: Shock Value, 1981; Crackpot: The Obsessions of John Waters, 1986; Satirical films (writer, director): Mondo Trasho, 1970; Pink Flamingos, 1972; Polyester, 1981; Hairspray, 1988; Others.

WATERS John Frederick, b. 27 Oct 1930, Somerville, Massachusetts, USA. Professional Writer. *Education:* BS, University of Massachusetts. *Publications Include:* Marine Animal Collectors (Grades 7 and Up), 1969; The Crab From Yesterday, Grades 2-5, 1970; The Sea Farmers, 1970; Saltmarshes and Shifting Dunes, 1970; Turtles, 1971; Neighborhood Puddle, 1971; Some Mammals Live in the Sea, 1972; Green Turtle: Mysteries, 1972; The Royal Potwasher, 1972; Seal Harbour, 1973; Hungry Sharks, 1973; Giant Sea Creatures, 1973; The Mysterious Eel, 1973; Camels: Ships of the Desert, 1974; Carnivorous Plants, 1974; Exploring New England Shores, 1974; The Continental Shelves, 1975; Creatures of Darkness, 1975; Victory Chimes, 1976; Maritime Careers, 1977; Fishing, 1978; Summer Seals, 1978; The Hatchlings, 1979; Crime Labs, 1979; A Jellyfish is Not a Fish, 1979; Flood, 1991; Watching Whales, 1991. *Contributions to:* Cape Cod Compass. *Honours:* Junior Literary Book Choice (twice); Outstanding Science books for Children Awards (6 times). *Memberships include:* Past President, Southeastern Massachusetts Creative Writers Club; Organizer, Cape Cod Writers; 12 O'Clock Scholars; Society of Children's Book Writers. *Address:* Box 735 Chatham, MA 02633, USA.

WATERTON Betty Marie, b. 31 Aug 1923, Oshawa, Ontario, Canada. Writer. Children's Books. m. Claude Waterton, 7 Apr 1942, 1 son, 2 daughters. *Publications:* A Salmon for Simon, 1978; Pettranella, 1980; Mustard, 1983; The White Moose, 1984; Quincy Rumpel, 1984; Orff, 27 Dragons (and a Snarkel !), 1984; The Dog Who Stopped the War, (adaptation and translation), 1985; Starring Quincy Rumpel, 1986; Quincy Rumpel, PI, 1988; Morris Rumpel and the Wings of Icasus, 1989; Plain Noodles, 1989. *Honours:* A Salmon for Simon, Co-winner, Canada Council Award for Children's Literature, 1978; Runner-up Book of the Year Award, CACL, 1978. *Memberships:* Canadian Society of Children's Authors, Illustrators and Performers; The Federation of BC Writers. *Address:* 10135 Tsaykum Road, RR1, Sidney BC, Canada V8L 3R9.

WATKINS Alan (Rhun), b. 3 Apr 1933, England. Journalist. m. Ruth Howard, 1955 (dec 1982), 1 son, 2 daughters (1 dec). *Education:* Queens College, Cambridge; Called to Bar, Lincoln's Inn, 1957. *Literary Appointments:* Editorial staff, Sunday Express, 1959-64; Political correspondent, Spectator 1964-67, New Statesman 1967-76; Political columnist, Sundary Mirror, 1968-69; Columnist, Evening Standard, 1974-75; Political columnist, Observer, 1976-; Rugby correspondent, Field, 1984-. *Publications:* The Liberal Dilemma, 1966; Co-author, The Left, 1966; The Making of the Prime Minister, with A. Alexander, 1970; Brief Lives, 1982; Co-author, The Queen Observed, 1986; Sportwriter's Eye, 1989; A Slight Case of Libel, 1990; A Conservative Coup, 2nd Edition, 1992; Take the Ball and Run, 1991 (contrib), 1991. *Honours:* Granada Award, political columnist, 1973; British Press Award, columnist 1982, commended 1984. *Address:* 54 Barnsbury Street, London N1 1ER, England.

WATKINS Floyd C, b. 19 Apr 1920, Cherokee County, Georgia, USA. Professor; Author; Farmer. m. Anna E Braziel, 14 June 1942, 1 son, 2 daughters. *Education:* BS, Georgia Southern, 1946; AM, Emory University, 1947; PhD, Vanderbilt University, 1952. *Appointments:* Instructor, Emory University, 1949, Professor 1961; Candler Professor, American Literature, 1980; Candler Professor Emeritus, 1988; Visiting Professor, Southeastern University, Oklahoma, summers 1961, 1970; Visiting Professor, Texas A & M University, 1980. *Publications:* Co-Editor, The Literature of the South, 1952; Thomas Wolfe's Characters, 1957; Co-author, Old Times in the Faulkner Country, 1961; The Flesh and the Word, 1971; In Time and Place, 1977; Then and Now : The Personal Past in the Poetry of Robert Penn Warren, 1982; Co-Author, Some Poems and Some Talk About Poetry, 1985.

Contributions to: Georgia Review; Southern Review; South Atlantic Quarterly; Sewanee Review; Mississippi Quarterly; Southern Literary Journal. *Honours:* Thomas Wolfe Memorial Award, 1957; Special Achievement Award, Georgia Writers Association, 1957; Thomas Jefferson Award, Emory University, 1968; Williams Distinguished Teacher of the Year Award, 1979; Scholar Teacher of the Year, Emory University, 1984-85. *Memberships:* Phi Beta Kappa; Modern Langage Association; Society for the Study of Southern Literature, Executive Committee. *Address:* 519 Durand Drive NE, Atlanta, GA 30307, USA.

WATKINS Gerrold. *See:* **MALZBERG Barry Norman.**

WATKINS Karen Christna, (Catrin Collier, Katherine John), b. 30 May 1948, Pontypridd, Wales. Writer. m. Trevor John Watkins, 28 Dec 1968, 2 sons, 1 daughter. *Education:* Teaching Certificate 1969, Swansea College. *Publications:* Without Trace, 1990; Hearts of Gold, 1992; One Blue Moon, 1993; Six Foot Under. *Memberships:* PEN; Society of Authors; Crime Writers' Association. *Literary Agent:* A M Heath & Co. *Address:* 31 Hen Parc Avenue, Upper Killay, Swansea SA2 7HA, Wales.

WATKINS-PITCHFORD Denys James (B B), b. 25 July 1905, England. Author; Artist; Broadcaster, natural history. m. Cecily Mary Adnitt, 1939 (dec.1974), 1 son, 1 daughter (1 dec.). *Education:* Royal College of Art, London, 1926-28. *Publications include:* Under pseudonym 'BB': Sportsman's Bedside Book, 1937; Wild Lone, 1939; Countryman's Bedside Book, 1941; Little Grey Men, 1941, TV serial 1975; The Idle Countryman, 1943; Brendon Chase, 1944, Radio & TV serial 1981; Fisherman's Bedside Book, 1945; The Wayfaring Tree, 1945; Down the Bright Stream, 1948; Shooting Man's Bedside Book, 1948; Letters from Compton Deverell, 1950; Tides Ending, 1950; Dark Estuary, 1952; The Forest of Boland Light Railway, 1955; Mr Bumstead, 1958; The Wizard of Boland, 1958; The Badgers of Bearshanks, 1961; September Road to Caithness, 1962; Lepus the Brown Hare, 1962; Pegasus Book of the Countryside, 1964; The Whopper, 1967; A Summer on the Nene, 1967; The Tyger Tray, 1971; Pool of the Black Witch, 1974; Recollections of a Longshore Gunner, 1976; A Child Alone, autobiography, 1978; Ramblings of a Sportsman Naturalist, 1979; The Quiet Fields, 1981; Best of 'BB' anthology, 1985. *Contributions to:* Field; Country Life; Shooting Times. *Honours:* Carnegie Medal, 1942; Honorary MA, Leicester University, 1986; MBE, Queens Birthday Honours, 1989. *Address:* The Round House, Sudborough, Kettering, Northants.

WATMOUGH David, b. 17 Aug 1926, London, England. Author. *Education:* Theology major, King's College, University of London, 1945- 49. *Appointments include:* War Service, Royal Naval Volunteer Reserve, 1944-45. *Publications:* Ashes for Easter, stories, 1972; Love and the Waiting Game, stories, 1975; From a Cornish Landscape, stories, 1975; No More into the Garden, novel, 1978; Fury, stories, 1984; The Connecticut Countess, stories, 1984; The Unlikely Pioneer, opera, 1985; Vibrations in Time, stories, 1986; The Year of Fears, novel, 1987; Families, novel, 1990; Thy Mother's Glass, novel, 1992. *Contributions to:* Encounter; Spectator; New York Times Book Review; Saturday Night, Canada; Canadian Literature; Dalhousie Review; Connoisseur, New York; Malahat Review; Vancouver Step. *Honours:* Senior Literary Arts Award, Canada Council, 1976, 1986l; Winner, Best Novel of Year Award, Giovanni's Room, Philadelphia, 1979. *Memberships:* The Writers Union of Canada, Chairman, British Columbia Branch; Founder, 1st Chairman, Federation of British Columbia Writers. *Literary Agent:* Robert Drake, Drake Literary Agency, 217 Hanover St 10, Annapolis, MD 21401, USA. *Address:* 3358 West First Avenue, Vancouver, British Columbia, Canada V6R 1G4.

WATNEY John Basil, Writer. *Publications:* The

Enemy Within, 1946; The Unexpected Angel, 1949; Common Love, 1954; Leopard with a Thin Skin, 1959; The Quarrelling Room, 1960; The Glass Facade, 1963; He Also Served, 1971; Clive of India, 1974; Beer is Best, 1974; Lady Hester Stanhope, 1975; Mervyn Peake, 1975; Mother's Ruin, 1976; The Churchills, 1977. *Address:* Flat 36, 5 Elm Park Gardens, London SW10 9QQ, England.

WATSON Ian, b. 20 Apr 1943, St Albans, Hertfordshire, England. Author. m. Judith Jackson, 1 Sept 1961, 1 daughter. *Education:* 1st Class Honours, English, 1963, Research Degree, 19th Century French and English Literature, 1965, Oxford University. *Appointments:* Lecturer, Literature, University College, Dar-es-Salaam, Tanzania, 1965-67; Lecturer, English Literature: Tokyo University of Education, Kejo University, Tokyo, Japan Women's University, 1967-70; Features Editor, Foundation: The Review of Science Fiction, 1974; European Editor, SFWA Bulletin, 1983. *Publications:* Japan: A Cat's Eye View, 1969; The Embedding, 1973; The Jonah Kit, 1975; Orgasmachine, 1976; Japan Tomorrow, 1977; Alien Embassy, 1977; The Martian Inca, 1977; Miracle Visitors, 1978; God's World, 1979; The Very Slow Time Machine: Science Fiction Stories, 1979; The Gardens of Delight, 1980; Under Heaven's Bridge (with Michael Bishop), 1981; Deathhunter, 1981; Sunstroke and Other Stories, 1982; The Book of the River, 1984; Converts, 1984; The Book of the Stars, 1984; The Book of Being, 1985; The Book of Ian Watson, collection, 1985; Slow Birds and Other Stories, 1985; Queenmagic, Kingmagic, 1986; Evil Water and Other Stories, 1987; The Power, 1987; The Fire Worm, 1988; Whores of Babylon, 1988; Meat, 1988; Salvage Rites and Other Stories, 1989; The Flies of Memory, 1990; Inquisitor, 1990; Stalin's Teardrops, collection, 1991; Several anthologies. *Contributions:* Literary criticism; Regular science fiction criticism. *Honours:* Scholarship, Balliol College, Oxford, 1959; Joint Winner, 2nd Prize, John W Campbell Memorial Award, 1974; Prix Apollo, 1975; British Science Fiction Orbit Award, 1976; British Science Fiction Association Award, 1977; Premios Zikkurath, best foreign novel in Spanish translation, 1978; Finalist: World Science Fiction Achievement Award, 1979, Hugo and Nebula Awards, 1984; Prix Europeen de Science Fiction, 1985. *Address:* c/o Victor Gollancz Ltd, 14 Henrietta St, London WC2E 8QJ, England.

WATSON James, b. 8 Nov 1936, Darwen, Lancashire, England. Author. m. Kitty Downey, 6 July 1963, 3 daughters. *Education:* BA, Honours, History, University of Nottingham; MA, Education, University of Sussex. *Publications:* Sign of the Swallow, 1967; The Bull Leapers, 1970; Legion of the White Tiger, 1973; The Freedom Tree, 1976; Talking in Whispers, 1983; Where Nobody Sees, 1987; A Dictionary of Communications & Media Studies, 1983; What is Communication Studies?, 1985; Make Your Move and Other Stories, 1988; No Surrender, 1991; Ticket to Prague, 1993. *Contributions to:* various journals. *Honours:* Winner, 'The Other Award' 1983; Highly Commended, Carnegie Medal Awards; Winner, Buxtehuder Bulle Prize for Young Fiction, 1987. *Address:* 9 Farmcombe Close, Tunbridge Wells, Kent TN2 5DG, England.

WATSON John Richard, b. 15 June 1934, Ipswich, England. Professor of English. m. Pauline Elizabeth Roberts, 21 July 1962, 1 son, 2 daughters. *Education:* BA (English) 1st Class, MA 1964, Magdalen College, Oxford, England; PhD, University of Glasgow, Scotland, 1966. *Publications:* Everyman's Book of Victorian Verse, 1982; English Poetry of the Romantic Period 1789-1830, 1985; Wordsworth's Vital Soul, 1982; The Poetry of Gerard Manley Hopkins, 1986; Wordsworth (British Council Pamphlet), 1983; Picturesque Landscape and English Romantic Poetry, 1970; Companion to Hymns and Psalms (with K Trickett), 1988. *Contributions:* Essays in: Critical Quarterly; Essays in Criticism; Collections of Essays. *Memberships:* Chairman, Modern Humanities Research Association; Director, Landscape Research Group; Public Orator, University of Durham.

Address: 3 Victoria Terrace, Durham DH1 4RW, England.

WATSON Julia (Jane De Vere, Julia Fitzgerald, Julia Hamilton), b. 18 Sept 1943, Bangor, North Wales. Author, Historical/Romance, Supernatural/Occult. m. 1 son, 1 daughter. *Education:* Self-taught historian, astrologer, nutritionist, Diploma, Nutrition. *Appointments include:* Consultant, series Golden Sovereigns, Sphere, 1972-73. *Publications include:* As Julia Watson: The Lovechild, 1967; Medici Mistress, 1968; A Mistress for the Valois, 1969; The King's Mistress, 1970; The Wolf and the Unicorn, 1971; Winter of the Witch, 1971; The Tudor Rose, 1972; Saffron, 1972; Love Song, 1981. As Jane de Vere: The Scarlet Women, 1986. As Julia Hamilton: The Last of the Tudos, 1971; Katharine of Aragon, 1972 (as Katherine the Tragic Tudor, 1974); Anne of Cleve, 1972; Son of York, 1973; The Changeling Queen, 1977; The Emperor's Daughter, 1978; The Pearl of Habsburgs, 1978; The Snow Queen, 1978; The Habsburg Inheritance, 1980. As Julia Fitzgerald: Royal Slave, 1978; Scarlet Woman, 1979; Slave Lady, 1980; Salamander, 1981; Fallen Woman, 1981; Venus Rising, 1982; The Princess and the Pagan, 1982; Firebird, 1983; The Jewelled Serpent, 1984; Taboo, 1984; Desert Queen, 1986; Daughter of the Gods, 1986; Flame of the East, 1986; Pasadoble, 1986; A Kiss From Aphrodite, 1986; Castle of the Enchantress, 1986; Beauty of the Devil, 1986; Healthy Signs (non-fiction), 1988; Earth Queen, Sky King, 1988; Jade Moon; Glade of Jewels; Temples of Butterflies. *Contributions to:* Regular column, reviews, Romantic Times; Articel, World of Books; Short story in Weekend magazine, 1989. *Honours:* Award, Historical Romance, Romantic Times, 1984; Nomination, most exotic book locale, ibid, 1985; Winner Romantic Times Reviewers Choice Award for Most Exotic Books for Taboo, 1988. *Memberships:* Romantics Novelists Association; Crime Writers Association; Society of Authors; Romance Writers of America. *Literary Agent:* June Hall. *Address:* c/o June Hall, 5th Floor, The Chambers, Chelsea Harbour, Lots Road, London SW10 0XF, England.

WATSON Lyall, b. 1939, South African/British. *Appointments:* Formerly apprenticed to Desmond Morris, London Zoo; worked in archaeology with American School of Oriental Research, Jordan and Saudi Arabia; an anthropological work in Northern Nigeria; Director of Johannesburg Zoo; Television producer, BBC, London; Founder of life science consultancy, Biologic of London; expeditions in marine biology, Indian Ocean. *Publications:* Omnivore, 1971; Supernature, 1973; The Romeo Error, 1975; Gifts of Unknown Things, 1977; Lifetide, 1979; Whales of the World, 1981; Lightning Bird, 1982; Heaven's Breath, 1984; Earthworks, 1985; Beyond Supernature, 1986; The Water Planet, 1987; Sumo, 1988; Neophilia, 1989; The Nature of Things, 1990. *Address:* c/o Murray Pollinger, 4 Garrick Street, London WC2E 9BH, England.

WATSON Lynn, b. 5 June 1948, Woodland, California, USA. Teacher; Writer. *Education:* University of California, Berkeley 1966-68; BA English 1975, Sonoma State University; MFA Fiction Writing 1977, University of Iowa, Writer's Workshop. *Appointments:* Freelance Writer for various print media and publications; Teacher, University of Iowa, College of the Desert, Sonoma State University, Santa Rosa Junior College. *Publications:* Alimony or Death of the Clock, novel, 1981; Amateur Blues, poetry, 1990; Catching the Devil, poetry, 1993. *Contributions to:* On the Bus; Chaminade Literary Review; Cyanosis; Avec; First Leaves; The Tomcat; Sonoma Review; and other literary publications. *Honours:* First Place, Poetry, National Poetry Association, San Francisco, 1990; Honorable Mention, World of Poetry Contest, Sacramento, 1991. *Membership:* California Poets in the Schools. *Address:* PO Box 1253, Occidental, CA 95465, USA.

WATSON Patricia Seets, b. 29 Nov 1930, Sharples, USA. Lawyer; Educator. m. Robert Patrick Watson, 11 Jan 1957, 2 daughters. *Education:* BA, 1977; Master of Criminal Justice, 1979; JD, 1982. *Appointments:*

Newspaper Reporter, 1950-75; Professor, Criminal Justice, 1982- . *Publications:* Guide to South Carolina Criminal Law and Procedure, 1984, 2nd edition 1987, 3rd edition, 1990; The Retarded Offender, 1982; Innovations in South Carolina Law Enforcement, 1981-84, Editor. *Contributions To:* various journals and magazines. *Honours:* Newspaper Feature Writing Awards, 1957, 1972, 1973; various other honours and awards. *Memberships:* South Carolina Bar, American Bar Associations; Academy of Criminal Justice Sciences; Phi Alpha Delta Law Fraternity. *Address:* 1520 Senate St., Columbia, SC 29201, USA.

WATSON Richard Allan, b. 23 Feb 1931, New Market, Iowa, USA. Professor of Philosophy. m. Patty Jo Andersen, 30 July 1955, 1 daughter. *Education:* BA, 1953, MA, 1957, PhD, 1961, Philosophy, University of Iowa; MS, Geology, University of Minnesota, 1959. *Publications:* The Downfall of Cartesianism, 1966; Man and Nature (with Patty Jo Watson), 1969; The Longest Cave (with Roger W Brucker), 1976; Under Plowman's Floor, novel, 1978; The Runner, novel, 1981; The Philosopher's Diet, 1985; The Breakdown of Cartesian Metaphysics, 1987; The Philosopher's Joke, 1990; Writing Philosophy, 1992; Niagara, novel, 1993. *Contributions to:* The Georgia Review; The Gettysburg Review; Numerous philosophy, anthropology and geology journals. *Honours:* American Health Top 10 Book Award for The Philosopher's Diet, 1985. *Membership:* Board Member, International Writers Center, Washington University. *Address:* Philosophy Box 1073, Washington University, St Louis, MO 63130, USA.

WATSON Steven Robert, b. 21 Dec 1947, Minneapolis, Minnesota, USA. Psychologist; Cultural Historian. *Education:* BA English 1970, Stanford University; PhD Counselling Psychology 1976, University of California at Santa Barbara. *Publications:* Artifacts at the End of a Decade, 1981; Strange Bedfellows: The First American Avant-Garde, 1991; Group Portrait: The First American Avant-Garde, 1991. *Contributions to:* Art and Antiques; The Village Voice. *Honour:* Phi Beta Kappa. *Address:* 603 West 111 Street, 6W, New York, NY 10025, USA.

WATSON Will. See: FLOREN Lee.

WATT Alick Angus, b. 22 July 1920, Wortley, Yorkshire, England. Former Golf Professional; Marketing Manager (retired). m. Elizabeth Richardson, 15 June 1949, 1 son. *Education:* North Berwick High School, East Lothian, Scotland, 1931-35. *Appointments:* Consultant on history of golf clubs and memorabilia, Golf Monthly. *Publications:* Collecting Old Golfing Clubs, 1985, revised 2nd edition, 1990. *Contributions to:* Golf Monthly; Golf articles to other magazines and papers; Lectures on history of golf; The Encyclopaedia of Golf, 1991. *Membership:* The Institute of Journalists. *Address:* 6 Musgrove Gardens, Alton, Hants GU34 2EQ, England.

WATT-EVANS Lawrence, b. 26 July 1954, Arlington, Massachusetts, USA. Freelance Writer. m. Julie F McKenna, 30 Aug 1977, 1 daughter, 1 son. *Education:* Princeton University, 1972-74, 1975-77. *Publications:* The Lure of the Basilisk, 1980; The Seven Altars of Dûsarra, 1981; The Cyborg and the Sorcerers, 1982; The Sword of Bheleu, 1983; The Book of Silence, 1984; The Chromosomal Code, 1984; The Misenchanted Sword, 1985; Shining Steel, 1986; With a Single Spell, 1987; The Wizard and the War Machine, 1987; Denner's Wreck, 1988; Nightside City, 1989; The Unwilling Warlord, 1989. *Contributions to:* Rayguns, Elves & Skin-Tight Suits, column for Comics Buyer's Guide, 1983-86; Comic Collector; Movie Collectors World; Starlog; Vintage Collectables; Sagebrush Journal. *Honours:* Isaac Asimov's Science Fiction Readers Poll Award, 1987; Nebula Award Nominee, 1987; Science Fiction Achievement Award (Hugo) for Best Short Story of 1987, 1988. *Memberships:* Science Fiction Writers of America; Mystery Writers of America; National Space

Society; SFWA. *Agent:* Russell Galen, Scott Meredith Literary Agency. *Address:* c/o Russell Galen, Scott Meredith Literary Agency, 845 Third Ave, New York, NY 10022, USA.

WATTS Nigel John, b. 24 June 1957, Winchester, England. Writer. m. Sahera Chohan, 10 Aug 1991. *Publications:* The Life Game, 1989; Billy Bayswater, 1990; We all Live in a House Called Innocence, 1992. *Honour:* Betty Trask Award, 1989. *Literary Agent:* Murray Pollinger. *Address:* 260 Ashburnham Road, Ham, Richmond, Surrey, England.

WATTS Victor Ernest, b. 18 Apr 1938, Bristol, England. University Teacher. m. Mary Curtis, 4 Apr 1964, 1 son, 2 daughters. *Education:* Merton College, Oxford, 1957-61; University College, London, 1961-62; MA, Oxford, 1964; FSA. *Appointments:* Lecturer in English, 1962, Senior Lecturer, 1974, Durham University; Master of Grey College, Durham University, 1989-. *Publications:* Boethius: the Consolation of Philosophy, 1969; The Cambridge Dictionary of English Place-names (editor), forthcoming. *Contributions to:* Medium Aevum; Nomina; Journal of the English Place-nam Society. *Memberships:* English Place-name Society, Honorary Director of English Place-name Survey; President, Architectural and Archaeological Society of Durham and Northumberland. *Address:* The Master's House, High Close, Hollingside Lane, Durham DH1 3TN, England.

WAUGH Auberon Alexander (Crispin de St Crispian), b. 17 Nov 1939, Dulverton, Somerset, England. Writer. m. Teresa Onslow, 1961, 2 sons, 2 daughters. *Education:* Downside School, Christ Church, Oxford. *Appointments:* Editorial Staff, Daily Telegraph, 1960-63; Special Writer, IPC Publications, 1964-67; Political Corrrespondent, Spectator, 1967-70, Chief Fiction Reviewer, 1970-73, Weekly Columnist, 1976-; Political Correspondent, Columnist, Private Eye, 1970-76; Columnist, The Times, 1970-71, The Sunday Telegraph, 1981-; Weekly Columnist, New Statesman, 1973-76; Chief Fiction Reviewer, Evening Standard, 1973-80; Monthly Columnist, Books and Bookmen, 1973-80; Chief Fiction Reviewer, Daily Mail, 1980-86; Chief Reviewer, Independent, 1986-; Editor, The Literary Review, Jan. 1986-. *Publications:* The Foxglove Saga, 1960; Consider the Lilies, 1968; Biafra: Britain's Shame (with S Cronje), 1969; Country Topics, 1974; Four Crowded Years, 1976; In the Lion's Den, 1979; The Last Word: The Trial of Jeremy Thorpe, 1980; Auberon Waugh's Yearbook, 1981; The Diaries of Auberon Waugh, A Turbulent Decade, 1976-85, 1985; Waugh on Wine, 1986; Another Voice (essays), 1986; Will This Do, 1992. *Honours:* British Press Award Commendation, Critic of the Year, 1977, 1978; Granada TV What the Papers Say, Columnist of the Year, 1979. *Address:* Combe Florey House, Combe Florey, Taunton, Somerset, England.

WAUGH Hillary Baldwin (Elissa Grandower, H Baldwin Taylor, Harry Walker), b. 22 June 1920, Author. m. (1) Diana Taylor, 16 June 1951, div 1980, 1 son, 2 daughters, (2) Shannon OCork, 11 June 1983. *Education:* BA, Yale University, 1942. *Publication:* Last Seen Wearing..., 1952; The Missing Man, 1964; and more recently, Rivergate House, 1980; The Glenna Powers Case, 1981; The Doria Rafe Case, 1981; The Billy Cantrell Case, 1982; The Nerissa Claire Case, 1983; The Veronica Dean Case, 1984; The Priscilla Copperwaite Case, 1985. *Honours:* Grand Master, Swedish Academy of detection, 1981; Grand Master, Mystery Writers of America, 1989. *Memberships:* Mystery Writers of America, Former President, Executive President, awards Chairman, Board of Directors; Crime Writers Association, England. *Address:* 9 Marshall Avenue, Guilford, CT 06437, USA.

WAWILOW Danuta, b. 14 Apr 1942, Kozmodemiansk, USSR. Writer; Translator. m. Oleg Usenko, 3 Feb 1967, 1 son, 1 daughter. *Education:* Warsaw University, 1959-63; MA, Russian Literature,

Moscow University, 1963-67. *Publications:* The Roopaks, 1977; An Awfully Important Thing, 1978; The Wandering, 1986; My Secret, 1985; A Story About a Prince, Kaleidoskopes and an Old Woman, (with Oleg Usenko), 1980; An Apple Flies into the Clouds, (with Oleg Usenko), 1982; Rhymes for Naughty Children, 1987; Wild Horses, TV Play, 1987; A Little Cherry Orchard, Polish Folk Erotic Poems, with Oleg Usenko, 1985; Radio & TV Series about poems by children, 1982-86. *Honours:* Premie Europee, Praveda, Italy, 1978; Peace Fund Award, USSR, 1987; Polish Prime Minister's Award, 1987. *Memberships:* Polish Writers Association. *Agent:* Polish Literary Agency. *Address:* ul Anieli Krzywon 2/129, 01-391 Warsaw, Poland.

WAYMAN Tom, b. 1945, Canadian. *Appointments:* Writer-in-Residence, University of Windsor, 1975-76; Assistant Professor of English, Wayne State University, Detroit, 1976-77; Writer-in-Residence, University of Alberta, Edmonton, 1978-79; Instructor, Kootenay School of Writing, David Thompson University Centre, Nelson, 1980-82; Writer-in-Residence, Simon Fraser University, Burnaby, 1983; Instructor, Kootenay School of Writing, Vancouver, 1984-87; Instructor, English Department, Kwantlen College, Surrey, BC, 1988-89; College Professor, English Department, Okanagan College, Kelowna, BC, 1990-91; Instructor, Kooteray School of the Arts, 1991-92; College Professor, Okanagan University College, 1992-. *Publications:* Mindscapes (with others), 1971; Waiting for Wayman, 1973; For and Against the Moon: Blues Yells and Chuckles, Beaton Abbott's Got the Contract: An Anthology of Working Poems (ed), 1974; Money and Rain: Tom Wayman Live!, 1975; Routines, Transport, A Government Job at Last: An Anthology of Working Poems Mainly Canadian (ed), 1976; Kitchener/Chicago/Saskatoon, Free Time: Industrial Poems, 1977; A Planet Mostly Sea, 1979; Living on the Ground: Tom Wayman Country, Introducing Tom Wayman: Selected Poems 1973-80, 1980; Going for Coffee: Poetry on the Job (ed), 1981; The Nobel Prize Acceptance Speech, 1981; Counting the Hours: City Poems, Inside Job: Essays on the New Work Writing, 1983; The Face of Jack Munro, 1986; In a Small House on the Outskirts of Heaven, 1989; East of Main: An Anthology of Poems from East Vancouver (edited jointly with Calvin Wharton), 1989; Paperwork: Contemporary Poems from the Job, 1991. *Address:* PO Box 163, Winlaw, BC, Canada V0G 2J0.

WEARNE Alan Richard, b. 23 July 1948, Melbourne, Australia. Poet; Verse Novelist. *Education:* BA, Latrobe University, 1973; DipEd, SCV Rusden, 1977. *Appointments:* Poetry Editor, Meanjin, 1984-87; Writer-in-Residence, University of Newcastle, New South Wales, 1989. *Publications:* Public Relations (poems), 1972; New Devil, New Parish (poems), 1976; The Nightmarkets (verse novel), 1986; Out Here (verse novella, 1987. *Contributions to:* Scripsi; Meanjin; Book Reviews in the Age. *Honours:* National Book Council Award, 1987; Gold Medal, Association for the Study of Australian Literature, 1987. *Address:* 83 Edgevale Road, Kew, Melbourne, Victoria 3101, Australia.

WEAVER Gordon Allison, b. 2 Feb. 1937, Moline, Illinois, USA. Professor. m. 14 Sept. 1961, 3 daughters. *Education:* BA, University of Wisconsin, 1961; MA, University of Illinois, 1962; PhD, University of Denver, 1970. *Publications:* A World Quite Round, 1986; Circling Byzantium, 1980; Getting Serious, 1980; Give Him a Stone, 1975; Such Waltzing Was Not Easy, 1975; The Entombed Man of Thule, 1972; Count a Lonely Cadence, 1968; Morality Play, 1985; The Eight Corners of the World, 1988. *Contributions to:* Antioch Review; Iowa Review; Sewanee Review; Mid American Review; Quarterly West; Kenyon Review; Southern Review. *Honours:* St Lawrence Award for Fiction, 1973; NEA Fellow, 1974; Quarterly West Story Prize, 1979; O Henry First Prize, 1979; Sherwood Anderson Short Story Prize, 1981; Quarterly West Novella Prize, 1984. *Memberships:* Associated Writing Programs. *Agent:* Nat Sobel, New York City. *Address:* English Dept., Oklahoma State University, Stillwater, OK 74078, USA.

WEAVER Michael D. b. 5 July 1961, Boston, MA, United States of America. m. Angela Renee Marshall, 18 Dec. 1987. *Education:* AAS, Community College of the Air Force, 1984. *Publications:* Wolf-Dreams (fantasy novel), 1987; Mercedes Nights (science fiction), 1987; Nightreaver (fantasy novel), 1988; My Father Immortal (science fiction), 1989; Bloodfang (fantasy novel), 1989. *Address:* c/o Susan Protter, 110 West 40th Street, New York, NY 10018, USA.

WEBB Bernice Larson, b. Ludell, Kansas, USA. Owner and Publisher, Spider Press; Writer; Adjunct University Professor. m. Robert MacHardy Webb, 14 July 1961, 1 son, 1 daughter. *Education:* BA, 1956, MA, 1957, PhD, 1961, University of Kansas, Lawrence; Doctoral Research, University of Aberdeen, Scotland, 1959-60. *Appointments:* Writing Contest Judge, 1960s-; Editor, Cajun Chatter, 1964-66; Editor, The Magnolia, 1967-71; Editor, Louisiana Poets, 1970-89; Professor of Creative Writing, World Campus Afloat, 1972; Coordinator, Poetry-in-the-Schools, 1974; Consultant, Writing of Poetry, Lafayette Parish School System, Louisiana, 1970s-; Poetry Consultant, Director, Poetry Workshops, Acadiana Arts Council, 1970s-; Director, Reading- Writing Laboratories, University of Southwestern Louisiana, summers 1977-79; Book Reviewer, Journal of Popular Culture, Journal of American Culture, 1980-87. *Publications:* The Basketball Man, 1973, Japanese translation, 1981; Beware of Ostriches, 1978; Poetry on the Stage, 1979; George Washington Cable, commissioned essay, in Critical Survey of Long Fiction, 1983; Lady Doctor on a Homestead, 1987; Two Peach Baskets, 1991; Born to Be a Loser (co-author Johnnie Allan), 1993. *Contributions to:* Many articles, short stories, 1-act plays, 100s of poems, to various publications. *Honours:* 8 Carruth Poetry Awards, 1946-61; Phi Beta Kappa, 1955; Fulbright Scholarship to France (alt), 1959; Foreign Exchange Scholar, Scotland, 1959-60; 3 research grants, 1978-86; Seaton Award, 1980; Coolidge Research Colloquium, 1985. *Memberships include:* Past President, Past Journal Editor, Louisiana State Poetry Society; President, Southwest Branch Poetry Society; Board Member, Deep South Writers Conference; Founder, Webb's Writers; Past President, South Central College English Association; Past President, Phi Beta Kappa Association; Fellow, Society for Values in Higher Education; Modern Language Association; College English Association; Conference on Christianity and Literature; American Folklore Society; National Federation of State Poetry Societies. *Address:* 159 Whittington Drive, Lafayette, LA 70503, USA.

WEBB Charles (John Paul), b. 1939, American. *Publications:* The Graduate, 1963; Love, Roger, 1967; The Marriage of a Young Stockbroker, 1969; Orphans and Other Children, 1974; The Abolitionist of Clark Gable Place, 1975; Elsinor, 1976; The Nose Collector, 1985. *Address:* C/o New American Library, 1633 Broadway, New York, NY 10019, USA.

WEBB Colin Thomas, b. 26 Mar.1939, England. Journalist. m. Margaret Frances Cheshire, 1970, 2 sons, 1 daughter. *Appointments:* Reporter, Portsmouth Evening News, Surrey Mirror, Press Association, Daily Telegraph, The Times; Home news editor, The Times, 1969-74; Editor, Cambridge Evening News, 1974-82; Deputy editor, The Times, 1982-86; Journalist director, Times Newspaper Holdings, 1983-86; Editor-in-Chief, Press Association, 1986-. *Publication:* Co-author, with Times news team, Black Man in Search of Power, 1968. *Memberships:* Core Committee, British Executive, International Press Institute, 1984-; Council, Commonwealth Press Union, 1985-. *Address:* 49 Winterbrook Road, London SE24, England.

WEBB Martha G. *See:* **WINGATE Martha Anne.**

WEBB Sharon Lynn, b. 29 Feb 1936, Tampa, Florida, USA, Writer. m. W Bryan Webb, 6 Feb 1956, 3 daughters. *Education:* Student, Florida Southern College, 1953-56; University of Miami, 1962; ADN,

Miami-Dade School of Nursing, 1972. *Appointments:* Freelance Writer, 1960-66; Registered Nurse, South Miami Hospital, 1972-73; Union General Hospital, Blairsville, Georgia, 1973-81. *Publications:* RN, 1981; Earthchild, 1982; Earth Song, 1983; Ram Song, 1984; Adventures of Terra Tarkington, 1985; Pestis 18, 1987; The Halflife, 1989; Over 40 short stories. *Memberships:* Authors Guild/League; Science Fiction Writers of America, South/Central division, Board of Directors. *Address:* Route 2, Box 2600, Blairsville, GA 30512, USA.

WEBB Stephen Barry, b. 14 May 1947, London, England. University Lecturer. *Education:* St Peter's College, Oxford 1965-69; BA Hons English Language and Literature 1968; Dip Theol 1969. *Publication:* Edmund Blunden: A Biography, 1990. *Address:* St Peter's College, Oxford OX1 2DL, England.

WEBER George Richard, b. 7 Feb. 1929, The Dalles, Oregon, USA. Certified Public Accountant. m. Nadine Hanson, 12 Oct. 1957, 3 daughters. *Education:* BS, Oregon State University, 1950; MBA, University of Oregon, 1962. *Publications:* Small Business Long-Term Finance, 1962; A History of the Coroner and Medical Examiner Offices, 1963; CPA Litigation Service References, 1991. *Contributions To:* Cost and Management; Hyacinths & Biscuits. *Honours:* Bronze Star Medal with V, US Army, 1953; Selected by AICPA as one of One Hundred Future Leaders of Accounting Profession in the USA, 1963; Knightly association of St George the Martyr, 1986. *Memberships:* American Institute of CPA's; Oregon Society of CPA's; Portland Committee on Foreign Relations. *Address:* 2603 NE 32 Ave., Portland, OR 97212, USA.

WEBER Hulda. *See:* **KATZ Hilda.**

WEBSTER Ernest, b. 24 Oct 1923, Habrough. Retired Director. m. 8 Oct 1942, 2 daughters. *Education:* London Matric, History and Economics. *Publications:* The Friulan Plot; Madonna of the Black Market; Cossack Hide-Out; Red Alert; The Venetian Spy-Glass; The Verratoli Inheritance; Million Dollar Stand-in; The Watchers. *Literary Agent:* Robert Hale. *Address:* 17 Chippendale Rise, Otley, West Yorkshire LS21 2BL, England.

WEBSTER Jan b.10 Aug 1924, Blantyre. Writer. m. 10 Aug 1946, 1 son, 1 daughter. *Education:* Hamilton Academy. *Publications:* Trilogy: Colliers Row, 1977, Saturday City, 1978, Beggarman's Country, 1979; Due South, 1981; Muckle Annie, 1985; One Little Room, 1987; Rags of Time, 1987; A Different Woman, 1989; Abercrombie's Aunt and Other Stories, 1990; I Only Can Dance With you, 1990. *Address:* c/o Robert Hale, 45-47 Clerkenwell Green, London EC1R 0HJ, England.

WEBSTER Jesse. *See:* **CASSILL Ronald Verlin.**

WEBSTER Norah. *See:* **KNOX William.**

WEBSTER Norman William, b. 21 Aug. 1920, Barrow-in-Furness, Cumbria, England. Retired Physicist. m. Phyllis Joan Layley, 17 Feb. 1945, 2 daughters. *Education:* BSc. Physics, University of London. *Publications include:* Joseph Locke, Railway Revolutionary, 1970; Britain's First Trunk Line; The Grand Junction Railway, 1972; Horace Reactor, 1972; The Great North Road, 1974; Blanche of Lancaster, 1990. *Contributions to:* Cumbria; Hertfordshire Countryside; numerous scientific journals. *Memberships:* Jane Austen Society; European Movement. *Address:* 15 Hillcrest Drive; Slackhead, Milnthorpe, Cumbria LA7 7BB, England.

WEDGWOOD C(icely) V(eronica) (Dame), b. 1910, British. *Appointments:* President, English Centre of International PEN, 1950-57, the English Association, 1955-56; Member, Royal Commission on Historical Manuscripts, 1952-78, Institute for Advanced Study, Princeton, NJ, 1953-68, Advisory Council, Victoria and

Albert Museum, 1959-69, Arts Council Literature Panel, 1965-67, London; Trustee, National Gallery, 1960-67, 1970-77. *Publications:* The Thirty Years War, 1938; The Emperor Charles V, by Karl Brandi (trans), 1939; William the Silent, 1944; Die Blendung, by Elias Canetti (in UK as Auto da Fe, in US as Tower of Babel) (trans), 1946; Richelieu and the French Monarchy, 1949; Seventeenth Century English Literature, 1950; Montrose, 1952; The King's Peace, 1955; The King's War, 1958; Poetry and Politics, 1960; Thomas Wentworth: A Reevaluation, 1961; Trial of Charles I (in US as A Coffin for King Charles), 1964; The World of Rubens, 1967; Milton and His World, 1970; Oliver Cromwell, 1973; The Political Career of Peter Paul Rubens, 1975; The Spoils of Time: A History of the World, volume 1, 1984; History and Hope, 1987. *Honours:* Member of Order of Merit; Dame British Empire; Officer, Order of Orange, Nassau, Goethe Medal, 1958; Hon LLD, Glasgow University; Hon DLitt, Sheffield, Smith, Harvard, Oxford, Keele, Sussex and Liverpool Universities; Honorary Fellow, Lady Margaret Hall, Oxford, 1962-; Hon Fellow, UC London and London School of Economics. *Memberships:* President, English PEN Centre, 1951-57; Fellow, Royal Society of Literature; Fellow, British Academy; Fellow, Royal Historical Society; Hon Member, American Academy of Arts and Science, American Philosophical Society, American Historical Association, and Massachusetts Historical Society; Society of Authors. *Address:* c/o Messrs W Harper Collins, Ophelia House, Fulham Palace Road, London W6, England.

WEHRLI Peter, b. 30 July 1939, Switzerland. Writer; TV Producer. *Education:* University of Zurich; University of Paris (Sorbonne) France. *Publications:* Aukunfte (Arrivals), 1970; Catalogue of the 134 most important observations during a long railway journey, 1974; Katalog von Allem (Catalogue of Everything), 1974; Donnerwetter das bin ja ich!, 1975; Zelluloid Paradies, 1978; Tingeltangel (novel), 1982; Charivari (theatre play), 1984; Alles von Allem, 1985; La Farandula, 1986; Co-Editor, This Book is Free of Chairge; Co-founder, Thearena (Zurich); Founder: Jurgendbuhne Leimbach (Switzerland) and Wort Circus Bramarbasani (Switzerland). *Contributions to:* Magazines and journals in Switzerland, UK, USA, Italy, Albania, Malta, Argentina, including Orte (Zurich); manuskripte (Graz); The Poets Encyclopedia (NYC). *Honours:* Recipient, several honours and awards including Award of the Government of Zurich; Distinguished Service Citation, World Poetry Society. *Memberships:* PEN Swiss Writers Association; Gruppe Olten; International Federation of Journalists; International Association of Art Critics. *Address:* Schifflande 16, 8001 Zurich, Switzerland.

WEIGEL George, b. 17 Apr 1951, Baltimore, Maryland, USA. Roman Catholic Theologian. m. Joan Balcombe, 21 June 1975, 1 son, 2 daughters. *Education:* BA Philosophy 1973, St Mary's Seminary & University, Baltimore; MA Theology 1975, University of St Michael's College, Toronto. *Appointments:* Fellow, Woodrow Wilson International Centre for Scholars 1984-85; Editorial Boards of: First Things, The Washington Quarterly, and Orbis. *Publications:* Tranquillitas Ordinis: The Present Failure and Future Promise of American Catholic Thought on War and Peace, 1987; Catholicism and the Renewal of American Democracy, 1989; American Interests, American Purpose: Moral Reasoning and US Foreign Policy, 1989; Freedom and Its Discontents, 1991; Just War and the Gulf War, Co-Author, 1991; The Final Revolution: The Resistance Church and the Collapse of Communism, 1992; 4 other volumes edited. *Contributions to:* Numerous and ongoing. *Memberships:* Catholic Theological Society of America; Council on Foreign Relations. *Address:* Ethics and Public Policy Centre, 1015-15th Street NW, Suite 900, Washington DC 20005, USA.

WEINBERG Florence M(ay), b. 1933, American. *Appointments:* Instructor 1967, Assistant Professor 1967-71, Associate Professor 1971-75, Chairman, Division of Modern Languages and Classical Studies 1972-79, Professor 1975-, St John Fisher College, Rochester, NY. *Publications:* The Wine and the Will:

Rabelais's Bacchic Christianity, 1972; Gargantua in a Convex Mirror, 1986; The Cave, 1987.

WEINER Jonathan David, b. 26 Nov 1953, New York City, New York, USA. Science Writer. m. 29 May 1981, 2 sons. *Education:* BA cum laude English and American Language and Literature 1977, Harvard College. *Appointments:* Assistant Editor, Moment magazine 1979; Associate Editor, The Sciences 1979-81; Senior Editor, The Sciences 1981-85. *Publications:* Planet Earth, 1986; The Next One Hundred Years, 1990. *Contributions to:* Field Notes column, The Sciences 1981-88. *Honours:* Year's Best Column, Society of National Association Publications, 1985, 1988; Annual Award of American Geophysical Union for Public Understanding of Geology, 1986. *Memberships:* Authors Guild; National Association of Science Writers. *Literary Agent:* Victoria Pryor, Arcadia Ltd, 20A Old NNeversink Road, Danbury, CT 06811, USA. *Address:* Buckingham, Pennsylvania, USA.

WEINREICH Beatrice, (Beatrice Silverman-Weinreich), b. 14 May 1928, New York City, USA. Folklorist. m. Uriel Weinreich, 26 June 1949, dec 1967, 1 son, 1 daughter. *Education:* BA 1949, Brooklyn College; One year of graduate work in Folklore and Ethnography, University of Zurich 1950; MA Anthropology 1956, Columbia University. *Publications:* Co-Editor, Volume II: Research Tools, The Language and Culture Atlas of Ashkenazic Jewry, 1993; Yiddish Folktales, 1988; Co-Editor, Yidisher folklor: A Journal of Yiddish folklore (in Yiddish), 1954; Co-Editor, Yiddish Language and Folklore: A Selective Bibliography for Research, 1959. *Contributions to:* Four Variants of the Yiddish Masterthief tale, The Field of Yiddish 1, 1954; Genres and Types of the Yiddish Folktales About the Prophet Elijah, The Field of Yiddish II, 1965; The Americanization of Passover, Studies in Biblical & Jewish Folklore, 1960. *Memberships:* American Folklore Society; New York Folklore Society; International Society for Folk Narrative Research. *Address:* c/o YIVO Institute for Jewish Research, 1048 Fifth Avenue, New York, NY 10028, USA.

WEINSTEIN Michael Alan, b. 24 Aug 1942, Brooklyn, New York, USA. Political Philosopher. m. Deena Schneiweiss, 31 May 1964. *Education:* BA summa cum laude 1964, New York University; MA 1965, PhD 1967, Western Reserve University. *Appointments:* Assistant Professor, Western Reserve University 1967; Assistant Professor, Virginia Polytechnic Institute 1967-68; Assistant Professor 1968-70, Associate Professor 1970-72, Professor 1972-, Purdue University; Milward Singson Distinguished Professor of Political Science, University of Wyoming 1979. *Publications:* The Polarity of Mexican Thought: Instrumentalism and Finalism, 1976; The Tragic Sense of Political Life, 1977; Meaning and Appreciation:Time and Modern Political Life, 1978; The Structure of Human Life: A Vitalist Ostology, 1979; The Wilderness and the City: American Classical Philosophy as a Moral Quest, 1982; Unity and Variety is the Philosophy of Samuel Alexander, 1984; Finite Perfection: Reflections on Virtue, 1985; Culture Critique: Fernand Dumont and the New Quebec Sociology, 1985. *Contributions to:* Over 100 articles to magazines and journals. *Honours:* Best Paper Prize, Midwest Political Science Association, 1969; Guggenheim Fellowship 1974-75; Rockefeller Foundation Humanities Fellowship, 1976. *Address:* Department of Political Science, Purdue University, West Lafayette, IN 47907, USA.

WEINTRAUB Stanley, b. 1929, USA. Professor. *Appointments:* Director of Institute for the Arts and Humanities Studies, 1970-90; Research Professor to 1986; Evan Pugh Professor of Arts and Humanities, Pennsylvania State University. *Publications:* Private Shaw and Public Shaw: A Dual Portrait of Lawrence of Arabia and George Bernard Shaw, 1963; The Ward in the Wards: Korea's Forgotten Battle, 1964, 1977; The Art of William Golding (with B S Oldsey), 1965; Reggie: A Portrait of Reginald Turner, 1965; Beardsley:

A Biography, 1967; The Last Great Cause: The Intellectuals and the Spanish Civil War, 1968; Evolution of a Revolt: Early Postwar Writings of T E Lawrence (with R Weintraub), 1968; Journey to Heartbreak: The Crucible Years of Bernard Shaw 1914-1918, 1971; Whistler: A Biography, 1974; Lawrence of Arabia: The Literary Impulse (with R Weintraub), 1975; Aubrey Beardsley: Imp of the Perverse, 1976; Four Rossettis: A Victorian Biography, 1977; The London Yankees: Portraits of American Writers and Artists in London 1894-1914, 1979; The Unexpected Shaw: Biographical Approaches to G B S and His Work, 1982; The End of the Great War, 1985; Bernard Shaw: The Diaries 1885-1897, 1986; Editor: An Unfinished Novel, by George Bernard Shaw, 1958; C P Snow: A Spectrum, 1963; The Yellow Book: Quintessence of the Nineties, 1964; The Savoy: Nineties Experiment, 1966; The Court Theatre, 1966; Biography & Truth, 1968; Cashel Byron's Profession, by Shaw, 1968; The Literary Criticism of Oscar Wilde, 1968; Shaw: An Autobiography, 2 vols, 1969-70; The Green Carnation, by Robert Hichens, 1970; Saint Joan, by Shaw, 1971; Bernard Shaw's Nondramatic Literary Criticism, 1972; Directions in Literary Criticism (with Philip Young), 1973; Saint Joan: Fifty Years After, 1973; The Portable Bernard Shaw, 1977; The Portable Oscar Wilde, 1981; Heartbreak House: A Facsimile of the Revised Typescript (with Anne Wright), 1981; Modern British Dramatists 1900-1945, 2 vols, 1982; The Playwright and the Pirate: Bernard Shaw and Frank Harris, a Correspondence, 1982; British Dramatists since World War II, 2 vols, 1982. *Address:* 202 Ihlseng Cottage, University Park, PA 16802, USA.

WEIR Ian Ralph, b. 3 Sept. 1956, Durham, North Carolina, USA. Writer. *Education:* BA, English, University of British Columbia; MA, English Language & Literature before 1525, King's College, University of London, England. *Publications:* The Idler, Stage Play, 1987; The Video Kid, Juvenile Novel, 1988; numerous plays produced professionally on stage, Radio (BBC & CBC), and CBC TV. *Honours:* Commonwealth Scholarship, 1982-83. *Memberships:* Playwrights Union of Canada; Alliance of Canadian Cinema, Television & Radio Artists. *Address:* Apartments 903, 1416 Harwood St., Vancouver, British Columbia, Canada U6G 1K5.

WEIR Joan Sherman, b. 21 Apr. 1928, Calgary, Alberta, Canada. Author; College English Instructor. m. Dr Ormond A Weir, 14 May 1955, 4 sons. *Education:* BA, Honours. *Appointments:* Writer in Residence, Thompson-Nicola Library Systems; Instructor, English, Cariboo College, 1977-. *Publications;* Three Day Challenge, juvenile novel, 1976; Sherman, biography, 1976; The Caledonians, history, 1977; Exile at the Rocking Seven, novel, 1977; Career Girl, juvenile novel, 1979; So, I'm Different, juvenile novel, 1981; Secret at Westwind, mystery, 1982; Walhachin, history, 1984; Canada's Gold Rush Church, history, 1986; Storm Rider, juvenile novel, 1987; Ski Lodge Mystery, juvenile mystery, 1988; Balloon Race Mystery, juvenile mystery, 1988; Sixteen is Spelled O-U-C-H, young adult novel, 1988; Backdoor to the Klondike, history, 1988. *Contributor to:* Discovery; The Friend; Trials; Kamloops Sentinel. *Honour:* Approved by Canada Council for giving readings & conducting creative writing workshops throughout Canada. *Memberships:* Writers Union of Canada; Federation of British Columbia Writers; Canadian Authors Association; CANSCAIP, Childrens Writers. *Agent:* J Kellock and Associates, Edmonton, Alberta. *Address:* 463 Greenstone Drive, Kamloops, British Columbia, Canada V2C 1N8.

WEIS Jack, b. 1 Oct. 1932, Tampa, Florida, USA. Motion Picture Producer & Director; Writer; Cinematographer. *Education:* BS, Notre Dame University; Master of Psychology, University of Chicago. *Publications:* Screen Plays: Quadroon, 1970; Storyville, 1972; Crypt of Dark Secrets, 1973; Mardi Gras Massacre, 1979; You Never Gave Me Roses, 1981; The Perfect Circle, 1982; Shooting Star of Pegasus, 1985; Witches Bayou; Cykwweck at Paytoua; Tia Chi The Fonec

Withio. *Address:* 6771 Marshal Foch, New Orleans, LA 70176, USA.

WEISMAN Alan Harley, b. 24 Mar 1947, Minneapolos, Minnesota, USA. Writer. *Education:* BA 1969, MS Journalism 1971, Northwestern University. *Appointments:* Professor of Writing, Prescott College 1982- 88; Escritor Residente, Altos de Chavon, Dominican Republic 1988. *Publications:* We Immortals, 1979; La Frontera: The United States Border With Mexico, 1986. *Contributions to:* New York Times Magazine; Los Angeles Times Magazine; The Atlantic; various others. *Honours:* John Farrar Fellow in Non Fiction, Bread Loaf 1986; Los Angeles Press Club Award 1987; Best in the West Journalism Award 1987; Fulbright Scholar 1988; Four Corners Book Award 1988; Unity Award 1992; Robert F Kennedy Journalism Award 1992. *Literary Agent:* Gina Maccoby Literary Agency. *Address:* HC32, Box 557, Groom Creek Route, Prescott, AZ 86303, USA.

WEISS Helen E Nitka, b. 26 Mar 1913, Malden, Massachusetts, USA. Poet; Former professional Cellist. m. Marvin D Weiss, 21 Sept 1946, 2 sons. *Education:* Longy School of Music, Cambridge, Massachusetts 1933-35; New England Conservatory, Boston, Massachusetts 1933-36; Manhattan School of Music, New York City 1936-40; Special Literature & Writing Classes, George Washington University, Washington DC 1940. *Publications:* Poetry: To Ask Myself, an Athology of Poetry for the Western World, 1989; Never Say Never II, collection of poetry, 1992; Wolfgang Amadeus Mozart; Family Tree; On Questioning Grandparents; Ode To Turner Centre's Writers' Groups. *Contributions to:* Heartland Journal; Missouri Review; 10 pages poetry to Bamboo Ridge Publishers of Honolulu, Hawaii. *Memberships:* Turner Centre Clinic of Geriatrics; University of Michigan Writers' Groups. *Address:* 3304 Platt Road, Ann Arbor, Michigan, 48108, USA.

WEISS Irving J, b. 11 Sept 1921, New York, USA. Writer. m. Anne de la Vergne, 14 Dec 1949, 1 son, 3 daughters. *Education:* BA English 1942, University of Michigan at Ann Arbor; MA Comparative Literature 1949, Columbia University at New York. *Appointments:* Instructor in English, Pennsylvania State University 1955-57; Assistant Professor English, Fashion Institute of Technology 1960-64; Professor English, SUNY at New Paltz 1964-85. *Publications:* American Authors and Books, 1640 to Present, 1962; Plastic Sense, 1972; Thesaurus of Book Digests 1950-1980, 1980; Sens-Plastique, 1980; Reflections on Childhood, 1991. *Contributions to:* Archae; Experiment in Words; NY Times Book Review; Marriage and Family; Gamut; Catalyst; Rohwedder; Prakalpana. *Honours:* SUNY Writing Award, 1972, 1984. *Literary Agent:* Julian Bach. *Address:* 319 Rosin Drive, Chestertown, MD 21620, USA.

WEISS Renee Karol, b. 11 Sept 1923, Allentown, Pennsylvania, USA, m. Theodore Weiss, 1941. *Education:* BA, Bard College; Connecticut Summer School of the Dance, 1950p; Instruction with Martha Graham and Jose Limon; Musical Education with Sascha Jacobinoff, Boris Koutzen, Emile Hauser and Ivan Galamian. *Appointments:* Teacher, modern dance to children, Bard College; Kindergarten, Tivoli, New York Public School, 1955-58; Poetry writing workshop, Hofstra College, summer, 1985; Princeton University academic year, 1985; Modern Poetry, Cooper Union, 1988; Violinist, member of Miami University Symphony Orchestra, 1941; North Carolina State Symphony, 1942-45; Oxford University Symphony and Opera Orchestras, England, 1953-54; Woodstock String Quartet, 1956-60; Bard College Ensemble, 1950-66; Hudson Valley Philharmonic, 1960-66; Touring public schools with Hudson Valley String Quartet, 1965; Orchestral, chamber and solo work, 1966-; Prionceton Chamber Orchestra, 1980-. *Publications:* To Win a Race, 1966; A Paper Zoo, 1968; The Bird From the Sea, 1970; David Schubert, Work and Days, biography, 1984. *Contributor to:* Various poems in journals; Co-editor, Quarterly review of Literature, 1945-. *Honours:* A Paper Zoo listed in Best Books for Children, New York Times and Book World, 1968; New Jersey Author's Award, 1968, 1970. *Address:* 26 Haslet Avenue, Princeton, NJ 08540, USA.

WEISSBERG Michael Peter, b. 14 July 1942, New York City, USA. Physician; Psychiatrist. m. Susan Patrice Dean, 14 Aug 1988, 1 son. *Education:* BA 1964, New York University; MD 1968, Tufts University School of Medicine; Residency, The Mount Sinai Hospital, New York City, Denver Institute for Psychoanalysis 1985-90. *Publications:* Clinical Psychiatry in Primary Care, 1978; Dangerous Secrets, 1983; The First Sin of Ross Michael Carlson, 1992. *Contributions to:* Over 50 articles, chapters and abstracts. *Memberships:* Fellow, American Psychiatric Association; American College of Psychiatry. *Literary Agent:* Regula Noetzli. *Address:* University of Colorado Health Sciences Centre, 4200 E 9th Avenue, Denver, CO 80262, USA.

WELBURN Ron, b. 30 Apr 1944, Berwyn, Pennsylvania, USA. Educator; Poet; Writer. m. Cheryl T Welburn, 16 Oct 1988, 2 sons, 1 daughter. *Education:* BA, Lincoln University, Pennsylvania, 1968; MA, University of Arizona, 1971; PhD, New York University, 1983. *Appointments:* For New York State Council on the Arts: Consultant, Workshop Teacher, Auburn State Prison, New York, 1972, Poet-in-Residence, Hartley House, New York City, 1982, Poet-in Residence, Schenectady County Public Library, New York, 1985; Poet-in-Residence, Lincoln University, Pennsylvania, 1973, 1974. *Publications:* Peripheries: Selected Poems 1966-1968, 1972; Brown-up, 1977; The Look in the Night Sky, 1978; Heartland, 1981; Council Decisions, 1991. *Contributions to:* Poems and fiction to over 75 literary magazines and anthologies; Jazz reviews and critical essays to: Nickel Review; Jazz Times; Scholarly music periodicals. *Honours:* Edward S Silvera Poetry Award, 1967, 1968; Fellow, Summer Institute in Jazz Criticism, Smithsonian Institution and Music Critics Association, 1975. *Memberships:* MELUS; ASAIL. *Address:* English Department, Bartlett Hall, University of Massachusetts, Amherst, MA 01003, USA.

WELCH Ann Courtenay, b. 20 May 1917, London, England. Aviation Writer. m. (1) 2 daughters (2) P P Lorne Elphinstone Welch, 23 June 1953, 1 daughter. *Appointments include:* Editor, Bulletin, Federation Aeronautique International 1979-89; Editor, Royal Aero Club Gazette, 1984-; Part-time Tutor AEI classes on Writing, 5 years. *Publications include:* The Woolacombe Bird, 1964; Story of Gliding, 1965; New Soaring Pilot, 1970; Pilot's Weather, 1973; Gliding, 1976; Hang Glider Pilot, 1977; Book of Air Sports, 1978; Accidents Happen, 1978; Soaring Hang Gliders, 1981; Complete Microlight Guide, 1983; Happy to Fly, autobiography, 1984; Complete Soaring Guide, 1986. *Contributions to:* Flight International, UK; Aeroplane, UK; Royal Aero Club Gazette. *Honours:* Officer, Order of British Empire (OBE); Silver Medal, Royal Aero Club; Gold, Lilienthal & Bronze Medals, Federation Aeronautique International; FAI Pelagia Majewska Medal, 1990. *Memberships:* Fellow; Royal Aeronautical Society, Chairman Light Aviation Group; Royal Meteorological Society. *Address:* 14 Upper Old Park Lane, Farnham, Surrey GU9 0AS, England.

WELCH (James) Colin (Ross), b. 23 Apr.1924, England. Journalist. m. Sybil Russell, 1950, 1 son, 1 daughter. *Education:* Peterhouse, Cambridge. *Appointments include:* Glasgow Herald, 1948; Colonial Office, 1949; Leader writer, columnist (Peter Simple, with Michael Wharton), parliamentary sketch writer 1950-64, deputy editor 1964-80, regular column 1981-83, Daily Telegraph; Editor-in-chief, Chief Executive magazine, 1980-82; Columnist, Spectator, 1982-; Parliamentary sketch writer, Daily Mail, 1984-92; Columnist, Independent, 1993. *Publications:* Editor, Sir Frederick Ponsonby: Recollections of Three Reigns, 1951; Translator, with Sybil Welch, Nestroy: Liberty Comes to Krahwinkel, 1954, BBC. *Contributions to:* Encounter; Spectator; New Statesman; etc. Various symposia, including The Future Doesn't Work, New York, 1977. *Honour:* Knight's Cross, Order of Polonia Restituta, 1972; Journalist of the Year, 1974; Special Writer of the Year, 1987. *Address:* 4 Goddard's Lane, Aldbourne, Wilts 5N8 2DL, England.

WELCH Liliane, b. 20 Oct. 1937, Luxembourg. Professor, French Literature. m. Cyril Welch, 1 daughter. *Education:* BA, 1960, MA 1961, University of Montana; PhD, Penn State University, 1964. *Appointments:* Assistant Professor, French, East Carolina University, 1965-66, Antioch College, 1966-67, Mount Allison University, 1967-71; Associate Professor, 1971-77, Professor, 1977-, French, Mount Allison University. *Publications:* Emergence : Baudelaire, Mallarme, Rimbaud, 1973; Winter Songs, 1973; *Address:* Rimbaud, Mallarme, Butor, 1979; Syntax of Ferment, 1979; Assailing Beats, 1979; October Winds, 1980; Brush and Trunks, 1981; From the Songs of the Artisans, 1983; Manstorna, 1985; Rest Unbound, 1985; Word-House of a Grandchild, 1987; Seismographs: Selected Essays and Reviews, 1988; Fire to the Looms Below, 1990; Life in Another Language, 1992. *Contributor to:* More than 50 USA, Canadian, European, Australian Journals; Literary articles in more than 20 International journals. *Memberships:* Writers Union of Canada; Federation of New Brunswick Writers; League of Canadian Poets; Association of Italian-Canadian Writers; Lëtzebuerger Schrëftsteller Verband. *Address:* Box 246, Sackville, NB EOA 3CO, Canada.

WELCH Rowland. *See:* **DAVIES Leslie Purnell.**

WELDON Fay, b. 22 Sept 1931. Writer. m. Ron Weldon, 12 June 1961, 4 sons. *Education:* MA, Economics, Psychology, St Andrews University, 1952. *Publications:* Fat Woman's Joke, 1968; Down Among the Women, 1971; Female Friends, 1975; Remember Me, 1976; Little Sister, 1977; Praxis, 1978; Puffball, 1980; Watching Me, Watching You, 1981; The President's Child, 1982; Letters to Alice, 1984; Life and Loves of a She-Devil, 1984; Polaris, 1984; Rebecca West, 1985; The Shrapnel Academy, 1986; The Heart of the Country, 1987; The Hearts and Lives of Men, 1987; The Rules of Life, 1987; Leader of the Band, 1988; Sackcloth and Ashes, 1989; Wolf of the Mechanical Dog (for children), 1989; The Cloning of Joanna May, 1989 (televised 1992); Pary Puddle, 1989; D'Arcy's Utopia, 1990; Stories 4: Green, 1990; Moon over Minneapolis or Why She Couldn't Stay (short stories), 1991; Life Force, 1992; Growing Rich, 1992. *Contributor to:* numerous journals and magazines. *Memberships:* Fellow, Royal Society of Literature; Management Committee, Society of Authors; Writers Guild of Great Britain. *Literary Agent:* Giles Gordon. *Address:* c/o Giles Gordon, 43 Doughty Street, London WC1N 2LF, England.

WELLAND Colin (b. Williams), b. 4 July 1934, Liverpool, England. Playwright; Actor. m. Patricia Sweeney, 1962, 1 son, 3 daughters. *Education:* Goldsmiths College, London. *Appointments:* Art Teacher, 1958-62; Entered Theatre, 1962-, Library Theatre, Manchester 1962-64; Director, Radio Aire, 1981-; Acted in Films: Kes; Villain; Stra Dogs; Sweeney. *Publications:* Plays: Say Goodnight to Grandma, 1973; Roll on Four O'Clock, 1981; TV Plays Include: Kisses at 50; Leeds United; Your Man from Six Counties; Plays: Roomful of Holes, 1972; Say Goodnight to Grandma, 1973; Northern Humour, 1982. *Honours:* Best TV Playwright, Writers Guild, 1970, 1973 and 1974; Best TV Writer, and Best Supporting Film Actor, BAFTA Awards, 1970; Broadcasting Press Guild Award (for writing), 1973; Oscar, Evening Standard and Broadcasting Press Guild Awards, 1982. *Address:* c/o Peters, Fraser and Dunlop, 5th Floor, The Chambers, Chelsea Harbour, Lots Road, London SW10 0XF, England.

WELLER Archie Irving Kirkwood, (R Chee, Kirk Weller), b. 13 July 1957, Western Australia, Australia. Writer. *Education:* Guildford Grammar School, 1968-1975; West Australian Institute of Technology (now Curtin Universdity), 1977-78. *Appointments:* Writer-in-

Residence, Australian National University, Canberra, 1984; Assistant Editor, Us Fellas anthology of Aboriginal writings and taped interviews, Artlook Books, 1988; Member, Panel of Judges, The Australia Centre, 1991; Writer-in-Residence, Black Swan Theatre, 1993. *Publications:* Day of the Dog, 1981, paperback, 1982, reprint, 1986; Going Home, short story collection, 1987, reprint, 1981-82; Short stories: Dead Dingo, 1977; Stolen Car, 1977; Pension Day, 1978; The Storm, 1979; Going Home, 1979; Mates, 1979; Sandcastles, 1979; Fish and Chips, 1980; Herbie, 1980; Johnny Blue, 1986; A Legend, 1987; It's Only a Game, 1988; Celebrations, 1988; Songs of the Sea, 1990; Millenium, 1990; Dead Roses, 1992; Lillies of the Valley, 1992; All the Pretty Little Horses, 1993; Poems include: Midgiegooroo, 1987; Frankie, My Man, 1988; Jimmy's Axe and Other Poems, 1989; For Kath Walker; Ngungalari; Willy-Willy Man; Oh Domjun; Plays: Sunset and Shadows, 1989; Nidjera, 1990; Voices in the Wind, 1993; Nuny's, 1993. *Contributions to:* Short stories, and poems to: Aboriginal and Islander Identity Magazine; Artlook Magazine; The Bulletin; Various anthologies; Articles to: Southern Hemisphere Review; Sydney Morning Herald; Cinema Papers; Aboriginal Australia Dictionary. *Honours:* 1st Prize, National Short Story Competition, 1977; Winner, Short Story, Canberra Times National Competition, 1979; Highly Commended, McGregor Literary Award, 1979, 1982; Commended, Lybndall Haddow Award, Fellowship of Writers, 1980; Commended, Bunbury Arts Council Award, 1981; 2nd Place, Vogel Literary Award, 1981; Winner, Western Australia Week Literary Awards, 1982; Writers Fellowship, Literature Board, Australia Council, 1983, 1991; Joint Winner, ABC Bi-Centennial Poetry Award, 1988. *Address:* PO Box 132, Northbridge PO, Northbridge 6001, Western Australia, Australia.

WELLER Kirk. *See:* **WELLER Archie Irving Kirkwood.**

WELLINGTON Monica Ann, b. 17 June 1957, London, England. Artist and Writer of Children's Picturebooks. 1 daughter. *Education:* BFA, University of Michigan School of Art, 1979. *Publications:* Writer, illustrator: Molly Chelsea and Her Calico Cat, 1988; All My Little Duckings, 1989; Seasons of Swans, 1990; The Sheep Follow, 1992; Mr Cookie Baker, 1992; Illustrator: Who is Tapping at My Window (A G Denning), 1988; In Between (Virginia Griest), 1989; Who Says That? (Arnold Shapiro), 1991; Forthcoming: What is Your Language? (Debra Leventhal). *Membership:* Society of Children's Book Writers and Illustrators. *Address:* 251 East 32nd St, New York, NY 10016, USA.

WELLS Allen, b. 26 Aug 1951, New York, New York, USA. History Professor. m. Katherine Conant, 1 May 1976, 1 son, 2 daughters. *Education:* BA 1973, State University of New York at Binghamton; MA 1974, PhD 1979, State University of New York at Stony Brook. *Publications:* Yucatan's Gilded Age, 1985; Yucatan y la International Harvester, 1986. *Contributions to:* Journal of Latin American Studies; Hispanic American Historical Review; Latin American Research Review; Mexican Studies; Revista de la Universidad de Yucatan. *Honours:* National Endowment for the Humanities Interpretive Research Grant 1987-89; American Philosophical Society, 1986; 2 articles won the Sturgis Leavitt Prizes for best article published in 1985 and 1987. *Memberships:* Academia Yucatanense de Ciencias y Artes, Merida, Yucatan, Conference on Latin American History, Nominating Committee; South Eastern Council of Latin American Studies, Executive Committee. *Address:* Department of History, Bowdoin College, Brunswick, ME 04011, USA.

WELLS Hondo. *See:* **WHITTINGDON Harry.**

WELLS Martin John b. 24 Aug. 1928, London, England. Zoologist; Educator. m. Joyce Finlay, 8 Sept. 1953, 2 sons. *Education:* BA 1952; MA, 1956; ScD, 1966, Cambridge University. *Publications:* Brain and Behaviour in Cephalopods, 1962; You, Me and the Animal World, 1964; Lower Animals, 1968; Octopus: Physiology and Behaviour of an Advanced Invertebrate, 1978. *Contributions to:* several journals. *Honours:* Silver Medal, Zoological Society, 1968; Fellow, Cambridge Philosophical Society. *Memberships:* Marine Biology Association. *Address:* The Bury Home End, Fulbourn, Cambridge, England.

WELLS Peter, b. 12 Jan 1919, London, England. Social Work Lecturer, 1978-80. m. (1) Elisabeth Vander Meulen, dec 1946, (2) Gillian Anne Hayes-Newington, 1988. 1 daughter. *Education:* Privately; Universities of London and Manchester; Dip Soc (London) 1970; Cert in Psychiatric Social Work (Manchester) 1973. *Publications:* Co-Editor, Poetry Folios, 1942-46, 1951; Short stories in Quarterly Review of Literature, USA, 1948, Dublin Magazine, Eire, 1947-49, Agonia Revista, Argentina, 1944, Points, Paris, 1955; Poetry in wartime anthologies Lyra, New Road 1942-43, Selected Writing, Crown and Sickle, 1944, Wartime Harvest, 1943; Contributor of fiction, criticism and poetry to New English Weekly 1944-47 and of poetry to Poetry, London, 1941-42, Poetry, Chicago, 1943, View, New York, 1942, Briarcliff Quarterly, USA, 1945, The Irish Times, including Poems from Ireland, 1943-44, Motive, Texas, 1940, The Townsman, UK, 1940, and other magazines; Occasional writer for The Adelphi, UK, 1939-42. *Memberships:* PEN; Society of Authors; Free Painters and Sculptors. *Address:* Model Farm, Linstead Magna, Halesworth, Suffolk, England.

WELLS Roger, b. 30 Jan 1947, London, England. University Lecturer. div., 1 daughter. *Education:* BA, History, Education, 1969, DPhil, History, 1978, University of York. *Appointments:* Lecturer, History: University of Wales, 1972-73; University of Exeter, 1973-75; University of York, 1975-76; Senior Lecturer, University of Brighton, 1976-. *Publications:* Dearth and Distress in Yorkshire 1793-1801, 1977; Insurrection: The British Experience 1795-1803, 1983, paperback, 1986; Riot and Political Disaffection in Nottinghamshire in the Age of Revolutions 1776-1803, 1983; Wretched Faces: Famine in Wartime England 1793-1801, 1988; Class, Conflict, and Protest in the English Countryside 1700-1880 (edited with M Reed), 1990; Victorian Village, 1992. *Contributions to:* Social History; Rural History; Southern History; Northern History; Policing and Society; Journal of Peasant Studies; Journal of Historical Geography; Local Historian; English Historical Review; Agricultural History Review; London Journal; Labour History Bulletin; Journals of Social Policy; Others. *Memberships:* Fellow, Royal Historical Society; Editor, Southern History, 1990-. *Address:* School of Historical and Critical Studies, University of Brighton, Grand Parade, Brighton BN2 2JY, England.

WELLS Stanley William, b. 21 May 1930, England. Professor; Editor; Shakespearean Scholar. m. Susan Elizabeth Hill, 1975, 3 daughters (1 dec.). *Education:* BA, University College, London; PhD, Shakespeare Institute, University of Birmingham. *Appointments include:* Fellow 1962-77, lecturer 1962, senior lecturer 1971, reader 1973-77, honorary fellow 1979-88, Director, 1988-, Shakespeare Institute; Consultant in English, Wroxton College, 1964-80; Director, Royal Shakespeare Theatre Summer School, 1971-; General editor, Oxford Shakespeare; Head of Shakespeare Department, Oxford University Press, 1978-88; Senior Research Fellow, Balliol College, Oxford, 1980-88; Professor of Shakespeare Studies, University of Birmingham, 1988-. *Publications include:* Editor, New Penguin Shakespeare, Midsummer Night's Dream 1967, Richard II 1969, Comedy of Errors 1972; Shakespeare: A Reading Guide, 1969, 1970; Literature & Drama, 1970; Editor, Select Bibliographical Guides, Shakespeare 1973, English Drama excluding Shakespeare 1975, Royal Shakespeare 1977, 1978; Compiler, 19th-Century Shakespeare Burlesques, 5 volumes, 1977; Shakespere: An Illustrated Dictionary, 1978, 1985; Shakespere: The Writer & His Work, 1978; Re-editing Shakespeare for the Modern Reader, 1984; General Editor, Shakespeares Complete Works, 1986; Editor, co-editor, author, numerous other publications on Shakespeare. *Honours include:* Honorary DLitt, Furman University, South Carolina, USA, 1978; Guest lecturer, British & overseas universities; British Academies Annual Shakespeare Lecture, 1987. *Memberships include:* President, Shakespeare Club of Stratford-upon-Avon, 1972-73; Council, Malone Society, 1967-; Governor 1974-, Executive Council 1976-, Royal Shakespeare Theatre. *Address:* Midsummer Cottage, Church Lane, Beckley, Oxford, England.

WELLS Tobias. *See:* **FORBES Deloris Stanton.**

WELLS Walter Newton, b. 15 Feb. 1943, South Carolina, USA. Journalist; Editor. m. Patricia Kleiber Raymer, 9 Sept. 1977. *Education:* BA, Presbyterian College, South Carolina, 1965; Virginia Commonwealth University, 1972; New School for Social Research, 1976; New York University, 1978. *Publications:* Assistant National Editor, New York Times, 1972-80; Deputy Editor, 1980-81, News Editor, 1981-93, International Herald Tribune. *Honour:* Doctor of Letters, Presbyterian College, 1987. *Address:* 18 Rue Daru, 75008, Paris, France.

WELLS William K. *See:* **GARSIDE Jack Clifford.**

WENTWORTH Wendy. *See:* **CHAPLIN Jenny.**

WERENSKIOLD Marit, b. 13 Dec 1942, Oslo, Norway. Art Historian; Professor. m. Yngvar Troim, 20 Aug 1970. *Education:* National College of Arts, Crafts and Design, Oslo, Norway 1961-62; Studies in History, Art History and Classical Archaeology, University of Oslo 1962-70 (1967-68 Universite de Paris, Sorbonne, Art History); Magister artium 1970; Doctor philosophiae, University of Oslo 1982; Passed examinations in basic Russian 1985. *Appointments:* Art Critic 1969-71, 1982-84 in Dagbladet, Morgenbladet, and Aftenposten, Oslo, Norway; Research Fellow, University of Oslo 1972-86; Assistant Professor 1986-91, Professor in Art History 1992, University of Oslo, Department of Archaeology, Numismatics and the History of Art. *Publications:* De norske Matisse-elevene, Laeretid og gjennombrudd 1908-1914 (The Norwegian Pupils of Matisse's: Apprenticeship and Breakthrough 1908-1914), 1972; The Concept of Expressionism: Origin and Metamorphoses, 1984. *Contributions to:* Kandinsky's Moscow, Art in America, 1989; Serge Diaghilev and Erik Werenskiold, Konsthistorisk tidskrift, 1991. *Honours:* Boursiere de l'Etat Francais, 1967-68; Grants from: Grinifangers Kulturfornd, 1970-71; Fondet for Svensk-Norsk Samarbeid, 1974; Det Norske Videnskaps-Akademi, 1975; Norsk Faglitteraer Forfatterforening 1992 (travelling grant). *Memberships:* Norsk Faglitteraer Forfatterforening (NFF), Oslo; VisitingMember of the Institute for Advanced Study, Princeton, New Jersey, USA, 1988; Corresponding member of the Anders Zorn Academy, Sweden, 1983-. *Literary Agent:* Universitetsforlaget, Oslo. *Address:* Ulsrudveien 6, 0690 Oslo, Norway.

WERSCHENSKA Galina, b. 21 Dec 1906, Sct Petersburg. Author; Pianist. 3 sons. *Publications:* My Russian Spring; My Life with Dore; Glimt Af Saelsomhed; Brogede Akkorder. *Membership:* The Danish Writers' Union. *Address:* C F Richs vej 122, DK-2000 Frederiksberg, Denmark.

WESCOTT Roger Williams, b. 28 April 1925, Philadelphia, Pennsylvania, USA. Anthropologist. m. 12 Apr 1964. *Education:* BA English and History 1945, MA Oriental Studies 1947, PhD Linguistic Science 1948, Princeton University; M Litt Social Anthropology 1953, Oxford University. *Appointments:* Director, University Playreaders, Ibadan, Nigeria 1955-56; Assistant Professor of English, MIT, USA 1956-57; Associate Professor of English, Michigan State University 1957-62; Evaluator, National Endowment for Humanities 1975-; Associate Editor, Thoughts for All Seasons, USA 1988-. *Publications:* The Divine Animal, 1969; Visions:

Selected Poems, 1975; Sound and Sense, 1980; Language Families, 1986; Getting it Together, 1990; Co-Author: The Creative Process, 1974; Poems for Children, 1975; Literary and Linguistic Studies, 1978; Anthropological Poetics, 1990. *Contributions:* Two Ibo Songs, Anthropological Linguistics, March 1962; From Proverb to Aphorism, Forum Linguisticum, 1981. *Honours:* Sophomore English Prize, Princeton University, 1943; Rhodes Scholar, Oxford University 1948-50; First Holder, Endowed Chair of Excellence in Humanities, University of Tennessee 1988-89. *Memberships:* President, Princeton University undergraduate Literary Society 1944; President, International Society for the Comparative Study of Civilsations 1992-; President, Linguistic Association of Canada and the US 1976-77. *Address:* 16-A Heritage Crest, Southbury, CT 06488, USA.

WESKER Arnold, b. 24 May 1932, London, England. Playwright; Director. m. Dusty Bicker, 14 Nov. 1958, 2 sons, 2 daughters. *Publications:* Chicken Soup with Barley, 1959; Roots, 1959; I'm Talking About Jerusalem, 1960; The Wesker Trilogy, 1960; The Kitchen, 1961; Chips with Everything, 1962; The Four Seasons, 1966; Their Very Own and Golden City, 1966; Fears of Fragmentation, 1970; Friends, 1970; Six Sundays in January, 1971; The Journalists, 1972; The Old Ones, 1973; Love Letters on Blue Paper, 1974; Say Goodbye! You May Never See Them Again, (with John Allin), 1974; The Wedding Feast, 1977; The Journalists, 1975; Shylock (formerly The Merchant), 1976; Journey into Journalism, 1977; Said the Old Man to the Young Man, 1978; Fatlips (story for young people), 1978; One More Ride on the Merry-go Round, 1978; Caritas, 1981; Distinctions, 1985; Bluey, 1985; Annie Wobbler/Yardsale/Flour Portraits/Whatever Happened to Betty Lemon. (Wesker's One Woman Plays), 1986; When God Wanted a Son, 1986; Badenheim 1939 (from novel by Aharon Appelfeld), 1987; Little Old Lady and Shoeshine (plays for young people), 1987; Lady Othello, 1987; A mini-biography, 1988; Caritas, 1988; Beorhtel's Hill, 1988; The Mistress, 1988; Shoeshine, 1989; Collected Plays, vols 1 and 5, 1989; Collected Plays, vols 2, 3, 4 and 6, 1990; Wild Spring, 1992; Forthcoming: Dance Me Through Flowers, (original film script); As Much As I Dare, (Autobiography). *Honours:* Most Promising Playwright, Evening Standard Drama Award, 1959; 1st Prize, Encyclopedia Britannica Award, 1960, 3rd Prize, 1961; Gold Medal, Prize of Critics and Spectators, Madrid, Spain, 1973, 1979. *Membership:* Fellow, Royal Society of Literature. *Literary Agent:* Nathan Joseph, Media Enterprises, London. *Address:* 37 Ashley Road, London N19 3AG, England.

WESLEY Elizabeth. *See:* **MCELFRESH (Elizabeth) Adeline .**

WESLEY James. *See:* **RIGONI Orlando Joseph.**

WESLEY Mary. *See:* **SIEPMANN Mary.**

WESLEY Richard Errol, b. 11 July 1945, Newark, New Jersey, USA. Screenwriter; Playwright. m. Valerie Deane Wilson, 22 May 1972, 2 daughters. *Education:* BFA, Howard University, Washington DC, 1967. *Appointments:* Adjunct Professor in Black Theatre History: African Cultural Institute, Wesleyan University, Middletown, Connecticut, 1974; Ethnic Studies Department, Borough of Manhattan Community College, 1980-82; Guest Lecturer in Black Theatre History: Rutgers University; South Carolina State University; Howard University; Morgan State University; Writing Workshop Coordinator: Frank Silvera Writers Workshop, New York; Ossining State Correctional Facility, Ossining, New York; Trenton State Penitentiary, Trenton, New Jersey; Board of Directors: Frank Silvera Writers Workshop, 1976- 84; Theatre of University Images, Newark, New Jersey; Member, Selection Committee for Newark Black Film Festival, Newark Museum; Panelist, Expansion Arts Programme (Theatre), National Endowment for the Arts. *Publications:* Plays: The Black Terror, 1971; Gettin' It

Together, 1972; Strike Heaven on the Face, 1973; The Past is the Present, 1974; Goin' thru Changes, 1974; The Sirens, 1974; The Last Street Play, 1977; The Mighty Gents, 1978; On the Road to Babylon, 1980; The Dream Team, 1984; The Talented Tenth, 1989; Films: Uptown Saturday Night, 1974; Let's Do It Again, 1975; Fast Forward, 1985; Native Son, 1986; TV: The House of Dies Drear, 1984. *Honours:* The Drama Desk, 1972; Rockefeller Grant, 1973; Audelco Award for Outstanding Playwrighting, 1974, 1977, 1989; National Association for the Advancement of Colored People Image Award, 1974, 1975; Richard Wesley Day, 1978, Richard Wesley Week, 1982, City of Newark; Richard Wesley Day, Washington, DC, 1984. *Address:* PO Box 43091, Upper Montclair, NJ 07043, USA.

WEST Douglas. *See:* **TUBB E C.**

WEST Morris (Langlo), (Morris East, Julian Morris), b. 26 Apr. 1916, Melbourne, Australia. Author. m. Joyce Lawford, 1953, 3 sons, 1 daughter. *Education:* University of of Melbourne. *Publications:* Gallows on the Sand, 1955; Kundu, 1956; Children of the Sun, 1957; The Crooked Road (English Title, The Big Story), 1957; The Concubine, 1958; Backlash (English Title The Second Victory), 1958; The Devil's Advocate, 1959 (filmed 1977); The Naked Country, 1960; Daughter of Silence (novel and play), 1961; The Shoes of the Fisherman, 1963; The Ambassador, 1965; The Tower of Babel, 1968; The Heretic, a Play in Three Acts, 1970; Scandal in the Assembly, with Robert Francis, 1970; Summer of the Red Wolf, 1971; The Salamander, 1973; Harlequin, 1974; The Navigator, 1976; Proteus, 1979; The Clowns of God, 1981; The World is Made of Glass, 1983, (play 1984); Cassidy, 1986; Masterclass, 1988; Lazarus. *Honours:* National Brotherhood Award, National Council of Christians and Jews, 1960; James Tait Black Memorial Prize, 1960; Royal Society of Literature, Heinemann award, 1960; Hon.D.Litt., Santa Clara University, 1969, Mercy College, New York, 1982; Order of Australia, 1985. *Memberships:* Fellow, Royal Society of Literature; World Academy of Arts and Science. *Address:* c/o Maurice Greenbaum, Rosenman Colin, Freund Lewis & Cohen, 587 Madison Avenue, New York, NY 10022, USA.

WEST Nicola. *See:* **BAKER Donna Anne.**

WEST Nigel, b. 8 Nov 1951, London, England. Historian. m. 15 June 1979, 1 son, 1 daughter. *Education:* University of Grenoble; University of Lille; London University. *Appointments:* BBC TV 1977-82. *Publications:* A Matter of Trust MI5 1945-72, 1982; Unreliable Witness, 1984; Garbo, MI5, 1981, MI6, 1983, 1985; GCHQ, 1986; Molehunt, 1986; The Friends, 1987; Games of Intelligence, 1990; Seven Spies who Changed the World, 1991; Secret War, 1992. *Contributions to:* The Times; Intelligence Quarterly. *Honour:* The Experts' Expert, 1989, The Observer. *Literary Agent:* Peters, Fraser and Dunlop. *Address:* Westintel Research Ltd, 310 Fulham Road, London SW10 9UG, England.

WEST William Alexander, (Anthony Worth), b. 30 May 1916, Pitlochry, Scotland. University Professor. m. (1) Kathleen Herring, 6 May 1942, (2) Marion Davies, 5 Sept 1963, 1 son, 4 daughters. *Education:* University College School; LLB, LLM, University of London, Kings College. *Appointments:* Leader Writer, Estates Gazette 1965-79; Planning Correspondent for The Spectator 1975-79. *Publications:* Consider Your Verdict, 1950; A number of books on legal subjects. *Contributions to:* Times; Spectator; Economist; Daily Telegraph. *Memberships:* Hurlingham Club; Royal Overseas Club; Landsdowne Club. *Address:* 13 St George's Court, London SW7 4QZ, England.

WESTCOTT (W)illiam (F)rancis, b. 4 Sept 1949, Toronto, Canada. Teacher; Author; Musician. m. (1) Christine McAra, 6 June 1970, divorced 1974, (2) Dawn Anne Jordan, 17 May 1978, divorced 1987, 1 daughter. *Education:* Teaching Certificate, Lakeshore Teacher's College, 1971; BA, McMaster University, 1974. *Appointment:* Former Associate Editor, Writer Lifeline, 1982; Research Board of Advisors, American Biographical Institute, 1987. *Publications:* Small Things, 1979; Basic Lessons In English Grammar, 1980; Being, 1981; Her Light Was Like Unto A Stone, 1981; The Old Man & the Hidden Forest, 1981; Captain Dreamer, 1982; So You Want to Be a Writer, 1983. *Contributions to:* Articles in professional journals. *Honours:* Recipient, various honours and awards. *Memberships:* Canadian Authors Association; Ontario Public School Teacher' Federation; Clear Lake Badminton Association, Honorary President. *Address:* PO Box 1326, Alliston, Ontario, Canada L0M 1A0.

WESTGATE John. *See:* **BLOOMFIELD Anthony John Westgate.**

WESTHEIMER David (Z Z Smith), b. 11 Apr 1917, Writer. m. Doris Rothstein Kahn, 9 Oct 1945, 2 sons. *Education:* BA, Rice Institute, 1937. *Publications:* Von Ryan's Express, 1964; My Sweet Charlie, 1965; Lighter than a Feather, 1971; The Auila Gold, 1974; The Olmec Head, 1974; Song of the Young Sentry, 1968; Summer on the Water, 1948; The Magic Fallacy, 1950 Watching Out For Dulie, 1960; This Time Next Year, 1963; Over the Edge, 1972; Von Ryan's return, 1980; Rider on the Wind, 1984; Going Public, 1973; Sitting It Out, 1992. *Memberships:* Writes Guild of America West; Authors Guild; PEN; California Writers Club, Advisory Board; Retired Officers Association. *Address:* 11722 Darlington No 2, Los Angeles, CA 90049, USA.

WESTLAKE Donald E (Curt Clark, Tucker Coe, Timothy J Culver, Richard Stark), b. 1933, USA. Author. *Publications:* The Mercenaries, 1960; Killing Time, 1961; 361, 1962; Killy, 1963; Pity Him Afterwards, 1964; The Fugitive Pigeon, 1965; The Busy Body, 1966; The Spy in the Ointment, 1966; Anarchaos (as Curt Clark), 1967; Philip, 1967; God Save the Mark, 1967; Once Against the Law (edited with W Tenn), 1968; The Curious Facts Preceding My Execution, 1968; Who Stole Sassi Manoon, 1969; Somebody Owes Me Money, 1969; Up Your Banners, 1969; Ex Officio (as Timothy J Culver), 1970; The Hot Rock, 1970; Adios Scheherezade, 1970; I Gave at the Office, 1971; Bank Shot, 1972; Under an English Heaven, 1972; Cops and Robbers, 1972; Comfort Station, 1973; Gangway (with B Garfield), 1973; Help I Am Being Held Prisoner, 1974; Jimmy the Kid, 1974; Brothers Keepers, 1975; Two Much, 1975; Dancing Aztecs, US Edition A New York Dance, 1976; Enough, 1977; Nobody's Perfect, 1977; Castle in the Air, 1980; Kahawa, 1982; Why Me, 1983; Levine, 1984; A Likely Story, 1984; High Adventure, 1985; Good Behaviour, 1986; As Richard Stark: The Hunter, 1962; The Man with the Getaway Face, 1963; The Outfit, 1963; The Mourner, 1963; The Score, 1964; The Jugger, 1965; The Handle, 1966; The Seventh, 1966; The Rare Coin Score, 1967; The Green Eagle Score, 1967; The Damsel, 1967; The Black Ice Score, 1968; The Sour Lemon Score, 1969; The Dame, 1969; The Blackbird, 1969; Slayground, 1971; Deadly Edge, 1971; Lemons Never Lie, 1971; Plunder Squad, 1972; Butcher's Moon, 1974; As Tucker Coe: Kinds of Love, Kinds of Death, 1966; Murder Among Children, 1967; A Jade in Aries, 1971; Don't Lie to Me, 1972. *Address:* c/o Knox Burger, 391 Washington Square South, New York, NY 10012, USA.

WESTON Helen Gray. *See:* **DANIELS Dorothy.**

WESTRICK Elsie Margaret Beyer, b. 12 Nov 1910, Fort William, Ontario, Canada. Writer, poetry, fiction. m. Roswell G. Westrick, 6 Oct 1945, 5 daughters, 2 step-sons, 1 step-daughter. *Education:* Diploma, Institute of Childrens Literature, 1976; Diploma, Writing for Young People, 1985; Diploma, Writing Self Fiction, 1989, Writers Digest School. *Publications include:* Poems, On This Holy Night, 1949; Tender Foliage of Summer, 1972; The Photograph, 1975; Beauty on a Beach, 1983; Memories of Childhood, 1983; Call of the Blue Jay, 1987; The Breath of Fall, 1986; My Last Love,

1989; The Old Lighthouse, 1990; Tender Foliage of Summer, World of Poetry's Anthology, Poems That Will Live Forever, 1991; Winter Magic, National Library of Poetry, 1992. *Honours:* One Hundred and One Best of Clover Publishers Award, 1970; Honorable Mention, International Poetry COmpetition, 1969; Golden Poet Award, World of Poetry, 1985. 1986; Award for Poetic Achievement, 1988; Silver Poet Award, World of Poetry, 1990. *Memberships include:* Charter member State of Liberty; Writers Digest Book Club; National Wildlife Federation; Wildlife Conservation International; Center for Marine Conservation, 1991-; ITAN, 1992; PETA, 1991-92. *Address:* 3751 Wheeler Road, Snover, MI 48472, USA.

WEXLER Richard, b. 21 Dec 1953, Bronx, New York, USA. Assistant Professor of Communications. m. Celia Viggo, 25 Feb 1984, 1 daughter. *Education:* BA summa cum laude 1975, Richmond College; MSJ 1976, Columbia University Graduate School of Journalism. *Appointments:* Associate Producer, Inside Albany, WMHT-TV, 1976; Reporter, Producer, Assistant News Director, Wisconsin Public Radio, 1977; News Director, Reporter, WGBY-TV, Springfield, Massachusetts, 1979; Reporter, Producer, WXXI Public Television, Rochester, New York 1981; Reporter, City Newspaper, Rochester 1985; Reporter, The Times Union, Albany, New York 1986; Assistant Professor of Communications, Penn State University-Beaver Campus, Monaca, Pennsylvania, 1993. *Publication:* Wounded Innocents: The Real Victims of the War Against Child Abuse, 1990. *Contributions of:* Invasion of the Child Savers, The Progressive, 1985. *Honours:* Pulitzer Travelling Fellowship from Columbia Graduate School of Journalism, 1976; Corporation for Public Broadcasting Local Radio Programme Awards, 1978; Milwaukee Press Club Award, 1978; National Press Club Consumer Journalism Citation, 1982; National Awards for Education Reporting Citation, 1986; New York Press Association Writer of the Year, 1986. *Address:* Penn State University-Beaver Campus, Brodhead Road, Monaca, Pennsylvania 15061, USA.

WEYL Brigitte Ruth, b. Munich, Germany. Publisher. *Education:* MD 1951, Freiburg/Br; Medical State Examination, 1950 Freiburg, Br; Medical Examination for Foreigners, corresponding to Swiss State examination, 1951, Basel. *Appointments:* Medizinische Tátigkeit, 1951-1956; Editor, Die Presse, Wien, 1957-58; Publisher, Sudkurier, Konstanz, 1959-89; Publisher, Südverlag, and Universitätsverlag Konstanz 1959- and 1963-. *Contributions to:* Die Presse; Südkurier; Publizistik, and within several books. *Honours:* Honorary President, Deutsch-Französische Vereinigung, Konstanz 1979-; Officier de l'Ordre National du Merite, 1982; Bundesverdienstkreuz I.K1, 1984. *Memberships:* International Press Institut; Gesellschaft der Freunde und Forderer der Universitat Konstanz, President; Stiftervereinigung der Presse e.V, Vice President; Stifterverband fur die Deutsche Wissenschaft, Landeskuratorium Baden-Wurttemberg; Vereinigung Deutsch-Französischer Gesellschaften in Deutschland und Frankreich, Kuratorium. *Address:* D-78420 Konstanz, POB 1020 51, Germany.

WHALEN Terry Anthony, b. 1 Feb 1944, Halifax, Nova Scotia, Canada, Professor of English; Editor. m. Maryann Antonia Walters, 30 Feb 1966, 2 sons, 2 daughters. *Education:* BA, Honours, Saint Mary's University, 1965; MA, Honours, University of Melbourne, 1968; International Graduate Seminar Certificate, Oxford University, 1970; PhD, University of Ottawa, 1980. *Appointments:* Tutor, University of Sydney, 1966; University of Melbourne, 1967; Lecturer, 1968-70, Assistant Professor, 1970-76, 1978-80, Associate Professor, 1981-85, Professor of English, 1985-, Saint Mary's University; Teaching Fellow, University of Ottawa, 1976-77; Editor, Atlantic Provinces Book Review, 1980-. *Publications:* Philip Larkin and English Poetry, 1986, reprinted 1990; Bliss Carman and His Works, 1983; The Atlantic Anthology: Criticism, (Editor and Introduction), 1985; Charles G D Roberts and His Works, 1989. *Contributor to:* Canadian

Literature; Canadian Poetry; Critical Quarterly; Critical Review; Conradiana; Dalhousie Review; The Fiddlehead; Canadian Review of American Studies; Quarry; Sift; Thalia; The Old Northwest; Times Higher Education Supplement; Modernist Studies; Australian Book Review; Contributor to books including: Canadian Poetry: New Press Canadian Classics, 1982; The New Canadian Anthology, 1988. *Honours:* British Commonwealth Scholarship, 1966-68; Election to Council Member Status, Writers' Federation of Nova Scotia; Grants: Canada Council; Social Sciences and Humanities Research Council of Canada; Canadian Federation for the Humanities. *Memberships:* Writers Federation of Nova Scotia; Association of Canadian University Teachers of English; Northeast Modern Language Association; Modern Language Association. *Address:* 26 Oceanview Drive, Purcell's Cove, Halifax, Nova Scotia, Canada B3P 2H3.

WHALLEY Peter, b. 12 Mar 1946. Writer. m. Ruth Whalley, 3 Jan 1970, 1 son, 1 daughter. *Education:* St Mary's College, Blackburn, Lancashire; BA (Hons), Philosophy, University of Lancaster; PGCE, University of London. *Publications:* Post Mortem, 1982; The Mortician's Birthday Party, 1983; Old Murders, 1984; Love and Murder, 1985; Robbers, 1986; Bandits, 1986; Villains, 1987; Blackmailer's Summer, 1990. *Memberships:* Writers Guild. *Literary Agent:* Stephen Durbridge, 24 Pottery Lane, London W11 4LZ, England. *Address:* Holly House, Green Lane, Lancaster, England.

WHAM David Buffington, b. 25 May 1937, Evanston, IL, USA. Political Writer. m. 3 Mar. 1968, 1 son, 1 daughter. *Education:* BA, Harvard. *Appointments:* Co-author, Official Report on Poor Peoples March for Jobs and Income, 1968; Speech Writer, Congressman James R. Mann, 1970-76; Speech Writer, Adlai E. Stevenson III, Democratic Candidate for Governor, Illinois, 1986. *Publication:* There is a Green Hill, 1967. *Contributions to:* December Magazine; Story Quarterly; Woodwind; The Fair Brandy, a Novella, 1966; Maelstrom; Means; PilgriMaGe; etc. *Honours:* 1st Prize, Maelstrom magazine, 1968. *Agent:* Gerald McCauley, New York City. *Address:* 8823 Dobson St., Evanston, IL 60202, USA.

WHARTON Annabel J Wharton, (Ann Wharton Epstein), b. 30 July 1944, New Rochelle, New York, USA. Associate Professor of Art History. 2 daughters. *Education:* BS, University of Wisconsin, Madison, 1966; MA, University of Chicago, 1969; PhD, Courtauld Institute of Art, London, 1975. *Appointments:* Research Fellow, Barber Institute, University of Birmingham, England, 1971-75; Assistant Professor, Oberlin College, Oberlin, Ohio, USA, 1975-79; Associate Professor, Department of Art and Art History, Duke University, Durham, North Carolina, 1979-; Byzantine Editor, Greek, Roman, and Byzantine Studies, 1985-. *Publications:* Change in Byzantine Culture in the Eleventh and Twelfth Centuries (with A P Kazhdan), 1985; Tokali Kilise. Tenth Century Metropolitan Art in Byzantine Cappadocia, 1986; Art of Empire: Painting and Architecture of the Byzantine Periphery. A Comparative Study of Four Provinces, 1988. *Contributions to:* Art, history and archaeology journals. *Honours:* Visiting Fellow, Dumbarton Oaks Center for Byzantine Studies, 1978-79; Fellow, American Council of Learned Societies, 1981-82; Fellow, National Humanities Center, 1985-86; Fellow, Center for the Advanced Study of the Visual Arts, National Gallery, Washington DC. *Memberships:* Editorial Board, Art Bulletin; Board of Directors, International Center for Medieval Art; Past President, Byzantine Studies Conference; Board of Directors, Institue of Architecture and Urban Studies, New York. *Address:* Department of Art, 112 East Duke Building, Duke University, Durham, NC 27706, USA.

WHARTON William, b. 7 Nov. 1925, USA. Artist; Author. m. Rosemary Henry, 26 Dec. 1949. 2 sons, 2 daughters, 1 deceased. *Education:* AB, MA, PhD, University of California, Los Angeles. *Publications:* Birdy, 1978; Dad, 1981; A Midnight Clear, 1982; Scumbler, 1984; Pride, 1985; Tidings; Franky Furdo, 1989. *Honour:*

NBA Award, Best First Novel, 1979. *Literary Agent:* Rosalie Siegel. *Address:* c/o Knopf, 201 East 50th Street, New York, NY 10022, USA.

WHEATCROFT Andrew Jonathan Maclean, b. 20 July 1944, Woking, England. Author m. Janet Margaret Wear, 25 July 1970, 2 sons, 2 daughters. *Education:* BA, MA, Christ's College, Cambridge; University of Madrid; Research Fellow, University of Edinburgh; Lecturer University of Stirling. *Literary Appointment:* Editor in Chief, The Heritage: Care - Preservation - Management Publishing Programme. *Publications:* The Habsburg Empire, 1972; Who's Who in Military History (with John Keegan) 1976, 2nd edition 1987; Russia in Original Photographs (with Marvin Lyons) 1977; The Tennyson Album 1980; The Covent Garden Album, 1981; Arabia in Original Photographs, 1982; Dolin: Friends and Memories, 1982; The World Atlas of Revolutions, 1775-1983, 1983; Zones of Conflict (with John Keegan) 1986; Bahrain in Original Photographs, 1880-1961, 1988; The Road to War (with Richard Overy) 1989; The Ottomans: Dissolving Images, 1993. *Contributions to:* Cambridge Review; Spectator; London Standard; Fontana Dictionary of Modern Thought, 1988; Sunday Times. *Honour:* Gold Medal, Outstanding Atlas, awarded to the World Atlas of Revolutions by the Geographical Society of Chicago, 1983. *Literary Agent:* Andrew Lownie Ltd. *Address:* Craigieburn House, by Moffat, Dumfriesshire, Scotland DG10 9LF.

WHEATCROFT John Stewart, b. 24 July 1925, Philadelphia, Pennsylvania, USA. College Professor; Writer. m. (1) Joan Mitchell Osborne, 10 Nov 1952, div. 1974, 2 sons, 1 daughter, (2) Katherine Whaley Warner, 14 Nov 1992. *Education:* BA, Bucknell University, 1949; MS, 1950, PhD, 1960, Rutgers University. *Appointments:* Currently Director, Stadler Center for Poetry, Bucknell University, Lewisbug, Pennsylvania. *Publications:* Books of poetry: Death of a Clown, 1963; Prodigal Son, 1967; A Voice from the Hump, 1977; Ordering Demons, 1981; The Stare on the Donkey's Face, 1990; Novels: Edie Tells, 1975; Catherine, Her Book, 1983; The Beholder's Eye, 1987; Killer Swan, 1992; Slow Exposures, stories, 1986; Our Other Voices (editor), interviews with poets, 1991. *Contributions to:* New York Times; Harper's Bazaar; Mademoiselle; Ladies' Home Journal; The Literary Review; New Letters; Criticism; Carleton Miscellany; Ohio Review; Agenda. *Honours:* Alcoa Playwriting Award, 1966; National Educational Television Award, 1967; Fellowships: Yaddo, 1972, 1985; MacDowell Colony, 1973; Virginia Cenger for the Creative Arts, 1976, 1978, 1980, 1982. *Memberships:* Academy of American Poets; Poetry Society of America. *Address:* Stadler Center for Poetry, Bucknell University, Lewisburg, PA 17837, USA.

WHEELWRIGHT Julie Diana, b. 2 June 1960, Farnborough, Kent, England. Writer; Broadcaster. *Education:* BA, University of British Columbia, Canada; MA, University of Sussex, England. *Appointments:* Reporter, Vancouver Sun 1980; President, Canadian University Press, 1981; Consultant, Open University, 1991. *Publications:* Amazons and Military Maids, 1989; The Fatal Lover: Mata Hari and the Myth of Women in Espionage, 1992 (to be translated into Dutch and Japanese). *Contributions to:* History Today; Newstatesman Society; Index on Censorship; Middle East; New African; Womens Studies International Forum; Gender and History; World Magazine; Women: a Cultural Review; The Guardian; The Times; Th TLS; The Financial Times; Queens Quarterly (Toronto); The Literary Review; New Internationalist; Radio: BBC World Service; Woman's Hour, (Radio 4); ABC (Australia). *Honours:* Nominated by Pandora Press for the Fawcett Award, 1989; Canada Council Non-Fiction Grant 1990-91. *Memberships:* Writers Guild; Institute of Historical Research. *Literary Agent:* Bill Hamilton, A.M. Heath.. *Address:* 5 Cleaver Street, London SE11 4DP, England.

WHICKER Alan Donald, b. 2 Aug 1925. Writer; Television Broadcaster. *Education:* Haberdasher's Aske's School. *Literary Appointments:* Director, Army Film and Photo Section, 8th Army and US 5th Army; War Correspondent in Korea; Foreign Correspondent; Novelist; Writer and Radio Broadcaster; Joined BBC TV 1957; Tonight Programme (appeared nightly in filmed reports from around the world, studio interviews, outside broadcasts, Eurovision and Telstar, including first Telstar two-way transmission at opening of UN Assembly, New York, 1962). TV Series: Whicker's World, 1959-60; Whicker Down Under, 1961; Whicker On Top of The World!, 1962; Whicker In Sweden, Whicker In The Heart of Texas, Whicker Down Mexico Way, 1963; Alan Whicker Report Series: The Solitary Billionaire (J Paul Getty); Wrote and appeared in own series of monthly documentaries under series title, Whicker's World, 1965-67; Left BBC, 1968; Various cinema films, including The Angry Silence; completed 110 documentaries for Yorkshire TV including Whicker's New World Series, and Specials on Gen. Stroessner of Paraguay, Count von Rosen, and Pres. Duvalier of Haiti; Whicker In Europe; Whicker's Walkabout; Broken Hill - Walled City; Gairy's Grenada; World of Whicker; Whicker's Orient; Whicker Within A Woman's World, 1972; Whicker's South Seas, Whicker Way Out West, 1973; Whicker's World Series on Cities, 1974-75; Whicker's World - Down Under, 1976; Whicker's World - US 1977 (4 programmes); India, 1978 (7 programmes); Indonesia, 1979; California. 1980 (6 programmes); Peter Sellers' Memorial Programme, 1980; Whicker's World Aboard The Orient Express, 1982; Around Whicker's World in 25 years (3 YTV Retrospective Programmes), 1982; Returned to BBC TV, 1982: Whicker's World - The First Million Miles (6 Retrospective Programmes), 1982; BBC Radio: chaired, Start The Week; Whicker's World (3 series), 1983; BBC 1: Whicker's World - A Fast Boat to China (4 QE2 Programmes), 1984; BBC 2: Whicker! Series of 10 talk shows, 1984, Whicker's World - Living With Uncle Sam (10 Programmes BBC1), 1985; Whicker's World Down Under, (10 programmes), 1987; Whicker's World, Hong Kong (8 programmes), 1989; Around Whicker's World (4 programmes), 1992; Whicker's World - Spain, (8 programmes), 1992; Returned to ITV: Around Whicker's World - the Ultimate Package (4 programmes), 1992; Whicker's World - the Absolute Monarch (the Sultan of Brunei), 1992. *Publications:* Some Rise By Sin, 1949; Away, with Alan Whicker, 1963; Within Whicker's World, 1982; Whicker's New World, 1985; Whicker's World Down Under, 1988. *Contributions to:* Articles for various publications; Sunday Newspaper Columns. *Honours:* Various Awards, 1963-, including Screenwriters' Guild, Best Documentary Scripts, 1963; Guild of Television Producers and Directors Personality of The Year, 1964; Silver Medal, Royal Television Society, 1968; Dumont Award, University of California, 1970; Best Interview Programme Award, Hollywood Fesitval, 1973; Dimbleby Award, BAFTA, 1978; First to be named in the Royal Television Society's new, Hall of Fame, for outstanding creative contribution to British Television, 1993. *Address:* Le Gallais Chambers, St. Helier, Jersey, Channel Islands.

WHIPPLE Addison Beecher Colvin, b. 15 July 1918, Glens Falls, New York, USA. Retired Journalist. m. Jane Mulvane Banks, 27 June 1942, 1 son, 1 daughter. *Education:* BA 1940, Yale; MA 1941, Harvard. *Publications:* Yankee Whalers in the South Seas; Vintage Nantucket; The Challenge; To the Shores of Tripoli; Fighting Sail; Pirate; Tall Ships and Great Captains; The Clipper Ships; The Whalers. *Contributions to:* Life; Smithsonian; Readers Digest; American Heritage. *Honour:* John Lyman Book Award, Honorable Mention for The Challenge, 1987. *Literary Agent:* Julian Bach, New York, USA. *Address:* Cove Road, Old Greenwich, CT 06870, USA.

WHITAKER Rodney William, (Nicholas Seare, Trevanian), b. 12 June 1931, Granville, New York, USA. Teacher; Novelist. m. Diane Brandon, 18 July 1958, 1 son, 2 daughters. *Education:* BA, MA, University of Washington, 1961; PhD, Northwestern University, 1966. *Publications:* The Language of Film, 1968; As Trevanian: The Eiger Sanction, 1970; The Loo Sanction, 1972; The Main, 1975; Shibumi, 1977; The Summer of Katya, 1982; As Nicholas Seare: 1339 Or So, 1975;

Rude Tales and Glorious, 1982. *Contributions to:* Academic journals in Theology, classic studies, law, esthetics; Yale Literary Magazine; Wyoming Sheepherder; Playboy; Harpers; etc. *Honours:* Edgar Allen Poe Award; Vatican City Award for The Main, Italy. *Agent:* William Morris Agency. *Address:* Windham County, Connecticut, USA & Somerset, England.

WHITBY Joy, b. 27 July 1930, Helsinki, Finland. Television Producer; Writer. m. Anthony Charles Whitby, (deceased 1975), 3 sons. *Education:* MA Honours, St Anne's College, Oxford University. *Appointments:* Studio Manager, 1956, Producer, Schools, Radio, 1957-60, Producer, Family Programmes, TV, 1960-68, BBC, London, England; Executive Producer, London Weekend TV, 1968-70; Freelance, Producer, Writer, Reviewer, 1970-76; Head of Children's Programmes, YTV, 1976-86; Freelance, Producer, Writer, 1986-. *Publications include:* Grasshopper Island, 1971; Emma and Grandpa, 1984; in TV Created Play School, and Jackanory for BBC; Notable Independent TV productions; Catweazle for London Weekend TV; The Book Tower; The Raggy Dolls, for Yorkshire TV; The EBU Drama Exchange for Children; Extraordinary; Two Way Ticket, Passport to Treasure, The Giddy Game Show, As Freelance through her own company Produced: Grasshopper Island, Pattern of Roses, Emma and Grandpa, East of the Moon, The Angel and the Soldier Boy. *Honours:* Guild of TV Producers and Directors Award, 1965; Prix Jeunesse, 1966, 1980, 1984, 1988; Eleanor Farjeon Award for Services to children's Books, 1979; BAFTA Award, 1980, 1983; Mifed Award, Spanish Platero Award, 1984; International Children's Film Festival of India Golden Elephant, 1985; Celtic Film Festival, Chicago Film Festival and Emmy Nomination, 1988. *Memberships:* Director, 1970-, Grasshopper Productions Limited; Founder Director, Board of Channel 4, 1980-84; Member, National Trust's Advisory Panel for Youth, 1985-; Member, Board of the Unicorn Theatre for Children; Member, IPPA, BAFTA, Royal Television Society. *Address:* 20 Peel Street, London W8 7PD, England.

WHITBY Sharon. *See:* **PETERS Maureen.**

WHITCOMBE Allan Ronald, b.25 June 1941, Senior Education Inspector; Writer. Married, 2 children. *Education:* Part 1 of London General External BSc, Bournemouth Municipal College, 1960-61; Part 2, London General External BSc, 1st Class Hons in Mathematics and Physics, Regent Street, Polytechnic, London, 1961-63; Part-time, Birkbeck College, London, 1961-63, MSc in Mathematical Physics, Relativity and Quantum Mechanics, 1965-67; Research Student, Nottingham University, 1968-70. *Appointments include:* Assistant Mathematics Master, Westminster City School, London, 1964-67; Research Student, Nottingham University, 1968-70; Lecturer in Mathematics, North Staffordshire Polytechnic, 1970-73; Head of Mathematics Department, Hagley Park School, Rugeley, Staffordshire 1973-77; Education Editor, W & R Chambers, Publishers, Edinburgh, 1977-81; Advisory Teacher for Mathematics, City of Birmingham, 1981-85; Education Adviser, Mathematics, London Borough of Barking and Dagenham, 1985-, Acting Senior Adviser, 1989-. *Publications include:* A-level Mathematics: A Course Companion, Charles Letts & Co, 1985; Author, Figurate Numbers: The Other Alternative, Mathematics in School, Mathematical Association, 1986; Author, Mathematics - Beauty, Creativity and Imagination, Mathematics in School, Mathematical Association, 1988; Co-author, Shongo Networks - a multicultural theme for the classroom. Mathematics in School. Mathematical Association, 1988; co-author, Maths Extra, 1991. *Address:* 59, Kingsley Gardens, Hornchurch, Essex RM11 2HY, England.

WHITE Aidan Patrick, b.2 Mar 1951, England. Journalist. *Appointments:* Deputy Group Editor, Stratford Express, 1977-79; Journalist, The Gurdian, 1980-. *Memberships:* Press Council, 1978-80; Executive Council 1974, 1976, 1977, Treasurer 1984-86, National Union of Journalists; Chairman, National Newspapers Council, 1981; Interntional Federation of Journalists Executive, 1986-; Vice Chairman, Campaign for Press & Broadcasting Freedom, 1983-84. *Address:* 92 Quilter Street, London E2, England.

WHITE Edgar Jewett, (Ned White), b. 27 Feb 1946, Boston, Massachusetts, USA. Writer. m. Martha Weeks, 3 Apr 1971, 1 son, 2 daughters. *Education:* BA 1968, Yale College, Scholar of the House. *Appointments:* Editor-in-Chief, Yale Literary Magazine, 1967. *Publications:* Inside Television, 1980; The Very Bad Thing, novel, 1990. *Literary Agent:* Margaret Ruley, Jane Rotrasen Agency, New York. *Address:* Sherborn, MA 01770, USA.

WHITE Edmund, b. 1940, American, Writer of novels/short stories, essays. Contributing Editor, HG magazine, New York City. Professor of English, Brown University, Providence, Rhode Island. Formerly Instructor of Literature and Creative Writing, Yale University, New Haven, Connecticut, Johns Hopkins University, Baltimore, Maryland, and George Mason University, Fairfax, Virginia; Visiting Writer, Columbia University, New York City, 1981-82; Executive Director, New York Institute for the Humanities, 1982-83. *Publications:* Forgetting Elena, 1973; Nocturnes for the King of Naples, 1978; States of Desire (non-fiction) 1980; A Boy's Own Story, 1982; Caracole, 1985; The Beautiful Room is Empty, 1988. *Address:* English Department, Brown University, Providence, RI 02906, USA.

WHITE Gillian Mary b. 13 Jan. 1936, Essex, England. University Professor. m. Colin A. Fraser, 1 Apr. 1978. *Education:* LLB, 1957; PhD, 1960, London; Barrister, Grays Inn, 1960. *Publications include:* Nationalization of Foreign Property, 1961; The Use of Experts by International Tribunals, 1965; Principles of International Economic Law: An Attempt to Map the Territory, 1988; International Economic Laws and Developing States: An Introduction, 1992; International Law in Transition: Essays in Memory of Judge Nagendra Singh, 1992. *Memberships include:* British Institute of International and Comparative Law; International Law Association; American Society of International Law; Hon. Life Fellow, New Hall, Cambridge. *Address:* 21 Wensley Drive, Manchester M20 9DD, England.

WHITE Harry. *See:* **WHITTINGTON Harry.**

WHITE James, b. 7 Apr. 1928, Belfast, Northern Ireland. Science Fiction Writer. m. Margaret Sarah Martin, 17 May 1955, 2 sons, 1 daughter. *Appointment:* Publicity officer, Short Brothers Ltd, 1966-84. *Publications Include:* The Secret Visitors, 1957; Second Ending, 1962; Star Surgeon, 1963; Open Prison, 1965; The Watch Below, 1968; All Judgment Fled, 1969; Tomorrow Is Too Far, 1971; Dark Inferno, 1972; The Dream Millennium, 1974; Deadly Litter, 1964; Ambulance Ship, 1979; Futures Past, 1982; Sector General, 1983; Code Blue - Emergency, 1987; Federation World, 1988; The Silent Stars Go By, 1991; The Genocidal Healer, 1992. *Contributions to:* Various science fiction magazines & anthologies. *Honour:* Europa Science Fiction Award, 1979. *Memberships:* Science Fiction Writers of America; World S-F; Council, British Science Fiction Association. *Literary Agent:* Carnell Literary Agency. *Address:* 2 West Drive, Portstewart, County Londonderry, N.Ireland BT55 7ND, UK.

WHITE Jon Manchip, b. 1924, England. Author. *Appointments:* Story Editor, BBC London 1950-51; Senior Executive Officer, UK Foreign Service 1952-56; Freelance Writer 1956-67; Professor of English, University of Texas, El Paso 1967-77; Lindsay Young Professor of English, University of Tennessee, Knoxville 1977-. *Publications:* Dragon, 1943; Salamander, 1943; The Rout of San Romano, 1952; Ancient Egypt, 1952, 1970; Mask of Dust (in USA as The Last Race), 1953;

Build Us A Dam, 1954; Anthropology, 1954; The Girl from Indiana, 1955; The Glory of Egypt, editor, 1955; No Home But Heaven, 1956; The Mercenaries, 1958; Hour of the Rat, 1962; Marshal of France: The Life and Times of Maurice, Comte de Saxe, 1962; Everyday Life in Ancient Egypt, 1963; The Rose in the Brandy Glass, 1965; Nightclimber, 1968; Diego Velazquez: Painter and Courtier, 1969; The Land God Made in Anger Reflections on a Journey Through South West Africa, 1969; Cortes and the Downfall of the Aztec Empire, 1971; Life in Ancient Egypt, by Adolf Erman, Editor, 1971; Tomb of Tutankhamen, by Howard Carter, Editor, 1971; The Game of Troy, 1971; The Mountain Lion, 1971; Manners and Customs of the Modern Egyptians, by E W Lane, Editor, 1972; The Garden Game, 1973; Send for Mr Robinson, 1974; A World Elsewhere: One Man's Fascination with the American Southwest, 1975 (in UK as The Great American Desert, 1977); Everyday Life of the North American Indian, 1979; The Moscow Papers, 1979; Death by Dreaming, 1981; Chills and Fevers: Three Extravagent Tales, 1983; The Last Grand Master: A Novel of Revolution, 1985; The Journeying Boy: Scenes from a Welsh Childhood, 1991; Whistling Past The Graveyard; Strange Tales from a Superstitious Welshman, 1992. *Address:* Department of English, University of Tennessee, Knoxville, TN 37916, USA.

WHITE Lucia Perry, b. Cleveland, Ohio, USA. Author; Research Assistant. m. Morton G White, 29 Aug 1940, 2 sons. *Education:* AB 1933, Vassar College; MS 1937, Columbia University School of Social Work. *Publications:* The Intellectual Versus the City, co-author, 1962; Journeys to the Japanese, co-author, 1986; both with Morton White. *Contributions to:* On a Passage by Hume Incorrectly Attributed to Jefferson, Journal of the History of Ideas, 1976. *Literary Agent:* Gerard McCauley, Katonah, New York, USA. *Address:* 25 Maxwell Lane, Princeton, NJ 08540, USA.

WHITE Ned. *See:* **WHITE Edgar Jewett.**

WHITE Robert Mitchell II, b. 6 Apr. 1915, Mexico, Missouri, USA. Newspaper Editor & Publisher. m. 14 Dec. 1983. 1 son, 3 daughters, previous marriage. *Education:* Graduate, Missouri Military Academy, 1933; AB, Washington & Lee University, Virginia, 1938. *Literary Appointments include:* Various duties, Mexico Ledger, 1930's, Kansas City Bureau, United Press, 1939-40; Army service including press conferences, White House, World War II; Mexico Ledger, 1946-56; Chicago Sun-Times, part-time, 1956-59. Owner, Mexico Ledger, 1950's-; Chief executive officer, New York Herald-Tribune, 1959-61. Currently board member: Thomson Newspapers Inc; World Press Freedom Committee; State Historical Society of Missouri; etc. *Honours include:* Pulitizer Prize, Ayers Cup, Page One Awards etc, NY Herald-Tribune; SDX Wells Key Award, 1970; Sigma Delta Chi Award, distinguished service to journalism, editorial writing, 1951, 1970; Silurian Award, 1959; Numerous other awards, journalism. *Memberships include:* Past chairman, Lovejoy Journalism Award Jury, Maine; Past chairman, Missouri Press-Bar Commission; Past chairman Freedom of Information Committee, past board member, American Society of Newspaper Editors; Past Juror, Pulitzer Prize, Journalism; Past national president, Society of Professional Journalists, Sigma Delta Chi; etc. *Address:* Box 8, Ledger Plaza, Mexico, Missouri 65265, USA.

WHITE Robert Rankin, b. 8 Feb 1942, Houston, Texas, USA. Historian; Writer. *Education:* BA, Geology, University of Texas, Austin, 1964; MS, Hydrology, University of Arizona, 1971; PhD, American Studies, University of New Mexico, 1993. *Publications:* The Taos Society of Artists, 1983; The Lithographs and Etchings of E Martin Hennings, 1978; Contributor to Pioneer Artists of Taos, revised edition 1984; co-author, Bert Geer Phillips and the Taos Art Colony, forthcoming. *Contributor to:* Southwest Art; Print Review; El Palacio; Rio Grande History; True West; Taos County Historical Society Bulletin; Southwest Profile; New Mexico Architecture; New Mexico Historical Review; Book Talk. *Memberships:* New Mexico Book League, 1993; First

Friday; President, Historical Society of New Mexico, 1991-93; Western History Association. *Address:* 1409 Las Lomas Road NE, Albuquerque, NM 87106, USA.

WHITE Robin. *See:* **WHITE William Robinson.**

WHITE (Herbert) Terence de Vere, b. 1912, Irish. Writer of Novels/Short stories, History, Travel/Exploration/Adventure, Biography. *Appointments:* Literary Editor, The Irish Times, 1961-77; Director, The Gate Theatre, Dublin, 1969-81; Solicitor and Senior Partner, McCann, Fitzgerald Roche Dudley until 1962. *Publications:* The Road of Excess: A Life of Isaac Butt, 1945; Kevin O'Higgins, 1948; The Story of the Royal Dublin Society, 1955; A Fretful Midge: An Autobiography, 1957; (ed)Letters and Diaries of George Egerton, 1958; A Leaf from the Yellow Book, 1958; An Affair with the Moon, 1959; Prenez Garde, 1962; The Remainder Man, 1963; Lucifer Falling, 1965; The Parents of Oscar Wilde, 1967; Tara, 1967; Lemster, 1968; Ireland, 1968; The Lambert Mile, 1969; The March Hare, 1970; Mr Stephen, 1971; The Anglo-Irish, 1972; The Distance and the Dark, 1973; The Radish Memoirs, 1974; Big Fleas and Little Fleas, 1976; Tom Moon, 1977; Chimes at Midnight and Other Stories, 1977; My Name is Norval, 1978; Birds of Prey, 1980; Johnny Cross, 1983; Chat Show, 1987. *Literary Agent:* Richard Scott Simon. *Address:* Davis Cottage, Torriano Cottages, London NW5 2TA, England.

WHITE William Robinson, (Robin White), b. 12 July 1928, India. Author. m. Marian Biesterfeld, 3 Feb 1948, 2 sons, 1 daughter. *Education:* BA, Yale University, USA; Bread Loaf Fellow, Middlebury College, 1956; Stegner Creative Writing Fellow, Stanford University, 1956-57; MA, California State Polytechnic University. *Appointments:* Editor-in-Chief, Per-Se International Quarterly, Stanford University Press, 1965-69; Instructor, Photojournalism, 1973, Director, Creative Writing Seminar, 1984, Mendocino Art Center; Lecturer, Writing Programme, Scripps College, 1984; Fiction Editor, West-word literary magazine, 1985-, Instructor, Writer's Programme, 1985-, University of California, Los Angeles; Research Reader, The Huntington Library, 1985-; Lecturer, Writing Programme and CompuWrite, California State Polytechnic University, 1985-. *Publications:* House of Many Rooms, 1958; Elephant Hill, 1959; Men and Angels, 1971; Foreign Soil, 1962; All in Favor Say No, 1964; His Own Kind, 1967; Be Not Afraid, 1972; The Special Child, 1978; The Troll of Crazy Mule Camp, 1979; Moses the Man, 1981. *Contributions to:* Harper's; The New Yorker; New York Times; Harper's Bazaar; Prism; Saturday Evening Post; Ladies' Home Journal; Seventeen; National Wildlife; McClean's, Canada; Mademoiselle; The Reporter; Saturday Review; Sunset Magazine; Lears; S F Focus; Camping Journal; Various learned journals and overseas periodicals; Anthlogies. *Honours include:* Curtis Essay Prize, Yale; Harper Prize, 1959; O Henry Prize, 1960; Coordinating Council of Literary Magazines Award, 1968; Distinguished Achievement Award, Educational Press, 1974; Fulbright nomination, 1987; Spring Harvest Poetry Award, 1992. *Membership:* Authors Guild. *Literary Agent:* Gina Maccoby Literary Agency Inc. *Address:* 1940 Fletcher Ave, South Pasadena, CA 91030, USA.

WHITEHEAD David Henry, (Ben Bridges, Matt Logan, Janet Whitehead), b. 3 Jan 1958, London, England. Writer. m. Janet Ann Smith, 2 Jan 1981. *Appointments:* Consultant, Western Magazine, IPC Magazines, 1979-80; Consultant, Twentieth Century Western Writers, St James Press, 1991. *Publications:* The Silver Trail, 1986; Hard As Nails, 1987; Mexico Breakout, 1987; The Deadly Dollars, 1988; Hangman's Noose, 1988; The Wilde Boys, 1988; Wilde Fire, 1988; Hang 'Em All, 1989; Squaw Man, 1989; Wilde's Law, 1990; North of the Border, 1990; Shoot To Kill, 1990; Heller, 1990; Starpacker, 1990; Riding for Justice, 1990; Tanner's Guns, 1991; Aces Wild, 1991; Law of the Gun, 1991; Yours for Eternity, 1991; Patterns in the Snow, 1991; Hell for Leather, 1992; Heller in the Rockies, 1992; Coffin Creek, 1992; Marked for Death, 1993; Trial by Fire, 1993; Far Eastern Promise, 1993; Gunsmoke Legend, 1993; Gunsmoke is Grey, 1993. *Contributions to:* Numerous to: Book and Magazine Collector; Books, Maps and Prints; Celebrity; Fear; Halls of Horror; London Calling; Making Better Movies; Paperback, Pulp and Comic Collector; TV Guide; Video Maker; Video-The Magazine; Video World; We Belong Dead. *Honours:* Best Actor, Cork International Film Fair, 1986, for performance in award-winning film Doll's House. *Address:* c/o Publicity Department, Robert Hale Limited, Clerkenwell House, 45-47 Clerkenwell Green, London EC1R OHT, England.

WHITEHEAD Edward Anthony, b. 3 Apr 1933, England. Playwright; Theatre & Film Reviewer. m. (1) Kathleen Horton, 1958 (div.1976), 2 daughters, (2) Gwenda Bagshaw, 1976. *Education:* MA, Christ's College, Cambridge. *Publications:* The Foursome, 1972; Alpha Beta, 1972; The Sea Anchor, 1975; Old Flames, 1976; The Punishment, 1976; Mecca, 1977; World's End, 1981; The Man Who Fell in Love with his Wife, 1984. *Honours:* Evening Standard Award, George Devine Award, 1971. *Address:* c/o Judy Daish Associates Ltd, 83 Eastbourne Mews, London W2 6LQ, England.

WHITEHEAD Janet. *See:* **WHITEHEAD David Henry.**

WHITEHEAD Phillip, b. 30 May 1937, England. Writer; Television Producer. m. Christine Usborne, 1967, 2 sons, 1 daughter. *Education:* Exeter College, Oxford. *Appointments include:* President, Oxford Union, 1961; BBC producer, 1961-67; Editor, This Week, Thames TV, 1967-70; Member of Parliament (Labour), 1970-83; Director, Brook Productions 1986, Goldcrest Film & Television Holdings. *Publications:* Co-author, Electoral Reform: Time for Change, 1982; The Writing on the Wall, 1985; (jointly) Stalin, A Time for Judgement, 1990. *Contributor to:* Fabian Essays in Socialist Thought, 1984. *Honours:* Guild of TV Producers Award, Factual Programmes, 1969. *Memberships include:* Chairman 1978-79, Centenary Director 1983-84, Fabian Society; Annan Committee on Future of Broadcasting, 1974-77; Council, Consumers Association, 1982-; Council of Europe Assembly, 1975-80; National Union of Journalists. *Address:* Mill House, Rowsley, Matlock, Derbyshire, England.

WHITEHORN Katharine (Elizabeth) (b. Landon). Writer. *Appointments:* Staff Writer, Picture Post, London, 1956-57; Staff Writer, Woman's Own, London, 1958; Editorial Staff, Spectator, London, 1959-61; Fashion Editor, 1960-63, Columnist, 1963-, The Observer, London. *Publications:* Cooking in a Bedsitter, 1960; Roundabout, 1961; Only on Sundays, 1966; Whitehorn's Social Survival, 1968; Observations, 1970; How To Survive in Hospital, 1972; How To Survive Children, 1975; Sunday Best, 1976; How to Survive in the Kitchen, 1979; View from a Column, 1981; How to Survive Your Money Problems, 1983. *Address:* The Observer, Chelsea Bridge House, Queenstown Road, London, SW8 4NN, England.

WHITEHOUSE David Bryn, b. 15 Oct 1941, Worksop, England. *Education:* BA 1963, MA 1965, PhD 1967, Cambridge University. *Appointments:* Correspondent, Archeologia Medievale; Scientific Committee: Storia Della Città; Enciclopedia dell'Arte Medievale; Arte Medievale; Editor, Journal of Glass Studies 1988-; Advisory Editor, American Early Medieval Studies 1991-. *Publications:* Co-Author: Archaeological Atlas of the World, 1975; Mohammed, Charlemagne and the Origins of Europe, 1983; Glass of the Caesars, 1987; The Portland Vase, monograph, 1990; Author, Siraf III, The Congregational Mosque, ND; Glass of the Roman Empire, 1988; Co- Author, Aspects of Medieval Lazio, 1982. *Contributions to:* Journal of Glass Studies, Editor; Medieval Archaeology; Archeologia Medievale, Iran; Papers of the British School at Rome; Arte Medievale; Antiquity; World Archaeology; and many others. *Memberships:*

International Association for the History of Glass, President 1991-; Unione Internazionale degli Istituti di Archeologia; Storia e Storia dell'Arte in Roma, President 1980- 81; Keats-Shelley Memorial Association, Rome, President 1982-83. *Address:* The Corning Museum of Glass, One Museum Way, Corning, NY 14830, USA.

WHITEMORE Hugh John, b. 16 June 1936, England. Author; Playwright. m. (1) Jill Brooke (div.), (2) Sheila Lemon, 1976, 1 son. *Education:* Royal Academy of Dramatic Art. *Publications/ Producations include:* Stage: Stevie, Vaudeville, 1977; Pack of Lies, Lyric, 1983; Breaking the Code, Haymarket, 1986; The Best of Friends, Apollo, 1988. Television: plays, dramatisations, including Elizabeth R, 1970; Cider with Rosie, 1971; Country Matters, 1972; Dummy, 1979; Concealed Enemies, 1984. Films: Stevie, 1980; Return of the Soldier, 1982; 84 Charing Cross Road, 1986; The Final Days, 1989. Books: Stevie, 1977, 1984; Pack of Lies, 1983; Breaking the Code, 1986; The Best of Friends, 1988; It's Ralph, 1991. *Contributions to:* Elizabeth R, 1972; My Drama School, 1978; Ah, Mischief!, 1982. *Honours:* Emmy Award, 1970, 1984; Writers Guild Award, 1971, 1972; RAI Prize, Prix Italia, 1979; Neil Simon Jury Award, 1984; The Scriptor Award, 1987. *Address:* c/o Judy Daish Associates, 83 Eastbourne Mews, London W2 6LQ, England.

WHITFIELD Stephen Jack, b. 3 Dec 1942, Houston, Texas, USA. Teacher. m. Lee Cone Hall, 15 Dec 1984. *Education:* BA 1964, Tulane University; MA 1966, Yale University; Doctorate 1972, Brandeis University. *Publications:* Scott Nearing: Apostle of American Radicalism, 1974; Into the Dark: Hannah Arendt and Totalitarianism, 1980; A Critical American: The Politics of Dwight Macdonald, 1984; Voices of Jacob, Hands of Esau: Jews in American Life and Thought, 1984; American Space, Jewish Time, 1988; A Death in the Delta: The Story of Emmett Till, 1988; The Culture of the Cold War, 1991. *Contributions to:* Contributing Editor, Moment Magazine 1980-87; Book Review Editor, American Jewish History, 1979-86. *Honours:* Kayden Prize for Best Book in the humanities published by an American Academic Press, 1981 for Into the Dark: Hannah Arendt and Totalitarianism; Rockefeller Foundation Fellow, Bellagio, Italy, 1991. *Memberships:* American Jewish Historical Society, member of Academic Council; American Studies Association; American Humour Studies Association. *Literary Agent:* Gerard McCauley Agency. *Address:* Department of American Studies, Brandeis University, Waltham, MA 02254, USA.

WHITNELL Barbara. *See:* **HUTTON Ann.**

WHITNEY Hallam. *See:* **WHITTINGTON Harry.**

WHITTAM SMITH Andreas, b. 13 June 1937, England. Financial Journalist, Editor. m. Valerie Catherine Sherry, 1964, 2 sons. *Education:* BA, Keble College, Oxford. *Appointments include:* Stock Exchange Gazette, 1962-63; Financial Times, 1963-64; The Times, 1964-66; Deputy City Editor, Daily Telegraph, 1966-69; City Editor, The Guardian, 1969-70; Editor, Investors Chronicle, Stock Exchange Gazette, and Director, Throgmorton Publications, 1970-77; City Editor, Daily Telegraph, 1977-85; Director, Newspaper Publishing Plc, 1986-; Editor of Independent, 1986-; Editor-in-Chief, Independent on Sunday, 1991-. *Honours include:* Wincott Award, 1975; Journalist of the Year, British Press Awards, 1987; Hemingway Europa Prize, 1988; Editor of the Year, Granada TV What The Papers Say Award, 1989. *Address:* 31 Brunswick Gardens, London W8 4AW, England.

WHITTEN Leslie H Jr, b. 21 Feb 1928, Jacksonville, Florida, USA. Writer; Journalist. m. Phyllis Webber, 11 Nov 1951. 3 sons, 1 daughter. *Education:* BA, English-Journalism, Lehigh University. *Publications:* Progeny of the Adder, 1965; Pinion, The Golden Eagle, 1968; Moon of the Wolf, 1967; The Abyss, 1970; F Lee Bailey, 1971;

The Alchemist, 1973; Conflict of Interest, 1976; Washington Cycle, poems, 1979; Sometimes a Hero, 1979; A Killing Pace, 1983; A Day Without Sunshine, 1985; The Lost Disciple, 1989. *Contributions to:* New York Times; Washington Post; Parade; Harper's Bazaar; Jack Anderson; The Progressive; Baltimore Sun. *Honours:* Doctor, Humane Letters, Lehigh University, 1989; Journalistic Awards, Edgerton Award, American Civil Liberties Union. *Memberships:* Former Director, Washington Independent Writers; Former Director, Investigative Reporters and Editors; Former Member: Washington Newspaper Guild; Authors Guild. *Address:* 114 Eastmoor Drive, Silver Spring, MD 20901, USA.

WHITTEN Norman E Jr, b. 23 May 1937, Orange, New Jersey, USA. Professor of Anthropology and Latin America. m. Dorothea S. Whitten, 4 Aug. 1962. *Education:* BA, Colgate University, 1959; MA, 1961, PhD, 1964, University of North Carolina, Chapel Hill. *Appointments:* Editor, Boletin de Antropologia Ecuatoriana, 1973-76; Editor, Anthropology Newsletter, Latin American Anthropology Group, 1973-76; Press Board, University of Illinois Press, 1978-82; Editor, American Ethnologist, Vols 7-11, 1979-84; Member, Editorial Boards: Latin American Research Review, 1979-83; Latin American Music Review, 1979-; Journal of Anthropological Linguistics, 1979-84; Smithsonian Series in Ethnography Inquiry, 1984-; Association of Black Anthropologists, 1987-. *Publications:* Class, Kinship, and Power in an Ecuadorian Town, 1965; Afro-American Anthropology (editor), 1970; Sacha Runa: Ethnicity and Adaptation of Ecuadorian Jungle Quichua, 1976; Cultural Transformations and Ethnicity in Modern Ecuador (editor), 1981; Amazonia Ecuatoria, La Otro Cara del Progreso, 1981; Black Frontiersmen: Afro-Hispanic Culture of Ecuador and Colombia, 1985; Sicuanga Runa: The Other Side of Development in Amazonian Ecuador, 1985; Art, Knowledge, and Health (with Dorothea S Whitten), 1985; From Myth to Creation: Art from Amazonian Ecuador (with Dorothea S Whitten), 1988; Imagery and Creativity: Ethnoaesthetics and Art Worlds in the Americas (with Dorothea S Whitten), 1993. *Contributions to:* American Anthropologist; Man; American Ethnologist; America Indigena; Journal of American Folklore; Journal of the Folklore Institute; Ethnology; Latin American Research Review; Journal of Ethnic Studies; Social Forces; American Sociological Review. *Honours:* Author's Award in Anthropology, New Jersey Teachers Association, 1966; Society of Sigma Xi. *Memberships:* American Anthropological Association, Executive Board 1975-78, Representative to American Association for the Advancement of Science 1990-95; American Ethnological Association, Executive Board 1980-84; Latin American Studies Associaton, Executive Board 1983-87; Society of Cultural Anthropology; Royal Anthropological Institute. *Address:* 507 Harding Drive, Urbana, IL 61801, USA.

WHITTINGTON Geoffrey, b. 21 Sept. 1938, Warsop, Nottinghamshire, England. University Teacher (Professor, University of Cambridge). m. Joyce Enid Smith, 7 Sept. 1963, 2 sons. *Education:* BSc (Econ), London School of Economics, 1959; PhD, Fitzwilliam College, Cambridge, 1971. *Appointments include:* Member, Editorial Boards: Journal of Business Finance and Accounting, 1976-79; Abacus, 1977-89; The Accounting Review, 1979-82; Accounting and Business Research, 1987-; The British Accounting Review, 1988-; Journal of Accounting and Public Policy, 1988-; The European Accounting Review, 1992-. *Publications:* Growth, Profitability and Valuation (with A Singh), 1968; The Prediction of Profitability, 1971; Inflation Accounting, 1983; The Debate on Inflation Accounting (with D Tweedie), 1984; Readings in the Concept and Measurement of Income (editor with R H Parker and G C Harcourt), 1986; An Introduction to the Elements of Accounting, 1992; Pamphlets and contributions to books. *Contributions to:* Numerous papers to academic and professional journals. *Memberships:* Fellow, Institute of Chartered Accountants in England and Wales; Part-time Member, Monopolies and Mergers Commission; Academic Adviser, Accounting Standards Board. *Address:* Faculty of Economics and Politics, Sidgwick Avenue, Cambridge CB3 9DD, England.

WHITTINGTON Harry Benjamin (Ashley Carter, Whit Harrison, Kel Holland, Harriet Kathryn Myers, Steve Philips, Blaise Stevens, Clay Stuart, Hondo Wells, Harry White, Hallam Whitney), b. 1915, USA. Author. *Appointments:* Advertising Copywriter, 1933-35; Editor, Advocate magazine, 1938-45; Screenwriter, Warner Brothers, 1957; Editor/Writer, Rural Electric Administration, US Department of Agriculture, 1968-75. *Publications:* As Harry Whittington: About 3 dozen, 1945-59; Face of the Phantom, screenplay, 1960; Journey into Violence, 1960; Guerrilla Girls, 1960; A Night for Screaming, 1960; Hell Can Wait, 1960; Connolly's Woman, 1960; Haven for the Damned, 1961; God's Back Was Turned, 1961; Searching Rider, 1961; Wild Sky, 1962; Don't Speak to Strange Girls, 1963; Fall of the Roman Empire, 1964; High Fury, 1964; Wild Lonesome, 1965; Pain and Pleasure, screenplay, 1966; Doomsday Mission, 1967; Doomsday Affair, 1967; Burden's Mission, 1968; Charro, 1969; As Whit Harrison: Swamp Kill, 1951; Violent Night, 1952; Body and Passion, 1952; Nature Girl, 1952; Sailor's Weekend, 1952; Army Girl, 1952; Girl on Parole, 1952; Rapture Alley, 1952; Shanty Road, 1953; Strip the Town Naked, 1953; Any Woman He Wanted, 1960; A Woman Possessed, 1960; As Hallam Whitney: Backwoods Hussy, 1952, as Lisa, 1965; Shack Road, 1953; Sinners Club, 1953; City Girl, 1953; Backwoods Shack, 1954; The Wild Seed, 1954; As Ashley Carter: Golden Stud (with Lance Horner), 1975; Master of Black Oaks, 1976; The Sword of the Golden Stud, 1977; Secret of Blackoaks, 1978; Panama, 1978; Taproots of Falconhurst, 1978; Scandal of Falconhurst, 1980; Heritage of Blackoaks, 1981; Against All Gods, 1982; Rogue of Falconhurst, 1983; Road to Falconhurst, 1983; Farewell to Blackoaks, 1984; As Blaine Stevens: The Outlanders, 1979; Embrace the Wind, 1982; As Tabor Evans: Longarm series, 6 vols, 1981-82. *Address:* 1909 First Street, Indian Rocks Beach, FL 33535, USA.

WHITTINGTON Peter. *See:* **MACKAY James Alexander.**

WHITTLE Tyler. *See:* **TYLER-WHITTLE Michael Sidney.**

WHYTE John Donaldson, b. 26 June 1940, Ontario, Canada. m. 12 Dec 1964, 3 daughters. *Education:* BA 1962, University of Toronto; LLB 1968, Queen's University; LLM 1969, Harvard University; Called to Bar: Ontario 1972, Saskatchewan 1981. *Publications:* Canadian Constitutional Law, 1975, 2nd ed 1977; Canada....Notwithstanding, 1984; The Death and Life of Constitutional Reform in Canada, 1990. *Contributions to:* Over 60 articles published in scholarly journals, collections and popular periodicals. *Address:* 418 Earl Street, Kingston, Ontario, Canada K7L 2J8.

WICK Carter. *See:* **WILCOX Collin.**

WICKERT Erwin, b. 7 Jan 1915, Bralitz, Germany. Author; Retired Ambassador. m. Ingeborg Weides, 2 Oct 1939, 2 sons, 1 daughter. *Education:* Friedrich-Wilhelm-University, Berlin 1934-35; BA 1936, Dickinson College, Carlisle, Pennsylvania, USA; PhD 1939, University of Heidelberg. *Appointments:* Lived as Writer after repatriation to Germany in 1947, as well as in the Foreign Service. *Publications:* Der Auftrag des Himmels, novel, 1961 (The Heavenly Mandate, 1964); Der Purpur, novel, 1966; Der verlassene Tempel, novel, 1985; China von innen gesehen, 1982 (The Middle Kingdom, 1983); Mut und Ubermut, biography, 1991; Der fremde Osten, 1988; Die Frage des Tigers, 1955-90; Der Kaiser und der Grosshistoriker, radio plays, 1987. *Contributions to:* Frankfurter Allgemeine Zeitung; Die Welt. *Honours:* Radio Play Award of WarBlinds, 1952; Grosses Bundesverdienstkreuz, 1979; State Prize of Literature by Government of Rhienland-Pfalz. *Memberships:* PEN Club, Germany; Academy of Sciences and Literature, Mainz, 1980; German Author's Council, Vice President; Free German Author's Association, Vice President; Chairman, German Society for East Asian Art. *Address:*

Rheinhohenweg 22, Oberwinter, D 53424 Remagen 2, Germany.

WICKHAM Glynne (William Gladstone), b. 1922. Writer; Broadcaster. *Appointments Include:* Editorial Committee, Shakespeare Survey, 1974-; Chairman, Radio West, 1979-84; Culture Advisory Panel, United Kingdom; National Commission to Unesco, 1984-86. *Publications:* The Relationship Between Universities and Radio, Film and Television, 1956; Early English Stages, vol I, 1959, 1963, vol 2 (part 1), 1963, vol 2 (part 2), 1972, 1980, vol 3, 1981; Drama in a World of Science, 1962; Shakespeare's Dramatic Heritage, 1969; The Medieval Theatre, 1974, 3rd edition, 1986; English Moral Interludes, 1975, 1985; The Theatre in Europe: Documents and Sources, 1979; A History of the Theatre, 1985, second edition, 1992. *Membership:* Polish Academy of Arts and Sciences, 1992-. *Address:* 6 College Road, Bristol 8, Avon, England.

WICKLEIN John Frederick, b. 20 July 1924, Reading, Pennsylvania, USA. Journalist, Educator. m. Myra Jane Winchester, 31 July 1948, 1 son, 2 daughters. *Education:* LittB, Rutgers University, 1947; MS, Journalism, Columbia University, 1948. *Publications:* Cable Television : A Guide for Citizen Action, 1972 (co-author); Electronic Nightmare : The New Communications and Freedom, 1981, revised paperback, 1982. *Contributions To:* The Atlantic Monthly; Washington Monthly; Progressive; Archeology; Journalism Quarterly; Columbia Journalism Review; Channels of Communication Australian Journalism Review; Short Stories: Collier's Story. *Honours:* Venice Film Festival Award, Best Documentary, 1968; George Polk Award, 1963; Armstrong (Dupont) Award, 1972; Brechner Freedom of Information Prize, 1987; Fulbright Fellowship, Australia, 1990. *Memberships:* Phi Beta Kappa; Investigative Reporters and Editors; Society of Professional Journalists. *Address:* John F Wicklein, 23200 Wilderness Walk, Gaithersburg, MD 20882, USA.

WIDDICOMBE Gillian Mary, b. 11 June 1943, Aldham, Suffolk, England. Journalist. *Education:* ARCM, 1964, Royal Academy of Music. *Literary Appointments:* Music Critic: Financial Times, 1970-75; Feature Writer: The Observer, 1976-. *Honour:* BP Arts Journalism Award, 1986. *Membership:* Critics' Circle, Secretary, Chairman, Music Section, 1970's. *Literary Agent:* A D Peters. *Address:* 80 New Concordia Wharf, Mill Street, Bermondsey, London SE1 2BB, England.

WIDDOWSON John David Allison, b. 22 June 1935, Sheffield, England. University Lecturer. m. Carolyn Lois Crawford, 1 Sept 1960, 2 sons, 1 daughter. *Education:* BA Hons 1959, MA 1963, Oxford; MA 1966, Leeds; PhD 1972, Newfoundland. *Appointments:* Editor, Lore and Language 1969-; Member Editorial Advisory Board, Rural History 1990-. *Publications:* Co-Author: Learning About Linguistics, 1974; The Linguistic Atlas of England, 1978; Dictionary of Newfoundland English, 1982; Word Maps, 1987; Author, If You Don't Be Good, 1977; Co-Editor: Language, Culture and Tradition, 1981; Studies in Linguistic Geography, 1985; Perspectives on Contemporary Legend, vol II, 1987; Studies in Newfoundland Folklore, 1991. *Contributions to:* Numerous articles and reviews 1962-. *Honours:* Certificate of Merit, Regional History Award, Canadian Historical Association, 1984, 1987. *Memberships:* The Devonshire Association; The Folklore Society, Vice President 1990-, President 1987-90; Societas Linguistica Europaeia; The American Folklore Society; The Oral History Society; The Canadian Oral History Society, Founder Treasurer; The Folklore Studies Association of Canada; The Yorkshire Dialect Society, Council Member 1970-. *Address:* The Centre for English Cultural Tradition and Language, The University, Sheffield S10 2TN, England.

WIDEMAN John Edgar, b. 1941, American. *Appointments:* Member of the English Department,

Howard University, WA, 1965; Instructor to Associate Professor of English, 1966-74; Assistant, Basketball Coach 1968- 72, Director of the Afro-American Studies Program 1971-73, University of Pennsylvania, Philadelphia; Professor of English, University of Wyoming, Laramie, 1975-. *Publications:* A Glance Away, 1967; Hurry Home, 1970; The Lynchers, 1973; Hiding Place, Damballah, 1981; Sent for You Yesterday, 1983; Brothers and Keepers, 1984. *Address:* Department of English, University of Wyoming, Laramie, WY 82071, USA.

WIEBE Rudy H, b. 4 Oct. 1934, Saskatchewan, Canada. Writer; Professor. m. Tena F. Isaak, 4 Mar. 1958, 2 sons, 1 daughter. *Education:* BA, 1956, MA, 1960, University of Alberta; BTh, Mennonite Brethren Bible College, Winnipeg, 1961; Other studies, University of Tuebingen, Federal Republic of Germany, 1957-58, University of Iowa, USA, 1964-65. *Appointments:* Professor of English and Creative Writing, University of Alberta, Edmonton, 1967-; Chair of Canadian Studies, University of Kiel, Federal Republic of Germany, 1984. *Publications:* Novels: Peace Shall Destroy Many, 1962; First and Vital Candle, 1966; The Blue Mountains of China, 1970; The Temptations of Big Bear, 1973; The Scorched-Wood People, 1977; The Mad Trapper, 1980; My Lovely Enemy, 1983. Stories: Where is the Voice Coming From, 1976; Alberta: A Celebration, 1979; The Angel of the Tar Sands, 1982; Playing Dead, essays, 1989; War in the West, history, 1985. *Honours:* Governor General's Award for Fiction for The Temptations of Big Bear, 1973; Honorary DLitt, University of Winnipeg, 1986; Lorne Peirce Medal, Royal Society of Canada, 1987. *Memberships:* Writers Union of Canada, President 1985-86; Writers Guild of Alberta, Founding President 1980-81. *Address:* c/o Department of English, University of Alberta, Edmonton, Canada T6G 2E5.

WIENER Allen Joel, b. 14 Aug. 1943, Newark, New Jersey, USA. Author; International Transportation Specialist. m. Katherine Ann Zantal, 22 June 1974. 1 daughter. *Education:* BA, Political Science, Fairleigh Dickinson University, 1968; MA, Political Science, Rutgers University, 1970; ABD, 1972. *Publication:* The Beatles: A Recording History, 1986, revised 1991. *Contributions to:* Goldmine Magazine. *Honour:* Fairleigh Dickinson University Honors College (Charter Member). *Literary Agent:* Carol Mann. *Address:* c/o Carol Mann Agency, 55 5th Avenue, New York, NY 10003, USA.

WIENER Joel Howard, b. 23 Aug. 1937, New York, USA. Professor of History. m. Suzanne Wolff, 4 Sept. 1961, 1 son, 2 daughters. *Education:* BA, New York University, 1959; Research Fellow, University of Glasgow, 1961-63; PhD, Cornell University, 1965. *Publications:* The War of the Unstamped, 1969; A Descriptive Finding List of Unstamped Periodicals 1830-36, 1970; Great Britain: Foreign Policy and the Span of Empire, (editor), 1972; Great Britain: The Lion at Home, (editor), 1974; Radicalism and Freethought in 19th Century Britain, 1983; Innovators and Preachers: The Role of the Editor in Victorian England, (editor), 1985; Papers for the Millions: The New Journalism in Britain c. 1850's - 1914, editor, 1988; William Lovett, 1989. *Contributions to:* Labor History; Journal of Social History; New Society; Victorian Periodicals Review; Albion; Journal of Modern History; Choice; English Literature In Transition; Victorian Studies; Listener. *Honours:* Fellow Royal Historical Society, 1974. *Memberships:* Research Society for Victorian Periodicals, President; American Historical Association; CUNY Academy for the Humanities and Sciences; American Journalism Historians Association; Conference on British Studies. *Address:* 267 Glen Court, Teaneck, NJ 07666, USA.

WIENERS John Joseph, b. 6 Jan 1934, Milton, Massachusetts, USA. Poet. m. 1 son. *Education:* BA, Boston College, 1954; Black Mountain College, North Carolina, 1955-56; Teaching Fellow, State University of New York, Buffalo, 1965-67. *Publications:* The Hotel Wentley Poems, 1958; Ace of Pentacles, 1964; Pressed

Wafer, 1967; Asylum Poems, 1969; Nerves, 1970; Behind the State Capitol or Cinncinnati Pike, 1975; Selected Poems, 1958-1984, 1986. *Contributions to:* Numerous works including: Semina; Yugen; Stylus; Floating Bear; Set; Blue Grass; Granta; Joglars; Sum; The Nation; Magazine of Further Studies; Intransit; Yale Literary Magazine; Niagara Frontier; Paris Review; Agenda; Wivenhoe Park Review; Boss; Evergreen Review; Film Culture; The World; Emerson Review; Gay Sunshine; Fag Rag; Mirage. *Honours:* Poet's Foundation, New York, 1961; New Hope Foundation Award, 1963; NEA, 1966, 1968; American Academy Award, 1968; Committee on Poetry Grant, 1970-72; Guggenheim Fellowship, 1985. *Agent:* Raymond Foye, New York. *Address:* 44 Joy Street, 10, Boston, MA 02114, USA.

WIESEL Elie, b. 1928, Rumania. Professor; Author; Journalist. *Appointments:* Distinguished Professor of Judaic Studies, City College, City University of New York, 1972-76; Andrew W Mellon Professor in the Humanities, Professor of Religion, Professor of Philosophy, Boston University, Massachusetts 1976-; Henry Luce Visiting Scholar in the Humanities and Social Thought, Whitney Humanities Centre, Yale University 1982-83; Distinguished Visiting Professor of Literature and Philosophy, Florida International University, 1982; Journalist for Israeli, French and US newspapers. *Publications:* Night, memoir, 1960; Dawn, novel, 1961; The Accident, novel, 1962; The Town Beyond the Wall, novel, 1964; The Gates of the Forest, novel, 1966; The Jews of Silence, personal testimony, 1966; Legends of Our Time, essays and stories, 1968; A Beggar in Jerusalem, novel, 1970; One Generation After, essays and stories, 1970; Souls on Fire: Portraits and Legends of the Hasidic Masters, 1972; The Oath, novel, 1973; Ani Maamin, cantata, 1973; Zalmen, or the Madness of God, play, 1974; Messengers of God: Portraits and Legends of Biblical Heroes, 1976; Four Hasidic Masters, 1978; A Jew Today, essays, stories, dialogues, 1978; The Trial of God, play, 1979; The Testament, novel, 1980; Images from the Bible, 1980; Five Biblical Portraits, 1981; Somewhere a Master, Hasidic tales, 1982; Paroles d'etranger, essays, stories, dialogues, 1982; The Golem, retelling of Legend, 1983; The Fifth Son, novel, 1985; Signes d'Exode, essays, stories, dialogues, 1985; Against Silence: The Voice and Vision of Elie Wiesel, collected writings, 1985; Job ou Dieu dans la Tempete, dialogue and commentary with Josy Eisenberg, 1986; A Song For Hipe, a cantata, 1987; The Nobel Address, 1987; Twilight, novel, 1988; The Six Days of Destruction, with Albert Friedlander, 1988; Silences et memoire d'hommes, essays, 1989; L'Oublie, novel, 1989; From the Kingdom of Memory , Reminiscences, 1990; Evil and Exile, dialogues with Philippe-Michael de Saint-Cheron, 1990; A Journey of Faith, with John Cardinal O'Connor, 1990; Sages and Dreamers, Portraits and Legends from the Bible, the Talmud and the Hasidic Tradition, 1991; Celebration Talmudique, Portraits of Talmudic Masters, 1991. *Honours include:* Recipient, Congressional Gold Medal, 1984; Nobel Peace Prize, 1986; Grand Officier, Legion of Honour, 1990, elevated from Commander, Legion of Honour, 1984. *Memberships:* Various literary societies including PEN. *Literary Agent:* Georges Borchardt, New York. *Address:* 745 Commonwealth Avenue, Boston, MA 02215, USA.

WIESENFARTH Joseph John, b. 20 Aug. 1933, Brooklyn, New York, USA. Professor of English. m. Louise Halpin, 21 Aug. 1971, 1 son. *Education:* BA, Catholic University of America, 1956; MA, University of Detroit, 1959; PhD, Catholic University of America, 1962. *Appointments:* Assistant Professor, La Salle College Philadelphia, USA, 1962-64; Assistant Professor, 1964-67, Associate Professor, 1967-70, Manhatten College New York; Associate Professor, 1970-76, Professor, 1976-, University of Wisconsin-Madison; Associate Editor, Renascence, 1972-76, 1992-; Chairman, Department of English, 1983-86, 1989-92; Chairman, Press Committee, University of Wisconsin Press, 1983-88. *Publications include:* Henry James and the Dramatic Analogy, 1963; The Errand of Form: An Essay of Jane Austen's Art, 1967; George Eliot's Mythmaking, 1977; George Eliot : A Writer's Notebook 1854-1879, 1981; Gothic Manners and the Classic English Novel, 1988; Ford Mador Ford and the Art, Contemprary Interature 3012, 1989. *Contributions to:* Numerous articles on British and American Fiction. *Honours:* Phi Beta Kappa, 1956; Fellow, National Endowment for the Humanities, 1967-68; Institute for Research in Humanities Fellow, 1975; Fulbright Fellow, 1981-82; Christian Gauss Prize Award Committee, 1986-88; 1989-90. *Memberships:* Modern Language Association; Jane Austen Society of North America; Henry James Society, Katherine Anne Porter Society. *Address:* Dept. of English, University of Wisconsin-Madison, 600 N. Park St., Madison, WI 53706, USA.

WIESENTHAL Simon b. 31 Dec 1908, Buczacz, Poland. Writer. m. Cyla, 1 daughter. *Education:* Dipl.Ing., Architectural Studies, Prague, Lvov. *Appointments:* Editor, Ausweg, 1960-. *Publications:* KZ Mauthausen, 1946; Head Mufti, 1947; Agent of the Axis, 1947; I Hunted Eichmann, 1961; Limitations, 1964; The Murderers Among Us, 1967; Sunflower, 1969; Sails of Hope, 1973; The Case of Krystyna Jaworska, 1975; Max and Helen, 1982; Every Day Remembrance Day, 1986; Justice, Not Vengeance, 1989. *Honours:* Recipient, numerous honours and awards including: Dutch medal for Freedom; Foundation of the Simon Wiesenthal Centre for Holocaust Studies, Yeshiva University of Los Angeles, California, 1977; Jean-Moulin-Medaille; Kaj-Munk-Medal; Commander, oranje-Nassau, Queen Juliana of the Netherlands, 1978; Justice Brandeis Award, Zionist Organization in USA, 1980; Jerusalem Medal; Doctor h.c., numerous colleges and universities throughout the World; Honorary Citizen, numerous cities including: Miami Beach, Memphis, Shelby County, etc; State of New York declared June 13th 1984 as Simon Wiesenthal Day; Great Medal of Merit, President German Federal Republic, 1985; Grand Silver Honorary Medal for Merits, Vienna, 1985; Knight, Honorary Legion of France, 1986; Honorary membership of the University of Appplied Arts, Vienna, 1989. Director of Documentation Centre. *Address:* Salztorgasse 6, 1010 Vienna, Austria.

WIGG T I G. *See:* **MCCUTCHAN Philip Donald.**

WIGHT J A (James Herriot). Author. *Publications:* If Only They Could Talk, 1970; It Shouldn't Happen to a Vet, 1972; All Creatures Great and Small, 1972; Vet in Harness, 1974; All Things Bright and Beautiful, 1974; Let Sleeping Vets Lie, 1974; Vets Might Fly, 1976; Vet in a Spin, 1977; All Things Wse and Wonderful, 1977; James Herriot's Yorkshire, 1979; The Lord God Made Them All, 1981; The Best of James Herriot, 1982; Moses the Kitten, 1984; Dog Stories, 1986; Christmas Day Kitten, 1986; Bonny's Big Day, 1987; Every Living Thing, 1992. *Honours:* OBE, 1979. *Address:* c/o Michael Joseph Limited, 44 Bedford Square, London WC1B 3DU, England.

WIGNELL Edel, b. 19 Oct 1936, Echuca, Victoria, Australia. Freelance Writer. m. Geoffrey Wignell, 7 Feb 1966. *Education:* Trained Infant Teachers Certificate, Toorak Teachers College, (3 year course) Certificate A (Upgraded to 4 year course 1973). *Appointments:* Teacher, Education Department of Victoria, 1957-61, 63, 64; Teacher, South Lambeth, London, 1962; Lecturer, Burwood State College - Teacher Education, English, 1965, 1967-72; 1962 and 1966 travelled in UK, Europe; Freelance Writer 1979 -. *Publications:* Reading: A Source Book, Nelson, Australia, Heinemann, London; A Boggle of Bunyips, 1981; Crutches are Nothing, 1982; The Ghostly Jigsaw, 1985; A Bluey of Swaggies, 1985; The Car Wash Monster, 1986; You'll Turn into a Rabbit!, 1988; What's in the Red Bag?, 1988; Spider in the Toilet, 1988; Escape by Deluge, 1989; A Gift of Squares; Marmalade, Jet and the Finnies; Rick's Magic; On the Track Series. *Contributions to:* Numerous journals and magazines including The Australian Author, The Age, The Educational Magazine, Primary Education, Reading Time, This Australia, The Writer's News, Magpies, Luna, Short Story International. *Honours:* McGregor Literary Competition S S Award - Commended 1982; Mary Grant Bruce S S Award -

Highly Commended, 1983, winner 1985, 2nd Prize and Commended 1986; Ballarat Literary Competition, Ballad Commended 1985; Macarthur FAW S S Competition - ghost story selected for anthology; Highly Commended, St George-Sutherland Branch FAW Short Story Competition, 1987; Open Poetry Prize, Mackay Arts Festival, 1987; Honour Award, Most Beautiful Books in All the World, Leipzig Book Fair, 1989; Escape by Deluge CBC (Australia) Notable Book, 1990. *Memberships:* Australian Society of Authors; Australian Writers Guild; Fellowship of Australian Writers; Society of Children's Book Writers and Illustrators, USA. Children's Book Council of Australia. *Address:* P. O. Box 135, Glen Iris, Victoria, 3146, Australia.

WIKSTRÖM Per-Olof Helge, b. 30 July 1955, Uppsala, Sweden. Criminologist. *Education:* BA, 1976, PhD, 1985, Docent in Criminology, 1988, University of Stockholm. *Publications:* Everyday Violence in Contemporary Sweden, 1985; Patterns of Crime in a Birth Cohort, 1987; Brott och stadsmiljo, 1987; Urban Crime, Criminals and Victims, 1990. *Contributions to:* Journal of Quantitative Criminology; The British Journal of Criminology; Criminal Behaviour and Mental Health; Contemporary Drug Problems; Alkoholpolitik - tidskrift for nordisk alkoholforskning. *Address:* BRA, Atlasmuren 1, 113 21 Stockholm, Sweden.

WILBUR Richard (Purdy), b. 1 Mar. 1921, New York City, USA. University Professor; Poet Laureate of the USA. *Education:* MA, Amherst College, Harvard University. *Publications include:* The Beautiful Changes and Other Poems, 1947; Things of this World, 1956; Tartuffe (translated from Moliere), 1963; Loudmouse (for children), 1963; poems of Shakespeare (with Alfred Harbage), 1966; Walking to Sleep (New Poems and translations), 1969; School for Wives (translation), 1971; Opposites (childrens verse illustrated by the author), 1973; The Mind Reader, 1976; Responses (essays), 1976; The Learned Ladies (translated from Moliere), 1978; Seven Poems, 1981; The Whale (translation), 1982; Racines Andromache, (translation), 1982; Moliere Four comedies, 1982; Racine's Phaedra (translation), 1986; new and Collected Poems, 1988; More Opposites, 1991; School for Husbands (translation from Moliere), 1992. *Honours:* Harriet Monroe Prize, 1948; Oscar Blumenthal Prize, 1950; prix de Rome, American Academy of Arts & Letters, 1954-55; Edna St Vincent Millay Memorial Award, 1956; Pulitzer Prize, 1957; National Book Award, 1957; prix Henri Desfeuilles, 1971; Brandeis Creative Arts Award, 1971; Shelley Mem prize, 1973; Harriet Monroe Poetry Award, 1983; Drama Desk Award, 1983; Chevalier, Ordre Des Palmes Academiques, 1983; Poet Laureate Consultant in Poetry to the Library of Congress, 1987-; Aiken-Taylor Award, 1988; Los Angeles Times Book Prize (Poetry), 1988; Pulitzer Prize, 1989; St Louis Literary Award, 1989. *Memberships:* Chancellor, Academy of American Poets; PEN; Former President, American Academy of Arts and Letters; Dramatists Guild; American Academy of Arts & Sciences. *Agent:* Gilbert Parker, William Morris Agency. *Address:* Dodwells Road, Cummington, MA 01026, USA.

WILBY Basil Leslie, (Gareth Knight), b. 1930, British. *Appointments:* University Sales Manager 1970-76, Longman Group Publishing Manager 1976-91; Freelance Publishing Consultant, 1991-. *Publications:* A Practical Guide to Qabalistic Symbolism (as G Knight), 1965; The New Dimensions Red Book (ed), 1968; The Practice of Ritual Magic (as G Knight), Occult Exercises and Practices (as G Knight), 1969; Meeting the Occult, 1973; Experience of the Inner Worlds (as G Knight), The Occult - An Introduction (as G Knight), 1975; A History of White Magic (as G Knight), 1979; The Secret Tradition in Arthurian Legend (as G Knight), 1983; The Rose Cross and the Goddess (as G Knight), The Gareth Knight Tarot Deck (as G Knight), 1985; The Treasure House of Images (as G Knight), 1986; The Magical World of the Inklings (as G Knight), 1990; The Magical World of the Tarot (as G Knight), 1991; Magic and the Western Mind (as G Knight), 1991. *Address:* PO Box 739, Braintree, Essex CM7 7JW, England.

WILCOX Collin (Carter Wick), b. 1924, American. *Appointments:* Teacher at the Town School, 1950-53; Partner, Amthor and Company, furniture store, 1953-55; Owner, Collin Wilcox Lamps, 1955-70; Full-time Writer, 1970-; Regional Vice-President, 1975, Member, Board of Directors, 1976, Mystery Writers of America. *Publications:* The Black Door, 1967; The Third Figure, 1968; The Lonely Hunter, 1969; The Disappearance, 1970; Dead Aim, 1971; Hiding Place, McCloud, 1973; Long Way Down, The New Mexico Connection, 1974; Aftershock, The Faceless Man (as Carter Wick), 1975; The Third Victim, 1976; Doctor, Lawyer ...., 1977; The Watcher, Twospot (with Bill Pronzini), 1978; Power Plays, 1979; Mankiller, Spellbinder, 1980; Stalking Horse, 1981; Dark House, Dark Road, 1982; Swallow's Fall, 1983; Victims, 1985; Night Games, 1986; The Pariah, 1987; Bernhardt's Edge, 1987; A Death Before Dying, 1988; Silent Witness, 1989; Hire A Hangman, 1990; Except for the Bones, 1991; Dead Center, 1992. *Address:* 4174 26th Street, San Francisco, CA 94131, USA.

WILDER Cherry. *See:* **GRIMM Barbara Lockett.**

WILDER John Richard, b. 3 Oct 1955, Council Bluff, Iowa, USA. Writer; Publisher; Justice Advocate. m. Laura Jean Hathaway, 18 Jan. 1973, divorced 1979, 3 daughters. *Education:* Specialist in Psychosynthesis, 1980; Bachelor of Philosophy, 1981; Master of Organizational Design & Administration, 1982; M.Div.C, 1982; Th.M, 1983; Sp.Psy, 1984; MFA, 1985; MUDA, 1986; Psy.D, 1988. *Appointments:* Governing Board, Windhover Press, University of Iowa, 1982; Editorial Review Board, University of Iowa Press, 1982; Director, Community Writers Association, 1982-87; Publisher, Writers House Press, 1983-; Publisher, The Peoples Press, 1986-; Producer/Writer, Eyes on Justice Documentary Consortium, 1989-. *Publications:* Only Silence is Shame, 1986; The Wilder Letters, 1987; Eyes on Justice (TV Programme), 1987-89; The Falling Torch: The Demise of Democracy, Ethics & Morality in America, forthcoming. *Contribution to:* various magazines & journals. *Honours:* Pushcart Press, Outstanding Small Press Recognition for Writers House Press, 1983-85; Grantee, Kaltenborn Foundation, 1985; Arts & Humanities Fellow, Institute for Human Potential, 1986. *Memberships:* International Platform Association; National Psychiatric Association; National Tribune Association; Alternative Press Association. *Address:* PO Box 3071, Iowa City, IA 52244, USA.

WILDING Eric. *See:* **TUBB E C.**

WILDING Griselda. *See:* **MCCUTCHEON Hugh.**

WILDING Michael, b. 1942, England. Professor in English,Australian Literature. *Education:* BA, 1963, MA, 1968, University of Oxford. *Appointments:* Lecturer in English, 1963-66; Senior Lecturer, 1969-72, Reader, 1972-92, Professor, 1993-, University of Sydney, New South Wales, Australia; Lecturer in English, University of Birmingham, England, 1967-68; Visiting Professor, University of California, Santa Barbara, USA, 1987. *Publications:* Fiction: Aspects of the Dying Process, 1972; Living Together, 1974; Short Story Embassy, 1975; West Midland Underground, 1975; Scenic Drive, 1976; The Phallic Forest, 1978; Pacific Highway, 1982; Reading the Signs, 1984; The Paraguyan Experiment, 1985; The Man of Slow Feeling; Selected Short Stories, 1985; Under Saturn, 1988; Great Climate, 1990; Non-fiction: Milton's Paradise Lost, 1969; Marcus Clarke, 1977; Political Fictions, 1980; Dragons Teeth: Literature in the English Revolution, 1987; Social Visions, 1993; The Radical Tradition: Lawson, Furphy, Stead, 1993 . *Honours:* Senior Fellowship, Literature Board, Australia Council, 1978; Elected Fellow, Australian Academy of the Humanities, 1988. *Address:* Department of English, University of Sydney, New South Wales 2006, Australia.

WILDSMITH Brian Lawrence, b. 22 Jan. 1930, Yorkshire, England. Artist; Author. m. Aurelie Ithurbide,

2 Apr. 1955, 1 son, 3 daughters. *Education:* Barnsley School of Art, 1946-49; Slade School of Fine Art, University College, London, 1949-52. *Publications include:* ABC, 1962; The Lion & The Rat, 1963; The Oxford Book of Poetry for Children, 1963; The North Wind and the Sun, 1964; Mother Goose, 1964; 1.2.3. 1965; The Rich Man and the Shoemaker, 1965; The Hare and the Tortoise, 1966; A Childs Garden of Verses, Illustrator, 1966; Birds, 1967; Wild Animals, 1967; Fishes, 1968; The Bible Story, Illustrator, 1968; The Miller The Boy and the Donkey, 1969; Circus, 1970; Puzzles, 1970; The Owl and the Woodpecker, 1971; The Twelve Days of Christmas, 1972; The Little Wood Duck, 1972; The Lazy Bear, 1973; Squirrels, 1974; Python's Party, 1974; Blue Bird, 1976; The True Cross, 1977; What the Moon Saw, 1978; Hunter and His Dog, 1979; Animal Games, 1980; Animal Homes, 1980; Animal Shapes, 1980; Animal Tricks, 1980; Seasons, 1980; Professor Noah's Space Ship, 1980; Bear's Adventure, 1981; The Trunk, 1981; Cat On the Mat, 198l; Pelican, 1982; The Island, The Apple Bird, All Fall Down, The Nest, 1983; Toot-Toot, Daisy, Who's Shoes, 1984; Give a Dog a Bone, 1985; My Dream, What a Tale, Goats Trail, 1986; If I Were You, Giddy Up, 1987; Carousel, 1988; A Christmas Story, 1989; The Snow Country Prince, 1990, The Cherry Tree, 1991, The Princess and the Moon, 1991, Over the Deep Blue Sea, 1992, with Daisaku Ikeda; The Easter Story, 1993; Wake Up Wake Up, 1993, Whose Hat Was That, 1993, What Did I Find, 1993, Look Closer, 1993, with Rebecca Wildsmith . *Honours:* Kate Greenaway Medal, 1962; Suka-Gakkai Education Medal, Japan, 1988. *Membership:* Reform Club. *Address:* 11 Castellaras, 06370 Mouans Sartoux, France.

WILFORD John Noble, b. 4 Oct 1933, Kentucky, USA. Journalist. m. Nancy Watts Paschall, 25 Dec 1966, 1 daughter. *Education:* BS, Journalism, University of Tennessee, 1955; MA, Political Science, Syracuse University, 1956; International Reporting Fellow, Columbia University, 1961- 62. *Appointments:* Science Reporter, 1965-73, 1979-, Assistant National Editor, 1973-75, Director of Science News, 1975-79, New York Times, New York City; McGraw Distinguished Lecturer in Writing, Princeton University, 1985; Professor of Science Journalism, University of Tennessee, 1989-90. *Publications:* We Reach the Moon, 1969; The Mapmakers, 1981; The Riddle of the Dinosaur, 1985; Mars Beckons, 1990; The Mysterious History of Columbus, 1991. *Contributions to:* Nature; Wilson Quarterly; New York Times Magazine; Science Digest; Popular Science. *Honours:* Westinghouse-American Association for the Advancement of Science Writing Award, 1983; Pulitzer Prize for National Reporting, 1984, shared 1987. *Memberships:* Century Club, New York City; National Association of Science Writers. *Address:* New York Times, 229 West 43rd Street, New York, NY 10036, USA.

WILKINSON Doris, b. Lexington, Kentucky, USA. University Professor. *Education:* BA Social Work & English 1958, University of Kentucky; MA Sociology 1960, Western Reserve University; PhD Medical Sociology 1968, Case Western Reserve University; MPH Public Health 1985, Johns Hopkins University; Post-doctoral study, History of Science, Harvard University, 1991. *Appointments:* Executive Associate, ASA 1977-80; Professor, Howard University, 1980-84; Visiting Professor, University of Virginia 1984-85; Professor, University of Kentucky 1985-; Ford Fellow, Harvard University 1989- 90. *Publications:* 6 books, 4 edited, 1 co-edited; Over 45 articles in professional journals; Over 25 major book reviews. *Honours:* Ford Fellow to Harvard 1989-90; Phi Beta Kappa; Public Humanities Award, 1990; Nominated for Great Teacher, 1990; Woman's History Month Award, 1991, Midway College; Elected Vice President of American Sociological Association, 1991-92; Elected President of the Eastern Sociological Society, 1991; Great Teacher Award, 1992. *Memberships:* American Sociological Association, Vice President Elect 1990-91; Eastern Sociological Society, ESS, Vice President 1983-84, President Elect 1990-91; Society for the Study of Social Problems, President 1987-88; District of Columbia Sociological Society,

President 1982-83. *Address:* Department of Sociology, University of Kentucky, Lexington, KY 40506, USA.

WILL Clifford Martin, b. 13 Nov 1946, Hamilton, Canada. Physicist. m. Leslie Carol Saxe, 26 June 1970, 2 daughters. *Education:* BSc, Applied Mathematics, Theoretical Physics, McMaster University, 1968; PhD, Physics, California Institute of Technology, 1971. *Publications:* Theory and Experiment in Gravitational Physics, 1981, 2nd Edition, 1993; Was Einstein Right?, 1986, 2nd Edition, 1993. *Contributions to:* 6 articles on general relativity (in German) to P M Magazin, 1989; The Renaissance of General Relativity to The New Physics, 1989; Twilight Time for the Fifth Force? to Sky and Telescope, 1990. *Honours:* Fellowship, Alfred P Sloan Foundation, 1975-79; Science Writing Award for Was Einstein Right?, American Institute of Physics, 1987. *Memberships:* Fellow, American Physical Society; American Astronomical Society; International Society on General Relativity and Gravitation. *Literary Agent:* Gerard F McCauley Agency. *Address:* Department of Physics, Campus Box 1105, Washington University, St Louis, MO 63130, USA.

WILL George Frederick, b. 4 May 1941, Champaign, Illinois, USA. Author; Syndicated Columnist. 2 sons, 1 daughter. *Education:* BA with honours, Trinity College, Hartford, Connecticut, 1962; Magdalen College, Oxford, England; BA (Oxon), Politics, Philosophy, Economics, 1964; PhD, Politics, Princeton University, New Jersey, 1967. *Appointments:* Editor, The National Review, Washington DC, 1973-76; Syndicated Columnist, The Washington Post, 1974-; Contributing Editor, Newsweek magazine, 1976-; Occasional Op-Ed Page Contributor, The London Daily Telegraph, 1987- . *Publications:* The Pursuit of Happiness and Other Sobering Thoughts, 1978; The Pursuit of Virtue and Other Tory Notions, 1982; Statecraft As Soulcraft: What Government Does, 1983; The Morning After: American Successes and Excesses, 1986; The New Season: A Spectator's Guide to the 1988 Election, 1987; Men at Work: The Craft of Baseball, 1990; Suddenly: The American Idea Abroad and At Home, 1990. *Honours:* Pulitzer Prize for Commentary, 1977; The Silurian Award, 1980; Weldon-Burckhardt Prize, Magdalen College, Oxford, 1964; Charlotte-Elizabeth Proctor Fellow, Princeton University; Honors Citation for Teaching Excellence, Michigan; Honorary degrees: LLD, University of San Diego, 1977; DLitt, Dickinson College, Carlisle, Pennsylvania, 1978; DLitt, Georgetown University, Washington DC, 1978; University of Illinois, 1988. *Memberships:* Emil Verban Society. *Address:* c/o Writers Group, The Washington Post, 1150 Fifteenth Street NW, Washington, DC 20071, USA.

WILLARD Nancy Margaret, b. Ann Arbor, Michigan, USA. Writer; Educator. m. Eric Lindbloom, 15 Aug 1964, 1 son. *Education:* BA 1958, PhD 1963, University of Michigan; Ma, Stanford University, 1960. *Appointment:* Lecturer, English, Vassar College, Poughkeepsie, New York, 1965-. *Publications include:* Poems: In His Country, 1966, Skin of Grace, 1967, A New Herball, 1968; Testimony of the Invisible Man: William Carlos Williams, Francis Ponge, Rainer Maria Rilke, Pablo Neruda, 1970; Nineteen Masks for the Naked Poet, 1971; Childhood of the Magician, 1973; The Carpenter of the Sun, 1974; A Visit to William Blake's Inn: Poems for Innocant and Experienced Travellers, 1981; Household Tales of Moon and Water, 1983; Water Walker, 1989; The ballad of Biddy Early, 1989. Play: East of the Sun, West of the Moon, 1989. Novel: Things Invisible to See, 1985. Stories: The Lively Anatomy of God. Essays: Angel in the Parlour, 1983. Short stories and books for juveniles. *Honours:* Hopwood Award, 1958; Devins Memorial Award, 1967; Woodrow Wilson Fellow, 1960; NEA Grantee, 1987, Newberry Medal 1982 for A Visit to William Blake's Inn: Poems for Innocent and Experienced Travellers. *Memberships:* Children's Literature Association; The Lewis Carroll Society; The George MacDonald Society. *Address:* 133 College Avenue, Poughkeepsie, NY 12603, USA.

WILLETT Frank, b. 18 Aug 1925, Bolton, Lancashire,

England. Museum Curator; Academic. m. M Constance Hewitt, 24 July 1950, 1 son, 3 daughters. *Education:* BA, 1947, MA, 1951, Oxford University; Diploma in Anthropology, 1949. *Appointments:* Editorial Secretary, Manchester Literary and Philosophical Society, 1950-58; Member, Editorial Board, West African Journal of Archaeology, 1970; Member, Editorial Board, Journal of African Studies, 1973-; Curator, Royal Society of Edinburgh, 1992-. *Publications:* Ife in the History of West African Sculpture, 1967; African Art: An Introduction, 1971; The Arts of the African Peoples, in Encyclopedia Britannica, 1974; Treasures of Ancient Nigeria (with Ekpo Eyo), 1980. *Contributions to:* Many articles on African art and archaeology especially on Ife and Benin, to various publications. *Honours:* Honorary Corresponding Member, Manchester Literary and Philosophical Society, 1958; Fellow, Royal Society of Edinburgh, 1979; Commander, Order of the British Empire, 1985. *Memberships:* Scottish Museums Council, Vice-Chairman 1985-88, Chairman, Advisory Committee on Education in Museums and Galleries, 1982-90, Member, Executive, 1980-90; Founder-Chairman, University Museums in Scotland; Fellow, Royal Anthropological Institute, Council Member 1982-85. *Address:* The Hunterian Museum, The University of Glasgow, Glasgow G12 8QQ, Scotland.

WILLETT John William Mills, b. 24 June 1917, Hampstead, London, England. Author; Translator; Journalist. m. 23 Feb 1951, 1 son, 1 daughter. *Education:* Christ Church, Oxford; MA, Philosophy, Politics and Economics, Oxford; Ruskin School of Art, Oxford. *Appointments:* Leader Writer, Manchester Guardian, 1948-51; Assistant Editor, Times Literary Supplement, 1960-72; Joint Editor (with the late Ralph Manheim), Brecht's Plays, Poetry and Prose, 1970-. *Publications:* Popski - A Life of Lt-Col Vladimir Peniakoff, 1954; The Theatre of Bertolt Brecht, 1959; Expressionism, 1970; The New Sobriety, 1978, US title, Arts and Politics in the Weimar Period; Brecht in Context, 1983; The Weimar Years, 1984; Caspar Neher, Brecht's Designer, 1986; The Theatre of the Weimar Republic, 1988. *Contributions to:* Guardian; Times Literary Supplement; New York Review of Books; Paese Sera, Rome; Theatre Publique, Paris; Ambit, London; Art Monthly, London, Canberra; Others. *Honours:* Zap Award for Dieppe Exhibition and catalogue, Brighton, 1992; Medal of City of Bourges, for contribution to discussion Brecht Aujourd'hui, 1992. *Membership:* Society of Authors. *Literary Agent:* Tessa Sayle Agency, London, England. *Address:* Volta House, Windmill Hill, London NW3 6SJ, England.

WILLIAMS J R. *See:* **WILLIAMS Jeanne.**

WILLIAMS Alan Moray (Robert the Rhymer), b. 17 June 1915, Petersfield, Hampshire, England. Foreign Correspondent; Literary Critic; Poet. m. Erkel Christiansen, 12 May 1965, 2 sons, 1 daughter. *Education:* MA, King's College, Cambridge University, 1934-37; Cand Mag in Russian, Copenhagen University, Denmark, 1969. *Appointments:* Foreign Correspondent for UK newspapers including especially The Sunday Times; News Chronicle; Guardian; Liverpool Daily Post and Books and the Media, positions for them held in Reykjavik, Oslo, Stockholm, Copenhagen and USSR. *Publications:* Russian Made Easy, 1943; The Road to the West (poems from Russian), 1945; Children of the Century (poems), 1945; Copenhagen - Praise and Protest, 1965; Denmark - Praise and Protest, 1969; Autumn in Copenhagen (poems), 1963; Translations: the Malachite Casket, by Bazhov, 1945; Man Overboard and other Sea Stories, by Stanyukovich 1945; Soren Kierkegaard, by Peter P Rohde. *Contributions to:* New Strand Magazine; John O'London's; Listener; Spectator; Time and Tide; Tribune; Lilliput; Oxford Magazine; Norseman; Woman's Own; Women and Home; Byron Journal; PEN International. *Memberships:* Society of Authors; National Union of Journalists; PEN International; Danish Authors Union; Interntional Federation of Journalists; London Press Club; The Byron Society. *Address:* Scandinavian Features Service, Box 4, 3450 Allerod pr Copenhagen, Denmark.

WILLIAMS Bert Nolan, b. 19 Aug 1930, Toronto, Ontario, Canada. Writer; Teacher. m. Angela Babando, 6 Dec 1952, 1 son. *Education:* Self-taught. *Publications:* Food for the Eagle, 1970; Master of Ravenspur, 1970; The Rocky Mountain Monster, 1972; Sword of Egypt, 1977; Brumaire, play in 3 acts, 1982; Poetry, Popular songs (music and lyrics), short stories, magazine articles. *Contributions to:* Well over 100 to assorted journals and magazines. *Address:* 10 Muirhead Road, Apt 504, North York, Ontario, Canada M2J 4P9.

WILLIAMS C.K. (Charles Kenneth), b. 4 Nov 1936, Newark, New Jersey, USA. Poet. m. Catherine Justine Mauger, 12 Apr 1975, 1 son, 1 daughter. *Education:* BA, University of Pennsylvania, USA, 1959. *Appointments:* Various Universities and Colleges including: George Mason University, University of California, Boston University, Wichita State University, Columbia University, Brooklyn College. *Publications:* Poems: Lies, 1969; I Am the Bitter Name, 1972; With Ignorance, 1977; Tar, 1983; Poems 1963-1983; Flesh and Blood, 1987; A Dream of Mind, 1992; Translator, with Gregory Dickerson, of Sophocles' Women of Trachis; Euripides' Bacchae. *Contribution to:* American Poetry Review; Antaeus; Atlantic; Chicago Review; Grand Street; Iowa Review; Mademoiselle. *Honours:* John Simon Guggenheim Fellowship, 1974; Nominee, National Book Critics Circle Award, 1983, winner 1987; Pushcart Press Prize, 1982, 1983, 1987; NEA Fellowship, 1985; National Book Critics Circle Award for Poetry, 1987; Morton Dauwen Zabel Prize of the American Academy of Arts and Letters, 1988; Lila Wallace Writer's Award, 1993. *Memberships:* PEN; Poetry Society of America. *Address:* 82 Rue D'Hautevill, 75010 Paris, France.

WILLIAMS Carol Elizabeth (Carol Fenner), b. 1929, USA. Children's Fiction Writer; Lecturer; Instructor. *Publications:* Tigers in the Cellar, 1963; Christmas Tree on the Mountain, 1966; Lagalag the Wanderer, 1968; Gorilla Gorilla, 1973; The Skates of Uncle Richard, 1978; Saving Amelia Earhart, 1982; Deer Flight, 1986; A Summer of Horses, 1989; Randall's Wall, 1991. *Address:* 190 Rebecca Road, Battle Creek, MI 49015, USA.

WILLIAMS David, b. 8 June 1926, Bridgend, Mid-Glamorgan, Wales. Novelist. m. Brenda Yvonne Holmes, 18 July 1952, 1 son, 1 daughter. *Education:* Cathedral School, Hereford, 1938-43; St John's College, Oxford, 1943-44, 1947-48; MA Hons. *Publications:* Unholy Writ; Murder for Treasure; Wedding Treasure; Murder in Advent; Treasure in Oxford; Holy Treasure; Treasure by Degrees; Treasure Up in Smoke; Copper, Gold & Treasure; Treasure Preserved; Advertise for Treasure; Treasure in Roubles; Divided Treasure; Prescription for Murder; Treasure by Post; Planning On Murder; Banking on Murder. *Contributions:* Numerous short stories. *Memberships:* Society of Authors; Crime Writers Association; Mystery Writers of America; Carlton Club; Wentworth G C; Detection Club. *Literary Agent:* Curtis Brown, 162-168 Regent Street, London W1, England. *Address:* Blandings, Pinewood Road, Virginia Water, Surrey GU25 4PA, England.

WILLIAMS David Larry, b. 22 June 1945, Souris, Manitoba, Canada. University Professor. m. Darlene Olinyk, 22 July 1967, 2 sons. *Education:* Pastor's Diploma, Briercrest Bible Institute, Saskatchewan, 1965; BA, Honours, University of Saskatchewan, 1968; MA, (Amherst), 1970, PhD, 1973, University of Massachusetts. *Appointments:* Lecturer, 1972-73, Assistant Professor, 1973-77, Associate Professor, 1977-83, Professor, 1983-, English, University of Manitoba, Winnipeg; Editorial Board, Canadian Review of American Studies, 1976-86. *Publications:* The Burning Wood, novel, 1975; Faulkner's Women: The Myth and the Muse, criticism, 1977; The River Horsemen, novel, 1982; Eye of the Father, novel, 1985; Chapter in Trace: Prairie Writers on Writing, 1986; To Run with Longboat: Twelve Stories of Indian Athletes in Canada (with Brenda Zeman), 1988; Confessional Fictions: A Portrait of the Artist in the Canadian Novel,

1990. *Contributions to:* Chapters in various books; Critical essays on Herman Melville, Harold Frederic, Margaret Laurence, Sinclair Ross, Rudy Wiebe, Robertson Davies, F.P. Grove, Ernest Hemingway, in CRevAS, DalREv, CanL, JCS, MSE, UTQ. *Honours:* Woodrow Wilson Fellow, 1968-69; Canada Council Fellow, 1969-72; Canada Council Arts Grant 'B' 1977-78, 1981-82; Manitoba Arts Council Grants, 1975, 1979; Touring Writer in Scandinavia for External Affairs, Canada, 1981; RH Institute Award for Research in Humanities, 1987. *Memberships:* Writers' Union of Canada; National Council of Prairie Region, 1978-79, 1984-85; Chairman, Search-for-a-New Manitoba-Novelist Competition, Manitoba Department of Cultural Affairs, 1981-83; PEN International. *Address:* Dept. of English, St Paul's College, University of Manitoba, Winnipeg, Canada R3T 2M6.

WILLIAMS Guy Richard, b. 23 Aug 1920, Mold, North Wales. Author; Schoolteacher. *Education:* St Edward's School, Oxford, 1934-37; Manchester College of Art, 1937-40; Hornsey College of Art, 1946-50; Art Teacher's Diploma, 1950. *Appointments:* Advisory Editor, Macmillan Education's Dramascripts and Dramascript Classics Series, 1969-90. *Publications:* The World of Models series, Deutsch, 1970-76; The Hidden World of Scotland Yard, 1972; The Age of Agony, 1975; The Age of Miracles, 1981; London Walks, 1981; Augustus Pugin versus Decimus Burton: A Victorian Architectural Duel, 1990; Numerous books on hobbies and handicrafts for young people. *Contributions to:* Numerous. *Honour:* Saxon Barton Prize, Royal Cambrian Academy, 1951. *Membership:* Savile Club, London. *Address:* 1A Earl Road, East Sheen, London SW14 7JH, England.

WILLIAMS Herbert Lloyd, b. 8 Sept 1932, Aberystwyth, Wales. Writer. m. Dorothy Maud Edwards, 13 Nov 1954, 4 sons, 1 daughter. *Publications:* The Trophy, 1967; A Lethal Kind of Love, 1968; Battles in Wales, 1975; Come Out Wherever You Are, 1976; Stage Coaches in Wales, 1977; The Welsh Quiz Book, 1978; Railways in Wales, 1981; The Pembrokeshire Coast National Park, 1987; Stories of King Arthur, 1990; Ghost Country, 1991; Davies The Ocean, 1991. *Contributions to:* New Welsh Review; The Anglo-Welsh Review; Planet; The Transatlantic Review; Poetry Wales; Cambrensis; Tribune; Acumen. *Honours:* Welsh Arts Council Short Story Prize, 1972; Welsh Arts Council Writing Bursary, 1988; Prize winner, Aberystwyth Open Poetry Competition, 1990. *Memberships:* The Writers Guild of Great Britain; The Welsh Academy, Welsh Union of Writers. *Literary Agent:* Juri Gabriel. *Address:* 20 Amesbury Road, Penylan, Cardiff CF2 5DW, Wales.

WILLIAMS Hugo Mordaunt, b. 20 Feb 1942, England. Writer, Poet. m. Hermine Demoriane, 1965, 1 daughter. *Appointments include:* Assistant editor, London Magazine, 1961-70; Television critic 1083-, poetry editor 1984-, New Statesman. *Publications:* Poems: Symptoms of Loss, 1965; Sugar Daddy, 1970; Some Sweet Day, 1975; Love-Life, 1979; Writing Home, 1985. Travel: All the Time in the World, 1966; No Particular Place to Go, 1981. *Honours:* Henfield Writers Fellowship, University of East Anglia, 1981. Poetry Awards: Eric Gregory, 1965; Cholmondeley, 1970; Geoffrey Faber Memorial Prize, 1979. *Address:* 3 Raleigh Street, London N1, England.

WILLIAMS Jeanne (Megan Castell, Jeanne Creasey, Jeanne Crecy, Jeanne Foster, Kristin Michaels, Deidre Rowan, J R Williams), b. 1930, USA. Author. *Publications:* To Buy a Dream, 1958; Promise of Tomorrow, 1959; Coyote Winter, 1965; Beasts with Music, 1967; Oil Patch Partners, 1968; New Medicine, 1971; Trails of Tears, 1972; Freedom Trail, 1973; Winter Wheat, 1975; A Lady Bought with Rifles, 1977; A Woman Clothed in Sun, 1978; Bride of Thunder, 1978; Daughter of the Sword, 1979; The Queen of a Lonely Country (as Megan Castell), 1980; The Valiant Women, 1981; Harvest of Fury, 1982; The Heaven Sword, 1983; A Mating of Hawks, 1984; The Care Dreamers, 1985; So Many Kingdoms, 1986; Texas Pride, 1987; Lady of

No Man's Land, 1988; No Roof but Heaven, 1990; Home Mountain, 1990; The Island Harp, 1991, The Longest Road, 1993. As J R Williams: Mission in Mexico, 1960; The Horsetalker, 1961; The Confederate Fiddle, 1962; River Guns, 1962; Oh Susanna, 1963; Tame the Wild Stallion, 1967. As Jeanne Crecy: Hands of Terror, UK Edition Lady Gift, 1972; The Lightning Tree, 1972; My Face Beneath Stone, 1975; The Winter-Keeper, 1975; The Night Hunters, 1975. As Deirdre Rowan: Dragon's Mount, 1973; Silver Wood, 1974; Shadow of the Volcano, 1975; Time of the Burning Mask, 1976; Ravensgate, 1976. As Kristin Michaels: To Begin with Love, 1975; Enchanted Twilight, 1975; A Special Kind of Love, 1976; Enchanted Journey, 1977; Song of the Heart, 1977; Make Believe Love, 1978. As Jeanne Foster: Deborah Leigh, 1981; Eden Richards, 1982; Woman of Three Worlds, 1984; The Island Harp, USA, 1991, England, 1992. *Contributions to:* Published over 70 stories in various magazines; Frequent reviews for Books of the Southwest. for Best West Childrens book, 1962 and 1973. *Honours:* Texas Institute of Letters Best Children's Book, 1958; for Best West Childrens book, 1962 and 1973; Four Western Writers of America Spur Awards; Best Novel of the West, 1981 and 1990; Lew Strauss Golden, Saddleman Award for Lifetime Achievment, 1988. *Memberships:* Author's Guild; Western Writers of America, Board Member, President, 1974-75. *Literary Agent:* Claire Smith of Harold Ober Associates. Address: Box 335, Portal, AZ 85632, USA.

WILLIAMS Joan, b. 26 Sept 1928, Memphis, Tennessee, USA. Fiction Writer. divorced, 2 sons. *Education:* BA, Bard College, 1950; MA, Fairfield University, 1985. *Publications:* The Morning and Evening, 1961; Old Powder Man, 1966; The Wintering, 1971; County Woman, 1982; Pariah and Other Stories, 1983; Novel: Pay the Piper with E.P. Dutton, 1988. *Honours:* J.P. Marquand First Novel Award, 1962; The National Institute of Arts & Letters, 1962; Guggenheim Foundation, 1986. *Memberships:* Authors Guild; PEN International. *Agent:* Harold Ober Associates. *Address:* 29 Olmstead Hill Road, Wilton, CT 06897, USA.

WILLIAMS John A(lfred), b. 1925, American. *Appointments:* Public Relations Officer, Doug Johnson Associations, Syracuse, 1952-54; with CBS Radio-Television Special Events, Hollywood and NYC, 1954-55; Publicity Director, Comet Press Books, 1955-56; Editor and Publisher, Negro Market Newsletter, 1956-57; Assistant to Publisher, Abelard-Schuman Incorporated, 1957-58; European Correspondent, Ebony magazine and Jet magazine, 1958-59; Correspondent, Newsweek magazine, Africa, 1964-65; Professor of English, Rutgers University, New Brunswick, NJ, 1979-; Chair, Paul Robeson Professor of English, 1990. *Publications:* The Angry Ones, 1960; Night Song, 1961; The Angry Black (ed), 1962; Africa: Her History, Lands and People, Sissie (in UK as Journey Out of Anger), 1963; The Protectors, 1964; This Is My Country, Too, 1965; The Man Who Cried I Am, Beyond the Angry Black (ed), 1967; Sons of Darkness, Sons of Light: A Novel of Some Probability, 1969; The Most Native of Sons, The King God Didn't Save, 1970; Amistad I and II (ed), 1970, 1971; The Ordeal of Abraham Blackman The Negro Soldier, Captain Blackman, 1971; Flashbacks: A Twenty-Year Diary of Article Writing, 1972; Romare Bearden, 1973; Mothersill and the Foxes, Minorities in the City, 1975; The Junior Bachelor Society, 1976; Click Song, 1982; The Berhama Account, 1985; Introduction to Literature, 1985; Jacobs Ladder, 1987; John A Williams Archive, 1987. *Address:* 693 Forest Avenue, Teaneck, NJ 07666, USA.

WILLIAMS John Hoyt, b. 26 Oct 1940, Darien, Connecticut, USA. Professor of History. m. 27 Jan 1963, 1 son, 1 daughter. *Education:* BA 1963, MA History 1965, University of Connecticut; PhD Latin American History 1969, University of Florida. *Appointments:* Assistant Professor History 1969-73, Associate Professor History 1973-78, Professor History 1978-, Indiana State University. *Publications:* Rise and Fall of the Paraguayon Republic 1800-1870, 1979; A Great and Shining Road, 1988; Sam Houston, A Biography of The Father of Texas, 1993. *Contributions to:* Atlantic Monthly; Christian Century; Americas; National Defense; Current History; Hispanic American Historical Review; and others. *Literary Agent:* Robert Gottlieb, William Morris Agency. *Address:* History Department, Indiana State University, Terre Haute, IN 47809, USA.

WILLIAMS John, b. 1922, American. *Appointments:* Instructor, University of Missouri, 1950-54; Editor, Twentieth Century Literature: A Scholarly and Critical Journal, 1954-56, and University of Denver Quarterly: A Journal of Modern Culture, 1965-70; Director, Workshop for Writers 1954-59, Creative Writing Program 1954-74, Assistant Professor 1954-60, Associate Professor 1960-64, Professor of English 1964-1985, University of Denver, CO. *Publications:* Nothing But the Night, 1948; The Broken Landscape, 1949; Butcher's Crossing, 1960; English Renaissance Poetry (ed), 1963; Stoner, 1965; The Necessary Lie, 1965; Augustus, 1972. *Honours:* American Academy and Institute of Arts and Letters Award in Literature, 1985; Guggenheim Fellowship, 1985; National Book Award.

WILLIAMS John Taylor, b. 19 June 1938, Cambridge, Massachusetts, USA. Attorney. m. Leonora Hall, 12 Nov 1967, 3 sons. *Education:* AB, Harvard College, LLB, University of Pennsylvania Law School. *Appointments:* National Endowment for the Arts, Literary Panel, 1989, 1990, 1991. *Publications:* Small Voices and Great Trumpets: Minorities and the Media, Contributing Editor, 1980 (Praeger); Legal Problems in Book Publishing, Contributing Author, 1981, 1984, 1986; The Publishing Law Handbook, co-Author, revised annually, Prentice Hall; Libel Defense Resource Centre: Annual 50 State Survey, LDRC, NYC Massachusetts Reporter; Rolf in the Woods, screenplay, 1987; Toussaint L'Overture, screenplay, 1989. *Contributions to:* The Lawyer's Role in the Acquisition and Exploitation of Life Story Rights, Boston Bar Journal, co-Author, 1987. *Memberships:* Authors Guild; American Bar Association, Section of Patent, Trademark and Copyright Law; Chairman, Committee on Authors 1978-81; Communications and Entertainment Law Forum Committees; Massachusetts Bar Association, Business Law and Computer Law Sections. *Literary Agent:* The Palmer & Dodge Agency, Boston, MA. *Address:* Palmer & Dodge, One Beacon Street, Boston, MA 02108, USA.

WILLIAMS Malcolm David, b. 9 Apr 1939, Cwmllynfell, Nr Swansea, South Wales. Author. Widower, 1 daughter. *Education:* Certificate in Education (Distinction), Birmingham University Institute, 1961. *Publications include:* Yesterdays Secret, 1980; Poor Little Rich Girl, 1981; Debt of Friendship, 1981; Another Time, Another Place, 1982; My Brother's Keeper, 1982; The Stuart Affair, 1983; The Cordillera Conspiracy, 1983; The Girl from Derry's Bluff, 1983; Sorrow's End, 1984; A Corner of Eden, 1984; A Stranger on Trust, 1987; Shadows From the Past, 1989. *Contributions to:* Several hundred short stories to various magazines, newspapers, in 13 different languages; poems; articles; radio play; 43 Serial Stories Published in Magazines, UK and Abroad. *Honours:* 1st prize, Short Story Competitions, City of Worcester College of Education, 1961; 1st Prize, Short Story Competition, Anglo-Welsh Review, 1969. *Memberships:* Society of Authors; West Country Writers Association; Fellow, World Literacy Academy. *Address:* 40 Longlands Road, Bishops Cleeve, Cheltenham, Glos. GL52 4JP, England.

WILLIAMS Margaret Frances Howell, b. 25 Jan 1912, Talladega County, USA. Retired Educator; Writer. m. Howard Eldridge Williams, 1 son, 1 daughter. *Education:* Andrew College, Cuthbert, Georgia, 1928-29; Abraham Baldwin College, Tifton, Georgia, 1930; AB, Valdosta State College, Valdosta, Georgia, 1932; Graduate work, University of Alabama, 1949, Birmingham Southern 1950. *Literary Appointments:* State President of Alabama Association National League of American Pen Women, 1986-88; First Vice President of Alabama State Poetry Society, 1984-86; Alabama

Reporter for STROPHES-WFSPS, 1980-93. *Publications:* International Who's Who in Poetry Anthology, 1972; Celebrating T S Eliot-On the Centennial of His Birth, 1888-1988, Wyndham Hall Press, Bristol Banner Books; Emily Dickinson - A Centennial Celebration 1890-1990 to appear in Nov 1990, Wyndham Hall Press; Contributor to ALALITCOM, publication of Alabama Writers Conclave, published annually; New Voices in the Wind, 1969; Yearbook of Modern Poetry, 1971. *Contributions to:* Journals, including Negative Capability, Dear Magnolia, Voices International, Tennessee Voices; Poem Published in Voices International, 1991; Poem to be published in Centennial Celebrating, Edna St Vincent Millay, 1992. *Honours include:* Many prizes from Alabama Writers Conclave, Birmingham Quill Club, Mid- South Poetry Club; First Prize Award in Poetry from Alabama Assoc, National League of American Pen Women, 1991. *Memberships include:* Alabama Writers Conclave; Birmingham Quill Club; Poetry Society of Tennessee; Birmingham Branch of NLAPW, President 1982-84; Birmingham Education Association; Alabama Education Association. *Address:* 215 West Linwood Drive, Birmingham AL 35209, USA.

WILLIAMS Masha, b. 23 May 1914, Petrograd, Russia. Writer. m. Sir Alan Williams, 17 Aug 1946, 1 son, 1 daughter. *Education:* Montreux College, Switzerland 1928-30; Responsions-Certificat D'Etudes Secondaires; Oxford Exhibitioner, LMH 1933-36; MA Oxon Hons degree. *Publications:* White Among the Reds, 1980; The Consul's Memsahib, 1985; Exiled to America, 1987; In the Bey's Palace, 1990. *Contributions to:* The Guardian; Britain-USSR, Planet Arcade; The Old Lady; LMH Brown Book; Hendon & Finckley Times; The Police Journal; Chronicle; The Nursing Mirror; Hampstead & Highgate Express; Anglia; Matrix; North Wales Weekly; Russian papers. *Memberships:* International PEN; Society of Authors; Diplomatic Service Wives' Association, Founder. *Address:* 1 Morland Close, Hampstead Way, London NW11 7JG, England.

WILLIAMS Miller, University Press Director. m. *Education:* BS, Biology, Arkansas State College, 1950; MS, Zoology, University of Arkansas, 1952. *Literary Appointments:* Founder, Editor, New Orleans Review, Loyola University, 1968-70; Advisory Editor, New Orleans Review, 1975- ; Contributing Editor, Translation Review, 1976-80. *Publications:* Books include: A Circle of Stone, 1964; Recital, 1964; 19 Poetas De Hoy En Los Estados, 1966; Southern Writing in The Sixties: Poetry 1966, Fiction 1966, (with J W Corrington); Poems & Antipoems (translation from Nicanor Parra), 1967; So Long at the Fair (Poems E P Dutton), 1968; Chile: An Anthology of New Writing, 1968; The Achievement of John Ciardi, 1968; The Only World There Is (Poems E P Dutton), 1968; The Poetry of John Crowe Ransom, 1971; Emergency Poems (translation from Nicanor Parra, New Directions), 1972; Contemporary Poetry in America, 1972; Halfway from Hoxie, New and Selected Poems, 1973; How Does a Poem Mean? (W John Ciardi), 1974; Railroad (with James Alan McPherson), 1976; Why God Permits Evil (poems), 1977; A Roman Collection, 1980; Sonnets of Guiseppe Belli (translation), 1981; Distration (poems), 1981; Ozark, Ozard: A Hillside Reader, 1981; The Boys on Their Bony Mules, 1983; Imperfect Love, 1986; Patterns of Poetry, 1986; Living On The Surface: New & Selected Poems, 1989; Adjusting to the Light (poems), 1992. *Contributions to:* Letras, Peru; Oberlin Quarterly; Saturday Review. *Honours include:* Henry Bellaman Poetry Award, 1957; Bread Loaf Fellowship in Poetry, 1961; Fulbright Lecturer in US Literature, National University of Mexico, 1970-; Prix de Rome, American Academy of Arts & Letters, 1976; DHum, Lander College, 1983; National Poets Prize, 1992. *Address:* University of Arkansas Press, Fayetteville, AR 72701, USA.

WILLIAMS Muriel E. (Betty) Rasmussen-Kay, b. 27 Nov 1920, Los Angeles, California, USA. Writer; Legal Executive Secretary; Independent Contractor. *Education:* Fellow of Religious Science, Ernest Holmes

College, 1985; Los Angeles Junior College of Business; Legal Research, El Camino College, Occidental College, Los Angeles City College, 1989. *Appointments:* Writer of action letters (confidential) to people in high places. *Publications:* Occasional poems. *Honours:* International Cultural Diploma of Honour, 1988; Deputy Life Governor, American Biographical Institute Research Association; Medal of Honour Commemorating Distinguished Lifelong Achievement; Biographical Roll of Honour; International Hall of leaders. *Memberships:* National Writers Union; League of Religious Science Practitioners; Republican Presidential Task Force; American Marketing Association; American Statistical Association. *Address:* 17102 Glenbury Avenue, Torrance, CA 90504, USA.

WILLIAMS Nigel, b. 1948. Author; Playwright. *Publications:* My Life Closed Twice (novel), 1977; Class Enemy, 1978; Jack Be Nimble (novel), 1980; Sugar and Spice and Trial Run, 1981; W.C.P.C., 1983; Johnny Jarvis (novel), 1983; Charlie (novel),1984; Star Turn (novel), 1985; My Brother's Keeper, 1985; Witchcraft (novel), 1987; Country Dancing, 1987. *Publications:* c/o Judy Daish Associates Limited, 83 Eastbourne Mews, London, W2 6LQ, England.

WILLIAMS Thomas, b. 15 Nov 1926, Duluth, Minnesota, USA. Writer. *Education:* BA, MA, University of New Hampshire. *Publications:* Ceremony of Love, 1955; Town Burning, 1959; The Night of Trees, 1961; A High New House, 1963; Whipple's Castle, 1969; The Hair of Harold Roux, 1974; Tsuaga's Children, 1977; The Followed Man, 1978; The Moon Pinnace, 1986. *Contributions To:* New Yorker; Esquire; Kenyon Review; Saturday Evening Post; Harpers. *Honours:* Guggenheim Fellowship, 1963; Dial Fellowship for Fiction, 1963; Rockefeller Fellowship for Fiction,1 968; National Book Award, 1975. *Memberships:* Authors' Guild. *Literary Agent:* RLR Associates Ltd. *Address:* 13 Orchard Drive, Durham, NH 03824, USA.

WILLIAMSON David Geoffrey, b. 25 Feb 1927, Haywards Heath, Sussex, England. Editor. *Appointments include:* Staff, Burke's Peerage Ltd, 1950-83; Co-editor, Debrett's Peerage, 1983-; Editor, Debrett's Distinguished People of Today, 1986-. *Publications include:* Debrett's Kings & Queens of Britain, 1986; Debrett's Book of the Royal Engagement, with Jean Goodman, 1986; The Counts Bobrinskoy, 1963. Also: Principal compiler, Burke's Guide to Royal Family, Burke's Presidential Families of USA (2 editions), Burke's Royal Families of the World (2 volumes); Debrett's Kings & Queens of Europe, 1988; Debrett's Presidents of the United States of America, 1989. *Contributions to:* Genealogists Magazine; Coat of Arms; Notes & Queries. *Memberships:* Fellow, Society of Genealogists; Fellow, Society of Antiquaries, Scotland; Association of Genealogists and Record Agents, Chairman of Council, 1985-89. *Address:* 7 Bonchurch Road, London W10 5SD, England.

WILLIAMSON David Keith, b. 24 Feb 1942, Melbourne, Victoria, Australia. Playwright; Screenwriter. m. Kristin Ingrid Lofven, 30 May 1974, 2 sons, 1 daughter. *Education:* BE, Monash University. *Publications:* Plays produced/published: The Removalists, 1972; Don's Party, 1972; The Department, 1974; a Handful of Friends, 1976; The Club, 1977; Travelling North, 1980; The Perfectionist, 1982; Sons of Cain, 1985; Emerald City, 1987; Top Silk, 1988; Siren, 1990; Screenplays for: Gallipoli, 1981; The Year of Living Dangerously (principal credit), 1983; Phar Lap, 1983; Travelling North, 1986; Emerald City, 1988. *Honours:* Co-Recipient, George Devine Award, London, 1972; Most Promising Playwright, London Evening Standard, 1973; 4 Australian Film Institute Awards; 11 Australian Writers Guild Awards; Officer of the Order of Australia, 1983; Honorary DLitt, Sydney University, 1988; Honorary DLitt, Monash University, 1990. *Memberships:* President, Australian Writers Guild; Trustee, Sydney Opera House Trust. *Literary Agent:* Anthony Williams Management. *Address:* c/o Anthony

Williams Management, 50 Oxford Street, Paddington, Sydney, New South Wales, Australia.

WILLIAMSON J. N. (Gerald), b. 18 Apr 1932, Indianapolis, Indiana, USA. Author; Editor. m. Mary Theresa Cavanaugh Welhoelter, 29 July 1960, 2 sons, 4 stepchildren. *Education:* Graduated Shortridge High School; Jordan College of Music; Butler University, Indianapolis. *Literary Appointment:* Associate Editor, Writer's Digest School. *Publications:* 27 novels including: Playmates, 1981, reprinted 1986; Horror House, 1981, reprinted 1987; Death-Coach, 1982; The Evil One, 1982, reprinted 1987; Ghost, 1984; The Longest Night, 1985; Evil Offspring, 1987; The Houngan; Ghost Mansion; Horror Mansion; The Ritual; The Offspring; Hour; Brotherkind; Noonspell; Dead to the World. Editor: Masques (anthology), 1984; Masques II (anthology), 1987; How To Write Tales of Horror, Fantasy and Science Fiction, 1988; Masques III (anthology), 1989; The Black School, 1989; Shadows of Death, 1989; Hell Storm, 1990; The Night Seasons, 1990. *Contributions to:* Over 100 short stories, articles and columns in various periodicals including: Twilight Zone; Night Cry; Ellery Queen's Mystery Magazine; Baker Street Journal; Sherlock Holmes Journal (London); Macabre (UK); Australian Horror and Fantasy; Borderland (Canada); Pursuit (Journal of Society for the Investigation of The Unexplained); Horrible Dictu column, Riverside Quarterly; The Dark Corner, 2AM; Pulphouse. *Honours:* Titular Investiture, Baker Street Irregulars, 1950; Bronze Award for Best Fantasy Novel, West Coast Review of Books, 1980; Best Professional Achievement Award, Balrog, 1984; 2 nominations for Balrog Awards, 1984; Dale Donaldson Memorial Award for Service, Small Press Writers and Artists Organization, 1985; Runner-up, Best Anthology or Collection, World Fantasy Awards, 1985, 1987; 2 short stories in preliminary ballot for Nebula Awards, Science Fiction Writers of America, 1986; Nomination for Dale Donaldson Memorial Award, 1987. *Memberships:* Science Fiction Writers of America; Secretary, Horror Writers of America; past member, Authors Guild and Mystery Writers of America. *Literary Agent:* Lori Perkins, Barbara Lowenstein Association Inc, 121 W 27th Street, New York, NY 10001, USA. *Address:* P.O. Box 26117, Indianapolis, IN 46226, USA.

WILLIAMSON Jack (John Stewart Williamson), b. 29 Apr 1908, Bisbee, Arizona, USA. Writer. m. Blanche Slaten Harp, 15 Aug 1947, dec 1985, 2 step-children. *Education:* BA, MA 1957, Eastern New Mexico University; LHD (hon) 1981; PhD 1964, University Colorado. *Appointments:* Professor English, Eastern New Mexico University, Portales 1960-77. *Publications include:* Science Fiction: The Legion of Space, 1947; Darker Than You Think, 1948; The Humanoids, 1949; The Green Girl, 1950; The Cometeers, 1950; One Against the Legion, 1950; Seetee Shock, 1950; Seetee Ship, 1950; Dragon's Island, 1951; The Legion of Time, 1952; Dome Around America, 1955; The Trial of Terra, 1962; Golden Blood, 1964; The Reign of Wizadry, 1965; Bright New Universe, 1967; Trapped in Space, 1968; The Pandora Effect, 1969; People Machines, 1971; The Moon Children, 1972; H G Wells: Critic of Progress, 1973; Teaching SF, 1975; The Early Williamson, 1975; The Power of Blackness, 1976; The Best of Jack Williamson, 1978; Brother to Demons, Brother to Gods, 1979; Teaching Science Fiction: Education for Tomorrow, 1980; The Alien Intelligence, 1980; The Humanoid Touch, 1980; Manseed, 1982; The Queen of a Legion, 1983; Wonder's Child: My Life in Science Fiction, 1984; Lifeburst, 1984; Firechild, 1986; Mazeway, 1990; Beachhead, 1992; Co-Author with Frederik Pohl: Undersea Quest, 1954; Undersea Fleet, 1955; Undersea City, 1956; The Reefs of Space, 1964; Starchild, 1965; Rogue Star, 1969; The Farthest Star, 1975; Wall Around a Star, 1983; Land's End, 1988; With James Gunn: Star Bridge, 1955; With Miles J Breuer: The Birth of an New Republic, 1981. *Honours:* Pilgrim Award 1968, Science Fiction Research Association; Grand Master Nebula Award 1976; Hugo Award for Wonder's Child: My Life in Science Fiction, 1985; *Memberships:* Science Fiction Writers of America, President 1978-80; Science Fiction Research

Association; World Science Fiction Planetary Society. *Address:* PO Box 761, Portales, NM 88130, USA.

WILLIAMSON John Gordon, b. 2 May 1949, Glasgow, Scotland. Lecturer in Music. m. Rosemary Ann Smith, 29 Mar 1979, 1 son, 1 daughter. *Education:* MA Hons Music & History 1970, University of Glasgow; D Phil 1975, Balliol College, Oxford. *Publications:* The Music of Hans Pfitzner, 1992; Richard Strauss: Also Sprach Zarathustra, 1993. *Contributions to:* Music Analysis; Music and Letters; Music Review; Musical Times; THES; New Hungarian Quarterly; The Consort. *Memberships:* Royal Musical Association; International Gustav Mahler Society, Vienna; Hans Pfitzner-Gesellschaft, member of the Praesidium. *Address:* Department of Music, The University, PO Box 147, Liverpool L69 3BX, England.

WILLIAMSON Robin, b. 24 Nov 1943, Edinburgh, Scotland. Writer; Musician; Storyteller. m. Bina Jasbinder Kaur Williamson, 2 Aug 1989, 1 son, 1 daughter. *Publications:* The Crandeskin Bag, 1989; Selected Writings 1980- 83, 1984; Five Denials on Merlins Grave, 1979; Home Thoughts from Abroad, 1972; various music books, spoken word cassettes and records. *Contributions to:* Poetry London, 1982. *Literary Agent:* Anthea Morton Stainer, Curtis Brown, London. *Address:* BCM 4797, London WC1N 3XX, England.

WILLIAMSON Tony (Anthony George Williamson), b. 1932, British. *Appointments:* Journalist, Kemsley/ Thomson newspaper, 1954-60, and CBC- TV, Montreal, 1960-63; Story Editor, BBC, London, 1966. *Publications:* Night Watch, 1972; The Connector, Counter Strike: Entebe, 1976; The Fabulous Assassin, Doomsday Contract, 1977; Technicians of Death, 1978; Breakthrough, Samson Strike, 1979, TV adaption, 1985; Night Without End, Slade's Marauders (as Steven Cade), 1980; Warhead, 1981; Barrington's Women (as Steven Cade), 1982; Ask Any Neighbour; Cage of Canvas; Victim; The Avengers; The Persuaders; Jason King; The Champions; Department S; Randall and Hopkirk; Z Cars; The Spies; Mask of Janus; Codename; Dr Finlay's Casebook; The Revenue Men; Spy Trap; Dixon of Dock Green; Counter-strike; The Adventurer; Strike the Devil, The Cabinet Mole, 1985. *Address:* C/o Robin Lowe, M L Representation, 194 Old Brompton Road, London, England.

WILLINGS David Richard, b. 16 May 1932, Cambridge, England. Director Willings Learning Clinic. *Education:* BA Hons Spanish 1957, University of Durham; MA Psychology 1962, University of London; PhD Guidance and Counselling 1972, University of Strathclyde. *Appointments:* Senior Advisory Editor, STI Publishers, Brockville, Ontario 1980-89; Contributing Editor, Roeper Review 1985-91; Editorial Board, Gifted Education International 1986-; Assistant to the Editor, Gifted Education International 1988-. *Publications:* Pseudo Scientific Thinking in Modern Psychology, 1962; The Creatively Gifted, book version of PhD thesis, 1980; Operation Counter Attack, charts and manual for teenage rape victims, 1990; Yerma 1990, adaptation and translation of Yerma by F Garcìa Lorca 1933, 1990; Minds Divorced, play on multi talented woman, co-author, 1992; Adventure in Creative Expression, 1993; Who am I, short story set in South Africa, 1993. *Contributions to:* Channel 4 TV: Roeper Review, Gifted Education International; Glasgow Herald; Teaching Exceptional Children; Social Service Quarterly; Sunday Express; International Journal for the Advancement of Counselling. *Honours:* Gold Medal for Outstanding Services to Canadian Fencing 1976, 1977, 1978; Sport Canada Award for Services to Amateur Sport, 1977; New Brunswick Minister of Youth Award for Services to Youth, 1984. *Memberships:* Fellow, World Literary Academy 1986-; Umpire and Coach various hockey clubs and fencing clubs 1950s-1992 (dropped due to severe heart attack); Director, World Federation of Innovators' Clubs 1986-92; President, International Winnie the Pooh Club 1988-92 (in 1992 both clubs were amalgamated). *Address:* Willings Learning Clinic, 116

Gaywood Road, King's Lynn, Norfolk PE30 2PX, England.

WILLIS Connie (Constance E), b. 31 Dec 1945, Denver, Colorado, USA, Writer, m. Courtney W Willis, 1967, 1 daughter. *Education:* BA, English and Elementary Education, 1967. *Appointments:* Artist in Residence for the Colorado Public Schools, 1986, 1987. *Publications Include:* Doomsday Book, 1992; Lincoln's Dreams, 1987; Fire Watch, 1985; Light Raid, (Co-author Cynthia Felice), 1989; Water Witch, (Co-author Cynthia Felice), 1982. *Contributions to:* Isaac Asimov's Science Fiction magazine; Asimov's. *Honours:* Nebula Award for short story, A Letter from the Clearys, 1982; Nebula Award for novelette, Fire Watch; Hugo Award for novelette Fire watch; Nebula Award, Best Novella, The Last of the Winnebagos, 1983; Hugo Award for The Last of the Winnebagos; Nebula Award Best Noveletle, At the Rialto, 1989; Best Short Story, Even the Queen, 1992. *Memberships:* Science Fiction Writers of America, Trustee, 2 years; Science Fiction Writers of America. *Literary Agent:* Ralph Vicinanza, 111 Eighth Avenue, New York, NY 10011, USA. *Address:* 1716 13th Avenue, Greeley, CO 80631, USA.

WILLIS Meredith Sue, b. 31 May 1946, West Virginia, USA. Writer; Teacher. m. Andrew B Weinberger, 9 May 1982, 1 son. *Education:* BA, Barnard College, 1969; MFA, Columbia University, 1972. *Publications:* A Space Apart, 1979; Higher Ground, 1981; Personal Fiction Writing, 1984; Only Great Changes, 1985; Blazing Pencils, 1991; Quilt Pieces, 1990. *Honours:* Fellowship, National Endowment for the Arts, 1978; New Jersey Literary Fellowship, 1989. *Memberships:* PEN; Authors Guild; National Writers Union. *Literary Agent:* Wendy Weil. *Address:* 311 Prospect St, South Orange, NJ 07079, USA.

WILLIS Valerie Joan, (Val), b. 29 June 1946, Stockport. Head Teacher; Writer. 1 son, 1 daughter. *Publications:* The Secreta in the Matchbox, 1988; Silly Little Chick, 1988; The Surprise in the Wardrobe, 1990; The Mystery in the Bottle, 1991. *Honours:* Runner Up to Mother Goose Award, 1989; Parents Choice Award, USA, 1992. *Address:* 4 Nearton End, Swanbourne, Nr Mursley, Bucks MK17 0SL, England.

WILLOUGHBY Cass. *See:* **OLSEN Theodore Victor.**

WILLOUGHBY Hugh. *See:* **HARVEY Nigel.**

WILLS Alfred John, b. 23 Nov 1927, Wickham, Hants., England. Retired Schoolmaster. *Education:* BA Hons, Trinity College, Oxford, 1949; Postgraduate Certificate in Education, London University Institute of Education, 1951. *Publications:* Introduction to the History of Central Africa, 1985; The Story of Africa, Book 1, 1968; Book 2, 1969. *Memberships:* P.E.N. International; Historical Association. *Address:* 28 Players Way, Norwich NR6 7AU, England.

WILLS Jean, b. 10 Feb 1929, West London, England. Author. m. Graham Boyce Wills, 15 Nov 1952, 2 sons, 1 daughter. *Publications:* The Sawdust Secret, 1973; The Sugar Trail, 1974; Who Wants a Job?, 1976; The Hope & Glory Band, 1978; Round the Twist, 1979; Sandy's Gargoyle, 1979; Nicky and the Genius, 1980; May Day Hullabaloo, 1981; Stargazers' Folly, 1982; The Railway Computer, 1983; When I Lived Down Cuckoo Lane..., 1988. *Membership:* Society of Authors. *Address:* 70 Highview Road, London W13 0HW, England.

WILMER Clive, b. 10 Feb 1945, Harrogate, Yorkshire, England. Freelance Teacher, Lecturer, Writer. m. Diane Redmond, 12 Sept 1971, 1 son, 1 daughter. *Education:* Kings College, Cambridge, 1964-67, 1968-71; BA 1st Class Hons, English, 1967; MA, 1970, Kings College, Cambridge. *Appointments:* Exhibition Committee, Pound's Artists, Tate Gallery, London and Kettle's Yard, Cambridge, 1984-85; Visitng Professor, Creative

Writing, University of California, Santa Barbara, 1986; Presenter of BBC Radio 3 Series, Poet of the Month, 1989-92. *Publications:* Poems: The Dwelling Place, 1977; Devotions, 1982; Of Earthly Paradise, 1992; Translated with G Gömöri: Miklós Radnóti, Forced March, 1979; György Petri, Night Song of the Personal Shadow, 1991; Editor of: Thom Gunn: The Occasions of Poetry, 1982; John Ruskin: Unto This Last and other writings, 1985; Dante Gabriel Rossetti: Selected Poems and Translations, 1991; William Morris: News From Nowhere and other writings, 1993. *Contributions to:* PN Review; Spectator; Southern Review; TLS; London Review of Books; Poetry Review; Agenda; Times; Poetry Durham; Guardian; Modern Painters; Daily Telegraph; New Statesman; Aquarius, and others. *Honours:* Cambridge University Chancellor's Medal for anEnglish Poem, 1967; Arts Council Grant GB, Writer's Grant, 1978; Artisjus (Budapest), translator's prize, 1980. *Membership:* Cambridge Poetry Festival Society, 1975-86; Cambridge Poetry Society, Chairman, 1981-83. *Literary Agent:* A.M. Heath. *Address:* 57 Norwich Street, Cambridge CB2 1ND, England.

WILOCH Thomas, b. 3 Feb 1953, Detroit, Michigan, USA. Writer; Editor. m. Denise Gottis, 10 Oct 1981. *Education:* BA, Wayne State University, 1978. *Appointments:* Associated with Gale Research Inc, 1977-; Freelance writing and editing; Columnist, Retrofuturism, 1991-; Book Reviewer, Anti-Matter Magazine, 1992-. *Publications:* Stigmata Junction, 1985; Paper Mask, 1988; The Mannikin Cypher, 1989; Tales of Lord Shantih, 1990; Decoded Factories of the Heart, 1991; Night Rain, 1991; Narcotic Signature, 1992; Lyrical Brandy, 1993. *Contributions to:* Over 200 magazines including: Bloomsbury Review; Small Press Review; Hawaii Review. *Honours:* Nomination, Pushcart Prize, 1988, 1990; Nomination, Rhysling Award, 1992. *Memberships:* Science Fiction Poetry Association; Creative Writers in the Schools; People Against Pluralities. *Address:* 43672 Emrick Dr, Canton, MI 48187, USA.

WILSON Alexander (Sandy) Galbraith, b. 19 May 1924, Sale, Cheshire, England. Writer; Composer. *Education:* Oxford University; Old Vic Theatre School. *Appointments:* Wrote Revues for: Watergate Theatre, London, See You Later, See You Again, 1951-52; Wrote Musical, The Boy Friend, for Players Club Theatre, 1953, transferred to Wyndhams Theatre and on Broadway, 1954, London Revival, 1984; The Buccaneer, 1955; Valmouth, Lyric Hammersmith, 1958, transferred to Saville, 1959, York Playhouse New York, 1960, revived Chichester, 1982; Divorce me Darling, 1965; Director, London revival of The Boy Friend, 1967; Composed music for As Dorothy Parker Once Said, London, 1969; Songs for BBC TV Charley's Aunt, 1969; Wrote & performed Sandy Wilson Thanks the Ladies (one man show), 1971; Wrote His Monkey Wife, 1971; The Clapham Wonder, 1978. *Publications:* This is Sylvia, 1954; The Poodle from Rome, 1962; I Could be Happy (autobiography), 1975; Ivor, 1975; The Roaring Twenties, 1977. *Address:* 2 Southwell Gardens, London, SW7, England.

WILSON Andrew James (Snoo Wilson), b. 2 Aug 1948, England. Writer. m. Ann McFerran, 1976, 2 sons, 1 daughter. *Education:* BA, English & American Studies, University of East Anglia. *Appointments include:* Associate director, Portable Theatre 1970-75; Dramaturge, Royal Shakespeare Company 1975-76; Script editor, Play for Today, 1976. *Publications include:* Plays: Co-author, Layby, 1972; Pignight, 1972; The Pleasure Principle, 1973; Blowjob, 1974; Soul of the White Ant, 1976; England England, 1978; Vampire, 1978; The Glad Hand, 1978; A Greenish Man, 1978; The Number of the Beast, 1982; Flaming Bodies, 1982; Grass Widow, 1983; Loving Reno, 1983; Hamlyn, 1984. Novels: Spaceache, 1984; Inside Babel, 1985. Opera: Orpheus in the Underworld (new version), 1984. Filmscript, Shadey, 1986. *Honours:* Henfield Fellow, 1978; US Bicentennial Fellow, Playwriting, 1981-82. *Address:* 41 The Chase, London SW4 0NP, England.

WILSON A(ndrew) N(orman), b. 27 Oct 1950, Stone, Staffordshire, England. Writer. m. Katherine Duncan-Jones, 1971, 2 daughters. *Education:* MA, New College, Oxford, c 1976. *Appointments:* Writer; Teacher at Oxford University and a tutorial agency, 1975; Schoolmaster, Merchant Taylor's School, Northwood, Middlesex, England, 1975-80; Lecturer in English, Oxford University, 1977-80; Teacher, Stanford University, 1978-80. *Publications:* Novels: The Sweets of Pimlico, 1977; Unguarded Hours, 1978; Kindly Light, 1979; The Healing Art; 1980; Who Was Oswald Fish? Secker & Warburg 1981, David & Charles, 1983; Wise Virgin, Secker & Warburg 1982, Viking 1983; Scandal; or Priscilla's Kindness, Hamish Hamilton, 1983, Viking, 1984; Gentleman in England: A Vision, 1985; Love Unknown, Hamish Hamilton, 1986, Viking 1987; Non-fiction: The Laird of Abbotsford: A View of Sir Walter Scott, 1980; The Life of John Milton, 1983; Hilaire Belloc, Hamish Hamilton 1984, Atheneum, 1984; How Can We Know? As Essay on the Christian Religion, 1985; (with Charles Moore and Gavin Stamp) The Church in Crisis, 1986; Tolstoy, 1988; Eminent Victorians, 1989; Penfriends from Porlock, 1989; C.S. Lewis (a biography), 1990; Against Religion, 1991; Jesus, 1992. *Honours:* Chancellor's Essay Prize from Oxford University, 1971; Ellerton Theological Prize from Oxford University, 1975; John Llewelyn Rhys Memorial Prize, 1978, for The Sweets of Pimlico; Somerset Maugham Award, Southern Arts Prize and Arts Council National Book Award, all 1981, all for The Healing Art; John Llewelyn Rhys Memorial Prize, 1981, for The Laird of Abbotsford: A View of Sir Walter Scott; W H Smith Literary Award, 1983, for Wise Virgin; Whitbread Biography Award, 1988 for Tolstoy. *Membership:* Fellow, Royal Society of Literature. *Literary Agent:* A D Peters Ltd, London. *Address:* c/o A D Peters Ltd, 10 Buckingham Street, London WC2N 6BU, England.

WILSON Barbara. *See:* **HARRIS Laurence Mark.**

WILSON Budge Marjorie, b. 2 May 1927, Halifax, Nova Scotia, Canada. Writer. m. Alan Wilson, 31 July 1953, 2 daughters. *Education:* BA, 1949, Diploma in Education, 1952, Dalhousie University. *Publications:* The Best-Worst Christmas Present Ever, 1984; A House Far from Home, 1986; Mr John Bertrand Nijinsky and Charlie, 1986; Mystery Lights at Blue Harbour, 1987; Breakdown, 1988; Going Bananas, 1989; Thirteen Never Changes, 1989; Madame Belzile and Ramsay Hitherton-Hobbs, 1990; Lorinda's Diary, 1991; The Leaving, adult and young adult, 1990; Oliver's Wars, 1992; Many adult and children's short stories. *Honours:* CBC Literary Competition, 1981; Atlantic Writing Competition, 1986; City of Dartmouth Book Award, 1991; Young Adult Book Award, Canadian Library Association, 1991; Marianna Dempster Award, Canadian Authors Association, 1992. *Memberships:* Past Vice-President, Writers Federation of Nova Scotia, Writers Federation; Secretary, Atlantic Representative, Canadian Society of Children's Authors, Illustrators and Performers. *Address:* North West Cove, RR 1 Hubbards, Nova Scotia, Canada B0J 1T0.

WILSON Carole. *See:* **WALLMANN Jeffrey M.**

WILSON Carter, b. 27 Dec 1941, Washington DC, USA. Writer. m. Ray Martinez, 29 Oct 1977. *Education:* BA, Harvard University, 1963; MA, Syracuse University, 1966. *Publications:* Treasures on Earth, 1981; Crazy February, 1966; On Firm Ice, 1970; I Have Fought the Good Fight, 1967; A Green Tree and a Dry Tree, 1971; narration The Times of Harvey Milk, (film), 1984. *Contributions to:* The Atlantic; Christopher Street; The Magazine of Fantasy and Science Fiction; The Nation. *Honour:* Member of the Order of Knights of Mark Twain, 1967. *Literary Agent:* Donadio and Ashworth, New York, USA. *Address:* 7229 Mesa Drive, Aptos, CA 95003, USA.

WILSON Catherine Warren, b. 28 Mar 1951, New York City, New York, USA. Philosopher. m. (1) Garry Hagberg, 14 Aug 1981, (2) Alexander Ruger, 4 June

1987, 1 son, 1 daughter. *Education:* Vassar College, 1968-69; BA, Yale University, 1972; BPhil, Oxford University, 1974; PhD, Princeton University, 1977. *Publications:* Leibniz's Metaphysics: A Historical and Comparative Study, 1989. *Contributions to:* Articles and translations to periodicals. *Address:* 10908 126 St., Edmonton, Alta, Canada, T5M OP3.

WILSON Charles, b. Aug 1935, Glasgow, Scotland. Journalist. m. (1) Anne Robinson, 1 daughter, (2) Sally O'Sullivan, 1 son, 2 daughters. *Appointments:* Copy Boy, The People, 1951; Later Reporter with Bristol Evening World, News Chronicle and Daily Mail; Sports Editor, Deputy Northern Editor, Daily Mail; Editor, Evening Times, Glasgow, 1976; later Editor, Glasgow Herald; Editor Sunday Standard, Glasgow, 1981-82; Executive Editor, The Times, 1982, Joint Deputy Editor, 1984-85, Editor, 1985-. *Address:* The Times, PO Box 481, Virginia Street, London E1 9DD, England.

WILSON Charles Presnell, b. 2 Aug 1939, Kennett, Missouri, USA. Author. m. Linda Fay George, 2 sons, 1 daughter. *Education:* Westminster College, Fulton, Missouri; University of Missouri, Columbia; Memphis State University, Memphis, Tennessee. *Publications:* Fiction: Nightwatches, 1990; Silent Witness, 1992; The Cassandra Prophecy, 1993. *Membership:* Author's Guild. *Address:* 119 Longwood, Brandon, MS 39042, USA.

WILSON Christine. *See:* **GEACH Christine.**

WILSON Christopher Richard Maclean, b. 6 Jan 1934, Minehead, Somerset, England. Educator. m. Alma Louis Oliver, 5 Sept 1964, 2 sons. *Education:* BA 1957, MA 1961, St Catharine's College, Cambridge; Clifton Theological School, Bristol; Episcopal Theological School, Cambridge, Mass USA; MA 1971, PhD 1977, University of Toronto. *Appointments:* Director, Board and Management Services, The Ontario Hospital Association 1978-92. *Publications:* Hospital-wide Quality Assurance, 1987; Governing with Distinction, 1988; New on Board, 1991; Strategies in Health Care Quality, 1992; Monographs: Quality Assurance-Getting Started, 1985; Annotated Bibliography on Hospital Governance, 1989; Risk Management for Canadian Health Care Facilities, 1990. *Contributions to:* Canadian, American, British & Australian' journals on management, quality and governance in health care, of over 50 articles. *Honours:* Writer of the Year, Canadian Association for Quality in Health Care 1990; 1992 Honorary Fellow of University of Manchester (1992-94 tenure). *Literary Agent:* MGA/McKnight Group Agency Inc. *Address:* c/o MGA, 10 St Mary Street, Toronto, Ontario M4Y 1P9, Canada.

WILSON Colin Henry, b. 26 July 1931, Leicester, England, Author. m. (1) Dorothy Betty Troop, 1 son, (2) Joy Stewart, 2 sons, 1 daughter. *Appointments:* Laboratory Assistant, Gateway School, 1948-49; Civil Servant, 1949-50; national Service, RAF, AC2, 1949-50; Writer, 1954-; Visiting Professor: Hollins College, Virginiam, 1966-67, niversity of Washington, Seattle, 1967, Dowling College, Majorca, 1969, Rutgers University, New Jersey, 1974. *Publications Include:* The Outsider, 1956; Religion and the Rebel, 1957; The Age of Defeat, 1959; Ritual in the Dark, 1960; The Strength to Dream, 1962; Origins of the Sexual Impulse, 1963; Necessary Doubt, 1964; Eagle and earwig, 1965; The Glass cage, 1966; Sex and the Intelligent Teenager, 1966; Voyage to a Beginning, 1969; Lingard, 1970; Tree by Tolkien, 1973; Hermann Hesse, 1973; Strange Powers, 1973; The Space vampires, 1976; Mysteries, 1978; Starseekers, 1980; Access to Inner Worldws, 1982; Psychic Detectives, 1983; The Essential Colin Wilson, 1984; The Personality Surgeon, 1986; Afterlife, 1986; Jung: The Lord of the Underworld, 1984; Rudolf Steiner: The Man and His Work, 1985; An Enclopedia of Scandal, (Co-author Donald Seaman), 1986; Spider World: The Tower, 1987; Aleister Crowley-The Man and the Myth, 1987; An Encyclopedia of Unsolved Mysteries, (Co-author Damon Wilson), 1987; Marx refuted, 1987;

Written in Blood, 1989; The Misfits- A Study of Sexual Outsiders, 1988; Beyond the Occult, 1988. *Contributions to:* The Spectator; Audio; Books and Bookmen; Hi-Fi News; Sunday Times; Sunday Telegraph. *Address:* Tetherdown, Trewallock Lane, Gorran Heath, Cornwall, England.

WILSON Dave. *See:* **FLOREN Lee.**

WILSON Des, b. 1941, New Zealand. Writer. *Appointments:* Journalist/Broadcaster, 1957-67; Director, Shelter: National Campaign for the Homeless, 1967-71; Columnist: The Guardian, 1968-70; The Observer, 1971- 75; Head of Public Affairs, Royal Shakespeare Company, London, 1974-76; Editor, Social Work Today, 1976-79; Deputy Editor, Illustrated London News, 1979-81; Chairman: Campaign for Lead-Free Air, 1981-85; Friends of the Earth, 1982-86; Campaign for Freedom of Information, 1984-91; President, Liberal Party, 1986-87; General Election Campaign Director, Liberal Democrats, 1991-92. *Publications:* I Know It Was the Place's Fault, 1970; Des Wilson's Minority Report: A Diary of Protest, 1973; So You Want to Be Prime Minister: A Personal View of British Politics, 1979; The Lead Scandal, 1982; Pressure: The A to Z of Campaigning in Britain, 1984; The Environmental Crisis, 1984; The Secrets File, 1984; Costa del Sol (novel), 1990; Campaign (novel), 1992. *Address:* Milestone House, 39 Main Road, Long Bennington, Nr Newark, Notts, NG23 8DJ, England.

WILSON Edward Osborne, b. 10 June 1929. Professor; Author. m. Irene Kelley, 30 Oct 1955, 1 daughter. *Education:* BS, 1949, MS, 1950, University of Alabama; PhD, Harvard University, 1955. *Publications:* The Insect Societies, 1971; Sociobiology: The New Synthesis, 1975; On Human Nature, 1978; Biophilia, 1984; The Ants (with Bert Holldobler), 1990. *Contributions:* 330 articles, mostly scientific. *Honours include:* National Medal of Science, 1977; Pulitzer Prize in General Non-Fiction, 1979; Tyler Prize for Environmental Achievement, 1984; Ingersoll Prize for Scholarly Letters, 1989; Crafoord Prize, Royal Swedish Academy of Sciences, 1990; Prix, Institut de Vie, Paris, 1990. *Memberships include:* National Academy of Sciences; Royal Society, England; American Philosophical Society; American Academy of Arts and Sciences; Royal Society of Sciences of Uppsala; Finnish Academy of Arts and Sciences. *Address:* Museum of Comparative Zoology, Harvard University, Cambridge, MA 02138, USA.

WILSON Elizabeth Jane (Morfitt), b. 29 Oct 1948, Toronto, Canada. Writer; Editor. m. George Norris Wilson, 24 Dec 1980, Toronto. 1 son, 1 daughter. *Education:* BA, English Literature; RN (Nursing diploma). *Appointments:* Managing Editor of The Ontario Appraisal Quarterly. *Publications:* Ottawa: More than a Capital City, 1989. *Contributions to:* Real Estate Apprasials in Canadian Banker, others in Newsletters, Magazines. *Honours:* International Association of Business Communications EXCEL Awards, 1990, 1991. *Memberships:* President, Ottawa Independent Writers. *Address:* 4 Mutchmor Road, Ottawa, Ontario K1S 1L5, Canada.

WILSON F(rancis) Paul, b. 1946, United States of America. Author. *Publications:* Novels: Healer, 1976; Wheels Within Wheels, 1979; An Enemy of the State, 1980; The Keep, 1981; The Tomb, 1984; The Touch, 1986; Black Wind, 1988; Soft & Others, 1989; Dydestown World, 1989; The Tery, 1990; Reborn, 1990; SIBS, 1991; Reprisal, 1991; Nightworld, 1992. *Address:* c/o Albert Zuckerman, Writers House, 21 W. 26th Street, New York, NY 10010, USA.

WILSON Gina, b. 1943. Children's Fiction Writer; Poet. *Appointments:* Assistant Editor, Scottish National Directory, 1967-73; Assistant Editor, Dictionary of the Older Scottish Tongue, Edinburgh, 1972-73. *Publications:* Cora Ravenwing, 1980; A Friendship of

Equals, 1981; The Whisper, 1982; All Ends Up, 1984; Family Feeling, 1986; Just Us, 1988; Polly Pipes Up, 1989; I Hope You Know..., 1989; Jim-Jam Pyjamas, 1990; Wompus Galumpus, 1990; Riding the Great White, forthcoming. *Address:* c/o Faber and Faber Limited, 3 Queen Square, London, WC1N 3AU, England.

WILSON Jacqueline, b. 17 Dec 1945, Bath, Somerset, England. Writer. m. William Millar Wilson, 28 Aug 1965, 1 daughter. *Appointment:* Journalist, D.C. Thomsons, 1963-65. *Publications include:* Nobody's Perfect, 1982; Waiting for the Sky to Fall, 1983; The Other Side, 1984; Amber, 1986; The Power of the Shade, 1987; This Girl, 1988; The School Trip, 1984; The Killer Tadpole, 1984; Stevie Day Series, 1987; Is There Anybody There?, 1990; The Story of Tracy Beaker, 1991; The Mum-Minder, 1993. *Honours:* Runner-up, Observer Teenage Novel Award, 1982, 1984; Shortlisted for the Smarties Award, 1992; Shortlisted for the Carnegie Medal, 1992; Winner of The Oak Tree Award, 1992. *Literary Agent:* Gina Pollinger. *Address:* 1B Beaufort Road, Kingston on Thames, Surrey KT1 2TH, England.

WILSON James Harold, of Rievaulx, b. 11 March 1916, Politician, Writer. m. Gladys Mary Baldwin, 1940, 2 sons. *Education:* Milnsbridge Council School and Royds Hall School, Huddersfield; Wirral Grammar School, Bebington, Cheshire; Jesus College, Oxford (Gladstone Memorial Prize, Webb Medley Economics Scholarship) First Class Hons, Philosophy, Politics and Economics. *Appointments:* Lecturer in Economics, New College, Oxford, 1937; Fellow of University College, 1938; Praelector in Economics and Domestic Bursar, 1945; Director of Economics and Statistics, Ministry of Fuel and Power, 1943-44; MP (Labour) Ormskirk 1945-50, Huyton, Lancs, 1950-83; Parliamentary Secretary to Ministry of Worls 1945-March 1947; Secretary for Overseas Trade, March-October 1947; President, Board of Trade, October 1947- April 1951; Chairman, Labour Party Executive Committee 1961-62; Public Accounts Committee 1959-63; Leader Labour Party 1963-76; Prime Minister and First Lord of the Treasury 1964-70, 1974-76; Leader of the Opposition, 1963- 64, 1970-74; Chairman, Committee to Review the Functioning of Financial Institutions, 1976-80; British Screen Advisory Council, 1985-; Chancellor, Bradford University, 1966-85. *Publications:* New Deal for Coal, 1945; In Place of Dollars, 1952; The War on World Poverty, 1953; The Relevance of British Socialism,1964; Purpose in Politics, 1964; The New Britain (Penguin) 1964; Purpose in Power, 1966; The Labour Government 1964-70'' 1971; The Governance of Britain, 1976; A Prime Minister on Prime Ministers, 1977; Final Term: the Labour Government 1974-76, 1979; The Chariot of Israel, 1981; Harold Wilson Memoirs 1916-64, 1986. *Honours:* KG 1976; OBE 1945; PC 1947; FRS 1969; President, Royal Statistical Society, 1972-73; An Elder Brother of Trinity House, 1968; Hon Fellow, Jesus and University Colleges, Oxford, 1963; Hon Freeman, City of London, 1975; Hon President, Great Britain-USSR Association, 1976-; President, Royal Shakespeare Theatre Company 1976-85; Hon LLD: Lancaster 1964, Liverpool 1965, Nottingham 1966, Sussex 1966, Hon DCL, Oxford, 1965, Hon DTech, Bradford, 1966, DUniv, Essex, 1967, Open 1974, Baron cr. 1983 (Life Peer) of Kirklees in the County of West Yorkshire. *Address:* House of Lords, London SW1, England.

WILSON Joyce Muriel (Joyce Stranger), b. 26 May 1921, Forest Gate, London, England. Writer; Dog Trainer. m. Dr Kenneth Bruce Wilson, 28 Feb 1944, 2 sons, 1 daughter. *Education:* BSc, University College, London, 1939-42. *Publications:* The Running Foxes, 1965; Rex, 1967; Flash, 1976; Walk in the Dark, 1977; Fox at Drummers Darkness, 1978; The Stallion, 1981; Josse: Breed of Giants; Casey; Zara; Never Tell A Secret; Kym; Three's A Pack; Two for Joy; A Dog in a Million; Dog Days; Double or Quit; How to Own a Sensible Dog; Midnight Magic; Animal Sanctuary Trilogy; The Hills Are Lonely; Souvenir; forthcoming, The Secret of Hunter's Keep, over 95 titles. *Contributions to:* Serials in My Weekly and Woman's Realm; Articles in: Our Dogs; Off

Lead (USA); Kennel Gazette: Dogs Monthly; Pet Dog; Cat World. *Honour:* Shortlisted for Trento Award, Italy for Fox at Drummers Darkness, 1978. *Memberships:* President, People and Dogs Society; Patron, The League Against Cruelty to Animals (The Humane Education Society). *Literary Agent:* Brian Stone, Aitken & Stone Ltd. *Address:* c/o Aitken & Stone Ltd, 29 Fernshaw Road, London SW10 0TG, England.

WILSON Keith, b. 26 Dec 1927, Clovis, New Mexico, USA. Poet; Writer. m. Heloise Brigham, 15 Feb 1958, 1 son, 4 daughters. *Education:* BA, US Navy Academy, 1950; MA, University of New Mexico, 1956. *Publications:* Graves Registry and Other Poems, 1969; Homestead, 1969; While Dancing Feet Shatter the Earth, 1978; Lion's Gate, 1988; The Winds of Pentecost, 1991; Graves Registry, 1992. *Honours:* Creative Writing Fellowship, National Endowment for the Arts; Fulbright-Hays Fellowship to Rumania; D H Lawrence Creative Writing Fellowship. *Address:* 1500 South Locust, Las Cruces, NM 88001, USA.

WILSON Lanford, b. 1937, USA. Dramatist. *Appointments:* Co-Founder, Circle Repertory Theatre Co, 1969; Currently Director and Designer, Caffe Cino and Cafe La Mama theatres, New York City, and others. *Publications:* Balm in Gilead and Other Plays, 1965; The Rimers of Eldritch and Other Plays, 1967; The Gingham Dog, 1968; Home Free, and The Madness of Lady Bright, 1968; Lemon Sky, 1970; Serenading Lottie, 1970; The Sand Castle and Three Other Plays, 1970; Summer and Smoke, adaptation, 1971; The Great Nebula in Orion and Three Other Plays, 1972; The Hot L Baltimore, 1972; The Mound Builders, 1975; The 5th of July, 1978; Talley's Folly, 1980; A Tale Told, 1981; Angels Fall, 1982; The Three Sisters by Chekhov, translation, 1984; Talley and Son, 1985; Burn This, 1987. *Honours:* Pulitzer Prize for Talley's Folly. *Address:* c/o Bridget Aschenberg, ICM, 40 West 57th Street, New York, NY 10019, USA.

WILSON Leslie Erica, b. 10 Aug 1952, Nottingham, England. Novelist. m. David Wilson, 20 July 1974, 2 daughters. *Education:* BA (Hons), German, Durham University; PGCE, Oxford. *Publications:* Mourning Is Not Permitted, 1990; Malefice, 1992, French translation, 1994, US publication, 1993. *Contributions to:* Orbis; Writing Women (poetry); Guardian. *Memberships:* Poetry Society; Society of Authors; PEN. *Literary Agent:* A M Heath. *Address:* 33 Surley Road, Caversham, Reading RG4 8ND, England.

WILSON Pat(ricia Elsie), b. 1910, United Kingdom. Dramatist; Poet. *Appointments:* Part-time Lecturer, Longlands College of Further Education, 1956-. *Publications:* N, My Darling Daughter; The Re-Union; Thy Kingdom Come; Little Miracle; A Summer's Tale, 1969; 3 Sheep 2-1/2 Kangaroos, US version One More Time; Four for a Boy, 1972; Jan Adamant, 1972; Rectors' Return, 1973; Enchanted Pantomime, 1973; The Snow Queen, 1973; Ballet Who, 1973; New Broom, 1973; Mixed Bag, 1973; The Teklite, 1973; Fairies at the Bottom of the Garden, 1973; Send Us Victorias, 1973; Funeral Tea, 1974; Hogmanay Hurrah, 1974; Get It All Together, 1974; The Rummage Rip-Off, 1974; Silver Wedding, 1974; Hairy Holiday, 1974; Queen Bee, 1975; Christmas Eve at the Mortuary, 1975; Ashes to Ashes, Crust to Crust, 1976; Christmas Cake and Chuppaties, 1976; Look Both Ways, 1976; I Was Here Before You, So Shove Up, 1977; You Too Can Be a Glamorous Gran, 1978; I Wish I'd Never Asked Them to Come, 1978; What Shall We Call the Baby, 1978; There Is a Fairy Upstairs in Our Attice, 1979; Things That Go Bump in the Night, 1979; Hi Jiminy, 1979; Medium Rare, 1980; Anybody Seen My Body, 1980; Back Door to Heaven, US version Heavenly Highrise, 1980; A Midsummer Nightmare, 1981; The Wok, 1982; Hurrah for Algie's Wedding (with O Wilson), 1986. *Address:* 66 Marwood Drive, Great Ayton, Cleveland TS9 6PD, England.

WILSON Robert Anton, b. 18 Jan 1932, Brooklyn, New York, USA. Author. m. Arlen Riley, 9 Dec 1959,

1 son, 3 daughters. *Education:* Brooklyn Polytechnic, 1952-55; New York University, 1956-57; PhD, Hawthorn Univerity, 1982. *Publications include:* Illuminatus, 1975; Cosmic Trigger, 1977; Masks of the Illuminati, 1981; Schrodinger's Cat, 1981; Right Where You Are Sitting Now, 1982; Prometheus Rising, 1983; The Earth Will Shake, 1985; The Widow's Son, 1985; New Inquisition, 1987. *Contributions to:* Playboy; Oui; New Age; James Joyce Review; Dublin Herald; Sphinx. *Honour:* Award, Classic of Science Fiction, Prometheus Hall of Fame, 1986. *Literary Agent:* Al Zuckerman, Writers House, 21 West 26th Street, New York, NY 10026. *Address:* Tigroney House, Avoca, County Wicklow, Ireland.

WILSON Snoo. *See:* **WILSON Andrew James.**

WINANS Christopher, b. 15 Dec 1950, Philadelphia, Pennsylvania, USA. Journalist. m. Kathy Ann Finch Winans, 10 Apr 1980, 2 sons. *Education:* BA English 1973, Pennsylvania State University. *Publication:* Malcolm Forbes: The Man Who Had Everything, 1990. *Membership:* Authors Guild. *Literary Agent:* Acton & Dystel, New York, New York. *Address:* 979 Iron Bridge Road, Asbury, NJ 08802, USA.

WINCH Donald Norman, b. 15 Apr 1935, London, England. University Professor. m. 5 Aug 1983. *Education:* BSc Economics 1956, London School of Economics; PhD 1960, Princeton University. *Publications:* Classical Political Economy & Colonies, 1965; Economics and Policy, 1969, 1972; Co-author, Economic Advisory Council, 1976; Adam Smith's Politics, 1978; That Noble Science of Politics, co-author, 1983; Malthus, 1987. *Contributions to:* Many learned journals. *Honours:* Fellow, British Academy, 1986; Fellow, Royal Historical Society, 1987. *Memberships:* Royal Economic Society; Review Editor, Economic Journal 1976-83; Publications Secretary, Royal Economic Society 1971-. *Address:* Arts E, University of Sussex, Falmer, Brighton, Sussex BN1 9QN, England.

WINCH Peter Guy, b. 14 Jan 1926, London, England. Professor of Philosophy. m. Jan 1947, 2 sons. *Education:* MA; BPhil, 1951, St. Edmund Hall, Oxford. *Publications:* The Idea of a Social Science, 1951; Ethics and Action, 1972; Trying to Make Sense, 1987; Simone Weil: The Just Balance, 1989; Editor: Studies in the Philosophy of Wittgenstein, 1969; Wittgenstein: Attention to Particulars, 1990; The Political Responsibility of Intellectuals, 1990; contributor to numerous journals and magazines. *Honours:* Senior Research Fellow, Leverhulme Trust, 1976-77; Corresponding Member, Institut fur die Wissenschaften vom Menschen, Vienna, 1986-; Fellow Kings College London, 1985-; Honorary Fellow University College of Swansea, 1990-. *Memberships:* Aristotelian Society, President 1980- 81; American Philosophical Association; Association of University Teachers; American Association of University Professors. *Address:* 310 W. Hill Street 3W, Champaign, IL 61820, USA.

WINDRUSH Elizabeth. *See:* **HARRIS Frida Elizabeth Ruth.**

WINDSOR Patricia (Colin Daniel), b. 21 Sept 1938, New York, USA. Author; Lecturer; Teacher. 1 son, 1 daughter. *Appointments:* Faculty Member, Institute of Children's Literature; University of Maryland Writers Institute; Editor-in-Chief, The Easterner, (Washington DC); Co-Director, Wordspring Literary Consultants. *Publications include:* The Summer Before, 1973; Diving for Roses, 1976; Mad Martin, 1976; Killing Time, 1980; The Sandman's Eyes, 1985; The Hero, 1988; Something's Waiting for You, Baker D., 1974; Home is Where your Feet are Standing, 1975; Just Like the Movies, 1990. *Contributions to:* Seventeen; Family Circle; Womans Journal; Fair Lady; New Idea; Damaras World, and others. *Honours:* Ala Best Book, 1973; Outstanding Books for Young Adults, N.Y. Times, 1976; Edgar Allan Poe Award, Mystery Writers of America,

1986. *Memberships:* The Authors Guild; The Childrens Book Guild; Mystery Writers of America; International Writing Guild; International Association of Business Communications. *Literary Agent:* Amy Berkower, USA; Patricia White, Rogers, Coleridge and White, England. *Address:* Writers House, 21 W. 26th St., New York, NY 10010, USA.

WINE Dick. *See:* **POSNER Richard.**

WINEAPPLE Brenda, b. 5 Feb 1949, Boston, Massachusetts, USA. Writer; Professor of English. m. Michael R Dellaira, 23 Mar 1986. *Education:* BA 1970, Brandeis University; MA 1972, PhD 1976, University of Wisconsin-Madison. *Publication:* Genet: A Biography of Janet Hanner, 1989, repeated 1992. *Contributions to:* Women's Review of Books; Dalhousie Review; Iowa Review; Belles Lettres, inter alia. *Honours:* National Endowment for the Humanities Travel Grant, 1985; National Endowment for the Humanities Fellowship 1986-87; Donald C Gallup Senior Fellow in American Literature, Yale University, 1991; Guggenheim Fellowship, 1992. *Memberships:* MLA; National Women's Council on Research; Biography Seminar, New York University; American Studies Association. *Literary Agent:* Elise Goodman, New York, New York. *Address:* English Department, Union College, Schenectady, NY 12308, USA.

WINEGARTEN Renee b. 23 June 1922, London, England. Literary Critic; Author. m. Asher Winegarten, (dec), 1946. *Education:* MA, 1943; PhD, 1950, Girton College, Cambridge. *Publications:* The Double Life of George Sand: Woman and Writer, 1978; French Lyric Poetry in the Age of Malherbe, 1954; Writers and Revolution, 1974; Madame de Staël, 1985; Simone de Beauvoir: A Critical View, 1988. *Contributions to:* French Studies; Modern Language Review; Encounter; Commentary; The American Scholar; The New Criterion, and others. *Memberships:* Friends of George Sand; Editorial Board, Jewish Quarterly; Society of Authors; The Authors Guild. *Literary Agent:* Georges Borchardt, New York, USA. *Address:* 12 Heather Walk, Edgware, Middlesex HA8 9TS, England.

WINETROUT Kenneth, b. 8 Sept 1912. College Professor. m. 6 May 1944, 1 son, 1 daughter. *Education:* AB, 1935, Ohio University; MA, 1939, PhD, 1947, Ohio State University. *Appointments:* Taught Creative Writing, Stephens College, Columbia, Missouri, Chairman, Department of Education, 1948-49; Margaret C Ells Professor, 1969-78, American International College, Springfield, Massachusetts. *Publications:* F. C. S. Schiller and the Dimensions of Prgamatis, 1967; Arnold Toynbee: The Ecumenical Vision, 1975; After One Is Dead: Arnold Toynbee As Prophet, 1989. *Contributions to:* Bulletin of the Atomic Scientists; Christian Century; ETC: The Journal of General Semantics; Journal of Higher Education; Journal of Individual Psychology; Journal of Thought; Personalist. *Memberships:* John Dewey Society; Philosophy of Education Society; International Society for the Comparative Study of Civilizations. *Address:* 10 Hickory Lane, Hampden, MA 01036, USA.

WINGATE John Allan, b. 15 Mar 1920, Cornwall, England. Author. m. Marie Watts, 25 Oct 1984, 1 son, 1 daughter. *Education:* Royal Naval College, Dartmouth. *Appointment:* Editor, Warship Profiles, 1970. *Publications include:* Submariner Sinclair, 1959; Above the Herison, 1974; Carrier, 1981; Submarine, 1982; Go Deep, 1985; Sub-Zero, 1963; The Sea Above Them, 1978; The Fighting Tenth, 1990. *Contributions to:* Warship Profiles. *Honours:* Admiralty History Prize, 1937; Mentioned in Dispatches, 1942; Distinguished Service Cross, 1943. *Membership:* Associate Member, The Nautical Institute. *Address:* Lloyds Bank Ltd., 16 St James Street, London SW1A 1EY, England.

WINGATE Martha Anne (Martha G Webb), b. 4 Sept 1943, Savannah, Georgia, USA. Writer. m. T Russell

Wingate, 25 May 1985, 1 son 3 daughters. *Education:* BS, Texas A&I University, 1967; MA, Texas Woman's University, 1981; PhD, University of Utah, 1989. *Appointment:* Investigative Reporter, Albany Journal, Albany, Georgia, 1971-72. *Publications:* As Anne Wingate: Death by Deception, 1988 (dissertation novel); The Eye of Anna, 1990; The Buzzards Must Also BE Fed, under negotiation; As Martha G Webb: Darling Corey's Dead, 1984; A White Male Running, 1985; Even Cops' Daughters, 1986; As Lee Martin: Too Sane a Murder, 1984, under option by Ralph Edwards for television production; A Conspiracy of Strangers, 1986; Murder at the Blue Owl, 1988; Death Warmed Over, 1988; Hal's Own Murder Case, 1989; Deficit Ending, 1989; The Mensa Murders, 1990. *Contributions to:* Numerous articles in journals such as Our Navy, The Writer and The Journal of Popular Culture. *Memberships:* Authors Guild; Mystery Writers of America; Modern Language Association. *Literary Agents:* For books: Scott Meredith; For films and television: Robert Goldfarb of the David Shapira Agency. *Address:* P O Box 16536, Salt Lake City, UT 84116, USA.

WINK Walter Philip, b. 21 May 1935, Dallas, Texas, USA. Professor. m. June Keener-Wink, 2 sons, 1 daughter. *Education:* BA magna cum laude 1956, Southern Methodist University; BD 1959, PhD 1963, Union Theological Seminary, New York. *Appointments include:* Professor, Auburn Theological Seminary 1976-. *Publications:* John the Baptist in the Gospel Tradition, 1968; The Bible in Human Transformation, 1973; Transforming Bible Study, 1980, 2nd ed 1990; Naming the Powers, 1984; Unmasking the Powers, 1986; Engaging the Powers, 1992. *Contributions to:* Sojourners; Christian Century; Theology Today; Witness; Fellowship; Weavings; Christianity and Crisis; Interpretation; Review and Expositor; Forum; Religious Studies Review. *Honour:* Peace Fellow, United States Institute of Peace, 1989-90. *Memberships:* Studiorum Novi Testamenti Societas; American Academy of Religion; Society of Biblical Literature. *Address:* HC66, Box 23, Sandisfield, MA 01255, USA.

WINSLOW Pauline Glen, b. London, England. Novelist. m. 18 May 1964. *Education:* High School in England; Studied at Hunter College, Columbia University and New School for Social Research, New York. *Publications:* Novels: The Strawberry Marten, Macmillan 1973, Readers Union 1974, under title Gallow Child, St Martin's 1978; The Windsor Plot, Arlington Books 1981, St Martin's 1985, Paperback 1986; I, Martha Adams, Arlington Books, 1982, St Martin's 1984, Detective Book Club, 1984, Baen Books 1986; The Kindness of Strangers, Arlington Books, 1983; Judgement Day, Arlington Books, 1984, St Martin's 1986 Haunts Book Club, Baen Books 1987; A Cry in the City, St Martin's Press, 1990, Piathus; Mystery Novels (Merle Capricorn Series) Death of an Angel, Macmillan 1975, St Martin's 1975; The Brandenburg Hotel, St Martin's 1976, Macmillan 1976, also published in Holland, Denmark and in US Murder Ink series Detective Book Club; The Witch Hill Murder, St Martin's Press 1977, Collins 1977, Detective Book Club Thriller Book Club, also published in Holland, St Martin's Fingerprint series 1983; Coppergold, St Martin's 1978, Collins 1978, Dell Murder Ink, 1981, Fontana 1982, Detective Book Club, Also published in Japan; The Counsellor Heart, St Martin's 1980, Collins 1980, Detective Book Club under title Sister Death, Fontana 1982; The Rockefeller Gift, St Martin's 1981, Collins 1982 Fontana 1983, Thorpe Detective Book Club; Romantic novels under name of Jane Sheridan. *Contributions to:* Article Anglo-American Conniving in Murderess, Ink, Workman Publishing. *Honours:* Grant award from Yaddo Foundation; Grant award from Huntington Hartford Foundation. *Literary Agent:* Bleecker Street Associates. *Address:* c/o Bleecker Street Associates, 88 Bleecker Street, New York City, NY 10012, USA.

WINSPEAR Violet, b. United Kingdom. Author. *Publications:* Lucifer's Angels, 1961; Wife Without Kisses, 1961; The Strange Waif, 1962; House of Strangers, 1963; Beloved Tyrant, 1964; Cap Flamingo, 1964, Canadian Edition, Nurse at Cap Flamingo, 1965; Love's Prisoner, 1964; Bride's Dilemma, 1965; Desert Doctor, 1965; The Tower of the Captive, 1966; The Viking Stranger, 1966; Tender Is the Tyrant, 1967; The Honey Is Bitter, 1967; Beloved Castaway, 1968; Court of the Veils, 1968; The Dangerous Delight, 1968; Pilgrim's Castle, 1969; The Unwilling Bride, 1969; Blue Jasmine, 1969; Dragon Bay, 1969; Palace of the Peacocks, 1969; The Chateau of St Avrell, 1970; The Cazalet Bride, 1970; Tawny Sands, 1970; Black Douglas, 1971; Dear Puritan, 1971; Bride to Lucifer, 1971; The Castle of the Seven Lilacs,, 1971; Raintree Valley, 1971; The Little Nobody, 1972; The Pagan Island, 1972; Rapture of the Desert, 1972; The Silver Slave, 1972; The Glass Castle, 1973; Devil in a Silver Room, 1973; Forbidden Rapture, 1973; The Kisses and the Wine, 1973; Palace of the Pomegranate, 1974; The Girl at Golden Hawk, 1974; The Noble Savage, 1974; Satan Took a Bride, 1975; Dearest Demon, 1975; The Devil's Darling, 1975; Darling Infidel, 1976; The Burning Sands, 1976; The Child of Judas, 1976; The Sun Tower, 1976; The Sin of Cynara, 1976; The Loved and the Feared, 1977; Love Battle, 1977; Love in a Stranger's Arms, 1977; Passionate Sinner, 1977; Time of the Temptress, 1977; The Valdez Marriage, 1978; The Awakening of Alice, 1978; Desire Has No Mercy, 1979; The Sheik's Captive, 1979; Love Is the Honey, 1980; A Girl Possessed, 1980; Love's Agony, 1981; The Man She Married, 1982; By Love Possessed, 1984; Secret Fire, 1984; Bride's Lace, 1985; House of Storms, 1985; The Honeymoon, 1986; A Silken Barbarity, 1987. *Address:* c/o Harlequin Enterprises, Duncan Mill Road, Don Mills, Ontario, Canada.

WINSTON Daoma, b. 1922, USA. Author. *Publications:* Tormented Lovers, 1962; Love Her, She's Yours, 1963; The Secrets of Cromwell Crossing, 1965; Sinister Stone, 1966; The Wakefield Witches, 1966; The Mansion of Smiling Masks, 1967; The Castle of Closing Doors, 1967; Shadow of an Unknown Woman, 1967; The Carnaby Curse, 1967; Shadow on Mercer Mountain, 1967; Pity My Love, 1967; The Traficante Treasure, 1968; Moderns, 1968; The Long and Living Shadow, 1968; Braken's World, 1069; Mrs Berrigan's Dirty Book, 1970; Beach Generation, 1970; Wild Country, 1970; Dennison Hill, 1970; House of Mirror Images, 1970; Sound Stage, 1970; The Love of Lucifer, 1970; The Vampire Curse, 1971; Flight of a Fallen Angel, 1971; The Devil's Daughter, The Devil's Princess, 1971; Seminar in Evil, 1972; The Victim, 1972; The Return, 1972; The Inheritance, 1972; Kingdom's Castle, 1972; Skeleton Key, 1972, as The Mayeroni Myth, 1979; Moorhaven, 1973; The Trap, 1973; The Unforgotten, 1973; The Haversham Legacy, 1974; Mills of the Gods, 1974; Emerald Station, 1974; The Golden Valley, 1975; Death Watch, 1975; A Visit after Dark, 1975; Walk Around the Square, 1975; Gallows Way, 1976; The Dream Killers, 1976; The Adventuress, 1978; The Lotteries, 1980; A Sweet Familiarity, 1981; Mira, 1982; The Fall River Line, 1984; Maybe This Time, 1988; The Sorcerers, 1988. *Address:* c/o Jay Garon-Brooke Associates, 415 Central Park West, New York, NY 10025, USA.

WINSTON Sarah, (Sarah E Lorenz), b. 15 Dec 1912, New York City, New York, USA. Writer. m. Keith Winston, 11 June 1932, 2 sons. *Education:* New York University, 1929, 1930; Philosophy and Appreciation of Art course, The Barnes Foundation, 1966, 1967; Art Seminars (research), 1967-89. *Publications:* And Always Tomorrow, 1963; Everything Happens for the Best, 1969, 1970; Our Son, Ken, 1969, 1970; Not Yet Spring, poems, 1976; V- Mail: Letters of the World War II Combat Medic, 1985; Summer Conference, 1990; Of Apples and Oranges, 1993. *Contributions to:* Literary Review, Fairleigh Dickenson College; Art Journal Vista, Barnes Foundation; New England Sampler; Guideposts. *Honours:* 1st Prize Award, Everything Happens for the Best, 1972, 1st Prize Award, Our Son, Ken, 1974, National League of American Pen Women; Recordings of Everything Happens for the Best, V-Mail, And Always Tomorrow, Library of Congress for

Blind; Tape recording, Our Son, Ken, Recording for the Blind Inc. *Membership:* National League of American Pen Women. *Literary Agent:* Dan Wright, Ann Wright Representatives Inc, New York City, New York, USA. *Address:* 1838 Rose Tree Lane, Havertown, PA 19083, USA.

WINTERSON Jeanette, b. 1958, England. Writer. *Education:* Oxford University. *Appointments:* Worked in Theatre and Publishing before becoming a full-time writer. *Publications:* Oranges are not the Only Fruit; Boating for Beginners; The Passion; Sexing the Cherry, 1989; Written of the Body, 1992. *Honour:* Whitbread First Novel Prize Winner (Oranges are not the Only Fruit), 1985. *Address:* c/o Bloomsbury.

WINTGENS Léo, b. 13 Nov 1938, Hergenrath, Belgium. Professor. m. Betty Pelzer, 13 Aug 1960, 3 sons, 1 daughter. *Education:* Licencié en philologie germanique, 1970, Docteur en Philosophie et Lettres, 1979, University of Liège. *Appointments:* Im Göhltal, Kelmis (per.), founder, 1966-; BRF, Belgian Radio German Sp., Brussels, 1966-; Obelit, 1976-, founder; Ostbelgische Studien, 1982-, founder; Honneur aux Passeurs, Chaiers du Centre de documentation de la Résistance au nazisme, 1990-, founder. *Publications:* Neutral-Moresnet, 1981; Sprachgeschichte des Herzogtums Limburg, 1982; Petrus Hebraicus, libretto, (with Henri Pousseur), 1983; Geschichte der Literatur in Ostbelgien, 1986; Le Pays de Herve, (co-author), 1987; Gewohnheitsrecht des Herzogtums Limburg, 1986; Weistümer des Herzogtums Limburg 14-18c, 1988. *Contributions to:* Numerous journals in Belgium, Germany, Austria, including: Le Journal des Poètes; Literatur und Kritik; Le Spantole Die Horen. *Honours:* Fellowship, University of Liège by the Fonds National de la Recherche Scientifique, Brussels 1977-78; Preis des Rates der Deutschsprachigen Gemeinschaft Belgiens-Bereich Philologis, Eupen, 1980; Kogge Studienpreis der Stadt Minden/Westfalen (D), 1987; Preis des Rates der Deutschsprachigen Gemeinschaft Belgiens-Bereich Geschichte, Eupen, 1989. *Memberships include:* PEN International (B); Board Member, BRF, 1977-85; Board Member, ISIB, 1982-; Member, Commission des Langues régionales endogènes, Cabinet du Ministre-President de la Communauté Française de Belgique; Consultant, Commission Royale de Toponymie et de Dialectologie, Brussels. *Address:* Rue d'Aix 9, B - 4671, Moresnet, Belgium.

WINTON John. See: PRATT John Clark.

WINTOUR Charles Vere, b. 18 May 1917, Wimborne, Dorset, England. Journalist. 2 sons, 2 daughters. *Education:* BA, 1939, MA 1946, Peterhouse, Cambridge. *Appointments:* Editor, Evening Standard, 1959- 76, 1978-80; Editor, Sunday Express Magazine, 1981-82; Editor, UK Press Gazette, 1985-86; Editorial Consultant, London Daily News, 1986-87. *Publication:* Pressure on the Press, 1972; The Rise and Fall of Fleet Street, 1989. *Honours:* MBE (Mil), 1945; CBE, 1978. *Membership:* Garrick Club. *Agent:* A.P. Watt. *Address:* 5 Alwyne Road, London N1 2HH, England.

WIRTHS Claudine (Turner) G(ibson), b. 9 May 1926, Covington, Georgia, USA. Writer; Adjunct faculty member. m. Theodore Wirths, 28 Dec 1945, 2 sons. *Education:* AB, cum laude, 1946, MA 1948, University of Kentucky; M Ed, American University, 1980; Doctoral study at University of North Carolina at Chapel Hill. *Appointments include:* Secretary and Research Assistant for departments of Psychology and Anthropology, Yale University, New Haven, Connecticut, 1946-47; Program Director, North Carolina League for Crippled Children and Adults, Chapel Hill, 1948-49; Research Psychologist with Savannah River Studies, Aiken, South Carolina for University of North Carolina, 1950-52; Police Psychologist, City Police Department, Aiken, 1952-56; Head Teacher in Special Education, Kirk School, Aiken, 1956- 58; Home-maker, Aiken, 1958-62; Social Science Consultant, Rockville,

Maryland, 1962-77; Elementary Schoolteacher, Green Acres School, Rockville, 1977-78; Special Education Intern at high school in Springfield, Virginia, 1978-79; Special Education Teacher, Gaithersburg High School, Gaithersburg, Maryland, 1979-81, Co-ordinator of Learning Center, 1981-84; Writer 1984-; Member, adjunct faculty, Frederick Community College, Frederick, Maryland, 1987-. *Publications:* (with Richard H Williams) Lives Through the Years, 1965; (with Mary Bowman-Kruhm) I Hate School: How to Hang In and When to Drop Out (juvenile) 1987; (with Mary Bowman-Kruhm) I Need a Job (juvenile) 1988. Work represented in anthologies, including Humpty Dumpty's Bedtime Stories, 1971. *Contributions to* Magazines and newspapers, including Law and Order, Maryland, Christian Ministry, Journal of Learning Disabilities, Parks and Recreation and Cat Fancy. *Honours:* Conservation Award from Maryland Environment Trust, 1973; award from Maryland-Delaware Press Association, 1979, for feature story writing; American Library Association listed I Hate School as a best book of 1986 and a recommended book for reluctant young adult readers. *Membership:* Phi Beta Kappa. *Address:* P O Box 335, Braddock Heights, MD 21714, USA.

WISE David, b. 10 May 1930, New York City, USA. Journalist; Author. m. Joan Sylvester, 16 Dec. 1962, 2 sons. *Education:* BA, Columbia College, 1951. *Appointments include:* Reporter 1951-66, Albany bureau chief 1956-57, Member Washington bureau 1958-66, chief 1963-66, New York Herald Tribune; Fellow, Woodrow Wilson International Centre for Scholars, 1970-71; Lecturer, Political Science, University of California, Santa Barbara, 1977-79. *Publications include:* Politics of Lying: Government Deception, Secrecy & Power, 1973; American Police State: Government Against the People, 1976; Spectrum, 1981; Children's Game, 1983; U-2 Affair, with Thomas B.Ross, 1962; Invisible Government, 1964; Espionage Establishment, 1967; Democracy Under Pressure: Introduction to American Political System, with Milton Cummings, 5th edition 1985; Samarkand Dimension, 1987; Contributing author, Kennedy Circle, 1961; None of Your Business: Government Secrecy in America, 1974; CIA File, 1976; etc. *Contributions:* Articles to national magazines. *Honours:* Page One Award, Newspaper Guild, New York, 1969; George Polk Memorial Award, 1974. *Memberships:* Washington Independent Writers; American Political Science Association; Various clubs. *Address:* c/o Sterling Lord Agency, 660 Madison Avenue, New York, NY 10021, USA.

WISEMAN Christopher Stephen, b. 31 May 1936, Hull, England. University Teacher. *Education:* MA, Cambridge University; PhD, University of Strathclyde. *Publications:* Waiting for the Barbarians, 1971; The Barbarian File, 1975; Beyond the Labyrinth : A Study of Edwin Muir's Poetry, 1978; The Upper Hand, 1981; An Ocean of Whispers, 1982; Postcards Home, 1988; Missing Persons, 1989. *Contributions To:* Poetry; Times Literary Supplement; Encounter; Critical Quarterly; Malahat Review; and others; Critical articles and reviews contributed to various journals. *Honours:* Alberta Achievement Award for Excellence, 1988; Writers Guild of Alberta Award for Poetry, 1988; Alberta Culture Poetry Prize, 1988. *Address:* Dept. of English, University of Calgary, Calgary, Alberta, Canada T2N 1N4.

WISEMAN David (Jane Julian), b. 13 Jan 1916, Manchester, England. Writer. m. Cicely Hilda Mary Richards, 2 Sept 1939, 2 sons, 2 daughters. *Education:* BA (Honours), History, 1937, Teaching Diploma, 1938, Manchester University. *Appointment:* Editor, Adult Education, 1947-50. *Publications:* Jeremy Visick, 1981, USA, published in UK as, The fate of Jeremy Visick, 1982; Thimbles, 1982 USA, 1983; Blodwen and the Guardians, 1983; Adam's Common, 1984; Pudding and Pie, 1986; Jumping Jack, 1988; Badge of Honour, published in USA as, A Tie To The Past, 1989; The Devil's Cauldron, 1989; Mum's Winning Streak, 1990; Moonglow, 1990; Goliath Takes the Bait, 1993; As Jane Julian: Ellen Bray, 1985; As Wind To Fire, 1989; The

Sunlit Days, 1990. *Membership:* Society of Authors. *Address:* 21 Treworder Road, Truro, Cornwall TR1 2JZ, England.

WITT Harold Vernon, b. 6 Feb 1923, Santa Ana, California, USA. Freelance Writer; Editor. m. Beth Hewitt, 8 Sept 1948, 1 son, 2 daughters. *Education:* BA 1943, BLS 1953, University of California, Berkeley; MA, University of Michigan, 1947. *Appointments:* Co-editor, California State Poetry Quarterly, 1976; Co-editor, Blue Unicorn, 1977-; Consulting editor, Poet Lore, 1976-1991. *Publications:* The Death of Venus, 1958; Beasts in Clothes, 1961; Now, Swim, 1974; Surprised by others at Fort Cronkhite, 1975; Winesburg by the Sea, 1979; The Snow Prince, 1982; Flashbacks and Reruns, 1985; The Light at Newport, 1992. *Contributions To:* Poems &/or stories: New Yorker; Poetry; The Atlantic; Harper's; Poetry Northwest; Southwest Review; Prairie Schooner; Wind; Fiction 83; Plains Poetry Journal; New Letters. *Honours:* Hopwood Award, poetry, 1947; Phelan Award, narrative poetry, 1960; 1st prize, San Francisco Poetry Centre poetic drama competition, 1963; Emily Dickinson Award, Poetry Society of America, 1972; Various awards, World Order of Narrative Poets. *Address:* 39 Claremont Avenue, Orinda, CA 94563, USA.

WITTLIN Thaddeus (Tadeusz), b. 1909, Warsaw, Poland. Lecturer; Radio Script Writer. *Education:* MA, LLM, University of Warsaw. *Appointments:* Editor, Barber of Warsaw satirical weekly, 1931-36. *Publications:* Trail to Parnassus, poetry, 1929; The Dreamer and the Guests, novel, 1932; The Hasbeen, novel, 1933; The Achilles Heel, short stories, 1939; The Broken Wings, novel, 1944; Happy Days, short stories, poetry, 1946; The Island of Lovers, short stories, 1950; A Reluctant Traveller in Russia, biography, English, French, Japanese, Polish versions, 1952; Modigliani-Prince of Montparnasse, biography, English, Dutch, Polish versions, 1964; Time Stopped at 6.30, historical account, 1965; Commissar, The Life and Death of Lavrenty Pavlovich Beria, biography, English, French, Spanish, Japanese versions, 1972; The Last Bohemians, 1974; The Songstress of Warsaw, 1985; On the Banks of the grey Vistula River, 1990. *Memberships:* PEN English Centre; PEN American Center; Societe Historique et Litteraire Polonaise, Paris. *Address:* 2020 F Street NW, Washington, DC 20006, USA.

WOESSNER Warren, b. 31 May 1944, New Brunswick, New Jersey, USA. Attorney. m. Iris Freeman, 6 Jan 1990. *Education:* BA 1966, Cornell University; PhD 1971, University of Wisconsin-Madison; JD 1981, University of Wisconsin Law School. *Appointments:* Founder, Editor and Publisher, Abraxas magazine 1968-81, Senior Editor 1981-; Board of Directors, Counsil of Small Magazine Editors and Publishers 1975-77; Member Wisconsin Arts Board Creative Writing Advisory Panel 1977-79; Board of Directors, Back Porch Radio Inc, Host, Visitors From Inner Space, programme of poetry, fiction and drama performance, 1975-78; Board of Directors, Coffee House Press 1988-1992, President 1989-1992. *Publications:* Books include: The Forest and the Trees, 1968; Landing, 1974; No Hiding Place, 1979; Storm Lines, 1987. *Contributions to:* Anthologies: Heartland II, 1975; Travelling America with Today's Poets, 1977; The Poets' Encyclopaedia, 1979; Anthology of Magazine Verse and Yearbook of American Poetry, 1980; The Point Riders Great Plains Poetry Anthology, 1982; The Journey Home, 1989; and others; Periodicals: Poetry, Chicago; Poetry Now; Poetry Northwest; The Nation; Ironwood; The Wormwood Review; Epoch; West Coast Poetry Review; The Beloit Poetry Journal; Prairie Schooner; Living Wilderness; Continental Drift; December; Lips; and others. *Honours include:* National Endowment for the Arts Individual Fellowship for Creative Writing, 1974; Wisconsin Arts Board Individual Fellowship for Creative Writing, 1975, 1976; Loft-McKnight Fellowship for Poetry, 1985; Minnesota Voices Competition, poetry, 1986. *Address:* 34 W Minnehaha Parkway, Minneapolis, MN 55419, USA.

WOJNA Ryszard, b. 2 July 1920, Sanok, Poland. Journalist. m. Elzbieta Wojna, 2 children. *Education:* Jagiellonian University; University of Grenoble. *Appointments:* Editor, Echo Krakowa, 1948-49; Foreign Editor, Glos Pracy, Warsaw, 1951-56; Permanent Correspondent, Middle East, 1957-61, Bonn 1963-67; Deputy Editor, Zycie Warszawy 1968-71, Editor 1971-72; Journalist, Trybuna Ludu, 1972-81; Political Commentator, Rzeczpospolita, 1983-90. *Publications:* Szkice Rozmowa z ojcem, 1978; Dojrzewanie, 1980; Komentarz do wspolczesnosci, 1988. *Honours:* Officers Cross of Order of Polonia Restituta, 1972; State Prize for Literature and Journalism, 1974; order of Banner of Labour, 1st Class; Cross of Valour. *Memberships:* Member Presidium, All Polish PeaceCommittee; various other professional organisations. *Address:* ul Dragonów 6/38, 00-467 Warsaw, Poland.

WOLASZ-RUHLAND Elizabeth Ann, b. 7 Mar 1949, Buffalo, USA. Micrographics Processor; Data Analyst; Systems Administrator. *Publications:* The Timeless Hour, 1986; Fall, 1984; Stage Chinaman, 1986; The Mover of My Heart, 1987; The Element That's Relevent, 1985; The Master Gardner, 1986; As It Is, 1986. *Contributions To:* Various journals and magazines. *Honours:* Golden Poet Award, World Poetry Association, 1987; Best of 87, Best of 86, American Poetry Association; Award of Merit, World Poetry Association. *Address:* 738 Niagara St., Apt. No. 5, Buffalo, NY 14213, USA.

WOLCOTT Leonard Thompson, b. 4 May, Buenos Aires, Argentina. m. Carolyn E. Muller, 31 Aug 1951, 1 daughter. *Education:* AB, Asbury College; MA, Indology, Hartford Seminary Foundation, 1939; MDiv, New Testament, 1943; PhD Program, 1952, Drew University; DPhil, Indology and New Testament, Oxford University, England, 1956. *Publications include:* Meditations on Ephesians, 1965; Religions Around the World, (with C.E. Wolcott), 1967; Hebrews and I,II Chronicles Basic Bible Commentaries, 1988; Wilderness Rider, (with C.E. Wolcott), 1984; Twelve Modern Disciples, 1963; We Go Forward, (with C.E. Wolcott), 1984; New Testament Odyssey, 1979; Iglesia en el Mundo, 1971; Introduction a l'étude du Nouveau Testament et de son message, 1983. *Contributions to:* Journal of Asiatic Studies; International Review of Mission; Christian Century; Christianity Today; Christian Action; Indian Witness; New World Outlook; United Methodist Reporter; Christian Advocate; Friends Journal. *Honours:* Book-of-the-Month, Meditation on Ephesians, Pulpit Digest, August, 1966; Ford Foundation Fellowship; Brookings Institute; Ezra Squier Tipple Fellowship; Stephen Green Fellowship. *Memberships:* International Association of Professors of Missions, Secretary-treasurer; Midwest Fellowship of Professors of Mission, President; International Fellowship of Reocnciliation, American Board of Directors; American Oriental Society; Society of Biblical Literature; American Association of University Professors; Nashville FOR, President; Commissioner, Nashville-Metropolitan Commission on Human Relations. *Address:* 3372 Mimosa Drive, Nashville, TN 37211, USA.

WOLDIN Judd, b. 30 May 1925. Composer; Librettist. *Education:* Black Mountain College (studied with Josef Albers and Henrich Jalowetz); University of New Mexico (studied with Ernst Krenek); BA 1958, MA 1960, Rutgers University, studied Theatre with Lehman Engel. *Publications:* Raisin (musical based on Lorraine Hansberry's play A Raisin in the Sun, 1973; King of Schnorrers (based on Zangwill Novella) 1979; Little Ham (based on Langston Hughes play) 1987; The Prince and the Pauper (based on Mark Twain novel) 1990; Jonah (a jazz fable); Filmscores: Nobody Ever Died of Old Age, 1964; Railway with a Heart of Gold, 1962. *Honours:* Antoinette Perry Award (Tony) 1973, Best Musical; NARAS Award (Grammy) Best Original Cast Album, 1974; N J Council of the Arts Award, 1979. *Memberships:* Dramatists Guild; Broadcast Music Inc; Songwriters Guild. *Address:* 310 Greenwich Street, Studio 39C, New York, NY 10013, USA.

WOLFE Christopher, b. 11 Mar 1949, Boston, Massachusetts, USA. College Professor; Writer. m. Anne McGowan Wolfe, 17 June 1972, 5 sons, 5 daughters. *Education:* BA, University of Notre Dame, 1971; PhD, Boston College (Political Science), 1978. *Publications:* The Rise of Modern Judicial Review, 1986; Essays on Faith and Liberal Democracy, 1987; Judicial Activism: Bulwark of Freedom or Precarious Security? 1990. *Contributor to:* Various articles included in journals: A Theory of US Consitutional History, Journal of Politics, 1981; How the Constitution was Taken Out of Constitutional Law in Harvard Journal of Law and Public Policy, Summer 1987; Abortion and Morally Acceptable Political Compromise; First Things, 1992. *Honour:* Benchmark Book of the Year Award for The Rise of Modern Judicial Review, 1987. *Memberships:* American Public Philosophy Institute, President 1989-; American Political Science Association; Fellowship of Catholic Scholars; The Federalist Society. *Address:* Department of Political Science, Marquette University, Milwaukee, WI 53233, USA.

WOLFE Gary Kent, b. 24 Mar 1946, Sedalia, Missouri, USA. Educator; Critic. *Education:* BA 1968, University of Kansas; MA 1969, PhD 1971, University of Chicago. *Appointments:* Editorial Board: Science-Fiction Studies 1984-; Journal of the Fantastic in the Arts 1988-. *Publications:* The Known and the Unknown: the Iconography of Science Fiction, 1979; David Lindsay, 1982; Critical Terms for Science Fiction and Fantasy, 1986; Co-author, Elements of Research, 1979; Editor, Science Fiction Dialogues, 1982. *Contributions to:* Over 200 essays and reviews in books, reference works, and journals; Currently Monthly Review Columnist for Locus magazine. *Honours:* Eaton Award for Science-Fiction Criticism, 1981; Pilgrim Award, Science Fiction Research Association, 1987; James Friend Memorial Award for Literary Criticism, Friends of Literature, 1992. *Memberships:* Committee Director, International Association for the Fantastic in the Arts, 1985-; Board of Directors, Friends of the Chicago Public Library, 1990-1993. *Address:* 1450 E 55th Pl, Apt 420 South, Chicago, IL 60637, USA.

WOLFE Gene (Rodman), b. 1931, United States of America. Author. *Publications:* Operation ARES, 1970; The Fifth Head of Cerberus (SF short stories), 1972; Peace (novel), 1975; The Devil in a Forest (juvenile Novel), 1976; The Island of Doctor Death and Other Stories, 1980; The Shadow of the Torturer, 1980; The Claw of the Conciliator, 1981; Gene Wolfe's Book of Days (short stories), 1981; The Sword of the Lictor, 1981; The Citadel of the Autarch, 1984; Free Live Free, 1984; Soldier of the Mist, 1986. *Address:* P.O. Box 69, Barrington, IL 60011, USA.

WOLFE Thomas Kennerly, b. 2 Mar 1930, Richmond, Virginia, United States of America. Author. m. Sheila Berger, 1978, 1 son, 1 daughter. *Education:* BA, Washington and Lee University, 1951; PhD, Yale University, 1957. *Appointments Include:* Reporter, Washington Post, New York Herald Tribune, 1959-66; Commission to write article for Esquire Magazine. *Publications:* The Kandy Kolored Tangerine-Flake Streamline Baby, 1965; The Electric Kool-Acid Test, 1968; Radical Chic and Mau-mauing the Flak Catchers, 1970; The Painted Word, 1975; The Right Stuff, 1979; From Bauhaus to Our House, 1981; The Bonfire of the Vanities, 1987. *Contributions to:* Esquire, New York, Harper's and Rolling Stone Magazines. *Honours:* American Book Award, for The Right Stuff; The Bonfire of the Vanities: New York Times Bestsellers List, 1987-88 (55 weeks). *Literary Agent:* Lynn Nesbit, Janklow & Nesbit Inc, New York. *Address:* Lynn Nesbit, Janklow & Nesbit Inc, 598 Madison Avenue, New York, NY 10022, USA.

WOLFERS Michael, b. 28 Sept 1938, London, England. Writer; Translator. *Education:* Wadham College, Oxford University, 1959-62; BA, Law, 1962, MA, 1965, Oxford; South Bank Polytechnic (now South Bank University), 1990-91; MSc with distinction, Intelligent Management Systems, 1991. *Appointments:*

Journalist, The Times, London, 1965-72 (latterly as Africa Correspondent); Visiting Senior Lecturer in African Politics and Government, University of Juba, Sudan, 1979-82. *Publications:* Black Man's Burden Revisited, 1974; Politics in the Organisation of African Unity, 1976; Luandino Vieira, The Real Life of Domingos Xavier, 1978; Poems from Angola (editor, translator), 1979; Amilcar Cabral, Unity and Struggle, 1979, 1980; Angola in the Front Line (with Jane Bergerol), 1983; Samir Amin, Delinking: Towards a Polycentric World, 1990; Hamlet and Cybernetics, 1991. *Contributions to:* Numerous publications. *Memberships:* Royal Institute of International Affairs; Associate Research Fellow, Gyosei Institute of Management, Gyosei International College, Reading. *Address:* 66 Roupell Street, London SE1 8SS, England.

WOLFF Edward Nathan, b. 10 Apr 1946, Long Branch, New Jersey, USA. Professor of Economics. m. Jane Zandra Forman, 27 Nov 1977, 1 son, 1 daughter. *Education:* AB 1968, Harvard College; M Phil 1972, PhD 1974, Yale University. *Appointments:* Managing Editor, Review of Income and Wealth 1987-; Associate Editor: Structural Change and Economic Dynamics 1989-; Journal of Population Economics 1990-. *Publications:* Growth, Accumulation and Unproductive Activity: An Analysis of the Post-War US Economy, 1987; Editor, International Comparisons of the Distribution of Household Wealth, 1987; Co-Author, Productivity and American Leadership: The Long View, 1989; Co-Author, The Information Economy: The Implications of Unbalanced Growth, 1989; Co-Editor, International Perspectives on Profitability and Accumulation, 1992. *Contributions to:* Over 75 articles published in professional economics journals and books. *Honours:* National Merit Scholarship, 1964-68; Magna Cum Laude in Economics, Harvard, 1968; Honorable Mention, Annual Awards for Excellence in Publishing, Social Sciences, 1989, by Association of American Publishers, Professional and Scholarly Publishing Division. *Memberships:* International Association for Research in Income and Wealth, Council Member 1987-94; American Economic Association; Conference on Research in Income and Wealth; International Institute of Public Finance. *Address:* 48 Morton Street, New York, NY 10014, USA.

WOLFF Geoffrey, b. 5 Nov 1937, Los Angeles, California, USA. Writer. m. 21 Aug 1965, 2 sons. *Education:* Eastbourne College, 1956; BA summa cum laude, Princeton University, 1961; Fulbright Scholar, Churchill College, Cambridge University, 1964. *Appointments:* Book Critic, The Washington Post, 1965-69; Book Editor, Newsweek, 1969-71; Writer-in-Residence: Princeton University, 1970-74, 1980, 1988; Columbia University, 1979; Brown University, 1981, 1988; Brandeis University, 1982-. *Publications:* Bad Debts, 1969; The Sightseer, 1974; Black Sun, 1976; Paklings, 1978; The Duke of Deception, 1979; Providence, 1986; The Final Club, 1990; A Day at the beach, 1992. *Contributions to:* Atlantic Monthly; Granta; Esquire; Newsweek; Paris Review; Triquarterly; Many others. *Honours:* Guggenheim Fellow, 1971, 1978; National Endowment for the Humanities, 1974; National Endowment for the Arts, 1979, 1987; Governor's Arts Award, 1992. *Membership:* PEN. *Literary Agent:* Amanda Urban, ICM, 40 West 57th St, New York, NY, USA. *Address:* 175 Narragansett Ave, Jamestown, RI 02835, USA.

WOLFF Tobias (Jonathan Ansell), b. 19 June 1945, Birmingham, Alabama, USA. Writer. m. Catherine Dolores Spohn, 1975, 2 sons, 1 daughter. *Education:* BA, 1972, MA, 1975, Oxford University; MA, Stanford University, 1978. *Publications:* In the Garden of the North American Martyrs, short stories, 1981; Editor, Matters of Life and Death: New American Stories, 1982; The Barracks Thief, 1984; Back in the World, 1985; Editor, A Doctor's Visit: The Short Stories of Anton Checkhov, 1987; This Boy's Life, a memoir, 1989. *Contributions to:* TriQuarterly; Missouri Review; Ploughshares; Atlantic Monthly; Esquire; Vanity Fair; Antaeus. *Honours:* Wallace Stegner Fellowship, 1975-

76; NEA Fellowship, 1978, 1985; Mary Roberts Rinehart Grant, 1979; Arizona Council on the Arts and Humanities Fellowship, 1980; O. Henry Short Story Prizes, 1980, 1981, 1985; Guggenheim Fellowship, 1982; St Lawrence Award for Fiction, 1982; PEN/Faulkner Award for Fiction, 1985; Rea Award for the Short Story, 1989; Whiting Foundation Award, 1989; Los Angeles Times Book Prize, 1989. *Memberships:* PEN; Associated Writing Programmes. *Address:* 214 Scott Avenue, Syracuse, NY 13224, USA.

WOLKSTEIN Diane, b. 11 Nov 1942, New Jersey, USA. Author; Storyteller. 1 daughter. *Education:* BA, Smith College, 1964; MA, Bank Street College of Education, 1967. *Publications:* The First Love Stories; The Magic Orange Tree, 1978; Inanna, Queen of Heaven and Earth, 1983; Oom Razoom, 1991; Little Mouse's Painting, 1992; The Banza; The Magic Wings; White Wave; Dream Songs; The Red Lion; Lazy Stories; Squirrel's Song; The Visit; Cool Ride in the Sky; 8,000 Stones. *Contributions to:* Many publications. *Honours:* Many books Notable, American Library Association; Featured on National Public Radio and on Charles Kurault, CBS Sunday Morning; Centennial Honours Award, Smith College Club, New York City. *Address:* 10 Patchin Pl, New York, NY 10011, USA.

WOLL Peter, b. 6 Jan 1933, Philadelphia, PA, USA. College Professor. m. Mary Jobes, 26 June 1954, 1 son, 1 daughter. *Education:* AB, Haversford College, 1957; PhD, Cornell University, 1958. *Publications:* American Government: Readings and Cases; Behind the Scenes in American Government; American Government: The Core; America's Political System; American Bureaucracy; Administrative Law; Constitutional Democracy; Debating American Government; Pulic Policy; Public Administration and Policy. *Contributions to:* The Nation; Washington Monthly; Western Political Quarterly; Cornell Law Quarterly; UCAL Law Review; World Book Encyclopedia. *Memberships:* American Political Science Association; Textbooks Author's Association. *Address:* 43 Oxbow Road, Weston, MA 02193, USA.

WOLLASTON Nicholas William, b. 23 June 1926, Gloucestershire, England. Writer. m. Deirdre Johnston, 11 Aug 1961, 2 sons, 1 daughter. *Education:* Winchester College; BA, Cambridge University. *Publications:* Handles of Chance, 1956; China in the Morning, 1960; Red Rumba, 1962; Winter in England, 1965; Jupiter Laughs, 1967; Pharaoh's Chicken, 1969; The Tale Bearer, 1972; Eclipse, 1974; The Man on the Ice Cap, 1980; Mr Thistlewood, 1985; The Stones of Bau, 1987; Cafe de Paris, 1988; Tilting at Don Quixote, 1990. *Contributions to:* The Observer; The Sunday Times; The Sunday Telegraph; The New Statesman; The Spectator; Times Literary Supplement. *Honours:* Heinemann Award for Fiction, 1970; Travelling Scholarship, Society of Authors, 1989; 3 Arts Council grants. *Memberships:* Fellow, Royal Society of Literature, 1970; Society of Authors; International PEN. *Literary Agent:* Gillon Aitken, England. *Address:* c/o Gillon Aitken, 29 Fernshaw Road, London SW10 0TG, England.

WOMACK Peter, b. 27 Jan 1952, Surrey, England. Lecturer. *Education:* BA 1973, Oxford University; PhD 1984, Edinburgh University. *Appointments:* Lectureship in English, University of East Anglia 1988-. *Publications:* Ben Jonson, 1986; Improvement and Romance, 1989. *Contributions to:* Textual Practice, 1987; New Theatre Quarterly, 1989; Culture and History 1350-1600, ed David Aers, 1992. *Address:* School of English and American Studies, University of East Anglia, Norwich NR4 7TJ, England.

WOMACK Steven James, b. 31 July 1952, Nashville, Tennessee, USA. Writer. m. Cathryn G Yarbrough, 5 May 1990. *Education:* Western Reserve Academy 1970; BA 1974, Tulane University. *Appointments:* Instructor, Tennessee State University 1988-91; Adjunct Professor of Writing, Nashville State Technical Institute 1991-. *Publications:* Murphy's Fault, 1990;

Smash Cut, 1991; Dead Folks Blues, 1992; The Software Bomb, 1993; Torch Town Boogie, 1993. *Contributions to:* Book Reviewer, Nashville Banner 1983-; Guest Columnist, USA Today, 1991. *Honour:* Murphy's Fault named to New York Times 1990 List of Notable Books. *Memberships:* Author's Guild; Author's League of America; Sisters-in-Crime; Tennessee Screenwriting Association, member Board of Directors; Mystery Writers of America. *Literary Agent:* Carole Abel Literary Agency. *Address:* 2109 Pontotoc Avenue, Nashville, TN 37206, USA.

WOOD Charles (Gerald), b. 1933, United Kingdom. Dramatist; Designer and Scenic Artist. *Appointments:* Stage Manager, 1957-62. *Publications:* Cockade, 1967; Dingo, 1969; Fill the Stage with Happy Hours, 1969; H: Being Monologues in Front of Burning Cities, 1970; Veterans, 1972; Has Washington Legs, and Dingo, 1978; Tumbledown, 1987. *Address:* c/o Fraser and Dunlop, 91 Regent Street, London W1R 8RU, England.

WOOD David Bernard, b. 21 Feb 1944, Sutton, England. Writer; Actor; Theatre producer; Director; Composer. m. Jacqueline Stanbury, 21 Jan 1975, 2 daughters. *Education:* BA, Honours, Worcester College, Oxford. *Publications:* Musical plays for children: The Owl and the Pussycat Went to See..... (with S. Ruskin), 1970; The Plotters of Cabbage Patch Corner, 1973; Flibberty and the Penguin, 1974; Hijack over Hygenia, 1974; The Papertown Paperchase, 1976; Larry The Lamb in Toytown (with S. Ruskin), 1976; Old Mother Hubbard, 1976; The Gingerbread Man, 1977; Old Father Time, 1977; Tickle, 1978; Babes in the Magic Wood, 1979; Nutcracker Sweet, 1979; Mother Goose's Golden Christmas, 1979; Cinderella, 1980; There Was an Old Woman, 1980; Aladdin, 1980; The Ideal Gnome Expedition, 1982; Dick Whittington and Wondercat, 1982; Meg and Mog Show (based on the books by Jan Pienkowski and Helen Nicoll), 1985; The Selfish Shellfish, 1986; Robin Hood (with Dave and Toni Arthur, 1985; The Old Man of Lochnagar (based on the book by H.R.H. The Prince of Wales), 1986; The See-Saw Tree, 1987; Dinosaurs and all that Rubbish (based on the book by Michael Foreman), 1986; (Books)The Operats of Rodent Garden (illustrated by Geoffrey Beitz), 1984; The Gingerbread Man (illustrated by Sally Anne Lambert), 1985; The Discorats (illustrated by Geoffrey Beitz), 1985; Play Theatres (with Richard Fowler), 1987; Chish 'N' Fips (illustrated by Don Seed), 1987; Sidney The Monster (illustrated by Clive Scruton), 1988; Happy Birthday, Mouse, 1991 (USA, 1990); Save the Human, 1991. *Memberships:* Society of Authors; British Actors' Equity Association; Green Room Club. *Honour:* Winner, Nottinghamshire Children's Book of the Year Award, 1989. *Literary Agent:* Margaret Ramsay Limited. *Address:* c/o Margaret Ramsay Limited, 14A Goodwin's Court, St Martin's Lane, London WC2, England.

WOOD Derek Harold, b. 19 Mar 1930, Croydon, England. Freelance Writer; Editor. m. Belinda Squire, 23 July 1955, 1 son, 1 daughter. *Literary Appointments:* Editor, Aerosphere, 1948-49; Editorial staff, British Trade Journal, Electrical Journal, 1950-53; London editor, then Managing Director, Interavia (UK) Ltd, 1953-83; Air correspondent, Liverpool Daily Post 1952-60, Westminster Newspapers 1954-60, Sunday Telegraph 1961-86; Editor-in-chief 1984-87, publisher 1987-89, Founder Editor/Publisher, 1989-, Jane's Defence Weekly; Head of Special Projects, Jane's Information Group, 1989-1990; Currently: UK Editor, Interavia and Freelance Writer. *Publications:* The Narrow Margin, 1961, revised 1969; Project Cancelled, 1975, revised 1990; Attack Warning Red, 1976; Jane's World Aircraft Recognition Handbook, 1979, 3rd edition 1985, 4th edition 1989, 5th edition, 1992; Target England, 1980. *Contributions to:* Air Pictorial; Air Force magazine, USA; Aero Digest, USA; Aviation Week, USA; Aviation magazine, France; Flight. *Honours:* C.P. Robertson Memorial Trophy, 1961; Honorary Companion, Royal Aeronautical Society. *Literary Agent:* Curtis Brown. *Address:* Stroods, Whitemans Green, Cuckfield, West Sussex RH17 5DA, England.

WOOD Edgar Allardyce (Kerry Wood), b. 1907, Canada. Author; Federal Migratory Bird Officer. *Appointments:* Correspondent and Columnist, newspapers including Edmonton Bulletin, Edmonton Journal, Calgary Herald and Calgary Albertan, 1926-73. *Publications:* Robbing the Roost: The Marquis of Roostburg Rules Governing the Ancient and Dishonourable Sport, 1938; I'm a Gaggle Man, Myself, 1940; Three Mile Bend, 1945; Birds and Animals in the Rockies, 1946; A Nature Guide for Farmers, 1947; The Magpie Menace, 1949; Cowboy Yarns for Young Folk, 1951; The Sanctuary, 1952; A Letter from Alberta, 1954; A Letter from Calgary, 1954; Wild Winter, autobiography, 1954; The Map-Maker: The Story of David Thompson, 1955; Willowdale, 1956; The Great Chief: Maskepetoon, Warrior of the Crees, 1957; The Queen's Cowboy: Colonel Macleod of the Mounties, 1960; Great Horned MacOwl, fiction, 1961; The Boy and the Buffalo, 1963; Mickey the Beaver and Other Stories, 1964; A Lifetime of Service: George Moon, 1966; A Corner of Canada: A Personalized History of the Red Deer River Country, 1966; A Time for Fun, 1967; The Medicine Man, 1968; Samson's Long Ride, 1968; The Creek, 1970; The Icelandic-Canadian Poet Stephan G Stephansson: A Tribute, 1974; Red Deer, A Love Story, 1975; Bessie, The Coo, 1975; A Legacy of Laughter, 1986. *Honours include:* Governor-General's Medals, Juvenile Literature, 1955, 1957; 1st Vicky Metcalf Award, 1963; Alberta Historical Society Award, 1965; Honorary Doctorate, University of Alberta, 1969; Honorary Life Member, Alberta Federation of Naturalists, 1970; Alberta Achievement Award, 1975; Loran L Goulden Memorial Award, 1987; Order of the Bighorn, Edmonton, Alberta, 1987; Distinguished Service Award, Interpretration, Red Deer, Alberta, 1988. *Memberships:* Board Member, Alberta Natural History Society, 1936-64. *Address:* Site 3, RR 2, Red Deer, Alberta, Canada T4N 5E2.

WOOD Fergus James, b. 13 May 1917, London, Ontario, Canada. Geophysical Consultant (Tidal Dynamics). m. Doris M. Hack, 14 Sept 1946, 2 daughters. *Education:* University of Oregon, USA, 1934-36; AB, University of California, Berkeley, 1938; Postgraduate, Universities of California, Chicago & Michigan, 1938-42; California Institute of Technology, 1946. *Appointments include:* Science editor, editorial board, Encyclopaedia Americana, 1955-60; Scientific & technical publications officer, US Coast & Geodetic Survey, 1962-66; Member, Interagency Coordinating Group, contributing author, 8-volume series, The Great Alaska Earthquake of 1964, National Academy of Sciences, 1968-73. *Publications include:* Tidal Dynamics: Coastal Flooding & Cycles of Gravitational Force, 1986; The Strategic Role of Perigean Spring Tides in Nautical History & North American Coastal Flooding, 1635-1976, 1978; Editor-in-chief, The Prince William Sound, Alaska, Earthquake of 1964 & Aftershocks, volumes 1-2A; scientific co-ordinator, volumes 2B, 2C & 3, ibid, 1966-69; Writer, technical director, documentary film, Pathfinders from the Stars, 1967. *Contributions to:* Contribution of more than 200 articles to 8 encyclopedias and reference sources the most recent being to The Encylopeadia of Beaches and Coastal Environments and The Encyclopedia of Planetary Sciences. *Honours:* Special achievement awards, National Oceanic & Atmospheric Administration, US Department of Commerce, 1970, 1974, 1976, 1977. *Memberships:* The American Geophysical Union. *Address:* 3103 Casa Bonita Drive, Bonita, CA 91902, USA.

WOOD John Cunningham, b. 12 July 1952. Perth, Western Australia, Australia. m. Caroline D'Cruz, 5 June 1976, 1 son, 2 daughters. *Education:* Bachelor of Economics with First Class Honours 1973, UWA; PhD in Economics 1978, Oxford University, England. *Publications:* British Economists and the Empire 1860-1914, 1983; Co-Author, International Economics: An Australian Perspective, 1983; Editor of 21 books on various great economists; 6 chapters in books; Author or co-Author of 9 articles in refereed journals; 24 other publications and conference papers. *Honours:* Shell Scholarship, University of Oxford 1975-78; Nuffield College Studentship, University of Oxford 1977-78; Visiting Professorship, J F Kennedy School of Government, Harvard University, Visiting Scholar, National University of Singapore 1981- 82; Visiting Fellowship, Nuffield College, Oxford, Visitor, OECD, Paris 1983- 84; Visiting Fellowship, Brookings Institute, Washington, Visiting Professorship, Berkeley Graduate School of Public Policy 1984-85; Duke of Edinburgh's Third Commonwealth Study Conference, Australia 1986. *Memberships:* Counsellor, CEDA; Counsellor, Economic Society of Western Australia; Counsellor, Royal Institute of Public Administration; Chairman of Directors, Helm Wood Publishers Pty Ltd. *Address:* 23 Simper Street, Wembley 6014, Western Australia, Australia.

WOOD Kerry. *See:* **WOOD Edgar Allandyce.**

WOOD Marguerite Noreen b. 27 Sept 1923, Ipswich, Suffolk, England, Poet; Physiotherapist, J.P. m. Douglas James Wood, 12 Apr 1947, 1 son, 1 daughter. *Education:* MCSP, School of Physiotherapy, Devonshire Royal Hospital, Buxton, 1944; BA, Honours, Open University, 1982; Justice of the Peace, 1968-93. *Appointment:* Assistant Editor, Envoi Poetry magazine, 1974-91. *Publications:* Stone of Vision, 1964; Windows are not Enough, 1971; Crack Me the Shell, 1975; A Line Drawn in Water, 1980; Jeanne La Pucelle, song cycle, 1987; Take Time, 1993. *Contributor to:* Various poetry magazines and anthologies. *Memberships:* The Poetry Society; Suffolk Poetry Society, Chairman, 1976-88; Chartered Society of Physiotherapy; Magistrates' Association. *Address:* Sandy Hill, Sandy Lane, Woodbridge, Suffolk, England.

WOOD Robin, b. 1931, United Kingdom. University Educator. Writer. *Appointments:* Lecturer in Film Studies, Queen's University, Canada, 1969-72; Lecturer in Film Studies, University of Warwick, England, 1973-77; Chairman, Department of Fine Arts, Atkinson College, York University, Toronto, Canada, 1977-. *Publications:* Hitchcock's Films, 1975; Howard Hawks, 1967, 2nd Edition, 1981; Arthur Penn, 1968; Antonioni (with Ian Cameron), 1968; Ingmar Bergman, 1969; Claude Chabrol (with Michael Walker), 1971; The Apu Trilogy, 1972; Personal Views: Explorations in Film, 1975; The American Nightmare: Essays on the Horror Film (edited with Richard Lippe, and contributor), 1979; Hollywood from Vietnam to Reagan, 1986. *Address:* Atkinson College, York University, Toronto, Ontario, Canada.

WOOD Ruzena Ariela Valda, b. 17 Mar 1937, Macclesfield, England. Music Archivist; Author; Poet; Composer. *Education:* Hon MA English Literature 1959, Edinburgh University. *Appointment:* Music Department, National Library of Scotland, Edinburgh. *Publications:* The Palace of the Moon, 1981; Other work in progress. *Contributions to:* Editor, Brio, 1964-74; The Edinburgh Star, 1990, 1991. *Membership:* Edinburgh Jewish Literary Society. *Address:* 50 Spottiswoode Street, Edinburgh EH9 1DG, Scotland.

WOOD Thomas Joseph, b. 8 Oct 1930, Hoxie, Arkansas, USA. Journalist; Aviator. *Appointments:* Editor/Publisher, AG-Pilot Magazine; Conservation Aeronautics Magazine; Canadian Aerial Applicator Association National Newsletter; International AG Aviation Foundation Newsletter. *Honours:* Appointed to Board of Nomination, National Aviation Hall of Fame (Dayton); FAA Accident Prevention Counselor; NPA Flight Proficiency Award; Member, Nominations AG Aviation Hall of Fame (Jackson). *Memberships:* Aviation/Space Writers Association; VFW (Life); American Legion; Rotary International; National Aviation Association; American Society of Agricultural Engineers; Canadian Aerial Applicators Association. *Address:* 405 Main Street, Mount Vernon, WA 98273, USA.

WOOD Victoria, b. 19 May 1953, Prestwich,

Lancashire, England. Writer; Comedienne. m. Geoffrey Durham, 1980, 1 son, 1 daughter. *Education:* BA, Drama, Theatre Arts, University of Birmingham. *Publications:* Victoria Wood Song Book, 1984; Lucky Bag, 1985; Up to You Porky, 1986; Barmy, 1987; Mens Sana in Thingummy Doodah, 1990. *Honours:* Recipient, BAFTA Awards, Broadcasting Press Awards; Variety Club BBC Personality of the Year, 1987; Hon D.Litt, Lancaster, 1989. *Agent:* Richard Stone. *Address:* c/o Richard Stone, 25 Whitehall, London, SW1, England.

WOOD William P, b. 23 Apr 1951, Bronxville, New York, USA. Lawyer. *Education:* BA, Political Science, Middlebury College, 1973; JD, University of the Pacific, 1976. *Publications:* Rampage, 1985; Gangland, forthcoming. Motion Picture, Rampage, released 1987; Season premiere, 2 additional episodes, CBS-TV series Kaz, 1978. *Contributions to:* America; Commonweal. *Literary Agent:* Michael Hamilburg, Mitchell Hamilburg Agency. *Address:* c/o Mitchell Hamilburg Agency, 292 South La Cienega Boulevard, Beverley Hills, CA 90211, USA.

WOODCOCK George, b. 8 May 1912, Winnipeg, Canada. Writer. m. Ingeborg Hedwig Linzer, 1949. *Publications:* The White Island, 1940; William Godwin, 1946; The Writer and Politics, 1948; The Anarchist Prince, 1950; Pierre Joseph Proudhon, 1956; Incas and Other Men, 1959; Anarchism, 1962; Faces of India, 1964; The Crystal Spirit, 1966; The Doukhobors, 1968; Odysseus Ever Returning, 1970; Canada and the Canadians, 1970; Herbert Read, 1972; The Rejection of Politics, 1972; Who Killed the British Empire?, 1974; Notes on Visitations, 1975; Gabrial Dumont, 1975; Peoples of the Coast, 1977; Thomas Merton, Monk and Poet, 1978; Faces from History, 1978; The Kestrel and Other Poems, 1978; The Canadians, 1979; The World of Canadian Writing, 1980; The George Woodcock Reader, 1980; The Mountain Road, poems, 1980; Taking It to the Letter, 1981; Ivan Eyre, 1985; Confederation Betrayed, 1981; The Benefactor, 1982; Letter to the Past, 1982; Collected Poems, 1983; British Columbia: a Celebration, 1983; Orwell's Message, 1984; Strange Bedfellows: The State and the Arts in Canada, 1985; Walls of India, 1985; The University of British Columbia: A Souvenir, 1986; Letters from Sooke, 1986; Northern Spring, 1987; Beyond the Blue Mountains, 1987; A Social History of Canada, 1988; Caves in the Desert, 1988; The Marvellous Century, 1988; The Century that Made Us, 1989; Powers of Observation, 1989; The Monk and His Message, 1991; Power To Us All, 1992; Letter for the Khyber Pass, 1992. *Contributions to:* Articles in many British, US and Canadian Journals; plays, documentaries & talks for CBC; film scripts. *Address:* 6429 McCleery Street, Vancouver, BC V6N 1G5, Canada.

WOODCOCK Joan, b. 6 Feb 1908, Bournemouth, England. Poet. m. Alexander Neville Woodcock, 18 Sept 1937, 2 sons, 1 daughter. *Appointments:* Secretary and Editorial Assistant to Chief Fiction Editor of the Associated Press, London; Secretary and Assistant to a Gaumont British film producer; Employed by Baird Television, worked with John Logie Baird on his projected biography; Extensive traveller; Exhibited Artist and Genealogist; Published Poet. *Publications:* The Wandering Years, 1990; Borrowing From Time, 1992. *Contributions to:* Envoi; Orbis; Iota; First Time; and others; Envoi Anthologies 1989, 90, 91; Fragments (2 anthologies for Calne Music and Arts Annual Festivals, Wiltshire); Has read her poems and been interviewed on BBC radio. *Honours:* Prizes: Envoi, Rhyme International (Orbis); World Order of Narrative and Formalist Poets, New York, 1991; Writers Forum. *Memberships:* The Poetry Society; Associate member, Peterloo Poets; Founder member, Calne Writers' Circle; Vese Writers Guild of Ohio, USA; National Federation of State Poetry Societies Inc, USA; Scottish Genealogy Society; Birmingham and Midland Society for Genealogy and Heraldry; Wiltshire and other Family History Societies. *Address:* 6 Hudson Road, Malmesbury, Wiltshire SN16 0BS, England.

WOODCOCK John Charles, b. 7 Aug 1926, Longparish, Hampshire, England. Cricket Writer. *Education:* Trinity College, Oxford; MA, Oxon. *Literary Appointments:* Staff, Manchester Guardian, 1952-54; Cricket Correspondent for The Times, 1954-; Editor, Wisden Cricketers' Almanack, 1980-86. *Publications:* The Ashes, 1956; Barclays World of Cricket (with E.W. Swanton), 1980. *Contributions to:* Country Life, 1962-92; The Cricketer (Board of Directors). *Honour:* Sportswriter of the Year Award, British Press Awards, 1987. *Address:* The Curacy, Longparish, Nr. Andover, Hants, SP11 6PB, England.

WOODCOTT Keith. *See:* **BRUNNER John Kilian Houston.**

WOODEN Rodney John, b. 16 July 1945, London, England. Playwright. *Publications:* Your Home in the West, 1991. Major Play Productions: High Brave Boy, Northern Stage, Newcastle Upon Tyne, 1990, Off The RSC, Fringe Festival, 1992; Woyzeck, an adaption from the German of Georg Buchner, Northern Stage, Newcastle Upon Tyne, 1990; Your Home in the West, Royal Exchange Theatre, Manchester, 1991, Steppenwolf Theatre, Chicago, 1991, Live Theatre, Newcastle Upon Tyne, 1992; Anti/Gone, Drama Centre, Darlington, 1992, The Other Place, Stratford Upon Avon, 1992. *Honours:* First Prizewinner, Mobil International Playwriting Competition, for Your Home in the West, 1990; Mobil Writer in Residence Bursary, Royal Exchange Theatre, Manchester, 1991-92; John Whiting Award, Arts Council of Great Britain, for Your Home in the West, 1991. *Membership:* PEN International. *Literary Agent:* Micheline Steinberg. *Address:* c/o Micheline Steinberg Playwrights, 110 Frognal, London NW3 6XU, England.

WOODFORD Peggy, b. 19 Sept 1937, Assam, India. Writer. m. Walter Aylen, 1 Apr 1967, 3 daughters. *Education:* MA, English, Hons., St. Anne's College, Oxford. *Publications:* Please Don't Go, 1972; Rise of the Raj, 1978; See You Tomorrow, 1979; Misfits, (editor and contributor, short stories), 1984; Monster in our Midst, 1987; Out of the Sun, 1990; Mozart, His Life and Times, 1977; Schubert, His Life and Times, 1978; The Girl with a Voice, 1981; Love Me, Love Rome, 1984. *Literary Agent:* Murray Pollinger. *Address:* c/o Murray Pollinger, 222 Old Brompton Road, London SW5 0BZ, England.

WOODFORDE John Edward Ffooks, b. 10 Apr 1925. Wrtier. Widower, 1 son, 2 daughters. *Education:* BA, Hons Englsih, Radley College, Cambridge. *Appointments:* Staff, Evening Standard; Daily Telegraph; Sunday Telegraph, 1956-87. *Publications:* The Strange Story of False Teeth, 1968; The Truth about Cottages, 1969; The Story of the Beagle, 1970; Georgian Homes for All; Farm Buildings. *Address:* New Hall, High Street, Ludd, Kent, England.

WOODHEAD Peter Anthony, b. 11 Nov 1944, Shipley, Yorkshire, England. m. Sylvia Ann, 24 Aug 1970, 1 son, 1 daughter. *Education:* BA Classics 1966, University College London; MA Librarianship 1969, University of Sheffield; M Phil Archaeology 1985, University of Leicester. *Publications:* Keyguide to Information Sources in Archaeology, 1985; Keyguide to Information Sources in Museum Studies, co-author, 1989. *Contributions to:* Various articles on library topics in librarianship periodicals. *Honour:* The Keyguide to Information Sources in Museum Studies was selected as an Outstanding Reference Book for 1990, by Choice, the major reviewing journal for reference publications in the United States. *Membership:* Associate member, Library Association. *Address:* 81 Uppingham Road, Houghton-on-the-Hill, Leicestershire LE7 9HL, England.

WOODMAN Richard Martin, b. 10 Mar 1944, London, England. Shipmaster. m. 15 Feb 1969, 1 son, 1 daughter. *Education:* Westminster City School 1955-60. *Publications:* The Nathaniel Drinkwater novels: An

Eye of the Fleet, 1981; A King's Cutter, 1982; A Brig of War, 1983; The Bomb Vessel, 1984; The Corvette, 1985; 1805, 1985; Baltic Mission, 1986; In Distant Waters, 1988; A Private Revenge, 1989; Under False Colours, 1991; The Flying Squadron, 1992; Also: Keepers of the Sea, 1983; View from the Sea, 1985; Voyage East, 1988; Wager, 1990; The Darkening Sea, 1991; Plays: Liberty of Death, 1990; The Trial of George Fox (co-author), 1991. *Honour:* Barbara Harmer Award given by The Marine Society, 1978. *Memberships:* The Society of Authors; Society for Nautical Research; Navy Records Society; Royal Institute of Navigation; Nautical Institute. *Literary Agent:* Barbara Levy. *Address:* Harwich, Essex CO12 3RS, England.

WOODRESS James (Leslie Jr), b. 1916, USA. Professor of English (retired 1987). *Appointments:* Assistant News Editor, KWK Radio, St Louis, Missouri, 1939-40; Rewrite Staff, UPI, New York City, 1941-43; Instructor, Grinnell College, Iowa, 1949-50; Assistant Professor, then Associate Professor, Butler University, Indianapolis, Indiana, 1950-58; Professor of English, 1958-66, Dean, 1963-64, San Fernando Valley State College, Northridge, California; Advisory Editor, College, English, 1961-63; Professor of English, University of California, Davis, 1966-. *Publications:* Howells and Italy, 1952; Booth Tarkington: Gentleman from Indiana, 1955; Dissertations in American Literature 1891-1955, 1957, 1962; A Yankee's Odyssey: The Life of Joel Barlow, 1958; Voices from America's Past series (edited with Richard B Morris), 1962- 63, 1975; American Literary Scholarship: An Annual (editor), 1963, 1965, later volumes; Willa Cather: Her Life and Art, 1970; Eight American Authors (editor), 1971; American Fiction 1900-1950, 1974; Willa Cather: A Literary Life, 1987. *Address:* Department of English, University of California, Davis, CA 95616, USA.

WOODS P F. *See:* **BAYLEY Barrington John.**

WOODS Kenneth, b. 23 Aug 1954, Richmond, Virginia, USA. Speaker; Writer; Teacher. m. Brenda Lee Roberts, 26 Feb 1983, 2 sons, 1 daughter. *Education:* Virginia State University, 1972-77. *Publications:* Life Goes On, 1982; Education is Attitude, 1984. *Contributions To:* various journals and magazines. *Honour:* Golden Poet Award, 1987. *Memberships:* International Society of Poets; Poet-National Library of Congress; International Platform Association. *Address:* 1312 S Indian Creek Drive, Stone Mountain, GA 30083, USA.

WOODS Stuart Chevalier, b. 9 Jan 1938, Manchester, Georgia, USA. Writer. m. Judy Nicholas Tabb, 27 Dec 1984, 1 stepdaughter. *Education:* BA, Sociology, University of Georgia, 1959. *Publications include:* Blue Water, Green Skipper, memoir, 1977; Romantic's Guide to Country Inns of Britain & Ireland, 1979. Novels: Chiefs, 1981; Run Before the Wind, 1983; Deep Lie, 1986; Under the Lake, 1987; White Cargo, 1988; Grass Roots, 1989; Palindrome, 1990. *Contributions to:* New York Times; Yachting; TV Guide; Yachting World. *Honour:* Edgar Allen Poe Award. *Memberships:* Century Association; PEN; Authors Guild; Writes Guild of America; New York Yacht Club; Royal Yacht Squadron, England. *Literary Agent:* Morton L. Janklow. *Address:* 4340 Tree Haven Drive NE, Atlanta, Georgia 30342, USA.

WOODWARD Bob, b. 26 Mar 1943, USA. Journalist; Author; Assistant Editor, the Washington Post. 1 daughter. *Education:* BA, Yale, 1965. *Publications:* All the President's Men, 1974; The Final Days, 1976; The Brethren, 1979; Wired, 1984; Veil, 1987. *Address:* 3027 Q Street, N W, Washington, DC 20007, USA

WOODWARD Douglas Powell, b. 16 Jan 1954, Rochester, New York, USA. Economist. m. 10 July 1981, 2 sons. *Education:* BA, State University of New York at Purchase; MA, New York University; PhD, University of Texas. *Publication:* The New Competitors.

Contributions to: Southern Economic Journal; Economic Development Quarterly; Journal of International Business Studies. *Honour:* Business Week's Top Ten Books of the Year 1989. *Memberships:* American Economic Association; Southern Economic Association. *Address:* 3118 Wilmot Avenue, Columbia, SC 29205, USA.

WOODWARD Gerard, b. 4 Dec 1961, London, England. Writer. m. Suzanne Anderson, 16 June 1983. *Education:* Fine Art, Falmouth School of ARt, 1981-83; BSc, Social Anthropology, London School of Economics, 1991. *Publications:* The Unwriter and Other Poems, 1989; Householder, 1991. *Contributions to:* Times Literary Supplement; Poetry Review; PN Review; Stand; London Magazine; Verese; Oxford Poetry; Orbis. *Honours:* Eric Gregory Award, 1991; Poetry Book Society Choice, 1991; Somerset Maugham Award, 1992; Shortlisted, J L Rhys Prize, Mail On Sunday, 1992. *Membership:* Society of Authors. *Address:* c/o Chatto and Windus, 20 Vauxhall Bridge Road, London SW1V 2SA, England.

WOODWORTH Steven Edward, b. 28 Jan 1961, Akron, Ohio, USA. College Professor. m. Leah Bunke, 13 Aug 1983, 3 sons. *Education:* BA 1982, Southern Illinois University; PhD 1987, Rice University. *Publication:* Jefferson Davis and His Generals, 1990. *Honour:* Fletcher Pratt Award, 1990. *Memberships:* American Historical Association; Southern Historical Association. *Address:* PO Box 800006, Toccoa Falls, GA 30598, USA.

WOOLF Douglas, b. 23 Mar 1922, New York City, New York, USA. Migrant Writer/Worker. *Publications:* The Hypocritic Days, 1955; Fade Out, 1959; Wall to Wall, 1961; Signs of a Migrant Worrier, 1965; Ya and John- Juan, 1971; On Us, 1977; HAD, 1977; Future Preconditional, 1978; The Timing Chain, 1985; Loving Ladies, 1986. *Contributions:* Numerous. *Address:* PO Box 215, Tacoma, WA 98401, USA.

WOOLF Rossetta, b. 30 Oct 1959, Kent, England. Artist. *Education:* State education; Travelled in Northern Spain and studied flamenco, trapeze and traditional arts, learning painting techniques on the way, via the Caribbean. *Publications:* Message in a Bottle, 1982; Under the Storyteller's Spell, 1989; Kamal Woolf Pack, 1990. *Contributions to:* AIN (monthly) 1989-. *Address:* 35D Hanley Road, London N4 3DU, England.

WORBOYS Anne Eyre. *See:* **WORBOYS Annette Isobel.**

WORBOYS Annette Isobel (Annette Eyre, Vicky Maxwell, Anne Eyre Warboys), b. New Zealand. Author. m. Walter Worboys, 2 daughters. *Publications:* A Kingdom for the Bold; Run, Sara, Run; The Bhunda Jewels; The Lion of Delos; Every Man a King; The Barrancourt Destiny; China Silk. *Honour:* Winner, Romantic Novelists Association, Romantic Novel of Year, 1976. *Memberships:* Crimewriters Association; Romantic Novelists Association; Society of Women Writers and Journalists; Tunbridge Wells and District Writers Circle; Society of Authors. *Literary Agent:* Jacqueline Korn, David Higham Associates. *Address:* The White House, Leigh, Tonbridge, Kent, England.

WORCESTER Richard Gray, b. 11 Mar 1917, Tilbury, England, Aerospace Counsel. m. 7 Jan 1956, 2 sons, 2 daughters. *Education:* George Washington University, Washington DC, USA, 1950. *Appointments:* Writer, Engineering Test Pilot, The Aeroplane, 1945; Editor, Design/Engineering, American Aviation, Washington DC, USA, 1950; Founder, Aviation Studies International, 1951. *Publications:* Roots of British Air Policy, 1966; Rationalization Measures for British Industry; Assessment of Rhodesian Air Force, 1969; Over 4000 Twice-weekly aviation reports and 16 other titles written quarterly, 1951-. *Contributor to:* The Times; Daily Mail; Spectator; Wall Street Journal; Numerous

Magazines. *Memberships:* Aviation and Space Writers Association, USA. *Address:* Sussex House, Parkside, Wimbledon, London, SW19 5NB, England.

WORSLEY Dale, b. 3 Nov 1948, Louisiana, USA. Writer. m. Elizabeth Fox, 14 July 1991. *Appointments:* The Writing Programme, Columbia University, New York City, 1992. *Publications:* The Focus Changes of August Previco, 1980; The Art of Science Writing, 1989; Plays: Cold Harbor, 1983; The Last Living Newspaper, 1993. *Honours:* Fellowships in Fiction, 1986, Fellowship in Playwriting, 1989, National Endowment for the Arts. *Membership:* Dramatists Guild. *Literary Agents:* Ellen Levine; Susan Schulman. *Address:* 150 Lafayette Ave 1, Brooklyn, NY 11238, USA.

WORSTHORNE Peregrine Gerard, b. 22 Dec 1923, Chelsea, London, England. Journalist. m. 1950, 1 daughter. *Education:* History Exhibitioner, Peterhouse, Cambridge; BA(hons) Cantabl Magdalen College, Oxford. *Literary Appointments:* Editorial Staff, Glasgow Herald, 1946-48; Editorial Staff, 1948-50, Washington Correspondent, 1950-52, Leader Writer, 1952-55, The Times; Leader Writer, Daily Telegraph, 1955-61; Assistant Editor, 1961-86, Editor, 1986-89, Editor, Comment Section, 1989-91, Columnist, 1991-, Sunday Telegraph. *Publications:* The Socialist Myth, 1972; Peregrinations, 1980; By The Right, 1987. *Contributions to:* Encounter; New York Times; Foreign Affairs; Twentieth Century; The Spectator; Washington Post; The American Spectator; Time and Tide. *Honour:* Granada Columnist of the Year, 1980. *Memberships:* Garrick Club; Beefsteak Club. *Literary Agent:* David Higham Limited. *Address:* c/o The Sunday Telegraph, 1 Canada Square, Canary Wharf, London E14 5DT, England.

WORTH Anthony. *See:* **WEST William Alexander.**

WOŚ Joanna Helena, b. 12 Dec 1951, Buffalo, New York, USA. Fiction Writer. m. Ray W Gonyea, 23 June 1984, 1 son. *Education:* Studio Arts, Rosary Hill College, 1969-71; BA, Art History, University of Pittsburgh, 1973; MA, Art History, Boston University, 1975. *Publications:* The One Sitting There, in Flash Fiction, 1992; Taken, in Loss of the Ground Note: Women Writing about the Loss of Their Mothers, 1992. *Contributions to:* Short stories to: Malahat Review; Kalliope; Ellipsis; Perma Frost; The Webster Review; The Old Red Kimono; The Little Magazine; Lost Creek Letters; Pleiades; Echoes; American Writing; Arts in Buffalo; The MacGuffin and Salmon Magazine. *Memberships:* PEN Center, USA West, PEN New Mexico Chapter, listed in Poets and Writers. *Address:* 1843 Otowi Drive, Santa Fe, NM 87501, USA.

WOUK Herman, b. 27 May 1915, New York City, USA. Writer. m. Betty Sarah Brown, 9 Dec 1945, 3 sons (1 deceased). *Education:* AB, Columbia University, 1934; LHD, Honorary, Yeshiva University, 1954; Ll.d. Honorary, Clark University, 1960; Litt.D., Honorary, American International College, 1979. *Appointments:* Visiting Professor, English, Yeshiva University, 1952-57; Scholar in Residence, Aspen Institute Humanistic Studies, 1973-74. *Publications:* The Caine Mutiny, 1951; The Winds of War, 1971; War and Remembrance, 1978; Marjorie Morningstar, 1955; The Caine-Mutiny Court-Martial, (Play), 1953; This Is My God, (non-fiction), 1959; Don't Stop the Carnival, 1965; Youngblood Hawke, 1962; City Boy, 1948; Inside, Outside, 1985; Aurora Dawn, 1947; Lomokome Papers, 1956; The Traitor (Play), 1949; Nature's Way (Play), 1957; Slattery's Hurricane, 1949; TV Screen-plays: The Winds of War, 1983; War and Remembrance, 1986; Latest novel: The Hope, 1993. *Honours:* Pulitzer Prize, for The Caine Mutiny, 1952; Columbia University Medal for Excellence, 1952; Alexander Hamilton medal, 1980; University of California Berkeley Medal, 1984; Washington Book Award, 1986; Golden Plate Award, American Academy of Achievement, 1986; US Naval Memorial Foundation "Lone Sailor Award", 1987. *Memberships:* PEN; Authors League; WGA. *Agent:*

B.S.W. Literary Agency. *Address:* c/o B.S.W. Literary Agency,3255 N. St., NW., Washington, DC 20007, USA.

WRACK Philip, b. 24 June 1929, Retford, Nottinghamshire, England. Journalist. 2 sons, 1 daughter. *Appointments:* Member, Press Council, 1986-88; Deputy Editor, News of the World, 1970-89. *Memberships:* Freeman of the City of London; Honorary Life Member, Wig & Pen. *Address:* 10 Alwyne Square, Canonbury, London N1 2JX, England.

WRIGHT A J. *See:* **WRIGHT Amos Jasper III.**

WRIGHT Amos Jasper III, (A J Wright), b. 3 Mar 1952, Gadsden, Alabama, USA. Medical Librarian. m. Margaret Dianne Vargo, 14 June 1980, 1 son, 1 daughter. *Education:* BA 1973, Auburn University; MLS 1983, University of Alabama. *Publications:* Frozen Fruit, poetry, 1978; Right Now I Feel Like Robert Johnson, poetry, 1981; Criminal Activity in the Deep South, 1700-1930, 1989. *Contributions to:* Anaesthesiology; Anaesthesia and Analgesia; Poem; Aura; Old West; and others. *Memberships:* Authors Guild; Poetry Society of America; Medical Library Association; Anaesthesia History Association. *Address:* 617 ValleyView Drive, Pelham, AL 35124, USA.

WRIGHT Anthony David, b. 9 June 1947, Oxford, England. Historian. *Education:* City of London School 1958-65; BA Hons (Class I) 1968, Merton College, Oxford; MA (Oxon) 1973, British School at Rome; D Phil (Oxon) 1973, Brasenose College, Oxford 1971-74. *Publications:* The Counter- Reformation, 1982; Catholicism and Spanish Society, 1991. *Contributions to:* English Historical Review; History; Historical Journal; Ecclesiastical History Journal; Historical Research; Studies in Church History; Northern History; Art History. *Honours:* Accademia Di San Carlo, member 1979; Fellowship, Royal Historical Society 1980; Visiting Fellowship, Edinburgh University, 1983. *Memberships:* Athenaeum; Ecclesiastical History Society, National Committee. *Address:* School of History, University of Leeds, Leeds LS2 9JT, England.

WRIGHT C D, b. 6 Jan 1949, Mountain Home, Arkansas, USA. Poet; Professor. m. Forrest Gander, 23 Sept 1983, 1 son. *Education:* BA 1971, Memphis State University; MFA 1976, University of Arkansas. *Publications:* Terrorism, 1979; Translations of the Gospel Back Into Tongues, 1981; Further Adventures with God, 1986; String Light, 1991; Just Whistle, 1992. *Contributions include:* Field; Ironwood; The New Yorker; Kenyon Review; Paris Review; Conjunctions; Sulfur; Tri-Quarterly. *Honours:* Fellowship from National Endowment for the Arts, 1981, 1987; Witter Bynner Prize for Poetry, 1986; Guggenheim Fellowship, 1987; Mary Ingraham Bunting Fellowship, 1987; GE Award for Younger Writers, 1988; Whiting Writers Award, 1989; Rhode Island Governors Award for Arts, 1990. *Address:* 351 Nayatt Road, Barrington, RI 02806, USA.

WRIGHT Charles Penzel, Jr, b. 25 Aug 1935, Pickwick Dam, Tennessee, USA. Writer; Teacher. m. Holly McIntire, 6 Apr 1969, 1 son. *Education:* BA, Davidson College, 1957; MFA, University of Iowa, 1963; Postgraduate, University of Rome, Italy, 1963-64. *Appointments include:* University of California, Irvine, 1966-83; University of Virginia, 1983-. *Publications include:* Grave of the Right Hand, 1970; Hard Freight, 1973; Bloodlines, 1975; China Trace, 1977; Southern Cross, 1981; Country Music, selected early poems, 1982; Other Side of the River, 1984; Zone Journals, 1988; The World of the 10,000 Things, 1990. Translations: The Storm, 1978; Orphic Songs, 1984. *Contributions to:* Numerous magazines & journals. *Honours:* Edgar Allen Poe Award, Academy of American Poets, 1976; PEN translation award, 1979; National Book Award, poetry, 1983; Brandeis Creative Arts Award, poetry, 1987; The Ruth Lilly Poetry Prize, 1993. *Memberships include:* PEN American Centre. *Address:*

940 Locust Avenue, Charlottesville, Virginia 22901, USA.

WRIGHT David, (John Murray), b. 1920, United Kingdom. Writer; Poet. *Appointments:* Staff Member, Sunday Times, London, 1942-47; Editor, Nimbus, London, 1955-56; Editor, X magazine, London, 1959-62; Gregory Fellow in Poetry, University of Leeds, 1965-1967. *Publications:* Poems, 1949; The Forsaken Garden: An Anthology of Poetry 1824-1909 (edited with John Heath-Stubbs), 1950; Moral Stories, 1952; The Faber Book of Twentieth Century Verse (edited with John Heath-Stubbs), 1953; Moral Stories, 1954; Beowulf, translation, 1957; Monologue of a Deaf Man, 1958; Roy Campbell, 1960; The Canterbury Tales, by Geoffrey Chaucer, translation, 1964; Seven Victorian Poets (editor), 1964; Adam at Evening, 1965; Algarve (with P Swift), 1965, 2nd Edition, 1971; The Mid-Century English Poetry 1940-60 (editor), 1965; Poems, 1966; Longer Contemporary Poems (editor), 1966; Minho and North Portugal: A Portrait and a Guide (with P Swift), 1968; The Penguin Book of English Romantic Verse (editor), 1968; Nerve Ends, 1969; Deafness: A Personal Account, 1969; Recollections of the Lakes and the Lake Poets, by Thomas de Quincey (editor), 1970; Lisbon: A Portrait and a Guide (with P Swift), 1971; Records of Shelley, Byron, and the Author, by Edward Trelawny (editor), 1973; A South African Album, 1975; A View of the North, 1976; To the Gods of the Shades: New and Collected Poems, 1976; The Penguin Book of Everyday Verse (editor), 1976; Under the Greenwood Tree, by Hardy (editor), 1978; Selected Poems, by Hardy (editor), 1979; Metrical Observations, 1980; Selected Poems, 1980; Edward Thomas: Selected Poems and Prose (editor), 1981; The Canterbury Tales, by Chaucer, verse translation, 1985; Selected Poems, 1988; Elegies, 1990; Deafness (New and Revised edition), 1990. *Literary Agent:* A D Peters Ltd, England. *Address:* c/o A D Peters Ltd, 10 Buckingham Street, Adelphi, London WC2N 6BU, England.

WRIGHT Elinor, (Elinor Lyon), b. 17 Aug 1921, Guisborough, Yorkshire, England. Housewife. m. Peter Wright, 19 Apr 1944, 2 sons, 2 daughters. *Education:* Headington School, Oxford, 1934-38; St George's School, Montreux, Switzerland, 1939; Lady Margaret Hall, Oxford, 1940-41 (cut short by volunteering for service in the WRNS). *Publications:* Children's Books: The Golden Shore, 1957; Daughters of Aradale, 1957; Green Grow the Rushes, 1964; Echo Valley, 1965; The Dream Hunters, 1966; Strangers at the Door, 1967; Hilary's Island, 1948; Wishing Watergate, 1949; The House in Hiding, 1950; We Daren't Go a-Hunting, 1951; Run Away Home, 1953; Sea Treasure, 1955; Dragon Castle, 1956; Rider's Rock, 1958; Cathie Runs Wild, 1960; Carver's Journey, 1962; The Day that Got Lost, 1968; The Wishing Pool, 1970; The King of Grey Corrie, 1975; The Floodmakers, 1976. *Address:* Bron Meini, Harlech, Gwynedd, Wales LL46 2YT.

WRIGHT Fred W Jr b. 21 Apr 1940, Nashville, Tennessee, USA, Writer; Teacher. *Education:* Davidson College, Davidson, North Carolina, 1958-60; BA, Eckerd College, St Petersburg, Florida, 1960-64; MA, University of South Florida, Tampa, 1969-71. *Appointments:* Feature Writer and Theatre and Film Critic, St Petersburg Evening Independent, Florida, 1964-75; Co-Editor, The Radiance Technique Journal, 1986-. *Publications:* The Radiance Technique on the Job, 1987; Insight Guides: Florida, (Florida Editor). *Contributions to:* Contributor of over 1000 nonfiction articles in dozens of publications including: GEO; Advertising Age; Variety; Next!; Moviegoer; The Floridian; Value and Retail News; Emergency. *Honours Include:* Awards for Poetry and Short Fiction and Non-fiction; 2nd Place, Columns, Florida Press Club, 1978; 1st Place, News, Florida Press Club, 1979. *Memberships:* Florida Freelance Writers Association, Board of Directors; Florida Suncoast Writers Conference, Founding Member, Board of Directors; Mensa; The Radiance Technique Association International Incorporated. *Address:* PO Box 86158, St Petersburg, FL 33738, USA.

WRIGHT Graeme Alexander, b. 23 Apr 1943, Wellington, New Zealand. Freelance editor and writer. *Appointments:* Managing Editor, Queen Anne Press, 1972-74; Editor and Freelance writer 1974-; Director, John Wisden & Co Ltd, 1983-87; Editor, Wisden Cricketers' Almanack, 1986-92. *Publications:* Great Moments in the Olympics, 1976; Phil Read - The Real Story, co-author with Phil Read, 1977; The Illustrated Handbook of Sporting Terms, 1978; Olympic Greats, 1980; Where Do I Go From Here? co-author with George Best, 1981; Test Decade 1972-1982, with Patrick Eagar, 1982; Botham, with Patrick Eagar, 1985; Brown Sauce, co-author with Joe Brown, 1986; Forty Vintage Years, Merrydown Wine plc, 1988; Betrayel: The Struggle for Cricket's Soul, 1993. *Address:* 14 Field End Road, Eastcote, Pinner, Middlesex HA5 2QL, England.

WRIGHT Laurali Rose, b. 5 June 1939, Saskatoon, Canada. Writer. m. 6 Jan. 1962, 2 daughters. *Education:* University of Calgary; Banff School of Fine Arts; University of British Columbia. *Publications:* The Suspect, 1985; The Favorite, 1982; Neighbours, 1979; Among Friends, 1984; Sleep While I Sing, 1986; Love in the Temperate Zone, 1988; Chill Rain in January, 1990; Prized Possessions, 1993. *Contributions to:* Journalist, Western Canadian Newspapers, 1968-77; Contributor to numerous professional journals, newspapers and magazines, 1977-. *Honours:* Alberta First Novel Award, 1978; Edgar Allan Poe Best Novel Award, Mystery Writers of America, 1986; Arthur Ellis Award from Crime Writers of Canada, 1991. *Memberships:* International PEN; Writers' Union of Canada; Authors Guild, USA. *Agent:* Virginia Barber. *Address:* c/o Virginia Barber Agency Inc., 101 Fifth Avenue, New York, NY 10003, USA.

WRIGHT Mary Morgan, (Mary Morgan), b. 27 Nov 1943, Searcy, Arkansas, USA. Writer; Programme Coordinator. m. (1) Clifford Councille, 1964, 1 daughter, (2) Benjamin Spock, 24 Oct 1976. *Education:* BA 1968, Hendrix College, Conway, Arkansas. *Appointments:* Self-employed Author, Programme Coordinator for Dr Spock's Lectures, Press and other speaking events, 1976-; Coordinator for speaking engagements for political causes, equal rights, civil disobedience for peace and disarmament 1976-86. *Publications:* Stepparenting, Experts Advise Parents, 1986; Spock on Spock, 1989. *Contributions to:* Loved Him First as a Teacher, My Marriage to Dr Spock, Parade: The Sunday Newspaper Magazine, 1984; Why I Married an Older Man, 1985. *Literary Agent:* Robert Lescher, Lescher & Lescher, New York. *Address:* PO Box 1268, Camden, ME 04843, USA.

WRIGHT Nancy Means, b. New Jersey, USA Author. m. 2 sons, 2 daughters. *Education:* AB, Vassar College; MA, Middlebury College. *Appointments:* Instructor English, various schools, 1960-87; Proctor Academy; Burlington College; Marist College, New York, 1990. *Publications:* The Losing, 1973; Down the Strings, 1982; Make Your Own Change, 1985; Vermonters At Their Craft, 1987; Tall Girls Don't Cry, 1990; Split Nipples, 1992. *Contributor to:* various journals and magazines. *Honours:* Scholar, Bread Loaf Writers Conference 1959; Grant for Novel in Progress Society of Children's Book Writers, 1987. *Memberships:* President, League of Vermont Writers, 1978-80; Poets and Writers; Authors League; Society of childens Book Writers. *Address:* Box 38, Bristol, VT 05443, USA.

WRIGHT (Mary) Patricia (Mary Napier), b. 1932, United Kingdom. Author; Previously Teacher of History and Economics (part-time); E Sussex County Councillor, 1981-. *Publications:* Conflict on the Nile: Study of Fashoda Incident 1897-1900, 1972; Space of the Heart, 1976, Paperback as Ilena, 1977; Journey into Fire, 1977; Shadow of the Rock, 1978; Storm Harvest, US Edition Heart of the Storm, 1979; Blind Chance, 1980; This, My City, 1981; While Paris Danced, 1982; History of Frant, 1982; I Am England, 1987; That Near & Distant Place, 1988. As Mary Napier: Woman's Estate, sketches, 1959; Forbidden Places, 1981; State of Fear, 1984; Heartsearch, 1987; Powers of Darkness, 1990. *Honour:*

Georgette Heyer Award, for I Am England, 1987. *Address:* Whitehill House, Frant, Sussex, TN3 9DX, England.

WRIGHT Peter, b. 30 Mar 1923, Fleetwood, Lancashire, England. Forensic Linguist. m. Patricia May Wright, 3 Apr 1956, 1 son, 3 daughters. *Education:* BA, English, 1949, PhD, English Language, 1954, Leeds University; Advanced Diploma in Education, London University, 1960. *Appointments:* Lecturer, English Language, 1965-70, Senior Lecturer, 1970-84, Honorary Senior Lecturer, Fellow in English Dialect Studies, 1984-1992, Salford University; Currently works when needed for Crown or defence, analysing from linguistic angles cases for trial or appeal. *Publications:* The Lanky Twang, 1974, various editions; Language of British Industry, 1974; The Yorkshire Yammer, 1976, various editions; Language at Work, 1978; Cockney Dialect and Slang, 1980; 8 other dialect books. *Contributions to:* Various magazines and journals. *Honours:* Queen's Award for Export Achievement, for examining work, with others of Cambridge Local Examinations Syndicate, 1992. *Memberships:* Life Member, Yorkshire Dialect Society; Life Member, Past Chairman, Past Editor, Past Secretary, Lancashire Dialect Society; Life Member, Lakeland Dialect Society. *Address:* 30 Broadoak Road, Stockport, Cheshire SK7 3BL, England.

WRIGHT Ronald, b. 12 Sept 1948, Surrey, England. *Education:* MA, Archaeology and Anthropology, Cambridge University. *Appointments:* Snider Lecturer, University of Toronto, 1992. *Publications include:* Cut Stones and Crossroads: A Journey in the Two Worlds of Peru, 1984; On Fiji Islands, 1986; Time Among The Maya, 1989; Quechua Phrasebook, 1989; Stolen Continents, 1992. *Contributions:* numerous articles and book reviews in journals including, Soho Square III, Times Literary Supplement; The Globe and Mail; New York Times Book Review; The Washington Post; Saturday Night, and others. *Honours:* Canadian Science Writers Association Award, 1986; Finalist, Trillium Book Award, 1990, 1993; Winner, CBC Literary Award (essay), 1991; Gordon Montador Award, 1993. *Memberships:* Royal Geographical Society, Fellow; Writers Union of Canada; International PEN, Board 1989-91; Latin American Indian Literatures Association; Survival International. *Literary Agents:* Blake Freidmann Ltd, 37-41 Gower Street, London WC1E 6HH, England; Bella Pomer Agency, 22 Shallmar Blvd, PH2, Toronto, Ontario M5N 2Z8. *Address:* R.R.1, Campbellcroft, Ontario, L0A 1B0, Canada.

WRIGHT Roy Kilner, b. 12 Mar 1926, England. Journalist. m. (1) (div), 2 daughters, (2) Jane Barnicoat (nee Selby), 1969. *Appointments include:* Junior reporter, St Helens Reporter, Lancashire, 1941; Sub-editor, Middlesbrough Gazette, 1947, Daily Express, Manchester 1951, Daily Mirror, London 1952; Features editor, deputy editor, Daily Express, London, 1976; Editor, ibid, 1976-77; Director, Beaverbrook Newspapers, 1976-77; Senior assistant editor, Daily Mail, 1977; Deputy editor, London Standard (formerly Evening Standard), 1979-. *Address:* 25 Foskett Road, London SW6, England.

WRIGHT Terence Roy, b. 12 Apr 1951, Rinteln, West Germany. University Lecturer. m. Gabriele Margarethe Hentrich, 2 Sept 1978, 1 son, 1 daughter. *Education:* BA 1973, Christ Church, Oxford; Princeton University 1976-77; PhD 1978, PGCE 1978, Christ Church, Oxford. *Appointments:* Associate Editor, Literature and Theology 1987-. *Publications:* The Religion of Humanity, 1986; Theology and Literature, 1988; Hardy and the Erotic, 1989; George Eliot's 'Middlemarch' 1991; Editor, John Henry Newman: A Man for Our Time?, 1983; Co-Editor, The Critical Spirit and the Will to Believe, 1988. *Contributions to:* Many magazines and journals. *Membership:* American Academy of Religion. *Address:* 14 Woodburn Avenue, Fenham, Newcastle-Upon-Tyne NE4 9EL, England.

WRIGHT MCKINNEY Judith Arundell, b. 31 May 1915, Armidale, New South Wales, Australia. Writer. m. Jack Philip McKinney. 1 daughter. *Education:* University of Sydney, 1935-37; DLitt, Universities of Queensland, New England, Sydney, Monash, New South Wales. *Publications:* Collected Poems, 1971; The Generations of Men (biography), 1959; Preoccupations in Australian Poetry (criticism), 1965; The Cry for the Dead (historical), 1981; The Double Tree (US collection) poems; We Call for a Treaty (historical), 1985, etc. *Contributions to:* Numerous journals and magazines. *Honours:* Grace Leven Prize, 1950; Encyclopedia Britannica Literature Prize, 1965; Robert Frost Memorial Medal, 1970; Alice Award (Australian Society of Women Writers), 1980. *Memberships:* Councillor, Australian Society of Authors; PEN Australia. *Literary Agent:* Angus and Robertson, Publishers. *Address:* PO Box 93, Braidwood, New South Wales 2622, Australia.

WROBLE Lisa Ann, b. 17 June 1963, Michigan, USA. Writer; Publicist. *Education:* Diploma, Writing for Children and Teenagers Course, Institute of Children's Literature, 1983; BA cum laude, English Language, Linguistics, 1985; Certificate, University of Toledo Continuing Education, 1991. *Appointments:* Editor, Publicist, Community Relations Department, Veterans Administration Medical Center, Ann Arbor, Michigan, 1984; Production Coordinator, The Community Crier Newspaper, Plymouth, Michigan, 1985; Publications Coordinator, Comma, Graphics, Plymouth, 1986; Documentation Specialist, National TechTeam, Dearborn, Michigan, 1989. *Publications:* Using Lotus 1-2-3, 1990; Using WordPerfect 5.0, 1990; Science Fair Projects Astronomy, 1992; Science Fair Projects Space Science, 1992; Natural Sciences, 1992. *Contributions to:* Regularly: Touch; Good Apple Newspaper; Contributing Editor, MetroParent; Computer software reviewer: Computel; PCM Magazine. *Memberships:* Certificate of Merit, National Dean's List, 1983; Silver Poet Award, World of Poetry, 1986; Certificate, English as a Second Language-Bilingual Programme, Community Literary Council, 1989; Prize Tested Recipe Winner, Better Homes and Gardens Magazine, 1992. *Memberships:* Society of Children's Book Writers; National Writers Club; Associated Business Writers of America; Literary Volunteers of America, Plymouth Community Literacy Council; Past Secretary, Sigma Tau Delta. *Address:* 14344 Princeton Drive, Plymouth, MI 48170, USA.

WUDUNN Sheryl, b. 16 Nov 1959, New York City, USA. Journalist. m. Nicholas D Kristof, 8 Oct 1988. *Education:* AB 1981, Cornell University; MBA 1986, Harvard Business School; MPA 1988, Princeton University, Woodrow Wilson School. *Appointments:* Reporter, The Wall Street Journal, Los Angeles 1986; Reporter, Reuters, Hong Kong 1987; Reporter, The South China Morning Post, Hong Kong 1987; Correspondent, The New York Times, Beijing Bureau 1989-. *Honours:* George Pobk Award, International Reporting 1989; Overseas Press Club Award 1989; Pulitzer Prize Award, International Reporting 1990. *Address:* c/o Foreign Desk, The New York Times, 229 West 43rd Street, New York, NY 10036, USA.

WUNSCH Josephine M, b. 1914, USA. Author. *Publications:* Flying Skis, 1962; Passport to Russia, 1965; Summer of Decision, 1968; Lucky in Love, 1970; The Aerie (as J Sloan McLean with Virginia Gillett), 1974; Girl in the Rough, 1981; Class Ring, 1983; Free as a Bird, 1984; Breaking Away, 1985; The Perfect Ten, 1986. *Address:* 830 Bishop Road, Grosse Pointe Park, MI 48230, USA.

WURSTER Michael, b. 8 Aug 1940, Moline, Illinois, USA. Poet. *Education:* BA, Dickinson College, 1962. *Appointments:* Poetry Editor, Stuff magazine, 1975-77; Director for Poetry Programmes, Lion Walk Performing Arts Center, 1978-80; Consultant/Facilitator, The Academy of Prison Arts at Western Penitentiary, SCI Pittsburgh, Pennsylvania, 1979-83; Director for Poetry Programmes, The Famous Rider Cultural Center, 1981-86; Coordinator, The Carson Street Gallery Poetry

Series, 1986-88; Advisory Board Member for Literature, The Three Rivers Arts Festival, 1987-90; Southwest Pennsylvania Correspondent, The All Muse Literary Network, 1987-; Consultant for Poetry, Carson Street Gallery, 1988-; Member, Literature Panel, Pennsylvania Council on the Arts, 1990-; Poetry Editor, Cafe Magazine, 1991-; Contributing Editor, The Endless Mountains Review, 1992-. *Publication:* The Cruelty of the Desert, 1989. *Contributions to:* The Bassettown Review; The Galley Sail Review; Poetry Canada Review; Golden Triangle; Flipside; The Greenfield Review; Pig Iron; The Northern Red Oak; 5 AM; Religious Humanism; Chapter Voice; 4th World Forum; Sunrust; The Blue Guitar; In Pittsburgh; Bone & Flesh; Pendulum; 5 AM; The Pittsburgh Quarterly; Violence/Visual Pleasure, others. *Honours:* Pittsburgh Award, Shaded Room magazine, 1970; Most Valuable Player Award, COSMEP Conference, 1980. *Memberships:* Founding Member, Co-Director, Pittsburgh Poetry Exchange; The Academy of American Poets; The Poetry Society of America; Canadian Poetry Association; Ligonier Valley Writers Association. *Address:* 3709 Perrysville Avenue, Pittsburgh, PA 15214, USA.

WYKES Alan, b. 1914, England. Freelance Writer & Journalist. m. 8 Nov 1939. *Appointments include:* Fiction Editor, Strand Magazine, 1947-49; Fiction Executive, Hulton Press, 1953-61. *Publications:* Biography, history, sociology, topography, recreation, literary criticism, novels. Titles include: Pursuit Till Morning, 1947; The Music Sleeping, 1948; Pen Friend, 1950; Happyland, 1952; Concise Survey of American Literature, 1955; Editor, Brabazon Story, 1956; Co-author with J.A.Hunter, Hunter's Tracks, 1957; Compiler, A Sex by Themselves, 1958; Co-author with W.H.Scott- Shaw, Mariner's Tale, 1959; Snake Man, 1960; Nimrod Smith, 1961; Party Games, 1963; Gambling, 1964; Doctor & His Enemy, 1964; Handbook of Amateur Dramatics, 1965, 1966; Great Yacht Race, with D.A. Rayner, 1966; Eye on the Thames, 1966; Siege of Leningrad, 1968; Royal Hampshire Regiment, 1968; Nuremberg Rallies, 1970; Reading: Biography of a Town, 1970; Lucrezia Borgia, 1970; Turning Point, 1972; Compiler, Abroad, 1973; Hitler's Bodyguards, 1974. *Contributions to:* Numerous magazines & Journals. *Membership:* Honorary secretary 1965-85, Savage Club. *Literary Agent:* Laurence Pollinger Ltd. *Address:* 382 Tilehurst Road, Reading, RG3 2NG, England.

WYLIE Betty Jane, b. 21 Feb 1931. Writer. m. William Tennent Wylie, 2 sons, 2 daughters. *Education:* BA, 1950, MA, 1952, University of Manitoba. *Appointments:* Consultant, Puppeteers of America, 1965-73; Writer-in-Library, Burlington, Ontario, 1987-88; Bunting Fellow, Radcliffe College, USA, 1989-90. *Publications:* Beginnings: A Book for Widows, 1977, 3rd Edition, 1985, US and UK editions; A Place on Earth, 1982; Every Woman's Money Book, 1984; The Book of Matthew, 1985; Something Might Happen, poetry, 1989; New Beginnings, 1991; 20 other books; 30 plays produced. *Contributions to:* Regularly, most Canadian magazines, 1973-85; Some US magazines. *Honours:* Education Award for Successfully Single, Ontario Psychology Foundation, 1988; Award for radio drama series Victorian Spice, Canadian Nursing Federation, 1989; University of Manitoba Alumni Jubilee Award, 1990. *Memberships:* Founding Member, Past Vice-Chair, Treasurer, Playwrights Union of Canada; Past Chair, Writers Union of Canada; ACTRA; US Dramatists Guild; CAPAC. *Literary Agent:* Farber Literary Agency, New York City, New York, USA. *Address:* c/o Writers Union of Canada, 24 Ryerson Ave, Toronto, Ontario, Canada M5T 2P3.

WYLIE Laura. *See:* **MATTHEWS Patricia Anne.**

WYN D Ham. *See:* **SHIHWARY Joan Olivia.**

WYND Oswald (Gavin Black), b. Tokyo, Japan. Novelist. m. *Education:* Edinburgh University, Scotland. *Publications:* Black Fountains; Thrillers (as Gavin Black).

Honours: Doubleday Prize for Black Fountains, 1947. *Address:* Crail, Scotland.

WYNDHAM Esther. *See:* **LUTYENS Mary.**

WYNDHAM Francis (Guy Percy), b. 2 July 1924, London, England. Editor; Journalist; Author. *Appointments:* Editor, Andre Deutsch, London, 1955-58; Literary Editor, Queen magazine, 1959-64; Assistant Editor, Staff Writer, Sunday Times, London, 1964-80. *Publications:* Trotsky: A Documentary (co-author), 1972; Out of the War, short stories, 1974; The Letters of Jean Rhys (co-editor), 1984; Mrs Henderson amd Other Stories, 1985; The Other Garden, 1987. *Honours:* Whitbread Literary Award for Best First Novel, 1987.

WYNN John Charles, b. 11 Apr 1920, Akron, Ohio, USA. Professor of Pastoral Theology. m. Rachel Linnell, 27 Aug 1943, 1 son, 2 daughters. *Education:* BA 1941, College of Wooster; BD 1944, Yale University; MA 1963, EdD 1964, Columbia University; Post doctoral fellowship, Cornell University, 1972. *Appointments:* Taught courses in religious journalism at Colgate Rochester Divinity School 1959-69. *Publications:* How Christian Parents Face Family Problems, 1955; Sermons on Marriage and the Family, 1956; Pastoral Ministry to Families, 1957; Families in the Church: A Protestant Survey, 1961; Sex, Family & Society in Theological Focus, 1966; Sex Ethics and Christian Responsibility, 1970; Education for Liberation and other Upsetting Ideas, 1977; The Family Therapist, 1987; Family Therapy in Pastoral Ministry, 1991. *Contributions to:* Over 300 articles in religious periodicals eg: Christian Century; Journal of Psychology and Theology; Ecumenische Rundschau; Presbyterian Life; The Episcopalian; Religious Education. *Honours:* Christian Education for Liberation and Other Upsetting Ideas judged best book of 1977 in category of religious education by Religious Media Today; Five of the listed books were bookclub selections by Religious Book Club, Pastoral Psychology Book Club and others. *Memberships:* The Presbyterian Writers Guild; American Association for Marriage and Family Therapy; Religious Education Association; National Council on Family Relations. *Address:* 717 Maiden Choice Lane 523, Catonsville, MD 21228, USA.

WYRWA-KRZYZANSKI Tadeusz, b. 21 Oct 1947, Poland. Writer and Art Grafik. 1 daughter. *Education:* Adam Mickiewicz University, Poznań, 1975-76. *Appointments:* Wa saw Autumn of Poetry, 1983-; Internation Society of Poetry, Poznań, 1984-; International Meeting of Writers, Duszanbe, USS, 1986; International Meeting of Poetry, Sarjewo, Yugoslavia, 1987. *Publications:* Poetry: Dom Ust, 1977; Drugi-dom, 1981; Fugi z popiołu, 1984; Adoracja śmietnika, 1987; Akt eretcyjny. Poemat tylko dla dorosłych, 1988; Całowanie klamek, 1989; Wyprawa przeciwko podfrozy, 1989; Siwe dziecko, 1990; Munchhausen z Czarnkowa, 1992, 1993; Short Stories: Amfiladowy trakt, 1979; Gumowe Obłoki, 1987; Novel: Kobieta anioł, 1983, 1986; Childrens Books: Cztery Katy a pies w piatym, 1984; Puchy puszki i poduszki, 1985; Wierszyki dookoła Dominiki, 1986; Złoty chłopiec, 1987; Zieolne konie, 1988; Juz idel, 1989; Strach sie bać, 1989; Nitka, wdzieki i rubinowa kropka, 1989; Exhibitions: Marginesy, Poznań, 1988; Ilustracyjność, Piła, 1988; Papierzastość, Piła, 1989; Papier i lustro, Czarnków, 1989; Tuszowanie, tuszowanie, Warszawa, 1989; Opozycje, Poznań, 1989; Kreskowanie, Wyrzysk, 1990; Miting, Poznań, 1991; Wspólnota utrat, Kraków, 1992; Czarne światoa, Piła, 1992, Graf-i-ka, Czarnków, 1992. Pictures for Books: St, eumert, Al. Rozenfeld, L. Zuliński. *Contributor To:* professional Journals and magazines. *Honours:* Ziemia Nadnotecka, 1977; Medal of New Arts 1980; Prix Wilhelm Mach, 1979; Prix Stanisław Pietak, 1984; Prix Ped Rose, 1987; Priz Ministers of Culture and Arts; many other honours and awards. *Membership:* Polish Writers Association. *Address:* ul. Łaczna 29 m. 7 64-920 Piła, Poland.

X

XIE Bingxin, b. 1900, Fu Zhou, People's Republic of China. Writer. m. Wu Wenzao, 15 June 1929. 1 son, 2 daughters. *Education:* Women's Union College, 1918-20; BA, Yenjing University, 1921-23; MA, Wellesley College, USA, 1923-26. *Literary Appointments:* Lecturer, Yenjing and Qinghua Universities, 1926-37; Adviser to China Writers' Association; Vice-Chairman of China Federation of Literary and Art Circles. *Publications:* Poetry: A Maze of Stars, 1922; Spring Water, 1922; Short Stories: Superman, 1923; Prose: Letters to Young Readers, 1923-26; More Letters to Young Readers, 1958-60; Feature Stories: On Women, 1943; Novel: Tao Qi's Diary, 1952; Novella: A Little Orange Lantern, 1957; We have Awoke Spring, 1950; Ode to Cherry Blossoms, 1961; Empty Nest, 1980; Translations of Tagore's Gitanjali, The Gardener, 1955; Gibran's The Prophet, 1931; Sand and Foam, 1963. *Contributions to:* People's Literature; Chinese Writers; World Literature; Harvest. *Honour:* Short Story Award for Empty Nest, 1980. *Address:* c/o China Writers Association, Shatan Beijie 2, Beijing, People's Republic of China.

Y

YAFFE James, b. 31 Mar 1927, Chicago, Illinois, USA. Writer; Teacher. m. 1 Mar 1964, 1 son, 2 daughters. *Education:* BA 1948, Yale University. *Publications:* Detective Novels: A Nice Murder for Mom, 1988; 3 others; The American Jews, non-fiction, 1968; The Voyage of Mr Franz- Joseph, novel, 1970; The Deadly Game, play, 1960; Cliff Hanger, play, 1985; Poor Cousin Evelyn, short stories; The Good-for-Nothing, novel; What's the Big Hurry?, novel; Mr Margolies, novel; Nothing But the Night, novel; Nobody Does You Any Favours, novel; So Sue Me!, non-fiction; Saul and Morris, Worlds Apart, novel; Ivory Tower, play. *Contributions to:* Esquire; Atlantic; Commentary; Saturday Review; New York Times; Ladies Home Journal; Ellery Queen's Mystery Magazine. *Honour:* National Arts Foundation Award, 1967 for Ivory Tower. *Memberships:* PEN; MWA; Writers Guild; Dramatists Guild; AAUP. *Literary Agent:* Curtis Brown Ltd; Robert Freedman. *Address:* 1215 N Cascade, Colorado Springs, CO 80903, USA.

YAJNIK Hasu, b. 13 Feb 1938, Rajkot, India. Secretary, Gujarat Sahitya Academy. m. Hasumati Yajnik, 7 Dec 1965, 1 son, 1 daughter. *Education:* MA, Gujarati Literature, 1962; PhD, 1972; Sangit Visharad, Violin, 1975. *Appointments:* Lecturer, Gujarati Literature, 1963-83; Secretary, State Academies for Gujarati, Sanskrit, Urdu, Sindhi and Folklore of Gujarat, 1983-. *Publications:* 16 novels; 5 short story collections; Edioted Folk Songs of Gujarati based on Krushna Charit and Rama Charit; Madhya Kalin Kathasahity (Medieval Narratives of Gujarati Literature); Thesis on Medieval Love Story of Gujarati Literature; Violine-Vadan, book on the violin; Kamkatha. *Contributions to:* 10 novels serialised in newspapers; Column on Ribald Stories (Kamkatha). *Honours:* Silver Medal for Short Story; Best Book Award, for Pachhitna pattharo and Diwal Pachhad ni Dunia. *Memberships:* Secretary, Literary State Academy, Gujarat State; Gujarati Sahity Parishad. *Address:* M-11-143 Vidyanagar, Ambawadi, Ahmedabad, India 382015.

YANIV Avner, b. 20 Dec 1942. Associate Professor of Political Science. m. Lo Michal, 3 children. *Education:* BA, Political Science, BA, English, Hebrew University of Jerusalem, 1967; Graduate study, London School of Economics and Political Science, London, England, 1968-69; DPhil, Linacre College, 1973. *Publications:* P L O: A Profile, 1974; Syria Under Assad: Domestic Constraints and Regional Risks (editor with Moshe Ma'oz, contributor), 1986; Deterrence Without the Bomb: The Politics of Israeli Strategy, 1987; Dilemmas of Security: Politics, Strategy, and the Israeli Experience in Lebanon, 1987; Israel Among the Nations: The Foreign Policy of the Jewish State, in progress; Contributor to: The Arab-Israeli Conflict: Risks and Opportunities, 1975; The Palestinians and the Middle East Conflict, 1978; The Elections in Israel, 1981; Security or Armageddon, 1985; The Middle East in Global Strategy, 1987; Syria at the Crossroads, 1988; The Arab-Israeli Conflict: Twenty Years After the Six Day War, 1988; Israel in the Post-Begin Era, 1988. *Contributions to:* Articles and reviews to periodicals including: Washington Quarterly; International Security; Journal of Politics. *Address:* Department of Political Science, University of Haifa, Haifa 31999 Israel.

YANKOWITZ Susan, b. Newark, New Jersey, USA. Writer. m. Herbert Leibowitz, 3 May 1978, 1 son. *Education:* BA, Sarah Lawrence College; MFA, Yale Drama School. *Publications:* Plays: Slaughterhouse Play, 1971; Boxes, 1973; Portrait of a Scientist, screenplay, 1974; Terminal, 1975; Alarms, 1988; Night Sky, 1992; Various unpublished stage plays, screenplays, teleplays; Silent Witness, novel, 1976-77; Taking the Fall, excerpt from novel, 1989. *Contributions to:* Short fiction, monologues, essays in: Gnosis; Solo!; Heresies; Interview with Contemporary Women Playwrights; Others. *Honours:* Joseph Levine Fellowship, Screenwriting, 1968; Vernon Rice Drama Desk Award, Most Promising Playwright, 1969; Grant, Rockefeller

Foundation, 1973; Award, 1974; Guggenheim Fellowship, 1975; Residencies, MacDowell Colony, 1975, 1984, 1987, 1990; Creative Writing Fellowship Grant, 1979, US-Japan Fellowship Grant, 1984, National Endowment for the Arts; Grant, Playwriting, NYFA, 1989; Finalist, Best Documentary for Sylvia Path teleplay, WGA, 1989; McKnight Fellowship, Playwriting, 1990; Collaboration Grant for NightSky play, TCG, 1990. *Memberships:* New Dramatists; PEN; Dramatists Guild; Authors Guild; WGA East. *Address:* 205 W 89th St, New York, NY 10024, USA.

YANO Shigeharu, (Rainbow), b. 11 Feb 1921, Ehime Prefecture, Japan. Professor Emeritus. m. Mizuya Ikeda, 22 Dec 1947, 3 daughters. *Education:* BA, Hosei University, Tokyo, 1950. *Appointments:* Professor Emeritus, Reitaku University, Chiba Prefecture, 1991; Guest Professor, Tokoha Gakuen University, Shizuoka City, 1991. *Publications:* Steinbeck's World, No 1, 1978, No 2, 1978, No 3, 1979, No 4, 1982, No 5, 1986; Editor: From Salinas to the World, 1986; John Steinbeck: Asian Perspectives, 1992. *Contributions to:* Steinbeck Quarterly, Ball State University, USA; Study of English, Tokyo; Newspaper of Education and Science, Tokyo; Reitaku University Journal, Chiba Prefecture. *Honours:* Recipient, Recognition Award, International Steinbeck Society, Ball State University, 1988, 1991; Honorary Citizen of Omaha, Nebraska, USA, 1990. *Memberships:* Consultant, International Steinbeck Society; Editor, Director, Steinbeck Society; Lecturer, Moralogy Institute, Chiba Prefecture. *Literary Agent:* Seibido Press, Tokyo, Japan. *Address:* Seibido Press, 3-22 Ogawa-cho, Kanda, Chiyoda-ku, Tokyo 101, Japan.

YAOS-KEST Itamar, b. 3 Aug 1934, Hungary. Poet; Author. m. Hanna Mercazy, 21 Aug 1958, 1 son, 1 daughter. *Appointments:* Founder, Eked Publishing House, 1958. *Publications:* Poems: Nof-Beashah, 1959; Eyes Heritage, 1966; Du-Shoresh, 1975; Toward Germany, 1980; Leshon Hanahar-Leshon Hayam, 1984; Tubes of Fire, 1986; Poems of the Prayer Book, 1991; Novels: In the Window of the Travelling House, 1970; The Shadow of the Bird, 1971; The Hold of Sand, 1972; Translations: Horazius 1970: Anthology of Jewish-Hungarian Poetry, 1960; Anthology of Hungarian Poetry, 1985; Anthology of Modern Hungarian Poetry, 1988; Jewish Fate in Hungarian Poetry, 1989. *Contributions to:* All Israeli literary magazines. *Honours:* Nordow Prize, 1961; Talpir Prize, 1969; Herzel Prize, 1972; Walenrode Prize, 1979; Chulon Prize, 1984; Werthime Prize, 1985; Lea Goldberg Prize, 1990; Prime Minister Prize, 1993. *Membership:* Association of Hebrew Writers, Israel. *Agent:* Eked, Tel Aviv. *Address:* Nahmani 51, Tel Aviv, Israel.

YARBRO Chelsea Quinn (Vanessa Pryor), b. 1942, USA. Author. *Appointments:* Manager, Playwright, Mirthmakers Children's Theatre, San Francisco, California, 1961-64; Children's Counsellor, 1963; Cartographer, C E Erickson and Associates, Oakland, California, 1963-70; Composer, Card and Palm Reader, 1974-78. *Publications:* Two Views of Wonder (edited with Thomas N Scortia), 1973; Time of the Fourth Horseman, science fiction, 1976; Ogilvie, Tallant, and Moon, 1976; Hotel Transylvania, 1978; False Down, science fiction, 1978; Cautionary Tales, science fiction short stories, 1978, 1980; Music When Sweet Voices Die, 1979; The Palace, 1979; Messages from Michael, occult, 1979; Blood Games, 1980; Sins of Omission, 1980; Ariosto, 1980; Dead and Buried, 1980; Path of the Eclipse, 1981; Tempting Fate, 1982; A Taste of Wine (as Vanessa Pryor), 1982; The Saint-Germain Chronicles, short stories, 1983; The Godforsaken, novel, 1983; Hyacinths, science fiction, 1983; The Making of Australia No 5: The Outback, 1983; Locadio's Apprentice, juvenile fiction, 1984; Nomads, screenplay novelization, 1984; Signs and Portents, short stories, 1984; Four Horses for Tishtry, juvenile fiction, 1985; A Mortal Glamour, novel, 1985; To the High Reboubt, novel, 1985; More Messages from Michael, 1986; A Baroque Fable, novel with music, 1986; Floating Illusions, juvenile fiction, 1986; Novels: A Flame in

Byzantium, 1987; Firecode, 1987; Michael's People (non-fiction), 1987; Crusader's Torch, 1988; Taji's Syndrome, 1988; Beastnights, 1989; A Candle for D'Artagnan, 1989; The Law in Charity, 1989; Out of the House of Life, 1990; Poison Fruit, 1991. *Memberships:* Secretary, Science Fiction Writers of America, 1970-72; President, Horror Writer's of America, 1988-90. *Address:* PO Box 7568, Berkeley, CA 94707, USA.

YARDLEY Jonathan, b. 27 Oct 1939, Pittsburgh, USA. Journalist. m. Susan L. Hartt, 23 Mar 1975, 2 sons by previous marriage. *Education:* AB, University of North Carolina, 1961. *Appointments:* Book Editor, The Miami Herald, 1974-78, The Washington Star, 1978-81; Book Critic, The Washington Post, 1981-. *Publications:* Ring : A Biography of Ring Lardner, 1977; Our Kind of People: The Story of an American Family, in progress. *Contributions to:* many major American Magazines & Newspapers. *Honours:* Nieman Fellow, Journalism, Harvard University, 1968-69; Pulitzer Prize for Criticism, 1981; LHD, George Washington University, 1987. *Agent:* Elizabeth Darhansoff, New York. *Address:* 223 Hawthorne Road, Baltimore, MD 21210, USA.

YATES J. Michael, b. 1938, Canada. Writer. *Appointments:* Promotional Director, Public Radio Corporation, Houston, Texas, USA, 1961- 62; Teaching Fellow, University of Michigan, Ann Arbor, 1962-63; Instructor in English and Creative Writing, Ohio University, Athens, 1964-65; Special Lecturer in Literature and Creative Writing, University of Alaska, Fairbanks, 1965-66; Associate Professor of Creative Writing, University of British Columbia, Vancouver, Canada, 1966-71; Editor-in-Chief, 1966-67, Poetry Editor, 1966-71, Prism International; Member, Editorial Board, Prism International Press, Mission, British Columbia, 1966-71; President, Sono Nis Press, Vancouver, 1971-. *Publications:* Subjunction, play, 1965; The Grand Edit, screenplay, 1966; Spiral of Mirrors, 1967; Hunt in an Unmapped Interior and Other Poems, 1967; Canticle for Electronic Music, 1967; Parallax (with B Frick), 1968; Night Freight, play, 1968; Man in the Glass Octopus, short stories, 1968; The Great Bear Lake Meditations, 1970; Contemporary Poetry of British Columbia (edited with A Schroder), 2 vols, 1970, 1972; The Abstract Beast, 1971; Volvox: Poetry from the Unoffical Languages of Canada in English Translations (edited with C Lillard), 1971; Contemporary Fiction of British Columbia, (editor), 1971; Exploding, novel, 1972; Nothing Speaks for the Blue Moraines: New and Selected Poems, 1973; Breath of the Snow Leopard, 1974; The Qualicum Physics, 1975; Quarks, radio plays, 1975; Fazes in Elsewhen: New and Selected Fiction, 1977; Esex Nobilion non Esox Lucius, 1978; Fugue Brancusi, 1983; Insel: The Queen Charlotte Islands Meditations, 1983; Completely Collapsible Portable Man, 1984; Oita Poems, 1984; Schedules of Silence, 1986.

YEATMAN Ted P, (Trezevant Player), b. 16 Dec 1951, Nashville, USA. Writer; Historical Researcher. *Education:* BA 1976, MLS 1977, George Peabody College for Teachers. *Appointments:* Senior Staff Writer, Peabody Post 1975-76; Editorial Board, Friends of the James Farm 1984-93; and others. *Publications:* Jesse James and Bill Ryan at Nashville, 1981; Alias Woodson and Howard: The Hidden years of Frank and Jesse James, 1995; The Tennessee Wild West: Historical and Cultural Links with the Western Frontier, co-author, 1995. *Contributions to:* Timeless Tennesseans, 1984; The Book of Days, 1987, 1988; Read More About It, 1989; Civil War Times Illustrated; North/South Trader; Show Me Libraries; James Farm Journal; True West; Book Page; Quarterly of the National Association & Centre for Outlaw and Lawmen History; The Late Milton F. Perry's, Press Agent to Outlaws. *Memberships:* potomac Corral of Westerners; Friends of the James Farm, Board of Directors 1982-93, Editorial Board 1984-93; Tennessee Western History & Folklore Society, Co-Director 1981-. *Address:* 1302 The Terrace, Hagerstown, MD 21742, USA.

YEHOSHUA Abraham B, b. 9 Dec 1936, Jerusalem, Israel. Professor. m. Rivka Kirsninski, 1960, 2 sons, 1 daughter. *Education:* BA, 1960; MA, 1962. *Appointments:* Co-Editor, Keshet, 1965-72; Siman Kria 1973-. *Publications:* Death of the Old Man, 1963; (short stories), Three Days and a Child, 1970; Early in the summer of 1970, 1973, (Novella); Two plays: (Novel), The Lover, 1978; Between Right and Right, 1981, Essays; (Novel), A Late Divorce, 1984; (Play), Possessions, 1986; (Novel), Five Seasons, 1988; (Novel), Mister Mani 1990. *Contributions to:* Esquire. *Honours:* Brener Prize; Alterman Prize; Bialik Prize; Winner of the National Jewish Book Award, USA, 1990, 1993; Winner of the Israeli Booker, 1992. *Agent:* Liepman, Zurich, Switzerland. *Address:* 102A Sea Road, Haifa, Israel, 34746.

YELDHAM Peter, b. Gladstone, New South Wales, Australia. Playwright; Screen-writer. m. Marjorie Crane, 27 Oct 1948, 1 son, 1 daughter. *Publications:* Stage Plays: Birds on the Wing, 1969-70; She Won't Lie Down, 1972; Fring Benefits, (co-author), 1973; Away Match, (co-author), 1974; Seven Little Australians, 1988. Feature Films include: The Comedy Man, 1963; The Liquidator, 1965; Age of Consent, 1968; Touch and Go, 1979; Television Plays include: Reunion Day; Stella; Thunder on the Snowy; East of Christmas; The Cabbage Tree Hat Boys; Television Series include: Run from the Morning, 1977; Golden Soak, 1978; Ride on, Stranger, 1979; The Timeless Land, 1979; Also: Levkas Man, 1980; Sporting Chance, 1981; 1915, 1982; All the Rivers Run, 1983; Flight into Hell, 1984; Tusitala, The Lancaster Miller Affair, 1985; The Far Country, 1985; Captain James Cook, 1986; The Alien Years, 1987; Naked Under Capricorn, 1988; The Heroes, 1988; The Heroes - The Return, 1991. *Honours:* Sammy Award, Best Television Series in Australia, 1979; Writers Guild, Best Adaption, 1980, 1983, 1986; Penguin Award, Best Script, 1982; Writers Guild, Best Original mini-series, 1989; Order of Australia Medal, 1991. *Memberships:* Writers Guild, Australia; British Writers Guild. *Literary Agent:* Lemon, Unna & Durbridge, (UK); Rick Raftos Management, Sydney, Australia. *Address:* 21 Glover Street, Mosman, Sydney, Australia.

YERBY Frank Garvin, b. 5 Sept 1916, Augusta, Georgia, USA. Novelist. m. (2) Blanca Calle Perez, 1956, 2 sons, 2 daughters (from previous marriage). *Education:* University of Chicago. *Publications:* The Foxes of Harrow, 1946; The Vixens, 1947; The Golden Hawk, 1948; Pride's Castle, 1949; Flood Tide, 1950; A Woman Called Fancy, 1951; The Saracen Blade, 1952; The Devil's Laughter, 1953; Benton's Row, 1954; The Treasure of Pleasant Valley, 1955; Captain Rebel, 1956; Fairoaks, 1957; The Serpent and the Staff, 1958; Jarrett's Jade, 1959; Gillian, 1960; The Garfield Honour, 1961; Griffin's Way, 1962; The Old Gods Laugh, 1964; An Odour of Sanctity, 1966; Goat Song, 1967; Judas My Brother, 1968; Speak Now, 1969; The Dahomean, 1971; The Girl from Storyville, 1972; The Voyage Unplanned, 1974; Tobias and the Angel, 1975; A Rose for Ana Maria, 1976; Hail the Conquering Hero, 1978; A Darkness at Ingraham's Crest, 1979; Western, A Saga of the Great Plains, 1982; Devilseed, 1984; McKenzie's Hundered, 1985. *Address;* c/o William Morris Agency, 1350 Avenue of the Americas, New York, NY 10019, USA.

YERMAKOV Nicholas, b. 1951, United States of America. Author. *Publications:* Journey from Flesh, 1981; Last Communion, 1981; Fall into Darkness, 1982; Clique, 1982; Epophany, 1982; Battlestar Galactic 6: The Living Legend (with Glen A. Larson), 1982; Battlestar Galactica 7: War of the Gods (with Glen A. Larson), 1982; Johad, 1984; Novels as Simon Hawkes: The Ivanhoe Gambit, 1984; The Timekeeper Conspiracy, 1984; The Pimpernel Plot, 1984; The Zenda Vendetta, 1985; The Nautilus Sanction, 1985.

YEVTUSHENKO Yevgenly Aleksandrovich, b. 18 July 1933, Zima, Irkutak Region, USSR. Poet. m. Jan Butler, 1978, 1 son. *Education:* Moscow Literary Institute; Geological Expeditions with father to

Kazakhstan, 1948, the Altai 1950. *Publications:* (Verse) Scouts of the Future (collected verse), 1952; The Third Snow, 1955; The Highway of Enthusiasts, 1956; Zima Junction, 1956; The Promise (collected verse), 1959; Conversation with a Count, Moscow Goods Station, At the Skorokhod Plant, The Nihilist, The Apple, 1960-61; A Sweep of the Arm, 1962; Tenderness, 1962; A Precocious Autobiography, 1963; Cashier, Woman, Mother, On the Banks of the Dnieper River, A Woman and a Girl, Do the Russians Want War?, Bratskaya Hydro-Electric Power Station, 1965; A Boat of Communication, 1966; Poems Chosen by the Author, 1966; Collection of Verses, 1967; That's What Is Happening to Me, 1968; It's Snowing White, 1969; Kazan University, 1971; I am of Siberian Stock, 1971; The Singing Domba, 1972; Stolen Apples, 1972; Under the Skin of the Statue of Liberty (play), 1972; Intimate Lyrics, 1973; A Father's Hearing, 1976; From Desire to Desire, 1976; Love Poems, 1977; People of the Morning, 1978; Heavy Soils, 1978; Winter Station, 1978; Selected Works, 1979; The Face Behind the Face, 1979; Ivan the Terrible and Ivan the Fool, 1979; Berries (novel), 1981; Ardabiola (short story), 1981; Almost at the End, 1987; Last Attempt, 1988; (essays) Politics - everybody's priviledge, 1990. *Address:* Union of USSR Writers, ul Vorovskogo 52, Moscow, Russia.

YEZHOV Valentin Ivanovich, b. 21 Jan 1921. Screenplay Writer. m. 1 son. *Publications:* Ballad of a Soldier, 1959; Co-Author, Scripts for Our Champions, 1954; World Champion, 1955; Liana, 1956; A Man from the Planet Earth, 1958; The House of Gold, 1959; The Volga Flows, 1962; Wings, 1966; Thirty Three, 1967; White Sun of the Desert, 1969; A Nest of Gentry, 1969; The Legend, 1971; This Sweet Word Liberty, 1973; Eleven Hopefuls, 1974; Siberiade, 1977; Meadow Flowers, 1981; The Girl and the Grand, 1982; Alexander the Small, 1982; Plays: Nightingale Night, 1969; Alesha, 1984; A Shot Over Sand-hills, 1985; Films: Moon Rainbow, 1983; Bow to the Ground, 1985; The Last Will, 1986; Igor Savvovich, 1987; Every time it's Different, 1987; Your Personal Correspondent, 1988; Esperansa, 1988. *Honours:* Lenin Prize, 1961; Honoured man, Arts of the Russian Federation, 1978. *Memberships:* Professor, All union Institute of Cinematography, 1988; Writers Union of USSR, 1962; Film-makers Union of USSR, 1957. *Address:* 121170 USSR, Moscow, Kutuzov av., 41-20.

YGLESIAS Jose, b. 29 Nob 1919, Florida, USA. Writer. 1 son. *Education:* Black Mountain College, 1946-47. *Appointments:* Regents Lecturer, University of California at Santa Barbara, 1973. *Publications:* A Wake in Ybor City, 1963; The Goodbye Land, 1967; In the Fist of the Revolution, 1968; An Orderly Life, 1968; Down There, 1970; The Truth About Them, 1971; Double Double, 1976; The Kill Price, 1977; The Franco Years, 1978; Home Again, 1987; Tristan and the Hispanics, 1989. *Contributions to:* The New Yorker; The Nation; New York Times Magazine; New York Review of Books; Esquire; The New Republic. *Honours:* Guggenheim Fellowship, 1970, 1976; National Endowment for the Arts, 1974. *Literary Agent:* Maria Carvainis Agency. *Address:* 55 W 11th St, New York, NY 10011, USA.

YGLESIAS Rafael, b. 12 May 1954, New York City, New York, USA. Novelist; Screenwriter. m. Margaret Joskow, 15 Oct 1977, 2 sons. *Publications:* Hide Fox, And All After, 1972; The Work Is Innocent, 1976; The Game Player, 1978; Hot Properties, 1986; Only Children, 1988; The Murderer Next Door, 1990; Fearless, 1993. *Contributions to:* New York Times Book Review. *Membership:* Authors Guild. *Literary Agent:* Gail Hochman, Brandt and Brandt. *Address:* 18 East 12th St, New York, NY 10003, USA.

YINLeslie Charles Bowyer (Leslie Charteris), b. 12 May 1907, Singapore. Author. m. (1) Pauline Schiskin, 1931, 1 daughter, (2) Barbara Meyer, 1939, (3) Elizabeth Borst, 1943, (4) Audrey Long, 1952. *Education:* King's College, Cambridge. *Appointments:* Editor, The Saint Magazine, 1953-67; Editorial Consultant, 1983-.

Publications: Meet the Tiger, 1929; Enter the Saint, 1931; the Last Hero, 1931; The Avenging Saint, 1931; Wanted for Murder, 1931; Angels of Doom, 1932; The Saint v Scotland Yard, 1932; Getaway, 1933; The Saint and Mr Teal, 1933; The Brighter Buccaneeer, 1933; The Misfortunes of Mr Teal, 1934; The Saint Intervenes, 1934; The Saint Goes on, 1935; The Saint in New York, 1935; Saint Overboard, 1936; The Ace of Knaves, 1937; Thieves Picnic, 1937; Juan Belmonte: Killer of Bulls (translated from Spanish), 1937; Follow the Saint, 1938; Prelude for War, 1938; The First Saint Omninus, 1939; The Saint in Miami, 1940; The Saint Goes West, 1942; The Saint Steps In, 1943; The Saint at Large, 1943; The Saint on Guard, 1944; The Saint Sees it Through, 1946; Call for the Saint, 1948; Saint Errant, 1948; The Second Saint Omnibus, 1951; The Saint in Europe, 1953; The Saint on the Spanish Main, 1955; The Saint Around the World, 1956; Thanks to the Saint, 1957; Senor Saint, 1958; The Saint to the Rescue, 1959; Trust the Saint, 1962; Saint in the Sun, 1963; Vendetta for the Saint, 1964; The Saint on TV, 1968; The Saint Returns, 1968; The Saint Abroad, 1969; The Saint and the Fiction Makers, 1969; The Saint in Pursuit, 1970; The Saint and the People Importers, 1971; Saint's Alive, 1974; Catch the Saint, 1975; The Saint and the Hapsburg Necklace, 1976; Send for the Saint, 1977; The Saint in Trouble, 1978; The Saint and the Templar Treasure, 1978; Count on the Saint, 1980; The Fantastic Saint, 1982; Salvage for the Saint, 1983. *Memberships:* Mensa; Council of International Foundation for Gifted Children; President, Saint Club; President, Arbour Youth Centre. *Address:* 3-4 Marlborough Street, London, W1V 2AR.

YOFFE Elkhonon, b. 16 Apr 1928, Riga, Latvia. Musicologist; Librarian. m. Lydia Yoffe, 27 Feb 1955, 1 son. *Education:* Jazep Medin Music School, Riga 1948; MA Percussion 1952, MA Musicology 1954, Latvian State Conservatoire 1954. *Appointments:* Lecturer, Music History, Riga Ballet School 1965-72; Lecturer, Latvian Philharmonia 1972-78; Assistant Librarian, The Juilliard School, New York City 1979-82; Librarian, Detroit Symphony Orchestra 1982-. *Publications:* Percussion Instruments, 1962; Marger Zarius, Ignoramus Suite, 1965; Tchaikovsky in America, 1986; Ruta U God I Wanted to Live, translation - Russian, 1989; K Kondrashin, Conductors Readings of Tchaikovsky's Symphonies, translation - English, unpublished. *Contributions to:* Sovetskaya Muzika, Moscow; Latviesu Muzika, Riga; Kontinent, Paris. *Memberships:* USSR Composers' Union 1967-78; Major Orchestra Librarian Association (MOLA), 1982. *Address:* 463 Coolidge Road, Birmingham, MI 48009, USA.

YOGMAN Michael, b. 1 Mar 1947, New Jersey, USA. Physician. m. Elizabeth Ascher, 9 June 1985, 2 daughters. *Education:* BA 1968, Williams College; MD 1972, Yale Medical School; MSc 1978, Harvard School of Public Health. *Publications:* Co-Editor: In Support of Families, 1986; Affective Development in Infancy, 1986; Follow Up Management of the High-Risk Infant, 1987. *Contributions to:* New England Journal of Medicine; Paediatrics; Journal of Paediatrics; Paediatric Research; American Journal of Public Health; Journal of American Academy of Child Psychiatry. *Memberships:* Society for Paediatric Research; American Academy of Paediatrics; Society for Research in Child Development; Ambulatory Paediatric Association; World Association for Infant Psychiatry; International Conference on Infant Studies. *Address:* 14 Wyman Road, Cambridge, MA 02138, USA.

YOLEN Jane, b. 11 Feb. 1939, USA. Author; Storyteller. m. 2 Sept. 1962, 2 sons, 1 daughter. *Education:* BA, English Literature, Smith College, 1960; M.Ed., University of Massachustts, 1976. *Appointments:* Editor-in-Chief of imprint Jane Yolen Books; Harcourt Brace Jovanovich Publishers, 1988. *Publications* Pirates in Petticoat, 1963; The Emperor & The Kite, 1968; The Girl Who Cried Flowers, 1974; Hundredth Dove, 1976; Commander Toad in Space, 1980; Dragon's Blood, 1982; Cards of Grief, 1985; Merlin's Books, 1986; Owl Moon, 1987; Sister Light, Sister Dark, 1989; Dove

Isabeau 1989; The Devils Authmetic, 1990; White Jenna, 1990; The Dragon's Boy, 1990; Encounter, 1991; Briar Rose, 1992; and 100 other books. *Contributions to:* New York Times Book Review; Horn Book; Washington Post; Fantasy and Science Fiction Magazine; Isaac Asimov's SF Magazine; Parabola Magazine; Parent's Choice Magazine; Children's Literature in Education. *Honours:* National Book Award Nomination, 1974; Mythopoeic Society Award, 1986; Golden Kite Award, 1974; Christopher Medal, 1979; Daedlus Award, 1987; World Fantasy Award, 1987; Kerlan Award, 1988; Smith College Medal, 1988; Caldecott Medal Book, 1988; Regina Medal, 1992; Honorary LLD. *Memberships:* Children's Literature Association, Board of Directors; Science Fiction Writers of America, President, 1986-88; Society of Children's Book Writers, Board of Directors. *Agent:* Curtis Brown Ltd., New York, USA. *Address:* Phoenix Farm, Box 27, Hatfield, MA 01038, USA.

YORK Alison. *See:* **NICOLE Christopher Robin.**

YORK Andrew. *See:* **NICOLE Christopher Robin.**

YORK Georgia. *See:* **HOFFMAN Lee.**

YORK Lorraine Mary, b. 21 Nov 1958, London, Ontario, Canada. English Professor. m. Michael Lawrence Ross, 23 May 1987, 1 daughter. *Education:* BA Hons 1981, MA 1982, PhD 1985, McMaster University. *Publications:* The Other Side of Dailiness: Photography in the Work of Alice Munro, Timothy Findley, Michael Ondaatje and Margaret Laurence, 1988; Front Lines: The Fiction of Timothy Findley, 1990. *Honour:* McMaster Humanities Faculty Teaching Award, 1990. *Memberships:* Association of Canadian College & University Teachers of English; Modern Languages Association; Association for Canadian Studies in the United States. *Address:* Department of English, McMaster University, Hamilton, Ontario, Canada L8S 4L9.

YORKE Katherine. *See:* **ELLERBECK Rosemary.**

YORKE Margaret. *See:* **NICHOLSON Margaret Beda.**

YOSHIMASU Gozo, b. 22 Feb 1939, Tokyo, Japan. Lecturer; Poet. m. Marilia, 17 Nov 1973. *Education:* BA, Keio University, 1963. *Appointments:* Chief Editor, Sensai Finer Arts)magazine), Tokyo, Japan, 1964-69; Freelance writer 1970-; Fulbright Visiting Writer, University of Iowa, 1970-71; Poet in Residence, Oakland University, 1979-81; Lecturer at institutions include Tama Art University, 1984-, and Asahi Cultural Center, has given poetry readings in the United States, Ireland, Netherlands, Brazil, India, Scotland, England and Canada. *Publications include:* A Thousand Steps and More: Selected Poems and Prose 1964-84, 1987; Poetry includes: Daibyoin waki ni sobietatsu kyojyu e no tegami (A Letter to the Tall Tree Standing Next to the Great Hospital) 1983; Oshirisu, ishi no kami, Shichosha, 1984, English edition published as Osiris, God of Stone, translated and edited by Hiroaki Sato, 1988; Doido na manha (Mad in the Morning) translated by Jp Takahashi, edited by Masao Ohno, 1986; Rasenka (Song of Tornado) 1989; Shinsen Yoshimasu Gozo shishu (New Selection of Popems by Gozo Yoshimasu) 1978. Also author of essays and other works. *Honours:* Takami Jun Prize from takami Jun Poetry Committee, 1971, for Shishu ogon Shihen; Rekitei Prize from Rekitei Group, 1979, for Neppu; Hanatsubaki Modern Poetry Prize from Shiseido, 1984 for Oshirisu ishi no kami. *Memberships:* Japan Writers Association; Japan Pen Club. *Literary Agent:* c/o Katydid Books, 5746 Bridgeview, West Bloomfield, MI 48033, USA. *Address:* 1-215-5 Kasumi- cho, Hachioji City 192, Japan.

YOST Elwy McMurran, b. 10 Jul 1925, Weston, Ontario, Canada. Television executive producer and host; Writer. m. Lila Ragnhild Melby, 16 June 1951, 2 sons. *Education:* BA (hons), University of Toronto, 1948. *Appointments:* in circulation department, Toronto Star, Toronto, Ontario, 1948-52; Human Relations Counselor, Avro Aircraft, Malton, Ontario, 1953-59; High School English Teacher, Toronto, 1959-64; Televison Panelist on Live a Borrowed Life, The Superior Sex and Flashback; host of radio show, It's Debatable and host of children's television show, Passport to Adventure for Canadian Broadcasting Corporation, 1959-68; Metropolitan Educational Television Association, Toronto, producer 1964-66, executive director 1967-70; TV Ontario, Toronto, superintendent of regional liaison 1970-73, 1970-73, executive producer and host of Saturday Night at the Movies, 1974-, Magic Shadows 1974-88 and Rough Cuts 1978-80; writer 1988-. Professional actor in summer stock with Midland Players and Niagara Born Players, 1946-53; Chairman, Conestoga College Film Advisory Council, 1979-81; Patron, Youth Without Shelter 1987-88; Canadian Army 1944-45. *Publications:* (Contributor)Walt McDayter, editor, The Media Mosaic, Holt c 1970; Magic Moments From the Movies, Doubleday 1978; Secret of the Lost Empire (juvenile) 1980; Billy and the Bubbleship (juvenile) 1982, published as The Mad Queen of Mordra, 1987. Author of radio scripts in the early 1960's. *Contributions to:* Bakka, Video Scene, Leisureways and Counsellor and Higher Literacy; contributor of film reviews to the Toronto Star. *Membership:* Alliance of Canadian Television and Radio Artists, Sons of the Desert. *Address:* 15 Sir Williams Lane, Islington, Ontario, Canada M9A 1T8.

YOUD Samuel (John Christopher, Hilary Ford, William Godfrey, Peter Graaf, Peter Nichols, Anthony Rye), b. 16 Apr 1922, Knowsley, Lancashire, England. Writer. m. Jessica Valerie, 24 Dec 1980, 1 son, 4 daughters (by previous marriage). *Publications:* As John Christopher: For Young People: The Lotus Caves, 1969; The Guardians, 1970; In The Beginning, 1972; Wild Jack, 1974; Empty World, 1978; The Tripods, Tetralogy: The White Mountains, 1967, The City of Gold and Lead, 1967, The Pool of Fire, 1968, When the Tripods Came, 1988; The Sword Trilogy: The Prince in Waiting, 1970, Beyond The Burning Lands, 1971, The Sword of the Spirits, 1972; The Fireball Trilogy: Fireball, 1981, New Found Land, 1983, Dragon Dance, 1986; Adult Fiction: The Twenty-Second Century, 1954; The Year of the Comet, 1955; The Death of Grass, 1956; The Caves of Night, 1958; A Scent of White Poppies, 1959; The Long Voyage, 1960; The World in Winter, 1962; Cloud on Silver, 1964; The Possessors, 1965; A Wrinkle in the Skin, 1965; The Little People, 1967; Pendulum, 1968; Dusk of Demons, 1993; many other books. *Memberships:* Society of Authors, Chairman Children's Writers Group, 1982-84. *Address:* c/o Society of Author, 84 Drayton Gardens, London SW10, England.

YOUMAN Roger Jacob, b. 25 Feb. 1932, New York, USA. Editor; Writer. m. Lillian Frank, 22 June 1958, 2 sons, 2 daughters. *Education:* BA, Swarthmore College, 1953. *Appointments:* Programme Editor, 1956, Regional Editor, 1956-57, Assistant Programming Editor, 1957-60, Associate Editor, 1960-65, Assistant Managing Editor, 1965-72, Managing Editor, 1972-76, Executive Editor, 1976-79, 1980-81, Co-Editor, 1981-, TV Guide; Editor, Panorama, 1979-80. *Publications:* How Sweet it Was, 1966; The Television Years, 1973. *Contributions to:* various magazines. *Memberships:* American Society of Magazine Editors; National Academy of Television Arts & Sciences. *Address:* 752 Mancill Road, Wayne, PA 19087, USA.

YOUNG Allan Edward, b. 21 June 1939, New York, USA. University Professor. m. Eleanor Podheiser, 16 Sept 1962, 1 son, 2 daughters. *Education:* BA 1961, SUNY at Binghamton, New York; MBA 1963, PhD 1967, Columbia University. *Publications:* The Contribution of the New York Based Securities Industry to the Economy of the City and State, 1985; The Financial Manager, 1987; Guidelines for the Financing of Industrial Investment Projects in Developing Countries, 1993.

Contributions to: Over 50 articles in leading academic and professional journals in the fields of Financial Management, Securities Markets & Investments. *Honour:* Alexander Hamilton Chair in Entrepreneurship, Budapest, Hungary (Fulbright Lectureship and Consultancy); Trust Bank Chair in Accounting and Finance, Lincoln University, Canterbury, New Zealand . *Memberships:* Many economic and finance societies. *Address:* 27 Ely Drive, Fayetteville, NY 13066, USA.

YOUNG Bertram Alfred, b. 20 Jan. 1912, London, England. Freelance Writer. *Appointments:* Assistant Editor, 1949-62, Drama Critic, 1962-64, Punch; Drama Critic, 1964-78, Arts Editor, 1971-77, Financial Times. *Publications:* Bechuanaland, 1966; Cabinet Pudding, 1967; The Rattigan Version, 1986; Tooth and Claw, 1958; The Mirror Up to Nature, 1982. *Contributions to:* Punch; numerous other professional journals and magazines. *Honour:* OBE, 1980. *Memberships:* Critics' Circle, President, 1978-80; Society of Authors; Garrick Club. *Address:* Clyde House, Station Street, Cheltenham, Glos GL50 3LX, England.

YOUNG Carter Travis. *See:* **CHARBONNEAU Louis (Henry).**

YOUNG Donald, b. 29 June 1933, Indianapolis, Indiana, USA. Editor; Writer. *Education:* BA, Indiana University; MA, Butler University. *Appointments:* Senior Editor, Encyclopedia Americana, 1967-77; Managing Editor, Aperture Foundation, 1986-87. *Publications:* American Roulette, 1965; Adventure in Politics (Editor), 1970; The Great American Desert (Author & Photography), 1980; The Sierra Club Guides to the National Parks, Volumes 3, 4, 5, (Editor), 1984-86; The Sierra Club Book of Our National Parks (co-author), 1990. *Contributions to:* Numerous magazines & journals. *Address:* 166 East 61st Street, Apt. 3-C, New York, NY 10021, USA.

YOUNG Hugo John Smelter, b. 13 Oct. 1938, England. Journalist. m. Helen Mason, 1966, 1 son, 3 daughters. *Education:* BA, Jurisprudence, Balliol College, Oxford. *Appointments include:* Yorkshire Post, 1961; Chief leader writer 1966-77, political editor 1973-84, joint deputy editor 1981-84, Sunday Times; Political columnist, The Guardian, 1984-; Director, The Tablet, 1985-; Chairman, Scott Trust, 1989. *Publications:* Co-author, The Zinoviev Letter 1966, Journey to Tranquillity 1969; The Crossman Affair, 1974; Co-author, No, Minister 1982, But, Chancellor 1984, The Thatcher Phenomenon 1986; One of Us, 1989. *Honours:* Harkness Fellow, 1963; Congressional Fellow, US Congress, 1964; Columnist of the Year, British Press Awards, 1980, 1983, 1985; What the Papers Say Award, Granada TV, 1985. *Address:* c/o The Guardian, 119 Farringdon Road, London EC1, England.

YOUNG Ian George, b. 5 Jan 1945, London, England. Writer; Editor. *Appointments:* Director, Catalyst Press 1969-80; Director, TMW Communications 1990-. *Publications:* Poetry: White Garland, 1969; Year of the Quiet Sun, 1969; Double Exposure, 1970, 1974; Cool Fire, 1970; Lions in the Stream, 1971; Some Green Moths, 1972; The Male Muse, 1973; Invisible Words, 1974; Common-or-Garden Gods, 1976; The Son of the Male Muse, 1983; Sex Magick, 1986. *Address:* 2483 Gerrard Street East, Scarborough, Ontario, Canada M1N 1W7.

YOUNG John Karl, b. 15 Aug 1951, Minneapolis, Minnesota, USA. Associate Professor of Anatomy. m. Paula Jean Spesock, 3 July 1977, 2 sons. *Education:* University South California 1968-69; BS 1972, Cornell University; PhD 1977, UCLA; Postdoctoral research appointment, University Minnesota 1977-79. *Publication:* Cells: Amazing Forms and Functions, 1990; Forthcoming: Hormones: Molecular Messengers; Plasticity in the Nervous System, by B Kotlyar, translated from Russian by J K Young, 1992; Forthcoming: Ageing, diseases, and disturbed neuroendocrine function, by V

Dilman, translated by J K Young. *Contributions to:* 27 papers in various scientific journals including: Oestrogen and the etiology of anorexia nervosa, Neuroscience and Biobehavioural Reviews 15, 1991. *Memberships:* American Association of Anatomists; American Physiological Society. *Address:* Department of Anatomy, Howard University, 520 W Street, NW, Washington DC 20059, USA.

YOUNG Michael Dunlop, (Lord Young of Dartington), b. 9 Aug 1915, Manchester, England, Sociologist, m. (1) Joan Lawson, 1945, 2 sons, 1 daughter, (2) Sasha Moorsom, 1960, 1 son, 1 daughter. *Education:* BSc, Economics, London School of Economics; MA, Cambridge University; PhD, London University. *Publications:* Family and Kinship in East London, (Co- author Peter Willmott), 1957; Rise of the Meritocracy, 1958; Metronomic Society-Naatural Rhythms and Human Timetables, 1988; family and Class in a London Suburb, (Co-author P Willmott), 1960; The Symmetrical Family, (Co- author Peter Willmott), 1973; Elmhirsts of Dartington, 1982; Innovation and Research in Education, 1965; Learning Begins at home, (Co-author Patrick McGeeney), 1968; Forecasting and the Social Sciences, (Editor), 1968; Poverty Reports, (Editor), 1974, 1975; The Metronomic Society, 1988; Life After Work, with Tom Schuller, 1990. *Contributions to:* New Society; New Statesman; Society; Samizdat. *Honours:* Honorary LittD, Sheffield, 1965; D Open University, 1973; Honorary DLitt, Adelaide, 1974; Honorary LLD, Exeter, 1982; Honorary fellow, Queen Mary College, 1983. *Address:* 18 Victoria Park Square, Bethnal Green, London E2 9PF, England.

YOUNG Robert Bruce, b. 30 June 1944, Sydney, Australia. University Lecturer. m. Helen Margaret Riley, 12 Aug 1967, 1 son, 1 daughter. *Education:* BEc (Sydney) 1965; BA (Sydney) 1968; PhD 1972, Flinders University of South Australia. *Publications:* Freedom, Responsibility and God, 1975; Personal Autonomy: Beyond Negative and Positive Liberty, 1986. *Contributions to:* more than 20 professional journals and over a dozen collections of articles. *Membership:* Editor, Australasian Journal of Philosophy. *Address:* 68 Empress Road, Surrey Hills, Victoria 3127, Australia.

YOUNG Rose. *See:* **HARRIS Marion Rose.**

YOUNG Scott Alexander, b. 14 Apr 1918, Glenboro, Manitoba, Canada, Author. m. (3) Margaret Hogan, 9 May 1980, 2 sons, 5 daughters. *Publications Include:* Neil and Me, 1984; Murder in a Cold Climate, 1988, 1989; Scrubs on Skates, 1952, 1985; Red Shield in Action, 1949; The Flood, 1956; The Clue of the Dead Duck, 1962; Big City Office Junior, 1964; The Leafs I Knew, 1966; Hockey is a Battle, 1969; The Face-off Series, 1972; Hockey Star Series, 1974; War On Ice, 1976; Best Talk in Town, 1980; Hello Canada!, 1985; Gordon Sinclair, 1988; Face-off in Moscow, 1989; 100 Years of Dropping the Puck, 1989; Home for Christmas, 1989; The Boys of Saturday Night, 1990. *Contributions to:* Numerous magazines and journals. *Honours:* National Newspaper award for sports writing, 1958; CBC Wilderness Award, TV Doc Script, 1962; US Eclipse Award, 1971; Canadian Sovereign Award, 1978; Elected Hockey Hall of Fame, 1988; Hon. Degree D. Letters 1990, Trent University. *Memberships:* Canadian Authors Association, Vice President, 1950s; Writers Union of Canada. *Literary Agent:* MGA Agency, 10 St Mary Street, Toronto, Canada. *Address:* 2 Clonross Close, Stillorgan Park, Blackrock, Co. Dublin, Ireland.

YOUNG-BRUEHL Elisabeth, b. 3 Mar 1946, Maryland, USA. Writer; Professor. *Education:* BA, MA & PhD in Philosophy, New School for Social Research, New York City. *Appointments:* Wesleyan University 1974-91; Haverford College 1991-. *Publications:* Hannah Arendt: For Love of the World, 1982; Anna Freud: A Biography, 1988; Mind and the Body Politic, 1989; Freud on Women, 1990; Creative Characters, 1991; Vigil, novel, 1983. *Honours:* Harcomt Award for Biography, 1982; Present Tense Literary Award, 1982;

National Endowment for the Humanities, 1985; Guggenheim Foundation, 1986. *Membership:* Authors Guild. *Literary Agent:* Georges Borchardt, New York City. *Address:* 82 Goose Hill Road, Chester, CT 06412, USA.

Z

ZACHARY Hugh (Ginny Gorman, Elizabeth Hughes, Zach Hughes, Peter Kanto, Derral Pilgrim, E R Rangely, Oliver Rangley, Marcus Van Heller), b. 1928. American, Writer of Mystery/Crime/Suspense, Historical/Romance/Gothic, Science fiction/Fantasy. Radio and TV broadcaster in Oklahoma, Tennessee, North Carolina and Florida, 1951-62. Publications include: How to Win at Wild Card Poker, 1976; (as Zach Hughes)For Texas and Zed, 1976; (as Zach Hughes)Tiger in the Stars, 1976; (as Zach Hughes) The St Francis Effect, 1976; Second Chance, 1976; (with Elizabeth Zachary)Dynasty of Desire, 1978; (with Elizabeth Zachary) The Land Rushers, 1978; (with Elizabeth Zachary) The Golden Dynasty, 1980; (with Elizabeth Zachary) Hotel Destiny, 1980; (with Elizabeth Zachary) Blitz Hotel, 1980; (as Zach Hughes) Killbird, 1980; To Guard the Right, 1980; (as Zach Hughes) Pressure Man, 1980; (with Elizabeth Zachary) Of Love and Battles, 1981; Bloodrush, 1981; Murder in White, 1981; Top Level Death, 1981; (as Zachary Hughes) The Hotel Destiny Series: The Adlon Link, Fortress London, The Fires of Paris, Tower of Treason, 1981; The Sierra Leone Series: Flight to Freedom, Freedom's Passion, Treasure of Hope, Freedom's Victory, 1981-82; (as Zach Hughes) Thunderworld, 1982; The Venus Venture, 1986. Address: 7 Pebble Beach Drive, Yaupon Beach, NC 28461, USA.

ZAHNISER E D. See: ZAHNISER Edward DeFrance.

ZAHNISER Edward DeFrance, (Ed Zahniser), b. 11 Dec 1945, Washington, District of Columbia, USA. Writer; Editor. m. Ruth Christine Hope Duewel, 13 July 1968, 2 sons. Education: AB, Greenville (Illinois) College, 1976; Officers Basic Course, Defense Information School, 1971. Appointments: Poetry Editor, The Living Wilderness Magazine, 1972-75; Founding Editor, Some Of Us Press, Washington, District of Columbia, 1972-75; Arts Editor, Good News Paper, 1981-; Editor, Arts and Kulchur, 1989-91; Curator, Public Hanging, Editor, Exhibit Catalog, 1989; Poetry Reader, Antietam Review, 1992. Publications: The Ultimate Double Play, poems, 1974; I Live In A Small Town (with Justin Duewel-Zahniser), 1984; The Way to Heron Mountain, poems, 1986, reprint, 1989; Sheenjek and Denali, poems, 1990; Jonathan Edwards..., artist book, 1991; Howard Zahniser's Where Wilderness Preservation Began: Adirondack Wilderness Writings (editor), 1992; Several handbooks of US National Parks and portions of illustrated books on natural history topics in North America. Contributions to: Hollins Critic; Journal of Western American Literature; Carolina Quarterly; Amicus Journal; Wilderness; Antietam Review; Rolling Coulter; Riverrun; December; Backcountry; North of Upstate; Trout; Moneysworth; Mother Earth News; Snowy Egret; Hobo Jungle; Metropolitan; Others. Honours: Woodrow Wilson Fellow, 1967; 1st and 2nd Prizes in Poetry Collection, Narrative Poetry, West Virginia Writers Annual Competitions, 1989, 1991, 1992. Address: c/o Atlantis Rising, ARC Box G, Shepherdstown, WV 25443, USA.

ZAHORSKI Kenneth James, b. 23 Oct 1939, Cedarville, Indiana, USA. Professor of English; Director of Faculty Development. m. Marijean Allen, 18 Aug 1962, 2 daughters. Publications: The Fantastic Imagination, vols I & II, 1977-78; Dark Imaginings, 1978; Fantasy Literature, 1979; The Phoenix Tree, 1980; Visions of Wonder, 1981; Alexander, Walton, Morris: A Primary and Secondary Bibliography, 1981; Fantasists on Fantasy, 1984; Peter S Beagle, 1988. Contributions to: College English; CLA Journal; Wisconsin English Journal; and others. Honours: Leonard Ledvina Outstanding Teacher Award, 1974; ALA Outstanding Reference Book Award, 1979; Mythopoeic Society Special Scholarship Award, 1985; Donald B King Distinguished Scholar Award, 1987. Memberships: Science Fiction Research Association; International Association for the Fantastic in the Arts; Modern Language Association of America; National Council of Teachers of English; American Association for Higher Education. Address: 1134 Stevens Street, DePere, WI 54115, USA.

ZAJACZKOWSKA-MITZNEROWA Larysa, b. 7 Aug. 1918, Kiev. Journalist; Writer. m. Zbigniew Mitzner, 8 Apr. 1950, deceased 1968, 1 son. Education: MA, Warsaw University, Higher School of Journalism, 1939. Publications: When You Return, 1958; Next Street, 1958; Blue Chincilla Fur, 1960; Writing to You, 1960; Unkown Addressee, 1962; Stars on Earth, 1962; Conjectural Prosecution, 1963; Clique, 1964; Date Under the Clock, 1965; Niobe, 1966; The Gentlemen in the Zodiac, 1967; King Priam's Vase, 1968; Cup of Coffee, 1970; No Trumps, 1970; Moths, 1976; Elusive, 1977; 18 moral and criminal books (novels); Childrens Books: Broken Next, 1946; On Pirate's Track, 1971; Co-operative Member Has Friends, 1972. Contributions To: numerous journals and magazines, 1936-76. Honours: Krzyz Kawalerski Orderu Odrodzenia Polski; Gold Silver and Bronze Crosses of Merit; Jubilee Medal. Memberships: Polish Writers Association; Polish Journalistic Association; International Organisation of Journalists. Address: Finlandzka 5/6, Warsaw 03-903, Poland.

ZALBEN BRESKIN Jane, b. 21 Apr. 1950, USA. Author; Artist; College Teacher. m. 25 Dec. 1969, 2 sons. Education: BA, Art, Queens College; Pratt Graphics Centre, 1972. Appointments: Assistant Art Director, Dial Press, 1971; Designer, Ty Crowell, 1974; Art Director, Scribners, 1975; Freelance, 1976-. Publications: Cecilia's Older Brother, 1973; Lyle and Humus, 1974; Jeremiah Knucklebones by Jan Wahl, 1974; Basil and Hillary, 1975; An Invitation to the Butterfly Ball: A Counting Rhyme, by Jane Yolen, 1976; Jabberwocky, by Lewis Carroll, 1977; Penny and the Captain, 1977; Norton's Nightime, 1979; Will You Count the Stars Without Me, 1979; Oliver and Alison's Week, 1980; Oh Simple!, 1981; Porcupine's Christmas Blues, 1982; Maybe it will Rain Tomorrow, 1982; Here's Looking at You, Kid, 1987; The Walrus and the Carpenter, by Lewis Carroll, 1986; Water from the Moon, 1987; Beni's First Chanukah, 1988; Earth to Andrew O Blechman, 1989; Happy Passover, Rosei, 1989; Leo and Blossom's Sukkah, 1990; Goldie's Purim, 1991; The Fourtune Teller in 5B, 1991. Contributions to: various journals and magazines including: Society of Children's Book Writers Bulletin Jewish World. Honours: International Reading Association, Children's Choice Award (twice); AIGA; Art Directors Club; Judge for Golden Kite Award, 1990. Memberships: Society of Children's Book Writers. Agent: Curtis Brown Ltd. 10 Astor Place, New York. Address: 70 South Road, Sands Point, NY 11050, USA.

ZALKA Miklos, b. 25 May 1928, Budapest, Hungary. Writer. Education: Degree by Correspondence, Zrinyi Miklos Military Academy, 1958. Publications: Author, many books including: A mi utcank, 1967; A borzekes, 1967; Mindenkihez, historical Essay, 1969; A Tavolban Kanaan, 1970; A dzungel vere, 1971; Rizs esbambusz (short stories from Vietnam), 1971; Es Lelno az elefant 1973; Csollima Szarnya (reports from the Democratic Peoples Republic of Korea), 1974; Roham 03.30 (historical essay, military & political outline of the military operations during WWII in Hungary), 1975; Fustkarikak (short stories), 1975; Az Asszony Akire Varnak, novel, 1975; Szamuely, 1979; Ostrom, novel, 1980; Vorosok es feherek, 1982; Fekete karacsony, novel, 1982; Zugnak a harangok, novel, 1984; Harmadik emelet jobbra, novel, 1985; Mindenfele historiak, short stories, 1988. Honours: Special prizes, 1962, 1969, 1974 (for Fustkarikak, 1975) (for Roham 03.30). Jozsef Attila Prize, 1984. Address: Abonyi u.27, 1146 Budapest XIV Hungary.

ZALL Paul M, b. 3 Aug 1922, Lowell, Massachusetts, USA. Author; Lecturer; Editor. m. Elisabeth Weisz, 21 June 1948, 3 sons. Education: AB, Swarthmore College, 1948; AM, 1950, PhD, 1951, Harvard University. Appointments: Lecturer, Harvard University, 1950-51; Assistant Professor, Cornell University, 1951-55;

Research Editor, Boeing Company, Seattle, Washington, 1955-56; Professor of English, California State University, Los Angeles, 1957-86; Consultant, Huntington Library, San Marino, California, 1986-. *Publications:* A Hundred Merry Tales, 1963, 2nd Edition, 1977; Literary Criticism of Wordsworth, 1969; Ben Franklin Laughing, 1980; Abe Lincoln Laughing, 1982; George Washington Laughing, 1989; Franklin's Autobiography: a Model Life, 1989; 14 others. *Contributions to:* 75 essays on history of Anglo-American humour and British Romantic poets in professional journals. *Address:* Huntington Library, 1151 Oxford Road, San Marino, CA 91108, USA.

ZALYGIN Sergey Pavlovich, b. 6 Dec 1913, Durasovka, Russia. Writer; Ecologist. *Education:* Omsk Agricultural Institute. *Appointments:* Editor-in-Chief, Novy Mir magazine 1986-; Chairman, Nongovernmental Ecological Organization of Scientists and Publicists, Association Ecology and Peace, 1987-. *Publications include:* Stories, 1941; Spring of 1954, 1955; Altai Paths, 1959; On the Irtich, 1964; The Saulty Ravine, 1967; My Poet, essay about Chehov, 1969; The Commission, 1975; After the Storm, 1985; many others. *Contributions to:* a series of articles on ecology. *Honours:* State Prize, 1968; Various others. *Membership:* Russian Union of Writers. *Address:* 28/3, The Lenin Prospect, Moscow, Russia.

ZAMAROVSKY Vojtech, b. 5 Oct 1919, Trencin, Slovakia. Writer. m. Mrie Nuslauer, 1952, 1 son, 1 daughter. *Education:* Dr iuris uts, Faculty of Law, Slovak University, Bratislava, 1943; High School of Economics, Prague, 1948. *Publications:* Books in Slovak, translated into Czech, Russian, Croatian, Polish, Lithuanian, Hungarian, Rumanian, German, Greek: Seven Wonders of the World, 1960, 8 editions; Discovery of Troy, 1962, 7 editions; History written by Rome, 1967, 4 editions; Greek Wonder, 1972, 4 editions; Goods and Kings of Ancient Egypt, 2 editions. *Memberships:* Union of Slovak Writers, Bratislava; Union of Classical Philologists, Prague. *Address:* Francouzski 22, 12000 Prague 2, CSFR.

ZAMINDAR Niranjan, b. 21 Mar 1923, Indore, India. Landlord. m. Vandawa Zamindar, 2 sons, 1 daughter. *Education:* MA; LLB. *Publications:* Aur Kshipra Bahati Raji, novel; Audhunik Bharat aur Gita; Everthing for a Smile; Samartha Ramdas Vani; Samay Sar; Vyakti Darshan; Rajaji; Dr Radha Krishnan; Nilkanth; Bolshevism; Bhagwad Gita; China Hamla; Yamraj ka Hridaya Parivartan; Chhatrapati Shivaji; Manav Samaj Niti aur Rajniti; Nirmalya, novel; Rosa Dobson, novel; Khuda Ko Phansi, poems; A Handbook of Modern Hindi Literature. *Contributions to:* Hundreds of articles and reviews to periodicals and papers including: Dharmayug; Vina; S Hindusthan Rang. *Honours:* University Gold Medallist; Bharat Bhasha Bhushah. *Memberships:* PEN; Authors Guild; Indian Society of Authors; Indian Philosophical Congress; Indian History Congress. *Address:* Bada Rawla, Indore City 452-004, India.

ZAND Roxane (Hakimzadeh), b. 21 Mar 1952, Tehran, Iran. Educator; Academic. m. Hakim Zadeh, 7 Nov 1978, 2 sons. *Education:* BA, Harvard University, USA, 1975; DPhil (Oxon), England, 1994. *Publication:* Persian Requiem, translation. *Contributions to:* Jaso; Feminist Review; Nimeye Digar Feminist Qaurterly. *Memberships:* Translators Society; Chairperson, Harvard Club of London. *Address:* 9 Templewood Ave, London NW3 7UY, England.

ZAPOEV Timur, (Timur Kibirov), b. 15 Feb 1955, Shepetovka, Ukraine. Writer; Poet. m. 25 Mar 1989, 1 daughter. *Education:* MA, Moscow Oblast Pedagogical Institute, 1981. *Publications:* Obschie Mesta, 1990; Lichnoe Delo (co-author), 1991; Poems in: Ponedelnik: Sem Poetor Samizdata, 1990; Kalendar, 1991; The Poetry of Perestroika, UK, 1991; Oktoberlegendernas land, Sweden, 1991; Third Wave: The New Russian Poetry, USA, 1992. *Contributions to:* Poetry selections to: Teatr, Moscow; Junost, Moscow; Ogonjok, Moscow;

Kontinent, Paris; Sintaksis, Paris; Vremia i My, New York; Novy Mir, Moscow; Others. *Address:* Ostrovitianova d 34 korp 1 kv 289, Moscow 117279, Russia.

ZAROKOSTA Katerina, b. 23 Apr 1951, Athens, Greece. Writer; Script Writer; Radio Journalist. m. Pantelis Gaganis, 25 Dec 1972, 1 daughter. *Education:* MA French Literature, University of Athens. *Appointments:* Teacher of French Language, University of Athens 1976- 79; Literary Programme on New Books, State Radio, A Programme 1979-92. *Publications:* Lecado, short Stories, 1986; Tomek, Short Stories, 1992; The Last Resort, Script Feature Film, 1984; Cochlias, scripts for TV series of dramatised documentary about modern Greek Writers 1981-83; As Lond as Cats Exist, novel for children, 1983; Translation into Greek of Le Coup de Grace, of Marg Yourcenar. *Contributions to:* Articles in French magazine Belvedere, 1991; Member of Editing Board Greek Literary magazine Currents, 1992-. *Address:* 6 Piniou Str, Psychico, Athens 15452, Greece.

ZASTROW Charles H, b. 30 July 1942, Wausau, Wisconsin, USA. Author; Professor. m. 28 June 1986, Kristine Kaneiss, 1 son. *Education:* BS Psychology 1964, MSW Social Work 1966, PhD Social Welfare 1971, University of Wisconsin-Madison. *Appointments:* Professor, University of Wisconsin-Whitewater 1971-; Social Work Consulting Editor, Nelson-Hall Publishers 1987-; Associate Editor, International Journal of Comparative and Applied Criminal Justice 1976-. *Publications:* The Personal Problem Solver, co-author, 1977; Talk to Yourself, 1979; Social Work with Groups, 2nd ed 1989; Introduction to Social Welfare, 4th ed 1990; Understanding Human Behaviour and the Social Environment, co-author, 2nd ed 1990; The Practice of Social Work, 4th ed, 1992; Social Problems, 3rd ed, 1992. *Contributions to:* 36 articles published in professional journals. *Honour:* Excellence in Teaching Award 1987 at University of Wisconsin-Whitewater. *Memberships:* National Association of Social Workers; Academy of Certified Social Workers; Council on Social Work Education; Register of Clinical Social Workers. *Address:* Social Work Department, University of Wisconsin-Whitewater, Whitewater, WI 53704, USA.

ZELAZNY Roger Joseph (Harrison Denmark), b. Cleveland, Ohio, USA Author. m. 20 Aug 1966, 2 sons, 1 daughter. *Education:* BA, Case Western Reserve University; MA, Columbia University. *Appointments:* Social Security Administration, Cleveland, Ohio, Baltimore, Maryland, 1962-69; Claims Representative, Cleveland, 1962-65; Claims Policy Specialist Baltimore, 1965- 69; Full-time writer, 1969-. *Publications include:* This Immortal, 1966; Four for Tomorrow, 1967; Isle of the Dead, 1969; Damnation Alley, 1969; Jack of Shadows, 1971, Today We Choose faces, 1973; Sign of the Unicorn, 1975; My Name is Legion, 1976; Bridge of Ashes, 1976; The Courts of Chaos, 1978; Roadmarks, 1979; Changeling, 1980; The Changing Land, 1981; Coils, 1982; Dilvish the damned, 1982; Trumps of Doom, 1985; Blood of Amber, 1986; A Dark Traveling, 1987; Sign of Chaos, 1987; Frost & Fire, 1989. *Contributor To:* Numerous short stories, articles and poems to magazines and anthologies including: Amazing Stories; Analog; Destinies; Fantastic Adventures; Heavy Metal; Isaac Asimovb's Science Fiction Adventure Magazine; Magzine of Horror; Satellite Orbit; Sorcerer's Apprentice; Unearth; Worlds of Tomorrow; The Writer; Writers Digest Yearbook. *Address:* c/o Kirby McCauley Limited, 155 E 77th Street, Suite 1A, New York, NY 10021, USA.

ZELENY Jindrich, b. 13 Nov 1922, Bitovany. Professor of Philosophy. m. Jirina Topicova, 21 Oct 1946, 2 daughters. *Education:* PhD in Philosophy & Sociology 1948, Charles University, Prague. *Publications:* The Logic of Marx, 1980, appeared also in German, Spanish and Swedish; Dialektik der Rationalitat, 1986, appeared also in Japanese; 5 books on epistemology in Czech. *Contributions to:* Many magazines and journals. *Honour:* State Prize for

Humanities 1988. *Memberships:* Steering Committee of Federation Internationale des Societes Philosophiques, 1983; Steering Committee of Internationale Gesellschaft fur Dialektische Philosophie, 1981; Vice President, Czechoslovakian Philosophical Society 1981-89. *Address:* Soukenicka 29, 11000 Prague 1, Czechoslovakia.

ZELINOVA Hana, b. 20 July 1914, Vrutky, Slovakia. Writer. m. Jan Havlat, 29 Apr. 1959, 1 daughter. *Education:* Teachers College, 1931. *Appointments:* Staff, Svojet Publishers, Kosice, 1947-51, Smena Publishing House, Bratislava, 1962-71. *Publications:* The Angel Land, 1946; The Diabolic Dance, 1956; The Young Jacob, 1959; The Elisabeth's Court (Trilogy), 1971, 1975, 1981; Time for Candle Lighting, 1979; The Silk Road, 1980; The Mirrored Bridge, 1941; The Port of Peace, 1943; The Mountain of Temptation, 1946; Stand-up Girl, 1948; The Grey Goose, 1960; Sinful Country Atlantis, 1961; Barfooted General, 1961; So Long Susanne, 1962; Hanibal Behind the Gate, 1963; I Do Not Come in the Evening, 1964; The Revenge is Mine, 1965; The Call of the Wind, 1973; The Thirst, 1981; The Flower of Horror, 1983; The Fan with Violets, 1984; The Voice of the Old Violin, 1987; Matthew and I, 1987; The Night Concert, 1989. *Contributions to:* Numerous professional journals. *Honours:* Czechoslovak Broadcasting Corporation Prize for Best Script, 1943; Prize, Czechoslovak Television, 1967; Prize, Union of Slovak Writers, 1973; Prize, Slovak Ministry of Culture for Literature, 1980; Prize, Frano Kral for Literature for Youth, 1984; many other honours and awards. *Memberships:* Union of Slovak Writers; Slovak Literary Fund. *Agent:* Slovak Literature Agency, Czechoslovakia. *Address:* Nabrezie Gen. Svobodu 44, 81102 Bratislava, Czechoslovakia.

ZELLER Frederic, b. 20 May 1924, Berlin (British Subject). Writer; Sculptor. m. (2) 21 Jan 1989. *Education:* BA, Birkbeck College, London University, England. *Publication:* When Time Ran Out: Coming of Age in the Third Reich, HB, US, UK, Germany, 1989, SB, US, Holland, 1989, 1990 US; Friendly Enemy Alien (The Fearful Forties). *Honours:* New American Writing Award by the National Endowment of the Arts 1989; Selected by the US Information Agency as part of 1990 exhibit, travelling to New Delhi, Buenos Aires, Cairo, Beijing, Moscow & Zurich. *Memberships:* Federation of Modern Painters & Sculptors, New York; Artists' Equity Association, New York. *Literary Agent:* Carole Mann Agency, NYC. *Address:* 775 Sixth Avenue, New York City NY 10001, USA.

ZELLERBACH Merla, b. 27 Aug 1930, San Francisco, California, USA. Writer. m. Fred Goerner, 4 Jan 1968, 1 son. *Education:* Stanford University 1949-50. *Appointments:* Featured Columnist, San Francisco Chronicle 1962-85; Lecture Leader, Creative Writing Seminars 1975-90. *Publications:* Love in a Dark House, 1961; Detox, 1984; The Wildes of Nob Hill, 1986; Cavett Manor, 1987; Love the Giver, 1987; Sugar, 1988; Ritten House Square, 1990; The type 1/type 2 Allergy Relief Programme 1983. *Contributions to:* Saturday Evening Post; Cosmopolitan; Travel & Leisure; Reader's Digest; Prevention; Town & Country. *Honour:* Permanent Panelist, ABC-TV Game Show Oh My Word 1965-70. *Literary Agent:* Frederick Hill Agency. *Address:* Presidio Terrace, San Francisco, CA 94118, USA.

ZEMANEK Alicja, b. 2 Aug 1949, Bielsko-Biata, Poland. Scientist; Poetess. m. Bogdan Zemanek, 30 July 1981. *Education:* Doctor of Biological Science (PbD) 1977, Assistant Professor (Dr hab) 1990, Jagiellonian University. *Publications:* Egzotyczny Ogród na Wesotej, 1986; Listopad w Bibliotece, 1988; Dién w Którym Zniknętam, 1990; Wakacje w Krakowie, 1991. *Contributions to:* Zycie Literackie; Poeja; Pismo Literacko- Artystyczne; Lektura; and others. *Memberships:* Zwiazek Literatów Polskich; Polskie Towarzystwo Botaniczne. *Address:* ul Kopernika 27, 31-501 Cracow, Poland.

ZENOFON Fonda, b. 31 Aug. 1953, Greece, Australian Nationality. Freelance Writer; Poet; Editor; Publisher. *Publications:* Editor, Brunwick Poetry Workshop Newsletter, 1972-79; Ode to a Child : Poetry Anthology, 1980; Matilda Literary & Arts Magazine, 1980-; The Wedding, 1980; Poetry Naked Wasp, 1981; Fly Dirt, 1981; Independance Voice, 1978; Books, Love Verse & Other Poems, 1974; Change, 1980; Anvil of Literature, 1982; Australia With Love, (play), 1979; World Poetry; Editor, Dr Krishna Srinivas, (anthology), 1991; TV and Radio appearances. *Contributions To:* Numerous professional journals, magazines and newspapers including: The Brunswick Sentinel; The Age; The New York Times of Australia; Australian Book Review; Melbourne Times; Brave New World; Access; Learning Exchange; Women's Weekly; Genii. *Honours Include:* Recipient, numerous honours and awards; Honorary Poet Laureate, City of Brunswick, 1983; 1 of Top 50 Poets invited to 1st Poets' Festival in Australia, 1976; various commissions. *Address:* 7 Mountfield Street, Brunswick, Victoria 3056, Australia.

ZETFORD Tully. *See:* **BULMER Henry Kenneth.**

ZETTERLING Mai (Elisabeth), b.24 May 1925, Vaesteras, Sweden, immigrated to England. Actress, screenwriter and director of motion pictures and stage and television productions, Author. m. 1. Tutte Lemkov, 1944, divorced 1953, 1 son, 1 daughter; 2. David Hughes, 1958, divorced 1977. *Education:* Graduated, Royal Theatre School of Drama, Stockholm, 1945. *Career:* Actress in stage productions including, The Wild Duck, 1948, The seagull, 1949 and A Doll's House, 1953; Actress in motion pictures, including Hets, 1944, The Girl in the Painting, 1948 and The Truth About Women, 1958. Contributing director to documentary Visions of Eight, 1973. *Publications include:* Books: (with husband David Hughes) The Cat's Tale (for children) 1965; Night Games (novel) 1966; In the Shadow of the Sun (short stories) 1975; Bird of Passage (novel) 1976; All Those Tomorrows (autobiography) J Cape, 1985, Grove, 1986; The Crystal Castle (for children) Norsteots (Sweden) 1985. Also author of children's book, The Rain's Hat adapted from Zetterling's television production, 1979; Screenplays (and director) include: (with David Hughes) Doktor Glas (adapted from Hjalmar Soderberg's novel) 1967, released in the United States as Doctor Glas, Twentieth Century-Fox, 1969; (with Hughes)Flickorna, 1968, released in the United States as The Girls, Goran Lindgren, 1972; (with Roy Minton and Jeremy Watt) Scrubbers, Orion Classics, 1984; Amorosa, Swedish Film Institute, 1986. Also writer or co-writer, and director of television features and documentaries; The History of Souls, 1991; Poems From Divinities, 1991; The Time of the Red Guards, 1992. *Honour:* Golden Lion from Venice Film Festival, 1963 for The War Game. *Literary Agent:* Douglas Rae Management Ltd, London. *Address:* c/o Douglas Rae Management Ltd, 28 Charing Cross Road, London W1, England.

ZHANG Chengzhi, b. 3 Sept. 1948, Beijing, China. Writer. m. 1 May 1977, 1 daughter. *Education:* History Diploma, Beijing University, 1975; Master of History, diplomas, Department of History & Languages, National Minorities, Chinese Academy of Social Sciences. *Literary Appointment:* Council 1984-, Chinese Writers Association; Member, Standing Council, Society of Beijing Moslem's Culture, 1989. *Publications include:* Old Bridge, 1984; Zhang Chengzhi, 1986; Tours to Inner Mongolian Grassland (Japanese), 1986; River of the North, 1987; Golden Farm, 1987; Yellow Mud House, 1987; Beautiful a Twinkling, 1987; Yellow Mud House, 1988; The Representative Works of Zhang Cheng-zhi, 1988; In the Norrth of the Great Wall, 1988; The Black Steed, 1989; The Green Land, 1989. *Contributions to:* Adviser to: The Chinese Western Novel; The Novel's Selected Readings. *Honours:* National Award, stories, 1978; National Awards, novellas, 1981-82, 1983-84. *Memberships:* Chinese Writers Association; Chinese Society for Mongolian History; Chinese Society for Central Asian Culture. *Address:* c/o Chinese Writers

Association, Sha-Tan-Bei-Jie no.2, 100720 Beijing, China.

ZHANG Jie. *Education:* BA Economics 1960, China People's University. *Publications:* Novels: Heavy Wings, 1982; Only One Sun, 1988; Collection of Short Stories and Novellas: The Ark, 1983; Emerald, 1985; Zhang Jie's Literature, 1986; Collection of Short Short Stories: Love Must Not Be Forgotten, 1980; Zhang Jie's Collection of Short Stories and Movie Scripts, 1980; On a Green Lawn, 1983; A Chinese Woman in Europe, 1989; You Are a Friend of My Soul, 1990; Published Abroad: Heavy Wings, novel, 1981; As Long As Nothing Happens, Nothing Will, collection of short stories; The Ark, novella; Love Must Not Be Forgotten; Only One Sun, novel, 1988; Smaragd, novella, 1984. *Honours:* National Short Story Awards in 1978, 1979, 1983; Maodun National Award for novels (granted once every 3 years), 1985; National Award for novellas (granted once every 2 years), 1985; Until Ihen, the only writer to win all three kinds of major national award on literature in China since 1949; Malaparte Literary Prize, Italy, 1989. *Memberships:* Chinese Association of Writers, Council Member; Beijing Association of Writers, Vice Chairman; International PEN, China Branch; Beijing Political Conference; American Academy and Institute of Arts and Letters, Honorary Membership. *Address:* International Department, China Writers' Association, 2 Shatan Beijie, Beijing 100720, China.

ZHANG Xian, b. 22 June 1934, Shanghai, China. Writer. m. Zhang Ling, 18 Nov. 1967, 1 son, 1 daughter. *Education:* Qinghua University, Beijing, 1953. *Publications:* The Unbreakable Red Silk Thread, 1983; The Selected Film Scenarios by Zhang Xian, 1984; The Collection of New Film Scenarios by Zhang Xian, 1987. *Contributions to:* People's Literature; Shanghai Literature; Harvest; Zhongshan; Wenhui Monthly Magazine. *Honours:* Award for Excellent National Short Stories, 1979, 1980. *Memberships:* Chinese Writers Association; Council of Jiangsu Branch of Chinese Writers Association. *Address:* Jiangsu Branch of Chinese Writers' Association, Nanjing, China.

ZHENG Zhao-Chang, b. 28 Apr. 1933, Jiangsu, China. Professor. m. Pei-Zhi Song, 1 July 1959, 1 son, 1 daughter. *Education:* Undergraduate study: Peking University, 1950-52; Tsinghua University, 1952-53; Graduate study, Engineering Mechanics Institute, Tsinghua University. *Appointments:* Associate Editor-in-Chief, Journal of Vibration and Shock; Associate Editor-in-Chief, Journal of Vibration Engineering; Editor, Chinese Journal of Applied Mechanics; Visiting Lecturer, several universities, USA, Japan, Federal Republic of Germany, France, Netherlands, UK; Vice-Chairman of Scientific Committee, Asia Vibration Conference, 1989; Vice-Chairman of local Organising Committee, ICVPE, 1990; Science and Technology Consultant to China National Offshore Corporation, Nanhai West Oil Company, Beihai Engineering and Design Company, Changcheng Institute of Metrology and Measurement. *Publications:* Editor-in-chief, major author: Mechanical Vibration, vol 1, 1980, vol 2, 1986. *Contributions to:* Over 50 papers in fields of Solid Mechanics, Computational Mechanics, Structural Dynamics, Rotor Dynamics, Linear and Nonlinear Vibration, in journals, Acta Mechanica Sinica, Acta Mechanica Solida Sinica, Applied Mathematics and Mechanics, Chinese Journal of Applied Mechanics, and Proceedings of ASME, CMVN, OMAE, ICVPE, ICMD, ICNM. *Honours:* Academic Achievement Award for Dynamic Response of Nonlinear Systems, Beijing Science Commission, 1984; Best Teaching Book Award for Mechanical Vibration, Vol 1, Chinese National Machinery Commission, 1987; Science and Technology Award, 2nd Class, for Theoretical and Applied Research for Modal Synthesis Technology, Chinese National Education Commission, 1988. *Memberships:* Vice-President, Chinese Society of Vibration Engineering; Vice-President, SCSVE SNV; Vice-President, CSVE SMA; CSTAM; SMEC; CSOE; CSAA. *Address:*

Department of Engineering Mechanics, Tsinghua University, Beijing, China.

ZICWARZ Lawrence Edward, b. 23 Dec 1942, Sault Ste Marie, Michigan, USA. m. Marilyn Sue Wood, 7 Dec 1968, 1 son, 1 daughter. *Education:* Graduate of Sault Ste Marie Loretto Catholic Central 1961; Michigan Tech Sault Branch 1961-63; BA 1965, MA 1966, PhD 1971, Michigan State University. *Publications:* Co-Author: Three Bullets Sealed His Lips; The Games They Played: Sports in American History 1865-1980; Michigan: A History of the Great Lakes State; Sport History; Chapters in: Wm J Baker/John M Carroll-Sports in Modern America; Gerald R Bay-The Evolution of Mass Culture; Richard J Hathaway-Michigan: Visions of Our Past. *Contributions to:* Michigan History & Sport Sociology Bulletin; The Journal of the Great Lakes History Conference; Sociological Viewpoints; Michigan Social Studies; Midwestern Miscellany; History Reviews of New Books. *Honours:* Phi Alpha Theta & Phi Kappa Phi academic honoraries; Number 1 Deans List, Michigan Tech, both campuses 1961-62, 1962-63, Honours College Graduate. *Memberships:* Society for Study of Midwestern Literature; American Culture/Popular Culture Association, Area Co-Chair Sports Sessions; American Historical Association; Organisation of American Historians. *Literary Agent:* Harold Smith. *Address:* Department of American Thought & Language, Michigan State University 229, Bessey, E Lansing, MI 48824, USA.

ZIEGLER Philip Sandeman, b. 24 Dec. 1929, Ringwood, Hampshire, England. Writer. *Education:* New College, Oxford; MA 1st Class Honours Oxon, Jurisprudence. *Publications:* The Black Death, 1968; Melbourne, 1976; Diana Cooper, 1981; Mountbatten, 1985; The Sixth Great Power Barings 1762-1929, 1988; Duchess of Dino; Addington; William IV; Omdurman; Crown and People; King Edward VIII, 1990; Harold Wilson, 1993. *Contributor to:* Reviews and articles: The Times; The Times Literary Supplement; The Daily Telegraph; The Spectator; Others. *Honours:* Fellow, Royal Society of Literature, 1975; W.H. Heinemann Award, 1976; Fellow Royal Historical Society, 1979; Hon DLitt, Westminster College, Fulton. *Memberships:* Council, Royal Society of Literature; General Committee, Royal Literary Fund; Committee of Management, Society of Authors, Chairman, Society of Authors. *Literary Agent:* Curtis Brown. *Address:* 22 Cottesmore Gardens, London, W8 5PR, England.

ZIMMERMAN Joanne, b. 14 Oct 1921, Chicago, Illinois, USA. Writer. m. Howard Zimmerman, 4 Aug 1943, 2 sons, 1 daughter. *Education:* Bachelor's degree, University of Chicago, 1942. *Publications:* Yours Very Truly, 1-act play; Smitty's Haven, in Best Little Magazine Fiction anthology, 1970; The Good Guy, short story, 1990. *Contributions to:* 56 stories to: Antioch Review; Apalachee Quarterly; Arizona Quarterly; Artesian; Chat Noir Review; Chicago Sheet; The Connecticut Writer; The Creative Woman; December; Descant; Florida Quarterly; Folio, Indiana University; Four Quarters; Forum, Ball State University; Forum, Houston, Texas; Glens Falls Review; Grande Ronde Review; The Husk; Kansas Quarterly; Karamu; Korone; The Literary Review; Mississippi Valley Review; Nit and Wit; Oyez Review; Quartet; Shooting Star Review; The University Review; Western Humanities Review; Whetstone; Habersham Review. *Honours:* Illinois Arts Council Award, 1991; Daniel Curley Award, 1991. *Address:* 18255 Perth Ave, Homewood, IL 60430, USA.

ZINDEL Bonnie, b. 3 May 1943, New York City, USA. Writer. m. Paul Zindel, 25 Oct. 1973, 1 son, 1 daughter. *Education:* BA, Psychology, Hofstra University, 1964. *Appointments include:* Public Relations Director, Cleveland Playhouse, 1969-72; Producer, Intermission Feature (Boston Symphony), Station WCLV-FM, Cleveland, 1970-72. *Publications:* A Star for the Latecomer, 1980; Hollywood Dream Machine, 1984. Plays: I Am A Zoo, 1976; Lemons in the Morning, 1983; The Latecomer, 1985; Adriana Earthlight, Student Shrink, 1987. *Memberships:* Playwrights Unit, Actors

Studio; Women in Film. *Literary Agent:* Curtis Brown. *Address:* c/o Curtis Brown, 10 Astor Place, New York, NY 10003, USA.

ZINDEL Paul, b. 1936, USA. Children's Fiction Writer; Dramatist; Former Chemistry Teacher. *Publications:* The Pigman, 1968; My Darling, My Hamburger, 1969; I Never Loved Your Mind, 1970; The Effects of Gamma Rays on Man-in-the-Moon Marigolds, play, 1971; And Miss Reardon Drinks a Little, play, 1972; The Secret Affairs of Mildred Wild, play, 1973; Let Me Hear You Whisper, play, 1974; I Love My Mother, 1975; Pardon Me, You're Stepping on My Eyeball, 1976; Confessions of a Teenage Baboon, 1977; The Undertaker's Gone Bananas, 1978; The Ladies Should Be in Bed, play, 1978; The Pigman's Legacy, 1980; A Star for the Latecomer (with Bonnie Zindel), 1980; The Girl Who Wanted a Boy, 1981; To Take a Dare (with Crescent Dragonwagon), 1982; When a Darkness Falls, 1984; Harry and Hortense at Hormone High, 1984; Maria's Lovers, 1985; Runaway Train, 1985. *Address:* Harper and Row, 10 East 53rd Street, New York, NY 10022, USA.

ZINOVIEV Alexandre, b. 29 Oct 1922, Russia. Scholar in Logic and Sociology; Writer. m. (1) Nina Kalinina, 1944, (2) Tamara Filatieva, 1951, (3) Olga Sorokina, 1967, 1 son, 3 daughters. *Education:* University of Moscow 1951, Postgraduate Course 1954; Candidate and Doctor of Science 1954 & 1962; Professor 1966. *Publications include:* Before the Gate of Paradise, 1979; The Yawning Heights, 1976; The Radiant Future, 1978; The Yellow House, 1980; Reality of Communism, 1981; Homo Sovieticus, 1982; The Wings of Our Youth, 1983; Go to the Calvary, 1985; Katastroika, 1990. *Contributions to:* Dozens of articles in many newspapers and magazines of Western Europe. *Honours:* Awarded number of prizes including: Prix Medicis Etranger, 1978; Alexis Tocqueville Prize, 1982; Prix Europeen de l'Essai, 1977; Several honorary medals. *Memberships:* PEN of some countries; Academy of Arts of Bayern and other societies; Finnish Academy of Sciences; Bavarian Academy of Arts; Italien Academy of Sciences. *Address:* Savitsstrasse 43, 8000 Munchen 81, Germany.

ZIOLKOWSKI Theodore Joseph, b. 30 Sept. 1932, USA. Professor of Comparative Literature, Princeton University; Scholar. m. Yetta B. Goldstein, 26 Mar, 1951, 2 sons, 1 daughter. *Education:* AB 1951, AM 1952, Duke University; University of Innsbruck, Austria, 1952-53; PhD, Yale University, USA, 1957. *Publications:* Novels of Hermann Hesse, 1965; Dimensions of the Modern Novel, 1969; Fictional Transfigurations of Jesus, 1972; Disenchanted Images, 1977; The Classical German Elegy, 1980; Varieties of Literary Thematics, 1983; German Romanticcism and It's Institutions, 1990; Virgil and the Moderns, 1993; Also: Der Schriftsteller Hermann Hesse, 1979; Hermann Broch, 1964. *Contributions:* Numerous articles & reviews, US & European journals. *Honours:* James Russell Lowell Prize, criticism, Modern Language Association, 1973; Howard T. Behrman Award, humanities, 1978; Wilbur Lucius Cross Medal, Yale University, 1982; Gold Medal, Goethe Institute, Federal Republic of Germany, 1987; Henry Allen Moe Prize, American Philosophical Society, 1988. *Memberships:* Academy of Literary Studies; American Philosophical Society; Past president, Modern Language Association; Gottingen Academy of Sciences; American Academy of Arts & Sciences. *Address:* 36 Bainbridge Street, Princeton, New Jersey 08540, USA.

ZIRAS Alexis, b. 12 Nov 1945, Athens, Greece. Literary Critic; Radio Producer. m. Ionna Hlabea, 25 Sept 1982, 2 sons. *Education:* Political and Social Sciences, University of Thessaloniki, 1967-71; Studies on Balkan Cultures and Languages, Institute of Balkan Studies, Thessaloniki. *Appointments:* Reviewer, Thessaloniki journal, 1968-1975; Reviewer, Kathimerini journal, 1976-82; Member, Board of National Literary Awards, 1982-92; Editorial, Grammata Ke Tehnes literary review, 1982-87; Editorial, Revmata literary review, 1990-92. *Publications:* Anatomia Epohis, 1973; Theoria

Morfon, 1978; Neoteri Elliniki Piisi, 1965-1980, 1980; Genealogika, on the poetry of the 70s, 1989; Poetry: In Searching of..., 1966; The Sleep of Eros, 1976. *Contributions to:* Journals: Argi, Ta Nea; Magazines: To Dendro, I Iexi, I Grafi, Entefktirion, To Tram, Porfiras, many others. *Membership:* Society of Writers, General Secretary 1984-86. *Address:* 4 Thisseos and Lydias, GR-15232 Halandri Attikis, Greece.

ZIVADIN Steven, b. 20 Nov 1908. Retired University Lecturer; Writer; Painter. *Education:* Lycee de nice, Real-Gymn, Zagreb and Belgrade, Yugoslavia; Graduate, Law & Economics, University of Paris, France; Doctor, Civil Law, University of Belgrade. *Appointments include:* Assistant Professor, Faculty of Subotica, University of Belgrade. *Publications:* The Anag-Rhyme, innovation, 1974; Metre, Rhyme and Freedom, 1975-76; Techniques in Surrealist Poetry, 1978; Biology of Nature, 1978; The Species and Biorbis, 1978. *Contributions to:* L'Impossible, Bilingual; Badrealisam DIO; Le Surrealisme ASDLR (Letter to Salvador Dali); Penine Platform; True Thomas; Orbis; Pall Mall Quarterly; Phoenix Special Supplement, reprints and translations in various books and periodicals; Main Innovations include: The Plural Automatic Text; Poetry of the Imaginery (Contents and others); the Ana Rhyme (non-chiming rhyme), in minor tonality; The Schoenberg Verse and the Poem with Cadenza. *Memberships:* Fellow, International Poetry Society; Museum for Modern Art, Oxford, England; Oxford Union Society. *Address:* Arthur Garrard House, 288 Iffley Road, Oxford OX4 4AE, England.

ZOLOTOW Charlotte, b. 1915, USA. Children's Fiction Writer; Poet; Editor. *Appointments:* Senior Editor, 1962-76, Vice-President, Associate Publisher, and Editorial Director, Harper Junior Books Division, 1976-81, Editorial Consultant, Editorial Director, Charlotte Zolotow Books, 1981-91, Publisher, Emerita and Editorial Advisor, 1991-, Harper & Collins Children's Books, New York City. *Publications:* The Park Book, 1944; But Not Billy, 1944, 1983; The Storm Book, 1952; The Magic Word, 1952; The City Boy and the Country Horse (as Charlotte Bookman), 1952; Indian, Indian, 1952; The Quiet Mother and the Noisy Little Boy, 1953, 1989; One Step, Two..., 1955; Over and Over, 1957; Not a Little Monkey, 1957, 1989; The Night Mother Was Away, 1958, The Summer Night, 1974; The Park Book, 1958; Do You Know What I'll Do, 1958; Sleepy Book, 1958, 1988; Bunny Who Found Easter, 1959; Aren't You Glad, 1960; Big Brother, 1960; The Three Funny Friends, 1961; The Sky Was Blue, 1963; The Quarreling Book, 1963; The White Marble, 1963, 1982; A Tiger Called Thomas, 1963; I Have a Horse of My Own, 1964; The Poodle Who Barked at the Wind, 1964, 1987; A Rose, a Bridge, and a Wild Black Horse, 1964, 1987; Mr Rabbit and the Lovely Present, 1964; When the Wind Stops, 1964, 1975; Flocks of Birds, 1965, 1983; Someday, 1965; When I Have a Little Girl, 1965; If It Weren't for You, 1966; Big Sister and Little Sister, 1966; I Like to be Little, 1966, 1980; Summer Is..., 1967, 1983; When I Have a Little Boy, 1967; All that Sunlight, 1967; The New Friend, 1968; Some Things Go Together, 1969, 1983; A Week in Yani's World: Greece, 1969; The Hating Book, 1969; Here Is Where I Begin (as Sarah Abbott), 1970; River Winding, 1970, 1978; A Week in Lateef's World: India, 1970; You and Me, 1971; A Father Like That, 1971; Wake Up and Goodnight, 1971; William's Doll, 1972; Hold My Hand, 1972; The Beautiful Christmas Tree, 1972; Janey, 1973; My Grandson Lew, 1974; An Overpraised Season (editor), 1974; The Unfriendly Book, 1975; The Little Black Pony, 1975; It's Not Fair, 1976; May I Visit, 1976; Someone New, 1978; If You Listen, 1980; Say it, 1980, I Know a Lady, 1984; Early Sorrow (editor), 1986; Everything Glistens and Everything Sings, 1987; Something is Going to Happen, 1988; The Summer Night, 1991; This Quiet Lady, 1992; The Seashore Book, 1992; Snippets, 1993; The Moon Was The Best, 1993. *Honours:* Carolyn W Field Award, Pennsylvania Library Association Youth Services Division, for Some Things Go Together, 1984; Redbrook Award for I Know a Lady, 1984 and for William's Doll, 1985; ALA tribute, 1991; Helen C White tribute, 1987; Kerlan Award, 1986; LMP Award, 1990. *Address:* c/

o Harper Collins Children's Books, 10 East 53rd Street, New York, NY 10022, USA.

ZOLTON Sumonyi. *See:* **SUMONYI PAPP Zolton.**

ZURAKOWSKI Boguslaw, b. 9 July 1939, Stanislawow, Poland. Poet; Literary Critic; Academic Lecturer. *Education:* Dr. Humanities and Philology, Wyzsza Szkola Pedagogiczna, 1975. *Appointment:* Taniec bez ludzi, Poetry, 1962. *Publications:* Piesn, 1971; Slowa czasu kazdego, 1975; Cialo i swiatlo, 1978; Wybor poezji, 1981; Paradoks poezji, 1982; Koncert ciszy, 1984; Grudy ziemi, 1966; Narzecze nadziei, 1980; W Swiecie poezji dla dzieci, 1981. *Contributions To:* Odra; Literatura; Poezja; Opole. *Honours:* Distinction, International Poetical Competition, PEN Club, London, England, 1965; Pietak award, Poland, 1979; Award Periodical Opole, Poland, 1980; Premio Internazionale Pinocchio, 1983. *Memberships:* PEN; SEC. *Address:* ul. Krupnicza 22/23, 31-123 Cracow, Poland.

ZUROWSKI Andrzej, b. 24 Sept. 1944, Poland. Essayist; Theatre Critic. m. Magda Oller, 23 Aug 1988, 3 daughters. *Education:* MA, Polish Philology, 1967; PhD, Arts, 1973. *Appointments:* Chief, Artistic Programmes, Polish TV, Gdansk, 1967-90; Commrntator, 1990-; Lecturer of Science of Theatrical matters, Gdansk University, 1975-77, 1986-. *Publications:* Spotkanie z mitem, 1976; Szekspiriady polskie, 1976; Teatr Wybrzeze, 1946-1976, 1976; Fatamorgana, 1979; Wieczory popremierowe, 1982; Ludzie w reflektorach, 1982; Zza kulis szeptem, 1982; Hebanowski, 1983; Myslenie Szekspirem, 1983; Latajacy fotel, 1987; Zasoby i sposoby, 1988; Czas przesilenia, 1990; Szajna, 1992Czytajaac Szekspira, 1993. *Contributions to:* Dialog; Kultura; Literatura; Zycie Literackie; Shakespeare Quarterly; Jeu; Shinhaz; Teatteri; New Theatre Quarterly; Teatr; Contemporary Review; Sipario; International Theatre Year Book. *Honours:* Polish Theatre Critics Club Award, 1970, 1977, 1988; Gdansk Voivode Award, 1981, 1984; Edward Csato Award, 1984; Fakty Award, 1984; Gdansk's Lord Mayor Award, 1988; Gdansk's Patron of Art Society, Artistic Prize, 1988; Medals. *Memberships:* Union of Polish Writers, President, Gdansk Section 1983-86; Theatre Critics Club, Vice President 1978-82, President 1982-, International Association of Theatre Critics, Vice-President, 1981-87, 1990-, Ex Com member, 1987-90. *Address:* Glogowa 21, 81-589 Gdynia, Poland.

ZUSPAN Frederick Paul, b. 20 Jan. 1922, Ohio, USA. Obstetrician & Gynaecologist. m. Mary Jane Cox, 23 Nov. 1943, 1 son, 2 daughters. *Education:* BA 1947, MD 1951, Ohio State University. *Appointments include:* J.B. Delee Professor & Chairman, Department of Obstetrics & Gynacology, University of Chicago, 1966-75; Professor & Department Chairman 1974-87, R. Meiling Professor 1984, 1989, Ohio State University. Also: Founding editor, Journal of Reproductive Medicine, 1967; Editor, American Journal of Obstetrics & Gynaecology 1969-91; Editor-in-Chief, American Journal of Obstetrics and Gynaecology, 1992-; Contemporary Obstetrics & Gynaecology Monograph Series 1970-83, Journal of Clinical & Experimental Hypertension in Pregnancy 1982-86, Reproductive Medicine Series 1982-; Editorial boards, various other journals. *Publications include:* Handbook of Obstetrics, with Quilligan, 1981-91; Operative Obstetrics, with Quilligan, 1982, 1987; Drug Therapy in Obstetrics & Gynaecology, with Rayburn, 1982, 1986, 1992; Clinical Procedures in Obstetrics & Gynaecology, 1983-84. *Contributions:* Over 200 original scientific articles, numerous professional journals. *Honours:* Research prize, South Atlantic Foundation, 1960; Armine Award, Lund, Sweden, 1978. *Address:* Department of Obstetrics & Gynaecology, Ohio State University, Columbus, Ohio 43210, USA.

Appendices

APPENDIX A

LITERARY AGENTS

The following list of agents does not claim to be exhaustive although every effort has been made to make it as comprehensive as possible. In all instances, authors are advised to send preliminary letters to agents before submitting manuscripts.

ARGENTINA

The Lawrence Smith Literary Agency
Aveni da de los Incas 3110
Buenos Aires 1426
Contact: Lawrence Smith, Mrs Nancy H Smith
Literary works accepted for translation into Spanish & Portuguese. Publications in Volume or Serial for, representation in Theatre, Film, Television or Radio.

AUSTRALIA

Australian Literary Management
2A Armstrong Street
Middlepark, Vic 3206
Contact: Caroline Lurie
Represents Australian writers in fields of fiction, non-fiction, children's books, theatre and film. Handles Australian/New Zealand rights only for a small number of American writers, in conjunction with other literary agents.

Curtis Brown (Aust) Pty Ltd
27 Union Street, Paddington
Sydney, NSW 2021
Contact: Tim Curnow
Fiction, Non-Fiction, Childrens' Writers, television, screen, radio & stage, also represents Directors.

Rick Raftos Pty Ltd
PO Box 445, Paddington
New South Wales 2021
Contact: Rick Raftos, Jane Rose
Represents Performing Arts Writers, television, screen, radio & stage, also represents Directors.

BRAZIL

Karin Schindler
Caixa Postal 19051
04599 Sao Paulo SP
Contact: Karin Schindler
Handles everything for the sale of Portuguese language rights in Brazil.

BULGARIA

The Bulgarian Copyright Agency JUSAUTOR
17 Ernst Telman Blvd
1463 Sofia
Contact: Mrs Yana Markova, Director General
Representative of Bulgarian authors, promoting work for publication & performance abroad.

CANADA

Authors' Marketing Services Ltd
217 Degrassi St
Toronto, Ontario, M4M 2K8
Contact: Larry Hoffman
Adult fiction and non-fiction, parental self-help, business and biography.

Bella Pomer Agency Inc
Shallmar Blvd, PH2
Toronto, Ontario, M5N 2Z8
Contact: Bella Pomer
International representation for full-length fiction & non-fiction. No cook books, how-to books or unsolicited manuscripts.

J Kellock & Associates Ltd
11017 - 80 Avenue
Edmonton, Alberta, T6G OR2
Contact: Joanne Kellock
Handles all non-fiction for trade market, all fiction, literary, commercial, genre, all works for children. Also acts for illustrators of books for children.

Peter Livingston Associates, Inc
1020 Bland St
Halifax, NS B3H 2S8
Contact: Peter W Livingston, David C Johnston
Handles serious non-fiction: business, politics, etc; popular non-fiction: self-help, how-to, literary & commercial fiction, film & television. No poetry or children's books.

CZECHOSLOVAKIA

Slovak Literary Agency, LITA
Zamocnicka 9
815 30 Bratislava
Contact: JUDr Matej Andras, Director
Protects rights of Slovak authors abroad, foreign authors in Slovakia.

DENMARK

Leonhardt Literary Agency Aps
35 Studiestraede
DK-1455 Copenhagan K
Handles all kinds of bookrights.

GERMANY

Buro fur Urheberrechte, Copyright Office, Copyright Information Center
Clara-Zetkin-Str 105
1080 Berlin
Contact: Dr Andreas Henselmann

Corry Theegarten-Schlotterer Verlags-und Autoren-Agentur
Kulmer Str 3
8 Munchen 81
Contact: Ms C Theegarten-Schlotterer
Co-production of books of international interest, fiction and non-fiction, biographies. No childrens' books.

Fralit Medium Agency
Brahmsallee 29
D-2000 Hamburg 13
Contact: Prof Fritz Kurt Albrecht
Manuscripts for newspapers and bookpublishers, of plays and features for theatre, broadcasting, television and film.

Geisenheyner & Crone International Literary Agents
Gymnasiumstrasse 31B
D-7000 Stuttgart 1
Contact: Mr Ernst W Geisenheyner
Representing German & foreign authors and publishers especially in the Socialist countries.

GPA Gerd Plesel Agentur & Verlags GmbH
Linprunstrasse 38
D-8000 Munchen 2
Contact: Gerd J Plessl
Represents publishers and literary agencies from the English language world in general and selected ones

from French and German. Also major American and British Studios for ancilliary rights.

Hans Hermann Hagedorn
Erikastr 142
2000 Hamburg 20
Contact: Hans Hermann Hagedorn

Literarische Agentur Brigitte Axster
Dreieichstr 43
D-6000 Frankfurt
Contacts: Brigitte Axster, Dr Petra Christina Hardt, Uta Angerer
Authors agent, representing English, Dutch, French and Italian publishers in German speaking countries.

Skandinavia Verlag, Marianne Weno - Michael Gunther
Ithweg 31
D-1000 Berlin 37
Contact: Michael Gunther
Handles plays for radio, stage and television. Represents contemporary Scandinavian playwrights.

FRANCE

Agence Strassova
4 Rue Git-le-Coeur
75006 Paris
Contact: Mrs Greta Strassova, Mme Monique Marie
Handles General Literature.

European American Information Services Inc
110 East 59th St
New York NY 10022
Paris address: 10 rue de l'Abreuvoir
92400 Courbevoie
Contact: Vera le Marie
Representing author Catherine Nay and French publishers in North America & North American publishers and agents in France.

Francoise Germain
8 Rue de la Paix
75002 Paris
Contact: Madame Francoise Germain
Representation of French and foreign authors.

La Nouvelle Agence
7 Rue Corneille
75006 Paris
Contact: Ms Mary Kling
Representation in France for US, English, Italian & German agents and publishers as well as French Authors.

Michelle Lapautre Literary Agency
6 rue Jean Carries
75007 Paris
Contact: Michelle Lapautre
Representing English-language publishers, agents and authors for the sale of French translation rights.

Promotion Litteraire
26 Rue Chalgrin
75116 Paris
Contact: M Giannetti
Publishers' consultants, representing leading American, French and Italian publishers, Internatioinal authors, scout service, general fiction and non-fiction books, film and TV scripts, movie rights and properties.

INDIA

Ajanta Books International
IUB Jawahar Nagar
Bungalow Road, Delhi 110007
Contact: S Balwant
Research work on Social Science & Humanity especially on Indian themes, oriental or modern.

ISRAEL

Rogan-Pikarski Literary Agency
200 Hayarkon Street
PO Box 4006, 61 040 Tel Aviv
Contact: Ilana Pikarski
Represents major US and European publishers and agents for Hebrew volume, serial and performance and merchandising rights, also has New York agency.

ITALY

Agenzia Letteraria Internazionale
3 Via Fratelli Gabba
Milano
Contact: Donatella Barbiere
Represent exclusively in Italy American, English and German publishers and agencies.

Natoli & Stefan
Galleria Buenos Aires 14
1-20124 Milano
Contact: Dott Gianni Natoli
Represents Fiction and Non-Fiction Authors Rights, Co-Editions, Translations.

JAPAN

Tuttle-Mori Agency
Fuji bldg 8th Floor
2-15 Kanda Jimbocho, Chiyoda-ku
Tokyo 101
Contact: Mr Takeshi Mori
Largest Literary Agency for foreign rights in Japan.

THE NETHERLANDS

Auteursbureau Greta Baars Jelgersma
Bovensteweg 46
NL-6585 KD Mook
Bovensteweg 46
Contact: Greta Baars Jelgersma
Represents authors and publishers, translations from the Scandinavian and modern languages. International co-printing of illustrated books and arranging profitable offers for bookproduction. Oldest international literary agency in The Netherlands.

Prins & Prins Literary Agents
Postbus 5400
1007 AK Amsterdam
Contact: Henk Prins
Representation in The Netherlands of foreign publishers.

NORWAY

Hanna-Kirsti Koch Literary Agency
PO Box 3043/Elisenberg
0207 Oslo 2
Contact: Mr Eilif Koch
Representing foreign authors in Norway.

Ulla Lohren Literary Agency
PO Box 150
Tasen, 0801 Oslo 8
Contact: Ulla Lohren
Represents agents and publishers from Canada, UK, USA and others for Scandinavian rights in fiction, non-fiction, and children's books.

POLAND

Authors' Agency
ul Hipoteczna 2
00-950 Warszawa
Contact: Wladyslaw Jakubowski
Handles Polish copyrights, foreign contracts, information.

PORTUGAL

Ilidio da Fonseca Matos Literary Agency
Rua de S Bernardo
68-30, 1200 Lisboa
Contact: Ilidio da Fonseca Matos
Represents in Portugal: Curtis Brown Ltd, Laurence Pollinger Ltd, The New American Library, Doubleday and Company, Inc, Rowohlt Verla - Diogenes Verlag.

SPAIN

Andres de Kramer
Castello 30
28001 Madrid
Handles only foreign writers and foreign rights of theatrical plays and production in Spain.

Bookbank S A
Rafael Calvo 13
28010 Madrid
Contact: Angela Gonzalez
Represent foreign publishers and/or agents and/or writers for the sale of Spanish language and Portuguese rights. Also Spanish language authors.

Julio F-Yanez Literary Agency
Via Augusta 139
08021 Barcelona
Contact: Mr Julio F-Yanez
Represents Publishers, Agencies and independent Authors from all countries and Spanish authors abroad. Covers Spain, Latin America, Portugal and Brazil.

Ute Korner de Moya Literary Agency
Ronda Guinardo 32-5-5
08025 Barcelona
Contact: Ute Korner
Represents foreign publishers, agents and authors in the Spanish and Portuguese speaking countries.

SWEDEN

D Richard Bowen
Post Box 30037
S-200 61 Malmo 30
Contact: D Richard Bowen
Publishers' Literary and Sales Agent, Translation Rights, etc., negotiated.

Lennart Sane Agency AB
Hollandareplan
537434 Karlshamn
Contact: Lennart Sane
Representing US, British and Scandinavian authors, publishers and agencies for translation rights in Continental Europe and Latin America.

Monica Heyum Literary Agency
PO Box 3300 Vendelso
S-13603 Haninge
Contact: Monica Heyum
Handles Fiction, Non-Fiction and Children's books.

SWITZERLAND

Dieter Breitsohl AG Literary Agency
PO Box 245, CH 8034 Zurich
OR: Heimatstr. 25, CH 8008 Zurich
Contact: Dr Jutta Motz
Handles Non-Fiction, Psychology, Psychosomatic, Religion, Theology, Mythology.

Liepman AG
Maienburgweg 23, Postfach 572
CH-8044 Zurich
Contact: Dr Ruth Liepman, Eva Koralnik, Ruth Weibel
Represents American, British, Canadian, French, Dutch, and Israeli publishers and agents for the German language rights, and authors from the manuscript on worldwide.

New Press Agency Society

Haus am Herterberg, Haldenstr 5
CH-8500 Frauenfeld, Herten
Contact: Rene Marti

Paul & Peter Fritz AG Literary Agency
Jupiterstrasse 1
Postfach 8032 Zurich
Contact: Peter S Fritz
Represents English language authors for the German language rights and authors for worldwide. No unsolicited manuscripts.

UNITED KINGDOM

Jacintha Alexander Associates
47 Emperor's Gate
London SW7 4HJ
Contact: Jacintha Alexander, Julian Alexander
Handles fiction and non-fiction.

Blake Friedman Literary Agency Ltd
37-41 Gower Street
London WC1E 6HH
Contact: Carol Blake, Julian Friedman
Worldwide representation of fiction and non-fiction, television and film rights and scripts. No juvenile projects or poetry.

Carnell Literary Agency
Danescroft, Goose Lane, Little Hallingbury
Bishop's Stortford, Herts CM22 7RG
Contact: Mrs Pamela Buckmaster
Specializes in science fiction and fantasy, also handles general fiction, non-fiction and children's fantasy.

Rosica Colin Limited
1 Clareville Grove Mews
London SW7 5AH
Contact: Joanna Marston
All full length manuscripts including theatre, films, television and sound broadcasting works in the USA, European countries and overseas.

Rupert Crew Limited
1A King's Mews
London WC1N 2JA
Contact: Doreen Montgomery, Shirley Russell
Representation offered to limited clientele, specialising in promoting major book projects: non-fiction, general and women's fiction.

Curtis Brown Ltd (London)
162-168 Regent Street
London W1R 5TB
Contact: Address material to company.

Felix de Wolfe
Manfield House, 376-378 The Strand
London WC2R 0LR
Contact: Felix de Wolfe
Handles quality fiction and scripts only. No non-fiction or children's. No unsolicited manuscripts. No reading fee.

Campbell Thomson and McLaughlin Limited
31 Newington Green
London N16 9PU
Contact: John McLaughlin, John Richard Parker, Charlotte Bruton
Handles book-length manuscripts, excluding children's science fiction and fantasy. No plays, films scripts, articles or poetry. Short stories from existing clients only. No reading fee.

Jonathan Clowes Ltd
Iron Bridge House
Bridge Approach
London NW1 8DB
Contact: Catherine Johnson, Brie Burkeman
Fiction and non-fiction, plus scripts. No textbooks or children's.

Elspeth Cochrane Agency
11-13 Orlando Road
London SW4 0LE
Contact: Donald Baker, Elspeth Cochrane
Authors handled for theatre, films, television. Books for all types of publication.

Eric Glass Ltd
28 Berkley Square
London W1X 6HD
Contact: Eric Glass, Janet Crowley
Books, plays, screenplays and television plays. Sole agents for the Societe des Auteurs et Compositeurs Dramatiques of Paris for the English speaking countries.

Elaine Green Ltd
37 Goldhawk Road
London W12 8QQ
Contact: Elaine Green, Carol Heaton
Handles novels, quality non-fiction and journalist's books. No original scripts for theatre, film or TV.

David Grossman Literary Agency Ltd
110-114 Clerkenwell Road
London EC1M 5SA
Contact: David Grossman
Fiction and general non-fiction. No verse or technical books for students. No original screenplays or teleplays.

A M Heath & Co Ltd
79 St Martins Lane
London WC2N 4AA
Contact: Sara Fisher, Mark Hamilton, William Hamilton, Michael Thomas
Full-length manuscripts handled in all markets.

David Higham Associates Ltd
5-8 Lower John Street
Golden Square
London W1R 4HA
Contact: Anthony Goff, John Rush, Elizabeth Cree
Representing professional authors and writers in all fields throughout the world.

International Copyright Bureau Ltd
22A Aubrey House
Maida Avenue
London W2 1TQ
Contact: Joy Westendarp
Scripts for theatre, TV, radio and film only. No books.

M B A Literary Agents
45 Fitzroy Street
London W1P 5HR
Contact: Diana Tyler, John Parker
Represent writers in all mediums: books, television, radio, screenplays.

William Morris Agency UK Ltd
31-32 Soho Square
London W1V 5DG
Contact: Stephen M Kenis, Jane Annakin, Lavinia Trevor
Scripts handled for theatre, film, TV and radio. Also fiction and general non-fiction.

The Penman Literary Agency
175 Pall Mall
Leigh-on-Sea
Essex SS9 1RE
Contact: Leonard G Stubbs
Full length novel manuscripts. Also theatre, films, television, sound broadcasting.

The Peters Fraser and Dunlop Group Ltd
503/4 The Chambers
Chelsea Harbour
London SW10 0XF
Contact: Kenneth Ewing, Tim Corrie
Agents for stage drama, TV plays and series, radio drama, fiction and non-fiction and children's books, representation for producers and directors of stage, TV and film.

Laurence Pollinger Limited
18 Maddox Street
London W1R OEU
Contact: Gerald J Pollinger
Author's agents for all material with the exception of original film stories, poetry and freelance journalistic articles.

Murray Pollinger
222 Old Brompton Road
London SW5 0BZ
Contact: Murray Pollinger, Gina Pollinger, Sara Menguc
Agents for all types of general fiction and non-fiction with the exception of plays, poetry and travel.

Shelley Power Literary Agency Limited
PO Box 149A
Surbiton
Surrey KT6 5JH
Contact: Shelley Power
General fiction and non-fiction. No poetry, plays or short pieces. Offers worldwide representation.

Margaret Ramsey Ltd
14A Goodwins Court
St Martin's Lane
London WC2N 4LL
Contact: Margaret Ramsey, Tom Erhardt, Sally Emmet
TV, film and theatre scripts.

Rogers Coleridge and White Ltd
20 Powis Mews
London W11 1JN
Contact: Deborah Rogers, Gill Coleridge, Patricia White, Ann Warnford Davis
Agents for fiction, non-fiction and children's books, No plays, poetry or children's books.

Vincent Shaw Associates
20 Jays Mews
Kensington Gore
London SW7 2EP
Contact: Vincent Shaw, Lester McGrath
Scripts for film, TV, theatre and radio only. Unsolicited manuscripts read.

Shiel Land Associates Ltd
43 Doughty Street
London WC1N 2LF
Contact: Anthony Shiel
Represents literary authors. Represents worldwide including translation, film, television and theatre.

Solo Syndication and Literary Agency Ltd
49-53 Kensington High Street
London W8 5ED
Contact: Don Short
Specialising in celebrity autobiographies and biographies. Non-fiction only except for established authors.

Tessa Sayle Agency
11 Jubilee Place
London SW3 3TE
Contact: Tessa Sayle, Penny Tackaberry
Full length manuscripts, plays, films, television, sound broadcasting. Represented in all foreign countries.

Peter Tauber Press Agency
94 East End Road
London N3 2SX
Contact: Peter Tauber, Robert Tauber
Full representation, specialising in well-researched epic women's saga fiction.

Ed Victor Ltd
162 Wardour Street
London W1V 3AT
Contact: Ed Victor, Maggie Phillips, Sophie Hicks
Commercial fiction and non-fiction. No scripts or academic books.

Watson Little Limited
12 Egbert Street
London NW1 8LJ
Contact: Mandy Little
Represents wide range of fiction and non-fiction. No poetry, short stories or articles, or books for very young children.

A P Watt Ltd
20 John Street
London WC1N 2DR
Contact: Hilary Rubinstein
Full length works for all media including plays and telescripts. No poetry. Representation throughout the world.

UNITED STATES OF AMERICA

ARIZONA

Bess Wallace Associates Literary Agency
1502 North Mitchell
Payson, AZ 85541
Contact: Bess D Wallace
Manuscripts sold, edited, typed, ghost-writing, typesetting for self publishers, writers for writing assignments, copy-editing for publishers. Query first.

CALIFORNIA

The Artists Agency
10000 Santa Monica Blvd, Suite 305
Los Angeles, CA 90067
Contact: Merrily Kane
Representation of novels and screenplays for motion pictures.

The Barskin Agency Inc
120 S Victory Boulevard
Burbank, CA 91502
Contact: Doovid Barskin
Submit to MP/TV studios. Only completed scripts for Motion Pictures and Television.

The Sandra Dijkstra Literary Agency
1155 Camino Del Mar
Del Mar, CA 92014
Contact: Sandra Dijkstra, Katherine Goodwin.
Handles quality and commercial adult fiction and non-fiction. Representation to major publishers in USA. British rights. Translation.

Renee Wayne Golden APLC
9601 Wilshire Blvd, Suite 506
Beverly Hills, CA 90210
Contact: Renee Wayne Golden
Representation of Selected Authors

Paul Kohner Inc
9169 Sunset Boulevard
Los Angeles, CA 90069
Contact: Gary Salt, Neal Stevens
Non-fiction preferred to fiction. No short stories, poetry, science fiction or gothic.

Michael Larson/Elizabeth Pomada Literary Agency
1029 Jones Street
San Francisco, CA 94109
Contact: Elizabeth Pomada
Handles general fiction and non-fiction for adults, self help, popular psychology.

Singer Media Corp
3164 Tyler Avenue
Anaheim, CA 92801
Contact: Dr Kurt Singer
Newspaper syndicate and literary agency, also photo bank. Handles sophisticated modern romance novels, biographies, mysteries, horror books.

New Age World Services and Books

62091 Valley View Circle
Joshua Tree, CA 92252
Contact: Rev Victoria E Vandertuin
Handles completed manuscripts dealing in the fields of the New Age, ie Occult, Astrology, Yoga.

Ernest J Oswald
128 Laguna Street
San Francisco, CA 94102
Contact: Ernest J Oswald
Supplies poetry evaluation to beginning poets. Send 5 poems, SASE & $25.00 for readings & evaluation.

The Rosen/Turtle Group
15010 Ventura Blvd, Suite No 219
Sherman Oaks, CA 91403
Contact: Michael Rosen, Cindy Turtle
Represents writers, directors and producers for television and film.

Jack Scagnetti Talent & Literary Agency
5330 Lankershim Blvd, No 210
North Hollywood, CA 91601
Contact: Jack Scagnetti
Handles screenplays, television scripts, treatments, books, major magazine articles. Franchised signatory to Writers Guild of America-West.

H N Swanson Inc
8523 Sunset Blvd
Los Angeles, CA 90069
Contact: Thomas Shanks, N V Swanson
Represents writers for novels, screenplays, television, theatre, worldwide representation.

CONNECTICUT

Sidney B Kramer, Mews Books Ltd
Bluewater Hill
Westford, CT 06880
Contact: Sidney B Kramer, Frank Pollack
Specializes in juvenile (pre-school - young adult), cookery, adult non-fiction and fiction, technical and medical software, film and TV rights etc. Prefers work of published/established authors, will accept small number of new/unpublished authors.

New England Publishing Associates Inc
PO Box 5
Chester, CT 06412
Contact: Elizabeth Frost Knappman, Edward W Knappman
Editorial Assistance and representation for non-fiction books for the adult market.

Van der Leun & Associates
464 Mill Hill Drive
Southport, CT 06490
Contact: Patricia Van der Leun
Handles fiction and non-fiction, specialize in illustrated books, art and science. No unsolicited manuscripts. Representation in all foreign countries.

DISTRICT OF COLUMBIA

The Sagalyn Literary Agency
2813 Bellvue Terrace, NW
Washington DC 20007
Contact: Raphael Sagalyn
Handles adult fiction and non-fiction.

HAWAII

Rhoes Literary Agency
2509 Ala Wai Blvd, Suite 806B
Honolulu, HI 96815
Contact: Fred C Pugarelli
Handles novels, non-fiction books, magazines, poetry books, single poems, religious materials, motion picture and television scripts, stage plays, juvenile books,

syndicated materials, radio scripts, textbooks, photos, books of cartoons etc.

ILLINOIS

Austin Wahl Agency Ltd
53 West Jackson Boulevard, Suite 342
Chicago, IL 60604
Contact: Thomas Wahl
Handles motion picture and TV scripts, novels and non-fiction books.

MASSACHUSETTS

The Otte Company
9 Goden Street
Belmont, MA 02178
Contact: Jane H Otte
Handles adult fiction and non-fiction full length books. Representation in all major markets and Hollywood.

Michael Snell Literary Agency
Box 655
Truro, MA 02666
Contact: Patricia Smith
Development and sale of adult non-fiction, primarily in business, computers, science, psychology and law.

Gunther Stuhlmann, Author's Representative
Post Office Box 276
Becket, MA 01223
Contact: Barbara Ward, Gunther Stuhlmann
Representation world wide of quality literature and non-fiction.

NEW JERSEY

Joseph Anthony Agency
8 Locust Court Road, 20 Mays Landing
New Jersey, NJ 08330
Contact: Joseph Anthony
Handles all types of novels and scripts for TV. No poetry, short stories or pornography.

Barbara Bauer Literary Agency
179 Washington Ave
Matawan, NJ 07747
Contact: Barbara Bauer
Specialize in new and unpublished authors, quality fiction and non-fiction for children and adults.

Rosalie Siegel, International Literary Agent, Inc
111 Murphy Drive
Pennington, NJ 08534
Contact: Rosalie Siegel, Pamela Walker
Adult fiction and non-fiction, particularly quality fiction. Also french fiction and non-fiction.

NEW YORK

Carole Abel Literary Agent
160 West 87th Street
New York, NY 10024
Contact: Carole Abel
Handles trade and mass market fiction and non-fiction books. No unsolicited manuscripts, query fist. Agents in Hollywood and most foreign countries.

Dominick Abel Literary Agency Inc
146 W 82 St, Suite 1B
New York, NY 10024
Contact: Dominick Abel.

Acton and Dystel
928 Broadway
New York, NY 10010
Contact: Jane Dystel
Non-fiction and novels.

Marcia Amsterdam Agency
41 West 82nd Street
New York, NY 10024
Contact: Marcia Amsterdam
Handles adult and young adult fiction, movie and TV rights, screenplays, teleplays.

Julian Bach Literary Agency Inc
747 Third Avenue
New York, NY 10017
Contact: Julian Bach, Emma Sweeney, Susan Merritt, Ann Rittenberg
Agents for fiction and non-fiction. No science fiction or fantasy, poetry or photography.

The Bethel Agency
Suite 1, 513 West 54 Street
New York, NY 10019
Contact: Lewis R Chambers
Handles fiction and non-fiction, plays for theatre, film and television, sub-division handles children's books.

The Boston Literary Agency
333 West 57th Street, Suite 404
New York, NY 10019
Contact: Justin K McDonough
Handles full length fiction and non-fiction, films, television. Query letter, synopsis and SAE essential.

Brandt & Brandt Literary Agency Inc
1501 Broadway
New York, NY 10036
Contact: Carl D Brandt, Gail Hochman
Handles fiction and non-fiction. No unsolicited manuscripts, query first, no reading fee. Agents in most foreign countries.

Pema Brown Ltd
Pine Road, HCR Box 104B
Neversink, NY 12765
Contact: Pema Brown, Perry Brown
Handles mass market fiction. Also scripts for film, TV, theatre and radio.

Hy Cohen Literary Agency Ltd
111 West 57th Street
New York, NY 10019
Contact: Hy Cohen
Novels and non-fiction. No scripts.

Connor Literary Agency
640 West 153rd Street
New York, NY 10031
Contact: Marlene K Connor
Handles commercial fiction and non-fiction, illustrated books, cookbooks, self-help, ethnic subjects, how-to. Foreign agents in major countries.

Curtis Brown Ltd
10 Astor Place, 3rd Floor
New York, NY 10003
Contact: Perry Knowlton, Peter Ginsberg
Handles fiction, non-fiction, science fiction, mystery, romance. Also children's fiction, non-fiction and theatrical, film and television. Handles general trade fiction, non-fiction, juvenile, and film & TV rights. Representatives in all major countries. No unsolicited manuscripts. Query first.

Joan Daves
21 West 26th Street
New York, NY 10010-1083
Contact: Joan Daves, Jennifer Lyons
Fiction and non-fiction. No scripts. No science fiction, romance or textbooks.

Anita Diamant Literary Agency
310 Madison Ave
New York, NY 10017
Contact: Anita Diamant, Robin Rae
Handles book manuscripts, fiction, non-fiction, foreign film rights.

The Jonathan Dolger Agency

49 East 96th Street, Suite 9B
New York, NY 10128
Contact: Mr Jonathan Dolger
Handles adult fiction and non-fiction, illustrated books.
No unsolicited material, query letter & SASE first.

Ethan Ellenberg, Literary Agency
548 Broadway, No 5-C
New York, NY 10012
Contact: Ethan Ellenberg
Handles quality fiction and non-fiction, first novels,
commercial fiction, military, history, sci-fi. Query before
submission of manuscripts.

Ann Elmo Agency Inc
60 East 42nd Street
New York, NY 10165
Contact: Ann Elmo, Lettie Lee, Mari Cronin
Handles all types of fiction, non-fiction, juveniles, plays
for book and magazine publication, as well as for film,
TV and stage use.

John Farquharson Ltd
Suite 1007, 250 West 57th Street
New York, NY 10107
Contact: Deborah Schneider
Works mostly with established authors. Specializes in
trade fiction and non-fiction.

Marje Fields/Rita Scott Inc
165 W 46, Suite 1205
New York, NY 10036
Contact: Ray Powers
Agent for fiction, non-fiction, plays, musicals. No poetry
or children's books.

Freida Fishbein Ltd
2556 Hubbard Street
Brooklyn, NY 11235
Contact: Janice Fishbein
Handles plays, books, motion picture and television
scripts. No short stories, poetry or young childrens'
books.

Samuel French Inc
45 West 25th Street
New York, NY 10010
Contact: Lawrence Harbison
Specializing in plays.

Jay Garon-Brooke Associates Inc
415 Central Park West, 17th Floor
New York, NY 10025
Fiction and non-fiction. No category romance, western
or mysteries.

Max Gartenberg Literary Agent
521 5th Avenue, Suite 1700
New York, NY 10175
Contact: Max Gartenberg
Handles book-length manuscripts of non-fiction and
fiction including all rights therein.

Gelles-Cole Literary Enterprises
320E 42 St, Suite 801
New York, NY 10017
Contact: Sordi Gelles-Cole
Handles commercial fiction and non-fiction.

John Hawkins & Associates Inc
71 West 23rd Street, Suite 1600
New York, NY 10010
Contact: J Hawkins, W Reiss
Provides all services of representation & limit works
to book-length manuscripts in prose. No theatrical, film
or TV scripts.

JCA Literary Agency Inc
27 West 20th Street, Suite 1103
New York, NY 10011
Contact: Jane C Cushman

Handles general fiction, non-fiction. No screen plays.
Query first with SASE.

JET Literary Associates Inc
124E 84th Street, Suite 4A
New York, NY 10028
Contact: James E Trupin
Handles book length fiction and non-fiction only.

Melanie Jackson Agency
250 W 57 Street, Suite 1119
New York, NY 10107
Contact: Melanie Jackson
Handles fiction and non-fiction.

Asher D Jason Enterprises Inc
111 Barrow Street
New York, NY 10014
Contact: Asher D Jason
Handles non-fiction and fiction. Representation to all
American publishers.

Lucy Kroll Agency
390 West End Avenue
New York, NY 10024
Contact: Lucy Kroll, Barbara Hogenson
Handles fiction and non-fiction including scripts for film,
TV and radio.

Peter Livingston Associates Inc
465 Park Avenue
New York, NY 10022
Contact: Peter W Livingston, David C Johnston, foreign
rights
Handles serious non-fiction, business, politics, popular
science etc. Literary and commercial fiction, film and
TV. No poetry or children's books.

Donald MacCampbell Inc
12 East 41st Street
New York, NY 10017
Women's fiction only. Specializes in romance.

McIntosh and Otis Inc
310 Madison Avenue
New York, NY 10017
Contact: Julie Fallowfield, Dorothy Markinko
Adult and juvenile fiction and non-fiction. No textbooks
or scripts.

Claudia Menza Literary Agency
237 West 11th Street
New York, NY 10014
Contact: Claudia Menza
Handles unique/avant-garde fiction, no genre novels.
Serious non-fiction. Represents writers through all
aspects of publishing.

Scott Meredith Literary Agency Inc
845 Third Avenue
New York, NY 10022
Contact: Jack Scovil, Scott Meredith
Handles general fiction and non-fiction, books and
magazines, juveniles, plays, TV scripts, motion picture
rights and properties. Accept unsolicited manuscripts,
reading fee. Agents in all principal countries.

Henry Morrison Inc
PO Box 235
Bedford Hills, NY 10507
Contact: Henry Morrison
Handles novels and non-fiction books, occasional
screenplays. Represent authors on a worldwide basis.
Query letters initially.

Jean V Naggar Literary Agency
216 E 75th Street
New York, NY 10021
Contact: Jean Naggar
Complete representation in all areas of general fiction
and non-fiction.

Pickering Associates Inc
432 Hudson Street
New York, NY 10014
Contact: John Pickering
Full service literary agency with co-agents in Hollywood
and all principal translation markets.

Susan Ann Protter Literary Agent
110 West 40th Street, Suite 1408
New York, NY 10018
Contact: Susan Protter
Principally hard and soft cover books and the various
rights involved. Fiction, non-fiction, health, science,
biography, history, science fiction etc.

The Robbins Office Inc
866 Second Avenue, 12th Floor
New York, NY 10017
Contact: Kathy P Robbins, Loretta Weingel-Fidel
Handles mainstream hardcover fiction and non-fiction
books.

Marie Rodell-Frances Collin Literary Agency
110 West 40th Street, Suite 1403
New York, NY 10018
Contact: Frances Collin
Full service representation and editorial guidance.
Handles everything from science fiction to classic
environmental works. No film treatments or scripts, or
short pieces. Please note no writers resident outside
continental US unless they have been recommended
by corresponding agents or American publisher.

Richard H Roffman Associates
697 West End Avenue, Suite 6A
New York, NY 10025
President: Richard Roffman
Primarily non-fiction.

Rosenstone/Wender
3 East 48th Street, 4th Floor
New York, NY 10017
Contact: Howard Rosenstone, plays, screenplays,
teleplays.
Contact: Phyllis Wender, fiction, non-fiction, plays,
screenplays and teleplays.

Russell and Volkening Inc
50 West 29th Street, No 7E
New York, NY 10001
Literary fiction and non-fiction.

The Shukat Company Ltd
340 West 55th Street, Ste 1-A
New York, NY 10019
Contact: Scott Shukat, Larry Weiss
Handles theatre musicals, plays, books (fiction and non-
fiction), TV and MP.

Evelyn Singer Literary Agency Inc
PO Box 594
White Plains, NY 10602
Contact: Evelyn Singer
Exclusive representation. Handles fiction, non-fiction,
for adults, young adults, children, first serial rights,
foreign rights, movie and TV rights with sub-agents.

Philip G Spitzer Literary Agency
788 Ninth Avenue
New York, NY 10019
Contact: Philip G Spitzer
Handles general fiction and non-fiction, also
screenplays.

Renee Spodheim
698 West End Avenue, No 58
New York, NY 10025
Contact: Renee Spodheim
All trade. Fiction and non-fiction. No juveniles.

Sterling Lord Literistic Inc
One Madison Avenue

New York, NY 10010
Contact: Peter Matson
Handles full length and short manuscripts, theatre,
films, TV, radio. Represented in Europe by
Intercontinental Literary Agency.

Gloria Stern Literary Agency
1230 Park Avenue
New York, NY 10128
Contact: Gloria Stern
Represent 90% trade, non-fiction, mostly biography,
education and women's and social issues. Also health,
some self-help and serious fiction.

2M Communications Ltd
121 West 27 Street, 601
New York, NY 10001
Contact: Madeleine Morel
Handles contemporary non-fiction, popular culture,
celebrity biographies.

Wecksler-Incomco
170 West End Avenue
New York, NY 10023
Contact: Sally Wecksler
Handles non-fiction, illustrated works, art and
photography, performing arts, humour.

Wieser & Wieser Inc
118 East 25th Street
New York, NY 10010
Contact: Olga Weiser
Handles literary & commercial fiction, general non-
fiction including all rights, film and TV rights.

Writers House Inc
21 West 26th Street
New York, NY 10010
Represents popular and literary fiction, mainstream and
genre, including thrillers, science fiction, fantasy and
romance. Also juvenile and young adult.

PENNSYLVANIA

**James Allen Literary Agent (in Association with
Virginia Kidd, Literary Agents)**
PO Box 278, 538 East Harford Street
Milford, PA 18337
Contact: Virginia Kidd
Handles fiction, specializing in science fiction, submit
to magazines & book publishers. Representation in
foreign countries & Hollywood.

Ray Peekner Literary Agency Inc
Box 3308
Bethlehem, PA 18017
Contact: Barbara Puechner
Handles general fiction, particularly mystery suspense.
Quality YA.

TEXAS

The Blake Group, Literary Agency
One Turtle Creek Village, Suite 600
Dallas, TX 75219
Contact: Lee B Halff
Represents limited number of published & unpublished
authors. Handles fiction, non-fiction, plays & poetry,
periodicals, publishers & producers. No reading fee.
SASE essential.

WISCONSIN

Lee Allan Agency
PO Box 18617
Milwaukee, WI 53218
Contact: Lee A Matthias
Handles book length novels, mysteries, thrillers,
westerns, science fiction, horror, romance & young adult
fiction. No TV material, non-fiction, poetry, magazine
articles or short stories.

APPENDIX B

LITERARY ORGANIZATIONS

Please note that while every effort has been made to include as many societies and organizations as possible, the editors acknowledge that the following lists are by no means exhaustive. Many societies are organized and administered by unpaid individuals from their own homes, not only do the addresses of secretaries change frequently, therefore, but these are difficult to trace. Secretaries of societies which have yet to be listed are consequently urged to send details for publication in future editions of the **INTERNATIONAL AUTHORS AND WRITERS WHO'S WHO** to the editors at the following address:

The International Authors and Writers Who's Who
International Biographical Centre
Cambridge CB2 3QP, England

The friendly co-operation of the listed societies is gratefully acknowledged, the future assistance of others is cordially invited.

AUSTRALIA

The Dickens Fellowship
29 Henley Beach Road
Henley Beach, Adelaide, SA 5022
Literary Society devoted to study & appreciation of the life and works of Charles Dickens. Approx. 120 members. Hon Sec: Dr A F Dilnot, Mrs G M Taylor, Mrs Barbara Barrett.

Australian Writers' Guild Ltd
60 Kellett Street
Kings Cross, Sydney, NSW 2011
Professional association for writers in areas of television, radio, screen & stage to promote and protect the professional interests. Approx 1800 members. Executive Officer: Angela Wales.

Bibliographical Society of Australia and New Zealand
c/o Secretary, Miss R T Smith
76 Warners Ave., Bondi Beach, NSW 2026
To encourage and promote research in all aspects of physical bibliography. Approx. 300 members. President: Mr Trevor Mills, Vice President: Mr John E Fletcher, Secretary: Miss R T Smith.

Children's Book Council of Australia
PO Box 420, Dickson, ACT 2602
President: Laurie Copping, Secretary: Lynn Fletcher

The Society of Editors
PO Box 176, Carlton South, Vic 3053
Professional association of book editors, regular training seminars, monthly meetings & newsletter. Approx. 300 members. President: Colin Jevons, Secretary: Susannah McFarlane.

Poetry Society of Australia
PO Box N110, Grosvenor St, Sydney, NSW 2000
Joint Secretaries: Robert Adamson; Debra Adamson
Publications: New Poetry (quarterly); also poems, articles, reviews, notes and comments, interviews.

BELGIUM

International P.E.N. Club, Belgian French Speaking Centre
76 Avenue de 11 Novembre, BP7
B-1040 Brussels
Receptions of foreign writers, defense of the liberty of thought of all writers, participation at the world-wide congresses of PEN. Approx. 230 members. President: Mr Georges Sion, General Secretary: Mr Raymond Quinot.

Koninklijke Academie voor Wetenschappen
Letteren en Schone Kunsten van Belgie
Paleis der Academien, Hertogsstr 1
B-1000 Brussels
Permanent Secretary: Gerard Verbeke

Societe de Langue et de Litterature Wallonnes
Universite de Liege, Place du XX Aout
B-4000 Liege
Hold meetings, lectures, exhibitions, library, media, archives, publications. Approx. 300 members. President: Jean Brumioul, Vice Presidents; Albert Maquet, Andre Goosse, Secretary: Victor George.

Societe Royale des Bibliophiles et Iconophiles de Belgique
4 Boulevard de l'Empereur, 1000 Brussels
Publication of "Le Livre et l'Estampe" (Semestrial), Expositions. Approx. 150 members. President: Baron de Sadeleer, Vice President: Michel Wittock, Secretary: Auguste Grisay.

BRAZIL

Academia Cearense di Letras
Palacio Senador Alencar, Rua Sao Paulo 51
60000 Fortaleza CE
To cultivate and develop literature and scientific achievement. Meets monthly, annual publication. Approx. 40 active members, unknown number of correspondent & honorary members. Secretary General: J Denizard Macedo de Alcantara.

Associacao Brasileira de Imprensa (Brazilian Press Association)
Rua Araujo Porto Alegre
71-Centro-Rio de Janeiro-RJ

Brazilian Translators Union (SINTRA)
Rua de Quitanda
194-sala 1005-Centro
CEP-20091-Rio de Janeiro-RJ

Companhia Editora Nacional
Rua Joli

294-Sao Paulo-SP

Sindicato de Escritores of Rio de Janeiro
Av. Heitor Beltrao
353-Rio de Janeiro-RJ
CEP 20550

CANADA

Association des Edituers Anglophones du Quebec
c/o Black Rose Books, 3981 St Laurent Blvd
Montreal, H2W 1YS Quebec
An association of book publishers in Quebec. Approx 8 members. President: Dimitrios Roussopoulos, Vice President: Simon Dardick, Secretary: Pamela Chichinskas.

Literary Translators Association
1030, rue Cherrier, Bureau 510
Montreal, Quebec H2L 1H9
Advice to members, legal services, link between authors and translators, John Glasso Translation Prize, International Translators Conferences. Approx. 110 members. President: Michael Buttiens, Co-president: Marie C Brasseur, Sherry Simon.

The Association of Canadian Publishers
260 King Street East, Toronto
Ontario M5A 1K3
Trade association representing the interest of the Canadian-owned and operated publishing industry. Approx. 150 members. President: Philip Cercone, Executive Director: Wayne Gilpin, Vice President: Diana Douglas, Director of Member Services: Joshua Samuel.

Canadian Authors Association
121 Avenue Road, Suite 104
Toronto, Ontario M5R 2G3
18 branches across Canada. Annual national conference, work to protect Canadian writers, spokesman to govt., sponsors awards programme, publishes periodicals. President: Mary E Dawe, National Vice President: Gail Corbett, Secretary: Fred Kerner, Treasurer: David Chilton.

Canadian Copyright Institute
34 Ross Street, Suite 200
Toronto, Ontario M5T 1Z9
Established to promote the use of copyright in the public interest. Membership: 12 organizations, 50 individuals. Chairman: John Irwin, Vice-President: Fred Kerner, Secretary: Barry Reese.

The Canada Council
99 Metcalfe St, Box 1047
Ottawa, Ontario K1P 5V8
Head, Writing & Pubn Section: Naim Kattan

The Canadian Centre (English-speaking) PEN
24 Ryerson Avenue, Toronto
Ontario M5T 2P3
Fosters understanding among writers of all nations, fights for freedom of expression, to work for the preservation of the world's literature. President: Graeme Gibson, Executive Director: Jan Bauer.

Federation Professionnelle des Journalistes du Quebec
1278 rue Panet
Montreal, Quebec H2L 2Y8
Representation and defense of journalists professional interest, freedom of the press, public's right to quality information etc. Approx 1000 members. President: R Barnaby.

Freeland Editors' Association of Canada (FEAC)
34 Ross St, Suite 200
Toronto, Ontario M5T 1Z9
Professional development seminars held twice yearly; Tom Fairley Award/award for editorial excellence by editor working/on a freelance basis. 150 members. President: Stephen K Rovey.

Periodical Writers' Association of Canada
24 Ryerson Ave., Toronto
Ontario M5T 2P3
To promote and protect the interests of Canadian periodical writers. Approx. 360 members. Director: Paulette Pelletier-Kelly.

League of Canadian Poets
24 Ryerson Ave, Toronto
Ontario M5T 2P3
President: Douglas Smith

Literary Press Group
Subs of Association of Canadian Publishers
260 Kings St E, Toronto
Ontario M5A 1K3
Director: John Ball, Sales Rep Mgr: Lisa Alward. Promote Canadian fiction, poetry, drama & literary criticism; sales representation across Canada. 45 members.

La Societé des Écrivains Canadiens de la Langue Française
1391 rue des Maristes
Chicoutimi
Quebec G7H 4K5

Writers' Union of Canada
24 Ryerson Avenue, Toronto
Ontario M5T 2P3
Professional association of published trade book writers. Approx 700 members. Executive Director: Penny Dickens.

CHINA

China Pen Centre
2 Shatan Beijie
Beijing
China

DENMARK

The Danish Society of Language and Literature
Frederiksholms Kanal 18A
DK-1220 Kobenhavn K
Scholarly editing in Danish language, literature & history, dictionaries c.150 titles, 750 volumes. Approx. 62 members. President: Iver Kjaer, Secretary: Dr Erik Dal.

Danish Writers' Association
Strandgade 6, St
1401 Kobenhavn K
Attending to social, artistic, professional & economic interests of Danish authors in Denmark & abroad. Approx. 1600 members. President: D Trier Morch.

Dansk Litteraturinformationscenter
Ameliegade 38
1256 Kobenhavn K

Nyt Dansk Litteraturselskab
Bibliotekscentralen
Tempovej 7-11
DK 2750 Ballerup
Works for re-publishing of titles missing in public libraries in co-operation with publishers. Approx. 276 members. Manager: Jorgen Rishoj

Danske Sprog-og Litteraturselskab
Frederiksholms Kanal 18A
DK-1220 Copenhagen
Administrator: Dr Erik Dal
Publications: Standard editions of literary, linguistic and historical texts, including diaries and correspondence.

FINLAND

Svenska Osterbottens Litteraturforening
Auroravagen 10, SF-65610 Smedsby

Co-owner of the publishers in Scriptum, publishes the journal Horisont, organizes writers' seminars, program evenings: lyrics, prose, music. Approx. 170 members. President: Torbjorn Ehrman, Vice President: Helge Englund, Secretary: Yvonne Hoffman.

Kirjallisuudentutkijain Seura
Fabianinkatu 33, SF-00170 Helsinki
Secretary: Paivi Karttunen
Publications: Kirjallisuudentutkijain Seuran Vousikirja (The Yearbook of the Literary Research Society).

Suomalaisen Kirjallisuuden Seura
PO Box 259, SF-00171 Helsinki
(Located at: Hallituskatu 1, Helsinki)
Secretary-General: Urpo Vento
Librarian: Henni Ilomaki
Dir, Folklore Archive: Pekka Laaksonen
Dir, Literature Archive: Kaarina Sala

Svenska Litteratursallskapet i Finland
Mariegatan 8, SF-00170 Helsinki
Publications: Skrifter (Writings)

FRANCE

Centre National des Lettres
53 rue de Verneuil, F-75007 Paris
To uphold and encourage the work of French writers, give financial help to writers, translators, publishers & public libraries, promote translation into French. President: Jean Gattegno, Secretary General: Veronique Chatenay-Dolto.

Societe des Gens de Lettres
Hotel de Massa, 38 rue du Faubourg Saint-Jacques
F-75014 Paris
Approx 11,000 members. President: Didier Decoin, Vice President: Michele Kahn, Secretary General: Jacques Bens.

Societe des Poetes Francais
Hotel de Massa, 38 rue du Faubourg Saint-Jacques
75014 Paris
Lectures, prizes, defending interests of members, loans to distinguished members in distress, quarterly bulleting. Approx. 1200 members. Honorary President: Pascal Bonetti, Marthe-Claire Fleury-Bonetti, Pierre Orsenat, Honorary Vice President: Roland Le Cordier, Presidents: Brigitte Level et Jacques Raphael-Leygues, Vice Presidents: Jean Bancal, Magdelein Labour, Francoise des Varennes.

GERMANY

P.E.N. Zentrum
Friedrichstrasse 194.199
Berlin 1080
Lectures, symposia, literary sessions. Approx. 86 members. President: Professor Dr Heinz Kamnitzer, Vice President: Walter Kaufmann.

Arbeitskreis fur Jugendliteratur e.V
Elisabeth Str 15, D-8000
Munich 40
Encourages and coordinates all efforts to support literature for children and young people. Approx. 45 member organisations, 175 individual members. Managing Director: F Meyer.

Deutsche Akademie fur Sprache und Dichtung
Alexandrakeg 23, 6100 Darmstadt
Approx. 144 members. President: Professor Dr Herbert Heckmann, General Secretary: Dr Gerhard Dette.

Deutsche Schillergesellschaft e.V
7142 Marbach am Neckar
Schillerhohe 8-10
Approx. 3600 members. President: Professor Dr Eberhard Lammert.

Deutsche Shakespeare-Gesellschaft West
Rathaus, D-4630 Bochum 1
Publication of a yearbook, Shakespeare Jahrbuch, yearly conferences. Approx 1850 members. President: Prof Dr Werner Habicht, Vice President: Prof Dr Ulrich Suerbaum, Chairman: Prof Dr Raimund Borgmeier, Treasurer: Claus Schmidt.

Deutsche Thomas-Mann-Gesellschaft
Sitz Lubeck, Konigstr 67a
D-2400 Lubeck
Chairman: Prof Dr Eckhard Heftrich

Literarischer Verein in Stuttgart eV
Postfach 102251, D-7000 Stuttgart 1
(Located at: Rosenbergstr 113, Stuttgart)
President: Karl G Hiersemann
Publications: Bibliothek des Literarischen Vereins in Stuttgart Vol 1 (1842) - Vol 311 (1987).

Maximilian-Gesellschaft e.V
Postfach 102251
D-7000 Stuttgart 1
Approx. 1200 members. President: Prof Dr Horst Gronemeyer, Vice-President: Prof Dr Paul Raabe.

GREECE

The Circle of the Greek Children's Books
Zalongou 7, GR-10678, Athens
Promoting Children's Literature in Greece, Seminars, information material, national contests for the writing of Children's books etc. Approx. 180 members. President: Constantinos P Demertzis, Vice President: Vito Angelopulu, Secretary: Loty Petrovits-Andrutsopulu.

HUNGARY

Artisjus
Agency for Literature and Theatre
V, Vorosmarty ter 1
H-1364 Budapest
POB 67

Institute of Literary Studies of the Hungarian Academy of Sciences
H-1118 Budapest, Menesi ut 11-13
Research of history of Hungarian literature, also research in literary theory, literary critisism to influence contemporary literature, source publications on the history of Hungarian literature, editing of reference books and bibliographies. Approx, 57 research professionals. Director: Prof Tibor Klaniczay, Deputy Director: Prof Gyorgy Bodnar.

ICELAND

Rithofundasambund Islands, The Writers' Union of Iceland
PO Box 949, IS-121 Rejkjavik
Union of Icelandic writers that guards copyrights, protects interests in field of literature & book-publishing, drama, textbooks, radio & television scripts etc. Approx 265 members. Chairman: Einar Karason, Managing Director: Rannveig G Agustsdottir.

INDIA

Indian Folklore Society
3 Abdul Hamid
Calcutta 700 069
To organise seminars, meetings, conference study groups & publish journals & books on Indian folklore & its allied disciplines in collaboration of Indian Publications. Approx. 218 members. President: Madame Sophia Wadia, Vice, President: Mr Sankar Sen Gupta.

The PEN All India Centre
Theosophy Hall, 40 New Marine Lines
Bombay 400 020

National centre of The International PEN. Publish The Indian PEN quarterly. Approx. 116 members. President: Annada Sankar Ray, Vice Presidents: Dr K R Srinivasa Iyengar, M R Masani, Secretary: Nissim Ezekiel.

The Poetry Society of India
L-67A Malaviya Nagar
New Delhi 110 017

Sahitya Akademi
Rabindrar Bhavan, 35 Ferozeshah Road
New Delhi 110 001
National organisation to work for the development of Indian letters, to set high literary standards, foster & co-ordinate literary activities in the Indian languages & promote through them all the cultural unity of the country. Secretary: Prof Indra Nath Choudhuri.

INDONESIA

PEN Centre
c/o Jl Cemara 6, Jakarta Pusat
Secretary: Dr Toeti Heraty Noerhadi

IRELAND

Irish Book Marketing GP
Book House Ireland
I65 Mid Abbey Street, Dublin 1
National association of book publishers, trade representation, training courses, national & international book fairs & promotions. Approx. 56 members. Chairman: Michael Gill.

Irish Academy of Letters
School of Irish Studies
Thomas Prior House, Merrion Rd, Dublin 4
Secretary: Evan Boland

Irish PEN
26 Rosslyn, Killarney Rd
Bray, Co Wicklow
President: Francis Stuart
Secretary: Arthur Flynn

Society of Irish Playwrights
Room 804, Liberty Hall, Dublin 1
To foster interest in & promote contemporary Irish drama. To guard the rights of Irish Playwrights. Approx. 120 members. Chairman: John Synch, Secretary: Patricia Martin.

ISRAEL

ACUM Ltd (Society of Authors, Composers and Music Publishers in Israel)
POB 14220, 61140 Tel Aviv
Approx; 1300 members. Chairman: Shlomo Tanny, Director General: Ran Kedar, Secretary General: Jochanan Ben-David.

The PEN Centre Israel
19 Shmaryahu Lewin St, Jerusalem 96664
Publishes a bulletin of information and translation of literature in European languages, meetings with members & receptions for guest writers. Approx. 70 members. President: Aharon Megged, Secretary Treasurer: Haim Toren.

ITALY

Istituto Lombardo Accademia di Scienze e Lettere
Via Brera 28, I-20121 Milan
Organization of conferences, meetings etc. Publications of literature and sciences, exchanged with similar associations all over the world. Approx. 80 science, 80 literary members. President: Prof Giancarlo Bolognesi.

Societa Italiana Autori Drammatici (SIAD) (Ente Morale)
00198 Roma

Via PO 10

JAPAN

The Dickens Fellowship
Bungei-Gakubu, Seijo University
6-1-20 Seiijo, Setagaya, Tokyo
Lectures, symposia, reading circles, publishing bulletins. President: Koichi Miyazaki, Vice Presidents: Shigerk Koike, Kazuhika Yoneda, Masaie V Matsumara, Hon Sec: Prof Koichi Miyazaki.

The English Literary Society of Japan
501 Kenkyusha Bldg., 9 Surugadai 2-Chome, Kanda Chiyoda-ku, Tokyo 101
An association of scholars in the fields of English and American literature and the English language. The Society's journal "Studies in English Literature" is published thrice yearly. Approx. 3800 members. President: Prof Yasunari Takahashi, Secretary: Prof Kenji Nakamura.

Japan Poets Association
c/o Eiji Kikai, 3-16-1, Minami
Azabu, Minato-Ku, Tokyo 105
To cultivate the mutual friendship among poets. To award H's Prize and Modern Poet Prize. Approx. 500 members.

KOREA

The Korean PEN Centre
186-210 Jangchung-dong 2-Ka
Jung-gu, Seoul 100
Bi-annual seminars. Annual literary prize awards, publication of quarterly bulletin. Takes part in annual International PEN Congress. Approx. 800 members. President: Mme Sook-Hee Chun, Vice Presidents: Chong-hyuk Yun, Eul- byung Chung, Geun-sam Lee, Secretary: Hyun-bok Lee.

MALAWI

The Writers' Group
PO Box 280, Zomba
Secretary: Dr A J M Nazombe
Publications: Odi The Muse

MOROCCO

L'Union des Ecrivains du Maroc
5 rue Ab Bakr Seddik
Rabat

NETHERLANDS

The Dickens Fellowship, Haarlem Branch
26-28 Marktsr, 1411 EA Naarden
Branch of The Dickens Fellowship, London. Organises lectures, editing "The Dutch Dickensian". Approx. 80 members. President: Professor Dr J H A Lukin, Vice President: Dr J J C Kabel, Hon Secretary: Mr J C Van Kessel.

Nederlandse Taalunie
Stadhoudersplantsoen 2
2517 JL Den Haag

Netherlands Centre of the International PEN
Meeweg 25, 1405 BC Bussum
Dutch branch of a world association of writers, poets, essayists, novelists, editors & playwrights. Approx. 350 members. President: Joost de Wit, Secretary: Rudolf Geel.

NEW ZEALAND

Arts Council of New Zealand
Old Public Trust Building
131-135 Lambton Quay

Wellington PO Box 3806
Wellington

Christchurch Dickens Fellowship
PO Box 6126, Christchurch
Study works of Dickens at regular monthly meetings.
Approx. 50 members. President: Gary Fox, Vice
President: Hubert Cocks, Thelma Conroy, Secretary:
Peter Oakley.

International Writers' Workshop N.Z. (Inc)
57 Baddeley Ave, Kohimarama, Auckland
Tutored workshops, group evaluation of work.
Workshops designed to interest & encourage writers.
Approx. 150 members. President: Mrs Joyce
Beumelburg, Vice President: Mrs Joyce Irving,
Secretary: Alison Tye.

New Zealand Women Writers' Society Inc
PO Box 11-352, Wellington
Stimulates & encourages creative work in literature,
foster comradeship among members. Approx. 280
members. President: Joy Tonks, Vice President: Betty
Bremner, Secretary: Barbara Wilkinson.

PEN (New Zealand Centre) Inc
PO Box 2283, Wellington
Promotion of cooperation & mutual support among
writers in all countries & encourage creative writing
in NZ. Approx. 600 members. President: Kevin Ireland,
Vice Presidents: Maurice Gee, Lynley Hood, Executive
Secretary: Jenny Jones.

NORWAY

Det Norske Videnskaps-Akademi
Drammensveien 78, Oslo 2
Secretary-General: Prof Dr A Semb-Johansson
Executive Secretary: Kjell Herlofsen
Publications: Skrifter Avhandlinger Arbok

NORLA - Norwegian Literature Abroad
PO Box 239, Sentrum
N-0103 Oslo 1
Information office for Norwegian literature. Managing
Director: Kristin Brudevoll.

PANAMA

Instituto Nacional de Cultura
Apartado 662
Panama 1

POLAND

Instytut Badan Literackich
Nowy Swiat 72, Palac Staszica, 00-330 Warsaw
Acting Directors: Prof Alina Witkowska, Dr Ryszard
Gorski, Dr Zbigniew Jaronsinski. Publications: Pamietnik
Literacki (Literary Journal, quarterly); Biuletyn
Polonistyczny (Bulletin of Polish Literary Scholarship).

Zwiazek Literatow Polskich (Union of Polish Writers)
Krakoweskie Przedmiescie 87
00-950 Warszawa

SOUTH AFRICA

English Academy of Southern Africa
PO Box 124
Witwatersrand 2050

Institute for the Study of English in Africa
Rhodes University, PO Box 94
Grahamston, 6140
Publishes English in Africa and New Coin Poetry.
Conducts research into needs of black pupils learning
English. Director: Prof L S Wright, National Director,
Molteno Project: Prof P S Walters, Secretary: Mrs C
M A Brown.

Nasionale Afrikaanse Letterkundige Museum en Navorsingsentrum
Private Bag X20543
Bloemfontein 9300

National English Literary Museum
Private Bag 1019
Grahamstown 6140

SWEDEN

Kungl Vitterhets Historie och Antikvitets Akademien
Villagatan 3, S-114 32 Stockholm
Secretary: Prof Erik Frykman
Publications: Fornvannen (journal), Handlingar
(memoirs), Arkiv (archives), Arsbok (Yearbook),
Monografier (monographs).

Svenska Osterbottens Litteraturforening
c/o Sven-Erik Klinkmann, Henriksgatan 7-9 4N
SF-65320 Vasa, Finland
Publications: Horisont

SWITZERLAND

PEN Club Centre
Postfach 1383, CH-3001 Bon
Approx. 200 members. President: Ernst Reinhardt,
Secretary General: Hans Erpf.

PEN Internazionale-Centro della Svizzera italiana e Romancia
PO Box 2126, CH-6901 Lugano 1
Organizes the Congresses etc. Organized the 50th
Congress of PEN in Lugano. Approx. 110 members.
President: Mr Grytzko Mascioni, Vice President: Mrs
Magda Kerenyi, Secretary General: Mrs Attilia Fiorenza
Venturini.

Schweizerischer Bund fur Jugendliteratur
Gewerbestr 8, CH-6330 Cham
Promotion and diffusion of literature for children &
young adults, distribution of specially developed
material, further education. Approx. 5000 members.
Secretary: Ursula Merz.

Schweizerischer Schriftsteller-verband
Kirchgasse 25
CH-8022 Zurich
Professional organisation, founded in 1912, for the
protection of writers' interests. Publications: FORUM der
Schriftsteller, Dictionary of Swiss authors. Approx. 630
members. President: Ernst Nef, Vice President: Janine
Massard, Secretary: Lou Pfluger.

Schweizer Autoren Gruppe Olten
Sekretariat, Siedlung Halen 43
CH-3047 Herrenschwanden
Author's Society. Approx. 220 members. President:
Lukas Hartmann, Secretary: Hans Muhlethaler.

THAILAND

The Siam Society
PO Box 65
Bangkok
Society promotes & tries to preserve artistic, scientific
and other Cultural affairs of Thailand & neighbouring
countries. Publishes Journal of the Siam Society & The
Siam Society Newsletter. Approx. 1250 members.
President: Mr Patanachai Jayant, Hon Secretary: Mrs
Virginia M Crocco.

UNITED KINGDOM

The Arvon Foundation
Totleigh Barton, Sheepwash
Beaworthy, Devon EX21 5NS
Offers residential writing courses. Chairman: Lawrence
Sail, Julia Wheadon, Co Secretary: Ted Hughes OBE

& Terry Hands, Co-Presidents: Stuart Delves, Marc Collett, Susan Burns.
Also at: Lumb Bank, Heptonstall
Hebden Bridge, W Yorks HX7 6DF

Association of British Science Writers
c/o British Association for the Advancement of Science
Fortress House, 23 Savile Row, London W1X 1AB
President: Sir David Phillips
Secretary: Dr Peter Briggs

Association for Scottish Literary Studies
Department of English, University of Aberdeen
Aberdeen AB9 2UB
Secretary: Dr D S Robb
Publications: Scottish Literary Journal; Scottish Literary Journal Supplement (both twice yearly).

Authors' Club
40 Dover Street, London W1X 3RB
Club for Writers. Approx. 75 members. Secretary: Mrs Huldine Ridgway.

Francis Bacon Society Inc
Canonbury Tower, Islington, London N1
Chairman: Noel Fermor
Publications: Baconiana (periodically); Jottings (periodically); booklets, pamphlets (list on request).

Birmingham & Midland Institute
9 Margaret Street
Cultural institute & library sponsoring musical, literary, poetical, art activities. Approx. 1200 members. President: The Viscountess Cobham, Senior Vice President: Nathan Myers, Junior Vice President: W Jarvis, Administrator: Mr J Hunt.

Book Trust
Book House, 45 East Hill
London SW18 2QZ
An independent charitable trust whose task is to promote reading & the using of books. Approx. 3000 members. Chief Executive: Keith McWilliams.

Books across the Sea
The English-Speaking Union, Dartmouth House
37 Charles St, London W1X 8AB
Librarian: Jean Huse
Publications: Ambassador Booklist (quarterly)

British Science Fiction Association
29 Thornville Road, Hartlepool
Cleveland TS26 8EW
Literary Criticism, News, Reviews, Serious Articles, Meetings, Writers Workshop, Lending Library & Magazine Chain. Approx. 1000 members. President: Maureen Porter, Secretary: Jo Raine.

Cambridge Bibliographical Society
University Library, Cambridge CB3 9DR
Honorary Secretary: F R Collieson
Publications: Transactions (annually); Monographs (irregular)

The Charles Lamb Society
1A Royston Road, Richmond
Surrey, TW10 6LT
To study the life, works & times of Charles Lamb & his circle, to stimulate the Elian spirit of friendliness & humour, form a collection of Eliana. Approx. 350 members. President: Prof John Beer, Chairman: Dr D G Wilson, OBE, Secretary: Mrs M R Huxstep.

The Dickens Fellowship
The Dickens House, 48 Doughty Street
London WC1N 2LF
HQ in London, over 60 branches worldwide, of Dickens enthusiasts. Organises talks, conferences, publishes 'The Dickensian' concerned with preservation of buildings associated with Dickens. Approx. 4000 members. President: Alan S Watts, Secretary: Hylton Craig.

Early English Text Society
c/o Dr H L Spencer, Department of English
University of Bristol, 3/5 Woodland Road
Bristol BS8 1TB
Publish 1 or more volumes per year of English texts earlier than 1558. Approx 1050 members. Director: Prof John Burrow, Editorial Secretary: Dr M R Godden, Executive Secretary: Dr H L Spencer.

Edinburgh Bibliographical Society
New College Library, Mound Place
Edinburgh EH1 2LU
Lectures & publications (Transaction, irregular, issued only to members) on all bibliographical matters. Approx. 200 members. President: Mr I C Cunningham, Secretary: Dr M C T Simpson.

The English Association
The Vicarage, Priory Gardens
London W4 1TT
To promote the understanding & appreciation of English Language & Literature. Approx. 900 members. Secretary: Ruth Fairbanks-Joseph.

The H G Wells Society
English Department, Nen College
Moulton Park, Northampton NN2 7AL
Circulate newsletter & journal, Wellsian, & organises lectures & conferences to promote an active interest in the life & work of H G Wells. Approx 300 members. President: John Harwood, Chairman: Michael Draper, Hon Secretary: Sylvia Mardt.

The Incorporated Bronte Society
Bronte Parsonage, Haworth
Keighley, West Yorkshire BD22 8DR
The preservation of the literary works of the Bronte family & of manuscripts and other objects related to the family. Approx. 3200 members worldwide. President: Lord Briggs of Lewes, Director: Ms Jane Sellars, Secretary: Mrs Eunice Skirrow.

Institute of Contemporary Arts
The Mall, London SW1
Galleries, performance, music, cinema, talks, conferences, restaurant, bar, 'Bookshop'. Approx. 6500 members. Director: Mik Flood, Director Talks: Linda Brandon.

The Johnson Society of London
Round Chimney, Playden, Rye
East Sussex TN31 7UR
To study the works of Dr Samuel Johnson, his circle, his contemporaries & his times through lectures & articles in 'The New Rambler'. Approx. 110 members. President: The Rev Dr E F Carpenter, KCVO, Secretary: Miss S B S Pigrome, MA.

Keats Shelley Memorial Association
c/o Leonora Collins, Flat 1
33 Aberdeen Road, London N5 2DG
To Promote the works of Keats, Shelley, Byron & Leigh Hunt & maintain the House in Rome where Keats died. Approx. 250 members. President: Lord De L'Isle And Dudley, Hon Secretary: Leonora Collins.

Kent & Sussex Poetry Society
Pendips, Furzefield Avenue
Speldhurst, Tunbridge Wells, Kent TN3 OLD
Readings, Workshops, Discussions to promote love & understanding of poetry. Approx 50 members. President: Laurence Lerner, Chairman: Mary Colloff, Secretary: Madeline Munro.

The Kipling Society
18 Northumberland Ave
London WC2N 5BJ
Promotion of Kipling studies, discussion meetings, annual luncheon, qtrly journal. Approx. 900 members. President: Sir Angus Wilson, CBE, Chairman: Mr G C G Philo, CMG, M, KMN, Secretary: Mr N Entract, Journal Editor: G H Webb, CMG, OBE.

Lancashire Authors' Association
Kings Fold, Pope Lane
Penwortham, Preston, Lancs PR1 9JN
Honorary General Secretary: J D Cameron MBE
Publications: The Record (quarterly)

London Writer Circle
c/o Cathy Smith, 23 Prospect Road
London NW2 2JU
Lectures and criticisms of manuscripts. Approx. 150 members. President: Gordon Wells, Vice President: Rosemary Wells, Secretary: Cathy Smith.

National Union of Journalists
Acorn House, 314 Grays Inn Rd
London WC1X 8DP

Northern Arts Poetry Library
The Willows, Morpeth
Northumberland NE61 1TA
Aims to collect all contemporary poetry in English published in Great Britain. Includes works by individual poets and has a huge range of anthologies. Also has a wide range of poetry magazines.

Oxford Bibliographical Society
Bodleian Library
Oxford OX1 3BG
Secretary: Dr P Bulloch
Publications: First Series, Vols I-VII, 1923-46; New Series, Vol I, 1948-.

PEN English Centre
7 Dilke St, Chelsea
London SW3 4JE
President: Lady Antonia Fraser
Publications: The Pen (broadsheet, twice a year)

PEN Scottish Centre
c/o Scott, 33 Drumsheugh Gardens
Edinburgh EH3 7RN
National Centre of the World Association of Writers PEN INTERNATIONAL, to promote friendly co-operation of writers in all countries through literary gatherings. Approx. 145 members. President: Prof A N Jeffares, Vice-Presidents: Paul H Scott, Mary Baxter, Honorary Secretary: Laura Fiorentini.

The Poetry Library
South Bank Centre
London SE1 8XX
Includes all 20th-Century poetry in English and a collection of all poetry magazines published in the UK. Also arranges functions and provides an information service.

The Poetry Society
22 Betterton St
London WC2H 9BU
Operates as a book club, quarterly members receive a new book of poetry, an annual anthology also part of membership. Approx. 1700 members. General Secretary: Paul Ralph.

Romantic Novelists' Association
The Secretary, 9 Hillside Road
Southport, Merseyside PR8 4QB
Aims to raise the prestige of romantic authorship. Open to published romantic & historical authors & probationers entering work for the Netta Muskett Award. Approx. 560 members. Chairman: Margaret Pemberton, Secretary: Marie Murray.

Royal Society of Literature of the United Kingdom
1 Hyde Park Gardens, London W2 2LT
Lectures, publications & awards. Approx 750 members. President: Lord Jenkins of Hillhead, Chairman of Council: John Mortimer QC, Secretary: Mrs P M Schute.

Shakespearean Authorship Trust
11 Old Square, Lincoln's Inn
London WC2A 3TS
Object of Trust is "The advancement of learning with particular reference to the social, political & literary history of England in the 16th century & authorship of the literary works commonly attributed to William Shakespeare". Trustees: Dr L L Ware, Dr D W T Vessey, Mr J H W Silberrad, Lord Vere of Hanworth.

Sherlock Holmes Society of London
3 Outram Road, Southsea
Hampshire PO5 1QP
Study of the life & works of Sherlock Holmes & Dr Watson. Approx 1000 members. Hon Secretary: Cdr G S Stavert.

Society of Civil Service Authors
8 Bawtree Close, Sutton
Surrey SM2 5LQ
Encourages authorship by past and present members of the Civil Service.

Surrey Poetry Centre, (Guildford & Wey Poets)
15 Woodside Road, Purley
Surrey CR8 4LQ
A poetry group that meets twice monthly for workshop, reading of members' works, discussion, poetry competition adjudication etc. Approx. 28 members. Hon General Secretary: Stella Stocker.

Swansea & District Writers' Circle
932 Carmathen Road, Fforestfach
Swansea SA5 4AB
To encourage 'writers' in an exchange of ideas & experience, 7 possibly help with problems encountered in creative writing. Approx. 40 members. President: Edith Courtney, Secretary: Beth Quinn.

The Thomas Hardy Society
Park Farm, Tolpuddle
Dorchester, Dorset DT2 7HG
Promotion & appreciation of works of T Hardy, summer conference, lectures, walks in Wessex. Approx. 900 members. Chairman: T R Wigtman, Secretary: Mrs K N Fowler.

The Tolkien Society
35 Amesbury Crescent, Hove
East Sussex, BN3 5RD
Furthering interest in the life & works of Prof J R R Tolkien. Newsletter. Approx. 700 members. Honorary President: Prof J R R Tolkien, CBE 'In perpetuo' Chairman: Brin Dunsire, Secretary: Anne Haward.

Ver Poets
Haycroft, 61/63 Chiswell Green Lane
St Albans, Herts AL2 3AL
Aim to promote poetry & help poets. Holds 6 competitions for members every year, 1 open international competition. Approx. 200 members. President: John Cotton, Vice-President: John Mole, Chairman: Ray Badman, Organiser: May Badman.

The Welsh Academy (Yr Academi Gymreig)
3rd Floor, Mount Stuart House
Mount Stuart Square, The Docks, Cardiff CF1 6DQ
Aims to promote Anglo-Welsh literature through readings, conferences, workshops, schools, projects. Organises Cardiff Literature Festival. Approx. 95 members. Chairman: Tony Curtis, Vice President: Roland Mathias, Secretary: Cathy Baker.

Women Writers Network (WWN)
23 Prospect Road
London NW2 2JU
Provides and exchanges information, support and opportunities for working women writers. Also arranges functions and provides a newsletter.

The Writer's Guild of Great Britain
430 Edgeware Road
London W2 1EH
Represents professional writers in film, radio, television, theatre and publishing. Regularly provides assistance

to members on items such as contracts and conditions of work.

UNITED STATES OF AMERICA

ARIZONA

The Authors Resource Centre (TARC Inc)
4001 East Fort Lowell Road
Tucson, AZ 85712-1011
Serves Writers etc, writers' research library, Literary agency, sponsors 40 workshops & seminars, publishes TARC Report for writers. Approx. 300 members. President/Executive Director: Martha R Gore, Secretary/Treasurer/Educational Director: Victor M Gore.

The Society of Southwestern Authors
Box 35220, Tuscon AZ 85740
Organization of pro. writers for supportive fellowship, recognition of member writers' professional achievement, & encouragement & assistance for persons striving to become writers. Approx 125 members. President: John Stickler, Corres. Secretary: Susy Smith.

Evangelical Christian Publishers Association
950 W Southern Ave, Suite 106B
Tempe, AZ 85282
Exec Dir: Douglas R Ross
Professional seminars, statistical studies & religious book awards

CALIFORNIA

International Black Writers & Artists, Inc
2318 25 Avenue, Oakland, CA 94601
Poetry readings, contests, pot lucks, workshops, annual conferences, writers picnic. Approx. 250 members. President: Edna Crutchfield, Chairman: Hazel Harrison, Vice Presidents: Donald Bakeer, Gene Williams, Secretary: Carl Crutchfield.

San Diego Writers Workshop
8431 Beaver Lake Dr, San Diego, CA 92119,
Dir: Chet Cunningham
For professional novel writers. Read & critique members' writing. Offer encouragement, aid & comfort. Semimonthly meetings. Members: 20.

Society of Children's Book Writers
PO Box 296, Mar Vista Station
Los Angeles, CA 90066
Offers bi-monthly 'Bulletin' MSS exchange, meetings, conferences, Golden Kite awards, insurance, grants, advise. Approx 5000 members. President: Stephen Mooser, Executive Director: Lin Oliver (Ms).

Women Writers West
Box 1637, Santa Monica, CA 90406
Support group, monthly meetings, offering workshops, seminars, speakers, etc. Approx. 150 members. President: Rita A White.

American Poetry Association
Box 1803, 250 A Potrero St
Santa Cruz, CA 95061
Outreach Mgr: Jennifer Manes
Anthology publication, poetry contest
Pubn(s): American Poetry Anthology (quarterly, $40)

Writers Guild of America, West, Inc
8955 Beverly Blvd, West Hollywood, CA 90048
Represents its membership in contract negotiation and compliance with the film and television industry. Approx. 7500 members. Executive Director: Brian Walton, President: George Kirgo, Vice President: Del Reisman, Secretary/Treasurer: Adam Rodman.

COLORADO

The Associated Business Writers of America
1450 S Havana Ste 620
Aurora, CO 80012
Association for business writers. Approx 150 members. Executive Director: James Lee Young.

The National Writers Club
1450 S Havana Ste 620
Aurora, CO 80012
Association for freelance writers. Approx 5000 members. Executive Director: James Lee Young.

DELAWARE

International Reading Association
800 Barksdale Road, PO Box 8139
Newark, DE 19714
Professional education association dedicated to the improvement of reading ability & development of the reading habit worldwide through publications, research, meetings, conferences & international congresses. Approx. 85,000 members. President: Patricia S Koppman, Executive Director: Ronald W Mitchell.

FLORIDA

Florida Freelance Writers Association
PO Box 9844, Fort Lauderdale, FL 33310
Regular seminars throughout Florida. Monthly freelance writers report. Annual guide to Florida writers. Approx 1300 members. Executive Director: Dan K Cassell.

International Society of Dramatists
Box 1310, Miami, FL 33153
Information clearinghouse for dramatists in all media: stage, screen, TV, radio, provides continually updated lists of script opportunities in English worldwide. Monthly publications. Annual playwriting award. Approx. 10,550 members. President: Andrew Delaplaine.

ILLINOIS

American Library Association
50 East Huron, Chicago, IL 60611
Provides leadership for the development, promotion, improvement of library & information services to enhance learning. Approx. 44,000 members. Director: Linda Chrismond, Editor: Arthur Plotnik.

Science Fiction Research Association Inc
855 S Harvard Dr, Palatine, IL 60067
Professional study of science fiction & fantasy; annual scholar award. Archives maintained at University of Kansas, Lawrence. Sponsor workshop awards & prizes. President: Elizabeth Anne Hull, Vice President: Neil Barron, Secretary: David Mead, Treasurer: Thomas Remington.

Independent Writers of Chicago
7855 Gross Point Rd, Suite G-4
Skokie, IL 60077
Monthly meetings & four workshops per year dealing with the business aspects of independent writing. Writers' line job referral; insurance. Members: 350. President: M A Porucznik.

Illinois Writers, Inc
PO Box 1087, Champaign, IL 61820
To promote the literary arts of Illinois poets, fiction writers, & small press publishers. Publish bi-annual review & bi-monthly newsletter. Approx. 5000 members. Chairperson: Deborah Bosley, Newsletter Editor: Mary Maddox.

Society of Midland Authors
840 East 87 St, Chicago IL 60619
To promote friendly contact & professional interchange among authors of the Midland, to explore topics of literary & professional interest in open monthly programmes, honour the best of Midland writing with

cash awards annually. Approx. 180 members. President: Dempsey J Travis, Vice President: Rick Kogan.

MARYLAND

The Lewis Carroll Society of North America
617 Rockford Road, Silver Spring, MD 20902
To Promote interests in & be a centre for Lewis Carroll studies. Approx. 300 members. President: Charles Lovett, Vice President: Alan Tannenbaum, Secretary: Maxine Schaefer.

NEW HAMPSHIRE

The MacDowell Colony Inc
100 High Street, Peterborough, NH 03458
Retreat for writers, composers, visual artists & filmmakers with professional standing in field. Board of Directors: 39, Staff: 10, Colony Fellows approx. 2000. Chairman: Vartan Gregorian, President: David W Helenaik, Executive Director: Mary Carswell.

NEW JERSEY

Baker Street Irregulars
34 Pierson Avenue, Norwood, NJ 07648
Keeping the memory of the Master green (Sherlock Holmes). Approx. 280 members plus scion societies. President: Thomas L Stix Jr, Wiggins, Vice President: John Bennett Shaw, Simpson.

NEW YORK

American Society of Journalists and Authors, Inc
1501 Broadway, Suite 1907
New York, NY 10036
Service organization providing exchange of ideas, market information. Regular meetings with speakers from the industry, annual writers conference; medical plans available. Professional referral service, annual membership directory; first amendment advocacy group. Approx. 750 members. President: Thomas Bedell, Executive Vice President: Katharine Davis Fishman, Secretary: Eleanor Dienstag.

The Academy of American Poets
177 E 87 St, New York, NY 10128
Sponsor The Lamont Poetry Selection, The Walt Whitman Award, The Harold Morton Landon Translation Award, The Lavan Younger Poets Award & annual college poetry prizes; workshops, classes & literary historical walking tours; award fellowships to American poets for distinguished poetic achievement. Members: 2000. President: Mrs Edward T Chase, Executive Director: William Wadsworth.

Brooklyn Writers' Network (BWN)
2509 Ave "K" Brooklyn, NY 11210
Seeks to improve contact between professional writers & publishing industry; newsletter; directory; conferences; workshops. Members: 500. Director: Ruth Schwartz.

Mystery Writers of America Inc
236 W 27th St, Rm 600
New York, NY 10001
To support & promote the mystery. Chapters around country hold monthly meetings with speakers, sponsors the Edgar Allan Poe Awards. Approx. 2500 members. Executive Secretary: Priscilla Ridgway.

International Association of Crime Writers Inc
JAF Box 1500, New York, NY 10116
President: Roger L Simon, Executive Director: Mary A Frisque, Sec-Treas: Thomas Adcock, Secretary: Jerome Charyn.

PEN American Center
568 Broadway, New York, NY 10012
An international organization of writers, poets, playwrights, essayists, editors, novelists & translators, whose purpose is to bring about better understanding among writers of all nations. Approx. 2100 members. President: Larry McMurtry, Intl Pres: Rene Tavernier, Executive Director: Karen Kennerly.

Poetry Society of America
15 Gramercy Park, New York, NY 10003
A service organization dedicated to the promotion of poets and poetry. Sponsors readings, lectures, contests/ houses the Van Voorhis Library. Approx 1700 members. President: Molly Peacock, Director: Elise Paschen.

Poets & Writers, Inc
72 Spring St, New York, NY 10012
National nonprofit information center for those interested in contemporary American literature. Publish magazine & information for writers on literary agents, sponsors, copyright & literary bookstores. Publish a directory of American poets & fiction writers; sponsor readings & workshops program. Executive Director: Elliot Figman.

Pushcart Press
PO Box 380, Wainscott, NY 11975
Literary publishers. President: Bill Henderson

The International Women's Writing Guild (IWWG)
Box 810, Gracie Sta
New York, NY 10028
A network for the empowerment of women through writing. Services include manuscript referral & exchange, writing conferences & retreats, group rates for health & life insurance, legal aid, regional clusters & job referrals. 5000 members. Executive Director: Hannelore Hahn.

Staten Island Poetry Society
25 Washington Place, Staten Island, NY 10302
Monthly meetings & workshops & periodic publication of mini-anthology. 12 members. President: Ted Lovington, Secretary: Louise Wright.

Teachers & Writers Collaborative
5 Union Square West, New York, NY 10003
Teachers & Writers sends professional artists into public schools to teach their art forms. Also publish books & a magazine about how to teach creative writing. Approx. 350 members. Executive Director: Nancy Larson Shapiro, Chairman of the Board: Steven Schrader, Associate Directors: Pat Padgett, Gary Lenhart, Publications Director: Ron Padgett, Programme Director: Elizabeth Fox.

Writers Guild Of America (WGA), East Inc
555 W 57 St, New York, NY 10019
Labor union representing professional writers in motion pictures, TV & radio. Membership available only through the sale of literary material or employment for writing services in one of these areas. Executive Director: Mona Mangan, President: Edward Adler, Vice President: Adrian J Meppen, Sec-Treas: Jane Bollinger.

Translation Center
412 Dodge Hall, Columbia University
New York, NY 10027
Publish a magazine bi-annually. Dedicated to finding and publishing the best translations of significant works of foreign contemporary literature. Director: Frank MacShane, Secretary: Elizabeth Koyama.

OHIO

Mariological Society of America
The Marian Library, University of Dayton
Dayton, OH 45469
To promote a more theological appreciation of the Blessed Virgin Mary & to further scientific research in the field of Marian Theology. Publishes Marian Studies annually. Approx. 500 members. President: Rev James McCurry, OFMConv, Vice President: Rev Matthew Morry, OP, Secretary: Rev Thomas A Thompson, SMM, Treasurer: Rev Charles R Costello.

Ohioana Library Association
65 S Front St, 1105 Ohio Depts Bldg
Columbus, OH 43215
Gives annual awards for books by Ohioans & about Ohio. Publishes 'Ohioana Quarterly'. Approx. 1000 members. President: Ruth Mount, Director: Linda Hengst, Vice President: Ann Bowers, Secretary: Kenneth Warren, Office Manager: Sandra Reed.

PENNSYLVANIA

Association of Professional Translators
Three Mellon Bank Centre - 2523
Pittsburgh, PA 15259
Holds bi-monthly meetings, members teach professional translation courses at University of Pittsburgh. Approx. 125 members. President: Gigliola Bisiana, Vice Presidents: Tom Clark, Marcella Martin, Mary Jo Bensasi, Secretary: Mary Jeanne Fredley, Permanent Officer: Josephine Thornton.

Catholic Library Association
461 W Lancaster Avenue
Haverford, PA 19041
An organization of professional librarians interested in providing service according to the Catholic philosophy. Approx. 3000 members. President: Emmett Corry, Executive Director: Natalie A Logan.

Outdoor Writers' Association of America
2017 Cato Ave, Suite 101
State College, PA 16801
Professional authors, journalists, broadcasters, photographers & artists who cover hunting, fishing, camping, canoeing & similar outdoor sports; workshops held at annual conference. Members: 1900. President: Joel Vance, Vice Presidents: Thomas Huggler, Lonnie Williamson, William Hilts, Executive Director: Sylvia G Bashline.

National Book Critics Circle
c/o Alida Becker, 756 South 10th Street
Philadelphia, PA 19147
Gives annual awards for Fiction, Poetry, Biography/Autobiography, General Nonfiction, Criticism. Purpose: to raise the standards of book criticism & enhance public appreciation of literature. Approx. 500 members. President: Nina King, Vice President & Treasurer: Eliot Fremont-Smith, Vice President & Secretary: Alida Becker.

The Philomathean Society of the University of Pennsylvania
Philomathean Society, Philomathean Halls
Box H, College Hall, University of Pennsylvania
Philadelphia, Pennsylvania 19104
Translated Rosetta Stone, offered first lectures in US history. Aim: to increase the knowledge of the members and to increase the academic prestige of the University. Approx. 2200 members. Moderator: Darren Rosenblum, First Censor: Jessica Cooperman, Secretary: James Bessin, Senior Member: Eugene A Bolt Jr.

SOUTH CAROLINA

Science Fiction Writers of America Inc
Box 4236, West Columbia, SC 29171
Professional association of SF/Fantasy writers, editors, agents, anthologists; presenters of the SFWA Nebula Awards. Approx. 1100 members. President: Greg Bear, Vice President: Michael Cassott, Secretary: Frank Catalano.

SOUTH DAKOTA

South Dakota State Poetry Society Inc
909 E 34th Street, Sioux Falls, SD 57105
Poetry Magazine 10 times a year, 'Pasque Petals'. Newsletter 'Serendipity'. Meetings, workshops, yearly contests. Approx 250 members. President: Verlyss V Jacobson, Vice President: Lois Bogue, Recording Secretary: Myra Osterberg, Treasurer: Emma Dinut.

TEXAS

Southwest Review
6410 Airline Road
Southern Methodist University, Dallas, TX 75275
Literary Quarterly. Editor: Willard Spiegelman, Associate Editor: Elizabeth Mills.

American Literary Translators Association (ALTA)
University of Texas, Dallas
Box 830688, Richardson, TX 75083
Sponsor the Gregory Rabassa Prize for the translation of fiction from any language into English & the Richard Wilbur Prize for the translation of poetry from any language into English. Awards, which consist of the publication of the winning mss are awarded biannually. Members: 1000. Executive Secretary: Sheryl St Germain.

VIRGINIA

Associated Writing Programs
AWP Old Dominion University
Norfolk, VA 23508
National, non-profit organization of writers & writers who teach. Approx. 4000 members. President: Joe David Bellamy, Vice President: Kate Daniels, Secretary: Alberto Rios.

Dog Writers' Association of America Inc
133 Chase Ave, Ivyland, PA 18974
Members are engaged in the publishing, writing, & broadcasting of dog news. Approx. 350 members.

VERMONT

Dorothy Canfield Fisher Children's Book Award Committee
Vermont Department of Libraries
Pavilion Office Building, 109 State Street
Montpelier, VT 05602
Chooses 30 books annually for children in grades 4-8 to read & vote on. Hosts an awards ceremony annually. 8 members. President: Gail Furnas.

WYOMING

Western Writers of America
1753 Victoria, Sheridan, WY 82801
An organization of professionals dedicated to the spirit & reality of the West, past & present. Approx. 600 members. President: David Dary, Vice President: Nancy Hamilton, Secretary: Barbara Ketcham.

APPENDIX C

LITERARY AWARDS AND PRIZES

The following list of Literary Awards and Prizes does not claim to be exhaustive although every effort has been made to make it as comprehensive as possible.

THE J R ACKERLEY PRIZE FOR AUTOBIOGRAPHY

English Pen, 7 Dilke Street
Chelsea, London SW3 4JE, England
Prize is awarded for Literary Autobiography, written in English and published in the year preceeding the Award. Annual prize of£500.00
Contact: Tom Aitken, Awards Secretary
1982 Shaky Relations by Edward Blishen
1983 Her People by Kathleen Dayus
     The High Path by Ted Walker
1984 Still Life by Richard Cobb
1985 Deceived with Kindness by Angelica Garnett
1986 Time and Time Again by Dan Jacobson
1987 After The Funeral by Diana Athill
1988 Little Wilson & Big God by Anthony Burgess
1989 The Grass Arena by John Healy

JANE ADDAMS CHILDREN'S BOOK AWARD

Jane Addams Peace Association
777 United Nations Plaza, New York, NY 10017, USA
Prize awarded for a book that best combines literary merit with themes stressing peace, social justice, world community & the equality of the sexes & all races. Award: Certificate presented annually
Contact: Ruth Chalmers
1980 The Road From Home by David Kherdian
1981 First Woman in Congress: Jeannette Rankin by Florence White
1982 A Spirit to Ride the Whirlwind by Athena V Lord
1983 Hiroshima No Pika by Toshi Maruki
1984 Rain of Fire by Marion Dane Bauer
1985 The Short Life of Sophie Scholl by Hermann Vink
1986 Ain't Gonna Study War No More: The Story of American Peace Seekers by Milton Meltzer
1987 Nobody Wants a Nuclear War, written and illustrated by Judith Vigna
1988 Waiting For The Rain: A Novel Of South Africa by Sheila Gordon
1989 Anthony Burns: The Defeat and Triumph of a Fugitive Slave by Virginia Hamilton.

THE AGE BOOK OF THE YEAR AWARD

c/o The Literary Editor, The Age
250 Spencer Street, Melbourne, Vic 3000, Australia
Prize is awarded to a published book of literary merit, written by living Australians. Award of $3000 to the author of a non-fiction book and $3000 to a work of imaginative writing

Contact: Literary Editor
1981 A Million Wild Acres by Eric Rolls
     Turtle Beach by Blanche d'Alpuget
1982 Fly Away Peter by David Malouf
     John Monash by Geoffrey Serle
1983 Mr Scobie's Riddle by Elizabeth Jolley
     A History of Tasmania, Vol I by Lloyd Robson
1984 The Bellarmine Jug by Nicholas Hasluck
     H B Higgins: The Rebel as Judge by John Rickard
1985 Illywhacker by Peter Carey
     Mapping the Paddocks by Chester Eagle
     Vietnam: A Reporter's War by Hugh Lunn
1986 Sister Ships by Joan London
     George Johnston: A Biography by Garry Kinnane
1987 Stories from the Warm Zone by Jessica Anderson
     The Fatal Shore by Robert Hughes
1988 Forty-Seventeen by Frank Moorhouse
     Big-Noting by Robin Gerster
1989 Mariners Are Warned! by Marsdern Hordern
     My Father's Moon by Elizabeth Jolley
1990 Blessed City by Gwen Harwood
     Longleg by Glenda Adams

THE ALICE LITERARY AWARD

c/o Federal President
Society of Women Writers (Australia)
GPO Box 2621, Sydney, NSW 2001, Australia
Presented by the Society of Women Writers (Australia) biennially for a distinguished and long-term contribution to literature by an Australian woman.
Contact: Marjorie Wilke, Federal President
1980 Dame Judith Wright
1982 Dame Mary Durack
1984 Kylie Tennant
1986 Ruth Park
1988 Nancy Cato

AMERICAN BOOK AWARD

Before Columbus Foundation
American Ethnic Studies, GN-80
Washington, Seattle, WA 98195, USA
Recognises outstanding literary achievement by contemporary American authors without restriction for race, sex, ethnic background, or genre. The purpose to acknowledge the excellence & multicultural diversity of American writing. The awards are non-profit. There are no categories & all winners are accorded equal status.
Contact: Gundars Strads
1980 Tortuga by Rudolfo Anaya

Random Possession by Mei-Mei Berssenbrugge

Mouth on Paper by Jayne Cortez

Hello, La Jolla by Ed Dorn

All I Asking to Is My Body by Milton Murayama

Ceremony by Leslie Silko

Snake-Back Solos by Quincy Troupe

Future Preconditional by Douglas Woolf

1981 Turn Again to Me & Other Poems by Helen Adam

On Call by Miguel Algarin

The Shameless Hussy by The American Library Trustee Association

The Salt Eaters by Toni Cade Bambara

Back Then Tomorrow by Peter Blue Cloud

The Choice by Rose Drachler

The Liberties by Susan Howe

In Time by Robert Kelly

Songs for Jadina by Alan Lau

Travelling Light by Lionel Mitchell

Felita by Nicholasa Mohr

A Scent of Apples by Ben Santos

Lifetime Achievement Awards for Frank Stanford & Larry Neal

1982 The Book of Jamaica by Russell Banks

Emplumada by Lorna Dee Cervantes

Chickencoop Chinaman and Year of the Dragon by Frank Chin

Enclave by Tato Laviera

Collected Poems by E L Mayo

Songs for the Harvester of Dreams by Duane Niatum

This Passover or Next I Will Never Be in Jerusalem by Hilton Obenzinger

Sangre by Leroy Quintana

Pre-Faces & Other Writings by Jerome Rothenberg

Shino Suite by Ronald Tanaka

Marked by Fire by Joyce Carol Thomas

Bodies & Soul by Al Young

Island: Poetry and History of Chinese Immigrants on Angel Island 1910-1949 by Him Mark Lai, Genny Lim, and Judy Yung (editors)

Lifetime Achievement Award for Chester Himes

1983 Not By the Sword by Nash Candelaria

Black Women Novelists by Barbara Christian

Queen of Wands by Judy Grahn

Lost Highway by Peter Guralnick

Pet Food & Tropical Apparitions by Jessica Hagedorn

Californians by James D Houston

Obasan by Joy Kogawa

Chinese Folk Poetry by Cecilia Liang

A Duanaire by Sean O'Tuama and Thomas Kinsella

The Legend of Foot Mountain by Harriet Rohmer

Iclick Song by John A Williams

Thirty An' Seen a Lot by Evangelina Vigil

Lifetime Achievement Award for Kay Boyle

1984 Confirmation: An Anthology of African-American Women by Amiri Baraka and Amina Baraka

The Heat Bird by Mei-mei Berssenbrugge

Days Without Weather by Cecil Brown

Breaking Silence: An Anthology of Contemporary Asian American Poets by Joseph Bruchac

A Puerto Rican in New York and Other Sketches by Jesus Colon

O Albany by William Kennedy

The Mama Poems by Maurice Kenny

Naked in Deccan by Venkatesh Kulkarni

Praisesong for the Widow by Paule Marshall

Pie-Biter by Ruthanne Lum McCunn (author), You-shan Tang (illustrator), and Ellen Lai-shan Yeung (trans)

Echoes Inside the Labyrinth by Thomas McGrath

Citizen 13660 by Mine Okubo

The Captive Soul of the Messiah: New Tales About Reb Nachman by Howard Schwartz

Axe Handles by Gary Snyder

Lifetime Achievement Award for Josephine Miles

1985 The House on Mango Street by Sandra Cisneros

Ground Work: Before the War by Robert Duncan

Love Medicine by Louise Erdrich

Justice at War by Peter Irons

Solo in the Box Car, Third Floor E by Angela Jackson

Say Ray by Ron Jones

Queen of the Ebony Isles by Collen J McElroy

Poets Behind Barbed Wire by Jiro Nakano and Kay Nakano

Round Valley Songs by William Oandasan

Amelia Earhart by Maureen Owen

Homegirls and Handgrenades by Sonia Sanchez

At Seventy: A Journal by May Sarton

Living Up the Street by Gary Soto

Genthe's Photographs of San Francisco's Old Chinatown by John Kuo Wei Tchen

The Book of Jerusalem by Julia Vinograd

Lifetime Achievement Award for Joe Flaherty

1986 Time's Now by Miguel Algarin

The Dream Book: An Anthology of Writing by Italian American Women by Helen Barolini (editor)

A Daughter of the Nobility by Natasha Borovsky

Smiles on Washington Square by Raymond Federman

I Hear You Knockin by Jeff Hannusch

Seeing Through the Sun by Linda Hogan

My Emily Dickinson by Susan Howe

This Bridge Called My Back: Writings by Radical Women of Color by Cherrie Moraga and Gloria Anzaldua

Yokohama, California by Toshio Mori

The Sun is Not Merciful by Anna Lee Walters

Irish Musicians/American Friends by Terence Winch

Close Your Eyes and Think of England by Michael Feingold

Lifetime Achievement Award for Hisaye Yamamoto

1987 Sin by Ai

liberazione della donna: feminism in Italy by Lucia Chiavola Birnbaum

Confessions of Madame Psyche by Dorothy Bryant

The Mixquiabuala Letters by Ana Castillo

Ready From Within by Septima Clark and Cynthia Stokes Brown (editor)
Celebrating Bird: The Triumph of Charlie Parker by Gary Giddins
Face Games by Juan Felipe Herrera
The Essential Etheridge Knight by Etheridge Knight
Practising Angels, A Contemporary Anthology of San Francisco Bay Area Poetry by Michael Mayo
Portrait of a Little Boy in Darkness by Daniel McGuire
Mama by Terry McMillan
American Splendor by Harvey Pekar
Selected Poems, 1958-1984 by John Wieners
Fools Crow by James Welch
Circumnavigation by Cyn Zarco
Lifetime Achievement Awards for Charles Blockson and Dennis Clark
1989 Eva Luna by Isabel Allende
Chinaman Pacific and Frisco R R Co by Frank Chin
Homemade Love by J California Cooper
Columbia Literary History of the United States by Emory Elliott (ed)
The Exiles of Erin: 19th Century Irish American Fiction by Charles Fanning
Memory of Fire by Eduardo Galeano
The Signifying Monkey: A Theory of Afro-American Literary Criticism by Henry L Gates Jr
The Right Thing To Do by Josephine Gattuso Hendin
Repairing America by William Hohri
Wode Shuofa (My Way of Speaking) by Carolyn Lau
A Burst of Light by Audre Lorde
Way by Leslie Scalapino
Stone's Throw by Jennifer Stone
Floating the River in Melancholy by Shuntaro Tanikawa
From the Pyramids to the Projects: Poems of Genocide and Resistance by Askia Muhammed Touré
The Ultraviolet Sky by Alma Luz Villanueva
Lifetime Achievement Award for Amiri Baraka and Ed Dorn
Editor/Publisher Award for Nicolás Kannellos

AMERICAN ACADEMY AND INSTITUTE OF ARTS AND LETTERS - GOLD MEDAL
633 West 155 St, New York,
NY 10032-6599, USA
Gold Medals are awarded each year for distinguished achievement in two of the following categories: belles letters & painting; biography & music; fiction & sculpture; history & architecture; poetry & music; drama & graphic art.
Award: Two medals
Contact: Jeanie Kim
1980 Edward Albee
Peggy Bacon
1981 Malcolm Cowley
Raphael Soyer
1982 William Schuman
Francis Steegmuller
1983 Bernard Malamud
Louise Nevelson

1984 Gordon Bunshart
George F Kennan
1985 Leonard Bernstein
Robert Penn Warren
1986 Edward Albee
Jasper Johns
1987 Jacques Barzun
Isabel Bishop

AMERICAN ACADEMY AND INSTITUTE OF ARTS AND LETTERS - LITERATURE
633 West 155 St, New York,
NY 10032-6599, USA
1980 Anne Beattie
William Dickey
Paul Fussell
Maxine Kumin
George Oppen
Robert Pinsky
Lewis Thomas
Larry Woiwode
1981 Louise Gluck
Gail Godwin
Howard Frank Mosher
James Salter
Elizabeth Sewell
William Stafford
Hilma Wolitzer
Jay Wright
1982 David H Bradley, Jr
Frederick Buechner
MacDonald Harris
Daryl Hine
Josephine Jacobsen
Donald Keene
Berton Roueche
Robert Stone
1983 Alfred Corn
Stephen Dixon
Robert Mezey
Mary Oliver
David Plante
George Starbuck
Leo Steinberg
Edmund White
1984 Amy Clampitt
Don De Lillo
Sanford Friedman
Robert Hass
Lincoln Kirstein
Romulus Linney
Bobbie Ann Mason
Craig Nova
1985 Alan Dugan
Maria Irene Fornes
George Garrett
Carolyn Kizer
Gilbert Sorrentino
Paul West
John Williams
Paul Zimmer
1986 Russell Banks
Frederick Busch
Robert A Caro
Robert Kelly
Barry Lopez
David Mamet
Marsha Norma
Lore Segal
1987 Evan S Connell

Ernest J Gaines
Ralph Manheim
Sandra McPherson
Steven Millhauser
Robert Phillips
Roger Shattuck
1988 William Barrett
David Bottoms
Rosellen Brown
David Cope
John Clellon Holmes
John McCormick
James Seay
William Weaver
Norman Williams
1989 Richard Ford
Martin Greenberg
Ron Hansen
Herbert Morris
Gregory Rabassa
David R Slavitt
Arturo Vivante
Joy Williams

ARVON INTERNATIONAL POETRY COMPETITION
Kilnhurst, Kilnhurst Road
Todmorden, Lancashire OL14 6AX, England
Poetry competition open to anyone in the world for poems of any length written in the English language. Biennial, first prize of £5000.00 with at least 15 other prizes.
1980 The Letter by Andrew Motion
1982 Ephraim Destiny's Perfectly Utter Darkness by John Hartley Williams
1985 Rorschach Writing by Oliver Reynolds
1987 The Notebook by Selima Hill
1989 Halfway Pond by Sheldon Flory

AUSTRALIAN LITERATURE SOCIETY GOLD MEDAL
Association for the Study of Australian Literature Ltd,
c/o English Department, University College, ADFA, Campbell, ACT 2600, Australia
Awarded annually for the most outstanding Australian literary work, or (occasionally), for outstanding services to Australian literature.
Contact: Susan McKernan, Secretary
1983 Child's Play; Fly Away Peter by David Malouf
1984 The People's Other World by Les Murray
1985 Archimedes and the Seagle by David Ireland
1986 Beachmasters by Thea Astley
1987 The Nightmarkets by Alan Wearne
1988 Louisa by Brian Matthews
1989 Forty-seventeen by Frank Moorhouse
1990 Possible Worlds, and Collected Poems by Peter Porter

BOLLINGEN PRIZE IN POETRY
Yale University, Beinecke Library,
Box 1603A, New Haven, CT 06520, USA
Prize is awarded for the best book of poetry by an American author during the preceding two years. Biennial prize of $10,000.00
1981 Howard Nemerov and May Swenson
1983 Anthony E Hecht and John Hollander
1985 John Ashbury and Fred Chappell
1987 Stanley Kunitz
1989 Edgar Bowers
1991 Laura (Riding) Jackson and Donald Justice

BOOKER PRIZE
Book Trust, Book House,
45 East Hill, London SW18 2QZ, England
Awarded for the best full-length novel published between 1 October and 30 September in UK. Novel must be written in English and written by a citizen of Britain, the Commonwealth, Republic of Ireland or South Africa. Annual prize of £20,000.00
Contact: Christine Shaw, Head of Publicity
1980 Rites of Passage by William Golding
1981 Midnight's Children by Salman Rushdie
1982 Schindler's Ark by Thomas Keneally
1983 Life & Times of Michael K by J M Coetzee
1984 Hotel du Lac by Anita Brookner
1985 The Bone People by Keri Hulme
1986 The Old Devils by Kingsley Amis
1987 Moon Tiger by Penelope Lively
1988 Oscar and Lucinda by Peter Carey
1990 Possession by A S Byatt
1991 The Famished Road by Ben Okri
1992 The English Patient by Michael Ondaatje and Sacred Hunger by Barry Unsworth

THE W H SMITH/BOOKS IN CANADA FIRST NOVEL AWARD
Books in Canada, 366 Adelaide Street E Suite 432, Toronto, Ontario M5A 3X9, Canada
Prize is awarded for the best Canadian first novel published in English during the calendar year. Annual prize of $1,000.00
Contact: Christopher Noxon, Editorial Assistant
1980 Gentle Sinners by W D Valgardson
1981 Obasan by Joy Kogawa
1982 Shoeless Joe by W P Kinsella
1983 Willie: A Romance by Heather Robertson
1984 Perdue: Or How The West Was Lost by Geoffrey Ursell
1985 The Story of Booby O'Malley by Wayne Johnston
1986 The Life of Helen Alone by Karen Lawrence
1987 The Butterfly Chair by Marion Quednau
1988 A Man of Little Faith by Rick Salutin
1989 The Missing Child by Sandra Birdsell

THE BUCKLAND AWARD
Trustees Executors and Agency Company of New Zealand Ltd,
24 Water St, PO Box 760,
Dunedin, New Zealand
Prize is awarded annually for work of the highest literary merit by a New Zealand writer.
1980 Living in the Maniototo by Janet Frame
1981 Various Poems by Elizabeth Smither
1982 Meg by Maurice Gee
1983 To the Island by Janet Frame
1984 The Bone People by Keri A Hulme
1985 Wednesday to Come by Renee G Taylor
1986 The Loop in Lone Kauri Road: Poems 1983-85 by Mr Allen Curnow
1987 Symmes Hole by Ian Wedde
1988 Dirty Work by Nigel Cox
1989 The Rock Garden by Fiona Farrell Poole

CNA Literary Award
The Director, Book Trade Association of South Africa, PO Box 326,
Howard Place 7450, South Africa
Established in 1961 for the best original works, one in English and one in Afrikaans, published for the first time during the calendar year of the competition. 7,500 rand each for the winner and

2,500 rand for the runners-up in both the English and Afrikaans categories, with an additional prize of 3,000 rand for the best designed book. Awarded annually.

1980 Waiting for the Barbarians by J M Coetzee
1981 July's People by Nadine Gordimer
1982 A Chain of Voices by André P Brink
1983 The Life & Times of Michael K by J M Coetzee
1984 Selected Poems by Douglas Livingstone
1985 Call Me Woman by Ellen Kuzwayo
1986 The 29th Parallel by David Robbins
1987 Phoebe & Nio by E M McPhail

RANDOLPH CALDECOTT MEDAL

Association for Library Service to Children, 50 E Huron St,
Chicago, IL 60611, USA
Prize is awarded to an illustrator of the most distinguished American picture book for children published in the preceding year. Annual prize of bronze medal.
Contact: Susan Roman, Executive Director

1980 Ox-Cart Man by Donald Hall
1981 Fables by Arnold Lobel
1982 Jumanji by Chris Van Allsburg
1983 Shadow by Blaise Cendrars
1984 The Glorious Flight: Across the Channel with Louis Bleriot by Alice Provensen and Martin Provensen
1985 Saint George and the Dragon Retold by Margaret Hodges
1986 The Polar Express by Chris Van Allsburg
1987 Hey, Al by Arthur Yorinks
1988 Owl Moon by Jane Yolen

THE BOOK OF THE YEAR FOR CHILDREN AWARD

200 Elgin St, Ste 206, Ottawa,
Ontario K2P 1L5, Canada
The award is presented to an author of an outstanding Childrens book published during previous calendar year. Suitable for children up to 14 years of age and published in Canada. Annual award

1980 River Runners by James Houston
1981 The Violin-Maker's Gift by Donn Kushner
1982 The Root Cellar by Janet Lunn
1983 Up to Low by Brian Doyle
1984 Sweetgrass by Jan Hudson
1985 Mama's Going to Buy You a Mockingbird by Jean Little
1986 Julie by Cora Taylor
1987 Shadow in Hawthorn Bay by Janet Lunn
1988 A Handful of Time by Kit Pearson
1989 Easy Avenue by Brian Doyle
1990 The Sky is Falling by Kit Pearson

CANADA - AUSTRALIA LITERARY AWARD

The Canada Council, PO Box 1047,
99 Metcalfe, Ottawa, Ontario, K1P 5V8, Canada
Prize is awarded alternately to an English-language Canadian writer or an Australian writer for his/her complete works. Annual prize of $3,000 and a journey to the hosting country where the prize is being awarded.
Contact: Naim Kattan, Administration Services Officer

1980 Roger McDonald
1981 Leon Rooke
1982 Barry Oakley

1983 Mavis Gallant
1984 Les A Murray
1985 Jack Hodgins
1986 Rodney Hall
1987 Sharon Pollock

CANADIAN AUTHORS ASSOCIATION LITERARY AWARDS

121 Avenue Road, Suite 104,
Toronto, Ontario M5R 2G3, Canada
Four categories; Fiction, Non-fiction; Poetry; Drama. Nominations apply to book length works by Canadian writers published or produced during the previous calendar year. One award per year in each category, $5,000 cash prize plus silver medal in each category.
Contact: Awards Chairman

Poetry
1980 There's A Trick With A Knife That I'm Learning To Do by Michael Ondaatje
1981 Land of the Peace by Leona Gom
1982 The Acid Test by Gary Geddes
1983 The Presence of Fire George Amabile
1984 Birding, or Desire by Don McKay
1985 Book of Mercy by Leonard Cohen
1986 The Glass Air by P K Page
1987 The Collected Poems, 1956-1986 by Al Purdy
1988 Selected Poems by Pat Lane
1989 Daniel by Bruce Rice
1990 Homeless Heart by Don Bailey

Drama
1980 Ned and Jack by Sheldon Rosen
1981 After Baba's Funeral and Sweet & Sour Pickles by Ted Galay
1982 Rexy! by Allan Stratton
1983 Back To Beulah by W O Mitchell
1984 Granite Point by W D Valgardson
1985 Gone The Burning Sun by Ken Mitchell
1986 Salt-Water Moon by David French
1987 Farther West by John Murrell
1988 Rock and Roll by John Gray
1989 Nothing Sacred by George F Walker
1990 Bordertown Cafe by Kelly Rebar

Fiction
1980 No award
1981 Voices in Time by Hugh MacLennan
1982 Obasan by Joy Kogawa
1983 Shoeless Joe by W P Kinsella
1984 Willie: A Romance by Heather Robertson
1985 Not Wanted On the Voyage by Timothy Findley
1986 What's Bred in the Bone by Robertson Davies
1987 No award
1988 The Color of Blood by Brian Moore
1989 The Victory of Geraldine Gull by Joan Clark
1990 Running West by James Houston

Non-fiction
1980 A Bloody War by Hal Lawrence
1981 The Invasion of Canada - 1812-13 by Pierre Berton
1982 The Young Vincent Massey by Claude T Bissell
1983 Grits by Christina McCall-Newman
1984 The Ghost Walker by R D Lawrence
1985 The Private Capital by Sandra Gwyn
1986 Company of Adventurers by Peter C Newman
1987 Meeting of Generals by Tony Foster

1988 My Father's House by Sylvia Fraser
1989 Caves in the Desert by George Woodcock
1990 Shadow of Heaven by John English

MELVILLE CANE AWARD
Poetry Society of America, 15 Gramercy Park,
New York, NY 10003, USA
For a published book on poetry (in even-numbered years) alternating (in odd-numbered years) with a book of poems published within the award year. Annual award $500.
Contact: Elise Paschen, Director
1980 Selected Poems by Richard Hugo
1981 The Poet's Calling in the English Ode by Paul Fry
1982 The Red Coal by Gerald Stern
1983 Robert Lowell by Ian Hamilton
1984 New and Collected Poems by Alan Dugan
1985 Kenneth Patchen and American Mysticism by Raymond Nelson
1986 Triumph of Achilles by Louis Gluck
1987 Visions and Revisions of American Poetry by Lewis Turco

CARNEGIE MEDAL
The Library Association, 7 Ridgmount St
London WC1E 7AE, England
Carnegie Medal is awarded annually for an outstanding book for children written in English and receiving its first publication in the United Kingdom during the preceding year.
1980 City of Gold by Peter Dickinson
1981 The Scarecrows by Robert Westall
1982 The Haunting by Margaret Mahy
1983 Handles by Jan Mark
1984 The Changeover by Margaret Mahy
1985 Storm by Kevin Crossley-Holland
1986 Granny was a Buffer Girl by Berlie Doherty
1987 The Ghost Drum by Susan Price
1988 A Pack of Lies by Geraldine McCaughrean
1989 Goggle-eyes by Anne Fine

CHOLMONDELEY AWARD FOR POETS
Society of Authors, 84 Drayton Gardens,
London SW10 9SB, England
The non-competitive award is for work generally, not for a specific book and submissions are not required. Annual prize of £6000.00
1980 George Barker
     Terence Tiller
     Roy Fuller
1981 Roy Fisher
     Robert Garioch
     Charles Boyle
1982 Basil Bunting
     Herbert Lomas
     William Scammell
1983 John Fuller
     Craig Raine
     Anthony Thwaite
1984 Michael Baldwin
     Michael Hoffmann
     Carol Rumens
1985 Dannie Abse
     Peter Redgrove
     Brian Taylor
1986 Lawrence Durrell
     James Fenton
     Selima Hill
1987 Wendy Cope
     Matthew Sweeney

     George Szirtes
1988 John Heath-Stubbs
     Sean O'Brien
     John Whitworth
1989 Peter Didsbury
     Douglas Dunn
     E J Scovell
1990 Kingsley Amis
     Elaine Feinstein
     Michael O'Neill
1991 James Berry
     Sujata Bhatt
     Michael Hulse
     Derek Mahon
1992 Allen Curnow
     Donald Davie
     Carol Ann Duffy
     Roger Woddis

ARTHUR C CLARKE AWARD
95 Finchley Lane,
London NW4 1BY, England
Prize is given to best science fiction novel of the year. Annual prize of £1000.00
Contact: Maxim Jakubowski, Chairman
1986 The Handmaid's Tale by Margaret Atwood
1987 The Sea and Summer by George Turner
1988 Unquenchable Fire by Rachel Pollock

THE COMMONWEALTH POETRY PRIZE AWARD
Commonwealth Institute, Kensington High Street,
London W8 6NQ, England
Awarded annually and open to all published Commonwealth (including UK) poets, in any officially recognized Commonwealth national language, if accompanied by English translation.
Contact: Rebecca Jewell
1980 Crossing the Peninsula by Shirley Lim
1981 The Silent Piano by Philip Salom
1982 Readings from Ecclesiases by Peter Goldsworthy
1983 I is a Long Memoried Woman by Grace Nichols
1984 Slave Song by David Dadydegn
1987 The Eye of the Earth by Niyi Osundare
     Holiday Girls by Vicki Raymond
     The Golden Gate by Vikram Seth
1988 Allen Curnow

COMMONWEALTH WRITERS' PRIZE
Commonwealth Foundation, Marlborough House,
Pall Mall, London SW1Y 5HY, England
Prize is awarded annually for a work of fiction, novel or collection of short stories - written in English by a citizen of the commonwealth and published in the preceding year. Sponsored by the Commonwealth Foundation. Prize of £10,000.00 for best book, £1,000.00 for best first published book, eight regional prizes of £500.00
Contact: Sandra Vince, Publicity Assistant
1987 Summer Lightning and Other Stories by Olive Senior
1988 Heroes by Festus Iyayi

THOMAS COOK TRAVEL BOOK AWARDS
The Thomas Cook Group, 45 Berkeley Street
London W1A 1EB, England
Three Awards for best travel book, best guide book and best illustrated travel book, published in the

current year. Annual Awards of £7,500 - best travel book, £2,500 - best guide book, and £1,000 - best illustrated travel book.

Travel
1980 Tracks by Robyn Davidson
1981 Old Glory by Jonathan Raban
1982 The Sindbad Voyage by Tim Severin
1983 From Heaven Lake by Vikram Seth
1984 To The Frontier by Geoffrey Moorhouse
1985 So Far From God by Patrick Marnham
1986/87 Between the Woods and the Water by Patrick Leigh Fermor
1988 Behind the Wall by Colin Thubron
1989 Riding the Iron Rooster by Paul Theroux
1990 Our Grandmothers' Drums by Mark Hudson

Guide
1980 The 1980 South American Handbook by John Brooks (ed)
1981 China Companion by Evelyn Garside
1982 India by G Crowther, Pa Raj, T Wheeler
1983 Companion Guide to New York by Michael Leapman
1984 Cruising French Waterways by Hugh McKnight
1985 Shell Guide to Nottinghamshire by Henry Thorold
1986/87 Fontana/Hatchette Guide to France 1986
1988 The Tibet Guide by Stephen Batchelor
1989 Landscapes of Madeira by John and Pat Underwood
1990 Blue Guide Turkey by Bernard McDonagh

Illustrated Guide
1988 Languedoc by Charlie Waite/James Bentley
1989 The Marco Polo Expedition by Richard B Fisher and Tom Ang
1990 What the Traveller Saw by Eric Newby

CRIME WRITERS' ASSOCIATION
CWA GOLD DAGGER
PO Box 172, Tring,
Herts HP23 5LP, England
Best crime novel of the year nominations by publishers only. Annual prize of Gold plated dagger and cheque (amount varies).
1980 The Murder of the Maharajah by H R F Keating
1981 Gorky Park by Martin Cruz Smith
1982 The False Inspector Dew by Peter Lovesey
1983 Accidental Crimes by John Hutton
1984 The Twelfth Juror by B M Gill
1985 Monkey Puzzle by Paula Gosling
1986 Live Flesh by Ruth Rendell
1987 A Fatal Inversion by Barbara Vine (Ruth Rendell)
1988 Ratking by Michael Dibdin
1989 The Wench is Dead by Colin Dexter
1990 Bones and Silence by Reginald Hill

CWA - CARTIER DIAMOND DAGGER
PO Box 172, Tring,
Herts HP23 5LP, England
Prize is awarded by Chairman and Committee for outstanding contribution to the genre. Annual prize of Diamond Dagger
1986 Eric Ambler
1987 P D James
1988 John le Carré
1989 Dick Francis
1990 Julian Symons
1991 Ruth Rendell

1992 Lesley Charteris
1993 Edith Pargeter

CWA JOHN CREASEY MEMORIAL AWARD
PO Box 172, Tring,
Herts HP23 5LP, England
Presented for the best crime novel by a previously unpublished author, this is in the form of an engraved magnifying glass, together with a bursary of £750 sponsored by Chivers Press.
Contact: The Secretary, Crime Writers' Association
1980 Dupe by Liza Cody
1981 The Ludi Victor by James Leigh
1982 Caroline Miniscule by Andrew Taylor
1983 The Ariadne Clue by Carol Clemeau
The Night the Gods Smiled by Eric Wright
1984 A Very Private Enterprise by Elizabeth Ironside
1985 The Latimer Mercy by Robert Richardson
1986 Tinplate by Neville Steed
1987 Dark Apostle by Denis Kilcommons
1988 Death's Bright Angel by Janet Neel
1989 A Real Shot in the Arm by Annette Roome
1990 Postmortem by Patricia Daniels Cornwell

DANISH ACADEMY PRIZE FOR LITERATURE
Rungstedlund, 109 Rungsted Strandvej,
DK-2960 Rungsted Kyst, Denmark
Prize is awarded bi-annually for an outstanding work of literature. Prize of DKr 100,000 awarded
Contact: Alan Philip
1980 Henrik Nordbrandt
1981 Dorrit Willumsen
1982 Per Højholt
1984 Jess Ornsbo
1986 Henrik Stangerup
1988 Halfdan Rasmussen
1990 Jens Smærup Sørensen

THE DUFF COOPER MEMORIAL PRIZE
24 Blomfield Road, London W9 1AD, England
Prize is awarded annually in memory of Alfred Duff Cooper, 1st Viscount Norwich (1890-1954). It consists of a specially bound and inscribed copy of his autobiography, Old Men Forget, together with a small cheque representing the interest on the money subscribed for the purpose by his friends after his death.
Contact: The Secretary
1980 Tennyson: The Unquiet Heart by Robert Bernard Martin
1981 Edith Sitwell: A Unicorn Among Lions by Victoria Glendinning
1982 James Joyce by Richard Ellmann
1983 Collected Poems by Peter Porter
1984 Ivy Compton-Burnett by Hilary Spurling
1985 Edmund Goose: A Literary Landscape by Ann Thwaite
1986 C R Ashbee: Architect, Designer and Romantic Socialist by Alan Crawford
1987 The Fatal Shore: History of the Transportation of Convicts to Australia, 1787-1868 by Robert Hughes
1988 Serious Character: Life of Ezra Pound by Humphrey Carpenter

THE ENCORE AWARD
The Society of Authors, 84 Drayton Gardens
London SW10 9SB
The Prize is awarded for a second published novel.
1990 A Lesser Dependency by Peter Benson

Calm At Sunset, Calm At Dawn by Paul Watkins
1991 Richard's Feet by Carey Harrison
1992 Downriver by Iain Sinclair

THE ENGLISH ACADEMY OF SOUTHERN AFRICA
PO Box 124, Witwatersrand 2050
South Africa
Thomas Pringle Awards
1985 Robert Greig
Karen Learmont-Batley
Patrick Cullinan
1986 Gus Silber
Jan Gorek
Njabulo Ndebele
1987 David Williams
Lionel Abrahams
Mark Swift
1988 John M Coetzee
Rosie Zwi
1989 Stephen Gray
Binkie Marwick
Douglas Livingstone
1990 Dorothy Driver
Patrick Cullinan
1991 Charlotte Bauer
Gregory Cunningham
Tatumkulu Afrika

Olive Schreiner Prize
1985 A State of Fear by Menan du Plessis
1986 Journal of a New Man by Lionel Abrahams
1987 No award
1988 The Arrowing of the Cane by John Conyngham
1989 Blood of Our Silence by Kelwyn Sole
1990 A Snake in the Garden by Norman Coombe
1991 Missing Persons by Ivan Vladislavic

THE GEOFFREY FABER MEMORIAL PRIZE
Faber and Faber Ltd, 3 Queen Square,
London WC1N 3AU, England
Awarded annually, alternate years prose and fiction. Given to a volume of verse or prose fiction first published originally in UK during 2 years preceding year of award. Eligible writers must be under 40 at time of publication, citizen of UK, Ireland, Commonwealth, or South Africa.
Contact: Sarah Gleadell/Belinda Matthews
1980 The Slant Door by George Szirtes
Love Life by Hugo Williams
1981 Waiting for the Barbarians by J M Coetzee
1982 Why Brownlee Left by Paul Muldoon
The Strange Museum by Tom Paulin
1983 Shuttlecock by Graham Swift
1984 In Memory of War by James Fenton
1985 Flaubert's Parrot by Julian Barnes
1986 A Quiet Gathering by David Scott
1987 Man Descending by Guy Vanderhaeghe
1988 Agrimony by Michael Hofmann
1989 Sea Music by David Profumo
1990 Shibboleth by Michael Donaghy

ELEANOR FARJEON AWARD
Children's Book Circle
c/o The Children's Book Foundation Book Trust
Book House, 45 East Hill, London SW18 2QZ
Prize awarded for distinguished service to children's books both in the UK and overseas.
1992 Stephnie Nettell

FAWCETT SOCIETY BOOKPRIZE
40-46 Harleyford Road,
London SE11 5AY, England
Prize is given to a fiction, non-fiction book in alternate years. Must offer enlightenment on women's position. Must have first been published in Britain, Commonwealth, Ireland. Annual prize of £500.00
Contact: Charlotte Burt/Julia Hubble
1982 Women, Power and Politics by Margaret Stacey and Marion Price
1983 Union Street by Pat Barker
Beka Lamb by Zee Edgell
1984 The Tidy House by Caroline Steedman
1985 Here Today by Zoe Fairbairns
1986 Monuments and Maidens by Marina Warner
1987 Redhill Rococo by Sheena MacKay
1988 Iron Ladies: Why Do Women Vote Tory by Beatrix Campbell
1989 Boy Blue by Stevie Davies
1990 The Long Road to Greenham by Jill Liddington

FELLOWSHIP OF THE ACADEMY OF AMERICAN POETS
177 East 87th Street,
NY 10128, USA
1980 Mona Van Duyn
1981 Richard Hugo
1982 John Ashbery
1983 Philip Booth
James Schuyler
1984 Robert Francis
Richmond Lattimore
1985 Amy Clampitt
Maxine Kumin
1986 Irving Feldman
Josephine Jacobsen
Howard Moss
1987 Alfred Corn
Josephine Jacobsen
1988 Donald Justice

THE KATHLEEN FIDLER AWARD
Book Trust Scotland, 15A Lynedoch St,
Glasgow G3 6EF, England
A novel of not less than 20,000 words for children aged 8-12. Author must not have had a novel published previously for this age group. Entries typewritten, double-spaced on one side of paper. Annual prize of £1000.00, entry published by Blackies Children's Books and a trophy - to be held for one year.
Contact: Dr Anne Smith, Chief Executive

FORWARD POETRY PRIZE
Book Trust, Book House
45 East Hill, London SW18 2QZ
First year of this award which is given for the best poem in English by a citizen of the UK or the Republic of Ireland.
1992 Thom Gunn
Simon Armitage (runner up)
Jackie Kay (runner up)

GLAXO PRIZES FOR MEDICAL WRITING AND ILLUSTRATION
The Society of Authors, Medical Writers Group
84 Drayton Gardens, London SW18 2QZ
Awards given annually for the categories medical textook and medical illustrated book.

Textbook

1989 Malaria: Principles and Practice of Malariology by W H Werndorfer and Sir I McGregor

1990 Immunology by Jan Klein

1991 Sports Injuries by Michael Hutson

Illustrated Book

1989 An Atlas of Clinical Nuclear Medicine by Ignac Fogelman and Michael Maisey

1990 Atlas of Serous Fluid Cytopathology by A I Spriggs and M M Boddington

1991 MRI Atlas of the Spine by Kenneth R Maravilla and Wendy A Cohen
Clinical Atlas of the Kidney by A William Asscher, David B Moffat and Eric Sanders

GOODMAN FIELDER WATTIE BOOK AWARD

PO Box 44-146, Auckland 2, New Zealand
Book published in New Zealand in the previous year by a New Zealand author (includes New Zealand residents and Pacific Island countries). Annual - 1st prize of NZ $20,000, 2nd prize of NZ $10,000, 3rd prize of NZ $5,000, Food Industry Book Award NZ $6,000
Contact: Gerard Reid

1980 Leaves of the Banyan Tree by Albert Wendt
New Zealand Adrift by Dr Graeme Stevens
Indirections by Charles Brasch

1981 Eruera by Eruera Stirling and Anne Salmond
Te Rauparaha by Patricia Burns
The Lovelock Version by Maurice Shadbolt

1982 Craft New Zealand by Doreen Blumhardt and Brian Brake Reeds
Other Halves by Sue McCauley
The South Island of New Zealand from the Road by Robin Morrison and Alister Taylor

1983 To the Is-Land by Janet Frame
Eagle's Trees & Shrubs of New Zealand - 2nd Series by Audrey Eagle
Historic Buildings of New Zealand: South Island

1984 Maori: A Photographic & Social History by Michael King
The New Zealand House by Michael Fowler
An Angel at My Table by Janet Frame

1985 The Envoy from Mirror City by Janet Frame
Bread & Roses Sonja Davies
The Natural World of the Maori by Margaret Orbell

1986 The Matriarch by Witi Ihimaera
From the Cradle to the Grave by Barry Gustafson
Potiki by Patricia Grace
Te Kaihau/The Windeater by Keri Hulme

1987 Season of the Jew by Maurice Shadbolt
Head and Shoulders by Virginia Myers
Nga Morehu: The Survivors by Judith Binney and Gillian Chaplin

1988 The Treaty of Waitangi by Claudia Orange
Oracles & Miracles by Stevan Eldred-Grigg
A Man's Country by Jock Phillips

1989 Sylvia by Lynley Hood
Wines & Vineyards of New Zealand by Michael Cooper
The Unfortunate Experiment by Sandra Coney

1990 Moriori by Michael King
Hanly: A New Zealand Artist by Russell Haley
The Forest Carpet by Bill & Nancy Malcolm

GOVERNOR GENERAL'S LITERARY AWARDS

Writing and Publishing Section, The Canada Council
99 Metcalfe Street, PO Box 1047
Ottawa, Ontario K1P 5V8, Canada
Awarded to Canadian authors of the best books in the English & French languages, in six categories: poetry, drama, fiction, nonfiction, translation & children's literature (text & illustration). Annual prize of $10,000
Contact: Gwen Hoover

Fiction

1980 Burning Water by George Bowering

1981 Home Truths: Selected Canadian Stories by Mavis Gallant

1982 Man Descending by Guy Vanderhaeghe

1983 Shakespeare's Dog by Leon Rooke

1984 The Engineer of Human Souls by Josef Skvorecky

1985 The Handmaid's Tale by Margaret Atwood

1986 The Progress of Love by Alice Munro

1987 A Dream Like Mine by M T Kelly

1988 Nights Below Station Street by David Adams Richards

1989 Whale Music by Paul Quarrington

1990 Lives of the Saints by Nino Ricci

1991 Such a Long Journey by Rohinton Mistry

Poetry

1980 McAlmon's Chinese Opera by Stephen Scobie

1981 The Collected Poems of F R Scott by F R Scott

1982 The Vision Tree: Selected Poems by Phyllis Webb

1983 Settlements by David Donnell

1984 Celestial Navigation by Paulette Jiles

1985 Waiting for Saskatchewan by Fred Wah

1986 The Collected Poems of Al Purdy by Al Purdy

1987 Afterworlds by Gwendolyn MacEwen

1988 Furious by Erin Mouré

1989 The Word for Sand by Heather Spears

1990 No Time by Margaret Avison

1991 Night Field by Don McKay

Drama

1980 McAlmon's Chinese Opera by Stephen Scobie

1981 Blood Relations by Sharon Pollock

1982 Billy Bishop Goes To War by John Gray

1983 Quiet in the Land by Anne Chislett

1984 White Biting Dog by Judith Thompson

1985 Criminals in Love by George F Walker

1986 Doc by Sharon Pollock

1987 Prague by John Krizanc

1988 Nothing Sacred by George F Walker

1989 The Other Side of the Dark by Judith Thompson

1990 Goodnight Desdemona (Good Morning Juliet) by Ann-Marie MacDonald

1991 Amigo's Blue Guitar by Joan MacLeod

Non-fiction

1980 Discipline of Power: The Conservative Interlude and the Liberal Restoration by Jeffrey Simpson

1981 Caribou and the Barren-lands by George Calef

1982 Louisbourg Portraits: Life in an Eighteenth-Century Garrison Town by Christopher Moore

1983 Byng of Vimy: General and Governor General by Jeffery Williams
1984 The Private Capital: Ambition and Love in the Age of Macdonald and Laurier by Sandra Gwyn
1985 The Regenerators: Social Criticism in Late Victorian English Canada by Ramsay Cook
1986 Northrop Frye on Shakespeare by Northrop Frye
1987 The Russian Album by Michael Ignatieff
1988 In the Sleep Room by Anne Collins
1989 Willie: The Life of W Somerset Maugham
1990 Trudeau and Our Times by Stephen Clarkson and Christina McCall
1991 Occupied Canada: A Young White Man Discovers His Unsuspected Past by Robert Hunter and Robert Calihoo

Children's Literature
1980 Petrouchka by Elizabeth Cleaver
Hebert Luee by Bertrand Gauthier
The Trouble with Princesses by Christie Harris
Les Gens de mon pays by Miyuki Tanobe
1981 The Gardian of Isis by Monica Hughes
Nos amis robots by Suzanne Martel
Les Papinachois by Joanne Ouellet
Ytek and the Arctic Orchid by Heather Woodall
1982 Fabien 1 and Fabien 2 by Ginette Anfousse
Hunter in the Dark by Monica Hughes
Agnes et le singulier bestiaire by Darcia Labrosse
ABC, 123, The Canadian Alphabet and Counting Book by Vlasta Van Kampen
1983 Petit Ours by Philippe Beha
Hockeyeurs cybernetiques by Denis Cote
Hans Christian Andersen's The Little Mermaid re-told by Margaret Crawford Maloney by Laszlo Gal
The Ghost of the Mounties by Sean O'Huigin
1984 Drole D'ecole by Marie-Louise Gay
Lizzy's Lion by Marie-Louise Gay
Sweetgrass by Jan Hudson
Le Cercle violet by Daniel Sernine
1985 Murdo's Story: A Legend from Northern Manitoba by Terry Gallagher
L'Alphabet by Roger Pare
Casse-tete chinois by Robert Soulieres
Julie by Cora Taylor
1986 Shadow in Hawthorn Bay by Janet Lunn
Le Dernier des raisins by Raymond Plante
Album de famille by Stephane Poulin
Have You Seen Birds by Barbara Reid
1987 Rainy Day Magic by Marie-Louise Gay
Venir au Monde by Darcia Labrosse
Gallahad Schwartz and the Cockroach Army by Morgan Nyberg
Le Don by David Schinkel and Yves Beauchesne
1988 Amos's Sweater by Kim LeFave
The Third Magic by Welwyn Wilton Katz
Le Jeux de Pic-mots by Phillippe Beha
Cassiopee ou L'Ete polonais by Michele Marineau
1989 The Magic Paintbrush by Robin Miller
Bad Boy by Diana Weiler
Benjamin et la saga des oreillers by Stephane Poulin
Temps mort by Charles Montpetit
1990 The Orphan Boy by Paul Morin

Redwork by Michael Bedard
Les Fantaisies de l'Oncle Henri by Pierre Pratt
Le Vraie Histoire du Chien de Clara Vic by Christiane Duchesne
1991 Doctor Kiss Says Yes by Joanne Fitzgerald
Pick-Up Sticks by Sarah Ellis
Un Champion by Sheldon Cohen
Deux Heures et Demi avant Jasmine

GRAND MASTER AWARD
Science Fiction Writers of America
PO Box 4236, West Columbia
SC 29171, USA
1984 Andre Norton
1986 Arthur C Clarke
1987 Isaac Asimov
1988 Alfred Bester

ERIC GREGORY TRUST FUND AWARD
The Society of Authors
84 Drayton Gardens, London SW10 9SB
For poets aged under 30 who are likely to benefit from more time given to writing.
1986 Mick North
Lachlan Mackinnon
Oliver Reynolds
Stephen Romer
1987 Peter McDonald
Maura Dooley
Stephen Knight
Steve Anthony
Jill Maughan
Paul Munden
1988 Michael Symmons Robert
Gwyneth Lewis
Adrian Blackledge
Simon Armitage
Robert Crawford
1989 Gerard Woodward
David Morley
Katrina Porteus
Paul Henry
1990 Nicholas Drake
Maggie Hannon
William Park
Jonathan Davidson
Lavinia Greenlaw
Don Paterson
John Wells
1991 Roddy Lumsden
Glyn Maxwell
Stephen Smith
Wayne Burrows
Jackie Kay
1992 Jill Dawson
Hugh Dunkerly
Christopher Greenhalgh
Marita Maddah
Stuart Paterson
Stuart Pickford

GUARDIAN CHILDREN'S FICTION AWARD
24 Weymouth St, London W1N 3FA, England
Work of fiction by a Commonwealth or British Author, published in Britain in previous year, excluding picture books and previous winners.
Annual prize of £500.00
Contact: Stephanie Nettell
1980 The Vandal by Ann Schlee
1981 The Sentinels by Peter Carter

1982 Goodnight Mister Tom by Michelle Magorian
1983 The Village by the Sea by Anita Desai
1984 The Sheep-Pig by Dick King-Smith
1985 What Is the Truth? by Ted Hughes
1986 Henry's Leg by Ann Pilling
1987 The True Story of Spit MacPhee by James Aldridge
1988 The Runaways by Ruth Thomas
1989 A Pack of Lies by Geraldine McCaughrean
1990 Goggle-eyes by Anne Fine

ERNEST HEMINGWAY FOUNDATION AWARD

PEN American Center, 568 Broadway
New York, NY 10012, USA
Prize is awarded for a distinguished first published book of fiction by an American author. Annual prize of $7500
Contact: John Morrone
1980 Mom Kills Kids and Self by Alan Saperstein
1981 Household Words by Joan Silber
1982 Housekeeping by Marilynne Robinson
1983 Shiloh and Other Stories by Bobbie Ann Mason
1984 During the Reign of the Queen of Persia by Joan Chase
1985 Dreams of Sleep by Josephine Humphreys
1986 Lady's Time by Alan V Hewat
1987 Tongues of Flame by Mary Ward Brown
1988 Imagining Argentina by Lawrence Thornton
1989 The Book of Ruth by Jane Hamilton

THE HAWTHORNDEN PRIZE

Hawthornden Castle, Lasswade
Midlothian E18 1EG, Scotland
For imaginative literature by a British subject under the age of 41 published during the previous year. Annual prize of £2000.00
1980 Arcadia by Christopher Reid
1981 St Kilda's Parliament by Douglas Dunn
1982 Sour Sweet by Timothy Mo
1983 Allegro Postillion by Jonathan Keats
1984-87 No awards
1988 Riding the Iron Rooster: by Train through China by Paul Theroux
1989 Talking Heads by Alan Bennett

DAVID HIGHAM PRIZE FOR FICTION

Book Trust, Book House,
45 East Hill, London SW18 2QZ, England
Award for first novel or book of short stories published in the UK in year of the award. Author must be citizen of Britain, Commonwealth, Republic of Ireland or South Africa. Annual prize of £1,000.00
Contact: Publicity Department
1980 Keep on Running by Ted Harriot
1981 A Separate Development by Christopher Hope
1982 Where I Used to Play on the Green by Glyn Hughes
1983 The Notebook of Gismondo Cavalletti by R M Lamming
1984 A Parish of Rich Women by James Buchan
1985 Family Myths and Legends by Patricia Ferguson
1986 Continent by Jim Crace
1987 The 13th House by Adam Zameenzad
1988 Life in the Palace by Carol Birch
1989 Motherland by Timothy O'Grady

1992 Halo by John Loveday

HISTORICAL NOVEL PRIZE IN MEMORY OF GEORGETTE HEYER

The Bodley Head, Random Century
20 Vauxhall Bridge Road, London SW1V 2SA, England
Awarded for full length previously unpublished historical novel set before 1939. Annual prize of £5000.00
Contact: Mrs J Black
1980 Children of Hachiman by Lynn Guest
1981 Zemindar by Valerie Fitzgerald
1982 No Prize Awarded
1983 Queen of the Lightning by Kathleen Herbert
1984 The Terioki Crossing by Alan Fisher
1985 Legacy by Susan Kay
1986 I Am England by Patricia Wright
1987 No Prize Awarded
1988 Trust and Treason by Margaret Birkhead
1989 A Fallen Land by Janet Broomfield

BOSTON GLOBE - HORN BOOK AWARD

Box 5378, Boston Globe, Boston
MA 02107-5378, USA
Prize is awarded for books published within the previous year. Three categories: fiction, non-fiction, and picture book. Annual prize of $500.00
Contact: Stephanie Loer
1980 Conrad's War by Andrew Davies
   Building: The Fight Against Gravity by Marion Salvador
   The Garden of Abdul Gasazi by Chris Van Allsburg
1981 The Leaving by Lynn Hall
   The Weaver's Gift by Kathryn Lasky
   Outside Over There by Maurice Sendak
1982 Playing Beatie Bow by Ruth Park
   Upon the Head of the Goat: A Childhood in Hungary 1939-1944 by Aranka Siegal
   A Visit to William Blake's Inn: Poems for Innocent and Experienced Travellers by Nancy Willard
1983 Sweet Whispers, Brother Rush by Virginia Hamilton
   Behind Barbed Wire: The Imprisonment of Japanese Americans During World War II by Daniel S Davis
   A Chair for My Mother by Vera B Williams
1984 A Little Fear by Patricia Wrightson
   The Double Life of Pochahontas by Jean Fritz
   Jonah and the Great Fish by Warwick Hutton
1985 The Moves Make the Man by Bruce Brooks
   Commodore Perry in the Land of the Shogun by Rhonda Blumberg
   Mama Don't Allow by Thacher Hurd
1986 In Summer Light by Zibby Oneal
   Auks, Rocks and the Odd Dinosaur: Tales from the Smithsonian's Museum of Natural History by Peggy Thomson
   The Paper Crane by Molly Bang
1987 Rabble Starkey by Lois Lowry
   The Pilgrims of Plimothi by Marcia Sewall
   Mufaro's Beautiful Daughters: An African Tale by John Steptoe

THE HUGO AWARDS

4705 Weddel St, Dearborn Heights,
MI 48125, USA
Established 1953 as Science Fiction Achievement

Awards for the best science fiction writing in several categories. Annual prize of chrome-plated rocket ship model.

Contact: Howard DeVore

Novels

1980 The Fountains of Paradise by Arthur C Clarke
1981 The Snow Queen by Joan D Vinge
1982 Downbelow Station by C J Cherryh
1983 Foundation's Edge by Isaac Asimov
1984 Startide Rising by David Brin
1985 Neuromancer by William Gibson
1986 Ender's Game by Orson Scott Card
1987 Speaker for the Dead by Orson Scott Card

Novella

1980 Enemy Mine by Barry B Longyear
1981 Lost Dorsai by Gordon R Dickson
1982 The Saturn Game by Paul Anderson
1983 Souls by Joanna Russ
1984 Cascade Point by Timothy Zahn
1985 Press Enter by John Varley
1986 Twenty-four Views of Mount Fuji by Hokusai by Roger Zelazny
1987 Gilgamesh in the Outback by Robert Silverberg

Novelette

1980 Sandkings by George R R Martin
1981 The Cloak and the Staff by Gordon R Dickson
1982 Unicorn Variation by Roger Zelazny
1983 Fire Watch by Connie Willis
1984 Blood Music by Greg Bear
1985 Bloodchild by Octavia Butler
1986 Paladin of the Lost Hour by Harlan Ellison
1987 Permafrost by Roger Zelazny

Short Story

1980 The Way of Cross and Dragon by George R R Martin
1981 Grotto of the Dancing Deer by Clifford D Simak
1982 The Pusher by John Varley
1983 Melancholy Elephants by Spider Robinson
1984 Speech Sounds by Octavia Butler
1985 The Crystal Spheres by David Brin
1986 Fermi and Frost by Frederik Pohl
1987 Tangents by Greg Bear

Non-fiction book

1980 The Science Fiction Encyclopedia by Peter Nicholls (ed)
1981 Cosmos by Carl Sagan
1982 Danse Macabre by Stephen King
1983 Isaac Asimov: The Foundations of Science Fiction by James Gunn
1984 Encyclopedia of Science Fiction and Fantasy, vol III by Donald Tuck
1985 Wonder's Child: My Life in Science Fiction by Jack Williamson
1986 Science Made Stupid by Tom Weller
1987 Trillion Year Spree by Brian Aldiss with David Wingrove

ALICE HUNT BARTLETT PRIZE

The Poetry Society, 21 Earls Court Sq
London SW5 9DE, England
Established in 1966 and awarded annually. Prize is awarded for a published collection of poetry, not less than 20 poems or 400 lines. Special consideration is given to younger or newly emerging poets. Annual prize of L500.00
Prize last awarded in 1988. Subsequently funding for the prize has run out.

Contact: Awards Administrator

1980 Unhistorical Fragments by John Whitworth
1981 The Sorrow Garden by Thomas McCarthy
     Unplayed Music by Carol Rumens
1982 The Flower Master by Medbh McGuckian
1983 Watching for Dolphins by David Constantine
1984 Kisses for Mayakovsky by Alison Fell
     The Stubborn Forest by Paul Hyland
1985 The Humble Administrator's Garden by Vikram Seth
     The Visitor's Book by John Davies
1986 The Sea Skater by Helen Dunmore
1987 Brunizem by Sujata Bhatt

IAN ST JAMES AWARDS

c/o PO Box 1371
London W5 2PN
Presented to previously unpublished authors for fictional short stories of between 5-10,000 words.

1990 Mothering Sunday by Annie Hedley
     A Seeing Lesson by William Walker
     A Whore's Vengeance by Louise Doughty
1992 Black Sky at Night by Jeremy Cain

THE INDEPENDENT FOREIGN FICTION AWARD

The Independent
40 City Road, London EC1Y 2DB
Contact: Veronica Youlton
Prize awarded for full length novel or a collection of short stories, translated into English and published in the preceding year.

1991 Immortality by Milan Kundera (trans by Peter Kussi)
     Rain In The Wind by Saiich Maruya (trans by Dennis Keene)
1992 The Death of Napoleon by Simon Leys (trans by Patricia Clancy)

THE INGERSOLL PRIZES

T S Eliot Award for Creative Writing

Ingersoll Foundation, 934 N Main St
Rockford, IL 61103, USA
For works in literature, including fiction, drama, poetry, essays & literary criticism. Annual prize of $15000

Contact: Thomas J Fleming, Exec Secretary

1983 Jorge Luis Borges
1984 Anthony Powell
1985 Eugene Ionesco
1986 V S Naipaul
1987 Octavio Paz
1988 Walker Percy
1989 George Garrett
1991 Mario Vargas Llosa
1992 Muriel Spark

Richard M Weaver Award for Scholarly Letters

Ingersoll Foundation, 934 N Main St
Rockford, IL 61103, USA
For a lifetime of distinguished achievements in the humanities, including philosophy, history, ethics & social & political science. Annual award of $15,000.

Contact: Thomas J Fleming, Secretary

1983 James Burnham
1984 Russell Kirk
1985 Robert Nisbet
1986 Andrew Lytle
1987 Josef Pieper
1988 Edward Shils
1989 Edward O Wilson

1990 Forrest McDonald
1991 John Lukacs
1992 Walter Burkert

THE IRISH TIMES/AER LINGUS INTERNATIONAL FICTION PRIZE

The Administrator, Gerard Cavnagh
11-15 D'Olier Street, Dublin 2, Eire
Awards for the categories of fiction and poetry, written in English or Irish.
1992 Mating by Norman Rush

THE JERUSALEM PRIZE

Binyaney Ha'ooma, POB 6001
Jerusalem 91060, Israel
The prestigious prize is awarded to a writer whose work expresses the idea of "the freedom of the individual in society". Prize of US $5,000 every two years
Contact: Zev Birger, Chairman & Managing Director
1981 Graham Greene
1983 V S Naipaul
1985 Milan Kundera
1987 J M Coetzee

THE KALINGA PRIZE

UNESCO, 7 Place de Fontenoy
75700 Paris, France
Annual prize of £1000.00
Contact: The Assistant Director-General for Science
1980 Aristides Bastidas
1981 David F Attenborough
       Dennis Flanagan
1982 Oswaldo Frota-Pessoa
1983 Abdullah Al Muti Sharafuddin
1984 Yves Coppens
       Igor Petryanov
1985 Sir Peter Medawar
1986 Nikolai G Basov
       David Suzuki
1987 Marcel Roche
1988 Björn Kurtén
1989 Saad Ahmed Shabaan

LAMONT POETRY SELECTION

177 E 87 St, New York
NY 10128, USA
Supports the publication of an American poet's second volume of poetry. Publishers in the United States are invited to submit to the Academy manuscripts by American poets who have already published one book of poems in a standard edition.
Annual prize of $1,000.00
1980 More Trouble with the Obvious by Michael Van Walleghen
1981 The Country Between Us by Carolyn Forche
1982 Long Walks in the Afternoon by Margaret Gibson
1983 The Dead and the Living by Sharon Olds
1984 Deep Within the Ravine by Philip Schultz
1985 Victims of the Latest Dance Craze by Cornelius Eady
1986 The Minute Hand by Jane Shore
1987 The River of Heaven by Garret Kaoru Hongo

THE PETER I B LAVAN YOUNGER POET AWARDS

The Academy of American Poets, 177 East 87th Street
New York, NY 10128, USA

Awarded to three poets under forty annually. Poet must be American citizen and have published at least one full length collection of poetry. Annual prize of $1,000.00
1983 Edward Hirsch
       Brad Leithauser
       Gjertrud Schnackenberg
1984 Vicki Hearne
       Cleopatra Mathis
       Katha Pollitt
1985 Diane Ackerman
       Michael Blumenthal
       Richard Kenney
1986 Rita Dove
       Rodney Jones
       Timothy Steele
1987 Jon Davis
       Debora Greger
       Norman Williams
1988 Marie Howe
       Naomi Shihab Nye
       John Yau
1989 Jeffrey Harrison
       Melissa Green
       William Logan

GRACE LEVEN PRIZE FOR POETRY

c/o Perpetual Trustee Company Ltd, 39 Hunter Street
Sydney, NSW 2000, Australia
For recognition of the best volume of poetry published during the twelve months immediately preceding the year in which the award is made. Writers must be Australian-born and writing as Australians, or naturalised in Australia and resident in Australia for not less than ten years.
Annual prize of Australian $200
Contact: M J O'Donnell, Charitable Trusts Manager
1980 The Boys Who Stole the Funeral by Leslie Allan Murray
1981 Nero's Poems by Geoffrey Lehmann
1982 Tide Country by Vivian Smith
1983 Collected Poems by Peter Porter
1984 The Three Gates and Other Poems by Rosemary Dobson
1985 Selected Poems by Robert Gray
       The Amorous Cannibal by Chris Wallace-Crabbe
1986 Washing the Money by Ryhll McMaster
1987 Occasions of Birds and other Poems by Elizabeth Riddell
1988 Under Berlin by John Tranter
1989 A Tremendous World in Her Head: Selected Poems by Dorothy Hewett
1990 Dog Fox Field by Les A Murray
1991 The Empire of Grass by Gary Catalano
       Peniel by Doctor Kevin Hart

THE MCKITTERICK PRIZE

Society of Authors
84 Drayton Gardens, London SW10 9SB
Contact: Awards Secretary
Annual award for a work first published in the UK or previously unpublished. Open to writers over 40 who have had no previous work published other than that submitted.
1990 Chimera by Simon Mawer
1991 A Summer to Halo by John Loveday
1992 News From a Foreign Country Came by Alberto Manguel

THE MAIL ON SUNDAY JOHN LLEWELLYN RHYS PRIZE

Book Trust, Book House
45 East Hill, London SW18 2QZ, England
Awarded for a work - fiction, non-fiction, poetry or drama - by an author under 35 at time of publication. Books must have been published in the UK in year of award in English by a citizen of Britain or the Commonwealth. Sponsored by the Mail on Sunday. Annual prize of £5,000.00
Contact: Publicity Department
1980 The Diamonds at the Bottom of the Sea by Desmond Hogan
1981 The Laird of Abbotsford by A N Wilson
1982 An Ice-Cream War by William Boyd
1983 The Slow Train to Milan by Lisa St Aubin de Teran
1984 Dangerous Play by Andrew Motion
1985 Out of the Blue by John Milne
1986 Loving Roger by Tim Parks
1987 The Passion by Jeanette Winterson
1988 The March Fence by Matthew Yorke
1989 Sylvia Townsend Warner by Claire Harman

SOMERSET MAUGHAM AWARDS

Somerset Maugham Trust Fund, The Society of Authors
84 Drayton Gardens, London SW10 9SB, England
1980 Bomber Command by Max Hastings
Arcadia by Christopher Reid
The Inklings by Humphrey Carpenter
1981 Metroland by Julian Barnes
Hearts of Gold by Clive Sinclair
The Healing Art by A N Wilson
1982 A Good Man in Africa by William Boyd
Lantern Lecture by Adam Mars-Jones
1983 Keepers of the House by Lisa St Aubin de Teran
1984 The Last Testament of Oscar Wilde by Peter Ackroyd
The Polish Revolution: Solidarity by Timothy Garton Ash
The Indoor Park by Sean O'Brien
1985 Dark Glasses by Blake Morrison
By the Fisheries by Jeremy Reed
Her Living Image by Jane Rogers
1986 Family Myths and Legends by Patricia Ferguson
Frontiers by Adam Nicolson
Tongues of Flame by Tim Parks
1987 The Cormorant by Stephen Gregory
Isaac Campion by Janni Howker
The Lamberts by Andrew Motion
1988 The Land that Lost its Heroes by Jimmy Burns
Selling Manhattan by Carol Ann Duffy
Whore Banquets by Matthew Kneale
1989 Romantic Affinities by Rupert Christiansen
The Swimming Pool Library by Alan Hollinghurst
The Birds of the Innocent Wood by Deirdre Madden
1990 Our Grandmothers' Drums by Mark Hudson
The Automatic Man by Sam North
The Vision of Elena Silves by Nicholas Shakespeare
1991 The Other Occupant by Peter Benson
Honour Thy Father by Lesley Glaister
Four Bare Legs in a Bed by Helen Simpson
1992 But Beautiful by Geoff Dyer

Lempriere's Dictionary by Lawrence Norfolk
Householder by Gerard Woodward

THE MILNER AWARD

The Friends of the Atlanta Fulton Public Library, One Margaret Mitchell Square
Atlanta, GA 30303, USA
Award to a living American author of children's books. The winning author is awarded a specially commissioned work of the internationally famous glass sculptor, Hans Frabel, and a $1,000.00 honorarium.
1983 Judy Blume
1984 Peggy Parish
1985 Paula Danziger
1986 Barbara Park
1987 Lois Lowry
1988 Francine Pascal
1989 John Steptoe
1990 Louis Sachar

NATIONAL BOOK AWARDS

264 Fifth Ave, 4th Fl
New York, NY 10001, USA
Award given to living American authors for books published in the USA; one fiction & one non-fiction. Annual first prize of $10,000.00 and $1,000.00 for short-listed works
Contact: Barbara Prete, Director
1980 By Myself by Lauren Bacall
Max Perkins: Editor of Genius by A Scott Berg
A Gathering of Days: A New England Girl's Journal 1830-32 by Joan W Blos
The Complete Directory to Prime Network TV Shows by Tim Brooks and Earle Marsh
Stained Glass by William F Buckley Jr
Julia Child and More Company by Julia Child
And I Worked at the Writer's Trade by Malcolm Cowley
Mandelstam's The Complete Critical Prose and Letters by Jane Gary Harris and Constance Link
Godel, Escher, Bach: An Eternal Golden Braid by Douglas Hofstadter
The World According to Garp by John Irving
White House Years by Henry Kissinger
Bendigo Shafter by Louis L'Amour
A Swiftly Tilting Planet by Madeleine L'Engle
The Culture of Narcissism by Christopher Lasćh
Ashes by Philip Levine
The Green Ripper John D MacDonald
The Rise of Theodore Roosevelt by Edmund Morris
The Gnostic Gospels by Elaine Pagels
Jem by Frederick Pohl
Sophie's Choice by William Styron
A Distant Mirror: The Calamitous 14th Century by Barbara W Tuchman
A Severe Mercy by Sheldon Vanauken
The Book of the Dun Cow by Walter Wangerin
Birdy by William Wharton
The Right Stuff by Tom Wolfe
The Dancing Wu Li Masters: An Overview of the New Physics by Gary Zukav
1981 Sister Wolf by Ann Arensberg
Samuel Beckett by Diedre Bair

Christianity, Social Tolerance and Homosexuality by John Boswell
The Night Swimmers by Betsy Byars
Ramona and Her Mother by Beverly Cleary
The Panda's Thumb by Stephen Jay Gould
Oh, Boy! Babies! by Alison Cragin Herzig and Jane Lawrence Mali
China Men by Maxine Hong Kingston
The Last Cowboy by Jane Kramer
Been in the Storm so Long: Aftermath of Slavery by Leon F Litwack
Plains Song by Wright Morris
The Need to Hold Still by Lisel Mueller
The Medusa and the Snail by Lewis Thomas
Evening Edged in Gold by John E Woods

1982 A Penguin Year by Susan Bonners
Life Supports by William Bronk
In the Shade of Spring Leaves by Robert Lyons Danly
Dale Loves Sophie to Death by Robb Forman Dew
Lucy: The Beginnings of Humankind by Donald C Johanson and A Maitland Edey
The Soul of a New Machine by Tracy Kidder
Ten Thousand Leaves by Ian Hideo Levy
So Long, See You Tomorrow by William Maxwell
Mornings on Horseback by David McCullough
Naming Names by Victor Navasky
People of the Sacred Mountain: A History of the Northern Cheyenne Chief and Warrior Societies by Father Peter John Powell
Words by Heart by Ouida Sebestyen
Outside Over There by Maurice Sendak
Noah's Ark by Peter Spier
Walter Lippman and the American Century by Ronald Steel
Rabbit is Rich by John Updike
The Generation of 1914 by Robert Wohl
Taking the Quantum Leap: The New Physics for Nonscientists by Fred Alan Wolf

1983 Voices of Protest: Huey Long, Father Coughlin and The Great Depression by Alan Brinkley
China: Alive in the Bitter Sea by Fox Butterfield
Miss Rumphius by Barbara Cooney
The Mathematical Experience by Philipp P Davis
National Defense by James Fallows
A Place Apart by Paula Fox
Homesick by Jean Fritz
Chimney Sweeps by James Cross Giblin
The Red Magician by Lisa Goldstein
A House is a House for Me by Mary Ann Hoberman
Baudelaire's Les Fleurs du Mal by Richard Howard
Selected Poems by Galway Kinnell
Utopian Thought in the Western World by Frank E Manuel and P Fritzie Manuel
Nathaniel Hawthorne in His Time by James Mellow
The Women of Brewster Place by Gloria Naylor
"Subtle is the Lord...." The Science and the life of Albert Einstein by Abraham Pais
Doctor De Soto by William Steig
Marked By Fire by Joyce Carol Thomas

Isaak Dinesen by Judith Thurman
The Color Purple by Alice Walker
The Collected Stories by Eudora Welty
Country Music by Charles Wright

1984 Stones for Ibarra by Harriet Doerr
Victory Over Japan by Ellen Gilchrist
Andrew Jackson and the Course of American Democracy 1833-1845 Vol III by Robert V Remini

1985 White Noise by Don Delillo
Common Ground: A Turbulent Decade in the Lives of Three American Families by J Anthony Lukas
Easy in the Islands by Bob Shacochis

1986 Arctic Dreams by Barry Lopez
World's Fair by E L Doctorow

1987 Paco's Story by Larry Heinemann
The Making of the Atomic Bomb by Richard Rhodes

NATIONAL BOOK CRITICS CIRCLE AWARDS

756 S Tenth St
Philadelphia, PA 19147, USA
For excellence in biography/autobiography, criticism, fiction, general nonfiction & poetry published for the first time during the previous year by American writers. Annual scroll & citations
Contact: Alida Becker

1980 The Transit of Venus by Shirley Hazzard
Sunrise by Frederick Seidel
Walter Lippmann and the American Century by Ronald Steel
Part of Nature, Part of Us: Modern American Poets by Helen Vendler

1981 Rabbit is Rich by John Updike
A Coast of Trees by A R Ammons
The Mismeasure of Man by Stephan Jay Gould
A Virgil Thomson Reader by Virgil Thomson

1982 George Mills by Stanley Elkin
Antarctic Traveller by Katha Pollitt
The Path to Power: The Years of Lyndon Johnson by Robert A Caro
The Second American Revolution and Other Essays 1976-82 by Gore Vidal
12-volume edition of Byron's Letters and Journals by Leslie A Marchand

1983 Ironweed by William Kennedy
The Price of Power: Kissinger in the Nixon White House by Seymour M Hersh
Minor Characters by Joyce Johnson
The Changing Light at Sandover by James Merrill
Hugging the Shore: Essays and Criticism by John Updike

1984 Love Medicine by Louise Erdrich
Dostoevsky: The Years of Ordeal 1850-1859 by Joseph Frank
Twentieth Century Pleasures by Robert Hass
Weapons and Hope by Freeman Dyson
The Dead and the Living by Sharon Olds

1985 The Accidental Tourist by Anne Tyler
The Triumph of Achilles by Louise Gluck
Henry James: A Life by Leon Edel
Common Ground by J Anthony Lukas
Habitations of the Word by William Gass

1986 Tombee: Portrait of a Cotton Planter by Theodore Rosengarten
Less Than One: Selected Essays by Joseph Brodsky

Kate Vaiden by Reynolds Price

War Without Mercy: Race and Power in the Pacific War by John W Dower

Wild Gratitude by Edward Hirsch

1987 Chaucer: His Life, His Works, His World by Donald Howard

Dance Writings by Edwin Denby

The Making of the Atomic Bomb by Richard Rhodes

The Counterlife by Philip Roth

Flesh and Blood by C K Williams

NATIONAL POETRY COMPETITION

The Poetry Society

21 Earls Court Square, London SW5 9DE

Prizes awarded for an unpublished poem of less than 40 lines by anyone over the age of 16.

1985 Jo Shapcott

Ian Keenan

William Palmer

1986 Carole Satyamurti

Adam Thorpe

Bill Turner

1987 Ian Duhig

Michael Donaghy

Harry Smart

1988 Martin Reed

Ian Caws

Rodney Pybus

1989 William Scammell

Patricia Pogson

Glyn Maxwell

1990 Nicky Rice

Frances Wilson

Geoffrey Constable

1991 John Levett

Jo Shapcott

Don Paterson

NCR BOOK AWARD FOR NON-FICTION

NCR Limited, 206 Marylebone Road

London NW1 6LY, England

For originality of thought, quality of writing and the ability of the author to communicate the subject to a wide readership. Books must be written in English by writers who are citizens of the British Commonwealth or the Republic of Ireland. Annual prize of £25,000

Contact: Michael Fenton Webster

1988 Nairn: In Darkness and Light by David Thomson

Katherine Mansfield: A Secret Life by Claire Tomalin

The Korean War by Max Hastings

The Life of Kenneth Tynan by Kathleen Tynan

The Russian Album by Michael Ignatieff

Thy Hand, Great Anarch! by Nirad C Chaudhuri

1989 Touching the Void by Joe Simpson

A Brief History of Time From the Big Bang to Black Holes by Stephen W Hawking

A Touch of Genius: The Life of T E Lawrence by Malcolm Brown and Julia Cave

Tolstoy by A N Wilson

1990 Citizens: A Chronicle of the French Revolution by Simon Schama

The Godwins and the Shelleys - The Biography of a Family by William St Clair

C S Lewis - A Biography by A N Wilson

Pity the Nation - Lebanon at War by Robert Fisk

SFWA NEBULA AWARDS

PO Box 4335, Spartanburg

SC 29305-4335, USA

Publication during the previous calendar year, and nomination by SFWA President. Annual trophy

Contact: Peter Dennis Pautz

Grand Master

1984 Andre Norton

1986 Arthur C Clarke

1987 Isaac Asimov

1988 Alfred Bester

1989 Ray Bradbury

Novel

1980 The Fountains of Paradise by Arthur C Clarke

1981 Timescape by Gregory Benford

1982 The Claw of the Conciliator by Gene Wolfe

1983 No Enemy But Time by Michael Bishop

1984 Startide Rising by David Brin

1985 Neuromancer by William Gibson

1986 Ender's Game by Orson Scott Card

1987 Speaker for the Dead by Orson Scott Card

1988 The Falling Woman by Pat Murphy

1989 Falling Free by Lois McMaster Bujold

1990 The Healer's War by Elizabeth Ann Scarborough

Novelet

1980 Sandkings by George R R Martin

1981 The Ugly Chickens by Howard Waldrop

1982 The Quickening by Michael Bishop

1983 Fire Watch by Connie Willis

1984 Blood Music by Greg Bear

1985 Bloodchild by Octavia E Butler

1986 Portraits of His Children by George R R Martin

1987 The Girl Who Fell into the Sky by Kate Wilhelm

1988 Rachael in Love by Pat Murphy

1989 Schrodinger's Kitten by George Alec Effinger

Novelette

1990 At the Rialto by Connie Willis

Novella

1980 Enemy Mine by Barry Longyear

1981 The Unicorn Tapestry by Suzy McKee Charnas

1982 The Saturn Game by Poul Anderson

1983 Another Orphan by John Kessel

1984 Hardfought by Greg Bear

1985 Press Enter by John Varley

1986 Sailing to Byzantium by Robert Silverberg

1987 R&R by Lucius Shepard

1988 The Blind Geometer by Kim Stanley Robinson

1989 The Last of the Winnebagos by Connie Willis

1990 The Mountains of Mourning by Lois McMaster Bujold

Short Story

1980 Giants by Edward Bryant

1981 Grotto of the Dancing Deer by Clifford D Simak

1982 The Bone Flute by Lisa Tuttle (declined)

1983 A Letter From the Clearys by Connie Willis

1984 The Peacemaker by Gardner Dozois

1985 Morning Child by Gardner Dozois

1986 Out of All Them Bright Stars by Nancy Kress

1987 Tangents by Greg Bear

1988 Forever Yours, Anna by Kate Wilhelm

1989 Bible Stories for Adults, No 17: The Deluge by James Morrow
1990 Ripples in the Dirac Sea by Geoffrey A Landis

NEUSTADT INTERNATIONAL PRIZE FOR LITERATURE

World Literature Today, 110 Monnet Hall, University of Oklahoma
Norman, OK 73019-0375, USA
The prize honours distinguished and outstanding achievement in fiction, poetry, or drama written in any language. Awarded only to living writers, and at least a representative sampling of the writer's work must be available in English or French. Nominations are made only by members of the international jury and the prize is not open to application. Biennial, awarded in even-numbered years, US $25,000 plus an eagle's feather in silver and a special certificate.
Contact: Dr Ivar Ivask, Editor
1980 Josef Skvorecký
1982 Octavio Paz
1984 Paavo Haavikko
1986 Max Frisch
1988 Raja Rao
1990 Tomas Tranströmer

JOHN NEWBERY MEDAL

American Library Association, 50 E Huron St
Chicago, IL 60611, USA
To the author of the most distinguished contribution to American literature for children published during the preceding year. Annual award: bronze medal
Contact: Susan Roman, Executive Director
1980 A Gathering of Days by Joan W Blos
1981 Jacob Have I Loved by Katherine Paterson
1982 A Visit to William Blake's Inn: Poems for Innocent and Experienced Travellers by Nancy Willard
1983 Dicey's Song by Cynthia Voight
1984 Dear Mr Henshaw by Beverly Cleary
1985 Hero and the Crown by Robin McKinley
1986 Sarah, Plain and Tall by Patricia MacLachlan
1987 The Whipping Boy by Sid Fleischman
1988 Lincoln: A Photobiography by Russell Freedman

NEW ZEALAND BOOK AWARDS

Advisorcorp House, 131-135 Lambton Quay
Wellington, New Zealand
Contact: Rosemary Wildblood, Programme Manager
1988 Fiona Kidman
1989 Benzina by Cilla McQueen
    Tarawera by Ronald Keam
    The Carpathians by Janet Frame
    The Fold of the Land by Bridget Williams

NOBEL PRIZE FOR LITERATURE

Nobel Committee of the Swedish Academy, Börshuset
S-111 29 Stockholm, Sweden
Based on the principle of competence and universality, in the field of literature the most outstanding work of an idealistic tendency. Annual prize
1980 Czeslaw Milosz
1981 Elias Canetti
1982 Gabriel Garcia Marquez

1983 William Golding
1984 Jaroslav Seifert
1985 Claude Simon
1986 Wole Soyinka
1987 Joseph Brodsky
1988 Naguib Mahfouz
1989 Camilo José Cela
1990 Octavio Paz

EDGAR ALLAN POE AWARDS

236 West 27 Street, New York
NY 10001, USA
Best Novel
1980 Whip Hand by Dick Francis
1981 Peregrine by William Bayer
1982 Billingsgate Shoal by Rick Boyer
1983 La Brava by Elmore Leonard
1984 Briar Patch by Ross Thomas
1985 The Suspect by L R Wright
    The Day the Senior Class Got Married by Charles Purpura (Children's live action
1986 A Dark-Adapted Eye by Barbara Vine
1988 Old Bones by Aaron Elkins
1989 A Cold Red Sunrise by Stuart M Kaminsky
Grand Master
1980 Stanley Ellin
1981 Julian Symons
1982 Margaret Millar
1983 John Le Carre
1984 Dorothy Salisbury Davis
1985 Ed McBain
1986 Michael Gilbert
1987 Phyliss A Whitney
1988 Hillary Waugh

PRIJS DER NEDERLANDSE LETTEREN (PRIZE FOR DUTCH LITERATURE)

Nederlandse Taalunie, Stadhoudersplantsoen 2
2517 JL Den Haag, Nederland
A literary prize to celebrate the entire oeuvre of a particular literary writer who writes in the Dutch language in the categories prose, poetry, essays and/or drama. Prize of f 30.000 every three years
Contact: Oscar de Wandel, De Algemeen Secretaris
1980 Maurice Gilliams
1983 Lucebert
1986 Hugo Claus
1989 Gerrit Kouwenaar

PRIX GONCOURT

Academie Goncourt, c/o Drouant
Pl Gaillon, F-75006, Paris, France
1980 Le Jardin d'Acclimatation by Yves Navarre
1981 Anne Marie by Lucien Bodard
1982 Dans la Main de l'Ange by Dominique Fernandez
1983 Les Egares by Frederick Tristan
1984 L'Amant by Marguerite Duras
1985 Les Noces Barbares by Yann Queffelec
1986 Valet de Nuit by Michel Host
1987 La Nuit by Tahar Ben Jelloun

THE PULITZER PRIZES

702 Journalism, Columbia University
New York, NY 10027, USA
21 prizes in newspaper journalism, letters, music and drama - for some of the prizes entrants must be American citizen. Annual prize of $3,000
Contact: Robert C Christopher, Administrator
Fiction

1980 The Executioner's Song by Norman Mailer
1981 A Confederacy of Dunces by the late John Kennedy Toole
1982 Rabbit is Rich by John Updike
1983 The Color Purple by Alice Walker
1984 Ironweed by William Kennedy
1985 Foreign Affairs by Alison Lurie
1986 Lonesome Dove by Larry McMurtry
1987 A Summons to Memphis by Peter Taylor
1988 Beloved by Toni Morrison
1989 Breathing Lessons by Anne Tyler
1990 The Mambo Kings Play Songs of Love by Oscar Hijuelos
1991 Rabbit at Rest by John Updike
1992 A Thousand Acres by Jane Smiley

Drama
1980 Talley's Folly by Lanford Wilson
1981 Crimes of the Heat by Beth Henley
1982 A Soldier's Play by Charles Fuller
1983 Night, Mother by Marsha Norman
1984 Glengarry Glen Ross by David Mamet
1985 Sunday in the Park with George by James Lapine
1986 No award
1987 Fences by August Wilson
1988 Driving Miss Daisy by Alfred Uhry
1989 The Heidi Chronicles by Wendy Wasserstein
1990 The Piano Lesson by August Wilson
1991 Lost in Yonkers by Neil Simon
1992 The Kentucky Cycle by Robert Schenkkan

History
1980 Been in the Storm So Long by Leon F Litwack
1981 American Education: The National Experience, 1783-1876 by Lawrence A Cremin
1982 Mary Chesnut's Civil War by C Vann Woodward (editor)
1983 The Transformation of Virginia, 1740-1790 by Rhys L Isaac
1984 No award
1985 Prophets of Regulation by Thomas K McCraw
1986 ....The Heavens and the Earth: A Political History of the Space Age by Walter A McDougall
1987 Voyagers to the West: A Passage in the Peopling of America on the Eve of the Revolution by Bernard Bailyn
1988 The Launching of Modern American Science 1846-1876 by Robert V Bruce
1989 Parting the Waters: America in the King Years 1954-63 by Taylor Branch
     Battle Cry of Freedom: the Civil War Era by James M McPherson
1990 In Our Image: America's Empire in the Philippines by Stanley Karnow
1991 A Midwife's Tale: The Life of Martha Ballard, Based on Her Diary, 1785-1812 by Laurel Thatcher Urich
1992 The Fate of Liberty: Abraham Lincoln and Civil Rights by Mark E Neely Jr

Biography
1980 The Rise of Theodore Roosevelt by Edmund Morris
1981 Peter the Great: His LIfe and World by Robert K Massie
1982 Grant: A Biography by William S McFeely
1983 Growing Up by Russell Baker
1984 Booker T Washington: The Wizard of Tuskegee, 1901-1915 by Louis R Harlan

1985 The Life and Times of Cotton Mather by Kenneth Silverman
1986 Louise Bogan: A Portrait by Elizabeth Frank
1987 Bearing the Cross: Martin Luther King, Jr and the Southern Christian Leadership Conference by David J Garrow
1988 Look Homeward: A Life of Thomas Wolfe by David Herbert Donald
1989 Oscar Wilde by the late Richard Ellmann
1990 Machiavelli in Hell by Sebastian de Grazia
1991 Jackson Pollock: An American Saga by Steven Naifeh and Gregory White Smith
1992 Fortunate Son: The Healing of a Vietnam Vet by Lewis B Puller Jr

Poetry
1980 Selected Poems by Donald Justice
1981 The Morning of the Poem by James Schuyler
1982 The Collected Poems by the late Sylvia Plath
1983 Selected Poems by Galway Kinnell
1984 American Primitive by Mary Oliver
1985 Yin by Carolyn Kizer
1986 The Flying Change by Henry Taylor
1987 Thomas and Beulah by Rita Dove
1988 Partial Accounts: New and Selected Poems by William Meredith
1989 New and Collected Poems by Richard Wilbur
1990 The World Doesn't End by Charles Simic
1991 Near Changes by Mona Van Duyn
1992 Selected Poems by James Tate

General Non-fiction
1980 Gödel, Escher, Bach: an Eternal Golden Braid by Douglas R Hofstadter
1981 Fin-de-Siècle Vienna: Politics and Culture by Carl E Schorske
1982 The Soul of A New Machine by Tracy Kidder
1983 Is There No Place on Earth for Me by Susan Sheehan
1984 The Social Transformation of American Medicine by Paul Starr
1985 The Good War: An Oral History of World War Two by Stods Terkel
1986 Move Your Shadow: South Africa, Black and White by Joseph Lelyveld
     Common Ground: A Turbulent Decade in the Lives of Three American Families by J Anthony Lukas
1987 Arab and Jew: Wounded Spirits in a Promised Land by David K Shipler
1988 The Making of the Atomic Bomb by Richard Rhodes
1989 A Bright Shining Lie: John Paul Vann and America in Vietnam by Neil Sheehan
1990 And Their Children After Them by Dale Maharidge
1991 The Ants by Bert Holldobler and Edward O Wilson
1992 The Prize: The Epic Quest for Oil, Money and Power by Daniel Yergin

THE QUEEN'S PRESENTATION MEDALS - POETRY
Buckingham Palace, London, England
The Medal is given for a book of verse published in the English Language, but translations of exceptional merit may be considered. It was originally awarded only to British citizens but the scope was widened in 1985 to make Her Majesty's subjects in Commonwealth Monarchies eligible for consideration. Awarded Gold Medal
1981 Dennis Joseph Enwright

1985 Norman MacCaig
1988 Derek Walcott
1989 Allen Curnow
1990 Sorley Maclean

THE ROMANTIC NOVELISTS' ASSOCIATION
20 First Avenue, Amersham
Bucks HP7 9BJ, England
Prize of £5,000.00
Contact: Dorothy Entwistle, Secretary
1982 Zemindar by Valerie Fitzgerald
      Flint and Roses by Brenda Jagger
      The Unreasoning Earth by Jean Chapman
      A Countess Below Stairs by Eva Ibbotson
      Emma Sparrow by Marie Joseph
      Mango Walk by Rhona Martin
      The Black Mountains by Janet Tanner
      The Avonhurst Inheritance by Sylvia Thorpe
1983 Magic Flutes by Eva Ibbotson
      Gemini Girls by Marie Joseph
      Antigua Kiss by Anne Weale
      Celebration by Rosie Thomas
      Rose Domino by Sheila Walsh
      The Ravensley Touch by Constance Heaven
1984 A Highly Respectable Marriage
      Margaret Normanby by Josephine Edgar
      Copper Kingdom by Iris Gower
      A London Season by Anthea Bell
      A Heritage of Shadows by Madeleine Brent
      The Silver Falcon by Sarah Hylton
      The Listening Silence by Marie Joseph
1985 Sunrise by Rosie Thomas
      A Winter's Child by Brenda Jagger
      Silk for a Lady by Rosina Pyatt
      A Fragile Peace by Teresa Crane
      The Merry Maid by Mollie Hardwick
      What the Heart Keeps by Rosalind Laker
      At the Going Down of the Sun by Elizabeth Darrell
1986 A Song Twice Over by Brenda Jagger
      Kessie by Joyce Marlow
      This Side of Christmas by Louise Elliott
      Company of Swans by Eva Ibbotson
      Here I Stay by Barbara Michaels
      Silver Shadows, Golden Dreams by Margaret Pemberton
      Rachael and the Viscount by Alanna Wilson
1987 A Better World Than This by Marie Joseph
      Just You Wait and See by Stan Barstow
      And in the Morning by Elizabeth Darrell
      Lady of Hay by Barbara Erskine
      The Lushai Girl by Roberta Forrest
      Tree of Gold by Rosalind Laker
      Jessica by Connie Monk
1988 The Juniper Bush by Audrey Howard
      Destiny by Sally Beauman
      The Lodestar by Pamela Belle
      Distinctions of Class by Anita Burgh
      The Raging Fire by Constance Heaven
      The Silver Touch by Rosalind Laker
      As It Was In the Beginning by Madeleine Pollard
1989 The Peacock's Feather by Sarah Woodhouse
      Daughters of the Storm by Elizabeth Buchan
      Dance of the Peacocks by Elizabeth de Guise
      Spring Imperial by Evelyn Hart
      The Shell Seekers by Rosamund Pilcher
      The Pink Stallion by Lucy Pinney

ROYAL SOCIETY OF LITERATURE'S W H HEINEMANN PRIZE

Royal Society of Literature
1 Hyde Park Gardens, London W2 2LT
Awards given for any kind of literature by living authors
1992 Goethe: The Poet and the Age-Volume I: The Poetry of Desire by Nicholas Boyle

THE SAGITTARIUS PRIZE
Society of Authors
84 Drayton Gardens, London SW10 9SB
Awarded for first published novels by authors over the age of 60.
1991 The Sea Has Many Voices by Judith Hubback
1992 Parnell and the English by Hugh Leonard

THE SCIENCE BOOK PRIZES
COPUS, c/o The Royal Society
6 Carlton House Terrace, London SW1Y 5AG, England
Awarded to the authors of the popular non-fiction, science and technology books, written in English and published during 1990, which are judged to contribute most to the public understanding of science. Annual prize of £10,000
Contact: Jill A Nelson, Copus Executive Committee
1988 Living With Risk by the British Medical Association Board of Science
1989 Bones of Contention by Roger Lewin
1990 The Emperor's New Mind by Roger Penrose

SMARTIES BOOK PRIZE
Book Trust, Book House
45 East Hill, London SW18 2QZ, England
Award given for a chidren's book written in English by a citizen of the UK, or an author resident in the UK, and published in the UK in the year ending 31 October. Annual prize for overall winner, £8,000 and two other category winners, £1,000 each.
Contact: Publicity Department
1985 Grand Prix and over 7's category winner
      Gaffer Samson's Luck by Jill Paton Walsh
      Under 7's category
      It's Your Turn Roger! by Susanna Gretz
      Innovation category
      Watch It Work! The Plane by Ray Marshall and John Bradley
1986 Grand Prix and 7-11 years category winner
      The Snow Spider by Jenny Nimmo
      6 years and under category
      The Goose That Laid the Golden Egg by Geoffrey Patterson
      Innovation category
      The Mirrorstone by Michael Palin, Alan Lee and Richard Seymour
      Village Heritage by Miss Pinnell and the children of Sapperton School
1987 Grand Prix and 7-11 category winner
      A Thief in the Village by James Berry
      6-8 years category
      Tangle and the Firesticks by Benedict Blathwayt
      Under 5 years category
      The Angel and the Soldier Boy by Peter Collington
1988 Grand Prix and Under 5 winner
      Can't You Sleep, Little Bear? by Martin Waddell
      6-8 years category
      Can It Be True? by Susan Hill

9-11 category
Rushavenn Time by Theresa Whistler & Brixworth Primary School

1989 Smarties Book Prize and Under 5 winner
We're Going on a Bear Hunt by Michael Rosen
6-8 years category
Bill's New Frock by Anne Fine
9-11 years category
Blitzcat by Robert Westall

W H SMITH LITERARY AWARD
Strand House, 7 Holbein Place
London SW1W 8NR, England
Presented for outstanding contribution to English literature in the year under review, to the author of a book written originally in English and published in the UK. Authors considered will be from the Commonwealth and Republic of Ireland. Annual award £10,000
Contact: Michael MacKenzie, Sponsorship Manager
1980 Selected Poems by Thom Gunn
1981 The Shooting Party by Isabel Colegate
1982 Last Waltz in Vienna by George Clare
1983 Wise Virgin by A N Wilson
1984 Required Writing (Miscellaneous Pieces 1955-1962) by Philip Larkin
1985 The Pork Butcher by David Hughes
1986 The Good Terrorist by Doris Lessing
1987 Collected Poems 1953-1985 by Elizabeth Jennings
1988 The Fatal Shore by Robert Hughes
1989 A Turbulent, Seditious and Factious People: John Bunyan and his Church (A Biography) by Christopher Hill
1990 A Careless Widow and Other Stories by Sir Victor Pritchett

SOUTH AFRICAN SUNDAY TIMES ALAN PATON AWARD
1992 The Scramble for Africa by Thomas Pakenham

SUNDAY EXPRESS BOOK OF THE YEAR AWARD
Graham Lord, Literary Editor
245 Blackfriars Road, London SE1 9UX
Prize awarded annually for the most stylish, literate and also the most readable work of fiction first published in Britain.
1992 A Place of Greater Safety by Hilary Mantel

JAMES TAIT BLACK MEMORIAL PRIZE
Department of English Literature, David Hume Tower
George Square, Edinburgh EH8 9JX, Scotland
Eligible works of fiction and biographies are those written in English, originating with a British publisher, and first published in Britain in the year of the award. The nationality of the writer is irrelevant. Two prizes, of £1,500 each are awarded annually: one for the best biography or work of that nature, the other for the best work of fiction, published during the calendar year.
Contact: Professor R D S Jack
Biography
1980 Tennyson: The Unquiet Heart by Robert B Martin
1981 Edith Sitwell: Unicorn among Lions by Victoria Glendinning

1982 James Joyce by Richard Ellmann
1983 Franz Liszt: The Virtuoso Years by Alan Walker
1984 Virginia Woolf: A Writer's Life by Lyndall Gordon
1985 Jonathan Swift: A Hypocrate Reversed by David Nokes
1986 Helen Waddell by D Felicitas Corrigan
1987 Victor Gollancz: A Biography by Ruth Dudley Edwards
1988 Wittgenstein: A Life: Young Ludwig (1889-1921) by Brian McGuinness
1989 Federico Garcia Lorca: A Life by Ian Gibson
Fiction
1980 Waiting for the Barbarians by J M Coetzee
1981 Midnight's Children by Salman Rushdie
The Mosquito Coast by Paul Theroux
1982 On the Black Hill by Bruce Chatwin
1983 Allegro Postillions by Jonathan Keates
1984 Empire of the Sun by J G Ballard
Nights at the Circus by Angela Carter
1985 Winter Garden by Robert Edric
1986 Persephone by Jenny Joseph
1987 The Golden Bird: Two Orkney Stories by George Mackay Brown
1988 A Season in the West by Piers Paul Read
1989 A Disaffection by James Kelman

TOM-GALLON AWARD
c/o Society of Authors
A biennial award for writers of limited means who have had at least one short story published.
1984 The Egg Man by Janni Howker
1986 The House of Funerals by Laurence Scott
1988 Taking Doreen Out of the Sky by Alan Beard
1990 Sister Monica's Last Journey by Richard Austin

TRANSLATORS ASSOCIATION TRANSLATION PRIZES
The Translator's Association
84 Drayton Gardens, London SW10 9SB
The Bernard Shaw Translation Prize (Swedish-English)
1991 (Inaugural Year) Tom Geddes for his translation of The Way of a Serpent by Torgny Lindgren
The Schlegel-Tieck Prize (German-English)
1989 Peter Tegel for his translation of The Snake Tree by Uwe Timm
Quintin Hoare for his translation of The Town Park and Other Stories by Herman Grab
1990 David McLintock for his translation of Women in a River Landscape by Heinrich Böll
1991 John Woods for his translation of The Last World by Christoph Ransmayr
Hugh Young for his translation of The Story of the Last Thought by Edgar Hilsenrath
1992 Geoffrey Skelton for his translation of Training Ground by Seigfried Lenz
The Scott Moncrieff Prize (French-English)
1989 Derek Mahon for his translation of The Selected Poems of Phillippe Jacottet
1990 John and Beryl Fletcher for their translation of The Georgics by Claude Simon
1991 Brian Pearce for his translation of Bread and Circuses by Paul Veyne
1992 Barbara Wright for her translation of The Midnight Love Feast by Michel Tournier

James Kirkup for his translation of Painted Shadows by Jean-Baptiste Niel

The Portuguese Translation Prize (Portuguese-English)

1992 (Inaugural Year) Margaret Jull Costa for her translation of The Book of Disquiet by Fernando Pesoa

Nicholas Round for his translation of Frei Luis de Sousa by Almeida Garrett

The John Florio Prize (Italian-English)

1989 Patrick Creagh for his translation of Danube by Claudio Magris

THE BETTY TRASK AWARDS

The Society of Authors, 84 Drayton Gardens London SW10 9SB, England

Awards are for authors under 35 and commonwealth citizens for a first novel of a traditional or romantic nature. Annual prize of £21,000

1984 Winter Journey by Ronald Frame
Cold Showers by Clare Nonhebel
A Parish of Rich Women by James Buchan
Playing Fields in Winter by Helen Harris
The Disinherited by Gareth Jones
The Devil's Looking Glass by Simon Rees
1985 Legacy by Susan Kay
A Season of Peace by Gary Armitage
A Very Private Enterprise by Elizabeth Ironside
Instead of Eden by Alice Mitchell
The Standing Hills by Caroline Stickland
The Earth Abides for Ever by George Schweiz
1986 Tongues of Flame by Tim Parks
Family Myths and Legends by Patricia Ferguson
Mzungu's Wife by Philippa Blake
(Keiko) Whore Banquets by Matthew Kneale
The Road to Dilmun by J F McLaughlin
The Prodigal Father by Kate Saunders
1987 Hard Luck by James Maw
The Levels by Peter Benson
Return Journey by Helen Flint
Lost Time by Catharine Arnold
Gestures by H S Bhabra
The Pink Stallion by Lucy Pinney
1988 The General Interruptor by Alex Martin
A Case of Knives by Candia McWilliam
Behind the Waterfall by Georgina Andrewes
Left of North by James Friel
Burning Your Own by Glenn Patterson
Small Tales of a Town by Susan Webster
1989 The Life Game by Nigel Watts
Watercolour Sky by William Riviere
Harry's Last Wedding by Paul Houghton
Uncle Harry's Last Stand by Alasdair McKee
1990 Ripley Bogle by Robert McLiam Wilson
The Wild Hunt by Elizabeth Chadwick
No Strange Land by Rosemary Cohen
The Vision of Elena Silves by Nicholas Shakespeare
1991 A Strange and Sublime Address by Amit Chaudhuri
Teaching Little Fang by Mark Swallow
Quite Contrary by Suzannah Dunn
Honour Thy Father by Lesley Glaister
Lives of the Saints by Nino Ricci
1992 The Dream Stone by Liane Jones

Kissing Through a Pane of Glass by Peter M Rosenberg
Under the Frog by Tibor Fisher
The Last of His Line by Eugene Mullen
Never Mind by Edward St Aubyn

THE TRAVELLING SCHOLARSHIP FUND

The Society of Authors
84 Drayton Gardens, London SW10 9SB
Non-competitive awards enabling British writers to travel abroad

1988 Sybille Bedford
David Harsent
Barry Hines
Nicholas Wollaston
1989 Roy Heath
Adrian Mitchell
Elizabeth North
1990 David Caute
Roy Fisher
David Hughes
Robert Nye
1991 Anne Devlin
Elaine Feinstein
Iain Sinclair
Emma Tennant

WHITBREAD BOOK OF THE YEAR

Booksellers Association, 272 Vauxhall Bridge Road, London SW1V 1BA, England
To promote and increase good English literature in each of the separate categories. Annual individual category award of £1750 and Whitbread Book of the Year award of £22,000
Contact: Elspeth Hyams, Assistant Director

Novels
1980 How Far Can You Go? by David Lodge
1981 Silver's City by Maurice Leitch
1982 Young Shoulders by John Wain
1983 Fools of Fortune by William Trevor
1984 Kruger's Alp by Christopher Hope
1985 Hawksmoor by Peter Ackroyd
1986 An Artist of the Floating World by Kazuo Ishiguro
1987 The Child in Time by Ian McEwan
1988 The Satanic Verses by Salman Rushdie
1989 The Chymical Wedding by Lindsay Clarke
1990 Hopeful Monsters by Nicholas Mosley (and Book of the Year)
1991 The Queen of Tambourine by Jane Gardam
1992 Poor Things by Alisdair Gray

Biography
1980 On the Edge of Paradise: AC Benson the Diarist by David Newsome
1981 Monty: The Making of a General by Nigel Hamilton
1982 Bismarck by Edward Crankshaw
1983 Vita by Victoria Glendinning
King George V by Kenneth Rose
1984 T S Eliot by Peter Ackroyd
1985 Hugh Dalton by Ben Pimlott
1986 Gilbert White by Richard Mabey
1987 Under the Eye of the Clock by Christopher Nolan (and Book of the Year)
1988 Tolstoy by A N Wilson
1989 Coleridge: Early Visions by Richard Holmes (and Book of the Year)
1990 A A Milne: His Life by Ann Thwaite
1991 A Life of Picasso by John Richardson (and Book of the Year)
1992 Trollope by Victoria Glendinning

Children's Novel
1980 John Diamond by Leon Garfield
1981 The Hollow Land by Jane Gardam
1982 The Song of Pentecost by W J Corbett
1983 The Witches by Roald Dahl
1984 The Queen of the Pharisees' Children by Barbara Willard
1985 The Nature of the Beast by Janni Howker
1986 The Coal House by Andrew Taylor
1987 A Little Lower Than the Angels by Geraldine McCaughrean
1988 Awaiting Developments by Judy Allen
1989 Why Weeps the Brogan? by Hugh Scott
1990 AK by Peter Dickinson
1991 Harvey Angell by Diana Hendry
1992 The Great Elephant Chase by Gillian Cross (and Book of the Year)

First Novel
1981 A Good Man in Africa by William Boyd
1982 On the Black Hill by Bruce Chatwin
1983 Flying to Nowhere by John Fuller
1984 A Parish of Rich Women by James Buchan
1985 Oranges are not the only Fruit by Jeanette Winterson
1986 Continent by Jim Crace
1987 The Other Garden by Francis Wyndham
1988 The Comforts of Madness by Paul Sayer (and Book of the Year)
1989 Gerontius by James Hamilton Paterson
1990 The Buddha of Suburbia by Hanif Kureishi
1991 Alma Cogan by Gordon Burn
1992 Swing Hammer Swing! by Jeff Torrington

Short Story
1984 Tomorrow is our Permanent Address by Diane Rowe

Poetry
1985 Elegies by Douglas Dunn (and Book of the Year)
1986 Stet by Peter Reading
1987 The Haw Lantern by Seamus Heaney
1988 The Automatic Oracle by Peter Porter
1989 Shibboleth by Michael Donaghy
1990 Daddy, Daddy by Paul Durcan
1991 Gorse Fires by Michael Longley
1992 The Gaze of the Gorgon by Tony Harrison

WHITING WRITERS' AWARDS
Mrs Giles Whiting Foundation, 30 Rockefeller Plaza Room 3500
New York, NY 10112, USA
Award to emergent writers in recognition of their writing achievement as well as promise for producing outstanding future work. Annual award of $30,000
Contact: Mrs Kellye Rosenheim, Assistant Director
Fiction
1985 Raymond Abbott
Stuart Dybeck
Wright Morris
Howard Norman
James Robison
Austin Wright
1986 Kent Haruf
Denis Johnson
Darryl Pinckney
Padgett Powell
Mona Simpson
1987 Joan Chase
Pam Durban
Deborah Eisenberg
Alice McDermott
David Foster Wallace
1988 Lydia Davis
Bruce Duffy
Jonathan Franzen
Mary La Chapelle
William T Vollmann
1989 Ellen Akins
Marianne Wiggins
Tobias Wolff
1990 Yannick Murphy
Lawrence Naumoff
Mark Richard
Christopher Tilghman
Stephen Wright
1991 Rebecca Goldstein
Allegra Goodman
John Holman
Cynthia Kadohata
Rick Rofihe
Anton Shammas

Poetry
1985 Douglas Crase
Jorie Graham
Linda Gregg
James Schuyler
1986 John Ash
Hayden Carruth
Frank Stewart
Ruth Stone
1987 Mark Cox
Michael Ryan
1988 Michael Burkard
Sylvia Moss
1989 Russell Edson
Mary Karr
C D Wright
1990 Emily Hiestand
Dennis Nurkse
1991 Thylias Moss
Franz Wright

Non-fiction
1985 Wright Morris
Austin Wright
1986 Darryl Pinckney
1987 Mindy Aloff
Gretel Ehrlich
1988 Gerald Early
Geoffrey O'Brien
1989 Ian Frazier
Natalie Kusz
Luc Sante
1990 Harriet Ritvo
Amy Wilentz
1991 Stanley Crouch
Anton Shammas

Plays
1986 August Wilson
1987 Reinaldo Povod
1989 Timberlake Wertenbaker
1990 Tony Kushner
1991 Scott McPherson

WRITER'S GUILD/MACALLAN AWARDS
The Writers Guild of Great Britain
430 Edgware Rd, London W2 1EH
Fiction
1992 Persistent Rumours by Lee Langley
Non-fiction
1992 Wild Swans by Jung Chang

Children's Book
1992 The Secret Summer of Daniel Lyons by Roy
Apps